STANDARD CATALOG of WORLD COINS

1981 EDITION • by CHESTER L. KRAUSE and CLIFFORD MISHLER

Colin R. Bruce II
Editor

James Vaughan
Market Analyst

Fred J. Borgmann
New Issues Editor

William A. Pettit
Research Specialist

Marian S. Moe
Production Coordinator

— Consulting Specialists —
Carl Allenbaugh, Jack F. Curtis, John S. Deyell, Alan Herbert, Robert F. Lemke, Joan Melum, Russell Rulau, Neil Shafer William F. Spengler and Robert Wilhite

— Photography —
David L. Heise and Teresa J. Wasrud

All valuations for gold or silver coins of the more common, basically bullion types, or those possessing only modest numismatic premiums, as presented in this edition are based on market levels of $650 per ounce for gold and $30 per ounce for silver. Where the letters BV — Bullion Value — appear in a value column, that particular issue, in the condition indicated, can be expected to trade at or near the bullion value of its precious metal content. For more information on utilizing this catalog to arrive at valuations for your gold or silver coins amid fluctuating precious metals market conditions, turn to page 25.

Seeing much, suffering much, and studying much, are the three pillars of learning.

—Benjamin Disraeli

Seventh Edition

Library of Congress Catalog Card Number: 79-640940
International Standard Book Number: 0-87341-054-8

INTRODUCTION

Substantially expanded and enhanced in both scope and detail of coverage, this seventh edition reaffirms the continued commitment of our editorial team to fully meet the many and varied needs of every coin collector. Presented herewith is the multitude of individual national coin issues which has been forthcoming from legally constituted governing authorities through a time frame of the past 225-odd years; be they issues intended for the transaction of everyday business, trade or other specialized intent coinages, or offerings of a commemorative nature.

Physically expanded to a count of 2,000 pages, this edition is nearly 150 pages larger than its immediate predecessor. The scope of coverage has been expanded to encompass more than 1,300 coin issuing entities, providing virtually complete documentation of the world's coinages commencing from the 1760s down to the present day. More than 79,000 coin issues are listed by date, with complete mintage statistics and values — including (where applicable) actual weight of fine gold or silver content. Over 39,000 original, full size coin photographs illustrate this wealth of listings.

Completely revised throughout, thousands of new and updated notations have again been appended to the listings to clarify design differences, production information, including the presence of restrike or other deceptive examples in the hobby marketplace, and the market values assigned, along with pertinent historical facts and related details. To facilitate the understanding of many of these notations, new enlarged illustrations of details described or custom line drawings, are featured.

Our editorial team has benefited from the cooperative efforts of some 300 active contributors whose roles in the ultimate presentation of this work have ranged from developing, revising and verifying listings to reviewing prices and loaning coins for photographing. Distilled and interleaved into the pages of this one-volume coin library is the digested knowledge, some of which had never previously been placed in print, which students of the numismatic science have contributed to the coin collecting hobby through many decades.

Assimilated into a single, coordinated package from such a multitude of sources, this unique numismatic study volume is arranged in a manner intended to provide the novice with an easy to use guide for the direction of his efforts, while at the same time setting forth the detailed information required by the advanced or specialized collector. The result is not a perfect book — a goal for which we reach, but which in reality will always remain beyond reach — but a contribution to scholarship which the staff seeks to constantly enhance and toward which end the assistance of all users is earnestly solicited.

This edition, like its predecessors, features numerous significant additions in the area of documenting earlier-dated coinages than were encompassed in the previous presentations. In several instances major revisions of established listings are introduced, most noticeably in the rearrangement of some countries by the mints of issue, where that system makes it easier for the reader than would be the case with listings presented in the usual sequencing by dates of issue.

An important new feature of this edition is the introduction of **ACTUAL SILVER WEIGHT** and **ACTUAL GOLD WEIGHT** figures for those coins with precious metals content. In combination with companion bullion value tables, these figures will enable the user to easily determine the gold or silver bullion value of a coin, in comparison to its numismatic value listings.

All silver and gold coin valuations in this edition are based on $30 per ounce silver and $650 gold bullion market conditions. For issues that possess only nominal numismatic values in the lower grades, the letters BV — Bullion Value — are used to indicate that issue in the indicated condition should trade for its approximate bullion value.

Important additions to the listings include comprehensive new material on Russia's Siberian and novodel coinages. The India Native States and Nepal listings have been completely revised to incorporate a wealth of new discoveries and earlier-dated issues. Also presented is a completely revised listing of Poland's prova issues.

Within the scope of each national listing featured in the catalog, every effort has been made to provide collectors with complete guides to the sometimes diverse and complex monetary issues of each, including popular tokens, commemoratives and special collector issue coins, without arbitrarily ruling on their status as commercially used coins. In carrying forth this objective, the compilations also incorporate most of the recorded pattern, emergency or other non-national, non-circulating, pretender or pseudo, and similar coin issues which are actively collected but have gone largely unrecognized in other catalogs.

This edition continues the historical-geographical arrangement of country listings, with the complete integration by denomination of non-circulating legal tender (NCLT) issues in the regular listings, as they have previously been handled in earlier editions. The basic arrangement of listings within countries continues to be by denominations from lowest to highest, with interruptions where major monetary reforms or coinage standard conversions are applicable, although exceptions have been made where particularly complicated coinages are concerned.

Our editorial team hopes you enjoy and benefit from using this catalog, and invite the reader to complete his world coin reference resources by subscribing to *World Coin News*, the only weekly periodical devoted exclusively to world numismatic subjects. Each issue includes a "World Coin Roundup" of newly issued or discovered world coin issues, along with frequent presentation of "SCWC Update," a special feature providing updated information on existing listings for Standard Catalog users. As an inducement to try this very useful adjunct to the SCWC, you will find a special money saving subscription coupon for yourself and a collecting friend bound between pages 64 and 65 following, or you may request a sample copy of the current issue by writing to World Coin News, 700 E. State St., Iola, WI 54945.

COUNTRY INDEX

B

C

D

ACKNOWLEDGMENTS

Many hundreds of individuals have contributed countless valuable contributions which have been incorporated in this seventh edition. While all can not be acknowledged, special appreciation is extended to the following principal contributors who have exhibited a special dedication — revising and verifying listings, reviewing prices and loaning coins for photographing — for this and previous editions.

Jan Olav Aamlid
Ed Ackerman
Bjarne Ahlstrom
Stephen Album
Carl H. Allenbaugh
Al Almanzar
Luis A. Asbun-Karmy
George Azuma
Clement Bailey
Frank J. Balcerzak
Herman Baron
Rolf G. Bau
George M. Beach
Lauren Benson
Newton M. Benzing
Jeff Bernberg
Dr. S. K. Bhatt
Milt Blackburn
Walter L. Blank
Maj. Joseph E. Boling
Q. David Bowers
Howard L. Bown
Bruce B. Braun
Ken Bressett
David G. Briggs
Glen W. Brogden
Gregory G. Brunk
Edward Busse, Jr.
Theodore V. Buttrey
Ray Byrne
Judy Cahn
Ralph A. Cannito
Michael D. Carter
K. S. Chang
Daniel K. E. Ching
Wm. B. Christensen
Conrado Ciriaco
Robert L. Clarke
John L. Cobb
M. Coeshaw
Edward E. Cohen
Delmar G. Cooke
Scott E. Cordry
Michael A. Cotta
Freeman Craig, Jr.
Maj. Chris. C. Currie
Maj. Raymond E. Czahor
Howard A. Daniel, III
Dolores H. Davis
Paul F. L. De Groot
Gordon De Mars
C. M. Desai
Daniel Diez-Canseco
Jean-Paul Divo
Peppe Dragoni
Frank Draskovic
Timothy M. Dunn
William M. Dwyer
Stephen D. Eccles
Lester J. Elliott
Wm. R. Elwell
Steve Eyer
Guvendik Fisekcioglu
Thomas F. Fitzgerald
Peter Flensborg
Richard Ford
Anton Fox
Marvin L. Fraley
Enrique Franke
Arthur Friedberg
Victor A. Gadoury
Edward J. Ganister
Wojciecm Gogolinski
Joseph J. Goldberg
Larry Goldberg
Mark Goldberg
Frank W. Gorsler
Dr. G. R. Gruber
Parmeshwari L. Gupta
Roger Haag
Nahum Hacohen
Larry Hannick
Brian Hannon
Dr. W. R. Hartsough
Dr. James A. Haxby
Melvin P. Hennisch
Steve Hochschild
Clyde Hubbard
Charles L. Huff
Granvyl G. Hulse, Jr.
Soli Icewalla
Dr. Norman Jacobs
Byron Johnson
Art Jorgensen
Robert W. Julian
Philip Keller
Mrs. Leona Kohl
Alex H. Kortiz
Andy Kornafel
Peter Kraneveld
Delbert R. Krause
Ernst Kraus
Kurt R. Krueger
Samuel Lachman
Jack R. Lamb
Adrien J. La Pointe
Charles La Rue
David Laties
M. Y. Law
Kenneth Liu
Raymond C. Lloyd
James Lorah
Dennis Luck
Odd Lund
Kenneth Mac Kenzie
Enrico Manara
Harrington Manville
Richard Margolis
Ivan Maxwell
Tom Mc Afee
Don Megill
M. Gutierrez Minera
Lazar Mishev
Robert Mish
Dr. Richard Montrey
Oen Nelson
Richard A. Nelson
Tony Lye Fong Nge
Tony Oliver
Dennis O'Neill
Charles Panish
John E. Paul
Nuri Pere
Robert A. Perrin
Jess Peters
William H. Pheatt
Marco G. Piattelli
Edward H. Pitts
Carol Plante
Stanley Pollard
Rick Ponterio
Major F. Pridmore
Sidky Rabie
Robert M. Ramsay
Jerome H. Remick
Dr. Jorge Emilio Restrepo
Nicholas Rhodes
Alistair F. Robb
Gerald N. Robbins
Dana Roberts
M. R. Roberts
Frank S. Robinson
Richard L. Rosenman
Godwin Said
Allen Schrock
David E. Seelye
Scott Semans
Robert R. Shaw
Ross B. Shields
James C. Shipley
Frovin Sieg
Ladislav Sin
Dr. Rungson Sittipong
W. B. Slate
Bruce Smith
Ward D. Smith
Lester D. Snell
R. C. Soxman
V. Clain-Stefanelli
LTC. G. O. Stenzel, Jr.
Larry Stevens
Jeffrey E. Stokes
Pierre Strauss
Curtis D. Stromme
Y. Sugiyama
William Swoger
Mario L. Tarizzo
M. Louis Teller
Albert A. Tom
Anastasios Tzamalis
Roberto Ulloa
J. J. Van Grover
E. J. Van Loon
E. D. J. Van Roekel
Holland Wallace
Verne R. Walrafen
Justin C. Wang
J. Brix Westergaard
Robert Westfall
R. B. White
R. E. Whyborn
William Williamson
Augusto Wing
Charles H. Wolfe
Fredrick R. Wolfe
Richard Wright
Richard S. Yeoman
Morty Zerder

American Numismatic Society

British Musuem

Evergreen House, Johns Hopkins University

Smithsonian Institution

HOW TO USE THIS CATALOG

This catalog is designed to serve the requirements of both novice and advanced collectors. Providing a comprehensive guide to more than 200 years of the world's coinage history, in most instances it is arranged in a manner that individuals possessing no more than a basic general knowledge of world history since the mid-1700s, and a casual acquaintance with coin collecting, can consult it with confidence and ease. The explanations which follow capsulize the general cataloging practices observed in the preparation of this catalog's listings, but because of specialized requirements which vary depending on country and era, they must not be considered ironclad. Where these standards are set aside, however, appropriate notations of the variations are incorporated.

ARRANGEMENT

A historical-geographic approach has been taken to the incorporation and grouping of all coin listings, which are alphabetically arranged according to the current identity of the sovereign government concerned; i.e., the coins of Persia can be located by referring to the listings for Iran, or the issues of Cambodia by turning to Kampuchea. This approach has also resulted in combining the coin listings for such issuing entities as Annam, French Cochin China, Tonkin, North and South Vietnam as sub-groupings under the historical-geographic identity of Vietnam, which has changed little through years of colonization, independence and strife. Likewise, coins of North and South Korea will be found grouped under Korea; those of the Congo Free State, Belgian Congo, Congo Democratic Republic, Katanga and Zaire under the latter identity.

The coins of each country or issuing entity are generally arranged by denomination from lowest to highest, except where arrangement by mint of issue, type or period makes a series easier to understand, with the non-circulating legal tender (NCLT) coins integrated (these issues are explained in another section of this introduction). The exceptions which were not readily adaptable to this traditional North American cataloging style are generally found in the more complicated series, most notably those encompassing the early issues of Afghanistan, the India Native States, Iran and Turkey.

Strict date sequencing of listings is also interrupted in a number of countries which have been subjected to major monetary reforms, or conversion to decimal or other new coinage standards. Where these considerations apply appropriate headings are incorporated to introduce the switch from one standard to another.

IDENTIFICATION

The most important step in the identification of a coin is the determination of the nation of origin. This task is generally accomplished easily where English speaking lands are concerned, although use of the country index is sometimes required, as the coin legends usually incorporate the name of the country exactly as it appears at the head of the individually grouped listings in this catalog. The coins of Great Britain are a major exception, as that country's issues traditionally do not carry the name of the nation in any form, but they are easily identified by the monarchial portraits, denominations and other familiar designs.

The coins of most countries beyond the English realm such as those possessing French, Italian and Spanish heritages are also quite easy to identify through reference to their legends, which appear in the national languages based on Western alphabets. In many instances the name is spelled exactly the same in English as in the national language, while in other cases, like Francaise for France, Italia for Italy, Belgique or Belgie for Belgium, Brasil for Brazil and Danmark for Denmark, it varies only slightly.

This is not always the case, however, as it is Norge for Norway, Espana for Spain, Sveriges for Sweden and Dansk Vestindien for Danish West Indies. Some other examples include:

DEUTSCHES REICH — Germany 1873-1945
BUNDESREPUBLIK DEUTSCHLAND — Federal Republic of Germany (West Germany)
DEUTSCHE DEMOKRATISCHE REPUBLIK — German Democratic Republic (East Germany)
EMPIRE CHERIFIEN or MAROC — Morocco
ESTADOS UNIDOS MEXICANOS — United Mexican States (Mexico)
ETAT DU GRAND LIBAN — State of Great Lebanon (Lebanon)

Thus, it can be seen that there are instances where a little schooling in the rudiments of foreign languages can be most helpful. In general, the colonial possessions of Western alphabet countries are similarly identifiable as they often carry the familiar lettering, sometimes in combination with a companion designation in the local language.

Those coins which cause the collector greatest difficulty are the ones which do not bear legends featuring the Western alphabet, and are also often devoid of Western numeral dating. These include coins bearing

Cyrillic lettering, which are attributable to the Russian lands, the Slavic states and Balkan area, or Mongolia; the Greek script peculiar to Greece, Crete and the Ionian Islands; the Amharic characters of Ethiopia or Hebrew in the case of Israel. Dragons and sunbursts, along with their distinctive word characters, attribute a coin to the Oriental countries of China, Japan, Korea, Vietnam, Tibet and their component parts.

The most difficult grouping of coins to identify are those bearing only Arabic script and its derivatives which are found on the issues of a number of nations stretching in a wide swath across North Africa and East Asia, from Morocco to Indonesia, and the Indian subcontinent coinages bearing Hindi and related language inscriptions. Although the task of identification is often eased on the more modern issues of these lands by the added presence of Western alphabet legends, a feature sometimes adopted as early as the late 19th Century, but generally not incorporated until well into the 20th Century, for the earlier pieces it is often necessary for the uninitiated to laboriously seek and find.

Except for the cruder issues, however, it will be found that certain characteristics and symbols featured in addition to the often predominating legends are typical of coins from a given country, or group of countries. The toughra monogram, for instance, occurs only on the coins of Afghanistan, Turkey, Egypt, the Sudan, Pakistan and some of the India native states. A predominant feature on early issues from several states and countries of the Indian subcontinent area is the trident, while other issues often appear quite similar in style to the Arab issues, even to the presence of Arabic legends, sometimes in combination with the more applicable Sanskrit and related characters.

As an aid to easier identification of the more difficult to attribute categories, we have assembled the *Instant Identifier* section presented on pages 12-17. It is designed to provide a point of beginning for collectors unfamiliar with the tough coinage series, by allowing him to compare unidentified coins with photographic extracts from typical issues. We also suggest reference to the alphabetical index of coin denominations presented on pages 18-19, or the comprehensive *Country Index*, where the country inscription will be found listed just as it appears on the coin for nations using the Western alphabet.

DENOMINATIONS

Denomination determination is the second basic consideration to be met in the attribution of a coin. As numeric designations of denominational value, rather then presentation in word form, generally prevail, arriving at this determination is usually quite easily accomplished on coins from countries which employ Western-type numerals, except in those instances where issues are devoid of any mention of face value, and thus the denomination is attributed by size, metal or weight. Coins listed in this volume are generally illustrated in actual size, and where actual size is critical to proper attribution, the coin's millimeter size is indicated.

The sphere of countries stretching from North Africa through the Orient, where symbols generally unfamiliar to Westerners are employed, often provide the collector with a much greater challenge. This is particularly true on nearly all of the pre-20th century issues, although on some of the more modern issues, and increasingly so as the years progress, Western-type numerals, generally presented in combination with the locally observed numeric system, are becoming more commonplace on their coins.

The determination of a coin's denomination can also be of value in attributing the issue to its country of origin. A comprehensive alphabetical index of denomination names applicable to the countries as cataloged in this volume, with the individual countries of use indicated for each, is presented on pages 18-19.

The table of *Standard International Numeral Systems* presented on page 20 charts the basic numeric designations found on coins of non-western origin. Although denomination numerals are generally prominently displayed on coins, it must be remembered that these are general representations of characters which individual coin engravers may have rendered in widely varying styles on various coin issues, much as do Western engravers. Where other numeric or script denominational designation forms peculiar to a given coin or country apply, such as the script used on some Persian (Iranian) issues, they are so indicated or illustrated in conjunction with the appropriate listing.

DATING

Coin dating is the final basic attribution consideration, and here the problem becomes more difficult, as the reading of dating is subject not only to the vagaries of numeric styling, but to variations in dating roots caused by the observance of various religious eras or regal periods from country to country, and in some instances even within a given country. Here again it will be found that most countries outside the North Africa through Orient sphere rely on Western date numerals and Christian era (AD) reckoning, although in a few instances coin dating has been tied to the year of a reign or government. The Vatican, with coin dating according to the year of the pope, is an example.

Countries of the Arabic sphere generally date their coins to the Mohammedan era (AH) which commenced on July 16, 622 AD, when the prophet Mohammed fled from Mecca to Medina. As their calendar is reckoned by the lunar year of 354 days, which is about three percent (precisely 3.03 percent) shorter than the Christian year, a formula is required to convert the dating to its Western equivalent. To convert an AH date to the approximate AD date, subtract three percent of the AH date (round to the closest whole number) from the AH date, then add 621. A chart of the equivalent Christian calendar beginning dates for all AH years from 1174 (Aug. 13, 1760) to 1409 (Aug. 14, 1988), which fully encompass the scope of this reference, is presented on page 2000 of this volume.

The Mohammedan calendar is not always based on the lunar year (AH), however, causing some confusion, particularly in Afghanistan and Iran (Persia) where a calendar based on the solar year (SH) was introduced around 1920. These dates can be converted to AD by simply adding 621. In 1976 the government of Iran implemented a new solar calendar based on the founding of the Iranian monarchy in 559 BC. The first year observed on the new calendar was 2535 (MS), which commenced on March 20, 1976. With the reversion to traditionalism a couple years later, the monarchical calendar was abadoned in favor of the former AH dating standards.

Several different eras of reckoning, including Christian and Mohammedan (AH), have been used to date coins of the Indian subcontinent. The two basic systems are the Vikrama Samvat (VS), which dates from Oct. 18, 58 BC, and the Saka era, the origin of which is reckoned from Mar. 3, 78 AD. Dating according to both eras appears on various coinages from the area.

Coins of Thailand (Siam) are found dated by three different eras. The most predominant is the Buddhist era (BE) which originated in 543 BC. Next is the Bangkok or Ratanakosind-sok era (RS) dating from 1781 AD (dates consist of only three numerals), followed by the Chula-Sakarat era (CS) dating from 638 AD. The latter era originated in Burma, and is used on that country's coins.

Other calendars include that of the Ethiopian era (EE) which commenced 7 years, 8 months after AD dating, and that of the Jewish people (AM) which commenced on Oct.7, 3761 BC. Korea claims a legendary dating from 2333 BC which is acknowledged in some of its coin dating, while some coin issues of the Indonesian area carry dates determined by the Javanese Aki Saka era (AS) a calendar of 354 days (100 Javanese years equal 97 Christian or Gregorian calendar years) which can be matched to AD dating by applying the basic formula for conversion of AH dating.

The following table indicates the year dating for the various eras which correspsond to 1981 by Christian calendar reckoning, but it must be remembered that there are overlaps between the eras in some instances:

Christian era (AD)	—	1981
Mohammedan era (AH)	—	AH1409
Solar year (SH)	—	SH1360
Monarchic Solar era (MS)	—	MS2540
Vikrama Samvat (VS)	—	VS2038
Saka era (SE)	—	Saka 1903
Buddhist era (BE)	—	BE 2524
Bangkok era (RS)	—	RS200
Chula-Sakarat era (CS)	—	CS1343
Ethiopian era (EE)	—	EE1973
Jewish era (AM)	—	5741
Korean era	—	4514
Javanese Aki Saka era (AS)	—	AS1913
Fasli era (FS)	—	FE1391

Coins of Oriental origin — principally Japan, Korea, China, Turkestan and Tibet — are generally dated to the year of the government (this also applies for some modern gold issues of Turkey), dynastical, regnal or cyclical eras, with the dates indicated in Oriental characters which usually read from right to left. In recent years, however, some dating has been according to the Christian calendar, and in Western numerals, while in Japan the Oriental character dating was rearranged to read from left to right in 1948AD (Showa year 23).

More detailed guides to other less prevalent coin dating systems, which are strictly local in nature, including the numeral designations employed, are presented in conjunction with the appropriate listings.

Some coins carry dating according to both the locally observed and Christian eras. This is particularly true in the Arabic sphere, where the Mohammedan date may be indicated in Arabic numerals and the Christian date in Western numerals, or both dates may be represented in either Arabic or Western numerals.

The date actually carried on a given coin as listed is generally indicated in the first column (Date) following the catalog number. If that date is not by AD reckoning, the next column (Year) indicates the date by the more conventional calendar which applies, generally Christian. If an AD date appears in either column, the AD is not necessarily indicated, while the era abbreviations appearing in the dating table which accompanies this section are generally presented in conjunction with the listings of coins dated in other eras.

Dating listed in either column which does not actually appear on a given coin is generally bracketed by parenthesis. Undated coin issues are indicated by the presence of the letters ND in the date column and the estimated year of issue in parenthesis in the year column.

Timing differentials between some eras of reckoning, particularly the 354-day Mohammedan and 365-day Christian years, cause situations whereby coins which carry dates for both eras exist bearing two year dates from one calendar combined with a single date from another.

One of the most interesting forms of dating to appear on coins involves the use of chronograms. A few pieces bearing this form of dating are chronicled in this volume, in particular some German thalers of the late 1700s. Chronogram dating presents the date hidden in a coin's Latin legends. Deciphering such dates requires removal and rearrangement of the large letters from the legends into a logical Roman numeral sequence. Thus, the letters XVIIIVVMIICLVDICIIVI would be rearranged to MDCCLXVVVVVIIIIIIIII, or 1794.

NUMBERING SYSTEM

The numeric identifications attached to the listings in this catalog are basically assigned from established references. This practice has been observed for two basic reasons: first, when world coins are listed on the date standard long observed in listing U.S. coins they are self-cataloging; second, there is no need to confuse collectors by infusing totally new numeric designations where appropriate systems already exist.

The majority of the coins listed in this catalog are identified by numbers assigned by R.S. Yeoman (Y#), or slight adaptations thereof, in his *Modern World Coins*, 12th edition, and *Current Coins of the World*, 7th edition, for the convenience of those collectors who maintain their collections by this numbering system. For the pre-Yeoman dated issues the numbers assigned by William D. Craig (C#) in his *Coins of the World* (1750-1850 period), 3rd edition, have generally been applied.

In some countries listings are also frequently attributed to Robert Freidberg's (Fr#) *Gold Coins of the World*, or *Coins of the British World*. Major Fred Pridmore's (P#) studies of British world coins are also referenced frequently, as are W.H. Valentine's (V#) references on the *Modern Copper Coins of the Muhammadan States* and *Copper Coins of India*. Coins issued under the Chinese sphere of influence are also frequently assigned numbers from E. Kann's (K#) *Illustrated Catalog of Chinese Coins* and T.K. Su's (S#) work of similar title. Listings attributed to Charles R. Hosch's (H#) studies of non-circulating legal tender coins are also incorporated in some countries.

Other more specialized works have also been consulted in the assignment of numbers, in which cases the origins of the applicable systems are noted. In a number of instances pieces are listed which have not received recognition in other standard works or specialized studies, at which points the authors have assigned numbers (KM#) distinctive to this volume.Many issues formerly listed by H# will be found reassigned by KM# or Fr# disignations in this edition.

INSTANT IDENTIFIER

Aachen (Germany)

Albania

Austria

Baden (Germany)

Brandenburg-Ansbach (Germany)

Finland

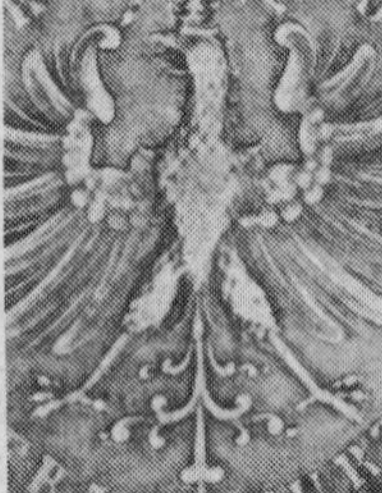
Frankfurt (Germany)

Furstenberg (Germany)

Geneva (Switzerland)

German Empire

Montenegro

Nurnberg (Germany)

Prussia

Russia (Czarist) Russian Poland

Schwarzburg-Rudolstadt (Germany)

Schwarzburg-Sondenhausen (Germany)

Serbia

Teutonic Order (Germany)

United Arab Republic (Egypt, Syria)

Yemen Democratic Republic

Bulgaria

Burma

Ethiopia

Finland

Gorizia (Italy)

Hannover (Germany)

Hesse-Darmstadt (Germany)

Hohenlohe-Neuenstein-Oehringen (Germany)

Iran (Persia)

Morocco

INSTANT IDENTIFIER

Nassau (Germany)

Norway

Sri Lanka (Ceylon)

Tibet

Utrecht (Netherlands)

Venice

China (Empire)

China (Empire)

Japan

Japan

African States

Bretzenheim (Germany)

Greenland

German New Guinea

Lithuania

Mongolia

Sudan

Algeria

Maldive Islands

Afghanistan

Eire

Israel

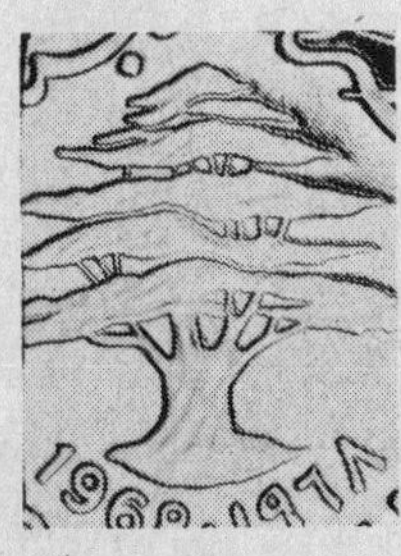
Lebanon

Papal States Vatican City

Sweden

North Korea

Russia (CCCP-USSR)

Russia (CCCP-USSR)

Yugoslavia

China (Formosa)

INSTANT IDENTIFIER

French Colonial

French Colonial

French Colonial

Bangladesh

Isle of Man
Sicily

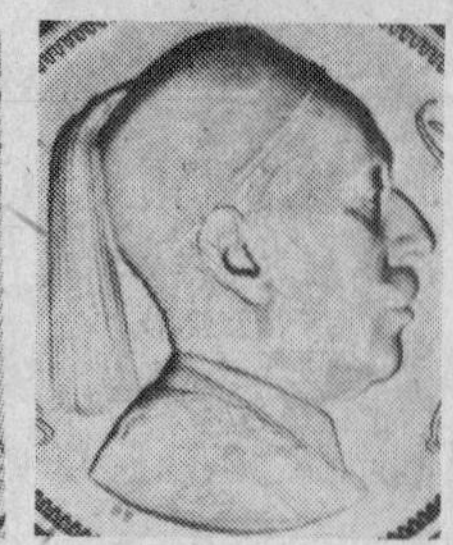
Libya

Aargau
(Switzerland)

Augsburg
(Germany)

Basel
(Switzerland)

Bavaria
(Germany)

Brazil

Bremen
(Germany)

Chur Pfalz
(Germany)

Fulda
(Germany)

Glarus
(Switzerland)

Grand Duchy
Of Warsaw
(Poland)

Graubunden
(Germany)

Hamburg
(Germany)

Hesse-Cassel
(Germany)

Hesse-
Homburg
(Germany)

Hildesheim
(Germany)

Hohenzollern-
Hechingen
(Germany)

Hungary

Julich-Berg
(Germany)

Lippe-
Detmold
(Germany)

Lubeck
(Germany)

Mecklenburg-
Strelitz
(Germany)

Oldenburg
(Germany)

Passau
(Germany)

Portugal

INSTANT IDENTIFIER

Prince Primate (Germany)

Reuss-Greiz (Germany)

Sardinia (Italy)

Saxony

Schaumburg-Lippe (Germany)

Schleswig-Holstein (Germany)

Slovakia

Solothurn (Switzerland)

Unterwalden (Ninwalden) (Switzerland)

Wurttemberg (Germany)

Wurzburg (Germany)

Zurich (Switzerland)

Iraq

Pakistan

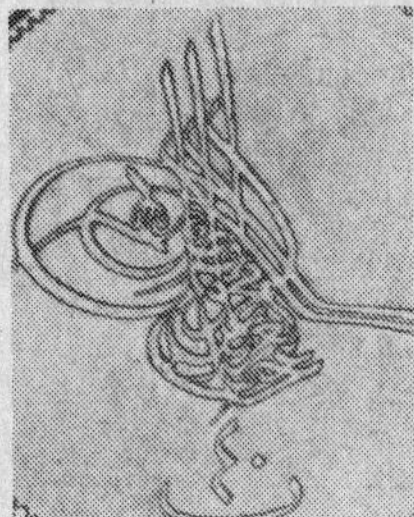
Turkey, Egypt

Muscat

Saudi Arabia

Tunisia

Hyderabad (Many India Native States dump coins resemble this style.)

Hyderabad (India)

Kutch (India)

Indore (India)

Tonk (India)

Travancore (India)

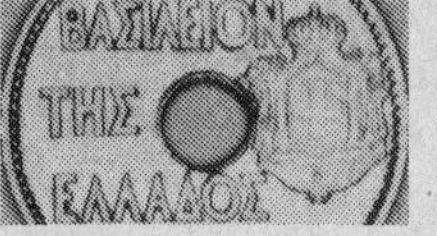

Greece

Serbia

Switzerland

Albania

Israel

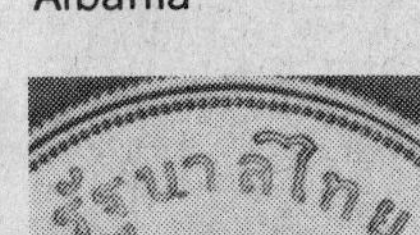

Thailand (Siam)

Japan (Dai Nippon)

South Korea

INSTANT IDENTIFIER

Dutch East India Co. (Netherlands Indies, Java)

English East India Co. (Sumatra)

China, Japan, Korea (All holed 'cash' coins look quite similar.)

Japan

Korea

Japan

Tibet

Tibet

Nepal

Morocco (AH1320=1902AD)

Morocco (AH1371=1952AD)

MONOGRAMS

A
Albert
Belgium

AF
Adolf Frederick
Sweden

B
Baudouin
Belgium

C
Cayenne
French Guiana

CL
Carl & Louise
Saxe-Meiningen

CR
Christian (Denmark)
Tranquebar

C7
Christian VII
Tranquebar

C7
Christian VII
Denmark

CIX
Christian IX
Denmark

CCX
Christian X
Denmark

CCXIII
Charles XIII
Sweden

CLXIV
Carl XIV Johann
Norway

EP
Elizabeth-Phillip
Great Britain

ERI
Edward Rex Imperator
(G.B.) New Guinea

EIIR
Elizabeth II Regina
(G.B.) Cook Isl.

FA
Friedrich August
Lubeck Bishopric

FF
Friedrich Franz
Mecklenburg-Schwerin

FJI
Franz Josef I
Austria

MONOGRAMS

F I
Frederick & Ingrid
Denmark

F VI R
Fred. VI Denmark
Tranquebar

FVII
Frederick VII
Denmark

FF8
Frederick VIII
Denmark

F IX R
Frederick IX
Denmark

FVII
Ferdinand VII
Mexico

FVII
Ferdinand VII
Mexico

FW
Friedrich Wilhelm
Prussia

GA IV
Gustav Adolf IV
Sweden

H I
Nicholas I
Russia

HC
Henri Christophe
Haiti

H VII
Haakon VII
Norway

J
Joachim (Murat)
Berg

E(K) I II
Katherine II
Russia

L
Ludwig
Hesse-Darmstadt

L
Leopold
Belgium

LL
Leopold
Belgium

LL
Louis XVIII
Antwerp

M
Morelos
Revolutionary
Mexico

M2R
Margrethe II
Denmark

N II
Nicholas
Russia

NI
Nicholas I
Russia

NFP
Nicholas Friedrich
Peter
Oldenburg

O II
Oscar II
Norway

O V
Olav V
Norway

(Pi) I
Paul I
Russia

(Pi) III
Peter III
Russia

R
Rainier
Monaco

WL
Wilhelm Landgraf
Hesse-Cassel

WR
William Rex
Hannover

ALPHABETICAL INDEX OF COIN DENOMINATIONS

ABAZE - Russian Caucasia
ABBASI - Afghanistan, Iran, Russian
ACKEY - Gold Coast (Ghana)
AGORA - Israel
AGOROT - Israel
AH - Kampuchea
AHMADI - Yemen
AHMADSHAHI - Afghanistan
AKCHE - Egypt
ALAD - Ethiopia
ALTIN - Egypt, Turkey
AMANI - Afghanistan
AMMAN CASH - Indian Native States
ANGSTER - Switzerland-Cantons
ANNA - Burma, India, Kenya, Muscat & Oman, Oman, Pakistan, Quaiti State
ARGENTINO - Argentina
ASHRAFI - India
ASPER - Algeria, Egypt, Tunisia, Turkey
ASSES - Luxembourg
ATIA - India-Portuguese
ATRIBUO - German States
ATT - Siam (Thailand)
AURAR - Iceland
AVOS - Macao, Timor
BAHT - Siam, Thailand
BAIOCCHI - Italian States, Papal States
BAIOCCO - Italian States, Papal States
BAIZAH - Muscat & Oman, Oman
BALBOA - Panama
BALKH - Afghanistan
BAN - Romania
BANI - Romania
BANU - Romania
BARILLA - Philippines
BATZEN - Switzerland - Cantons
BAZARUCOS - India-Portuguese
BELGA - Belgium
BENDUQI - Morocco
BESA - Ethiopia, Italian Somaliland
BESE - Ethiopia, Italian Somaliland
BICHE - India-French
BIR - Ethiopia
BISTI - Russian Caucasia
BIT - Danish West Indies, Essequibo & Demerary (Guyana)
BOALA - Ethiopia
BOGACH - Yemen
BOLIVAR - Venezuela
BOLIVIANO - Bolivia
BU - Japan
BUDJU - Algeria
BUQSHA - Yemen
BURBE - Tunisia
BUTUT - Gambia
CACHE - India-French
CAGLIARESI - Italian States
CANDAREENS - China
CARLINI - Italian States
CARLINO - Italian States
CAROLIN - Sweden
CASH - China, Hong Kong, Indian Native States
CASSATHALER - German States
CAURIS - Guinea
CAVALLI - Italian States
CENT - Australia, Bahamas, Barbados, Belize, Bermuda, Botswana, British East Caribbean Territories, British Honduras, British North Borneo, British Virgin Islands, Brunei, Canada, Cayman Islands, Ceylon, China, Cocos-Keeling Islands, Cook Islands, Curacao, Danish West Indies, East Africa, Ethiopia, Fiji, Guyana, Hawaii, Hong Kong, Indonesia, Jamaica, Kenya, Kiao Chau, Kiribati, Liberia, Malaya, Malaya & British Borneo, Malaysia, Malta, Mauritius, Netherlands, Netherlands Antilles, Netherlands East Indies, New Zealand, Newfoundland, Nova Scotia, Prince Edward Island, Rhodesia, Sarawak, Seychelles, Sierra Leone, Singapore, South Africa, Sri Lanka, Straits Settlement, Surinam, Swaziland, Tanzania, Trinidad & Tobago, Uganda, United States of America, Zanzibar
CENTAI - Lithuania
CENTAS - Lithuania
CENTAVO - Angola, Argentina, Bolivia, Brazil, Cape Verde Island, Chile, Colombia, Costa Rica, Cuba, Dominican Republic, Ecuador, Guatemala, Guinea-Bissau, Honduras, India-Portuguese, Mexico, Mozambique, Nicaragua, Paraguay, Peru, Philippines, Portugal, Portuguese Guinea, Puerto Rico, Salvador, St. Thomas & Prince Islands, Timor, Venezuela
CENTECIMO - Bolivia
CENTESIMI - Eritrea (Ethiopia), Italy, Italian States, San Marino, Somalia, Vatican City
CENTESIMO - Bolivia, Chile, Dominican Republic, Italy, Italian States, Panama, Paraguay, Somalia, Uruguay, Vatican City
CENTIME - Algeria, Antwerp, Belgian Congo, Belgium, Cambodia, Cameroon, Comoro Islands, France, French Cochin China, French Equatorial Africa, French Guiana, French Indo China, French Oceania, French Polynesia, French West Africa, Germany, Ghent, Guadeloupe, Haiti, Isle of Bourbon, Khmer, Laos, Luxembourg, Madagascar, Malagasy Republic, Martinique, Monaco, Morocco, New Caledonia, Reunion, Switzerland, Togo, Tunisia, Vietnam, Yugoslavia, Zaire, Zara
CENTIMO - Costa Rica, Paraguay, Philippines, St. Thomas & Prince Islands, Spain, Venezuela
CENTU - Lithuania
CHETRUM - Bhutan
CHIAO - China, Manchukuo
CHIEN - China
CHIO - China
CHOMSIH - Ghurfah, Tarim (Yemen)
CHOMSIHI - Mukalla (Yemen)
CHON - Korea, Korea-North
CHRISTIAN D'OR - Denmark
CHUCKRAM - Indian Native States
COLON - Costa Rica, Salvador
CONDOR - Chili, Ecuador
CORDOBA - Nicaragua
CORONA - Austria
CROCIONE - Italian States
CROWN - Ascension, Australia, Bermuda, Gibraltar, Great Britain, Ireland, Isle of Man, Malawi, New Zealand, Rhodesia & Nyasaland, Southern Rhodesia, Turks & Caicos Island
CRUZADO - Portugal
CRUZEIRO - Brazil
DAK - Nepal
DALA - Hawaii
DALASI - Gambia
DALER - Danish West Indies
DECIME - France, Monaco
DECIMO - Argentina, Chile, Colombia, Ecuador, Galapagos Islands
DENARI - Switzerland, Italian States
DENGA - Russia
DENIERS - Haiti, Switzerland - Cantons
DEUTSCHE MARK - Germany
DHINGLA - Indian Native States
DHUFARI - Muscat & Oman, Oman
DIME - United States of America
DINAR - Afghanistan, Algeria, Bahrain, Hejaz, Iran, Iraq, Jordan, Kuwait, Persia, Serbia, Tunisia, Yugoslavia, United Arab Emirates
DINARA - Serbia, Yugoslavia
DINERO - Peru, Spain
DIRHAM - Ras Al Khaima, United Arab Emirates
DIRHEM - Morocco, Qatar, Qatar & Dubai
DIU, DIO - India-Portuguese
DOBRA - St. Thomas & Prince Islands
DOIT - Indonesia
DOKDA - Indian Native States
DOKDO - Indian Native States
DOLLAR - Anguilla, Antigua, Bahamas, Barbados, Belize, Bermuda, British Virgin Islands, British West Indies, Brunei, Canada, Cayman Islands, China, Cook Islands, Danish West Indies, Dominica, Ehtiopia, Fiji, Great Britain, Grenada, Guyana, Hawaii, Hong Kong, Indonesia, Jamaica, Japan, Kiribati, Liberia, Malaysia, Mauritius, New Zealand, Newfoundland, Saint Kitts, Saint Lucia, Saint Vincent, Sierra Leone, Singapore, Straits Settlements, Trinidad & Tobago, United States of America
DONG - Annam, Vietnam, Vietnam-North, Vietnam-South
DOPPIA - Italian States
DOUBLE - Guernsey
DOU DOU - India-French
DRACHMA - Crete, Greece
DRACHMAI - Crete, Greece
DREILING - German States
DUB - Indian Native States
DUCAT - Austria, Austrian States, Czechoslovakia, German States, Hungary, Indonesia, Liege, Netherlands, Olmutz, Poland, Sweden
DUCATI - Italian States
DUCATO - Ragusa
DUCATON - Netherlands
DUIT - Indonesia, Netherlands
DUKAT - Hungary, Sweden, Yugoslavia
DUPLONE - Switzerland - Cantons
DURO - Spain
ECU - France
EKUELE - Equatorial Guinea
EMALANGENI - Swaziland
ESCALIN - Liege
ESCUDO - Angola, Argentina, Bolivia, Cape Verde Island, Chile, Colombia, Costa Rica, Ecuador, Guatemala, Guinea-Bissau, India-Portuguese, Mexico, Peru, Portugal, Portuguese Guinea, Spain, St. Thomas & Prince Islands, Timor
EYRIR - Iceland
FALS - Iraq
FALUS - Iran, Morocco, Russian Turkestan
FANAM - Ceylon (Sri Lanka), India
FANO - India-Danish
FANON - India-French
FARTHING - Antigua, Ceylon (Sri Lanka), Great Britain, Ireland, Isle of Man, Jamaica, Malta, South Africa
FEN - China, Manchukuo
FENIG - Poland
FENIGOW - Poland
FILS - Bahrain, Iraq, Jordan, Kuwait, South Arabia, United Arab Emirates, Yemen
FILLER - Hungary
FIORINO - Italian States
FLORIN - Australia, Austria, Austrian Netherlands, East Africa, Fiji, Great Britain, Ireland, Malawi, Netherlands, New Zealand, South Africa
FORINT - Hungary
FRANC - Algeria, Austria, Belgian Congo, Belgium, Benin, Burma, Burundi, Cambodia, Cameroon, Cattaro, Central African Republic, Chad, Comoro Islands, Congo, Dahomey, Danish West Indies, Ecuador, Equatorial African States, France, French Afars & Issas, French Equatorial Africa, French Oceania, French Polynesia, French Somaliland, French West Africa, Gabon, Guadeloupe, Guinea, Ivory Coast, Katanga, Khmer, Luxembourg, Madagascar, Malagasy Republic, Mali, Martinique, Monaco, Morocco, New Caledonia, New Hebrides, Reunion, Rwanda, Rwanda & Burundi, St. Pierre & Miquelon, Senegal, Somalia, Sweden, Switzerland, Togo, Tunisia, West African States, Yugoslavia
FRANCESCONE - Italian States
FRANCHI - Switzerland - Cantons
FRANCO - Dominican Republic, Switzerland - Cantons
FRANG - Luxembourg
FRANK - German States, Liechtenstein
FRANGA ARI - Albania
FRANKEN - Ghent, Liechtenstein, Saarland (Germany-West), Switzerland - Cantons
FREDERIK D'OR - Denmark
FUANG - Burma, Siam, Thailand
FUENG - Siam, Thailand
FUN - Korea
GAZETTA - Ionian Islands
GERSH - Ethiopia
GHAZNI - Afghanistan
GHIRSH - Sudan
GIRSH - Hejaz, Saudi Arabia
GIULIO - Italian States
GOLDE - Sierra Leone
GOLDGULDEN - German States
GOURDE - Haiti
GRANO - Italian States
GROAT - Great Britain
GROESCHL - Bohemia
GROSCHEL - German States
GROSHEN - Austria, Danzig, East Prussia, German States, Poland, Posen
GROSSETTI - Ragusa
GROSSO - Italian States
GROSSUS - Poland
GROSZ - Poland
GROSZE - Poland
GROSZY - Krakow, Poland, Zamosc
GROTE - German States
GUARANI - Paraguay
GUARANIES - Paraguay
GUERCHE - Egypt
GUILDERS - British Guiana, Essequibo & Demerary (Guyana)
GUINEA - Great Britain, Saudi Arabia
GULDEN - Austria, Curacao, Danzig, German States, Indonesia, Netherlands, Netherlands Antilles, Netherlands East Indies, Surinam
GUTERPFENNIG - German States
HABIBI - Afghanistan
HALALA - Saudi Arabia, Yemen
HALBAG - German States
HALER - Czechoslovakia
HALERE - Czechoslovakia
HALERU - Bohemia & Moravia, Czechoslovakia
HALIEROV - Slovakia (Czechoslovakia)
HALLER - Switzerland - Cantons
HAO - China, Vietnam-North
HAPALUA - Hawaii
HAU - Tonga
HAYRIYE ALTIN - Iraq
HELLER - Austria, German East Africa (Tanzania), German States
HERAT - Afghanistan
HSIEN - China
HWAN - Korea-South
IMADI - Yemen
KAPANG - Malaysia, Sarawak
KAROLIN - German States
KAS - India-Danish
KEPING - Indonesia, Malaysia
KHANABAD - Afghanistan
KHARUB - Algeria, Tunisia
KHARUBA - Algeria
KHAYRIYA - Egypt
KHOUM - Mauritania
KIN - Japan
KINA - Papua New Guinea
KIP - Laos
KOBAN - Japan
KOBO - Nigeria
KOPECK - Germany, Poland, Russia, Spitzbergen, Tanna Tuva
KOPEJEK - Russia, Tanna Tuva
KORI - India
KORONA - Hungary
KORUN - Czechoslovakia
KORUNA - Bohemia & Moravia, Czechoslovakia, Slovakia
KORUNY - Czechoslovakia
KOULA - Tonga
KRAJCZAR - Hungary
KRAN - Iran, Persia
KREUZER - Austria, Czechoslovakia, German States, Hungary, Olmutz, Switzerland
KRONA - Iceland, Sweden
KRONE - Austria, Denmark, German States, Greenland, Liechtenstein, Norway
KRONEN - Austria, Liechtenstein
KRONER - Denmark, Greenland, Norway
KRONOR - Sweden
KRONUR - Iceland
KROON - Estonia
KROONI - Estonia
KRUGERRAND - South Africa
KUNA - Croatia, Yugoslavia
KUPANG - malaysia
KURUS - Turkey
KWACHA - Malawi, Zambia
KWANZA - Angola
KYAT - Burma
LANG - Annam (Vietnam)
LARI - Maldive Islands
LARIN - Maldive Islands
LATI - Latvia
LATS - Latvia
LEI - Romania
LEK - Albania
LEKE - Albania
LEKU - Albania
LEMPIRA - Honduras
LEONE - Sierra Leone
LEPTA - Crete, Greece, Ionian Islan

LEPTON - Crete, Greece, Ionian Islands
LEU - Romania
LEV - Bulgaria
LEVA - Bulgaria
LI - China, Manchukuo
LIANG - China
LIARD - Austrian Netherlands
LIBRA - Peru
LICENTE - Lesotho
LIKUTA - Congo (Zaire)
LILANGENI - Swaziland
LION D'OR - Austrian Netherlands
LIRA - Eritrea, Ethiopia, Israel, Italian States, Italy, San Marino, Syria, Turkey, Vatican City
LIRE - Eritrea (Ethiopia), Israel, Italian Somaliland, Italian States, Italy, San Marino, Somalia, Turkey, Vatican City
LITAI - Lithuania
LITAS - Lithuania
LITU - Lithuania
LIVRE - France, Lebanon
LOUIS D'OR - France
LWEI - Angola
MACE - China
MACUTA - Angola
MAHALLAK - Harar (Ethiopia)
MAHBUB - Egypt, Turkey
MAHMUDI - Mecca (Saudi Arabia)
MAHMUDIYE - Turkey
MAKUTA - Congo (Zaire)
MALOTI - Lesotho
MARAVEDI - Spain
MARK - Estonia, German States, German New Guinea (Papua New Guinea), Germany, Germany-East, Germany-West
MARKA - Estonia
MARKKA - Finland
MARKKAA - Finland
MAS - Malaysia
MASRIYA - Egypt
MAT - Burma
MATHBU - Morocco
MATICAES - Mozambique
MATONAS - Ethiopia
MAZUNA - Morocco
MEI - China
MELGAREJO - Bolivia
METICA - Mozambique
MIL - Cyprus, Hong Kong, Israel, Malta, Palestine
MILESIMA - Spain
MILLIEME - Egypt, Libya
MILLIM - Sudan
MILLIME - Tunisia
MILREIS - Brazil
MISCALS - China
MITKAL - Morocco
MOHAR - Nepal
MOHUR - Afghanistan, India, Indonesia
MOMME - Japan
MON - Japan, Ryukyu Islands (Japan)
MONGO - Mongolia
MU - Burma
MUDRA - Indian Native States
MUN - Korea
MUZUNA - Algeria
NAYA PAISA - Bhutan, India
NEUGROSCHEN - German States
NEW PENCE - Gibraltar, Great Britain, Guernsey, Jersey
NEW PENNY - Great Britain
NEW PESO - Uruguay
NGULTRUM - Bhutan
NGWEE - Zambia
NISFIYA - Egypt
NOUSE - Egypt
OBAN - Japan
OBOL - Greece, Ionian Islands
OCHAVO - Spain
OCTAVO - Mexico, Philippines
ONCA - Mozambique
ONZA - Bolivia, Chile, Costa Rica, Mexico
ORE - Denmark, Faeroe Islands, Greenland, Norway, Sweden
OUGUIYA - Mauritania
PA'ANGA - Tonga
PAGODA - Indian Native States
PAHLEVI - Persia (Iran)
PAI - India, Siam, Thailand
PAISA - Afghanistan, Bhutan, India, Nepal, Pakistan
PANCHIA - India
PAOLI - Italian States
PARA - Egypt, Hejaz, Iraq, Montenegro, Nejd, Saudi Arabia, Serbia, Sudan, Turkey, Yugoslavia
PARDAO - India-Portuguese
PARE - Montenegro, Serbia (Yugoslavia)
PATACA - Macao
PATACO - Portugal
PATAGON - Liege
PE - Burma, Cambodia
PECA - Portugal
PENCE - Australia, Biafra, British Guiana, British West Africa, Ceylon, Falkland Islands, Fiji Islands, Gambia, Ghana, Great Britain, Guernsey, Guyana, Ireland, Isle of Man, Jamaica, Jersey, Malawi, New Guinea, New Zealand, Nigeria, Rhodesia & Nyasaland, St. Helena, St. Kitts, South Africa, Southern Rhodesia, Sri Lanka, Zambia
PENGO - Hungary
PENNI - Finland
PENNIA - Finland
PENNY - Australia, Bahamas, Barbados, Bermuda, British West Africa, Canada, Falkland Islands, Fiji Islands, Gambia, Ghana, Great Britain, Guernsey, Ireland, Isle of Man, Jamaica, Malawi, New Guinea, New Zealand, Nigeria, Rhodesia & Nyasaland, St. Helena, Sierra Leone, South Africa, Southern Rhodesia, Zambia
PERPER - Montenegro (Yugoslavia)
PERPERA - Montenegro (Yugoslavia)
PERPERO - Ragusa
PESA - German East Africa (Tanzania)
PESETA - Equatorial Guinea, Peru, Spain
PESEWA - Ghana
PESO - Argentina, Bolivia, Chile, Colombia, Costa Rica, Cuba, Dominican Republic, Guatemala, Honduras, Mexico, Paraguay, Peru, Philippines, Puerto Rico, Salvador, Uruguay, Venezuela
PESO BOLIVIANO - Bolivia
PESSA - Lahej, Yemen
PFENNIG - Danzig (Poland), German New Guinea (Papua New Guinea), German States, Germany, Germany-East, Germany-West, Salzburg, Switzerland
PFENNING - German States
PHOENIX - Greece
PIASTRA - Italian States
PIASTRE - Annam, Cambodia, Cyprus, Egypt, French Cochin China, French Indo China, Hejaz, Iraq, Khmer, Lebanon, Libya, Nejd, Saudi Arabia, Sudan, Tonkin, Tunisia, Turkey, Vietnam, Yemen
PICE - Bhutan, East Africa, India, Kenya, Malaysia, Mombasa, Pakistan
PIE - Pakistan
PINTO - Portugal
PISO - Philippines
PISTOLE - German States
PITIS - Brunei, Indonesia, Malaysia
POISHA - Bangladesh
POLTINA - Russia
POLTURA - Hungary
POLUPOLTINNIK - Russia
POLUSHKA - Russia
POND - Zuid Afrikaansche Republic
POUND - Australia, Biafra, Egypt, Ghana, Great Britain, Isle of Man, Israel, Malta, Nigeria, Rhodesia, Saudi Arabia, South Africa, Syria
PRUTA - Israel
PUFFIN - Lundy
PUL - Afghanistan
PULA - Botswana
PULI - Russian Caucasia
PYA - Burma
PYSA - Zanzibar, (Tanzania)
QANDAHAR - Afghanistan
QINDARAR - Albania
QINDARARI - Albania
QINDARKA - Albania
QIRAN - Afghanistan
QUAN - Annam (Vietnam)
QUART - Gibraltar
QUARTER DOLLAR - United States of America
QUARTINHO - Portugal
QUARTO - Mexico, Philippines, Spain
QUATTRINO - Italian States
QUETZAL - Guatemala
RAND - South Africa
RAPPEN - Switzerland - Cantons
REAAL - Curacao (Netherlands Antilles)
REAL - Argentina, Bolivia, Central American Republic, Chile, Colombia, Costa Rica, Dominican Republic, Ecuador, Guatemala, Honduras, Mexico, Paraguay, Peru, Salvador, Santo Domingo, Spain, Venezuela
REAL DE VELLON - Spain, Valencia (Spain)
REALES - Argentina, Bolivia, Central American Republic, Chile, Colombia, Costa Rica, Dominican Republic, Ecuador, Guatemala, Honduras, Mexico, Paraguay, Peru, Salvador, Santo Domingo, Spain, Venezuela
REICHSMARK - Germany
REICHSPFENNING - Germany
REIS - Angola, Azores, Brazil, India-Portuguese, Madeira, Mozambique, Portugal
RENTENPFENNIG - Germany
RIAL - Iran, Morocco, Muscat & Oman, Oman, Persia
RIEL - Khmer
RIGSBANKDALER - Denmark
RIGSBANKSKILLING - Denmark
RIGSDALER - Denmark
RIGSDALER SPECIES - Denmark
RIGSMONTSKILLING - Denmark
RIJKSDAALER - Netherlands
RIKSDALER - Sweden
RIKSDALER RIKSMYNT - Sweden
RIKSDALER SPECIE - Sweden
RIN - Japan
RINGGIT - Malaya & British Borneo, Malaysia
RIXDOLLAR - Ceylon (Sri Lanka)
RIYAL - Ajman, Fujairah, Iran, Iraq, Ras Al Khaima, Saudi Arabia, Sharjah, Umm Al Qaiwan, United Arab Emirates.
ROUBLE - Russia, Russian Caucasia, Russian Turkestan
ROYALIN - India-Danish, India-French
RUB - Ethiopia
RUBIYA - Egypt
RUBLE - Poland
RUFIYAA - Maldive Islands
RUPEE - Afghanistan, Andaman Islands, Bhutan, Burma, Ceylon, China, Cocos-Keeling Islands, India, India-French, Indonesia, Iran, Kenya, Mauritius, Mombasa, Nejd, Nepal, Pakistan, Quaiti State, Saudi Arabia, Seychelles, Sharjah, Sri Lanka, Tibet
RUPIA - India-Portuguese, Italian Somaliland (Somalia)
RUPIAH - Indonesia
RUPIE - German East Africa (Tanzania)
RUPIEN - German East Africa (Tanzania)
RUSPONE - Italian States
RYAL - Hejaz, Iran, Muscat & Oman, Nejd, Oman, Persia, Quaiti State, Saudi Arabia, Yemen, Zanzibar (Tanzania)
RYO - Japan
SALU'NG - Siam, Thailand
SANAR - Afghanistan
SANTIMI - Latvia
SANTIMS - Latvia
SANTIMU - Latvia
SAPEQUE - Annam (Vietnam), French Cochin China, French Indo China
SAR - Sinkiang (China)
SATANG - Siam, Thailand
SCELLINO - Somalia
SCHILLING - Austria, Danzig, East Prussia, German States, Poland, Swtizerland
SCHWAREN - German States
SCUDO - Bolivia, Italian States, Mexico, Order of Malta, Papal States (Vatican City), Peru, San Marino
SECHSLING - German States
SEN - Brunei, Cambodia, China, Indonesia, Irian Barat, Japan, Khmer, Malaya & British Borneo, Malaysia, Riau Archipelago, West Irian, West New Guinea
SENE - Western Samoa
SENGI - Congo (Zaire)
SENITI - Tonga
SENT - Estonia
SENTI - Estonia, Tanzania
SENTIMO - Philippines
SERTUM - Bhutan
SESINO - Italian States
SHAHI - Afghanistan, Iran, Persia
SHEKEL - Israel
SHILIN - Somalia
SHILINGI - Tanzania
SHILLING - Australia, Biafra, British West Africa, Cyprus, East Africa, Fiji Islands, Gambia, Ghana, Great Britain, Guernsey, Ireland, Jamaica, Jersey, Kenya, Malawi, New Guinea, New Zealand, Nigeria, Rhodesia, Rhodesia & Nyasaland, Scotland, Somalia, South Africa, Southern Rhodesia, Uganda, Zambia
SHO - Tibet (China)
SHU - Japan, Ryukyu Islands
SIK - Siam, Thailand
SKAR - Tibet (China)
SKILLING - Danish West Indies, Denmark, Norway, Sweden
SKILLINGRIGSMONT - Denmark
SOL - Argentina, Bolivia, France, Haiti, Luxembourg, Peru, Switzerland - Cantons
SOLDI - Switzerland - Cantons, Vatican City
SOLES - Argentina, Bolivia, Peru
SOLIDUS - Poland
SOMALO - Somalia
SOUS - Canada, French Guiana, Mauritius, Spain
SOUVERAIN D'OR - Austrian Netherlands
SOVEREIGN - Australia, Canada, Great Britain, India, Isle of Man, Saudi Arabia, South Africa
SOVRANO - Italian States
SPECIEDALER - Norway
SPECIESDALER - Denmark
SRANG - Tibet (China)
STIVER - Essequibo & Demerary (Guyana) Indonesia
STOTINKA - Bulgaria
STOTINKI - Bulgaria
STUBER - German States
STUIVER - Ceylon (Sri Lanka), Curacao, Indonesia, Netherlands
SU - Vietnam-South
SUCRE - Ecuador, Galapagos Islands
SUELDO - Bolivia
SUKUS - Indonesia
SULTANI - Algeria
SYLI - Guinea
TACA - Indian Native States
TACKOE - Gold Coast (Ghana)
TAEL - China
TAKA - Bangladesh
TALA - Tokelau, Western Samoa
TALAR - Poland
TALARI - Ethiopia
TALLERO - Eritrea (Ethiopia)
TAMBALA - Malawi
TAMLUNG - Siam, Thailand
TANGA - India-Portuguese
TANGKA - Tibet (China)
TARI - Order of Malta
TASHQURGHAN - Afghanistan
TENGA - Russian Turkestan
THALER - Austria, Austrian States, German States, Liechtenstein, Olmutz (Czechoslovakia)
THEBE - Botswana
THELER - German States
TICAL - Siam, Thailand
TIEN - Annam (Vietnam)
TILLA - Afghanistan, Russian Turkestan
TIMASHA - Indian Native States
TOASTAO - Portugal
TOEAS - Papua New Guinea
TOMAN - Iran, Persia, Russian Caucasia
TORNESI - Italian States
TRADE DOLLAR - Japan, United States of America
TRAH - Malaysia
TRAMBIYO - Indian Native States
TUGRUG - Mongolia
TUKHRIK - Mongolia
UNGHERO - Italian States
UNIT - French West Africa
VENEZOLANO - Venezuela
VINTEM - Portugal
WERK - Ethiopia
WARN - Korea
WEN - China
WHAN - Korea
WON - Korea, Korea-South
XERAFIM - India-Portuguese
XU - Vietnam-North, Vietnam-South (Vietnam)
YANG - Korea
YEN - Japan
YUAN - China
ZECCHINO - Italian States
ZELAGH - Morocco
ZLOTE - Poland
ZLOTY - Krakow, Poland, Zamosc
ZLOTYCH - Poland

STANDARD INTERNATIONAL NUMERAL SYSTEMS

WESTERN	0	½	1	2	3	4	5	6	7	8	9	10	50	100	500	1000
ROMAN			I	II	III	IV	V	VI	VII	VIII	IX	X	L	C	D	M
ARABIC-TURKISH	٠	١/٢	١	٢	٣	٤	٥	٦	٧	٨	٩	١٠	٥٠	١٠٠	٥٠٠	١٠٠٠
MALAY—PERSIAN	٠	١/٢	١	٢	٣	۴	۵	٦ or ۶	٧	٨	٩	١٠	۵٠	١٠٠	۵٠٠	١٠٠٠
EASTERN ARABIC	0	½	۱	۲	۳	۴	۵	۶	۷	۸	۹	۱0	۵0	۱00	۵00	۱000
HYDERBAD ARABIC	0	١/٢	١	٢	٣	۴	۵	۶	٧	٨	٩	١0	۵0	١00	۵00	١000
INDIAN (Sanskrit)	०	१/२	१	२	३	४	५	६	७	८	९	१०	५०	१००	५००	१०००
ASSAMESE	০	১/২	১	২	৩	৪	৫	৬	৭	৮	৯	১০	৫০	১০০	৫০০	১০০০
BENGALI	০	১/২	১	২	৩	৪	৫	৬	৭	৮	৯	১০	৫০	১০০	৫০০	১০০০
GUJARATI	૦	૧/૨	૧	૨	૩	૪	૫	૬	૭	૮	૯	૧૦	૫૦	૧૦૦	૫૦૦	૧૦૦૦
KUTCH	0	1/२	1	२	३	४	५	६	७	८	९	10	५0	100	५00	1000
NAVANAGAR	૦	૧/૨	૧	૨	૩	૪	૫	૬ or ૬	૭	૮	૯ or ૯	૧૦	૫૦	૧૦૦	૫૦૦	૧૦૦૦
NEPALESE	०	१/२	१ or १	२	३	४	५ or ५	६	७	८ or ८	९ or ९ or ९	१०	५०	१००	५००	१०००
TIBETAN	༠	༡/༢	༡	༢	༣	༤	༥	༦	༧	༨	༩	༡༠	༥༠	༡༠༠	༥༠༠	༡༠༠༠
MONGOLIAN	᠐	᠑/᠒	᠑	᠒	᠓	᠔	᠕	᠖	᠗	᠘	᠙	᠑᠐	᠕᠐	᠑᠐᠐	᠕᠐᠐	᠑᠐᠐᠐
BURMESE	၀	၁/၂	၁	၂	၃	၄	၅	၆	၇	၈	၉	၁၀	၅၀	၁၀၀	၅၀၀	၁၀၀၀
THAI-LAO	๐	๑/๒	๑	๒	๓	๔	๕	๖	๗	๘	๙	๑๐	๕๐	๑๐๐	๕๐๐	๑๐๐๐
JAVANESE	꧐		꧑	꧒	꧓	꧔	꧕	꧖	꧗	꧘	꧙	꧑꧐	꧕꧐	꧑꧐꧐	꧕꧐꧐	꧑꧐꧐꧐
ORDINARY CHINESE JAPANESE-KOREAN	另	半	一	二	三	四	五	六	七	八	九	十	十五	百	百五	千
OFFICIAL CHINESE-JAPANESE	零	半	壹	貳	叁	肆	伍	陸	柒	捌	玖	拾	拾伍	佰	佰伍	仟
COMMERCIAL CHINESE			〡	〢	〣	〤	〥	〦	〧	〨	〩	十	〥十	〡百	〥百	〡千
KOREAN		반	일	이	삼	사	오	육	칠	팔	구	십	오십	백	오백	천
GEORGIAN			ა	ბ	გ	დ	ე	ვ	ზ	ჱ	თ	ი	ნ	რ	ფ	ჩ
			11 ლ	20 კ	30 ლ	40 მ	50 ნ	60 ჲ	70 ო	80 პ	90 ჟ	100 რ	200 ს 300 ტ	400 უ	600 ქ 700 ღ	800 ყ
ETHIOPIAN	◆		፩	፪	፫	፬	፭	፮	፯	፰	፱	፲	፶	፻	፭፻	፲፻
				20 ፳	30 ፴	40 ፵		60 ፷	70 ፸	80 ፹	90 ፺					
HEBREW			א	ב	ג	ד	ה	ו	ז	ח	ט	י	נ	ק	תק	
				20 כ	30 ל	40 מ		60 ס	70 ע	80 פ	90 צ		200 ר 300 ש	400 ת	600 תר 700 תש	800 תת
GREEK			Α	Β	Γ	Δ	Ε	ΣΤ	Ζ	Η	Θ	Ι	Ν	Ρ	Ο	Α
				20 Κ	30 Λ	40 Μ	60 Ξ	70 Ο	80 Π		200 Σ	300 Τ	400 Υ	600 Χ	700 Ψ	800 Ω

METALS

The metal of issue for each coin denomination is indicated at the beginning of the date listing thereof, and thereafter whenever a coin type change encompasses a change in metal. The traditional coinage metals and their symbolic chemical abbreviations follow:

Platinum	— (Pt)	Brass	—
Gold	— (Au)	Copper-nickel	— (CN)
Silver	— (Ag)	Lead	— (Pb)
Billon	—	Steel	—
Nickel	— (Ni)	Tin	— (Sn)
Zinc	— (Zn)	Aluminum	— (Al)
Bronze) Copper)	— (Ae) or (Cu)	Cupro-nickel) Clad Copper)	—

During the 18th and 19th centuries most of the world's coins were struck of copper, silver or gold. Commencing in the early years of the 20th century, however, numerous new coinage metals, primarily non-precious metal alloys, were introduced. Gold has not been widely used for circulation issue coinages since World War I, although silver remained a popular coinage metal in most areas until after World War II. With the exit of silver, numerous additional metallic compositions were introduced to coinage applications, many of which are difficult to distinguish. Brief descriptions of the characteristics of prevalent coinage alloys follow:

COPPER is a relatively soft metal, which in its base state with slight impurities is pink in color. Coins struck of "pure" copper generally toned to a dark brown after extended exposure to the air. Copper has seldom been used in its "pure" form as a coinage metal since the mid-1800s, but continues as a basic coinage metal alloyed with hard metals in contents generally ranging from 75- to 98-percent.

BRONZE is an alloy obtained by mixing copper with other metals, generally zinc or tin at content levels of 2- to 10-percent. The resulting coins, varying in color from a shiny pink to rich goldene when newly minted, tone to darker brownish colorings following extended exposure to the air. Cannon bronze is a distinctive coinage metal, employed mainly for French coinage following various wars, which takes its name from the fact that the source of the metal was captured and melted enemy cannons. This heavily alloyed copper is pale yellow in color.

BRASS is an alloy of copper and zinc, with the copper content generally not greater than 80-percent, at which level the resulting metal is a bright golden color. Brass containing less than 50-percent copper ranges down the color spectrum from pale yellow to near white.

NICKEL-BRASS is another copper alloy, containing a small percentage of nickel for hardness, which runs a similar color spectrum to brass, but has a slightly bolder surface texture.

ALUMINUM-BRONZE is an alloy of copper (generally about 92-percent), aluminum and a third metal, usually nickel, which provides hardness. The color may range from dark yellow to pale pink.

NICKEL was first used for regular coinage in 1881. The hard, dark silver-colored metal is magnetic, and although used for coinage in its pure form by some countries, it has most often been used alloyed with copper at a ratio of 75-percent copper, 25-percent nickel to produce cupronickel, a non-magnetic metal with a color almost identical to that of pure nickel. A similar alloy, with the addition of a small amount of zinc, is known as nickel-silver, or German silver, although it contains no silver. The nickel-copper alloys vary in color from white (30-per cent nickel) to a pale, brassy yellow (7-percent).

ALUMINUM was first used for coinage in 1907, This metal is easily identified by its extremely light weight and varies in color from grey to near white, depending on the amount and nature of the metal it is alloyed with.

STAINLESS STEEL is an alloy containing 10 to 30 percent chromium, up to 22 percent nickel, and iron, which generally results in a magnetic metal, although some alloys are not. Similar in color to cupronickel, the metal has a smoother, seemingly oily, surface.

IRON and STEEL have both been used for coinage, sometimes with a plating applied, but not widely because the coins are subject to heavy corrosion. Grey in color when new, the magnetic coins rapidly become a very dark reddish-brown.

ZINC, TIN and LEAD range from grey to white in color and are seldom used in their pure state as coinage metals. The surfaces of coins struck in these metals corrode rapidly and take on the appearance of being covered with a white powder. Being much heavier than the other two metals, lead is readily distinguished and possesses a very soft texture.

SILVER ranges in color from grey to white, depending on the amount and nature of the base metals to which it is alloyed for coinage. Silver is generally combined with copper in percentages ranging up to a fineness of .925 (sterling); when the fineness is less than .500, the resulting metal is known as billon. Sulphur in the air causes a chemical reaction which tones the surface of silver coins, often causing them to display varying shades of blue, purple and yellow. Extended exposure of silver coins to open air may cause them to turn almost black.

GOLD is the most precious of coinage metals, and is generally used alloyed with copper at a ratio of 9-to-1. Gold is the heaviest of the traditional coinage metals, and in its refined state may range in color from a very pale to a very rich yellow. Depending on the nature of the alloy and the color of the originally refined gold, the coinage metal can vary in color from a very pale yellow to a reddish-yellow. Gold in its pure state, and generally as alloyed for coinage, is not subject to tarnishing or corrosion, and seldom tones.

PLATINUM has occasionally been used for coinage in the place of gold. It possesses similar weight properties to those of gold, but has a dull silver-grey color.

PALLADIUM, a member of the platinum family of metals, has been infrequently utilized for coinage. It possesses dull silver-grey color qualities similar to those of platinum.

CLAD METALS have been employed in coinage since the early 1900s, in a number of forms, but their application has widened in the years since World War II. In most instances examination of the edge of a clad coin will reveal a base metal in the center to which has been bonded, by heat and pressure, to thin outer layers of a different metal. Brass-clad-steel coins possess brass colored surfaces and are magnetic, as are copper-clad-steel coins which have copper colored surfaces, while nickel or cupronickel-clad-steel coins bear surfaces characteristic of the properties of the claddings. Cupronickel-clad-copper looks like cupronickel on the surface, but the edge evidences a copper color, and nickel-clad-cupronickel coins appear to be cupronickel and are slightly magnetic.

STANDARD INTERNATIONAL GRADING TERMINOLOGY AND ABBREVIATIONS

U.S. and ENGLISH SPEAKING LANDS	PROOF	UNCIRCULATED	EXTREMELY FINE	VERY FINE	FINE	VERY GOOD	GOOD	POOR
Abbreviation	PF	UNC	EF or XF	VF	F	VG	G	PR
BRAZIL	—	(1) FDC or FC	(3) S	(5) MBC	(7) BC	(8) BC/R	(9) R	UTGeG
DENMARK	M	O	O1	1+	1	1÷	2	3
FINLAND	—	0	01	1+	1	1÷ or 1?	2	3
FRANCE	FB	FDC	SUP	TTB or TB	TB or B	B	TBC	BC
GERMANY	P	I/STGL	II / VZGL	III / SS	IV / S	V / S.g.E.	VI / G.e.	G.e.s.
ITALY	FS	FDC	SPL	BB	MB	B	M	—
JAPAN	—	未使用	極美品	美品	並品	—	—	—
NETHERLANDS	—	FDC	Pr.	Z.F.	Fr.	Z.g.	G	—
NORWAY	M	0	01	1+	1	1÷	2	3
PORTUGAL	—	Novo	Soberbo	Muito bo	—	—	—	—
SPAIN	Prueba	Lujo	SC, IC or EBC	MBC	BC	—	RC	MC
SWEDEN	Polerad	0	01	1+	1	1?	—	2

WEIGHTS AND FINENESSES

Where the information is of value in differentiating between types, weights of coins are indicated in grams (abbreviated "gm." or occasionally "gr."), along with fineness. These weights are based on the 31.103 grams in a troy (scientific) ounce, as opposed to the aviordupois (commercial) standard of 28.350 grams. Actual coin weights are generally shown in tenths or thousandths of a gram; for example: .500 SILVER, 2.92 gm.

As the silver and gold bullion markets have advanced sharply in recent years, the fineness and total fine metal content of coins has become especially significant where bullion coins — issues which trade in bulk quantities based on their metallic content rather than numismatic value — are concerned. In many instances such issues have become worth much more in bullion form than their monetary or nominal collector values indicate.

Establishing the weight of a coin can be valuable for determining its denomination. After determining this factor the result can be used to ascertain the specific gravity of the coin's metallic content, an important factor considered when checking the authenticity of an issue, as the specific gravity of the piece can be compared to a chart known standards to determine the fineness of the metallic content. Specific gravity is determined by weighing a coin both in water and dry on a laboratory scale, subtracting the wet weight from the dry weight and dividing the difference into the dry weight. In the interest of accuracy the result should be carried out at least three places beyond the decimal point and an average result of at least three tests should be considered.

TROY WEIGHT STANDARDS
24 Grains = 1 Pennyweight
480 Grains = 1 Ounce
31.103 Grams = 1 Ounce

AVIORDUPOIS STANDARDS
27 11/32 Grains = 1 Dram
437½ Grains = 1 Ounce
28.350 Grams = 1 Ounce

UNIFORM WEIGHTS
15.432 Grains = 1 Gram
0.0648 Gram = 1 Grain

BRAZIL

FC (FDC) — Flor De Cunho
S — Soberba
MBC — Muito Bem Conservada
BC — Bem Conservada
R — Regular
UTGeG — Um Tanto Gasto e Gasto

DENMARK

M — Medaillepraeg
0 — Ucirkuleret
01 — Meget Paent Eksemplar
1+ — Paent Eksemplar
1 — Acceptabelt Eksemplar
1÷ — Noget Slidt Eksemplar
2 — Darligt Eksemplar
3 — Meget Darligt Eksemplar

FINLAND

0 — Stampelglans
01 — Mycket Vacker
1+ — Vacker
1 — Fullgod
1÷ or 1? — Ej Fullgod
2 — Svag
3 — Dalig

FRANCE

FB — Flan Bruni
FDC — Fleur de Coin
SUP — Superbe
TTB — Tres Tres Beau
TB — Tres Beau
B — Beau
TBC — Tres Bien Conserve
BC — Bien Conserve

GERMANY

P — Polierte Platte
STGL — Stempelglanz
VZGL — Vorzuglich
SS — Sehr Schon
S — Schon
S.g.E. — Sehr Gut Erhalten
G.e. — Gut Erhalten
G.e.s. — Gering Erhalten Schlecht

ITALY

FS — Fondo Specchio
FDC — Fior di Conio
SPL — Splendido
BB — Bellissimo
MB — Molto Bello
B — Bello
M — Mediocre

JAPAN

未使用 — Mishiyo
極美品 — Goku Bihin
美 品 — Bihin
並 品 — Futuhin

NETHERLANDS

FDC — Fleur de Coin
Pr. — Prachtig
Z.F. — Zeer Fraai
Fr. — Fraai
Z.g. — Zeer Goed
G — Goed

NORWAY

0 — Ocirkulerat
01 — Mycket Vackert Exemplar
1+ — Fullgott Exemplar Med Spar av Forslitning
1 — Fullgott Exemplar Men Mera Forslitet
1÷ — Alla Detaljer Bar Spar av Forslitning
2 — Daliga Exemplar

SPAIN

EBC — Extraordinariamente Bien Conservada
SC — Sin Circular
IC — Incirculante
MBC — Muy Bien Conservada
BC — Bien Conservada
RC — Regular Conservada
MC — Mala Conservada

SWEDEN

0 — Ocirkulerat Exemplar
01 — Mycket Vackert Exemplar
1+ — Vackert Exemplar
1 — Fullgott Exemplar
1? — Ej Fullgott Exemplar
2 — Daligt Exemplar

CONDITIONS

Valuations for coins cataloged in this work are generally provided in three grades of preservation. Although they cannot be universally applied, and thus the incorporation of variations as appropriate will be noted, the following standards have been observed to provide continuity in grouping grade ranges observed throughout this work: 1) Good, Very Good and Fine; crude "dump" and similar non-machine struck issues. 2) Very Good, Fine and Very Fine; early machine-minted issues of Europe (early 1800s), Latin America (up to the mid-1800s), the Middle East and Asia (as late as the close of the 19th century). 3) Fine, Very Fine and Extremely Fine; most machine-minted issues from the mid-1800s through the early 1900s. 4) Very Fine, Extremely Fine and Uncirculated; modern issues from the late 1800s through the present. 5) Extremely Fine, Uncirculated and Proof; modern commemorative issues.

In this edition listings will frequently be found presented in four grades of preservation, usually in the cases of more popular countries and issues. Three grade range groupings have been introduced to accommodate this expansion: 1) Good, VG, Fine, VF; 2) VG, Fine, VF, XF; 3) Fine, VF, XF, Unc.

In the lower grades it is not practical to apply sharply defined guidelines to these conditions, because of wide variances in coin quality/detail outside Europe and North America prior to the early 1900s (except for overseas issues produced by the European colonial powers). Accordingly, collectors interested in particular series should acquaint themselves with any of its peculiar grading characteristics.

Proof coins are the finest obtainable specimens, having been struck under special quality control conditions, generally for presentation purposes or to be offered for sale to collectors. Uncirculated (Unc) coins are the highest quality production-run issues minted for circulation. In the cases of Arab, Asian and sometimes South and Central American coinages, such coins often have poorly defined detail, particularly on the high points, which may make them appear worn. Coins are not priced in uncirculated condition in instances where they are rarely encountered in that quality.

Coins in Extremely Fine (XF) condition evidence only the slightest degree of wear on the highest points of the design, particularly in the hair lines of portraits and on the central figures of armorial bearings. Very Fine (VF) coins reflect a fair degree of wear at the fine points of the design, although in a relative sense they remain sharp overall. Coins in Fine condition, perhaps the most widely collected grade, have become lightly worn on all high points of the design, although all elements of the design and lettering remain distinct.

Coins in Very Good (VG) condition show considerable wear, with most high points of design detail worn smooth. Lettering near the rim, although worn down, remains quite distinct. Good condition world coins generally grade somewhat higher than the comparably graded U.S. coins. Although most points of detail are worn smooth, and lettering near the rim is often worn nearly smooth on the outer edges, all major portions of the design remain readily distinguishable.

Assigning any of the above condition labels to crudely executed coins, should be done with care and only following careful study of the series concerned, as the original quality of their production must be considered.

Coins in poor or other inferior conditions are generally identifiable by date and mint, but otherwise badly worn, with only parts of the design and lettering distinguishable. Specimens of this quality may evidence mutilation, and are of value only as space fillers unless they are of extreme rarity.

VALUATIONS

The valuations quoted in this catalog represent market averages compiled from recommendations provided and verified through various source documents and specialized panelists. However, it should be stressed that this book is intended to serve only as an aid for evaluating coins; actual market conditions are constantly changing and additional influences, such as particularly strong local demand for some coin series, and worldwide collecting patterns must also be considered. Publication of this catalog is not intended as a solicitation by the publisher, authors, editors or contributors to buy or sell the listed coins at the prices indicated.

All valuations are stated in U.S. dollars, based on careful assessment of the varied international money market. Valuations for coins priced below $1,000.00 are generally stated in full amounts — i.e.; 37.50 or 950.00 — while valuations at or above that figure are rounded off in even dollars with the cents assumed — i.e.; $1250.00 is expressed as 1250. — and a comma is added to indicate tens of thousands in value.

For the convenience of overseas collectors using this volume and for U.S. collectors purchasing from overseas dealers, a comprehensive table of foreign exchange rates covering 13 of the world's major currencies in graduated increments from five cents through $500, is presented on page 24. Those using this table are reminded, however, that although the rates were current on the day this edition was completed, they are subject to economic fluctuations. The base exchange rates for the national currencies of approximately 150 additional countries are presented in a companion table on the adjoining page.

It should also be noted that when particularly select uncirculated or proof examples of most listed coins become available, they can be expected to command proportionately higher premiums than those listed for normally encountered coins in those high grades.

Valuations assigned for listings of common gold and silver coins were based on market values of $650 per ounce for gold and $30 for silver. While issues of substantial numismatic value will not be influenced significantly as market conditions fluctuate above and below these levels, coins closely balanced in their numismatic and intrinsic values will be seriously affected, although to a lesser degree than most common, or bullion issues.

UNLISTED VARIETIES

Users of this work should be mindful that unlisted regular date, overdate, mintmark and assayer mark varieties of listed coin issues undoubtedly await discovery. We are interested in hearing from any collector who uncovers a variety which he believes has gone unrecorded. All such reports received will be considered for listing in subsequent editions, and reported in the special "Variety Logbook", "World Coin Roundup" and "SCWC Update" columns of *World Coin News.*

TABLE OF FOREIGN EXCHANGE RATES

(Courtesy Anne Diane Augustyne of Manfra, Tordella & Brookes of New York City)

U.S. Dollars	Australia Dollar 1.15600	Canada Dollar .86950	England Sterling 2.32900	France Franc .24370	W. German Mark .56710	Hong Kong Dollar .20360	Israel Shekel .21300	Japan Yen .00462	Mexico Peso .04380	Netherlands Guilder .51760	S. Africa Rand 1.29100	Switz. Franc .61480	Venezuela Bolivar .23300	U.S. Dollars
.05	.04	.06	.02	.21	.09	.25	.23	10.82	1.14	.10	.04	.08	.21	.05
.10	.09	.12	.04	.41	.18	.49	.47	21.65	2.28	.19	.08	.16	.43	.10
.15	.13	.17	.06	.62	.26	.74	.70	32.47	3.42	.29	.12	.24	.64	.15
.20	.17	.23	.09	.82	.35	.98	.94	43.29	4.57	.39	.15	.33	.86	.20
.25	.22	.29	.11	1.03	.44	1.23	1.17	54.11	5.71	.48	.19	.41	1.07	.25
.30	.26	.35	.13	1.23	.53	1.47	1.41	64.94	6.85	.58	.23	.49	1.29	.30
.35	.30	.40	.15	1.44	.62	1.72	1.64	75.76	7.99	.68	.27	.57	1.50	.35
.40	.35	.46	.17	1.64	.71	1.96	1.88	86.58	9.13	.77	.31	.65	1.72	.40
.45	.39	.52	.19	1.85	.79	2.21	2.11	97.40	10.27	.87	.35	.73	1.93	.45
.50	.43	.58	.21	2.05	.88	2.46	2.35	108.23	11.42	.97	.39	.81	2.15	.50
.55	.48	.63	.24	2.26	.97	2.70	2.58	119.05	12.56	1.06	.43	.89	2.36	.55
.60	.52	.69	.26	2.46	1.06	2.95	2.82	129.87	13.70	1.16	.46	.98	2.58	.60
.65	.56	.75	.28	2.67	1.15	3.19	3.05	140.69	14.84	1.26	.50	1.06	2.79	.65
.70	.61	.81	.30	2.87	1.23	3.44	3.29	151.52	15.98	1.35	.54	1.14	3.00	.70
.75	.65	.86	.32	3.08	1.32	3.68	3.52	162.34	17.12	1.45	.58	1.22	3.22	.75
.80	.69	.92	.34	3.28	1.41	3.93	3.76	173.16	18.26	1.55	.62	1.30	3.43	.80
.85	.74	.98	.36	3.49	1.50	4.17	3.99	183.98	19.41	1.64	.66	1.38	3.65	.85
.90	.78	1.04	.39	3.69	1.59	4.42	4.23	194.81	20.55	1.74	.70	1.46	3.86	.90
.95	.82	1.09	.41	3.90	1.68	4.67	4.46	205.63	21.69	1.84	.74	1.55	4.08	.95
1.00	.87	1.15	.43	4.10	1.76	4.91	4.69	216.45	22.83	1.93	.77	1.63	4.29	1.00
1.25	1.08	1.44	.54	5.13	2.20	6.14	5.87	270.56	28.54	2.41	.97	2.03	5.36	1.25
1.50	1.30	1.73	.64	6.16	2.65	7.37	7.04	324.68	34.25	2.90	1.16	2.44	6.44	1.50
1.75	1.51	2.01	.75	7.18	3.09	8.60	8.22	378.79	39.95	3.38	1.36	2.85	7.51	1.75
2.00	1.73	2.30	.86	8.21	3.53	9.82	9.39	432.90	45.66	3.86	1.55	3.25	8.58	2.00
2.25	1.95	2.59	.97	9.23	3.97	11.05	10.56	487.01	51.37	4.35	1.74	3.66	9.66	2.25
2.50	2.16	2.88	1.07	10.26	4.41	12.28	11.74	541.13	57.08	4.83	1.94	4.07	10.73	2.50
2.75	2.38	3.16	1.18	11.28	4.85	13.51	12.91	595.24	62.79	5.31	2.13	4.47	11.80	2.75
3.00	2.60	3.45	1.29	12.31	5.29	14.73	14.08	649.35	68.49	5.80	2.32	4.88	12.88	3.00
3.25	2.81	3.74	1.40	13.34	5.73	15.96	15.26	703.46	74.20	6.28	2.52	5.29	13.95	3.25
3.50	3.03	4.03	1.50	14.36	6.17	17.19	16.43	757.58	79.91	6.76	2.71	5.69	15.02	3.50
3.75	3.24	4.31	1.61	15.39	6.61	18.42	17.61	811.69	85.62	7.24	2.90	6.10	16.09	3.75
4.00	3.46	4.60	1.72	16.41	7.05	19.65	18.78	865.80	91.32	7.73	3.10	6.51	17.17	4.00
4.25	3.68	4.89	1.82	17.44	7.49	20.87	19.95	919.91	97.03	8.21	3.29	6.91	18.24	4.25
4.50	3.89	5.18	1.93	18.47	7.94	22.10	21.13	974.03	102.74	8.69	3.49	7.32	19.31	4.50
4.75	4.11	5.46	2.04	19.49	8.38	23.33	22.30	1,028.14	108.45	9.18	3.68	7.73	20.39	4.75
5.00	4.33	5.75	2.15	20.52	8.82	24.56	23.47	1,082.25	114.16	9.66	3.87	8.13	21.46	5.00
5.50	4.76	6.33	2.36	22.57	9.70	27.01	25.82	1,190.48	125.57	10.63	4.26	8.95	23.61	5.50
6.00	5.19	6.90	2.58	24.62	10.58	29.47	28.17	1,298.70	136.99	11.59	4.65	9.76	25.75	6.00
6.50	5.62	7.48	2.79	26.67	11.46	31.93	30.52	1,406.93	148.40	12.56	5.03	10.57	27.90	6.50
7.00	6.06	8.05	3.01	28.72	12.34	34.38	32.86	1,515.15	159.82	13.52	5.42	11.39	30.04	7.00
7.50	6.49	8.63	3.22	30.78	13.23	36.84	35.21	1,623.38	171.23	14.49	5.81	12.20	32.19	7.50
8.00	6.92	9.20	3.43	32.83	14.11	39.29	37.56	1,731.60	182.65	15.46	6.20	13.01	34.33	8.00
8.50	7.35	9.78	3.65	34.88	14.99	41.75	39.91	1,839.83	194.06	16.42	6.58	13.83	36.48	8.50
9.00	7.79	10.35	3.86	36.93	15.87	44.20	42.25	1,948.05	205.48	17.39	6.97	14.64	38.63	9.00
9.50	8.22	10.93	4.08	38.98	16.75	46.66	44.60	2,056.28	216.89	18.35	7.36	15.45	40.77	9.50
10.00	8.65	11.50	4.29	41.03	17.63	49.12	46.95	2,164.50	228.31	19.32	7.75	16.27	42.92	10.00
11.00	9.52	12.65	4.72	45.14	19.40	54.03	51.64	2,380.95	251.14	21.25	8.52	17.89	47.21	11.00
12.00	10.38	13.80	5.15	49.24	21.16	58.94	56.34	2,597.40	273.97	23.18	9.30	19.52	51.50	12.00
13.00	11.25	14.95	5.58	53.34	22.92	63.85	61.03	2,813.85	296.80	25.12	10.07	21.15	55.79	13.00
14.00	12.11	16.10	6.01	57.45	24.69	68.76	65.73	3,030.30	319.63	27.05	10.84	22.77	60.09	14.00
15.00	12.98	17.25	6.44	61.55	26.45	73.67	70.42	3,246.75	342.47	28.98	11.62	24.40	64.38	15.00
16.00	13.84	18.40	6.87	65.65	28.21	78.59	75.12	3,463.20	365.30	30.91	12.39	26.02	68.67	16.00
17.00	14.71	19.55	7.30	69.76	29.98	83.50	79.81	3,679.65	388.13	32.84	13.17	27.65	72.96	17.00
17.50	15.14	20.13	7.51	71.81	30.86	85.95	82.16	3,787.88	399.54	33.81	13.56	28.46	75.11	17.50
18.00	15.57	20.70	7.73	73.86	31.74	88.41	84.51	3,896.10	410.96	34.78	13.94	29.28	77.25	18.00
19.00	16.44	21.85	8.16	77.96	33.50	93.32	89.20	4,112.55	433.79	36.71	14.72	30.90	81.55	19.00
20.00	17.30	23.00	8.59	82.07	35.27	98.23	93.90	4,329.00	456.62	38.64	15.49	32.53	85.84	20.00
22.50	19.46	25.88	9.66	92.33	39.68	110.51	105.63	4,870.13	513.70	43.47	17.43	36.60	96.57	22.50
25.00	21.63	28.75	10.73	102.59	44.08	122.79	117.37	5,411.26	570.78	48.30	19.36	40.66	107.30	25.00
27.50	23.79	31.63	11.81	112.84	48.49	135.07	129.11	5,952.38	627.85	53.13	21.30	44.73	118.03	27.50
30.00	25.95	34.50	12.88	123.10	52.90	147.35	140.85	6,493.51	684.93	57.96	23.24	48.80	128.76	30.00
32.50	28.11	37.38	13.95	133.36	57.31	159.63	152.58	7,034.63	742.01	62.79	25.17	52.86	139.48	32.50
35.00	30.28	40.25	15.03	143.62	61.72	171.91	164.32	7,575.76	799.09	67.62	27.11	56.93	150.21	35.00
37.50	32.44	43.13	16.10	153.88	66.13	184.18	176.06	8,116.88	856.16	72.45	29.05	61.00	160.94	37.50
40.00	34.60	46.00	17.17	164.14	70.53	196.46	187.79	8,658.01	913.24	77.28	30.98	65.06	171.67	40.00
42.50	36.76	48.88	18.25	174.39	74.94	208.74	199.53	9,199.13	970.32	82.11	32.92	69.13	182.40	42.50
45.00	38.93	51.75	19.32	184.65	79.35	221.02	211.27	9,740.26	1,027.40	86.94	34.86	73.19	193.13	45.00
47.50	41.09	54.63	20.40	194.91	83.76	233.30	223.00	10,281.39	1,084.47	91.77	36.79	77.26	203.86	47.50
50.00	43.25	57.50	21.47	205.17	88.17	245.58	234.74	10,822.51	1,141.55	96.60	38.73	81.33	214.59	50.00
55.00	47.58	63.25	23.62	225.69	96.98	270.14	258.22	11,904.76	1,255.71	106.26	42.60	89.46	236.05	55.00
60.00	51.90	69.01	25.76	246.20	105.80	294.70	281.69	12,987.01	1,369.86	115.92	46.48	97.59	257.51	60.00
65.00	56.23	74.76	27.91	266.72	114.62	319.25	305.16	14,069.26	1,484.02	125.58	50.35	105.73	278.97	65.00
70.00	60.55	80.51	30.06	287.24	123.44	343.81	328.64	15,151.52	1,598.17	135.24	54.22	113.86	300.43	70.00
75.00	64.88	86.26	32.20	307.76	132.25	368.37	352.11	16,233.77	1,712.33	144.90	58.09	121.99	321.89	75.00
80.00	69.20	92.01	34.35	328.27	141.07	392.93	375.59	17,316.02	1,826.48	154.56	61.97	130.12	343.35	80.00
85.00	73.53	97.76	36.50	348.79	149.89	417.49	399.06	18,398.27	1,940.64	164.22	65.84	138.26	364.81	85.00
90.00	77.85	103.51	38.64	369.31	158.70	442.04	422.54	19,480.52	2,054.79	173.88	69.71	146.39	386.27	90.00
95.00	82.18	109.26	40.79	389.82	167.52	466.60	446.01	20,562.77	2,168.95	183.54	73.59	154.52	407.73	95.00
100.00	86.51	115.01	42.94	410.34	176.34	491.16	469.48	21,645.02	2,283.11	193.20	77.46	162.65	429.18	100.00
125.00	108.13	143.76	53.67	512.93	220.42	613.95	586.85	27,056.28	2,853.88	241.50	96.82	203.32	536.48	125.00
150.00	129.76	172.51	64.41	615.51	264.50	736.74	704.23	32,467.53	3,424.66	289.80	116.19	243.98	643.78	150.00
175.00	151.38	201.27	75.14	718.10	308.59	859.53	821.60	37,878.79	3,995.43	338.10	135.55	284.65	751.07	175.00
200.00	173.01	230.02	85.87	820.68	352.67	982.32	938.97	43,290.04	4,566.21	386.40	154.92	325.31	858.37	200.00
225.00	194.64	258.77	96.61	923.27	396.76	1,105.11	1,056.34	48,701.30	5,136.99	434.70	174.28	365.97	965.67	225.00
250.00	216.26	287.52	107.34	1,025.85	440.84	1,227.90	1,173.71	54,112.55	5,707.76	483.00	193.65	406.64	1,072.96	250.00
275.00	237.89	316.27	118.08	1,128.44	484.92	1,350.69	1,291.08	59,523.81	6,278.54	531.30	213.01	447.30	1,180.26	275.00
300.00	259.52	345.03	128.81	1,231.02	529.01	1,473.48	1,408.45	64,935.06	6,849.32	579.60	232.38	487.96	1,287.55	300.00
325.00	281.14	373.78	139.54	1,333.61	573.09	1,596.27	1,525.82	70,346.32	7,420.09	627.90	251.74	528.63	1,394.85	325.00
350.00	302.77	402.53	150.28	1,436.19	617.18	1,719.06	1,643.19	75,757.58	7,990.87	676.20	271.11	569.29	1,502.15	350.00
375.00	324.39	431.28	161.01	1,538.78	661.26	1,841.85	1,760.56	81,168.83	8,561.64	724.50	290.47	609.95	1,609.44	375.00
400.00	346.02	460.03	171.75	1,641.36	705.34	1,964.64	1,877.93	86,580.09	9,132.42	772.80	309.84	650.62	1,716.74	400.00
425.00	367.65	488.79	182.48	1,743.95	749.43	2,087.43	1,995.31	91,991.34	9,703.20	821.10	329.20	691.28	1,824.03	425.00
450.00	389.27	517.54	193.22	1,846.53	793.51	2,210.22	2,112.68	97,402.60	10,273.97	869.40	348.57	731.95	1,931.33	450.00
475.00	410.90	546.29	203.95	1,949.12	837.59	2,333.01	2,230.05	102,813.85	10,844.75	917.70	367.93	772.61	2,038.63	475.00
500.00	432.53	575.04	214.68	2,051.70	881.68	2,455.80	2,347.42	108,225.11	11,415.53	966.00	387.30	813.27	2,145.92	500.00

The exchange rates for the national currencies of approximately 150 countries not encompassed in the comprehensive table of foreign exchange rates for the world's major trade currencies presented on the facing page are detailed in the currency rate table which follows. In this table the approximate prevailing rates in effect for bank transfers and related transactions as of June 11, 1980, or the median rate in the case of rigidly controlled or "soft" currencies, are quoted.

Country, Currency	Rate
AMERICAS	
Argentina, New Peso	.0006
Bahamas, Dollar	1.00
Barbados, Dollar	.50
Belize (Br. Hond.), Dollar	.50
Bermuda, Dollar	1.00
Bolivia, Peso	.04
Brazil, New Cruzeiro	.0197
Cayman Islands, Dollar	1.20
Chile, New Peso	.0256
Colombia, Peso	.0278
Costa Rica, Colon	.1167
Cuba, Peso*	1.38
Curacao, Guilder	.555
Dominican Republic, Peso	1.00
E. Caribbean Terr., Dollar	.3711
Ecuador, Sucre	.0375
El Salvador, Colon*	.40
Falkland, Pound	2.27
Guatemala, Quetzal	1.00
Guyana, Dollar*	.40
Haiti, Gourde	.2006
Honduras Rep., Lempira	.50
Jamaica, Dollar	.56
Nicaragua, Cordoba	.1000
Paraguay, Guarani	.0073
Peru, Sol	.0037
Surinam, Guilder*	—
Trinidad & Tobago, Dollar	.416
Uruguay, New Peso	.1147
EUROPE	
Austria, Schilling	.0797
Belgium, Franc	.0353
Bulgaria, Leva*	.86
Czechoslovakia, Koruna*	.1088
Denmark, Krone	.1829
Finland, Markka	.2751
Germany (E.), Ostmark*	.5558
Gibraltar, Pound	2.329
Greece, Drachma	.0234
Hungary, Forint	.0499
Iceland, Krona	.0028
Ireland, Rep., Pound	2.114
Ireland, North., £ Sterling	2.329
Italy, Lira	.0012
Luxembourg, Franc	.0353
Malta, Pound	2.93
Norway, Krone	.2065
Poland, Zloty*	.0332
Portugal, Escudo	.0202
Roumania, Lei*	.0795
Russia, Rouble*	1.58
Scotland, £ Sterling	2.329
Spain, Peseta	.0144
Sweden, Krona	.2405
Turkey, Lira	.013
Yugoslavia, New Dinar	.0502
ASIA, AUSTRALIA	
Afghanistan, Afghani*	.0225
Bahrain, Dinar	2.65
Brunei, Dollar	.4491
Burma, Kyat	.1497
China (Peoples Republic), Renminbi*	.6855
Cyprus, Pound	2.70
Fiji, Dollar	1.1975
India, Rupee	.128
Indonesia, Rupiah	.0016
Iran, Rial*	—
Iraq, Dinar	3.40
Jordan, Dinar	3.39
Korea (South), Won	.0017
Kuwait, Dinar	3.727
Lebanon, Pound	.2953
Macao, Pataca	.1885
Malaysia, Ringgit	.4688
Nepal, Rupee*	.0836
New Caledonia, CFP-Franc	.013
New Zealand, Dollar	.991
Oman, Rial	2.89
Pakistan, Rupee	.1015
Papua, Kina	1.45
Philippines, Piso	.136
Qatar, Riyal	.2718
Western Samoa, Tala	1.05
Saudi Arabia, Riyal	.3004
Singapore, Dollar	.4733
Solomon Islands, Dollar	1.148
Sri Lanka, Rupee*	.064
Syria, Pound	.2545
Tahiti, CFP-Franc	.013
Taiwan, Dollar	.0278
Thailand, Baht	.05
Tonga, Pa'anga	1.10
United Arab Emirates, Dirham	.2686
Yemen (Arab Rep.), Rial*	.2186
Yemen (South), Dinar*	2.93
AFRICA	
Algeria, Dinar*	.2609
Angola, Kwanza*	—
Benin, CFA-Franc West	.0048
Botswana, Pula	1.37
Burundi, Franc	.0111
Cameroon, CFA-Franc Eq.	.0048
Central African Republic CFA-Franc Eq.	.0048
Chad, CFA-Franc Eq.	.0048
Cong (Brazzaville), CFA-Franc Eq.	.0048
Djibouti, Franc	.006
Egypt, Pound	1.45
Ethiopia, Birr*	.479
Gabon, CFA-Franc Eq.	.0048
Gambia, Dalasi	.5778
Ghana, New Cedi*	.3637
Guinea, Syli*	.052
Ivory Coast, CFA-Fr. West	.0048
Kenya, Shilingi	.1332
Libya, Dinar*	3.37
Malagasy Rep., Franc	.0047
Malawi, Kwacha*	1.23
Mali, Franc	.0023
Mauritania, Ouguiya	.0234
Mauritius, Rupee	.1302
Morocco, Dirham	.2583
Mozambique, Escudo*	.035
Niger, CFA-Franc West	.0048
Nigeria, Naira	1.72
Reunion Isl., French Franc	.238
Rhodesia, Dollar*	1.44
Rwanda, Franc	.0108
Senegal, CFA-Franc West	.0048
Seychelles, Rupee	.1706
Sierra Leone, Leone	.976
Somalia, Somali Shilling*	.1661
Sudan, Pound*	2.00
Swaziland, Lilangeni	1.25
Tanzania, Schilling*	.1212
Togo, CFA-Franc West	.0048
Tunisia, Dinar	2.42
Uganda, Schilling*	.133
Upper Volta, CFA-Franc West	.0048
Zaire, Zaire*	—
Zambia, Kwacha*	1.235

*** This is a controlled currency that is not regularly traded by currency brokers. The rate quoted is significantly higher than the rate at which the currency will trade in foreign exchange transactions.**

SILVER AND GOLD WEIGHTS

A new feature in this edition is the listing of weight, fineness and actual silver (ASW) or gold (AGW) content of most machine-struck silver and gold coins. These new designations — ASW stands for **Actual Silver Weight** and AGW stands for **Actual Gold Weight** — will be found incorporated in the listings immediately beneath illustrations or in conjunction with type changes wherever these factors could be determined.

The ASW and AGW figures were determined by multiplying the total (gross) weight of a given coin by its known or tested fineness and converting the resulting gram or grain weight to troy ounces, rounded to the nearest ten thousandth of an ounce — i.e.; a silver coin with a 24.25 gram weight and a .875 fineness would have a fine weight of approximately 21.2188 grams, or a .6822 ASW — a factor that can be used to accurately determine the intrinsic value for multiple examples.

The ASW or AGW figure can be multiplied by the spot price of silver or gold to determine the actual current intrinsic value of any coin accompanied by these designations. Using the example above, if the market value of one ounce of silver is $26.50, the coin's precious metal content would be worth approximately $18.08.

BULLION VALUE CHARTS

Also new to this edition are a pair of universal silver and gold bullion value charts, provided for use in combination with the ASW and AGW factors to determine approximate intrinsic values of listed silver and gold coins. By adding the component weights as shown in troy ounces on each chart, a determination of the approximate intrinsic value of the precious metal content of any silver or gold coin can be easily made.

Again referring to the example presented in the above section, the intrinsic value of a silver coin with a .6822 ASW would be indicated as $18.073+ based on the application of the silver bullion chart. This result is obtained by following across the top to the $26.50 column, then moving down to the line indicated 0.680 in the far right hand column, which reveals a bullion value of $18.02. To determine the value of the remaining .0022 of ASW, return up the same column to the 0.002 line, the closest factor available, where a $0.053 value is indicated. The two factors total to $18.073, which would be slightly less than the actual value.

The silver bullion charts presented on pages 26-27 provide silver values in thousandths from .001 to .009 troy ounce, and in hundredths from .01 to 1.00, in 50¢ value increments from $15 to $30. If the market value of silver exceeds $30, doubling the increments presented will provide valuations in $1 steps from $31 to $60.

The gold bullion charts presented on pages 28-29 are similarly arranged in $20 increments from $500 to $1,000, and by doubling the increments presented, $40 steps from $1,040 to $2,000 can be determined. On the gold bullion charts "Per $10" figures are indicated to the left of the $500 and to the right of the $1,000 columns, for figuring intermediate steps.

Most of the silver and gold coin valuations assigned in this edition are based on assumed market values of $30 per troy ounce for silver, and $650 for gold. To arrive at accurate current market indications for these issues, increase or decrease the valuations appropriately based on any bullion price variations.

Silver Bullion Chart

Oz.	$15.00	$15.50	$16.00	$16.50	$17.00	$17.50	$18.00	$18.50	$19.00	$19.50	$20.00	$20.50	$21.00	$21.50	$22.00	$22.50	Oz.
0.001	0.015	0.016	0.016	0.017	0.017	0.018	0.018	0.019	0.019	0.020	0.020	0.021	0.021	0.022	0.022	0.023	0.001
0.002	0.030	0.031	0.032	0.033	0.034	0.035	0.036	0.037	0.038	0.039	0.040	0.041	0.042	0.043	0.044	0.045	0.002
0.003	0.045	0.047	0.048	0.050	0.051	0.053	0.054	0.056	0.057	0.059	0.060	0.062	0.063	0.065	0.066	0.068	0.003
0.004	0.060	0.062	0.064	0.066	0.068	0.070	0.072	0.074	0.076	0.078	0.080	0.082	0.084	0.086	0.088	0.090	0.004
0.005	0.075	0.078	0.080	0.083	0.085	0.088	0.090	0.093	0.095	0.098	0.100	0.103	0.105	0.108	0.110	0.113	0.005
0.006	0.090	0.093	0.096	0.099	0.102	0.105	0.108	0.111	0.114	0.117	0.120	0.123	0.126	0.129	0.132	0.135	0.006
0.007	0.105	0.109	0.112	0.116	0.119	0.123	0.126	0.130	0.133	0.137	0.140	0.144	0.147	0.151	0.154	0.158	0.007
0.008	0.120	0.124	0.128	0.132	0.136	0.140	0.144	0.148	0.152	0.156	0.160	0.164	0.168	0.172	0.176	0.180	0.008
0.009	0.135	0.140	0.144	0.149	0.153	0.158	0.162	0.167	0.171	0.176	0.180	0.185	0.189	0.194	0.198	0.203	0.009
0.010	0.150	0.155	0.160	0.165	0.170	0.175	0.180	0.185	0.190	0.195	0.200	0.205	0.210	0.215	0.220	0.225	0.010
0.020	0.300	0.310	0.320	0.330	0.340	0.350	0.360	0.370	0.380	0.390	0.400	0.410	0.420	0.430	0.440	0.450	0.020
0.030	0.450	0.465	0.480	0.495	0.510	0.525	0.540	0.555	0.570	0.585	0.600	0.615	0.630	0.645	0.660	0.675	0.030
0.040	0.600	0.620	0.640	0.660	0.680	0.700	0.720	0.740	0.760	0.780	0.800	0.820	0.840	0.860	0.880	0.900	0.040
0.050	0.750	0.775	0.800	0.825	0.850	0.875	0.900	0.925	0.950	0.975	1.000	1.025	1.050	1.075	1.100	1.125	0.050
0.060	0.900	0.930	0.960	0.990	1.020	1.050	1.080	1.110	1.140	1.170	1.200	1.230	1.260	1.290	1.320	1.350	0.060
0.070	1.050	1.085	1.120	1.155	1.190	1.225	1.260	1.295	1.330	1.365	1.400	1.435	1.470	1.505	1.540	1.575	0.070
0.080	1.200	1.240	1.280	1.320	1.360	1.400	1.440	1.480	1.520	1.560	1.600	1.640	1.680	1.720	1.760	1.800	0.080
0.090	1.350	1.395	1.440	1.485	1.530	1.575	1.620	1.665	1.710	1.755	1.800	1.845	1.890	1.935	1.980	2.025	0.090
0.100	1.500	1.550	1.600	1.650	1.700	1.750	1.800	1.850	1.900	1.950	2.000	2.050	2.100	2.150	2.200	2.250	0.100
0.110	1.650	1.705	1.760	1.815	1.870	1.925	1.980	2.035	2.090	2.145	2.200	2.255	2.310	2.365	2.420	2.475	0.110
0.120	1.800	1.860	1.920	1.980	2.040	2.100	2.160	2.220	2.280	2.340	2.400	2.460	2.520	2.580	2.640	2.700	0.120
0.130	1.950	2.015	2.080	2.145	2.210	2.275	2.340	2.405	2.470	2.535	2.600	2.665	2.730	2.795	2.860	2.925	0.130
0.140	2.100	2.170	2.240	2.310	2.380	2.450	2.520	2.590	2.660	2.730	2.800	2.870	2.940	3.010	3.080	3.150	0.140
0.150	2.250	2.325	2.400	2.475	2.550	2.625	2.700	2.775	2.850	2.925	3.000	3.075	3.150	3.225	3.300	3.375	0.150
0.160	2.400	2.480	2.560	2.640	2.720	2.800	2.880	2.960	3.040	3.120	3.200	3.280	3.360	3.440	3.520	3.600	0.160
0.170	2.550	2.635	2.720	2.805	2.890	2.975	3.060	3.145	3.230	3.315	3.400	3.485	3.570	3.655	3.740	3.825	0.170
0.180	2.700	2.790	2.880	2.970	3.060	3.150	3.240	3.330	3.420	3.510	3.600	3.690	3.780	3.870	3.960	4.050	0.180
0.190	2.850	2.945	3.040	3.135	3.230	3.325	3.420	3.515	3.610	3.705	3.800	3.895	3.990	4.085	4.180	4.275	0.190
0.200	3.000	3.100	3.200	3.300	3.400	3.500	3.600	3.700	3.800	3.900	4.000	4.100	4.200	4.300	4.400	4.500	0.200
0.210	3.150	3.255	3.360	3.465	3.570	3.675	3.780	3.885	3.990	4.095	4.200	4.305	4.410	4.515	4.620	4.725	0.210
0.220	3.300	3.410	3.520	3.630	3.740	3.850	3.960	4.070	4.180	4.290	4.400	4.510	4.620	4.730	4.840	4.950	0.220
0.230	3.450	3.565	3.680	3.795	3.910	4.025	4.140	4.255	4.370	4.485	4.600	4.715	4.830	4.945	5.060	5.175	0.230
0.240	3.600	3.720	3.840	3.960	4.080	4.200	4.320	4.440	4.560	4.680	4.800	4.920	5.040	5.160	5.280	5.400	0.240
0.250	3.750	3.875	4.000	4.125	4.250	4.375	4.500	4.625	4.750	4.875	5.000	5.125	5.250	5.375	5.500	5.625	0.250
0.260	3.900	4.030	4.160	4.290	4.420	4.550	4.680	4.810	4.940	5.070	5.200	5.330	5.460	5.590	5.720	5.850	0.260
0.270	4.050	4.185	4.320	4.455	4.590	4.725	4.860	4.995	5.130	5.265	5.400	5.535	5.670	5.805	5.940	6.075	0.270
0.280	4.200	4.340	4.480	4.620	4.760	4.900	5.040	5.180	5.320	5.460	5.600	5.740	5.880	6.020	6.160	6.300	0.280
0.290	4.350	4.495	4.640	4.785	4.930	5.075	5.220	5.365	5.510	5.655	5.800	5.945	6.090	6.235	6.380	6.525	0.290
0.300	4.500	4.650	4.800	4.950	5.100	5.250	5.400	5.550	5.700	5.850	6.000	6.150	6.300	6.450	6.600	6.750	0.300
0.310	4.650	4.805	4.960	5.115	5.270	5.425	5.580	5.735	5.890	6.045	6.200	6.355	6.510	6.665	6.820	6.975	0.310
0.320	4.800	4.960	5.120	5.280	5.440	5.600	5.760	5.920	6.080	6.240	6.400	6.560	6.720	6.880	7.040	7.200	0.320
0.330	4.950	5.115	5.280	5.445	5.610	5.775	5.940	6.105	6.270	6.435	6.600	6.765	6.930	7.095	7.260	7.425	0.330
0.340	5.100	5.270	5.440	5.610	5.780	5.950	6.120	6.290	6.460	6.630	6.800	6.970	7.140	7.310	7.480	7.650	0.340
0.350	5.250	5.425	5.600	5.775	5.950	6.125	6.300	6.475	6.650	6.825	7.000	7.175	7.350	7.525	7.700	7.875	0.350
0.360	5.400	5.580	5.760	5.940	6.120	6.300	6.480	6.660	6.840	7.020	7.200	7.380	7.560	7.740	7.920	8.100	0.360
0.370	5.550	5.735	5.920	6.105	6.290	6.475	6.660	6.845	7.030	7.215	7.400	7.585	7.770	7.955	8.140	8.325	0.370
0.380	5.700	5.890	6.080	6.270	6.460	6.650	6.840	7.030	7.220	7.410	7.600	7.790	7.980	8.170	8.360	8.550	0.380
0.390	5.850	6.045	6.240	6.435	6.630	6.825	7.020	7.215	7.410	7.605	7.800	7.995	8.190	8.385	8.580	8.775	0.390
0.400	6.000	6.200	6.400	6.600	6.800	7.000	7.200	7.400	7.600	7.800	8.000	8.200	8.400	8.600	8.800	9.000	0.400
0.410	6.150	6.355	6.560	6.765	6.970	7.175	7.380	7.585	7.790	7.995	8.200	8.405	8.610	8.815	9.020	9.225	0.410
0.420	6.300	6.510	6.720	6.930	7.140	7.350	7.560	7.770	7.980	8.190	8.400	8.610	8.820	9.030	9.240	9.450	0.420
0.430	6.450	6.665	6.880	7.095	7.310	7.525	7.740	7.955	8.170	8.385	8.600	8.815	9.030	9.245	9.460	9.675	0.430
0.440	6.600	6.820	7.040	7.260	7.480	7.700	7.920	8.140	8.360	8.580	8.800	9.020	9.240	9.460	9.680	9.900	0.440
0.450	6.750	6.975	7.200	7.425	7.650	7.875	8.100	8.325	8.550	8.775	9.000	9.225	9.450	9.675	9.900	10.125	0.450
0.460	6.900	7.130	7.360	7.590	7.820	8.050	8.280	8.510	8.740	8.970	9.200	9.430	9.660	9.890	10.120	10.350	0.460
0.470	7.050	7.285	7.520	7.755	7.990	8.225	8.460	8.695	8.930	9.165	9.400	9.635	9.870	10.105	10.340	10.575	0.470
0.480	7.200	7.440	7.680	7.920	8.160	8.400	8.640	8.880	9.120	9.360	9.600	9.840	10.080	10.320	10.560	10.800	0.480
0.490	7.350	7.595	7.840	8.085	8.330	8.575	8.820	9.065	9.310	9.555	9.800	10.045	10.290	10.535	10.780	11.025	0.490
0.500	7.500	7.750	8.000	8.250	8.500	8.750	9.000	9.250	9.500	9.750	10.000	10.250	10.500	10.750	11.000	11.250	0.500
0.510	7.650	7.905	8.160	8.415	8.670	8.925	9.180	9.435	9.690	9.945	10.200	10.455	10.710	10.965	11.220	11.475	0.510
0.520	7.800	8.060	8.320	8.580	8.840	9.100	9.360	9.620	9.880	10.140	10.400	10.660	10.920	11.180	11.440	11.700	0.520
0.530	7.950	8.215	8.480	8.745	9.010	9.275	9.540	9.805	10.070	10.335	10.600	10.865	11.130	11.395	11.660	11.925	0.530
0.540	8.100	8.370	8.640	8.910	9.180	9.450	9.720	9.990	10.260	10.530	10.800	11.070	11.340	11.610	11.880	12.150	0.540
0.550	8.250	8.525	8.800	9.075	9.350	9.625	9.900	10.175	10.450	10.725	11.000	11.275	11.550	11.825	12.100	12.375	0.550
0.560	8.400	8.680	8.960	9.240	9.520	9.800	10.080	10.360	10.640	10.920	11.200	11.480	11.760	12.040	12.320	12.600	0.560
0.570	8.550	8.835	9.120	9.405	9.690	9.975	10.260	10.545	10.830	11.115	11.400	11.685	11.970	12.255	12.540	12.825	0.570
0.580	8.700	8.990	9.280	9.570	9.860	10.150	10.440	10.730	11.020	11.310	11.600	11.890	12.180	12.470	12.760	13.050	0.580
0.590	8.850	9.145	9.440	9.735	10.030	10.325	10.620	10.915	11.210	11.505	11.800	12.095	12.390	12.685	12.980	13.275	0.590
0.600	9.000	9.300	9.600	9.900	10.200	10.500	10.800	11.100	11.400	11.700	12.000	12.300	12.600	12.900	13.200	13.500	0.600
0.610	9.150	9.455	9.760	10.065	10.370	10.675	10.980	11.285	11.590	11.895	12.200	12.505	12.810	13.115	13.420	13.725	0.610
0.620	9.300	9.610	9.920	10.230	10.540	10.850	11.160	11.470	11.780	12.090	12.400	12.710	13.020	13.330	13.640	13.950	0.620
0.630	9.450	9.765	10.080	10.395	10.710	11.025	11.340	11.655	11.970	12.285	12.600	12.915	13.230	13.545	13.860	14.175	0.630
0.640	9.600	9.920	10.240	10.560	10.880	11.200	11.520	11.840	12.160	12.480	12.800	13.120	13.440	13.760	14.080	14.400	0.640
0.650	9.750	10.075	10.400	10.725	11.050	11.375	11.700	12.025	12.350	12.675	13.000	13.325	13.650	13.975	14.300	14.625	0.650
0.660	9.900	10.230	10.560	10.890	11.220	11.550	11.880	12.210	12.540	12.870	13.200	13.530	13.860	14.190	14.520	14.850	0.660
0.670	10.050	10.385	10.720	11.055	11.390	11.725	12.060	12.395	12.730	13.065	13.400	13.735	14.070	14.405	14.740	15.075	0.670
0.680	10.200	10.540	10.880	11.220	11.560	11.900	12.240	12.580	12.920	13.260	13.600	13.940	14.280	14.620	14.960	15.300	0.680
0.690	10.350	10.695	11.040	11.385	11.730	12.075	12.420	12.765	13.110	13.455	13.800	14.145	14.490	14.835	15.180	15.525	0.690
0.700	10.500	10.850	11.200	11.550	11.900	12.250	12.600	12.950	13.300	13.650	14.000	14.350	14.700	15.050	15.400	15.750	0.700
0.710	10.650	11.005	11.360	11.715	12.070	12.425	12.780	13.135	13.490	13.845	14.200	14.555	14.910	15.265	15.620	15.975	0.710
0.720	10.800	11.160	11.520	11.880	12.240	12.600	12.960	13.320	13.680	14.040	14.400	14.760	15.120	15.480	15.840	16.200	0.720
0.730	10.950	11.315	11.680	12.045	12.410	12.775	13.140	13.505	13.870	14.235	14.600	14.965	15.330	15.695	16.060	16.425	0.730
0.740	11.100	11.470	11.840	12.210	12.580	12.950	13.320	13.690	14.060	14.430	14.800	15.170	15.540	15.910	16.280	16.650	0.740
0.750	11.250	11.625	12.000	12.375	12.750	13.125	13.500	13.875	14.250	14.625	15.000	15.375	15.750	16.125	16.500	16.875	0.750
0.760	11.400	11.780	12.160	12.540	12.920	13.300	13.680	14.060	14.440	14.820	15.200	15.580	15.960	16.340	16.720	17.100	0.760
0.770	11.550	11.935	12.320	12.705	13.090	13.475	13.860	14.245	14.630	15.015	15.400	15.785	16.170	16.555	16.940	17.325	0.770
0.780	11.700	12.090	12.480	12.870	13.260	13.650	14.040	14.430	14.820	15.210	15.600	15.990	16.380	16.770	17.160	17.550	0.780
0.790	11.850	12.245	12.640	13.035	13.430	13.825	14.220	14.615	15.010	15.405	15.800	16.195	16.590	16.985	17.380	17.775	0.790
0.800	12.000	12.400	12.800	13.200	13.600	14.000	14.400	14.800	15.200	15.600	16.000	16.400	16.800	17.200	17.600	18.000	0.800
0.810	12.150	12.555	12.960	13.365	13.770	14.175	14.580	14.985	15.390	15.795	16.200	16.605	17.010	17.415	17.820	18.225	0.810
0.820	12.300	12.710	13.120	13.530	13.940	14.350	14.760	15.170	15.580	15.990	16.400	16.810	17.220	17.630	18.040	18.450	0.820
0.830	12.450	12.865	13.280	13.695	14.110	14.525	14.940	15.355	15.770	16.185	16.600	17.015	17.430	17.845	18.260	18.675	0.830
0.840	12.600	13.020	13.440	13.860	14.280	14.700	15.120	15.540	15.960	16.380	16.800	17.220	17.640	18.060	18.480	18.900	0.840
0.850	12.750	13.175	13.600	14.025	14.450	14.875	15.300	15.725	16.150	16.575	17.000	17.425	17.850	18.275	18.700	19.125	0.850
0.860	12.900	13.330	13.760	14.190	14.620	15.050	15.480	15.910	16.340	16.770	17.200	17.630	18.060	18.490	18.920	19.350	0.860
0.870	13.050	13.485	13.920	14.355	14.790	15.225	15.660	16.095	16.530	16.965	17.400	17.835	18.270	18.705	19.140	19.575	0.870
0.880	13.200	13.640	14.080	14.520	14.960	15.400	15.840	16.280	16.720	17.160	17.600	18.040	18.480	18.920	19.360	19.800	0.880
0.890	13.350	13.795	14.240	14.685	15.130	15.575	16.020	16.465	16.910	17.355	17.800	18.245	18.690	19.135	19.580	20.025	0.890
0.900	13.500	13.950	14.400	14.850	15.300	15.750	16.200	16.650	17.100	17.550	18.000	18.450	18.900	19.350	19.800	20.250	0.900
0.910	13.650	14.105	14.560	15.015	15.470	15.925	16.380	16.835	17.290	17.745	18.200	18.655	19.110	19.565	20.020	20.475	0.910
0.920	13.800	14.260	14.720	15.180	15.640	16.100	16.560	17.020	17.480	17.940	18.400	18.860	19.320	19.780	20.240	20.700	0.920
0.930	13.950	14.415	14.880	15.345	15.810	16.275	16.740	17.205	17.670	18.135	18.600	19.065	19.530	19.995	20.460	20.925	0.930
0.940	14.100	14.570	15.040	15.510	15.980	16.450	16.920	17.390	17.860	18.330	18.800	19.270	19.740	20.210	20.680	21.150	0.940
0.950	14.250	14.725	15.200	15.675	16.150	16.625	17.100	17.575	18.050	18.525	19.000	19.475	19.950	20.425	20.900	21.375	0.950
0.960	14.400	14.880	15.360	15.840	16.320	16.800	17.280	17.760	18.240	18.720	19.200	19.680	20.160	20.640	21.120	21.600	0.960
0.970	14.550	15.035	15.520	16.005	16.490	16.975	17.460	17.945	18.430	18.915	19.400	19.885	20.370	20.855	21.340	21.825	0.970
0.980	14.700	15.190	15.680	16.170	16.660	17.150	17.640	18.130	18.620	19.110	19.600	20.090	20.580	21.070	21.560	22.050	0.980
0.990	14.850	15.345	15.840	16.335	16.830	17.325	17.820	18.315	18.810	19.305	19.800	20.295	20.790	21.285	21.780	22.275	0.990
1.000	15.000	15.500	16.000	16.500	17.000	17.500	18.000	18.500	19.000	19.500	20.000	20.500	21.000	21.500	22.000	22.500	1.000

Silver Bullion Chart

Oz.	$23.00	$23.50	$24.00	$24.50	$25.00	$25.50	$26.00	$26.50	$27.00	$27.50	$28.00	$28.50	$29.00	$29.50	$30.00	Oz.
0.001	0.023	0.024	0.024	0.025	0.025	0.026	0.026	0.027	0.027	0.028	0.028	0.029	0.029	0.030	0.030	0.001
0.002	0.046	0.047	0.048	0.049	0.050	0.051	0.052	0.053	0.054	0.055	0.056	0.057	0.058	0.059	0.060	0.002
0.003	0.069	0.071	0.072	0.074	0.075	0.077	0.078	0.080	0.081	0.083	0.084	0.086	0.087	0.089	0.090	0.003
0.004	0.092	0.094	0.096	0.098	0.100	0.102	0.104	0.106	0.108	0.110	0.112	0.114	0.116	0.118	0.120	0.004
0.005	0.115	0.118	0.120	0.123	0.125	0.128	0.130	0.133	0.135	0.138	0.140	0.143	0.145	0.148	0.150	0.005
0.006	0.138	0.141	0.144	0.147	0.150	0.153	0.156	0.159	0.162	0.165	0.168	0.171	0.174	0.177	0.180	0.006
0.007	0.161	0.165	0.168	0.172	0.175	0.179	0.182	0.186	0.189	0.193	0.196	0.200	0.203	0.207	0.210	0.007
0.008	0.184	0.188	0.192	0.196	0.200	0.204	0.208	0.212	0.216	0.220	0.224	0.228	0.232	0.236	0.240	0.008
0.009	0.207	0.212	0.216	0.221	0.225	0.230	0.234	0.239	0.243	0.248	0.252	0.257	0.261	0.266	0.270	0.009
0.010	0.230	0.235	0.240	0.245	0.250	0.255	0.260	0.265	0.270	0.275	0.280	0.285	0.290	0.295	0.300	0.010
0.020	0.460	0.470	0.480	0.490	0.500	0.510	0.520	0.530	0.540	0.550	0.560	0.570	0.580	0.590	0.600	0.020
0.030	0.690	0.705	0.720	0.735	0.750	0.765	0.780	0.795	0.810	0.825	0.840	0.855	0.870	0.885	0.900	0.030
0.040	0.920	0.940	0.960	0.980	1.000	1.020	1.040	1.060	1.080	1.100	1.120	1.140	1.160	1.180	1.200	0.040
0.050	1.150	1.175	1.200	1.225	1.250	1.275	1.300	1.325	1.350	1.375	1.400	1.425	1.450	1.475	1.500	0.050
0.060	1.380	1.410	1.440	1.470	1.500	1.530	1.560	1.590	1.620	1.650	1.680	1.710	1.740	1.770	1.800	0.060
0.070	1.610	1.645	1.680	1.715	1.750	1.785	1.820	1.855	1.890	1.925	1.960	1.995	2.030	2.065	2.100	0.070
0.080	1.840	1.880	1.920	1.960	2.000	2.040	2.080	2.120	2.160	2.200	2.240	2.280	2.320	2.360	2.400	0.080
0.090	2.070	2.115	2.160	2.205	2.250	2.295	2.340	2.385	2.430	2.475	2.520	2.565	2.610	2.655	2.700	0.090
0.100	2.300	2.350	2.400	2.450	2.500	2.550	2.600	2.650	2.700	2.750	2.800	2.850	2.900	2.950	3.000	0.100
0.110	2.530	2.585	2.640	2.695	2.750	2.805	2.860	2.915	2.970	3.025	3.080	3.135	3.190	3.245	3.300	0.110
0.120	2.760	2.820	2.880	2.940	3.000	3.060	3.120	3.180	3.240	3.300	3.360	3.420	3.480	3.540	3.600	0.120
0.130	2.990	3.055	3.120	3.185	3.250	3.315	3.380	3.445	3.510	3.575	3.640	3.705	3.770	3.835	3.900	0.130
0.140	3.220	3.290	3.360	3.430	3.500	3.570	3.640	3.710	3.780	3.850	3.920	3.990	4.060	4.130	4.200	0.140
0.150	3.450	3.525	3.600	3.675	3.750	3.825	3.900	3.975	4.050	4.125	4.200	4.275	4.350	4.425	4.500	0.150
0.160	3.680	3.760	3.840	3.920	4.000	4.080	4.160	4.240	4.320	4.400	4.480	4.560	4.640	4.720	4.800	0.160
0.170	3.910	3.995	4.080	4.165	4.250	4.335	4.420	4.505	4.590	4.675	4.760	4.845	4.930	5.015	5.100	0.170
0.180	4.140	4.230	4.320	4.410	4.500	4.590	4.680	4.770	4.860	4.950	5.040	5.130	5.220	5.310	5.400	0.180
0.190	4.370	4.465	4.560	4.655	4.750	4.845	4.940	5.035	5.130	5.225	5.320	5.415	5.510	5.605	5.700	0.190
0.200	4.600	4.700	4.800	4.900	5.000	5.100	5.200	5.300	5.400	5.500	5.600	5.700	5.800	5.900	6.000	0.200
0.210	4.830	4.935	5.040	5.145	5.250	5.355	5.460	5.565	5.670	5.775	5.880	5.985	6.090	6.195	6.300	0.210
0.220	5.060	5.170	5.280	5.390	5.500	5.610	5.720	5.830	5.940	6.050	6.160	6.270	6.380	6.490	6.600	0.220
0.230	5.290	5.405	5.520	5.635	5.750	5.865	5.980	6.095	6.210	6.325	6.440	6.555	6.670	6.785	6.900	0.230
0.240	5.520	5.640	5.760	5.880	6.000	6.120	6.240	6.360	6.480	6.600	6.720	6.840	6.960	7.080	7.200	0.240
0.250	5.750	5.875	6.000	6.125	6.250	6.375	6.500	6.625	6.750	6.875	7.000	7.125	7.250	7.375	7.500	0.250
0.260	5.980	6.110	6.240	6.370	6.500	6.630	6.760	6.890	7.020	7.150	7.280	7.410	7.540	7.670	7.800	0.260
0.270	6.210	6.345	6.480	6.615	6.750	6.885	7.020	7.155	7.290	7.425	7.560	7.695	7.830	7.965	8.100	0.270
0.280	6.440	6.580	6.720	6.860	7.000	7.140	7.280	7.420	7.560	7.700	7.840	7.980	8.120	8.260	8.400	0.280
0.290	6.670	6.815	6.960	7.105	7.250	7.395	7.540	7.685	7.830	7.975	8.120	8.265	8.410	8.555	8.700	0.290
0.300	6.900	7.050	7.200	7.350	7.500	7.650	7.800	7.950	8.100	8.250	8.400	8.550	8.700	8.850	9.000	0.300
0.310	7.130	7.285	7.440	7.595	7.750	7.905	8.060	8.215	8.370	8.525	8.680	8.835	8.990	9.145	9.300	0.310
0.320	7.360	7.520	7.680	7.840	8.000	8.160	8.320	8.480	8.640	8.800	8.960	9.120	9.280	9.440	9.600	0.320
0.330	7.590	7.755	7.920	8.085	8.250	8.415	8.580	8.745	8.910	9.075	9.240	9.405	9.570	9.735	9.900	0.330
0.340	7.820	7.990	8.160	8.330	8.500	8.670	8.840	9.010	9.180	9.350	9.520	9.690	9.860	10.030	10.200	0.340
0.350	8.050	8.225	8.400	8.575	8.750	8.925	9.100	9.275	9.450	9.625	9.800	9.975	10.150	10.325	10.500	0.350
0.360	8.280	8.460	8.640	8.820	9.000	9.180	9.360	9.540	9.720	9.900	10.080	10.260	10.440	10.620	10.800	0.360
0.370	8.510	8.695	8.880	9.065	9.250	9.435	9.620	9.805	9.990	10.175	10.360	10.545	10.730	10.915	11.100	0.370
0.380	8.740	8.930	9.120	9.310	9.500	9.690	9.880	10.070	10.260	10.450	10.640	10.830	11.020	11.210	11.400	0.380
0.390	8.970	9.165	9.360	9.555	9.750	9.945	10.140	10.335	10.530	10.725	10.920	11.115	11.310	11.505	11.700	0.390
0.400	9.200	9.400	9.600	9.800	10.000	10.200	10.400	10.600	10.800	11.000	11.200	11.400	11.600	11.800	12.000	0.400
0.410	9.430	9.635	9.840	10.045	10.250	10.455	10.660	10.865	11.070	11.275	11.480	11.685	11.890	12.095	12.300	0.410
0.420	9.660	9.870	10.080	10.290	10.500	10.710	10.920	11.130	11.340	11.550	11.760	11.970	12.180	12.390	12.600	0.420
0.430	9.890	10.105	10.320	10.535	10.750	10.965	11.180	11.395	11.610	11.825	12.040	12.255	12.470	12.685	12.900	0.430
0.440	10.120	10.340	10.560	10.780	11.000	11.220	11.440	11.660	11.880	12.100	12.320	12.540	12.760	12.980	13.200	0.440
0.450	10.350	10.575	10.800	11.025	11.250	11.475	11.700	11.925	12.150	12.375	12.600	12.825	13.050	13.275	13.500	0.450
0.460	10.580	10.810	11.040	11.270	11.500	11.730	11.960	12.190	12.420	12.650	12.880	13.110	13.340	13.570	13.800	0.460
0.470	10.810	11.045	11.280	11.515	11.750	11.985	12.220	12.455	12.690	12.925	13.160	13.395	13.630	13.865	14.100	0.470
0.480	11.040	11.280	11.520	11.760	12.000	12.240	12.480	12.720	12.960	13.200	13.440	13.680	13.920	14.160	14.400	0.480
0.490	11.270	11.515	11.760	12.005	12.250	12.495	12.740	12.985	13.230	13.475	13.720	13.965	14.210	14.455	14.700	0.490
0.500	11.500	11.750	12.000	12.250	12.500	12.750	13.000	13.250	13.500	13.750	14.000	14.250	14.500	14.750	15.000	0.500
0.510	11.730	11.985	12.240	12.495	12.750	13.005	13.260	13.515	13.770	14.025	14.280	14.535	14.790	15.045	15.300	0.510
0.520	11.960	12.220	12.480	12.740	13.000	13.260	13.520	13.780	14.040	14.300	14.560	14.820	15.080	15.340	15.600	0.520
0.530	12.190	12.455	12.720	12.985	13.250	13.515	13.780	14.045	14.310	14.575	14.840	15.105	15.370	15.635	15.900	0.530
0.540	12.420	12.690	12.960	13.230	13.500	13.770	14.040	14.310	14.580	14.850	15.120	15.390	15.660	15.930	16.200	0.540
0.550	12.650	12.925	13.200	13.475	13.750	14.025	14.300	14.575	14.850	15.125	15.400	15.675	15.950	16.225	16.500	0.550
0.560	12.880	13.160	13.440	13.720	14.000	14.280	14.560	14.840	15.120	15.400	15.680	15.960	16.240	16.520	16.800	0.560
0.570	13.110	13.395	13.680	13.965	14.250	14.535	14.820	15.105	15.390	15.675	15.960	16.245	16.530	16.815	17.100	0.570
0.580	13.340	13.630	13.920	14.210	14.500	14.790	15.080	15.370	15.660	15.950	16.240	16.530	16.820	17.110	17.400	0.580
0.590	13.570	13.865	14.160	14.455	14.750	15.045	15.340	15.635	15.930	16.225	16.520	16.815	17.110	17.405	17.700	0.590
0.600	13.800	14.100	14.400	14.700	15.000	15.300	15.600	15.900	16.200	16.500	16.800	17.100	17.400	17.700	18.000	0.600
0.610	14.030	14.335	14.640	14.945	15.250	15.555	15.860	16.165	16.470	16.775	17.080	17.385	17.690	17.995	18.300	0.610
0.620	14.260	14.570	14.880	15.190	15.500	15.810	16.120	16.430	16.740	17.050	17.360	17.670	17.980	18.290	18.600	0.620
0.630	14.490	14.805	15.120	15.435	15.750	16.065	16.380	16.695	17.010	17.325	17.640	17.955	18.270	18.585	18.900	0.630
0.640	14.720	15.040	15.360	15.680	16.000	16.320	16.640	16.960	17.280	17.600	17.920	18.240	18.560	18.880	19.200	0.640
0.650	14.950	15.275	15.600	15.925	16.250	16.575	16.900	17.225	17.550	17.875	18.200	18.525	18.850	19.175	19.500	0.650
0.660	15.180	15.510	15.840	16.170	16.500	16.830	17.160	17.490	17.820	18.150	18.480	18.810	19.140	19.470	19.800	0.660
0.670	15.410	15.745	16.080	16.415	16.750	17.085	17.420	17.755	18.090	18.425	18.760	19.095	19.430	19.765	20.100	0.670
0.680	15.640	15.980	16.320	16.660	17.000	17.340	17.680	18.020	18.360	18.700	19.040	19.380	19.720	20.060	20.400	0.680
0.690	15.870	16.215	16.560	16.905	17.250	17.595	17.940	18.285	18.630	18.975	19.320	19.665	20.010	20.355	20.700	0.690
0.700	16.100	16.450	16.800	17.150	17.500	17.850	18.200	18.550	18.900	19.250	19.600	19.950	20.300	20.650	21.000	0.700
0.710	16.330	16.685	17.040	17.395	17.750	18.105	18.460	18.815	19.170	19.525	19.880	20.235	20.590	20.945	21.300	0.710
0.720	16.560	16.920	17.280	17.640	18.000	18.360	18.720	19.080	19.440	19.800	20.160	20.520	20.880	21.240	21.600	0.720
0.730	16.790	17.155	17.520	17.885	18.250	18.615	18.980	19.345	19.710	20.075	20.440	20.805	21.170	21.535	21.900	0.730
0.740	17.020	17.390	17.760	18.130	18.500	18.870	19.240	19.610	19.980	20.350	20.720	21.090	21.460	21.830	22.200	0.740
0.750	17.250	17.625	18.000	18.375	18.750	19.125	19.500	19.875	20.250	20.625	21.000	21.375	21.750	22.125	22.500	0.750
0.760	17.480	17.860	18.240	18.620	19.000	19.380	19.760	20.140	20.520	20.900	21.280	21.660	22.040	22.420	22.800	0.760
0.770	17.710	18.095	18.480	18.865	19.250	19.635	20.020	20.405	20.790	21.175	21.560	21.945	22.330	22.715	23.100	0.770
0.780	17.940	18.330	18.720	19.110	19.500	19.890	20.280	20.670	21.060	21.450	21.840	22.230	22.620	23.010	23.400	0.780
0.790	18.170	18.565	18.960	19.355	19.750	20.145	20.540	20.935	21.330	21.725	22.120	22.515	22.910	23.305	23.700	0.790
0.800	18.400	18.800	19.200	19.600	20.000	20.400	20.800	21.200	21.600	22.000	22.400	22.800	23.200	23.600	24.000	0.800
0.810	18.630	19.035	19.440	19.845	20.250	20.655	21.060	21.465	21.870	22.275	22.680	23.085	23.490	23.895	24.300	0.810
0.820	18.860	19.270	19.680	20.090	20.500	20.910	21.320	21.730	22.140	22.550	22.960	23.370	23.780	24.190	24.600	0.820
0.830	19.090	19.505	19.920	20.335	20.750	21.165	21.580	21.995	22.410	22.825	23.240	23.655	24.070	24.485	24.900	0.830
0.840	19.320	19.740	20.160	20.580	21.000	21.420	21.840	22.260	22.680	23.100	23.520	23.940	24.360	24.780	25.200	0.840
0.850	19.550	19.975	20.400	20.825	21.250	21.675	22.100	22.525	22.950	23.375	23.800	24.225	24.650	25.075	25.500	0.850
0.860	19.780	20.210	20.640	21.070	21.500	21.930	22.360	22.790	23.220	23.650	24.080	24.510	24.940	25.370	25.800	0.860
0.870	20.010	20.445	20.880	21.315	21.750	22.185	22.620	23.055	23.490	23.925	24.360	24.795	25.230	25.665	26.100	0.870
0.880	20.240	20.680	21.120	21.560	22.000	22.440	22.880	23.320	23.760	24.200	24.640	25.080	25.520	25.960	26.400	0.880
0.890	20.470	20.915	21.360	21.805	22.250	22.695	23.140	23.585	24.030	24.475	24.920	25.365	25.810	26.255	26.700	0.890
0.900	20.700	21.150	21.600	22.050	22.500	22.950	23.400	23.850	24.300	24.750	25.200	25.650	26.100	26.550	27.000	0.900
0.910	20.930	21.385	21.840	22.295	22.750	23.205	23.660	24.115	24.570	25.025	25.480	25.935	26.390	26.845	27.300	0.910
0.920	21.160	21.620	22.080	22.540	23.000	23.460	23.920	24.380	24.840	25.300	25.760	26.220	26.680	27.140	27.600	0.920
0.930	21.390	21.855	22.320	22.785	23.250	23.715	24.180	24.645	25.110	25.575	26.040	26.505	26.970	27.435	27.900	0.930
0.940	21.620	22.090	22.560	23.030	23.500	23.970	24.440	24.910	25.380	25.850	26.320	26.790	27.260	27.730	28.200	0.940
0.950	21.850	22.325	22.800	23.275	23.750	24.225	24.700	25.175	25.650	26.125	26.600	27.075	27.550	28.025	28.500	0.950
0.960	22.080	22.560	23.040	23.520	24.000	24.480	24.960	25.440	25.920	26.400	26.880	27.360	27.840	28.320	28.800	0.960
0.970	22.310	22.795	23.280	23.765	24.250	24.735	25.220	25.705	26.190	26.675	27.160	27.645	28.130	28.615	29.100	0.970
0.980	22.540	23.030	23.520	24.010	24.500	24.990	25.480	25.970	26.460	26.950	27.440	27.930	28.420	28.910	29.400	0.980
0.990	22.770	23.265	23.760	24.255	24.750	25.245	25.740	26.235	26.730	27.225	27.720	28.215	28.710	29.205	29.700	0.990
1.000	23.000	23.500	24.000	24.500	25.000	25.500	26.000	26.500	27.000	27.500	28.000	28.500	29.000	29.500	30.000	1.000

Gold Bullion Chart

Oz.	Per $10	$500.00	$520.00	$540.00	$560.00	$580.00	$600.00	$620.00	$640.00	$660.00	$680.00	$700.00	$720.00	$740.00	Oz.
0.001	0.01	0.50	0.52	0.54	0.56	0.58	0.60	0.62	0.64	0.66	0.68	0.70	0.72	0.74	0.001
0.002	0.02	1.00	1.04	1.08	1.12	1.16	1.20	1.24	1.28	1.32	1.36	1.40	1.44	1.48	0.002
0.003	0.03	1.50	1.56	1.62	1.68	1.74	1.80	1.86	1.92	1.98	2.04	2.10	2.16	2.22	0.003
0.004	0.04	2.00	2.08	2.16	2.24	2.32	2.40	2.48	2.56	2.64	2.72	2.80	2.88	2.96	0.004
0.005	0.05	2.50	2.60	2.70	2.80	2.90	3.00	3.10	3.20	3.30	3.40	3.50	3.60	3.70	0.005
0.006	0.06	3.00	3.12	3.24	3.36	3.48	3.60	3.72	3.84	3.96	4.08	4.20	4.32	4.44	0.006
0.007	0.07	3.50	3.64	3.78	3.92	4.06	4.20	4.34	4.48	4.62	4.76	4.90	5.04	5.18	0.007
0.008	0.08	4.00	4.16	4.32	4.48	4.64	4.80	4.96	5.12	5.28	5.44	5.60	5.76	5.92	0.008
0.009	0.09	4.50	4.68	4.86	5.04	5.22	5.40	5.58	5.76	5.94	6.12	6.30	6.48	6.66	0.009
0.010	0.10	5.00	5.20	5.40	5.60	5.80	6.00	6.20	6.40	6.60	6.80	7.00	7.20	7.40	0.010
0.020	0.20	10.00	10.40	10.80	11.20	11.60	12.00	12.40	12.80	13.20	13.60	14.00	14.40	14.80	0.020
0.030	0.30	15.00	15.60	16.20	16.80	17.40	18.00	18.60	19.20	19.80	20.40	21.00	21.60	22.20	0.030
0.040	0.40	20.00	20.80	21.60	22.40	23.20	24.00	24.80	25.60	26.40	27.20	28.00	28.80	29.60	0.040
0.050	0.50	25.00	26.00	27.00	28.00	29.00	30.00	31.00	32.00	33.00	34.00	35.00	36.00	37.00	0.050
0.060	0.60	30.00	31.20	32.40	33.60	34.80	36.00	37.20	38.40	39.60	40.80	42.00	43.20	44.40	0.060
0.070	0.70	35.00	36.40	37.80	39.20	40.60	42.00	43.40	44.80	46.20	47.60	49.00	50.40	51.80	0.070
0.080	0.80	40.00	41.60	43.20	44.80	46.40	48.00	49.60	51.20	52.80	54.40	56.00	57.60	59.20	0.080
0.090	0.90	45.00	46.80	48.60	50.40	52.20	54.00	55.80	57.60	59.40	61.20	63.00	64.80	66.60	0.090
0.100	1.00	50.00	52.00	54.00	56.00	58.00	60.00	62.00	64.00	66.00	68.00	70.00	72.00	74.00	0.100
0.110	1.10	55.00	57.20	59.40	61.60	63.80	66.00	68.20	70.40	72.60	74.80	77.00	79.20	81.40	0.110
0.120	1.20	60.00	62.40	64.80	67.20	69.60	72.00	74.40	76.80	79.20	81.60	84.00	86.40	88.80	0.120
0.130	1.30	65.00	67.60	70.20	72.80	75.40	78.00	80.60	83.20	85.80	88.40	91.00	93.60	96.20	0.130
0.140	1.40	70.00	72.80	75.60	78.40	81.20	84.00	86.80	89.60	92.40	95.20	98.00	100.80	103.60	0.140
0.150	1.50	75.00	78.00	81.00	84.00	87.00	90.00	93.00	96.00	99.00	102.00	105.00	108.00	111.00	0.150
0.160	1.60	80.00	83.20	86.40	89.60	92.80	96.00	99.20	102.40	105.60	108.80	112.00	115.20	118.40	0.160
0.170	1.70	85.00	88.40	91.80	95.20	98.60	102.00	105.40	108.80	112.20	115.60	119.00	122.40	125.80	0.170
0.180	1.80	90.00	93.60	97.20	100.80	104.40	108.00	111.60	115.20	118.80	122.40	126.00	129.60	133.20	0.180
0.190	1.90	95.00	98.80	102.60	106.40	110.20	114.00	117.80	121.60	125.40	129.20	133.00	136.80	140.60	0.190
0.200	2.00	100.00	104.00	108.00	112.00	116.00	120.00	124.00	128.00	132.00	136.00	140.00	144.00	148.00	0.200
0.210	2.10	105.00	109.20	113.40	117.60	121.80	126.00	130.20	134.40	138.60	142.80	147.00	151.20	155.40	0.210
0.220	2.20	110.00	114.40	118.80	123.20	127.60	132.00	136.40	140.80	145.20	149.60	154.00	158.40	162.80	0.220
0.230	2.30	115.00	119.60	124.20	128.80	133.40	138.00	142.60	147.20	151.80	156.40	161.00	165.60	170.20	0.230
0.240	2.40	120.00	124.80	129.60	134.40	139.20	144.00	148.80	153.60	158.40	163.20	168.00	172.80	177.60	0.240
0.250	2.50	125.00	130.00	135.00	140.00	145.00	150.00	155.00	160.00	165.00	170.00	175.00	180.00	185.00	0.250
0.260	2.60	130.00	135.20	140.40	145.60	150.80	156.00	161.20	166.40	171.60	176.80	182.00	187.20	192.40	0.260
0.270	2.70	135.00	140.40	145.80	151.20	156.60	162.00	167.40	172.80	178.20	183.60	189.00	194.40	199.80	0.270
0.280	2.80	140.00	145.60	151.20	156.80	162.40	168.00	173.60	179.20	184.80	190.40	196.00	201.60	207.20	0.280
0.290	2.90	145.00	150.80	156.60	162.40	168.20	174.00	179.80	185.60	191.40	197.20	203.00	208.80	214.60	0.290
0.300	3.00	150.00	156.00	162.00	168.00	174.00	180.00	186.00	192.00	198.00	204.00	210.00	216.00	222.00	0.300
0.310	3.10	155.00	161.20	167.40	173.60	179.80	186.00	192.20	198.40	204.60	210.80	217.00	223.20	229.40	0.310
0.320	3.20	160.00	166.40	172.80	179.20	185.60	192.00	198.40	204.80	211.20	217.60	224.00	230.40	236.80	0.320
0.330	3.30	165.00	171.60	178.20	184.80	191.40	198.00	204.60	211.20	217.80	224.40	231.00	237.60	244.20	0.330
0.340	3.40	170.00	176.80	183.60	190.40	197.20	204.00	210.80	217.60	224.40	231.20	238.00	244.80	251.60	0.340
0.350	3.50	175.00	182.00	189.00	196.00	203.00	210.00	217.00	224.00	231.00	238.00	245.00	252.00	259.00	0.350
0.360	3.60	180.00	187.20	194.40	201.60	208.80	216.00	223.20	230.40	237.60	244.80	252.00	259.20	266.40	0.360
0.370	3.70	185.00	192.40	199.80	207.20	214.60	222.00	229.40	236.80	244.20	251.60	259.00	266.40	273.80	0.370
0.380	3.80	190.00	197.60	205.20	212.80	220.40	228.00	235.60	243.20	250.80	258.40	266.00	273.60	281.20	0.380
0.390	3.90	195.00	202.80	210.60	218.40	226.20	234.00	241.80	249.60	257.40	265.20	273.00	280.80	288.60	0.390
0.400	4.00	200.00	208.00	216.00	224.00	232.00	240.00	248.00	256.00	264.00	272.00	280.00	288.00	296.00	0.400
0.410	4.10	205.00	213.20	221.40	229.60	237.80	246.00	254.20	262.40	270.60	278.80	287.00	295.20	303.40	0.410
0.420	4.20	210.00	218.40	226.80	235.20	243.60	252.00	260.40	268.80	277.20	285.60	294.00	302.40	310.80	0.420
0.430	4.30	215.00	223.60	232.20	240.80	249.40	258.00	266.60	275.20	283.80	292.40	301.00	309.60	318.20	0.430
0.440	4.40	220.00	228.80	237.60	246.40	255.20	264.00	272.80	281.60	290.40	299.20	308.00	316.80	325.60	0.440
0.450	4.50	225.00	234.00	243.00	252.00	261.00	270.00	279.00	288.00	297.00	306.00	315.00	324.00	333.00	0.450
0.460	4.60	230.00	239.20	248.40	257.60	266.80	276.00	285.20	294.40	303.60	312.80	322.00	331.20	340.40	0.460
0.470	4.70	235.00	244.40	253.80	263.20	272.60	282.00	291.40	300.80	310.20	319.60	329.00	338.40	347.80	0.470
0.480	4.80	240.00	249.60	259.20	268.80	278.40	288.00	297.60	307.20	316.80	326.40	336.00	345.60	355.20	0.480
0.490	4.90	245.00	254.80	264.60	274.40	284.20	294.00	303.80	313.60	323.40	333.20	343.00	352.80	362.60	0.490
0.500	5.00	250.00	260.00	270.00	280.00	290.00	300.00	310.00	320.00	330.00	340.00	350.00	360.00	370.00	0.500
0.510	5.10	255.00	265.20	275.40	285.60	295.80	306.00	316.20	326.40	336.60	346.80	357.00	367.20	377.40	0.510
0.520	5.20	260.00	270.40	280.80	291.20	301.60	312.00	322.40	332.80	343.20	353.60	364.00	374.40	384.80	0.520
0.530	5.30	265.00	275.60	286.20	296.80	307.40	318.00	328.60	339.20	349.80	360.40	371.00	381.60	392.20	0.530
0.540	5.40	270.00	280.80	291.60	302.40	313.20	324.00	334.80	345.60	356.40	367.20	378.00	388.80	399.60	0.540
0.550	5.50	275.00	286.00	297.00	308.00	319.00	330.00	341.00	352.00	363.00	374.00	385.00	396.00	407.00	0.550
0.560	5.60	280.00	291.20	302.40	313.60	324.80	336.00	347.20	358.40	369.60	380.80	392.00	403.20	414.40	0.560
0.570	5.70	285.00	296.40	307.80	319.20	330.60	342.00	353.40	364.80	376.20	387.60	399.00	410.40	421.80	0.570
0.580	5.80	290.00	301.60	313.20	324.80	336.40	348.00	359.60	371.20	382.80	394.40	406.00	417.60	429.20	0.580
0.590	5.90	295.00	306.80	318.60	330.40	342.20	354.00	365.80	377.60	389.40	401.20	413.00	424.80	436.60	0.590
0.600	6.00	300.00	312.00	324.00	336.00	348.00	360.00	372.00	384.00	396.00	408.00	420.00	432.00	444.00	0.600
0.610	6.10	305.00	317.20	329.40	341.60	353.80	366.00	378.20	390.40	402.60	414.80	427.00	439.20	451.40	0.610
0.620	6.20	310.00	322.40	334.80	347.20	359.60	372.00	384.40	396.80	409.20	421.60	434.00	446.40	458.80	0.620
0.630	6.30	315.00	327.60	340.20	352.80	365.40	378.00	390.60	403.20	415.80	428.40	441.00	453.60	466.20	0.630
0.640	6.40	320.00	332.80	345.60	358.40	371.20	384.00	396.80	409.60	422.40	435.20	448.00	460.80	473.60	0.640
0.650	6.50	325.00	338.00	351.00	364.00	377.00	390.00	403.00	416.00	429.00	442.00	455.00	468.00	481.00	0.650
0.660	6.60	330.00	343.20	356.40	369.60	382.80	396.00	409.20	422.40	435.60	448.80	462.00	475.20	488.40	0.660
0.670	6.70	335.00	348.40	361.80	375.20	388.60	402.00	415.40	428.80	442.20	455.60	469.00	482.40	495.80	0.670
0.680	6.80	340.00	353.60	367.20	380.80	394.40	408.00	421.60	435.20	448.80	462.40	476.00	489.60	503.20	0.680
0.690	6.90	345.00	358.80	372.60	386.40	400.20	414.00	427.80	441.60	455.40	469.20	483.00	496.80	510.60	0.690
0.700	7.00	350.00	364.00	378.00	392.00	406.00	420.00	434.00	448.00	462.00	476.00	490.00	504.00	518.00	0.700
0.710	7.10	355.00	369.20	383.40	397.60	411.80	426.00	440.20	454.40	468.60	482.80	497.00	511.20	525.40	0.710
0.720	7.20	360.00	374.40	388.80	403.20	417.60	432.00	446.40	460.80	475.20	489.60	504.00	518.40	532.80	0.720
0.730	7.30	365.00	379.60	394.20	408.80	423.40	438.00	452.60	467.20	481.80	496.40	511.00	525.60	540.20	0.730
0.740	7.40	370.00	384.80	399.60	414.40	429.20	444.00	458.80	473.60	488.40	503.20	518.00	532.80	547.60	0.740
0.750	7.50	375.00	390.00	405.00	420.00	435.00	450.00	465.00	480.00	495.00	510.00	525.00	540.00	555.00	0.750
0.760	7.60	380.00	395.20	410.40	425.60	440.80	456.00	471.20	486.40	501.60	516.80	532.00	547.20	562.40	0.760
0.770	7.70	385.00	400.40	415.80	431.20	446.60	462.00	477.40	492.80	508.20	523.60	539.00	554.40	569.80	0.770
0.780	7.80	390.00	405.60	421.20	436.80	452.40	468.00	483.60	499.20	514.80	530.40	546.00	561.60	577.20	0.780
0.790	7.90	395.00	410.80	426.60	442.40	458.20	474.00	489.80	505.60	521.40	537.20	553.00	568.80	584.60	0.790
0.800	8.00	400.00	416.00	432.00	448.00	464.00	480.00	496.00	512.00	528.00	544.00	560.00	576.00	592.00	0.800
0.810	8.10	405.00	421.20	437.40	453.60	469.80	486.00	502.20	518.40	534.60	550.80	567.00	583.20	599.40	0.810
0.820	8.20	410.00	426.40	442.80	459.20	475.60	492.00	508.40	524.80	541.20	557.60	574.00	590.40	606.80	0.820
0.830	8.30	415.00	431.60	448.20	464.80	481.40	498.00	514.60	531.20	547.80	564.40	581.00	597.60	614.20	0.830
0.840	8.40	420.00	436.80	453.60	470.40	487.20	504.00	520.80	537.60	554.40	571.20	588.00	604.80	621.60	0.840
0.850	8.50	425.00	442.00	459.00	476.00	493.00	510.00	527.00	544.00	561.00	578.00	595.00	612.00	629.00	0.850
0.860	8.60	430.00	447.20	464.40	481.60	498.80	516.00	533.20	550.40	567.60	584.80	602.00	619.20	636.40	0.860
0.870	8.70	435.00	452.40	469.80	487.20	504.60	522.00	539.40	556.80	574.20	591.60	609.00	626.40	643.80	0.870
0.880	8.80	440.00	457.60	475.20	492.80	510.40	528.00	545.60	563.20	580.80	598.40	616.00	633.60	651.20	0.880
0.890	8.90	445.00	462.80	480.60	498.40	516.20	534.00	551.80	569.60	587.40	605.20	623.00	640.80	658.60	0.890
0.900	9.00	450.00	468.00	486.00	504.00	522.00	540.00	558.00	576.00	594.00	612.00	630.00	648.00	666.00	0.900
0.910	9.10	455.00	473.20	491.40	509.60	527.80	546.00	564.20	582.40	600.60	618.80	637.00	655.20	673.40	0.910
0.920	9.20	460.00	478.40	496.80	515.20	533.60	552.00	570.40	588.80	607.20	625.60	644.00	662.40	680.80	0.920
0.930	9.30	465.00	483.60	502.20	520.80	539.40	558.00	576.60	595.20	613.80	632.40	651.00	669.60	688.20	0.930
0.940	9.40	470.00	488.80	507.60	526.40	545.20	564.00	582.80	601.60	620.40	639.20	658.00	676.80	695.60	0.940
0.950	9.50	475.00	494.00	513.00	532.00	551.00	570.00	589.00	608.00	627.00	646.00	665.00	684.00	703.00	0.950
0.960	9.60	480.00	499.20	518.40	537.60	556.80	576.00	595.20	614.40	633.60	652.80	672.00	691.20	710.40	0.960
0.970	9.70	485.00	504.40	523.80	543.20	562.60	582.00	601.40	620.80	640.20	659.60	679.00	698.40	717.80	0.970
0.980	9.80	490.00	509.60	529.20	548.80	568.40	588.00	607.60	627.20	646.80	666.40	686.00	705.60	725.20	0.980
0.990	9.90	495.00	514.80	534.60	554.40	574.20	594.00	613.80	633.60	653.40	673.20	693.00	712.80	732.60	0.990
1.000	10.00	500.00	520.00	540.00	560.00	580.00	600.00	620.00	640.00	660.00	680.00	700.00	720.00	740.00	1.000

Gold Bullion Chart

Oz.	$760.00	$780.00	$800.00	$820.00	$840.00	$860.00	$880.00	$900.00	$920.00	$940.00	$960.00	$980.00	$1000.00	Per $10	Oz.
0.001	0.76	0.78	0.80	0.82	0.84	0.86	0.88	0.90	0.92	0.94	0.96	0.98	1.00	0.01	0.001
0.002	1.52	1.56	1.60	1.64	1.68	1.72	1.76	1.80	1.84	1.88	1.92	1.96	2.00	0.02	0.002
0.003	2.28	2.34	2.40	2.46	2.52	2.58	2.64	2.70	2.76	2.82	2.88	2.94	3.00	0.03	0.003
0.004	3.04	3.12	3.20	3.28	3.36	3.44	3.52	3.60	3.68	3.76	3.84	3.92	4.00	0.04	0.004
0.005	3.80	3.90	4.00	4.10	4.20	4.30	4.40	4.50	4.60	4.70	4.80	4.90	5.00	0.05	0.005
0.006	4.56	4.68	4.80	4.92	5.04	5.16	5.28	5.40	5.52	5.64	5.76	5.88	6.00	0.06	0.006
0.007	5.32	5.46	5.60	5.74	5.88	6.02	6.16	6.30	6.44	6.58	6.72	6.86	7.00	0.07	0.007
0.008	6.08	6.24	6.40	6.56	6.72	6.88	7.04	7.20	7.36	7.52	7.68	7.84	8.00	0.08	0.008
0.009	6.84	7.02	7.20	7.38	7.56	7.74	7.92	8.10	8.28	8.46	8.64	8.82	9.00	0.09	0.009
0.010	7.60	7.80	8.00	8.20	8.40	8.60	8.80	9.00	9.20	9.40	9.60	9.80	10.00	0.10	0.010
0.020	15.20	15.60	16.00	16.40	16.80	17.20	17.60	18.00	18.40	18.80	19.20	19.60	20.00	0.20	0.020
0.030	22.80	23.40	24.00	24.60	25.20	25.80	26.40	27.00	27.60	28.20	28.80	29.40	30.00	0.30	0.030
0.040	30.40	31.20	32.00	32.80	33.60	34.40	35.20	36.00	36.80	37.60	38.40	39.20	40.00	0.40	0.040
0.050	38.00	39.00	40.00	41.00	42.00	43.00	44.00	45.00	46.00	47.00	48.00	49.00	50.00	0.50	0.050
0.060	45.60	46.80	48.00	49.20	50.40	51.60	52.80	54.00	55.20	56.40	57.60	58.80	60.00	0.60	0.060
0.070	53.20	54.60	56.00	57.40	58.80	60.20	61.60	63.00	64.40	65.80	67.20	68.60	70.00	0.70	0.070
0.080	60.80	62.40	64.00	65.60	67.20	68.80	70.40	72.00	73.60	75.20	76.80	78.40	80.00	0.80	0.080
0.090	68.40	70.20	72.00	73.80	75.60	77.40	79.20	81.00	82.80	84.60	86.40	88.20	90.00	0.90	0.090
0.100	76.00	78.00	80.00	82.00	84.00	86.00	88.00	90.00	92.00	94.00	96.00	98.00	100.00	1.00	0.100
0.110	83.60	85.80	88.00	90.20	92.40	94.60	96.80	99.00	101.20	103.40	105.60	107.80	110.00	1.10	0.110
0.120	91.20	93.60	96.00	98.40	100.80	103.20	105.60	108.00	110.40	112.80	115.20	117.60	120.00	1.20	0.120
0.130	98.80	101.40	104.00	106.60	109.20	111.80	114.40	117.00	119.60	122.20	124.80	127.40	130.00	1.30	0.130
0.140	106.40	109.20	112.00	114.80	117.60	120.40	123.20	126.00	128.80	131.60	134.40	137.20	140.00	1.40	0.140
0.150	114.00	117.00	120.00	123.00	126.00	129.00	132.00	135.00	138.00	141.00	144.00	147.00	150.00	1.50	0.150
0.160	121.60	124.80	128.00	131.20	134.40	137.60	140.80	144.00	147.20	150.40	153.60	156.80	160.00	1.60	0.160
0.170	129.20	132.60	136.00	139.40	142.80	146.20	149.60	153.00	156.40	159.80	163.20	166.60	170.00	1.70	0.170
0.180	136.80	140.40	144.00	147.60	151.20	154.80	158.40	162.00	165.60	169.20	172.80	176.40	180.00	1.80	0.180
0.190	144.40	148.20	152.00	155.80	159.60	163.40	167.20	171.00	174.80	178.60	182.40	186.20	190.00	1.90	0.190
0.200	152.00	156.00	160.00	164.00	168.00	172.00	176.00	180.00	184.00	188.00	192.00	196.00	200.00	2.00	0.200
0.210	159.60	163.80	168.00	172.20	176.40	180.60	184.80	189.00	193.20	197.40	201.60	205.80	210.00	2.10	0.210
0.220	167.20	171.60	176.00	180.40	184.80	189.20	193.60	198.00	202.40	206.80	211.20	215.60	220.00	2.20	0.220
0.230	174.80	179.40	184.00	188.60	193.20	197.80	202.40	207.00	211.60	216.20	220.80	225.40	230.00	2.30	0.230
0.240	182.40	187.20	192.00	196.80	201.60	206.40	211.20	216.00	220.80	225.60	230.40	235.20	240.00	2.40	0.240
0.250	190.00	195.00	200.00	205.00	210.00	215.00	220.00	225.00	230.00	235.00	240.00	245.00	250.00	2.50	0.250
0.260	197.60	202.80	208.00	213.20	218.40	223.60	228.80	234.00	239.20	244.40	249.60	254.80	260.00	2.60	0.260
0.270	205.20	210.60	216.00	221.40	226.80	232.20	237.60	243.00	248.40	253.80	259.20	264.60	270.00	2.70	0.270
0.280	212.80	218.40	224.00	229.60	235.20	240.80	246.40	252.00	257.60	263.20	268.80	274.40	280.00	2.80	0.280
0.290	220.40	226.20	232.00	237.80	243.60	249.40	255.20	261.00	266.80	272.60	278.40	284.20	290.00	2.90	0.290
0.300	228.00	234.00	240.00	246.00	252.00	258.00	264.00	270.00	276.00	282.00	288.00	294.00	300.00	3.00	0.300
0.310	235.60	241.80	248.00	254.20	260.40	266.60	272.80	279.00	285.20	291.40	297.60	303.80	310.00	3.10	0.310
0.320	243.20	249.60	256.00	262.40	268.80	275.20	281.60	288.00	294.40	300.80	307.20	313.60	320.00	3.20	0.320
0.330	250.80	257.40	264.00	270.60	277.20	283.80	290.40	297.00	303.60	310.20	316.80	323.40	330.00	3.30	0.330
0.340	258.40	265.20	272.00	278.80	285.60	292.40	299.20	306.00	312.80	319.60	326.40	333.20	340.00	3.40	0.340
0.350	266.00	273.00	280.00	287.00	294.00	301.00	308.00	315.00	322.00	329.00	336.00	343.00	350.00	3.50	0.350
0.360	273.60	280.80	288.00	295.20	302.40	309.60	316.80	324.00	331.20	338.40	345.60	352.80	360.00	3.60	0.360
0.370	281.20	288.60	296.00	303.40	310.80	318.20	325.60	333.00	340.40	347.80	355.20	362.60	370.00	3.70	0.370
0.380	288.80	296.40	304.00	311.60	319.20	326.80	334.40	342.00	349.60	357.20	364.80	372.40	380.00	3.80	0.380
0.390	296.40	304.20	312.00	319.80	327.60	335.40	343.20	351.00	358.80	366.60	374.40	382.20	390.00	3.90	0.390
0.400	304.00	312.00	320.00	328.00	336.00	344.00	352.00	360.00	368.00	376.00	384.00	392.00	400.00	4.00	0.400
0.410	311.60	319.80	328.00	336.20	344.40	352.60	360.80	369.00	377.20	385.40	393.60	401.80	410.00	4.10	0.410
0.420	319.20	327.60	336.00	344.40	352.80	361.20	369.60	378.00	386.40	394.80	403.20	411.60	420.00	4.20	0.420
0.430	326.80	335.40	344.00	352.60	361.20	369.80	378.40	387.00	395.60	404.20	412.80	421.40	430.00	4.30	0.430
0.440	334.40	343.20	352.00	360.80	369.60	378.40	387.20	396.00	404.80	413.60	422.40	431.20	440.00	4.40	0.440
0.450	342.00	351.00	360.00	369.00	378.00	387.00	396.00	405.00	414.00	423.00	432.00	441.00	450.00	4.50	0.450
0.460	349.60	358.80	368.00	377.20	386.40	395.60	404.80	414.00	423.20	432.40	441.60	450.80	460.00	4.60	0.460
0.470	357.20	366.60	376.00	385.40	394.80	404.20	413.60	423.00	432.40	441.80	451.20	460.60	470.00	4.70	0.470
0.480	364.80	374.40	384.00	393.60	403.20	412.80	422.40	432.00	441.60	451.20	460.80	470.40	480.00	4.80	0.480
0.490	372.40	382.20	392.00	401.80	411.60	421.40	431.20	441.00	450.80	460.60	470.40	480.20	490.00	4.90	0.490
0.500	380.00	390.00	400.00	410.00	420.00	430.00	440.00	450.00	460.00	470.00	480.00	490.00	500.00	5.00	0.500
0.510	387.60	397.80	408.00	418.20	428.40	438.60	448.80	459.00	469.20	479.40	489.60	499.80	510.00	5.10	0.510
0.520	395.20	405.60	416.00	426.40	436.80	447.20	457.60	468.00	478.40	488.80	499.20	509.60	520.00	5.20	0.520
0.530	402.80	413.40	424.00	434.60	445.20	455.80	466.40	477.00	487.60	498.20	508.80	519.40	530.00	5.30	0.530
0.540	410.40	421.20	432.00	442.80	453.60	464.40	475.20	486.00	496.80	507.60	518.40	529.20	540.00	5.40	0.540
0.550	418.00	429.00	440.00	451.00	462.00	473.00	484.00	495.00	506.00	517.00	528.00	539.00	550.00	5.50	0.550
0.560	425.60	436.80	448.00	459.20	470.40	481.60	492.80	504.00	515.20	526.40	537.60	548.80	560.00	5.60	0.560
0.570	433.20	444.60	456.00	467.40	478.80	490.20	501.60	513.00	524.40	535.80	547.20	558.60	570.00	5.70	0.570
0.580	440.80	452.40	464.00	475.60	487.20	498.80	510.40	522.00	533.60	545.20	556.80	568.40	580.00	5.80	0.580
0.590	448.40	460.20	472.00	483.80	495.60	507.40	519.20	531.00	542.80	554.60	566.40	578.20	590.00	5.90	0.590
0.600	456.00	468.00	480.00	492.00	504.00	516.00	528.00	540.00	552.00	564.00	576.00	588.00	600.00	6.00	0.600
0.610	463.60	475.80	488.00	500.20	512.40	524.60	536.80	549.00	561.20	573.40	585.60	597.80	610.00	6.10	0.610
0.620	471.20	483.60	496.00	508.40	520.80	533.20	545.60	558.00	570.40	582.80	595.20	607.60	620.00	6.20	0.620
0.630	478.80	491.40	504.00	516.60	529.20	541.80	554.40	567.00	579.60	592.20	604.80	617.40	630.00	6.30	0.630
0.640	486.40	499.20	512.00	524.80	537.60	550.40	563.20	576.00	588.80	601.60	614.40	627.20	640.00	6.40	0.640
0.650	494.00	507.00	520.00	533.00	546.00	559.00	572.00	585.00	598.00	611.00	624.00	637.00	650.00	6.50	0.650
0.660	501.60	514.80	528.00	541.20	554.40	567.60	580.80	594.00	607.20	620.40	633.60	646.80	660.00	6.60	0.660
0.670	509.20	522.60	536.00	549.40	562.80	576.20	589.60	603.00	616.40	629.80	643.20	656.60	670.00	6.70	0.670
0.680	516.80	530.40	544.00	557.60	571.20	584.80	598.40	612.00	625.60	639.20	652.80	666.40	680.00	6.80	0.680
0.690	524.40	538.20	552.00	565.80	579.60	593.40	607.20	621.00	634.80	648.60	662.40	676.20	690.00	6.90	0.690
0.700	532.00	546.00	560.00	574.00	588.00	602.00	616.00	630.00	644.00	658.00	672.00	686.00	700.00	7.00	0.700
0.710	539.60	553.80	568.00	582.20	596.40	610.60	624.80	639.00	653.20	667.40	681.60	695.80	710.00	7.10	0.710
0.720	547.20	561.60	576.00	590.40	604.80	619.20	633.60	648.00	662.40	676.80	691.20	705.60	720.00	7.20	0.720
0.730	554.80	569.40	584.00	598.60	613.20	627.80	642.40	657.00	671.60	686.20	700.80	715.40	730.00	7.30	0.730
0.740	562.40	577.20	592.00	606.80	621.60	636.40	651.20	666.00	680.80	695.60	710.40	725.20	740.00	7.40	0.740
0.750	570.00	585.00	600.00	615.00	630.00	645.00	660.00	675.00	690.00	705.00	720.00	735.00	750.00	7.50	0.750
0.760	577.60	592.80	608.00	623.20	638.40	653.60	668.80	684.00	699.20	714.40	729.60	744.80	760.00	7.60	0.760
0.770	585.20	600.60	616.00	631.40	646.80	662.20	677.60	693.00	708.40	723.80	739.20	754.60	770.00	7.70	0.770
0.780	592.80	608.40	624.00	639.60	655.20	670.80	686.40	702.00	717.60	733.20	748.80	764.40	780.00	7.80	0.780
0.790	600.40	616.20	632.00	647.80	663.60	679.40	695.20	711.00	726.80	742.60	758.40	774.20	790.00	7.90	0.790
0.800	608.00	624.00	640.00	656.00	672.00	688.00	704.00	720.00	736.00	752.00	768.00	784.00	800.00	8.00	0.800
0.810	615.60	631.80	648.00	664.20	680.40	696.60	712.80	729.00	745.20	761.40	777.60	793.80	810.00	8.10	0.810
0.820	623.20	639.60	656.00	672.40	688.80	705.20	721.60	738.00	754.40	770.80	787.20	803.60	820.00	8.20	0.820
0.830	630.80	647.40	664.00	680.60	697.20	713.80	730.40	747.00	763.60	780.20	796.80	813.40	830.00	8.30	0.830
0.840	638.40	655.20	672.00	688.80	705.60	722.40	739.20	756.00	772.80	789.60	806.40	823.20	840.00	8.40	0.840
0.850	646.00	663.00	680.00	697.00	714.00	731.00	748.00	765.00	782.00	799.00	816.00	833.00	850.00	8.50	0.850
0.860	653.60	670.80	688.00	705.20	722.40	739.60	756.80	774.00	791.20	808.40	825.60	842.80	860.00	8.60	0.860
0.870	661.20	678.60	696.00	713.40	730.80	748.20	765.60	783.00	800.40	817.80	835.20	852.60	870.00	8.70	0.870
0.880	668.80	686.40	704.00	721.60	739.20	756.80	774.40	792.00	809.60	827.20	844.80	862.40	880.00	8.80	0.880
0.890	676.40	694.20	712.00	729.80	747.60	765.40	783.20	801.00	818.80	836.60	854.40	872.20	890.00	8.90	0.890
0.900	684.00	702.00	720.00	738.00	756.00	774.00	792.00	810.00	828.00	846.00	864.00	882.00	900.00	9.00	0.900
0.910	691.60	709.80	728.00	746.20	764.40	782.60	800.80	819.00	837.20	855.40	873.60	891.80	910.00	9.10	0.910
0.920	699.20	717.60	736.00	754.40	772.80	791.20	809.60	828.00	846.40	864.80	883.20	901.60	920.00	9.20	0.920
0.930	706.80	725.40	744.00	762.60	781.20	799.80	818.40	837.00	855.60	874.20	892.80	911.40	930.00	9.30	0.930
0.940	714.40	733.20	752.00	770.80	789.60	808.40	827.20	846.00	864.80	883.60	902.40	921.20	940.00	9.40	0.940
0.950	722.00	741.00	760.00	779.00	798.00	817.00	836.00	855.00	874.00	893.00	912.00	931.00	950.00	9.50	0.950
0.960	729.60	748.80	768.00	787.20	806.40	825.60	844.80	864.00	883.20	902.40	921.60	940.80	960.00	9.60	0.960
0.970	737.20	756.60	776.00	795.40	814.80	834.20	853.60	873.00	892.40	911.80	931.20	950.60	970.00	9.70	0.970
0.980	744.80	764.40	784.00	803.60	823.20	842.80	862.40	882.00	901.60	921.20	940.80	960.40	980.00	9.80	0.980
0.990	752.40	772.20	792.00	811.80	831.60	851.40	871.20	891.00	910.80	930.60	950.40	970.20	990.00	9.90	0.990
1.000	760.00	780.00	800.00	820.00	840.00	860.00	880.00	900.00	920.00	940.00	960.00	980.00	1000.00	10.00	1.000

CHART OF COIN SIZES BY MILLIMETERS

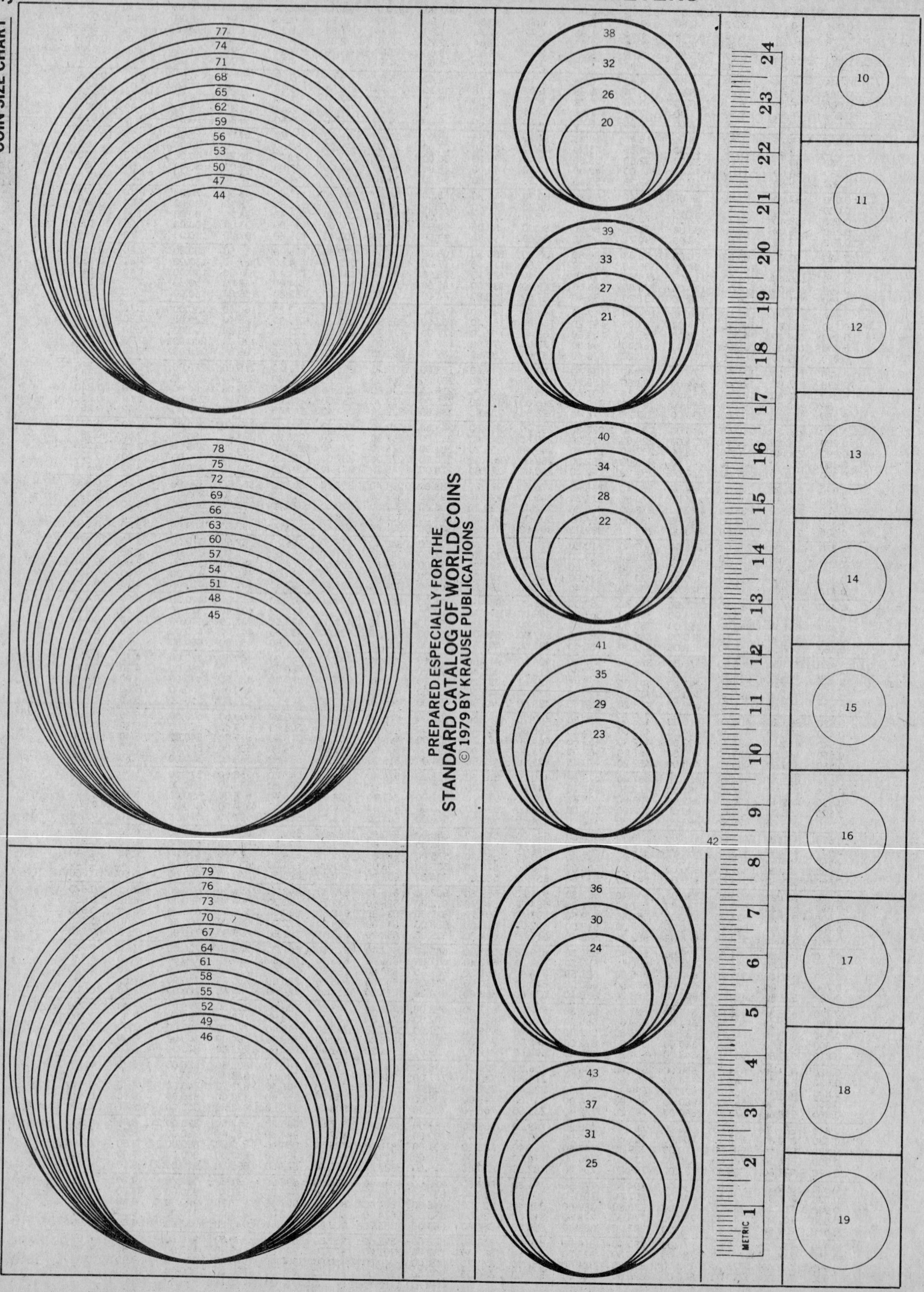

77
74
71
68
65
62
59
56
53
50
47
44

78
75
72
69
66
63
60
57
54
51
48
45

79
76
73
70
67
64
61
58
55
52
49
46

PREPARED ESPECIALLY FOR THE
STANDARD CATALOG OF WORLD COINS

38
32
26
20

39
33
27
21

40
34
28
22

41
35
29
23

42
36
30
24

43
37
31
25

METRIC 1 2 3 4 5 6 7 8 9 10 11 12 13 14 15 16 17 18 19 20 21 22 23 24

10
11
12
13
14
15
16
17
18
19

PHOTOGRAPHS

As an aid to minimizing the problems involved in coin identification every effort has been made to acquire and present actual size photographs of each type listed. Both obverse and reverse are illustrated, except in instances where a change in coinage type is restricted to just the obverse or reverse and the coin has a diameter of 30mm or larger, in which situations only the side required for identification of the type is generally illustrated. All coin type photographs up to 60mm diameter are illustrated actual size; to the nearest 1/2mm up to 25mm, and to the nearest 1mm thereafter. Coins larger than 60mm diameter are illustrated in reduced size, with the actual size noted thereunder. Where slight changes in size are important to coin type identification, actual millimeter measurements are stated.

MINT MARKS

The mints of issue for many of the coin issues listed in this catalog are indicated by the presence of distinctive, but frequently inconspicuously placed mintmarks. Their presence on the actual coins is usually noted by incorporating an appropriate designation in the listings.

The date listings generally indicate the presence of a mint letter(s) on a given coin by incorporating it adjoining the date; i.e., 1950D or 1927R, as in the German and Italian listings. The presence of mint and/or mintmasters privy marks on a coin in non-letter form is indicated by the incorporation of a mint letter in lower case within parenthesis ( ) adjoining the date listing; i.e., 1927(a) or 1948(a) as in the French and French territorial listings.

A listing format by mints of issue has been adopted for some countries — examples include Spain, South and Central American countries — where that cataloging style allows for a more logical arrangement. In these instances the name of the mint and its mintmark letter(s) is presented at the beginning of each series of date listings.

Where listings incorporate mintmaster initials, they are always presented in caps separated from the date; i.e., 1850 MF, as will be found on the coins of Mexico. The different mintmark and mintmaster letters found on the coins of any country, state or city of issue are always defined at the beginning of the listings.

COIN vs. MEDAL ALIGNMENT

Coins are traditionally struck with the obverse and reverse dies aligned at a rotation of 180 degrees, one to the other; i.e., if you hold a coin for vertical viewing with the obverse designs aligned upright and the index finger and thumb at the top and bottom when it is rotated left to right for viewing the reverse, the latter will appear upside down. Such a piece is termed to have been struck in "coin rotation." Some coins are struck with the obverse and reverse designs mated on an alignment of zero or 360 degrees; i.e., if such a piece is held and rotated as described, the reverse will appear at the proper attitude for viewing. This is the alignment which is generally observed in the striking of medals, and for that reason coins presented in this manner are termed to have been struck in "medal rotation." In some instances certain coin issues have been struck to both alignment standards, creating interesting collectible varieties which will be found noted in some listings.

MINTAGES

The quantities minted of each date are indicated where that information is available, with quantiites generally stated in millions, rounded off to the nearest 10,000 pieces. On quantities of a few thousand or less, actual mintages are generally indicated, a fact that can be determined by the presence of a comma, rather than decimal point, in the stated figure. The following mintage conversion formulas have been observed:

10,000,000 —	10.000	9,999 — 9,999	
1,000,000 —	1.000	1,000 — 1,000	
100,000 —	.100	842 — 842 pcs.)	
10,000 —	.010	27 — 27 pcs.)	— Pieces

RESTRIKES AND FAKES

Deceptive restrike and counterfeit examples exist of some coins issues, the latter in both contemporary and modern versions. Where possible the existence of restrikes is noted. Warnings are also incorporated in instances where particularly deceptive counterfeits are known to exist. Collectors who are uncertain about the authenticity of a scarce coin held in their collection, or available for purchase, should take the precaution of having it tested by the American Numismatic Association Certification Service, 818 North Cascade, Colorado Springs, CO 80903. Their reasonably priced certification tests are widely recognized by collectors and dealers alike.

TRADE COINS

The period from approximately 1850 to 1940 found a number of nations, particularly the European colonial powers and commercial traders, minting trade coins, the intended purpose of which was to facilitate trade with the local populace in Africa, the Arab countries, the Indian sub-continent, Southeast Asia and the Far East. These coins generally passed from hand to hand at a value based on the weight and quality of their silver and gold contents in preference to any consideration of denomination. Included are such issues as the silver British Trade Dollar and the Gold Ducat issues of the German States, Austria, Hungary and the Netherlands, which will be found listed in special categories at the end of the homeland issues.

HOMELAND TYPES

The era of global empires established by Europe's colonial powers found the homeland coinage types, particularly in the case of Great Britain, of specific dates and denominations being minted exclusively or primarily for circulation in certain overseas possessions. Identical in design and indistinguishable except for the date of issue from the homeland coinages, these issues also circulated freely, if on a somewhat restricted basis, in other colonies, ports of call and even the homeland.

In a departure from established cataloging practice, which incorporated listings of these issues under the designated area of issue, in this volume they will be found incorporated under the homelands. Appropriate references note the intended areas of distribution for these sometimes puzzling issues, which range in date from the early 1800s until after World War II.

NON-CIRCULATING LEGAL TENDER COINS

Coins of non-circulating legal tender (NCLT) origin will be found individually listed and integrated by denomination into the regular listings for each country, or grouped as essais, proofs or pieforts, along with mint and proof sets at the end of national listings as appropriate. These issues fall outside the customary definitions of circulating legal tender, coin-of-the-realm issues, but all were created and marketed by or under the authorization of agencies of sovereign governments expressly for collector purposes. These are primarily individual coins and sets of a commemorative nature which generally are released at prices substantially in excess of their face values, and often do not have counterparts in the same or a base metal which were released to circulation.

Eight basic criteria have been applied in considering the assignment of coins other than regular issue mint and proof sets to the NCLT category. They are: 1) The metallic content of the coin is of greater value than its denominational value. 2) Both proof and "circulation," if any, issues are of very low mintage. 3) All specimens are distributed at prices in excess of the coin's face value. 4) The metallic composition is unsuitable for circulation use. 5) General use would be unlikely because of excessively high face value or physical size. 6) The currency unit is not in general use. 7) Prohibitions prevent circulation of the coin in country of issue. 8) Only non-governmental agencies distribute the coin.

Also grouped under the NCLT identity are all special sets of regular issue coins, which may be variously described by issuing authorities as proof, proof-like, fleur de coin, specimen or mint sets, or are similarly designated, produced in special packaging for presentation or collector marketing purposes by or in the name of the government concerned.

When individual and NCLT issue sets were originally recognized with listings in the SCWC they were designated by distinctive catalog numbers — assigned by Charles R. Hosch and designated H# — which will still be found attached to many of the issues grouped under this general identity. In this edition some of the listings have been switched to KM# designations, or other appropriate applicable numbering systems, in order to continue providing an orderly system for cataloging these varied, but related issues, for which the last detailed study by Hosch was published in 1975.

Within the NCLT section of national listings, prefix letters are used in combination with the catalog numbers assigned to designate the nature of the various types of entries. Thus, the letter "E" denotes essais and "Pr" probas (trial strike tests of regular designs, generally in standard metals of issue, with the word "essai" or "proba" added). The letter "P" designates piefort strikes (specimens struck on planchets double the normal coin thickness for a given issue, or more, in standard or precious metals), and "Pe" pieforts with the word "essai" present. Mint sets are designated with three digit hundred series KM# assignments with a "S" prefix, proof sets with regular KM#s. Proofs of regular issue coins, and patterns as entered in combination with the regular coin listings, are assigned catalog numbers consistent with the established cataloging sequence for the country, being individually designated as appropriate.

TOKEN COINAGE

When local economic conditions forced regular coinage from circulation or found the mints unable to cope with the demands for small change, issues such as the British tokens of the early 1800s and the French Chamber of Commerce emissions of the 1920s were also issued and freely accepted in monetary transactions over wide areas. Tokens were likewise introduced to satisfy specific, restricted needs, such as the issues produced to satisfy monetary requirements in the leper colonies of Colombia and the Phillippines.

This reference incorporates introductory or detailed listings of many of these and similar token coinage issues, particularly those which enjoyed wide circulation and where the series were limited in their diversity. The more complex series, and those issues which were somewhat more restricted in the scope of their circulation, are generally not listed, although a representative example may be illustrated and a reference provided to comprehensive works which fully catalog the series.

OFF-METAL STRIKES

A new feature in this edition is the designation of known off-metal strikes. In this context the term will be understood to include the wide range of coinage issues struck in other than their officially authorized compositions for purposes of presentation, sale to collectors and trade. The designation is not meant to cover those issues struck as true patterns or as genuine minting errors.

Off-metal strikes will be designated by an (OMS) following the listed metal; i.e., Brass (OMS).

Examples of off-metal strikes include the Dutch duits, struck normally in copper, but also produced in limited quantities in gold and silver for collectors.

Collectors of Germanic coinage may be familiar with off-metal strikes of small denomination iron coins in gold; often a method used to give a stamp of legitimacy to a gold planchet, allowing it to circulate as a trade piece.

MEDALLIC ISSUES

This and the last edition have featured a new listing category segregating a class of issues designated as medallic issues. Grouped in this category, placed following the regular issue listings or at the beginning of the NCLT listings of national coinages, are coin-type issues which can generally be identified as commemoratives produced to the country's established coinage standards, along with related issues, but with the absence of the usual indicator of denomination. These pieces may or may not feature one or both designs adapted from the country's regular issue or commemorative coinage.

Grouped under the new medallic issues heading are such diverse offerings as France's popular "mint visit" pieces and Iceland's "Althing" commemoratives — designated by their traditional Y# assignments — along with Denmark's "royal" commemorative proofs and a variety of commemoratives issued in recent years by British Commonwealth nations — designated by KM# assignments prefixed by the letter "M" — and other items of similar nature. These listings will be expanded in future editions as additional pieces which merit inclusion are brought to the editor's attention.

The Democratic Republic of Afghanistan, which occupies a mountainous region of Southwest Asia, has an area of 260,000 sq. mi. (673,397 sq. km.) and a population of 12.7 million. Capital: Kabul. It is bordered by Iran, Pakistan, the USSR, and China's Sinkiang Province. Agriculture and herding are the principal industries; textile mills and cement factories are recent additions to the industrial sector. Cotton, wool, fruits, nuts, sheepskin coats and hand-woven carpets are exported.

Because of its strategic position astride the ancient land route to India, Afghanistan – formerly known as Aryana and Khorasan – was conquered by Darius I, Alexander the Great, various Scythian tribes, the Arabs, Genghis Khan, Tamerlane, and in more recent times by Great Britain. Its history as an independent state dates only from the middle of the 18th century when Ahmad Shah Abdali declared independence from Persia AH1160 (1747AD) and established his Durrani Dynasty: Later, family feuds plagued his successors and resulted in a new dynasty, the Barakzai.

A constitution approved by the General Assembly in 1964 established Afghanistan as a constitutional monarchy, and began moving the country toward parliamentary democracy. The last king was Mohammad Zahir Shah, who ascended the throne Nov. 8, 1933. On July 17, 1973, Mohammad Daud, the king's cousin, seized power in a coup d'etat, and proclaimed Afghanistan a republic with himself as president and premier. Daud was killed in a military coup which established a Marxist regime on April 28, 1978. Integral conflict mounted and in December, 1979 the U.S.S.R. invaded and occupied the country, installing a puppet regime.

Coinage reflects Persian, Turkish and Indian influences. Inscriptions are in Persian and Pushtu, with Pushtu being employed exclusively after A.D. 1950. Dating is by the Mohammadan lunar calendar (A.H.) and solar calendar (S.H.), the lunar calendar being employed prior to A.D. 1920 and during A.D. 1929-31. Decimal coinage was introduced in 1926.

RULERS

DURRANI DYNASTY:

Ahmad Shah:
AH1160-86 (AD1747-72)

Taimur Shah, as Nizam:
AH1170-86 (AD1757-72)

Sulaiman Shah, pretender:
AH1186 (AD1772)

Taimur Shah, as King:
AH1186-1207 (AD1772-93)

Humayun (at Qandahar):
AH1207 (AD1793)

Shah Zaman:
AH1207-16 (AD1793-1801)

Shah Shuja al-Mulk, 1st reign:
AH1216 (AD1801) (no coins)

Mahmud Shah, 1st reign:
AH1216-18 (AD1801-03)

Qaisar Shah (at Qandahar):
AH1218 (AD1803)

Shah Shuja al-Mulk, 2nd reign:
AH1218-24 (AD1803-08)

Mahmud Shah, 2nd reign:
AH1224-33 (AD1808-17)

Ayyub Shah (puppet of Dost Muhammad):
AH1233-1245 (AD1817-26)
(at Peshawar after 1239)

Sultan Muhammad (at Peshawar):
AH1247-50 (AD1831-34)

Kohandil Khan (at Qandahar):
AH1256-69 (AD1840-53)

Shah Shuja al-Mulk (as puppet of British East India Co.), 3rd reign:
AH1255-58 (AD1839-42)

Fath Jang:
AH1258 (AD1842)

Shahpur Shah:
AH1258 (AD1842)

Succession at Kashmir between 1221 and 1234:

Qaisar Shah:
AH1221-23 (AD1806-08)

Ata Muhammad (called Shah Nur al—din on coins):
AH1223-28 (AD1808-13)

Azim Khan (coins in name of Mahmud Shah):
AH1228-34 (AD1813-18)

Succession at Herat, 1216-98:

Mahmud Shah:
AH1216-45 (AD1801-29)

Kamran Shah:
AH1245-58 (AD1829-42)

Yar Muhammad Khan Barakzai:
AH1258-67 (AD1842-51)

Muhammad Yusuf Khan Sadozai:
AH1267-72 (AD1851-56)

Iranian occupation (coins in name of Nasir al-din Shah):
AH1272-80 (AD1856-63)

Sher Ali:
AH1280-96 (AD1863-79)

Muhammad Yaqub:
AH1296-98 (AD1879-81)

thereafter, as in the rest of Afghanistan

BARAKZAI DYNASTY:

Dost Muhammad, 1st reign:
AH1239-55 (AD1824-39)

(British occupation:
AH1255-58)

Dost Muhammad, 2nd reign:
AH1258-80 (AD1842-63)

Sher Ali, 1st reign:
AH1280-83 (AD1863-66)

Muhammad Afzal:
AH1283-84 (AD1866-67)

Muhammad A'zam:
AH1283-85 (AD1866-68)

Sher Ali, 2nd reign:
AH1285-96 (AD1868-79)

Muhammad Yaqub:
AH1296-97 (AD1879-80)
(in Herat until 1298)

Wali Muhammad (at Kabul):
AH1297 (AD1880)

Wali Sher Ali (at Qandahar):
AH1297 (AD1880)

Abdur Rahman
AH1297-1319 (AD1880-1901)

Muhammad Ishaq, rebel at Balkh:
AH1305-06 (AD1889)

Habibullah
AH1319-37 (AD1901-19)

Amanullah:
AH1337, SH1298-1307 (AD1919-29)

Habibullah Ghazi, rebel, known as Baccha-i-Saqao:
AH1347-48 (AD1929)

Nadir Shah:
AH1348-50, SH1310-12 (AD1929-33)

Muhammad Zahir Shah:
SH1312-52 (AD1933-73)

Republic, SH1352- (AD1973-)

MINTS

Hammered coins were struck at numerous mints in Afghanistan and adjacent lands. These are listed below, together with their honorific titles, and shown in the style ordinarily found on the coins. Additional mints were located in India, and are listed under INDIA: DURRANI EMPIRE.

Ahmadpur Mint احمدپور

Ahmadshahi Mint احمدشاهی

'Ashraf al-Bilad' اشرف البلاد

Bahawalpur Mint بهاولپور

'Dar as-Surur' دارالسرور

Balkh Mint بلخ

'Umm al-Bilad' ام البلاد

Bhakhar Mint بکهر بهکر

Dera Mint دیره

Derajat Mint دیره جات

Ghazni Mint غزنین

Herat Mint هرات ہرات

'Dar as-Saltanat' دارالسلطنه

Kabul Mint كابل

'Dar al-Mulk' دارالملك

'Dar al-Saltanat' (as at Herat)

Khanabad Mint خاناباد

Multan Mint ملتان

'Dar al-Aman' دارالامان

Peshawar Mint پشاور

Qandahar Mint قندهار

Rikab Mint رکاب

Sar-i Pol Mint سرپل

Tashqurghan Mint تاشقرغان

ANONYMOUS HAMMERED COPPER COINAGE

Afghan Copper Coins, prior to the beginning of machine-struck coinage in 1891, were not regulated by the central authorities. Mintmasters produced many types of machine-struck coinage including the use of old Afghan coins as blanks. Consequently, weights are quite random, and there are no denominations in the true sense of the term. All were known as 'Falus', and lots of mixed sizes were accounted by weight. Every few years-sometimes every year-coppers were recalled and recoined, at a fee, often substantial, which was paid to the mintmaster and formed his salary. This accounts for the large number of overstruck pieces, which are generally less desirable than clear singly struck specimens.

Hundreds of varieties were issued at the principal mints of Kabul and Qandahar, and the following listing is only a representation of what exists. A more detailed, but still very fragmentary listing is given by W. H. Valentine, in 'Modern Copper Coins of the Muhammadan States.' No attempt at a complete listing has ever been undertaken. 'V' numbers refer to Valentine.

Prices are for well-struck specimens with clear design and date. Partial or overstruck coins are worth considerably less. Unrepresented types are worth about the same as listed pieces of the same mint.

IMPORTANT: Most types were used at one time or other at all mints. The type cannot therefore be used to determine the mint, which can ordinarily only be ascertained by reading the Persian inscription.

NOTE: For later issues, see the local coppers after the machine-struck coinage.

AHMADSHAHI
(See also Qandahar)

Sword and Star

V#	Date	Year	VG	Fine	VF	XF
50	AH1190	—	2.50	5.00	8.00	12.00

Sword between two leaves

V#	Date	Year	VG	Fine	VF	XF
48/49	AH1257	—	2.50	5.00	8.00	12.00

Lion

V#	Date	Year	VG	Fine	VF	XF
64	AH1227		2.00	4.00	7.00	11.00

Sunface

V#	Date	Year	VG	Fine	VF	XF
24	AH1227		1.50	3.00	5.00	8.00
36-37	1253		1.50	3.00	5.00	8.00

Flower

V#	Date	Year	VG	Fine	VF	XF
34-35	AH1252		2.00	4.00	7.00	11.00

Crossed swords

V#	Date	Year	VG	Fine	VF	XF
39	ND		2.50	5.00	8.00	12.00

Bird

V#	Date	Year	VG	Fine	VF	XF
69	ND		2.00	4.00	7.00	11.00

BALKH

Flower between two swords

V#	Date	Year	VG	Fine	VF	XF
2	AH1228		2.00	4.00	7.00	11.00
3	1233		2.00	4.00	7.00	11.00
4-5	1234		2.00	4.00	7.00	11.00
—	1238		2.00	4.00	7.00	11.00

Lion

V#	Date	Year	VG	Fine	VF	XF
—	AH1267		2.50	5.00	8.00	12.00

Small lion and inscriptions

V#	Date	Year	VG	Fine	VF	XF
7-8	AH1295		1.50	3.00	5.00	8.00

Plant between two swords.

V#	Date	Year	VG	Fine	VF	XF
6	AH1274	—	3.00	6.00	10.00	15.00

NOTE: This type struck over a number of years without change of date.

GHAZNI

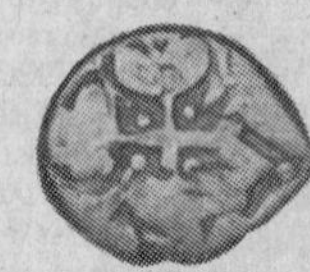

Floral design

V#	Date	Year	VG	Fine	VF	XF
—	ND	—	3.00	6.00	10.00	15.00

HERAT

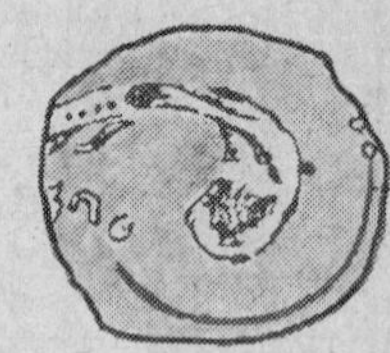

Fish ?

V#	Date	Year	VG	Fine	VF	XF
7	AH1261	—	2.00	4.00	7.00	11.00

NOTE: Illustrated example of P#7 is double-struck.

Leaf and two swords

V#	Date	Year	VG	Fine	VF	XF
2-3	AH1135		2.00	4.00	7.00	11.00
5	1224		2.00	4.00	7.00	11.00
	1226		2.00	4.00	7.00	11.00

Sunface

V#	Date	Year	VG	Fine	VF	XF
10	AH1227		2.00	4.00	7.00	11.00

KABUL

Leaf and swords, 'J' in center, large size

V#	Date	Year	VG	Fine	VF	XF
10	AH1229		2.50	5.00	8.00	12.00

Sword and floral ornaments

V#	Date	Year	VG	Fine	VF	XF
14-18	AH1254		2.00	4.00	7.00	11.00

Flower

V#	Date	Year	VG	Fine	VF	XF
24-25	AH1254		2.00	4.00	7.00	11.00

Flower and swords

V#	Date	Year	VG	Fine	VF	XF
26-29	AH1254-1258		2.00	4.00	7.00	11.00

Flower and swords

V#	Date	Year	VG	Fine	VF	XF
37	AH1261		2.50	5.00	8.00	12.00

Floral pattern

V#	Date	Year	VG	Fine	VF	XF
43-46	AH12xx	—	2.00	4.00	7.00	11.00
	ND	—	2.00	4.00	7.00	11.00

Sword and stars

V#	Date	Year	VG	Fine	VF	XF
48	AHxx52		2.00	4.00	7.00	11.00
47	126x		2.00	4.00	7.00	11.00
53	ND		2.00	4.00	7.00	11.00

KHANABAD

V#	Date	Year	VG	Fine	VF	XF
—	AH1301		10.00	18.50	28.50	40.00
	1302		10.00	18.50	28.50	40.00

QANDAHAR

(See also Ahmadshahi)

Large date and legend

V#	Date	Year	VG	Fine	VF	XF
25	AH1228		2.00	4.00	7.00	11.00

Four petaled flower

V#	Date	Year	VG	Fine	VF	XF
60	ND		2.00	4.00	7.00	11.00

Crown

V#	Date	Year	VG	Fine	VF	XF
55	AH1296		75.00	100.00	150.00	250.00

NOTE: Issued during the British occupation of Qandahar 1878-79.

Hand of Ali

V#	Date	Year	VG	Fine	VF	XF
84	AH1295		2.25	4.50	7.50	11.50

Adl (-justice) in 6-pointed star

V#	Date	Year	VG	Fine	VF	XF
88-90	AH1296		1.00	2.00	3.50	6.00

Peacock

V#	Date	Year	VG	Fine	VF	XF
91	AH1297		1.50	2.50	3.50	5.50

SAR-I POL

Lion

V#	Date	Year	VG	Fine	VF	XF
—	AH1297	—	10.00	15.00	20.00	30.00
	ND	—	10.00	15.00	20.00	30.00

TASHQURGHAN

Stem with leaves

V#	Date	Year	VG	Fine	VF	XF
—	AH1300	—	10.00	18.50	28.50	40.00

NAMED HAMMERED COINAGE

Unlike the anonymous copper coinage, which was purely local, the silver and gold coins, as well as some of the early copper coins, bear the name or characteristic type of the ruler. Because the sequence of rulers often varied at different mints, each ruled by different princes, the coins are best organized according to mint. Each mint employed characteristic types and calligraphy, which continued from one ruler to the next. It is hoped that this system will facilitate identification of these coins.

The following listings include only the mints situated in contiguous territories under Durrani and Barakzai rule for extended periods of time. They do not include mints in Kashmir or in other parts of India which the Afghans occupied for relatively brief intervals. For these mints, see the section under INDIA: DURRANI EMPIRE.

COUNTERMARKED ISSUES

Large numbers of Durrani silver coins from the reigns of Ahmad Shah, Taimur Shah, and Shah Zaman are found countermarked with the word RAYIJ ('current') and a date, observed years ranging from 1180 until 1213. These were formerly attributed to the Rohilla tribes of north—central India, but recent evidence suggests they were stamped by the Durranis themselves, possibly in Peshawar or Attock. The counterstamps are occasionally found on contemporary Persian coins, and more rarely on Indian rupees. Counterstamped coins are worth 15-25 percent more than pieces without the stamp.

AHMADPUR

(In Bahawalpur)

RUPEE

SILVER
Mahmud Shah

C#	Date	Year	VG	Fine	VF	XF
541	AH1217	48	11.50	13.50	17.50	25.00
	—	49	11.50	13.50	17.50	25.00

Probably posthumous issue. Reverse only shown.

AHMADSHAHI/QANDAHAR

'Ashraf-al-Bilad'

Until AH1273, this mint was almost always given on the coins as Ahmadshahi, a name given it by Ahmad Shah in honor of himself in AH1171, often with the honorific 'Ashraf al-Bilad' (meaning 'Most Noble of Cities'). On later issues, the traditional name Qandahar is generally used. These variations are indicated by the symbols 'Ah' or 'Qr' after the dates.

Although Qandahar was Ahmad Shah's capital throughout his reign, he did not issue coins from there until AH1171 (1758AD).

1/4 RUPEE

SILVER
Shah Zaman

C#	Date	Year	VG	Fine	VF	XF
441	AH1214Ah	8	20.00	30.00	50.00	75.00

Shah Shuja al-Mulk, 2nd reign

C#	Date	Year	VG	Fine	VF	XF
521	AH1218Ah	—	10.00	16.50	23.50	35.00

1/2 RUPEE

SILVER

Anonymous (Kohandil Khan)

C#	Date	Year	VG	Fine	VF	XF
850	AH1260Ah	—	6.50	8.00	10.00	15.00
	1261Ah	—	6.50	8.00	10.00	15.00
	1262Ah	—	6.50	8.00	10.00	15.00
	1263Ah	—	Reported, not confirmed			
	1264Ah	—	6.50	8.00	10.00	15.00
	1268Ah	—	6.50	8.00	11.00	17.50
	1269Ah	—	6.50	8.00	11.00	17.50

NOTE: Both obverse and reverse have legends differently arranged in different years.

Dost Muhammad

C#	Date	Year	VG	Fine	VF	XF
891	AH1270Ah	—	6.50	7.00	8.50	11.50
	1271Ah	—	6.50	7.00	8.50	11.50
	1272Ah	—	6.50	7.00	8.50	11.50
	1273Ah	—	6.50	7.00	8.50	11.50

C#	Date	Year	VG	Fine	VF	XF
880	AH1272Qr	—	6.50	7.00	8.50	11.50
	1273Qr	—	6.50	7.00	8.50	11.50
	1274Qr	—	6.50	7.00	8.50	11.50
	1275Qr	—	6.50	7.00	8.50	11.50
	1278Qr	—	6.50	7.00	9.00	12.50
	1279Qr	—	Reported, not confirmed			

Sher Ali, 1st reign

C#	Date	Year	VG	Fine	VF	XF
901	AH1280Qr	—	6.50	7.00	8.50	11.50
	1281Qr	—	6.50	7.00	8.50	11.50
	1282Qr	—	6.50	7.00	8.50	11.50
	1283Qr	—	6.50	7.00	9.00	12.50

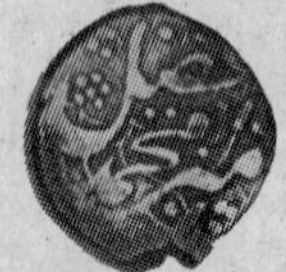

Muhammad Afzal

C#	Date	Year	VG	Fine	VF	XF
911	AH1283Ah	—	8.50	13.50	22.50	35.00

Muhammad A'zam

C#	Date	Year	VG	Fine	VF	XF
917	AH1283Qr	—	8.50	12.50	20.00	30.00
	1284Qr	—	8.50	12.50	20.00	30.00

Sher Ali, 2nd reign

C#	Date	Year	VG	Fine	VF	XF
921	AH1285Qr	—	6.50	9.00	15.00	25.00

C#	Date	Year	VG	Fine	VF	XF
922	AH1277Qr (error for 1288)					
		—	6.50	8.50	12.00	15.00
	1288Qr	—	6.50	7.00	9.00	13.00
	1289Qr	—	6.50	8.50	12.00	15.00

C#	Date	Year	VG	Fine	VF	XF
921	AH1290Qr	—	6.50	7.00	8.00	12.00
	1291Qr	—	—	Reported, not confirmed		
	1292Qr	—	6.50	7.00	8.00	12.00
	1293Qr	—	6.50	7.00	8.00	12.00
	1294Qr	—	6.50	7.00	8.00	12.00
	1295Qr	—	6.50	7.00	8.00	12.00

Muhammad Yaqub Khan

C#	Date	Year	VG	Fine	VF	XF
943	AH1296Qr	—	6.50	7.50	10.00	15.00
	1297Qr	—	6.50	7.50	10.00	15.00

Wali Sher Ali

C#	Date	Year	VG	Fine	VF	XF
957	AH1297Qr	—	6.50	8.50	15.00	20.00

Anonymous (Issuer Unknown)

C#	Date	Year	VG	Fine	VF	XF
—	AH1297Qr	—	7.50	12.50	22.50	35.00

RUPEE

SILVER

Ahmad Shah

C#	Date	Year	VG	Fine	VF	XF
241	AH1171Ah	11	11.50	13.50	17.50	25.00
	1172Ah	12	11.50	13.50	17.50	25.00
	1172Ah	13	11.50	13.50	17.50	25.00
	-Ah	16	11.50	13.50	17.50	25.00
	-Ah	17	11.50	13.50	17.50	25.00
	1178Ah	18	11.50	13.50	17.50	25.00
	1180Ah	20	11.50	13.50	17.50	25.00
	1182Ah	22	11.50	13.50	17.50	25.00
	1183Ah	23	11.50	13.50	17.50	25.00
	1184Ah	23	11.50	13.50	17.50	25.00
	-Ah	25	11.50	13.50	17.50	25.00
	-Ah	26	11.50	13.50	17.50	25.00

Sulaiman Shah

C#	Date	Year	VG	Fine	VF	XF
341	AH1186Ah	1	25.00	40.00	65.00	90.00

Taimur Shah

C#	Date	Year	VG	Fine	VF	XF
381	AH1187Ah	2	11.50	13.50	16.50	22.50
	1187Ah	3	11.50	13.50	16.50	22.50
	1189Ah	—	11.50	13.50	16.50	22.50
	1191Ah	—	11.50	13.50	16.50	22.50
	1192Ah	—	11.50	13.50	16.50	22.50
	1193Ah	21	11.50	13.50	16.50	22.50
	1194Ah	9	11.50	13.50	16.50	22.50
	1195Ah	—	11.50	13.50	16.50	22.50
	1197Ah	12	11.50	13.50	16.50	22.50

C#	Date	Year	VG	Fine	VF	XF
381	1198Ah	—	11.50	13.50	16.50	22.50
	1204Ah	18	11.50	13.50	16.50	22.50
	1205Ah	19	11.50	13.50	16.50	22.50
	1206Ah	19	11.50	13.50	16.50	22.50
	1206Ah	20	11.50	13.50	16.50	22.50
	1207Ah	21	11.50	13.50	16.50	22.50

Humayun Shah

C#	Date	Year	VG	Fine	VF	XF
421	AH1207Ah	(1)	25.00	40.00	65.00	90.00

Shah Zaman

C#	Date	Year	VG	Fine	VF	XF
461	AH1207Ah	—	11.50	13.50	16.50	22.50
	1208Ah	—	11.50	13.50	16.50	22.50
	1209Ah	2	11.50	13.50	16.50	22.50
	1211Ah	4	11.50	13.50	16.50	22.50
	1212Ah	5	11.50	13.50	16.50	22.50
	1213Ah	5	11.50	13.50	16.50	22.50
	1214Ah	7	11.50	13.50	16.50	22.50
	1214Ah	8	11.50	13.50	16.50	22.50
	1215Ah	8	11.50	13.50	16.50	22.50

Mahmud Shah, 1st reign

C#	Date	Year	VG	Fine	VF	XF
541	AH1216Ah	—	11.50	13.00	15.00	20.00
	1217Ah	2	11.50	13.00	15.00	20.00
	1218Ah	3	11.50	13.00	15.00	20.00

Qaisar Shah

C#	Date	Year	VG	Fine	VF	XF
670	AH1218Ah	—	17.50	25.00	40.00	60.00

Shah Shuja al-Mulk, 2nd reign

C#	Date	Year	VG	Fine	VF	XF
621	AH1218Ah	—	11.50	13.00	15.00	20.00
	1219Ah	—	11.50	13.00	15.00	20.00
	1220Ah	—	11.50	13.00	15.00	20.00
	1221Ah	—	11.50	13.00	15.00	20.00
	1222Ah	—	11.50	13.00	15.00	20.00
	1223Ah	—	11.50	13.00	15.00	20.00
	1224Ah	—	11.50	13.00	15.00	20.00

Mahmud Shah, 2nd reign

Reverse in cartouche

C#	Date	Year	VG	Fine	VF	XF
541.1	AH1222 (error date)					
		—	11.50	13.00	15.00	20.00
	1224Ah	—	11.50	13.00	15.00	20.00
	1225Ah	—	11.50	13.00	15.00	20.00
	1226Ah	—	11.50	13.00	15.00	20.00

Reverse in toughra.

C#	Date	Year	VG	Fine	VF	XF
541.2	1229Ah	—	11.50	13.00	15.00	20.00
	1230Ah	—	11.50	13.00	15.00	20.00
	1231Ah	—	11.50	13.00	15.00	20.00
	1232Ah	—	11.50	13.00	15.00	20.00

C#	Date	Year	VG	Fine	VF	XF
541.2	1233Ah	—	11.50	13.00	15.00	20.00
	1234Ah	—	11.50	13.50	16.50	22.50

NOTE: Several varieties of type during this reign.

Ayyub Shah

C#	Date	Year	VG	Fine	VF	XF
811	ND	—	12.50	16.50	22.50	30.00
	AH1235Ah	—	12.50	16.50	22.50	30.00
	1236Ah	—	Reported, not confirmed			
	1239Ah	—	12.50	16.50	22.50	30.00

Dost Muhammad
Anonymous, with Kalimah

C#	Date	Year	VG	Fine	VF	XF
826	AH1243Ah	—	11.50	13.00	16.50	22.50
	1244Ah		11.50	13.00	16.50	22.50
	1245Ah	—	11.50	13.00	16.50	22.50
	1246Ah	—	11.50	13.00	16.50	22.50
	1247Ah	—	11.50	13.00	16.50	22.50
	1248Ah	—	11.50	13.00	16.50	22.50
	1249Ah	—	11.50	13.00	15.00	20.00
	1250Ah	—	11.50	13.00	15.00	20.00
	1251Ah	—	11.50	13.00	15.00	20.00
	1252Ah	—	11.50	13.00	15.00	20.00
	1253Ah	—	11.50	13.00	16.50	22.50
	1254Ah	—	11.50	13.00	16.50	22.50

NOTE: Varieties of reverse exist.

Shah Shuja al-Mulk, 3rd reign

C#	Date	Year	VG	Fine	VF	XF
621	AH1255Ah	—	12.50	15.00	18.50	25.00
	1256Ah	—	12.50	15.00	18.50	25.00

Fath Jang

C#	Date	Year	VG	Fine	VF	XF
861	AH1258Ah	—	15.00	25.00	40.00	60.00

Anonymous (Kohandil Khan)

C#	Date	Year	VG	Fine	VF	XF
851	AH1259Ah	—	13.50	18.50	25.00	40.00

Dost Muhammad

C#	Date	Year	VG	Fine	VF	XF
882b	AH1272Ah	—	11.50	13.50	16.50	22.50
	1273Ah	—	11.50	13.50	16.50	22.50

Wali Sher Ali
Type of half rupee

C#	Date	Year	VG	Fine	VF	XF
959	AH1297Qr	—	13.50	18.50	27.50	45.00

Muhammad Yaqub Khan

C#	Date	Year	VG	Fine	VF	XF
945a	AH1298Qr	—	12.50	15.00	22.50	35.00

Abdur Rahman Khan

C#	Date	Year	VG	Fine	VF	XF
977.1	AH1298Qr	—	11.50	13.00	15.00	18.50

C#	Date	Year	VG	Fine	VF	XF
977.2	AH1299Qr	—	11.50	13.00	15.00	18.50
	1300Qr	—	11.50	13.00	15.00	18.50
	1302Qr	—	Reported, not confirmed			
	1305Qr	—	11.50	13.50	16.50	22.50
	1306Qr	—	11.50	13.50	16.50	22.50
	1307Qr	—	11.50	13.50	16.50	22.50
	1308Qr	—	11.50	13.50	16.50	22.50

2 RUPEES

SILVER
Shah Zamon

C#	Date	Year	VG	Fine	VF	XF
475	AH -Ah	7	40.00	60.00	85.00	120.00
	1214Ah	8	40.00	60.00	85.00	120.00

ASHRAFI

GOLD, 3.5 gm.
Ahmad Shah

C#	Date	Year	VG	Fine	VF	XF
261	AH1171Ah	11	—	—	—	—
	Ah	22	—	—	—	—
	Ah	23	—	—	—	—

Mahmud Shah, 1st reign

C#	Date	Year	VG	Fine	VF	XF
574	AH1218Ah	3	200.00	300.00	400.00	550.00

Shah Shuja al-Mulk, 2nd reign

C#	Date	Year	VG	Fine	VF	XF
641	AH1222Ah	—	150.00	175.00	200.00	350.00

Mahmud Shah, 2nd reign

C#	Date	Year	VG	Fine	VF	XF
575	AH1224Ah	—	150.00	175.00	200.00	350.00

TILLA

GOLD
Sher Ali

C#	Date	Year	VG	Fine	VF	XF
932	AH1283Qr	—	150.00	175.00	200.00	300.00
	1284Qr	—	150.00	175.00	200.00	300.00
	1285Qr	—	150.00	175.00	200.00	300.00

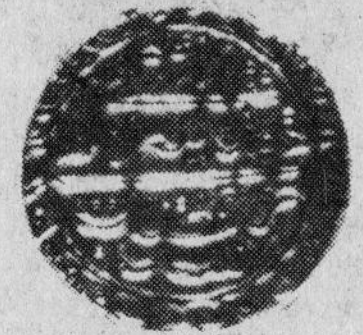 

Wali Sher Ali

C#	Date	Year	VG	Fine	VF	XF
965	AH1297Qr	—	200.00	250.00	325.00	350.00

Abdur Rahman Khan

C#	Date	Year	VG	Fine	VF	XF
981	AH1298Ah	—	100.00	140.00	170.00	275.00

MOHUR

GOLD, 10.9 gm.
Ahmad Shah

C#	Date	Year	VG	Fine	VF	XF
271	AH -Ah	22	—	—	—	—

Taimur Shah

C#	Date	Year	VG	Fine	VF	XF
321	AH1186Ah	1	—	—	—	
	1190Ah	—	—	—	—	—
	1197Ah	12	—	—	—	—
	-Ah	14	—	—	—	—
	1204Ah	18	—	—	—	—
	1207Ah	21	—	—	—	—

Humayun Shah

C#	Date	Year	VG	Fine	VF	XF
425	AH1207Ah	—	—	—	—	—

Shah Zaman

C#	Date	Year	VG	Fine	VF	XF
481	AH1209Ah	2	—	—	—	—
	1215Ah	7	—	—	—	—
	1215Ah	8	—	—	—	—

Similar, with mint name 'Qandahar'

C#	Date	Year	VG	Fine	VF	XF
482	AH1211Qr	5	—	—	—	—

Mahmud Shah, 1st reign

C#	Date	Year	VG	Fine	VF	XF
581	AH1218Ah	3	225.00	260.00	300.00	350.00

Qaisar Shah

C#	Date	Year	VG	Fine	VF	XF
670	AH1218Ah	—	300.00	350.00	400.00	500.00

Shah Shuja, al-Mulk, 2nd reign

C#	Date	Year	VG	Fine	VF	XF
645	AH1220Ah	—	225.00	260.00	300.00	350.00
	1222Ah	—	225.00	260.00	300.00	350.00

ATTOCK

NOTE: Attock Fort, on the Indus River, fell to the Sikhs in AH1202 (1788AD).

RUPEE

SILVER
Ahmad Shah

C#	Date	Year	VG	Fine	VF	XF
241	AH—	9	12.50	15.00	18.50	25.00
	1170	11	12.50	15.00	18.50	25.00
	1171	11	12.50	15.00	18.50	25.00
	1172	12	12.50	15.00	18.50	25.00
	—	13	12.50	15.00	18.50	25.00
	1174	14	12.50	15.00	18.50	25.00
	—	19	12.50	15.00	18.50	25.00
	—	21	12.50	15.00	18.50	25.00
	—	22	12.50	15.00	18.50	25.00
	1182	22	12.50	15.00	18.50	25.00

Taimur Shah

C#	Date	Year	VG	Fine	VF	XF
381	AH1186	1	11.50	13.50	16.50	22.50
	1187	2	11.50	13.50	16.50	22.50
	1188	2	11.50	13.50	16.50	22.50
	1188	4	11.50	13.50	16.50	22.50
	1192	4	(error year)			
			11.50	13.50	16.50	22.50
	1193	8	11.50	13.50	16.50	22.50
	1196	10	11.50	13.50	16.50	22.50
	1197	11	11.50	13.50	16.50	22.50
	1198	—	11.50	13.50	16.50	22.50
	—	14	11.50	13.50	16.50	22.50
	—	16	11.50	13.50	16.50	22.50

MOHUR

GOLD, 10.9 gm.
Ahmad Shah

C#	Date	Year	VG	Fine	VF	XF
271	AH1175	15	—	—	—	—
	1181	21	—	—	—	—
		Taimur Shah				
401	AH1188	2	—	—	—	—

BAHAWALPUR

Dar as-Surur'

RUPEE

SILVER
Mahmud Shah, 1st reign

C#	Date	Year	VG	Fine	VF	XF
541	AH1217	1	12.50	16.50	21.50	27.50
	1217	2	12.50	16.50	21.50	27.50
	1218	2	12.50	16.50	21.50	27.50

NOTE: Most Bahawalpur coins have oblique milling on the edge.

Shah Shuja al-Mulk, 2nd reign

C#	Date	Year	VG	Fine	VF	XF
621	AH1218	1	12.50	16.50	21.50	27.50
	1218	2	12.50	16.50	21.50	27.50
	1219	1	12.50	16.50	21.50	27.50
	1222	—	12.50	16.50	21.50	27.50
	1212 (error for 1221 ?)					
		—	12.50	16.50	22.50	27.50
		Mahmud Shah, 2nd reign				
541	AH1224	1	12.50	16.50	22.50	30.00
	1239	—	12.50	16.50	21.50	27.50
	1240	—	12.50	16.50	21.50	27.50
	1241	—	12.50	16.50	21.50	27.50
	1242	—	12.50	16.50	21.50	27.50
	1244	—	12.50	16.50	21.50	27.50
	1244 (1245 on reverse)					
		—	7.50	12.50	20.00	27.50
	1249	—	7.50	12.50	20.00	27.50
	1249 (1250 on reverse)					
		—	7.50	12.50	20.00	27.50
	1250	—	7.50	12.50	20.00	27.50

NOTE: Coins dated after AH1233 are struck in Mahmud's name by the virtually independent Nawabs of Bahawalpur.

2 RUPEES

SILVER
Mahmud Shah, 1st reign

C#	Date	Year	VG	Fine	VF	XF
561	AH1217	1	75.00	125.00	175.00	250.00

Shah Shuja al-Mulk, 2nd reign

C#	Date	Year	VG	Fine	VF	XF
635	AH1218	1	60.00	90.00	125.00	175.00

MOHUR

GOLD
Mahmud Shah, 1st reign

C#	Date	Year	VG	Fine	VF	XF
581	AH1218	2	225.00	265.00	325.00	400.00
		Shah Shuja al-Mulk, 2nd reign				
645	AH—	1	225.00	265.00	325.00	400.00
		Mahmud Shah, 2nd reign				
581	AH1225	1	225.00	265.00	325.00	400.00

2 MOHURS

GOLD
Mahmud Shah, 1st reign

C#	Date	Year	VG	Fine	VF	XF
591	AH1217	1	500.00	600.00	750.00	900.00
	1217	2	500.00	600.00	750.00	900.00
	1218	2	500.00	600.00	750.00	900.00

Shah Shuja al-Mulk, 2nd reign

C#	Date	Year	VG	Fine	VF	XF
650	AH1218	1	700.00	850.00	1000.	1200.

BALKH

'Umm al-Bilad'

Located in northern Afghanistan, Balkh bore the honorary epithet of 'Umm al-Bilad', 'Mother of Cities', because of its great age. It was taken by Ahmad Shah from the Amir of Bukhara in AH1180 (1765AD) and lost by Taimur Shah to the Uzbeks in AH1206 (1792AD).

FALUS

COPPER
Taimur Shah
Single sword on reverse

C#	Date	Year	Good	VG	Fine	VF
361	AH1202	—	2.00	4.00	7.00	10.00
	1205	—	2.00	4.00	7.00	10.00

NOTE: AH1202 is ordinarily found written as AH1220.

Double sword on reverse

C#	Date	Year	Good	VG	Fine	VF
361a	AH1206	—	3.00	6.00	9.00	13.50

RUPEE

SILVER
Ahmad Shah

C#	Date	Year	VG	Fine	VF	XF
240	AH1180	—	30.00	50.00	75.00	100.00
		Taimur Shah				
381	AH1195	—	20.00	30.00	40.00	60.00
	1198	—	20.00	30.00	40.00	60.00

BHAKHAR

NOTE: The mint is found variously spelled, as Bhakhar (most common), Bakhar, and Bakkar.

FALUS

COPPER
Ahmad Shah

C#	Date	Year	Good	VG	Fine	VF
201	AH1162	1	2.50	5.00	9.00	13.50
	1163	3	2.50	5.00	9.00	13.50
	—	7	2.50	5.00	9.00	13.50
	1168	8	2.50	5.00	9.00	13.50
	1169	8	2.50	5.00	9.00	13.50

Taimur Shah

C#	Date	Year	Good	VG	Fine	VF
361	AH—	8	2.50	5.00	9.00	13.50
	—	9	2.50	5.00	9.00	13.50
	1194	—	2.50	5.00	9.00	13.50
	1198	—	2.50	5.00	9.00	13.50
		Shah Zaman				
431	ND	—	3.00	6.00	10.00	15.00

RUPEE

SILVER
Ahmad Shah

C#	Date	Year	VG	Fine	VF	XF
241	AH—	3	12.50	15.00	18.50	25.00
	1164	4	12.50	15.00	18.50	25.00
	1165	5	12.50	15.00	18.50	25.00
	1166	7	12.50	15.00	18.50	25.00
	—	8	12.50	15.00	18.50	25.00
	1169	9	12.50	15.00	18.50	25.00
	1170	—	12.50	15.00	18.50	25.00
	1171	—	12.50	15.00	18.50	25.00
	1172	—	12.50	15.00	18.50	25.00
	1173	—	12.50	15.00	18.50	25.00
	1174	—	12.50	15.00	18.50	25.00
	1175	—	12.50	15.00	18.50	25.00
	1177	—	12.50	15.00	18.50	25.00

C#	Date	Year	VG	Fine	VF	XF
241	1178	—	12.50	15.00	18.50	25.00
	1179	—	12.50	15.00	18.50	25.00
	1180	—	12.50	15.00	18.50	25.00
	1183	—	12.50	15.00	18.50	25.00
	1184	—	12.50	15.00	18.50	25.00

Taimur Shah, as Nizam

C#	Date	Year	VG	Fine	VF	XF
301	AH1173	2	13.50	16.50	22.50	30.00
	1177	3	13.50	16.50	22.50	30.00
	1178	3	13.50	16.50	22.50	30.00
	1181	7	13.50	16.50	22.50	30.00
	1182	—	13.50	16.50	22.50	30.00
	1183	—	13.50	16.50	22.50	30.00
	1184	—	13.50	16.50	22.50	30.00
	1185	—	13.50	16.50	22.50	30.00
	1186	—	13.50	16.50	22.50	30.00

NOTE: Coins of Taimur Shah as Nizam (Governor) were struck concurrently at Bhakhar with those of his father Ahmad Shah.

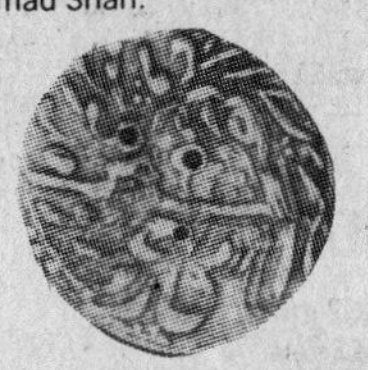

Taimur Shah, as King

C#	Date	Year	VG	Fine	VF	XF
381	AH1186	—	12.50	16.00	17.50	22.50
	1187	—	12.50	16.00	17.50	22.50
	1188	—	12.50	16.00	17.50	22.50
	1189	—	12.50	16.00	17.50	22.50
	1190	—	12.50	16.00	17.50	22.50
	1191	—	12.50	16.00	17.50	22.50
	1192	—	12.50	16.00	17.50	22.50
	1193	—	12.50	16.00	17.50	22.50
	1195	—	12.50	16.00	17.50	22.50
	1196	—	12.50	16.00	17.50	22.50
	1197	—	12.50	16.00	17.50	22.50
	1198	—	12.50	16.00	17.50	22.50
	1199	—	12.50	16.00	17.50	22.50
	1200	—	12.50	16.00	17.50	22.50
	1201	—	12.50	16.00	17.50	22.50
	1202	—	12.50	16.00	17.50	22.50
	1203	—	12.50	16.00	17.50	22.50
	1205	—	12.50	16.00	17.50	22.50
	1206	—	12.50	16.00	17.50	22.50
	1207	—	12.50	16.00	17.50	22.50

(A rupee with error date AH1172 on reverse has been reported)

Shah Zaman

C#	Date	Year	VG	Fine	VF	XF
461	AH1215?	—	12.50	15.00	22.50	30.00
	ND	—	11.50	14.00	21.50	27.50

Mahmud Shah

C#	Date	Year	VG	Fine	VF	XF
541	ND	—	12.50	15.00	17.50	22.50

Shah Shuja al-Mulk, 2nd reign

C#	Date	Year	VG	Fine	VF	XF
621	AH1218	—	13.50	16.50	22.50	27.50

NOTE: For later rupees of Bhakhar, struck in the name of Shah Mahmud and dated AH1241-67, see the Indian Native State of Sind.

ASHRAFI

GOLD
Ahmad Shah

C#	Date	Year	VG	Fine	VF	XF
261	AH1168	8	—	—	—	—

MOHUR

GOLD
Ahmad Shah

C#	Date	Year	VG	Fine	VF	XF
271	AH1177	—	—	—	—	—

Taimur Shah

C#	Date	Year	VG	Fine	VF	XF
401a	AH1196	—	—	—	—	—
	1204	—	—	—	—	—
401b	AH1204	18	—	—	—	—

Shah Zaman

C#	Date	Year	VG	Fine	VF	XF
481	AH—	2	—	—	—	—

DERA

Dera Ghazi Khan

FALUS

COPPER
Ahmad Shah

C#	Date	Year	Good	VG	Fine	VF
201	AH1161	1	3.25	6.50	10.00	14.00
	1162	1	3.25	6.50	10.00	14.00
	1165	5	3.25	6.50	10.00	14.00
	1167	7	3.25	6.50	10.00	14.00
	1168	7	3.25	6.50	10.00	14.00
	—	10	3.25	6.50	10.00	14.00

Taimur Shah, as Nizam

C#	Date	Year	Good	VG	Fine	VF
291	AH1172	3	5.00	10.00	17.50	25.00

Taimur Shah, as King

C#	Date	Year	Good	VG	Fine	VF
361	AH1199	—	2.50	5.00	8.00	12.50
	—	6	2.50	5.00	8.00	12.50
	1201	16	2.50	5.00	8.00	12.50
	—	18	2.50	5.00	8.00	12.50

Shah Zaman

C#	Date	Year	Good	VG	Fine	VF
431	AH1209	2	3.75	7.50	11.50	15.00

RUPEE

SILVER
Ahmad Shah

C#	Date	Year	VG	Fine	VF	XF
241	AH—	1	12.50	15.00	18.50	25.00
	1166	5	12.50	15.00	18.50	25.00
	1167	6	12.50	15.00	18.50	25.00
	1167	7	12.50	15.00	18.50	25.00
	1168	7	12.50	15.00	18.50	25.00
	1168	8	12.50	15.00	18.50	25.00
	1169	9	12.50	15.00	18.50	25.00
	1170	10	12.50	15.00	18.50	25.00
	1173	13	12.50	15.00	18.50	25.00
	1173	14	12.50	15.00	18.50	25.00
	1174	14	12.50	15.00	18.50	25.00
	1175	15	12.50	15.00	18.50	25.00
	1175	16	12.50	15.00	18.50	25.00
	1177	17	12.50	15.00	18.50	25.00
	1178	18	12.50	15.00	18.50	25.00
	1179	19	12.50	15.00	18.50	25.00
	1180	20	12.50	15.00	18.50	25.00
	1180	21	12.50	15.00	18.50	25.00
	1182	23	12.50	15.00	18.50	25.00
	1182	24	12.50	15.00	18.50	25.00
	1184	24	12.50	15.00	18.50	25.00
	1184	25	12.50	15.00	18.50	25.00
	1184	26	12.50	15.00	18.50	25.00

NOTE: Obverse & reverse dies are often carelessly paired, which accounts for the discrepancies between AH dates and regnal years.

Taimur Shah, as Nizam

C#	Date	Year	VG	Fine	VF	XF
301	AH1170	1	13.50	18.50	28.50	40.00
	—	2	13.50	18.50	28.50	40.00
	—	3	13.50	18.50	28.50	40.00

Sulaiman Shah
Obv: Full couplet.

C#	Date	Year	VG	Fine	VF	XF
341a	AH1186	1	30.00	45.00	70.00	100.00

Obv: 'Durri-i-Durran'.

C#	Date	Year	VG	Fine	VF	XF
341b	AH1186	1	30.00	45.00	70.00	100.00

Taimur Shah, as King

C#	Date	Year	VG	Fine	VF	XF
381	AH1186	1	11.50	13.50	15.00	20.00
	1188	2	11.50	13.50	15.00	20.00
	1188	3	11.50	13.50	15.00	20.00
	1189	3	11.50	13.50	15.00	20.00
	1190	4	11.50	13.50	15.00	20.00
	1191	5	11.50	13.50	15.00	20.00
	1192	6	11.50	13.50	15.00	20.00
	1193	7	11.50	13.50	15.00	20.00
	1194	8	11.50	13.50	15.00	20.00
	1195	9	11.50	13.50	15.00	20.00
	1196	10	11.50	13.50	15.00	20.00
	1197	11	11.50	13.50	15.00	20.00
	1198	12	11.50	13.50	15.00	20.00
	1199	13	11.50	13.50	15.00	20.00
	1200	14	11.50	13.50	15.00	20.00
	1200	15	11.50	13.50	15.00	20.00
	1201	16	11.50	13.50	15.00	20.00
	1202	17	11.50	13.50	15.00	20.00
	1203	18	11.50	13.50	15.00	20.00
	1204	19	11.50	13.50	15.00	20.00
	1205	20	11.50	13.50	15.00	20.00
	1206	21	11.50	13.50	15.00	20.00
	1207	21	11.50	13.50	15.00	20.00

Shah Zaman

C#	Date	Year	VG	Fine	VF	XF
461	AH1208	1	12.50	15.00	18.50	25.00
	1208	2	12.50	15.00	18.50	25.00
	1210	3	12.50	15.00	18.50	25.00
	1211	4	12.50	15.00	18.50	25.00
	1213	5	12.50	15.00	18.50	25.00
	1214	6	12.50	15.00	18.50	25.00
	1215	7	12.50	15.00	18.50	25.00

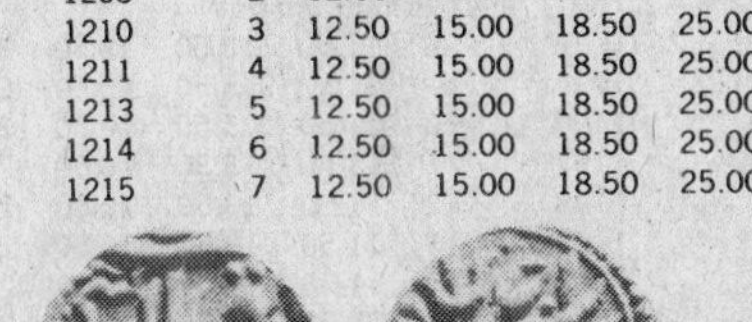

Mahmud Shah, 1st reign

C#	Date	Year	VG	Fine	VF	XF
541	AH1216	1	11.50	13.50	16.50	22.50
	—	2	11.50	13.50	16.50	22.50

Shah Shuja al-Mulk, 2nd reign

C#	Date	Year	VG	Fine	VF	XF
621	—	1	12.50	15.00	18.50	25.00
	—	4	12.50	15.00	18.50	25.00
	—	5	12.50	15.00	18.50	25.00

MOHUR

GOLD
Ahmad Shah

C#	Date	Year	VG	Fine	VF	XF
271	AH1166	5	—	—	—	—
	—	8	—	—	—	—
	—	9	—	—	—	—
	1170	10	—	—	—	—
	1175	15	—	—	—	—
	1175	16	—	—	—	—
	1184	25	—	—	—	—

Taimur Shah, as Nizam

C#	Date	Year	VG	Fine	VF	XF
321	AH1170	1	—	—	—	—
	117x	3	—	—	—	—

Taimur Shah, as King

C#	Date	Year	VG	Fine	VF	XF
401	AH—	1	—	—	—	—
	1202	17	—	—	—	—
	1204	19	—	—	—	—

Shah Zaman

C#	Date	Year	VG	Fine	VF	XF
481	AH1208	1	—	—	—	—
	1208	2	—	—	—	—
	1210	3	—	—	—	—

Shah Shuja al-Mulk, 2nd reign

C#	Date	Year	VG	Fine	VF	XF
645	AH1218	—	225.00	250.00	300.00	400.00

NOTE: The mint of Dera was located at Dera Ghazi Khan, taken by the Sikhs in AH1235 (1819AD), and now within Pakistan.

DERAJAT

Dera Ismail Khan

RUPEE

SILVER
Ahmad Shah

C#	Date	Year	VG	Fine	VF	XF
241	AH1168	—	12.50	15.00	18.50	25.00
	1173	—	12.50	15.00	18.50	25.00
	1180	—	12.50	15.00	18.50	25.00
	1181	—	12.50	15.00	18.50	25.00
	1183	23	12.50	15.00	18.50	25.00

Taimur Shah

C#	Date	Year	VG	Fine	VF	XF
381	AH1192	8	11.50	13.50	16.50	22.50
	1194	—	11.50	13.50	16.50	22.50
	1196	10	11.50	13.50	16.50	22.50
	1197	11	11.50	13.50	16.50	22.50
	1198	12	11.50	13.50	16.50	22.50
	1199	13	11.50	13.50	16.50	22.50
	1199	15	11.50	13.50	16.50	22.50
	1200	15	11.50	13.50	16.50	22.50
	1201	16	11.50	13.50	16.50	22.50
	1202	17	11.50	13.50	16.50	22.50
	1202	18	11.50	13.50	16.50	22.50
	1203	18	11.50	13.50	16.50	22.50
	1204	18	11.50	13.50	16.50	22.50
	1205	19	11.50	13.50	16.50	22.50
	1206	19	11.50	13.50	16.50	22.50
	1206	20	11.50	13.50	16.50	22.50
	1207	20	11.50	13.50	16.50	22.50
	—	21	11.50	13.50	16.50	22.50
	1207	22	11.50	13.50	16.50	22.50
	1208	—	12.50	15.00	18.50	25.00
	1209	—	12.50	15.00	18.50	25.00

NOTE: The issues of AH1208 & 1209 are posthumous issues, bearing no regnal year.

Shah Zaman

C#	Date	Year	VG	Fine	VF	XF
461	1207	1	12.50	15.00	18.50	25.00
	1208	—	12.50	15.00	18.50	25.00
	1209	2	12.50	15.00	18.50	25.00
	1210	2	12.50	15.00	18.50	25.00
	1211	2	12.50	15.00	18.50	25.00
	1212	2	12.50	15.00	18.50	25.00
	1212	6	12.50	15.00	18.50	25.00
	1213	7	12.50	15.00	18.50	25.00
	1214	7	12.50	15.00	18.50	25.00
	1215	8	12.50	15.00	18.50	25.00

NOTE: The regnal year 2 was retained for five years, for reasons unknown today.

Mahmud Shah, 1st reign

C#	Date	Year	VG	Fine	VF	XF
541.1	AH1216	1	11.50	13.50	16.50	22.50
	1217	2	11.50	13.50	16.50	22.50

Shah Shuja al-Mulk, 2nd reign

C#	Date	Year	VG	Fine	VF	XF
621	AH1218	1	12.50	15.00	18.50	25.00
	1218	2	12.50	15.00	18.50	25.00
	1219	2	12.50	15.00	18.50	25.00
	1220	2	12.50	15.00	18.50	25.00
	1220	3	12.50	15.00	18.50	25.00
	1221	4	12.50	15.00	18.50	25.00
	1221	5	12.50	15.00	18.50	25.00
	—	6	12.50	15.00	18.50	25.00

Shah Mahmud, 2nd reign

C#	Date	Year	VG	Fine	VF	XF
541.2	AH1224	1	13.50	16.50	21.50	27.50
	1226	3	13.50	16.50	21.50	27.50
	1227	3	13.50	16.50	21.50	27.50
	1228	4	13.50	16.50	21.50	27.50
	1234	—	13.50	16.50	21.50	27.50
	1236	—	13.50	16.50	21.50	27.50
	1237	—	13.50	16.50	21.50	27.50
	1240	—	13.50	16.50	21.50	27.50
	1241	—	13.50	16.50	21.50	27.50
	1242	—	13.50	16.50	21.50	27.50
	1244	—	13.50	16.50	21.50	27.50
	1245	—	13.50	16.50	21.50	27.50
	1246	—	13.50	16.50	21.50	27.50
	1247	—	13.50	16.50	21.50	27.50
	1248	—	13.50	16.50	21.50	27.50
	1250	—	13.50	16.50	21.50	27.50
	1251	—	13.50	16.50	21.50	27.50

NOTE: The mint of Derajat was located at Dera Ismail Khan, which fell to the Sikhs in AH1236 (1820-21AD). Issues in the name of Mahmud Shah dated AH1236 and later are actually Sikh issues. For other and later issues, see the Indian States of Punjab and Derajat.

MOHUR

GOLD
Ahmad Shah

C#	Date	Year	VG	Fine	VF	XF
271	AH1161	—	—	—	—	—
	117x	—	—	—	—	—
	1180	—	—	—	—	—
	—	23	—	—	—	—

Shah Zaman

C#	Date	Year	VG	Fine	VF	XF
481	AH1211	2	—	—	—	—

HERAT

'Dar as-Sultanat'

1/12 RUPEE

SILVER, 0.9 gm.
Mahmud Shah

C#	Date	Year	VG	Fine	VF	XF
517	AH1230	—	15.00	25.00	40.00	60.00

1/8 RUPEE

SILVER, 13mm
Abdur Rahman

C#	Date	Year	VG	Fine	VF	XF
971	AH1307	—	15.00	22.50	35.00	50.00

1/6 RUPEE

SILVER, 1.8 gm.
Mahmud Shah

C#	Date	Year	VG	Fine	VF	XF
519	AH12xx	—	13.50	18.50	28.50	40.00

C#	Date	Year	VG	Fine	VF	XF
836	AH1257	—	25.00	35.00	50.00	65.00

Yaqub Khan, 11mm

C#	Date	Year	VG	Fine	VF	XF
940	AH1297	—	—	—	Rare	—

1/4 RUPEE

SILVER, 2.7 gm.
Mahmud Shah

C#	Date	Year	VG	Fine	VF	XF
521	AH1242	—	10.00	16.50	23.50	35.00

Kamran Shah

C#	Date	Year	VG	Fine	VF	XF
831	AH1248	—	20.00	30.00	45.00	60.00

1/2 RUPEE

SILVER
Mahmud Shah

C#	Date	Year	VG	Fine	VF	XF
531	AH1242	—	12.50	17.50	27.50	35.00
	1243	—	12.50	17.50	27.50	35.00

Kamran Shah

C#	Date	Year	VG	Fine	VF	XF
837	AH125x	—	20.00	30.00	45.00	60.00

Yar Muhammad (anonymous)

C#	Date	Year	VG	Fine	VF	XF
878	AH1261	—	8.00	12.50	20.00	25.00
	1263	—	7.00	10.00	16.50	22.50
	1265	—	8.00	12.50	20.00	25.00

Muhammad Yusuf Khan Sadozai (anonymous)

C#	Date	Year	VG	Fine	VF	XF
896	AH1271	—	20.00	30.00	45.00	60.00

Sher Ali
Obv: AMIR at top. Rev: Date.

C#	Date	Year	VG	Fine	VF	XF
906.1	AH1281	—	7.00	11.00	17.50	22.50

Sher Ali
Obv: AMIR at bottom, date both sides.

C#	Date	Year	VG	Fine	VF	XF
906	AH1281	—	6.50	10.00	15.00	20.00
	1282	—	6.50	10.00	15.00	20.00

C#	Date	Year	VG	Fine	VF	XF
924a	AH1295	—	6.50	7.00	8.50	10.00

Muhammad Yaqub

C#	Date	Year	VG	Fine	VF	XF
943a	AH1296	—	6.50	7.00	8.50	10.00
	1297	—	6.50	7.00	8.50	10.00
	1298	—	6.50	7.00	8.50	10.00

Abdur Rahman

C#	Date	Year	VG	Fine	VF	XF
975	AH1297	—	6.50	7.00	8.50	10.00
	1298	—	6.50	7.00	8.50	10.00
	1299	—	6.50	7.00	8.50	10.00
	1300	—	6.50	7.00	8.50	10.00
	1301	—	6.50	7.00	8.50	10.00
	1302	—	6.50	7.00	8.50	10.00
	1303	—	6.50	7.00	8.50	10.00
	1304	—	6.50	7.00	8.50	10.00
	1305	—	6.50	7.00	8.50	10.00
	1306	—	6.50	7.00	8.50	10.00
	1307	—	6.50	7.00	8.50	10.00
	1308	—	6.50	7.00	8.50	10.00

NOTE: Many coins of this type C#975 are found with blundered dates. Such coins are worth the same as normal dates.

RUPEE

SILVER
Ahmad Shah

C#	Date	Year	VG	Fine	VF	XF
241	AH1168	8	14.50	21.50	30.00	40.00
	1171	—	14.50	21.50	30.00	40.00

Taimur Shah

C#	Date	Year	VG	Fine	VF	XF
381	AH1184	—	11.50	13.50	16.50	22.50
	1187	—	11.50	13.50	16.50	22.50
	1188	—	11.50	13.50	16.50	22.50
	1189	—	11.50	13.50	16.50	22.50
	1190	—	11.50	13.50	16.50	22.50
	1191	—	11.50	13.50	16.50	22.50
	1192	—	11.50	13.50	16.50	22.50
	1193	—	11.50	13.50	16.50	22.50
	1194	—	11.50	13.50	16.50	22.50
	1195	—	11.50	13.50	16.50	22.50
	1196	—	11.50	13.50	16.50	22.50
	1197	—	11.50	13.50	16.50	22.50
	1198	—	11.50	13.50	16.50	22.50
	1199	—	11.50	13.50	16.50	22.50

C#	Date	Year	VG	Fine	VF	XF
381	1200	—	11.50	13.50	16.50	22.50
	1201	—	11.50	13.50	16.50	22.50
	1202	—	11.50	13.00	15.00	20.00
	1203	—	11.50	13.00	15.00	20.00
	1204	—	11.50	13.00	15.00	20.00
	1205	—	11.50	13.00	15.00	20.00
	1206	—	11.50	13.00	15.00	20.00
	1207	—	11.50	13.00	15.00	20.00
381a	AH1208	—	12.50	15.00	18.50	25.00
	1209	—	12.50	15.00	18.50	25.00
	1210	—	12.50	15.00	18.50	25.00
	1211	—	12.50	15.00	18.50	25.00
381b	AH1216	—	13.50	16.50	22.50	30.00

NOTE: Posthumous Taimur Shah rupees dated AH1208-1211 were struck by his son, Mahmud Shah, during his first reign at Herat. Those dated 1216 are from his 2nd reign at Herat.

NOTE: Rupees dated AH1221 are probably crudely engraved AH1202 or 1212 dates.

Shah Zaman

C#	Date	Year	VG	Fine	VF	XF
461	AH1212	—	11.50	13.50	16.50	22.50
	1213	—	11.50	13.50	16.50	22.50
	1214	—	11.50	13.50	16.50	22.50
	1215	—	11.50	13.50	16.50	22.50

NOTE: Some AH1213 rupees are muled with AH1214 and 1212 reverses. These command no premium.

Mahmud Shah

C#	Date	Year	VG	Fine	VF	XF
541	AH1216	—	11.50	13.00	15.00	18.50
	1217	—	11.50	13.00	15.00	18.50
	1218	—	11.50	13.00	15.00	18.50
	1219	—	11.50	13.00	15.00	18.50
	1220	—	11.50	13.00	15.00	18.50
	1221	—	11.50	13.00	15.00	18.50
	1222	—	11.50	13.00	15.00	18.50
	1223	—	11.50	13.00	15.00	18.50
	1224	—	11.50	13.00	15.00	18.50
	1225	—	11.50	13.00	15.00	18.50
	1226	—	11.50	13.00	15.00	18.50
	1227	—	11.50	13.00	15.00	18.50
	1228	—	11.50	13.00	15.00	18.50
	1229	—	11.50	13.00	15.00	18.50
	1230	—	11.50	13.00	15.00	18.50
	1231	—	11.50	13.00	15.00	18.50
	1232	—	11.50	13.00	15.00	18.50
	1233	—	11.50	13.50	16.50	20.00
	1234	—	11.50	13.50	16.50	20.00
	1235	—	11.50	13.50	16.50	20.00
	1236	—	11.50	13.50	16.50	20.00
	1237	—	11.50	13.50	16.50	20.00
	1238	—	11.50	13.50	16.50	20.00
	1240	—	11.50	13.50	17.50	22.50
	1242	—	11.50	13.50	17.50	22.50
	1254 (error date)					
		—	11.50	13.50	17.50	22.50

Kamran Shah

C#	Date	Year	VG	Fine	VF	XF
839	AH1248	—	Reported, not confirmed			
	1252	—	15.00	23.50	32.50	45.00

NOTE: After 1254, rupees ceased to be coined at Herat. Later emissions, beginning with anonymous issues of Yar Muhammad Khan, were half rupees. From AH1272-1280 (1856-63AD), Herat was occupied by the Persians, who struck coins there in the name of Nasir Al-Din Shah. The mint was closed in AH1308 (1891AD).

TILLA

GOLD
Muhammad Yusuf Khan Sadozai

C#	Date	Year	VG	Fine	VF	XF
898	AH1272	—	200.00	250.00	300.00	400.00

NOTE: A tilla dated AH1284 of Sher Ali has been reported.

MOHUR

GOLD
Ahmad Shah

C#	Date	Year	VG	Fine	VF	XF
271	ND	—	—	—	—	—

Taimur Shah

C#	Date	Year	VG	Fine	VF	XF
401	AH1192	—	—	—	—	—
	1194	—	—	—	—	—
	1195	—	—	—	—	—
	1200	—	—	—	—	—
	1203	—	—	—	—	—
	1205	—	—	—	—	—
	1206	—	—	—	—	—
	1207	—	—	—	—	—

Shah Zaman

C#	Date	Year	VG	Fine	VF	XF
481	AH1212	—	—	—	—	—
	1214	—	—	—	—	—

KABUL

'Dar al-Mulk' (until AH1163)
'Dar as-Sultanat' (after AH1164)

1/16 RUPEE

SILVER, 1.5 gm.
Sher Ali Khan

C#	Date	Year	VG	Fine	VF	XF
440	AH1287		25.00	35.00	50.00	75.00

1/4 RUPEE

SILVER
Shah Zaman

C#	Date	Year	VG	Fine	VF	XF
441	ND	—	10.00	17.50	27.50	40.00

1/3 RUPEE

SILVER, 16mm
Muhammad Yaqub

C#	Date	Year	VG	Fine	VF	XF
941	AH1296	—	11.50	18.50	25.00	35.00

Abdur Rahman
15mm

C#	Date	Year	VG	Fine	VF	XF
973	AH1298	—	11.50	18.50	25.00	35.00

1/2 RUPEE

SILVER
Shah Zaman

C#	Date	Year	VG	Fine	VF	XF
451	AH1212	—	12.50	18.50	27.50	40.00
	—	5	12.50	18.50	27.50	40.00

Sher Ali

C#	Date	Year	VG	Fine	VF	XF
924	AH1288KI	—	6.50	7.50	9.00	12.00
	1292KI	—	6.50	7.50	9.00	12.00
	1293KI	—	6.50	7.50	9.00	12.00
	1294KI	—	6.50	7.50	9.00	12.00

Large, thin planchet; fine engraving

C#	Date	Year	VG	Fine	VF	XF
925.1	AH1292KI	—	7.00	8.50	12.50	16.50

Small, thick planchet; coarse engraving

C#	Date	Year	VG	Fine	VF	XF
925.2	AH1295KI	—	6.50	7.50	9.00	11.00

RUPEE

SILVER

Ahmad Shah

C#	Date	Year	VG	Fine	VF	XF
241	AH—	1	11.50	13.50	16.50	22.50
	—	3	11.50	13.50	16.50	22.50
	—	5	11.50	13.50	16.50	22.50
	—	8	11.50	13.50	16.50	22.50
	1170	—	11.50	13.50	16.50	22.50
	1170 dated 1173 on reverse					
			12.50	15.00	18.50	25.00
	1171	—	11.50	13.50	16.50	22.50
	1173	—	11.50	13.50	16.50	22.50
	1174	—	11.50	13.50	16.50	22.50
	1175	15	11.50	13.50	16.50	22.50
	1176	16	11.50	13.50	16.50	22.50
	1177	17	11.50	13.50	16.50	22.50
	1178	18	11.50	13.50	16.50	22.50
	1180	20	11.50	13.50	16.50	22.50
	1181	—	11.50	13.50	16.50	22.50
	1182	22	11.50	13.50	16.50	22.50
	1183	23	11.50	13.50	16.50	22.50
	1184	23	11.50	13.50	16.50	22.50
	1184	24	11.50	13.50	16.50	22.50
	1185	24	11.50	13.50	16.50	22.50
	1186	25	11.50	13.50	16.50	22.50

Sulaiman Shah

C#	Date	Year	VG	Fine	VF	XF
341	AH1186	1	30.00	45.00	60.00	75.00

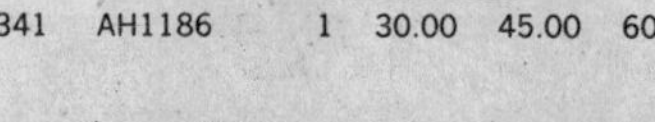

Taimur Shah

C#	Date	Year	VG	Fine	VF	XF
381	AH1186	1	11.50	13.50	16.00	20.00
	1187	1	11.50	13.50	16.00	20.00
	1187	2	11.50	13.50	16.00	20.00
	1188	2	11.50	13.50	16.00	20.00
	1188	3	11.50	13.50	16.00	20.00
	1189	3	11.50	13.50	16.00	20.00
	1190	4	11.50	13.50	16.00	20.00
	1191	4	11.50	13.50	16.00	20.00
	1191	5	11.50	13.50	16.00	20.00
	1192	6	11.50	13.50	16.00	20.00
	1193	7	11.50	13.50	16.00	20.00
	1194	8	11.50	13.50	16.00	20.00
	1195	9	11.50	13.50	16.00	20.00
	1197	11	11.50	13.50	16.00	20.00
	—	12	11.50	13.50	16.00	20.00
	1200	13	11.50	13.50	16.00	20.00
	1201	—	11.50	13.50	16.00	20.00
	—	15	11.50	13.50	16.00	20.00
	—	16	11.50	13.50	16.00	20.00
	1203	17	11.50	13.50	16.00	20.00
	1204	18	11.50	13.50	16.00	20.00
	1204	19	11.50	13.50	16.00	20.00
	1205	19	11.50	13.50	16.00	20.00
	1205	20	11.50	13.50	16.00	20.00
	1206	20	11.50	13.50	16.00	20.00
	1207	20	11.50	13.50	16.00	20.00
	1207	21	11.50	13.50	16.00	20.00

Shah Zaman

C#	Date	Year	VG	Fine	VF	XF
461	AH1207	1	11.50	13.00	15.00	17.50
	1208	1	11.50	13.00	15.00	17.50
	1208	2	11.50	13.00	15.00	17.50
	1209	2	11.50	13.00	15.00	17.50
	1209	3	11.50	13.00	15.00	17.50
	1210	4	11.50	13.00	15.00	17.50
	1211	4	11.50	13.00	15.00	17.50
	1211	5	11.50	13.00	15.00	17.50
	1212	4	(muling with old die)			
			11.50	13.50	16.50	22.50
	1212	5	11.50	13.00	15.00	17.50
	1212	6	11.50	13.00	15.00	17.50
	1213	6	11.50	13.00	15.00	17.50
	1213	7	11.50	13.00	15.00	17.50
	1215	7	11.50	13.00	15.00	17.50
	1215	8	11.50	13.00	15.00	17.50

Mahmud Shah, 1st reign

C#	Date	Year	VG	Fine	VF	XF
541.1	AH1216	1	11.50	13.50	16.50	22.50
	1217	1	11.50	13.50	16.50	22.50
	1217	2	11.50	13.50	16.50	22.50
	1218	2	11.50	13.50	16.50	22.50

Shah Shuja al-Mulk, 2nd reign

C#	Date	Year	VG	Fine	VF	XF
621	AH1218	1	12.50	15.00	18.50	25.00
	1219	2	12.50	15.00	18.50	25.00
	1222	—	12.50	15.00	18.50	25.00
	1223	—	12.50	15.00	18.50	25.00

Qaisar Shah (as rebel)

C#	Date	Year	VG	Fine	VF	XF
670	AH1222	1	20.00	30.00	42.50	55.00

Mahmud Shah, 2nd reign

C#	Date	Year	VG	Fine	VF	XF
541.2	AH1225	2	12.50	15.00	18.50	25.00
	1228	5	12.50	15.00	18.50	25.00
	—	8	12.50	15.00	18.50	25.00

NOTE: Several varieties of type.

C#	Date	Year	VG	Fine	VF	XF
541.3	AH1226	3	13.50	16.50	22.50	35.00

Ayyub Shah

C#	Date	Year	VG	Fine	VF	XF
811	AH1234	1	12.50	18.50	26.50	35.00
	1234	2	12.50	18.50	26.50	35.00
	1235	2	12.50	18.50	26.50	35.00
	1237	3	12.50	18.50	26.50	35.00

Dost Muhammad, 1st reign

In the name of Mahmud Shah Durrani

C#	Date	Year	VG	Fine	VF	XF
824.1	AH1239	—	12.50	15.00	20.00	27.50

Anonymous, with title Sultan al-Zaman

C#	Date	Year	VG	Fine	VF	XF
824.2	AH1239	—	11.50	13.50	17.50	25.00

Anonymous, with title Sahib al-Zaman

C#	Date	Year	VG	Fine	VF	XF
824a.1						
	AH1240	1	11.50	13.50	16.50	20.00
	1241	2	11.50	13.50	16.50	20.00

C#	Date	Year	VG	Fine	VF	XF
824a.2						
	AH1241	—	11.50	13.00	15.00	18.50
	1242	—	11.50	13.00	15.00	18.50
	1243	—	11.50	13.00	15.00	18.50
	1244	—	11.50	13.00	15.00	18.50

C#	Date	Year	VG	Fine	VF	XF
824a.3						
	AH1243	—	11.50	13.00	15.00	18.50
	1244	—	11.50	13.00	15.00	18.50
	1245	—	11.50	13.00	15.00	18.50

In the name of his father, Payinda Khan.

C#	Date	Year	VG	Fine	VF	XF
825	AH1245	—	11.50	13.00	15.00	18.50
	1246	—	11.50	13.00	15.00	18.50
	1247	—	11.50	13.00	15.00	18.50
	1248	—	11.50	13.00	15.00	18.50
	1249	—	11.50	13.00	15.00	18.50
	1250	—	11.50	13.00	15.00	18.50

NOTE: Four varieties known.

In his own name

C#	Date	Year	VG	Fine	VF	XF
827	AH1250	—	11.50	13.00	15.00	18.50
	1251	—	11.50	13.00	15.00	18.50
	1252	—	11.50	13.00	15.00	18.50
	1253	—	11.50	13.00	15.00	18.50
	1254	—	11.50	13.00	15.00	18.50

C#	Date	Year	VG	Fine	VF	XF
827	1255	—	11.50	13.00	15.00	18.50
	ND, KI	—	11.50	13.00	15.00	18.50

Shah Shuja al-Mulk, 3rd reign
Obv: Long inscription.

C#	Date	Year	VG	Fine	VF	XF
621.1	AH1255	—	12.50	15.00	23.50	30.00

Obv: Short inscription, title SULTAN.

C#	Date	Year	VG	Fine	VF	XF
621.2	AH1255	—	11.50	13.00	15.00	18.50
	1256	—	11.50	13.00	15.00	18.50
	1257	—	11.50	13.50	16.50	20.00

Anonymous type in name of Sahib al-Zaman

C#	Date	Year	VG	Fine	VF	XF
858	AH1257	—	12.50	20.00	30.00	40.00

Struck by Shah Shuja al-Mulk in the name of Shah Zaman

C#	Date	Year	VG	Fine	VF	XF
461a	AH1258	—	12.50	16.50	25.00	35.00

Fath Jang

C#	Date	Year	VG	Fine	VF	XF
861	AH1258	—	15.00	22.50	32.50	45.00

NOTE: 4 varieties are known.

Shahpur Shah

C#	Date	Year	VG	Fine	VF	XF
871	AH1258	—	20.00	30.00	45.00	60.00

Dost Muhammad, 2nd reign
Anonymous, with Kalimah

C#	Date	Year	VG	Fine	VF	XF
826a	AH1258	—	11.50	13.50	16.50	22.50

In the name of Shuja al-Mulk Durrani
With title SULTAN

C#	Date	Year	VG	Fine	VF	XF
621.3	AH1258	—	12.50	15.00	20.00	27.50
	1259	—	12.50	15.00	20.00	27.50

In the name of Shuja al-Mulk Durrani
With title Durr-i-Durran

C#	Date	Year	VG	Fine	VF	XF
621.4	AH1259	—	12.50	15.00	20.00	27.50

In his own name, obv: long couplet.

C#	Date	Year	VG	Fine	VF	XF
882.1	AH1259	—	13.50	16.50	22.50	30.00

In his own name, obv: couplet ending 'Khaliq-i-Akbar'.
Many varieties

C#	Date	Year	VG	Fine	VF	XF
882	AH1263	—	11.50	13.50	16.50	20.00
	1265	—	11.50	13.00	15.00	18.50
	1266	—	11.50	13.00	15.00	18.50
	1267	—	11.50	13.00	15.00	18.50
	1268	—	11.50	13.00	15.00	18.50
	1269	—	11.50	13.00	15.00	18.50
	1270	—	11.50	13.00	15.00	18.50
	1271	—	11.50	13.00	15.00	18.50
	1272	—	11.50	13.00	15.00	18.50
	1273	—	11.50	13.00	15.00	18.50
	1274	—	11.50	13.00	15.00	18.50
	1275	—	11.50	13.00	15.00	18.50
	1276	—	11.50	13.00	15.00	18.50
	1277	—	11.50	13.00	15.00	18.50
	1277/8	—	11.50	13.00	15.00	18.50
	1278	—	11.50	13.00	15.00	18.50
	1279	—	11.50	13.00	15.00	18.50

Shir, Ali, 1st reign
Obv: Couplet starting 'Za Aini Marhamat...'

C#	Date	Year	VG	Fine	VF	XF
903	AH1280	—	11.50	12.50	14.00	16.50
	1281	—	11.50	12.50	14.00	16.50
	1282	—	11.50	12.50	14.00	16.50

NOTE: Two varieties of obv. exist.

Anonymous, with title Sahib al-Zaman

C#	Date	Year	VG	Fine	VF	XF
	AH1282	—	12.50	15.00	20.00	30.00

Muhammad Afzal

C#	Date	Year	VG	Fine	VF	XF
913	AH1283	—	11.50	13.50	16.50	22.50
	1284	—	11.50	13.50	18.50	25.00

NOTE: 2 varieties are known dated AH1283.

Muhammad A'zam

C#	Date	Year	VG	Fine	VF	XF
919	AH1284	—	11.50	13.50	18.50	25.00

NOTE: 2 varieties are known.

C#	Date	Year	VG	Fine	VF	XF
919a	AH1285	—	12.50	16.50	22.50	30.00

Sher Ali, 2nd reign
Obv: Couplet starting 'Za Iltifat-i...'

C#	Date	Year	VG	Fine	VF	XF
927	AH1285	—	11.50	13.00	15.00	18.50

With 3-stem toughra

C#	Date	Year	VG	Fine	VF	XF
928	AH1285	—	11.50	13.00	15.00	18.00
	1286	—	11.50	13.00	15.00	18.00
	1287	—	11.50	13.00	15.00	18.00

With 5-stem toughra.

C#	Date	Year	VG	Fine	VF	XF
928a	AH1286	—	25.00	40.00	60.00	80.00

C#	Date	Year	VG	Fine	VF	XF
929	AH1287	—	11.50	12.50	14.50	16.50
	1288	—	11.50	12.50	14.50	16.50
	1289	—	11.50	12.50	14.50	16.50
	1290	—	11.50	12.50	14.50	16.50
	1291	—	11.50	12.50	14.50	16.50
	1292	—	11.50	12.50	14.50	16.50
	1293	—	11.50	12.50	14.50	16.50
	1294	—	11.50	12.50	14.50	16.50
	1295	—	11.50	12.50	14.50	16.50
	1295 (dated 1296 on rev.)					
		—	11.50	13.50	16.50	21.50
	1296 date on both sides					
		—	11.50	12.50	14.50	16.50

NOTE: Other examples bearing different obverse and reverse dates probably exist, and would be worth the same as the example given.

Fine style

C#	Date	Year	VG	Fine	VF	XF
930.1	AH1292	—	11.50	12.50	16.50	20.00
	1293	—	11.50	12.50	16.50	20.00

Coarse style

C#	Date	Year	VG	Fine	VF	XF
930.2	AH1293	—	11.50	12.50	14.00	16.50
	1294	—	11.50	12.50	14.00	16.50
	1295	—	11.50	12.50	14.00	16.50

Muhammad Yaqub

C#	Date	Year	VG	Fine	VF	XF
945	AH1296	—	11.50	12.50	14.00	16.50
	1297	—	11.50	12.50	14.00	16.50

Wali Muhammad

C#	Date	Year	VG	Fine	VF	XF
951	AH1297	—	11.50	13.50	17.50	22.50

C#	Date	Year	VG	Fine	VF	XF
976	AH1297	—	15.00	21.50	30.00	40.00

Abdur Rahman Khan
Many varieties

C#	Date	Year	VG	Fine	VF	XF
977	AH1297	—	11.50	13.00	15.00	17.50
	1298	—	11.50	13.00	15.00	17.50
	1299	—	11.50	13.00	15.00	17.50
	1300	—	11.50	13.00	15.00	17.50
	1301	—	11.50	13.00	15.00	17.50
	1302	—	11.50	13.00	15.00	17.50
	1302/1298	—	11.50	13.00	15.00	17.50
	1303	—	11.50	13.00	15.00	17.50
	1304	—	11.50	13.00	15.00	17.50
	1304/5	—	11.50	13.00	15.00	17.50
	1305	—	11.50	13.00	15.00	17.50
	1306	—	11.50	13.00	15.00	17.50
	1307	—	11.50	13.00	15.00	17.50
	1308/7	—	11.50	13.00	15.00	17.50
	1308	—	11.50	13.00	15.00	17.50

NOTE: Obverses are often muled with reverses bearing a different date.

NOTE: The year 1297 has been observed struck over an 1876 British India 1/4 Rupee, probably a mint sport.

Muhammad Ishak
Struck at Balkh, but inscribed KABUL.

C#	Date	Year	VG	Fine	VF	XF
968	AH1305	—	18.50	28.50	40.00	60.00
	1306	—	18.50	28.50	40.00	60.00

NOTE: 2 varieties in name exist.

2 RUPEES

SILVER
Shah Zaman

C#	Date	Year	VG	Fine	VF	XF
475	AH1212	5	45.00	60.00	80.00	100.00
	1212	6	45.00	60.00	80.00	100.00
	1213	6	45.00	60.00	80.00	100.00

Mahmud Shah, 2nd reign

C#	Date	Year	VG	Fine	VF	XF
561	AH1225	1	50.00	75.00	100.00	140.00

TILLA

GOLD
Dost Muhammad

C#	Date	Year	VG	Fine	VF	XF
887	AH1269	—	125.00	160.00	200.00	250.00

Sher Ali, 2nd reign

C#	Date	Year	VG	Fine	VF	XF
935	AH1294	—	140.00	180.00	225.00	300.00
	1295	—	130.00	165.00	200.00	250.00
	1296	—	130.00	165.00	200.00	250.00

MOHUR

GOLD
Ahmad Shah

C#	Date	Year	VG	Fine	VF	XF
271	AH1161	1	—	—	—	—
	1170	10	—	—	—	—
	1181	21	—	—	—	—
	1185	25	—	—	—	—
	1186	25	—	—	—	—

Sulaiman Shah

C#	Date	Year	VG	Fine	VF	XF
351	AH1186	1	225.00	240.00	265.00	300.00

Taimur Shah

C#	Date	Year	VG	Fine	VF	XF
401	AH1186	1	225.00	240.00	265.00	300.00
	1189	3	225.00	240.00	265.00	300.00
	1190	4	225.00	240.00	265.00	300.00
	1192	6	225.00	240.00	265.00	300.00
	1194	8	225.00	240.00	265.00	300.00
	1197	11	225.00	240.00	265.00	300.00
	1199	13	225.00	240.00	265.00	300.00
	1201	15	225.00	240.00	265.00	300.00
	1204	18	225.00	240.00	265.00	300.00
	1209	21	225.00	240.00	265.00	300.00

Shah Zaman

C#	Date	Year	VG	Fine	VF	XF
481	AH1208	1	—	—	—	—
	1209	2	—	—	—	—
	1209	3	—	—	—	—
	1211	4	—	—	—	—
	12xx	5	—	—	—	—
	1213	6	—	—	—	—

Qaisar Shah

C#	Date	Year	VG	Fine	VF	XF
	AH1222	—	—	—	—	—

Shah Shuja al-Mulk, 2nd reign

C#	Date	Year	VG	Fine	VF	XF
645	AH1223	—	225.00	240.00	265.00	300.00

Mahmud Shah, 2nd reign

C#	Date	Year	VG	Fine	VF	XF
581	AH1224	2	225.00	240.00	265.00	300.00
	122x	8	225.00	240.00	265.00	300.00

Shah Shuja al-Mulk, 3rd reign

C#	Date	Year	VG	Fine	VF	XF
645	AH1255	—	225.00	250.00	285.00	325.00
	1258	—	225.00	250.00	285.00	325.00

Sher Ali

C#	Date	Year	VG	Fine	VF	XF
933	AH1288KI	—	235.00	265.00	300.00	350.00

MULTAN

Known as 'Dar al-Aman', ('Abode of Security'), Multan was annexed by Ahmad Shah in AH1165/AD1752, and held under Afghan rule until lost to the Sikhs in AH1233/AD1818, except for an interval of Sikh control from AH1185-1194/AD1771-1780.

FALUS

COPPER
Ahmad Shah

C#	Date	Year	Good	VG	Fine	VF
201	AH1170	10	5.00	7.50	11.50	16.50
	1172	12	3.75	7.50	11.50	17.50

Taimur Shah

C#	Date	Year	Good	VG	Fine	VF
361	AH1181 (error date)					
		—	2.75	5.50	7.50	11.50
	1194	3	2.75	5.50	7.50	11.50
	1196	—	2.75	5.50	7.50	11.50
	1197	6	2.75	5.50	7.50	11.50
	1200	7	2.75	5.50	7.50	11.50
	—	8	2.75	5.50	7.50	11.50
	1201	10	2.75	5.50	7.50	11.50
	1202	10	2.75	5.50	7.50	11.50
	1203	10	2.75	5.50	7.50	11.50
	1204	—	2.75	5.50	7.50	11.50
	1205	19	2.75	5.50	7.50	11.50
	1206	19	2.75	5.50	7.50	11.50
	1206	20	2.75	5.50	7.50	11.50
	1207	19	2.75	5.50	7.50	11.50

NOTE: AH dates & regnal years are frequently mismatched.

Shah Zaman

C#	Date	Year	Good	VG	Fine	VF
431	AH1211	4	3.25	6.50	9.00	13.50
	1212	5	3.25	6.50	9.00	13.50
	1215	8	3.25	6.50	9.00	13.50

Mahmud Shah, 2nd reign

C#	Date	Year	Good	VG	Fine	VF
531	AH1226	1	3.75	7.50	10.00	15.00
	1231	—	3.75	7.50	10.00	15.00

RUPEE

SILVER
Ahmad Shah

C#	Date	Year	VG	Fine	VF	XF
241.1	AH1165	5	11.50	12.50	15.00	18.50
	1166	5	11.50	12.50	15.00	18.50
	1166	6	11.50	12.50	15.00	18.50
	1167	6	11.50	12.50	15.00	18.50
	1167	7	11.50	12.50	15.00	18.50
	1168	7	11.50	12.50	15.00	18.50
	1168	8	11.50	12.50	15.00	18.50
	1169	8	11.50	12.50	15.00	18.50

C#	Date	Year	VG	Fine	VF	XF
241.2	AH1169	9	11.50	12.50	15.00	18.50
	1170	9	11.50	12.50	15.00	18.50
	1170	10	11.50	12.50	15.00	18.50

Taimur Shah as Nizam

C#	Date	Year	VG	Fine	VF	XF
301	AH1170	1	11.50	13.50	16.50	20.00
	1171	1	11.50	13.50	16.50	20.00
	1172	2	11.50	13.50	16.50	20.00
	1173	2	11.50	13.50	16.50	20.00
	1173	3	11.50	13.50	16.50	20.00
	1174	3	11.50	13.50	16.50	20.00
	1174	4	11.50	13.50	16.50	20.00
	1175	4	11.50	13.50	16.50	20.00
	1175	5	11.50	13.50	16.50	20.00
	1176	5	11.50	13.50	16.50	20.00
	1176	6	11.50	13.50	16.50	20.00
	1177	7	11.50	13.50	16.50	20.00
	1177	8	11.50	13.50	16.50	20.00
	1178	8	11.50	13.50	16.50	20.00
	1178	9	11.50	13.50	16.50	20.00
	1179	9	11.50	13.50	16.50	20.00
	1179	10	11.50	13.50	16.50	20.00
	1180	10	11.50	13.50	16.50	20.00
	1180	11	11.50	13.50	16.50	20.00
	1181	11	11.50	13.50	16.50	20.00
	1181	12	11.50	13.50	16.50	20.00
	1182	12	11.50	13.50	16.50	20.00
	1182	13	11.50	13.50	16.50	20.00
	1183	13	11.50	13.50	16.50	20.00
	1183	14	11.50	13.50	16.50	20.00
	1184	14	11.50	13.50	16.50	20.00
	1184	15	11.50	13.50	16.50	20.00
	1185	15	11.50	13.50	16.50	20.00
	1185	16	11.50	13.50	16.50	20.00

Taimur Shah, as King

C#	Date	Year	VG	Fine	VF	XF
381	AH1194	3	11.50	12.50	14.00	16.50
	1195	4	11.50	12.50	14.00	16.50
	1197	5	11.50	12.50	14.00	16.50
	1198	5	11.50	12.50	14.00	16.50
	1198	6	11.50	12.50	14.00	16.50
	1198	7	11.50	12.50	14.00	16.50
	1199	7	11.50	12.50	14.00	16.50
	1200	7	11.50	12.50	14.00	16.50
	1201	7	11.50	12.50	14.00	16.50
	1203	9	11.50	12.50	14.00	16.50
	1203	10	11.50	12.50	14.00	16.50
	1204	10	11.50	12.50	14.00	16.50

With normal regnal years

C#	Date	Year	VG	Fine	VF	XF
381a	AH1204	18	11.50	12.50	14.00	16.50
	1205	18	11.50	12.50	14.00	16.50
	1205	19	11.50	12.50	14.00	16.50
	1206	19	11.50	12.50	14.00	16.50
	1207	20	11.50	12.50	14.00	16.50

NOTE: Rupees of AH1194-1204 (C#381) are struck on small, thick flans, and have mismatched regnal years, due to the Sikh occupation of Multan from AH1185-94. In AH1204, the flan was made broader, the design changed, and the regnal years made to conform with Taimur's other mints.

Shah Zaman

C#	Date	Year	VG	Fine	VF	XF
461	AH1207	1	11.50	13.50	16.50	22.50
	1208	1	11.50	13.50	16.50	22.50
	1209	1	11.50	13.50	16.50	22.50
	1210	1	11.50	13.50	16.50	22.50
	1215	8	11.50	13.50	16.50	22.50

NOTE: It is not known why the first regnal year was retained so long at Multan.

Mahmud Shah, 1st reign

C#	Date	Year	VG	Fine	VF	XF
541	AH1216	1	11.50	13.50	16.50	22.50
	1218	1	11.50	13.50	16.50	22.50

Shah Shuja al-Mulk, 2nd reign

C#	Date	Year	VG	Fine	VF	XF
621	AH1218	1	11.50	13.50	18.50	22.50
	1219	—	11.50	13.50	18.50	22.50

MOHUR

GOLD
Ahmad Shah

C#	Date	Year	VG	Fine	VF	XF
271	AH1165	5	—	—	—	—
	1166	5	—	—	—	—
	1167	6	—	—	—	—
	—	8	—	—	—	—
	1169	9	—	—	—	—
	1170	9	—	—	—	—
	1170	10	—	—	—	—

Taimur Shah, as Nizam

C#	Date	Year	VG	Fine	VF	XF
321	AH1170	1	—	—	—	—
	1173	2	—	—	—	—
	1176	6	—	—	—	—
	—	9	—	—	—	—
	1182	12	—	—	—	—

Taimur Shah, as King

C#	Date	Year	VG	Fine	VF	XF
401	AH1203	9	—	—	—	—
	1203	10	—	—	—	—

Shah Zaman

C#	Date	Year	VG	Fine	VF	XF
481	AH1210	1	—	—	—	—

Shah Shuja al-Mulk, 2nd reign

C#	Date	Year	VG	Fine	VF	XF
645	AH1218	1	225.00	250.00	285.00	375.00
	1224	8	225.00	250.00	285.00	375.00

NOTE: Multan fell to the Sikhs in AH1233 (1818AD). For later issues, as well as coins issued during the Sikh occupation of AH1185-94, see India: Sikhs.

PESHAWAR

Peshawar was inherited by Ahmad Shah from Nadir Shah Afshar, who had seized it from the Mughals in AH1151 (1738AD). It was lost to the Sikhs in AH1250 (1834AD). Although the winter capital of the Durranis, it was never granted an honorific epithet.

FALUS

COPPER
Ahmad Shah

C#	Date	Year	Good	VG	Fine	VF
201	AH—	7	4.50	7.50	12.50	16.50
	1177	17	4.50	7.50	12.50	16.50

Taimur Shah

C#	Date	Year	Good	VG	Fine	VF
361	AH1186	1	4.50	7.50	12.50	16.50
	—	4	4.50	7.50	12.50	16.50
361	—	8	4.50	7.50	12.50	16.50

Ayyub Shah

C#	Date	Year	Good	VG	Fine	VF
801	AH1237	—	5.00	8.50	14.00	18.50

1/10 RUPEE

SILVER
Ahmad Shah

C#	Date	Year	VG	Fine	VF	XF
221	AH1167	7	15.00	22.50	35.00	50.00

RUPEE

SILVER
Ahmad Shah

C#	Date	Year	VG	Fine	VF	XF
241	AH1161	1	12.50	15.00	18.50	25.00
	1161	2	12.50	15.00	18.50	25.00
	1162	2	12.50	15.00	18.50	25.00
	1164	3	12.50	15.00	18.50	25.00
	—	4	12.50	15.00	18.50	25.00
	1166	6	12.50	15.00	18.50	25.00
	1170	10	12.50	15.00	18.50	25.00
	1171	11	12.50	15.00	18.50	25.00
	—	12	12.50	15.00	18.50	25.00
	—	14	12.50	15.00	18.50	25.00
	—	15	12.50	15.00	18.50	25.00
	1176	16	12.50	15.00	18.50	25.00
	1177	17	12.50	15.00	18.50	25.00
	—	18	12.50	15.00	18.50	25.00
	—	19	12.50	15.00	18.50	25.00
	—	22	12.50	15.00	18.50	25.00
	1183	23	12.50	15.00	18.50	25.00
	1184	24	12.50	15.00	18.50	25.00
	1185	25	12.50	15.00	18.50	25.00
	1186	26	12.50	15.00	18.50	25.00

Sulaiman Shah

C#	Date	Year	VG	Fine	VF	XF
341	AH1186	1	40.00	60.00	85.00	110.00

Taimur Shah

C#	Date	Year	VG	Fine	VF	XF
381	AH1186	1	11.50	12.50	14.50	17.50
	1187	1	11.50	12.50	14.50	17.50
	1187	2	11.50	12.50	14.50	17.50
	1188	2	11.50	12.50	14.50	17.50
	1188	3	11.50	12.50	14.50	17.50
	1189	4	11.50	12.50	14.50	17.50
	1190	5	11.50	12.50	14.50	17.50
	1194	8	11.50	12.50	14.50	17.50
	1195	9	11.50	12.50	14.50	17.50
	1196	10	11.50	12.50	14.50	17.50
	1196	11	11.50	12.50	14.50	17.50
	1197	10 (muling)	11.50	13.00	15.00	20.00
	1197	11	11.50	12.50	14.50	17.50
	1197	12	11.50	12.50	14.50	17.50
	1198	12	11.50	12.50	14.50	17.50
	1199	12	11.50	12.50	14.50	17.50
	1199	13	11.50	12.50	14.50	17.50
	1200	13	11.50	12.50	14.50	17.50
	1201	15	11.50	12.50	14.50	17.50
	1203	17	11.50	12.50	14.50	17.50
	—	18	11.50	12.50	14.50	17.50
	—	19	11.50	12.50	14.50	17.50
	1206	20	11.50	12.50	14.50	17.50
	1207	20	11.50	12.50	14.50	17.50

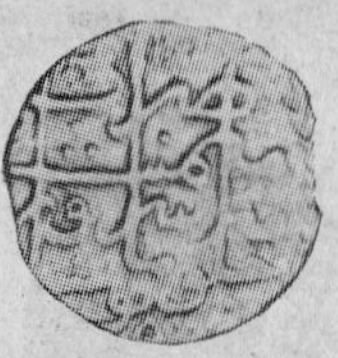

Shah Zaman
Obv: Couplet in 3 lines.

C#	Date	Year	VG	Fine	VF	XF
461.1	AH1208	1	11.50	12.50	14.50	17.50
	1207	2	11.50	12.50	14.50	17.50
	—	2	11.50	12.50	14.50	17.50
	1211	3	11.50	12.50	14.50	17.50
	1211	4	11.50	12.50	14.50	17.50
	1211	5	11.50	12.50	14.50	17.50
	1212	4	11.50	12.50	14.50	17.50
	1212	5	11.50	12.50	14.50	17.50
	1213	6	11.50	12.50	14.50	17.50

Obv: Couplet in circle.

C#	Date	Year	VG	Fine	VF	XF
461.2	AH1215	8	11.50	12.50	14.50	17.50
	1215	9	11.50	12.50	14.50	17.50
	1216	9	11.50	12.50	14.50	17.50

Mahmud Shah, 1st reign

C#	Date	Year	VG	Fine	VF	XF
541	AH1216	1	11.50	13.50	16.00	20.00
	1217	2	11.50	13.50	16.00	20.00
	1218	3	11.50	13.50	16.00	20.00

NOTE: Varieties exist.

Shah Shuja al-Mulk, 2nd reign

C#	Date	Year	VG	Fine	VF	XF
621	AH1218	1	11.50	13.50	16.50	22.50
	1219	2	11.50	13.50	16.50	22.50
	1220	3	11.50	13.50	16.50	22.50
	1221	4	11.50	13.50	16.50	22.50
	1223	6	11.50	13.50	16.50	22.50

As Local Ruler at Peshawar

C#	Date	Year	VG	Fine	VF	XF
621c	AH1227	1	13.50	20.00	30.00	45.00

Mahmud Shah, 2nd reign
Obv: Linear

C#	Date	Year	VG	Fine	VF	XF
541.1	AH1226	2	11.50	13.50	16.00	20.00
	1227	3	11.50	13.50	16.00	20.00
	1227	4	11.50	13.50	16.00	20.00
	1228	4	11.50	13.50	16.00	20.00
	1228	5	11.50	13.50	16.00	20.00
	1229	6	11.50	13.50	16.00	20.00
	1230	6	11.50	13.50	16.00	20.00
	1230	7	11.50	13.50	16.00	20.00
	1231	7	11.50	13.50	16.00	20.00
541.1	1231	8	11.50	13.50	16.00	20.00

Obv: Cartouche

C#	Date	Year	VG	Fine	VF	XF
541.2	AH1232	8	11.50	13.50	16.00	20.00
	1232	9	11.50	13.50	16.00	20.00
	1233	9	11.50	13.50	16.00	20.00
	1233	10	11.50	13.50	16.00	20.00

Shah Shuja briefly at Peshawar in AH1233/AD1818.

C#	Date	Year	VG	Fine	VF	XF
621d	AH1233	1	17.50	30.00	45.00	65.00

NOTE: This coin may be distinguished from C#621 and C#621c by the cartouche and calligraphy of the reverse.

Ayyub Shah
Obv: Name in triple diamond.

C#	Date	Year	VG	Fine	VF	XF
811.1	AH1233	1	15.00	30.00	50.00	75.00

Obv: Couplet in 3 lines.

C#	Date	Year	VG	Fine	VF	XF
811.2	AH1233	2	12.50	15.00	18.50	25.00
	1234	2	12.50	15.00	18.50	25.00
	1235	2	12.50	15.00	18.50	25.00
	1235	3	12.50	15.00	18.50	25.00
	1236	3	12.50	15.00	18.50	25.00
	1237	4	12.50	15.00	18.50	25.00
	1238	5	12.50	15.00	18.50	25.00
	1238	6	12.50	15.00	18.50	25.00
	1239	6	12.50	15.00	18.50	25.00
	1239	7	12.50	15.00	18.50	25.00
	1240	7	12.50	15.00	18.50	25.00
	1240	8	12.50	15.00	18.50	25.00
	1241	7	12.50	15.00	18.50	25.00
	1243	10	12.50	15.00	18.50	25.00
	124x)	11	12.50	15.00	18.50	25.00

Obv: Name in foliated diamond.

C#	Date	Year	VG	Fine	VF	XF
811.3	AH124x	12	15.00	25.00	40.00	60.00

Dost Muhammad, 1st reign

C#	Date	Year	VG	Fine	VF	XF
828	AH1246	—	12.50	15.00	20.00	27.50

Sultan Muhammad
(Anonymous)

C#	Date	Year	VG	Fine	VF	XF
830	AH1247	—	12.50	15.00	20.00	27.50
	1248	—	12.50	15.00	20.00	27.50
	1249	—	12.50	15.00	20.00	27.50

NOTE: Peshawar fell to the Sikhs in AH1250 (AD1834). For later issues, see India: Sikhs.

MOHUR

GOLD
Ahmad Shah

C#	Date	Year	VG	Fine	VF	XF
271	AH1161	1	225.00	250.00	285.00	325.00
	—	9	225.00	250.00	285.00	325.00
	1177	17	225.00	250.00	285.00	325.00

Taimur Shah

C#	Date	Year	VG	Fine	VF	XF
401	AH1186	1	—	—	—	—
	1194	8	—	—	—	—
	1196	11	—	—	—	—
	—	12	—	—	—	—

C#	Date	Year	VG	Fine	VF	XF
401	1202	15	—	—	—	—
	1204	17	—	—	—	—
	1204	18	—	—	—	—
	1205	18	—	—	—	—
	1209	21	Posthumous		—	—
			—	—	—	—

Shah Zaman

C#	Date	Year	VG	Fine	VF	XF
481	AH—	2	—	—	—	—
	—	3	—	—	—	—
	1215	8	—	—	—	—

Ayyub Shah

C#	Date	Year	VG	Fine	VF	XF
821	—	6	225.00	250.00	285.00	325.00
	—	7	225.00	250.00	285.00	325.00

QANDAHAR

Issues of this mint are listed together with those of Ahmadshahi, which was a name of Qandahar granted in honor of Ahmad Shah, founder of the Durrani Kingdom.

RIKAB

The Camp mint, brought with the royal entourage on campaign entitled 'Mubarak', 'Auspicious'.

RUPEE

SILVER
Taimur Shah
Rev: Full legend.

C#	Date	Year	VG	Fine	VF	XF
381a	—	11	30.00	40.00	60.00	85.00

Rev: Short legend in circle.

C#	Date	Year	VG	Fine	VF	XF
381b	ND	—	25.00	35.00	50.00	75.00

MOHUR

GOLD
Ahmad Shah

C#	Date	Year	Fine	VF	XF	Unc
271	AH1173	—	—	—	—	—

Taimur Shah

C#	Date	Year	Fine	VF	XF	Unc
401	AH1191	5	—	—	—	—

Shah Shuja al-Mulk, 2nd reign

C#	Date	Year	Fine	VF	XF	Unc
645	AH1219	—	225.00	250.00	285.00	325.00

Uncertain Mint

1/2 RUPEE

SILVER
Sher Ali

C#	Date	Year	VG	Fine	VF	XF
924b	AH1287	—	6.50	9.00	13.50	17.50

MACHINE-STRUCK COINAGE

MONETARY SYSTEM

10 Dinar = 1 Paisa
5 Paisa = 1 Shahi
2 Shahi = 1 Sanar
2 Sanar = 1 Abbasi
1-1/2 Abbasi = 1 Qiran
2 Qiran = 1 Kabuli Rupee

PAISA

BRONZE, 24-25mm

Y#	Date	Mintage	VG	Fine	VF	XF
1.1	AH1309	—	13.50	22.50	35.00	50.00

Size reduced, 20mm

Y#	Date	Mintage	VG	Fine	VF	XF
1.2	AH1309	—	7.50	13.50	23.50	30.00

BRONZE or BRASS 20-22mm

Y#	Date	Mintage	VG	Fine	VF	XF
2	AH1309	—	1.50	3.00	5.50	10.00
	1312	—	1.25	2.50	5.00	8.50
	1313	—	1.75	3.50	7.00	12.00
	1314	—	1.00	2.50	5.00	8.50
	1316	—	1.75	3.50	6.00	11.00
	1317	—	2.50	4.00	6.50	11.50

NOTE: Coins dated AH1313 and 1317 are known in two varieties. 3 varieties are known for AH1314.

20mm

Y#	Date	Mintage	VG	Fine	VF	XF
5	AH1317	—	3.00	5.00	8.50	14.00

NOTE: 2 varieties are known.

Mule. Obv. of Y#5. Rev. of Y#2.

Y#	Date	Mintage	VG	Fine	VF	XF
6	AH1317	—	3.00	6.00	10.00	15.00

Y#	Date	Mintage	VG	Fine	VF	XF
20	AH1329	—	3.50	7.50	12.50	17.50
	1329/17 on Y#6 obverse die					—
		—	3.50	7.50	12.50	17.50

21mm

Y#	Date	Mintage	VG	Fine	VF	XF
26.1	AH1329	—	1.25	2.75	4.50	6.00
	1331	—	1.25	2.75	4.50	6.00
	1332	—	1.50	3.00	5.00	7.00
	1334	—	1.75	3.25	5.50	7.50

Thick flan, reduced size: 19mm

Y#	Date	Mintage	VG	Fine	VF	XF
26.2	AH1336	—	1.50	2.75	4.00	5.50

Thin flan

Y#	Date	Mintage	VG	Fine	VF	XF
26.3	AH1336	—	.75	1.50	3.00	4.50
	1337	—	.75	1.50	3.00	4.50

Thick flan, 20mm

Y#	Date	Mintage	VG	Fine	VF	XF
32.1	AH1337	—	3.50	6.50	10.00	14.00

Thin flan, 19-20mm

Y#	Date	Year	VG	Fine	VF	XF
32.2	AH1337	—	1.50	3.00	5.00	7.00
	SH1298	1919	2.00	4.00	6.00	8.00

NOTE: 3 varieties are known dated AH1337.

20mm

Y#	Date	Year	VG	Fine	VF	XF
33	SH1299	(1920)	1.25	3.00	5.00	7.00
	1300	(1921)	1.75	3.50	6.00	7.50
	1301	(1922)	1.75	3.50	6.00	7.50
	1302	(1923)	1.25	3.00	5.00	6.00
	1303	(1924)	1.25	3.00	5.00	6.00

SHAHI (5 Paisa)

COPPER or BRASS, 31mm

Y#	Date	Mintage	VG	Fine	VF	XF
3	AH1309	—	7.00	12.50	20.00	35.00

Thick flan, 25mm

Y#	Date	Mintage	VG	Fine	VF	XF
34.1	AH1337	—	4.50	8.50	15.00	25.00

Thin flan

Y#	Date	Mintage	VG	Fine	VF	XF
34.2	AH1337	—	4.50	8.50	15.00	25.00

100 DINAR (10 Paisa)

COPPER, 41mm

Y#	Date	Mintage	VG	Fine	VF	XF
4	AH1311	—	75.00	110.00	175.00	350.00

SANAR (10 PAISA)

SILVER, 13mm

Obv: Date in loop of toughra.

Y#	Date	Mintage	Fine	VF	XF	Unc
7.1	AH1315	—	7.00	10.00	15.00	25.00

Similar, but with date under mosque

Y#	Date	Mintage	Fine	VF	XF	Unc
7.2	AH1315	—	8.50	13.50	18.50	27.50

Y#	Date	Mintage	Fine	VF	XF	Unc
21	AH1325	—	Reported, not confirmed			
	1326	—	5.00	7.50	12.50	20.00
	1328	—	5.00	7.50	12.00	17.50
	1329	—	5.75	8.50	14.00	25.00

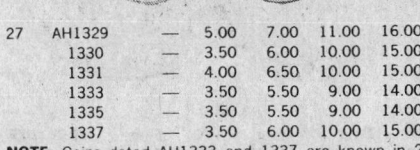

Y#	Date	Mintage	Fine	VF	XF	Unc
27	AH1329	—	5.00	7.00	11.00	16.00
	1330	—	3.50	6.00	10.00	15.00
	1331	—	4.00	6.50	10.00	15.00
	1333	—	3.50	5.50	9.00	14.00
	1335	—	3.50	5.50	9.00	14.00
	1337	—	3.50	6.00	10.00	15.00

NOTE: Coins dated AH1333 and 1337 are known in 2 varieties.

COPPER or BRASS, 29-30mm

Thick flan

Y#	Date	Mintage	Fine	VF	XF	Unc
35.1	AH1337	—	4.50	8.50	15.00	22.50

Thin flan

Y#	Date	Mintage	Fine	VF	XF	Unc
35.2	AH1337	—	4.50	8.50	15.00	22.50

10 PAISA

COPPER, 22mm

Y#	Date	Mintage	Fine	VF	XF	Unc
66	AH1348	—	6.50	12.50	17.50	25.00

3 SHAHI (15 Paisa)

COPPER, 32-33mm

Without Al-Ghazi

Y#	Date	Year	VG	Fine	VF	XF
36.1	AH1337	—	3.50	6.50	10.00	13.50
	SH1298 with SHAMSI					
		(1919)	1.75	4.00	7.50	10.00

NOTE: SHAMSI (= Solar) is an additional word written on some of the coins dated SH1298, to show the change from a lunar to solar calendar. 2 varieties are known with AH1337 date.

Rev: AL-GHAZI at top, mosque in 8-pointed star.

Y#	Date	Year	VG	Fine	VF	XF
36.2	SH1298 without SHAMSI					
		(1919)	1.75	4.00	7.50	10.00
	1298 with SHAMSI					
		(1919)	1.75	4.00	7.50	10.00
	1299	(1920)	1.25	3.50	7.00	9.00
	1300	(1921)	1.25	3.50	7.00	9.00

Rev: Mosque in 7-pointed star.

Y#	Date	Year	VG	Fine	VF	XF
36.3	SH1298 with SHAMSI					
		(1919)	1.75	4.00	7.50	10.00
	1299	(1920)	1.25	3.50	7.00	9.00
	1300	(1921)	1.25	3.50	7.00	9.00

NOTE: Varieties of obverse exist for coins dated SH1300.

Obv. and rev: 8 stars around perimeter.

Y#	Date	Year	VG	Fine	VF	XF
36.4	SH1300	(1921)	—	—	—	—

BRASS

Y#	Date	Year	VG	Fine	VF	XF
36a	SH1300	(1921)	3.50	7.25	10.00	15.00

COPPER

Y#	Date	Year	VG	Fine	VF	XF
43	SH1300	(1921)	1.25	3.00	5.00	7.00
	1301 (2 vars.)	(1922)	1.25	3.00	5.00	7.00

ABBASI (20 Paisa)

SILVER, 15-16mm
Obv: Date over toughra.

Y#	Date	Mintage	Fine	VF	XF	Unc
8.1	AH1313	—	3.50	5.50	8.50	12.50

Rev: Date under mosque.

8.2	AH1313	—	10.00	17.50	27.50	40.00

Rev: New style mosque.

8.3	AH1314	—	3.50	5.50	8.00	12.50

15	AH1320	—	12.50	22.50	35.00	50.00
22	AH1324	—	7.50	12.50	17.50	25.00
	1328	—	7.50	12.50	17.50	25.00

28	AH1329	—	6.50	11.50	16.50	22.50
	1330	—	4.00	7.00	10.00	15.00
	1333	—	3.50	5.50	8.00	13.50
	1334	—	3.50	6.00	8.50	13.50
	1335	—	3.50	5.50	8.00	12.50
	1337	—	3.50	5.50	8.00	12.50

BILLON, 20mm

Y#	Date	Year	Fine	VF	XF	Unc
37	SH1298	(1919)	30.00	50.00	75.00	100.00

Similar, but larger (25mm)

38	SH1299	(1920)	12.50	20.00	30.00	45.00

COPPER or BILLON, 25mm

44	SH1299	(1920)	1.25	2.50	4.00	6.50
	1300	(1921)	1.50	3.00	5.00	7.50
	1301	(1922)	1.50	3.00	5.00	7.50
	1302	(1923)	1.50	3.00	5.00	7.50
	1303	(1924)	1.50	3.00	5.00	7.50

20 PAISA

BRONZE OR BRASS, 25mm

Y#	Date	Mintage	Fine	VF	XF	Unc
62	AH1347	—	3.00	5.00	7.50	12.50

QIRAN (1/2 Rupee)

SILVER, 18mm
Rev: Star over mosque.

9.1	AH1308	—	6.50	7.50	8.50	11.00
	1309	—	6.50	8.50	11.00	17.50
	1310	—	6.50	7.50	9.00	12.50

Rev: KABUL over mosque.

9.2	AH1313	—	6.50	7.50	8.50	11.00

Rev: YAK MESQHAL over mosque.

9.3	AH1314	—	6.50	7.50	8.50	11.00

Rev: Crossed swords and cannons under mosque.

9.4	AH1316	—	6.50	7.50	8.50	10.00
	1317	—	Reported, not confirmed			
	1318	—	Reported, not confirmed			

Rev: Crossed cannons under mosque.

9.5	AH1319	—	7.50	12.50	20.00	27.50

(The half rupee dated 1314 bears the denomination of '1 Qiran'; all others have 'Half Rupee').

Obv: Date beneath toughra, 19mm.

16.1	AH1320	—	7.50	13.50	22.50	30.00
	1325	—	7.00	11.00	16.50	25.00

Obv: Date at upper right of toughra.

16.2	AH1321	—	6.50	9.00	13.50	20.00

Rev: Dated AH1320

23	AH1323	—	6.50	7.50	9.00	12.50
	1324	—	6.50	7.50	8.50	11.50
	1326	—	6.50	7.50	8.50	11.50
	1327	—	6.50	7.50	8.50	11.50
	1328	—	6.50	7.50	8.50	11.50
	1329	—	6.50	7.50	9.00	12.50

NOTE: 2 varieties are known.

20mm

29	AH1329	—	6.50	7.50	8.50	10.00
	1333	—	6.50	7.50	8.50	10.00
	1334	—	6.50	7.50	8.50	11.00
	1335	—	6.50	7.50	8.50	10.00
	1337	—	6.50	7.50	8.50	10.00

Obv: Circled inscription, 5 gms.

39.1	AH1337	—	—	—	—	—

Obv: Uncircled inscription.

Y#	Date	Year	Fine	VF	XF	Unc
39.2	AH1337	—	6.50	7.50	8.50	11.00

NOTE: 5 varieties are known.

Obv: Star over inscription.

39.3	SH1298 (1919) with SHAMSI		6.50	7.50	8.50	10.00

NOTE: 2 varieties are known.

Obv: AL-GHAZI over inscription.

39.4	SH1298 with SHAMSI	—	—	—	—	—
	1299	(1920)	6.50	7.50	8.50	10.00
	1300	(1921)	6.50	7.50	8.50	10.00

NOTE: 2 varieties are known dated 1299.

45	SH1300	(1921)	6.50	7.50	8.50	11.00
	1301	(1922)	6.50	7.50	8.50	10.00
	1302	(1923)	6.50	7.50	8.50	10.00
	1303	(1924)	6.50	7.50	8.50	10.00

21mm

Y#	Date	Mintage	Fine	VF	XF	Unc
63	AH1347	—	6.50	8.50	12.50	17.50

67	AH1348	—	10.00	20.00	30.00	45.00

RUPEE

SILVER, 24mm

A10	AH1304(1303 on rev.)	—	25.00	35.00	50.00	65.00
	1304(1304 on rev.)	—	25.00	35.00	50.00	65.00

NOTE: These Rupees may have been intended as patterns. The silver rupee was the standard trade and hoarding coin of Afghanistan, and as a result was issued in larger quantities than any other denomination. Consequently, there are many variations of type.

23-25mm, 10 gms.
Obv: Star above mosque.
Rev: KABUL below mosque, error date AH1391.

Toughra of Abdur Rahman Khan. Above the toughra between the ends of the wreath, appear stars, a single star, the name 'Kabul' or a blank space.

10.1	AH1308	—	11.50	13.00	15.00	20.00

Y#	Date	Mintage	Fine	VF	XF	Unc
10.1	1309	—	11.50	13.00	15.00	18.50
	1310	—	11.50	13.00	15.00	18.50
	1311	—	11.50	13.00	15.00	18.50
	1312	—	11.50	13.00	15.00	18.50
	1313	—	11.50	13.00	15.00	18.50

NOTE: 2 varieties are known with dates AH1311 and 1312.

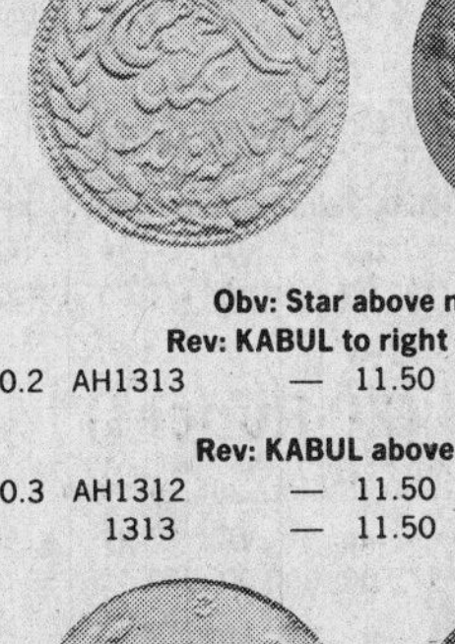

Obv: Star above mosque.
Rev: KABUL to right of mosque.

Y#	Date	Mintage	Fine	VF	XF	Unc
10.2	AH1313	—	11.50	13.00	15.00	20.00

Rev: KABUL above mosque.

Y#	Date	Mintage	Fine	VF	XF	Unc
10.3	AH1312	—	11.50	13.00	15.00	18.50
	1313	—	11.50	13.00	15.00	18.50

Rev: DU MESQAL above mosque.

Y#	Date	Mintage	Fine	VF	XF	Unc
10.4	AH1314	—	11.50	13.00	15.00	20.00

Obv: KABUL above toughra.

Y#	Date	Mintage	Fine	VF	XF	Unc
10.5	AH1314	—	11.50	13.00	15.00	18.50
	1315	—	11.50	13.00	15.00	18.50
	1316	—	11.50	13.00	15.00	18.50
	1317	—	11.50	13.00	15.00	20.00

Obv: 3 stars over toughra.

Y#	Date	Mintage	Fine	VF	XF	Unc
10.6	AH1317	—	11.50	13.00	15.00	20.00

Rev: New style mosque.

Y#	Date	Mintage	Fine	VF	XF	Unc
10.7	AH1318	—	11.50	13.00	15.00	18.50

Obv: Toughra of Habibullah in wreath, star above, 25mm.

Y#	Date	Mintage	Fine	VF	XF	Unc
17.1	AH1319	—	11.50	13.00	15.00	20.00

NOTE: 2 varieties are known.

Obv: AFGHANISTAN above small toughra.

Y#	Date	Mintage	Fine	VF	XF	Unc
17.2	AH1319	—	11.50	13.00	15.00	20.00
	1320	—	11.50	13.00	15.00	20.00
	1325	—	11.50	13.00	15.00	21.50

NOTE: 2 varieties are known for dates AH1319 and 1325. 3 varieties are known dated AH1320.

Obv: AFGHANISTAN above large toughra.

Y#	Date	Mintage	Fine	VF	XF	Unc
17.3	AH1320	—	11.50	13.00	15.00	20.00
	1321	—	11.50	13.00	15.00	20.00
	1325	—	11.50	13.00	15.00	21.50

Rev: Small dome mosque.

Y#	Date	Mintage	Fine	VF	XF	Unc
17.4	AH1320	—	11.50	13.00	15.00	21.50

Obv: Name and titles of Habibullah in wreath.

Y#	Date	Mintage	Fine	VF	XF	Unc
24.1	AH1321	—	11.50	13.00	15.00	18.50
	1322	—	11.50	13.00	15.00	18.50
	1324	—	11.50	13.00	15.00	18.50
	1325	—	11.50	13.00	15.00	18.50
	1326	—	11.50	13.00	15.00	18.50
	1327	—	11.50	13.00	15.00	18.50
	1328	—	11.50	13.00	15.00	21.50
	1329	—	11.50	13.00	15.00	20.00

NOTE: 2 varieties are known for dates AH1321 and 1322. 3 varieties are known dated AH1328.

Rev: Large dome mosque.

Y#	Date	Mintage	Fine	VF	XF	Unc
24.2	AH1328	—	11.50	13.00	15.00	20.00

Obv: Name and titles of Habibullah in wreath.
Rev: Mosque with pulpit within sunburst.

Y#	Date	Mintage	Fine	VF	XF	Unc
30	AH1329	—	11.50	13.00	15.00	20.00
	1330	—	11.50	13.00	15.00	18.50
	1331	—	11.50	13.00	15.00	18.50
	1332	—	11.50	13.00	15.00	18.50
	1333	—	11.50	13.00	15.00	18.50
	1334	—	11.50	13.00	15.00	18.50
	1335	—	11.50	13.00	15.00	18.50
	1337	—	11.50	13.00	15.00	20.00

NOTE: 2 varieties are known for dates AH1330, 1331, 1333 and 1337.

Similar to Y#30, but name and titles of Amanullah on obverse, star above inscription.

Y#	Date	Year	Fine	VF	XF	Unc
40.1	AH1337	—	11.50	13.00	15.00	20.00

NOTE: 7 varieties are known.

Obv: AL-GHAZI above inscription.

Y#	Date	Year	Fine	VF	XF	Unc
40.2	SH1298	(1919)	11.50	13.00	15.00	20.00
	1299	(1920)	11.50	13.00	15.00	20.00

NOTE: 4 varieties are known dated 1298. 2 varieties are known dated 1299.

Obv: Toughra of Amanullah.

Y#	Date	Year	Fine	VF	XF	Unc
46	SH1299	(1920)	11.50	13.00	15.00	18.50
	1300	(1921)	11.50	13.00	15.00	18.50
	1301	(1922)	11.50	13.00	15.00	18.50
	1302	(1923)	11.50	13.00	15.00	18.50
	1303	(1924)	11.50	13.00	15.00	18.50

Obv: Name and titles of 'Amir Habibullah' (the usurper).

Y#	Date	Mintage	Fine	VF	XF	Unc
64	AH1347	—	12.50	15.00	20.00	28.50

Obv: Title in circle.

Y#	Date	Mintage	Fine	VF	XF	Unc
68	AH1347	—	20.00	30.00	40.00	55.00

2-1/2 RUPEES

SILVER, 34mm, 25 gms.

Y#	Date	Year	Fine	VF	XF	Unc
47	SH1298	(1919)	25.00	35.00	50.00	75.00
	1299	(1920)	22.50	27.50	32.50	45.00
	1300	(1921)	22.50	27.50	32.50	45.00
	1301	(1922)	21.50	25.00	30.00	40.00
	1302	(1923)	21.50	25.00	30.00	40.00
	1303	(1924)	21.50	25.00	30.00	40.00

NOTE: 2 varieties are known for dates SH1298 and 1300. 3 varieties are known dated SH1299.

5 RUPEES

SILVER, 39mm, 45 gms., Thick Flan

Y#	Date	Mintage	Fine	VF	XF	Unc
11	AH1314	—	42.50	50.00	60.00	90.00

45mm

Y#	Date	Mintage	Fine	VF	XF	Unc
12	AH1316	—	42.50	47.50	60.00	75.00

45-46mm (2 vars.)
Rev: Similar to Y#12

Y#	Date	Mintage	Fine	VF	XF	Unc
18	AH1319	—	42.50	47.50	60.00	75.00

45mm

Y#	Date	Mintage	Fine	VF	XF	Unc
25	AH1322	—	42.50	47.50	55.00	70.00
	1323	—	Reported, not confirmed			
	1324	—	42.50	47.50	55.00	70.00
	1326	—	42.50	47.50	55.00	65.00
	1327	—	42.50	47.50	55.00	65.00
	1328	—	42.50	47.50	55.00	65.00
	1329	—	42.50	47.50	55.00	65.00

NOTE: Most dates are recut dies. 2 varieties are known for dates AH1324 and 1327.

1/2 AMANI (5 Rupees)

2.2750 gm., .900 GOLD, 16mm, .0658 oz AGW

Y#	Date	Year	Fine	VF	XF	Unc
48	SH1299	(1920)	60.00	75.00	100.00	125.00

TILLA (10 Rupees)

4.6000 gm., .900 GOLD, 22mm, .1331 oz AGW
Rev: ALLAH AKBAR above mosque.

Y#	Date	Mintage	Fine	VF	XF	Unc
A13	AH1309	—	125.00	150.00	200.00	275.00
	19mm					
13.1	AH1313	—	150.00	200.00	300.00	400.00

21mm
Rev: Date below mosque.

Y#	Date	Mintage	Fine	VF	XF	Unc
13.2	AH1314	—	90.00	110.00	130.00	150.00
	1316	—	100.00	120.00	140.00	170.00

Obv: Date below toughra.

Y#	Date	Mintage	Fine	VF	XF	Unc
13.3	AH1314	—	100.00	120.00	140.00	170.00
	1316	—	90.00	110.00	130.00	150.00
	Obv: Star above toughra.					
19.1	AH1319	—	110.00	125.00	150.00	185.00
	Obv: AFGHANISTAN above toughra, 21mm.					
19.2	AH1319	—	100.00	120.00	140.00	170.00
	1320	—	90.00	110.00	130.00	150.00

Obv: Name of Habibullah.

Y#	Date	Mintage	Fine	VF	XF	Unc
31	AH1336	—	100.00	120.00	140.00	175.00
	1337	—	110.00	125.00	150.00	200.00

Obv: Name of Amanullah.

Y#	Date	Mintage	Fine	VF	XF	Unc
41	AH1337(2 vars.)	—	90.00	100.00	110.00	130.00

AMANI (10 Rupees)

4.5500 gm., .900 GOLD, 22mm, .1316 oz AGW

Y#	Date	Year	Fine	VF	XF	Unc
49	SH1299	(1920)	90.00	100.00	110.00	130.00

2 TILLAS (20 Rupees)

9.2000 gm., .900 GOLD, 22mm, .2661 oz AGW

Y#	Date	Mintage	Fine	VF	XF	Unc
14	AH1309	—	175.00	200.00	225.00	250.00

23mm

Y#	Date	Year	Fine	VF	XF	Unc
42	SH1298	(1919)	170.00	185.00	200.00	225.00

2 AMANI (20 Rupees)

9.1000 gm., .900 GOLD, 24mm, .2633 oz AGW

Y#	Date	Year	Fine	VF	XF	Unc
50	SH1299	(1920)	175.00	190.00	210.00	235.00
	1300	(1921)	175.00	190.00	225.00	250.00
	1301	(1922)	175.00	190.00	225.00	250.00
	1302	(1923)	175.00	190.00	210.00	235.00
	1303	(1924)	175.00	190.00	225.00	250.00

HABIBI (30 Rupees)

4.6000 gm., .900 GOLD, 21mm, .1331 oz AGW

Y#	Date	Mintage	Fine	VF	XF	Unc
65.1	AH1347	—	150.00	175.00	250.00	350.00
	Obv: Small star replaces '30 RUPEES' in legend					
65.2	AH1347	—	150.00	175.00	250.00	350.00

5 AMANI (50 Rupees)

22.7500 gm., .900 GOLD, .6583 oz AGW
Obv: 5 above toughra, 34mm.

Y#	Date	Year	Fine	VF	XF	Unc
51.1	SH1299	(1920)	450.00	550.00	750.00	1000.

Rev: 5 above mosque.

Y#	Date	Year	Fine	VF	XF	Unc
51.2	SH1299	(1920)	450.00	550.00	750.00	1000.

DECIMAL COINAGE

100 Pul = 1 Afghani
20 Afghani = 1 Amani

PUL

BRONZE or BRASS, 16mm

Y#	Date	Year	Fine	VF	XF	Unc
69	AH1349	—	.75	1.25	1.75	2.50

NOTE: On this and many other Afghan copper coins, various alloys were used quite indiscriminately, depending upon what was immediately at hand. Thus one finds bronze, brass, and various shades in between. For this reason, bronze and brass coins are not given separate types, but are indicated as a single listing.

NOTE: A similar coin also dated AH 1349, but with toughra on obverse, as on Y#70, is believed to be a pattern.

2 PUL

BRONZE or BRASS, 18mm

Y#	Date	Year	Fine	VF	XF	Unc
52	SH1304	(1925)	2.00	3.00	4.50	6.00
	1305	(1926)	2.00	3.00	4.50	6.00

Y#	Date	Year	Fine	VF	XF	Unc
70	AH1348	—	1.25	2.50	3.50	5.00

 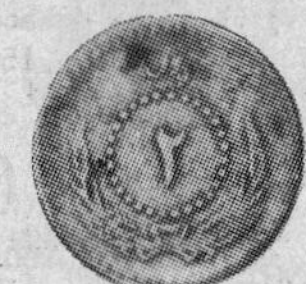

Y#	Date	Year	Fine	VF	XF	Unc
80	SH1311	(1932)	2.00	3.00	4.00	6.00
	1312	(1933)	1.50	2.25	3.00	5.00
	1313	(1934)	1.75	2.75	3.75	5.50
	1314	(1935)	2.00	3.00	4.00	6.00

BRONZE, 15mm

Y#	Date	Year	Fine	VF	XF	Unc
90	SH1316	(1937)	.15	.20	.35	.60

3 PUL

BRONZE, 16mm

Y#	Date	Year	Fine	VF	XF	Unc
91	SH1316	(1937)	.50	.75	1.00	1.50

5 PUL

BRONZE or BRASS, 22mm

Y#	Date	Year	Fine	VF	XF	Unc
53	SH1304	(1925)	1.75	3.50	6.00	7.50
	1305	(1926)	1.50	3.00	5.50	7.50

Y#	Date	Year	Fine	VF	XF	Unc
71	AH1349	—	1.75	2.75	4.50	5.50
	1350	—	1.25	2.25	3.50	5.00

NOTE: 2 varieties are known dated 1350.

 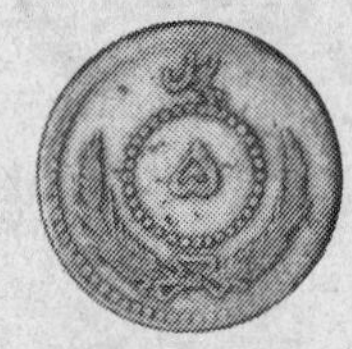

Y#	Date	Year	Fine	VF	XF	Unc
81	SH1311	(1932)	2.00	3.50	5.00	7.00
	1312	(1933)	2.00	3.50	5.00	7.00
	1313	(1934)	2.00	3.50	5.00	7.00
	1314	(1935)	2.00	3.50	5.00	7.00

BRONZE, 17mm

Y#	Date	Year	Fine	VF	XF	Unc
92	SH1316	(1937)	.25	.30	.40	.60

10 PUL

COPPER, 24mm

Y#	Date	Year	Fine	VF	XF	Unc
54	SH1304	(1925)	2.00	3.50	5.50	8.00
	1305	(1926)	2.50	4.00	6.00	9.00
	1306	(1927)	2.50	4.00	6.00	9.00
	ND	—	Reported, not confirmed			

COPPER or BRASS, 25mm

Y#	Date	Year	Fine	VF	XF	Unc
72	AH1348	—	2.00	3.50	5.00	8.00
	1349(2 vars.)		2.25	4.00	5.50	8.50

NOTE: Illustration shows an example struck off-center; prices are for properly struck specimens.

BRASS, 23mm

Y#	Date	Year	Fine	VF	XF	Unc
82	SH1311	(1932)	1.50	2.50	4.00	6.00
	1312	(1933)	1.50	2.50	4.00	6.00
	1313	(1934)	1.50	2.50	4.00	6.00
	1314	(1935)	1.50	2.50	4.00	6.00

COPPER-NICKEL, 18mm

Y#	Date	Year	Fine	VF	XF	Unc
93	SH1316	(1937)	.40	.60	.90	1.30

20 PUL

BILLON, 19mm

Y#	Date	Year	Fine	VF	XF	Unc
55	SH1304	(1925)	75.00	95.00	125.00	160.00
	ND	—	60.00	85.00	110.00	150.00

COPPER or BRASS, 24-25mm

Y#	Date	Year	Fine	VF	XF	Unc
73	AH1348	—	2.00	4.00	5.50	7.50
	1349	—	2.25	4.50	6.00	8.00

25 PUL

COPPER or BRASS, 25mm

Y#	Date	Mintage	Fine	VF	XF	Unc
74	AH1349	—	2.00	3.50	5.00	7.50

BRONZE or BRASS, 24-25mm

Y#	Date	Year	Fine	VF	XF	Unc
85	SH1312	(1933)	1.50	2.50	3.50	5.00
	1313	(1934)	1.50	2.50	3.50	5.00
	1314	(1935)	1.75	2.75	4.00	6.00
	1315	(1936)	Reported, not confirmed			
	1316	(1937)	1.75	2.75	4.00	6.00

COPPER-NICKEL, 20mm

Y#	Date	Year	Fine	VF	XF	Unc
94	SH1316	(1937)	.60	.75	1.00	1.50

BRONZE, 20mm

Y#	Date	Year	Fine	VF	XF	Unc
95	SH1330	(1951)	.15	.25	.50	.75
	1331	(1952)	.15	.25	.50	.75
	1332	(1953)	.15	.25	.50	.75

NICKEL-CLAD STEEL, 20mm, reeded edge

Y#	Date	Year	Fine	VF	XF	Unc
95a	SH1331	(1952)	1.00	2.00	3.50	6.00
	1332	(1953)	1.50	3.00	5.00	7.50

Plain edge

Y#	Date	Year	Fine	VF	XF	Unc
	SH1331	(1952)	.30	.50	.60	.75
	1332	(1953)	.30	.50	.60	.75
	1333	(1954)	.30	.50	.60	.75
	1334	(1955)	.30	.50	.60	1.00

ALUMINUM, 24mm

Y#	Date	Year	Fine	VF	XF	Unc
95b	SH1331	(1952)	.50	.75	1.25	2.00

NOTE: Struck on oversize 2 Afghani Y#98 planchets in 1970.

BRASS CLAD STEEL

Y#	Date	Mintage	Fine	VF	XF	Unc
103	SH1352(1973)					
		32.000	.15	.20	.35	.50
	1352(1975)					
		13.950	.15	.20	.35	.50

ALUMINUM-BRONZE, 2,5000 gms.

Y#	Date	Mintage	Fine	VF	XF	Unc
109	SH1357(1978)	—	—	—	—	—

1/2 AFGHANI (50 Pul)

SILVER, 25mm, 5 gms.
Obv: Date under toughra.

Y#	Date	Year	Fine	VF	XF	Unc
56.1	SH1304	7	6.50	7.50	8.50	11.50
	1305	8	6.50	7.50	8.50	11.50
	1306	9	6.50	7.50	8.50	11.50

NOTE: 2 varieties are known dated 1304.

Rev: Date under mosque.

Y#	Date	Year	Fine	VF	XF	Unc
56.2	SH1307	10	6.50	7.50	8.50	12.50

24mm

Y#	Date	Year	Fine	VF	XF	Unc
75	AH1348	1	5.00	6.00	7.00	9.00
	1349	2	5.00	6.00	7.00	9.00
	1350	3	5.00	6.00	7.00	9.00

Y#	Date	Year	Fine	VF	XF	Unc
83	SH1310	(1931)	5.00	6.00	7.00	9.00
	1311	(1932)	5.00	6.00	7.00	9.00
	1312	(1933)	5.00	6.00	7.00	9.00

Y#	Date	Year	Fine	VF	XF	Unc
86	SH1312	(1933)	5.00	6.00	7.00	9.00
	1313	(1934)	5.00	6.00	7.00	9.00
	1314	(1935)	5.00	6.00	7.00	9.00
	1315	(1936)	5.00	6.00	7.00	9.00
	1316	(1937)	5.00	6.00	7.00	9.00

BRONZE, 22mm
Obv: Denomination in numerals.

Y#	Date	Year	Fine	VF	XF	Unc
96	SH1330	(1951)	.35	.50	.75	1.25

NICKEL-CLAD STEEL, 22mm
Obv: Denomination in words.

Y#	Date	Year	Fine	VF	XF	Unc
97	SH1331	(1952)	.40	.65	.85	1.25

Type of Y#96, but nickel-clad steel.

Y#	Date	Year	Fine	VF	XF	Unc
96a	SH1331	(1952)	.15	.25	.40	.75
	1332	(1953)	.15	.25	.40	.75
	1333	(1954)	.20	.30	.50	.80
	1334	(1955)	.15	.25	.40	.75

COPPER CLAD STEEL

Y#	Date	Mintage	Fine	VF	XF	Unc
104	SH1352(1973)					
		24.000	.15	.25	.50	1.00
	1352(1975)					
		.750	.15	.25	.50	1.00

ALUMINUM-BRONZE, 3.000 gms.

Y#	Date	Mintage	Fine	VF	XF	Unc
110	SH1357(1978)	—	—	—	—	—

AFGHANI (100 Pul)

SILVER
Obv: Date under toughra.

Y#	Date	Year	Fine	VF	XF	Unc
57.1	SH1304	7	11.50	13.00	15.00	17.50
	1305	8	11.50	13.00	15.00	17.50
	1305	9	11.50	13.00	15.00	17.50
	1306	9	11.50	13.00	15.00	17.50

NOTE: 3 varieties are known dated SH1304. 2 varieties are known for dates SH1305 and 1306.

Rev: Date under mosque.

57.2 SH1307 (1928) Reported, not confirmed

30mm

Y#	Date	Year	Fine	VF	XF	Unc
76	AH1348	1	11.50	13.00	15.00	18.50
	1349	2	11.50	13.00	15.00	18.50
	1350	3	11.50	13.00	15.00	18.50

27mm

Y#	Date	Year	Fine	VF	XF	Unc
84	SH1310	(1931)	60.00	75.00	90.00	120.00

NICKEL-CLAD STEEL, 23mm

Y#	Date	Year	Fine	VF	XF	Unc
100	SH1340	(1961)	.15	.20	.30	.50

2 AFGHANI

ALUMINUM, 24mm

Y#	Date	Year	Fine	VF	XF	Unc
98	SH1337	(1958)	.60	1.00	1.50	2.00

NOTE: The above issue was withdrawn and demonitized due to extensive counterfeiting.

NICKEL-CLAD STEEL, 25mm

Y#	Date	Year	Fine	VF	XF	Unc
101	SH1340	(1961)	.20	.30	.50	.75

2 varieties, normal coin type and medallic die orientation.

2-1/2 AFGHANI

SILVER, 38mm, 25 gms.

Y#	Date	Year	Fine	VF	XF	Unc
58	SH1305	8	23.50	28.50	35.00	50.00
	1306	9	25.00	30.00	37.50	55.00

NOTE: 2 varieties are known for above dates.

5 AFGHANI

ALUMINUM, 26mm

Y#	Date		Fine	VF	XF	Unc
99	SH1337	(1958)	1.00	1.75	2.25	3.00

NOTE: The above issue was withdrawn and demonitized due to extensive counterfeiting.

NICKEL-CLAD STEEL, 29mm

Y#	Date		Fine	VF	XF	Unc
102	SH1340	AH1381	.25	.40	.75	1.50

COPPER-NICKEL CLAD STEEL

Y#	Date	Mintage	Fine	VF	XF	Unc
105	SH1352(1973)					
		20.000	.20	.35	.50	.80
	1352(1975)					
		14.750	.20	.35	.50	.80

COPPER-NICKEL, 7.4000 gms.

Y#	Date	Mintage	Fine	VF	XF	Unc
111	SH1357(1978)	—	—	—	—	—

1/2 AMANI

3.0000 gm., .900 GOLD, 18mm, .0087 oz AGW

Y#	Date	Year	Fine	VF	XF	Unc
59	SH1304	7	60.00	70.00	80.00	100.00
	1305	8	60.00	70.00	80.00	100.00
	1306	9	60.00	70.00	80.00	100.00

4 GRAMS

4.0000 gm., .900 GOLD, 19mm, .1157 oz AGW

Y#	Date	Year	Fine	VF	XF	Unc
88	SH1315	(1936)	100.00	110.00	130.00	150.00
	1317	(1938)	100.00	110.00	130.00	150.00
A102	SH1339	AH1380	—	—	—	—

AMANI

4.5500 gm., .900 GOLD, .1316 oz AGW

Y#	Date	Year	Fine	VF	XF	Unc
60	SH1304	7	90.00	110.00	135.00	165.00
	1305	8	100.00	125.00	150.00	185.00
	1306	9	90.00	110.00	135.00	165.00

20 AFGHANI

6.0000 gm., .900 GOLD, 22mm, .1736 oz AGW

Y#	Date	Year	Fine	VF	XF	Unc
78	AH1349	2	150.00	170.00	210.00	250.00
	1350	3	150.00	170.00	210.00	250.00

6 GRAMS

Y#	Date	Year	Fine	VF	XF	Unc
87	SH1313	(1934)	135.00	150.00	175.00	200.00

8 GRAMS

8.0000 gm., .900 GOLD, 22mm, .2314 oz AGW

Y#	Date	Year	Fine	VF	XF	Unc
89	SH1314	(1935)	165.00	185.00	210.00	250.00
	1315	(1936)	165.00	185.00	210.00	250.00
	1317	(1938)	165.00	185.00	210.00	250.00

Y#	Date	Year	Fine	VF	XF	Unc
B102	SH1339	AH1380	200 pcs.	—	300.00	450.00

NOTE: Struck for royal presentation purposes.

2-1/2 AMANI

15.0000 gm., .900 GOLD, 30mm, .4340 oz AGW

Y#	Date	Year	Fine	VF	XF	Unc
61	SH1306	9	300.00	450.00	700.00	1000.

250 AFGHANI

.925 SILVER, 28.28 gms.
Conservation Series

Y#	Date	Mintage	Fine	VF	XF	Unc
106	1978	—	—	BV	BV	25.00
	1978	—	—	—	Proof	30.00

500 AFGHANI

.925 SILVER, 35 gms.
Conservation Series
Obv: Similar to 250 Afghani, Y#106.

Y#	Date	Mintage	Fine	VF	XF	Unc
107	1978	—	—	BV	BV	40.00
	1978	—	—	—	Proof	50.00

10,000 AFGHANI

.900 GOLD
Conservation Series

Y#	Date	Mintage	Fine	VF	XF	Unc
108	1978	—	—	BV	BV	650.00
	1978	—	—	—	Proof	750.00

LOCAL COPPER COINS

With the inception of machine struck coinage in AH1308/AD1891, the provincial mints were closed and all minting was centralized at Kabul. However, few base metal coins were struck at Kabul, and old copper coins, as well as foreign copper coins, circulated in Afghanistan. After nine years, the Kabul Mint suspended the production of copper coins (AH1317/AD1900), the consequent was the sanctioning of private striking at Herat and Qandahar, where coins were struck from about AH1322 until AH1333. Royal coinage in copper and brass resumed in AH1329/AD1911, and the private mints were soon afterwards suppressed. Further private strikings took place in AH1337-38/SH1298-99. The minting place, probably Kabul, is not shown on these coins. The local coinage is quite crude, and is usually counterstruck on older Afghan and foreign coins. The listings below are incomplete.

Herat

PAISA

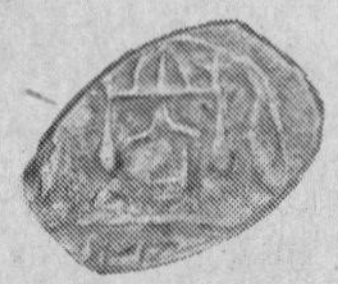

COPPER, round or irregular flan

KM#	Date	Mintage	VG	Fine	VF
1	AH1322	—	4.00	7.50	12.50
	1328	—	4.00	7.50	12.50
	1330	—	4.00	7.50	12.50
	1331	—	4.00	7.50	12.50
	1332	—	4.00	7.50	12.50
	Date off flan	—	2.50	5.00	8.00

Struck over Iran, 50 Dinars (Y#4).

KM#	Date	Mintage	VG	Fine	VF
1a	AH1328	—	5.00	10.00	12.50

Obv: "Dar al-Nu-Shat" added.

KM#	Date	Mintage	VG	Fine	VF
1b		—	4.00	7.50	12.50

2 PAISA

COPPER
Similar to Paisa, KM#1, but inscribed DO PAISA below mosque.

KM#	Date	Mintage	VG	Fine	VF
2	AH1329	—	5.00	8.50	13.50

Qandahar

PAISA

COPPER

KM#	Date	Mintage	VG	Fine	VF
10	AH1322	—	7.50	12.50	17.50

Struck over Iran, 50 Dinars (Y#4).

KM#	Date	Mintage	VG	Fine	VF
10a	AH1321	—	6.00	10.00	15.00
	1322	—	5.00	8.00	12.50

Struck over Muscat & Oman, 1/4 Anna (Y#3).

KM#	Date	Mintage	VG	Fine	VF
10b	AH1322	—	6.50	10.00	15.00

Struck over British East India Co., 1/4 Anna.

KM#	Date	Mintage	VG	Fine	VF
10c	AH1322	—	6.50	10.00	15.00

KM#	Date	Mintage	VG	Fine	VF
11	AH1333	—	3.50	6.00	10.00

Without Mint Name

Believed struck at Kabul

PAISA

COPPER, 15-17mm. Crudely struck.

KM#	Date	Year	Mintage	VG	Fine	VF
20	SH1298	(1919)	—	7.50	12.50	20.00
	1299	(1920)	—	7.50	12.50	20.00

Rev: With name of Amanullah.

KM#	Date	Year	Mintage	VG	Fine	VF
21	SH1299	(1920)	—	10.00	16.50	24.00

5 PAISA (SHAHI)

COPPER, Crude-struck, about 20mm.

KM#	Date	Year	Mintage	VG	Fine	VF
25	SH1298	AH1338	—	10.00	16.50	24.00
	1299	1339	—	10.00	16.50	24.00

Rev: With name of Amanullah.

KM#	Date	Year	Mintage	VG	Fine	VF
26	SH1299	(1920)	—	10.00	16.50	24.00

BRASS, 17mm
In name of Baccha-i-Saqao

KM#	Date	Mintage	VG	Fine	VF
31	AH1347	—	8.00	14.00	22.50

10 PAISA

BRASS, 21-22mm
In name of Baccha-i-Saqao

KM#	Date	Mintage	VG	Fine	VF
32	AH1347	—	10.00	16.50	25.00

15 PAISA

BRASS, 22-23mm
In name of Baccha-i-Saqao

KM#	Date	Mintage	VG	Fine	VF
33	AH1347	—	12.50	20.00	30.00

20 PAISA

BRASS, 25mm
In name of Baccha-i-Saqao

KM#	Date	Mintage	VG	Fine	VF
34	AH1347	—	12.50	20.00	30.00

Listings For

AJMAN: refer to United Arab Emirates

ALBANIA

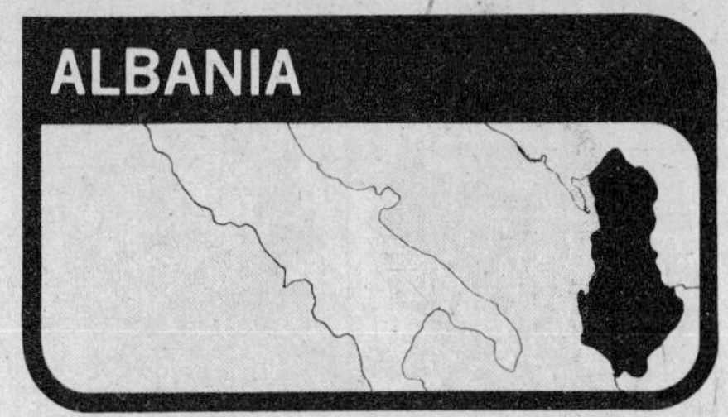

The People's Socialist Republic of Albania, a Balkan communist republic bounded by Yugoslavia, Greece, and the Adriatic Sea, has an area of 11,000 sq. mi. (28,489 sq. km.) and a population of 2.5 million. Capital: Tirana. The country is predominantly agricultural, although recent progress has been made in the manufacturing and mining sectors. Petroleum, chrome, iron, copper, cotton textiles, tobacco and wood products are exported.

Since it had been part of the Greek and Roman empires, little is known of the early history of Albania. After the disintegration of the Roman Empire, Albania was overrun by Goths, Byzantines, Venetians, and Turks. Skanderbeg, the national hero, resisted the Turks and established an independent Albania in 1443, but in 1468 the country again fell to the Turks and remained part of the Ottoman empire for more than 400 years.

Independence was restablished by revolt in 1912, and the present borders established in 1913 by a conference of European powers which, in 1914, placed Prince William of Wied on the throne; popular discontent forced his abdication within months. In 1920, following World War I occupancy by several nations, a republic was set up. Ahmed Zogu seized the presidency in 1925, and in 1928 proclaimed himself king with the title of Zog I. King Zog fled when Italy occupied Albania in 1939 and enthroned King Victor Emanuel of Italy. Upon the surrender of Italy to the Allies in 1943, German troops occupied the country. They withdrew in 1944, and communist partisans seized power, naming Gen. Enver Hoxha provisional president. In 1946, following a victory by the communist front in the 1945 elections, a new constitution modeled on that of the USSR was adopted. In accordance with the constitution of Dec. 28, 1976, the official name of Albania was changed from the People's Republic of Albania to the People's Socialist Republic of Albania.

RULERS

Amet Zogu - King Zog I, 1928-1939
Vittorio Emanuele III, 1939-1943

MINTMARKS

L - London
R - Rome
V - Valona

MONETARY SYSTEM

100 Qindar Leku = 1 Lek
100 Qindar Ari = 1 Franga Ari
= 5 Lek

5 QINDAR LEKU

BRONZE

Y#	Date	Mintage	Fine	VF	XF	Unc
1	1926R	.512	7.50	12.50	20.00	37.50

QINDAR ARI

BRONZE

Y#	Date	Mintage	Fine	VF	XF	Unc
14	1935R	2.000	1.75	3.00	5.00	10.00

10 QINDAR LEKU

BRONZE

Y#	Date	Mintage	Fine	VF	XF	Unc
2	1926R	.511	10.00	17.50	22.50	37.50

2 QINDAR ARI

BRONZE

Y#	Date	Mintage	Fine	VF	XF	Unc
15	1935R	1.500	1.75	3.00	5.00	12.00

1/4 LEKU

NICKEL

Y#	Date	Mintage	Fine	VF	XF	Unc
3	1926R	.506	2.75	4.50	8.50	12.50
	1927R	.756	2.50	4.00	6.50	10.00

1/2 LEKU

NICKEL

Y#	Date	Mintage	Fine	VF	XF	Unc
4	1926R	1.002	2.50	4.00	6.50	10.00

Y#	Date	Mintage	Fine	VF	XF	Unc
13	1930V	.500	2.00	3.50	6.50	10.00
	1931L	.500	2.00	3.50	5.00	10.00

LEK

NICKEL

Y#	Date	Mintage	Fine	VF	XF	Unc
5	1926R	1.004	2.00	3.50	5.50	11.00
	1927R	.506	2.50	4.00	6.50	13.50
	1930V	1.250	2.00	3.50	6.50	11.00
	1931L	1.000	2.00	3.50	5.50	11.00

FRANGA ARI

5.0000 gm., .835 SILVER, .1342 oz ASW

Y#	Date	Mintage	Fine	VF	XF	Unc
6	1927R	.100	40.00	65.00	90.00	135.00
	1927V	.050	—Reported, Not Confirmed.			
	1928R	.060	42.50	70.00	95.00	145.00

Y#	Date	Mintage	Fine	VF	XF	Unc
16	1935R	.700	BV	BV	8.50	12.50
	1937R	.600	BV	BV	8.50	12.50

Independence Commemorative

Y#	Date	Mintage	Fine	VF	XF	Unc
18	1937R	.050	8.50	12.50	22.50	32.50

2 FRANGA ARI

10.0000 gm., .835 SILVER, .2684 oz ASW

Y#	Date	Mintage	Fine	VF	XF	Unc
7	1926R	.050	50.00	82.50	125.00	165.00
	1927R	.050	60.00	100.00	150.00	200.00
	1928R	.060	50.00	82.50	125.00	165.00

Y#	Date	Mintage	Fine	VF	XF	Unc
17	1935R	.150	BV	BV	22.50	32.50

Independence Commemorative

Y#	Date	Mintage	Fine	VF	XF	Unc
19	1937R	.025	BV	21.00	32.50	45.00

5 FRANGA ARI

25.0000 gm., .900 SILVER, .7234 oz ASW

Y#	Date	Mintage	Fine	VF	XF	Unc
8	1926R	.060	100.00	175.00	250.00	325.00
	1926R star below bust	Inc. Ab.	110.00	190.00	275.00	350.00

10 FRANGA ARI

3.2258 gm., .900 GOLD, .0933 oz AGW

Y#	Date	Mintage	Fine	VF	XF	Unc
9	1927R	6,000	65.00	75.00	125.00	175.00

20 FRANGA ARI

6.4516 gm., .900 GOLD, .1867 oz AGW
Obv.: Head left. Rev.: Double-headed eagle.

Y#	Date	Mintage	Fine	VF	XF	Unc
10	1926R	—	125.00	150.00	175.00	225.00
	1927R	6,000	125.00	150.00	175.00	225.00

Skanderberg Commemorative

Y#	Date	Mintage	Fine	VF	XF	Unc
12	1926R	6,000	125.00	150.00	175.00	200.00
	1926Fasces	Inc.Ab.	135.00	175.00	200.00	250.00
	1927V	5,053	125.00	150.00	175.00	200.00

Independence Commemorative

Y#	Date	Mintage	Fine	VF	XF	Unc
20	1937R	2,500	125.00	150.00	200.00	250.00

King Zog Marriage Commemorative

Y#	Date	Mintage	Fine	VF	XF	Unc
22	1938R	2,500	125.00	150.00	200.00	250.00

King Zog 10th Anniversary

Y#	Date	Mintage	Fine	VF	XF	Unc
24	1938R	1,000	150.00	200.00	225.00	275.00

NOTE: This piece was restruck in 1969 from new dies and is possibly counterfeit.

50 FRANGA ARI

16.1290 gm., .900 GOLD, .4667 oz AGW
King Zog 10th Anniversary

Y#	Date	Mintage	Fine	VF	XF	Unc
25	1938R	600 pcs.	325.00	350.00	375.00	450.00

NOTE: This piece was restruck in 1969 from new dies and is possibly counterfeit.

100 FRANGA ARI

32.2580 gm., .900 GOLD, .9335 oz AGW

Y#	Date	Mintage	Fine	VF	XF	Unc
11	1926R	6,614	625.00	650.00	700.00	800.00
11.1	1926R star below bust	Inc. Ab.	625.00	650.00	700.00	800.00

Y#	Date	Mintage	Fine	VF	XF	Unc
11.2	1926R two stars below bust	Inc. Ab.	625.00	650.00	700.00	800.00

Obv: Similar to Y#11.

Y#	Date	Mintage	Fine	VF	XF	Unc
11a	1927R	5,000	625.00	650.00	700.00	800.00
11a.1	1927R star below bust	Inc. Ab.	625.00	650.00	700.00	800.00
11a.2	1927R two stars below bust	Inc. Ab.	625.00	650.00	700.00	800.00

Independence Commemorative

Y#	Date	Mintage	Fine	VF	XF	Unc
21	1937R	500 pcs.	650.00	700.00	900.00	1200.

King Zog Marriage Commemorative
Obv: Similar to Y#21.

Y#	Date	Mintage	Fine	VF	XF	Unc
23	1938R	500 pcs.	650.00	700.00	850.00	1100.

King Zog 10th Anniversary
Obv: Similar to Y#21.

Y#	Date	Mintage	Fine	VF	XF	Unc
26	1938R	500 pcs.	625.00	650.00	850.00	1000.

NOTE: This piece was restruck in 1969 from new dies and is possibly counterfeit.

ITALIAN OCCUPATION

MONETARY SYSTEM

1 Lek = 1 Lira

.05 LEK

ALUMINUM-BRONZE

Y#	Date	Mintage	Fine	VF	XF	Unc
27	1940R	1.400	.85	2.00	3.00	5.00
	1941R	.200	2.50	5.00	12.00	20.00

.10 LEK

ALUMINUM-BRONZE

Y#	Date	Mintage	Fine	VF	XF	Unc
28	1940R	.800	1.00	2.50	5.00	7.00
	1941R	.250	25.00	50.00	70.00	100.00

.20 LEK

NOTE: Y29, 30, 31, 32 exist in two types, magnetic and non-magnetic, the latter being the scarcer.

STAINLESS STEEL

Y#	Date	Mintage	Fine	VF	XF	Unc
29	1939R	.900	.85	1.50	2.25	4.00
	1940R	.700	1.00	1.75	2.75	4.50
	1941R	1.400	1.25	2.25	3.50	6.00

.50 LEK

STAINLESS STEEL

Y#	Date	Mintage	Fine	VF	XF	Unc
30	1939R	.100	1.00	1.75	2.50	4.00
	1940R	.500	1.25	2.00	3.00	5.00
	1941R	.900	1.50	2.50	3.50	6.00

LEK

STAINLESS STEEL

Y#	Date	Mintage	Fine	VF	XF	Unc
31	1939R	2.100	.85	2.00	3.00	5.00
	1940R	—	—	—	—	—
	1941R	—	—	—	—	—

NOTE: Coins dated after 1939 were not struck for circulation.

2 LEK

STAINLESS STEEL

Y#	Date	Mintage	Fine	VF	XF	Unc
32	1939R	1.300	1.50	3.00	5.00	10.00
	1940R	—	—	—	—	—
	1941R	—	—	—	—	—

NOTE: Coins dated after 1939 were not struck for circulation.

5 LEK

5.0000 gm., .835 SILVER, .1342 oz ASW

Y#	Date	Mintage	Fine	VF	XF	Unc
33	1939R	1.350	BV	10.00	16.50	24.00

10 LEK

10.0000 gm., .835 SILVER, .2684 oz ASW

Y#	Date	Mintage	Fine	VF	XF	Unc
34	1939R	.175	20.00	37.50	55.00	80.00

REPUBLIC

MONETARY SYSTEM

100 Qindarka = 1 Lek

5 QINDARKA

ALUMINUM

Y#	Date	Mintage	Fine	VF	XF	Unc
39	1964	—	.10	.25	.45	.75

Liberation Commemorative

Y#	Date	Mintage	Fine	VF	XF	Unc
44	1969	—	.10	.20	.30	.50

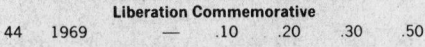

10 QINDARKA

ALUMINUM

Y#	Date	Mintage	Fine	VF	XF	Unc
40	1964	—	.15	.30	.50	.85

Liberation Commemorative

Y#	Date	Mintage	Fine	VF	XF	Unc
45	1969	—	.10	.20	.35	.60

20 QINDARKA

ALUMINUM

Y#	Date	Mintage	Fine	VF	XF	Unc
41	1964	—	.20	.35	.60	1.00

Liberation Commemorative

Y#	Date	Mintage	Fine	VF	XF	Unc
46	1969	—	.15	.25	.50	1.00

1/2 LEKU

ZINC

Y#	Date	Mintage	Fine	VF	XF	Unc
35	1947	—	.25	.50	1.00	2.00
	1957	—	.20	.50	.85	1.75

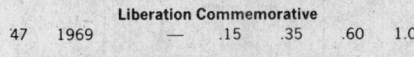

50 QINDARKA

ALUMINUM

Y#	Date	Mintage	Fine	VF	XF	Unc
42	1964	—	.25	.50	.90	1.50

Liberation Commemorative

Y#	Date	Mintage	Fine	VF	XF	Unc
47	1969	—	.15	.35	.60	1.00

LEK

ZINC

Y#	Date	Mintage	Fine	VF	XF	Unc
36	1947	—	.25	.60	1.00	3.50
	1957	—	.25	.60	1.00	2.00

ALUMINUM

Y#	Date	Mintage	Fine	VF	XF	Unc
43	1964	—	.50	1.00	2.00	3.00

Liberation Commemorative

Y#	Date	Mintage	Fine	VF	XF	Unc
48	1969	—	.35	.75	1.25	2.00

2 LEKE

ZINC

Y#	Date	Mintage	Fine	VF	XF	Unc
37	1947	—	.35	.75	1.50	2.50

Y#	Date	Mintage	Fine	VF	XF	Unc
37	1957	—	.25	.60	1.35	2.00

5 LEKE

ZINC

Y#	Date	Mintage	Fine	VF	XF	Unc
38	1947	—	.60	1.25	2.25	3.00
	1957	—	.50	1.00	2.00	2.50

16.1600 gm., .999 SILVER, .5190 oz ASW

H#	Date	Mintage	XF	Unc	Proof
1	1968	8,540	—	—	30.00
	1969	1,500	—	—	35.00
	1970	500 pcs.	—	—	50.00

10 LEKE

33.3300 gm., .999 SILVER, 1.0706 oz ASW
Rev: Similar to 5 Leke, H#1.

H#	Date	Mintage	XF	Unc	Proof
2	1968	8,540	—	—	60.00
	1969	1,500	—	—	70.00
	1970	500 pcs.	—	—	80.00

20 LEKE

3.9500 gm., .900 GOLD, .1143 oz AGW
Rev: Similar to 5 Leke, H#1.

Fr#	Date	Mintage	XF	Unc	Proof
22	1968	1,540	—	—	100.00
	1969	—	—	—	120.00
	1970	—	—	—	140.00

25 LEKE

83.3300 gm., .999 SILVER, 2.6767 oz ASW
Rev: Similar to 5 Leke, H#1.

H#	Date	Mintage	XF	Unc	Proof
3	1968	8,540	—	—	160.00
	1969	1,500	—	—	200.00
	1970	500 pcs.	—	—	240.00

50 LEKE

9.8700 gm., .900 GOLD, .2856 oz AGW
Rev: Similar to 5 Leke, H#1.

Fr#	Date	Mintage	XF	Unc	Proof
21	1968	1,540	—	—	250.00
	1969	—	—	—	300.00
	1970	—	—	—	350.00

100 LEKE

19.7500 gm., .900 GOLD, .5715 oz AGW
Rev: Similar to 5 Leke, H#1.

Fr#	Date	Mintage	XF	Unc	Proof
20	1968	1,540	—	—	500.00
	1969	—	—	—	600.00
	1970	—	—	—	700.00

200 LEKE

39.4900 gm., .900 GOLD, 1.1427 oz AGW
Rev: Similar to 5 Leke, H#1.

Fr#	Date	Mintage	XF	Unc	Proof
19	1968	1,540	—	—	1000.
	1969	—	—	—	1200.
	1970	—	—	—	1400.

500 LEKE

98.7400 gm., .900 GOLD, 2.8574 oz AGW
Rev: Similar to 5 Leke, H#1.

Fr#	Date	Mintage	XF	Unc	Proof
18	1968	1,540	—	—	2500.
	1969	—	—	—	3000.
	1970	—	—	—	3500.

NCLT ISSUES

PROVAS (Pr)

(PROVA on reverse)

Standard metals unless otherwise stated

Y#	Date	Mintage	Identification	Issue Price	Mkt Val.
Pr8	1926R	—	5 Franga Ari	—	400.00
Pr8	1926R	—	5 Franga Ari, Copper	—	—
Pr8	1926R star	—	5 Franga Ari	—	400.00
Pr8	1926R star	—	5 Franga Ari, Copper	—	—
Pr12	1926R	—	20 Franga Ari	—	200.00
Pr12	1926 Fasces	—	20 Franga Ari	—	225.00
Pr11	1926R	—	100 Franga Ari	—	750.00
Pr11.1	1926R	—	100 Franga Ari, star	—	750.00
Pr11.2	1926R	—	100 Franga Ari, two stars	—	750.00
Pr6	1927R	—	1 Franga Ari	—	200.00
Pr8	1927V	—	5 Franga Ari	—	400.00
Pr9	1927R	—	10 Franga Ari	—	400.00
Pr12	1927V	—	20 Franga Ari	—	250.00
Pr12	1927R	—	20 Franga Ari, Gold	—	225.00
Pr11a	1927R	—	100 Franga Ari	—	750.00
Pr11a.1	1927R	—	100 Franga Ari, star	—	750.00
Pr11a.2	1927R	—	100 Franga Ari, two stars	—	750.00
Pr28	1928R	—	2 Lek, Copper-Nickel	—	150.00
Pr6	1928R	—	1 Franga Ari	—	150.00
Pr7	1928R	—	2 Franga Ari	—	200.00

Y#	Date	Mintage	Identification	Issue Price	Mkt Val.
PrF7	1928R	—	100 Franga Ari, Gold	—	1000.

Y#	Date	Mintage	Identification	Issue Price	Mkt Val.
PrF8	1928R	—	100 Franga Ari, Gold	—	1250.

Y#	Date	Mintage	Identification	Issue Price	Mkt Val.
PrF9	1928R	—	100 Franga Ari, Gold	—	1250.

Y#	Date	Mintage	Identification	Issue Price	Mkt Val.
PrF10	1929R	—	100 Franga Ari, Gold	—	1250.
Pr20	1937R	—	20 Franga Ari	—	300.00
Pr21	1937R	—	100 Franga Ari	—	1500.
Pr22	1938R	—	20 Franga Ari, Zog Marriage	—	300.00
Pr24	1938R	—	20 Franga Ari, Zog 10th Anniv.	—	350.00
Pr25	1938R	—	50 Franga Ari	—	500.00
Pr23	1938R	—	100 Franga Ari, 10th Anniv.	—	1350.
Pr26	1938R	—	100 Franga Ari, Marriage	—	1250.

NOTE: Modern copies of 5 Frangi Ari Pr#8 exist in copper and bronze. Beware of counterfeits.

PROOF SETS
STANDARD METALS

KM#	Date	Mintage	Identification	Issue Price	Mkt. Val.
101	1968(5)	1,540	Fr18-21	470.00	4250.
102	1968(3)	8,540	H1-3	44.00	225.00
103	1969(5)	—	Fr18-21	470.00	5000.
104	1969(3)	1,500	H1-3	45.00	275.00
105	1970(5)	—	Fr18-21	516.00	5500.
106	1970(3)	500	H1-3	45.00	335.00

ALGERIA

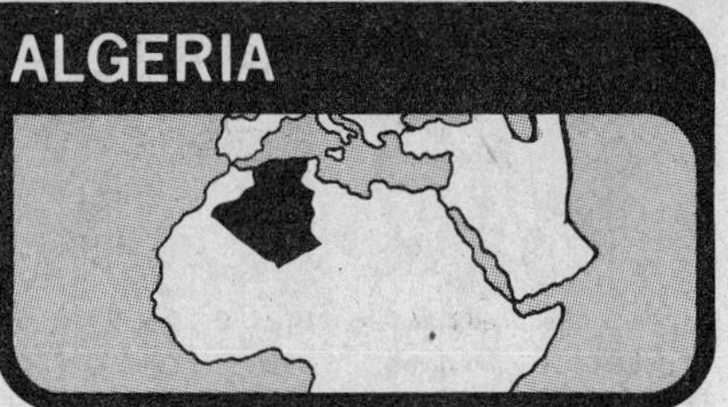

The Democratic and Popular Republic of Algeria, a North African country fronting on the Mediterranean Sea between Tunisia and Morocco, has an area of 919,590 sq. mi. (2,381,727 sq. km.) and a population of 16.3 million. Capital: Algiers. Most of the country's working population is engaged in agriculture although a recent industrial diversification, financed by oil revenues, is making steady progress. Wines, fruits, iron and zinc ores, phosphates, tobacco products, liquified natural gas, and petroleum are exported.

Algiers, the capital and chief seaport of Algeria, was the site of Phoenician and Roman settlements before the present Moslem city was founded about 950. Nominally part of the sultanate of Tlemcen, Algiers had a large measure of independence under amirs of its own. In 1492 the Jews and Moors who had been expelled from Spain settled in Algiers and enjoyed an increasing influence until the imposition of Turkish control in 1518. For the following three centuries Algiers was the headquarters of the notorious Barbary pirates. The French took Algiers in 1830, and after a long and wearisome war completed the conquest of Algeria and annexed it to France, 1848. The inability to obtain equal rights with Frenchmen led to an organized revolt which began on Nov. 1, 1954 and lasted until a ceasefire was signed on July 1, 1962. Independence was proclaimed on July 5, 1962, following a self-determination referendum.

RULERS

Sultan Abdul Hamid I,
AH1187-1203, AD1774-89
Sultan Selim III,
AH1203-22, AD1789-1807
Sultan Mustafa IV
AH1222-23, AD1807-08
Sultan Mahmud II
AH1223-55 (AD1808-39)
Abd-el-Kader (rebel), AH1250-64
(AD1834-47)

ALGIERS

Algiers ('Jaza'Ir')
Until AH1246/AD1830

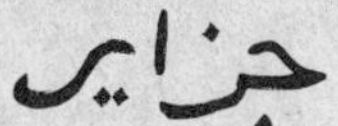

Constantine ("Qusantinah")
AH1246-1253/AD1830-36

قسنطينة

Taqidemt and Mascara
During revolt of Abd-el-Kader
AH1250-64/AD1834-47

تاقدمت

NOTE: The dots above and below the letters are integral parts of the letters, but for stylistic reasons, are occasionally omitted.

MONETARY SYSTEM
(Until 1847)

14-1/2 Asper (Akcheh, Dirham Saghir) = 1 Kharuba
2 Kharuba = 1 Muzuna
24 Muzuna = 1 Budju

NOTE: Coin denominations are not expressed on the coins, and are best determined by size and weight. The silver Budju weighed about 13.5 gm. until AH1236/AD1821, when it was reduced to about 10.0 gm. The fractional pieces varied in proportion to the Budju. They had secondary names, which are given in the text. In 1829 three new silver coins were introduced and Budju became tugrali-rial, tugrali-batlaka = 1/3 rial = 8 mazunas and tugrali- nessflik = 1/2 batlaka = 4 mazunas. The gold sultani was officially valued at 108 muzuna, but varied in accordance with the market price of gold expressed in silver. It weighed 3.2 gm.

MAHMUD II (of Turkey)
(AH1223-1253/1808-1837AD)

ASPER
(Akcheh or Dirham Saghir)

COPPER, square, often silver washed
UNKNOWN MINT
Inscribed 'ALLAH' faintly on one or both faces.

C#	Date	Mintage	VG	Fine	VF
84	ND	—	—	—	—

2 ASPERS

COPPER, 12mm., 0.8 gm.
ALGIERS MINT

C#	Date	Mintage	VG	Fine	VF
85	AH1237	—	4.50	7.00	15.00
	1238	—	4.50	7.00	15.00
	1240	—	4.50	7.00	15.00
	1242	—	4.50	7.00	15.00
	1243	—	4.50	7.00	15.00
	1244	—	4.00	6.00	12.50

CONSTANTINE MINT

C#	Date	Mintage	VG	Fine	VF
138	AH1247	—	25.00	50.00	75.00

5 ASPERS
(Valued at 1/3 Kharuba)

COPPER, 17mm., 1.8-2.2 gm.
ALGIERS MINT

C#	Date	Mintage	VG	Fine	VF
90	AH1237	—	4.00	6.50	11.50
	1238	—	4.00	6.50	11.50
	1239	—	4.00	6.50	11.50
	1240	—	4.00	7.00	12.50
	1244	—	3.50	5.50	10.00

NOTE: The 5 Aspers formerly listed as C#140 is probably an example of the 1/8 Budju, C#148, of very base metal.

KHARUB

BILLON, 14mm., 0.7-0.8 gm.
ALGIERS MINT

C#	Date	Mintage	VG	Fine	VF
95	AH1237	—	11.50	18.50	28.50
	1238	—	11.50	20.00	30.00
	1240	—	11.50	18.50	28.50
	1242	—	11.50	18.50	28.50

18mm., 0.7-0.9 gm.
CONSTANTINE MINT

C#	Date	Mintage	VG	Fine	VF
145	AH1245	—	30.00	50.00	70.00
	1246	—	30.00	50.00	70.00
	1247	—	30.00	50.00	70.00
	1250	—	30.00	50.00	70.00
	1252	—	30.00	50.00	70.00

1/8 BUDJU
(Temin Budju = 3 Muzuna)

SILVER, 18-20mm., 1.65-1.70 gm.

ALGIERS MINT

C#	Date	Mintage	VG	Fine	VF
100	AH1225	—	10.00	20.00	35.00
	1226	—	10.00	20.00	35.00
	1228	—	10.00	20.00	35.00
	1229	—	10.00	20.00	35.00
	1230	—	10.00	20.00	35.00
	1231	—	10.00	20.00	35.00
	1232	—	10.00	20.00	35.00
	1233	—	10.00	20.00	35.00

Reduced standard, 16mm., 1.20-1.30 gm.

C#	Date	Mintage	VG	Fine	VF
102	AH1237	—	4.00	7.50	12.50
	1238	—	4.00	7.50	12.50
	1239	—	4.00	7.50	12.50
	1240	—	5.00	9.00	15.00
	1242	—	4.00	7.50	12.50
	1243	—	4.00	7.50	12.50
	1244	—	4.00	7.50	12.50
	1245	—	5.00	10.00	15.00

NOTE: The dates AH1232,1234, and 1235 are reported, with weights conforming to the standard only adopted in AH1236. These need to be confirmed.

1/6 BUDJU

('Tugrali-ness-flik')

(4 Muzuna = 1/2 Batlaka)

SILVER, 18mm., 1.5 gm.

ALGIERS MINT

Tughra type

C#	Date	Mintage	VG	Fine	VF
105	AH1245	—	7.50	15.00	25.00

SILVER or BILLON, 18-19mm., 1.4-1.5 gm.

CONSTANTINE MINT

Tughra type

C#	Date	Mintage	VG	Fine	VF
150	AH1247	—	30.00	60.00	90.00
	1248	—	30.00	60.00	90.00
	1252	—	30.00	60.00	90.00

1/4 BUDJU

(6 Muzuna = Rebi Budju)

SILVER, 20mm., 3.4 gm.

ALGIERS MINT

Octagram type

C#	Date	Mintage	VG	Fine	VF
108.1	AH1223	—	20.00	40.00	60.00
	1224	—	20.00	40.00	60.00

C#	Date	Mintage	VG	Fine	VF
108.2	AH1225	—	15.00	25.00	37.50
	1226	—	12.50	20.00	32.50
	1227	—	12.50	20.00	32.50
	1228	—	12.50	20.00	32.50
	1229	—	12.50	20.00	32.50
	1230	—	12.50	20.00	32.50
	1231	—	12.50	20.00	32.50
	1232	—	12.50	20.00	32.50
	1233	—	12.50	20.00	32.50
	1234	—	12.50	20.00	32.50
	1235	—	12.50	20.00	32.50

Reduced standard, 21mm., 2.4 gm.

C#	Date	Mintage	VG	Fine	VF
110	AH1236	—	4.00	7.50	13.50
	1237	—	4.00	7.50	13.50
	1238	—	4.00	7.50	13.50
	1239	—	4.00	7.50	13.50
	1240	—	4.00	7.50	13.50
	1241	—	4.00	7.50	13.50
	1242	—	4.00	7.50	13.50
	1243	—	4.00	7.50	13.50
	1244	—	4.00	7.50	13.50
	1245	—	5.00	8.50	15.00
	1246	—	6.50	12.00	20.00

1/3 BUDJU

('Tugrali-batlaka')

SILVER, 23mm., 3.1 gm.

ALGIERS MINT

Tughra type

C#	Date	Mintage	VG	Fine	VF
112	AH1245	—	10.00	20.00	35.00

BUDJU

SILVER, 29-30mm., 9.8-10.1 gm.

C#	Date	Mintage	VG	Fine	VF
115	AH1236	—	7.00	15.00	22.50
	1237	—	6.00	12.00	20.00
	1238	—	6.00	12.00	20.00
	1239	—	6.00	12.00	20.00
	1240	—	6.00	12.00	20.00
	1241	—	6.00	12.00	20.00
	1242	—	7.00	15.00	22.50
	1243	—	7.00	15.00	22.50
	1244	—	7.00	15.00	22.50
	1245	—	Reported, Not Confirmed		

('Tugrali-rial')

Tughra type

C#	Date	Mintage	VG	Fine	VF
117	AH1245	—	100.00	175.00	275.00

SILVER or BILLON, 30-31mm., 7.9-9.8 gm.

CONSTANTINE MINT

C#	Date	Mintage	VG	Fine	VF
155	AH1248	—	150.00	250.00	375.00
	1249	—	150.00	250.00	375.00
	1253	—	150.00	250.00	375.00

2 BUDJU

(Zudj Budju)

SILVER, 38mm., 19.5-20 gm.

C#	Date	Mintage	VG	Fine	VF
120	AH1237	—	25.00	40.00	50.00
	1238	—	25.00	40.00	50.00
	1239	—	25.00	40.00	50.00
	1240	—	27.50	40.00	55.00
	1241	—	25.00	40.00	50.00
	1242	—	27.50	40.00	55.00
	1243	—	27.50	40.00	55.00

NOTE: Varieties exist.

1/4 SULTANI

GOLD, 14-15mm., 0.8 gm.

ALGIERS MINT

Obv: SULTAN MAHMUD

C#	Date	Mintage	Fine	VF	XF
125	AH1228	—	125.00	160.00	200.00
	1234	—	125.00	160.00	200.00

Obv: SULTAN MAHMUD HAN

C#	Date	Mintage	Fine	VF	XF
125a	1231	—	110.00	140.00	180.00
	1240	—	110.00	140.00	180.00
	1243	—	110.00	140.00	180.00

1/2 SULTANI

GOLD, 16-18mm., 1.6 gm.

ALGIERS MINT

C#	Date	Mintage	Fine	VF	XF
128	AH1231	—	125.00	160.00	200.00
	1232	—	125.00	160.00	200.00
	1236	—	125.00	160.00	200.00
	1237	—	125.00	160.00	200.00
	1238	—	125.00	160.00	200.00
	1239	—	125.00	160.00	200.00
	1240	—	125.00	160.00	200.00

SULTANI

GOLD, 24mm., 3.2 gm.

ALGIERS MINT

Rev: Year in fourth line

C#	Date	Mintage	Fine	VF	XF
132	AH1223	—	150.00	200.00	275.00
	1224	—	150.00	200.00	275.00
	1225	—	150.00	200.00	275.00
	1226	—	150.00	200.00	275.00
	1228	—	150.00	200.00	275.00
	1231	—	150.00	200.00	275.00

Rev: Year in third line

C#	Date	Mintage	Fine	VF	XF
132a	1235	—	125.00	175.00	225.00
	1236	—	125.00	175.00	225.00
	1237	—	125.00	175.00	225.00
	1238	—	125.00	175.00	225.00
	1239	—	125.00	175.00	225.00
	1240	—	125.00	175.00	225.00
	1241	—	125.00	175.00	225.00
	1243	—	125.00	175.00	225.00
	3421(Error)	—	125.00	175.00	225.00
	1244	—	125.00	175.00	225.00

2.4 gm.

CONSTANTINE MINT

Denomination uncertain

C#	Date	Mintage	Fine	VF	XF
—	AH1246	—	—	—	—

Revolt Of Abdel-Kader

AH1250-64/1834-47AD

5 ASPERS

COPPER, 15-17mm.

TAQIDEMT MINT

C#	Date	Mintage	VG	Fine	VF
170	AH1250	—	10.00	17.50	25.00
	1252	—	10.00	17.50	25.00
	1253	—	10.00	17.50	25.00
	1254, Arabic '4'	—	6.00	10.00	15.00
	1254, Persian '4'	—	6.00	10.00	15.00
	1255	—	5.00	8.50	12.50
	1256	—	5.00	8.50	12.50
	1257	—	7.50	12.50	20.00

KHARUBA

BILLON, 14mm., 0.7 gm.

TAQIDEMT MINT

175	AH1254 Persian '4'	—	17.50	30.00	50.00
	1254 Arabic '4'	—	17.50	30.00	50.00
	1258	—	17.50	30.00	50.00

MASCARA MINT

C#	Date	Mintage	Good	VG	Fine
176	AH125x	—	70.00	100.00	150.00

1/8 BUDJU

(3 Muzuna)

BILLON, 16mm., 1.0 gm.

C#	Date	Mintage	VG	Fine	VF
178	Undated	—	40.00	75.00	125.00

BUDJU

BILLON, 24mm., 5.5 gm.
Denomination uncertain

180	1256	—	125.00	200.00	300.00

NOTE: This coin has also been considered a 1/2 Budju, but its weight apparently indicates a reduced Budju in debased metal.

ALGERIA

MINTMARKS

(a) Paris - Privy marks only

MONETARY SYSTEM

100 Centimes = 1 Franc

20 FRANCS

COPPER-NICKEL

Y#	Date	Mintage	Fine	VF	XF
1	1949(a)	25.566	.25	.50	1.25
	1956(a)	7.500	.25	.50	1.25

50 FRANCS

COPPER-NICKEL

Y#	Date	Mintage	Fine	VF	XF
2	1949(a)	18.000	.25	.50	1.25

100 FRANCS

COPPER-NICKEL

3	1950(a)	22.189	.35	.75	1.50
	1952(a)	12.000	.35	.75	1.50

NOTE: During World War II homeland coins were struck at the Paris Mint and France, 2 Francs, Y#89 was struck at the Philadelphia Mint for use in Africa.

MONETARY REFORM

100 Centimes = 1 Dinar

CENTIME

ALUMINUM

Y#	Date	Year	Mintage	VF	XF	Unc
4	AH1383	1964	—	—	—	.10

2 CENTIMES

ALUMINUM

5	AH1383	1964	—	—	—	.15

5 CENTIMES

ALUMINUM

6	AH1383	1964	—	—	.10	.15

F.A.O. Issue

Y#	Date	Mintage	VF	XF	Unc
11	1970	50.000	—	.10	.25

F.A.O. Issue

Y#	Date	Mintage	VF	XF	Unc
12	1974	10.000	—	.10	.20

10 CENTIMES

ALUMINUM-BRONZE

Y#	Date	Year	Mintage	VF	XF	Unc
7	AH1383	1964	—	—	.20	.25

20 CENTIMES

ALUMINUM-BRONZE

8	AH1383	1964	—	—	.25	.50

BRASS
F.A.O. Issue

Y#	Date	Mintage	VF	XF	Unc
13	1972	50.000	—	.25	.50

ALUMINUM-BRONZE
F.A.O. Issue

19	1975	50.000	.50	1.00	1.50

50 CENTIMES

ALUMINUM-BRONZE

Y#	Date	Year	Mintage	VF	XF	Unc
9	AH1383	1964	—	.20	.30	.65

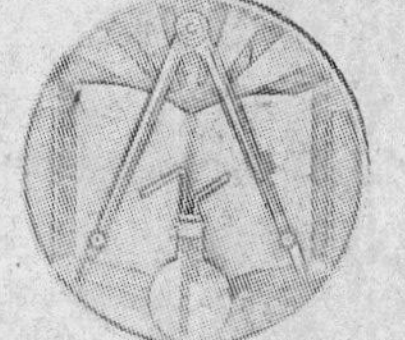

COPPER-NICKEL-ZINC

16	AH1391	1971	10.000	—	.20	.40
		1973	—	—	.15	.30

BRASS
30th Anniversary French-Algerian Clash

Y#	Date	Mintage	VF	XF	Unc
18	ND(1975)	18.000	—	.75	1.25

DINAR

COPPER-NICKEL

Y#	Date	Year	Mintage	VF	XF	Unc
10	AH1383	1964	—	.35	.60	1.00

F.A.O. Issue

Y#	Date	Mintage	VF	XF	Unc
14	1972	75.000	.65	1.00	1.50

Legend touches inner circle.

Y#	Date	Mintage	VF	XF	Unc
14.1	1972	Inc. Ab.	.65	1.00	1.50

5 DINARS

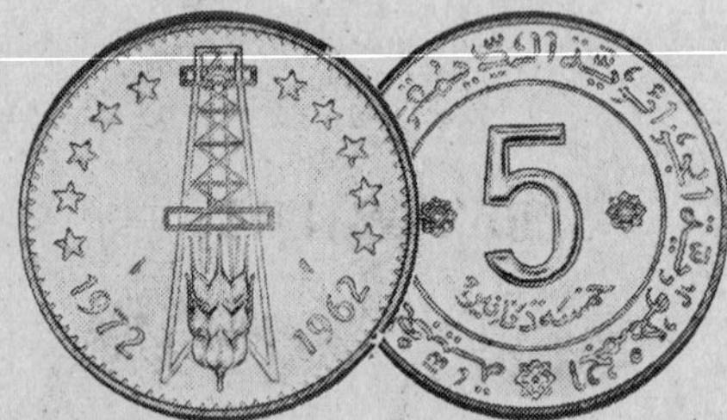

12.0000 gm., .750 SILVER, .2893 oz ASW
10th Anniversary & F.A.O. Commemorative

Y#	Date	Mintage	VF	XF	Unc
15	1972(a)	—	BV	Bv	12.00

NICKEL
10th Anniversary & F.A.O. Commemorative

Y#	Date	Mintage	VF	XF	Unc
15a	1972(a)	—	4.00	7.50	12.50

20th Anniversary of Revolution

Y#	Date	Mintage	VF	XF	Unc
17	1974	—	1.50	2.00	3.00

10 DINARS

BRONZE, 11.37 gm.

Y#	Date	Mintage	VF	XF	Unc
20	1979	—	2.50	2.75	3.50

TOKEN ISSUES

ALGER

Chamber of Commerce

5 CENTIMES

ALUMINUM

KM#	Date	Mintage	Fine	VF	XF
1	1916	—	3.00	6.00	9.00
	1918	—	1.50	3.00	4.50
	1919	—	1.00	2.00	3.00
	1921	—	1.25	2.50	3.75
	IRON				
2	1916	—	10.00	20.00	30.00
	ZINC				
3	1917	—	1.50	3.00	4.50
	1919	—	—	Unc	30.00

NOTE: The year 1919 is not a regular issue.

BRASS

KM#	Date	Mintage	Fine	VF	XF
4	1921	—	—	Unc	30.00

NOTE: Not a regular issue.

10 CENTIMES

ALUMINUM

KM#	Date	Mintage	Fine	VF	XF
5	1916	—	2.50	5.00	7.50
	1918	—	.75	1.50	2.25
	1919	—	1.50	3.00	4.50
	1921	—	.75	1.50	2.25
	IRON				
6	1916	—	4.50	9.00	13.50
	ZINC				
7	1917	—	2.00	4.00	6.00
	1918	—	—	Unc	30.00
	1919	—	—	Unc	30.00

NOTE: 1918 and 1919 are not regular issues.

BRASS

KM#	Date	Mintage	Fine	VF	XF
8	1919	—	—	Unc	12.50
	1921	—	—	Unc	30.00

NOTE: Not a regular issue.

BONE

Chamber of Commerce

5 CENTIMES

ALUMINUM

KM#	Date	Mintage	Fine	VF	XF
9	1915	—	2.00	3.00	4.00
	ND	—	2.00	3.00	4.00
	BRASS				
10	ND	—	2.25	3.25	4.50

10 CENTIMES

ALUMINUM

KM#	Date	Mintage	Fine	VF	XF
11	1915	—	2.00	3.00	4.50
	ND	—	2.00	3.00	4.50
	BRASS				
12	ND	—	2.50	3.50	5.00

50 CENTIMES

BRASS

KM#	Date	Mintage	Fine	VF	XF
13	ND	—	3.50	5.50	7.50
	COPPER-NICKEL				
14	ND	—	3.50	5.50	7.50

FRANC

BRASS

KM#	Date	Mintage	Fine	VF	XF
15	ND	—	5.00	7.50	10.00
	COPPER-NICKEL				
16	ND	—	5.00	7.50	10.00

BOUGIE

Chamber of Commerce

5 CENTIMES

ALUMINUM

KM#	Date	Mintage	Fine	VF	XF
17	1915	—	2.00	3.00	4.50

10 CENTIMES

ALUMINUM

KM#	Date	Mintage	Fine	VF	XF
18	1915	—	2.00	3.00	4.50
	ZINC				
18a	1915	—	25.00	35.00	50.00

CONSTANTINE

Chamber of Commerce

5 CENTIMES

ALUMINUM

KM#	Date	Mintage	Fine	VF	XF
19	1922	—	3.00	4.50	6.00

10 CENTIMES

ALUMINUM

KM#	Date	Mintage	Fine	VF	XF
20	1922	—	2.00	3.00	4.50

ORAN

Chamber of Commerce

5 CENTIMES

ALUMINUM

KM#	Date	Mintage	Fine	VF	XF
21	1921	—	3.00	4.50	6.50
	1922	—	3.00	4.50	6.50

10 CENTIMES

ALUMINUM

KM#	Date	Mintage	Fine	VF	XF
22	1921	—	2.50	3.50	5.00
	1922	—	2.50	3.50	5.00

25 CENTIMES

ALUMINUM

KM#	Date	Mintage	Fine	VF	XF
23	1921	—	3.50	5.50	7.50
	1922	—	3.50	5.50	7.50

NOTE: For further listings of private token issues refer to the catalogue of French Emergency Tokens of 1914-1922 by Robert Lamb.

NCLT ISSUES

ESSAIS (E)

Standard metals unless otherwise noted

Y#	Date	Mintage	Identification	Issue Price	Mkt Val.
—	1919	—	10 Centimes, Alger, KM#8	—	37.50
—	1921	—	5 Centimes, Alger, KM#4	—	37.50
E1	1949(a)	1,500	20 Francs	—	17.50
E2	1949(a)	1,500	50 Francs	—	20.00
E3	1950(a)	1,500	100 Francs	—	22.50
E15	1972(a)	—	5 Dinars	—	16.00
E17	1974(a)	—	5 Dinars	—	—

PIEFORTS WITH ESSAI (PE)

(Double Thickness)

Standard metals unless otherwise noted

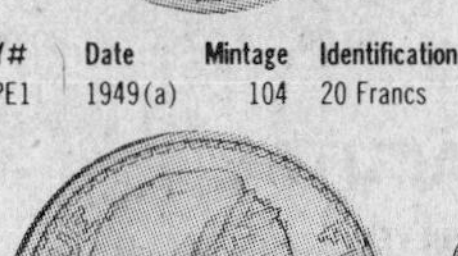

Y#	Date	Mintage	Identification	Issue Price	Mkt Val.
PE1	1949(a)	104	20 Francs	—	70.00

Y#	Date	Mintage	Identification	Issue Price	Mkt Val.
PE2	1949(a)	104	50 Francs	—	75.00

Y#	Date	Mintage	Identification	Issue Price	Mkt Val.
PE3	1950(a)	104	100 Francs	—	80.00

Listings For

ANDAMAN ISLANDS: refer to India Native States

ANGOLA

The People's Republic of Angola, a country on the west coast of southern Africa bounded by Zaire, Zambia, and Namibia (South-West Africa), has an area of 481,351 sq. mi. (1,246,699 sq. km.) and a population of 6.1 million, predominantly Bantu in origin. Capital: Luanda. Most of the people are engaged in subsistence agriculture. However, important oil and mineral deposits make Angola potentially one of the richest countries in Africa. Iron and diamonds are exported.

Angola was discovered by Portuguese navigator Diogo Cao in 1482. Portuguese settlers arrived in 1491, and established Angola as a major slaving center which sent about 3 million slaves to the New World.

A revolt, characterized by guerrilla warfare, against Portuguese rule began in 1961 and continued until 1974, when a new regime in Portugal offered independence. The independence movement was actively supported by three groups, the National Front, based in Zaire, the Soviet-backed Popular Movement, and the moderate National Union. Independence was proclaimed on Nov. 11, 1975, and the Portuguese departed, leaving the Angolan people to work out their own political destiny. Within hours, each of the independence groups proclaimed itself Angola's sole ruler. A bloody intertribal civil war erupted in which the communist Popular Movement, assisted by Soviet arms and Cuban mercenaries, was the eventual victor.

RULERS

Portuguese until 1975

MONETARY SYSTEM

(Until 1860)

50 Reis = 1 Macuta

(Commencing 1910)

100 Centavos = 20 Macutas
= 1 Escudo

1/4 MACUTA

COPPER

Obv: Legend around crowned arms.
Rev: Legend around denomination in circle, date above.

C#	Date	Mintage	VG	Fine	VF
14	1785	—	5.00	10.00	20.00
	Similar to C#14, but MARIA I D.G., etc.				
23.5	1789	—	6.00	12.00	22.50
33	1814	—	15.00	25.00	40.00
	1815	—	20.00	30.00	50.00

1/2 MACUTA

COPPER

Similar to 1/4 Macuta, C#14.

C#	Date	Mintage	VG	Fine	VF
15	1785	—	5.00	10.00	20.00
	1786	—	5.00	10.00	20.00
	Similar to 1/4 Macuta, C#23.5.				
24	1789	—	6.00	12.00	22.50
34	1814	—	12.50	17.50	25.00
	1815	—	20.00	45.00	75.00
	1819	.018	Reported, Not Confirmed		

C#	Date	Mintage	VG	Fine	VF
75	1848	.417	5.00	8.00	12.50
	1851	.104	7.50	12.50	17.50
	1853	.143	6.00	10.00	15.00
76	1858	.226	3.00	5.50	8.00
	1860	.398	4.00	7.50	10.00

MACUTA

COPPER

Similar to 1/4 Macuta, C#14.

C#	Date	Mintage	VG	Fine	VF
16	1783	—	6.00	12.00	22.50
	1784	—	6.00	12.00	22.50
	1785	—	6.00	12.00	22.50
	1786	—	6.00	12.00	22.50

Similar to 1/4 Macuta, C#23.5.

C#	Date	Mintage	VG	Fine	VF
25	1789	—	7.50	14.00	27.50

C#	Date	Mintage	VG	Fine	VF
35	1814	—	7.50	10.00	12.50
	1816	—	10.00	17.50	25.00
	1819	6,110	Reported, Not Confirmed		

NOTE: Lightweight coins dated 1814 exist weighing 10.96 gm.

Similar to 1/2 Macuta, C#75.

C#	Date	Mintage	VG	Fine	VF
77	1860	—	7.50	12.50	20.00

2 MACUTAS

SILVER

Similar to 1/4 Macuta, C#14.

C#	Date	Mintage	VG	Fine	VF
18	1783	—	20.00	40.00	55.00

Similar to 1/4 Macuta, C#23.5.

C#	Date	Mintage	VG	Fine	VF
27	1796	—	20.00	40.00	55.00

COPPER

C#	Date	Mintage	VG	Fine	VF
36	1815	—	75.00	100.00	135.00
	1816	—	90.00	125.00	165.00
	1819	3,175	Reported, Not Confirmed		

4 MACUTAS

SILVER

Similar to 1/4 Macuta, C#14.

C#	Date	Mintage	VG	Fine	VF
19	1783	—	30.00	45.00	85.00
	1784	—	30.00	45.00	85.00

Similar to 1/4 Macuta, C#23.5.

C#	Date	Mintage	VG	Fine	VF
28	1789	—	30.00	45.00	85.00
	1796	—	30.00	45.00	85.00

6 MACUTAS

SILVER

Similar to 1/4 Macuta, C#14.

C#	Date	Mintage	VG	Fine	VF
20	1784	—	40.00	60.00	100.00

Similar to 1/4 Macuta, C#23.5.

C#	Date	Mintage	VG	Fine	VF
29	1789	—	40.00	60.00	100.00
	1796	—	40.00	60.00	80.00

8 MACUTAS

SILVER

Similar to 1/4 Macuta, C#14.

C#	Date	Mintage	VG	Fine	VF
21	1783	—	60.00	100.00	150.00

Similar to 1/4 Macuta, C#23.5.

C#	Date	Mintage	VG	Fine	VF
30	1789	—	60.00	100.00	150.00
	1796	—	60.00	100.00	150.00

10 MACUTAS

SILVER

Similar to 1/4 Macuta, C#14.

C#	Date	Mintage	VG	Fine	VF
22	1783	—	100.00	175.00	250.00

C#	Date	Mintage	VG	Fine	VF
31	1796	—	100.00	175.00	250.00

12 MACUTAS

SILVER

Similar to 1/4 Macuta, C#14.

C#	Date	Mintage	VG	Fine	VF
23	1783	—	170.00	275.00	375.00

C#	Date	Mintage	VG	Fine	VF
32	1796	—	170.00	275.00	375.00

COUNTERSTAMP ISSUES

In 1814 various copper coins were counterstamped with the crowned arms of Portugal to double their face value.

20 REIS

COPPER

c/s: Crowned arms on X Reis, C#2.

C#	Date	Mintage	VG	Fine	VF
2a	1753	—	9.00	15.00	25.00
	1757	—	11.50	17.50	27.50

1/2 MACUTA

COPPER

c/s: Crowned arms on 1/4 Macuta, C#5.

C#	Date	Mintage	VG	Fine	VF
5a	1762	—	12.00	18.00	30.00
	1763	—	10.00	15.00	25.00
	1770	—	9.00	13.00	20.00
	1771	—	10.00	15.00	25.00

c/s: Crowned arms on 1/4 Macuta, C#14.

C#	Date	Mintage	VG	Fine	VF
14a	1785	—	15.00	22.00	35.00
	1786	—	15.00	22.00	35.00

c/s: Crowned arms on 1/4 Macuta, C#25.

C#	Date	Mintage	VG	Fine	VF
25a	1789	—	14.00	20.00	32.50

40 REIS

COPPER

c/s: Crowned arms on XX Reis, C#3.

C#	Date	Mintage	VG	Fine	VF
3a	1752	—	7.50	12.50	20.00
	1753	—	6.50	10.00	20.00

MACUTA

COPPER

c/s: Crowned arms on 1/2 Macuta, C#6.

C#	Date	Mintage	VG	Fine	VF
6a	1762	—	15.00	22.00	35.00
	1763	—	15.00	22.00	35.00
	1770	—	10.00	15.00	25.00

c/s: Crowned arms on 1/2 Macuta, C#15.

C#	Date	Mintage	VG	Fine	VF
15a	1785	—	15.00	22.00	35.00
	1786	—	20.00	27.50	50.00

c/s: Crowned arms on 1/2 Macuta, C#25.

C#	Date	Mintage	VG	Fine	VF
25a	1789	—	15.00	22.00	35.00

80 REIS

COPPER

c/s: Crowned arms on XL Reis, C#4.

C#	Date	Mintage	VG	Fine	VF
4a	1753	—	9.00	17.50	25.00
	1757	—	9.00	17.50	25.00

2 MACUTAS

COPPER

c/s: Crowned arms on 1 Macuta, C#7.

C#	Date	Mintage	VG	Fine	VF
7a	1762	—	15.00	22.50	35.00
	1763	—	17.50	25.00	37.50
	1770	—	12.50	18.50	30.00

c/s: Crowned arms on 1 Macuta, C#16.

C#	Date	Mintage	VG	Fine	VF
16a	1783	—	20.00	27.50	50.00
	1785	—	17.50	25.00	37.50
	1786	—	15.00	22.50	35.00

Now that you've got this huge catalog, how about some fresh news and advertising?

Tolbert Topples, Page 8

world coin news

60¢

VOL. 7, NO. 20 IOLA, WISCONSIN • MAY 13, 1980 ONE YEAR $11.50

Kumar Uncovers Mangrol Cardboards

Discovery of the cash coupons of another Indian Native state has just been reported by dealer Santosh Kumar, New Delhi, India. The cardboard notes, emanating from the World War II period, have never before been published or even suspected, Kumar pointed out.

The one-anna cardboards were issued during the war by Mangrol State, a small Muslim principality in Gujerat. The capital city of Mangrol is a port on the Arabian Sea, midway between the port cities of Porbandar and Diu, the latter a former Portuguese enclave.

The small cardboard notes are square, 50 by 50 millimeters in size.

The face side contains Gujarati script meaning ONE ANNA VALUE and a serial number in Indian numerals, as well as an autograph signature. The reverse carries the value in Gujarati, ONE 1 ANNA at top, and at center is a wreath of leaves enclosing the flag-supported coat of arms of the state. Prominent in the arms are three crescent-and-star emblems of Islam, crossed scimitars and a sailing ship.

One the face side is the English phrase ONE ANNA and on reverse the English spelling MANGROL. Otherwise all script is in the Gujarati language.

Kumar said he values the one-anna cardboard at U.S. $150 each. Only a few specimens have been found.

Cash coupons are small, usually cardboard, substitutes for coins which became popular in India during the hoarding of coin period in 1942-1943 as the Japanese army overran Burma and crossed the Indian frontier near Imphal and Kohima. A number of these scarce numismatic items are illustrated and listed in the 3rd edition of the *Standard Catalog of World Paper Money*, now being supplied to distributors and dealers.

The tiny state of Mangrol is on the Kathiawar peninsula in western India. The peninsula is the site of many small states which issued cash coupons in World War II – Junagadh, Gondal, Jasdan, Navanagar, Muli, Palitana, Rajkot and Vithalgadh among them. Indian scholars believe that even more states' notes may still come to light as collectors search for them.

Mangrol State in the Kathiawar peninsula in western India issued cardboard one-anna cash coupons during a change shortage in World War II, reports Santosh Kumar, New Delhi, India. The tiny Arabian Sea coastal state has never previously been reported to have issued any coins, notes or postage stamps.

Ecuador has just issued 1980-dated 20-centavo coins in a new alloy, Nickel-Bonded-Steel, struck at the Sherritt Mint, Fort Saskatchewan, Canada. (Courtesy Rex F. Pearce, Toronto)

Gold Deak Fivepiece Debuts

A new bullion token minted for the Gold Standard Corp. will bear the effigy of Nicholas L. Deak, the founder and moving force behind Deak-Perera Group, the United States' largest retailer of gold and a worldwide network of foreign exchange houses.

Dubbed the "Deak Fivepiece," the token contains 1/20th of a troy ounce of fine gold, in response to a growing demand for practical bullion pieces of smaller value. It carries the inscription INTERNATIONALIZATION OF SOUND MONEY.

Deak was presented with the first strike Fivepiece at the American economic conference in Beverly Hills, Calif., on March 9.

"The future depends on those who quietly provide solutions, and it is in this spirit that we hope always to emulate Mr. Deak," said Conrad J. Braun, president of Gold Standard Corp. in Kansas City, Mo., one of the largest private gold minters in North America.

"It's possible the Deak Fivepiece could become the largest privately circulated gold piece in existence, and we fully anticipate difficulty in keeping it in stock," Braun added.

Gold Standard Corp. is planning on marketing more than 50,000 gold Fivepieces, the fifth in its series of gold tokens regularly offered. Other pieces include the ounce, half ounce, quarter ounce and tenth ounce, the latter called a Tenpiece. The Fivepiece bears the date 1980 and is struck in pure (.999 fine) gold.

'Deak Fivepiece' is the name given the new 1980 gold bullion tokens being distributed by Gold Standard Corp., each containing 1/20th troy ounce of fine gold. They portray Nicholas L. Deak, founder of Deak-Perera Group and a long-time advocate of sound money.

New Coinage Material

A new type of coinage material will soon be produced on a large scale in Canada by Sherritt Gordon Mines Ltd. The company recently announced plans to build a new plant on the site of its Sherritt Mint, refinery and rolling mill at Fort Saskatchewan, Alberta.

Sherritt officials predict their Nickel-Bonded-Steel coins and coin blanks will go a long way toward solving the problem that ever-increasing metal prices have created in the world's coinage industry.

During the 1960's pure nickel and copper-nickel alloys replaced silver as the basic coinage material in most countries, but nickel and copper are now becoming too costly for low-denomination coins. In some cases the costs exceed the coin's face value – as the current Canadian 5-cent piece, which costs 6 cents to produce.

Sherritt's NBS, developed at the company's research center in Fort Saskatchewan, meets all the requirements for a coinage material that is physically attractive yet has a low cost. NBS has a bright, lustrous appearance and the heft of pure nickel coinage at about half the cost, and is completely corrosion-resistant, officials say.

The alloy is magnetic. It has a steel core completely

(NICKEL, Page 16)

Ken L. Davies, new assistant marketing director for Canada's Sherritt Mint

CNA Releases Basic Primer Book

A basic primer on coin collecting was included in the April issue of the *Canadian Numismatic Journal*. The primer on money and money-related items was prepared under the direction of Jack Veffer, president of the Canadian Numismatic Association, publisher of the magazine.

"We at the CNA felt a need to reexamine the subject," Veffer told readers. "We wanted to put it into words simple enough for anyone to understand. While these pages are directed especially towards the novice and the young collector, they should be of great interest to long-time numismatists as well."

Contributors include some of Canada's best known experts, R. C. Willey, David Ashe, Lloyd T. Smith, Grant Monck, James E. Charlton, Major Sheldon S. Carroll, Stanley H. Clute, Bruce R. Brace, Ross W. Irwin, and Veffer himself.

The 60-page special issue of

(CNA, Page 16)

Bright red cover of the special issue of Canadian Numismatic Journal which includes a primer on coins and other forms of money. The April 1980 edition is in the mails to CNA members.

Introducing World Coin News, the weekly newspaper devoted exclusively to world coins and world paper money.

If you collect world coins, or if you're interested in reading about world coins . . . this newspaper is for you!

From country to country . . . and around the world, World Coin News will give you the latest news of hobby people, places and events. You'll learn of unusual sales, discoveries and transactions within our hobby.

You'll enjoy feature articles complete with photos and lots of historical information. And, of course, you'll enjoy special features in World Coin News, including:

News Front — a brief look at events important to you and your hobby.

Readers' Soapbox — an open "letters" page where you can vent your opinions on anything hobby related.

Question Forum — the column to write to for well-researched answers to your tough hobby questions.

World Coin Roundup — a periodic listing of new coin types and dates, complete with photos and descriptions — a good companion to your Standard Catalog of World Coins.

Special subscription offer for catalog buyers. Save $2.00!

Save $2.00 on a one year (52 issue) subscription to World Coin News. The regular rate is $13.50. Use this special offer and you'll pay only $11.50. That's more than a 14% discount off the regular rate! Use one of the order blanks on back to enter your subscription. Then give the other order blank to a friend . . . so they can enjoy a discount too.

The classified and display advertising in World Coin News will give you an excellent opportunity to buy and sell coins and notes from around the world. You'll have the opportunity to mail order your coins and notes from trustworthy dealers who will hold your satisfaction as an important goal.

If you enjoy reading about world coins, if you enjoy building a collection and if you want the perfect companion to your Standard Catalog of World Coins, don't hesitate . . . enter your subscription to World Coin News. Use one order blank on the backside. Give the other order blank to a friend.

Your money-back guarantee

If for some reason you decide to cancel your World Coin News subscription, here's all you need to do. Notify us before you receive your fourth issue, and we'll refund your entire payment. After the fourth issue, we'll refund on all issues not yet mailed. Your initial risk is very little when you subscribe to World Coin News.

See the subscription order blanks on back.

World Coin News subscription order blank

Please mail with payment to World Coin News, 700 E. State St., Iola, Wisconsin 54945.

☐ Please enter my one year (52 issue) subscription to World Coin News. I understand the cost to me is only $11.50 (I'm saving $2.00 off the regular rate of $13.50). My method of payment is checked below.

☐ new subscription ☐ renewal/extension

☐ Check or money order enclosed.

☐ Charge to my Master Charge/Visa account.

account no. ______________________

expiration date mo. __________ yr. __________

signature ______________________

name ______________________

address ______________________

city ______________________

state __________ zip __________

Addresses outside the U.S., including Canada and Mexico, please send $15. Thank you. This special rate offer expires July 1, 1981. Offer good with this order blank only.

AKX

The Standard Catalog of World Coins.

World Coin News.

Use and enjoy the perfect companions!

Subscribe to World Coin News now and save $2.00.

Give this order blank to a friend!

World Coin News subscription order blank

Please mail with payment to World Coin News, 700 E. State St., Iola, Wisconsin 54945.

☐ Please enter my one year (52 issue) subscription to World Coin News. I understand the cost to me is only $11.50 (I'm saving $2.00 off the regular rate of $13.50). My method of payment is checked below.

☐ new subscription ☐ renewal/extension

☐ Check or money order enclosed.

☐ Charge to my Master Charge/Visa account.

account no. ______________________

expiration date mo. __________ yr. __________

signature ______________________

name ______________________

address ______________________

city ______________________

state __________ zip __________

Addresses outside the U.S., including Canada and Mexico, please send $15. Thank you. This special rate offer expires July 1, 1981. Offer good with this order blank only. AKY

Subscription information you'll want to know . . .

How often will I receive World Coin News?

A copy of World Coin News will be mailed t you each week of your subscription.

How much of World Coin News is devoted to coins, and how much to paper money?

While it's difficult to establish an actual ratic it's safe to say the majority of features will b devoted to world coins.

Who publishes World Coin News?

World Coin News is published by Krause Pub lications, the same people who bring you th popular Standard Catalog of World Pape Money, Standard Catalog of World Coins anc many other fine hobby publications.

How large is a typical issue of World Coin News?

Most issues of World Coin News have in the neighborhood of 28-32 pages. Just the right amount of material to consume in a week! And World Coin News is a convenient tabloid size — great for reading on the bus, on the train or curled up in your favorite easy chair.

How much of a refund will I receive if I decide to cancel?

If you decide to cancel your subscription here's all you need do. Drop us a note before you receive your fourth issue and we'll refund your entire payment. After the fourth issue is received, we'll refund on all undelivered issues. That's our guarantee to you!

c/s: Crowned arms on 1 Macuta, C#25.

C#	Date	Mintage	VG	Fine	VF
25a	1789	—	12.50	18.50	30.00

c/s: Crowned arms on 1 Macuta, C#35.

C#	Date	Mintage	VG	Fine	VF
35b	1814	—	—	Rare	—

c/s: Crowned arms on 1 Macuta, C#35a.

C#	Date	Mintage	VG	Fine	VF
35b	1814	—	—	Rare	—
	1816	—	—	Rare	—

4 MACUTAS

COPPER

c/s: Crowned arms on 2 Macutas, C#36.

C#	Date	Mintage	VG	Fine	VF
36a	1815	—	—	Rare	—
	1816	—	—	Rare	—

DECIMAL COINAGE

100 Centavos = 1 Escudo

CENTAVO

BRONZE

Y#	Date	Mintage	VF	XF	Unc
12	1921	1.360	12.50	20.00	35.00

2 CENTAVOS

BRONZE

Y#	Date	Mintage	VF	XF	Unc
13	1921	.530	12.50	20.00	35.00

5 CENTAVOS

BRONZE

Y#	Date	Mintage	VF	XF	Unc
14	1921	.720	12.50	17.50	25.00
	1922	5.680	10.00	15.00	22.50
	1923	5.840	10.00	15.00	22.50
	1924	—	25.00	45.00	75.00

NICKEL-BRONZE

Y#	Date	Mintage	VF	XF	Unc
18	1927	2.002	3.00	7.50	12.50

10 CENTAVOS

COPPER-NICKEL

Y#	Date	Mintage	VF	XF	Unc
15	1921	.160	10.00	15.00	25.00
	1922	.340	7.50	12.50	20.00
	1923	2.960	4.50	7.50	15.00

Y#	Date	Mintage	VF	XF	Unc
19	1927	2.003	4.00	7.50	15.00
	1928	1.000	4.00	7.50	15.00

BRONZE

Y#	Date	Mintage	VF	XF	Unc
22	1948	10.000	.20	.35	.65
	1949	10.000	.25	.40	.65

ALUMINUM

Y#	Date	Mintage	VF	XF	Unc
22a	1974	4.000	—	—	30.00

NOTE: Not released for circulation.

20 CENTAVOS

COPPER-NICKEL

Y#	Date	Mintage	VF	XF	Unc
16	1921	2.115	6.00	10.00	17.50
	1922	1.730	7.50	12.50	20.00

NICKEL-BRONZE

Y#	Date	Mintage	VF	XF	Unc
20	1927	2.001	5.00	8.50	15.00
	1928	.500	6.00	10.00	20.00

BRONZE

Y#	Date	Mintage	VF	XF	Unc
23	1948	7.850	.35	.75	1.50
	1949	2.150	.75	1.50	3.00

Y#	Date	Mintage	VF	XF	Unc
23a	1962	3.000	—	.15	.50

50 CENTAVOS

NICKEL

Y#	Date	Mintage	VF	XF	Unc
17	1922	6.000	4.00	6.50	12.50
	1923	4.780	4.00	7.50	15.00

NICKEL-BRONZE

Y#	Date	Mintage	VF	XF	Unc
21	1927	1.608	5.00	7.50	15.00
	1928	1.600	6.00	8.00	17.50

Y#	Date	Mintage	VF	XF	Unc
24	1948	4.000	.50	1.25	2.00
	1950	4.000	1.25	1.50	2.50

BRONZE

Y#	Date	Mintage	VF	XF	Unc
25	1953	5.000	.15	.25	.60
	1954	11.731	.15	.25	.60
	1955	1.126	.40	.75	1.25
	1957	8.873	.15	.30	.65
	1958	17.520	.10	.15	.35
	1961	8.750	.15	.20	.40
	1962	5.861	.15	.20	.40

COPPER-NICKEL

Y#	Date	Mintage	VF	XF	Unc
25a	1974	—	1.50	2.50	4.00

ESCUDO

BRONZE

Y#	Date	Mintage	VF	XF	Unc
26	1953	2.001	.25	1.00	3.00
	1956	2.989	.20	.35	.75
	1963	5.000	.20	.35	.75
	1965	5.000	.20	.35	.75
	1972	10.000	.20	.35	.75
	1974	6.214	.75	1.50	3.00

2-1/2 ESCUDOS

COPPER-NICKEL

Y#	Date	Mintage	VF	XF	Unc
27	1953	6.008	.25	.40	.75
	1956	9.992	.25	.35	.75
	1967	6.000	.25	.40	.85
	1968	5.000	.25	.40	.85
	1969	5.000	.25	.40	.85
	1974	19.999	1.50	3.00	6.00

5 ESCUDOS

COPPER-NICKEL

A28	1972	8.000	3.50	6.00	10.00
	1974	3.343	—	—	—

NOTE: Not released for circulation.

10 ESCUDOS

5.0000 gm., .720 SILVER, .1157 oz ASW

28	1952	2.023	BV	3.50	5.00
	1955	1.977	BV	3.50	5.00

COPPER-NICKEL

28a	1969	3.022	.65	1.00	2.00
	1970	.978	.75	1.25	2.50

20 ESCUDOS

10.0000 gm., .720 SILVER, .2315 oz ASW

29	1952	1.003	BV	7.00	8.50
	1955	.997	BV	7.00	8.50

COPPER-NICKEL

Y#	Date	Mintage	VF	XF	Unc
30	1971	1.572	.75	2.00	3.00
	1972	.428	1.00	2.00	3.00

NCLT ISSUES

PATTERNS

KM#	Date	Mintage	Identification	Mkt.Val.
1	1831	—	1/4 Macuta, Copper, C#71	180.00
2	1831	—	1/2 Macuta, Copper, C#72	180.00
3	1831	—	1 Macuta, Copper, C#73	180.00
4	1831	—	2 Macutas, Copper, C#74	180.00

PROVAS PR

STANDARD METALS

Raised or stamped 'PROVA' in field.

Y#	Date	Mintage	Identification	Issue Price	Mkt Val.
Pr12	1921	—	1 Centavo	—	20.00
Pr13	1921	—	2 Centavos	—	20.00
Pr14	1921	—	5 Centavos	—	20.00
Pr14	1922	—	5 Centavos	—	20.00
Pr14	1923	—	5 Centavos	—	20.00
Pr14	1924	—	5 Centavos	—	100.00
Pr15	1921	—	10 Centavos	—	35.00
Pr15	1922	—	10 Centavos	—	30.00
Pr15	1923	—	10 Centavos	—	30.00
Pr16	1921	—	20 Centavos	—	30.00
Pr16	1922	—	20 Centavos	—	30.00
Pr16	1923	—	20 Centavos	—	30.00
Pr18	1927	—	5 Centavos	—	20.00
Pr19	1927	—	10 Centavos	—	20.00
Pr19	1928	—	10 Centavos	—	20.00
Pr20	1927	—	20 Centavos	—	20.00
Pr20	1928	—	20 Centavos	—	20.00
Pr21	1927	—	50 Centavos	—	20.00
Pr21	1928	—	50 Centavos	—	20.00
Pr22	1948	—	10 Centavos	—	20.00
Pr22	1949	—	10 Centavos	—	20.00
Pr23	1948	—	20 Centavos	—	20.00
Pr23	1949	—	20 Centavos	—	20.00
Pr23a	1962	—	20 Centavos	—	20.00
Pr24	1948	—	50 Centavos	—	20.00
Pr24	1949	—	50 Centavos	—	20.00
Pr24	1950	—	50 Centavos	—	20.00
Pr25	1953	—	50 Centavos	—	20.00
Pr25	1954	—	50 Centavos	—	20.00
Pr25	1955	—	50 Centavos	—	20.00
Pr25	1956	—	50 Centavos	—	20.00
Pr25	1957	—	50 Centavos	—	20.00
Pr25	1958	—	50 Centavos	—	20.00
Pr25	1959	—	50 Centavos	—	20.00
Pr25	1960	—	50 Centavos	—	20.00
Pr25	1961	—	50 Centavos	—	20.00
Pr26	1953	—	1 Escudo	—	20.00
Pr26	1954	—	1 Escudo	—	20.00
Pr26	1955	—	1 Escudo	—	20.00
Pr26	1956	—	1 Escudo	—	20.00
Pr26	1957	—	1 Escudo	—	20.00
Pr26	1958	—	1 Escudo	—	20.00
Pr26	1959	—	1 Escudo	—	20.00
Pr26	1960	—	1 Escudo	—	20.00
Pr26	1961	—	1 Escudo	—	20.00
Pr26	1962	—	1 Escudo	—	20.00
Pr26	1963	—	1 Escudo	—	20.00
Pr26	1964	—	1 Escudo	—	20.00
Pr26	1965	—	1 Escudo	—	20.00
Pr26	1966	—	1 Escudo	—	20.00
Pr26	1967	—	1 Escudo	—	20.00
Pr26	1968	—	1 Escudo	—	20.00
Pr26	1969	—	1 Escudo	—	20.00
Pr26	1970	—	1 Escudo	—	20.00
Pr26	1971	—	1 Escudo	—	20.00
Pr26	1972	—	1 Escudo	—	20.00
Pr26	1974	—	1 Escudo	—	20.00
Pr27	1953	—	2-1/2 Escudos	—	30.00
Pr27	1954	—	2-1/2 Escudos	—	30.00
Pr27	1955	—	2-1/2 Escudos	—	30.00
Pr27	1956	—	2-1/2 Escudos	—	30.00
Pr27	1957	—	2-1/2 Escudos	—	30.00
Pr27	1958	—	2-1/2 Escudos	—	30.00
Pr27	1959	—	2-1/2 Escudos	—	30.00
Pr27	1960	—	2-1/2 Escudos	—	30.00
Pr27	1961	—	2-1/2 Escudos	—	30.00
Pr27	1962	—	2-1/2 Escudos	—	30.00
Pr27	1963	—	2-1/2 Escudos	—	30.00
Pr27	1964	—	2-1/2 Escudos	—	30.00
Pr27	1965	—	2-1/2 Escudos	—	30.00
Pr27	1966	—	2-1/2 Escudos	—	30.00
Pr27	1967	—	2-1/2 Escudos	—	30.00
Pr27	1968	—	2-1/2 Escudos	—	30.00
Pr27	1969	—	2-1/2 Escudos	—	30.00
Pr27	1970	—	2-1/2 Escudos	—	30.00
Pr27	1971	—	2-1/2 Escudos	—	30.00
Pr27	1972	—	2-1/2 Escudos	—	30.00
Pr28	1952	—	10 Escudos	—	45.00
Pr28	1955	—	10 Escudos	—	45.00
Pra28	1972	—	5 Escudos	—	30.00
Pr28a	1969	—	5 Escudos	—	30.00
Pr28a	1970	—	5 Escudos	—	30.00
Pr29	1952	—	20 Escudos	—	45.00
Pr29	1955	—	20 Escudos	—	45.00
Pr30	1971	—	20 Escudos	—	30.00
Pr30	1972	—	20 Escudos	—	30.00

PEOPLE'S REPUBLIC

MONETARY SYSTEM

100 Lwei = 1 Kwanza

50 LWEI

COPPER-NICKEL

Y#	Date	Mintage	VF	XF	Unc
31	1975	—	.25	.50	1.00

KWANZA

COPPER-NICKEL

32	1975	—	.35	.75	1.50

2 KWANZAS

COPPER-NICKEL

33	1975	—	.75	1.25	2.50

5 KWANZAS

COPPER-NICKEL

34	1975	—	.85	1.75	3.50

10 KWANZAS

COPPER-NICKEL

Y#	Date	Mintage	VF	XF	Unc
35	1975	—	1.25	2.25	4.50

20 KWANZAS

COPPER-NICKEL

Y#	Date	Mintage	VF	XF	Unc
36	1978	—	2.00	3.00	5.50

ANGUILLA

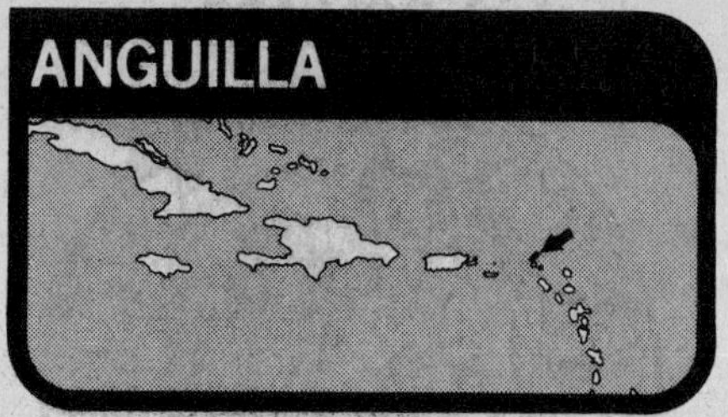

The British Colony of Anguilla, a self-governing British territory situated in the east Caribbean Sea about 60 miles (100 km.) northwest of St. Kitts, has an area of 35 sq. mi. (91 sq. km.) and a population of 6,600. Capital: The Valley. Fishing, stock raising, salt production and tourism are the main industries.

Anguilla was discovered by Columbus in 1493 and became a British colony in 1650. In March 1967 Anguilla was joined politically with St. Christopher (St. Kitts) and Nevis to form a British associated state.

On June 16, 1967, Anguilla unilaterally declared its independence and seceded from the Federation. Britain refused to accept the declaration (nor did any other country recognize it), and appointed a British administrator whom Anguilla accepted. However, in Feb. 1969 Anguilla ousted the British emissary, voted to sever all ties with Britain, and established the Republic of Anguilla. The following month Britain landed a force of paratroopers and policemen, and in a bloodless counteraction ended the self-proclaimed republic and installed a commissioner to govern. The troops were withdrawn in Sept. 1969. and the Anguilla Act of July 1971 placed Anguilla directly under British control. A new constitution in 1976 established Anguilla as a self-governing British colony. Britain retains power over defense, police and civil service, and foreign affairs.

RULERS

British

1/2 DOLLAR

3.5700 gm., 1.000 SILVER, .1147 oz ASW

H#	Date	Mintage	XF	Unc	Proof
15	1967	.010	—	—	10.00
	1969	—	—	—	12.50
	1970	—	—	—	12.50

DOLLAR

7.1400 gm., 1.000 SILVER, .2295 oz ASW

H#	Date	Mintage	XF	Unc	Proof
16	1967	.010	—	—	12.50
	1969	—	—	—	15.00
	1970	—	—	—	15.00

LIBERTY DOLLARS

c/s: ANGUILLA LIBERTY DOLLAR JULY 11, 1967 on various crown-sized coins. Mintages are estimates.

KM#	Date	Mintage	Identification	Issue Price	Mkt. Val.
1	1967	6,000	c/s on Mexico KM#467	10.00	20.00

NOTE: 4,000 of the above pieces were remelted.

KM#	Date	Mintage	Identification	Issue Price	Mkt. Val.
2	1967	1,500	c/s on Mexico KM#465	10.00	30.00
3	1967	1,500	c/s on Peru Y#41	10.00	30.00

KM#	Date	Mintage	Identification	Issue Price	Mkt. Val.
3a	1967	Inc. #4	c/s on Yemen Y#31	10.00	65.00
4	1967	500 pcs.	c/s on Yemen Y#17	10.00	200.00
5	1967	340 pcs.	c/s on Philippines Y#25	10.00	125.00

KM#	Date	Mintage	Identification	Issue Price	Mkt. Val.
6	1967	250 pcs.	c/s on Mexico KM#474	10.00	150.00
7	1967	90 pcs.	c/s on Panama Y#16	10.00	200.00
8	1967	21 pcs.	c/s on Ecuador Y#56	—	275.00
9	1967	15 pcs.	c/s on Mexico KM#409	—	350.00
10	1967	10 pcs.	c/s on China, assorted Yuan Shih Kai Dollars	—	400.00
11	1967	2 pcs.	c/s on Mexico KM#468	—	750.00
12	1967	2 pcs.	c/s on Gr. Britain Y#T1	—	—

2 DOLLARS

14.2800 gm., 1.000 SILVER, .4591 oz ASW

H#	Date	Mintage	XF	Unc	Proof
17	1967	.010	—	—	20.00
	1969	—	—	—	22.50
	1970	—	—	—	22.50

4 DOLLARS

28.570

18 196

5 DOLLARS

2.4600 gm., .900 GOLD, .0711 oz AGW

Date	Mintage	XF	Unc	Proof
1967	680 pcs.	—	—	50.00
1970	—	—	—	50.00

10 DOLLARS

4.9300 gm., .900 GOLD, .1426 oz AGW

	Date	Mintage	XF	Unc	Proof
21	1967	680 pcs.	—	—	100.00

20 DOLLARS

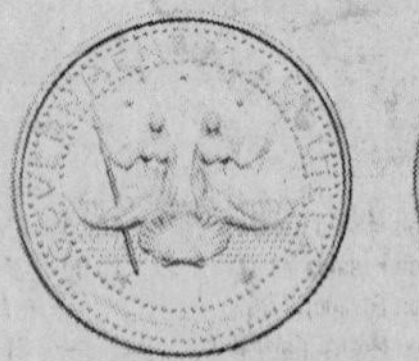

9.8700 gm., .900 GOLD, .2856 oz AGW

	Date	Mintage	XF	Unc	Proof
22	1967	680 pcs.	—	—	200.00

25 DOLLARS

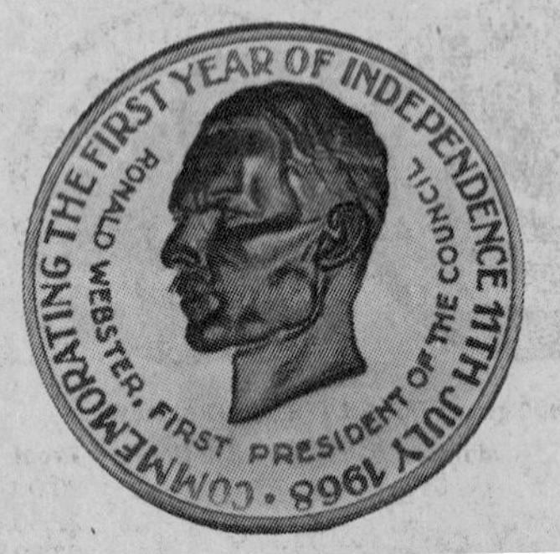

31.000 gm., SILVER
R. Webster Commemorative

	Date	Mintage	XF	Unc	Proof
26	1974	—	—	—	—

NOTE: The above is not an official issue.

100 DOLLARS

49.3700 gm., .900 GOLD, 1.4287 oz AGW

H#	Date	Mintage	XF	Unc	Proof
23	1967	680 pcs.	—	—	1000.

100 LIBERTY DOLLARS

GOLD
c/s: 100 LIBERTY DOLLARS

KM#	Date	Mintage	Identification	Issue Price	Mkt. Val.
14	1967	2 pcs.	c/s on Mexico KM#481	—	3000.

NCLT ISSUES

PROOF SETS

STANDARD METALS

101	1967(8)	—	H15-23	225.50	800.00
102	1967(4)	10,000	H15-18	25.50	70.00
103	1967(4)	680	H20-23	200.00	730.00
104	1969(4)	—	H15-18	25.50	60.00
105	1970(4)	—	H15-18	25.50	60.00

Listings For

ANNAM: refer to Vietnam

ANTIGUA

The Associated State of Antigua, located on the eastern edge of the Leeward Islands in the Caribbean Sea, has an area of 171 sq. mi. (422 sq. km.) and a population of 70,000. Capital: St. John's. Prior to 1967 Antigua and its dependencies, Barbuda and Redonda, comprised a presidency of the Leeward Islands. The mountainous island produces sugar, molasses, rum, cotton and fruit. Tourism is making an increasingly valuable contribution to the economy.

Antigua was discovered by Columbus in 1493, settled by the British in 1632, occupied by the French in 1666, and ceded to Britain in 1667. It became an associated state in 1967.

The three piece numismatic history of Antigua includes the 1836- dated copper farthing token of Hannay & Coltart, a half dollar Franklinium gambling token issued by the Reef Casino in 1969, and a 4-dollar cupro-nickel FAO coin issued in 1970. Coins and banknotes of the British Caribbean Territories (Eastern Group) are used on the island.

RULERS

British

FARTHING

COPPER

C#	Date	Mintage	Fine	VF	XF	Unc
1	1836	—	40.00	65.00	100.00	175.00
	1836	—	—	—	Proof	175.00

NOTE: Although dated 1836, this was issued in 1850 by Hannay and Coltart, merchants of St. John. Five die varieties exist. Occasionally counterstamped with numerals.

4 DOLLARS

COPPER-NICKEL
F.A.O. Issue

Y#	Date	Mintage	VF	XF	Unc
1*	1970	.020	3.50	5.00	7.50
	1970	2,000	—	Proof	50.00

NOTE: *This number refers to Yeoman's East Caribbean Territories listings, where seven companion 4-dollar issues are listed.

Listings For

ANTWERP: refer to Belgium
ANVERS: refer to Belgium

ARGENTINA

The Argentine Republic, located in southern South America, has an area of 1,073,700 sq. mi. (2,780,870 sq. km.) and a population of 25.1 million. Capital: Buenos Aires. Its varied topography ranges from the subtropical lowlands of the north to the towering Andean Mountains in the west and the wind- swept Patagonian steppe in the south. The rolling, fertile pampas of central Argentina are ideal for agriculture and grazing, and support most of the republic's population. Meat packing, flour milling, textiles, sugar refining and dairy products are the principal industries. Oil is found in Patagonia, but most mineral requirements must be imported.

Argentina was discovered in 1516 by the Spanish navigator Juan de Solis. A permanent Spanish colony was established at Buenos Aires in 1580, but the colony developed slowly. When Napoleon conquered Spain, the Argentines set up their own government in the name of the Spanish king on May 25, 1810. Independence was formally declared on July 9, 1816. A strong tendency toward local autonomy, fostered by difficult communication, resulted in a federalized union with much authority left to the states or provinces, which resulted in the issues of 1817-1867.

A monetary reform undertaken in June, 1970, devalued the peso to a rate of 100 old pesos to 1 new peso.

Internal conflict through the first half century of Argentine independence resulted in a limited national coinage supplemented by provincial issues.

MINTMARKS

BA, Bs = Buenos Aires Mint
Potosi Monogram (Bolivia) Mint
R, RA-RIOJA (Argentina) Mint

MONETARY SYSTEM

8 Reales = 8 Soles = 100 Centavos = 1 Peso
2 Pesos = 1 Scudo
100 Decimos = 10 Real = 1 Escudo
5 Pesos = 1 Argentino (Commencing 1970)
100 Old Pesos = 1 New Peso

FIRST NATIONAL COINAGE

1/2 REAL

SILVER

MINTMARK: Potosi monogram

Obv: Facing sun, leg: 'PROVINCIAS DEL RIO DE LA PLATA'. Rev: Arms in branches.

C#	Date	Mintage	Good	VG	Fine	VF
11	1813 J	—	5.00	10.00	20.00	40.00
	1815 F	—	5.00	10.00	20.00	40.00

1/2 SOL

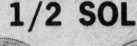

SILVER

MINTMARK: Potosi monogram

C#	Date	Mintage	Good	VG	Fine	VF
16	1815 FL	—	7.50	15.00	30.00	60.00

REAL

SILVER

MINTMARK: Potosi monogram

Similar to 1/2 Sol, C#16.

C#	Date	Mintage	Good	VG	Fine	VF
12	1813 J	—	5.00	10.00	20.00	40.00
	1815 F	—	5.00	10.00	20.00	40.00

MINTMARK: RA

C#	Date	Mintage	Good	VG	Fine	VF
23	1824 DS	—	3.50	7.50	12.50	25.00
	1825 CA	—	25.00	50.00	75.00	100.00

SOL

SILVER

MINTMARK: Potosi monogram

Similar to 1/2 Sol, C#16.

C#	Date	Mintage	Good	VG	Fine	VF
17	1815 FL	—	7.50	15.00	35.00	60.00

2 REALES

SILVER

MINTMARK: Potosi monogram

C#	Date	Mintage	Good	VG	Fine	VF
13	1813 J	—	5.00	10.00	20.00	40.00
	1815 F	—	5.00	10.00	20.00	40.00

MINTMARK: R

Crude workmanship

C#	Date	Mintage	Good	VG	Fine	VF
23.5	1821	Unique	—	—	—	—

2 SOLES

SILVER

MINTMARK: Potosi monogram

Similar to 2 Reales, C#13.

C#	Date	Mintage	Good	VG	Fine	VF
18	1815 FL	—	7.50	15.00	35.00	60.00

MINTMARK: RA

C#	Date	Mintage	Good	VG	Fine	VF
24	1824 DS	—	4.00	8.00	12.50	20.00
	1825 CA	—	10.00	20.00	40.00	75.00
	1825 CA. DE B. AS.	—	5.00	10.00	20.00	35.00
	1826 P	—	4.00	8.00	12.50	20.00
	1826 'P' omitted from rev. legend	—	6.50	12.50	22.50	40.00

4 REALES

SILVER

MINTMARK: Potosi monogram

Similar to 2 Soles, C#24.

C#	Date	Mintage	Good	VG	Fine	VF
14	1813 J	—	15.00	30.00	50.00	75.00
	1815 F	—	15.00	30.00	55.00	80.00

4 SOLES

SILVER

MINTMARK: Potosi monogram

C#	Date	Mintage	Good	VG	Fine	VF
19	1815 FL	—	22.50	45.00	65.00	125.00

MINTMARK: RA

C#	Date	Mintage	Good	VG	Fine	VF
25	1828 P	—	17.50	35.00	55.00	100.00
	1832 P	—	17.50	35.00	55.00	100.00

8 REALES

SILVER

MINTMARK: Potosi monogram

C#	Date	Mintage	VG	Fine	VF	XF
15	1813 J	—	35.00	55.00	100.00	150.00
	1815 F	—	35.00	55.00	100.00	150.00

SILVER

MINTMARK: RA

Obv: Similar to C#15.

C#	Date	Mintage	VG	Fine	VF	XF
26	1826 P	—	65.00	110.00	200.00	250.00
	1827 P	—	55.00	90.00	160.00	200.00
	1828 P	—	55.00	85.00	150.00	200.00
	1830 P	—	65.00	150.00	300.00	350.00
	1831/0 P	—	65.00	150.00	300.00	350.00
	1831 P	—	65.00	150.00	300.00	350.00
	1832 P	—	55.00	110.00	200.00	250.00
	1833 P	—	45.00	85.00	175.00	225.00
	1834 P	—	45.00	85.00	175.00	225.00
	1835 P	—	40.00	80.00	150.00	200.00
	1836 P	—	35.00	70.00	140.00	200.00
	1837 P	—	35.00	70.00	140.00	200.00

8 SOLES

SILVER

MINTMARK: Potosi monogram

Obv: Similar to 8 Reales, C#20.

C#	Date	Mintage	VG	Fine	VF	XF
20	1815 FL	—	40.00	65.00	125.00	175.00

ESCUDO

3.3750 gm., .875 SILVER, .0949 oz AGW

MINTMARK: Potosi monogram

C#	Date	Mintage	VG	Fine	VF	XF
21	1813 J	—	700.00	1000.	1500.	2000.

2 ESCUDOS

6.7500 gm., .875 GOLD, .1899 oz AGW

MINTMARK: Potosi monogram

C#	Date	Mintage	VG	Fine	VF	XF
21.5	1813 J	—	700.00	1000.	1500.	2000.

MINTMARK: RA

C#	Date	Mintage	VG	Fine	VF	XF
27	1824 DS	—	150.00	225.00	350.00	500.00
	1825 CA. DE B. AS.	—	150.00	200.00	350.00	550.00
	1826 P	—	150.00	200.00	350.00	550.00
	1826 'P' omitted from rev. legend	—	150.00	200.00	350.00	550.00

4 ESCUDOS

13.5000 gm., .875 GOLD, .3798 oz AGW

MINTMARK: Potosi monogram

C#	Date	Mintage	VG	Fine	VF	XF
21.6	1813 J	—	— Reported, not confirmed			

8 ESCUDOS

27.0000 gm., .875 GOLD, .7596 oz AGW

MINTMARK: Potosi monogram

C#	Date	Mintage	VG	Fine	VF	XF
22	1813 J	—	2000.	4000.	7000.	12,000.

MINTMARK: RA

C#	Date	Mintage	VG	Fine	VF	XF
28	1826 P	—	750.00	1350.	2150.	2750.
	1828 P	—	750.00	1350.	2150.	2750.
	1829 P	—	1000.	1850.	2500.	3000.
	1830 P	—	750.00	1350.	2150.	2750.
	1831 P	—	750.00	1350.	2150.	2750.
	1832 P	—	650.00	1200.	1850.	2300.
	1833 P	—	650.00	1200.	1850.	2300.
	1834 P	—	750.00	1350.	2150.	2500.
	1835 P	—	750.00	1350.	2150.	2500.

CONFEDERATION ARGENTINA

CENTAVO

COPPER

C#	Date	Mintage	VG	Fine	VF	XF
31	1854	—	3.50	5.00	10.00	20.00

2 CENTAVOS

COPPER

C#	Date	Mintage	VG	Fine	VF	XF
32	1854	—	5.00	7.50	15.00	25.00

4 CENTAVOS

COPPER

C#	Date	Mintage	VG	Fine	VF	XF
33	1854	—	4.00	6.00	12.50	22.00

PROVINCIAL ISSUES

BUENOS AIRES

Buenos Aires, a city and province in eastern Argentina, was the first province to have their coins made outside the country. Governor Martin Rodriguez initiated negotiations with Robert Boulton of the Birmingham Mint in 1821 for coins. The quinto is known only as a pattern but the decimos was made the following 2 years. These coins were retired in 1827 to make way for a new locally produced coin issue of the National Bank. Four denominations were made ending in 1831. The National Bank was disolved in 1836 and the Casa de Moneda took its place. Various denominations were made starting in 1840 and ending in 1861.

DECIMO

COPPER

C#	Date	Mintage	VG	Fine	VF	XF
41	1822	—	1.50	2.50	3.50	6.50
	1823	—	1.00	1.75	3.00	5.50

1/4 REAL

COPPER

Obv: Fraction in shaded circle.
Rev: 'BUENOS AYRES 1827' within branches.

C#	Date	Mintage	VG	Fine	VF	XF
42	1827	—	10.00	20.00	35.00	70.00

5/10 REAL

COPPER

C#	Date	Mintage	VG	Fine	VF	XF
43	1827	—	1.50	2.25	4.00	10.00
	1828	—	1.50	2.25	4.00	10.00
	1830	—	2.00	3.00	6.00	15.00
	1831	—	1.50	2.25	4.00	10.00

C#	Date	Mintage	VG	Fine	VF	XF
48	1840	—	7.00	15.00	35.00	70.00

10 DECIMOS

COPPER

C#	Date	Mintage	VG	Fine	VF	XF
45	1827	—	4.00	7.50	12.50	20.00
	1828	—	22.50	30.00	50.00	80.00
	1830	—	4.00	7.50	12.50	20.00

REAL

COPPER

C#	Date	Mintage	VG	Fine	VF	XF
49	1840	—	1.50	3.00	5.00	10.00

C#	Date	Mintage	VG	Fine	VF	XF
51	1854	—	7.50	15.00	25.00	50.00

20 DECIMOS

COPPER

C#	Date	Mintage	VG	Fine	VF	XF
47	1827	—	4.50	7.50	12.50	20.00
	1830	—	3.50	6.00	11.50	20.00
	1831	—	30.00	45.00	80.00	130.00

2 REALES

COPPER

C#	Date	Mintage	VG	Fine	VF	XF
50	1840	—	3.00	4.50	8.00	15.00
	1844	—	3.00	4.50	8.00	15.00

C#	Date	Mintage	VG	Fine	VF	XF
52	1853	—	1.50	2.50	4.50	10.00
	1854	—	1.50	2.50	4.50	10.00
	1855	—	1.50	2.50	4.50	10.00
	1856	—	3.50	6.00	12.50	20.00

C#	Date	Mintage	VG	Fine	VF	XF
53	1860	—	1.50	2.50	4.50	10.00
	1861	—	1.50	2.50	4.50	10.00

CORDOBA

Cordoba, a city and province in central Argentina, was the most prolific of the provincial issuers. The provincial government contracted with individuals for the making of their coins. The issuers of the mid-1830's are not known. Beginning in 1839 Pedro Nolasco Pizarro made the coins for the next two years. There are numerous die varieties and Pizarro's initials appear on most. In 1841 Jose Policarpo Patino began the coinage series. Again his initials appeared on the numerous types and varieties.

On February 2, 1844 a provincial mint was authorized by Governor Manuel Lopez. It was to make the distinctive Cordoba coinage until closed by a law of June 19, 1855.

CONCESSIONARES:

PP, PNP - Pedro Nolasco Pizarro
JPP - Jose Policarpo Patino

1/4 REAL

SILVER

Obv: Castle; date below.
Rev: Sun; no legends.

C#	Date	Mintage	VG	Fine	VF	XF
61	1833	—	7.50	12.50	20.00	35.00
	1838	—	7.50	12.50	20.00	35.00

Obv: Castle flanked by Ps; date below.
Rev: Sun face.

C#	Date	Mintage	VG	Fine	VF	XF
62	1839 PP	—	5.00	7.50	13.50	22.50
	1839 PP rosette above castle	—	5.00	7.50	13.50	22.50
	1839 PP X above castle	—	10.00	15.00	27.50	45.00
	1839 PP banners from top of castle	—	5.00	7.50	13.50	22.50
	1839 PP banner and rosette over castle	—	10.00	15.00	27.50	45.00
	1840 PP	—	12.50	20.00	35.00	55.00
	1841 PP banner over castle	—	12.50	20.00	35.00	55.00

Obv: Fraction

C#	Date	Mintage	VG	Fine	VF	XF
63	ND(1853-54) 8 pointed sun	—	5.00	8.00	17.50	30.00
	ND(1853-54) 10 pointed sun	—	40.00	65.00	110.00	165.00

1/2 REAL

SILVER

Obv. leg: EN UNION Y LIBERTAD, arms in wreath.
Rev. leg: PROVINCIA DE CORDOVA, sun face.

C#	Date	Mintage	VG	Fine	VF	XF
64	1839 PNP	—	45.00	85.00	110.00	150.00
	1839 PNP LIVERTAD	—	55.00	95.00	125.00	175.00
	1839 PNP CORDOBA on rev.	—	55.00	95.00	125.00	175.00
	1840 PNP	—	30.00	65.00	95.00	125.00

Obv. leg: EN UNION Y LIVERTAD
Rev. leg: CONFEDERADA

C#	Date	Mintage	VG	Fine	VF	XF
64a	1839 PNP	—	45.00	85.00	110.00	150.00

Obv. leg: CONFEDERADA
Rev. leg: PROVINCIA DE CORDOVA

C#	Date	Mintage	VG	Fine	VF	XF
64b	1840 PNP	—	55.00	85.00	110.00	150.00

Obv. leg: PROVINCIA DE CORDOV
Rev. leg: CONFEDERADA

C#	Date	Mintage	VG	Fine	VF	XF
64c	1841 PNP	—	45.00	85.00	110.00	150.00
	1841	—	45.00	85.00	110.00	150.00

Obv: Banner over castle; date below. Leg: CORDOVA.
Rev: Sun face. Leg: CONFEDERADA.

C#	Date	Mintage	VG	Fine	VF	XF
64.5a	1840 PNP crossed lances below castle	—	55.00	95.00	125.00	175.00
	1841 PNP	—	45.00	85.00	110.00	150.00
	1841	—	45.00	85.00	110.00	150.00

Obv: Denomination. Rev: Sun face.

C#	Date	Mintage	VG	Fine	VF	XF
65	1850 large letters	—	4.00	8.00	17.50	30.00
	1850 small letters	—	4.00	8.00	17.50	30.00
	1850 error: CONFEDRRADA	—	4.00	8.00	17.50	30.00
	1851	—	30.00	65.00	95.00	125.00
	1853	—	4.00	8.00	17.50	30.00
	1854	—	4.00	8.00	17.50	30.00

REAL

SILVER

Obv: Arms (shaded) in wreath; date below,
leg: PROVINCIA DE CORDOVA.
Rev: Sun face, leg: CONFEDERADA.

C#	Date	Mintage	VG	Fine	VF	XF
66	1840 PNP	—	3.00	5.00	8.50	13.50
	1841 PNP	—	3.00	5.00	8.50	13.50
	1841 PNP 2 dots in arms	—	5.00	10.00	15.00	25.00
	1841 PNP CORDOBA	—	55.00	75.00	100.00	135.00
	1841 PNP CORDOBA & inverted 4	—	55.00	75.00	100.00	135.00
	1841 JPP	—	3.00	5.00	8.50	13.50
	1842 JPP	—	3.00	5.00	8.50	13.50
	1842 JPP PROVINCI	—	5.00	10.00	15.00	25.00
	1842 JPP PROVINCA	—	5.00	10.00	15.00	25.00
	1843 JPP	—	3.00	5.00	8.50	13.50
66	1843 JPP inverted 3	—	3.00	6.00	10.00	15.00
	3481 JPP (error for 1843)	—	6.00	10.00	15.00	25.00
	1843 JPP PROVICIA	—	5.00	10.00	15.00	25.00
	1843 JPP CORDOV	—	3.00	5.00	8.50	13.50
	1843 JPP 2 dots in arms	—	5.00	10.00	15.00	25.00
	4481 JPP (error for 1844)	—	50.00	65.00	95.00	125.00

Obv. leg: PROVINCIA DE CORDOVA
Rev. leg: PROVINCIA DE CORDOVA

C#	Date	Mintage	VG	Fine	VF	XF
66d	1840 PNP	—	25.00	50.00	75.00	110.00
	1841 PNP	—	25.00	50.00	75.00	110.00

Obv. leg: PROVINCIA DE CORDOVA
Rev. leg: EN UNION Y LIBERTAD

C#	Date	Mintage	VG	Fine	VF	XF
66a	1840 PNP	—	5.00	10.00	15.00	25.00
	1841 PNP	—	5.00	10.00	15.00	25.00
	1841 PNP CORDOBA	—	50.00	65.00	95.00	125.00

Obv. leg: CONFEDERADA
Rev. leg: CONFEDERADA

C#	Date	Mintage	VG	Fine	VF	XF
66e	1840 PNP	—	55.00	75.00	100.00	135.00

Obv. leg: CONFEDERADA
Rev. leg: PROVINCIA DE CORDOVA

C#	Date	Mintage	VG	Fine	VF	XF
66f	1840 PNP	—	55.00	75.00	100.00	135.00

Obv. leg: EN UNION Y LIVERTAD
Rev. leg: PROVINCIA DE CORDOVA

C#	Date	Mintage	VG	Fine	VF	XF
66b	1840 PNP	—	55.00	75.00	100.00	135.00

Obv. leg: EN UNION Y LIVERTAD
Rev. leg: CONFEDERADA

C#	Date	Mintage	VG	Fine	VF	XF
66g	1840 PNP	—	55.00	75.00	100.00	135.00

Obv. leg: PROVINCIA DE CORDOVA, arms w/o shading and 2 rosettes. Rev. leg: CONFEDERADA, sun face.

C#	Date	Mintage	VG	Fine	VF	XF
66h	1841 PNP	—	3.00	5.00	8.50	13.50
	1843 JPP	—	3.00	5.00	8.50	13.50
	1843 JPP PROVINCI	—	3.00	5.00	8.50	13.50
	1843 JPP CONFEDERDA	—	3.00	5.00	8.50	13.50
	1843 JPP CORDOV	—	3.00	5.00	8.50	13.50

Rev. leg: LIBRE YNDEPENDIENTE

C#	Date	Mintage	VG	Fine	VF	XF
66c	1843 JPP	—	6.00	10.00	15.00	25.00

Obv. leg: PROVINCIA DE CORDOVA; banner over castle.
Rev. leg: CONFEDERADA, sun face.

C#	Date	Mintage	VG	Fine	VF	XF
67	1840 PNP crossed lances below castle	—	65.00	95.00	125.00	175.00
	1840 PNP rosette above lances	—	65.00	95.00	125.00	175.00
	1841 PNP crossed lances below castle	—	5.00	10.00	15.00	25.00
	1841 PNP CORDOBA	—	50.00	65.00	95.00	125.00
	1841 PNP CORDOBA, rosette above lances	—	50.00	65.00	95.00	125.00
	1841 PNP flowers, rosette & dot below castle	—	5.00	10.00	15.00	25.00
	1841 PNP horizontal lines below castle	—	5.00	10.00	15.00	25.00
	1841 PNP horizontal lines below castle, CORDOV in leg., inverted 4	—	5.00	10.00	15.00	25.00
	1841 PNP rosette below castle	—	5.00	10.00	15.00	25.00
	1841 PNP rosette below castle, inverted 4	—	5.00	10.00	15.00	25.00
	1841 inverted 4	—	5.00	10.00	15.00	25.00
	1841 CORDOV	—	9.50	15.00	25.00	40.00
	1841	—	5.00	10.00	15.00	25.00

Obv. leg: PROVINCIA DE CORDOVA
Rev. leg: EN UNION Y LIBERTAD

C#	Date	Mintage	VG	Fine	VF	XF
66i	1841 PNP	—	12.50	20.00	32.50	45.00

Obv. leg: PROVINCIA DE CORDOVA
Rev. leg: PROVINCIA DE CORDOVA

C#	Date	Mintage	VG	Fine	VF	XF
66j	1841 PNP rosette below castle	—	25.00	50.00	75.00	110.00

Obv. leg: PROVINCIA DE CORDOVA, arms w/o shading; date below. Rev. leg: CONFEDERADA, sun face.

C#	Date	Mintage	VG	Fine	VF	XF
66k	1843 JPP 2 dots in arms	—	3.00	5.00	8.50	13.50
	1843 JPP 2 dots in arms, CONFEDERDA	—	3.00	6.00	10.00	15.00
	1843 JPP 2 dots in arms, CORDOV	—	3.00	5.00	8.50	13.50
	1843 JPP 2 dots in arms, CORDOV & CONFEDERDA	—	3.00	6.00	10.00	15.00
	1843 JPP 2 dots in arms, CORDOV & PROVINCI	—	5.00	10.00	15.00	25.00
	1843 JPP 2 dots in arms, CORDO	—	3.00	5.00	8.50	13.50
	1843 JPP 2 dots in arms, CORDO & CONFEDERDA	—	3.00	5.00	8.50	13.50
	1843 JPP 2 crosses in arms	—	3.00	5.00	8.50	13.50
	1843 JPP 2 crosses in arms, CONFEDERDA	—	3.00	6.00	10.00	15.00
	1843 JPP 2 crosses in arms, CORDOV	—	3.00	6.00	10.00	15.00
	1843 JPP 2 spear heads in arms	—	—	—	Rare	—
	1844 JPP 2 dots in arms	—	25.00	50.00	75.00	110.00
	1844 JPP 2 dots in arms, CORDOV	—	25.00	50.00	75.00	110.00

Obv. leg: PROVINCIA DE CORDOVA
Rev. leg: LIBRE YNDEPENDIENTE

C#	Date	Mintage	VG	Fine	VF	XF
	1843 JPP 2 rosettes in arms	—	6.00	10.00	15.00	25.00
	1843 JPP 2 dots in arms	—	6.00	10.00	15.00	25.00
	1843 JPP 2 crosses in arms	—	6.00	10.00	15.00	25.00

Obv. leg: PROVINCIA DE CORDOBA, denomination. Rev. leg: CONFEDERADA, sun face; date below.

C#	Date	Mintage	VG	Fine	VF	XF
68	1848 w/8 pointed sun	—	5.00	7.50	12.50	20.00
	1848 w/9 pointed sun	—	5.00	7.50	12.50	20.00
	1848 w/10 pointed sun	—	5.00	7.50	12.50	20.00
	1848 medallic rev.	—	10.00	20.00	35.00	50.00

2 REALES

SILVER
Obv. leg: PROVINCIA DE CORDOBA, castle among flags in sprays.
Rev. leg: CONFEDERADA, sun face in sprays; date below.

C#	Date	Mintage	VG	Fine	VF	XF
69	1844	—	6.00	7.50	10.00	13.50
	1844 CONFEDRADA	—	25.00	50.00	75.00	110.00
	1845 8 pointed sun	—	6.00	7.50	10.00	15.00
	1845 12 pointed sun	—	25.00	50.00	75.00	110.00

C#	Date	Mintage	VG	Fine	VF	XF
69	1846 8 pointed sun	—	6.00	7.50	10.00	15.00
	1846 10 pointed sun	—	6.00	10.00	15.00	25.00
	1848	—	—	—	Rare	—

C#	Date	Mintage	VG	Fine	VF	XF
	1849 7 pointed sun	—	6.00	7.50	10.00	13.50

C#	Date	Mintage	VG	Fine	VF	XF
	1849 8 pointed sun	—	6.00	7.50	10.00	13.50
	1850 large letters	—	6.00	10.00	15.00	25.00
	1850 small letters	—	6.00	7.50	10.00	13.50

Similar to 4 Reales, C#79a.

C#	Date	Mintage	VG	Fine	VF	XF
69a	1852	—	20.00	30.00	40.00	65.00
	1854	—	20.00	30.00	40.00	65.00

4 REALES

.750 SILVER
Obv: Castle among flags over spray.
Rev: Sun face; date below.

C#	Date	Mintage	VG	Fine	VF	XF
70	1844	—	165.00	275.00	450.00	625.00
	1845 gate in castle	—	50.00	65.00	95.00	125.00
	1845 no gate in castle	—	35.00	50.00	75.00	100.00
	1846 die of 1845	—	125.00	150.00	175.00	250.00
	1846 rayed edge	—	65.00	95.00	125.00	165.00
	1846 laureate edge	—	65.00	95.00	125.00	165.00
	1847	—	25.00	35.00	50.00	85.00
	1850	—	25.00	35.00	50.00	85.00
	1851 large sun	—	25.00	35.00	50.00	85.00
	1851 small sun	—	25.00	35.00	50.00	85.00

Finer die work.

C#	Date	Mintage	VG	Fine	VF	XF
79a	1852	—	65.00	95.00	125.00	165.00

8 REALES

.750 SILVER

C#	Date	Mintage	VG	Fine	VF	XF
71	1852	—	50.00	70.00	100.00	155.00

ENTRE RIOS

entre rios (colonia san jose) was a settlement of Swiss and Italian families in northeast Argentina on the Uruguay border. General Urguiza (deposer of Rosas) was a political power in the province and served as its governor at one time. In 1867 during the war with Paraguay, Urguiza authorized an Italian by the name of Pablo Cataldi to make some coins for circulation in the settlement due to a coin shortage.

1/2 REAL

SILVER

C#	Date	Mintage	VG	Fine	VF
81	1867	—	40.00	70.00	95.00

LA RIOJA

La Rioja, a city and province in northwest Argentina, was the source of rich mineral wealth. Governor Nicolas Davila, at the end of 1820, gave consideration to a mint at Chilecito to take advantage of the rich mines at Famatina. The mint made cob pieces of two types -- those with and without the name RIOXA. These were made from 1821 to 1823 and retired in 1824.

Also made at this time in Chilecito were gold 1 Escudo and silver 1 Reales in 1823. With the making of these pieces the mint was transferred to La Rioja in 1824. From this time until 1860 the coinage was almost continuous and of many denominations and types.

1/2 REAL

SILVER
Cob type with "RIOXA".

C#	Date	Mintage	Good	VG	Fine	VF
—	1822	—	—	—	Rare	—

Obv: Arms in branches. Rev: Sun over mountain.

C#	Date	Mintage	Good	VG	Fine	VF
95	1844 B	—	4.00	8.00	15.00	25.00

Obv: REPUB. ARGENT. CONFEDERADA
Rev. leg: PROV. DE LA. RIOJA

C#	Date	Mintage	Good	VG	Fine	VF
96	1854 B	—	2.50	5.00	9.00	15.00

Rev. leg: CRED. PUB. DE LA RIOJA

C#	Date	Mintage	Good	VG	Fine	VF
96a	1854 B	—	3.50	6.50	12.50	20.00

Obv: CONFEDERACION ARGENTINA
Rev: PROV. DE LA. RIOJA

C#	Date	Mintage	Good	VG	Fine	VF
97	1854 B	—	2.50	5.00	9.00	15.00

C#	Date	Mintage	Good	VG	Fine	VF
97a	1854 B	—	2.50	5.00	9.00	15.00
	1860 B	—	5.00	10.00	17.50	30.00

REAL

SILVER
Cob type with "RIOXA".

C#	Date	Mintage	Good	VG	Fine	VF
—	1822	—	—	—	Rare	—

NOTE: 1821 dated coins are false.

Obv: Sun, arms. Rev: SVR AMERICA RIOXA

C#	Date	Mintage	Good	VG	Fine	VF
91	ND (1823)	—	90.00	175.00	275.00	400.00

Rev. leg: SUD AMERICA 1823 RIOXA

C#	Date	Mintage	Good	VG	Fine	VF
92	1823	—	—	—	Rare	—

NOTE: Above 3 coins minted in Chilecito.

2 REALES

SILVER
Cob Type

C#	Date	Mintage	Good	VG	Fine	VF
93	(1)821	*	90.00	175.00	275.00	400.00
	(1)822	—	90.00	175.00	275.00	400.00
	(1)823	—	—	—	Rare	—

***NOTE:** Counterfeits exist.

C#	Date	Mintage	Good	VG	Fine	VF
98	1842	—	11.50	22.50	40.00	70.00

Mountain type

C#	Date	Mintage	Good	VG	Fine	VF
99	1843 RB	—	6.50	12.50	22.50	35.00

Mountain and sun type

C#	Date	Mintage	Good	VG	Fine	VF
100	1843 RB	—	12.50	25.00	40.00	70.00
	1844 RB	—	8.50	17.50	27.50	45.00

C#	Date	Mintage	Good	VG	Fine	VF
101	1859 B	—	30.00	60.00	100.00	175.00
	1860 B	—	6.00	10.00	17.50	30.00

4 REALES

SILVER
Obv: Castles & lions. Rev: Pillars, RIOXA, date.

C#	Date	Mintage	Good	VG	Fine	VF
94	(1)821	—	175.00	350.00	500.00	700.00
	(1)822	*	—	—	Rare	—
	(1)823 w/o RIOXA	—	175.00	350.00	500.00	700.00

C#	Date	Mintage	VG	Fine	VF	XF
102	1846 RV	—	12.00	17.50	25.00	50.00
	1849 RB	—	12.00	17.50	25.00	50.00
	1850 RB	—	13.50	25.00	35.00	60.00

C#	Date	Mintage	VG	Fine	VF	XF
103	1852 B	—	85.00	125.00	175.00	225.00

8 REALES

SILVER

C#	Date	Mintage	VG	Fine	VF	XF
104	1838 R	—	30.00	55.00	125.00	180.00
	1839 R	—	30.00	55.00	125.00	180.00
	1840 R	—	35.00	60.00	140.00	200.00

C#	Date	Mintage	VG	Fine	VF	XF
105	1840 R	—	225.00	350.00	500.00	750.00

ESCUDO

3.3750 gm., .875 GOLD, .0949 oz AGW
Obv: Sun over arms in branches.
Rev. leg: SUD AMERICA 1823 RIOXA in wreath.

C#	Date	Mintage	VG	Fine	VF	XF
105.5	1823	Unique	—	—	—	—

2 ESCUDOS

6.7500 gm., .875 GOLD, .1899 oz AGW

C#	Date	Mintage	VG	Fine	VF	XF
106	1842	—	325.00	500.00	700.00	1000.

C#	Date	Mintage	VG	Fine	VF	XF
107	1843 B	—	300.00	450.00	600.00	900.00

8 ESCUDOS

27.0000 gm., .875 GOLD, .7596 oz AGW

C#	Date	Mintage	VG	Fine	VF	XF
109	1838	—	600.00	1000.	1500.	2000.
	1840	—	750.00	1150.	1750.	2250.
	Obv. leg: REPUBLICA ARGENTINA.					
110	1840	—	850.00	1250.	1850.	2350.
	Bust type					
111	1842	—	3000.	4000.	5000.	6000.

C#	Date	Mintage	VG	Fine	VF	XF
112	1845 B	—	1350.	1850.	2350.	3000.

MENDOZA

Mendoza, a province in western Argentina, was one of the first independent groups to make cobs after the style of the Spanish cobs of the Potosi mint. During the term of governor Pedro Molina, a mint was established in 1822. By a law of December 12, 1823 the local cobs were put in circulation. In a year or less these coins were retired from circulation.

In 1835 Molina again saw need for locally made coins but decided to award contracts for production rather than having the provincial mint make them. Abel Bucci made a copper 1/8 Real in 1835 and Manuel Espeys, who had the contract for all silver and gold, made a silver 1/4 Real in 1836. These two pieces saw virtually no circulation and were retired in 1836.

1/8 REAL

COPPER
Obv: Provincial arms, date below.
Rev: Fraction in dotted circle in wreath.

C#	Date	Mintage	VG	Fine	VF
115	1835	Unique	—	—	—

1/4 REAL

SILVER
Obv: Arms divide value.
Rev: Small animal.

C#	Date	Mintage	VG	Fine	VF
119	1836	Unique	—	—	—

1/2 REAL

SILVER
Obv: Cross with castles and lions in angles.
Rev: PM monogram, date below.

C#	Date	Mintage	VG	Fine	VF
120	1823	—	250.00	350.00	—
	1824	—	225.00	325.00	—

REAL

SILVER

C#	Date	Mintage	VG	Fine	VF
121	(18)23	—	55.00	75.00	100.00
	(18)24	—	100.00	150.00	200.00

2 REALES

SILVER

C#	Date	Mintage	VG	Fine	VF
122	(1)823	—	—	Rare	—
	(1)824	—	—	Rare	—

4 REALES

SILVER

C#	Date	Mintage	VG	Fine	VF
123	(18)23	—	200.00	300.00	500.00
	(18)24	—	200.00	300.00	500.00

COUNTERSTAMP ISSUES

2 REALES

SILVER
c/s: "FIDELIDAD" around scales on Cob 2 Reales.

C#	Date	Mintage	VG	Fine	VF
125	(1)821	—	—	Rare	—
	(1)822	—	—	Rare	—
	(1)823	—	—	Rare	—

4 REALES

SILVER
c/s: "FIDELIDAD" around scales on Cob 4 Reales.

C#	Date	Mintage	VG	Fine	VF
126	(18)21	—	—	Rare	—
	(18)22	—	—	Rare	—
	(18)23	—	—	Rare	—

SANTIAGO DEL ESTERO

Santiago del Estero is a province in north central Argentina. In 1823 during the governorship of Felipe Ibarra a coinage was begun to take the place of the fast-disappearing cob coins of the Potosi mint. The coins were not well received and were terminated quickly. Another effort was made in 1836 with no better luck.

1/2 REAL

SILVER
Obv: SoEo in angles of crossed arrows, date below.
Rev: Sun in branches.

C#	Date	Mintage	VG	Fine	VF
131.1	(1)823 So Eo	Unique	—	—	—
	Obv: S E in angles of crossed arrows, date below.				
131.2	(1)823	—	125.00	200.00	300.00

REAL

SILVER
Obv: SoEo in angles of crossed arrows, date below.
Rev: Cross.

C#	Date	Mintage	VG	Fine	VF
132.1	(1)823	Unique	—	—	—
	Rev: Sun in branches.				
132.2	(1)823	—	200.00	350.00	600.00
	Obv: S E in angles of crossed arrows, date below.				
132.3	(1)823	—	100.00	150.00	250.00
	Rev: Sun over Liberty cap in branches.				
133.1	(1)836	—	—	—	—
133.2	(1)836	—	75.00	125.00	200.00

DE SALTA

Salta is a province in northwest Argentina that was a popular battleground during the War of Independence for control of northern Argentina. Governor Martin Guemes issued a proclamation on October 26, 1817 authorizing the countermarking of Potosi cobs then in circulation. This plan was in effect until the National Congress passed a law invalidating it on May 24, 1818.

2 REALES

SILVER
c/s: Monogram 'PATRIA' in wreath on Spanish Colonial pillar cobs.

C#	Date	Mintage	VG	Fine	VF
—	(1817)	—	100.00	150.00	—

4 REALES

SILVER
Similar to above

C#	Date	Mintage	VG	Fine	VF
—	1817	—	—	Rare	—

TUCUMAN

Tucuman is a province in northwest Argentina. Due to a large quantity of false Potosi cobs in circulation in the province governor Bernabi Araioz established a mint to make cobs that would be distinctive to the area. The brief circulation was terminated because of the introduction of confederation coins.

2 REALES

SILVER
MINTMARK: TN
Similar to Potosi 'cob' 2 Reales.

C#	Date	Mintage	VG	Fine	VF
152	(1823)	—	75.00	100.00	125.00

NOTE: Similar coins without TN mintmark having ficticious dates, i.e.: 257, 577, 752 or 758 are attributed to Venezuela.

REPUBLIC

DECIMAL COINAGE

100 Centavos = 1 Peso
5 Pesos = 1 Argentino

CENTAVO

BRONZE

Y#	Date	Mintage	VF	XF	Unc
1	1882	.110	15.00	25.00	35.00
	1883	.790	1.00	3.00	5.50
	1884	4.600	1.00	3.00	5.50
	1885	1.310	1.00	3.00	5.50
	1886	.440	1.00	3.00	5.50
	1888	.410	1.00	3.00	5.50
	1889	.590	1.00	3.00	5.50
	1890	2.140	1.00	3.00	6.00
	1891	.610	1.00	3.00	6.00
	1892	.210	1.00	3.00	6.00
	1893	.750	1.00	3.00	6.00
	1894	.530	1.00	2.50	5.50
	1895	.420	2.00	2.50	5.50
	1896	.170	12.50	17.50	25.00

Y#	Date	Mintage	VF	XF	Unc
12	1939	3.490	.25	.40	.75
	1940	3.140	.25	.40	.75
	1941	4.570	.25	.40	.75
	1942	.500	.75	1.25	2.00
	1943	1.290	.50	.70	1.00
	1944	3.100	.25	.40	.75

CRUDE COPPER

Y#	Date	Mintage	VF	XF	Unc
12a	1945	.420	.50	.70	1.00
	1946	4.450	.35	.50	.75
	1947	5.630	.35	.50	.75
	1948	4.420	.25	.50	.75

ALUMINUM
100 Old Centavos - 1 New Centavo

Y#	Date	Mintage	VF	XF	Unc
36	1970	54.590	—	.10	.15
	1971	44.640	—	.10	.20
	1972	92.430	—	.10	.15
	1973	29.515	—	.10	.15
	1974	5.162	—	.10	.15
	1975	3.840	—	.30	.50

2 CENTAVOS

BRONZE

Y#	Date	Mintage	VF	XF	Unc
2	1882	.090	15.00	25.00	45.00
	1883	1.390	1.50	2.75	5.50
	1884	5.670	2.00	3.50	5.50
	1885	3.070	2.00	3.50	5.50
	1887	.360	12.00	17.50	25.00
	1888	.660	2.00	3.50	7.00
	1889	2.390	2.00	3.50	5.50
	1890	3.610	2.00	3.50	5.50
	1891	8.050	2.00	3.50	5.50
	1892	3.500	2.00	3.50	5.50
	1893	5.470	2.00	3.50	5.50
	1894	2.230	1.00	2.25	5.50
	1895	.590	4.00	6.00	8.00
	1896	.600	5.00	8.00	20.00

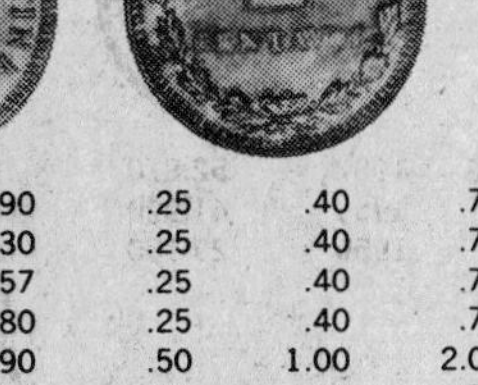

Y#	Date	Mintage	VF	XF	Unc
13	1939	5.490	.25	.40	.75
	1940	4.630	.25	.40	.75
	1941	4.57	.25	.40	.75
	1942	2.080	.25	.40	.75
	1944	.390	.50	1.00	2.00
	1945	4.590	.25	.40	.75
	1946	3.400	.25	.40	.75
	1947	4.400	.25	.40	.75

CRUDE COPPER

Y#	Date	Mintage	VF	XF	Unc
13a	1947	Inc.Ab.	.30	.40	.75
	1948	3.650	.30	.40	.75
	1949	7.290	.30	.40	.75
	1950	.900	.65	1.25	2.00

5 CENTAVOS

COPPER-NICKEL

Y#	Date	Mintage	VF	XF	Unc
7	1896	1.500	.75	1.50	10.00
	1897	3.980	.35	.75	7.00
	1898	2.660	.35	.75	7.00
	1899	2.840	.35	.75	6.50
	1903	2.500	.35	.75	6.50
	1904	2.520	.35	.75	6.50
	1905	4.360	.35	.75	6.50
	1906	3.940	.35	.75	6.50
	1907	1.680	.50	1.00	10.00
	1908	1.690	.50	1.00	10.00
	1909	4.650	.35	.75	6.50
	1910	1.470	.50	1.00	8.50
	1911	1.430	.35	.75	6.50
	1912	2.380	.35	.75	6.50
	1913	1.480	.40	1.00	8.50
	1914	1.100	1.00	2.50	10.00
	1915	1.900	.35	.75	1.50
	1916	1.310	.75	1.25	2.00
	1917	1.010	1.50	2.25	3.50
	1918	2.390	.35	.75	1.00
	1919	2.480	.35	.75	1.00
	1920	5.240	.35	.75	1.00
	1921	7.040	.35	.75	1.00
	1922	9.430	.35	.75	1.00
	1923	6.260	.35	.75	1.00
	1924	6.360	.35	.75	1.00
	1925	3.960	.35	.75	1.00
	1926	3.560	.35	.75	1.00
	1927	5.650	.35	.75	1.00
	1928	6.380	.35	.75	1.00
	1929	11.380	.35	.75	1.00
	1930	7.110	.35	.75	1.00
	1931	.510	2.00	3.00	4.50
	1933	5.540	.25	.45	.75
	1934	1.290	.25	.45	.75
	1935	3.050	.25	.45	.75
	1936	7.180	.25	.45	.75
	1937	7.060	.25	.45	.75
	1938	10.250	.25	.45	.75
	1939	7.170	.25	.45	.75
	1940	10.190	.25	.45	.75
	1941	.950	.50	1.00	2.00
	1942	8.690	.25	.45	.75

ALUMINUM-BRONZE

Y#	Date	Mintage	VF	XF	Unc
15	1942	2.130	.35	.60	1.00
	1943	15.780	.25	.35	.50
	1944	21.080	.25	.35	.50
	1945	21.600	.25	.35	.50
	1946	20.460	.25	.35	.50
	1947	22.520	.25	.35	.50
	1948	42.790	.25	.35	.50
	1949	35.470	.25	.35	.50
	1950	13.500	.25	.35	.50

COPPER-NICKEL

Y#	Date	Mintage	VF	XF	Unc
18	1950	3.460	.50	.75	1.00

Reeded edge

Y#	Date	Mintage	VF	XF	Unc
21	1951	34.990	.20	.30	.40
	1952	33.110	.20	.30	.40
	1953	20.130	.20	.30	.40

NICKEL-CLAD STEEL
Plain edge

Y#	Date	Mintage	VF	XF	Unc
21a	1953	56.300	.15	.20	.25

Head size reduced slightly

Y#	Date	Mintage	VF	XF	Unc
21b	1954	50.640	.15	.20	.25
	1955	42.200	.15	.20	.25
	1956	36.870	.15	.20	.25

Y#	Date	Mintage	VF	XF	Unc
25	1957	26.930	.10	.15	.25
	1958	13.110	.10	.15	.25
	1959	14.970	.10	.15	.25

ALUMINUM
100 Old Centavos - 1 New Centavo

Y#	Date	Mintage	VF	XF	Unc
37	1970	56.170	.10	.15	.25
	1971	3.800	.20	.35	.50
	1972	84.250	.10	.15	.25
	1973	113.912	.10	.15	.25
	1974	18.150	.10	.15	.25
	1975	6.940	.10	.15	.25

10 CENTAVOS

2.5000 gm., .900 SILVER, .0723 oz ASW

Y#	Date	Mintage	Fine	VF	XF	Unc
3	1881	1,020	100.00	200.00	250.00	300.00
	1882	.780	BV	2.25	4.00	7.50
	1883	2.790	BV	2.25	4.00	7.50

COPPER-NICKEL

Y#	Date	Mintage	VF	XF	Unc
8	1896	1.880	1.50	2.75	5.00
	1897	8.580	.35	.50	1.50
	1898	8.530	.35	.50	1.50
	1899	8.890	.35	.50	1.50
	1905	7.790	.35	.50	1.50
	1906	3.850	.75	1.00	2.00
	1907	2.360	.75	1.00	2.00
	1908	2.280	.75	1.00	2.00
	1909	3.740	.35	.50	1.25
	1910	3.030	.35	.50	1.25
	1911	2.140	.35	.50	1.25
	1912	2.990	.35	.50	1.25
	1913	1.830	.35	.50	1.25
	1914	.750	1.00	1.50	2.50
	1915	2.610	.35	.50	1.25
	1916	.840	1.00	1.75	3.00
	1918	3.900	.25	.40	1.00
	1919	2.520	.35	.50	1.00
	1920	7.510	.25	.40	1.00
	1921	11.560	.25	.40	1.00
	1922	6.540	.25	.40	1.00
	1923	5.300	.25	.40	1.00
	1924	3.490	.25	.40	1.00
	1925	5.420	.25	.40	1.00
	1926	5.060	.25	.40	1.00
	1927	5.210	.25	.40	1.00
	1928	8.260	.25	.40	1.00
	1929	2.500	.25	.40	1.00
	1930	14.590	.25	.40	1.00
	1931	.890	1.00	1.75	3.00
	1933	5.390	.25	.40	1.00
	1934	3.320	.25	.40	1.00
	1935	1.020	.75	1.00	1.50
	1936	3.000	.25	.40	1.00
	1937	11.770	.25	.40	.75
	1938	10.500	.25	.40	.75
	1939	5.590	.25	.40	.75
	1940	3.960	.25	.40	.75
	1941	4.100	.50	.80	1.50
	1942	2.960	.20	.30	.50

ALUMINUM-BRONZE

Y#	Date	Mintage	VF	XF	Unc
16	1942	15.540	.20	.30	.50
	1943	13.920	.20	.30	.50
	1944	16.410	.20	.30	.50
	1945	12.500	.20	.30	.50
	1946	15.790	.20	.30	.50
	1947	36.430	.20	.30	.50
	1948	54.690	.20	.30	.50
	1949	57.740	.20	.30	.50
	1950	42.830	.20	.30	.50

COPPER-NICKEL

Y#	Date	Mintage	VF	XF	Unc
19	1950	17.270	.75	1.00	1.25

Y#	Date	Mintage	VF	XF	Unc
22	1951	98.520	.20	.30	.50
	1952	67.330	.20	.30	.50

NICKEL-CLAD STEEL

Y#	Date	Mintage	VF	XF	Unc
22a	1952	33.240	.10	.15	.25
	1953	106.690	.10	.15	.20

Head size reduced slightly

Y#	Date	Mintage	VF	XF	Unc
22b	1954	117.200	.10	.15	.20
	1955	97.050	.10	.15	.20
	1956	122.630	.10	.15	.20

Y#	Date	Mintage	VF	XF	Unc
26	1957	52.810	.10	.15	.20
	1958	41.920	.10	.15	.20
	1959	29.180	.10	.15	.20

BRASS

100 Old Centavos - 1 New Centavo

Y#	Date	Mintage	VF	XF	Unc
38	1970	64.950	.10	.15	.20
	1971	135.620	.10	.15	.20
	1973	19.930	.10	.15	.20
	1974	79.156	.10	.15	.20
	1975	31.270	.10	.15	.20
	1976	.730	—	—	—

20 CENTAVOS

5.0000 gm., .900 SILVER, .1446 oz ASW

Y#	Date	Mintage	Fine	VF	XF	Unc
4	1881	2,018	45.00	60.00	80.00	125.00
	1882	.760	BV	5.00	8.50	15.00
	1883	1.510	BV	4.50	7.00	12.50

COPPER-NICKEL

Y#	Date	Mintage	VF	XF	Unc
9	1896	2.030	1.50	2.50	4.50
	1897	5.260	.50	.90	1.75
	1898	1.260	1.00	2.00	3.50
	1899	.840	4.50	6.00	10.50
	1905	4.460	.40	.75	1.50
	1906	4.330	.40	.75	1.50
	1907	3.730	.40	.75	1.50
	1908	.720	3.50	5.00	8.50
	1909	1.330	.50	1.00	2.00
	1910	1.850	.50	1.00	2.00
	1911	1.110	.50	1.00	2.00
	1912	2.400	.50	1.00	2.00
	1913	1.580	1.00	1.50	2.50
	1914	.530	3.00	5.00	8.00
	1915	1.920	.35	.80	1.50
	1916	.990	.75	1.25	2.00
	1918	1.640	.35	.60	1.00
	1919	2.280	.35	.60	1.00
	1920	7.570	.35	.60	1.00
	1921	5.290	.35	.60	1.00
	1922	2.320	.35	.60	1.00
	1923	4.420	.25	.40	.75
	1924	3.680	.25	.40	.75
	1925	3.800	.25	.40	.75
	1926	3.250	.25	.40	.75
	1927	2.880	.25	.40	.75
	1928	2.890	.25	.40	.75
	1929	8.360	.25	.40	.75
	1930	8.280	.25	.40	.75
	1931	.320	3.50	5.50	8.50

Y#	Date	Mintage	VF	XF	Unc
9	1933	—	.25	.40	.75
	1934	—	.25	.40	.75
	1935	1.130	.25	.40	.75
	1936	.860	.75	1.25	2.50
	1937	.200	.30	.50	1.00
	1938	6.450	.20	.30	.50
	1939	3.560	.20	.30	.50
	1940	4.470	.20	.30	.50
	1941	.600	1.00	1.50	2.50
	1942	4.840	.25	.35	.50

ALUMINUM-BRONZE

Y#	Date	Mintage	VF	XF	Unc
17	1942	10.260	.20	.30	.50
	1943	13.780	.20	.30	.50
	1944	12.230	.20	.30	.50
	1945	13.340	.20	.30	.50
	1946	14.630	.20	.30	.50
	1947	23.170	.20	.30	.50
	1948	32.250	.20	.30	.50
	1949	67.120	.20	.30	.50
	1950	40.070	.20	.30	.50

COPPER-NICKEL

Y#	Date	Mintage	VF	XF	Unc
20	1950	86.770	.70	1.00	1.50

Y#	Date	Mintage	VF	XF	Unc
23	1951	85.780	.20	.30	.50
	1952	69.800	.20	.30	.50

NICKEL CLAD STEEL

Y#	Date	Mintage	VF	XF	Unc
23a	1952	12.860	.15	.25	.30
	1953	36.890	.15	.20	.30

Head size reduced slightly

Y#	Date	Mintage	VF	XF	Unc
23b	1954	52.560	.15	.20	.25
	1955	46.950	.15	.20	.25
	1956	36.000	.15	.20	.25

Y#	Date	Mintage	VF	XF	Unc
27	1957	89.370	.15	.20	.25
	1958	52.710	.15	.20	.25
	1959	56.590	.15	.20	.25
	1960	21.250	.15	.20	.25
	1961	2.080	.15	.20	.50

BRASS

100 Old Centavos - 1 New Centavo

Y#	Date	Mintage	VF	XF	Unc
39	1970	27.030	.10	.15	.25
	1971	33.210	.10	.15	.25
	1972	.220	—	Rare	—
	1973	9.676	.10	.15	.25
	1974	41.024	.10	.15	.25
	1975	26.540	.10	.15	.20

Y#	Date	Mintage	VF	XF	Unc
39	1976	.960	—	—	—

50 CENTAVOS

12.5000 gm., .900 SILVER, .3617 oz ASW

Y#	Date	Mintage	Fine	VF	XF	Unc
5	1881	1,020	150.00	225.00	275.00	350.00
	1882	.476	BV	12.50	15.00	20.00
	1883	2.273	BV	11.00	12.50	17.50

NICKEL

Y#	Date	Mintage	VF	XF	Unc
14	1941	10.960	1.00	1.25	2.00

NICKEL-CLAD STEEL

Y#	Date	Mintage	VF	XF	Unc
24	1952	29.740	.20	.35	.60
	1953	62.810	.20	.35	.60
	1954	132.220	.20	.35	.60
	1955	75.490	.20	.35	.60
	1956	19.120	.20	.35	.60

Y#	Date	Mintage	VF	XF	Unc
28	1957	18.140	.10	.25	.30
	1958	51.750	.20	.30	.40
	1959	14.000	.10	.20	.30
	1960	26.040	.20	.30	.40
	1961	11.110	.10	.20	.35

BRASS
100 Old Centavos - 1 New Centavo

Y#	Date	Mintage	VF	XF	Unc
40	1970	56.100	.15	.30	.50
	1971	34.950	.15	.30	.50
	1972	40.960	.15	.30	.50
	1973	69.472	.15	.30	.50
	1974	63.063	.15	.30	.50
	1975	64.859	.15	.30	.50
	1976	9.768	.15	.30	.40

PESO

25.0000 gm., .900 SILVER, .7234 oz ASW

Y#	Date	Mintage	Fine	VF	XF	Unc
6	1881	.060	75.00	115.00	175.00	250.00
	1882	.410	50.00	90.00	125.00	225.00
	1883	.100	75.00	115.00	190.00	300.00

NICKEL-CLAD STEEL

Y#	Date	Mintage	VF	XF	Unc
29	1957	118.120	.20	.30	.40
	1958	118.150	.20	.30	.50
	1959	237.730	.20	.30	.40
	1960	75.050	.20	.30	.40
	1961	76.900	.20	.30	.40
	1962	30.010	.20	.30	.40

Y#	Date	Mintage	VF	XF	Unc
30	1960	98.750	.50	.75	1.25

ALUMINUM BRASS
100 Old Pesos - 1 New Peso

Y#	Date	Mintage	VF	XF	Unc
41	1974	77.292	—	.25	.50
	1975	658.200	—	.20	.50

Slightly modified design.

Y#	Date	Mintage	VF	XF	Unc
41a	1975	Inc. Ab.	—	.20	.50
	1976	365.075	—	.25	.50

1/2 ARGENTINO

4.0322 gm., .900 GOLD, .1167 oz AGW

Y#	Date	Mintage	VF	XF	Unc
10	1881	9 pcs.	—	Rare	—
	1884	421 pcs.	600.00	900.00	1250.

5 PESOS

NICKEL-CLAD STEEL

Y#	Date	Mintage	VF	XF	Unc
31	1961	37.420	.20	.30	.50
	1962	42.360	.20	.30	.50
	1963	71.770	.20	.25	.50
	1964	7.220	.20	.35	.50
	1965	19.730	.20	.25	.35
	1966	17.270	.20	.30	.50
	1967	17.600	.20	.25	.35
	1968	13.000	.20	.25	.35

ALUMINUM-BRONZE
100 Old Pesos - 1 New Peso

Y#	Date	Mintage	VF	XF	Unc
42	1976	118.353	.10	.20	.60
	1977	—	—	—	—

Brown Commemorative

Y#	Date	Mintage	VF	XF	Unc
50	1977	—	.15	.25	.50

ARGENTINO

8.0645 gm., .900 GOLD, .2333 oz AGW

Y#	Date	Mintage	Fine	VF	XF	Unc
11	1881	.037	BV	200.00	275.00	350.00
	1882	.252	BV	160.00	200.00	250.00
	1883	.906	BV	155.00	175.00	200.00
	1884	.448	BV	155.00	175.00	200.00
	1885	.204	BV	160.00	200.00	250.00
	1886	.398	BV	155.00	175.00	200.00
	1887	1.835	BV	155.00	175.00	200.00
	1888	1.663	BV	155.00	175.00	200.00
	1889	.404	BV	200.00	275.00	350.00
	1896	.197	BV	160.00	200.00	250.00

10 PESOS

NICKEL-CLAD STEEL

Y#	Date	Mintage	VF	XF	Unc
32	1962	57.400	.20	.30	.50
	1963	136.790	.20	.30	.50
	1964	73.900	.20	.30	.50
	1965	40.540	.15	.30	.50
	1966	50.330	.20	.30	.50
	1967	43.150	.20	.30	.75
	1968	51.270	.15	.30	.50

Y#	Date	Mintage	VF	XF	Unc
34	1966	Inc.Ab.	.15	.35	.75

ALUMINUM-BRONZE
100 Old Pesos - 1 New Peso

Y#	Date	Mintage	VF	XF	Unc
43	1976	128.965	.15	.35	.80
	1977	—	.15	.50	1.00
	1978	—	—	—	—

Brown Commemorative

51	1977	—	.15	.50	1.00

20 PESOS

COPPER-ALUMINUM-NICKEL
World Soccer Championship 1978

44	1977	1.500	.35	.75	1.25
	1978	2.000	.25	.50	1.00

25 PESOS

NICKEL-CLAD STEEL

33	1964	20.490	.25	.60	1.00
	1965	15.060	.25	.65	1.00
	1966	16.610	.25	.75	1.00
	1967	15.900	.25	.60	.90
	1968	20.250	.25	.60	.90

35	1968	Inc. Ab.	.60	.85	1.25

50 PESOS

COPPER-ALUMINUM-NICKEL
World Soccer Championship 1978

45	1977	1.500	.35	.75	1.25
	1978	2.000	.25	.50	1.00

Jose de San Martin

Y#	Date	Mintage	VF	XF	Unc
52	1978	—	.50	1.00	2.00

ALUMINUM-BRONZE
Jose de San Martin

54	1979	—	.25	.75	1.50

Conquest of Patagonia Centennial

56	1979	—	.25	.75	1.50

100 PESOS

COPPER-ALUMINUM-NICKEL
World Soccer Championship 1978

46	1977	1.500	.50	1.00	1.50
	1978	2.000	.50	1.00	1.50

Jose de San Martin

53	1978	—	.50	1.00	2.00

ALUMINUM-BRONZE
Jose de San Martin

55	1979	—	.25	.75	1.50

Conquest of Patagonia Centennial

Y#	Date	Mintage	VF	XF	Unc
57	1979	—	.25	.75	1.50

1000 PESOS

10.0000 gm., .900 SILVER, .2893 oz ASW
World Soccer Championship 1978

47	1977	.100	BV	8.75	10.00
	1977	1,000	—	Proof	—
	1978	.200	BV	8.75	10.00
	1978	1,750	—	Proof	—

2000 PESOS

15.0000 gm., .900 SILVER, .4340 oz ASW
World Soccer Championship 1978

48	1977	.100	BV	13.50	15.00
	1977	1,000	—	Proof	—
	1978	.200	BV	13.50	15.00
	1978	1,750	—	Proof	—

3000 PESOS

25.0000 gm., .900 SILVER, .7234 oz ASW
World Soccer Championship 1978

49	1977	.100	BV	22.00	25.00
	1977	1,000	—	Proof	—
	1978	.200	BV	22.00	25.00
	1978	1,750	—	Proof	—

NCLT ISSUES

PATTERNS

KM#	Date	Mintage	Identification	Mkt.Val.
1	1822	—	Decimo, Province of Buenos Aires, Copper, Medallic Rev.	—
2	1823	—	Octavo, Copper	—
3	1824	—	Quinto, Copper	—
4	1826	—	Real, Silver	—
4a	1826	—	Real, Copper	—
5	1827	—	Real, Silver	—
5a	1827	—	Real, Copper	—

KM#	Date	Mintage	Identification	Mkt.Val.
6	1876	—	Peso, Silver	

KM#	Date	Mintage	Identification	Mkt.Val.
7	1878	—	Centavo, Copper, ESSAI	50.00

KM#	Date	Mintage	Identification	Mkt.Val.
8	1878	—	2 Centavos, Copper, ESSAI	60.00

KM#	Date	Mintage	Identification	Mkt.Val.
9	1879	—	20 Centavos, Fuertes, Silver, ESSAI	275.00
9a	1879	—	20 Centavos, Fuertes, Bronze, ESSAI	—

KM#	Date	Mintage	Identification	Mkt.Val.
10	1879	—	40 Centavos, Fuertes, Silver, ESSAI	400.00
10a	1879	—	40 Centavos, Fuertes, Bronze, ESSAI	—

KM#	Date	Mintage	Identification	Mkt.Val.
11	1879	—	80 Centavos, Fuertes, Silver, ESSAI	650.00
11a	1879	—	80 Centavos, Fuertes, Bronze, ESSAI	100.00
11b	1879	—	80 Centavos, Fuertes, Copper, ESSAI	—

KM#	Date	Mintage	Identification	Mkt.Val.
12	1879	—	Patacon, Silver, ESSAI	1250.
12a	1879	—	Patacon, Copper, ESSAI	

KM#	Date	Mintage	Identification	Mkt.Val.
13	1879	—	Peso, Silver	—
13a	1879	—	Peso, Copper	—
13b	1879	—	Peso, Tin	—
14	1880	—	Centavo, Copper	—
15	1880	—	2 Centavos, Copper	—
16	1880	—	50 Centavos, Silver	—
17	1880	—	Peso, Silver	—
18	1880	—	Peso, UN PESO PLATA, Silver	—
19	18xx	—	Centavo, Copper	—
20	18xx	—	Centavo, Silver	—
21	18xx	—	Centavo, Gold	—
22	18xx	—	20 Centavos, Silver	—
23	18xx	—	50 Centavos, Silver	—
24	1881	—	1/2 Argentino, Gold	—
25	1887	—	20 Centavos, Nickel	—
26	1892	—	Centavo, UN CENTAVO, Aluminum	65.00
27	1892	—	Centavo, 1 CENTAVO, Aluminum	65.00

KM#	Date	Mintage	Identification	Mkt.Val.
28	1892	—	Centavo, Nickel	65.00
29	19xx	—	Centavo, Copper	—
30	19xx	—	2 Centavos, Copper	—
31	1925	—	2 Centavos, Copper	—
31a	1925	—	2 Centavos, Bronze	—
32	1932	—	Argentino, Copper	—
32a	1932	—	Argentino, Bronze	—
33	1934	—	Argentino, Copper	—
33a	1934	—	Argentino, Bronze	—
34	1935	—	Centavo, Copper	—
35	1935	—	2 Centavos, Copper	—
36	1936	—	50 Centavos, Bronze	—
36a	1936	—	50 Centavos, Nickel	—
37	1936	—	Peso, Bronze	—
37a	1936	—	Peso, Nickel	—
38	1938	—	Centavo, Copper	—
39	1938	—	2 Centavos, Copper	—
40	1940	—	50 Centavos, Bronze	—
41	1940	—	50 Centavos, Nickel, Head by Oudine	—
42	1940	—	50 Centavos, Nickel, Head by L.Bazor	—
43	1941	—	50 Centavos, Nickel	—
44	1943	—	Peso, Bronze	—
44a	1943	—	Peso, Nickel	—
45	1943	—	Peso, Bronze, Condor Rev.	—
46	1945	—	Peso, Bronze	—
46a	1945	—	Peso, Nickel	—
47	1946	—	Peso, Bronze	—
47a	1946	—	Peso, Nickel	—

MINT SETS

KM#	Date	Mintage	Identification	Issue Price	Mkt. Val.
S1	1978(6)	—	Y44-49	—	50.00

PROOF SETS
STANDARD METALS

KM#	Date	Mintage	Identification	Issue Price	Mkt. Val.
101	1978(3)	1,750	Y47-49	153.00	—

ASCENSION

An island of volcanic origin, Ascension Island lies in the South Atlantic 700 miles (1,100 km.) northwest of St. Helena. It has an area of 34 square miles (88 sq. km.) on an island 9 miles (14 km.) long and 6 miles (10 km.) wide. Approximate population: 1,230. Although having little vegetation and scant rainfall, the island has a very healthy climate. The island is the nesting place for large numbers of sea turtles and sooty terns. Phosphates and guano are the chief natural sources of income.

The island was discovered on Ascension Day, 1501, by Joao da Nova, a Portuguese navigator. It lay unoccupied until 1815 when occupied by the British. It was under Admiralty rule until 1922 when it was annexed as a dependency of St. Helena. During World War II an airfield was built that has been used as a fueling stop for transatlantic flights to Southern Europe, North Africa and the Near East. Ascension Island also has cable connections with Europe and Africa. Its advance into the Space Age came with the construction of a U.S. tracking station.

RULERS

British

MINTMARKS

PM - Popjoy Mint

CROWN

COPPER-NICKEL
25th Anniversary of Coronation

Y#	Date	Mintage	VF	XF	Unc
1	1978PM	—	1.25	1.75	2.50

28.2800 gm., .925 SILVER, .8411 oz ASW

Y#	Date	Mintage	VF	XF	Unc
1a	1978PM	.070	—	25.00	30.00
	1978PM	.025	—	Proof	50.00

Obv: Isle of Man crown. Rev: Ascension Y#1.

Y#	Date	Mintage	VF	XF	Unc
1b	1978PM (error)	—	—	Proof	350.00

AUSTRALIA

The Commonwealth of Australia, the smallest continent and largest island in the world, is located south of Indonesia between the Indian and Pacific oceans. It has an area of 2,967,909 sq. mi. (7,686,849 sq. km.) and a population of 14 million. Capital: Canberra. Due to its early and sustained isolation, Australia is the habitat of such curious and unique fauna as the kangaroo, koala bear, platypus, wombat and barking lizard. The continent possesses extensive mineral deposits, the most important of which are gold, coal, silver, nickel, uranium, lead and zinc. Livestock raising, mining and manufacturing are the principal industries. Chief exports are wool, meat, wheat, iron ore, coal and nonferrous metals.

The first whites to see Australia probably were Portuguese and Spanish navigators of the late 16th century. In 1770, Captain James Cook explored the east coast and annexed it for Great Britain. The Colony of New South Wales was founded by Capt. Arthur Phillip on January 26, 1788, a date now celebrated as Australia Day. Dates of creation of the six colonies that now comprise the states of the Australian Commonwealth are: New South Wales, 1823; Tasmania, 1825; Western Australia, 1838; South Australia, 1842; Victoria, 1851; Queensland, 1859. A constitution providing for federation of the colonies was approved by the British Parliament in 1900; the Commonwealth of Australia came into being in 1901. Australia passed the Statute of Westminster Adoption Act on October 9, 1942, which officially established Australia's complete autonomy in external and internal affairs, thereby formalizing a situation that had existed for years. Australia is a member of the Commonwealth of Nations. The Queen of England is Chief of State.

Australia's currency system was changed from Pounds-Shillings- Pence to a decimal system of Dollars and Cents on Feb. 14, 1966.

RULERS

British

MINTMARKS

Abbr.	Mint	Mint Marks and Locations
(b)	Bombay	"I" under bust; dots before and after HALF PENNY
(b)	Bombay	"I" under bust dots before and after PENNY
(c)	Calcutta	"I" above date, 1916-18
none	Canberra	None, 1966-date
D	Denver	"D" above date 1/-& 2/-, under date on 3d
H	Heaton	"H" below date on silver coins
H	Heaton	"H" above date on bronze coins
PL	London	"PL" after PENNY in 1951
PL	London	"PL" on bottom folds of ribbon, 1951 threepence
PL	London	"PL" over date on sixpence, 1951
(L)	London	none, 1910-1915
M	Melbourne	"M" under date on silver coins, 1916-21
(m)	Melbourne	Dot Below scroll on penny 1919-20
(m)	Melbourne	Two dots; under lower scroll and above upper, 1919-20
none	Melbourne	None 1922-1964
(p)	Perth	Dot between KG (designer's initials), 1940-41
(p)	Perth	Dot after PENNY, 1941-51, 1954-63
(p)	Perth	Dot after AUSTRALIA, 1952-53
(p)	Perth	Dot before SHILLING, 1946
(p)	Perth	None, 1922 penny
S	San Francisco	"S" above or below date
(sy)	Sydney	Dot above bottom scroll on penny. 1920
none	Sydney	None, 1919-1926

Mint designations are shown in ( ). Ex. 1878 (m).
Mint marks are shown after date. Ex. 1878M.

MONETARY SYSTEM

12 Pence = 1 Shilling
2 Shillings = 1 Florin
5 Shillings = 1 Crown
20 Shillings = 1 Pound

NEW SOUTH WALES COINAGE

15 PENCE

.903 SILVER
Struck over the center plugs of cut 8 Reales.

C#	Date	Mintage	Good	VG	Fine	VF
1	1813	*1,000	90.00	225.00	500.00	800.00

*Estimated remaining specimens.

HOLEY DOLLAR

(5 Shillings)

SILVER
c/s. on Spanish and Colonial 8 Reales.

C#	Date	Mintage	Good	VG	Fine	VF
2	1813	*200	1200.	2500.	3500.	7000.

*Estimated remaining specimens.

NOTE: The following Spanish and Colonial 8 Reales have been recorded cut and c/s. into "Holey Dollars": The no. known of each date is shown in ( ).

2.1 - BOLIVIA - Potosi Mint, C#18: 1783PR (1); 1786PR (1); 1789PR (2).

2.2 BOLIVIA - Potosi Mint, C#37: 1792PR (1); 1794PR (1); 1796PP (1); 1799PP (1); 1801PP (2); 1802PP (2); 1803PJ (1); 1804PJ (2); 1805PJ (2); 1806PJ (2); 1807PJ (1); 1808PJ (3).

2.3 MEXICO - Mexico City Mint, KM#104: 1757MM (1).

2.4 MEXICO - Mexico City Mint, KM#106: 1773FM (3); 1777FM (1); 1780FF (1); 1782FF (1); 1783FF (1); 1784FF (1); 1784FM (1); 1785FM (2); 1786FM (2); 1788FM (1); 1789FM (1).

2.5 MEXICO - Mexico City Mint, KM#107: 1789FM (2); 1790FM (6).

2.6 MEXICO - Mexico City Mint, KM#109: 1791FM (4); 1792FM (5); 1793FM (7); 1794FM (6); 1795FM (1); 1796FM (5); 1797FM (3); 1798FM (9); 1799FM (7); 1800FM (4); 1801FT (3); 1802FT (6); 1803FT (9); 1804TH (13); 1805TH (16); 1806TH (4); 1807TH (3); 1808TH (6).

2.7 MEXICO - Mexico City Mint, KM#110: 1809TH (11); 1810HJ (2).

2.8 PERU - Lima Mint, C#45: 1782MI (1); 1786MI (1).

2.9 PERU - Lima Mint, C#76: 1795IJ (1); 1796IJ (1); 1798IJ (1); 1800IF (1); 1801IF (2); 1803IJ (2); 1805JP (1); 1806JP (3); 1807JP (1); 1808JP (5).

2.10 PERU - Lima Mint, C#96: 1810JP (2).

2.11 SPAIN - Madrid Mint, C#71.1: 1799FA (1); 1802FA (2).

2.12 SPAIN - Seville Mint, C#71.2: 1793CN (1).

TRADESMENS' TOKENS

The first copper token of penny value was issued in Melbourne in 1849. With the increase in population following the discovery of gold in the early 1850's a large number of traders tokens were used in the colonies. Most of these were of copper and were valued as pennies or halfpennies. A few were of silver and valued at a higher rate. The greatest number appeared between 1857 and 1863. The total number exceeded 530 and they were issued by some 126 firms. About 1860 British bronze coins began to arrive in the colonies in quantity and with their use the tokens became unpopular. Victoria declared tokens illegal in 1863 and the other colonies took similar action in the following years, the last being Tasmania in 1876. these are listed in 'The Coins and Tokens of British Oceania' by Robert L. Clarke.

Another reference is Dr. Andrews 'Australasian Coins and Tokens'.

COMMONWEALTH

1/2 PENNY

BRONZE

Y#	Date	Mintage	Fine	VF	XF	Unc
5	1911(L)	2.832	.50	2.50	15.00	60.00
	1912H	2.400	.50	2.50	20.00	80.00
	1913(L)	2.160	1.00	5.00	40.00	200.00
	1914(L)	1.440	3.00	7.00	40.00	225.00
	1914H	1.200	3.00	7.00	35.00	200.00
	1915H	.720	20.00	50.00	175.00	500.00
	1916I(c)	3.600	.25	1.00	5.00	35.00
	1916I(c) (muled to obv. of India 1/4 Anna)					
		*10	2750.	3500.	—	—
	1917-I(c)	5.760	.25	1.00	5.00	29.50
	1918-I(c)	1.440	5.00	20.00	80.00	375.00
	1919(sy)	3.326	.25	1.00	9.00	40.00
	1920(sy)	4.114	.50	3.50	30.00	120.00
	1921(sy)	5.280	.25	1.00	6.00	40.00
	1922(sy)	6.924	.25	2.00	15.00	60.00
	1923(sy)					
		Disputed	175.00	250.00	750.00	2500.
	1923(sy)	—	—	—	Proof	3500.
	1924(m)	.682	1.50	5.00	30.00	200.00
	1925(m)	1.147	1.00	2.50	25.00	150.00
	1925(m)	—	—	—	Proof	300.00
	1926(m&sy)					
		4.139	.25	1.00	5.00	55.00
	1926(m)	—	—	—	Proof	150.00
	1927(m)	3.072	.25	1.00	6.00	55.00
	1927(m)	50 pcs.	—	—	Proof	175.00
	1928(m)	2.318	.75	1.75	20.00	150.00
	1928(m)	—	—	—	Proof	200.00
	1929(m)	2.635	.25	1.00	12.50	55.00
	1929(m)	—	—	—	Proof	200.00
	1930(m)	.638	3.75	6.00	35.00	350.00

Y#	Date	Mintage	Fine	VF	XF	Unc
	1930(m)	—	—	—	Proof	800.00
	1931(m)	.370	3.75	6.00	35.00	300.00
	1932(m)	2.554	.25	.50	5.00	30.00
	1933(m)	4.608	.25	.50	3.75	25.00
	1933(m)	—	—	—	Proof	125.00
	1934(m)	3.816	.25	.50	5.00	25.00
	1934(m)	100 pcs.	—	—	Proof	150.00
	1935(m)	2.916	.25	.50	5.00	25.00
	1935(m)	100 pcs.	—	—	Proof	200.00
	1936(m)	2.562	.25	.50	3.00	20.00
	1936(m)	—	—	—	Proof	125.00

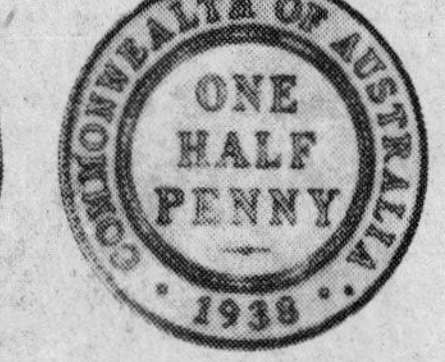

Y#	Date	Mintage	Fine	VF	XF	Unc
13	1938(m)	3.014	.15	.25	2.00	10.00
	1938(m)	250 pcs.	—	—	Proof	150.00
	1939(m)	4.382	.20	.45	4.00	15.00
	1939(m)	—	—	—	Proof	125.00

Y#	Date	Mintage	Fine	VF	XF	Unc
14	1939(m)	.504	6.00	10.00	25.00	120.00
	1939(m)	100 pcs.	—	—	Proof	150.00
	1940(m)	2.294	.75	1.50	6.50	30.00
	1941(m)	5.011	.25	.50	2.00	15.00
	1941(P)	—	—	—	Proof	125.00
	1942(m)	.720	2.00	3.00	10.00	50.00
	1942(m)	—	—	—	Proof	150.00
	1942(p) 'Y.'	4.334	.15	.25	1.00	15.00
	1942-I(b)	6.000	.15	.25	1.00	10.00
	1943(m)	33.989	.15	.25	.75	7.50
	1943-I(b)	6.000	.25	.50	2.00	15.00
	1943(b) no dot	—	—	—	—	—
	1944(m)	.720	3.00	5.00	20.00	60.00
	1945(p)	3.033	.50	1.00	5.00	20.00
	1945(p) no dot		—			
		Inc. Ab.	.50	1.00	1.50	12.50
	1945(p)	—	—	—	Proof	125.00
	1946(p)	13.747	.15	.25	1.00	7.50
	1946(p) 'Y.'	—	—	—	Proof	125.00
	1947(p) 'Y.'	9.293	.15	.25	1.00	6.50
	1947(p)	—	—	—	Proof	125.00
	1948(m)	4.608	.40	.75	4.00	20.00
	1948(p) 'Y.'	25.553	.15	.25	.95	5.50
	1948(p)	—	—	—	Proof	125.00

Obv: IND:IMP: dropped from legend

Y#	Date	Mintage	Fine	VF	XF	Unc
21	1949(p)'Y.'	22.310	.15	.25	1.00	6.50
	1949(p)'Y.'	—	—	—	Proof	125.00
	1950(p)'Y.'	12.014	.20	.95	3.50	15.00
	1950(p)'Y.'	—	—	—	Proof	125.00
	1951(p)'Y.'	29.422	.15	.25	.75	3.50
	1951(p)'Y.'	—	—	—	Proof	125.00
	1951(p) no dot	I.A.	.15	.25	1.00	3.50
	1951PL	12.000	.25	.60	2.25	7.50
	1951(I)	—	—	—	Proof	150.00
	1952(p)'A.'	1.832	1.25	2.00	6.50	22.50
	1952(p)'A.'	—	—	—	Proof	—

Y#	Date	Mintage	Fine	VF	XF	Unc
28	1953(p)'A.'	23.967	.15	.25	.90	3.50
	1953(p)'A.'	—	—	—	Proof	—
	1954(p)'Y.'	21.963	.15	.25	.90	3.50

Y#	Date	Mintage	Fine	VF	XF	Unc
28	1954(p)'Y.'	—	—	—	Proof	125.00
	1955(p)	9.343	.15	.25	.90	3.50
	1955(p)	301 pcs.	—	—	Proof	125.00

Obv: F:D: added to legend

Y#	Date	Mintage	Fine	VF	XF	Unc
35	1959(m)	10.166	.15	.25	.50	2.00
	1959(m)	1,506	—	—	Proof	15.00
	1960(p)'Y.'	17.812	.15	.25	.45	1.00
	1960(p)	1,030	—	—	Proof	15.00
	1961(p)'Y.'	20.183	.15	.25	.45	1.00
	1961(p)	1,040	—	—	Proof	12.50
	1962(p)'Y.'	10.259	.30	.50	1.25	2.00
	1962(p)	1,064	—	—	Proof	12.50
	1963(p)'Y.'	16.410	.15	.25	.25	1.00
	1963(p)	1,060	—	—	Proof	12.50
	1964(p)'Y.'	18.230	.15	.25	.25	1.00

PENNY

Bronze

Y#	Date	Mintage	Fine	VF	XF	Unc
6	1911(L)	3.768	1.00	3.00	10.00	75.00
	1912H	3.600	1.50	4.00	15.00	100.00
	1913(L)	2.520	2.75	6.75	20.00	150.00
	1914(L)	.720	6..0	17.50	60.00	300.00
	1915(L)	.960	5.00	12.50	50.00	250.00
	1915H	1.320	2.50	7.00	25.00	250.00
	1916-I(c)	3.324	.35	1.00	6.00	85.00
	1917-I(c)	6.240	.35	.75	5.00	70.00
	1918-I(c)	1.200	3.00	10.00	35.00	300.00
	1919(m) no dots					
		5.810	.35	1.00	5.00	125.00
	1919(m) dot under bottom scroll					
		Inc. Ab.	.75	1.25	5.00	100.00
	1919(m) dots under lower scroll and above upper					
		Inc. Ab.	5.00	8.00	—	—
	1920(m&sy) no dots					
		8.250	.50	3.25	50.00	200.00
	1920(m) dot under bottom scroll					
		Inc. Ab.	2.50	4.50	25.00	200.00
	1920(sy) dot over bottom scroll					
		Inc. Ab.	2.50	5.00	25.00	200.00
	1920(m) dots under lower scroll and above upper					
		Inc. Ab.	4.00	7.50	80.00	400.00
	1921(m&sy)	7.438	.25	1.00	6.50	140.00
	1922(m&p)	12.697	.25	1.00	6.00	145.00
	1923(m)	5.654	.40	1.05	7.50	—
	1923(m)	—	—	—	Proof	300.00
	1924(m&sy)	4.656	.35	1.00	4.00	60.00
	1925(m)	1.639	25.00	45.00	150.00	1000.
	1925(m)	—	—	—	Proof	1200.
	1926(m&sy)	1.859	.85	2.00	15.00	150.00
	1926(m)	—	—	—	Proof	200.00
	1927(m)	4.922	.25	.75	5.00	100.00
	1927(m)	50 pcs.	—	—	Proof	200.00
	1928(m)	3.038	.25	1.50	10.00	130.00
	1928(m)	—	—	—	Proof	200.00
	1929(m)	2.599	.50	2.00	20.00	300.00
	1929(m)	—	—	—	Proof	400.00
	1930(m)	Est. 3,000	2500.	3500.	6000.	15,000.
	1930(m)	—	—	—	Proof	25,000.
	1931(m)	.494	2.50	5.00	40.00	450.00
	1932(m)	2.117	.50	1.00	10.00	90.00
	1933/2(m)	5.818	4.00	6.00	15.00	90.00
	1933(m)	Inc. Ab.	.25	.50	4.00	60.00
	1933(m)	—	—	—	Proof	110.00
	1934(m)	5.808	.25	.50	3.00	50.00
	1934(m)	100 pcs.	—	—	Proof	170.00
	1935(m)	3.725	.25	.50	2.50	40.00
	1935(m)	100 pcs.	—	—	Proof	200.00
	1936(m)	9.890	.25	.50	2.50	40.00
	1936(m)	—	—	—	Proof	110.00

Y#	Date	Mintage	Fine	VF	XF	Unc
15	1938(m)	5.552	.25	.75	5.00	15.00
	1938(m)	250 pcs.	—	—	Proof	175.00
	1939(m)	6.240	.25	.75	5.00	15.00
	1939(m)	—	—	—	Proof	400.00
	1940(m)	4.075	.50	1.00	10.00	30.00
	1940(p)'K.G.'	—				
		1.114	4.00	8.00	40.00	200.00
	1941(m)	1.588	.75	1.50	10.00	35.00
	1941(p)'K.G.'	—				
		12.794	1.50	4.00	15.00	35.00
	1941(p) 'Y.'	I.A.	.25	.50	5.00	15.00
	1941(p)	2 pcs.	—	—	Proof	3,225.
	1941 high dot after 'Y'	—				
		Inc. Ab.	2.00	3.50	8.50	65.00
	1942(p)'Y.'	12.245	.15	.30	5.00	22.50
	1942-I(b)	9.000	.20	.40	4.00	15.00
	1942(b) w/o 'I'					
		Inc. Ab.	3.00	5.00	13.50	35.00
	1943(m)	11.112	.20	.40	3.00	12.50
	1943(p) 'Y.'	33.086	.15	.30	2.00	10.00
	1943(p)	—	—	—	Proof	110.00
	1943-I(b)	9.000	.30	.65	5.00	20.00
	1943-I(b) type 2					
		Inc. Ab.	.80	1.50	6.00	25.00
	1944(m)	2.112	1.00	2.50	15.00	75.00
	1944(p)'Y.'	27.830	.15	.30	1.75	10.00
	1944(p)'Y.'	—	—	—	Proof	150.00
	1945(p)'Y.'	15.173	.35	.60	6.00	20.00
	1945(p)'Y.'	—	—	—	Proof	125.00
	1945-I(b)	6 pcs.	—	—	Rare	—
	1945M	—	—	—	Rare	—
	1946(m)	.240	12.50	18.00	40.00	200.00
	1947M	6.864	.15	.20	1.50	10.00
	1947(p)'Y.'	4.49	1.25	2.50	7.50	20.00
	1947(p)'Y.'	—	—	—	Proof	110.00
	1948(m)	26.616	.15	.20	1.50	5.00
	1948(p)'Y.'	1.534	1.50	4.00	35.00	175.00
	1948(p)'Y.'	—	—	—	Proof	200.00

Obv: IND:IMP. dropped from legend

Y#	Date	Mintage	Fine	VF	XF	Unc
22.1	1949(m)	27.065	.10	.25	1.00	6.00
	1950(m)	36.359	.10	.25	1.00	5.00
	1950(P)'Y.'	21.488	.30	.75	6.00	16.50
	1950(P)'Y.'	—	—	—	Proof	110.00
	1951(m)	21.240	.10	.15	1.00	4.00
	1951(P)'Y.'	12.888	.50	1.00	3.50	10.00
	1951(P)'Y.'	—	—	—	Proof	110.00
	1951PL	18.000	.10	.15	1.00	4.00
	1951(L)	—	—	—	Proof	150.00
	1952(m)	12.408	.15	.25	.50	3.00
	1952(p)'A.'	45.514	.15	.25	1.50	5.00
	1952(p)'A.'	—	—	—	Proof	—

Obv: Legend reengraved

Y#	Date	Mintage	Fine	VF	XF	Unc
22.2	1952(P)	Inc. Ab.	—	—	—	—

Y#	Date	Mintage	Fine	VF	XF	Unc
29	1953(m)	6.936	.45	.95	3.00	10.00
	1953(p)	—	—	—	Proof	—
	1953(p)'A.'	6.203	.20	.45	1.00	5.00

Obv: F.D. added to legend

Y#	Date	Mintage	Fine	VF	XF	Unc
36	1955(m)	6.336	.75	1.25	4.50	12.50
	1955(m)	1,200	—	—	Proof	45.00
	1955(p)'Y.'	11.110	.10	.25	1.00	4.00
	1955(p)	301 pcs.	—	—	Proof	125.00
	1956(m)	13.872	.20	.75	1.75	4.00
	1956(m)	1,500	—	—	Proof	30.00
	1956(p)'Y.'	12.121	.10	.25	1.00	4.00
	1956(p)	417 pcs.	—	—	Proof	110.00
	1957(p)'Y.'	15.978	.10	.15	.50	2.00
	1957(p)	1,112	—	—	Proof	25.00
	1958(m)	10.012	.20	.35	1.00	4.00
	1958(m)	1,506	—	—	Proof	25.00
	1958(p)'Y.'	14.428	.10	.15	1.00	3.00
	1958(p)	1,028	—	—	Proof	20.00
	1959(m)	1.617	2.00	3.25	6.00	20.00
	1959(m)	1,506	—	—	Proof	30.00
	1959(p)'Y.'	14.428	.10	.15	1.00	3.00
	1959(p)	1,030	—	—	Proof	20.00
	1960(p)'Y.'	20.515	.10	.15	.50	2.00
	1960(p)'Y.'	1,030	—	—	Proof	15.00
	1961(p)'Y.'	30.607	.10	.15	.50	1.50
	1961(p)'Y.'	1,040	—	—	Proof	15.00
	1962(p)'Y.'	34.851	.10	.15	.50	1.00
	1962(p)'Y.'	1,064	—	—	Proof	10.00
	1963(p)'Y.'	10.258	.10	.25	.60	1.50
	1963(p)'Y.'	1,100	—	—	Proof	10.00
	1964(p)'Y.'	54.590	.10	.15	.50	1.00
	1964(m)	49.130	.10	.15	.30	1.00

THREEPENCE

1.4000 gm., .925 SILVER, .0416 oz ASW

Y#	Date	Mintage	Fine	VF	XF	Unc
1	1910(L)	4.000	5.00	7.50	20.00	35.00

Y#	Date	Mintage	Fine	VF	XF	Unc
9	1911(L)	2.000	6.00	12.00	45.00	85.00
	1911(L)	—	—	—	Proof	300.00
	1912(L)	2.400	10.00	25.00	75.00	225.00
	1914(L)	1.600	12.50	35.00	125.00	300.00
	1915(L)	.800	25.00	60.00	200.00	400.00
	1916M	1.913	6.00	15.00	60.00	175.00
	1916M	25 pcs.	—	—	Proof	325.00
	1917M	3.808	3.00	7.50	10.00	50.00
	1918M	3.119	3.00	10.00	25.00	65.00
	1919M	3.201	3.00	10.00	35.00	75.00
	1920M	4.196	7.50	20.00	75.00	175.00
	1921M	7.378	1.50	3.00	10.00	30.00
	1921(m)plain	I.A.	5.00	15.00	40.00	100.00
	1922/1(m)	5.531	600.00	1500.	2000.	—
	1922(m)	Inc. Ab.	3.00	6.00	20.00	45.00
	1923(m)	.815	10.00	25.00	95.00	225.00
	1924(m&sy)	2.014	3.00	10.00	30.00	75.00
	1925(m)	—	—	—	Proof	200.00
	1925(m&sy)	4.347	1.50	3.50	12.50	30.00
9	1926(m&sy)	6.158	1.50	3.00	11.00	22.50
	1926(m)	—	—	—	Proof	200.00
	1927(m)	6.720	1.50	3.00	11.00	22.50
	1927(m)	50 pcs.	—	—	Proof	200.00
	1928(m)	5.000	1.50	3.00	11.00	25.00
	1928(m)	—	—	—	Proof	200.00
	1934(m)	1.616	1.50	2.00	5.00	25.00
	1934(m)	100 pcs.	—	—	Proof	170.00
	1934/3(m)	Inc. Ab.	15.00	30.00	75.00	225.00
	1935(m)	2.800	1.50	3.50	5.00	25.00
	1936(m)	3.600	1.50	2.00	3.50	15.00
	1936(m)	—	—	—	Proof	110.00

Y#	Date	Mintage	Fine	VF	XF	Unc
16	1938(m)	4.560	2.25	3.50	6.00	12.00
	1938(m)	250 pcs.	—	—	Proof	175.00
	1939(m)	3.856	2.25	3.50	5.00	10.00
	1940(m)	3.840	2.25	3.00	4.25	9.00
	1941(m)	7.584	1.25	2.50	4.00	8.00
	1942(m)	.528	10.00	15.00	35.00	80.00
	1942D	16.000	BV	BV	1.35	2.50
	1942S	8.000	BV	BV	1.35	2.50
	1943(m)	24.912	BV	BV	1.35	3.00
	1943D	16.000	BV	BV	1.35	2.50
	1943S	8.000	BV.	BV	1.35	2.75
	1944S	32.000	BV	BV	1.35	2.00

1.4000 gm., .500 SILVER, .0225 oz ASW

Y#	Date	Mintage	Fine	VF	XF	Unc
16a	1947(m)	4.176	2.50	4.75	12.00	25.00
	1948(m)	26.208	BV	BV	1.00	3.00

Obv: IND:IMP. dropped from legend.

Y#	Date	Mintage	Fine	VF	XF	Unc
24	1949(m)	26.400	BV	BV	1.00	2.00
	1950(m)	35.456	BV	BV	1.00	2.00
	1951(m)	15.856	BV	BV	2.00	4.00
	1951PL	40.000	BV	BV	.75	2.50
	1951(L)	—	—	—	Proof	150.00
	1952(m)	21.560	BV	BV	1.00	3.00

Y#	Date	Mintage	Fine	VF	XF	Unc
30	1953(m)	7.664	1.00	1.50	3.00	6.00
	1954(m)	2.672	2.00	4.00	7.00	12.00

Obv: F:D: added to legend.

Y#	Date	Mintage	Fine	VF	XF	Unc
37	1955(m)	27.088	BV	BV	.75	2.00
	1955(m)	1,040	—	—	Proof	12.50
	1956(m)	14.088	BV	BV	1.00	2.00
	1956(m)	1,500	—	—	Proof	12.50
	1957(m)	26.704	BV	BV	.75	2.00
	1957(m)	1,256	—	—	Proof	12.50
	1958(m)	11.248	BV	BV	.75	1.00
	1958(m)	1,506	—	—	Proof	10.00
	1959(m)	19.888	BV	BV	.75	1.00
	1959(m)	1,508	—	—	Proof	10.00
	1960(m)	19.600	BV	BV	.75	1.00
	1960(m)	1,509	—	—	Proof	10.00
	1961(m)	33.840	BV	BV	.75	1.00
	1961(m)	1,506	—	—	Proof	8.00
	1962(m)	15.968	BV	BV	.75	1.00
	1962(m)	1,500	—	—	Proof	8.00
	1963(m)	44.016	BV	BV	.75	1.00
	1963(m)	1,500	—	—	Proof	8.00
	1964(m)	20.320	BV	BV	.75	1.00

SIXPENCE

2.8000 gm., .925 SILVER, .0832 oz ASW

Y#	Date	Mintage	Fine	VF	XF	Unc
2	1910(L)	3.046	6.00	12.00	25.00	50.00

Y#	Date	Mintage	Fine	VF	XF	Unc
10	1911(L)	1.000	10.00	25.00	65.00	175.00
	1911(L)	—	—	—	Proof	300.00
	1912(L)	1.600	20.00	40.00	150.00	350.00
	1914(L)	1.800	10.00	20.00	75.00	200.00
	1916M	1.769	15.00	35.00	100.00	275.00
	1916M	25 pcs.	—	—	Proof	325.00
	1917M	1.632	15.00	35.00	100.00	275.00
	1918M	.915	25.00	50.00	175.00	375.00
	1919M	1.521	5.00	10.00	50.00	150.00
	1920M	1.476	12.50	25.00	75.00	250.00
	1921(m)	—	—	—	Proof	250.00
	1921(m&sy)	3.795	4.00	8.00	25.00	75.00
	1922(sy)	1.488	12.00	30.00	125.00	400.00
	1923(m&sy)	1.458	8.00	20.00	75.00	200.00
	1924(m&sy)	1.038	8.00	20.00	75.00	200.00
	1925(m&sy)	3.266	3.75	7.50	25.00	75.00
	1926(m)	—	—	—	Proof	150.00
	1926(m&sy)	3.609	BV	6.00	20.00	50.00
	1927(m)	3.592	BV	6.50	17.50	40.00
	1927(m)	50 pcs.	—	—	Proof	150.00
	1928(m)	2.721	BV	6.50	12.50	40.00
	1928(m)	—	—	—	Proof	150.00
	1934(m)	1.024	3.75	7.50	25.00	75.00
	1934(m)	100 pcs.	—	—	Proof	200.00
	1935(m)	.392	5.00	12.00	45.00	150.00
	1936(m)	1.800	BV	3.00	10.00	30.00
	1936(m)	—	—	—	Proof	110.00

Y#	Date	Mintage	Fine	VF	XF	Unc
17	1938(m)	2.864	BV	3.00	5.00	15.00
	1938(m)	250 pcs.	—	—	Proof	160.00
	1939(m)	1.600	BV	3.50	7.00	25.00
	1940(m)	1.600	BV	3.00	5.00	12.00
	1941(m)	2.912	BV	BV	3.00	8.00
	1942(m)	8.968	BV	BV	4.00	10.00
	1942D	12.000	BV	BV	2.75	4.00
	1942S	4.000	BV	BV	2.75	4.00
	1943D	8.000	BV	BV	2.75	4.00
	1943S	4.000	BV	BV	2.75	4.00
	1944S	4.000	BV	BV	2.75	4.00
	1945(m)	10.096	BV	BV	2.75	6.00

2.8000 gm., .500 SILVER, .0450 oz ASW

Y#	Date	Mintage	Fine	VF	XF	Unc
17a	1946(m)	10.024	BV	1.50	2.00	5.00
	1948(m)	1.584	BV	2.00	6.00	12.00

Obv: IND:IMP dropped from legend.

Y#	Date	Mintage	Fine	VF	XF	Unc
25	1950(m)	10.272	BV	2.00	5.00	10.00
	1951(m)	13.760	BV	BV	3.00	5.00
	1951(L)	—	—	—	Proof	125.00
	1951PL	20.024	BV	BV	2.00	4.00
	1952(m)	2.112	3.00	6.50	20.00	50.00

Y#	Date	Mintage	Fine	VF	XF	Unc
31	1953(m)	1.152	4.00	6.00	15.00	25.00
	1954(m)	7.672	BV	BV	1.50	3.00

Obv: F:D: added to legend.

Y#	Date	Mintage	Fine	VF	XF	Unc
38	1955(m)	14.248	BV	BV	1.50	2.50
	1955(m)	1,200	—	—	Proof	12.00
	1956(m)	7.904	BV	3.00	6.00	15.00
38	1956(m)	1,500	—	—	Proof	12.00
	1957(m)	13.752	BV	BV	BV	2.00
	1957(m)	1,256	—	—	Proof	10.00
	1958(m)	17.944	BV	BV	BV	2.00
	1958(m)	1,506	—	—	Proof	10.00
	1959(m)	11.728	BV	BV	1.50	2.50
	1959(m)	1,506	—	—	Proof	10.00
	1960(m)	18.592	BV	BV	1.50	2.50
	1960(m)	1,509	—	—	Proof	10.00
	1961(m)	9.152	BV	BV	1.50	2.50
	1961(m)	1,506	—	—	Proof	8.00
	1962(m)	44.816	BV	BV	BV	1.75
	1962(m)	2,016	—	—	Proof	8.00
	1963(m)	25.056	BV	BV	BV	1.75
	1963(m)	2,000	—	—	Proof	8.00

SHILLING

5.6500 gm., .925 SILVER, .1680 oz ASW

Y#	Date	Mintage	Fine	VF	XF	Unc
3	1910(L)	2.536	12.00	25.00	65.00	100.00

Y#	Date	Mintage	Fine	VF	XF	Unc
11	1911(L)	1.700	15.00	30.00	90.00	225.00
	1911(L)	—	—	—	Proof	300.00
	1912(L)	1.000	35.00	100.00	300.00	750.00
	1913(L)	1.200	25.00	70.00	200.00	450.00
	1914(L)	3.300	7.50	20.00	50.00	150.00
	1915(L)	.800	35.00	100.00	250.00	500.00
	1915H	.500	40.00	125.00	300.00	750.00
	1916M	5.141	BV	7.50	25.00	75.00
	1916M	25 pcs.	—	—	Proof	450.00
	1917M	5.274	BV	7.50	25.00	75.00
	1918M	3.761	6.00	12.00	35.00	100.00
	1919M	6 pcs.	—	—	—	Rare
	1920M	.520	7.00	20.00	75.00	200.00
	1921Star(sy)	1.641	30.00	90.00	300.00	800.00
	1922(m)	2.040	BV	15.00	45.00	150.00
	1924(m&sy)	.674	10.00	30.00	125.00	300.00
	1925/3(m&sy)	1.448	BV	7.00	25.00	75.00
	1926(m)	—	—	—	Proof	150.00
	1926(m&sy)	2.352	BV	10.00	40.00	100.00
	1927(m)	1.146	BV	8.00	30.00	75.00
	1927(m)	50 pcs.	—	—	Proof	150.00
	1928(m)	.664	7.00	25.00	125.00	400.00
	1928(m)	—	—	—	Proof	200.00
	1931(m)	1.000	BV	8.50	35.00	80.00
	1933(m)	.220	35.00	90.00	300.00	750.00
	1934(m)	.480	10.00	20.00	75.00	225.00
	1934(m)	100 pcs.	—	—	Proof	300.00
	1935(m)	.500	BV	12.00	35.00	100.00
	1936(m)	2.000	BV	6.50	20.00	75.00
	1936(m)	—	—	—	Proof	110.00

Y#	Date	Mintage	Fine	VF	XF	Unc
18	1938(m)	1.484	BV	7.00	12.00	25.00
	1938(m)	250 pcs.	—	—	Proof	125.00
	1939(m)	1.520	BV	6.00	10.00	20.00
	1940(m)	.760	7.50	12.00	20.00	60.00
	1941(m)	3.040	BV	BV	7.00	10.00
	1942(m)	1.380	BV	BV	6.00	8.00
	1942'.S'	4.000	BV	BV	6.00	8.00
	1943(m)	2.720	6.00	8.00	15.00	40.00
	1943'.S'	16.000	BV	BV	5.50	8.00
	1944(m)	14.576	BV	BV	7.00	15.00
	1944'.S'	8.000	BV	BV	5.50	8.00

5.6500 gm., .500 SILVER, .0908 oz ASW

Y#	Date	Mintage	Fine	VF	XF	Unc
18a	1946(m)	10.072	BV	BV	6.00	12.00
	1946(p)'.S'	1.316	6.00	8.00	20.00	50.00
	1948(m)	4.132	BV	BV	6.00	16.00

Obv: IND:IMP. dropped from legend.

Y#	Date	Mintage	Fine	VF	XF	Unc
26	1950(m)	7.188	BV	BV	5.00	12.50
	1952(m)	19.644	BV	BV	5.00	10.00

Y#	Date	Mintage	Fine	VF	XF	Unc
32	1953(m)	12.204	BV	BV	4.00	8.00
	1954(m)	16.188	BV	BV	3.00	6.00

Obv: F:D: added to legend.

Y#	Date	Mintage	Fine	VF	XF	Unc
39	1955(m)	7.492	BV	BV	3.00	6.00
	1955(m)	1,200	—	—	Proof	15.00
	1956(m)	6.064	BV	BV	3.00	6.00
	1956(m)	1,500	—	—	Proof	15.00
	1957(m)	12.668	BV	BV	3.00	5.00
	1957(m)	1,256	—	—	Proof	15.00
	1958(m)	7.412	BV	BV	3.00	4.00
	1958(m)	1,506	—	—	Proof	15.00
	1959(m)	10.876	BV	BV	3.00	4.00
	1959(m)	1,506	—	—	Proof	15.00
	1960(m)	14.512	BV	BV	3.00	4.00
	1960(m)	1,509	—	—	Proof	15.00
	1961(m)	31.864	BV	BV	3.00	4.00
	1961(m)	1,506	—	—	Proof	10.00
	1962(m)	6.592	BV	BV	3.50	4.50
	1962(m)	2,016	—	—	Proof	10.00
	1963(m)	10.072	BV	BV	BV	3.50
	1963(m)	2,000	—	—	Proof	10.00

FLORIN

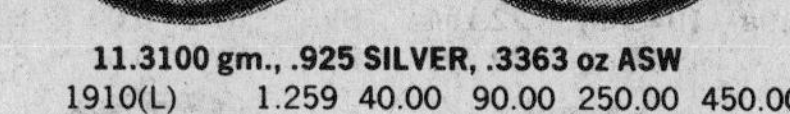

11.3100 gm., .925 SILVER, .3363 oz ASW

Y#	Date	Mintage	Fine	VF	XF	Unc
4	1910(L)	1.259	40.00	90.00	250.00	450.00

Y#	Date	Mintage	Fine	VF	XF	Unc
12	1911(L)	.950	40.00	100.00	300.00	950.00
	1911(L)	—	—	—	Proof	600.00
	1912(L)	1.000	50.00	125.00	375.00	1100.
	1913(L)	1.200	40.00	90.00	275.00	800.00
	1914(L)	2.300	12.00	25.00	75.00	200.00
	1914H	.500	75.00	200.00	600.00	1500.
	1915(L)	.500	75.00	200.00	600.00	1500.
	1915H	.750	45.00	90.00	275.00	575.00
	1916(m)	2.752	12.00	15.00	60.00	175.00
	1916(m)	25 pcs.	—	—	Proof	550.00
	1917(m)	4.305	12.00	15.00	50.00	150.00
	1918(m)	2.095	15.00	25.00	80.00	250.00
	1919(m)	1.677	25.00	75.00	225.00	650.00
	1921(m)	1.247	20.00	70.00	200.00	600.00
	1922(m)	2.058	15.00	35.00	150.00	400.00
	1923(m)	1.038	15.00	40.00	175.00	450.00

Y#	Date	Mintage	Fine	VF	XF	Unc
12	1924(m&sy)	1.582	15.00	35.00	150.00	400.00
	1925(m&sy)	2.960	BV	15.00	45.00	125.00
	1926(m&sy)	2.487	BV	15.00	60.00	175.00
	1927(m)	3.420	BV	15.00	40.00	125.00
	1927(m)	50 pcs.	—	—	Proof	150.00
	1928(m)	1.962	BV	15.00	40.00	125.00
	1931(m)	3.129	BV	12.00	30.00	100.00
	1932(m)	.188	175.00	500.00	1500.	3500.
	1933(m)	.488	35.00	100.00	300.00	1000.
	1934(m)	1.674	BV	12.00	40.00	150.00
	1934(m)	100 pcs.	—	—	Proof	300.00
	1935(m)	.915	BV	12.00	35.00	125.00
	1936(m)	2.382	BV	12.00	25.00	75.00
	1936(m)	—	—	—	Proof	150.00

(m) Parliment Commemorative

Y#	Date	Mintage	Fine	VF	XF	Unc
7	1927(m)	2.000	BV	12.00	16.00	25.00
	1927(m)	75 pcs.	—	—	Proof	200.00

Centennial Of Victoria And Melbourne

Y#	Date	Mintage	Fine	VF	XF	Unc
8	"1934-35"	*.054	125.00	150.00	175.00	225.00

***NOTE:** 21,000 pcs. were remelted.

Y#	Date	Mintage	Fine	VF	XF	Unc
19	1938(m)	2.990	BV	BV	18.00	25.00
	1939(m)	.630	12.00	25.00	50.00	125.00
	1940(m)	8.410	BV	BV	12.00	20.00
	1941(m)	7.614	BV	BV	12.00	20.00
	1942(m)	17.986	BV	BV	12.00	15.00
	1942S	6.000	BV	BV	12.00	17.50
	1943(m)	12.762	BV	BV	12.00	15.00
	1943S	11.000	BV	BV	12.00	15.00
	1944(m)	22.440	BV	BV	12.00	17.50
	1944S	11.000	BV	BV	14.00	20.00
	1945(m)	11.970	BV	BV	14.00	22.50

11.3100 gm., .500 SILVER, .1818 oz ASW

Y#	Date	Mintage	Fine	VF	XF	Unc
19a	1946(m)	22.154	BV	BV	6.00	8.00
	1947(m)	39.292	BV	BV	6.00	8.00

50th Year Jubilee

Y#	Date	Mintage	Fine	VF	XF	Unc
23	1951(m)	2.000	BV	BV	6.50	10.00

Obv: IND:IMP. dropped from legend.

Y#	Date	Mintage	Fine	VF	XF	Unc
27	1951(m)	10.068	BV	BV	7.00	10.00
	1952(m)	10.044	BV	BV	7.00	12.50

Y#	Date	Mintage	Fine	VF	XF	Unc
33	1953(m)	12.658	BV	BV	6.00	12.00
	1954(m)	15.366	BV	BV	6.00	10.00

Royal Visit Commemorative

Y#	Date	Mintage	Fine	VF	XF	Unc
34	1954(m)	4.000	BV	BV	6.00	8.50

Obv: F:D: added to legend.

Y#	Date	Mintage	Fine	VF	XF	Unc
40	1956(m)	8.090	BV	6.00	10.00	15.00
	1956(m)	1,500	—	—	Proof	20.00
	1957(m)	9.278	BV	BV	BV	7.50
	1957(m)	1,256	—	—	Proof	15.00
	1958(m)	8.972	BV	BV	BV	7.50
	1958(m)	1,506	—	—	Proof	15.00
	1959(m)	3.500	BV	BV	BV	7.50
	1959(m)	1,506	—	—	Proof	15.00
	1960(m)	15.760	BV	BV	BV	7.50
	1960(m)	1,509	—	—	Proof	15.00
	1961(m)	9.452	BV	BV	BV	7.50
	1961(m)	1,506	—	—	Proof	10.00
	1962(m)	13.748	BV	BV	BV	7.50
	1962(m)	2,016	—	—	Proof	10.00
	1963(m)	12.002	BV	BV	BV	7.50
	1963(m)	2,000	—	—	Proof	10.00

CROWN

28.2800 gm., .925 SILVER, .8411 oz ASW

Y#	Date	Mintage	Fine	VF	XF	Unc
20	1937(m)	1.008	BV	27.50	35.00	45.00
	1937(m)	100 pcs.	—	—	Proof	500.00
	1938(m)	.102	45.00	65.00	90.00	125.00
	1938(m)	250 pcs.	—	—	Proof	1000.

TRADE COINS

1/2 SOVEREIGN

3.9940 gm., .917 GOLD, .1177 oz AGW

C#	Date	Mintage	Fine	VF	XF	Unc
3	1855(sy)	.021	2500.	8500.	13,500.	18,500.
	1856(sy)	.478	1000.	2500.	4000.	7000.

Obv: Smaller bust, hair tied with oak wreath.

C#	Date	Mintage	Fine	VF	XF	Unc
3a	1857(sy)	.537	150.00	350.00	800.00	4500.
	1857(sy)	—	—	—	Proof	5000.
	1858(sy)	.483	350.00	600.00	1500.	4500.
	1859(sy)	.341	175.00	400.00	800.00	4500.
	1860(sy)	.156	225.00	500.00	1000.	4500.
	1861(sy)	.186	175.00	400.00	800.00	4500.
	1862(sy)	.210	350.00	600.00	1500.	4500.
	1863(sy)	.348	300.00	600.00	1500.	4500.
	1864(sy)	.141	250.00	500.00	1000.	4500.
	1865(sy)	.062	250.00	500.00	1000.	4500.
	1866(sy)	.154	150.00	350.00	800.00	4500.

HALF SOVEREIGN MINTMARKS

Y#A1: S or M on reverse below shield.

Y#D1: S or M on reverse below shield.

All others have S, M or P (from 1900) on reverse on ground below dragon.

Obv: Young head.

Y#	Date	Mintage	Fine	VF	XF	Unc
A1	1871S	.180	100.00	150.00	300.00	450.00
	1871S	—	—	—	Proof	2500.
	1872S	.356	100.00	150.00	300.00	450.00
	1873M	.165	100.00	160.00	300.00	450.00
	1875S	.252	100.00	150.00	300.00	450.00
	1877M	.080	100.00	150.00	300.00	450.00
	1879S	.220	100.00	150.00	300.00	500.00
	1880S	.080	100.00	150.00	300.00	450.00
	1880S	—	—	—	Proof	2500.
	1881S	.062	100.00	150.00	350.00	550.00
	1881M	.042	150.00	200.00	500.00	750.00
	1881M	—	—	—	Proof	2500.
	1882S	.052	100.00	150.00	350.00	550.00
	1882M	.106	125.00	200.00	400.00	650.00
	1883S	.220	90.00	135.00	275.00	400.00
	1883S	—	—	—	Proof	2500.
	1884M	.048	125.00	200.00	400.00	650.00
	1884M	—	—	—	Proof	2500.
	1885M	.011	500.00	1200.	2500.	3500.
	1886S	.082	90.00	135.00	275.00	400.00
	1886M	.038	125.00	200.00	400.00	650.00
	1886M	—	—	—	Proof	2500.
	1887S	.013	100.00	150.00	300.00	500.00
	1887S	—	—	—	Proof	2500.
	1887M	.060	150.00	250.00	425.00	650.00

Obv: Jubilee head.

Y#	Date	Mintage	Fine	VF	XF	Unc
D1	1887S	Inc. Ab.	90.00	125.00	250.00	300.00
	1887S	—	—	—	Proof	2500.
	1887M	Inc. Ab.	100.00	150.00	275.00	325.00
	1887M	—	—	—	Proof	2000.
	1888M	—	—		Proof Only	2500.
	1889S	.064	100.00	150.00	250.00	300.00
	1889M	—	—		Proof Only	2500.
	1890M	—	—		Proof Only	2500.
	1891S	.154	90.00	125.00	200.00	250.00
	1891M	—	—		Proof Only	2500.
	1892S	—	—		Proof Only	2500.
	1892M	—	—		Proof Only	2500.
	1893S	—	—		Proof Only	3500.
	1893M	.110	90.00	125.00	200.00	250.00
	1893M	—	—		Proof	2000.

Obv: Old head.

Y#	Date	Mintage	Fine	VF	XF	Unc
F1	1893S	.250	85.00	110.00	135.00	175.00
	1893S	—	—	—	Proof	2500.
	1893M	—	—		Proof Only	2500.
	1894M	—	—		Proof Only	2500.
	1895M	—	—		Proof Only	2500.
	1896M	.218	85.00	110.00	135.00	175.00
	1896M	—	—	—	Proof	2000.
	1897S	.230	85.00	110.00	150.00	250.00
	1897M	—	—		Proof Only	2500.
	1898M	—	—		Proof Only	2500.
	1899M	.090	85.00	110.00	150.00	275.00
	1899M	—	—	—	Proof	2000.
	1899P	One known		—	Proof	7500.
	1900S	.260	85.00	110.00	150.00	250.00
	1900M	.113	85.00	110.00	150.00	275.00
	1900M	—	—	—	Proof	2000.
	1900P	.119	85.00	110.00	150.00	250.00
	1901M	—	—		Proof Only	3500.
	1901P	—	—		Proof Only	3000.
A5	1902S	.084	85.00	110.00	125.00	175.00
	1902S	—	—	—	Proof	2500.
	1903S	.231	85.00	100.00	120.00	150.00
	1904P	.060	100.00	150.00	250.00	300.00
	1906S	.308	85.00	100.00	120.00	150.00
	1906M	.082	85.00	100.00	120.00	150.00
	1907M	.400	85.00	100.00	120.00	150.00
	1908S	.538	85.00	100.00	120.00	150.00
	1908M	Inc. 1907M	85.00	100.00	120.00	150.00
	1908P	.025	150.00	250.00	400.00	500.00
	1909M	.186	85.00	100.00	120.00	150.00
	1909P	.044	125.00	175.00	225.00	350.00
	1910S	.474	85.00	100.00	120.00	150.00

Y#	Date	Mintage	Fine	VF	XF	Unc
A13	1911S	.252	85.00	100.00	120.00	140.00
	1911S	—	—	—	Proof	1200.
	1911P	.130	85.00	100.00	120.00	150.00
	1912S	.278	85.00	100.00	120.00	140.00
	1914S	.322	85.00	100.00	120.00	140.00
	1915S	.892	85.00	100.00	120.00	140.00
	1915M	.125	85.00	100.00	120.00	150.00
	1915P	.138	85.00	100.00	120.00	140.00
	1916S	.448	85.00	100.00	120.00	140.00
	1918P	*15-20 pcs.	950.00	1000.	1500.	2500.

ADELAIDE POUND

.917 GOLD

Rev: Type 1, value in plain circle.

C#	Date	Mintage	VG	Fine	VF	XF
5	1852	*20-50 pcs.	6000.	8000.	15,000.	25,000.

Rev: Type 2, value in dentilated circle.

C#	Date	Mintage	VG	Fine	VF	XF
5	1852	.025	1000.	1800.	3000.	4500.

SOVEREIGN

7.9881 gm., .917 GOLD, .2354 oz AGW

C#	Date	Mintage	Fine	VF	XF	Unc
4	1855(sy)	.502	1750.	3000.	6000.	10,000.
	1856(sy)	.981	1750.	3000.	6000.	10,000.

Obv: Smaller bust, oak laureate hair tie.

C#	Date	Mintage	Fine	VF	XF	Unc
4a	1857(sy)	.499	200.00	400.00	1350.	2000.
	1857(sy)	—	—	—	Proof	8000.
	1858(sy)	1.101	200.00	450.00	1300.	2000.
	1859(sy)	1.050	185.00	400.00	1150.	2000.
	1860(sy)	1.573	300.00	625.00	1600.	2200.
	1861(sy)	1.626	185.00	325.00	850.00	2000.
	1862(sy)	2.477	225.00	500.00	1275.	2000.
	1863(sy)	1.255	200.00	375.00	900.00	2000.
	1864(sy)	2.698	175.00	310.00	600.00	2000.
	1865(sy)	2.130	175.00	325.00	600.00	2000.
	1866(sy)	2.911	250.00	350.00	500.00	1000.
	1867(sy)	2.370	175.00	250.00	500.00	1000.
	1868(sy)	2.319	175.00	250.00	475.00	1000.
	1869(sy)	—	—	—	—	—
	1870(sy)	1.220	175.00	225.00	375.00	1000.
	1870(sy)	—	—	—	Proof	5000.

SOVEREIGN MINTMARKS

Y#B1: S or M on reverse below shield.

Y#C1: S or M on obverse below head.

All others have S, M or P from 1899 on reverse on ground below dragon.

Obv: Young head.

NOTE: Mintage figures include St. George and shield types. No separate mintage figures are known.

Y#	Date	Mintage	Fine	VF	XF	Unc
C1	1871S	2.814	BV	BV	175.00	200.00
	1871S	—	—	—	Proof	4000.
	1872S	1.815	BV	BV	175.00	225.00
	1872/1M	.748	300.00	425.00	650.00	—
	1872M	Inc. Ab.	BV	BV	175.00	225.00
	1873S	1.478	BV	BV	175.00	225.00
	1873M	.752	BV	BV	175.00	225.00
	1874S	1.899	BV	BV	175.00	225.00
	1874M	1.373	BV	BV	175.00	225.00
	1875S	2.122	BV	BV	175.00	225.00
	1875M	1.888	BV	BV	175.00	225.00
	1876S	1.613	BV	BV	175.00	225.00
	1876M	2.124	BV	BV	175.00	225.00
	1877M	1.487	BV	BV	175.00	225.00
	1878M	2.171	BV	BV	175.00	225.00
	1879S	1.366	BV	BV	175.00	225.00
	1879M	2.740	BV	BV	175.00	225.00
	1880S	1.459	BV	BV	175.00	225.00
	1880S	—	—	—	Proof	3000.
	1880M	3.053	BV	BV	175.00	225.00
	1881S	1.360	BV	BV	175.00	225.00
	1881M	2.324	BV	BV	175.00	225.00
	1881M	—	—	—	Proof	2000.
	1882S	1.298	BV	BV	175.00	225.00
	1882M	2.466	BV	BV	175.00	225.00
	1883S	1.108	BV	BV	175.00	225.00
	1883M	2.050	BV	BV	175.00	225.00
	1884S	1.595	BV	BV	175.00	225.00
	1884M	2.942	BV	BV	175.00	225.00
	1884M	—	—	—	Proof	2000.
	1885M	2.957	BV	BV	175.00	225.00
	1885M	—	—	—	Proof	2000.
	1886S	1.677	BV	BV	175.00	225.00
	1886M	2.902	BV	BV	175.00	225.00
	1887S	1.000	BV	BV	175.00	225.00
	1887M	1.915	BV	BV	175.00	225.00
	1887M	—	—	—	Proof	2000.

Obv: Young head.

NOTE: Mintage figures include St. George and shield types. No separate mintage figures are known.

Y#	Date	Mintage	Fine	VF	XF	Unc
B1	1871S	2.814	BV	BV	175.00	225.00
	1871S	—	—	—	Proof	4000.
	1872S	1.815	BV	BV	175.00	225.00
	1872M	.748	BV	BV	175.00	225.00
	1873S	1.478	BV	BV	175.00	225.00
	1874M	1.373	BV	BV	175.00	225.00
	1875S	2.122	BV	BV	175.00	225.00
	1875S	—	—	—	Proof	4000.
	1877S	1.590	BV	BV	175.00	200.00
	1878S	1.259	BV	BV	175.00	200.00
	1879S	1.366	BV	BV	175.00	200.00
	1880S	1.459	BV	BV	175.00	225.00
	1880S	—	—	—	Proof	4000.
	1880M	3.053	1000.	1500.	2000.	3250.
	1881S	1.360	BV	BV	185.00	225.00
	1881M	2.324	BV	175.00	250.00	325.00
	1882S	1.298	BV	BV	175.00	200.00
	1882M	2.466	BV	BV	175.00	200.00
	1883S	1.108	BV	BV	175.00	200.00
	1883S	—	—	—	Proof	4000.
	1883M	2.050	500.00	800.00	1250.	2000.
	1884S	1.595	BV	BV	175.00	200.00
	1884M	2.942	BV	BV	175.00	200.00
	1885S	1.486	BV	BV	175.00	200.00
	1885M	2.957	BV	BV	175.00	200.00
	1885M	—	—	—	Proof	2000.
	1886S	1.677	BV	BV	175.00	200.00
	1886S	—	—	—	Proof	3000.
	1886M	2.902	2000.	2500.	3500.	5000.
	1886M	—	—	—	Proof	2000.
	1887S	1.000	BV	175.00	200.00	250.00
	1887S	—	—	—	Proof	3000.
	1887M	1.915	750.00	1250.	1750.	2500.

NOTE: Designer's initials omitted on 1880S, 1881S, 1882M, 1883M, 1884M and 1885M.

Obv: Jubilee head.

Y#	Date	Mintage	Fine	VF	XF	Unc
E1	1887S	1.002	BV	BV	175.00	225.00
	1887S	—	—	—	Proof	3000.
	1887M	.940	BV	BV	175.00	200.00
	1887M	—	—	—	Proof	2000.
	1888S	2.187	BV	BV	175.00	200.00
	1888M	2.830	BV	BV	175.00	200.00
	1888M	—	—	—	Proof	2000.
	1889S	3.262	BV	BV	175.00	200.00
	1889M	2.732	BV	BV	175.00	200.00
	1889M	—	—	—	Proof	2000.
	1890S	2.808	BV	BV	175.00	200.00
	1890M	2.473	BV	BV	175.00	200.00
	1890M	—	—	—	Proof	2000.
	1891S	2.596	BV	BV	175.00	200.00
	1891M	2.749	BV	BV	175.00	200.00
	1892S	2.837	BV	BV	175.00	200.00
	1892M	3.488	BV	BV	175.00	200.00
	1893S	1.498	BV	BV	175.00	200.00
	1893S	—	—	—	Proof	3000.
	1893M	1.649	BV	BV	175.00	200.00
	1893M	—	—	—	Proof	2000.

Obv: Old head.

Y#	Date	Mintage	Fine	VF	XF	Unc
G1	1893S	1.346	BV	BV	175.00	200.00
	1893S	—	—	—	Proof	3000.
	1893M	1.914	BV	BV	175.00	200.00
	1893M	—	—	—	Proof	2000.
	1894S	3.067	BV	BV	175.00	200.00
	1894S	—	—	—	Proof	2000.
	1894M	4.166	BV	BV	175.00	200.00
	1894M	—	—	—	Proof	2000.
	1895S	2.758	BV	BV	175.00	200.00
	1895M	4.165	BV	BV	175.00	200.00
	1895M	—	—	—	Proof	2000.
	1896S	2.544	BV	BV	175.00	200.00
	1896M	4.456	BV	BV	175.00	200.00
	1896M	—	—	—	Proof	2000.
	1897S	2.532	BV	BV	175.00	200.00
	1897M	5.130	BV	BV	175.00	200.00
	1897M	—	—	—	Proof	2000.

Y#	Date	Mintage	Fine	VF	XF	Unc
G1	1898S	2.548	BV	BV	175.00	200.00
	1898M	5.509	BV	BV	175.00	200.00
	1898M	—	—	—	Proof	2000.
	1899S	3.259	BV	BV	175.00	200.00
	1899M	5.579	BV	BV	175.00	200.00
	1899M	—	—	—	Proof	2000.
	1899P	.690	BV	BV	175.00	250.00
	1899P	—	—	—	Proof	3500.
	1900S	3.586	BV	BV	175.00	200.00
	1900M	4.305	BV	BV	175.00	200.00
	1900M	—	—	—	Proof	2000.
	1900P	1.886	BV	BV	175.00	200.00
	1901S	3.012	BV	BV	175.00	200.00
	1901M	3.987	BV	BV	175.00	200.00
	1901M	—	—	—	Proof	2000.
	1901P	2.889	BV	BV	175.00	200.00
	1901P	—	—	—	Proof	1400.
B5	1902S	2.813	BV	BV	175.00	200.00
	1902S	—	—	—	Proof	2000.
	1902M	4.267	BV	BV	175.00	200.00
	1902P	4.289	BV	BV	175.00	200.00
	1902P	—	—	—	Proof	1400.
	1903S	2.806	BV	BV	175.00	200.00
	1903M	3.521	BV	BV	175.00	200.00
	1903P	4.674	BV	BV	175.00	200.00
	1904S	2.986	BV	BV	175.00	200.00
	1904M	3.743	BV	BV	175.00	200.00
	1904M	—	—	—	Proof	2000.
	1904P	4.506	BV	BV	175.00	200.00
	1905S	2.778	BV	BV	175.00	200.00
	1905M	3.633	BV	BV	175.00	200.00
	1905P	4.876	BV	BV	175.00	200.00
	1906S	2.792	BV	BV	175.00	200.00
	1906M	3.657	BV	BV	175.00	200.00
	1906P	4.829	BV	BV	175.00	200.00
	1907S	2.539	BV	BV	175.00	200.00
	1907M	3.332	BV	BV	175.00	200.00
	1907P	4.972	BV	BV	175.00	200.00
	1908S	2.017	BV	BV	175.00	200.00
	1908M	3.080	BV	BV	175.00	200.00
	1908P	4.875	BV	BV	175.00	200.00
	1909S	2.057	BV	BV	175.00	200.00
	1909M	3.029	BV	BV	175.00	200.00
	1909P	4.524	BV	BV	175.00	200.00
	1910S	2.135	BV	BV	175.00	200.00
	1910M	3.054	BV	BV	175.00	200.00
	1910M	—	—	—	Proof	1400.
	1910P	4.690	BV	BV	175.00	200.00
B13.1	1911S	2.519	BV	BV	175.00	200.00
	1911S	—	—	—	Proof	2500.
	1911M	2.851	BV	BV	175.00	200.00
	1911M	—	—	—	Proof	1400.
	1911P	4.373	BV	BV	175.00	200.00
	1912S	2.227	BV	BV	175.00	200.00
	1912M	2.467	BV	BV	175.00	200.00
	1912P	4.278	BV	BV	175.00	200.00
	1913S	2.249	BV	BV	175.00	200.00
	1913M	2.323	BV	BV	175.00	200.00
	1913P	4.635	BV	BV	175.00	200.00
	1914S	1.774	BV	BV	175.00	200.00
	1914S	—	—	—	Proof	2000.
	1914M	2.012	BV	BV	175.00	200.00
	1914P	4.815	BV	BV	175.00	200.00
	1915S	1.346	BV	BV	175.00	200.00
	1915M	1.637	BV	BV	175.00	200.00
	1915P	4.373	BV	BV	175.00	200.00
	1916S	1.242	BV	BV	175.00	200.00
	1916M	1.277	BV	BV	175.00	200.00
	1916P	4.906	BV	BV	175.00	200.00
	1917S	1.666	BV	BV	175.00	200.00
	1917M	.934	BV	BV	175.00	200.00
	1917P	4.110	BV	BV	175.00	200.00
	1918S	3.716	BV	BV	175.00	200.00
	1918M	4.969	BV	BV	175.00	200.00
	1918P	3.812	BV	BV	175.00	200.00
	1919S	1.835	BV	BV	175.00	200.00
	1919M	.514	BV	BV	185.00	210.00
	1919P	2.995	BV	BV	175.00	200.00
	1920S	.360	2500.	3500.	5000.	—
	1920M	.530	1500.	2000.	2250.	—
	1920P	2.421	BV	BV	175.00	200.00
	1921S	.839	900.00	1400.	1600.	2000.
	1921M	.240	3000.	4000.	5000.	6500.
	1921P	2.314	BV	BV	175.00	200.00
	1922S	.578	3000.	4000.	5000.	—
	1922M	.608	2000.	3000.	3500.	—
	1922P	2.298	BV	BV	175.00	200.00
B13.1	1923S	.416	1500.	2000.	2750.	—
	1923M	.510	BV	BV	175.00	200.00
	1923P	2.124	BV	BV	175.00	200.00
	1924S	.394	900.00	1400.	1600.	2000.
	1924M	.278	BV	BV	185.00	210.00
	1924P	1.464	BV	BV	175.00	200.00
	1925S	5.632	BV	BV	175.00	200.00
	1925M	3.311	BV	BV	175.00	200.00
	1925P	1.837	BV	BV	175.00	200.00
	1926S	1.031	3500.	4500.	5500.	7000.
	1926S	—	—	—	Proof	7500.
	1926M	.211	BV	BV	175.00	200.00
	1926P	1.131	BV	BV	175.00	200.00
	1927P	1.383	BV	BV	175.00	200.00
	1928M	.413	1200.	1800.	2200.	3000.
	1928P	1.333	BV	BV	175.00	200.00
	Smaller head					
B13.2	1929M	.436	1200.	1600.	2000.	2500.
	1929M	—	—	—	Proof	3500.
	1929P	1.606	BV	BV	175.00	200.00
	1930M	.077	BV	BV	185.00	250.00
	1930M	—	—	—	Proof	2500.
	1930P	1.915	BV	BV	175.00	200.00
	1931M	.057	200.00	300.00	350.00	450.00
	1931M	—	—	—	Proof	2500.
	1931P	1.173	BV	BV	175.00	200.00

DECIMAL COINAGE

100 Cents = 1 Dollar

CENT

BRONZE

Y#	Date	Mintage	Fine	VF	XF	Unc
41	1966	146.457	—	—	—	.15
	1966	.018	—	—	Proof	10.00
	1966(m) blunted whisker on right					
		238.990	—	—	—	.15
	1966(p) blunted second whisker from right					
		26.620	—	—	—	.15
	1967	110.055	—	—	—	.15
	1968	19.930	—	—	—	.15
	1969	87.680	—	—	—	.15
	1969	.013	—	—	Proof	11.00
	1970	72.560	—	—	—	.15
	1970	.015	—	—	Proof	10.00
	1971	102.455	—	—	—	.15
	1971	.005	—	—	Proof	10.00
	1972	30.300	—	—	—	.15
	1972	.006	—	—	Proof	10.00
	1973	84.530	—	—	—	.15
	1973	.010	—	—	Proof	10.00
	1974	50.500	—	—	—	.15
	1974	.010	—	—	Proof	10.00
	1975	101.495	—	—	—	.15
	1975	.025	—	—	Proof	6.00
	1976	172.935	—	—	—	.15
	1976	.023	—	—	Proof	6.00
	1977	—	—	—	—	.15
	1977	.055	—	—	Proof	5.00
	1978	—	—	—	—	.15
	1978	—	—	—	Proof	—
	1979	—	—	—	—	.15
	1979	—	—	—	Proof	—
	1980	—	—	—	—	.15
	1980	—	—	—	Proof	—

2 CENTS

BRONZE

Y#	Date	Mintage	Fine	VF	XF	Unc
42	1966	145.226	—	—	.10	1.00
	1966	.018	—	—	Proof	15.00
	1966(m) blunted third left claw					
		66.575	—	—	.10	1.00
	1966(p) blunted first right claw					
		217.735	—	—	.10	1.00
	1967	73.250	—	—	.10	1.00
	1968	17.000	—	—	.15	.75
42	1969	12.940	—	—	.15	.75
	1969	.013	—	—	Proof	12.00
	1970	39.870	—	—	.10	.15
	1970	.015	—	—	Proof	15.00
	1971	67.170	—	—	.10	.15
	1971	.005	—	—	Proof	15.00
	1972	65.370	—	—	.10	.15
	1972	.006	—	—	Proof	15.00
	1973	83.315	—	—	.10	.15
	1973	.010	—	—	Proof	15.00
	1974	58.705	—	—	.10	.15
	1974	.010	—	—	Proof	15.00
	1975	74.925	—	—	—	.15
	1975	.025	—	—	Proof	7.00
	1976	107.883	—	—	—	.15
	1976	.023	—	—	Proof	7.00
	1977	—	—	—	—	.15
	1977	.055	—	—	Proof	6.00
	1978	—	—	—	—	.15
	1978	—	—	—	Proof	—
	1979	—	—	—	—	.15
	1979	—	—	—	Proof	—
	1980	—	—	—	—	.15
	1980	—	—	—	Proof	—

5 CENTS

COPPER-NICKEL

Y#	Date	Mintage	Fine	VF	XF	Unc
43	1966	45.427	—	—	.20	.30
	1966	.018	—	—	Proof	20.00
	1966(L)	30.000	—	—	.20	.30
	1966(L)	—	—	—	Proof	15.00
	1967	62.144	—	—	.15	.25
	1968	67.336	—	—	.15	.25
	1969	36.170	—	—	.15	.25
	1969	.013	—	—	Proof	12.00
	1970	45.058	—	—	.15	.25
	1970	.015	—	—	Proof	15.00
	1971	39.516	—	—	.15	.25
	1971	.005	—	—	Proof	15.00
	1972	8.256	—	—	.15	.25
	1972	.006	—	—	Proof	15.00
	1973	29.352	—	—	.15	.25
	1973	.010	—	—	Proof	15.00
	1974	28.800	—	—	.15	.25
	1974	.010	—	—	Proof	15.00
	1975	14.400	—	—	—	.40
	1975	—	—	—	Proof	7.00
	1976	113.180	—	—	—	.25
	1976	—	—	—	Proof	7.00
	1977	—	—	—	—	.25
	1977	.055	—	—	Proof	6.00
	1978	—	—	—	—	.25
	1978	—	—	—	Proof	—
	1979	—	—	—	—	.25
	1979	—	—	—	Proof	—
	1980	—	—	—	—	.25
	1980	—	—	—	Proof	—

10 CENTS

COPPER-NICKEL

Y#	Date	Mintage	Fine	VF	XF	Unc
44	1966	13.700	—	.20	.30	.50
	1966	.018	—	—	Proof	20.00
	1966(L)	30.000	—	.20	.30	.50
	1966(L)	—	—	—	Proof	20.00
	1967	49.316	—	.20	.30	.35
	1968	57.194	—	.20	.30	.35
	1969	22.146	—	.20	.30	.35
	1969	.013	—	—	Proof	15.00
	1970	22.306	—	.20	.30	.35
	1970	.015	—	—	Proof	20.00
	1971	20.726	—	.20	.30	.35
	1971	.005	—	—	Proof	20.00
	1972	12.502	—	.20	.30	.35
	1972	.006	—	—	Proof	20.00
	1973	15.246	—	.20	.30	.35
	1973	.010	—	—	Proof	20.00
	1974	8.000	—	.20	.30	.35

Y#	Date	Mintage	Fine	VF	XF	Unc
44	1974	.010	—	—	Proof	20.00
	1975	43.500	—	—	—	.35
	1975	.025	—	—	Proof	6.00
	1976	57.060	—	—	—	.35
	1976	.023	—	—	Proof	6.00
	1977	—	—	—	—	.35
	1977	.055	—	—	Proof	5.00
	1978	—	—	—	—	.35
	1978	—	—	—	Proof	—
	1979	—	—	—	—	.35
	1979	—	—	—	Proof	—
	1980	—	—	—	—	.35
	1980	—	—	—	Proof	—

20 CENTS

COPPER-NICKEL

Y#	Date	Mintage	Fine	VF	XF	Unc
45	1966	28.223	—	.45	.60	.75
	1966	.018	—	—	Proof	25.00
	1966(L)	30.000	—	.45	.60	.75
	1966(L)	—	—	—	Proof	25.00
	1967	83.848	—	.30	.35	.40
	1968	40.537	—	.30	.35	.40
	1969	16.502	—	.30	.35	.40
	1969	.013	—	—	Proof	30.00
	1970	23.271	—	.30	.35	.40
	1970	.015	—	—	Proof	30.00
	1971	8.947	—	.30	.35	.40
	1971	.005	—	—	Proof	30.00
	1972	16.643	—	.30	.35	.40
	1972	.006	—	—	Proof	30.00
	1973	23.356	—	.30	.35	.40
	1973	.010	—	—	Proof	30.00
	1974	35,036	—	.30	.35	.40
	1974	.010	—	—	Proof	30.00
	1975	46.400	—	—	—	.40
	1975	.025	—	—	Proof	9.00
	1976	59.700	—	—	—	.40
	1976	.023	—	—	Proof	9.00
	1977	—	—	—	—	.40
	1977	.055	—	—	Proof	8.00
	1978	—	—	—	—	.40
	1978	—	—	—	Proof	—
	1979	—	—	—	—	.40
	1979	—	—	—	Proof	—
	1980	—	—	—	—	.40
	1980	—	—	—	Proof	—

50 CENTS

13.2800 gm., .800 SILVER, .3416 oz ASW

Y#	Date	Mintage	Fine	VF	XF	Unc
46	1966	36.450	BV	BV	BV	12.00
	1966	.018	—	—	Proof	60.00

COPPER-NICKEL

Y#	Date	Mintage	Fine	VF	XF	Unc
47	1969	14.020	—	.70	.80	1.50
	1969	.013	—	—	Proof	45.00
	1971	7.530	—	.70	1.00	1.50
	1971	5,080	—	—	Proof	60.00
	1972	8.030	—	.70	.80	1.00
	1972	5,861	—	—	Proof	60.00
	1973	4.230	—	.70	.80	1.00
	1973	.010	—	—	Proof	50.00
	1974	1.287	—	.70	.80	1.00
	1974	.010	—	—	Proof	50.00
	1975	14.680	—	—	—	1.00
	1975	.013	—	—	Proof	15.00
	1976	27.280	—	—	—	1.00
	1976	—	—	—	Proof	15.00
	1978	—	—	—	—	1.00
	1978	—	—	—	Proof	—
	1979	—	—	—	—	1.00
	1979	—	—	—	Proof	—
	1980	—	—	—	—	1.00
	1980	—	—	—	Proof	—

Cook Commemorative
Obv: Similar to Y#47.

Y#	Date	Mintage	Fine	VF	XF	Unc
48	1970	17.100	—	.80	1.75	4.50
	1970	.015	—	—	Proof	60.00

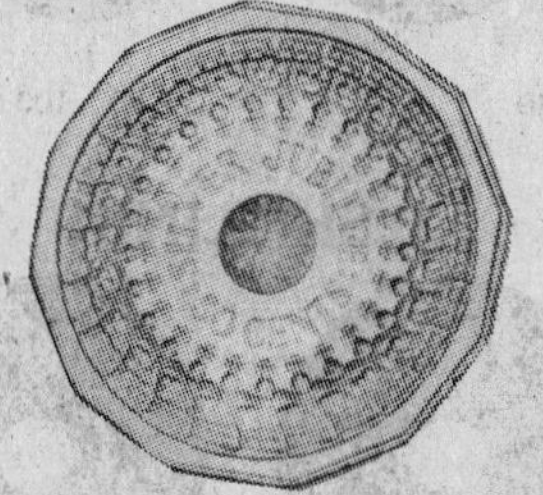

Queen's Silver Jubilee
Obv: Similar to Y#47.

Y#	Date	Mintage	Fine	VF	XF	Unc
49	1977	4.000	—	—	—	2.50
	1977	.055	—	—	Proof	20.00

NCLT ISSUES

PATTERNS

KM#	Date	Mintage	Identification	Mkt.Val.
1	1853	—	1/4 Ounce-Port Philip, Gold	—
1a	1853	—	1/4 Ounce-Port Philip, Gilt Copper (Restrike)	—
2	1853	—	1/2 Ounce-Port Philip, Gold	—
2a	1853	—	1/2 Ounce-Port Philip, Gilt Copper (Restrike)	—
3	1853	—	1 Ounce-Port Philip, Gold	—
3a	1853	—	1 Ounce-Port Philip, Gilt Copper (Restrike)	—
4	1853	—	2 Ounces-Port Philip, Gold	—
4a	1853	—	2 Ounces-Port Philip, Gilt Copper (Restrike)	—
5	1853	—	1/2 Sovereign, Gold T.1	6500.
6	1853	—	Sovereign, Gold T.1	7500.

KM#	Date	Mintage	Identification	Mkt.Val.
7	ND(1855)	—	6 Pence, Copper, Milled Edge	250.00
7a	ND(1855)	—	6 Pence, Copper, Plain Edge	200.00
7b	ND(1855)	—	6 Pence, Pewter, Milled Edge	200.00
7c	ND(1855)	—	6 Pence, Pewter, Plain Edge	200.00
7d	ND(1855)	—	6 Pence, Silver, Milled Edge	375.00
7e	ND(1855)	—	6 Pence, Silver, Plain Edge	300.00
7f	ND(1855)	—	6 Pence, Gold, Milled Edge	1000.
7g	ND(1855)	—	6 Pence, Gold, Plain Edge	750.00

KM#	Date	Mintage	Identification	Mkt.Val.
8	ND(1855)	—	Shilling, Copper, Milled Edge	300.00
8a	ND(1855)	—	Shilling, Copper, Plain Edge	200.00
8b	ND(1855)	—	Shilling, Pewter, Milled Edge	300.00
8c	ND(1855)	—	Shilling, Pewter, Plain Edge	200.00
8d	ND(1855)	—	Shilling, Silver, Milled Edge	375.00
8e	ND(1855)	—	Shilling, Silver, Plain Edge	300.00
8f	ND(1855)	—	Shilling, Gold, Milled Edge	1000.
8g	ND(1855)	—	Shilling, Gold, Plain Edge	750.00
9	1855	—	1/2 Sovereign, Gold, T.2, Milled Edge	6500.
9a	1856	—	1/2 Sovereign, Gold, T.2, Plain Edge	5500.

KM#	Date	Mintage	Identification	Mkt.Val.
10	1855	—	Sovereign, Gold, T.2, Milled Edge	7500.
10a	1856	—	Sovereign, Gold, T.2, Plain Edge	7500.

KM#	Date	Mintage	Identification	Mkt.Val.
11	ND(1860)	—	Shilling, Copper, Milled Edge	650.00
11a	ND(1860)	—	Shilling, Copper, Plain Edge	500.00
11b	ND(1860)	—	Shilling, Silver, Milled Edge	650.00
11c	ND(1860)	—	Shilling, Silver, Plain Edge	500.00
11d	ND(1860)	—	Shilling, Gold	750.00
11e	ND(1860)	—	Shilling, Gold, Plain Edge	750.00
12	1909	—	Florin	—
13	1919	—	Penny, 60 grns., Copper-Nickel, T.3	1250.
13a	1919	—	Penny, 65 grns., Copper-Nickel, T.3	1250.
13b	1919	—	Penny, 70 grns., Copper-Nickel, T.3	1250.
14	1919	—	Penny, 60 grns., Copper-Nickel, T.4	1250.
14	1919	—	Penny, 72 grns., Sterling Silver, T.4	3000.

KM#	Date	Mintage	Identification	Mkt.Val.
15	1919	—	Penny, 60 grns., Copper-Nickel, T.5	1250.
15a	1919	—	Penny, 72 grns., Sterling Silver, T.5	3000.

KM#	Date	Mintage	Identification	Mkt.Val.
16	1919	—	Penny, 60 grns., Copper-Nickel, T.6	1250.
16a	1919	—	Penny, 68 grns., Sterling Silver, T.6	2500.
17	1920	—	1/2 Penny, 28 grns., Copper-Nickel, T.1	3000.

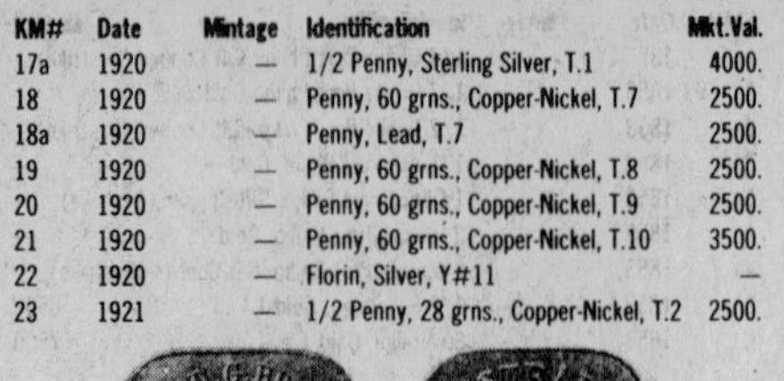

KM#	Date	Mintage	Identification	Mkt.Val.
17a	1920	—	1/2 Penny, Sterling Silver, T.1	4000.
18	1920	—	Penny, 60 grns., Copper-Nickel, T.7	2500.
18a	1920	—	Penny, Lead, T.7	2500.
19	1920	—	Penny, 60 grns., Copper-Nickel, T.8	2500.
20	1920	—	Penny, 60 grns., Copper-Nickel, T.9	2500.
21	1920	—	Penny, 60 grns., Copper-Nickel, T.10	3500.
22	1920	—	Florin, Silver, Y#11	—
23	1921	—	1/2 Penny, 28 grns., Copper-Nickel, T.2	2500.

KM#	Date	Mintage	Identification	Mkt.Val.
24	1921	—	Penny, 60 grns., Copper-Nickel, T.11	1500.
24a	1921	—	Penny, 65 grns., Copper-Nickel, T.11	1500.
24b	1921	—	Penny, 70 grns., Copper-Nickel, T.11	1500.
24c	1921	—	Penny, Nickel, T.11	2000.

KM#	Date	Mintage	Identification	Mkt.Val.
25	1921	—	Penny, 60 grns., Copper-Nickel, T.12	1500.
25a	1921	—	Penny, 65 grns., Copper-Nickel, T.12	1500.
25b	1921	—	Penny, 70 grns., Copper-Nickel, T.12	1500.
26	1937	8 pcs.	Penny, Bronze, Uniface-Rev.	8000.
26a	1937	12 pcs.	Penny, Bronze	16,000.
27	1937	15 pcs.	3 Pence, Silver, Uniface-Rev.	6000.
27a	1937	7 pcs.	3 Pence, Silver	10,000.
28	1937	20 pcs.	Shilling, Silver, Uniface-Rev.	3500.
28a	1937	6 pcs.	Shilling, Silver	6000.
29	1937	15 pcs.	Florin, Silver, Uniface-Rev.	5000.
30	1967	—	50 Cents, Silver, Y#46	—
31	1968	—	50 Cents, Copper-Nickel, Y#47	—

MINT SETS

KM#	Date	Mintage	Identification	Issue Price	Mkt. Val.
S1	1966(6)	—	Y41-46	2.00	25.00
S2	1969(6)	31,176	Y41-45,47	2.50	25.00
S3	1970(6)	40,230	Y41-45,48	2.50	25.00
S4	1971(6)	28,572	Y41-45,47	2.50	25.00
S5	1972(6)	14,355	Y41-45,47	2.75	25.00
S6	1973(6)	—	Y41-45,47	3.40	25.00
S7	1974(6)	—	Y41-45,47	3.60	10.00
S8	1975(6)	45,151	Y41-45,47	3.30	10.00
S9	1976(6)	40,004	Y41-45,47	3.80	10.00
S10	1977(6)	—	Y41-45,49	—	10.00
S11	1978(6)	—	Y41-45,47	—	5.00
S12	1979(6)	—	Y41-45,47	—	5.00
S13	1980(6)	—	Y41-45,47	5.75	—

PROOF SETS
STANDARD METALS

KM#	Date	Mintage	Identification	Issue Price	Mkt. Val.
101	1911L(4)	—	Y9-12	—	5000.
102	1916M(4)	25	Y9-12	—	3500.
103	1925M(3)	—	Y5,6,9	—	2500.
104	1926M(5)	—	Y5,6,9-11	—	1200.
105	1927M(6)	50	Y5,6,9-12	—	1400.
106	1928M(5)	—	Y5,6,9-11	—	1550.
107	1929M(2)	—	Y5,6	—	800.00
108	1930M(2)	—	Y5,6	—	37,500.
109	1933M(2)	—	Y5,6	—	450.00
110	1934M(6)	100	Y5,6,9-12	—	1275.
111	1935M(2)	100	Y5,6	—	360.00
112	1936M(6)	—	Y5,6,9-12	—	1050.
113	1938M(6)	250	Y13,15-19	—	1800.
114	1939M(2)	—	Y14,15	—	700.00
115	1941P(2)	—	Y14,15	—	4500.
116	1945P(2)	—	Y14,15	—	350.00
117	1947P(2)	—	Y14,15	—	350.00
118	1948P(2)	—	Y14,15	—	400.00
119	1950P(2)	—	Y21,22	—	335.00
120	1951L(4)	—	Y21,22,24,25	—	675.00
121	1951P(2)	—	Y21,22	—	335.00
122	1952P(2)	—	Y21,22	—	750.00
123	1953P(2)	—	Y28,29	—	3000.
124	1955M(4)	1,200	Y36-39	—	75.00
125	1955P(2)	301	Y35,36	—	350.00
126	1956M(5)	1,500	Y36-40	—	80.00
127	1957M(4)	1,256	Y37-40	—	70.00
128	1958M(5)	1,506	Y36-40	—	75.00
129	1959M(6)	1,506	Y35-40	—	90.00
130	1960M(4)	1,509	Y37-40	—	60.00
131	1960P(2)	1,030	Y35,36	—	35.00
132	1961M(4)	1,506	Y37-40	—	42.50
133	1961P(2)	1,040	Y35,36	—	35.00
134	1962M(4)	2,016	Y37-40	—	42.50
135	1962P(2)	1,064	Y35,36	—	35.00
136	1963M(4)	5,042	Y37-40	—	42.50
137	1963P(2)	1,064	Y35,36	—	35.00
138	1966C(6)	18,000	Y41-46	15.70	550.00
139	1969C(6)	13,031	Y41-45,47	11.25	350.00
140	1970C(6)	15,339	Y41-45,48	11.30	425.00
141	1971C(6)	10,000	Y41-45,47	11.30	350.00
142	1972C(6)	10,000	Y41-45,47	14.00	350.00
143	1973C(6)	10,090	Y41-45,47	15.50	350.00
144	1974(6)	10,918	Y41-45,47	18.00	350.00
145	1975(6)	34,011	Y41-45,47	17.00	70.00
146	1976(6)	21,200	Y41-45,47	20.20	70.00
147	1977(6)	55,000	Y41-45,49	20.20	70.00
148	1978(6)	—	Y41-45,47	—	60.00
149	1979(6)	—	Y41-45,47	—	60.00
150	1980(6)	—	Y41-45,47	—	50.00

TOKEN ISSUES

POW INTERNMENT CAMP TOKENS

PENNY

BRASS

KM#	Date	Mintage	VF	XF	Unc
1	ND	—	60.00	75.00	95.00

3 PENCE

BRONZE

KM#	Date	Mintage	VF	XF	Unc
2	ND	—	70.00	85.00	125.00

SHILLING

BRONZE

KM#	Date	Mintage	VF	XF	Unc
3	ND	—	77.50	100.00	140.00

2 SHILLINGS

BRONZE

KM#	Date	Mintage	VF	XF	Unc
4	ND	—	100.00	145.00	200.00

5 SHILLINGS

BRONZE

KM#	Date	Mintage	VF	XF	Unc
5	ND	—	900.00	1200.	1500.

KEELING COCOS

The Territory of Cocos (Keeling) Islands, an Australian territory, comprises a group of 27 coral islands located in the Indian Ocean 1,300 miles northwest of Australia. Only Direction and Home Islands are regularly inhabited. The group has an area of 5 sq. mi. and a population of about 618. Calcium, phosphate, and coconut products are exported.

The islands were discovered by Capt. William Keeling of the British East India Co. in 1609. Alexander Hare, an English adventurer, established a settlement on one of the southern islands in 1823, but it lasted less than a year. A permanent settlement was established on Direction Island in 1827 by Hare and Capt. John Clunies Ross, a Scot, for the purpose of storing East Indian spices for reshipment to Europe during periods of shortage. When the experiment in spice futures did not develop satisfactorily, Hare left the islands (1829 or 1830), leaving Ross as sole owner. The coral group became a British protectorate in 1856; was attached to the colony of Ceylon in 1878; and was placed under the administration of the Straits Settlements in 1882. In 1903 the group was annexed to the Straits Settlements and incorporated into the colony of Singapore until Nov. of 1955, when it was placed under the administration of Australia.

RULERS

British

MONETARY SYSTEM

100 Cents = 1 Rupee

TOKEN ISSUES

Plastic 'Ivory' Tokens

5 CENTS

4736
C.5
J.S. CLUNIES ROSS
1913

KM#	Date	Mintage	VG	Fine	VF	XF
1	1913	5,000	90.00	125.00	185.00	250.00

10 CENTS

KM#	Date	Mintage	VG	Fine	VF	XF
2	1913	5,000	80.00	110.00	160.00	225.00

25 CENTS

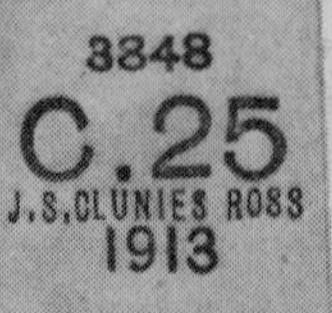

KM#	Date	Mintage	VG	Fine	VF	XF
3	1913	5,000	13.50	23.50	35.00	55.00

50 CENTS

KM#	Date	Mintage	VG	Fine	VF	XF
4	1913	2,000	125.00	165.00	235.00	300.00

RUPEE

KM#	Date	Mintage	VG	Fine	VF	XF
5	1913	2,000	13.50	23.50	35.00	55.00

2 RUPEES

KM#	Date	Mintage	VG	Fine	VF	XF
6	1913	1,000	15.00	25.00	35.00	55.00

5 RUPEES

KM#	Date	Mintage	VG	Fine	VF	XF
7	1913	1,000	15.00	25.00	37.50	60.00

NOTE: The above were all issued with individual serial numbers.

Modern Plastic Tokens

Colors: Cent Values, Aqua - Rupee Values, Red

CENT

KM#	Date	Mintage	Fine	VF	XF	Unc
8	1968	—	—	.10	.20	30.00

5 CENTS

KM#	Date	Mintage	Fine	VF	XF	Unc
9	1968	—	—	.10	.25	40.00

10 CENTS

KM#	Date	Mintage	Fine	VF	XF	Unc
10	1968	—	—	.15	.35	50.00

25 CENTS

KM#	Date	Mintage	Fine	VF	XF	Unc
11	1968	—	—	.30	.60	90.00

50 CENTS

KM#	Date	Mintage	Fine	VF	XF	Unc
12	1968	—	—	.40	.85	1.25

RUPEE

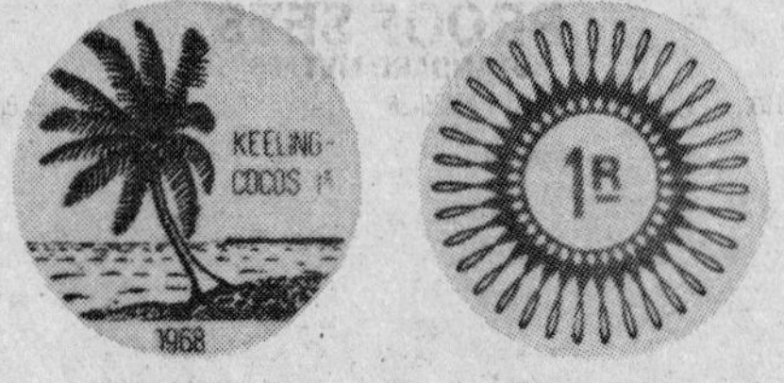

KM#	Date	Mintage	Fine	VF	XF	Unc
13	1968	—	—	.75	1.25	1.85

2 RUPEES

KM#	Date	Mintage	Fine	VF	XF	Unc
14	1968	—	—	1.00	1.75	2.50

5 RUPEES

KM#	Date	Mintage	Fine	VF	XF	Unc
15	1968	—	—	1.50	3.00	4.50

10 RUPEES

KM#	Date	Mintage	Fine	VF	XF	Unc
16	1968	—	—	3.00	4.50	6.50

25 RUPEES

KM#	Date	Mintage	Fine	VF	XF	Unc
17	1968	—	—	7.00	9.00	12.50

REGULAR COINAGE

5 CENTS

BRONZE

KM#	Date	Mintage	VF	XF	Unc
18	1977	—	—	—	.25

10 CENTS

BRONZE

KM#	Date	Mintage	VF	XF	Unc
19	1977	—	—	—	.35

25 CENTS

BRONZE

KM#	Date	Mintage	VF	XF	Unc
20	1977	—	—	—	.50

50 CENTS

BRONZE

KM#	Date	Mintage	VF	XF	Unc
21	1977	—	—	—	1.00

RUPEE

COPPER-NICKEL

KM#	Date	Mintage	VF	XF	Unc
22	1977	—	—	—	2.00

2 RUPEES

COPPER-NICKEL

KM#	Date	Mintage	VF	XF	Unc
23	1977	—	—	—	3.00

5 RUPEES

COPPER-NICKEL

KM#	Date	Mintage	VF	XF	Unc
24	1977	—	—	—	5.00

10 RUPEES

6.5000 gm., .925 SILVER, .1933 oz ASW

KM#	Date	Mintage	VF	XF	Unc
25	1977	6,000	—	—	10.00
	1977	4,000	—	Proof	15.00

25 RUPEES

16.2500 gm., .925 SILVER, .4833 oz ASW

KM#	Date	Mintage	VF	XF	Unc
26	1977	6,000	—	—	15.00
	1977	4,000	—	Proof	20.00

150 RUPEES

.750 GOLD

KM#	Date	Mintage	VF	XF	Unc
27	1977	2,000	—	—	—
	1977	2,000	—	—	—

NOTE: The entire issue of KM#27 was stolen with only 290 pieces being recovered.

8.4800 gm., .916 GOLD, .2497 oz AGW

KM#	Date	Mintage	VF	XF	Unc
27a	1977	2,000	—	—	175.00
	1977	2,000	—	Proof	175.00

NCLT ISSUES

MINT SETS

KM#	Date	Mintage	Identification	Issue Price	Mkt. Val.
S1	1977(7)	—	KM18-24	—	10.00
S2	1977(2)	6,000	KM25,26	—	25.00

PROOF SETS

STANDARD METALS

KM#	Date	Mintage	Identification	Issue Price	Mkt. Val.
101	1977(2)	4,000	KM25-26	28.00	35.00

AUSTRIA

The Republic of Austria, a parliamentary democracy located in mountainous central Europe, has an area of 32,369 sq. mi. (83,835 sq. km.) and a population of 7.6 million. Capital: Vienna. Austria is primarily an industrial country. Machinery, iron and steel, textiles, yarns and timber are exported.

The territories later to be known as Austria were overrun in pre-Roman times by various tribes, including the Celts. Upon the fall of the Roman Empire, the country became a margravate of Charlemagne's Empire. Ottokar, King of Bohemia, gained possession in 1252, only to lose the territory to Rudolf of Hapsburg in 1276. Thereafter, until World War I, the story of Austria was that of the ruling Hapsburgs.

During World War I, the Austro-Hungarian Empire was one of the Central Powers with Germany, Bulgaria and Turkey. At the end of the war, the Empire was dismembered and Austria established as an independent republic. In March, 1938, Austria was incorporated into Hitler's short- lived Greater German Reich. Allied forces of both East and West liberated Austria in April, 1945, and subsequently divided it into four zones of military occupation. On May 15, 1955, the four powers formally recognized Austria as a 'sovereign', independent democratic state'.

A number of coin-issuing entities that were or are a part of Austria continue to be of interest to collectors of world coins.

RULERS

Maria Theresa, 1740-1780
Widow, 1765-1780
Joseph II, joint with his Mother 1765-1780
Alone, 1780-1790
Leopold II, 1790-1792
Franz II (I), 1792-1835
(as Franz II, 1792-1806)
(as Franz I , 1806-1835)
Ferdinand I, 1835-1848
Franz Joseph, 1848-1916
Karl I, 1916-1918

MINTMARKS

A - Vienna
B,K,K-B - Kremnitz
C - Prague
D - Salzburg
E - Carlsburg
F - Hall
G - Nagybanya
GM - Mantua
H - Gunzburg
M - Milan (Lombardy)
N-B-Nagybanya-Hungary
O - Oravicza (Hungary)
S - Schmollnitz (Hungary)
V - Venice (Venetia)

MONETARY SYSTEM

Before 1857
60 Kreuzer = 1 Florin (Gulden)
2 Florin = 1 Species or Convention Thaler

1857-1892
100 Kreuzer = 1 Florin (Gulden)
1-1/2 Florin = 1 Vereinsthaler

1892-1924
100 Heller = 1 Krone
100 Groschen = 1 Schilling
10,000 Kronen = 1 Schilling

HELLER

COPPER

Obv: Crowned arms. Rev: Value and date.

C#	Date	Mintage	VG	Fine	VF
5a	1777A	—	1.75	3.50	5.00
	1778A	—	1.75	3.50	5.00
	1779A	—	1.75	3.50	5.00

1/4 KREUZER

COPPER

Obv: Veiled head right.
Rev: Value and date in cartouche.

C#	Date	Mintage	VG	Fine	VF
10a	1777S	—	3.50	5.00	8.50
	1779	—	3.50	5.00	8.50
	1779K	—	3.50	5.00	8.50
	1780K	—	3.50	5.00	8.50

Rev: Value and date in wreath.

C#	Date	Mintage	VG	Fine	VF
10b	1780W	—	6.00	9.50	12.50

Obv: Head of Joseph right, as joint ruler.
Rev: Value and date.

C#	Date	Mintage	VG	Fine	VF
110	1772W	—	2.50	4.50	7.50
	1777S	—	2.50	4.50	7.50

As sole ruler.

C#	Date	Mintage	VG	Fine	VF
126	1781A	—	3.00	5.00	7.50
	1781B	—	3.00	5.00	7.50
	1781F	—	9.50	13.50	17.50
	1781S	—	3.00	5.00	7.50
	1782A	—	3.00	5.00	7.50
	1782B	—	3.00	5.00	7.50
	1782F	—	3.00	5.00	7.50
	1782S	—	3.00	5.00	7.50
	1783A	—	9.50	13.50	17.50
	1783F	—	3.00	5.00	7.50
	1785F	—	9.50	13.50	17.50
	1790F	—	3.00	5.00	7.50

C#	Date	Mintage	Fine	VF	XF	Unc
147	1800A	—	3.75	7.50	17.50	35.00
	1800B	—	—	—	Rare	—
171	1812A	—	1.75	5.00	8.50	15.00
	1812B	—	2.50	6.25	12.50	20.00
175	1816A	—	1.00	2.00	4.00	10.00
	1816B	—	1.00	2.00	4.00	10.00
	1816E	—	—	—	Rare	—
	1816G	—	—	—	Rare	—
	1816O	—	1.75	4.00	8.00	15.00
	1816S	—	1.00	2.00	4.00	10.00
197	1851A	—	.50	2.25	5.00	7.50
	1851B	—	1.00	3.25	6.50	10.00
	1851G	—	—	6.00	12.00	20.00

1/2 KREUZER

COPPER

Obv: Veiled head right.
Rev: Value and date in cartouche.

C#	Date	Mintage	VG	Fine	VF
13	1772W	—	2.25	4.50	6.50
	1775W	—	2.25	4.50	6.50
	1776S	—	2.25	4.50	6.50
	1777S	—	2.25	4.50	6.50
	1779	—	2.25	4.50	6.50
	1779K	—	2.25	4.50	6.50

Rev: Value and date in wreath.

C#	Date	Mintage	VG	Fine	VF
13a	1780	—	2.00	3.75	6.00

Obv: Head of Joseph right, as joint ruler.
Rev: Value and date.

C#	Date	Mintage	VG	Fine	VF
111	1772W	—	2.25	4.50	6.50
	1773S	—	2.25	4.50	6.50
	1774S	—	2.25	4.50	6.50
	1775S	—	2.25	4.50	6.50
	1776S	—	2.25	4.50	6.50
	1779	—	2.25	4.50	6.50

As sole ruler.

C#	Date	Mintage	VG	Fine	VF
127	1780W	—	9.50	12.50	20.00
	1781A	—	4.50	6.00	10.00
	1781W	—	10.00	15.00	25.00
	1781B	—	4.50	6.00	10.00
	1781G	—	10.00	15.00	25.00
	1781S	—	4.50	6.00	10.00
	1782A	—	4.50	6.00	10.00
	1782B	—	4.50	6.00	10.00
	1782F	—	4.50	6.00	10.00
	1782S	—	4.50	6.00	10.00
	1783A	—	4.50	6.00	10.00
	1783F	—	4.50	6.00	10.00
	1790F	—	4.50	6.00	10.00

C#	Date	Mintage	Fine	VF	XF	Unc
148	1800A	—	1.00	1.75	10.00	20.00
	1800B	—	10.00	20.00	40.00	75.00
	1800C	—	2.50	5.00	25.00	50.00
	1800D	—	10.00	20.00	40.00	75.00
	1800E	—	10.00	20.00	40.00	75.00
	1800F	—	7.50	15.00	30.00	60.00
	1800G	—	—	—	Rare	—
	1800S	—	—	—	Rare	—
172	1812A	—	2.00	6.00	15.00	30.00
	1812B	—	—	—	Rare	—
	1812S	—	2.50	7.50	20.00	40.00
176	1816A	—	1.00	2.00	4.50	10.00
	1816B	—	2.00	6.00	15.00	30.00
	1816E	—	—	—	Rare	—
	1816O	—	2.50	7.50	20.00	40.00
	1816S	—	2.50	7.50	20.00	40.00
198	1851A	—	1.00	3.00	6.25	8.50
	1851B	—	.75	2.00	5.00	9.00
	1851C	—	30.00	60.00	100.00	140.00
	1851G	—	7.50	15.00	30.00	60.00

5/10 KREUZER

COPPER, 1.67 gm.

Obv: Small eagle

Y#	Date	Mintage	Fine	VF	XF	Unc
6	1858A	—	1.75	3.25	6.25	8.50
	1858B	—	2.00	3.75	8.50	10.00
	1858E	—	10.00	20.00	40.00	80.00
	1858M	—	3.75	7.50	15.00	30.00
	1858V	—	5.00	10.00	20.00	40.00
	1859A	—	.75	1.50	4.00	6.00
	1859B	—	3.25	6.50	10.00	20.00
	1859E	—	3.50	7.00	12.50	22.50
	1859M	—	8.00	16.00	23.50	40.00
	1859V	—	15.00	30.00	60.00	100.00
	1860A	—	1.50	2.50	5.00	10.00
	1860E	—	18.50	27.50	55.00	100.00
	1860V	—	6.00	12.50	25.00	50.00
	1861A	—	5.00	10.00	20.00	40.00
	1861B	—	3.75	7.50	15.00	30.00
	1863B	—	8.50	13.50	25.00	50.00
	1864A	—	4.00	8.00	16.50	32.50
	1864B	—	2.50	5.00	10.00	20.00
	1865A	—	3.25	6.50	12.50	25.00
	1865B	—	6.50	13.50	27.50	50.00
	1866A	—	3.00	6.00	12.50	25.00

Reduced weight, 1.6 gm.

Y#	Date	Mintage	Fine	VF	XF	Unc
6a	1877	—	5.00	10.00	15.00	25.00
	1881	4.200	2.00	4.00	6.00	10.00
	1885	2.000	.75	1.75	3.75	7.00

Obv: Large eagle.

Y#	Date	Mintage	Fine	VF	XF	Unc
6b	1885	Inc. Ab.	.75	1.50	3.00	4.50
	1891	2.000	3.25	6.50	8.50	13.50

KREUZER

COPPER

Obv: Veiled head right.
Rev: Value and date in cartouche.

C#	Date	Mintage	VG	Fine	VF
17	1772W	—	3.50	6.00	9.50
	1775W	—	3.50	6.00	9.50
	1775S	—	3.50	6.00	9.50
	1779	—	3.50	6.00	9.50
	1779G	—	3.50	6.00	9.50
	1779H	—	3.50	6.00	9.50
	1780	—	3.50	6.00	9.50
	1780W	—	3.50	6.00	9.50
	1780H	—	3.50	6.00	9.50
	1780K	—	3.50	6.00	9.50
	1780N	—	3.50	6.00	9.50

Rev: Value and date in wreath.

C#	Date	Mintage	VG	Fine	VF
17a	1780S	—	2.50	4.00	6.50

Obv: Head of Joseph right, as joint ruler.
Rev: Value and date in cartouche.

C#	Date	Mintage	VG	Fine	VF
112	1772W	—	4.50	7.50	11.50
	1773S	—	4.50	7.50	11.50
	1774S	—	4.50	7.50	11.50
	1775S	—	4.50	7.50	11.50
	1779	—	4.50	7.50	11.50
	1780W	—	4.50	7.50	11.50
	1780N	—	4.50	7.50	11.50

Rev: Value and date in wreath.

C#	Date	Mintage	VG	Fine	VF
112a	1780S	—	4.50	7.50	11.50

As sole ruler.

C#	Date	Mintage	VG	Fine	VF
128	1780W	—	7.50	12.50	20.00
	1780B	—	3.00	5.00	7.50
	1780G	—	3.00	5.00	7.50
	1781A	—	3.00	5.00	7.50
	1781B	—	3.00	5.00	7.50
	1781C	—	3.00	5.00	7.50
	1781F	—	3.00	5.00	7.50
	1781G	—	7.50	12.50	20.00
	1781H	—	3.00	5.00	7.50
	1781S	—	3.00	5.00	7.50
	1782A	—	3.00	5.00	7.50
	1782B	—	3.00	5.00	7.50
	1782C	—	3.00	5.00	7.50
	1782G	—	3.00	5.00	7.50
	1782H	—	3.00	5.00	7.50
	1782S	—	3.00	5.00	7.50
	1788A	—	7.50	12.50	20.00
	1790A	—	3.00	5.00	7.50
	1790B	—	7.50	12.50	20.00
	1790F	—	3.00	5.00	7.50
	1790G	—	3.00	5.00	7.50
	1790S	—	3.00	5.00	7.50

C#	Date	Mintage	Fine	VF	XF	Unc
149	1800A	—	.50	3.00	9.00	15.00
	1800B	—	.75	3.00	9.00	15.00
	1800C	—	.75	3.00	9.00	15.00
	1800D	—	11.50	22.50	42.50	75.00
	1800E	—	5.50	12.50	22.50	35.00
	1800F	—	5.50	12.50	22.50	35.00
	1800G	—	6.00	13.50	25.00	40.00
	1800S	—	.75	2.25	5.00	10.00

C#	Date	Mintage	Fine	VF	XF	Unc
173	1812A	—	2.00	10.00	20.00	30.00
	1812B	—	1.25	6.00	12.50	18.50
	1812E	—	1.75	2.50	5.00	10.00
	1812G	—	2.25	10.00	20.00	30.00
	1812O	—	4.00	16.50	30.00	45.00
	1812S	—	1.00	5.00	10.00	17.50

C#	Date	Mintage	Fine	VF	XF	Unc
177	1816A	—	.50	1.00	3.00	10.00
	1816B	—	.75	1.50	5.00	15.00
	1816E	—	6.50	15.00	25.00	40.00
	1816G	—	2.50	5.00	10.00	20.00
	1816O	—	2.50	5.00	10.00	20.00
	1816S	—	2.50	5.00	10.00	20.00

C#	Date	Mintage	Fine	VF	XF	Unc
199	1851A	—	.25	.50	1.50	3.00
	1851B	—	.50	1.00	2.50	3.75
	1851C	—	30.00	60.00	90.00	125.00
	1851E	—	4.50	10.00	20.00	30.00
	1851G	—	2.00	4.00	7.50	11.50

Obv: Small eagle

Y#	Date	Mintage	Fine	VF	XF	Unc
7.1	1858A	—	.60	1.25	2.00	3.75
	1858B	—	1.00	2.00	3.00	5.00
	1858E	—	6.25	12.50	25.00	45.00
	1858M	—	4.50	8.50	17.50	35.00
	1858V	—	11.00	21.50	42.50	75.00
	1859A	—	.60	1.25	2.00	3.75
	1859B	—	1.00	2.00	4.00	6.00
	1859E	—	2.50	6.25	10.00	17.50
	1859M	—	3.75	7.50	12.50	18.50
	1859V	—	8.00	16.00	23.50	40.00
	1860A	—	.60	1.25	2.00	4.00
	1860B	—	.60	1.25	2.00	3.75
	1860E	—	10.00	20.00	30.00	45.00
	1860V	—	6.50	13.50	20.00	32.50
	1861A	—	.75	1.75	2.25	5.00
	1861B	—	.60	1.25	2.00	3.25
	1861E	—	6.25	13.50	20.00	32.50
	1862B	—	8.50	17.50	25.00	40.00
	1862E	—	10.00	20.00	30.00	45.00
	1863E	—	17.50	37.50	55.00	85.00
	1873A	—	2.25	4.50	6.50	10.00
	1878	—	.60	1.00	2.00	3.00
	1879	—	.75	1.25	2.75	4.00
	1881	37.900	.40	.75	1.75	2.50

Obv: Large eagle.

Y#	Date	Mintage	Fine	VF	XF	Unc
7.2	1885	29.000	.30	.50	1.50	2.50
	1891	23.800	.30	.50	1.50	3.00

2 KREUZER

COPPER
Revolution 1848-1849

C#	Date	Mintage	Fine	VF	XF	Unc
196	1848A	7.755	3.00	6.00	15.00	30.00

C#	Date	Mintage	Fine	VF	XF	Unc
200	1851A	—	3.00	6.00	11.50	17.50
	1851B	—	3.50	7.00	13.50	22.50
	1851G	—	8.00	16.50	30.00	42.50

3 KREUZER

BILLON
Obv: Veiled head of Maria Theresa right.
Rev: Crowned imperial eagle.

C#	Date	Mintage	VG	Fine	VF
26	1765	—	3.50	6.00	10.00
	1766 C-K	—	3.50	6.00	10.00
	1767 C-K	—	3.50	6.00	10.00
	1768 C-K	—	3.50	6.00	10.00
	1769 C-K	—	3.50	6.00	10.00
	1770 C-K	—	3.50	6.00	10.00
	1771 C-K	—	3.50	6.00	10.00
	1772 C-K	—	3.50	6.00	10.00
	1773 C-K	—	3.50	6.00	10.00
	1774 C-K	—	3.50	6.00	10.00
	1775 C-A	—	3.50	6.00	10.00
	1776 C-A	—	3.50	6.00	10.00
	1777 C-A	—	3.50	6.00	10.00
	1778 C-A	—	3.50	6.00	10.00
	1779 C-A	—	3.50	6.00	10.00
	1780 C-A	—	3.50	6.00	10.00

Obv: Bust of Joseph right, as joint ruler.
Rev: Crowned imperial eagle; value on breast.

C#	Date	Mintage	VG	Fine	VF
113	1766B EVM-D	—	3.50	6.00	10.00
	1767A C-K	—	5.00	8.50	12.50
	1767B EVM-D	—	3.50	6.00	10.00
	1768A C-K	—	5.00	8.50	12.50
	1768B EVM-D	—	3.50	6.00	10.00
	1769B EVM-D	—	3.50	6.00	10.00
	1770A C-K	—	5.00	8.50	12.50
	1771A C-K	—	5.00	8.50	12.50
	1771B EVM-D	—	3.50	6.00	10.00
	1773A C-K	—	5.00	8.50	12.50
	1773B EVM-D	—	3.50	6.00	10.00
	1773E H-G	—	5.00	8.50	12.50
	1774A C-A	—	5.00	8.50	12.50
	1774E H-G	—	5.00	8.50	12.50
	1775A C-A	—	5.00	8.50	12.50
	1775C VS-K	—	5.00	8.50	12.50
	1776A C-A	—	5.00	8.50	12.50
	1776C VS-K	—	5.00	8.50	12.50
	1777A C-K	—	5.00	8.50	12.50
	1777A C-A	—	5.00	8.50	12.50
	1777C VS-K	—	5.00	8.50	12.50
	1777E H-G	—	5.00	8.50	12.50

C#	Date	Mintage	VG	Fine	VF
	1778A C-A	—	5.00	8.50	12.50
	1778C VS-K	—	5.00	8.50	12.50
	1779A C-A	—	5.00	8.50	12.50
	1779C VS-K	—	5.00	8.50	12.50
	1780A C-A	—	5.00	8.50	12.50

Obv: Bust of Joseph right.

C#	Date	Mintage	VG	Fine	VF
129a	1780A	—	7.50	11.50	15.00
	1781A	—	7.50	11.50	15.00
	1781B	—	7.50	11.50	15.00
	1781E	—	7.50	11.50	15.00
	1781F	—	7.50	11.50	15.00
	1782B	—	7.50	11.50	15.00
	1783B	—	7.50	11.50	15.00
	1783F	—	7.50	11.50	15.00
	1784B	—	7.50	11.50	15.00

Obv: Head of Joseph right.

C#	Date	Mintage	VG	Fine	VF
129	1780A	—	7.50	11.50	15.00
	1781A	—	7.50	11.50	15.00
	1782A	—	7.50	11.50	15.00
	1783A	—	7.50	11.50	15.00
	1783E	—	7.50	11.50	15.00
	1783G	—	7.50	11.50	15.00
	1784A	—	7.50	11.50	15.00
	1785E	—	7.50	11.50	15.00
	1786A	—	7.50	11.50	15.00
	1786B	—	7.50	11.50	15.00
	1786E	—	7.50	11.50	15.00
	1787A	—	7.50	11.50	15.00
	1787B	—	7.50	11.50	15.00
	1787G	—	7.50	11.50	15.00
	1788A	—	7.50	11.50	15.00
	1788B	—	7.50	11.50	15.00
	1789A	—	7.50	11.50	15.00
	1790A	—	7.50	11.50	15.00
	1790B	—	7.50	11.50	15.00

.346 SILVER
Obv: Head of Leopold right.

C#	Date	Mintage	Fine	VF	XF	Unc
138	1790A	—	10.00	25.00	55.00	110.00
	1791A	—	12.50	30.00	62.50	125.00
	1791B	—	10.00	25.00	55.00	110.00
	1792A	—	12.50	30.00	62.50	125.00
	1792B	—	12.50	30.00	62.50	125.00
	1792G	—	15.00	35.00	75.00	150.00

COPPER, 17 gm.

C#	Date	Mintage	Fine	VF	XF	Unc
150	1799A	—	7.50	15.00	30.00	50.00
	1799B	—	7.50	17.50	30.00	50.00
	1799C	—	8.50	20.00	35.00	60.00

Reduced weight, 9 gm.

C#	Date	Mintage	Fine	VF	XF	Unc
150a	1800A	—	1.50	5.00	10.00	20.00
	1800B	—	2.50	7.50	15.00	30.00
	1800C	—	2.50	7.50	15.00	30.00
	1800D	—	—	—	Rare	—
	1800E	—	3.50	10.00	20.00	40.00
	1800F	—	1.50	5.00	10.00	20.00
	1800G	—	2.50	7.50	15.00	30.00
	1800S	—	1.50	4.25	8.50	17.50
	1801E	—	8.50	20.00	35.00	60.00
	1801F	—	8.50	20.00	35.00	60.00
	1803F	—	5.00	15.00	30.00	60.00

.346 SILVER
Obv: Head right, Rev: Imperial eagle

C#	Date	Mintage	Fine	VF	XF	Unc
152	1792B	—	12.00	30.00	50.00	80.00
	1792G	—	—	—	Rare	—
	1793B	—	12.00	30.00	50.00	80.00
	1793F	—	15.00	37.50	60.00	100.00
	1793G	—	—	—	Rare	—
	1794A	—	12.00	30.00	50.00	80.00

C#	Date	Mintage	Fine	VF	XF	Unc
152	1794B	—	17.50	42.50	70.00	115.00
	1795B	—	18.50	45.00	75.00	125.00
	1796A	—	—	—	Rare	—
	1796B	—	12.00	30.00	50.00	80.00
	1796E	—	20.00	50.00	80.00	135.00
	1796F	—	15.00	36.50	60.00	100.00
	1796G	—	—	—	Rare	—
	1797A	—	—	—	Rare	—
	1798A	—	15.00	36.50	60.00	100.00
	1799A	—	15.00	36.50	60.00	100.00
	1801E	—	17.50	42.50	70.00	110.00

COPPER

C#	Date	Mintage	Fine	VF	XF	Unc
174	1812A	—	10.00	25.00	50.00	75.00
	1812B	—	1.25	3.75	7.50	15.00
	1812E	—	6.50	12.50	25.00	50.00
	1812G	—	5.00	10.00	20.00	40.00
	1812O	—	5.00	10.00	20.00	40.00
	1812S	—	1.25	2.50	5.00	15.00

.346 SILVER

C#	Date	Mintage	Fine	VF	XF	Unc
180	1814A	—	—	—	Rare	—
	1815A	—	6.50	12.50	25.00	50.00
	1815B	—	8.50	20.00	40.00	80.00
	1815V	—	6.50	12.50	25.00	50.00
180a	1817A	—	—	—	Rare	—
	1818B	—	10.00	22.50	45.00	80.00
	1818V	—	—	—	Rare	—
	1819A	—	20.00	40.00	60.00	100.00
	1820A	—	7.50	15.00	30.00	60.00
	1820B	—	6.50	12.50	25.00	50.00
	1820G	—	—	—	Rare	—
	1821A	—	5.50	11.50	22.50	45.00
	1821B	—	7.50	15.00	30.00	60.00
	1821E	—	30.00	60.00	100.00	140.00
	1821G	—	22.50	45.00	75.00	115.00
	1822A	—	17.50	35.00	60.00	90.00
	1823A	—	30.00	60.00	100.00	140.00
	1823B	—	—	—	Rare	—
	1824A	—	—	—	Rare	—
	1824G	—	30.00	60.00	100.00	140.00
180b	1825A	—	20.00	40.00	65.00	100.00
	1826A	—	5.00	10.00	20.00	27.50
	1826B	—	5.00	10.00	20.00	40.00
	1826E	—	10.00	20.00	45.00	90.00
	1827A	—	—	—	Rare	—
	1827B	—	—	—	Rare	—
	1828A	—	5.00	10.00	20.00	40.00
	1828B	—	4.00	8.50	17.50	35.00
	1828E	—	20.00	40.00	65.00	100.00
	1828G	—	—	—	Rare	—
	1829A	—	4.00	8.50	17.50	35.00
	1829B	—	10.00	20.00	45.00	90.00
	1829E	—	15.00	30.00	60.00	120.00
	1829G	—	—	—	Rare	—
	1830A	—	5.50	11.50	22.50	45.00
	1830B	—	—	—	Rare	—
	1830E	—	—	—	Rare	—

Struck in a collar.

C#	Date	Mintage	Fine	VF	XF	Unc
180d	1831A	—	25.00	60.00	80.00	125.00

Obv: Larger head

C#	Date	Mintage	Fine	VF	XF	Unc
180c	1832A	—	5.00	10.00	20.00	40.00
	1833A	—	5.00	10.00	20.00	37.50
	1833C	—	8.50	17.50	35.00	65.00
	1834A	—	12.50	25.00	45.00	80.00
	1834C	—	—	—	Rare	—
	1835A	—	12.50	25.00	45.00	80.00

Obv: Head of Ferdinand right.
Rev: Eagle, value on chest.

C#	Date	Mintage	Fine	VF	XF	Unc
188	1835A	—	10.00	20.00	40.00	75.00
	1835E	—	—	—	—	—
	1836A	—	12.50	25.00	50.00	100.00
	1836E	—	17.50	37.50	75.00	150.00
188a	1837A	—	3.00	6.50	12.50	25.00
	1837C	—	—	—	—	—
	1837E	—	—	—	—	—
	1838A	—	5.00	10.00	22.50	45.00
	1838B	—	10.00	17.50	35.00	65.00
	1838C	—	12.50	21.50	42.50	75.00
	1838E	—	15.00	25.00	50.00	90.00
	1839A	—	3.00	6.50	12.50	25.00
	1839C	—	15.00	25.00	50.00	90.00
	1839E	—	9.00	15.00	30.00	55.00
	1840A	—	3.50	6.50	12.50	20.00
	1840E	—	15.00	25.00	50.00	90.00
	1841A	—	9.00	22.50	45.00	85.00
	1841E	—	—	—	—	—
	1842A	—	13.50	22.50	45.00	85.00
	1842E	—	13.50	22.50	45.00	85.00
	1843A	—	8.50	17.50	35.00	65.00
	1843E	—	8.50	17.50	35.00	65.00
	1844A	—	7.50	12.50	25.00	50.00
	1844E	—	13.50	22.50	45.00	85.00
	1845A	—	6.50	11.50	22.50	45.00
	1845E	—	13.50	22.50	45.00	85.00
	1846A	—	3.50	5.50	8.50	15.50
	1846E	—	13.50	22.50	45.00	85.00
	1847A	—	2.75	5.00	8.50	15.50
	1847C	—	6.00	12.50	25.00	45.00
	1847E	—	10.00	16.50	32.50	60.00
	1848A	—	2.25	4.50	8.50	17.50
	1848E	—	15.00	30.00	60.00	110.00
188b	1848GM	—	200.00	400.00	800.00	1250.

NOTE: The above issue was struck in Mantua by the Austrian garrison under General Josef Radetzky during the siege of March 18-22, 1848 by Italian rebels.

COPPER

C#	Date	Mintage	Fine	VF	XF	Unc
201	1851A	—	10.00	21.50	35.00	55.00
	1851B	—	13.50	28.50	40.00	60.00
	1851G	—	13.50	28.50	40.00	60.00

4 KREUZER

COPPER

Y#	Date	Mintage	Fine	VF	XF	Unc
8	1860A	—	4.50	10.00	17.50	26.50
	1860B	—	3.75	8.50	15.00	21.50
	1860E	—	13.00	27.50	50.00	72.50
	1861A	—	3.75	7.50	13.50	20.00
	1861B	—	3.75	8.50	16.50	22.50
	1861E	—	14.00	28.50	45.00	70.00
	1864B	6.666	4.00	8.50	15.00	22.50

5 KREUZER

BILLON

Obv: Veiled head of Maria Theresa right in wreath.
Rev: Crowned imperial eagle over value.

C#	Date	Mintage	VG	Fine	VF
28a	1772 C-K	—	7.50	12.50	16.50
	1778 C-A	—	7.50	12.50	16.50
	1779 C-A	—	7.50	12.50	16.50

Obv: Head of Joseph right in wreath.

C#	Date	Mintage	VG	Fine	VF
130	1783A	—	7.50	12.50	16.50
	1788A	—	7.50	12.50	16.50
	1790A	—	7.50	12.50	16.50

.438 SILVER

C#	Date	Mintage	Fine	VF	XF	Unc
181	1815A	—	10.00	25.00	37.50	50.00
181a	1817A	—	30.00	60.00	80.00	135.00
	1818A	—	7.50	15.00	30.00	60.00
	1818B	—	7.50	15.00	30.00	60.00
	1819A	—	—	—	Rare	—
	1820A	—	6.50	12.50	25.00	50.00
	1820B	—	5.50	11.50	22.50	45.00
	1820G	—	—	—	Rare	—
	1820V	—	12.50	25.00	50.00	100.00
	1821A	—	10.00	20.00	40.00	75.00
	1821B	—	7.50	15.00	30.00	60.00
	1821E	—	17.50	35.00	70.00	140.00
	1821G	—	15.00	30.00	60.00	120.00
	1822E	—	—	—	Rare	—
	1822G	—	—	—	Rare	—
	1823A	—	20.00	40.00	75.00	150.00
	1824A	—	—	—	Rare	—
	1824G	—	—	—	Rare	—

Obv: Bust with short hair

C#	Date	Mintage	Fine	VF	XF	Unc
181b	1825A	—	—	—	Rare	—
	1826A	—	50.00	100.00	165.00	225.00
	1826E	—	—	—	Rare	—
	1827A	—	—	—	Rare	—
	1828A	—	50.00	100.00	165.00	225.00

Obv: Larger head

C#	Date	Mintage	Fine	VF	XF	Unc
181c	1832A	—	20.00	32.50	65.00	130.00
	1833A	—	13.50	27.50	55.00	100.00
	1834A	—	15.00	27.50	57.50	115.00
	1835A	—	12.50	25.00	50.00	100.00

Obv: Head of Ferdinand right.
Rev: Eagle, value below.

C#	Date	Mintage	Fine	VF	XF	Unc
189	1835A	—	15.00	30.00	60.00	115.00
	1836A	—	10.00	20.00	42.50	75.00
189a	1837A	—	5.00	10.00	20.00	35.00
	1838A	—	5.00	10.00	20.00	35.00
	1839A	—	5.00	11.50	22.50	40.00
	1839C	—	5.00	11.50	22.50	40.00
	1840A	—	8.50	18.50	37.50	70.00
	1840C	—	3.75	7.50	15.00	25.00
	1842A	—	8.50	18.50	37.50	70.00
	1844A	—	8.50	17.50	35.00	60.00
	1846A	—	3.75	7.50	15.00	25.00
	1847A	—	3.50	7.00	13.50	22.50
	1848A	—	4.00	7.50	15.00	25.00

1.3333 gm., .375 SILVER, .0161 oz ASW

Y#	Date	Mintage	Fine	VF	XF	Unc
9	1858A	—	1.50	3.00	7.50	15.00
	1858B	—	55.00	75.00	100.00	130.00
	1858V	—	55.00	75.00	100.00	130.00
	1859A	—	1.25	2.00	4.00	7.50
	1859M	—	10.00	17.50	30.00	40.00
	1859V	—	8.50	16.50	27.50	37.50
	1860V	—	55.00	75.00	100.00	130.00
	1863A	—	10.00	17.50	30.00	40.00
	1864A	1.013	3.00	4.50	6.50	10.00

Obv: Head with heavier whiskers.

Y#	Date	Mintage	Fine	VF	XF	Unc
9a	1867A	1.923	75.00	175.00	250.00	375.00

6 KREUZER

.250 SILVER

Obv: Value above branches, Rev: Imperial eagle

C#	Date	Mintage	Fine	VF	XF	Unc
153	1795A	—	4.50	10.00	20.00	40.00
	1795B	—	6.50	12.50	25.00	50.00
	1795C	—	—	—	Rare	—
	1795E	—	45.00	90.00	150.00	250.00
	1795F	—	6.50	12.50	25.00	50.00
	1795G	—	8.50	17.50	35.00	70.00

COPPER

C#	Date	Mintage	Fine	VF	XF	Unc
151	1800A	—	1.75	3.50	12.50	25.00
	1800B	—	1.50	3.00	7.50	15.00
	1800C	—	2.00	4.00	8.00	17.50
	1800D	—	15.00	30.00	50.00	80.00
	1800E	—	2.50	5.00	11.50	22.50
	1800F	—	2.50	5.00	11.50	22.50
	1800G	—	—	—	Rare	—
	1800S	—	1.50	3.00	10.00	17.50
	1803F	—	—	—	—	—

.428 SILVER

Revolution 1848-1849

C#	Date	Mintage	Fine	VF	XF	Unc
202	1848A	—	2.50	5.00	10.00	17.50
	1848C	—	3.75	7.50	15.00	27.50

C#	Date	Mintage	Fine	VF	XF	Unc
202a	1849A	—	1.25	2.50	5.00	7.50
	1849B	—	10.00	20.00	32.50	50.00
	1849C	—	7.50	10.00	20.00	35.00

7 KREUZER

BILLON

Obv: Veiled head of Maria Theresa right.
Rev: Crowned imperial eagle over value.

C#	Date	Mintage	VG	Fine	VF
32	1768 C-K	—	15.00	22.50	35.00
	1769 C-K	—	15.00	22.50	35.00
	1770 C-K	—	15.00	22.50	35.00
	1771 C-K	—	15.00	22.50	35.00
	1772 C-K	—	15.00	22.50	35.00
	1773 C-K	—	15.00	22.50	35.00
	1774 C-A	—	15.00	22.50	35.00
	1775 C-A	—	15.00	22.50	35.00
	1776 C-A	—	15.00	22.50	35.00
	1777 C-A	—	15.00	22.50	35.00

Obv: Bust of Joseph right, as joint ruler.

C#	Date	Mintage	VG	Fine	VF
114	1768A C-K	—	10.00	15.00	25.00
	1769A C-K	—	10.00	15.00	25.00
	1770A C-K	—	10.00	15.00	25.00
	1771A C-K	—	10.00	15.00	25.00
114	1776	—	10.00	15.00	25.00

SILVER

C#	Date	Mintage	VF	XF	Unc
154	1802A	—	10.00	17.50	35.00
	1802B	—	10.00	17.50	35.00
	1802C	—	10.00	17.50	35.00
	1802E	—	25.00	35.00	60.00
	1802F	—	30.00	55.00	100.00
	1802G	—	20.00	35.00	65.00

10 KREUZER

SILVER

Obv: Veiled head of Maria Theresa right in wreath.
Rev: Crowned imperial eagle over value.

C#	Date	Mintage	Fine	VF	XF
33a	1768 C-K	—	5.00	8.50	12.50
	1769 C-K	—	5.00	8.50	12.50
	1769 IC-SK	—	5.00	8.50	12.50
	1770 C-K	—	5.00	8.50	12.50
	1771 C-K	—	5.00	8.50	12.50
	1772 C-K	—	5.00	8.50	12.50
	1773 C-K	—	5.00	8.50	12.50
	1773 IC-SK	—	5.00	8.50	12.50
	1774 C-A	—	5.00	8.50	12.50
	1775	—	5.00	8.50	12.50
	1776 C-A	—	5.00	8.50	12.50
	1777 C-A	—	5.00	8.50	12.50
	1778 C-A	—	5.00	8.50	12.50
	1779 C-A	—	5.00	8.50	12.50
	1780 C-A	—	5.00	8.50	12.50

Obv: Bust of Joseph right in wreath, as joint ruler.

C#	Date	Mintage	Fine	VF	XF
115	1765B EVM D	—	7.50	12.50	20.00
	1766B EVM D	—	7.50	12.50	20.00
	1767A C-K	—	7.50	12.50	20.00
	1767B EVM-D	—	7.50	12.50	20.00
	1768A C-K	—	7.50	12.50	20.00
	1768B EVM-D	—	7.50	12.50	20.00
	1769A C-K	—	7.50	12.50	20.00
	1769B EVM-D	—	7.50	12.50	20.00
	1770A C-K	—	7.50	12.50	20.00
	1771A C-K	—	7.50	12.50	20.00
	1772A C-K	—	7.50	12.50	20.00
	1773A C-K	—	7.50	12.50	20.00
	1778A C-A	—	7.50	12.50	20.00
	1779A C-A	—	7.50	12.50	20.00
	1779G IB-IV	—	7.50	12.50	20.00

Similar to above, sole ruler.

C#	Date	Mintage	Fine	VF	XF
131a	1781C	—	7.50	12.50	20.00
	1782C	—	7.50	12.50	20.00
	1782E	—	7.50	12.50	20.00
	1783E	—	7.50	12.50	20.00
	1783G	—	7.50	12.50	20.00
	1783H	—	7.50	12.50	20.00
	1784H	—	7.50	12.50	20.00
	1785F	—	7.50	12.50	20.00
	1785H	—	7.50	12.50	20.00
	1787F	—	7.50	12.50	20.00
	1787H	—	7.50	12.50	20.00
	1788H	—	7.50	12.50	20.00

Obv: Head of Joseph right in wreath.
Rev: Crowned imperial eagle over date.

C#	Date	Mintage	Fine	VF	XF
131	1782A	—	7.50	12.50	20.00
	1783A	—	7.50	12.50	20.00
	1784A	—	7.50	12.50	20.00
	1785A	—	7.50	12.50	20.00
	1786A	—	7.50	12.50	20.00
	1787A	—	7.50	12.50	20.00
	1787B	—	7.50	12.50	20.00
	1787E	—	7.50	12.50	20.00
	1788A	—	7.50	12.50	20.00
	1788B	—	7.50	12.50	20.00
	1788E	—	7.50	12.50	20.00
	1789A	—	7.50	12.50	20.00
	1789B	—	7.50	12.50	20.00
	1789E	—	7.50	12.50	20.00
	1790A	—	7.50	12.50	20.00
	1790B	—	7.50	12.50	20.00
	1790E	—	7.50	12.50	20.00

.500 SILVER

Obv: Head of Leopold right in wreath.
Rev: Crowned imperial eagle over value.

C#	Date	Mintage	Fine	VF	XF	Unc
139	1790A	—	30.00	62.50	125.00	225.00
	1791A	—	27.50	55.00	110.00	200.00
	1791B	—	30.00	62.50	125.00	225.00
	1791H	—	—	—	Rare	—
	1792A	—	30.00	62.50	125.00	225.00
	1792B	—	22.50	45.00	85.00	150.00
	1792E	—	—	—	Rare	—

Obv: Head right. Rev: Imperial eagle.

C#	Date	Mintage	VF	XF	Unc
155	1792A	—	35.00	75.00	130.00
	1792B	—	35.00	75.00	130.00
	1792E	—	—	Rare	—
	1792F	—	—	Rare	—
	1793A	—	30.00	60.00	115.00
	1794B	—	30.00	60.00	115.00
	1794E	—	35.00	75.00	130.00
	1795B	—	—	Rare	—
	1795C	—	—	Rare	—
	1795E	—	35.00	75.00	130.00
	1795G	—	—	Rare	—
	1796B	—	35.00	75.00	130.00
	1796E	—	30.00	60.00	115.00
	1797E	—	35.00	75.00	115.00

Rev. leg. ends: D. LO. SAL. WIRC.

C#	Date	Mintage	VF	XF	Unc
182	1809A	—	45.00	80.00	150.00
	1810A	—	35.00	75.00	125.00

Rev. leg. ends: LO: WI: ET IN FR: D:

C#	Date	Mintage	VF	XF	Unc
182a	1814A	—	—	Rare	—
	1815A	—	10.00	20.00	37.00
	1815B	—	12.00	25.00	50.00
	1815C	—	20.00	40.00	75.00

Rev. leg. ends: GAL. LOD. IL. REX. A. A.

C#	Date	Mintage	VF	XF	Unc
182b	1817A	—	40.00	80.00	150.00
	1818A	—	—	Rare	—
	1818B	—	—	Rare	—
	1818G	—	—	Rare	—
	1818V	—	35.00	70.00	125.00
	1819A	—	—	Rare	—
	1820A	—	—	Rare	—
	1820B	—	—	Rare	—
	1820G	—	—	Rare	—
	1821B	—	—	Rare	—
	1821G	—	45.00	90.00	150.00
	1821V	—	—	Rare	—
	1822G	—	—	Rare	—
	1823A	—	35.00	70.00	125.00
	1823G	—	35.00	70.00	125.00
	1824A	—	30.00	60.00	115.00
	1824G	—	—	Rare	—

Obv: Older head of Francis right.
Rev: Eagle, value below.

C#	Date	Mintage	VF	XF	Unc
182c	1825A	—	—	Rare	—
	1826A	—	30.00	60.00	115.00
	1827A	—	45.00	90.00	165.00
	1828A	—	45.00	90.00	165.00
	1828E	—	45.00	90.00	165.00
	1829A	—	—	Rare	—
	1829E	—	40.00	80.00	150.00
	1830A	—	40.00	80.00	150.00
	1830B	—	45.00	90.00	165.00
	1830E	—	45.00	90.00	165.00

Obv: Larger head

C#	Date	Mintage	VF	XF	Unc
182d	1832A	—	25.00	45.00	85.00
	1833A	—	30.00	55.00	100.00
	1834A	—	25.00	45.00	85.00
	1835A	—	30.00	55.00	100.00

Obv: Head of Ferdinand right.
Rev: Eagle, value below.

C#	Date	Mintage	Fine	VF	XF	Unc
190	1835A	—	15.00	30.00	60.00	130.00
	1835E	—	—	—	—	—
	1836A	—	10.00	20.00	40.00	85.00
	1836E	—	—	—	—	—

C#	Date	Mintage	Fine	VF	XF	Unc
190a	1837A	—	5.00	8.50	18.50	35.00
	1837C	—	8.50	17.50	35.00	65.00
	1837E	—	10.00	20.00	40.00	75.00
	1838A	—	12.50	25.00	50.00	90.00

C#	Date	Mintage	Fine	VF	XF	Unc
190a	1838C	—	5.00	10.00	21.50	42.50
	1839A	—	12.50	25.00	50.00	100.00
	1839C	—	4.00	8.50	17.50	30.00
	1839E	—	10.00	20.00	40.00	75.00
	1840A	—	8.00	16.50	32.50	60.00
	1840E	—	10.00	21.50	42.50	80.00
	1841E	—	9.00	17.50	35.00	65.00
	1842A	—	3.25	8.50	17.50	33.50
	1842E	—	9.00	18.50	37.50	70.00
	1843A	—	6.50	13.50	27.50	50.00
	1843E	—	9.00	18.50	37.50	70.00
	1844A	—	7.50	15.00	27.50	50.00
	1844E	—	9.00	18.50	37.50	70.00
	1845A	—	8.00	16.50	32.50	60.00
	1845E	—	8.50	17.50	35.00	65.00
	1846A	—	6.50	12.50	25.00	45.00
	1846E	—	9.00	18.50	37.50	70.00
	1847A	—	6.50	12.50	25.00	45.00
	1847E	—	9.00	18.50	35.00	70.00
	1848A	—	12.50	25.00	50.00	90.00
	1848E	—	13.50	28.50	55.00	110.00

.900 SILVER
Obv: Young head of Franz Josef right.
Rev: Eagle, value.

C#	Date	Mintage	Fine	VF	XF	Unc
206	1852A	—	10.00	20.00	40.00	60.00
	1853A	—	7.50	15.00	30.00	50.00
	1853B	—	25.00	50.00	100.00	150.00
	1854A	—	10.00	20.00	40.00	60.00
	1855A	—	7.50	15.00	37.50	42.50

2.0000 gm., .500 SILVER, .0322 oz ASW

Y#	Date	Mintage	Fine	VF	XF	Unc
10	1858A	—	6.00	14.00	25.00	37.50
	1858B	1,354	—	—	Rare	—
	1858V	—	35.00	75.00	110.00	150.00
	1859M	—	5.00	11.00	22.50	32.50
	1859V	—	8.00	16.50	35.00	55.00
	1860V	—	7.50	18.00	30.00	45.00
	1861V	—	15.00	30.00	57.50	90.00
	1862V	—	32.50	65.00	100.00	130.00
	1863A	—	7.50	15.00	30.00	45.00
	1864A	1.050	10.00	21.50	42.50	65.00
	1864V	.036	35.00	70.00	100.00	135.00
	1865V	1.198	10.00	20.00	40.00	60.00

Obv: Head of Franz Josef right with heavier whiskers.

Y#	Date	Mintage	Fine	VF	XF	Unc
10a	1867A	—	110.00	200.00	300.00	450.00

1.6667 gm., .400 SILVER, .0214 oz ASW

Y#	Date	Mintage	Fine	VF	XF	Unc
11	1868	12.000	1.00	2.50	4.25	7.00
	1869	30.000	1.00	2.00	4.00	6.00
	1870	35.000	1.00	2.00	3.00	5.00
	1871	2.000	10.00	22.50	47.50	65.00
	1872	70.000	1.00	1.50	2.00	4.50

12 KREUTZER

SILVER

C#	Date	Mintage	VF	XF	Unc
156	1795A	—	10.00	17.50	35.00
	1795B	—	10.00	17.50	35.00
	1795C	—	10.00	20.00	40.00
	1795E	—	12.00	25.00	50.00
	1795F	—	10.00	20.00	40.00
	1795G	—	12.00	25.00	50.00

15 KREUTZER

COPPER

C#	Date	Mintage	VF	XF	Unc
178	1807A	—	5.00	10.00	20.00
	1807B	—	5.00	10.00	20.00
	1087B (error for 1807B)	—	—	100.00	150.00
	1807E	—	12.50	25.00	50.00
	1807G	—	12.50	25.00	50.00
	1807S	—	5.00	10.00	20.00

20 KREUTZER

SILVER
Obv: Veiled head of Maria Theresa right in wreath.
Rev: Crowned imperial eagle over value.

C#	Date	Mintage	Fine	VF	XF
39b	1765	—	5.00	8.50	12.50
	1766 IC-SK	—	5.00	8.50	12.50
	1767 IC-SK	—	5.00	8.50	12.50
	1768 IC-SK	—	5.00	8.50	12.50
	1769 IC-SK	—	5.00	8.50	12.50
	1771 IC-SK	—	5.00	8.50	12.50
	1772 IC-SK	—	5.00	8.50	12.50
	1774 IC-SK	—	5.00	8.50	12.50
	1774 IC-FA	—	5.00	8.50	12.50
	1775 IC-FA	—	5.00	8.50	12.50
	1776 IC-FA	—	5.00	8.50	12.50
	1777 IC-FA	—	5.00	8.50	12.50
	1779 IC-FA	—	5.00	8.50	12.50
	1780 IC-FA	—	5.00	8.50	12.50

As Joint Ruler

C#	Date	Mintage	Fine	VF	XF
116	1765A	—	5.00	8.50	12.50
	1766A IC-SK	—	5.00	8.50	12.50
	1767A IC-SK	—	5.00	8.50	12.50
	1767B EVM-D	—	5.00	8.50	12.50
	1767G IB-FL	—	5.00	8.50	12.50
	1768A IC-SK	—	5.00	8.50	12.50
	1768A C-K	—	5.00	8.50	12.50
	1768B EVM-D	—	5.00	8.50	12.50
	1768G IB-FL	—	5.00	8.50	12.50
	1769A IC-SK	—	5.00	8.50	12.50
	1769B EVM-D	—	5.00	8.50	12.50
	1769G IB-FL	—	5.00	8.50	12.50
	1770A IC-SK	—	5.00	8.50	12.50
	1770B EVM-D	—	5.00	8.50	12.50
	1770G IB-FL	—	5.00	8.50	12.50
	1771A IC-SK	—	5.00	8.50	12.50
	1771B EVM-D	—	5.00	8.50	12.50
	1771G IB-FL	—	5.00	8.50	12.50
	1772A IC-SK	—	5.00	8.50	12.50
	1772B EVM-D	—	5.00	8.50	12.50
	1772G IB-FL	—	5.00	8.50	12.50
	1772G IB-IV	—	5.00	8.50	12.50
	1773B EVM-D	—	5.00	8.50	12.50
	1773G IB-IV	—	5.00	8.50	12.50
	1773G B-V	—	5.00	8.50	12.50
	1774A IC-SK	—	5.00	8.50	12.50
116	1774A IC-FA	—	5.00	8.50	12.50
	1774B EVM-D	—	5.00	8.50	12.50
	1774B SK-PD	—	5.00	8.50	12.50
	1774G IB-IV	—	5.00	8.50	12.50
	1774G B-V	—	5.00	8.50	12.50
	1775A IC-FA	—	5.00	8.50	12.50
	1775B SK-PD	—	5.00	8.50	12.50
	1775G IB-IV	—	5.00	8.50	12.50
	1776A IC-FA	—	5.00	8.50	12.50
	1776B SK-PD	—	5.00	8.50	12.50
	1776G IB-IV	—	5.00	8.50	12.50
	1777A IC-FA	—	5.00	8.50	12.50
	1777B SK-PD	—	5.00	8.50	12.50
	1777G IB-IV	—	5.00	8.50	12.50
	1778A IC-FA	—	5.00	8.50	12.50
	1778B SK-PD	—	5.00	8.50	12.50
	1778G IB-IV	—	5.00	8.50	12.50
	1779A IC-FA	—	5.00	8.50	12.50
	1779B SK-PD	—	5.00	8.50	12.50
	1779G IB-IV	—	5.00	8.50	12.50
	1779G B-V	—	5.00	8.50	12.50
	1780A IC-FA	—	5.00	8.50	12.50
	1780B SK-PD	—	5.00	8.50	12.50
	1780G IB-IV	—	5.00	8.50	12.50

As Sole Ruler
Obv: Armored bust of Joseph right.

C#	Date	Mintage	Fine	VF	XF
132a	1780A	—	8.50	12.50	20.00
	1781A	—	8.50	12.50	20.00
	1781B	—	8.50	12.50	20.00
	1781C	—	8.50	12.50	20.00
	1781E	—	8.50	12.50	20.00
	1781F	—	8.50	12.50	20.00
	1781G	—	8.50	12.50	20.00
	1782B	—	8.50	12.50	20.00
	1782C	—	8.50	12.50	20.00
	1782E	—	8.50	12.50	20.00
	1782F	—	8.50	12.50	20.00
	1782G	—	8.50	12.50	20.00
	1782H	—	8.50	12.50	20.00
	1783B	—	8.50	12.50	20.00
	1783F	—	8.50	12.50	20.00
	1784F	—	8.50	12.50	20.00
	1785F	—	8.50	12.50	20.00
	1786F	—	8.50	12.50	20.00
	1786H	—	8.50	12.50	20.00
	1787F	—	8.50	12.50	20.00
	1787H	—	8.50	12.50	20.00

Obv: Head of Joseph right.

C#	Date	Mintage	Fine	VF	XF
132	1781A	—	7.50	11.50	15.00
	1782A	—	7.50	11.50	15.00
	1782C	—	7.50	11.50	15.00
	1782E	—	7.50	11.50	15.00
	1783A	—	7.50	11.50	15.00
	1783B	—	7.50	11.50	15.00
	1783C	—	7.50	11.50	15.00
	1783E	—	7.50	11.50	15.00
	1783G	—	7.50	11.50	15.00
	1784A	—	7.50	11.50	15.00
	1784B	—	7.50	11.50	15.00
	1784C	—	7.50	11.50	15.00
	1784E	—	7.50	11.50	15.00
	1784G	—	7.50	11.50	15.00
	1785A	—	7.50	11.50	15.00
	1785B	—	7.50	11.50	15.00
	1785E	—	7.50	11.50	15.00
	1785G	—	7.50	11.50	15.00
	1786A	—	7.50	11.50	15.00
	1786B	—	7.50	11.50	15.00
	1786E	—	7.50	11.50	15.00
	1786G	—	7.50	11.50	15.00
	1787A	—	7.50	11.50	15.00
	1787B	—	7.50	11.50	15.00
	1787E	—	7.50	11.50	15.00
	1787F	—	7.50	11.50	15.00
	1787G	—	7.50	11.50	15.00
	1787H	—	7.50	11.50	15.00
	1788A	—	7.50	11.50	15.00
	1788B	—	7.50	11.50	15.00
	1788E	—	7.50	11.50	15.00
	1788F	—	7.50	11.50	15.00
	1788G	—	7.50	11.50	15.00
	1788H	—	7.50	11.50	15.00
	1789A	—	7.50	11.50	15.00

C#	Date	Mintage	Fine	VF	XF
	1789E	—	7.50	11.50	15.00
	1789F	—	7.50	11.50	15.00
	1789G	—	7.50	11.50	15.00
	1789H	—	7.50	11.50	15.00
	1790A	—	7.50	11.50	15.00
	1790E	—	7.50	11.50	15.00
	1790F	—	7.50	11.50	15.00
	1790G	—	7.50	11.50	15.00

.583 SILVER

Obv: Head of Leopold right in wreath.

C#	Date	Mintage	Fine	VF	XF	Unc
140	1790A	—	17.50	35.00	62.50	125.00
	1791A	—	18.50	37.50	75.00	130.00
	1791B	—	10.00	20.00	40.00	80.00
	1791E	—	15.00	30.00	60.00	100.00
	1791F	—	16.50	32.50	60.00	100.00
	1791G	—	15.00	30.00	55.00	100.00
	1791H	—	15.00	30.00	55.00	100.00
	1792A	—	16.50	32.50	60.00	100.00
	1792B	—	13.50	27.50	50.00	90.00
	1792E	—	18.50	37.50	70.00	125.00
	1792F	—	15.00	30.00	55.00	100.00
	1792G	—	13.50	27.50	50.00	90.00
	1792H	—	16.50	32.50	60.00	100.00

C#	Date	Mintage	VF	XF	Unc
157	1792A	—	8.00	15.00	45.00
	1792B	—	7.00	13.00	40.00
	1792E	—	8.00	15.00	45.00
	1792H	—	6.00	10.00	35.00
	1793A	—	4.50	9.00	30.00
	1793B	—	4.50	9.00	30.00
	1793E	—	—	Rare	—
	1793F	—	6.00	10.00	35.00
	1793G	—	10.00	20.00	45.00
	1793H	—	6.00	10.00	35.00
	1794B	—	4.50	9.00	30.00
	1794E	—	10.00	20.00	45.00
	1794F	—	4.50	9.00	30.00
	1794G	—	10.00	20.00	45.00
	1794H	—	10.00	20.00	45.00
	1795B	—	4.50	9.00	30.00
	1795C	—	10.00	20.00	50.00
	1795E	—	10.00	20.00	45.00
	1795F	—	10.00	20.00	45.00
	1795G	—	6.00	12.00	40.00
	1795H	—	—	Rare	—
	1796B	—	4.00	8.00	30.00
	1796C	—	8.00	15.00	45.00
	1796E	—	10.00	20.00	45.00
	1796F	—	5.00	10.00	30.00
	1796G	—	10.00	20.00	45.00
	1796H	—	10.00	20.00	45.00
	1797B	—	10.00	20.00	45.00
	1797C	—	10.00	20.00	45.00
	1797E	—	8.00	15.00	40.00
	1797F	—	10.00	20.00	45.00
	1797G	—	8.00	15.00	40.00
	1797H	—	5.00	10.00	35.00
	1802A	—	8.00	15.00	40.00
	1802B	—	8.00	15.00	40.00
	1802C	—	5.00	10.00	30.00
	1802E	—	10.00	20.00	50.00
	1802G	—	10.00	20.00	45.00
	1802H	—	5.00	10.00	30.00
	1803A	—	6.00	15.00	40.00
	1803B	—	5.00	10.00	30.00
	1803C	—	5.00	10.00	30.00
	1803E	—	8.00	15.00	40.00
	1803F	—	5.00	10.00	30.00
	1803G	—	5.00	10.00	30.00
	1803H	—	10.00	20.00	45.00
	1804A	—	10.00	20.00	45.00
	1804B	—	5.00	10.00	30.00
	1804C	—	8.00	15.00	40.00
	1804E	—	8.00	15.00	40.00
	1804F	—	7.50	15.00	30.00
	1804G	—	7.50	15.00	30.00

Rev. leg. ends: D. LOTH. VEN. SAL.

C#	Date	Mintage	VF	XF	Unc
166	1804A	—	—	Rare	—
	1804H	—	—	Rare	—
	1805A	—	5.00	10.00	35.00
	1805B	—	6.00	11.00	35.00
	1805C	—	7.00	14.00	40.00
166	1805E	—	5.00	10.00	30.00
	1805G	—	7.00	14.00	40.00
	1806A	—	7.50	10.00	25.00
	1806B	—	7.50	10.00	25.00
	1806C	—	15.00	10.00	35.00
	1806D	—	6.00	12.00	40.00
	1806E	—	—	Rare	—
	1806G	—	6.50	13.00	40.00

Rev. leg. ends: D. LO. SAL. WIRC

C#	Date	Mintage	VF	XF	Unc
183	1806A	—	5.00	10.00	35.00
	1806B	—	8.00	12.00	40.00
	1806C	—	—	Rare	—
	1807A	—	5.00	10.00	35.00
	1807B	—	10.00	20.00	45.00
	1807C	—	10.00	20.00	45.00
	1807D	—	9.00	18.00	40.00
	1808A	—	6.00	12.00	25.00
	1808B	—	6.00	12.00	25.00
	1808D	—	6.00	12.00	25.00
	1808E	—	7.50	15.00	30.00
	1808G	—	9.00	18.00	40.00
	1809A	—	9.00	18.00	40.00
	1809B	—	9.00	18.00	40.00
	1809C	—	6.00	13.00	30.00
	1809D	—	7.50	15.00	30.00
	1809E	—	9.00	18.00	40.00
	1809G	—	7.50	15.00	30.00
	1810A	—	6.00	12.00	25.00
	1810E	—	—	Rare	—
	1810G	—	10.00	20.00	45.00
	1814C	—	20.00	30.00	75.00

Rev. leg. ends: LO WI: ET IN FR D

C#	Date	Mintage	VF	XF	Unc
183a	1811A	—	7.00	14.00	30.00
	1811B	—	6.00	13.00	30.00
	1811E	—	7.00	14.00	30.00
	1812A	—	6.00	13.00	30.00
	1812B	—	8.00	16.00	35.00
	1812E	—	10.00	20.00	45.00
	1812G	—	8.00	16.00	35.00
	1813A	—	6.00	12.00	25.00
	1813B	—	6.00	13.00	30.00
	1813E	—	6.00	13.00	30.00
	1813G	—	—	Rare	—
	1814A	—	6.00	12.00	25.00
	1814B	—	6.00	13.00	28.00
	1814C	—	7.50	15.00	30.00
	1814E	—	7.50	15.00	30.00
	1814G	—	7.50	15.00	30.00
	1815	—	15.00	30.00	50.00
	1815A	—	7.50	10.00	25.00
	1815B	—	7.50	10.00	25.00
	1815C	—	7.50	10.00	25.00
	1815E	—	8.00	17.00	35.00
	1815G	—	7.50	10.00	25.00
	1816B	—	5.00	10.00	25.00
	1816C	—	Reported, Not Confirmed		

Rev. leg. ends: GAL. LOD. UL. REX. A. A.

C#	Date	Mintage	VF	XF	Unc
183b	1817A	—	7.50	10.00	25.00
	1818A	—	6.00	12.00	26.00
	1818B	—	6.00	13.00	28.00
	1818C	—	7.50	15.00	30.00
	1818E	—	8.00	17.00	32.00
183b	1818G	—	8.00	17.00	32.00
	1818V	—	6.00	13.00	28.00
	1818V (Error FNANCISCUS)				
		—	30.00	60.00	125.00
	1819A	—	4.00	8.00	20.00
	1819C	—	—	Rare	—
	1819E	—	7.50	15.00	30.00
	1819M	—	7.50	10.00	25.00
	1820A	—	6.00	13.00	28.00
	1820B	—	11.00	22.00	40.00
	1820C	—	7.50	15.00	30.00
	1820E	—	6.00	12.00	25.00
	1820G	—	5.00	11.00	25.00
	1821A	—	6.00	13.00	28.00
	1821B	—	6.00	13.00	28.00
	1821C	—	8.00	16.00	30.00
	1821E	—	6.00	13.00	28.00
	1821G	—	—	Rare	—
	1822A	—	7.50	15.00	30.00
	1822B	—	8.00	16.00	32.00
	1822C	—	7.50	15.00	30.00
	1822E	—	7.50	15.00	30.00
	1822G	—	8.00	16.00	32.00
	1823A	—	6.00	13.00	28.00
	1823B	—	8.00	16.00	32.00
	1823C	—	—	Rare	—
	1823E	—	8.00	16.00	32.00
	1823G	—	6.00	13.00	28.00
	1824A	—	6.00	13.00	28.00
	1824B	—	—	Rare	—
	1824E	—	6.00	12.00	25.00
	1824G	—	7.50	15.00	30.00

Obv: Small bust with short hair

C#	Date	Mintage	VF	XF	Unc
183c	1825A	—	7.50	10.00	25.00
	1825B	—	9.00	18.00	35.00
	1825E	—	7.50	15.00	30.00
	1826A	—	4.50	9.00	25.00
	1826B	—	6.00	12.00	25.00
	1826E	—	7.50	10.00	25.00
	1826G	—	—	Rare	—
	1827A	—	7.50	10.00	25.00
	1827B	—	5.00	10.00	25.00
	1827C	—	5.00	10.00	25.00
	1827E	—	7.50	15.00	30.00
	1827G	—	7.50	15.00	30.00
	1828A	—	7.50	10.00	25.00
	1828B	—	9.00	18.00	32.00
	1828E	—	7.50	15.00	30.00

Obv: Large bust with short hair

C#	Date	Mintage	VF	XF	Unc
183e	1829A	—	7.50	10.00	25.00
	1829B	—	7.50	10.00	25.00
	1829E	—	5.00	11.00	26.00
	1830A	—	7.50	10.00	25.00
	1830B	—	7.50	10.00	25.00
	1830C	—	7.50	10.00	25.00
	1830E	—	7.50	10.00	25.00

Obv: Ribbons on wreath forward across neck

C#	Date	Mintage	VF	XF	Unc
183d	1831A	—	65.00	90.00	140.00

Obv: Ribbons on wreath behind neck

C#	Date	Mintage	VF	XF	Unc
183f	1831A	—	7.50	10.00	25.00
	1831C	—	13.00	20.00	35.00

C#	Date	Mintage	VF	XF	Unc
183f	1831M	—	8.00	15.00	30.00
	1831V	—	8.00	15.00	30.00
	1832A	—	7.50	10.00	25.00
	1832B	—	—	Rare	—
	1832C	—	8.00	15.00	30.00
	1832M	—	11.00	16.00	32.00
	1833A	—	8.00	15.00	30.00
	1833B	—	9.00	18.00	34.00
	1833C	—	8.00	16.00	30.00
	1833E	—	10.00	20.00	37.00
	1834A	—	8.00	16.00	32.00
	1834B	—	9.00	18.00	34.00
	1834C	—	8.00	16.00	32.00
	1834E	—	8.00	16.00	32.00
	1835A	—	8.00	16.00	32.00
	1835B	—	8.00	16.00	32.00
	1835C	—	6.00	12.00	25.00
	1835E	—	6.00	12.00	25.00

Obv: Head of Ferdinand right.
Rev: Eagle, value below.

C#	Date	Mintage	Fine	VF	XF	Unc
191	1835A	—	15.00	30.00	55.00	100.00
	1835C	—	15.00	30.00	55.00	100.00
	1835E	—	25.00	50.00	100.00	200.00
	1836A	—	8.50	17.50	35.00	65.00
	1836E	—	25.00	50.00	100.00	200.00

C#	Date	Mintage	Fine	VF	XF	Unc
191a	1837A	—	5.00	10.00	20.00	35.00
	1837B	—	6.50	12.50	25.00	45.00
	1837C	—	6.50	12.50	25.00	45.00
	1837E	—	7.00	13.50	27.50	50.00
	1837M	—	17.50	36.50	72.50	140.00
	1838A	—	5.00	10.00	20.00	35.00
	1838B	—	4.00	8.00	16.00	28.50
	1838C	—	8.00	16.00	30.00	55.00
	1838E	—	5.50	11.00	20.00	36.50
	1838M	—	18.50	37.50	75.00	145.00
	1839A	—	4.25	9.00	18.50	37.50
	1839B	—	5.50	11.50	22.50	45.00
	1839C	—	6.50	13.50	27.50	55.00
	1839E	—	5.50	11.50	22.50	45.00
	1840A	—	3.75	5.00	8.00	16.50
	1840C	—	4.25	6.50	12.50	25.00
	1840E	—	7.50	15.00	30.00	55.00
	1840M	—	15.00	30.00	60.00	100.00
	1841A	—	3.75	5.00	8.00	15.00
	1841C	—	4.25	8.50	17.50	37.50
	1841E	—	5.50	10.00	21.50	45.00
	1842A	—	3.75	5.00	10.00	20.00
	1842C	—	4.50	8.00	16.00	30.50
	1842E	—	7.50	15.00	30.00	55.00
	1842M	—	10.00	20.00	40.00	65.00
	1843A	—	7.50	15.00	30.00	55.00
	1843C	—	4.25	8.75	17.50	30.00
	1843E	—	6.50	12.50	25.00	45.00
	1843M	—	6.50	12.50	25.00	45.00
	1844A	—	3.75	5.00	8.00	15.00
	1844C	—	4.25	8.50	16.50	30.00
	1844E	—	8.50	17.50	35.00	65.00
	1844M	—	6.00	12.00	24.00	42.50
	1845A	—	3.75	5.00	8.50	15.00
	1845C	—	3.75	5.00	10.00	20.00
	1845E	—	8.50	17.50	35.00	65.00
	1845M	—	6.50	12.50	25.00	45.00
	1846A	—	3.75	5.00	10.00	20.00
	1846C	—	3.75	5.00	10.00	20.00
	1846E	—	12.50	25.00	50.00	100.00
	1846M	—	6.50	12.50	25.00	50.00
	1847A	—	3.75	5.00	8.50	17.50
	1847C	—	3.75	5.00	8.50	17.50
	1847E	—	6.50	13.50	27.50	50.00
	1847M	—	8.50	17.50	35.00	65.00
	1848A	—	3.75	5.00	9.00	18.50
	1848C	—	3.75	5.00	8.00	15.00
	1848E	—	7.50	15.00	32.50	60.00

Obv: Head of Ferdinand right.

C#	Date	Mintage	VF	XF	Unc
191b	1848GM	7,799	140.00	250.00	350.00

NOTE: The above issue was struck in Mantua by the Austrian garrison under General Josef Radetzky during the siege of March 18-22, 1848 by Italian rebels.

.584 SILVER
Obv: Young head of Franz Josef left.

C#	Date	Mintage	Fine	VF	XF	Unc
203	1852A	—	35.00	60.00	120.00	150.00
	1852C	—	65.00	115.00	225.00	400.00

.900 SILVER

C#	Date	Mintage	Fine	VF	XF	Unc
207	1852A	—	5.00	10.00	15.00	30.00
	1852B	—	5.00	10.00	17.50	35.00
	1852C	—	70.00	125.00	240.00	400.00
	1852E	—	32.50	55.00	110.00	165.00
	1853A	—	5.00	8.50	15.00	35.00
	1853C	—	8.50	13.50	25.00	50.00
	1853E	—	25.00	50.00	75.00	100.00
	1854A	—	4.50	7.50	13.50	27.50
	1854B	—	5.00	10.00	20.00	40.00
	1854C	—	7.50	15.00	25.00	45.00
	1854E	—	16.50	30.00	50.00	80.00
	1855A	—	7.50	13.50	21.50	30.00
	1855B	—	5.00	10.00	15.00	22.50
	1855C	—	11.50	22.50	36.50	50.00
	1855E	—	8.50	16.50	25.00	37.50
	1856A	—	27.50	45.00	70.00	120.00
	1856B	—	5.00	10.00	16.50	22.50
	1856C	—	35.00	75.00	100.00	135.00
	1856E	—	8.50	16.50	32.50	65.00

2.6667 gm., .500 SILVER, .0429 oz ASW

Y#	Date	Mintage	Fine	VF	XF	Unc
12	1868	30.000	1.50	3.00	5.00	8.50
	1869	30.000	1.75	3.50	5.00	10.00
	1870	30.000	1.50	3.00	5.00	8.00
	1872	—	16.50	32.50	65.00	120.00

24 KREUTZER

SILVER

C#	Date	Mintage	VF	XF	Unc
158	1800A	—	150.00	225.00	325.00
	1800B	—	150.00	225.00	325.00
	1800C	—	150.00	225.00	325.00

NOTE: Most of the above coins were overstruck as 2 Lire coins for the occupation of Venice in 1801.

1/4 FLORIN

5.3450 gm., .520 SILVER, .0893 oz ASW

Y#	Date	Mintage	Fine	VF	XF	Unc
13	1857A	—	7.50	15.00	25.00	40.00
	1857B	—	12.00	22.50	36.50	60.00
	1857E	—	32.50	65.00	100.00	125.00
	1857M	—	30.00	60.00	90.00	120.00
	1857V	—	25.00	50.00	75.00	110.00
	1858A	—	5.00	8.50	12.50	20.00
	1858B	—	7.50	15.00	30.00	55.00
	1858E	—	7.50	15.00	25.00	40.00
	1858M	—	27.50	50.00	90.00	150.00
	1858V	—	15.00	32.50	65.00	100.00

Y#	Date	Mintage	Fine	VF	XF	Unc
13	1859M	—	50.00	85.00	135.00	200.00

Y#	Date	Mintage	Fine	VF	XF	Unc
14	1859A	—	2.75	6.00	10.00	15.00
	1859B	—	2.75	4.00	10.00	16.50
	1859E	—	4.25	8.50	15.00	20.00
	1859M	—	25.00	50.00	75.00	100.00
	1859V	—	11.50	21.50	42.50	60.00
	1860A	—	10.00	15.00	30.00	50.00
	1860B	—	2.75	4.50	7.50	12.50
	1860E	—	45.00	70.00	112.50	150.00
	1860V	—	20.00	30.00	50.00	75.00
	1861A	—	7.50	15.00	22.50	30.00
	1861B	—	15.00	37.50	55.00	75.00
	1861E	—	90.00	185.00	275.00	400.00
	1861V	—	12.50	25.00	50.00	72.50
	1862A	—	7.50	15.00	22.50	30.00
	1862B	—	11.50	22.50	45.00	80.00
	1862E	—	12.50	20.00	40.00	65.00
	1862V	—	11.00	21.50	42.50	70.00
	1863A	—	15.00	30.00	60.00	100.00
	1863V	—	20.00	40.00	80.00	125.00
	1864A	—	5.00	10.00	20.00	30.00
	1864V	—	20.00	35.00	50.00	65.00
	1865A	—	35.00	70.00	120.00	165.00

Obv: Head of Franz Josef right with heavier side whiskers.
Rev: Eagle, value below.

Y#	Date	Mintage	Fine	VF	XF	Unc
14a	1866A	—	75.00	150.00	300.00	600.00
	1866V	—	100.00	200.00	425.00	750.00

Rev. leg: HUNGAR, BOHEN. GAL. - LOD. ILL. REX. A.A.

Y#	Date	Mintage	Fine	VF	XF	Unc
14b	1867A	—	85.00	150.00	275.00	575.00
	1868A	—	35.00	70.00	125.00	165.00
	1869A	—	45.00	90.00	135.00	225.00
	1870A	7,956	100.00	200.00	400.00	550.00
	1871A	—	75.00	150.00	250.00	450.00
14c	1872	.100	50.00	100.00	180.00	300.00
	1873	.050	50.00	110.00	185.00	325.00
	1874	.100	75.00	150.00	250.00	425.00
	1875	.020	110.00	225.00	325.00	550.00

30 KREUTZER

SILVER
Obv: Veiled head right in diamond.
Rev: Crowned imperial eagle in diamond.

C#	Date	Mintage	Fine	VF	XF
41a	1766 IC-SK	—	35.00	50.00	75.00
	1767 IC-SK	—	35.00	50.00	75.00
	1768 IC-SK	—	35.00	50.00	75.00
	1769 IC-SK	—	35.00	50.00	75.00
	1770 IC-SK	—	35.00	50.00	75.00
	1773 IC-SK	—	35.00	50.00	75.00

Obv: Bust of Joseph, as joint ruler.

C#	Date	Mintage	Fine	VF	XF
117	1767A IC-SK	—	40.00	55.00	85.00
	1768A IC-SK	—	40.00	55.00	85.00
	1768A	—	40.00	55.00	85.00
	1769A IC-SK	—	40.00	55.00	85.00

COPPER

C#	Date	Mintage	VF	XF	Unc
179	1807A	—	7.50	15.00	30.00
	1807B	—	7.50	15.00	30.00
	1807B (Error inverted C in ERBLAENDISCH)				
		—	40.00	60.00	120.00
	1807E	—	7.50	15.00	40.00
	1807G	—	10.00	20.00	40.00
	1807S	—	7.50	15.00	30.00

GULDEN

.900 SILVER

C#	Date	Mintage	Fine	VF	XF	Unc
210	1854A	—	35.00	50.00	75.00	125.00

FLORIN

12.3400 gm., .900 SILVER, .3571 oz ASW

Y#	Date	Mintage	Fine	VF	XF	Unc
15	1857A	—	12.50	20.00	42.50	60.00
	1857B	—	85.00	150.00	285.00	475.00
	1857E	—	75.00	175.00	300.00	500.00
	1857V	—	135.00	250.00	500.00	750.00
	1858A	—	BV	BV	12.50	20.00
	1858B	—	BV	12.50	18.50	30.00
	1858E	—	12.50	25.00	37.50	50.00
	1858M	—	12.50	25.00	37.50	50.00
	1858V	—	15.00	35.00	70.00	115.00
	1859A	—	BV	BV	12.50	18.00
	1859B	—	BV	12.50	20.00	35.00
	1859E	—	12.50	17.50	35.00	60.00
	1859M	—	12.50	27.50	50.00	75.00
	1859V	—	10.00	25.00	45.00	70.00
	1860A	—	BV	BV	12.50	18.00
	1860B	—	12.50	25.00	37.50	50.00
	1860E	—	12.50	17.50	32.50	45.00
	1860V	—	17.50	35.00	70.00	110.00
	1861A	—	BV	BV	12.50	16.00
	1861B	—	100.00	200.00	350.00	600.00
	1861E	—	17.50	35.00	70.00	135.00
	1861V	—	17.50	35.00	70.00	135.00
	1862A	—	BV	BV	12.50	20.00
	1862B	—	15.00	30.00	62.50	100.00
	1862E	—	32.50	65.00	110.00	185.00
	1862V	—	30.00	60.00	100.00	165.00
	1863A	—	BV	12.50	17.50	35.00
	1863B	—	16.50	32.50	65.00	110.00
	1863E	—	16.50	35.00	60.00	100.00
	1863V	—	20.00	40.00	60.00	90.00
	1864A	—	16.50	27.50	45.00	75.00
	1864B	—	55.00	110.00	200.00	325.00
	1864E	—	55.00	80.00	150.00	240.00
	1864V	—	60.00	120.00	200.00	325.00
	1865A	—	15.00	25.00	42.50	70.00
	1865B	—	16.50	32.50	65.00	100.00
	1865E	—	17.50	35.00	70.00	110.00
15	1865V	—	100.00	200.00	325.00	550.00

Obv: Head of Franz Josef right with heavier side whiskers. Rev: Eagle, value below.

Y#	Date	Mintage	Fine	VF	XF	Unc
15a	1866A	—	20.00	37.50	62.50	100.00
	1866B	—	27.50	55.00	85.00	125.00
	1866E	—	75.00	150.00	250.00	425.00
	1866V	—	60.00	110.00	175.00	300.00

Rev. leg: HUNGAR, BOHEN. GAL. - LOD. ILL. REX. A.A.

Y#	Date	Mintage	Fine	VF	XF	Unc
15b	1867A	—	17.50	32.50	55.00	85.00
	1867B	—	14.00	27.50	45.00	75.00
	1867E	—	150.00	250.00	400.00	550.00
	1868A	—	27.50	55.00	110.00	140.00
	1869A	—	14.00	27.50	55.00	90.00
	1870A	—	12.50	22.50	45.00	75.00
	1871A	—	12.00	20.00	32.50	50.00
	1872A	—	100.00	210.00	350.00	600.00

Y#	Date	Mintage	Fine	VF	XF	Unc
15c	1872	3.000	12.50	16.50	32.50	50.00
	1873	8.000	BV	12.50	20.00	40.00
	1874	2.000	25.00	50.00	80.00	135.00
	1875	5.000	BV	BV	17.50	35.00
	1876	7.000	BV	BV	12.50	25.00
	1877	14.000	BV	BV	12.50	20.00
	1878	20.000	BV	BV	12.50	20.00
	1879	35.000	BV	BV	12.50	20.00
	1880	6.000	BV	BV	12.50	25.00
	1881	6.000	BV	BV	12.50	22.50
	1882	2.000	12.50	17.50	25.00	45.00
	1883	7.000	BV	BV	12.50	20.00
	1884	4.000	BV	BV	12.50	20.00
	1885	3.000	BV	12.50	17.50	25.00
	1886	7.000	BV	BV	12.50	20.00
	1887	6.000	BV	BV	12.50	20.00
	1888	6.000	BV	12.50	15.00	25.00
	1889	5.000	BV	12.50	15.00	25.00
	1890	4.000	BV	12.50	15.00	25.00
	1891	4.000	BV	12.50	15.00	25.00
	1892	3.000	12.50	17.50	35.00	60.00

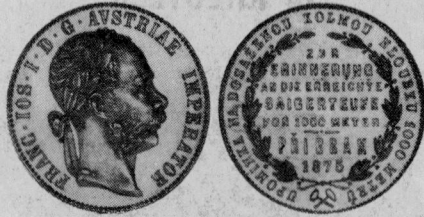

Pribram Mine

Y#	Date	Mintage	Fine	VF	XF	Unc
17	1875	*.010	75.00	165.00	240.00	350.00

1/2 THALER

(Convention)

SILVER

Obv: Veiled head right.
Rev: Crowned imperial eagle.

C#	Date	Mintage	Fine	VF	XF
45	1766 IC-SK	—	40.00	55.00	85.00
	1767 IC-SK	—	40.00	55.00	85.00
	1768 IC-SK	—	40.00	55.00	85.00
	1769 IC-SK	—	40.00	55.00	85.00
	1770 IC-SK	—	40.00	55.00	85.00
	1771 IC-SK	—	40.00	55.00	85.00
	1772 IC-SK	—	40.00	55.00	85.00
	1773 IC-SK	—	40.00	55.00	85.00
	1774 IC-FA	—	40.00	55.00	85.00
	1775 IC-FA	—	40.00	55.00	85.00
	1776 IC-FA	—	40.00	55.00	85.00
	1777 IC-FA	—	40.00	55.00	85.00
	1778 IC-FA	—	40.00	55.00	85.00
	1779 IC-FA	—	40.00	55.00	85.00
	1780 IC-FA	—	40.00	55.00	85.00

Obv: Bust of Joseph right, as joint ruler.

C#	Date	Mintage	Fine	VF	XF
118	1768A IC-SK	—	100.00	150.00	225.00

Obv: Laureated head of Joseph right, sole ruler.

C#	Date	Mintage	Fine	VF	XF
133	1781A	—	125.00	175.00	250.00
	1782A	—	125.00	175.00	250.00
	1784A	—	125.00	175.00	250.00
133	1785A	—	125.00	175.00	250.00
	1786A	—	125.00	175.00	250.00
	1787A	—	125.00	175.00	250.00
	1788A	—	125.00	175.00	250.00
	1789A	—	125.00	175.00	250.00
	1790A	—	125.00	175.00	250.00

.833 SILVER

Obv: Laureated head of Leopold right.

C#	Date	Mintage	Fine	VF	XF	Unc
141	1790A	—	225.00	550.00	900.00	1500.
	1792A	—	180.00	450.00	750.00	1250.

Obv. leg: FRANCISCVS II. D. G. R. IMP., etc.

C#	Date	Mintage	VF	XF	Unc
159	1792A	—	Reported, Not Confirmed		
	1793A	—	135.00	225.00	300.00
	1794A	—	135.00	225.00	300.00
	1795A	—	70.00	125.00	175.00
	1796A	—	—	Rare	—
	1797A	—	135.00	225.00	300.00
	1798A	—	70.00	125.00	175.00
	1799A	—	60.00	112.00	150.00
	1800A	—	135.00	225.00	300.00
	1801A	—	70.00	125.00	175.00
	1802A	—	70.00	125.00	175.00
	1803A	—	135.00	225.00	300.00
	1804A	—	70.00	125.00	175.00

Obv. leg: FRANCISCVS II. D. G. ROM ET, etc.

C#	Date	Mintage	VF	XF	Unc
167	1804A	—	—	Rare	—
	1805A	—	200.00	450.00	675.00
	1806A	—	185.00	400.00	600.00

Obv. leg: FRANCISCVS I. D. G. AVSTRIAE, etc.
Rev. leg. ends: D. LO. SAL. WIRC.

C#	Date	Mintage	VF	XF	Unc
184	1807A	—	—	Rare	—
	1808A	—	200.00	450.00	675.00
	1809A	—	200.00	450.00	675.00
	1809C	—	225.00	500.00	750.00
	1810A	—	225.00	500.00	750.00

Rev. leg. ends: LO: WI: ET IN. FR: DVX

C#	Date	Mintage	VF	XF	Unc
184a	1811A	—	100.00	167.00	250.00
	1812A	—	110.00	175.00	275.00
	1813A	—	110.00	175.00	275.00
	1814A	—	80.00	125.00	225.00
	1815A	—	50.00	85.00	125.00
	1815B	—	70.00	130.00	200.00

Rev. leg. ends: GAL. LOD. IL. REX. A. A.

C#	Date	Mintage	VF	XF	Unc
184b	1817A	—	70.00	115.00	175.00
	1818A	—	80.00	125.00	185.00
	1818B	—	80.00	125.00	185.00
	1818V	—	60.00	100.00	150.00
	1819A	—	65.00	110.00	165.00
	1819B	—	—	Rare	—
	1819C	—	75.00	125.00	185.00
	1819E	—	—	Rare	—
	1819G	—	80.00	135.00	200.00
	1820A	—	70.00	115.00	175.00
	1820B	—	—	Rare	—
	1820C	—	70.00	115.00	175.00
	1820E	—	80.00	125.00	185.00
	1820G	—	—	Rare	—
	1821A	—	70.00	115.00	175.00
	1821B	—	70.00	115.00	175.00
	1821C	—	60.00	100.00	150.00
	1821E	—	80.00	125.00	185.00
	1821G	—	80.00	125.00	185.00
	1821V	—	—	Rare	—
	1822A	—	60.00	100.00	150.00
	1822B	—	—	Rare	—
	1822C	—	70.00	115.00	175.00
	1822E	—	80.00	125.00	185.00
	1822G	—	80.00	125.00	185.00
	1823A	—	60.00	100.00	150.00
	1823B	—	80.00	125.00	185.00
	1823C	—	80.00	125.00	185.00
	1823E	—	80.00	125.00	185.00
	1823G	—	65.00	110.00	165.00
	1824A	—	60.00	100.00	150.00
	1824B	—	70.00	115.00	175.00
	1824C	—	55.00	100.00	135.00
	1824G	—	115.00	150.00	225.00

Obv: Bust with short hair

C#	Date	Mintage	VF	XF	Unc
184c	1825A	—	80.00	125.00	185.00
	1825B	—	80.00	125.00	185.00
	1825C	—	80.00	125.00	185.00
	1826A	—	50.00	82.50	125.00
	1826B	—	70.00	115.00	175.00
	1826C	—	60.00	100.00	150.00
	1826G	—	150.00	300.00	450.00
	1827A	—	40.00	60.00	120.00
	1827B	—	—	Rare	—
	1827C	—	100.00	175.00	250.00
	1828A	—	55.00	87.50	130.00

C#	Date	Mintage	VF	XF	Unc
184c	1829A	—	50.00	82.00	125.00
	1830A	—	45.00	75.00	112.00
	1830E	—	—	Rare	—

Obv: Ribbons on wreath forward across neck

C#	Date	Mintage	VF	XF	Unc
184d	1831A	—	100.00	165.00	225.00

Obv: Ribbons on wreath behind neck

C#	Date	Mintage	VF	XF	Unc
184e	1832A	—	75.00	125.00	200.00
	1832A plain edge	—	—	—	—
	1833A	—	75.00	125.00	200.00
	1833A plain edge	—	—	—	—
	1833E	—	—	Rare	—
	1834A	—	75.00	125.00	200.00
	1835A	—	60.00	100.00	175.00

Obv: Head of Ferdinand right. Rev: Eagle.

C#	Date	Mintage	Fine	VF	XF	Unc
192	1835A	—	125.00	250.00	500.00	750.00
	1836A	—	125.00	200.00	325.00	500.00
192a	1837A	—	30.00	60.00	125.00	235.00
	1838A	—	30.00	60.00	125.00	235.00
	1839A	—	27.50	55.00	110.00	200.00
	1840A	—	20.00	42.50	85.00	165.00
	1841A	—	30.00	62.50	110.00	200.00
	1842A	—	25.00	50.00	100.00	180.00
	1843A	—	25.00	50.00	100.00	185.00
	1844A	—	30.00	62.00	110.00	200.00
	1845A	—	25.00	50.00	100.00	180.00
	1846A	—	22.50	45.00	90.00	160.00
	1847A	—	20.00	40.00	80.00	140.00
	1848A	—	30.00	60.00	110.00	210.00

C#	Date	Mintage	Fine	VF	XF	Unc
192b	1848GM	3,947	150.00	275.00	450.00	800.00

NOTE: The above issue was struck in Mantua by the Austrian garrison under General Josef Radetzky during the siege of March 18-22, 1848 by Italian rebels.

.833 SILVER
Obv: Young head of Franz Josef left.

C#	Date	Mintage	Fine	VF	XF	Unc
204	1848A	—	200.00	350.00	600.00	900.00
	1849A	—	400.00	600.00	950.00	1450.
	1850A	—	500.00	750.00	1100.	1650.
	1851A	—	500.00	750.00	1100.	1650.

.900 SILVER
Obv: Young head of Franz Josef right.

C#	Date	Mintage	Fine	VF	XF	Unc
208	1852A	—	85.00	175.00	300.00	500.00
	1853A	—	135.00	275.00	450.00	750.00
	1854A	—	135.00	275.00	450.00	750.00
	1855A	—	115.00	235.00	375.00	650.00
	1856A	—	115.00	235.00	375.00	650.00

Edge lettering: VIRIBVS-VIRIBVS

C#	Date	Mintage	Fine	VF	XF	Unc
208a	1856A	—	100.00	225.00	350.00	600.00

ZWEI (2) GULDEN

SILVER
Denomination on edge

C#	Date	Mintage	Fine	VF	XF	Unc
211	1854A	—	60.00	100.00	160.00	250.00

2 FLORINS

24.6900 gm., .900 SILVER, .7145 oz ASW

Y#	Date	Mintage	Fine	VF	XF	Unc
16	1859A	—	75.00	125.00	175.00	250.00
	1859B	—	40.00	70.00	125.00	165.00
	1860A	—	500.00	900.00	1400.	2000.
	1860V	—	275.00	450.00	700.00	1000.
	1862A	—	70.00	165.00	235.00	350.00
	1863A	—	45.00	90.00	150.00	225.00
	1864A	—	45.00	90.00	150.00	225.00
	1865A	—	42.50	85.00	140.00	210.00

Obv: Head of Franz Josef right with heavier side whiskers.
Rev: Similar to Y#16.

Y#	Date	Mintage	Fine	VF	XF	Unc
16a	1866A	.011	85.00	150.00	235.00	335.00

Rev: Similar to Y#16.

Y#	Date	Mintage	Fine	VF	XF	Unc
16b	1867A	—	60.00	100.00	140.00	200.00
	1868A	—	50.00	85.00	125.00	180.00
	1869A	—	50.00	80.00	120.00	175.00
	1870A	—	50.00	80.00	120.00	175.00
	1871A	—	42.50	75.00	100.00	150.00
	1872A	—	100.00	175.00	250.00	350.00

Y#	Date	Mintage	Fine	VF	XF	Unc
16c	1872	.045	50.00	85.00	120.00	175.00
	1873	.099	55.00	90.00	140.00	200.00
	1874	.079	35.00	55.00	110.00	165.00
	1875	.106	35.00	55.00	100.00	150.00
	1876	.092	42.50	60.00	110.00	160.00
	1877	.105	35.00	55.00	100.00	135.00
	1878	.147	42.50	70.00	100.00	150.00
	1879	.501	35.00	55.00	90.00	130.00
	1880	.083	42.50	70.00	100.00	150.00
	1881	.104	42.50	70.00	100.00	150.00
	1882	.121	42.50	70.00	100.00	150.00
	1883	.070	45.00	75.00	110.00	150.00
	1884	.087	55.00	55.00	90.00	130.00
	1885	.078	35.00	55.00	90.00	135.00
	1886	.093	35.00	55.00	90.00	135.00
	1887	.117	32.50	50.00	80.00	115.00
	1888	.073	35.00	55.00	90.00	135.00
	1889	.147	35.00	55.00	90.00	135.00
	1890	.104	35.00	55.00	90.00	135.00
	1891	.117	40.00	65.00	100.00	150.00
	1892	.032	35.00	55.00	90.00	135.00

Vienna Shooting Fest
Rev: F. GAUL below eagle, 22gm.

Y#	Date	Mintage	Fine	VF	XF	Unc
18	1873	—	500.00	800.00	1125.	1400.
	1873	—	—	—	Proof	1600.

NOTE: The Kremnica Mint struck reproductions with 'R.1973-KOLARSKY' below eagle, 24.31gm.

Silver Wedding Anniversary

Y#	Date	Mintage	Fine	VF	XF	Unc
19	1879	.275	25.00	35.00	55.00	75.00

First Federal Shooting Festival

Y#	Date	Mintage	Fine	VF	XF	Unc
—	1880	—	100.00	135.00	175.00	225.00

Reopening Of Kuttenberg Mines

Y#	Date	Mintage	Fine	VF	XF	Unc
20	1887	400 pcs.	1000.	1500.	2250.	3000.
	1887	—	—	—	Proof	3500.

BRONZE

Y#	Date	Mintage	Fine	VF	XF	Unc
20a	1887	—	450.00	750.00	1100.	1600.

THALER

(Convention)

SILVER

Obv: Veiled head right.
Rev: Crowned imperial eagle.

C#	Date	Mintage	Fine	VF	XF
50	1765A	—	65.00	100.00	150.00
	1766	—	65.00	100.00	150.00
	1766A	—	65.00	100.00	150.00
	1766 IC-SK	—	65.00	100.00	150.00
	1766 EC-SK	—	65.00	100.00	150.00
	1767 IC-SK	—	65.00	100.00	150.00

Obv: Different veiled head right.

C#	Date	Mintage	Fine	VF	XF
50.1	1767 IK-SC	—	65.00	100.00	150.00
	1768 IC-SK	—	65.00	100.00	150.00
	1769 IC-SK	—	65.00	100.00	150.00
	1770 IC-SK	—	65.00	100.00	150.00
50.1	1771 IC-SK	—	65.00	100.00	150.00
	1772 IC-SK	—	65.00	100.00	150.00

Obv: Smaller veiled head right.

C#	Date	Mintage	Fine	VF	XF
50.2	1772 IC-SK	—	65.00	100.00	150.00
	1773 IC-SK	—	65.00	100.00	150.00
	1774 IC-SK	—	65.00	100.00	150.00
	1774 IC-FA	—	65.00	100.00	150.00
	1775 IC-FA	—	65.00	100.00	150.00
	1776 IC-FA	—	65.00	100.00	150.00
	1777 IC-FA	—	65.00	100.00	150.00
	1778 IC-FA	—	65.00	100.00	150.00
	1779 IC-FA	—	65.00	100.00	150.00

Obv: Larger veiled head right.

C#	Date	Mintage	Fine	VF	XF
50.3	1780 IC-FA	—	65.00	100.00	150.00

Obv: Armored bust of Joseph right, as joint ruler.

C#	Date	Mintage	Fine	VF	XF
119	1765A	—	135.00	175.00	225.00
	1766A	—	135.00	175.00	225.00
	1766A IC-SK	—	135.00	175.00	225.00
	1767A IC-SK	—	135.00	175.00	225.00
	1769A IC-SK	—	135.00	175.00	225.00
	1770A IC-SK	—	135.00	175.00	225.00
	1771A IC-SK	—	135.00	175.00	225.00
	1772A IC-SK	—	135.00	175.00	225.00

Obv: Older head of Joseph right, as joint ruler.

C#	Date	Mintage	Fine	VF	XF
119.1	1773 IC-SK	—	135.00	175.00	225.00
	1774 IC-SK	—	135.00	175.00	225.00
	1774A IC-FA	—	135.00	175.00	225.00
	1775A IC-FA	—	135.00	175.00	225.00
	1776A IC-FA	—	135.00	175.00	225.00
	1778A IC-FA	—	135.00	175.00	225.00
	1779A IC-FA	—	135.00	175.00	225.00
	1780A IC-FA	—	135.00	175.00	225.00

(Ordens)

Obv: Armored bust of Joseph with order sash over shoulder, as joint ruler.

C#	Date	Mintage	Fine	VF	XF
119a	1768A IC-SK	—	225.00	300.00	400.00
	1769A IC-SK	—	225.00	300.00	400.00

Obv: Laureated head of Joseph right, as sole ruler.

C#	Date	Mintage	Fine	VF	XF
134	1781A	—	200.00	275.00	350.00
	1782A	—	200.00	275.00	350.00
	1784A	—	200.00	275.00	350.00
	1785A	—	200.00	275.00	350.00
	1786A	—	200.00	275.00	350.00
	1787A	—	200.00	275.00	350.00
	1788A	—	200.00	275.00	350.00
	1789A	—	200.00	275.00	350.00
	1790A	—	200.00	275.00	350.00

.833 SILVER
Leopold II as King of Hungary and Bohemia
Rev: Similar to C#160.

C#	Date	Mintage	Fine	VF	XF	Unc
142	1790A	—	225.00	550.00	850.00	1250.

Leopold II as Emperor
Rev: Crowned imperial eagle.

C#	Date	Mintage	Fine	VF	XF	Unc
143	1790A	—	325.00	550.00	900.00	1500.
	1791A	—	375.00	650.00	1000.	1750.
	1792A	—	325.00	550.00	900.00	1500.

Obv. leg: FRANCISCVS D. G. HVNGAR., etc.

C#	Date	Mintage	VF	XF	Unc
160	1792A	—	700.00	1250.	1650.

Obv. leg: FRANCISCVS II. D. G. R. IMP. S. A., etc.

C#	Date	Mintage	Fine	VF	XF
161	1792A	—	200.00	375.00	600.00
	1793A	—	200.00	475.00	750.00
	1794A	—	200.00	425.00	675.00
	1795A	—	225.00	475.00	750.00
	1796A	—	—	Rare	—
	1797A	—	—	Rare	—
	1798A	—	225.00	475.00	750.00
	1799A	—	200.00	375.00	600.00
	1800A	—	225.00	475.00	750.00
	1801A	—	225.00	475.00	750.00
	1802A	—	225.00	475.00	750.00
	1803A	—	225.00	475.00	750.00
	1804A	—	200.00	425.00	675.00

Obv. leg: FRANCISCVS II D. G. ROM. ET, etc.

C#	Date	Mintage	Fine	VF	XF
168	1804A	—	200.00	375.00	600.00
	1805A	—	150.00	275.00	450.00
	1806A	—	125.00	250.00	400.00

Obv. leg: FRANCISCVS I. D. G. AVSTRIAE, etc.
Rev. leg. ends: D. LO. SAL. WIRC

C#	Date	Mintage	Fine	VF	XF
185	1806A	—	—	Rare	—
	1807A	—	60.00	120.00	200.00
	1808A	—	60.00	120.00	200.00
	1809A	—	60.00	120.00	200.00
	1809B	—	—	Rare	—
	1809B (Restrike 1841)	—	—	—	—
	1809C	—	60.00	120.00	200.00
	1810A	—	65.00	130.00	225.00

NOTE: 1810A exists as a klippe.

Rev. leg. ends: LO: WI: ET IN. FR: DVX

C#	Date	Mintage	Fine	VF	XF
185a	1811A	—	60.00	120.00	175.00
	1811C	—	60.00	120.00	175.00
	1812A	—	—	Rare	—
	1812C	—	125.00	250.00	400.00
	1813A	—	125.00	250.00	400.00
	1813C	—	125.00	250.00	400.00
	1813G	—	75.00	150.00	200.00
	1814A	—	50.00	100.00	150.00
	1814B	—	—	Rare	—
	1814C	—	75.00	150.00	200.00
	1814G	—	75.00	150.00	200.00
	1815A	—	45.00	90.00	140.00
	1815B	—	75.00	150.00	200.00
	1815C	—	50.00	100.00	150.00

Rev. leg. ends: GAL. LOB. IL. REX. A. A.

C#	Date	Mintage	VF	XF	Unc
185b	1817A	—	70.00	140.00	200.00
	1818A	—	70.00	140.00	200.00
	1818B	—	45.00	87.00	135.00
	1818V	—	40.00	80.00	125.00
	1819A	—	30.00	50.00	90.00
	1819B	—	—	Rare	—
	1819C	—	50.00	100.00	155.00
	1819E	—	70.00	140.00	200.00
	1819G	—	50.00	100.00	150.00
	1819M	—	50.00	100.00	150.00
	1820A	—	30.00	60.00	100.00
	1820B	—	—	Rare	—
	1820C	—	40.00	80.00	125.00
	1820E	—	50.00	100.00	155.00
	1820G	—	70.00	140.00	200.00
	1820M	—	45.00	87.50	135.00
	1821A	—	50.00	100.00	150.00
	1821B	—	45.00	87.50	135.00
	1821C	—	40.00	80.00	125.00
	1821E	—	50.00	100.00	150.00
	1821G	—	70.00	140.00	200.00
	1821M	—	50.00	100.00	155.00
	1821V	—	60.00	115.00	170.00
	1822A	—	30.00	60.00	100.00
	1822B	—	40.00	80.00	125.00
	1822C	—	45.00	87.50	135.00
	1822E	—	50.00	100.00	155.00
	1822G	—	50.00	100.00	150.00
	1822M	—	50.00	100.00	155.00
	1822V	—	—	—	—
	1823A	—	40.00	80.00	125.00
	1823B	—	70.00	140.00	200.00
	1823C	—	50.00	100.00	155.00
	1823E	—	50.00	100.00	155.00
	1823G	—	35.00	70.00	100.00
	1824A	—	40.00	80.00	125.00
	1824B	—	35.00	70.00	115.00
	1824C	—	30.00	60.00	100.00
	1824E	—	90.00	175.00	250.00
	1824G	—	50.00	100.00	155.00

Rev: Similar to C#185b.

C#	Date	Mintage	VF	XF	Unc
185c	1824A	—	45.00	90.00	135.00
	1825A	—	45.00	90.00	135.00
	1825B	—	35.00	75.00	115.00
	1825C	—	35.00	75.00	115.00
	1825G	—	45.00	90.00	135.00
	1826A	—	35.00	67.50	110.00
	1826B	—	38.00	75.00	115.00
	1826C	—	45.00	90.00	135.00
	1826G	—	45.00	90.00	135.00
	1827A	—	60.00	115.00	170.00
	1827B	—	—	Rare	—
	1827C	—	50.00	100.00	150.00
	1828A	—	32.50	65.00	110.00
	1828B	—	40.00	85.00	125.00
	1829A	—	45.00	75.00	117.00
	1830A	—	32.50	65.00	110.00
	1830E	—	60.00	115.00	170.00

Obv: Ribbons on wreath forward across neck

C#	Date	Mintage	VF	XF	Unc
185d	1831A	—	80.00	150.00	225.00

Obv: Ribbons on wreath behind neck

C#	Date	Mintage	VF	XF	Unc
185e	1831A	—	500.00	800.00	1200.
	1832A	—	90.00	175.00	250.00
	1833A	—	75.00	150.00	225.00
	1833A (error edge reads: FUNDAMENIUM)				
		—	60.00	120.00	240.00
	1833B	—	—	Rare	—
	1833E	—	100.00	200.00	300.00
	1834A	—	90.00	175.00	250.00
	1835A	—	90.00	175.00	250.00

Ferdinandus I

Obv: Oval loop in knot of wreath.

C#	Date	Mintage	Fine	VF	XF	Unc
193	1835A	—	175.00	300.00	500.00	800.00
	1835C	—	—	Proof only		—
	1836A	—	85.00	175.00	300.00	600.00
	1836C	—	300.00	550.00	900.00	1250.

Obv: Sharp cornered loop in knot of wreath.

C#	Date	Mintage	Fine	VF	XF	Unc
193b	1835A	—	375.00	650.00	1150.	1650.

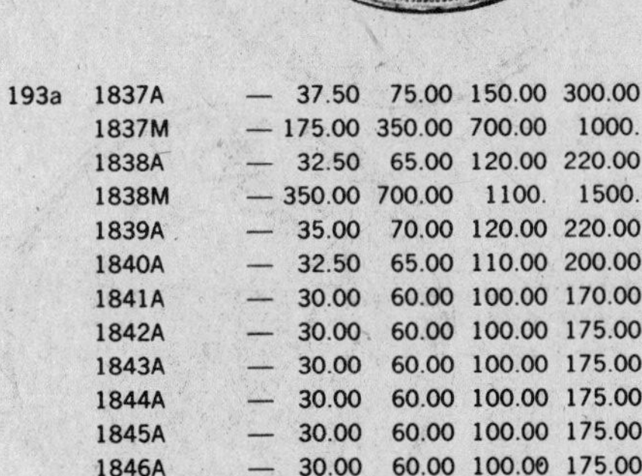

C#	Date	Mintage	Fine	VF	XF	Unc
193a	1837A	—	37.50	75.00	150.00	300.00
	1837M	—	175.00	350.00	700.00	1000.
	1838A	—	32.50	65.00	120.00	220.00
	1838M	—	350.00	700.00	1100.	1500.
	1839A	—	35.00	70.00	120.00	220.00
	1840A	—	32.50	65.00	110.00	200.00
	1841A	—	30.00	60.00	100.00	170.00
	1842A	—	30.00	60.00	100.00	175.00
	1843A	—	30.00	60.00	100.00	175.00
	1844A	—	30.00	60.00	100.00	175.00
	1845A	—	30.00	60.00	100.00	175.00
	1846A	—	30.00	60.00	100.00	175.00
	1847A	—	30.00	60.00	100.00	175.00
	1848A	—	27.50	55.00	90.00	160.00

Rev: Similar to C#193a.

C#	Date	Mintage	Fine	VF	XF	Unc
205	1848A	—	500.00	1000.	1500.	2250.
	1849A	—	500.00	1000.	1500.	2250.
	1850A	—	500.00	1000.	1500.	2250.
	1851A	—	350.00	750.00	1000.	1500.

Rev: Similar to C#193a.

C#	Date	Mintage	Fine	VF	XF	Unc
205a	1852A	—	625.00	1250.	1750.	2500.

Rev: Similar to C#193a.

C#	Date	Mintage	Fine	VF	XF	Unc
209	1852A	—	50.00	100.00	225.00	350.00
	1853A	—	50.00	100.00	200.00	325.00
	1853B	—	135.00	275.00	500.00	850.00
	1854A	—	50.00	100.00	200.00	325.00
	1855A	—	50.00	100.00	185.00	300.00
	1856A	—	45.00	90.00	170.00	285.00

Edge lettering: VIRIBUS-VIRIBUS

C#	Date	Mintage	Fine	VF	XF	Unc
209a	1856A	—	—	—	—	—

(Vereins)

18.5186 gm., .900 SILVER, .5359 oz ASW

Y#	Date	Mintage	Fine	VF	XF	Unc
1	1857A	—	17.50	35.00	65.00	100.00
	1857B	—	75.00	150.00	300.00	500.00
	1857E	—	60.00	120.00	225.00	375.00
	1857V	—	110.00	225.00	400.00	650.00
	1858A	—	17.50	35.00	65.00	100.00
	1858B	—	22.50	45.00	85.00	150.00
	1858E	—	75.00	150.00	300.00	500.00
	1858M	—	55.00	110.00	225.00	350.00
	1858V	—	55.00	110.00	225.00	350.00
	1859A	—	26.50	50.00	85.00	150.00
	1859B	—	27.50	55.00	110.00	165.00
	1859E	—	60.00	120.00	225.00	400.00
	1859M	—	55.00	110.00	225.00	375.00
	1860A	—	25.00	50.00	100.00	165.00
	1860V	—	55.00	110.00	225.00	375.00
	1861A	—	27.50	50.00	100.00	165.00
	1861B	—	27.50	50.00	100.00	165.00
	1861E	—	27.50	50.00	100.00	165.00
	1861V	—	45.00	90.00	175.00	250.00
	1862A	—	20.00	40.00	80.00	150.00
	1862B	—	25.00	50.00	100.00	175.00
	1862V	—	32.50	62.50	125.00	200.00
	1863A	—	21.50	42.50	85.00	160.00
	1863B	—	30.00	60.00	120.00	185.00
	1863E	—	32.50	65.00	130.00	200.00
	1863V	—	32.50	62.50	125.00	200.00
	1864A	—	17.50	32.50	65.00	125.00
	1864B	—	30.00	60.00	120.00	185.00
	1864E	—	17.50	32.50	65.00	125.00
	1864V	—	100.00	185.00	325.00	500.00
	1865A	—	18.50	35.00	70.00	135.00
	1865B	—	18.50	35.00	70.00	120.00
	1865E	—	18.50	33.50	62.50	110.00
	1865V	—	100.00	200.00	375.00	600.00

Obv: Head with heavier whiskers.
Rev: Similar to Y#1.

Y#	Date	Mintage	Fine	VF	XF	Unc
1a	1866A	—	22.50	40.00	75.00	125.00
	1866B	—	20.00	37.50	70.00	110.00
	1866E	—	27.50	55.00	110.00	190.00
	1867A	—	25.00	50.00	100.00	175.00
	1867B	—	27.50	55.00	110.00	190.00
	1867E	—	27.50	55.00	110.00	190.00

(FEIN)

3rd German Shooting Fest

Y#	Date	Mintage	VF	XF	Unc
A16	1868	—	50.00	100.00	175.00

(GEDENK)

Opening Of Mt. Raxalpe Inn

Y#	Date	Mintage	VF	XF	Unc
A20	1877	100 pcs.	1000.	1800.	4000.

2 THALERS
(Vereins)

37.0371 gm., .900 SILVER, 1.0718 oz ASW
Opening of Vienna-Trieste Railway

Y#	Date	Mintage	Fine	VF	XF	Unc
3	1857A	1,644	450.00	700.00	1000.	1300.

Rev: Similar to Y#2a.

Y#	Date	Mintage	Fine	VF	XF	Unc
2	1865A	—	575.00	1000.	1350.	1900.

Y#	Date	Mintage	Fine	VF	XF	Unc
2a	1866A	—	225.00	350.00	600.00	900.00
	1867A	—	225.00	350.00	600.00	1000.

1/2 KRONE

5.5555 gm., .900 GOLD, .1608 oz AGW

Y#	Date	Mintage	VF	XF	Unc
4	1858A	.020	500.00	1000.	1500.
	1858E	.025	450.00	850.00	1250.
	1858V	947 pcs.	1250.	1750.	2500.
	1859A	.400	350.00	750.00	1000.
	1859B	.065	500.00	1000.	1500.
	1859E	.017	500.00	1000.	1500.
	1860A	.200	250.00	500.00	900.00
	1860B	.045	500.00	1000.	1500.
	1861A	3,000	750.00	1250.	1750.
	1861B	.018	500.00	1000.	1500.
	1861E	.055	500.00	1000.	1500.
	1863A	40 pcs.	2500.	5000.	7500.
	1864A	980 pcs.	1000.	1600.	2000.
	1865A	2,690	750.00	1250.	1750.

Y#	Date	Mintage	VF	XF	Unc
4a	1866A	4,000	550.00	1100.	1600.

KRONE

11.1111 gm., .900 GOLD, .3215 oz AGW

Y#	Date	Mintage	VF	XF	Unc
5	1858A	.050	550.00	1100.	1600.
	1858E	.030	500.00	1000.	1250.
	1858V	600 pcs.	1500.	2250.	2750.
	1859A	10,000	500.00	1000.	1250.
	1859M	4,000	750.00	1400.	1900.
	1859V	1,000	1000.	1750.	2350.
	1860A	557 pcs.	1250.	2000.	2500.
	1861A	2,010	1000.	1750.	2250.
	1863A	1,000	1000.	1750.	2350.
	1864A	1,530	1000.	1750.	2250.
	1865A	2,800	900.00	1650.	2150.

Obv: Large bust.

Y#	Date	Mintage	VF	XF	Unc
5a	1866A	3,000	1250.	2000.	2500.

MONETARY REFORM

100 Heller = 1 Krone, 1892-1923
10,000 Kronen = 1 Schilling, 1923-1924

HELLER

BRONZE

Y#	Date	Mintage	Fine	VF	XF	Unc
26	1892	—	150.00	250.00	350.00	550.00
	1893	29.000	.25	.60	2.50	5.00
	1894	30.100	.25	.60	2.50	5.00
	1895	49.500	.20	.40	.75	2.00
	1896	15.600	.50	2.50	5.00	10.00
	1897	12.400	1.00	4.00	7.50	15.00
	1898	6.780	6.50	11.50	22.50	37.50
	1899	1.900	7.50	13.50	27.50	50.00
	1900	26.900	.25	.60	2.50	5.00
	1901	52.000	.20	.40	.75	1.50
	1902	20.500	.30	.75	1.50	3.00
	1903	13.700	.20	.40	.75	2.00
	1909	12.600	.20	.40	.75	2.00
	1910	21.900	.20	.40	.75	2.00
	1911	18.300	.20	.40	.75	2.00
	1912	27.000	.20	.40	.75	2.00
	1913	8.780	.25	.50	1.00	2.50
	1914	9.900	.20	.40	.75	1.50
	1915	5.670	.25	.50	1.00	2.00
	1916	12.400	.50	1.00	2.00	4.00

Obv: With Austrian shield on eagle's breast.

Y#	Date	Mintage	Fine	VF	XF	Unc
27	1916	Inc. Ab.	3.50	6.00	10.00	16.50

2 HELLER

BRONZE

Y#	Date	Mintage	Fine	VF	XF	Unc
28	1892	.260	150.00	200.00	275.00	400.00
	1893	41.500	.50	1.00	2.50	5.00
	1894	78.000	.25	.50	1.00	2.50
	1895	25.600	.60	1.25	3.00	6.50
	1896	43.000	.25	.40	.75	2.50
	1897	98.000	.25	.40	.75	2.00
	1898	10.700	1.50	3.00	6.00	9.00
	1899	42.700	.25	.40	1.00	2.50
	1900	7.940	1.00	2.00	4.00	8.00
	1901	12.100	3.00	6.00	10.00	12.50
	1902	18.700	.25	.60	2.00	3.00
	1903	26.900	1.00	2.00	4.00	8.00
	1904	12.800	.35	1.00	2.50	4.00
	1905	6.670	1.75	3.50	7.50	12.50
	1906	20.100	1.00	2.00	4.00	8.00
	1907	23.800	.20	.40	1.00	2.00
	1908	21.900	.20	.40	1.00	1.75
	1909	25.900	.20	.40	1.00	1.75
	1910	28.400	1.00	2.00	4.00	8.00
	1911	50.000	.20	.40	.60	1.50
	1912	74.200	.15	.25	.50	1.50
	1913	27.400	.75	1.50	3.00	6.00
	1914	60.600	.15	.25	.50	1.50
	1915	7.870	.15	.25	.50	1.50

IRON

Obv: With Austrian shield on eagle's breast.

Y#	Date	Mintage	Fine	VF	XF	Unc
33	1916	61.900	.50	1.25	2.50	4.00
	1917	81.100	.15	.25	.50	.75
	1918	66.300	.15	.25	.50	.75

10 HELLER

NICKEL

Y#	Date	Mintage	Fine	VF	XF	Unc
29	1892	—	250.00	350.00	475.00	625.00
	1893	43.500	.20	.50	1.50	2.00
	1894	45.500	.20	.50	1.25	1.75
	1895	79.900	.20	.50	1.00	1.50
	1907	8.660	.20	.50	1.00	1.50
	1908	7.770	.75	1.50	3.00	5.00
	1909	20.400	.15	.25	.60	1.00
	1910	10.100	.15	.25	.60	1.00
	1911	3.630	1.00	2.00	5.00	7.50

COPPER-NICKEL-ZINC

Y#	Date	Mintage	Fine	VF	XF	Unc
31	1915	18.300	.15	.25	.50	1.00
	1916	27.400	.15	.25	.50	1.00

Obv: With Austrian shield on eagle's breast.

Y#	Date	Mintage	Fine	VF	XF	Unc
32	1916	14.800	.75	1.25	2.50	3.75

20 HELLER

NICKEL

Y#	Date	Mintage	Fine	VF	XF	Unc
30	1892	1.500	15.00	30.00	65.00	100.00
	1892	—	—	—	Proof	200.00
	1893	41.400	.50	.75	2.00	4.00
	1894	50.100	.50	.75	2.00	4.00
	1895	32.900	.40	.60	1.00	2.75
30	1907	7.650	2.00	3.00	7.50	15.00
	1908	7.460	1.25	2.50	5.00	10.00
	1909	7.590	2.00	4.00	7.50	15.00
	1911	19.500	.25	.50	.75	1.25
	1914	2.340	7.50	18.50	25.00	40.00

IRON

Obv. with Austrian shield on eagle's breast.

Y#	Date	Mintage	Fine	VF	XF	Unc
34	1916	130.700	.50	1.00	1.50	3.00
	1917	127.400	.50	1.00	1.50	3.00
	1918	100.200	.15	.25	.75	2.00

KRONE

5.0000 gm., .835 SILVER, .1342 oz ASW

Y#	Date	Mintage	Fine	VF	XF	Unc
35	1892	.230	67.50	135.00	225.00	325.00
	1893	50.100	BV	BV	4.50	7.50
	1894	28.000	BV	BV	4.50	8.50
	1895	15.100	BV	6.50	13.50	22.50
	1896	3.060	BV	5.00	15.00	30.00
	1897	2.140	18.50	30.00	60.00	90.00
	1898	5.850	BV	4.50	10.00	20.00
	1899	11.800	BV	BV	4.50	8.50
	1900	3.060	BV	BV	7.50	15.00
	1901	10.300	BV	BV	4.50	8.50
	1902	2.940	BV	BV	7.50	15.00
	1903	2.190	BV	BV	7.50	15.00
	1904	.990	BV	8.50	17.50	35.00
	1905	.500	10.00	25.00	50.00	80.00
	1906	.160	100.00	150.00	250.00	350.00
	1907	.240	32.50	65.00	100.00	150.00

60th Anniversary of Reign

Y#	Date	Mintage	Fine	VF	XF	Unc
36	1908	4.780	BV	BV	4.50	6.00

Y#	Date	Mintage	Fine	VF	XF	Unc
37	1912	8.450	BV	BV	4.00	5.00
	1913	9.340	BV	BV	4.00	4.50
	1914	37.800	BV	BV	4.00	4.50
	1915	23.000	BV	BV	4.00	4.50
	1916	12.400	BV	BV	4.00	4.50

2 KRONEN

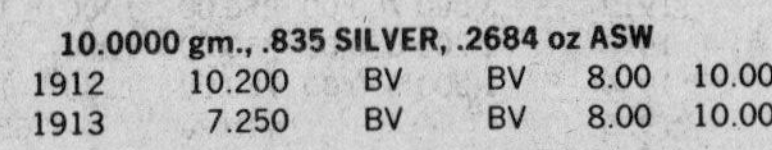

10.0000 gm., .835 SILVER, .2684 oz ASW

Y#	Date	Mintage	Fine	VF	XF	Unc
38	1912	10.200	BV	BV	8.00	10.00
	1913	7.250	BV	BV	8.00	10.00

5 KRONEN

24.0000 gm., .900 SILVER, .6945 oz ASW

Y#	Date	Mintage	Fine	VF	XF	Unc
39	1900	8.960	BV	22.50	30.00	50.00
	1907	1.530	BV	25.00	35.00	65.00
	1907	—	—	—	Proof	650.00

60th Anniversary of Reign

Y#	Date	Mintage	Fine	VF	XF	Unc
40	1908	3.940	BV	22.50	30.00	50.00

Obv: Large head.
Rev: Similar to Y#39.

Y#	Date	Mintage	Fine	VF	XF	Unc
41	1909	1.700	BV	25.00	35.00	55.00

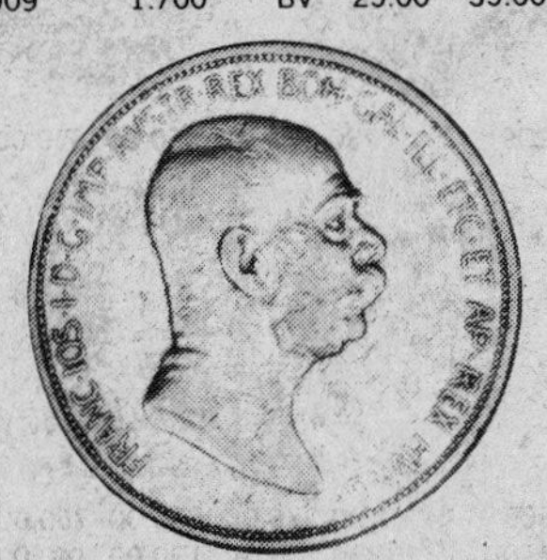

Obv: Small head.

Rev: Similar to Y#39.

Y#	Date	Mintage	Fine	VF	XF	Unc
A41	1909	1.770	BV	25.00	35.00	65.00

10 KRONEN

3.3875 gm., .900 GOLD, .0980 oz AGW
Obv: Laureate head of Franz Josef right.
Rev: Eagle with value and date below.

Y#	Date	Mintage	Fine	VF	XF	Unc
42	1892	—	500.00	800.00	1350.	1850.
	1896	.210	BV	65.00	70.00	75.00
	1897	1.800	BV	65.00	70.00	75.00
	1905	1.930	BV	65.00	70.00	75.00
	1906	1.080	BV	65.00	70.00	75.00

Jubilee
Obv: Small plain head of Franz Josef right.
Rev: Eagle, value below, 2 dates above.

Y#	Date	Mintage	Fine	VF	XF	Unc
44	1908	.650	BV	65.00	75.00	95.00

Obv: Small head.
Rev: Eagle, value and date below.

Y#	Date	Mintage	Fine	VF	XF	Unc
47	1909	2.320	BV	65.00	75.00	85.00

Obv: Large head.

Y#	Date	Mintage	Fine	VF	XF	Unc
49	1909	.200	BV	65.00	75.00	85.00
	1910	1.000	BV	65.00	70.00	75.00
	1911	1.280	BV	65.00	70.00	75.00
	1912	Restrike	BV	BV	BV	70.00

20 KRONEN

6.7751 gm., .900 GOLD, .1960 oz AGW

Y#	Date	Mintage	Fine	VF	XF	Unc
43	1892	.650	BV	130.00	140.00	150.00
	1893	7.870	BV	130.00	140.00	150.00
	1894	6.710	BV	130.00	140.00	150.00
	1895	2.960	BV	130.00	140.00	150.00
	1896	6.860	BV	130.00	140.00	150.00
	1897	5.130	BV	130.00	140.00	150.00
	1898	1.870	BV	130.00	140.00	150.00
	1899	.100	BV	140.00	150.00	175.00
	1900	.030	130.00	160.00	200.00	250.00
	1901	.050	130.00	160.00	200.00	250.00
	1902	.440	BV	130.00	140.00	160.00
	1903	.320	BV	130.00	140.00	160.00
	1904	.500	BV	130.00	140.00	150.00
	1905	.150	BV	130.00	140.00	160.00

Jubilee
Rev. with 2 dates above eagle.

Y#	Date	Mintage	Fine	VF	XF	Unc
45	1908	.190	130.00	160.00	225.00	275.00

Y#	Date	Mintage	Fine	VF	XF	Unc
48	1909	.230	375.00	550.00	850.00	1100.

Y#	Date	Mintage	Fine	VF	XF	Unc
50	1909	.100	375.00	550.00	750.00	1000.
	1910	.390	BV	130.00	140.00	160.00
	1911	.060	130.00	175.00	225.00	275.00

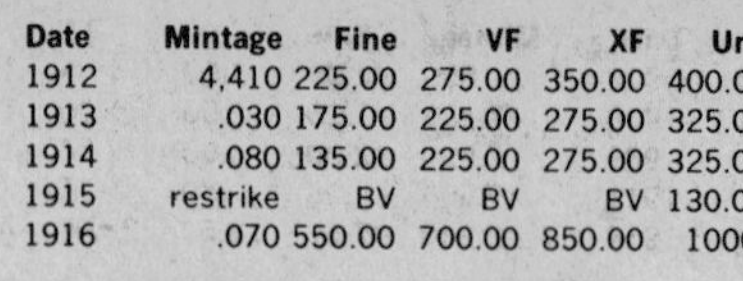

Y#	Date	Mintage	Fine	VF	XF	Unc
50	1912	4,410	225.00	275.00	350.00	400.00
	1913	.030	175.00	225.00	275.00	325.00
	1914	.080	135.00	225.00	275.00	325.00
	1915	restrike	BV	BV	BV	130.00
	1916	.070	550.00	700.00	850.00	1000.

Rev: Austrian shield on eagle.

Y#	Date	Mintage	Fine	VF	XF	Unc
52	1916	Inc. Ab.	250.00	450.00	600.00	750.00

Y#	Date	Mintage	Fine	VF	XF	Unc
80	1923	6,988	—	700.00	1000.	1500.
	1924	10,337	—	700.00	1000.	1500.

100 KRONEN

33.8753 gm., .900 GOLD, .9803 oz AGW
Jubilee

Y#	Date	Mintage	Fine	VF	XF	Unc
46	1908	.016	650.00	1100.	1500.	1750.
	1908	—	—	—	Proof	1500.

Y#	Date	Mintage	Fine	VF	XF	Unc
51	1909	3,200	650.00	750.00	1250.	1600.
	1910	3,070	700.00	800.00	1350.	1750.
	1911	11,160	650.00	750.00	1250.	1600.
	1912	3,590	700.00	850.00	1400.	1750.
	1913	2,700	650.00	750.00	1250.	1600.
	1914	1,200	650.00	750.00	1250.	1600.
	1915	—		Restrike	—	650.00

Y#	Date	Mintage	Fine	VF	XF	Unc
81	1923	617 pcs.	—	2000.	2750.	3500.
	1923	—	—	—	Proof	4000.
	1924	2,851	—	2000.	2750.	3500.

BRONZE

Y#	Date	Mintage	Fine	VF	XF	Unc
56	1923	6.404	4.50	8.50	15.00	27.50
	1924	42.899	.25	.50	1.75	3.75

200 KRONEN

BRONZE

Y#	Date	Mintage	Fine	VF	XF	Unc
57	1924	57.160	.50	1.00	2.50	4.50

1000 KRONEN

COPPER-NICKEL

Y#	Date	Mintage	Fine	VF	XF	Unc
58	1924	72.353	.75	1.75	4.00	7.50

Careful attention should be given to the grade headings of Austrian coins. Early coins are priced in VF, XF, and Unc and the current coins at XF, Unc. and Proof.

TRADE COINS

THALER

28.0668 gm., .833-1/3 SILVER Restrike, .7520 oz ASW

Y#	Date	Mintage	XF	Unc	Proof
55	1780SF	—	BV	24.00	25.00

An unofficial trade dollar, the final date of the famous Maria Theresa Thaler has been struck intermittently to modern times at many world mints. It has been used in many areas that lacked a firm local coinage, particularly in north and east Africa and The Near East. The Gunzburg mint was where the original talers were struck. (Listings for these can be found under Burgau-Austrian States). Since then the talers have been restruck at the following mints, Vienna, Prague, Milan, Venice, Gunzburg, London, Paris, Brussels, Lenningrad, Rome, Bombay and Florence with an estimated 800 million struck to date. For original Thaler listings refer to BURGAU.

Period	Mintage	Mint
1935-1939	19,496,729	Rome
1935-1957	11,809.956	Paris
1936-1961	19,835,054	London
1937-1957	10,994,524	Bruxelles
1940-1941	18,864,676	Bombay
1949-1955	3,428,500	Birmingham
1956-1975	9,924,151	Vienna

1/4 DUCAT

.8750 gm., .986 GOLD, .0277 oz AGW
Obv: Laureated bust of Joseph right, as joint ruler.
Rev: Crowned imperial eagle.

C#	Date	Mintage	Fine	VF	XF
120	1765NB	—	175.00	225.00	300.00
	1777G B-V	—	175.00	225.00	300.00

4 FLORIN-10 FRANCS

3.2258 gm., .900 GOLD, .0933 oz AGW

Y#	Date	Mintage	Fine	VF	XF	Unc
21	1870	7,440	75.00	115.00	145.00	185.00
	1871	6,665	75.00	115.00	145.00	185.00
	1872	4,960	65.00	110.00	150.00	190.00
	1877	3,004	75.00	135.00	190.00	235.00
	1878	6,820	65.00	90.00	120.00	150.00
	1881	8,370	65.00	90.00	120.00	150.00
	1883	3,720	75.00	135.00	190.00	225.00
21	1884	7,518	65.00	90.00	120.00	150.00
	1885	.038	65.00	80.00	100.00	120.00
	1888	4,145	65.00	100.00	135.00	175.00
	1889	5,707	65.00	100.00	135.00	175.00
	1890	2,947	75.00	135.00	190.00	235.00
	1891	.011	65.00	90.00	120.00	200.00
	1892	Restrike	BV	BV	BV	65.00

DUCAT

3.4909 gm., .986 GOLD, .1106 oz AGW

C#	Date	Mintage	Fine	VF	XF
55	1765	—	350.00	450.00	600.00
	1766 C-K	—	350.00	450.00	600.00
	1767	—	350.00	450.00	600.00
	1768 C-K	—	350.00	450.00	600.00
	1769	—	350.00	450.00	600.00
	1770 C-K	—	350.00	450.00	600.00
	1771 C-K	—	350.00	450.00	600.00
	1772 C-K	—	350.00	450.00	600.00
	1773 C-K	—	350.00	450.00	600.00
	1774 C-A	—	350.00	450.00	600.00
	1775 C-A	—	350.00	450.00	600.00
	1776 C-A	—	350.00	450.00	600.00
	1777 C-A	—	350.00	450.00	600.00
	1778 C-A	—	350.00	450.00	600.00
	1779 C-A	—	350.00	450.00	600.00
	1780 C-A	—	350.00	450.00	600.00

Royal Title Only
Obv: Laureated bust of Joseph right.
Rev: Crowned arms supported by griffons.

C#	Date	Mintage	Fine	VF	XF
121	1764	—	400.00	650.00	950.00

Rev: Similar to C#121.

C#	Date	Mintage	Fine	VF	XF
122	1765A	—	400,00	650.00	950.00

C#	Date	Mintage	Fine	VF	XF
123	1768A C-K	—	350.00	475.00	650.00
	1768E H-G	—	350.00	475.00	650.00
	1769A C-K	—	350.00	475.00	650.00
	1769C vS-S	—	350.00	475.00	650.00
	1769E H-G	—	350.00	475.00	650.00
	1769F A-S	—	350.00	475.00	650.00
	1769G B-L	—	350.00	475.00	650.00
	1770C vs-S	—	350.00	475.00	650.00
	1770D G-K	—	350.00	475.00	650.00
	1770E H-G	—	350.00	475.00	650.00
	1771C vS-S	—	350.00	475.00	650.00
	1771D G-K	—	350.00	475.00	650.00
	1771E H-G	—	350.00	475.00	650.00
	1772A C-K	—	350.00	475.00	650.00
	1772C vS-S	—	350.00	475.00	650.00
	1772E H-G	—	350.00	475.00	650.00
	1772G B-L	—	350.00	475.00	650.00
	1772G B-V	—	350.00	475.00	650.00
	1773A C-K	—	350.00	475.00	650.00
	1773C vS-S	—	350.00	475.00	650.00
	1773E H-G	—	350.00	475.00	650.00
	1773G B-V	—	350.00	475.00	650.00
	1774E H-G	—	350.00	475.00	650.00
	1774G B-V	—	350.00	475.00	650.00
	1775A C-A	—	350.00	475.00	650.00
	1775E H-G	—	350.00	475.00	650.00
	1775G B-V	—	350.00	475.00	650.00
	1776A C-A	—	350.00	475.00	650.00
	1776C VS-K	—	350.00	475.00	650.00
	1776E H-G	—	350.00	475.00	650.00
	1776G B-V	—	350.00	475.00	650.00
	1777C VS-K	—	350.00	475.00	650.00
	1777E H-G	—	350.00	475.00	650.00
	1777E H-S	—	350.00	475.00	650.00
	1777F VC-S	—	350.00	475.00	650.00
	1777G B-V	—	350.00	475.00	650.00
	1778A C-A	—	350.00	475.00	650.00
	1778C VS-K	—	350.00	475.00	650.00
	1778G B-V	—	350.00	475.00	650.00
	1779A C-A	—	350.00	475.00	650.00
	1779C vS-K	—	350.00	475.00	650.00
	1779E H-S	—	350.00	475.00	650.00
	1779G B-V	—	350.00	475.00	650.00
123	1780E H-S	—	350.00	475.00	650.00
	1780F VC-S	—	350.00	475.00	650.00
	1780G IB-IV	—	350.00	475.00	650.00

Obv: Younger laureate military bust of Joseph, as sole ruler.

C#	Date	Mintage	Fine	VF	XF
135.1	1781C	—	250.00	300.00	400.00
	1781F	2,143	250.00	300.00	400.00
	1782C	—	250.00	300.00	400.00
	1782F	1,731	250.00	300.00	400.00
	1783C	—	250.00	300.00	400.00
	1783F	3,989	250.00	300.00	400.00
	1784C	—	—	Unique	—
	1784F	—	250.00	300.00	400.00
	1785F	3,145	250.00	300.00	400.00
	1786F	—	250.00	300.00	400.00

Obv: Balding bust of Joseph right.

C#	Date	Mintage	Fine	VF	XF
135.2	1780A	—	250.00	300.00	400.00
	1781A	—	250.00	300.00	400.00
	1781E	—	250.00	300.00	400.00
	1781G	—	250.00	300.00	400.00
	1782E	—	250.00	300.00	400.00
	1782G	—	250.00	300.00	400.00

Obv: Laureated head of Joseph right.

C#	Date	Mintage	Fine	VF	XF
135a	1780A	—	225.00	275.00	350.00
	1782A	—	225.00	275.00	350.00
	1783A	—	225.00	275.00	350.00
	1783E	—	225.00	275.00	350.00
	1783G	—	225.00	275.00	350.00
	1784A	—	225.00	275.00	350.00
	1784E	—	225.00	275.00	350.00
	1784G	—	225.00	275.00	350.00
	1785A	—	225.00	275.00	350.00
	1786A	—	225.00	275.00	350.00
	1786B	—	225.00	275.00	350.00
	1786E	—	225.00	275.00	350.00
	1786G	—	225.00	275.00	350.00
	1787A	—	225.00	275.00	350.00
	1787B	—	225.00	275.00	350.00
	1787E	—	225.00	275.00	350.00
	1787F	—	225.00	275.00	350.00
	1787G	—	225.00	275.00	350.00
	1788A	—	225.00	275.00	350.00
	1788B	—	225.00	275.00	350.00
	1788E	—	225.00	275.00	350.00
	1788F	—	225.00	275.00	350.00
	1788G	—	225.00	275.00	350.00
	1789A	—	225.00	275.00	350.00
	1789B	—	225.00	275.00	350.00
	1789E	—	225.00	275.00	350.00
	1789F	—	225.00	275.00	350.00
	1789G	—	225.00	275.00	350.00
	1790A	—	225.00	275.00	350.00
	1790B	—	225.00	275.00	350.00
	1790E	—	225.00	275.00	350.00
	1790F	8,171	225.00	275.00	350.00
	1790G	—	225.00	275.00	350.00

As King of Hungary and Bohemia
Obv: Laureated head of Leopold right.
Rev: Crowned arms in collar of the Golden Fleece.

C#	Date	Mintage	Fine	VF	XF	Unc
144	1790A	—	250.00	550.00	800.00	1150.

C#	Date	Mintage	Fine	VF	XF	Unc
145	1790A	—	175.00	350.00	525.00	700.00
	1791A	—	225.00	450.00	650.00	850.00
	1791B	—	200.00	400.00	600.00	800.00
	1791E	—	175.00	350.00	525.00	700.00
	1791F	—	225.00	450.00	650.00	850.00
	1791G	—	200.00	400.00	600.00	800.00
	1792E	—	175.00	350.00	525.00	700.00

C#	Date	Mintage	Fine	VF	XF	Unc
145	1792F	1,417	225.00	450.00	650.00	850.00
	1792G	—	185.00	375.00	550.00	750.00

Obv: Bust right. Rev: Crowned shield.

C#	Date	Mintage	VF	XF	Unc
192	1792A	—	1200.	1800.	2250.

Obv: Legend FRANC. II. D. G. R., etc.

C#	Date	Mintage	VF	XF	Unc
163	1792A	—	150.00	225.00	325.00
	1792B	—	150.00	225.00	325.00
	1792E	—	125.00	200.00	300.00
	1793A	—	125.00	200.00	300.00
	1793B	—	165.00	250.00	350.00
	1793E	—	125.00	200.00	300.00
	1793G	—	125.00	200.00	300.00
	1794A	—	165.00	250.00	350.00
	1794B	—	165.00	250.00	350.00
	1794E	—	125.00	200.00	300.00
	1794G	—	165.00	250.00	350.00
	1795A	—	165.00	250.00	350.00
	1795E	—	125.00	200.00	300.00
	1795G	—	150.00	225.00	325.00
	1796A	—	165.00	250.00	350.00
	1796B	—	165.00	250.00	350.00
	1796E	—	165.00	250.00	350.00
	1796G	—	150.00	225.00	325.00
	1797A	—	165.00	250.00	350.00
	1797B	—	200.00	300.00	400.00
	1797C	—	165.00	250.00	350.00
	1797E	—	125.00	200.00	300.00
	1797G	—	165.00	250.00	350.00
	1798A	—	150.00	225.00	325.00
	1798B	—	165.00	250.00	350.00
	1798C	—	Existence Doubtful		—
	1798E	—	125.00	200.00	300.00
	1798G	—	200.00	300.00	400.00
	1799A	—	165.00	250.00	350.00
	1799B	—	Existence Doubtful		—
	1799E	—	165.00	250.00	350.00
	1799G	—	150.00	225.00	325.00
	1800A	—	165.00	250.00	350.00
	1800E	—	125.00	200.00	300.00
	1800G	—	150.00	225.00	325.00
	1801A	—	180.00	275.00	375.00
	1802A	—	165.00	250.00	350.00
	1802B	—	150.00	225.00	325.00
	1802G	—	150.00	225.00	325.00
	1803A	—	180.00	275.00	375.00
	1804A	—	150.00	225.00	325.00
	1804E	—	125.00	200.00	300.00

Obv. leg: FRANCISCVS II D. G. ROM., etc.
Rev. leg. ends: D. LOTH. VEN. SAL.

C#	Date	Mintage	VF	XF	Unc
169	1804A	—	300.00	450.00	550.00
	1805A	—	300.00	450.00	550.00
	1806A	—	250.00	400.00	500.00
	1806B	—	300.00	450.00	550.00
	1806D	—	300.00	450.00	550.00

Rev. leg. ends: D. LO. SAL. WIRC.

C#	Date	Mintage	VF	XF	Unc
186	1806A	—	165.00	250.00	350.00
	1806D	—	225.00	325.00	425.00
	1807A	—	145.00	225.00	325.00
	1807C	—	200.00	300.00	400.00
	1808A	—	140.00	225.00	300.00
	1808D	—	—	Rare	—
	1809A	—	140.00	200.00	300.00
	1809B	—	180.00	275.00	375.00
	1809D	—	180.00	275.00	375.00
	1810A	—	140.00	200.00	300.00

Rev. leg. ends: LO: WI: ET IN. FR: DVX.

C#	Date	Mintage	VF	XF	Unc
186a	1811A	—	110.00	150.00	190.00
	1811B	—	100.00	140.00	175.00
	1812A	—	110.00	150.00	190.00
	1812B	—	110.00	150.00	190.00
	1812G	—	—	Rare	—
	1813A	—	135.00	175.00	225.00
	1813B	—	125.00	170.00	200.00
	1813E	—	135.00	175.00	225.00
	1813G	—	—	Rare	—

C#	Date	Mintage	VF	XF	Unc
186a	1814A	—	110.00	150.00	190.00
	1814B	—	135.00	175.00	225.00
	1814E	—	135.00	175.00	225.00
	1814G	—	—	Rare	—
	1815A	—	110.00	150.00	190.00
	1815B	—	110.00	150.00	190.00
	1815E	—	110.00	150.00	190.00
	1815G	—	135.00	175.00	225.00

Rev. leg. ends: GAL. LOB. IL. REX. A. A.

C#	Date	Mintage	VF	XF	Unc
186b	1816A	—	125.00	165.00	200.00
	1817A	—	100.00	140.00	180.00
	1818A	—	100.00	140.00	180.00
	1818B	—	100.00	140.00	180.00
	1818E	—	110.00	150.00	190.00
	1818G	—	135.00	175.00	225.00
	1819A	—	110.00	150.00	190.00
	1819B	—	135.00	175.00	225.00
	1819E	—	110.00	150.00	190.00
	1819G	—	135.00	175.00	225.00
	1819V	—	325.00	400.00	475.00
	1820A	—	100.00	145.00	185.00
	1820B	—	110.00	150.00	190.00
	1820E	—	100.00	145.00	185.00
	1820G	—	110.00	150.00	190.00
	1821A	—	100.00	145.00	185.00
	1821B	—	100.00	145.00	185.00
	1821E	—	100.00	145.00	185.00
	1821G	—	110.00	150.00	190.00
	1822A	—	100.00	145.00	185.00
	1822B	—	110.00	150.00	190.00
	1822E	—	100.00	145.00	185.00
	1822G	—	110.00	150.00	190.00
	1823A	—	100.00	145.00	185.00
	1823B	—	100.00	145.00	185.00
	1823E	—	100.00	140.00	180.00
	1823G	—	100.00	145.00	185.00
	1824A	—	100.00	140.00	180.00
	1824B	—	100.00	145.00	185.00
	1824E	—	100.00	145.00	185.00
	1824G	—	135.00	175.00	225.00
	1824V	—	185.00	225.00	275.00

Obv: Ribbons on wreath forward across neck

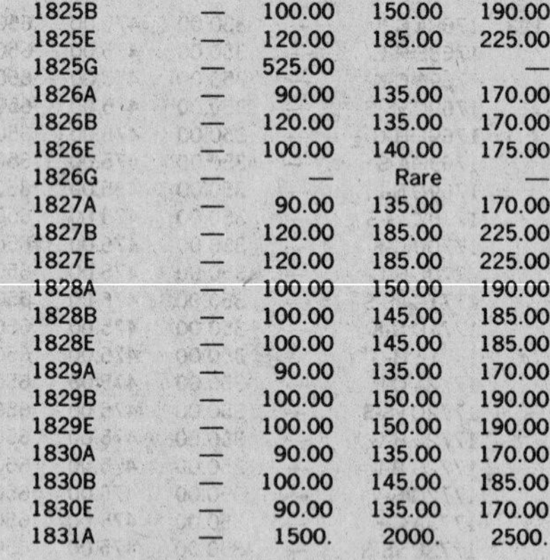

C#	Date	Mintage	VF	XF	Unc
186c	1825A	—	100.00	140.00	175.00
	1825B	—	100.00	150.00	190.00
	1825E	—	120.00	185.00	225.00
	1825G	—	525.00	—	—
	1826A	—	90.00	135.00	170.00
	1826B	—	120.00	135.00	170.00
	1826E	—	100.00	140.00	175.00
	1826G	—	—	Rare	—
	1827A	—	90.00	135.00	170.00
	1827B	—	120.00	185.00	225.00
	1827E	—	120.00	185.00	225.00
	1828A	—	100.00	150.00	190.00
	1828B	—	100.00	145.00	185.00
	1828E	—	100.00	145.00	185.00
	1829A	—	90.00	135.00	170.00
	1829B	—	100.00	150.00	190.00
	1829E	—	100.00	150.00	190.00
	1830A	—	90.00	135.00	170.00
	1830B	—	100.00	145.00	185.00
	1830E	—	90.00	135.00	170.00
	1831A	—	1500.	2000.	2500.

Obv: Ribbons on wreath behind neck

C#	Date	Mintage	VF	XF	Unc
186d	1831A	—	135.00	175.00	225.00
	1832A	—	100.00	140.00	180.00
	1832B	—	110.00	150.00	190.00
	1833A	—	100.00	140.00	180.00
	1833B	—	100.00	145.00	185.00
	1833E	—	135.00	175.00	225.00
	1834A	—	100.00	145.00	185.00
	1834B	—	110.00	150.00	190.00
	1834E	—	135.00	175.00	225.00
	1835A	—	100.00	145.00	185.00
	1835B	—	100.00	145.00	185.00
	1835E	—	135.00	175.00	225.00

Obv. leg. ends: AVSTRIAE IMPERATOR

C#	Date	Mintage	Fine	VF	XF	Unc
194	1835A	—	180.00	300.00	500.00	750.00
	1835E	—	180.00	300.00	500.00	750.00
	1836A	—	100.00	165.00	275.00	400.00
	1836E	—	120.00	200.00	325.00	500.00

Obv. leg. ends: AVSTRI. IMP.

C#	Date	Mintage	Fine	VF	XF	Unc
194a	1837A	—	BV	85.00	110.00	150.00
	1837B	—	BV	100.00	150.00	225.00
	1837E	—	BV	100.00	150.00	225.00
	1838A	—	BV	85.00	150.00	225.00
	1838B	—	BV	100.00	150.00	225.00
	1838E	—	BV	100.00	150.00	225.00
	1839A	—	BV	85.00	110.00	150.00
	1839B	—	BV	100.00	150.00	225.00
	1839E	—	BV	100.00	150.00	225.00
	1840A	—	BV	85.00	110.00	150.00
	1840B	—	BV	85.00	110.00	150.00
	1840E	—	BV	85.00	110.00	165.00
	1840V	—	400.00	550.00	750.00	1000.
	1841A	—	BV	85.00	110.00	150.00
	1841B	—	BV	85.00	100.00	130.00
	1841E	—	BV	85.00	100.00	130.00
	1841V	—	200.00	300.00	400.00	550.00
	1842A	—	BV	100.00	135.00	200.00
	1842B	—	BV	100.00	150.00	275.00
	1842E	—	BV	80.00	100.00	135.00
	1842V	—	175.00	300.00	500.00	750.00
	1843A	—	BV	80.00	100.00	135.00
	1843B	—	BV	85.00	110.00	150.00
	1843E	—	BV	85.00	110.00	150.00
	1843V	—	250.00	425.00	700.00	950.00
	1844A	—	BV	80.00	100.00	135.00
	1844B	—	BV	80.00	100.00	135.00
	1844E	—	BV	80.00	100.00	135.00
	1844V	—	300.00	450.00	700.00	900.00
	1845A	—	BV	75.00	100.00	135.00
	1845B	—	BV	75.00	100.00	135.00
	1845E	—	BV	80.00	110.00	150.00
	1845V	—	300.00	450.00	700.00	900.00
	1846A	—	BV	80.00	110.00	150.00
	1846B	—	BV	80.00	110.00	150.00
	1846E	—	BV	80.00	110.00	150.00
	1846V	—	275.00	400.00	600.00	800.00
	1847A	—	BV	75.00	100.00	135.00
	1847B	—	BV	75.00	100.00	135.00
	1847E	—	BV	100.00	135.00	200.00
	1847V	—	225.00	300.00	450.00	600.00
	1848A	—	BV	75.00	100.00	135.00
	1848B	—	BV	80.00	110.00	150.00
	1848E	—	BV	80.00	110.00	150.00
	1848V	—	225.00	300.00	450.00	600.00

C#	Date	Mintage	Fine	VF	XF	Unc
212	1852A	—	BV	85.00	140.00	200.00
	1853A	—	BV	85.00	140.00	200.00
	1853B	—	BV	100.00	175.00	235.00
	1853E	—	BV	100.00	175.00	235.00
	1854A	—	BV	80.00	110.00	160.00
	1854B	—	BV	90.00	150.00	210.00
	1854E	—	BV	80.00	140.00	200.00
	1854V	—	250.00	350.00	600.00	850.00
	1855A	—	BV	80.00	110.00	150.00
	1855B	—	150.00	200.00	300.00	500.00
	1855E	—	BV	80.00	110.00	150.00
	1855V	—	350.00	500.00	850.00	1250.
	1856A	—	BV	75.00	100.00	135.00
	1856B	—	BV	80.00	110.00	150.00
	1856E	—	BV	75.00	100.00	135.00
	1856V	—	500.00	750.00	1250.	1750.
	1857A	—	BV	75.00	100.00	135.00
	1857B	—	BV	75.00	100.00	150.00
	1857E	—	125.00	175.00	275.00	450.00
	1857V	—	500.00	750.00	1250.	1750.
	1858A	—	BV	75.00	100.00	135.00
	1858B	—	BV	75.00	100.00	150.00
	1858E	—	BV	75.00	100.00	135.00
	1858M	—	250.00	350.00	600.00	850.00
	1858V	—	500.00	750.00	1250.	1750.
	1859A	—	BV	75.00	100.00	135.00
	1859B	—	BV	75.00	100.00	150.00
	1859E	—	BV	75.00	100.00	135.00

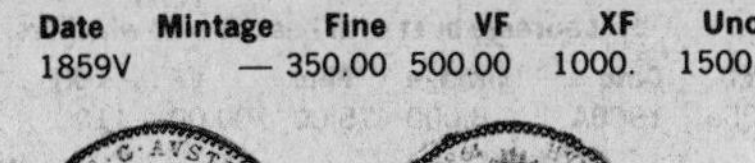

C#	Date	Mintage	Fine	VF	XF	Unc
212	1859V	—	350.00	500.00	1000.	1500.

Y#	Date	Mintage	Fine	VF	XF	Unc
23	1860A	—	BV	75.00	100.00	140.00
	1860B	—	BV	75.00	100.00	150.00
	1860E	—	75.00	100.00	160.00	275.00
	1860V	—	350.00	500.00	1000.	1500.
	1861A	—	BV	75.00	85.00	110.00
	1861B	—	BV	75.00	85.00	125.00
	1861E	—	75.00	100.00	165.00	275.00
	1861V	—	150.00	275.00	450.00	750.00
	1862A	—	BV	75.00	100.00	140.00
	1862B	—	BV	75.00	100.00	150.00
	1862E	—	BV	80.00	125.00	175.00
	1862V	—	150.00	225.00	450.00	750.00
	1863A	—	BV	75.00	85.00	110.00
	1863B	—	BV	75.00	85.00	110.00
	1863E	—	BV	75.00	85.00	110.00
	1863V	—	375.00	450.00	1000.	1500.
	1864A	—	BV	75.00	100.00	135.00
	1864B	—	BV	75.00	100.00	140.00
	1864E	—	BV	80.00	110.00	175.00
	1864V	—	150.00	275.00	450.00	750.00
	1865A	—	BV	75.00	100.00	135.00
	1865B	—	BV	75.00	100.00	135.00
	1865E	—	BV	80.00	120.00	165.00
	1865V	—	350.00	500.00	1000.	1500.

Obv: Head of Franz Josef right with heavier side whiskers.

Y#	Date	Mintage	Fine	VF	XF	Unc
23a	1866A	—	75.00	100.00	150.00	235.00
	1866B	—	75.00	125.00	175.00	300.00
	1866E	—	75.00	125.00	175.00	300.00
	1866V	—	350.00	500.00	1000.	1500.

Y#	Date	Mintage	Fine	VF	XF	Unc
23b	1867A	—	BV	75.00	100.00	135.00
	1867B	—	BV	75.00	100.00	135.00
	1867E	—	BV	75.00	110.00	160.00
	1868A	—	BV	75.00	100.00	135.00
	1869A	—	BV	75.00	100.00	135.00
	1870A	—	BV	75.00	100.00	135.00
	1871A	—	BV	75.00	100.00	135.00
	1872A	—	BV	75.00	100.00	135.00

Y#	Date	Mintage	Fine	VF	XF	Unc
23c	1872	.460	BV	75.00	100.00	125.00
	1873	.516	BV	75.00	100.00	125.00
	1874	.353	BV	75.00	100.00	125.00
	1875	.184	BV	75.00	100.00	125.00
	1876	.680	BV	75.00	100.00	125.00
	1877	.823	BV	75.00	100.00	125.00
	1878	.281	BV	75.00	100.00	125.00
	1879	.381	BV	75.00	100.00	125.00
	1880	.341	BV	85.00	110.00	150.00
	1881	.477	BV	75.00	100.00	125.00
	1882	.390	BV	85.00	110.00	135.00
	1883	.409	BV	75.00	100.00	125.00
	1884	.238	BV	80.00	110.00	130.00
	1885	.257	BV	75.00	100.00	125.00
	1886	.291	BV	75.00	100.00	125.00
	1887	.223	BV	75.00	90.00	110.00
	1888	.309	BV	75.00	90.00	110.00
	1889	.335	BV	75.00	90.00	110.00
	1890	.374	BV	75.00	90.00	110.00
	1891	.325	BV	75.00	90.00	110.00
	1892	.361	BV	75.00	90.00	110.00
	1893	.285	BV	75.00	90.00	110.00
	1894	.292	BV	75.00	90.00	110.00
	1895	.330	BV	75.00	90.00	110.00
	1896	.414	BV	75.00	90.00	110.00
	1897	.263	BV	75.00	90.00	110.00
	1898	.350	BV	75.00	90.00	110.00
	1899	.412	BV	75.00	90.00	110.00
	1900	.361	BV	75.00	90.00	110.00
	1901	.349	BV	75.00	90.00	110.00

Y#	Date	Mintage	Fine	VF	XF	Unc
23c	1902	.311	BV	75.00	90.00	110.00
	1903	.380	BV	85.00	110.00	135.00
	1904	.517	BV	85.00	110.00	135.00
	1905	.392	BV	85.00	110.00	135.00
	1906	.492	75.00	90.00	125.00	150.00
	1907	.554	85.00	110.00	150.00	200.00
	1908	.409	BV	85.00	110.00	135.00
	1909	.366	BV	75.00	90.00	110.00
	1910	.440	BV	75.00	90.00	110.00
	1911	.591	BV	75.00	90.00	110.00
	1912	.495	BV	75.00	90.00	110.00
	1913	.320	BV	75.00	90.00	110.00
	1914	.378	BV	75.00	90.00	110.00
	1915	Restrike	BV	BV	BV	75.00
	1951 (error for 1915)					
		—	—	—	100.00	150.00

50th Jubilee
Rev: Second date below eagle.

Y#	Date	Mintage	Fine	VF	XF	Unc
24	1848/1898A		—			
		.025	—	350.00	450.00	650.00
	1849/1898A		—			
		2,300	—	1200.	1600.	2200.
	1850/1898A		—			
		2,300	—	1200.	1600.	2200.
	1851/1898A		—			
		2,300	—	1200.	1600.	2200.

8 FLORIN-20 FRANCS

6.4516 gm., .900 GOLD, .1867 oz AGW

Y#	Date	Mintage	Fine	VF	XF	Unc
22	1870	.025	BV	BV	125.00	160.00
	1871	.034	BV	BV	125.00	150.00
	1872	5,185	125.00	175.00	250.00	335.00
	1873	.023	BV	BV	125.00	160.00
	1874	.042	BV	BV	125.00	150.00
	1875	.086	BV	BV	125.00	150.00
	1876	.146	BV	BV	125.00	150.00
	1877	.125	BV	BV	125.00	150.00
	1878	.125	BV	BV	125.00	150.00
	1879	.043	BV	BV	125.00	150.00
	1880	.062	BV	BV	125.00	150.00
	1881	.062	BV	BV	125.00	150.00
	1882	.115	BV	BV	125.00	150.00
	1883	.031	BV	BV	125.00	150.00
	1884	.091	BV	BV	125.00	150.00
	1885	.178	BV	BV	125.00	150.00
	1886	.140	BV	BV	125.00	150.00
	1887	.174	BV	BV	125.00	150.00
	1888	.114	BV	BV	125.00	150.00
	1889	.208	BV	BV	125.00	150.00
	1890	.043	BV	BV	125.00	150.00
	1891	.019	125.00	150.00	200.00	250.00
	1892	Restrike	BV	BV	BV	125.00

2 DUCATS

7.0000 gm., .986 GOLD, .2219 oz AGW

C#	Date	Mintage	Fine	VF	XF
124	1768E H-G	—	450.00	600.00	850.00
	1769E H-G	—	450.00	600.00	850.00
	1770E H-G	—	450.00	600.00	850.00
	1771E H-G	—	450.00	600.00	850.00
	1772E H-G	—	450.00	600.00	850.00
	1773E H-G	—	450.00	600.00	850.00
	1774E H-G	—	450.00	600.00	850.00
	1775E H-G	—	450.00	600.00	850.00
	1776E H-G	—	450.00	600.00	850.00
	1777E H-G	—	450.00	600.00	850.00

C#	Date	Mintage	Fine	VF	XF
124	1777E H-S	—	450.00	600.00	850.00
	1778E H-S	—	450.00	600.00	850.00
	1779E H-S	—	450.00	600.00	850.00
	1780E H-S	—	450.00	600.00	850.00

Obv: Balding bust of Joseph right, as sole ruler.

C#	Date	Mintage	Fine	VF	XF
136	1781E	—	500.00	700.00	950.00
	1782E	—	500.00	700.00	950.00

C#	Date	Mintage	Fine	VF	XF
136a	1783E	—	450.00	600.00	850.00
	1784A	—	450.00	600.00	850.00
	1786A	—	450.00	600.00	850.00
	1786B	—	450.00	600.00	850.00
	1786E	—	450.00	600.00	850.00
	1787A	—	450.00	600.00	850.00
	1787B	—	450.00	600.00	850.00
	1787E	—	450.00	600.00	850.00

C#	Date	Mintage	VF	XF	Unc
164	1799A	.068	800.00	1200.	1700.

3 DUCATS

10.5000 gm., .986 GOLD, .3329 oz AGW

C#	Date	Mintage	Fine	VF	XF
125	1773E H-G	—	1500.	2500.	3500.
	1776E H-G	—	1500.	2500.	3500.
	1778E H-S	—	1500.	2500.	3500.

4 DUCATS

13.9636 gm., .986 GOLD, .4430 oz AGW
Obv: Veiled head of Maria Theresa right.
Rev: Crowned imperial eagle, value below.

C#	Date	Mintage	Fine	VF	XF
58	1778 IC-FA	—	1500.	2500.	3500.
	1779 IC-FA	—	1500.	2500.	3500.

Obv: Laureated bust of Joseph right.

C#	Date	Mintage	Fine	VF	XF
137	1786A	—	1500.	2500.	3500.

Obv: Laureated head of Leopold right.

C#	Date	Mintage	Fine	VF	XF
146	1790A	—	—	Rare	—

Obv. leg: FRANCISCVS II. D. G. R. IMP....
Rev: Legend ends LOTH. M. D. HET.

C#	Date	Mintage	VF	XF	Unc
165	1793A	—	1000.	1500.	2000.
	1794A	—	1200.	1700.	2200.
	1795A	—	950.00	1350.	1750.
	1796A	—	1000.	1500.	2000.
	1797A	—	1000.	1500.	2000.
	1798A	—	1200.	1700.	2200.
	1799A	—	1000.	1500.	2000.

C#	Date	Mintage	VF	XF	Unc
165	1800A	—	1000.	1500.	2000.
	1801A	—	900.00	1350.	1800.
	1802A	—	1000.	1500.	2000.
	1803A	—	950.00	1400.	1850.
	1804A	—	900.00	1350.	1800.
	1853A	—	—No Specimens Known		

Obv. leg: FRANCISCVS II. D. G. ROM. ET....
Rev. leg. ends: D. LOTH. VEN. SAL.

C#	Date	Mintage	VF	XF	Unc
170	1804A	—	1000.	1500.	2000.
	1805A	—	1000.	1500.	2000.
	1806A	—	800.00	1200.	1600.

Obv. leg. ends: AVSTRIAE IMPERATOR
Rev. leg. ends: D. LO. SAL. WIRC.

C#	Date	Mintage	VF	XF	Unc
187	1807A	—	1200.	1800.	2300.
	1808A	—	1000.	1500.	2000.
	1809A	—	900.00	1300.	1750.
	1810A	—	1200.	1800.	2300.

Rev. leg. ends: LO: WI: ET IN. FR: DVX.

C#	Date	Mintage	VF	XF	Unc
187a	1811A	—	900.00	1200.	1500.
	1812A	—	1000.	1400.	1700.
	1813A	—	900.00	1200.	1500.
	1814A	—	1000.	1400.	1700.
	1815A	—	900.00	1200.	1500.

Rev. leg. ends: GAL. LOD. IL. REX. A. A.

C#	Date	Mintage	VF	XF	Unc
187b	1816A	—	700.00	1200.	1800.
	1817A	—	700.00	1200.	1800.
	1818A	—	800.00	1400.	2000.
	1819A	—	700.00	1200.	1800.
	1820A	—	700.00	1200.	1800.
	1821A	—	700.00	1200.	1800.
	1822A	—	700.00	1200.	1800.
	1823A	—	700.00	1200.	1800.
	1824A	—	700.00	1200.	1800.
	1825A	—	500.00	950.00	1400.
	1826A	—	700.00	1200.	1800.
	1827A	—	700.00	1200.	1800.
	1828A	—	600.00	1000.	1500.
	1829A	—	600.00	1000.	1500.
	1830A	—	600.00	1000.	1500.

C#	Date	Mintage	Fine	VF	XF	Unc
195	1837A	—	400.00	650.00	1100.	1500.
	1838A	—	400.00	650.00	1100.	1500.
	1839A	—	400.00	650.00	1100.	1500.
	1840A	—	400.00	650.00	1100.	1500.
	1841A	—	400.00	650.00	1100.	1500.
	1842A	—	400.00	650.00	1100.	1500.
	1843A	—	400.00	650.00	1100.	1500.
	1844A	—	400.00	650.00	1100.	1500.
	1845A	—	400.00	650.00	1100.	1500.
	1846A	—	400.00	650.00	1100.	1500.
	1847A	—	400.00	650.00	1100.	1500.
	1848A	—	400.00	650.00	1100.	1500.
	1848E	—	450.00	750.00	1200.	1600.

C#	Date	Mintage	Fine	VF	XF	Unc
213	1852A	—	—	No specimens known		
	1853A	—	—	No specimens known		
	1854A	—	500.00	900.00	1350.	1750.
	1855A	—	500.00	900.00	1350.	1750.
	1856A	—	500.00	900.00	1350.	1750.
	1857A	—	475.00	800.00	1200.	1500.
	1857V	—	1400.	1850.	2500.	3000.
	1858A	—	400.00	750.00	1100.	1400.
	1859A	.013	400.00	750.00	1100.	1400.

Rev: Similar to C#25b.

Y#	Date	Mintage	Fine	VF	XF	Unc
25	1860A	6,303	800.00	1250.	1700.	2000.
	1861A	7,664	800.00	1250.	1700.	2000.
	1862A	8,944	500.00	800.00	1300.	1650.
	1863A	.022	500.00	800.00	1200.	1500.
	1864A	.045	500.00	800.00	1200.	1500.
	1864V	4,463	1000.	1500.	1750.	2000.
	1865A	.013	500.00	800.00	1200.	1500.
	1865V	.010	500.00	800.00	1200.	1500.

Obv: Laureate bust with heavier side whiskers.

Y#	Date	Mintage	Fine	VF	XF	Unc
25a	1866A	8,000	475.00	700.00	1100.	1600.

Y#	Date	Mintage	Fine	VF	XF	Unc
25b	1867A	.016	500.00	800.00	1200.	1500.
	1868A	.017	500.00	800.00	1200.	1500.
	1869A	.019	500.00	800.00	1200.	1500.
	1870A	.012	500.00	800.00	1300.	1650.
	1871A	.019	500.00	800.00	1200.	1500.
	1872A	*.012	500.00	800.00	1300.	1650.

Y#	Date	Mintage	Fine	VF	XF	Unc
A18	1873	—	1000.	1500.	2000.	2500.
	1873	—	—	—	Proof	4500.

Obv: W/o mintmark.

Y#	Date	Mintage	Fine	VF	XF	Unc
25c	1872	*.012	400.00	700.00	1000.	1350.
	1873	.024	400.00	700.00	1000.	1350.
	1874	.015	350.00	500.00	800.00	1150.
	1875	.012	350.00	500.00	800.00	1150.
	1876	5,243	375.00	600.00	1000.	1450.
	1877	5,970	375.00	600.00	1000.	1450.
	1878	.023	BV	400.00	700.00	1000.
	1879	.029	BV	400.00	700.00	1000.
	1880	.023	BV	400.00	700.00	1000.
	1881	.035	BV	400.00	700.00	1000.
	1882	.029	BV	400.00	700.00	1000.
	1883	.037	BV	400.00	700.00	1000.
	1884	.035	BV	400.00	700.00	1000.
	1885	.028	BV	400.00	700.00	1000.
	1886	.018	BV	400.00	700.00	1000.
	1887	.027	BV	400.00	700.00	1000.
	1888	.036	BV	400.00	700.00	1000.
	1889	.031	BV	400.00	700.00	1000.
	1890	.047	BV	375.00	650.00	950.00
	1891	.054	BV	350.00	600.00	850.00
	1892	.058	BV	350.00	600.00	850.00
	1893	.054	BV	375.00	650.00	950.00
	1894	.035	BV	375.00	650.00	950.00
	1895	.040	BV	375.00	650.00	950.00
	1896	.049	BV	375.00	650.00	950.00
	1897	.035	BV	375.00	650.00	950.00
	1898	.054	BV	375.00	600.00	850.00
	1899	.054	BV	375.00	500.00	700.00
	1900	.048	BV	400.00	525.00	700.00
	1901	.052	BV	400.00	525.00	700.00
	1902	.069	BV	375.00	500.00	650.00
	1903	.073	BV	375.00	500.00	650.00
	1904	.080	BV	375.00	500.00	650.00
	1905	.091	BV	375.00	500.00	600.00
	1906	.123	BV	325.00	375.00	450.00
	1907	.104	BV	325.00	375.00	450.00
	1908	.080	BV	400.00	525.00	700.00
	1909	.084	BV	375.00	500.00	575.00
	1910	.101	BV	325.00	375.00	450.00
	1911	.142	BV	325.00	375.00	450.00
	1912	.151	BV	325.00	375.00	450.00
	1913	.119	BV	325.00	375.00	450.00
	1914	.102	BV	300.00	350.00	425.00
	1915	Restrike	BV	BV	BV	300.00

5 DUCATS

17.5000 gm., .986 GOLD, .5548 oz AGW

C#	Date	Mintage	Fine	VF	XF
62	1777 IC-FA	—	2000.	3000.	4500.

DECIMAL COINAGE

100 Groschen = 1 Schilling

GROSCHEN

BRONZE

Y#	Date	Mintage	Fine	VF	XF	Unc
60	1925	30.400	.10	.20	.50	1.50
	1926	15.400	.10	.30	1.00	2.00
	1927	9.310	.10	.30	1.00	2.00
	1928	17.100	.10	.30	1.00	2.00
	1929	11.400	.10	.30	1.00	2.00
	1930	8.890	.10	.30	1.00	2.00
	1931	.970	15.00	32.50	50.00	80.00
	1932	3.040	1.00	2.50	5.00	7.50
	1933	3.940	.50	1.50	3.75	6.00
	1934	4.230	.15	.75	2.00	4.00
	1935	3.740	.15	.75	2.00	4.00
	1936	6.020	.60	2.00	4.50	9.00
	1937	5.830	.50	1.50	3.75	7.50
	1938	1.650	2.00	4.50	7.50	17.50

ZINC

Y#	Date	Mintage	Fine	VF	XF	Unc
86	1947	23.515	—	.10	.20	.35

2 GROSCHEN

BRONZE

Y#	Date	Mintage	Fine	VF	XF	Unc
61	1925	29.800	.10	.25	.75	1.50
	1926	17.700	.10	.30	1.00	1.75
	1927	7.750	.15	.75	3.50	5.00
	1928	19.400	.10	.30	1.00	1.75
	1929	16.100	.10	.30	1.00	1.75
	1930	5.700	.15	.60	2.50	3.50
	1934	.810	8.50	12.50	17.50	25.00
	1935	3.140	.15	.60	2.50	3.50
	1936	4.410	.10	.30	1.25	2.00
	1937	3.790	.10	.50	1.75	2.50
	1938	.860	2.50	4.50	8.00	13.50

ALUMINUM

Y#	Date	Mintage	VF	XF	Unc
89	1950	21.600	.10	.25	.50
	1950	—	—	Proof	10.00
	1951	7.370	.10	.50	1.00
	1951	—	—	Proof	10.00
	1952	37.800	.10	.25	.50
	1952	—	—	Proof	10.00
	1954	20.000	.10	.20	.40
	1957	21.300	.10	.25	.50
	1957	—	—	Proof	8.00
	1962	5.430	.10	.25	.50
	1962	—	—	Proof	11.00
	1964	.173	—	Proof	1.00
	1965	14.475	.10	.15	.40
	1965	—	—	Proof	1.00
	1966	7.454	.10	.15	.40
	1966	—	—	Proof	3.00
	1967	.013	—	Proof	50.00
	1968	1.803	.10	.40	.75
	1968	.022	—	Proof	1.50
	1969	.057	—	Proof	2.00
	1970	.260	—	Proof	1.00
	1971	.145	—	Proof	1.25
	1972	2.763	—	.10	.15
	1972	.132	—	Proof	.75
	1973	5.883	—	.10	.15
	1973	.149	—	Proof	.50
	1974	1.387	—	.10	.20
	1974	.093	—	Proof	.50
	1975	1.394	—	.10	.20
	1975	.052	—	Proof	.50
89	1976	2.710	—	—	.10
	1976	.045	—	Proof	.50
	1977	1.790	—	—	.10
	1977	.047	—	Proof	.50
	1978	—	—	—	.10
	1978	—	—	Proof	.50
	1979	—	—	—	—
	1979	—	—	Proof	—

5 GROSCHEN

COPPER-NICKEL

Y#	Date	Mintage	Fine	VF	XF	Unc
62	1931	16.600	.15	.50	1.25	2.50
	1932	4.700	.25	1.00	3.00	5.00
	1934	3.210	.40	1.25	3.75	6.50
	1936	1.240	2.50	7.50	12.50	15.00
	1937	1.540	20.00	40.00	60.00	100.00
	1938	.870	150.00	200.00	300.00	450.00

ZINC

Y#	Date	Mintage	VF	XF	Unc
87	1948	17.200	.15	.75	1.25
	1950	19.400	.15	.75	1.25
	1951	12.400	.15	.75	1.25
	1951	—	—	Proof	11.50
	1953	84.900	.10	.50	1.00
	1955	17.000	.10	.50	1.00
	1957	20.700	.10	.50	1.00
	1961	3.420	.15	.85	1.50
	1962	5.990	.15	.85	1.50
	1963	13.295	.10	.50	1.00
	1963	—	—	Proof	3.00
	1964	4.659	.10	.50	1.00
	1964	—	—	Proof	.50
	1965	13.704	.10	.15	.25
	1965	—	—	Proof	.50
	1966	9.348	.10	.15	.25
	1966	—	—	Proof	6.50
	1967	4.404	.10	.15	.25
	1967	—	—	Proof	6.50
	1968	31.422	—	.10	.15
	1968	.016	—	Proof	6.50
	1969	.040	—	Proof	9.00
	1970	.144	—	Proof	1.00
	1971	.125	—	Proof	1.00
	1972	10.879	—	—	.10
	1972	.116	—	Proof	.75
	1973	10.336	—	—	.10
	1973	.120	—	Proof	.50
	1974	2.911	—	—	.10
	1974	.087	—	Proof	.50
	1975	7.559	—	—	.10
	1975	.051	—	Proof	.50
	1976	8.034	—	—	.10
	1976	.045	—	Proof	.50
	1977	1.555	—	—	.10
	1977	.045	—	Proof	.50
	1978	—	—	—	.10
	1978	—	—	Proof	.50
	1979	—	—	—	—
	1979	—	—	Proof	—

10 GROSCHEN

COPPER-NICKEL

Y#	Date	Mintage	Fine	VF	XF	Unc
63	1925	66.100	.10	.25	.75	2.00
	1928	11.400	.50	1.00	5.00	10.00
	1929	12.000	.40	.75	2.00	3.75

ZINC

Y#	Date	Mintage	Fine	VF	XF	Unc
88	1947	6.840	1.00	2.50	5.00	8.50
	1947	—	—	—	Proof	12.50
	1948	66.200	—	.10	.50	2.00
	1948	—	—	—	Proof	3.75
	1949	51.200	—	.10	.50	1.50
	1949	—	—	—	Proof	8.50

ALUMINUM

Y#	Date	Mintage	VF	XF	Unc
90	1951	9.570	.20	.50	1.25
	1951	—	—	Proof	8.00
	1952	45.900	.10	.25	1.00
	1952	—	—	Proof	7.50
	1953	39.000	.10	.25	1.00
	1955	27.500	.10	.25	1.00
	1957	33.500	.10	.25	1.00
	1959	80.700	.10	.25	.75
	1961	11.100	.10	.25	.75
	1962	24.600	.10	.20	.75
	1963	38.062	.10	.20	.60
	1963	—	—	Proof	7.50
	1964	34.928	.10	.20	.30
	1964	—	—	Proof	.50
	1965	40.615	.10	.20	.50
	1965	—	—	Proof	1.50
	1966	24.991	.10	.20	.50
	1966	—	—	Proof	5.00
	1967	32.553	—	.10	.25
	1967	—	—	Proof	5.00
	1968	42.396	—	.10	.25
	1968	.016	—	Proof	7.50
	1969	19.953	—	.10	.25
	1969	.027	—	Proof	1.50
	1970	36.998	—	.10	.25
	1970	.102	—	Proof	.50
	1971	57.450	—	.10	.25
	1971	.082	—	Proof	.50
	1972	75.661	—	.10	.25
	1972	.081	—	Proof	.50
	1973	60.244	—	.10	.25
	1973	.097	—	Proof	.50
	1974	55.924	—	.10	.15
	1974	.078	—	Proof	.50
	1975	70.196	—	.10	.15
	1975	.049	—	Proof	.50
	1976	39.313	—	.10	.15
	1976	.044	—	Proof	.50
	1977	53.610	—	.10	.15
	1977	.044	—	Proof	.50
	1978	—	—	.10	.50
	1978	—	—	Proof	.15
	1979	—	—	—	—
	1979	—	—	Proof	—

20 GROSCHEN

ALUMINUM-BRONZE

Y#	Date	Mintage	Fine	VF	XF	Unc
95	1950	1.610	.50	1.00	2.50	5.00
	1950	—	—	—	Proof	20.00
	1951	7.780	.10	.25	.50	1.25
	1951	—	—	—	Proof	12.50
	1954	5.340	.10	.25	.50	1.25
	1954	—	—	—	Proof	15.00

1/2 SCHILLING

3.0000 gm., .640 SILVER, .0617 oz ASW

Y#	Date	Mintage	Fine	VF	XF	Unc
67	1925	18.300	2.00	3.00	4.50	7.50
	1926	12.300	3.00	6.00	11.50	15.00

50 GROSCHEN

COPPER-NICKEL

Y#	Date	Mintage	Fine	VF	XF	Unc
64	1934	8.220	15.00	30.00	50.00	75.00
	1934	Inc. Ab.	—	—	Proof	100.00

Y#	Date	Mintage	Fine	VF	XF	Unc
65	1935	11.400	1.00	2.25	5.50	10.00
	1935	Inc. Ab.	—	—	Proof	70.00
	1936	1.000	25.00	55.00	75.00	110.00
	1936	Inc. Ab.	—	—	Proof	165.00

ALUMINUM

Y#	Date	Mintage	Fine	VF	XF	Unc
91	1946	13.000	.10	.25	.75	1.50
	1946	—	—	—	Proof	20.00
	1947	26.900	.10	.25	.60	1.25
	1947	—	—	—	Proof	20.00
	1952	7.450	.40	1.00	3.50	5.00
	1952	—	—	—	Proof	20.00
	1955	10.500	.20	.50	2.00	3.75
	1955	—	—	—	Proof	25.00

ALUMINUM-BRONZE

Y#	Date	Mintage	VF	XF	Unc
103	1959	14.100	.10	.25	.75
	1959	—	—	Proof	7.50
	1960	22.400	.10	.25	.75
	1961	19.800	.10	.25	.75
	1962	10.000	.10	.30	1.00
	1963	9.483	.10	.25	.75
	1963	—	—	Proof	20.00
	1964	5.331	.10	.35	1.00
	1964	—	—	Proof	2.00
	1965	15.007	.10	.20	.40
	1965	—	—	Proof	2.50
	1966	7.322	.10	.20	.40
	1966	—	—	Proof	10.00
	1967	8.237	.10	.15	.20
	1967	—	—	Proof	11.00
	1968	7.742	—	.10	.15
	1968	.015	—	Proof	7.50
	1969	7.076	—	.10	.15
	1969	.026	—	Proof	4.50
	1970	2.994	—	.10	.15
	1970	.129	—	Proof	2.00
	1971	14.217	—	.10	.15
	1971	.084	—	Proof	1.00
	1972	17.367	—	.10	.15
	1972	.080	—	Proof	.75
	1973	17.902	—	.10	.15

Y#	Date	Mintage	VF	XF	Unc
103	1973	.090	—	Proof	.50
	1974	15.852	—	.10	.15
	1974	.076	—	Proof	.50
	1975	9.916	—	.10	.15
	1975	.049	—	Proof	.50
	1976	11.052	—	.10	.15
	1976	.044	—	Proof	.50
	1977	7.214	—	.10	.15
	1977	.044	—	Proof	.50
	1978	—	—	.10	.15
	1978	—	—	Proof	.50
	1979	—	—	—	—
	1979	—	—	Proof	—

SCHILLING

7.0000 gm., .800 SILVER, .1800 oz ASW

Y#	Date	Mintage	Fine	VF	XF	Unc
59	1924	11.086	BV	BV	6.00	7.50

6.0000 gm., .640 SILVER, .1235 oz ASW

Y#	Date	Mintage	Fine	VF	XF	Unc
68	1925	38.200	3.75	4.25	5.00	7.50
	1926	20.100	4.00	5.00	7.00	10.00
	1932	.700	32.50	55.00	80.00	125.00

COPPER-NICKEL

Y#	Date	Mintage	Fine	VF	XF	Unc
66	1934	30.600	.75	1.50	3.50	6.50
	1935	11.900	4.00	8.50	17.50	30.00

ALUMINUM

Y#	Date	Mintage	Fine	VF	XF	Unc
92	1946	27.300	.20	.35	1.00	1.75
	1947	35.800	.20	.35	1.00	1.75
	1947	—	—	—	Proof	32.50
	1952	23.300	.25	.50	1.25	3.00
	1952	—	—	—	Proof	25.00
	1957	28.600	.25	.50	1.25	3.00
	1957	—	—	—	Proof	50.00

ALUMINUM-BRONZE

Y#	Date	Mintage	VF	XF	Unc
104	1959	46.700	.15	.25	.75
	1959	—	—	Proof	8.00
	1960	46.100	.15	.25	.75
	1960	—	—	Proof	—
	1961	51.100	.15	.25	.75
	1962	9.300	.20	.35	1.00
	1963	24.845	.15	.25	.75
	1963	—	—	Proof	20.00
	1964	11.709	.20	.35	1.00

Y#	Date	Mintage	VF	XF	Unc
104	1964	—	—	Proof	.50
	1965	23.925	.15	.20	.40
	1965	—	—	Proof	2.50
	1966	18.688	.15	.20	.40
	1966	—	—	Proof	10.00
	1967	22.214	.10	.15	.20
	1967	—	—	Proof	11.00
	1968	30.860	.10	.15	.20
	1968	.017	—	Proof	7.50
	1969	10.285	.10	.15	.20
	1969	.028	—	Proof	4.50
	1970	10.679	.10	.15	.20
	1970	.100	—	Proof	2.00
	1971	27.974	—	.15	.20
	1971	.082	—	Proof	1.00
	1972	54.577	—	.15	.20
	1972	.078	—	Proof	.75
	1973	41.332	—	.15	.20
	1973	.090	—	Proof	.50
	1974	43.712	—	.15	.20
	1974	.077	—	Proof	.50
	1975	18.564	—	.15	.20
	1975	.049	—	Proof	.50
	1976	28.704	—	.15	.20
	1976	.044	—	Proof	.50
	1977	19.544	—	.15	.20
	1977	.044	—	Proof	.50
	1978	—	—	.10	.20
	1978	—	—	Proof	.50
	1979	—	—	—	—
	1979	—	—	Proof	—

2 SCHILLING

12.0000 gm., .640 SILVER, .2469 oz ASW
Schubert

Y#	Date	Mintage	Fine	VF	XF	Unc
69	1928	6.900	7.50	8.50	10.00	15.00
	1928	Inc. Ab.	—	—	Proof	400.00

Dr. Billroth

Y#	Date	Mintage	Fine	VF	XF	Unc
70	1929	2.000	10.00	20.00	30.00	40.00

Vogelweide

Y#	Date	Mintage	Fine	VF	XF	Unc
71	1930	.500	7.50	8.50	12.00	20.00
	1930	Inc. Ab.	—	—	Proof	200.00

Mozart

Y#	Date	Mintage	Fine	VF	XF	Unc
72	1931	.500	15.00	20.00	32.00	60.00
72	1931	Inc. Ab.	—	—	Proof	300.00

Haydn

Y#	Date	Mintage	Fine	VF	XF	Unc
73	1932	.300	50.00	75.00	100.00	150.00
	1932	Inc. Ab.	—	—	Proof	400.00

Dr. Seipel

Y#	Date	Mintage	Fine	VF	XF	Unc
74	1932	.400	15.00	30.00	40.00	75.00
	1932	Inc. Ab.	—	—	Proof	350.00

Dollfuss

Y#	Date	Mintage	Fine	VF	XF	Unc
75	1934	1.500	10.00	20.00	30.00	45.00
	1934	Inc. Ab.	—	—	Proof	250.00

Lueger

Y#	Date	Mintage	Fine	VF	XF	Unc
76	1935	.500	12.50	25.00	40.00	60.00
	1935	Inc. Ab.	—	—	Proof	250.00

Prince Eugen

Y#	Date	Mintage	Fine	VF	XF	Unc
77	1936	.500	7.50	15.00	20.00	40.00
	1936	Inc. Ab.	—	—	Proof	225.00

St. Charles Church

Y#	Date	Mintage	Fine	VF	XF	Unc
78	1937	.500	7.50	15.00	20.00	40.00
	1937	Inc. Ab.	—	—	Proof	225.00

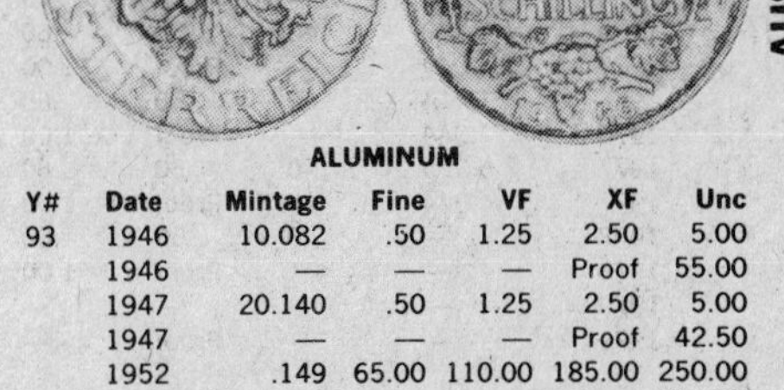

ALUMINUM

Y#	Date	Mintage	Fine	VF	XF	Unc
93	1946	10.082	.50	1.25	2.50	5.00
	1946	—	—	—	Proof	55.00
	1947	20.140	.50	1.25	2.50	5.00
	1947	—	—	—	Proof	42.50
	1952	.149	65.00	110.00	185.00	250.00
	1952	—	—	—	Proof	600.00

5 SCHILLING

15.0000 gm., .835 SILVER, .4027 oz ASW
Madonna

Y#	Date	Mintage	Fine	VF	XF	Unc
79	1934	3.066	15.00	22.50	28.50	42.50
	1935	5.377	13.50	21.50	27.50	42.50
	1936	1.557	45.00	75.00	120.00	200.00

ALUMINUM

Y#	Date	Mintage	Fine	VF	XF	Unc
94	1952	29.873	2.00	3.50	5.00	8.50
	1952	—	—	—	Proof	35.00
	1957	.240	100.00	175.00	250.00	340.00
	1957	—	—	—	Proof	450.00

5.2000 gm., .640 SILVER, .1070 oz ASW
Reeded edge

Y#	Date	Mintage	VF	XF	Unc
106	1960	12.618	BV	3.50	4.25
	1960	1,000	—	Proof	12.50
	1961	17.902	BV	3.50	4.25
	1961	—	—	Proof	12.50
	1962	6.771	BV	3.50	4.25
	1962	—	—	Proof	8.00
	1963	1.811	BV	5.00	8.00
	1963	—	—	Proof	8.50
	1964	4.030	BV	3.50	4.25
	1964	—	—	Proof	4.50
	1965	4.759	BV	3.50	4.25
	1965	—	—	Proof	4.50
	1966	4.481	BV	3.50	4.00
	1966	—	—	Proof	5.50
	1967	1.900	BV	4.00	4.50
	1967	—	—	Proof	7.50
	1968	4.792	BV	3.50	4.00
	1968	.020	—	Proof	5.50

COPPER-NICKEL
Plain edge

Y#	Date	Mintage	VF	XF	Unc
106a	1968	2.075	.50	1.00	1.75
	1969	41.222	.40	.50	.75
	1969	.021	—	Proof	4.50
	1970	15.771	.40	.50	.75
	1970	.092	—	Proof	3.25
	1971	21.422	.40	.50	.75
	1971	.084	—	Proof	2.00

Y#	Date	Mintage	VF	XF	Unc
106a	1972	5.430	.40	.50	.60
	1972	.075	—	Proof	1.50
	1973	8.259	.40	.50	.60
	1973	.087	—	Proof	1.00
	1974	17.973	.40	.50	.60
	1974	.076	—	Proof	1.00
	1975	6.898	.40	.50	.60
	1975	.049	—	Proof	1.00
	1976	1.414	.40	.50	.60
	1976	.044	—	Proof	1.00
	1977	6.379	.40	.50	.60
	1977	.044	—	Proof	1.00
	1978	—	.40	.50	.60
	1978	—	—	Proof	1.00
	1979	—	—	—	—
	1979	—	—	Proof	—

10 SCHILLING

7.5000 gm., .640 SILVER, .1543 oz ASW

Y#	Date	Mintage	VF	XF	Unc
99	1957	15.636	BV	BV	7.50
	1957	—	—	Proof	50.00
	1958	27.280	BV	BV	7.50
	1959	4.740	BV	BV	10.00
	1959	—	—	Proof	25.00
	1960	1,000	—	Proof	35.00
	1961	—	—	Proof	35.00
	1962	—	—	Proof	35.00
	1963	—	—	Proof	35.00
	1964	.187	12.50	17.50	25.00
	1964	—	—	Proof	27.50
	1965	1.721	BV	BV	5.00
	1965	—	—	Proof	5.50
	1966	3.392	BV	BV	5.00
	1966	—	—	Proof	8.50
	1967	1.394	BV	BV	5.50
	1967	—	—	Proof	9.00
	1968	1.525	BV	BV	5.00
	1968	—	—	Proof	8.00
	1969	1.200	BV	BV	5.50
	1969	—	—	Proof	8.00
	1970	4.600	BV	BV	5.00
	1970	—	—	Proof	6.00
	1971	7.100	BV	BV	5.00
	1971	—	—	Proof	5.50
	1972	14.300	BV	BV	5.00
	1972	—	—	Proof	5.50
	1973	14.600	BV	BV	5.00
	1973	—	—	Proof	5.50

COPPER-NICKEL

Y#	Date	Mintage	VF	XF	Unc
A99	1974	79.000	.85	1.00	1.35
	1974	—	—	Proof	2.50
	1975	16.941	.85	1.00	1.35
	1975	.049	—	Proof	2.50
	1976	13.459	.85	1.00	1.35
	1976	.044	—	Proof	2.50
	1977	3.804	.85	1.00	1.35
	1977	.044	—	Proof	2.50
	1978	—	.85	1.00	1.35
	1978	—	—	Proof	2.50
	1979	—	—	—	—
	1979	—	—	Proof	—

25 SCHILLING

5.8810 gm., .900 GOLD, .1702 oz AGW

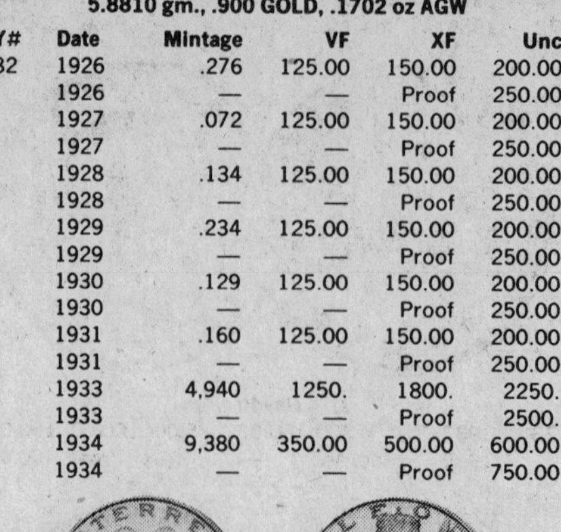

Y#	Date	Mintage	VF	XF	Unc
82	1926	.276	125.00	150.00	200.00
	1926	—	—	Proof	250.00
	1927	.072	125.00	150.00	200.00
	1927	—	—	Proof	250.00
	1928	.134	125.00	150.00	200.00
	1928	—	—	Proof	250.00
	1929	.234	125.00	150.00	200.00
	1929	—	—	Proof	250.00
	1930	.129	125.00	150.00	200.00
	1930	—	—	Proof	250.00
	1931	.160	125.00	150.00	200.00
	1931	—	—	Proof	250.00
	1933	4,940	1250.	1800.	2250.
	1933	—	—	Proof	2500.
	1934	9,380	350.00	500.00	600.00
	1934	—	—	Proof	750.00

St. Leopold

Y#	Date	Mintage	VF	XF	Unc
84	1935	2,880	650.00	800.00	1000.
	1935	—	—	Proof	1200.
	1936	7,260	650.00	800.00	1000.
	1936	—	—	Proof	1200.
	1937	7,660	700.00	850.00	1050.
	1937	—	—	Proof	1250.
	1938	1,360	10,000.	12,500.	13,500.
	1938	—	—	Proof	15,000.

13.0000 gm., .800 SILVER, 13.3344 oz ASW

Reopening of the National Theater in Vienna

Y#	Date	Mintage	VF	XF	Unc
96	1955	1.499	20.00	35.00	50.00
	1955	1,000	—	Proof	150.00

Mozart

Y#	Date	Mintage	VF	XF	Unc
97	1956	4.999	BV	11.00	12.00
	1956	1,000	—	Proof	300.00

Maria Zell Cathedral

Y#	Date	Mintage	VF	XF	Unc
98	1957	4.999	BV	11.00	12.00
	1957	1,000	—	Proof	300.00

von Welsbach

Y#	Date	Mintage	VF	XF	Unc
100	1958	4.999	BV	11.00	12.00
	1958	1,000	—	Proof	1500.

Archduke Johann

Y#	Date	Mintage	VF	XF	Unc
102	1959	1.899	BV	11.00	12.00
	1959	1,000	—	Proof	350.00

Carinthian Plebescite

Y#	Date	Mintage	VF	XF	Unc
105	1960	1.599	12.00	15.00	20.00
	1960	1,000	—	Proof	375.00

Burgenland

Y#	Date	Mintage	VF	XF	Unc
107	1961	1.399	17.50	25.00	40.00
	1961	1,000	—	Proof	250.00

Bruckner

Y#	Date	Mintage	VF	XF	Unc
108	1962	2.399	BV	11.00	12.00
	1962	1,000	—	Proof	200.00

Prince Eugene Of Savoy

Y#	Date	Mintage	VF	XF	Unc
109	1963	1.994	BV	12.00	15.00
	1963	5,931	—	Proof	125.00

Grillparzer

Y#	Date	Mintage	VF	XF	Unc
112	1964	1.630	BV	12.00	15.00
	1964	.070	—	Proof	16.00

9 shield obverse (error)

Y#	Date	Mintage	VF	XF	Unc
112a	1964	3,660	—	Proof	350.00

Vienna Technical School

Y#	Date	Mintage	VF	XF	Unc
113	1965	1.563	BV	12.00	15.00
	1965	.037	—	Proof	20.00

Raimund

Y#	Date	Mintage	VF	XF	Unc
115	1966	1.388	7.50	10.00	20.00
	1966	11,800	—	Proof	80.00

Maria Theresa

Y#	Date	Mintage	VF	XF	Unc
117	1967	2.472	BV	12.00	13.50
	1967	.028	—	Proof	35.00

Von Hildebrandt

Y#	Date	Mintage	VF	XF	Unc
119	1968	1.258	17.50	25.00	30.00
	1968	.042	—	Proof	35.00

Rosegger

Y#	Date	Mintage	VF	XF	Unc
121	1969	1.356	BV	12.00	16.50
	1969	.044	—	Proof	20.00

Lehar

Y#	Date	Mintage	VF	XF	Unc
123	1970	1.661	BV	12.00	13.50
	1970	.139	—	Proof	15.00

Vienna Bourse

Y#	Date	Mintage	VF	XF	Unc
126	1971	1.804	BV	12.00	13.50
	1971	.196	—	Proof	15.00

Ziehrer

Y#	Date	Mintage	VF	XF	Unc
128	1972	1.955	BV	12.00	13.50
	1972	.145	—	Proof	15.00

Centennial Birth of Max Reinhardt

Y#	Date	Mintage	VF	XF	Unc
131	1973	2.323	BV	12.00	13.50
	1973	.177	—	Proof	15.00

50 SCHILLING

20.0000 gm., .900 SILVER, .5787 oz ASW

Andreas Hofer

Y#	Date	Mintage	VF	XF	Unc
101	1959	2.999	BV	17.50	20.00
	1959	1,000	—	Proof	500.00

Union with Tirol

Y#	Date	Mintage	VF	XF	Unc
110	1963	2.994	BV	17.50	20.00
	1963	6,000	—	Proof	150.00

Winter Olympics

Obv: Similar to Y#110

Y#	Date	Mintage	VF	XF	Unc
111	1964	2.832	BV	17.50	20.00
	1964	.068	—	Proof	30.00

600th Anniversary Vienna University

Y#	Date	Mintage	VF	XF	Unc
114	1965	2.163	BV	17.50	20.00
	1965	.037	—	Proof	25.00

National Bank Sesquicentennial

Obv: Similar to Y#114

Y#	Date	Mintage	VF	XF	Unc
116	1966	1.782	BV	20.00	25.00
	1966	17,400	—	Proof	75.00

Blue Danube Waltz
Obv: Similar to Y#114

Y#	Date	Mintage	VF	XF	Unc
118	1967	2.974	BV	17.50	20.00
	1967	.026	—	Proof	65.00

50th Anniversary Republic
Obv: Similar to Y#114
Matte surface between pillars

Y#	Date	Mintage	VF	XF	Unc
120	1968	1.660	BV	20.00	25.00
	1968	.040	—	Proof	45.00

Proof surface between pillars

Y#	Date	Mintage	VF	XF	Unc
120v	1968	1,000	—	Proof	175.00

Maximilian I
Obv: Similar to Y#114

Y#	Date	Mintage	VF	XF	Unc
122	1969	2.045	BV	17.50	20.00
	1969	.055	—	Proof	25.00

University Of Innsbruck
Obv: Similar to Y#114

Y#	Date	Mintage	VF	XF	Unc
124	1970	2.087	BV	17.50	20.00
	1970	.113	—	Proof	25.00

Dr. Karl Renner
Obv: Similar to Y#114

Y#	Date	Mintage	VF	XF	Unc
125	1970	2.214	BV	17.50	20.00
	1970	.286	—	Proof	22.00

Julius Raab
Obv: Similar to Y#114

Y#	Date	Mintage	VF	XF	Unc
127	1971	2.317	BV	17.50	20.00
	1971	.183	—	Proof	22.00

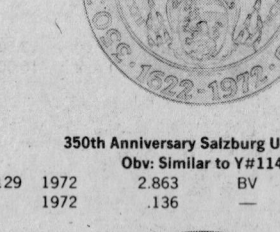

350th Anniversary Salzburg University
Obv: Similar to Y#114

Y#	Date	Mintage	VF	XF	Unc
129	1972	2.863	BV	17.50	20.00
	1972	.136	—	Proof	22.00

100th Anniversary Agricultural University
Obv: Similar to Y#114

Y#	Date	Mintage	VF	XF	Unc
130	1972	1.891	BV	17.50	20.00
	1972	.109	—	Proof	22.00

500th Anniversary of Bummerlhaus
Obv: Similar to Y#114

Y#	Date	Mintage	VF	XF	Unc
132	1973	2.842	BV	17.50	20.00
	1973	.158	—	Proof	22.00

Centennial Birth of Dr. Theodor Korner
Obv: Similar to Y#114

Y#	Date	Mintage	VF	XF	Unc
133	1973	2.868	BV	17.50	20.00
	1973	.132	—	Proof	22.00

20.0000 gm., .640 SILVER, .4115 oz ASW
International Garden Exhibition
Obv: Similar to Y#114

Y#	Date	Mintage	VF	XF	Unc
134	1974	2.279	BV	12.50	13.50
	1974	.221	—	Proof	15.00

Austrian Police Force
Obv: Similar to Y#114

Y#	Date	Mintage	VF	XF	Unc
135	1974	2.259	BV	12.50	13.50
	1974	.241	—	Proof	15.00

Salzburg Cathedral
Obv: Similar to Y#114

Y#	Date	Mintage	VF	XF	Unc
136	1974	2.293	BV	12.50	13.50
	1974	.207	—	Proof	15.00

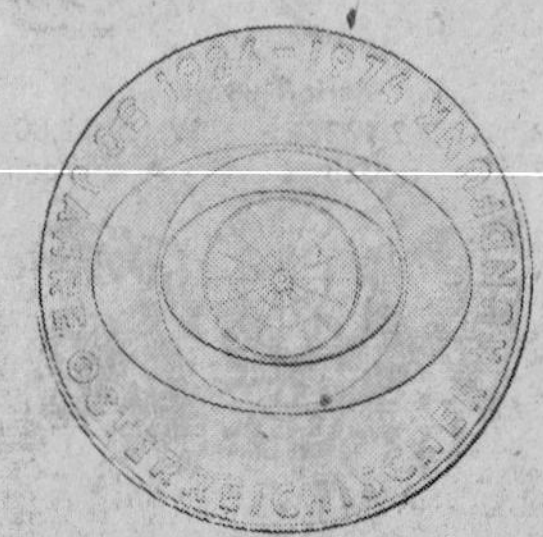

50th Year Austrian Broadcasting
Obv: Similar to Y#114

Y#	Date	Mintage	VF	XF	Unc
137	1974	2.290	BV	12.50	13.50
	1974	.210	—	Proof	15.00

150th Anniversary of Death of Schubert
Obv: Similar to Y#114

Y#	Date	Mintage	VF	XF	Unc
152	1978	—	BV	12.50	13.50
	1978	—	—	Proof	16.00

100 SCHILLING

23.5245 gm., .900 GOLD, .6807 oz AGW

Y#	Date	Mintage	VF	XF	Unc
83	1926	.064	450.00	550.00	650.00
	1926	Inc. Ab.	—	Proof	750.00
	1927	.069	450.00	550.00	650.00
	1927	Inc. Ab.	—	Proof	750.00
	1928	.040	450.00	600.00	700.00
	1928	Inc. Ab.	—	Proof	750.00
	1929	.074	450.00	550.00	650.00
	1929	Inc. Ab.	—	Proof	750.00
	1930	.025	450.00	600.00	700.00
	1930	Inc. Ab.	—	Proof	750.00
	1931	.102	450.00	550.00	650.00
	1931	Inc. Ab.	—	Proof	750.00
	1933	4,700	—	1500.	1750.
	1933	Inc. Ab.	—	Proof	2000.
	1934	9.400	—	600.00	700.00
	1934	Inc. Ab.	—	Proof	800.00

Madonna of Maria Zell

Y#	Date	Mintage	VF	XF	Unc
85	1935	900 pcs.	—	2750.	3000.
	1935	Inc. Ab.	—	Proof	3500.
	1936	.012	—	1500.	1750.
	1936	Inc. Ab.	—	Proof	2000.
	1937	2,900	—	2000.	2250.
	1937	Inc. Ab.	—	Proof	2500.
	1938	1,400	—	10,000.	12,000.
	1938	Inc. Ab.	—	Proof	15,000.

24.0000 gm., .640 SILVER, .4938 oz ASW
Johann Strauss

Y#	Date	Mintage	VF	XF	Unc
138	1975	2.646	BV	15.00	16.00
	1975	.209	—	Proof	18.50

20th Anniversary, State Treaty

Y#	Date	Mintage	VF	XF	Unc
139	1975	3.215	BV	15.00	16.00
	1975	.225	—	Proof	18.50

50th Anniversary of Schilling
Obv: Similar to Y#139

Y#	Date	Mintage	VF	XF	Unc
140	1975	3.234	BV	15.00	16.00
	1975	.201	—	Proof	18.50

Winter Olympics I
Obv: Similar to Y#138

Y#	Date	Mintage	VF	XF	Unc
141	1976	2.826	BV	15.00	16.00
	1976	.374	—	Proof	18.50

NOTE: The above coins were issued in 1974.

Winter Olympics II
Obv: Similar to Y#139

Y#	Date	Mintage	VF	XF	Unc
142	1976H	2.692	BV	15.00	16.00
	1976H	.223	—	Proof	18.50
	1976V	2.718	BV	15.00	16.00
	1976V	.232	—	Proof	18.50

NOTE: The above coins were issued in 1975.

Winter Olympics III
Obv: Similar to Y#139

Y#	Date	Mintage	VF	XF	Unc
143	1976H	2.636	BV	15.00	16.00
	1976H	.179	—	Proof	18.50
	1976V	2.641	BV	15.00	16.00
	1976V	.184	—	Proof	18.50

NOTE: The above coins were issued in 1975.

Winter Olympics IV
Obv: Similar to Y#139

Y#	Date	Mintage	VF	XF	Unc
144	1976H	2.611	BV	15.00	16.00
	1976H	.179	—	Proof	18.50
	1976V	2.631	BV	15.00	16.00
	1976V	.184	—	Proof	18.50

Burgtheater Centennial
Obv: Similar to Y#138

Y#	Date	Mintage	VF	XF	Unc
145	1976	1.630	BV	15.00	16.00
	1976	.220	—	Proof	18.50

1000th Anniversary of Carinthia

Obv: Similar to Y#139

Y#	Date	Mintage	VF	XF	Unc
146	1976	1.632	BV	15.00	16.00
	1976	.168	—	Proof	18.50

Johann Nestroy

Y#	Date	Mintage	VF	XF	Unc
147	1976	1.762	BV	15.00	16.00
	1976	.138	—	Proof	20.00

1200th Anniversary of Kremsmunster Monastery
Obv: Similar to Y#138

Y#	Date	Mintage	VF	XF	Unc
149	1977	1.865	BV	15.00	16.00
	1977	.135	—	Proof	20.00

900th Anniversary of Hohensalzburg Fortress
Obv: Similar to Y#139

Y#	Date	Mintage	VF	XF	Unc
150	1977	1.878	BV	15.00	16.00
	1977	.122	—	Proof	18.50

500th Anniversary of Mint at Hall

Y#	Date	Mintage	VF	XF	Unc
151	1977	1.868	BV	15.00	16.00
	1977	.132	—	Proof	60.00

700th Anniversary of Gmunden
Obv: Similar to Y#139.

Y#	Date	Mintage	VF	XF	Unc
153	1978	1.870	BV	15.00	16.00
	1978	.130	—	Proof	18.50

700th Anniversary Battle of Durnkrut and Jedenspeigen

Y#	Date	Mintage	VF	XF	Unc
154	1978	—	BV	15.00	16.00
	1978	—	—	Proof	18.50

1100th Anniversary of Founding of Villach
Obv: Similar to Y#139.

Y#	Date	Mintage	VF	XF	Unc
155	1978	—	BV	15.00	16.00
	1978	—	—	Proof	18.50

Opening of Arlberg Tunnel

Y#	Date	Mintage	VF	XF	Unc
156	1978	—	BV	15.00	16.00
	1978	—	—	Proof	18.50

Cathedral of Wiener Neustadt

Y#	Date	Mintage	VF	XF	Unc
157	1979	1.780	BV	15.00	16.00
	1979	.150	—	Proof	18.50

200th Anniversary of Inn District

Y#	Date	Mintage	VF	XF	Unc
158	1979	1.790	BV	15.00	16.00
	1979	.135	—	Proof	18.50

Vienna International Center

Y#	Date	Mintage	VF	XF	Unc
159	1979	1.790	BV	15.00	16.00
	1979	.135	—	Proof	18.50

Festival and Congress Hall at Bregenz

Y#	Date	Mintage	VF	XF	Unc
160	1979	1.490	—	—	—
	1979	.135	—	Proof	—

500 SHILLING

.640 SILVER

Millenium of City of Steyr

Y#	Date	Mintage	VF	XF	Unc
161	1980	—	—	—	—

1000 SCHILLING

13.5000 gm., .900 YELLOW GOLD, .3906 oz AGW

1000 Austrian Anniversary

Y#	Date	Mintage	VF	XF	Unc
148	1976	1.800	250.00	260.00	275.00

13.5000 gm., .900 RED GOLD, .3906 oz AGW

Y#	Date	Mintage	VF	XF	Unc
—	1976	Inc. Ab.	250.00	260.00	275.00

NCLT ISSUES

PATTERNS

KM#	Date	Mintage	Identification	Mkt.Val.
1	1796E	—	1/2 Ducat, Gold	1250.
2	1851C	—	1/4 Kreuzer, C#197	—
3	1851C	—	2 Kreuzer, C#200	1850.
4	1851C	—	3 Kreuzer, C#201	2500.
5	1851E	—	1/4 Kreuzer, C#197	900.00
6	1851E	—	1/2 Kreuzer, C#198	1500.
7	1851E	—	2 Kreuzer, C#200	—
8	1851E	—	3 Kreuzer, C#201	2000.
9	1858A	—	3 Kreuzer	—
10	1858B	—	3 Kreuzer	—
11	1924	—	1/2 Schilling, C#67	—

SPECIAL SELECTS (S/S)

NOTE: These are proof like in appearance.

Y#	Date	Mintage	Identification	Issue Price	Mkt Val.
138	1975	—	100 Schilling, Strauss	—	16.50
139	1975	—	100 Schilling, State Treaty	—	16.50
140	1975	—	100 Schilling, 50th Anniversary of Schilling	—	16.50
142	1976	—	100 Schilling, Winter Olympics II, Hall Mint	—	16.50
142	1976	—	100 Schilling, Winter Olympics II, Vienna Mint	—	16.50
143	1976	—	100 Schilling, Winter Olympics III, Hall Mint	—	16.50
143	1976	—	100 Schilling, Winter Olympics III, Vienna Mint	—	16.50
144	1976	—	100 Schilling, Winter Olympics IV, Vienna Mint	—	16.50
144	1976	—	100 Schilling, Winter Olympics IV, Hall Mint	—	16.50
145	1976	—	100 Schilling, Burgtheater	—	16.50
146	1976	—	100 Schilling, Herzogstuhl	—	16.50
147	1976	—	100 Schilling, Nestroy	—	16.50
149	1977	—	100 Schilling, Kremsmunster	—	16.50
150	1977	—	100 Schilling, Hohensalzb	—	16.50
151	1977	—	100 Schilling, Hall Mint	—	16.50
153	1978	—	100 Schilling, Gmunder	—	16.50
154	1978	—	100 Schilling, Durnkrut	—	16.50
155	1978	—	100 Schilling, Villach	—	16.50
156	1978	80,000	100 Schilling, Arlberg	—	16.50
157	1979	70,000	100 Schilling, Weiner Neustadt	—	16.50
158	1979	75,000	100 Schilling, Inn District	8.50	16.50
159	1979	75,000	100 Schilling, Vienna Center	—	16.50
160	1979	75,000	100 Schilling, Bregenz Hall	—	16.50

PROOF SETS

STANDARD METALS

KM#	Date	Mintage	Identification	Issue Price	Mkt. Val.
101	1959(2)	1,000	Y101,102	—	850.00
102	1960(8)	1,000	Y87,89,90,99,103-106	—	60.00
103	1963(9)	5,931	Y87,89,90,99,103, 104,106,109,110.	—	65.00
104	1964(9)	69,731	Y87,89,90,99,103, 104,106,111,112.	—	80.00
105	1964(9)	2,700	Y87,89,90,99,103,104, 106,111,112a (error set)	—	400.00
106	1964(7)	—	Y87,89,90,99,103,104,106	—	30.00
106	1965(7)	83,000	Y87,89,90,99,103,104,106	—	15.00
107	1965(4)	38,000	Y99,106,113,114	5.00	50.00
108	1966(9)	1,765	Y87,89,90,99,103, 104,106,115,116.	—	180.00
109	1966(7)	—	Y87,89,90,99,103,104,106	—	45.00
110	1967(9)	1,163	Y87,89,90,99,103, 104,106,117,118.	5.50	200.00
111	1967(7)	—	Y87,89,90,99,103,104,106	—	90.00
112	1968(9)	15,200	Y87,89,90,99,103, 104,106a,119,120.	5.75	110.00
113	1968(7)	—	Y87,89,90,99,103,104,106	—	40.00
114	1969(9)	20,000	Y87,89,90,99,103, 104,106a,121,122.	7.50	70.00
115	1969(7)	—	Y87,89,90,99,103,104,106a	—	30.00
116	1970(10)	—	Y87,89,90,99,103,104, 106a,123,124,125.	8.25	70.00
117	1970(7)	—	Y87,89,90,99,103,104,106a	—	15.00
118	1970(3)	—	Y123,124,125	7.00	55.00
119	1971(9)	—	Y87,89,90,99,103, 104,106a,126,127.	8.25	45.00
120	1971(7)	—	Y87,89,90,99,103,104,106a	—	10.00
121	1972(9)	—	Y87,89,90,99,103, 104,106a,128,129.	8.50	42.00
122	1972(9)	—	Y87,89,90,99,103, 104,106a,128,130.	8.50	42.00
123	1972(7)	—	Y87,89,90,99,103,104,106a	—	10.00
124	1972(3)	—	Y128,129,130	7.50	52.00
125	1973(10)	—	Y87,89,90,99,103, 104,106a,131,132,133.	—	65.00
126	1973(7)	—	Y87,89,90,99,103,104,106a	—	10.00
127	1973(3)	—	Y131,132,133	—	55.00
128	1974(12)	—	Y87,89,90,99,103, 104,106a,134-138	29.70	75.00
129	1974(7)	—	Y87,89,90,99,103,104,106a	—	5.00
130	1974(5)	—	Y134-138	27.00	70.00
131	1975(10)	—	Y87,89,90,99,103,104,106a 139-141	30.00	55.00
132	1975(7)	—	Y87,89,90,99,103,104,106a	—	5.00
133	1975(3)	—	Y139-141	27.00	50.00
134	1976(7)	—	Y87,89,90,99,103,104,106a	3.00	5.00
135	1977(7)	—	Y87,89,90,99,103,104,106a	3.15	5.00
136	1977(6)	—	Y145-147,149-151	27.00	150.00
137	1978(7)	—	Y87,89,90,A99,103,104,106a	—	5.00
138	1979(7)	—	Y87,89,90,A99,103,104,106a	—	—

AUERSPERG

Auersperg (Auersberg): The Auersperg princes were princes of estates in Austrian Carniola, a former duchy with estates in Laibach and Silesia, a former province in southwestern Poland; and Swabia, one of the stem—duchies of medieval Germany. They were elevated to princely rank in 1653, and the following year were made dukes of Muensterberg, which they ultimately sold to Prussia.

RULERS

Wilhelm, 1800-1822

THALER

(Convention)

SILVER

C#	Date	Mintage	Fine	VF	XF
3	1805	—	125.00	250.00	450.00

BATTHYANI

Batthyani is the name of a royal Hungarian family, princes of domains in Austria, Styria and Bohemia, who were granted the coining privilege in 1763.

RULERS

Ludwig, 1788-1806

MONETARY SYSTEM

120 Kreuzer = 1 Convention Thaler

20 KREUZER

SILVER
Obv: Bust. Rev: Crowned mantled arms.

C#	Date	Mintage	Fine	VF	XF
6	1790	—	75.00	100.00	175.00

1/2 THALER
(Convention)

SILVER
Obv: Bust. Rev: Crowned mantled arms.

C#	Date	Mintage	Fine	VF	XF
7	1789	—	125.00	165.00	225.00

NOTE: Refer to 5 Ducats for gold strike of C#7.

THALER
(Convention)

SILVER
Obv: Bust. Rev: Crowned mantled arms.

C#	Date	Mintage	Fine	VF	XF
8	1788	—	200.00	275.00	350.00

TRADE COINS

DUCAT

3.500 gm., .986 GOLD, .1109 oz AGW
Obv: Bust. Rev: Crowned mantled arms.

C#	Date	Mintage	VF	XF	Unc
9	1791/0	—	275.00	450.00	600.00

5 DUCATS

17.5000 gm., .986 GOLD, .5548 oz AGW
Obv: Bust. Rev: Crowned mantled arms.

C#	Date	Mintage	VF	XF	Unc
9.5	1789	—	1000.	1250.	1750.

10 DUCATS

35.000 gm., .986 GOLD, 1.1095 oz AGW
Obv: Bust. Rev: Crowned mantled arms.

C#	Date	Mintage	VF	XF	Unc
10	1788	—	—	Rare	—

BURGAU

Austrian possession near Ulm in Germany. In Austrian possession from 1618 to 1805 at which time it passed to Bavaria. Gunzburg Mint located in Burgau.

MINTMARKS

G,H - Gunzburg

MINTMASTER'S INITIALS

C - J.H.V. Clotz
F, IF - J. Faby
S, TS - T. Schobl

HELLER

COPPER
Obv: Arms of Austria-Burgau.
Rev: Value and date.

C#	Date	Mintage	Fine	VF	XF	Unc
1	1768G	—	4.50	6.50	10.00	25.00
	1772G	—	4.50	6.50	10.00	25.00
	1773G	—	4.50	6.50	10.00	25.00
	1774G	—	4.50	6.50	10.00	25.00
	1777G	—	4.50	6.50	10.00	25.00
	1778G	—	4.50	6.50	10.00	25.00
	1780G	—	4.50	6.50	10.00	25.00

1/4 KREUZER

COPPER
Obv: Arms of Austria-Burgau.
Rev: Value and date.

C#	Date	Mintage	Fine	VF	XF	Unc
2	1772G	—	4.50	6.50	10.00	25.00
	1774G	—	4.50	6.50	10.00	25.00
	1776G	—	4.50	6.50	10.00	25.00
	1777G	—	4.50	6.50	10.00	25.00
	1778G	—	4.50	6.50	10.00	25.00

1/2 KREUZER

COPPER
Obv: Arms of Austria-Burgau.
Rev: Value and date.

C#	Date	Mintage	Fine	VF	XF	Unc
3	1772G	—	2.75	4.50	7.50	30.00

KREUZER

COPPER
Obv: Crowned arms of Austria-Burgau.
Rev: Value, date and mintmark in cartouche.

C#	Date	Mintage	Fine	VF	XF	Unc
4	1772G	—	2.75	4.50	7.50	20.00
	1773G	—	2.75	4.50	7.50	20.00
	1774G	—	2.75	4.50	7.50	20.00
	1779G	—	2.75	4.50	7.50	20.00

48 EIN (1/48) THALER
(Convention)

(2-1/2 KREUZER)

BILLON
Obv: Crowned arms of Austria-Burgau.
Rev: Value, date and mintmark.

C#	Date	Mintage	Fine	VF	XF	Unc
5	1772G	—	30.00	42.50	60.00	100.00
	1773G	—	30.00	42.50	60.00	100.00
	1774G	—	30.00	42.50	60.00	100.00

5 KREUZER
(Convention)

SILVER
Obv: Head in branches.
Rev: Crowned imperial eagle; value below; sprays at sides.

C#	Date	Mintage	Fine	VF	XF	Unc
8	1770 SC	—	15.00	25.00	37.50	100.00
	1772 SC	—	15.00	25.00	37.50	100.00
	1773 SC	—	15.00	25.00	37.50	125.00
	1774 SC	—	15.00	25.00	37.50	125.00
	1775 SF	—	15.00	25.00	37.50	125.00

10 KREUZER
(Convention)

SILVER
Obv: Head in branches.
Rev: Crowned imperial eagle; value below; sprays at sides.

C#	Date	Mintage	Fine	VF	XF	Unc
10	1772 SC	—	10.00	15.00	25.00	75.00
	1774 SC	—	10.00	15.00	25.00	75.00
	1775 SF	—	10.00	15.00	25.00	75.00
	1776 SF	—	10.00	15.00	25.00	75.00
	1777 SF	—	10.00	15.00	25.00	75.00

20 KREUZER
(Convention)

SILVER
Obv: Head in branches.
Rev: Crowned imperial eagle; value below; sprays at sides.

C#	Date	Mintage	Fine	VF	XF	Unc
12	1772 SC	—	10.00	15.00	25.00	75.00
	1773 SC	—	10.00	15.00	25.00	75.00
	1774 SF	—	10.00	15.00	25.00	75.00
	1775 SF	—	10.00	15.00	25.00	75.00
	1777 SF	—	10.00	15.00	25.00	75.00
	1778 SF	—	10.00	15.00	25.00	75.00
	1779 SF	—	10.00	15.00	25.00	75.00
	1780 SF	—	10.00	15.00	25.00	75.00

THALER
(Convention)

SILVER

C#	Date	Mintage	Fine	VF	XF	Unc
6	1766	—	50.00	75.00	100.00	200.00
	1766 SC	—	50.00	75.00	100.00	200.00
	1767 SC	—	50.00	75.00	100.00	200.00

Obv: Veiled head right.
Rev: Crowned imperial eagle.

C#	Date	Mintage	Fine	VF	XF	Unc
14	1765 SC	—	65.00	100.00	150.00	225.00
	1767 SC	—	65.00	100.00	150.00	225.00
	1768 SC	—	65.00	100.00	150.00	225.00
	1769 SC	—	65.00	100.00	150.00	225.00
	1770 SC	—	65.00	100.00	150.00	225.00
	1771 SC	—	65.00	100.00	150.00	225.00
	1772 SC	—	65.00	100.00	150.00	225.00

Obv: Head with smaller veil right.

C#	Date	Mintage	Fine	VF	XF	Unc
14a	1773 SC	—	65.00	100.00	150.00	225.00
	1774 SC	—	65.00	100.00	150.00	225.00
	1776 SF	—	65.00	100.00	150.00	225.00
	1777 SF	—	65.00	100.00	150.00	225.00

Obv: Larger head right.

C#	Date	Mintage	Fine	VF	XF	Unc
14b	1780 SF	—	30.00	50.00	75.00	125.00
	1780 FS	—	30.00	50.00	75.00	125.00
	1780 TS-IF	—	30.00	50.00	75.00	125.00
	1780 SF-ST	—	30.00	50.00	75.00	125.00
	1780 PS-IF	—	30.00	50.00	75.00	125.00

NOTE: C#14b is similar to Y#55, the popular Maria Theresa Taler restrike, found listed under Trade Coins/Austria.

COLLOREDO-MANSFELD

Colloredo-Mansfeld: The Colloredos, a German-Italian family, attained the rank of count of the Austro-Hungarian Empire in 1724, and of prince in 1763. Prince Franz Gundacker acquired the titles of the predominant German Mansfeld family, (which was seated at Mansfeld in Saxony from the 11th to the 18th century), in 1780, by marriage.

RULERS

Franz Gundacker, 1788-1807

THALER
(Convention)

SILVER
Obv: St. George on horseback slaying dragon
Rev: Crowned, draped arms

C#	Date	Mintage	VF	XF	Unc
1	1794		Restrike	300.00	400.00

TRADE COINS

DUCAT

3.5000 gm., .986 GOLD, .1109 oz AGW
Similar to Thaler, C#1.

C#	Date	Mintage	VF	XF	Unc
2	1792	—	300.00	500.00	750.00

Restrike with curved die break

C#	Date	Mintage	VF	XF	Unc
2a	(1792)	—	150.00	200.00	275.00

ESZTERHAZY

A rich and famous old Hungarian family. The name Eszterhazy established in 1584. Became Princes in 1687.

Nikolas Joseph was a patron of Haydn for 30 years and the only member of the family to exercise the coinage right.

RULERS

Nicolas Joseph, 1762-1790

1/2 THALER
(Convention)

SILVER
Obv: Armored bust of Nicholas right.
Rev: Crowned arms in collar of the Golden Fleece.

C#	Date	Mintage	Fine	VF	XF	Unc
1	1770	—	125.00	175.00	275.00	500.00

THALER
(Convention)

SILVER
Obv: Armored bust of Nicholas right.
Rev: Crowned arms in collar of the Golden Fleece.

C#	Date	Mintage	Fine	VF	XF	Unc
2	1770	406 pcs.	350.00	500.00	750.00	1200.

TRADE COINS

DUCAT

3.5000 gm., .986 GOLD, .1109 oz AGW

C#	Date	Mintage	Fine	VF	XF	Unc
3	1770	—	500.00	750.00	1250.	1750.

GURK

Gurk, a bishopric in the Austrian Alpine province of Carinthia, was founded in 1071. In 1806 it was mediatized and assigned to Austria.

RULERS

Franz Xavier, Count V. Salm - Reifferscheid (Later Prince) 1783-1822

20 KREUZER

SILVER

C#	Date	Mintage	VG	Fine	VF	XF
1	1806	—	50.00	75.00	100.00	125.00

THALER
(Convention)

SILVER

C#	Date	Mintage	VG	Fine	VF	XF
2	1801	—	100.00	175.00	275.00	350.00

TRADE COINS

DUCAT

3.5000 gm., .986 GOLD, .1109 oz AGW
Similar to 20 Kreuzer, C#1.

C#	Date	Mintage	VG	Fine	VF	XF
3	1801	—	400.00	650.00	800.00	1200.

KHEVENHULLER

A prominent family of Carinthia. Became counts in 1673. Elevated to Princes in 1763.

RULERS

Johann Joseph
As Count 1742-1763
As Prince 1763-1776

THALER
(Convention)

SILVER
Obv: Bust of Johann Joseph right.
Rev: Helmed and supported arms.

C#	Date	Mintage	Fine	VF	XF	Unc
1	1761	—	300.00	500.00	850.00	1250.

C#	Date	Mintage	Fine	VF	XF	Unc
2	1771	200 pcs.	275.00	400.00	650.00	1250.

TRADE COINS

DUCAT

3.5000 gm., .986 GOLD, .1109 oz AGW

C#	Date	Mintage	Fine	VF	XF	Unc
3	1761	—	650.00	1000.	1500.	3000.

LOBKOWITZ

The Lobkowitz family of Bohemia, an ancient kingdom in central Europe, held the title of prince, and in the 17th century occupied high imperial office in the Austro-Hungarian Empire.

RULERS

Franz Joseph Maximillian, 1784-1816

(Under regency of his mother, Maria Gabriele of Savoy-Carignan, and his cousin, August, until 1794.)

20 KREUZER

SILVER
Similar to Thaler, C#2.

C#	Date	Mintage	Fine	VF	XF
1	1794	—	100.00	150.00	225.00

THALER
(Convention)

SILVER

C#	Date	Mintage	Fine	VF	XF
2	1794	300 pcs.	275.00	400.00	600.00

TRADE COINS

DUCAT

3.5000 gm., .986 GOLD, .1109 oz AGW
Similar to Thaler, C#2.

C#	Date	Mintage	Fine	VF	XF
3	1794	—	650.00	800.00	1400.

NETHERLANDS

Netherlands (Austrian): The Austrian Netherlands, which corresponds roughly to present-day Belgium, came into being on April 11, 1713, when the Treaty of Utrecht awarded the lands to Austria as part settlement following war with Spain. It passed to France in 1795, was part of the Kingdom of Netherlands from 1815 to 1830, and became present Belgium as the result of the revolution of 1830 against William I, Prince of Orange and King of the Netherlands.

RULERS

Joseph II, 1780-90
Insurrection, 1790
Leopold II, 1790-92
Franz II, 1792-1835

MINTMARKS

A - Vienna
(b) - Brussels (angelface)
B - Kremnitz
C - Prague
E - Karlsburg
F - Hall
G - Nagybanya
H - Gunzburg
V - See note after C#49-50.

NOTE: For similar coins with M mintmark refer to Italian States - Milan.

MINTMASTERS

Brussels

R - J. Roettiers

Vienna

IC - J.A. Cronberg
SK - S. A. Klemmer
FA - F. Aycherau

MONETARY SYSTEM

4 Liards = 1 Sol
254 Liards = 1 Kronentaler

LIARD

COPPER

Obv: Veiled head right.
Rev: 4-line legend over date and mintmark.

C#	Date	Mintage	VG	Fine	VF	XF
1b	1776	—	5.00	8.50	13.50	30.00
	1777	—	3.50	6.50	10.00	17.50
	1778	—	3.50	6.50	10.00	17.50
	1780	—	3.50	6.50	10.00	17.50

Obv: Laureated bust right.

C#	Date	Mintage	VG	Fine	VF	XF
19	1781	—	4.00	6.50	10.00	17.50
	1782	—	4.00	6.50	10.00	17.50
	1787	.135	5.00	7.50	13.50	22.50
	1788	1,185	4.00	6.50	10.00	17.50
	1789	.655	4.00	6.50	10.00	17.50

Similar to C#19.

C#	Date	Mintage	VG	Fine	VF	XF
34	1791	.480	11.50	22.50	35.00	50.00
	1792	.266	12.50	25.00	37.50	55.00

Obv: Bust right. Rev. leg: AD USUM BELGII AUSTR.

C#	Date	Mintage	VG	Fine	VF	XF
43	1792(b)	.128	7.50	15.00	30.00	45.00
	1793(b)	—	2.50	5.00	10.00	15.00
	1794(b)	—	2.50	5.00	10.00	15.00

2 LIARDS

COPPER

Obv: Veiled head right.
Rev: 4-line legend over date and mintmark in wreath.

C#	Date	Mintage	VG	Fine	VF	XF
2a	1777	—	5.00	7.50	12.50	20.00
	1778	—	5.00	7.50	12.50	20.00
	1780	—	5.00	7.50	12.50	20.00

Obv: Laureated head right.

C#	Date	Mintage	VG	Fine	VF	XF
20	1781	—	5.00	7.50	12.50	20.00
	1782	—	5.00	7.50	12.50	20.00
	1787	.067	6.50	10.00	20.00	35.00
	1788	.728	5.00	7.50	12.50	20.00
	1789	.195	5.00	7.50	13.50	20.00

C#	Date	Mintage	VG	Fine	VF	XF
35	1791	.210	12.50	22.50	45.00	60.00
	1792	.083	15.00	25.00	55.00	70.00

Obv: Bust right.
Rev. leg: AD USUM BELGII AUSTR., wreath around.

C#	Date	Mintage	VG	Fine	VF	XF
44	1792(b)	—	—	—	Rare	—
	1793(b)	—	2.00	6.50	12.50	20.00
	1794(b)	—	2.00	6.50	12.50	20.00

10 LIARDS

BILLON

Obv: X cross, legend around border.
Rev: Crowned arms in order collar.

C#	Date	Mintage	VG	Fine	VF	XF
21	1788	.206	11.50	22.50	35.00	45.00
	1789	.225	10.00	20.00	32.50	40.00

Similar to C#21.

C#	Date	Mintage	VG	Fine	VF	XF
36	1791	.106	32.50	47.50	60.00	80.00

.416 BILLON

Obv: Ornate cross. Rev: Crowned shield within chain.

C#	Date	Mintage	VG	Fine	VF	XF
44.5	1792(b)	.061	175.00	350.00	600.00	850.00

NOTE: Patterns exist.

XIV (14) LIARDS

BILLON

Obv: X cross separates value; crown above, mintmark below. Rev: Crowned imperial eagle.

C#	Date	Mintage	VG	Fine	VF	XF
22	1788	.079	12.50	22.50	40.00	70.00
	1789	.265	11.50	20.00	35.00	55.00

Similar to C#22.

C#	Date	Mintage	VG	Fine	VF	XF
37	1790	.063	55.00	100.00	180.00	300.00
	1791	.297	25.00	40.00	60.00	90.00
	1792	.272	25.00	40.00	60.00	90.00

.538 SILVER

Obv: Two crossed scepters. Rev: Crowned imperial eagle displayed, with shield on breast.

C#	Date	Mintage	VG	Fine	VF	XF
45	1792(b)	.052	60.00	100.00	175.00	225.00
	1793(b)	.642	10.00	22.50	45.00	90.00
	1794(b)	.374	10.00	22.50	45.00	90.00

1/4 KRONENTHALER

7.3600 gm., .873 SILVER, .2066 oz ASW

C#	Date	Mintage	VG	Fine	VF	XF
23	1788A	—	10.00	17.50	27.50	45.00
	1788B	—	10.00	17.50	27.50	45.00
	1788H	—	17.50	25.00	40.00	55.00
	1789A	—	12.50	20.00	30.00	45.00
	1789B	—	13.50	22.50	30.00	45.00
	1790A	—	12.50	20.00	30.00	35.00
	1790B	—	12.50	20.00	30.00	35.00

C#	Date	Mintage	VG	Fine	VF	XF
38	1790A	—	22.50	35.00	45.00	65.00
	1791A	—	22.50	35.00	45.00	65.00
	1791B	—	22.50	35.00	50.00	65.00
	1791H	—	22.50	35.00	45.00	65.00
	1792A	—	27.50	45.00	70.00	100.00
	1792B	—	22.50	35.00	50.00	65.00
	1792H	—	27.50	45.00	70.00	100.00

C#	Date	Mintage	VG	Fine	VF	XF
46	1792A	—	10.00	25.00	50.00	80.00
	1792B	—	12.50	32.50	65.00	100.00
	1793A	—	8.50	25.00	50.00	85.00
	1793B	—	7.50	15.00	30.00	50.00
	1794A	—	7.50	16.50	30.00	50.00
	1794B	—	10.00	40.00	80.00	120.00
	1795A	—	7.50	16.50	30.00	50.00
	1795B	—	7.50	16.50	30.00	50.00
	1795C	—	10.00	22.50	40.00	65.00
	1795G	—	12.50	55.00	125.00	200.00
	1796A	—	10.00	25.00	50.00	80.00
	1796B	—	7.50	30.00	60.00	100.00
	1796C	—	10.00	40.00	80.00	120.00
	1797A	—	15.00	75.00	150.00	250.00
	1797B	—	7.50	16.50	30.00	50.00
	1797C	—	8.50	20.00	40.00	65.00
	1797E	—	12.50	32.50	65.00	100.00
	1797G	—	15.00	30.00	60.00	110.00

1/2 KRONENTHALER

14.7200 gm., .873 SILVER, .4132 oz ASW

Similar to Kronenthaler, C#25.

C#	Date	Mintage	VG	Fine	VF	XF
24	1786(b)	—	150.00	300.00	800.00	1000.
	1788(b)	.014	200.00	400.00	900.00	1200.
	1788A	—	17.50	32.50	50.00	65.00
	1788B	—	22.50	37.50	60.00	75.00
	1789(b)	.024	100.00	250.00	600.00	900.00
	1789A	—	17.50	32.50	50.00	65.00
	1790A	—	17.50	32.50	50.00	65.00

Similar to Kronenthaler, C#25.

C#	Date	Mintage	VG	Fine	VF	XF
39	1790A	—	27.50	50.00	85.00	125.00
	1791H	—	27.50	45.00	70.00	90.00
	1792H	—	27.50	50.00	85.00	125.00

Edge: LEGE ET FIDE
Rev: Similar to Kronenthaler, C#48.

C#	Date	Mintage	VG	Fine	VF	XF
47	1792A	—	30.00	65.00	125.00	225.00
	1792H	—	35.00	85.00	160.00	250.00
	1793A	—	20.00	65.00	130.00	190.00
	1795A	—	20.00	35.00	65.00	100.00
	1795C	—	35.00	55.00	90.00	140.00
	1795G	—	60.00	125.00	250.00	350.00
	1796A	—	20.00	35.00	60.00	90.00
	1796C	—	40.00	80.00	150.00	200.00
	1796F	—	40.00	65.00	125.00	175.00
	1797A	—	15.00	27.50	55.00	100.00
	1797C	—	12.50	20.00	35.00	65.00
	1797E	—	40.00	60.00	120.00	170.00
	1797F	—	75.00	150.00	300.00	500.00
	1797G	—	50.00	100.00	200.00	300.00

Edge: FIDE ET LEGE

C#	Date	Mintage	VG	Fine	VF	XF
47	1793B	—	15.00	25.00	50.00	80.00
	1794B	—	15.00	55.00	110.00	150.00
	1795B	—	40.00	80.00	150.00	250.00
	1796B	—	12.50	17.50	25.00	45.00
	1797B	—	12.50	20.00	30.00	45.00

KRONENTHALER

29.4400 gm., .873 SILVER, .8264 oz ASW

C#	Date	Mintage	VG	Fine	VF	XF
25	1781(b)	.044	35.00	75.00	100.00	175.00
	1782(b)	.030	40.00	80.00	200.00	275.00
	1783A	—	25.00	35.00	60.00	125.00
	1783(b)	.172	30.00	60.00	100.00	175.00
	1784A	—	25.00	35.00	60.00	125.00
	1784B	—	25.00	35.00	60.00	125.00
	1784(b)	.928	25.00	35.00	60.00	125.00
	1785(b)	1,351	25.00	35.00	60.00	125.00
	1786(b)	1,386	25.00	35.00	60.00	125.00
	1787(b)	.256	30.00	50.00	90.00	150.00
	1788A	—	25.00	35.00	60.00	125.00
	1788B	—	25.00	35.00	60.00	125.00
	1788(b)	.087	40.00	80.00	200.00	275.00
	1789A	—	25.00	35.00	60.00	125.00
	1789(b)	.356	30.00	50.00	90.00	150.00
	1790A	—	25.00	35.00	60.00	125.00

Similar to C#25.

C#	Date	Mintage	VG	Fine	VF	XF
40	1790A	—	55.00	90.00	175.00	225.00
	1791H	—	50.00	85.00	150.00	200.00
	1792H	—	50.00	85.00	150.00	200.00

C#	Date	Mintage	VG	Fine	VF	XF
48	1792A	—	30.00	50.00	125.00	225.00
	1793A	—	25.00	35.00	70.00	140.00
48	1793H	—	30.00	55.00	125.00	200.00
	1794A	—	35.00	50.00	75.00	135.00
	1794(b)	.281	150.00	225.00	425.00	625.00
	1794H	—	25.00	40.00	75.00	135.00
	1795A	—	25.00	40.00	75.00	135.00
	1795C	—	25.00	30.00	50.00	85.00
	1795F	—	60.00	125.00	225.00	350.00
	1795H	—	25.00	30.00	50.00	85.00
	1796A	—	25.00	30.00	50.00	85.00
	1796C	—	25.00	30.00	50.00	85.00
	1796F	—	30.00	80.00	135.00	200.00
	1796H	—	25.00	30.00	65.00	110.00
	1797A	—	30.00	85.00	150.00	225.00
	1797C	—	30.00	45.00	75.00	125.00
	1797E	—	30.00	70.00	125.00	225.00
	1797F	—	30.00	70.00	125.00	200.00
	1797G	—	30.00	55.00	110.00	165.00
	1797H	—	25.00	30.00	50.00	75.00
	1798A	—	—	—	Rare	—

Edge lettering: FIDE ET LEGE

C#	Date	Mintage	VG	Fine	VF	XF
48a	1793B	—	30.00	50.00	100.00	170.00
	1794B	—	25.00	35.00	65.00	120.00
	1795B	—	25.00	60.00	110.00	190.00
	1796B	—	25.00	30.00	50.00	75.00
	1797B	—	25.00	30.00	50.00	75.00

TRADE COINS

1/2 SOVERAIN D'OR

5.5300 gm., .919 GOLD, .1634 oz AGW

C#	Date	Mintage	Fine	VF	XF
15c	1770(b)R	—	750.00	1500.	2500.
	1773(b)R	—	700.00	1200.	2000.
	1774(b)R	—	450.00	900.00	1500.
	1775(b)	—	450.00	900.00	1400.
	1776(b)	—	450.00	900.00	1400.
	1777(b)	—	450.00	900.00	1400.

C#	Date	Mintage	Fine	VF	XF
26	1786	2,186	4000.	6000.	10,000.
	1786A	—	200.00	300.00	500.00
	1786F	—	300.00	400.00	1000.
	1787A	—	250.00	350.00	600.00
	1787F	—	300.00	400.00	1000.
	1788	986 pcs.	—	Rare	—
	1788A	—	250.00	350.00	600.00
	1788F	4,847	500.00	700.00	1200.
	1789A	—	250.00	350.00	600.00
	1789F	1,382	600.00	1000.	1800.
	1790A	—	300.00	400.00	1000.
	1790F	1,350	600.00	1000.	1800.

Similar to C#26.

C#	Date	Mintage	Fine	VF	XF
41	1791A	—	300.00	350.00	600.00
	1792A	—	300.00	350.00	600.00
	1792B	—	300.00	350.00	600.00
	1792E	—	300.00	350.00	600.00

Obv. leg: FRANC. II. D.G.R. IMP. S.A.GE.

C#	Date	Mintage	Fine	VF	XF
49	1792A	—	225.00	350.00	525.00
	1793A	—	200.00	300.00	500.00
	1793B	—	—	Rare	—
	1793H	.060	250.00	400.00	600.00
	1793V	—	200.00	300.00	500.00
	1794A	—	250.00	400.00	600.00
	1794B	—	200.00	300.00	500.00
	1795B	—	200.00	300.00	500.00
	1798A	—	225.00	350.00	525.00

NOTE: Coins dated 1793V were struck in 1823 at Gunzburg. For similar coins with M mintmark, refer to Milan.

Obv. leg: FRANC.II.D.G.R. IMP. S.A. GER., head right.
Rev: Crowned oval arms.

C#	Date	Mintage	Fine	VF	XF
49a	1793F	1,892	250.00	400.00	750.00
	1794F	1,636	400.00	600.00	800.00
	1795F	1,503	500.00	800.00	1000.
	1796F	3,355	250.00	400.00	750.00

SOVERAIN D'OR

11.0600 gm., .916 GOLD, .3268 oz AGW
Obv: Veiled head right.
Rev: Crowned oval arms.

C#	Date	Mintage	Fine	VF	XF
16c	1767(b)R	—	1000.	1500.	2500.
	1768(b)R	—	1000.	1500.	2500.
	1769(b)R	—	1000.	1500.	2500.
	1771(b)R	—	1000.	1500.	2500.
	1772(a)I.CSK	—	1000.	1500.	2500.
	1772(b)R	—	1000.	1500.	2500.
	1773(b)R	—	1000.	1500.	2500.
	1778(b)	—	750.00	1000.	1500.
	1779	—	750.00	1000.	1500.
	1780	—	1000.	1500.	2500.

Rev: Arms in cartouche.

C#	Date	Mintage	Fine	VF	XF
16d	1772(a)IC-SK	—	1000.	1500.	2500.
	1773(a)IC-SK	—	1000.	1500.	2500.
	1780(a)IC-FA	—	1000.	1500.	2500.

Similar to C#16c.

C#	Date	Mintage	Fine	VF	XF
27	1781	4,338	900.00	1500.	2500.
	1782	3,012	900.00	1500.	2500.
	1783	5,309	900.00	1600.	2500.
	1783A	—	500.00	900.00	1200.
	1784	5,944	900.00	1500.	2500.
	1784A	—	400.00	600.00	900.00
	1785	3,949	900.00	1500.	2500.
	1785A	—	400.00	600.00	900.00
	1786	16,071	900.00	1500.	2500.
	1786A	—	400.00	600.00	800.00
	1786F	—	400.00	600.00	1800.
	1787	1,053	—	Rare	—
	1787A	—	400.00	600.00	900.00
	1788	8,632	900.00	1600.	2500.
	1788A	—	400.00	600.00	900.00
	1789	—	800.00	1400.	2200.
	1789A	—	700.00	1000.	1600.

Similar to C#16c.

C#	Date	Mintage	Fine	VF	XF
42	1790A	—	500.00	700.00	900.00
	1791A	—	500.00	700.00	900.00
	1792B	—	500.00	700.00	900.00
	1792E	—	700.00	1000.	1500.
	1792F	1,250	800.00	1200.	2000.

C#	Date	Mintage	Fine	VF	XF
50	1792A	—	600.00	750.00	1150.
	1793A	—	500.00	600.00	1000.
	1793(b)	1,763	4000.	5000.	7000.
	1793H	.060	500.00	600.00	1000.
	1794A	—	400.00	500.00	800.00
	1795A	—	400.00	500.00	800.00
	1795B	—	450.00	550.00	900.00
	1796A	—	450.00	550.00	900.00
	1796B	—	400.00	500.00	800.00
	1797A	—	450.00	550.00	800.00
	1798A	—	—	Rare	—

NOTE: Coins dated 1793V were struck in 1823 at Gunzburg. For similar coins with M mintmark, refer to Milan.

Obv. legend: FRANCISC. II.

C#	Date	Mintage	Fine	VF	XF
50a	1796F	2,357	500.00	700.00	1000.

1790 INSURRECTION

LAIRD

COPPER
Obv: Lion holding liberty cap on staff.
Rev: 4-line legend over date and mintmark.

Date	Mintage	VG	Fine	VF	XF
1790	.359	5.00	7.50	11.50	17.50

2 LAIRDS

COPPER

Date	Mintage	VG	Fine	VF	XF
1790	.763	9.00	12.50	17.50	27.50

10 SOLS

SILVER
Obv. leg: MON.NOV.ARG.PROV.FOED.BELG.

C#	Date	Mintage	VG	Fine	VF	XF
30	1790	.053	45.00	80.00	140.00	225.00

Obv. leg: DOMINI EST AEGNUM.

C#	Date	Mintage	VG	Fine	VF	XF
30a	1790	8,162	75.00	150.00	250.00	450.00

FLORIN

SILVER
Obv. leg: MON.NOV.ARG.PROV.FOED.BELG.

C#	Date	Mintage	VG	Fine	VF	XF
31	1790	.052	150.00	175.00	225.00	350.00

Obv. leg: DOMINI EST REGNUM.

C#	Date	Mintage	VG	Fine	VF	XF
31a	1790	.015	125.00	175.00	300.00	450.00

3 FLORINS

SILVER

C#	Date	Mintage	VG	Fine	VF	XF
32	1790	.044	250.00	300.00	550.00	825.00

.986 GOLD
Similar to C#32, 26mm.

C#	Date	Mintage	VG	Fine	VF	XF
33	1790	3,805	1000.	2000.	3000.	4500.

NCLT ISSUES

PATTERNS

KM#	Date	Mintage	Identification	Mkt.Val.
1	1794B	—	1 Sovereign d'or, C#50, .916 Gold	—
2	1795E	—	1/2 Sovereign d'or, C#49	—

SALZBURG

Salzburg: Salzburg, a town on the Austro-Bavarian frontier, grew up about a monastery and bishopric founded circa 700. It was raised to the rank of archbishopric in 798. In 1803 Salzburg was secularized and given to the archduke of Austria. In 1805 it was annexed to Austria but four years later passed to Bavaria, returning to Austria in 1813. It became a crownland in 1849, remaining so until becoming part of the Austrian republic in 1918.

RULERS

Hieronymus, 1772-1803
Ferdinand, Elector, 1803-1805

MINTMASTERS

F.M., F.M.F., F.M.K., M. - Franz Xavier Matzenkopf

MONETARY SYSTEM

4 Pfenning = 1 Kreutzer
120 Kreutzer = 1 Convention Thaler

EIN (1) PFENNING

COPPER

C#	Date	Mintage	VG	Fine	VF	XF
86	1775	—	3.00	5.00	7.50	15.00
	1777	—	3.00	5.00	7.50	15.00
	1778	—	3.00	5.00	7.50	15.00
	1779	—	3.00	5.00	7.50	15.00
	1780	—	3.00	5.00	7.50	15.00
	1781	—	3.00	5.00	7.50	15.00

C#	Date	Mintage	VG	Fine	VF	XF
86a	1783	—	5.00	6.50	9.00	17.50
	1784	—	5.00	6.50	9.00	17.50

C#	Date	Mintage	VG	Fine	VF	XF
87	1786	—	3.00	5.00	7.50	15.00
	1789	—	3.00	5.00	7.50	15.00
	1790	—	3.00	5.00	7.50	15.00

C#	Date	Mintage	VG	Fine	VF	XF
87a	1792	—	6.50	10.00	20.00	30.00

C#	Date	Mintage	VG	Fine	VF	XF
87b	1792	—	3.00	5.00	7.50	15.00
	1793	—	3.00	5.00	7.50	15.00
	1794	—	3.00	5.00	7.50	15.00
	1795	—	3.00	5.00	7.50	15.00
	1796	—	3.00	5.00	7.50	15.00
	1797	—	3.00	5.00	7.50	15.00
	1798	—	3.00	5.00	7.50	15.00
	1799	—	3.00	5.00	7.50	15.00
	1800	—	3.00	5.00	7.50	15.00
	1801	—	3.00	5.00	7.50	15.00
	1802	—	3.00	5.00	7.50	15.00

C#	Date	Mintage	VG	Fine	VF	XF
88	1802	—	5.00	7.00	10.00	20.00

Rev: 1 PFENNING

C#	Date	Mintage	VG	Fine	VF	XF
115	1804	—	2.00	5.00	7.50	20.00

Rev: EIN PFENNING

C#	Date	Mintage	VG	Fine	VF	XF
115a	1804	—	1.50	3.00	5.00	15.00
	1805	—	1.50	3.00	5.00	15.00

ZWEI (2) PFENNING

COPPER

C#	Date	Mintage	VG	Fine	VF	XF
89	1777	—	4.50	6.50	10.00	20.00
	1781	—	4.50	6.50	10.00	20.00
	1782	—	4.50	6.50	10.00	20.00

C#	Date	Mintage	VG	Fine	VF	XF
90	1786	—	4.00	6.00	8.50	17.50
	1791	—	4.00	6.00	8.50	17.50

C#	Date	Mintage	VG	Fine	VF	XF
90a	1791	—	3.00	4.50	6.50	12.50
	1793	—	3.00	4.50	6.50	12.50
	1794	—	3.00	4.50	6.50	12.50
	1795	—	3.00	4.50	6.50	12.50
	1796	—	3.00	4.50	6.50	12.50
	1797	—	3.00	4.50	6.50	12.50
	1798	—	3.00	4.50	6.50	12.50
	1799	—	3.00	4.50	6.50	12.50
	1800	—	3.00	4.50	6.50	12.50
	1801	—	3.00	4.50	6.50	12.50

C#	Date	Mintage	VG	Fine	VF	XF
91	1802	—	4.50	6.50	10.00	—

Rev: II PFENNING

C#	Date	Mintage	VG	Fine	VF	XF
116	1804	—	2.00	4.00	6.00	12.50

Rev: ZWEI PFENNING

C#	Date	Mintage	VG	Fine	VF	XF
116a	1805	—	1.50	3.00	5.00	12.50
	1806	—	1.50	3.00	5.00	12.50

EIN (1) KREUTZER

COPPER

C#	Date	Mintage	VG	Fine	VF	XF
92	1782	—	4.50	6.50	10.00	20.00
	1783	—	4.50	6.50	10.00	20.00
	1784	—	4.50	6.50	10.00	20.00

C#	Date	Mintage	VG	Fine	VF	XF
93	1786	—	4.00	6.00	8.50	17.50
	1790	—	4.00	6.00	8.50	17.50

C#	Date	Mintage	VG	Fine	VF	XF
93a	1790	—	4.00	6.00	8.50	17.50
	1793	—	4.00	6.00	8.50	17.50
	1794	—	4.00	6.00	8.50	17.50
	1795	—	4.00	6.00	8.50	17.50
	1797	—	4.00	6.00	8.50	17.50
	1798	—	4.00	6.00	8.50	17.50
	1799	—	4.00	6.00	8.50	17.50
	1800	—	4.00	6.00	8.50	17.50
	1801	—	4.00	6.00	8.50	17.50
	1802	—	4.00	6.00	8.50	17.50

C#	Date	Mintage	VG	Fine	VF	XF
93b	1802	—	4.50	6.50	10.00	20.00

C#	Date	Mintage	VG	Fine	VF	XF
117	1804	—	1.25	2.50	4.50	8.50
	1805	—	1.25	2.50	4.50	8.50
	1806	—	1.25	2.50	4.50	8.50

3 KREUTZER

BILLON

C#	Date	Mintage	VG	Fine	VF	XF
119	1803	—	1.75	3.50	6.50	12.50
	1804	—	1.75	3.50	6.50	12.50

Rev: Date in lozenge

C#	Date	Mintage	VG	Fine	VF	XF
119a	1805	—	1.75	3.50	6.50	15.00

5 KREUZER

BILLON

C#	Date	Mintage	VG	Fine	VF	XF
96	1773	—	7.50	10.00	15.00	25.00
	1775	—	7.50	10.00	15.00	20.00
	1778	—	7.50	10.00	15.00	20.00
	1781	—	7.50	10.00	15.00	20.00
	1784	—	7.50	10.00	15.00	20.00

Obv: Oval arms.

C#	Date	Mintage	VG	Fine	VF	XF
96a	1786	—	8.50	12.50	20.00	25.00
	1788	—	8.50	12.50	20.00	25.00

Obv: Square arms.

C#	Date	Mintage	VG	Fine	VF	XF
96b	1792	—	8.50	12.50	20.00	25.00

C#	Date	Mintage	VG	Fine	VF	XF
96c	1793	—	7.50	10.00	15.00	20.00
	1794	—	7.50	10.00	15.00	20.00
	1795	—	7.50	10.00	15.00	20.00
	1796	—	7.50	10.00	15.00	20.00
	1797	—	7.50	10.00	15.00	20.00
	1798	—	7.50	10.00	15.00	20.00
	1799	—	7.50	10.00	15.00	20.00
	1800	—	7.50	10.00	15.00	20.00
	1801	—	7.50	10.00	15.00	20.00
	1802	—	7.50	10.00	15.00	20.00

6 KREUTZER

BILLON

C#	Date	Mintage	VG	Fine	VF	XF
121	1803	—	2.25	4.50	8.50	15.00
	1804	—	2.25	4.50	8.50	15.00
	1805	—	2.25	4.50	8.50	15.00

Rev: Date in lozenge

C#	Date	Mintage	VG	Fine	VF	XF
121a	1805	—	2.25	4.50	8.50	15.00
	1806	—	2.25	4.50	8.50	15.00

10 KREUZER
(Convention)

3.8900 gm., .500 SILVER, .0625 oz ASW

C#	Date	Mintage	VG	Fine	VF	XF
99	1772 M	—	8.50	12.50	20.00	30.00
	1773 M	—	8.50	12.50	20.00	30.00
	1774 M	—	8.50	12.50	20.00	30.00
	1775 M	—	8.50	12.50	20.00	30.00

C#	Date	Mintage	VG	Fine	VF	XF
	1776 M	—	8.50	12.50	20.00	30.00
	1777 M	—	8.50	12.50	20.00	30.00
	1778 M	—	8.50	12.50	20.00	30.00
	1779 M	—	8.50	12.50	20.00	30.00
	1780 M	—	8.50	12.50	20.00	30.00
	1782 M	—	8.50	12.50	20.00	30.00
	1784 M	—	8.50	12.50	20.00	30.00
	1786 M	—	8.50	12.50	20.00	30.00

C#	Date	Mintage	VG	Fine	VF	XF
99a	1788 M	—	8.50	12.50	20.00	30.00
	1791 M	—	8.50	12.50	20.00	30.00
	1792 M	—	8.50	12.50	20.00	30.00

C#	Date	Mintage	VG	Fine	VF	XF
99a	1793 M	—	8.50	12.50	20.00	30.00
	1794 M	—	8.50	12.50	20.00	30.00
	1795 M	—	8.50	12.50	20.00	30.00
	1796 M	—	8.50	12.50	20.00	30.00
	1797 M	—	8.50	12.50	20.00	30.00
	1798 M	—	8.50	12.50	20.00	30.00
	1799 M	—	8.50	12.50	20.00	30.00
	1800 M	—	8.50	12.50	20.00	30.00
	1801 M	—	8.50	12.50	20.00	30.00
	1802 M	—	8.50	12.50	20.00	30.00

20 KREUTZER

(Convention)

6.6800 gm., .583 SILVER, .1252 oz ASW

C#	Date	Mintage	VG	Fine	VF	XF
103	1772 M	—	10.00	15.00	20.00	32.50
	1773 M	—	10.00	15.00	20.00	32.50
	1774 M	—	10.00	15.00	20.00	32.50
	1775 M	—	10.00	15.00	20.00	32.50
	1776 M	—	10.00	15.00	20.00	32.50
	1777 M	—	10.00	15.00	20.00	32.50
	1778 M	—	10.00	15.00	20.00	32.50
	1779 M	—	10.00	15.00	20.00	32.50
	1780 M	—	10.00	15.00	20.00	32.50
	1781 M	—	10.00	15.00	20.00	32.50
	1782 M	—	10.00	15.00	20.00	32.50
	1783 M	—	10.00	15.00	20.00	32.50
	1784 M	—	10.00	15.00	25.00	37.50
	1785 M	—	10.00	15.00	25.00	37.50
	1786 M	—	10.00	15.00	25.00	37.50

NOTE: Varieties exist.

C#	Date	Mintage	VG	Fine	VF	XF
103a	1787 M	—	10.00	15.00	25.00	37.50
	1788 M	—	10.00	15.00	25.00	37.50
	1789 M	—	10.00	15.00	25.00	37.50
	1790 M	—	10.00	15.00	25.00	37.50
	1791 M	—	10.00	15.00	25.00	37.50
	1792 M	—	10.00	15.00	25.00	37.50
	1793 M	—	10.00	15.00	25.00	37.50
	1794 M	—	10.00	15.00	25.00	37.50
	1795 M	—	10.00	15.00	25.00	37.50
	1796 M	—	10.00	15.00	25.00	37.50
	1797 M	—	10.00	15.00	25.00	37.50
	1798 M	—	10.00	15.00	25.00	37.50
	1799 M	—	10.00	15.00	25.00	37.50
	1800 M	—	10.00	15.00	25.00	37.50
	1801 M	—	10.00	15.00	25.00	37.50
	1802 M	—	10.00	15.00	25.00	37.50
	1803 M	—	10.00	15.00	25.00	37.50

NOTE: Varieties exist.

C#	Date	Mintage	Fine	VF	XF	Unc
123	1804 M	—	5.00	12.00	25.00	50.00

C#	Date	Mintage	Fine	VF	XF	Unc
123a	1805 M	—	5.00	12.00	25.00	50.00
	1806 M	—	5.00	12.00	25.00	50.00

1/2 THALER

(Convention)

14.0300 gm., .833 SILVER, .3757 oz ASW

C#	Date	Mintage	VG	Fine	VF	XF
104	1772 FM	—	20.00	50.00	95.00	150.00
	1773 M	—	20.00	50.00	95.00	150.00
	1775 M	—	20.00	50.00	95.00	150.00
	1778 M	—	20.00	50.00	95.00	150.00
	1779 M	—	20.00	50.00	95.00	150.00
	1780 M	—	20.00	50.00	95.00	150.00
	1782 M	—	20.00	50.00	95.00	150.00

C#	Date	Mintage	VG	Fine	VF	XF
104a	1787 M	—	25.00	65.00	110.00	175.00
	1792 M	—	25.00	65.00	110.00	175.00
	1797 M	—	25.00	65.00	110.00	175.00
	1802 M	—	25.00	65.00	110.00	175.00

THALER

(Convention)

28.0600 gm., .833 SILVER, .7515 oz ASW

C#	Date	Mintage	VG	Fine	VF	XF
106	1772 F.M. close date	—	50.00	110.00	150.00	225.00
106	1772 FMF wide date	—	50.00	110.00	150.00	225.00

C#	Date	Mintage	VG	Fine	VF	XF
106a	1772 FMF	—	50.00	110.00	150.00	225.00

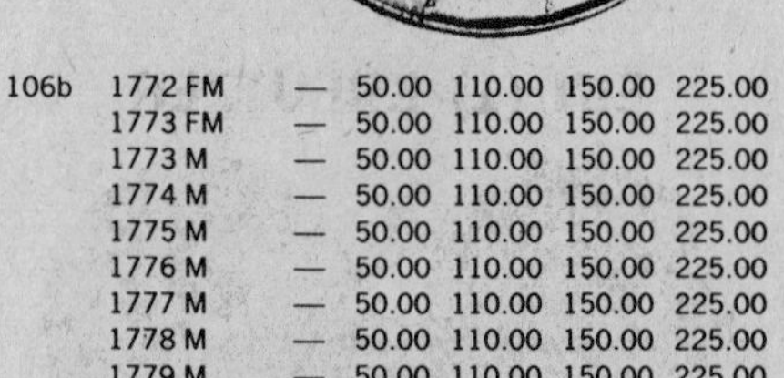

C#	Date	Mintage	VG	Fine	VF	XF
106b	1772 FM	—	50.00	110.00	150.00	225.00
	1773 FM	—	50.00	110.00	150.00	225.00
	1773 M	—	50.00	110.00	150.00	225.00
	1774 M	—	50.00	110.00	150.00	225.00
	1775 M	—	50.00	110.00	150.00	225.00
	1776 M	—	50.00	110.00	150.00	225.00
	1777 M	—	50.00	110.00	150.00	225.00
	1778 M	—	50.00	110.00	150.00	225.00
	1779 M	—	50.00	110.00	150.00	225.00

Obv: Similar to C#106b.

C#	Date	Mintage	VG	Fine	VF	XF
106c	1780 M	—	50.00	110.00	150.00	225.00

C#	Date	Mintage	VG	Fine	VF	XF
106c	1781 M	—	50.00	110.00	150.00	225.00
	1782 M	—	50.00	110.00	150.00	225.00
	1783 M	—	50.00	110.00	150.00	225.00
	1784 M	—	50.00	110.00	150.00	225.00
	1785 M	—	50.00	110.00	150.00	225.00
	1786 M	—	50.00	110.00	150.00	225.00

NOTE: Varieties exist.

Rev: Crowned baroque arms with larger mantle; close date below.

C#	Date	Mintage	VG	Fine	VF	XF
107	1787 M	—	50.00	110.00	150.00	225.00
	1788 M	—	50.00	110.00	150.00	225.00
	1789 M	—	50.00	110.00	150.00	225.00

Rev: Crowned and mantled spade arms.

C#	Date	Mintage	VG	Fine	VF	XF
107a	1789	—	50.00	110.00	150.00	225.00
	1789 M	—	50.00	110.00	150.00	225.00
	1790 M	—	50.00	110.00	150.00	225.00
	1791 M	—	50.00	110.00	150.00	225.00
	1792 M	—	50.00	110.00	150.00	225.00
	1793 M	—	50.00	110.00	150.00	225.00
	1794 M	—	50.00	110.00	150.00	225.00
	1795 M	—	50.00	110.00	150.00	225.00
	1796 M	—	50.00	110.00	150.00	225.00
	1797 M	—	50.00	110.00	150.00	225.00
	1798 M	—	50.00	110.00	150.00	225.00
	1799 M	—	50.00	110.00	150.00	225.00
	1800 M	—	50.00	110.00	150.00	225.00
	1801 M	—	60.00	110.00	150.00	225.00
	1802 M	—	60.00	110.00	150.00	225.00
	1803 M	—	60.00	110.00	150.00	225.00

NOTE: Varieties exist.

Rev: Crowned arms with lion supporters; garland and date below.

C#	Date	Mintage	VG	Fine	VF	XF
—	1790 FM	7 pcs.	—	—	Rare	—

C#	Date	Mintage	Fine	VF	XF	Unc
125	1803	—	30.00	60.00	100.00	200.00

C#	Date	Mintage	Fine	VF	XF	Unc
125a	1805 M	—	25.00	50.00	75.00	150.00

Rev: Legend...PAS ETBER S R IP ELECTOR

C#	Date	Mintage	Fine	VF	XF	Unc
125b	1806 M	—	25.00	50.00	75.00	175.00

TRADE COINS

1/4 DUCAT

.8750 gm., .986 GOLD, .0277 oz AGW

C#	Date	Mintage	VG	Fine	VF	XF
109	1776	—	100.00	175.00	250.00	325.00
	1777	—	100.00	175.00	250.00	325.00
	1782	—	100.00	175.00	250.00	325.00

1/2 DUCAT

1.7500 gm., .986 GOLD, .0555 oz AGW

C#	Date	Mintage	VG	Fine	VF	XF
110	1776	—	200.00	300.00	375.00	600.00

DUCAT

3.5000 gm., .986 GOLD, .1109 oz AGW

C#	Date	Mintage	VG	Fine	VF	XF
111	1772 M	—	175.00	350.00	450.00	650.00
	1773 M	—	175.00	350.00	450.00	650.00
	1774 M	—	175.00	350.00	450.00	650.00
	1775 M	—	175.00	350.00	450.00	650.00
	1776 M	—	175.00	350.00	450.00	650.00
	1777 M	—	175.00	350.00	450.00	650.00
	1778 M	—	175.00	350.00	450.00	650.00
	1779 M	—	175.00	350.00	450.00	650.00
	1780 M	—	175.00	350.00	450.00	650.00
	1781 M	—	175.00	350.00	450.00	650.00
	1782 M	—	175.00	350.00	450.00	650.00
	1783 M	—	175.00	350.00	450.00	650.00
	1784 M	—	175.00	350.00	450.00	650.00
	1785 M	—	175.00	350.00	450.00	650.00
	1786 M	—	175.00	350.00	450.00	650.00

C#	Date	Mintage	VG	Fine	VF	XF
111a	1787 M	—	175.00	350.00	450.00	650.00
	1788 M	—	175.00	350.00	450.00	650.00
	1789 M	—	175.00	350.00	450.00	650.00
	1790 M	—	175.00	350.00	450.00	650.00
	1791 M	—	175.00	350.00	450.00	650.00
	1792 M	—	175.00	350.00	450.00	650.00
	1793 M	—	175.00	350.00	450.00	650.00
	1794 M	—	175.00	350.00	450.00	650.00
	1795 M	—	175.00	350.00	450.00	650.00
	1796 M	—	175.00	350.00	450.00	650.00
	1797 M	—	175.00	350.00	450.00	650.00
	1798 M	—	175.00	350.00	450.00	650.00
	1799 M	—	175.00	350.00	450.00	650.00
	1800 M	—	175.00	350.00	450.00	650.00
	1801 M	—	175.00	350.00	450.00	650.00
	1802 M	—	175.00	350.00	450.00	650.00
111b	1803 M	—	—	—	Rare	—

NOTE: Varieties exist.

1200th Anniversary of the Bishopric

C#	Date	Mintage	VG	Fine	VF	XF
112	1782 M	—	400.00	600.00	950.00	1500.

C#	Date	Mintage	Fine	VF	XF	Unc
126	1803 M	—	350.00	500.00	650.00	850.00
	1804 M	—	350.00	500.00	650.00	850.00

C#	Date	Mintage	Fine	VF	XF	Unc
126a	1805 M	—	300.00	450.00	600.00	800.00
	1806 M	—	300.00	450.00	600.00	800.00

2 DUCATS

7.0000 gm., .986 GOLD, .2219 oz AGW
Obv: Bust right.
Rev: Crowned and mantled oval arms, value below.

C#	Date	Mintage	VG	Fine	VF	XF
113	1773 M	—	1000.	1250.	1950.	2750.

1200th Anniversary of the Bishopric
Rev: Temple.

C#	Date	Mintage	VG	Fine	VF	XF
114	1782 M	—	1000.	1350.	2000.	3000.

STYRIA

A mountainous region of southeastern Austria. It became a duchy in 1180, later became a part of the Hapsburg lands in 1246. The Graz Mint is located in Styria.

RULERS

Maria Theresa, 1740-1780
Widow, 1765-1780

MINTMASTER'S INITIAL

CG,CvG,G - Carl Geramb
AK,K - J.A. Kollmann

20 KREUZER

SILVER
Obv: Veiled head right.
Rev: Crowned imperial eagle on pedestal; value in pedestal.

C#	Date	Mintage	Fine	VF	XF	Unc
11a	1767CG-AK	—	10.00	12.00	15.00	25.00
	1768CvG-AK	—	10.00	12.00	15.00	25.00
	1769CvG-AK	—	10.00	12.00	15.00	25.00
	1770CvG-AK	—	10.00	12.00	15.00	25.00
	1771CvG-AK	—	10.00	12.00	15.00	25.00
	1772CvG-AK	—	10.00	12.00	15.00	25.00

TRADE COINS

DUCAT

3.5000 gm., .986 GOLD, .1109 oz AGW
Obv: Veiled head right.
Rev: Crowned imperial eagle; arms on breast.

C#	Date	Mintage	Fine	VF	XF	Unc
18a	1768G-K	—	250.00	375.00	500.00	1000.
	1769G-K	—	250.00	375.00	500.00	1000.

TRANSYLVANIA

A plateau region of northwestern Romania. It was made a principality in 1540. Buffer between Austria and Turkey from 1660 to 1683. After the defeat of the Turks before Vienna in 1683 the Transylvanian princes looked to Austria for guidance and protection. The last independent prince abdicated in 1697 and the lands became completely Austrian after the Peace of Szatmar in 1711. The mints of Karlsburg and Nagybanya are located in Transylvania.

RULERS

Maria Theresa, 1740-1780
Widow, 1765-1780

MINTMARKS

E - Karlsburg

MINTMASTERS

HG - A.J. Hammerschmidt and A. deGagia
H.S. - A.J. Hammerschmidt and G. Schickmayer

3 KREUZER

BILLON

C#	Date	Mintage	VG	Fine	VF	XF
8	1774 HG	—	12.50	17.50	25.00	50.00
	1774E-HG	—	12.50	17.50	25.00	50.00
	1774B-HG	—	12.50	17.50	25.00	50.00
	1777 HG	—	12.50	17.50	25.00	50.00
	1777E-HG	—	12.50	17.50	25.00	50.00
	1780 HS	—	12.50	17.50	25.00	50.00

10 KREUZER

SILVER
Similar to 20 Kreuzer, C#16.

C#	Date	Mintage	VG	Fine	VF	XF
12	1776 HG	—	15.00	17.50	22.50	35.00
	1780 HS	—	15.00	17.50	22.50	35.00

20 KREUZER

SILVER

C#	Date	Mintage	VG	Fine	VF	XF
16	1767 HG	—	20.00	27.50	37.50	50.00
	1768 HG	—	20.00	27.50	37.50	50.00
	1769 HG	—	20.00	27.50	37.50	50.00
	1770 HG	—	20.00	27.50	37.50	50.00
	1771 HG	—	20.00	27.50	37.50	50.00
	1772 HG	—	20.00	27.50	37.50	50.00
	1773 HG	—	20.00	27.50	37.50	50.00
	1774 HG	—	20.00	27.50	37.50	50.00
	1776 HG	—	20.00	27.50	37.50	50.00
	1777 HG	—	20.00	27.50	37.50	50.00
	1777 HS	—	20.00	27.50	37.50	50.00
	1778 HS	—	20.00	27.50	37.50	50.00
	1779 HS	—	20.00	27.50	37.50	50.00
	1780 HS	—	20.00	27.50	37.50	50.00

TRADE COINS

1/16 DUCAT

.2188 gm., .986 GOLD, .0069 oz AGW

C#	Date	Mintage	VG	Fine	VF	XF
26	1778 HS	—	100.00	175.00	225.00	300.00

1/8 DUCAT

.4375 gm., .986 GOLD, .0139 oz AGW

C#	Date	Mintage	VG	Fine	VF	XF
28	1778 HS	—	125.00	175.00	250.00	400.00

1/4 DUCAT

.8750 gm., .986 GOLD, .0277 oz AGW

C#	Date	Mintage	VG	Fine	VF	XF
30a	1768 HG	—	125.00	185.00	250.00	325.00
	1772 HG	—	125.00	185.00	250.00	325.00
	1776 HG	—	125.00	185.00	250.00	325.00
	1778 HS	—	125.00	185.00	250.00	325.00
	1780 HS	—	125.00	185.00	250.00	325.00

1/2 DUCAT

1.7500 gm., .986 GOLD, .0555 oz AGW

C#	Date	Mintage	VG	Fine	VF	XF
31a	1770 HG	—	200.00	250.00	350.00	500.00
	1774 HG	—	200.00	250.00	350.00	500.00
	1775 HG	—	200.00	250.00	350.00	500.00
	1780 HS	—	200.00	250.00	350.00	500.00

DUCAT

3.5000 gm., .986 GOLD, .1109 oz AGW

C#	Date	Mintage	VG	Fine	VF	XF
33a	1765 HG	—	300.00	425.00	600.00	850.00
	1767 HG	—	300.00	425.00	600.00	850.00
	1768 HG	—	300.00	425.00	600.00	850.00
	1769 HG	—	300.00	425.00	600.00	850.00
	1770 HG	—	300.00	425.00	600.00	850.00
	1771 HG	—	300.00	425.00	600.00	850.00
	1772 HG	—	300.00	425.00	600.00	850.00
	1773 HG	—	300.00	425.00	600.00	850.00
	1774 HG	—	300.00	425.00	600.00	850.00
	1775	—	300.00	425.00	600.00	850.00
	1776 HG	—	300.00	425.00	600.00	850.00
	1777 HG	—	300.00	425.00	600.00	850.00
	1777 HS	—	300.00	425.00	600.00	850.00
	1778 HS	—	300.00	425.00	600.00	850.00
	1779 HS	—	300.00	425.00	600.00	850.00
	1780 HS	—	300.00	425.00	600.00	850.00

2 DUCATS

7.0000 gm., .986 GOLD, .2219 oz AGW

C#	Date	Mintage	VG	Fine	VF	XF
34a	1768 HG	—	450.00	700.00	1000.	1750.
	1769 HG	—	450.00	700.00	1000.	1750.
	1770 HG	—	450.00	700.00	1000.	1750.
	1771 HG	—	450.00	700.00	1000.	1750.
	1772 HG	—	450.00	700.00	1000.	1750.
	1773 HG	—	450.00	700.00	1000.	1750.
	1774 HG	—	450.00	700.00	1000.	1750.
	1775 HG	—	450.00	700.00	1000.	1750.
	1776 HG	—	450.00	700.00	1000.	1750.
	1777 HG	—	450.00	700.00	1000.	1750.
	1777 HS	—	450.00	700.00	1000.	1750.
	1778 HS	—	450.00	700.00	1000.	1750.
	1779 HS	—	450.00	700.00	1000.	1750.
	1780 HS	—	450.00	700.00	1000.	1750.

4 DUCATS

14.0000 gm., .986 GOLD, .4438 oz AGW
Obv: Veiled head right.
Rev: Crowned imperial eagle; date in legend.

C#	Date	Mintage	VG	Fine	VF	XF
35a	1779 HS	—	1750.	2250.	3000.	4500.

TYROL

Tyrol (Tirol) was a prince-bishopric situated in Austria between Germany and Italy. In 1363 Margaret Maultasch, countess of Tyrol, handed over Tyrol to Rudolph, duke of Austria. Except for a period of Bavarian occupation, 1805-14, Tyrol remained a Hapsburg possession until the breakup of the Austrian Empire at the end of World War I. The world's first dollar-size silver crown was struck at Hall, Tyrol, in 1486.

RULERS

Maria Theresa, 1740-1780
Widow, 1765-1780
Napoleon, (France) 1805-1809
Maximilian Joseph I, (Bavaria) 1805-1814
Andreas Hofer, Rebellion, 1809
Franz I, (Austria), 1814-1835
Ferdinand, (Austria), 1835-1848
Franz Joseph, (Austria), 1848-1916

MINTMARKS

F - Hall

MINTMASTER'S INITIALS

A - L. Aschpacher
VC - J.H. von Clotz
S - J.J. Stockner

EIN (1) KREUZER

COPPER
Insurrection Issue of Andreas Hofer

C#	Date	Mintage	VG	Fine	VF	XF
41	1809	—	11.50	17.50	45.00	75.00

10 KREUZER

SILVER
Obv: Veiled head right in wreath.
Rev: Crowned imperial eagle, arms on breast; value below date in legend.

C#	Date	Mintage	VG	Fine	VF	XF
20a	1770 AS	—	5.00	6.00	10.00	15.00
	1771 AS	—	5.00	6.00	10.00	15.00
	1772 AS	—	5.00	6.00	10.00	15.00
	1773 AS	—	5.00	6.00	10.00	15.00
	1774 AS	—	5.00	6.00	10.00	15.00
	1774VC-S	—	5.00	6.00	10.00	15.00
	1775VC-S	—	5.00	6.00	10.00	15.00
	1776VC-S	—	5.00	6.00	10.00	15.00
	1777VC-S	—	5.00	6.00	10.00	15.00
	1778VC-S	—	5.00	6.00	10.00	15.00
	1779VC-S	—	5.00	6.00	10.00	15.00
	1780VC-S	—	5.00	6.00	10.00	15.00

20 KREUZER

SILVER
Insurrection Issue of Andreas Hofer
Obv: Veiled head right in wreath.
Rev: Crowned imperial eagle, arms on breast; value below date in legend.

C#	Date	Mintage	VG	Fine	VF	XF
26a	1768 AS	—	4.00	6.00	8.50	15.00
	1769 AS	—	4.00	6.00	8.50	15.00
	1770 AS	—	4.00	6.00	8.50	15.00
	1771 AS	—	4.00	6.00	8.50	15.00
	1772 AS	—	4.00	6.00	8.50	15.00
	1773 AS	—	4.00	6.00	8.50	15.00
	1774 AS	—	4.00	6.00	8.50	15.00
	1774 VC-S	—	4.00	6.00	8.50	15.00
	1775 VC-S	—	4.00	6.00	8.50	15.00
	1776 VC-S	—	4.00	6.00	8.50	15.00
	1777 VC-S	—	4.00	6.00	8.50	15.00
	1778 VC-S	—	4.00	6.00	8.50	15.00
	1779 VC-S	—	4.00	6.00	8.50	15.00
	1780 VC-S	—	4.00	6.00	8.50	15.00

Insurrection Issue of Andreas Hofer

C#	Date	Mintage	VG	Fine	VF	XF
42	1809	—	—	25.00	45.00	75.00

NOTE: Three varieties exist.

1/2 THALER
(Convention)

SILVER

C#	Date	Mintage	VG	Fine	VF	XF
31	1767 AS	—	25.00	35.00	65.00	100.00
	1767 AS	—	25.00	35.00	65.00	100.00
	1768 AS	—	25.00	35.00	65.00	100.00
	1769 AS	—	25.00	35.00	65.00	100.00
	1770 AS	—	25.00	35.00	65.00	100.00
	1771 AS	—	25.00	35.00	65.00	100.00
	1772 AS	—	25.00	35.00	65.00	100.00
	1773 AS	—	25.00	35.00	65.00	100.00
	1774 VC-S	—	25.00	35.00	65.00	100.00
	1775 VC-S	—	25.00	35.00	65.00	100.00
	1776 VC-S	—	25.00	35.00	65.00	100.00
	1777 VC-S	—	25.00	35.00	65.00	100.00

THALER
(Convention)

SILVER
Similar to 1/2 Thaler, C#31.

C#	Date	Mintage	VG	Fine	VF	XF
34	1765 F	—	40.00	65.00	125.00	165.00
	1765 AS	—	40.00	65.00	125.00	165.00
	1766 AS	—	40.00	65.00	125.00	165.00
	1767 AS	—	40.00	65.00	125.00	165.00
	1768 AS	—	40.00	65.00	125.00	165.00
	1768 S	—	40.00	65.00	125.00	165.00
	1769 AS	—	40.00	65.00	125.00	165.00
	1771 AS	—	40.00	65.00	125.00	165.00
	1772 AS	—	40.00	65.00	125.00	165.00

Obv: Veiled head right with smaller veil.
Rev: Initials.

C#	Date	Mintage	VG	Fine	VF	XF
34a	1773 AS	—	40.00	65.00	125.00	165.00
	1774 AS	—	40.00	65.00	125.00	165.00
	1774 VC-S	—	40.00	65.00	125.00	165.00
	1775 VC-S	—	40.00	65.00	125.00	165.00
	1776 VC-S	—	40.00	65.00	125.00	165.00

TRADE COINS

DUCAT

3.5000 gm., .986 GOLD, .1109 oz AGW
Obv: Veiled head right.
Rev: Crowned imperial eagle with Tyrol arms on breast.

C#	Date	Mintage	VG	Fine	VF	XF
37	1768 AS	—	175.00	250.00	375.00	600.00
	1770 AS	—	175.00	250.00	375.00	600.00
	1771 AS	—	175.00	250.00	375.00	600.00
	1773 AS	—	175.00	250.00	375.00	600.00
	1774 VC-S	—	175.00	250.00	375.00	600.00
	1775 VC-S	—	175.00	250.00	375.00	600.00
	1777 VC-S	—	175.00	250.00	375.00	600.00
	1778 VC-S	—	175.00	250.00	375.00	600.00
	1779 VC-S	—	175.00	250.00	375.00	600.00

VIENNA (WIEN)

Vienna became a bishopric in 1471. The bishop became a prince in 1631 and Vienna was made an archbishopric is 1722.

Archbishopric

RULERS

Christoph Anton,
Graf. v. Migazzi, 1757-1803

THALER
(Convention)

SILVER

C#	Date	Mintage	VG	Fine	VF	XF
1	1781	—	150.00	200.00	275.00	400.00

TRADE COINS

DUCAT

3.5000 gm., .986 GOLD, .1109 oz AGW
Similar to Thaler C#1.

C#	Date	Mintage	VG	Fine	VF	XF
2	1781	—	400.00	600.00	850.00	1150.

WINDISCHGRATZ

A family descended from the counts of Weimar with holdings in Styria. Made "free barons" in 1551. They became counts during the reign of Emperor Leopold I and received the coin right in 1730. First coins were made in 1732, the last in 1777.

RULERS

Joseph Nicholas, 1744-1802

20 KREUZER

SILVER

C#	Date	Mintage	Fine	VF	XF	Unc
1	1777	—	50.00	70.00	100.00	150.00

1/2 THALER
(Convention)

SILVER

C#	Date	Mintage	Fine	VF	XF	Unc
2	1777	—	75.00	100.00	175.00	250.00

TRADE COINS

DUCAT

3.5000 gm., .986 GOLD, .1109 oz AGW
Similar to 1/2 Thaler C#2.

C#	Date	Mintage	Fine	VF	XF	Unc
3	1777	—	500.00	650.00	850.00	1000.

5 DUCATS

17.5000 gm., .986 GOLD, .5548 oz AGW
Similar to 1/2 Thaler C#2.

C#	Date	Mintage	Fine	VF	XF	Unc
4	1777	—	—	—	Rare	—

AZORES

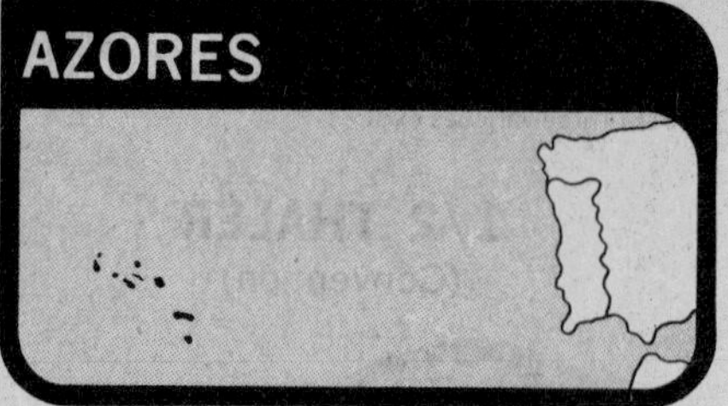

The Azores, an archipelago of nine islands of volcanic origin, are located in the Atlantic Ocean 740 miles (1,190 km.) west of Cape de Roca, Portugal. They are under the administration of Portugal, and have an area of 902 sq. mi. (2,335 sq. km.) and a population of 337,000. Principal City: Ponta Delgada. The natives are mainly of Portuguese descent and earn their livelihood by fishing, wine making, basket weaving, and the growing of fruit, grains and sugar cane. Pineapples are the chief item of export. The climate is particularly temperate, making the islands a favorite winter resort.

The Azores were discovered about 1427 by the Portuguese navigator Diago de Silves. Portugal secured the islands in the 15th century and established the first settlement, on Santa Maria, about 1432. From 1580 to 1640 the Azores were subject to Spain.

Angra on Terceira Island became the capital of the captaincy-general of the Azores in 1766 and it was here in 1826 that the constitutionalists set up a pro-Pedro government in opposition to King Miguel in Lisbon. The whole Portuguese fleet attacked Terceira and was repelled at Praia, after which Azoreans, Brazilians and British mercenaries defeated Miguel in Portugal. Maria de Gloria, Pedro's daughter, was proclaimed queen of Portugal on Terceira in 1828.

A U.S. naval base was established at Ponta Delgada in 1917.

After World War II, the islands acquired a renewed importance as a refueling stop for transatlantic air transport. The United States maintains defense bases in the Azores as part of the collective security program of NATO.

RULERS
Portuguese

MONETARY SYSTEM
1000 Reis (Insulanos) = 1 Milreis

TERCEIRA ISLAND

INSURRECTION OF 1826

On the death of John VI in 1826 the constitutionalists on Terceira supported Pedro, the Brazilian emperor and oldest son of John VI, for the Portuguese throne in opposition to Miguel, Pedro's younger brother who was proclaimed king in 1828.

After repelling the attack of the entire Portuguese fleet at Praia, the constitutionalists with their British mercenaries invaded Portugal and defeated Miguel in 1834. Maria da Gloria, daughter of Pedro, was then proclaimed Queen of Portugal.

LXXX (80) REIS

COPPER
"AZORES INDEPENDEN. ILHA TERCEIRA"

C#	Date	Mintage	Good	VG	Fine	VF
9.5	1826	—	—	Rare	—	—

MARIA II IN EXILE, 1828-1833

In 1828 Pedro declined the Portuguese throne in favor of his daughter, Maria da Gloria, who was therefore forced to live in exile 1828-1834 until Miguel was completely defeated.

20 REIS

CAST GUN OR BELL METAL

C#	Date	Mintage	Good	VG	Fine	VF
10	1829	—	—	Rare	—	—

40 REIS

CAST GUN OR BELL METAL

C#	Date	Mintage	Good	VG	Fine	VF
11	1829	—	—	—	Rare	—

80 REIS

CAST GUN OR BELL METAL

C#	Date	Mintage	Good	VG	Fine	VF
12	1829	—	6.00	12.50	25.00	35.00

AZORES

5 REIS

COPPER
Obv: Legend, MARIA I, arms.
Rev: Value in wreath, legend.

C#	Date	Mintage	Good	VG	Fine	VF
4	1795	—	3.00	5.00	7.50	12.50
	1796	—	5.00	10.00	18.50	28.50
	1797	—	4.00	7.00	13.50	20.00
	1798	—	3.50	6.50	12.50	18.50
	1799	—	—	—	—	—

C#	Date	Mintage	VG	Fine	VF	XF
13	1843	—	1.75	3.50	7.50	12.50

Y#	Date	Mintage	Fine	VF	XF	Unc
1	1865	.090	1.25	2.50	6.00	12.50
	1866	.060	1.75	3.50	7.50	15.00
	1880	.400	1.25	2.50	6.00	12.50

Y#	Date	Mintage	Fine	VF	XF	Unc
4	1901	.800	.75	1.50	3.50	7.50

10 REIS

COPPER
Obv: Legend, MARIA I, arms.
Rev: Value in wreath, legend.

C#	Date	Mintage	Good	VG	Fine	VF
5	1793	—	12.00	20.00	37.50	60.00
	1795	—	3.00	5.00	9.00	14.00
	1796	—	3.50	6.50	12.50	18.50

C#	Date	Mintage	VG	Fine	VF	XF
14	1843	—	2.50	5.00	7.50	10.00

Y#	Date	Mintage	Fine	VF	XF	Unc
2	1865	.525	1.75	3.50	7.50	15.00
	1866	Inc. Ab.	25.00	35.00	50.00	75.00

Y#	Date	Mintage	Fine	VF	XF	Unc
5	1901	.600	2.00	4.00	7.50	10.00

20 REIS

COPPER
Obv: Legend, MARIA I, arms.
Rev: Value in wreath, legend.

C#	Date	Mintage	Good	VG	Fine	VF
6	1790	—	20.00	30.00	50.00	80.00
	1795	—	3.00	5.00	9.00	14.50
	1796	—	3.50	6.00	12.00	19.00

NOTE: Sometimes found overstruck on Portuguese 10 Reis, C#34.

Error Dates

C#	Date	Mintage	Good	VG	Fine	VF
6a	1190(1790)	—	30.00	50.00	75.00	115.00
	1196(1796)	—	20.00	30.00	50.00	80.00

C#	Date	Mintage	VG	Fine	VF	XF
15	1843	—	2.50	5.00	7.50	10.00

Y#	Date	Mintage	Fine	VF	XF	Unc
3	1865	.178	.75	1.50	4.50	15.00
	1866	.273	.75	1.50	5.50	17.50

75 REIS

SILVER
Obv: MARIA I DG. PORT. Et ALG. REGINA, denomination. Rev: IN HOC. etc., cross.

C#	Date	Mintage	Good	VG	Fine	VF
7	1794	—	7.00	12.00	20.00	35.00
	1795	—	8.00	15.00	25.00	40.00

150 REIS

SILVER
Obv: Legend MARIA I D.G. PORT. ET ALG. REGINA, denomination. Rev: Legend IN HOC....., cross.

C#	Date	Mintage	Good	VG	Fine	VF
8	1794	—	10.00	15.00	20.00	35.00
	1795	—	12.00	17.50	25.00	40.00
	1797	—	60.00	85.00	125.00	175.00
	1798	—	25.00	35.00	50.00	75.00

300 REIS

SILVER
Obv: Legend MARIA I DG PORT. ET ALG. REGINA, denomination. Rev: Legend IN HOC...., cross.

C#	Date	Mintage	Good	VG	Fine	VF
9	1794	—	25.00	35.00	50.00	75.00
	1795	—	20.00	30.00	45.00	60.00
	1797	—	40.00	50.00	70.00	100.00

NOTE: Portugal's 50-Centavos (Y#54) and 1 Escudo (Y#55) dated 1935 were minted solely for use in the Azores.

COUNTERSTAMP ISSUES

Decree of June 14, 1871

This first decree ordained that the circulating Brazilian Patacas of 2000 Reis including the fractions of 1000, 500 and 200 Reis which at the time locally had a value of 1200, 600, 300 and 120 Reis (Portuguese) respectively were to be counterstamped with a royal crown. These were eventually to be replaced or exchanged by current Portuguese coinage upon their entry into the public treasury. This countermark is also known on copper coins and on various silver coins of other nations that were circulating at the time. The following list is a basic guide with samples of known examples. Grades noted are for the basic coin as the countermark is normally found in better condition.

20 REIS

COPPER
c/s: Crown on Portuguese and Colonies X (10) Reis

KM#	Date	Mintage	Good	VG	Fine	VF
3	ND	—	9.00	15.00	25.00	40.00

40 REIS

COPPER
c/s: Crown on Mozambique 40 Reis

KM#	Date	Mintage	Good	VG	Fine	VF
4	ND	—	9.00	15.00	25.00	40.00

600 REIS

SILVER
c/s: Crown on Brazilian 1000 Reis

KM#	Date	Mintage	Good	VG	Fine	VF
9	ND	—	17.50	25.00	45.00	85.00

1200 REIS

SILVER
c/s: Crown on Austrian Maria Theresa Thaler

KM#	Date	Mintage	Good	VG	Fine	VF
10	ND(1780)	—	25.00	35.00	70.00	110.00

c/s: Crown on Brazilian 2000 Reis

KM#	Date	Mintage	Good	VG	Fine	VF
11	ND	—	25.00	35.00	70.00	110.00

Decree of March 31, 1887

Countermark crowned G.P., 8mm.
Illustration is twice normal size.

This second decree ordained that all foreign silver and copper coinage circulating in the Azores was to be counterstamped with a crowned G.P. (Governo Portugues) within a circle. These also were eventually to be replaced or exchanged by current Portuguese coinage upon their entry into the public treasury. This counterstamp for general use is found on a profusion of Portuguese, Brazilian, and foreign issues. The largest crown or dollar size includes the Portuguese 1000 Reis, Brazilian 2000 Reis, obsolete 960 Reis, 1200 Reis, Austrian Thaler, English 5 Shilling or crown, Spanish American 8 Reales and Spanish 2 Escudos for comparison to the United States dollar. This countermark has been heavily counterfeited and should be approached with caution. The following list is a basic guide with samples of known examples. Grades noted are for the basic coin and the countermark is normally found in better condition than the coin bearing it.

15 REIS

COPPER

c/s: Crowned G.P. on Portuguese India (Goa) 15 Reis, C#338.2.

Y#	Date	Mintage	Good	VG	Fine	VF
C1	ND	—	12.50	20.00	30.00	45.00

120 REIS

SILVER

c/s: Crowned G.P. on Portuguese 80 Reis, C#7.

C2	ND	—	10.00	15.00	25.00	35.00

300 REIS

SILVER

c/s: Crowned G.P. on Spanish or Spanish Colonial 2 Reales.

C3	ND	—	8.50	12.50	20.00	30.00

600 REIS

SILVER

c/s: Crowned G.P. on Bolivia 4 Reales, C#17.

C4.1	ND(1773-89)	—	22.50	32.50	50.00	75.00

c/s: Crowned G.P. on Portuguese 400 Reis, C#59a.

C4.2	ND(1802-16)	—	22.50	32.50	50.00	75.00

1200 REIS

SILVER

c/s: Crowned G.P. on Brazilian 960 Reis

Y#	Date	Mintage	VG	Fine	VF	XF
C5.1	ND(1809-18)	—	30.00	50.00	75.00	110.00

c/s: Crowned G.P. on Peru 8 Reales, C#132-1a.

C5.2	ND(1828-40)	—	30.00	50.00	70.00	100.00

c/s: Crowned G.P. on Spain 20 Reales, C#92.

Y#	Date	Mintage	VG	Fine	VF	XF
C5.3	ND(1808-13)	—	45.00	75.00	125.00	200.00

NOTE: The above examples as noted are listed only to determine relative size and do not reflect a current price for other foreign types found with genuine counterstamps.

Copper Series of 1795-8

5 REIS

COPPER

c/s: 5 on Portuguese III Reis, C#17.

C#	Date	Mintage	Good	VG	Fine	VF
6.4	ND(1777-8)	—	40.00	75.00	125.00	200.00

10 REIS

COPPER

c/s: 10 on Portuguese V Reis, C#33.

6.7	ND(1791-)	—	40.00	75.00	125.00	200.00

NCLT ISSUES

PATTERNS

C#	Date	Mintage	Identification	Issue Price	Mkt Val.
—	1798	—	40 Reis, Maria I, Copper	—	300.00

BAHAMAS

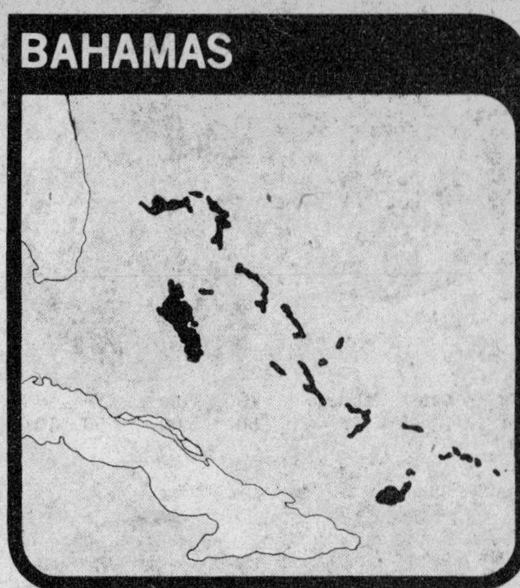

The Commonwealth of the Bahamas is an archipelago of about 3,000 islands, cays and rocks located in the Atlántic Ocean east of Florida and north of Cuba. The total land area of the 800 mile (1,287 km.) long chain of islands is 5,380 sq. mi. (13,934 sq. km.). They have a population of 216,000. Capital: Nassau. The Bahamas import most of their food and manufactured products and export cement, refined oil, pulpwood and lobsters. Tourism is the principal industry.

The Bahamas were discovered by Columbus in October, 1492, but Spain made no attempt to settle them. British influence began in 1626 when Charles I granted them to the lord proprietors of Carolina. They continued under British proprietors until 1717, when the civil and military governments were surrendered to the King and the islands designated a British Crown Colony. The Bahamas obtained complete internal self-government under the constitution of Jan. 7, 1964. Full independence was achieved on July 10, 1973. The Bahamas is a member of the Commonwealth of Nations. The Queen of England is Chief of State.

The coinage of Great Britain was legal tender in the Bahamas prior to the issuing of a definitive coinage in 1966.

RULERS

British

MINTMARKS

Through 1969 all decimal coinage of the Bahamas was executed at the Royal Mint in England. Since that time issues have been struck at both the Royal Mint (RM) and at the Franklin Mint (FM) in the U.S.A. While the mintmark of the latter appears on coins dated 1971 and subsequently, it is missing from the 1970 issues.

JP - John Pinches, London
RM - Royal Mint (no mintmark)
(t) - Tower of London
FM - Franklin Mint, U.S.A.*

***NOTE:** During 1975-77 the Franklin Mint produced coinage in up to 3 different qualities. Qualities of issue are designated in ( ) after each date and are defined as follows:

(M) MATTE - Normal circulation strike or a dull finish produced by sandblasting special uncirculated (polish finish) or proof quality dies.

(U) SPECIAL UNCIRCULATED - Polished or proof-like in appearance without any frosted features.

(P) PROOF - The highest quality obtainable having mirror-like fields and frosted features.

MONETARY SYSTEM

100 Cents = 1 Dollar

PENNY

COPPER

C#	Date	Mintage	VG	Fine	VF	XF
1	1806 engrailed edge					
		.120	15.00	25.00	40.00	65.00

C#	Date	Mintage	VG	Fine	VF	XF
1	1806 engrailed edge				Proof	350.00
	1806 plain edge				—	250.00
	1806 plain edge				Proof	350.00
	1807 engrailed edge			Restrike Proof		2000.

CENT

NICKEL BRASS

Y#	Date	Mintage	VF	XF	Unc
1	1966	7.312	.20	.30	.50
	1968	.800	.45	.70	1.25
	1969	4.036	.10	.15	.25
	1969	.010	—	Proof	1.00

NOTE: The obverse of the above also comes muled with the reverse of a New Zealand 2-cent piece (Y#37). The undated (1967) error is listed as New Zealand Y#37a.

Y#	Date	Mintage	VF	XF	Unc
1a	1970	.125	.10	.15	.25
	1970	.023	—	Proof	1.00

NOTE: Proof specimens of this date are struck in 'special brass' which looks like a pale bronze.

Y#	Date	Mintage	VF	XF	Unc
14	1971FM	1.007	.10	.25	.75
	1971FM(P)	.031	—	Proof	1.00
	1972FM	1.037	.10	.15	.50
	1972FM(P)	.035	—	Proof	1.00
	1973RM	7.000	.10	.15	.50
	1973FM	1.040	.10	.15	.50
	1973FM(P)	.035	—	Proof	1.00

BRASS

Y#	Date	Mintage	VF	XF	Unc
33	1974RM	.011	.15	.25	.50
	1974FM	.071	.10	.15	.50
	1974FM(P)	.094	—	Proof	1.00
	1975FM(M)	.060	—	.10	.20
	1975FM(U)	3,845	—	.20	.30
	1975FM(P)	.029	—	Proof	1.00
	1976FM(M)	.060	—	.10	.20
	1976FM(U)	1,453	—	.10	.20
	1976FM(P)	.023	—	Proof	1.00
	1977FM(M)	.060	—	.10	.20
	1977FM(U)	713 pcs.	—	.35	.75
	1977FM(P)	.011	—	Proof	1.00
	1978FM(M)	.060	—	—	.20
	1978FM(U)	767 pcs.	—	—	—
	1978FM(P)	6,931	—	Proof	1.00

5 CENTS

COPPER-NICKEL

Y#	Date	Mintage	VF	XF	Unc
2	1966	2.571	.20	.30	.50
	1968	.600	1.00	1.25	15.00
	1969	2.026	.20	.30	.50
	1969	.075	—	Proof	1.25
	1970	.026	.20	.30	.50
	1970	.023	—	Proof	1.25

Y#	Date	Mintage	VF	XF	Unc
15	1971FM	.013	.15	.40	1.00
	1971FM(P)	.031	—	Proof	1.25
	1972FM	.011	.15	.40	1.00
	1972FM(P)	.035	—	Proof	1.25
	1973FM	.021	.15	.40	1.00
	1973FM(P)	.035	—	Proof	1.25

Y#	Date	Mintage	VF	XF	Unc
15a	1973RM	1.000	.15	.35	2.00

Y#	Date	Mintage	VF	XF	Unc
34	1974FM	.023	.15	.40	1.00
	1974FM(P)	.094	—	Proof	1.25
	1975FM(M)	.012	.15	.40	1.00
	1975FM(U)	3,845	—	.20	.35
	1975FM(P)	.029	—	Proof	1.25
	1976FM(M)	.012	.10	.20	.35
	1976FM(U)	1,453	—	.20	.35
	1976FM(P)	.023	—	Proof	1.25
	1977FM(M)	.012	.10	.20	.35
	1977FM(U)	713 pcs.	—	.50	1.00
	1977FM(P)	.011	—	Proof	1.25
	1978FM(M)	.012	—	—	.35
	1978FM(U)	767 pcs.	—	—	—
	1978FM(P)	6,931	—	Proof	1.25

10 CENTS

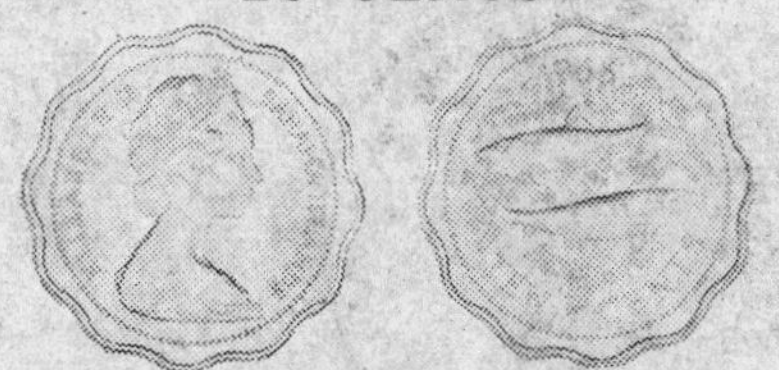

COPPER-NICKEL

Y#	Date	Mintage	VF	XF	Unc
3	1966	2.198	.25	.40	.60
	1968	.550	1.50	2.25	10.00
	1969	2.026	.25	.40	.85
	1969	.010	—	Proof	1.50
	1970	.027	.25	.40	.65
	1970	.023	—	Proof	1.50

Y#	Date	Mintage	VF	XF	Unc
16	1971FM	.013	.35	.75	1.50
	1971FM	.031	—	Proof	1.50
	1972FM	.011	.35	.75	1.50
	1972FM	.035	—	Proof	1.50
	1973FM	.015	.35	.75	1.50
	1973FM	.035	—	Proof	1.50

Obv: THE COMMONWEALTH OF THE BAHAMAS

Y#	Date	Mintage	VF	XF	Unc
16a	1973RM	—	.50	2.00	3.00

Y#	Date	Mintage	VF	XF	Unc
35	1974FM	.017	.25	.50	1.00
35	1974FM(P)	.094	—	Proof	1.50
	1975	3.000	.20	.40	.75
	1975FM(M)	6,000	.20	.35	.75
	1975FM(U)	3,845	—	.45	.90
	1975FM(P)	.029	—	Proof	1.50
	1976FM(M)	6,000	.20	.35	.75
	1976FM(U)	1,453	—	.50	1.00
	1976FM(P)	.023	—	Proof	1.50
	1977FM(M)	6,000	.20	.35	.75
	1977FM(U)	713 pcs.	—	.75	1.50
	1977FM(P)	.011	—	Proof	1.50
	1978FM(M)	6,000	—	—	.75
	1978FM(U)	.767	—	—	—
	1978FM(P)	6,931	—	Proof	2.00

15 CENTS

COPPER-NICKEL

Y#	Date	Mintage	VF	XF	Unc
4	1966	.930	.50	.60	.80
	1969	1.026	.30	.50	1.00
	1969	.010	—	Proof	2.00
	1970	.028	.30	.50	.75
	1970	.023	—	Proof	2.00

Y#	Date	Mintage	VF	XF	Unc
17	1971FM	.013	—	—	2.00
	1971FM(P)	.031	—	Proof	2.00
	1972FM	.011	—	—	2.00
	1972FM(P)	.035	—	Proof	2.00
	1973FM	.014	—	—	2.00
	1973FM(P)	.035	—	Proof	2.00

Y#	Date	Mintage	VF	XF	Unc
36	1974FM	.015	—	—	1.00
	1974FM(P)	.094	—	Proof	2.00
	1975FM(M)	3,500	.85	1.75	3.50
	1975FM(U)	3,845	—	1.75	3.25
	1975FM(P)	.029	—	Proof	2.00
	1976FM(M)	3,500	.85	1.75	3.50
	1976FM(U)	1,453	—	1.75	3.25
	1976FM(P)	.023	—	Proof	2.00
	1977FM(M)	3,500	.85	1.75	3.50
	1977FM(U)	713 pcs.	—	2.25	4.50
	1977FM(P)	.011	—	Proof	2.00
	1978FM(M)	3,500	—	—	3.50
	1978FM(U)	767 pcs.	—	—	—
	1978FM(P)	6,931	—	Proof	2.50

25 CENTS

NICKEL

Y#	Date	Mintage	VF	XF	Unc
5	1966	3.685	.50	.65	1.00
	1969	1.026	.50	.75	2.00
	1969	.010	—	Proof	2.50
	1970	.026	.40	.65	1.00
	1970	.023	—	Proof	2.50

Y#	Date	Mintage	VF	XF	Unc
18	1971FM	.013	.65	1.25	2.50
	1971FM(P)	.031	—	Proof	2.50
	1972FM	.011	.65	1.25	2.50
	1972FM(P)	.035	—	Proof	2.50
	1973FM	.012	.65	1.25	2.50
	1973FM(P)	.035	—	Proof	2.50

Y#	Date	Mintage	VF	XF	Unc
37	1974FM	.013	.35	.75	1.50
	1974FM(P)	.094	—	Proof	2.50
	1975FM(M)	2,400	1.25	2.25	4.50
	1975FM(U)	3,845	—	1.35	2.75
	1975FM(P)	.029	—	Proof	2.50
	1976FM(M)	2,400	1.00	2.00	4.00
	1976FM(U)	1,453	—	1.75	3.25
	1976FM(P)	.023	—	Proof	2.50
	1977FM(M)	2,400	1.00	2.00	4.00
	1977FM(U)	713 pcs.	—	2.75	5.50
	1977FM(P)	.011	—	Proof	2.50
	1978FM(M)	2,400	—	—	4.00
	1978FM(U)	767 pcs.	—	—	—
	1978FM(P)	6,931	—	Proof	3:25

50 CENTS

10.3700 gm., .800 SILVER, .2667 oz ASW

Y#	Date	Mintage	VF	XF	Unc
6	1966	.701	BV	8.00	10.00
	1969	.026	BV	8.00	10.00
	1969	.010	—	Proof	12.00
	1970	.025	BV	8.00	10.00
	1970	.023	—	Proof	12.00

COPPER-NICKEL

Y#	Date	Mintage	VF	XF	Unc
19	1971FM	.014	1.00	2.00	3.00
	1972FM	.012	1.00	2.00	3.00
	1973FM	.011	1.00	2.00	3.00

10.3700 gm., .800 SILVER, .2667 oz ASW

Y#	Date	Mintage	VF	XF	Unc
19a	1971FM(P)	.031	—	Proof	12.00
	1972FM(P)	.035	—	Proof	12.00
	1973FM(P)	.035	—	Proof	12.00

COPPER-NICKEL

Y#	Date	Mintage	VF	XF	Unc
38	1974FM	.012	.50	1.00	2.00
	1975FM(M)	1,200	1.75	3.25	6.50
	1975FM(U)	3,828	—	1.75	3.50
	1976FM(M)	1,200	1.75	3.25	6.50
	1976FM(U)	1,453	—	3.00	6.00
	1977FM(M)	1,200	1.75	3.25	6.50
	1977FM(U)	713 pcs.	—	3.75	7.50
	1978FM(M)	1,200	—	—	6.50
	1978FM(U)	767 pcs.	—	—	—

10.3700 gm., .800 SILVER, .2667 oz ASW

Y#	Date	Mintage	VF	XF	Unc
38a	1974FM(P)	.094	—	Proof	12.00
	1975FM(P)	.029	—	Proof	12.00
	1976FM(P)	.023	—	Proof	12.00
	1977FM(P)	.011	—	Proof	12.00
	1978FM(P)	6,931	—	Proof	15.00

DOLLAR

18.1400 gm., .800 SILVER, .4666 oz ASW

Y#	Date	Mintage	VF	XF	Unc
7	1966	.406	BV	15.00	17.50
	1969	.026	BV	15.00	17.50
	1969	.010	—	Proof	20.00
	1970	.027	BV	15.00	17.50
	1970	.023	—	Proof	20.00

Y#	Date	Mintage	VF	XF	Unc
20	1971FM	.015	BV	15.00	17.50
	1972FM	.018	BV	15.00	17.50
	1973FM	.010	BV	15.00	17.50
20a	1971FM(P)	.031	—	Proof	20.00
	1972FM(P)	.035	—	Proof	20.00
	1973FM(P)	.035	—	Proof	20.00

COPPER-NICKEL

Y#	Date	Mintage	VF	XF	Unc
39	1974FM	.012	1.50	2.50	4.00
	1975FM(M)	600 pcs.	15.00	25.00	40.00
	1975FM(U)	3,845	—	5.50	9.00
	1976FM(M)	600 pcs.	15.00	25.00	40.00
	1976FM(U)	1,453	—	6.50	11.00
	1977FM(M)	600 pcs.	15.00	25.00	40.00
	1977FM(U)	713 pcs.	—	9.00	15.00
	1978FM(U)	1,367	—	—	12.50

18.1400 gm., .800 SILVER, .4666 oz ASW

Y#	Date	Mintage	VF	XF	Unc
39a	1974FM(P)	.094	—	Proof	20.00
	1975FM(P)	.029	—	Proof	20.00
	1976FM(P)	.023	—	Proof	20.00
	1977FM(P)	.011	—	Proof	20.00
	1978FM(P)	6,931	—	Proof	22.00

2 DOLLARS

29.8000 gm., .925 SILVER, .8863 oz ASW

Y#	Date	Mintage	VF	XF	Unc
8	1966	.104	BV	27.00	32.50
	1969	.026	BV	27.00	32.50
	1969	.010	—	Proof	35.00
	1970	.032	BV	27.00	32.50
	1970	.023	—	Proof	32.50

Rev: Similar to Y#8.

Y#	Date	Mintage	VF	XF	Unc
21	1971FM	.088	BV	27.00	32.50
	1971FM(P)	.060	—	Proof	32.50
	1972FM	.065	BV	27.00	32.50
	1972FM(P)	.059	—	Proof	32.50
	1973FM	.043	BV	27.00	32.50
	1973FM(P)	.050	—	Proof	32.50

COPPER-NICKEL
Rev: Similar to Y#8.

Y#	Date	Mintage	VF	XF	Unc
40	1974FM	.037	2.50	4.00	6.50
	1975FM(M)	300 pcs.	40.00	65.00	110.00
	1975FM(U)	8,810	—	4.50	7.50
	1976FM(M)	300 pcs.	40.00	65.00	110.00
	1976FM(U)	4,381	—	6.00	10.00
	1977FM(M)	300 pcs.	40.00	65.00	110.00
	1977FM(U)	946 pcs.	—	15.00	25.00
	1978FM	1,067	—	—	22.50

29.8000 gm., .925 SILVER, .8863 oz ASW

Y#	Date	Mintage	VF	XF	Unc
40a	1974FM(P)	.129	—	Proof	32.50
	1975FM(P)	.045	—	Proof	32.50
	1976FM(P)	.035	—	Proof	32.50
	1977FM(P)	.015	—	Proof	32.50
	1978FM(P)	.011	—	Proof	35.00

5 DOLLARS

42.1200 gm., .925 SILVER, 1.2527 oz ASW

Y#	Date	Mintage	VF	XF	Unc
9	1966	.100	BV	37.50	40.00
	1969	.036	BV	37.50	40.00
	1969	.010	—	Proof	42.50
	1970	.043	BV	37.50	40.00
	1970	.023	—	Proof	40.00

Rev: Similar to Y#9.

Y#	Date	Mintage	VF	XF	Unc
22	1971FM	.029	BV	37.50	40.00
22	1971FM(P)	.031	—	Proof	40.00

Obv: Similar to Y#22

Y#	Date	Mintage	VF	XF	Unc
22a	1972FM	.032	BV	37.50	40.00
	1972FM(P)	.035	—	Proof	40.00
	1973FM	.032	BV	37.50	40.00
	1973FM(P)	.035	—	Proof	40.00

COPPER-NICKEL

Y#	Date	Mintage	VF	XF	Unc
41	1974FM	.032	6.00	7.50	10.00
	1975FM(M)	200 pcs.	60.00	100.00	160.00
	1975FM(U)	7,058	—	6.00	10.00
	1976FM(M)	200 pcs.	60.00	100.00	155.00
	1976FM(U)	2,591	—	11.00	18.00
	1977FM(M)	200 pcs.	55.00	90.00	150.00
	1977FM(U)	801 pcs.	—	—	—
	1978FM(M)	1,244	—	—	30.00

42.1200 gm., .925 SILVER, 1.2527 oz ASW

Y#	Date	Mintage	VF	XF	Unc
41a	1974FM(P)	.094	—	Proof	40.00
	1975FM(P)	.029	—	Proof	40.00
	1976FM(P)	.023	—	Proof	45.00
	1977FM(P)	.011	—	Proof	40.00
	1978FM(P)	6,931	—	Proof	45.00

10 DOLLARS

3.9943 gm., .917 GOLD, .1177 oz AGW

Y#	Date	Mintage	VF	XF	Unc
10	1967	6,200	BV	80.00	100.00
	1967	850 pcs.	—	Proof	150.00
23.1	1971	9,835	BV	80.00	100.00
	1971(t)	1,250	—	Proof	125.00

Rev: Hallmark and fineness stamped near bottom.

Y#	Date	Mintage	VF	XF	Unc
23.2	1971	—	BV	80.00	100.00

NOTE: The above coins were struck by the Gari & Zucchi Mint, Italy.

Y#	Date	Mintage	VF	XF	Unc
23	1972	9,906	BV	80.00	100.00
	1972	1,250	—	Proof	125.00

1.4500 gm., .750 GOLD, .0349 oz AGW
No fineness on reverse.

Y#	Date	Mintage	VF	XF	Unc
29.1	1973	—	25.00	30.00	40.00

1.4500 gm., Gold fineness, .585, stamped on rev., .0272 oz AGW

Y#	Date	Mintage	VF	XF	Unc
29.2	1973	—	20.00	22.50	35.00
	1973	—	—	Proof	40.00

48.6000 gm., .925 SILVER, 1.4454 oz ASW
Independence Commemorative

Y#	Date	Mintage	VF	XF	Unc
27	1973FM	.028	BV	45.00	55.00
	1973FM(P)	.029	—	Proof	60.00

COPPER-NICKEL
First Anniversary of Independence
Obv: Similar to 5 Dollars, Y#41.

Y#	Date	Mintage	VF	XF	Unc
42	1974FM	4,825	12.50	16.50	22.50

48.6000 gm., .925 SILVER, 1.4454 oz ASW

Y#	Date	Mintage	VF	XF	Unc
42a	1974FM(P)	.043	—	Proof	60.00

COPPER-NICKEL
Second Anniversary of Independence
Obv: Similar to 5 Dollars, Y#41.

Y#	Date	Mintage	VF	XF	Unc
48	1975FM(M)	100 pcs.	75.00	125.00	200.00
	1975FM(U)	5,325	—	20.00	30.00
	1976FM(M)	100 pcs.	75.00	325.00	450.00
	1976FM(U)	100 pcs.	—	200.00	300.00
	1977FM(M)	100 pcs.	125.00	175.00	250.00
	1977FM(U)	250 pcs.	—	85.00	125.00

48.6000 gm., .925 SILVER, 1.4454 oz ASW

48a	1975FM(P)	.063	—	Proof	60.00
	1976FM(P)	.010	—	Proof	60.00
	1977FM(P)	4,424	—	Proof	60.00

45.3500 gm., .500 SILVER, .729 oz ASW
Fifth Anniversary of Independence
Obv: Arms.

50	1978	.050	Proof only	40.00

Fifth Anniversary of Independence
Obv: Arms.

52	1978	.050	Proof only	40.00

20 DOLLARS

7.9880 gm., .917 GOLD, .2355 oz AGW

11	1967	6,200	BV	155.00	175.00
	1967	850 pcs.	—	Proof	225.00
24.1	1971	8,786	BV	155.00	175.00
	1971(t)	1,250	—	Proof	200.00

Rev: Hallmark and fineness stamped at bottom

Y#	Date	Mintage	VF	XF	Unc
24.2	1971	—	BV	155.00	175.00

NOTE: The above coins were struck by the Gari & Zucchi Mint, Italy.

24	1972	9,259	BV	155.00	175.00
	1972	1,250	—	Proof	200.00

2.9000 gm., .750 GOLD, .0699 oz AGW
No fineness on reverse

30.1	1973	—	BV	50.00	65.00

Gold, fineness, .585, stamped on rev., .0545 oz AGW.

30.2	1973	—	BV	40.00	45.00
	1973	—	—	Proof	70.00

25 DOLLARS

37.38 gm., .925 SILVER, 1.1117 oz ASW
250th Anniversary of Parliament

54	1979FM	—	—	—	55.00

50 DOLLARS

19.9710 gm., .917 GOLD, .5888 oz AGW

12	1967	1,200	BV	400.00	500.00
	1967	850 pcs.	—	Proof	800.00

25.1	1971	3,754	BV	400.00	450.00
	1971(t)	1,250	—	Proof	600.00

Rev: Hallmark and fineness stamped at bottom

25.2	1971	—	BV	400.00	450.00

NOTE: The above coins were struck by the Gari & Zucchi Mint, Italy.

25	1972	3,180	BV	400.00	450.00
	1972	1,250	—	Proof	500.00

7.2700 gm., .750 GOLD, .1753 oz AGW
Rev: No fineness, date below lobster.

31.1	1973	—	BV	115.00	135.00

7.2700 gm., .585 GOLD, .1367 oz AGW

Fineness to left, date to right.

Y#	Date	Mintage	VF	XF	Unc
31.2	1973	—	BV	90.00	115.00
	1973	—	—	Proof	135.00

Rev: No date or fineness

31.3	1973	—	—	—	—

15.6448 gm., .500 GOLD, .2515 oz AGW
Independence Commemorative

28	1973JP	.023	BV	BV	165.00
	1973JP	.018	—	Proof	175.00

2.7300 gm., .917 GOLD, .0804 oz AGW
Rev: No fineness

44.1	1974	—	BV	55.00	60.00
	1974	—	—	Proof	75.00
	1975	.026	BV	55.00	60.00
	1975	.015	—	Proof	65.00
	1976	—	BV	55.00	60.00
	1976	—	—	Proof	65.00
	1977	—	BV	55.00	60.00

GOLD, fineness, .917, stamped on reverse.

44.2	1974	—	—	60.00	65.00

100 DOLLARS

39.9400 gm., .917 GOLD, 1.1776 oz AGW

13	1967	1,200	BV	775.00	800.00
	1967	850 pcs.	—	Proof	1100.

26.1	1971	4,760	BV	775.00	800.00
	1971(t)	1,250	—	Proof	850.00

Rev: Hallmark and fineness at bottom right.

Y#	Date	Mintage	VF	XF	Unc
26.2	1971	—	BV	775.00	800.00

NOTE: The above coins were struck by the Gari & Zucchi Mint, Italy.

Y#	Date	Mintage	VF	XF	Unc
26	1972	3,180	BV	775.00	800.00
	1972	1,250	—	Proof	850.00

The 1972 proof $100 is serially numbered on the edge.

14.5400 gm., .750 GOLD, .3506 oz AGW
Rev: No fineness, date at bottom.

Y#	Date	Mintage	VF	XF	Unc
32.1	1973	—	BV	230.00	250.00

14.5400 gm., .585 GOLD, .2735 oz AGW
Rev: Fineness to left, date to right.

Y#	Date	Mintage	VF	XF	Unc
32.2	1973	—	BV	200.00	250.00
	1973 Serial no. on edge		—	Proof	375.00

18.0145 gm., .500 GOLD, .2896 oz AGW
Independence Commemorative

Y#	Date	Mintage	VF	XF	Unc
43	1974	4,486	BV	200.00	225.00
	1974	4,153	—	Proof	250.00

5.4600 gm., .917 GOLD, .1609 oz AGW
Broken waves behind flamingos legs

Y#	Date	Mintage	VF	XF	Unc
45.1	1974	—	BV	110.00	130.00
	1975	—	BV	110.00	130.00

Unbroken waves behind flamingos legs

Y#	Date	Mintage	VF	XF	Unc
45.2	1974	—	—	Proof	225.00
	1975	—	—	Proof	250.00
	1976	—	BV	110.00	130.00
	1976	—	—	Proof	400.00
	1977	—	BV	110.00	130.00
	1977	—	—	Proof	150.00

Fineness, .917, stamped on rev.

Y#	Date	Mintage	VF	XF	Unc
45.3	1974	—	BV	135.00	150.00

18.0145 gm., .500 GOLD, .2896 oz AGW
Second Anniversary Of Independence

Y#	Date	Mintage	VF	XF	Unc
49	1975	3,694	BV	200.00	250.00
	1975	3,145	—	Proof	275.00
	1976	761 pcs.	—	Proof	350.00

13.6000 gm., .963 GOLD, .4211 oz AGW
Fifth Anniversary of Independence
Obv: Arms. Rev: Portrait of H.R.H. Prince Charles.

Y#	Date	Mintage	VF	XF	Unc
51	1978	.025		Proof only	275.00

Fifth Anniversary of Independence
Obv: Arms. Rev: Portrait of Sir Milo B. Butler.

Y#	Date	Mintage	VF	XF	Unc
53	1978	.025		Proof only	275.00

150 DOLLARS

8.1900 gm., .917 GOLD, .2414 oz AGW

Y#	Date	Mintage	VF	XF	Unc
46.1	1974	—	BV	160.00	175.00
	1974	—	—	Proof	250.00
	1975	3,141	—	—	—
	1975	2,770	—	—	—
	1977	—	—	—	—

Waves under crawfish extend to its two front legs

Y#	Date	Mintage	VF	XF	Unc
46.2	1974	—	—	Proof	250.00

Fineness, .917, stamped on rev.

Y#	Date	Mintage	VF	XF	Unc
46.3	1974	—	—	175.00	200.00

200 DOLLARS

10.9200 gm., .917 GOLD, .3219 oz AGW

Y#	Date	Mintage	VF	XF	Unc
47.1	1974	—	—	225.00	275.00
	1974	—	—	Proof	450.00
	1975	1,545	—	—	250.00
	1975	1,570	—	—	—
	1977	—	—	—	—

Y#	Date	Mintage	VF	XF	Unc
47.2	1974	—	—	Proof	450.00

Fineness, .916, stamped on reverse.

Y#	Date	Mintage	VF	XF	Unc
47.3	1974	—	—	225.00	250.00

Fineness, .916, stamped to left, serial number stamped below arms.

Y#	Date	Mintage	VF	XF	Unc
47.4	1974	—	—	—	400.00

Rev: No fineness, serial number to left.

Y#	Date	Mintage	VF	XF	Unc
47.5	1974	—	—	—	400.00

250 DOLLARS

10.5800 gm., .900 GOLD, .3061 oz AGW
250th Anniversary of Parliament

Y#	Date	Mintage	VF	XF	Unc
55	1979	—	—	—	400.00

2500 DOLLARS

407.2600 gm., .917 GOLD, 12.0082 oz AGW
Obv: Similar to 5 Dollars, Y#41.
Illustration is reduced, actual size: 72mm

Y#	Date	Mintage	VF	XF	Unc
—	1974	250 pcs.	—	Proof	8000.
	1977	250 pcs.	—	Proof	8000.

NCLT ISSUES

MINT SETS

KM#	Date	Mintage	Identification	Issue Price	Mkt. Val.
S1	1966(9)	75,050	Y1-9	16.00	100.00
S2	1966(7)	500,000	Y1-7	5.25	30.00
S3	1967(4)	1,200	Y10-13	180.00	1100.
S4	1969(9)	26,221	Y1-9	20.25	100.00
S5	1970(9)	25,135	Y1-9	20.25	100.00
S6	1971(9)	12,895	Y14-22	20.25	100.00

KM#	Date	Mintage	Identification	Issue Price	Mkt. Val.
S7	1971(4)	1,250	Y23-26	185.00	800.00
S8	1972(9)	10,128	Y14-21,22A	22.75	100.00
S9	1972(4)	—	Y23-26	185.00	800.00
S10	1973(9)	9,853	Y14-21,22a	23.75	100.00
S11	1973(4)	—	Y29.1-32.1	—	350.00
S12	1973(2)	—	Y29.1,30.1	—	50.00
S13	1974(9)	11,004	Y33-41	22.50	35.00
S14	1974(4)	—	Y43,44.1-46.1	—	450.00
S15	1974(2)	—	Y43,44.1	—	200.00
S16	1975(9)	3,845	Y33-41	27.00	35.00
S17	1975(4)	1,545	Y43,44.1-46.1	—	450.00
S18	1976(9)	1,453	Y33-41	27.00	35.00
S19	1977(9)	731	Y33-41	27.00	75.00
S20	1978(9)	767	Y33-41	27.00	75.00

PROOF SETS

STANDARD METALS

KM#	Date	Mintage	Identification	Issue Price	Mkt. Val.
101	1967(4)	850	Y10-13	252.00	1300.
102	1969(9)	10,381	Y1-9	35.00	100.00
103	1970(9)	22,827	Y1a,2-9	35.00	100.00
104	1971(9)	30,507	Y14-18,19a,20a,21,22	35.00	100.00
105	1971(4)	1,250	Y23.1-26.1	298.00	1500.
106	1972(9)	34,789	Y14-18,19a,20a,21,22a	35.00	100.00
107	1972(4)	2,820	Y23-26	565.00	1000.
108	1973(9)	34,815	Y14-18,19a,20a,21,22a	35.00	100.00
109	1973(4)	—	Y29.1-32.1	Reported, Not Confirmed	
110	1973(4)	1,260	Y29.2-32.2	402.00	575.00
111	1974(9)	93,776	Y33-37,38a-41a	45.00	100.00
112	1974(4)	—	Y44.1-47.1	500.00	1000.
113	1975(9)	29,095	Y33-37,38a-41a	59.00	100.00
114	1975(4)	1,570	Y44.1-47.1	400.00	—
115	1976(9)	22,570	Y33-37,38a-41a	59.00	100.00
116	1976	—	Y44.1-47.1	500.00	—
117	1977(9)	10,812	Y33-37,38a-41a	59.00	110.00
118	1978(9)	6,931	Y33-37,38a-41a	59.00	125.00
119	1979(9)	—	Y33-37,38a-41a	115.00	—
120	1979(2)	—	Y54,55	445.00	—

BAHRAIN

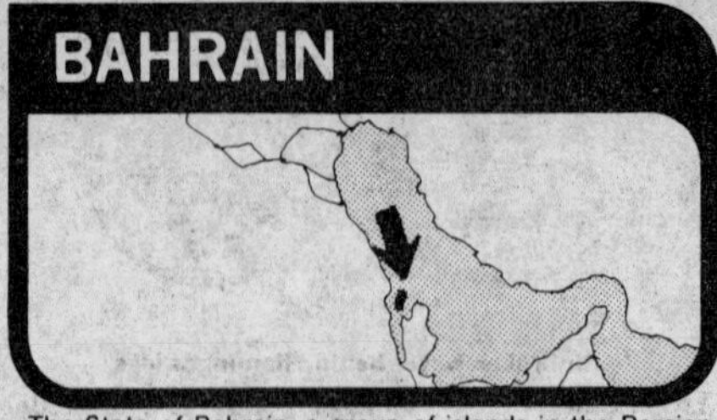

The State of Bahrain, a group of islands in the Persian Gulf off Saudi Arabia, has an area of 260 sq. mi. (673 sq. km.) and a population of 305,000. Capital: Manama. Prior to the depression of the 1930s, the economy was based on pearl fishing. Petroleum and aluminum industries and transit trade are the vital factors in the economy today.

The Portuguese occupied the islands in 1507 but were driven out in 1602 by Arab subjects of Persia. They in turn were ejected by Arabs of the Ataiba tribe from the Arabian mainland who have maintained possession up to the present time. The ruling sheikh of Bahrain entered into relations with Great Britain in 1805 and concluded a binding treaty of protection in 1861. In 1968 Great Britain decided to terminate treaty relations with the Persian Gulf sheikhdoms. Unable to agree on terms of union with the other skeikhdoms, Bahrain decided to seek independence as a separate entity and became fully independent on August 14, 1971.

The coinage of the State of Bahrain was struck at the Royal Mint, London, England.

RULERS

Isa Bin Sulman, 1961-

MONETARY SYSTEM

1000 Fils = 1 Dinar

FIL

BRONZE

Y#	Date	Year	Mintage	VF	XF	Unc
1	AH1385	1965	1.500	—	.10	.25
	1385	1965	—	—	Proof	1.00
	1386	1966	1.500	—	.10	.25

5 FILS

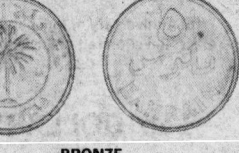

BRONZE

Y#	Date	Year	Mintage	VF	XF	Unc
2	AH1385	1965	7.000	—	.15	.35
	1385	1965	—	—	Proof	1.25

10 FILS

BRONZE

Y#	Date	Year	Mintage	VF	XF	Unc
3	AH1385	1965	7.500	.10	.20	.50
	1385	1965	—	—	Proof	1.50

25 FILS

COPPER NICKEL

Y#	Date	Year	Mintage	VF	XF	Unc
4	AH1385	1965	7.500	.15	.30	.75
	1385	1965	—	—	Proof	1.75

50 FILS

COPPER-NICKEL

Y#	Date	Year	Mintage	VF	XF	Unc
5	AH1385	1965	3.709	.20	.40	1.00
	1385	1965	—	—	Proof	2.00

100 FILS

COPPER-NICKEL

Y#	Date	Year	Mintage	VF	XF	Unc
6	AH1385	1965	3.300	.30	.60	1.50
	1385	1965	—	—	Proof	3.00

250 FILS

COPPER-NICKEL
F.A.O. Issue

Y#	Date	Year	Mintage	VF	XF	Unc
9	AH1389	1969	.050	.60	1.25	3.00
	1389	1969	—	—	Proof	6.00

500 FILS

18.3000 gm., .800 SILVER, .4707 oz ASW
Opening of Isatown Commemorative

Y#	Date	Year	Mintage	VF	XF	Unc
7	AH1388	1968	.050	BV	BV	15.00
	1388	1968	—	—	Proof	20.00

10 DINARS

16.0000 gm., .917 GOLD, .4717 oz AGW
Opening of Isatown Commemorative

Y#	Date	Year	Mintage	XF	Unc	Proof
8	AH1388	1968	3,000	325.00	400.00	550.00

100 DINARS

6.2100 gm., .917 GOLD, .1831 oz AGW
Independence Commemorative

Y#	Date	Year	Mintage	XF	Unc	Proof
—	AH1385	1971	3,000	—	—	550.00

NCLT ISSUES

PROOF SETS
STANDARD METALS

KM#	Date	Mintage	Identification	Issue Price	Mkt. Val.
101	Mixed (8)	20,000	Y1-6,1965;Y9,1969;Y7,1968	32.00	42.00

BANGLADESH

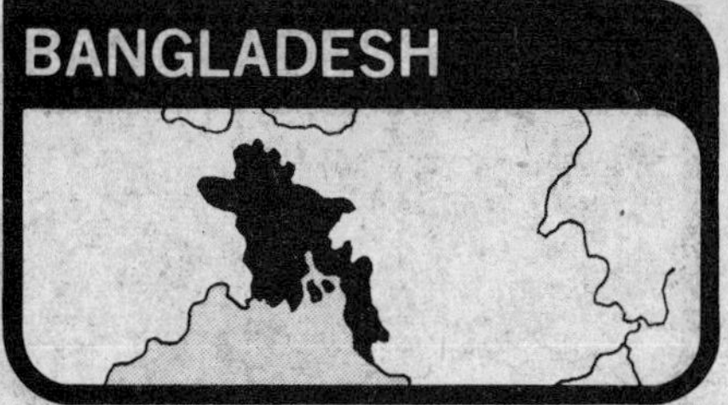

The People's Republic of Bangladesh (formerly East Pakistan), a parliamentary democracy located on the Bay of Bengal bordered by India and Burma, has an area of 55,548 sq. mi. (142,775 sq. km.) and a population of 85 million. Capital: Dacca. The economy is predominantly agricultural. Jute products, jute and tea are exported.

British rule over the vast Indian sub-continent ended in 1947 when British India attained independence and was partitioned into the two successor states of India and Pakistan. Pakistan consisted of East and West Pakistan, two areas united by the Moslem religion but separated by culture and 1,000 miles of Indian territory. Restive under the de facto rule of the militant but fewer West Pakistanis, the East Pakistanis unsuccessfully demanded greater economic benefits and political reforms. The inability of the leaders of East and West Pakistan to resolve a political breakdown occasioned by the East Pakistan success in the general elections of 1970 precipitated massive civil disobedience in East Pakistan which West Pakistan sought to suppress militarily. East Pakistan seceded from Pakistan, March 26, 1971, and with the support of India declared an independent People's Republic of Bangladesh.

Bangladesh is a member of the Commonwealth of Nations. The president is the Head of State and of Government.

MONETARY SYSTEM

100 Poisha = 1 Taka

POISHA

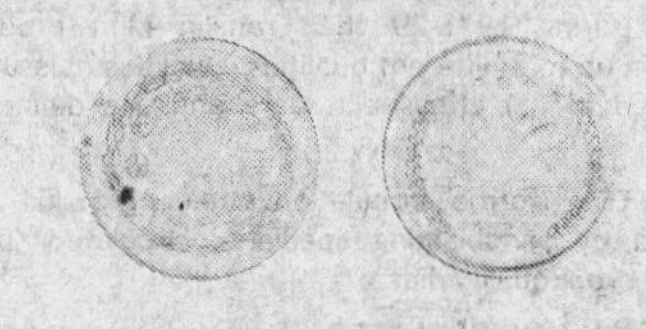

ALUMINUM

Y#	Date	Mintage	VF	XF	Unc
A1	1974	300.000	—	—	.20

5 POISHA

ALUMINUM

Y#	Date	Mintage	VF	XF	Unc
1	1973	*47.088	—	.10	.25

F.A.O. Issue

Y#	Date	Mintage	VF	XF	Unc
5	1974	5.000	—	.10	.25
	1975	3.000	—	.10	.25
	1976	3.000	—	—	—

F.A.O. Issue

Y#	Date	Mintage	VF	XF	Unc
9	1977	3.000	—	.10	.20
	1978	—	—	.10	.25

10 POISHA

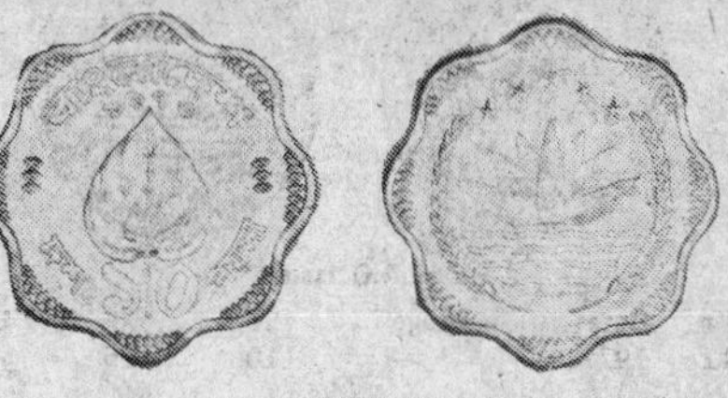

ALUMINUM

Y#	Date	Mintage	VF	XF	Unc
2	1973	*21.500	—	.10	.35

F.A.O. Issue

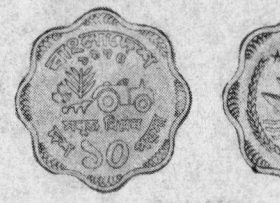

Y#	Date	Mintage	VF	XF	Unc
6	1974	5.000	—	.20	.35
	1975	4.000	—	.20	.40
	1976	4.000	—	.20	.40
	1977	4.000	—	.20	.40
	1979	—	—	.20	.40

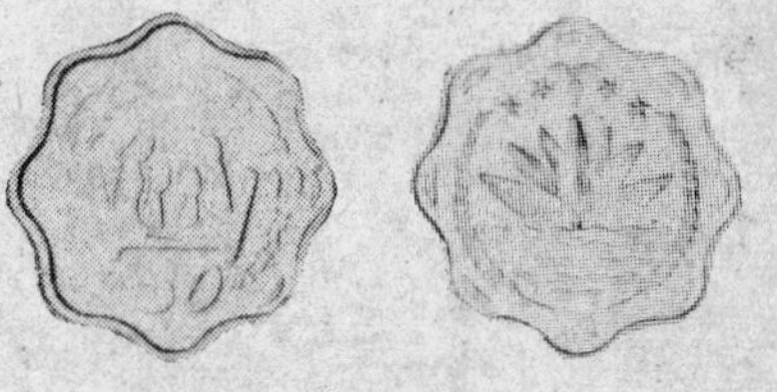

F.A.O. Issue

Y#	Date	Mintage	VF	XF	Unc
10	1977	—	—	.20	.40

25 POISHA

STEEL

Y#	Date	Mintage	VF	XF	Unc
3	1973	*25.072	.10	.15	.50

F.A.O. Issue

Y#	Date	Mintage	VF	XF	Unc
7	1974	5.000	.10	.20	.50
	1975	6.000	.10	.20	.50
	1976	6.000	.10	.20	.50
	1977	6.000	.10	.20	.50

COPPER-NICKEL

Y#	Date	Mintage	VF	XF	Unc
11	1977	—	.10	.20	.60

50 POISHA

COPPER-NICKEL

Y#	Date	Mintage	VF	XF	Unc
4	1973	18.000	.10	.25	.65

F.A.O. Issue

Y#	Date	Mintage	VF	XF	Unc
12	1977	—	.10	.25	.75

TAKA

COPPER-NICKEL
F.A.O. Issue

Y#	Date	Mintage	VF	XF	Unc
8	1975	4.000	.20	.35	1.00
	1976	—	.20	.35	1.00

BARBADOS

Barbados, an independent state within the British Commonwealth, is located in the Windward Islands of the West Indies east of St. Vincent. The coral island has an area of 166 sq. mi. (430 sq. km.) and a population of 244,000. Capital: Bridgetown. The economy is based on sugar and tourism. Sugar, petroleum products, molasses, and rum are exported.

Barbados was named by the Portuguese who achieved the first landing on the island in 1563. British sailors landed at the site of present-day Holetown in 1624. Barbados was under uninterrupted British control from the time of the first British settlement in 1627 until it obtained independence on Nov. 30, 1966. It is a member of the Commonwealth of Nations. The Queen of England is Chief of State.

Unmarked 'side cut' pieces of Spanish and Spanish Colonial 1, 2 and 8 reales were the principal coinage medium of 18th-century Barbados. The "Neptune" tokens issued by Sir Phillip Gibbs, a local plantation owner, circulated freely but were never established as legal coinage. The coinage and banknotes of the British Caribbean Territories (Eastern Group) were employed prior to 1973 when Barbados issued a decimal coinage.

RULERS

British, until 1966

MINTMARKS

FM - Franklin Mint, U.S.A.*

***NOTE:** During 1975-79 the Franklin Mint produced coinage in up to 3 different qualities. Qualities of issue are designated in ( ) after each date and are defined as follows:

(M) MATTE - Normal circulation strike or a dull finish produced by sandblasting special uncirculated (polish finish) or proof quality dies.

(U) SPECIAL UNCIRCULATED - Polished or proof-like in appearance without any frosted features.

(P) PROOF - The highest quality obtainable having mirror-like fields and frosted features.

MONETARY SYSTEM

12 Pence = 1 Shilling

COUNTERSTAMP ISSUES

2 REALES

SILVER
c/s: Pineapple in relief on plugged Spanish or Spanish Colonial 2 Reales.

P#	Date	Year	Mintage	VG	Fine	VF
9	ND	(1791-99)	—	600.00	800.00	1000.

8 REALES

SILVER
c/s: Pineapple in relief on plugged Spanish or Spanish Colonial 8 Reales.

P#	Date	Year	Mintage	VG	Fine	VF
8	ND	(1791-99)	—	600.00	800.00	1000.

TOKEN ISSUES

1/2 PENNY

COPPER

C#	Date	Mintage	VG	Fine	VF	XF
2	1792	.047	10.00	20.00	30.00	45.00
2a	1792	—		Restrike	Proof	60.00

PENNY

COPPER

C#	Date	Mintage	VG	Fine	VF	XF
	Type I, small head, small pineapple, P#10.					
1	1788	—	—		Proof only	100.00
	Type II, small head, larger pineapple, P#11.					
1.1	1788	5,476	20.00	35.00	45.00	60.00
	Obv: With I MILTON F in relief on truncation, P#19.					
1a	1788	—		Restrike	Proof	55.00
	Obv: With M incuse on truncation, P#18.					
1a.1	1788	—		Restrike	Proof	60.00

C#	Date	Mintage	VG	Fine	VF	XF
	Type III: Large head, large pineapple, wiry hair, P#14.					
1a.2	1788	.200	5.00	9.00	15.00	25.00
	Obv: Similar to C#3. Rev: Small pineapple, P#20.					
1a.3	1788	—	—		Proof only	75.00

C#	Date	Mintage	VG	Fine	VF	XF
3	1792	.039	7.50	12.50	20.00	40.00
	1792	—		Restrike	Proof	55.00

NOTE: Restrikes of CR#1-3 were struck in collared dies while originals were not.

DECIMAL COINAGE

100 Cents = 1 Dollar

CENT

BRONZE

Y#	Date	Mintage	VF	XF	Unc
1	1973	5.000	.10	.15	.25
	1973FM(M)	7,500	.25	.50	1.00
	1973FM(P)	.097	—	Proof	1.00
	1974	7.000	.10	.15	.25
	1974FM(M)	8,708	.20	.35	.75
	1974FM(P)	.036	—	Proof	1.00
	1975	8.000	.10	.15	.25
	1975FM(M)	5,000	.20	.35	.75
	1975FM(U)	1,360	—	.50	1.00
	1975FM(P)	.020	—	Proof	1.00
	1977FM(M)	2,102	.20	.35	.75
	1977FM(U)	468 pcs.	—	—	.75
	1977FM(P)	5,014	—	Proof	1.00
	1978	—	.20	.35	.75
	1978FM(U)	2,517	—	—	.75
	1978FM(P)	4,436	—	Proof	1.00
	1979FM(M)	1,500	.10	.15	.30
	1979FM(U)	523 pcs.	—	—	—
	1979FM(P)	4,126	—	Proof	1.00
	1980FM(U)	—	—	—	.75
	1980FM(P)	—	—	Proof	1.00

10th Anniversary of Independence

Y#	Date	Mintage	VF	XF	Unc
10	1976	6.406	—	.10	.15
	1976FM(M)	5,000	.15	.25	.50
	1976FM(U)	996 pcs.	—	3.00	5.00
	1976FM(P)	.012	—	Proof	1.00

5 CENTS

BRASS

Y#	Date	Mintage	VF	XF	Unc
2	1973	3.000	.10	.20	.50
	1973FM(M)	7,500	.35	.65	1.25
	1973FM(P)	.097	—	Proof	1.25
	1974	4.600	.10	.20	.50
	1974FM(M)	8,708	.25	.50	1.00
	1974FM(P)	.036	—	Proof	1.25
	1975FM(M)	5,000	.25	.50	1.00
	1975FM(U)	1,360	—	.65	1.25
	1975FM(P)	.020	—	Proof	1.25
	1977FM(M)	2,100	.15	.30	.60
	1977FM(U)	468 pcs.	—	—	.60
	1977FM(P)	5,014	—	Proof	1.25
	1978FM(U)	2,517	—	—	.75
	1978FM(P)	4,436	—	Proof	1.25
	1979FM(M)	1,500	.20	.50	.75
	1979FM(U)	523 pcs.	—	—	—
	1979FM(P)	4,126	—	Proof	1.25
	1980FM(U)	—	.20	.50	.75
	1980FM(P)	—	—	Proof	2.00

10th Anniversary of Independence
Obv: '1966 - 1976' beside arms.

Y#	Date	Mintage	VF	XF	Unc
11	1976FM(M)	5,000	.35	.65	1.25
	1976FM(U)	996 pcs.	—	3.00	5.00
	1976FM(P)	.012	—	Proof	1.25

10 CENTS

COPPER-NICKEL

Y#	Date	Mintage	VF	XF	Unc
3	1973	4.000	.15	.25	.50
	1973FM(M)	5,000	.35	.65	1.25
	1973FM(P)	.097	—	Proof	1.50
3	1974	4.000	.15	.30	.75
	1974FM(M)	6,208	.25	.50	1.00
	1974FM(P)	.036	—	Proof	1.50
	1975FM(M)	2,500	.25	.50	1.00
	1975FM(U)	1,360	—	.75	1.50
	1975FM(P)	.020	—	Proof	1.50
	1977FM(M)	2,100	.35	.65	1.25
	1977FM(U)	468 pcs.	—	—	1.25
	1977FM(P)	5,014	—	Proof	1.50
	1978FM(U)	2,517	—	—	1.25
	1978FM(P)	4,436	—	Proof	1.50
	1979FM(M)	1,500	—	—	—
	1979FM(U)	523 pcs.	—	—	—
	1979FM(P)	4,126	—	Proof	1.50
	1980FM(U)	—	—	—	1.00
	1980FM(P)	—	—	Proof	3.00

10th Anniversary of Independence
Obv: '1966 - 1976' beside arms.

Y#	Date	Mintage	VF	XF	Unc
12	1976FM(M)	2,500	.20	.35	.75
	1976FM(U)	996 pcs.	—	3.00	5.00
	1976FM(P)	.012	—	Proof	1.50

25 CENTS

COPPER-NICKEL

Y#	Date	Mintage	VF	XF	Unc
4	1973	6.000	.20	.40	1.00
	1973FM(M)	4,300	.35	.75	1.50
	1973FM(P)	.097	—	Proof	2.50
	1974	1.000	.25	.60	1.25
	1974FM(M)	5,508	.35	.65	1.25
	1974FM(P)	.036	—	Proof	2.50
	1975FM(M)	1,800	.35	.65	1.25
	1975FM(U)	1,360	.40	.85	1.75
	1975FM(P)	.020	—	Proof	2.50
	1977FM(M)	2,100	.25	.50	1.00
	1977FM(U)	468 pcs.	—	—	1.00
	1977FM(P)	5,014	—	Proof	2.50
	1978FM(U)	2,517	—	—	1.00
	1978FM(P)	4,436	—	Proof	2.75
	1979FM(M)	1,500	—	—	—
	1979FM(U)	523 pcs.	—	—	2.75
	1979FM(P)	4,126	—	Proof	2.75
	1980FM(U)	—	—	—	3.00
	1980FM(P)	—	—	Proof	5.00

10th Anniversary of Independence
Obv: '1966-1976' beside arms.

Y#	Date	Mintage	VF	XF	Unc
13	1976FM(M)	1,800	.35	.65	1.25
	1976FM(U)	996 pcs.	—	3.00	5.00
	1976FM(P)	.012	—	Proof	2.50

DOLLAR

COPPER-NICKEL

Y#	Date	Mintage	VF	XF	Unc
5	1973	—	1.00	1.50	2.50
	1973FM(M)	3,000	1.00	1.50	2.50
	1973FM(P)	.097	—	Proof	2.50
	1974	2.000	1.00	1.50	2.00
	1974FM(M)	4,208	1.00	1.50	2.50
	1974FM(P)	.036	—	Proof	3.00
	1975FM(M)	500 pcs.	2.00	3.00	5.00
	1975FM(U)	1,360	1.25	2.00	3.50
	1975FM(P)	.020	—	Proof	3.50
	1977FM(M)	600 pcs.	—	—	4.50
	1977FM(U)	468 pcs.	—	—	4.50
	1977FM(P)	5,014	—	Proof	4.50
	1978FM(U)	1,017	—	—	4.50
	1978FM(P)	4,436	—	Proof	4.50
	1979FM(M)	600 pcs.	—	—	—
	1979FM(U)	523 pcs.	—	—	—
	1979FM(P)	4,126	—	Proof	4.50
	1980FM(U)	—	—	—	4.50
	1980FM(P)	—	—	Proof	10.00

10th Anniversary of Independence
Obv: '1966 - 1976' beside arms.

Y#	Date	Mintage	VF	XF	Unc
14	1976FM(M)	500 pcs.	—	6.00	10.00
	1976FM(U)	996 pcs.	—	5.00	7.50
	1976FM(P)	.012	—	Proof	4.50

2 DOLLARS

COPPER-NICKEL

Y#	Date	Mintage	VF	XF	Unc
6	1973FM(M)	3,000	2.00	3.00	5.00
	1973FM(P)	.097	—	Proof	3.00
	1974FM(M)	4,208	1.50	2.50	4.00
	1974FM(P)	.036	—	Proof	4.00
	1975FM(M)	500 pcs.	6.00	8.50	12.50
	1975FM(U)	1,360	—	—	7.00
	1975FM(P)	.020	—	Proof	6.50
	1977FM(M)	600 pcs.	4.50	7.50	11.50
	1977FM(U)	468 pcs.	—	—	11.00
	1977FM(P)	5,014	—	Proof	10.00
	1978FM(U)	1,017	—	—	11.00
	1978FM(P)	4,436	—	Proof	10.00
	1979FM(M)	600 pcs.	—	—	—
	1979FM(U)	523 pcs.	—	—	—
	1979FM(P)	4,126	—	Proof	10.00
	1980FM(U)	4,126	—	—	11.00
	1980FM(P)	—	—	Proof	15.00

10th Anniversary of Independence
Obv: '1966 - 1976' beside arms.

Y#	Date	Mintage	VF	XF	Unc
15	1976FM(M)	500 pcs.	6.00	10.00	15.00
	1976FM(U)	996 pcs.	—	6.00	10.00
	1976FM(P)	.012	—	Proof	7.50

4 DOLLARS

COPPER-NICKEL
F.A.O. Issue

Y#	Date	Mintage	VF	XF	Unc
2*	1970	.035	—	3.50	5.00
	1970	5,000	—	Proof	27.50

***NOTE:** This number refers to Yeoman's East Caribbean Territories listings, where seven companion 4-Dollar issues are listed.

5 DOLLARS

COPPER NICKEL
Obv: Similar to 2 Dollars, Y#6.

Y#	Date	Mintage	VF	XF	Unc
7	1973FM(M)	2,750	3.50	6.00	10.00
	1974FM(M)	3,958	3.00	5.00	8.50
	1975FM(M)	250 pcs.	25.00	40.00	60.00
	1975FM(U)	1,360	—	11.50	17.50
	1977FM(M)	600 pcs.	12.50	20.00	27.50
	1977FM(U)	468 pcs.	—	20.00	27.50
	1978FM(U)	1,017	—	—	—
	1979FM(M)	600 pcs.	4.00	10.00	20.00
	1979FM(U)	523 pcs.	4.00	12.00	25.00
	1980FM(U)	—	4.00	12.00	25.00
	29.4700 gm., .800 SILVER, .7580 oz ASW				
7a	1973FM(P)	.097	—	Proof	25.00
	1974FM(P)	.036	—	Proof	25.00
	1975FM(P)	.020	—	Proof	25.00
	1976FM(P)	.012	—	Proof	25.00
	1977FM(P)	5,014	—	Proof	27.50
	1978FM(P)	4,436	—	Proof	27.50
	1979FM(P)	4,126	—	Proof	27.50
	1980FM(P)	—	—	Proof	25.00

COPPER NICKEL
10th Anniversary of Independence
Rev: Similar to Y#7.

Y#	Date	Mintage	VF	XF	Unc
16	1976FM(M)	250 pcs.	25.00	40.00	60.00
	1976FM(U)	996 pcs.	—	20.00	35.00
	29.4700 gm., .800 SILVER, .7580 oz ASW				
16a	1976FM(P)	.012	—	Proof	25.00

10 DOLLARS

COPPER NICKEL
Obv: Similar to 2 Dollars, Y#6.

Y#	Date	Mintage	VF	XF	Unc
8	1973FM(M)	2,750	7.50	11.50	15.00
	1974FM(M)	3,958	6.00	10.00	13.50
	1975FM(M)	250 pcs.	30.00	45.00	75.00
	1975FM(U)	1,360	—	17.50	25.00
	1977FM(M)	600 pcs.	15.00	22.50	32.50
	1977FM(U)	468 pcs.	15.00	22.50	32.50
	1978FM(U)	1,017	—	—	30.00
	1979FM(M)	523 pcs.	15.00	20.00	30.00
	1979FM(U)	600 pcs.	15.00	20.00	30.00
	1980FM(U)	—	15.00	20.00	30.00

35.5200 gm., .925 SILVER, 1.0564 oz ASW

Y#	Date	Mintage	VF	XF	Unc
8a	1973FM(P)	.097	—	Proof	35.00
	1974FM(P)	.057	—	Proof	35.00
	1975FM(P)	.029	—	Proof	35.00
	1977FM(P)	7,212	—	Proof	40.00
	1978FM(P)	7,079	—	Proof	40.00
	1979FM(P)	6,534	—	Proof	50.00
	1980FM(P)	—	—	Proof	55.00

COPPER NICKEL
10th Anniversary of Independence
Rev: Similar to Y#8.

Y#	Date	Mintage	VF	XF	Unc
17	1976FM(M)	250 pcs.	27.50	45.00	75.00
	1976FM(U)	996 pcs.	—	25.00	35.00
	35.5200 gm., .925 SILVER, 1.0564 oz ASW				
17a	1976FM(P)	.016	—	Proof	40.00

25 DOLLARS

27.2800 gm., .925 SILVER, .8113 oz ASW
Coronation Jubilee
Obv: Portrait of Queen Elizabeth II.

Y#	Date	Mintage	VF	XF	Unc
18	1978FM(M)	300 pcs.	—	—	—
	1978FM(U)	69 pcs.	—	—	—
	1978FM(P)	8,728	—	Proof	45.00

100 DOLLARS

6.2100 gm., .500 GOLD, .0998 oz AGW
350th Anniversary Commemorative

Y#	Date	Mintage	VF	XF	Unc
9	1975FM(M)	.016	BV	65.00	75.00
	1975FM(U)	50 pcs.	—	—	—
	1975FM	.023	—	Proof	85.00

4.0600 gm., .900 GOLD, .1174 oz AGW
Human Rights Commemorative

Y#	Date	Mintage	VF	XF	Unc
—	1978	—	—	—	—
	5.0500 gm., .900 GOLD, .1461 oz AGW				
	1978	—	—	Proof	—

200 DOLLARS

8.1200 gm., .900 GOLD, .2349 oz AGW
Year of the Child

Y#	Date	Mintage	VF	XF	Unc
—	1979	—	—	—	—
	10.1000 gm., .900 GOLD, .2922 oz AGW				
	1979	—	—	Proof	—

NCLT ISSUES

MINT SETS

KM#	Date	Mintage	Identification	Issue Price	Mkt. Val.
S1	1973(8)	2,500	Y1-8	25.00	45.00
S2	1974(8)	3,708	Y1-8	25.00	30.00
S3	1975(8)	1,360	Y1-8	27.50	35.00
S4	1976(8)	996	Y10-17	27.50	80.00
S5	1977(8)	468	Y1-8	27.50	85.00
S6	1978(8)	517	Y1-8	29.00	85.00
S7	1979(8)	523	Y1-8	29.00	—
S8	1980(8)	—	Y1-8	30.00	80.00
S9	1980(2)	—	Y7a,8a	115.00	125.00

PROOF SETS

STANDARD METALS

KM#	Date	Mintage	Identification	Issue Price	Mkt. Val.
101	1973(8)	97,454	Y1-6,7a,8a	37.50	70.00
102	1974(8)	35,600	Y1-6,7a,8a	50.00	70.00
103	1975(8)	20,458	Y1-6,7a,8a	55.00	70.00
104	1976(8)	11,929	Y10-15,16a,17a	55.00	80.00
105	1977(8)	5,014	Y1-6,7a,8a	55.00	80.00
106	1978(8)	4,436	Y1-6,7a,18a	58.00	90.00
107	1979(8)	4,126	Y1-6,7a,18a	60.00	90.00
108	1980(8)	—	Y1-6,7a,8a	117.00	135.00

Listings For

BELGIAN CONGO: refer to Zaire

BELGIUM

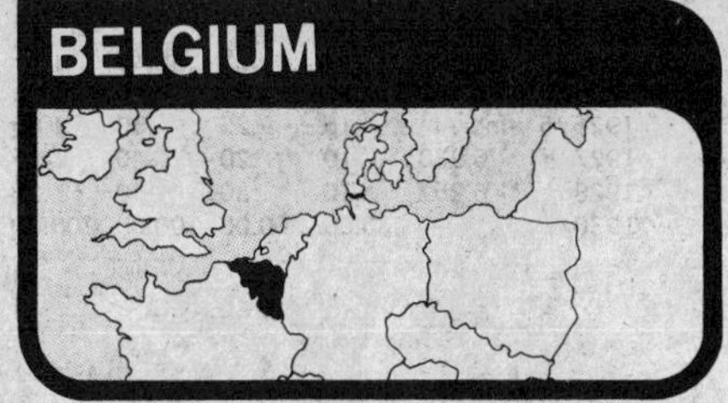

The Kingdom of Belgium, a constitutional monarchy in northwest Europe, has an area of 11,779 sq. mi. (30,559 sq. km.) and a population of 9.8 million, chiefly Dutch-speaking Flemish and French-speaking Walloons. Capital: Brussels. Agriculture, dairy farming, and the processing of raw materials for re-export are the principal industries. Beurs voor Diamant in Antwerp is the world's largest diamond trading center. Iron and steel, machinery, motor vehicles, chemicals, textile yarns and fabrics comprise the principal exports.

The Celtic tribe called 'Belgae', from which Belgium derived its name, was described by Caesar as the most courageous of all the tribes of Gaul. The Belgae eventually capitulated to Rome and the area remained for centuries as a part of the Roman Empire known as Belgica.

As Rome began its decline Frankish tribes migrated westward and established the Merovingian, and subsequently, the Carolingian empires. At the death of Charlemagne Europe was divided among his three sons Karl, Lothar and Ludwig. The eastern part of today's Belgium lay in the Duchy of Lower Lorraine while much of the western parts eventually became the County of Flanders. After further divisions the area was absorbed into the Duchy of Burgundy from whence it passed into Hapsburg control when Marie of Burgundy married Maximilian of Austria. Phillip I (the Fair), son of Maximilian and Marie then added Spain to the Hapsburg empire by marrying Johanna, daughter of Ferdinand and Isabella. Charles and Ferdinand, sons of Phillip and Johanna, began the separate Spanish and Austrian lines of the Hapsburg family. The Burgundian lands, along with the northern provinces which make up present day Netherlands, became the Spanish Netherlands. The northern provinces successfully rebelled and broke away from Hapsburg rule in the late 16th century and early 17th century. The southern provinces along with the Duchy of Luxembourg remained under the influence of Spain until the year 1700 when Charles II, last of the Spanish Hapsburg line, died without leaving an heir and the Spanish crown went to the Bourbon family of France. The Spanish Netherlands then reverted to the control of the Austrian line of Hapsburgs and became the Austrian Netherlands. The Austrian Netherlands along with the Bishopric of Liege fell to the French Republic in 1794.

At the Congress of Vienna in 1815 the area was united with the Netherlands, but in 1830 independence was gained and the constitutional monarchy of Belgium was established. A large part of the Duchy of Luxembourg was incorporated into Belgium and the first king was Leopold I of Saxe-Coburg-Gotha.

Belgian coins are inscribed either in Flemish, French or both. The language used is best told by noting the spelling of the name of the country.

LEGENDS:

(Fr) French: BELGIQUE or BELGES
(Fl) Flemish: BELGIE or BELGEN

RULERS

Leopold I, 1831-1865
Leopold II, 1865-1909
Albert I, 1909-1934
Leopold III, 1934-1950
Baudouin I, 1951-

MONETARY SYSTEM

100 Centimes = 1 Franc

CENTIME

COPPER

C#	Date	Mintage	VG	Fine	VF	XF
1	1832	—	27.50	65.00	140.00	250.00
	1833/2	5.007	6.00	15.00	50.00	90.00
	1833	Inc. Ab.	5.00	12.50	40.00	75.00
	1835/2	4.367	7.50	18.50	55.00	100.00
	1835	Inc. Ab.	6.00	15.00	45.00	85.00

NOTE: Until 1836 these were commonly struck over Netherlands 1/2 and 1 Cents.

Modified design

C#	Date	Mintage	VG	Fine	VF	XF
1.1	1835	—	2.50	5.00	12.50	25.00
	1836/2	4.256	2.50	5.00	12.50	25.00
	1836	Inc. Ab.	3.00	7.00	20.00	35.00
	1837	—	50.00	125.00	250.00	400.00
	1838	—	50.00	125.00	250.00	400.00
	1841	—	50.00	125.00	250.00	400.00
	1844	1.822	6.00	12.50	37.50	75.00
	1845	8.324	1.00	3.00	9.00	18.50
	1846	8.241	1.00	2.50	7.00	15.00
	1847	5.138	1.25	3.00	10.00	18.50
	1848	.383	125.00	250.00	500.00	1000.
	1849	1.218	4.00	9.00	27.50	60.00
	1850	2.309	3.00	6.00	18.50	35.00
	1855	—	50.00	100.00	175.00	300.00
	1856	2.428	3.00	6.00	18.50	35.00
	1857	.948	5.00	12.50	35.00	70.00
	1858	.916	6.00	15.00	40.00	80.00
	1859	.982	5.00	12.50	35.00	75.00
	1860	1.581	1.75	3.50	9.00	20.00
	1861	1.696	1.75	3.50	9.00	20.00
	1862	11.907	.75	1.50	3.00	7.00
	1863	—	50.00	100.00	200.00	400.00

Obv. French leg: DES BELGES

Y#	Date	Mintage	Fine	VF	XF	Unc
1	1869	5.064	1.50	4.00	10.00	18.50
	1870	3.930	.50	2.00	4.50	7.50
	1873	2.036	.50	2.50	5.00	8.50
	1874	3.907	.50	2.00	4.50	7.50
	1875	2.970	.50	2.00	4.50	7.50
	1876	2.966	.75	2.50	5.00	8.50
	1882	5.000	.30	1.00	3.00	4.50
	1899	2.500	.25	1.00	3.00	4.50
	1901/801 near 1					
		3.743	.30	.90	1.80	4.50
	1901/801 far 1					
		3.743	.30	.90	1.80	4.50
	1901/899	Inc. Ab.	.30	.90	1.80	4.50
	1901	Inc. Ab.	.25	.50	1.25	2.50
	1902/802 near 2		—			
		2.847	.25	.75	1.50	3.50
	1902/802 far 2					
		Inc. Ab.	.25	.75	1.50	3.50
	1902/801					
		Inc. Ab.	.25	.75	1.50	3.50
	1902/1	Inc. Ab.	.25	.75	1.25	2.50
	1902	Inc. Ab.	.20	.50	1.25	2.50
	1907	3.967	.20	.50	1.25	2.75

Obv. Flemish leg: DER BELGEN

Y#	Date	Mintage	Fine	VF	XF	Unc
1.1	1882	Inc. Ab.	60.00	150.00	250.00	400.00
	1887	5.000	.20	.75	1.40	3.50
	1892	—	60.00	150.00	250.00	400.00
	1894	5.000	.20	.75	1.50	3.50
	1899	2.500	.20	.75	1.50	3.50
	1901	3.738	.35	.75	1.25	2.50
	1902/1	2.482	.25	.90	1.50	3.00
	1902	Inc. Ab.	.20	.75	1.25	2.50
	1907	3.966	.20	.75	1.60	2.50

Obv. French leg: DES BELGES

Y#	Date	Mintage	Fine	VF	XF	Unc
22	1912	2.540	.15	.40	.60	1.75
	1914	.870	.50	.90	1.25	3.75

Obv. Flemish leg: DER BELGEN

Y#	Date	Mintage	Fine	VF	XF	Unc
22.1	1912	2.542	.20	.30	.60	1.75

2 CENTIMES

COPPER

C#	Date	Mintage	VG	Fine	VF	XF
2	1833	16.748	1.75	4.00	12.50	22.50
	1834	3.268	5.00	12.50	27.50	55.00
	1835	26.774	10.00	15.00	37.50	75.00

NOTE: Until 1836 these were commonly struck over Netherlands 1/2 and 1 Cents.

Modified design

C#	Date	Mintage	VG	Fine	VF	XF
2.1	1835	Inc. Ab.	.75	1.25	3.00	9.00
	1836	27.084	.75	1.25	3.00	9.00
	1837	—	35.00	75.00	200.00	375.00
	1838	—	35.00	75.00	175.00	350.00
	1841	2.226	1.65	4.50	12.50	30.00
	1842	2.823	2.00	5.50	15.00	32.50
	1844	1.802	1.25	3.50	10.00	25.00
	1845	8.324	.75	2.00	6.00	12.50
	1846	8.088	.75	2.00	6.00	12.50
	1847	3.432	1.25	2.50	8.50	17.50
	1848	.420	7.50	20.00	55.00	120.00
	1849	3.690	1.25	2.75	8.50	17.50
	1850	.404	6.00	16.50	45.00	90.00
	1851	2.407	.65	1.60	4.50	14.00
	1852	.731	3.50	7.50	20.00	60.00
	1853	.466	17.50	35.00	75.00	150.00
	1855	.171	40.00	80.00	200.00	300.00
	1856	6.255	.65	1.75	4.00	11.50
	1857	4.612	1.00	2.00	6.00	18.50
	1858/47	3.177	1.00	2.50	7.50	22.50
	1858/7	Inc. Ab.	1.00	2.50	7.50	22.50
	1858	Inc. Ab.	.90	2.00	6.00	18.50
	1859	4.074	1.00	2.00	6.00	18.50
	1860	3.070	1.00	2.00	6.00	18.50
	1861	2.924	.50	.90	2.75	6.50
	1862	6.589	.30	.65	2.25	4.00
	1863/2	18.621	.60	.90	1.50	3.00
	1863	Inc. Ab.	.50	.75	1.25	2.50
	1864	16.840	.20	.60	1.40	3.00
	1865	2.447	.75	2.00	5.00	13.50

Obv. French leg: DES BELGES

Y#	Date	Mintage	Fine	VF	XF	Unc
2	1869	2.972	6.50	17.50	37.50	70.00
	1870/1 close 0					
		5.654	.60	1.80	5.00	10.00
	1870	Inc. Ab.	.50	1.50	4.00	7.50
	1871	Inc. 1870	1.00	3.00	8.50	14.00
	1873	7.491	.40	1.50	4.00	7.50
	1874	7.876	.50	1.50	4.00	7.50
	1875	7.932	.40	1.50	4.00	7.50
	1876	10.472	.25	1.00	3.00	5.00
	1902	2.490	.25	.75	2.00	4.00
	1905	4.981	.25	.75	1.50	3.00
	1909/0	4.983	—	—	—	—
	1909	Inc. Ab.	.25	.75	1.50	3.00

Obv. Flemish leg: DER BELGEN

Y#	Date	Mintage	Fine	VF	XF	Unc
2.1	1902	2.488	.25	.75	2.00	4.00
	1905	4.986	.25	.75	1.50	3.00
	1909	.565	1.00	2.50	5.00	10.00

Obv. French leg: DES BELGES

Y#	Date	Mintage	Fine	VF	XF	Unc
23	1911	.645	1.50	2.50	6.50	15.00
	1912	4.928	.40	.50	1.00	2.50
	1914	.491	1.50	2.50	6.50	15.00
	1919/4	5.000	.30	.60	1.20	3.50
	1919	Inc. Ab.	.25	.50	1.00	2.50

Obv. Flemish leg: DER BELGEN

Y#	Date	Mintage	Fine	VF	XF	Unc
23.1	1910	1.248	.25	.50	1.00	3.00
	1911	6.441	.20	.30	.75	2.00
	1912	16.013	.25	.50	1.00	3.00
	1919	4.998	.20	.30	.75	2.00

5 CENTIMES

COPPER

C#	Date	Mintage	VG	Fine	VF	XF
3	1811 (error)	—	55.00	150.00	450.00	750.00
	1832	—	55.00	150.00	450.00	750.00
	1833	4.437	1.50	4.00	11.00	25.00
	1834	2.515	1.50	4.00	11.00	25.00
	1835	—	55.00	150.00	450.00	750.00
	1837	12.038	1.00	3.50	10.00	22.50
	1838	—	50.00	150.00	450.00	750.00
	1841/11	2.509	2.00	5.00	12.50	30.00
	1841 narrow 1					
		Inc. Ab.	2.00	4.00	10.00	25.00
	1841 wide 1					
		Inc. Ab.	1.25	5.00	12.00	25.00
	1842	5.537	1.00	4.00	10.00	25.00
	1847	1.131	2.25	7.00	16.50	45.00
	1848	1.845	1.25	4.50	10.00	22.50
	1849	1.447	2.00	6.00	17.50	32.50
	1850 5 w/ball top, round 0 w/wide center					
		2.689	1.50	3.50	10.00	20.00
	1850 5 w/less curved top, 0 tall w/narrow center					
		Inc. Ab.	1.50	3.50	10.00	20.00
	1851	2.381	1.00	2.25	10.00	20.00
	1852	1.943	1.00	2.25	10.00	20.00
	1853	.705	6.50	20.00	65.00	140.00
	1855	.265	35.00	90.00	200.00	400.00
	1856	5.656	.55	1.25	8.50	10.00
	1857	2.299	.75	2.25	8.50	20.00
	1858	2.712	.75	2.25	8.50	20.00
	1859	2.591	.75	2.25	8.50	20.00
	1860	.199	75.00	150.00	500.00	850.00
	1861	—	70.00	200.00	600.00	1000.

COPPER-NICKEL

C#	Date	Mintage	VG	Fine	VF	XF
6	1861	8.259	.35	.70	2.25	4.50
	1862/1	14.149	.30	.60	1.50	2.75
	1862	Inc. Ab.	.25	.50	1.25	2.25
	1863/2	16.055	.30	.85	2.50	5.50
	1863	Inc. Ab.	.25	.70	2.00	4.00
	1864	2.513	12.00	30.00	50.00	75.00

Obv. French leg: DES BELGES

Y#	Date	Mintage	Fine	VF	XF	Unc
3	1894	3.111	3.00	4.00	6.00	10.00
	1895	3.693	3.00	4.00	6.00	10.00
	1898	1.004	20.00	30.00	40.00	55.00
	1900	1.666	15.00	20.00	30.00	45.00

Rev: Lion of different design.

Y#	Date	Mintage	Fine	VF	XF	Unc
3.1	1901	2.494	15.00	20.00	30.00	45.00

Obv. Flemish leg: DER BELGEN

Y#	Date	Mintage	Fine	VF	XF	Unc
3.2	1894	1.658	3.00	4.00	6.00	10.00
	1895	4.957	3.00	4.00	6.00	10.00
	1898	.985	25.00	35.00	50.00	70.00
	1900/891	1.670	15.00	20.00	30.00	45.00
	1900/890	Inc. Ab.	15.00	20.00	30.00	45.00
	1900	Inc. Ab.	15.00	20.00	30.00	45.00

Rev: Lion of different design

Y#	Date	Mintage	Fine	VF	XF	Unc
3.3	1901	2.491	15.00	20.00	30.00	45.00

Obv. French leg: BELGIQUE, small date

Y#	Date	Mintage	Fine	VF	XF	Unc
12	1901	.202	35.00	60.00	100.00	150.00
	1902/1	1.416	.50	.75	1.50	4.00
	1902	Inc. Ab.	.40	.60	1.40	3.00
	1903	.864	.60	1.00	2.50	7.50

Obv: Large date

Y#	Date	Mintage	Fine	VF	XF	Unc
12.1	1904	5.814	.15	.25	.90	2.50
	1905/4	9.575	.20	.30	1.10	3.50
	1905	Inc. Ab.	.15	.25	.90	2.50
	1906/5	8.463	.30	.50	1.10	4.00
	1906	Inc. Ab.	.25	.40	.90	3.00
	1907	.993	.25	.50	1.50	3.50

Obv. Flemish leg: BELGIE, small date

Y#	Date	Mintage	Fine	VF	XF	Unc
12.2	1902	1.485	.25	.50	1.50	3.50
	1903	1.002	.25	1.00	2.50	7.50

Obv: Large date

Y#	Date	Mintage	Fine	VF	XF	Unc
12.3	1904	5.812	.15	.25	.90	3.00
	1905/3	7.002	.20	.30	1.10	4.00
	1905/4	Inc. Ab.	.20	.30	1.10	4.00
	1905	Inc. Ab.	.15	.25	.90	3.00
	1906/5	11.016	.15	.25	.90	3.00
	1906	Inc. Ab.	.15	.25	.90	3.00
	1907	.998	.25	1.00	2.50	7.50

Obv. French leg: BELGIQUE

Y#	Date	Mintage	Fine	VF	XF	Unc
24	1910	8.011	.15	.20	.50	1.50
	1913/0	5.005	.20	.25	.60	2.00
	1913	Inc. Ab.	.15	.20	.50	1.50
	1914	1.004	1.50	3.00	7.50	12.50
	1920	10.040	.10	.20	.50	1.25
	1922/12	12.640	.15	.25	.60	1.65
	1922/0	Inc. Ab.	.15	.25	.60	1.65
	1922	Inc. Ab.	.10	.20	.50	1.25
	1923/13	9.000	.15	.25	.60	1.65
	1923	Inc. Ab.	.10	.20	.50	1.25
	1925/13	15.860	.20	.25	.50	1.65
	1925	Inc. Ab.	.15	.20	.40	1.25
	1926/5	7.000	.20	.25	.60	1.65
	1926	Inc. Ab.	.15	.20	.50	1.25
	1927	2.000	.10	.50	.80	2.00
	1928	12.507	.10	.20	.50	1.25
	1932	—	30.00	60.00	100.00	200.00

Obv. Flemish leg: BELGIE

Y#	Date	Mintage	Fine	VF	XF	Unc
24.1	1910	8.033	.15	.20	.40	1.50
	1914	6.040	.10	.20	.40	1.50
	1920/10	10.030	.20	.25	.50	1.65
	1920	Inc. Ab.	.15	.20	.40	1.25
	1921/11	4.200	.20	.25	.50	1.65
	1921/2	Inc. Ab.	.20	.25	.50	1.65
	1921	Inc. Ab.	.10	.20	.40	1.25
	1922/12	13.180	.15	.25	.50	1.65
	1922/0	Inc. Ab.	.15	.25	.50	1.65
	1922	Inc. Ab.	.10	.20	.40	1.25
	1923/13	3.530	.15	.25	.50	1.65
	1923	Inc. Ab.	.10	.20	.40	1.25
	1924/11	5.260	.15	.25	.50	1.65
	1924/14	Inc. Ab.	.15	.25	.50	1.65
	1924	Inc. Ab.	.10	.20	.40	1.25
	1925/15 high 2					
		13.000	.15	.25	.50	1.65
24.1	1925/15 level 2					
		Inc. Ab.	.15	.25	.50	1.65
	1925	Inc. Ab.	.10	.20	.40	1.25
	1926/5	Inc. Ab.	.15	.25	.50	1.65
	1927	6.938	.10	.20	.40	1.25
	1928	6.252	.10	.20	.40	1.25
	1930	—	30.00	60.00	100.00	200.00

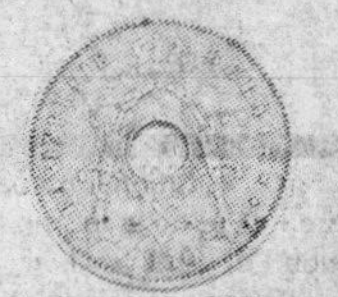

NICKEL-BRASS
Obv. French leg: BELGIQUE
Rev: Star added above 5

Y#	Date	Mintage	Fine	VF	XF	Unc
24a	1932	5.520	.15	.30	.50	3.00

The dates 1906 (sic) and 1922 are restrikes.

Obv. Flemish leg: BELGIE

Y#	Date	Mintage	Fine	VF	XF	Unc
24a.1	1930	3.000	.15	.40	.65	3.00
	1931	7.430	.15	.25	.50	3.00

ZINC
German Occupation WW I
Obv. French leg: BELGIQUE-BELGIE

Y#	Date	Mintage	Fine	VF	XF	Unc
38	1915	10.199	.15	.50	1.20	3.25
	1916	45.464	.10	.30	1.00	2.50

NICKEL-BRASS
Obv. French leg: BELGIQUE-BELGIE

Y#	Date	Mintage	Fine	VF	XF	Unc
42	1938	4.970	.15	.25	.60	1.50

Obv. Flemish leg: BELGIE-BELGIQUE

Y#	Date	Mintage	Fine	VF	XF	Unc
42.1	1939	3.000	.15	.25	.60	1.50
	1940	1.970	.20	.50	1.25	2.25

ZINC
German Occupation WW II
Obv. French leg: BELGIQUE-BELGIE

Y#	Date	Mintage	Fine	VF	XF	Unc
51	1941	10.000	.10	.20	.30	1.25
	1943	7.606	.10	.20	.30	1.50

Obv. Flemish leg: BELGIE-BELGIQUE

Y#	Date	Mintage	Fine	VF	XF	Unc
51.1	1941	4.000	.15	.20	.30	1.50
	1942	18.430	.15	.20	.30	1.00

10 CENTIMES

COPPER-NICKEL

C#	Date	Mintage	VG	Fine	VF	XF
4	1832	.993	15.00	35.00	90.00	200.00
	1833	.994	15.00	40.00	100.00	225.00
	1835	—	125.00	225.00	550.00	1100.
	1838	—	100.00	225.00	550.00	1100.
	1841	—	125.00	225.00	550.00	1100.
	1847/37	.135	40.00	75.00	150.00	275.00
	1847	Inc. Ab.	30.00	60.00	130.00	250.00
	1848/38	.777	30.00	50.00	125.00	250.00
	1848	Inc. Ab.	15.00	30.00	115.00	200.00
	1849	Inc. Ab.	100.00	250.00	550.00	1100.
	1855	.191	50.00	100.00	225.00	425.00
	1856	Inc. Ab.	125.00	250.00	550.00	1100.

NOTE: The dates 1835 and 1841 were not released officially into circulation.

C#	Date	Mintage	VG	Fine	VF	XF
7	1861	9.080	.25	.75	1.25	2.00
	1862	15.129	.25	.75	1.25	2.00
	1863	14.482	.25	.75	1.25	2.00
	1864	3.202	5.00	10.00	15.00	22.50

Obv. French leg: DES BELGES

Y#	Date	Mintage	Fine	VF	XF	Unc
4	1894	18.886	1.75	2.50	3.50	9.00
	1895	.736	60.00	80.00	110.00	175.00
	1898	3.499	3.00	4.50	7.50	15.00
	1901/601	.556	95.00	135.00	195.00	275.00
	1901	Inc. Ab.	90.00	125.00	175.00	250.00

Obv. Flemish leg: DER BELGEN

Y#	Date	Mintage	Fine	VF	XF	Unc
4.1	1894	9.209	1.75	2.50	3.50	8.00
	1895/4	3.529	3.50	5.00	7.50	17.50
	1895	Inc. Ab.	3.00	4.50	7.50	15.00
	1898	3.500	3.00	4.50	7.50	15.00
	1901	.556	90.00	125.00	175.00	250.00

Obv. French leg: BELGIQUE, small date.

Y#	Date	Mintage	Fine	VF	XF	Unc
13	1901	.582	7.50	12.00	18.00	35.00
	1902/1	5.866	.30	.70	1.65	4.00
	1902	Inc. Ab.	.25	.60	1.25	3.00
	1903	.763	2.00	4.00	6.00	10.00

Obv: Large date

Y#	Date	Mintage	Fine	VF	XF	Unc
13.1	1904	16.354	.20	.55	1.10	3.00
	1905	14.392	.20	.55	1.10	3.00
	1906/5	1.483	.35	.85	2.25	6.00
	1906	Inc. Ab.	.30	.70	1.75	4.50

Obv. Flemish leg: BELGIE, small date.

Y#	Date	Mintage	Fine	VF	XF	Unc
13.2	1902	1.560	.30	.75	1.75	4.50
	1903	5.658	.25	.60	1.10	2.75

Obv: Large date

Y#	Date	Mintage	Fine	VF	XF	Unc
13.3	1904	16.834	.25	.60	1.10	2.75
	1905/3	13.758	.30	.70	1.30	3.50
	1905	Inc. Ab.	.25	.60	1.10	2.75
	1906/5 point above center of 6					
		2.017	.30	.70	2.00	5.50
	1906/5 point above right side of 6					
		Inc. Ab.	.30	.70	2.00	5.50
	1906	Inc. Ab.	.25	.60	1.60	4.25

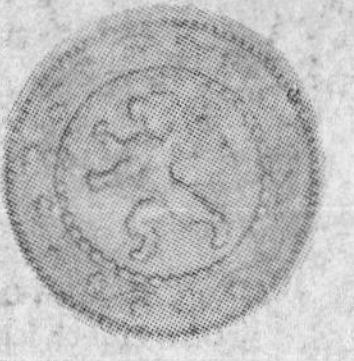

ZINC
German Occupation
Obv. French leg: BELGIQUE-BELGIE

Y#	Date	Mintage	Fine	VF	XF	Unc
39	1915	9.681	.20	.50	1.50	3.25
	1916	37.382	.20	.40	.90	2.75
	1917	1.447	20.00	35.00	55.00	80.00

COPPER-NICKEL
Obv. French leg: BELGIQUE

Y#	Date	Mintage	Fine	VF	XF	Unc
25	1920	6.520	.15	.20	.40	1.25
	1921	7.215	.15	.20	.40	1.25
	1923	20.625	.10	.20	.40	1.25
	1926/3	6.916	.20	.25	.50	1.65
	1926/5	Inc. Ab.	.20	.25	.50	1.65
	1926	Inc. Ab.	.15	.20	.40	1.25
	1927	8.125	.15	.20	.40	1.25
	1928/3	6.895	.20	.25	.50	1.65
	1928	Inc. Ab.	.15	.20	.40	1.25
	1929	12.260	.15	.20	.40	1.25

Obv. Flemish leg: BELGIE

Y#	Date	Mintage	Fine	VF	XF	Unc
25.1	1920	5.050	.15	.20	.40	1.25
	1921	7.580	.15	.20	.40	1.25
	1922	6.250	.15	.20	.40	1.25
	1924	5.825	.15	.20	.40	1.25
	1925/4	8.160	.15	.25	.50	1.65
	1925	Inc. Ab.	.10	.20	.40	1.25
	1926/5	6.250	.20	.25	.50	1.65
	1926	Inc. Ab.	.15	.20	.40	1.25
	1927	10.625	.15	.20	.40	1.25
	1928	6.750	.15	.20	.40	1.25
	1929	4.668	.15	.20	.40	1.25

NICKEL-BRASS
Obv. French leg: BELGIQUE
Rev: Star added above 10

Y#	Date	Mintage	Fine	VF	XF	Unc
25a	1930	2.000	50.00	75.00	125.00	225.00
	1931	6.270	2.25	5.50	11.50	17.50
	1932	1.270	75.00	125.00	175.00	275.00

Obv. Flemish leg: BELGIE

Y#	Date	Mintage	Fine	VF	XF	Unc
25a.1	1930	1.581	.30	.50	1.25	3.00
	1931	5.000	50.00	75.00	125.00	225.00

Obv. French leg: BELGIQUE-BELGIE

Y#	Date	Mintage	Fine	VF	XF	Unc
43	1938	6.000	.10	.25	.75	2.00
	1939	7.000	.10	.35	1.00	3.00

Obv. Flemish leg: BELGIE-BELGIQUE

Y#	Date	Mintage	Fine	VF	XF	Unc
43.1	1939	8.425	.10	.25	.75	2.00

ZINC
German Occupation WW II
Obv. French leg: BELGIQUE-BELGIE

Y#	Date	Mintage	Fine	VF	XF	Unc
52	1941	10.000	.15	.25	.50	1.25
	1942	17.000	.15	.25	.50	1.25
	1943	22.500	.15	.25	.50	1.25
	1946	5.000	.15	.25	.50	1.25

Obv. Flemish leg: BELGIE-BELGIQUE

Y#	Date	Mintage	Fine	VF	XF	Unc
52.1	1941	7.000	.15	.25	.50	1.25
	1942	21.000	.15	.25	.50	1.25
	1943	22.000	.15	.25	.50	1.25
	1944	28.140	.15	.25	.50	1.25
	1945	8.000	.15	.25	.50	1.25
	1946	5.370	.15	.25	.50	1.25

20 CENTIMES

.900 SILVER

C#	Date	Mintage	VG	Fine	VF	XF
14	1852	.301	10.00	25.00	50.00	100.00
	1853	1.965	2.00	7.50	22.50	45.00
	1858/7	.865	75.00	175.00	400.00	800.00
	1858	Inc. Ab.	75.00	175.00	400.00	800.00

COPPER-NICKEL

C#	Date	Mintage	VG	Fine	VF	XF
8	1860	1.804	15.00	25.00	50.00	100.00
	1861	Inc. Ab.	1.25	2.25	6.00	12.50

BRONZE
Obv. French leg: BELGIQUE

Y#	Date	Mintage	Fine	VF	XF	Unc
62	1953	14.150	—	—	.15	.35
	1954	—	150.00	325.00	500.00	750.00
	1957	13.300	—	—	.20	.35
	1958	8.700	—	—	.20	.35
	1959	19.670	—	—	.20	.35
	1962	.410	.80	1.50	2.50	5.00
	1963	2.550	—	—	.15	.25

Obv. Flemish leg: BELGIE

Y#	Date	Mintage	Fine	VF	XF	Unc
62.1	1954	50.130	—	—	.10	.30
	1959	—	—	—	.15	.25
	1960	7.530	—	—	.20	.30

1/4 FRANC

1.2500 gm., .900 SILVER, .0362 oz ASW

C#	Date	Mintage	VG	Fine	VF	XF
9	1834 w/signature					
		.762	12.50	27.50	75.00	130.00
	1834 w/o signature					
		Inc. Ab.	20.00	45.00	150.00	250.00
	1835 w/signature					
		.640	12.50	35.00	100.00	200.00
	1835 w/o signature					
		Inc. Ab.	25.00	85.00	250.00	500.00
	1841	—	150.00	375.00	1250.	2250.

C#	Date	Mintage	VG	Fine	VF	XF
9	1843	8,000	50.00	90.00	250.00	425.00
	1844	.966	8.50	25.00	75.00	125.00

NOTE: Coins dated 1841 were not released officially into circulation.

C#	Date	Mintage	VG	Fine	VF	XF
15	1849	—	140.00	300.00	750.00	1350.
	1850	.101	100.00	225.00	600.00	1150.

25 CENTIMES

COPPER-NICKEL
Obv. French leg: BELGIQUE

Y#	Date	Mintage	Fine	VF	XF	Unc
14	1908	4.007	.50	1.50	5.00	17.50
	1909	1.998	.50	1.75	6.00	20.00

Obv. Flemish leg: BELGIE

Y#	Date	Mintage	Fine	VF	XF	Unc
14.1	1908	4.011	.50	1.50	5.00	17.50

Obv. French leg: BELGIQUE

Y#	Date	Mintage	Fine	VF	XF	Unc
26	1913	2.011	.15	.30	1.25	3.50
	1920	2.844	.15	.25	1.00	2.50
	1921	7.464	.10	.15	.50	1.25
	1922	7.600	.10	.20	.50	1.25
	1923	11.356	.15	.25	.50	1.25
	1926/3	1.300	.60	.90	3.50	13.50
	1926	Inc. Ab.	.50	.75	3.00	10.00
	1927/3	8.800	.20	.30	.60	1.65
	1927/6	Inc. Ab.	.20	.30	.60	1.65
	1927	Inc. Ab.	.15	.25	.50	1.25
	1928	4.351	.10	.15	.50	1.25
	1929	9.600	.10	.15	.50	1.25

Obv. Flemish leg: BELGIE

Y#	Date	Mintage	Fine	VF	XF	Unc
26.1	1910	2.006	.15	.30	1.25	3.50
	1913	2.010	.15	.30	1.00	2.50
	1921	11.173	.15	.25	.50	1.25
	1922	14.200	.15	.25	.50	1.25
	1926	6.400	.10	.20	.50	1.25
	1927	3.799	.10	.15	.50	1.25
	1928	9.200	.15	.25	.50	1.25
	1929	8.980	.15	.25	.50	1.25
	1930/20	—	.20	.30	.60	1.65

ZINC
German Occupation WW I
Obv. French leg: BELGIQUE-BELGIE

Y#	Date	Mintage	Fine	VF	XF	Unc
40	1915	8.080	.25	1.00	2.50	8.00
	1916	10.671	.20	1.00	2.50	8.00
	1917	3.555	3.50	6.00	9.00	20.00
	1918	5.489	1.50	2.50	4.50	10.00

NICKEL-BRASS
Obv. French leg: BELGIQUE-BELGIE

Y#	Date	Mintage	Fine	VF	XF	Unc
44	1938	7.200	—	.15	.75	1.75
	1939	7.732	—	.15	.75	1.75

Obv. Flemish leg: BELGIE-BELGIQUE

Y#	Date	Mintage	Fine	VF	XF	Unc
44.1	1938	14.932	—	.15	.75	1.75

ZINC
German Occupation WW II
Obv. French leg: BELGIQUE-BELGIE

Y#	Date	Mintage	Fine	VF	XF	Unc
53	1942	14.400	—	.10	.50	1.50
	1943	21.600	—	.10	.50	1.50
	1946	21.428	—	.10	.50	1.50
	1947	.300	—	—	—	—

Obv: Flemish leg: BELGIE BELGIQUE

Y#	Date	Mintage	Fine	VF	XF	Unc
53.1	1942	14.400	—	.10	.50	1.50
	1943	21.600	—	.10	.50	1.50
	1944	25.960	—	.10	.50	1.50
	1945	8.200	—	.10	.50	1.25
	1946	11.652	—	.10	.50	1.50
	1947	.316	—	—	—	—

COPPER-NICKEL
Obv. French leg: BELGIQUE

Y#	Date	Mintage	Fine	VF	XF	Unc
66	1964	21.770	—	—	.10	.15
	1965	11.440	—	—	.10	.15
	1966	19.990	—	—	.10	.15
	1967	6.820	—	—	.10	.15
	1968	25.250	—	—	.10	.15
66	1969	7.670	—	—	.10	.15
	1970	27.000	—	—	.10	.15
	1971	16.000	—	—	.10	.15
	1972	20.000	—	—	.10	.15
	1973	12.500	—	—	.10	.15
	1974	20.000	—	—	.10	.15
	1975	12.000	—	—	.10	.15
	1976	—	—	—	.10	.15

Obv. Flemish leg: BELGIE

Y#	Date	Mintage	Fine	VF	XF	Unc
66.1	1964	21.300	—	—	—	.10
	1965	7.900	—	—	.10	.15
	1966	23.420	—	—	.10	.15
	1967	7.720	—	—	.10	.15
	1968	22.750	—	—	.10	.15
	1969	25.190	—	—	.10	.15
	1970	12.000	—	—	.10	.15
	1971	16.000	—	—	.10	.15
	1972	20.000	—	—	.10	.15
	1973	12.500	—	—	.10	.15
	1974	20.000	—	—	.10	.15
	1975	12.000	—	—	.10	.15
	1976	—	—	—	.10	.15

1/2 FRANC

2.5000 gm., .900 SILVER, .0723 oz ASW

C#	Date	Mintage	VG	Fine	VF	XF
10	1833	.058	75.00	200.00	600.00	1000.
	1834	1.578	15.00	35.00	100.00	175.00
	1835	.805	25.00	55.00	175.00	275.00
	1838	.550	35.00	90.00	225.00	400.00
	1840	.347	35.00	100.00	275.00	450.00
	1841	—	150.00	400.00	1150.	2250.
	1843	.346	35.00	90.00	225.00	400.00
	1844	1.584	15.00	35.00	100.00	160.00

C#	Date	Mintage	VG	Fine	VF	XF
16	1849	—	150.00	350.00	800.00	1500.
	1850	.210	120.00	250.00	600.00	1150.

50 CENTIMES

2.5000 gm., .835 SILVER, .0671 oz ASW
Obv. French leg: DES BELGES

Y#	Date	Mintage	Fine	VF	XF	Unc
5	1866	6.906	2.50	10.00	50.00	125.00
	1867	1.014	25.00	75.00	150.00	300.00
	1868	1.076	100.00	250.00	500.00	1000.
	1881/61	.200	75.00	175.00	500.00	1200.
	1881/66	Inc. Ab.	75.00	175.00	500.00	1200.
	1881	Inc. Ab.	80.00	200.00	450.00	1200.
	1886/1	1.250	3.00	10.00	35.00	100.00
	1886	Inc. Ab.	3.00	10.00	35.00	100.00
	1898	.499	3.00	10.00	40.00	100.00
	1899	.500	3.00	10.00	40.00	100.00

Obv. Flemish leg: DER BELGEN

Y#	Date	Mintage	Fine	VF	XF	Unc
5.1	1886	3.750	2.25	7.50	25.00	75.00
	1898	.501	3.00	10.00	40.00	100.00
	1899/86	Inc. Ab.	3.00	12.50	40.00	100.00
	1899	.500	3.00	10.00	40.00	100.00

Obv. French leg: DES BELGES

Y#	Date	Mintage	Fine	VF	XF	Unc
15	1901	3.000	2.25	7.50	15.00	30.00

Obv. Flemish leg: DER BELGEN

Y#	Date	Mintage	Fine	VF	XF	Unc
15.1	1901	3.000	2.25	7.50	15.00	30.00

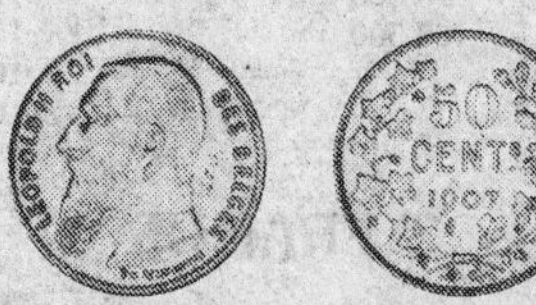

Obv. French leg: DES BELGES

Y#	Date	Mintage	Fine	VF	XF	Unc
16	1907	.545	2.25	5.00	12.50	20.00
	1909	2.503	BV	2.25	4.50	10.00

Obv. Flemish leg: DER BELGEN

Y#	Date	Mintage	Fine	VF	XF	Unc
16.1	1907	.545	2.25	5.00	12.50	20.00
	1909	2.510	BV	2.25	4.50	10.00

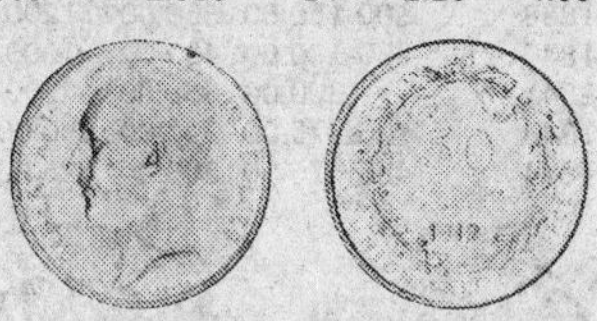

Obv. French leg: DES BELGES

Y#	Date	Mintage	Fine	VF	XF	Unc
33	1910	1.900	BV	2.25	3.50	6.00
	1911	2.063	BV	2.25	3.50	6.00
	1912	1.000	BV	2.25	3.50	6.00
	1914	.240	7.50	12.50	20.00	30.00

Obv. Flemish leg: DER BELGEN

Y#	Date	Mintage	Fine	VF	XF	Unc
33.1	1910	1.900	BV	2.25	3.50	6.00
	1911	2.063	BV	2.25	3.50	6.00
	1912	1.000	BV	2.25	3.50	6.00

ZINC
German Occupation WW I
Obv. Flemish leg: BELGIE-BELGIQUE

Y#	Date	Mintage	Fine	VF	XF	Unc
41	1918	7.394	1.20	2.00	5.00	11.50

NICKEL
Obv. French leg: BELGIQUE

Y#	Date	Mintage	Fine	VF	XF	Unc
27	1922	6.180	.15	.25	.50	1.00
	1923	8.820	.15	.25	.50	1.00
	1927	7.000	.15	.30	.50	1.00
	1928	3.000	.15	.25	.75	1.50
	1929	1.000	.25	1.00	2.00	5.00
	1930	1.000	.25	1.00	2.00	5.00
	1932	2.530	.15	.30	.75	1.50
	1933	2.861	.15	.25	.75	1.50

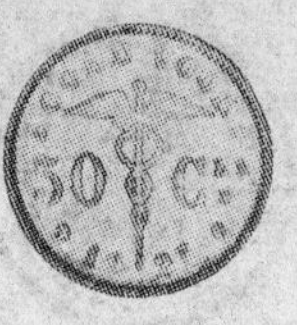

Obv. Flemish leg: BELGIE

Y#	Date	Mintage	Fine	VF	XF	Unc
27.1	1923	15.000	.20	.25	.50	1.00
	1928	10.000	.20	.25	.50	1.00
	1930/20	—	.25	.35	.90	2.25
	1930	2.252	.20	.30	.75	1.75
	1932	2.000	.20	.30	.75	1.75
	1933	3.139	.25	1.00	2.50	7.50
	1934	.935	125.00	150.00	200.00	250.00

Obv. French leg: BELGIQUE-BELGIE

Y#	Date	Mintage	Fine	VF	XF	Unc
27.2	1939	—	—	175.00	325.00	425.00

NOTE: Striking interrupted by the war. Never officially released into circulation.

BRONZE
Obv. French leg: BELGIQUE. Rev: Large head.

Y#	Date	Mintage	Fine	VF	XF	Unc
63	1952	3.520	—	.10	.20	.30
	1953	22.620	—	—	—	.20

Rev: Smaller head

Y#	Date	Mintage	Fine	VF	XF	Unc
63.1	1955	29.160	—	—	—	.20
	1958	9.750	—	—	—	.20
	1959	17.350	—	—	—	.15
	1962	6.160	—	—	—	.15
	1964	5.860	—	—	—	.15
	1965	10.320	—	—	—	.15
	1966	11.040	—	—	—	.15
	1967	7.200	—	—	—	.15
	1968	2.000	—	—	—	.20
	1969	10.000	—	—	—	.15
	1970	16.000	—	—	—	.15
	1971	1.250	—	—	—	.20
	1972	3.000	—	—	—	.15
	1973	3.000	—	—	—	.15
	1974	5.000	—	—	—	.15
	1975	7.000	—	—	—	.15
	1976	8.000	—	—	—	.15
	1977	13.000	—	—	—	.15
	1978	—	—	—	—	.15
	1979	—	—	—	—	.15

Obv. Flemish leg: BELGIE. Rev: Large head.

Y#	Date	Mintage	Fine	VF	XF	Unc
63.2	1952	5.830	—	.10	.20	.30
	1953	22.930	—	—	—	.20
	1954	15.730	—	—	—	.20

Rev: Smaller head

Y#	Date	Mintage	Fine	VF	XF	Unc
63.3	1956	5.640	—	—	—	.20
	1957	13.800	—	—	—	.20
	1958	19.480	—	—	—	.15
	1962	4.150	—	—	—	.15
	1963	1.110	—	—	—	.15
	1964	10.340	—	—	—	.15
	1965	9.590	—	—	—	.15
	1966	6.930	—	—	—	.15
	1967	6.970	—	—	—	.15
	1968	2.000	—	—	—	.20
	1969	10.000	—	—	—	.15
	1970	12.000	—	—	—	.15
	1971	1.250	—	—	—	.20
	1972	7.000	—	—	—	.15
	1973	3.000	—	—	—	.15
	1974	5.000	—	—	—	.15
	1975	7.000	—	—	—	.15
	1976	8.000	—	—	—	.15
	1977	13.000	—	—	—	.15
	1978	—	—	—	—	.15
	1979	—	—	—	—	.15

FRANC

5.0000 gm., .900 SILVER, .1447 oz ASW

C#	Date	Mintage	VG	Fine	VF	XF
11	1833	.061	80.00	200.00	600.00	1000.
	1834	.482	35.00	50.00	125.00	250.00
	1835	.861	45.00	100.00	275.00	450.00
	1838	.525	50.00	110.00	300.00	525.00
	1840	.261	55.00	140.00	350.00	550.00
	1841	—	250.00	650.00	1650.	2250.
	1843	—	150.00	400.00	1000.	1500.
	1844	2.196	22.50	50.00	125.00	225.00

C#	Date	Mintage	VG	Fine	VF	XF
17	1849	.041	225.00	450.00	1250.	2250.
	1850	.162	150.00	300.00	1000.	2000.

5.0000 gm., .835 SILVER, .1342 oz ASW
Obv. French leg: DES BELGES

Y#	Date	Mintage	Fine	VF	XF	Unc
6	1866	3.041	4.25	15.00	50.00	200.00
	1867	6.652	4.25	12.50	40.00	150.00
	1868	.675	400.00	1000.	1750.	2500.
	1869	1.394	6.00	15.00	50.00	250.00
	1881	.119	100.00	250.00	550.00	1500.
	1886/66	Inc. Ab.	4.25	17.50	50.00	150.00
	1886	1.250	4.25	8.50	35.00	125.00

Obv. Flemish leg: DER BELGEN

Y#	Date	Mintage	Fine	VF	XF	Unc
6.1	1886	1.026	4.25	17.50	50.00	150.00
	1887	2.724	4.25	8.50	35.00	125.00

50th Anniversary Independence

Y#	Date	Mintage	Fine	VF	XF	Unc
9	1880	.545	8.50	25.00	60.00	150.00

Obv. French leg: DES BELGES

Y#	Date	Mintage	Fine	VF	XF	Unc
17	1904	.803	4.25	7.50	15.00	40.00
	1909	2.250	BV	4.25	7.50	20.00

Obv. Flemish leg: DER BELGEN

Y#	Date	Mintage	Fine	VF	XF	Unc
17.1	1904	.803	4.25	7.50	15.00	40.00
	1909	2.250	BV	4.25	7.50	20.00

Obv. French leg: DES BELGES

Y#	Date	Mintage	Fine	VF	XF	Unc
34	1910	2.190	BV	4.25	6.00	8.50

Y#	Date	Mintage	Fine	VF	XF	Unc
34	1911	2.810	BV	4.25	6.00	8.50
	1912	3.250	BV	4.25	6.00	8.50
	1913	3.000	BV	4.25	6.00	8.50
	1914	11.222	BV	4.25	6.00	8.50
	1917	—	175.00	400.00	1150.	2250.
	1918	—	175.00	400.00	1150.	2000.

Obv. Flemish leg: DER BELGEN

Y#	Date	Mintage	Fine	VF	XF	Unc
34.1	1910	2.750	BV	4.25	6.00	8.50
	1911	2.250	BV	4.25	6.00	8.50
	1912	3.250	BV	4.25	6.00	8.50
	1913	3.000	BV	4.25	6.00	8.50
	1914	10.222	BV	4.25	6.00	8.50
	1918	—	175.00	400.00	1150.	2000.

NICKEL
Obv. French leg: BELGIQUE

Y#	Date	Mintage	Fine	VF	XF	Unc
28	1922	14.000	.15	.25	.50	1.50
	1923	22.500	.15	.25	.50	1.50
	1928/3	5.000	.20	.50	.75	2.00
	1928	Inc. Ab.	.15	.25	.50	1.50
	1929	7.415	.15	.25	.50	1.50
	1930	5.365	.20	.50	.75	1.75
	1931	—	225.00	700.00	1150.	2000.
	1933	2.000	.60	1.00	2.00	4.00
	1934	10.362	.15	.25	.50	1.50

Obv. Flemish leg: BELGIE

Y#	Date	Mintage	Fine	VF	XF	Unc
28.1	1922	19.000	.15	.25	.50	1.50
	1923/2	17.500	.20	.30	.60	2.00
	1923	Inc. Ab.	.15	.25	.50	1.50
	1928/3	4.975	.20	.30	.60	2.00
	1928	Inc. Ab.	.15	.25	.50	1.50
	1929	10.365	.15	.25	.50	1.50
	1931	2.340	—	—	Rare	—
	1933	.002	275.00	375.00	600.00	1000.
	1934/24	8.025	.20	.30	.60	2.00
	1934	Inc. Ab.	.15	.25	.50	1.50
	1935/23	—	.35	.60	1.50	4.00
	1935	2.338	.30	.50	1.25	3.00

Obv. French leg: BELGIQUE-BELGIE

Y#	Date	Mintage	Fine	VF	XF	Unc
45	1939	46.865	.15	.25	.50	1.25

Obv. Flemish leg: BELGIE-BELGIQUE

Y#	Date	Mintage	Fine	VF	XF	Unc
45.1	1939	36.000	.15	.25	.50	1.25
	1940	10.865	.20	.40	.75	1.75

ZINC
German Occupation WW II
Obv. French leg: BELGIQUE-BELGIE

Y#	Date	Mintage	Fine	VF	XF	Unc
54	1941	16.000	.15	.30	.80	2.00
	1942	25.000	.20	.30	.80	2.00
	1943	28.000	.20	.30	.80	2.00
	1947	3.175	150.00	300.00	375.00	500.00

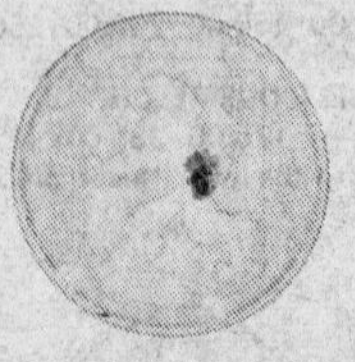

Obv. Flemish leg: BELGIE-BELGIQUE

Y#	Date	Mintage	Fine	VF	XF	Unc
54.1	1942	42.000	.20	.30	.60	2.00
	1943	28.000	.15	.30	.60	2.00
	1944	24.190	.20	.30	.60	2.00
	1945	15.930	.15	.30	.60	2.00
	1946	36.000	.10	.25	.50	1.75
	1947	3.000	50.00	75.00	100.00	150.00

COPPER-NICKEL
Obv. French leg: BELGIQUE

Y#	Date	Mintage	Fine	VF	XF	Unc
57	1950	13.630	—	—	.10	.25
	1951	51.025	—	—	.10	.25
	1952	52.205	—	—	.10	.20
	1954	4.940	—	.10	.25	.45
	1955	3.960	—	.10	.25	.45
	1956	10.000	—	—	.10	.15
	1958	31.750	—	—	.10	.15
	1959	9.000	—	—	.10	.15
	1960	10.000	—	—	.10	.15
	1961	5.030	—	—	.10	.15
	1962	12.250	—	—	.10	.15
	1963	18.700	—	—	.10	.15
	1964	10.110	—	—	.10	.15
	1965	10.185	—	—	.10	.15
	1966	16.430	—	—	.10	.15
	1967	32.945	—	—	.10	.15
	1968	8.000	—	—	.10	.15
	1969	21.950	—	—	.10	.15
	1970	35.500	—	—	.10	.15
	1971	10.000	—	—	.10	.15
	1972	35.000	—	—	.10	.15
	1973	42.500	—	—	.10	.15
	1974	30.000	—	—	.10	.15
	1975	80.000	—	—	.10	.15
	1976	18.000	—	—	.10	.15
	1977	68.500	—	—	.10	.15
	1978	—	—	—	—	—
	1979	—	—	—	—	—

Obv. Flemish leg: BELGIE

Y#	Date	Mintage	Fine	VF	XF	Unc
57.1	1950	10.000	—	—	.10	.25
	1951	53.750	—	—	.10	.25
	1952	49.150	—	—	.10	.25
	1953	9.920	—	—	.10	.25
	1954	4.940	—	.10	.25	.45
	1955	3.960	—	.10	.25	.45
	1956	10.040	—	—	.10	.15
	1957	18.320	—	—	.10	.15
	1958	17.370	—	—	.10	.15
	1959	5.830	—	—	.10	.15
	1960	5.560	—	—	.10	.15
	1961	9.350	—	—	.10	.15
	1962	10.720	—	—	.10	.15
57.1	1963	23.460	—	—	.10	.15
	1964	7.430	—	—	.10	.15
	1965	11.190	—	—	.10	.15
	1966	20.990	—	—	.10	.15
	1967	27.470	—	—	.10	.15
	1968	8.170	—	—	.10	.15
	1969	21.730	—	—	.10	.15
	1970	35.730	—	—	.10	.15
	1971	10.000	—	—	.10	.15
	1972	35.000	—	—	.10	.15
	1973	42.500	—	—	.10	.15
	1974	30.000	—	—	.10	.15
	1975	80.000	—	—	.10	.15
	1976	18.000	—	—	.10	.15
	1977	68.500	—	—	.10	.15
	1978	—	—	—	.10	.15
	1979	—	—	—	.10	.15

2 FRANCS

10.000 gm., .900 SILVER, .2894 oz ASW

C#	Date	Mintage	VG	Fine	VF	XF
12	1834	.276	150.00	250.00	650.00	1400.
	1835	.225	150.00	300.00	700.00	1500.
	1838	.300	150.00	350.00	1200.	2250.
	1840	.236	130.00	400.00	1000.	1800.
	1841	—	300.00	650.00	2250.	3250.
	1843	.735	75.00	200.00	550.00	1250.
	1844	.483	75.00	200.00	525.00	1250.

C#	Date	Mintage	VG	Fine	VF	XF
18	1848	—	300.00	700.00	2000.	3500.
	1849	—	350.00	1200.	2500.	4500.
	1865	—	400.00	1200.	2800.	5000.

NOTE: The above dates were not officially released into circulation.

10.0000 gm., .835 SILVER, .2685 oz ASW
Obv. French leg: DES BELGES

Y#	Date	Mintage	Fine	VF	XF	Unc
7	1866	1.942	10.00	25.00	125.00	400.00
	1867	3.789	10.00	20.00	100.00	350.00
	1868	2.164	12.00	35.00	175.00	500.00

Obv. Flemish leg: DER BELGEN

Y#	Date	Mintage	Fine	VF	XF	Unc
7.1	1887	.150	100.00	300.00	900.00	1500.

50th Anniversary Independence
Rev. French leg: DE BELGIQUE

Y#	Date	Mintage	Fine	VF	XF	Unc
10	1880	.118	40.00	80.00	200.00	400.00

Obv. French leg: DES BELGES

Y#	Date	Mintage	Fine	VF	XF	Unc
18	1904	.400	12.50	22.50	35.00	70.00
	1909	1.088	BV	8.00	12.50	30.00

Obv. Flemish leg: DER BELGEN

Y#	Date	Mintage	Fine	VF	XF	Unc
18.1	1904	.400	12.50	22.50	35.00	70.00
	1909	1.088	BV	8.00	12.50	30.00

Obv. French leg: DES BELGES

Y#	Date	Mintage	Fine	VF	XF	Unc
35	1910	.800	BV	8.00	12.50	30.00
	1911	1.000	BV	8.00	12.50	30.00
	1912	.375	8.00	12.00	20.00	40.00

Obv. Flemish leg: DER BELGEN

Y#	Date	Mintage	Fine	VF	XF	Unc
35.1	1911	1.775	BV	8.00	12.50	30.00
	1912	.375	8.00	12.00	20.00	40.00

NICKEL
Obv. French leg: BELGIQUE

Y#	Date	Mintage	Fine	VF	XF	Unc
29	1923	7.500	.20	.40	1.00	2.25
	1930	1.250	25.00	40.00	50.00	75.00

Obv. Flemish leg: BELGIE

Y#	Date	Mintage	Fine	VF	XF	Unc
29.1	1923	6.500	.20	.40	1.00	2.25
	1924	1.000	25.00	40.00	50.00	80.00
	1930/20	1.252	30.00	45.00	55.00	85.00
	1930	Inc. Ab.	25.00	40.00	50.00	75.00

ZINC COATED STEEL
Allied Occupation Issue
Obv. French leg: BELGIQUE-BELGIE

Y#	Date	Mintage	Fine	VF	XF	Unc
56	1944	25.000	.30	.50	1.00	1.50

NOTE: Made in U.S.A. on blanks for 1943 cents.

2-1/2 FRANCS

.900 SILVER

Obv. French leg: ROI DES BELGES

C#	Date	Mintage	VG	Fine	VF	XF
19	1848	.559	55.00	110.00	250.00	500.00
	1849	2.003	35.00	75.00	200.00	350.00

Larger head

C#	Date	Mintage	VG	Fine	VF	XF
19.1	1848	Restrikes	175.00	450.00	1500.	2250.
	1849	—	50.00	90.00	250.00	400.00
	1850	.159	150.00	400.00	1100.	2000.
	1865	—	300.00	1250.	2500.	4000.

NOTE: Coins dated 1865 were not released into circulation.

5 FRANCS

25.0000 gm., .900 SILVER, .7234 oz ASW

C#	Date	Mintage	VG	Fine	VF	XF
13	1832	.037	125.00	300.00	600.00	900.00
	1833	1.126	25.00	60.00	125.00	225.00
	1834	.350	75.00	275.00	500.00	700.00
	1835	.370	75.00	275.00	500.00	700.00
	1838	5,203	2000.	3000.	6000.	7500.
	1840	—	2000.	3000.	6000.	7500.
	1841	—	2000.	3000.	6000.	7500.
	1844	.080	125.00	350.00	650.00	1000.
	1847	.700	35.00	125.00	200.00	500.00
	1848	2.516	22.00	35.00	70.00	160.00
	1849	3.014	22.00	35.00	60.00	125.00

NOTE: Coins dated 1838, 1840 and 1841 were not officially released into circulation.

C#	Date	Mintage	VG	Fine	VF	XF
20	1849	3.909	BV	35.00	50.00	80.00
	1850 with dot above date					
		5.265	BV	35.00	50.00	80.00
	1850 w/o dot above date					
		Inc. Ab.	—	—	—	—
	1851/50	3.708	BV	35.00	50.00	80.00
	1851 with dot above date					
		Inc. Ab.	BV	35.00	50.00	80.00
	1851 w/o dot above date					
		Inc. Ab.	—	—	—	—
	1852/1	4.605	BV	35.00	50.00	80.00
	1852	Inc. Ab.	BV	35.00	50.00	80.00
	1853	2.427	25.00	40.00	65.00	100.00
	1858	.018	100.00	200.00	400.00	700.00
	1865/55 broken M in PREMIER					
		.907	25.00	45.00	60.00	120.00
	1865/55	Inc. Ab.	25.00	45.00	60.00	130.00
	1865	Inc. Ab.	25.00	45.00	60.00	100.00
	1865 with dot after F on reverse					
		Inc. Ab.	25.00	50.00	75.00	125.00

Obv: Smaller head, engravers name near rim, below truncation. Rev: Similar to C#20.

Y#	Date	Mintage	Fine	VF	XF	Unc
8	1865	Inc. 1867	350.00	450.00	650.00	1100.
	1866	Inc. 1867	375.00	550.00	750.00	1200.
	1866 with dot after F on reverse					
		Inc. 1867	375.00	550.00	750.00	1200.
	1867	3.693	22.00	35.00	50.00	85.00
	1867 with dot after F on reverse					
		Inc. Ab.	25.00	50.00	75.00	125.00
	1868	6.751	BV	22.00	30.00	60.00
	1869	12.658	BV	22.00	30.00	60.00
	1870	10.468	BV	22.00	30.00	60.00
	1871	4.783	BV	22.00	30.00	60.00
	1872	2.045	BV	25.00	40.00	75.00
	1873	22.341	BV	22.00	30.00	60.00
	1874	2.400	BV	25.00	40.00	75.00
	1875	2.980	BV	22.00	35.00	70.00
	1876	2.160	BV	25.00	40.00	75.00

Obv: Larger head, engravers name below truncation.

Y#	Date	Mintage	Fine	VF	XF	Unc
8.1	1865	—	300.00	800.00	1350.	1800.
	1866	—	375.00	1000.	1900.	2650.
	1867	—	250.00	700.00	1250.	1650.
	1868	—	350.00	850.00	1600.	2300.

5 FRANCS

(= Un (1) Belga)

NICKEL
Obv. French leg: DES BELGES
Rev: Value UN BELGA

Y#	Date	Mintage	Fine	VF	XF	Unc
30	1930	1.600	2.00	3.00	4.00	9.00
	1931	9.032	1.00	1.50	2.50	7.50

Y#	Date	Mintage	Fine	VF	XF	Unc
30	1932	3.600	3.00	4.00	5.00	10.00
	1933	1.387	7.50	10.00	12.50	20.00
	1934	1.000	50.00	80.00	115.00	150.00

Obv. Flemish leg: DER BELGEN
Rev: Value EEN BELGA

Y#	Date	Mintage	Fine	VF	XF	Unc
30.1	1930	5.086	1.00	1.50	2.50	7.50
	1931	5.336	1.00	1.50	2.50	7.50
	1932	3.683	3.00	4.00	5.00	10.00
	1933	2.514	7.50	10.00	12.50	20.00

5 FRANCS

NICKEL
Rev. French leg: BELGIQUE

Y#	Date	Mintage	Fine	VF	XF	Unc
47	1936	.650	12.50	15.00	20.00	40.00
	1937	1.847	10.00	12.50	17.50	35.00

Rev. Flemish leg: BELGIE

Y#	Date	Mintage	Fine	VF	XF	Unc
47.1	1936	2.498	7.50	10.00	12.50	25.00

Obv. French leg: BELGIQUE-BELGIE

Y#	Date	Mintage	Fine	VF	XF	Unc
46	1938 with incuse edge lettering under milling					
		11.419	.35	.60	1.00	2.00
	1938 milled edge without lettering					
		Inc. Ab.	40.00	75.00	150.00	250.00

Obv. Flemish leg: BELGIE-BELGIQUE

Y#	Date	Mintage	Fine	VF	XF	Unc
46.1	1938 edge lettering separated by a crown					
		3.200	20.00	30.00	50.00	75.00
	1938 edge lettering separated by a star					
		Inc. Ab.	25.00	35.00	55.00	85.00
	1939 edge lettering separated by a crown					
		8.219	25.00	35.00	55.00	85.00
	1939 edge lettering separated by a star					
		Inc. Ab.	.30	.50	1.00	2.00

ZINC
German Occupation WW II
Obv. French leg: DES BELGES

Y#	Date	Mintage	Fine	VF	XF	Unc
55	1941	15.200	.40	.75	2.00	4.50
	1943	16.236	.40	.75	2.00	4.50
	1944	1.868	3.00	4.00	6.00	15.00
	1945	3.200	1.00	1.50	3.00	7.50
	1946	4.452	.65	1.50	3.00	7.50
	1947	3.100	15.00	27.50	50.00	100.00

Obv. Flemish leg: DER BELGEN

Y#	Date	Mintage	Fine	VF	XF	Unc
55.1	1941	27.544	.30	.65	1.50	3.50
	1945	3.200	35.00	45.00	60.00	100.00
	1946	4.000	150.00	250.00	400.00	650.00
	1947	.036	140.00	235.00	375.00	600.00

COPPER-NICKEL
Obv. French leg: BELGIQUE

Y#	Date	Mintage	Fine	VF	XF	Unc
58	1948	5.304	—	.15	.25	3.00
	1949	38.752	—	.15	.25	1.00
	1950	23.948	—	.15	.25	1.00
	1958	9.088	—	.15	.25	1.00
	1961	6.000	—	.15	.25	1.00
	1962	6.576	—	.15	.25	1.00
	1963	11.144	—	.15	.25	.40
	1964	3.520	—	.15	.25	.40
	1965	11.988	—	.15	.25	.35
	1966	6.772	—	.15	.25	.40
	1967	13.268	—	.15	.25	.40
	1968	5.192	—	.15	.25	.35
	1969	22.235	—	.15	.25	.40
	1970	2.000	—	.15	.25	.45
	1971	15.000	—	.15	.25	.40
	1972	17.500	—	.15	.25	.40
	1973	10.000	—	.15	.25	.40
	1974	25.000	—	.20	.30	.40
	1975	34.000	—	.20	.30	.40
	1976	7.500	—	.20	.30	.40
	1977	22.500	—	.20	.30	.40
	1978	—	—	.20	.30	.40
	1979	—	—	.20	.30	.40

Obv. Flemish leg: BELGIE

Y#	Date	Mintage	Fine	VF	XF	Unc
58.1	1948	4.800	—	.15	.25	3.00
	1949	31.500	—	.15	.25	1.00
	1950	34.728	—	.15	.25	1.00
	1958	2.672	—	.15	.25	3.00
	1960	5.896	—	.15	.25	1.00
	1961	4.120	—	.15	.25	1.00
	1962	7,624	—	.15	.25	1.00
	1963	6.136	—	.15	.25	.40
	1964	8.128	—	.15	.25	.35
	1965	9.956	—	.15	.25	.35
	1966	7.136	—	.15	.25	.40
	1967	16.132	—	.15	.25	.40
	1968	3.200	—	.15	.25	.40
	1969	21.500	—	.15	.25	.40
	1970	2.000	—	.15	.25	.45
	1971	15.000	—	.15	.25	.40
	1972	17.500	—	.15	.25	.40
	1973	10.000	—	.15	.25	.40
	1974	25.000	—	.20	.30	.40
	1975	34.000	—	.20	.30	.40
	1976	7.500	—	.20	.30	.40
	1977	22.500	—	.20	.30	.40
	1978	—	—	—	—	—
	1979	—	—	—	—	—

10 FRANCS

3.2258 gm., .900 GOLD, .0933 oz AGW

C#	Date	Mintage	Fine	VF	XF	Unc
24	1849	.037	500.00	1250.	2000.	2750.
	1850	.063	450.00	1100.	1850.	2600.

NOTE: 54,890 pcs. dated 1849 and 1850 were withdrawn from circulation.

(= Twee (2) Belga)

NICKEL
Independence Centennial Commemorative
Rev. French leg: BELGIQUE

Y#	Date	Mintage	Fine	VF	XF	Unc
31	1930	2.699	60.00	100.00	125.00	175.00

Rev. Flemish leg: BELGIE

Y#	Date	Mintage	Fine	VF	XF	Unc
31.1	1930	3.000	65.00	120.00	150.00	200.00

Rev. French leg: BELGIQUE

Y#	Date	Mintage	Fine	VF	XF	Unc
67	1969	22.235	.25	.35	.55	.75
	1970	9.500	.25	.35	.55	.75
	1971	15.000	.25	.35	.55	.75
	1972	10.000	.25	.35	.55	.75
	1973	10.000	.25	.35	.55	.75
	1974	5.000	.40	.50	.60	.75
	1975	5.000	.40	.50	.60	.75
	1976	7.500	.40	.50	.60	.75
	1977	7.000	.40	.50	.60	.75
	1978	—	—	—	—	—
	1979	—	—	—	—	—

Rev. Flemish leg: BELGIE

Y#	Date	Mintage	Fine	VF	XF	Unc
67.1	1969	21.500	.25	.35	.55	.75
	1970	10.000	.25	.35	.55	.75
	1971	15.000	.25	.35	.55	.75
	1972	10.000	.25	.35	.55	.75
	1973	10.000	.25	.35	.55	.75
	1974	5.000	.40	.50	.60	.75
	1975	5.000	.40	.50	.60	.75
	1976	7.500	.40	.50	.60	.75
	1977	7.000	.40	.50	.60	.75
	1978	—	—	—	—	—
	1979	—	—	—	—	—

20 FRANCS

6.4516 gm., .900 GOLD, .1867 oz AGW

C#	Date	Mintage	Fine	VF	XF	Unc
26	1864	—	1750.	3000.	3750.	5000.
	1865	1.026	BV	BV	125.00	140.00

Y#	Date	Mintage	Fine	VF	XF	Unc
19	1866	—	1000.	1500.	2500.	3500.
	1867	1.341	BV	BV	125.00	140.00
	1868	1.382	BV	BV	125.00	140.00
	1869	1.234	BV	BV	125.00	140.00
	1870	3.191	BV	BV	125.00	140.00
		Obv: Smaller bust				
19.1	1870	Inc. Ab.	BV	BV	125.00	140.00
	1871	2.259	BV	BV	125.00	140.00
	1874	3.046	BV	BV	125.00	140.00
	1875	4.134	BV	BV	125.00	140.00
	1876	2.070	BV	BV	125.00	140.00
	1877	5.906	BV	BV	125.00	140.00
	1878	2.505	BV	BV	125.00	140.00
	1882	.522	BV	BV	125.00	140.00

Obv. French leg: DES BELGES

Y#	Date	Mintage	Fine	VF	XF	Unc
37	1914	.125	BV	125.00	135.00	150.00

Obv. Flemish leg: DER BELGEN

Y#	Date	Mintage	Fine	VF	XF	Unc
37.1	1914	.125	BV	125.00	135.00	150.00

(= Quatre (4) Belgas)

NICKEL
Obv. French leg: DES BELGES

Y#	Date	Mintage	Fine	VF	XF	Unc
32	1931	3.957	60.00	100.00	125.00	175.00
	1932	5.472	60.00	100.00	125.00	175.00
		Obv. Flemish leg: DER BELGEN				
32.1	1931	2.600	60.00	100.00	125.00	175.00
32.1	1932	6.950	60.00	100.00	125.00	175.00

11.0000 gm., .680 SILVER, .2405 oz ASW
Obv. French leg: DES BELGES

Y#	Date	Mintage	Fine	VF	XF	Unc
36	1933	.200	50.00	75.00	100.00	125.00
	1934	12.300	BV	BV	7.50	8.50

Obv. Flemish leg: DER BELGEN

Y#	Date	Mintage	Fine	VF	XF	Unc
36.1	1933	.200	50.00	75.00	100.00	125.00
	1934	12.300	BV	BV	7.50	8.50

Y#	Date	Mintage	Fine	VF	XF	Unc
49	1934	1.250	BV	7.50	10.00	20.00
	1935	10.760	BV	BV	7.50	8.50

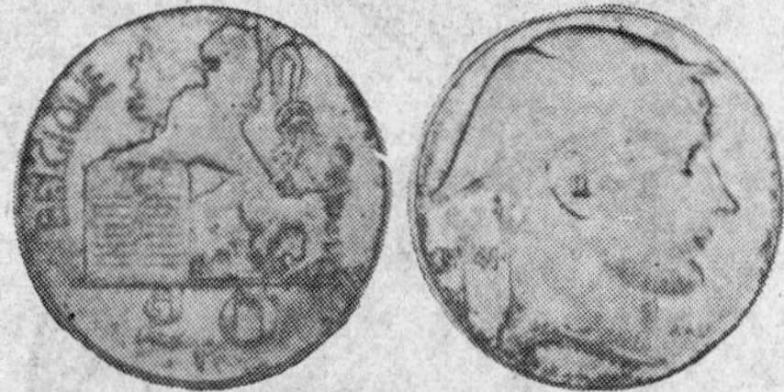

8.0000 gm., .835 SILVER, .2148 oz ASW
Obv: French leg: BELGIQUE

Y#	Date	Mintage	Fine	VF	XF	Unc
59	1949	4.600	BV	BV	6.50	7.50
	1950	12.957	BV	BV	6.50	7.50
	1953	3.952	BV	BV	7.50	12.50
	1954	4.835	15.00	20.00	40.00	60.00
	1955	1.730	200.00	500.00	700.00	1000.

Obv. Flemish leg: BELGIE

Y#	Date	Mintage	Fine	VF	XF	Unc
59.1	1949	5.545	BV	BV	6.50	7.50
	1950	—	300.00	450.00	700.00	1000.
	1951	7.885	BV	BV	6.50	7.50
	1953	6.625	BV	BV	6.50	10.00
	1954	5.323	15.00	20.00	40.00	60.00
	1955	2.760	20.00	40.00	75.00	125.00

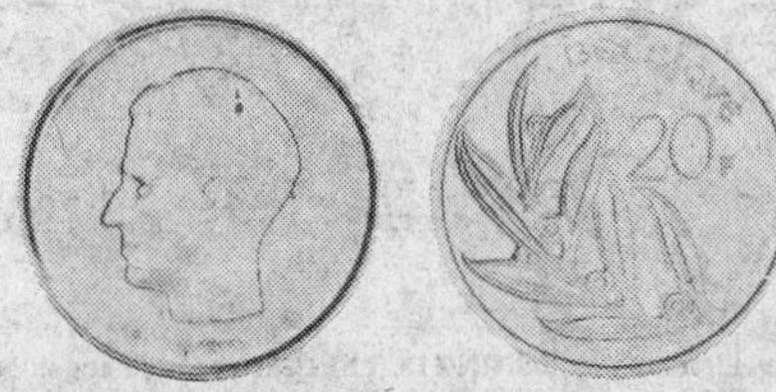

BRONZE
Rev. French leg: BELGIQUE

Y#	Date	Mintage	Fine	VF	XF	Unc
A67	1980	—	—	1.00	1.40	2.00

Rev. Flemish leg: BELGIE

Y#	Date	Mintage	Fine	VF	XF	Unc
A67.1	1980	—	—	1.00	1.40	2.00

25 FRANCS

8.0645 gm., .900 GOLD, .2333 oz AGW

C#	Date	Mintage	Fine	VF	XF	Unc
25	1848	.321	400.00	800.00	1500.	2000.
	1849	.150	450.00	1000.	1650.	2000.
	1850	.074	550.00	1250.	2000.	2500.

50 FRANCS

22.0000 gm., .680 SILVER, .4810 oz ASW
Brussels Exposition And Railway Centennial
Obv. French leg: DE FER BELGES
Rev. leg: DE BELGIQUE

Y#	Date	Mintage	Fine	VF	XF	Unc
48	1935	.140	100.00	140.00	200.00	300.00

Obv. Flemish leg: DER BELGISCHE
Rev. leg: BELGIE

Y#	Date	Mintage	Fine	VF	XF	Unc
48a	1935	.140	125.00	225.00	300.00	400.00

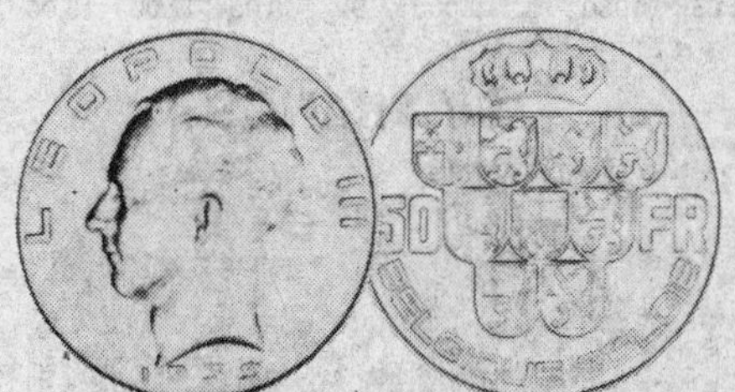

12.5000 gm., .835 SILVER, .3356 oz ASW
Obv. French leg: BELGIQUE: BELGIE

Y#	Date	Mintage	Fine	VF	XF	Unc
50	1939	1.000	10.00	12.00	15.00	20.00
	1940	.631	12.00	15.00	20.00	30.00
		Obv. Flemish leg: BELGIE: BELGIQUE				
50a	1939	1.000	10.00	12.00	15.00	20.00
	1940	.631	12.00	15.00	20.00	30.00

Obv. French leg: BELGIQUE

Y#	Date	Mintage	Fine	VF	XF	Unc
60	1948	2.000	BV	BV	10.00	12.50
	1949	4.354	BV	BV	10.00	12.50
	1951	2.904	BV	BV	10.00	12.50
	1954	3.232	BV	BV	10.00	15.00

Obv. Flemish leg: BELGIE

Y#	Date	Mintage	Fine	VF	XF	Unc
60a	1948	3.000	BV	BV	10.00	12.50
	1950	4.110	BV	BV	10.00	12.50
	1951	1.698	BV	BV	10.00	12.50
	1954	2.978	BV	BV	10.00	12.50

Brussels Fair
Obv. French leg: DES BELGES

Y#	Date	Mintage	Fine	VF	XF	Unc
64	1958	.476	BV	10.00	12.00	15.00

Obv. Flemish leg: DER BELGEN

Y#	Date	Mintage	Fine	VF	XF	Unc
64a	1958	.382	BV	10.00	12.00	15.00

King Baudouin Marriage

Y#	Date	Mintage	Fine	VF	XF	Unc
65	1960	.500	BV	10.00	12.00	15.00

100 FRANCS

18.0000 gm., .835 SILVER, .4832 oz ASW
Obv. French leg: BELGIQUE

Y#	Date	Mintage	Fine	VF	XF	Unc
61	1948	1.000	BV	BV	15.00	17.50
61	1949	.106	25.00	50.00	65.00	80.00
	1950	2.807	BV	BV	15.00	17.50
	1954	2.517	BV	BV	15.00	17.50

Obv. Flemish leg: BELGIE

Y#	Date	Mintage	Fine	VF	XF	Unc
61a	1948	1.000	BV	BV	15.00	17.50
	1949	2.271	BV	BV	15.00	17.50
	1950	—	250.00	500.00	1000.	1250.
	1951	4.691	BV	BV	15.00	17.50

250 FRANCS

25.2000 gm., .835 SILVER, .6765 oz ASW
Obv. French leg: ROI DES BELGIES, reeded edge.

Y#	Date	Mintage	Fine	VF	XF	Unc
68	1976	1.000	BV	21.00	22.50	25.00

Stars on edge

Y#	Date	Mintage	Fine	VF	XF	Unc
68b	1976	.100	—	—	Proof	35.00

Obv. Flemish leg: KONING DER BELGEN, reeded edge.

Y#	Date	Mintage	Fine	VF	XF	Unc
68a	1976	1.000	BV	21.00	22.50	25.00

Stars on edge

Y#	Date	Mintage	Fine	VF	XF	Unc
68c	1976	.100	—	—	Proof	35.00

NCLT ISSUES

MEDALLIC ISSUES

5 CENTIMES

COPPER
25th Anniversary of Independence
Rev. French leg: .....DE L'INAUGURATION DU ROI.

KM#	Date	Mintage	VG	Fine	VF	XF
M1	1856	.214	2.00	3.50	10.00	15.00

Rev. Flemish leg: .....VAN B'KONINGS.

KM#	Date	Mintage	VG	Fine	VF	XF
M2	1856	3,000	15.00	60.00	150.00	300.00

BRONZE
Rev. French LEG: .....DE L'INAUGURATION DU ROI.
DU ROI.

KM#	Date	Mintage	VG	Fine	VF	XF
M3	1856	4,776	12.50	50.00	120.00	250.00

Rev. Flemish leg: .....VAN B'KONINGS.

KM#	Date	Mintage	VG	Fine	VF	XF
M4	1856	1,160	30.00	150.00	300.00	500.00

10 CENTIMES

COPPER
Marriage of Duke and Duchess of Brabant

KM#	Date	Mintage	VG	Fine	VF	XF
M5	1853	.104	2.00	5.00	10.00	17.50

2 FRANCS

SILVER
25th Anniversary of Independence
Rev. French leg: .....DE L'INAUGURATION DU ROI.

KM#	Date	Mintage	VG	Fine	VF	XF
M6	1856	.012	50.00	80.00	175.00	300.00

Rev. Flemish leg: .....VAN B'KONINGS.

KM#	Date	Mintage	VG	Fine	VF	XF
M7	1856	1,898	150.00	450.00	900.00	1900.

5 FRANCS

.900 SILVER
Marriage of the Duke and Duchess of Brabant
Obv: Bare head of Leopold I left.
Rev: Accolated busts of the Duke and Duchess of Brabant.

KM#	Date	Mintage	VG	Fine	VF	XF
M8	1853	.032	25.00	75.00	140.00	250.00

SILVER

Y#	Date	Mintage	Fine	VF	XF	Unc
M9	1880	—	85.00	150.00	250.00	350.00
			COPPER			
M9a	1880	—	20.00	30.00	50.00	80.00
			GOLD			
M9b	1880	—	—	—	Rare	—

40 FRANCS

GOLD
25th Anniversary of Independence
Rev. French leg: .....DE L'INAUGURATION.

KM#	Date	Mintage	VG	Fine	VF	XF
M10	1856	449 pcs.	1000.	1750.	3500.	5500.

100 FRANCS

.900 GOLD
Marriage of Duke and Duchess of Brabant
Similar to 5 Francs, KM#2.

KM#	Date	Mintage	Fine	VF	XF	Unc
M11	1853	482 pcs.	2000.	2750.	4000.	6000.

PATTERNS

KM#	Date	Mintage	Identification	Mkt.Val.
1	1832	—	1 Centime, Copper	—
2	1834	—	20 Francs, .900 Gold	6000.
3	1834	*10pcs.	40 Francs, .900 Gold, lettered edge	10,000.
4	1834	*50 pcs.	40 Francs, .900 Gold, plain edge	7500.
5	1835	—	5 Centimes, Copper	—
6	1835	—	10 Centimes, Copper	—

KM#	Date	Mintage	Identification	Mkt.Val.
7	1835	—	20 Francs, .900 Gold	8000.

KM#	Date	Mintage	Identification	Mkt.Val.
8	1835	*10 pcs.	40 Francs, .900 Gold, lettered edge	10,000.
9	1835	*50 pcs.	40 Francs, .900 Gold, plain edge	—
10	1837	—	1 Centime, Copper	—
11	1837	—	2 Centimes, Copper	—
12	1838	—	1 Centime, Copper	—
13	1838	—	2 Centimes, Copper	—
14	1838	—	5 Centimes, Copper	—
15	1838	—	10 Centimes, Copper	—
16	1838	—	1/4 Franc, Silver	—
17	1838	—	20 Francs, .900 Gold	12,000.
18	1838	*10 pcs.	40 Francs, .900 Gold, lettered edge	12,000.
19	1838	*50 pcs.	40 Francs, .900 Gold, plain edge	10,000.
20	1840	—	5 Francs, Silver	—
21	1841	—	1 Centime, Copper	—
22	1841	—	10 Centimes, Copper	—
23	1841	—	1/4 Franc, Silver	—
24	1841	—	1/2 Franc, Silver	—
25	1841	—	1 Franc, Silver	—
26	1841	—	2 Francs, Silver	—
27	1841	—	5 Francs, Silver	—
28	1841	—	20 Francs, .900 Gold	10,000.
29	1841	*10 pcs.	40 Francs, .900 Gold, lettered edge	—
30	1841	*50 pcs.	40 Francs, .900 Gold, plain edge	—
31	1842	—	5 Francs, Silver	—
32	1843	—	1 Franc, Silver	—

KM#	Date	Mintage	Identification	Mkt.Val.
33	1847	—	5 Francs, Gilt Copper	—
34	1847	—	5 Francs, Silver	—

KM#	Date	Mintage	Identification	Mkt.Val.
35	1847	—	5 Francs, Gilt Copper	—
36	1847	—	5 Francs, Gilt Copper	—

KM#	Date	Mintage	Identification	Mkt.Val.
37	1847	—	5 Francs, Gilt Copper	—
38	1847	—	25 Francs, .900 Gold	—
39	1849	—	1/4 Franc, Silver	—
40	1849	—	2 Francs, Silver	—
41	1855	—	1 Centime, Copper	—
42	1859	—	2 Centimes, Aluminum	—

KM#	Date	Mintage	Identification	Mkt.Val.
43	1859	—	20 Centimes, Silver, Piefort	—
44	1859	—	20 Centimes, Silver, Double Piefort	—

KM#	Date	Mintage	Identification	Mkt.Val.
45	1859	—	1 Franc, Silver	—
46	1860	—	20 Centimes, Bronze, Rev. Uniface	—
47	1860	—	20 Centimes, Brass Coated Nickel	—
48	1860	—	20 Centimes, Nickel	—
49	1861	—	5 Centimes, Copper	—
50	1861	—	20 Centimes, Copper	—
51	1861	—	20 Centimes, Nickel by Breamt	—
52	1861	—	20 Centimes, Nickel by Wiener	—
53	1865	—	2 Francs, Silver	—
54	ND(1866)	—	2 Francs, Copper, Obv. Uniface	—
55	1867	—	10 Francs, Gold	3000.
56	1870	—	10 Francs, Gold	3000.
57	1872	—	2 Centimes, Copper	—
58	1872	—	2 Centimes, Pewter, Obv. Uniface	—
59	1872	—	2 Centimes, Pewter, Rev. Uniface	—
60	1882	—	1 Centime, Copper	—
61	1887	—	1 Centime, Copper	—
62	1892	—	1 Centime, Copper	—
63	1892	—	5 Centime, Copper-Nickel	—
64	1894	—	10 Centimes, Nickel	—

KM#	Date	Mintage	Identification	Mkt.Val.
65	1901	—	5 Centimes, Pewter	—
66	1901	—	5 Centimes, Brass Plated Nickel	—
67	1901	—	10 Centimes, Copper-Nickel	—
68	1901	—	50 Centimes, Silver	—
69	1901	—	1 Franc, Silver	—
70	1901	—	2 Francs, Silver	—
71	1903	—	1 Franc, Pewter, Rectangle Planchet, Rev. Uniface	—
72	1904	—	1 Franc, Pewter, Rectangle Planchet, Rev. Uniface	—
73	1907	—	25 Centimes, Copper-Nickel	—
74	1911	—	10 Centimes, Copper, Not Holed	—
75	1911	—	10 Centimes, Brass, Holed	—
76	1911	—	10 Centimes, Copper-Nickel, Not Holed	—
77	1911	—	10 Francs, Gold	2000.

KM#	Date	Mintage	Identification	Mkt.Val.
78	1911	—	20 Francs, Brass Plated Copper	—
79	1911	—	20 Francs, Nickel	—
80	1911	—	20 Francs, Gold, Error Obv.	—
81	1911	—	20 Francs, Aluminum, Error Obv.	—
82	1911	—	20 Francs, Gold	—
83	1911	—	20 Francs, Pewter	—
84	1911	—	100 Francs, Aluminum-Nickel	—

KM#	Date	Mintage	Identification	Mkt.Val.
85	1912	—	100 Francs, Gold	20,000.
86	ND(1915)	—	1 Centime, Zinc	—
87	1915	—	25 Centimes, Composition	—
88	1922	—	50 Centimes, Bronze	—

KM#	Date	Mintage	Identification	Mkt.Val.
89	1926	—	5 Francs, Red Bronze	—
90	1929	—	5 Francs, Nickel	—
91	1929	—	5 Francs, Similor (Copper and Zinc)	—
92	1930	—	20 Francs, Silver	—
93	1931	—	1 Franc, Nickel	—
94	1931	—	20 Francs, Bronze	—
95	1932	—	5 Centimes, Copper-Nickel	—

KM#	Date	Mintage	Identification	Mkt.Val.
96	1935	—	40 Francs, .680 Silver	4000.
97	1936	—	5 Francs, Nickel	—

KM#	Date	Mintage	Identification	Mkt.Val.
98	1938	—	20 Francs, Silver	—
99	1949	—	50 Francs, Bronze	—
100	1949	—	100 Francs, Silver	—
101	1949	—	100 Francs, Silver	—
102	1949	—	1000 Francs, Red Copper, Obv. Klippe	—
103	1949	—	1000 Francs, Yellow Copper, Obv. Klippe	—
104	1949	—	1000 Francs, Red Copper, Rev. Klippe	—
105	1949	—	1000 Francs, Yellow Copper, Rev. Klippe	—
106	1949	—	1000 Francs, Silver, Rev. Klippe	—
107	1949	—	1000 Francs, Bronze, plain edge	—
108	1949	—	1000 Francs, Silver	—
109	1949	—	1000 Francs, Gold	—
110	ND(1949)	—	1000 Francs, Bronze	—
111	1949	—	1000 Francs, Bronze, milled edge	—

FLEUR DE COIN SETS

STANDARD METALS

KM#	Date	Mintage	Identification	Issue Price	Mkt. Val.
—	1976(5)	15,000	Y57,58,63,66,67FL	17.50	—
—	1976(5)	Inc. Ab.	Y57,58,63,66,67FR	17.50	—
—	1977(8)	50,000	Y57,57a,58,58a,63,63a,67,67a	—	—
—	1978(8)	50,000	Y57,57a,58,58a,63,63a,67,67a	4.00	—
—	1979(8)	50,000	Y57,57a,58,58a,63,63a,67,67a	4.00	—

MINT SETS

STANDARD METALS

KM#	Date	Mintage	Identification	Issue Price	Mkt. Val.
S1	1970(5)	10,000	Y57,58,63,66,67 FL	.60	20.00
S2	1970(5)	10,000	Y57,58,63,66,67 FR	.60	20.00
S3	1971(5)	20,000	Y57,58,63,66,67 FL	.63	8.00
S4	1971(5)	20,000	Y57,58,63,66,67 FR	.63	8.00
S5	1972(5)	10,000	Y57,58,63,66,67 FL	.70	8.00
S6	1972(5)	10,000	Y57,58,63,66,67 FR	.70	8.00
S7	1973(5)	31,773	Y57,58,63,66,67 FL	.80	8.00
S8	1973(5)	31,773	Y57,58,63,66,67 FR	.80	8.00
S9	1974(5)	39,609	Y57,58,63,66,67 FL	1.10	6.00
S10	1974(5)	39,609	Y57,58,63,66,67 FR	1.10	5.50
S11	1975(10)	100,000	Y57,58,63,66,67 FL & FR	2.50	3.00
S12	1976(10)	15,000	Y57,58,63,67,68 FL & Fr	20.75	35.00
S13	1977(8)	50,000	Y57,58,63,67 FL & Fr	2.65	3.00
S14	1978(8)	50,000	Y57,58,63,67 Fl & Fr	—	—
S15	1979(8)	50,000	Y57,58,63,67 Fl & Fr	—	—

PROOF SETS

STANDARD METALS

KM#	Date	Mintage	Identification	Issue Price	Mkt. Val.
101	1976(2)	15,000	Y68b & 68c	36.75	70.00

ANTWERP (ANVERS)

Antwerp, the second largest town in Belgium, grew from a tiny walled marquisate under Godfrey of Bouillon one of the leaders of the First Crusade in the 11th century to the chief port and commercial center of 15th-century western Europe. Not only was it an acknowledged leader in trade and commerce, but also in the arts. The following centuries carried as much tragedy as triumph. Antwerp was plundered by Spain and its Protestant citizens murdered during the religious troubles of the 16th century. It served as the chief military harbor of Napoleon during the fall of the First Empire. It was the scene of the most famous siege of World War I, and was repeatedly battered by V-bombs during World War II. The French-auspice Antwerp coins of 1814-15 were a necessity money issued while Antwerp, under General Carnot, was besieged by the Allies.

The following coins were minted by the French while besieged in Anvers, Belgium. Some have the monogram N for Napoleon, others have a double L monogram for Louis XVIII of France.

5 CENTIMES

NAPOLEON

COPPER, 34mm

Obv: N in wreath, date below. Rev: Value.

C#	Date	Mintage	VG	Fine	VF	XF
1.1	1814	180 pcs.	100.00	250.00	500.00	1000.
		29mm				
1.2	1814	—	6.00	15.00	35.00	75.00
		Obv: V above ribbon.				
1.3	1814	.011	4.50	12.50	30.00	60.00
		Obv: V below ribbon bow.				
1.4	1814	2,820	10.00	27.50	70.00	150.00
		Obv: JLGN on ribbon				
1.5	1814	.017	7.00	15.00	40.00	75.00

LOUIS XVIII

C#	Date	Mintage	VG	Fine	VF	XF
		Type I obv: Ornate LL monogram.				
3.1	1814	.010	10.00	22.50	50.00	100.00
		Obv: V below ribbon bow.				
3.2	1814	—	15.00	37.50	85.00	175.00
		Obv: JLGP on ribbon				
3.3	1814	.031	6.50	17.50	45.00	80.00

C#	Date	Mintage	VG	Fine	VF	XF
		Type II obv: Plain LL monogram, JLGP on ribbon.				
3.4	1814	—	6.00	14.00	32.50	80.00
		Obv: V below ribbon				
3.5	1814	—	6.00	14.00	32.50	80.00

10 CENTIMES

NAPOLEON

COPPER
JEAN LOUIS GAGNEPAIN on ribbon, pearls on N.

C#	Date	Mintage	VG	Fine	VF	XF
2.1	1814	.018	7.50	20.00	70.00	140.00

Obv: Shading on N. Rev: Similar to C#2.1.

C#	Date	Mintage	VG	Fine	VF	XF
2.2	1814	7,500	10.00	22.50	55.00	150.00

Obv: R below ribbon bow.

C#	Date	Mintage	VG	Fine	VF	XF
2.3	1814	.066	5.00	12.50	30.00	70.00

Obv: W above ribbon bow. Rev: Similar to C#2.1.

C#	Date	Mintage	VG	Fine	VF	XF
2.4	1814	.029	3.50	8.00	22.50	60.00

LOUIS XVIII

Type I obv: Ornate LL monogram.

C#	Date	Mintage	VG	Fine	VF	XF
4.1	1814	.020	6.50	16.50	40.00	90.00

Type II obv: Plain LL monogram.

C#	Date	Mintage	VG	Fine	VF	XF
4.2	1814	—	6.50	14.00	35.00	90.00

Obv: R below ribbon bow.

C#	Date	Mintage	VG	Fine	VF	XF
4.3	1814	.053	6.00	13.50	32.50	75.00

Obv: JEAN LOUIS GAGNEPAIN on ribbon, R below bow.

C#	Date	Mintage	VG	Fine	VF	XF
4.4	1814	.035	9.00	22.50	60.00	110.00

GHENT

A city in northwest Belgium dating from the 7th century. The center of the textile industry in Belgium. During the German occupation of World War I numerous emergency coins were made for the city and environs. Four denominations were made in various metals and shapes.

MONETARY SYSTEM

100 Centimes = 1 Franken

GERMAN OCCUPATION

1914-1918

50 CENTIMES

IRON
Obv: Brass and Iron. Rev: Copper plated.
Similar to KM#1a, thin '50'

KM#	Date	Mintage	Fine	VF	XF	Unc
1	1915	.512	3.00	5.00	9.00	15.00

Rev: Thick 50

KM#	Date	Mintage	Fine	VF	XF	Unc
1a	1915	Inc. Ab.	3.00	5.00	9.00	15.00

Both sides Iron, Brass-plated.

KM#	Date	Mintage	Fine	VF	XF	Unc
1b	1915	Inc. Ab.	3.00	5.00	9.00	15.00

FRANKEN

IRON
Obv: Brass. Rev: Copper plated.

KM#	Date	Mintage	Fine	VF	XF	Unc
2	1915	.370	2.75	6.00	9.00	16.00

Rev: 11. 1919 instead of 1.1. 1919.

KM#	Date	Mintage	Fine	VF	XF	Unc
2a	1915	Inc. Ab.	3.00	6.50	10.00	20.00

GILT COPPER
Square planchet, 20mm. Obv: Lion in circle, STAD GENT VILLE DE GAND around. Rev: 1915 1 FR in circle, UIT BETAALBAAR 1 JANUARI 1918 REMBOURSABLE 1 JANVIER 1920 along sides of square.

KM#	Date	Mintage	Fine	VF	XF	Unc
3	1915	—	10.00	20.00	40.00	60.00

NOTE: This coin was struck for the benefit of charity.

2 FRANKEN

IRON
Obv: Brass and Iron. Rev: Copper plated.

KM#	Date	Mintage	Fine	VF	XF	Unc
4	1915	.314	5.00	10.00	17.50	30.00

GILT COPPER
Obv: Arms in circle, STAD GENT FIDES ET AMOR around. Rev: 1928 2 FRANK in circle, UIT BETAAL BAAR JANUARI 1922 PAX ET LABOR around.

KM#	Date	Mintage	Fine	VF	XF	Unc
5	1918	—	40.00	60.00	100.00	150.00

NOTE: This coin was struck for the benefit of charity.

5 FRANKEN

IRON
Obv: Brass and Iron. Rev: Copper plated.

KM#	Date	Mintage	Fine	VF	XF	Unc
6	1917	.108	10.00	18.50	30.00	50.00

Both sides Brass plated

KM#	Date	Mintage	Fine	VF	XF	Unc
6a	1917	Inc. Ab.	10.00	18.50	30.00	50.00

Obv: As above. Rev: 1918 5 FRANK in circle, BETAAL BAAR JANUARI 1922 PAX ET LABOR around.

KM#	Date	Mintage	Fine	VF	XF	Unc
7	1918	.339	9.00	15.00	25.00	40.00

LIEGE

Bishopric

Liege was founded as a bishopric in 930. Liege received the coinage right in the 11th century. The considerable holdings of the bishopric were secularized in 1802 and are in what is now Belgium.

After the death of Johann Theodor (Bishop, 1744-1763) there were no issues of the bishops. The only coin issues were the Sede Vacante issues of 1763, 1771, 1784 and 1792.

MONETARY SYSTEM

6 Sols = 1 Escalin
48 Sols = 1 Patagon

ESCALIN

(6 Sols)

SILVER

C#	Date	Mintage	Fine	VF	XF	Unc
13	1763	1,000	35.00	50.00	100.00	250.00

C#	Date	Mintage	Fine	VF	XF	Unc
13a	1771	500 pcs.	35.00	50.00	100.00	250.00

C#	Date	Mintage	Fine	VF	XF	Unc
13b	1784	500 pcs.	35.00	50.00	100.00	250.00

C#	Date	Mintage	Fine	VF	XF	Unc
13c	1792	150 pcs.	50.00	75.00	125.00	300.00

PATAGON

(48 Sols)

SILVER

C#	Date	Mintage	Fine	VF	XF	Unc
14	1763	300 pcs.	850.00	1250.	1750.	2500.

C#	Date	Mintage	Fine	VF	XF	Unc
14a	1771	150 pcs.	500.00	850.00	1250.	2000.

C#	Date	Mintage	Fine	VF	XF	Unc
14b	1784	150 pcs.	450.00	650.00	1000.	1500.
14c	1792	150 pcs.	450.00	650.00	1000.	1500.

TRADE COINS

DUCAT

.986 GOLD

C#	Date	Mintage	Fine	VF	XF	Unc
15	1763	300 pcs.	475.00	750.00	1250.	2500.

Obv: Bust of St. Lambert in mitre left.
Rev: Crowned and mantled arms.

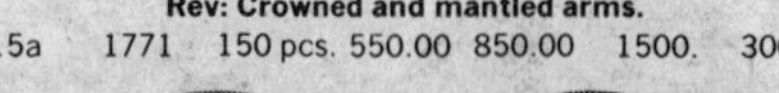

C#	Date	Mintage	Fine	VF	XF	Unc
15a	1771	150 pcs.	550.00	850.00	1500.	3000.

C#	Date	Mintage	Fine	VF	XF	Unc
15b	1784	150 pcs.	550.00	850.00	1500.	3000.

C#	Date	Mintage	Fine	VF	XF	Unc
15c	1792	150 pcs.	550.00	850.00	1500.	3000.

NCLT ISSUES

PATTERNS

KM#	Date	Mintage	Identification	Mkt.Val.
1	1843	—	Escalin, Silver, Cornelius Van Bommel	350.00
2	1852	—	Escalin, Silver, Sede Vacante	325.00
3	1852	—	Ducat, Gold, Sede Vacante	1250.

KM#	Date	Mintage	Identification	Mkt.Val.
4	1852	—	Escalin, Bronze, Theodore De Montpellier	125.00
5	1852	—	Escalin, Silver, Theodore De Montpellier	250.00

BELIZE

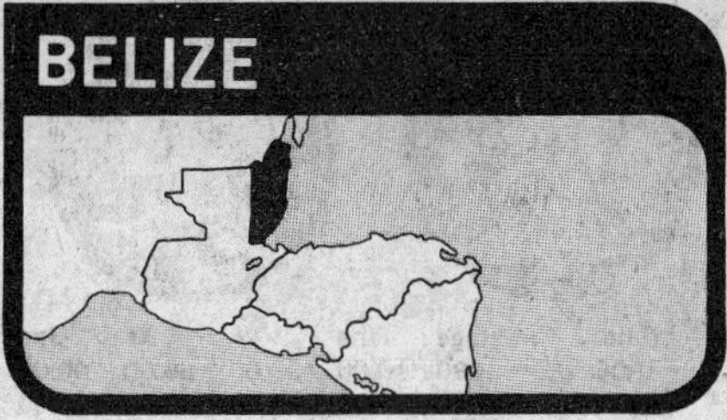

The British colony of Belize, formerly British Honduras, a self- governing dependency of the United Kingdom situated in Central America south of Mexico and east and north of Guatemala, has an area of 8,866 sq. mi. (22,963 sq. km.) and a population of 140,000. Capital: Belmopan. Sugar, citrus fruits, chicle and hard woods are exported.

The area, site of the ancient Mayan civilization, was sighted by Columbus in 1502, and settled by shipwrecked English seamen in 1638. British buccaneers settled the former capital of Belize in the 17th century. Britain claimed administrative right over the area after the emancipation of Central America from Spain, and declared it a colony subordinate to Jamaica in 1862. It was established as the separate Crown Colony of British Honduras in 1884. The anti-British People's United Party, which attained power in 1954, won a constitution, effective in 1964 which established self-government under a British appointed governor. British Honduras became Belize on June 1, 1973, following the passage of a surprise bill by the People's United Party, but the constitutional relationship with Britain remained unchanged.

In Dec. 1975, the U.N. General Assembly adopted a resolution supporting the right of the people of Belize to self-determination, and asking Britain and Guatemala to renew their negotiations on the future of Belize.

RULERS

British

MINTMARKS

H - Birmingham Mint

MONETARY SYSTEM

Circa 1810

6 Shillings 8 Pence (Jamaican)
= 8 Reales

Commencing 1884

100 Cents = 1 Dollar

BRITISH HONDURAS

Counterstamp Issues

8 REALES

(6 Shillings 8 Pence)

(1810-1818)

SILVER

c/s: Crowned script GR in rectangular indent on Mexico City 8 Reales, KM#109.

C#	Date	Mintage	Good	VG	Fine	VF
1	(1791-1808)	—	45.00	75.00	125.00	200.00

c/s: Crowned script GR in oval indent on Mexico City 8 Reales, KM#111.

C#	Date	Mintage	Good	VG	Fine	VF
2	(1811-1816)	—	45.00	75.00	125.00	200.00

c/s: Crowned script GR in oval indent on France 5 Francs, C#138.

C#	Date	Mintage	Good	VG	Fine	VF
2a	(L'An 4-11)	—	180.00	300.00	400.00	500.00

c/s: Incuse crowned script GR on Mexico City 8 Reales, KM#111.

C#	Date	Mintage	Good	VG	Fine	VF
3	(1811-1816)	—	60.00	100.00	150.00	225.00

c/s: Incuse crowned script GR on other Spanish Colonial 8 Reales.

C#	Date	Mintage	Good	VG	Fine	VF
3a	—	—	20.00	35.00	65.00	100.00

NOTE: C#3 and 3a are considered local issues. The c/s crowned GR in octagonal indent is considered a modern fabrication.

MODERN COINAGE

CENT

BRONZE

Y#	Date	Mintage	Fine	VF	XF	Unc
1	1885	.072	3.50	8.50	22.50	45.00
	1885	—	—	—	Proof	100.00
	1888	.100	4.75	12.00	20.00	55.00
	1888	—	—	—	Proof	125.00
	1889	.050	7.00	17.50	35.00	65.00
	1889	—	—	—	Proof	125.00
	1894	.050	10.00	23.50	50.00	100.00
	1894	*25 pcs.	—	—	Proof	200.00

Y#	Date	Mintage	Fine	VF	XF	Unc
6	1904	.050	10.00	25.00	35.00	60.00
	1904	—	—	—	Proof	150.00
	1906	.050	10.00	25.00	45.00	100.00
	1909	.025	30.00	75.00	150.00	275.00

Y#	Date	Mintage	Fine	VF	XF	Unc
10	1911	.050	32.50	80.00	150.00	425.00
	1912H	.050	100.00	225.00	350.00	650.00
	1913	.025	100.00	225.00	300.00	600.00

Y#	Date	Mintage	Fine	VF	XF	Unc
11	1914	.175	4.00	10.00	22.50	65.00
	1916H	.125	2.75	7.00	22.50	65.00
	1918	.040	4.50	11.50	30.00	65.00
	1919	.050	5.00	12.50	32.50	85.00
	1924	.050	4.00	10.00	35.00	70.00
	1924	—	—	—	Proof	150.00
	1926	.050	4.00	10.00	37.50	80.00
	1926	—	—	—	Proof	110.00
	1936	.040	1.80	4.50	18.50	40.00
	1936	50 pcs.	—	—	Proof	100.00

Y#	Date	Mintage	Fine	VF	XF	Unc
16	1937	.080	.80	2.00	6.50	45.00
	1937	—	—	—	Proof	100.00
	1939	.050	1.10	2.75	4.50	17.50
	1939	—	—	—	Proof	90.00
	1942	.050	1.80	4.50	6.50	50.00
	1943	.100	.80	2.00	13.50	45.00
	1944	.100	.80	2.00	9.00	40.00
	1944	—	—	—	Proof	90.00
	1945	.130	.40	1.00	6.50	30.00
	1945	—	—	—	Proof	90.00
	1947	.100	.40	1.00	5.00	25.00
	1947	—	—	—	Proof	90.00

Obv. leg: W/o EMPEROR OF INDIA

Y#	Date	Mintage	Fine	VF	XF	Unc
19	1949	.100	.60	1.50	5.00	15.00
	1949	—	—	—	Proof	90.00
	1950	.100	.40	1.00	2.50	5.00
	1950	—	—	—	Proof	90.00
	1951	.100	.60	1.50	4.00	20.00
	1951	—	—	—	Proof	90.00

Y#	Date	Mintage	Fine	VF	XF	Unc
22	1954	.200	.30	.80	1.75	6.50
	1954	—	—	—	Proof	80.00

Y#	Date	Mintage	Fine	VF	XF	Unc
23	1956	.200	.10	.25	.50	2.50
	1956	—	—	—	Proof	75.00
	1958	.400	.50	1.00	4.00	25.00
	1958	—	—	—	Proof	75.00
	1959	.200	.50	1.00	4.00	25.00

Y#	Date	Mintage	Fine	VF	XF	Unc
23	1959	—	—	—	Proof	90.00
	1961	.800	—	.15	.25	1.00
	1961	—	—	—	Proof	75.00
	1964	.300	—	.10	.30	.90
	1965	.400	—	—	.10	.50
	1966	.100	—	—	.10	.20
	1967	.400	—	—	.10	.50
	1968	.200	—	—	.10	.50
	1969	.520	—	—	.10	.40
	1970	.120	—	—	.10	.40
	1971	.800	—	—	.10	.20
	1972	.800	—	—	.10	.20
	1973	.400	—	—	.10	.40

5 CENTS

1.1620 gm., .925 SILVER, .0346 oz ASW

Y#	Date	Mintage	Fine	VF	XF	Unc
2	1894	.128	5.00	12.00	27.50	65.00
	1894	*25 pcs.	—	—	Proof	300.00

COPPER-NICKEL

Y#	Date	Mintage	Fine	VF	XF	Unc
7	1907	.010	15.00	35.00	60.00	130.00
	1909	.010	16.50	40.00	85.00	170.00

Y#	Date	Mintage	Fine	VF	XF	Unc
12	1911	.010	10.00	25.00	40.00	90.00
	1912H	.020	7.50	17.50	37.50	75.00
	1916H	.020	7.50	17.50	30.00	70.00
	1918	.020	6.00	15.00	25.00	65.00
	1919	.020	6.00	15.00	20.00	70.00
	1936	.060	1.60	4.00	10.00	45.00
	1936	50 pcs.	—	—	Proof	100.00

Y#	Date	Mintage	Fine	VF	XF	Unc
17	1939	.020	2.00	5.00	10.00	35.00
	1939	—	—	—	Proof	90.00

NICKEL-BRASS

Y#	Date	Mintage	Fine	VF	XF	Unc
17a	1942	.030	3.50	9.00	25.00	100.00
	1942	—	—	—	Proof	120.00
	1943	.040	2.00	5.00	16.50	50.00
	1944	.050	3.00	7.50	16.50	65.00
	1945	.065	2.00	5.00	12.50	45.00
	1947	.040	3.00	7.50	15.00	55.00

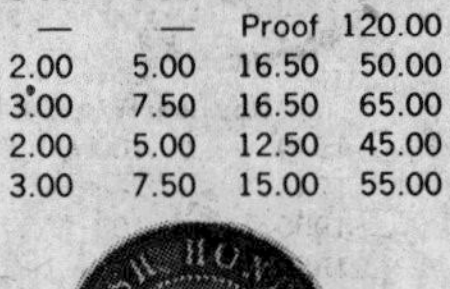

Obv. leg: W/o EMPEROR OF INDIA

Y#	Date	Mintage	Fine	VF	XF	Unc
20	1949	.040	1.00	2.50	7.50	25.00
	1949	—	—	—	Proof	90.00
	1950	.225	.40	1.00	2.50	25.00
	1952	.100	.80	2.00	3.50	20.00

Y#	Date	Mintage	Fine	VF	XF	Unc
24	1956	.100	.20	.50	2.00	30.00
	1956	—	—	—	Proof	80.00
	1957	.100	.30	.75	1.50	10.00
	1958	.200	.30	.75	3.50	45.00
	1959	.100	.30	.75	3.50	40.00

Y#	Date	Mintage	Fine	VF	XF	Unc
24	1961	.100	.30	.75	2.50	20.00
	1962	.200	.15	.35	.65	2.00
	1962	—	—	—	Proof	110.00
	1963	.100	—	.20	.50	1.50
	1963	—	—	—	Proof	75.00
	1964	.100	—	.15	.35	1.00
	1965	.150	—	.10	.25	.75
	1966	.150	—	.10	.20	.60
	1968	.200	—	.10	.15	.50
	1969	.540	—	.10	.15	.40
	1970	.240	—	.10	.15	.35
	1971	.450	—	.10	.15	.40
	1972	.200	—	.10	.15	.40
	1973	.210	—	.10	.15	.75

10 CENTS

2.3240 gm., .925 SILVER, .0691 oz ASW

Y#	Date	Mintage	Fine	VF	XF	Unc
3	1894	.126	7.50	18.50	30.00	65.00
	1894	*25 pcs.	—	—	Proof	375.00

Y#	Date	Mintage	Fine	VF	XF	Unc
13	1918	.010	8.50	20.00	50.00	150.00
	1919	.010	8.50	20.00	45.00	145.00
	1936	.030	4.00	10.00	20.00	60.00
	1936	50 pcs.	—	—	Proof	120.00

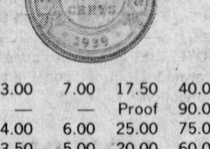

Y#	Date	Mintage	Fine	VF	XF	Unc
18	1939	.020	3.00	7.00	17.50	40.00
	1939	—	—	—	Proof	90.00
	1942	.010	4.00	6.00	25.00	75.00
	1943	.020	3.50	5.00	20.00	60.00
	1944	.030	2.50	4.00	17.50	60.00
	1946	.010	3.00	7.50	22.50	70.00

COPPER-NICKEL

Y#	Date	Mintage	Fine	VF	XF	Unc
25	1956	.100	.40	1.00	2.00	7.50
	1956	—	—	—	Proof	80.00
	1959	.100	.60	1.50	2.00	27.50
	1961	.050	.30	.75	1.25	5.00
	1963	.050	.20	.50	.75	2.50
	1964	.060	—	.25	.50	1.00
	1965	.200	—	.15	.35	.75
	1966	—	—	Reported, not confirmed		
	1968	—	—	Reported, not confirmed		
	1969	—	—	Reported, not confirmed		
	1970	—	—	Reported, not confirmed		
	1971	—	—	Reported, Not Confirmed		

25 CENTS

5.8100 gm., .925 SILVER, .1728 oz ASW

Y#	Date	Mintage	Fine	VF	XF	Unc
4	1894	.048	7.50	20.00	50.00	125.00
	1894	*25 pcs.	—	—	Proof	350.00
	1895	.047	8.00	20.00	65.00	150.00
	1897	.040	10.00	25.00	60.00	150.00
	1901	.020	12.00	30.00	85.00	250.00
	1901	30 pcs.	—	—	Proof	250.00

Y#	Date	Mintage	Fine	VF	XF	Unc
8	1906	.030	10.00	30.00	85.00	200.00
	1907	.060	8.00	20.00	70.00	175.00

Y#	Date	Mintage	Fine	VF	XF	Unc
14	1911	.014	10.00	25.00	60.00	190.00
	1919	.040	6.00	12.00	45.00	150.00

COPPER-NICKEL

Y#	Date	Mintage	Fine	VF	XF	Unc
21	1952	.075	1.40	3.50	11.50	70.00
	1952	—	—	—	Proof	100.00

Y#	Date	Mintage	Fine	VF	XF	Unc
26	1955	.075	.40	1.00	2.50	15.00
	1955	—	—	—	Proof	100.00
	1960	.075	.40	1.00	5.00	40.00
	1962	.050	.30	.75	1.50	3.25
	1963	.050	.30	.75	1.50	5.00
	1964	.100	.30	.75	1.50	2.75
	1965	.075	—	.50	1.00	2.75
	1966	.075	.30	.75	1.50	5.50
	1968	.125	—	.50	1.00	2.25
	1969	—	—	Reported, not confirmed		
	1970	—	—	.35	.75	1.50
	1971	.150	—	.30	.50	1.25
	1972	.200	—	.30	.50	1.25
	1973	.100	—	.30	.60	1.40

50 CENTS

11.6200 gm., .925 SILVER, .3456 oz ASW

Y#	Date	Mintage	Fine	VF	XF	Unc
5	1894	.038	12.00	25.00	65.00	250.00
	1894	*25 pcs.	—	—	Proof	900.00
	1895	.036	12.00	25.00	80.00	200.00
	1897	.020	12.00	25.00	65.00	250.00
	1901	.010	18.50	45.00	90.00	300.00
	1901	30 pcs.	—	—	Proof	400.00

Y#	Date	Mintage	Fine	VF	XF	Unc
9	1906	.015	15.00	35.00	85.00	225.00
	1907	.019	15.00	35.00	85.00	200.00

Y#	Date	Mintage	Fine	VF	XF	Unc
15	1911	.012	18.50	45.00	70.00	225.00
	1919	.040	12.00	20.00	45.00	170.00
	1919	—	—	—	Proof	275.00

COPPER-NICKEL

Y#	Date	Mintage	Fine	VF	XF	Unc
27	1954	.075	—	1.00	2.00	5.00
	1954	—	—	—	Proof	125.00
	1962	.050	—	1.00	2.00	4.50
	1964	.050	—	1.00	2.00	3.50
	1965	.025	1.20	3.00	5.00	20.00
	1966	.025	.60	1.50	3.00	12.50
	1968	—	— Reported, Not Confirmed			
	1969	—	— Reported, Not Confirmed			
	1970	—	— Reported, Not Confirmed			
	1971	.030	—	.75	1.25	2.25

NCLT ISSUES

PROOF SETS

STANDARD METALS

KM#	Date	Mintage	Identification	Issue Price	Mkt. Val.
101	1894(5)	25*	Y1-5	—	1500.
102	1901(2)	30	Y4, 5	—	600.00
103	1936(3)	50	Y11-13	—	450.00
104	1939(3)	—	Y16-18	—	325.00
105	1949(2)	—	Y19-20	—	175.00
106	1954(2)	—	Y22,27	—	175.00
107	1956(3)	—	Y23-25	—	200.00

*Estimate

BELIZE

MINTMARKS

FM - Franklin Mint, U.S.A.*

***NOTE:** From 1975 until mid-1977 the Franklin Mint produced coinage in 3 different qualities. Qualities of issue are designated in ( ) after each date and are defined as follows:

(M) MATTE - Normal circulation strike or a dull finish produced by sandblasting special uncirculated (polish finish) or proof quality dies.

(U) SPECIAL UNCIRCULATED - Polished or proof-like in appearance without any frosted features.

(P) PROOF - The highest quality obtainable having mirror-like fields and frosted features.

CENT

BRONZE

Y#	Date	Mintage	VF	XF	Unc
1	1973	.400	—	.10	.25
	1974	2.000	—	.10	.20
	1975	Inc. Ab.	—	—	.10
	1976	—	—	—	.10

ALUMINUM

Y#	Date	Mintage	VF	XF	Unc
1a	1976	1.800	—	—	.15
	1979	2.005	—	—	.15

BRONZE

Y#	Date	Mintage	VF	XF	Unc
6	1974FM(M)	.225	—	—	.25
	1974FM(P)	.021	—	Proof	1.00

3.5000 gm., .925 SILVER, .1040 oz ASW

Y#	Date	Mintage	VF	XF	Unc
6a	1974FM(P)	.031	—	Proof	3.50

BRONZE

Y#	Date	Mintage	VF	XF	Unc
14	1975FM(M)	.118	—	.10	.40
	1975FM(U)	1,095	—	1.00	2.00
	1975FM(P)	8,794	—	Proof	1.00
	1976FM(M)	.126	—	—	.10
	1976FM(U)	759 pcs.	—	—	.60
	1976FM(P)	4,893	—	Proof	1.25

3.5000 gm., .925 SILVER, .1040 oz ASW

Y#	Date	Mintage	VF	XF	Unc
14a	1975FM(P)	.013	—	Proof	4.00
	1976FM(P)	5,897	—	Proof	6.00
	1977FM(P)	3,197	—	Proof	7.00
	1978FM(P)	3,342	—	Proof	6.25
	1979FM(P)	—	—	Proof	—
	1980FM(P)	—	—	Proof	12.00

ALUMINUM

Y#	Date	Mintage	VF	XF	Unc
14b	1977FM(M)	.125	—	—	.15
	1977FM(U)	520 pcs.	—	—	.15
	1977FM(P)	2,107	—	Proof	1.00
	1978FM(U)	.125	—	—	.15
	1978FM(P)	1,671	—	Proof	1.00
	1979FM(U)	—	—	—	.15
	1979FM(P)	—	—	Proof	1.00
	1980FM(U)	—	—	—	.15
	1980FM(P)	—	—	Proof	1.00

5 CENTS

NICKEL-BRASS

Y#	Date	Mintage	VF	XF	Unc
2	1973	.210	.10	.20	.40
	1974	.210	—	.15	.35
	1975	.420	—	—	.15
	1976	.570	—	—	.40

ALUMINUM

Y#	Date	Mintage	VF	XF	Unc
2a	1976	—	—	—	.40
	1979	2.000	—	—	—

NICKEL-BRASS

Y#	Date	Mintage	VF	XF	Unc
7	1974FM(M)	.050	.15	.35	.75
	1974FM(P)	.021	—	Proof	1.25

4.2900 gm., .925 SILVER, .1275 oz ASW

Y#	Date	Mintage	VF	XF	Unc
7a	1974FM(P)	.031	—	Proof	4.00

NICKEL-BRASS

Y#	Date	Mintage	VF	XF	Unc
15	1975FM(M)	.024	.25	.50	1.00
	1975FM(U)	1,095	—	.90	1.50
	1975FM(P)	8,794	—	Proof	1.25
	1976FM(M)	.025	.10	.25	.50
	1976FM(U)	759 pcs.	—	.75	1.25
	1976FM(P)	4,893	—	Proof	1.25

.925 SILVER

Y#	Date	Mintage	VF	XF	Unc
15a	1975FM(P)	.013	—	Proof	5.50
	1976FM(P)	5,897	—	Proof	7.00
	1977FM(P)	3,197	—	Proof	8.50
	1978FM(P)	3,342	—	Proof	7.50
	1979FM(P)	—	—	Proof	—
	1980FM(P)	—	—	Proof	15.00

ALUMINUM

Y#	Date	Mintage	VF	XF	Unc
15b	1977FM(M)	.025	.15	.20	.40
	1977FM(U)	520 pcs.	—	.20	.40
	1977FM(P)	2,107	—	Proof	1.25
	1978FM(U)	.025	—	—	.40
	1978FM(P)	1,671	—	Proof	1.25
	1979FM(U)	—	—	—	.40
	1979FM(P)	—	—	Proof	1.25
	1980FM(U)	—	—	—	.40
	1980FM(P)	—	—	Proof	1.25

10 CENTS

COPPER-NICKEL

Y#	Date	Mintage	VF	XF	Unc
3	1974	.100	.15	.30	.60
	1975	.200	.10	.20	.40
	1976	.450	.10	.15	.40
	1979	.800	—	—	—

Y#	Date	Mintage	VF	XF	Unc
8	1974FM(M)	.027	.25	.50	.75
	1974FM(P)	.021	—	Proof	1.50

2.7700 gm., .925 SILVER, .0823 oz ASW

Y#	Date	Mintage	VF	XF	Unc
8a	1974FM(P)	.031	—	Proof	3.75

COPPER-NICKEL

Y#	Date	Mintage	VF	XF	Unc
16	1975FM(M)	.012	.75	1.25	2.00
	1975FM(U)	1,095	—	1.25	2.00
	1975FM(P)	8,794	—	Proof	1.50
	1976FM(M)	.013	.25	.50	1.00
	1976FM(U)	759 pcs.	—	.90	1.50
	1976FM(P)	4,893	—	Proof	1.50
	1977FM(M)	.013	.55	.90	1.50
	1977FM(U)	520 pcs.	—	.90	1.50
	1977FM(P)	2,107	—	Proof	2.25
	1978FM(U)	.013	—	—	1.50
	1978FM(P)	1,671	—	Proof	3.00
	1979FM(U)	—	—	—	1.50
	1979FM(P)	—	—	Proof	3.00
	1980FM(U)	—	—	—	1.50
	1980FM(P)	—	—	Proof	3.00

2.7700 gm., .925 SILVER, .0823 oz ASW

Y#	Date	Mintage	VF	XF	Unc
16a	1975FM(P)	.013	—	Proof	6.50
	1976FM(P)	5,897	—	Proof	7.50
	1977FM(P)	3,197	—	Proof	8.25

Y#	Date	Mintage	VF	XF	Unc
16a	1978FM(P)	3,342	—	Proof	8.00
	1979FM(P)	—	—	Proof	8.00
	1980FM(P)	—	—	Proof	16.00

25 CENTS

COPPER-NICKEL

Y#	Date	Mintage	VF	XF	Unc
4	1974	.100	.35	.65	1.25
	1975	.200	.20	.35	.75
	1976	.290	.20	.35	.75
	1979	.500	—	—	—

Y#	Date	Mintage	VF	XF	Unc
9	1974FM(M)	.013	.65	1.25	2.50
	1974FM(P)	.021	—	Proof	2.50

6.5400 gm., .925 SILVER, .1945 oz ASW

Y#	Date	Mintage	VF	XF	Unc
9a	1974FM(P)	.031	—	Proof	6.75

COPPER-NICKEL

Y#	Date	Mintage	VF	XF	Unc
17	1975FM(M)	4,716	1.25	2.50	5.00
	1975FM(U)	1,095	—	2.00	3.50
	1975FM(P)	8,794	—	Proof	2.50
	1976FM(M)	5,000	.65	1.25	3.00
	1976FM(U)	759 pcs.	—	1.25	2.50
	1976FM(P)	4,893	—	Proof	2.50
	1977FM(M)	5,000	.75	1.25	2.00
	1977FM(U)	520 pcs.	—	1.25	2.00
	1977FM(P)	2,107	—	Proof	2.75
	1978FM(U)	5,458	—	—	2.00
	1978FM(P)	1,671	—	Proof	3.00
	1979FM(U)	—	—	—	2.00
	1979FM(P)	—	—	Proof	3.00
	1980FM(U)	—	—	—	2.00
	1980FM(P)	—	—	Proof	3.00

6.5400 gm., .925 SILVER, .1945 oz ASW

Y#	Date	Mintage	VF	XF	Unc
17a	1975FM(P)	.013	—	Proof	8.50
	1976FM(P)	5,897	—	Proof	11.50
	1977FM(P)	3,197	—	Proof	12.50
	1978FM(P)	3,342	—	Proof	11.00
	1979FM(P)	—	—	Proof	11.00
	1980FM(P)	—	—	Proof	22.00

50 CENTS

COPPER-NICKEL

Y#	Date	Mintage	VF	XF	Unc
5	1974	.123	.75	1.25	2.25
	1975	Inc. Ab.	.60	1.00	2.50
	1976	.187	.60	1.00	2.00
	1979	.125	—	—	1.50

Y#	Date	Mintage	VF	XF	Unc
10	1974FM(M)	8,806	1.00	2.00	4.00
	1974FM(P)	.021	—	Proof	3.50

10.4900 gm., .925 SILVER, .3120 oz ASW

Y#	Date	Mintage	VF	XF	Unc
10a	1974FM(P)	.031	—	Proof	10.00

COPPER-NICKEL

Y#	Date	Mintage	VF	XF	Unc
18	1975FM(M)	2,358	3.00	5.50	10.00
	1975FM(U)	1,095	—	3.50	6.50
	1975FM(P)	8,794	—	Proof	3.50
	1976FM(M)	3,259	.75	1.50	3.00
	1976FM(U)	759 pcs.	—	2.50	5.00
	1976FM(P)	4,893	—	Proof	3.50
	1977FM(M)	3,020	.90	1.50	6.50
	1977FM(U)	520 pcs.	—	1.50	6.50
	1977FM(P)	2,107	—	Proof	6.00
	1978FM(U)	2,958	—	—	7.00
	1978FM(P)	1,671	—	Proof	6.50
	1979FM(U)	—	—	—	6.50
	1979FM(P)	—	—	Proof	6.50
	1980FM(U)	—	—	—	6.50
	1980FM(P)	—	—	Proof	6.50

10.4900 gm., .925 SILVER, .3120 oz ASW

Y#	Date	Mintage	VF	XF	Unc
18a	1975FM(P)	.013	—	Proof	10.00
	1976FM(P)	5,897	—	Proof	13.50
	1977FM(P)	3,197	—	Proof	10.00
	1978FM(P)	3,342	—	Proof	13.50
	1979FM(P)	—	—	Proof	13.50
	1980FM(P)	—	—	Proof	27.00

DOLLAR

COPPER-NICKEL

Y#	Date	Mintage	VF	XF	Unc
11	1974FM(M)	6,656	4.50	6.00	7.50
	1974FM(P)	.021	—	Proof	5.00
	1975FM(M)	1,182	12.50	20.00	25.00
	1975FM(U)	1,095	—	6.00	7.50
	1975FM(P)	8,794	—	Proof	12.50
	1976FM(M)	1,250	—	10.00	12.50
	1976FM(U)	759 pcs.	—	12.00	25.00
	1976FM(P)	4,893	—	Proof	10.00
	1977FM(M)	1,250	7.00	11.50	12.50
	1977FM(U)	520 pcs.	—	11.50	12.50
	1977FM(P)	2,107	—	Proof	16.50
	1978FM(U)	1,708	—	—	6.00
	1978FM(P)	1,671	—	Proof	22.50
	1979FM(U)	—	—	—	6.00
11	1979FM(P)	—	—	Proof	22.50
	1980FM(U)	—	—	—	6.00
	1980FM(P)	—	—	Proof	22.50

19.6200 gm., .925 SILVER, .5835 oz ASW

Y#	Date	Mintage	VF	XF	Unc
11a	1974FM(P)	.031	—	Proof	17.50
	1975FM(P)	.013	—	Proof	17.50
	1976FM(P)	5,897	—	Proof	22.50
	1977FM(P)	3,197	—	Proof	22.50
	1978FM(P)	3,342	—	Proof	20.00
	1979FM(P)	—	—	Proof	20.00
	1980FM(P)	—	—	Proof	40.00

5 DOLLARS

COPPER-NICKEL
Obv: Similar to Dollar, Y#11.

Y#	Date	Mintage	VF	XF	Unc
12	1974FM(M)	4,936	3.50	15.00	22.50
	1974FM(P)	.021	—	Proof	6.50
	1975FM(M)	237 pcs.	45.00	75.00	125.00
	1975FM(U)	1,095	—	16.50	27.50
	1975FM(P)	8,794	—	Proof	5.50
	1976FM(M)	250 pcs.	32.50	55.00	90.00
	1976FM(U)	759 pcs.	—	20.00	35.00
	1976FM(P)	4,893	—	Proof	12.50
	1977FM(M)	200 pcs.	12.50	20.00	35.00
	1977FM(U)	520 pcs.	—	20.00	35.00
	1977FM(P)	2,107	—	Proof	10.00
	1978FM(U)	708 pcs.	—	—	35.00
	1978FM(P)	1,671	—	Proof	10.00
	1979FM(U)	—	—	—	35.00
	1979FM(P)	—	—	Proof	10.00
	1980FM(U)	—	—	—	35.00
	1980FM(P)	—	—	Proof	10.00

26.7000 gm., .925 SILVER, .7941 oz ASW

Y#	Date	Mintage	VF	XF	Unc
12a	1974FM(P)	.031	—	Proof	30.00
	1975FM(P)	.013	—	Proof	30.00
	1976FM(P)	5,897	—	Proof	30.00
	1977FM(P)	3,197	—	Proof	37.50
	1978FM(P)	3,342	—	Proof	37.50
	1979FM(P)	—	—	Proof	30.00
	1980FM(P)	—	—	Proof	60.00

10 DOLLARS

COPPER-NICKEL
Obv: Similar to 1 Dollar, Y#11.

Y#	Date	Mintage	VF	XF	Unc
13	1974FM(M)	4,726	—	25.00	50.00
	1974FM(P)	.021	—	Proof	13.50
	1975FM(M)	117 pcs.	—	175.00	250.00
	1975FM(U)	1,095	—	25.00	40.00
	1975FM(P)	8,794	—	Proof	10.00
	1976FM(M)	125 pcs.	—	175.00	250.00
	1976FM(U)	759 pcs.	—	32.50	55.00
	1976FM(P)	4,893	—	Proof	12.50
	1977FM(M)	125 pcs.	—	40.00	60.00
	1977FM(U)	520 pcs.	—	40.00	60.00
	1977FM(P)	2,107	—	Proof	20.00
	1978FM(U)	583 pcs.	—	—	60.00
	1978FM(P)	1,671	—	Proof	20.00

29.8000 gm., .925 SILVER, .8863 oz ASW

Y#	Date	Mintage	VF	XF	Unc
13a	1974FM(P)	.031	—	Proof	35.00
	1975FM(P)	.013	—	Proof	35.00
	1976FM(P)	5,897	—	Proof	40.00
	1977FM(P)	3,197	—	Proof	55.00

Y#	Date	Mintage	VF	XF	Unc
13a	1978FM(P)	3,342	—	Proof	50.00

COPPER-NICKEL
Jabiru
Obv: Similar to 1 Dollar, Y#11.

Y#	Date	Mintage	VF	XF	Unc
25	1979FM(U)	—	—	—	60.00
	1979FM(P)	—	—	Proof	20.00

29.8000 gm., .925 SILVER, .8863 oz ASW

Y#	Date	Mintage	VF	XF	Unc
25a	1979FM(P)	—	—	Proof	—

COPPER-NICKEL
Scarlet Ibis

Y#	Date	Mintage	VF	XF	Unc
28	1980FM(M)	—	—	—	60.00
	1980FM(U)	—	—	—	20.00

25.8000 gm., .925 SILVER, .7673 oz ASW

Y#	Date	Mintage	VF	XF	Unc
28a	1980FM(P)	—	—	—	40.00

25 DOLLARS

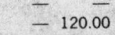

27.2800 gm., .925 SILVER, .8113 oz ASW
Coronation Jubilee

Y#	Date	Mintage	VF	XF	Unc
24	1978FM(U)	352 pcs.	—	—	50.00
	1978FM(P)	8,438	—	Proof	50.00

100 DOLLARS

6.2100 gm., .500 GOLD, .0998 oz AGW
30th Anniversary of United Nations

Y#	Date	Mintage	VF	XF	Unc
19	1975FM(M)	100 pcs.	—	—	425.00
	1975FM(U)	2,028	—	75.00	100.00
	1975FM(P)	8,126	—	Proof	75.00

Ancient Mayan Symbols

Y#	Date	Mintage	VF	XF	Unc
20	1976FM(M)	216 pcs.	—	250.00	400.00
	1976FM(P)	.011	—	Proof	80.00

Kinich Ahau, Mayan Sun God

Y#	Date	Mintage	VF	XF	Unc
21	1977FM(M)	200 pcs.	—	250.00	400.00
	1977FM(U)	51 pcs.	—	500.00	700.00
	1977FM(P)	7,859	—	Proof	85.00

Itzamna Mayan God

Y#	Date	Mintage	VF	XF	Unc
22	1978FM(U)	351 pcs.	—	165.00	225.00
	1978FM(P)	7,178	—	Proof	85.00

Queen Angelfish

Y#	Date	Mintage	VF	XF	Unc
26	1979FM(U)	—	—	—	—
	1979FM(P)	—	—	Proof	95.00

6.4700 gm., .1040 oz AGW
Star of Bethlehem

Y#	Date	Mintage	VF	XF	Unc
27	1979FM(U)	—	—	—	—
	1979FM(P)	—	—	—	120.00

6.2100 gm., .0998 oz AGW
Moorish Idols

Y#	Date	Mintage	VF	XF	Unc
29	1980FM(P)	—	—	Proof	125.00

250 DOLLARS

8.8100 gm., .900 GOLD, .2549 oz AGW
Jaguar Commemorative

Y#	Date	Mintage	VF	XF	Unc
23	1978FM(U)	200 pcs.	—	—	300.00
	1978FM(P)	*3,399	—	Proof	200.00

***NOTE:** 1,712 pieces were used in First Day Covers.

NCLT ISSUES

MINT SETS

KM#	Date	Mintage	Identification	Issue Price	Mkt. Val.
S1	1974(8)	4,506	Y3-10	20.00	60.00
S2	1975(8)	1,095	Y11-18	27.50	85.00
S3	1976(8)	759	Y11-18	27.50	100.00
S4	1977(8)	520	Y11-18	27.50	125.00
S5	1978(8)	458	Y11-18	28.50	95.00
S6	1979(8)	—	Y14b,15b,16-18,11,12,25	28.50	60.00
S7	1980(8)	—	Y14b,15b,16-18,11,12,28,	29.50	—

PROOF SETS

STANDARD METALS

KM#	Date	Mintage	Identification	Issue Price	Mkt. Val.
101	1974(8)	21,470	Y6-13	35.00	75.00
102	1974(8)	31,368	Y6a-13a	100.00	75.00
103	1975(8)	8,794	Y11-18	37.50	75.00
104	1975(8)	13,275	Y11a-18a	110.00	80.00
105	1976(8)	4,893	Y11-18	37.50	75.00
106	1976(8)	5,897	Y11a-18a	110.00	120.00
107	1977(8)	2,107	Y11-18	37.50	75.00
108	1977(8)	3,197	Y11a-18a	110.00	120.00
109	1978(8)	1,671	Y11-18	39.50	75.00
110	1978(8)	3,342	Y11a-18a	110.00	125.00
111	1978(8)	—	Y11-18	39.50	—
112	1978(8)	—	Y11a-18a	110.00	—
113	1979(8)	—	Y14b,15b,16-18,11,12,25	41.50	—
114	1979(8)	—	Y14a-18a,11a,12a,25a	112.00	—
115	1980(8)	—	Y14b,15b,16-18,11,12,28	41.50	—
116	1980(8)	—	Y15a-18a,11a-12a,28a	222.00	—

BENIN (Dahomey)

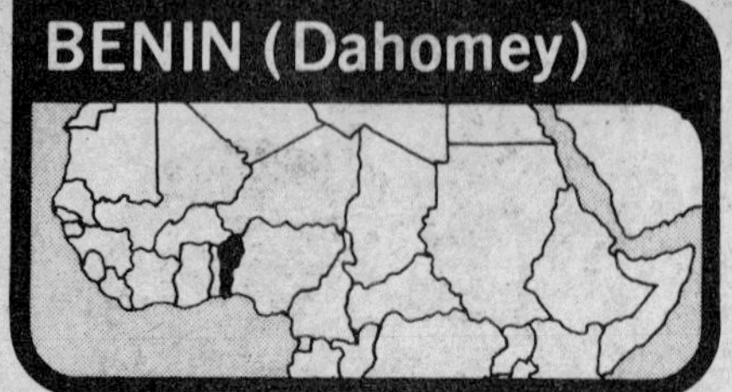

The People's Republic of Benin (formerly the Republic of Dahomey), located on the south side of the African bulge between Togo and Nigeria, has an area of 43,483 sq. mi. (112,620 sq. km.) and a population of 3.4 million. Capital: Porto-Novo. The principal industry of Benin, one of the poorest countries of West Africa, is the processing of palm oil products. Palm kernel oil, peanuts, cotton, and coffee are exported.

Porto-Novo, on the Bight of Benin, was founded as a trading post by the Portuguese in the 17th century. At that time, Benin was composed of an aggregation of mutually suspicious tribes, the majority of which were tributary to the powerful northern Kingdom of Abomey. In 1863, the King of Porto-Novo petitioned France for protection from Abomey. The French subjugated other militant tribes as well, and in 1892 organized the area as a protectorate of France; in 1904 it was incorporated into French West Africa as the Territory of Dahomey. After the establishment of the Fifth French Republic, the Territory of Dahomey became an autonomous state within the French community. On Aug. 1, 1960, it became the fully independent Republic of Dahomey. In 1974, the republic began a transition to a socialist society with Marxism-Leninism as its revolutionary philosophy. On Nov. 30, 1975, the name of the Republic of Dahomey was changed to the People's Republic of Benin.

DAHOMEY

100 FRANCS

5.1000 gm., .999 SILVER, .1638 oz ASW

H#	Date	Mintage	XF	Unc	Proof
1	1971	—	—	—	15.00

200 FRANCS

10.3000 gm., .999 SILVER, .3308 oz ASW

H#	Date	Mintage	XF	Unc	Proof
2	1971	—	—	—	20.00

500 FRANCS

25.7000 gm., .999 SILVER, .8255 oz ASW

H#	Date	Mintage	XF	Unc	Proof
3	1971	—	—	—	35.00

1000 FRANCS

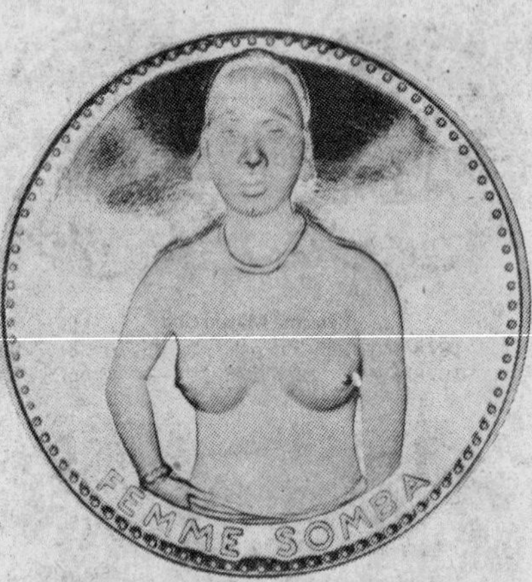

51.5000 gm., .999 SILVER, 1.6542 oz ASW

H#	Date	Mintage	XF	Unc	Proof
4	1971	—	—	—	65.00

2500 FRANCS

8.8800 gm., .900 GOLD, .2569 oz AGW

H#	Date	Mintage	XF	Unc	Proof
6	1971	2,000	—	—	175.00

5000 FRANCS

17.7700 gm., .900 GOLD, .5142 oz AGW
Obv: Similar to 2500 Francs, H#6.

H#	Date	Mintage	XF	Unc	Proof
7	1971	2,000	—	—	350.00

10,000 FRANCS

35.5500 gm., .900 GOLD, 1.0287 oz AGW
Obv: Similar to 2500 Francs, H#6.

H#	Date	Mintage	XF	Unc	Proof
8	1971	2,000	—	—	675.00

25,000 FRANCS

88.8800 gm., .900 GOLD, 2.5720 oz AGW
Obv: Similar to 2500 Francs, H#6.

H#	Date	Mintage	XF	Unc	Proof
9	1971	2,000	—	—	1700.

NCLT ISSUES

PROOF SETS
STANDARD METALS

KM#	Date	Mintage	Identification	Issue Price	Mkt. Val.
101	1971(4)	—	H1-4	36.00	135.00
102	1971(4)	2,000	H6-9	—	2900.

BERMUDA

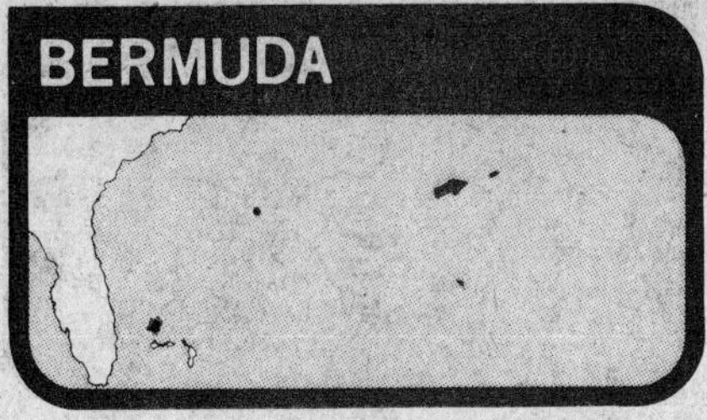

The Parliamentary British Colony of Bermuda, situated in the western Atlantic Ocean 660 miles (1,062 km.) east of North Carolina, has an area of 20.5 sq. mi. (53 sq. km.) and a population of 55,000. Capital: Hamilton. Concentrated essences, beauty preparations, and cut flowers are exported. Most Bermudians derive their livelihood from tourism.

Bermuda was discovered by Juan de Bermudez, a Spanish navigator, in 1503. British influence dates from 1609 when a group of Virginia-bound British colonists under the command of Sir George Somers was shipwrecked on the islands for 10 months. The islands were settled in 1612 by 60 British colonists from the Virginia Colony and became a crown colony in 1684. Internal autonomy was obtained by the constitution of June 8, 1968.

In February, 1970, Bermuda converted from its former currency, termed a pound, to a decimal currency, termed a dollar, which is equal to one U.S. dollar. On July 31, 1972, Bermuda severed its monetary link with the British pound sterling and pegged its dollar to be the same gold value as the U.S. dollar.

RULERS

British

MONETARY SYSTEM

12 Pence = 1 Shilling

PENNY

COPPER

C#	Date	Mintage	Fine	VF	XF	Unc
1	1793	.082	17.50	30.00	55.00	125.00

NOTE: Similar restrikes (ca. 1880) exist. They are valued at about $65.00 Unc.

CROWN

28.2800 gm., .925 SILVER, .8411 oz ASW

Y#	Date	Mintage	Fine	VF	XF	Unc
1	1959	.100	BV	BV	30.00	40.00

Y#	Date	Mintage	VF	XF	Unc
1	1959	2 pcs.	—	Proof	—

22.6200 gm., .500 SILVER, .3636 oz ASW

Y#	Date	Mintage	Fine	VF	XF	Unc
2	1964	.470	BV	BV	12.00	
	1964	.030	—	Proof	17.50	

DECIMAL COINAGE

100 Cents = 1 Dollar

CENT

BRONZE

Y#	Date	Mintage	VF	XF	Unc
3	1970	5.500	—	—	.20
	1970	.011	—	Proof	2.00
	1971	4.256	—	—	.15
	1972	—	Reported, Not Confirmed		
	1973	3.144	—	—	.15
	1974	.856	—	—	.10
	1975	1.000	—	—	.10
	1976	1.000	—	—	.10
	1977	—	—	—	.15

5 CENTS

COPPER-NICKEL

Y#	Date	Mintage	VF	XF	Unc
4	1970	2.200	—	—	.25
	1970	.011	—	Proof	2.25
	1974	.300	—	—	.15
	1975	.500	—	—	.15
	1977	—	—	—	—

10 CENTS

COPPER-NICKEL

Y#	Date	Mintage	VF	XF	Unc
5	1970	2.500	—	.15	.25
	1970	.011	—	Proof	2.75
	1971	2.000	—	.15	.25
	1978	—	—	—	—

25 CENTS

COPPER-NICKEL

Y#	Date	Mintage	VF	XF	Unc
6	1970	1.500	.30	.40	.50
	1970	.011	—	Proof	3.75
	1973	1.000	.50	.75	1.00

50 CENTS

COPPER-NICKEL

Y#	Date	Mintage	VF	XF	Unc
7	1970	1.000	.60	.70	.85
	1970	.011	—	Proof	4.50

DOLLAR

28.6000 gm., .800 SILVER, .7356 oz ASW

Y#	Date	Mintage	VF	XF	Unc
8	1970	.011	—Proof Only		75.00

28.2800 gm., .500 SILVER, .4546 oz ASW
Silver Wedding Anniversary
Obv: Similar to Y#8

Y#	Date	Mintage	VF	XF	Unc
10	1972	.075	BV	BV	15.00

28.2800 gm., .925 SILVER, .8411 oz ASW

Y#	Date	Mintage	VF	XF	Unc
10a	1972	.015	—	Proof	35.00

20 DOLLARS

7.9881 gm., .917 GOLD, .2355 oz AGW

Y#	Date	Mintage	VF	XF	Unc
9	1970	1,000	—	Proof	800.00

25 DOLLARS

COPPER-NICKEL
Royal Visit Commemorative
Obv: Bust of Queen Elizabeth

11	1975FM(M)	1,193	28.50	33.50	45.00
	1975FM(U)	100 pcs.	—	—	—

48.3000 gm., .925 SILVER, 1.4365 oz ASW

11a	1975FM(P)	.015	—	Proof	65.00

Queen's Silver Jubilee Commemorative

13	1977	.060	BV	45.00	50.00
	1977	Inc. Ab.	—	Proof	60.00

50 DOLLARS

4.0500 gm., .900 GOLD, .1172 oz AGW
Queen's Silver Jubilee Commemorative

Y#	Date	Mintage	VF	XF	Unc
14	1977	.060	BV	BV	80.00
	1977	—	—	Proof	100.00

100 DOLLARS

7.0300 gm., .900 GOLD, .2034 oz AGW
Royal Visit Commemorative

12	1975FM(M)	.019	BV	135.00	140.00
	1975FM(U)	25 pcs.	—	—	—
	1975FM(P)	.027	—	Proof	150.00

Queen's Silver Jubilee Commemorative

15	1977	.030	BV	135.00	140.00
	1977	—	—	Proof	160.00

NCLT ISSUES

MINT SETS

KM#	Date	Mintage	Identification	Issue Price	Mkt. Val.
S1	1970(5)	10,000	Y3-7	3.25	4.00

PROOF SETS

STANDARD METALS

101	1970(6)	10,000	Y3-8	24.00	90.00
102	1970(7)	1,000	Y3-9	216.00	825.00
103	1977(3)	—	Y13-15	—	300.00

BHUTAN

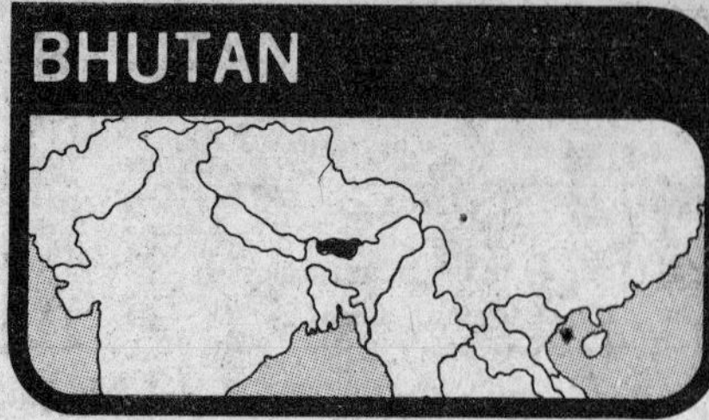

The Kingdom of Bhutan, a landlocked Himalayan country bordered by Tibet, India, and Sikkim, has an area of 18,000 sq. mi. (46,620 sq. km.) and a population of 1.2 million. Capital: Thimphu; Paro is the administrative capital. Virtually the entire population is engaged in agricultural and pastoral activities. Rice, wheat, barley, and yak butter are produced in sufficient quantity to make the country self-sufficient in food. The economy of Bhutan is primitive and many transactions are conducted on a barter basis.

Bhutan's early history is obscure, but is thought to have resembled that of rural medieval Europe. The country was conquered by Tibet, which still claims sovereignty over Bhutan, in the 9th century, and subjected to a dual temporal and spiritual rule until the mid-19TH century, when the southern part of the country was occupied by the British and annexed to British India. Bhutan was established as a hereditary monarchy in 1907, and in 1910 agreed to British control of its external affairs. In 1949, India and Bhutan concluded a treaty whereby India assumed Britain's role in subsidizing Bhutan and conducting its foreign affairs.

RULERS

Jigme Wangchuk, 1926-1952
Jigme Dorji Wangchuk, 1952-1972
Jigme Singye Wangchuk, 1972-

DEB (1/2) RUPEE

NOTE: Prior to their own issues the coins (1/2 Rupees) of Cooch-Behar circulated freely followed by their own coinage. As time went on these coins were remelted and increasing amounts of debasing alloys were used until we have a copper or brass issue, some with a slight silver wash.

Period I

1790-1835 AD

'Ma' 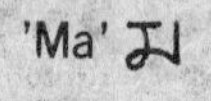

SILVER

KM#	Date	Mintage	Good	VG	Fine	VF
1	ND	—	BV	5.50	6.50	8.50

'Sa'

2	ND	—	BV	5.50	6.50	8.50

1820-1850 AD

'Sa'

SILVER, LEAD alloying

3	ND	—	3.50	4.50	6.00	8.00

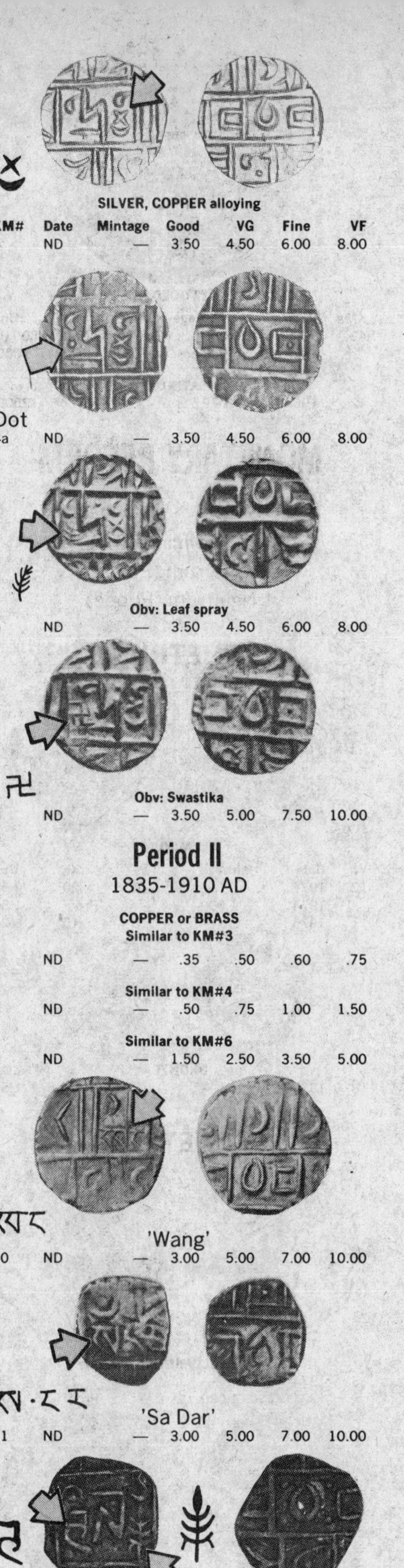

SILVER, COPPER alloying

KM#	Date	Mintage	Good	VG	Fine	VF
4	ND	—	3.50	4.50	6.00	8.00

Dot

KM#	Date	Mintage	Good	VG	Fine	VF
4a	ND	—	3.50	4.50	6.00	8.00

Obv: Leaf spray

KM#	Date	Mintage	Good	VG	Fine	VF
5	ND	—	3.50	4.50	6.00	8.00

Obv: Swastika

KM#	Date	Mintage	Good	VG	Fine	VF
6	ND	—	3.50	5.00	7.50	10.00

Period II

1835-1910 AD

COPPER or BRASS
Similar to KM#3

KM#	Date	Mintage	Good	VG	Fine	VF
7	ND	—	.35	.50	.60	.75

Similar to KM#4

KM#	Date	Mintage	Good	VG	Fine	VF
8	ND	—	.50	.75	1.00	1.50

Similar to KM#6

KM#	Date	Mintage	Good	VG	Fine	VF
9	ND	—	1.50	2.50	3.50	5.00

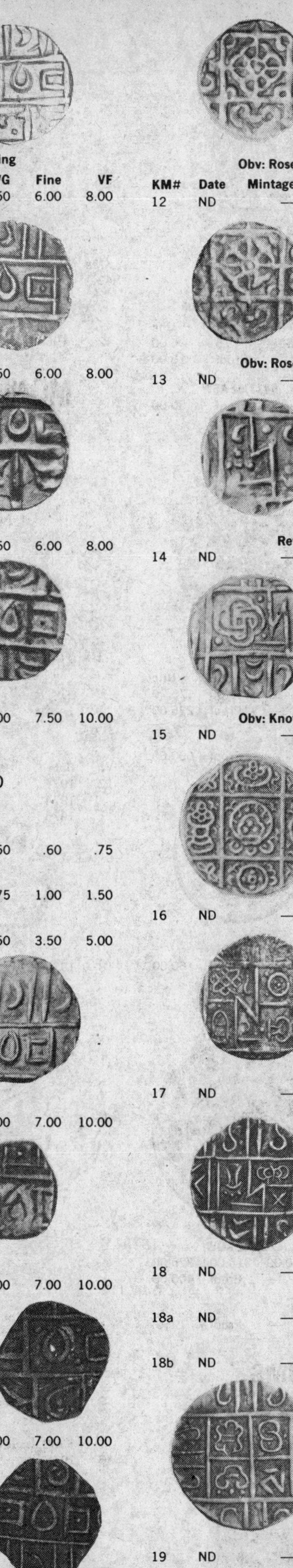

'Wang'

KM#	Date	Mintage	Good	VG	Fine	VF
10	ND	—	3.00	5.00	7.00	10.00

'Sa Dar'

KM#	Date	Mintage	Good	VG	Fine	VF
11	ND	—	3.00	5.00	7.00	10.00
11a	ND	—	3.00	5.00	7.00	10.00
11b	ND	—	3.00	5.00	7.00	10.00

Obv: Rosette. Rev: Swastika.

KM#	Date	Mintage	Good	VG	Fine	VF
12	ND	—	3.00	5.00	7.00	10.00

Obv: Rosette. Rev: Two fish.

KM#	Date	Mintage	Good	VG	Fine	VF
13	ND	—	3.00	5.00	7.00	10.00

Rev: Two fishes

KM#	Date	Mintage	Good	VG	Fine	VF
14	ND	—	1.50	2.50	3.50	5.00

Obv: Knot. Rev: Conch shell.

KM#	Date	Mintage	Good	VG	Fine	VF
15	ND	—	1.50	2.50	3.50	5.00
16	ND	—	2.00	3.50	5.00	7.50

SILVER

KM#	Date	Mintage	Good	VG	Fine	VF
17	ND	—	3.00	4.50	6.00	8.50
18	ND	—	2.00	3.50	5.00	7.50

COPPER

KM#	Date	Mintage	Good	VG	Fine	VF
18a	ND	—	2.00	3.50	5.00	7.50

BRASS

KM#	Date	Mintage	Good	VG	Fine	VF
18b	ND	—	2.00	3.50	5.00	7.50

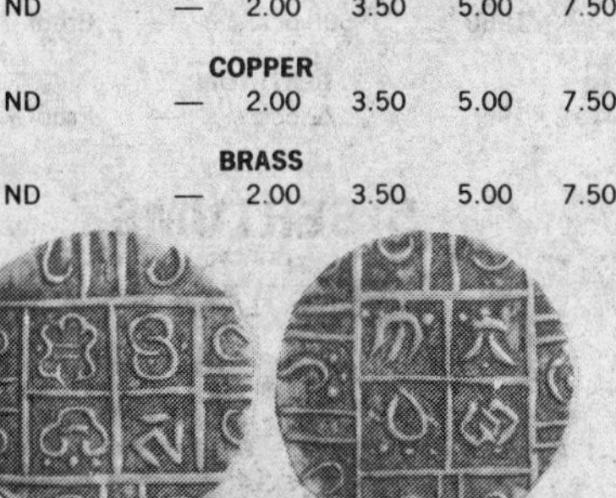

SILVER

KM#	Date	Mintage	Good	VG	Fine	VF
19	ND	—	3.00	4.50	6.00	8.50

COPPER

KM#	Date	Mintage	Good	VG	Fine	VF
19a	ND	—	2.00	3.50	5.00	7.50

SILVER

KM#	Date	Mintage	Good	VG	Fine	VF
20	ND	—	2.00	3.50	5.00	7.50

COPPER

KM#	Date	Mintage	Good	VG	Fine	VF
20a	ND	—	3.00	4.50	6.00	8.50

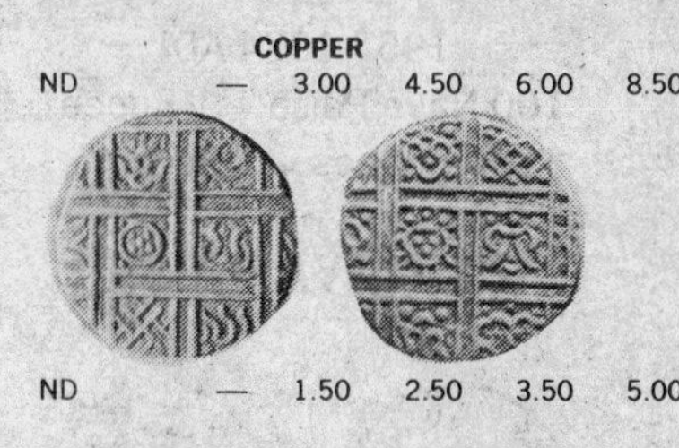

KM#	Date	Mintage	Good	VG	Fine	VF
21	ND	—	1.50	2.50	3.50	5.00

MODERN COINAGE

64 Pice (Paisa) = 1 Rupee

PICE

BRONZE

Y#	Date	Mintage	Fine	VF	XF	Unc
1	1928	.010	30.00	40.00	50.00	75.00
	1928	—	—	—	Proof	100.00

Y#	Date	Mintage	Fine	VF	XF	Unc
3	ND	*1.260	.60	.75	1.25	1.75

***NOTE:** Struck 1951 and 54.

1/2 RUPEE

SILVER

Y#	Date	Mintage	Fine	VF	XF	Unc
4.1	1928*	.050	10.00	15.00	22.50	35.00
	1928	—	—	—	Proof	100.00

***NOTE:** Actually struck in 1929 with the cyclical date of earth-dragon.

Y#	Date	Mintage	Fine	VF	XF	Unc
4.2	1928*	Inc. Ab.	10.00	15.00	22.50	35.00

NOTE: Actually struck in 1930 with the cyclical date of the earth-dragon.

COPPER-NICKEL, 5.78-5.82 gm.

Y#	Date	Year	Mintage	VF	XF	Unc
4a	1928*	.020	2.00	3.00	4.50	7.00
	1950**	.202	1.75	2.50	3.00	4.25

***NOTE:** Actually struck in 1951 with the cyclical date of earth-dragon.

****NOTE:** Actually struck in 1954/55with the cyclical date of iron-tiger.

NICKEL, reduced wgt., 5.08 gm.

Y#	Date	Mintage	Fine	VF	XF	Unc
4b	1950***	10,000	.60	.75	.90	1.40

***NOTE: Still having the cyclical date of the iron-tiger year (1950) but struck in 1967.

DECIMAL COINAGE

1957-1974 AD
100 Naye Paisa = 1 Rupee
100 Rupees = 1 Sertum

25 NAYA PAISA

COPPER-NICKEL
40th Anniversary Accession of Jigme Wangchuk

Y#	Date	Mintage	VF	XF	Unc
6	1966	.010	.20	.50	1.00
	1966	6,000	—	Proof	2.50

50 NAYA PAISA

COPPER-NICKEL
40th Anniversary Accession of Jigme Wangchuk

Y#	Date	Mintage	VF	XF	Unc
7	1966	.010	.25	.50	1.00
	1966	6,000	—	Proof	3.50

RUPEE

COPPER-NICKEL
40th Anniversary Accession of Jigme Wangchuk

Y#	Date	Mintage	VF	XF	Unc
8	1966	.010	.50	.75	1.50
	1966	6,000	—	Proof	5.00

3 RUPEES

COPPER-NICKEL
40th Anniversary Accession of Jigme Wangchuk

Y#	Date	Mintage	VF	XF	Unc
9	1966	5,826	3.50	4.75	6.00
	1966	6,000	—	Proof	15.00

28.2800 gm., .925 SILVER, .8411 oz ASW

Y#	Date	Mintage	VF	XF	Unc
9a	1966	2,000	—	Proof	50.00

SERTUM

7.9800 gm., .917 GOLD, .2352 oz AGW

KM#	Date	Mintage	VF	XF	Unc
40	1966	2,300	BV	160.00	175.00
	1966	598 pcs.	—	Proof	225.00

PLATINUM

KM#	Date	Mintage	VF	XF	Unc
40a	1966	72 pcs.	—	Proof	600.00

7.9800 gm., .917 GOLD, .2352 oz AGW

KM#	Date	Mintage	VF	XF	Unc
43	1970	—	BV	155.00	160.00

2 SERTUMS

15.9800 gm., .917 GOLD, .4711 oz AGW

KM#	Date	Mintage	VF	XF	Unc
41	1966	800 pcs.	310.00	315.00	325.00
	1966	598 pcs.	—	Proof	400.00

PLATINUM

KM#	Date	Mintage	VF	XF	Unc
41a	1966	72 pcs.	—	Proof	1250.

5 SERTUMS

39.9400 gm., .917 GOLD, 1.1776 oz AGW

KM#	Date	Mintage	VF	XF	Unc
42	1966	800 pcs.	765.00	775.00	800.00
	1966	598 pcs.	—	Proof	1000.

PLATINUM

KM#	Date	Mintage	VF	XF	Unc
42a	1966	72 pcs.	—	Proof	2500.

MONETARY REFORM

Commencing 1974
100 Chetrum (Paisa) =
1 Ngultrum (Rupee)

5 CHETRUMS

ALUMINUM

Y#	Date	Mintage	VF	XF	Unc
12	1974	—	.10	.20	.50
	1974	1,000	—	Proof	1.50
	1975	—	.10	.15	.20

BRONZE

Y#	Date	Mintage	VF	XF	Unc
18	1979	—	—	Proof	1.50

10 CHETRUMS

ALUMINUM

Y#	Date	Mintage	VF	XF	Unc
13	1974	—	.15	.25	.50
	1974	1,000	—	Proof	2.00

F.A.O. Issue and International Women's Year

Y#	Date	Mintage	VF	XF	Unc
16	1975	4,000	.15	.25	.75

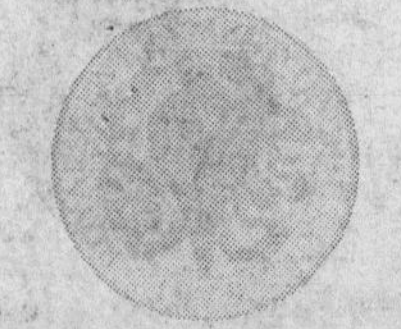

BRONZE

Y#	Date	Mintage	VF	XF	Unc
19	1979	—	—	Proof	2.50

20 CHETRUMS

ALUMINUM-BRONZE
F.A.O. Issue

Y#	Date	Mintage	VF	XF	Unc
10	1974	1.194	.15	.25	.50
	1974	1,000	—	Proof	2.50

25 CHETRUMS

COPPER-NICKEL

Y#	Date	Mintage	VF	XF	Unc
14	1974	—	.10	.20	.75
	1974	1,000	—	Proof	3.50
	1975	—	—	—	.50
	1975	—	—	Proof	3.50

Y#	Date	Mintage	VF	XF	Unc
20	1979	—	—	Proof	5.00

50 CHETRUMS

COPPER-NICKEL

Y#	Date	Mintage	VF	XF	Unc
21	1979	—	—	Proof	15.00

NGULTRUM

COPPER-NICKEL

Y#	Date	Mintage	VF	XF	Unc
15	1974	—	.25	.50	1.25
	1974	1,000	—	Proof	5.00
	1975	—	—	—	1.00
	1975	—	—	Proof	5.00

Y#	Date	Mintage	VF	XF	Unc
22	1979	—	—	Proof	8.00

3 NGULTRUM

28.2800 gm., SILVER

Y#	Date	Mintage	VF	XF	Unc
23	1979	—	—	—	—
	1979	—	—	Proof	50.00

15 NGULTRUMS

22.5000 gm., .500 SILVER, .3617 oz ASW
F.A.O. Issue

Y#	Date	Mintage	VF	XF	Unc
11	1974	.030	BV	11.00	12.50
	1974	1,000	—	Proof	15.00

30 NGULTRUMS

22.5000 gm., .500 SILVER, .3617 oz ASW
F.A.O. Issue and International Women's Year

Y#	Date	Mintage	VF	XF	Unc
17	1975	.014	BV	11.00	12.50
	1975	—	—	Proof	17.50

MONETARY REFORM

1 SERTUM

7.9800 gm., .917 GOLD, .2352 oz AGW
Similar to 3 Ngultrum, Y#23.

Y#	Date	Mintage	VF	XF	Unc
24	1979	1,000	—	—	200.00
	1979	1,000	—	Proof	280.00

9.8500 gm., PLATINUM

Y#	Date	Mintage	VF	XF	Unc
24a	1979	—	—Proof Only		—

2 SERTUM

15.9800 gm., .917 GOLD, .4711 oz AGW
Similar to 3 Ngultrum, Y#23.

Y#	Date	Mintage	VF	XF	Unc
25	1979	1,000	—	—	400.00
	1979	1,000	—	Proof	550.00

19.7000 gm., PLATINUM

Y#	Date	Mintage	VF	XF	Unc
25a	1979	—	—Proof Only		—

5 SERTUM

39.9400 gm., .917 GOLD, 1.1776 oz AGW
Similar to 3 Ngultrum, Y#23.

Y#	Date	Mintage	VF	XF	Unc
26	1979	1,000	—	—	1000.
	1979	1,000	—	Proof	1300.

49.2000 gm., PLATINUM

Y#	Date	Mintage	VF	XF	Unc
26a	1979	—	—Proof Only		—

NCLT ISSUES

MINT SETS

KM#	Date	Mintage	Identification	Issue Price	Mkt. Val.
S1	1966(3)	300	KM40-42	175.00	1300.
S2	1974(2)	—	Y10-11	4.00	13.00
S3	1974(4)	—	Y12-15	6.00	3.00
S4	1979(3)	1,000	Y24-26	1579.	—

PROOF SETS

STANDARD METALS

KM#	Date	Mintage	Identification	Issue Price	Mkt. Val.
101	1966(4)	6,000	Y6-9	11.50	22.50
102	1966(3)	598	KM40-42	300.00	1600.
103	1966(3)	72	KM40a-42a	685.00	4250.
104	1974(6)	1,000	Y10-15	18.00	35.00
105	1979(5)	.020	Y18,22	30.00	35.00
106	1979(3)	1,000	Y24-26	2107.	—
107	1979(3)	—	Y24a-26a	2410.	—

Listings For

BIAFRA: refer to Nigeria

BOHEMIA & MORAVIA: refer to Czechoslovakia

The Republic of Bolivia, a landlocked country in west—central South America, has an area of 424,162 sq. mi. (1,098,580 sq. km.) and a population of 5.5 million. Capital: La Paz (administrative); Sucre (constitutional). Mining is the principal industry and tin the most important metal. Minerals, petroleum, natural gas, cotton and coffee are exported.

The Incas, who ruled one of the world's greatest imperial dynasties, incorporated the area that is now Bolivia into their empire about 1200 A.D. Their control was maintained until the Spaniards arrived in 1535 and reduced the predominantly Indian population to slavery. When Napoleon occupied Madrid in 1808 and placed his brother Joseph on the Spanish throne, a fervor of revolutionary activity quickened in Bolivia, culminating with the 1809 proclamation of independence. Sixteen years of struggle ensued before the republic, named for the famed liberator Simon Bolivar, was established on August 6, 1825. Since then, Bolivia has had more than 60 revolutions, 70 presidents and 11 constitutions.

Most pre-decimal coins of independent Bolivia carry the assayer's initials which generally appear near the rim on the reverse to the right of the date between the 4 and 5 o'clock positions. The mintmark appears in the 7 to 8 o'clock position.

RULERS

Spanish until 1825

MINTMARKS

P or POTOSI monogram - Potosi

MONETARY SYSTEM

16 Reales = 1 Escudo

COLONIAL COINAGE

1/4 REAL

.8500 gm., .903 SILVER, .0250 oz ASW

MINTMARK: (POTOSI) monogram

Obv: Castle. Rev: Lion.

C#	Date	Mintage	VG	Fine	VF	XF
32	1796	—	7.50	10.00	20.00	50.00
	1797	—	7.50	12.50	20.00	50.00
	1798	—	7.50	12.50	20.00	50.00
	1799	—	7.50	12.50	20.00	50.00
	1800	—	10.00	15.00	30.00	65.00
	1801	—	10.00	15.00	30.00	65.00
	1802	—	7.50	12.50	20.00	50.00
	1803	—	10.00	15.00	30.00	65.00
	1804	—	20.00	50.00	150.00	300.00
	1805	—	20.00	50.00	150.00	300.00
	1806	—	7.50	12.50	32.50	60.00
	1807	—	12.50	25.00	50.00	125.00
	1808	—	7.50	12.50	20.00	60.00

GOLD

C#	Date	Mintage	VG	Fine	VF	XF
32a	1808	—		—	Rare	—

.8500 gm., .903 SILVER, .0250 oz ASW

Similar to C#32

C#	Date	Mintage	VG	Fine	VF	XF
42	1809	—	12.50	20.00	70.00	90.00
	1825	—	50.00	80.00	200.00	300.00

1/2 REAL

1.6500 gm., .917 SILVER, .0486 oz ASW

MINTMARK: P

Crude, 'Cob' Coinage

Obv: CAROLUS III monogram. Rev: Arms.

C#	Date	Mintage	Good	VG	Fine	VF
6	1760 V	—	10.00	17.50	55.00	100.00
	1761 V	—	10.00	17.50	55.00	100.00
	1762 V	—	10.00	17.50	55.00	100.00
	1763 V	—	10.00	17.50	55.00	100.00
	1764 V	—	10.00	17.50	55.00	100.00
	1765 V	—	10.00	17.50	55.00	100.00
	1766 V	—	10.00	17.50	55.00	100.00
	Date Off Flan	—	8.50	15.00	20.00	55.00

MINTMARK: POTOSI (monogram)

Obv. leg: CAR III...., arms. Rev: Pillars.

C#	Date	Mintage	VG	Fine	VF	XF
9	1767 JR	—	8.50	15.00	25.00	65.00
	1768 JR	—	8.00	15.00	25.00	50.00
	1769 JR	—	8.00	15.00	25.00	40.00
	1770 JR	—	8.00	15.00	25.00	40.00
	1771 JR	—	—	—	Rare	—

1.6500 gm., .903 SILVER, .0479 oz ASW

Obv. leg: CAROLUS III...., bust.

C#	Date	Mintage	VG	Fine	VF	XF
14	1773 JR	—	6.50	10.00	20.00	50.00
	1774 JR	—	5.00	8.50	17.50	40.00
	1775 JR	—	5.00	7.00	15.00	32.50
	1776 JR	—	10.00	15.00	35.00	75.00
	1776 PR	—	5.00	8.50	20.00	50.00
	1777 PR	—	5.00	8.50	17.50	40.00
	1778 PR	—	5.00	8.50	17.50	40.00
	1779/7 PR	—	8.50	13.00	30.00	55.00
	1779/8 PR	—	8.50	13.00	30.00	55.00
	1779 PR	—	5.00	8.50	17.50	40.00
	1780 PR	—	5.00	8.50	17.50	40.00
	1781 PR	—	5.00	7.50	15.00	35.00
	1782 PR	—	6.00	9.00	17.50	32.50
	1783/2 PR	—	10.00	15.00	25.00	30.00
	1783 PR	—	5.00	8.00	12.50	32.50
	1784 PR	—	5.00	8.50	15.00	32.50
	1785 PR	—	5.00	8.50	15.00	32.50
	1786 PR	—	5.00	7.50	15.00	30.00
	1787 PR	—	6.00	10.00	20.00	42.50
	1788 PR	—	6.00	10.00	20.00	55.00
	1789 PR	—	6.00	10.00	25.00	40.00

Obv. leg: CAROLUS IV...., bust of Charles III.

C#	Date	Mintage	VG	Fine	VF	XF
23	1789 PR	—	6.00	13.50	30.00	60.00
	1790 PR	—	6.00	12.50	25.00	50.00
	1791 PR	—	6.00	12.50	25.00	50.00

Obv. leg: CAROLUS IIII...., bust.

C#	Date	Mintage	VG	Fine	VF	XF
33	1791 PR	—	6.00	10.00	20.00	55.00
	1792 PR	—	6.00	10.00	20.00	55.00
	1793 PR	—	6.50	10.00	20.00	55.00
	1794 PR	—	6.50	10.00	20.00	55.00
	1795 PR	—	12.50	20.00	35.00	80.00
	1795 PP	—	6.00	10.00	15.00	42.50
	1796 PP	—	6.50	10.00	20.00	42.50
	1797 PP	—	6.50	10.00	20.00	42.50
	1798 PP	—	6.50	10.00	20.00	42.50
	1799 PP	—	6.50	10.00	20.00	42.50
	1800 PP	—	6.50	10.00	20.00	42.50
	1801 PP	—	6.50	10.00	20.00	45.00
	1802 PP	—	6.50	10.00	20.00	45.00
	1803 PJ	—	6.50	10.00	20.00	45.00
	1804 PJ	—	6.50	10.00	20.00	42.50
	1805 PJ	—	6.50	10.00	20.00	42.50
	1806 PJ	—	6.50	10.00	20.00	42.50
	1807 PJ	—	6.50	10.00	20.00	50.00
	1808 PJ	—	6.50	10.00	20.00	40.00
	1809 PJ	—	20.00	32.50	45.00	85.00

Obv. leg: FERDIN VII...., bust.

C#	Date	Mintage	VG	Fine	VF	XF
43	1814 PJ	—	12.50	20.00	75.00	100.00
	1815 PJ	—	10.00	17.50	70.00	100.00
	1816 PJ	—	6.50	10.00	35.00	55.00
	1817 PJ	—	5.00	8.50	18.50	35.00
	1818 PJ	—	4.50	7.50	17.50	35.00
	1819 PJ	—	4.50	7.50	17.50	35.00
	1820 PJ	—	4.50	7.50	17.50	35.00
	1821 PJ	—	4.50	7.50	17.50	35.00
	1822 PJ	—	4.50	7.50	17.50	35.00
	1823 PJ	—	4.50	7.50	17.50	35.00
	1823 JL	—	4.50	7.50	20.00	50.00
	1824 PJ	—	4.50	7.50	17.50	35.00
	1825 JL	—	4.50	7.50	17.50	35.00

REAL

3.2500 gm., .917 SILVER, .0958 oz ASW

MINTMARK: P

Crude, 'Cob' Coinage

(PLV-) SVL (-TRA')/date within pillars

C#	Date	Mintage	Good	VG	Fine	VF
7	1760 V	—	10.00	22.50	50.00	85.00
	1761 V	—	10.00	22.50	50.00	85.00
	1762 V	—	10.00	22.50	50.00	85.00
	1763 V	—	10.00	22.50	50.00	85.00
	1764 V	—	10.00	22.50	50.00	85.00
	1765 V	—	10.00	22.50	50.00	85.00
	1767 V	—	10.00	22.50	50.00	85.00
	1768 V	—	10.00	22.50	50.00	85.00
	1769 V	—	10.00	22.50	50.00	85.00
	1770 V	—	10.00	22.50	50.00	85.00
	1771 V	—	10.00	22.50	50.00	85.00
	1771/0 V	—	12.50	25.00	60.00	100.00
	1772 V	—	10.00	22.50	50.00	85.00
	1773 V	—	10.00	22.50	50.00	85.00
	Date Off Flan	—	4.50	10.00	15.00	25.00

3.2500 gm., .903 SILVER, .0943 oz ASW

MINTMARK: POTOSI (monogram)

Obv. leg: CAR. III...., arms. Rev: Pillars.

C#	Date	Mintage	VG	Fine	VF	XF
10	1767 JR	—	20.00	35.00	55.00	80.00
	1768 JR	—	20.00	35.00	55.00	80.00
	1769 JR	—	20.00	35.00	55.00	80.00
	1770 JR	—	20.00	35.00	55.00	80.00
	1771 JR	—	45.00	65.00	100.00	135.00
	1772 JR	—	45.00	65.00	100.00	135.00
	1773 JR	—	45.00	65.00	100.00	135.00

Obv. leg: CAROLUS III...., bust.

C#	Date	Mintage	VG	Fine	VF	XF
15	1773 JR	—	7.50	12.50	20.00	42.50
	1774 JR	—	6.50	10.00	15.00	35.00
	1775 JR	—	6.50	10.00	15.00	35.00
	1776 JR	—	10.00	17.50	35.00	70.00
	1776 PR	—	4.00	6.50	10.00	35.00
	1776 PR/JR	—	7.50	12.50	30.00	70.00
	1777 PR	—	6.50	10.00	20.00	35.00
	1778 PR	—	6.50	10.00	20.00	35.00
	1779 PR	—	6.50	10.00	20.00	35.00
	1780 PR	—	6.50	10.00	20.00	35.00
	1781 PR	—	6.50	10.00	20.00	35.00
	1782 PR	—	6.50	10.00	20.00	35.00
	1783 PR	—	6.50	10.00	20.00	35.00
	1784/3 PR	—	6.50	10.00	20.00	27.50
	1784 PR	—	6.50	10.00	20.00	35.00
	1785 PR	—	10.00	15.00	27.50	50.00
	1786 PR	—	6.50	10.00	20.00	35.00
	1787 PR	—	6.50	10.00	20.00	35.00
	1788 PR	—	6.50	10.00	20.00	35.00
	1789 PR	—	10.00	15.00	30.00	65.00

Obv. leg: CAROLUS IV...., bust of Charles III.

C#	Date	Mintage	VG	Fine	VF	XF
24	1789 PR	—	10.00	16.50	35.00	65.00
	1790 PR	—	6.50	10.00	17.50	55.00
	1791/81 PR	—	8.50	12.50	27.50	65.00
	1791 PR	—	6.50	10.00	20.00	42.50

Obv. leg: CAROLUS IIII...., bust.

C#	Date	Mintage	VG	Fine	VF	XF
34	1791 PR	—	6.50	10.00	17.50	40.00
	1792 PR	—	6.50	10.00	12.50	27.50
	1793 PR	—	5.00	7.50	12.50	27.50
	1794 PR	—	5.00	7.50	15.00	42.50
	1795 PR	—	10.00	17.50	27.50	65.00
	1795 PP	—	6.50	10.00	15.00	42.50
	1796 PP	—	6.50	10.00	15.00	45.00
	1797 PP	—	5.00	7.50	12.50	27.50
	1798 PP	—	5.00	7.50	12.50	27.50
	1799 PP	—	6.00	8.50	15.00	45.00
	1800 PP	—	5.00	7.50	12.50	37.50
	1801 PP	—	5.00	7.50	12.50	37.50
	1802 PP	—	6.00	8.50	15.00	45.00
	1803 PP	—	6.50	10.00	25.00	60.00
	1803 PJ	—	5.00	8.50	15.00	35.00
	1804 PJ	—	5.00	7.50	12.50	27.50
	1805 PJ	—	5.00	8.50	15.00	40.00
	1806 PJ	—	5.00	8.50	15.00	40.00
	1807 PJ	—	5.00	8.50	15.00	40.00
	1808 PJ	—	5.00	7.50	15.00	35.00
	1808/9 PJ	—	17.50	30.00	60.00	125.00
	1809 PJ	—	22.50	40.00	75.00	100.00
44	1813 PJ	—	6.50	10.00	25.00	40.00
	1816 PJ	—	4.00	6.50	12.50	25.00
	1817 PJ	—	4.00	6.50	12.50	25.00
	1818 PJ	—	4.00	6.50	12.50	25.00
	1819 PJ	—	4.00	6.50	12.50	25.00
	1820 PJ	—	4.00	6.50	12.50	25.00
	1821 PJ	—	4.00	6.50	12.50	25.00
	1822 PJ	—	4.00	6.50	12.50	25.00
	1823 PJ	—	4.00	6.50	12.50	25.00
	1824 PJ	—	4.00	6.50	12.50	25.00
	1825 JL	—	4.00	6.50	12.50	25.00

2 REALES

6.5000 gm., .917 SILVER, .1916 oz ASW

MINTMARK: P

Crude, 'Cob' Coinage

(PLV-) SVL (-TRA)/date within pillars

C#	Date	Mintage	Good	VG	Fine	VF
7.5	1759 Q	—	20.00	50.00	75.00	125.00
	1760 V	—	17.50	35.00	65.00	125.00
	1761 V	—	17.50	35.00	70.00	125.00
	1762 V	—	16.00	30.00	65.00	125.00
	1763 V	—	16.00	30.00	70.00	125.00
	1764 V	—	16.00	30.00	70.00	125.00
	1765 V	—	16.00	30.00	70.00	125.00
	1766 V	—	15.00	25.00	65.00	125.00
	1767 V	—	15.00	25.00	65.00	125.00
	1768 V	—	15.00	25.00	65.00	125.00
	1768 Y	—	20.00	45.00	90.00	150.00
	1769 V	—	15.00	25.00	65.00	125.00
	1770 V	—	15.00	25.00	65.00	125.00

6.5000 gm., .903 SILVER, .1887 oz ASW

C#	Date	Mintage	Good	VG	Fine	VF
	1771 V	—	17.50	35.00	85.00	150.00
	1772 V	—	17.50	30.00	65.00	125.00
	1773 V	—	19.00	32.50	65.00	125.00
	Date Off Flan					
		—	10.00	15.00	27.50	45.00

6.5000 gm., .917 SILVER, .1916 oz ASW

MINTMARK: POTOSI (monogram)

Obv. leg: CAR.III..., arms. Rev: Pillars.

C#	Date	Mintage	VG	Fine	VF	XF
11	1767 JR	—	15.00	25.00	55.00	110.00
	1768 JR	—	15.00	27.50	55.00	100.00
	1769 JR	—	17.50	32.50	60.00	110.00
	1770 JR	—	15.00	25.00	50.00	100.00

6.5000 gm., .903 SILVER, .1887 oz ASW

C#	Date	Mintage	VG	Fine	VF	XF
11a	1771 JR	—	40.00	65.00	110.00	200.00
16	1773 JR	—	7.50	10.00	20.00	50.00
	1774 JR	—	7.50	10.00	17.50	42.50
	1775 JR	—	7.50	10.00	17.50	42.50
	1776 JR	—	10.00	17.50	22.50	65.00
	1776 PR	—	8.50	14.00	20.00	32.50
	1777 PR	—	8.50	14.00	20.00	32.50
	1778 PR	—	8.50	14.00	22.50	32.50
	1779 PR	—	8.50	13.50	22.50	45.00
	1780/79 PR	—	8.50	14.00	20.00	25.00
	1780 PR	—	8.50	13.50	20.00	32.50
	1781 PR	—	8.50	13.50	20.00	32.50
	1782/81 PR	—	10.00	15.00	25.00	50.00
	1782 PR	—	8.50	13.50	20.00	30.00
	1783 PR	—	8.50	13.50	20.00	30.00
	1784/3 PR	—	10.00	17.50	30.00	60.00
	1784 PR	—	8.50	13.50	20.00	30.00
	1785/4PR	—	9.50	15.00	22.50	35.00
	1785 PR	—	8.50	13.50	20.00	30.00
	1786 PR	—	8.50	13.50	20.00	30.00
	1787 PR	—	8.50	13.50	20.00	30.00
	1788 PR	—	8.50	13.50	20.00	30.00
	1789 PR	—	10.00	17.50	20.00	65.00

Obv. leg: CAROLUS IV...., bust of Charles III.

C#	Date	Mintage	VG	Fine	VF	XF
24	1789 PR	—	12.50	20.00	30.00	70.00
	1790 PR	—	12.50	20.00	30.00	70.00
	1791 PR	—	7.50	10.00	20.00	60.00

Obv. leg: CAROLUS IIII...., bust.

C#	Date	Mintage	VG	Fine	VF	XF
35	1791 PR	—	7.50	10.00	22.50	55.00
	1792 PR	—	7.50	10.00	17.50	40.00
	1793 PR	—	6.50	8.50	15.00	35.00
	1794 PR	—	6.50	8.50	13.50	30.00
	1795 PR	—	10.00	17.50	25.00	65.00
	1795 PP	—	6.50	8.50	13.50	30.00
	1796 PP	—	6.50	8.50	13.50	30.00
	1797 PP	—	6.50	8.50	13.50	30.00
	1798 PP	—	6.50	8.50	13.50	30.00
	1799 PP	—	6.50	8.50	13.50	30.00
	1800 PP	—	6.50	8.50	13.50	30.00
	1801 PP	—	6.50	8.50	13.50	30.00
	1802 PP	—	12.50	20.00	90.00	165.00
	1802 PJ	—	6.50	8.50	13.50	30.00
	1803/2 PJ	—	6.50	8.50	15.00	40.00
	1803 PJ	—	6.50	8.50	13.50	30.00
	1804 PJ	—	6.50	8.50	13.50	30.00
	1805 PJ	—	6.50	8.50	13.50	30.00
	1806 PJ	—	6.50	8.50	13.50	30.00
	1807 PJ	—	6.50	8.50	13.50	30.00
	1808 PJ	—	6.50	8.50	13.50	30.00

Obv. leg: FERDIN VII...., bust.

C#	Date	Mintage	VG	Fine	VF	XF
45	1808 PJ	—	10.00	15.00	25.00	40.00
45	1809 PJ	—	7.50	12.50	16.50	25.00
	1813 PJ	—	7.50	12.50	16.50	27.50
	1814 PJ	—	8.50	13.50	20.00	25.00
	1816 PJ	—	7.50	12.50	16.50	32.50
	1817 PJ	—	7.50	12.50	16.50	32.50
	1818 PJ	—	7.50	12.50	16.50	32.50
	1819 PJ	—	7.50	12.50	16.50	27.50
	1820 PJ	—	7.50	12.50	16.50	32.50
	1821 PJ	—	7.50	12.50	16.50	27.50
	1822 PJ	—	7.50	12.50	16.50	27.50
	1823 PJ	—	7.50	12.50	16.50	27.50
	1824 PJ	—	7.50	12.50	16.50	27.50
	1825 PJ	—	10.00	17.50	27.50	60.00
	1825 J	—	40.00	60.00	125.00	200.00
	1825 JL	—	10.00	15.00	25.00	50.00

4 REALES

13.0000 gm., .917 SILVER, .3833 oz ASW

MINTMARK: P

Crude, 'Cob' Coinage

(PL)V-SVL-T(RA)/date within pillars

C#	Date	Mintage	Good	VG	Fine	VF
8	1760 V	—	50.00	80.00	125.00	200.00
	1761 V	—	50.00	80.00	125.00	200.00
	1762 V	—	50.00	80.00	125.00	200.00
	1763 Q	—	65.00	140.00	175.00	250.00
	1763 V	—	50.00	80.00	125.00	200.00
	1764 V	—	50.00	80.00	125.00	200.00
	1765 V	—	50.00	80.00	125.00	200.00
	1766 V	—	50.00	80.00	125.00	200.00
	1767 V	—	50.00	80.00	125.00	200.00
	1768 V	—	50.00	80.00	125.00	200.00
	1769 V	—	50.00	80.00	125.00	200.00
	1770 V	—	50.00	80.00	125.00	200.00

13.0000 gm., .903 SILVER, .3774 oz ASW

C#	Date	Mintage	Good	VG	Fine	VF
8a	1771 V	—	50.00	80.00	125.00	200.00
	1772 H	—	90.00	135.00	200.00	300.00
	1772 V	—	50.00	80.00	125.00	200.00
	1773 V	—	50.00	80.00	125.00	200.00
	Date off flan					
		—	20.00	37.50	55.00	100.00

13.0000 gm., .917 SILVER, .3833 oz ASW

MINTMARK: POTOSI (monogram)

Obv. leg: CAROLUS III...., arms.

C#	Date	Mintage	VG	Fine	VF	XF
12	1767 JR	—	60.00	110.00	200.00	475.00
	1768 JR	—	50.00	75.00	125.00	250.00
	1769/8 JR	—	75.00	125.00	200.00	500.00
	1769 JR	—	70.00	115.00	175.00	475.00
	1770 JR(lg)	—	50.00	75.00	130.00	200.00
	1770 JR(sm)	—	55.00	80.00	150.00	275.00

13.0000 gm., .903 SILVER, .3774 oz ASW

C#	Date	Mintage	VG	Fine	VF	XF
12a	1771 JR	—	275.00	400.00	600.00	800.00
	1772 JR	—	350.00	500.00	650.00	950.00
	1773 JR	—	500.00	750.00	1150.	1500.

Obv: Bust. Rev: Pillars.

C#	Date	Mintage	VG	Fine	VF	XF
17	1773 JR	—	22.50	35.00	60.00	100.00
	1774 JR	—	22.50	35.00	55.00	90.00
	1775 JR	—	22.50	35.00	60.00	100.00
	1776 JR	—	55.00	80.00	110.00	190.00
	1776 PR	—	22.50	35.00	60.00	100.00
	1777 PR	—	22.50	35.00	60.00	100.00
	1778/7 PR	—	45.00	65.00	80.00	200.00
	1778 PR	—	22.50	35.00	60.00	100.00
	1778 JR Nex.	—	75.00	120.00	300.00	825.00
	1779 PR	—	22.50	35.00	55.00	100.00
	1780 PR	—	22.50	35.00	50.00	85.00
17	1781 PR	—	22.50	35.00	50.00	85.00
	1782/1 PR	—	25.00	37.50	55.00	120.00
	1782 PR	—	22.50	35.00	50.00	85.00
	1783 PR	—	20.00	30.00	50.00	100.00
	1784/3 PR	—	25.00	37.50	55.00	100.00
	1784 PR	—	22.50	35.00	50.00	115.00
	1785/4 PR	—	25.00	40.00	65.00	100.00
	1785 PR	—	22.50	35.00	50.00	90.00
	1786/4 PR	—	22.50	35.00	55.00	90.00
	1786 PR	—	22.50	35.00	55.00	85.00
	1787 PR	—	22.50	35.00	50.00	80.00
	1788 PR	—	22.50	35.00	50.00	100.00
	1789 PR	—	25.00	40.00	120.00	200.00

Obv. leg: CAROLUS IV...., bust of Charles III.

C#	Date	Mintage	VG	Fine	VF	XF
26	1789 PR	—	25.00	45.00	90.00	200.00

Obv. leg: CAROLUS IIII...., bust of Charles III.

C#	Date	Mintage	VG	Fine	VF	XF
26a	1790 PR	—	25.00	40.00	80.00	175.00

Obv. leg: CAROLUS IIII....., bust.

C#	Date	Mintage	VG	Fine	VF	XF
36	1791 PR	—	15.00	25.00	35.00	90.00
	1792 PR	—	12.50	15.00	25.00	50.00
	1793 PR	—	12.50	15.00	25.00	60.00
	1794 PR	—	12.50	15.00	25.00	50.00
	1795/4 PR	—	15.00	20.00	30.00	80.00
	1795 PR	—	17.50	25.00	35.00	80.00
	1795 PP	—	12.50	15.00	25.00	60.00
	1796 PP	—	12.50	15.00	25.00	40.00
	1797 PP	—	12.50	15.00	25.00	60.00
	1798 PP	—	12.50	15.00	25.00	55.00
	1799 PP	—	12.50	15.00	25.00	40.00
	1800 PP	—	12.50	15.00	25.00	40.00
	1801 PP	—	12.50	15.00	25.00	40.00
	1802 PP	—	12.50	15.00	25.00	40.00
	1803 PJ	—	12.50	15.00	25.00	40.00
	1804 PJ	—	12.50	15.00	25.00	40.00
	1805 PJ	—	12.50	15.00	25.00	60.00
	1806 PJ	—	12.50	15.00	25.00	40.00
	1807 PJ	—	15.00	20.00	30.00	70.00
	1808 PJ	—	12.50	15.00	25.00	45.00
	1809 PJ	—	20.00	35.00	50.00	100.00

Obv. leg: FERDIN...., bust.

C#	Date	Mintage	VG	Fine	VF	XF
46	1809 PJ	—	17.50	25.00	35.00	70.00
	1813 PJ	—	35.00	55.00	75.00	100.00
	1814 PJ	—	15.00	22.50	35.00	65.00
	1815 PJ	—	15.00	20.00	30.00	50.00
	1816 PJ	—	15.00	20.00	32.50	80.00
	1817 PJ	—	12.50	15.00	37.50	90.00
	1818 PJ	—	12.50	15.00	32.50	90.00
	1819 PJ	—	12.50	15.00	32.50	80.00
	1820 PJ	—	12.50	15.00	32.50	80.00
	1821 PJ	—	14.00	17.50	37.50	100.00
	1822 PJ	—	12.50	15.00	32.50	80.00
	1823 PJ	—	12.50	15.00	32.50	80.00
	1824 PJ	—	14.00	17.50	37.50	100.00
	1825 PJ	—	20.00	35.00	90.00	140.00
	1825 JL	—	14.00	17.50	40.00	100.00
	1825 J	—	20.00	35.00	80.00	200.00

8 REALES

25.0000 gm., .917 SILVER, .7371 oz ASW

MINTMARK: P

Crude, 'Cob' Coinage

PLV-SVL-TRA/date within pillars

C#	Date	Mintage	Good	VG	Fine	VF
8.5	1760 V	—	37.50	70.00	115.00	165.00
	1761 V	—	32.50	55.00	100.00	125.00
	1762 V	—	32.50	55.00	100.00	125.00
	1763 V	—	32.50	55.00	100.00	125.00
	1764 V	—	32.50	55.00	100.00	125.00
	1765 V	—	32.50	55.00	100.00	125.00
	1766 V	—	32.50	55.00	100.00	125.00

C#	Date	Mintage	Good	VG	Fine	VF
8.5	1767 V	—	32.50	55.00	100.00	125.00
	1768 V	—	30.00	50.00	75.00	110.00
	1768 E	—	30.00	50.00	75.00	110.00
	1769/8 V	—	50.00	75.00	175.00	300.00
	1769 V	—	32.50	55.00	100.00	125.00
	1770/62 V	—	35.00	60.00	125.00	200.00
	1770 V	—	32.50	55.00	100.00	125.00
	1770 J	—	—	Rare	—	—

25.0000 gm., .903 SILVER, .7258 oz ASW

C#	Date	Mintage	Good	VG	Fine	VF
8.5a	1771/0 V	—	60.00	75.00	115.00	175.00
	1771 V	—	32.50	55.00	100.00	125.00
	1772 V	—	30.00	70.00	115.00	175.00
	1773/2 V	—	45.00	90.00	175.00	300.00
	1773 V	—	75.00	110.00	140.00	200.00
	Date Off Flan	—	30.00	50.00	75.00	125.00

25.0000 gm., .917 SILVER, .7371 oz ASW

MINTMARK: POTOSI (monogram)

C#	Date	Mintage	VG	Fine	VF	XF
13	1767 JR	—	250.00	500.00	900.00	2500.
	1768 JR	—	125.00	225.00	300.00	750.00
	1769 JR w/rounded 9	—	125.00	250.00	350.00	500.00
	1769 JR w/fancy 9	—	125.00	250.00	350.00	500.00
	1769/70 JR	—	125.00	250.00	350.00	500.00
	1770 JR	—	125.00	200.00	325.00	450.00

25.0000 gm., .903 SILVER, .7258 oz ASW

C#	Date	Mintage	VG	Fine	VF	XF
	1771 JR	—	150.00	275.00	400.00	550.00
	1772 JR	—	150.00	275.00	450.00	600.00
	1773 JR	—	200.00	300.00	500.00	750.00

Obv. leg: CAROLUS III....

C#	Date	Mintage	VG	Fine	VF	XF
18	1772 JR	—	400.00	600.00	750.00	1000.
	1773 JR	—	40.00	80.00	150.00	250.00
	1774 JR	—	27.50	45.00	75.00	125.00
	1775 JR	—	27.50	40.00	55.00	85.00
	1776 JR	—	35.00	50.00	65.00	125.00
	1776 PR	—	40.00	55.00	100.00	175.00
	1777 PR	—	30.00	45.00	60.00	100.00
	1778 PR	—	27.50	40.00	55.00	100.00
	1778 PR-NEX	—	65.00	100.00	125.00	200.00
	1779 PR	—	30.00	45.00	80.00	160.00
	1780 PR	—	30.00	45.00	60.00	100.00
	1781 PR	—	27.50	40.00	55.00	100.00
	1782/1 PR	—	35.00	50.00	65.00	125.00
	1782 PR	—	35.00	50.00	100.00	150.00
	1783/2 PR	—	40.00	55.00	160.00	225.00
	1783 PR	—	30.00	45.00	100.00	150.00
	1784 PR	—	30.00	45.00	110.00	175.00
	1785/4 PR	—	35.00	50.00	100.00	150.00
	1785 PR	—	35.00	50.00	100.00	140.00
	1786/5 PR	—	40.00	55.00	85.00	125.00
	1786 PR	—	30.00	45.00	60.00	100.00
	1787 PR	—	30.00	45.00	60.00	100.00
	1788/7 PR	—	27.50	40.00	55.00	85.00
	1788 PR	—	27.50	40.00	55.00	85.00
	1789 PR	—	50.00	75.00	200.00	450.00

Obv. leg: CAROLUS IV...., bust of Charles III.
Rev: Similar to C#18.

C#	Date	Mintage	VG	Fine	VF	XF
27	1789 PR	—	40.00	55.00	100.00	150.00
	1790 PR	—	35.00	50.00	80.00	135.00
	1791 PR	—	250.00	375.00	750.00	1300.

Obv. leg: CAROLUS IIII...., bust. Rev: Pillars.

C#	Date	Mintage	VG	Fine	VF	XF
37	1791 PR	—	35.00	60.00	100.00	140.00
	1792 PR	—	27.50	40.00	65.00	120.00
	1793 PR	—	27.50	40.00	55.00	85.00
	1794 PR	—	27.50	40.00	55.00	85.00
	1795/4 PR	—	40.00	65.00	115.00	175.00
	1795 PR	—	50.00	75.00	125.00	175.00
	1795 PP	—	27.50	40.00	55.00	85.00
	1796 PP	—	27.50	40.00	55.00	85.00
	1797 PP	—	27.50	40.00	55.00	85.00
	1798 PP	—	27.50	40.00	55.00	85.00
	1799 PP	—	27.50	40.00	55.00	85.00
	1800 PP	—	27.50	40.00	55.00	85.00
	1801 PP	—	27.50	40.00	55.00	85.00
	1802 PP	—	27.50	40.00	55.00	85.00
	1803 PJ	—	27.50	40.00	55.00	85.00
	1804 PJ	—	27.50	40.00	55.00	85.00
	1805 PJ	—	27.50	40.00	55.00	85.00
	1806 PJ	—	27.50	40.00	55.00	85.00
	1807 PJ	—	27.50	40.00	55.00	85.00
	1808 PJ	—	27.50	40.00	55.00	85.00

Rev: Similar to C#18.

C#	Date	Mintage	VG	Fine	VF	XF
47	1808 PJ	—	35.00	60.00	100.00	200.00
	1809 PJ	—	35.00	60.00	100.00	135.00
	1813 PJ	—	27.50	40.00	55.00	100.00
	1813 PJ (error) legend: FERDIN IIV	—	250.00	400.00	750.00	1200.
	1814/13 PJ	—	27.50	40.00	60.00	110.00
	1814 PJ	—	27.50	40.00	55.00	85.00
	1815 PJ	—	35.00	45.00	60.00	100.00
	1816 PJ	—	27.50	40.00	55.00	85.00
	1817 PJ	—	27.50	40.00	55.00	85.00
	1818 PJ	—	27.50	40.00	55.00	85.00

C#	Date	Mintage	VG	Fine	VF	XF
47	1819 PJ	—	27.50	40.00	60.00	100.00
	1820 PJ	—	35.00	45.00	60.00	100.00
	1821 PJ	—	27.50	40.00	55.00	85.00
	1822 PJ	—	27.50	40.00	55.00	85.00
	1823 PJ	—	27.50	40.00	55.00	85.00
	1823 JP	—	30.00	45.00	85.00	175.00
	1824 PJ	—	27.50	40.00	55.00	85.00
	1824 J	—	150.00	300.00	450.00	1200.
	1825 J	—	65.00	100.00	150.00	350.00
	1825 JL	—	27.50	40.00	55.00	85.00

ESCUDO

3.4000 gm., .875 GOLD, .0956 oz AGW

MINTMARK: POTOSI (monogram)

Obv. leg: CAROL III...., bust. Rev: Arms.

C#	Date	Mintage	VG	Fine	VF	XF
19	1780 PR	—	85.00	110.00	150.00	300.00
	1781 PR	—	85.00	110.00	150.00	300.00
	1782 PR	—	85.00	110.00	135.00	200.00
	1783 PR	—	85.00	110.00	150.00	300.00
	1784 PR	—	75.00	100.00	125.00	175.00
	1785 PR	—	75.00	100.00	125.00	150.00
	1786 PR	—	75.00	100.00	125.00	175.00
	1787 PR	—	75.00	100.00	125.00	150.00
	1788 PR	—	—	—	Rare	—

Obv. leg: CAROLUS IV...., bust of Charles III.

C#	Date	Mintage	VG	Fine	VF	XF
28	1789 PR	—	85.00	120.00	190.00	275.00
	1790 PR	—	85.00	110.00	165.00	250.00
	1791 PR	—	75.00	100.00	125.00	200.00

Obv. leg: CAROL IIII...., bust of Charles III.

C#	Date	Mintage	VG	Fine	VF	XF
28a	1791 PR	—	125.00	200.00	250.00	450.00

Obv. leg: CAROL IIII...., bust.

C#	Date	Mintage	VG	Fine	VF	XF
38	1791 PR	—	85.00	110.00	135.00	250.00
	1792 PR	—	85.00	110.00	135.00	250.00
	1793 PR	—	85.00	110.00	135.00	225.00
	1794 PR	—	85.00	110.00	135.00	300.00
	1795 PP	—	85.00	110.00	135.00	225.00
	1796 PP	—	85.00	110.00	135.00	225.00
	1797 PP	—	85.00	110.00	135.00	200.00
	1798 PP	—	85.00	110.00	135.00	250.00
	1799 PP	—	75.00	100.00	125.00	250.00
	1800 PP	—	75.00	100.00	125.00	250.00
	1801 PP	—	75.00	100.00	125.00	200.00
	1802 PP	—	75.00	100.00	125.00	250.00
	1803 PJ	—	75.00	100.00	125.00	300.00
	1804 PJ	—	75.00	100.00	125.00	300.00
	1805 PJ	—	75.00	100.00	125.00	300.00
	1806 PJ	—	75.00	100.00	125.00	300.00
	1807 PJ	—	75.00	100.00	125.00	300.00
	1808 PJ	—	75.00	100.00	125.00	300.00

Obv. leg: FERDIN VII...., bust.

C#	Date	Mintage	VG	Fine	VF	XF
48	1822 PJ	—	100.00	150.00	200.00	600.00
	1823 PJ	—	125.00	200.00	300.00	800.00
	1824 PJ	—	150.00	250.00	375.00	900.00

2 ESCUDOS

6.8000 gm., .875 GOLD, .1913 oz AGW

MINTMARK: POTOSI (monogram)

Obv. leg: CAROL III...., bust. Rev: Arms.

C#	Date	Mintage	VG	Fine	VF	XF
20	1778 PR	—	350.00	525.00	775.00	1100.
	1780 PR	—	350.00	500.00	700.00	1075.
	1781/0 PR	—	350.00	525.00	750.00	1100.
	1781 PR	—	300.00	450.00	675.00	1000.
	1782 PR	—	500.00	725.00	1000.	1300.
	1783 PR	—	150.00	250.00	475.00	700.00
	1784 PR	—	150.00	225.00	350.00	700.00
	1785 PR	—	200.00	300.00	450.00	800.00
	1786 PR	—	225.00	325.00	400.00	750.00
	1787 PR	—	350.00	500.00	650.00	1100.
	1788 PR	—	300.00	450.00	700.00	1200.

Obv. leg: CAROL IV...., bust of Charles III.

C#	Date	Mintage	VG	Fine	VF	XF
29	1789 PR	—	300.00	425.00	675.00	900.00
	1790 PR	—	350.00	500.00	675.00	1100.

Obv. leg: CAROL IIII...., bust of Charles III.

C#	Date	Mintage	VG	Fine	VF	XF
29a	1791 PR	—	—	600.00	750.00	1100.

Obv. leg: CAROL IIII, bust.

C#	Date	Mintage	VG	Fine	VF	XF
39	1791 PR	—	250.00	350.00	450.00	625.00
	1793 PR	—	250.00	350.00	450.00	625.00
	1794 PR	—	200.00	325.00	375.00	625.00
	1795 PP	—	150.00	225.00	450.00	800.00
	1796 PP	—	250.00	350.00	450.00	800.00
	1798 PP	—	250.00	350.00	400.00	700.00
	1799 PP	—	200.00	300.00	350.00	625.00
	1800 PP	—	150.00	225.00	275.00	425.00
	1801 PP	—	150.00	250.00	275.00	550.00
	1802 PP	—	250.00	350.00	400.00	675.00
	1804 PJ	—	200.00	275.00	300.00	575.00

C#	Date	Mintage	VG	Fine	VF	XF
	1805 PJ	—	200.00	300.00	400.00	700.00
	1806 PJ	—	250.00	350.00	450.00	700.00
	1807 PJ	—	150.00	225.00	275.00	400.00
	1808 PJ	—	200.00	300.00	400.00	525.00

4 ESCUDOS

13.5000 gm., .875 GOLD, .3798 oz AGW

MINTMARK: POTOSI (monogram)

Obv. leg: CAROL III...., bust. Rev: Arms.

C#	Date	Mintage	VG	Fine	VF	XF
21	1778 PR	—	450.00	600.00	1000.	1500.
	1779 PR	—	450.00	600.00	850.00	1300.
	1780 PR	—	450.00	600.00	900.00	1300.
	1781 PR	—	350.00	500.00	800.00	1200.
	1783 PR	—	350.00	500.00	800.00	1200.
	1784/3 PR	—	350.00	500.00	800.00	1200.
	1784 PR	—	350.00	500.00	800.00	1200.
	1785 PR	—	350.00	500.00	800.00	1200.
	1786 PR	—	350.00	500.00	800.00	1200.
	1787 PR	—	350.00	500.00	800.00	1200.
	1788 PR	—	350.00	500.00	800.00	1200.

Obv. leg: CAROL IV...., bust of Charles III.

C#	Date	Mintage	VG	Fine	VF	XF
30	1789 PR	—	650.00	1000.	1500.	2000.
	1790 PR	—	500.00	750.00	1000.	1500.

Obv. leg: CAROL IIII...., bust of Charles III.

C#	Date	Mintage	VG	Fine	VF	XF
30a	1791 PR(lg)	—	500.00	750.00	1100.	1500.
	1791 PR(sm)	—	450.00	650.00	1000.	1400.

Obv. leg: CAROL IIII...., bust.

C#	Date	Mintage	VG	Fine	VF	XF
40	1791 PR	—	300.00	400.00	575.00	925.00
	1792 PR	—	300.00	400.00	575.00	925.00
	1793 PR	—	300.00	400.00	575.00	925.00
	1794 PR	—	350.00	450.00	550.00	1000.
	1795 PP	—	300.00	375.00	450.00	900.00
	1796 PF	—	300.00	375.00	450.00	900.00
	1797 PP	—	250.00	325.00	450.00	900.00
	1798 PP	—	250.00	325.00	450.00	900.00
	1799 PP	—	250.00	325.00	450.00	900.00
	1800 PP	—	250.00	325.00	450.00	900.00
	1801 PP	—	250.00	325.00	450.00	900.00
	1802 PP	—	300.00	375.00	475.00	700.00
	1803 PP	—	500.00	700.00	900.00	1500.
	1804 PJ	—	600.00	825.00	900.00	1500.
	1804 PP	—	600.00	825.00	900.00	1500.
	1805 PJ	—	350.00	450.00	550.00	850.00
	1806 PJ	—	250.00	325.00	450.00	825.00
	1807 PJ	—	300.00	375.00	450.00	825.00
	1808 PJ	—	300.00	375.00	450.00	825.00

8 ESCUDOS

27.0000 gm., .875 GOLD, .7596 oz AGW

MINTMARK: POTOSI (monogram)

Obv. leg: CAROL III.... Rev: Similar to C#41.

C#	Date	Mintage	VG	Fine	VF	XF
22	1778 PR	—	650.00	800.00	2000.	3000.
	1779 PR	—	600.00	750.00	1000.	1800.
	1780 PR	—	500.00	600.00	750.00	1500.
	1781 PR	—	500.00	600.00	800.00	1650.
	1782 PR	—	600.00	750.00	1000.	1750.
	1783 PR	—	600.00	750.00	1000.	1600.
	1784/3 PR	—	600.00	750.00	1000.	1700.
	1784 PR	—	600.00	750.00	1000.	1600.
	1785 PR	—	500.00	600.00	750.00	1600.
	1786 PR	—	600.00	750.00	1000.	1600.
	1787/86 PR	—	600.00	750.00	1000.	1850.
	1787 PR	—	600.00	750.00	1000.	1600.
	1788 PR	—	600.00	750.00	1000.	1600.

Obv. leg: CAROL IV...., bust of Charles III.

C#	Date	Mintage	VG	Fine	VF	XF
31	1789 PR	—	600.00	750.00	1000.	1500.
	1790 PR	—	500.00	600.00	750.00	1250.

Obv. leg: CAROL IIII...., bust of Charles III.

C#	Date	Mintage	VG	Fine	VF	XF
31a	1791 PR	—	650.00	1000.	1500.	2000.

Obv. leg: CAROL IIII....

C#	Date	Mintage	VG	Fine	VF	XF
41	1791 PR	—	600.00	800.00	1200.	1750.
	1792 PR	—	500.00	600.00	750.00	1200.
	1793 PR	—	500.00	600.00	750.00	1200.
	1794 PR	—	500.00	600.00	750.00	1200.
	1795 PP	—	500.00	600.00	750.00	1150.
	1796 PP	—	500.00	600.00	750.00	1100.
	1797 PP	—	500.00	600.00	750.00	1100.
	1798 PP	—	500.00	600.00	750.00	1100.
	1799 PP	—	500.00	600.00	750.00	1100.
	1800 PP	—	500.00	600.00	750.00	1100.
	1801 PP	—	500.00	600.00	750.00	1100.
	1802 PP	—	500.00	600.00	750.00	1100.
	1803 PJ	—	500.00	600.00	750.00	1100.
	1804 PJ	—	500.00	600.00	750.00	1100.
	1805 PJ	—	500.00	600.00	750.00	1100.
	1806 PJ	—	500.00	600.00	750.00	1100.
	1807 PJ	—	500.00	600.00	750.00	1100.
	1808 PJ	—	500.00	600.00	750.00	1100.

Obv. leg: FERDIN VII...., uniformed bust.

C#	Date	Mintage	VG	Fine	VF	XF
49	1809 PJ	—	1650.	4000.	12,000.	15,000.

Obv. leg: FERDIN. VII...., bust.

C#	Date	Mintage	VG	Fine	VF	XF
50	1817 PJ	—	650.00	1000.	1500.	4000.
	1822 PJ	—	500.00	600.00	750.00	1300.
	1823 PJ	—	650.00	1000.	1500.	4000.
	1824 PJ	—	550.00	675.00	1200.	1600.

REPUBLIC COINAGE

MINTMARKS

A - Paris
(a) - Paris, privy marks only
Potosi (monogram)
PAZ - La Paz

MONETARY SYSTEM

8 Soles (Sueldos) = 1 Peso
2 Pesos = 1 Escudo (Scudo)

1/4 SOL

.8500 gm., .900 SILVER, .0245 oz ASW

Llama in plain field/POTOSI

Y#	Date	Mintage	VG	Fine	VF	XF
1 (13)	1852	—	4.50	6.50	10.00	35.00

Branches flank llama

Y#	Date	Mintage	VG	Fine	VF	XF
1a (A13)	1853	—	25.00	35.00	60.00	100.00

1/2 SOL

1.6500 gm., .900 SILVER, .0477 oz ASW

MINTMARK: POTOSI (monogram)

C#	Date	Mintage	VG	Fine	VF	XF
51	1827 JM	—	3.50	5.00	9.00	17.50
	1828/7 JM	—	4.00	6.00	10.00	20.00
	1828 JM	—	2.50	4.00	7.00	15.00
	1829 JM	—	3.00	4.50	8.00	16.00
	1830 JL	—	1.75	2.50	3.50	7.50
	1830 J	—	4.00	5.50	10.00	20.00
	1830 JF	—	6.50	10.00	15.00	35.00

Obv: W/o denomination.

Y#	Date	Mintage	VG	Fine	VF	XF
2	1853 FP	—	3.00	7.50	12.50	20.00
(14)	1854 MJ	—	2.50	4.00	8.50	13.50
	1855 MJ	—	3.00	7.50	12.50	20.00
	1856 FP	—	4.00	6.00	12.50	20.00
	1856 FJ	—	4.75	7.00	15.00	25.00
	1856 MJ	—	5.25	8.00	15.00	25.00

Obv: Denomination added.

Y#	Date	Mintage	VG	Fine	VF	XF
2a	1856 FJ	—	3.50	7.50	12.50	20.00
(14a)	1857 FJ	—	2.25	4.50	10.00	15.00
	1857/6 FJ	—	4.00	8.50	15.00	22.50
	1858 FJ	—	3.00	7.50	12.50	20.00

MINTMARK: PAZ

Obv: Crude "La Paz style" head.

Y#	Date	Mintage	VG	Fine	VF	XF
17	1855 F	—	8.00	12.00	20.00	30.00
(39)	1855 P	—	10.00	15.00	35.00	50.00
	1856/5 P	—	12.50	17.50	40.00	60.00
	1856 P	—	10.00	15.00	35.00	50.00

Obv: Crude so-called "ugly head".

Y#	Date	Mintage	VG	Fine	VF	XF
17b	1858/7 P	—	12.50	20.00	45.00	70.00
(39)	1858 P	—	11.50	17.50	40.00	60.00

MINTMARK: POTOSI (monogram)

Obv: Laureate head of Bolivar left.
Rev: 2 llamas under palm tree, date below.

Y#	Date	Mintage	VG	Fine	VF	XF
2b	1859	—	11.50	17.50	37.50	55.00
(19)	1859 (error) BOLIVAR spelled BOLIVRA					
		—	13.50	20.00	45.00	65.00

1/16 PESO

1.3800 gm., .900 SILVER, .0399 oz ASW

Y#	Date	Mintage	VG	Fine	VF	XF
7 (24)	1859 FJ	—	10.00	15.00	35.00	60.00

W/o denomination, only weight indicated as 25 GS.

Y#	Date	Mintage	VG	Fine	VF	XF
7a	1859 FJ	—	Reported, Not Confirmed			
(27)	1860 FJ	—	3.00	5.00	7.50	10.00
	1861 FJ	—	3.00	5.00	7.50	10.00
	1862 FP	—	20.00	30.00	65.00	110.00
	1863 FP	—	20.00	30.00	55.00	100.00

SOL

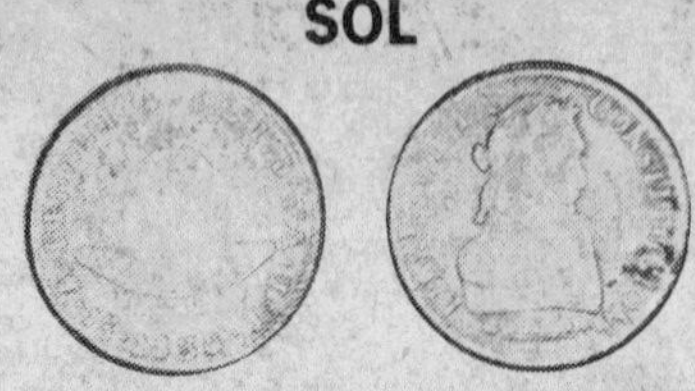

3.1000 gm., .900 SILVER, .0897 oz ASW

MINTMARK: POTOSI (monogram)

C#	Date	Mintage	VG	Fine	VF	XF
52	1827 JM	—	4.00	6.00	10.00	17.50
	1828 JM	—	5.00	7.50	12.50	20.00
	1829 JM	—	5.50	8.50	15.00	25.00
	1830 JL	—	2.75	3.50	6.00	10.00
	1830 J	—	6.50	10.00	20.00	30.00

Obv: W/o denomination.

Y#	Date	Mintage	VG	Fine	VF	XF
3	1853 FP	—	4.00	6.00	12.00	20.00
(15)	1854 MJ	—	5.00	10.00	17.50	30.00

Obv: Denomination added.

Y#	Date	Mintage	VG	Fine	VF	XF
3a	1855 MJ	—	6.00	10.00	20.00	30.00
(15a)	1856/5 FJ/MJ	15.00	20.00	35.00	60.00	
	1856 FJ	—	3.50	8.50	15.00	25.00
	1857 FJ	—	5.50	12.00	20.00	30.00
	1858/7 FJ	—	6.00	10.00	20.00	30.00
	1858 FJ	—	5.25	12.00	20.00	30.00

MINTMARK: PAZ

Obv: "Potosi style" laureate head.

Y#	Date	Mintage	VG	Fine	VF	XF
18	1853 P	—	Reported, not confirmed			
(40)	1855 P	—	11.50	15.00	35.00	50.00

Obv: Crude "La Paz style" head.

Y#	Date	Mintage	VG	Fine	VF	XF
18a	1855 F	—	25.00	55.00	90.00	125.00
(40)	1856 P	—	9.25	14.00	30.00	50.00

Obv: Crude so-called "ugly head".

Y#	Date	Mintage	VG	Fine	VF	XF
18b	1857 P	—	25.00	55.00	100.00	125.00
(40)	1859/7 P	—	30.00	75.00	150.00	200.00
	1859 P	—	17.00	25.00	50.00	75.00

MINTMARK: POTOSI (monogram)

Y#	Date	Mintage	VG	Fine	VF	XF
3b	1859	—	13.50	20.00	45.00	65.00
(20)						

1/8 PESO

2.6000 gm., .900 SILVER, .0752 oz ASW

Y#	Date	Mintage	VG	Fine	VF	XF
8	1859 FJ	—	10.00	15.00	35.00	60.00
(A24)						

W/o denomination, only weight indicated as 50 GS.

Y#	Date	Mintage	VG	Fine	VF	XF
8a	1859 FJ	—	Reported, Not Confirmed			

Y#	Date	Mintage	VG	Fine	VF	XF
(28)	1860 FJ	—	3.00	5.00	7.50	12.50
	1861 FJ	—	3.00	5.00	7.50	12.50
	1862 FJ	—	—	—	—	—
	1862 FP	—	3.00	5.00	7.50	12.50
	1863/2 FP	—	4.00	6.00	10.00	16.50
	1863 FP	—	3.00	5.00	7.50	12.50

2 SOLES

6.5000 gm., .900 SILVER, .1881 oz ASW

MINTMARK: POTOSI (monogram)

C#	Date	Mintage	VG	Fine	VF	XF
53	1827 JM	—	13.50	20.00	40.00	60.00
	1828/7 JM	—	30.00	50.00	80.00	125.00
	1828 JM	—	6.50	10.00	20.00	30.00
	1829 JM	—	17.00	25.00	45.00	60.00
	1830 JL	—	6.00	8.50	12.50	17.50
	1830 J	—	8.50	12.50	20.00	30.00
	1830 JV	—	—	—	—	—
	1830 JF	—	17.00	25.00	45.00	60.00

Obv: W/o denomination.

Y#	Date	Mintage	VG	Fine	VF	XF
4	1853 FP	—	10.00	15.00	30.00	45.00
(16)						

Obv: Denomination added.

Y#	Date	Mintage	VG	Fine	VF	XF
4a	1854 MJ	—	7.50	12.50	25.00	40.00
(16a)	1855 MJ	—	7.50	12.50	25.00	40.00
	1856 FJ	—	10.00	17.50	35.00	50.00
	1856/5 MJ	—	15.00	20.00	35.00	50.00
	1856 MJ	—	6.50	10.00	20.00	30.00
	1857 FJ	—	7.50	10.00	25.00	35.00
	1858 FJ	—	10.00	15.00	35.00	50.00

MINTMARK: PAZ

Obv: Bare head

Y#	Date	Mintage	VG	Fine	VF	XF
15	1853	—	—	Rare	—	
(A43)						

Obv: "Potosi style" laureate head.

Y#	Date	Mintage	VG	Fine	VF	XF
19	1854 F	—	30.00	100.00	150.00	225.00
(41)						

Obv: Crude "La Paz style" head.

Y#	Date	Mintage	VG	Fine	VF	XF
19a	1855 F	—	55.00	85.00	150.00	200.00
(41)	1856 P	—	50.00	75.00	140.00	200.00

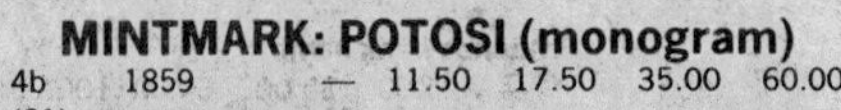

MINTMARK: POTOSI (monogram)

Y#	Date	Mintage	VG	Fine	VF	XF
4b	1859	—	11.50	17.50	35.00	60.00
(21)						

1/4 PESO

4.5000 gm., .900 SILVER, .1302 oz ASW

Y#	Date	Mintage	VG	Fine	VF	XF
9	1859 FJ	—	15.00	22.50	45.00	75.00
(25)						

W/o denomination, only weight indicated as 100 GS.

Y#	Date	Mintage	VG	Fine	VF	XF
9a	1859 FJ	—	Reported, not confirmed			
(29)	1860 FJ	—	5.00	8.50	12.50	20.00
	1861 FJ	—	7.50	12.50	20.00	30.00
	1862 FJ	—	5.00	8.50	12.50	20.00
	1862 FP	—	4.50	7.50	10.00	15.00
	1863/2 FP	—	4.50	7.50	10.00	15.00
	1863 FP	—	5.00	8.50	12.50	20.00

4 SOLES

13.5000 gm., .900 SILVER, .3906 oz ASW

MINTMARK: POTOSI (monogram)

C#	Date	Mintage	VG	Fine	VF	XF
54	1827 JM	—	27.00	40.00	75.00	100.00
	1828 JM	—	27.00	40.00	75.00	100.00
	1829 JM	—	20.00	30.00	60.00	100.00
	1830/27 JL	—	15.00	25.00	50.00	90.00
	1830 JL	—	12.00	15.00	20.00	27.50
	1830 J	—	15.00	20.00	25.00	35.00

NOTE: Many die varieties exist.

Obv: W/o denomination

Y#	Date	Mintage	VG	Fine	VF	XF
5	1853 FP	—	20.00	35.00	65.00	100.00
(17)						

Obv: Denomination added

Y#	Date	Mintage	VG	Fine	VF	XF
5a	1853 MF	—	12.00	17.50	22.50	35.00
(17a)	1854 MF	—	12.00	15.00	20.00	27.50
	1854 MJ	—	12.00	15.00	20.00	27.50
	1855 MJ	—	12.00	15.00	20.00	27.50
	1855 FJ	—	12.00	17.50	22.50	35.00
	1856 FJ	—	12.00	15.00	20.00	27.50
	1856/5 MJ	—	15.00	25.00	40.00	60.00
	1856 MJ	—	12.00	17.50	25.00	35.00
	1857 FJ	—	12.00	15.00	20.00	27.50
	1857 FJ (error) V in BOLIVIANA is inverted A					
		—	—	—	—	—
	1858 FJ	—	12.00	15.00	20.00	30.00

MINTMARK: PAZ

Y#	Date	Mintage	VG	Fine	VF	XF
16	1853 J	—	55.00	85.00	135.00	175.00
(43)						

Obv: "Potosi style" laureate head.

20	1853 J	—	27.50	40.00	75.00	110.00
(42)	1854 J	—	Reported, not confirmed			
	1854 F	—	30.00	55.00	100.00	125.00
	1855 F	—	30.00	60.00	100.00	150.00

Obv: Crude "La Paz style" head.

20a	1855 F	—	17.50	32.50	50.00	75.00
(42)	1856/5 P/F	—	20.00	35.00	65.00	90.00
	1856 P	—	17.50	32.50	55.00	80.00
	1857/6 P	—	45.00	75.00	120.00	150.00
	1857 P	—	225.00	275.00	375.00	500.00
	1858 P	—	300.00	375.00	450.00	600.00
20b	1859 P	—	225.00	275.00	375.00	500.00
(42)	1859 J	—	—	Reported, not confirmed		

NOTE: Several distinct bust varieties exist.

MINTMARK: POTOSI (monogram)

5b	1859 MJ	—	35.00	50.00	75.00	100.00
(22)	1859 FJ	—	12.00	17.50	30.00	50.00

1/2 PESO

27.0000 gm., .900 SILVER, .7813 oz ASW
W/o denomination, only weight indicated as 200 GS.

10	1860 FJ	—	30.00	50.00	65.00	100.00
(30)						

8 SOLES

27.0000 gm., .900 SILVER, .7813 oz ASW

C#	Date	Mintage	VG	Fine	VF	XF
55	1827 JM	—	27.50	37.50	65.00	100.00
	1828 JM	—	25.00	32.50	55.00	85.00
	1829 JM	—	25.00	32.50	60.00	90.00
	1830 JF	—	30.00	40.00	60.00	90.00
	1830 J	—	35.00	45.00	70.00	100.00
	1830/20 JF	—	35.00	45.00	70.00	100.00
	1831 JF	—	25.00	35.00	50.00	75.00
	1831 JL	—	25.00	35.00	50.00	75.00
	1832 J	—	27.50	35.00	50.00	75.00
	1833 L	—	200.00	300.00	450.00	600.00
	1833 LM	—	27.50	35.00	60.00	100.00
	1834 LM	—	30.00	40.00	60.00	100.00
	1835 LM	—	30.00	40.00	70.00	100.00
	1836/5 LM	—	45.00	60.00	75.00	100.00
	1836 LM	—	30.00	40.00	70.00	100.00
	1837 LM	—	25.00	35.00	50.00	75.00
	1838 LM	—	25.00	35.00	50.00	75.00
	1839 LM	—	25.00	35.00	50.00	75.00
	1839 LR	—	35.00	45.00	70.00	100.00
	1840 LR	—	25.00	35.00	50.00	75.00

Obv: Similar to C#55.

61	1841 LR	—	25.00	35.00	37.50	55.00
	1841 LR (error: CONSTITUCIN)					
		—	—	Rare	—	—
	1842	—	25.00	35.00	50.00	—
	1842 LR	—	25.00	35.00	50.00	75.00
	1843/2 LR	—	35.00	50.00	65.00	90.00
	1843 LR	—	30.00	45.00	60.00	75.00
	1844 R	—	27.50	37.50	60.00	85.00
	1845 R	—	25.00	35.00	50.00	70.00
	1846/45 R	—	75.00	100.00	150.00	225.00
	1846 R	—	30.00	45.00	60.00	85.00
	1847 R	—	30.00	45.00	60.00	85.00
	1848 R	—	50.00	85.00	125.00	250.00
	1848 M	—	200.00	450.00	650.00	950.00

Obv: w/o denomination.

C#	Date	Mintage	VG	Fine	VF	XF
62	1848 FM	—	35.00	50.00	100.00	150.00
	1849 FM	—	35.00	50.00	100.00	150.00
	1850 FM	—	30.00	45.00	75.00	100.00
	1851/50 FM	—	45.00	65.00	85.00	110.00
	1851 FM	—	30.00	50.00	90.00	115.00
	1851 FR	—	30.00	45.00	75.00	125.00

Obv: Similar to C#62

Y#	Date	Mintage	VG	Fine	VF	XF
6	1852 FM	—	37.50	65.00	100.00	175.00
(18)	1852 M	—	50.00	75.00	100.00	150.00
	1853 FP	—	50.00	100.00	165.00	250.00
	1854 M	—	100.00	130.00	150.00	225.00
	1854 FM	—	60.00	120.00	225.00	350.00
	1856 FJ	—	60.00	110.00	200.00	300.00

Obv: Denomination added. Rev: Similar to Y#6.

6a	1854 MJ	—	27.50	35.00	50.00	65.00
(18a)	1855 MJ	—	25.00	32.50	60.00	90.00

Obv: Similar to Y#6a.

6b	1859 FJ	—	375.00	550.00	1200.	1700.
(23)						

PESO

20.0000 gm., .903 SILVER, .5807 oz ASW

MINTMARK: POTOSI (monogram)

Rev: Peso

Y#	Date	Mintage	VG	Fine	VF	XF
11	1859 F.J.	—	25.00	70.00	115.00	150.00
(26.1)	1859 FJ.	—	42.50	60.00	125.00	250.00

Space between CONSTITUCION 400 Gs wider.
Rev: PESO over Po

Y#	Date	Mintage	VG	Fine	VF	XF
11c (26.2)	1859F.J.	—	25.00	50.00	85.00	125.00

Rev: PESO changed to Po

Y#	Date	Mintage	VG	Fine	VF	XF
11a (26.3)	1859F.J.	—	200.00	350.00	800.00	1500.

Rev: Without PESO or Po

Y#	Date	Mintage	VG	Fine	VF	XF
— (26.4)	1859F.J.	—	200.00	375.00	800.00	1500.

Obv: Tree now divides 10DS-20Gs. Rev. leg: Po without L10D20GS.

Y#	Date	Mintage	VG	Fine	VF	XF
11b (26.5)	1860F.J.	—	135.00	200.00	375.00	500.00

Obv: Tree divides 10DS.-20GS. Rev. leg: W/o Po.

Y#	Date	Mintage	VG	Fine	VF	XF
11d	1859 FJ	—	100.00	150.00	250.00	350.00
(31)	1860 FJ	—	17.50	22.50	40.00	70.00
	1861 FJ	—	17.50	22.50	40.00	70.00
	1862 FJ	—	17.50	22.50	40.00	70.00
	1862 FP	—	20.00	25.00	60.00	90.00
	1863/2 FP	—	17.50	22.50	30.00	90.00
	1863 FP	—	20.00	25.00	60.00	90.00

1/2 ESCUDO

1.7000 gm., .875 GOLD, .0478 oz AGW

C#	Date	Mintage	VG	Fine	VF	XF
56	1834 LM	—	—	—	Rare	—
	1838 LM	—	100.00	150.00	200.00	325.00
	1839 LM	—	100.00	135.00	180.00	325.00
	1840 LR	—	100.00	150.00	200.00	325.00

C#	Date	Mintage	VG	Fine	VF	XF
63	1841 LR	—	50.00	75.00	100.00	140.00
	1842 LR	—	50.00	75.00	100.00	160.00
	1843 LR	—	50.00	75.00	100.00	160.00
63	1844 R	—	50.00	75.00	100.00	140.00
	1845 R	—	50.00	75.00	100.00	140.00
	1846 R	—	50.00	75.00	100.00	130.00
	1847 R	—	50.00	75.00	100.00	150.00

Y#	Date	Mintage	Fine	VF	XF	Unc
12	1852 MJ	—	65.00	110.00	160.00	200.00
(50)	1852 FP	—	60.00	85.00	110.00	185.00
	1853 FP	—	50.00	75.00	100.00	175.00
	1854 FP	—	65.00	110.00	160.00	200.00
	1855 M	—	60.00	85.00	120.00	175.00
	1855 FS	—	60.00	85.00	120.00	175.00
	1856 FS	—	50.00	75.00	110.00	155.00
	1857 FP	—	200.00	300.00	400.00	500.00

Y#	Date	Mintage	Fine	VF	XF	Unc
30 (53)	1868 FE	—	400.00	600.00	1000.	1300.

ESCUDO

3.4000 gm., .875 GOLD, .0956 oz AGW

C#	Date	Mintage	VG	Fine	VF	XF
57	1831 JL	—	100.00	175.00	250.00	325.00
	1832 JL	—	100.00	165.00	200.00	250.00
	1833 JL	—	100.00	165.00	250.00	300.00
	1834 JL	—	75.00	100.00	150.00	225.00
	1837 LM	—	100.00	165.00	250.00	300.00
	1838 LM	—	100.00	165.00	250.00	300.00
	1839 LM	—	100.00	165.00	250.00	300.00

C#	Date	Mintage	VG	Fine	VF	XF
64	1841 LR	—	75.00	100.00	125.00	175,00
	1842 LR	—	75.00	100.00	125.00	175.00
	1846 R	—	75.00	100.00	125.00	175.00

Y#	Date	Mintage	Fine	VF	XF	Unc
13	1852 FP	—	75.00	100.00	150.00	200.00
(51)	1853 FP	—	75.00	100.00	150.00	200.00
	1855 LM/J	—	75.00	100.00	150.00	200.00
	1856 FJ	—	75.00	100.00	150.00	200.00

Y#	Date	Mintage	Fine	VF	XF	Unc
31 (54)	1868 FE	—	150.00	225.00	350.00	550.00

2 ESCUDOS

6.8000 gm., .875 GOLD, .1913 oz AGW

C#	Date	Mintage	VG	Fine	VF	XF
58	1834 LM	—	200.00	300.00	450.00	600.00
58	1835 JM	—	Reported, Not Confirmed			
	1835 LM	—	175.00	250.00	350.00	450.00
	1839 JM	—	Reported, Not Confirmed			
	1839 LM	—	Reported, Not Confirmed			

C#	Date	Mintage	VG	Fine	VF	XF
65	1841 LR	—	350.00	475.00	600.00	1000.

4 ESCUDOS

13.5000 gm., .875 GOLD, .3798 oz AGW

C#	Date	Mintage	VG	Fine	VF	XF
59	1834 JL	—	500.00	700.00	900.00	2000.

C#	Date	Mintage	VG	Fine	VF	XF
66	1841 LR	—	750.00	1000.	1250.	2500.

8 ESCUDOS

27.0000 gm., .875 GOLD, .7596 oz AGW

C#	Date	Mintage	VG	Fine	VF	XF
60	1831 JL	—	BV	550.00	650.00	950.00
	1832 JL	—	BV	550.00	650.00	950.00
	1833 JL	—	BV	550.00	650.00	950.00
	1833 LM	—	BV	550.00	650.00	950.00
	1834 JL	—	BV	550.00	650.00	950.00
	1834 JM	—	550.00	650.00	750.00	1000.
	1834 LM	—	BV	550.00	650.00	950.00
	1835 JM	—	BV	550.00	650.00	950.00
	1835 LM	—	BV	550.00	650.00	950.00
	1836 LM	—	550.00	650.00	750.00	1000.
	1837 LM	—	BV	600.00	650.00	950.00
	1838 LM	—	BV	600.00	650.00	950.00
	1839 LM	—	BV	600.00	650.00	950.00
	1840 LR	—	BV	600.00	650.00	950.00

Obv: Similar to C#60

C#	Date	Mintage	VG	Fine	VF	XF
67	1841 LR	—	550.00	625.00	675.00	800.00
	1842 LR	—	550.00	625.00	675.00	800.00
	1843 LR	—	BV	550.00	600.00	725.00
	1844 LR	—	BV	550.00	600.00	725.00
	1844 R	—	600.00	700.00	750.00	950.00
	1845 R	—	600.00	700.00	750.00	950.00
	1846 R	—	600.00	700.00	750.00	950.00
	1847 R	—	600.00	700.00	750.00	950.00
	Obv: Bare head of Bolivar left.					
69	1851 MF	—	700.00	850.00	1000.	1400.

Y#	Date	Mintage	Fine	VF	XF	Unc
14	1852 FP	—	BV	550.00	650.00	900.00
(52)	1853 FP	—	BV	550.00	650.00	900.00
	1854 M	—	BV	550.00	650.00	900.00
	1854 MJ	—	BV	550.00	650.00	900.00
	1855 LM	—	BV	550.00	650.00	900.00
	1855 MJ	—	BV	550.00	650.00	900.00
	1856 FJ	—	BV	550.00	650.00	900.00
	1857 FJ	—	BV	550.00	650.00	900.00

ONZA

35.9991 gm., .900 GOLD, 1.0417 oz AGW
Obv: Value in wreath.
Rev: Arms set against weapons and flags.

Y#	Date	Mintage	Fine	VF	XF	Unc
32	1868 FE	—	2500.	5200.	6500.	7000.
(55)	1868 FP	—	2000.	4000.	6000.	6750.

MELGAREJO ISSUES

1/4 MELGAREJO

.666 SILVER

Y#	Date	Mintage	VG	Fine	VF	XF
21	1865	—	5.00	8.00	12.50	30.00
(A49)						

1/2 MELGAREJO

.666 SILVER

Y#	Date	Mintage	VG	Fine	VF	XF
22	1865*	—	6.00	8.00	12.00	20.00
(B49)	1868	—	—	—	Rare	—

***NOTE:** Varieties exist.

MELGAREJO

.666 SILVER

Y#	Date	Mintage	Fine	VF	XF	Unc
23	1865 FP small letters					
(C49)		—	30.00	45.00	75.00	150.00
	1865 FP thicker letters					
		—	20.00	35.00	50.00	90.00
	1866	—		—	Rare	—

DECIMAL COINAGE

100 Centecimos = 1 Boliviano
100 Centavos = 1 Boliviano

In 1870 the weight of the silver coins was modified by adjusting it to the metric system.

CENTECIMO

COPPER

Y#	Date	Mintage	Fine	VF	XF	Unc
24	1864	.010	40.00	60.00	90.00	150.00
(44)						

CENTAVO

COPPER

Y#	Date	Mintage	Fine	VF	XF	Unc
37	1878	—	40.00	65.00	125.00	175.00
(65)						
	Obv: Denomination under eagle. Rev: 'LA UNION ES LA FUERZA' in wreath, date below.					
37a	1878	—	—	—	—	—
(65a)						

Y#	Date	Mintage	Fine	VF	XF	Unc
39	1883A	.500	3.50	4.50	6.00	16.50
(67)						

2 CENTECIMOS

COPPER

Y#	Date	Mintage	Fine	VF	XF	Unc
25	1864	.150	60.00	125.00	190.00	275.00
(45)						

2 CENTAVOS

COPPER

Y#	Date	Mintage	Fine	VF	XF	Unc
38	1878	—	50.00	85.00	140.00	200.00
(66)						
	Denomination under eagle.					
38a	1878	—	—	—	—	—
(66a)						

Y#	Date	Mintage	Fine	VF	XF	Unc
40	1883A	.250	4.00	7.50	11.50	20.00
(68)						

1/20 BOLIVIANO

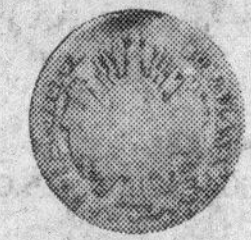

1.2500 gm., .900 SILVER, .0361 oz ASW

Y#	Date	Mintage	Fine	VF	XF	Unc
26	1864 FP	—	7.50	12.50	20.00	65.00
(46)	1865/4 FP	—	10.00	17.50	27.50	100.00
	1865 FP	—	10.00	15.00	22.50	70.00

5 CENTAVOS

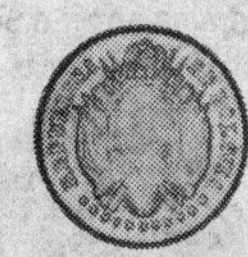

1.2500 gm., .900 SILVER, .0361 oz ASW
Obv: 11 stars at bottom.
Rev. leg: LA UNION HACE LA FUERZA, with weight.

Y#	Date	Mintage	Fine	VF	XF	Unc
33	1871 ER	—	10.00	15.00	35.00	60.00
(56)	1871 FP	—	50.00	80.00	120.00	200.00

Obv: 11 stars at bottom. Rev: Without weight.

Y#	Date	Mintage	Fine	VF	XF	Unc
33a	1871 ER	—	6.50	10.00	20.00	42.50
(56a)	1872 ER	—	—	—	Rare	—
	1872/1 FE	—	5.00	8.00	12.50	25.00
	1872 FE	—	6.50	10.00	20.00	42.50

Obv: 9 stars at bottom.

Y#	Date	Mintage	Fine	VF	XF	Unc
33b (56b)	1872 FE	—	6.50	10.00	15.00	32.50

Rev. leg: LA UNION ES LA FUERZA

Y#	Date	Mintage	Fine	VF	XF	Unc
47	1872 FE	—	2.00	3.50	5.00	12.50
(60)	1873 FE	—	1.50	2.50	4.50	7.00
	1874 FE	—	3.00	4.00	6.00	8.00
	1875 FE	—	1.50	2.50	4.50	7.00
	1876 FE	—	2.00	3.00	5.00	9.00
	1877 FE	—	2.00	3.00	5.00	9.00
	1878 FE	—	2.50	3.50	5.00	10.00
	1879 FE	—	3.50	5.00	10.00	17.50
	1880 FE	—	3.00	7.50	11.50	27.50
	1881 FE	—	2.00	3.50	5.00	12.50
	1882 FE	—	3.75	6.50	10.00	25.00
	1883 FE	—	3.50	4.75	9.25	12.50
	1884 FE	—	4.00	6.00	8.00	20.00
	1884/3 FE	—	7.00	12.50	22.50	55.00

Reduced size lettering

Y#	Date	Mintage	Fine	VF	XF	Unc
47a	1885 FE		3.00	5.00	7.00	17.50
(60a)	1886 FE	—	2.75	4.50	6.00	15.00
	1887 FE	—	3.00	4.00	8.00	15.00
	1888 FE	—	5.00	7.50	12.50	20.00
	1889/8 FE	—	7.50	10.00	15.00	25.00
	1889 FE	—	5.00	8.00	11.50	20.00
	1890 CB	—	3.00	4.00	6.50	12.50
	1891 CB	—	4.00	6.50	10.00	17.50
	1893 CB	.070	2.00	2.75	3.75	10.00
	1895 ES	.020	8.50	15.00	20.00	35.00
	1899 MM	—	2.00	2.75	3.75	8.00
	1900 MM	.050	3.00	4.00	5.00	9.00

COPPER-NICKEL

Y#	Date	Mintage	Fine	VF	XF	Unc
41 (69)	1883 A	1.420	6.00	10.00	15.00	35.00

Y#	Date	Mintage	Fine	VF	XF	Unc
41a (69a)	1883 A	.390	2.50	3.50	6.50	18.00

Y#	Date	Mintage	Fine	VF	XF	Unc
43 (73)	1892 H	2.500	1.00	1.75	3.00	7.00

Y#	Date	Mintage	Fine	VF	XF	Unc
45	1893	2.500	2.00	3.00	10.00	17.50
(75)	1895	2.000	.35	.50	1.50	4.50
	1897	1.500	.35	.50	1.50	4.50
	1899	2.000	.35	.50	1.50	4.50
	1902	2.000	.35	.50	1.50	4.50
	1907	2.000	1.25	3.00	4.00	7.50
	1908	3.000	.35	.50	1.50	4.50
	1909	4.000	.35	.50	1.50	4.50
	1918	.530	.50	.75	1.75	4.50
	1919	5.370	3.00	4.50	7.50	12.50

Y#	Date	Mintage	Fine	VF	XF	Unc
57 (83)	1935	5.000	1.50	2.50	4.00	6.75

1/10 BOLIVIANO

2.5000 gm., .900 SILVER, .0723 oz ASW

Y#	Date	Mintage	VG	Fine	VF	XF
27	1864 FP	—	4.00	6.50	10.00	20.00
(47)	1865 FP	—	4.00	6.00	10.00	20.00
	1866 FP	—		Reported, Not Confirmed		
	1867 FP	—	22.50	45.00	75.00	125.00

10 CENTAVOS

.900 SILVER
Obv: 11 stars at bottom.
Rev. leg: LA UNION HACE LA FUERZA, weight in grams.

Y#	Date	Mintage	VG	Fine	VF	XF
34	1870 ER	—	3.00	5.00	8.00	12.00
(57)	1871 ER	—	5.00	7.50	12.50	18.00
	1871 FP	—	7.50	10.00	16.50	22.50

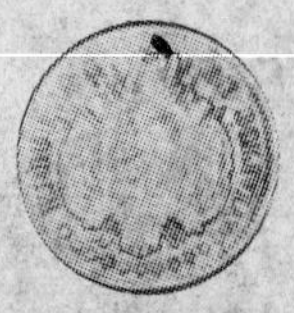

Obv: 11 stars at bottom. Rev: Without weight.

Y#	Date	Mintage	VG	Fine	VF	XF
34a (57a)	1871 ER	—	3.00	5.00	11.50	20.00

Obv: 9 stars at bottom.

Y#	Date	Mintage	VG	Fine	VF	XF
34b (57b)	1872 FE	—	3.00	5.00	15.00	25.00

Rev. leg: LA UNION ES LA FUERZA, line below CENTS.

Y#	Date	Mintage	VG	Fine	VF	XF
48	1872 FE	—	2.50	3.50	6.50	16.00
(61)	1873 FE	—	2.25	3.25	6.00	15.00
	1883 FE	—	2.50	3.50	6.75	15.00
	1884 FE	—	2.25	3.25	6.00	15.00
(61)	1884/3 FE	—	6.50	10.00	15.00	27.50

No line below CENTS.

Y#	Date	Mintage	VG	Fine	VF	XF
48.1	1872 FE	—	—	—	—	—
(61)	1873 FE	—	2.50	3.50	6.50	14.00
	1874 FE	—	2.50	3.50	6.50	14.00
	1875 FE	—	2.50	3.50	6.50	13.50
	1876 FE	—	2.25	3.25	6.75	13.75
	1877 FE	—	2.50	3.50	6.75	13.75
	1878 FE	—	2.25	3.25	6.00	17.50
	1879 FE	—	2.25	3.25	6.00	16.00
	1880 FE	—	2.50	3.50	6.00	16.00
	1881 FE	—	2.25	3.25	6.00	14.50
	1882 FE	—	3.00	4.00	6.50	18.50
	1883 FE	—	—	—	—	—
	1884/3 FE	—	—	—	—	—

Reduced size lettering

Y#	Date	Mintage	VG	Fine	VF	XF
48a	1885 FE	—	2.50	3.75	6.75	12.50
(61a)	1886 FE	—	2.25	3.25	6.75	12.50
	1887 FE	—	5.00	8.00	12.00	20.00
	1888 FE	—	6.00	9.00	14.00	25.00
	1889 FE	—	3.00	5.00	9.00	15.00
	1890 FE	—	3.00	4.00	7.50	12.50
	1890 CB	—	4.00	6.00	9.00	14.00
	1891 CB	—	3.00	5.00	9.00	20.00
	1893 CB	.050	3.00	5.00	9.00	15.00
	1895 ES	.020	6.00	9.00	13.50	20.00
	1899 MM	—	3.00	5.00	9.00	15.00
	1900 MM	.030	5.50	8.00	11.50	15.00

COPPER-NICKEL

Y#	Date	Mintage	Fine	VF	XF	Unc
42 (70)	1883 A	.140	3.00	4.00	7.00	20.00

Y#	Date	Mintage	Fine	VF	XF	Unc
42a (70a)	1883 A	.320	2.50	3.50	6.00	17.50

Y#	Date	Mintage	Fine	VF	XF	Unc
44 (74)	1892 H	1.250	1.50	2.25	5.50	15.00

Y#	Date	Mintage	Fine	VF	XF	Unc
46	1893	1.250	2.00	3.00	10.00	17.50
(76)	1895	1.000	.50	1.00	2.00	5.00
	1897	2.250	.50	1.00	2.00	5.00
	1899	3.000	.50	1.00	2.00	5.00
	1901	—	3.00	5.00	7.50	12.50
	1902	8.500	.50	1.00	1.50	5.00
	1907/2	4.000	1.00	1.50	2.50	7.50
	1907	Inc. Ab,	.50	1.00	2.00	5.00
	1908	6.000	.50	1.00	2.00	5.00
	1909	8.000	.50	1.00	2.00	5.00
	1918	1.330	.50	1.00	2.00	5.00
	1919	6.160	.50	1.00	2.00	5.00

Y#	Date	Mintage	Fine	VF	XF	Unc
58	1935	10.000	.50	1.00	2.50	3.25
(84)	1936	10.000	.50	1.00	2.50	3.75
	1939	—	.50	1.00	1.35	2.00

Y#	Date	Mintage	Fine	VF	XF	Unc
60	1937	20.000	.50	.90	1.50	2.50
(85)						

ZINC

Y#	Date	Mintage	Fine	VF	XF	Unc
57a	1942	10.000	.50	.75	1.25	2.00
(89)						

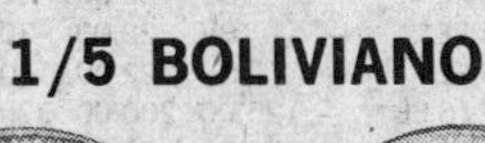

1/5 BOLIVIANO

5.0000 gm., .900 SILVER, .1446 oz ASW

Y#	Date	Mintage	VG	Fine	VF	XF
28	1864 FP	—	10.00	18.50	25.00	45.00
(48)	1865 FP	—	6.50	10.00	20.00	40.00
	1866 FP	—	6.50	10.00	20.00	40.00
	1866/5 FP	—	—	17.50	35.00	60.00

20 CENTAVOS

5.0000 gm., .900 SILVER, .1446 oz ASW
Obv: 11 stars at bottom.
Rev. leg: LA UNION HACE LA FUERZA, weight.

Y#	Date	Mintage	VG	Fine	VF	XF
35	1870 ER	—	10.00	15.00	25.00	40.00
(58)	1871 ER	—	15.00	25.00	50.00	90.00

Obv: 11 stars. Rev: Without weight.

Y#	Date	Mintage	VG	Fine	VF	XF
35a	1871 ER	—	10.00	18.50	35.00	60.00
(58a)						

Obv: 9 stars at bottom

Y#	Date	Mintage	VG	Fine	VF	XF
35b	1870 ER	—	7.50	12.50	20.00	35.00
(58b)	1871 ER	—	6.50	10.00	20.00	35.00
	1872 ER	—	7.50	12.50	20.00	35.00
	1872 FE	—	10.00	15.00	30.00	50.00

Rev. leg: LA UNION ES LA FUERZA

Y#	Date	Mintage	VG	Fine	VF	XF
49	1872 FE	—	BV	BV	5.00	10.00
(62)	1873 FE	—	BV	4.50	7.50	16.50
	1874 FE	—	BV	4.50	7.00	15.00
	1875 FE	—	BV	4.50	7.00	13.00
	1876 FE	—	BV	4.50	7.00	13.00
	1877 FE	—	BV	4.50	7.00	13.00
	1878 FE	—	BV	4.50	7.00	12.75
	1879 FE	—	BV	4.50	7.00	12.75
	1880 FE	—	BV	4.50	7.00	12.75
	1881 FE	—	BV	4.50	7.50	12.50
	1882 FE	—	BV	4.50	7.50	12.50
	1883 FE	—	BV	4.50	7.50	12.50
	1883 EF	—	10.00	15.00	25.00	35.00
	1884 FE	—	BV	4.50	7.50	12.50
	1884/3 FE	—	—	—	—	—
	1885 FE	—	5.00	7.00	10.00	15.00

Daza Commemorative

Y#	Date	Mintage	VG	Fine	VF	XF
53	1879	—	22.50	37.50	55.00	80.00
(A64)						

Reduced size lettering

Y#	Date	Mintage	VG	Fine	VF	XF
49a	1885 FE	—	BV	4.50	7.00	13.00
(62a)	1886 FE	—	BV	4.50	7.00	13.00
	1887 FE	—	BV	4.50	7.00	13.00
	1888 FE	—	BV	4.50	7.50	13.00
	1889 FE	—	BV	4.50	7.50	13.00
	1889/8 FE	—	—	—	—	—
	1890 FE	—	BV	4.50	7.50	13.50
	1890 CB	—	BV	4.50	7.00	13.00
	1891 CB	—	BV	4.50	7.00	15.00
	1892/82 CB	—	—	—	—	—
	1892 CB	—	BV	4.50	7.50	13.50
	1893 CB	.500	BV	4.50	7.00	13.50
	1894 ES	.490	BV	4.50	7.00	14.00
	1895 ES	—	BV	4.50	7.00	15.00
	1896 ES	—	BV	4.50	7.00	18.00
	1896 CB	.100	10.00	15.00	25.00	35.00
	1897 CB	.170	BV	4.50	7.00	15.00
	1898 CB	—	10.00	15.00	25.00	35.00
	1899 CB	—	—	Rare	—	—
	1899 MM	—	BV	4.50	6.25	10.00
	1900 MM	.170	BV	4.50	6.00	10.00
	1901 MM	.040	BV	4.50	8.50	12.00
	1902 MM	—	6.50	10.00	20.00	30.00
	1903 MM	.010	10.00	15.00	25.00	35.00
	1904 MM	—	7.00	11.00	17.50	30.00
	1907 MM	—	—	Rare	—	—

4.0000 gm., .833 SILVER, .1071 oz ASW

Y#	Date	Mintage	VG	Fine	VF	XF
55	1909 H	1.500	BV	BV	3.50	6.00
(81)						

ZINC

Y#	Date	Mintage	VG	Fine	VF	XF
58a	1942	10.000	.65	1.00	1.50	2.00
(90)						

50 CENTAVOS

(1/2 Boliviano)

12.5000 gm., .900 SILVER, .3617 oz ASW
Rev. leg: 12 GS. 500 MS. 9 DS. FINO

Y#	Date	Mintage	VG	Fine	VF	XF
51	1873 FE	—	BV	BV	13.50	20.00
(63)						

Rev. leg: 15 GMS 500 MMS

Y#	Date	Mintage	VG	Fine	VF	XF
	1873 FE	—	30.00	50.00	80.00	120.00

Rev: Without 50 Cents and weight.

Y#	Date	Mintage	VG	Fine	VF	XF
50	1879 FE	—	75.00	125.00	200.00	275.00
(A63)	1882 FE	—	75.00	125.00	200.00	275.00
	1884 FE	—	BV	BV	12.50	17.50

Rev: Reduced size lettering with weight.

Y#	Date	Mintage	VG	Fine	VF	XF
51a	1887 FE	—	—	—	Rare	—
(63a)	1889 MM	—	—	—	Rare	—
	1891 CB	—	40.00	60.00	90.00	150.00
	1891 MM	—	—	Reported, not confirmed		

Rev: Reduced size lettering without weight.

Y#	Date	Mintage	VG	Fine	VF	XF
51b	1891 CB	—	BV	BV	12.50	17.50
(A63a)	1892 CB	—	BV	BV	12.50	17.50
	1893 CB	3.150	BV	BV	12.50	17.50
	1894/1 CB	—	BV	12.50	17.50	25.00
	1894 CB	2.470	BV	BV	12.50	16.50
	1894 ES	I.A.	BV	BV	12.50	16.50
	1895 ES	3.390	BV	BV	12.50	17.50
	1896 ES	2.980	BV	12.50	15.00	20.00
	1897 CB	2.300	BV	12.50	15.00	20.00
	1897 ES	—	12.50	17.50	35.00	45.00
	1898 CB	—	BV	12.50	17.50	25.00
	1899 CB	—	BV	12.50	17.50	25.00
	1899 MM	—	BV	BV	12.50	17.50
	1900 MM	3.820	BV	BV	12.50	17.50

Y#	Date	Mintage	VG	Fine	VF	XF
54	1900 MM	I.A.	BV	BV	12.00	20.00
(80)	1901 MM	2.000	BV	BV	10.00	20.00
	1901/0 MM	—		—	35.00	50.00
	1902 MM	1.530	BV	BV	10.00	20.00
	1903 MM	.690	BV	BV	10.00	20.00
	1904 MM	1.290	BV	BV	10.00	20.00
	1905 MM	1.690	BV	BV	17.50	30.00
	1905 AB	—	BV	BV	10.00	20.00
	1906 MM	.630	BV	BV	10.00	20.00
	1906 AB	5.500	BV	BV	15.00	30.00
	1907 MM	.050	12.50	17.50	32.50	50.00
	1908 MM	—	20.00	30.00	75.00	110.00
	1908 MM					
		—	65.00	100.00	200.00	275.00

BOLIVIANO

Y#	Date	Mintage	VG	Fine	VF	XF
54.1 (80a)	1900 So	.900	BV	12.50	17.50	30.00

.900 GOLD

Y#	Date	Mintage	VG	Fine	VF	XF
	1900 So	—		—	3500.	5000.

10.0000 gm., .833 SILVER, .2678 oz ASW

Y#	Date	Mintage	Fine	VF	XF	Unc
56 (82)	1909 H	1.400	BV	BV	8.50	17.50

COPPER-NICKEL

Y#	Date	Mintage	Fine	VF	XF	Unc
61 (86)	1937	8.000	30.00	50.00	75.00	100.00

Y#	Date	Mintage	Fine	VF	XF	Unc
59 (88)	1939	—	.50	.75	1.25	2.25

BRONZE

Y#	Date	Mintage	Fine	VF	XF	Unc
59a (91)	1942	10.000	.65	1.00	1.75	3.25

Restrike-poor detail

Y#	Date	Mintage	Fine	VF	XF	Unc
59b (91a)	1942	5.310	.65	1.00	1.75	3.00

25.0000 gm., .900 SILVER, .7234 oz ASW
Obv: 9 stars

Y#	Date	Mintage	VG	Fine	VF	XF
29 (49)	1864 FP	—	22.00	30.00	50.00	110.00
	1864 FP larger shield	—	40.00	60.00	100.00	150.00
	1865/1 FP	—	—	—	—	—
	1865 FP	—	BV	22.00	45.00	90.00
	1866/5 FP	—	—	—	—	—
	1866 FP	—	BV	22.00	45.00	90.00
	1867 FP	—	22.00	30.00	55.00	110.00
	1868 FP	—		—	Rare	—

Obv: 11 stars. Rev: Similar to Y#29.

Y#	Date	Mintage	VG	Fine	VF	XF
29a (49a)	1867/6 FP	—	BV	22.00	35.00	45.00
	1867/6 FE/P	—	22.00	30.00	40.00	60.00
	1867 FE	—	BV	22.00	27.50	40.00
	1867 FP	—	22.00	30.00	40.00	70.00
	1868/7 FE	—	25.00	40.00	65.00	100.00
	1868 FE	.720	BV	22.00	25.00	40.00
	1869 FE	.260	BV	22.00	30.00	50.00

Obv: Similar to Y#29a.
Rev. leg: LA UNION HACE LA FUERZA

Y#	Date	Mintage	VG	Fine	VF	XF
36a (59)	1870 ER*	—	22.00	25.00	35.00	60.00
	1871 ER*	—	22.00	27.50	45.00	70.00
	1871 FP*	—	22.00	25.00	35.00	60.00

Rev: Large wreath, leg: 25 GMS 9DS FINO.

Y#	Date	Mintage	VG	Fine	VF	XF
36 (59)	1870 ER*	—	BV	22.00	25.00	30.00

Obv: 9 stars at bottom. Rev: Similar to Y#36.

Y#	Date	Mintage	VG	Fine	VF	XF
36b (59a)	1870 ER*	—	22.00	27.50	40.00	80.00
	1871 ER*	—	BV	22.00	27.50	60.00
	1871 FP*	—	BV	22.00	27.50	60.00
	1871 EF	—	BV	22.00	27.50	60.00
	1872 FE	—	BV	BV	22.00	40.00

***NOTE:** Several varieties exist.

Obv: Similar to Y#36b.
Rev. leg: LA UNION ES LA FUERZA

Y#	Date	Mintage	VG	Fine	VF	XF
52 (64)	1872 FE	—	BV	22.00	30.00	65.00
	1873 FE	—	BV	22.00	30.00	65.00
	1874 FE*	—	BV	22.00	30.00	65.00
	1875 FE	—	BV	22.00	30.00	65.00
	1877/6 FE	—	125.00	200.00	325.00	550.00
	1877 FE	—	50.00	75.00	125.00	200.00

Rev. leg: 25 GS instead of GMS.

Y#	Date	Mintage	VG	Fine	VF	XF
52.1	1879 F.E.	—	75.00	125.00	200.00	325.00
	1884 FE	—	—	—	Rare	—
	1887 FE	—	—	—	Rare	—
	1893 CB	—	—	—	Rare	—
	1893 FE	—	50.00	75.00	125.00	200.00

BRONZE

Y#	Date	Mintage	Fine	VF	XF	Unc
62 (92)	1951	10.000	.50	.75	1.25	1.75
	1951H	15.000	.75	1.00	1.75	2.75
	1951KN	15.000	1.00	1.25	2.25	3.75

5 BOLIVIANOS

BRONZE

Y#	Date	Mintage	Fine	VF	XF	Unc
63 (93)	1951	7.000	.50	.75	1.10	1.50
	1951H	15.000	.65	1.00	1.50	2.50
	1951KN	15.000	1.00	1.25	2.25	3.50

10 BOLIVIANOS

BRONZE

Y#	Date	Mintage	Fine	VF	XF	Unc
64 (94)	1951	40.000	.85	1.25	2.00	5.00

MONETARY REFORM

100 Centavos = 1 Peso Boliviano

5 CENTAVOS

COPPER-CLAD STEEL

Y#	Date	Mintage	Fine	VF	XF	Unc
66	1965	10.000	.50	.85	1.25	2.00
(95)	1966	—	— Reported, Not Confirmed			
	1967	—	—	—	—	.10
	1968	—	— Reported, Not Confirmed			
	1969	—	— Reported, Not Confirmed			
	1970	.100	—	—	.65	1.00

10 CENTAVOS

COPPER-CLAD STEEL

Y#	Date	Mintage	Fine	VF	XF	Unc
67	1965	10.000	1.00	1.50	2.00	3.00
(96)	1966	—	— Reported, Not Confirmed			
	1967	—	.65	1.00	1.50	2.00
	1968	—	— Reported, Not Confirmed			
	1969	5.700	—	.45	.75	1.25
	1971	.200	—	—	—	.50
	1972	.100	—	—	—	.30
	1973	6.000	—	—	—	.15

20 CENTAVOS

NICKEL-CLAD STEEL

Y#	Date	Mintage	Fine	VF	XF	Unc
68	1965	5.000	1.00	1.50	2.00	3.00
(97)	1966	—	— Reported, Not Confirmed			
	1967	—	.65	1.00	1.50	2.00
	1968	—	— Reported, Not Confirmed			
	1969	—	— Reported, Not Confirmed			
	1970	.400	—	—	—	.50
	1971	.400	—	—	—	.20
	1973	5.000	—	—	—	.20

25 CENTAVOS

NICKEL-CLAD STEEL

Y#	Date	Mintage	Fine	VF	XF	Unc
71	1971	—	.35	.50	.75	1.25
(101)	1972	9.998	—	—	—	.50

50 CENTAVOS

NICKEL-CLAD STEEL

Y#	Date	Mintage	Fine	VF	XF	Unc
69	1965	10.000	.10	.25	.35	2.50
(98)	1967	—	—	.10	.15	1.50
	1972	—	—	.10	.15	.50
	1973	5.000	—	.10	.15	.50

Y#	Date	Mintage	Fine	VF	XF	Unc
(98)	1974	15.000	— Reported, Not Confirmed			

PESO BOLIVIANO

NICKEL-CLAD STEEL
F.A.O. Issue

Y#	Date	Mintage	Fine	VF	XF	Unc
72 (99)	1968	.025	2.00	3.25	5.00	7.50

Y#	Date	Mintage	Fine	VF	XF	Unc
70	1968	10.000	.20	.35	.75	2.00
(100)	1969	—	.20	.35	.75	1.75
	1970	10.000	.15	.25	.35	.75
	1972	—	.20	.35	.75	1.75
	1973	5.000	.15	.25	.35	.75
	1974	15.000	.15	.25	.35	.75

5 PESOS BOLIVIANOS

NICKEL-CLAD STEEL

Y#	Date	Mintage	Fine	VF	XF	Unc
76	1976	20.000	.40	.75	1.50	4.50

3-1/2 GRAMOS

(5 Bolivianos)

3.8900 gm., .900 GOLD, .1125 oz AGW
1952 Revolution Commemorative

KM#	Date	Mintage	Fine	VF	XF	Unc
1	1952(a)	.029	BV	BV	75.00	100.00

7 GRAMOS

(10 Bolivianos)

7.7800 gm., .900 GOLD, .2251 oz AGW
1952 Revolution Commemorative

KM#	Date	Mintage	Fine	VF	XF	Unc
2	1952(a)	.079	BV	BV	150.00	175.00

14 GRAMOS

(20 Bolivianos)

15.5600 gm., .900 GOLD, .4502 oz AGW
1952 Revolution Commemorative

KM#	Date	Mintage	Fine	VF	XF	Unc
3	1952(a)	7,142	BV	BV	300.00	400.00

35 GRAMOS

(50 Bolivianos)

38.9000 gm., .900 GOLD, 1.1257 oz AGW
1952 Revolution Commemorative

KM#	Date	Mintage	Fine	VF	XF	Unc
4	1952(a)	2,857	BV	BV	730.00	800.00

100 PESOS BOLIVIANOS

9.9500 gm., .933 SILVER, .2985 oz ASW
Sesquicentenario Commemorative

Y#	Date	Mintage	Fine	VF	XF	Unc
73 (102)	1975	.160	BV	9.00	10.50	12.50

250 PESOS BOLIVIANOS

15.0100 gm., .933 SILVER, .4503 oz ASW
Sesquicentenario Commemorative

Y#	Date	Mintage	Fine	VF	XF	Unc
74 (103)	1975	.140	BV	15.00	18.50	25.00

500 PESOS BOLIVIANOS

22.0300 gm., .933 SILVER, .6609 oz ASW
Sesquicentenario Commemorative

Y#	Date	Mintage	Fine	VF	XF	Unc
75 (104)	1975	.100	BV	27.50	35.00	40.00

NCLT ISSUES

ESSAIS (E)

Standard metals unless otherwise noted

Y#	Date	Mintage	Identification	Issue Price	Mkt Val.
E39	1883A	—	1 Centavo	—	40.00
E39	1883	—	1 Centavo, EG	—	—
E40	1883A	—	2 Centavos	—	45.00
E41	1883A	—	5 Centavos	—	50.00
E42	1883A	—	10 Centavos	—	55.00

PATTERNS

MINTMARK: Potosi (monogram)

KM#	Date	Mintage	Identification	Mkt.Val.
1	1827 JM	—	4 Soles, Silver, bare head right	—
2	1865 FP	—	1 Onza, Gold	—

KM#	Date	Mintage	Identification	Mkt.Val.
3	1868 CT	—	1 Boliviano, Silver, reeded edge	—
4	1868 CT	—	1 Boliviano, Silver, plain edge	—
5	1868 FE	—	1 Onza, Silver	—
6	1868 FP	—	1 Onza, Gold	—
7	1878	—	1 Centavo, Copper	—
8	1902 MM	—	50 Centavos, Brass	—

MINTMARK: PAZ

KM#	Date	Mintage	Identification	Mkt.Val.
9	1868	—	5 Centavos, Silver	—
10	1868 CT	—	5 Centavos, Silver	—

KM#	Date	Mintage	Identification	Mkt.Val.
11	1868 CT	—	10 Centavos, Silver	—
12	1868 CT	—	10 Centavos, Gold	—
13	1868 CT	—	20 Centavos, Copper	—
14	1868 CT	—	20 Centavos, Silver	—

KM#	Date	Mintage	Identification	Mkt.Val.
15	1868 CT	—	Un Boliviano, Copper, plain edge	—
16	1868 CT	—	Un Boliviano, Copper, reeded edge	—
17	1868 CT	—	Un Boliviano, Silver, reeded edge	—
18	1868 CT	—	1 Boliviano, Copper, reeded edge	—
19	1868 CT	—	1 Boliviano, Silver, plain edge	—
20	1868 CT	—	Un Boliviano, Gold, reeded edge	—

KM#	Date	Mintage	Identification	Mkt.Val.
21	1868	—	Un Boliviano, Copper, plain edge	—
22	1868	—	1 Boliviano, Copper, plain edge	—
23	1868	—	1 Boliviano, Silver, reeded edge	—

MINT SETS

KM#	Date	Mintage	Identification	Issue Price	Mkt. Val.
S1	1952(4)	—	KM1-4	—	1300.

BOTSWANA

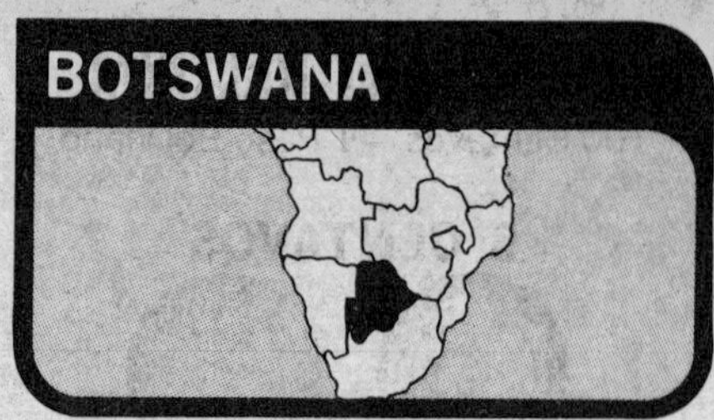

The Republic of Botswana (formerly Bechuanaland), located in south central Africa between South Africa and Rhodesia, has an area of 220,000 sq. mi. (569,797 sq. km.) and a population of 719,000. Capital: Gaborone. Botswana is a member of a customs union with South Africa, Lesotho, and Swaziland. The economy is primarily pastoral with a rapidly developing mining industry, of which diamonds and copper-nickel are the chief elements. Meat products and diamonds comprise 85 percent of the exports.

Little is known of the origin of the peoples of Botswana. The early inhabitants, the Bushmen, did not develop a recorded history and are now dying out. The ancestors of the present Botswana probably arrived about 1600 A.D. in Bantu migrations from the north and east. Bechuanaland was first united early in the 19th century under Chief Khama III to more effectively resist incursions by the Boer trekkers from Transvaal and by the neighboring Matabeles. As the Boer threat intensified, appeals for protection were made to the British Government, which proclaimed the whole of Bechuanaland a British protectorate in 1885. In 1895, the southern part of the protectorate was annexed to Cape Province. The northern part, known as the Bechuanaland Protectorate, remained under British administration until it became the independent Republic of Botswana on Sept. 30, 1966. Botswana is a member of the Commonwealth of Nations. The president is Chief of State and Head of Government.

MINTMARKS

B - Berne

MONETARY SYSTEM

100 Cents = 1 Thebe

50 CENTS

10.0000 gm., .800 SILVER, .2572 oz ASW
Independence Commemorative

Y#	Date	Mintage	VF	XF	Unc
1	1966B	40,200	BV	8.00	10.00
	1966B	—	—	Proof	12.50

10 THEBE

11.3000 gm., .900 GOLD, .3270 oz AGW

Y#	Date	Mintage	XF	Unc	Proof
2	1966B	5,100	—	—	225.00

MONETARY REFORM

100 Thebe = 1 Pula

THEBE

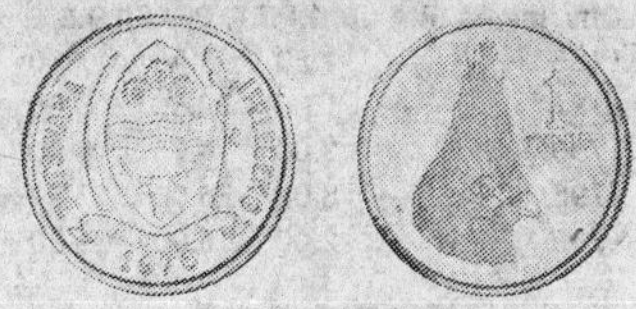

ALUMINUM
F.A.O. Issue

Y#	Date	Mintage	VF	XF	Unc
3	1976	15.000	.10	.15	.20
	1976	.020	—	Proof	1.25

5 THEBE

BRONZE
F.A.O. Issue

Y#	Date	Mintage	VF	XF	Unc
4	1976	3.000	.10	.20	.40
	1976	.020	—	Proof	1.75
	1977	.250	.10	.20	.40

10 THEBE

COPPER-NICKEL
F.A.O. Issue

Y#	Date	Mintage	VF	XF	Unc
5	1976	1.500	.15	.25	.50
	1976	.020	—	Proof	2.25
	1977	.500	.15	.25	.50

25 THEBE

COPPER-NICKEL
F.A.O. Issue

Y#	Date	Mintage	VF	XF	Unc
6	1976	1.500	.50	.75	1.25
	1976	.020	—	Proof	3.00
	1977	.250	.50	.75	1.25

50 THEBE

COPPER-NICKEL
F.A.O. Issue

Y#	Date	Mintage	VF	XF	Unc
7	1976	.266	.75	1.25	2.00
	1976	.020	—	Proof	4.50
	1977	.300	.75	1.25	2.00

PULA

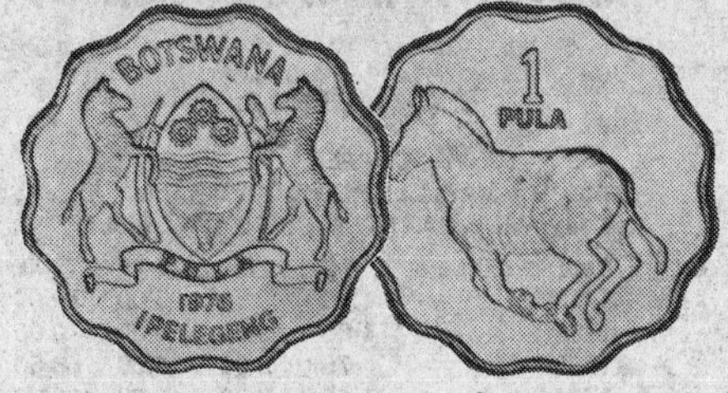

COPPER-NICKEL
F.A.O. Issue

Y#	Date	Mintage	VF	XF	Unc
8	1976	.166	1.50	2.25	3.50
	1976	.020	—	Proof	6.50
	1977	.500	1.50	2.25	3.50

5 PULA

28.5000 gm., .500 SILVER, .4581 oz ASW
10th Anniversary of Independence

Y#	Date	Mintage	VF	XF	Unc
9	1976	.025	BV	13.75	15.00

28.5000 gm., .925 SILVER, .8476 oz ASW

Y#	Date	Mintage	VF	XF	Unc
9a	1976	.020	—	Proof	25.00

28.5000 gm., .500 SILVER, .4581 oz ASW
Conservation Series

Y#	Date	Mintage	VF	XF	Unc
11	1978	.030	BV	13.75	15.00

28.5000 gm., .925 SILVER, .8476 oz ASW

Y#	Date	Mintage	VF	XF	Unc
11a	1978	.010	—	Proof	25.00

10 PULA

35.6000 gm., .500 SILVER, .5723 oz ASW
Conservation Series
Obv: Similar to 5 Pula, Y#11.

Y#	Date	Mintage	VF	XF	Unc
12	1978	.030	BV	21.50	30.00

35.6000 gm., .925 SILVER, 1.0588 oz ASW

Y#	Date	Mintage	VF	XF	Unc
12a	1978	.010	—	Proof	40.00

150 PULA

15.9800 gm., .917 GOLD, .4711 oz AGW
10th Anniversary of Independence
Obv: Similar to 5 Pulas, Y#9.

Y#	Date	Mintage	VF	XF	Unc
10	1976	2,500	BV	310.00	350.00
	1976	2,000	—	Proof	425.00

15.9800 gm., .900 GOLD, .4624 oz AGW
Conservation Series
Obv: Similar to 5 Pula, Y#11.

Y#	Date	Mintage	VF	XF	Unc
13	1978	.010	—	350.00	450.00
	1978	1,000	—	Proof	800.00

NCLT ISSUES

MINT SETS

KM#	Date	Mintage	Identification	Issue Price	Mkt. Val.
S1	1978(2)	—	Y11,12	—	45.00

PROOF SETS

STANDARD METALS

KM#	Date	Mintage	Identification	Issue Price	Mkt. Val.
101	1976(6)	20,000	Y3-8	18.00	18.00
102	1978(2)	—	Y11a,12a	—	65.00

BRAZIL

The Federative Republic of Brazil, which comprises half the continent of South America and is the only Latin American country deriving its culture and language from Portugal, has an area of 3,290,000 sq. mi. (8,521,100 sq. km.) and a population of 111.7 million. Capital: Brasilia. The economy of Brazil is as varied and complex as any in the developing world. Agriculture is a mainstay of the economy, although but 4 percent of the area is under cultivation. Known mineral resources are almost unlimited in variety and size of reserves. A large, relatively sophisticated industry ranges from basic steel and chemical production to finished consumer goods. Coffee, cotton, iron ore and cocoa are the chief exports.

Brazil was discovered and claimed for Portugal by Admiral Pedro Alvares Cabral in 1500. Portugal established a settlement in 1532 and proclaimed the area a royal colony in 1549. During the Napoleonic Wars, Dom Joao VI established the seat of Portuguese government in Rio de Janeiro. when he returned to Portugal, his son Dom Pedro I declared Brazil's independence on Sept. 7, 1822, and became emperor of Brazil. The Empire of Brazil was maintained until 1889 when the federal republic was established. The Federative Republic that exists today was established in 1946 by terms of a constitution drawn up by a constituent assembly.

RULERS

Maria I and Pedro III, 1777-1786
Maria I, Widow 1786-1805
Maria I as Regent 1799-1805
John, Prince Regent 1799-1810
John VI 1818-1822
Pedro I, 1822-1831
Pedro II, 1831-1889

MINTMARKS

(a) - Paris, privy marks only
A - Berlin 1913
B - Bahia 1714-1831
C - Cuiaba (Mato Grosso) 1823-1833
G - Goias 1823-1833
M - Minas Gerais 1823-1828
P - Pernambuco (supposedly all counterfeit)
R - Rio De Janeiro 1703-1834
RS - Rio de Janeiro 1869
RS. - Brussels 1869
SP - Sao Paulo 1825-1832

MONETARY SYSTEM

(Until 1833)
1 Peca (Dobra = Johannes (Joe) = 4 Escudos
(1833-1942)
1000 Reis = 1 Milreis
(1942-1967)
100 Centavos = 1 Cruzeiro

COLONIAL COINAGE

V (5) REIS

COPPER
Obv. leg: MARIA.I.E.PETRUS.III.D.G.P.E....
Rev. leg: PECUNIA.TOTUM.CIRCUMIT.... globe.

C#	Date	Mintage	VG	Fine	VF	XF
41	1778	—	1.00	2.50	5.00	10.00
	1781	—	1.00	2.50	5.00	10.00
	1782	—	.75	2.00	4.00	8.50
	1784	—	1.25	3.00	6.00	12.00

Obv. leg: MARIA.I.D.G.P.ET.BRASILIAE.....

C#	Date	Mintage	VG	Fine	VF	XF
60	1786	—	5.00	12.50	22.50	40.00
	1787	—	.75	2.00	4.00	8.50
	1790	—	.75	2.00	4.00	8.50
	1791	—	.75	2.00	4.00	8.50
	1797	—	4.00	10.00	17.50	35.00

Reduced size

C#	Date	Mintage	VG	Fine	VF	XF
64	1799	—	4.00	10.00	17.50	27.50

X (10) REIS

COPPER
Obv. leg: MARIA.I.E.PETRUS.III....
Rev. leg: PECUNIA.TOTUM.CIRCUM IT...,globe.

C#	Date	Mintage	VG	Fine	VF	XF
42	1778	—	1.25	3.00	6.00	8.50
	1781	—	1.50	4.00	7.50	10.00
	1782	—	1.50	4.00	7.50	10.00
	1784	—	1.50	4.00	7.50	10.00
	1785	—	1.50	4.00	7.50	10.00

Obv. leg: MARIA.I.D.G.P.ET. BRASILIAE......

C#	Date	Mintage	VG	Fine	VF	XF
61	1786	—	1.25	3.00	5.00	12.00
	1787	—	1.25	3.00	5.00	12.00
	1790	—	1.75	4.50	8.50	17.50
	1796	—	7.50	17.50	25.00	40.00

Reduced size

C#	Date	Mintage	VG	Fine	VF	XF
65	1799	—	1.25	3.00	4.50	10.00

Obv. leg: JOANNES.D.G.P.E. BRASILIAE....

C#	Date	Mintage	VG	Fine	VF	XF
80	1802	—	.75	2.00	3.75	8.50
	1803	—	.75	2.00	3.75	8.50
	1805	—	.75	2.00	3.75	8.50
	1805R	—	.75	2.00	3.75	8.50
	1806R	—	2.50	6.00	10.00	15.00
	1812R	—	—	—	Rare	—
	1814R	—	2.50	6.00	10.00	20.00
	1815	—	1.00	2.50	4.50	10.00
	1815R	—	.75	2.00	3.75	8.50
	1816	—	1.00	2.50	4.50	10.00
	1818	—	1.25	3.00	6.00	12.50

Obv. leg: JOANNES VI.D.G.PORT....

C#	Date	Mintage	VG	Fine	VF	XF
105	1818R	—	1.10	2.75	4.75	11.50
	1819R	—	.75	2.00	3.75	8.50
	1820R	—	.75	2.00	3.75	8.50
	1821	—	.75	2.00	3.75	8.50
	1821R	—	.65	1.75	3.25	7.50
	1822	—	1.25	3.00	4.75	11.50
	1822R	—	.65	1.75	3.25	7.50
	1823	—	1.10	2.75	4.75	11.50

XX (20) REIS

COPPER
Obv. leg: MARIA.I.E. PETRUS.III....
Rev. leg: PECUNIA.TOTUM.CIRCUMIT....globe.

C#	Date	Mintage	VG	Fine	VF	XF
43	1778	—	1.00	2.50	4.50	10.00
	1781	—	1.25	3.25	6.00	12.00
	1782	—	1.25	3.25	6.00	12.00
43	1784	—	1.25	3.25	6.00	12.00

Obv. leg: MARIA.I.D.G.P.ET. BRASILIAE....

C#	Date	Mintage	VG	Fine	VF	XF
62	1786	—	1.50	3.50	7.50	15.00
	1787	—	1.00	2.50	5.00	10.00
	1790	—	2.00	4.75	8.50	17.50
	1796	—	8.00	20.00	27.50	50.00
	1799	—	2.00	5.00	9.00	17.50

High crown over X.

C#	Date	Mintage	VG	Fine	VF	XF
62.1	1799	—	—	30.00	40.00	75.00

Reduced size

C#	Date	Mintage	VG	Fine	VF	XF
66	1799	—	1.50	3.75	7.50	15.00

Obv. leg: JOANNES D.G.P(ORT).E.BRASILIAE.P.REGENS

C#	Date	Mintage	VG	Fine	VF	XF
81	1802	—	1.10	2.75	4.50	10.00
	1803	—	1.10	2.75	4.50	10.00
	1812B	—	1.50	3.75	7.50	15.00
	1812R	—	2.50	6.00	10.00	20.00
	1813B	—	1.10	2.75	5.00	10.00
	1813R	—	1.50	3.75	7.50	12.00
	1814R	—	1.50	3.75	7.50	12.00
	1815B	—	1.25	3.00	5.00	10.00
	1815R	—	1.50	3.75	7.50	12.00
	1816B	—	1.25	3.00	5.00	10.00
	1817R	—	2.50	6.00	10.00	20.00
	1818R	—	2.50	6.00	10.00	20.00

Obv. leg: JOANNES D.G.PORT.BRAS.ET ALG.

C#	Date	Mintage	VG	Fine	VF	XF
82	1816R	—	2.50	6.00	10.00	20.00

Minted for Goias and Mato Grosso
Obv. leg: JOANNES D.G.P.E.....crowned value.
Rev. leg: PECUNIA.TOTUM.CIRCUMIT....globe.

C#	Date	Mintage	VG	Fine	VF	XF
86	1818R	—	2.00	5.00	8.25	15.00

Obv. leg: JOANNES. VI. D.G.PORT.....

C#	Date	Mintage	VG	Fine	VF	XF
106	1818R	—	1.50	3.75	7.50	15.00
	1819R	—	1.00	2.50	5.00	10.00
	1820B	—	1.50	3.75	7.50	15.00
	1820R	—	1.00	2.50	5.00	10.00
	1821B	—	1.50	3.75	7.50	15.00
	1821R	—	2.50	6.00	10.00	20.00
	1822R	—	1.00	2.50	5.00	10.00

37-1/2 REIS

COPPER
Minted for Minas Gerais
Obv. leg: JOANNES.VI.D.G.PORT.BRAS...crowned value
Rev. leg: PECUNIA.TOTUM.CIRCUMIT...globe

C#	Date	Mintage	VG	Fine	VF	XF
109	1818M	—	2.50	6.00	10.00	20.00
	1818R	—	5.00	12.50	20.00	30.00

XL (40) REIS

COPPER
Obv: Crowned XL, leg: MARIA.I.E. PETRUS.III....
Rev: Globe, leg: PECUNIA.TOTUM.CIRCUMIT....

C#	Date	Mintage	VG	Fine	VF	XF
44	1778	—	2.00	5.00	10.00	20.00
	1781	—	2.75	7.00	12.50	25.00
	1784	—	5.00	12.50	17.50	35.00

Obv: Low crown over XL, leg: MARIA.I.D.G......

C#	Date	Mintage	VG	Fine	VF	XF
63	1786	—	2.00	5.00	10.00	22.50
	1787	—	2.75	6.50	12.00	27.50
	1790	—	2.75	6.50	12.00	27.50
	1791	—	16.50	40.00	75.00	125.00
	1796	—	3.00	7.50	15.00	30.00

Obv: High crown over XL.

C#	Date	Mintage	VG	Fine	VF	XF
63.1	1790	—	—	30.00	40.00	85.00
	1791	—	3.00	7.50	15.00	30.00

Reduced size

C#	Date	Mintage	VG	Fine	VF	XF
67	1799	—	2.00	5.00	10.00	20.00

Rev: Similar to 10 Reis, C#80.

C#	Date	Mintage	VG	Fine	VF	XF
83	1802	—	1.50	3.75	7.50	15.00
	1803	—	1.50	3.75	7.50	15.00
	1809B	—	2.50	6.00	10.00	20.00
	1810B	—	2.50	6.00	10.00	20.00
	1811B	—	1.75	4.50	8.50	17.50
	1812B	—	1.50	3.75	7.50	15.00
	1812R	—	2.50	6.00	10.00	20.00
	1813R	—	2.50	6.00	10.00	20.00
	1814B	—	1.50	3.75	7.50	15.00
	1815R	—	2.50	6.00	12.50	25.00
	1816B	—	1.50	3.75	7.50	15.00
	1816R	—	2.50	6.00	10.00	20.00
	1817R	—	6.00	15.00	25.00	45.00

Obv. leg: JOANNES D.G.P.ET.BRAS.P.REGENS., smaller crown.

C#	Date	Mintage	VG	Fine	VF	XF
83.1	1816B	—	—	—	—	—

Obv. leg: JOANNES D.G. PORT.BRAS....

C#	Date	Mintage	VG	Fine	VF	XF
84	1816R	—	3.00	7.50	15.00	30.00

Minted for Goias and Mato Grosso
Obv. leg: JOANNES.D.G.P.E....crowned value.
Rev. leg: PECUNIA.TOTUM.CIRCUMIT....globe.

C#	Date	Mintage	VG	Fine	VF	XF
87	1818R	—	10.00	25.00	35.00	45.00

Similar to 20 Reis, C#106.

C#	Date	Mintage	VG	Fine	VF	XF
107	1818R	—	1.50	3.50	6.00	12.00
	1819R	—	3.00	7.50	15.00	30.00
	1820B	—	3.00	7.50	15.00	30.00
	1820R	—	1.25	3.00	6.00	12.00
	1821B	—	3.50	8.50	17.50	35.00
	1821R	—	1.25	3.00	6.00	12.00
	1822B	—	3.50	8.50	17.50	35.00
	1822R	—	1.25	3.00	6.00	12.00
	1823B	—	3.50	8.50	17.50	35.00

Minted for Goias and Mato Grosso
Obv. leg: JOANNES.VI.D.G.PORT.BRAS.

C#	Date	Mintage	VG	Fine	VF	XF
111	1820	—	5.00	12.50	18.50	35.00

75 REIS

COPPER
Minted for Minas Gerais
Obv. leg: JOANNES.VI.D.G.PORT.BRAS...crowned value
Rev. leg: PECUNIA.TOTUM.CIRCUMIT..arms on globe.

C#	Date	Mintage	VG	Fine	VF	XF
110	1818M	—	2.00	5.00	8.25	15.00
	1819M	—	2.50	6.00	10.00	18.50
	1821M	—	2.00	5.00	8.25	15.00

LXXX (80) REIS

2.2200 gm., .917 SILVER, .0654 oz ASW
Obv. leg: MARIA.I.E.PETRUS.III.; crowned arms.
Rev. leg: SUBQ. SIGN.NATA.STAB..,globe.

C#	Date	Mintage	VG	Fine	VF	XF
45	1778	—	3.75	7.50	12.50	25.00
	1779	—	3.75	7.50	12.50	25.00
	1780	—	2.25	4.50	10.00	20.00
	1781	—	3.75	7.50	12.50	25.00
	1782	—	3.75	7.50	12.50	25.00
	1785	—	3.75	7.50	12.50	25.00
	1786	—	3.75	7.50	12.50	25.00

Obv. leg: MARIA.I.D.G.PORT.REGINA....

C#	Date	Mintage	VG	Fine	VF	XF
70	1787	—	2.50	5.00	10.00	20.00
	1788	—	3.25	6.50	12.50	25.00
	1790	—	5.00	10.00	17.50	30.00
	1796	—	2.50	5.00	10.00	20.00

2.2400 gm., .917 SILVER, .0660 oz ASW
Obv. leg: JOANNES.D G.PORT.P.REGENS.....

C#	Date	Mintage	VG	Fine	VF	XF
90	1810R	—	50.00	100.00	140.00	200.00
	1814R	—	17.50	35.00	50.00	75.00
	1816R	—	37.50	75.00	125.00	175.00

COPPER
Similar to 10 Reis, C#80.

C#	Date	Mintage	VG	Fine	VF	XF
85	1811R	—	7.50	17.50	27.50	50.00
	1812R	—	5.00	12.50	20.00	40.00

Minted for Goias and Mato Grosso
Obv. leg: JOANNES D.G.PORT...crowned value.
Rev. leg: PECUNIA.TOTUM.CIRCUMIT...globe.

C#	Date	Mintage	VG	Fine	VF	XF
88	1818B	—	1.50	4.00	7.50	15.00
	1818R	—	4.00	10.00	17.50	30.00

Minted for Goias and Mato Grosso
Obv. leg: JOANNES.VI.D.G.PORT...crowned value.
Rev: Arms on globe.

C#	Date	Mintage	VG	Fine	VF	XF
112	1820	—	4.00	10.00	17.50	30.00

2.2400 gm., .917 SILVER, .0660 oz ASW
Obv: Crowned 80 within wreath, leg: JOANNES.VI. D.G.PORT. BRAS.....

C#	Date	Mintage	VG	Fine	VF	XF
113	1818R	—	17.50	35.00	50.00	75.00
	1821B	—	20.00	40.00	60.00	100.00

COPPER

C#	Date	Mintage	VG	Fine	VF	XF
108	1820B	—	1.50	4.00	8.50	20.00
	1821B	—	1.50	4.00	8.50	20.00
	1821R	—	1.25	3.00	7.50	17.50
	1822B	—	2.50	6.00	10.00	22.50
	1822R	—	1.50	4.00	8.50	20.00
	1823B	—	2.50	6.00	10.00	22.50

160 REIS

4.4400 gm., .917 SILVER, .1309 oz ASW
Obv. leg: MARIA.I.E. PETRUS.III....
Rev. leg: SUBQ.SIGN.NATA.STAB....

C#	Date	Mintage	VG	Fine	VF	XF
46	1778	—	4.50	6.50	10.00	20.00
	1779	—	4.50	6.50	10.00	20.00
	1780	—	4.50	6.50	10.00	20.00
	1781	—	5.00	7.50	13.00	25.00
	1783	—	8.50	17.50	35.00	60.00
	1785	—	4.50	6.50	10.00	20.00
	1786	—	6.00	10.00	17.00	35.00

Obv. leg: MARIA.I.D.G.PORT.REGINA.....

C#	Date	Mintage	VG	Fine	VF	XF
71	1787	—	4.50	5.50	8.50	15.00
	1790	—	6.00	10.00	15.00	25.00
	1795	—	4.50	6.50	10.00	20.00
	1797	—	5.00	7.50	13.00	25.00

4.4800 gm., .917 SILVER, .1320 oz ASW
Obv. leg: JOANNES.D.G.PORT.P. REGENS....

C#	Date	Mintage	VG	Fine	VF	XF
91	1810R	—	17.50	35.00	45.00	75.00
	1811B	—	42.50	85.00	115.00	165.00
	1812B	—	20.00	40.00	60.00	100.00
	1813R	—	6.00	10.00	17.50	35.00
	1813R/B	—	8.50	17.50	25.00	40.00
	1815R	—	12.50	25.00	32.50	45.00

Obv. leg: JOANNES.III.D.G.PORT.BRAS....

C#	Date	Mintage	VG	Fine	VF	XF
114	1818R	—	10.00	20.00	40.00	60.00
	1820R	—	20.00	40.00	60.00	100.00
	1821B	5,639	50.00	100.00	175.00	250.00

320 REIS

8.8900 gm., .917 SILVER, .2621 oz ASW
Obv. leg: MARIA.I.E.PETRUS.III...

C#	Date	Mintage	VG	Fine	VF	XF
47	1778	—	9.00	15.00	20.00	35.00
	1779	—	9.00	15.00	20.00	35.00
	1780	—	9.00	15.00	20.00	35.00
	1782	—	9.00	15.00	20.00	35.00
	1783	—	9.00	15.00	20.00	35.00
	1784	—	9.00	15.00	20.00	35.00
	1785	—	9.00	15.00	20.00	35.00
	1786	—	9.00	15.00	20.00	35.00

Obv. leg: MARIA.I.D.G.PORT.REGINA....

C#	Date	Mintage	VG	Fine	VF	XF
72	1787	—	10.00	17.50	22.50	37.50
	1788	—	10.00	17.50	22.50	37.50
	1790	—	17.50	35.00	45.00	60.00
	1793	—	10.00	17.50	22.50	37.50
	1797	—	10.00	17.50	22.50	37.50
	1800R	—	11.00	20.00	27.50	40.00
	1802R	—	11.00	20.00	27.50	40.00

8.9600 gm., .917 SILVER, .2641 oz ASW
Obv. leg: JOANNES.D.G.PORT.P.REGENS....

C#	Date	Mintage	VG	Fine	VF	XF
92	1809R	—	11.50	22.50	30.00	45.00
	1810B	—	11.00	20.00	25.00	40.00
	1812M	—	17.50	35.00	45.00	60.00
	1812R	—	9.00	15.00	20.00	30.00
	1813R	—	9.00	15.00	20.00	30.00
	1814M	—	20.00	40.00	55.00	85.00
	1816B	—	20.00	40.00	55.00	85.00
	1816M	—	22.50	45.00	65.00	110.00
	1817R	—	15.00	30.00	50.00	75.00

Obv. leg: JOANNES.III.D.G.PORT.BRAS....

C#	Date	Mintage	VG	Fine	VF	XF
115a	1818M	—	75.00	150.00	225.00	325.00
115	1818R	—	11.00	20.00	25.00	40.00
	1819R	—	17.50	35.00	45.00	60.00
	1820R	—	9.00	15.00	20.00	30.00
	1821B	—	18.50	37.50	55.00	100.00

640 REIS

17.7800 gm., .917 SILVER, .5242 oz ASW
Obv. leg: MARIA.I.E.PETRUS.III...
Rev. leg: SUBQ.SIGN.NATA.STAB......

C#	Date	Mintage	VG	Fine	VF	XF
48	1778	—	17.50	22.50	27.50	40.00
	1779	—	17.50	22.50	27.50	40.00
	1780	—	17.50	22.50	27.50	40.00
	1781	—	17.50	22.50	27.50	40.00
	1782	—	17.50	22.50	27.50	40.00
	1783	—	17.50	22.50	27.50	40.00
	1784	—	17.50	22.50	27.50	40.00
	1785	—	17.50	22.50	27.50	40.00
	1786	—	17.50	22.50	27.50	40.00

Obv. leg: MARIA.I.D.G.PORT.REGINA....

C#	Date	Mintage	VG	Fine	VF	XF
73	1787	—	18.50	25.00	35.00	50.00
	1790	—	20.00	40.00	60.00	85.00
	1791R	—	22.50	45.00	65.00	90.00
	1792	—	21.50	40.00	60.00	85.00
	1792R	—	21.50	40.00	60.00	85.00
	1793	—	20.00	35.00	45.00	65.00
	1793R	—	22.50	45.00	65.00	100.00
	1794R	—	18.50	25.00	35.00	50.00
	1795	—	21.50	40.00	60.00	85.00
	1799B	—	18.50	25.00	35.00	50.00
	1800R	—	17.00	20.00	30.00	40.00
	1802R	—	20.00	35.00	45.00	65.00

17.9200 gm., .917 SILVER, .5283 oz ASW

C#	Date	Mintage	VG	Fine	VF	XF
73.1	1799B	—	25.00	50.00	75.00	150.00
	1800/1799B	—	19.00	30.00	40.00	60.00
	1800B	—	18.50	25.00	35.00	50.00
	1801B	—	18.50	25.00	35.00	50.00
	1802B	—	18.50	25.00	35.00	50.00
	1803B	—	18.50	25.00	35.00	50.00
	1804B	—	18.50	25.00	35.00	50.00
	1805B	—	21.50	40.00	60.00	85.00

Obv. leg: JOANNES.D.G.PORT.P.REGENS....

C#	Date	Mintage	VG	Fine	VF	XF
93	1806B	—	18.50	35.00	45.00	65.00
	1807B	—	18.50	35.00	45.00	65.00
	1808/7B	—	17.00	27.50	47.50	60.00
	1808B	—	16.50	25.00	35.00	50.00
	1809B	—	16.50	25.00	35.00	50.00
	1809R	—	18.50	35.00	45.00	65.00
	1810B	—	16.50	25.00	35.00	50.00
	1810M	—	125.00	250.00	325.00	425.00
	1811M	—	16.50	25.00	35.00	50.00
	1811R	—	18.50	35.00	45.00	65.00
	1812M	—	21.50	40.00	60.00	85.00
	1812R	—	18.50	35.00	45.00	65.00
	1813M	—	18.50	35.00	45.00	65.00
	1813R	—	18.50	35.00	45.00	65.00
	1814R	—	19.00	37.50	50.00	70.00
	1815R	—	18.50	35.00	45.00	65.00
	1816M	—	18.50	35.00	45.00	65.00
	1816R	—	21.50	40.00	60.00	90.00

Obv. leg: JOANNES.III.

C#	Date	Mintage	VG	Fine	VF	XF
116a	1818M	—	75.00	150.00	225.00	325.00
116	1818R	—	16.50	25.00	35.00	50.00
	1819R	—	18.50	35.00	45.00	65.00
	1820R	—	16.00	18.50	25.00	35.00
	1821B	—	21.50	40.00	60.00	85.00
	1821R	—	16.00	18.50	25.00	35.00
	1822R	—	21.50	40.00	60.00	85.00

800 REIS

1.7900 gm., .917 GOLD, 16mm, .0527 oz AGW
Obv. leg: MARIA.I.ET.PETRUS.III., jugate busts
Rev: Stylized arms.

C#	Date	Mintage	Fine	VF	XF	Unc
50	1782B	—	100.00	200.00	300.00	400.00
	1786B	—	100.00	200.00	300.00	400.00

960 REIS

26.8900 gm., .917 SILVER, .7928 oz ASW

C#	Date	Mintage	VG	Fine	VF	XF
94	1810B	—	BV	25.00	30.00	40.00
	1810B (small crown)					
		—	25.00	45.00	65.00	120.00
	1810B (..P.REGENES...)					
		—	27.50	40.00	60.00	120.00
	1810M	—	75.00	150.00	225.00	300.00
	1810R	—	BV	25.00	30.00	40.00
	1811B	—	25.00	30.00	35.00	45.00
	1811R	—	BV	25.00	30.00	40.00
	1812B	—	BV	25.00	30.00	40.00
	1812R	—	BV	25.00	30.00	40.00
	1813B	—	BV	25.00	30.00	40.00
	1813B (..P.REGENES..)					
		—	27.50	40.00	60.00	120.00
	1813R	—	BV	25.00	30.00	40.00
	1814B	—	BV	25.00	30.00	40.00
	1814R	—	BV	25.00	30.00	40.00
	1815B	—	BV	25.00	30.00	40.00
	1815R	—	BV	25.00	30.00	40.00
	1815R (..STAB.NATA..)					
		—	27.50	40.00	65.00	100.00
	1816B	—	BV	25.00	30.00	40.00
	1816M	—	200.00	350.00	500.00	700.00
	1816R	—	BV	25.00	30.00	40.00
	1817R	—	BV	25.00	30.00	40.00

Obv. leg. ends: .BRAS.ET.ALG.P.REGENS.....
Rev: Similar to C#94.

C#	Date	Mintage	VG	Fine	VF	XF
94a	1816R	—	26.50	35.00	50.00	75.00
	1817R	—	BV	25.00	30.00	40.00
	1818R	—	BV	25.00	30.00	40.00

C#	Date	Mintage	VG	Fine	VF	XF
117	1818R	—	BV	25.00	30.00	40.00
	1819B	—	—	—	Rare	—
117	1819R	—	BV	25.00	30.00	40.00
	1820B	—	BV	25.00	30.00	40.00
	1820B (...BARS.ET...)					
		—	26.50	35.00	50.00	75.00
	1820R	—	BV	25.00	30.00	40.00
	1820R (small castle within zero of denomination)					
		—	100.00	175.00	250.00	350.00
	1821/0B	—	26.50	35.00	50.00	75.00
	1821B	—	BV	25.00	30.00	40.00
	1821R	—	BV	25.00	30.00	40.00
	1822B	—	150.00	250.00	400.00	600.00
	1822R	—	25.00	30.00	40.00	50.00

NOTE: C#117 was usually struck over Spanish Colonial 8 Reales. Specimens having the original date and mintmark still visible command a premium.

1000 REIS

2.0100 gm., .917 GOLD, .0592 oz AGW
Obv. leg: MARIA.I.E.PETRUS.III....

C#	Date	Mintage	Fine	VF	XF	Unc
54	1778	2,816	75.00	100.00	150.00	200.00
	1779	3,000	75.00	100.00	150.00	200.00
	1781	5,800	75.00	100.00	150.00	200.00
	1782	—	100.00	175.00	275.00	350.00

Obv. leg: MARIA I D.G......

C#	Date	Mintage	Fine	VF	XF	Unc
76	1787	6,000	75.00	100.00	150.00	200.00

1600 REIS

3.5800 gm., .917 GOLD, .1055 oz AGW
Obv. leg: MARIA.I.ET.....jugate busts.
Rev: Stylized crowned arms.

C#	Date	Mintage	Fine	VF	XF	Unc
51	1780B	—	225.00	350.00	400.00	475.00
	1781B	—	225.00	350.00	400.00	475.00
	1782B	—	225.00	350.00	400.00	475.00
	1784B	—	300.00	500.00	575.00	650.00

2000 REIS

4.0300 gm., .917 GOLD, .1188 oz AGW
Obv. leg: MARIA.I.E.PETRUS.III....

C#	Date	Mintage	Fine	VF	XF	Unc
55	1778	7,800	135.00	225.00	275.00	325.00
	1781	3,500	165.00	275.00	350.00	425.00
	1782	—	135.00	225.00	275.00	325.00
	1783	—	165.00	275.00	350.00	425.00

Obv. leg: MARIA I.D.G....

C#	Date	Mintage	Fine	VF	XF	Unc
77	1787	1,500	165.00	275.00	350.00	425.00
	1792	2,251	165.00	275.00	350.00	425.00
	1793	1,500	165.00	275.00	350.00	425.00

3200 REIS

7.1700 gm., .917 GOLD, .2114 oz AGW
Obv. leg: MARIA.I.ET....jugate busts
Rev: Stylized crowned arms.

C#	Date	Mintage	Fine	VF	XF	Unc
52	1780	—	200.00	350.00	425.00	550.00
	1781	—	200.00	350.00	425.00	550.00
	1782	—	200.00	350.00	425.00	550.00
	1783	—	200.00	350.00	425.00	550.00
	1784	—	200.00	350.00	425.00	550.00
	1785	—	200.00	350.00	425.00	550.00
	1786	—	275.00	450.00	575.00	650.00

4000 REIS

8.0600 gm., .917 GOLD, .2376 oz AGW

C#	Date	Mintage	Fine	VF	XF	Unc
56	1778	2,741	225.00	275.00	325.00	400.00
	1779	5,150	225.00	275.00	325.00	400.00
	1781	4,250	225.00	275.00	325.00	400.00
	1783	2,000	275.00	350.00	400.00	500.00
	1786	3,000	225.00	275.00	325.00	400.00

Obv. leg: MARIA I.D.G...

C#	Date	Mintage	Fine	VF	XF	Unc
78	1787	2,000	225.00	275.00	325.00	400.00
	1790	1,250	—	—	Rare	—
	1792	2,050	—	—	Rare	—
	1801	3,705	225.00	260.00	300.00	375.00
	1802	7,738	225.00	260.00	300.00	375.00
	1803	7,807	225.00	260.00	300.00	375.00
	1804	Inc. Ab.	225.00	260.00	300.00	375.00
	1805	Inc. Be.	225.00	260.00	300.00	375.00

BAHIA MINT

Obv. leg: JOANNES,.....
Rev: Dots on either side of date.

C#	Date	Mintage	Fine	VF	XF	Unc
101	1805	10,219	250.00	300.00	375.00	450.00
	1806	11,567	250.00	300.00	375.00	450.00
	1807	7,725	250.00	300.00	375.00	450.00
	1808	.032	250.00	300.00	375.00	450.00
	1809/8	.019	—	—	—	—
	1809	Inc. Ab.	250.00	300.00	375.00	450.00
	1810	.018	250.00	300.00	375.00	450.00
	1811	.019	250.00	300.00	375.00	450.00
	1812	—	250.00	300.00	375.00	450.00
	1813	.011	250.00	300.00	375.00	450.00
	1814	9,494	250.00	300.00	375.00	450.00
	1815	—	350.00	400.00	475.00	600.00
	1816	—	300.00	375.00	450.00	575.00

RIO DE JANEIRO MINT

Rev: Flower on either side of date.

C#	Date	Mintage	Fine	VF	XF	Unc
101b	1808	.128	275.00	325.00	400.00	550.00
	1809	.094	275.00	325.00	400.00	550.00
	1810	.066	275.00	325.00	400.00	550.00
	1811	.087	275.00	325.00	400.00	550.00
	1812	.124	275.00	325.00	400.00	550.00
	1813	.148	275.00	325.00	400.00	550.00
	1814	.102	275.00	325.00	400.00	550.00
	1815	.083	275.00	325.00	400.00	550.00
	1816	.091	275.00	325.00	400.00	550.00

Rev. leg: ...PRINCEPS.REGENS....

C#	Date	Mintage	Fine	VF	XF	Unc
101a	1816	Inc. Ab.	325.00	400.00	550.00	700.00
	1817	.071	275.00	325.00	400.00	550.00

BAHIA MINT

Similar to C#119. Rev: Date between crosses.

C#	Date	Mintage	Fine	VF	XF	Unc
119a	1819	1,864	350.00	425.00	500.00	625.00
	1820	4,374	350.00	425.00	500.00	625.00

RIO DE JANEIRO MINT

Rev: 6-petal flower on either side of date.

C#	Date	Mintage	Fine	VF	XF	Unc
119	1818	.064	225.00	275.00	325.00	400.00
	1819	.049	225.00	275.00	325.00	400.00
	1820	.087	225.00	275.00	325.00	400.00
	1821/0	.035	—	—	—	—
	1821	Inc. Ab.	225.00	275.00	325.00	400.00
	1822	.054	225.00	275.00	325.00	400.00

Rev: 4 petal flower on either side of date

C#	Date	Mintage	Fine	VF	XF	Unc
119b	1819	Inc. Ab.	225.00	350.00	450.00	650.00

6400 REIS

14.3400 gm., .917 GOLD, .4228 oz AGW

C#	Date	Mintage	Fine	VF	XF	Unc
53	1777B	—	650.00	800.00	1000.	1200.
	1777R	—	650.00	800.00	1000.	1200.
	1778B	—	300.00	350.00	425.00	550.00
	1778B '...PORT.ALG...'	—	350.00	425.00	575.00	700.00
	1778R	.378	325.00	375.00	425.00	550.00
	1779B	—	300.00	350.00	425.00	550.00
	1779R	.408	325.00	375.00	425.00	550.00
	1780B	.019	300.00	350.00	425.00	550.00
	1780R	.343	325.00	375.00	425.00	550.00
	1781B	.034	300.00	350.00	425.00	550.00
	1781R	.375	325.00	375.00	425.00	550.00
	1782B	.060	300.00	350.00	425.00	550.00
	1782R	.324	325.00	375.00	425.00	550.00
	1783B	.030	300.00	350.00	425.00	550.00
	1783R	.322	325.00	375.00	425.00	550.00
	1784B	.024	300.00	350.00	425.00	550.00
	1784R	.327	325.00	375.00	425.00	550.00
	1785B	.023	300.00	350.00	425.00	550.00
	1785R	.282	325.00	375.00	425.00	550.00
	1786B	.020	300.00	350.00	425.00	550.00
	1786R	.294	325.00	375.00	425.00	550.00

C#	Date	Mintage	Fine	VF	XF	Unc
74	1786R	Inc. Ab.	450.00	500.00	600.00	725.00
	1787B	.016	375.00	425.00	525.00	650.00
	1787R	.276	300.00	375.00	450.00	575.00
	1788B	.014	375.00	425.00	525.00	650.00
	1788R	.263	300.00	375.00	450.00	575.00
	1789B	.021	375.00	425.00	525.00	650.00
	1789R	.247	300.00	375.00	450.00	575.00
	1790B	.012	400.00	600.00	800.00	1100.

Obv: Bejeweled headdress

C#	Date	Mintage	Fine	VF	XF	Unc
75	1789R	Inc. Ab.	300.00	375.00	450.00	550.00
	1790B	Inc. Ab.	600.00	800.00	1000.	1200.
	1790R	.211	300.00	375.00	450.00	550.00
	1791B	.015	300.00	375.00	450.00	550.00
	1791R	.231	300.00	375.00	450.00	550.00
	1792B	.024	300.00	375.00	450.00	550.00
	1792R	.230	300.00	375.00	450.00	550.00
	1793B	.015	300.00	375.00	450.00	550.00
	1793R	.237	300.00	375.00	450.00	550.00
	1794B	.014	325.00	400.00	475.00	575.00
	1794R	.246	300.00	375.00	450.00	550.00
	1795B	.016	325.00	400.00	475.00	575.00
	1795R	.226	300.00	375.00	450.00	550.00
	1796B	.011	325.00	400.00	475.00	575.00
	1796R	.219	300.00	375.00	450.00	550.00
	1797B	9,775	600.00	750.00	850.00	1000.
	1797R	.214	300.00	375.00	450.00	550.00
	1798B	7,864	325.00	425.00	525.00	625.00
	1798R	.204	300.00	375.00	450.00	550.00
	1799B	.012	325.00	400.00	475.00	575.00
	1799R	.189	300.00	375.00	450.00	550.00
	1800B	9,567	325.00	425.00	525.00	625.00
	1800R	.214	300.00	375.00	450.00	550.00
	1801B	.012	325.00	400.00	475.00	575.00
	1801R	.185	300.00	375.00	450.00	550.00
	1802B	3,324	600.00	750.00	850.00	1000.
	1802R	.168	300.00	375.00	450.00	550.00
	1803B	3,743	350.00	500.00	625.00	750.00
	1803R	.176	300.00	375.00	450.00	550.00
	1804B	3,539	350.00	500.00	625.00	750.00
	1804R	.128	300.00	375.00	450.00	550.00
	1805R	.109	300.00	375.00	450.00	550.00

Obv. leg: JOANNES.D.G.PORT.ET.ALG.P.REGENS.

C#	Date	Mintage	Fine	VF	XF	Unc
100	1805R	Inc. Ab.	325.00	400.00	500.00	600.00
	1806R	.096	325.00	400.00	500.00	600.00
	1807R	.059	375.00	450.00	550.00	650.00
	1808R	.133	325.00	450.00	500.00	600.00
	1809R	.188	325.00	450.00	500.00	600.00
	1810R	.159	325.00	450.00	500.00	600.00
	1811R	.082	325.00	450.00	500.00	600.00
	1812R	.064	325.00	450.00	500.00	600.00
	1813R	.053	325.00	400.00	500.00	600.00
	1814R	.042	375.00	450.00	550.00	650.00
	1815R	.040	550.00	650.00	800.00	950.00
	1816R	.039	600.00	750.00	850.00	1000.

Obv. leg. ends: ...PORT.BRAS.ET.ALG.P.REG.

C#	Date	Mintage	Fine	VF	XF	Unc
100a	1816R	Inc. Ab.	800.00	1000.	1200.	1350.
	1817R	.032	550.00	650.00	800.00	950.00

Obv. leg: JOANNES.VI,D.G.PORT.BRAS.ET.ALG.REX.

C#	Date	Mintage	Fine	VF	XF	Unc
118	1818R	.014	525.00	600.00	750.00	900.00
	1819R	9,227	525.00	600.00	800.00	950.00
	1820R	3,286	650.00	750.00	1000.	1250.
	1821R	2,122	1250.	1750.	2250.	2850.
	1822R	599 pcs.	1350.	2000.	2500.	3500.

COUNTERSTAMP ISSUES

Shield Countermark

Authorized on April 18, 1809.

The purpose of the shield countermark was to double the value of the earlier Colonial copper coinage and raise the value of the earlier silver coinage. Other Portuguese and Portuguese Colonial coins are known with this countermark.

75 = 80 Reis   300 = 320 Reis
150 = 160 Reis   600 = 640 Reis

10 REIS

COPPER

c/s: Shield on V (5) Reis, C#1 (Lisbon Mint).

C#	Date	Year	Good	VG	Fine	VF
1a	(1809)	1752	7.50	12.50	17.50	25.00
		1753	2.00	3.50	5.50	10.00
		1768	1.00	2.00	3.50	6.00
		1773	1.00	2.00	3.50	6.00
		1774	1.00	2.00	3.50	6.00

c/s: Shield on V (5) Reis, C#2.

C#	Date	Year	Good	VG	Fine	VF
2a	(1809)	1762B	2.50	4.50	7.50	12.50
		1763B	2.50	4.50	7.50	12.50
		1764B	2.00	3.50	5.50	8.50
		1766B	2.00	3.50	5.50	8.50
		1767B	1.50	2.50	4.50	7.50
		1768B	1.50	2.50	4.50	7.50
		1769B	1.50	2.50	4.50	7.50

c/s: Shield on V (5) Reis, C#41.

C#	Date	Year	Good	VG	Fine	VF
41a	(1809)	1778	1.25	2.00	3.50	6.00
		1781	1.25	2.00	3.50	6.00
		1782	.75	1.25	2.50	4.50
		1784	1.25	2.00	3.50	6.00

c/s: Shield on V (5) Reis, C#60.

C#	Date	Year	Good	VG	Fine	VF
60a	(1809)	1786	4.50	7.50	15.00	25.00
		1787	.75	1.25	2.50	4.50
		1790	.75	1.25	2.50	4.50
		1791	.75	8.50	12.50	4.50
		1797	5.00	8.50	12.50	20.00

20 REIS

COPPER

c/s: Shield on X (10) Reis, C#3 (Rio Mint).

C#	Date	Year	Good	VG	Fine	VF
3a	(1809)	1751	15.00	25.00	35.00	50.00

c/s: Shield on X (10) Reis, C#4 (Lisbon Mint).

C#	Date	Year	Good	VG	Fine	VF
4a	(1809)	1752	2.00	3.50	5.00	8.00
		1753	1.00	1.75	3.00	5.00
		1773	3.00	5.00	8.00	12.50
		1774	.75	1.25	2.50	4.50
		1775	.85	1.50	3.00	5.00
		1776	.85	1.50	3.00	5.00

c/s: Shield on X (10) Reis, C#5.

C#	Date	Year	Good	VG	Fine	VF
5a	(1809)	1762B	1.25	2.00	3.50	6.00

c/s: Shield on X (10) Reis, C#42.

C#	Date	Year	Good	VG	Fine	VF
42a	(1809)	1778	.75	1.25	2.50	4.00
		1781	.85	1.50	3.00	5.00
		1782	.85	1.50	3.00	5.00
		1784	.85	1.50	3.00	5.00
		1785	.85	1.50	3.00	5.00

c/s: Shield on X (10) Reis, C#61.

C#	Date	Year	Good	VG	Fine	VF
61a	(1809)	1786	1.25	2.00	3.50	6.00
		1787	1.25	2.00	3.50	6.00
		1790	1.75	3.00	5.50	8.50
		1796	7.50	12.50	17.50	25.00

c/s: Shield on X (10) Reis, C#65.

C#	Date	Year	Good	VG	Fine	VF
65a	(1809)	1799	.85	1.50	2.50	4.50

40 REIS

COPPER

c/s: Shield on XX (20) Reis, C#6 (Rio Mint).

C#	Date	Year	Good	VG	Fine	VF
6a	(1809)	1751	5.00	8.50	12.50	20.00
		1752	2.50	4.00	6.50	10.00

c/s: Shield on XX (20) Reis, C#7 (Lisbon Mint).

C#	Date	Year	Good	VG	Fine	VF
7a	(1809)	1752	2.00	3.50	6.00	10.00
		1753	1.00	1.75	3.00	5.00
		1774	1.00	1.75	3.00	5.00
		1775	1.00	1.75	3.00	5.00
		1776	1.00	1.75	3.00	5.00

c/s: Shield on XX (20) Reis, C#8.

C#	Date	Year	Good	VG	Fine	VF
8a	(1809)	1761B	.75	1.25	2.00	3.50

c/s: Shield on XX (20) Reis, C#43.

C#	Date	Year	Good	VG	Fine	VF
43a	(1809)	1778	.75	1.25	2.25	4.00
		1781	1.25	2.00	3.50	6.00
		1782	1.25	2.00	3.50	6.00
		1784	1.25	2.00	3.50	6.00

c/s: Shield on XX (20) Reis with low crown, C#62.

C#	Date	Year	Good	VG	Fine	VF
62a	(1809)	1786	1.50	2.50	4.00	6.50
		1787	1.00	1.75	3.00	5.00
		1790	2.00	3.50	5.50	8.50
		1796	7.50	12.50	20.00	30.00
		1797	2.00	3.50	5.50	8.50

c/s: Shield on XX 20 Reis with high crown, C#62.1.

C#	Date	Year	Good	VG	Fine	VF
62c	(1809)	1799	15.00	23.50	30.00	40.00

c/s: Shield on XX (20) Reis, C#66.

C#	Date	Year	Good	VG	Fine	VF
66a	(1809)	1799	1.50	2.50	4.00	6.50

c/s: Shield on XX (20) Reis, C#81 (Lisbon Mint).

C#	Date	Year	Good	VG	Fine	VF
81a	(1809)	1802	.75	1.25	2.25	4.00
		1803	.75	1.25	2.25	4.00

80 REIS

COPPER

c/s: Shield on XL (40) Reis, C#9.

C#	Date	Year	Good	VG	Fine	VF
9a	(1809)	1753	.85	1.50	3.00	5.00
		1760	.85	1.50	3.00	5.00
		1774	2.00	3.50	5.00	8.00

c/s: Shield on XL (40) Reis, C#10.

C#	Date	Year	Good	VG	Fine	VF
10a	(1809)	1762B	3.00	5.00	8.00	11.50

c/s: Shield on XL (40) Reis, C#44.

C#	Date	Year	Good	VG	Fine	VF
44a	(1809)	1778	2.00	3.50	5.00	8.00
		1781	3.00	5.00	8.00	11.50
		1784	5.00	8.50	13.50	20.00

c/s: Shield on XL (40) Reis with low crown, C#63.

C#	Date	Year	Good	VG	Fine	VF
63a	(1809)	1786	2.75	4.50	6.50	10.00
		1787	3.25	5.50	8.50	13.50
		1790	3.25	5.50	8.50	13.50
		1791	18.50	30.00	40.00	60.00
		1796	3.25	5.50	8.50	13.50

c/s: Shield on XL 40 Reis with high crown, C#63.1.

C#	Date	Year	Good	VG	Fine	VF
63a.1	(1809)	1790	13.50	22.50	30.00	40.00
		1791	3.00	5.00	8.50	13.50

c/s: Shield on XL (40) Reis, C#67.

C#	Date	Year	Good	VG	Fine	VF
67a	(1809)	1799	1.50	2.50	4.00	7.00

c/s: Shield on XL (40) Reis, C#83.

C#	Date	Year	Good	VG	Fine	VF
83a	(1809)	1802	.85	1.50	3.00	5.00
		1803	.85	1.50	3.00	5.00

2.2600 gm., .917 SILVER, .0666 oz ASW
c/s: Shield on 75 Reis, C#21.

C#	Date	Year	Good	VG	Fine	VF
21a	(1809)	1752B	4.50	7.50	12.50	20.00
		1753B	3.50	6.00	10.00	15.00
		1754B	3.50	6.00	10.00	15.00

c/s: Shield on 75 Reis, C#22.

C#	Date	Year	Good	VG	Fine	VF
22a	(1809)	1754R	3.50	6.00	10.00	15.00
		1755R	3.50	6.00	10.00	15.00
		1760R	4.50	7.50	12.50	20.00

160 REIS

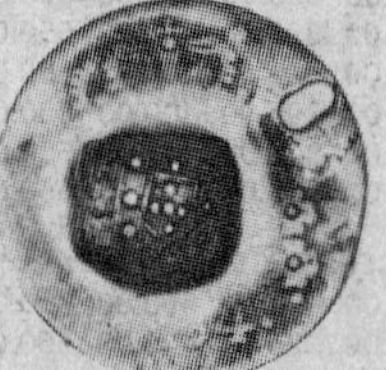

4.5200 gm., .917 SILVER, .1332 oz ASW
c/s: Shield on 150 Reis, C#23.

C#	Date	Year	Good	VG	Fine	VF
23a	(1809)	1752B	6.00	10.00	16.50	25.00
		1753B	5.50	9.00	15.00	22.50

C#	Date	Year	Good	VG	Fine	VF
23a		1754B	5.50	9.00	15.00	22.50
		1756B	6.00	10.00	16.50	25.00
		1768B	6.00	8.50	18.50	30.00

c/s: Shield on 150 Reis, C#24.

24a	(1809)	1754R	5.50	9.00	15.00	22.50
		1755R	5.50	9.00	15.00	22.50
		1758R	5.50	9.00	15.00	22.50
		1760R	7.00	11.50	18.50	30.00
		1771R	6.00	10.00	16.50	25.00

320 REIS

9.0500 gm., .917 SILVER, .2668 oz ASW
c/s: Shield on 300 Reis, C#25.

25a	(1809)	1752B	8.50	12.50	20.00	33.50
		1753B	8.50	12.50	20.00	33.50
		1754B	8.50	12.50	20.00	33.50
		1756B	8.50	12.50	20.00	33.50
		1757B	8.50	12.50	20.00	33.50
		1768B	11.50	18.50	27.50	40.00

c/s: Shield on 300 Reis, C#26.

26a	(1809)	1754R	8.50	12.50	20.00	33.50
		1755R	8.50	12.50	20.00	33.50
		1756R	8.50	12.50	20.00	33.50
		1757R	8.50	12.50	20.00	33.50
		1758R	8.50	12.50	20.00	33.50
		1764R	8.50	12.50	20.00	33.50
		1771R	8.00	11.50	18.50	30.00

620 REIS

18.1100 gm., .917 SILVER, .5339 oz ASW
c/s: Shield on 600 Reis, C#27.

27a	(1809)	1752B	20.00	30.00	35.00	60.00
		1754B	18.50	21.50	26.50	37.50
		1756B	17.50	21.50	27.50	35.00
		1757B	17.50	21.50	27.50	35.00
		1758B	17.50	21.50	27.50	35.00
		1760B	18.50	26.50	27.50	35.00
		1768B	18.50	21.50	26.50	37.50

c/s: Shield on 600 Reis, C#28.

28a	(1809)	1754R	18.50	25.00	30.00	45.00
		1755R	18.50	25.00	30.00	45.00
		1756R	18.50	25.00	30.00	45.00
		1758R	18.50	25.00	30.00	45.00
		1760R	22.50	35.00	40.00	60.00
		1764R	18.50	25.00	30.00	45.00
		1765R	18.50	25.00	30.00	45.00
		1770R	18.50	25.00	30.00	45.00
		1771R	18.50	25.00	30.00	45.00
		1774R	18.50	25.00	30.00	45.00

REGIONAL ISSUES

CUIABA

Cuiaba is the present capitol of the Mato Grosse state. In 1820 this city name appeared as "CUYABA" or "C" on a counterstamp appearing on Spanish-American 8 reales coins. This is the rarest Brazilian counterstamp.

Authorized 1820
Obv. c/s: Crowned shield above CUYABA.
Rev. c/s: Banded globe.

960 REIS

SILVER
c/s: On Spanish Colonial 8 Reales.

C#	Date	Year	Good	VG	Fine	VF
98	(1820)	—	—	—	Rare	—

MATO GROSSO

A large state in the center of Brazil. One of the issuers of the counterstamps of the 1808 law. The name of the province appears under the arms on the obverse.

TYPE A
Authorized November 4, 1818
c/s: Crowned shield above MATO GROSSO.
Rev. c/s: Banded globe.

NOTE: The c/s having the crown made up of close large pearls is considered a counterfeit.

960 REIS

SILVER
c/s: Type A on Argentina 8 Reales, C#15.

97.1	ND	(1813-15)	250.00	400.00	600.00	850.00

c/s: Type A on Bolivia 8 Reales, C#37.

97.2	ND	(1791-1808)	250.00	400.00	600.00	850.00

TYPE B
Authorized in January, 1821.
Obv. c/s: Crowned 960/C within branches.
Rev. c/s: Shield on globe.

TYPE C
Obv. c/s: Crowned 960/C. within branches.
Rev. c/s: Shield on globe.

TYPE D
Obv. c/s: Crowned 960/.C. within branches.
Rev. c/s: Shield on globe.

c/s: Type B on Bolivia 8 Reales, C#37.

99.1	ND	(1791-1808)	150.00	250.00	400.00	550.00

c/s: Type C on Argentina 8 Reales, C#15.

C#	Date	Year	Good	VG	Fine	VF
99.2	ND	(1813-15)	—	—	—	—

c/s: Type C on Bolivia 8 Reales, C#47

99.3	ND	(1808-1820)	175.00	275.00	450.00	600.00

c/s: Type D on Spanish Colonial 8 Reales.

99.4	ND	—	150.00	250.00	400.00	550.00

MINAS GERAIS

Minas Gerais is a state in eastern Brazil. In September of 1808 an edict was issued for the authorization of various counterstamps to be used on the many circulating Spanish 8 reales in the country. The Minas Gerais counterstamp was issued both with and w/o the M on the reverse. The silver value was 750 to 800 Reis per coin but they were marked and passed at 960 reis giving the government a nice profit.

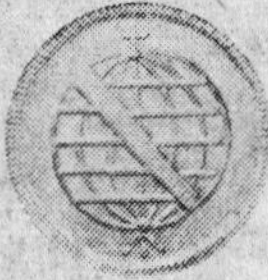

Authorized Sept. 1, 1808 until 1810
Obv. c/s: Crowned shield in branches/960.
Rev. c/s: Banded globe with cross.

960 REIS

SILVER
c/s: On Bolivia 8 Reales, C#18.

96.1	ND	(1773-89)	100.00	175.00	300.00	500.00

c/s: On Bolivia 8 Reales, C#27.

C#	Date	Year	Good	VG	Fine	VF
96.2	ND	(1789-91)	45.00	65.00	100.00	150.00

c/s: On Bolivia 8 Reales, C#37.

96.3	ND (1791-1808)		35.00	50.00	75.00	110.00

c/s: On Chile 8 Reales.

96.4	ND		—	—	—	Rare	—

c/s: On Guatemala 8 Reales.

96.5	ND		—	—	—	Rare	—

c/s: On Mexico City 8 Reales, KM#105 (C#35).

96.6	ND	(1760-72)	40.00	65.00	100.00	150.00

c/s: On Mexico City 8 Reales, KM#106 (C#40).

96.7	ND	(1772-89)	35.00	50.00	75.00	110.00

c/s: On Mexico City 8 Reales, KM#107 (C#73).

96.8	ND	(1789-90)	45.00	65.00	100.00	150.00

c/s: On Mexico City 8 Reales, KM#109 (C#81).

96.9	ND (1791-1808)		35.00	50.00	75.00	110.00

c/s: On Peru 8 Reales, C#45.

96.10	ND	(1772-89)	35.00	50.00	75.00	110.00

c/s: On Peru 8 Reales, C#69.

C#	Date	Year	Good	VG	Fine	VF
96.11	ND	(1789-91)	45.00	65.00	100.00	150.00

c/s: On Peru 8 Reales, C#76.

96.12	ND (1791-1808)		30.00	45.00	75.00	100.00

c/s: On Spanish 8 Reales.

96.13	ND		—	—	—	Rare	—

UNITED KINGDOM

Copper Coinage

The imperial copper coins of Brazil (1823-1833) were struck to several different standards simultaneously, each intended for a different part of the empire. The following table shows the standards used at each mint:

Weights of Imperial Brazilian copper coins in oitavos:

MINTMARK DENOMINATION (REIS)

	MARK	10	20	40	80	37½	75
Rio De Janeiro	R	1	2	4	8	—	—
Bahia	B	1	2	4	8	—	—
Goias	G	—	1	2	4	—	4
Cuiaba	C	—	1	2	4	—	—
Minas Gerais	M	—	—	—	—	2	—
Sao Paulo	SP	—	—	—	5⅓	—	—

NOTE: 1 Oitavo - 3.586 gm.; 8 Oitavos - 1 Onza (28.68 gm.); thus 5-1/3 Oitavos (5 Oitavos plus 1 Escropalo) is precisely 2/3 Onza (ounce).

Lightweight coins: Many coppers are found as much as 15 percent or more below the official weights, and even heavy specimens are occasionally observed. Most of the above coins were counterfeited, as their face value exceeded the cost of the metal and minting. Though usually crude and carelessly engraved, some counterfeits are of decent workmanship, and entirely undistinguishable from government issues. Brazilian collectors generally accept these contemporary counterfeits as collectable, due to their historical value. Before Pedro I began his regular coinage, colonial coppers were revalued with a special countermark, probably in 1822.

Imperial Countermarks

These countermarks consist of a crowned 20, 40 or 80 within a wreath in a circle and opposite a shield in a circle is used.

20 REIS

COPPER

20 countermarked on various Colonial X (10) Reis coins.

120	Various	—	—	—	Rare	—

NOTE: Many authorities consider all known examples of C#120 to be counterfeit.

40 REIS

COPPER

40 countermarked on various Colonial XX (20) Reis.

121	Various	—	—	—	Rare	—

NOTE: Three of eight known dies believed counterfeit.

80 REIS

COPPER

80 countermarked on various Colonial XL (40) Reis.

C#	Date	Year	Good	VG	Fine	VF
122	Various	—	—	—	Rare	—

NOTE: One of 11 known dies believed counterfeit.

Regular Coinage

CAUTION: Prices are for specimens without any countermark. Countermarked pieces follow these listings.

10 REIS

COPPER

C#	Date	Mintage	Good	VG	Fine	VF
125	1824R	.235	.75	2.00	7.00	10.00
	1827B	.104	4.00	10.00	25.00	40.00
	1828B	.728	1.75	4.00	10.00	17.50

20 REIS

COPPER

PEDRO I, weight: 2 oitavos, 7.17 gm.

C#	Date	Mintage	Good	VG	Fine	VF
126	1822R		Counterfeit		—	—
	1823R	1.700	.60	1.50	4.00	7.50
	1824R	4.956	.75	1.25	2.00	4.50
	1825B	.582	1.60	4.00	7.50	12.50
	1825R	9.054	.50	1.25	2.00	4.50
	1826R	4.419	.50	1.25	2.00	4.50
	1827B	.044	5.00	12.50	25.00	40.00
	1827R	4.648	4.50	11.50	22.50	37.50
	1828B	.585	1.50	3.50	7.00	10.00
	1828R	4.474	.75	1.75	3.00	5.00
	1829R	6.806	.50	1.25	2.00	4.50
	1830B	.316	1.65	4.00	7.50	12.50
	1830R	—	.50	1.25	2.00	4.50
	1831R		Counterfeit		—	—

PEDRO I, reduced weight: 1 oitavo - 3.59 gm.

129	1825C	—	16.50	40.00	70.00	100.00
	1829G		Counterfeit		—	—

PEDRO II, reduced weight: 2 oitavos - 7.17 gm.

145	1832R	.014	12.00	30.00	60.00	95.00

37-1/2 REIS

COPPER

PEDRO I, weight: 2 oitavos - 7.17 gm.

130	1823M	—	4.00	10.00	25.00	40.00

C#	Date	Mintage	Good	VG	Fine	VF
	1824M	—	4.00	10.00	25.00	40.00
	1825M	—	7.50	17.50	37.50	55.00
	1826M	—	7.50	17.50	37.50	55.00
	1827M	—	7.50	17.50	37.50	55.00
	1828M	—	7.50	17.50	37.50	55.00

40 REIS

COPPER

PEDRO I, weight: 4 oitavos - 14.34 gm.

C#	Date	Mintage	Good	VG	Fine	VF
127	1823R	.920	.50	1.25	2.50	6.00
	1824B	.230	3.00	7.50	15.00	25.00
	1824R	9.170	.50	1.25	2.50	6.00
	1825B					
		Inc. w/1824B	3.50	8.50	17.50	30.00
	1825R	6.774	.75	2.00	4.00	8.00
	1826R	10.507	1.25	3.00	5.00	10.00
	1827B	.161	3.00	7.50	15.00	25.00
	1827R	17.892	.75	2.00	4.00	8.00
	1828B	.051	1.00	2.50	6.00	12.00
	1828R	15.570	.75	2.00	4.00	8.00
	1829B	2.052	.65	1.75	4.00	8.00
	1829R	8.924	.75	2.00	4.00	8.00
	1830B	1.032	1.10	2.75	5.00	8.50
	1830R	—	1.00	2.50	4.50	8.00
	1831R	—	1.25	3.00	5.00	8.25

NOTE: Most known examples of 1828R, 1829R, and 1830R are counterfeit!

PEDRO I, reduced weight: 2 oitavos - 7.17 gm.

C#	Date	Mintage	Good	VG	Fine	VF
131	1823C	—	6.00	15.00	35.00	50.00
	1823G	—	9.00	22.50	50.00	75.00
	1824C	—	1.25	3.00	6.00	10.00
	1825C	—	1.00	2.50	5.00	10.00
	1825G	—	3.50	8.50	17.50	32.50
	1826C	—	1.25	3.00	6.00	10.00
	1826G	—	3.50	8.50	17.50	32.50
	1827C	—	1.25	3.00	6.00	10.00
	1827G	—	1.25	3.00	6.00	10.00
	1828C	—	1.00	2.50	4.50	10.00
	1828G	—	1.25	3.00	6.00	10.00
	1829C	—	3.50	8.50	17.50	32.50
	1829G	—	1.25	3.00	6.00	10.00
	1830C	—	3.50	8.50	17.50	32.50
	1830G	—	1.25	3.00	6.00	10.00
	1831C	—	3.50	8.50	17.50	32.50

NOTE: 1823C is considered a counterfeit by many authorities.

PEDRO II, weight: 4 oitavos - 14.34 gm.

C#	Date	Mintage	Good	VG	Fine	VF
146	1831R	—	— Counterfeit issue			—
	1832R	.816	2.00	5.00	10.00	16.50

NOTE: 1833R exists as a pattern.

PEDRO II, reduced weight: 2 oitavos - 7.17 gm.

C#	Date	Mintage	Good	VG	Fine	VF
148	1832G Petrus II					
		—	3.00	7.50	15.00	25.00
	1832G Petrus 20					
		—	2.00	5.00	10.00	16.50
	1833C	—	6.00	15.00	25.00	37.50

75 REIS

COPPER

PEDRO I, weight: 4 oitavos - 14.34 gm.

C#	Date	Mintage	Good	VG	Fine	VF
132	1823G	—	10.00	25.00	50.00	80.00

80 REIS

COPPER

PEDRO I, weight: 8 oitavos - 28.69 gm.

C#	Date	Mintage	Good	VG	Fine	VF
128	1823R	.100	.75	2.00	3.50	6.00
	1824B	.879	1.25	3.00	4.50	8.00
	1824R	.825	.65	1.75	3.00	6.00
	1825B					
		Inc. 1824B	1.25	3.00	5.00	8.75
	1825R	1.027	.75	2.00	3.50	6.00
	1826B	.695	1.35	3.50	6.00	10.00
	1826R	10.507	.65	1.75	3.00	6.00
	1827B	.352	2.75	4.50	7.50	12.00
	1827R	17.892	.60	1.50	3.00	6.00
	1828B	2.539	.75	2.00	3.50	6.00
	1828R	26.524	.60	1.50	3.00	6.00
	1829B	3.993	.75	2.00	3.25	6.00
	1829R	20.180	.60	1.50	3.00	6.00
	1830B	.359	1.25	3.00	4.75	8.25
	1830R	—	.65	1.75	3.00	6.00
	1831B	—	Counterfeits exist.			—
	1831R	—	.75	2.00	3.50	8.00

NOTE: Coins with P mintmark are all counterfeit.

PEDRO I, weight: 5 1/3 oitavos - 19.13 gm.

C#	Date	Mintage	Good	VG	Fine	VF
128b	1825SP	—	10.00	25.00	50.00	80.00
	1828SP	—	4.00	10.00	20.00	36.50
	1829SP	—	5.00	12.50	25.00	40.00

NOTE: Many varieties of the Sao Paulo coins exist.

PEDRO I, weight: 4 oitavos - 14.34 gm.

C#	Date	Mintage	Good	VG	Fine	VF
133	1826C	—	2.00	5.00	10.00	16.50
	1826G	—	16.50	40.00	80.00	120.00
	1827C	—	20.00	50.00	100.00	140.00
	1828C	—	2.00	5.00	15.00	20.00
	1828G	—	1.65	4.00	12.00	18.00
	1829G	—	2.25	5.50	15.00	20.00
	1830C	—	16.50	40.00	80.00	120.00
	1830G	—	2.75	7.00	15.00	25.00
	1831G	—	3.25	8.50	20.00	26.00

NOTE: Coins dated 1826G are believed to be all counterfeit.

PEDRO II, weight: 8 oitavos - 28.69 gm.
Rev: Similar to C#128.

C#	Date	Mintage	Good	VG	Fine	VF
147	1831R	—	1.25	3.00	5.00	8.50
	1832R	6.119	.60	1.50	2.50	5.00
	1833R	—	Reported, Not Confirmed			

PEDRO II, weight: 5 1/3 oitavos - 19.13 gm.

C#	Date	Mintage	Good	VG	Fine	VF
147b	1832SP	—	—	—	—	—

NOTE: The 1832SP is considered a counterfeit by many authorities.

PEDRO II, weight: 4 oitavos - 14.34 gm.

C#	Date	Mintage	Good	VG	Fine	VF
149	1832G	—	6.00	15.00	40.00	55.00
	1833G	—	3.25	8.50	20.00	35.00
	1833G Petrus I (error)					
		—	6.00	15.00	40.00	55.00

COUNTERSTAMP ISSUES

Regional

NOTE: Due to variations in value from one part of the country to another, copper coins tended to flow to areas where their buying power was greatest. To prevent the outflow, some districts ordered coinage countermarked and reduced in value. There is speculation that silver coins were also ordered to be counterstamped, but no documentation is available to substantiate this claim. The following issues are recognized as genuine. Prices are for countermarks on common coins of each variety. Countermarked rare dates bring a premium.

CEARA

Ceara is a state in northeastern Brazil. Due to coin shortages a law was passed October 3, 1833 that copper coins would be counterstamped and pass for 1/2 of their face value. In November of 1834 legislation was passed to stop the star counterstamps.

Coins of 20, 40, and 80 reis were countermarked CEARA in a 5-pointed star to indicate a 50 percent reduction in value (to 10, 20, and 40 reis).

10 REIS

COPPER

c/s: Star on various 20 Reis.

C#	Date	Year	Good	VG	Fine	VF
150	ND	(1834)	7.50	15.00	25.00	37.50

20 REIS

COPPER

c/s: Star on various 40 Reis.

C#	Date	Year	Good	VG	Fine	VF
151	ND	(1834)	4.50	8.00	12.50	18.50

40 REIS

COPPER

c/s: Star on various 80 Reis.

C#	Date	Year	Good	VG	Fine	VF
152	ND	(1834)	4.50	8.00	12.50	18.50

NOTE: All silver coins bearing this c/s are considered fantasies.

MARANHAO

Maranhao is a state in northeastern Brazil. Coin shortages caused 2 issues of counterstamped coins. The first was to make the coins pass for 1/4 their face value. These had M and the new value. The second issue was to make the coins pass for 1/2 the face value. These were counterstamped with an M. These, too, were soon recalled.

FIRST SERIES (1834)

M and denomination in Roman numerals within a rectangle.

5 REIS

COPPER

c/s: M/V on various 20 Reis.

C#	Date	Year	Good	VG	Fine	VF
154	ND	(1834)	4.00	10.00	20.00	35.00

10 REIS

COPPER

c/s: M/X on various 40 Reis.

C#	Date	Year	Good	VG	Fine	VF
155	ND	(1834)	1.60	4.00	7.50	12.00

20 REIS

COPPER

c/s: M/XX on various 80 Reis.

C#	Date	Year	Good	VG	Fine	VF
156	ND	(1834)	1.40	3.50	6.00	10.00

SECOND SERIES (1835)

Large M on reverse of coin.

10 REIS

COPPER

c/s: M on various 20 Reis.

C#	Date	Mintage	Good	VG	Fine	VF
157	ND	(1835)	7.50	15.00	25.00	37.50

20 REIS

COPPER

c/s: M on various 40 Reis.

C#	Date	Mintage	Good	VG	Fine	VF
158	ND	(1835)	4.00	7.50	12.50	18.50

40 REIS

COPPER

c/s: M on various 80 Reis.

C#	Date	Mintage	Good	VG	Fine	VF
159	ND	(1835)	5.00	8.50	15.00	22.50

NOTE: Second series countermarks are found struck over coins which already have the first series countermark. They are worth about 50 percent more than ordinary second series coins.

PARA

Para is a state in northern Brazil. Two series of counterstamps were issued from this state. On January 14, 1835 Governor Malcher authorized a law for the counterstamping of the recently withdrawn Mato Grosso coppers to 1/4 of their previous value. On March 6, 1835 Governor Vinagre authorized the counterstamping of coppers at 1/2 their face value. Although heavily counterfeited because of their crudeness these coins stayed in circulation until 1868 and even later.

Crude Arabic 10, 20, or 40 countermarked on obverse of coins weighing 2, 4, and 8 oitavos, respectively. The numerals are quite crude and styles vary and are easily distinguished from the general counterstamps. Examples of the Para marks are:

10 20 40

10 REIS

COPPER

c/s: 10 on various Colonial XX (20) Reis.

C#	Date	Year	Good	VG	Fine	VF
160	(1835)	—	1.50	2.25	4.00	6.00

c/s: 10 on Imperial 20 Reis, R or B mints.

C#	Date	Year	Good	VG	Fine	VF
160	(1835)	—	1.50	2.25	4.00	6.00

c/s: 10 on Imperial 40 Reis, C or G mints.

C#	Date	Year	Good	VG	Fine	VF
161	(1835)	—	2.00	3.00	5.00	7.50

20 REIS

COPPER

c/s: 20 on Colonial XL (40) Reis.

C#	Date	Year	Good	VG	Fine	VF
162	(1835)	—	1.50	2.25	4.00	6.00

c/s: 20 on Imperial 40 Reis, R or B mints.

C#	Date	Year	Good	VG	Fine	VF
164	(1835)	—	1.50	2.25	4.00	6.00

c/s: 20 on Imperial 80 Reis, C or G mints.

C#	Date	Year	Good	VG	Fine	VF
163	(1835)	—	2.00	3.00	6.00	9.00

40 REIS

COPPER

c/s: 40 on Colonial LXXX (80) Reis.

C#	Date	Year	Good	VG	Fine	VF
165	(1835)	—	1.50	2.25	4.00	6.00

c/s: 40 on Imperial 80 Reis, R or B mints.

C#	Date	Year	Good	VG	Fine	VF
165	(1835)	—	1.50	2.25	4.00	6.00

REPUBLIC OF PIRATINI

As a result of a revolt in 1835 in the southern Brazilian state of Rio Grande do Sol the "Republic of Piratini" was briefly established and all coins then circulating in the province were counterstamped with the arms of the new republic. This series is probably the most counterfeited of all of the elaborate counterstamps.

(1835)

Two hands grasping a curved sword with Liberty cap on point within oval. Similar c/s with the date 1835 are considered counterfeit.

960 REIS

SILVER

c/s: On Brazil 960 Reis, C#94.

KM#	Date	Mintage	Fine	VF	XF
1	(1835)	—	—	Rare	—

ICO

Ico is a city in the state of Ceara in northeastern Brazil. It was the center of a revolutionary movement from 1829-1832. Various copper and silver coins countermarked ICO, YCO, JGO, and IGO are all considered counterfeit, countermarked after the suppression of the revolt. They have little value, but are collected as curiosities. Average value, about $4.00.

NOTE: In addition to local countermarks, over 280 private countermarks are known. A list of these is given by Kurt Prober, in his "Catalogo das Moedas Brasileiras."

National Countermarks

In order to prevent chaotic conditions resulting from local and private countermarking, the government passed law #54 of 6 October 1835 ordering all coppers countermarked according to the following standards:

2 Oitavos = 7.18 gm. = 10 Reis
4 Oitavos = 14.34 gm. = 20 Reis
8 Oitavos = 28.69 gm. = 40 Reis

The countermarks consist of neat numerals within a circle, having a plain or shaded field. These countermarks were applied to various Brazilian coinage from 1799 to 1833. In addition, wrong countermarks are occasionally found, as well as various Portuguese, Angolan, San Tome, Mozambiquean and pre-1799 Brazilian coins.

10 REIS

COPPER

c/s: 10 on XX (20) Reis, C#66.

C#	Date	Year	Good	VG	Fine	VF
66b	ND	1799	1.50	2.50	4.00	6.00

c/s: 10 on XX (20) Reis, C#81 (Lisbon Mint).

C#	Date	Year	Good	VG	Fine	VF
81b	ND	1802	1.00	2.00	3.50	5.50
		1803	1.00	2.00	3.50	5.50
		1805	1.00	2.00	3.50	5.50
		1812B	1.75	3.00	5.00	6.50
		1812R	3.50	5.00	8.50	11.50
		1813B	1.25	2.25	3.50	4.75
		1813R	1.25	2.50	4.50	6.50
		1814R	1.25	2.50	4.50	6.50
		1815B	1.25	2.25	3.50	4.75
		1815R	1.25	2.50	4.50	6.00
	ND	1816B	1.25	2.25	3.50	4.75

COPPER

c/s: 10 on XX (20) Reis, C#82.

C#	Date	Year	Good	VG	Fine	VF
82a	ND	1816R	2.25	3.50	6.50	10.00
		1817R	2.25	3.50	6.50	10.00

C#	Date	Year	Good	VG	Fine	VF
82a		1818R	2.25	3.50	6.50	10.00

c/s: 10 on XL (40) Reis, C#87.

C#	Date	Year	Good	VG	Fine	VF
87a	ND	1818R	12.50	18.50	27.50	40.00

c/s: 10 on XX (20) Reis, C#106.

C#	Date	Year	Good	VG	Fine	VF
106a	ND	1818R	1.75	3.00	5.50	8.50
		1819R	.50	1.00	1.75	2.75
		1820B	1.50	3.00	5.50	8.50
		1820R	.50	1.00	1.75	2.75
		1821B	1.50	3.00	5.50	8.50
		1821R	.50	1.00	1.75	2.75
		1822R	.50	1.00	1.75	2.75

c/s: 10 on 37-1/2 Reis, C#109.

C#	Date	Year	Good	VG	Fine	VF
109a	ND	1818M	3.00	5.00	8.50	13.50
		1818R	6.50	10.00	16.50	25.00

c/s: 10 on XL (40) Reis, C#111.

C#	Date	Year	Good	VG	Fine	VF
111a	ND	1820	5.00	8.50	15.00	22.50

c/s: 10 on 20 Reis, Pedro I, C#126.

C#	Date	Year	Good	VG	Fine	VF
126a	ND	1823R	.75	1.50	3.00	4.50
		1824R	.50	1.00	2.00	3.50
		1825B	1.00	1.85	3.50	5.00
		1825R	.50	1.00	2.00	3.50
		1826R	.50	1.00	2.00	3.50
		1827B	3.00	5.00	8.00	12.50
		1827R	.60	1.25	2.75	4.25
		1828B	1.25	2.00	3.75	6.00
		1828R	.75	1.50	3.00	4.50
		1829R	.75	1.50	3.00	4.50
		1830B	1.25	2.00	3.50	5.50
		1830R	.75	1.50	3.00	4.50

c/s: 10 on 20 Reis of Pedro I, C#129.

C#	Date	Year	Good	VG	Fine	VF
129a	ND	1825C	50.00	100.00	150.00	225.00
		1827G	20.00	32.50	50.00	75.00

NOTE: The above two pieces were not supposed to have been countermarked, as they only weigh one oitavo-3.59 gm.

c/s: 10 on 20 Reis of Pedro II, C#145.

C#	Date	Year	Good	VG	Fine	VF
145a	ND	1832R	30.00	60.00	100.00	150.00

c/s: 10 on 37-1/2 Reis of Pedro I.

C#	Date	Year	Good	VG	Fine	VF
130a	ND	1823M	12.50	22.50	35.00	52.50
		1824M	10.00	20.00	30.00	45.00
		1825M	5.00	10.00	16.50	25.00
		1826M	7.50	15.00	23.50	35.00
		1827M	7.50	15.00	23.50	35.00
		1828M	9.00	17.50	27.50	42.50

c/s: 10 on 40 Reis of Pedro I, C#131.

C#	Date	Year	Good	VG	Fine	VF
131a	ND	1823C	12.50	25.00	50.00	75.00
		1823G	6.50	12.50	25.00	37.50
		1824C	1.00	1.50	4.00	6.00
		1825C	1.00	1.50	4.00	6.00
		1825G	1.75	2.50	6.00	9.00
		1826C	1.75	2.50	6.00	9.00
		1826G	1.35	2.00	5.00	7.50
		1827C	1.00	1.50	4.00	6.00
		1827G	1.00	1.50	4.00	6.00
		1828C	1.00	1.50	4.00	6.00
		1828G	1.00	1.50	4.00	6.00
		1829C	1.00	1.50	4.00	6.00
		1829G	2.00	4.00	8.00	12.00
		1830C	1.00	1.50	4.00	6.00
		1830G	1.00	1.50	4.00	6.00
		1831C	1.00	1.50	4.00	6.00

c/s: 10 on 40 Reis of Pedro II, C#148.

C#	Date	Year	Good	VG	Fine	VF
148a	ND	1832G	Petrus II			11.50
			3.00	4.50	7.50	
		1832G	Petrus 20			
			2.00	3.00	5.00	7.50
		1833C	2.50	4.00	6.00	9.00

c/s: 10 On Mozambique 40 Reis, C#55.

C#	Date	Year	Good	VG	Fine	VF
55a	ND	1819	2.50	5.00	7.50	11.50
		1820	1.75	3.50	5.00	7.50
		1821	2.50	5.00	7.50	11.50
		1821	1.50	3.00	4.50	6.50
		1822	2.00	4.00	6.00	9.00
		1825	2.00	4.00	6.00	9.00

NOTE: The above Craig # refers to the Mozambique listing, not Brazil.

20 REIS

COPPER

c/s: 20 on XL (40) Reis, C#67.

C#	Date	Year	Good	VG	Fine	VF
67b	ND	1799	1.00	1.50	2.50	3.75

c/s: 20 on XL (40) Reis, C#83.

C#	Date	Year	Good	VG	Fine	VF
83b	ND	1802	1.00	1.50	3.00	4.50
		1803	1.00	1.50	3.00	4.50
		1809B	2.50	4.00	7.00	11.50
		1810B	2.50	4.00	7.00	11.50
		1811B	2.00	3.50	6.00	9.00
		1812B	1.00	1.50	3.00	4.50
		1812R	1.25	2.00	4.00	6.00
		1813R	1.00	1.50	3.00	4.50
		1814B	1.00	1.50	3.00	4.50
		1815R	.75	1.25	2.50	3.75
		1816B	1.00	1.50	3.00	4.50

c/s: 20 on XL (40) Reis, C#84.

C#	Date	Year	Good	VG	Fine	VF
84a	ND	1816R	2.00	3.00	6.00	9.00
	ND	1817R	1.50	2.50	5.00	7.50

c/s: 20 on XL (40) Reis, C#107.

C#	Date	Year	Good	VG	Fine	VF
107a	ND	1818R	1.00	1.50	3.00	4.50
		1819R	2.00	3.50	6.50	10.00
		1820B	1.50	2.50	5.00	7.50
		1820R	.75	1.25	2.50	3.75
		1821B	2.00	3.50	6.50	10.00
		1821R	.75	1.25	2.50	3.75
		1822B	2.00	3.50	6.50	10.00
		1822R	.75	1.25	2.50	3.75
		1823B	2.00	3.50	6.50	10.00

c/s: 20 on 75 Reis, C#110.

C#	Date	Year	Good	VG	Fine	VF
110a	ND	1818M	2.50	4.00	7.00	11.50
		1819M	3.00	5.00	8.50	13.50
		1821M	2.50	4.00	7.00	11.50

c/s: 20 on LXXX (80) Reis, C#112.

C#	Date	Year	Good	VG	Fine	VF
112a	ND	1820	5.00	8.50	15.00	22.50

c/s: 20 on 40 Reis of Pedro I, C#127.

C#	Date	Year	Good	VG	Fine	VF
127a	ND	1823R	1.00	1.50	2.25	3.50
		1824B	2.50	4.50	7.50	11.50
		1824R	1.00	1.50	2.25	3.50
		1825B	2.50	4.50	7.50	11.50
		1825R	1.00	1.75	2.25	3.50
		1826R	1.00	1.50	2.75	3.50
		1827B	3.50	6.00	10.00	15.00
		1827R	1.00	1.50	2.25	3.50
		1828B	1.00	1.75	3.00	4.50
		1828R	1.00	1.75	2.25	3.50
		1829B	1.00	1.75	3.00	4.50
		1829R	1.00	1.50	3.00	4.50
		1830B	1.00	1.75	3.00	4.50
		1830R	1.00	1.75	2.25	3.50
		1831R	1.00	1.50	2.75	4.25

c/s: 20 on 40 Reis of Pedro II, C#146.

C#	Date	Year	Good	VG	Fine	VF
146a	ND	1831R	15.00	30.00	60.00	90.00
		1832R	.75	1.50	3.00	4.50

c/s: 20 on 75 Reis of Pedro I, C#132.

C#	Date	Year	Good	VG	Fine	VF
132a	ND	1823G	10.00	18.50	30.00	45.00

c/s: 20 on 80 Reis of Pedro I, C#133.

C#	Date	Year	Good	VG	Fine	VF
133a	ND	1826C	1.75	3.00	4.75	7.00
		1826G	17.50	35.00	50.00	75.00
		1827C	40.00	80.00	130.00	200.00
		1828C	3.00	5.00	8.50	12.50
		1828G	1.00	2.00	3.00	4.50
		1829G	1.50	2.50	4.00	6.00
		1830C	2.50	4.50	7.50	11.50
		1830G	1.50	2.50	4.00	6.00
		1831G	2.00	3.50	6.00	9.00

c/s: 20 on 80 Reis of Pedro II, C#149.

C#	Date	Year	Good	VG	Fine	VF
149a	ND	1832G	7.00	12.50	20.00	30.00
		1833G	2.00	3.25	4.50	7.00
		1833G Petrus I				
			4.00	7.50	12.50	18.50

c/s: 20 On Mozambique 80 Reis, C#56.

C#	Date	Year	Good	VG	Fine	VF
56a	ND	1819	4.50	8.50	12.50	18.50
		1820	3.50	6.50	10.00	15.00
		1825	2.75	5.50	8.00	12.00

NOTE: The above Craig # refers to the Mozambique listing, not Brazil.

40 REIS

COPPER

c/s: 40 on LXXX (80) Reis, C#85.

C#	Date	Year	Good	VG	Fine	VF
85a	ND	1811R	12.50	16.50	22.50	35.00
		1812R	8.50	12.50	18.50	27.50

c/s: 40 on LXXX (80) Reis, C#108.

C#	Date	Year	Good	VG	Fine	VF
108a	ND	1820B	1.00	1.50	3.00	4.50
		1821B	1.00	1.50	3.00	4.50
		1821R	1.25	2.00	3.50	5.25
		1822B	1.50	2.50	5.00	7.50
		1822R	1.25	2.00	3.50	5.25
		1823B	2.00	3.50	6.50	10.00

c/s: 40 on 80 Reis of Pedro I, C#128.

C#	Date	Year	Good	VG	Fine	VF
128a	ND	1823R	.80	1.25	2.25	3.25
		1824B	1.00	1.75	3.00	4.50
		1824R	.80	1.00	3.00	4.50
		1825B	1.00	1.75	3.00	4.50
		1825R	.80	1.00	2.00	3.00
		1826B	1.00	1.75	3.00	4.50
		1826R	.85	1.50	2.75	4.00
		1827B	1.00	1.75	3.00	4.50
		1827R	.80	1.00	2.00	3.00
		1828B	1.00	1.75	3.00	4.50
		1828R	.80	1.00	2.00	3.00
		1829B	1.00	1.75	3.00	4.50
		1829R	.80	1.00	2.00	3.00
		1830B	1.25	2.00	3.50	5.50
		1830R	.80	1.00	2.00	3.00
		1831B	Counterfeit			—
		1831R	.85	1.50	2.75	4.00

c/s: 40 on 80 Reis of Pedro I, C#128b.

C#	Date	Year	Good	VG	Fine	VF
128c	ND	1825SP	25.00	50.00	75.00	110.00
		1828SP	5.00	10.00	17.50	27.50
		1829SP	6.00	12.50	20.00	30.00

c/s: 40 on 80 Reis of Pedro II, C#147.

C#	Date	Year	Good	VG	Fine	VF
147a	ND	1831R	1.00	2.00	5.00	7.50
		1832R	.50	2.00	5.00	7.50

c/s: 40 on 80 Reis of Pedro II, C#147b.

C#	Date	Year	Good	VG	Fine	VF
147c	ND	1832SP	35.00	60.00	100.00	150.00

SILVER & GOLD ISSUES

Old Monetary System

(1822 - 1834)

80 REIS

SILVER
Obv: Value in floral circle. Titles of Pedro I.
Rev: Crowned arms in branches.

C#	Date	Mintage	Fine	VF	XF	Unc
134	1824R	—	60.00	100.00	150.00	250.00
	1826R	—	60.00	100.00	150.00	250.00
	Obv: Titles of Pedro II.					
178	1833R	418 pcs.		575.00	800.00	1000.00

160 REIS

SILVER

C#	Date	Mintage	Fine	VF	XF	Unc
135	1824R	—	9.00	15.00	25.00	45.00
	1826R	—	350.00	550.00	750.00	950.00

Obv: Value in floral circle. Titles of Pedro II.
Rev: Crowned arms in branches.

C#	Date	Mintage	Fine	VF	XF	Unc
179	1833R	492 pcs.		400.00	550.00	750.00

320 REIS

SILVER
Obv: Value in floral circle. Titles of Pedro I.
Rev: Crowned arms in branches.

C#	Date	Mintage	Fine	VF	XF	Unc
136	1824R	642 pcs.	60.00	100.00	150.00	250.00
	1825R	.018	35.00	60.00	90.00	125.00
	1826R	—	42.50	75.00	150.00	250.00
	1827R	—		—	Unique	—
	1830R	8,542	—	—	Rare	—
	Obv: Titles of Pedro II.					
180	1833R	22 pcs.	—	—	Rare	—

640 REIS

SILVER
Obv: Value in floral circle. Titles of Pedro I.
Rev: Crowned arms in branches.

C#	Date	Mintage	Fine	VF	XF	Unc
137	1823R	—	—		Counterfeit	—
	1824/3	—	50.00	85.00	110.00	150.00
	1824R	.080	17.50	27.50	50.00	75.00
	1825R	.353	15.00	25.00	45.00	70.00
	1826R	9,472	175.00	300.00	500.00	700.00
	1827R	Inc. Ab.	175.00	300.00	500.00	700.00
	Obv: Titles of Pedro II.					
181	1832R	118 pcs.	—	—	Rare	—
	1833R	5 pcs.	—	—	Rare	—

960 REIS

SILVER

C#	Date	Mintage	Fine	VF	XF	Unc
138	1823R	.395	25.00	30.00	40.00	60.00
	1824B	—	27.50	35.00	60.00	100.00
	1824R	.600	25.00	30.00	40.00	60.00
	1825B	—	30.00	50.00	100.00	150.00
	1825R	.600	25.00	30.00	40.00	60.00
	1826B	—	100.00	175.00	300.00	500.00
	1826R	.500	25.00	30.00	40.00	60.00
	1827R	.018	90.00	150.00	275.00	450.00
	1828R	—	—		Counterfeit	—

C#	Date	Mintage	Fine	VF	XF	Unc
182	1832R	3,039	250.00	400.00	600.00	850.00
	1833R	Inc. Ab.	275.00	450.00	700.00	1000.
	1834R	154 pcs.	350.00	600.00	1000.	1500.

4000 REIS

8.2000 gm., .917 GOLD, .2417 oz AGW

C#	Date	Mintage	Fine	VF	XF	Unc
140	1823R	.021	325.00	375.00	450.00	550.00
	1824R	.038	300.00	350.00	425.00	525.00
	1825B	—	400.00	650.00	1000.	1300.
	1825R	.020	300.00	350.00	425.00	525.00
	1826B	—	450.00	700.00	1100.	1500.
	1826R	8,966	375.00	450.00	650.00	850.00
	1827B	7,771	700.00	1000.	1500.	1850.
	1828B	—	550.00	800.00	1200.	1500.
	Obv: Nothing below bust.					
202	1832R	64 pcs.	—	—	Rare	—
	Obv: AZEVEDO below bust.					
202	1832R	Inc. Ab.	—	—	Rare	—
	1833R	257 pcs.	—	—	Rare	—

6400 REIS

14.3400 gm,, .917 GOLD, .4228 oz AGW
Pedro I Coronation Issue
Obv: Bare bust

C#	Date	Mintage	Fine	VF	XF	Unc
139	1822R	64 pcs.	—	—	Rare	—
	Obv: Military bust					
141	1823R	931 pcs.	600.00	1000.	1350.	1600.
	1824R	235 pcs.	750.00	1200.	1500.	1850.
	1825B	—	600.00	1000.	1350.	1600.
	1825R	776 pcs.	600.00	1000.	1350.	1600.
	1826B	—	750.00	1200.	1600.	2000.
	1827R	637 pcs.	600.00	1000.	1400.	1700.
	1828B	423 pcs.	600.00	1000.	1400.	1700.
	1828R	650 pcs.	600.00	1000.	1350.	1600.
	1830R	—	—	—	Unique	—

NOTE: Counterfeits of 1830R exist.

Obv: Boy head of Pedro II, nothing below bust.
Rev: Crowned arms in branches.

C#	Date	Mintage	Fine	VF	XF	Unc
203	1832R	.030	350.00	425.00	575.00	700.00
	1833R	.011	400.00	500.00	650.00	750.00

Obv: AZEVEDO below bust.

C#	Date	Mintage	Fine	VF	XF	Unc
203	1832R	4,101	600.00	850.00	1200.	1600.

MONETARY REFORM

(All denominations in Reis)

Numbers in parentheses indicate previous Craig numbers.

10 REIS

BRONZE

Y#	Date	Mintage	Fine	VF	XF	Unc
A11	1868	—	.50	1.25	2.50	6.00
(169)	1869 Rs. (Brussels)					
		Inc. Ab.	.50	1.25	2.50	6.00
	1869 Rs (no period, Rio de Janeiro)					
		Inc. Ab.	.75	1.50	3.00	8.00
	1870	—	1.75	3.50	6.00	15.00

20 REIS

BRONZE

Y#	Date	Mintage	Fine	VF	XF	Unc
A12	1868	90.360	1.50	2.25	4.00	10.00
(170)	1869 Rs. (Brussels)					
		Inc. Ab.	1.50	2.25	4.00	10.00
	1869 Rs (no period, Rio de Janeiro)					
		Inc. Ab.	1.75	2.75	5.00	12.50
	1870	—	1.75	2.75	5.50	15.00

40 REIS

BRONZE

Y#	Date	Mintage	Fine	VF	XF	Unc
A13	1873	3.750	.60	1.50	4.00	10.00
(171)	1874	.890	.75	2.00	5.50	15.00
	1875	1.208	1.00	1.75	4.50	12.50
	1876	.549	1.25	3.00	8.50	20.00
	1877	.465	.75	2.00	5.50	15.00
	1878	1.223	.70	1.75	4.50	12.50
	1879	2.771	.70	1.75	4.50	12.50
	1880	1.569	.70	1.75	4.50	12.50

50 REIS

COPPER-NICKEL

Y#	Date	Mintage	Fine	VF	XF	Unc
A16	1886	.590	.75	2.00	5.00	13.50
(175)	1887	Inc. Ab.	1.00	2.50	6.00	15.00
	1888	.153	2.25	5.50	12.50	25.00

100 REIS

SILVER
Obv: Value in floral circle.
Rev: Crowned arms in branches.

C#	Date	Mintage	Fine	VF	XF	Unc
183	1834	7,709	8.00	20.00	50.00	100.00
	1835	Inc. Ab.	8.00	20.00	50.00	100.00
	1836	5,592	60.00	150.00	300.00	500.00
	1837	9,562	8.00	20.00	50.00	100.00
	1840	—	30.00	50.00	125.00	250.00
	1844	—	—	—	Rare	—
	1846	4,699	8.00	20.00	50.00	100.00
	1847	—	20.00	50.00	125.00	250.00
	1848	—	60.00	150.00	300.00	500.00

COPPER-NICKEL

Y#	Date	Mintage	Fine	VF	XF	Unc
A14	1871	4.000	.50	1.00	3.00	6.00
(173)	1872	100 Pcs.	60.00	150.00	250.00	400.00
	1874	—	2.75	5.00	15.00	30.00
	1875	—	10.00	20.00	50.00	100.00
	1876	—	4.00	10.00	20.00	40.00
	1877	—	.75	3.00	8.00	16.00
	1878	—	.75	3.00	8.00	16.00
	1879	—	2.75	5.00	15.00	30.00
	1880	—	2.75	5.00	15.00	30.00
	1881	—	.75	3.00	8.00	16.00
	1882	—	.75	3.00	8.00	16.00
	1883	—	.50	1.00	4.00	8.00
	1884	—	.75	2.00	6.00	12.00
	1885	—	.50	1.00	4.00	8.00

Y#	Date	Mintage	Fine	VF	XF	Unc
A17	1886	.877	1.00	2.00	5.00	15.00
(176)	1887	—	1.00	2.00	5.00	15.00
	1888	1.696	1.00	2.00	5.00	15.00
	1889	Inc. w/Y#3	2.00	3.50	6.50	20.00

200 REIS

SILVER
Obv: Value in floral circle.
Rev: Crowned arms in branches.

C#	Date	Mintage	Fine	VF	XF	Unc
184	1835	4,894	20.00	40.00	75.00	150.00
	1837	5.007	20.00	40.00	75.00	150.00
	1840	—	100.00	175.00	250.00	500.00
	1844	—	30.00	50.00	100.00	200.00
	1846	—	100.00	175.00	250.00	500.00
	1847	2,936	45.00	75.00	100.00	200.00
	1848/47	501	250.00	400.00	600.00	1200.
	1848	—	100.00	175.00	250.00	500.00

Y#	Date	Mintage	Fine	VF	XF	Unc
A6	1854	.037	12.50	20.00	35.00	70.00
(191)	1855	.228	3.50	7.50	15.00	30.00
	1856/5	—	—	—	—	—
	1856	.103	3.00	5.00	10.00	20.00
	1857	.128	3.00	5.00	10.00	20.00
	1858	.245	5.00	10.00	17.50	35.00
	1859	.152	3.75	7.50	12.50	25.00
	1860	.028	3.00	5.00	7.50	15.00
	1861	—	3.75	7.50	12.50	25.00
	1862	—	3.00	5.00	7.50	15.00
	1863	—	3.00	5.00	7.50	15.00
	1864	—	3.00	5.00	7.50	15.00
	1865	—	3.00	5.00	7.50	15.00
	1866	—	5.00	7.50	12.50	25.00
	1867	—	5.00	7.50	12.50	25.00

2.5000 gm., .835 SILVER, .0671 oz ASW

Y#	Date	Mintage	Fine	VF	XF	Unc
A19	1867	—	2.50	4.00	7.50	12.50
(195)	1868	—	2.50	4.00	8.50	15.00
	1869	—	8.50	15.00	25.00	35.00

COPPER-NICKEL

Y#	Date	Mintage	Fine	VF	XF	Unc
A15	1871	3.650	.50	1.25	3.50	7.00
(174)	1874	—	1.00	2.00	8.00	16.00
	1875	—	3.00	10.00	20.00	40.00
	1876	—	1.00	2.00	8.00	16.00
	1877	—	1.00	2.00	8.00	16.00
	1878	—	1.25	2.50	10.00	20.00
	1880	—	1.25	3.00	12.50	25.00
	1882	—	1.25	3.50	15.00	30.00
	1884	—	.50	1.25	4.00	8.00

Y#	Date	Mintage	Fine	VF	XF	Unc
A18	1886	.177	3.75	7.50	15.00	35.00
(177)	1887	—	1.00	2.00	4.00	12.50
	1888	.967	1.00	2.00	4.00	12.50
	1889	Inc. w/Y#4	1.00	2.00	4.00	12.50

400 REIS

SILVER
Obv: Value in floral circle.
Rev: Crowned arms in branches.

C#	Date	Mintage	Fine	VF	XF	Unc
185	1834	6,197	30.00	60.00	125.00	200.00
	1835	Inc. Ab.	100.00	150.00	200.00	350.00
	1837	7,837	100.00	150.00	200.00	350.00
	1840	—	200.00	300.00	450.00	625.00
	1841	—	300.00	450.00	650.00	900.00
	1843	161 pcs.	1000.	1750.	2500.	3250.
	1844	—	125.00	200.00	350.00	475.00
	1845	—	200.00	300.00	450.00	625.00
	1847/0	—	60.00	100.00	150.00	200.00
	1847	878 pcs.	50.00	85.00	125.00	175.00
	1848	—	175.00	275.00	425.00	600.00

500 REIS

SILVER

Y#	Date	Mintage	Fine	VF	XF	Unc
A1	1848	—	—	Rare	—	
(188)	1849	.026	32.50	50.00	75.00	150.00
	1850	.067	10.00	15.00	25.00	40.00
	1851	.095	6.50	10.00	13.50	20.00
	1852	.167	6.00	8.50	11.50	17.50

Y#	Date	Mintage	Fine	VF	XF	Unc
A7	1853	.241	6.00	8.50	11.50	17.50
(192)	1854	.317	6.00	8.50	11.50	17.50
	1855	.212	6.00	8.50	11.50	17.50
	1856	.223	6.00	8.50	11.50	17.50
	1857	.265	6.00	8.50	11.50	17.50
	1858	.791	6.00	8.50	11.50	17.50
	1859	.152	6.00	8.50	11.50	17.50

Y#	Date	Mintage	Fine	VF	XF	Unc
(192)	1860/50	*.108	6.00	8.50	11.50	17.50
	1860	Inc. Ab.	6.00	8.50	11.50	17.50
	1861	—	6.00	8.50	11.50	17.50
	1862	—	6.00	8.50	11.50	17.50
	1863	—	6.00	8.50	11.50	17.50
	1864	—	6.00	8.50	11.50	17.50
	1865	—	6.00	8.50	11.50	17.50
	1866	—	6.00	8.50	11.50	17.50
	1867	—	6.00	8.50	11.50	17.50

***NOTE:** The 1860 mintage figure includes only first six month's production.

6.2500 gm., .835 SILVER, .1678 oz ASW

Y#	Date	Mintage	Fine	VF	XF	Unc
A20	1867	—	5.50	7.50	10.00	15.00
(196)	1868	—	5.50	7.50	10.00	15.00

6.3750 gm., .917 SILVER, .1879 oz ASW

Y#	Date	Mintage	Fine	VF	XF	Unc
A23	1876	.076	6.50	8.50	11.50	17.50
(199)	1886	5,283	60.00	100.00	175.00	250.00
	1887	769 pcs.	450.00	750.00	1000.	1250.
	1888	.333	6.50	9.00	12.50	20.00
	1889	Inc. w/Y#5	6.50	9.00	12.50	20.00

800 REIS

SILVER

C#	Date	Mintage	Fine	VF	XF	Unc
186	1835	1,698	500.00	750.00	1200.	1900.
	1838	497 pcs.	550.00	800.00	1250.	2000.
	1840	—	600.00	850.00	1300.	2100.
	1843	—	1500.	2200.	3200.	4000.
	1844	628 pcs.	500.00	750.00	1200.	1900.
	1846	—	800.00	1250.	1600.	2400.

1000 REIS

SILVER

Y#	Date	Mintage	Fine	VF	XF	Unc
A2	1849	965 pcs.	300.00	500.00	750.00	1250.
(189)	1850	.169	12.00	15.00	20.00	27.50
	1851	.099	12.00	15.00	20.00	27.50
	1852	.196	12.00	15.00	20.00	27.50

Y#	Date	Mintage	Fine	VF	XF	Unc
A8	1853	.266	12.00	15.00	20.00	27.50
(193)	1854	.228	12.00	15.00	20.00	27.50
	1855	.312	12.00	15.00	20.00	27.50
	1856	.426	12.00	15.00	20.00	27.50
	1857	.512	12.00	15.00	20.00	27.50
	1858	.430	12.00	15.00	20.00	27.50
	1859	.996	12.00	15.00	20.00	27.50
	1860/50	—	—	—	—	—
	1860	.387	12.00	15.00	20.00	27.50
	1861	—	12.00	15.00	20.00	27.50
	1862	—	12.00	15.00	20.00	27.50
	1863	—	12.00	15.00	20.00	27.50
	1864	—	12.00	15.00	20.00	27.50
	1865	—	12.00	15.00	20.00	27.50
	1866	—	12.00	15.00	20.00	27.50

12.5000 gm., .835 SILVER, .3356 oz ASW

Y#	Date	Mintage	Fine	VF	XF	Unc
A21 (197)	1869	—	20.00	35.00	55.00	85.00

12.7500 gm., .917 SILVER, .3759 oz ASW

Y#	Date	Mintage	Fine	VF	XF	Unc
A24	1876	8.659	12.00	15.00	25.00	27.50
(200)	1877	.194	20.00	35.00	50.00	80.00
	1878	.047	17.50	25.00	37.50	60.00
	1879	.035	15.00	22.50	35.00	50.50
	1880	.020	25.00	45.00	75.00	150.00
	1881	.020	25.00	45.00	75.00	150.00
	1882	.018	27.50	50.00	80.00	160.00
	1883	.031	15.00	22.50	30.00	50.00
	1884	5,360	25.00	40.00	60.00	100.00
	1885	.011	50.00	70.00	100.00	160.00
	1886	.048	13.50	20.00	30.00	50.00
	1887	9,875	50.00	70.00	90.00	125.00
	1888	.100	12.00	15.00	20.00	27.50
	1889	—	50.00	70.00	90.00	125.00

1200 REIS

SILVER

C#	Date	Mintage	Fine	VF	XF	Unc
187	1834	841 pcs.	100.00	175.00	225.00	400.00
	1835	.010	100.00	175.00	225.00	400.00
	1837	6,300	100.00	175.00	225.00	400.00
	1839	186 pcs.	—	—	Rare	—
	1840/30	—	—	—	—	500.00
	1840	633 pcs.	125.00	200.00	300.00	450.00
	1843	—	100.00	175.00	225.00	400.00
	1845	—	250.00	400.00	700.00	1000.
	1846	—	150.00	250.00	500.00	800.00
	1847	—	100.00	175.00	225.00	400.00

NOTE: The above coins dated 1841 and 1842 are counterfeit.

2000 REIS

SILVER
Rev: Similar to 1200 Reis, C#187.

Y#	Date	Mintage	Fine	VF	XF	Unc
A3	1851	.256	20.00	30.00	40.00	60.00
(190)	1852	.277	20.00	30.00	40.00	60.00

Obv: Similar to Y#A3.

Y#	Date	Mintage	Fine	VF	XF	Unc
A9	1853	.145	20.00	30.00	40.00	60.00
(194)	1854	.086	21.50	31.50	42.50	65.00
	1855	.300	20.00	30.00	40.00	60.00
	1856	.229	20.00	30.00	40.00	60.00
	1857	.105	20.00	30.00	40.00	60.00
	1858	.022	35.00	60.00	85.00	125.00
	1859	.041	125.00	200.00	300.00	450.00
	1863	—	20.00	30.00	40.00	60.00
	1864	—	35.00	60.00	85.00	125.00
	1865	—	20.00	30.00	40.00	60.00
	1866	—	100.00	175.00	250.00	400.00
	1867	—	650.00	1000.	1500.	2750.

25.0000 gm., .835 SILVER, .6712 oz ASW

Y#	Date	Mintage	Fine	VF	XF	Unc
A22	1868	—	25.00	35.00	65.00	100.00
(198)	1869	—	22.50	32.50	40.00	55.00

25.5000 gm., .917 SILVER, .7518 oz ASW

Y#	Date	Mintage	Fine	VF	XF	Unc
A22a	1875	—	25.00	35.00	42.50	60.00
(198a)	1876	—	85.00	150.00	275.00	400.00

Obv: Similar to Y#A22.
Rev. leg: With DECRETO DE 1870.

Y#	Date	Mintage	Fine	VF	XF	Unc
A25	1886	1,190	125.00	200.00	300.00	450.00
(201)	1887	.043	25.00	35.00	42.50	60.00
	1888	.906	25.00	32.50	40.00	55.00
	1889	—	25.00	32.50	40.00	55.00

5000 REIS

4.4824 gm., .917 GOLD, .1321 oz AGW

Y#	Date	Mintage	Fine	VF	XF	Unc
A26	1854	.021	100.00	150.00	200.00	275.00
(209)	1855	.047	100.00	150.00	200.00	275.00
	1856	.027	100.00	150.00	200.00	275.00
	1857	4,631	150.00	225.00	325.00	400.00
	1858	1,146	300.00	450.00	600.00	750.00
	1859	493	600.00	750.00	1000.	1350.

10,000 REIS

.917 GOLD

C#	Date	Mintage	Fine	VF	XF	Unc
204	1833	7,304	275.00	350.00	500.00	600.00
	1834	5,617	275.00	350.00	500.00	600.00
	1835	.013	275.00	350.00	500.00	600.00
	1836	.011	275.00	350.00	500.00	600.00
	1838	482 pcs.	300.00	450.00	600.00	700.00
	1839	567 pcs.	375.00	550.00	750.00	1000.
	1840	1,008	350.00	500.00	650.00	750.00

Obv: Military bust

C#	Date	Mintage	Fine	VF	XF	Unc
205	1841	—	300.00	450.00	600.00	700.00
	1842	—	300.00	450.00	600.00	700.00
205	1843	—	300.00	450.00	600.00	700.00
	1844	—	450.00	650.00	850.00	1200.
	1845	—	300.00	450.00	600.00	700.00
	1847	—	275.00	350.00	500.00	600.00
	1848	—	275.00	350.00	500.00	600.00

8.9648 gm., .917 GOLD, .2643 oz AGW
Obv: Court dress, size reduced to 26mm.

Y#	Date	Mintage	Fine	VF	XF	Unc
A4	1849	1,678	300.00	450.00	600.00	800.00
(206)	1850	7,359	275.00	350.00	500.00	600.00
	1851	.011	275.00	350.00	500.00	600.00

Y#	Date	Mintage	Fine	VF	XF	Unc
A27	1853	.040	175.00	225.00	275.00	350.00
(210)	1854	.163	175.00	225.00	275.00	350.00
	1855	.041	175.00	225.00	275.00	350.00
	1856	.208	175.00	225.00	275.00	350.00
	1857	.098	200.00	250.00	300.00	375.00
	1858	.055	175.00	225.00	275.00	350.00
	1859	.016	400.00	550.00	900.00	1350.
	1861	—	175.00	225.00	275.00	350.00
	1863	—	400.00	550.00	900.00	1350.
	1865	—	175.00	225.00	275.00	350.00
	1866	—	175.00	225.00	275.00	350.00
	1867	—	175.00	225.00	275.00	350.00
	1871	—	200.00	250.00	300.00	400.00
	1872	—	200.00	250.00	300.00	400.00
	1873	—	200.00	250.00	300.00	400.00
	1874	—	200.00	250.00	300.00	400.00
	1875	—	200.00	250.00	300.00	400.00
	1876	—	200.00	250.00	300.00	400.00
	1877	.020	200.00	250.00	300.00	400.00
	1878	.019	200.00	250.00	300.00	400.00
	1879	6,431	200.00	250.00	300.00	400.00
	1880	9,806	200.00	250.00	300.00	400.00
	1882	4,671	200.00	250.00	300.00	400.00
	1883	5,358	200.00	250.00	300.00	400.00
	1884	3,733	200.00	250.00	300.00	400.00
	1885	7,955	200.00	250.00	300.00	400.00
	1886	5,021	200.00	250.00	300.00	400.00
	1887	1,861	250.00	325.00	400.00	550.00
	1888	6,914	225.00	300.00	350.00	475.00
	1889	Inc. Ab.	200.00	250.00	300.00	475.00

20,000 REIS

17.9296 gm., .917 GOLD, .5286 oz AGW

Y#	Date	Mintage	Fine	VF	XF	Unc
A5	1849	6,464	450.00	550.00	700.00	850.00
(207)	1850	.042	400.00	500.00	600.00	700.00
	1851	.303	375.00	450.00	550.00	675.00

Y#	Date	Mintage	Fine	VF	XF	Unc
A10	1851	Inc. Ab.	375.00	425.00	500.00	600.00
(208)	1852	.186	375.00	425.00	500.00	600.00

Obv: Larger bust

Y#	Date	Mintage	Fine	VF	XF	Unc
A28	1853	.246	375.00	425.00	500.00	600.00
(211)	1854	.026	375.00	425.00	500.00	600.00
	1855	.048	375.00	425.00	500.00	600.00
	1856	.262	375.00	425.00	500.00	600.00
	1857	.315	375.00	425.00	500.00	600.00
	1858	.032	400.00	450.00	525.00	625.00
	1859	.047	400.00	450.00	525.00	625.00
	1860	—	400.00	450.00	525.00	625.00
	1861	—	400.00	450.00	525.00	625.00
	1862	—	750.00	1000.	1250.	1600.
	1863	—	450.00	500.00	575.00	675.00
	1864	—	425.00	475.00	550.00	650.00
	1865	—	375.00	425.00	500.00	600.00
	1867	—	375.00	425.00	500.00	600.00
	1889	—	375.00	425.00	500.00	600.00

REPUBLIC COINAGE

20 REIS

BRONZE

Y#	Date	Mintage	Fine	VF	XF	Unc
1	1889	.630	.35	.75	2.50	6.00
	1893	.250	.35	.75	2.50	6.00
	1894	Inc. Ab.	.75	1.50	3.00	8.50
	1895	2.118	.50	1.00	2.75	8.00
	1896	.490	1.75	3.50	10.00	25.00
	1897	.273	1.00	2.00	3.50	10.00
	1898	.300	1.00	2.00	3.50	10.00
	1899	1.065	1.00	2.00	3.50	10.00
	1900	1.718	.35	.75	2.50	6.00
	1901	.713	.50	1.00	2.75	8.00
	1904	.850	.50	1.00	2.75	8.00
	1905	1.075	2.50	5.00	10.00	14.00
	1906	.215	.50	1.00	2.75	8.00
	1908	4.558	.35	.75	2.00	6.00
	1909	1.215	2.50	5.00	15.00	25.00
	1910	.828	.75	1.50	3.00	8.50
	1911	1.545	.75	1.50	3.00	8.50
	1912	.480	.85	1.75	3.50	10.00

COPPER-NICKEL

Y#	Date	Mintage	Fine	VF	XF	Unc
27	1918	.373	.25	.40	1.00	2.50
	1919	2.870	.25	.40	1.00	2.50
	1920	.825	.25	.40	1.00	2.50
	1921	1.020	.25	.40	1.00	2.50
	1927	.053	2.50	6.00	12.00	25.00
	1935	100 pcs.	75.00	125.00	175.00	250.00

40 REIS

BRONZE

Y#	Date	Mintage	Fine	VF	XF	Unc
2	1889	1.781	.40	1.00	2.00	8.50

Y#	Date	Mintage	Fine	VF	XF	Unc
2	1893	1.085	.40	1.00	2.00	8.50
	1894	.770	.40	1.00	2.00	8.50
	1895	Inc. Ab.	.40	1.00	2.00	8.50
	1896	.191	15.00	40.00	60.00	100.00
	1897	1.236	.40	1.00	3.00	10.00
	1898	.300	10.00	25.00	45.00	75.00
	1900	2.115	.40	1.00	2.00	8.50
	1901	.525	.40	1.00	2.00	4.00
	1907	.218	.40	1.00	2.00	8.50
	1908	4.639	.40	1.00	2.00	8.50
	1909	4.226	.40	1.00	2.00	8.50
	1910	.848	.40	1.00	3.00	10.00
	1911	1.660	.40	1.00	3.00	10.00
	1912	.819	.60	1.50	4.00	15.00

50 REIS

COPPER-NICKEL

Y#	Date	Mintage	Fine	VF	XF	Unc
28	1918	.558	.15	.35	.75	3.00
	1919	.558	.15	.35	.75	3.00
	1920	.072	.40	1.00	2.00	5.50
	1921	.682	.15	.35	.75	3.00
	1922	.176	.40	1.00	2.00	5.50
	1925	.128	.40	1.00	2.00	5.50
	1926	.194	.40	1.00	2.00	5.50
	1931	.020	2.00	5.00	10.00	20.00
	1935	100 pcs.	75.00	125.00	150.00	250.00

100 REIS

COPPER-NICKEL

Y#	Date	Mintage	Fine	VF	XF	Unc
3	1889	*8.554	3.00	7.50	12.50	20.00
	1893	3.589	.40	1.00	1.75	8.00
	1894	1.881	.40	1.00	1.75	8.00
	1895	2.308	.40	1.00	1.50	5.50
	1896	3.390	.40	1.00	1.50	5.50
	1897	2.875	.40	1.00	1.50	5.50
	1898	3.685	1.75	4.50	10.00	15.00
	1899	2.990	.75	2.00	3.00	7.50
	1900	.539	4.00	10.00	17.50	35.00

***NOTE:** Mintage figure includes C#176 dated 1889.

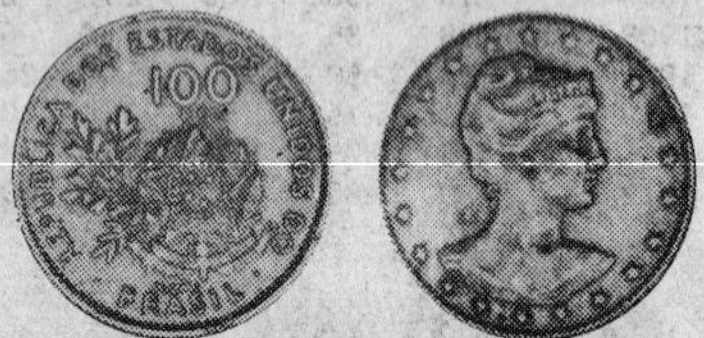

Date: MCMI - 1901.

Y#	Date	Mintage	Fine	VF	XF	Unc
12	1901	75.000	.20	.50	1.00	4.00

Y#	Date	Mintage	Fine	VF	XF	Unc
29	1918	.600	.40	1.00	1.45	2.50
	1919	1.219	.40	1.00	1.45	2.50
	1920	1.251	.40	1.00	1.45	2.50
	1921	.853	.40	1.00	1.45	2.50
	1922	.347	1.00	2.50	4.00	12.50
	1923	.956	.30	.75	1.25	2.25
	1924	1.478	.75	2.00	3.50	8.00
	1925	2.502	.30	.75	1.25	2.25
	1926	1.807	.30	.75	1.25	2.25
	1927	1.451	.30	.75	1.25	2.25
	1928	1.514	.25	.65	1.10	2.25
	1929	2.503	.25	.65	1.10	2.25
	1930	2.398	.25	.65	1.10	2.25
	1931	2.500	.20	.50	1.00	2.00
	1932	.948	.20	.50	1.00	2.00
	1933	1.314	.20	.50	1.00	2.00
	1934	3.614	.20	.50	1.00	2.00

Y#	Date	Mintage	Fine	VF	XF	Unc
29	1935	3.442	.20	.50	1.00	2.00

Cazique Tibercia
400th Anniversary of Colonization

Y#	Date	Mintage	Fine	VF	XF	Unc
39	1932	1.012	.75	3.00	6.25	

Tamandare Commemorative

Y#	Date	Mintage	Fine	VF	XF	Unc
45	1936	3.928	.20	.50	1.75	4.00
	1937	7.905	.30	.75	1.50	3.50
	1938	8.618	.10	.25	1.35	3.00

Getulio Vargas Government

Y#	Date	Mintage	Fine	VF	XF	Unc
57	1938	8.106	.10	.25	.80	1.50
	1940	8.797	.10	.25	1.00	2.00
	1942	1.285	.10	.25	1.00	2.00

NOTE: The 1942 issue has a yellow cast due to higher copper content.

200 REIS

COPPER-NICKEL

Y#	Date	Mintage	Fine	VF	XF	Unc
4	1889	*5.340	.60	1.50	2.50	5.50
	1893	2.586	.60	1.50	2.50	5.50
	1894	1.562	.60	1.50	2.50	5.50
	1895	1.633	.60	1.50	2.50	5.50
	1896	2.850	.60	1.50	2.50	5.50
	1897	2.405	.65	1.75	3.00	10.00
	1898	3.925	.80	2.00	4.00	12.00
	1899	2.724	1.00	2.50	5.00	15.00
	1900	.330	6.00	15.00	30.00	75.00

***NOTE:** Mintage figure includes C#177 dated 1889.

Date: MCMI - 1901.

Y#	Date	Mintage	Fine	VF	XF	Unc
13	1901	60.000	.60	1.50	2.00	5.00

Y#	Date	Mintage	Fine	VF	XF	Unc
30	1918	.625	.30	.75	1.25	3.50
	1919	.882	.30	.75	1.00	3.00
	1920	1.657	.30	.75	1.00	3.00
	1921	1.135	.30	.75	1.00	3.00
	1922	.678	.40	1.00	1.75	4.00
	1923	1.655	.30	.75	1.00	3.00
	1924	1.750	.30	.75	1.00	3.00
	1925	2.082	.30	.75	1.00	3.00
	1926	.324	1.00	2.50	6.00	15.00
	1927	1.806	.30	.75	1.00	3.00
	1928	.782	.30	.75	1.00	3.00
	1929	2.440	.20	.50	.75	2.75
	1930	1.697	.20	.50	.75	2.75
	1931	1.830	.20	.50	.75	2.75
	1932	.761	.20	.50	.75	2.75
	1933	.173	1.00	2.50	5.00	12.50
	1934	.612	.20	.50	.75	2.75
	1935	1.329	.20	.50	.75	2.75

400th Anniversary of Colonization

Y#	Date	Mintage	Fine	VF	XF	Unc
40	1932	.596	.75	1.75	3.00	7.00

Maua Commemorative

Y#	Date	Mintage	Fine	VF	XF	Unc
46	1936	2.256	.20	.50	1.50	3.00
	1937	6.506	.20	.50	2.00	4.00
	1938	5.787	.20	.50	2.00	4.00

Getulio Vargas Government

Y#	Date	Mintage	Fine	VF	XF	Unc
58	1938	7.666	.15	.40	1.00	2.00
	1940	10.161	.15	.40	1.00	2.00
	1942	1.966	.20	.50	1.00	2.50

NOTE: The 1942 issue has a yellow cast due to higher copper content.

300 REIS

COPPER-NICKEL
Gomes Commemorative

Y#	Date	Mintage	Fine	VF	XF	Unc
47	1936	3.029	.30	.75	1.50	4.00
	1937	4.507	.30	.75	2.00	4.50
	1938	3.753	.30	.75	2.00	4.50

Getulio Vargas Government

Y#	Date	Mintage	Fine	VF	XF	Unc
59	1938	12.080	.10	.30	.50	1.50
	1940	8.124	.10	.30	.50	2.00
	1942	2.020	.15	.35	.75	2.50

NOTE: The 1942 issue has a yellow cast due to higher copper content.

400 REIS

5.1000 gm., .917 SILVER, .1503 oz ASW
400th Anniversary of Discovery

8	1900	.055	20.00	35.00	50.00	75.00

COPPER-NICKEL
Date: MCMI - 1901.

14	1901	26.250	—	7.50	12.50	20.00

B14	1914	.646	40.00	100.00	165.00	200.00

NOTE: This is considered a pattern by many authorities.

31	1918	.491	.75	1.75	3.00	6.00
	1919	.891	.50	1.25	3.00	5.00
	1920	1.521	.50	1.25	3.00	5.00
	1921	.871	.50	1.25	3.00	5.00
	1922	1.275	.50	1.25	3.00	5.00
	1923	.764	.50	1.25	3.00	4.50
	1925	2.048	.50	1.25	3.00	4.50
	1926	1.034	.80	2.00	3.75	7.50
	1927	.738	.80	2.00	3.75	7.50
	1929	.869	.50	1.25	3.00	4.50
	1930	1.031	.50	1.25	3.00	4.50
	1931	1.431	.50	1.25	3.00	4.50
	1932	.588	.50	1.25	3.00	4.50
	1935	.225	.50	1.25	3.00	6.00

400th Anniversary of Colonization

41	1932	.416	1.10	5.00	10.00

Cruz Commemorative

Y#	Date	Mintage	Fine	VF	XF	Unc
48	1936	2.079	.50	1.25	2.00	3.00
	1937	3.111	.50	1.25	2.00	4.50
	1938	2.681	.50	1.25	2.00	5.00

Getulio Vargas Government

60	1938	10.620	.20	.50	1.00	1.75
	1940	7.312	.20	.50	1.00	2.50
	1942	1.496	.20	.50	1.00	2.50

NOTE: The 1942 issue has a yellow cast due to higher copper content.

500 REIS

6.3750 gm., .917 SILVER, .1879 oz AGW

5	1889	*4.541	6.50	10.00	13.50	18.50

***NOTE:** Mintage figure includes C#199 dated 1889.

5.0000 gm., .900 SILVER, .1446 oz ASW

15	1906	.352	BV	BV	6.00	8.50
	1907	1.282	BV	6.00	10.00	17.50
	1908	.498	BV	BV	6.00	8.50
	1911	8,000	6.00	10.00	17.50	35.00
	1912	*.222	30.00	50.00	100.00	150.00

18	1912	*Inc. Ab.	BV	8.50	12.00	25.00

21	1913A	—	BV	BV	6.00	10.00

ALUMINUM-BRONZE
Independence Centennial

34	1922	13.744	.25	.60	1.25	5.00

Error: BBASIL instead of BRASIL

Y#	Date	Mintage	Fine	VF	XF	Unc
34a	1922	Inc. Ab.	15.00	32.50	55.00	85.00

32	1924	7.400	.30	.75	1.25	3.50
	1927	2.725	.30	.75	1.25	3.50
	1928	9.432	.30	.75	1.25	3.50
	1930	.146	.60	1.50	2.50	6.50

Ramalho
400th Anniversary of Colonization

42	1932	.034	2.00	5.00	8.75	14.50

Feijo Commemorative
4 gm.

49	1935	.014	1.50	3.75	5.00	8.75

5 gm.

50	1936	1.326	.60	1.50	2.00	4.00
	1937	Inc. Ab.	.60	1.50	2.00	4.00
	1938	—	.60	1.50	2.00	4.00

Assis Commemorative

61	1939	5.928	.50	1.25	2.00	3.00

1000 REIS

12.7500 gm., .917 SILVER, .3758 oz ASW

6	1889	.296	12.50	16.50	25.00	45.00

400th Anniversary of Discovery

Y#	Date	Mintage	Fine	VF	XF	Unc
9	1900	.033	50.00	85.00	125.00	200.00

10.0000 gm., .900 SILVER, .2894 oz ASW

Y#	Date	Mintage	Fine	VF	XF	Unc
16	1906	.420	BV	BV	10.00	17.50
	1907	1.282	BV	BV	10.00	17.50
	1908	1.624	BV	BV	10.00	17.50
	1909	.816	BV	BV	10.00	17.50
	1910	2.354	BV	BV	10.00	17.50
	1911	2.810	BV	BV	10.00	17.50
	1912	*1.570	BV	BV	10.00	17.50

Y#	Date	Mintage	Fine	VF	XF	Unc
19	1912	*Inc. Ab.	BV	10.00	15.00	25.00
	1913	2.525	BV	10.00	15.00	25.00

Y#	Date	Mintage	Fine	VF	XF	Unc
22	1913A	—	BV	BV	10.00	15.00

ALUMINUM-BRONZE
Independence Centennial

Y#	Date	Mintage	Fine	VF	XF	Unc
35	1922	16.698	.40	1.00	2.00	5.00

Error: BBASIL instead of BRASIL

Y#	Date	Mintage	Fine	VF	XF	Unc
35a	1922	Inc. Ab.	—	5.00	10.00	15.00

Y#	Date	Mintage	Fine	VF	XF	Unc
33	1924	9.354	.50	1.25	2.50	6.50
	1925	6.205	.50	1.25	2.50	7.00

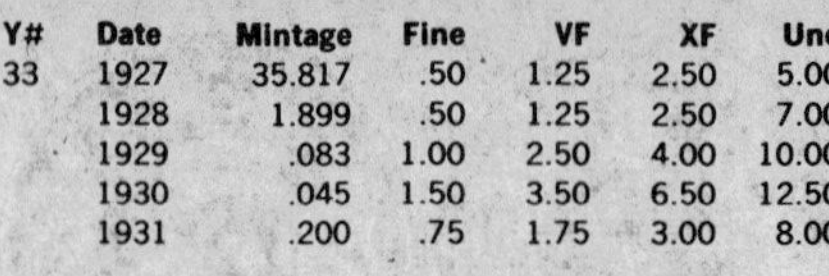

Y#	Date	Mintage	Fine	VF	XF	Unc
33	1927	35.817	.50	1.25	2.50	5.00
	1928	1.899	.50	1.25	2.50	7.00
	1929	.083	1.00	2.50	4.00	10.00
	1930	.045	1.50	3.50	6.50	12.50
	1931	.200	.75	1.75	3.00	8.00

Da Sousa
400th Anniversary of Colonization

Y#	Date	Mintage	Fine	VF	XF	Unc
43	1932	.056	2.00	5.00	9.00	15.00

Anchieta Commemorative

Y#	Date	Mintage	Fine	VF	XF	Unc
51	1935	.138	1.25	3.00	5.00	7.50

Size reduced

Y#	Date	Mintage	Fine	VF	XF	Unc
52	1936	.926	.40	1.00	3.50	7.00
	1937	Inc. Ab.	.40	1.00	3.00	6.00
	1938	—	.40	1.00	3.00	6.00

Barreto Commemorative

Y#	Date	Mintage	Fine	VF	XF	Unc
62	1939	9.586	.50	1.25	2.00	4.00

2000 REIS

25.5000 gm., .917 SILVER, .7518 oz ASW

Y#	Date	Mintage	Fine	VF	XF	Unc
7	1891	.040	300.00	500.00	800.00	1200.
	1896	.010	325.00	550.00	900.00	1500.
	1897	.160	250.00	400.00	600.00	900.00

400th Anniversary of Discovery

Y#	Date	Mintage	Fine	VF	XF	Unc
10	1900	.020	90.00	150.00	225.00	300.00

20.0000 gm., .900 SILVER, .5787 oz ASW

Y#	Date	Mintage	Fine	VF	XF	Unc
17	1906	.256	BV	BV	17.50	25.00
	1907	2.863	BV	BV	17.50	25.00
	1908	1.707	BV	BV	17.50	25.00
	1910	.585	BV	BV	17.50	25.00
	1911	1.929	BV	BV	17.50	25.00
	1912	.741	BV	BV	17.50	25.00

Y#	Date	Mintage	Fine	VF	XF	Unc
20	1912	Inc. Ab.	BV	BV	20.00	32.50
	1913	.395	BV	BV	20.00	32.50

Y#	Date	Mintage	Fine	VF	XF	Unc
23	1913A	—	BV	BV	17.50	25.00

8.0000 gm., .900 SILVER, .2315 oz ASW
Independence Centennial

Y#	Date	Mintage	Fine	VF	XF	Unc
38	1922	1.560	BV	BV	7.50	12.50

8.0000 gm., .500 SILVER, .1286 oz ASW

Y#	Date	Mintage	Fine	VF	XF	Unc
38a	1922	Inc. Ab.	BV	BV	4.50	7.50

***NOTE:** Struck in both .900 and .500 fine silver, but can only be distinguished by analysis (and color, on worn specimens).

Y#	Date	Mintage	Fine	VF	XF	Unc
24	1924	9.147	BV	BV	4.50	6.50
	1925	.723	BV	BV	5.00	7.50
	1926	1.787	BV	BV	4.50	6.50
	1927	1.009	BV	BV	5.00	7.50
	1928	1.250	BV	BV	4.50	6.50
	1929	1.744	BV	BV	4.50	6.50
	1930	1.240	BV	BV	5.00	7.50
	1931	.546	BV	BV	4.50	6.50
	1934	.938	BV	BV	4.50	6.50

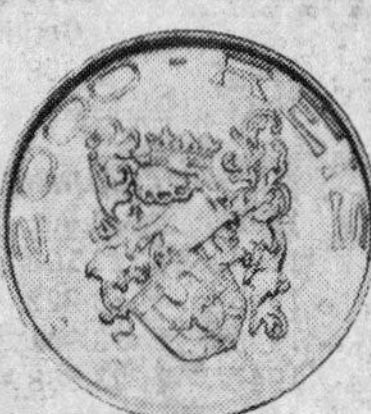

John III
400th Anniversary of Colonization

Y#	Date	Mintage	Fine	VF	XF	Unc
44	1932	.695	BV	5.00	7.50	12.00

Caxias Commemorative

Y#	Date	Mintage	Fine	VF	XF	Unc
55	1935	2.131	BV	BV	4.50	7.50

ALUMINUM-BRONZE
Caxias Commemorative
Reeded edge.

Y#	Date	Mintage	Fine	VF	XF	Unc
53	1936	.665	.75	1.75	3.00	7.00
	1937	Inc. Ab.	.75	1.75	3.00	7.00
	1938	—	5.00	12.50	20.00	40.00

Plain edge, polygonal planchet

Y#	Date	Mintage	Fine	VF	XF	Unc
54	1938	11.151	1.25	3.00	5.00	10.00

Peixoto Commemorative

Y#	Date	Mintage	Fine	VF	XF	Unc
63	1939	5.048	.30	.75	1.75	5.00

4000 REIS

51.0000 gm., .917 SILVER, 1.5030 oz ASW
400th Anniversary of Discovery

Y#	Date	Mintage	Fine	VF	XF	Unc
11	1900	6,850	225.00	375.00	500.00	700.00

5000 REIS

10.0000 gm., .600 SILVER, .1929 oz ASW
Santos Dumont Commemorative

Y#	Date	Mintage	Fine	VF	XF	Unc
56	1936	1.986	BV	BV	6.00	7.50
	1937	.414	BV	BV	6.00	8.50
	1938	.994	BV	BV	6.00	7.50

10,000 REIS

8.9645 gm., .917 GOLD, .2643 oz AGW

Y#	Date	Mintage	Fine	VF	XF	Unc
25	1889	7,302	250.00	400.00	500.00	650.00
	1892	2,289	500.00	800.00	1000.	1250.
	1893	—	400.00	650.00	800.00	1000.
	1895	306 pcs.	300.00	500.00	650.00	800.00
	1896	383 pcs.	1350.	2250.	3000.	3500.
	1897	421 pcs.	275.00	450.00	550.00	700.00
	1898	216 pcs.	1350.	2250.	3000.	3500.
	1899	238 pcs.	350.00	650.00	800.00	1000.
	1901	111 pcs.	275.00	450.00	550.00	700.00
	1903	391 pcs.	300.00	500.00	650.00	800.00
	1904	541 pcs.	250.00	400.00	500.00	650.00
	1906	572 pcs.	425.00	700.00	900.00	1100.
	1907	878 pcs.	250.00	400.00	500.00	650.00
	1908	689 pcs.	250.00	400.00	500.00	650.00
	1909	1,069	250.00	400.00	500.00	650.00
	1911	137 pcs.	400.00	650.00	800.00	1000.
	1914	969 pcs.	1350.	2250.	3000.	3500.
	1915	4,314	1350.	2250.	3000.	3500.
	1916	4,720	250.00	400.00	500.00	650.00
	1919	526 pcs.	300.00	500.00	600.00	750.00

Y#	Date	Mintage	Fine	VF	XF	Unc
25	1921	2,435	250.00	400.00	500.00	650.00
	1922	6 pcs.	3000.	5000.	6000.	7500.

NOTE: More than 6 pcs. are known dated 1922.

20,000 REIS

17.9290 gm., .917 GOLD, .5286 oz AGW

Y#	Date	Mintage	Fine	VF	XF	Unc
26	1889	.091	375.00	475.00	600.00	750.00
	1892	7,738	1500.	2500.	3000.	4000.
	1893	4,303	375.00	475.00	600.00	800.00
	1894	4,267	375.00	475.00	600.00	800.00
	1895	4,811	375.00	475.00	600.00	800.00
	1896	7,043	375.00	525.00	700.00	900.00
	1897	.011	375.00	525.00	700.00	900.00
	1898	.014	375.00	475.00	600.00	800.00
	1899	9,558	425.00	575.00	800.00	1000.
	1900	7,551	375.00	475.00	600.00	800.00
	1901	784 pcs.	450.00	600.00	900.00	1100.
	1902	884 pcs.	700.00	900.00	1100.	1350.
	1903	675 pcs.	700.00	850.00	1000.	1350.
	1904	444 pcs.	450.00	600.00	900.00	1100.
	1906	396 pcs.	1500.	2500.	3000.	4000.
	1907	3,310	375.00	475.00	600.00	800.00
	1908	6.001	375.00	475.00	600.00	800.00
	1909	4,427	375.00	475.00	600.00	800.00
	1910	5,119	375.00	525.00	700.00	900.00
	1911	8,467	375.00	525.00	700.00	900.00
	1912	4,878	425.00	575.00	800.00	1000.
	1913	5,182	375.00	525.00	700.00	900.00
	1914	1,980	375.00	575.00	800.00	1000.
	1917	2,269	375.00	575.00	800.00	1000.
	1918	1,216	475.00	600.00	900.00	1100.
	1921	5,924	375.00	525.00	700.00	900.00
	1922	2,681	375.00	575.00	800.00	1000.

DECIMAL COINAGE

(1942-1967)
100 Centavos = 1 Cruzeiro
(Commencing 1967)
100 Old Cruzeiros = 1 New Cruzeiro

CENTAVO

STAINLESS STEEL

Y#	Date	Mintage	VF	XF	Unc
87	1967	57.499	—	—	.10

Thinner planchet

Y#	Date	Mintage	VF	XF	Unc
87a	1969	243.855	—	—	.10
	1975	—	—	—	.10

F.A.O. Issue

Y#	Date	Mintage	VF	XF	Unc
98	1975	31.700	—	—	.20
	1976	18.355	—	—	.10
	1977	.100	—	—	.10
	1978	.050	—	—	.15

2 CENTAVOS

STAINLESS STEEL

Y#	Date	Mintage	VF	XF	Unc
88	1967	65.226	—	—	.10
		Thinner planchet			
88a	1969	134.298	—	—	.10
	1975	—	—	—	.20

***NOTE:** Mintage figure includes coins struck through 1974 dated 1969.

F.A.O. Issue

Y#	Date	Mintage	VF	XF	Unc
99	1975	31.400	—	—	.10
	1976	18.754	—	—	.10
	1977	.100	—	—	.10
	1978	.050	—	—	.15

5 CENTAVOS

STAINLESS STEEL

Y#	Date	Mintage	VF	XF	Unc
89	1967	69.304	—	—	.15
		Thinner planchet			
89a	1969	345.071	—	—	.15

***NOTE:** Mintage figure includes coins struck through 1974 dated 1969.

F.A.O. Issue

Y#	Date	Mintage	VF	XF	Unc
100	1975	Plain 5			
		44.500	—	.10	.15
	1975	w/5 over wavy lines			
		Inc. Ab.	—	.10	.15
	1976	134.267	—	.10	.15
	1978	50.000	—	.10	.20

10 CENTAVOS

COPPER-NICKEL
Getulio Vargas

Y#	Date	Mintage	VF	XF	Unc
64	1942	3.826	.35	.50	1.00
	1943	13.565	.25	.35	.75
		ALUMINUM-BRONZE			
64a	1943	Inc. Ab.	.25	.35	.75
	1944	12.617	.25	.60	1.00
	1945	24.674	.25	.60	1.00
	1946	35.159	.25	.60	1.00
	1947	20.664	.25	.35	.75

Jose Bonifacio

Y#	Date	Mintage	VF	XF	Unc
73	1947	Inc. Ab.	.15	.20	.35
	1948	45.041	.15	.20	.35
	1949	21.763	.15	.20	.35
	1950	16.330	.15	.20	.35
	1951	15.561	—	.15	.35
	1952	10.966	—	.15	.35
	1953	25.883	—	.15	.35
	1954	17.031	—	.15	.35
	1955	25.172	—	.15	.35

ALUMINUM

Y#	Date	Mintage	VF	XF	Unc
76	1956	.741	—	.15	.50
	1957	25.311	—	.15	.25
	1958	5.813	—	.15	.25
	1959	2.611	—	.15	.25
	1960	.624	—	.15	.40
	1961	.951	—	.15	.40

COPPER-NICKEL

Y#	Date	Mintage	VF	XF	Unc
90	1967	22.420	—	.10	.30
		Thinner planchet			
90a	1970	*134.070	—	.10	.20

***NOTE:** Mintage figure includes coins struck through 1974 dated 1970.

STAINLESS STEEL

Y#	Date	Mintage	VF	XF	Unc
90b	1974	114.598	—	.10	.20
	1975	—	—	.10	.20
	1976	—	—	.10	.20
	1977	—	—	.10	.20
	1978	—	—	.10	.20

20 CENTAVOS

COPPER-NICKEL
Getulio Vargas

Y#	Date	Mintage	VF	XF	Unc
65	1942	3.007	.25	.50	1.00
	1943	13.392	.15	.40	.75
		ALUMINUM-BRONZE			
65a	1943	Inc. Ab.	.15	.35	.75
	1944	12.673	.15	.35	.75
	1945	61.632	.15	.35	.60
	1946	31.526	.15	.35	.60
	1947	36.422	.15	.35	.75
	1948	39.671	.15	.35	.75

Rui Barbosa

Y#	Date	Mintage	VF	XF	Unc
74	1948	Inc. Ab.	.15	.25	.50
	1949	24.805	.15	.25	.50
	1950	15.145	.15	.25	.50
	1951	14.964	.15	.25	.50
	1952	10.942	.15	.25	.50
	1953	25.585	.15	.25	.50
	1954	16.477	.15	.25	.50
	1955	25.122	.15	.25	.50
	1956	6.716	.15	.25	.50

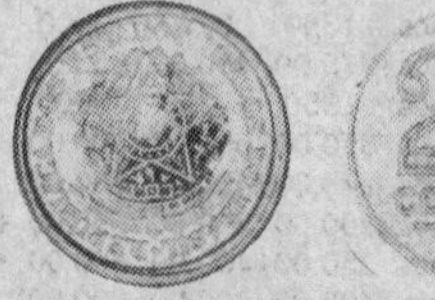

ALUMINUM
National arms

Y#	Date	Mintage	VF	XF	Unc
77	1956	Inc. Ab.	.10	.25	.50
	1957	27.110	.10	.20	.40
	1958	8.552	.10	.20	.40
	1959	4.810	.10	.20	.40
	1960	.510	.10	.20	.40
	1961	2.332	.10	.20	.40

COPPER-NICKEL

Y#	Date	Mintage	VF	XF	Unc
91	1967	123.610	—	.10	.25
		Thinner planchet			
91a	1970	384.894	—	.10	.30

***NOTE:** Mintage figure includes coins struck through 1974 dated 1970.

STAINLESS STEEL

Y#	Date	Mintage	VF	XF	Unc
91b	1975	102.367	—	.10	.25
	1976	—	—	.10	.25
	1977	—	—	.10	.25
	1978	—	—	.10	.25

50 CENTAVOS

COPPER-NICKEL
Getulio Vargas

Y#	Date	Mintage	VF	XF	Unc
66	1942	2.358	.40	.75	1.50
	1943	13.392	.35	.50	1.00
		ALUMINUM-BRONZE			
66a	1943	Inc. Ab.	.30	.50	1.00
	1944	12.102	.30	.50	1.00
	1945	73.222	.30	.50	1.00
	1946	13.941	.30	.50	1.00
	1947	23.588	.20	.50	1.00

Presidente Dutra

Y#	Date	Mintage	VF	XF	Unc
75	1948	32.023	.15	.25	.50
	1949	11.392	.15	.25	.50
	1950	7.804	.15	.35	.75
	1951	7.523	.15	.35	.75
	1952	6.863	.15	.35	.75
	1953	17.372	.15	.25	.50
	1954	11.353	.15	.25	.50
	1955	27.150	.15	.25	.50
	1956	32.130	.15	.25	.50

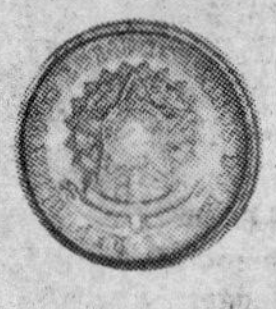

National arms

Y#	Date	Mintage	VF	XF	Unc
78	1956	Inc. Ab.	.10	.20	.40

ALUMINUM

Y#	Date	Mintage	VF	XF	Unc
81	1957	49.350	.10	.20	.35
	1958	59.815	.10	.20	.35
	1959	32.891	.10	.20	.35
	1960	15.997	.10	.20	.35
	1961	18.456	.10	.15	.25

NICKEL

Y#	Date	Mintage	VF	XF	Unc
92	1967	12.987	.25	.50	1.25
		COPPER-NICKEL			
92a	1970	503.895	.20	.35	.75
	1975	—	.20	.35	.75
		STAINLESS STEEL			
92b	1975	79.062	.20	.35	.75
	1976	—	.20	.35	.75
	1977	—	.20	.35	1.00
	1978	—	—	—	.75

CRUZEIRO

ALUMINUM-BRONZE

Y#	Date	Mintage	VF	XF	Unc
67	1942	.381	.40	.75	2.00
	1943	2.728	.25	.50	1.00
	1944	3.820	.25	.50	1.00
	1945	32.544	.25	.50	.75
	1946	49.794	.25	.50	1.00
	1947	15.391	.25	.50	1.00
	1949	7.889	.25	.50	1.00
	1950	5.163	.25	.50	1.00
	1951	3.757	.25	.50	1.00
	1952	1.769	.50	1.00	2.00
	1953	5.195	.25	.50	1.00
	1954	1.145	.25	.50	1.50
	1955	1.758	.25	.50	1.00
	1956	.668	3.00	5.00	8.50

Y#	Date	Mintage	VF	XF	Unc
79	1956	Inc. Ab.	.15	.50	1.00

ALUMINUM

Y#	Date	Mintage	VF	XF	Unc
82	1957	11.849	—	.15	.30
	1958	15.443	—	.15	.30
	1959	25.010	—	.15	.30
	1960	35.267	—	.15	.30
	1961	22.181	—	.15	.30

NICKEL

Y#	Date	Mintage	VF	XF	Unc
93	1970	*48.930	.25	.50	1.50
	1970	.018	—	Proof	3.00
	1974	24.135	.20	.35	.75
		COPPER-NICKEL			
93a	1975	21.613	.20	.35	.75
	1976	—	.20	.35	.75

***NOTE:** Mintage figure includes coins struck through 1972 dated 1970.

NICKEL
150 Year Commemorative

Y#	Date	Mintage	VF	XF	Unc
94	1972	5.600	.35	.75	1.25
	1972	—	—	Proof	3.00
		STEEL F.A.O. Issue			
101	1979	—	—	—	.50
	1979	—	—	Proof	—

2 CRUZEIROS

ALUMINUM-BRONZE

Y#	Date	Mintage	VF	XF	Unc
68	1942	.276	.75	1.50	3.00
	1943	1.929	.25	.50	1.00
	1944	3.820	.25	.50	1.00
	1945	32.544	.20	.40	1.00
	1946	33.650	.20	.40	1.00
	1947	9.908	.20	.40	1.00
	1949	11.252	.20	.40	1.00
	1950	7.754	.25	.50	1.00
	1951	.390	.40	1.00	3.00
	1952	1.456	1.00	2.00	5.00
	1953	3.582	.20	.40	1.00
	1954	1.197	.25	1.00	2.00
	1955	1.838	.20	.50	1.00
	1956	—	.35	1.00	2.00

Y#	Date	Mintage	VF	XF	Unc
80	1956	Inc. Ab.	.20	.40	1.50

ALUMINUM

Y#	Date	Mintage	VF	XF	Unc
83	1957	.194	.25	.50	1.50
	1958	13.687	.15	.25	.50
	1959	20.894	.15	.25	.50
	1960	19.624	.15	.25	.50
	1961	24.924	.15	.25	.50

5 CRUZEIROS

ALUMINUM-BRONZE

Y#	Date	Mintage	VF	XF	Unc
69	1942	.115	.75	1.50	4.50
	1943	.222	.50	1.00	3.25

10 CRUZEIROS

ALUMINUM

Y#	Date	Mintage	VF	XF	Unc
84	1965	19.656	—	.15	.25

11.4900 gm., .800 SILVER, .2955 oz ASW

Y#	Date	Mintage	VF	XF	Unc
97	1975	.020	12.50	25.00	50.00
		STAINLESS STEEL			
102	1980	—	—	.40	.50

20 CRUZEIROS

ALUMINUM

Y#	Date	Mintage	VF	XF	Unc
85	1965	25.930	.15	.20	.35

18.0100 gm., .900 SILVER, .5211 oz ASW
150th Year Commemorative

Y#	Date	Mintage	VF	XF	Unc
95	1972(a)	.250	BV	BV	17.50

50 CRUZEIROS

COPPER-NICKEL

Y#	Date	Mintage	VF	XF	Unc
86	1965	18.001	.15	.25	.50

300 CRUZEIROS

16.6500 gm., .920 GOLD, .4925 oz AGW
150th Year Commemorative

Y#	Date	Mintage	VF	XF	Unc
96	1972(a)	.030	BV	325.00	350.00

NCLT ISSUES

PROVAS

KM#	Date	Mintage	Identification	Mkt.Val.
PR1	1972	—	20 Cruzeiros, Y95	—

COMMEMORATIVE COUNTERSTAMPS

The following listing is an initial attempt to familiarize the numismatic fraternity with the various counterstamps found on Brazilian coins. The specific coins listed are only samples of the many types of coins found counterstamped. The market value in VF is approximately $10.00 to $25.00 over the normal value of the parent coin unless otherwise noted.

1932 Revolution

Type I

c/s: Helmet/1932/C.O.
Companha do Ouro
da Revolucao Constitucionalista

KM#	Date	Mintage	Identification	Mkt.Val.
CC1	1816B	—	960 Reis, C94	40.00
	1817R	—	960 Reis, C94a	40.00
	1824B	—	960 Reis, C138	55.00
	1852	—	1000 Reis, YA2	25.00
	1853	—	1000 Reis, YA8	23.50
	1853	—	2000 Reis, YA9	35.00
	1860	—	500 Reis, YA7	27.50
	1862	—	200 Reis, YA6	21.50
	1865	—	500 Reis, YA7	27.50
	1869	—	200 Reis, YA19	35.00
	1876	—	500 Reis, YA23	23.50

KM#	Date	Mintage	Identification	Mkt.Val.
	1888	—	500 Reis, YA23	23.50
	1888	—	1000 Reis, YA24	28.50

KM#	Date	Mintage	Identification	Mkt.Val.
	1889	—	500 Reis, Y5	27.50

KM#	Date	Mintage	Identification	Mkt.Val.
	1889	—	1000 Reis, Y6	35.00

KM#	Date	Mintage	Identification	Mkt.Val.
	1887	—	2000 Reis, YA25	35.00
	1888	—	2000 Reis, YA25	35.00
	1889	—	2000 Reis, YA25	35.00
	1922	—	2000 Reis, Y34	20.00

Type II

December 15, 1937
Obv. c/s: 2A EXPOSICAO NUMISMATICA around triangle.
Rev. c/s: BELLO HORIZONTE. MINAS GERAES. around sun behind a mountain.

KM#	Date	Mintage	Identification	Mkt.Val.
CC2	1936	50 pcs.	5000 Reis, Y56	75.00

NOTE: These are found with an additional control number c/s.

TYPE III

December, 1949
Obv. c/s: Crowned shield/S-A-N-P-E-X
Rev. c/s: "SANPEX" on globe over date.

KM#	Date	Mintage	Identification	Mkt.Val.
CC3	1812	—	960 Reis, C94	—
	1817	—	960 Reis, C94a	—
	1819	—	960 Reis, C117	—
	1820	—	960 Reis, C117	—
	1889	—	2000 Reis, C201	—

NOTE: These are found with an additional control number c/s.

Type IV

December, 1949
c/s: "SANPEX" in fish-like outline.

KM#	Date	Mintage	Identification	Mkt.Val.
CC4	1889	—	2000 Reis, C201	—

NOTE: These are found with an additional control number c/s.

Type V

May 31, 1950
c/s: JUPEX over date

KM#	Date	Mintage	Identification	Mkt.Val.
CC5	1888	—	2000 Reis, C201	—
	1889	—	2000 Reis, C201	—
	1911	—	2000 Reis, Y17	—

NOTE: These are found with an additional control number c/s.

Type VI

1954
400th Anniversary of Sao Paulo
Brazil Numismatic Society

KM#	Date	Mintage	Identification	Mkt.Val.
CC6	1812	—	960 Reis, C94	—
	1813	—	960 Reis, C94	—
	1815	—	960 Reis, C94	—
	1817	—	960 Reis, C94a	—
	1818	—	960 Reis, C117	—
	1821	—	960 Reis, C117	—
	1888	—	8 Reales, Mexico City, KM377.10	—
	1889	—	2000 Reis, C201	—

Type VII

1954
400th Anniversary of Sao Paulo
Brazil Philatelic Society

KM#	Date	Mintage	Identification	Mkt.Val.
CC7	1810	—	960 Reis, C94	—
	1816	—	960 Reis, C94	—
	1817	—	960 Reis, C94a	—
	1818	—	960 Reis, C117	—
	1819	—	960 Reis, C117	—

KM#	Date	Mintage	Identification	Mkt.Val.
	1820	—	960 Reis, C117	—
	1823	—	960 Reis, C138	—

TYPE VIII

January 26-31, 1955
Obv. c/s: Sailing ship
Rev. c/s: SANPEX II, date around fish.

KM#	Date	Mintage	Identification	Mkt.Val.
CC8	1816	—	960 Reis, C94	—
	1817	—	960 Reis, C94a	—
	1818	—	960 Reis, C117	—
	1820	—	960 Reis, C117	—
	1853	—	1000 Reis, C193	—

Type IX

1955
36th Eucharistic Congress

KM#	Date	Mintage	Identification	Mkt.Val.
CC9	1814	—	960 Reis, C94	—
	1818	—	960 Reis, C117	—
	1819	—	960 Reis, C117	—
	1820	—	960 Reis, C117	—
	1821	—	960 Reis, C117	—

TYPE X

1955
XXIII Anniversary of the 1932 Revolution

KM#	Date	Mintage	Identification	Mkt.Val.
CC10	1813	—	960 Reis, C94	—
	1814	—	960 Reis, C94	—
	1815	—	960 Reis, C94	—
	1816	—	960 Reis, C94	—
	1817	—	960 Reis, C94a	—
	1823	—	960 Reis, C138	—

TYPE XI

September, 1956
Obv. c/s: Sailing ship, leg:999EXPO DG TURISMO
Rev. c/s: SANPEX III-ANO SANTOS DUMONT around date and fish.

KM#	Date	Mintage	Identification	Mkt.Val.
CC11	1810	—	960 Reis, C94	—
	1815	—	960 Reis, C94	—
	1816	—	960 Reis, C94	—
	1820	—	960 Reis, C117	—
	1821	—	960 Reis, C117	—
	1912	—	2000 Reis, Y17	—

Type XII

1956
50th Anniversary of flight of Santos Dumont

KM#	Date	Mintage	Identification	Mkt.Val.
CC12	1815	—	960 Reis, C94	—
	1819	—	960 Reis, C117	—
	1824	—	960 Reis, C138	—

Type XIII

October, 1957
Opening of Santos Dumont Museum

KM#	Date	Mintage	Identification	Mkt.Val.
CC13	1815	—	960 Reis, C94	—
	1818	—	960 Reis, C117	—
	1907	—	2000 Reis, Y17	—

SANTA TEREZA LEPER COLONY

All the following tokens have plain edges. Obverse letters C.S.T. abbreviation for Colonia Santa Tereza.

100 REIS

BRASS

KM#	Date	Mintage	VF	XF	Unc
T1	ND	—	—	Rare	—

200 REIS

BRASS

KM#	Date	Mintage	VF	XF	Unc
T2	ND	—	—	Rare	—

300 REIS

BRASS

KM#	Date	Mintage	VF	XF	Unc
T3	ND	—	—	Rare	—

500 REIS

BRASS

KM#	Date	Mintage	VF	XF	Unc
T4	ND	—	—	Rare	—

1000 REIS

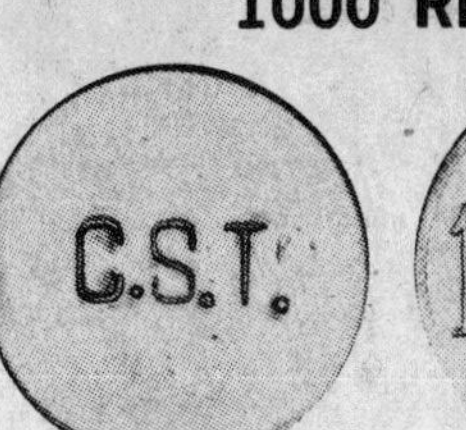

BRASS

KM#	Date	Mintage	VF	XF	Unc
T5	ND	—	—	Rare	—

GOLD BARS

CUYABA

C/S: Crown over "CUYABA" in branches.

Known dates: 1821, 1822.

GOIAS

C/S: "GOIAS": in an incuse rectangle.

Known dates: 1790, 1811, 1813, 1814, 1819, 1820, 1821, 1822, 1823.

MATO GROSSO

C/S: Crown over "MATO GROSSO" in branches.

Known dates: 1784, 1811, 1812, 1813, 1815, 1816, 1817, 1818, 1820.

RIO DAS MORTES

C/S: Arms in branches; "RIO DAS M" below.

Known dates: 1796, 1800, 1804, 1811, 1817.

SABARA

C/S: "SABARA" below arms.

Known dates: 1778, 1792, 1794, 1796, 1801, 1804, 1805, 1806, 1807, 1808, 1809, 1810, 1811, 1812, 1813, 1814, 1815, 1816, 1817, 1818, 1819, 1828, 1832, 1833.

SERRO FRIO

C/S: AAB monogram in beaded circle.

Known dates: 1809, 1810, 1811, 1812, 1813, 1814, 1816, 1818, 1820, 1829, 1830, 1831, 1832.

VILA RICA

C/S: Script VR. Known dates: 1786, 1799, 1804, 1807, 1808, 1809, 1810, 1811, 1812, 1813, 1814, 1815, 1816, 1818, 1828.

SILVER BARS

1932 Sao Paulo Gold Department.
Quantity issued: 40 pcs.

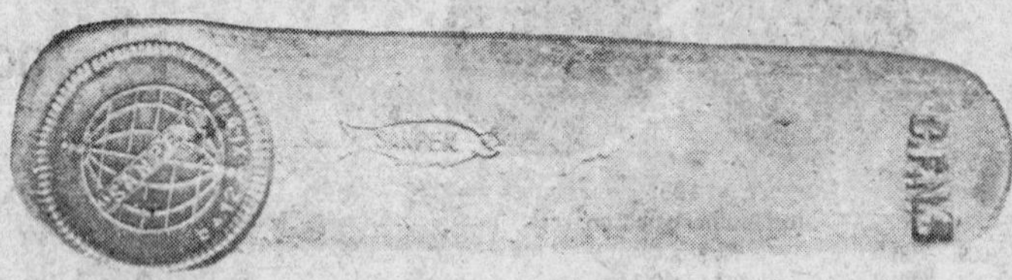

1949 Sanpex I.
Quantity issued: 261 pcs.

1954 400th Anniversary of Sao Paulo – Numismatic Exposition.
Quantity issued: 45 pcs.

1954 400th Anniversary of Sao Paulo – Philatelic Exposition.
Quantity issued: 6 pcs.

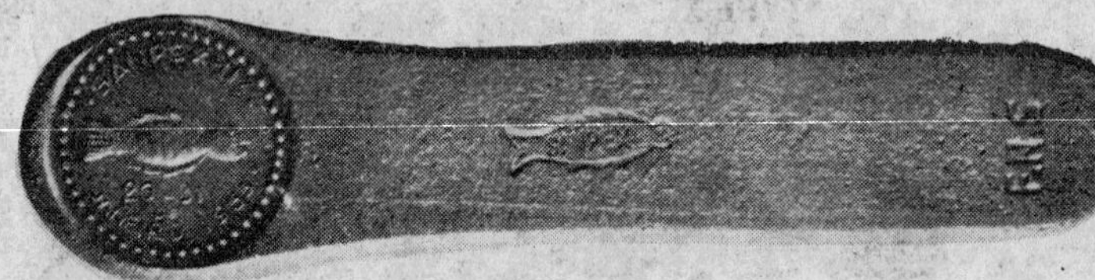

1955 Sanpex II.
Quantity issued: 45 pcs.

1955 36th Eucharistic Congress.
Quantity issued: 45 pcs.

1955 Revolution of 1932 in Sao Paulo Commemorative.
Quantity issued: 45 pcs.

1956 Santos Dumont-Sao Paulo.
Quantity issued: N.A.

1956 Sanpex III.
Quantity issued: N.A.

1957 Presidential Visit to Santos.
Quantity issued: 10 pcs.

1958 Santos Dumont Museum.
Quantity issued: 25 pcs.

BRITISH EAST CARIBBEAN TER.

The British Caribbean Territories (Eastern Group), a currency board formed in 1950, comprised the British West Indies territories of Trinidad and Tobago; Barbados; the Leeward Islands of Anguilla, Saba, St. Christopher, Nevis and Antigua; the Windward Islands of St. Lucia, Dominica, St. Vincent and Grenada; British Guiana and the British Virgin Islands.

The union was without political connotation and was intended to provide the constituent territories with a common currency, thereby permitting the withdrawal of the regular British currency in use.

RULERS

British

MONETARY SYSTEM

100 Cents = 1 Br. W. Indies Dollar

1/2 CENT

BRONZE

Y#	Date	Mintage	Fine	VF	XF	Unc
1	1955	.500	.30	.50	.75	1.00
	1955	2,000	—	—	Proof	2.00
	1958	.200	2.00	3.00	4.00	6.50
	1958	20 pcs.	—	—	Proof	250.00

NOTE: Most 1958 coins were melted.

CENT

BRONZE

Y#	Date	Mintage	Fine	VF	XF	Unc
2	1955	8.000	.15	.25	.60	1.00
	1955	2,000	—	—	Proof	3.00
	1957	3.000	.15	.25	1.75	3.00
	1958	1.500	.35	.50	4.50	7.50
	1958	20 pcs.	—	—	Proof	275.00
	1959	.500	.40	.60	5.75	9.50
	1960	2.500	.15	.25	.60	1.25
	1960	—	—	—	Proof	30.00
	1961	2.280	.25	.35	.75	1.25
	1962	2.000	.15	.25	.50	1.25
	1962	—	—	—	Proof	125.00
	1963	.750	.45	.70	1.20	2.00
	1963	—	—	—	Proof	125.00
	1964	2.500	—	—	.20	.35
	1965	4.800	—	—	—	.35

2 CENTS

BRONZE

Y#	Date	Mintage	Fine	VF	XF	Unc
3	1955	5.500	.15	.25	.50	.85
	1955	2,000	—	—	Proof	4.00
	1957	1.250	.15	.25	1.25	2.50
	1958	1.250	.15	.25	2.50	5.00
	1958	20 pcs.	—	—	Proof	300.00
	1960	.750	.15	.25	1.75	3.00
	1960	—	—	—	Proof	—
	1961	.788	.15	.25	1.75	3.00
	1962	1.060	.10	.20	.30	.75
	1962	—	—	—	Proof	30.00
	1963	.250	.50	.75	1.50	5.00
	1964	1.188	.10	.20	.30	.65
	1965	2.001	—	.10	.20	.40

5 CENTS

NICKEL-BRASS

Y#	Date	Mintage	Fine	VF	XF	Unc
4	1955	8.600	.15	.25	.60	1.25
	1955	2,000	—	—	Proof	5.00
	1956	2.000	.15	.25	.60	1.00
	1960	1.000	.20	.30	.90	1.50
	1962	1.300	.15	.25	.50	1.00
	1963	.200	.25	.35	1.20	2.00
	1964	1.350	—	.10	.30	.75
	1964	—	—	—	Proof	125.00
	1965	2.400	—	.10	.20	.50
	1965	—	—	—	Proof	—

10 CENTS

COPPER-NICKEL

Y#	Date	Mintage	Fine	VF	XF	Unc
5	1955	5.000	.15	.25	.45	.75
	1955	2,000	—	—	Proof	5.00
	1956	4.000	.15	.25	.45	.75
	1959	2.000	.15	.25	.60	1.00
	1961	1.260	.20	.30	.50	1.00
	1962	1.200	.15	.25	.50	1.00
	1964	1.400	.15	.25	.35	.65
	1965	3.200	.15	.25	.30	.50

25 CENTS

COPPER-NICKEL

Y#	Date	Mintage	Fine	VF	XF	Unc
6	1955	7.000	.35	.50	.70	1.00
	1955	2,000	—	—	Proof	10.00
	1957	.800	.75	1.00	2.25	4.50
	1959	1.000	.35	.50	1.25	2.25
	1961	.744	.50	.75	2.50	5.00
	1962	.480	.25	.50	1.25	2.50
	1963	.480	.25	.50	1.25	2.50
	1964	.480	.25	.50	1.00	1.75
	1965	1.280	.25	.50	.75	1.00

50 CENTS

COPPER-NICKEL

Y#	Date	Mintage	Fine	VF	XF	Unc
7	1955	1.500	.75	1.25	1.75	3.00
	1955	2,000	—	—	Proof	20.00
	1965	.100	—	—	—	—

NCLT ISSUES

PROOF SETS

STANDARD METALS

KM#	Date	Mintage	Identification	Issue Price	Mkt. Val.
101	1955(7)	2,000	Y1-7	—	45.00
102	1958(3)	20	Y1-3	—	800.00

Listings For

BRITISH GUIANA: refer to Guyana

BRITISH HONDURAS: refer to Belize

BRITISH NORTH BORNEO: refer to Malaysia

BRITISH VIRGIN IS.

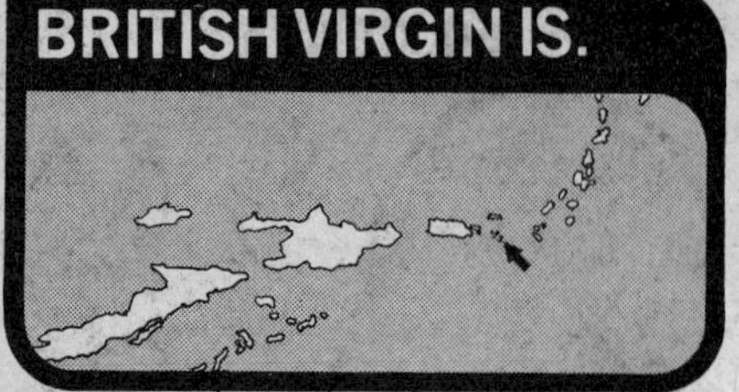

The Colony of the Virgin Islands, a British colony situated in the Caribbean Sea northeast of Puerto Rico and west of the Leeward Islands, has an area of 59 sq. mi. (163 sq. km.) and a population of 11,000. Capital: Road Town. The principal islands of the 36-island group are Tortola, Virgin Gorda, Anegada, and Jost Van Dyke. The chief industries are fishing and stock raising. Fish, livestock and bananas are exported.

The Virgin Islands were discovered by Columbus in 1493, and named, by him Las Virgenes, in honor of St. Ursula and her companions. The British Virgin Islands were formerly part of the administration of the Leeward Islands, but received a separate administration as a Crown Colony in 1950. A new constitution promulgated in 1967 provided for a ministerial form of government headed by the Governor.

The Government of the British Virgin Islands issued the first official coinage in its history on June 30, 1973, in honor of 300 years of constitutional government in the islands. U.S. coins and currency continue to be accepted as a medium of exchange.

TORTOLA

Tortola, which has an area of about 24 sq. mi. (62 sq. km), is the largest of thirty—six islands which comprise the British Virgin Islands. It was settled by the Dutch in 1648 and was occupied by the British in 1666. They have held it ever since.

MONETARY SYSTEM

8 Shillings, 3 Pence = 11 Bits
= 8 Reales

1-1/2 PENCE

BILLON
c/s: Incuse 'T' on French Colonial 2 Sous

C#	Date	Year	Good	VG	Fine	VF
3	ND	(1801)	22.50	32.50	45.00	75.00

TORTOLA COUNTERMARKS

TORTOLA in odd shaped rectangle.

9 PENCE or 1 BIT

SILVER
c/s: 'TORTOLA' on 1/2 cut of Spanish 2 Reales

C#	Date	Year	Good	VG	Fine	VF
5	ND	(1801)	60.00	85.00	125.00	175.00

SHILLING

SILVER
c/s: 'TORTOLA' on 1/8 cut of Spanish 8 Reales

C#	Date	Year	Good	VG	Fine	VF
6	ND	(1801)	75.00	100.00	140.00	190.00

2 SHILLINGS

SILVER
c/s: 'TORTOLA' on 1/4 cut of Spanish 8 Reales

C#	Date	Year	Good	VG	Fine	VF
7	ND	(1801)	50.00	75.00	115.00	165.00

4 SHILLINGS, 1-1/2 PENCE

SILVER
c/s: 'TORTOLA' on 1/2 cut of Spanish 8 Reales

C#	Date	Year	Good	VG	Fine	VF
8	ND	(1801)	65.00	90.00	130.00	185.00

TORTOLA in rectangle

SHILLING

SILVER
c/s: 'TORTOLA' on 1/8 cut of Spanish 8 Reales

C#	Date	Year	Good	VG	Fine	VF
10	ND	(1801-05)	50.00	75.00	115.00	165.00

2 SHILLINGS

SILVER
c/s: 'TORTOLA' on 1/4 cut of Spanish 8 Reales

C#	Date	Year	Good	VG	Fine	VF
11	ND	(1801-05)	40.00	65.00	100.00	150.00

4 SHILLINGS, 1-1/2 PENCE

SILVER
c/s: 'TORTOLA' on 1/2 cut of Spanish 8 Reales

C#	Date	Year	Good	VG	Fine	VF
12	ND	(1801-05)	40.00	65.00	100.00	150.00

TIRTILA COUNTERMARKS

Private Issues

9 PENCE or 1 BIT

SILVER
c/s: 'TIRTILA' on 1/2 cut of Spanish 2 Reales

C#	Date	Year	Good	VG	Fine	VF
13	ND	(1805-24)	22.50	32.50	50.00	75.00

SHILLING

SILVER
c/s: 'TIRTILA' on 1/8 cut of Spanish 8 Reales

C#	Date	Year	Good	VG	Fine	VF
17	ND	(1805-24)	22.50	32.50	50.00	75.00

2 SHILLINGS

SILVER
c/s: 'TIRTILA' on 1/4 cut of Spanish 8 Reales

C#	Date	Year	Good	VG	Fine	VF
19	ND	(1805-24)	22.50	32.50	50.00	75.00

4 SHILLINGS, 1-1/2 PENCE

SILVER
c/s: 'TIRTILA' on 1/2 cut of Spanish 8 Reales

C#	Date	Mintage	VG	Fine	VF
20	ND (1805-24)	—	30.00	40.00	50.00

Prices listed for Tortola issues are just for the Tortola c/s and do not take into consideration any other counterstamps that may be found on the same piece.

BRITISH VIRGIN ISLANDS

RULERS

British

MINTMARKS

FM - Franklin Mint, U.S.A.*

***NOTE:** During 1975-78 the Franklin Mint produced coinage in up to 3 different qualities. Qualities of issue are designated in ( ) after each date and are defined as follows:

(M) MATTE -Normal circulation strike or a dull finish produced by sandblasting special uncirculated (polish finish) or proof quality dies.

(U) SPECIAL UNCIRCULATED - Polished or proof-like in appearance without any frosted features.

(P) PROOF - The highest quality obtainable having mirror-like fields and frosted features.

MONETARY SYSTEM

100 Cents = 1 Dollar

CENT

BRONZE

Y#	Date	Mintage	VF	XF	Unc
1	1973FM	.053	—	—	.10
	1973FM(P)	.181	—	Proof	1.00
	1974FM	.022	—	.10	.25
	1974FM(P)	.094	—	Proof	1.00
	1975FM(M)	6,000	.35	.75	1.50
	1975FM(U)	2,351	—	.75	1.75
	1975FM(P)	.032	—	Proof	1.25
	1976FM(M)	.012	.25	.50	.75
	1976FM(U)	996 pcs.	—	1.50	2.50
	1976FM(P)	.015	—	Proof	1.50
	1977FM(M)	500 pcs.	—	1.25	2.00
	1977FM(U)	782 pcs.	—	1.25	2.00
	1977FM(P)	7,218	—	Proof	2.00
	1978FM(U)	1,443	—	—	1.00
	1978FM(P)	7,059	—	Proof	2,00
	1979FM(U)	—	—	—	1.00
	1979FM(P)	—	—	Proof	2.00
	1980FM(U)	—	—	—	1.00
	1980FM(P)	—	—	Proof	4.00

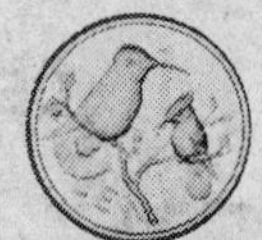

1.5300 gm., .925 SILVER, .0455 oz ASW
Queen's Silver Jubilee

Y#	Date	Mintage	VF	XF	Unc
9	1977FM(P)	.017	—	Proof	4.00

Coronation Jubilee
Similar to Y#1.

Y#	Date	Mintage	VF	XF	Unc
1a	1978FM(P)	6,196	—	Proof	—

5 CENTS

COPPER-NICKEL

Y#	Date	Mintage	VF	XF	Unc
2	1973FM	.026	.10	.25	.50
	1973FM(P)	.181	—	Proof	1.00
	1974FM	.018	.15	.35	.75
	1974FM(P)	.094	—	Proof	1.25
	1975FM(M)	3,800	.75	1.25	2.50
	1975FM(U)	2,351	—	1.00	2.25

Y#	Date	Mintage	VF	XF	Unc
2	1975FM(P)	.032	—	Proof	1.25
	1976FM(M)	4,800	.50	1.00	2.25
	1976FM(U)	996 pcs.	—	2.00	3.50
	1976FM(P)	.015	—	Proof	2.00
	1977FM(M)	500 pcs.	—	1.75	3.00
	1977FM(U)	782 pcs.	—	1.75	3.00
	1977FM(P)	7,218	—	Proof	2.50
	1978FM(U)	1,443	—	—	2.00
	1978FM(P)	7,059	—	Proof	2.50
	1979FM(U)	—	—	—	—
	1979FM(P)	—	—	Proof	2.50
	1980FM(U)	—	—	—	2.00
	1980FM(P)	—	—	Proof	5.00

3.3300 gm., .925 SILVER, .0990 oz ASW
Queen's Silver Jubilee

Y#	Date	Mintage	VF	XF	Unc
10	1977FM	.017	—	Proof	5.00

Coronation Jubilee
Similar to Y#2.

Y#	Date	Mintage	VF	XF	Unc
2a	1978FM(P)	6,196	—	Proof	—

10 CENTS

COPPER-NICKEL

Y#	Date	Mintage	VF	XF	Unc
3	1973FM	.023	.15	.35	.75
	1973FM(P)	.181	—	Proof	1.25
	1974FM	.013	.25	.50	1.00
	1974FM(P)	.094	—	Proof	1.25
	1975FM(M)	2,000	.75	1.50	3.25
	1975FM(U)	2,351	—	1.50	3.00
	1975FM(P)	.032	—	Proof	1.25
	1976FM(M)	3,000	.75	1.25	2.50
	1976FM(U)	996 pcs.	—	2.50	4.00
	1976FM(P)	.015	—	Proof	2.50
	1977FM(M)	500 pcs.	1.25	2.00	3.50
	1977FM(U)	782 pcs.	—	2.00	3.50
	1977FM(P)	7,218	—	Proof	2.50
	1978FM(U)	1,443	—	—	2.50
	1978FM(P)	7,059	—	Proof	2.50
	1979FM(U)	—	—	—	—
	1979FM(P)	—	—	Proof	2.50
	1980FM(U)	—	—	—	3.00
	1980FM(P)	—	—	Proof	6.00

5.9200 gm., .925 SILVER, .1760 oz ASW
Queen's Silver Jubilee

Y#	Date	Mintage	VF	XF	Unc
11	1977FM(P)	.017	—	Proof	7.00

Coronation Jubilee
Similar to Y#3.

Y#	Date	Mintage	VF	XF	Unc
3a	1978FM(P)	6,196	—	Proof	—

25 CENTS

COPPER-NICKEL

Y#	Date	Mintage	VF	XF	Unc
4	1973FM	.021	.35	.60	1.00
	1973FM(P)	.181	—	Proof	1.50
	1974FM	.012	.35	.75	1.50
	1974FM(P)	.094	—	Proof	1.50
4	1975FM(M)	1,000	1.50	3.00	6.00
	1975FM(U)	2,351	—	2.00	4.00
	1975FM(P)	.032	—	Proof	1.75
	1976FM(M)	2,000	1.00	2.00	3.75
	1976FM(U)	996 pcs.	—	3.00	5.00
	1976FM(P)	.015	—	Proof	3.00
	1977FM(M)	500 pcs.	—	3.00	5.00
	1977FM(U)	782 pcs.	—	3.00	5.00
	1977FM(P)	7,218	—	Proof	3.25
	1978FM(U)	1,443	—	—	3.50
	1978FM(P)	7,059	—	Proof	3.25
	1979FM(U)	—	—	—	—
	1979FM(P)	—	—	Proof	3.25
	1980FM(U)	—	—	—	4.00
	1980FM(P)	—	—	Proof	8.00

8.5600 gm., .925 SILVER, .2545 oz ASW
Queen's Silver Jubilee

Y#	Date	Mintage	VF	XF	Unc
12	1977FM(P)	.017	—	Proof	10.00

Coronation Jubilee
Similar to Y#4.

Y#	Date	Mintage	VF	XF	Unc
4a	1978FM(P)	6,196	—	Proof	—

50 CENTS

COPPER-NICKEL

Y#	Date	Mintage	VF	XF	Unc
5	1973FM	.020	.75	1.00	2.00
	1973FM(P)	.181	—	Proof	2.00
	1974FM	.012	.85	1.75	3.50
	1974FM(P)	.094	—	Proof	2.00
	1975FM(M)	1,000	1.50	2.50	5.00
	1975FM(U)	2,351	—	2.00	4.00
	1975FM(P)	.032	—	Proof	3.00
	1976FM(M)	2,000	1.00	1.75	4.50
	1976FM(U)	996 pcs.	—	4.00	6.50
	1976FM(P)	.015	—	Proof	4.50
	1977FM(M)	600 pcs.	—	3.50	6.00
	1977FM(U)	782 pcs.	—	3.50	6.00
	1977FM(P)	7,218	—	Proof	5.00
	1978FM(U)	1,543	—	—	4.50
	1978FM(P)	7,059	—	Proof	5.00
	1979FM(U)	—	—	—	—
	1979FM(P)	—	—	Proof	5.00
	1980FM(U)	—	—	—	5.00
	1980FM(P)	—	—	Proof	12.00

16.3500 gm., .925 SILVER, .4862 oz ASW
Queen's Silver Jubilee

Y#	Date	Mintage	VF	XF	Unc
13	1977FM(P)	.017	—	Proof	17.50

Coronation Jubilee
Similar to Y#5.

Y#	Date	Mintage	VF	XF	Unc
5a	1978FM(P)	6,196	—	Proof	—

DOLLAR

COPPER-NICKEL
Obv: Similar to 50 Cents, Y#5.

Y#	Date	Mintage	VF	XF	Unc
6	1973FM	.020	—	7.50	12.50
	1974FM	.012	1.50	3.00	7.50
	1975FM(M)	800 pcs.	7.50	15.00	30.00
	1975FM(U)	2,151	4.50	8.50	16.50
	1976FM(M)	1,800	6.50	12.50	20.00
	1976FM(U)	996 pcs.	—	13.50	22.50
	1977FM(M)	800 pcs.	7.50	15.00	30.00
	1977FM(U)	782 pcs.	7.50	15.00	30.00
	1978FM(U)	1,743	—	—	27.50
	1979FM(M)	—	—	—	—
	1979FM(U)	—	—	—	—
	1980FM(U)	—	—	—	7.50

25.1000gm., .925 SILVER, .7465 oz ASW

Y#	Date	Mintage	VF	XF	Unc
6a	1973FM(U)	—	—	—	—
	1973FM(P)	.181	—	Proof	25.00
	1974FM(P)	.094	—	Proof	25.00
	1975FM(P)	.032	—	Proof	25.00
	1976FM(P)	.015	—	Proof	27.50
	1977FM(P)	7,218	—	Proof	30.00
	1978FM(P)	7,059	—	Proof	30.00
	1978FM(P)	6,196	—	Proof	—
	1979FM(P)	—	—	Proof	25.00
	1980FM(P)	—	—	Proof	25.00

*Coronation Jubilee

Queen's Silver Jubilee
Rev: Similar to Y#6.

Y#	Date	Mintage	VF	XF	Unc
14	1977FM(P)	.017	—	Proof	30.00

5 DOLLARS

COPPER-NICKEL
Snowy Egret Commemorative

Y#	Date	Mintage	VF	XF	Unc
18	1979FM(U)	—	—	—	—

40.1400 gm., .925 SILVER, 1.1938 oz ASW

Y#	Date	Mintage	VF	XF	Unc
18a	1979FM(P)	—	—	Proof	40.00

COPPER-NICKEL
Great Blue Heron

Y#	Date	Mintage	VF	XF	Unc
20	1980FM(U)	—	—	—	10.00
	.925 SILVER				
20a	1980FM(P)	—	—	Proof	45.00

25 DOLLARS

27.2800 gm., .925 SILVER, .8113 oz ASW
Coronation Jubilee
Obv: Portrait of Queen.

Y#	Date	Mintage		Unc
16	1978FM(P)	8,438	Proof only	50.00

.500 GOLD

Y#	Date	Mintage		Unc
21	1980FM(P)	—	Proof only	50.00

100 DOLLARS

7.1000 gm., .900 GOLD, .2054 oz AGW

Y#	Date	Mintage	VF	XF	Unc
7	1975FM(M)	10 pcs.	—	—	1250.
	1975FM(U)	.013	BV	150.00	175.00
	1975FM(P)	*.023	—	Proof	150.00

*NOTE: Includes 8,754 in First Day Covers.

50th Birthday Commemorative

Y#	Date	Mintage	VF	XF	Unc
8	1976FM(M)	10 pcs.	—	—	1250.
	1976FM(U)	1,752	—	175.00	225.00
	1976FM(P)	.012	—	Proof	175.00

Queen's Silver Jubilee

Y#	Date	Mintage	VF	XF	Unc
15	1977FM(U)	10 pcs.	—	—	1500.
	1977FM(P)	6,715	—	Proof	150.00

25th Anniversary of Coronation.

Y#	Date	Mintage	VF	XF	Unc
17	1978FM(P)	5,772	—	Proof	175.00

Sir Francis Drake Commemorative

Y#	Date	Mintage	VF	XF	Unc
19	1979FM(P)	3,216	—	Proof	185.00

400th Anniversary of Drake's Voyage

Y#	Date	Mintage	VF	XF	Unc
22	1980FM(P)	—	—	Proof	210.00

NCLT ISSUES

MINT SETS

KM#	Date	Mintage	Identification	Issue Price	Mkt. Val.
S1	1973(6)	18,402	Y1-6	11.50	15.00
S2	1974(6)	9,474	Y1-6	10.00	20.00
S3	1975(6)	2,351	Y1-6	12.50	40.00
S4	1976(6)	996	Y1-6	13.50	45.00
S5	1977(6)	782	Y1-6	12.50	50.00
S6	1978(6)	943	Y1-6	13.00	45.00
S7	1979(7)	—	Y1-6,18	20.00	30.00
S8	1980(7)	—	Y1-6,20	21.00	30.00

PROOF SETS
STANDARD METALS

KM#	Date	Mintage	Identification	Issue Price	Mkt. Val.
101	1973(6)	*146,581	Y1-5,6A	15.00	20.00

*NOTE: Includes 34,418 proofs in First Day Covers.

KM#	Date	Mintage	Identification	Issue Price	Mkt. Val.
102	1974(6)	93,555	Y1-5,6a	20.00	20.00
103	1975(6)	32,244	Y1-5,6a	25.00	30.00
104	1976(6)	15,003	Y1-5,6a	25.00	35.00
105	1977(6)	7,218	Y1-5,6a	26.00	40.00
106	1977(6)	17,366	Y9-14	60.00	70.00
107	1978(6)	7,059	Y1-5,6a	25.00	40.00
108	1979(7)	—	Y1-5,6a,18a	39.50	90.00
109	1980(7)	—	Y1-5,6a,20a	97.00	100.00

BRITISH WEST AFRICA

British West Africa was an administrative grouping of the four former British West African colonies of Gambia, Sierra Leone, Nigeria and Gold Coast (now Ghana). All are now independent republics and members of the British Commonwealth of Nations. See separate entries for individual statistics and history.

The four colonies were supplied with a common coinage and banknotes by the West African Currency Board from 1907 through 1958. From 1907 through 1911, the coinage bore the inscription, NIGERIA-BRITISH WEST AFRICA; from 1912 through 1958, BRITISH WEST AFRICA. The coinage, which includes three coins of 1936 bearing the name of Edward VIII, is obsolete.

RULERS

British until 1952

MINTMARKS

G-J.R. Gaunt & Sons, Birmingham
H - Heaton Mint, Birmingham
K, KN - King's Norton, Birmingham
SA - Pretoria, South Africa
No mm - Royal Mint

MONETARY SYSTEM

12 Pence = 1 Shilling
20 Shillings = 1 Pound

1/10 PENNY

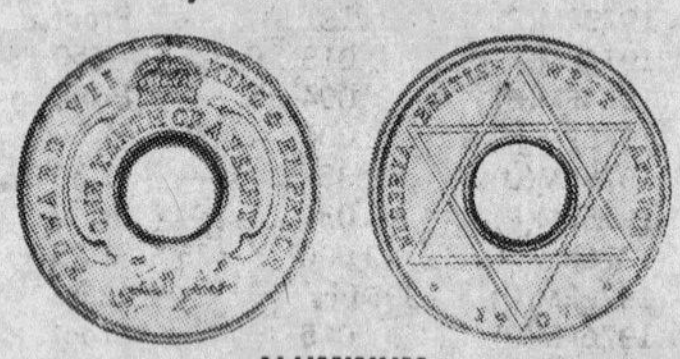

ALUMINUM

Y#	Date	Mintage	Fine	VF	XF	Unc
3	1907	1.254	.75	1.75	3.00	6.00
	1908	8.363	.75	1.75	3.50	7.00

COPPER-NICKEL

Y#	Date	Mintage	Fine	VF	XF	Unc
1	1908	9.600	.30	.50	1.25	3.00
	1909	4.800	.40	.75	1.50	4.00
	1910	7.200	.60	1.00	2.50	6.00

Y#	Date	Mintage	Fine	VF	XF	Unc
4	1911H	7.200	1.75	3.00	5.00	10.00

Rev. leg: W/o NIGERIA

Y#	Date	Mintage	Fine	VF	XF	Unc
7	1912H	10.800	.60	1.00	2.00	4.00
	1913	4.632	3.00	5.00	10.00	20.00
	1913H	1.080	1.00	1.75	3.75	7.50
	1914	1.200	3.00	5.00	10.00	20.00
	1914H	20.288	1.00	1.75	3.75	7.50
	1915H	10.032	.75	1.25	2.50	5.00
	1916H	.480	60.00	80.00	100.00	135.00
	1917H	9.384	3.00	5.00	10.00	20.00

Y#	Date	Mintage	Fine	VF	XF	Unc
7	1919H	.912	1.25	2.00	4.00	7.50
	1919KN	.480	12.50	20.00	40.00	75.00
	1920H	1.560	5.00	8.00	15.00	25.00
	1920KN	12.996	.40	.75	1.25	2.50
	1920KN	Inc. Ab.	—	—	Proof	125.00
	1922KN	7.265	1.00	1.75	3.75	7.50
	1923KN	12.000	.60	1.00	2.00	4.00
	1925	2.400	5.00	8.00	15.00	25.00
	1925H	12.000	2.50	4.50	7.50	15.00
	1925KN	12.000	1.25	2.00	4.00	8.00
	1926	12.000	1.25	2.00	4.00	8.00
	1927	3.984	.20	.35	.75	2.00
	1928	11.760	.20	.35	.75	2.00
	1928H	2.964	.20	.35	.75	2.00
	1928KN	3.151	3.00	5.00	10.00	17.50
	1930	9.600	1.75	3.00	5.50	10.00
	1931	9.840	.20	.35	.75	2.00
	1932	3.600	.20	.35	.75	2.00
	1933	7.200	.20	.35	.75	2.00
	1934	4.800	1.75	3.00	5.50	10.00
	1935	13.200	1.50	2.50	4.00	8.00
	1936	9.720	.20	.35	.75	1.50

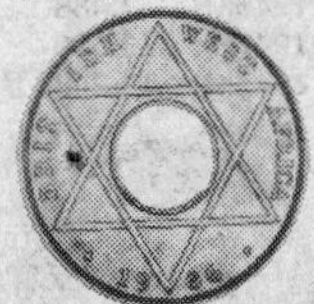

Y#	Date	Mintage	Fine	VF	XF	Unc
18	1936	5.880	.25	.50	1.00	2.00
	1936	Inc. Ab.	—	—	Proof	125.00
	1936H	1.404	50.00	90.00	120.00	175.00
	1936KN	3.000	1.75	3.00	7.50	20.00

Y#	Date	Mintage	Fine	VF	XF	Unc
22	1938	12.000	.25	.50	1.00	2.00
	1938	—	—	—	Proof	125.00
	1938H	1.596	10.00	18.00	25.00	50.00
	1938H	—	—	—	Proof	125.00
	1939	9.840	.25	.50	1.00	2.50
	1940	13.920	.25	.50	1.00	2.00
	1941	16.560	1.50	3.00	5.00	10.00
	1942	12.360	1.50	3.00	5.00	10.00
	1943	22.560	1.50	3.00	5.00	10.00
	1944	10.440	.50	1.00	1.75	3.00
	1945	25.706	.50	1.00	1.75	3.00
	1946	2.803	1.00	2.00	4.00	7.00
	1946H	6.004	1.00	2.00	4.00	7.00
	1946KN	1.152	.15	.25	.50	1.50
	1947	4.202	.50	1.00	2.50	4.00
	1947KN	3.900	75.00	125.00	200.00	300.00

Obv. leg: W/o IND: IMP:

Y#	Date	Mintage	Fine	VF	XF	Unc
29	1949H	3.700	1.00	2.00	3.50	6.00
	1949KN	3.036	3.50	7.00	12.00	18.00
	1950KN	13.200	.35	.75	1.25	2.00

BRONZE

Y#	Date	Mintage	Fine	VF	XF	Unc
29a	1952	15.060	.50	1.00	2.50	4.00
	1952	Inc. Ab.	—	—	Proof	100.00

Y#	Date	Mintage	Fine	VF	XF	Unc
38	1954	4.800	.50	1.00	1.25	1.75
	1954	Inc. Ab.	—	—	Proof	100.00
	1956	1 Known	—	—	—	—
	1957	7.200	15.00	30.00	50.00	80.00

1/2 PENNY

COPPER-NICKEL

Y#	Date	Mintage	Fine	VF	XF	Unc
5	1911H	3.360	5.00	10.00	20.00	40.00

Rev. leg: W/o NIGERIA

Y#	Date	Mintage	Fine	VF	XF	Unc
8	1912H	3.120	1.75	3.50	6.50	13.50
	1913	—	100.00	150.00	250.00	—
	1913H	.216	6.00	12.00	18.00	35.00
	1914	1.622	9.00	18.00	25.00	50.00
	1914H	.585	9.00	18.00	25.00	50.00
	1914K	3.360	3.00	6.00	12.50	25.00
	1915H	3.577	1.00	2.00	4.00	8.00
	1916H	4.046	1.00	2.00	4.00	8.00
	1917H	.214	3.75	7.50	15.00	25.00
	1918H	.490	2.50	5.00	10.00	20.00
	1919H	4.950	1.25	2.50	4.00	8.00
	1919KN	3.861	1.25	2.50	4.00	8.00
	1920H	26.285	1.50	3.00	6.00	12.00
	1920KN	13.844	.75	1.25	2.50	5.00
	1922KN	5.800	350.00	750.00	1000.	1500.
	1927	.528	3.00	6.00	12.50	25.00
	1929	.336	2.75	5.50	11.00	22.00
	1931	.096	15.00	30.00	42.50	65.00
	1932	.960	2.75	5.50	11.00	20.00
	1933	2.122	1.50	3.00	5.00	10.00
	1934	1.694	1.50	3.00	5.00	10.00
	1935	3.271	1.50	3.00	6.00	12.00
	1936	5.400	2.00	4.00	15.00	25.00

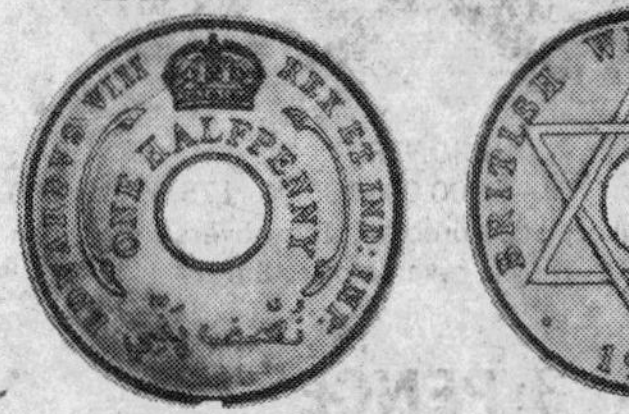

Y#	Date	Mintage	Fine	VF	XF	Unc
19	1936	14.760	.25	.50	1.00	2.50
	1936	Inc. Ab.	—	—	Proof	65.00
	1936H	2.400	.75	1.50	4.00	7.00
	1936KN	2.298	.65	1.25	2.75	3.50

Y#	Date	Mintage	Fine	VF	XF	Unc
23	1937H	4.022	.40	.85	1.50	3.00
	1937KN	5.577	.40	.85	1.50	3.00
	1940KN	2.410	1.25	2.50	4.00	7.00
	1941H	2.400	.40	.85	1.50	3.00
	1942	4.800	.40	.85	1.25	4.00
	1943	3.360	.35	.75	3.00	6.00
	1944	3.600	.65	1.25	3.50	7.00
	1944	—	—	—	Proof	125.00
	1946	3.600	.25	.50	1.00	2.00
	1947H	15.218	.35	.75	1.25	2.50
	1947KN	12.000	.40	.85	1.50	3.00

Obv. leg: W/o IND: IMP:

Y#	Date	Mintage	Fine	VF	XF	Unc
30	1949H	4.859	1.25	2.50	7.50	25.00
30	1949KN	3.413	1.25	2.50	7.50	25.00
	1951	3.468	1.00	2.00	7.50	25.00
	1951	—	—	—	Proof	250.00

BRONZE

Y#	Date	Mintage	Fine	VF	XF	Unc
30a	1952	11.332	.25	.50	1.00	4.00
	1952	—	—	—	Proof	150.00
	1952H	27.603	.20	.35	.75	1.75
	1952KN	4.800	.85	1.75	3.75	5.00

PENNY

COPPER-NICKEL

Y#	Date	Mintage	Fine	VF	XF	Unc
2	1906	—	—	—	Rare	—
	1907	.863	1.35	2.75	5.50	11.00
	1908	3.217	1.35	2.75	5.50	11.00
	1909	.960	2.50	5.00	10.00	20.00
	1910	2.520	1.50	3.00	6.00	12.00

Y#	Date	Mintage	Fine	VF	XF	Unc
6	1911H	1.920	15.00	30.00	50.00	90.00

Rev. leg: W/o NIGERIA

Y#	Date	Mintage	Fine	VF	XF	Unc
9	1912H	1.560	1.50	3.00	5.00	10.00
	1913	1.680	10.00	20.00	30.00	50.00
	1913H	.144	5.00	10.00	17.50	35.00
	1914	3.000	1.50	3.00	5.00	10.00
	1914H	.072	20.00	40.00	65.00	100.00
	1915H	3.295	1.35	2.75	5.50	11.00
	1916H	3.461	1.50	3.00	5.00	10.00
	1917H	.444	2.50	5.00	10.00	20.00
	1918H	.994	8.50	17.50	27.50	45.00
	1919H	21.864	1.25	2.50	5.00	10.00
	1919KN	.264	7.50	14.50	25.00	40.00
	1920H	37.870	1.00	2.00	4.50	9.00
	1920KN	20.685	1.00	2.00	4.50	9.00
	1922KN	3.971	300.00	600.00	800.00	1500.
	1926	8.040	2.00	4.00	8.00	16.00
	1927	.792	10.00	20.00	45.00	75.00
	1928	6.672	3.00	7.50	30.00	60.00
	1929	.636	2.00	4.00	7.00	15.00
	1933	2.806	1.00	2.50	8.00	20.00
	1934	2.640	7.50	14.50	22.50	35.00
	1935	8.551	1.25	3.00	17.50	30.00
	1936	7.368	1.25	3.00	17.50	30.00

BRASS (OMS)

Y#	Date	Mintage	Fine	VF	XF	Unc
9a	1920KN	Inc. Ab.	40.00	75.00	110.00	150.00

COPPER-NICKEL

Y#	Date	Mintage	Fine	VF	XF	Unc
20	1936	7.992	.50	1.00	3.50	8.00

Y#	Date	Mintage	Fine	VF	XF	Unc
20	1936	Inc. Ab.	—	—	Proof	80.00
	1936H	12.600	.35	.75	1.50	2.50
	1936KN	12.512	.35	.75	1.50	2.50

Y#	Date	Mintage	Fine	VF	XF	Unc
24	1937H	6.112	.75	1.25	2.50	5.00
	1937KN	11.999	.50	1.00	2.00	4.00
	1940	3.840	.50	1.00	2.00	4.00
	1940H	2.400	.50	1.00	3.00	6.00
	1940KN	2.400	.50	1.00	3.00	6.00
	1941	6.960	.35	.75	1.50	3.75
	1942	18.840	.30	.60	1.00	3.00
	1943	28.920	.30	.60	1.00	3.00
	1943H	7.200	1.25	2.25	4.50	9.00
	1944	19.440	.30	.60	1.00	3.00
	1945	6.072	.45	.90	1.75	4.00
	1945H	9.000	1.00	2.00	4.50	9.00
	1945KN	9.557	.75	1.50	3.00	7.00
	1946H	10.446	.85	1.75	3.75	8.00
	1946KN	11.976	.30	.60	1.00	3.00
	1946SA	1.020	125.00	200.00	300.00	500.00
	1947	—	—	—	—	—
	1947H	12.443	.30	.60	1.00	3.00
	1947KN	9.829	.30	.60	1.00	3.00
	1947SA	58.980	.30	.60	1.00	2.75

COPPER (OMS)

Y#	Date	Mintage	Fine	VF	XF	Unc
24a	1937H	—	—	—	—	350.00

Obv. leg: W/o IND: IMP:

Y#	Date	Mintage	Fine	VF	XF	Unc
31	1951	1.258	—	12.00	20.00	35.00
	1951KN	2.692	6.50	12.50	22.50	37.50

BRONZE

Y#	Date	Mintage	Fine	VF	XF	Unc
31a	1952	10.542	.75	1.50	3.00	7.00
	1952	—	—	—	Proof	175.00
	1952H	30.794	.20	.40	.60	1.50
	1952KN	45.398	.20	.40	.60	1.50

Y#	Date	Mintage	Fine	VF	XF	Unc
39	1956H	13.503	.75	1.50	3.00	7.00
	1956KN	13.500	.30	.60	1.00	6.00
	1957	9.000	.75	1.50	3.00	7.00
	1957H	5.340	.75	1.50	3.00	7.00
	1957KN	5.600	.50	1.00	2.00	7.00
	1958	12.200	.75	1.50	3.00	7.00
	1958	—	—	—	Proof	75.00
	1958KN	Inc. Ab.	.75	1.50	3.00	7.00

PENNY MULES

COPPER-NICKEL

Y#	Date	Mintage	Fine	VF	XF	Unc
21	1936H	—	75.00	125.00	200.00	275.00

NOTE: The above piece combines the obverse of East Africa Y#26 with the reverse of British West Africa Y#20.

Y#	Date	Mintage	Fine	VF	XF	Unc
A24	1945H	—	900.00	1500.	2000.	2750.

NOTE: The above piece combines the obverse of British West Africa Y#20 with the reverse of Y#24.

BRONZE

Y#	Date	Mintage	Fine	VF	XF	Unc
A39	1956H	—	100.00	135.00	175.00	225.00

NOTE: The above piece combines the obverse of British West Africa Y#31 with the reverse of Y#39.

3 PENCE

1.4138 gm., .925 SILVER, .0420 oz ASW

Y#	Date	Mintage	Fine	VF	XF	Unc
14	1913	.240	3.50	7.50	12.50	25.00
	1913	Inc. Ab.	—	—	Proof	75.00
	1913H	.496	2.25	4.50	7.50	15.00
	1914H	1.560	1.50	2.50	4.50	9.00
	1915H	.270	5.00	10.00	18.50	30.00
	1916H	.820	5.00	10.00	18.50	30.00
	1917H	3.600	1.50	2.50	5.00	10.00
	1918H	1.722	1.75	3.50	6.50	11.50
	1919H	19.826	1.50	2.50	3.75	7.50

1.4138 gm., .500 SILVER, .0227 oz ASW

Y#	Date	Mintage	Fine	VF	XF	Unc
	1920H	3.616	15.00	23.50	40.00	85.00

NICKEL-BRASS

Y#	Date	Mintage	Fine	VF	XF	Unc
14a	1920KN	19.000	.75	1.50	3.00	25.00
	1920KN	Inc. Ab.	—	—	Proof	70.00
	1925	8.800	.85	1.75	3.75	25.00
	1926	1.600	6.50	12.50	22.50	50.00
	1927	.800	11.50	22.50	35.00	90.00
	1928	1.760	11.50	22.50	35.00	75.00
	1928	—	—	—	Proof	125.00
	1933	2.800	1.00	2.00	4.00	25.00
	1933	Inc. Ab.	—	—	Proof	125.00
	1934	6.400	1.00	2.00	4.00	25.00
	1934	—	Proof	Reported, not confirmed		
	1935	11.560	1.00	2.00	4.00	25.00
	1936	17.160	1.00	2.00	4.00	25.00
	1936H	1.000	30.00	55.00	85.00	140.00
	1936KN	2.038	10.00	20.00	30.00	50.00

COPPER-NICKEL

Y#	Date	Mintage	Fine	VF	XF	Unc
25	1938H	7.000	.30	.60	1.50	3.00
	1938KN	9.056	.35	.75	1.75	3.50
	1939H	17.500	.30	.60	1.50	3.00
	1939KN	15.500	.30	.60	1.50	3.00
	1940H	1.496	.40	.85	2.00	4.00
	1940KN	10.000	.30	.60	1.50	3.00
	1941H	5.032	1.00	2.00	3.75	6.00
	1943H	5.106	1.00	2.00	3.75	6.00
	1943KN	9.502	1.00	2.25	4.50	8.00
	1944KN	2.536	1.00	2.25	4.50	8.00
	1945H	.998	1.25	2.50	5.00	10.00
	1945KN	3.000	1.00	2.25	4.50	8.00
	1946KN	7.488	.40	.85	2.00	4.00
	1947H	10.000	.35	.75	1.75	3.50
	1947KN	11.248	.40	.85	2.00	4.00

Y#	Date	Mintage	Fine	VF	XF	Unc
40	1957H	.800	12.50	25.00	50.00	100.00

6 PENCE

2.8276 gm., .925 SILVER, .0841 oz ASW

Y#	Date	Mintage	Fine	VF	XF	Unc
15	1913	.560	3.00	5.00	10.00	20.00
	1913	Inc. Ab.	—	—	Proof	100.00
	1913H	.400	3.00	5.00	10.00	20.00
	1914H	.952	2.75	4.00	8.00	15.00
	1916H	.400	3.00	5.00	10.00	20.00
	1917H	2.400	3.00	5.00	10.00	20.00
	1918H	1.160	3.00	5.00	10.00	20.00
	1919H	8.676	2.75	4.00	8.00	12.50

2.8276 gm., .500 SILVER, .0454 oz ASW

Y#	Date	Mintage	Fine	VF	XF	Unc
15b	1920H	2.948	8.50	17.50	30.00	60.00

NICKEL-BRASS

Y#	Date	Mintage	Fine	VF	XF	Unc
15a	1920KN	12.000	1.00	2.00	4.00	20.00
	1920KN	Inc. Ab.	—	—	Proof	75.00
	1923H	2.000	5.00	10.00	20.00	50.00
	1924	1.000	10.00	20.00	30.00	50.00
	1924H	1.000	10.00	20.00	30.00	50.00
	1924KN	1.000	10.00	20.00	30.00	50.00
	1925	2.800	3.50	6.50	13.50	25.00
	1928	.400	25.00	45.00	65.00	150.00
	1928	—	—	—	Proof	175.00
	1933	1.000	17.50	35.00	60.00	150.00
	1935	4.000	2.50	5.00	10.00	20.00
	1936	10.400	10.00	20.00	30.00	45.00
	1936H	.480	22.50	45.00	70.00	100.00
	1936H	—	—	—	Proof	—
	1936KN	2.696	10.00	20.00	30.00	50.00

BRASS

Y#	Date	Mintage	Fine	VF	XF	Unc
26	1938	12.114	.50	1.00	2.00	10.00
	1940	17.829	.75	1.50	3.50	10.00
	1942	1.600	1.75	3.50	7.50	15.00
	1943	10.586	.75	1.75	4.00	10.00
	1944	1.814	3.50	7.50	15.00	25.00
	1945	4.000	2.50	5.00	8.50	15.00
	1946	4.000	3.00	6.00	15.00	40.00
	1947	6.120	.75	1.50	3.50	10.00
	1947	—	—	—	Proof	175.00

Obv. leg: W/o IND: IMP:

Y#	Date	Mintage	Fine	VF	XF	Unc
32	1952	2.544	2.00	4.00	9.00	15.00
	1952	—	—	—	Proof	175.00

SHILLING

5.6552 gm., .925 SILVER, .1682 oz ASW

Y#	Date	Mintage	Fine	VF	XF	Unc
16	1913	8.800	BV	5.50	10.00	30.00
	1913	Inc. Ab.	—	—	Proof	150.00
	1913H	3.540	BV	5.50	10.00	30.00
	1914	3.000	BV	5.50	10.00	30.00
	1914H	11.292	BV	5.50	10.00	30.00
	1915H	.254	7.50	13.50	20.00	45.00
	1916H	11.838	BV	5.50	10.00	30.00
	1917H	15.018	BV	5.50	10.00	30.00
	1918H	9.486	BV	5.50	10.00	30.00
	1919	2.000	7.50	13.50	20.00	45.00
	1919H	.992	12.00	20.00	35.00	75.00
	1920	.828	17.50	30.00	50.00	100.00
			NICKEL-BRASS			
16a	1920G	.016	500.00	1000.	1500.	2000.
	1920KN/G	—	—	—	—	—
	1920KN	38.800	1.50	3.00	6.00	30.00
	1920KN	—	—	—	Proof	100.00
	1922KN	32.324	1.50	3.00	20.00	50.00
	1923H	24.384	3.00	6.00	12.00	30.00
	1923KN	5.000	3.50	7.00	14.00	35.00
	1924	17.000	1.50	3.00	6.00	30.00
	1924H	9.567	9.00	18.00	30.00	45.00
	1924KN	7.000	5.00	10.00	17.50	35.00
	1925	19.800	3.50	7.00	13.00	30.00
	1926	19.952	1.50	3.00	6.00	30.00
	1927	22.248	5.00	10.00	17.00	35.00
	1928	10.000	9.00	18.00	28.00	40.00
	1928	—	—	—	Proof	175.00
	1936	70.200	1.50	3.00	6.00	30.00
	1936H	10.920	11.50	22.50	35.00	50.00
	1936KN	14.962	6.50	12.50	22.50	45.00
			SILVER (OMS)			
16b	1936KN	—	—	—	Proof	325.00

BRASS

Y#	Date	Mintage	Fine	VF	XF	Unc
27	1938	57.806	.50	1.25	2.50	10.00
	1939	55.472	.50	1.25	2.50	10.00
	1940	40.311	.50	1.25	2.50	10.00
	1942	42.000	.50	1.25	2.50	10.00
	1943	133.600	.50	1.25	2.50	10.00
	1945	8.010	1.25	2.75	5.50	25.00
	1945H	12.864	1.25	2.50	5.00	15.00
	1945KN	11.120	1.00	2.00	3.50	15.00
	1946	37.350	1.00	2.00	3.50	20.00
	1946H	—	—	—	—	—
	1947	99.200	.50	1.00	2.50	10.00
	1947H	10.000	1.25	2.75	5.00	15.00
	1947KN	10.384	.50	1.00	2.50	10.00

Obv. leg: W/o IND: IMP:

Y#	Date	Mintage	Fine	VF	XF	Unc
33	1949	70.000	.50	1.00	2.00	8.50
	1949	Inc. Ab.	—	—	Proof	175.00
33	1949H	10.000	1.25	2.50	5.00	9.00
	1949KN	10.016	1.25	2.50	5.00	9.00
	1951	35.346	1.25	2.50	5.00	12.00
	1951H	10.000	1.25	2.50	5.00	12.00
	1951KN	16.832	1.25	2.50	5.00	12.00
	1952	98.654	.50	1.00	1.75	4.00
	1952H	44.096	.50	1.00	1.75	4.00
	1952KN	41.653	.50	1.00	1.75	4.00
	1952KN	Inc. Ab.	—	—	Proof	55.00

2 SHILLINGS

11.3104 gm., .925 SILVER, .3364 oz ASW

Y#	Date	Mintage	Fine	VF	XF	Unc
17	1913	2.100	BV	12.00	15.00	35.00
	1913	Inc. Ab.	—	—	Proof	175.00
	1913H	1.180	BV	12.00	15.00	35.00
	1914	.330	17.50	27.50	42.50	90.00
	1914H	.637	BV	12.00	15.00	35.00
	1915H	.066	12.00	15.00	20.00	40.00
	1916H	9.824	BV	12.00	15.00	35.00
	1917H	1.059	15.00	20.00	27.50	60.00
	1918H	7.294	BV	12.00	15.00	35.00
	1919	2.000	BV	12.00	15.00	40.00
	1919H	10.866	BV	12.00	15.00	35.00
	1920	.683	20.00	30.00	60.00	125.00
			11.3104 gm., .500 SILVER, .1818 oz ASW			
	1920H	1.926	10.00	25.00	50.00	150.00
			NICKEL-BRASS			
17a	1920KN	15.856	2.50	5.00	10.00	35.00
	1920KN	—	—	—	Proof	200.00
	1922	10.000	2.50	5.00	10.00	35.00
	1922KN	5.500	6.00	12.00	20.00	40.00
	1922KN	Inc. Ab.	—	—	Proof	250.00
	1923H	12.698	5.00	10.00	17.50	35.00
	1924	1.500	4.50	9.00	17.50	40.00
	1925	3.700	2.50	5.00	10.00	40.00
	1926	11.500	3.25	6.50	12.50	35.00
	1927	11.100	3.25	6.50	12.50	35.00
	1928	7.900	600.00	1000.	1500.	2000.
	1928	—	—	—	Proof	2000.
	1936	32.940	4.50	9.00	17.50	35.00
	1936H	8.703	16.50	32.50	50.00	75.00
	1936KN	8.794	10.00	20.00	35.00	60.00

BRASS

Y#	Date	Mintage	Fine	VF	XF	Unc
28	1938H	32.000	1.00	2.00	4.00	30.00
	1938KN	27.852	1.00	2.00	4.00	30.00
	1939H	5.750	1.25	2.50	5.50	35.00
	1939KN	6.250	1.00	2.00	4.00	32.50
	1942KN	10.000	1.25	2.50	5.50	35.00
	1946H	11.242	1.25	2.50	5.50	35.00
	1946KN	4.800	1.25	2.75	7.00	37.50
	1947H	4.758	1.00	2.00	4.50	32.50
	1947KN	4.200	1.25	2.50	5.50	35.00

NICKEL-BRASS
Obv. leg: W/o IND: IMP:

Y#	Date	Mintage	Fine	VF	XF	Unc
34	1949H	7.500	1.25	2.50	5.50	20.00
	1949KN	7.576	1.25	2.50	5.50	20.00
	1951H	6.566	1.25	2.50	5.50	20.00
	1952H	4.410	1.25	2.75	7.00	20.00
	1952KN	1.236	1.25	2.75	7.00	20.00

NOTE: For later coinage see Gambia, Ghana, Sierra Leone, and Nigeria.

NCLT ISSUES

PATTERNS

KM#	Date	Mintage	Identification	Mkt.Val.
1	1925	—	1 Shilling, Nickel-Brass, ROYAL MINT 1925 on edge	1500.
2	1952KN	—	2 Shillings, Nickel-Brass, raised word "SPECIMEN" in field	600.00

SPECIMEN SETS

KM#	Date	Mintage	Identification	Issue Price	Mkt. Val.
SS1	1913(4)	—	Y14-17	—	425.00
SS2	1913(8)	—	Y14-17 Double Set	—	800.00
SS3	1920KN(8)	12	Y14a,15a,16a,17a,double set	—	900.00
SS4	1928(4)	—	Y14a, 15a, 16a, 17a	—	3000.

BRITISH WEST INDIES

The 'Anchor Coins' catalogued under this heading do not bear a particular place identification. They were issued for use in various British colonies in both the New World and the Orient. Coins of this type dated 1820 are traditionally assigned to Mauritius and other holdings in the Indian Ocean. Those of 1822 were initially struck for Mauritius but found their widest circulation in Canada and colonies in the Caribbean Sea.

RULERS

George IV, 1820-1830

ANCHOR COINAGE

NOTE: Coins dated 1820 were struck for Mauritius, while issues of 1822 were common to Mauritius and colonies of the British West Indies. These circulated in Mauritius until 1826 when they were shipped to the British West Indies.

1/16 DOLLAR

.892 SILVER

C#	Date	Mintage	Fine	VF	XF	Unc
1	1820	.162	15.00	25.00	35.00	75.00
	1820	—	—	—	Proof	150.00
	1822/1	.704	20.00	27.50	35.00	75.00
	1822/1	—	—	—	Proof	450.00
	1822	Inc. Ab.	7.50	10.00	20.00	60.00
	1822	—	—	—	Proof	100.00

1/8 DOLLAR

.892 SILVER

C#	Date	Mintage	Fine	VF	XF	Unc
2	1820	.120	20.00	27.50	35.00	75.00
	1820	—	—	—	Proof	150.00
	1822/0	.557	15.00	20.00	30.00	65.00
	1822/1	Inc. Ab.	12.50	17.50	25.00	50.00
	1822	Inc. Ab.	10.00	15.00	20.00	45.00
	1822	—	—	—	Proof	125.00

1/4 DOLLAR

.892 SILVER

C#	Date	Mintage	Fine	VF	XF	Unc
3	1820	.100	40.00	50.00	75.00	150.00
	1820	—	—	—	Proof	225.00
	1822/1	.434	12.50	17.50	25.00	50.00
	1822	Inc. Ab.	10.00	15.00	22.50	45.00
	1822	—	—	—	Proof	125.00

1/2 DOLLAR

.892 SILVER

C#	Date	Mintage	Fine	VF	XF	Unc
4	1821	Unique	—	—	—	—
	1822/1	.089	—	—	Rare	—
	1822/1	—	—	—	Proof	—
	1822	Inc. Ab.	100.00	150.00	200.00	350.00
	1822	—	—	—	Proof	500.00

NCLT ISSUES

PATTERNS

KM#	Date	Mintage	Identification	Mkt.Val.
1	1823	—	1/100 Dollar, Bronze	500.00

KM#	Date	Mintage	Identification	Mkt.Val.
2	1823	—	1/50 Dollar, Bronze	600.00

BRUNEI

The state of Brunei (Negeri Brunei), a British protected state on the northwest coast of the island of Borneo, has an area of 2,226 sq. mi. (5,765 sq. km.) and a population of 144,000. Capital: Bandar Seri Begawan. Crude oil and rubber are exported.

Magellan was the first European to visit Brunei in 1521. It was a powerful state, ruling over northern Borneo and adjacent islands from the 16th to the 19th century. Brunei became a British protectorate in 1888 and a British dependency in 1905. The Consitiution of 1959 restored control over internal affairs to the sultan, while delegating responsibility for defense and foreign affairs to Britain.

The island of Labuan (formerly Sultana), located 6 miles off the northwest coast of Borneo, has an area of 35 sq. mi. and a population of 10,000. It is now part of Sabah (British North Borneo), and consequently of Malaysia. The East India Co. sought to make Labuan a trading station in 1775, but the island reverted to a pirate refuge. In 1846 it was ceded by the sultan of Brunei to Britain. Labuan was a crown colony from 1848 to 1890, when its administration was handed over to British North Borneo, which ruled it until 1905, when it became part of the Straits Settlements. Labuan became a part of Sabah in 1946.

RULERS

Sultan Abdul Mumin, 1852-1885
Sultan Hashim Jelal, 1885-1906
British 1906-1950
Sultan Sir Omar Ali Saifuddin, 1950-1967
Sultan Hassanal Bolkiah I, 1967-

MONETARY SYSTEM

100 Cents = 1 Straits Dollar
100 Sen = 1 Dollar

1/2 PITIS

TIN, 24mm

KM#	Date	Mintage	Good	VG	Fine	VF
20	AH1285	—	17.50	27.50	40.00	70.00

PITIS

TIN

KM#	Date	Mintage	Good	VG	Fine	VF
21	AH1285	—	12.50	30.00	40.00	50.00

CENT

BRONZE

Y#	Date	Mintage	Fine	VF	XF	Unc
1	AH1304	1.000	7.50	20.00	30.00	60.00
	1304	—	—	—	Proof	250.00

DECIMAL COINAGE

100 Sen = 1 Dollar (Ringgit)

SEN

BRONZE

Y#	Date	Mintage	VF	XF	Unc
2	1967	1.000	—	.10	.20

Y#	Date	Mintage	VF	XF	Unc
7	1968	.060	—	.20	.30
	1970	.140	—	.25	.40
	1970	4,000	—	Proof	3.00
	1971	.400	—	.10	.20
	1973	.120	—	—	.15
	1974	.920	—	—	.10
	1976	.140	—	—	.10

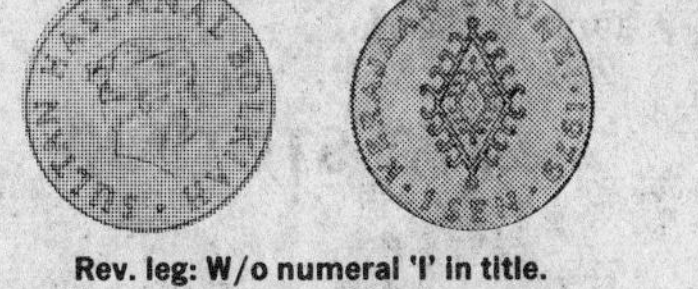

Rev. leg: W/o numeral 'I' in title.

Y#	Date	Mintage	VF	XF	Unc
7a	1977	.140	—	—	.10
	1978	.269	—	—	.10
	1979	.060	—	—	.25
	1979	—	—	Proof	2.00

5 SEN

COPPER-NICKEL

Y#	Date	Mintage	VF	XF	Unc
3	1967	1.160	—	.10	.20

Y#	Date	Mintage	VF	XF	Unc
8	1968	.320	—	.10	.25
	1970	.760	—	.10	.40
	1970	4,000	—	Proof	3.00
	1971	.320	—	.10	.20
	1973	.128	—	—	.15
	1974	.832	—	—	.10
	1976	.384	—	—	.10

Rev. leg: W/o numeral 'I' in title.

Y#	Date	Mintage	VF	XF	Unc
8a	1977	.384	—	—	.10
	1978	.640	—	—	.10
	1979	.120	—	—	—
	1979	—	—	Proof	3.00

10 SEN

COPPER-NICKEL

Y#	Date	Mintage	VF	XF	Unc
4	1967	3.510	—	.20	.30

Y#	Date	Mintage	VF	XF	Unc
9	1968	.580	—	.25	.40
	1970	1.360	—	.30	.60
	1970	4,000	—	Proof	4.00
	1971	.420	—	.10	.25
	1973	.300	—	.10	.20
	1974	1.760	—	.10	.20
	1976	.920	—	.10	.20

Rev. leg: W/o numeral 'I' in title.

Y#	Date	Mintage	VF	XF	Unc
9a	1977	.920	—	.10	.20
	1978	1.080	—	.10	.20
	1979	1.080	—	—	—
	1979	—	—	Proof	4.00

20 SEN

COPPER-NICKEL

Y#	Date	Mintage	VF	XF	Unc
5	1967	2.130	.15	.25	.40

Y#	Date	Mintage	VF	XF	Unc
10	1968	.510	.25	.50	.75
	1970	.850	.25	.50	.75
	1970	4,000	—	Proof	4.25
	1971	.450	.15	.25	.60
	1973	.450	.15	.25	.50
	1974	.900	.15	.20	.35
	1976	.640	.15	.20	.35

Rev. leg: W/o numeral 'I' in title.

Y#	Date	Mintage	VF	XF	Unc
10a	1977	.640	—	.20	.30
	1978	.720	—	.20	.30
	1979	.410	—	—	—
	1979	—	—	Proof	5.00

50 SEN

COPPER-NICKEL

Y#	Date	Mintage	VF	XF	Unc
6	1967	.788	.30	.60	1.00

Y#	Date	Mintage	VF	XF	Unc
11	1968	.212	.50	1.00	1.60
	1970	.300	.50	1.00	1.80
	1970	4,000	—	Proof	5.25
	1971	.320	.30	.60	1.00
	1973	.140	.35	.60	1.00
	1974	.324	.30	.50	.75
	1976	.240	.30	.50	.75

Rev. leg: W/o numeral 1 in title.

Y#	Date	Mintage	VF	XF	Unc
11a	1977	.240	.30	.50	.75
	1978	.264	.30	.50	.75
	1979	.480	—	—	—
	1979	—	—	Proof	6.00

DOLLAR

COPPER-NICKEL

Y#	Date	Mintage	VF	XF	Unc
12	1970	5,000	—	Proof	35.00

Rev. leg: W/o numeral 1 in title.

Y#	Date	Mintage	VF	XF	Unc
12a	1979	—	—	Proof	15.00

10 DOLLARS

28.2800 gm., .925 SILVER, .8411 oz ASW
10th Anniversary of Dollar

Y#	Date	Mintage	VF	XF	Unc
13	1977	.010	— Proof only		40.00
	10th Anniversary of Sultan's Coronation				
14	1978	—	—	—	—

1000 DOLLARS

50.0000 gm., .917 GOLD, 1.4742 oz AGW
10th Anniversary of Sultan's Coronation

Y#	Date	Mintage	VF	XF	Unc
15	1978	1,000	— Proof only		1200.

NCLT ISSUES

PROOF SETS
STANDARD METALS

KM#	Date	Mintage	Identification	Issue Price	Mkt. Val.
101	1970(5)	4,000	Y#7-11	6.60	18.00
102	1979(6)	—	Y#7a-12a	30.00	35.00

Listings For

BUKHARA: refer to Russian Turkestan

BULGARIA

The People's Republic of Bulgaria, a Balkan country on the Black Sea in southeastern Europe, has an area of 42,758 sq. mi. (110,743 sq. km.) and a population of 8.9 million. Capital: Sofia. Agriculture remains a key component of the economy but industrialization, particularly heavy industry, has been emphasized since the late 1940s. Machinery, tobacco and cigarettes, wines and spirits, clothing and metals are the chief exports.

The area now occupied by Bulgaria was conquered by the Bulgars, an Asiatic tribe, in the 7th century. Bulgarian kingdoms continued to exist on the Bulgarian peninsula until it came under Turkish rule in 1395. In 1878, after nearly 500 years of Turkish rule, Bulgaria was made a principality under Turkish suzerainty. Union seven years later with Eastern Rumelia created a Balkan state with borders approximating those of present-day Bulgaria. A Bulgarian kingdom fully independent of Turkey was proclaimed Sept. 22, 1908. That monarchy was abolished by plebiscite in 1946 and Bulgaria became a people's republic on the Soviet pattern.

Coinage of the People's Republic features a number of politically oriented commemoratives.

RULERS

Alexander I, 1879-1886
Ferdinand I, as Prince, 1887-1908
As King, 1908-1918
Boris III, 1918-1943

MINTMARKS

A - Berlin
(a) Cornucopia & torch - Paris
BP - Budapest
H - Heaton Mint, Birmingham
KB - Kormoczbanya
Poissy - Thunderbolt

MONETARY SYSTEM

100 Stotinki = 1 Lev

STOTINKA

BRONZE

Y#	Date	Mintage	VF	XF	Unc
16	1901	20.000	1.25	2.50	4.50
	1912	20.000	1.25	2.50	4.50

BRASS

Y#	Date	Mintage	VF	XF	Unc
46	1951	—	—	—	.15

Currency Revision 1962

Y#	Date	Mintage	VF	XF	Unc
53	1962	—	—	—	.15
	1971	—	—	—	—

Obv: 2 dates on arms, '681-1944'

Y#	Date	Mintage	VF	XF	Unc
53a	1974	—	—	—	.15
	1979	2,000	—	Proof	—

2 STOTINKI

BRONZE
Rev: HEATON below wreath

Y#	Date	Mintage	VF	XF	Unc
1	1881	4.996	4.50	7.00	12.50

Y#	Date	Mintage	VF	XF	Unc
17	1901(a)	40.000	1.25	2.25	4.50
	1912	40.000	1.25	1.85	4.00

BRASS
Currency Revision 1962

Y#	Date	Mintage	VF	XF	Unc
54	1962	—	—	—	.15

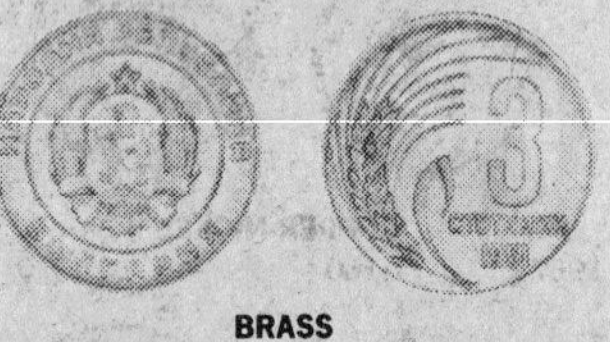

Obv: 2 dates on arms, '681-1944'

Y#	Date	Mintage	VF	XF	Unc
54a	1974	—	—	—	.15
	1979	2,000	—	Proof	—

2-1/2 STOTINKI

COPPER-NICKEL

Y#	Date	Mintage	VF	XF	Unc
8	1888	12.000	3.75	5.50	9.00

3 STOTINKI

BRASS

Y#	Date	Mintage	VF	XF	Unc
47	1951	—	—	.10	.25

5 STOTINKI

BRONZE
Rev: HEATON below wreath

Y#	Date	Mintage	VF	XF	Unc
2	1881	10.000	3.50	5.00	10.00

COPPER-NICKEL

Y#	Date	Mintage	VF	XF	Unc
9	1888	14.000	.75	1.50	3.00

Y#	Date	Mintage	VF	XF	Unc
18	1906	14.000	.25	.75	1.75
	1912	14.000	.25	.75	1.75
	1913	20.850	.25	.75	1.75

ZINC

Y#	Date	Mintage	VF	XF	Unc
18a	1917	53.200	.75	1.50	3.50

BRASS

Y#	Date	Mintage	VF	XF	Unc
48	1951	—	.15	.20	.25

Currency Revision 1962

Y#	Date	Mintage	VF	XF	Unc
55	1962	—	—	.10	.20

Obv: 2 dates on arms '681-1944'

Y#	Date	Mintage	VF	XF	Unc
55a	1974	—	—	.10	.20
	1979	2,000	—	Proof	—

10 STOTINKI

BRONZE
Rev: HEATON below wreath

Y#	Date	Mintage	VF	XF	Unc
3	1881	15.000	3.00	5.00	10.00

COPPER-NICKEL

Y#	Date	Mintage	VF	XF	Unc
10	1888	10.000	1.00	2.00	4.00

Y#	Date	Mintage	VF	XF	Unc
19	1906	13.000	.30	.75	2.00
	1912	13.000	.30	.75	2.00
	1913	20.000	.25	.75	2.00

ZINC

Y#	Date	Mintage	VF	XF	Unc
19a	1917	59.100	1.00	1.50	3.50

COPPER-NICKEL

Y#	Date	Mintage	VF	XF	Unc
49	1951	—	.10	.20	.30

NICKEL-BRASS
Currency Revision 1962

Y#	Date	Mintage	VF	XF	Unc
56	1962	—	.10	.15	.25

Obv: 2 dates on arms, '681-1944'

Y#	Date	Mintage	VF	XF	Unc
56a	1974	—	.10	.15	.25
	1979	2,000	—	Proof	—

20 STOTINKI

COPPER-NICKEL

Y#	Date	Mintage	VF	XF	Unc
11	1888	5.000	1.25	2.50	5.00

Y#	Date	Mintage	VF	XF	Unc
20	1906	10.000	.40	.75	2.00
	1912	10.000	.40	.75	2.00
	1913	5.000	.40	.75	2.00

ZINC

Y#	Date	Mintage	VF	XF	Unc
20a	1917	40.000	1.25	2.50	5.00

COPPER-NICKEL

Y#	Date	Mintage	VF	XF	Unc
A49	1952	—	.35	.60	1.00
	1954	—	.10	.20	.50

NICKEL-BRASS
Currency Revision 1962

Y#	Date	Mintage	VF	XF	Unc
57	1962	—	.20	.30	.50

Obv: 2 dates on arms, '681-1944'

Y#	Date	Mintage	VF	XF	Unc
57a	1974	—	.20	.30	.50
	1979	2,000	—	Proof	—

25 STOTINKI

COPPER-NICKEL

Y#	Date	Mintage	VF	XF	Unc
50	1951	—	.20	.35	.60

50 STOTINKI

2.5000 gm., .835 SILVER, .0671 oz ASW

Y#	Date	Mintage	VF	XF	Unc
4	1883	3.000	2.50	4.50	7.00

Y#	Date	Mintage	VF	XF	Unc
12	1891KB	2.000	2.50	4.50	7.00

Y#	Date	Mintage	VF	XF	Unc
24	1910	.400	3.00	6.00	10.00

Y#	Date	Mintage	VF	XF	Unc
27	1912	5.000	2.25	3.00	5.00
	1913	2.282	2.50	4.00	6.00
	1916	4.526	50.00	75.00	100.00

ALUMINUM-BRONZE

Y#	Date	Mintage	VF	XF	Unc
41	1937	30.000	.20	.30	.75

COPPER-NICKEL

Y#	Date	Mintage	VF	XF	Unc
51	1959	—	.20	.50	.75

NICKEL-BRASS
Currency Revision 1962

Y#	Date	Mintage	VF	XF	Unc
58	1962	—	.40	.65	1.00

Obv: 2 dates on arms, '681-1944'

Y#	Date	Mintage	VF	XF	Unc
58a	1974	—	.40	.65	1.00
	1979	2,000	—	Proof	—

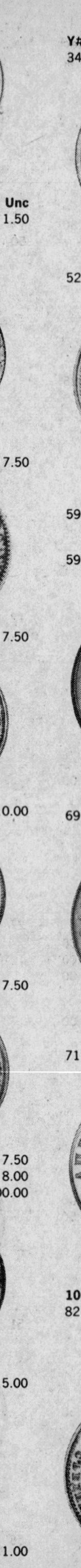

COPPER-NICKEL
Sofia University

Y#	Date	Mintage	VF	XF	Unc
86	1977	—	.50	.75	1.50

LEV

5.0000 gm., .835 SILVER, .1342 oz ASW

Y#	Date	Mintage	VF	XF	Unc
5	1882	4.500	4.50	6.00	7.50
13	1891KB	4.000	4.50	6.00	7.50
13a	1894	1.000	4.50	6.00	10.00
25	1910	3.000	4.50	6.00	7.50
28	1912	5.500	4.50	6.00	7.50
	1913	2.282	4.50	6.00	8.00
	1916	4.568	200.00	250.00	300.00

ALUMINUM

Y#	Date	Mintage	VF	XF	Unc
32	1923	40.000	5.00	7.00	15.00

COPPER-NICKEL

Y#	Date	Mintage	VF	XF	Unc
34	1925	35.000	.20	.50	1.00
	1925 (Poissy)	35.000	.20	.50	1.00

NOTE: The Poissy issue bears the thunderbolt mintmark.

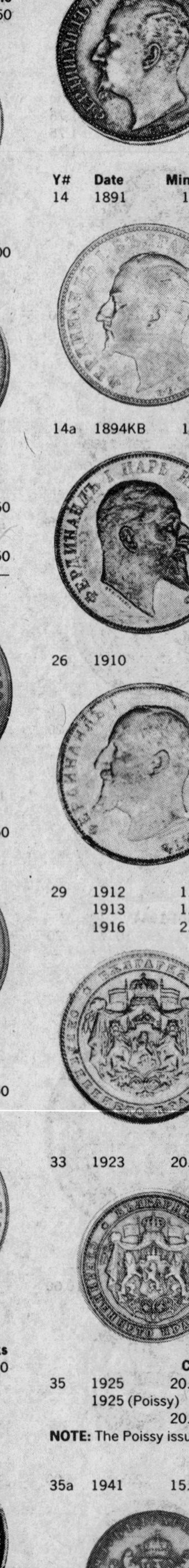

IRON

Y#	Date	Mintage	VF	XF	Unc
34a	1941	10.000	5.00	7.50	13.50

COPPER-NICKEL

Y#	Date	Mintage	VF	XF	Unc
52	1960	—	.20	.35	1.00

NICKEL-BRASS
Currency Revision 1962

Y#	Date	Mintage	VF	XF	Unc
59	1962	—	.85	1.00	1.50

Obv: 2 dates on arms, '681-1944'

Y#	Date	Mintage	VF	XF	Unc
59a	1974	—	.85	1.00	1.50
	1979	2,000	—	Proof	—

25th Anniversary of Socialist Revolution

Y#	Date	Mintage	VF	XF	Unc
69	1969	4.000	.85	1.00	1.50

90th Anniversary Liberation From Turks

Y#	Date	Mintage	VF	XF	Unc
71	1969	—	.85	1.00	1.50

COPPER-NICKEL
100th Anniversary of the April Uprising Against the Turks

Y#	Date	Mintage	VF	XF	Unc
82	1976	*.300	.85	1.00	1.50

2 LEVA

10.0000 gm., .835 SILVER, .2685 oz ASW

Y#	Date	Mintage	VF	XF	Unc
6	1882	2.000	8.50	10.00	15.00

Y#	Date	Mintage	VF	XF	Unc
14	1891	1.500	8.50	10.00	15.00
14a	1894KB	1.000	8.50	10.00	15.00
26	1910	.400	8.50	10.00	15.00
29	1912	1.500	8.50	10.00	15.00
	1913	1.141	8.50	10.00	15.00
	1916	2.286	—	—	—

ALUMINUM

Y#	Date	Mintage	VF	XF	Unc
33	1923	20.000	7.50	10.00	20.00

COPPER-NICKEL

Y#	Date	Mintage	VF	XF	Unc
35	1925	20.000	.35	.50	1.00
	1925 (Poissy)	20.000	.35	.50	1.00

NOTE: The Poissy issue bears thunderbolt mintmark.

IRON

Y#	Date	Mintage	VF	XF	Unc
35a	1941	15.000	1.00	2.00	5.00

Y#	Date	Mintage	VF	XF	Unc
A45	1943	—	1.00	2.00	6.00

8.8900 gm., .900 SILVER, .2572 oz ASW
1100th Anniversary Slavic Alphabet

Y#	Date	Mintage	VF	XF	Unc
60	1963	5,000	—	Proof	12.00

20th Anniversary People's Republic

Y#	Date	Mintage	VF	XF	Unc
64	1964	.010	—	Proof	10.00

COPPER-NICKEL
1050th Anniversary Death of Ochridsky

Y#	Date	Mintage	VF	XF	Unc
68	1966	.500	2.00	2.50	3.50

25th Anniversary of Socialist Revolution

Y#	Date	Mintage	VF	XF	Unc
70	1969	2.000	1.75	2.25	3.50

90th Anniversary Liberation From Turks

Y#	Date	Mintage	VF	XF	Unc
72	1969	—	1.75	2.25	3.50

NICKEL-BRASS
100th Anniversary of Birth of Dobri Chintu Lov

Y#	Date	Mintage	VF	XF	Unc
75	1972	—	1.75	2.25	3.50

COPPER-NICKEL

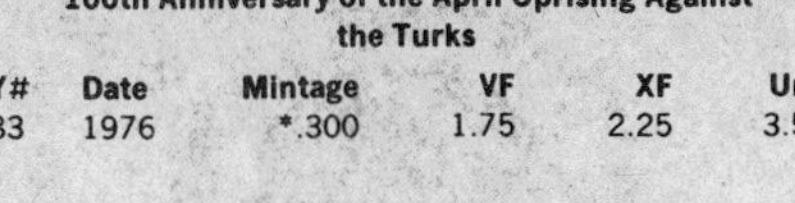

100th Anniversary of the April Uprising Against the Turks

Y#	Date	Mintage	VF	XF	Unc
83	1976	*.300	1.75	2.25	3.50

5 LEVA

25.0000 gm., .900 SILVER, .7234 oz ASW

Y#	Date	Mintage	VF	XF	Unc
7	1884	.512	22.50	27.50	40.00
	1885	1.426	25.00	30.00	50.00

Y#	Date	Mintage	VF	XF	Unc
15	1892	1.000	22.50	27.50	40.00

Obv. leg. rearranged.

Y#	Date	Mintage	VF	XF	Unc
15a	1894	1.800	22.50	27.50	40.00

COPPER-NICKEL

Y#	Date	Mintage	VF	XF	Unc
36	1930	20.001	1.00	1.75	3.00

IRON

Y#	Date	Mintage	VF	XF	Unc
36a	1941	15.000	4.00	7.50	15.00

NICKEL-CLAD STEEL

Y#	Date	Mintage	VF	XF	Unc
36b	1943	—	1.00	1.75	3.25

16.6700 gm., .900 SILVER, .4824 oz ASW
1100th Anniversary Slavic Alphabet

Y#	Date	Mintage	VF	XF	Unc
61	1963	5,000	—	Proof	20.00

20th Anniversary People's Republic

Y#	Date	Mintage	VF	XF	Unc
65	1964	.010	—	Proof	20.00

120th Anniversary Ivan Vazov

Y#	Date	Mintage	VF	XF	Unc
73	1970	—	—	7.00	10.00
	1970	—		Proof	18.50

Rakovski

Y#	Date	Mintage	VF	XF	Unc
74	1971	—	—	Proof	18.50

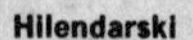

Hilendarski

Y#	Date	Mintage	VF	XF	Unc
76	1972	.200	—	Proof	15.00

Alexander Stamboliiski

Y#	Date	Mintage	VF	XF	Unc
79	1974	.200	—	Proof	15.00

20.5000 gm., .500 SILVER, .3295 oz ASW
100th Anniversary of the April Uprising Against the Turks

Y#	Date	Mintage	VF	XF	Unc
85	1976	.200	—	Proof	15.00

Levski

Y#	Date	Mintage	VF	XF	Unc
77	1973	—	—	Proof	18.50

30th Anniversary Socialist Revolution

Y#	Date	Mintage	VF	XF	Unc
80	1974	.200	—	Proof	18.50

Petko Slaveykov

Y#	Date	Mintage	VF	XF	Unc
87	1977	—	—	Proof	15.00

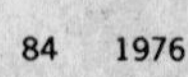

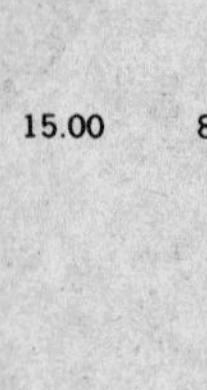

50th Anniversary Anti-Fascist Uprising

Y#	Date	Mintage	VF	XF	Unc
78	1973	.200	—	Proof	15.00

Khristo Botev

Y#	Date	Mintage	VF	XF	Unc
84	1976	—	—	Proof	15.00

Pelo Javoroff

Y#	Date	Mintage	VF	XF	Unc
88	1978	.200	—	Proof	15.00

100th Anniversary of National Library

Y#	Date	Mintage	VF	XF	Unc
90	1978	—	—	Proof	15.00

100th Anniversary of Communications Systems

Y#	Date	Mintage	VF	XF	Unc
91	1979	.035	—	—	—
	1979	.015	—	Proof	16.50

10 LEVA

3.2258 gm., .900 GOLD, .0933 oz AGW

Y#	Date	Mintage	VF	XF	Unc
21	1894KB	.075	100.00	125.00	150.00

COPPER-NICKEL

Y#	Date	Mintage	VF	XF	Unc
37	1930	15.001	.90	1.50	3.50

IRON

Y#	Date	Mintage	VF	XF	Unc
37a	1941	2.200	15.00	22.50	50.00

NICKEL-CLAD STEEL

Y#	Date	Mintage	VF	XF	Unc
37b	1943	—	1.50	3.00	7.50

8.4444 gm., .900 GOLD, .2443 oz AGW
1100th Anniversary Slavic Alphabet

Y#	Date	Mintage	VF	XF	Unc
62	1963	7,000	—	Proof	200.00

20th Anniversary People's Republic

Y#	Date	Mintage	VF	XF	Unc
66	1964	.010	—	Proof	175.00

30.1700 gm., .900 SILVER, .8730 oz ASW
10th Olympic Congress

Y#	Date	Mintage	VF	XF	Unc
81	1975 with edge inscription in Latin				
		.050	—	Proof	35.00
81a	1975 with edge inscription in Cyrillic				
		.050	—	Proof	35.00

30.1700 gm., .500 SILVER, .4850 oz ASW
100th Anniversary Liberation from Turks

Y#	Date	Mintage	VF	XF	Unc
89	1978	.200	BV	15.00	17.50
	1978	—	—	Proof	30.00

20 LEVA

6.4516 gm., .900 GOLD, .1867 oz AGW

Y#	Date	Mintage	VF	XF	Unc
22	1894KB	.175	150.00	175.00	200.00

25th Year Jubilee

Y#	Date	Mintage	VF	XF	Unc
30	1912	.075	—	Proof	250.00

4.0000 gm., .500 SILVER, .0643 oz ASW

Y#	Date	Mintage	VF	XF	Unc
38	1930BP	10.008	2.25	3.50	6.00

COPPER-NICKEL

Y#	Date	Mintage	VF	XF	Unc
42	1940A	—	1.00	1.75	2.75

16.8889 gm., .900 GOLD, .4887 oz AGW
1100th Anniversary Slavic Alphabet

Y#	Date	Mintage	VF	XF	Unc
63	1963	3,000	—	Proof	350.00

20th Anniversary People's Republic

Y#	Date	Mintage	VF	XF	Unc
67	1964	5,000	—	Proof	340.00

32.0000 gm., .900 SILVER, .9260 oz ASW

Centennial of Sophia as Capital

Y#	Date	Mintage	VF	XF	Unc
92	1979	5,000	—	Proof	—

50 LEVA

10.0000 gm., .500 SILVER, .1607 oz ASW

39	1930BP	9.029	5.00	6.00	7.50

Similar to 100 Leva, Y#45

44	1934	3.000	5.00	6.50	8.50

COPPER-NICKEL

43	1940A	4.000	1.50	2.00	4.00

NICKEL-CLAD STEEL

43a	1943A	—	2.00	3.50	6.00

100 LEVA

32.2580 gm., .900 GOLD, .9334 oz AGW

23	1894KB	2.502	650.00	800.00	1000.

25th Year Jubilee

31	1912	5,000	—	Proof	1250.

20.0000 gm., .500 SILVER, .3215 oz ASW

Y#	Date	Mintage	VF	XF	Unc
40	1930BP	1.556	BV	11.00	17.50

45	1934	2.500	BV	10.00	14.00
	1937	2.200	BV	10.00	14.00

TRADE COINS

4 DUKAT

13.9600 gm., .900 GOLD, .4039 oz AGW
c/s: Crown and government mark

Fr#	Date	Mintage	VF	XF	Unc
7	1910	—	BV	275.00	350.00
	1911	—	BV	300.00	375.00
	1912	—	BV	275.00	350.00
	1914	—	BV	600.00	700.00

Fr#	Date	Mintage	VF	XF	Unc
7	1918	—	BV	300.00	375.00

Obv: Uniformed bust left. Rev: Coat of arms.
c/s: Crown and government mark

8	1926	—	300.00	425.00	525.00

NOTE: Values above are for holed or holed and plugged specimens. Unholed specimens are rare.

NCLT ISSUES

PATTERNS

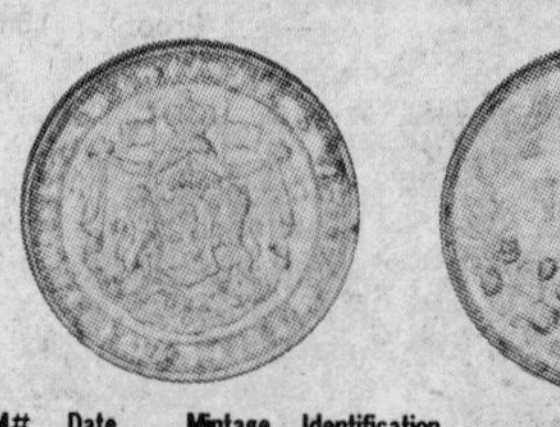
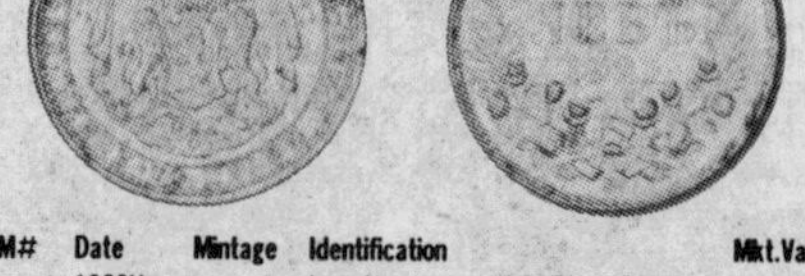

KM#	Date	Mintage	Identification	Mkt.Val.
1	1923H	—	Lev, Aluminum	—

2	1923H	—	2 Lev, Aluminum	—

PROOF SETS

STANDARD METALS

KM#	Date	Mintage	Identification	Issue Price	Mkt. Val.
101	1912(2)	5,000	Y30,31	—	1500.
102	1963(2)	5,000	Y60,61	—	32.00
103	1964(2)	10,000	Y64,65	—	30.00
104	1979(7)	2,000	Y53a-59a	—	—

BURMA

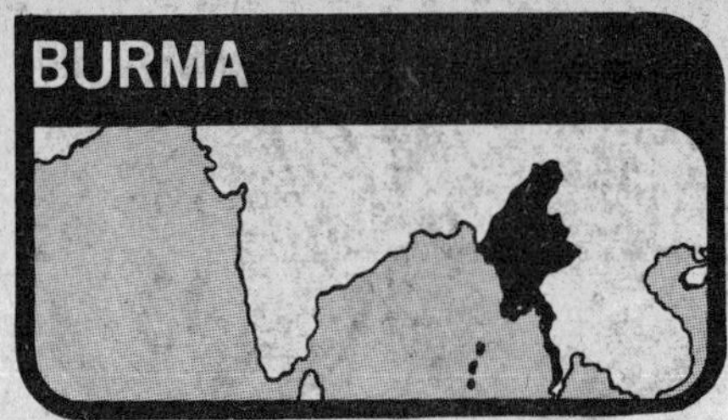

The Socialist Republic of the Union of Burma, a country of Southeast Asia fronting on the Bay of Bengal and the Andaman Sea, has an area of 262,000 sq. mi. (678,576 sq. km.) and a population of 31.9 million. Capital: Rangoon. Burma is an agricultural country heavily dependent on its leading product (rice) which occupies two-thirds of the cultivated area and accounts for 40 per cent of the value of exports. Mineral resources are extensive, but production is low. Petroleum, lead, tin, silver, zinc, nickel cobalt, and precious stones are exported.

The first European to reach Burma, about 1435, was Nicolo Di Conti, a merchant of Venice. During the beginning of the reign of Bodawpaya (1781-1819AD) the kingdom comprised most of the same area as it does today including Arakan which was taken over in 1784-85. The British East India Company, while unsuccessful in its 1612 effort to establish posts along the Bay of Bengal, was enabled by the Anglo-Burmese Wars of 1824-86 to expand to the whole of Burma and to secure its annexation to British India. In 1937, Burma was separated from India, becoming a separate British colony with limited self-government. Burma became an independent nation outside the British Commonwealth on Jan. 4, 1948, the constitution of 1948 providing for a parliamentary democracy and the nationalization of certain industries. However, political and economic problems persisted, and on March 2, 1962, Gen. Ne Win took over the government, suspended the constitution, installed himself as chief of state, and pursued a socialistic program with nationalization of nearly all industry and trade. On Jan. 4, 1974, a new constitution adopted by referendum established Burma as a 'socialist republic' under one-party rule.

The coins issued by kings Mindon and Thibaw between 1852 and 1885 circulated in Upper Burma. Indian coins were current in Lower Burma, which was annexed in 1852. Burmese coins are frequently known by the equivalent Indian denominations, although their values are inscribed in Burmese units. Upper Burma was annexed in 1885 and the Burmese coinage remained in circulation until 1889, when Indian coins became current throughout Burma. Coins were again issued in the old Burmese denominations after independence in 1948, but these were replaced by decimal issues in 1952. The Chula-Sakarat (CS) dating began in 638 AD.

RULERS

Bodawpaya, BE1143-1181
1782-1819AD
Bagyidaw, BE1181-1198
1819-1837AD
Tharawaddy, BE1198-1207 = 1837-46AD
Pagan, BE1207-1214 = 1846-53AD
Mindon, BE1214-1240 = 1853-78AD
Thibaw, BE1240-1248 = 1880-85AD

MONETARY SYSTEM

(Until 1952)

4 Pyas = 1 Pe
2 Pe = 1 Mu
2 Mu = 1 Mat
5 Mat = 1 Kyat

NOTE: Originally 10 light Mu = 1 Kyat but later on 8 heavy Mu = 1 Kyat.

Indian Equivalents

1 Silver Kyat = 1 Rupee = 16 Annas
1 Gold Kyat = 1 Mohur = 16 Rupees

ARAKAN

A coastal region of Burma on the Bay of Bengal. The Buddhist Arakanese trace their history back 4500 years.

Arakan surrendered to the Burmese King Bodawpaya in 1784 and coins were issued by the king's governor in Arakan, bearing the following inscription "Amarapura, Kingdom of the Lord of Many White Elephants".

Thaditha Dhammarit Raja
AD1777-1782

RUPEE

SILVER, 29mm

C#	Date	Year	Good	VG	Fine	VF
10	CS1140	(1778)	20.00	30.00	42.50	55.00

Maha Thamada Raja
AD1782-1784

RUPEE

SILVER

C#	Date	Year	Good	VG	Fine	VF
15	CS1144	(1782)	25.00	35.00	50.00	75.00

Amarapura Lord (Bodawpaya)
AD1784

RUPEE

SILVER, 33mm, 9.98 gm.
Reverse as Obverse

C#	Date	Year	Good	VG	Fine	VF
20	CS1146	(1784)	30.00	50.00	75.00	100.00

35mm, 9.87 gm.
Reverse as Obverse

C#	Date	Year	Good	VG	Fine	VF
21	CS1146	(1784)	30.00	50.00	75.00	100.00

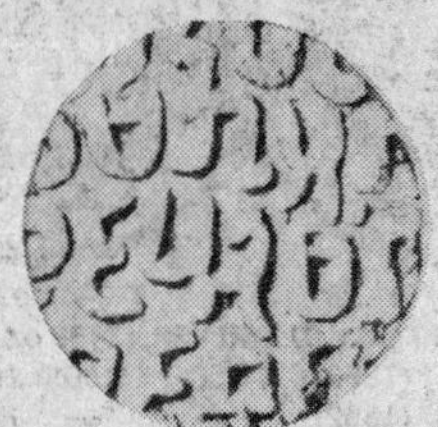

Reverse as Obverse

C#	Date	Year	Good	VG	Fine	VF
22	CS1146	(1784)	25.00	35.00	50.00	75.00

GOLD, 27mm, 10.11 gm.
Reverse as Obverse

C#	Date	Year	Good	VG	Fine	VF
30	CS1146	(1784)	—	—	Rare	—

BURMA

1/8 PYA

LEAD, 20-21mm

Y#	Date	Year	Good	VG	Fine	VF
C1	CS1231	(1869)	17.50	27.50	45.00	75.00

1/4 PYA

LEAD, 21-22mm
Obv: Hare crouching left. Rev: Legends in wreath.

Y#	Date	Year	Good	VG	Fine	VF
D1	CS1231	(1869)	15.00	25.00	35.00	60.00

1/2 PYA (1/2 PICE)

COPPER, 22mm
Obv: 2 fish. Rev: Burmese legends.

Y#	Date	Year	Good	VG	Fine	VF
E1	BE1143	(1782)	25.00	40.00	60.00	85.00

1/4 PE (1 PICE)

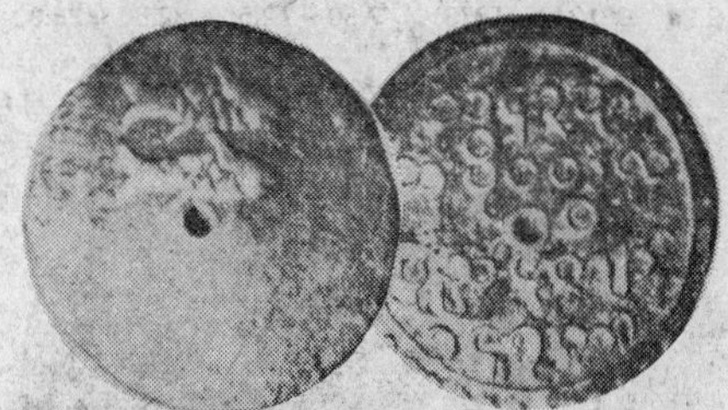

COPPER, 31-32mm
With center hole.

Y#	Date	Year	Good	VG	Fine	VF
F1	BE1143	(1782)	30.00	50.00	70.00	100.00

Without hole

Y#	Date	Year	Good	VG	Fine	VF
F1.1	BE1143	(1782)	30.00	50.00	70.00	100.00

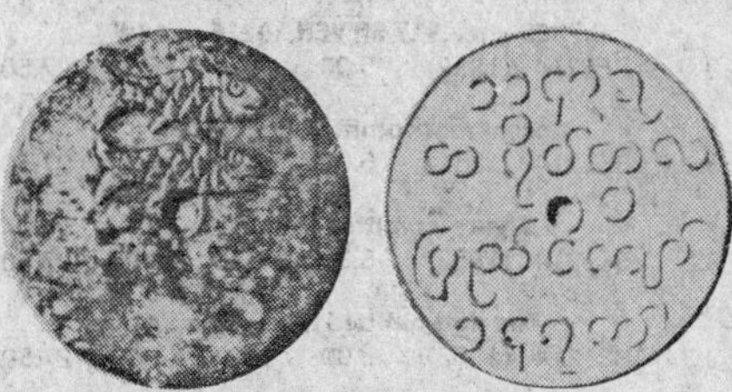

With center hole, 27-28mm.

Y#	Date	Year	Good	VG	Fine	VF
G1	BE1143	(1782)	25.00	40.00	60.00	85.00

Without hole

Y#	Date	Year	Good	VG	Fine	VF
G1.1	BE1143	(1782)	25.00	40.00	60.00	85.00

Y#	Date	Year	Good	VG	Fine	VF
1	BE1227	(1865)	2.50	4.50	7.50	13.50

Rev: W/o stars above and below legend.

Y#	Date	Year	Good	VG	Fine	VF
1.1	BE1227	(1865)	—	—	—	—

IRON

Y#	Date	Year	Good	VG	Fine	VF
1a	BE1227	(1865)	22.50	35.00	55.00	85.00

COPPER
Rev: Flower petals at top of wreath upright.

Y#	Date	Year	Good	VG	Fine	VF
9	BE1240	(1878)	2.50	4.50	7.50	13.50

Rev: Flower petals at top of wreath diagonal.

Y#	Date	Year	Good	VG	Fine	VF
9.1	BE1240	(1878)	6.00	10.00	17.50	25.00

BRASS

Y#	Date	Year	Good	VG	Fine	VF
9.2a	BE1240	(1878)	7.50	12.50	22.50	35.00

2 PYAS

COPPER

Y#	Date	Year	Good	VG	Fine	VF
2	BE1231	(1869)	17.50	30.00	50.00	75.00

PE

0.7300 gm., .917 SILVER, .0215 oz ASW

Y#	Date	Year	Good	VG	Fine	VF
3	BE1214	(1852)	5.00	8.50	15.00	27.50

Accent mark omitted from value.

Y#	Date	Year	Good	VG	Fine	VF
3.1	BE1214	(1852)	5.00	8.50	15.00	27.50

Figure J omitted from date.

Y#	Date	Year	Good	VG	Fine	VF
3.2	BE1214	(1852)	5.00	8.50	15.00	27.50

Two dots omitted from value.

Y#	Date	Year	Good	VG	Fine	VF
3.3	BE1214	(1852)	5.00	8.50	15.00	27.50

Accent marks and two dots omitted.

Y#	Date	Year	Good	VG	Fine	VF
3.4	BE1214	(1852)	5.00	8.50	15.00	27.50

MU

1.4600 gm., .917 SILVER, .0430 oz ASW

Y#	Date	Year	Good	VG	Fine	VF
4	BE1214	(1852)	5.00	8.50	13.50	22.50
	1214	(1852)	—	—	Proof	—

MAT

SILVER, 17mm, 3.45 gm.

Y#	Date	Year	Good	VG	Fine	VF
H1	ND	(1797)	30.00	50.00	70.00	100.00

2.9200 gm., .917 SILVER, .0860 oz ASW

Y#	Date	Year	Good	VG	Fine	VF
5	BE1214	(1852)	5.00	8.50	13.50	20.00
	1214	(1852)	—	—	Proof	—

Tail omitted from last digit of date.

Y#	Date	Year	Good	VG	Fine	VF
5.1	BE1214	(1852)	5.00	8.50	13.50	20.00

5 MU (= 1/2 Rupee)

5.8300 gm., .917 SILVER, .1719 oz ASW

Y#	Date	Year	Good	VG	Fine	VF
6	BE1214	(1852)	6.00	8.50	11.50	17.50
	BE1214	(1852)	—	—	Proof	—

KYAT (= 1 Rupee)

SILVER, 30mm, 9.98 gm.

Y#	Date	Year	Good	VG	Fine	VF
J1	ND	(1797)	—	100.00	140.00	200.00

11.6600 gm., .917 SILVER, .3438 oz ASW

Y#	Date	Year	Good	VG	Fine	VF
7	BE1214	(1852)	11.50	13.50	16.50	21.50
	BE1214	(1852)	—	—	Proof	—

GOLD

Y#	Date	Year	Good	VG	Fine	VF
7a	BE1214	(1852) restrike	Reported, not confirmed			

SILVER, 29.5 mm, 16.23 gm.
Obv: Peacock with spread tail, flanked by two groups of 5 rosettes.

Y#	Date	Year	Good	VG	Fine	VF
A7	BE1214	(1852)	—	—	—	—

SILVER, 39mm, 16.45 gm.
Obv: Shwepyizoe bird. Rev: Legend over date.

Y#	Date	Year	Good	VG	Fine	VF
B7	NE2396	(1853)	—	—	—	—

SILVER, 32mm, 15.75 gm.
Obv: Peacock with folded tail flanked by floral garlands.

Y#	Date	Year	Good	VG	Fine	VF
C7	BE1222	(1860)	—	—	—	—

PE

.900 GOLD
Obv: Facing peacock. Rev: Value in wreath.

Y#	Date	Year	Good	VG	Fine	VF
10	BE1214	(1852)	35.00	60.00	85.00	125.00

GOLD, 67 gm.

Y#	Date	Year	Good	VG	Fine	VF
A8	BE1228	(1866)	35.00	60.00	85.00	125.00

MU

.900 GOLD
Obv: Facing peacock. Rev: Value in wreath.

Y#	Date	Year	Good	VG	Fine	VF
11	BE1214	(1852)	60.00	100.00	150.00	200.00

2 MU 1 PE

GOLD, 2.75 gm.

Y#	Date	Year	Good	VG	Fine	VF
8	BE1228	(1866)	75.00	125.00	175.00	235.00

5 MU (= 1/2 Mohur)

GOLD, 5.85 gm.

Y#	Date	Year	Good	VG	Fine	VF
C8	BE1240	(1878)	75.00	125.00	150.00	200.00

KYAT (= 1 Mohur)

GOLD, 11.94 gm.

Y#	Date	Year	Good	VG	Fine	VF
B8	BE1228	(1866)	225.00	350.00	450.00	600.00

REPUBLIC ISSUES

2 PYAS

COPPER-NICKEL

Y#	Date	Mintage	Fine	VF	XF	Unc
13	1949	7.000	.25	.50	1.00	2.00
	1949	100 pcs.	—	—	Proof	100.00

PE

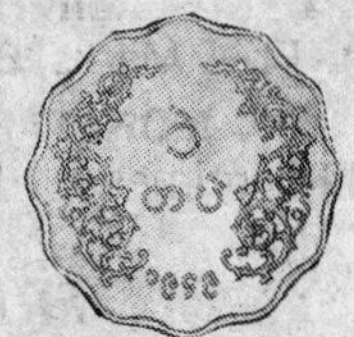

COPPER-NICKEL

Y#	Date	Mintage	Fine	VF	XF	Unc
14	1949	8.000	.35	.75	1.50	3.00
	1949	100 pcs.	—	—	Proof	100.00
	1950	9.500	.35	.75	1.50	3.00
	1951	6.500	.50	1.00	2.00	4.00

2 PE

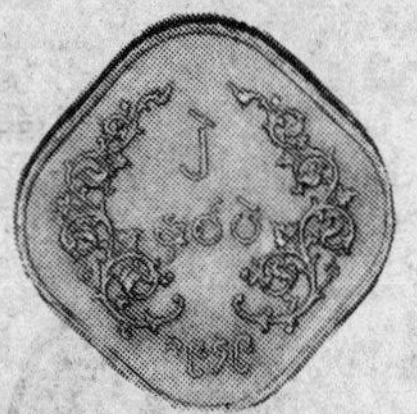

COPPER-NICKEL

Y#	Date	Mintage	Fine	VF	XF	Unc
15	1949	7.100	.50	1.00	2.00	4.00
	1949	100 pcs.	—	—	Proof	100.00
	1950	8.500	.50	1.00	2.00	4.00
	1951	7.480	.50	1.00	2.00	4.00

4 PE

NICKEL

Y#	Date	Mintage	Fine	VF	XF	Unc
16	1949	6.500	1.25	2.50	5.00	10.00
	1949	100 pcs.	—	—	Proof	100.00
	1950	6.120	1.00	2.00	4.00	8.00

8 PE

NICKEL

Y#	Date	Mintage	Fine	VF	XF	Unc
17	1949	3.270	1.50	3.00	6.00	12.00
	1949	100 pcs.	—	—	Proof	100.00
	1950	3.900	1.25	2.50	5.00	10.00

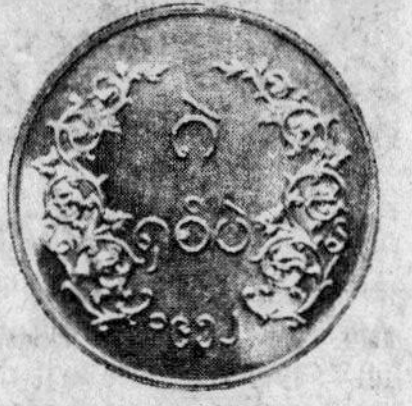

COPPER-NICKEL
Obv: Similar to 50 Pyas, Y#22.

Y#	Date	Year	Fine	VF	XF	Unc
17a	Be1314	(1952)	50.00	100.00	150.00	200.00

DECIMAL COINAGE

100 Pyas = 1 Kyat

PYA

BRONZE

Y#	Date	Mintage	Fine	VF	XF	Unc
18	1952	.500	.10	.15	.20	.35
	1952	100 pcs.	—	—	Proof	60.00
	1953	14.000	.10	.15	.20	.35
	1955	30.000	.10	.15	.20	.35
	1955	—	—	—	Proof	—
	1962	—	—	—	Proof	50.00
	1965	7.000	.10	.15	.20	.35
	1966	8.000	.10	.15	.20	.35

ALUMINUM

Y#	Date	Mintage	Fine	VF	XF	Unc
24	1966	8.000	.10	.15	.25	.50
	1970	—Reported, Not Confirmed				

5 PYAS

COPPER-NICKEL

Y#	Date	Mintage	Fine	VF	XF	Unc
19	1952	20.000	.10	.15	.25	.50
	1952	100 pcs.	—	—	Proof	65.00
	1953	59.700	.10	.15	.35	.50
	1953	—	—	—	Proof	—
	1955	40.200	.10	.15	.25	.50
	1956	20.000	.10	.15	.25	.50
	1961	12.000	.10	.15	.25	.50
	1962	10.000	.10	.15	.25	.50
	1962	—	—	—	Proof	55.00
	1963	40.400	.10	.15	.25	.50
	1965	43.600	.10	.15	.20	.30
	1966	20.000	.10	.15	.20	.30

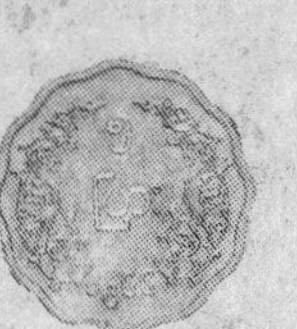

ALUMINUM

Y#	Date	Mintage	Fine	VF	XF	Unc
25	1966	20.000	.10	.20	.35	.60
	1970	—	Reported, not confirmed			

10 PYAS

COPPER-NICKEL

Y#	Date	Mintage	Fine	VF	XF	Unc
20	1952	20.000	.10	.25	.35	.60
	1952	100 pcs.	—	—	Proof	70.00
	1953	37.000	.10	.25	.35	.60
	1955	22.750	.10	.25	.35	.60
	1956	35.000	.10	.25	.35	.75
	1956	35.000	.10	.15	.35	.75
	1962	—	—	—	Proof	60.00
	1963	21.500	.10	.15	.35	.60
	1965	32.620	.10	.15	.35	.60

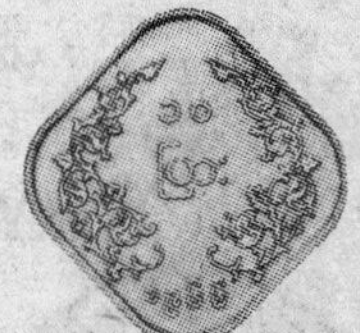

ALUMINUM

Y#	Date	Mintage	Fine	VF	XF	Unc
26	1966	—	—	.30	.50	1.00
	1970	—	Reported, not confirmed			

25 PYAS

COPPER-NICKEL

Y#	Date	Mintage	Fine	VF	XF	Unc
21	1952	13.540	.10	.20	.50	1.00
	1952	100 pcs.	—	—	Proof	75.00
	1953	Inc. Ab.	.10	.20	.50	1.00
	1954	18.000	.10	.20	.50	1.00
	1955	—	—	—	Proof	75.00
	1956	14.000	.10	.20	.50	1.00
	1959	6.000	.10	.20	.50	1.00
	1961	4.000	.10	.20	.50	1.00
	1962	3.200	.10	.20	.50	1.00
	1962	—	—	—	Proof	65.00
	1963	16.000	.10	.15	.30	.60
	1965	26.000	.10	.15	.30	.60

ALUMINUM

Y#	Date	Mintage	Fine	VF	XF	Unc
27	1966	—	.10	.20	.50	1.00
	1970	—	Reported, not confirmed			

F.A.O. Issue

Y#	Date	Mintage	Fine	VF	XF	Unc
—	1976	—	Reported, not confirmed			

50 PYAS

COPPER-NICKEL

Y#	Date	Mintage	Fine	VF	XF	Unc
22	1952	4.140	.20	.50	.75	1.50
	1952	100 pcs.	—	—	Proof	80.00
	1954	12.000	.20	.50	.75	1.50
	1954	—	—	—	Proof	—
	1956	8.000	.20	.50	.75	1.50
	1961	2.000	.15	.40	.75	1.50
	1962	.600	.25	.75	1.25	2.25
	1962	—	—	—	Proof	70.00
	1963	4.800	.20	.50	.75	1.50
	1965	2.800	.15	.40	.75	1.50
	1966	3.400	.10	.30	.75	1.50

ALUMINUM

Y#	Date	Mintage	Fine	VF	XF	Unc
28	1966	—	.15	.35	1.00	2.00
	1970	—	Reported, not confirmed			

F.A.O. Issue

Y#	Date	Mintage	Fine	VF	XF	Unc
—	1976	—	Reported, not confirmed			

KYAT

COPPER-NICKEL

Y#	Date	Mintage	VF	XF	Unc	
23	1952	2.500	.35	.75	1.50	
	1952	100 pcs.	—	—	Proof	85.00
	1953	7.500	.35	.75	1.50	3.00
	1956	3.500	.35	.75	1.50	3.00
	1962	—	—	—	Proof	75.00
	1963	—	Reported, not confirmed			
	1964	1.000	Reported, not confirmed			
	1965	1.000	.35	.75	1.50	3.00
	1970	—	Reported, not confirmed			

F.A.O. Issue

Y#	Date	Mintage	Fine	VF	XF	Unc
34	1975	20.000	.25	.50	1.00	2.00

UNION OF BURMA

(Government In Exile)

MU

GOLD, 2 gm.
Obv: 'UNION OF BURMA GOVERNMENT 1970-1971' around peacock. Rev: 'SHWE MUZI'.

Y#	Date	Mintage	VF	XF	Unc
29	1971	—	—	50.00	60.00

2 MU

GOLD, 4 gm.
Similar to Mu, Y#29

Y#	Date	Mintage	VF	XF	Unc
30	1971	—	—	100.00	120.00

4 MU

GOLD, 8 gm.
Similar to Mu, Y#29

Y#	Date	Mintage	VF	XF	Unc
31	1971	—	Reported, not confirmed		

NCLT ISSUES

PROOF SETS

STANDARD METALS

KM#	Date	Mintage	Identification	Issue Price	Mkt. Val.
101	1949(5)	100	Y13-17	—	450.00
102	1952(6)	100	Y18-23	—	400.00
103	1956(6)	100	Y18-23	—	350.00

BURUNDI

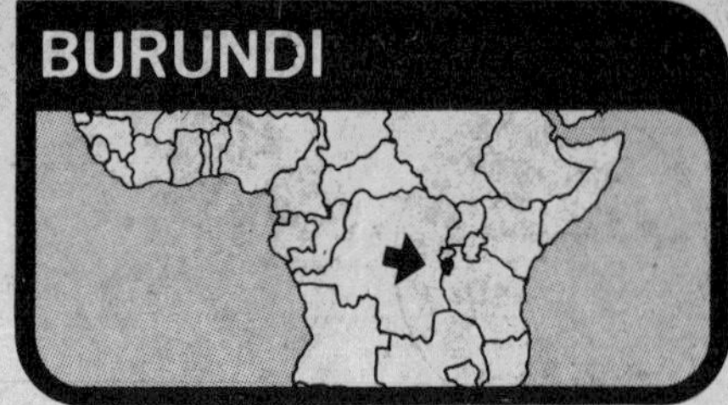

The Republic of Burundi, a landlocked country in central Africa, was a kingdom with a feudalistic society, caste system and Mwami (king) for more than 400 years before independence. It has an area of 10,747 sq. mi. (27,834 sq. km.) and a population of 3.9 million. Capital: Bujumbura. Plagued by poor soil, irregular rainfall and a single-crop economy -coffee- Burundi is barely able to feed itself. Coffee and tea are exported.

Although the area was visited by European explorers and missionaries in the latter half of the 19th century, it wasn't until the 1890s that it, together with Rwanda, fell under European domination as part of German East Africa. Following World War I, the territory was mandated to Belgium by the League of Nations and administered with the Belgian Congo. After World War II it became a U.N. Trust Territory. Limited self-government was established by U.N.-supervised elections in 1961. Burundi gained independence as a kingdom under Mwami Mwambutsa IV on July 1, 1962. The republic was established by military coup in 1966.

NOTE: For earlier coinage see Belgian Congo, and Rwanda and Burundi.

RULERS

Mwambutsa IV, 1962-1966
Ntare V, 1966

MINTMARKS

(b) - Privy Marks, Brussels

MONETARY SYSTEM

100 Centimes = 1 Franc

FRANC

BRASS

Y#	Date	Mintage	VF	XF	Unc
1	1965	10.000	.15	.35	.75

ALUMINUM

Y#	Date	Mintage	VF	XF	Unc
A2	1970	10.000	.20	.35	.75

Y#	Date	Mintage	VF	XF	Unc
4	1976	5.000	—	—	—

5 FRANCS

COPPER-NICKEL
Mwambutsa IV

KM#	Date	Mintage	VF	XF	Unc
1	1962	—	—	—	—
	1962	—	—	Proof	—

ALUMINUM

Y#	Date	Mintage	VF	XF	Unc
2	1968(b)	2.000	.25	.60	1.00
	1969(b)	2.000	.25	.60	1.00
	1970	2.000	.25	.60	1.25
	1971(b)	2.000	.25	.60	1.00
	1976	2.000	—	—	—

10 FRANCS

COPPER-NICKEL
F.A.O. Issue

Y#	Date	Mintage	VF	XF	Unc
3	1968	2.000	.40	.85	1.25
	1971	2.000	.35	.75	1.25

3.2000 gm., .900 GOLD, .0926 oz AGW

Fr#	Date	Mintage	VF	XF	Unc
4	1962	7,500	—	Proof	75.00
	3.0000 gm., .900 GOLD, .0868 oz AGW				
8	1965	—	BV	65.00	70.00
	1965	5,000	—	Proof	100.00
	Micombero Commemorative				
13	1967	—	BV	65.00	70.00

20 FRANCS

.900 GOLD
Micombero Commemorative

Fr#	Date	Mintage	VF	XF	Unc
12	1967	—	BV	140.00	150.00

25 FRANCS

8.0000 gm., .900 GOLD, .2315 oz AGW

Fr#	Date	Mintage	VF	XF	Unc
3	1962	15,000	—	Proof	175.00
	7.5000 gm., .900 GOLD, .2170 oz AGW				
7	1965	—	BV	150.00	160.00
	1965	5,000	—	Proof	175.00
	Micombero Commemorative				
11	1967	—	BV	150.00	170.00

50 FRANCS

16.0000 gm., .900 GOLD, .4630 oz AGW

Fr#	Date	Mintage	VF	XF	Unc
2	1962	3,500	—	Proof	325.00
	15.0000 gm., .900 GOLD, .4340 oz AGW				
6	1965	—	BV	300.00	315.00
	1965	5,000	—	Proof	325.00
	Micombero Commemorative				
10	1967	—	BV	300.00	325.00

100 FRANCS

32.0000 gm., .900 GOLD, .9260 oz AGW

Fr#	Date	Mintage	VF	XF	Unc
1	1962	2,500	—	Proof	650.00

30.0000 gm., .900 GOLD, .8681 oz AGW

Fr#	Date	Mintage	VF	XF	Unc
5	1965	—	BV	575.00	600.00
	1965	5,000	—	Proof	625.00

Ntare V

Fr#	Date	Mintage	VF	XF	Unc
2	1966	—	—	—	—
	Micombero Commemorative				
9	1967	—	BV	575.00	600.00

500 FRANCS

SILVER
Mwambutsa IV

KM#	Date	Mintage	VF	XF	Unc
3	1966	—	BV	15.00	20.00

Ntare V

KM#	Date	Mintage	VF	XF	Unc
4	1966	—	BV	15.00	20.00

NCLT ISSUES

PROOF SETS

STANDARD METALS

KM#	Date	Mintage	Identification	Issue Price	Mkt. Val.
101	1962(4)	2,500	Fr1-4	—	1275.
102	1965(4)	5,000	Fr5-8	—	1200.

Listings For
CAMBODIA: refer to Kampuchia

CAMEROON

The United Republic of Cameroon, located in west-central Africa on the Gulf of Guinea, has an area of 183,568 sq. mi. (475,439 sq. km.) and a population of 7.6 million. Capital: Yaounde. About 90 per cent of the labor force is employed on the land; cash crops account for 80 per cent of the country's export revenue. Cocoa, coffee, aluminum, cotton, rubber, and timber are exported.

European contact with what is now the United Republic of Cameroon began in the 16th century with the voyage of Portuguese navigator Fernando Po. The following three centuries saw continuous activity by Spanish, Dutch, and British traders and missionaries. The land was spared colonial rule until 1884, when treaties with tribal chiefs brought German domination. In 1919, the League of Nations divided the Cameroons between Great Britain and France, with the larger eastern area going to France. The French and British mandates were converted into United Nations trusteeships in 1946. French Cameroon became the independent Cameroon Republic on Jan. 1, 1960. The federation of East (French) and West (British) Cameroon was established in 1961 when the southern part of British Cameroon voted for reunification with the Cameroon Republic, and the northern part for union with Nigeria.

Coins of French Equatorial Africa and of the monetary unions identified as the Equatorial African States and Central African States are also current in Cameroon.

MONETARY SYSTEM

100 Centimes = 1 Franc

MINTMARKS

(a) - Paris, privy marks only
SA - Pretoria, 1943

50 CENTIMES

ALUMINUM-BRONZE

Y#	Date	Mintage	Fine	VF	XF
1	1924(a)	4.000	1.00	1.50	4.00
	1925(a)	2.500	1.00	1.75	5.50
	1926(a)	7.800	1.00	1.50	4.00

BRONZE

Y#	Date	Mintage	VF	XF	Unc
4	1943	4.000	1.00	3.00	10.00

Obv. leg: LIBRE added

Y#	Date	Mintage	VF	XF	Unc
6	1943	4.000	4.50	8.00	15.00

FRANC

ALUMINUM-BRONZE

Y#	Date	Mintage	Fine	VF	XF
2	1924(a)	3.000	1.50	3.00	7.50
	1925(a)	1.722	2.75	5.00	10.00
	1926(a)	11.928	1.25	2.50	6.00

BRONZE

Y#	Date	Mintage	VF	XF	Unc
5	1943	3.000	5.00	10.00	20.00

Obv. leg: LIBRE added

Y#	Date	Mintage	VF	XF	Unc
7	1943	3.000	5.00	15.00	25.00

ALUMINUM

Y#	Date	Mintage	VF	XF	Unc
8	1948(a)	8.000	.25	.75	1.75

2 FRANCS

ALUMINUM-BRONZE

Y#	Date	Mintage	Fine	VF	XF
3	1924(a)	.500	2.00	5.00	10.00
	1925(a)	.100'	3.00	6.00	14.00

ALUMINUM

Y#	Date	Mintage	VF	XF	Unc
9	1948(a)	5.000	.30	.90	2.00

50 FRANCS

COPPER-NICKEL
Independence Commemorative

Y#	Date	Mintage	VF	XF	Unc
13	1960(a)	1.154	1.50	2.75	6.50

100 FRANCS

NICKEL

Y#	Date	Mintage	VF	XF	Unc
14	1966(a)	9.950	1.50	2.25	6.00
	1967(a)	10.000	1.50	2.25	6.00
	1968(a)	11.000	1.50	2.25	6.00

NOTE: Y#14 was issued double thick and should not be considered a Piefort.

Y#	Date	Mintage	VF	XF	Unc
15	1971(a)	15.000	1.25	1.75	3.25
	1972(a)	20.000	1.00	1.25	2.50

NOTE: For earlier issues of similar coinage with 'Cameroun' in the legends see French Equatorial Africa. Refer also to Equatorial African States and Central African States.

Mule. Obv: Y#16 with Rev: Y#15

Y#	Date	Mintage	VF	XF	Unc
15a	1972(a)	—	1.00	2.00	3.00

Y#	Date	Mintage	VF	XF	Unc
16	1975(a)	—	.75	1.00	2.00

1000 FRANCS

3.5000 gm., .900 GOLD, .1012 oz AGW
10th Anniversary of Independence

Fr#	Date	Mintage	XF	Unc	Proof
5	1970	4,000	—	—	85.00

3000 FRANCS

10.5000 gm., .900 GOLD, .3038 oz AGW
10th Anniversary of Independence

Fr#	Date	Mintage	XF	Unc	Proof
4	1970	4,000	—	—	225.00

5000 FRANCS

17.5000 gm., .900 GOLD, .5064 oz AGW
10th Anniversary of Independence

Fr#	Date	Mintage	XF	Unc	Proof
3	1970	4,000	—	—	375.00

10,000 FRANCS

35.0000 gm., .900 GOLD, 1.0128 oz AGW
10th Anniversary of Independence

Fr#	Date	Mintage	XF	Unc	Proof
2	1970	4,000	—	—	750.00

20,000 FRANCS

70.0000 gm., .900 GOLD, 2.0257 oz AGW
10th Anniversary of Independence

Fr#	Date	Mintage	XF	Unc	Proof
1	1970	4,000	—	—	1500.

NCLT ISSUES

ESSAIS (E)

Standard metals unless otherwise noted

Y#	Date	Mintage	Identification	Issue Price	Mkt Val.
E1	1924(a)	—	50 Centimes	—	100.00
E2	1924(a)	—	1 Franc	—	110.00

Y#	Date	Mintage	Identification	Issue Price	Mkt Val.
E3	1924(a)	—	2 Francs	—	120.00
E8	1948(a)	2,000	1 Franc, Copper-Nickel	—	15.00
E9	1948(a)	2,000	2 Francs, Copper-Nickel	—	15.00
E13	1960(a)	1,500	50 Francs	—	25.00
E14	1966(a)	—	100 Francs	—	35.00
E Fr5	1970(a)	—	1000 Francs, Bronze	—	—
E15	1971(a)	—	100 Francs	—	30.00
E15a	1972(a)	—	100 Francs	—	25.00
E16	1972(a)	—	100 Francs	—	20.00

PIEFORTS with ESSAI (PE)

(DOUBLE THICKNESS)

Standard metals unless otherwise noted

Y#	Date	Mintage	Identification	Issue Price	Mkt Val.
PE8	1948(a)	104	1 Franc	—	100.00
PE9	1948(a)	104	2 Francs	—	110.00

PROOF SETS

STANDARD METALS

KM#	Date	Mintage	Identification	Issue Price	Mkt. Val.
101	1970(5)	4,000	Fr1-5	—	2750.

CANADA

Jacques Cartier, a French explorer, took possession of Canada for France in 1534, and for more than a century the history of Canada was that of a French colony. Samuel de Champlain helped to establish the first permanent French colony in North America, in 1604 at Port Royal, Acadia - now Annapolis Royal, Nova Scotia. Four years later he founded the settlement of Quebec.

The British settled along the coast to the south while the French, motivated by a grand design, pushed into the interior. France's plan for a great American empire was to occupy the Mississippi heartland of the country, and from there to press in upon the narrow strip of English coastal settlements from the rear. Inevitably, armed conflict erupted between the French and the British, as a consequence of which Britain acquired Hudson Bay, Newfoundland, and Nova Scotia from the French in 1713. British control of the rest of New France was secured in 1763, largely because of James Wolfe's great victory over Montcalm near Quebec in 1759.

During the American Revolution, Canada became a refuge for great numbers of American loyalists, most of whom settled in Ontario, thereby creating an English majority west of the Ottawa River. This ethnic imbalance contravened the effectiveness of the prevailing French type of government, and in 1791 the Constitutional act was passed by the British parliament, dividing Canada at the Ottawa River into two parts, each with its own government: Upper Canada, chiefly English and consisting of the southern section of what is now Ontario; and Lower Canada, chiefly French and consisting principally of the southern section of Quebec. Subsequent revolt by dissidents in both sections caused the British government to pass the Union act, July 23, 1840, which united Lower and Upper Canada (as Canada East and Canada West) to form the Province of Canada, with one council and one assembly in which the two sections had equal numbers.

The union of the two provinces did not encourage political stability; the equal strength of the French and British made the task of government all but impossible. A further change was made with the passage of the British North American act, which took effect on July 1, 1867, and established Canada as the first federal union in the British Empire. Four provinces entered the union at first: Upper Canada as Ontario, Lower Canada as Quebec, Nova Scotia and New Brunswick. The Hudson's Bay Company's territories were acquired in 1869 out of which were formed the provinces of Manitoba, Saskatchewan and Alberta. British Colombia joined in 1871 and Prince Edward Island in 1873. Canada took over the Arctic Archipelego in 1895. In 1949 Newfoundland came into the confederation. Canada is a member of the Commonwealth of Nations. The Queen of England is Chief of State.

RULERS

British

MONETARY SYSTEM

2 Sous = 1 Penny (Pence)
12 Pence = 1 Shilling
5 Shillings = 1 Dollar

(COMMENCING 1858)

100 Cents = 1 Dollar

LOWER CANADA

The Colonial coinages of Canada began with the copper deniers, billon marques and half-marques, and silver sols issued under the French Regime. Of these, only the 5 and 10 sols of 1670, the 9 deniers of 1721 and 1722, and the marques and half-marques of 1738-60 saw actual circulation.

Unfortunately for local commerce, gold and silver coins passed out of the colonies faster than they could be brought in. France, and to a lesser extent Great Britain, endeavored to supply their colonies with coin, but mercantilism operated to see that coined money was exported. After 1800 private initiative began to issue halfpenny and penny coppers, particularly the basic halfpenny token, to alleviate the shortage of copper coin. When these were issued in such quantities as to discredit them in the public mind, the government stepped in and replaced the private issues with authorized bank and regal tokens which had most of the characteristics of coins yet remained in circulation.

The first Bank Tokens (1835-37) appeared because the banks refused to accept the trashy pieces in circulation except by weight. In 1835 the Bank of Montreal issued half- penny coppers of good weight on which the value was inscribed incorrectly as SOUS, rather than SOU. The bank received permission from the government to strike its coppers in 1836 and added its name to the reverse inscription. The denomination error was not corrected because the people had come to regard it as a mark of authenticity. The bank of Montreal Sous were struck in Birmingham.

An interesting variety of this token known as the 'Rebellion sou' was issued in 1837 by the Banque du Peuple. It received its name when an accountant who favored the cause of the rebels of 1837 surreptitiously caused a small star and liberty cap to be added to the design.

'Bouquet Sous'

UN (1) SOU

COPPER
Rev: BANK TOKEN, MONTREAL

C#	Date	Mintage	Fine	VF	XF	Unc
1	ND(1835)	—	2.00	5.00	10.00	40.00

Rev: BANK OF MONTREAL TOKEN

C#	Date	Mintage	Fine	VF	XF	Unc
2	ND(1836)	—	2.00	5.00	10.00	40.00

Rev: Star - BANK DU PEUPLE - Liberty cap.

C#	Date	Mintage	Fine	VF	XF	Unc
3	ND(1837)	—	3.00	10.00	20.00	60.00

Rev: Without star and liberty cap.

C#	Date	Mintage	Fine	VF	XF	Unc
4	ND(1838)	—	2.25	5.50	11.50	45.00

BRASS
Without star and Liberty cap.

C#	Date	Mintage	Fine	VF	XF	Unc
4a	ND(1838)	—	4.00	11.50	21.50	70.00

COPPER
Rev: TOKEN/MONTREAL

C#	Date	Mintage	Fine	VF	XF	Unc
4.5	ND(1837-8)	—	1.75	4.00	8.00	32.50

NOTE: Many varieties of C#4.5 exist. All are inscribed TOKEN/MONTREAL, and were privately struck during the period 1837-38.

Quebec Token Issues

The Bouquet Sous of 1835-37 were followed by the Quebec Habitant tokens of 1837, the Bank of Montreal tokens of 1842-45, and the Quebec Bank tokens of 1852.

The Habitant tokens were so named because they show on obverse a Canadian habitant in traditional winter garb. For years the habitant was popularly identified with the rebel and politician Louis Joseph Papineau and the tokens known as 'Papineaus,' but there is no valid reason for the association. The Habitants were struck by Boulton & Watt in denominations of penny and halfpenny.

After Upper and Lower Canada were united as the Province of Canada, the Bank of Montreal was granted the right to coin copper and ordered the 'Side View' tokens bearing a side view of the bank in 1837-38 which were rejected being returned to the Mint of Cotterill, Hill & Co. of Walsall, England. It later issued in 1842-45, a series of tokens bearing a front view of the bank, and commonly known as the 'Front View' tokens. The tokens were struck by Boulton & Watt in denominations of penny and halfpenny.

In 1852 the Quebec Bank was granted the authority to coin copper because of a severe shortage of copper coin in the province, and issued an exceptionally attractive Colonial issue with the habitant obverse and reverse depicting the arms of the city of Quebec. They were struck by Ralph Heaton & Sons in denominations of penny and halfpenny.

UN (1) SOU-1/2 PENNY

COPPER
Obv. legend: PROVINCE DU BAS CANADA
Rev: 'CITY BANK' on ribbon

C#	Date	Mintage	Fine	VF	XF	Unc
5	1837	.240	1.50	3.00	7.50	30.00

Rev: 'QUEBEC BANK' on ribbon

C#	Date	Mintage	Fine	VF	XF	Unc
5a	1837	.240	1.50	3.00	7.50	30.00

Rev: 'BANQUE DU PEUPLE' on ribbon.

C#	Date	Mintage	Fine	VF	XF	Unc
5b	1837	.240	2.00	5.00	10.00	40.00

Rev: 'BANK OF MONTREAL' on ribbon

C#	Date	Mintage	Fine	VF	XF	Unc
5c	1837	.480	2.00	5.00	10.00	40.00

Obv: Side view of bank
Obv. legend: BANK OF MONTREAL
Rev: 'BANK OF MONTREAL' on ribbon

C#	Date	Mintage	Fine	VF	XF	Unc
7	1838	*.240	125.00	200.00	300.00	450.00
	1839	*.240	100.00	150.00	200.00	300.00

***NOTE:** The above issues were not officially released.

Obv. leg: PROVINCE OF CANADA-BANK OF MONTREAL

C#	Date	Mintage	Fine	VF	XF	Unc
13	1842	.480	1.25	2.50	5.00	25.00
	1844	1.440	1.00	2.00	4.00	22.50
	1845	2 Known		—	Rare	—

NOTE: 3 varieties of trees exist for 1842 and 1844 tokens.

Obv. legend: PROVINCE DU CANADA
Rev. legend: QUEBEC BANK TOKEN

C#	Date	Mintage	Fine	VF	XF	Unc
15	1852	—	1.75	3.50	7.00	35.00

DEUX (2) SOUS - PENNY

COPPER
Obv. legend: PROVINCE DU BAS CANADA
Rev: 'CITY BANK' on ribbon

C#	Date	Mintage	Fine	VF	XF	Unc
6	1837	.120	2.50	5.00	10.00	40.00

Rev: 'QUEBEC BANK' on ribbon

C#	Date	Mintage	Fine	VF	XF	Unc
6a	1837	.120	2.50	5.00	10.00	40.00

Rev: 'BANQUE DU PEUPLE' on ribbon

C#	Date	Mintage	Fine	VF	XF	Unc
6b	1837	.120	2.50	5.00	10.00	40.00

Rev: 'BANK OF MONTREAL' on ribbon

C#	Date	Mintage	Fine	VF	XF	Unc
6c	1837	.240	2.00	4.00	8.00	32.50

Obv: Side view of bank
Obv. legend: BANK OF MONTREAL
Rev: 'BANK OF MONTREAL' on ribbon

C#	Date	Mintage	Fine	VF	XF	Unc
8	1838	*.120	200.00	325.00	450.00	600.00
	1839	*.120	200.00	325.00	450.00	600.00

Rev: 'BANQUE DU PEUPLE' on ribbon.

C#	Date	Mintage	Fine	VF	XF	Unc
8a	1839	*—	1000.	1500.	2250.	—

NOTE: The C#8 and 8a were not officially released.

COPPER
Obv: Leg. PROVINCE OF CANADA-BANK OF MONTREAL
Rev: 'CITY BANK' on ribbon

C#	Date	Mintage	Fine	VF	XF	Unc
14a	1837	—	40.00	60.00	85.00	125.00

NOTE: The authenticity of the above issue is doubtful.

Rev: 'BANK OF MONTREAL' on ribbon

C#	Date	Mintage	Fine	VF	XF	Unc
14	1842	.240	2.00	5.00	10.00	40.00

Obv. legend: PROVINCE DU CANADA
Rev. legend: QUEBEC BANK TOKEN

C#	Date	Mintage	Fine	VF	XF	Unc
16	1852	—	2.50	6.50	13.50	50.00

UPPER CANADA

Province of Upper Canada

1/2 PENNY

COPPER

KM#	Date	Mintage	Fine	VF	XF	Unc
1	1832	—	11.50	21.50	42.50	85.00

Bank of Upper Canada

In 1849, rioting mobs, angered by the passage of the French Rebellion Losses bill, burned the Parliament Buildings at Montreal. The capital was then transferred to Toronto and the Bank of Upper Canada was granted the right to coin copper. Penny and halfpenny tokens struck by Ralph Heaton and Sons were issued during the period of 1850-57. Because of their design, these attractive tokens are frequently called the 'St. George' tokens. The initials R K & CO on obverse are those of Rowe, Kentish & Co., the agents through whom the token orders were placed.

1/2 PENNY

COPPER

C#	Date	Mintage	Fine	VF	XF	Unc
17	1850	1.500	.75	1.75	3.50	17.50
	1852	1.500	.75	1.75	3.50	17.50
	1854	1.500	.75	1.75	3.50	17.50
	1854 crosslet 4					
		Inc. Ab.	10.00	20.00	35.00	70.00
	1857	3.000	.50	1.00	2.00	10.00

PENNY

COPPER
Similar to 1/2 Penny, C#17.

C#	Date	Mintage	Fine	VF	XF	Unc
18	1850	.750	1.25	2.50	5.00	25.00
	1850 with dot between the cornucopias					
		Inc. Ab.	3.75	7.50	15.00	40.00
	1852	*.750	1.25	2.50	5.00	20.00
	1854	.750	1.25	2.50	5.00	20.00
	1854 crosslet 4					
		Inc. Ab.	3.75	7.50	15.00	40.00
	1857	1.500	1.25	2.50	5.00	20.00
	1857	—	—	—	Proof	225.00

NOTE: 4 varieties exist in '2' of 1852.

MAGDALEN ISLANDS

A group of 13 islands in the Gulf of St. Lawrence north of Prince Edward Island and west of Newfoundland. The island was awarded to Sir Isaac Coffin after the American Revolution. In an effort to exercise his authority on his property Coffin had 1 penny tokens made at Birmingham, England in 1815. The British government felt this was overstepping his authority and revoked his grant of the island. Today it is a part of the province of Quebec.

PENNY

COPPER

KM#	Date	Mintage	Fine	VF	XF	Unc
1	1815	—	15.00	30.00	60.00	120.00

NOTE: Issued by Sir Isaac Coffin while the islands were under the administration of Newfoundland. In 1825 the islands were transferred under the administration of Lower Canada (Quebec).

PRINCE EDWARD ISLAND

An island in the Gulf of St. Lawrence off the coast of New Brunswick and Nova Scotia. In 1813, due to a coin shortage, Governor Smith authorized the perforation of Spanish-American dollars. The centre was to pass for 1 shilling, the balance of the coin 5 shillings. They circulated until 1824 despite wide spread counterfeiting.

SHILLING

(ca.1813)

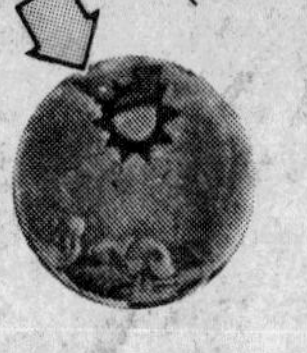

.903 SILVER
c/s: Sunburst on center plug of Spanish or Spanish Colonial 8 Reales.

C#	Date	Mintage	Good	VG	Fine	VF
41	ND	1,000	500.00	850.00	1250.	1850.

5 SHILLINGS

(ca.1813)

.903 SILVER

c/s: Sunburst on holed Lima 8 Reales, C#96.

C#	Date	Mintage	Good	VG	Fine	VF
42.1	(1808-11)	1,000	450.00	750.00	1150.	1750.

c/s: Sunburst on holed Mexico City 8 Reales, KM#109.

C#	Date	Mintage	Good	VG	Fine	VF
42.2	(1791-1808)					
		Inc. Ab.	450.00	750.00	1150.	1750.

1858-59 (5¢ & 10¢ to 1901) 1870-1901

VICTORIA

1902-1910

EDWARD VII

1911 1912-1936

GEORGE V

1937-1947 1948-1952

GEORGE VI

1953-1964

(without straps) (with straps) 1965 to Date

ELIZABETH II

1973 Olympics 1978 Games

CANADIAN COINS

Royal Canadian Mint in Ottawa, Ontario.

The history of Canadian coinage parallels that of the United States in many respects, although in several aspects it also contrasts quite sharply. Canadian coins are widely collected in the U.S., particularly in the northern tier of states, where at times the issues of our northern neighbors have been encountered in substantial circulating quantities.

This is a most logical situation, as when the dollar was established as the monetary unit of Canada, in 1857 it was given the same intrinsic value as the U.S. dollar. Through the years the Canadian dollar has traded on an approximate par with the U.S. dollar, although from time to time one or the other units has traded at a slight premium.

The first Canadian decimal coins were issued in 1858 — 1, 5, 10 and 20 cents — in the name of the Province of Canada (Upper and Lower Canada, or the provinces of Ontario and Quebec as we know them today). The first truly Canadian coinage was offered in 1870 — 5, 10, 25 and 50 cents — following the confederation of these provinces with Nova Scotia and New Brunswick in 1867. Both of the latter had offered their own distinctive coinages in the early 1860s.

Prince Edward Island also offered a single issue of a one cent coin in 1871, prior to its 1873 entry into the confederation. A coinage of Newfoundland was also initiated during this period, in 1865, which continued through 1947, with the British dependency moving into the confederation in 1949.

In contrast to the .900 fine standard of American silver coins, Canada's coinage was originally launched with a .925 fine silver content, and as a result slightly smaller coin sizes. In 1920 the standard was reduced to .800 fine, remaining there until mid-1967 when it was lowered to .500 fine, then abandoned in favor of pure nickel a year later. Another contrast with U.S. coinage was evident in the issue of the large cent from 1858 to 1920, when a small cent of similar size, content and weight to the U.S. cent was introduced.

When Canada's dominion coin issue of 1870 was introduced, the 1858 provincial issue of a decimal 20 cent piece was abandoned in favor of a quasi-decimal 25 cent piece. This move was made, in part, because of the confusion between the 20 cent piece and the U.S. 25 cent piece, which also circulated in Canada, forecasting the similar fate which would befall the U.S. 20 cent piece a few years later. Although tentative steps aimed at the creation of a dollar coin were instituted in 1911, it was not until 1935, the year the issue of silver dollars was halted in the U.S., that Canada launched the issue of a silver dollar.

The first dollar was a commemorative of the silver jubilee of the reign of George V, while the other George V dollar coin (1936) utilized dies which had been prepared at the Royal Mint in

London in anticipation of the 1911 dollar which did not materialize. From the beginning, Canada's dollar series has been frequently employed as a vehicle for the commemoration of national events. In addition, a 1951 nickel commemorated the 200th anniversary of the isolation of nickel, of which Canada is the world's leading producer, while the entire 1967 series commemorates the centennial of Canadian confederation.

In the early years, Canada's coins were struck in England at London's Royal Mint or at the Heaton Mint in Birmingham. Issues struck at the Royal Mint do not bear a mintmark, but those produced by Heaton carry an "H". All Canadian coins have been struck at the Royal Canadian Mint in Ottawa since January 2, 1908, excepting some 1968 pure nickel dimes struck at the U.S. Mint in Philadelphia, and do not bear mint marks. Ottawa's mintmark (C) does appear on some 20th century Newfoundland issues, however, as it does on English type sovereigns struck there from 1908 through 1918.

Canadian coins are graded on standards similar to those used for the U.S. series. The points of greatest wear are generally found on the obverses in the bands of the crowns, the sprays of laurel around the head and in the hairlines above or over the ear. The susceptibility of these varying points to wear has decreed that Canadian coins are almost exclusively graded accordingly, with little concentration on the reverses, unless they are abnormally worn.

Those who become seriously interested in the collecting of Canadian coins will find membership in the Canadian Numismatic Association benefical. The organization publishes a scholarly monthly journal for its members. Full details on membership may be obtained by writing to:

General Secretary
Canadian Numismatic Association
P.O. Box 226
Barrie, Ontario, L4M 4T2 Canada

LARGE CENTS

1858-1910

1911-1920

BRONZE

Y#	Date	Mintage	VG	Fine	VF	XF	Unc	BU
1	1858	421,000	21.00	26.00	35.00	60.00	170.00	270.00
	1859/8 Narrow 9	Inc. Ab.	45.00	65.00	105.00	190.00	235.00	340.00
	1859/8 Wide 9	Inc. Ab.	17.00	23.00	38.00	50.00	75.00	180.00
	1859 Reengraved Date, Narrow 9	Inc. Ab.	30.00	38.00	50.00	75.00	210.00	300.00
	1859 Reengraved Date, Wide 9	Inc. Ab.	21.00	25.00	35.00	60.00	70.00	150.00
	1859 Narrow 9	9,579,000	1.25	2.35	2.75	3.80	16.00	65.00
	1881H	2,000,000	1.00	2.00	3.50	6.75	20.00	60.00
	1882H	4,000,000	1.00	1.50	3.40	6.00	15.00	42.00
	1884	2,500,000	1.50	2.00	3.40	5.00	21.00	50.00
	1886	1,500,000	1.00	2.00	5.00	8.00	30.00	75.00
	1887	1,500,000	1.00	2.50	5.00	8.00	25.00	75.00
	1888	4,000,000	.75	1.25	1.50	3.50	18.00	40.00
	1890H	1,000,000	4.25	6.00	8.50	13.00	30.00	85.00
	1891 Large Date	1,452,000	4.25	5.00	7.00	13.00	38.00	110.00
	1891 Small Date, Large Leaves	Inc. Ab.	30.00	40.00	50.00	75.00	210.00	600.00
	1891 Small Date, Small Leaves	Inc. Ab.	25.00	35.00	45.00	65.00	150.00	350.00
	1892	1,200,000	2.00	3.00	5.00	7.50	20.00	55.00
	1893	2,000,000	1.00	2.00	3.00	5.00	13.00	50.00
	1894	1,000,000	5.00	7.00	8.50	12.00	45.00	130.00
	1895	1,200,000	2.00	3.25	5.00	8.00	20.00	50.00
	1896	2,000,000	1.00	2.00	2.50	4.50	21.00	55.00
	1897	1,500,000	1.90	2.75	3.40	5.00	17.00	51.00
	1898H	1,000,000	3.40	4.50	7.50	10.00	34.00	105.00
	1899	2,400,000	1.00	1.70	2.25	4.00	15.00	50.00
	1900	1,000,000	5.00	6.00	10.00	14.00	42.00	110.00
	1900H	2,600,000	1.50	1.90	3.00	4.50	15.00	35.00
	1901	4,100,000	1.25	1.70	2.50	3.50	12.50	30.00

Y#	Date	Mintage	VG	Fine	VF	XF	Unc	BU
10	1902	3,000,000	1.25	1.70	2.50	3.50	12.50	30.00
	1903	4,000,000	1.70	2.25	3.00	3.75	12.50	30.00
	1904	2,500,000	1.70	2.50	3.50	5.00	17.00	35.00
	1905	2,000,000	3.50	5.00	6.50	7.65	21.00	40.00
	1906	4,100,000	1.50	1.90	2.50	3.60	12.50	30.00
	1907	2,400,000	2.00	2.75	3.80	6.00	17.00	50.00
	1907H	800,000	7.50	10.00	12.75	21.00	75.00	190.00
	1908	2,401,506	1.70	2.10	3.00	5.00	17.00	30.00
	1909	3,973,339	1.00	1.25	2.00	3.40	9.00	34.00
	1910	5,146,487	1.00	1.25	2.00	3.00	8.00	20.00

Y#	Date	Mintage	VG	Fine	VF	XF	Unc	BU
15a	1911	4,663,486	1.25	1.90	3.25	6.25	18.50	38.00

Y#	Date	Mintage	VG	Fine	VF	XF	Unc	BU
15	1912	5,107,642	.75	1.00	1.50	2.50	7.00	21.00
	1913	5,735,405	.75	1.00	1.50	2.50	7.00	21.00
	1914	3,405,958	1.00	1.50	2.25	3.40	8.50	30.00
	1915	4,932,134	.85	1.15	1.90	2.50	6.75	21.00
	1916	11,022,367	.75	1.00	1.50	2.50	7.50	17.00
	1917	11,899,254	.60	.85	1.40	2.25	5.50	15.00
	1918	12,970,798	.50	.85	1.25	2.25	5.50	15.00
	1919	11,279,634	.50	.85	1.25	2.25	5.50	15.00
	1920	6,762,247	.60	1.00	1.50	2.50	6.00	17.00

SMALL CENTS

Bronze

Y#	Date	Mintage	VG	Fine	VF	XF	Unc	BU
16	1920	15,483,923	.25	.35	1.25	1.70	6.75	15.00
	1921	7,601,627	.50	.80	2.10	3.40	10.00	27.00
	1922	1,243,635	11.00	12.75	15.00	24.00	80.00	300.00
	1923	1,019,002	17.00	21.00	27.00	38.00	150.00	400.00
	1924	1,593,195	5.00	5.75	8.00	12.00	38.00	150.00
	1925	1,000,622	12.75	15.00	17.00	27.00	90.00	315.00
	1926	2,143,372	1.90	3.00	3.50	6.50	24.00	55.00
	1927	3,553,928	1.00	1.50	2.75	4.75	15.00	40.00
	1928	9,144,860	.25	.35	.75	1.50	6.50	18.00
	1929	12,159,840	.25	.35	.75	2.00	6.75	18.00
	1930	2,538,613	1.50	2.00	3.00	5.00	15.00	42.00
	1931	3,842,776	1.25	1.75	2.00	3.75	19.00	50.00
	1932	21,316,190	.15	.25	.50	1.00	5.00	18.00
	1933	12,079,310	.15	.25	.50	1.00	5.00	16.00
	1934	7,042,358	.25	.35	.50	1.50	6.00	14.00
	1935	7,526,400	.25	.35	.50	1.50	6.00	14.00
	1936	8,768,769	.25	.35	.50	1.50	4.25	13.00

Y#	Date	Mintage	VG	Fine	VF	XF	Unc	BU
16	1936 Dot Below Date	678,823		Specimen		—	—	3400.00

MAPLE LEAVES

Maple Leaf

Y#	Date	Mintage	VG	Fine	VF	XF	Unc	BU
26	1937	10,040,231	.15	.25	.35	.75	1.50	3.00
	1938	18,365,608	.15	.25	.35	.75	1.50	3.50
	1939	21,600,319	.15	.25	.35	.75	1.50	3.00
	1940	85,740,532	.05	.10	.15	.50	1.50	3.00
	1941	56,336,011	.05	.15	.25	.35	3.00	15.00
	1942	76,113,708	.05	.10	.25	.50	2.75	12.50
	1943	89,111,969	.05	.10	.15	.35	1.00	3.00
	1944	44,131,216	.05	.10	.15	.85	2.00	6.00
	1945	77,268,591	.05	.10	.15	.35	.75	2.00
	1946	56,662,071	—	.10	.15	.25	.75	2.00
	1947	31,093,901	—	.05	.10	.25	1.00	2.00
	1947ML	47,855,448	—	.05	.10	.60	1.00	2.25

Y#	Date	Mintage	VG	Fine	VF	XF	Unc	BU
35	1948	25,767,779	.20	.30	.40	.50	1.00	3.75
	1949	33,128,933	—	.05	.15	.20	.70	1.50
	1950	60,444,992	—	—	.10	.15	.50	1.75
	1951	80,430,379	—	—	.10	.15	.50	1.75
	1952	67,631,736	—	—	.10	.15	.50	1.50

Y#	Date	Mintage	VG	Fine	VF	XF	Unc	BU
43	1953 No Strap	67,806,016	—	—	—	.10	.30	1.50
	1953 With Strap	Inc. Ab.	1.00	1.25	1.70	2.50	11.00	38.00

Y#	Date	Mintage	VG	Fine	VF	XF	Unc	BU
43	1954 With Strap	22,181,760	.20	.30	.40	.50	1.70	3.75
	1954 No Strap	Inc. Ab.	Proof-Like Only			—	40.00	100.00
	1955 With Strap	56,403,193	—	—	—	.10	.25	1.00
	1955 No Strap	Inc. Ab.	—	15.00	20.00	30.00	65.00	210.00

Y#	Date	Mintage	Unc	BU
43	1956	78,658,535	.35	.75
	1957	100,601,792	.20	.40
	1958	59,385,679	.15	.50
	1959	83,615,343	.15	.50
	1960	75,772,775	.10	.20
	1961	139,598,404	.10	.20
	1962	227,244,069	.10	.20
	1963	279,076,334	.10	.20
	1964	484,655,322	.10	.20
	NEW ELIZABETH II EFFIGY			
53	1965 Sm. Beads, Pointed 5	304,441,082	.10	.20
	1965 Small Beads, Blunt 5	Inc. Ab.	.10	.20
	1965 Lg. Beads, Pointed 5	Inc. Ab.	6.50	8.50
	1965 Large Beads, Blunt 5	Inc. Ab.	.10	.20
	1966	184,151,087	.10	.20
59	1967 Dove, Confederation Centennial	345,140,645	.10	.20
	MAPLE LEAF REVERSE RESUMED			
53	1968	329,695,772	.10	.20

Y#59

Y#	Date	Mintage	Unc	BU
53	1969	335,240,929	.10	.20
	1970	311,145,010	.10	.20
	1971	298,228,936	.10	.20
	1972	451,304,591	—	.10
	1973	457,059,852	—	.10
	1974	692,058,489	—	.10
	1975	642,318,000	—	.10
	1976	701,122,890	—	.10
	1977	453,762,670	—	.10
	1978	914,375,639	—	.10
	1979	—	—	.10
	Reduced Size			
53a	1980	—	—	.10

FIVE CENTS

Round 0's

Oval 0's

1.1620 gm. .925 SILVER .0346 oz ASW

Y#	Date	Mintage	VG	Fine	VF	XF	Unc	BU
2	1858 Small Date	1,500,000	7.50	12.75	17.00	30.00	95.00	130.00
	1858 Large Date Over Small Date	Inc. Ab.	95.00	130.00	190.00	250.00	550.00	675.00
	1870 Flat Rim	2,800,000	6.25	9.25	14.50	25.00	95.00	105.00
	1870 Wire Rim	Inc. Ab.	6.75	10.00	17.00	30.00	100.00	130.00
	1871	1,400,000	6.00	8.50	12.50	22.50	95.00	105.00
	1872H	2,000,000	5.50	7.50	12.50	22.50	105.00	130.00
	1874H Plain 4	800,000	10.00	13.50	25.00	50.00	160.00	190.00
	1874H Crosslet 4	Inc. Ab.	6.00	8.50	15.00	30.00	130.00	170.00
	1875H Large Date	1,000,000	64.00	105.00	150.00	250.00	600.00	765.00
	1875 Small Date	Inc. Ab.	51.00	85.00	105.00	210.00	425.00	725.00
	1880H	3,000,000	2.75	4.25	6.00	15.00	105.00	135.00
	1881H	1,500,000	3.25	5.00	9.00	17.50	85.00	110.00
	1882H	1,000,000	4.25	6.00	10.00	22.50	85.00	110.00
	1883H	600,000	6.75	13.00	19.00	34.00	130.00	170.00
	1884	200,000	42.50	68.00	100.00	190.00	510.00	650.00
	1885	1,000,000	5.00	6.75	10.00	20.00	85.00	110.00
	1886	1,700,000	2.00	4.25	6.75	13.50	85.00	110.00
	1887	500,000	7.50	12.75	19.50	34.00	170.00	210.00
	1888	1,000,000	3.40	4.25	8.50	21.00	85.00	110.00
	1889	1,200,000	12.75	21.00	34.00	60.00	210.00	250.00
	1890H	1,000,000	3.00	5.00	8.50	17.00	85.00	110.00
	1891	1,800,000	2.50	4.25	6.00	12.75	85.00	110.00
	1892	860,000	4.25	6.00	10.00	17.00	85.00	110.00
	1893	1,700,000	2.50	3.25	5.00	12.50	85.00	110.00
	1894	500,000	8.50	12.50	17.00	34.00	105.00	135.00
	1896	1,500,000	2.50	3.25	6.00	11.00	85.00	110.00
	1897	1,319,283	2.50	3.25	6.00	11.00	65.00	85.00
	1898	580,717	6.75	13.50	21.00	34.00	105.00	135.00
	1899	3,000,000	1.70	2.50	4.00	8.50	65.00	85.00
	1900 Oval 0's	1,800,000	1.70	2.50	4.00	8.50	65.00	85.00
	1900 Round 0's	Inc. Ab.	12.50	19.00	25.00	42.50	170.00	210.00
	1901	2,000,000	1.70	2.50	3.50	6.00	65.00	85.00
11a	1902	2,120,000	1.25	1.70	2.50	4.50	25.00	42.50
	1902 Lg. Broad H	2,200,000	1.70	2.50	3.50	6.00	30.00	47.00
	1902 Sm. Narrow H	Inc. Ab.	6.75	8.50	12.50	21.00	65.00	85.00
11	1903	1,000,000	2.50	4.50	8.50	12.50	85.00	110.00
	1903H	2,640,000	1.70	2.50	4.25	6.75	42.50	65.00
	1904	2,400,000	2.50	3.50	4.50	8.50	42.50	65.00
	1905	2,600,000	2.50	3.50	4.50	8.50	42.50	65.00
	1906	3,100,000	1.70	2.50	3.50	6.00	42.50	65.00
	1907	5,200,000	1.70	2.50	3.50	6.00	42.50	65.00
	1908	1,220,524	4.25	6.75	10.00	17.00	85.00	130.00
	1909	1,983,725	2.50	3.50	5.00	8.50	50.00	70.00
	1910	3,850,325	1.70	2.50	3.50	6.00	42.50	65.00
17a	1911	3,692,350	1.70	3.50	5.50	12.50	70.00	100.00
17	1912	5,863,170	1.25	2.10	3.40	5.00	34.00	42.50
	1913	5,488,048	1.25	2.10	3.40	5.00	34.00	42.50
	1914	4,202,179	1.70	2.50	4.50	6.00	42.50	65.00
	1915	1,172,258	4.25	8.50	12.75	25.50	95.00	130.00
	1916	2,481,675	2.00	3.50	5.50	8.50	42.50	65.00
	1917	5,521,373	1.25	1.70	2.50	4.25	30.00	42.50
	1918	6,052,298	1.25	1.70	2.50	4.25	30.00	42.50
	1919	7,835,400	1.25	1.70	2.50	4.25	30.00	42.50

1.1664 gm. .800 SILVER .0300 oz ASW

Y#	Date	Mintage	VG	Fine	VF	XF	Unc	BU
17	1920	10,649,851	1.25	1.70	2.50	4.25	30.00	42.50
	1921	2,582,495	Approximately 100 Known; Balance Remelted					
			950.00	1500.	1850.	2250.	4000.	—

MAPLE LEAVES

Nickel

Y#	Date	Mintage	VG	Fine	VF	XF	Unc	BU
21	1922	4,794,119	.25	.50	2.00	5.00	25.00	30.00
	1923	2,502,279	.40	1.00	3.00	8.00	40.00	50.00
	1924	3,105,839	.35	.75	2.50	7.00	40.00	45.00
	1925	201,921	25.00	30.00	70.00	170.00	340.00	510.00

Near 6

Far 6

Y#	Date	Mintage	VG	Fine	VF	XF	Unc	BU
21	1926 Near 6	938,162	2.50	3.75	12.00	42.50	110.00	130.00
	1926 Far 6	Inc. Ab.	68.00	85.00	120.00	300.00	850.00	1275.
	1927	5,285,627	.30	.55	2.50	6.50	31.00	38.00
	1928	4,577,712	.30	.55	2.50	6.50	29.00	38.00
	1929	5,611,911	.30	.55	2.50	6.50	31.00	38.00
	1930	3,704,673	.30	.55	2.50	6.50	31.00	38.00
	1931	5,100,830	.30	.55	2.50	6.50	31.00	38.00
	1932	3,198,566	.35	.55	2.50	6.75	34.00	42.50
	1933	2,597,867	.45	.85	3.00	7.25	30.00	42.50
	1934	3,827,304	.30	.60	2.75	6.25	30.00	38.00
	1935	3,900,000	.35	.60	2.75	6.25	30.00	38.00
	1936	4,400,450	.30	.60	2.75	6.00	25.00	34.00

BEAVER

Y#	Date	Mintage	VG	Fine	VF	XF	Unc	BU
27	1937 Dot	4,593,263	.25	.50	1.50	3.00	16.00	17.50
	1938	3,898,974	.30	.75	3.00	7.75	54.00	70.00
	1939	5,661,123	.20	.40	1.25	4.50	29.00	40.00
	1940	13,920,197	.20	.35	1.00	3.00	18.50	21.00
	1941	8,681,785	.15	.35	1.00	4.00	23.00	26.00
	1942 Round	6,847,544	.15	.30	1.00	4.00	21.00	23.00
28	1942 Tombac, 12 Sided	3,396,234	.75	1.00	1.25	2.00	3.00	4.00

VICTORY

Y#	Date	Mintage	VG	Fine	VF	XF	Unc	BU
29	1943 Tombac	24,760,256	.30	.50	.75	1.00	3.00	4.00
29a	1944 Steel	11,532,784	.15	.25	.45	.75	2.00	3.00
	1945 Steel	18,893,216	.15	.25	.45	.60	1.70	2.25

NICKEL, BEAVER REVERSE RESUMED

Y#	Date	Mintage	VG	Fine	VF	XF	Unc	BU
28a	1946	6,952,684	.10	.20	.50	2.50	7.25	8.50
	1947	7,603,724	.10	.25	.50	1.25	6.25	7.75
	1947 Dot	Inc. Ab.	10.00	15.00	25.00	65.00	650.00	850.00
	1947 Maple Leaf	9,595,124	.10	.25	.50	1.25	6.00	7.75
36	1948	1,810,789	.75	1.00	2.00	4.25	17.50	19.00
	1949	13,037,090	.10	.25	.45	.70	4.25	5.25
	1950	11,970,521	.10	.25	.45	.70	4.25	5.25

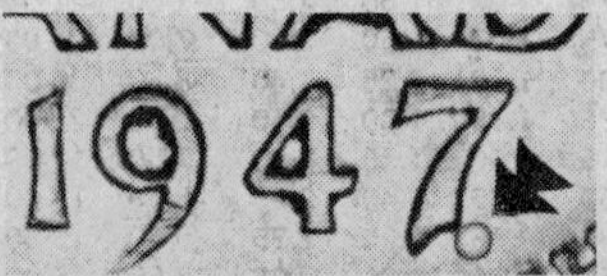

1947 Dot

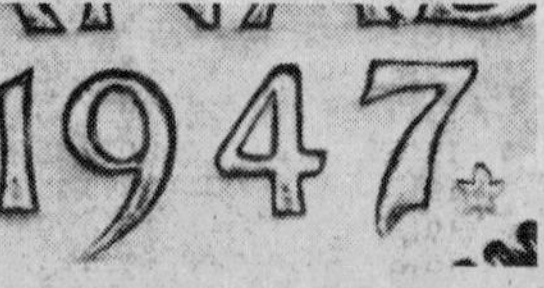

Maple Leaf

Y#	Date	Mintage	Unc	BU
37	1951	Nickel Commemorative		
		9,028,507	2.00	2.50

Y#	Date	Mintage	Unc	BU
	New Elizabeth II Effigy			
54	1965	84,876,018	—	.15
	1966	27,976,648	—	.15

Y#	Date	Mintage	Unc	BU
	CHROMIUM PLATED STEEL			
36a	1951	4,313,410	1.25	6.00
	1952	10,891,148	.60	3.25
44	1953 Without Strap	16,635,552	1.00	3.50
	1953 With Strap	Inc. Ab.	1.50	4.75
	1954	6,998,662	1.75	6.75
	NICKEL			
45	1955	5,355,028	.75	5.00
	1956	9,399,854	.50	2.00
	1957	7,387,703	.50	1.75
	1958	7,607,521	.50	1.75
	1959	11,552,523	.20	.75
	1960	37,157,433	.25	.40
	1961	47,889,051	—	.35
	1962	46,307,305	—	.25
45a	1963	43,970,320	—	.20
	1964	78,075,068	—	—

Y#	Date	Mintage	Unc	BU
60	1967	Rabbit, Confederation Centennial 36,876,574	—	.25
	Beaver Reverse Resumed			
54	1968	101,930,379	—	.25
	1969	27,830,229	—	.15
	1970	5,726,010	.10	.40
	1971	27,312,609	—	.10
	1972	62,417,387	—	.10
	1973	53,507,435	—	.10
	1974	94,704,645	—	.10
	1975	138,882,000	—	.10
	1976	55,140,213	—	.10
	1977	89,120,791	—	.10
	1978	137,077,187	—	.10
	1979	—	—	.10
	1980	—	—	.10

TEN CENTS

2.3240 gm. .925 SILVER .0691 oz ASW

Y#	Date	Mintage	VG	Fine	VF	XF	Unc	BU
3	1858	1,250,000	9.25	15.00	35.00	70.00	235.00	340.00
	1870 Narrow O	1,600,000	6.75	13.50	35.00	70.00	210.00	300.00
	1870 Wide O	Inc. Ab.	8.50	17.00	35.00	70.00	235.00	340.00
	1871	800,000	10.00	19.00	38.00	72.00	275.00	380.00
	1871H	1,870,000	15.00	21.00	38.00	75.00	250.00	340.00
	1872H	1,000,000	50.00	85.00	130.00	210.00	500.00	680.00
	1874H	600,000	6.00	13.00	25.00	50.00	210.00	340.00
	1875H	1,000,000	130.00	190.00	340.00	600.00	1700.	3000.
	1880H	1,500,000	5.00	9.00	21.00	50.00	250.00	360.00
	1881H	950,000	7.00	15.00	25.00	55.00	235.00	340.00
	1882H	1,000,000	5.00	9.00	21.00	50.00	235.00	340.00
	1883H	300,000	15.00	34.00	70.00	150.00	425.00	600.00
	1884	150,000	68.00	170.00	340.00	765.00	2100.	3400.
	1885	400,000	9.00	20.00	50.00	105.00	300.00	510.00
	1886 Small 6	800,000	9.00	18.00	42.00	85.00	255.00	425.00
	1886 Large 6	Inc. Ab.	9.00	18.00	42.00	85.00	255.00	425.00
	1887	350,000	13.00	21.00	75.00	170.00	680.00	1000.
	1888	500,000	4.50	6.75	17.00	42.50	210.00	300.00
	1889	600,000	300.00	470.00	1050.	1700.	3000.	5950.
	1890H	450,000	8.50	17.00	38.00	85.00	300.00	425.00
	1891 21 Leaves	800,000	8.50	17.00	38.00	68.00	210.00	300.00
	1891 22 Leaves	Inc. Ab.	8.50	17.00	38.00	68.00	255.00	380.00
	1892	520,000	6.75	13.50	30.00	60.00	170.00	255.00
	1893 Flat Top 3	500,000	9.00	19.00	38.00	68.00	210.00	425.00
	1893 Rd. Top 3	92 Pcs. Known	300.00	680.00	1000.	2500.	10,000.	14,500.
	1894	500,000	6.00	10.00	20.00	45.00	210.00	300.00
	1896	650,000	5.00	10.00	20.00	45.00	170.00	255.00
	1898	720,000	5.00	10.00	20.00	45.00	210.00	300.00
	1899 Small 9's	1,200,000	4.25	6.75	18.00	42.50	170.00	255.00
	1899 Large 9's	Inc. Ab.	6.75	12.00	34.00	72.00	250.00	380.00
	1900	1,100,000	3.00	6.00	17.00	34.00	150.00	250.00
	1901	1,200,000	3.00	6.00	18.00	35.00	150.00	250.00
12	1902	720,000	3.50	6.75	12.50	34.00	190.00	250.00
	1902H	1,100,000	3.00	6.00	10.00	25.00	105.00	190.00
	1903	500,000	5.00	12.00	30.00	65.00	210.00	340.00
	1903H	1,320,000	2.50	6.00	12.00	30.00	130.00	190.00
	1904	1,000,000	6.00	12.00	28.00	55.00	190.00	300.00
	1905	1,000,000	4.75	10.00	21.00	47.00	190.00	300.00
	1906	1,700,000	3.00	6.75	17.00	34.00	160.00	210.00
	1907	2,620,000	2.50	6.00	12.00	25.00	130.00	190.00
	1908	776,666	3.00	6.75	13.50	30.00	150.00	250.00
	1909 With Large Leaves, Similar To 1902-1908 Coinage							
		1,697,200	4.25	6.75	13.50	32.00	130.00	190.00

Y#	Date	Mintage	VG	Fine	VF	XF	Unc	BU
12	1909 With Broad Leaves Similar To 1910-1912 Coinage							
		Inc. Ab.	4.50	8.50	24.00	42.50	150.00	210.00
	1910	4,468,331	2.50	4.25	8.50	25.00	105.00	150.00
18a	1911	2,737,584	10.00	13.50	25.00	60.00	200.00	275.00
18	1912	3,235,557	1.80	2.50	6.00	11.00	85.00	130.00

Small Leaves **Broad Leaves**

Y#	Date	Mintage	VG	Fine	VF	XF	Unc	BU
18	1913 Small Leaves	3,613,937	1.80	2.50	6.00	8.50	85.00	130.00
	1913 Large Leaves	Inc. Ab.	72.00	105.00	235.00	625.00	1275.	1700.
	1914	2,549,811	1.80	3.50	7.50	17.00	68.00	85.00
	1915	688,057	6.00	10.00	34.00	95.00	340.00	500.00
	1916	4,218,114	1.80	2.50	6.00	13.00	60.00	68.00
	1917	5,011,988	1.80	3.50	5.00	12.00	50.00	60.00
	1918	5,133,602	1.80	3.50	6.00	12.00	50.00	60.00
	1919	7,877,722	1.80	3.50	6.00	12.00	50.00	68.00

2.3328 gm. .800 SILVER .0600 oz ASW

Y#	Date	Mintage	VG	Fine	VF	XF	Unc	BU
	1920	6,305,345	1.80	3.50	6.75	12.00	50.00	68.00
	1921	2,469,562	1.80	3.50	6.75	13.00	55.00	72.00
	1928	2,458,602	1.80	3.50	6.75	10.00	50.00	68.00
	1929	3,253888	1.80	3.50	6.75	10.00	50.00	68.00
	1930	1,831,043	1.80	3.50	6.75	10.00	55.00	72.00
	1931	2,067,421	1.80	3.50	6.75	10.00	50.00	68.00
	1932	1,154,317	1.80	3.50	8.50	12.00	70.00	85.00
	1933	672,368	1.80	3.50	10.00	22.00	85.00	105.00
	1934	409,067	1.80	3.50	10.00	22.00	130.00	170.00
	1935	384,056	3.80	5.00	19.00	34.00	250.00	340.00
	1936	2,460,871	1.80	3.50	7.50	12.00	50.00	68.00
	1936 Dot On Reverse	—	Only 4 Known		—		4000.	—

BLUENOSE

Maple Leaf

Y#	Date	Mintage	VG	Fine	VF	XF	Unc	BU
30	1937	2,500,095	3.50	5.00	6.75	12.00	30.00	42.50
	1938	4,197,323	2.50	2.75	6.75	10.00	60.00	76.00
	1939	5,501748	BV	2.50	6.75	10.00	60.00	76.00
	1940	16,526,470	BV	2.50	3.50.	6.00	12.50	21.00
	1941	8,716,386	BV	2.50	6.75	13.00	68.00	85.00
	1942	10,214,011	BV	2.50	5.00	8.50	42.50	51.00
	1943	21,143,229	BV	2.50	5.00	7.50	21.00	30.00
	1944	9,383,582	BV	2.50	6.00	7.50	34.00	50.00
	1945	10,979,570	BV	2.50	5.00	6.75	17.00	25.00
	1946	6,300,066	BV	2.50	5.00	7.50	34.00	50.00
	1947	4,431,926	BV	2.50	6.75	7.50	50.00	68.00
	1947 Maple leaf	9,638,793	BV	2.50	5.00	6.00	17.00	30.00
38	1948	422,741	5.00	6.00	12.00	21.00	85.00	130.00
	1949	11,336,172	BV	BV	2.50	3.40	8.50	17.00
	1950	17,823,075	BV	BV	2.50	3.40	8.50	17.00
	1951	15,079,265	BV	BV	2.50	3.40	8.50	17.00
	1952	10,474,455	BV	BV	2.50	3.40	8.50	17.00
46	1953 No Straps	17,706,395	BV	BV	2.50	3.40	10.00	19.00
	1953 With Straps	Inc. Ab.	BV	2.50	3.40	4.25	12.00	22.00
	1954	4,493,150	BV	2.50	3.40	4.25	12.00	22.00
	1955	12,237,294	BV	BV	2.50	3.40	5.00	7.00
	1956	16,732,844	BV	BV	2.50	3.40	4.25	6.00
	1956 Dot Below Date	Inc. Ab.	3.40	4.25	5.00	6.75	17.00	25.00

Y#	Date	Mintage	Unc	BU
	1957	16,110,229	BV	2.00
	1958	10,621,236	BV	2.00
	1959	19,691,433	BV	2.00
	1960	45,446,835	BV	1.80
	1961	26,850,859	BV	1.80
	1962	41,864,335	BV	1.80
	1963	41,916,208	BV	1.80
	1964	49,518,549	BV	1.80
	NEW ELIZABETH II EFFIGY			
55	1965	56,965,392	BV	1.80
	1966	34,567,898	BV	1.80

Y#	Date	Mintage	Unc	BU
61	1967	Mackerel, Confederation		
	Centennial	62,998,215	BV	1.80

2.3328 gm., .500 SILVER, .0375 oz ASW
Mackerel, Confederation Centennial

Y#	Date	Mintage	Unc	BU
	2.3328 gm., .500 SILVER, .0375 oz ASW			
61a	1968	Ottawa		
		70,460,000	BV	1.20
	NICKEL			
55a	1968	Ottawa		
		87,412,930	—	.25

OTTAWA-REEDING-PHILADELPHIA

Y#	Date	Mintage	Unc	BU
55a	1968	Philadelphia	—	.25
		85,170,000	—	.25
	1969 Large Date, Large Ship	Inc.Be.	—	Rare
	REDESIGNED SMALLER SHIP			
55b	1969	55,833,929	—	.25
	1970	5,249,296	.15	.50
	1971	41,016,968	—	.25
	1972	60,169,387	—	.25
	1973	167,715,435	—	.20
	1974	201,566,565	—	.20
	1975	207,680,000	—	.20
	1977	128,452,206	—	.20

TWENTY CENTS

4.6480 gm. .925 SILVER .1382 oz ASW

Y#	Date	Mintage	VG	Fine	VF	XF	Unc	BU
4	1858	750,000	42.50	60.00	85.00	130.00	680.00	1000.

TWENTY-FIVE CENTS

1870-1901 5.8100 gm., .925 SILVER .1728 oz ASW 1902-1936

Y#	Date	Mintage	VG	Fine	VF	XF	Unc	BU
8	1870	900,000	9.00	15.00	32.50	68.00	340.00	600.00
	1871	400,000	12.00	19.00	40.00	75.00	380.00	765.00
	1871H	748,000	11.00	18.00	40.00	75.00	425.00	850.00
	1872H	2,240,000	5.00	10.00	19.00	40.00	250.00	500.00
	1874H	1,600,000	5.00	10.00	19.00	40.00	250.00	500.00
	1875H	1,000,000	110.00	210.00	600.00	1200.	3400.	5100.
	1880H Narrow 0	400,000	13.00	25.00	55.00	115.00	600.00	1000.
	1880H Wide 0	Inc. Ab.	42.50	85.00	170.00	340.00	850.00	1700.
	1881H	820,000	8.50	17.00	47.00	100.00	425.00	850.00
	1882H	600,000	10.00	21.00	47.00	210.00	425.00	850.00
	1883H	960,000	6.75	13.00	30.00	65.00	380.00	850.00
	1885	192,000	42.50	72.00	135.00	275.00	1100.	2100.
	1886	540,000	9.00	17.00	42.50	85.00	500.00	1000.
	1887	100,000	38.00	65.00	100.00	250.00	765.00	1700.
	1888	400,000	7.50	17.00	42.50	90.00	340.00	680.00
	1889	66,324	45.00	90.00	170.00	350.00	1350.	2550.
	1890H	200,000	11.00	21.00	42.50	85.00	500.00	1000.
	1891	120,000	21.00	42.50	85.00	170.00	600.00	1275.
	1892	510,000	7.50	15.00	34.00	68.00	340.00	680.00
	1893	100,000	25.00	50.00	105.00	210.00	625.00	1275.
	1894	220,000	8.50	17.00	38.00	75.00	380.00	750.00
	1899	415,580	5.00	7.50	17.00	38.00	210.00	425.00
	1900	1,320,000	4.50	7.00	16.00	30.00	210.00	425.00
	1901	640,000	5.00	8.50	17.50	34.00	210.00	425.00
13	1902	464,000	6.00	10.00	21.00	42.50	190.00	425.00
	1902H	800,000	BV	7.50	19.00	38.00	170.00	340.00
	1903	846,150	6.00	12.00	34.00	65.00	275.00	550.00
	1904	400,000	10.00	21.00	50.00	100.00	550.00	1100.
	1905	800,000	6.00	12.00	34.00	68.00	340.00	680.00
	1906	1,237,843	6.00	12.00	25.00	60.00	250.00	500.00
	1907	2,088,000	6.00	12.00	25.00	60.00	210.00	425.00
	1908	495,016	6.00	12.00	30.00	70.00	210.00	425.00
	1909	1,335,929	5.00	7.50	21.00	70.00	255.00	510.00
	1910	3,577,569	BV	6.00	14.00	42.50	190.00	380.00
19a	1911	1,721,341	13.00	28.00	55.00	130.00	380.00	765.00
19	1912	2,544,199	BV	BV	11.00	30.00	150.00	300.00
	1913	2,213,595	BV	BV	11.00	30.00	150.00	300.00
	1914	1,215,397	BV	5.00	13.50	34.00	170.00	340.00
	1915	242,382	8.50	21.00	85.00	190.00	850.00	1700.
	1916	1,462,566	BV	5.00	13.00	25.00	130.00	250.00
	1917	3,365,644	BV	BV	10.00	21.00	130.00	250.00
	1918	4,175,649	BV	BV	10.00	21.00	100.00	170.00
	1919	5,852,262	BV	BV	10.00	21.00	100.00	170.00

5.8319 gm., .800 SILVER .1500 oz ASW

Y#	Date	Mintage	VG	Fine	VF	XF	Unc	BU
19	1920	1,975,278	BV	BV	10.00	25.00	130.00	250.00
	1921	597,337	6.75	17.00	45.00	105.00	750.00	1700.
	1927	468,096	17.00	34.00	72.00	150.00	650.00	1275.
	1928	2,114,178	BV	BV	10.00	21.00	140.00	170.00
	1929	2,690,562	BV	BV	10.00	21.00	140.00	210.00
	1930	968,748	BV	BV	13.00	34.00	210.00	425.00
	1931	537,815	BV	6.00	17.00	36.00	230.00	470.00
	1932	537,994	BV	6.75	21.00	42.50	230.00	470.00
	1933	421,282	BV	6.75	21.00	42.50	230.00	470.00
	1934	384,350	BV	6.75	21.00	42.50	230.00	470.00
	1935	537,772	BV	6.00	17.00	34.00	190.00	380.00
	1936	972,094	BV	BV	10.00	25.00	100.00	200.00

Y#	Date	Mintage	VG	Fine	VF	XF	Unc	BU
	1936 Dot	153,322	21.00	42.50	105.00	190.00	850.00	1500.

1938-

1967

1973

Y#	Date	Mintage	VG	Fine	VF	XF	Unc	BU
31	1937	2,690,176	BV	BV	5.00	8.50	25.00	50.00
	1938	3,149,245	BV	BV	6.00	10.00	75.00	150.00
	1939	3,532,495	BV	BV	6.00	10.00	75.00	150.00
	1940	9,583,650	BV	BV	6.00	10.00	75.00	150.00
	1941	6,654,672	BV	BV	BV	6.75	21.00	42.50
	1942	6,935,871	BV	BV	BV	6.75	21.00	42.50
	1943	13,559,575	BV	BV	BV	6.75	21.00	42.50
	1944	7,216,237	BV	BV	BV	6.75	42.50	65.00
	1945	5,296,495	BV	BV	BV	6.75	21.00	42.50
	1946	2,210,810	BV	BV	5.00	12.50	65.00	95.00
	1947	1,524,554	BV	BV	5.00	12.50	85.00	150.00
	1947 Dot After 7	Inc. Ab.	17.00	25.00	42.50	72.50	425.00	650.00
	1947 Maple Leaf	4,393,938	BV	BV	BV	5.00	19.00	30.00

Maple Leaf Variety

Y#	Date	Mintage	VG	Fine	VF	XF	Unc	BU
39	1948	2,564,424	BV	BV	5.00	7.50	45.00	72.00
	1949	7,988,830	BV	BV	BV	BV	12.50	21.00
	1950	9,673,335	BV	BV	BV	BV	12.00	19.00
	1951	8,290,719	BV	BV	BV	BV	10.00	12.50
	1952	8,859,642	BV	BV	BV	BV	8.50	12.50
47	1953 Large Date	10,546,769	BV	BV	BV	BV	8.50	12.50
	1953 Small Date	Inc. Ab.	BV	BV	BV	BV	9.00	12.50
	1954	2,318,891	BV	BV	5.00	12.00	50.00	68.00
	1955	9,552,505	BV	BV	BV	BV	8.50	12.50
	1956	11,269,353	BV	BV	BV	BV	5.00	6.75
	1957	12,770,190	BV	BV	BV	BV	BV	5.00
	1958	9,336,910	BV	BV	BV	BV	BV	5.00

Y#	Date	Mintage	Unc	BU	Y#	Date	Mintage	Unc	BU
47	1959	13,503,461	BV	5.00	56a	1969	133,037,929	—	1.00
	1960	22,835,327	BV	5.00		1970	10,302,010	—	1.00
	1961	18,164,368	BV	5.00		1971	48,170,428	—	.55
	1962	29,559,266	BV	5.00		1972	43,743,387	—	.55
	1963	21,180,652	BV	5.00	70	1973 Mountie, 120 beads obv.			
	1964	36,479,343	BV	5.00			134,958,587	—	.55
56	1965	44,708,869	BV	4.75		1973 132 Beads Obv.		125.00	200.00
	1966	25,626,315	BV	4.75		CARIBOU REVERSE RESUMED			
62	1967 Wildcat, Confederation Cen-				56a	1974	192,360,598	—	.55
	tennial	48,855,500	BV	4.75		1975	141,148,000	—	.50
	5.8319 gm., .500 SILVER, .0937 oz ASW					1976	86,898,261	—	.35
62a	1967 Wildcat, Confederation Cen-					1977	99,634,555	—	.35
	tennial	Inc. Ab.	BV	3.00		1978	175,953,351	—	.35
	CARIBOU REVERSE RESUMED					1979	—	—	.35
56	1968	71,464,000	BV	3.00		1980	—	—	.35
	NICKEL								
56a	1968	88,686,931	—	.70					

FIFTY CENTS

1870-1901 11.6200 gm., .925 SILVER .3456 oz ASW 1902-1936

Y#	Date	Mintage	VG	Fine	VF	XF	Unc	BU
9	1870	450,000	210.00	425.00	680.00	1500.	3400.	4250.
	1870 LCW	Inc. Ab.	42.50	85.00	170.00	250.00	1275.	1700.
	1871	200,000	42.50	68.00	150.00	325.00	1500.	2700.
	1871H	45,000	60.00	105.00	190.00	340.00	1500.	2700.
	1872H	80,000	30.00	60.00	130.00	240.00	2100.	3000.
	1872H Inverted A for V in VICTORIA							
		—	50.00	105.00	170.00	300.00	2500.	3400.
	1881H	150,000	30.00	50.00	130.00	230.00	1700.	2500.
	1888	60,000	72.00	135.00	275.00	500.00	1900.	2700.
	1890H	20,000	340.00	600.00	1000.	1900.	6800.	10,000.
	1892	151,000	34.00	68.00	130.00	210.00	1500.	1900.
	1894	29,036	120.00	210.00	425.00	1275.	6800.	10,000.
	1898	100,000	30.00	60.00	120.00	235.00	1275.	2400.
	1899	50,000	55.00	95.00	190.00	400.00	3000.	3800.
	1900	118,000	25.00	45.00	100.00	235.00	1200.	2200.
	1901	80,000	35.00	55.00	130.00	360.00	1500.	2300.
14	1902	120,000	17.00	42.50	130.00	235.00	680.00	1275.
	1903H	140,000	21.00	42.50	130.00	340.00	1000.	1700.
	1904	60,000	60.00	130.00	255.00	600.00	2550.	3800.
	1905	40,000	68.00	130.00	300.00	765.00	2550.	4250.
	1906	350,000	12.50	30.00	75.00	190.00	850.00	1350.
	1907	300,000	12.00	30.00	75.00	190.00	680.00	1060.
	1908	128,119	17.00	42.50	95.00	175.00	680.00	1500.
	1909	302,118	15.00	38.00	75.00	190.00	680.00	1000.

Victorian Leaves

Edwardian Leaves

Y#	Date	Mintage	VG	Fine	VF	XF	Unc	BU
14	1910 Victorian Leaves	649,521	10.00	25.00	75.00	160.00	600.00	1100.
	1910 Edwardian Leaves	Inc. Ab.	10.00	25.00	75.00	160.00	600.00	1100.
20a	1911	209,972	15.00	75.00	340.00	1000.	1700.	2550.
20	1912	285,867	BV	17.00	50.00	135.00	1700.	2550.
	1913	265,889	BV	17.00	50.00	135.00	1700.	2550.
	1914	160,128	25.00	50.00	135.00	340.00	1900.	2550.
	1916	459,070	BV	15.00	42.50	105.00	425.00	850.00
	1917	752,213	BV	13.50	30.00	105.00	340.00	600.00
	1918	754,989	BV	13.50	30.00	105.00	340.00	600.00
	1919	1,113,429	BV	17.00	30.00	105.00	340.00	425.00

11.6638 gm., .800 SILVER .3000 oz ASW

Y#	Date	Mintage	VG	Fine	VF	XF	Unc	BU
20	1920	584,691	BV	14.00	42.50	130.00	500.00	750.00
	1921	Abt. 50 Known	4250.	5500.	8100.	13,000.	17,000.	27,000.
	1929	228,328	BV	17.00	34.00	85.00	425.00	550.00
	1931	57,581	10.00	20.00	50.00	135.00	850.00	1500.
	1932	19,213	45.00	68.00	210.00	400.00	1500.	2100.
	1934	39,539	15.00	30.00	70.00	210.00	680.00	850.00
	1936	38,550	15.00	30.00	55.00	190.00	600.00	750.00

ARMS OF CANADA

1937-1958

1959-

Y#	Date	Mintage	VG	Fine	VF	XF	Unc	BU
32	1937	192,016	BV	BV	15.00	30.00	72.00	85.00
	1938	192,018	BV	BV	15.00	72.00	250.00	300.00
	1939	287,976	BV	BV	15.00	30.00	105.00	150.00
	1940	1,996,566	BV	BV	13.00	17.00	25.00	30.00
	1941	1,714,874	BV	BV	13.00	17.00	34.00	42.50
	1942	1,974,164	BV	BV	13.00	17.00	34.00	42.50
	1943	3,109,583	BV	BV	13.00	17.00	34.00	42.50
	1944	2,460,205	BV	BV	13.00	17.00	34.00	42.50
	1945	1,959,528	BV	BV	13.00	17.00	34.00	42.50
	1946	950,235	BV	BV	13.00	21.00	68.00	120.00
	1946 Hoof in 6	Inc. Ab.	17.00	25.00	42.50	105.00	500.00	680.00
	1947 Straight 7	424,885	BV	BV	13.00	25.00	105.00	150.00
	1947 Curved 7	Inc. Ab.	BV	BV	13.00	25.00	105.00	150.00
	1947ML, Straight 7	38,433	35.00	45.00	60.00	85.00	210.00	250.00
	1947ML, Curved 7	Inc. Ab.	1200.	1500.	1900.	2200.	3400.	4250.
40	1948	37,784	50.00	60.00	85.00	115.00	235.00	325.00
	1949	858,991	BV	BV	13.00	25.00	55.00	85.00
	1949 Hoof over 9	Inc. Ab.	13.00	17.00	30.00	55.00	425.00	680.00
	1950	2,384,179	BV	BV	10.00	12.00	17.00	25.00
	1950 Lines in 0	Inc. Ab.	10.00	13.50	17.00	34.00	255.00	425.00
	1951	2,421,730	BV	BV	10.00	12.00	17.00	22.00
	1952	2,596,465	BV	BV	10.00	12.00	17.00	22.00
48	1953 Small Date	1,630,429	BV	BV	BV	BV	13.00	17.00
	1953 Lg. Date, Straps	Inc. Ab.	BV	BV	10.00	21.00	50.00	70.00
	1953 Lg. Date, No Straps	I.A.	15.00	33.00	41.00	47.00	255.00	425.00
	1954	506,305	BV	BV	10.00	21.00	50.00	70.00
	1955	753,511	BV	BV	10.00	19.00	34.00	42.50

Y#	Date	Mintage	Unc	BU
48	1956	1,379,499	BV	10.00
	1957	2,171,689	BV	10.00
	1958	2,957,266	BV	10.00
51	1959	3,095,535	BV	10.00
	1960	3,488,897	BV	10.00
	1961	3,584,417	BV	10.00
	1962	5,208,030	BV	10.00
	1963	8,348,871	BV	10.00
	1964	9,377,676	BV	10.00
	NEW ELIZABETH II EFFIGY			
57	1965	12,629,974	BV	10.00
	1966	7,920,496	BV	10.00
63	1967 Wolf, Confederation Centennial	4,211,392	BV	10.00
	NICKEL			
57a	1968	3,966,932	—	1.00
	1969	7,113,929	—	1.00
	1970	2,429,526	—	1.25
	1971	2,166,444	—	—
	1972	2,515,632	—	1.00
	1973	2,546,096	—	1.00
	1974	3,436,650	—	.85

Y#	Date	Mintage	Unc	BU
57a	1975	3,710,000	—	.85
	1977	709,839	—	4.25
	1978 Square Beads	3,327,337	—	.70
	1978 Round Beads	Inc. Ab.	2.50	8.50
	1979	—	—	.70
	1980	—	—	.70

Dollar

(Canoe design except for dates illustrated.)

23.3276 gm., .800 SILVER .6000 oz ASW

Y#	Date	Mintage	Fine	VF	XF	AU	Unc	BU
22	1935 Jubilee	428,707	BV	BV	20.00	30.00	51.00	70.00
A22	1936	306,100	BV	BV	20.00	34.00	60.00	75.00
33	1937	241,002	BV	19.00	22.00	34.00	60.00	75.00
	1938	90,304	BV	34.00	42.50	70.00	130.00	170.00

1939 Parliament

1949 Newfoundland

Y#	Date	Mintage	Fine	VF	XF	AU	Unc	BU
34	1939 Parliament	1,363,816	BV	BV	BV	19.00	21.00	25.00
33	1945	38,391	90.00	130.00	150.00	210.00	350.00	385.00
	1946	93,055	18.00	29.00	34.00	55.00	105.00	170.00
	1947 Blunt 7	65,595	45.00	60.00	75.00	105.00	130.00	170.00
	1947 Pointed 7	Inc. Ab.	90.00	130.00	150.00	210.00	600.00	850.00
	1947 Maple Leaf	21,135	100.00	150.00	170.00	235.00	500.00	650.00

Maple Leaf

Y#	Date	Mintage	Fine	VF	XF	AU	Unc	BU
41	1948	18,780	325.00	490.00	600.00	680.00	1000.	1650.
42	1949 Newfoundland	672,218	BV	19.00	22.00	30.00	34.00	38.00
41	1950	261,002	BV	BV	BV	21.00	30.00	38.00
	1950 Arnprior	Inc. Ab.	19.00	21.00	30.00	50.00	70.00	85.00
	1951	416,395	BV	BV	BV	19.00	20.00	22.00
	1951 Arnprior	Inc. Ab.	25.00	40.00	50.00	85.00	105.00	170.00
	1952 Water Lines	406,148	BV	BV	BV	BV	19.00	21.00
	1952 No Water Lines	Inc. Ab.	BV	BV	BV	21.00	25.00	34.00
49	1953 No Strap	1,074,578	BV	BV	BV	BV	19.00	21.00
	1953 With Strap	Inc. Ab.	BV	BV	BV	BV	19.00	21.00
	1954	246,606	BV	BV	BV	BV	19.00	22.00
	1955	268,105	BV	BV	BV	BV	19.00	22.00
	1955 Arnprior	Inc. Ab.	55.00	70.00	85.00	105.00	130.00	170.00
	1956	209,092	BV	BV	BV	20.00	22.00	27.00
	1957	496,389	BV	BV	BV	BV	19.00	21.00
	1957 One Water Line	Inc. Ab.	BV	BV	BV	21.00	25.00	34.00

1958 British Columbia

1964 Charlottetown

Y#	Date	Mintage	Fine	VF	XF	AU	Unc	BU
50	1958 Br. Columbia	3,039,630	BV	BV	BV	BV	BV	18.50
49	1959	1,443,502	BV	BV	BV	BV	BV	18.50
	1960	1,420,486	BV	BV	BV	BV	BV	18.50
	1961	1,262,231	BV	BV	BV	BV	BV	18.50
	1962	1,884,789	BV	BV	BV	BV	BV	18.50
	1963	4,179,981	BV	BV	BV	BV	BV	18.50
52	1964 Charlottetown	7,296,832	BV	BV	BV	BV	BV	18.50

Small Beads

Medium Beads

Large Beads

New Elizabeth II Effigy

Y#	Date	Mintage	BU
58	1965 Small beads, pointed 5	10,768,569	BV
	1965 Small beads, blunt 5	Inc. Ab.	BV
	1965 Large beads, blunt 5	Inc. Ab.	BV
	1965 Large beads, pointed 5	Inc. Ab.	BV
	1965 Medium beads, pointed 5	Inc. Ab.	20.00

Pointed

Blunt

Y#	Date	Mintage	BU	P/L	Proof
58	1966 Canoe (Silver, 36mm), large beads	9,912,178	18.50	19.00	—
	1966 Canoe, small beads	*485 pcs.	1,100.	—	—
64	1967 Goose, Confederation Centennial	6,767,496	18.50	19.00	—
	1967 (error) 'diving goose'	Inc. Ab.	275.00	—	—
58a	1968 Canoe (Nickel, 32mm)	5,579,714	1.50	2.50	—
	1969 Canoe (Nickel, 32mm)	4,809,313	1.50	2.00	—
66	1970 Manitoba (Nickel, 32mm)	4,140,058	1.50	(c) 4.00	—

23.5000 gm., NICKEL

.500 SILVER .3778 oz ASW

Y#	Date	Mintage	BU	P/L	Proof
67	1971 Br. Columbia (Nickel, 32mm)	4,260,781	1.50	(c) 4.00	—
68	1971 Br. Columbia (.500 Silver, 36mm)	555,564	—	—	(c) 15.00
58a	1972 Canoe (Nickel, 32mm)	2,676,041	1.50	(c) 4.00	—
58	1972 Canoe (.500 Silver, 36mm)	350,109	—	—	(c) 15.00

Y#	Date	Mintage	BU	P/L	Proof
69	1973 Pr. Edward Island (Nickel, 32mm)	3,196,452	1.50	(c) 4.00	—
71	1973 Mountie (.500 Silver, 36mm)	904,795	—	—	(c) 11.50
71a	1973 Mountie, with metal crest on case	Inc. Ab.	—	—	(c) 27.50

.500 SILVER

Y#	Date	Mintage	BU	P/L	Proof
100	1974 Winnipeg (Nickel, 32mm)	2,799,363	1.50	(c) 4.00	—
100a	1974 Winnipeg (.500 Silver, 36mm)	628,183	—	—	(c) 11.50
58a	1975 Canoe (Nickel, 32mm)	3,256,000	1.50	(c) 4.00	—
101	1975 Calgary (.500 Silver, 36mm)	833,095	—	—	(c) 11.50

Y#	Date	Mintage	BU	P/L	Proof
58a	1976 Canoe (Nickel, 32mm)	2,498,204	1.50	(c) 4.00	—
	1976 Mule, with 1975 reverse	—	—	—	—
102	1976 Parliament (.500 Silver, 36mm)	483,722	—	—	(c) 14.00

Y#	Date	Mintage	BU	P/L	Proof
58a	1977 Canoe (Nickel, 32mm, attached Jewel)	1,393,745	12.50	—	—
	1977 Canoe (Nickel, 32mm, detached jewel)	Inc. Ab.	2.00	4.00	—
	1977 (error) 'dipping canoe'	Inc. Ab.	35.00	—	—
103	1977 Silver Jubilee (.500 Silver, 36mm)	847,194	—	—	(c) 11.50
58a	1978 Canoe (Nickel, 32mm)	2,920,337	1.50	4.00	—
	1978 (error) 'dipping canoe'	Inc. Ab.	15.00	—	—
106	1978 XI Games (.500 Silver, 36mm)	709,602	—	—	(c) 11.50
58a	1979 Canoe (Nickel, 32mm)	—	1.50	4.00	—

Y#	Date	Mintage	BU	P/L	Proof
107	1979 Griffon (.500 Silver, 36mm)	—	—	—	(c) 13.00
58a	1980 Canoe, Nickel, 32mm	—	1.50	—	—
110	1980 Artic Territories .500 SILVER, 36mm	—	—	—	(c) 20.00

(c) Individually cased Proof-likes (P/L) or Proofs or from broken up Proof-like or Proof sets.

5 DOLLARS

8.3592 gm., .900 GOLD .2419 oz AGW

Y#	Date	Mintage	Fine	VF	XF	AU	Unc	BU
23	1912	165,680	BV	200.00	240.00	275.00	300.00	450.00
	1913	98,832	BV	200.00	240.00	275.00	300.00	450.00
	1914	31,122	325.00	600.00	700.00	750.00	800.00	1000.

OLYMPIC COMMEMORATIVES

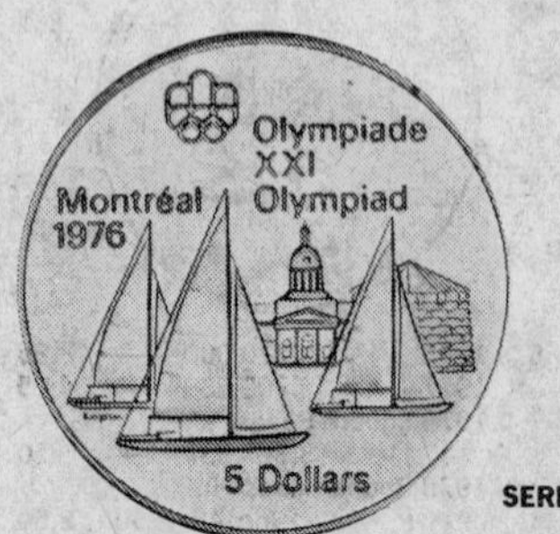

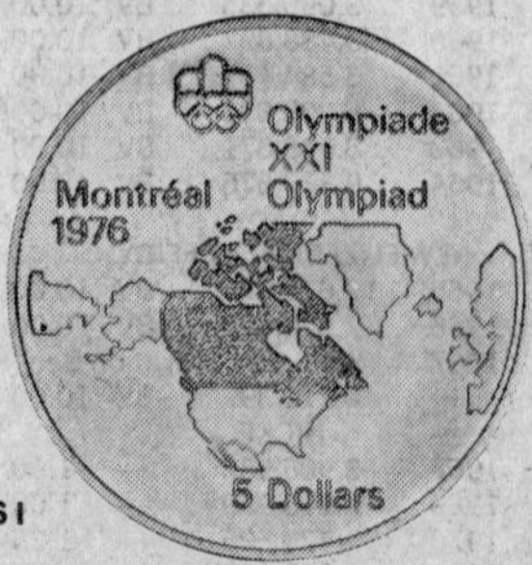

SERIES I

24.3000 gm., .925 SILVER .7227 oz ASW

Y#	Date	Mintage	BU	Proof
72	1973 Sailboats (Kingston)	—	25.00	28.50
73	1973 North America Map	—	25.00	28.50

SERIES II

Y#	Date	Mintage	BU	Proof
76	1974 Olympic Rings	—	25.00	28.50
77	1974 Athlete with torch	—	25.00	28.50

SERIES III

Y#	Date	Mintage	BU	Proof
80	1974 Rowing	—	25.00	28.50
81	1974 Canoeing	—	25.00	28.50

SERIES IV

Y#	Date	Mintage	BU	Proof
84	1975 Marathon	—	25.00	28.50
85	1975 Ladies' javelin	—	25.00	28.50

SERIES V

Y#	Date	Mintage	BU	Proof
88	1975 Swimmer	—	25.00	28.50
89	1975 Diver	—	25.00	28.50

SERIES VI

Y#	Date	Mintage	BU	Proof
92	1976 Fencing	—	25.00	28.50
93	1976 Boxing	—	25.00	28.50

SERIES VII

Y#	Date	Mintage	BU	Proof
96	1976 Olympic Village	—	25.00	28.50
97	1976 Olympic flame	—	25.00	28.50

10 DOLLARS

16.7185 gm., .900 GOLD .4838 oz AGW

Y#	Date	Mintage	Fine	VF	XF	AU	Unc	BU
24	1912	74,759	350.00	500.00	600.00	650.00	765.00	875.00
	1913	149,232	350.00	575.00	650.00	700.00	765.00	900.00
	1914	140,068	350.00	600.00	725.00	775.00	850.00	950.00

OLYMPIC COMMEMORATIVES

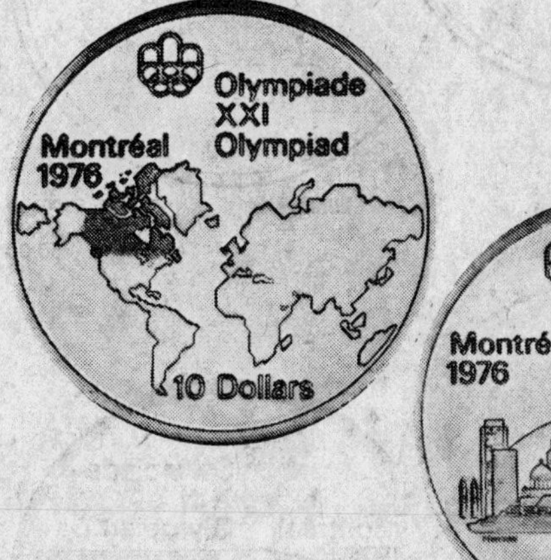

Series I

48.6000 gm., .925 SILVER 1.4454 oz ASW

Y#	Date	Mintage	BU	Proof
74	1973 World Map	—	45.00	50.00
74a	1974 World Map (Error-Mule)	—	550.00	—
75	1973 Montreal Skyline	—	45.00	50.00

SERIES II

Y#	Date	Mintage	BU	Proof
78	1974 Head of Zeus	—	45.00	50.00
79	1974 Temple of Zeus	—	45.00	50.00

SERIES III

Y#	Date	Mintage	BU	Proof
82	1974 Cycling	—	45.00	50.00
83	1974 Lacrosse	—	45.00	50.00

SERIES IV

Y#	Date	Mintage	BU	Proof
86	1975 Men's hurdles	—	45.00	50.00
87	1975 Ladies' shot put	—	45.00	50.00

SERIES V

Y#	Date	Mintage	BU	Proof
90	1975 Sailing	—	45.00	50.00
91	1975 Paddler	—	45.00	50.00

SERIES VI

Y#	Date	Mintage	BU	Proof
94	1976 Football	—	45.00	50.00
95	1976 Field Hockey	—	45.00	50.00

SERIES VII

Y#	Date	Mintage	BU	Proof
98	1976 Olympic Stadium	—	45.00	50.00
99	1976 Olympic Velodrome	—	45.00	50.00

20 DOLLARS

18.2733 gm., .900 GOLD .5288 oz AGW

CENTENNIAL COMMEMORATIVE

Y#	Date	Mintage	BU	Proof
65	1967	337,688	—	350.00

50 DOLLARS

31.1000 gm., .999 GOLD 1.0000 oz AGW

Y#	Date	Mintage	BU	Proof
109	1979 Maple leaf, 30mm	—	—	—

100 DOLLARS

OLYMPIC COMMEMORATIVES

13.3000 gm., .583 GOLD .2493 oz AGW

Y#	Date	Mintage	BU
A100	1976 Beaded borders	650,000	175.00

15.5000 gm., .917 GOLD .4570 oz AGW

Y#	Date	Mintage	BU	Proof
A100a	1976 Reduced size, 25mm, plain borders	350,000	—	350.00

QUEEN'S SILVER JUBILEE

Y#	Date		Mintage	BU	Proof
104	1977	Proof only	180,396	—	350.00

CANADIAN UNIFICATION

Y#	Date	Mintage	BU	Proof
107	1978	176,080	—	350.00

YEAR OF THE CHILD

Y#	Date	Mintage	BU	Proof
108	1979	—	—	350.00

ARCTIC TERRITORIES CENTENNIAL

Y#	Date	Mintage	BU	Proof
111	1980	—	—	—

SOVEREIGN

1908-1910 **7.9881 gm., .917 GOLD .2354 oz AGW** **1911-1919**
with C mintmark below horses' rear hoofs

Y#	Date	Mintage	Fine	VF	XF	AU	Unc	BU
14	1908C	636	750.00	1350	1800.	2200.	2450.	2900.
	1909C	16,273	BV	230.00	320.00	360.00	425.00	550.00
	1910C	28,012	BV	220.00	300.00	340.00	380.00	425.00
25	1911C	256,946	BV	BV	BV	BV	180.00	190.00
	1913C	3,715	300.00	470.00	530.00	680.00	850.00	1200.
	1914C	14,871	BV	210.00	275.00	320.00	360.00	425.00
	1916C	Rare	*Less than 10 known			17,000.	—	22,000.
	1917C	58,845	BV	BV	BV	BV	180.00	190.00
	1918C	106,516	BV	BV	BV	BV	180.00	190.00
	1919C	135,889	BV	BV	BV	BV	180.00	190.00

*Charlton, March, 1977 Auction

PROOF-LIKE DOLLARS

23.3276 gm., .800 SILVER .6000 oz ASW

KM#	Date	Mintage	Identification	Issue Price	Mkt Value
D3	1953	6,900	Y49, Canoe	—	—
D4	1954	1,268	Y49, Canoe	1.25	170.00
D5	1955	5,501	Y49, Canoe	1.25	95.00
D5a	1955	Inc. Ab.	Y49, Arnprior	1.25	250.00
D6	1956	6,154	Y49, Canoe	1.25	75.00
D7	1957	4,379	Y49, Canoe	1.25	34.00
D8	1958	14,978	Y50, British Columbia	1.25	34.00
D9	1959	13,583	Y49, Canoe	1.25	18.00
D10	1960	18,631	Y49, Canoe	1.25	18.00
D11	1961	22,555	Y49, Canoe	1.25	18.00
D12	1962	47,591	Y49, Canoe	1.25	18.00
D13	1963	290,529	Y49, Canoe	1.25	18.00
D14	1964	1,209,279	Y52, Charlottetown	1.25	18.00
D15	1965	—	Y58, Canoe	—	18.00
D16	1966	—	Y58, Canoe	—	18.00
D17	1967	—	Y64, Confederation	—	18.00

NICKEL

KM#	Date	Mintage	Identification	Issue Price	Mkt Value
D18	1968	885,124	Y58a, Canoe	1.25	2.00
D19	1969	221,112	Y58a, Canoe	1.25	2.00
D20	1970	297,547	Y66, Manitoba	2.00	(c)3.50
D21	1971	181,901	Y67, Br. Columbia	2.00	(c)3.50
D22	1972	143,392	Y58a, Canoe	2.00	(c)3.25
D23	1973	174,810	Y69, Pr. Edward Island	2.00	(c)3.00
D24	1974	—	Y100, Winnipeg	2.50	(c)3.50
D25	1975	88,102	Y58a, Canoe	2.50	(c)3.50
D26	1976	74,207	Y58a, Canoe	2.50	(c)3.50
D27	1977	—	Y58a, Canoe	—	3.50
D28	1978	—	Y58a, Canoe	—	3.50

Mint Sets

OLYMPIC COMMEMORATIVES

KM#	Date	Mintage	Identification	Issue Price	Mkt Value
S1	1973(4)	—	Y72-75, Series I	45.00	130.00
S2	1974(4)	—	Y76-79, Series II	48.00	130.00
S3	1974(4)	—	Y80-83, Series III	48.00	130.00
S4	1975(4)	—	Y84-87, Series IV	48.00	130.00
S5	1975(4)	—	Y88-91, Series V	60.00	130.00
S6	1976(4)	—	Y92-95, Series VI	60.00	130.00
S7	1976(4)	—	Y96-99, Series VII	60.00	130.00

SPECIMEN SETS

NOTE: Some authorities list these as proof sets. However, the Canadian Mint does not. The coins are double struck with higher than usual pressure, but are considered to have the same quality as proof issue from the Royal Mint, London.

KM#	Date	Mintage	Identification	Issue Price	Mkt Value
SS1	1858(4)	—	Y1-4 Reeded Edge	—	3,500.
SS2	1858(4)	—	Y1-4 Plain Edge	—	3,500.
SS3	1858(8)	—	Y#1-4 Double Set	—	6,000.
SS4	1870(4)	100*	Y2,3,8,9	—	6,500.
SS5	1902(5)	100*	Y10,11a,12-14	—	6,000.
SS6	1908(5)	1,000*	Y10-14	—	900.00
SS7	1911(5)	1,000*	Y15a,17a-20a	—	2,750.
SS8	1911/12(8)	5 Pcs.	Y15a,17a-20a,23-25	—	—
SS9	1921(5)	—	Y16-20	—	35,000.
SS10	1934(5)	—	Y16,18-21	—	4,000.
SS11	1936(5)	—	Y16,18-21	—	5,250.
SS12	1937(6)	1025*	Y26,27,30-33 Matte Proof	—	500.00
SS13	1937(6)	75*	Y26,27,30-33 Polished Proof	—	1,250.
SS14	1938(6)	—	Y26,27,30-33 Brilliant	—	7,500.
SS15	1944(5)	3	Y26,29a,30-33	—	2,500.
SS16	1945(6)	6	Y26,29a,30-33	—	2,000.
SS17	1946(5)	15	Y26,28a,30-33	—	4,000.
SS18	1947(6)	20	Y26,28a,30-33	—	3,500.
SS19	1947(6)	—	Y26,28a,30-32(7 curved left) 33	—	4,000.
SS20	1947ML(6)	—	Y26,28a,30-32(7 curved left) 33	—	4,000.
SS21	1947ML(6)	—	Y26,28a,30-32(7 curved right) 33	—	6,500.
SS22	1948(6)	30	Y35,36,38-41	—	4,000.
SS23	1949(6)	20	Y35,36,38-40,42	—	—
SS24	1950(6)	12	Y35,36,38-41	—	1,500.
SS25	1951(6)	12	Y35,36a,38-41	—	1,500.
SS26	1952(6)	2,317	Y35,36a,38-41	—	300.00
SS27	1953(6)	28	Y43 No Straps,44,46-49	—	2,500.
SS28	1953(6)	—	Y43 With Straps,44,46-49	—	1,400.
SS29	1965(6)	—	Y53-58	—	200.00
SS30	1970(5)	—	Y53,54,55b,56a,66	—	425.00

NOTES: *Estimated. A 1903H double set has been reported on display in Bombay, India.

PROOF SETS

NOTE: These sets have been struck and issued by the Mint as proof sets.

KM#	Date	Mintage	Identification	Issue Price	Mkt Value
P1	1967(7)	337,514	Y59-65	40.00	325.00
P2	1967(6)	Inc. Ab.	Y59-64 With silver medal	12.00	50.00
P3	1970(6)	50	Y53,54,55b,56a,57a,66,V.I.P.	—	500.00
P4	1971(7)	66,860	Y53,54,55b,56a,57a,67(2 pcs.)	12.00	22.50
P5	1972(7)	36,349	Y53,54,55b,56a,57a,58a(2 pcs.)	12.00	50.00
P6	1973(7)	119,819	Y53,54,55b,57a,69-71	12.00	22.50
P7	1973(7)	Inc. Ab.	As above, large bust quarter,132 beads	—	225.00
P8	1974(7)	85,230	Y53,54,55b,56a-57a,100,100a	15.00	22.50
P9	1975(7)	97,263	Y53,54,55b,56a-58a,101	15.00	22.50
P10	1976(7)	87,744	Y53,54,55b,56a-58a,102	16.00	30.00
P11	1977(7)	142,577	Y53,54,55b,56a-58a,103	16.50	37.50
P12	1978(7)	—	Y53,54,55b,56a-58a,106	16.50	25.00
P13	1979(7)	—	Y53,54,55b,56a-58a,107	18.50	37.50
P14	1980(7)	—	Y53,54,55b,56a-58a,110	30.50	32.50

OLYMPIC COMMEMORATIVES

KM#	Date	Mintage	Identification	Issue Price	Mkt Value
OCP1	1973(4)	—	Y72-75,Series I	78.50	130.00
OCP2	1974(4)	—	Y76-79,Series II	88.50	130.00
OCP3	1974(4)	—	Y80-83,Series III	88.50	130.00
OCP4	1975(4)	—	Y84-87,Series IV	88.50	130.00
OCP5	1975(4)	—	Y88-91,Series V	88.50	130.00
OCP6	1976(4)	—	Y92-95,Series VI	88.50	130.00
OCP7	1976(4)	—	Y96-99,Series VII	88.50	130.00

CUSTOM PROOF-LIKE SETS

Each set contains two 1 cent pieces.

KM#	Date	Mintage	Identification	Issue Price	Mkt Value
CPL1	1971(7)	33,517	Y53(2 .Pcs.),54,55b,56a-57a	6.50	8.50
CPL2	1972(7)	38,198	Y53(2 Pcs.),54,55b,56a-58a	6.50	8.50
CPL3	1973(7)	35,676	Y53 (2 Pcs.),54,55b,57a,69,70	6.50	8.50
CPL4	1974(7)	44,296	Y53(2 Pcs.),54,55b,56a-57a,100	8.00	8.50
CPL5	1975(7)	36,851	Y53(2 Pcs.),54,55b,56a-58a	8.00	8.50
CPL6	1976(7)	28,162	Y53(2 pcs.),54,55b,56a-58a	8.00	13.50
CPL7	1977(7)	44,198	Y53 (2 pcs.),54,55b,56a-58a	8.15	13.50
CPL8	1978(7)	—	Y53(2 pcs.),54,55b,56a-58a	—	11.50
CPL9	1979(7)	—	Y53(2 pcs.),54,55b,56a-58a	10.75	12.50
CPL10	1980(7)	—	Y53 2 pcs., 54,55b,56a-58a	10.75	11.50

PROOF-LIKE SETS

NOTE: These sets do not have the quality of the Proof or Specimen Set, but will consist of selected pieces from uncirculated coinage.

KM#	Date	Mintage	Identification	Issue Price	Mkt Value
PL1	1953(6)	—	Y43,44,46-49	2.20	1000.
PL2	1954(6)	7,426	Y43,44,46-49	2.50	350.00
PL3	1954(6)	Inc. Ab.	Y43 No Straps,44,46-49	2.50	490.00
PL4	1955(6)	6,301	Y43,45-49	2.50	220.00
PL5	1955(6)	Inc. Ab.	Y43,45-49,Arnprior	2.50	470.00
PL6	1956(6)	9,018	Y43,45-49	2.50	175.00
PL7	1957(6)	11,862	Y43,45-49	2.50	90.00
PL8	1958(6)	18,259	Y43,45-48,50	2.50	82.00
PL9	1959(6)	31,577	Y43,45-47,49,51	2.50	37.50
PL10	1960(6)	64,097	Y43,45-47,49,51	3.00	34.00
PL11	1961(6)	98,373	Y43,45-47,49,51	3.00	33.50
PL12	1962(6)	200,950	Y43,45-47,49,51	3.00	33.50
PL13	1963(6)	673,006	Y43,45a,46,47,49,51	3.00	33.50
PL14	1964(6)	1,653,162	Y43,45a,46,47,51,52	3.00	33.50
PL15	1965(6)	2,904,352	Y53-58	4.00	33.50
PL16	1966(6)	672,514	Y53-58	4.00	33.50
PL17	1967(6)	963,714	Y59-64	4.00	33.50
PL18	1968(6)	521,641	Y53,54,55a-58a	4.00	2.50
PL19	1969(6)	326,203	Y53,54,55b,56a-58a	4.00	3.50
PL20	1970(6)	349,120	Y53,54,55b,56a-57a,66	4.00	9.50
PL21	1971(6)	253,311	Y53,54,55b,56a-57a,67	4.00	5.50
PL22	1972(6)	224,275	Y53,54,55b,56a-58a	4.00	4.00
PL23	1973(6)	243,695	Y53,54,55b,56a-57a,69,70, sm. bust quarter	4.00	6.00
PL24	1973(6)	Inc. Ab.	Y53,54,55b,56a-57a,69,70, lg. bust quarter	4.00	250.00
PL25	1974(6)	213,589	Y53,54,55b,56a-57a,100	5.00	6.00
PL26	1975(6)	197,372	Y53,54,55b,56a-58a	5.00	6.00
PL27	1976(6)	171,737	Y53,54,55b,56a-58a	5.15	12.00
PL28	1977(6)	225,307	Y53,54,55b,56a-58a	5.15	12.50
PL29	1978(6)	—	Y53,54,55b,56a-58a	—	7.00
PL30	1979(6)	—	Y53,54,55b,56a-58a	6.25	7.50

NEWFOUNDLAND

LARGE CENTS

1865-1896 Bronze 1904-1936

Y#	Date	Mintage	VG	Fine	VF	XF	Unc	BU
1	1865	240,000	1.70	2.50	4.50	10.00	75.00	125.00
	1872H	200,000	1.70	2.50	4.50	10.00	75.00	100.00
	1872H	—	—	—	—	—	Proof	500.00
	1873	200,025	1.70	2.50	4.50	10.00	75.00	150.00
	1876H	200,000	1.70	2.50	4.50	10.00	75.00	300.00
	1880 Round O, Even Date	400,000	1.25	2.25	4.50	7.50	75.00	650.00
	1880 Round O, Low O	Inc. Ab.	2.00	3.50	7.50	11.00	81.00	130.00
	1880 oval O	Inc. Ab.	50.00	70.00	85.00	130.00	425.00	680.00
	1885	40,000	12.50	18.00	22.50	38.00	160.00	300.00
	1888	50,000	12.00	15.00	20.00	25.00	130.00	300.00
	1890	200,000	1.25	2.00	4.00	7.50	50.00	105.00
	1894	200,000	1.25	2.00	4.00	7.50	50.00	110.00
	1896	200,000	1.25	2.00	4.00	7.50	50.00	110.00
7	1904H	100,000	4.25	6.75	14.00	22.00	90.00	210.00
	1907	200,000	1.25	2.00	4.00	8.50	45.00	150.00
	1909	200,000	1.25	2.00	4.00	8.50	45.00	130.00
	1909	—	—	—	—	—	Proof	250.00
12	1913	400,000	.50	1.00	1.70	3.50	25.00	42.50
	1917C	702,350	.40	.75	1.70	3.50	25.00	42.50
	1919C	300,000	.50	1.00	1.70	3.50	25.00	45.00
	1919C	—	—	—	—	—	Proof	275.00
	1920C	302,184	.50	1.00	1.70	3.50	25.00	50.00
	1929	300,000	.40	.75	1.70	3.50	25.00	50.00
	1929	—	—	—	—	—	Proof	250.00
	1936	300,000	.40	.75	1.70	3.50	21.00	38.00
	1936	—	—	—	—	—	Proof	250.00

SMALL CENTS

Y#	Date	Mintage	VG	Fine	VF	XF	Unc	BU
18	1938	500,000	.40	.75	1.25	2.25	13.00	17.00
	1938	—	—	—	—	—	Proof	75.00
	1940C	300,000	2.25	3.00	5.00	8.00	34.00	42.50
	1940 Re-engraved date	—	10.00	13.00	18.00	25.00	90.00	110.00
	1941C	827,662	.30	.50	1.00	1.25	8.50	10.00
	1942	1,996,889	.30	.50	1.00	1.25	8.50	10.00
	1943C	1,239,732	.30	.50	1.00	1.25	4.50	8.50
	1944C	1,328,776	1.25	2.25	2.75	4.00	25.00	32.00
	1947C	313,772	.75	1.00	1.50	2.75	13.00	17.00

FIVE CENTS

1.1782 gm., .925 SILVER .0350 oz ASW

Y#	Date	Mintage	VG	Fine	VF	XF	Unc	BU
2	1865	80,000	25.00	35.00	50.00	85.00	130.00	250.00
	1870	40,000	25.00	35.00	50.00	85.00	130.00	250.00
	1870	—	—	—	—	—	Proof	650.00
	1872H	40,000	21.00	30.00	42.50	85.00	130.00	300.00
	1873	44,260	25.00	35.00	50.00	85.00	130.00	320.00
	1873H	Inc. Ab.	340.00	550.00	725.00	1000.	1700.	3000.
	1876H	20,000	40.00	50.00	85.00	135.00	680.00	1500.
	1880	40,000	22.00	32.00	55.00	85.00	130.00	320.00
	1881	40,000	17.00	25.00	38.00	100.00	130.00	340.00
	1882H	60,000	15.00	25.00	42.50	100.00	130.00	340.00
	1885	16,000	70.00	95.00	140.00	235.00	300.00	725.00
	1888	40,000	15.00	25.00	40.00	60.00	105.00	275.00
	1890	160,000	9.00	18.00	35.00	50.00	85.00	210.00
	1890	—	—	—	—	—	Proof	500.00
	1894	160,000	9.00	18.00	35.00	50.00	85.00	210.00
	1896	400,000	7.50	13.50	30.00	42.50	75.00	200.00
8	1903	100,000	3.00	5.50	14.50	34.00	65.00	190.00
	1904H	100,000	3.00	5.50	13.00	30.00	65.00	170.00
	1908	400,000	2.25	4.50	8.50	21.00	42.50	105.00
13	1912	300,000	1.25	2.75	5.50	13.00	25.00	105.00
	1917C	300,319	2.50	4.25	6.75	17.00	34.00	105.00
	1919C	100,844	2.50	4.25	8.50	17.00	34.00	105.00
	1929	300,000	BV	1.75	3.50	8.50	30.00	105.00
19	1938	100,000	BV	BV	1.70	3.50	13.00	42.50
	1938	—	—	—	—	—	Proof	165.00
	1940C	200,000	BV	BV	1.70	2.50	8.50	30.00
	1941C	612,641	BV	BV	1.70	2.50	9.00	21.00
	1942C	298,348	1.50	1.70	2.25	3.50	16.00	21.00
	1943C	351,666	BV	BV	1.70	2.50	10.00	21.00

1.1664 gm., .800 SILVER .0300 oz ASW

Y#	Date	Mintage	VG	Fine	VF	XF	Unc	BU
19a	1944C	286,504	BV	1.25	1.70	3.00	5.00	17.00
	1945C	203,828	BV	BV	1.70	2.50	4.25	17.00
	1945C	—	—	—	—	—	Proof	150.00
	1946C	2,041	110.00	120.00	210.00	425.00	850.00	1275.
	1947C	38,400	4.00	6.00	7.00	10.00	25.00	50.00
	1947C	—	—	—	—	—	Proof	150.00

TEN CENTS

1865-1896 2.3564 gm., .925 SILVER .0701 oz ASW 1903-1947

Y#	Date	Mintage	VG	Fine	VF	XF	Unc	BU
3	1865	80,000	11.00	17.00	30.00	70.00	300.00	425.00
	1865 plain edge	—	—	—	—	—	Proof	700.00
	1870	30,000	115.00	170.00	250.00	425.00	1275.	1700.
	1872H	40,000	10.00	17.00	30.00	65.00	300.00	600.00
	1873	23,614	17.00	25.00	42.50	75.00	350.00	750.00
	1876H	10,000	22.00	38.00	75.00	150.00	500.00	1000.
	1880/70	10,000	22.00	38.00	75.00	150.00	475.00	950.00
	1882H	20,000	10.00	17.00	38.00	75.00	250.00	500.00
	1885	8,000	42.50	70.00	150.00	250.00	625.00	1275.
	1888	30,000	13.00	17.50	38.00	75.00	250.00	500.00
	1890	100,000	5.00	13.00	24.00	50.00	210.00	500.00
	1890	—	—	—	—	—	Proof	600.00
	1894	100,000	5.00	13.00	24.00	50.00	210.00	500.00
	1896	230,000	4.50	10.50	24.00	50.00	150.00	380.00
9	1903	100,000	3.50	7.50	18.00	45.00	150.00	340.00
	1904H	100,000	3.50	7.50	18.00	45.00	150.00	340.00
14	1912	150,000	2.50	5.50	11.00	22.50	135.00	250.00
	1917C	250,805	2.00	4.00	8.50	18.00	105.00	210.00
	1919C	54,342	3.00	6.00	13.50	30.00	85.00	150.00
20	1938	100,000	BV	2.00	3.00	6.75	25.00	50.00
	1938	—	—	—	—	—	Proof	175.00
	1940	100,000	BV	2.00	3.00	6.75	25.00	50.00
	1941C	483,630	BV	2.00	3.00	4.50	25.00	50.00
	1942C	292,736	BV	2.00	3.00	4.50	25.00	50.00
	1943C	104,706	BV	2.00	3.00	4.50	25.00	50.00

2.3328 gm., .800 SILVER .0600 oz ASW

Y#	Date	Mintage	VG	Fine	VF	XF	Unc	BU
20	1944C	151,471	BV	2.00	3.00	4.50	25.00	50.00
	1945C	175,833	BV	2.00	3.00	4.25	23.00	45.00
	1946C	38,400	5.00	7.00	8.50	17.00	85.00	130.00
	1947C	61,988	2.25	2.50	3.50	4.25	24.00	47.00

TWENTY CENTS

1865-1900 4.7127 gm., .925 SILVER .1401 oz ASW 1904-1912

Y#	Date	Mintage	VG	Fine	VF	XF	Unc	BU
4	1865	100,000	7.50	12.00	21.00	55.00	340.00	425.00
	1865 Plain Edge	—	—	—	—	—	Proof	750.00
	1870	50,000	10.00	20.00	28.00	70.00	340.00	425.00
	1872H	90,000	5.00	8.50	17.00	34.00	425.00	600.00
	1873	45,797	6.75	10.00	20.00	40.00	425.00	600.00
	1876H	50,000	10.00	18.00	35.00	47.00	500.00	850.00
	1880/70	30,000	11.00	20.00	35.00	50.00	680.00	850.00
	1881	60,000	4.25	6.00	10.00	25.00	340.00	500.00
	1882H	100,000	4.25	6.00	10.00	25.00	340.00	500.00
	1885	40,000	4.25	6.00	10.00	25.00	340.00	500.00
	1888	75,000	4.25	6.00	8.50	25.00	340.00	500.00
	1890	100,000	BV	5.00	8.50	25.00	340.00	500.00
	1890	—	—	—	—	—	Proof	650.00
	1894	100,000	BV	5.00	8.50	25.00	340.00	500.00
	1896 Narrow Date	125,000	BV	5.00	8.50	25.00	340.00	500.00
	1896 Wide Date	Inc. Ab.	BV	5.00	9.50	25.00	340.00	500.00
	1899 Wide Date	125,000	4.25	6.00	8.50	25.00	250.00	475.00
	1899 Narrow Date	Inc. Ab.	BV	5.00	8.50	25.00	250.00	425.00
	1900	125,000	BV	5.00	8.50	25.00	250.00	425.00
10	1904H	75,000	13.00	21.00	40.00	120.00	680.00	1000.
	1904H	—	—	—	—	—	Proof	1250.
15	1912	350,000	BV	5.00	12.00	17.00	250.00	425.00

TWENTY-FIVE CENTS

5.8319 gm., .925 SILVER .1734 oz ASW

Y#	Date	Mintage	VG	Fine	VF	XF	Unc	BU
16	1917C	464,779	BV	BV	BV	6.75	50.00	70.00
	1919C	163,939	BV	BV	BV	6.75	50.00	70.00

FIFTY CENTS

1870-1900 11.7818 gm., .925 SILVER .3504 oz ASW 1904-1919

Y#	Date	Mintage	VG	Fine	VF	XF	Unc	BU
5	1870	50,000	BV	17.00	25.00	75.00	500.00	680.00
	1870 Plain Edge	—	—	—	—	—	Proof	1000.
	1872H	48,000	BV	17.00	25.00	75.00	500.00	680.00
	1873	37,675	BV	17.00	35.00	85.00	500.00	680.00
	1874	80,000	BV	16.00	30.00	75.00	500.00	680.00
	1876H	28,000	21.00	25.00	55.00	135.00	850.00	1275.
	1880	24,000	19.00	26.00	55.00	130.00	500.00	680.00
	1881	50,000	BV	17.00	30.00	80.00	775.00	1000.
	1882H	100,000	BV	15.00	25.00	70.00	775.00	950.00
	1885	40,000	BV	25.00	40.00	110.00	1200.	1700.
	1888	20,000	BV	24.00	42.50	115.00	1200.	1700.
	1894	40,000	BV	BV	15.00	60.00	1275.	1900.
	1896	60,000	BV	BV	16.00	55.00	850.00	1700.
	1898	79,607	BV	BV	15.00	55.00	850.00	1700.
	1899 Wide 9's	150,000	BV	BV	15.00	55.00	850.00	1700.
	1899 Narrow 9's	Inc. Ab.	BV	BV	15.00	55.00	850.00	1700.
	1900	150,000	BV	BV	15.00	55.00	250.00	425.00
11	1904H	140,000	BV	BV	BV	30.00	250.00	425.00
	1907	100,000	BV	BV	BV	25.00	170.00	250.00
	1908	160,000	BV	BV	BV	25.00	170.00	250.00
	1909	200,000	BV	BV	BV	23.00	170.00	210.00
	1911	200,000	BV	BV	BV	23.00	130.00	210.00
17	1917C	375,560	BV	BV	BV	17.00	130.00	210.00
	1918C	294,824	BV	BV	BV	17.00	130.00	210.00
	1919C	306,267	BV	BV	BV	17.00	130.00	210.00

Two Dollars

3.3284 gm., .917 GOLD .0981 oz AGW

Y#	Date	Mintage	Fine	VF	XF	AU	Unc	BU
6	1865	10,000	120.00	195.00	220.00	255.00	330.00	610.00
	1865 Plain Edge	—	—	—	—	—	Proof	5500.
	1870	10,000	120.00	195.00	210.00	255.00	330.00	610.00
	1870 Plain Edge	—	—	—	—	—	Proof	6500.
	1872	6,050	175.00	300.00	360.00	400.00	560.00	850.00
	1880	2,500	750.00	1100.	1350.	1500.	1600.	2550.
	1881	10,000	115.00	190.00	210.00	255.00	300.00	600.00
	1882H	25,000	115.00	190.00	210.00	255.00	300.00	600.00
	1885	10,000	115.00	190.00	210.00	255.00	300.00	600.00
	1888	25,000	115.00	190.00	210.00	255.00	300.00	600.00

New Brunswick

HALF PENNY

COPPER

Y#	Date	Mintage	VG	Fine	VF	XF	Unc	BU
1	1843	480,000	1.50	2.25	4.00	7.00	15.00	30.00
	1843	—	—	—	—	—	Proof	225.00

Y#	Date	Mintage	VG	Fine	VF	XF	Unc	BU
3	1854	480,000	1.75	2.50	4.50	8.00	20.00	35.00
	1854	—	—	—	—	—	Proof	250.00

ONE PENNY

COPPER

Y#	Date	Mintage	VG	Fine	VF	XF	Unc	BU
2	1843	480,000	2.00	3.00	5.00	8.00	15.00	30.00
	1843	—	—	—	—	—	Proof	250.00

Y#	Date	Mintage	VG	Fine	VF	XF	Unc	BU
4	1854	480,000	2.50	3.50	5.50	9.00	20.00	35.00

HALF CENT

BRONZE

Y#	Date	Mintage	VG	Fine	VF	XF	Unc	BU
5	1861	222,800	35.00	45.00	55.00	65.00	135.00	225.00
	1861	—	—	—	—	—	Proof	1200.

ONE CENT

BRONZE

Y#	Date	Mintage	VG	Fine	VF	XF	Unc	BU
6	1861	1,000,000	1.00	2.00	4.00	9.00	22.50	55.00
	1861	—	—	—	—	—	Proof	650.00
	1864 Short 6	1,000,000	1.00	2.60	4.00	9.00	22.50	55.00
	1864 Long 6	Inc. Ab.	1.00	2.00	4.00	9.00	22.50	55.00

FIVE CENTS

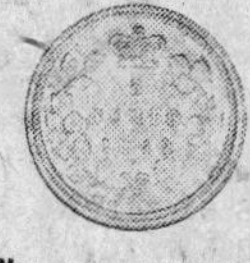

1.1620 gm., .925 SILVER .0346 oz ASW

Y#	Date	Mintage	VG	Fine	VF	XF	Unc	BU
7	1862	100,000	25.00	35.00	55.00	75.00	175.00	275.00
	1864 Small 6	100,000	20.00	30.00	45.00	70.00	175.00	275.00
	1864 Large 6	Inc. Ab.	25.00	45.00	70.00	100.00	225.00	325.00

TEN CENTS

2.3240 gm., .925 SILVER .0691 oz ASW

Y#	Date	Mintage	VG	Fine	VF	XF	Unc	BU
8	1862	150,000	20.00	30.00	45.00	90.00	200.00	300.00
	1862 Recut 2	Inc. Ab.	18.00	27.50	40.00	80.00	175.00	275.00
	1864	100,000	18.00	27.50	40.00	90.00	300.00	450.00

TWENTY CENTS

4.6480 gm., .925 SILVER .1382 oz ASW

Y#	Date	Mintage	VG	Fine	VF	XF	Unc	BU
9	1862	150,000	10.00	15.00	20.00	35.00	175.00	275.00
	1864	150,000	12.00	18.00	25.00	40.00	175.00	275.00

Nova Scotia

HALF PENNY

COPPER

C#	Date	Mintage	VG	Fine	VF	XF	Unc	BU
31	1823	400,000	2.50	3.50	6.00	9.00	25.00	50.00
	1824	118,636	3.00	6.00	9.00	15.00	35.00	70.00
	1832	800,000	2.00	3.00	6.00	8.00	20.00	40.00
31a	1382(Error)	Inc. Ab.	265.00	380.00	500.00	725.00	1150.	—
	1832/1382	Inc. Ab.	8.00	12.00	18.00	25.00	35.00	70.00

Y#	Date	Mintage	VG	Fine	VF	XF	Unc	BU
3	1840	300,000	2.00	2.50	4.00	10.00	25.00	50.00
	1843	300,000	2.00	2.50	4.00	8.00	20.00	40.00

Y#	Date	Mintage	VG	Fine	VF	XF	Unc	BU
5	1856 W/o LCW	300,000	2.25	3.50	6.00	8.00	27.50	55.00
	1856 W/ LCW	Inc. Ab.	—	—	100.00	125.00	150.00	225.00

PENNY

COPPER

C#	Date	Mintage	VG	Fine	VF	XF	Unc	BU
32	1824	217,776	4.00	6.00	8.00	15.00	35.00	70.00
	1832	200,000	2.25	3.50	7.00	10.00	25.00	50.00

Y#	Date	Mintage	VG	Fine	VF	XF	Unc	BU
4	1840	150,000	2.25	3.50	7.00	10.00	25.00	50.00
	1843	150,000	4.00	6.00	9.00	15.00	30.00	60.00

Y#	Date	Mintage	VG	Fine	VF	XF	Unc	BU
6	1856 W/o LCW	150,000	3.00	4.50	7.00	9.00	25.00	50.00
	1856 W/ LCW	Inc. Ab.	2.50	4.00	7.00	9.50	20.00	40.00

HALF CENT

BRONZE

Y#	Date	Mintage	VG	Fine	VF	XF	Unc	BU
7	1861	400,000	4.00	6.00	8.00	12.00	25.00	80.00
	1864	400,000	4.00	6.00	8.00	12.00	25.00	80.00

ONE CENT

BRONZE

Y#	Date	Mintage	VG	Fine	VF	XF	Unc	BU
8	1861	800,000	1.00	2.00	5.00	8.00	25.00	80.00
	1862	(Est.) 100,000	12.50	20.00	30.00	50.00	125.00	300.00
	1864	800,000	1.25	2.50	5.00	9.00	27.50	90.00

Prince Edward Is.

ONE CENT

BRONZE

Y#	Date	Mintage	VG	Fine	VF	XF	Unc	BU
1	1871	1,000,000	1.00	3.50	6.00	10.00	50.00	150.00
	1871	—	—	—	—	—	Proof	1250.

CANADA

PATTERNS

KM#	Date	Mintage	Identification	Mkt.Val.
1	1858	—	1 Cent, bronze, rev. uniface, wide date	1000.
2	1858	—	1 Cent, bronze, rev. uniface, close date	1000.

KM#	Date	Mintage	Identification	Mkt.Val.
3	1858	—	1 Cent, bronze	1000.

KM#	Date	Mintage	Identification	Mkt.Val.
4	1858	—	20 Cents, silver	1500.

KM#	Date	Mintage	Identification	Mkt.Val.
5	1859	—	1 Cent, bronze, mule with Great Britain 1/2 penny rev.	1500.

KM#	Date	Mintage	Identification	Mkt.Val.
6	1870	—	50 Cents, bronze	2000.
7	1871	—	20 Cents, plain edge, silver	2000.
8	1871	—	20 Cents, reeded edge, silver	2000.
9	1875	—	5 Cents, no H, silver	—

KM#	Date	Mintage	Identification	Mkt.Val.
10	1876	—	1 Cent, no H, bronze	700.00
11	1876-H	—	1 Cent, copper-nickel	1500.
12	1876-H	—	1 Cent, Head of '58, bronze	1500.
13	ND	—	10 Cents, bronze, obverse uniface	—
14	1911	—	1 Cent, bronze, type as 1912-1920	—

KM#	Date	Mintage	Identification	Mkt.Val.
15	1911	—	1 Dollar, silver	160,000
16	1911	—	1 Dollar, lead	—

KM#	Date	Mintage	Identification	Mkt.Val.
17	1911	—	5 Dollars, gold	2500.
18	1911	—	10 Dollars, gold	2500.
19	1928	—	5 Dollars, bronze	1500.

KM#	Date	Mintage	Identification	Mkt.Val.
20	1928	—	10 Dollars, bronze	1500.
21	1928	—	5 Dollars, bronze, reverse uniface	—
22	1928	—	10 Dollars, bronze, reverse uniface	—
23	1964	—	1 Dollar, tin, Piefort	—
24	1967	—	1 Dollar, silver	—

TRIAL STRIKES

KM#	Date	Mintage	Identification	Mkt.Val.
T1	1858	—	1 Cent, copper-nickel, double thickness	—
T2	1858	—	1 Cent, copper-nickel	1500.
T3	1937	—	1 Cent, brass, thick planchet	500.00
T4	1937	—	5 Cents, brass, thick planchet	500.00
T5	1937	—	10 Cents, brass, thick planchet	500.00
T6	1937	—	25 Cents, brass, thick planchet	—
T7	1937	—	25 Cents, bronze	—
T8	1937	—	50 Cents, brass, thick planchet	1500.
T9	1942	—	5 Cents, nickel, 12 sided	—
T10	1943	—	1 Cent, copper-plated steel	500.00
T11	1943	—	5 Cents, steel	500.00
T12	1944	—	5 Cents, tombac	—
T13	1951	—	5 Cents, chrome-plated steel	—
T14	1952	—	5 Cents, white metal (?)	—
T15	1959	—	50 Cents, uniface, tin, oversize planchet	—

BRITISH COLUMBIA

PATTERNS

KM#	Date	Mintage	Identification	Mkt.Val.
1	1862	—	10 Dollars, gold	—
2	1862	—	10 Dollars, silver	8000.
3	1862	—	20 Dollars, gold	—

KM#	Date	Mintage	Identification	Mkt.Val.
4	1862	—	20 Dollars, silver	7500.

NEW BRUNSWICK

PATTERNS

KM#	Date	Mintage	Identification	Mkt.Val.
1	1861	—	1 Cent, bronze	700.00

KM#	Date	Mintage	Identification	Mkt.Val.
2	1862	—	10 Cents, silver	1500.
3	1870	—	5 Cents, silver	1500.
4	1870	—	10 Cents, silver	1500.
5	1871	—	10 Cents, silver	1500.

KM#	Date	Mintage	Identification	Mkt.Val.
6	1871	—	20 Cents, silver	1500.

KM#	Date	Mintage	Identification	Mkt.Val.
7	1875	—	5 Cents, silver	1500.
8	1875-H	—	5 Cents, silver	—

TRIAL STRIKES

KM#	Date	Mintage	Identification	Mkt.Val.
T1	1862	—	1 Cent, bronze	—

NOTE: Struck for 1862 proof sets.

NEWFOUNDLAND

PATTERNS

KM#	Date	Mintage	Identification	Mkt.Val.
1	1864	—	1 Cent, bronze	500.00
2	1864	—	1 Cent, bronze	500.00
3	1864	—	5 Cents, bronze	1000.
4	1864	—	10 Cents, bronze	1000.

KM#	Date	Mintage	Identification	Mkt.Val.
5	1864	—	20 Cents, bronze	1500.

KM#	Date	Mintage	Identification	Mkt.Val.
6	1864	—	2 Dollars, bronze	9000.
7	1865	—	1 Cent, bronze	500.00

KM#	Date	Mintage	Identification	Mkt.Val.
8	1865	—	5 Cents, silver	500.00
9	1865	—	5 Cents, silver	500.00

KM#	Date	Mintage	Identification	Mkt.Val.
10	1865	—	10 Cents, silver	850.00
11	1865	—	10 Cents, silver	850.00

KM#	Date	Mintage	Identification	Mkt.Val.
12	1865	—	20 Cents, silver	900.00
13	1865	—	20 Cents, silver	900.00

KM#	Date	Mintage	Identification	Mkt.Val.
14	1865	—	2 Dollars, gold	7000.
15	1865	—	2 Dollars, gold	7000.

KM#	Date	Mintage	Identification	Mkt.Val.
16	1870	—	50 Cents, bronze	2000.

KM#	Date	Mintage	Identification	Mkt.Val.
17	1870	—	2 Dollars, gold	7000.

TRIAL STRIKES

KM#	Date	Mintage	Identification	Mkt.Val.
T1	1864	—	1 Cent, bronze	500.00
T2	1882	—	50 Cents, no H, silver	—
T3	1945C	—	10 Cents, nickel	—

NOVA SCOTIA

PATTERNS

KM#	Date	Mintage	Identification	Mkt.Val.
1	186—	—	1/2 Cent, bronze	850.00

KM#	Date	Mintage	Identification	Mkt.Val.
2	1861	—	1/2 Cent, bronze	850.00
3	1861	—	1/2 Cent, bronze	500.00
4	1861	—	1/2 Cent, bronze	700.00
5	186—	—	1 Cent, bronze	750.00
6	1861	—	1 Cent, bronze	750.00
7	1861	—	1 Cent, bronze	550.00

KM#	Date	Mintage	Identification	Mkt.Val.
8	1861	—	1 Cent, bronze	750.00
9	1861	—	1 Cent, bronze	500.00

CAPE VERDE ISLANDS

The Republic of Cape Verde, Africa's smallest republic, is located in the Atlantic Ocean, about 370 miles (595 km.) west of Dakar, Senegal, off the coast of Africa. The 14-island republic has an area of 1,557 sq. mi. (4,033 sq. km.) and a population of 320,000. Capital: Praia. The refueling of ships and aircraft is the chief economic function of the country. Fishing is important and agriculture is widely practiced, but the Cape Verdes are not self-sufficient in food. Fish products, salt, bananas, and shellfish are exported.

The date of discovery of the islands is uncertain. Possibly they were visited by Venetian captain Alvise Cadamosto in 1456. Portuguese navigator Diogo Gomes claimed them for Portugal in May of 1460. Settlement began two years later. The early importance and wealth of the islands, which caused them to be attacked by Sir Francis Drake and the Dutch, resulted from the monopoly of the Guinea slave trade granted the inhabitants in 1466. Poverty and famine occasioned by frequent periods of severe drought have marked the history of the country since abolition of the slave trade in 1876.

After 500 years of Portuguese rule, the Cape Verdes became independent on July 5, 1975. At the first general election, all seats of the new national assembly were won by the Party for the Independence of Guinea—Bissau and Cape Verde (PAIGC). The PAIGC plans to link the two former colonies into one state.

RULERS

Portuguese, until 1975.

MONETARY SYSTEM

100 Centavos = 1 Escudo

5 CENTAVOS

BRONZE

Y#	Date	Mintage	VF	XF	Unc
1	1930	1.000	1.00	1.75	3.50

10 CENTAVOS

BRONZE

Y#	Date	Mintage	VF	XF	Unc
2	1930	1.500	1.00	2.00	4.00

20 CENTAVOS

BRONZE

Y#	Date	Mintage	VF	XF	Unc
3	1930	1.500	1.00	2.50	5.00

ALUMINUM

Y#	Date	Mintage	VF	XF	Unc
13	1977	—	.25	.50	1.00

50 CENTAVOS

NICKEL-BRONZE

Y#	Date	Mintage	Fine	VF	XF
4	1930	1.000	2.25	5.00	10.00

Y#	Date	Mintage	VF	XF	Unc
6	1949	1.000	.50	1.00	3.00

BRONZE

Y#	Date	Mintage	VF	XF	Unc
A8	1968	1.000	.25	.50	1.00

ALUMINUM

Y#	Date	Mintage	VF	XF	Unc
14	1977	—	.35	.75	1.50

ESCUDO

NICKEL-BRONZE

Y#	Date	Mintage	Fine	VF	XF
5	1930	.050	10.00	17.50	25.00

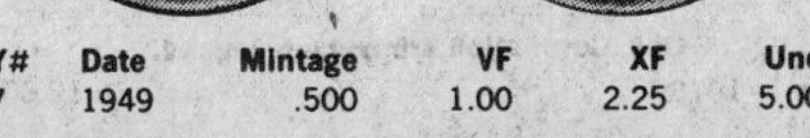

Y#	Date	Mintage	VF	XF	Unc
7	1949	.500	1.00	2.25	5.00

BRONZE

Y#	Date	Mintage	VF	XF	Unc
8	1953	.250	1.25	2.50	4.00
	1968	.500	.50	1.00	1.75

NICKEL-BRONZE
F.A.O. Issues

Y#	Date	Mintage	VF	XF	Unc
15	1977	1.000	.50	1.00	2.00

2-1/2 ESCUDOS

NICKEL-BRONZE

Y#	Date	Mintage	VF	XF	Unc
9	1953	.500	.60	1.25	2.00
	1967	.400	.50	.75	1.75

F.A.O. Issues

Y#	Date	Mintage	VF	XF	Unc
16	1977	1.200	.25	1.40	2.00

5 ESCUDOS

NICKEL-BRONZE

Y#	Date	Mintage	VF	XF	Unc
A10	1968	.200	.75	1.25	2.00

10 ESCUDOS

10.0000 gm., .720 SILVER, .2315 oz ASW

Y#	Date	Mintage	VF	XF	Unc
10	1953	.400	BV	7.50	10.00

COPPER-NICKEL

Y#	Date	Mintage	VF	XF	Unc
17	1977	—	.50	1.75	2.50

20 ESCUDOS

COPPER-NICKEL

Y#	Date	Mintage	VF	XF	Unc
18	1977	—	1.00	2.50	3.00

50 ESCUDOS

COPPER-NICKEL

Y#	Date	Mintage	VF	XF	Unc
19	1977	—	2.00	3.50	5.00

250 ESCUDOS

16.7000 gm., .900 SILVER, .4832 oz ASW
1st Anniversary of Independence

Y#	Date	Mintage	VF	XF	Unc
11	1976	.013	BV	17.50	22.50
	1976	500 Pcs.	—	Proof	50.00

2500 ESCUDOS

8.0000 gm., .900 GOLD, .2315 oz AGW
Similar to 250 Escudos, Y#11.

Y#	Date	Mintage	VF	XF	Unc
12	1976	3,000	—	Proof	300.00

NCLT ISSUES

PROVAS (Pr)

STANDARD METALS
Stamped 'PROVA' in field

Y#	Date	Mintage	Identification	Issue Price	Mkt Val.
Pr1	1930	—	5 Centavos	—	20.00
Pr2	1930	—	10 Centavos	—	20.00
Pr3	1930	—	20 Centavos	—	20.00
Pr4	1930	—	50 Centavos	—	20.00
Pr5	1930	—	1 Escudo	—	20.00
Pr6	1949	—	50 Centavos	—	20.00
Pr7	1949	—	1 Escudo	—	20.00
PrA8	1968	—	50 Centavos	—	20.00
Pr8	1953	—	1 Escudo	—	20.00
Pr8	1954	—	1 Escudo	—	20.00
Pr8	1955	—	1 Escudo	—	20.00
Pr8	1956	—	1 Escudo	—	20.00
Pr8	1957	—	1 Escudo	—	20.00
Pr8	1958	—	1 Escudo	—	20.00
Pr8	1959	—	1 Escudo	—	20.00
Pr8	1960	—	1 Escudo	—	20.00
Pr8	1961	—	1 Escudo	—	20.00
Pr8	1962	—	1 Escudo	—	20.00
Pr8	1963	—	1 Escudo	—	20.00
Pr8	1964	—	1 Escudo	—	20.00
Pr8	1965	—	1 Escudo	—	20.00
Pr8	1966	—	1 Escudo	—	20.00
Pr8	1967	—	1 Escudo	—	20.00
Pr8	1968	—	1 Escudo	—	20.00
Pr9	1953	—	2-1/2 Escudos	—	30.00
Pr9	1954	—	2-1/2 Escudos	—	30.00
Pr9	1955	—	2-1/2 Escudos	—	30.00
Pr9	1956	—	2-1/2 Escudos	—	30.00
Pr9	1957	—	2-1/2 Escudos	—	30.00
Pr9	1958	—	2-1/2 Escudos	—	30.00
Pr9	1959	—	2-1/2 Escudos	—	30.00
Pr9	1960	—	2-1/2 Escudos	—	30.00
Pr9	1961	—	2-1/2 Escudos	—	30.00
Pr9	1962	—	2-1/2 Escudos	—	30.00
Pr9	1963	—	2-1/2 Escudos	—	30.00
Pr9	1964	—	2-1/2 Escudos	—	30.00
Pr9	1965	—	2-1/2 Escudos	—	30.00
Pr9	1966	—	2-1/2 Escudos	—	30.00
Pr9	1967	—	2-1/2 Escudos	—	30.00
PrA10	1968	—	5 Escudos	—	30.00
Pr10	1953	—	10 Escudos	—	45.00

Listings For

CATTARO: refer to Yugoslavia

CAYMAN ISLANDS

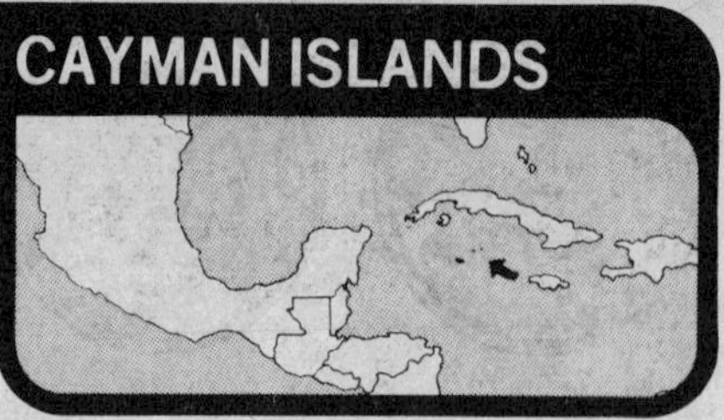

The Cayman Islands, a British dependency situated about 180 miles (290 km.) northwest of Jamaica, consists of three islands: Grand Cayman, Little Cayman, and Cayman Brac. The islands have an area of 118 sq. mi. (306 sq. km.) and a population of 14,000. Capital: Georgetown. Seafaring, commerce, banking, and tourism are the principal industries. Rope, turtle shells, and shark skins are exported.

The islands were discovered by Columbus in 1503, and named by him Tortugas (Spanish for 'turtles') because of the great number of turtles in the nearby waters. They were colonized from Jamaica by the British and remained dependencies of Jamaica until 1959, when they became a unit territory within the West Indies Federation. They became a separate colony when the Federation was dissolved in 1962.

Cayman issued its first national coinage in 1972. The $25 gold and silver commemorative coins issued in 1972 to celebrate the silver wedding anniversary of Queen Elizabeth II and Prince Philip are the first coins in 300 years of Commonwealth coinage to portray a member of the British royal family other than the reigning monarch.

RULERS
British

MONETARY SYSTEM
100 Cents = 1 Dollar

CENT

BRONZE

Y#	Date	Mintage	VF	XF	Unc
1	1972	2.155	—	—	.15
	1972	.011	—	Proof	1.25
	1973	9,988	—	Proof	1.25
	1974	.030	—	Proof	1.00
	1975	7,175	—	Proof	1.25
	1976	3,044	—	Proof	1.50
	1977	—	—	—	.25
	1977	1,970	—	Proof	1.50
	1979FM(P)	—	—	Proof	2.50
	Obv: Coronation Anniversary legend.				
1a	1978	—	—	Proof	2.50

5 CENTS

COPPER-NICKEL

Y#	Date	Mintage	VF	XF	Unc
2	1972	.300	—	.10	.25
	1972	.012	—	Proof	2.00
	1973	.200	—	.15	.30
	1973	9,988	—	Proof	2.00
	1974	.030	—	Proof	2.00
	1975	7,175	—	Proof	2.00
	1976	3,044	—	Proof	2.25
	1977	—	—	—	.20
	1977	1,970	—	Proof	2.50
	1979FM(P)	—	—	Proof	4.00

NOTE: 1973 Uncs. were not put into circulation.

Y#	Date	Mintage	VF	XF	Unc
	Obv: Coronation Anniversary legend.				
2a	1978	—	—	Proof	4.00

10 CENTS

COPPER-NICKEL

Y#	Date	Mintage	VF	XF	Unc
3	1972	.550	.15	.25	.50
	1972	.011	—	Proof	3.00
	1973	.200	.15	.30	.60
	1973	9,988	—	Proof	3.00
	1974	.030	—	Proof	3.00
	1975	7,175	—	Proof	3.00
	1976	3,044	—	Proof	3.00
	1977	—	.15	.30	.60
	1977	1,970	—	Proof	4.00
	1979FM(P)	—	—	Proof	5.00

NOTE: 1973 Uncs. were not put into circulation.

Y#	Date	Mintage	VF	XF	Unc
	Obv: Coronation Anniversary legend.				
3a	1978	—	—	Proof	5.00

25 CENTS

COPPER-NICKEL

Y#	Date	Mintage	VF	XF	Unc
4	1972	.350	.35	.50	1.00
	1972	.011	—	Proof	2.50
	1973	.100	.35	.50	1.25
	1973	9,988	—	Proof	2.50
	1974	.030	—	Proof	2.50
	1975	7,175	—	Proof	2.50
	1976	3,044	—	Proof	3.00
	1977	—	.35	.50	1.00
	1977	1,970	—	Proof	4.00
	1979FM(P)	—	—	Proof	6.00

NOTE: 1973 Uncs. were not put into circulation.

Y#	Date	Mintage	VF	XF	Unc
	Obv: Coronation Anniversary legend.				
4a	1978	—	—	—	—

50 CENTS

10.6100 gm., .925 SILVER, .3155 oz ASW

Y#	Date	Mintage	VF	XF	Unc
5	1972	500 pcs.	12.50	17.50	25.00
	1972	.011	—	Proof	12.00
	1973	9,988	—	Proof	12.00
	1974	.030	—	Proof	12.00
	1975	7,175	—	Proof	12.00
	1976	3,044	—	Proof	12.00
	1977	1,970	—	Proof	15.00
	1979FM(P)	—	—	Proof	12.00
	Obv: Coronation Anniversary legend.				
5a	1978	—	—	Proof	12.00

DOLLAR

18.4100 gm., .925 SILVER, .5475 oz ASW
Obv: Similar to 50 Cents, Y#5.

Y#	Date	Mintage	VF	XF	Unc
6	1972	500 pcs.	17.50	22.50	27.50
	1972	.011	—	Proof	20.00
	1973	9,988	—	Proof	20.00
	1974	.030	—	Proof	20.00
	1975	7,175	—	Proof	20.00
	1976	3,044	—	Proof	20.00
	1977	1,970	—	Proof	25.00
	1979FM(P)	—	—	Proof	20.00
	Obv: Coronation Anniversary legend.				
6a	1978	—	—	Proof	20.00

2 DOLLARS

29.9200 gm., .925 SILVER, .8899 oz ASW
Obv: Similar to 50 Cents, Y#5.

Y#	Date	Mintage	VF	XF	Unc
7	1972	500 pcs.	27.50	35.00	45.00
	1972	.011	—	Proof	30.00
	1973	9,988	—	Proof	30.00
	1974	.030	—	Proof	30.00
	1975	5,390	—	Proof	30.00
	1976	3,044	—	Proof	30.00
	1977	1,970	—	Proof	35.00
	1979FM(P)	—	—	Proof	35.00
	Obv: Coronation Anniversary legend.				
7a	1978	—	—	Proof	30.00

5 DOLLARS

35.8700 gm., .925 SILVER, 1.0668 oz ASW
Obv: Similar to 50 Cents, Y#5.

Y#	Date	Mintage	VF	XF	Unc
8	1972	500 pcs.	35.00	45.00	60.00
	1972	.011	—	Proof	40.00
	1973	.017	—	Proof	40.00
	1974	.026	—	Proof	40.00
	1975	7,753	—	Proof	40.00
	1976	5,177	—	Proof	40.00
	1977	3,525	—	Proof	45.00
	1979FM(P)	—	—	Proof	50.00
	Obv: Coronation Anniversary legend.				
8a	1978	—	—	Proof	50.00

25 DOLLARS

51.5000 gm., .925 SILVER, 1.5317 oz ASW
Silver Wedding Anniversary
Obv: Similar to 50 Cents, Y#5.

Y#	Date	Mintage	VF	XF	Unc
9	1972	.186	BV	50.00	60.00
	1972	.026	—	Proof	70.00

15.7500 gm., .500 GOLD, .2532 oz AGW
Silver Wedding Anniversary

Y#	Date	Mintage	VF	XF	Unc
9a	1972	7,706	BV	165.00	175.00
	1972	.021	—	Proof	175.00

51.5000 gm., .925 SILVER, 1.5317 oz ASW
Churchill Commemorative

Y#	Date	Mintage	VF	XF	Unc
10	1974	1,200	BV	50.00	60.00
	1974	.012	—	Proof	55.00

NOTE: 4300 sets were issued in proof containing Y#10 and Turks & Caicos Islands 20 Crowns Y#2 with an issue price of $80.00.

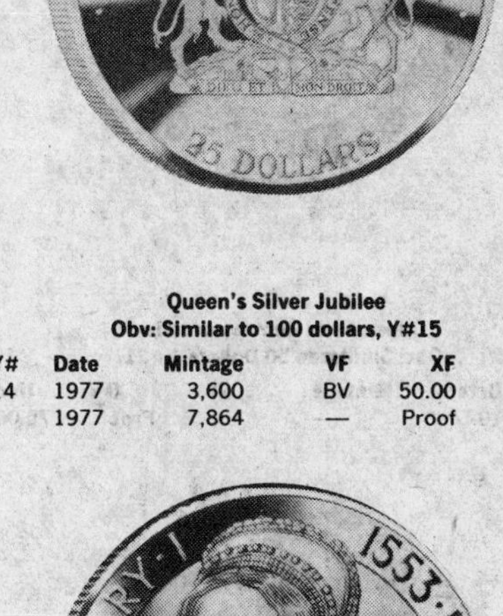

Queen's Silver Jubilee
Obv: Similar to 100 dollars, Y#15

Y#	Date	Mintage	VF	XF	Unc
14	1977	3,600	BV	50.00	60.00
	1977	7,864	—	Proof	70.00

Queen Mary I Commemorative
Obv: Similar to 50 Dollars, Y#21.

Y#	Date	Mintage	VF	XF	Unc
16	1977	—	—	Proof	75.00

Queen Elizabeth I Commemorative
Obv: Similar to 50 Dollars, Y#21.

Y#	Date	Mintage	VF	XF	Unc
17	1977	—	—	Proof	75.00

Queen Mary II Commemorative
Obv: Similar to 50 Dollars, Y#21.

Y#	Date	Mintage	VF	XF	Unc
18	1977	—	—	Proof	75.00

Queen Anne Commemorative
Obv: Similar to 50 Dollars, Y#21.

Y#	Date	Mintage	VF	XF	Unc
19	1977	—	—	Proof	75.00

Queen Victoria Commemorative
Obv: Similar to 50 Dollars, Y#21.

Y#	Date	Mintage	VF	XF	Unc
20	1977	—	—	Proof	75.00

25th Anniversary of Coronation
Obv: Similar to 50 Dollars, Y#21.
Rev: Ampulla.

Y#	Date	Mintage	VF	XF	Unc
26	1978	5,000	—	Proof	75.00

25th Anniversary of Coronation
Obv: Similar to 50 Dollars, Y#21. Rev: Orb.

Y#	Date	Mintage	VF	XF	Unc
27	1978	5,000	—	Proof	75.00

25th Anniversary of Coronation
Obv: Similar to 50 Dollars, Y#21.
Rev: St. Edward's crown.

Y#	Date	Mintage	VF	XF	Unc
28	1978	5,000	—	Proof	75.00

25th Anniversary of Coronation
Obv: Similar to 50 Dollars, Y#21.
Rev: Coronation chair.

Y#	Date	Mintage	VF	XF	Unc
29	1978	5,000	—	Proof	75.00

25th Anniversary of Coronation
Obv: Similar to 50 Dollars, Y#21.
Rev: Royal scepter.

Y#	Date	Mintage	VF	XF	Unc
30	1978	5,000	—	Proof	75.00

25th Anniversary of Coronation
Obv: Similar to 50 Dollars, Y#21. Rev: Spoon.

Y#	Date	Mintage	VF	XF	Unc
31	1978	5,000	—	Proof	75.00

50 DOLLARS

64.9400 gm., .925 SILVER, 1.9314 oz ASW
Sovereign Queens of England
Obv: Similar to 50 cents, Y#5

Y#	Date	Mintage	VF	XF	Unc
12	1975	.033	BV	65.00	80.00
	1975	7,800	—	Proof	125.00
	1976	1,292	BV	75.00	100.00
	1976	2,843	—	Proof	125.00
	1977	—	BV	65.00	80.00
	1977	—	—	Proof	100.00

Rev: Coronation Anniversary legend.

Y#	Date	Mintage	VF	XF	Unc
38	1978	5,000	—	Proof	—

11.3400 gm., .500 GOLD, .1823 oz AGW
Queen Mary I Commemorative

Y#	Date	Mintage	VF	XF	Unc
21	1977	—	—	Proof	225.00

Queen Elizabeth I Commemorative

Y#	Date	Mintage	VF	XF	Unc
22	1977	—	—	Proof	225.00

Queen Mary II Commemorative

Y#	Date	Mintage	VF	XF	Unc
23	1977	—	—	Proof	225.00

Queen Anne Commemorative

Y#	Date	Mintage	VF	XF	Unc
24	1977	—	—	Proof	225.00

Queen Victoria Commemorative

Y#	Date	Mintage	VF	XF	Unc
25	1977	—	—	Proof	225.00

25th Anniversary of Coronation
Obv: Similar to Y#21. Rev: Ampulla.

Y#	Date	Mintage	VF	XF	Unc
32	1978	5,000	—	Proof	225.00

25th Anniversary of Coronation
Obv: Similar to Y#21. Rev: Orb.

Y#	Date	Mintage	VF	XF	Unc
33	1978	5,000	—	Proof	225.00

25th Anniversary of Coronation
Obv: Similar to Y#21. Rev: St. Edward's crown.

Y#	Date	Mintage	VF	XF	Unc
34	1978	5,000	—	Proof	225.00

25th Anniversary of Coronation
Obv: Similar to Y#21. Rev: Chair.

Y#	Date	Mintage	VF	XF	Unc
35	1978	5,000	—	Proof	225.00

25th Anniversary of Coronation
Obv: Similar to Y#21. Rev: Scepter.

Y#	Date	Mintage	VF	XF	Unc
36	1978	5,000	—	Proof	225.00

25th Anniversary of Coronation
Obv: Similar to Y#21. Rev: Spoon.

Y#	Date	Mintage	VF	XF	Unc
37	1978	5,000	—	Proof	225.00

100 DOLLARS

22.6801 gm., .500 GOLD, .3646 oz AGW
Churchill Commemorative

Y#	Date	Mintage	VF	XF	Unc
11	1974	1,400	BV	250.00	275.00
	1974	6,300	—	Proof	300.00

Sovereign Queens of England
Obv: Similar to 50 Cents, Y#5.

Y#	Date	Mintage	VF	XF	Unc
13	1975	8,053	BV	250.00	275.00
	1975	4,950	—	Proof	300.00
	1976	1,164	BV	250.00	275.00
	1976	2,105	—	Proof	300.00
	1977	—	BV	250.00	275.00
	1977	—	—	Proof	1300.

Queen's Silver Jubilee

Y#	Date	Mintage	VF	XF	Unc
15	1977	562 pcs.	250.00	275.00	300.00
	1977	2,420	—	Proof	325.00

Rev: Coronation Anniversary legend.

Y#	Date	Mintage	VF	XF	Unc
39	1978	5,000	—	—	—

NCLT ISSUES

PROOF SETS
STANDARD METALS

KM#	Date	Mintage	Identification	Issue Price	Mkt. Val.
101	1972(8)	10,757	Y1-8	40.00	100.00
102	1973(8)	9,988	Y1-8	40.00	100.00
103	1974(8)	15,387	Y1-8	40.00	100.00
104	1974(2)	2,400	Y10-11	245.00	350.00
105	1975(8)	5,390	Y1-8	54.50	100.00
106	1975(6)	1,785	Y1-6	31.50	40.00
107	1975(2)	3,650	Y12,13	293.00	425.00
108	1976(8)	3,044	Y1-8	54.50	100.00
109	1976(2)	1,531	Y12,13	293.00	425.00
111	1977(8)	1,970	Y1-8	52.50	125.00
112	1977(6)	2,445	Y12, 16-20	315.00	475.00
113	1977(6)	1,932	Y13, 21-25	651.00	1400.
114	1977(2)	223	Y14,15	290.00	395.00
115	1978(6)	5,000	Y26-31	306.00	450.00
116	1978(6)	5,000	Y32-37	600.00	1350.
117	1979(8)	—	Y1-8	117.00	120.00

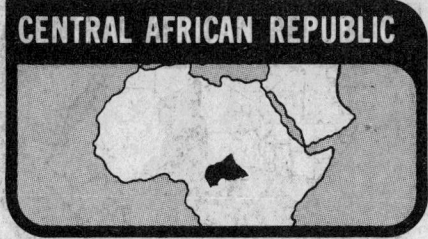

CENTRAL AFRICAN REPUBLIC

The Central African Republic, a landlocked country in Central Africa, bounded by Chad on the north, Cameroon on the west, Congo (Brazzaville) and Zaire on the south, and The Sudan on the east, has an area of 242,000 sq. mi. (626,777 sq. km.) and a population of 2.2 million. Capital: Bangui. Deposits of uranium, iron ore, manganese and copper remain to be developed. Diamonds, cotton, timber and coffee are exported.

The area that is now the Central African Republic was constituted as the French territory of Ubangi-Shari in 1894. It was united with Chad in 1905 and joined with Middle Congo and Gabon in 1910, becoming one of the four territories of French Equatorial Africa. Upon dissolution of the federation on Dec. 1, 1958, the constituent territories became fully autonomous members of the French Community. Ubangi-Shari proclaimed its complete independence as the Central African Republic on Aug. 13, 1960.

On Jan. 1, 1966, Col. Jean-Bedel Bokassa, Chief of Staff of the Armed Forces, overthrew the government of President David Dacko and assumed power as president of the republic. President Bokassa abolished the constitution of 1959 and dissolved the National Assembly. In 1975 the Congress of the sole political party appointed Bokassa president for life. The republic became a constitutional monarchy on Dec. 4, 1976; President Bokassa was named Emperor Bokassa I. Bokassa was ousted as Central African emperor in a bloodless takeover of the government led by former president David Dacko on Sept. 20, 1979, and the African nation proclaimed once again a republic.

NOTE: Also see French Equatorial Africa and Equatorial African States.

RULERS

French, until 1960
Marshal Jean-Bedel Bokassa,
1976-1979

MINTMARKS

(a) - Paris, privy marks only

MONETARY SYSTEM

100 Centimes = 1 Franc

100 FRANCS

NICKEL

Y#	Date	Mintage	Fine	VF	XF	Unc
1	1971(a)	3.500	.75	1.00	1.25	2.00
	1972(a)	—	.75	1.00	1.25	2.00
	1974(a)	—	.75	1.00	1.25	2.00

Y#	Date	Mintage	Fine	VF	XF	Unc
2	1975(a)	—	.75	1.00	1.25	2.00
	1976(a)	—	—	—	—	2.00

Central African Empire

Y#	Date	Mintage	Fine	VF	XF	Unc
	1978(a)	—	—	—	—	—

1000 FRANCS

3.5000 gm., .900 GOLD, .1012 oz AGW
10th Anniversary of Independence
Obv: Bust of Pres. Jean Bedel Bokasso. Rev: Arms.

H#	Date	Mintage	XF	Unc	Proof
1	1970	4,000	—	—	75.00

3000 FRANCS

10.5000 gm., .900 GOLD, .3038 oz AGW
10th Anniversary of Independence

H#	Date	Mintage	XF	Unc	Proof
2	1970	4,000	—	—	225.00

5000 FRANCS

17.5000 gm., .900 GOLD, .5064 oz AGW
10th Anniversary of Independence

H#	Date	Mintage	XF	Unc	Proof
3	1970	4,000	—	—	350.00

10,000 FRANCS

35.0000 gm., .900 GOLD, 1.0128 oz AGW
10th Anniversary of Independence
Obv: Bust of Pres. Jean Bedel Bokassa.
Rev: Globe with figures above.

H#	Date	Mintage	XF	Unc	Proof
4	1970	4,000	—	—	700.00

6.1400 gm., .900 GOLD, .1776 oz AGW

Y#	Date	Mintage	VF	XF	Unc
—	ND(1979)	—	—	—	—

20,000 FRANCS

70.0000 gm., .900 GOLD, 2.0257 oz AGW
10th Anniversary of Independence

H#	Date	Mintage	XF	Unc	Proof
5	1970	4,000	—	—	1400.

25,000 FRANCS

15.3500 gm., .900 GOLD, .4442 oz AGW
Obv: Similar to 10,000 Francs, Y#

Y#	Date	Mintage	VF	XF	Unc
—	ND(1979)	—	—	—	—

NCLT ISSUES

ESSAIS (E)

Standard metals unless otherwise noted

Y#	Date	Mintage	Identification	Issue Price	Mkt Val.
E1	1971(a)	—	100 Francs	—	22.50
E2	1975(a)	—	100 Francs	—	22.50
E3	1978(a)	—	100 Francs	—	—

PROOF SETS

STANDARD METALS

KM#	Date	Mintage	Identification	Issue Price	Mkt. Val.
1	1970(5)	4,000	H1-5	376.35	2750.

CENTRAL AFRICAN STATES

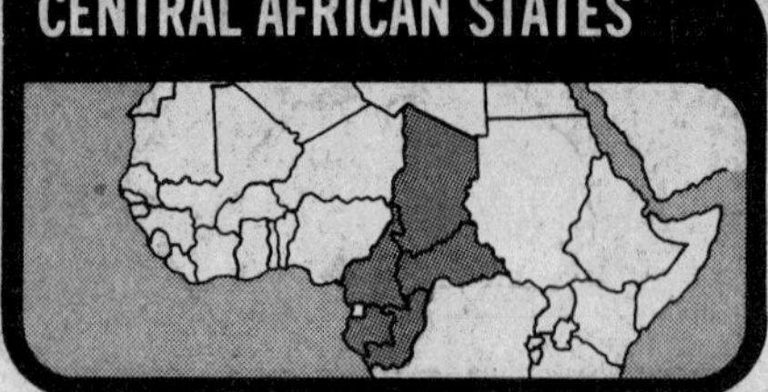

The Central African States, a monetary union comprising the former French possessions and now independent states of the Republic of Congo (Brazzaville), Gabon, Central African Republic, Chad and Cameroon, issues a common currency for the member states from a common central bank. The monetary unit, the African Financial Community Franc, is tied to and supported by the French franc.

In 1960, an abortive attempt was made to form a union of the newly independent republics of Chad, Congo, Central Africa and Gabon. The proposal was discarded when Chad refused to become a constituent member. The four countries then linked into an Equatorial Customs Unit, to which Cameroon became an associate member in 1961. A more extensive cooperation of the five republics, identified as the Central African Customs and Economic Union, was entered into force at the beginning of 1966.

In 1974 the Central Bank of the Equatorial African States, which had issued coins and paper currency in its own name and with the names of the constituent member nations, changed its name to the Bank of the Central African States.

NOTE: For earlier coinage see French Equatorial Africa.

EQUATORIAL AFRICAN STATES

MINT MARKS

(a) - Paris, privy marks only

MONETARY SYSTEM

100 Centimes = 1 Franc (C.F.A.)

FRANC

ALUMINUM

Y#	Date	Mintage	Fine	VF	XF	Unc
A1	1967(a)	—	.10	.25	.50	1.00
	1969(a)	2.500	.10	.15	.20	.40
	1971(a)	3.000	.10	.15	.20	.35

5 FRANCS

ALUMINUM-BRONZE

Y#	Date	Mintage	Fine	VF	XF	Unc
1	1961(a)	10.000	.10	.15	.20	.40
	1962(a)	5.000	.10	.15	.20	.50
	1965(a)	2.010	.10	.15	.25	.60
	1967(a)	5.795	.10	.15	.20	.50
	1968(a)	5.000	.10	.15	.20	.50
	1969(a)	—	.10	.15	.20	.50
	1970(a)	9.000	.10	.15	.20	.50
	1972(a)	5.010	.10	.15	.20	.50
	1973(a)	5.010	.10	.15	.20	.50
	1974(a)	26.000	.10	.15	.20	.40

10 FRANCS

ALUMINUM-BRONZE

Y#	Date	Mintage	Fine	VF	XF	Unc
2	1961(a)	10.000	.10	.15	.25	.50
	1962(a)	5.000	.10	.15	.25	.50
	1965(a)	7.000	.10	.15	.25	.50
	1967(a)	8.000	.10	.15	.25	.50
	1968(a)	2.000	.10	.20	.35	.65
	1969(a)	10.000	.10	.15	.25	.50
	1972(a)	5.000	.10	.15	.25	.50
	1973(a)	5.000	.10	.15	.25	.50
	1974(a)	18.500	.10	.15	.25	.50

25 FRANCS

ALUMINUM-BRONZE

Y#	Date	Mintage	Fine	VF	XF	Unc
3	1962(a)	6.000	.20	.30	.50	1.00
	1968(a)	—	.20	.30	.50	1.00
	1969(a)	—	.20	.30	.50	1.00
	1970(a)	3.019	.20	.30	.50	1.00
	1972(a)	5.016	.20	.30	.50	1.00
	1973(a)	—	.20	.30	.50	1.00
	1974(a)	13.500	.20	.30	.50	1.00

50 FRANCS

COPPER-NICKEL

Y#	Date	Mintage	Fine	VF	XF	Unc
4	1961(a)	5.000	.75	1.25	2.00	3.50
	1963(a)	5.000	1.00	2.00	3.50	5.00

100 FRANCS

NICKEL

Y#	Date	Mintage	Fine	VF	XF	Unc
5	1966(a)	9.948	1.00	1.50	2.00	2.50
	1967(a)	11.000	1.00	1.50	2.00	2.50
	1968(a)	—	1.00	1.50	2.50	4.00

NOTE: For later 100-Francs issues see individual listings under Central African Republic. Congo Peoples' Republic, Gabon, Chad and Cameroun.

NCLT ISSUES

ESSAIS (E)

Standard metals unless otherwise noted.

Y#	Date	Mintage	Identification	Issue Price	Mkt Val.
EA1	1969(a)	—	1 Franc	—	20.00
E1	1961(a)	—	5 Francs	—	20.00
E2	1961(a)	—	10 Francs	—	25.00
E3	1962(a)	—	25 Francs*	—	35.00
E4	1961(a)	1,550	50 Francs	—	25.00
E4a	1961(a)	6 pcs.	50 Francs, Gold	—	—
E5	1966(a)	—	100 Francs	—	25.00

NOTE: The 25 Francs, 1962(a) ESSAI is a mule having an old reverse die with wing privy mark.

CENTRAL AFRICAN STATES

FRANC

ALUMINUM

Y#	Date	Mintage	VF	XF	Unc
6	1974(a)	—	.10	.15	.35
	1976(a)	—	.10	.15	.35

5 FRANCS

ALUMINUM-BRONZE

Y#	Date	Mintage	VF	XF	Unc
7	1973(a)	—	.10	.20	.40
	1975(a)	—	.10	.20	.40
	1976(a)	—	.10	.20	.40

10 FRANCS

ALUMINUM-BRONZE

Y#	Date	Mintage	VF	XF	Unc
8	1975(a)	—	.15	.25	.65
	1976(a)	—	.15	.25	.65
	1977(a)	—	.15	.25	.65

25 FRANCS

ALUMINUM-BRONZE

Y#	Date	Mintage	VF	XF	Unc
9	1975(a)	—	.20	.40	1.00

50 FRANCS

NICKEL

Y#	Date	Mintage	VF	XF	Unc
10	1976(a)	10.000	.40	.75	1.25
	1977(a)	—	.40	.75	1.25

NOTE: Coins have letter A, B, C, D, or E on reverse above value near rim.

500 FRANCS

COPPER NICKEL

Y#	Date	Mintage	VF	XF	Unc
11	1976(a)	4.000	3.50	5.00	8.00

NOTE: Coins have letter A, B, C, D or E on reverse above value near rim.

NCLT ISSUES

ESSAIS (E)

Standard metals unless otherwise noted.

Y#	Date	Mintage	Identification	Issue Price	Mkt Val.
E6	1974(a)	—	1 Franc	—	25.00
E8	1974(a)	—	10 Francs	—	25.00
E9	1975(a)	—	25 Francs	—	—
E10	1976(a)	—	50 Francs*	—	25.00
E11	1976(a)	—	500 Francs*	—	25.00

***NOTE:** Essais exist with each letter - A, B, C, D and E. Believed to indicate the five constituent nations of the Central African States.

CENTRAL AMERICAN REP.

The Central American Republic (Provincias Unidas del Centro de America, Republic of the United States of Central America, Central American Union) was an 1823-39 confederation of the former departments of the Captaincy General of Guatemala - Guatemala, Honduras, El Salvador, Nicaragua and Costa Rica - formed after the downfall of the short-lived Mexican empire of Augustin de Iturbide. The confederation, which occupied all of Central America between Mexico and Panama, had a population of fewer than 1.5 million. There was no permanent capital.

On Sept. 15, 1821, the leaders of the Captaincy General that governed the five provinces of Central America for Spain, declared Central America independent from Spain. The following year, Iturbide crowned himself Augustin I of Mexico and invited the Central Americans to join his empire. Guatemala, Honduras, Nicaragua and Costa Rica did so. El Salvador, which desired to become a part of the United States, refused and was invaded and conquered for Mexico by Vicente Filisola, the military governor Iturbide had sent to Guatemala. But almost before El Salvador had been forced into the Mexican empire, Iturbide was ousted and sent into exile by Antonio Lopez de Santa Anna. Filisola then reconvened the National Constituent Assembly that had been called into existence by the Central American declaration of independence of 1821. On July 1, 1823, the Assembly issued a second declaration of independence, from Mexico as well as Spain, and established the Central American Republic.

Historically the confederation, which lasted 15 years, was a triumph of rhetoric over reality. It had neither permanent capital, army nor treasury and was all but powerless to raise funds. The political leaders managed to write a constitution, but it was as ineffectual as the first constitution of the United States, the Articles of Confederation. The citizens of the Central American Republic had no sense of nationhood and were divided by religious and class animosity. By 1827 the entire confederation was embroiled in a civil war. By the end of 1838 every province but El Salvador had seceded from the ill-advised union, however both Costa Rica and Guatemala continued to strike coins of the same style until 1850 and 1851 respectively.

MINTMARKS

CR - San Jose, Costa Rica
G - Guatemala
NG - Guatemala
T - Tegucigalpa, Honduras

MONETARY SYSTEM

16 Reales = 1 Escudo

1/4 REAL

.8500 gm., .903 SILVER, .0246 oz ASW

MINTMARK: CR

C#	Date	Mintage	VG	Fine	VF	XF
1	1845	—	25.00	45.00	75.00	125.00

MINTMARK: G

C#	Date	Mintage	VG	Fine	VF	XF
91	1824	—	5.50	11.50	22.50	37.50
	1826	—	3.50	7.50	15.00	25.00
	1828	—	—	—	Rare	—
	1831	—	3.50	7.50	15.00	25.00
	1833	—	6.50	13.50	26.50	42.50
	1837	—	3.00	6.50	13.50	22.50
	1838	—	4.50	10.00	20.00	35.00
	1840/30	—	2.50	6.00	12.00	20.00
	1841	—	—	—	Rare	—

C#	Date	Mintage	VG	Fine	VF	XF
91	1842/29	—	2.50	6.00	12.00	20.00
	1842/31	—	2.50	6.00	12.00	20.00
	1842	—	2.50	6.00	12.00	20.00
	1843	—	2.50	6.00	12.00	20.00
	1844	—	2.50	6.00	12.00	20.00
	1845	—	6.50	15.00	30.00	50.00
	1846	—	2.50	6.00	12.00	20.00
	1847	—	—	—	Rare	—
	1850	—	8.00	17.50	35.00	60.00
	1851	—	8.00	17.50	35.00	60.00

1/2 REAL

1.6500 gm., .903 SILVER, .0479 oz ASW

MINTMARK: CR

C#	Date	Mintage	VG	Fine	VF	XF
2	1831 E	—	7.00	15.00	30.00	50.00
	1831 F	—	6.00	12.50	25.00	40.00
	1843 M	—	6.00	12.50	25.00	40.00
	1845 B	—	8.50	17.50	35.00	60.00
	1846 JB 'CRESCA'	—	6.50	13.50	27.50	45.00
	1846 JB 'CREZCA'	—	11.50	22.50	40.00	75.00
	1847 JB	—	6.50	13.50	27.50	45.00
	1848 JB	—	4.50	10.00	20.00	35.00
	1849 JB	—	14.50	30.00	50.00	85.00

MINTMARK: NG

C#	Date	Mintage	VG	Fine	VF	XF
92	1824 M	—	7.50	15.00	30.00	50.00

MINTMARK: T

Obv: Sun to left of 3 mountains.
Rev: Ceiba tree divides value, in circle.

C#	Date	Mintage	VG	Fine	VF	XF
21	1830 F	—	—	—	Rare	—
	1831 F	—	—	—	Rare	—

REAL

3.2500 gm., .903 SILVER, .0943 oz ASW

MINTMARK: CR

C#	Date	Mintage	VG	Fine	VF	XF
3	1831 E	—	8.50	17.50	35.00	60.00
	1831 F	—	7.50	15.00	30.00	50.00
	1848 JB	—	21.50	42.50	85.00	140.00
	1849 JB	—	11.50	22.50	45.00	75.00

MINTMARK: NG

C#	Date	Mintage	VG	Fine	VF	XF
93	1824 M	—	7.50	15.00	30.00	50.00
	1828 M	—	22.50	45.00	90.00	150.00

MINTMARK: T

Obv: Sun to left of 3 mountains.
Rev: Ceiba tree divides value, in circle.

C#	Date	Mintage	VG	Fine	VF	XF
22	1830 F	—	5.00	10.00	20.00	35.00
	1831 F	—	—	—	Rare	—

2 REALES

6.5000 gm., .903 SILVER, .1887 oz ASW

MINTMARK: CR

C#	Date	Mintage	VG	Fine	VF	XF
4	1848 JB	—		Reported, not confirmed		
	1849 JB	—	—	—	Rare	—

MINTMARK: T

C#	Date	Mintage	VG	Fine	VF	XF
23	1825 M	—	—	—	Rare	—
	1830 F	—		Reported, not confirmed		
	1831 F	—	6.00	10.00	20.00	35.00
	1832 F	—	7.50	12.50	25.00	40.00

8 REALES

25.0000 gm., .903 SILVER, .7258 oz ASW

MINTMARK: CR

C#	Date	Mintage	VG	Fine	VF	XF
5	1831 E	—	750.00	1250.	2500.	4000.
	1831 F	—	250.00	500.00	750.00	1200.

MINTMARK: NG

Obv: Similar to C#5.

C#	Date	Mintage	VG	Fine	VF	XF
95	1824 M	—	30.00	50.00	90.00	150.00
	1825 M	—	25.00	35.00	75.00	135.00
	1826 M	—	25.00	35.00	75.00	135.00
	1827 M	—	25.00	35.00	75.00	135.00
	1828 M	—	30.00	40.00	100.00	175.00
	1829 M	—	25.00	35.00	75.00	135.00
	1830 M	—	175.00	250.00	450.00	700.00
	1831 M	—	275.00	400.00	650.00	1500.
	1834 M	—	175.00	250.00	450.00	700.00
	1835 M	—	25.00	35.00	75.00	135.00
	1836 M	—	25.00	35.00	75.00	135.00
	1836 BA	—	25.00	35.00	75.00	135.00
	1837 BA	—	25.00	35.00	75.00	135.00
	1838 BA	—	—	—	Rare	—
	1839/7 MA/BA		25.00	35.00	65.00	125.00
	1839 BA		25.00	35.00	80.00	150.00
	1840/37 MA/BA		25.00	35.00	65.00	125.00
	1840 MA	—	35.00	70.00	125.00	275.00
	1841/37 MA/BA		40.00	75.00	150.00	250.00
	1841 MA	—	65.00	110.00	280.00	450.00
	1842/37 MA/BA		25.00	35.00	65.00	125.00
95	1842 MA	—	25.00	35.00	65.00	125.00
	1846 MA	—	35.00	60.00	125.00	250.00
	1846 AE/MA with CREZCA over CRESCA	—	25.00	35.00	70.00	125.00
	1846 A	—	25.00	35.00	75.00	135.00
	1847/6 A	—	25.00	35.00	70.00	125.00
	1847 A	—	25.00	35.00	70.00	125.00

1/2 ESCUDO

1.6875 gm., .875 GOLD, .0474 oz AGW

MINTMARK: CR

Provisional Issue

C#	Date	Mintage	VG	Fine	VF	XF
5.1	1825	2 known	—	—	Rare	—
	1826	—	—	—	—	—

C#	Date	Mintage	VG	Fine	VF	XF
6	1828 F	4,435	40.00	75.00	100.00	135.00
	1843 M	593	75.00	150.00	200.00	300.00
	1846 JB	.013	35.00	60.00	85.00	125.00
	1847 JB	.023	35.00	60.00	85.00	125.00
	1848 JB	.014	35.00	60.00	85.00	125.00
	1849 JB	Inc. Ab.	75.00	150.00	200.00	300.00

MINTMARK: NG

C#	Date	Mintage	VG	Fine	VF	XF
111	1824 M	—	50.00	100.00	175.00	250.00
	1825 M	—	35.00	60.00	85.00	125.00
	1826 M	—	35.00	60.00	85.00	125.00
	1843 M	—	50.00	100.00	175.00	250.00

ESCUDO

3.3750 gm., .875 GOLD, .0949 oz AGW

MINTMARK: CR

C#	Date	Mintage	VG	Fine	VF	XF
7	1833 E	.010	65.00	100.00	125.00	175.00
	1833 F	Inc. Ab.	75.00	125.00	150.00	225.00
	1844 M	6,353	65.00	100.00	125.00	175.00
	1845 JB	8,672	75.00	125.00	175.00	300.00
	1846 JB	2,722	65.00	100.00	125.00	175.00
	1847 JB	3,510	75.00	125.00	150.00	200.00
	1848 JB	.010	75.00	125.00	150.00	200.00
	1849 JB	.013	75.00	125.00	150.00	200.00

MINTMARK: NG

Obv: Sun over 5 mountains.
Rev: Ceiba tree dividing value, in circle.

C#	Date	Mintage	VG	Fine	VF	XF
112	1824 M	—	85.00	175.00	250.00	350.00
	1825 M	—	85.00	175.00	250.00	350.00

2 ESCUDOS

6.7500 gm., .875 GOLD, .1899 oz AGW

MINTMARK: CR

C#	Date	Mintage	VG	Fine	VF	XF
8	1828 F	2,750	150.00	200.00	275.00	375.00
	1835 F	5,452	150.00	200.00	275.00	375.00
	1843 F	4,482	150.00	200.00	300.00	400.00
	1846 JB	—	150.00	200.00	350.00	450.00
	1850 JB	7,432	150.00	200.00	275.00	375.00

MINTMARK: NG

C#	Date	Mintage	VG	Fine	VF	XF
113	1825 M	—	150.00	200.00	275.00	375.00
	1826 M	—	150.00	200.00	275.00	375.00
	1827 M	—	150.00	200.00	275.00	375.00
	1828 M	—	150.00	200.00	275.00	375.00
	1830 M	—	200.00	250.00	325.00	450.00
	1835 M	—	150.00	200.00	275.00	375.00
	1836 M	—	175.00	225.00	325.00	425.00
	1837 BA	—	175.00	225.00	350.00	600.00
	1842 MA	—	175.00	225.00	325.00	575.00
	1846 A	—	175.00	225.00	325.00	450.00
	1847 A	—	175.00	225.00	325.00	500.00

4 ESCUDOS

13.5000 gm., .875 GOLD, .3798 oz AGW

MINTMARK: CR

C#	Date	Mintage	VG	Fine	VF	XF
9	1828 F	3,048	350.00	600.00	1200.	1750.
	1835 F	697	325.00	550.00	1100.	1600.
	1837 E	.011	300.00	475.00	850.00	1250.
	1837 F	Inc. Ab.	400.00	700.00	1200.	1750.
	1849 JB	441	425.00	750.00	1400.	2000.

MINTMARK: NG

Similar to 2 Escudos, C#113.

C#	Date	Mintage	VG	Fine	VF	XF
114	1824 M	—	900.00	1500.	2750.	4500.
	1825 M	—	1000.	1750.	3000.	5000.
	1826 M	—	—	—	Rare	—

8 ESCUDOS

27.0000 gm., .875 GOLD, .7596 oz AGW

MINTMARK: CR

C#	Date	Mintage	VG	Fine	VF	XF
10	1828 F	5,302	750.00	1250.	2250.	3250.
	1833 F	4,459	750.00	1250.	2250.	3250.
	1837 E	2,028	800.00	1300.	2500.	3500.
	1837 F	Inc. Ab.	1000.	1750.	3000.	4000.

MINTMARK: NG

C#	Date	Mintage	VG	Fine	VF	XF
115	1824 M	—	2000.	3500.	5500.	9000.
	1825 M	—	2250.	4000.	6000.	10,000.

Listings For

CEYLON: refer to Sri Lanka

CHAD

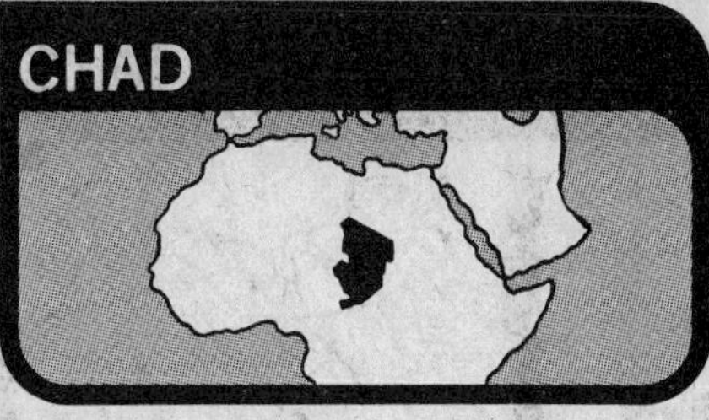

The Republic of Chad, a landlocked country of central Africa, is the largest country of former French Equatorial Africa. It has an area of 496,000 sq. mi. (1,284,634 sq. km.) and a population of 4 million. Capital: N'Djamena. An expanding livestock industry produces camels, cattle and sheep. Cotton (the chief product), ivory and palm oil are important exports.

Although supposedly known to Ptolemy, the Chad area was first visited by white men in 1823. Exaggerated estimates of its economic importance led to a race for its possession (1890-93) which resulted in the territory being divided by treaty between Great Britain, France and Germany. As a consequence of World War I, the German area was mandated to France in 1919. Chad was absorbed into the colony of French Equatorial Africa, as part of Ubangi-Shari, in 1910 and became a separate colony in 1920. Upon dissolution of French Equatorial Africa in 1959, the component states became autonomous members of the French Union. Chad became an independent republic on Aug. 11, 1960.

NOTE: For earlier and related coinage see French Equatorial Africa and the Equatorial African States.

MINTMARKS

(a) - Paris, privy marks only

100 FRANCS

3.2200 gm., .925 SILVER, .0957 oz ASW
Robert Francis Kennedy

KM#	Date	Mintage	XF	Unc	Proof
7	1970	975 pcs.	—	—	12.50

NICKEL

Y#	Date	Mintage	Fine	VF	XF	Unc
1	1971(a)	5.000	.75	1.25	2.00	3.50
	1972(a)	5.000	.75	1.25	2.00	3.50

Y#	Date	Mintage	Fine	VF	XF	Unc
2	1975(a)	—	.75	1.00	1.25	2.00

200 FRANCS

15.0000 gm., .925 SILVER, .4461 oz ASW
Martin Luther King, Jr.

KM#	Date	Mintage	XF	Unc	Proof
8	1970	952 pcs.	—	—	25.00

.800 SILVER
General De Gaulle

KM#	Date	Mintage	XF	Unc	Proof
10	1970	877 pcs.	Reported, Not Confirmed		

President Nasser

KM#	Date	Mintage	XF	Unc	Proof
11	1970	Inc. Ab.	Reported, Not Confirmed		

300 FRANCS

30.0000 gm., .925 SILVER, .8922 oz ASW
John Fitzgerald Kennedy

KM#	Date	Mintage	XF	Unc	Proof
9	1970	504 pcs.	—	—	50.00

1000 FRANCS

3.5000 gm., .900 GOLD, .1012 oz AGW
Commandant Lamy

KM#	Date	Mintage	XF	Unc	Proof
1	1970	4,000	—	—	75.00

3000 FRANCS

10.5000 gm., .900 GOLD, .3038 oz AGW
Governor Eboue

KM#	Date	Mintage	XF	Unc	Proof
2	1970	4,000	—	—	225.00

5000 FRANCS

17.5000 gm., .900 GOLD, .5064 oz AGW
General Leclerc

KM#	Date	Mintage	XF	Unc	Proof
3	1970	4,000	—	—	350.00

10,000 FRANCS

35.0000 gm., .900 GOLD, 1.0128 oz AGW
General DeGaulle

KM#	Date	Mintage	XF	Unc	Proof
4	1970	4,000	—	—	700.00

20,000 FRANCS

70.0000 gm., .900 GOLD, 2.0257 oz AGW
Francois Tombalbaye

KM#	Date	Mintage	XF	Unc	Proof
5	1970	4,000	—	—	1400.

NCLT ISSUES

ESSAIS (E)

Standard metals unless otherwise noted

Y#	Date	Mintage	Identification	Issue Price	Mkt Val.
E1	1971(a)	—	100 Francs	—	20.00
E2	1975(a)	—	100 Francs	—	20.00

PROOF SETS

STANDARD METALS

KM#	Date	Mintage	Identification	Issue Price	Mkt. Val.
101	1970(5)	4,000	KM1-5	412.50	2750.
102	1970(3)	—	KM7-9	33.00	80.00

CHILE

The Republic of Chile, a ribbonlike country on the Pacific coast of southern South America, has an area of 292,258 sq. mi. (756,945 sq. km.) and a population of 10.7 million. Capital: Santiago. Historically, the economic base of Chile has been the rich mineral deposits of its northern provinces. Copper, of which Chile has 25 percent of the free world's reserves, has accounted for more than 75 percent of Chile's export earnings in recent years. Other important exports are iron ore, iodine and nitrate of soda.

Diego de Almargo was the first Spaniard to attempt to wrest Chile from the Incas and Araucanian tribes in 1536. He failed, and was followed by Pedro de Valdivia, a favorite of Pizarro, who founded Santiago in 1541. When the Napoleonic Wars involved Spain, leaving the constituent parts of the Spanish Empire to their own devices, Chilean patriots formed a national government and proclaimed the country's independence, Sept. 18, 1810. Independence, however, was not secured until Feb. 12, 1818, after a bitter struggle led by Bernardo O'Higgins and San Martin.

In 1960, the peso was replaced by the escudo, valued at 1,000 pesos. In 1975, the peso was reintroduced, valued at 1,000 escudos.

RULERS

Spanish until 1818

MINTMARKS

So - Santiago

MONETARY SYSTEM

16 Reales = 1 Escudo

COLONIAL COINAGE

1/4 REAL

.903 SILVER

SANTIAGO MINT (So)

Obv. leg: CAROL IV, bust of Charles III. Rev: Castles within wreath.

C#	Date	Mintage	VG	Fine	VF	XF
36	1790	.322	18.50	30.00	50.00	80.00
	1791/0	.253	20.00	32.50	55.00	70.00
	1791	Inc. Ab.	15.00	25.00	40.00	65.00

Obv. leg: CAROL IIII..., bust of Charles III.

C#	Date	Mintage	VG	Fine	VF	XF
46	1791	Inc. Ab.	16.50	27.50	45.00	75.00
	1792	.229	16.50	27.50	45.00	75.00

Obv. leg: CAROL IIII, bust of Charles IIII.

C#	Date	Mintage	VG	Fine	VF	XF
55	1792	Inc. Ab.	16.50	27.50	45.00	75.00
	1793	.240	16.50	27.50	45.00	75.00

Obv: Lion. Rev: Castle, date below.

C#	Date	Mintage	VG	Fine	VF	XF
56	1796	.063	6.50	13.50	22.50	50.00
	1797	.066	6.50	13.50	22.50	50.00
	1798	.050	6.50	13.50	22.50	50.00
	1799	.042	6.50	13.50	22.50	50.00
	1800	.072	6.50	13.50	22.50	50.00
	1801	.057	6.50	13.50	22.50	50.00
	1802	.056	6.50	13.50	22.50	50.00
	1803	.054	6.50	13.50	22.50	50.00
	1804	.056	6.50	13.50	22.50	50.00
	1805	.056	6.50	13.50	22.50	50.00
	1806/5	.054	6.50	15.00	25.00	55.00
	1806	Inc. Ab.	6.50	13.50	22.50	50.00
	1807	.057	6.50	13.50	22.50	50.00
	1808	.057	6.00	12.00	22.50	50.00

Similar to C#56.

C#	Date	Mintage	VG	Fine	VF	XF
64	1809	.054	7.50	15.00	37.50	55.00
	1810	.054	6.50	13.50	30.00	55.00
	1811	.054	6.50	13.50	30.00	55.00
	1812	.071	6.50	13.50	30.00	55.00
	1813	.063	6.00	12.00	25.00	50.00
	1814	.067	6.50	13.50	30.00	50.00
	1815	.054	6.50	13.50	37.50	50.00
	1816	.082	6.50	13.50	30.00	50.00
	1817	—	13.50	22.50	35.00	55.00

1/2 REAL

.917 SILVER

SANTIAGO MINT (So)

Obv. leg: CRL III D.G...., arms. Rev: 2 hemispheres between pillars.

C#	Date	Mintage	VG	Fine	VF	XF
15	1760J	—	—	2000.	3000.	—

.903 SILVER

Obv. leg: CAROLUS III...., bust. Rev: Arms, pillars.

C#	Date	Mintage	VG	Fine	VF	XF
20	1773 DA	9,000	17.50	30.00	70.00	100.00
	1775 DA	.065	15.00	25.00	40.00	85.00
	1776 DA	.020	16.50	27.50	40.00	90.00
	1777 DA	.020	16.50	27.50	40.00	90.00
	1778 DA	.150	15.00	25.00	40.00	85.00
	1779 DA	.049	15.00	25.00	40.00	85.00
	1780 DA	.061	15.00	25.00	40.00	85.00
	1781 DA	.071	15.00	25.00	40.00	85.00
	1782 DA	.054	15.00	25.00	40.00	85.00
	1783 DA	.054	15.00	25.00	40.00	85.00
	1784 DA	.109	15.00	25.00	40.00	85.00
	1785 DA	.080	15.00	25.00	40.00	85.00
	1786 DA	.125	15.00	25.00	40.00	85.00
	1787/6 DA	.079	15.00	25.00	40.00	85.00
	1787 DA	I.A.	15.00	25.00	40.00	85.00
	1788 DA	.175	15.00	25.00	40.00	85.00
	1789 DA	.186	15.00	25.00	40.00	85.00

Obv. leg: CAROLUS IV, bust of Charles III.

C#	Date	Mintage	VG	Fine	VF	XF
37	1789 DA	I.A.	10.00	20.00	35.00	65.00
	1790 DA	.110	8.50	17.50	30.00	60.00
	1791 DA	.139	8.50	17.50	30.00	60.00

Obv. leg: CAROLUS IIII...., bust of Charles III.

C#	Date	Mintage	VG	Fine	VF	XF
47	1791 DA	I.A.	10.00	20.00	30.00	70.00

Obv. leg: CAROLUS IIII...., bust of Charles IIII.

C#	Date	Mintage	VG	Fine	VF	XF
57	1792 DA	.074	7.50	15.00	25.00	50.00
	1793 DA	.163	6.50	12.50	20.00	45.00
	1794/3 DA	.207	8.50	17.50	30.00	55.00
	1794 DA	I.A.	6.50	12.50	20.00	45.00
	1795 DA	.094	6.50	12.50	20.00	45.00
	1796 DA	.126	6.50	12.50	20.00	45.00
	1797 DA	.125	6.50	12.50	20.00	45.00
	1798 DA	.109	6.50	12.50	20.00	45.00
	1799 DA	.061	6.50	12.50	20.00	45.00
	1800 AJ	.075	6.50	12.50	20.00	45.00
	1801 AJ	.059	6.50	12.50	20.00	45.00
	1802 JJ	.078	6.50	12.50	20.00	45.00
	1803 FJ	.036	—	—	Rare	—
	1804/3 FJ	.058	8.50	17.50	30.00	55.00
	1804 FJ	I.A.	6.50	12.50	20.00	45.00
	1805 FJ	.028	—	—	Rare	—
	1806 FJ	.059	6.50	12.50	20.00	45.00
	1807 FJ	.040	6.50	12.50	20.00	45.00
	1808/7 FJ	.058	8.50	17.50	30.00	55.00
	1808 FJ	I.A.	6.50	12.50	20.00	45.00

Obv. leg: FERDIN VII, bust of Charles IV.

C#	Date	Mintage	VG	Fine	VF	XF
65	1808 FJ	Inc. Ab.	17.50	15.00	30.00	55.00
	1809 FJ	.051	10.00	20.00	35.00	60.00
	1810 FJ	.050	10.00	20.00	35.00	60.00
	1811 FJ	.018	10.00	20.00	35.00	65.00
	1812 FJ	.125	10.00	20.00	35.00	60.00
	1813 FJ	.218	10.00	20.00	35.00	60.00
	1814 FJ	.077	5.00	10.00	16.50	35.00
	1815 FJ	.099	5.00	10.00	16.50	37.50
	1816 FJ	.119	5.00	10.00	16.50	32.50
	1817 FJ	—	5.00	10.00	16.50	32.50
	1817 FD	—	8.50	16.50	40.00	70.00
	1817 FI	—	—	—	Rare	—

REAL

.903 SILVER

SANTIAGO MINT (So)

Obv. leg: CAROLUS III...., BUST. Rev: Arms, pillars.

C#	Date	Mintage	VG	Fine	VF	XF
21	1773 DA	.014	35.00	60.00	75.00	140.00
	1775 DA	.027	25.00	40.00	65.00	125.00
	1776 DA	.010	30.00	50.00	75.00	140.00
	1777 DA	.020	25.00	40.00	65.00	125.00
	1778 DA	.095	20.00	30.00	60.00	115.00
	1779 DA	.042	15.00	25.00	50.00	100.00

C#	Date	Mintage	VG	Fine	VF	XF
21	1780 DA	.031	15.00	25.00	50.00	100.00
	1781 DA	.068	15.00	25.00	50.00	100.00
	1782 DA	.032	17.50	30.00	55.00	100.00
	1783 DA	.027	15.00	25.00	50.00	100.00
	1784 DA	.054	15.00	25.00	50.00	100.00
	1785 DA	.048	15.00	25.00	50.00	100.00
	1786/5 DA	.102	17.50	30.00	55.00	110.00
	1786 DA	I.A.	15.00	25.00	50.00	100.00
	1787 DA	.060	15.00	25.00	50.00	100.00
	1788 DA	.112	10.00	20.00	35.00	75.00
	1789 DA	.109	30.00	50.00	65.00	125.00

Obv. leg: CAROLUS IV..., bust of Charles III.

C#	Date	Mintage	VG	Fine	VF	XF
38	1789 DA	I.A.	15.00	25.00	50.00	100.00
	1790 DA	.039	10.00	30.00	40.00	65.00
	1791 DA	.020	10.00	20.00	40.00	65.00

Obv. leg: CAROLUS IIII...., bust of Charles III.

C#	Date	Mintage	VG	Fine	VF	XF
48	1791 DA	I.A.	10.00	20.00	50.00	90.00

Obv. leg: CAROLUS IIII...., bust of Charles IIII.

C#	Date	Mintage	VG	Fine	VF	XF
58	1792 DA	.024	7.50	15.00	30.00	55.00
	1793 DA	.077	7.50	15.00	30.00	60.00
	1794 DA	.054	7.50	15.00	30.00	50.00
	1795 DA	.089	7.50	15.00	30.00	50.00
	1796 DA	.064	7.50	15.00	30.00	50.00
	1797 DA	.085	7.50	15.00	35.00	60.00
	1798 DA	.034	7.50	15.00	25.00	45.00
	1799 DA	.048	5.00	10.00	25.00	40.00
	1800 AJ	.048	6.50	12.50	25.00	50.00
	1801 AJ	.053	6.50	12.50	25.00	50.00
	1802 JJ	.081	5.00	10.00	25.00	40.00
	1803 FJ	.018	—	—	Rare	—
	1804 FJ	.035	6.50	12.50	25.00	50.00
	1804 FJ/AJ	I.A.	6.50	12.50	25.00	50.00
	1805 FJ	.019	6.50	12.50	25.00	50.00
	1806 FJ	.038	6.50	12.50	25.00	50.00
	1807 FJ	.023	6.50	12.50	25.00	50.00
	1808/7 FJ	.034	—	—	—	—
	1808 FJ	I.A.	7.50	15.00	25.00	55.00

Obv. leg: FERDIN. VII...., bust of Charles IV.

C#	Date	Mintage	VG	Fine	VF	XF
66	1808 FJ	I.A.	—	—	Rare	—
	1809/8 FJ	.029	5.00	10.00	22.50	40.00
	1809 FJ	I.A.	5.00	10.00	22.50	40.00
	1810 FJ	.079	5.00	10.00	22.50	40.00
	1811 FJ	.020	5.00	10.00	22.50	40.00
	1812 FJ	.043	5.00	10.00	22.50	40.00
	1813 FJ	.213	5.00	10.00	22.50	40.00
	1814 FJ	.054	5.00	10.00	22.50	40.00
	1815 FJ	.041	5.00	10.00	22.50	40.00
	1816 FJ	.123	5.00	10.00	22.50	40.00
	1817 FJ	—	5.00	10.00	22.50	40.00

2 REALES

.903 SILVER

SANTIAGO MINT (So)

Obv. leg: CAROLUS III..., bust. Rev: Arms, pillars.

C#	Date	Mintage	VG	Fine	VF	XF
22	1773 DA	.014	65.00	110.00	200.00	250.00
	1774 DA	—	90.00	150.00	300.00	425.00
	1775 DA	.034	20.00	35.00	75.00	120.00
	1776 DA	.007	75.00	125.00	200.00	325.00
	1777 DA	.007	75.00	125.00	200.00	325.00
	1778/6 DA	.068	17.50	30.00	45.00	100.00
	1778 DA	I.A.	17.50	30.00	45.00	90.00
	1779 DA	.048	10.00	20.00	40.00	85.00
	1780 DA	.034	10.00	20.00	40.00	85.00
	1781 DA	.044	10.00	20.00	40.00	85.00
	1782 DA	.021	15.00	25.00	40.00	75.00
	1783/2 DA	.034	15.00	25.00	45.00	85.00
	1783 DA	I.A.	10.00	20.00	40.00	75.00
	1784 DA	.054	10.00	20.00	40.00	75.00
	1785 DA	.027	10.00	20.00	40.00	75.00
	1786 DA	.051	10.00	20.00	40.00	75.00
	1787 DA	.031	10.00	20.00	40.00	75.00
	1788 DA	.066	10.00	20.00	40.00	75.00
	1789 DA	.067	16.50	27.50	45.00	90.00

Obv. leg: CAROLUS IV...., bust of Charles III.

C#	Date	Mintage	VG	Fine	VF	XF
39	1789 DA	I.A.	10.00	20.00	40.00	65.00
	1790 DA	.047	10.00	20.00	40.00	65.00
	1791 DA	.054	30.00	50.00	70.00	110.00

Obv. leg: CAROLUS IIII...., bust of Charles III.

C#	Date	Mintage	VG	Fine	VF	XF
49	1791 DA	I.A.	10.00	20.00	40.00	65.00
	1792 DA	.014	10.00	20.00	40.00	65.00

Obv. leg: CAROLUS IIII...., bust of Charles IIII.

C#	Date	Mintage	VG	Fine	VF	XF
59	1792 DA	I.A.	7.50	15.00	30.00	55.00
	1793 DA	.053	7.50	15.00	30.00	55.00
	1794 DA	.058	7.50	15.00	30.00	55.00
	1795 DA	.058	7.50	15.00	30.00	55.00
	1796 DA	.066	7.50	15.00	30.00	55.00
	1797 DA	.049	7.50	15.00	30.00	55.00
	1798/7 DA	.030	8.50	17.50	35.00	60.00
	1798 DA	I.A.	7.00	14.00	30.00	50.00
	1799 DA	.041	7.00	14.00	30.00	50.00
	1799 DA/inverted MM	Inc. Ab.	12.50	20.00	40.00	65.00
	1800 AJ	.034	7.50	15.00	30.00	50.00
	1801 AJ	.039	7.50	15.00	30.00	50.00
	1802 JJ	.028	8.00	16.00	30.00	50.00
	1803 FJ	.025	7.50	15.00	30.00	55.00
	1803 FJ/JJ	I.A.	7.50	15.00	30.00	55.00
	1804 FJ	.028	7.00	14.00	30.00	50.00
	1804 FJ/inverted MM	Inc. Ab.	12.50	20.00	40.00	65.00
	1805 FJ	.024	6.50	12.50	22.50	45.00
	1806/5 FJ	.066	8.00	16.00	30.00	55.00
	1806 FJ	I.A.	7.00	14.00	30.00	50.00
	1807 FJ	.042	7.50	15.00	30.00	55.00
	1808 FJ	.054	7.50	15.00	30.00	55.00

Obv. leg: FERDIN. VII...., bust of Charles IV.

C#	Date	Mintage	VG	Fine	VF	XF
67	1808 FJ	I.A.	14.00	27.50	40.00	75.00
	1809 FJ	.041	10.00	20.00	35.00	55.00

Obv. leg: FERDIN. VII...., imaginary laureate military bust.

C#	Date	Mintage	VG	Fine	VF	XF
78	1810 FJ	.045	13.50	22.50	35.00	55.00
	1811 FJ	.027	10.00	20.00	35.00	55.00

Obv. leg: FERDIN. VII...., bust of Ferdinand.

C#	Date	Mintage	VG	Fine	VF	XF
80	1812 FJ	.069	7.50	15.00	35.00	55.00
	1813 FJ	.136	7.50	15.00	35.00	55.00
	1813 FJ/inverted MM	Inc. Ab.	12.50	20.00	40.00	65.00
	1814 FJ	.004	25.00	40.00	70.00	135.00
	1815 FJ	.024	5.00	10.00	20.00	40.00
	1816 FJ	.067	7.50	15.00	30.00	55.00
	1817 FJ	—	8.50	17.50	30.00	55.00

4 REALES

.917 SILVER

SANTIAGO MINT (So)

Obv. leg: CAROLUS III..., arms.
Rev: 2 hemispheres between pillars.

C#	Date	Mintage	VG	Fine	VF	XF
18	1760 J	—	—	—	Rare	—

.903 SILVER

Obv. leg: CAROLUS III..., bust. Rev: Arms, pillars.

C#	Date	Mintage	VG	Fine	VF	XF
23	1775 DA	3,000	250.00	300.00	650.00	1150.
	1776 DA	3,000	250.00	300.00	650.00	1150.
	1777 DA	3,000	250.00	300.00	650.00	1150.
	1778 DA	.015	250.00	300.00	650.00	1150.
	1779 DA	.010	150.00	250.00	475.00	900.00
	1780 DA	9,000	150.00	250.00	475.00	900.00
	1781 DA	.014	150.00	250.00	450.00	900.00
	1782 DA	7,000	150.00	250.00	475.00	900.00
	1783 DA	.010	165.00	275.00	450.00	900.00
	1784 DA	.040	150.00	250.00	425.00	850.00
	1785 DA	.030	150.00	250.00	425.00	850.00
	1786 DA	.036	150.00	250.00	425.00	850.00
	1787 DA	.025	150.00	250.00	425.00	850.00
	1788 DA	.041	150.00	250.00	425.00	850.00
	1789/8 DA	.045	160.00	275.00	475.00	1000.
	1789 DA	I.A.	165.00	275.00	500.00	1150.

Obv. leg: CAROLUS IV...., bust of Charles III.

C#	Date	Mintage	VG	Fine	VF	XF
40	1789 DA	I.A.	180.00	300.00	450.00	900.00
	1790 DA	9,000	180.00	300.00	425.00	900.00
	1791/0 DA	—	—	—	—	—
	1791 DA	6,000	180.00	300.00	450.00	1000.

Obv. leg: CAROLUS IIII...., bust of Charles III.

C#	Date	Mintage	VG	Fine	VF	XF
50	1791 DA	I.A.	180.00	300.00	500.00	1000.
	1792 DA	4,000	150.00	250.00	350.00	825.00

Obv. leg: CAROLUS IIII...., bust of Charles IV.

C#	Date	Mintage	VG	Fine	VF	XF
60	1792 DA	I.A.	135.00	225.00	350.00	600.00
	1793 DA	.015	60.00	100.00	175.00	350.00
	1794 DA	.017	75.00	120.00	200.00	400.00
	1795 DA	.011	60.00	100.00	165.00	275.00
	1796 DA	.011	60.00	100.00	165.00	275.00
	1797 DA	.012	60.00	100.00	175.00	300.00
	1798 DA	3,000	100.00	140.00	250.00	500.00
	1799 DA	8,000	100.00	140.00	250.00	500.00
	1800 AJ	5,000	100.00	165.00	275.00	550.00
	1801 AJ	2,000	150.00	250.00	475.00	725.00
	1802 JJ	.018	75.00	110.00	150.00	300.00
	1803 FJ	9,000	75.00	110.00	150.00	275.00
	1804 FJ	6,000	90.00	150.00	225.00	450.00
	1805 FJ	9,000	45.00	75.00	100.00	200.00
	1806 FJ	.020	40.00	65.00	100.00	200.00
	1807 FJ	.048	35.00	60.00	90.00	175.00
	1808/7 FJ	.025	65.00	110.00	130.00	175.00
	1808 FJ	I.A.	45.00	75.00	100.00	120.00

Obv. leg: FERDIN. VII...., bust of Charles IV.

C#	Date	Mintage	VG	Fine	VF	XF
68	1808 FJ	I.A.	50.00	80.00	150.00	300.00
	1808 FJ/inverted J	Inc. Ab.		150.00	200.00	400.00
	1809 FJ	.015	60.00	100.00	180.00	325.00
	1810 FJ	.010	40.00	65.00	115.00	200.00
	1811 FJ	6,000	35.00	60.00	100.00	200.00
	1811 FJ/inverted J	Inc. Ab.	60.00	85.00	120.00	225.00
	1812 FJ	.027	45.00	70.00	100.00	170.00
	1813 FJ	.034	30.00	50.00	75.00	130.00
	1813 FJ/inverted J	Inc. Ab.	35.00	55.00	90.00	150.00
	1814 FJ	850 pcs.	—	—	Rare	—
	1815 FJ	.010	35.00	55.00	90.00	150.00

8 REALES

.917 SILVER

SANTIAGO MINT (So)

Obv. leg: CAROLUS III..., arms.

C#	Date	Mintage	VG	Fine	VF	XF
19	1760 J	—	1850.	3000.	5000.	8500.
	1762 J	—	1850.	3000.	5000.	8500.
	1763 J	—	1850.	3000.	5000.	8500.
	1764 J	—	1850.	3000.	5000.	8500.
	1765 J	—	1850.	3000.	5000.	8500.
	1766 J	—	1850.	3000.	5000.	8500.
	1767 J	—	1850.	3000.	5000.	8500.
	1768 A	—	1850.	3000.	5000.	8500.
	1768 J	—	1850.	3000.	5000.	8500.
	1769(J)	—	2500.	4000.	7000.	11,000.
	1771 J	—	2150.	3500.	6000.	10,000.

.903 SILVER

Obv. leg: CAROLUS III...., bust. Rev: Arms, pillars.

C#	Date	Mintage	VG	Fine	VF	XF
24	1773 DA	.027	450.00	750.00	1100.	1800.
	1774 DA	—	600.00	1000.	1800.	2650.
	1775 DA	8,500	525.00	875.00	2000.	3250.
	1776 DA	.018	450.00	750.00	1250.	1750.
	1777 DA	.026	400.00	650.00	1000.	1650.
	1778 DA	.074	375.00	625.00	900.00	1500.
	1779 DA	.099	350.00	600.00	800.00	1350.
	1780 DA	.075	350.00	600.00	875.00	1350.
	1781 DA	.105	300.00	500.00	750.00	1100.
	1782 DA	.060	300.00	500.00	750.00	1100.
	1783 DA	.074	375.00	625.00	875.00	1300.
	1784 DA	.128	325.00	525.00	750.00	1100.
	1785 DA	.130	325.00	525.00	750.00	1100.
	1786 DA	.149	325.00	525.00	750.00	1100.
	1787 DA	.183	325.00	525.00	750.00	1100.
	1788 DA	.187	325.00	525.00	750.00	1100.
	1789 DA	.188	350.00	600.00	875.00	1250.

Obv. leg: CAROLUS IV...., bust of Charles III.

C#	Date	Mintage	VG	Fine	VF	XF
41	1789 DA	I.A.	500.00	850.00	1250.	2000.
	1790 DA	.147	475.00	800.00	1000.	1350.
	1791 DA	.167	500.00	850.00	1250.	2000.

Obv. leg: CAROLUS IIII...., bust of Charles III.

C#	Date	Mintage	VG	Fine	VF	XF
51	1790 DA	I.A.	600.00	1000.	1750.	2650.

Obv. leg: CAROLUS IIII...., bust of Charles IIII.

C#	Date	Mintage	VG	Fine	VF	XF
61	1791 DA	I.A.	750.00	1250.	2400.	3250.
	1792 DA	.161	300.00	500.00	650.00	900.00
	1793 DA	.206	180.00	300.00	450.00	625.00
	1794 DA	.161	200.00	325.00	450.00	650.00
	1795 DA	.200	200.00	350.00	550.00	775.00
	1796/5 DA	.199	—	—	—	—
	1796 DA	I.A.	225.00	375.00	500.00	700.00
61	1797 DA	.195	225.00	375.00	500.00	700.00
	1798 DA	.174	225.00	375.00	500.00	700.00
	1799 DA	.170	225.00	375.00	500.00	700.00
	1800 AJ	.184	250.00	425.00	550.00	750.00
	1801 AJ	.185	250.00	400.00	500.00	675.00
	1802 JJ	.160	225.00	375.00	500.00	675.00
	1803/2 FJ/JJ	.111	275.00	450.00	575.00	675.00
	1803 FJ	I.A.	300.00	500.00	625.00	900.00
	1804 FJ	.129	180.00	300.00	400.00	500.00
	1805 FJ	.159	250.00	400.00	500.00	700.00
	1806/5 FJ	.155	275.00	450.00	550.00	750.00
	1806 FJ	I.A.	250.00	400.00	500.00	700.00
	1807 FJ	.094	300.00	500.00	550.00	1000.
	1808 FJ	.134	300.00	500.00	625.00	800.00

Obv. leg: FERDIN. VII..., imaginary military bust. Rev: Similar to C#61.

C#	Date	Mintage	VG	Fine	VF	XF
73	1808 FJ	I.A.	180.00	300.00	350.00	500.00
	1809 FJ	.123	115.00	190.00	250.00	400.00

Obv. leg: FERDIN. VII...., imaginary laureate military bust. Rev: Similar to C#61.

C#	Date	Mintage	VG	Fine	VF	XF
79	1810 FJ	.126	75.00	125.00	190.00	300.00
	1811 FJ	.097	75.00	125.00	190.00	300.00

Obv. leg: FERDIN. VII.., bust of Ferdinand. Rev: Similar to C#61.

C#	Date	Mintage	VG	Fine	VF	XF
81	1812 FJ	.307	75.00	120.00	150.00	240.00
	1813 FJ	.415	75.00	120.00	150.00	240.00
	1814 FJ	.368	75.00	120.00	150.00	240.00
	1815 FJ	.388	75.00	120.00	150.00	240.00
	1816 FJ	.386	75.00	120.00	150.00	240.00
	1817 FJ	*.132	600.00	1000.	1500.	2250.

*Beware of counterfeits.

ESCUDO

.875 GOLD

SANTIAGO MINT (So)

Obv. leg: CAROLUS III...., bust of Ferdinand VI. Rev: 4 fold arms.

C#	Date	Mintage	VG	Fine	VF	XF
25	1760 J	—	125.00	200.00	325.00	650.00
	1761 J	—	125.00	200.00	300.00	525.00
	1762 J	968 pcs.	125.00	200.00	300.00	525.00

Obv. leg: CAR.III...., bust of Charles III.

C#	Date	Mintage	VG	Fine	VF	XF
28	1763 J	540 pcs.	150.00	250.00	350.00	575.00
	1764 J	—	150.00	250.00	350.00	575.00
28	1766 J	—	150.00	250.00	350.00	575.00

Obv. leg: CAROL III..., bust of Charles III. Rev: Arms, order chain.

C#	Date	Mintage	VG	Fine	VF	XF
32	1772 DA	384 pcs.	100.00	175.00	250.00	475.00
	1773 DA	3,400	90.00	150.00	200.00	425.00
	1774 DA	4,488	75.00	125.00	200.00	425.00
	1775 DA	3,128	100.00	175.00	300.00	525.00
	1776 DA	5,372	90.00	150.00	200.00	425.00
	1777 DA	5,780	75.00	125.00	200.00	425.00
	1778 DA	5,508	75.00	125.00	200.00	425.00
	1779 DA	6,324	75.00	125.00	200.00	425.00
	1780 DA	4,080	75.00	125.00	200.00	425.00
	1781 DA	3,332	75.00	125.00	200.00	425.00
	1782 DA	3,332	75.00	125.00	200.00	425.00
	1783 DA	2,584	75.00	125.00	200.00	425.00
	1784 DA	3,264	75.00	125.00	200.00	425.00
	1785 DA	2,448	75.00	125.00	200.00	425.00
	1786 DA	2,652	75.00	125.00	200.00	425.00
	1787 DA	3,060	75.00	125.00	200.00	425.00
	1788 DA	3,672	90.00	150.00	250.00	500.00

Obv. leg: CAROL IV..., bust of Charles III. Rev: AUS PICE...., arms.

C#	Date	Mintage	VG	Fine	VF	XF
42	1790 DA	3,772	135.00	225.00	300.00	550.00

Obv. leg: CAROL IIII...., bust of Charles III.

C#	Date	Mintage	VG	Fine	VF	XF
52	1791 DA	.016	135.00	225.00	300.00	550.00

Obv. leg. CAROL IIII..., bust of Charles IIII.

C#	Date	Mintage	VG	Fine	VF	XF
62	1792 DA	.027	100.00	175.00	300.00	475.00
	1793 DA	.014	100.00	175.00	250.00	425.00
	1794 DA	.021	100.00	175.00	250.00	425.00
	1795 DA	.021	135.00	225.00	300.00	475.00
	1796 DA	.015	100.00	175.00	250.00	425.00
	1797 DA	.023	100.00	175.00	250.00	425.00
	1798 DA	.015	100.00	175.00	250.00	425.00
	1799 DA	6,596	100.00	175.00	250.00	425.00
	1800 DA	1,836	100.00	175.00	250.00	425.00
	1801 AJ	1,088	100.00	175.00	250.00	425.00
	1802 JJ	748 pcs.	100.00	175.00	250.00	425.00
	1803 FJ	1,156	100.00	175.00	250.00	425.00
	1804 FJ	1,428	90.00	150.00	200.00	400.00
	1805 FJ	816 pcs.	90.00	150.00	200.00	400.00
	1806 FJ	544 pcs.	90.00	150.00	200.00	400.00
	1807 FJ	544 pcs.	90.00	150.00	200.00	400.00
	1808 FJ	2,448	90.00	150.00	200.00	400.00

Obv. leg: FERDIN, VII..., imaginary military bust. Rev: Arms.

C#	Date	Mintage	VG	Fine	VF	XF
74	1808	3,986	—	—	Rare	—
	1809	5,026	—	—	Rare	—

Obv. leg: FERDIN. VII.D.G...., bust of Charles IV.

C#	Date	Mintage	VG	Fine	VF	XF
69	1810 FJ	816 pcs.	85.00	140.00	200.00	425.00
	1811 FJ	680 pcs.	85.00	140.00	200.00	425.00
	1812 FJ	952 pcs.	75.00	100.00	160.00	325.00
	1813 FJ	4,556	85.00	140.00	200.00	425.00
	1814 FJ	1,152	85.00	140.00	200.00	425.00
	1815 FJ	816 pcs.	85.00	140.00	200.00	425.00
	1816 FJ	408 pcs.	75.00	120.00	200.00	375.00
	1817 FJ	.022	110.00	180.00	250.00	475.00
	1817 JF	Inc. Ab.	150.00	250.00	325.00	750.00

NOTE: An additional 17,860 pcs. were struck between 1818-1823, the actual date on the coin is unknown.

2 ESCUDOS

.875 GOLD

SANTIAGO MINT (So)

Obv. leg: CAROLUS III...., bust. Rev: 4 fold arms.

C#	Date	Mintage	VG	Fine	VF	XF
29	1764 J	143 pcs.	500.00	850.00	1500.	2500.

Obv. leg: CAROL III.D.G..., bust. Rev: Arms, order chain.

C#	Date	Mintage	VG	Fine	VF	XF
33	1773 DA	850 pcs.	325.00	525.00	850.00	1500.
	1774 DA	3,026	250.00	425.00	575.00	1100.
	1775 DA	2,482	275.00	450.00	725.00	1300.
	1776 DA	2,890	275.00	450.00	725.00	1300.

C#	Date	Mintage	VG	Fine	VF	XF
33	1777 DA	2,856	275.00	450.00	725.00	1300.
	1778 DA	2,652	275.00	450.00	725.00	1300.
	1779 DA	3,196	275.00	450.00	725.00	1300.
	1780 DA	1,904	275.00	450.00	725.00	1300.
	1781 DA	1,666	275.00	450.00	725.00	1300.
	1782 DA	1,632	275.00	450.00	725.00	1300.
	1783 DA	1,292	275.00	450.00	725.00	1300.
	1784 DA	1,632	275.00	450.00	725.00	1300.
	1785 DA	1,632	250.00	400.00	575.00	1100.
	1786 DA	1,394	250.00	400.00	575.00	1100.
	1787 DA	1,768	250.00	400.00	575.00	1100.
	1788 DA	2,380	180.00	300.00	450.00	850.00

Obv. leg: CAROL IV...., bust of Charles III.
Rev: Arms, legend: AUSPICE.....

C#	Date	Mintage	VG	Fine	VF	XF
43	1789 DA	1,632	475.00	800.00	1300.	1900.
	1790 DA	5,508	350.00	600.00	850.00	1100.

Obv. leg: CAROL IIII..., bust of Charles III.

C#	Date	Mintage	VG	Fine	VF	XF
53	1791 DA	6,698	250.00	400.00	525.00	850.00
	1792 DA	7,760	275.00	475.00	650.00	875.00
	1793 DA	7,820	275.00	450.00	600.00	850.00
	1794 DA	7,832	275.00	450.00	600.00	850.00
	1795 DA	.010	250.00	400.00	500.00	800.00
	1796 DA	.014	250.00	400.00	525.00	800.00
	1797 DA	.011	275.00	475.00	650.00	900.00
	1798 DA	8,500	275.00	475.00	650.00	900.00
	1799 DA	4,148	350.00	600.00	750.00	1000.
	1800 AJ	986 pcs.	275.00	475.00	650.00	900.00
	1801 AJ	680 pcs.	275.00	475.00	650.00	900.00
	1802 JJ	374 pcs.	275.00	475.00	650.00	900.00
	1803 FJ	578 pcs.	275.00	475.00	650.00	900.00
	1804 FJ	544 pcs.	275.00	475.00	650.00	900.00
	1805 FJ	646 pcs.	250.00	400.00	525.00	800.00
	1806 FJ	306 pcs.	275.00	450.00	575.00	900.00
	1807 FJ	340 pcs.	350.00	600.00	725.00	1000.
	1808 FJ	1,020	250.00	400.00	525.00	800.00
	1810 FJ	510 pcs.	275.00	450.00	600.00	850.00
	1811 FJ	340 pcs.	275.00	450.00	600.00	850.00
	1812 FJ	476 pcs.	180.00	300.00	425.00	725.00
	1813 FJ	2,958	180.00	300.00	425.00	725.00

Obv. leg: FERDIN.VII., imaginary military bust.

C#	Date	Mintage	VG	Fine	VF	XF
75	1808 FJ	Inc. Ab.	—	—	Rare	—
	1809 FJ	Inc. Ab.	—	—	Rare	—
	1810 FJ	Inc. Ab.	—	—	Rare	—
	1811 FJ	Inc. Ab.	—	—	Rare	—

Obv. leg: FERDIN. VII...., bust of Charles IV.

C#	Date	Mintage	VG	Fine	VF	XF
70	1814 FJ	682 pcs.	180.00	300.00	400.00	650.00
	1815 FJ	408 pcs.	150.00	250.00	375.00	550.00
	1816 FJ	608 pcs.	200.00	350.00	475.00	725.00
	1817 FJ	168 pcs.	150.00	250.00	375.00	725.00

NOTE: An additional 19,876 pcs. were struck between 1818-1823, the actual date on the coin is unknown.

4 ESCUDOS

.875 GOLD

SANTIAGO MINT (So)

Obv. leg: CAROLUS III...., bust of Ferdinand VI.
Rev: 4 fold arms.

C#	Date	Mintage	VG	Fine	VF	XF
26	1762 J	—	400.00	675.00	1200.	2250.
	1763 J	—	375.00	625.00	925.00	1500.

Obv. leg: CAROLUS III..., bust of Charles III.

C#	Date	Mintage	VG	Fine	VF	XF
30	1763 J	—	450.00	750.00	1300.	2400.
	1764 J	372 pcs.	400.00	675.00	1200.	2000.
	1765 J	.011	400.00	675.00	1200.	2000.

Obv. leg: CAROL.III..., bust. Rev: Arms, order chain.

C#	Date	Mintage	VG	Fine	VF	XF
34	1773DA	170 pcs.	350.00	575.00	900.00	1600.
	1774DA	1,275	300.00	500.00	825.00	1300.
	1775DA	1,190	300.00	500.00	825.00	1300.
	1776DA	1,615	300.00	500.00	825.00	1300.
	1777DA	1,462	300.00	500.00	825.00	1300.
	1778DA	1,294	425.00	700.00	1300.	2500.
	1779DA	1,683	425.00	700.00	1300.	2500.
	1780DA	918 pcs.	425.00	700.00	1300.	2500.
	1781DA	850 pcs.	425.00	700.00	1300.	2500.
	1782DA	901 pcs.	425.00	700.00	1300.	2500.
	1783DA	612 pcs.	425.00	700.00	1300.	2500.
	1784DA	816 pcs.	350.00	600.00	925.00	1600.
	1785DA	816 pcs.	250.00	350.00	500.00	850.00
	1786DA	697 pcs.	250.00	350.00	500.00	850.00
	1787DA	952 pcs.	250.00	350.00	475.00	825.00
	1788DA	1,020	250.00	400.00	700.00	1100.
	1789DA	850 pcs.	350.00	600.00	925.00	1600.

Obv. leg: CAROL IV...., bust of Charles III.
Rev: Arms, legend: AUSPICE....

C#	Date	Mintage	VG	Fine	VF	XF
44	1789 DA	I.A.	275.00	450.00	625.00	1100.
	1790 DA	3,332	275.00	450.00	625.00	1100.
	1791 DA	4,879	375.00	625.00	850.00	1400.

Obv. leg: CAROL IIII..., bust of Charles IIII.

C#	Date	Mintage	VG	Fine	VF	XF
63	1792 DA	4,680	350.00	600.00	750.00	1100.
	1793 DA	6,238	350.00	600.00	750.00	1100.
	1794 DA	7,140	350.00	600.00	750.00	1100.
	1795 DA	6,808	350.00	600.00	750.00	1100.
	1796 DA	6,970	350.00	600.00	750.00	1100.
	1797 DA	5,950	250.00	400.00	550.00	925.00
	1798 DA	4,471	350.00	600.00	750.00	1100.
	1799 DA	2,754	350.00	600.00	750.00	1100.
	1800 AJ	646 pcs.	350.00	600.00	750.00	1100.
	1801 AJ	340 pcs.	250.00	300.00	375.00	750.00
	1802 JJ	374 pcs.	250.00	400.00	500.00	925.00
	1803 FJ	476 pcs.	325.00	525.00	750.00	1100.
	1804 FJ	255 pcs.	250.00	400.00	500.00	925.00
	1805 FJ	323 pcs.	250.00	400.00	500.00	925.00
	1806 FJ	204 pcs.	250.00	425.00	700.00	1100.
	1807 FJ	187 pcs.	250.00	425.00	700.00	1100.
	1808/7 FJ	1,207	250.00	350.00	500.00	925.00
	1808 FJ	I.A.	250.00	350.00	450.00	750.00

Obv. leg: FERDIN. VII..., bust of Ferdinand. Rev: Arms.

C#	Date	Mintage	VG	Fine	VF	XF
76	1808 FJ	Inc. Ab.	—	—	Rare	—
	1809 FJ	Inc. Ab.	—	—	Rare	—

Obv. leg: FERDIN. VII...., bust of Charles IV.

C#	Date	Mintage	VG	Fine	VF	XF
71	1810 FJ	272 pcs.	350.00	600.00	925.00	1300.
	1811 FJ	170 pcs.	425.00	700.00	1250.	2000.
	1812 FJ	254 pcs.	400.00	650.00	1000.	1400.
	1813 FJ	1,462	325.00	525.00	750.00	1150.
	1814 FJ	340 pcs.	—	Reported, not confirmed		
	1815 FJ	290 pcs.	—	Reported, not confirmed		
	1816 FJ	100 pcs.	—	Reported, not confirmed		
	1817 FJ	68 pcs.	300.00	500.00	800.00	1150.

NOTE: An additional 6,560 pcs. were struck between 1818-1823; the actual date on the coin is unknown.

8 ESCUDOS

.875 GOLD

SANTIAGO MINT (So)

Obv. leg: CAROLUS III...., bust of Ferdinand VI.

C#	Date	Mintage	VG	Fine	VF	XF
27	1760 J	—	650.00	850.00	1500.	2750.
	1761 J	—	650.00	850.00	1000.	2000.
	1762 J	.032	650.00	850.00	1200.	2400.
	1763 J	.041	650.00	850.00	1200.	2400.

Obv. leg: CAROLUS III...., bust of Charles III.

C#	Date	Mintage	VG	Fine	VF	XF
31	1764 J	.036	650.00	850.00	1200.	2250.
	1765 J	.035	650.00	850.00	1500.	3000.
	1766 J	.023	650.00	850.00	1500.	3000.
	1767 J	—	650.00	850.00	1500.	3000.
	1768 A	—	650.00	850.00	1200.	2500.
	1769 A	—	650.00	850.00	1800.	3500.
	1770 A	—	650.00	850.00	1800.	3500.
	1771 A	—	650.00	850.00	1800.	3500.
	1772 A	.017	650.00	1000.	2000.	2750.

Obv. leg: CAROL III...., bust of Charles III.

C#	Date	Mintage	VG	Fine	VF	XF
35	1772 DA	I.A.	550.00	650.00	800.00	1250.
	1773 DA	.033	550.00	650.00	800.00	1250.
	1774 DA	.042	550.00	650.00	800.00	1250.
	1775 DA	.036	550.00	650.00	800.00	1250.
	1776 DA	.041	550.00	650.00	800.00	1250.
	1777 DA	.041	550.00	650.00	800.00	1250.
	1778 DA	.042	550.00	650.00	800.00	1250.
	1778 DA TE in legend reversed					
		Inc. Ab.	—	—	—	—
	1779 DA	.044	575.00	700.00	900.00	1250.
	1780 DA	.042	550.00	650.00	800.00	1200.
	1781 DA	.043	550.00	650.00	800.00	1200.
	1782 DA	.040	550.00	650.00	800.00	1200.
	1783 DA	.034	550.00	650.00	800.00	1200.
	1784 DA	.037	550.00	650.00	800.00	1200.
	1785 DA	.034	550.00	650.00	800.00	1200.
	1786 DA	.034	550.00	650.00	800.00	1200.
	1787 DA	.037	550.00	650.00	800.00	1200.
	1788 DA	.042	550.00	650.00	800.00	1200.
	1789 DA	.041	650.00	850.00	1200.	1750.

Obv. leg: CAROL IV...., bust of Charles III.
Rev: Similar to C#35.

C#	Date	Mintage	VG	Fine	VF	XF
45	1789 DA	I.A.	550.00	650.00	850.00	1000.
	1790 DA	.042	550.00	650.00	850.00	1000.
	1791 DA	.042	600.00	750.00	1000.	1200.

Obv. leg: CAROL IIII...., bust of Charles III.
Rev: Similar to C#35.

C#	Date	Mintage	VG	Fine	VF	XF
54	1791 DA	I.A.	550.00	650.00	800.00	1200.
	1792 DA	.038	550.00	650.00	800.00	1200.
	1793 DA	.034	550.00	650.00	800.00	1200.
	1794 DA	.040	550.00	650.00	800.00	1200.
	1795 DA	.043	550.00	650.00	800.00	1200.
	1796 DA	.044	550.00	650.00	800.00	1200.
	1797 DA	.043	550.00	650.00	800.00	1200.
	1798 DA	.043	550.00	650.00	800.00	1200.
	1799 DA	.041	550.00	650.00	800.00	1200.
	1800 DA	.054	600.00	750.00	900.00	1350.
	1800 JA	I.A.	600.00	750.00	900.00	1350.
	1800 AJ	I.A.	600.00	750.00	900.00	1350.
	1801 AJ	.046	550.00	650.00	800.00	1200.
	1802 JJ	.049	550.00	650.00	800.00	1200.
	1803 FJ	.044	550.00	650.00	800.00	1200.
	1804 FJ	.040	550.00	650.00	800.00	1200.
	1805 FJ	.044	550.00	650.00	800.00	1200.
	1806 FJ	.040	550.00	650.00	800.00	1200.
	1806 JF	I.A.	750.00	1000.	1500.	2500.
	1807 FJ	.039	600.00	750.00	900.00	1350.
	1807 JF	I.A.	600.00	750.00	900.00	1350.
	1808 FJ	.039	550.00	650.00	800.00	1200.

Obv. leg: FERDIN. VIII..., imaginary military bust.
Rev: Similar to C#35.

C#	Date	Mintage	VG	Fine	VF	XF
77	1808 FJ	I.A.	700.00	1200.	1500.	2500.
	1809 FJ	.041	550.00	800.00	1200.	2000.

Similar to C#77.

C#	Date	Mintage	VG	Fine	VF	XF
77a	1810 FJ	.055	550.00	800.00	1200.	1750.

Obv. leg: FERDIN. VII...., bust of Charles IIII.
Rev: Similar to C#35.

C#	Date	Mintage	VG	Fine	VF	XF
72	1811 FJ	.044	900.00	1500.	2400.	4500.
	1812 FJ	.048	550.00	650.00	800.00	1200.
	1813 FJ	.037	550.00	650.00	800.00	1200.
	1814 FJ	.029	550.00	650.00	800.00	1200.
	1815 FJ	.039	550.00	650.00	800.00	1200.
	1816 FJ	.030	550.00	650.00	800.00	1200.
	1817 FJ	.011	550.00	650.00	800.00	1200.

ROYALIST ISSUES

CHILOE

An island off the southwest coast of Chile. The island was the last outpost of the Spanish in their war with Chile. Antonio Quintanilla had the emergency coins cast to show that the empire of Ferdinand VII of Spain still exerted power in the New World.

(Issued by Antonio Quintanilla)

8 REALES

SILVER

LIMA MINT

c/s: Chi - loe on cast 8 Reales of Ferdinand VII

C#	Date	Mintage	Good	VG	Fine
N1.1	1818	—	350.00	500.00	750.00

POTOSI MINT

c/s: Chi-loe on cast 8 Reales of Ferdinand VII.

C#	Date	Mintage	Good	VG	Fine
N1.2	1822	—	350.00	500.00	750.00
	1825	—	350.00	500.00	750.00

VALDIVIA

REAL

BILLON

C#	Date	Mintage	Good	VG	Fine	VF
N31	1822	—	75.00	100.00	150.00	250.00

2 REALES

BILLON

C#	Date	Mintage	Good	VG	Fine	VF
N32	1822	—	75.00	100.00	150.00	250.00

8 REALES

BILLON

C#	Date	Mintage	Good	VG	Fine	VF
N34	1822	—	275.00	400.00	500.00	800.00

REPUBLIC ISSUES

MONETARY SYSTEM

8 Reales = 1 Peso
16 Reales = 1 Escudo

UN QUART (1/4) REAL

.903 SILVER
Similar to 1/4 Real, C#56.

C#	Date	Mintage	VG	Fine	VF	XF
64.1	1818/6	.104	25.00	40.00	65.00	110.00
	1818	Inc. Ab.	25.00	40.00	65.00	110.00

NOTE: Dies of C#64 used by Republic.

.900 SILVER

C#	Date	Mintage	Good	VG	Fine	VF
82	1832/1	.054	5.00	10.00	25.00	50.00
	1832	Inc. Ab.	5.00	10.00	25.00	50.00
	1833	.082	5.00	10.00	25.00	50.00
	1834	.134	7.50	15.00	40.00	80.00

1/2 REAL

.900 SILVER

SANTIAGO MINT (So)

C#	Date	Mintage	Good	VG	Fine	VF
83	1833	.014	6.50	12.50	20.00	25.00
	1834/3	.022	7.00	13.50	22.50	27.50
	1834	Inc. Ab.	7.50	15.00	25.00	30.00

C#	Date	Mintage	Good	VG	Fine	VF
96	1838 IJ	.015	10.00	20.00	30.00	40.00
	1840 IJ	.014	10.00	20.00	30.00	40.00
	1841 IJ	.016	15.00	25.00	35.00	50.00
	1842 IJ	.027	7.50	15.00	25.00	35.00

C#	Date	Mintage	Good	VG	Fine	VF
96a	1844	—	2.00	4.00	7.50	12.50
	1844 IJ	—	—	—	—	—
	1845 IJ	—	2.00	4.00	9.00	15.00
	1846 IJ	—	3.00	6.00	12.00	25.00
	1847 IJ	—	3.00	6.00	12.00	25.00
	1848 JM	—	5.00	10.00	15.00	25.00
	1849 ML	—	3.00	6.00	12.00	20.00
	1850 LA	—	5.00	10.00	15.00	25.00
	1851 LA	—	3.00	6.00	10.00	17.50

UN (1) REAL

.900 SILVER

C#	Date	Mintage	Good	VG	Fine	VF
84	1834 IJ	.016	6.50	12.50	20.00	30.00

C#	Date	Mintage	Good	VG	Fine	VF
97	1836	5,100	4.00	6.00	9.00	12.50
	1837	6,800	4.00	6.00	9.00	12.50
	1838 IJ	Inc. Ab.	12.50	20.00	30.00	45.00
	1839	Inc. Be.	4.00	6.00	9.00	12.50
	1840 IJ	6,800	5.00	10.00	15.00	25.00
	1841 IJ	7,928	7.50	15.00	30.00	40.00
	1842	4,768	5.00	10.00	15.00	25.00

C#	Date	Mintage	Good	VG	Fine	VF
97a	1843 IJ	—	4.00	6.00	8.00	12.50
	1844 IJ	—	4.00	6.00	8.00	12.50
	1845 IJ	—	4.00	6.00	8.00	12.50
	1846 IJ	—	4.00	6.00	8.00	12.50
	1847 IJ	—	5.00	10.00	15.00	20.00
	1848/7/6 JM	—	—	—	—	—
	1848/7 JM	—	—	—	—	—
	1848 JM	—	5.00	10.00	15.00	20.00
	1849	—	5.00	10.00	15.00	20.00
	1850 LA	—	5.00	10.00	15.00	20.00
	1851	—	—	—	—	—

2 REALES

.900 SILVER

C#	Date	Mintage	Good	VG	Fine	VF
85	1834 IJ	3,740	10.00	15.00	25.00	45.00

24.5 mm.

C#	Date	Mintage	Good	VG	Fine	VF
98	1839	—	— Reported, Not Confirmed			

23 mm.

C#	Date	Mintage	Good	VG	Fine	VF
98a	1843 IJ	—	5.75	6.50	10.00	15.00
	1844 IJ	—	5.75	6.50	10.00	15.00
	1845 IJ	—	5.75	6.50	10.00	15.00
	1846/5 IJ	—	—	—	—	—
	1846 IJ	—	5.75	6.50	10.00	15.00
	1847 IJ	—	5.75	6.50	10.00	15.00
	1848	—	6.50	10.00	15.00	20.00
	1848 JM	—	—	—	—	—
	1849 ML	—	6.50	10.00	15.00	20.00
	1850 LA	—	5.75	6.50	10.00	15.00
	1851 LA	—	5.75	6.50	10.00	15.00
	1852	—	7.50	12.00	20.00	30.00

UN (1) PESO

.900 SILVER

C#	Date	Mintage	Good	VG	Fine	VF
86	1817	—	75.00	125.00	200.00	300.00
	1817 FJ	—	30.00	50.00	80.00	110.00
	1817 FD	—	45.00	70.00	90.00	125.00
	1818/7 FD	—	60.00	100.00	150.00	225.00
	1818 FD	—	65.00	110.00	130.00	150.00
	1819 FD	—	55.00	90.00	110.00	150.00
	1820 FD	—	45.00	70.00	85.00	125.00
	1821 FD	—	120.00	200.00	300.00	400.00
	1822 FI	—	45.00	70.00	85.00	110.00
	1823 FI	—	60.00	100.00	150.00	225.00
	1824 I	—	100.00	175.00	225.00	450.00
	1825 I	—	120.00	200.00	300.00	600.00
	1826 I	—	—	—	Rare	—
	1830 I	—	120.00	200.00	300.00	600.00
	1831 I	—	60.00	100.00	150.00	200.00
	1832 I	—	60.00	100.00	150.00	200.00
	1833 I	—	45.00	70.00	85.00	110.00
	1834 I	—	60.00	100.00	125.00	250.00
	1834 IJ	—	75.00	125.00	200.00	350.00

COQUIMBO MINT

C#	Date	Mintage	Good	VG	Fine	VF
88	1828TH	—	—	—	—	5000.

8 REALES

.900 SILVER, 39mm

SANTIAGO MINT (So)

C#	Date	Mintage	Good	VG	Fine	VF
100	1837 IJ	—	—	—	Rare	—
	1839 IJ	—	30.00	45.00	75.00	125.00
	1840 IJ	—	—	—	Rare	—

Reduced size, 38.5mm

C#	Date	Mintage	Good	VG	Fine	VF
100a	1848 JM	—	35.00	50.00	85.00	110.00
	1849 ML	—	35.00	50.00	85.00	110.00

ESCUDO

3.4000 gm., .875 GOLD, .0956 oz AGW
Obv: Sun over mountains in wreath.
Rev: Crossed flags behind pillar in wreath, date below.

C#	Date	Mintage	VG	Fine	VF	XF
89	1824 I	3,400	100.00	135.00	175.00	225.00
	1825 I	2,920	100.00	135.00	175.00	225.00
	1826 I	4,280	100.00	135.00	175.00	225.00
	1827 I	408 pcs.	100.00	135.00	175.00	225.00
	1828 I	4,488	100.00	135.00	175.00	225.00
	1830 I	3,328	100.00	135.00	175.00	225.00
	1832 I	2,338	100.00	135.00	175.00	225.00
	1833/0 I	2,620	150.00	200.00	250.00	300.00
	1833 I	Inc. Ab.	125.00	175.00	225.00	275.00
	1834 I	10,614	125.00	175.00	225.00	275.00

Obv: Plumed and supported arms, date below.
Rev: Hand on book under sun rays.

C#	Date	Mintage	VG	Fine	VF	XF
101	1838 IJ	6,122	125.00	175.00	225.00	275.00

Rev: Liberty standing, column at left, fasces and cornucopia at right.

C#	Date	Mintage	VG	Fine	VF	XF
105	1839 IJ	4,946	100.00	135.00	175.00	225.00
	1840 IJ	4,312	100.00	135.00	175.00	225.00
	1841 IJ	3,992	100.00	135.00	175.00	225.00
	1842 IJ	5,076	100.00	135.00	175.00	225.00
	1843 IJ	4,632	100.00	135.00	175.00	225.00
	1844 IJ	—	100.00	135.00	175.00	225.00
	1845 IJ	—	100.00	135.00	175.00	225.00

Rev: Liberty standing scene rendered on smaller scale.

C#	Date	Mintage	VG	Fine	VF	XF
105a	1847 IJ	—	125.00	175.00	225.00	275.00
	1848 JM	—	100.00	135.00	200.00	250.00
	1849 ML	—	100.00	135.00	200.00	250.00
	1850 LA	—	100.00	135.00	200.00	250.00
	1851 LA	—	125.00	175.00	225.00	275.00

2 ESCUDOS

6.8000 gm., .875 GOLD, .1913 oz AGW

C#	Date	Mintage	VG	Fine	VF	XF
90	1824 I	1,700	165.00	225.00	300.00	400.00
	1825 I	1,460	165.00	225.00	300.00	400.00
	1826 I	1,936	165.00	225.00	300.00	400.00
	1827 I	204 pcs.	225.00	325.00	400.00	550.00
	1832 I	493 pcs.	225.00	325.00	400.00	550.00
	1833 I	224 pcs.	165.00	225.00	325.00	400.00
	1834 IJ	4,648	165.00	225.00	325.00	400.00

C#	Date	Mintage	VG	Fine	VF	XF
102	1837 IJ	331 pcs.	180.00	250.00	350.00	500.00
	1838 IJ	3,449	150.00	200.00	250.00	450.00

C#	Date	Mintage	VG	Fine	VF	XF
106	1839 IJ	3,064	165.00	225.00	300.00	400.00
	1840 IJ	2,396	150.00	225.00	300.00	400.00
	1841 IJ	2,552	150.00	200.00	250.00	350.00
	1842 IJ	2,986	150.00	200.00	250.00	350.00
	1843 IJ	2,464	150.00	200.00	250.00	350.00
	1844 IJ	—	150.00	200.00	250.00	350.00
	1845 IJ	—	150.00	200.00	250.00	350.00

Rev: Liberty standing scene rendered on smaller scale.

C#	Date	Mintage	VG	Fine	VF	XF
106a	1846 IJ	—	150.00	200.00	250.00	350.00
	1847 IJ	—	150.00	200.00	250.00	350.00
	1848 JM	—	150.00	200.00	250.00	350.00
	1849 ML	—	150.00	200.00	250.00	350.00
	1850 LA	—	150.00	200.00	250.00	350.00
	1851 LA	—	150.00	200.00	250.00	350.00

4 ESCUDOS

13.5000 gm., .875 GOLD, .3798 oz AGW

C#	Date	Mintage	VG	Fine	VF	XF
91	1824 FD	1,530	275.00	325.00	400.00	700.00
	1825 I	986 pcs.	275.00	325.00	400.00	700.00
	1826 I	1,326	275.00	325.00	400.00	700.00
	1833 IJ	321 pcs.	300.00	350.00	425.00	750.00
	1834 IJ	2,564	275.00	325.00	400.00	700.00

C#	Date	Mintage	VG	Fine	VF	XF
103	1836 IJ	1,389	325.00	375.00	450.00	800.00
	1837 IJ	321 pcs.	350.00	400.00	475.00	800.00

Rev: Liberty standing, column left, fasces and cornucopia right.

C#	Date	Mintage	VG	Fine	VF	XF
107	1839 IJ	—	—	—	Rare	—
	1840 IJ	108 pcs.	—	—	Rare	—
	1841 IJ	100 pcs.	—	—	Rare	—

8 ESCUDOS

27.0000 gm., .875 GOLD, .7596 oz AGW

C#	Date	Mintage	VG	Fine	VF	XF
92	1818 FD	.029	550.00	600.00	700.00	900.00
	1819 FD	.037	550.00	600.00	700.00	900.00
	1820 FD	.035	550.00	600.00	700.00	900.00
	1821 FD	.016	550.00	600.00	700.00	900.00
	1822 FD	.031	550.00	600.00	700.00	900.00
	1823 FD	.019	550.00	600.00	700.00	900.00
	1824 FD	.010	550.00	600.00	700.00	900.00
	1825 I	8,483	525.00	575.00	675.00	800.00
	1826 I	7,607	525.00	575.00	675.00	800.00
	1827 I	2,176	525.00	575.00	675.00	800.00
	1828/7 I	4,250	750.00	1000.	1500.	2500.
	1828 I	Inc. Ab.	525.00	575.00	675.00	800.00
	1829 I	—	525.00	575.00	675.00	800.00
	1830 I	3,068	525.00	575.00	675.00	800.00
	1831 I	1,745	550.00	600.00	700.00	800.00
	1832 I	.011	525.00	575.00	675.00	800.00
	1833 I	.025	525.00	575.00	675.00	800.00
	1834 IJ	.031	525.00	575.00	675.00	800.00

C#	Date	Mintage	VG	Fine	VF	XF
104	1835 IJ	.028	525.00	575.00	675.00	900.00
	1836 IJ	.027	525.00	575.00	675.00	900.00
	1837 IJ	.017	525.00	575.00	675.00	900.00
	1838 IJ	.033	525.00	575.00	675.00	900.00

Reeded edge

C#	Date	Mintage	VG	Fine	VF	XF
108	1839 IJ	.027	525.00	575.00	675.00	900.00
	1840 IJ	.025	525.00	575.00	675.00	900.00
	1841 IJ	.025	525.00	575.00	675.00	900.00
	1842 IJ	.027	525.00	575.00	675.00	900.00

C#	Date	Mintage	VG	Fine	VF	XF
108	1843 IJ	.027	525.00	575.00	675.00	900.00
	Lettered edge					
108a	1844 IJ	—	575.00	625.00	750.00	1000.
	1845 IJ	—	575.00	625.00	750.00	1000.

C#	Date	Mintage	VG	Fine	VF	XF
108b	1846 IJ	—	550.00	600.00	700.00	900.00
	1847 IJ	—	550.00	600.00	700.00	900.00
	1848 JM	—	550.00	600.00	700.00	900.00
	1849 ML	—	550.00	600.00	700.00	900.00
	1850 LA	—	550.00	600.00	700.00	900.00
	1851 LA	—	550.00	600.00	700.00	900.00

COUNTERSTAMP ISSUES

NOTE: On March 29, 1833, the government ordered the legal circulation of the Argentinian 8 Reales struck at Potosi. The coins struck at Potosi must have the counterstamp of the coat of arms of Chile and the abbreviation of the place where the counterstamp was applied.

8 REALES

SILVER

COUNTERSTAMP: Uniface counterstamp of 3 mountains with abbreviation of place below, designating where the counterstamp was applied.

KM#	Mint	Mintage	VG	Fine	VF
1	CHIL (Chiloe)		1750.	2250.	2750.
2	CON (Conception)		1500.	2000.	2500.
3	SAN (Santiago)		1750.	2250.	2750.
4	SER (Serena)		225.00	375.00	550.00
5	VALD (Valdivia)		300.00	550.00	900.00
6	VALP (Valparaiso)		300.00	550.00	900.00

DECIMAL COINAGE

10 Centavos = 1 Decimo
10 Decimos = 1 Peso
10 Pesos = 1 Condor

MEDIO (1/2)CENTAVO

COPPER

C#	Date	Mintage	VG	Fine	VF	XF
93	1835	2.000	1.75	3.50	4.50	9.00
	1835	Inc. Ab.	—	—	Proof	—

Flat star; stars flank date

Y#	Date	Mintage	VG	Fine	VF	XF
1	1851	1.625	2.25	4.50	6.00	12.00

Raised star; dots flank date

Y#	Date	Mintage	VG	Fine	VF	XF
3	1851	2.200	1.50	3.00	8.00	15.00

Y#	Date	Mintage	VG	Fine	VF	XF
3a	1853	2.667	1.00	2.00	3.50	7.00

COPPER-NICKEL

Y#	Date	Mintage	VG	Fine	VF	XF
10	1871	.133	1.75	3.50	6.00	12.00
	1872/1	.506	1.75	3.50	6.00	12.00
	1872	Inc. Ab.	1.75	3.50	6.00	12.00
	1873	1.265	1.75	3.50	6.00	12.00

COPPER

Y#	Date	Mintage	VG	Fine	VF	XF
10a	1883/73	.714	1.75	3.50	5.00	10.00
	1883	Inc. Ab.	1.25	2.50	4.00	8.00
	1884	.104	1.75	3.50	6.00	12.00
	1885	.132	1.25	2.50	4.00	8.00
	1886	.469	1.25	2.50	4.00	8.00
	1888/78	.294	1.50	3.00	5.00	10.00
	1888	Inc. Ab.	1.75	3.50	6.00	12.00
	1890	.070	4.00	8.50	15.00	30.00
	1893	.071	2.25	4.50	7.00	14.00
	1894	.251	1.25	2.50	4.00	8.00

UN(1)CENTAVO

COPPER

C#	Date	Mintage	VG	Fine	VF	XF
94	1835	2.000	1.75	3.50	5.00	10.00
	1835	Inc. Ab.	—	—	Proof	—

Obv: Flat star; stars flank date.
Rev: No diamond below wreath.

Y#	Date	Mintage	VG	Fine	VF	XF
2	1851	2.438	2.50	5.00	7.50	15.00

Obv: Raised star; dots flank date.
Rev: Diamond below wreath.

Y#	Date	Mintage	VG	Fine	VF	XF
4	1851	3.300	3.00	6.00	10.00	20.00

Y#	Date	Mintage	VG	Fine	VF	XF
4a	1853	2.667	1.25	2.50	2.50	5.00

COPPER-NICKEL

Y#	Date	Mintage	VG	Fine	VF	XF
11	1871	1.687	1.00	2.00	3.00	6.00
	1872/1	.690	1.75	3.50	5.00	10.00
	1872	Inc. Ab.	1.50	3.00	4.00	8.00
	1873/2	.779	—	—	—	—
	1873	Inc. Ab.	1.50	3.00	4.00	8.00
	1874	.363	1.90	3.75	4.00	8.00
	1875	.113	2.25	4.50	5.00	10.00
	1876	.022	3.25	6.50	10.00	20.00
	1877	.016	3.50	7.00	10.00	20.00

COPPER

Y#	Date	Mintage	VG	Fine	VF	XF
11a	1878	.177	1.50	3.00	5.00	10.00
	1879	.793	1.10	2.25	3.75	7.50
	1880/70	.478	—	—	—	—
	1880	Inc. Ab.	1.10	2.25	3.75	7.50
	1881	.318	1.25	2.50	4.00	8.00
	1882	.492	1.10	2.25	3.75	7.50
	1883	.274	1.50	3.00	5.00	10.00
	1884/3	.171	1.75	3.50	6.00	12.50
	1884	Inc. Ab.	1.50	3.00	5.00	10.00
	1885	.205	1.10	2.25	3.75	7.50
	1886	.510	1.10	2.25	3.75	7.50
	1887	.231	1.10	2.25	3.50	7.00
	1888	.141	1.50	3.00	5.00	10.00
	1890	.047	4.25	8.50	15.00	30.00
	1891	.099	2.50	5.00	10.00	20.00
	1893	.115	1.00	2.00	3.75	7.50
	1894	.244	.75	1.50	3.00	6.00
	1895	.449	.75	1.50	2.50	5.00
	1896	.139	1.25	2.50	4.00	8.00
	1898	1.605	.50	1.00	1.50	4.00

Y#	Date	Mintage	VG	Fine	VF	XF
27	1904	.970	.50	1.00	2.00	4.00
	1908	.174	.65	1.25	2.00	4.00
	1919	.173	.25	.50	2.00	4.00

DOS (2) CENTAVOS

COPPER-NICKEL

Y#	Date	Mintage	Fine	VF	XF	Unc
12	1871	.639	2.50	6.00	9.00	18.00
	1872	.207	2.50	6.00	9.00	18.00
	1873	.461	2.50	6.00	9.00	18.00
	1874	.263	2.50	6.00	9.00	18.00
	1875	.294	2.50	6.00	9.00	18.00
	1876	.108	6.00	10.00	17.50	30.00
	1877	.021	15.00	35.00	50.00	100.00

COPPER

Y#	Date	Mintage	Fine	VF	XF	Unc
12a	1878	.112	3.00	7.50	11.00	22.00
	1879	.479	1.60	4.00	6.00	12.50
	1880	.278	1.60	4.00	6.00	12.50
	1881	.172	2.00	5.00	7.50	15.00
	1882	.361	2.00	5.00	7.50	15.00
	1883	.405	1.80	4.50	6.75	13.50
	1884	.182	2.00	5.00	7.50	15.00
	1885	.146	2.00	5.00	7.50	15.00
	1886	.494	1.60	4.00	6.00	12.50
	1887	.106	2.00	5.00	7.50	15.00
	1888	.186	2.50	6.00	9.00	18.00
	1890	.155	3.00	7.50	11.00	22.00
	1891	.089	8.00	20.00	30.00	60.00
	1893/1	.141	1.60	4.00	6.00	12.50
	1893	Inc. Ab.	1.50	3.50	5.00	10.00
	1894	.190	2.50	6.00	9.00	18.00

Y#	Date	Mintage	Fine	VF	XF	Unc
28	1919	.147	1.00	2.50	4.00	5.00

DOS I MEDIO (2-1/2) CENTAVOS

COPPER

Y#	Date	Mintage	Fine	VF	XF	Unc
13	1886	.381	1.60	4.00	10.00	17.50
	1887	.500	2.00	5.00	7.50	15.00
	1895	.366	1.60	4.00	6.00	12.50
	1896	.172	2.00	5.00	7.50	15.00
	1898	2.177	1.60	4.00	6.00	12.50

Y#	Date	Mintage	Fine	VF	XF	Unc
29	1904	.277	1.60	4.00	7.00	10.00
	1906	.161	2.00	5.00	7.50	10.00
	1907	.262	1.60	4.00	7.00	10.00
	1908	.201	1.20	3.00	6.50	10.00

MEDIO (1/2) DECIMO

1.2000 gm., .900 SILVER, .0347 oz ASW

Y#	Date	Mintage	VG	Fine	VF	XF
5	1851	.233	—	—	Rare	—
	1853	Inc. Ab.	2.00	3.75	6.00	12.00
	1854	.122	3.25	6.50	10.00	20.00
	1855	1.257	2.00	3.75	6.00	12.00
	1856/5	.767	2.75	5.50	9.50	35.00
	1856	Inc. Ab.	2.50	5.00	8.00	16.00
	1857	1.655	2.00	3.75	6.00	12.00
	1858	.318	2.25	4.50	7.50	15.00
	1859/8	.041	—	—	—	—
	1859	Inc. Ab.	9.00	18.00	30.00	60.00

Y#	Date	Mintage	VG	Fine	VF	XF
5a	1860/50	.372	10.00	20.00	27.50	55.00
	1860	Inc. Ab.	8.50	17.50	25.00	50.00
	1861	.338	7.50	15.00	22.50	45.00
	1862	4.400	—	—	Rare	—

Y#	Date	Mintage	VG	Fine	VF	XF
14	1865	.040	18.50	30.00	45.00	90.00
	1866	.082	10.00	20.00	32.50	50.00

Y#	Date	Mintage	VG	Fine	VF	XF
14a	1867	.028	4.00	8.00	12.50	25.00
	1868	.181	2.00	4.00	7.50	15.00
	1869	.293	1.50	3.00	4.75	9.50
	1870/69	.540	1.25	2.50	4.00	7.50
	1870	Inc. Ab.	1.25	2.00	3.25	6.50
	1871/0	.171	1.50	3.00	5.00	10.00
	1871	Inc. Ab.	2.00	4.00	7.50	15.00
	1872	.286	1.25	2.00	3.25	6.50
	1873	.170	2.00	4.00	7.50	15.00
	1874	.588	1.25	2.00	3.25	6.50
	1875	.097	3.75	7.50	10.00	20.00
	1876	.082	2.50	5.00	8.00	16.00
	1877	.327	1.25	2.50	4.00	8.00
	1878	.306	1.50	3.00	4.75	9.50
	1880	.194	2.50	5.00	8.00	16.00
	1881	.264	2.50	5.00	8.00	16.00

1.2500 gm., .500 SILVER, .0200 oz ASW
Rev. leg: 0.5 added

Y#	Date	Mintage	Fine	VF	XF	Unc
14b	1879	.916	1.25	2.50	4.00	8.00
	1880	1.205	1.00	2.00	3.50	5.00
	1881/0	1.687	1.10	2.25	3.50	5.00
	1881	Inc. Ab.	1.10	2.25	3.50	5.00
	1882	.235	2.50	5.00	8.00	12.50
	1883	.117	3.75	7.50	12.50	20.00
	1884	.664	1.25	2.50	4.00	8.00
	1885	.489	1.25	2.50	4.00	8.00
	1887	3.081	1.00	2.00	3.00	4.00
	1888/7	2.448	1.50	3.00	4.00	8.00
	1888	Inc. Ab.	1.00	2.00	3.00	4.00
	1892	1.684	1.00	2.00	3.00	4.00
	1893	.850	1.00	2.00	3.00	4.00
	1894/84	.784	1.75	3.50	7.50	12.50
	1894	Inc. Ab.	1.50	3.00	6.50	10.00

Mule: Obv. of Y#14b, rev. of Y#14a.

Y#	Date	Mintage	Fine	VF	XF	Unc
A49	1884	—	—	—	—	—

CINCO (5) CENTAVOS

1.0000 gm., .835 SILVER, .0268 oz ASW

Y#	Date	Mintage	Fine	VF	XF	Unc
30	1896	.888	3.00	6.00	10.00	15.00

1.0000 gm., .500 SILVER, .0160 oz ASW

Y#	Date	Mintage	Fine	VF	XF	Unc
30a	1899	1.794	1.00	2.00	3.50	5.00
	1901	2.109	1.00	2.00	3.50	5.00
	1904	2.527	1.00	2.00	3.50	5.00
	1906	.713	1.00	2.00	3.50	8.00
	1907	2.791	1.00	2.00	3.50	5.00
	1909/899	—	1.00	2.00	3.50	8.00

1.0000 gm., .400 SILVER, .0128 oz ASW

Y#	Date	Mintage	Fine	VF	XF	Unc
30b	1908	3.642	.65	1.25	2.75	4.50
	1909	1.177	1.25	2.50	4.00	6.00
	1910	1.587	1.00	2.00	3.50	5.00
	1911	.847	1.75	3.50	6.00	10.00
	1913	2.573	.65	1.00	1.50	2.00
	1919	Inc. Bl.	.75	1.50	2.00	3.00

1.0000 gm., .450 SILVER, .0144 oz ASW
Obv: 0.45 added below Condor

Y#	Date	Mintage	Fine	VF	XF	Unc
30c	1915	2.250	.75	1.50	2.00	2.50
	1916/1	4.337	.90	1.75	2.50	4.00
	1916	Inc. Ab.	.75	1.50	2.00	2.50
	1919	1.494	1.50	3.00	4.50	6.00

COPPER-NICKEL

Y#	Date	Mintage	Fine	VF	XF	Unc
41	1920	.718	.75	1.50	3.00	5.00
	1921	2.406	—	.75	1.00	1.50
	1922	3.872	—	.75	1.00	1.50
	1923	2.150	—	.75	1.00	1.50
	1925	.994	—	.75	1.00	1.50
	1926	.594	1.25	2.50	3.00	5.00
	1927	1.276	.65	1.25	1.75	3.00
	1928	5.197	—	.75	1.00	1.50
	1933	3.000	—	—	Rare	—
	1934	Inc. Ab.	—	.75	1.00	1.50
	1936	2.000	—	.75	1.00	1.50
	1937	2.000	—	.75	1.00	1.50
	1938	2.000		.75	1.00	1.50

UN (1) DECIMO

2.5000 gm., .900 SILVER, .0723 oz ASW

Y#	Date	Mintage	VG	Fine	VF	XF
6	1852	.211	3.75	7.50	12.50	25.00
	1853	Inc. Ab.	2.50	5.00	8.00	16.00
	1855	.585	2.50	5.00	8.00	16.00
	1856/5	.580	2.75	5.50	9.00	17.50
	1856	Inc. Ab.	2.50	5.00	8.00	16.00
	1857	1.481	2.50	5.00	8.00	16.00
	1858	.540	2.50	5.00	8.00	16.00
	1859	.020	7.50	15.00	25.00	45.00
	1860/59	—	—	—	—	—

2.3000 gm., .900 SILVER, .0665 oz ASW

Y#	Date	Mintage	VG	Fine	VF	XF
6a	1860	.382	3.25	5.00	7.50	15.00
	1861	.236	3.25	5.00	7.50	15.00
	1862	.095	4.00	6.00	10.00	20.00

Y#	Date	Mintage	VG	Fine	VF	XF
15	1864	.096	5.50	9.00	15.00	30.00
	1865	.222	4.75	7.50	12.50	25.00
	1866	.096	5.50	9.00	15.00	30.00

Y#	Date	Mintage	VG	Fine	VF	XF
15a	1867	.020	7.00	12.00	20.00	40.00
	1868	.207	2.00	2.50	4.00	6.00
	1869	.245	2.00	2.50	4.00	6.00
	1870/60	.192	2.75	3.75	6.00	12.50
	1870	Inc. Ab.	2.50	3.50	5.00	10.00
	1871	.091	2.50	3.50	5.00	10.00
	1872	.288	2.00	2.50	4.00	6.00
	1873	.305	2.00	2.50	4.00	6.00
	1874	.271	2.00	2.50	4.00	6.00
	1875	.050	3.25	5.00	8.00	16.00
	1876	.100	2.25	2.75	4.50	7.50
	1877	.096	2.25	2.75	4.50	7.50
	1878	.512	2.00	2.50	4.00	6.00
	1880	.243	2.00	2.50	4.00	6.00

2.5000 gm., .500 SILVER, .0401 oz ASW
Rev. leg: 0.5 added

Y#	Date	Mintage	Fine	VF	XF	Unc
15b	1879	1.268	BV	1.25	2.50	3.75
	1880	.705	BV	1.25	2.50	3.75
	1881	2.186	BV	1.25	2.50	3.75
	1882	.233	BV	1.75	3.50	5.00
	1883	.178	BV	1.75	3.50	5.00
	1884	.319	BV	1.25	2.25	3.75
	1885	.116	3.00	6.00	9.00	12.50
	1887	1.514	BV	1.25	2.00	3.00
	1892/82	.994	BV	1.25	2.00	3.00
	1892/90	Inc. Ab.	5.00	10.00	17.50	27.50
	1892	Inc. Ab.	BV	1.25	2.00	3.00
	1893	.516	BV	1.25	2.00	3.00
	1894/3	.826	BV	1.25	2.00	3.00
	1894	Inc. Ab.	BV	1.25	2.00	3.00

2.0000 gm., .500 SILVER, .0321 oz ASW

Y#	Date	Mintage	Fine	VF	XF	Unc
15c	1891	.264	1.00	1.75	2.75	3.75

DIEZ (10) CENTAVOS

2.0000 GM., .835 SILVER, .0536 oz ASW

Y#	Date	Mintage	Fine	VF	XF	Unc
31	1896	2.561	BV	BV	3.75	7.50

2.0000 gm., .500 SILVER, .0321 oz ASW

Y#	Date	Mintage	Fine	VF	XF	Unc
31a	1899	2.013	1.00	1.50	2.00	3.00
	1900	.104	10.00	20.00	25.00	35.00
	1901	Inc. Ab.	6.50	12.50	15.00	20.00
	1904	.779	1.00	1.50	2.00	3.00
	1906	.139	1.75	3.50	5.00	9.00
	1907	3.151	1.00	1.50	2.00	3.00

1.5000 gm., .400 SILVER, .0192 oz ASW

Y#	Date	Mintage	Fine	VF	XF	Unc
31b	1908	4.149	.75	1.00	1.50	2.00
	1909	2.964	.75	1.00	1.50	2.00
	1913	1.269	1.50	3.00	5.00	7.50
	1919	.883	2.50	5.00	7.50	10.00
	1920	2.109	.75	1.00	1.50	2.00

1.5000 gm., .450 SILVER, .0217 oz ASW

Y#	Date	Mintage	Fine	VF	XF	Unc
31c	1915	1.620	.75	1.25	2.00	3.50
	1916	2.855	.75	1.25	2.00	3.50
	1917	.736	1.25	2.50	4.00	6.00
	1918	Inc. Ab.	1.25	2.50	4.00	6.00

COPPER-NICKEL

Y#	Date	Mintage	Fine	VF	XF	Unc
42	1920	.451	1.00	2.00	3.00	4.00
	1921	2.654	—	.75	1.00	1.50
	1922	4.017	—	.75	1.00	1.50
	1923	3.356	—	.75	1.00	1.50
	1924	1.445	—	.75	1.00	1.50
	1925	2.665	—	.75	1.00	1.50
	1927	.523	.75	1.50	2.50	3.50
	1928	3.052	—	.75	1.00	1.50
	1932	1.500	—	.75	1.00	1.50
	1933	5.800	—	.50	.75	1.00
	1934	.900	—	.75	1.00	1.25
	1935	1.500	—	.75	1.00	1.25
	1936	3.300	—	.50	.75	1.00
	1937	2.000	—	.50	.75	1.25
	1938	5.000	—	.50	.75	1.25
	1939	1.200	—	.50	.75	1.25
	1940	6.100	—	.50	.75	1.25
	1941	.900	.75	1.50	2.50	5.00

VEINTE (20) CENTAVOS

5.0000 gm., .900 SILVER, .1446 oz ASW

Y#	Date	Mintage	VG	Fine	VF	XF
7	1852	.077	7.50	10.00	15.00	25.00
	1853	.906	4.50	6.00	8.00	12.50
	1854	.417	4.50	6.00	8.00	12.50
	1855	.325	4.50	6.00	8.00	12.50
	1856/5	.396	4.50	6.00	8.00	12.50
	1856	Inc. Ab.	4.50	6.00	8.00	12.50
	1857	.748	4.50	6.00	8.00	12.50
	1858	.532	7.50	10.00	15.00	25.00
	1859/8	.120	7.50	10.00	15.00	25.00
	1859	Inc. Ab.	7.50	10.00	15.00	25.00

4.60000 gm., .900 SILVER, .1331 oz ASW

Y#	Date	Mintage	VG	Fine	VF	XF
7a	1860/59	.388	5.00	7.50	10.00	20.00
	1860	Inc. Ab.	4.50	6.00	9.00	17.50
	1861/91	1.471	4.50	6.00	8.00	15.00
	1861	Inc. Ab.	4.50	6.00	8.00	15.00
	1862	.324	5.00	7.50	10.00	20.00

Y#	Date	Mintage	VG	Fine	VF	XF
16	1863	.160	5.00	7.50	10.00	20.00
	1864	.226	4.50	6.00	9.00	16.00
	1865	1.505	BV	BV	4.50	7.50
	1866	4.298	BV	BV	4.50	7.50
	1867	Inc. Be.	27.50	45.00	75.00	100.00

Smaller wreath

Y#	Date	Mintage	VG	Fine	VF	XF
16a	1867	.286	4.50	6.00	8.50	15.00
	1868	.197	BV	BV	4.50	6.00
	1869/8	.163	BV	BV	4.50	6.00
	1869	Inc. Ab.	BV	BV	4.50	6.00
	1870/60	.992	BV	BV	4.50	6.00
	1870	Inc. Ab.	BV	BV	4.50	6.00
	1871	1.144	BV	BV	4.50	6.00
	1872	1.979	BV	BV	4.50	6.00
	1873	.846	BV	BV	4.50	6.00
	1874	1.256	BV	BV	4.50	6.00
	1875	.120	5.00	7.50	12.50	25.00
	1876	.749	4.00	4.50	6.00	7.50
	1877	.549	4.00	4.50	6.00	7.50
	1878	2.639	4.00	4.50	6.00	7.50
	1879	9.645	60.00	100.00	175.00	250.00

5.0000 gm., .500 SILVER, .0803 oz ASW
Rev. leg: 0.5 added

Y#	Date	Mintage	VG	Fine	VF	XF
16b	1879	5.073	2.50	4.00	6.50	10.00
	1880/70	6.846	2.75	4.50	7.50	12.50
	1880/79	Inc. Ab.	2.75	4.50	7.50	12.50
	1880	Inc. Ab.	2.50	4.00	6.50	10.00
	1881	6.408	2.50	4.00	6.50	10.00
	1892	3.719	2.50	4.00	6.50	10.00
	1893	1.397	2.50	4.00	6.50	10.00

4.0000 gm., .500 SILVER, .0643 oz ASW

Y#	Date	Mintage	VG	Fine	VF	XF
16c	1891	2.953	2.50	4.50	7.50	15.00

5.0000 gm., .200 SILVER, .0321 oz ASW

Y#	Date	Mintage	VG	Fine	VF	XF
16d	1891	.787	7.50	15.00	25.00	50.00

4.0000 gm., .835 SILVER, .0321 oz ASW

Y#	Date	Mintage	VG	Fine	VF	XF
32	1895	.146	15.00	25.00	40.00	80.00

4.0000 gm., .500 SILVER, .0643 oz ASW

Y#	Date	Mintage	VG	Fine	VF	XF
32a	1899	4.343	BV	BV	2.25	3.50
	1900	.334	3.75	7.50	12.50	25.00
	1906	.866	BV	2.25	3.00	5.00
	1907	7.625	BV	BV	2.25	3.50

3.0000 gm., .400 SILVER, .0385 oz ASW
Obv: 0.5 eliminated below Condor

Y#	Date	Mintage	VG	Fine	VF	XF
32b	1907	1.201	BV	1.25	1.75	3.00
	1908	5.869	BV	1.25	1.75	3.00
	1909	1.080	BV	1.25	1.75	3.00
	1913/1	3.507	BV	1.25	2.00	4.00
	1913	Inc. Ab.	BV	1.25	1.75	3.00
	1919	3.749	BV	1.25	1.75	3.00
	1920	4.189	BV	1.25	1.75	3.00

3.0000 gm., .450 SILVER, .0434 oz ASW

Y#	Date	Mintage	VG	Fine	VF	XF
32c	1916	3.377	BV	1.75	2.00	3.00

COPPER-NICKEL
Obv: Without designer's name. Rev: Large 20.

Y#	Date	Mintage	VG	Fine	VF	XF
43.1	1920	.499	—	1.00	1.75	3.00
	1921	6.547	—	.60	1.00	2.00
	1922	8.261	—	.60	1.00	2.00
	1923	5.439	—	.60	1.00	2.00
	1924	16.096	—	.60	1.00	2.00
	1925	9.830	—	.60	1.00	2.00
	1929	9.685	—	.60	1.00	2.00

Rev: Small 20

Y#	Date	Mintage	VG	Fine	VF	XF
43.2	1932	—	—	.60	1.00	2.00
	1933	5.900	—	.60	1.00	2.00

Obv: With O. Roty.

Y#	Date	Mintage	VG	Fine	VF	XF
43.3	1932	—	—	.60	1.00	2.00
	1933	1.000	—	.60	1.00	2.00
	1937	1.000	—	.60	1.00	2.00
	1938	3.043	—	.60	1.25	2.00
	1939	5.283	—	.50	1.25	2.00
	1940	9.300	—	.60	1.25	2.00
	1941	3.000	—	.60	1.25	2.00

COPPER

Y#	Date	Mintage	VG	Fine	VF	XF
50	1942	30.000	—	.15	.25	.50
	1943	39.600	—	.15	.25	.50
	1944	29.100	—	.15	.25	.50
	1945	11.400	—	.15	.25	.50
	1946	13.800	—	.15	.25	.50
	1947	15.700	—	.15	.25	.50
	1948	15.200	—	.15	.25	.50
	1949	14.700	—	.15	.25	.50
	1950	15.200	—	.15	.25	.50
	1951	14.700	—	.15	.25	.40
	1952	15.500	—	.15	.25	.40
	1953	7.800	—	.15	.25	.40

40 CENTAVOS

6.0000 gm., .400 SILVER, .0771 oz ASW

Y#	Date	Mintage	VG	Fine	VF	XF
33	1907	.056	3.50	5.00	7.50	15.00
	1908	1.452	2.75	4.00	6.00	10.00

50 CENTAVOS

12.5000 gm., .900 SILVER, .3617 oz ASW

Y#	Date	Mintage	VG	Fine	VF	XF
8	1853	.769	12.50	15.00	20.00	30.00
	1854	.551	12.50	15.00	22.50	35.00
	1855	1.354	12.50	15.00	22.50	35.00
	1856	.606	12.50	15.00	22.50	35.00
	1858	.245	17.50	25.00	40.00	75.00
	1859	.489	12.50	15.00	25.00	50.00
	1860	.020	—	—	Rare	—
	1862	.123	17.50	25.00	40.00	75.00

Obv: Large wreath. Rev: Eagle with shield.

Y#	Date	Mintage	VG	Fine	VF	XF
17	1862	Inc. Ab.	22.50	30.00	50.00	80.00
	1863	.080	17.50	25.00	35.00	60.00
	1864/3	.068	17.50	25.00	35.00	60.00
	1864	Inc. Ab.	17.50	25.00	35.00	60.00
	1865	.287	12.50	15.00	22.50	35.00
	1866/5	—	12.50	15.00	22.50	35.00
	1866	.200	12.50	15.00	22.50	35.00
	1867	Inc. Bl.	25.00	40.00	60.00	100.00

Obv: Smaller wreath

Y#	Date	Mintage	VG	Fine	VF	XF
17a	1867	.047	17.50	25.00	35.00	60.00
	1868	.147	12.50	15.00	20.00	30.00
	1870	.271	12.50	15.00	20.00	30.00
	1872/0	.104	12.50	15.00	20.00	30.00
	1872	Inc. Ab.	12.50	15.00	20.00	30.00

10.0000 gm., .700 SILVER, .2250 oz ASW

Y#	Date	Mintage	Fine	VF	XF	Unc
34	1902	2.022	BV	7.50	12.50	20.00
	1903	1.111	BV	7.50	12.50	20.00
	1905	1.075	BV	7.50	12.50	20.00
	1906	.142	10.00	15.00	20.00	30.00

COPPER

Y#	Date	Mintage	Fine	VF	XF	Unc
51	1942	4.715	—	1.00	3.00	5.00

UN (1) PESO

25.0000 gm., .900 SILVER, .7234 oz ASW

Y#	Date	Mintage	VG	Fine	VF	XF
9	1853	.394	30.00	35.00	50.00	90.00
	1854	.567	25.00	35.00	45.00	75.00
	1855	.683	25.00	35.00	45.00	75.00
	1856/5	.406	27.50	37.50	47.50	80.00
	1856	Inc. Ab.	25.00	35.00	45.00	70.00
	1858	.051	75.00	125.00	200.00	300.00
	1859/8	.330	27.50	40.00	60.00	75.00
	1859	Inc. Ab.	25.00	35.00	45.00	70.00
	1862	.103	60.00	100.00	200.00	300.00

1.5235 gm., .900 GOLD, .0441 oz AGW

Y#	Date	Mintage	Fine	VF	XF	Unc
19	1860	.156	35.00	45.00	65.00	110.00
	1861	.176	35.00	45.00	65.00	110.00
	1862	.011	40.00	50.00	70.00	125.00
	1863	.055	35.00	45.00	65.00	110.00
	1864	.029	40.00	50.00	70.00	125.00
	1867	949 pcs.	75.00	100.00	150.00	250.00
	1873	.016	40.00	50.00	70.00	125.00

25.0000 gm., .900 SILVER, .7234 oz ASW
Obv. value: 1 PESO. Rev: Eagle with shield.

Y#	Date	Mintage	VG	Fine	VF	XF
18	1867	Inc. Bl.	475.00	800.00	1000.	1500.

Obv. value: UN PESO

Y#	Date	Mintage	VG	Fine	VF	XF
18a	1867	.220	35.00	50.00	75.00	100.00
	1868	1.037	BV	25.00	30.00	45.00
	1869	.467	BV	27.50	32.50	45.00
	1870/69	.556	BV	27.50	32.50	45.00
	1870	Inc. Ab.	BV	27.50	32.50	45.00
	1871	.795	50.00	75.00	125.00	175.00
	1872	Inc. Ab.	BV	27.50	32.50	45.00

Y#	Date	Mintage	Fine	VF	XF	Unc
	1873	.323	BV	27.50	32.50	50.00
	1874	1.204	BV	25.00	30.00	45.00
	1875	2.128	BV	25.00	30.00	45.00
	1876	1.508	BV	25.00	30.00	45.00
	1877	1.930	BV	25.00	30.00	45.00
	1878	.950	BV	25.00	30.00	45.00
	1879	.780	BV	25.00	30.00	45.00
	1880	.693	BV	25.00	30.00	45.00
	1881	1.420	BV	25.00	30.00	45.00
	1882/1	1.648	BV	27.50	32.50	45.00
	1882	Inc. Ab.	BV	25.00	30.00	45.00
	1883 round top 3					
		1.397	BV	25.00	30.00	45.00
	1884	1.812	BV	25.00	30.00	45.00
	1885/3	.528	BV	27.50	40.00	60.00
	1885	Inc. Ab.	BV	25.00	30.00	45.00
	1886	.966	BV	27.50	32.50	45.00
	1887	.023	250.00	400.00	700.00	1000.00
	1889	.241	25.00	35.00	45.00	60.00
	1890/89	.109	30.00	45.00	65.00	150.00
	1890	Inc. Ab.	25.00	40.00	70.00	125.00
	1891	.109	50.00	80.00	150.00	225.00

Flat top 3, obv. not inverted with respect to rev.

Y#	Date	Mintage	Fine	VF	XF	Unc
18b	1883(1925)	.150	50.00	75.00	100.00	150.00

Flat top 3, obv. inverted with respect to rev.

Y#	Date	Mintage	Fine	VF	XF	Unc
18c	1883(1926)	I.A.	100.00	150.00	200.00	300.00

Above issue minted in 1925-6 and most coins were subsequently melted down.

20.0000 gm., .835 SILVER, .5369 oz ASW

Y#	Date	Mintage	Fine	VF	XF	Unc
35	1895	6.086	BV	17.50	25.00	35.00
	1896	1.556	BV	17.50	25.00	35.00
	1897	.037	22.50	35.00	50.00	75.00

20.0000 gm., .700 SILVER, .4501 oz ASW
Rev: Similar to Y#35.

Y#	Date	Mintage	Fine	VF	XF	Unc
35a	1902	.178	BV	17.50	25.00	40.00
	1903	.372	BV	15.00	20.00	35.00
	1905	.429	BV	15.00	20.00	35.00

12.0000 gm., .900 SILVER, .3472 oz ASW

Y#	Date	Mintage	Fine	VF	XF	Unc
35b	1910	2.166	BV	11.50	13.00	15.00

9.0000 gm., .720 silver, .2083 oz asw

Y#	Date	Mintage	Fine	VF	XF	Unc
35c	1915	6.032	BV	BV	7.00	10.00
	1917	3.033	BV	BV	8.50	12.50

9.0000 gm., .500 SILVER, .1446 oz ASW

Y#	Date	Mintage	Fine	VF	XF	Unc
35d	1921	2.287	BV	BV	5.00	7.50
	1922	2.718	BV	BV	5.00	7.50
	1924	1.748	BV	BV	5.00	7.50
	1925	2.037	BV	BV	5.00	7.50

Y#	Date	Mintage	Fine	VF	XF	Unc
35e	1927	4.099	5.00	8.00	12.00	18.00

6.0000 gm., .400 SILVER, .0771 oz ASW

Y#	Date	Mintage	Fine	VF	XF	Unc
35f	1932	4.000	BV	2.75	3.50	5.00
	1933	—	—	Reported, Not Confirmed		

COPPER-NICKEL

Y#	Date	Mintage	Fine	VF	XF	Unc
35g.1	1933	29.976	—	.50	1.00	1.50

Obv: O Roty incuse on rock base.

Y#	Date	Mintage	Fine	VF	XF	Unc
35g.2	1940	.150	1.50	3.00	3.50	4.00

COPPER

Y#	Date	Mintage	Fine	VF	XF	Unc
52	1942	15.150	.10	.35	1.00	1.50
	1943	16.900	.10	.35	1.00	1.50
	1944	12.050	.10	.35	1.25	2.00
	1945	7.600	.10	.35	1.25	2.00
	1946	2.050	.10	.35	1.75	3.00
	1947	2.200	.10	.35	1.75	3.00
	1948	5.900	.10	.25	.75	1.25
	1949	7.100	.10	.20	.45	.75
	1950	7.250	.10	.20	.45	.75
	1951	8.150	.10	.20	.45	.75
	1952	10.400	.10	.20	.45	.75
	1953	17.200	.10	.20	.40	.50
	1954	7.566	.10	.20	.40	.50

ALUMINUM

Y#	Date	Mintage	Fine	VF	XF	Unc
52a	1954	43.550	.10	.15	.25	.40
	1955	69.050	.10	.15	.25	.40
	1956	58.250	.10	.15	.25	.40
	1957	49.250	.10	.15	.25	.40
	1958	29.900	.10	.15	.25	.40

DOS (2) PESOS

3.0506 gm., .900 GOLD, .0882 oz AGW

Y#	Date	Mintage	Fine	VF	XF	Unc
20	1857	.207	65.00	75.00	85.00	100.00
	1858/7	.056	75.00	100.00	125.00	150.00
	1858	Inc. Ab.	65.00	75.00	85.00	100.00
	1859	.097	65.00	75.00	85.00	100.00
	1860	.078	65.00	75.00	85.00	100.00
	1862	.010	65.00	75.00	85.00	100.00
	1865	—	—	—	Rare	—
	1867	841 pcs.	—	—	Rare	—
	1873	.054	65.00	75.00	85.00	100.00
	1874	.061	65.00	75.00	85.00	100.00
	1875	.037	65.00	75.00	85.00	100.00

18.0000 gm., .500 SILVER, .2893 oz ASW

Y#	Date	Mintage	Fine	VF	XF	Unc
45	1927	1.112	BV	BV	10.00	12.50

CINCO (5) PESOS

7.6265 gm., .900 GOLD, .2207 oz AGW

Y#	Date	Mintage	Fine	VF	XF	Unc
21	1851	3,735	BV	170.00	210.00	275.00
	1852	.020	BV	160.00	200.00	250.00
	1853	5,987	BV	170.00	210.00	275.00
	1854	953 pcs.	—	—	Rare	—
	1855	7,609	BV	170.00	210.00	275.00
	1856	4,753	BV	170.00	210.00	275.00
	1857	.025	BV	160.00	200.00	250.00
	1858	1.100	BV	160.00	200.00	250.00
	1859/8	.066	BV	160.00	200.00	275.00
	1859	Inc. Ab.	BV	150.00	190.00	250.00
	1862	6,738	BV	170.00	210.00	275.00
	1865	5,110	BV	170.00	210.00	275.00
	1866	6,249	BV	170.00	210.00	275.00
	1867	.010	BV	160.00	200.00	190.00
	1868	4,065	BV	170.00	210.00	275.00

Y#	Date	Mintage	Fine	VF	XF	Unc
	1869	5,913	BV	170.00	210.00	275.00
	1870	.013	BV	160.00	200.00	250.00
	1872	.023	BV	150.00	190.00	225.00
	1873	.050	BV	150.00	190.00	225.00

2.9955 gm., .917 GOLD, .0883 oz AGW

Y#	Date	Mintage	Fine	VF	XF	Unc
36	1895	3.026	75.00	100.00	125.00	150.00
	1896	—	175.00	300.00	425.00	600.00

Y#	Date	Mintage	Fine	VF	XF	Unc
38	1898	.426	90.00	125.00	150.00	200.00
	1900	1.267	85.00	115.00	140.00	175.00
	1916/1	—	—	—	—	—

25.0000 gm., .900 SILVER, .7234 oz ASW

Y#	Date	Mintage	Fine	VF	XF	Unc
46	1927	.976	BV	25.00	30.00	37.50

ALUMINUM

Y#	Date	Mintage	Fine	VF	XF	Unc
53	1956	1.600	.15	.30	.50	.75

22.0500 gm., 1.000 SILVER, .7090 oz ASW
Rev: Similar to 200 pesos, FR#58.

H#	Date	Mintage	XF	Unc	Proof
1	1968	12,000	—	—	35.00

DIEZ (10) PESOS

15.2530 gm., .900 GOLD, .4414 oz AGW

Y#	Date	Mintage	Fine	VF	XF	Unc
22.1	1851	.050	300.00	350.00	375.00	450.00
	1852	.135	300.00	350.00	375.00	450.00
	1853	.206	300.00	350.00	375.00	450.00
	1854	.195	300.00	350.00	375.00	450.00
	1855	.061	300.00	350.00	375.00	450.00
	1856	.066	300.00	350.00	375.00	450.00
	1857	.020	300.00	350.00	375.00	450.00
	1858	.052	300.00	350.00	375.00	450.00
	1859	.281	300.00	350.00	375.00	450.00
	1860	.031	300.00	350.00	375.00	450.00
	1861	.015	300.00	350.00	375.00	450.00
	1862	.021	300.00	350.00	375.00	450.00
	1863	.025	300.00	350.00	375.00	450.00
	1864	.026	300.00	350.00	375.0	450.00
	1865	.045	300.00	350.00	375.00	450.00
	1866	.066	300.00	350.00	375.00	450.00
	1867	.121	300.00	350.00	375.00	450.00

Obv: Modified arms design.

Y#	Date	Mintage	Fine	VF	XF	Unc
22.2	1868	.054	300.00	350.00	375.00	450.00
	1869	.036	300.00	350.00	375.00	450.00
	1870	.076	300.00	350.00	375.00	450.00
	1871	.041	300.00	350.00	375.00	450.00
	1872	.235	300.00	350.00	375.00	450.00
	1873	.112	300.00	350.00	375.00	450.00
	1874	1,277	325.00	375.00	400.00	475.00
	1876	2,106	325.00	375.00	400.00	475.00
	1877	8,208	325.00	375.00	400.00	475.00
	1878	7,983	325.00	375.00	400.00	475.00
	1879	9,805	325.00	375.00	400.00	475.00
	1880	.011	300.00	350.00	375.00	450.00
	1881	.013	300.00	350.00	375.00	450.00
	1882	.014	300.00	350.00	375.00	450.00
	1883	8,381	325.00	375.00	400.00	475.00
	1884	9,888	325.00	375.00	400.00	475.00
	1885	7,758	325.00	375.00	400.00	475.00
	1886	3,721	325.00	375.00	400.00	475.00
	1887	5,236	325.00	375.00	400.00	475.00
	1888	4,217	325.00	375.00	400.00	475.00
	1889	4,650	325.00	375.00	400.00	475.00
	1890	2,344	325.00	375.00	400.00	475.00
	1892	1,192	325.00	375.00	400.00	475.00

5.9910 gm., .917 GOLD, .1766 oz AGW

Y#	Date	Mintage	Fine	VF	XF	Unc
37	1895	.808	125.00	150.00	175.00	225.00

Y#	Date	Mintage	Fine	VF	XF	Unc
39	1896	1.438	125.00	150.00	175.00	225.00
	1898	—	150.00	200.00	250.00	425.00
	1900	—	—	Reported, Not Confirmed		
	1901	1.651	125.00	150.00	175.00	225.00

ALUMINUM

Y#	Date	Mintage	Fine	VF	XF	Unc
54	1956	13.100	—	.35	.50	1.00
	1957	28.800	—	.35	.50	1.00
	1958	44.500	—	.35	.50	1.00
	1959	10.220	—	.35	.50	.75

1.000 SILVER

H#	Date	Mintage	XF	Unc	Proof
2	1968	.012	—	—	30.00

VEINTE (20) PESOS

11.9821 gm., .917 GOLD, .3532 agw

Y#	Date	Mintage	Fine	VF	XF	Unc
40	1896	.149	250.00	275.00	300.00	325.00
	1906	.041	250.00	275.00	300.00	325.00
	1907	.012	250.00	275.00	300.00	325.00
	1908	.025	250.00	275.00	300.00	325.00
	1910	.027	250.00	275.00	300.00	325.00
	1911	.017	250.00	275.00	300.00	325.00
	1913/11	.018	—	—	—	—
	1913	Inc. Ab.	250.00	275.00	300.00	325.00
	1914	.022	250.00	275.00	300.00	325.00
	1915	.065	250.00	275.00	300.00	325.00
	1916	.035	250.00	275.00	300.00	325.00
	1917	.717	250.00	275.00	300.00	325.00

4.0679 gm., .900 GOLD, .1177 oz AGW

Y#	Date	Mintage	Fine	VF	XF	Unc
47	1926	.085	100.00	120.00	140.00	160.00
(98)	1958	500 pcs.	150.00	200.00	275.00	375.00

Y#	Date	Mintage	Fine	VF	XF	Unc
(98)	1959	.025	100.00	120.00	150.00	200.00
	1961	.020	100.00	120.00	150.00	200.00

CINCUENTA (50) PESOS

10.1698 gm., .900 GOLD, .2943 oz AGW

Y#	Date	Mintage	Fine	VF	XF	Unc
48	1926	.126	BV	200.00	210.00	225.00
(99)	1958	.010	BV	200.00	210.00	225.00
	1961	.020	BV	200.00	210.00	225.00
	1962	.030	BV	200.00	210.00	225.00
	1965	—	— Reported, Not Confirmed			
	1967	—	BV	200.00	210.00	225.00
	1968	—	BV	200.00	210.00	225.00
	1974	—	BV	200.00	210.00	225.00

.900 GOLD
Rev: Similar to 200 Pesos, Fr#58.

Fr#	Date	Mintage	XF	Unc	Proof
60	1968	.012	—	—	200.00

CIEN (100) PESOS

20.3397 gm., .900 GOLD, .5886 oz AGW

Y#	Date	Mintage	Fine	VF	XF	Unc
49	1926	.678	BV	400.00	420.00	450.00

Y#	Date	Mintage	Fine	VF	XF	Unc
49a	1932	9.315	BV	425.00	450.00	500.00
(100)	1946	.380	BV	400.00	420.00	450.00
	1947	.500	BV	400.00	420.00	450.00
	1948	.405	BV	400.00	420.00	450.00
	1949	.245	BV	400.00	420.00	450.00
	1950	.020	BV	400.00	420.00	450.00
	1951	.190	BV	400.00	420.00	450.00
	1952	.240	BV	400.00	420.00	450.00
	1953	.150	BV	400.00	420.00	450.00
	1954	.250	BV	400.00	420.00	450.00
	1955	.085	BV	400.00	420.00	450.00
	1956	.070	BV	400.00	420.00	450.00
	1957	.020	BV	400.00	420.00	450.00
	1958	.178	BV	400.00	420.00	450.00
	1959	.100	BV	400.00	420.00	450.00
	1960	.345	BV	400.00	420.00	450.00
	1961	.195	BV	400.00	420.00	450.00
	1962	.250	BV	400.00	420.00	450.00
	1963	.145	BV	400.00	420.00	450.00

.900 GOLD

Fr#	Date	Mintage	XF	Unc	Proof
59	1968	.012	—	—	400.00

200 PESOS

40.6700 gm., .900 GOLD, 1.1769 oz AGW

Fr#	Date	Mintage	XF	Unc	Proof
58	1968	.012	—	—	800.00

500 PESOS

101.6900 gm., .900 GOLD, 2.9427 oz AGW
Obv: Liberty facing left with flag.
Rev: Similar to 200 Pesos, Fr#58.

Fr#	Date	Mintage	XF	Unc	Proof
57	1968	.012	—	—	2000.

CURRENCY REVALUATION

10 Pesos = 1 Centesimo
100 Centesimos = 1 Escudo

1/2 CENTESIMO

ALUMINUM

Y#	Date	Mintage	VF	XF	Unc
55	1962	3.750	.10	.30	.50
	1963	8.100	.10	.30	.50

CENTESIMO

ALUMINUM

Y#	Date	Mintage	VF	XF	Unc
56	1960	20.160	.35	.75	1.25
	1961	Inc. Ab.	.15	.30	.50
	1962	26.320	.15	.30	.50
	1963	51.360	.15	.30	.50

2 CENTESIMOS

ALUMINUM-BRONZE

Y#	Date	Mintage	VF	XF	Unc
57	1964	4.050	—	.10	.25
	1965	32.550	—	.10	.25
	1966	31.800	—	.10	.20
	1967	34.750	—	.10	.20
	1968	29.400	—	.10	.25
	1969	—	—	.10	.25
	1970	20.250	—	.10	.25

5 CENTESIMOS

ALUMINUM-BRONZE

Y#	Date	Mintage	VF	XF	Unc
58	1960	—	—	Rare	—
	1961	.012	—	4.50	10.00
	1962	Inc. Bl.	—	.15	.30
	1963	17.280	—	.15	.30
	1964	16.628	—	.15	.25
	1965	37.680	—	.15	.25
	1966	32.360	—	.15	.25
	1967	17.640	—	.15	.30
	1968	4.338	—	.15	.30
	1969	—	—	.15	.25
	1970	30.680	—	.15	.25

10 CENTESIMOS

ALUMINUM-BRONZE

Y#	Date	Mintage	VF	XF	Unc
59	1960	—	2.00	3.50	6.50
	1961	57.068	.10	.20	.40
	1962	1.480	.10	.20	.40
	1963	10.920	.10	.20	.40
	1964	27.020	.10	.20	.40
	1965	49.480	.10	.20	.40
	1966	60.360	.10	.20	.40
	1967	60.680	.10	.25	.40
	1968	8.040	.10	.20	.40
	1969	—	.10	.20	.40
	1970	42.080	.10	.20	.40

Y#	Date	Mintage	VF	XF	Unc
60	1971	99.700	—	—	.10
(113)					

20 CENTESIMOS

ALUMINUM-BRONZE

Y#	Date	Mintage	VF	XF	Unc
61	1971	89.200	—	.10	.20
(114)	1972	—	—	—	—

50 CENTESIMOS

ALUMINUM-BRONZE

Y#	Date	Mintage	VF	XF	Unc
62	1971	58.300	—	.10	.25
(115)					

ESCUDO

COPPER-NICKEL

Y#	Date	Mintage	VF	XF	Unc
63	1971	160.900	.10	.20	.40
(116)	1972	inc. Ab.	.10	.20	.40
	1973	.150	Reported, Not Confirmed		

NOTE: 1973 coinage not released for circulation.

2 ESCUDOS

COPPER-NICKEL

Y#	Date	Mintage	VF	XF	Unc
64	1971	—	—	Rare	—
(117)					

NOTE: Not released for circulation.

5 ESCUDOS

COPPER-NICKEL

Y#	Date	Mintage	VF	XF	Unc
65	1971	—	.10	.25	.75
(118)	1972	—	—	—	.75
	1973	41.100	Reported, Not Confirmed		

ALUMINUM

Y#	Date	Mintage	VF	XF	Unc
65a	1972	—	.10	.15	.20
(118a)	1974	8.000	.10	.15	.20

10 ESCUDOS

ALUMINUM

Y#	Date	Mintage	VF	XF	Unc
66	1974	33.750	.10	.20	.50
(119)	1975	31.600	.10	.20	.50

50 ESCUDOS

NICKEL-BRASS

Y#	Date	Mintage	VF	XF	Unc
67	1974	6.000	.15	.25	.60
(120)	1975	20.300	.15	.20	.50

100 ESCUDOS

NICKEL-BRASS

Y#	Date	Mintage	VF	XF	Unc
68	1974	32.100	.20	.35	.75
(121)	1975	65.600	.20	.35	.75

MONETARY REFORM

100 Centavos = 1 Peso
1 Peso = 1000 Old Escudos

CENTAVO

ALUMINUM

Y#	Date	Mintage	VF	XF	Unc
69	1975	2.000	—	—	.10
(122)					

5 CENTAVOS

ALUMINUM-BRONZE

Y#	Date	Mintage	VF	XF	Unc
70	1975	5.400	—	—	.10
(123)	1976	6.600	—	—	—

ALUMINUM

Y#	Date	Mintage	VF	XF	Unc
70a	1976	5.000	—	—	.25
123a					

10 CENTAVOS

ALUMINUM-BRONZE

Y#	Date	Mintage	VF	XF	Unc
71	1975	8.600	—	—	.15
(124)	1976	9.000	—	—	—

ALUMINUM

Y#	Date	Mintage	VF	XF	Unc
71a	1976	6.600	—	—	.25
(124a)	1977	—	—	—	.25
	1978	—	—	—	.25

50 CENTAVOS

COPPER-NICKEL

Y#	Date	Mintage	VF	XF	Unc
72	1975	38.000	—	—	.20
(125)	1976	1.000	—	—	.20
	1977	—	—	—	.40
	1978	—	—	—	.25

ALUMINUM-BRONZE

Y#	Date	Mintage	VF	XF	Unc
72a	1978	—	—	—	—
(125a)					

PESO

COPPER-NICKEL

Y#	Date	Mintage	VF	XF	Unc
73	1975	51.000	.10	.15	.25
(126)					

LIBERTADOR legend change

Y#	Date	Mintage	VF	XF	Unc
73a	1976	30.000	.10	.15	.50
(126a)	1977	—	.10	.15	.50
	1978	—	.10	.15	.40

ALUMINUM-BRONZE

Y#	Date	Mintage	VF	XF	Unc
73b	1978	—	—	—	—

5 PESOS

COPPER-NICKEL
3rd Anniversary of New Government

Y#	Date	Mintage	VF	XF	Unc
74	1976	2.100	.20	.30	.60
(127)	1977	—	.20	.30	.60
	1978	—	.20	.30	.60

10 PESOS

COPPER-NICKEL
3rd Anniversary of New Government

Y#	Date	Mintage	VF	XF	Unc
75	1976	2.100	.40	.60	1.00
(128)	1977	—	.40	.60	1.00
	1978	—	.40	.60	1.00

44.8000 gm., .999 SILVER
3rd Anniversary of New Government
Obv: Arms. Rev: Woman with wings with raised arms below dates.

Y#	Date	Mintage			
75a	1976	1,000	—	Proof	125.00

50 PESOS

10.1500 gm., .900 GOLD'
3rd Anniversary of New Government
Similar to 10 Pesos, Y#75a.

Y#	Date	Mintage			
76	1976	1,000	—	Proof	300.00
	1976	Inc. Ab.	—	Proof	250.00

100 PESOS

.900 GOLD
3rd Anniversary of New Government

Y#	Date	Mintage			
77	1976	2,900	—	170.00	190.00
	1976	100 pcs.	—	Proof	—

500 PESOS

102.2700 gm., .900 GOLD
3rd Anniversary of New Government
Similar to 10 Pesos, Y#75a.

Y#	Date	Mintage			
78	1976	1,000	—	—	—
	1976	Inc. Ab.	—	Proof	2200.

1 ONZA

31.1000 gm., .999 GOLD

Y#	Date				
79	1979	—	—	—	650.00

NCLT ISSUES

PATTERNS

KM#	Date	Mintage	Identification	Mkt.Val.
1	1828	—	1/2 Real, Silver, Coquimbo Mint, C#87	—

PROOF SETS

STANDARD METALS

KM#	Date	Mintage	Identification	Issue Price	Mkt. Val.
101	1968(6)*	—	H1,2,F57-60	560.00	1950.
102	1968(4)*	—	F57-60	528.00	1900.
103	1968(2)*	12,000	H1, 2	31.50	50.00

*Total of 12,000 coins struck for each denomination, including those available singly.

NECESSITY COINAGE

COPIAPO

REVOLUTION OF 1859

50 CENTAVOS

SILVER
Uniface; obv: star in shield, value below.

Y#	Date	Mintage	VG	Fine	VF	XF
23 (N11)	ND	—	27.50	32.50	50.00	65.00

PESO

SILVER
Uniface. Obv: Star in shield, value below.

Y#	Date	Mintage	VG	Fine	VF	XF
24 (N12)	ND	—	25.00	30.00	40.00	50.00

WAR OF 1865 WITH SPAIN

Blockade of Puerto de Caldera

50 CENTAVOS

SILVER, uniface
Obv: COPIAPO-CHILE around shield. Rev: Date.

Y#	Date	Mintage	VG	Fine	VF	XF
25 (N13)	1865	—	—	37.50	55.00	65.00

NOTE: All known specimens are restrikes made from original dies circa 1909 by Medina.

PESO

SILVER, uniface

Y#	Date	Mintage	VG	Fine	VF	XF
26 (N14)	1865	—	27.50	37.50	55.00	75.00

SAN BERNARDO DE MAYPO

1/4 REAL

COPPER
Obv: Mountains (volcano in center) in circle.
Rev: View of Canal de San Bernardo.

C#	Date	Mintage	Good	VG	Fine	VF
N21	1821	—	125.00	200.00	300.00	475.00

NOTE: Struck to pay canal workers.

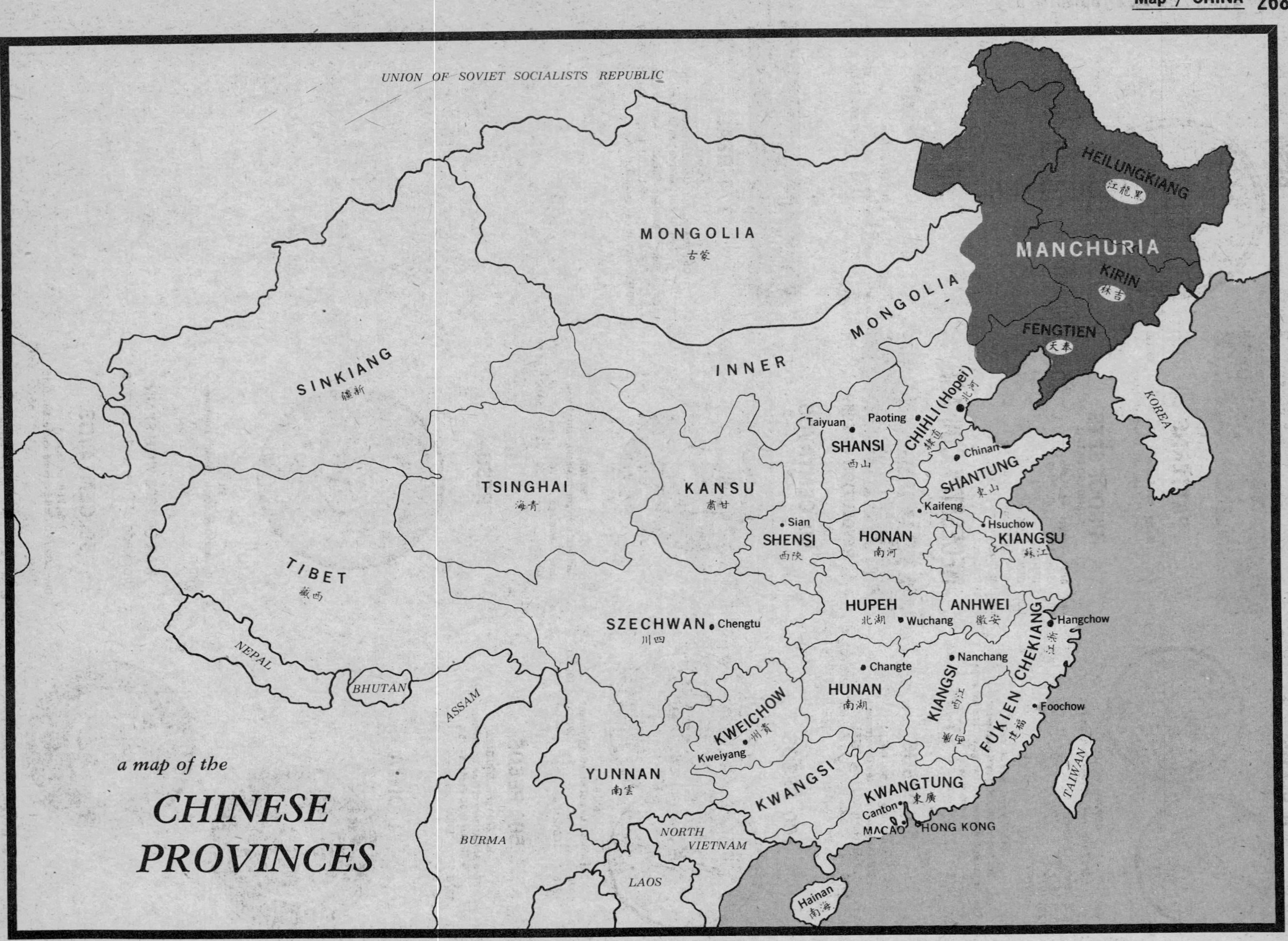
UNION OF SOVIET SOCIALISTS REPUBLIC
MONGOLIA
古蒙
INNER MONGOLIA
MANCHURIA
HEILUNGKIANG
江龍黑
KIRIN
林吉
FENGTIEN
天奉
KOREA
SINKIANG
疆新
TIBET
藏西
TSINGHAI
海青
KANSU
肅甘
SHANSI
西山
Taiyuan
Paoting
CHIHLI (Hopei)
北河
SHANTUNG
東山
Chinan
Kaifeng
Hsuchow
KIANGSU
蘇江
SHENSI
西陝
Sian
HONAN
南河
HUPEH
北湖
Wuchang
ANHWEI
徽安
Hangchow
CHEKIANG
江浙
SZECHWAN
川四
Chengtu
Changte
Nanchang
HUNAN
南湖
KIANGSI
Foochow
FUKIEN
建福
KWEICHOW
州貴
Kweiyang
YUNNAN
南雲
KWANGSI
KWANGTUNG
東廣
Canton
MACAO
HONG KONG
TAIWAN
Hainan
南海
NEPAL
BHUTAN
ASSAM
BURMA
NORTH VIETNAM
LAOS
a map of the
CHINESE PROVINCES

CHINA

Before 1912, China was ruled by an imperial government. The republican administration which replaced it was itself supplanted on the Chinese mainland by a communist government in 1949, but it has remained in control of Taiwan and other offshore islands in the China Sea with a land area of approximately 14,000 square miles and a population of more than 14 million. The People's Republic of China administers some 3.7 million square miles and an estimated 942 million people. This communist government, officially established on October 1, 1949, was admitted to the United Nations, replacing its nationalist predecessor, the Republic of China, in 1971.

Cast coins in base metals were used in China many centuries before the Christian era, but locally struck coinages of the western type in gold, silver, copper and other metals did not appear until 1889. In spite of the relatively short time that modern coins were in use, the number of varieties is exceptionally large.

Both nationalist and communist China, as well as the prerevolutionary imperial government and numerous provincial or other agencies, including some foreign administered agencies and governments, have issued coins in China. Most of these have been in dollar or dollar fraction denominations, based on the internationally used silver crown, but coins in tael denominations were issued in the 1920's and earlier. The striking of coins nearly ceased in the late 1930's through the 1940's due to the war effort and a period of uncontrollable inflation while vast amounts of paper currency was issued by the nationalist and Japanese occupation institutions.

EMPERORS

高宗 KAO TSUNG
1736-1795

Reign title: Ch'ien Lung 乾 隆
乾 隆 通 寶 Ch'ien-lung t'ung-pao.

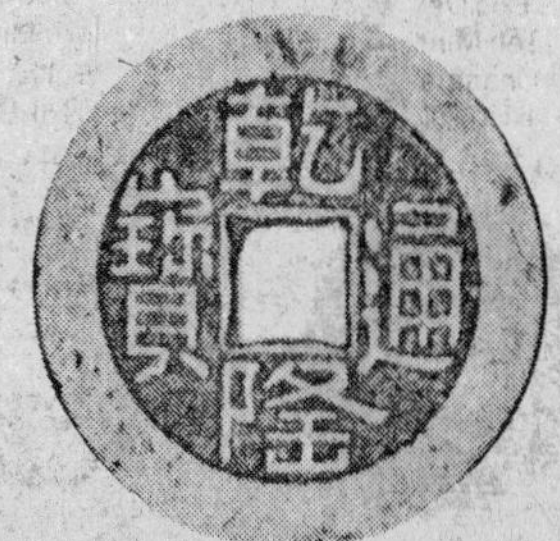

Variety of Ch'ien Lung issue having the bottom character written in a different style. This is commonly refered to as a "Shan Lung" commemorative issue.

仁宗 JEN TSUNG
1796-1820

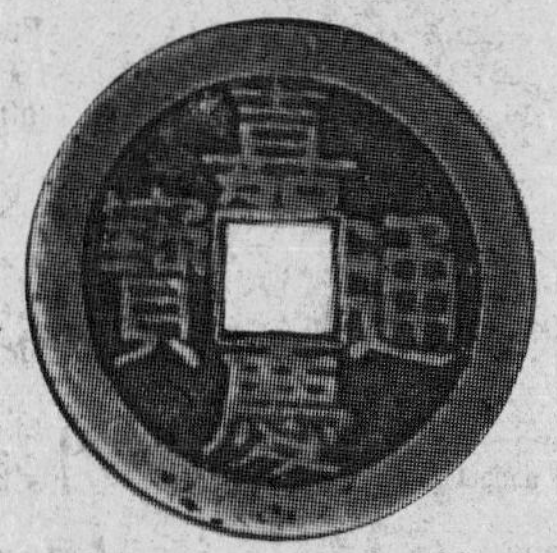

Reign title: Chia Ching 嘉 慶
嘉 慶 通 寶 Chia-ch'ing t'ung-pao.

宣宗 HSUAN TSUNG
1821-1851

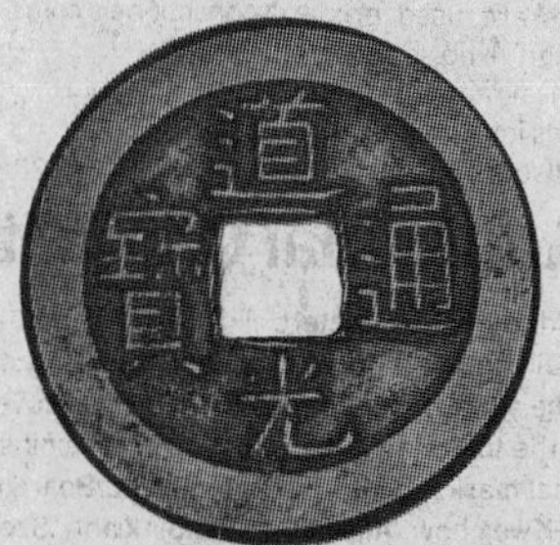

Reign title: Tao Kuang 道 光
道 光 通 寶 Tao-kuang t'ung-pao.

文宗 WEN TSUNG
1851-1861

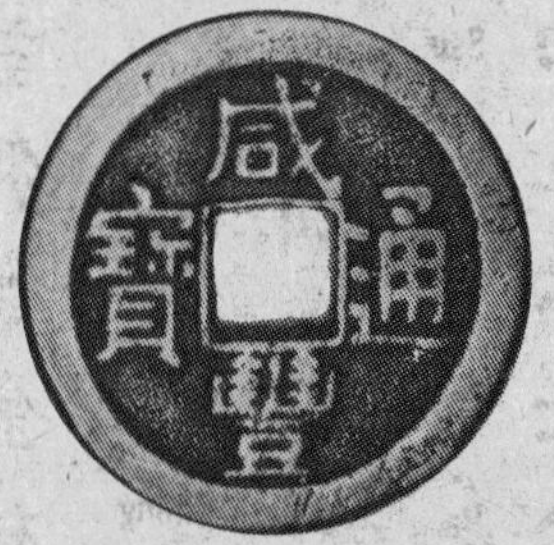

Reign title: Hsien Feng 咸 豐
咸 豐 通 寶 Hsien-feng t'ung-pao.

穆宗 MU TSUNG
1861*

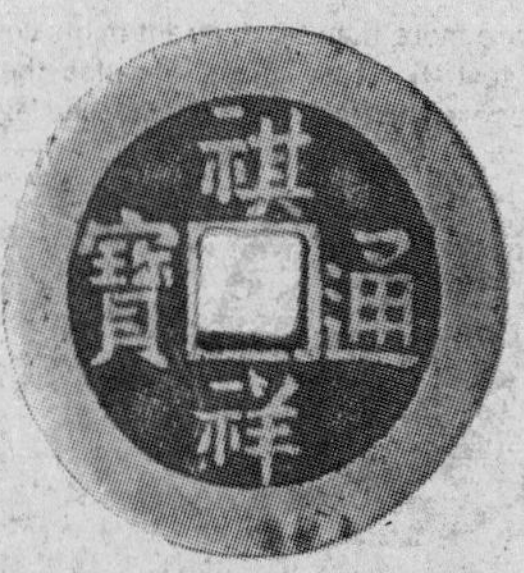

1st reign title: Ch'i-hsiang 祺 祥
祺 祥 通 寶 Ch'i'hsiang t'ung-pao.

穆宗 MU TSUNG
1862-1875

2nd reign title: T'ung Chih 同 治
同 治 通 寶 T'ung-chih t'ung-pao.

He first chose reign-title "Ch'i-hsiang" and a few coins were so struck. His mother, Dowagner Empress Tz'u-hsi, made him change to nien-hao "T'ung-chih."

德宗 TE TSUNG
1875-1908

Reign title: Kuang Hsu 光 緒
光 緒 通 寶 Kuang-hsu t'ung-pao.

宣統帝 HSUAN T'UNG
遜帝 TI (HsunTi)
1908-1911

Reign title: Hsuan T'ung 宣 統
宣 統 通 寶 Hsuan-t'ung t'ung-pao.

1915-1916

Reign title: Hung Hsein 憲 洪

*Dec. 15, 1915 - March 21, 1916.

PROVINCIAL NAMES
(and other source indicators)

Province		Single Character (1)	Full Names (Right to left reading)
ANHWEI Also: An-hwei, Anhui	(Huan)	皖	安徽
CHEKIANG Also: Cheh-kiang	(Che)	浙	浙江
CHIHLI Also: Hopei (after 1928)	(Chih)	直	直隸
CH'ING DYNASTY			大清 (2)
CHING-KIANG Also: Tsing Kiang	(Huai)	淮	清江
FUKIEN Also: Foo-kien, F.K.	(Min)	閩	福建
FENGTIEN Also: Fung-tien, Fun-tien Manchurian Provinces	(Feng)	奉	奉天
HEILUNGKIANG Also: Hei Lung Kiang			黑龍江
HONAN Also: Ho-nan	(Pien)	汴	河南
HUNAN Also: Hu-nan	(Hsiang)	湘	湖南
HUPEH Also: Hupei, Hu-peh		鄂	湖北
HU PU (Board of Revenue) Also: Hu Poo	(Hu)	户	户部
KANSU			甘肅
KIANGNAN Also: Kiang Nan	(Ning)	寗	江南
KIANGSI Also: Kiang-si, Kiang-see	(Kan)	贛	江西
KIANGSI (Alternate)		贑	
KIANGSU Also: Kiang-soo	(Su)	蘇	江蘇
KIRIN	(Chi)	吉	吉林
KWANGSI Also: Kwang-si	(Kuei)	桂	廣西
KWANGTUNG Also: Kwang-tung	(Yueh)	粤	廣東
KWEICHOW Also: Kweichou	(Ch'ien)	黔	貴州
PEIYANG MINT (Tientsin) Also: Pei-yang, Pei Yang			北洋
SINKIANG (Chinese Turkestan) (4) Also: Sin-kiang, Sungarei			新疆
SHANSI	(Shan)	山	山西
SHENSI Also: Shen-si	(Shan)	陝	陝西
SHANTUNG, SHAN-TUNG, Also: Shang-tung	(Tung)	東	山東
SZECHUAN	(Ch'uan)	川	四川
TAIWAN Also: Tai-wan		臺	臺灣
TAIWAN (Alternate)			台灣
YUNNAN Also: Yun-nan	(Yun)	雲	雲南
YUNNAN (Alternate)	(Tien)	滇	雲南
YUNNAN-SZECHUAN		滇川	

PROVINCIAL NAMES
(and other source indicators)

	Full Names (Right to left reading)
Chitung (Japanese puppet)	冀東政府
Chinese Soviet Republic	中華蘇維埃共和國
Manchukuo (Japanese puppet)	大滿洲國
Mengchiang (Japanese puppet)	(2) 蒙疆銀行
Peoples Republic of China (Communist) (3)	中華人民共和國
Republic of China (Nationalist)	中華民國
North China (Japanese puppet)	中國聯合準備銀行

(1) Single-character designators for provincial or regional mints are used primarily on copper coins of the Tai Ching Ti Kuo series.
(2) Vertical readings predominate.
(3) Reads left to right.
(4) For list of mints in Sinkiang, see that section.

Additional Characters

The additional characters illustrated and defined below are usually found on the reverse of cast bronze cash coins above the square center hole. In the period covered by this catalog the following mints produced cash coins with these additional marks: Board of Revenue and Board of Works in Peking, Kweichow, Aksu and Ili in Sinkiang, Szechuan, and all three mints listed in Yunnan.

一	Yi	十一	Shih yi	大	Ta
二	Erh	合	Ho	心	Sin
三	San	工	Kung	宇	Yü
四	Ssu	主	Chu	宙	Chou
五	Wu	川	Ch'uan	來	Lai
六	Liu	之	Chih	往	Wang
七	Chi	正	Cheng	金	Chin
八	Pa	又	Yu	村	Tsun
九	Chiu	山	Shan	日	Jih
十	Shih			列	Lieh

MINTMARK IDENTIFIER

There are more than 30 different mints covered in the following text. For ease in identification the more common varieties are illustrated with the Manchu legend.

Boo - Ciowan (Peking) BOARD OF REVENUE

Boo Yuwan (Peking) BOARD OF PUBLIC WORKS

Boo Hu Hu Mint ANHWEI

Boo Je Che Mint Hang chow CHEKIANG

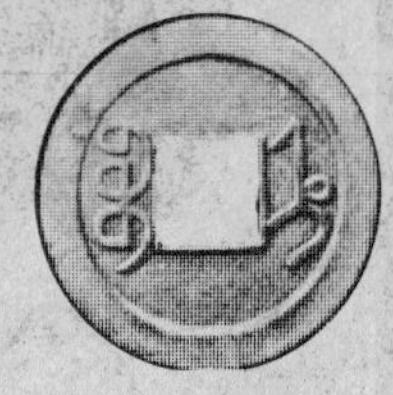

Boo Ji Chihli Mint Paoting CHIHLI

Boo Gi Chi Mint Chichow CHIHLI

Boo Jiyen Ching Mint Tientsin CHIHLI

Boo Fung FENGTIEN

Boo Fu Fu Mint Fuchou FUKIEN

Boo Ho Ho Mint K'aifeng HONAN

Boo Ho Ho Mint K'aifeng HUNAN

Boo De Teh Mint Changte HUNAN

Boo U Wu Mint Wuch'ang HUPEH

Boo Gung Kungchang KANSU

Nanchang KIANGSI

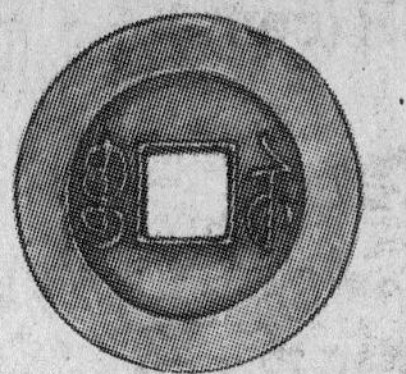
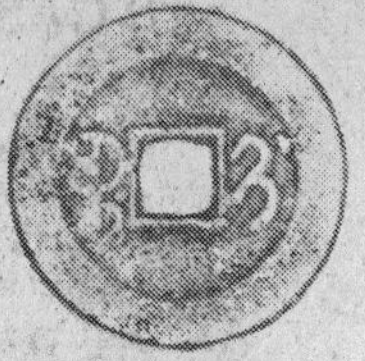

Boo Su
Su Mint
Suchow
KIANGSU

Boo Gi
Chi Mint
KIRIN

Kuche
SINKIANG

Boo Gui
Kuelin
KWANGSI

Boo Guwang
Canton
KWANGTUNG

Khotan
SINKIANG

Tihwa
SINKIANG

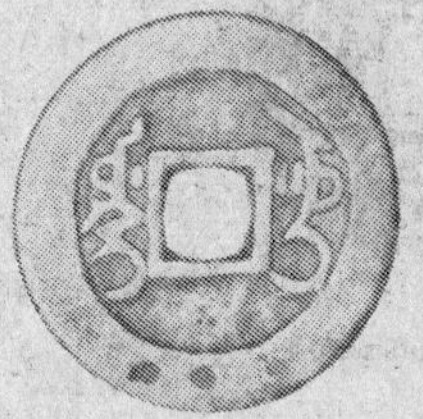

Boo Giyan
Kweiyang
KWEICHOW

Boo Jin
Taiyuan
SHANSI

Wushih
SINKIANG

Yerkim
SINKIANG

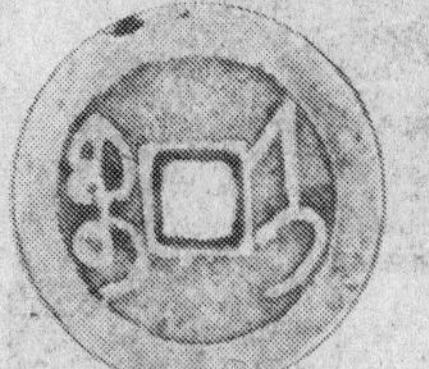

Boo Ji
Chinan
SHANGTUNG

Boo Cuwan
Chengtu
SZECHUAN

Yarkand
SINKIANG

Tai Mint
TAIWAN

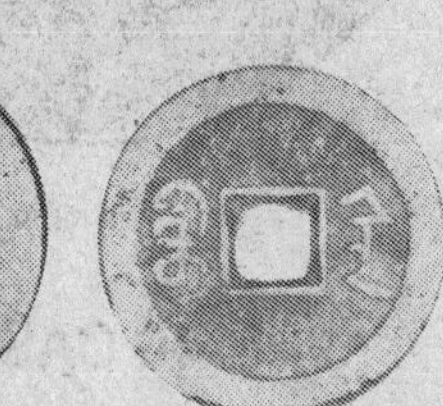

Boo San
Shan Mint
Sian
SHENSI

Boo Yon
Yun Mint
Yunnan Fu
YUNNAN

Boo Dong
Tung Mint
Tung ch'uan
YUNNAN

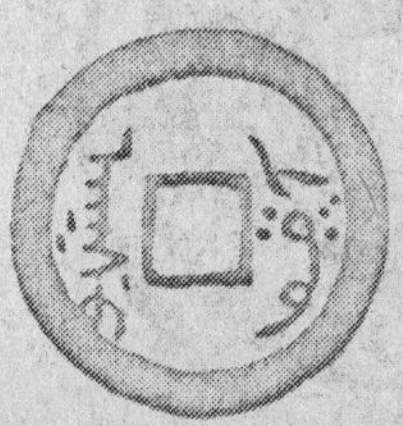

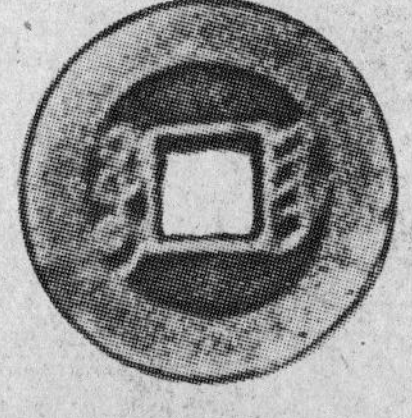

Aksu
SINKIANG

Ili
SINKIANG

Ching Mint
Location unknown.

Fu Mint
Location uncertain.
(Refer to Yunnan)

NON-CIRCULATING ISSUES

Along with regular circulation coinage produced by the various mints certain cash types were cast with the emperor's reign title on the obverse but with various characters and/or symbols not found in our mint identifiers. This listing is not complete but it will benefit the collector as an aide to proper identification.

PALACE ISSUES

Tien-hsia T'ai-p'ing

"An Empire at peace."
Market value: VF $40.00-60.00

Obv: Chia Ching
Tao Kuang
Hsien Feng
Mu Tsung
Kuang Hsu

I-t'ung T'ien-hsia

"One Government (altogether) at peace."
Market value: VF $50.00-70.00.

Obv: Hsien Feng

BIRTHDAY CASH

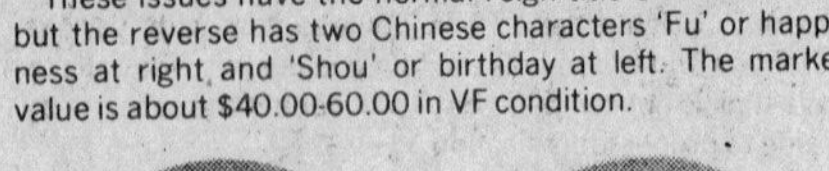

These issues have the normal reign title on the obverse but the reverse has two Chinese characters 'Fu' or happiness at right and 'Shou' or birthday at left. The market value is about $40.00-60.00 in VF condition.

Hsien Feng

Mu Tsung

Kuang Hsu

AMULETS

"The Eight Trigrams"

Hsien Feng

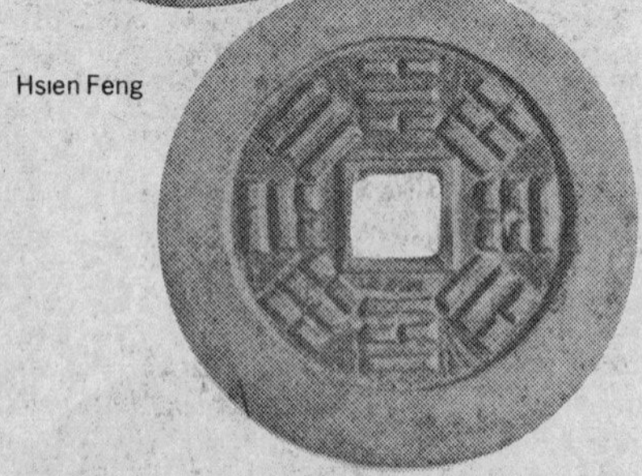

The eight trigrams (Pa Kua) of the Book of Changes (I Ching). This book, one of the Five Classics consists of a set of sixty-four figures known as "trigrams". The trigram is composed of combinations of pairs of eight trigrams each of which represents some power in nature, either active or passive, such as fire, water, thunder, earth, etc. These trigrams are said to have been invented 2000 years and more B.C. by the legendary monarch Fu Hsi, who copied them from the back of a tortoise. Attached to each hexagram are explanatory notes and expository comments. The notes are said to have been written by the Chou King Wen Wang and the comments by Confucius. The notes are made in symbolic language which only mystics could understand, but the comments are written in plain language. These comments have lifted the Book of Changes from a primitive book of divination and oracles to an ethical and philosophical importance. The market value is about $30.00-40.00 in VF condition.

MULTIPLE CASH

The size and weight of multiple cash coins cannot be used to determine the correct denomination as these were issued on various standards. The weights decreased considerably in later years. The values are given in various manners.

4 CASH

Ili, Sinkiang

5 CASH

Board of Public Works

8 CASH

Tihwa, Sinkiang

10 CASH

Official Ten
Board of Revenue, Peking

10 CASH (cont.)

Fukien

20 CASH

Fukien

30 CASH

Kiangsu

40 CASH

Chekiang

50 CASH

Fukien

100 CASH

Board of Revenue, Peking

500 CASH

Board of Revenue, Peking

1000 CASH

Board of Revenue, Peking

MONETARY UNITS

Dollar Amounts		
DOLLAR (*Yuan*)	元 or 員	圓 or 圜
HALF DOLLAR (*Pan Yuan*)	圓 半	元中
50¢ (*Chiao/Hao*)	角伍	毫伍
10¢ (*Chiao/Hao*)	角壹	毫壹
1¢ (*Fen/Hsien*)	分壹	仙壹

Copper and Cash Coin Amounts			
COPPER (*Mei*)	枚	CASH (*Wen*)	文

Tael Amounts	
1 TAEL (*Liang*)	兩
HALF TAEL (*Pan Liang*)	兩半
5 MACE (*Wu Ch'ien*)	錢伍
1 MACE (*I Ch'ien*)	錢壹
1 CANDEREEN (*I Fen*)	分壹

Common Prefixes			
COPPER (*T'ung*)	銅	GOLD (*Chin*)	金
SILVER (*Yin*)	銀	Ku Ping (*Tael*)*	平庫

*Standard (Treasury) tael: 37.3 grams (approx.)

NUMBER	CONVENTIONAL		FORMAL		COMMERCIAL
1	一	元	壹	弌	〡
2	二		弍	貳	〢
3	三		叁	弎	〣
4	四		肆		〤
5	五		伍		〥
6	六		陸		〦
7	七		柒		〧
8	八		捌		〨
9	九		玖		〩
10	十		拾	什	十
20	十二	廿	拾貳		〢十
25	五十二	五廿	伍拾貳		〢十〥
30	十三	卅	拾叁		〣十
100	百一		佰壹		〡百
1,000	千一		仟壹		〡千
10,000	萬一		萬壹		〡万
100,000	萬十	億一	萬拾	億壹	十万
1,000,000	萬百一		萬佰壹		〡百万

This and preceding tables adapted from "Chinese Banknotes" by Ward Smith and Brian Matravers.

MONETARY SYSTEM

Cash Coin System

800-1600 Cash = 1 Tael

In theory, 1000 cash were equal to a tael of silver, but in actuality the rate varied from time to time and place to place.

Dollar System

10 Cash (wen, ch'ien) = 1 Cent (fen, hsien)
10 Cents = 1 Chiao (hao)
100 Cents = 1 Dollar (yuan)
1 Dollar = 0.72 Tael

Imperial silver coins normally bore no denomination, but were inscribed with their weights as follows:

Dollar	7 Mace and Candareens
50 Cents	3 Mace and 6 Candareens
20 Cents	1 Mace and 4.4 Candareens
10 Cents	7.2 Candareens
5 Cents	3.6 Candareens

Tael System

10 Li=1 Fen (candareen)
10 Fen (candareen)=1 Ch'ien (mace)
10 Ch'ien (mace)=1 Liang (tael)

DATING

Most struck Chinese coins are dated by year within a given period, such as the regnal eras or the republican periods. A 1907 issue, for example, would be dated in the 33rd year of the Kuang Hsu era (1875 + 33 - 1 = 1907) or a 1926 issue is dated in the 15th year of the Republic (1912 + 15 - 1 = 1926). The mathematical discrepancy in both instances is accounted for by the fact that the first year is included in the elapsed time. Modern Chinese Communist coins are dated in western numerals using the western calendar, but earlier issues use conventional Chinese numerals. Still another method is a 60-year, repeating cycle, outlined in the table below. The date is shown by the combination of two characters, the first from the top row and the second from the column at left. In this catalog, when a cyclical date is used, the abbreviation CD appears before the AD date.

CYCLICAL DATES

	庚	辛	壬	癸	甲	乙	丙	丁	戊	己
戌	1850 1910		1862 1922		1874 1934		1886 1946		1838 1898	
亥		1851 1911		1863 1923		1875 1935		1887 1947		1839 1899
子	1840 1900		1852 1912		1864 1924		1876 1936		1888 1948	
丑		1841 1901		1853 1913		1865 1925		1877 1937		1889 1949
寅	1830 1890		1842 1902		1854 1914		1866 1926		1878 1938	
卯		1831 1891		1843 1903		1855 1915		1867 1927		1879 1939
辰	1880 1940		1832 1892		1844 1904		1856 1916		1868 1928	
巳		1881 1941		1833 1893		1845 1905		1857 1917		1869 1929
午	1870 1930		1882 1942		1834 1894		1846 1906		1858 1918	
未		1871 1931		1883 1943		1835 1895		1847 1907		1859 1919
申	1860 1920		1872 1932		1884 1944		1836 1896		1848 1908	
酉		1861 1921		1873 1933		1885 1945		1837 1897		1849 1909

Dates not in parenthesis are those which appear on the coins. For undated coins, dates appearing in parenthesis are the years in which the coin was actually minted. Undated coins for which the year of minting is unknown are listed with ND (No Date) in the date or year column.

GRADING

Chinese coins should not be graded entirely by western standards. In addition to Fine, Very Fine, Extremely Fine (XF), and Uncirculated, the type of strike should be considered: weak, medium or sharp struck. China had no rigid minting rules as we know them. For instance, Kirin Province used some dies made of iron — hence, they wore out rapidly. Some communist army issues were apparently struck by crude hand methods on soft dies (it is hard to find two coins of the same die!) In general, especially for some minor coins, dies were used until they were worn well beyond western standards. Subsequently, one could have an uncirculated coin struck from worn dies with little of the design or letters still visible, but still uncirculated! All prices quoted are for well struck (sharp struck) well centered specimens. Most silver coins can be found from very fine to uncirculated. Some copper coins are difficult to find except in poorer grades.

NOTE: The following refences have been used for this section:

K — Edward Kann — Illustrated Catalog of Chinese Coins.

S — T. K. Su — Illustrated Catalog of Chinese Coins 1975 edition.

IDENTIFICATION

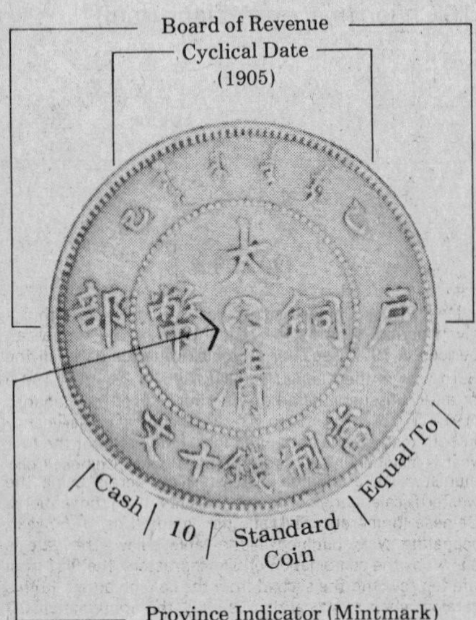

DRAGON TYPES

(Chinese Imperial Coins)

Side View Dragon (Silver Coins)

First used by the Kwangtung Mint in 1889. This was the standard (though not the only) dragon used on silver coins. Normally there is no circle around the dragon. Note the fireball beneath the dragon's chin. Normally there are seven flames on the fireball.

Side View Dragon (Copper Coins)

First used on copper coins in 1901 or 1902. The dragon may be circled or uncircled. Many varieties exist, with three to seven flames on the fireball.

Flying Dragon

Introduced in 1901. Copied from the dragon on Japanese coins, China used this dragon only on copper coins (with one rare exception). Note that the clouds around the dragon's body are curly and snake-like instead of puffy like those around the side view dragon. The fireball now appears as a pearl which the dragon is about to grasp, and normally has no flames. This dragon is normally circled.

Front View Dragon

Introduced about 1904, this type of dragon was not used by many mints. The dragon is usually uncircled and has few clouds around its body. Note the tiny mountain under the cloud beneath the fireball.

Tai Ch'ing Ti Kuo Dragon

In 1905 China carried out a coinage reform which standardized the designs of copper coins. All mints were ordered to use the same obverse and reverse designs, but to place a mintmark in the center of the obverse.

SYCEE (INGOTS)

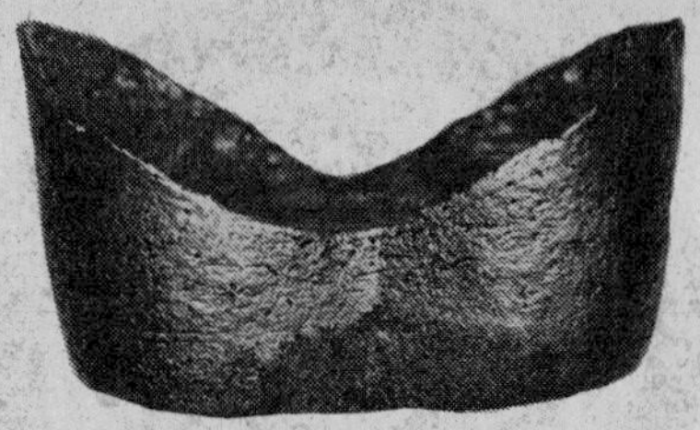

Prior to 1889 the only coinage issued by the Chinese government was the brass cash coin. Despite occasional shortlived experiments with silver and gold coinage, and disregarding paper money which tended to be unreliable, the government expected the people to get by solely with cash coins. This system worked well for individuals making purchases for themselves, but was unsatisfactory for trade and large business transactions, since a dollar's worth of cash coins weighed about four pounds. As a result, a private currency consisting of silver ingots crudely stamped by the firm which made them came into use. These were the sycee ingots.

It is not known when these ingots first came into use. Some sources date them to the Yuan (Mongol) dynasty but they are certainly much older. Examples are known from as far back as the Han dynasty (206 BC — 220 AD) but prior to the Sung era (960 - 1280 AD) they were used mainly for hoarding wealth. The development of commerce by the Sung dynasty, however, required the use of silver or gold to pay for large purchases. By the Mongol period (1280-1368) silver ingots and paper money had become the dominant currencies, especially for trade. The western explorers who traveled to China during this period (such as Marco Polo) mention both paper money and sycee but not a single one refers to cash coins.

During the Ming dynasty (1368-1644) trade fell off and the use of silver decreased. But towards the end of that dynasty, Dutch and British ships began a new China trade and sycee once again became common. During the 19th and early 20th centuries, the trade in sycee became enormous. Most of the sycee around today are from this period. In 1935 the Chinese government banned the use of sycee and it soon disappeared.

The word sycee (pronounced "sigh - see") is a western corruption of the Chinese words hsi ssu ("fine silk") or sai ssu ("fine silver") and is first known to have appeared in the English language in the late 1600's. By the early 1700's the word appeared regularly in the records of the British East India Company. Westerners also called these ingots "boat money" or "shoe money" due to the fact that the most common type of ingot resembles a Chinese shoe. The Chinese, however, called the ingots by a variety of names, the most common of which were yuan pao, wen yin and yin ting.

The ingots were cast in molds (giving them their characteristic shapes) and while the metal was still semi-liquid, the inscription was impressed. It was due to this procedure that the sides of some sycee are higher than the center. The manufacturers were usually silver firms, often referred to as lu fang's, and after the sycee was finished it was tested and marked by the kung ku (public assayer).

Sycee were not circulated as we understand it. One didn't usually carry a sycee to market and spend it. Usually the ingots were used as a means of carrying a large amount of money on trips (as we would carry $100 bills instead of $5 bills) or for storing wealth. Large transactions between merchants or banks were paid by means of crates of sycee — each containing 60 fifty tael ingots.

Sycee are known in a variety of shapes the most common of which are the shoe or boat shaped, drum shaped, and loaf shaped (rectangular or hourglass-shaped, with a generally flat surface). Other shapes include one that resembles a double headed axe (this is the oldest type known), one that is square and flat, and others that are "fancy" (in the form of fish, butterflies, leaves, etc.).

Sycee have no denominations as they were simply ingots that passed by weight. Most are in more or less standard weights, however, the most common being 1, 5, 10 and 50 taels. Other weights known include 1/10, 1/5, 1/4, 1/3, 1/2, 2/3, 72/100 (this is the weight of a dollar), 3/4, 2, 3, 4, 6, 7 and 8 taels. Most of the pieces weighing less than 5 taels were used as gifts or souvenirs.

The actual weight of any given value of sycee varied considerably due to the fact that the tael was not a single weight but a general term for a wide range of local weight standards. The weight of the tael varied depending upon location and type of tael in question. For example in one town, the weight of a tael of rice, of silver and of stones may each be different. In addition, the fineness of silver also varied depending upon location and type of tael in question. It was not true, as westerners often wrote, that sycee were made of pure silver. For most purposes, a weight of 37 grams may be used for the tael.

Weights and Current Market Value of Sycee
(Weights are approximate)

Weight	Grams	Value
1/2 tael	17 - 19 grams	6.50
72/100 tael	25 - 27 grams	7.50
1 tael	35 - 38 grams	8.50
2 taels	70 - 75 grams	16.50
3 taels	100 - 140 grams	25.00
5 taels	175 - 190 grams	40.00
7 taels	240 - 260 grams	65.00
10 taels	350 - 380 grams	85.00
50 taels	1790 - 1850 grams	700.00

GENERAL ISSUE

EMPIRE

Board Of Revenue Mint

(Peking)

CASH

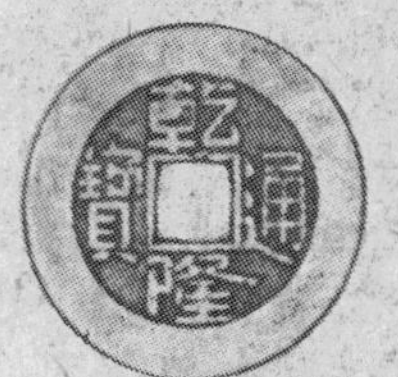

C#	Date	Emperor	Good	VG	Fine	VF
CAST BRASS, 21-26mm						
1-1	(1736-95)	Ch'ien Lung	.10	.15	.20	.25
28-30mm						
1-1.1	(1736-95)	Ch'ien Lung	1.75	3.00	4.00	6.00
Rev: Dot above.						
1-1.2	(1736-95)	Ch'ien Lung	1.25	2.00	3.00	4.50
Rev: Dot below.						
1-1.3	(1736-95)	Ch'ien Lung	1.25	2.00	3.00	4.50

C#	Date	Emperor	Good	VG	Fine	VF
Shan Lung Commemorative						
1-1.4	(1796-1802)	Chia Ch'ing	.75	2.00	3.00	5.00
21-26mm						
1-2	(1796-1820)	Chia Ch'ing	.10	.20	.35	.65
28-30mm						
1-2.1	(1796-1820)	Chia Ch'ing	1.50	3.00	4.00	6.00
Rev: Dot Above.						
1-2.2	(1796-1820)	Chia Ch'ing	1.25	2.00	3.00	5.00
Rev: Dot below.						
1-2.3	(1796-1820)	Chia Ch'ing	1.25	2.00	3.00	5.00

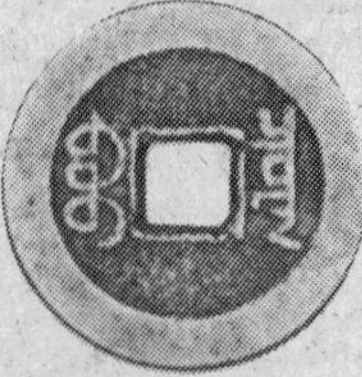

C#	Date	Emperor	Good	VG	Fine	VF
20-26 mm						
1-3	(1821-51)	Tao Kuang	.15	.25	.40	.75
28-30mm						
1-3.1	(1821-51)	Tao Kuang	1.75	3.00	4.00	6.00
Rev: Dot above.						
1-3.2	(1821-51)	Tao Kuang	1.75	3.00	4.00	6.00
Rev: Dot below.						
1-3.3	(1821-51)	Tao Kuang	1.75	3.00	4.00	6.00

C#	Date	Emperor	Good	VG	Fine	VF
1-4	(1851-61)	Hsien Feng	.60	1.00	2.00	3.50
CAST IRON						
1-4a	(1851-61)	Hsien Feng	7.50	12.50	17.50	25.00
CAST ZINC						
1-4b	(1851-61)	Hsien Feng	—	—	Rare	—
Obv: Character 'Pao' in different form.						
1-4.1	(1851-61)	Hsien Feng	—	—	—	—

C#	Date	Emperor	Good	VG	Fine	VF
CAST BRASS						
1-12	(1861)	Ch'i Hsiang	—	—	Rare	—

C#	Date	Emperor	Good	VG	Fine	VF
1-14	(1862-74)	T'ung Chih	3.50	5.50	8.50	15.00

C#	Date	Emperor	Good	VG	Fine	VF
1-16	(1875-1908)	Kuang Hsu	1.75	2.00	3.00	5.00
Rev: Character 'Chih' above.						
1-16.1	(1875-1908)	Kuang Hsu	6.00	9.00	13.50	18.50
Rev: Character 'Chou' above.						
1-16.2	(1875-1908)	Kuang Hsu	6.00	9.00	13.50	18.50
Rev: Character 'Jih' above.						
1-16.3	(1875-1908)	Kuang Hsu	6.00	9.00	13.50	18.50
Rev: Character 'Lai' above.						
1-16.4	(1875-1908)	Kuang Hsu	6.00	9.00	13.50	18.50
Rev: Character 'Lieh' above.						
1-16.5	(1875-1908)	Kuang Hsu	Reported, not confirmed			
Rev: Character 'Wang' above.						
1-16.6	(1875-1908)	Kuang Hsu	6.00	9.00	13.50	18.50

C#	Date	Emperor	Good	VG	Fine	VF
Rev: Character 'Yu' above.						
1-16.7	(1875-1908)	Kuang Hsu	9.00	13.50	18.50	25.00

NOTE: Refer to the 'Additional Characters' chart in the introduction to China.

C#	Date	Emperor	Good	VG	Fine	VF
Rev: Dot below.						
1-16.8	(1875-1908)	Kuang Hsu	1.75	3.00	4.00	6.00
Rev: Dot above.						
1-16.9	(1875-1908)	Kuang Hsu	1.75	3.00	4.00	6.00

C#	Date	Emperor	Good	VG	Fine	VF
19mm						
1-19	(1909-11)	Hsuan T'ung	3.50	6.00	8.00	12.50
24mm						
1-19.1	(1909-11)	Hsuan T'ung	5.50	9.00	13.50	18.50

5 CASH

C#	Date	Emperor	Good	VG	Fine	VF
CAST BRASS						
1-5	(1851-61)	Hsien Feng	—	—	Rare	—

10 CASH

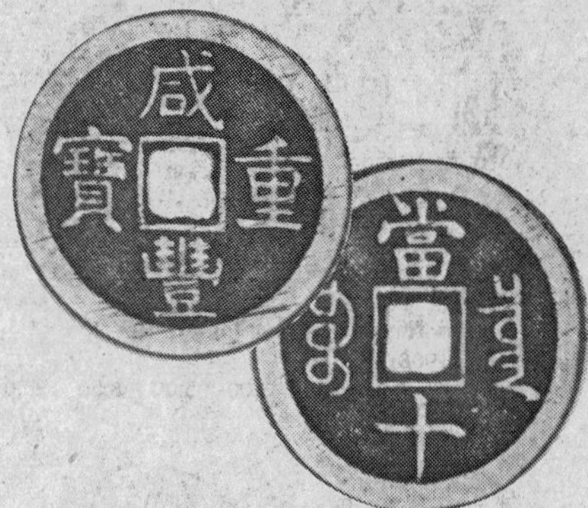

C#	Date	Emperor	Good	VG	Fine	VF
CAST BRASS, 36-39mm						
1-6	(1851-61)	Hsien Feng	3.00	5.00	7.50	11.50
CAST IRON, 37.5mm						
1-6a	(1851-61)	Hsien Feng	20.00	30.00	40.00	60.00
CAST BRASS, 29-34mm						
1-6.1	(1851-61)	Hsien Feng	2.50	4.00	6.00	8.50
CAST IRON, 29-34mm						
1-6.1a	(1851-61)	Hsien Feng	15.00	25.00	35.00	50.00

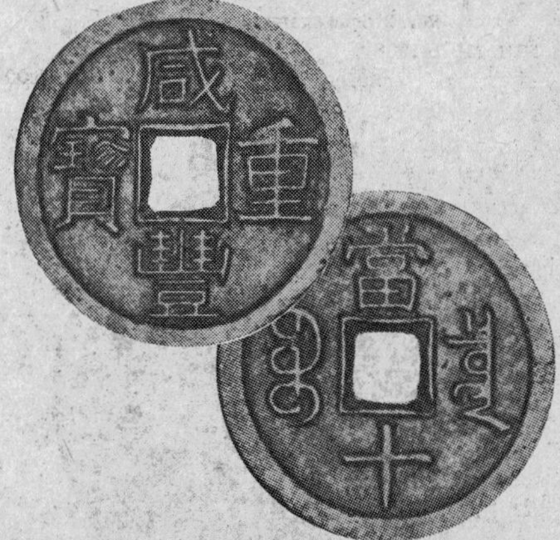

C#	Date	Emperor	Good	VG	Fine	VF
Obv: Character 'Pao' in different form.						
1-6.2	(1851-61)	Hsien Feng	—	—	—	—

CAST BRASS

C#	Date	Emperor	Good	VG	Fine	VF
1-13	(1861)	Ch'i Hsiang	200.00	300.00	450.00	600.00

28-33mm

1-15	(1862-74)	T'ung Chih	2.50	4.00	7.00	10.00

23-26mm

1-15.1	(1862-74)	T'ung Chih	1.75	3.00	5.50	8.50

Rev: Normal character for 10 below.

1-17	(1875-1908)	Kuang Hsu	3.00	5.00	8.50	12.50

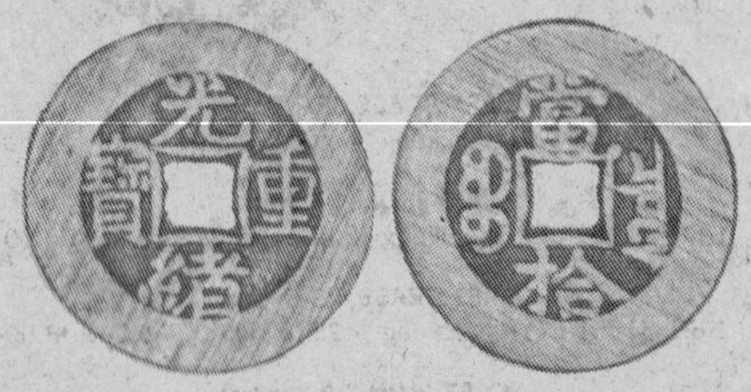

Rev: Official character for 10 below.

1-18	(1875-1908)	Kuang Hsu	4.50	7.50	11.00	15.00

50 CASH

CAST BRASS, 54-58mm

C#	Date	Emperor	Good	VG	Fine	VF
1-7	(1851-61)	Hsien Feng	11.50	15.00	20.00	27.50

40-48mm

1-7.1	(1851-61)	Hsien Feng	12.50	16.50	21.50	30.00

Obv: Similar to C#1-7.1.
Rev: Dot to upper right and crescent to upper left.

1-7.2	(1851-61)	Hsien Feng	15.00	25.00	40.00	60.00

NOTE: This is one of a series of coins from this mint marked with a dot and crescent to indicate that they were issued by Ching Hui, the Hereditary Prince of K'o Ch'in.

100 CASH

CAST BRASS

1-8	(1851-61)	Hsien Feng	11.50	16.50	22.50	30.00

Rev: Dot and crescent similar to 50 Cash, C#1-7.3.

1-8.1	(1851-61)	Hsien Feng	18.50	30.00	50.00	75.00

200 CASH

CAST BRASS

1-9	(1851-61)	Hsien Feng	22.50	37.50	60.00	90.00

Rev: Dot and crescent similar to 50 Cash, C#1-7.3.

1-9.1	(1851-61)	Hsien Feng	30.00	50.00	80.00	120.00

500 CASH

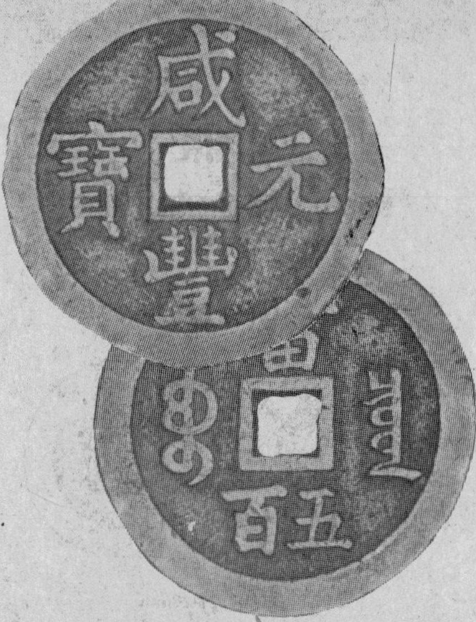

CAST BRASS
Obv: Similar to 100 cash, C#1-8.1.

C#	Date	Emperor	Good	VG	Fine	VF
1-10	(1851-61)	Hsien Feng	20.00	32.50	50.00	75.00

Rev: Dot and crescent similar to 50 Cash, C#1-7.3.

1-10.1	(1851-61)	Hsien Feng	22.50	35.00	55.00	85.00

1000 CASH

CAST BRASS

1-11	(1851-61)	Hsien Feng	25.00	37.50	50.00	80.00

Rev: Dot and crescent similar to 50 Cash, C#1-7.3.

1-11.1	(1851-61)	Hsien Feng	25.00	40.00	60.00	90.00

FANTASY ISSUES

NOTE: Coins of this mint in denominations of 6, 9, 20, 90, 300, 400, 4000 and 5000 Cash are considered fantasy issues.

Board Of Public Works Mint

(Peking)

CASH

CAST BRASS

2-1	(1736-95)	Ch'ien Lung	.10	.15	.25	.35

Rev: Dot above.

2-1.1 (1736-95) Ch'ien Lung 1.50 2.50 3.50 5.00

Rev: Dot below.

2-1.2 (1736-95) Ch'ien Lung 1.50 2.50 3.50 5.00

Obv: Bottom character written differently.

C#	Date	Emperor	Good	VG	Fine	VF
2-1.3	(1796-1802)	Chia Ch'ing	1.25	2.00	3.00	5.00

NOTE: Though bearing the reign title of Emperor Ch'ien Lung, this coin is a special issue cast during the reign of his successor, the Chia Ch'ing emperor.

2-2 (1796-1820) Chia Ch'ing .15 .25 .40 .75

Rev: Dot above.

2-2.1 (1796-1820) Chia Ch'ing 2.50 4.00 6.00 7.50

Rev: Dot below.

2-2.2 (1796-1820) Chia Ch'ing 2.50 4.00 6.00 7.50

2-3 (1821-51) Tao Kuang .15 .25 .40 .75

Rev: Dot above.

2-3.1 (1821-51) Tao Kuang 2.50 4.00 6.00 7.50

Rev: Dot below.

2-3.2 (1821-51) Tao Kuang 2.50 4.00 6.00 7.50

Large size coin, about 27mm.

2-4 (1851-61) Hsien Feng 3.00 5.00 8.00 12.50

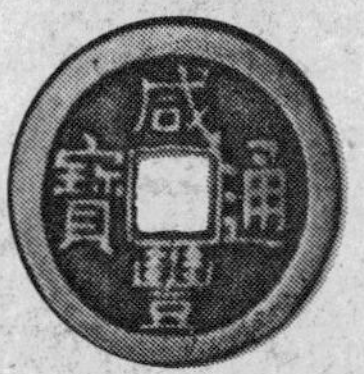
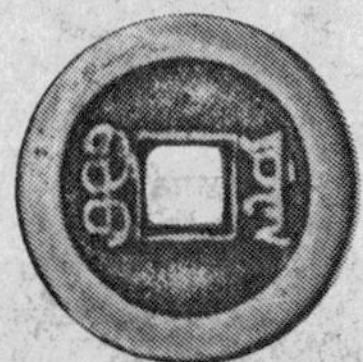

20-24mm

2-4.1 (1851-61) Hsien Feng .85 1.50 3.00 4.00

CAST ZINC

2-4.2 (1851-61) Hsien Feng — — Rare —

CAST IRON

2-4.3 1851-61 Hsien Feng — — Rare —

CAST BRASS

2-11 (1861) Ch'i Hsiang 30.00 50.00 75.00 100.00

2-13 (1862-74) T'ung Chih 1.75 3.00 5.00 6.00

C#	Date	Emperor	Good	VG	Fine	VF
2-15	(1875-1908)	Kuang Hsu	1.50	2.50	4.00	5.00

Rev: Character 'Chou' above.

2-15.1 (1875-1908) Kuang Hsu 6.00 10.00 15.00 20.00

Rev: Character 'Lai' above.

2-15.2 (1875-1908) Kuang Hsu 6.00 10.00 15.00 20.00

Rev: Character 'Lieh' above.

2-15.3 (1875-1908) Kuang Hsu 6.00 10.00 15.00 20.00

Rev: Character 'Yu' above.

2-15.4 (1875-1908) Kuang Hsu 6.00 10.00 15.00 20.00

Rev: Character 'Jih' above.

2-15.5 (1875-1908) Kuang Hsu 6.00 10.00 15.00 20.00

NOTE: For a machine-struck cash with this mintmark, refer to Szechuan.

5 CASH

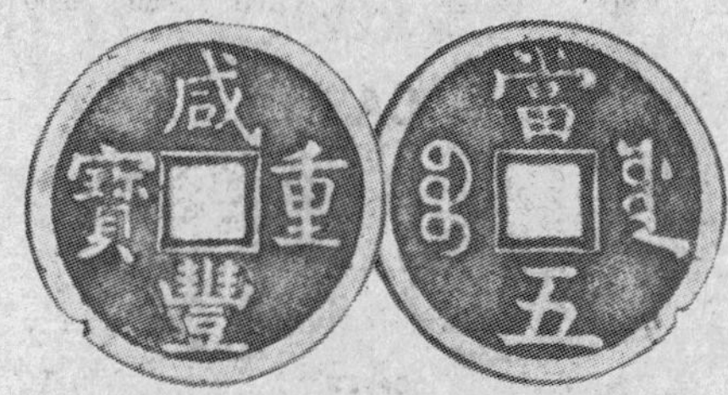

CAST BRASS, 28-32mm

2-5 (1851-61) Hsien Feng 10.00 17.50 25.00 40.00

23-25mm

2-5.1 (1851-61) Hsien Feng 10.00 17.50 25.00 40.00

CAST IRON

2-5a (1851-61) Hsien Feng Reported, not confirmed

CAST BRASS

2-16 (1875-1908) Kuang Hsu — — Rare —

10 CASH

CAST BRASS, 33-38mm

2-6 (1851-61) Hsien Feng 3.00 5.00 7.50 12.50

29-31mm

2-6.1 (1851-61) Hsien Feng 3.00 5.00 7.50 12.50

CAST IRON

2-6a (1851-61) Hsien Feng — — Rare —

CAST BRASS

C#	Date	Emperor	Good	VG	Fine	VF
2-12	(1861)	Ch'i Hsiang	400.00	500.00	700.00	850.00

2-14 (1862-74) T'ung Chih 4.50 7.50 11.50 17.50

Rev: Normal character for 10 below.

2-17 (1875-1908) Kuang Hsu 4.50 7.50 10.00 15.00

Rev: Official character for 10 below.

2-18 (1875-1908) Kuang Hsu 6.00 10.00 15.00 20.00

50 CASH

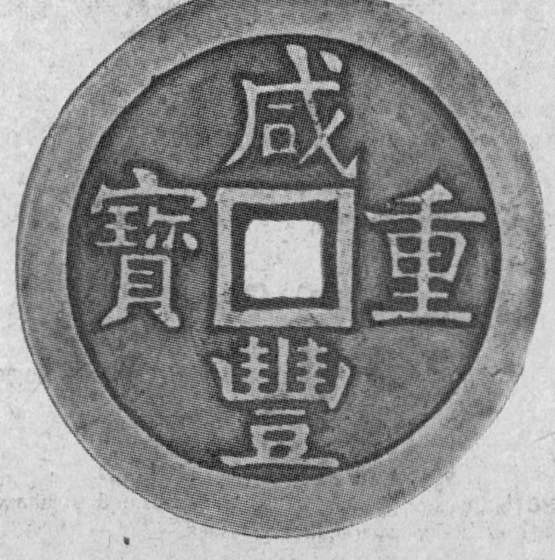

CAST BRASS, 51-55mm

C#	Date	Emperor	Good	VG	Fine	VF
2-7	(1851-61)	Hsien Feng	11.50	16.50	22.50	30.00
	42-45mm					
2-7.1	(1851-61)	Hsien Feng	11.50	16.50	22.50	30.00

100 CASH

CAST BRASS

C#	Date	Emperor	Good	VG	Fine	VF
2-8	(1851-61)	Hsien Feng	13.50	21.50	28.50	37.50

500 CASH

CAST BRASS

C#	Date	Emperor	Good	VG	Fine	VF
2-9	(1851-61)	Hsien Feng	20.00	30.00	50.00	75.00
	CAST COPPER					
2-9.1	(1851-61)	Hsien Feng	20.00	30.00	50.00	75.00

1000 CASH

CAST BRASS

C#	Date	Emperor	Good	VG	Fine	VF
2-10	(1851-61)	Hsien Feng	25.00	40.00	55.00	90.00

FANTASY ISSUES

NOTE: Coins of this mint in denominations of 6, 9, 30 and 90 Cash are considered fantasy issues.

STRUCK COINAGE

CASH

BRASS, struck
Obv: Four Chinese characters "Kuang-hsu T'ung-pao"
Rev: Two Manchu characters "Pao-chuan"
(Board of Revenue Mint)

Su#	Date	Mintage	Fine	VF	XF	Unc
2	ND*	—	—	—	Rare	—

***NOTE:** Believed to have been minted in 1899.

Y#	Date	Mintage	VG	Fine	VF	XF
7	CD1908	—	1.20	3.00	5.00	12.00

Y#	Date	Mintage	VG	Fine	VF	XF
18	CD1909	Inc. Y25	12.50	30.00	50.00	80.00

Y#	Date	Mintage	VG	Fine	VF	XF
25	ND	92.126	.75	2.00	3.50	5.00

2 CASH

COPPER

Y#	Date	Mintage	VG	Fine	VF	XF
8	CD1905	—	1.60	4.00	8.00	15.00
	CD1906	—	2.75	7.00	10.00	20.00
	CD1907	—	10.00	25.00	40.00	80.00
A18	CD1909	13.353	—	—	Rare	—

5 CASH

COPPER

Y#	Date	Mintage	VG	Fine	VF	XF
3	(1903-05)	3.671	5.00	10.00	15.00	25.00

Rev: Legend with smaller English letters.

Y#	Date	Mintage	VG	Fine	VF	XF
3.1	(1903-05)	—	Reported, Not Confirmed			

Y#	Date	Mintage	VG	Fine	VF	XF
9	CD1905	—	4.00	8.00	12.00	20.00
	CD1906	—	Reported, Not Confirmed			
	CD1907	—	16.50	40.00	60.00	80.00
19	CD1909	2.170	—	—	Rare	—

10 CASH

COPPER

Y#	Date	Mintage	VG	Fine	VF	XF
4	(1903-05)	281.171	.40	1.00	2.00	3.50

Rev: Smaller English letters and different rosettes.

Y#	Date	Mintage	VG	Fine	VF	XF
4.1	(1903-05)	I.A.	.40	1.00	2.00	3.50
10	CD1905	Inc. Ab.	.60	1.50	3.00	5.00

Similar, but larger English letters and different dragon.

Y#	Date	Mintage	VG	Fine	VF	XF
10.1	CD1905	—	8.00	20.00	40.00	70.00

Y#	Date	Mintage	VG	Fine	VF	XF
10.2	CD1906	—	.30	.75	1.50	3.00

Obv: Without dots. Rev. leg: without dot after KUO.

Y#	Date	Mintage	VG	Fine	VF	XF
10.3	CD1907	—	.20	.50	1.00	2.00

Obv: Without dots. Rev. leg: with dot after KUO.

Y#	Date	Mintage	VG	Fine	VF	XF
10.4	CD1907	—	.20	.50	1.00	2.00

20 CASH

BRASS

Obv: Without dots.

Y#	Date	Mintage	VG	Fine	VF	XF
10.4a	CD1907	—	2.00	5.00	10.00	20.00

COPPER

Obv: With dots.

Y#	Date	Mintage	VG	Fine	VF	XF
10.5	CD1907	—	.20	.50	1.00	2.00

BRASS

Y#	Date	Mintage	VG	Fine	VF	XF
10.5a	CD1907	—	2.00	5.00	10.00	20.00

COPPER

W277 CD1907 -Mule, with Kiangnan reverse.

Y#	Date	Mintage	VG	Fine	VF	XF
W277	CD1907	—	25.00	60.00	100.00	150.00

NOTE: Other mules exist. Refer to Kiangnan.

Waves under dragon.

Y#	Date	Mintage	VG	Fine	VF	XF
20	CD1909	—	.40	1.00	2.00	4.00

Rosette under dragon.

Y#	Date	Mintage	VG	Fine	VF	XF
20.1	CD1909	—	2.00	5.00	10.00	20.00

Y#	Date	Mintage	VG	Fine	VF	XF
20x	CD1909	—	6.00	15.00	25.00	50.00

NOTE: Although this coin bears no indication of its origin, it was minted in Kirin Province.

BRONZE

Y#	Date	Mintage	Fine	VF	XF	Unc
27	Yr.3 (1911)	95.585	2.50	4.00	7.00	25.00

COPPER

Y#	Date	Mintage	Fine	VF	XF	Unc
27a	Yr.3 (1911)	I.A.	50.00	100.00	145.00	225.00

COPPER

Y#	Date	Mintage	VG	Fine	VF	XF
5	(1917)	—	.20	.50	1.50	5.00

NOTE: This coin was struck in 1917 from unused dies made in 1903.

Obv: 4-point rosette in center.

Y#	Date	Mintage	VG	Fine	VF	XF
5.1	ND	—	2.00	5.00	10.00	20.00

Obv: Dot in center.

Rev: Head of dragon and clouds redesigned.

Y#	Date	Mintage	VG	Fine	VF	XF
5.2	ND	—	2.00	5.00	10.00	20.00

Rev: Dragon in circle of dots.

Y#	Date	Mintage	VG	Fine	VF	XF
5a	(1903-05)	—	8.00	20.00	40.00	100.00

COPPER

Y#	Date	Mintage	VG	Fine	VF	XF
11	CD1905	—	12.50	30.00	40.00	50.00

Y#	Date	Mintage	VG	Fine	VF	XF
11.1	CD1906	—	12.50	30.00	40.00	60.00

Obv: Dots around date, 1.2-1.7mm thick.

Y#	Date	Mintage	VG	Fine	VF	XF
11.2	CD1907	—	.60	1.50	2.00	3.50

2.0-2.3mm thick

Y#	Date	Mintage	VG	Fine	VF	XF
11.3	CD1907	—	2.00	5.00	10.00	20.00

Obv: Without dots around date.

11.4 CD1907 — — Reported, not confirmed

Obv: Waves beneath dragon.

Rev: Legend with dot between KUO and COPPER.

Y#	Date	Mintage	VG	Fine	VF	XF
21	CD1909	—	.75	2.00	3.00	5.00

1.2-1.7mm thick

Rev: Legend without dot between KUO and copper. Six waves beneath dragon.

Y#	Date	Mintage	VG	Fine	VF	XF
21.1	CD1909	—	1.20	3.00	5.00	8.00

2.0-2.3mm thick

Y#	Date	Mintage	VG	Fine	VF	XF
21.2	CD1909	—	—	—	—	—

Rev: Rosette beneath dragon.

Y#	Date	Mintage	VG	Fine	VF	XF
21.3	CD1909	—	3.00	7.50	11.50	17.50

Similar, but dot below dragon's chin.

Y#	Date	Mintage	VG	Fine	VF	XF
21.4	CD1909	—	3.50	8.50	13.50	20.00

Rev: Five crude waves beneath dragon.
Redesigned forehead.
Inner circle of large dots on obverse and reverse.

Y#	Date	Mintage	VG	Fine	VF	XF
21.5	CD1909	—	1.20	3.00	5.00	12.00

10 CENTS

SILVER, 2.7000 gm.
Similar to Y#12.

K#	Date	Mintage	Fine	VF	XF	Unc
215	CD1907	—	30.00	75.00	125.00	225.00

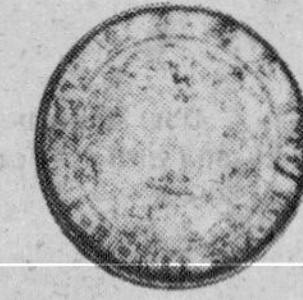

Y#	Date	Mintage	VG	Fine	VF	XF
12	(1908)	—	20.00	45.00	60.00	100.00

Similar to 50 Cents, Y#23.

K#	Date	Mintage	Fine	VF	XF	Unc
222	(1910)	—	50.00	85.00	175.00	325.00

Y#	Date	Mintage	Fine	VF	XF	Unc
28	Yr.3 (1911)	—	8.00	17.50	30.00	60.00

NOTE: Refer to Hunan Republic 10 Cents, K#762.

20 CENTS

SILVER, 5.5 gm.

K#	Date	Mintage	Fine	VF	XF	Unc
214	CD1907	—	30.00	75.00	150.00	300.00

Y#	Date	Mintage	Fine	VF	XF	Unc
13	(1908)	—	85.00	115.00	150.00	200.00

Y#	Date	Mintage	Fine	VF	XF	Unc
29	Yr.3 (1911)	—	8.00	20.00	35.00	75.00

25 CENTS

SILVER

K#	Date	Mintage	Fine	VF	XF	Unc
221	(1910)	1.410	40.00	100.00	165.00	350.00

50 CENTS

SILVER, 13.6 gm.

K#	Date	Mintage	Fine	VF	XF	Unc
213	CD1907	—	60.00	150.00	250.00	400.00

Y#	Date	Mintage	Fine	VF	XF	Unc
23	(1910)	1.571	28.50	65.00	95.00	145.00

Y#	Date	Mintage	Fine	VF	XF	Unc
30	Yr.3 (1911)	I.A.	100.00	250.00	500.00	800.00

DOLLAR

SILVER, 26.9 gm.

K#	Date	Mintage	Fine	VF	XF	Unc
212	CD1907	—	160.00	400.00	500.00	700.00

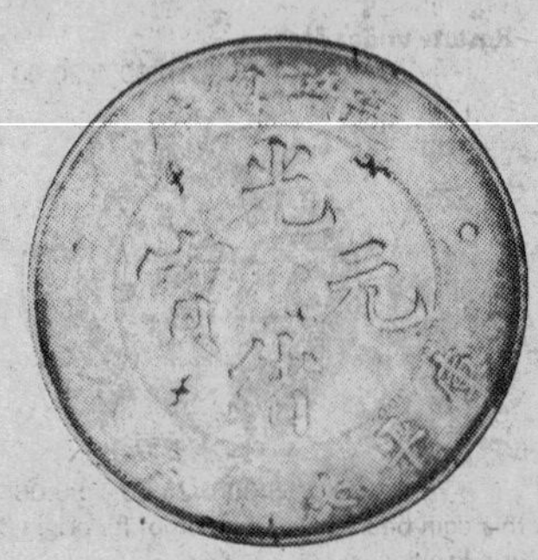

Y#	Date	Mintage	VG	Fine	VF	XF
14	(1908)	—	22.50	37.50	60.00	100.00

K#	Date	Mintage	Fine	VF	XF	Unc
219	(1910)	—	150.00	275.00	350.00	500.00

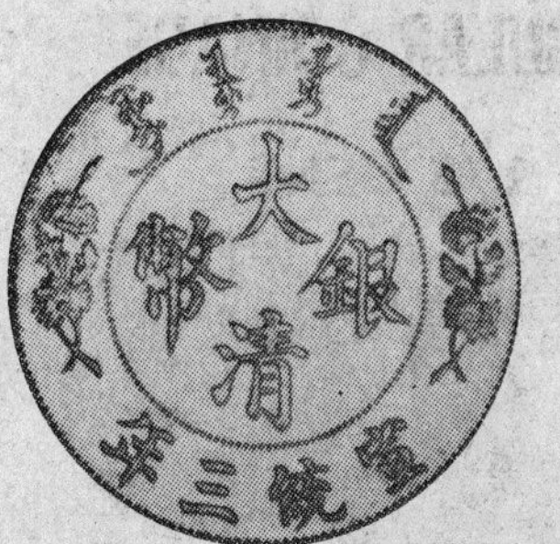

Y#	Date	Mintage	Fine	VF	XF	Unc
31	Yr.3 (1911)	77.153	13.50	18.50	30.00	75.00

NOTE: Other pieces with similar design are patterns.

NCLT ISSUES

PATTERNS

KM#	Date	Mintage	Identification	Mkt.Val.
1	ND	—	1 Cash, Brass, Su 4	—
2	ND	—	1 Cash, Brass, square hole, Su 4a	—
3	ND	—	1 Cash, Brass, no hole, Su 4b	—
4	ND	—	1 Cash, Brass, no hole, Y25.2	—
5	ND	—	1 Cash, Copper, no hole, Su 4	—
6	ND	—	1 Cash, Copper, no hole, Y8	—

KM#	Date	Mintage	Identification	Mkt.Val.
7	(1910)	—	1 Cash, Copper, Su 33	300.00

KM#	Date	Mintage	Identification	Mkt.Val.
8	(1910)	—	2 Cash, Copper, Su 13	—
9	(1910)	—	2 Cash, Brass, with hole, Su 13	—

KM#	Date	Mintage	Identification	Mkt.Val.
10	Yr.1 (1910)	—	5 Cash, Copper, Su 34	—

KM#	Date	Mintage	Identification	Mkt.Val.
11	Yr.1 (1910)	—	1 Fen, Copper, Su 35	500.00

KM#	Date	Mintage	Identification	Mkt.Val.
12	Yr.1 (1910)	—	2 Fen, Copper, Su 36	600.00

KM#	Date	Mintage	Identification	Mkt.Val.
13	Yr.3 (1911)	—	5 Cash, Copper, Y26	500.00

KM#	Date	Mintage	Identification	Mkt.Val.
14	Yr.3 (1911)	—	20 Cash, Bronze, Su 32	600.00

PEKING ISSUES

KM#	Date	Mintage	Identification	Mkt.Val.
15	CD1900	—	5 Cents, Silver, K237	1000.
16	CD1900	—	10 Cents, Silver, K236	700.00

KM#	Date	Mintage	Identification	Mkt.Val.
17	CD1900	—	20 Cents, Silver, K235	700.00
18	CD1900	—	50 Cents, Silver, K234	2000.

KM#	Date	Mintage	Identification	Mkt.Val.
19	CD1900	—	1 Dollar, Silver, K233	3000.

NOTE: There are two theories concerning the origin of the Peking coins. One asserts that a few sets of all five denominations were minted during 1900 at the mint erected in Peking the previous year, with equipment partly from the Hangchow, Chekiang Mint, and partly from Germany. The second theory alledges that some 10 and 20 cent pieces may have been minted in 1900, but that the rest of the set was restruck sometime later by private parties using original dies looted from the mint during the Boxer uprising. There is a similar 10 Cash in copper also dated 1900, which is believed to be a fantasy.

TAEL SYSTEM

KM#	Date	Mintage	Identification	Mkt.Val.
20	Yr.29 (1903)	—	5 Fen, Silver, K931	500.00
21	Yr.29 (1903)	—	1 Ch'ien, silver, k930	500.00

KM#	Date	Mintage	Identification	Mkt.Val.
22	Yr.29 (1903)	—	2 Ch'ien, silver	500.00

KM#	Date	Mintage	Identification	Mkt.Val.
23	Yr.29 (1903)	—	5 Ch'ien, silver, k928	1000.
24	Yr.29 (1903)	—	1 Liang, Silver, K927	3500.
25	CD1906	—	1 Ch'ien, Silver, K937	350.00

26	CD1906	—	2 Ch'ien, Silver, K936	550.00

27	CD1906	—	5 Ch'ien, Silver, K935	850.00

KM#	Date	Mintage	Identification	Mkt.Val.
28	CD1906	—	1 Liang, Silver, K934	1850.

29	CD1906	—	1 Liang, Gold, K1540	5000.
30	CD1907	—	1 Liang, Gold, K1541	4000.

REPUBLIC

Transitional Issues

In the name of the Republic:

CASH

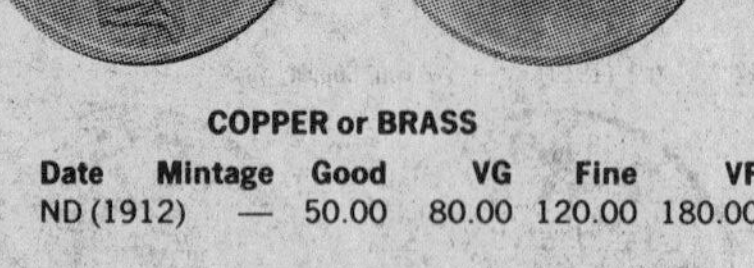

COPPER or BRASS

KM#	Date	Mintage	Good	VG	Fine	VF
3	ND (1912)	—	50.00	80.00	120.00	180.00
	ZINC					
3a	ND (1912)	—	—	—	—	—

10 CASH

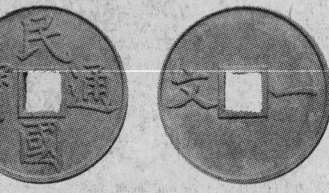

BRASS

4	ND (1912)	—	—	—	Rare	—

In the name of Hung Hsien:

5 CASH

COPPER

KM#	Date	Mintage	Good	VG	Fine	VF
1	ND (1916)	—	—	—	Rare	—

10 CASH

COPPER or BRASS
Rev: Blank

2	ND (1916)	—	350.00	450.00	550.00	700.00

REGULAR COINAGE

1/2 CENT

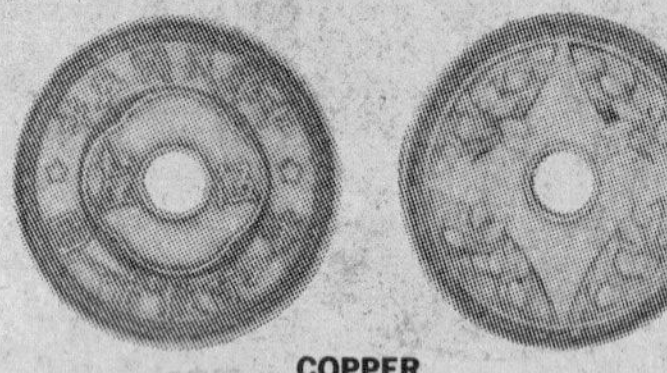

COPPER

Y#	Date	Mintage	Fine	VF	XF	Unc
323	Yr.5 (1916)	—	7.50	12.50	20.00	40.00

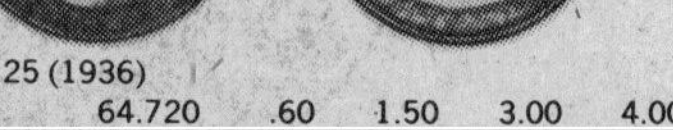

346	Yr.25 (1936)	64.720	.60	1.50	3.00	4.00

10 CASH (1 CENT or 1 FEN)

NOTE: Some sources date these 10 Cash pieces bearing crossed flags ca. 1912, but many were not struck until the 1920's.

COPPER
Rev: Double circle with small rosettes separating legend.

301	ND	—	.20	.50	1.00	6.00

Obv: Second character from right in bottom legend is rounded. Rev: Double circle with three dots separating legend.

Y#	Date	Mintage	Fine	VF	XF	Unc
301.1	ND	—	.40	1.00	2.00	8.50

Obv: Second character from right in bottom legend rounded. Rev: Double circle with two dots separating legend.

Y#	Date	Mintage	Fine	VF	XF	Unc
301.2	ND	—	.30	.75	1.50	7.50

Obv: Small star on flag. Rev: Double circle with six-pointed stars separating legend.

Y#	Date	Mintage	Fine	VF	XF	Unc
301.3	ND	—	.60	1.50	3.00	12.50

Obv: Large star on flag extending to edges of flag. Rev: Double circle with six-pointed stars separating legend.

Y#	Date	Mintage	Fine	VF	XF	Unc
301.4	ND	—	.60	1.50	3.00	12.50

Obv: Flower with many stems. Rev: Single circle.

Y#	Date	Mintage	Fine	VF	XF	Unc
301.5	ND	—	.20	.50	1.00	6.00

Obv: Flower with fewer stems. Rev: Single circle.

Y#	Date	Mintage	Fine	VF	XF	Unc
301.6	ND	—	.20	.50	1.00	6.00

Rev: Vine above leaf at 12 o'clock. Wreath tied at bottom. M-shaped leaves at base of wheat ears.

Y#	Date	Mintage	Fine	VF	XF	Unc
302	ND	—	.40	1.00	2.00	8.50

BRASS

Y#	Date	Mintage	Fine	VF	XF	Unc
302a	ND	—	—	—	—	—

COPPER
Wheat ears larger.

Y#	Date	Mintage	Fine	VF	XF	Unc
302b	ND	—	1.20	3.00	7.50	20.00

Rev: Vine beneath leaf at 12 o'clock. Wreath not tied at bottom. Without M-shaped leaves at base of wheat ears.

Y#	Date	Mintage	Fine	VF	XF	Unc
302.1	ND	—	1.60	4.00	8.00	20.00

Rev: Leaves pointing clockwise.

Y#	Date	Mintage	Fine	VF	XF	Unc
302.2	ND	—	20.00	50.00	80.00	150.00

Obv: Small star shaped rosettes. Rev: Small four-pointed rosettes separating legend.

Y#	Date	Mintage	Fine	VF	XF	Unc
303	ND	—	.20	.50	1.00	6.50

Left flag redesigned.

Y#	Date	Mintage	Fine	VF	XF	Unc
303.1	ND	—	.20	.50	1.00	6.50

BRASS
Obv: Similar to Y#303.3, but stars replace resettes.

Y#	Date	Mintage	Fine	VF	XF	Unc
303.2	ND	—	1.60	4.00	8.00	20.00

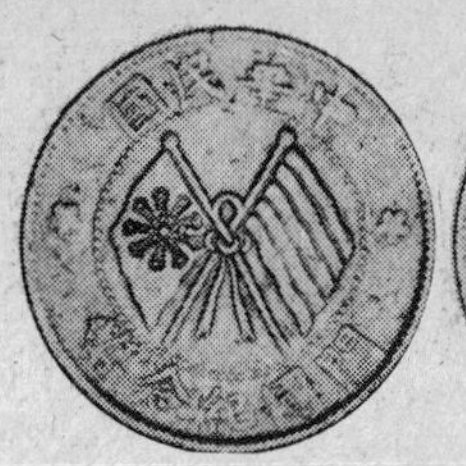

COPPER
Obv: Large rosettes replace stars. Rev: Stars separating legend.

Y#	Date	Mintage	Fine	VF	XF	Unc
303.3	ND	—	.75	2.00	4.00	15.00

Obv: Very small pentagonal rosettes.

Y#	Date	Mintage	Fine	VF	XF	Unc
303.4	ND	—	.60	1.50	3.00	10.00

BRASS

Y#	Date	Mintage	Fine	VF	XF	Unc
303.4a	ND	—	2.00	5.00	10.00	25.00

COPPER
Obv: Circled flag flanked by pentagonal rosettes.

Y#	Date	Mintage	Fine	VF	XF	Unc
304	ND	—	12.50	30.00	40.00	85.00

Rev: Chrysanthemum reverse.

Y#	Date	Mintage	Fine	VF	XF	Unc
305	ND	—	15.00	25.00	40.00	100.00

Y#	Date	Mintage	Fine	VF	XF	Unc
306.1	ND	—	.20	.50	1.00	6.00

BRASS

Y#	Date	Mintage	Fine	VF	XF	Unc
306.1a	ND	—	.80	2.00	4.00	15.00

COPPER
Obv: Y#306.1, Rev: Y#306.4

Y#	Date	Mintage	Fine	VF	XF	Unc
306.1b	ND	—	1.20	3.00	5.00	15.00

Obv: Dot on either side of upper legend.

Y#	Date	Mintage	Fine	VF	XF	Unc
306.2	ND	—	.80	2.00	3.00	8.00

BRASS

Y#	Date	Mintage	Fine	VF	XF	Unc
306.2a	ND	—	1.20	3.00	5.00	15.00

COPPER

Obv: Star between flags.

Y#	Date	Mintage	Fine	VF	XF	Unc
306.3	ND	—	4.00	10.00	20.00	50.00

Obv: Elongated rosettes. Different characters in bottom legend. Rev: Thin leaf blade between lower wheat ears.

Y#	Date	Mintage	Fine	VF	XF	Unc
306.4	ND	—	6.00	15.00	25.00	60.00

Obv: Five characters in lower legend.

Y#	Date	Mintage	Fine	VF	XF	Unc
306a	ND	—	2.75	7.00	12.50	30.00

Obv: One large rosette on either side. Rev: Slender leaves and short ribbon.

Y#	Date	Mintage	Fine	VF	XF	Unc
307	ND	421.138	.40	1.00	2.00	8.00

Rev: Larger leaves and longer ribbon.

Y#	Date	Mintage	Fine	VF	XF	Unc
307.1	ND	Inc. Ab.	4.00	10.00	18.50	40.00

Obv: Three rosettes on either side. Rev: Long ribbon.

Y#	Date	Mintage	Fine	VF	XF	Unc
307a	ND	Inc. Ab.	.80	2.00	4.00	12.50

Rev: Short ribbon and smaller wheat ears.

Y#	Date	Mintage	Fine	VF	XF	Unc
307A.1	ND	Inc. Ab.	20.00	50.00	85.00	150.00

Y#	Date	Mintage	Fine	VF	XF	Unc
309	ND	—	8.00	20.00	35.00	75.00

NOTE: Pieces with L. GIORGI near rim are patterns.

Y#	Date	Mintage	Fine	VF	XF	Unc
324	Yr.5 (1916)	—	.80	2.00	3.75	10.00

NOTE: Pieces with L. GIORGI near rim are patterns.

Y#	Date	Mintage	Fine	VF	XF	Unc
311	Yr.13 (1924)	—	40.00	100.00	150.00	250.00

NOTE: This coin is probably a pattern.

BRASS

Y#	Date	Mintage	Fine	VF	XF	Unc
337	Yr.17 (1928)	—	90.00	145.00	200.00	300.00

NOTE: This coin is always found with small punchmarks near center on obverse and reverse.

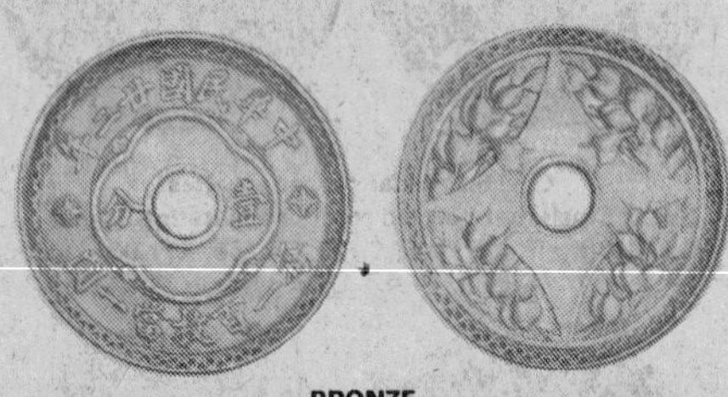

BRONZE

Y#	Date	Mintage	Fine	VF	XF	Unc
324a	Yr.22 (1933)	—	8.00	20.00	40.00	75.00

Y#	Date	Mintage	Fine	VF	XF	Unc
347	Yr.25 (1936)	311.780	.20	.50	.75	1.50
	Yr.26 (1937)	307.198	.25	.60	.85	1.75
	Yr.27 (1938)	—	.60	1.50	3.00	5.00
	Yr.28 (1939)	—	1.00	2.50	5.00	7.50

Y#	Date	Mintage	Fine	VF	XF	Unc
353	Yr.28 (1939)	—	14.00	35.00	50.00	75.00

ALUMINUM

Y#	Date	Mintage	Fine	VF	XF	Unc
355	Yr.29 (1940)	150.000	.10	.25	.50	1.00

BRASS

Y#	Date	Mintage	Fine	VF	XF	Unc
357	Yr.29 (1940)	—	.30	.75	1.00	2.50

BRONZE

Y#	Date	Mintage	Fine	VF	XF	Unc
363	Yr.37 (1948)	—	4.00	10.00	15.00	20.00

'PORTRAIT' TEN CASH

NOTE: A number of ten Cash pieces exist with portraits of Yuan Shih-kai, Sun Yat-sen, Li Yuan-hung or Ni Su-chung. These are patterns, presentation issues or fantasies which saw little if any circulation and are rare.

20 CASH (2 CENTS or 2 FEN)

NOTE: Some sources date these 20 Cash pieces bearing crossed flags ca. 1912, but many were not struck until the 1920's.

COPPER

Y#	Date	Mintage	Fine	VF	XF	Unc
308	Yr.8 (1919)	200.861	1.00	2.50	6.00	20.00

Y#	Date	Mintage	Fine	VF	XF	Unc
308a	Yr.10 (1921)	I.A.	1.00	2.50	6.00	20.00

Obv: Same as Y#308a. Rev: Same as Y#308.

Y#	Date	Mintage	Fine	VF	XF	Unc
308b	Yr.10 (1921)	I.A.	16.50	40.00	65.00	150.00

Y#	Date	Mintage	Fine	VF	XF	Unc
310	ND	—	12.50	30.00	50.00	110.00

NOTE: This coin is usually found weakly struck.

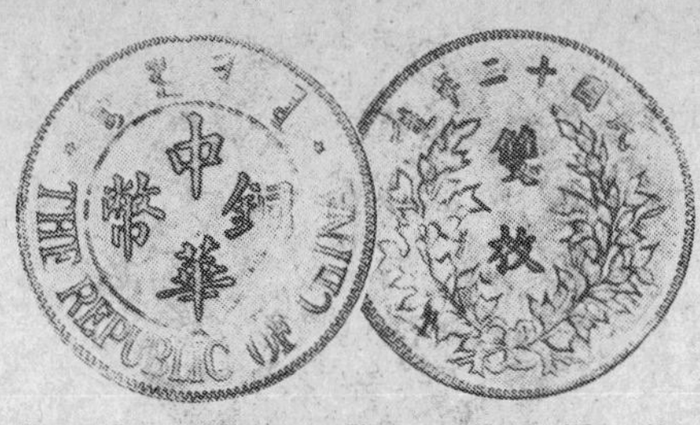

Y#	Date	Mintage	Fine	VF	XF	Unc
312	Yr.13 (1924)	—	4.00	10.00	20.00	50.00

NOTE: This coin is usually found weakly struck.

BRASS

Y#	Date	Mintage	Fine	VF	XF	Unc
338	Yr.17 (1928)	—	70.00	175.00	200.00	300.00

NOTE: This coin has always been found with small punchmarks near center on obverse and reverse.

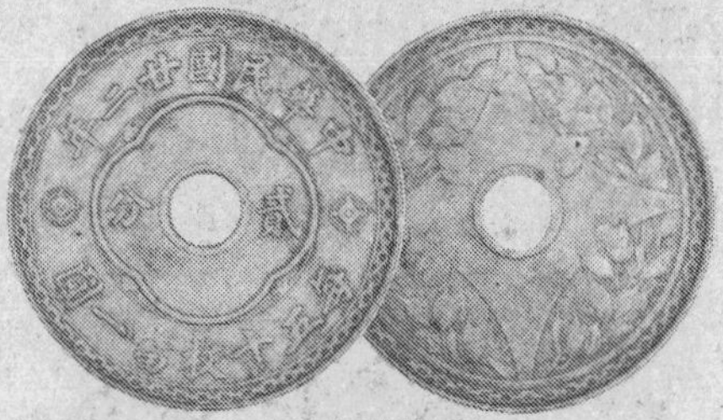

BRONZE

Y#	Date	Mintage	Fine	VF	XF	Unc
325a	Yr.22 (1933)	—	50.00	125.00	175.00	225.00

BRASS

Y#	Date	Mintage	Fine	VF	XF	Unc
354	Yr.28 (1939)	—	1.60	4.00	6.00	12.00

Y#	Date	Mintage	Fine	VF	XF	Unc
358	Yr.29 (1940)	—	.20	.50	.75	1.50

5 CENTS (5 FEN)

NICKEL

Y#	Date	Mintage	Fine	VF	XF	Unc
348	Yr.25 (1936)	72.844	.25	.60	1.00	3.00
	Yr.27 (1938)	34.325	.80	2.00	4.00	6.00
	Yr.28 (1939)	I.A.	4.00	10.00	15.00	25.00

NOTE: Pieces dated 1935 are patterns.

Rev: A mintmark below spade (Vienna)

Y#	Date	Mintage	Fine	VF	XF	Unc
348.1	Yr.25 (1936)	20.000	.40	1.00	2.00	5.00

Obv: Character "P'ing" on both sides of portrait.

Y#	Date	Mintage	Fine	VF	XF	Unc
348.2	Yr.25 (1936)	—	20.00	50.00	100.00	150.00

Obv: Character "Ch'ing" on both sides of portrait.

Y#	Date	Mintage	Fine	VF	XF	Unc
348.3	Yr.25 (1936)	—	20.00	50.00	100.00	150.00

ALUMINUM

Y#	Date	Mintage	Fine	VF	XF	Unc
356	Yr.29 (1940)	350.000	.10	.25	.50	1.00

COPPER-NICKEL

Y#	Date	Mintage	Fine	VF	XF	Unc
359	Yr.29 (1940)	—	.20	.50	2.00	3.00
	Yr.30 (1941)	—	.20	.50	2.00	3.00

10 CENTS (10 FEN)

SILVER, 2.3 gm.
Similar to Dollar, Y#318, vertical reeding.

K#	Date	Mintage	Fine	VF	XF	Unc
602	ND(1912)	—	80.00	200.00	300.00	400.00

Edge engrailed with circles.

K#	Date	Mintage	Fine	VF	XF	Unc
602b	ND(1912)	—	—	220.00	350.00	500.00

.700 SILVER, 2.7 gm.

Y#	Date	Mintage	Fine	VF	XF	Unc
326	Yr.3 (1914)	—	BV	2.50	4.50	11.50
	Yr.5 (1916)	—	10.00	25.00	50.00	125.00

SILVER
Pu Yi Wedding Commemorative

Y#	Date	Mintage	Fine	VF	XF	Unc
334	Yr.15 (1926)	—	2.00	4.00	8.00	22.50

2.5 gm.
Death of Sun Yat-Sen Commemorative

Y#	Date	Mintage	Fine	VF	XF	Unc
339	Yr.16 (1927)	—	13.50	30.00	50.00	75.00

NOTE: Two different copper-nickel pieces dated 1929 with Sun Yat-sen obverse and a junk reverse exist. Both are rare patterns. A similar pattern in silver dated 1932 also exists.

NICKEL

Y#	Date	Mintage	Fine	VF	XF	Unc
349	Yr.25 (1936)	73.866	.40	1.00	1.50	2.50
	Yr.27 (1938)	110.203	.80	2.00	4.00	6.00
	Yr.28 (1939)	I.A.	.80	2.00	4.00	6.00

NON-MAGNETIC NICKEL ALLOY

Y#	Date	Mintage	Fine	VF	XF	Unc
349a	Yr.25 (1936)	1.000	8.00	20.00	35.00	50.00

All of the Y#349 coins were supposed to have been minted in pure nickel at the Shanghai Mint. However in 1936 the Tientsin Mint produced about one million 10 Cent pieces of heavily alloyed nickel. The result is that the Shanghai pieces are attracted to a magnet while the Tientsin pieces are not.

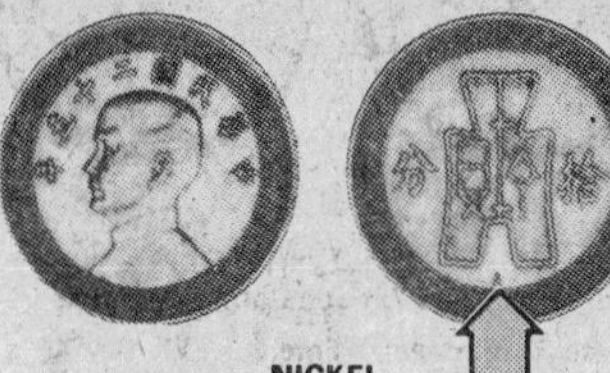

NICKEL
Rev: A mintmark below spade (Vienna Mint)

Y#	Date	Mintage	Fine	VF	XF	Unc
349.1	Yr.25 (1936)A	60.000	.40	1.00	2.00	5.00

Obv: Character "Ch'ing" in field or on portrait.

Y#	Date	Mintage	Fine	VF	XF	Unc
349.2	Yr.25 (1936)	—	20.00	50.00	100.00	150.00

Obv: Character "P'ing" in field or on portrait.

Y#	Date	Mintage	Fine	VF	XF	Unc
349.3	Yr.25 (1936)	—	40.00	100.00	150.00	200.00

Obv: Character Ch'ing on side of portrait.

Y#	Date	Mintage	Fine	VF	XF	Unc
349.4	Yr.25 (1936)	—	40.00	100.00	150.00	200.00

Obv: Character P'ing on side of portrait.

Y#	Date	Mintage	Fine	VF	XF	Unc
349.5	Yr.25 (1936)	—	60.00	150.00	200.00	300.00

COPPER-NICKEL
Reeded edge.

Y#	Date	Mintage	Fine	VF	XF	Unc
360	Yr.29 (1940)	—	.30	.75	1.25	6.00
	Yr.30 (1941)	—	.40	1.00	2.00	4.00
	Yr.31 (1942)	—	6.00	15.00	25.00	50.00

Unreeded edge.

Y#	Date	Mintage	Fine	VF	XF	Unc
360.1	Yr.29 (1940)	—	—	—	Rare	—
	Yr.30 (1941)	—	2.00	5.00	7.50	12.50

Rev: Character "Kuei" below the spade.

Y#	Date	Mintage	Fine	VF	XF	Unc
360.2	Yr.31 (1942)	—	—	—	Rare	—

20 CENTS (20 FEN)

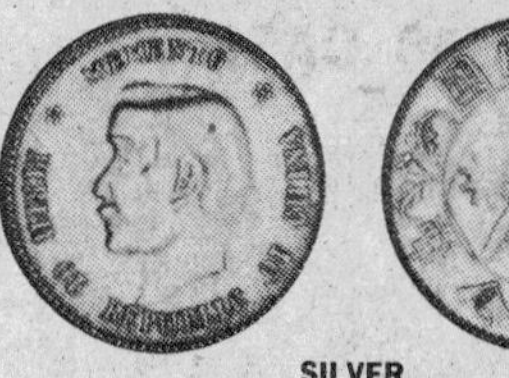

SILVER
Founding of the Republic

Y#	Date	Mintage	Fine	VF	XF	Unc
317	(1912)	.155	12.50	18.50	32.50	60.00

GOLD, 19.3 gm.

K#	Date	Mintage	Fine	VF	XF	Unc
1551	1912	—	—	—	1000.	1500.

.700 SILVER, 5.4 gm.

Y#	Date	Mintage	Fine	VF	XF	Unc
327	Yr.3 (1914)	—	BV	4.00	6.50	13.50
	Yr.5 (1916)	—	5.00	10.00	20.50	40.00
	Yr.9 (1920)	—	40.00	100.00	135.00	200.00

5.2 gm.
Pu Yi Wedding Commemorative

Y#	Date	Mintage	Fine	VF	XF	Unc
335	Yr.15 (1926)	—	4.00	6.50	12.50	25.00

5.3 gm.
Death of Sun Yat-Sen Commemorative

Y#	Date	Mintage	Fine	VF	XF	Unc
340	Yr.16 (1927)	—	12.00	20.00	35.00	70.00

NICKEL

Y#	Date	Mintage	Fine	VF	XF	Unc
350	Yr.25 (1936)	49.620	.20	.50	1.00	2.50
	Yr.27 (1938)	61.248	.80	2.00	4.00	6.00
	Yr.28 (1939)	I.A.	.80	2.00	4.00	7.50

Rev: A mintmark below spade (Vienna Mint)

Y#	Date	Mintage	Fine	VF	XF	Unc
350.1	Yr.25 (1936)	40.000	.40	1.00	2.00	5.00

COPPER-NICKEL

Y#	Date	Mintage	Fine	VF	XF	Unc
361	Yr.31 (1942)	—	.40	1.00	2.25	4.00

Rev: Character "Kuei" below spade

Y#	Date	Mintage	Fine	VF	XF	Unc
361.1	Yr.31 (1942)	—	—	—	Rare	—

500 CASH

COPPER

Y#	Date	Mintage	Fine	VF	XF	Unc
—	ND (C.1928)	—	450.00	800.00	1100.	1500.

NOTE: Formerly designated Y#460. Provincial attribution is uncertain.

50 CENTS

.700 SILVER, 13.6 gm.

Y#	Date	Mintage	Fine	VF	XF	Unc
328	Yr.3 (1914)	—	BV	15.00	25.00	50.00

.720 SILVER, 10 gm.

K#	Date	Mintage	Fine	VF	XF	Unc
633	Yr.25 (1936)	*6.480	160.00	400.00	500.00	700.00

***NOTE:** All but,a few pieces were remelted.

COPPER-NICKEL

Y#	Date	Mintage	Fine	VF	XF	Unc
362	Yr.31 (1942)	—	.40	1.00	2.00	3.00
	Yr.32 (1943)	—	2.00	5.00	8.00	15.00

Rev: Character "Kuei" below spade

Y#	Date	Mintage	Fine	VF	XF	Unc
362.1	Yr.31 (1942)	—	—	—	Rare	—

DOLLAR (YUAN)

.900 SILVER, 26.9 gm.
Sun Yat-sen Founding of the Republic Commemorative
Rev: Five-pointed stars dividing legend.

Y#	Date	Mintage	Fine	VF	XF	Unc
318	ND(1912)	—	100.00	150.00	200.00	350.00

GOLD

K#	Date	Mintage	Fine	VF	XF	Unc
1552	ND(1912)	—	—	—	—	—

NOTE: For similar issue with rosettes see Y#318a (1927).

.900 SILVER, 27.3 gm.
Obv: Similar to Y#318.
Rev: Different English legend.

Y#	Date	Mintage	Fine	VF	XF	Unc
319	ND(1912)	—	47.50	85.00	135.00	250.00

GOLD

K#	Date	Mintage	Fine	VF	XF	Unc
1550	ND(1912)	—	—	—	—	—

SILVER, 26.5 gm.
Li Yuan-hung Founding of Republic

Y#	Date	Mintage	Fine	VF	XF	Unc
320	ND(1912)	—	175.00	275.00	350.00	450.00

Rev. legend: OE for OF

Y#	Date	Mintage	Fine	VF	XF	Unc
320.1	ND(1912)	—	125.00	200.00	400.00	600.00

Li Yuan-hung Founding of Republic

Y#	Date	Mintage	Fine	VF	XF	Unc
321	ND(1912)	—	30.00	50.00	80.00	135.00

Rev: H of 'THE' written as I I, without crossbar.

Y#	Date	Mintage	Fine	VF	XF	Unc
321.1	ND(1912)	—	50.00	85.00	150.00	200.00

Yuan Shih-kai Founding of Republic
Diameter 39mm. Thickness 2.5mm.

322	ND(1914)	.020	75.00	125.00	175.00	250.00

As above, but diameter 39.5mm and thickness 3.25mm.

322.1	ND	—	65.00	110.00	150.00	225.00

A restrike made about 1918 for collectors.

.890 SILVER, 26.4 gm.
Vertical reeding.

329	Yr.3 (1914)	—	BV	BV	25.00	32.50
	Yr.8 (1919)	—	BV	BV	35.00	45.00
	Yr.9 (1920)	—	BV	BV	25.00	32.50
	Yr.10 (1921)	—	BV	BV	25.00	32.50

GOLD

K#	Date	Mintage	Fine	VF	XF	Unc
1556	Yr.3 (1914)	—	—	—	—	—

SILVER
Edge engrailed with circles.

Y#	Date	Mintage	Fine	VF	XF	Unc
329.1	Yr.3 (1914)	—	30.00	75.00	100.00	125.00

Edge ornamented with alternating T's.

329.2	Yr.3 (1914)	—	30.00	75.00	100.00	125.00

Plain edge.

329.3	Yr.3 (1914)	—	27.50	40.00	60.00	80.00

Tiny circle in ribbon bow. This is a mintmark, but it is not clear what mint is indicated.

329.4	Yr.3 (1914)	—	BV	35.00	65.00	90.00

Oblique edge reeding.

329.5	Yr.10 (1921)	—	BV	30.00	35.00	50.00

NOTE: Although bearing dates of 1914 through 1921,these Yuan Shi-Kai Dollars were struck for years afterwards. Coins dated yr. 3 (1914) were struck continuously through 1919 and were also later restruck by the Chinese Soviets. Later again in the 1950's this coin was struck for use in Tibet. Coins with dates 1920 and 1921 were struck at least until 1929. The total mintage of all four dates of Y#329 is estimated at more than 750 million pieces.

26.8 gm.
Hung Hsien

332	Yr.1 (1916)	—	150.00	275.00	425.00	600.00

GOLD

K#	Date	Mintage	Fine	VF	XF	Unc
1560	Yr.1 (1916)	—	—	—	3500.	5000.

SILVER, 26.5 gm.
President Hsu Shih-chang
Reeded edge

676	Yr.10 (1921)	—	175.00	300.00	500.00	900.00

Unreeded edge

K#	Date	Mintage	Fine	VF	XF	Unc
676.1	Yr.10 (1921)	—	80.00	200.00	325.00	700.00

26.7 gm.
President Tsao Kun

677	ND(1923)	.050	60.00	150.00	250.00	450.00

GOLD, 37.5 gm.

1572	ND(1923)	—	—	—	3500.	5000.

SILVER, 26.7 gm.
President Tsao Kun

678	ND(1923)	—	80.00	200.00	275.00	450.00

GOLD, 37.5 gm.

1573	ND(1923)	—	—	—	3500.	5000.

SILVER, 26.8 gm.
Pu Yi Wedding Commemorative
Rev: Value in small characters.

Y#	Date	Mintage	Fine	VF	XF	Unc
336	Yr.12 (1923)	—	250.00	400.00	600.00	800.00

GOLD

K#	Date	Mintage	Fine	VF	XF	Unc
1575	Yr.12 (1923)	—	—	—	3500.	5000.

SILVER
Rev: Value in large characters.

Y#	Date	Mintage	Fine	VF	XF	Unc
336.1	Yr.12 (1923)	—	175.00	300.00	500.00	600.00

GOLD

K#	Date	Mintage	Fine	VF	XF	Unc
1575.1	Yr.12 (1923)	—	—	—	3500.	5000.

SILVER
President Tuan Chi-Jui

Y#	Date	Mintage	Fine	VF	XF	Unc
683	ND(1924)	—	150.00	250.00	325.00	500.00

GOLD

K#	Date	Mintage	Fine	VF	XF	Unc
1577	ND(1924)	—	—	—	3500.	5000.

.890 SILVER, 27 gm.
Incuse edge reeding
Rev: Rosettes dividing legends.

Y#	Date	Mintage	Fine	VF	XF	Unc
318.1	ND(1927)	—	BV	BV	25.00	32.50

GOLD, 42 gm.

K#	Date	Mintage	Fine	VF	XF	Unc
1553	ND(1927)	—	—	—	3500.	5000.

.890 SILVER, 27 gm.
Edge reeding in relief.

Y#	Date	Mintage	Fine	VF	XF	Unc
318.2	ND(1927)	—	BV	BV	25.00	32.50

NOTE: Varieties exist with errors in the English legend. For similar coins with 5 pointed stars dividing legends, see Y#318 (1912).

26.5 gm.
General Chu Yu-pu

K#	Date	Mintage	Fine	VF	XF	Unc
690	Yr.16 (1927)	—	400.00	1000.	1600.	2500.

27 gm.

Sun Yat-Sen Memorial

K#	Date	Mintage	Fine	VF	XF	Unc
609	Yr.16 (1927)	480 pcs.	400.00	900.00	1100.	1600.

Rev: Birds over junk

Y#	Date	Mintage	Fine	VF	XF	Unc
344	Yr.21 (1932)	2.260	80.00	125.00	165.00	225.00

Obv: Similar to Y#344.

Y#	Date	Mintage	Fine	VF	XF	Unc
345	Yr.22 (1933)	46.400	BV	BV	27.50	35.00
	Yr.23 (1934)	128.740	BV	BV	25.00	32.50

NOTE: In 1949, three U.S. Mints restruck a total of 30 million junk Dollars dated 1934.

.720 SILVER, 20 gm.

K#	Date	Mintage	Fine	VF	XF	Unc
632	Yr.25 (1936)	3.240	—	—	1000.	1750.

10 DOLLARS

RED GOLD, 7.05 gm.
Hung Hsien Commemorative

Y#	Date	Mintage	Fine	VF	XF	Unc
333	Yr.1 (1916)	—	600.00	1000.	1750.	2500.
	YELLOW GOLD, 7.05 gm.					
333a	Yr.1 (1916)	—	600.00	1000.	1750.	2500.

.850 GOLD, 8.15 gm.

Y#	Date	Mintage	Fine	VF	XF	Unc
330	Yr.8 (1919)	—	450.00	700.00	1000.	1350.

20 DOLLARS

.850 GOLD, 16.3 gm.

Y#	Date	Mintage	Fine	VF	XF	Unc
331	Yr.8 (1919)	—	750.00	1150.	1650.	2250.

NCLT ISSUES

PATTERNS

KM#	Date	Mintage	Identification	Mkt.Val.
1	ND	—	10 Cash, Copper, w/L. Giorgi, Y309	500.00

KM#	Date	Mintage	Identification	Mkt.Val.
2	ND(1912)	—	10 Cash, Copper	400.00
3	(1913)	—	1 Cash, Iron, square hole in center	—
4	(1914)	—	5 Cents, Nickel, yr. 3, K815	—
5	(1914)	—	5 Cents, Nickel, yr.3, unmilled, essay, K815a	—
6	(1914)	—	5 Cents, Nickel, yr.3, milled, w/G.L.,essay, K815b	—
7	(1914)	—	5 Cents, Silver, yr.3, milled, w/G.L., essay, K815c	—
8	(1914)	—	5 Cents, Copper, yr.3, essay, K815x	—
9	(1914)	—	5 Cents, Pewter, yr.3, essay, unmilled, essay, K815y	—
10	(1914)	—	5 Cents, Copper, yr.3, w/G.L., essay, K815z	—
11	Yr.3 (1914)	—	10 Cents, Silver, w/L.G., K659a	400.00
12	Yr.3 (1914)	—	20 Cents, Silver, w/L.G., K657a	400.00
13	Yr.3 (1914)	—	50 Cents, Silver, w/L.Giorgi K655a	200.00
14	(1914)	—	1 Dollar, Silver, w/L.Giorgi, Y322.3	500.00

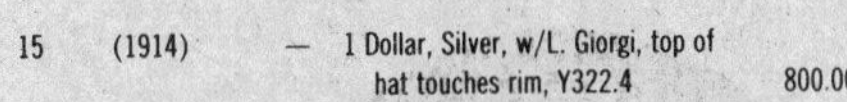

KM#	Date	Mintage	Identification	Mkt.Val.
15	(1914)	—	1 Dollar, Silver, w/L. Giorgi, top of hat touches rim, Y322.4	800.00

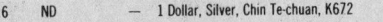

KM#	Date	Mintage	Identification	Mkt.Val.
16	ND	—	1 Dollar, Silver, Chin Te-chuan, K672	2500.

KM#	Date	Mintage	Identification	Mkt.Val.
17	Yr.3 (1914)	—	1 Dollar, Silver, K643.1	2000.
18	Yr.3 (1914)	—	1 Dollar, Silver, w/L.Giorgi K643.2	2200. 900.00

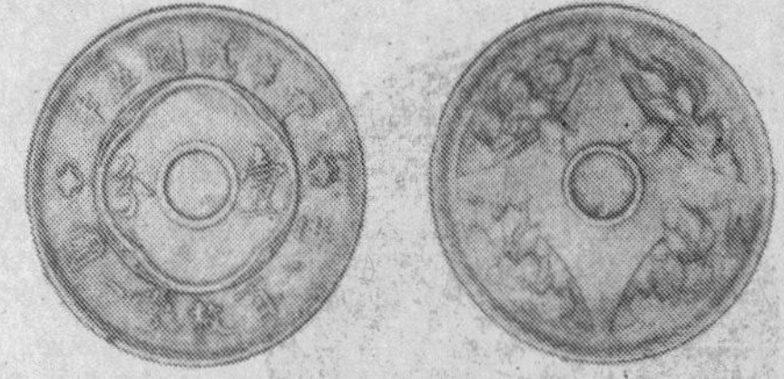

KM#	Date	Mintage	Identification	Mkt.Val.
19	(1916)	—	10 Cash, Copper, Y324.2	275.00
20	(1916)	—	10 Cash, Copper, w/L.Giorgi, Y324.3	—

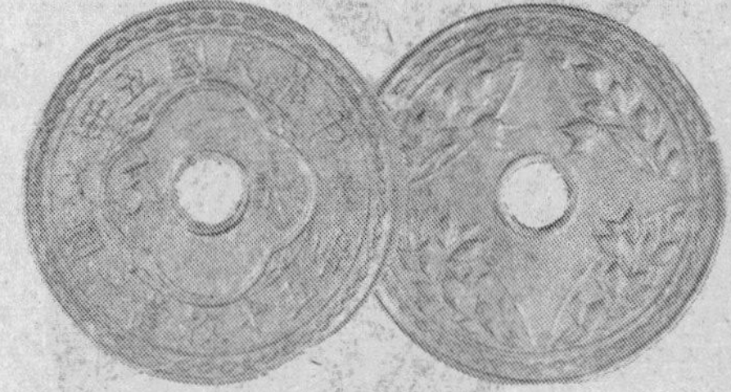

KM#	Date	Mintage	Identification	Mkt.Val.
21	Yr.5 (1916)	—	20 Cash, Copper, Su44	—
22	(1916)	—	1 Dollar, Silver, w/L.Giorgi, K663	—

KM#	Date	Mintage	Identification	Mkt.Val.
23	Yr.10 (1921)	—	1 Dollar, Silver, reeded edge K676a.1	600.00
24	Yr.10 (1921)	—	Dollar, Gold, reeded edge, K1570	—
25	Yr.10 (1921)	—	1 Dollar, Silver, plain edge, K676a.2	600.00
26	Yr.10 (1921)	—	Dollar, Gold, plain edge, K1570a	—

KM#	Date	Mintage	Identification	Mkt.Val.
27	Yr.15 (1926)	—	1 Dollar, Silver, K685	6000.
28	(1927)	—	1 Dollar, Silver, K687	4500.
29	Yr.16 (1927)	—	1 Dollar, Silver, K686	4500.

30	(c.1928)	—	20 Cash, Copper	—

KM#	Date	Mintage	Identification	Mkt.Val.
31	Yr.17 (1928)	—	1 Dollar, Silver, K688	2500.
32	Yr.18 (1929)	—	10 Cents, Copper-Nickel, Vienna, K617 Y VI	850.00

33	Yr.18 (1929)	—	20 Cents, Copper-Nickel, Vienna, K617yV	1000.

34	Yr.18 (1929)	—	50 Cents, Copper-Nickel Vienna, K617yIV	1000.

35	Yr.18 (1929)	—	1 Dollar, Silver, Italian, K614	1100.
36	Yr.18 (1929)	—	1 Dollar, Silver, Italian, w/designer's name, K614a	1400.

KM#	Date	Mintage	Identification	Mkt.Val.
37	Yr.18 (1929)	—	1 Dollar, Silver, English, K615	600.00

38	Yr.18 (1929)	—	1 Dollar, Silver, American, K616	700.00

39	Yr.18 (1929)	—	1 Dollar, Silver, Austrian, K617	500.00
40	Yr.18 (1929)	—	10 Cents, Silver, K617 III	850.00

KM#	Date	Mintage	Identification	Mkt.Val.
41	Yr.18 (1929)	—	20 Cents, Silver, K617 II	850.00
42	Yr.18 (1929)	—	50 Cents, Silver, K617 I	850.00

43	Yr.18 (1929)	—	1 Dollar, Silver, K610	4000.

44	Yr.18 (1929)	—	1 Dollar, Silver, Italian, K614	600.00
45	Yr.18 (1929)	—	1 Dollar, Silver, Japanese, K618	600.00

In 1929 China invited several mints to submit designs for a new Sun Yat-sen Dollar, with his bust on one side and a junk on the other. All of the designs were very much alike, differing mainly in the details of the portrait, the waves, and the junk. Coin illustrated is the Italian design.

46	Yr.21 (1932)	—	20 Cents, Silver Trial, K630	950.00

KM#	Date	Mintage	Identification	Mkt.Val.
47	Yr.21 (1932)	—	1/2 Dollar, Silver Essay, K629	1500.

48	Yr.21 (1932)	—	1 Dollar, Silver, K628	1500.

Minted as part of a gold standard coinage, but not adopted. Though inscribed "One Yuan Dollar", the proposed unit was called a sun. Similar 1/2, 1/5 and 1/10 sun patterns were also made in silver and 1/20 and 1/50 sun patterns were made in nickel and 1/100 in bronze with and without hole punched. A brass pattern yuan dated year 18 (1929) exists.

49	Yr.24 (1935)	—	5 Cents, Nickel, K833	—

50	Yr.21 (1935)	—	10 Cents, Nickel, K832	150.00

51	Yr.24 (1935)	—	20 Cents, Nickel, K831	160.00
52	Yr.24 (1935)	—	1 Dollar, Silver, K625	—

53	(1936)	—	10 Cash, Copper, W161	—
54	(1936)	—	20 Cents, Nickel, K633	—
55	Yr.25 (1936)	—	1 Dollar, Silver, K634	—
56	Yr.26 (1937)	—	5 Cents, Nickel, Y348.2	—
57	Yr.26 (1937)	—	10 Cents, Nickel, w/P'ing on side of portrait, Y349.7	—
58	Yr.26 (1937)	—	20 Cents, Nickel, Y350.1	—

KM#	Date	Mintage	Identification	Mkt.Val.
59	Yr.26 (1937)	—	50 Cents, Silver, K637	—
60	Yr.26 (1937)	—	1 Dollar, Silver, K636	—
61	Yr.37 (1948)	—	1 Dollar, Silver, K637-II	—
62	Yr.37 (1948)	—	2 Dollars, Silver, K637-I	—

PROVINCIAL ISSUES

ANHWEI PROVINCE

A province located in eastern China. Made a separate province during the Manchu dynasty in the 17th century. Principally agricultural with some mining of coal and iron ore. Spanish-American 8 Reales saw wide circulation in this province until the end of World War I. The provincial mint at Anking began operations in 1897, closed in 1899, and later reopened in 1902. The primary production of the mint was Cash coins but included a series of silver coinage.

EMPIRE

CASH

CAST BRASS

C#	Date	Emperor	Good	VG	Fine	VF
—	(1796-1820)	Chia Ch'ing	—	—	Rare	—

NOTE: Not to be confused with similar coins from the Changsha Mint in Hunan Province. The Changsha Mint coins have an extra dot or vertical stroke to the left of the mintmark at right of the center hole.

3-1	(1875-1908)	Kuang Hsu	15.00	27.50	37.50	50.00

3-1.1	(1875-1908)	Kuang Hsu	15.00	27.50	37.50	50.00

CAST ZINC

3-1.1a	(1875-1908)	Kuang Hsu	—	—	Rare	—

STRUCK COINAGE

5 CASH

COPPER
Rev: Circled dragon, AN-HWEI.

Y#	Date	Mintage	VG	Fine	VF	XF
35	(1902)	—	50.00	100.00	150.00	225.00

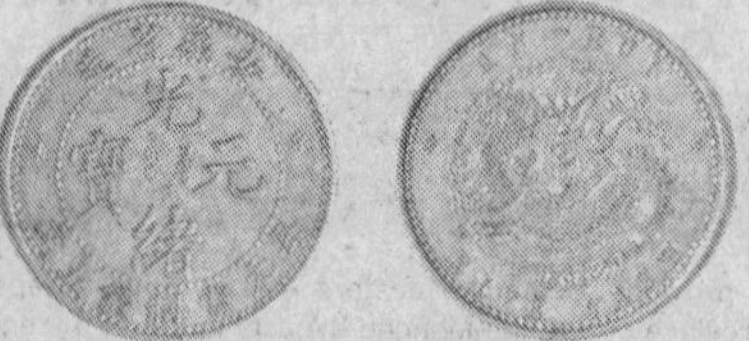

Rev: Uncircled dragon, AN-HUI.

Y#	Date	Mintage	VG	Fine	VF	XF
35.1	ND	—	—	—	Rare	—

10 CASH

COPPER
Rev: Letter A inverted, denomination ONE SEN.

Y#	Date	Mintage	VG	Fine	VF	XF
34a	(1902)	—	16.50	40.00	60.00	90.00

Letter A corrected.

Y#	Date	Mintage	VG	Fine	VF	XF
34a.1	(1902)	—	16.50	40.00	60.00	90.00

Rev. denomination: ONE CEN

Y#	Date	Mintage	VG	Fine	VF	XF
34	(1902)	—	12.50	30.00	40.00	75.00

NOTE: May show various stages of recutting of 'C' in CEN.

Rev: Rosettes around dragon close together.
Letter N backwards in AN-HWEI.

Y#	Date	Mintage	VG	Fine	VF	XF
36	(1902-06)	—	4.00	10.00	15.00	25.00

Obv: Small Manchu characters in center.
Rev: Rosettes close together. Letter N corrected.

Y#	Date	Mintage	VG	Fine	VF	XF
36.1	(1902-06)	—	.75	2.00	3.00	5.00

Obv: Smaller redesigned rosettes.
Larger Manchu characters in center.
Rev: Rosettes close together.
Larger clouds around redesigned dragon.

Y#	Date	Mintage	VG	Fine	VF	XF
36.2	(1902-06)	—	.75	2.00	3.00	5.00

Obv: Rosettes crude and heavy.
Rev: Rosettes close together. Dragon's head redesigned.

Y#	Date	Mintage	VG	Fine	VF	XF
36.3	(1902-06)	—	4.00	10.00	15.00	25.00

Reverse rosettes far apart.

Y#	Date	Mintage	VG	Fine	VF	XF
36.4	(1902-06)	—	.75	2.00	3.00	5.00

Obv: Small rosette at center with five characters at bottom. Rev: Large English legend above dragon.

Y#	Date	Mintage	VG	Fine	VF	XF
36a	(1902-06)	—	.75	2.00	3.00	5.00

Obv: Small rosette.
Rev: Small English legend above dragon.

Y#	Date	Mintage	VG	Fine	VF	XF
36a.1	(1902-06)	—	1.50	3.50	7.00	12.00

Rev: Small English legend with larger clouds around dragon and only one cloud below dragon's tail.

Y#	Date	Mintage	VG	Fine	VF	XF
36a.2	(1902-06)	—	1.50	3.50	7.00	12.00

Obv: Large rosette at center with two characters at bottom.

Y#	Date	Mintage	VG	Fine	VF	XF
36a.3	(1902-06)	—	.75	2.00	3.00	5.00

Obv: Large rosette at center with five characters at bottom.

Y#	Date	Mintage	VG	Fine	VF	XF
36a.4	(1902-06)	—	1.25	2.50	3.50	6.00

Obv: Two characters at bottom.
Rev: Small English legend above dragon.

Y#	Date	Mintage	VG	Fine	VF	XF
36a.5	(1902-06)	—	3.00	7.50	12.50	20.00

Obv: Slightly smaller rosette at center with right Manchu character slightly higher than on 36a.5.
Rev: Small English legend above dragon.

Y#	Date	Mintage	VG	Fine	VF	XF
36a.6	(1902-06)	—	.75	2.00	3.50	6.00

Obv: With two characters at bottom.
Rev: Ten spelled TOEN.

Y#	Date	Mintage	VG	Fine	VF	XF
38a	(1902-06)	—	3.00	7.50	15.00	25.00

Obv: With five characters at bottom.
Rev: Ten spelled TOEN.

Y#	Date	Mintage	VG	Fine	VF	XF
38a.1	(1902-06)	—	4.00	10.00	20.00	30.00

Obv: With two characters at bottom.
Rev: Without Ten Cash.

Y#	Date	Mintage	VG	Fine	VF	XF
38b	(1902-06)	—	4.00	10.00	20.00	30.00

Obv: With five characters at bottom.

38b.1	(1902-06)	—	12.50	30.00	40.00	60.00

Rev: With rosettes at sides and AN-HUI above dragon.

39	(1902-06)	—	—	—	Rare	—

Rev: With stars at sides and AN-HUI above dragon.

39.1	(1902-06)	—	—	—	Rare	—

Obv: With large mintmark at center.

10a	CD1906	—	.75	2.00	3.00	5.00

Obv: With small mintmark at center.

10a.1	CD1906	—	.60	1.50	2.50	5.00

Obverse and reverse more finely engraved.

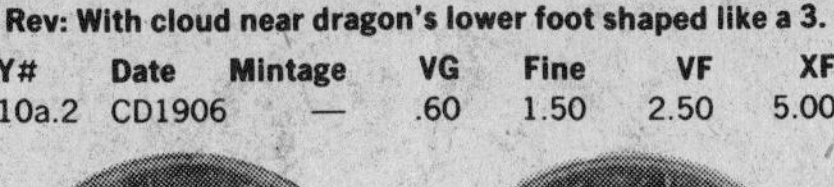

Rev: With cloud near dragon's lower foot shaped like a 3.

Y#	Date	Mintage	VG	Fine	VF	XF
10a.2	CD1906	—	.60	1.50	2.50	5.00

20a	CD1909	—	10.00	25.00	40.00	70.00

Rev: Dot after coin

20a.1	CD1909	—	30.00	75.00	100.00	150.00

20 CASH

COPPER

37	(1902)	—	300.00	625.00	875.00	1200.

11a	CD1906	—	40.00	100.00	140.00	185.00

5 CENTS

.820 SILVER, 1.33 gm.

Y#	Date	Mintage	Fine	VF	XF	Unc
41	(1897)	—	25.00	60.00	100.00	200.00

41.1	Yr.25 (1899)	—	15.00	31.50	62.50	125.00

10 CENTS

.820 SILVER, 2.65 gm.
Obv: With rosettes dividing legends.

42	(1897)	—	10.00	17.50	35.00	75.00

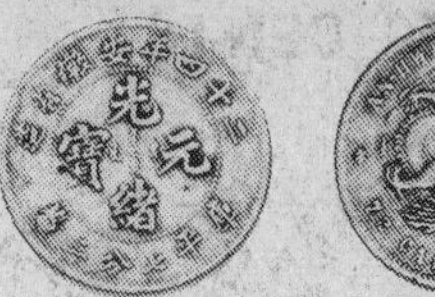

Obv: Without rosettes dividing legends.

Y#	Date	Mintage	Fine	VF	XF	Unc
42.1	Yr.24 (1898)	—	8.50	15.00	27.50	60.00

Obv: With rosettes dividing legends.

42.2	Yr.24 (1898)	—	8.50	15.00	27.50	60.00

Obv: A S T C in field.

42.3	Yr.24 (1898)	—	8.50	15.00	28.50	70.00

Obv: With six characters at top.

42.4	CD1898	—	10.00	17.50	35.00	75.00

20 CENTS

.820 SILVER, 5.3 gm.
Rev: With large dragon and small English legends.

43	(1897)	—	18.50	30.00	50.00	150.00

Rev: With smaller dragon and larger English legends.

43.1	(1897)	—	18.50	30.00	50.00	150.00
43.2	Yr.23 (1897)		One known		—	—

43.3	Yr.24 (1898)	—	15.00	28.50	45.00	135.00

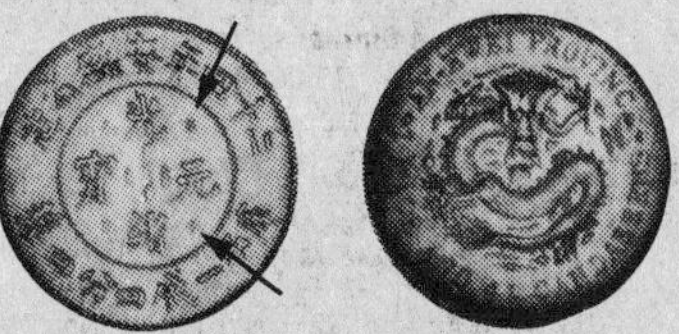

Obv: A S T C in field.

43.4	Yr.24 (1898)	—	15.00	28.50	45.00	135.00

43.5	Yr.27 (1901)		One known		—	—

50 CENTS

SILVER, 13.5 gm.

Y#	Date	Mintage	Fine	VF	XF	Unc
44	Yr.24 (1898)	—	60.00	100.00	165.00	500.00

Obv: A S T C in field.

Y#	Date	Mintage	Fine	VF	XF	Unc
44.1	Yr.24 (1898)	—	35.00	60.00	120.00	400.00

DOLLAR

.900 SILVER, 27.1 gm.

Y#	Date	Mintage	Fine	VF	XF	Unc
45	ND (1897)	—	100.00	150.00	250.00	500.00
45.1	Yr.23 (1897)	3 known		2000.	—	

Rev: Similar to Y#45.

Y#	Date	Mintage	Fine	VF	XF	Unc
45.2	Yr.24 (1898)	—	75.00	125.00	200.00	325.00

Obv: A S T C in field.
Rev: Similar to Y#45.

Y#	Date	Mintage	Fine	VF	XF	Unc
45.3	Yr.24 (1898)	—	75.00	125.00	200.00	325.00

26.9 gm.
Obv: With six characters at top.
Rev: Similar to Y#45.1

Y#	Date	Mintage	Fine	VF	XF	Unc
45.4	CD1898	—	65.00	110.00	185.00	300.00

NCLT ISSUES

PATTERNS

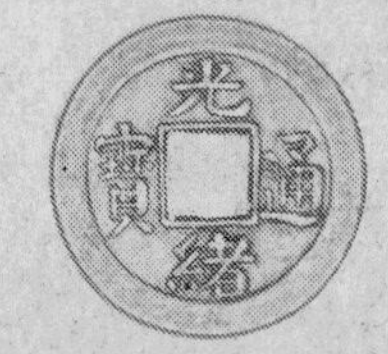

KM#	Date	Mintage	Identification	Mkt.Val.
1	ND	—	Cash, Copper, C3.2	225.00

CHEKIANG PROVINCE

A province located along the east coast of China. Although the smallest of the Chinese provinces, it is one of the most densely populated. Mostly agricultural with iron and coal mining and some fishing. The mint opened at Hangchow in 1898, but closed shortly thereafter. Another opened in 1903 and still another in 1905, both of which closed in 1906. Chekiang coins dated prior to 1898 were possibly produced at the Hangchow Arsenal Mint.

EMPIRE

CASH

CAST BRASS

C#	Date	Emperor	Good	VG	Fine	VF
4-1	(1736-95)	Ch'ien Lung	.25	.50	.75	1.00

Rev: Mintmark written differently.

C#	Date	Emperor	Good	VG	Fine	VF
4-1.1	(1736-95)	Ch'ien Lung	.25	.50	.75	1.00

Rev: Dot at top.

C#	Date	Emperor	Good	VG	Fine	VF
4-1.2	(1736-95)	Ch'ien Lung	2.00	3.50	5.00	7.00

Rev: Large mintmark and normal rims.

C#	Date	Emperor	Good	VG	Fine	VF
4-2	(1796-1820)	Chia Ch'ing	.25	.50	.75	1.00

Rev: Small mintmark and wide rims.

C#	Date	Emperor	Good	VG	Fine	VF
4-2.1	(1796-1820)	Chia Ch'ing	.25	.50	.75	1.00

CAST IRON

C#	Date	Emperor	Good	VG	Fine	VF
4-2.1a	(1796-1820)	Chia Ch'ing	—	—	Rare	—

CAST BRASS
Rev: Dot at bottom.

C#	Date	Emperor	Good	VG	Fine	VF
4-2.2	(1796-1820)	Chia Ch'ing	2.00	3.50	5.00	7.00

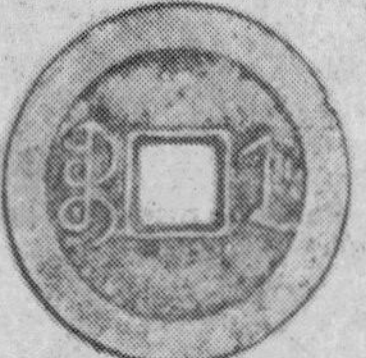

Rev: Large mintmark. 23-25mm.

C#	Date	Emperor	Good	VG	Fine	VF
4-3	(1820-51)	Tao Kuang	.25	.50	.75	1.00

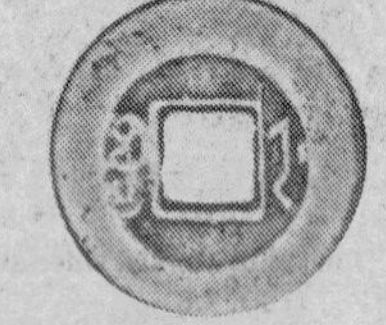

Rev: Small mintmark. 21-23mm.

C#	Date	Emperor	Good	VG	Fine	VF
4-3.1	(1820-51)	Tao Kuang	.25	.50	.75	1.00

21-25mm

C#	Date	Emperor	Good	VG	Fine	VF
4-3.5	(1851-61)	Hsien Feng	1.00	2.00	3.00	4.50

16-20mm

C#	Date	Emperor	Good	VG	Fine	VF
4-3.6	(1851-61)	Hsien Feng	1.00	2.00	3.00	4.50

CAST IRON

C#	Date	Emperor	Good	VG	Fine	VF
4-3.6a	(1851-61)	Hsien Feng	10.00	17.50	25.00	35.00

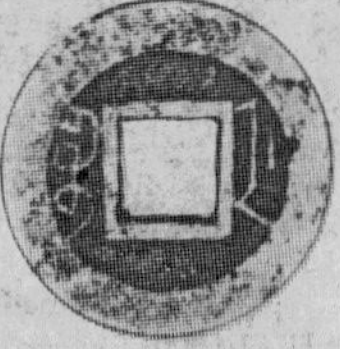

CAST BRASS

C#	Date	Emperor	Good	VG	Fine	VF
4-17	(1862-74)	T'ung Chih	1.00	2.00	3.00	5.50

Rev: Mintmark as C#4-1.

4-19 (1875-1908)

C#	Date	Emperor	Good	VG	Fine	VF
4-19		Kuang Hsu	1.00	2.00	3.00	4.50

CAST ZINC

C#	Date	Emperor	Good	VG	Fine	VF
4-19a	(1875-1908)	Kuang Hsu	—	—	Rare	—

CAST BRASS
Rev: Mintmark as C#4-1.1.

C#	Date	Emperor	Good	VG	Fine	VF
4-19.1	(1875-1908)	Kuang Hsu	1.00	2.00	3.00	4.50

NOTE: For similar coinage refer to "Rebel Issues".

10 CASH

CAST BRASS
Rev: Manchu mintmark to right as above. Denomination at bottom in Chinese.

C#	Date	Emperor	Good	VG	Fine	VF
4-4	(1851-61)	Hsien Feng	5.00	7.50	12.50	20.00

Rev: As above but with numeral 10 at top in Chinese.

C#	Date	Emperor	Good	VG	Fine	VF
4-9	(1851-61)	Hsien Feng	15.00	25.00	40.00	60.00

Rev: Manchu mintmark left and Chinese mintmark right. Denomination at bottom.

C#	Date	Emperor	Good	VG	Fine	VF
4-11	(1851-61)	Hsien Feng	20.00	35.00	60.00	90.00
4-18	(1862-74)	T'ung Chih	—	—	Rare	—

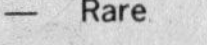

C#	Date	Emperor	Good	VG	Fine	VF
4-20	(1875-1908)	Kuang Hsu	—	—	Rare	—

20 CASH

CAST BRASS
Rev: Similar to 10 Cash, C#4-4.

C#	Date	Emperor	Good	VG	Fine	VF
4-5	(1851-61)	Hsien Feng	20.00	35.00	60.00	90.00

Rev: Similar to 10 Cash, C#4-11.

C#	Date	Emperor	Good	VG	Fine	VF
4-12	(1851-61)	Hsien Feng	20.00	35.00	60.00	90.00

30 CASH

CAST BRASS
Rev: Similar to 10 Cash, C#4-4.

C#	Date	Emperor	Good	VG	Fine	VF
4-6	(1851-61)	Hsien Feng	35.00	65.00	110.00	165.00

Rev: Similar to 10 Cash, C#4-11.

C#	Date	Emperor	Good	VG	Fine	VF
4-13	(1851-61)	Hsien Feng	35.00	65.00	110.00	165.00

40 CASH

CAST BRASS
Rev: Similar to 10 Cash, C#4-4.

C#	Date	Emperor	Good	VG	Fine	VF
4-7	(1851-61)	Hsien Feng	35.00	65.00	110.00	165.00

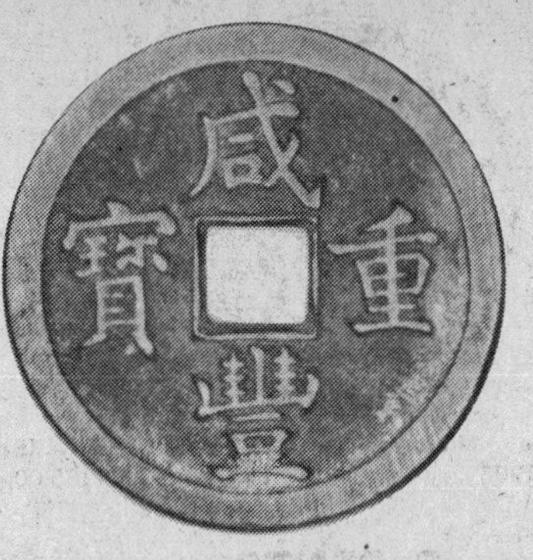

Rev: Similar to 10 Cash, C#4-11.

C#	Date	Emperor	Good	VG	Fine	VF
4-14	(1851-61)	Hsien Feng	35.00	65.00	110.00	165.00

50 CASH

CAST BRASS
Rev: Similar to 10 Cash, C#4-4.

C#	Date	Emperor	Good	VG	Fine	VF
4-8	(1851-61)	Hsien Feng	25.00	40.00	65.00	90.00

Rev: Similar to 10 Cash, C#4-11.

C#	Date	Emperor	Good	VG	Fine	VF
4-15	(1851-61)	Hsien Feng	25.00	40.00	65.00	90.00

100 CASH

CAST BRASS
Rev: Similar to 10 Cash, C#4-11.

C#	Date	Emperor	Good	VG	Fine	VF
4-16	(1851-61)	Hsien Feng	25.00	40.00	65.00	90.00

FANTASY ISSUES

NOTE: Coins of this mint in denominations of 400 Cash are considered fantasy issues.

STRUCK COINAGE

CASH

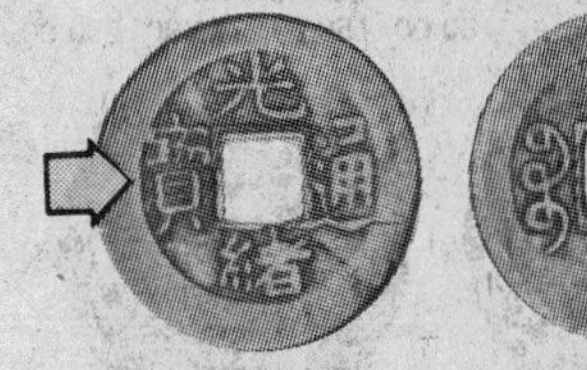

BRASS, struck
Obv: Large character at left.

Su#	Date	Mintage	VG	Fine	VF	XF
151	ND(1897-8)	—	18.50	30.00	40.00	60.00

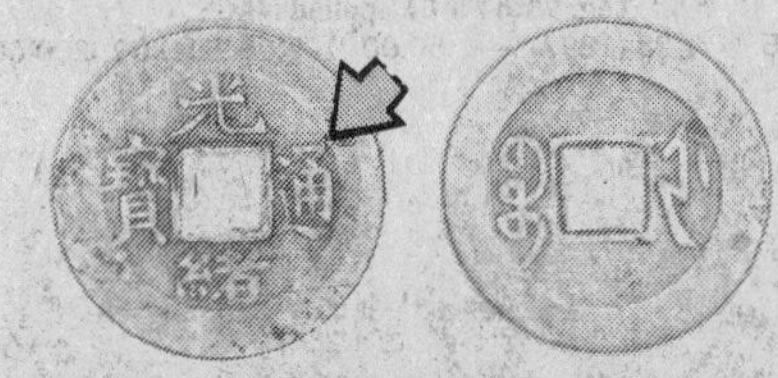

Obv: Top part of right character shaped like a triangle.

Su#	Date	Mintage	VG	Fine	VF	XF
151.1	ND(1897-8)	—	16.50	27.50	35.00	50.00

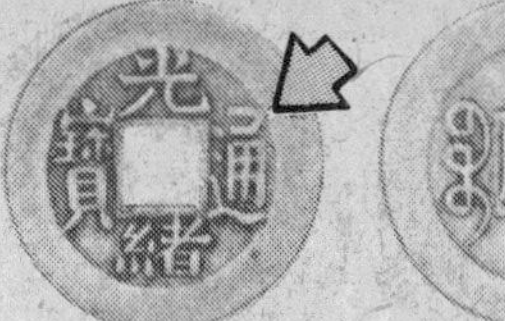

Obv: Top part of right character shaped like a box.

Su#	Date	Mintage	VG	Fine	VF	XF
151.2	ND(1897-8)	—	16.50	27.50	35.00	50.00

2 CASH

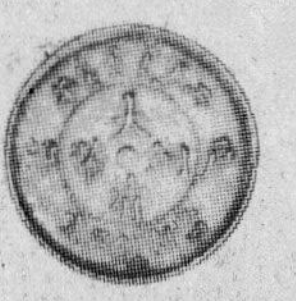

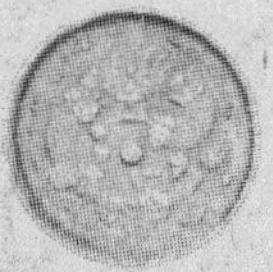

COPPER

Y#	Date	Mintage	VG	Fine	VF	XF
8b	CD1906	—	6.50	13.50	22.50	40.00

5 CASH

COPPER

Y#	Date	Mintage	VG	Fine	VF	XF
9b	CD1906	—	4.50	8.50	13.50	25.00

10 CASH

COPPER
Obv: With ball in circle in center.

Y#	Date	Mintage	VG	Fine	VF	XF
49	(1903-06)	—	.40	1.00	2.00	3.00

Obv: With rosette at center and large Manchu character at left.

Y#	Date	Mintage	VG	Fine	VF	XF
49.1	(1903-06)	—	.20	.50	1.00	2.00

BRASS

Y#	Date	Mintage	VG	Fine	VF	XF
49.1a	(1903-06)	—	1.40	3.50	6.00	10.00

Similar to Y#49.1a

Y#	Date	Mintage	VG	Fine	VF	XF
49.2	(1903-06)	—	.75	2.00	3.00	5.00

COPPER
Obv: Rosette at center and small Manchu character at left. Rev: Small cramped dragon with few clouds around body.

Y#	Date	Mintage	VG	Fine	VF	XF
49.3	(1903-06)	—	1.00	2.00	3.00	5.00

Rev: Without ball at center of circle.

Y#	Date	Mintage	VG	Fine	VF	XF
49.4	(1903-06)	—	1.25	3.00	5.00	8.50

BRASS
Obv: Four characters at bottom.

49a	(1903-06)	—	2.00	5.00	9.00	15.00

COPPER

49b	(1903-06)	—	6.00	15.00	20.00	30.00

Rev. legend: KIIO

10b	CD1906	—	.60	1.50	3.00	5.50

Rev. legend: KUO

10b.1	CD1906	—	2.00	5.00	10.00	20.00

NOTE: Chekiang and other 10 Cash designs struck over Korean 5 Fun coins are counterfeits.

20 CASH

COPPER

50	(1903-04)	—	75.00	110.00	150.00	200.00

NOTE: Exists in two different size planchets.

Y#	Date	Mintage	VG	Fine	VF	XF
11b	CD1906	—	35.00	65.00	90.00	135.00

5 CENTS

SILVER, 1.35 gm.
Rev. leg: CHEH-KIANG

Y#	Date	Mintage	Fine	VF	XF	Unc
51	(1898-99)	—	12.50	22.50	40.00	75.00

10 CENTS

SILVER, 2.7 gm.
Rev. leg: CHEH-KIANG

52	Yr.22 (1896)	—	50.00	80.00	125.00	200.00

Rev. leg: N's backwards.

52.1	Yr.22 (1896)	—	60.00	90.00	150.00	250.00

Rev: Denomination reads 2.7 instead of 7.2.

52.2	Yr.22 (1896)	—	50.00	80.00	125.00	200.00
52.3	Yr.23 (1897)	—	65.00	110.00	175.00	250.00

52.4	(1898-99)	—	10.00	20.00	40.00	70.00

20 CENTS

SILVER, 5.4 gm.
Six rows of scales on dragon.

53	Yr.22 (1896)	—	60.00	150.00	200.00	250.00

Rev. leg: Has letter E backwards in CHEH-KIANG.

53.1	Yr.22 (1896)	—	60.00	150.00	200.00	250.00

Rev. leg: Has additional cross-strokes in letter H IN CHEH-KIANG. Eight rows of scales on dragon.

53.2	Yr.22 (1896)	—	60.00	150.00	200.00	250.00

Rev. leg: Without hyphen in CHEH KIANG.

53.3	Yr.22 (1896)	—	60.00	150.00	200.00	250.00

Rev. leg: With dot in CHEH.KIANG.

53.4	Yr.22 (1896)	—	60.00	150.00	200.00	250.00

Rev: Rosettes made of seven dots dividing legends.

53.5	Yr.23 (1897)	—	50.00	125.00	150.00	200.00

Rev: Rosettes replaced by a cross;
Leg: With MACE spelled NACE.

53.6	Yr.23 (1897)	—	50.00	125.00	150.00	200.00

Rev. leg: CHEH-KIANG

Y#	Date	Mintage	Fine	VF	XF	Unc
53.7	(1898-99)	—	10.00	18.50	30.00	60.00

50 CENTS

SILVER, 13.5 gm.
Rev. leg: CHEH-KIANG

54	(1898-99)	—	100.00	200.00	450.00	600.00

REPUBLIC

10 CENTS

SILVER, 2.65 gm.

371	Yr.13 (1924)	4.464	5.00	10.00	20.00	40.00

20 CENTS

SILVER, 5.3 gm.
Rev: With large 20

373	Yr.13 (1924)	—	250.00	400.00	550.00	750.00

NCLT ISSUES

PATTERNS

KM#	Date	Mintage	Identification	Mkt.Val.
1	Yr.23 (1897)	—	5 Cents, Brass	—
2	(1897)	—	1 Dollar, Silver	—

KM#	Date	Mintage	Identification	Mkt.Val.
3	(1898-99)	—	1 Dollar, Silver, Cheh-Kiang, Y55	4000.

NOTE: This Dollar pattern has been found circulated and with chop marks.

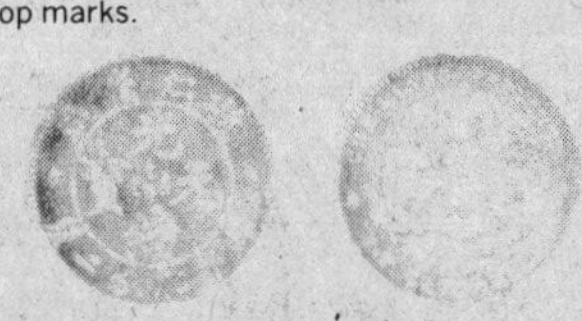

KM#	Date	Mintage	Identification	Mkt.Val.
5	(1902)	—	5 Cents, Silver, Che-Kiang, K123-I	—

KM#	Date	Mintage	Identification	Mkt.Val.
6	(1902)	—	10 Cents, Silver, Che-Kiang, K122-I	—
7	(1902)	—	20 Cents, Silver, Che-Kiang, K121-I	—
8	(1902)	—	50 Cents, Silver, Che-Kiang, K120-I	—

KM#	Date	Mintage	Identification	Mkt.Val.
9	(1902)	—	1 Dollar, Silver, Che-Kiang, K119-I	5000.

KM#	Date	Mintage	Identification	Mkt.Val.
10	(1903-06)	—	10 Cash, Copper, Y49	150.00
11	Yr.13 (1924)	—	20 Cents, Silver, Y372	750.00

CHIHLI PROVINCE

A province located in northeastern China. The eastern end of the Great Wall. An important producer of coal and some iron ore. In 1928 the provincial name was changed from Chihli to Hopei. The Paoting mint was established in 1745 and only produced cast cash coins. Mint for struck coinage was established in the arsenal at Tientsin in 1896. A larger mint was built in 1901 and started production in 1904. It burned down during the revolution (1912) and was later rebuilt in 1914.

EMPIRE

Included here are coins inscribed PEI YANG. These were produced by a mint in the Peiyang Arsenal in Tientsin. For coins inscribed PEKING, see general issues.

Paoting Mint

CASH

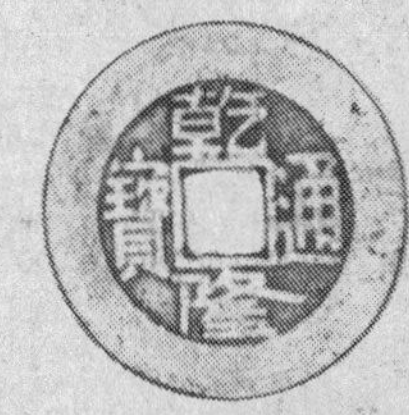

CAST BRASS

C#	Date	Emperor	Good	VG	Fine	VF
5-1	(1736-95)	Ch'ien Lung	.15	.35	.50	.75
		Rev: Dot above				
5-1.1	(1736-95)	Ch'ien Lung	1.60	4.00	5.00	8.00
5-2	(1796-1820)	Chia Ch'ing	.20	.50	.75	1.00
5-3	(1820-51)	Tao Kuang	.20	.50	.75	1.00
		Rev: Dot below				
5-3.1	(1820-51)	Tao Kuang	1.60	4.00	5.00	8.00
5-4	(1851-61)	Hsien Feng	1.60	4.00	5.00	8.00
		CAST IRON				
5-4a	(1851-61)	Hsien Feng	7.50	15.00	25.00	40.00
		CAST BRASS				
5-8	(1862-74)	T'ung Chih	2.00	5.00	7.00	10.00
5-10	(1875-1908)	Kuang Hsu	2.00	4.00	7.00	10.00
		Rev: Dot above.				
5-10.1	(1875-1908)	Kuang Hsu	3.00	6.00	9.00	13.00
		Rev: Crescent above.				
5-10.2	(1875-1908)	Kuang Hsu	4.00	7.00	10.00	15.00

NOTE: The crescent is known in various positions above the center hole.

C#	Date	Emperor	Good	VG	Fine	VF
		Rev: Circle above.				
5-10.3	(1875-1908)	Kuang Hsu	4.00	7.00	10.00	15.00
		Rev: Dot below.				
5-10.4	(1875-1908)	Kuang Hsu	3.00	6.00	9.00	13.00
		Rev: Circle below.				
5-10.5	(1875-1908)	Kuang Hsu	4.00	7.00	10.00	15.00
		Rev: Dash above.				
5-10.6	(1875-1908)	Kuang Hsu	4.00	7.00	10.00	15.00
		Rev: Dash below.				
5-10.7	(1875-1908)	Kuang Hsu	4.00	7.00	10.00	15.00

10 CASH

CAST BRASS

C#	Date	Emperor	Good	VG	Fine	VF
5-5	(1851-61)	Hsien Feng	10.00	15.00	25.00	35.00
		CAST IRON				
5-5a	(1851-61)	Hsien Feng	—	—	Rare	—
		CAST BRASS				
		Rev: Dot above.				
5-5.1	(1851-61)	Hsien Feng	11.50	16.50	27.50	38.50
5-9	(1862-74)	T'ung Chih	—	—	Rare	—
5-11	(1875-1908)	Kwang Hsu	—	—	Rare	—

50 CASH

CAST BRASS

C#	Date	Emperor	Good	VG	Fine	VF
5-6	(1851-61)	Hsien Feng	15.00	25.00	35.00	45.00
		Rev: Dot to upper right; crescent upper left.				
5.6.1	(1851-61)	Hsien Feng	17.50	27.50	37.50	55.00

100 CASH

CAST BRASS

C#	Date	Emperor	Good	VG	Fine	VF
5-7	(1851-61)	Hsien Feng	17.50	27.50	37.50	55.00

Chichow Mint

5 CASH

CAST BRASS

C#	Date	Emperor	Good	VG	Fine	VF
7-1	(1851-61)	Hsien Feng	17.50	27.50	37.50	55.00
		CAST IRON				
7-1a	(1851-61)	Hsien Feng	25.00	40.00	65.00	100.00

10 CASH

CAST BRASS

C#	Date	Emperor	Good	VG	Fine	VF
		Large size, 35mm.				
7-2	(1851-61)	Hsien Feng	17.50	27.50	37.50	55.00
		Small size, 27mm.				
7-2.1	(1851-61)	Hsien Feng	17.50	27.50	37.50	55.00
		CAST IRON				
7-2a	(1851-61)	Hsien Feng	25.00	40.00	65.00	100.00

50 CASH

CAST BRASS

C#	Date	Emperor	Good	VG	Fine	VF
7-3	(1851-61)	Hsien Feng	25.00	40.00	60.00	90.00

100 CASH

CAST BRASS

C#	Date	Emperor	Good	VG	Fine	VF
7-4	(1851-61)	Hsien Feng	25.00	40.00	65.00	100.00

NOTE: This mintmark was later transferred to the Kirin Mint; the Chichow Mint operated only during the reign of Hsien Feng.

Changte Mint

(Refer to Hunan Province)

Peiyang Mint
(Tientsin)

CASH

CAST BRASS

C#	Date	Emperor	Good	VG	Fine	VF
8-1	(1875-1908)					
		Kuang Hsu	2.00	3.50	5.00	7.00
		Rev: Dot above.				
8-1.1	(1875-1908)					
		Kuang Hsu	2.50	4.00	5.50	8.00
		Rev: Dot below.				
8-1.2	(1875-1908)					
		Kuang Hsu	2.50	4.00	5.50	8.00
		Rev: Two dots below.				
8-1.3	(1875-1908)					
		Kuang Hsu	3.00	5.00	7.00	10.00
		Rev: Circle above.				
8-1.4	(1875-1908)					
		Kuang Hsu	3.00	5.00	7.00	10.00

C#	Date	Emperor	Good	VG	Fine	VF
		Rev: Circle below.				
8-1.5	(1875-1908)					
		Kuang Hsu	3.00	5.00	7.00	10.00

C#	Date	Emperor	Good	VG	Fine	VF
		Rev: Crescent above.				
8-1.6	(1875-1908)					
		Kuang Hsu	3.00	5.00	7.00	10.00

C#	Date	Emperor	Good	VG	Fine	VF
		Rev: Crescent below.				
8-1.7	(1875-1908)					
		Kuang Hsu	3.00	5.00	7.00	10.00

C#	Date	Emperor	Good	VG	Fine	VF
		Rev: Dash below.				
8-1.8	(1875-1908)					
		Kuang Hsu	3.00	5.00	7.00	10.00

NOTE: 4 other varieties exist, each with dot in a different corner on reverse.

STRUCK COINAGE

CASH

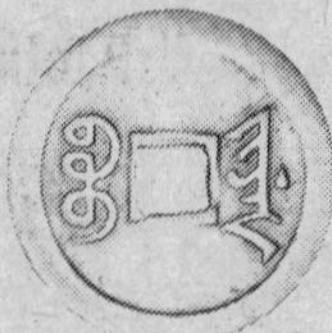

BRASS, struck

Su#	Date	Mintage	VG	Fine	VF	XF
410	(1888-89)	—	20.00	35.00	60.00	100.00

NOTE: Four varieties are known.

Y#	Date	Mintage	VG	Fine	VF	XF
66	ND	—	1.50	3.00	4.50	7.50

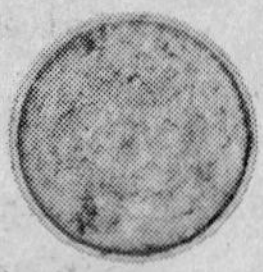

Y#	Date	Mintage	VG	Fine	VF	XF
7c	CD1908	—	2.50	4.50	7.50	12.50

5 CASH

COPPER

Y#	Date	Mintage	VG	Fine	VF	XF
9c	CD1906	—	4.50	8.50	13.50	22.50

10 CASH

COPPER

Y#	Date	Mintage	VG	Fine	VF	XF
		Rev: Hole in center of rosettes. Square mouth dragon.				
67	ND	—	.50	1.00	1.75	3.00
		Rev: Round mouth dragon.				
67.1	ND	—	.50	1.00	1.75	3.00

Y#	Date	Mintage	VG	Fine	VF	XF
		Rev: Dot in center of rosettes. Square mouth dragon.				
67.2	ND	—	.50	1.00	1.75	3.00
		Rev: Round mouth dragon.				
67.3	ND	—	.50	1.00	1.75	3.00

Rev: Redesigned dragon with smaller body and smaller English legends.

Y#	Date	Mintage	VG	Fine	VF	XF
67.4	ND	—	1.50	3.50	7.00	13.00
		BRASS				
67.4a	ND	—	2.00	4.50	9.00	15.00

COPPER

Y#	Date	Mintage	VG	Fine	VF	XF
10c	CD1906	—	.40	1.00	2.00	4.00

20 CASH

Y#	Date	Mintage	VG	Fine	VF	XF
		COPPER				
68	ND	—	6.00	15.00	25.00	40.00
		BRASS				
68a	ND	—	8.00	20.00	32.50	55.00
		COPPER Rev: Smaller lettering.				
68.1	ND	—	8.00	20.00	32.50	55.00

Y#	Date	Mintage	VG	Fine	VF	XF
11c	CD1906	—	12.50	30.00	45.00	75.00

5 CENTS

SILVER, 1.3200 gm.

Y#	Date	Mintage	Fine	VF	XF	Unc
61	Yr.22 (1896)	7,000	17.50	45.00	80.00	175.00
	Yr.23 (1897)	Inc. Ab.	7.00	17.50	35.00	65.00

Rev: Redesigned dragon.

Y#	Date	Mintage	Fine	VF	XF	Unc
61.1	Yr.23 (1897)	.039	10.00	20.00	40.00	80.00
	Yr.24 (1898)	.231	7.50	15.00	30.00	60.00

Y#	Date	Mintage	Fine	VF	XF	Unc
69	Yr.25 (1899)	.097	10.00	20.00	40.00	80.00
	Yr.26 (1900)	—	80.00	200.00	300.00	600.00

10 CENTS

SILVER, 2.6500 gm.

Y#	Date	Mintage	Fine	VF	XF	Unc
62	Yr.22 (1896)	5,000	16.50	40.00	60.00	100.00
	Yr.23 (1897)	.148	10.00	20.00	30.00	60.00
	Yr.24 (1898)	.614	9.00	13.50	25.00	50.00
70	Yr.25 (1899)	.153	10.00	20.00	30.00	60.00
	Yr.26 (1900)	—	— Reported, Not Confirmed			

20 CENTS

SILVER, 5.3000 gm.

Y#	Date	Mintage	Fine	VF	XF	Unc
63	Yr.22 (1896)	.012	100.00	200.00	400.00	600.00
	Yr.23 (1897)	.147	10.00	20.00	35.00	70.00
	Yr.24 (1898)	.350	10.00	20.00	35.00	70.00

Y#	Date	Mintage	Fine	VF	XF	Unc
71	Yr.25 (1899)	.152	15.00	25.00	37.50	75.00
	Yr.26 (1900)	—	—	600.00	750.00	900.00

Y#	Date	Mintage	Fine	VF	XF	Unc
71a	Yr.31 (1905)	.161	45.00	80.00	120.00	160.00

50 CENTS

SILVER, 13.3000 gm.

Y#	Date	Mintage	Fine	VF	XF	Unc
64	Yr.22 (1896)	2,500	500.00	800.00	1175.	1375.
	Yr.23 (1897)	.021	20.00	35.00	55.00	125.00
	Yr.24 (1898)	I.A.	18.50	30.00	50.00	125.00

Rev: Redesigned dragon.

Y#	Date	Mintage	Fine	VF	XF	Unc
64.1	Yr.24 (1898)	.176	17.50	27.50	45.00	100.00

Y#	Date	Mintage	Fine	VF	XF	Unc
72	Yr.25 (1899)	.056	20.00	60.00	150.00	400.00

DOLLAR

.900 SILVER, 26.7 gm.

Y#	Date	Mintage	Fine	VF	XF	Unc
65	Yr.22 (1896)	3,000	1000.	1500.	2200.	4000.
	Yr.23 (1897)	1.120	50.00	80.00	115.00	150.00

Rev: Redesigned dragon.

Y#	Date	Mintage	Fine	VF	XF	Unc
65.1	Yr.24 (1898)	2.806	82.50	150.00	200.00	275.00

Obv: Similar to Y#73.1.

Y#	Date	Mintage	Fine	VF	XF	Unc
73	Yr.25 (1899)	1.566	BV	BV	40.00	100.00
	Yr.26 (1900)	—	BV	BV	50.00	150.00
	Yr.29 (1903)	22.018	BV	BV	32.50	65.00

Rev: Thinner dragon.

Y#	Date	Mintage	Fine	VF	XF	Unc
73.1	Yr.33 (1907)	—	BV	BV	32.50	65.00
	Yr.34 (1908)	—	BV	BV	30.00	55.00

NOTE: The 1907 issue has the year as '33th'. The 34th year (1908) issue was restruck during Republican times.

TAEL SYSTEM

TAEL

SILVER

Y#	Date	Mintage	Fine	VF	XF	Unc
74	Yr.33 (1907)	—	—	—	4000.	4500.

CHINGKIANG

For coins of CHINGKIANG refer to listings under KIANGSU.

FENGTIEN AND/ MANCHURIAN PROVINCES

Since the 17th century, Manchuria has been divided into three provinces. The two northern provinces were called Heilungkiang and Kirin. The southernmost province was known by a variety of names including Fengtien, Shengching, and Liaoning. Together the three provinces of Manchuria were known as the Manchurian Provinces in English or the Three Eastern Provinces in Chinese.

EMPIRE

CASH

CAST BRASS
Mintmark similar to Su#456.1 in Pattern listing.

C#	Date	Emperor	Good	VG	Fine	VF
9-1	(1875-1908) Kuang-Hsu		—	—	Rare	—

STRUCK COINAGE

5 CASH

COPPER

Y#	Date	Mintage	VG	Fine	VF	XF
19e	CD1909	—	32.50	75.00	100.00	135.00

10 CASH

COPPER

Y#	Date	Mintage	VG	Fine	VF	XF
W250a	ND	—	—	—	Rare	—

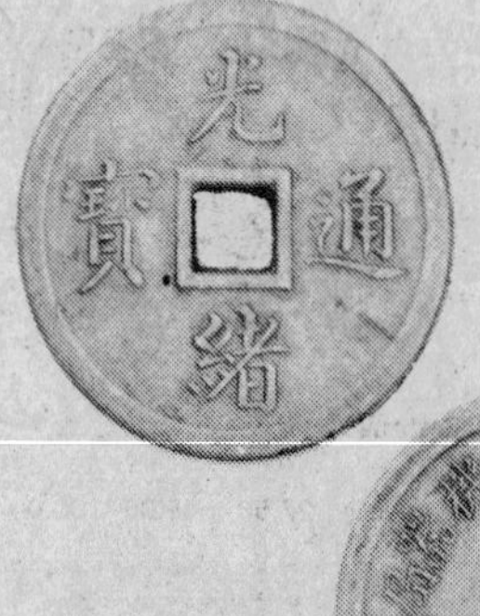

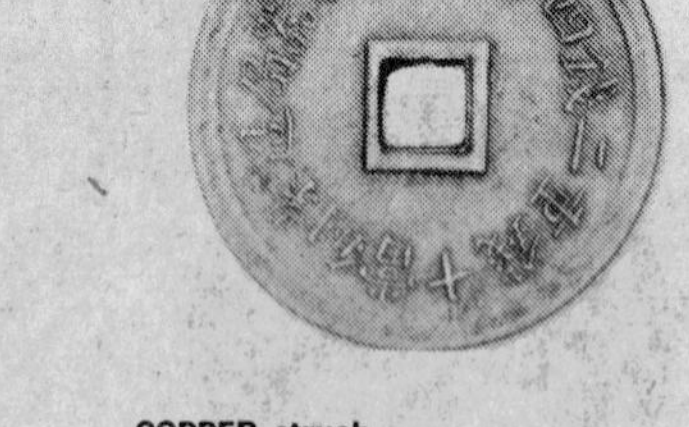

COPPER, struck

Y#	Date	Mintage	VG	Fine	VF	XF
81	ND	—	25.00	40.00	65.00	90.00

NOTE: Several varieties exist.

BRASS
Province spelled FEN-TIEN.

Y#	Date	Mintage	VG	Fine	VF	XF
88	CD1903	—	30.00	75.00	125.00	175.00

Province spelled FUNG-TIEN.

Y#	Date	Mintage	VG	Fine	VF	XF
89	CD1903	—	3.00	7.50	15.00	25.00
	CD1904	—	1.50	2.50	4.50	8.00
	CD1905	—	1.25	2.50	4.50	8.00
	CD1906	35.036	2.50	5.00	10.00	20.00

Y#	Date	Mintage	VG	Fine	VF	XF
	Obv: Manchu characters in center reversed.					
89.1	CD1903	—	4.00	10.00	15.00	30.00
	COPPER					
89a	CD1904	—	—	—	Rare	—
	CD1905	—	—	—	Rare	—
	BRASS					
	Rev: Large pearl.					
89.2	CD1905	—	.70	1.75	3.00	6.00

Y#	Date	Mintage	VG	Fine	VF	XF
	COPPER					
	Rev: Small pearl.					
10e	CD1905	—	1.20	3.00	7.00	12.50
	Rev: Large pearl.					
10e.1	CD1905	—	1.20	3.00	7.00	12.50

Obv: Mintmark on spherical disc in center.

Y#	Date	Mintage	VG	Fine	VF	XF
10e.2	CD1907	130.000	.60	1.50	2.50	5.00

Obv: Mintmark on flat disc in center.

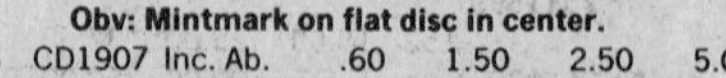

Y#	Date	Mintage	VG	Fine	VF	XF
10e.3	CD1907	Inc. Ab.	.60	1.50	2.50	5.00

Y#	Date	Mintage	VG	Fine	VF	XF
20e	CD1909	—	2.00	5.00	10.00	15.00

20 CASH

COPPER

Y#	Date	Mintage	VG	Fine	VF	XF
90	CD1903	—	25.00	45.00	70.00	100.00

BRASS

Y#	Date	Mintage	VG	Fine	VF	XF
90a	CD1903	—	25.00	40.00	60.00	90.00
	CD1904	—	7.50	12.50	17.50	30.00
	CD1905	—	7.00	11.00	15.00	25.00

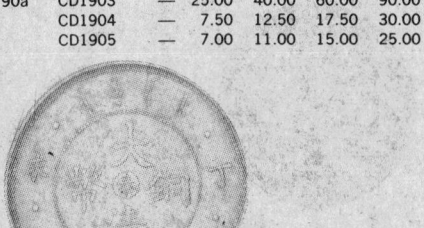

COPPER

Y#	Date	Mintage	VG	Fine	VF	XF
11e	CD1905	—	7.00	11.00	15.00	27.50
	CD1907	—	8.00	12.50	20.00	35.00

Y#	Date	Mintage	VG	Fine	VF	XF
21e	CD1909	—	20.00	50.00	75.00	125.00

5 CENTS

SILVER, 1.2000 gm.

Y#	Date	Mintage	Fine	VF	XF	Unc
83	Yr.25 (1899)	—	8.00	20.00	50.00	100.00

10 CENTS

SILVER

Y#	Date	Mintage	Fine	VF	XF	Unc
84	Yr.24 (1898)	—	12.50	22.50	40.00	80.00

Y#	Date	Mintage	Fine	VF	XF	Unc
209	Yr.33 (1907)	1.079	10.00	18.50	37.50	75.00

20 CENTS

SILVER, 2.6000 gm.
Rev: 4 rows of scales on dragon.
Clockwise spiral on pearl.

Y#	Date	Mintage	Fine	VF	XF	Unc
85	Yr.24 (1898)	—	7.50	18.50	37.50	85.00

Rev: 5 rows of scales on dragon.
Counter-clockwise spiral on pearl.

Y#	Date	Mintage	Fine	VF	XF	Unc
85.1	Yr.24 (1898)	—	7.50	18.50	37.50	85.00

24mm, 8 rows of scales on dragon.

Y#	Date	Mintage	Fine	VF	XF	Unc
91	CD1904	—	6.50	12.50	25.00	50.00

25mm, 5 rows of scales on dragon.

Y#	Date	Mintage	Fine	VF	XF	Unc
91.1	CD1904	—	7.50	15.00	30.00	60.00

Obv: One rosette at either side.

Y#	Date	Mintage	Fine	VF	XF	Unc
210	Yr.33 (1907)	—	5.00	10.00	20.00	40.00

Obv: Three rosettes at either side.

Y#	Date	Mintage	Fine	VF	XF	Unc
210.1	Yr.33 (1907)	—	7.50	15.00	30.00	60.00

Obv: Dots replace rosettes.

Y#	Date	Mintage	Fine	VF	XF	Unc
210.2	Yr.33 (1907)	—	12.50	25.00	50.00	100.00

Hsuan T'ung
Obv: Two small stars flanking one large star at either side.
Rev: Date given as FIRST YEAR.

Y#	Date	Mintage	Fine	VF	XF	Unc
213	Yr.1 (1909)	249.219	3.50	6.50	12.50	20.00

Obv: One small star at sides.

Y#	Date	Mintage	Fine	VF	XF	Unc
213.1	Yr.1 (1909)	I. A.	3.75	7.50	15.00	30.00

Obv: One large six-pointed rosette at either side.
Rev: Date as 1ST YEAR.

Y#	Date	Mintage	Fine	VF	XF	Unc
213.2	(1909)	Inc. Ab.	3.50	6.50	13.50	26.50

Obv: Manchu characters at center.

Y#	Date	Mintage	Fine	VF	XF	Unc
213a	(1910)	Inc. Ab.	3.50	6.50	13.50	26.50

Obv: Five-petalled rosette in center with dot in center of rosette. Dot under side rosettes.

Y#	Date	Mintage	Fine	VF	XF	Unc
213a.1	(1914)	Inc. Ab.	3.50	6.50	13.50	26.50

Obv: No dot under side rosettes.

Y#	Date	Mintage	Fine	VF	XF	Unc
213a.2	(1914)	Inc. Ab.	3.50	6.50	13.50	26.50

As above, but no dot in center of 5-petalled rosette.

Y#	Date	Mintage	Fine	VF	XF	Unc
213a.3	(1914)	Inc. Ab.	3.50	6.50	13.50	26.50

Obv: No rosette in center.
Rev: Few clouds around dragon.

Y#	Date	Mintage	Fine	VF	XF	Unc
213a.4	(1912)	Inc. Ab.	3.75	7.50	15.00	30.00

Provinces spelled PROVIENCES.

Y#	Date	Mintage	Fine	VF	XF	Unc
213a.5	(1912)	Inc. Ab.	3.75	7.50	15.00	30.00

Head of dragon redesigned. Heavier clouds around dragon. Rosettes to sides of dragon elongated.

Y#	Date	Mintage	Fine	VF	XF	Unc
213a.6	(1912)	Inc. Ab.	3.75	7.50	15.00	30.00

NOTE: These 20 Cent pieces (Y213 and Y231a) are relatively common in higher grades. Y213a.1-213a.3 were struck in 1914. Y213a.4-213a.6 were struck during 1912 and 1913.

50 CENTS

SILVER, 13.1000 gm.

Y#	Date	Mintage	Fine	VF	XF	Unc
86	(1898)	—	85.00	150.00	250.00	400.00
	(1899)	—	275.00	400.00	600.00	900.00
	(1906)	—	80.00	200.00	350.00	600.00

NOTE: (Error) date should read 23rd year (1897).

Y#	Date	Mintage	Fine	VF	XF	Unc
211	(1907)	—	60.00	150.00	210.00	300.00

ONE DOLLAR

Obv: Double circle around two center Chinese characters.

Y#	Date	Mintage	Fine	VF	XF	Unc
87.1	Yr.25 (1899)	—	16.50	40.00	80.00	200.00

Y#	Date	Mintage	Fine	VF	XF	Unc
92	CD1903	.262	72.50	120.00	185.00	300.00

Obv: Manchu characters in center are reversed.

Y#	Date	Mintage	Fine	VF	XF	Unc
92.1	CD1903	Inc. Ab.	85.00	135.00	165.00	200.00

SILVER, 26.4000 gm.

Y#	Date	Mintage	Fine	VF	XF	Unc
87	Yr.24 (1898)	—	60.00	125.00	225.00	400.00
	Yr.25 (1899)	—	80.00	150.00	275.00	500.00
212	Yr.33 (1907)	—	100.00	175.00	250.00	350.00

REPUBLIC

CENT

COPPER

Y#	Date	Mintage	Fine	VF	XF	Unc
434	Yr.18 (1929)	—	.60	1.50	5.00	15.00

TOKEN ISSUES

DOLLAR

COPPER

Obv: Rev. of Y#10e. Small spiral on pearl.

Rev: Two Chinese characters meaning: worth a Dollar.

Y#	Date	Mintage	Fine	VF	XF	Unc
W242	ND	—	—	—	Rare	—

Large spiral on pearl.

Y#	Date	Mintage	Fine	VF	XF	Unc
W243	ND	—	—	—	Rare	—

NCLT ISSUES

PATTERNS

KM#	Date	Mintage	Identification	Mkt.Val.
1	ND	—	1 Cash, Copper, Fen 4 below hold, Su456.1	—
2	ND	—	1 Cash, Copper, w/o characters below hole, Su456.2	—
3	ND	—	20 Cents, Brass, regular provincial design	—
4	ND	—	20 Cents, Silver	—
5	ND	—	50 Cents, Brass, (error) TENG-TIEN	—
6	ND	—	1 Dollar, White Metal, regular provincial design	—

KM#	Date	Mintage	Identification	Mkt.Val.
7	CD1903	—	1 Tael, Silver, K931-I	4500.

FUKIEN PROVINCE

A province located on the southeastern coast of China. Important agricultural area, also forestry and some mining, particularly iron ore and coal. The Foochow Mint operated throughout the Manchu dynasty. For struck coinage a private mint was opened in 1901. This later became a government mint in 1904. Also in 1904 two more minting facilities were opened at arsenals in the area but later closed down because of an over abudance of copper coins. It reopened again in 1924 to strike silver coins. In 1924 a mint was put in operation at Amoy.

EMPIRE

Fuchow Mint

CASH

CAST BRASS

C#	Date	Emperor	Good	VG	Fine	VF
10-1	(1736-95)	Ch'ien Lung	.15	.35	.50	.75
10-2	(1796-1820)	Chia Ch'ing	.30	.75	1.25	2.00

NOTE: Varieties of mintmark known.

C#	Date	Emperor	Good	VG	Fine	VF
10-3	(1821-51)	Tao Kuang	1.00	2.50	4.00	6.00

Rev: Dot right of mintmark. 22-24mm.

C#	Date	Emperor	Good	VG	Fine	VF
10-4	(1851-61)	Hsien Feng	1.00	2.50	4.00	6.00

Rev: Line right of mintmark. 26mm.

C#	Date	Emperor	Good	VG	Fine	VF
10-4.1	(1851-61)	Hsien Feng	2.50	5.00	7.50	12.50

CAST IRON

C#	Date	Emperor	Good	VG	Fine	VF
10-4a	(1851-61)	Hsien Feng	10.00	20.00	30.00	40.00

CAST BRASS

C#	Date	Emperor	Good	VG	Fine	VF
10-22	(1862-74)	T'ung Chih	1.25	2.50	4.00	6.00
10-25	(1875-1908)	Kuang Hsu	1.00	2.00	3.00	4.50

Rev: Dot at top of hole.

C#	Date	Emperor	Good	VG	Fine	VF
10-25.1	(1875-1908)	Kuang Hsu	1.50	3.00	4.50	7.00

5 CASH

BRASS, 31mm

Rev: Weight on the rim similar to 20 Cash, C#10-12.

C#	Date	Emperor	Good	VG	Fine	VF
10-5	(1851-61)	Hsien Feng	20.00	35.00	55.00	75.00

10 CASH

CAST BRASS, 35-40mm.

Obv: Legend reads "Hsien Feng T'ung Pao."

C#	Date	Emperor	Good	VG	Fine	VF
10-6	(1851-61)	Hsien Feng	5.00	10.00	16.50	25.00

Rev: Characters 'Ta Ching' appear to upper left and right.

C#	Date	Emperor	Good	VG	Fine	VF
10-6.1	(1851-61)	Hsien Feng	—	—	Rare	—

Obv: Legend reads "Hsien Feng Chung Pao"

Rev: Similar to C#10-6.

C#	Date	Emperor	Good	VG	Fine	VF
10-7	(1851-61)	Hsien Feng	7.00	12.00	18.50	30.00

Obv: Similar to C#10-7.

C#	Date	Emperor	Good	VG	Fine	VF
10-8	(1851-61)	Hsien Feng	12.50	20.00	30.00	50.00

IRON

C#	Date	Emperor	Good	VG	Fine	VF
10-8a	(1851-61)	Hsien Feng	—	—	Rare	—

CAST BRASS

Obv: Similar to C#10-7.

C#	Date	Emperor	Good	VG	Fine	VF
10-9	(1851-61)	Hsien Feng	25.00	40.00	60.00	90.00

42mm

Rev: Four characters at top, four different characters at bottom. Mintmark (to right) has a crescent to right instead of a dot.

C#	Date	Emperor	Good	VG	Fine	VF
10-9.1	(1851-61)	Hsien Feng	—	—	Rare	—

35mm. Rev: Chinese mintmark at right, and Manchu mintmark at left.

C#	Date	Emperor	Good	VG	Fine	VF
10-9.2	(1851-61)	Hsien Feng	—	—	Rare	—
10-23	(1862-74)	T'ung Chih	—	—	Rare	—
10-26	(1875-1908)	Kuang Hsu	—	—	Rare	—

20 CASH

CAST BRASS, 45-46mm

C#	Date	Emperor	Good	VG	Fine	VF
10-10	(1851-61)	Hsien Feng	8.50	15.00	21.50	32.50

CAST IRON

C#	Date	Emperor	Good	VG	Fine	VF
10-10a	(1851-61)	Hsien Feng	Reported, not confirmed			

CAST BRASS, 44mm

Obv: Hsien Feng Chung Pao. Rev: Similar to C#10-10.

C#	Date	Emperor	Good	VG	Fine	VF
10-11	(1851-61)	Hsien Feng	10.00	18.50	27.50	40.00

Rev: With four characters appearing on rim.

C#	Date	Emperor	Good	VG	Fine	VF
10-12	(1851-61)	Hsien Feng	12.50	20.00	32.50	50.00

CAST IRON

10-12a	(1851-61)	Hsien Feng	Reported, not confirmed			

CAST COPPER, 46mm
Obv: Similar to C#10-11. Rev: Eight characters in the field.

10-13	(1851-61)	Hsien Feng	25.00	45.00	65.00	90.00

CAST IRON

10-13a	(1851-61)	Hsien Feng	Reported, not confirmed			

50 CASH

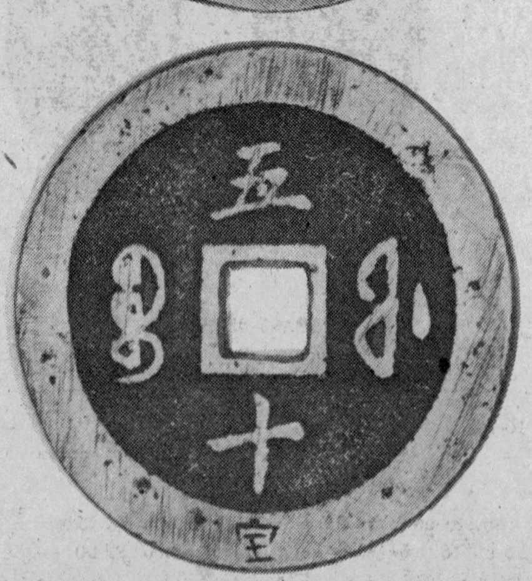

CAST COPPER, 55mm
Obv: Hsien Feng T'ung Pao. Rev: Four characters.

C#	Date	Emperor	Good	VG	Fine	VF
10-14	(1851-61)	Hsien Feng	12.50	20.00	30.00	45.00

65mm
Rev: Mintmark has a long vertical stroke to the right instead of a dot.

10-14.1	(1851-61)	Hsien Feng	—	—	Rare	—

Obv: Hsien Feng Chung Pao. Rev: Four characters.

10-15	(1851-61)	Hsien Feng	20.00	30.00	45.00	65.00

Obv: Similar to C#10-15. Rev: With four characters appearing on rim.

10-16	(1851-61)	Hsien Feng	20.00	35.00	50.00	75.00

Obv: Similar to C#10-15. Rev: Eight characters in the field.

10-17	(1851-61)	Hsien Feng	25.00	45.00	60.00	90.00

100 CASH

CAST COPPER, 70mm
Obv: Hsien Feng T'ung Pao. Rev: Four characters.

10-18	(1851-61)	Hsien Feng	16.50	25.00	35.00	60.00

74mm
Rev: Mintmark has long vertical stroke to right instead of dot.

10-18.1	(1851-61)	Hsien Feng	—	—	Rare	—

CAST ZINC
Obv: Hsien Feng T'ung Pao. Rev: Four characters.

10-18a	(1851-61)	Hsien Feng	—	—	Rare	—

NOTE: Composition of this coin is reportedly a mixture of zinc, lead and tin. The coin is blue-gray in color and has a large mintmark, written differently from any of the above.

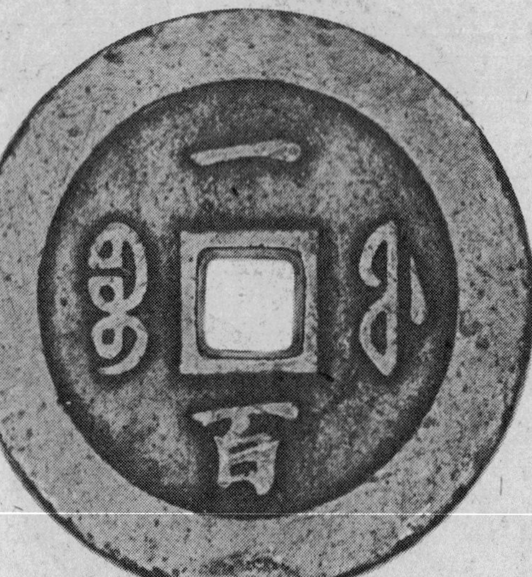

CAST COPPER
Obv: Hsien Feng Chung Pao. Rev: Four characters.

10-19	(1851-61)	Hsien Feng	17.50	27.50	37.50	60.00

72mm. Obv: Similar to C#10-19. Rev: With four characters appearing on rim and small characters in field.

10-20	(1851-61)	Hsien Feng	25.00	45.00	65.00	90.00

78mm
Obv: Similar to C#10-19. Rev: Larger characters in field.

10-20.1	(1851-61)	Hsien Feng	20.00	30.00	42.50	70.00

Obv: Hsien Feng Chung Pao.
Rev: Eight characters in the field.

10-21	(1851-61)	Hsien Feng	Reported, not confirmed			

FANTASY ISSUES

NOTE: 30, 40, 500 and 1000 Cash pieces are reported for this mint, but their existence is doubtful and would most likely be considered fantasies.

STRUCK COINAGE

CASH

BRASS

Y#	Date	Mintage	VG	Fine	VF	XF
95	ND	—	8.00	20.00	32.50	50.00

NOTE: Minted during Kuang Hsu reign 1875-1908.

Tai Ching Ti Kuo type, Su#259.

7f	CD1908	—	30.00	75.00	100.00	150.00

106	ND	—	17.50	40.00	65.00	80.00

NOTE: Minted during Hsuan T'ung reign 1909-1911.

2 CASH

BRASS

8f	CD1906	—	2.00	5.00	8.00	15.00

5 CASH

COPPER

99	(1901-03)	.590	5.00	10.00	15.00	22.50

BRASS

99a	(1901-03)	—	10.00	20.00	40.00	60.00

10 CASH

COPPER
Obv: Large characters to left and right.

97	(1901-05) 417.031		.60	1.50	2.50	5.00

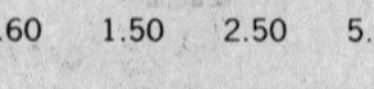

Obv: Small characters to left and right sides.

97.1	(1901-05)	I. A.	.80	2.00	4.00	7.00

Rev: FOO-KIEN CUSTOM.

Y#	Date	Mintage	VG	Fine	VF	XF
98	(1901-05)	I. A.	40.00	100.00	125.00	175.00

Rev: One cloud left of pearl.

100	(1901-05)	I. A.	.80	2.00	4.00	7.00

Rev: Three clouds left of pearl and without cloud above tip of dragons tail.

100.1	(1901-05)	I. A.	.80	2.00	4.00	7.00

Rev: Three clouds left of pearl and a cloud above tip of dragon's tail.

100.2	(1901-05)	I. A.	.40	1.00	2.00	4.00

Rev. denomination: 10 CASHES.

100.3	(1901-05)	I. A.	5.00	12.50	20.00	35.00

10f	CD1906	—	.30	.75	1.00	2.00

20f	CD1909	—	20.00	50.00	75.00	100.00

20 CASH

COPPER

Y#	Date	Mintage	VG	Fine	VF	XF
101	(1901-02)	.018	10.00	25.00	35.00	50.00

5 CENTS

SILVER, 1.3500 gm.
Obv: Five characters at top.

Y#	Date	Mintage	Fine	VF	XF	Unc
102	(1896-03)	—	BV	6.00	10.00	20.00

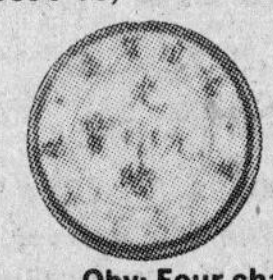
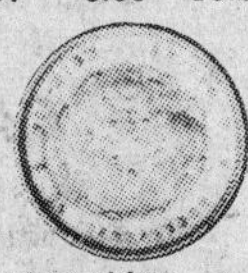

Obv: Four characters at top.
Rev: Rosette at either side of redesigned dragon.

102.1	(1898-03)	—	BV	5.00	8.00	15.00

Rev: Rosette above dragon.

102.2	(1898-03)	—	BV	10.00	18.50	30.00

10 CENTS

SILVER, 2.7000 gm.
Obv: Five characters at top.
Rev: Rosette at either side of dragon.

103	(1896-08) 13.425		4.00	8.00	15.00	30.00

Rev: Dot at either side of dragon.

103.1	(1896-08)	I.A.	7.50	15.00	25.00	50.00

Obv: Four characters at top.

103.2	(1898-08)	I.A.	BV	4.00	8.00	15.00

20 CENTS

SILVER, 5.4000 gm.

Obv: Five characters at top.
Rev: Dot at either side of dragon.

Y#	Date	Mintage	Fine	VF	XF	Unc
104	(1896-08)	31.772	BV	6.00	12.00	20.00

Rev: Rosette at either side of dragon.

104.1	(1898-08)	I.A.	BV	6.00	12.00	20.00

Obv: Four characters at top. Rev: Redesigned dragon.

104.2	(1898-08)	I.A.	BV	6.00	12.00	20.00

DOLLAR

SILVER, 25.7000 gm.
Obv: Four characters at top.

K#	Date	Mintage	VG	Fine	VF	XF
6	(ca.1844)	—	50.00	125.00	200.00	300.00

27.2000 gm.
Obv: Different flourish below legend.

5	(ca.1844)	—	350.00	550.00	750.00	900.00

26.2000 gm.
Obv: Two characters at top.
Two rosettes obv. and rev.

K#	Date	Mintage	VG	Fine	VF	XF
7	(ca.1844)	—	65.00	150.00	250.00	400.00

Four rosettes obv. and rev.

K#	Date	Mintage	VG	Fine	VF	XF
7c	(ca.1844)	—	65.00	150.00	250.00	400.00

Kann #5-7 above were issued by military authorities at the city of Chang Chow. Though Kann dates these pieces in the 1860's they were already circulating in the 1840's.

25.0000 gm.
Djia Ih Hsien Dzou

K#	Date	Mintage	VG	Fine	VF	XF
3	Yr.1 (1861)	—	1500.	2500.	3500.	4500.

NOTE: Prices for the dollar coins above are for specimens with a few light chops. For unchopped specimens, add 10 per cent and for heavily chopped specimens deduct 20 per cent.

27.0000 gm.

Y#	Date	Mintage	Fine	VF	XF	Unc
105	(ca.1899)	—	1250.	3000.	4000.	5000.

REPUBLIC

CASH

CAST BRASS
Rev: Five stripes on right flag.

Y#	Date	Mintage	Good	VG	Fine	VF
374	ND(c.1912)	—	60.00	150.00	300.00	400.00

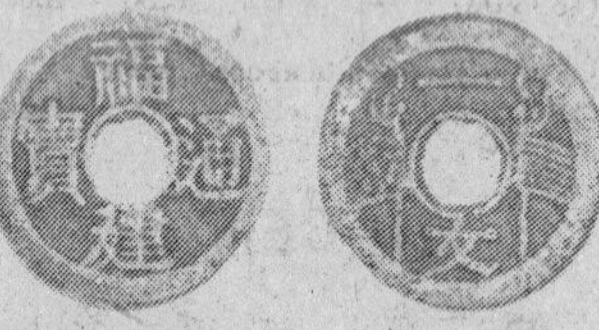

Rev: Six stripes on right flag.

Y#	Date	Mintage	Good	VG	Fine	VF
374.1	ND(c.1912)	—	60.00	150.00	300.00	400.00

2 CASH

CAST BRASS
Rev: Five stripes on right flag.

Y#	Date	Mintage	Good	VG	Fine	VF
375	ND(c.1912)	—	10.00	20.00	30.00	50.00

Rev: Six stripes on right flag, left flag redesigned.

Y#	Date	Mintage	Good	VG	Fine	VF
375.1	ND(c.1912)	—	20.00	35.00	50.00	80.00

STRUCK COINAGE

10 CASH

COPPER

Y#	Date	Mintage	Fine	VF	XF	Unc
379	ND(ca.1912)	—	2.50	6.00	10.00	20.00

10 CENTS

SILVER, 2.6000 gm.

Y#	Date	Mintage	Fine	VF	XF	Unc
380	ND(ca.1912)	—	10.00	25.00	35.00	50.00

Y#	Date	Mintage	Fine	VF	XF	Unc
382	ND(ca.1913)	—	BV	BV	7.00	15.00

Similar to Y#380. Obv: With different legend in center.

Y#	Date	Mintage	Fine	VF	XF	Unc
380a	CD1924	—	8.00	20.00	30.00	40.00

Canton Martyrs Commemorative

Y#	Date	Mintage	Fine	VF	XF	Unc
388	Yr.17 (1928)	—	6.00	15.00	25.00	45.00
	Yr.20 (1931)	—	8.00	20.00	30.00	55.00

Canton Martyrs Commemorative

Y#	Date	Mintage	Fine	VF	XF	Unc
390	Yr.21 (1932)	—	60.00	150.00	225.00	275.00

20 CENTS

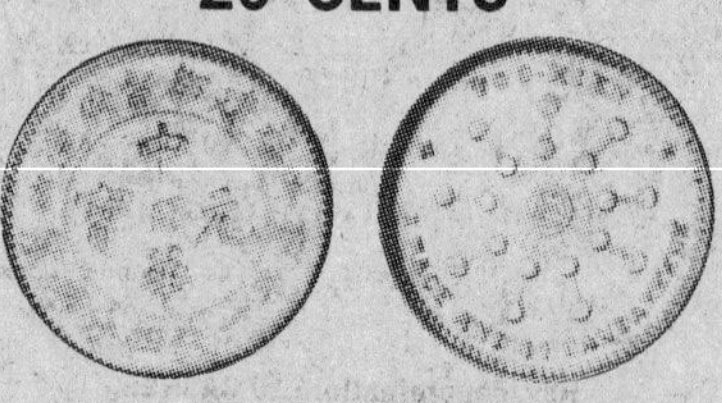

SILVER, 5.0000 gm.

Y#	Date	Mintage	Fine	VF	XF	Unc
377	CD1911	—	6.00	15.00	20.00	40.00

Y#	Date	Mintage	Fine	VF	XF	Unc
381	(1912)	—	BV	BV	10.00	20.00

Y#	Date	Mintage	Fine	VF	XF	Unc
383	ND	—	BV	BV	7.50	15.00

NOTE: Kann dates this coin 1913, but evidence suggests that it was struck in 1923.

Y#	Date	Mintage	Fine	VF	XF	Unc
383a	Yr.13 (1924)	—	30.00	40.00	60.00	80.00

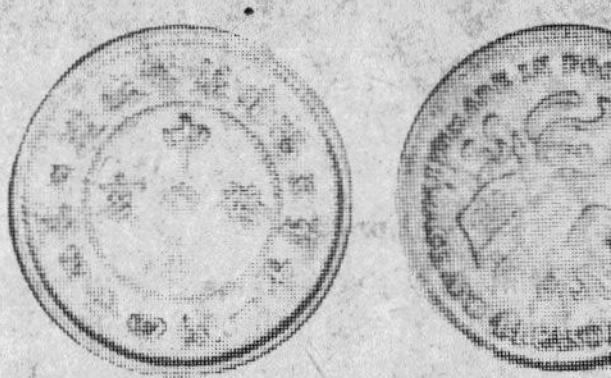

Obv. and rev: Rosettes at sides.
Obv: Dot in middle of rosette center.

381.1	CD1923	—	BV	8.50	13.50	20.00

Made spelled MAIE.

381.2	CD1923	—	BV	9.00	15.00	22.50

Rev. leg: MADEIN FOO-KIENMINT.

381.3	CD1923	—	BV	9.00	15.00	22.50

Obv: No dot in middle of center rosette, Five-pointed star at sides in place of rosette.

381.4	CD1923	—	10.00	15.00	25.00	40.00

Obv: Different legend in center.

381.5	CD1924	—	BV	10.00	15.00	22.50

Northern Expedition Commemorative

384	Yr.16 (1927)	—	200.00	275.00	400.00	600.00

Northern Expedition Commemorative

385	Yr.16 (1927)	—	250.00	325.00	450.00	650.00

Canton Martyrs Commemorative

389	Yr.17 (1928)	—	BV	11.50	22.50	32.50
	Yr.20 (1931)	—	BV	13.50	25.00	35.00

Canton Martyrs Commemorative

391	Yr.21 (1932)	—	90.00	150.00	200.00	300.00

HEILUNGKIANG PROVINCE

The northwestern-most of the former Three Eastern Provinces, bordering on Siberia. Though very large in extent, it is only sparsely populated, for wide areas are desert land. Economically the district was always backward. Heilungkiang Province had no mint of its own, and seemingly no silver money bearing its name was ever placed in circulation. During the beginning of the 20th century it was suggested to order silver coins with the province's name for circulation there. At present only a brass pattern is known.

NCLT ISSUES

PATTERNS

KM#	Date	Mintage	Identification	Mkt.Val.
1	ND (1903)	—	50 Cents, Brass, K584x	—

HONAN PROVINCE

A province in east central China. As well as being one of the most densely populated provinces it is also one of the most important argiculturally. It is the area of earliest settlement in China and has housed the capitol during various dynasties. The Kaifeng Mint issued coins from its opening in 1647 through most of the rulers of the Manchu dynasty.

EMPIRE

CASH

CAST BRASS

C#	Date	Emperor	Good	VG	Fine	VF
11-1	(1851-61)	Hsien Feng	5.00	9.00	13.50	20.00

Rev: Crescent above.

11-1.1	(1851-61)	Hsien Feng	5.00	9.00	13.50	20.00

Rev: Circle above.

11-1.2	(1851-61)	Hsien Feng	5.00	9.00	13.50	20.00

CAST IRON

11-1a	(1851-61)	Hsien Feng	Reported, not confirmed

CAST BRASS

11-9	(1875-1908)	Kuang Hsu	5.00	9.00	13.50	20.00

Rev: Circle above.

11-9.1	(1875-1908)	Kuang Hsu	5.00	9.00	13.50	20.00

Rev: Circle below.

11-9.2	(1875-1908)	Kuang Hsu	5.00	9.00	13.50	20.00

Rev: Crescent above.

C#	Date	Emperor	Good	VG	Fine	VF
11-9.3	(1875-1908)	Kuang Hsu	5.00	9.00	13.50	20.00

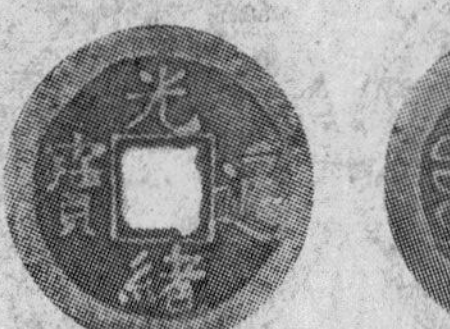

Rev: Crescent below.

11-9.4	(1875-1908)	Kuang Hsu	5.00	9.00	13.50	20.00

Rev: Crescent above, dot below.

11-9.5	(1875-1908)	Kuang Hsu	5.00	9.00	13.50	20.00

Rev: Dot above.

11-9.6	(1875-1908)	Kuang Hsu	5.00	9.00	13.50	20.00

Rev: Dot below.

11-9.7	(1875-1908)	Kuang Hsu	5.00	9.00	13.50	20.00

10 CASH

BRASS

11-2	(1851-61)	Hsien Feng	15.00	21.50	32.50	45.00

50 CASH

BRASS

11-5	(1851-61)	Hsien Feng	20.00	30.00	45.00	70.00

100 CASH

BRASS

11-6	(1851-61)	Hsien Feng	20.00	30.00	45.00	70.00

500 CASH

BRASS

11-7	(1851-61)	Hsien Feng	25.00	40.00	60.00	90.00

1000 CASH

BRASS

11-8	(1851-61)	Hsien Feng	40.00	60.00	85.00	125.00

FANTASY ISSUES

Coins of this mint in denominations of 20, 30, 40 and 70 Cash are considered fantasy issues.

STRUCK COINAGE

CASH

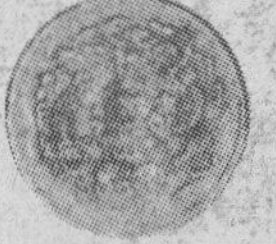

BRASS

Date	Mintage	VG	Fine	VF	XF
CD1908	—	8.50	15.00	25.00	35.00

5 CASH

BRASS

Date	Mintage	VG	Fine	VF	XF
CD1909	—	—	—	—	—

10 CASH

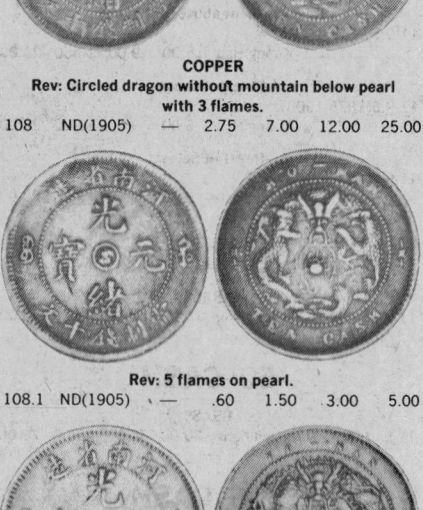

BRASS
Obv: Raised sphere (yin-yang) in center.
Rev: Uncircled dragon, Honan spelled HOU-NAN.

Y#	Date	Mintage	VG	Fine	VF	XF
108a	ND(1905)	—	—	—	Rare	—

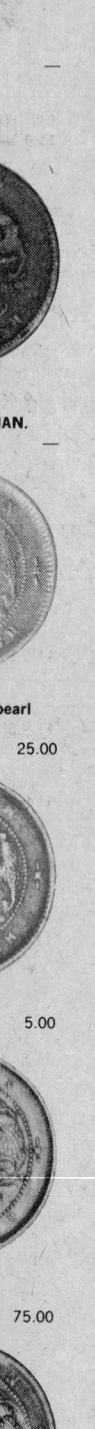

COPPER
Rev: Circled dragon without mountain below pearl with 3 flames.

Y#	Date	Mintage	VG	Fine	VF	XF
108	ND(1905)	—	2.75	7.00	12.00	25.00

Rev: 5 flames on pearl.

Y#	Date	Mintage	VG	Fine	VF	XF
108.1	ND(1905)	—	.60	1.50	3.00	5.00

Rev: Mountain below pearl. and very small English lettering.

Y#	Date	Mintage	VG	Fine	VF	XF
108.2	ND(1905)	—	10.00	25.00	50.00	75.00

Rev: Large English legend.

Y#	Date	Mintage	VG	Fine	VF	XF
108.3	ND(1905)	—	2.00	5.00	8.00	15.00

Rev: Uncircled dragon.

Y#	Date	Mintage	VG	Fine	VF	XF
108a.1	ND(1905)	—	.80	2.00	3.50	7.00

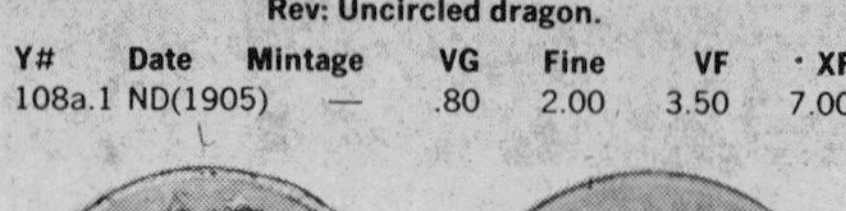

Curved line on raised Yin-Yang slanted more.

Y#	Date	Mintage	VG	Fine	VF	XF
108a.2	ND(1905)	—	.80	2.00	3.50	7.00

Obv: Flat Yin-Yang. Rev: Plain pearl.

Y#	Date	Mintage	VG	Fine	VF	XF
108a.3	ND(1905)	—	.40	1.00	2.00	3.50

BRASS

Y#	Date	Mintage	VG	Fine	VF	XF
108a.3a	ND(1905)	—	1.20	3.00	5.00	8.00

COPPER
Incuse swirl in pearl.

Y#	Date	Mintage	VG	Fine	VF	XF
108a.4	ND(1905)	—	.60	1.50	2.50	4.50

Rev: Period after COIN.

Y#	Date	Mintage	VG	Fine	VF	XF
10g	CD1906	132.000	.60	1.50	2.50	5.00

Rev: Period after COPPER.

Y#	Date	Mintage	VG	Fine	VF	XF
10g.1	CD1906	—	1.20	3.00	6.00	10.00

Y#	Date	Mintage	VG	Fine	VF	XF
20g	CD1909	—	4.00	10.00	15.00	25.00

Y#	Date	Mintage	VG	Fine	VF	XF
—	CD1911	—	1.00	2.50	5.00	10.00

REPUBLIC

10 CASH

COPPER

Y#	Date	Mintage	VG	Fine	VF	XF
A392	ND(ca.1913)	—	.40	1.00	2.00	6.00

Obv: Without lines above and below rosettes.

Y#	Date	Mintage	VG	Fine	VF	XF
A392.1	ND(ca.1913)	—	.40	1.00	2.00	6.00

Rev: TEN CASH in larger letters

Y#	Date	Mintage	VG	Fine	VF	XF
392	ND	—	.30	.75	1.50	4.00

Obv: Rosette in center higher in relation to heart shaped leaves below.

Y#	Date	Mintage	VG	Fine	VF	XF
392.1	ND	—	.80	2.00	3.50	6.00

Letter S in CASH backwards.

Y#	Date	Mintage	VG	Fine	VF	XF
392.2	ND	—	3.25	8.00	13.50	22.50

20 CASH

COPPER
Obv: Six characters at bottom.

Y#	Date	Mintage	Good	VG	Fine	VF
393	ND	—	1.00	2.50	5.00	10.00

Obv: Five characters at bottom.

Y#	Date	Mintage	Good	VG	Fine	VF
393.1	ND	—	.80	2.00	3.00	6.00

Rev: CHINA replaces HO-NAN.

Y#	Date	Mintage	Good	VG	Fine	VF
393a	ND	—	10.00	20.00	40.00	60.00

50 CASH

COPPER

Y#	Date	Mintage	Good	VG	Fine	VF
394	ND	—	1.00	2.50	5.00	8.50

BRASS

Y#	Date	Mintage	Good	VG	Fine	VF
394.1	ND	—	20.00	40.00	60.00	100.00

Rev: CHINA replaces HONAN.

Y#	Date	Mintage	Good	VG	Fine	VF
394a	ND	—	6.50	12.50	20.00	35.00

Y#	Date	Mintage	Good	VG	Fine	VF
397	Yr.20 (1931)	—	22.50	40.00	65.00	100.00

100 CASH

COPPER

Obv: Small star in right flag.

Rev: Tassels 4mm long.

Y#	Date	Mintage	Good	VG	Fine	VF
395	ND	—	1.60	4.00	8.00	15.00

Rev: Tassels 5mm long.

Y#	Date	Mintage	Good	VG	Fine	VF
395.1	ND	—	2.00	5.00	8.50	17.50

Obv: Large star in right flag.

Y#	Date	Mintage	Good	VG	Fine	VF
395.2	ND	—	—	—	—	—

Y#	Date	Mintage	Good	VG	Fine	VF
398	Yr.20 (1931)	—	7.50	18.50	25.00	45.00

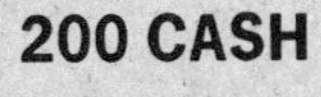

200 CASH

COPPER

Obv: Large square inside right flag.

Y#	Date	Mintage	Good	VG	Fine	VF
396	ND	—	2.50	4.00	12.50	20.00

Rev: Small square and small star inside right flag.

Y#	Date	Mintage	Good	VG	Fine	VF
396.1	ND	—	2.00	3.50	8.00	15.00

Rev: Small square and large star inside right flag.

Y#	Date	Mintage	Good	VG	Fine	VF
396.2	ND	—	2.00	3.50	8.00	15.00

BRASS

Y#	Date	Mintage	Good	VG	Fine	VF
396a	ND	—	6.00	15.00	25.00	50.00

NOTE: The Republican coins of Honan are usually found weakly struck. Crudely struck specimens with die variations are war lord issues.

NCLT ISSUES

PATTERNS

KM#	Date	Mintage	Identification	Mkt.Val.
1	CD1909	—	20 Cash, Copper, Y21g	—

HUNAN PROVINCE

A province in south-central China. Mining of coal, antimony, tungsten and tin as well as having varied agricultural products. The Changsha Mint produced Cash coins from early in the Manchu dynasty. Its facility for struck coinage opened in 1901 to produce coppers. It issued large numbers and many of questionable composition. Coins bearing dates earlier than 1901 are probably arsenal issues.

EMPIRE

Changsha Mint

CASH

CAST BRASS
Rev: Type 1 mintmark.

C#	Date	Emperor	Good	VG	Fine	VF
12.1	(1736-95)	Ch'ien Lung	.20	.50	1.00	2.00

NOTE: There are additional minor varieties in the mintmark for this reign.

C#	Date	Emperor	Good	VG	Fine	VF
12-2	(1796-1820)	Chia Ch'ing	.40	1.00	1.50	2.50
12-3	(1821-50)	Tao Kuang	2.00	4.00	5.00	7.00
12-4	(1851-61)	Hsien Feng	2.00	4.00	5.00	7.00
12-5	(1862-74)	T'ung Chih	2.50	5.00	6.00	8.00
12-7	(1875-1908)	Kuang Hsu	2.50	5.00	6.00	8.00

10 CASH

CAST BRASS

C#	Date	Emperor	Good	VG	Fine	VF
12-6	(1862-74)	T'ung Chih	—	—	Rare	—
12-8	(1875-1908)	Kuang Hsu	—	—	Rare	—

Changte Mint

NOTE: Craig erroneously places this in Chihli Province.

CASH

CAST BRASS

C#	Date	Emperor	Good	VG	Fine	VF
6-1	(1851-61)	Hsien Feng	7.50	12.50	20.00	30.00

5 CASH

CAST BRASS

C#	Date	Emperor	Good	VG	Fine	VF
6-2	(1851-61)	Hsien Feng	12.50	22.50	35.00	50.00

CAST IRON

C#	Date	Emperor	Good	VG	Fine	VF
6-2a	(1851-61)	Hsien Feng	20.00	35.00	50.00	75.00

10 CASH

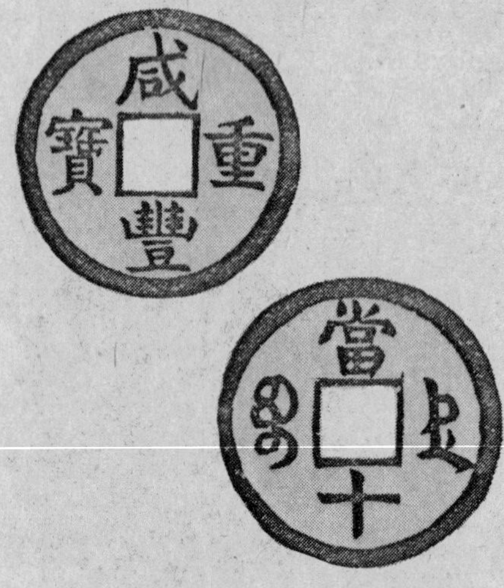

CAST BRASS

C#	Date	Emperor	Good	VG	Fine	VF
6-3	(1851-61)	Hsien Feng	8.50	17.50	25.00	40.00

CAST IRON

C#	Date	Emperor	Good	VG	Fine	VF
6-3a	(1851-61)	Hsien Feng	20.00	35.00	55.00	80.00

30 CASH

CAST BRASS

C#	Date	Emperor	Good	VG	Fine	VF
12-4.5	(1851-61)	Hsien Feng	—	—	—	—

50 CASH

CAST BRASS

C#	Date	Emperor	Good	VG	Fine	VF
6-4	(1851-61)	Hsien Feng	15.00	25.00	40.00	60.00

100 CASH

CAST BRASS

C#	Date	Emperor	Good	VG	Fine	VF
6-5	(1851-61)	Hsien Feng	20.00	32.50	45.00	65.00

MACHINE STRUCK COINAGE

NOTE: 2, 5 and 20 Cash Tai Ching type patterns are reported, not confirmed.

10 CASH

COPPER
Obv: Rosette in center with center of petals depressed. Manchu characters at sides.
Rev: Narrow spacing in HU-NAN above dragon.

Y#	Date	Mintage	VG	Fine	VF	XF
112	(1902-06)	—	.40	1.00	2.00	5.00

Rev: Wide spacing in HU-NAN.

Y#	Date	Mintage	VG	Fine	VF	XF
112.1	(1902-06)	—	.50	1.25	2.00	5.00

Obv: Petals of rosette not depressed.

Y#	Date	Mintage	VG	Fine	VF	XF
112.2	(1902-06)	—	.60	1.50	2.50	6.00

Obv: Two Manchu characters in center.

Y#	Date	Mintage	VG	Fine	VF	XF
112.3	(1902-06)	—	1.20	3.00	6.00	10.00

Rev: Narrow spacing in HU-NAN.

Y#	Date	Mintage	VG	Fine	VF	XF
112.4	(1902-06)	—	.60	1.50	2.50	6.00

Obv: Rosette in center. Rev: Ring around pearl.

Y#	Date	Mintage	VG	Fine	VF	XF
112.5	(1902-06)	—	.50	1.25	2.00	4.00

Obv: Centers of petals on rosette depressed.

Y#	Date	Mintage	VG	Fine	VF	XF
112.6	(1902-06)	—	.60	1.50	2.50	6.00

Obv: Two Manchu characters in center.
Rev: Ring around pearl.

Y#	Date	Mintage	VG	Fine	VF	XF
112.7	(1902-06)	—	.60	1.50	2.50	6.00

Obv: Larger characters at left and right, and different characters below. Rev: Dragon redesigned and small star to either side.

Y#	Date	Mintage	VG	Fine	VF	XF
112.8	(1902-06)	—	2.00	5.00	8.00	15.00

Obv: Rosette in center, four characters at bottom.
Rev: Redesigned dragon without pearl; rosette at either side.

Y#	Date	Mintage	VG	Fine	VF	XF
112.9	(1902-06)	—	2.00	5.00	10.00	15.00

Obv: Two Manchu characters in center with dot between; two characters at bottom.

Y#	Date	Mintage	VG	Fine	VF	XF
112.10	(1902-06)	—	.40	1.00	2.00	4.00

Obv: Without dot between Manchu characters.

Y#	Date	Mintage	VG	Fine	VF	XF
112.11	(1902-06)	—	.40	1.00	2.00	4.00

With smaller inner circle.

Y#	Date	Mintage	VG	Fine	VF	XF
112.12	(1902-06)	—	16.50	40.00	65.00	100.00

Obv: Six characters at bottom.
Rev: Flying dragon. Reeded edge.

Y#	Date	Mintage	VG	Fine	VF	XF
113	(1902-06)	—	1.60	4.00	8.00	12.50

Inverted U in HU-NAN.
Reeded edge.

Y#	Date	Mintage	VG	Fine	VF	XF
113.1	(1902-06)	—	4.00	10.00	20.00	35.00

BRASS

Obv: Three characters at bottom.

Y#	Date	Mintage	VG	Fine	VF	XF
113.2	(1904-06)	—	1.40	3.50	6.00	12.50

COPPER

Obv: Upper and lower parts of character HU connected.
Rev: Dot among Chinese characters above dragon.

Y#	Date	Mintage	VG	Fine	VF	XF
10h	CD1906	—	4.00	10.00	18.50	30.00

Obv: Upper and lower part of Hu not connected. Rev: Dot among Chinese at top.

Y#	Date	Mintage	VG	Fine	VF	XF
10h.1	CD1906	—	4.00	10.00	18.50	30.00

Rev: Seven flames on plain pearl.

Y#	Date	Mintage	VG	Fine	VF	XF
10h.2	CD1906	—	.80	2.00	4.00	6.00

Rev: 7-flame pearl ornamented with toothlike projections.

Y#	Date	Mintage	VG	Fine	VF	XF
10h.3	CD1906	—	.40	1.00	2.00	4.00

Rev: Four flames on fireball.

Y#	Date	Mintage	VG	Fine	VF	XF
10h.4	CD1906	—	.80	2.00	4.00	6.00

Rev: Redesigned dragon with high waves beneath.

Y#	Date	Mintage	VG	Fine	VF	XF
10h.5	CD1906	—	4.00	10.00	18.50	30.00

Rev: Redesigned dragon: dot between COPPER COIN; HU connected.

Y#	Date	Mintage	VG	Fine	VF	XF
10h.6	CD1906	—	4.00	10.00	18.50	30.00

Rev: Redesigned dragon, with five flames on pearl (Woodward #342 and 343).

Y#	Date	Mintage	VG	Fine	VF	XF
10h.7	CD1906	—	10.00	25.00	35.00	50.00

5 CENTS

SILVER

Similar to 20 Cents, Y#116.

Y#	Date	Mintage	Fine	VF	XF	Unc
—	(1897)	1 Known	—	—	Rare	—

10 CENTS

SILVER, 2.5000 gm.

Obv: With two rosettes to either side.

Y#	Date	Mintage	Fine	VF	XF	Unc
115	(1897)	—	6.00	15.00	22.50	40.00

Obv: With one rosette to either side.

Y#	Date	Mintage	Fine	VF	XF	Unc
115.1	ND(1897)	—	6.00	15.00	22.50	40.00
	CD1898	—	11.50	27.50	45.00	75.00
	CD1899	—	16.50	40.00	65.00	120.00

20 CENTS

SILVER, 5.3000 gm.

116	ND(1897)	—	10.00	25.00	35.00	50.00

TAEL SYSTEM

The following coins, in Tael and Mace (Liang and Ch'ien) denominations, are often called Hunan cakes because of their thickness. Three basic series exist: those issued under provincial authority, those issued by the Ta Ch'ing Bank, and those issued by Changsha merchants. Because of their simple designs and unreeded edges, they were easily counterfeited.

CH'IEN (MACE)

SILVER, 3.7000 gm.
Provincial Type
Obv: Four characters. Rev: Two characters.

K#	Date	Mintage	VG	Fine	VF	XF
951	(1906)	—	25.00	40.00	60.00	100.00

3.8000 gm.
Merchant Type
Obv: Six characters vertical. Rev: 6 characters horizontal.

971	(C.1908)	—	15.00	25.00	35.00	50.00

Merchant Type
Obv: 4 characters. Rev: 2 vertical characters.

973	(C.1908)	—	15.00	25.00	35.00	50.00

Merchant Type
Obv: Six characters horizontal.
Rev: Two characters vertical.

985	(C.1908)	—	15.00	25.00	35.00	50.00

2 CH'IEN (MACE)

SILVER, 7.3000 gm.
Provincial Type
Obv: Four characters. Rev: Four characters.

950	(C.1906)	—	20.00	30.00	40.00	60.00

Provincial Type
Obv: Six characters vertical. Rev: Four characters.

960	(C.1906)	—	20.00	30.00	40.00	60.00

Ta Ch'ing Bank Type
Obv: Six characters vertical.
Rev: Six characters horizontal.

970	(C.1908)	—	20.00	30.00	40.00	60.00

Merchant Type
Obv. and rev: 4 characters.

K#	Date	Mintage	VG	Fine	VF	XF
972	(C.1908)	—	20.00	30.00	40.00	60.00

Merchant Type
Obv: Six characters horizontal. Rev: Four characters.

982	(C.1908)	—	20.00	30.00	40.00	60.00

3 CH'IEN (MACE)

SILVER, 10.7000 gm.
Provincial Type
Obv. and rev: Six characters horizontal.

949	(C.1906)	—	25.00	35.00	45.00	65.00

Provincial Type
Obv: Six characters vertical.
Rev: Six characters horizontal.

959	(C.1906)	—	25.00	35.00	45.00	65.00

Ta Ch'ing Bank Type
Obv: Six characters vertical.
Rev: Six characters horizontal.

969	(C.1908)	—	25.00	35.00	45.00	65.00

Merchant Type
Obv. and rev: Six characters horizontal.

981	(C.1908)	—	25.00	35.00	45.00	65.00

Merchant Type
As above, but "official" character for "three".

981a	(C.1908)	—	25.00	35.00	45.00	65.00

4 CH'IEN (MACE)

SILVER, 14.3000 gm.
Provincial Type
Obv. and rev: Six characters horizontal.

948	(C.1906)	—	30.00	40.00	50.00	70.00

Provincial Type
Obv: Six characters vertical.
Rev: Six characters horizontal.

958	(C.1906)	—	30.00	40.00	50.00	70.00

Ta Ch'ing Bank Type
Obv: Six characters vertical.
Rev: Six characters horizontal.

968	(C.1908)	—	30.00	40.00	50.00	70.00

Merchant Type
Obv. and rev: Six characters horizontal.

980	(C.1908)	—	30.00	40.00	50.00	70.00

5 CH'IEN (MACE)

SILVER, 18.3000 gm.
Provincial Type
Obv. and rev: Six characters horizontal.

947	(C.1906)	—	35.00	45.00	55.00	75.00

Provincial Type
Obv: Six characters vertical.
Rev: Six characters horizontal.

957	(C.1906)	—	35.00	45.00	55.00	75.00

Ta Ch'ing Bank Type
Obv: Six characters vertical.
Rev: Six characters horizontal.

967	(C.1908)	—	35.00	45.00	55.00	75.00

Merchant Type
Obv. and rev: Six characters horizontal.

K#	Date	Mintage	VG	Fine	VF	XF
979	(C.1908)	—	35.00	45.00	55.00	75.00

6 CH'IEN (MACE)

SILVER, 21.4000 gm.
Provincial Type
Obv. and rev: Six characters horizontal.

946	(C.1906)	—	40.00	50.00	60.00	80.00

Provincial Type
Obv: Six characters vertical.
Rev: Six characters horizontal.

956	(C.1906)	—	40.00	50.00	60.00	80.00

Ta Ch'ing Bank Type
Obv: Six characters vertical.
Rev: Six characters horizontal.

966	(C.1908)	—	40.00	50.00	60.00	80.00

Merchant Type
Obv. and rev: Six characters horizontal.

978	(C.1908)	—	40.00	50.00	60.00	80.00

7 CH'IEN (MACE)

SILVER, 25.9000 gm.
Provincial Type
Obv. and rev: Six characters horizontal.

945	(C.1906)	—	40.00	50.00	60.00	80.00

Provincial Type
Obv: Six characters vertical.
Rev: Six characters horizontal.

955	(C.1906)	—	40.00	50.00	60.00	80.00

Ta Ch'ing Bank Type
Obv: Six characters vertical.
Rev: Six characters horizontal.

965	(C.1908)	—	40.00	50.00	60.00	80.00

Merchant Type
Obv. and rev: Six characters horizontal.

977	(C.1908)	—	40.00	50.00	60.00	80.00

8 CH'IEN (MACE)

SILVER, 29.2000 gm.
Provincial Type
Obv. and rev: Six characters horizontal.

K#	Date	Mintage	VG	Fine	VF	XF
944	(C.1906)	—	45.00	55.00	65.00	85.00

Provincial Type
Obv: Six characters vertical.
Rev: Six characters horizontal.

954	(C.1906)	—	45.00	55.00	65.00	85.00

Ta Ch'ing Bank Type
Obv: Six characters vertical.
Rev: Six characters horizontal.

964	(C.1908)	—	45.00	55.00	65.00	85.00

Merchant Type
Obv. and rev: Six characters horizontal.

976	(C.1908)	—	45.00	55.00	65.00	85.00

9 CH'IEN

SILVER, 32.7000 gm.
Provincial Type
Obv. and rev: Six characters horizontal.

943	(C.1906)	—	50.00	60.00	70.00	90.00

Provincial Type
Obv: Six characters vertical.
Rev: Six characters horizontal.

953	(C.1906)	—	50.00	60.00	70.00	90.00

Ta Ch'ing Bank Type
Obv: Six characters vertical.
Rev: Six characters horizontal.

963	(C.1908)	—	50.00	60.00	70.00	90.00

Merchant Type
Obv. and rev: Six characters horizontal.

975	(C.1908)	—	50.00	60.00	70.00	90.00

LIANG (TAEL)

SILVER, 35.9000 gm.
Provincial Type
Obv. and rev: Six characters horizontal.

942	(C.1906)	—	50.00	85.00	125.00	180.00

Obv: 12 characters. Rev: Blank.

942r	C.1908	—	—	—	Rare	—

Provincial Type
Obv: Six characters vertical.
Rev: Six characters horizontal.

K#	Date	Mintage	VG	Fine	VF	XF
952	(C.1906)	—	40.00	60.00	100.00	150.00

Ta Ch'ing Bank Type
Obv: Six characters vertical.
Rev: Six characters horizontal.

962	(C.1908)	—	40.00	55.00	70.00	100.00

Merchant Type
Obv. and rev: Six characters horizontal.

974	(C.1908)	—	85.00	150.00	200.00	275.00

REPUBLIC

10 CASH

COPPER
Obv: Large rosette. Rev: Center of star convex.

Y#	Date	Mintage	VG	Fine	VF	XF
399	ND	—	.80	2.00	3.50	6.00

BRASS

399a	ND	—	1.80	4.50	7.50	12.50

COPPER
Obv: Small rosette. Rev: Center of star convex.

399.1	ND	—	.80	2.00	3.50	6.00

Rev: Center of star concave.
Star outlined.

399.2	ND	—	.80	2.00	4.00	8.00

Rev: Same star not outlined.

Y#	Date	Mintage	VG	Fine	VF	XF
399.3	ND	—	.80	2.00	4.00	8.00

Obv: Large rosette. Rev: Center of star concave.

399.4	ND	—	.80	2.00	4.00	8.00

Hung Hsien Commemorative

401	Yr.1 (1915)	—	7.00	17.50	25.00	40.00

NOTE: This coin is dated first year of Hung Hsien which corresponds to 1915.

Rev: Rosette above flags.
Provincial Constitution Commemorative

402	Yr.11 (1922)	—	7.00	17.50	25.00	40.00

Rev: Star above flags.

402.1	Yr.11 (1922)	—	5.50	13.50	20.00	30.00

20 CASH

COPPER
Obv: Rosette above flags, 5 characters at bottom.

400	ND	—	1.20	3.00	7.50	15.00

BRASS

400.1	ND	—	1.60	4.00	10.00	20.00

Obv: Dot in rosette above flags, 6 characters at bottom.
Rev: Large rice grains, thick ribbon at base of plant.

Y#	Date	Mintage	VG	Fine	VF	XF
400.2	ND	—	.40	1.00	2.00	4.00

Obv: No dot in rosette above flags.

Y#	Date	Mintage	VG	Fine	VF	XF
400.3	ND	—	.40	1.00	2.00	4.00

Obv: Floral ornament to left smaller.
Rev: Smaller rice grains.

Y#	Date	Mintage	VG	Fine	VF	XF
400.4	ND	—	.40	1.00	2.00	4.00

Rev: Thin ribbon at base of plant.

Y#	Date	Mintage	VG	Fine	VF	XF
400.5	ND	—	.40	1.00	2.00	4.00

Small pentagontal rosette above flags.

Y#	Date	Mintage	VG	Fine	VF	XF
400.6	ND	—	.40	1.00	2.00	4.00

Small star-shaped rosette above flags.

Y#	Date	Mintage	VG	Fine	VF	XF
400.7	ND	—	.80	2.00	3.00	5.00

BRASS

Y#	Date	Mintage	VG	Fine	VF	XF
400.7a	ND	—	1.60	4.00	8.00	15.00

Larger star-shaped rosette above flags.

Y#	Date	Mintage	VG	Fine	VF	XF
400.8	ND	—	1.00	2.50	4.00	6.00

Sharp-pointed star above flags.

Y#	Date	Mintage	VG	Fine	VF	XF
400.9	ND	—	1.00	2.50	4.00	6.00

Sharp pointed star over rosette above flags.

Y#	Date	Mintage	VG	Fine	VF	XF
400.10	ND	—	2.00	5.00	7.50	10.00

Rev. denomination: 20 CASH.

Y#	Date	Mintage	VG	Fine	VF	XF
400a	ND	—	20.00	50.00	75.00	100.00

NOTE: May also exist in brass.

Provincial Constitution
Rev: Small characters

Y#	Date	Mintage	VG	Fine	VF	XF
403	Yr.11 (1922)	—	9.00	22.50	32.00	55.00

10 CENTS

SILVER
Hung Hsien

K#	Date	Mintage	Fine	VF	XF	Unc
762	(1915)	—	200.00	500.00	800.00	1000.

Though Kann calls this coin an Essay, contemporary reports indicate that the coin actually circulated briefly in 1915. Not to be confused with Y#28, the obverse of which has a different legend in Chinese. (See General Issues - Empire).

DOLLAR

SILVER, 27.4 gm.
Provincial Constitution

Y#	Date	Mintage	Fine	VF	XF	Unc
404	Yr.11 (1922)	—	150.00	300.00	500.00	800.00

NCLT ISSUES

PATTERNS

KM#	Date	Mintage	Identification	Mkt.Val.
1	(1897)	—	50 Cents, Silver	—

KM#	Date	Mintage	Identification	Mkt.Val.
2	(1897)	—	1 Dollar, Silver	—

NOTE: The dollar and half dollar above were produced at the Heaton Mint, Birmingham, England as trials before sending the dies and machinery to China.

KM#	Date	Mintage	Identification	Mkt.Val.
3	Yr.11 (1922)	—	20 Cash, Copper, Y403.2	150.00

HUPEH PROVINCE

A province located in east-central China. Hilly, with some lakes and swamps it has rich coal and iron deposits plus a varied agricultural program. The Wuchang Mint had been active from early in the Manchu dynasty and its modern equipment began operations in 1895. The last coin issue at the Wuchang Mint was a Yuan Shih Kai 20 cent piece dated in the year 9 (1920).

EMPIRE

CASH

CAST BRASS

C#	Date	Emperor	Good	VG	Fine	VF
13-1	(1736-95)	Ch'ien Lung	.20	.40	.75	1.00

NOTE: Minor varieties in mintmarks exist in this reign.

Rev: Type 1 mintmark. Large dot below.

C#	Date	Emperor	Good	VG	Fine	VF
13-1.1	(1736-95)	Ch'ien Lung	1.50	3.00	5.00	7.50

Rev: Dot above.

C#	Date	Emperor	Good	VG	Fine	VF
13-1.2	(1736-95)	Ch'ien Lung	1.50	3.00	5.00	7.50

Rev: Crescent below.

C#	Date	Emperor	Good	VG	Fine	VF
13-1.3	(1736-95)	Ch'ien Lung	2.50	4.50	7.00	10.00
13-2	(1796-1820)	Chia Ch'ing	1.00	2.00	3.00	5.00

Rev: Crescent above.

C#	Date	Emperor	Good	VG	Fine	VF
13-2.1	(1796-1820)	Chia Ch'ing	2.50	5.00	6.00	8.50
13-3	(1821-50)	Tao Kuang	.75	1.50	2.50	4.00
13-4	(1851-61)	Hsien Feng	1.60	4.00	5.00	7.50
13-9	(1862-74)	T'ung Chih	3.50	7.50	11.50	16.50
13-11	(1875-1908)	Kuang Hsu	3.50	7.50	11.50	16.50

5 CASH

CAST BRASS

C#	Date	Emperor	Good	VG	Fine	VF
13-5	(1851-61)	Hsien Feng	20.00	35.00	50.00	65.00

10 CASH

CAST BRASS

C#	Date	Emperor	Good	VG	Fine	VF
13-6	(1851-61)	Hsien Feng	10.00	15.00	20.00	30.00

Rev: Crescent in upper right corner.

C#	Date	Emperor	Good	VG	Fine	VF
13-6.1	(1851-61)	Hsien Feng	15.00	27.50	40.00	60.00
13-10	(1862-74)	T'ung Chih	—	—	Rare	—
13-12	(1875-1908)	Kuang Hsu	—	—	Rare	—

50 CASH

CAST BRASS

C#	Date	Emperor	Good	VG	Fine	VF
13-7	(1851-61)	Hsien Feng	17.50	27.50	37.50	50.00

Rev: Crescent in upper right corner.

C#	Date	Emperor	Good	VG	Fine	VF
13-7.1	(1851-61)	Hsien Feng	18.50	30.00	40.00	60.00

100 CASH

CAST BRASS

C#	Date	Emperor	Good	VG	Fine	VF
13-8	(1851-61)	Hsien Feng	17.50	27.50	37.50	50.00

Rev: Crescent in upper right corner.

C#	Date	Emperor	Good	VG	Fine	VF
13-8.1	(1851-61)	Hsien Feng	20.00	35.00	50.00	70.00

Ching Chow Mint

CASH

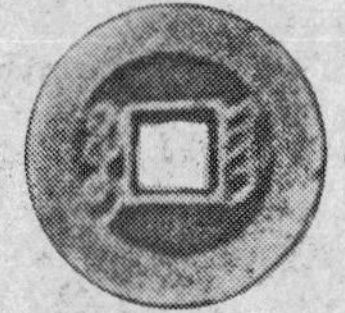

CAST BRASS

C#	Date	Emperor	Good	VG	Fine	VF
13-11.1	(1875-1908)	Kuang Hsu	—	—	Rare	—

STRUCK COINAGE

CASH

BRASS, struck
Obv: Small characters, 22.5mm.

Su#	Date	Mintage	VG	Fine	VF	XF
181	(1898)	—	20.00	35.00	40.00	50.00

Obv: Larger characters, 20.5mm.

Su#	Date	Mintage	VG	Fine	VF	XF
182	(1898)	—	15.00	20.00	30.00	45.00

Y#	Date	Mintage	VG	Fine	VF	XF
121	(1906)	66.474	2.50	4.50	7.50	12.50

Obv: Small mintmark on small disc in center.

Y#	Date	Mintage	VG	Fine	VF	XF
7j	CD1908	Inc. Ab.	2.75	7.00	14.00	20.00

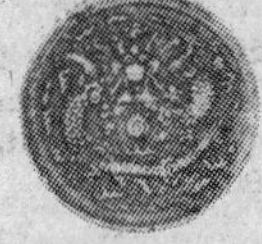

Obv: Large mintmark on small disc in center.

Y#	Date	Mintage	VG	Fine	VF	XF
7j.1	CD1908	Inc. Ab.	2.50	6.50	10.00	20.00

2 CASH

COPPER

Y#	Date	Mintage	VG	Fine	VF	XF
8j	CD1906	.844	25.00	42.50	65.00	85.00

5 CASH

COPPER, 24mm

Y#	Date	Mintage	VG	Fine	VF	XF
9j	CD1906	9.846	4.50	7.50	13.50	22.50

Dragon redesigned, 23mm.

Y#	Date	Mintage	VG	Fine	VF	XF
9j.1	CD1906	Inc. Ab.	5.00	8.50	15.00	25.00

10 CASH

COPPER
Obv: Eight-petal rosette. Rev: Circled dragon.

Y#	Date	Mintage	VG	Fine	VF	XF
120	(1902-05)	4.475	2.00	5.00	8.00	15.00

Rev: Small English letters.

Y#	Date	Mintage	VG	Fine	VF	XF
120a	(1902-05)	I.A.	1.40	3.50	7.00	12.50

Rev: Slightly larger English letters; wide face on dragon.

Y#	Date	Mintage	VG	Fine	VF	XF
120a.1	(1902-05)	I.A.	.20	.50	.75	1.50

Rev: Large pearl with many spines.
Narrower face on dragon.

Y#	Date	Mintage	VG	Fine	VF	XF
120a.2	(1902-05)	I.A.	.20	.50	.75	1.50

Rev: Smaller pearl with fewer spines on dragon.

Y#	Date	Mintage	VG	Fine	VF	XF
120a.3	(1902-05)	I.A.	.20	.50	.75	1.50

Obv: Five-petal rosette, small Manchu character to right. Rev: Four dots in shape of cross at either side of dragon. Province spelled PHOVINCE, with V as inverted A.

120a.4 (1902-05) I.A. .30 .75 1.00 2.00

Obv: Large Manchu at right.

120a.5 (1902-05) I.A. .30 .75 1.00 2.00

Rev: Six-pointed star at either side of dragon. Hyphen in HU-PEH.

120a.6 (1902-05) I.A. .30 .75 1.00 2.00

Rev: No hyphen in HU PEH.

120a.7 (1902-05) I.A. .60 1.50 2.50 5.00

Obv: Five-petal rosette and small Manchu. Rev: Very small pearl.

120a.8 (1902-05) I.A. .60 1.50 2.50 5.00

Obv: Square in circle. Rev: Hyphen in HU-PEH.

120a.9 (1902-05) I.A. .60 1.50 2.50 5.00

Rev: No hyphen in HU PEH.

Y#	Date	Mintage	VG	Fine	VF	XF
120a.10	(1902-05)	I.A.	.60	1.50	2.50	5.00

Obv: Second character from right at top is larger. Rev: Front view dragon.

122 (1902-05) I.A. .20 .50 .75 1.50

Obv: 2nd character from right 'Pei' smaller.

122.1 (1902-05) I.A. .20 .50 .75 1.50

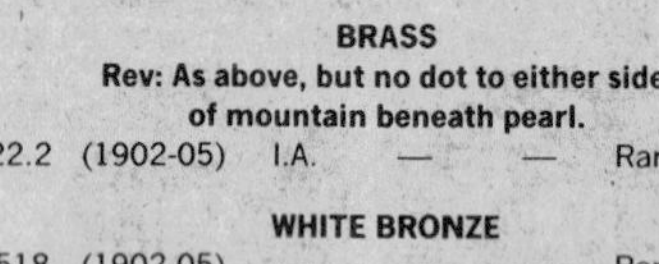

BRASS

Rev: As above, but no dot to either side of mountain beneath pearl.

122.2 (1902-05) I.A. — — Rare —

WHITE BRONZE

W518 (1902-05) — — — Rare —

COPPER

Rev: Clouds above dragons head; two clouds below pearl instead of one.

122.3 (1902-05) I.A. .80 2.00 5.00 10.00

Rev: Small circle around lower part of pearl; without dots on either side of mountain.

122.4 (1902-05) I.A. .80 2.00 5.00 10.00

Rev: Larger circle around larger pearl; larger English letters.

122.5 (1902-05) I.A. .80 2.00 5.00 10.00

Rev: Circled front view dragon.

122a (1902-05) — 60.00 150.00 200.00 250.00

Rev: Tai Ch'ing Ti Kuo dragon. Seven flames on pearl.

Y#	Date	Mintage	VG	Fine	VF	XF
10j	CD1906					
		1865.558	.30	.75	1.00	2.00

Rev: Redesigned dragon with wide lips; cloud shaped bar under pearl with five flames, 28 to 29mm.

10j.1 CD1906 Inc. Ab. .80 2.00 5.00 10.00

30mm

10j.2 CD1906 Inc. Ab. .80 2.00 5.00 10.00

Rev: Different dragon with hook-shaped cloud beneath. pearl with four flames; large incuse swirl on pearl.

10j.3 CD1906 Inc. Ab. .20 .50 .75 1.50

Rev: Small incuse swirl on pearl with four flames.

10j.4 CD1906 Inc. Ab. .20 .50 .75 1.50

Rev: Swirl on pearl in relief having four flames.

10j.5 CD1906 Inc. Ab. .30 .75 1.00 2.00

Rev: Large incuse swirl on pearl.

20j CD1909 371.577 .60 1.50 3.00 5.00

Rev: Small swirl in relief on pearl.

Y#	Date	Mintage	VG	Fine	VF	XF
20j.1	CD1909	Inc. Ab.	.60	1.50	3.00	5.00

Obv: CD1909 over CD1906.

20j.2	CD1909/1906	—	40.00	100.00	150.00	200.00

Rev: Characters Hsuan T'ung' re-engraved over characters 'Kuang Hsu'.

20j.3	CD1909	—	40.00	100.00	150.00	200.00

20 CASH

COPPER

11j	CD1906	3.710	80.00	175.00	325.00	475.00

5 CENTS

SILVER, 1.3500 gm.

Y#	Date	Mintage	Fine	VF	XF	Unc
123	(1895-1905)	4.278	50.00	125.00	300.00	600.00

10 CENTS

SILVER, 2.7000 gm.
Rev: Character at either side of the dragon (Pen Sheng) indicating the coin was for provincial use.

124	(1894)	—	250.00	600.00	1000.	1500.

Rev: Without the characters beside the dragon. Two varieties of edge milling.

Y#	Date	Mintage	Fine	VF	XF	Unc
124.1	(1895-1907)	—	3.50	7.50	15.00	30.00

Obv: Similar to Y#124.1 with different characters in center.

129	(1909)	—	10.00	25.00	50.00	90.00

20 CENTS

SILVER, 5.3000 gm.
Rev: Character at either side of the dragon (Pen Sheng) indicating that the coin was for provincial use.

125	(1894)	—	1200.	3000.	3250.	3500.

Rev: Without characters beside dragon.

125.1	(1895-1907)	—	BV	7.50	15.00	25.00

Numerals 4.4 backwards and letter D in CANDAREENS backwards.

125.2	(1895-1907)	—	BV	7.50	15.00	25.00

Obv: Different center characters.

130	(1909)	—	120.00	300.00	400.00	500.00

50 CENTS

SILVER, 13.5000 gm.

126	(1895-1905)	—	27.50	55.00	110.00	250.00

DOLLAR

SILVER, 26.7000 gm.
Obv: Similar to Y#127.1.
Rev: Characters at either side of dragon 'Pen Sheng' indicating the coin was for provincial use.

Y#	Date	Mintage	Fine	VF	XF	Unc
127	(1894)	—	—	—	—	6500.

Rev: Without 'Pen Sheng' at either side of dragon.

127.1	(1895-1907)	19.935	BV	30.00	45.00	125.00

Obv: Hsuan Tung' in center legend.
Rev: Similar to Y#127.1

131	(1909-11)	2.703	50.00	80.00	130.00	300.00

TAEL SYSTEM

TAEL

SILVER

Y#	Date	Mintage	Fine	VF	XF	Unc
128	Yr.30 (1904)	.648	150.00	200.00	250.00	300.00

NOTE: Minor varieties of obv. legends exist.

REPUBLIC

20 CASH

BRASS

Y#	Date	Mintage	VG	Fine	VF	XF
A405	ND	—	35.00	75.00	100.00	150.00

Attribution is uncertain. Probably minted in Szechuan. Former Y#471.

50 CASH

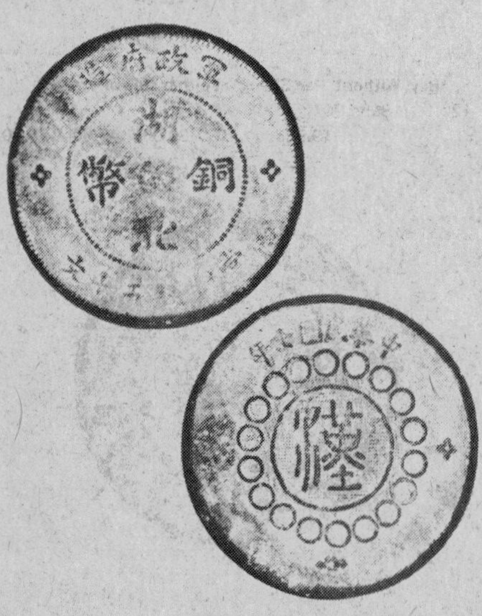

COPPER OR BRASS

Y#	Date	Mintage	VG	Fine	VF	XF
405	Yr.3 (1914)	—	75.00	150.00	250.00	500.00
	Yr.7 (1918)	—	75.00	150.00	250.00	500.00

NOTE: NOT to be confused with Szechuan Y#449.

20 CENTS

SILVER, 5.2000 gm.
Obv: Characters at left and right of bust.

Y#	Date	Mintage	Fine	VF	XF	Unc
406	Yr.9 (1920)	—	100.00	200.00	250.00	350.00

NOTE: Do not confuse with Y#327 (See Republic-General Issues.

NCLT ISSUES

PATTERNS

KM#	Date	Mintage	Identification	Mkt.Val.
1	Yr.1 (1916)	—	10 Cents, White Metal, K764x	—

KANSU PROVINCE

A province located in north central China with a contrast of mountains and scandy plains. The west end of the Great Wall with its branches lies in Kansu. Kansu was the "Silk Road" that led to central and western Asia. Two mints issued Cash coins. It has been reported, but not confirmed, that the Lanchow Mint operated as late as 1949.

EMPIRE

CASH

CAST BRASS

C#	Date	Emperor	Good	VG	Fine	VF
14-1	(1851-61)	Hsien Feng	5.00	10.00	15.00	22.50
14-8	(1862-74)	T'ung Chih	6.00	12.00	18.00	25.00

5 CASH

CAST BRASS

C#	Date	Emperor	Good	VG	Fine	VF
14-2	(1851-61)	Hsien Feng	20.00	30.00	45.00	65.00
14-9	(1862-74)	T'ung Chih	25.00	37.50	55.00	75.00

10 CASH

CAST BRASS

C#	Date	Emperor	Good	VG	Fine	VF
14-3	(1851-61)	Hsien Feng	15.00	25.00	35.00	50.00
14-10	(1862-74)	T'ung Chih	20.00	30.00	40.00	55.00

50 CASH

CAST BRASS. 48mm.

C#	Date	Emperor	Good	VG	Fine	VF
14-4	(1851-61)	Hsien Feng	20.00	30.00	45.00	65.00

43mm

C#	Date	Emperor	Good	VG	Fine	VF
14-4.1	(1851-61)	Hsien Feng	20.00	30.00	45.00	65.00

100 CASH

CAST BRASS

C#	Date	Emperor	Good	VG	Fine	VF
14-5	(1851-61)	Hsien Feng	20.00	30.00	45.00	65.00

500 CASH

CAST BRASS

C#	Date	Emperor	Good	VG	Fine	VF
14-6	(1851-61)	Hsien Feng	30.00	50.00	75.00	100.00

1000 CASH

CAST BRASS

C#	Date	Emperor	Good	VG	Fine	VF
14-7	(1851-61)	Hsien Feng	35.00	60.00	90.00	150.00

REPUBLIC

STRUCK COINAGE

50 CASH

COPPER

Y#	Date	Mintage	VG	Fine	VF	XF
408	Yr.15 (1926)	2.564	65.00	135.00	185.00	250.00

100 CASH

COPPER

Y#	Date	Mintage	VG	Fine	VF	XF
409	Yr.15 (1926)	—	45.00	85.00	135.00	185.00

DOLLAR

SILVER, 26.6000 gm.

Y#	Date	Mintage	Fine	VF	XF	Unc
407	Yr.3 (1914)	—	250.00	500.00	750.00	1350.

410	Yr.17 (1928)	—	125.00	225.00	400.00	700.00

NCLT ISSUES

PATTERNS

KM#	Date	Mintage	Identification	Mkt.Val.
1	ND	—	5 Cash, Copper, Su385	300.00
2	ND	—	10 Cash, Copper	—

KM#	Date	Mintage	Identification	Mkt.Val.
3	ND	—	5 Fen, Copper, Su383	150.00
4	Yr.17 (1928)	—	50 Cash, Copper	—
5	ND	—	10 Fen, Copper, Su384	200.00

KIANGNAN PROVINCES

A district in eastern China made up of Anhwei and Kiangsu provinces. In 1667 the province of Kiangnan was divided into the present provinces of Anhwei and Kiangsu. In 1723 Nanking, formerly the capital of Kiangnan, was made the capital of Liang-Chiang (an administrative area consisting of Anhwei, Kiangsu and Kiangsi provinces.

Always highly regarded because of location, agriculture and manufacturing, Kiangnan has always been sought after by contending forces.

The Nanking Mint had been active during imperial times. Modern minting facilities began operations in 1897 at the Kiangnan Arsenal in Nanking. A second mint was opened in 1905 in northern Kiangsu for the production of coppers only. A third mint opened in Shanghai in 1921 and a fourth at Soochow saw limited service. The Nanking Mint, the most important of the group, burned down in 1929.

EMPIRE

STRUCK COINAGE

CASH

COPPER

Su#	Date	Mintage	VG	Fine	VF	XF
261	(1898)	—	20.00	35.00	60.00	100.00

***NOTE:** Mintage reported, but questionable.

Obv: Smaller character. Mintmark written differently.

Y#	Date	Mintage	VG	Fine	VF	XF
—	ND	—	—	—	—	—

NOTE: This coin has been erroneously attributed to Ning Po in Chekiang and to Changchow in Fukien.

BRASS
Bottom horizontal stroke in mintmark extends beyond outside vertical strokes.

Y#	Date	Mintage	VG	Fine	VF	XF
7k	CD1908	25.450	2.50	4.50	8.50	16.00

Bottom horizontal stroke in mintmark does not extend beyond outside vertical strokes.

Y#	Date	Mintage	VG	Fine	VF	XF
7k.1	CD1908	Inc. Ab.	3.50	6.50	12.50	21.50

5 CASH

COPPER
Mintmark incused on raised disk.

Y#	Date	Mintage	VG	Fine	VF	XF
9k.1	CD1906	—	30.00	55.00	85.00	125.00

BRASS

Y#	Date	Mintage	VG	Fine	VF	XF
9k.1a	CD1906	—	37.50	75.00	110.00	150.00

COPPER
Obv: Mintmark in relief at center without disc.

Y#	Date	Mintage	VG	Fine	VF	XF
9k.2	CD1906	—	37.50	75.00	100.00	135.00

10 CASH

COPPER
Reeded edge

Y#	Date	Mintage	VG	Fine	VF	XF
135	ND	—	8.00	20.00	30.00	45.00

Plain edge.

Y#	Date	Mintage	VG	Fine	VF	XF
135.1	ND	—	8.00	20.00	30.00	45.00

Obv: Small Manchu characters in center.

Y#	Date	Mintage	VG	Fine	VF	XF
135.2	CD1902	—	.60	1.50	3.00	5.00

Obv: Large Manchu characters in center.

Y#	Date	Mintage	VG	Fine	VF	XF
135.3	CD1902	—	2.00	5.00	10.00	20.00

Y#	Date	Mintage	VG	Fine	VF	XF
135.4	CD1903	—	.40	1.00	2.00	3.00

Rev: Cloud above letter T looks like the number 3.

Y#	Date	Mintage	VG	Fine	VF	XF
135.5	CD1904	351.974	.40	1.00	2.00	3.00

Rev: Cloud above T redesigned.
Cash spelled GASH.

Y#	Date	Mintage	VG	Fine	VF	XF
135.6	CD1904	I. A.	1.60	4.00	8.00	15.00

Rev: Third design of cloud above letter T.
Thin tailed dragon.

Y#	Date	Mintage	VG	Fine	VF	XF
135.7	CD1904	I. A.	.40	1.00	2.00	3.00

Rev: Fewer clouds around dragon.

Scales on dragons body different. Pearl smaller.

Y#	Date	Mintage	VG	Fine	VF	XF
135.8	CD1904	I. A.	1.60	4.00	8.00	15.00

NOTE: The above coin is believed to be counterfeit.

Rev: Small rosette at either side of dragon.

Y#	Date	Mintage	VG	Fine	VF	XF
135.9	CD1905	496.020	.30	.75	1.50	3.00

Rev: With large oblong rosettes at either side of dragon.

Y#	Date	Mintage	VG	Fine	VF	XF
135.10	CD1905	I. A.	.60	1.50	3.00	5.00

Obv: Rosette in center. Rev. denomination: TEN-CASH.

Y#	Date	Mintage	VG	Fine	VF	XF
138	CD1905	I. A.	1.20	3.00	5.00	10.00

Rev: Without hyphen in TEN CASH.

Y#	Date	Mintage	VG	Fine	VF	XF
138.1	CD1905	I. A.	.30	.75	1.50	3.00

Mule. Y#10k obv. and Y#138 rev., raised or incused mintmark.

Y#	Date	Mintage	VG	Fine	VF	XF
140	CD1906	I. A.	1.20	3.00	7.50	15.00

Mule. Y#10k.2 obv. and Y#138 rev.

Y#	Date	Mintage	VG	Fine	VF	XF
140.1	CD1906	I. A.	8.00	20.00	35.00	50.00

Mule. Y#138 obv. and Y#10k rev.

Y#	Date	Mintage	VG	Fine	VF	XF
140.2	CD1905	I. A.	8.00	20.00	35.00	50.00

Mule. Kiangnan obv. and Kiangsu rev. often confused with Y#162.

Y#	Date	Mintage	VG	Fine	VF	XF
140.3	ND	—	50.00	75.00	125.00	200.00

Mule. Y#138.1 obv. and Y#135 rev.

Y#	Date	Mintage	VG	Fine	VF	XF
140.4	CD1905	I. A.	—	—	Rare	—

Other Kiangnan mules exist, dated 1902 and 1903.

Obv: Mintmark in relief on raised disc.
Rev: Dragon with wide face and incuse eyes.

Y#	Date	Mintage	VG	Fine	VF	XF
10k	CD1906	504.800	.40	1.00	1.75	3.50

Rev: Dragon with narrower face and raised dots for eyes.

Y#	Date	Mintage	VG	Fine	VF	XF
10k.1	CD1906	I. A.	.30	.75	1.50	3.50

Obv: Mintmark in relief in field (no raised disc).
Rev: Dragon with wide face and incuse eyes.

Y#	Date	Mintage	VG	Fine	VF	XF
10k.2	CD1906	I. A.	.20	.50	1.00	2.50

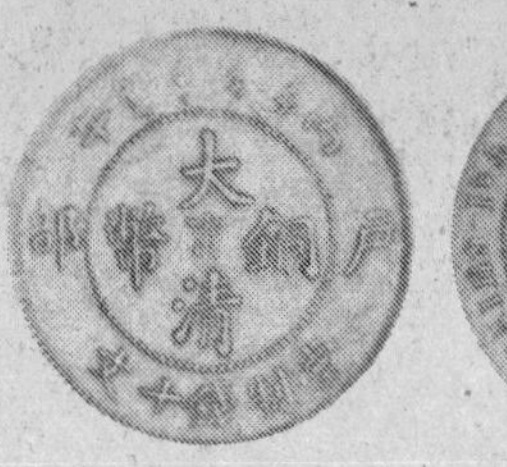

Rev: Dragon with narrow face and raised dots for eyes.

Y#	Date	Mintage	VG	Fine	VF	XF
10k.3	CD1906	I. A.	.20	.50	1.00	2.50

Obv: Mintmark incuse on raised disc.

10k.4	CD1906	I. A.	4.00	10.00	20.00	35.00

Obv: Mintmark incuse on raised disc.
Rev: Dragon with wide face. Seven flames on pearl.

10k.5	CD1907	552.000	.60	1.50	3.00	5.00

Rev: Different dragon with narrow face and small mouth. Five flames on pearl. Dot after coin.

10k.6	CD1907	I. A.	.20	.50	1.00	2.50

BRASS

10k.6a	CD1907	I. A.	3.00	7.50	15.00	25.00

COPPER
Rev: Dragon with large mouth and redesigned head. Flame below pearl has long tail which touches dragon's body. KUO spelled KIIO.

10k.7	CD1907	I. A.	.20	.50	1.00	2.50

Rev: Tail of flame below pearl does not touch body. Dash after word COIN. Kuo spelled KUO.

10k.8	CD1907	I. A.	.20	.50	1.00	2.50

Rev: Dragon with square mouth. Letter K in KUO larger than other letters. No dot or dash after COIN.

Y#	Date	Mintage	VG	Fine	VF	XF
10k.9	CD1907	I. A.	.20	.50	1.00	2.50

Large, flat faced dragon.

10k.9a	CD1907	—	—	—	—	—

Obv: Mintmark incuse on raised disc. Rev: Dragon with small mouth. Five-flame pearl. Dot after coin. Kuo spelled KUO.

10k.10	CD1908	442.750	.20	.50	1.00	2.50

Rev: Dragon has large mouth and redesigned head. Tail on cloud beneath pearl touches dragon's body. Kuo spelled KIIO.

10k.11	CD1908	I. A.	.40	1.00	2.00	3.50

Rev: Dash after COIN. Kuo spelled KUO.

10k.12	CD1908	I. A.	.20	.50	1.00	2.50

Rev: Dragon's head redesigned. No dot or dash after COIN. Kuo spelled KIIO.

10k.13	CD1908	I. A.	.40	1.00	2.00	3.50

NOTE: Most of the 1907 and 1908 ten Cash above have copper spelled GOPPER.

5 CENTS

SILVER, 1.3000 gm.
Rev: Circled dragon.

Y#	Date	Mintage	Fine	VF	XF	Unc
141	ND(1898)	.100	12.50	25.00	50.00	125.00
	ND(1898)	—	—	—	Proof	600.00

Rev: No circle around dragon.

Y#	Date	Mintage	Fine	VF	XF	Unc
141a	ND(1898)	I. A.	4.00	10.00	17.50	35.00
	CD1899	3,812	7.50	18.50	25.00	50.00
	CD1900	—	4.00	10.00	17.50	35.00
	CD1901	—	8.00	20.00	30.00	60.00

10 CENTS

SILVER, 2.6 gm.
Rev: Circled dragon.

Y#	Date	Mintage	Fine	VF	XF	Unc
142	ND(1898)	—	10.00	20.00	40.00	100.00
	ND(1898)	—	—	—	Proof	600.00

142.1	CD1898	Inc. Ab.	6.00	12.00	20.00	35.00

Rev: No circle around dragon with small rosettes at sides.

142a	CD1898	I. A.	BV	4.50	9.00	18.00

Rev: Large rosettes at sides of dragons.

142a.1	CD1898	I. A.	BV	4.50	9.00	18.00

Obv: Large characters in center, small characters in outer ring.

142a.2	CD1899	10.784	BV	4.50	9.00	18.00

Obv: Small characters center, large characters in outer ring.

142a.3	CD1899	I. A.	BV	4.50	9.00	18.00

142a.4	CD1900	—	BV	5.00	10.00	20.00

Obv: No initials. Rev: Large English.

142a.5	CD1901	—	BV	4.50	9.00	18.00

Rev: Small English.

142a.6	CD1901	—	BV	4.50	9.00	18.00

Obv: With initials HAH.
Rev: Large rosettes beside dragon.

142a.7	CD1901	—	3.50	6.50	12.50	25.00

Rev: Small rosettes beside dragon.

142a.8	CD1901	—	3.50	6.50	12.50	25.00

Rev: Large stars beside dragon.

142a.9	CD1902	—	BV	4.50	9.00	18.00

Rev: Small stars beside dragon.

Y#	Date	Mintage	Fine	VF	XF	Unc
142a.10	CD1902	—	BV	4.50	9.00	18.00

Obv: Large rosette.

Y#	Date	Mintage	Fine	VF	XF	Unc
142a.11	CD1903	—	3.50	6.50	12.50	25.00

Obv: Small rosette.

Y#	Date	Mintage	Fine	VF	XF	Unc
142a.12	CD1903	—	3.50	6.50	12.50	25.00
142a.13	CD1904	.897	3.75	7.50	15.00	30.00

Obv: With initials SY upside down.

Y#	Date	Mintage	Fine	VF	XF	Unc
142a.14	CD1905	.681	3.50	6.50	12.50	25.00

Obv: Without initials.

Y#	Date	Mintage	Fine	VF	XF	Unc
142a.15	CD1905	I. A.	3.50	6.50	12.50	25.00

Y#	Date	Mintage	Fine	VF	XF	Unc
146	ND(1911)	*.820	7.50	15.00	30.00	60.00

***NOTE:** Includes 590,000 pieces struck in debased silver in 1916.

20 CENTS

SILVER, 5.3000 gm.
Obv: Rosettes at 2 and 10 o'clock.
Rev: Circle around dragon.

Y#	Date	Mintage	Fine	VF	XF	Unc
143	ND(1898)	7.000	15.00	35.00	60.00	100.00

Y#	Date	Mintage	Fine	VF	XF	Unc
143.1	CD1898	I. A.	13.50	32.50	55.00	90.00

Obv: Large characters in outer ring. Rev: Large English, no circle around dragon.

Y#	Date	Mintage	Fine	VF	XF	Unc
143a	CD1898	I. A.	BV	5.50	11.50	22.50

Obv: Small char. in outer ring. Rev: Small English.

Y#	Date	Mintage	Fine	VF	XF	Unc
143a.1	CD1898	I. A.	BV	5.50	11.50	22.50

Rev: Old type dragon with long face, flanked by short rosettes.

Y#	Date	Mintage	Fine	VF	XF	Unc
143a.2	CD1899	11.096	BV	5.00	10.00	21.50

Rev: New type dragon with shorter face and larger forehead, flanked by long rosettes.

Y#	Date	Mintage	Fine	VF	XF	Unc
143a.3	CD1899	I. A.	BV	5.00	10.00	21.50

Rev: Old type dragon with long face forehead, flanked by long rosettes.

Y#	Date	Mintage	Fine	VF	XF	Unc
143a.4	CD1900	—	5.00	10.00	17.50	35.00

Rev: New type dragon with shorter face and larger forehead.

Y#	Date	Mintage	Fine	VF	XF	Unc
143a.5	CD1900	—	5.00	10.00	18.50	37.50

Obv: No initials.

Y#	Date	Mintage	Fine	VF	XF	Unc
143a.6	CD1901	—	BV	5.00	10.00	21.50

Obv: With initials HAH.

Y#	Date	Mintage	Fine	VF	XF	Unc
143a.7	CD1901	—	BV	5.00	10.00	21.50
143a.8	CD1902	—	BV	6.50	12.50	25.00

Obv: With rosette in outer legend.

Y#	Date	Mintage	Fine	VF	XF	Unc
143a.9	CD1903	—	6.00	15.00	25.00	45.00

Obv: Without rosette

Y#	Date	Mintage	Fine	VF	XF	Unc
143a.10	CD1903	—	8.00	20.00	30.00	55.00

Y#	Date	Mintage	Fine	VF	XF	Unc
143a.11	CD1904	1.172	12.50	30.00	45.00	75.00

Obv: Without initials

Y#	Date	Mintage	Fine	VF	XF	Unc
143a.12	CD1905	.828	6.00	15.00	25.00	45.00

Obv: With initials SY

Y#	Date	Mintage	Fine	VF	XF	Unc
143a.13	CD1905	I. A.	8.00	20.00	30.00	50.00

Y#	Date	Mintage	Fine	VF	XF	Unc
147	(1911)	*2.320	10.00	25.00	40.00	75.00

***NOTE:** Includes 2,005,000 pieces struck in debased silver in 1916.

50 CENTS

SILVER, 13.2000 gm.
Rev: Circled dragon

Y#	Date	Mintage	Fine	VF	XF	Unc
144	(1898)	.100	45.00	110.00	150.00	300.00
	(1898)	—	—	—	Proof	800.00

Rev: Without circle around dragon

Y#	Date	Mintage	Fine	VF	XF	Unc
144a	CD1899	155 pcs.	—	550.00	850.00	1000.
	CD1900	—	250.00	500.00	750.00	900.00

DOLLAR

SILVER, 27.0000 gm.
Rev: Circled dragon. Normal edge reeding.

Y#	Date	Mintage	Fine	VF	XF	Unc
145	(1898)	1.603	25.00	50.00	100.00	250.00
		Ornamented edge				
145.1	(1898)	Inc. Ab.	80.00	150.00	250.00	350.00
		Plain edge				
145.2	(1898)	—	—	—	—	*3500.

*1975 Paramount sale.

Rev: Without circle around old style dragon.

Y#	Date	Mintage	Fine	VF	XF	Unc
145a	CD1898	I. A.	BV	25.00	45.00	90.00
	CD1899	2.039	BV	25.00	40.00	80.00

Rev: Redesigned dragon with shorter face and larger forehead, similar to 1900.

Y#	Date	Mintage	Fine	VF	XF	Unc
145a.1	CD1899	I. A.	BV	25.00	40.00	80.00

Y#	Date	Mintage	Fine	VF	XF	Unc
145a.2	CD1900	—	BV	25.00	40.00	80.00
		Obv: Without initials				
145a.3	CD1901	—	BV	25.00	40.00	80.00

Obv: With initials HAH without rosette.
Rev: Petals of rosettes separated from each other.

Y#	Date	Mintage	Fine	VF	XF	Unc
145a.4	CD1901	—	BV	27.50	45.00	90.00

Obv: With initials HAH and rosette.
Rev: Petals of rosettes run together.

Y#	Date	Mintage	Fine	VF	XF	Unc
145a.5	CD1901	—	BV	28.50	50.00	110.00

Obv: Small date, small HAH.
Rev: Similar to Y#145a.4

Y#	Date	Mintage	Fine	VF	XF	Unc
145a.6	CD1902	—	BV	26.50	42.50	85.00
		Obv: Larger date, larger HAH.				
145a.7	CD1902	—	BV	26.50	42.50	85.00

Obv: With rosette in outer ring.

Y#	Date	Mintage	Fine	VF	XF	Unc
145a.8	CD1903	—	BV	26.50	42.50	85.00
		Obv: Without rosette in outer ring.				
145a.9	CD1903	—	26.50	42.50	80.00	125.00

Obv: With initials HAH and CH, without dots or rosettes.

Y#	Date	Mintage	Fine	VF	XF	Unc
145a.10	CD1904	44.725	BV	25.00	40.00	80.00
		With dot at either side.				
145a.11	CD1904	I. A.	BV	25.00	40.00	80.00
		Rev: Dot to left of numeral 7.				
145a.12	CD1904	I. A.	BV	25.00	40.00	80.00
		Obv: Four point rosette at either side HAH and CH.				
145a.13	CD1904	I. A.	BV	26.50	42.50	85.00
		Obv: With initials HAH and TH.				
145a.14	CD1904	I. A.	BV	30.00	50.00	100.00

Obv: With initials SY.
Rev: Similar to Y#145a.10.

Y#	Date	Mintage	Fine	VF	XF	Unc
145a.15	CD1905	I. A.	BV	25.00	40.00	80.00

NOTE: The initials HAH, SY, CH and TH are those of mint officials and were placed on the coins as a guarantee of the coins fineness. The 5, 10 and 20 Cent coins are often found without a decimal point between the numbers on the reverse.

NCLT ISSUES

PATTERNS

KM#	Date	Mintage	Identification	Mkt.Val.
1	CD1906	—	2 Cash, Copper, Y8k	1750.

KIANGSI / KIANGSEE PROVINCE

A province located in southeastern China. Mostly hilly with some mountains on borders that produce coal and tungsten. Some of China's finest porcelain comes from this province. Kiangsi was visited by Marco Polo. A mint was opened in Nanchang in 1729, closed in 1733, reopened in 1736 and operated with reasonable continuity from that time. Modern machinery was introduced in 1901 although it only produced copper coins. The mint closed amidst internal problems in the 1920's.

EMPIRE

CASH

CAST BRASS

C#	Date	Emperor	Good	VG	Fine	VF
15-1	(1736-95)	Ch'ien Lung	.15	.35	.60	.75
15-2	(1796-1820)	Chia Ch'ing	.20	.50	1.00	1.50

Rev: Dot in upper left corner.

C#	Date	Emperor	Good	VG	Fine	VF
15-2.1	(1796-1820)	Chia Ch'ing	1.20	3.00	4.00	5.00
15-3	(1821-51)	Tao Kuang	.35	.85	1.50	2.00

CAST ZINC

C#	Date	Emperor	Good	VG	Fine	VF
15-3a	(1821-51)	Tao Kuang	—	—	Rare	—

CAST BRASS

C#	Date	Emperor	Good	VG	Fine	VF
15-4	(1851-61)	Hsien Feng	.80	2.00	3.00	4.00
15-7	(1862-74)	T'ung Chih	1.20	3.00	4.00	5.00
15-9	(1875-1908)	Kuang Hsu	2.00	5.00	7.50	10.00

10 CASH

CAST BRASS

C#	Date	Emperor	Good	VG	Fine	VF
15-5	(1851-61)	Hsien Feng	10.00	17.50	27.50	40.00
15-8	(1862-74)	T'ung Chih	—	—	Rare	—
15-10	(1875-1908)	Kuang Hsu	—	—	Rare	—

50 CASH

CAST BRASS

C#	Date	Emperor	Good	VG	Fine	VF
15-6	(1851-61)	Hsien Feng	20.00	30.00	40.00	55.00

STRUCK COINAGE

10 CASH

COPPER

Obv: Vertical rosette at center.
Rev: Name of province spelled KIANG-SEE.

Y#	Date	Mintage	VG	Fine	VF	XF
149	ND	—	2.75	7.00	12.00	20.00

Obv: Horizontal rosette at center.

Y#	Date	Mintage	VG	Fine	VF	XF
149.1	ND	—	2.75	7.00	12.00	20.00

Obv: Different Manchu character to right. Rev: Circled dragon.

Y#	Date	Mintage	VG	Fine	VF	XF
149.2	ND	—	—	—	Rare	—

NOTE: May be a pattern.

Obv: Manchu reading Pao Yuan.
Rev: Name of province spelled KIANG-SI, two stars to either side of dragon.

Y#	Date	Mintage	VG	Fine	VF	XF
150	ND	—	2.00	5.00	9.00	15.00

Obv: Manchu reading Pao Ch'ang at center and Chinese reading Ku P'ing at 3 and 9 o'clock.

Y#	Date	Mintage	VG	Fine	VF	XF
150.1	ND	—	1.20	3.00	5.00	10.00

Obv: Manchu reading Pao Ch'ang at 3 and 9 o'clock. Horizontal rosette in center.

Y#	Date	Mintage	VG	Fine	VF	XF
150.2	ND	—	.40	1.00	2.00	4.00
	ND	double die reverse		—	Rare	—

BRASS

Y#	Date	Mintage	VG	Fine	VF	XF
150.2a	ND	—	1.60	4.00	7.00	12.00

COPPER

Obv: Vertical rosette in center.

Y#	Date	Mintage	VG	Fine	VF	XF
150.3	ND	—	.40	1.00	2.00	4.00

Obv: Horizontal rosette. Rev: One star at either side of dragon, large English lettering.

Y#	Date	Mintage	VG	Fine	VF	XF
150.4	ND	—	.40	1.00	2.00	4.00

BRASS

Y#	Date	Mintage	VG	Fine	VF	XF
150.4a	ND	—	1.40	3.50	6.50	11.50

Obv: Vertical rosette.

Y#	Date	Mintage	VG	Fine	VF	XF
150.5	ND	—	.40	1.00	2.00	4.00

Rev: Smaller English lettering, one star at either side of dragon.

Y#	Date	Mintage	VG	Fine	VF	XF
150.6	ND	—	.40	1.00	2.00	4.00

Obv: Small rosette center.
Rev: One star at either side of dragon.

Y#	Date	Mintage	VG	Fine	VF	XF
150.7	ND	—	2.00	5.00	10.00	15.00

Rev: Three stars at either side of dragon.

Y#	Date	Mintage	VG	Fine	VF	XF
150.8	ND	—	4.00	10.00	15.00	22.50

Obv: Manchu for Pao Ch'ang at 3 and 9 o'clock.
Rev: Name of province spelled KIANG-SI. Front view dragon, with mountain below pearl.

Y#	Date	Mintage	VG	Fine	VF	XF
152	ND	—	2.00	5.00	7.50	10.00

Obv: Horizontal rosette in center and Manchu for Pao Ch'ang K'u Ping at 3 and 9 o'clock.

Y#	Date	Mintage	VG	Fine	VF	XF
152.1	ND	—	2.00	5.00	7.50	10.00

Obv: Horizontal rosette in center and Manchu for Pao Ch'ang at 3 and 9 o'clock, small character '10'.

Y#	Date	Mintage	VG	Fine	VF	XF
152.2	ND	—	4.00	10.00	15.00	22.50

Obv: Horizontal rosette in center and Manchu Pao Chang at 3 and 9 o'clock, large character '10'.
Rev: Without mountain below dragon.

Y#	Date	Mintage	VG	Fine	VF	XF
152.3	ND	—	2.75	7.00	10.00	15.00

Obv: Small character '10'.

Y#	Date	Mintage	VG	Fine	VF	XF
152.4	ND	—	2.75	7.00	10.00	15.00

Obv: Manchu for Pao Ch'ang in center, Chinese K'u P'ing at 3 and 9 o'clock. Rev: Without mountain below pearl, dragon's body repositioned.

Y#	Date	Mintage	VG	Fine	VF	XF
152.5	ND	—	2.75	7.00	10.00	15.00

Rev: With mountain under dragon.

Y#	Date	Mintage	VG	Fine	VF	XF
152.6	ND	—	2.50	6.50	10.00	15.00

Rev: Front view dragon with KIANG-SEE PROVINCE above.

Y#	Date	Mintage	VG	Fine	VF	XF
153	ND	—	1.60	4.00	6.00	9.00

Obv: Manchu for Pao Ch'ang at center and Chinese K'u P'ing at 3 and 9 o'clock.

153.1	ND	—	.60	1.50	2.75	6.00

Obv: Manchu for Pao Ch'ang at 3 and 9 o'clock and horizontal rosette in center.

153.2	ND	—	.60	1.50	2.75	6.00

Obv: With small vertical rosette in center.

153.3	ND	—	.60	1.50	2.75	6.00

NOTE: All four varieties of Y#153 are found with and without a swirl on the pearl below dragon's mouth.

Rev: Flying dragon with KIANG-SI above.

154	ND	—	15.00	35.00	60.00	85.00

Rev: Eyes of dragon in relief

10m	CD1906	—	1.00	2.50	5.00	10.00

Rev: Dragon's eyes incuse

10m.1	CD1906	—	1.00	2.50	5.00	10.00

Rev: Dragon redesigned, small faint cloud beneath pearl.

Y#	Date	Mintage	VG	Fine	VF	XF
10m.2	CD1906	—	4.00	10.00	15.00	25.00

REPUBLIC

10 CASH

COPPER

Obv: Mintmark incused on raised-disc center, with Chinese characters on four sides reading Ta Han T'ung Pi. Five character value in outer ring at bottom. Rev: Ring of nine balls no inscription.

411	CD1911	—	—	—	Rare	—

Obv: Date appears at 3 and 9 o'clock. Rev: Nine pointed star inside circle and five-petal rosette at 3 and 9 o'clock.

412	CD1912	—	100.00	150.00	200.00	300.00

Obv: Horizontal rosette in center, with Chinese characters Chiang Hsi above and below. Rev: Six-petal rosette to either side.

412a	CD1912	—	1.00	2.50	4.00	8.50

Obv: Small vertical rosette in center.

412a.1	CD1912	—	1.00	2.50	4.00	8.50

Obv: Large vertical rosette, thick, large center characters. Rev: Five-petal rosette either side.

412a.2	CD1912	—	5.00	10.00	15.00	22.50

Obv: Large vertical rosette in center, thin center characters.

Y#	Date	Mintage	VG	Fine	VF	XF
412a.3	CD1912	—	1.00	2.50	4.00	8.50

NOTE: Many Kiangsi coins have a six-petal rosette in the center of the obverse, arranged so that two sides of the rosette are formed by two petals in line with each other. The remaining two sides have a single petal, standing out from the rest. The direction that these single petals point, determines whether the rosette is horizontal or vertical. A horizontal rosette has the single petals pointing left and right, while the single petals of the vertical rosette point up and down.

KIANGSU / KIANGSOO PROVINCE

A province located on the east coast of China. One of the smallest and most densely populated of all Chinese provinces. A mint opened in Soochow in 1667, but closed shortly after in 1670. A new mint opened in 1734 for producing Cash coins and had continuous operation until about 1870. Modern equipment was introduced in 1898 and a second mint was opened in 1904. Both mints closed down production in 1906. Taels were produced in Shanghai by local silversmiths as early as 1856. These saw limited circulation in the immediate area.

EMPIRE

Kiangsu Issues

CASH

CAST BRASS

C#	Date	Emperor	Good	VG	Fine	VF
16-1	(1736-95)	Ch'ien Lung	.20	.50	.85	1.25

NOTE: MINOR varieties of the mintmark exist.

16-2	(1796-1820)	Chia Ch'ing	.20	.50	1.00	1.75

Narrow rims.

16-3	(1821-51)	Tao Kuang	.75	1.50	2.50	3.50

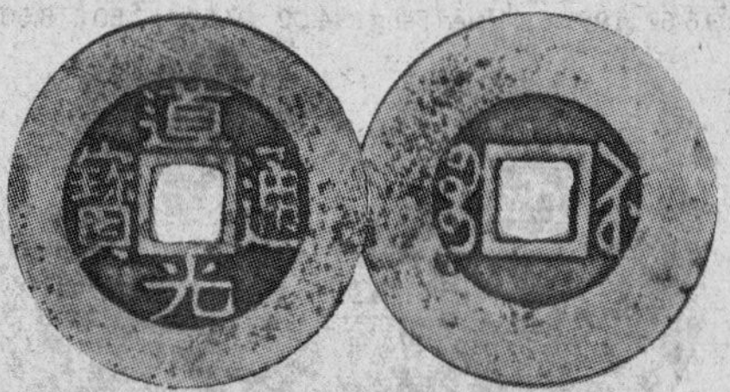

Wide rims.

16-3.1	(1821-51)	Tao Kuang	.75	1.50	2.50	3.50

Narrow rims.

C#	Date	Emperor	Good	VG	Fine	VF
16-4	(1851-61)	Hsien Feng	1.00	2.00	3.00	4.00

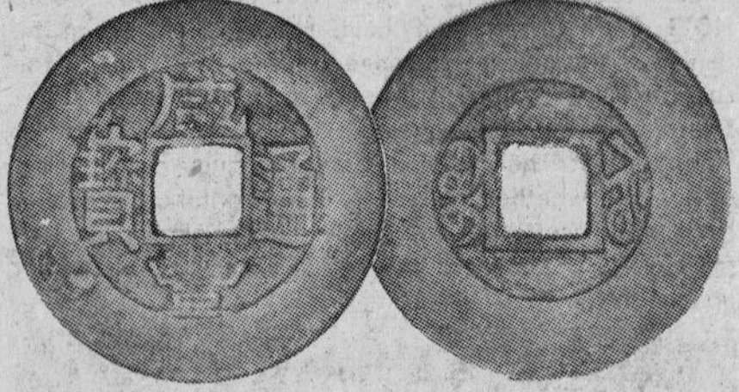

Wide rims.

C#	Date	Emperor	Good	VG	Fine	VF
16-4.1	(1851-61)	Hsien Feng	2.00	4.00	7.00	10.00

Rev: Crescent above.

C#	Date	Emperor	Good	VG	Fine	VF
16-4.2	(1851-61)	Hsien Feng	2.00	4.00	7.00	10.00
16-11	(1862-74)	T'ung Chih	1.00	2.00	3.00	4.00
16-12	(1875-1908)	Kuang Hsu	1.20	3.00	4.00	5.00

Rev: Circle above.

C#	Date	Emperor	Good	VG	Fine	VF
16-12.1	(1875-1908)	Kuang Hsu	3.00	7.50	10.00	13.50

Rev: Crescent above.

C#	Date	Emperor	Good	VG	Fine	VF
16-12.2	(1875-1908)	Kuang Hsu	3.00	7.50	10.00	13.50

5 CASH

CAST BRASS

C#	Date	Emperor	Good	VG	Fine	VF
16-5	(1851-61)	Hsien Feng	20.00	30.00	45.00	70.00

CAST IRON

C#	Date	Emperor	Good	VG	Fine	VF
16-5a	(1851-61)	Hsien Feng	30.00	45.00	65.00	100.00

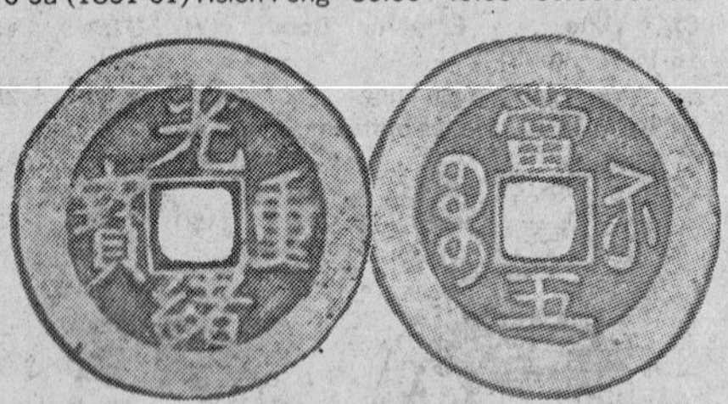

CAST BRASS

C#	Date	Emperor	Good	VG	Fine	VF
16-13	(1875-1908)	Kuang Hsu	12.50	20.00	30.00	45.00

10 CASH

CAST BRASS, 36-40mm

C#	Date	Emperor	Good	VG	Fine	VF
16-6	(1851-61)	Hsien Feng	4.00	7.50	12.50	18.50

30-34mm

C#	Date	Emperor	Good	VG	Fine	VF
16-6.1	(1851-61)	Hsien Feng	4.00	7.50	12.50	18.50

CAST IRON

C#	Date	Emperor	Good	VG	Fine	VF
16-6a	(1851-61)	Hsien Feng	27.50	50.00	75.00	100.00

CAST BRASS

C#	Date	Emperor	Good	VG	Fine	VF
16-14	(1875-1908)	Kuang Hsu	—	—	Rare	—

20 CASH

CAST BRASS

C#	Date	Emperor	Good	VG	Fine	VF
16-7	(1851-61)	Hsien Feng	13.50	25.00	35.00	50.00

30 CASH

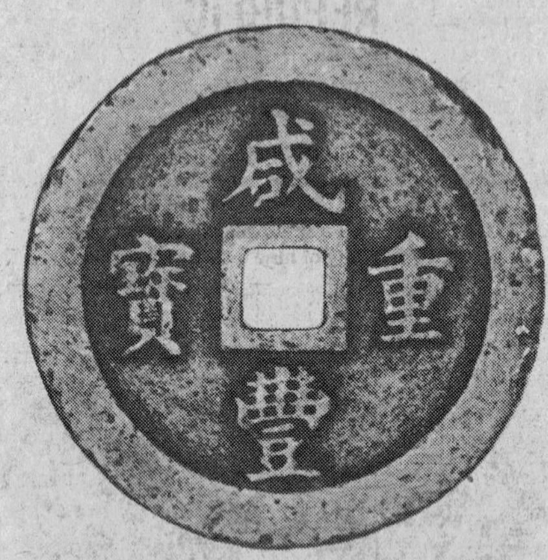

CAST BRASS

C#	Date	Emperor	Good	VG	Fine	VF
16-8	(1851-61)	Hsien Feng	22.50	40.00	55.00	75.00

Rev: Crescent in upper left and right corners; dot in lower left and right corners.

C#	Date	Emperor	Good	VG	Fine	VF
16-8.1	(1851-61)	Hsien Feng	25.00	45.00	60.00	85.00

50 CASH

CAST BRASS

C#	Date	Emperor	Good	VG	Fine	VF
16-9	(1851-61)	Hsien Feng	17.50	27.50	37.50	55.00

100 CASH

CAST BRASS

C#	Date	Emperor	Good	VG	Fine	VF
16-10	(1851-61)	Hsien Feng	17.50	30.00	45.00	65.00

Chiang-ning Mint

5 CASH

CAST BRASS

C#	Date	Emperor	Good	VG	Fine	VF
16-12	(1851-61)	Hsien Feng	—	—	Rare	—

STRUCK COINAGE

CASH

BRASS, 21-23mm

Su#	Date	Mintage	VG	Fine	VF	XF
85	ND	—	18.50	28.50	42.50	70.00

5 CASH

COPPER

Rev: Side view dragon, EIVE for FIVE.

Y#	Date	Mintage	VG	Fine	VF	XF
158	(1901)	—	20.00	40.00	65.00	100.00

BRASS

Y#	Date	Mintage	VG	Fine	VF	XF
9n	CD1906	—	27.50	60.00	100.00	150.00

10 CASH

BRASS

Y#	Date	Mintage	Fine	VF	XF	Unc
—	ND(1898)	—	—	—	Rare	—

COPPER

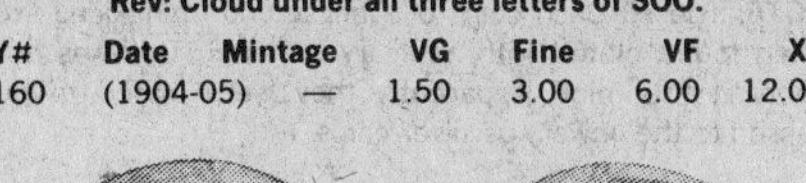

Rev: Cloud under all three letters of SOO.

Y#	Date	Mintage	VG	Fine	VF	XF
160	(1904-05)	—	1.50	3.00	6.00	12.00

Rev: Cloud under first two letters of SOO. Manchu character at 9 o'clock higher, dragons body thinner.

Y#	Date	Mintage	VG	Fine	VF	XF
160.1	(1904-05)	—	1.50	3.00	6.00	12.00

Obv: Manchu characters at center, no rosettes. Reeded edge.

Y#	Date	Mintage	VG	Fine	VF	XF
162	ND	—	.40	1.00	2.00	3.00

Obv: Manchu in center, rosettes at 2 and 10 o'clock.

Y#	Date	Mintage	VG	Fine	VF	XF
162.1	ND	—	.40	1.00	2.00	3.00

Unreeded edge.

Y#	Date	Mintage	VG	Fine	VF	XF
162.2	ND	—	.40	1.00	2.00	3.00

Obv. and rev: Tiny rosettes. Reeded edge.

Y#	Date	Mintage	VG	Fine	VF	XF
162.3	ND	—	.60	1.50	2.50	4.00

Obv: Rosette center, Manchu at 3 and 9 o'clock.

Y#	Date	Mintage	VG	Fine	VF	XF
162.4	ND	—	.30	.75	1.50	3.00

Plain edge.

Y#	Date	Mintage	VG	Fine	VF	XF
162.5	ND	—	.30	.75	1.50	3.00

Obv: Rosette center, large Manchu at 3 and 9 o'clock, higher than on 162.4. Reeded edge.

Y#	Date	Mintage	VG	Fine	VF	XF
162.6	ND	—	.60	1.50	2.50	4.00

Plain edge.

Y#	Date	Mintage	VG	Fine	VF	XF
162.7	ND	—	.60	1.50	2.50	4.00

BRASS

Y#	Date	Mintage	VG	Fine	VF	XF
162.7a	ND	—	—	—	Rare	—

COPPER

Obv: Manchu characters at center, reeded edge.

Y#	Date	Mintage	VG	Fine	VF	XF
162.8	CD1902	—	.80	2.00	4.00	7.50

Obv: Manchu characters at center, reeded edge.

Y#	Date	Mintage	VG	Fine	VF	XF
162.9	CD1903	—	2.00	5.00	7.50	12.00

Obv: Rosette center, small Manchu at 3 and 9 o'clock. Unreeded edge.

Y#	Date	Mintage	VG	Fine	VF	XF
162.10	CD1905	—	.40	1.00	2.00	4.00

Obv: Larger Manchu characters.

Y#	Date	Mintage	VG	Fine	VF	XF
162.11	CD1905	—	1.00	2.50	5.00	8.00

Rev: Kiangsu spelled KIANG-COO.

Y#	Date	Mintage	VG	Fine	VF	XF
162.12	CD1905	—	100.00	250.00	500.00	750.00

NOTE: Y#162.10 is considered a contemporary counterfeit by some authorities.

Mule: Kiangsu obv. Y#162 and Kiangnan rev. Y#135.

Y#	Date	Mintage	VG	Fine	VF	XF
162.13	ND	—	50.00	75.00	125.00	200.00

Mule. Kiangsu obv. Y#162.8 and Kiangnan rev. Y#135.

Y#	Date	Mintage	VG	Fine	VF	XF
162.14	CD1902	—	50.00	75.00	125.00	200.00

Mule. Kiangsu obv. Y#162.9 and Kiangnan rev. Y#135.

Y#	Date	Mintage	VG	Fine	VF	XF
162.15	CD1903	—	50.00	75.00	125.00	200.00

Mintmark incused on raised disc. Plain edge.

Y#	Date	Mintage	VG	Fine	VF	XF
10n	CD1906	—	1.00	2.50	5.00	10.00

Reeded edge.

Y#	Date	Mintage	VG	Fine	VF	XF
10n.1	CD1906	—	2.00	5.00	10.00	15.00

Mintmark in relief in field at center; no raised disc. Plain edge.

Y#	Date	Mintage	VG	Fine	VF	XF
10n.2	CD1906	—	2.00	5.00	10.00	15.00

20 CASH

COPPER

Y#	Date	Mintage	VG	Fine	VF	XF
163	ND	—	15.00	27.50	37.50	60.00

BRASS

Y#	Date	Mintage	VG	Fine	VF	XF
163a	ND	—	25.00	40.00	60.00	90.00

COPPER

Y#	Date	Mintage	VG	Fine	VF	XF
11n.1	CD1906	—	20.00	32.50	50.00	75.00

BRASS

Y#	Date	Mintage	VG	Fine	VF	XF
11n.1a	CD1906	—	30.00	50.00	75.00	125.00

Chingkiang Issues

Chingkiang was a city in Kiangsu province. Some of

the coins issued by the mint have the name spelled Tsing-Kiang in English. This is not an error as both spellings were acceptable at the time.

10 CASH

COPPER
Obv: Large character at 3 o'clock. Reeded edge.

Y#	Date	Mintage	VG	Fine	VF	XF
77	(1905)	—	1.00	2.50	4.00	7.50
Plain edge.						
77.1	(1905)	—	1.00	2.50	4.00	7.50
Obv: Ring around the center dot in the rosette. Reeded edge.						
77.2	(1905)	—	1.20	3.00	5.00	10.00
Plain edge.						
77.3	(1905)	—	1.20	3.00	5.00	10.00

Obv: Smaller character at 3 o'clock. Reeded edge.

Y#	Date	Mintage	VG	Fine	VF	XF
77.4	(1905)	—	1.40	3.50	6.00	12.00
Plain edge.						
77.5	(1905)	—	1.40	3.50	6.00	12.00

Obv: No rosette. Reeded edge.

Y#	Date	Mintage	VG	Fine	VF	XF
77.6	(1905)	—	1.20	3.00	5.00	10.00
Plain edge.						
77.7	(1905)	—	1.20	3.00	5.00	10.00

Obv: Large character at 3 o'clock. Reeded edge.

Y#	Date	Mintage	VG	Fine	VF	XF
78	(1905)	—	.60	1.50	3.00	5.00
Plain edge.						
78.1	(1905)	—	1.20	3.00	5.00	10.00

Obv: Small character at 3 o'clock. Reeded edge.

Y#	Date	Mintage	VG	Fine	VF	XF
78.2	(1905)	—	.40	1.00	2.00	4.50
Plain edge.						
78.3	(1905)	—	.30	.75	1.50	4.00

Obv: No rosette. Reeded edge.

Y#	Date	Mintage	VG	Fine	VF	XF
78.4	(1905)	—	1.40	3.50	6.00	15.00

Obv: Small mintmark in center, no center raised disc.
Rev: Five flames on pearl. No hyphen in TI KUO.

Y#	Date	Mintage	VG	Fine	VF	XF
10d	CD1906	—	15.00	25.00	50.00	100.00

Obv: Small mintmark. Rev: Seven flames on pearl, hyphen in TI-KUO.

Y#	Date	Mintage	VG	Fine	VF	XF
10d.1	CD1906	—	.60	1.50	2.50	5.00
Rev: Nine flames on pearl, no hyphen in TI KUO.						
10d.2	CD1906	—	.40	1.00	2.00	4.00

Obv: Large mintmark. Rev: Five flames on pearl, no hyphen in TI KUO.

Y#	Date	Mintage	VG	Fine	VF	XF
10d.3	CD1906	—	.60	1.50	2.50	5.00

Rev: Seven flames on pearl, hyphen in TI-KUO.

Y#	Date	Mintage	VG	Fine	VF	XF
10d.4	CD1906	—	.60	1.50	2.50	5.00

Rev: Nine flames on pearl, hyphen in TI-KUO.

Y#	Date	Mintage	VG	Fine	VF	XF
10d.5	CD1906	—	.60	1.50	2.50	5.00
Mintmark incused on raised disc.						
10d.6	CD1906	—	—	—	Rare	—

NOTE: A trial piece.

NOTE: The 10 Cash coins of Kiangsu and Chingkiang are often found plated with a silvery material. This was not done at the mint. Apparently they were plated to be passed to the unwary as silver coins.

Shanghai Issues

NOTE: An important port city in Kiangsu province. Although there was no mint in Shanghai prior to the 1930's a number of coins were minted for Shanghai. Of these only the 1856 Silversmith Taels ever circulated. The Kwanping series was struck by the Royal Mint, London about 1858, while the 1867 series was struck at the Hong Kong mint. Refer to FOREIGN ENCLAVES - SHANGHAI.

5 CH'IEN

SILVER, 18.4 gm.
Issued by Wang Yung-sheng. Engraved by Wan Ch'uan.
Similar to K#902.

K#	Date	Mintage	VG	Fine	VF	XF
908	Yr.6 (1856)	—	80.00	200.00	250.00	325.00

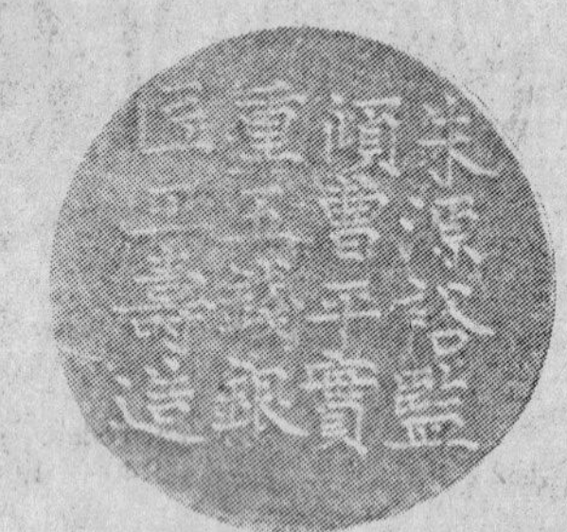

Issued by Yu Shen-sheng. Engraved by Wang Shou.

K#	Date	Mintage	VG	Fine	VF	XF
907	Yr.6 (1856)	—	60.00	150.00	200.00	275.00

Issued by Ching Cheng-chi. Engraved by Wan Ch'uan.

K#	Date	Mintage	VG	Fine	VF	XF
910	Yr.6 (1856)	—	60.00	150.00	200.00	275.00

LIANG (TAEL)

SILVER, 36.7 gm.
Issued by Wang Yung-sheng. Engraved by Wan Ch'uan.
Similar to K#902.

K#	Date	Mintage	VG	Fine	VF	XF
900	Yr.6 (1856)	—	125.00	275.00	375.00	550.00

Issued by Yu Shen-sheng. Engraved by P'ing Cheng.

902	Yr.6 (1856)	—	100.00	225.00	275.00	400.00

Issued by Yu Shen-sheng. Engraved by Feng Nien.

K#	Date	Mintage	VG	Fine	VF	XF
901	Yr.6 (1856)	—	100.00	225.00	275.00	400.00

Issued by Ching Cheng-chi. Engraved by Feng Nien.

903	Yr.6 (1856)	—	60.00	150.00	200.00	275.00

K#900-910 above are known as Silversmith Taels because each bears the name of a silver smelting firm in Shanghai. The coins were authorized by the taotai (a government official) of Shanghai to facilitate foreign trade and to replace the vanishing Mexican 8 Reales which had become very scarce due to hoarding.

NCLT ISSUES

PATTERNS

KM#	Date	Mintage	Identification	Mkt.Val.
1	ND	—	2 Cash, Brass, Y159	225.00

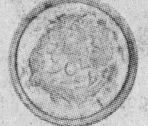

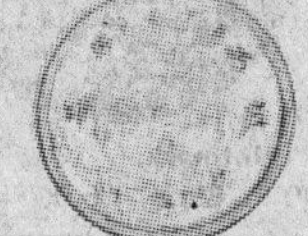

2	CD1906	—	2 Cash, Brass, Y8n	135.00

3	ND	—	5 Cash, Brass, EIVE for five, Y161.1	250.00
4	ND	—	5 Cash, Copper, EIVE for five, Y161.1a	250.00

KM#	Date	Mintage	Identification	Mkt.Val.
5	CD1906	—	20 Cash, Copper, Y11d	Rare

KIRIN

A province of northeast China that was formed in 1945. Before that it was one of the three original provinces of Manchuria. Besides growing corn, wheat and tobacco, there is also coal mining. An arsenal in Kirin opened in 1881 and was chosen as a source for coinage attempts. In 1884 Tael trials were and regular coinage began in 1895. Modern equipment was installed in a new mint in Kirin in 1901. The issues of this mint were very prolific and many varieties exist due to the poor iron dies used for striking the earlier issues. The mint burned down in 1911.

EMPIRE

CASH

CAST BRASS

C#	Date	Emperor	Good	VG	Fine	VF
17-1	(1875-1908)	Kuang Hsu	8.50	13.50	20.00	30.00

10 CASH

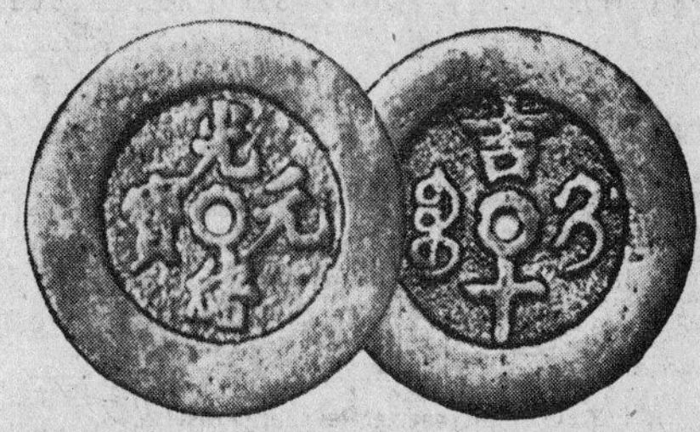

CAST BRASS

17-2	(1875-1908)	Kuang Hsu	—	—	Rare	—

STRUCK COINAGE

NOTE: It has been estimated there are 2500 varieties of Kirin silver coins and 1000 varieties of copper 10 Cash. Listed here are basic types and major varieties only.

CASH

BRASS, struck

Su#	Date	Mintage	Fine	VF	XF	Unc
481	ND	—	—	—	Rare	—

NOTE: This coin is sometimes erroneously attributed to Chichou in Chihli province.

2 CASH

COPPER

Y#	Date	Mintage	VG	Fine	VF	XF
175	ND	—	60.00	100.00	150.00	200.00

10 CASH

COPPER

Y#	Date	Mintage	VG	Fine	VF	XF
174	ND	—	20.00	35.00	65.00	100.00

Y#	Date	Mintage	VG	Fine	VF	XF
176	ND	—	20.00	35.00	50.00	75.00

Thinner dragon.

Y#	Date	Mintage	VG	Fine	VF	XF
176.1	ND	—	20.00	35.00	50.00	75.00

Obv: Small rosette. Rev: Large rosette.

Y#	Date	Mintage	VG	Fine	VF	XF
177	ND	—	3.50	6.00	12.00	20.00

Rev: Small star.

Y#	Date	Mintage	VG	Fine	VF	XF
177.1	ND	—	3.00	5.00	10.00	15.00

Obv: Small star. Rev: Large rosette.

Y#	Date	Mintage	VG	Fine	VF	XF
177.2	ND	—	4.00	7.50	15.00	25.00

Obv. & Rev: Small stars.

Y#	Date	Mintage	VG	Fine	VF	XF
177.3	ND	—	3.00	6.00	10.00	15.00

BRASS

Y#	Date	Mintage	VG	Fine	VF	XF
177.3a	ND	—	3.75	7.00	12.00	18.00

COPPER

Obv. and rev: Large stars.

Y#	Date	Mintage	VG	Fine	VF	XF
177.4	ND	—	3.50	6.00	10.00	15.00

Obv: Large star. Rev: Large rosette.

Y#	Date	Mintage	VG	Fine	VF	XF
177.5	ND	—	3.50	6.00	10.00	15.00

Obv: Medium rosettes.

Y#	Date	Mintage	VG	Fine	VF	XF
177.6	ND	—	3.50	6.00	10.00	15.00

Rev. legend: Denomination spelled: CASHIS

Y#	Date	Mintage	VG	Fine	VF	XF
177.7	ND	—	60.00	100.00	160.00	250.00

NOTE: It is difficult to differentiate the stars and rosettes on worn coins. The rosettes have a dot in the center while the stars have a hole in the center. It has been estimated that 1000 varieties of Y#177 exist.

Obv: Very small mintmark.

Y#	Date	Mintage	VG	Fine	VF	XF
20p	CD1909	—	5.00	8.50	15.00	25.00

Obv: Larger mintmark. Rev: Head of dragon redesigned with more whiskers.

Y#	Date	Mintage	VG	Fine	VF	XF
20p.1	CD1909	—	6.00	10.00	17.50	30.00

Obv: Larger mintmark. Rev: Dragon as Y#20p.

Y#	Date	Mintage	VG	Fine	VF	XF
20p.2	CD1909	—	6.00	10.00	17.50	30.00

NOTE: For Y 20x refer to General Issues-Empire.

20 CASH

COPPER

Y#	Date	Mintage	VG	Fine	VF	XF
178	ND	—	30.00	50.00	75.00	110.00

Obv: Manchu in center, eight characters below.

Y#	Date	Mintage	VG	Fine	VF	XF
A176	ND	—	35.00	60.00	100.00	150.00

Obv: Rosette in center, three characters below.

Y#	Date	Mintage	VG	Fine	VF	XF
A176.1	ND	—	35.00	60.00	120.00	180.00

Y#	Date	Mintage	VG	Fine	VF	XF
21p	CD1909	—	60.00	90.00	140.00	200.00

50 CASH

BRASS

Y#	Date	Mintage	Good	VG	Fine	VF
B176	CD1901	(3 known)	500.00	1000.	2000.	—

NOTE: A similar 20 Cash and silver 50 Cent have been reported.

5 CENTS

SILVER, 1.2700 gm.
Obv: Flower vase center.
Rev: Cross before and after denomination.

Y#	Date	Mintage	Fine	VF	XF	Unc
179	ND	—	9.00	18.50	37.50	75.00
	Rev: No crosses.					
179.1	ND	—	5.00	10.00	20.00	40.00
	CD1899	—	6.50	12.50	25.00	50.00
	CD1900	—	7.50	15.00	30.00	60.00
	CD1906	—	6.50	12.50	25.00	50.00
	CD1907	—	6.50	12.50	25.00	50.00
	CD1908	One known	—	—	—	—

Obv: Yin-Yang center.

Y#	Date	Mintage	Fine	VF	XF	Unc
179a	CD1900	—	7.50	15.00	30.00	60.00
	CD1901	—	5.50	11.50	22.50	45.00
	CD1902	—	6.50	12.50	25.00	50.00
	CD1903	—	12.50	25.00	50.00	100.00
	CD1904	—	5.50	11.50	22.50	45.00
	CD1905	—	7.50	15.00	30.00	60.00

10 CENTS

SILVER, 2.5500 gm.
Obv: Small flower vase center.
Rev: Cross before and after denomination.

Y#	Date	Mintage	Fine	VF	XF	Unc
180	ND	—	5.50	11.50	22.50	45.00
	Obv: Large flower vase center. Rev: No cross flanking denomination.					
180.1	ND	—	5.50	11.50	22.50	45.00
	CD1899	—	6.50	12.50	25.00	50.00
	CD1900	—	6.50	12.50	25.00	50.00
	CD1906	—	6.50	12.50	25.00	50.00
	CD1907	—	45.00	90.00	150.00	250.00

Obv: Yin-Yang center.

Y#	Date	Mintage	Fine	VF	XF	Unc
180a	CD1900	—	7.50	15.00	30.00	60.00
	CD1901	—	5.50	11.50	22.50	45.00
	CD1902	—	7.50	15.00	30.00	60.00
	CD1903	—	9.00	18.50	37.50	75.00
	CD1904	—	10.00	20.00	40.00	80.00
	CD1905	—	5.50	11.50	22.50	45.00

Obv: Numeral 1 in center.

Y#	Date	Mintage	Fine	VF	XF	Unc
180c	CD1908	—	27.50	55.00	90.00	150.00

20 CENTS

SILVER, 5.1000 gm.
Obv: Flower vase center.

Y#	Date	Mintage	Fine	VF	XF	Unc
181	ND	—	7.50	15.00	30.00	60.00
	CD1899	—	6.50	12.50	25.00	50.00
	CD1900	—	7.50	15.00	30.00	60.00
	CD1906	Inc. Be.	6.50	12.50	25.00	50.00
	CD1907	Inc. Be.	6.50	12.50	25.00	50.00
	CD1908	Inc. Be.	87.50	175.00	300.00	500.00

Obv: Yin-Yang center.

Y#	Date	Mintage	Fine	VF	XF	Unc
181a	CD1900	—	7.50	15.00	30.00	60.00
	CD1901	22.508	6.50	12.50	25.00	50.00
	CD1902	Inc.Ab.	6.50	12.50	25.00	50.00
	CD1903	Inc.Ab.	6.50	12.50	25.00	50.00
	CD1904	Inc.Ab.	6.50	12.50	25.00	50.00
	CD1905	Inc.Ab.	6.50	12.50	25.00	50.00

Obv: Manchu characters center.

Y#	Date	Mintage	Fine	VF	XF	Unc
181b	CD1908	Inc.Ab.	30.00	60.00	100.00	160.00

Obv: Numeral 2 center.

Y#	Date	Mintage	Fine	VF	XF	Unc
181c	CD1908	Inc.Ab.	20.00	40.00	70.00	120.00

Obv: Mintmark in relief on raised disc at center.

Y#	Date	Mintage	Fine	VF	XF	Unc
22	(1909)	—	30.00	60.00	100.00	175.00
	Mintmark incuse on raised disc at center.					
22.1	(1909)	—	30.00	60.00	100.00	175.00

50 CENTS

SILVER, 13.1000 gm.
Obv.: Flower vase center with rosette to either side. Rev.: No crosses flanking denomination.

Y#	Date	Mintage	Fine	VF	XF	Unc
182	ND	—	16.50	27.50	47.50	80.00
	Obv.: Rosette either side. Rev.: Crosses before and after denomination.					
182.1	ND	—	16.50	27.50	47.50	80.00
	Obv.: No rosettes. Rev.: No crosses.					
182.2	ND	—	16.50	27.50	47.50	80.00
	CD1899	—	27.50	47.50	80.00	135.00
	CD1900	—	20.00	32.50	55.00	90.00
	CD1906	—	20.00	32.50	55.00	90.00

Y#	Date	Mintage	Fine	VF	XF	Unc
182.3	CD1907	—	20.00	32.50	55.00	90.00

Y#	Date	Mintage	Fine	VF	XF	Unc
182.3	CD1908	—	47.50	80.00	135.00	225.00

Obv: Yin-Yang in center.

182a	CD1900	—	20.00	32.50	55.00	90.00

Obv: Redesigned Yin-Yang in center.

182a.1	CD1901	—	20.00	32.50	55.00	90.00
	CD1902	—	20.00	32.50	55.00	90.00
	CD1903	—	21.50	35.00	60.00	100.00
	CD1904	—	20.00	32.50	55.00	90.00
	CD1905	—	17.50	30.00	50.00	80.00

Obv: Manchu characters in center.

182b	CD1908	—	65.00	110.00	185.00	300.00

DOLLAR

SILVER, 26.1000 gm.
Obv: Flower vase center.
Rev: Crosses or rosettes before and after denomination.

Y#	Date	Mintage	Fine	VF	XF	Unc
183	ND	—	47.50	80.00	135.00	225.00
	CD1899	—	55.00	90.00	150.00	250.00
	CD1900	—	47.50	80.00	135.00	225.00
	CD1906	—	47.50	80.00	135.00	225.00
	CD1907	—	47.50	80.00	135.00	225.00
	CD1908	—	120.00	200.00	350.00	600.00

Rev: No crosses flanking denomination.

183.1	ND	—	47.50	80.00	135.00	225.00

Obv: Yin-Yang in center.
Rev: Similar to Y#183.1

183a	CD1900	—	72.50	120.00	200.00	350.00
	CD1901	—	65.00	110.00	185.00	325.00
	CD1902	—	65.00	110.00	185.00	325.00
	CD1903	—	65.00	110.00	185.00	325.00
	CD1904	—	65.00	110.00	185.00	325.00
	CD1905	—	65.00	110.00	185.00	325.00

Obv: Manchu characters in center.

183b	CD1908	—	150.00	250.00	400.00	650.00

Obv: Numeral II in center.

Y#	Date	Mintage	Fine	VF	XF	Unc
183c	CD1908	—	175.00	275.00	450.00	750.00

NOTE: Errors in the English legends are common on Kirin coins. Kirin Dollars are frequently found with chopmarks. For coins which have a few light chops, subtract 20 percent from prices shown.

TAEL SERIES

CH'IEN (MACE)

SILVER, 3.6000 gm.
Rev.: Numeral 1 in simple Chinese.

K#	Date	Mintage	Fine	VF	XF	Unc
919	Yr.10 (1884)	—	125.00	200.00	350.00	600.00

Rev: Different, more complicated character for 1.

920	Yr.10 (1884)	—	75.00	125.00	200.00	350.00

3 CH'IEN

SILVER, 10.8000 gm.
Vertical edge reeding.

918	Yr.10 (1884)	—	75.00	125.00	200.00	350.00

Diagonal edge reeding.

918b	Yr.10 (1884)	—	75.00	125.00	200.00	350.00

5 CH'IEN

(= 1/2 Tael)

SILVER, 17.8000 gm.

917	Yr.10 (1884)	—	125.00	200.00	350.00	600.00

7 CH'IEN

SILVER, 25.4000 gm.

K#	Date	Mintage	Fine	VF	XF	Unc
916	Yr.10 (1884)	—	150.00	250.00	425.00	700.00

TAEL

SILVER, 35.5000 gm.

K#	Date	Mintage	Fine	VF	XF	Unc
915	Yr.10 (1884)	—	550.00	900.00	1500.	2500.

NCLT ISSUES

PATTERNS

KM#	Date	Mintage	Identification	Mkt.Val.
1	Yr.8 (1882)	—	1 Tael, Silver, K914	—

KWANGSI/KWANGSEA

Autonomous region in southeast China. Hilly with many forests. Large amounts of rice grown adjacent to the many rivers. A mint opened in Kweilin in 1667, closed in 1670, reopened in 1679, closed again in 1681. It reopened in the mid-1700's and was a rather prolific issuer of cash coins. In 1905 the government allowed modern mints to be established in some of the southern regions. Three were established in Kwangsi-Nannung (1905), Kweilin (1905), and Winchow (1920). The Nanning Mint began operation in 1919 and closed in 1921. The nature and amount of activity of the other two mints is questionable.

EMPIRE

CASH

CAST BRASS

C#	Date	Emperor	Good	VG	Fine	VF
18-1	(1736-95)	Ch'ien Lung	.15	.40	.65	.85
18-2	(1796-1820)	Chia Ch'ing	.20	.50	.85	1.25
18-3	(1821-51)	Tao Kuang	.30	.85	1.50	2.50

C#	Date	Emperor	Good	VG	Fine	VF
		Rev: Dot below.				
18-3.1	(1821-51)	Tao Kuang	.60	1.00	2.00	3.00
18-4	(1851-61)	Hsien Feng	1.00	2.00	3.00	5.00
18-7	(1862-74)	T'ung Chih	2.50	4.50	6.50	9.00
		Rev: Circle above.				
18-7.1	(1862-74)	T'ung Chih	3.50	6.50	9.00	13.50
18-9	(1875-1908)	Kuang Hsu	3.50	6.50	9.00	13.50

10 CASH

CAST BRASS

C#	Date	Emperor	Good	VG	Fine	VF
18-5	(1851-61)	Hsien Feng	10.00	20.00	30.00	45.00
18-8	(1862-74)	T'ung Chih	—	—	Rare	—
18-10	(1875-1908)	Kuang Hsu	—	—	Rare	—

50 CASH

CAST BRASS

C#	Date	Emperor	Good	VG	Fine	VF
18-6	(1851-61)	Hsien Feng	17.50	27.50	37.50	55.00

STRUCK COINAGE

REPUBLIC

CENT

BRASS
Rev. leg: KWANG-SEA.

Y#	Date	Mintage	Fine	VF	XF	Unc
413	Yr.8 (1919)	—	40.00	100.00	175.00	300.00

Y#	Date	Mintage	Fine	VF	XF	Unc
	Rev. leg: KWANG-SI.					
413a	Yr.8 (1919)	—	15.00	35.00	60.00	125.00
	Large Kuei mintmark.					
347	Yr.28 (1939)	6 known	—	—	Rare	—
	Small Kuei mintmark.					
347.1	Yr.28 (1939)	3 known	—	—	Rare	—

10 CENTS

SILVER

Y#	Date	Mintage	Fine	VF	XF	Unc
414	Yr.9 (1920)	—	35.00	85.00	110.00	175.00

20 CENTS

SILVER, 5.3000 gm.
Rev: KWANG-SEA.

Y#	Date	Mintage	Fine	VF	XF	Unc
415	Yr.8 (1919)	—	35.00	60.00	100.00	175.00
	Yr.9 (1920)	—	55.00	90.00	150.00	250.00
	Yr.13 (1924)	—	55.00	90.00	150.00	250.00
	Rev: KWANG-SI.					
415a	Yr.8 (1919)	—	—	—	—	—
	Yr.9 (1920)	—	17.50	35.00	70.00	140.00
	Yr.11 (1922)	—	17.50	35.00	70.00	140.00
	Yr.12 (1923)	—	12.50	25.00	50.00	100.00
	Yr.13 (1924)	—	12.50	25.00	50.00	100.00
	Yr.14 (1925)	—	12.50	25.00	50.00	100.00

Y#	Date	Mintage	Fine	VF	XF	Unc
	Rev: Wreath added around '20'.					
415b	Yr.15 (1926)	—	6.50	12.50	25.00	50.00

Y#	Date	Mintage	Fine	VF	XF	Unc
415b	Yr.16 (1927)	—	6.50	12.50	25.00	50.00

Character 'Kuei' in center instead of dot.

Y#	Date	Mintage	Fine	VF	XF	Unc
415a.1	Yr.13 (1924)	—	50.00	75.00	125.00	200.00

Y#	Date	Mintage	Fine	VF	XF	Unc
416	Yr.38 (1949)	—	60.00	100.00	175.00	300.00

NCLT ISSUES

PATTERNS

KM#	Date	Mintage	Identification	Mkt.Val.
1	(1905)	—	10 Cash, Copper	—
2	CD1906	—	10 Cash, Copper	—
3	Yr.10 (1921)	—	10 Cents, Copper, Y414a	75.00
4	Yr.10 (1921)	—	10 Cents, Brass, Y414b	—
5	Yr.10 (1921)	—	10 Cents, Bronze, Y414c	—
6	Yr.10 (1921)	—	10 Cents, Silver, Y414f	—
7	Yr.10 (1921)	—	20 Cents, Copper, Y415c	100.00
8	Yr.10 (1921)	—	20 Cents, Bronze, Y415d	—
9	Yr.10 (1921)	—	20 Cents, Brass, Y415e	—
10	Yr.10 (1921)	—	20 Cents, Silver, Y415f	—

KWANGTUNG

A province located on the southeast coast of China. Kwangtung lies mostly in the tropics and has both mountains and plains. Its coastline is nearly 800 miles long and provides many good harbors. Because of the location of Canton in the province Kwangtung was the first to be visited by foreign traders. Hong Kong was ceded to Great Britain after First Opium War in 1841. Kowloon was later ceded to Britain in 1860 (100 year lease in 1898) and Macao to Portugal in 1887. Kwangchowan was leased to France in 1898 (a property that was restored in 1946). A modern mint opened in Canton in 1889 with Edward Wyon as superintendent. The mint was a large issuer of coins until it closed in 1931. The Nationalists reopened the mint briefly in 1949, striking a few silver dollars, before abandoning the mainland for their retreat to Taiwan.

EMPIRE

CASH

CAST BRASS

C#	Date	Emperor	Good	VG	Fine	VF
19-1	(1736-95)	Ch'ien Lung	.30	.75	1.25	2.00
19-2	(1796-1820)	Chia Ch'ing	.30	.75	1.50	2.00

CAST IRON

C#	Date	Emperor	Good	VG	Fine	VF
19-2a	(1796-1820)	Chia Ch'ing	—	—	Rare	—

CAST BRASS

C#	Date	Emperor	Good	VG	Fine	VF
19-3	(1821-51)	Tao Kuang	.20	.50	1.00	1.50

C#	Date	Emperor	Good	VG	Fine	VF
19-4	(1851-61)	Hsien Feng	1.50	2.50	3.50	5.00
19-5	(1862-74)	T'ung Chih	2.00	3.00	4.00	6.00
19-7	(1875-1908)	Kuang Hsu	5.00	8.00	11.00	15.00

10 CASH

CAST BRASS

C#	Date	Emperor	Good	VG	Fine	VF
19-6	(1862-74)	T'ung Chih	—	—	Rare	—
19-8	(1875-1908)	Kuang Hsu	—	—	Rare	—

STRUCK COINAGE

CASH

BRASS, struck

Y#	Date	Mintage	Fine	VF	XF	Unc
189	ND(1889)	—	.10	.20	.40	1.25

Obv: 'Kuang' in a different style.

Y#	Date	Mintage	Fine	VF	XF	Unc
189.1	ND(1889)	—	—	—	—	—

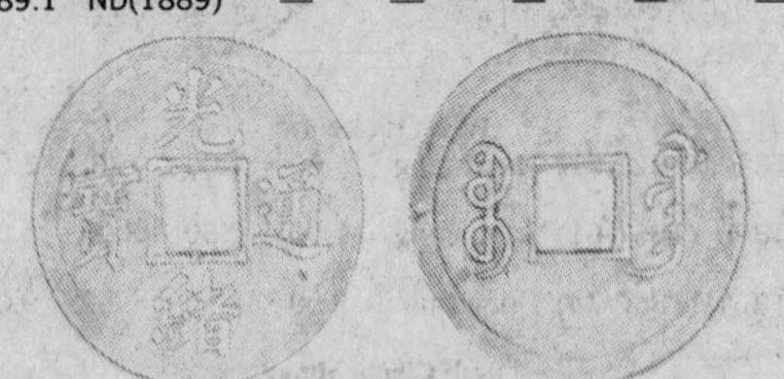

Y#	Date	Mintage	Fine	VF	XF	Unc
190	(1890-98)	1059.253	—	.10	.20	.50
191	ND	—	—	.10	.20	.50
204	(1909)	—	.15	.40	.75	1.50

CENT (10 CASH)

COPPER
Obv: Six characters at bottom. Rev: ONE CENT.

Y#	Date	Mintage	VG	Fine	VF	XF
192	(1900-06)	—	.30	.75	1.50	3.00

Obv: Seven characters at bottom. Rev: TEN CASH.

Y#	Date	Mintage	VG	Fine	VF	XF
193	(1900-06)	—	.30	.75	1.50	3.00

NOTE: Mulings exist with obverse of Y#192 and reverse of Y#193 and with obverse of Y#193 with reverse of Y#192.

Y#	Date	Mintage	VG	Fine	VF	XF
W896	—	—	65.00	100.00	150.00	225.00

Y#	Date	Mintage	VG	Fine	VF	XF
10r	CD1906	79.000	.40	1.00	2.00	4.00
	CD1907	46.000	.40	1.00	2.00	4.00
	CD1908	62.736	.40	1.00	2.00	4.00

Y#	Date	Mintage	VG	Fine	VF	XF
20r	CD1909	—	.60	1.50	3.00	5.00

5 CENTS

.820 SILVER, 1.3000 gm.
Obv: 3.65 CANDAREENS.
Rev: Chinese characters around dragon.

Y#	Date	Mintage	Fine	VF	XF	Unc
194	(1889)	—	125.00	250.00	375.00	500.00

Obv: 3.6 CANDAREENS.

Y#	Date	Mintage	Fine	VF	XF	Unc
194.1	(1889)	—	250.00	500.00	750.00	1000.

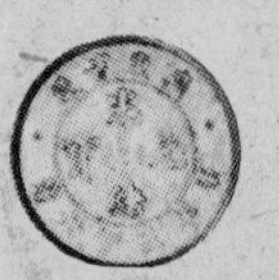

Rev: English legend around dragon.

Y#	Date	Mintage	Fine	VF	XF	Unc
199	(1890-1905)	—	2.00	3.50	6.00	10.00

10 CENTS

.820 SILVER, 2.7000 gm.
Obv: 7 3/10 CANDAREENS.

Y#	Date	Mintage	Fine	VF	XF	Unc
195	(1889)	—	75.00	125.00	200.00	350.00
	Obv: 7.2 CANDAREENS.					
195.1	(1889)	—	125.00	200.00	350.00	600.00

Rev: English legends around dragon.

Y#	Date	Mintage	Fine	VF	XF	Unc
200	(1890-1900)	—	BV	BV	3.00	6.50

20 CENTS

.820 SILVER, 5.3000 gm.
Obv: 1 MACE AND 4 3/5 CANDAREENS.

Y#	Date	Mintage	Fine	VF	XF	Unc
196	(1889)	—	100.00	175.00	300.00	500.00
	Obv: 1 MACE AND 4.4 CANDAREENS.					
196.1	(1889)	—	150.00	275.00	450.00	750.00

Rev: English legends around dragon.

Y#	Date	Mintage	Fine	VF	XF	Unc
201	(1890-1908)	—	BV	BV	5.50	8.50

.800 SILVER, 5.5000 gm.

Y#	Date	Mintage	Fine	VF	XF	Unc
205	(1909-11)	94.774	BV	BV	7.50	15.00

NOTE: Two varieties of edge reeding known.

50 CENTS

.820 SILVER, 13.8000 gm.
Obv: 3 MACE AND 6-1/2 CANDAREENS.

Y#	Date	Mintage	Fine	VF	XF	Unc
197	(1889)	—	300.00	450.00	600.00	850.00

Obv: 3 MACE AND 6 CANDAREENS.

Y#	Date	Mintage	Fine	VF	XF	Unc
197.1	(1889)	—	350.00	500.00	700.00	1000.

13.5000 gm.
Rev: English legends around dragon.

Y#	Date	Mintage	Fine	VF	XF	Unc
202	(1890-1905)	—	25.00	45.00	75.00	125.00

DOLLAR

.900 SILVER, 27.4000 gm.
Obv: 7 MACE AND 3 CANDAREENS.

Y#	Date	Mintage	Fine	VF	XF	Unc
198	(1889)	—	400.00	1000.	1500.	2000.

Obv: 7 MACE AND 2 CANDAREENS.

Y#	Date	Mintage	Fine	VF	XF	Unc
198.1	(1889)	—	800.00	2000.	3000.	4000.

27.0000 gm.
Rev: English legends around dragon.

Y#	Date	Mintage	Fine	VF	XF	Unc
203	(1890-08)	—	BV	BV	30.00	60.00
	Obv: Different characters at top and bottom.					
206	(1909-11)	—	BV	BV	37.50	75.00

REPUBLIC

CENT

COPPER

Y#	Date	Mintage	Fine	VF	XF	Unc
417	Yr.1 (1912)	18.836	1.20	3.00	6.00	20.00
	Yr.3 (1914)	14.750	1.20	3.00	6.00	20.00
	Yr.4 (1915)	6.350	1.60	4.00	8.00	25.00
	Yr.5 (1916)	18.388	1.60	4.00	8.00	25.00
	Yr.7 (1918)	—	3.25	8.00	15.00	35.00
	BRASS					
417.1	Yr.3 (1914)	I.A.	.70	1.75	3.50	15.00
	Yr.4 (1915)	I.A.	1.00	2.50	5.00	20.00
	Yr.5 (1916)	I.A.	.60	1.50	3.00	12.50
	Yr.7 (1918)	—	2.00	5.00	10.00	25.00

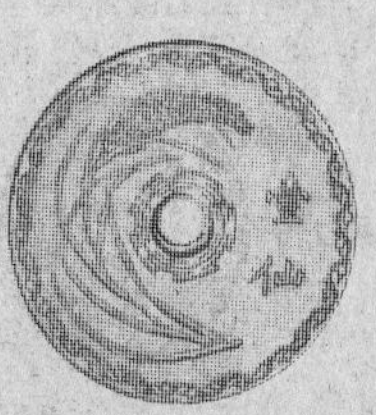

COPPER

Y#	Date	Mintage	Fine	VF	XF	Unc
427	Yr.25 (1936)	—	60.00	100.00	140.00	200.00

2 CENTS

BRASS

Y#	Date	Mintage	Fine	VF	XF	Unc
418	Yr.7 (1918)	—	25.00	45.00	85.00	150.00

COPPER

Y#	Date	Mintage	Fine	VF	XF	Unc
418a	Yr.7 (1918)	—	—	—	Rare	—

5 CENTS

COPPER-NICKEL

Y#	Date	Mintage	Fine	VF	XF	Unc
420	Yr.8 (1919)	.916	.50	1.25	2.25	4.00

Y#	Date	Mintage	Fine	VF	XF	Unc
421	Yr.10 (1921)	.666	.80	2.00	3.50	6.50

Y#	Date	Mintage	Fine	VF	XF	Unc
420a	Yr.12 (1923)	.480	.50	1.25	2.25	4.00

10 CENTS

SILVER, 2.7000 gm.

Y#	Date	Mintage	Fine	VF	XF	Unc
422	Yr.2 (1913)	8.798	BV	3.00	4.00	7.50
	Yr.3 (1914)	I.A.	BV	3.50	4.50	8.50
	Yr.11 (1922)	—	BV	4.50	6.50	12.50

2.5000 gm.

Y#	Date	Mintage	Fine	VF	XF	Unc
425	Yr.18 (1929)	48.960	BV	BV	3.50	7.00

20 CENTS

SILVER, 5.4000 gm.

Y#	Date	Mintage	Fine	VF	XF	Unc
423	Yr.1 (1912)	88.000	BV	BV	6.00	7.50
	Yr.2 (1913)	109.974	BV	BV	6.00	7.50
	Yr.3 (1914)	41.691	BV	BV	6.00	7.50
	Yr.4 (1915)	22.332	6.00	10.00	15.00	27.50
	Yr.7 (1918)	—	BV	BV	6.00	7.50
	Yr.8 (1919)	195.000	BV	BV	6.00	7.50
	Yr.9 (1920)	197.000	BV	BV	6.00	7.50
	Yr.10 (1921)	402.250	BV	BV	6.00	7.50
	Yr.11 (1922)	350.000	BV	BV	6.00	7.50
	Yr.12 (1923)	4.400	BV	BV	7.00	10.00
	Yr.13 (1924)	55.109	BV	BV	7.00	10.00

NOTE: The fineness of many of these 20 cent pieces especially those dated yr.13 (1924) is as low as .500. In 1924 the Anhwei Mint secretly produced quantities of Kwangtung 20 cent pieces which were only .400 fine.

Y#	Date	Mintage	Fine	VF	XF	Unc
424	Yr.13 (1924)	I.A.	6.00	10.00	20.00	40.00

GOLD

Y#	Date	Mintage	Fine	VF	XF	Unc
424a	Yr.13 (1924)	—	—	—	—	—

SILVER

Y#	Date	Mintage	Fine	VF	XF	Unc
426	Yr.17 (1928)	28.530	8.00	20.00	30.00	50.00
	Yr.18 (1929)	779.738	BV	BV	6.00	7.50

NCLT ISSUES

PATTERNS

KM#	Date	Mintage	Identification	Mkt.Val.
1	ND	—	5 Cash, Brass	—
2	ND	—	1/2 Cent, Copper	—

KM#	Date	Mintage	Identification	Mkt.Val.
3	ND	—	10 Cash, Brass	—
4	Yr.25 (1936)	—	1 Cent, Bronze, Sun Yat-Sen	—

SPECIMEN SETS

STANDARD METALS

KM#	Date	Mintage	Identification	Issue Price	Mkt. Val.
1	1889(10)	—	Y189,195.1-198.1 (2 each)	—	10,000.

NOTE: 'PRESENTATION' sets exist in odd shaped wooden cases containing first strikes of Y#189,190,199-203. If coins are proof or proof-like the market value is about $1000.

KWEICHOW

A province located in southern China. It is basically a plateau region that is somewhat remote from the general traffic of China. The Kweichow Mint opened in 1730 and produced Cash coins until the end of the reign of Kuang Hsu. The Republic issues for this province are enigmatic as to their origin, as a mint supposedly did not exist in Kweichow at this time.

EMPIRE

CASH

CAST BRASS

C#	Date	Emperor	Good	VG	Fine	VF
20-1	(1736-95)	Ch'ien Lung	.20	.50	1.00	1.50

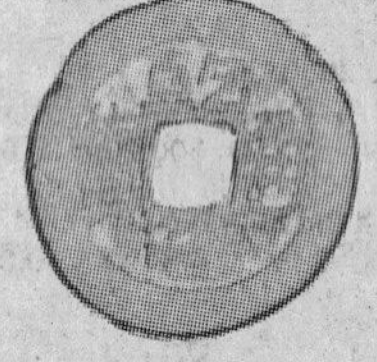 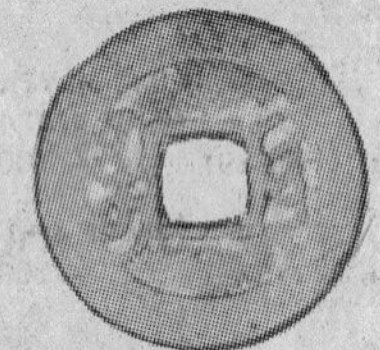

Shan Lung Commemorative

C#	Date	Emperor	Good	VG	Fine	VF
20-1.1	(1796-1820)	Chia Ch'ing	1.00	2.00	3.00	5.00

CAST IRON

C#	Date	Emperor	Good	VG	Fine	VF
20-1.1a	(1736-95)	Ch'ien Lung	—	—	Rare	—

CAST BRASS

C#	Date	Emperor	Good	VG	Fine	VF
20-2	(1796-1820)	Chia Ch'ing	.40	1.00	1.25	1.75
		Rev: Dot above.				
20-2.1	(1796-1820)	Chia Ch'ing	.80	2.00	3.00	4.00
		Rev: Character 'Erh' (two) above.				
20-2.2	(1796-1820)	Chia Ch'ing	2.00	5.00	7.00	10.00
20-3	(1820-50)	Tao Kuang	.60	1.50	2.00	3.00
		Rev: Crescent above.				
20-3.1	(1820-50)	Tao Kuang	2.50	5.00	6.50	9.00
		Rev: Circle above.				
20-3.2	(1820-50)	Tao Kuang	2.50	5.00	6.50	9.00
		Rev: Dot inside circle above.				
20-3.3	(1820-50)	Tao Kuang	2.50	5.00	6.50	9.00
		Rev: Dot above.				
20-3.4	(1820-50)	Tao Kuang	2.50	5.00	6.50	9.00
		Rev: An X above.				
20-3.5	(1820-50)	Tao Kuang	3.00	5.50	8.00	11.50
		Rev: A triangle above.				
20-3.6	(1820-50)	Tao Kuang	3.00	5.50	8.00	11.50
		Rev: Character 'Yi' (meaning one) above.				
20-3.7	(1820-50)	Tao Kuang	3.00	5.50	8.00	11.50
		Rev: Character 'Ta' (meaning large) above.				
20-3.8	(1820-50)	Tao Kuang	3.00	5.50	8.00	11.50
		Rev: Crescent below.				
20-3.9	(1820-50)	Tao Kuang	3.00	5.50	8.00	11.50

Rev: An X below.

C#	Date	Emperor	Good	VG	Fine	VF
20-3.10	(1820-50)	Tao Kuang	3.00	5.50	8.00	11.50

Rev: Dot below.

C#	Date	Emperor	Good	VG	Fine	VF
20-3.11	(1820-50)	Tao Kuang	3.00	5.50	8.00	11.50

Rev: Triangle below.

C#	Date	Emperor	Good	VG	Fine	VF
20-3.12	(1820-50)	Tao Kuang	3.00	5.50	8.00	11.50

Rev: 'Yi' below.

C#	Date	Emperor	Good	VG	Fine	VF
20-3.13	(1820-50)	Tao Kuang	3.00	5.50	8.00	11.50
20-4	(1851-61)	Hsien Feng	1.50	2.50	4.00	6.00

Rev: Dot above.

C#	Date	Emperor	Good	VG	Fine	VF
20-4.1	(1851-61)	Hsien Feng	2.50	4.00	5.00	7.00

Rev: Two vertical lines above.

C#	Date	Emperor	Good	VG	Fine	VF
20-4.2	(1851-61)	Hsien Feng	3.00	5.50	8.00	11.50

Rev: Three vertical lines above.

C#	Date	Emperor	Good	VG	Fine	VF
20-4.3	(1851-61)	Hsien Feng	3.00	5.50	8.00	11.50

Rev: An X above.

C#	Date	Emperor	Good	VG	Fine	VF
20-4.4	(1851-61)	Hsien Feng	3.00	5.50	8.00	11.50

Rev: Character "Chi" (meaning seven) above.

C#	Date	Emperor	Good	VG	Fine	VF
20-4.5	(1851-61)	Hsien Feng	3.00	5.50	8.00	11.50

Rev: Character 'Shih' (meaning ten) above.

C#	Date	Emperor	Good	VG	Fine	VF
20-4.6	(1851-61)	Hsien Feng	3.00	5.50	8.00	11.50

Rev: Character "Wen" (meaning unit) laying on its side above.

C#	Date	Emperor	Good	VG	Fine	VF
20-4.7	(1851-61)	Hsien Feng	3.00	5.50	8.00	11.50

Rev: Character 'Shih' above and crescent below.

C#	Date	Emperor	Good	VG	Fine	VF
20-4.8	(1851-61)	Hsien Feng	3.00	5.50	8.00	11.50
20-7	(1862-74)	T'ung Chih	—	—	Rare	—
20-9	(1875-1908)	Kuang Hsu	4.00	7.50	10.00	14.00

Rev: Dot above.

C#	Date	Emperor	Good	VG	Fine	VF
20-9.1	(1875-1908)	Kuang Hsu	5.00	9.00	12.50	17.50

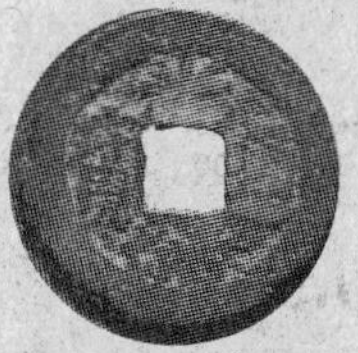

Rev: Character 'Kung' above.

C#	Date	Emperor	Good	VG	Fine	VF
20-9.2	(1875-1905)	Kuang Hsu	5.00	9.00	12.50	17.50

10 CASH

CAST BRASS, 38mm

C#	Date	Emperor	Good	VG	Fine	VF
20-5	(1851-61)	Hsien Feng	17.50	27.50	37.50	50.00

25mm

C#	Date	Emperor	Good	VG	Fine	VF
20-5.1	(1851-61)	Hsien Feng	17.50	27.50	37.50	50.00
20-8	(1862-74)	T'ung Chih	—	—	Rare	—
20-10	(1875-1908)	Kuang Hsu	—	—	Rare	—

50 CASH

CAST BRASS

C#	Date	Emperor	Good	VG	Fine	VF
20-6	(1851-61)	Hsien Feng	35.00	45.00	60.00	80.00

STRUCK COINAGE

50 CENTS

SILVER

Obv: Curled dragon in small circle surrounded by legend in Chinese. Rev. Wreath around two Chinese characters. Similar to K#13.

K#	Date	Mintage	VG	Fine	VF	XF
10	Yr.14 (1888)	—	325.00	800.00	1200.	1800.

DOLLAR

SILVER, 24.8000 gm.

K#	Date	Mintage	VG	Fine	VF	XF
9	Yr.14 (1888)	—	600.00	1500.	2000.	2500.

22.6000 gm.

K#	Date	Mintage	VG	Fine	VF	XF
12	Yr.16 (1890)	—	400.00	1000.	1500.	2000.

NOTE: The Kweichow coins above, obviously copied from contemporary Japanese coins, are still a mystery. Even as late as the 1920's Kweichow was a very primitive area. It is highly unlikely that the coins were made in Kweichow in the 1880's and 1890's. It is possible that they were minted elsewhere, possibly in one of the central coastal provinces.

REPUBLIC

10 CENTS

ANTIMONY

Y#	Date	Mintage	VG	Fine	VF	XF
429	Yr.20 (1931)	—	250.00	450.00	650.00	850.00

20 CENTS

SILVER

Y#	Date	Mintage	Fine	VF	XF	Unc
430	Yr.38 (1949)	—	125.00	200.00	350.00	600.00

Y#	Date	Mintage	Fine	VF	XF	Unc
431	Yr.38 (1949)	—	175.00	275.00	450.00	750.00

50 CENTS

SILVER

Y#	Date	Mintage	Fine	VF	XF	Unc
432	Yr.38 (1949)	—	175.00	275.00	450.00	750.00

DOLLAR

SILVER, 25.8000 gm.

First Road In Kweichow Commemorative

Y#	Date	Mintage	Fine	VF	XF	Unc
428	Yr.17 (1928)	*.648	250.00	350.00	550.00	1250.

*This coin is commonly known as the 'Auto Dollar' as it portrays the governor's automobile.

26.4000 gm.

Y#	Date	Mintage	Fine	VF	XF	Unc
433	Yr.38 (1949)	—	—	2500.	3500.	5000.

Possibly a pattern. This coin is known as the 'Bamboo Dollar.'

SHANSI

A province located in northeastern China that has some of the richest coal deposits in the world. Parts of the Great Wall cross the province. Extensive agriculture of early China started here. Cited as a "model province" in the new Chinese Republic. Intermittently active mint from 1645. The modern mint was established in 1919. It operated until the mid-1920's and closed because of the public's resistance against the coins that were being produced.

EMPIRE

CASH

CAST BRASS

C#	Date	Emperor	Good	VG	Fine	VF
21-1	(1736-95)	Ch'ien Lung	.25	.65	1.00	1.55
21-2	(1796-1820)	Chia Ch'ing	.50	1.00	2.00	4.00

C#	Date	Emperor	Good	VG	Fine	VF
21-3	(1821-50)	Tao Kuang	2.50	5.00	7.50	12.50
21-4	(1851-61)	Hsien Feng	9.00	17.50	25.00	35.00
21-6	(1862-74)	T'ung Chih	6.00	11.50	17.50	25.00
21-8	(1875-1908)	Kuang Hsu	3.50	7.00	10.00	15.00

10 CASH

CAST BRASS

C#	Date	Emperor	Good	VG	Fine	VF
21-5	(1851-61)	Hsien Feng	17.50	30.00	45.00	60.00
21-7	(1862-74)	T'ung Chih	—	—	Rare	—
21-9	(1875-1908)	Kuang Hsu	—	—	Rare	—

STRUCK COINAGE

REPUBLIC

10 CASH (1 CENT)

COPPER

Y#	Date	Mintage	Fine	VF	XF	Unc
A435	ND	—	90.00	150.00	250.00	350.00

20 CENTS

SILVER, 4.8000 gm.

Y#	Date	Mintage	VG	Fine	VF	XF
217	(1913)	—	85.00	150.00	250.00	350.00

NOTE: Several varieties exist similar to Y#217, but struck cruder, base metal and with different Chinese legends at top of obverse. English legends are usually blundered. Struck about 1913 and thought to be war lord issues. Do not confuse with coins of Fengtien, from which this was copied.

NCLT ISSUES

PATTERNS

KM#	Date	Mintage	Identification	Mkt.Val.
1	Yr.16 (1890)	—	Tael, Silver, K922	—

SHANTUNG

A province located on the northeastern coast of China. Confucius was born in this province. Parts of the province were leased to Great Britain and to Germany. Farming, fishing and mining are the chief occupations. A mint was opened at Tsinan in 1647 and was an intermittent producer for the empire. A modern mint was opened at Tsinan in 1905, but later closed in 1906. Patterns were prepared between 1926-1933 in anticipation of a new coinage, but none were struck for circulation.

EMPIRE

CASH

CAST BRASS

C#	Date	Emperor	Good	VG	Fine	VF
22-1	(1736-95)	Ch'ien Lung	5.00	9.00	13.50	20.00
22-2	(1851-61)	Hsien Feng	16.50	30.00	45.00	60.00
22-5	(1862-74)	T'ung Chih	5.00	9.00	13.50	20.00
22-6	(1875-1908)	Kuang Hsu	5.00	9.00	13.50	20.00

10 CASH

CAST BRASS

C#	Date	Emperor	Good	VG	Fine	VF
22-7	(1851-61)	Hsien Feng	20.00	30.00	40.00	55.00

50 CASH

CAST BRASS

C#	Date	Emperor	Good	VG	Fine	VF
22-3	(1851-61)	Hsien Feng	27.50	37.50	50.00	75.00

100 CASH

CAST BRASS

C#	Date	Emperor	Good	VG	Fine	VF
22-4	(1851-61)	Hsien Feng	30.00	40.00	60.00	85.00

STRUCK COINAGE

CASH

COPPER, struck

Y#	Date	Mintage	VG	Fine	VF	XF
—	ND	—	—	—	Rare	—

NOTE: Authenticity is in doubt. Two other Shantung struck Cash exist, but are also doubtful.

2 CASH

COPPER

Y#	Date	Mintage	VG	Fine	VF	XF
8s	CD1906	—	10.00	20.00	30.00	50.00

10 CASH

COPPER

Y#	Date	Mintage	VG	Fine	VF	XF
220	(1904-05)	—	4.00	8.00	12.50	25.00

Obv: Thin Manchu characters in center. Rev: SHANTUNG.

Y#	Date	Mintage	VG	Fine	VF	XF
221	(1904-05)	—	3.00	6.00	9.00	15.00

Obv: Thick Manchu in center.

Y#	Date	Mintage	VG	Fine	VF	XF
221.1	(1904-05)	—	1.50	3.00	5.00	10.00
	Obv: Smaller stars.					
221.2	(1904-05)	—	1.50	3.00	5.00	10.00

Obv: As Y#220. Rev: As Y#221.

Y#	Date	Mintage	VG	Fine	VF	XF
221.3	(1904-05)	—	50.00	100.00	160.00	250.00

Obv: Thick Manchu in center. Rev: SHANG-TUNG.

Y#	Date	Mintage	VG	Fine	VF	XF
221a	(1904-05)	—	1.25	2.50	4.00	8.00

Obv: Thin Manchu.

Y#	Date	Mintage	VG	Fine	VF	XF
221a.1	(1904-05)	—	2.00	4.00	8.00	15.00

BRASS
Rev: Six large waves under dragon.

Y#	Date	Mintage	VG	Fine	VF	XF
10s	CD1906	—	2.50	5.00	8.00	15.00

COPPER
Rev: Five small waves under dragon.

Y#	Date	Mintage	VG	Fine	VF	XF
10s.1	CD1906	—	2.00	4.00	8.00	15.00
	BRASS					
10s.1a	CD1906	—	3.00	6.00	10.00	20.00

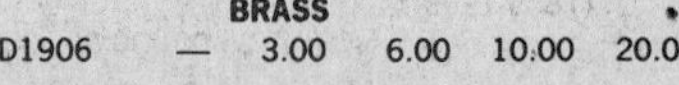

COPPER
Rev: Dragon with larger forehead and narrower face. Pearl redesigned.

Y#	Date	Mintage	VG	Fine	VF	XF
10s.2	CD1906	—	3.00	6.00	10.00	20.00

NCLT ISSUES

PATTERNS

KM#	Date	Mintage	Identification	Mkt.Val.
1	Yr.16 (1890)	—	5 Mace, Silver, K924	—
1a	Yr.16 (1890)	—	5 Mace, Copper, K924x	—

KM#	Date	Mintage	Identification	Mkt.Val.
2	Yr.16 (1890)	—	Tael, Silver, K923	—
3	Yr.15 (1926)	—	10 Dollars, Gold, K1536	2000.
4	Yr.15 (1926)	—	20 Dollars, Gold, K1535	2500.

KM#	Date	Mintage	Identification	Mkt.Val.
5	(1932)	—	20 Cash, Copper	—
6	Yr.22 (1933)	—	20 Cash, Copper, Yr. 22	—

SHENSI

A province located in central China that is a rich agricultural area. A very important province in the early development of China. An active imperial mint was located at Sian.

EMPIRE

CASH

CAST BRASS
Rev: Type 1 mintmark.

C#	Date	Emperor	Good	VG	Fine	VF
23-1	(1736-95)	Ch'ien Lung	.30	.75	1.50	2.50

Rev: Type 2 mintmark.

C#	Date	Emperor	Good	VG	Fine	VF
23-1.1	(1736-95)	Ch'ien Lung	.40	1.00	2.00	3.50

Rev: Type 3 mintmark.

C#	Date	Emperor	Good	VG	Fine	VF
23-1.2	(1736-95)	Ch'ien Lung	.30	.75	1.50	2.50
23-2	(1796-1820)	Chia Ch'ing	1.50	3.00	4.00	6.00
23-3	(1821-50)	Tao Kuang	2.00	4.00	6.00	8.50
23-4	(1851-61)	Hsien Feng	2.50	5.00	7.50	12.50
	CAST IRON					
23-4a	(1851-61)	Hsien Feng	—	—	Rare	—

CAST BRASS

C#	Date	Emperor	Good	VG	Fine	VF
23-11	(1862-74)	T'ung Chih	—	—	Rare	—
23-13	(1875-1908)	Kuang Hsu	—	—	Rare	—

10 CASH

CAST BRASS, 43mm

C#	Date	Emperor	Good	VG	Fine	VF
23-5	(1851-61)	Hsien Feng	17.50	27.50	37.50	50.00
	36mm					
23-5.1	(1851-61)	Hsien Feng	17.50	27.50	37.50	50.00
	Rev: Character "Shen" (for Shensi) above center hole.					
23-6	(1851-61)	Hsien Feng	25.00	35.00	45.00	65.00
23-12	(1862-74)	T'ung Chih	—	—	Rare	—
23-14	(1875-1908)	Kuang Hsu	—	—	Rare	—

50 CASH

CAST BRASS

C#	Date	Emperor	Good	VG	Fine	VF
23-7	(1851-61)	Hsien Feng	20.00	30.00	40.00	60.00

100 CASH

CAST BRASS

C#	Date	Emperor	Good	VG	Fine	VF
23-8	(1851-61)	Hsien Feng	25.00	40.00	55.00	75.00

500 CASH

CAST BRASS

C#	Date	Emperor	Good	VG	Fine	VF
23-9	(1851-61)	Hsien Feng	35.00	55.00	75.00	100.00

Rev: Character 'Kuan' (meaning official) stamped on rim.

C#	Date	Emperor	Good	VG	Fine	VF
23-9.1	(1851-61)	Hsien Feng	35.00	55.00	75.00	100.00

1000 CASH

CAST BRASS

C#	Date	Emperor	Good	VG	Fine	VF
23-10	(1851-61)	Hsien Feng	40.00	75.00	125.00	175.00

CAST COPPER

C#	Date	Emperor	Good	VG	Fine	VF
23-10a	(1851-61)	Hsien Feng	40.00	75.00	125.00	175.00

Rev: Character "Kuan" stamped on rim.

C#	Date	Emperor	Good	VG	Fine	VF
23-10.1	(1851-61)	Hsien Feng	40.00	75.00	125.00	175.00

STRUCK COINAGE

REPUBLIC

IMTYPIF; I MEY TA YUAN PI I FEN
(One Piece Great Dollar Coin - 1 Cent)
IMTYPEF: Ehr Fen or 2 Fen

CENT

COPPER

Y#	Date	Mintage	VG	Fine	VF	XF
435	ND	—	65.00	135.00	200.00	275.00

2 CENTS

Obv: Star between flags.

Y#	Date	Mintage	VG	Fine	VF	XF
436	ND	—	40.00	75.00	110.00	175.00

Obv: No star between flags.

Y#	Date	Mintage	VG	Fine	VF	XF
436.1	ND	—	32.50	65.00	100.00	160.00

NOTE: Y#435 and Y#436 have an English legend IMTYPIF or IMTYPEF on the obverse. Several minor varieties are known.

NCLT ISSUES

PATTERNS

KM#	Date	Mintage	Identification	Mkt.Val.
1	(1898)	—	5 Cents, Silver, K159	2500.
2	(1898)	—	10 Cents, Silver, K158	—

KM#	Date	Mintage	Identification	Mkt.Val.
3	(1898)	—	20 Cents, Silver, K157	3000.
4	(1898)	—	50 Cents, Silver, K156	3500.

KM#	Date	Mintage	Identification	Mkt.Val.
5	(1898)	—	1 Dollar, Silver, K155	22,500.

NOTE: The Shensi patterns above were made at the Heaton Mint, Birmingham, England as samples to be sent, along with the dies and machinery, to Shensi. The machinery never reached the province, having been diverted instead to the Hupeh Mint. Beware of forgeries.

SINKIANG

An autonomous region in western China. High mountains surround 2000 ft. tableland on three sides with a large desert in center of this province. Many salt lakes, mining and some farming and oil. Inhabited by early man and was referred to as the "Silk Route" to the West.

Sinkiang has been historically, under the control of many factions, including Genghis Khan. It becamse a province in 1884. China has made claim to Sinkiang for many, many years. This rule has been more nominal than actual. Sinkiang had eight imperial mints, only three of which were in operation towards the end of the reign of Kuang Hsu. Only two mints operated during the early years of the republic. In 1949, due to a drastic coin shortage and lack of confidence in the inflated paper money, it was planned to mint some dollars in Sinkiang. These did not see much circulation however due to the defeat of the nationalists.

MONETARY SYSTEM

2 Pul = 1 Cash
4 Cash = 1 Fen
25 Cash = 1 Miscal
10 Fen = 1 Ch'ien (Mace)
1 Ch'ien = 1 Miscal (Tanga)
10 Miscals (Mace) = 1 Liang Tael or Sar
20 Miscals (Tangas) = 1 Tilla

GENERAL ISSUES

EMPIRE

10 CASH

CAST COPPER

Rev: Pao Yuan? (right-left) with K'a (Kashgar) above.

KM#	Date	Emperor	Good	VG	Fine	VF
1	(1736-96)	Ch'ien Lung	25.00	30.00	35.00	75.00

Rev: Pao Yuan with K'u (Kuche) above.

KM#	Date	Emperor	Good	VG	Fine	VF
2	(1736-96)	Ch'ien Lung	25.00	30.00	35.00	75.00

Rev: Pao Yuan with Hsin (new) above.

KM#	Date	Emperor	Good	VG	Fine	VF
3	(1821-50)	Tao Kuang	25.00	30.00	35.00	75.00

Rev: Pao Yuan with K'u (Kuche) above.

KM#	Date	Emperor	Good	VG	Fine	VF
4	(1862-74)	T'ung Chih	25.00	30.00	35.00	75.00

Rev: Pao Yuan with Hsin (new) above.

KM#	Date	Emperor	Good	VG	Fine	VF
5	(1862-74)	T'ung Chih	25.00	30.00	35.00	75.00

NOTE: All Of The Above Were Probably Cast In The reign of Kuang Hsu (1875-1908).

Rev: Pao Yuan with K'a (Kashgar) above.

KM#	Date	Emperor	Good	VG	Fine	VF
6	(1875-1908)	Kuang Hsu	25.00	30.00	35.00	75.00

Rev: Pao Yuan with K'u (Kuche) above.

KM#	Date	Emperor	Good	VG	Fine	VF
7	(1875-1908)	Kuang Hsu	25.00	30.00	35.00	75.00

Rev: Pao Yuan with Hsin (new) above.

KM#	Date	Emperor	Good	VG	Fine	VF
8	(1875-1908)	Kuang Hsu	25.00	30.00	35.00	75.00

Rev: Pao Hsin (Sinkiang - New Territory) with Hsin (new) over hole.

KM#	Date	Emperor	Good	VG	Fine	VF
33-24	(1875-1908)	Kuang Hsu	25.00	30.00	35.00	75.00

STRUCK COINAGE

FEN, 5 LI

COPPER
Obv: Large dots in circle, reemed rims.

Y#	Date	Mintage	VG	Fine	VF	XF
1	ND	—	65.00	135.00	165.00	275.00

NOTE: Two varieties are reported.

Obv: Small dots in circle, dotted rims.

Y#	Date	Mintage	Fine	VF	XF	Unc
1a	ND	(restrike)		—	25.00	40.00

NOTE: The legend on this coin states that it is valued at 1 Fen 5 Li of silver (about 15 Cash). The coin is the size of a normal 10 Cash piece of Sinkiang, but these pieces are usually larger than those of the other provinces. For this reason, it is assumed the coin was overvalued to benefit the government.

10 CASH

Y#	Date	Mintage	VG	Fine	VF	XF
2	ND	—	65.00	125.00	175.00	300.00

Obv: Small characters within center circle.
Rev: Chinese leg. w/date added above dragon.

Y#	Date	Mintage	VG	Fine	VF	XF
2.1	CD1910	—	75.00	135.00	200.00	350.00

Obv: Large characters within center circle.

Y#	Date	Mintage	Fine	VF	XF	Unc
2a	CD1910	(restrike)	—	—	25.00	40.00

Obv: Rosette in center.

Y#	Date	Mintage	VG	Fine	VF	XF
2a.1	CD1911	—	50.00	125.00	175.00	300.00

Obv: Double ring around star in center.

Y#	Date	Mintage	VG	Fine	VF	XF
2a.2	CD1911	—	50.00	90.00	150.00	250.00

NOTE: Other varieties are reported.

1/2 MISCAL (5 FEN)

SILVER
Obv: 'On gumush'.

Rev: 'Besh Fen' - (5) Fen, without mint name.

Y#	Date	Mintage	Good	VG	Fine	VF
A7.2	AH1294	—	7.50	15.00	25.00	40.00
	1295	—	7.50	15.00	25.00	40.00

Obv: 'Kang Hsu Beg'.
Rev: 'Fourth year' in Turki script.

Y#	Date	Mintage	Good	VG	Fine	VF
A7.3	ND Yr.4 (1878)		6.50	13.50	22.50	32.50

Obv. leg: Turki. Rev. leg: Manchu.

K#	Date	Mintage	VG	Fine	VF	XF
995	ND	—	7.50	15.00	25.00	40.00

MISCAL (MACE)

SILVER

1000	ND	—	85.00	165.00	225.00	375.00

Kann 1000 was minted at the Arsenal of Lanchowfu (Kansu) by order of General Tso Tsung-tang when he was campaigning against Yakub Beg's Sinkiang armies.

3.5000 gm.
Obv. leg: Turki w/o dot in center.
Rev: W/o Turki legends.

Y#	Date	Mintage	VG	Fine	VF	XF
3	ND	—	27.50	55.00	90.00	150.00

Obv. leg: Turki w/ dot in center.
Rev: W/o Turki legends.

3.1	ND	—	62.50	125.00	200.00	325.00

Obv: W/o Turki legends. Rev. leg: Turki.

3.2	ND	—	87.50	175.00	300.00	500.00

Obv. & rev: W/o Turki legends.

3.3	ND	—	20.00	40.00	65.00	110.00

Rev. leg: SUNGAREI above dragon, 1 MACE below.

10	ND	—	100.00	200.00	350.00	600.00

2 MISCALS (2 MACE)

SILVER, 7.2000 gm.
Obv. leg: Turki. Rev: W/o Turki legends.

Y#	Date	Mintage	VG	Fine	VF	XF
4	ND	—	17.50	35.00	60.00	100.00

Obv. leg: Continuous Turki. Rev: W/o Turki legends.

Y#	Date	Mintage	VG	Fine	VF	XF
4.1	ND	—	21.50	42.50	70.00	120.00

Obv: W/o Turki legends. Rev. leg: Turki.

Y#	Date	Mintage	VG	Fine	VF	XF
4.2	ND	—	—	—	Rare	—

Rev. leg: SUNGAREI above dragon, 2 MACE below.

Y#	Date	Mintage	VG	Fine	VF	XF
11	ND	—	175.00	300.00	500.00	850.00

4 MISCALS (4 MACE)

SILVER, 14.2000 gm.

Y#	Date	Mintage	VG	Fine	VF	XF
5	ND	—	35.00	60.00	120.00	200.00

5 MISCALS (5 MACE)

SILVER, 17.9000 gm.
Obv: No dot or rosette in center.
Rev: Uncircled dragon.

Y#	Date	Mintage	VG	Fine	VF	XF
6	ND	—	37.50	75.00	125.00	200.00

Rev: Circled dragon, no rosettes.

Y#	Date	Mintage	VG	Fine	VF	XF
6.1	ND	—	18.50	30.00	50.00	85.00

Rev: Large rosettes at sides of dragon.

Y#	Date	Mintage	VG	Fine	VF	XF
6.2	ND	—	20.00	32.50	55.00	90.00

Obv: Dot in center. Rev: No rosettes, circled dragon.

Y#	Date	Mintage	VG	Fine	VF	XF
6.3	ND	—	18.50	30.00	50.00	85.00

Obv: Cross in center.

Y#	Date	Mintage	VG	Fine	VF	XF
6.4	ND	—	18.50	30.00	50.00	85.00

Obv: Large rosette in center, middle of which is depressed.

Y#	Date	Mintage	VG	Fine	VF	XF
6.5	ND	—	18.50	30.00	50.00	85.00

Obv: Eight-petal rosette in center, middle of which is raised. Rev: Small rosettes at sides of dragon.

Y#	Date	Mintage	VG	Fine	VF	XF
6.6	ND	—	20.00	32.50	55.00	90.00

Rev: Bat above dragon's head, K#1012-I.

Y#	Date	Mintage	VG	Fine	VF	XF
6.7	ND	—	150.00	250.00	400.00	650.00

Rev: Turki legends around dragon.

Y#	Date	Mintage	VG	Fine	VF	XF
6.8	ND	—	—	—	Rare	—

Rev. leg: SUNGAREI above uncircled dragon, 5 MACE below.

Y#	Date	Mintage	VG	Fine	VF	XF
6.9	ND	—	—	—	Rare	—

NOTE: Authenticity in doubt. Some authorities say this is a fantasy.

SAR (TAEL)

SILVER, 35.5000 gm.
Obv: W/o Turki legends. Rev: W/o Turki legends, w/rosettes at sides of uncircled dragon.

Y#	Date	Mintage	VG	Fine	VF	XF
7	ND	—	50.00	100.00	175.00	300.00

Obv: W/dot in center.
Rev: Circled dragon w/Turki legends, w/o rosettes.

Y#	Date	Mintage	VG	Fine	VF	XF
7.1	ND	—	90.00	180.00	300.00	500.00

Obv: W/o Turki legends, w/dot in center.
Rev: W/Turki legends around uncircled dragon.

Y#	Date	Mintage	VG	Fine	VF	XF
7.2	ND	—	—	—	Rare	—

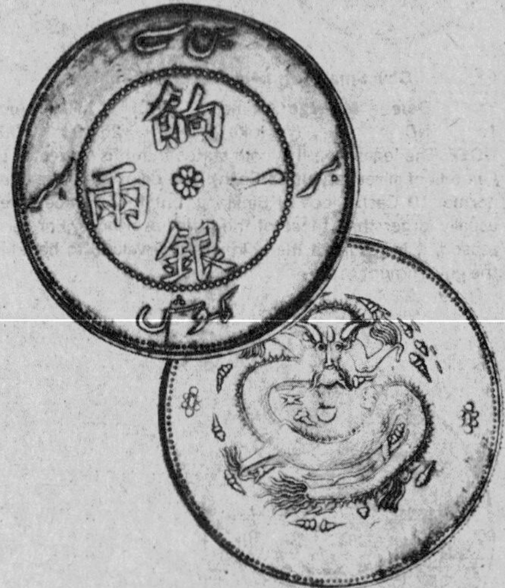

Obv: W/Turki legends, rosette in center.
Rev: W/o Turki legends, w/rosettes at sides of uncircled dragon.

Y#	Date	Mintage	VG	Fine	VF	XF
7.3	ND	—	75.00	150.00	250.00	400.00

GOLD MISCAL (MACE)

GOLD
Rev: W/Turki legends around dragon.

Y#	Date	Mintage	Fine	VF	XF	Unc
8	ND	—	325.00	550.00	900.00	1500.

Rev: W/o Turki legends.

Y#	Date	Mintage	Fine	VF	XF	Unc
8.1	ND	—	350.00	600.00	1000.	1600.

2 MISCALS

GOLD, 7.8000 gm.

Y#	Date	Mintage	Fine	VF	XF	Unc
9	ND	—	160.00	400.00	550.00	750.00

Similar to 2 Miscals (silver) Y#11.

Y#	Date	Mintage				
1505	ND	—	Reported, not confirmed			

REPUBLIC

10 CASH

COPPER
Obv: Small characters.

Y#	Date	Mintage	VG	Fine	VF	XF
B39	ND	—	75.00	150.00	250.00	375.00

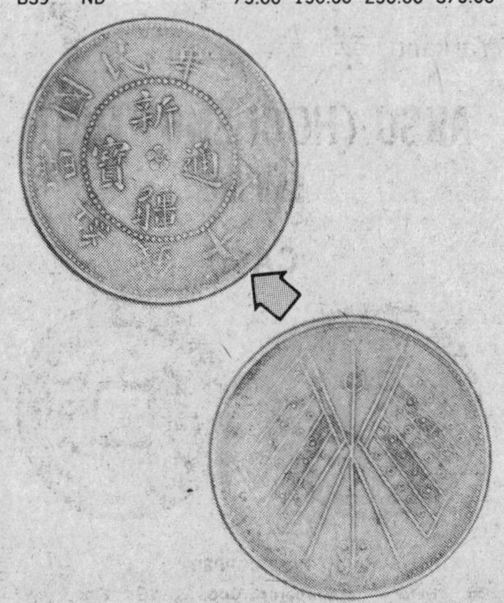

Obv: Large character 'ten'.

Y#	Date	Mintage	VG	Fine	VF	XF
B39.1	ND	—	37.50	75.00	125.00	200.00

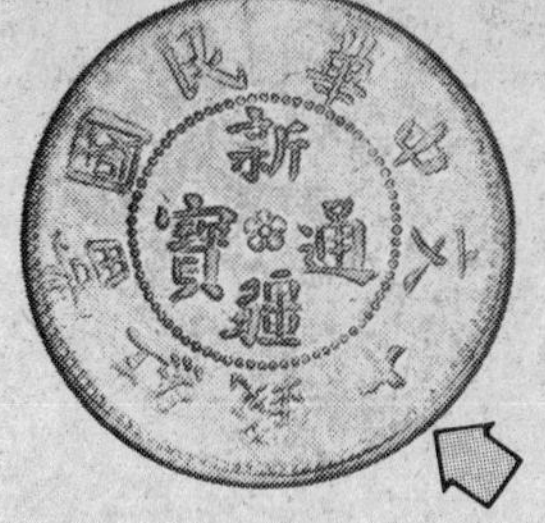

Obv: Small character 'ten'.
Rev: Small crossed flags.

Y#	Date	Mintage	VG	Fine	VF	XF
A39	1912	—	85.00	175.00	275.00	400.00

Rev: Large crossed flags.

Y#	Date	Mintage	VG	Fine	VF	XF
A39.1	1912	—	75.00	150.00	200.00	300.00

Y#	Date	Mintage	VG	Fine	VF	XF
40	1929	—	125.00	250.00	400.00	600.00

Flags in reversed order.

Y#	Date	Mintage	VG	Fine	VF	XF
40.1	1929	—	125.00	250.00	400.00	600.00

20 CASH

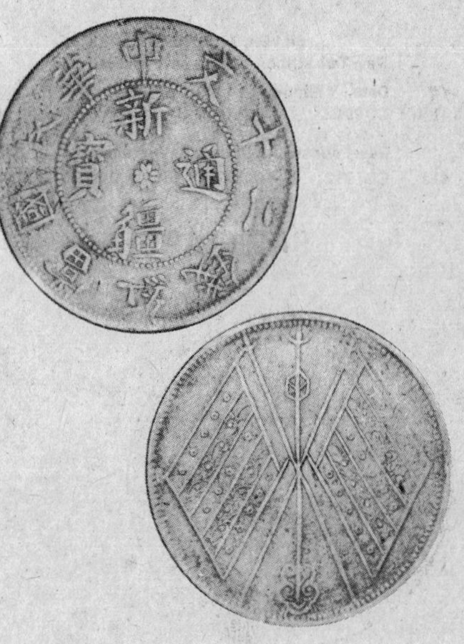

COPPER
Obv: Eight-pointed rosette in center.

Y#	Date	Mintage	VG	Fine	VF	XF
39	ND	—	100.00	175.00	275.00	400.00

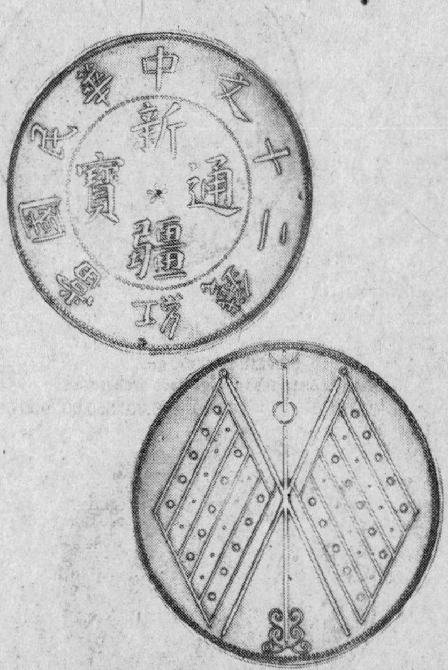

Obv: Five-pointed rosette in center.

Y#	Date	Mintage	VG	Fine	VF	XF
39.1	ND	—	—	—	—	—

Authenticity in doubt.

5 MISCALS (5 MACE)

SILVER, 17.9000 gm.
Rev: Two stripes in flags have arabesques.

Y#	Date	Mintage	VG	Fine	VF	XF
41	CD1912	—	60.00	120.00	200.00	350.00
	Rev: Four stripes in flags have arabesques.					
41a	CD1912	—	32.50	65.00	125.00	200.00

SAR (TAEL)

SILVER, 35.9000 gm.
Rev: Two stripes in flags have arabesques.

Y#	Date	Mintage	VG	Fine	VF	XF
42	CD1912	—	165.00	325.00	550.00	900.00

Rev: Four stripes in flags have arabesques.

Y#	Date	Mintage	VG	Fine	VF	XF
42a	CD1912	—	165.00	325.00	550.00	900.00

Obv: Solid characters for denomination within wreath.

K#	Date	Mintage	Fine	VF	XF	Unc
1275	Yr.38 (1949)	38	150.00	300.00	500.00	800.00

Obv: Outline characters for denomination within wreath.

K#	Date	Mintage	Fine	VF	XF	Unc
1276	Yr.38 (1949)	38	150.00	300.00	500.00	800.00

NCLT ISSUES

PATTERNS

KM#	Date	Mintage	Identification	Mkt.Val.
1	ND	—	4 Miscals, Silver	—
2	ND	—	4 Miscals, Brass	—
3	ND	—	5 Miscals, Silver, w/o bats around dragon, Y6.9	—
4	ND	—	5 Miscals, Silver, w/bats around dragon, Y6.10	—
5	ND	—	1 Dollar, Silver, Y12	3000.

LOCAL ISSUES

MINT NAMES AND MARKS

MINT	CHINESE	ARABIC	MANCHU
Aksu	阿	اقصو	
Ili	伊		
Kashgar	喀	كاشغر	
Khotan		خوتن	
Kuche			
Tihwa	迪	اورمچى	
Wushih	烏	[illegible]	
Yanghissar			
Yarkand	葉	يارقند	

AKSU (HOCHENG) MINT

EMPIRE

CASH

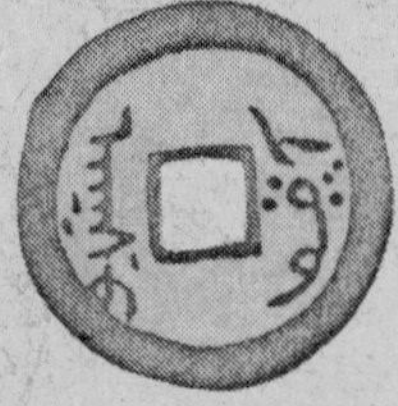

CAST COPPER

C#	Date	Emperor	Good	VG	Fine	VF
30-1	(1736-95)	Ch'ien Lung	18.50	30.00	50.00	85.00

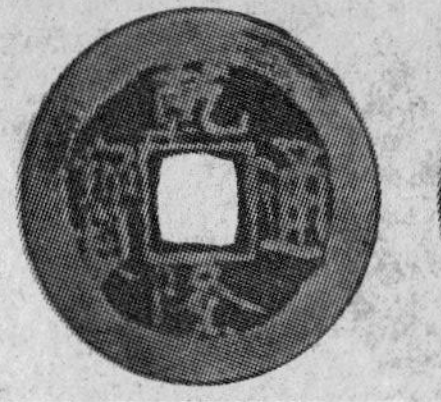

Rev: Circle sun above.

C#	Date	Emperor	Good	VG	Fine	VF
30-1.1	(1736-95)	Ch'ien Lung	27.50	45.00	75.00	125.00

Rev: Character "Hiu" (meaning nine) above.

C#	Date	Emperor	Good	VG	Fine	VF
30-4	(1736-95)	Ch'ien Lung	18.50	30.00	50.00	85.00
30-5	(1796-1820)	Chia Ching	20.00	32.50	55.00	90.00
30-6	(1821-50)	Tao Kuang	18.50	30.00	50.00	85.00

CAST BRASS

C#	Date	Emperor	Good	VG	Fine	VF
30-9	(1851-61)	Hsien Feng	—	—	—	100.00

C#	Date	Emperor	Good	VG	Fine	VF
30-14	(1862-74)	T'ung Chih	—	—	—	100.00

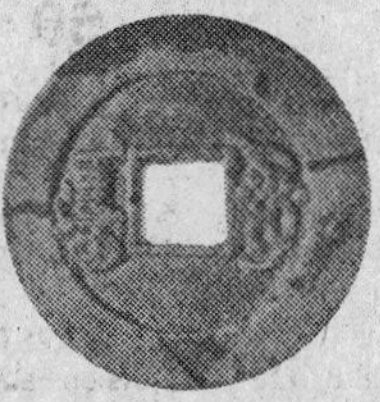

C#	Date	Emperor	Good	VG	Fine	VF
30-16	(1875-1908)	Kuang Hsu	—	—	—	100.00

NOTE: C#30-9, 30-14 and 30-6 are special castings made at Peking.

5 CASH

CAST COPPER
Rev: Characters 'Pa Nien' above.

C#	Date	Emperor	Good	VG	Fine	VF
30-7	Yr.8 (1828)	Tao Kuang	30.00	50.00	75.00	125.00
30-10	(1851-61)	Hsien Feng	30.00	50.00	75.00	125.00

10 CASH

CAST COPPER
Rev: "K'a" (Kashgan) above.

C#	Date	Emperor	Good	VG	Fine	VF
30-2	(1736-95)	Ch'ien Lung	20.00	35.00	60.00	100.00

Rev: Character 'A' (for Aksu) above.

C#	Date	Emperor	Good	VG	Fine	VF
30-3	(1736-95)	Ch'ien Lung	20.00	35.00	60.00	100.00

NOTE: C#30-2, 30-3 and 30-4 (1 Cash) though bearing the reign title of Ch'ien Lung, were cast during the Kuang Hsu era, (1875-1908).

Rev: Characters 'Pa Nien' (- year 8 - 1828) above.

C#	Date	Emperor	Good	VG	Fine	VF
30-8	Yr.8 (1828)	Tao Kuang	30.00	50.00	75.00	125.00

NOTE: C#30-7 and 30-8 are commemoratives marking the supression of a revolt in Sinkiang in 1828.

25 mm

C#	Date	Emperor	Good	VG	Fine	VF
30-11	(1851-61)	Hsien Feng	20.00	30.00	40.00	60.00

CAST BRASS, 38mm

C#	Date	Emperor	Good	VG	Fine	VF
30-11a	(1851-61)	Hsien Feng	—	—	—	100.00

CAST COPPER, 25mm

C#	Date	Emperor	Good	VG	Fine	VF
30-15	(1862-74)	T'ung Chih	20.00	35.00	60.00	100.00

CAST BRASS, 33mm

C#	Date	Emperor	Good	VG	Fine	VF
30-15a	(1862-74)	T'ung Chih	—	—	—	100.00

C#	Date	Emperor	Good	VG	Fine	VF
30-17	(1875-1908)	Kuang Hsu	—	—	—	100.00

CAST COPPER
Rev: Character "A" (for Aksu) above center hole.

C#	Date	Emperor	Good	VG	Fine	VF
30-18	(1875-1908)	Kuang Hsu	20.00	35.00	60.00	100.00

Rev: Character 'K'e' (for Kashgar) above.

C#	Date	Emperor	Good	VG	Fine	VF
30-19	(1875-1908)	Kuang Hsu	20.00	35.00	60.00	100.00

50 CASH

CAST COPPER, 37mm

C#	Date	Emperor	Good	VG	Fine	VF
30-12	(1851-61)	Hsien Feng	45.00	75.00	120.00	200.00

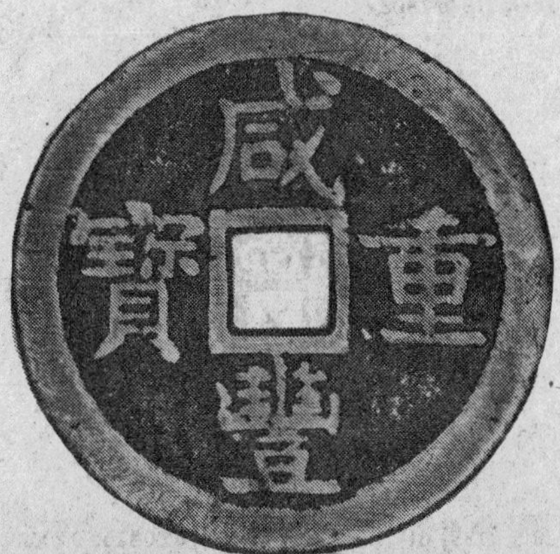

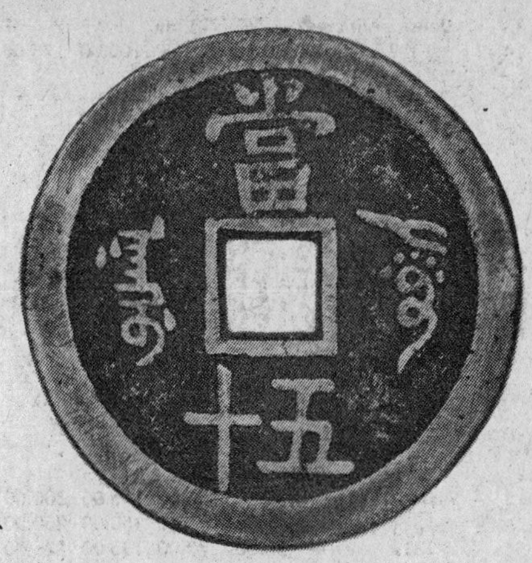

CAST BRASS, 54mm

C#	Date	Emperor	Good	VG	Fine	VF
30-12a	(1851-61)	Hsien Feng	—	—	—	200.00

100 CASH

CAST COPPER, 45mm

C#	Date	Emperor	Good	VG	Fine	VF
30-13	(1851-61)	Hsien Feng	47.50	80.00	135.00	225.00

40mm

C#	Date	Emperor	Good	VG	Fine	VF
30-13.1	(1851-61)	Hsien Feng	47.50	80.00	135.00	225.00

STRUCK COINAGE

1/2 MISCAL (5 FEN)

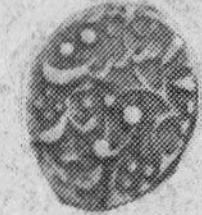

SILVER, 1.6000 gm.
Obv. and Rev: Turki script.

Y#	Date	Mintage	VG	Fine	VF	XF
A7.5	ND	—	7.50	15.00	25.00	40.00
	AH1296	—	7.50	15.00	25.00	40.00

Obv: Square in center. Rev: Turki legend.

Y#	Date	Mintage	VG	Fine	VF	XF
A7	AH1297	—	12.50	25.00	40.00	65.00
	1298	—	12.50	25.00	40.00	65.00

MISCAL (MACE)

SILVER, 3.6000 gm.
Similar to 3 Miscals, Y#14.

Y#	Date	Mintage	VG	Fine	VF	XF
A13	AH1311	—	—	—	Rare	—

2 MISCALS (2 MACE)

SILVER, 6.5000 gm.
Similar to 3 Miscals, Y#14.

Y#	Date	Mintage	VG	Fine	VF	XF
13	AH1310	—	37.50	75.00	125.00	200.00
	1311	—	27.50	55.00	90.00	150.00
	1312	—	37.50	75.00	125.00	200.00

3 MISCALS (3 MACE)

SILVER, 9.0000-10.5000 gm.

Y#	Date	Mintage	VG	Fine	VF	XF
14	AH1310	—	37.50	75.00	125.00	200.00
	1311	—	30.00	60.00	100.00	175.00

Y#	Date	Mintage	VG	Fine	VF	XF
14	1313	—	30.00	60.00	100.00	175.00

5 MISCALS (5 MACE)

SILVER, 17.0000-17.5000 gm.

Y#	Date	Mintage	VG	Fine	VF	XF
15	AH1310	—	50.00	100.00	175.00	300.00
	1311	—	45.00	90.00	150.00	250.00
	1312	—	35.00	70.00	135.00	225.00

REPUBLIC

10 CASH

CAST COPPER, 32mm.

Y#	Date	Mintage	Good	VG	Fine	VF
37	ND	—	150.00	250.00	400.00	600.00

Reduced size, 29mm.

Y#	Date	Mintage	Good	VG	Fine	VF
37.1	ND	—	150.00	250.00	400.00	600.00

COPPER
Obv: Similar to 10 Cash, Y#B38.
Rev: Crossed national flags.

Y#	Date	Mintage	Good	VG	Fine	VF
40.3	CD1930	—	100.00	175.00	300.00	500.00

ILI MINT

EMPIRE

CASH

CAST COPPER

C#	Date	Emperor	Good	VG	Fine	VF
28-1	(1736-95)	Ch'ien Lung	22.50	35.00	60.00	100.00

Rev: Dot above.

C#	Date	Emperor	Good	VG	Fine	VF
28-1.1	(1736-95)	Ch'ien Lung	25.00	40.00	65.00	110.00
28-2	(1796-1820)	Chia Ch'ing	20.00	32.50	55.00	90.00

Rev: Vertical line below.

C#	Date	Emperor	Good	VG	Fine	VF
28-2.1	(1796-1820)	Chia Ch'ing	22.50	35.00	60.00	100.00
28-3	(1821-50)	Tao Kuang	20.00	32.50	55.00	90.00

Rev: Dot above.

C#	Date	Emperor	Good	VG	Fine	VF
28-3.1	(1821-50)	Tao Kuang	22.50	35.00	60.00	100.00

Rev: Vertical line above.

C#	Date	Emperor	Good	VG	Fine	VF
28-3.2	(1821-50)	Tao Kuang	22.50	35.00	60.00	100.00

Rev: Character 'Shih' (meaning 10) above.

C#	Date	Emperor	Good	VG	Fine	VF
28-3.3	(1821-50)	Tao Kuang	22.50	35.00	60.00	100.00

CAST BRASS

C#	Date	Emperor	Good	VG	Fine	VF
28-4	(1851-61)	Hsien Feng	22.50	—	—	80.00
28-8a	(1862-74)	T'ung Chih	—	—	—	80.00

C#	Date	Emperor	Good	VG	Fine	VF
28-9a	(1875-1908)	Kuang Hsu	—	—	—	80.00

4 CASH

CAST COPPER

C#	Date	Emperor	Good	VG	Fine	VF
28-5	(1851-61)	Hsien Feng	45.00	75.00	125.00	200.00

C#	Date	Emperor	Good	VG	Fine	VF
28-9	(1862-74)	T'ung Chih	45.00	75.00	125.00	200.00

10 CASH

CAST COPPER

C#	Date	Emperor	Good	VG	Fine	VF
28-6	(1851-61)	Hsien Feng	27.50	45.00	75.00	125.00
28-8b	(1862-74)	T'ung Chih	—	—	Rare	—
28-10	(1875-1908)	Kuang Hsu	—	—	Rare	—

50 CASH

CAST COPPER

C#	Date	Emperor	Good	VG	Fine	VF
28-7	(1851-61)	Hsien Feng	45.00	75.00	125.00	200.00

100 CASH

CAST COPPER

C#	Date	Emperor	Good	VG	Fine	VF
28-8	(1851-61)	Hsien Feng	65.00	110.00	175.00	300.00

KASHGAR MINT

2 varieties of the Arabic mintmark are known.

EMPIRE

CASH

CAST COPPER

C#	Date	Emperor	Good	VG	Fine	VF
32-1	(1736-95)	Ch'ien Lung	—	—	Rare	—

5 CASH

CAST COPPER

32-1a (1851-61) Hsien Feng Reported, not confirmed

10 CASH

CAST COPPER

C#	Date	Emperor	Good	VG	Fine	VF
32-2	(1851-61)	Hsien Feng	30.00	40.00	60.00	120.00

Rev: Kashgar in Turki at left; in Manchu at right.

C#	Date	Emperor	Good	VG	Fine	VF
32-6	(1875-1908)	Kuang Hsu	—	—	Rare	—

Rev: Pao Kashgar (right-left).

C#	Date	Emperor	Good	VG	Fine	VF
32-6.1	(1875-1908)	Kuang Hsu	—	—	Rare	—

50 CASH

CAST COPPER

C#	Date	Emperor	Good	VG	Fine	VF
32-3	(1851-61)	Hsien Feng	55.00	90.00	150.00	250.00

100 CASH

CAST COPPER, 52mm

C#	Date	Emperor	Good	VG	Fine	VF
32-4	(1851-61)	Hsien Feng	—	—	—	—

Authenticity in doubt.

40mm

C#	Date	Emperor	Good	VG	Fine	VF
32-4.1	(1851-61)	Hsien Feng	120.00	200.00	325.00	550.00

1000 CASH

CAST COPPER

C#	Date	Emperor	Good	VG	Fine	VF
32-5	(1851-61)	Hsien Feng	—	—	—	—

Authenticity in doubt.

STRUCK COINAGE

1/2 MISCAL (5 FEN)

SILVER, 1.6000 gm.
Obv. leg: Manchu and Chinese with outer border of S's at rim w/o square in center.
Rev: Turki legends.

Y#	Date	Mintage	VG	Fine	VF	XF
A7.1	ND	—	6.50	12.50	25.00	40.00
	AH(12)95	—	6.50	12.50	25.00	40.00

Obv. & rev: Square in center.

Rev. leg: In Manchu, Chinese and Turki.

Y#	Date	Mintage	VG	Fine	VF	XF
A7.2	ND	—	6.50	12.50	25.00	40.00
	AH(12)95	—	6.50	12.50	25.00	40.00

Obv. & rev: W/o square in center.
Obv. leg: Turki. Rev. leg: Chinese for 5 Fen.

K#	Date	Mintage	VG	Fine	VF	XF
1064	AH1313	—	50.00	100.00	165.00	275.00

K#	Date	Mintage	VG	Fine	VF	XF
1064A	ND	—	50.00	100.00	165.00	275.00

Obv: Arabesque, wreath and flower replaces Turki legend.
Rev. leg: Chinese for 5 Fen.

K#	Date	Mintage	VG	Fine	VF	XF
1064B	ND	—	50.00	100.00	165.00	275.00

MISCAL (MACE)

SILVER, 3.5000-3.6000 gm.
Rev. leg: In Chinese, Turki and Manchu.

Y#	Date	Mintage	VG	Fine	VF	XF
B7	1295	—	21.50	42.50	75.00	125.00

Obv: Six characters. Rev: Wreath around Turki legends.

Y#	Date	Mintage	VG	Fine	VF	XF
16	ND	—	27.50	55.00	90.00	150.00
	AH1309	—	27.50	55.00	90.00	150.00
	1311	—	27.50	55.00	90.00	150.00

Obv: Four characters. Rev: No wreath.

Y#	Date	Mintage	VG	Fine	VF	XF
A16	ND	—	27.50	55.00	90.00	150.00
	AH1310	—	27.50	55.00	90.00	150.00

Obv: W/Kashgar to right.

Y#	Date	Mintage	VG	Fine	VF	XF
B16	AH1322	—	27.50	55.00	90.00	150.00

Obv: Kashgar in Chinese to right and left.

Y#	Date	Mintage	VG	Fine	VF	XF
C16	AH1322	—	32.50	65.00	110.00	175.00

Obv: Date at lower left. Rev: Dragon w/o legends.

Y#	Date	Mintage	VG	Fine	VF	XF
A20	AH1323	—	75.00	150.00	250.00	400.00

Obv: Date at lower right. Rev: Dragon w/o legends.

Y#	Date	Mintage	VG	Fine	VF	XF
A20.1	AH1323	—	75.00	150.00	250.00	400.00

2 MISCALS (2 MACE)

SILVER, 6.2000 gm.

Y#	Date	Mintage	VG	Fine	VF	XF
17	AH1310	—	9.50	18.50	30.00	50.00
	1311	—	8.50	17.50	27.50	45.00
	1312	—	11.50	22.50	37.50	60.00
	1313	—	12.50	25.00	40.00	65.00

Obv: Chinese characters K'e Shih to right.

Y#	Date	Mintage	VG	Fine	VF	XF
17a	AH1313	—	8.50	17.50	27.50	45.00
	1314	—	8.50	17.50	27.50	45.00
	1315	—	8.50	17.50	27.50	45.00
	1319	—	8.50	17.50	27.50	45.00
	1320	—	12.50	25.00	40.00	65.00

Obv: Chinese characters K'e Tsao to right.

Y#	Date	Mintage	VG	Fine	VF	XF
17a.1	AH1320	—	—	—	Rare	—
	1321	—	12.50	25.00	40.00	65.00
	1322	—	15.00	30.00	50.00	85.00

Obv: Chinese and Turki legends.
Rev: Dragon, w/o legends.

Y#	Date	Mintage	VG	Fine	VF	XF
B20	AH1323	—	60.00	120.00	200.00	325.00

Rev: Dragon in circle surrounded by wreath.

Y#	Date	Mintage	VG	Fine	VF	XF
23	AH1325	—	17.50	35.00	60.00	100.00
	1326	—	17.50	35.00	60.00	100.00
	1329	—	30.00	60.00	100.00	165.00

Obv: Turki legends around Chinese within a beaded circle. Rev: Double ring around small dragon, floral pattern outside, w/o legends.

Y#	Date	Mintage	VG	Fine	VF	XF
29	AH1329	—	22.50	45.00	90.00	150.00

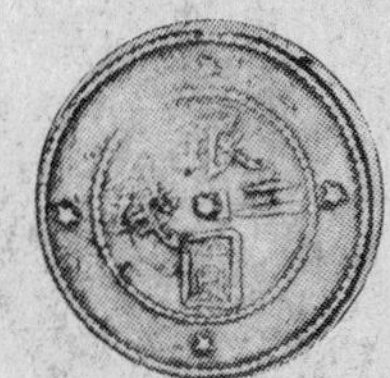 

Obv: Chinese legends within circle w/o Turki legends. Rev: Turki legends around larger dragon within single circle.

Y#	Date	Mintage	VG	Fine	VF	XF
29.1	AH1329	—	60.00	120.00	200.00	350.00

3 MISCALS

SILVER, 10.2000 gm.

Y#	Date	Mintage	VG	Fine	VF	XF
—	AH1307	—	—	—	Rare	—

Y#	Date	Mintage	VG	Fine	VF	XF
18	AH1310	—	12.50	25.00	40.00	65.00
	1311	—	12.50	25.00	40.00	65.00
	1312	—	15.00	30.00	50.00	85.00

Obv: Chinese characters K'e Shih to right.

Y#	Date	Mintage	VG	Fine	VF	XF
18a	AH1313	—	10.00	20.00	32.50	55.00
	1314	—	10.00	20.00	32.50	55.00
	1315	—	11.00	21.50	35.00	60.00
	1317	—	13.50	27.50	45.00	70.00
	1319	—	11.00	21.50	35.00	60.00
	1320	—	11.00	21.50	35.00	60.00

Obv: Chinese characters K'e Tsao to right.

Y#	Date	Mintage	VG	Fine	VF	XF
18a.1	AH1320	—	11.00	21.50	35.00	60.00
	1321	—	10.00	20.00	32.50	55.00
	1322	—	11.00	21.50	35.00	60.00

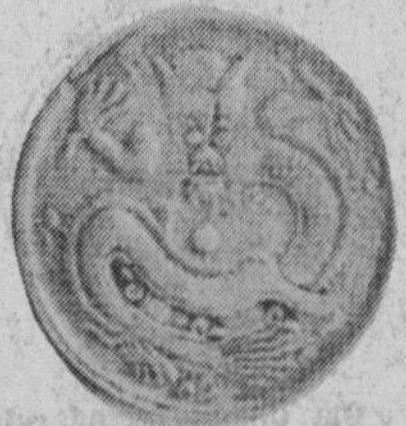

Obv: Simple 3 in Chinese at bottom.

Y#	Date	Mintage	VG	Fine	VF	XF
20	AH1323	—	75.00	150.00	250.00	400.00

Obv: Official 3 in Chinese at bottom, date at upper left.

Y#	Date	Mintage	VG	Fine	VF	XF
20.1	AH1323	—	87.50	175.00	300.00	500.00

Obv: Official 3 in Chinese at bottom, date at lower right.

Y#	Date	Mintage	VG	Fine	VF	XF
20.2	AH1323	—	87.50	175.00	300.00	550.00

Rev: Small, circled dragon, Arabic legend.

Y#	Date	Mintage	VG	Fine	VF	XF
30	AH1329	—	75.00	150.00	250.00	400.00

5 MISCALS

SILVER, 17.2000 gm.
Obv: Legends in Turki, Chinese and Manchu.

K#	Date	Mintage	VG	Fine	VF	XF
1040	AH1307	—	225.00	450.00	700.00	1250.

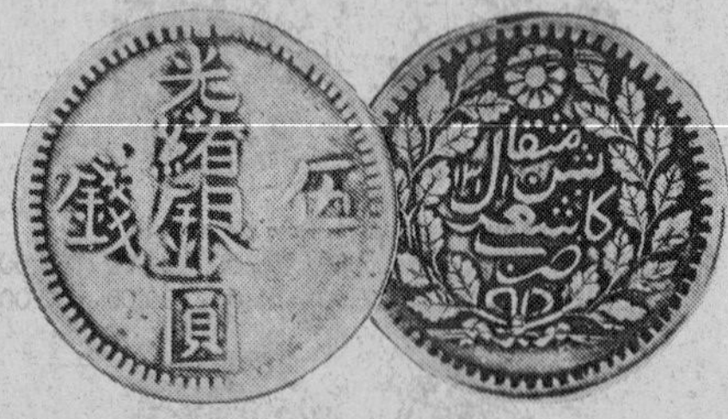

Y#	Date	Mintage	VG	Fine	VF	XF
19	AH1310	—	18.50	35.00	60.00	100.00
	1311	—	16.50	30.00	50.00	85.00
	1312	—	16.50	30.00	50.00	85.00
	1313	—	16.50	30.00	50.00	85.00

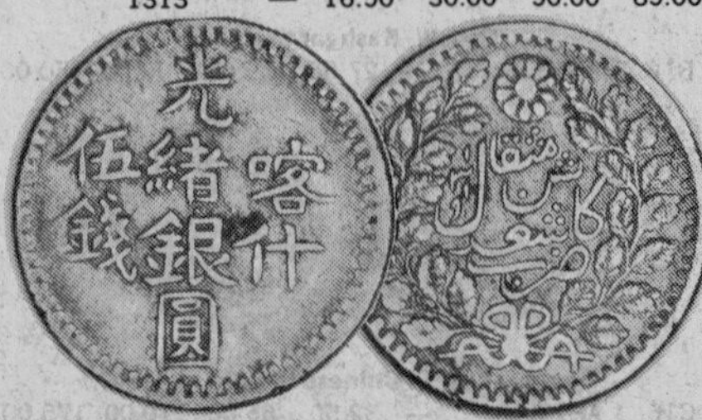

Obv: Chinese characters K'e Shih to right.

Y#	Date	Mintage	VG	Fine	VF	XF
19a	AH1313	—	BV	20.00	35.00	60.00
	1314	—	BV	20.00	35.00	60.00
	1315	—	BV	20.00	35.00	60.00
	1316	—	BV	20.00	35.00	60.00
	1317	—	BV	20.00	35.00	60.00

Y#	Date	Mintage	VG	Fine	VF	XF
19a	1319	—	BV	20.00	35.00	60.00
	1320	—	BV	20.00	35.00	60.00

Obv: Chinese characters K'e Tsao to right.

Y#	Date	Mintage	VG	Fine	VF	XF
19a.1	AH1321	—	BV	20.00	35.00	60.00
	1322	—	BV	20.00	35.00	60.00

Obv: Official Chinese and standard Turki legends. Date at upper left.
Rev: Dragon's tail points to right.

Y#	Date	Mintage	VG	Fine	VF	XF
21	AH1323	—	BV	25.00	40.00	65.00

Obv: Date at lower right.

Y#	Date	Mintage	VG	Fine	VF	XF
21.1	AH1323	—	BV	25.00	40.00	65.00

Obv: Inverted Turki legends, date at lower right.

Y#	Date	Mintage	VG	Fine	VF	XF
21.2	AH1323	—	17.50	32.50	55.00	90.00

Obv: Simple 5 in Chinese, date at lower right.

Y#	Date	Mintage	VG	Fine	VF	XF
21.3	AH1323	—	—	—	Rare	—

Obv: Official Chinese and standard Turki legends, date at upper left.
Rev: Dragon's tail points to left.

Y#	Date	Mintage	VG	Fine	VF	XF
21.4	AH1323	—	17.50	32.50	55.00	90.00

Obv: Date at lower right.

Y#	Date	Mintage	VG	Fine	VF	XF
21.5	AH1323	—	17.50	32.50	55.00	90.00

Obv: Inverted Turki legends, date at lower right.

Y#	Date	Mintage	VG	Fine	VF	XF
21.6	AH1323	—	17.50	32.50	55.00	90.00

Obv: Three Chinese characters at top between standard Turki legends.

Y#	Date	Mintage	VG	Fine	VF	XF
25	ND	—	18.50	35.00	60.00	100.00

Similar to Y#21 w/date at upper left.

Y#	Date	Mintage	VG	Fine	VF	XF
25.1	AH1326	—	18.50	35.00	60.00	100.00

Similar to Y#21.1 w/date at lower right.

Y#	Date	Mintage	VG	Fine	VF	XF
25.2	AH1327	—	18.50	35.00	60.00	100.00

Obv: W/inverted Turki legends, date at lower right.

Y#	Date	Mintage	VG	Fine	VF	XF
25.3	AH1325	—	BV	20.00	35.00	60.00
	1328	—	BV	20.00	35.00	60.00

Obv: Two Chinese characters at top between standard Turki legends w/date at upper right.

Y#	Date	Mintage	VG	Fine	VF	XF
25.4	AH1325	—	45.00	90.00	150.00	250.00

Obv: Three Chinese characters at top, star in center.

Y#	Date	Mintage	VG	Fine	VF	XF
27	AH1327	—	BV	25.00	40.00	65.00
	1328	—	22.50	45.00	75.00	125.00

Obv: Official 5 at right, dot in center.

Y#	Date	Mintage	VG	Fine	VF	XF
27.1	AH1328	—	30.00	60.00	100.00	165.00

Obv: Rosette in center.

Y#	Date	Mintage	VG	Fine	VF	XF
27.2	AH1329	—	45.00	90.00	150.00	250.00

Obv: Two Chinese characters at top, simple 5 at right, star in center.

Y#	Date	Mintage	VG	Fine	VF	XF
27.3	AH1329	—	BV	20.00	35.00	60.00

Obv: Dot in center.

Y#	Date	Mintage	VG	Fine	VF	XF
27.4	AH1329	—	BV	25.00	40.00	65.00

Obv: Rosette in center.

Y#	Date	Mintage	VG	Fine	VF	XF
27.5	AH1329	—	BV	20.00	35.00	60.00

Obv: Official 5 at right.

Y#	Date	Mintage	VG	Fine	VF	XF
27.6	AH1329	—	BV	20.00	35.00	60.00

Obv: Dot in center.

Y#	Date	Mintage	VG	Fine	VF	XF
31	AH1329	—	22.50	45.00	75.00	125.00

Obv: Star in center. Rev: Stars in outer field.

Y#	Date	Mintage	VG	Fine	VF	XF
31.1	AH1329	—	18.50	35.00	60.00	100.00
	1330	—	18.50	35.00	60.00	100.00
	1331	—	18.50	35.00	60.00	100.00

Rev: Rosettes in outer field.

Y#	Date	Mintage	VG	Fine	VF	XF
31.2	AH1329	—	45.00	90.00	150.00	250.00

Obv: Rosette in center.

Y#	Date	Mintage	VG	Fine	VF	XF
31.3	AH1329	—	18.50	35.00	60.00	100.00

SAR (TAEL)

SILVER, 35.2000 gm.
Obv: Two Chinese characters at top.

Y#	Date	Mintage	VG	Fine	VF	XF
26	AH1325	—	135.00	275.00	450.00	750.00

Obv: Three Chinese characters at top.

Y#	Date	Mintage	VG	Fine	VF	XF
26.1	AH1325	—	400.00	1000.	1500.	2000.

REPUBLIC

5 CASH

COPPER
Obv: Similar to 10 Cash, Y#B36.
Rev: W/one flag in center.

Y#	Date	Mintage	VG	Fine	VF	XF
A36	ND	—	60.00	120.00	200.00	350.00

Y#	Date	Mintage	VG	Fine	VF	XF
36	AH1331	—	45.00	90.00	150.00	250.00

10 CASH

COPPER
Rev: One flag in center.

Y#	Date	Mintage	VG	Fine	VF	XF
B36	ND	—	100.00	200.00	350.00	600.00

Rev: Smaller Turki legends around flag.

Y#	Date	Mintage	VG	Fine	VF	XF
B36.1	ND	—	—	—	—	—

Obv: Chinese legends, w/o Chinese date.
Rev: Crossed flags dividing Turki legend.

Y#	Date	Mintage	VG	Fine	VF	XF
38	AH1331	—	75.00	150.00	250.00	400.00
	1332	—	75.00	150.00	250.00	400.00

Rev: Modified Turki legends.

Y#	Date	Mintage	VG	Fine	VF	XF
38.1	AH133-4	—	40.00	80.00	135.00	225.00

Rev: Turki legends similar to Y#38a.

Y#	Date	Mintage	VG	Fine	VF	XF
38.2	AHxxx-4	—	40.00	80.00	135.00	225.00

Y#	Date	Mintage	VG	Fine	VF	XF
A38	AH1334	—	100.00	175.00	300.00	500.00

NOTE: This coin was issued for the brief reign of Yuan Shih-kai as Emperor Hung Hsien (1916).

Obv: Chinese date at top.
Obv: Rosette at right edge.

Y#	Date	Mintage	VG	Fine	VF	XF
38a	Yr.10 (1921)	—	37.50	75.00	125.00	200.00
	Yr.11 (1922)	—	37.50	75.00	125.00	200.00

Obv. leg. in dotted circle: MIN KUO TUNG YUAN.

Y#	Date	Mintage	VG	Fine	VF	XF
38b	—	—	—	—	Rare	—

Y#	Date	Mintage	VG	Fine	VF	XF
B38	CD1928	—	—	—	Rare	—

Design similar to Y#38. Rev: Turki legends.

Y#	Date	Mintage	VG	Fine	VF	XF
B38a	CD1929	—	—	—	350.00	500.00

Obv: Crossed flags, one of which is triangular.

Y#	Date	Mintage	VG	Fine	VF	XF
D38	AH1352	—	100.00	225.00	350.00	500.00

NOTE: This coin was issued under the short-lived Uighuristan Republic (1933-1934).

20 CASH

COPPER

Y#	Date	Mintage	VG	Fine	VF	XF
—	ND	—	—	—	Rare	—

NOTE: Authenticity in doubt.

Struck over 1929 10 Cash, Y#40.

Y#	Date	Mintage	VG	Fine	VF	XF
E38	AH1352	—	175.00	350.00	600.00	1000.

NOTE: This coin was issued under the short-lived Uighuristan Republic (1933-1934).

5 MISCALS

SILVER, 17.3000 gm.
Obv: Stars dividing Chinese legends.
Rev: Crossed flags dividing Turki legends.

Y#	Date	Mintage	VG	Fine	VF	XF
43	AH1331	—	BV	30.00	50.00	85.00
	1332	—	BV	30.00	50.00	85.00

Obv: Rosettes dividing Chinese legends.

Y#	Date	Mintage	VG	Fine	VF	XF
43.1	AH1331	—	BV	25.00	40.00	65.00
	1332	—	BV	25.00	40.00	65.00
	13-32	—	BV	25.00	40.00	65.00

Obv: Rosettes dividing Chinese legends.
Rev: Different Turki legends.

Y#	Date	Mintage	VG	Fine	VF	XF
43.2	AH1334	—	20.00	35.00	60.00	100.00
	133-4	—	20.00	35.00	60.00	100.00

Obv: Rosette in center, floral arrangements dividing Chinese legends.

Y#	Date	Mintage	VG	Fine	VF	XF
43.3	AH13-32	—	BV	30.00	50.00	85.00
	133-4	—	20.00	35.00	60.00	100.00

KHOTAN (HOTIEN) MINT

EMPIRE

CASH

CAST COPPER
Shan Lung Commemorative

C#	Date	Emperor	Good	VG	Fine	VF
31-1	1736-95	Ch'ien Ling	—	—	Rare	—

500 CASH

CAST COPPER

C#	Date	Emperor	Good	VG	Fine	VF
31-1a	1851-61	Hsien Feng	Reported, not confirmed			

1000 CASH

CAST COPPER

C#	Date	Emperor	Good	VG	Fine	VF
31-2	1851-61	Hsien Feng	—	—	Rare	—

STRUCK COINAGE

1/2 MISCAL

SILVER
Rev: 'Kho-tan' in Arabic.

K#	Date	Mintage	VG	Fine	VF	XF
1184	ND (1875-1908)		15.00	30.00	50.00	85.00

Rev: 'Zarb Khotan' in Arabic.

K#	Date	Mintage	VG	Fine	VF	XF
1184v	ND (1875-1908)		15.00	30.00	50.00	85.00

KUCHE MINT

(Also called Kuchar and Kuldja)

Empire

CASH

CAST COPPER

C#	Date	Emperor	Good	VG	Fine	VF
33-1	(1736-95)	Ch'ien Lung	20.00	35.00	60.00	100.00

NOTE: This coin was cast during a later reign.

5 CASH

CAST COPPER

C#	Date	Emperor	Good	VG	Fine	VF
33-8	(1851-61)	Hsien Feng	32.50	55.00	90.00	150.00

10 CASH

CAST COPPER

C#	Date	Emperor	Good	VG	Fine	VF
33-2	(1736-95)	Ch'ien Lung	32.50	55.00	90.00	150.00

NOTE: This coin was cast during a later reign. 4 varieties are reported.

Rev: Character 'K'u (Kuche) above.

C#	Date	Emperor	Good	VG	Fine	VF
33-6	(1821-50)	Tao Kuang	20.00	35.00	60.00	100.00

Rev: Character 'Hsin' (Sinkiang) above.

C#	Date	Emperor	Good	VG	Fine	VF
33-7	(1821-50)	Tao Kuang	Reported, Not Confirmed			

NOTE: C#33-6 and 33-7 were cast during a later reign.

C#	Date	Emperor	Good	VG	Fine	VF
33-9	(1851-61)	Hsien Feng	20.00	35.00	60.00	100.00
33-13	(1862-74)	T'ung Chih	20.00	35.00	60.00	100.00

Rev: Character 'K'u' (Kuche) above.

C#	Date	Emperor	Good	VG	Fine	VF
33-14	(1862-74)	T'ung Chih	20.00	35.00	60.00	100.00
33-16	(1875-1908)	Kuang Hsu	20.00	35.00	60.00	100.00

Rev: Characters "Chiu Nien" (meaning year 9 - 1883) above.

C#	Date	Emperor	Good	VG	Fine	VF
33-17	(1883)	Kuang Hsu	20.00	35.00	60.00	100.00

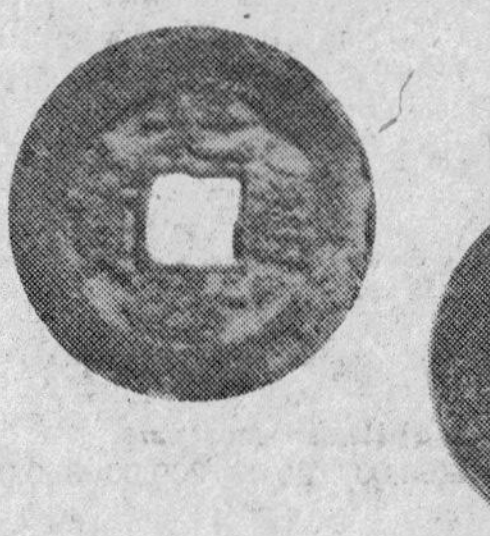

Rev: Character 'K'u' above.

C#	Date	Emperor	Good	VG	Fine	VF
33-18	(1875-1908)	Kuang Hsu	20.00	35.00	60.00	100.00

NOTE: Other varieties are reported for T'ung Chih and Kuang Hsu reigns.

50 CASH

CAST COPPER

C#	Date	Emperor	Good	VG	Fine	VF
33-10	(1851-61)	Hsien Feng	55.00	90.00	150.00	250.00

100 CASH

CAST COPPER

C#	Date	Emperor	Good	VG	Fine	VF
33-11	(1851-61)	Hsien Feng	60.00	100.00	175.00	300.00

1000 CASH

CAST COPPER

C#	Date	Emperor	Good	VG	Fine	VF
33-12	(1851-61)	Hsien Feng	Reported, Not Confirmed			

STRUCK COINAGE

1/2 MISCAL (5 FEN)

SILVER

#	Date					
—	ND (1875-1908)	—	—	—	Rare	—

TIHWA (URUMCHI) MINT

EMPIRE

8 CASH

CAST COPPER

C#	Date	Emperor	Good	VG	Fine	VF
29-1	(1851-61)	Hsien Feng	45.00	75.00	125.00	200.00

10 CASH

CAST COPPER

C#	Date	Emperor	Good	VG	Fine	VF
29-2	(1851-61)	Hsien Feng	35.00	60.00	100.00	175.00

50 CASH

CAST COPPER

C#	Date	Emperor	Good	VG	Fine	VF
29-3	(1851-61)	Hsien Feng	Reported, Not Confirmed			

100 CASH

CAST COPPER

C#	Date	Emperor	Good	VG	Fine	VF
29-4	(1851-61)	Hsien Feng	—	—	Rare	—

STRUCK COINAGE

2 MISCALS (= 2 MACE)

SILVER, 6.6000 gm.
Obv: Simple two in Chinese.

Y#	Date	Mintage	VG	Fine	VF	XF
33	AH1321	—	10.00	20.00	35.00	60.00
	1322	—	10.00	20.00	35.00	60.00
	1323	—	12.50	25.00	42.50	70.00

Obv: Official two in Chinese.

Y#	Date	Mintage	VG	Fine	VF	XF
33.1	AH1323	—	10.00	20.00	35.00	60.00
	1324	—	10.00	20.00	35.00	60.00
	1325	—	10.00	20.00	35.00	60.00

3 MISCALS

SILVER, 10.3000 gm.
Obv: Simple three in Chinese.

Y#	Date	Mintage	VG	Fine	VF	XF
34	AH1321	—	12.50	25.00	40.00	65.00
	1322	—	12.50	25.00	40.00	65.00
	1323	—	12.50	25.00	40.00	65.00

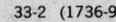

Obv: Official three in Chinese.

Y#	Date	Mintage	VG	Fine	VF	XF
34a	AH1322	—	12.50	25.00	40.00	65.00
	1323	—	12.50	25.00	40.00	65.00
	1324	—	12.50	25.00	40.00	65.00
	1325	—	12.50	25.00	40.00	65.00

5 MISCALS

SILVER, 17.9000 gm.
Obv: Simple five in Chinese.

Y#	Date	Mintage	VG	Fine	VF	XF
35	AH1321	—	BV	30.00	50.00	85.00
	1322	—	BV	30.00	50.00	85.00
	1323	—	BV	32.50	55.00	90.00

Obv: Official five in Chinese.

Y#	Date	Mintage	VG	Fine	VF	XF
35a	AH1322	—	BV	30.00	50.00	85.00
	1323	—	18.50	32.50	55.00	90.00
	1324	—	BV	30.00	50.00	85.00
	1325	—	BV	30.00	50.00	85.00

REPUBLIC

SAR (TAEL)

SILVER, 35.0000 gm.
Obv: Large characters.
Rev: Rosette at top between wheat ears.

Y#	Date	Mintage	VG	Fine	VF	XF
45	1917	—	37.50	75.00	125.00	200.00

Obv: Small characters. Rev: No rosette at top.

Y#	Date	Mintage	VG	Fine	VF	XF
45.1	1917	—	40.00	80.00	135.00	225.00

Rev: Rosette at top between wheat ears.

Y#	Date	Mintage	VG	Fine	VF	XF
45a	1918	—	60.00	120.00	200.00	350.00

WUSHIH MINT

EMPIRE

CASH

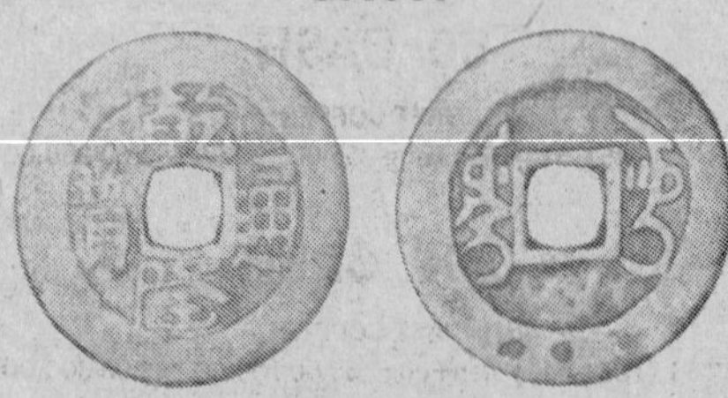

CAST COPPER
Shan Lung Commemorative

C#	Date	Emperor	Good	VG	Fine	VF
34-1	(1736-95)	Ch'ien Lung	20.00	35.00	60.00	100.00

YANGHISSAR MINT

EMPIRE

1/2 MISCAL

SILVER

K#	Date	Mintage	VG	Fine	VF	XF
998	ND (1875-1908)		15.00	30.00	50.00	85.00

NOTE: Error in Kann, correct illustration is K#999.

YARKAND MINT

EMPIRE

CASH

CAST COPPER
Rev: Manchu reads "Yerkim."

C#	Date	Emperor	Good	VG	Fine	VF
35-1	(1759-61)	Ch'ien Lung	20.00	30.00	50.00	85.00

Rev: Manchu reads "Yerkiyang."

C#	Date	Emperor	Good	VG	Fine	VF
35-2	(1761-95)	Ch'ien Lung	20.00	30.00	50.00	85.00

10 CASH

CAST COPPER

C#	Date	Emperor	Good	VG	Fine	VF
35-3	(1851-61)	Hsien Feng	22.50	35.00	60.00	100.00
35-7	(1862-74)	T'ung Chih	27.50	45.00	75.00	125.00

50 CASH

CAST COPPER

C#	Date	Emperor	Good	VG	Fine	VF
35-4	(1851-61)	Hsien Feng	60.00	90.00	150.00	250.00

100 CASH

CAST COPPER, 50-54mm

C#	Date	Emperor	Good	VG	Fine	VF
35-5	(1851-61)	Hsien Feng	65.00	110.00	180.00	300.00

45mm

C#	Date	Emperor	Good	VG	Fine	VF
35-5.1	(1851-61)	Hsien Feng	65.00	110.00	180.00	300.00

500 CASH

CAST COPPER

35-5a (1851-61) Hsien Feng Reported, not confirmed

1000 CASH

CAST COPPER

35-6 (1851-61) Hsien Feng Reported, not confirmed

STRUCK COINAGE

1/2 MISCAL

SILVER
Rev: Turki and Chinese legends.

K#	Date	Mintage	VG	Fine	VF	XF
998b	ND (1875-1908)		10.00	20.00	35.00	60.00

Rev: Date at left.

K#	Date	Mintage	VG	Fine	VF	XF
1180	AH1295	—	15.00	30.00	50.00	85.00

Rev: Date at right.

K#	Date	Mintage	VG	Fine	VF	XF
1180v	AH1295	—	15.00	30.00	50.00	85.00

Rev: Turki, Chinese and Manchu legends.

K#	Date	Mintage	VG	Fine	VF	XF
1181	ND (1875-1908)		8.50	17.50	30.00	50.00

REBEL ISSUES

Ghazi Rashid

A rebel in Sinkiang about whom little is known. He was in power from 1862 until his death in 1867.

PUL

CAST COPPER

C#	Date	Emperor	Good	VG	Fine	VF
36-7	ND	Yarkand	45.00	75.00	125.00	200.00

CASH

COPPER
Small legends

C#	Date	Emperor	Good	VG	Fine	VF
36-1	AH1280	K'u-Ch'e	45.00	75.00	125.00	200.00

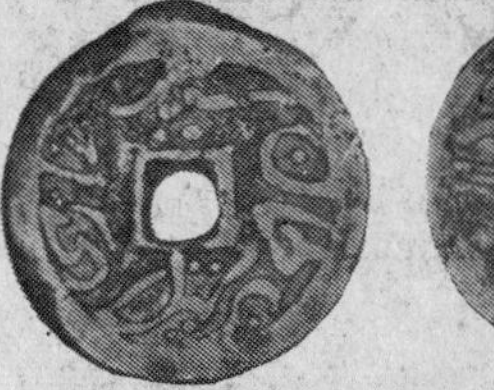

Large legends

C#	Date	Emperor	Good	VG	Fine	VF
36-2	AH1280	K'u-Ch'e	45.00	75.00	125.00	200.00
36-3	—	Aksu	—	—	Rare	—

TENGA

SILVER

C#	Date	Mint	VG	Fine	VF	XF
36-5	AH1283	Khotan	22.50	45.00	75.00	125.00

Yakub Beg

These coins were struck at Kashgar in the name of the Ottoman Sultan Abdul Aziz by the rebel Yakub Beg, who controlled much of Sinkiang between 1865 and 1877.

FALUS

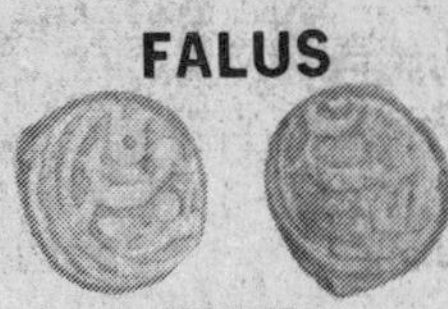

COPPER

C#	Date	Mintage	Good	VG	Fine	VF
—	ND	—	6.50	11.50	18.50	30.00
	AH1292	—	6.50	11.50	18.50	30.00
—	1293	—	6.50	11.50	18.50	30.00

1/2 MISCAL (MACE)

SILVER

C#	Date	Mintage	VG	Fine	VF	XF
37-1	AH1291	—	10.00	18.50	30.00	50.00
	1292	—	10.00	18.50	30.00	50.00
	1293	—	10.00	18.50	30.00	50.00
	1294	—	10.00	18.50	30.00	50.00

Legends arranged differently.

C#	Date	Mintage	VG	Fine	VF	XF
37-1.1	AH1292	—	10.00	18.50	30.00	50.00
	1293	—	10.00	18.50	30.00	50.00
	1294	—	10.00	18.50	30.00	50.00

Mule obv. with 1293 date, rev. with 1294 date.

C#	Date	Mintage	VG	Fine	VF	XF
37-1.2	AH1293/94	—	17.50	30.00	50.00	85.00

TILLA

GOLD, 3.7600 gm.
Segmented double circle around Turki legends.

C#	Date	Mintage	VG	Fine	VF	XF
37-2	AH1291	—	85.00	125.00	175.00	250.00

Single circle around legend

C#	Date	Mintage	VG	Fine	VF	XF
37-2.1	AH1290	—	—	—	Rare	—
	1291	—	100.00	150.00	210.00	300.00
	1292	—	90.00	140.00	200.00	285.00
	1293	—	125.00	175.00	250.00	350.00

SZECHUAN

A province located in south central China. The largest of the Chinese provinces, Szechuan is a plateau region watered by many rivers. These rivers carry much trading traffic. Agriculture or mining are the occupational choices of most of the populace. In World War II the national capitol was moved to Chungking in Szechuan. Chengtu was an active imperial mint that opened in 1732 and was in practically continuous operation until the advent of modern equipment. Modern minting was introduced in the province when Chengtu began struck coinage in 1898. A mint was authorized for Chungking in 1905 but it did not begin operations until 1913. The Chengtu Mint was looted by soldiers in 1925. The last republic issues from Szechuan were dated 1932.

EMPIRE

CASH

CAST BRASS

C#	Date	Emperor	Good	VG	Fine	VF
24-1	(1736-95)	Ch'ien Lung	.25	.60	1.00	1.20

CAST ZINC

C#	Date	Emperor	Good	VG	Fine	VF
24-1a	(1736-95)	Ch'ien Lung	—	—	Rare	—

CAST BRASS

C#	Date	Emperor	Good	VG	Fine	VF
24-2	(1796-1820)	Chia Ch'ing	.40	1.00	1.50	2.00
24-3	(1821-50)	Tao Kuang	.40	1.00	2.00	3.00
24-4	(1851-61)	Hsien Feng	1.20	3.00	4.00	5.00
	Rev: Character 'Shih' (meaning ten) above.					
24-4.1	(1851-61)	Hsien Feng	5.00	8.00	12.50	20.00
	Rev: Character "Wen" (meaning unit) above.					
24-4.2	(1851-61)	Hsien Feng	5.00	8.00	12.50	20.00
	Rev: Character "Kung" (meaning work) above.					
24-4.3	(1851-61)	Hsien Feng	5.00	8.00	12.50	20.00
	Rev: Character "Erh" (meaning two) above.					
24-4.4	(1851-61)	Hsien Feng	5.00	8.00	12.50	20.00
	Rev: Circle above.					
24-4.5	(1851-61)	Hsien Feng	5.00	8.00	12.50	20.00
	Rev: Crescent standing on end above.					
24-4.6	(1851-61)	Hsien Feng	5.00	8.00	12.50	20.00
	Rev: Two horizontal and one vertical lines above.					
24-4.7	(1851-61)	Hsien Feng	5.00	8.00	12.50	20.00
	Rev: Two figures above, possibly meaning 15.					
24-4.8	(1851-61)	Hsien Feng	5.00	8.00	12.50	20.00
	Rev: Crescent below.					
24-4.9	(1851-61)	Hsien Feng	5.00	8.00	12.50	20.00
24-8	(1862-74)	T'ung Chih	5.00	8.00	12.50	20.00
	Rev: Character "Shih" (ten) above and dot below.					
24-8.1	(1862-74)	T'ung Chih	5.00	8.00	12.50	20.00
	Rev: Character "Shih" above and crescent on edge below.					
24-8.2	(1862-74)	T'ung Chih	5.00	8.00	12.50	20.00
	Rev: Character "Shih" above and "Lin" below.					
24-8.3	(1862-74)	T'ung Chih	5.00	8.00	12.50	20.00
	Rev: Character "Wen" (meaning unit) above and "Yi" below.					
24-8.4	(1862-74)	T'ung Chih	5.00	8.00	12.50	20.00
	Rev: Character "Wen" above and "Chi" below.					
24-8.5	(1862-74)	T'ung Chih	5.00	8.00	12.50	20.00
	Rev: Character "Wen" above and "Chuan" below.					
24-8.6	(1862-74)	T'ung Chih	5.00	8.00	12.50	20.00
24-9	(1875-1908)	Kuang Hsu	4.50	7.50	11.50	17.50

NOTE: Refer to "Additional Characters" chart in the introduction to China.

10 CASH

CAST BRASS

Rev: Type I mintmark.

C#	Date	Emperor	Good	VG	Fine	VF
24-5	(1851-61)	Hsien Feng	15.00	25.00	35.00	50.00

Rev: Type II mintmark.

C#	Date	Emperor	Good	VG	Fine	VF
24-5.1	(1851-61)	Hsien Feng	15.00	25.00	35.00	50.00
24-10	(1875-1908)	Kuang Hsu	—	—	Rare	—

50 CASH

CAST BRASS

C#	Date	Emperor	Good	VG	Fine	VF
24-6	(1851-61)	Hsien Feng	20.00	30.00	40.00	60.00

100 CASH

CAST BRASS

C#	Date	Emperor	Good	VG	Fine	VF
24-7	(1851-61)	Hsien Feng	25.00	35.00	45.00	60.00

STRUCK COINAGE

5 CASH

COPPER
Side view dragon.

Y#	Date	Mintage	VG	Fine	VF	XF
225	(1903-04)	.085	75.00	150.00	225.00	300.00

Flying dragon.

Y#	Date	Mintage	VG	Fine	VF	XF
228	(1903-04)	I.A.	55.00	110.00	150.00	200.00

10 CASH

COPPER
Obv: Thick Manchu characters in center. Large rosettes.

Y#	Date	Mintage	VG	Fine	VF	XF
226	(1903-05)	95.960	15.00	30.00	60.00	100.00

Obv: Thin Manchu characters. Small rosettes.

Y#	Date	Mintage	VG	Fine	VF	XF
226.1	(1903-05)	I.A.	15.00	30.00	60.00	100.00

Obv: Large rosettes.

Y#	Date	Mintage	VG	Fine	VF	XF
226.2	(1903-05)	I.A.	15.00	30.00	60.00	100.00

Obv: Two characters at bottom, 6-9mm apart. Rev: Trident-shaped flame on dragons body under letters CHU.

Y#	Date	Mintage	VG	Fine	VF	XF
229	(1903-05)	I.A.	3.50	6.00	8.00	15.00

Obv: Characters at bottom 4-5mm apart.

Y#	Date	Mintage	VG	Fine	VF	XF
229.1	(1903-05)	I.A.	3.50	6.00	8.00	15.00

Obv: Manchu at 3 o'clock is lower in relation to center characters.

Y#	Date	Mintage	VG	Fine	VF	XF
229.2	(1903-05)	I.A.	3.50	6.00	8.00	15.00

Obv: Characters 6-9mm apart. Rev: Trident-shaped flame under letters HUE.

Y#	Date	Mintage	VG	Fine	VF	XF
229.3	(1903-05)	I.A.	3.50	6.00	8.00	15.00

BRASS

Y#	Date	Mintage	VG	Fine	VF	XF
229.3a	(1903-05)	I.A.	3.50	6.00	8.00	15.00

Obv: Characters 4-5mm apart.

Y#	Date	Mintage	VG	Fine	VF	XF
229.4	(1903-05)	I.A.	3.50	6.00	8.00	15.00

Obv: Bottom characters 6-9mm apart. Rev: No trident—shaped flame, instead a cloud pointing to the letter U.

Y#	Date	Mintage	VG	Fine	VF	XF
229.5	(1903-05)	I.A.	2.00	3.50	6.00	10.00

COPPER

Y#	Date	Mintage	VG	Fine	VF	XF
229.5a	(1903-05)	I.A.	2.50	4.00	8.00	12.00

BRASS
Obv: Characters 4-5mm apart.

Y#	Date	Mintage	VG	Fine	VF	XF
229.6	(1903-05)	I.A.	3.25	5.00	8.00	15.00

COPPER

Y#	Date	Mintage	VG	Fine	VF	XF
229.6a	(1903-05)	I.A.	1.50	2.50	4.50	7.50

BRASS
Obv: Manchu at 3 o'clock is lower.

Y#	Date	Mintage	VG	Fine	VF	XF
229.7	(1903-05)	I.A.	3.25	5.00	8.00	15.00

COPPER

Y#	Date	Mintage	VG	Fine	VF	XF
229.7a	(1903-05)	I.A.	1.50	2.50	4.50	7.50

BRASS
Obv: Characters 4-5mm apart. Rev: No cloud under CHU. High point of dragon's body under letter C. Tail joins body over letter S in CASH.

Y#	Date	Mintage	VG	Fine	VF	XF
229.8	(1903-05)	I.A.	3.25	5.00	8.00	15.00

COPPER

Y#	Date	Mintage	VG	Fine	VF	XF
229.8a	(1903-05)	I.A.	1.50	2.50	4.50	7.50

Rev: High point of dragons body under letter H. Tail joins body over letter C in CASH.

Y#	Date	Mintage	VG	Fine	VF	XF
229.9	(1903-05)	I.A.	1.50	2.50	4.50	7.50

Y#	Date	Mintage	VG	Fine	VF	XF
231	(1903-05)	I.A.	85.00	150.00	200.00	250.00

Y#	Date	Mintage	VG	Fine	VF	XF
10t	CD1906	337.748	1.00	1.50	2.50	5.00

Bottom of Manchu character at 11 o'clock curls to left.

Y#	Date	Mintage	VG	Fine	VF	XF
20t.1	CD1909	231.930	1.00	1.50	2.50	5.00

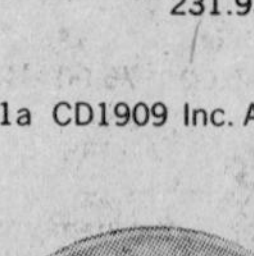

BRASS

Y#	Date	Mintage	VG	Fine	VF	XF
20t.1a	CD1909	Inc. Ab.	2.50	4.00	7.00	12.50

COPPER
Bottom of Manchu character at 11 o'clock curls to right.

Y#	Date	Mintage	VG	Fine	VF	XF
20t.2	CD1909	Inc. Ab.	4.00	7.50	10.00	15.00

20 CASH

COPPER

Y#	Date	Mintage	VG	Fine	VF	XF
227	(1903-05)	25.319	35.00	60.00	90.00	150.00

Obv: Small Manchu at 3 and 9 o'clock.
Rev: Trident flame points to E of SZE.

230	(1903-05)	I.A.	10.00	18.50	30.00	50.00

Obv: Large Manchu at 3 and 9 o'clock. Rev: Large trident flame points to C of CHUEN.

230.1	(1903-05)	I.A.	10.00	18.50	30.00	50.00

BRASS
Obv: Small Manchu. Rev: Larger cloud under CHUEN.

Y#	Date	Mintage	VG	Fine	VF	XF
230.2	(1903-05)	I.A.	12.50	22.50	35.00	60.00

Obv: Large Manchu. Rev: Trident flame under ZE.

230.3	(1903-05)	I.A.	13.50	25.00	40.00	70.00

Rev: Trident flame under CHU of CHUEN, large letters.

230.4	ND	—	—	—	—	—

Rev: Trident flame points to E of CHUEN, small letters.

230.5	(1903-05)	I.A.	—	—	—	—

Front view dragon.

232 ND — — Reported, Not Confirmed

COPPER

Y#	Date	Mintage	VG	Fine	VF	XF
11t	CD1906	51.028	8.50	15.00	22.50	40.00

Bottom of Manchu character at 11 o'clock curls right.

21t.1	CD1909	33.414	12.50	22.50	35.00	60.00

Bottom of Manchu character at 11 o'clock curls left.

21t.2	CD1909	—	12.50	22.50	35.00	60.00

BRASS

21t.1a	CD1909	Inc. Ab.	20.00	30.00	45.00	75.00

30 CASH

COPPER
Obv: Front view dragon
Rev: Flying dragon.

Y#	Date	Mintage	Fine	VF	XF	Unc
233	ND	—	—	—	Rare	—

5 CENTS

SILVER, 1.3000 gm.

234	(1898; 1901-08)	.671	10.00	15.00	25.00	50.00

Errors in the English legend.

234.1	(1901-08)	I.A.	11.50	17.50	30.00	60.00

239	(1910)	.566	16.50	25.00	40.00	75.00

10 CENTS

SILVER, 2.6000 gm.

235	(1898; 1901-08)	1.274	11.50	17.50	27.50	50.00

Y#	Date	Mintage	Fine	VF	XF	Unc
240	(1909-11)	.278	15.00	22.50	40.00	65.00

20 CENTS

.820 SILVER, 5.3000 gm.
Rev: Five flames on pearl.

Y#	Date	Mintage	Fine	VF	XF	Unc
236	(1898; 1901-08)	.897	10.00	15.00	25.00	50.00
	Rev: Six flames on pearl.					
236.1	(1898; 1901-08)	Inc. Ab.	10.00	15.00	25.00	50.00
	Seven flames on pearl.					
236.2	(1898; 1901-08)	Inc. Ab.	10.00	15.00	25.00	50.00
	Various errors in English legend.					
236.3	(1901-08)	I.A.	11.50	17.50	30.00	60.00
	Rev: Head of dragon redesigned, longer moustache. Oblong rosette to either side od dragon. Snakelike cloud near upper right claw. PAO at 9 o'clock inside circle) written differently.					
236.5	(1901-08)	I.A.	35.00	90.00	150.00	250.00
—	(1909-11)	.041	—	—	Rare	—

50 CENTS

.860 SILVER, 13.2 gm.
Rev: Dragon with narrow face, with small cross to either side. Large fireball.

Y#	Date	Mintage	Fine	VF	XF	Unc
237	(1898; 1901-08)	.474	20.00	35.00	60.00	120.00
	Various errors in English legend.					
237.1	(1901-08)	I.A.	21.50	37.50	70.00	140.00

Rev: Dragon with tapering face and small chin. Small fireball. Small cross to either side of dragon.

Y#	Date	Mintage	Fine	VF	XF	Unc
237.2	(1901-08)	I.A.	22.50	40.00	75.00	150.00

Rev: Dragon with wide face and smaller fireball, thicker spines on top of dragon's head, small cross at either side of dragon.

Y#	Date	Mintage	Fine	VF	XF	Unc
237.3	(1901-08)	I.A.	22.50	45.00	75.00	150.00
	Rev: Dragon with redesigned head, oblong rosette at either side of dragon and a snakelike cloud near right claw. Pao (at 9 o'clock inside circle) written differently.					
237.4	(1901-08)	I.A.	150.00	200.00	250.00	500.00

Y#	Date	Mintage	Fine	VF	XF	Unc
242	(1909-11)	.038	60.00	85.00	125.00	250.00
	Rev. legend: Inverted A in place of V in PROVINCE.					
242.1	(1909-11)	I.A.	60.00	85.00	125.00	250.00

DOLLAR

.900 SILVER, 26.8000 gm.
Rev: Dragon with narrow face and large fireball, small cross to either side of dragon.

Y#	Date	Mintage	Fine	VF	XF	Unc
238	(1898; 1901-08)	6.487	BV	27.50	37.50	90.00
	Inverted A instead of V in PROVINCE.					
238.1	(1901-08)	I.A.	BV	32.50	50.00	120.00
	Rev: Dragon with wider face and flatter pearl, small cross to either side of dragon.					
238.2	(1901-08)	I.A.	BV	27.50	37.50	90.00
	As above, but 7 MACE and 3 CANDAREENS instead of 2 CANDAREENS.					
238.3	(1901-08)	I.A.	BV	32.50	50.00	120.00
	Obv: Pao (at 9 o'clock inside circle) written differently. Rev: Dragon with redesigned head, oblong rosette at either side of dragon, snakelike cloud near right claw.					
238.4	(1901-08)	I.A.	—	—	1500.	2000.

Y#	Date	Mintage	Fine	VF	XF	Unc
243	(1909-11)	2.846	BV	27.50	37.50	90.00
	Inverted A instead of V in PROVINCE.					
243.1	(1909-11)	I.A.	BV	32.50	50.00	120.00

NOTE: The machinery for the first Szechuan mint was produced in New Jersey and the dies were engraved in Philadelphia. The mint was opened in 1898, but closed within a few months and did not reopen until 1901. There is no doubt now that K#145 -149 were the first issues of this mint, contrary to the Kann listings.

REPUBLIC

Many coins in silver and minor metals, issued by warlords and Chinese Communists, circulated in such provinces as Kansu, Szechuan and Yunnan. These coins were struck or sometimes cast of silver or copper, but also of debased metals of cruder craftsmanship. Some coins in this category include Y#217, Y#459.3 and many pieces among Y#446 through Y#464. Y#447 through 450 come in differing degrees of copper: red copper, debased (yellow) copper and greenish yellow brass. To classify as copper, the color of the coin must be red to brown-red.

5 CASH

COPPER

Y#	Date	Mintage	VG	Fine	VF	XF
441	Yr.1 (1912)	.471	25.00	60.00	90.00	125.00

NOTE: Many varieties.

BRASS

Y#	Date	Mintage	VG	Fine	VF	XF
441a	Yr.1 (1912)	I.A.	—	—	—	—

COPPER

Y#	Date	Mintage	VG	Fine	VF	XF
443	Yr.1 (1912)	I.A.	35.00	65.00	110.00	145.00

Y#	Date	Mintage	VG	Fine	VF	XF
446	Yr.1 (1912)	I.A.	45.00	110.00	150.00	225.00

BRASS

Y#	Date	Mintage	VG	Fine	VF	XF
446a	Yr.1 (1912)	I.A.	—	—	—	—

10 CASH

COPPER
Obv: Two rosettes

Y#	Date	Mintage	VG	Fine	VF	XF
447	Yr.1 (1912)					
		108.618	1.50	3.00	10.00	20.00
	Yr.2 (1913)	I.A.	6.00	15.00	25.00	50.00

BRASS

Y#	Date	Mintage	VG	Fine	VF	XF
447a	Yr.1 (1912)	I.A.	.60	1.50	2.50	5.00
	Yr.2 (1913)	I.A.	1.60	4.00	8.00	20.00

Obv: Three rosettes.

Y#	Date	Mintage	VG	Fine	VF	XF
447.1	Yr.2 (1913)	I.A.	—	—	Rare	—

20 CASH

COPPER
Obv: Two rosettes.

Y#	Date	Mintage	VG	Fine	VF	XF
448	Yr.1 (1912)					
		115.061	1.00	2.50	5.00	10.00
	Yr.2 (1913)	I.A.	— Reported, not confirmed			

BRASS

Y#	Date	Mintage	VG	Fine	VF	XF
448a	Yr.1 (1912)	I.A.	.60	1.50	2.50	6.00
	Yr.2 (1913)	I.A.	.80	2.00	3.50	7.00

COPPER
Obv: Three rosettes.

Y#	Date	Mintage	VG	Fine	VF	XF
448.1	Yr.2 (1913)	I.A.	6.00	15.00	25.00	40.00
	Yr.3 (1914)	I.A.	— Reported, Not Confirmed			

BRASS

Y#	Date	Mintage	VG	Fine	VF	XF
448.1a	Yr.2 (1913)	I.A.	2.00	5.00	10.00	20.00
	Yr.3 (1914)	I.A.	2.00	5.00	10.00	20.00

NOTE: There are many varieties of this 20 Cash; small and large rosettes; open and closed size characters and exaggerated size character with horns.

2 CENTS

COPPER

Y#	Date	Mintage	VG	Fine	VF	XF
476	Yr.19 (1930)	—	70.00	175.00	250.00	400.00

BRASS

Y#	Date	Mintage	VG	Fine	VF	XF
476a	Yr.19 (1930)	—	—	—	—	—

50 CASH

COPPER
Rev: Small rosette in center.

Y#	Date	Mintage	VG	Fine	VF	XF
449	Yr.1 (1912)					
		489.382	1.50	3.50	6.00	12.00

BRASS

Y#	Date	Mintage	VG	Fine	VF	XF
449a	Yr.1 (1912)	I.A.	1.25	3.00	5.00	10.00

COPPER
Rev: Larger rosette in center.

Y#	Date	Mintage	VG	Fine	VF	XF
449.1	Yr.1 (1912)	I.A.	2.00	5.00	10.00	20.00

BRASS

Y#	Date	Mintage	VG	Fine	VF	XF
449.1a	Yr.1 (1912)	I.A.	2.50	6.00	12.50	25.00

COPPER
Obv: Three rosettes.

Y#	Date	Mintage	VG	Fine	VF	XF
449.2	Yr.2 (1913)	I.A.	2.00	5.00	10.00	20.00

BRASS

Y#	Date	Mintage	VG	Fine	VF	XF
449.2a	Yr.2 (1913)	I.A.	2.00	5.00	10.00	20.00
	Yr.3 (1914)	I.A.	2.00	5.00	10.00	20.00

COPPER

Y#	Date	Mintage	VG	Fine	VF	XF
462	Yr.15 (1926)					
		.090	15.00	35.00	50.00	75.00

BRASS

Y#	Date	Mintage	VG	Fine	VF	XF
462a	Yr.15 (1926)	I.A.	15.00	35.00	50.00	75.00

100 CASH

COPPER
Obv: Two rosettes.

Y#	Date	Mintage	VG	Fine	VF	XF
450	Yr.2 (1913)					
		399.212	2.00	5.00	7.50	15.00
	Yr.3 (1914)	—	6.00	15.00	22.50	45.00
	BRASS					
450a	Yr.2 (1913)	I.A.	1.00	2.50	5.00	9.00

Obv: Three rosettes.

Y#	Date	Mintage	VG	Fine	VF	XF
450.1	Yr.2 (1913)	I.A.	3.00	7.50	12.50	20.00
	Yr.3 (1914)	—	—	—	—	—

COPPER or BRASS
200 Cash, Y#459 cut in half.

Y#	Date	Mintage	VG	Fine	VF	XF
459x	ND	2	3.50	7.50	13.50	20.00

NOTE: It has been reported that the 200 Cash, Y#459 was cut in half and circulated locally as 100 Cash.

COPPER

Y#	Date	Mintage	VG	Fine	VF	XF
463	Yr.15 (1926)					
		7.055	3.25	8.00	12.50	20.00
	BRASS					
463a	Yr.15 (1926)					
		Inc. Ab.	3.25	8.00	12.50	20.00

NOTE: Two reverse varieties known.

COPPER

Y#	Date	Mintage	VG	Fine	VF	XF
466	Yr.15 (1926)					
		Inc. Ab.	140.00	200.00	335.00	375.00
	Yr.19 (1930)	—	30.00	75.00	100.00	150.00
	BRASS					
466a	Yr.19 (1930)	—	—	—	—	—

200 CASH

COPPER

Y#	Date	Mintage	VG	Fine	VF	XF
459	Yr.2 (1913)					
		360.274	— Reported, not confirmed			
	BRASS					
459a	Yr.2 (1913)	I.A.	16.50	40.00	65.00	100.00

COPPER
Obv: Tassels draped over flag poles.

Y#	Date	Mintage	VG	Fine	VF	XF
459.1	Yr.2 (1913)	I.A.	3.50	8.50	17.50	30.00
	BRASS					
459.1a	Yr.2 (1913)	—	3.50	8.50	17.50	30.00
	COPPER					
	Rev: Smaller star to sides.					
459.2	Yr.2 (1913)	I.A.	3.50	8.50	17.50	30.00

Obv: Mirror image of normal coin.

Y#	Date	Mintage	VG	Fine	VF	XF
459.3	Yr.2 (1913)	—	8.00	20.00	35.00	60.00

NOTE: Possibly a warlord issue. Authenticity is doubtful.

Plain edge.

Y#	Date	Mintage	VG	Fine	VF	XF
464	Yr.15 (1926)					
		404.644	4.00	10.00	15.00	20.00

Reeded edge.

Y#	Date	Mintage	VG	Fine	VF	XF
464.1	Yr.15 (1926)					
		Inc. Ab.	6.00	15.00	25.00	35.00

BRASS
Plain edge.

464a	Yr.15 (1926)					
		Inc. Ab.	4.75	12.00	17.00	22.00

Reeded edge

464.1a	Yr.15 (1926)	I.A.	—	—	—	—

NOTE: Many varieties: Open and closed buds; overstruck on earlier pieces and on virgin flans; different sizes and thicknesses.

10 CENTS

SILVER, 2.6000 gm.

Y#	Date	Mintage	Fine	VF	XF	Unc
453	Yr.1 (1912)	.370	15.00	25.00	40.00	75.00

		NICKEL				
468	ND	—	30.00	75.00	90.00	125.00
		SILVER				
468a	ND	—	20.00	50.00	75.00	100.00
		IRON				
468b	ND	—	16.50	40.00	60.00	100.00
		COPPER-NICKEL				
468c	ND	—	10.00	25.00	38.00	50.00

20 CENTS

SILVER, 5.2000 gm.

454	Yr.1 (1912)	.095	25.00	40.00	70.00	125.00

Tibetan War Commemorative

K#	Date	Mintage	Fine	VF	XF	Unc
795	1932	—	40.00	100.00	150.00	200.00

NOTE: Authenticity not established.

50 CENTS

SILVER, 12.9000 gm.

Y#	Date	Mintage	Fine	VF	XF	Unc
455	Yr.1 (1912)					
		37.942	BV	15.00	37.50	75.00
	Yr.2 (1913)	I.A.	—	—	Rare	—

Sun Yat-sen

473	Yr.17 (1928)					
		1.594	40.00	100.00	150.00	250.00

DOLLAR

SILVER, 25.6000 gm.

456	Yr.1 (1912)					
		55.670	BV	30.00	35.00	50.00
	Yr.3 (1914)	I.A.	—	—	Rare	—

Sun Yat-sen
Similar to 50 Cents, Y#473.

474	Yr.17 (1928)					
		7.684	125.00	200.00	275.00	400.00

NCLT ISSUES

PATTERNS

KM#	Date	Mintage	Identification	Mkt.Val.
—	(1897)	—	1 Cash, Brass, w/center hole	100.00
1	(1897)	—	1 Cash, Brass, w/o hole	200.00

NOTE: This coin was struck in New Jersey as a sample by the company which made the machinery for the Szechuan Mint. The dies for this coin, however, were not used because of the erroneous mintmark which reads PAO YUAN, indicating the Board of Works Mint in Peking. Trial strikes exist, uniface of both obverse and reverse.

2	CD1908	—	1 Cash, Brass, Y#7t	300.00

3	ND	—	30 Cash, Copper, front views dragon, Y233.1	Rare
4	ND	—	30 Cash, Copper, flying dragon, Y232.2	Rare

TAIWAN

For historical information refer to introductory paragraph of the Republic of China following the People's Republic of China listings.

EMPIRE

CASH

CAST BRASS

C#	Date	Emperor	Good	VG	Fine	VF
25-1	(1736-95)					

C#	Date	Emperor	Good	VG	Fine	VF
		Ch'ien Lung	10.00	20.00	30.00	45.00
25-2	(1796-1820)	Chia Ch'ing	—	—	Rare	—

C#	Date	Emperor	Good	VG	Fine	VF
25-6	(1851-61)	Hsien Feng	10.00	20.00	30.00	45.00

10 CASH

CAST BRASS

25-7 (1851-61) Hsien Feng Reported, Not Confirmed

STRUCK COINAGE

Made in Taiwan 造製灣臺

Made in Tai Province 造製省臺

5 CENTS

SILVER, 1.3000 gm.
Similar to 10 Cents, Y#247.

Y#	Date	Mintage	Fine	VF	XF	Unc
246	(1893-94)	—	50.00	100.00	150.00	225.00

10 CENTS

SILVER, 2.7000 gm.
Obv: Four Chinese characters above meaning: Made in Taiwan. Large characters in outside circle; small characters inside.

Y#	Date	Mintage	Fine	VF	XF	Unc
247	(1893-94)	—	12.50	25.00	50.00	100.00

Smaller characters in outside circle and larger characters inside circle.

Y#	Date	Mintage	Fine	VF	XF	Unc
247.1	(1893-94)	—	13.50	27.50	55.00	110.00

Four Chinese characters above meaning: Made in Tai Province.

Y#	Date	Mintage	Fine	VF	XF	Unc
247.2	(1893-94)	—	16.50	32.50	65.00	130.00

20 CENTS

SILVER, 5.4000 gm.
Obv: Four Chinese characters above, meaning Made in Taiwan.

Y#	Date	Mintage	VG	Fine	VF	XF
248	(1894)	—	—	—	Rare	—

Obv: Four Chinese characters above, meaning: Made in Tai Province.

Y#	Date	Mintage	VG	Fine	VF	XF
248.1	(1894)	—	—	—	Rare	—

DOLLAR

SILVER, 26.8000 gm.

C#	Date	Mintage	VG	Fine	VF	XF
25-3	(1837-1845)	—	125.00	200.00	300.00	500.00

NOTE: This coin is known as the Old Man Dollar. Many varieties exist.

25.0000 gm.
Rev: Crossed lotus flowers.

C#	Date	Mintage	VG	Fine	VF	XF
25-4	ND	—	100.00	175.00	275.00	450.00

Rev: Crossed brushes.

C#	Date	Mintage	VG	Fine	VF	XF
25-5	ND	—	125.00	200.00	300.00	500.00

NOTE: The market values shown for C#25-3/25-5 are for coins which have been lightly chopmarked. Attribution of C#25-4 and C#25-5 to Taiwan is not fully accepted. Other sources attribute these coins to Chihli Province.

YUNNAN

A province located in south China bordering Burma. It is very mountainous with many lakes. Yunnan was the home of various active imperial mints. A modern mint was established at Kunming in 1905 and the first struck copper coins were issued in 1906 and the first struck silver coins in 1908. General Tang Chi-Yao issued coins in gold, silver and copper with his portrait in 1919. The last Republican coins were struck here in 1949.

EMPIRE

Yunnanfu Mint

CASH

CAST BRASS

C#	Date	Emperor	Good	VG	Fine	VF
26-1	(1736-95)	Ch'ien Lung	.20	.50	1.00	1.25
26-2	(1796-1820)	Chia Ch'ing	.10	.25	.50	.75
Rev: Crescent above.						
26-2.1	(1796-1820)	Chia Ch'ing	1.00	2.00	3.00	5.00

C#	Date	Emperor	Good	VG	Fine	VF
26.3	(1821-50)	Tao Kuang	.10	.25	.50	.75
Rev: Crescent above.						
26.3.1	(1821-50)	Tao Kuang	1.00	2.00	3.00	5.00
Rev: Horizontal line above.						
26-3.2	(1821-50)	Tao Kuang	1.50	3.00	4.00	6.00
26.4	(1851-61)	Hsien Feng	.50	1.00	1.50	2.50
Rev: Crescent above.						
26.4.1	(1851-61)	Hsien Feng	2.50	5.00	7.50	11.50
Rev: Crescent below.						
26.4.2	(1851-61)	Hsien Feng	2.50	5.00	7.50	11.50
Rev: Crescent standing on end above.						
26-4.3	(1851-61)	Hsien Feng	2.50	5.00	7.50	11.50
Rev: Dot within crescent above.						
26-4.4	(1851-61)	Hsien Feng	2.50	5.00	7.50	11.50
Rev: Circle above.						
26-4.5	(1851-61)	Hsien Feng	2.50	5.00	7.50	11.50
Rev: Circle below.						
26-4.6	(1851-61)	Hsien Feng	2.50	5.00	7.50	11.50
Rev: Dot within circle above.						
26-4.7	(1851-61)	Hsien Feng	2.50	5.00	7.50	11.50
Rev: Dot within circle below.						
26-4.8	(1851-61)	Hsien Feng	2.50	5.00	7.50	11.50
Rev: An X above the center.						
26-4.9	(1851-61)	Hsien Feng	2.50	5.00	7.50	11.50
Rev: Character "Ho" above and circle below.						
26-4.10	(1851-61)	Hsien Feng	2.50	5.00	7.50	11.50
Rev: Character "Ho" above and dot within circle below.						
26-4.11	(1851-61)	Hsien Feng	2.50	5.00	7.50	11.50

Rev: Character "Kung" above.

C#	Date	Emperor	Good	VG	Fine	VF
26-4.12	(1851-61)	Hsien Feng	2.50	5.00	7.50	11.50
Rev: Character "Yi" (one) above.						
26-4.13	(1851-61)	Hsien Feng	2.50	5.00	7.50	11.50
Rev: Character "Erh" (two) above.						
26-4.14	(1851-61)	Hsien Feng	Reported, Not Confirmed			
Rev: Character "San" (three) above.						
26-4.15	(1851-61)	Hsien Feng	2.50	5.00	7.50	11.50
Rev: Character 'Ssu' (four) above.						
26-4.16	(1851-61)	Hsien Feng	2.50	5.00	7.50	11.50
Rev: Character above probably meaning "five".						
26-4.17	(1851-61)	Hsien Feng	2.50	5.00	7.50	11.50
Rev: Character "Shih" (ten) above and a crescent below.						
26-4.18	(1851-61)	Hsien Feng	2.50	5.00	7.50	11.50
Rev: Character "Chin" above and dot in circle below.						
26-4.19	(1851-61)	Hsien Feng	2.50	5.00	7.50	11.50
Rev: Manchu character above.						
26-4.20	(1851-61)	Hsien Feng	2.50	5.00	7.50	11.50
26-7	(1862-74)	T'ung Chih	1.50	3.00	4.00	6.00
Rev: Circle above.						
26-7.1	(1862-74)	T'ung Chih	2.50	5.00	7.50	11.50
Rev: Dot within circle above.						
26-7.2	(1862-74)	T'ung Chih	2.50	5.00	7.50	11.50
Rev: Dot within crescent above.						
26-7.3	(1862-74)	T'ung Chih	2.50	5.00	7.50	11.50
Rev: Crescent below.						
26-7.4	(1862-74)	T'ung Chih	2.50	5.00	7.50	11.50
Rev: Vertical line above.						
26-7.5	(1862-74)	T'ung Chih	2.50	5.00	7.50	11.50
Rev: Vertical line below.						
26-7.6	(1862-74)	T'ung Chih	2.50	5.00	7.50	11.50
Rev: Character 'Kung' above center.						
26-7.7	(1862-74)	T'ung Chih	2.50	5.00	7.50	11.50
Rev: Character 'Ho' above.						
26-7.8	(1862-74)	T'ung Chih	2.50	5.00	7.50	11.50
Rev: Character 'Ta' above.						
26-7.9	(1862-74)	T'ung Chih	2.50	5.00	7.50	11.50
Rev: Character 'Shan' above.						
26-7.10	(1862-74)	T'ung Chih	2.50	5.00	7.50	11.50
Rev: Character 'Chuan' below.						
26-7.11	(1862-74)	T'ung Chih	2.50	5.00	7.50	11.50
Rev: Character 'Yi' (one) above.						
26-7.12	(1862-74)	T'ung Chih	2.50	5.00	7.50	11.50
Rev: Character 'Wu' (five) below.						
26-7.13	(1862-74)	T'ung Chih	2.50	5.00	7.50	11.50
Rev: Character 'Liu' (six) above.						
26-7.14	(1862-74)	T'ung Chih	2.50	5.00	7.50	11.50

Rev: Characters "Liu" (six) above, but sideways.

C#	Date	Emperor	Good	VG	Fine	VF
26-7.15	(1862-74)	T'ung Chih	2.50	5.00	7.50	11.50
Rev: Character 'Pa' (eight) above.						
26-7.16	(1862-74)	T'ung Chih	2.50	5.00	7.50	11.50
Rev: Character 'Shih' (ten) above.						
26-7.17	(1862-74)	T'ung Chih	2.50	5.00	7.50	11.50
Rev: Characters "Shih Yi" (eleven) above.						
26-7.18	(1862-74)	T'ung Chih	2.50	5.00	7.50	11.50
Rev: Characters "Shih" above and "Yi" below.						
26-7.19	(1862-74)	T'ung Chih	2.50	5.00	7.50	11.50
Rev: Character 'Jen' above.						
26-7.20	(1862-74)	T'ung Chih	2.50	5.00	7.50	11.50
26-9	(1875-1908)	Kuang Hsu	2.00	4.00	5.00	7.00
Rev: Character "Kung" above.						
26-9.1	(1875-1908)	Kuang Hsu	2.00	5.00	7.50	10.00
Rev: Character "Ssu" (four) above.						
26-9.2	(1875-1908)	Kuang Hsu	2.50	5.00	7.50	10.00
Rev: Character "Chin" (nine) above.						
26-9.3	(1875-1908)	Kuang Hsu	2.50	5.00	7.50	10.00

Refer to "Additional Characters" chart in the introduction to China.

10 CASH

CAST BRASS

C#	Date	Emperor	Good	VG	Fine	VF
26-5	(1851-61)	Hsien Feng	10.00	17.50	27.50	40.00
37mm						
26-8	(1862-74)	T'ung Chih	12.50	22.50	32.50	45.00
35mm						
26-8.1	(1862-74)	T'ung Chih	12.50	22.50	32.50	45.00
26-10	(1875-1908)	Kuang Hsu	—	—	Rare	—

50 CASH

CAST BRASS

C#	Date	Emperor	Good	VG	Fine	VF
26-6	(1851-61)	Hsien Feng	25.00	35.00	50.00	70.00

Tungchuan Mint

CASH

CAST BRASS

Rev: Type 1 mintmark.

C#	Date	Emperor	Good	VG	Fine	VF
27-1	(1796-1820)	Chia Ch'ing	.50	1.00	2.00	4.00
Rev: Type 2 mintmark.						
27-1.1	1796-1820	Chia Ch'ing	2.50	5.00	7.50	11.50

Rev: Type 1 mintmark.

C#	Date	Emperor	Good	VG	Fine	VF
27-2	(1821-50)	Tao Kuang	.50	1.00	1.50	2.50

Rev: Type 3 mintmark.

C#	Date	Emperor	Good	VG	Fine	VF
27-2.1	(1821-50)	Tao Kuang	.50	1.00	1.50	2.50
27-3	(1851-61)	Hsien Feng	1.50	3.00	4.00	6.00
Rev: Character 'Cheng' above.						
27-3.1	(1851-61)	Hsien Feng	2.50	5.00	7.50	11.50
27-5	(1862-74)	T'ung Chih	1.50	3.00	4.00	6.00

Rev: Character "Cheng" above and crescent below.

C#	Date	Emperor	Good	VG	Fine	VF
27-5.1	(1862-74)	T'ung Chih	2.50	5.00	7.50	11.50
Rev: Character 'Cheng' above, dot below.						
27-5.2	(1862-74)	T'ung Chih	2.50	5.00	7.50	11.50
27-6	(1875-1908)	Kuang Hsu	2.50	5.00	7.50	11.50

Rev: Character 'Chin' above.

C#	Date	Emperor	Good	VG	Fine	VF
27-6.1	(1875-1908)	Kuang Hsu	2.50	5.00	7.50	11.50

Rev: Characters 'Ts'un' below.

C#	Date	Emperor	Good	VG	Fine	VF
27-6.2	(1875-1908)	Kuang Hsu	2.50	5.00	7.50	11.50

10 CASH

BRASS

C#	Date	Emperor	Good	VG	Fine	VF
27-4	(1851-61)	Hsien Feng	10.00	17.50	25.00	35.00

Uncertain Mint

The following coins bear a Manchu mintmark, different from Fukien which reads, 'FU'. Though previously attributed to Fukien, they are now believed to have been produced in Yunnan.

CASH

CAST BRASS

Rev: Crescent above.

KM#	Date	Emperor	Good	VG	Fine	VF
1	(1862-74)	T'ung Chih	3.50	6.00	9.00	13.50

Rev: Horizontal line above.

KM#	Date	Emperor	Good	VG	Fine	VF
1.1	(1862-74)	T'ung Chih	5.00	8.50	12.50	16.50

KM#	Date	Emperor	Good	VG	Fine	VF
Rev: Vertical line above.						
1.2	(1862-74)	T'ung Chih	5.00	8.50	12.50	16.50
Rev: Character 'Ta' above.						
1.3	(1862-74)	T'ung Chih	5.00	8.50	12.50	16.50
Rev: Character 'Ho' above.						
1.4	(1862-74)	T'ung Chih	5.00	8.50	12.50	16.50
Rev: Character 'Chuan' above.						
1.5	(1862-74)	T'ung Chih	5.00	8.50	12.50	16.50
Rev: Character 'Chih' above.						
1.6	(1862-74)	T'ung Chih	5.00	8.50	12.50	16.50
Rev: Character 'Chung' above.						
1.7	(1862-74)	T'ung Chih	5.00	8.50	12.50	16.50
Rev: Character 'Yu' above.						
1.8	(1862-74)	T'ung Chih	5.00	8.50	12.50	16.50
Rev: Character 'Kung' above.						
1.9	(1862-74)	T'ung Chih	5.00	8.50	12.50	16.50

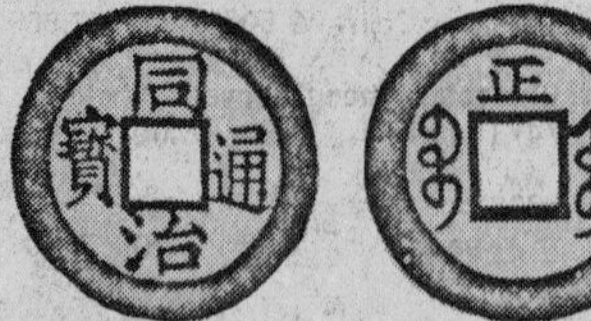

KM#	Date	Emperor	Good	VG	Fine	VF
Rev: Character 'Cheng' above.						
1.10	(1862-74)	T'ung Chih	5.00	8.50	12.50	16.50
Rev: Character 'Cheng' above and circle below.						
1.11	(1862-74)	T'ung Chih	5.00	8.50	12.50	16.50
Rev: With X above.						
1.12	(1862-74)	T'ung Chih	5.00	8.50	12.50	16.50

Rev: Character 'Chu' above.

KM#	Date	Emperor	Good	VG	Fine	VF
1.13	(1862-74)	T'ung Chih	5.00	8.50	12.50	16.50

Rev: Character 'Shih' above.

KM#	Date	Emperor	Good	VG	Fine	VF
1.14	(1862-74)	T'ung Chih	5.00	8.50	12.50	16.50

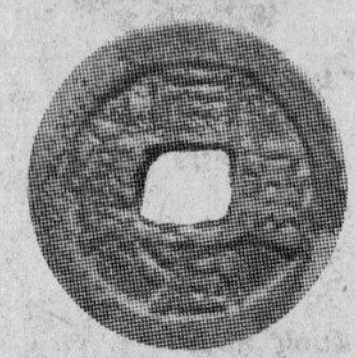

Rev: Character 'Feng' above.

KM#	Date	Emperor	Good	VG	Fine	VF
1.15	(1862-74)	T'ung Chih	5.00	8.50	12.50	16.50

NOTE: Other varieties probably exist. Refer to "Additional Characters" chart in the introduction.

STRUCK COINAGE

10 CASH

COPPER

Obv: Large mintmark in center.

Y#	Date	Mintage	VG	Fine	VF	XF
10u	CD1906	36.701	8.00	20.00	30.00	50.00

Obv: Small mintmark.

Y#	Date	Mintage	VG	Fine	VF	XF
10u.1	CD1906	Inc. Ab.	20.00	50.00	75.00	110.00

Obv: Different mintmark in center.

Y#	Date	Mintage	VG	Fine	VF	XF
10v	CD1906	Inc. Ab.	10.00	25.00	35.00	55.00

20 CASH

COPPER

Large mintmark

Y#	Date	Mintage	VG	Fine	VF	XF
11u	CD1906	.645	30.00	75.00	100.00	150.00

Obv: Smaller mintmark

Y#	Date	Mintage	VG	Fine	VF	XF
11u.1	CD1906	—	30.00	75.00	100.00	150.00

Obv: Different mintmark.

Y#	Date	Mintage	VG	Fine	VF	XF
11v.1	CD1906	Inc. Ab.	125.00	250.00	350.00	450.00
BRASS						
11v.1a	CD1906	Inc.Ab.	150.00	300.00	400.00	500.00

10 CENTS

SILVER, 2.6000 gm.

Y#	Date	Mintage	VG	Fine	VF	XF
255	(1908)	.902	12.50	20.00	30.00	50.00

20 CENTS

SILVER, 5.3000 gm.

Y#	Date	Mintage	VG	Fine	VF	XF
252	(1908)	.532	12.50	20.00	30.00	60.00

Rev: Two circles beneath pearl.

Y#	Date	Mintage	VG	Fine	VF	XF
256	(1908)	Inc. Ab.	10.00	15.00	22.50	40.00

Rev: Three circles beneath pearl.

Y#	Date	Mintage	VG	Fine	VF	XF
256.1	(1908)	Inc. Ab.	10.00	15.00	22.50	40.00

50 CENTS

SILVER, 13.2000 gm.

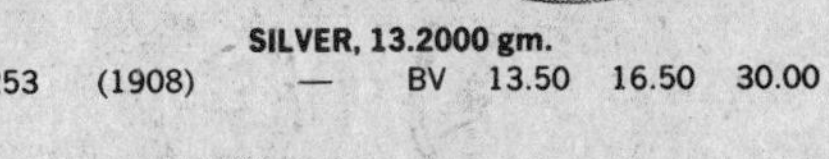

Y#	Date	Mintage	VG	Fine	VF	XF
253	(1908)	—	BV	13.50	16.50	30.00

Two circles under pearl.

Y#	Date	Mintage	VG	Fine	VF	XF
257	(1908)	—	BV	BV	BV	13.50

Three circles under pearl.

Y#	Date	Mintage	VG	Fine	VF	XF
257.1	(1908)	—	BV	BV	BV	13.50

Four circles under pearl.

Y#	Date	Mintage	VG	Fine	VF	XF
257.2	(1908)	—	BV	BV	BV	13.50

NOTE: There are more than 30 varieties of Y#257. In 1949 this coin was restruck in large numbers, but in reduced fineness.

Rev: Seven flames on pearl.

Y#	Date	Mintage	VG	Fine	VF	XF
259	(1909-11)	—	BV	13.50	18.50	35.00

Rev: Nine flames on pearl.

Y#	Date	Mintage	VG	Fine	VF	XF
259.1	(1909-11)	—	BV	13.50	18.50	35.00

DOLLAR

SILVER, 26.8000 gm.

Y#	Date	Mintage	VG	Fine	VF	XF
254	(1908)	—	BV	28.50	38.50	75.00

One circle under pearl.

Y#	Date	Mintage	VG	Fine	VF	XF
258	(1908)	—	BV	27.50	33.50	60.00

Four circles under pearl.

Y#	Date	Mintage	VG	Fine	VF	XF
258.1	(1908)	—	BV	27.50	33.50	60.00

NOTE: Y#258 was restruck in 1949.

Obv: Four characters at top.

Y#	Date	Mintage	VG	Fine	VF	XF
260	(1909-11)	—	BV	28.50	38.50	75.00

Obv: Seven characters at top.

Y#	Date	Mintage	VG	Fine	VF	XF
260.1	CD1910	—	—	—	Rare	—

REPUBLIC

CENT

BRASS
Similar to 2 Cents, Y#489.

Y#	Date	Mintage	VG	Fine	VF	XF
488	Yr.21 (1932)	—	60.00	150.00	210.00	275.00

2 CENTS

BRASS

Y#	Date	Mintage	VG	Fine	VF	XF
489	Yr.21 (1932)	—	175.00	350.00	550.00	750.00

50 CASH

BRASS

Y#	Date	Mintage	VG	Fine	VF	XF
478	ND	—	8.00	15.00	22.50	40.00

COPPER

Y#	Date	Mintage	VG	Fine	VF	XF
478a	ND	—	10.00	17.50	27.50	50.00

5 CENTS

BRASS

Y#	Date	Mintage	VG	Fine	VF	XF
490	Yr.21 (1932)	—	120.00	195.00	265.00	330.00

COPPER-NICKEL

Y#	Date	Mintage	Fine	VF	XF	Unc
485	Yr.12 (1923)	—	25.00	40.00	70.00	125.00

10 CENTS

COPPER-NICKEL
Reeded edge.

Y#	Date	Mintage	Fine	VF	XF	Unc
486	Yr.12 (1923)	—	2.00	3.50	6.00	15.00

Unreeded edge.

Y#	Date	Mintage	Fine	VF	XF	Unc
486.1	Yr.12 (1923)	—	2.50	5.00	10.00	20.00

20 CENTS

SILVER, 5.6000 gm.

Y#	Date	Mintage	Fine	VF	XF	Unc
491	Yr.21 (1932)	—	6.00	10.00	17.50	30.00

Y#	Date	Mintage	Fine	VF	XF	Unc
493	Yr.38 (1949)	—	37.50	60.00	85.00	125.00

50 CENTS

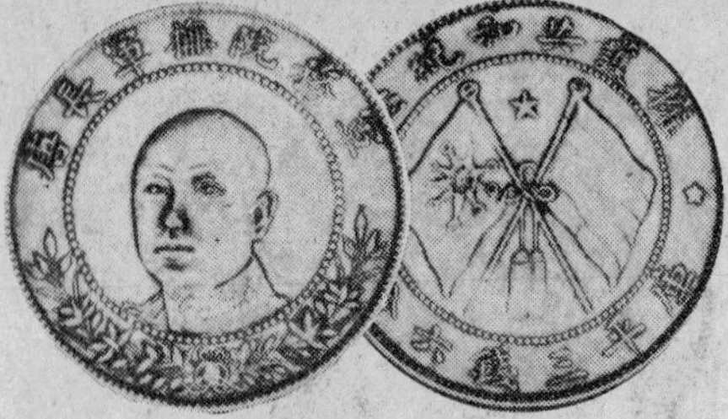

SILVER, 13.1000 gm.
Gen. T'ang Chi-yao

Y#	Date	Mintage	Fine	VF	XF	Unc
479	ND	—	BV	BV	13.50	25.00

Gen. T'ang Chi-yao

Y#	Date	Mintage	Fine	VF	XF	Unc
480	ND	—	15.00	25.00	50.00	85.00

Y#	Date	Mintage	Fine	VF	XF	Unc
492	Yr.21 (1932)	—	BV	BV	BV	13.50

5 DOLLARS

GOLD, 4.5000 gm.
Gen. T'ang Chi-yao
Rev: Numeral 2 below flags.

Y#	Date	Mintage	Fine	VF	XF	Unc
481	(1919)	Est .060	225.00	350.00	500.00	700.00

Rev: No numeral 2 below flags.

Y#	Date	Mintage	Fine	VF	XF	Unc
481.1	(1919)	Inc. Ab.	Reported, Not Confirmed			

K#	Date	Mintage	Fine	VF	XF	Unc
1529	ND	—	300.00	500.00	650.00	850.00

10 DOLLARS

RED GOLD, 8.5000 gm.
Gen. T'ang Chi-yao Commemorative

Y#	Date	Mintage	Fine	VF	XF	Unc
482	(1919)	.090	350.00	550.00	750.00	1000.

YELLOW GOLD

Y#	Date	Mintage	Fine	VF	XF	Unc
482a	(1919)	Inc. Ab.	350.00	550.00	750.00	1000.

Rev: Numeral 1 below flags.

Y#	Date	Mintage	Fine	VF	XF	Unc
482.1	(1919)	Inc. Ab.	250.00	450.00	650.00	850.00

K#	Date	Mintage	Fine	VF	XF	Unc
1528	ND	—	275.00	400.00	525.00	650.00

YUNNAN-BURMA

The 'Yunnan-Burma' coins were produced during World War II, but it is not known exactly when, where nor by whom. The coins are normally weakly struck.

1/2 LIANG (TAEL)

SILVER, 18.3000 gm.
Obv. leg: Laotian and Chinese.

Y#	Date	Mintage	Fine	VF	XF	Unc
495	ND	—	BV	BV	18.50	30.00

TAEL

SILVER, 36.6000 gm.
Obv. leg: Laotian and Chinese.

Y#	Date	Mintage	Fine	VF	XF	Unc
496	ND	—	BV	BV	35.00	45.00

Obv. leg: Laotian and Chinese.

Y#	Date	Mintage	Fine	VF	XF	Unc
497	ND	—	BV	BV	37.50	50.00

Obv: Stags head larger and antlers more developed.

Y#	Date	Mintage	Fine	VF	XF	Unc
497.1	ND	—	—	—	—	—

YUNNAN—SZECHUAN

These two coins have a 2 character mintmark in the center of the obverse, indicating the provinces of Yunnan and Szechuan.

EMPIRE

10 CASH

COPPER

Y#	Date	Mintage	VG	Fine	VF	XF
10w	CD1906	—	12.50	25.00	45.00	85.00

20 CASH

COPPER

Y#	Date	Mintage	VG	Fine	VF	XF
11w	CD1906	—	30.00	60.00	110.00	185.00

REBEL COINS

Chao Ch'in Lung

CASH

CAST COPPER or BRASS

KM#	Date	Emperor	Good	VG	Fine	VF
1	(1832)	—	—	—	Rare	—

T'AI P'ING REBELLION

A radical political and religious upheaval that lasted from 1850 to 1864. It ravaged 17 provinces and took an estimated 20,000,000 lives. The rebellion began under the leadership of Hung Hsiu-Ch'uan (1814-64), a disappointed civil service examination candidate who believed himself to be the son of God, the younger brother of Jesus Christ, sent to reform China.

Their slogan -- to share property in common -- attracted many famine-stricken peasants, workers, and miners, as did their propaganda against the foreign Manchu rulers of China. Under the Taipings, the Chinese language was simplified, and equality between men and women was decreed. All property was to be held in common, and equal distribution of the land according to a form of communism was planned. Both the Chinese Communists and the Chinese Nationalists trace their origin to the Taipings.

Hung Hsiu-Ch'uan

CASH

CAST COPPER or BRASS
Obv: T'at P'ing T'ien Kuo (top-bottom-right-left).
Rev: Sheng Pao (right-left). 24-25mm.

C#	Date	Emperor	Good	VG	Fine	VF
38-8	(1853-64)	—	7.00	10.00	15.00	20.00
	31-35mm					
38-7	(1853-64)	—	10.00	15.00	25.00	35.00
	42-45mm					
38-6	(1853-64)	—	15.00	25.00	40.00	65.00

Rev: Sheng Pao (top-bottom).
24-26mm. Narrow rims.

C#	Date	Emperor	Good	VG	Fine	VF
38-5	(1853-64)	—	7.00	10.00	15.00	20.00
	28mm. Wide rims.					
38-5.1	(1853-64)	—	7.00	10.00	15.00	20.00
	31-33mm. Narrow rims.					
38-4	(1853-64)	—	10.00	15.00	25.00	35.00

C#	Date	Emperor	Good	VG	Fine	VF
	35mm. Wide rims.					
38-4.1	(1853-64)	—	12.50	20.00	35.00	55.00
	38-42mm. Narrow rims.					
38-3	(1853-64)	—	15.00	25.00	40.00	65.00
	47-48mm. Wide rims.					
38-3.1	(1853-64)	—	25.00	35.00	60.00	90.00
	54-56mm. Narrow rims.					
38-2	(1853-64)	—	30.00	45.00	75.00	110.00

Obv: T'ai P'ing Sheng Pao (top-bottom-right-left).
Rev: T'ien Kuo (right-left).

C#	Date	Emperor	Good	VG	Fine	VF
38-12	(1853-64)	—	7.00	10.00	15.00	20.00

Obv: T'ien Kuo T'ai P'ing (top-bottom-right-left).

Rev: Sheng Pao (right-left). 25-26mm.

C#	Date	Emperor	Good	VG	Fine	VF
38-14	(1853-64)	—	10.00	15.00	25.00	40.00

Obv: T'ien Kuo Sheng Pao (top-bottom-right-left).
Rev: T'ai P'ing (right-left). 21-23mm.

38-13	(1853-64)	—	10.00	15.00	25.00	40.00

Obv: T'ien Kuo (top-bottom)
Rev: Sheng Pao (top-bottom). 24-25mm.

38-11	(1853-64)	—	12.50	20.00	30.00	50.00

38mm. Large characters.

38-10	(1853-64)	—	15.00	25.00	40.00	60.00

36mm. Small characters.

38-10.1	(1853-64)	—	15.00	25.00	40.00	60.00

BRASS

Obv: T'ai P'ing T'ung Pao
Rev: Crescent above and character Ming below.

39-1	(1853-64)	—	10.00	15.00	25.00	40.00

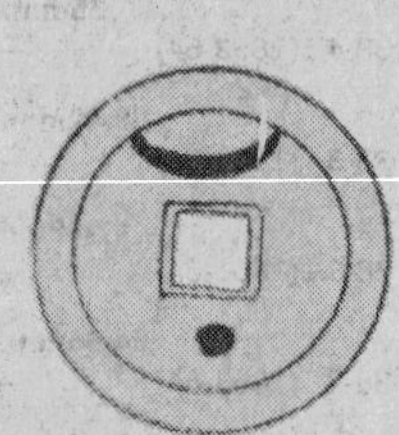

Rev: Dot above and crescent below.

39-2	(1853-64)	—	10.00	15.00	25.00	40.00

Rev: Character "Wen" above.

39-3	(1853-64)	—	10.00	15.00	25.00	40.00

Rev: Character "Wen" to the right of the hole.

39-4	(1853-64)	—	10.00	15.00	25.00	40.00

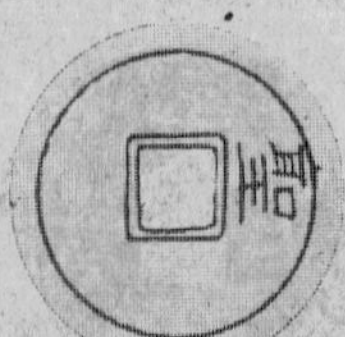

Obv: Huang Ti T'ung Pao.
Rev: Character Sheng at right (sideways).

39-5	(1853-64)	—	10.00	15.00	25.00	40.00

Obv: Huang Ti T'ung Pao.
Rev: Characters Che-Pao (Right-Left).

39-6	(1853-64)	—	10.00	15.00	25.00	40.00

NOTE: There are numerous other Cash coins issued by Taiping supporters and military units.

1/4 TAEL

SILVER

KM#	Date	Mintage	Good	VG	Fine	VF
2	(1853-64)	5 known	—	—	—	—

1/2 TAEL

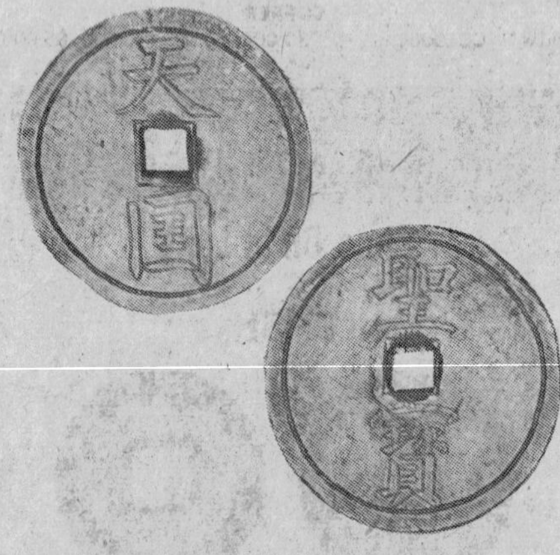

SILVER

3	(1853-64)	3 known	—	—	—	—

5 TAELS

GOLD

4	(1853-64)	1 known	—	—	—	—

NOTE: For additional listings of rebel coins, refer to Sinkiang Province.

CHINA-JAP. PUPPET STATES

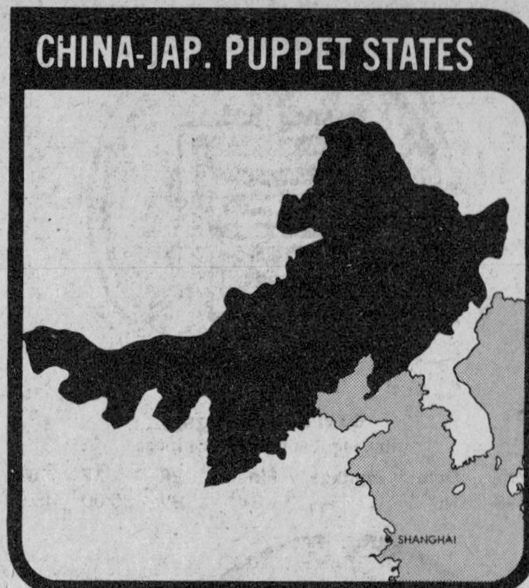

The greatest external threat to the territorial integrity of China was posed by Japan, which urgently needed room for an expanding population and raw materials for its industrial and military machines, and which recognized the necessity of controlling all of China if it was to realize its plan of dominating the rest of the Asiatic and South Sea countries. The Japanese had large investments in Manchuria (a name given by non-Chinese to the three northeastern provinces of China) which allowed them privileges that compromised Chinese sovereignty. The articulate of China remained unreconciled to Japan's growing power in Manchuria, and the resultant friction occasioned a series of vexing incidents which Japan decided to eliminate by direct action. On the night of Sept. 18-19, 1931, with a contrived incident for an excuse, Japanese forces seized the city of Mukden, and within a few weeks completely demolished Chinese power north of the Great Wall.

In Feb. 1932, after the Japanese occupation of Manchuria, they set up Manchukuo as an independent republic. Jehol was occupied by the Japanese in 1933 and added to Manchukuo. Manchukuo was established as an empire in 1934 with the deposed Manchu emperor Hsuan Tung (now Henry Pu yi) as the puppet emperor Kang Te. Lacking the means to face the Japanese armies in the field, the Chinese could only trade space for time.

Not content with confining its control of China to the areas north of the Great Wall, the Japanese launched a major campaign in 1937, and by the fall of 1938 had occupied in addition to Manchuria the provinces of Hopei and Chahar, most of the port cities, and the major cities as far west as Hankow. In addition, they dominated or threatened the provinces of Suiyan, Shansi and Shantung.

Still the Chinese did not yield. The struggle was prolonged until the advent of World War II, which brought about the defeat of Japan and the return of the puppet states to Chinese control.

As the victorious Japanese armies swept deeper into China, Japan established central banks under control of the Bank of Japan in the conquered provinces for the purpose of establishing control over banking and finance in the puppet states, and eventually in all of China. These included the Chi Tung Bank which had its main office in Tientsin with branches in Peking, Chinan and Tangshan; the Federal Reserve Bank of China with main office in Peking and branches in 37 other cities; and the Hua Hsing Bank with main office in Shanghai and two branches. The puppet states of Manchukuo, previously detailed in this introduction, and Meng Chiang, which comprised a greater part of Inner Mongolia, were also major coin-issuing entities.

EAST HOPEI

AUTONOMOUS

Chi Tung Bank

The Chi Tung Bank was the banking institution of the "East Hopei Autonomous Government" established by the Japanese in 1936 to undermine the political position of China in the northwest provinces. It issued both coins and notes between 1937 and 1939 with a restraint uncharacteristic of the puppet banks of the China-Japanese puppet states.

5 LI

COPPER

Y#	Date	Mintage	Fine	VF	XF	Unc
516	Yr.26 (1937)	—	7.50	13.50	22.50	45.00

FEN

COPPER

Y#	Date	Mintage	Fine	VF	XF	Unc
517	Yr.26 (1937)	—	3.00	6.00	10.00	20.00

5 FEN

COPPER-NICKEL

Y#	Date	Mintage	Fine	VF	XF	Unc
518	Yr.26 (1937)	—	2.50	5.00	7.50	15.00

CHIAO

COPPER-NICKEL

Y#	Date	Mintage	Fine	VF	XF	Unc
519	Yr.26 (1937)	—	2.50	5.00	7.50	15.00

2 CHIAO

COPPER-NICKEL

Y#	Date	Mintage	Fine	VF	XF	Unc
520	Yr.26 (1937)	—	3.00	6.00	10.00	20.00

MANCHUKUO

The former Japanese puppet state of Manchukuo (largely Manchuria), comprising the northeastern Chinese provinces of Liaoning, Kirin, Heilungkiang and Jehol, had an area of 503,143 sq. mi. (1,303,134 sq. km.) and a population of 43.3 million. Capital: Changchun, renamed Hsinking. The area is rich in fertile soil, timber and mineral resources, including coal, iron and gold.

Until the closing years of the 19th century when Chinese influence became predominant, Manchuria was chiefly a domain of the tribal Manchus and their Mongol allies. Coincident with the rise of Chinese influence, foreign imperialistic powers began to appreciate the value of the area to their expansionist philosophy. Japan, overpopulated and poor in resources, desired it as a source of raw materials and for increased living area. Russia wanted it as the eastern terminus of the Trans-Siberian railway that was to unite its Asian empire. The inevitable conflict of Japanese, Chinese and Russian interests required that one or more of the powers be eliminated. Japan eliminated China on the night of Sept. 18, 1931, when, on the pretext of a contrived incident, it moved militarily to seize control of the Three Eastern Provinces. Early in 1932 Japan declared Manchuria independent by virtue of a voluntary separatist movement and established the state of Manchukuo. To give the puppet state an aura of legitimacy, the deposed Emperor of the former Manchu dynasty was recalled from retirement and designated "chief executive". The area was restored to China at the end of World War II.

RULERS

Ta Tung, 1932-1934
Kang Teh, 1934-1945

MONETARY SYSTEM

10 Li = 1 Fen
10 Fen = 1 Chiao

The puppet emperor under the assumed name of Kang Teh was previously the last emperor of China (Pu-Yi, or Hsuan T'ung, 1909-11).

IDENTIFICATION OF REIGN CHARACTERS

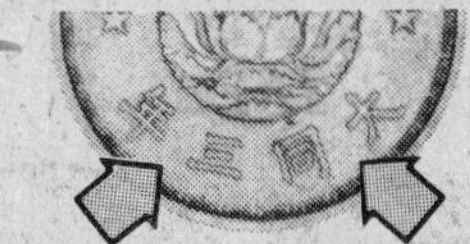

'Nien' Year 1932-1934 Ta Tung

'Nien' Year 1934-1945 K'ang Te

DATE ABBREVIATIONS
TT - Ta T'ung
KT - K'ang Te

NOTE: Uncirculated aluminum coins without any planchet defects are worth up to twice the market valuations given.

5 LI

BRONZE

Y#	Date	Mintage	Fine	VF	XF	Unc
1	TT 2 (1933)	—	8.50	20.00	30.00	75.00
	TT 3 (1934)	—	4.00	10.00	20.00	40.00

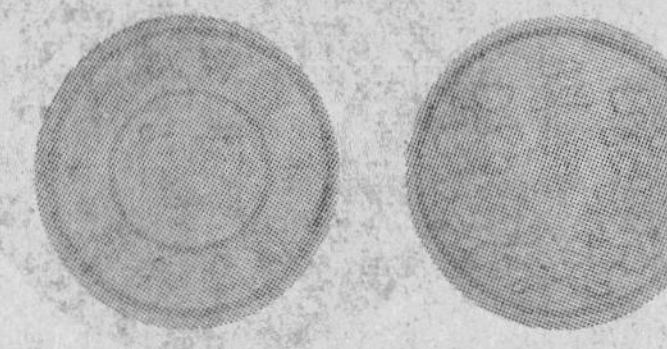

Y#	Date	Mintage	Fine	VF	XF	Unc
5	KT 1 (1934)	—	3.00	7.50	10.00	25.00
	KT 2 (1935)	—	3.00	7.50	10.00	25.00
	KT 3 (1936)	—	20.00	30.00	50.00	75.00
	KT 4 (1937)	—	4.00	10.00	12.50	25.00
	KT 6 (1939)	—	100.00	200.00	375.00	750.00

FEN

BRONZE

Y#	Date	Mintage	Fine	VF	XF	Unc
2	TT 2 (1933)	—	1.50	3.50	7.50	20.00
	TT 3 (1934)	—	.80	2.00	3.50	10.00

Y#	Date	Mintage	Fine	VF	XF	Unc
6	KT 1 (1934)	—	.60	1.50	3.50	8.50
	KT 2 (1935)	—	.60	1.50	3.50	8.50
	KT 3 (1936)	—	.60	1.50	3.50	8.50
	KT 4 (1937)	—	.60	1.50	3.50	8.50
	KT 5 (1938)	—	.60	1.50	3.50	8.50
	KT 6 (1939)	—	.60	1.50	3.50	8.50

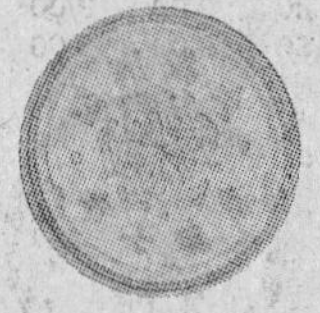

ALUMINUM

Y#	Date	Mintage	Fine	VF	XF	Unc
9	KT 6 (1939)	—	.40	1.00	3.00	6.00
	KT 7 (1940)	—	.40	1.00	3.00	6.00
	KT 8 (1941)	—	.40	1.00	3.00	6.00
	KT 9 (1942)	—	.80	2.00	5.00	7.50
	KT 10 (1943)	—	.40	1.00	3.00	6.00

Y#	Date	Mintage	Fine	VF	XF	Unc
13	KT 10 (1943)	—	.40	1.00	3.00	8.00
	KT 11 (1944)	—	.40	1.00	3.00	8.00

BRIGHT RED FIBER

Y#	Date	Mintage	VG	Fine	VF	XF
13a	KT 12 (1945)	—	1.20	3.00	4.00	6.00

DARK RED FIBER

Y#	Date	Mintage	VG	Fine	VF	XF
13a.1	KT 12 (1945)	—	4.00	10.00	15.00	20.00

5 FEN

COPPER-NICKEL

Y#	Date	Mintage	Fine	VF	XF	Unc
3	TT 2 (1933)	—	.60	1.50	3.00	12.50
	TT 3 (1934)	—	.40	1.00	2.00	10.00

Rim border varieties:

Narrow Design **Wide Design**

Y#	Date	Mintage	Fine	VF	XF	Unc
7	KT 1 (1934)	—	.60	1.50	3.00	6.00
	KT 2 (1935)	—	.60	1.50	3.00	6.00
	KT 3 (1936) w/narrow border design					
		—	.60	1.50	3.00	6.00

Y#	Date	Mintage	Fine	VF	XF	Unc
7	KT 3 (1936) w/wide border design					
		—	1.25	3.00	6.00	12.00
	KT 4 (1937)	—	.60	1.50	3.00	6.00
	KT 6 (1939)	—	.60	1.50	3.00	6.00

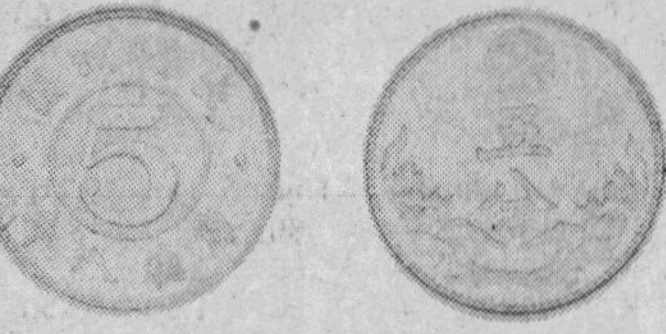

ALUMINUM

Y#	Date	Mintage	Fine	VF	XF	Unc
11	KT 7 (1940)	—	1.00	2.50	4.00	10.00
	KT 8 (1941)	—	.80	2.00	3.00	7.50
	KT 9 (1942)	—	.80	2.00	3.00	7.50
	KT 10 (1943)	—	.80	2.00	3.00	7.50

Y#	Date	Mintage	Fine	VF	XF	Unc
A13	KT 10 (1943)	—	1.00	2.50	4.00	10.00
	KT 11 (1944)	—	1.00	2.50	4.00	10.00

BRIGHT RED FIBER

Y#	Date	Mintage	Fine	VF	XF	Unc
A13a						
	KT 11 (1944)	—	.80	2.00	3.00	4.00

DARK RED FIBER

Y#	Date	Mintage	Fine	VF	XF	Unc
A13a.1						
	KT 11 (1944)	—	4.00	10.00	15.00	20.00

CHIAO

COPPER-NICKEL

Y#	Date	Mintage	Fine	VF	XF	Unc
4	TT 2 (1933)	—	1.00	2.50	4.00	10.00
	TT 3 (1934)	—	.80	2.00	3.00	8.00

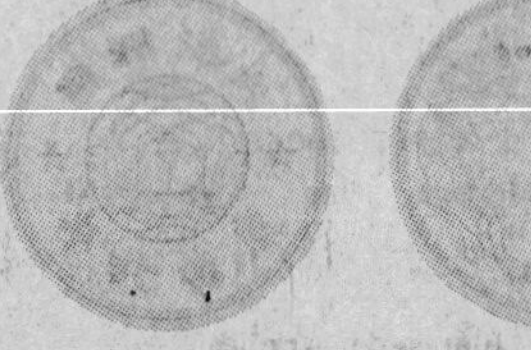

Y#	Date	Mintage	Fine	VF	XF	Unc
8	KT 1 (1934)	—	.80	2.00	3.00	7.50
	KT 2 (1935)	—	.80	2.00	3.00	7.50
	KT 5 (1938)	—	.80	2.00	3.00	7.50
	KT 6 (1939)	—	.80	2.00	3.00	7.50

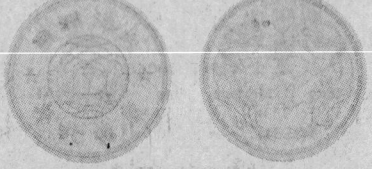

Y#	Date	Mintage	Fine	VF	XF	Unc
10	KT 7 (1940)	—	1.75	4.50	8.50	15.00

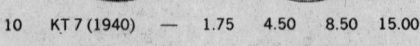

ALUMINUM

Y#	Date	Mintage	Fine	VF	XF	Unc
12	KT 7 (1940)	—	.80	2.00	3.00	7.50

Y#	Date	Mintage	Fine	VF	XF	Unc
12	KT 8 (1941)	—	.80	2.00	3.00	7.50
	KT 9 (1942)	—	.80	2.00	3.00	7.50
	KT 10 (1943)	—	200.00	350.00	600.00	1000.

Y#	Date	Mintage	Fine	VF	XF	Unc
14	KT 10 (1943)	—	1.00	2.50	3.50	10.00

GOLD INGOTS

These ingots, issued under the authority of the Japanese military, were issued and held by the Bank of Manchukuo in the early 1930's. Although they carry Chinese legends they were not made by or for the Chinese market.

TAEL

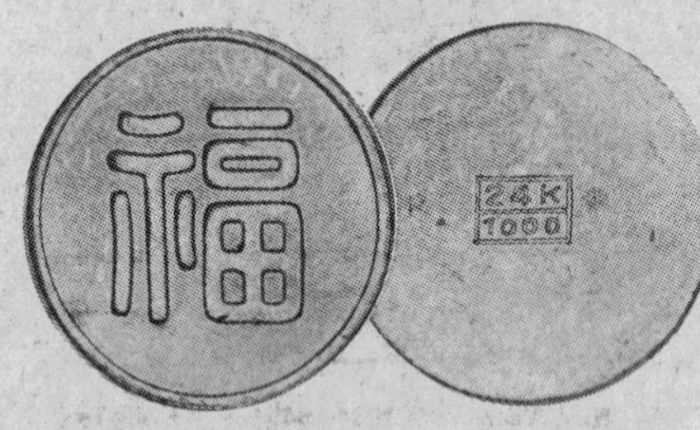

31.25 gm., 1.0000 GOLD, 1.0048 oz AGW
Obv: Character Fu "happiness".

KM#	Date	Mintage	Fine	VF	XF	Unc
1	ND (1932)	—	BV	BV	675.00	750.00

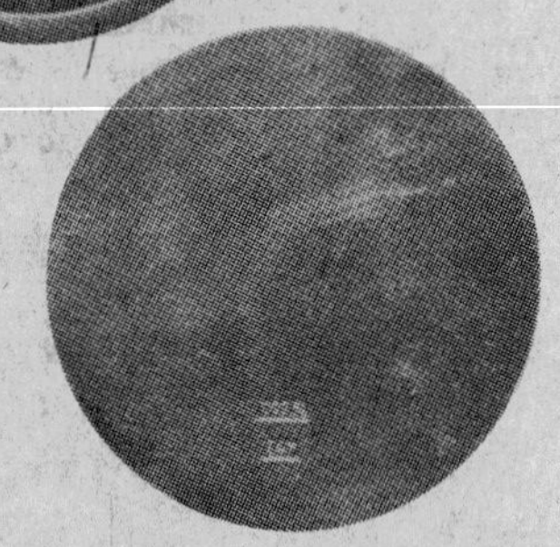

Obv: Character Fu

KM#	Date	Mintage	Fine	VF	XF	Unc
2	ND (1932)	—	BV	BV	675.00	750.00

Obv: Character Shang Hsi "double happiness".

KM#	Date	Mintage	Fine	VF	XF	Unc
3	ND (1932)	—	BV	BV	675.00	750.00

Obv: Character Fu in center.
Characters Fu Kuei Wan Nien (top-bottom-left-right)
"richness, honor (for) 10,000 years."

KM#	Date	Mintage	Fine	VF	XF	Unc
4	ND (1932)	—	BV	BV	675.00	750.00

Obv: Similar to KM#4, different rev.

KM#	Date	Mintage	Fine	VF	XF	Unc
5	ND (1932)	—	BV	BV	675.00	750.00

Obv: Character Shou "longevity".

KM#	Date	Mintage	Fine	VF	XF	Unc
6	ND (1932)	—	BV	BV	675.00	750.00

Obv: Similar to KM#6, different rev.

KM#	Date	Mintage	Fine	VF	XF	Unc
7	ND (1932)	—	BV	BV	675.00	750.00

Obv: Character Lu "prosperity".

KM#	Date	Mintage	Fine	VF	XF	Unc
8	ND (1932)	—	BV	BV	675.00	750.00

MENG CHIANG

As Japanese troops moved into North China in 1937, the political situation became fluid in several provinces bordering on Manchukuo. On September 27, 1937 the Chanan Bank was established. As the situation became more settled the Japanese effected the merger of two local banks with the Bank of Chanan under a new title, Meng Chiang (Mongolian Borderlands or Mongol Territory) Bank. The Meng Chiang Bank was organized on November 27 and opened on December 1, 1937 with headquarters in Kalgan and branch offices in about a dozen locations throughout the region. Its notes were declared the exclusive currency for the area. The bank closed at the end of the war. Issue dates are known for only the early series.

5 CHIAO

COPPER-NICKEL

Y#	Date	Mintage	Fine	VF	XF	Unc
521	Yr.27 (1938)	—	1.75	3.00	6.00	12.50

NCLT ISSUES

PATTERNS

KM#	Date	Mintage	Identification	Mkt.Val.
1	Yr.27 (1938)	—	1 Fen, Aluminum, ram's head	—
2	Yr.27 (1938)	—	5 Fen, Aluminum, ram's head	—
3	Yr.27 (1938)	—	1 Chiao, Aluminum, ram's head	—
4	(1943)	—	1 Fen, Aluminum	—
5	(1943)	—	5 Fen, Aluminum	1500.
6	(1943)	—	1 Chiao, Aluminum	1000.

PROVISIONAL GOVT. OF CHINA

In late 1937 the Japanese North China Expeditionary Army established the "Provisional Government of China" at Peking.

Federal Reserve Bank

The Federal Reserve Bank of China was opened in 1938 by Japanese military authorities in Peking. It was the puppet financial agency of the Japanese in northeast China. This puppet bank issued both coins and currency, but in modest amounts.

FEN

ALUMINUM

Y#	Date	Mintage	Fine	VF	XF	Unc
523	Yr.30 (1941)	—	.80	2.00	4.00	7.50
	Yr.31 (1942)	—	.80	2.00	4.00	7.50
	Yr.32 (1943)	—	7.50	15.00	25.00	50.00

5 FEN

ALUMINUM

Y#	Date	Mintage	Fine	VF	XF	Unc
524	Yr.30 (1941)	—	.40	1.00	2.50	8.00
	Yr.31 (1942)	—	.40	1.00	2.50	8.00
	Yr.32 (1943)	—	6.00	15.00	20.00	35.00

NOTE: The 5 Fen pieces were struck on both thick and thin planchets.

CHIAO

ALUMINUM

Y#	Date	Mintage	Fine	VF	XF	Unc
525	Yr.30 (1941)	—	.40	1.00	2.00	6.00
	Yr.31 (1942)	—	.40	1.00	2.00	6.00
	Yr.32 (1943)	—	1.50	3.00	6.00	15.00

NOTE: The 1 Chiao pieces were struck on both thick and thin planchets.

REFORMED GOVERNMENT REPUBLIC OF CHINA

On March 28, 1938 the Japanese Central China Expeditionary Army established the Reformed Government of the Republic of China at Nanking.

Hua Hsing Commercial Bank

The Hua Hsing Commercial Bank was a financial agency created and established by the government of Japan and its puppet authorities in Shanghai in May 1939. Notes and coins were issued until sometime in 1941, with the quantities restricted by Chinese aversion to accepting them.

10 FEN

COPPER-NICKEL

Y#	Date	Mintage	Fine	VF	XF	Unc
522	Yr.29 (1940)	—	1.00	1.50	2.00	3.50

NOTE: Once thought to be a pattern, Y#522 turned up large quantities in the 1950's and 1960's.

NCLT ISSUES

PATTERNS

KM#	Date	Mintage	Identification	Mkt.Val.
1	Yr.29 (1940)	—	1 Fen, Copper-Nickel, K863II	500.00
1a	Yr.29 (1940)	—	1 Fen, Copper	500.00
2	Yr.29 (1940)	—	5 Fen, Copper-Nickel, K863I	500.00
3	Yr.29 (1940)	—	20 Fen, Copper-Nickel, K862	500.00

TIBET

Tibet, an autonomous region of China located in central Asia between the Himalayan and Kunlun Mts. has an area of 471,660 sq. mi. (1,221,599 sq. km.) and a population of 1.3 million. Capital: Lhasa. The economy is based on agriculture and livestock raising. Wool, livestock, salt and hides are exported.

Lamaism, a form of Buddhism, developed in Tibet in the 8th century. From that time until the 1900s, the Dalai Lama virtually isolated the country from the outside world. The British in India achieved some influence in the early 20th century, and encouraged Tibet to declare its independence from China in 1913. The Communist revolution in China marked a new era in Tibetan history. Chinese Communist troops invaded Tibet in Oct., 1950. After a token resistance. Tibet signed an agreement with China in which China recognized the spiritual and temporal leadership of the Dalai Lama, and Tibet recognized the suzerainty of China. In 1959, a nationwide revolt triggered by Communist-initiated land reform broke out. The revolt was ruthlessly crushed. The Dalai Lama fled to India, and on Sept. 1, 1965, the Chinese made Tibet an autonomous region of China.

The first coins to circulate in Tibet were those of neighboring Nepal about 1570. Shortly after 1720, the Nepalese government began striking specific issues for use in Tibet; they were exchanged with the Tibetans for an equal weight in silver bullion. The first Tibetan government mint opened in 1791, but operations were suspended two years later. The Chinese opened a second mint in Lhasa in 1792. It produced a coinage until 1836. Shortly thereafter, the Tibetan mint was reopened and the government of Tibet continued to strike coins until 1953.

MONETARY SYSTEM

15 Skar = 1-1/2 Sho = 1 Tangka

10 Sho = 1 Srang

DATING

Based on the Tibetan calendar, Tibetan coins are dated by the cycle which contains 60 years. Example 15th cycle 25th year - 1891 AD.

13/40 - 1786	14/40 - 1846	15/40 - 1906
13/60 - 1806	14/60 - 1866	15/60 - 1926
14/20 - 1826	15/20 - 1886	16/20 - 1946

Certain Sino-Tibetan issues are dated in the year of reign of the Emperor of China.

TANGKA

6 x 10 = 60th YEAR = 1795 AD
CHINESE EMPEROR CH'IEN LUNG
1736-1796 AD

The word CYCLE is written:

Or:

The word YEAR is written: 

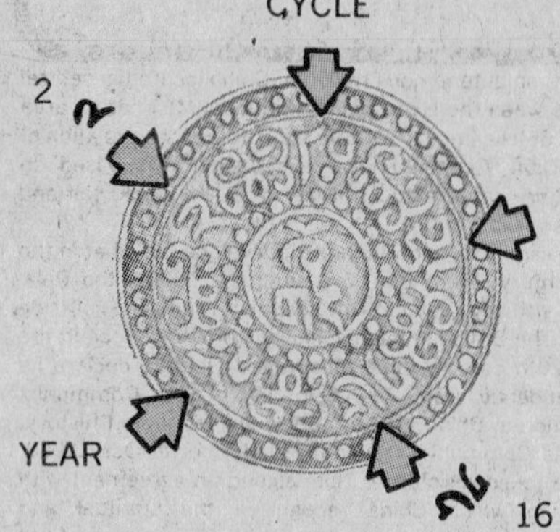

16(th)CYCLE 2(nd)YEAR = 1928AD

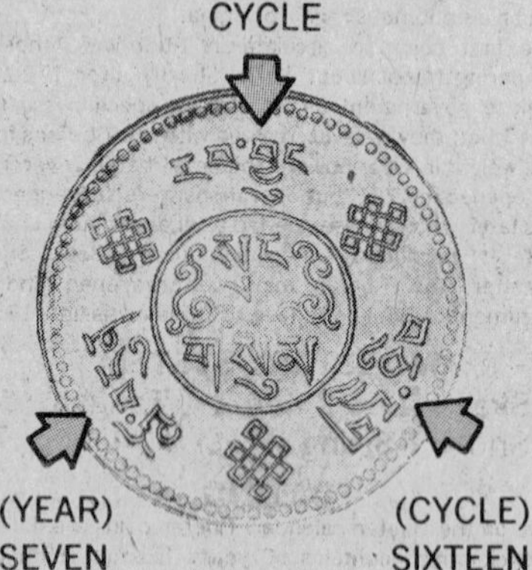

16(th) CYCLE 7(th) YEAR = 1933AD

SINO-TIBETAN ISSUES

RULERS

Ch'ien Lung 1735-1796
Chia Ch'ing 1796-1820
Tao Kuang 1820-1851
Hsuan T'ung 1909-1911

Early Period: 1792-1836

1/2 SHO

SILVER, 21mm, 1.8000-1.9000 gm.

C#	Date	Year	Good	VG	Fine	VF
71	Yr. 57	(1792)	—	—	Rare	—
	Yr. 58	(1793)	30.00	50.00	85.00	125.00

NOTE: Two varieties exist; one with 24 dots and the other with 32.

82	Yr. 3	(1798)	Reported, not confirmed

NOTE: The only evidence for this issue is this photograph from China.

1/2 TANGKA (3/4 SHO)

SILVER, 2.8000 gm.

C#	Date	Year	Good	VG	Fine	VF
—	Yr. 58	(1793)	50.00	85.00	125.00	185.00

SHO

SILVER, 3.4000-3.8000 gm.
MINT: LHASA

—	Yr. 57	(1792)	—	—	Rare	—

26-27mm

72	Yr. 58	(1793)	10.00	20.00	30.00	40.00
	Yr. 59	(1794)	10.00	20.00	30.00	40.00
	Yr. 60	(1795)	18.50	27.50	37.50	50.00
	Yr. 61	(1796)	25.00	45.00	60.00	90.00

NOTE: Two varieties of year 59 exist; one with 28 dots and the other with 32.

23-24mm

72.1	Yr. 58	(1793)	30.00	45.00	65.00	100.00

29-30mm

72.2	Yr. 60	(1795)	17.50	30.00	40.00	60.00

25-29mm

83	Yr. 1	(1796)	18.50	45.00	60.00	90.00
	Yr. 2	(1797)	—	—	Rare	—
	Yr. 4	(1799)	30.00	75.00	120.00	150.00
	Yr. 8	(1803)	12.50	30.00	45.00	65.00
	Yr. 9	(1804)	12.50	30.00	45.00	65.00
	Yr. 24	(1819)	12.50	25.00	35.00	50.00
	Yr. 25	(1820)	10.00	20.00	27.50	37.50

'One Miscal' in Manchu script added.

—	Yr. 6	(1801)	—	—	Rare	—

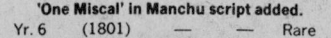

26-28mm

C#	Date	Year	Good	VG	Fine	VF
93	Yr. 1	(1821)	16.50	40.00	55.00	80.00
	Yr. 2	(1822)	12.50	22.50	32.50	45.00
	Yr. 3	(1823)	12.50	22.50	32.50	45.00
	Yr. 4	(1824)	15.00	30.00	40.00	60.00
	Yr. 15	(1835)	15.00	30.00	40.00	60.00
	Yr. 16	(1836)	15.00	30.00	40.00	60.00

TANGKA

SILVER, 5.3000-5.6000 gm.

K#	Date	Mintage	Good	VG	Fine	VF
1455	Yr.57 (1792)	—	—	—	Rare	—

29-31mm, 5.3000-5.7000 gm.

C#	Date	Year	Good	VG	Fine	VF
73	Yr. 58	(1793)	20.00	40.00	55.00	80.00

In the name of Hsuan Tung:

1/2 SKAR

COPPER

Y#	Date	Mintage	Good	VG	Fine	VF
A4	(1910)	—	35.00	60.00	80.00	100.00

SKAR

COPPER

4	(1910)	—	30.00	50.00	75.00	100.00

SHO

BASE SILVER

Y#	Date	Mintage	Good	VG	Fine	VF
5	(1910)	—	30.00	30.00	40.00	60.00

NOTE: A variety exists, having the inner circle of dots, on the Chinese side, connected by lines.

2 SHO

SILVER

6	(1910)	—	25.00	35.00	50.00	75.00

LOCAL ISSUES

Lukuan (Kang Ting) City

RUPEE

SILVER

—	ND	—	250.00	350.00	500.00	750.00

TIBETAN ISSUES

'Kong-par' TANGKA

BILLON, 4.9000-5.3000 gm.
MINT: DODPAL
Rev: Two circles around lotus.

C#	Date	Year	Good	VG	Fine	VF
60	Yr. 13-45	(1791)	10.00	15.00	20.00	30.00
	Yr. 13-46	(1792)	10.00	15.00	20.00	30.00

5.0000-5.8000 gm.
Rev: One circle around lotus.

60.1	Yr. 13-46	(1792)	6.50	10.00	15.00	25.00
	Yr. 13-47	(1793)	15.00	25.00	35.00	50.00

5.0000-5.6000 gm.
Sun and moon above date arch.

C#	Date	Year	Good	VG	Fine	VF
60.2	*Yr. 13-46	—	6.50	10.00	15.00	25.00

NOTE: IT is believed that this type was struck in the 1820's.

4.2000-5.6000 gm.
Crescent and 3 dots above date arch.

60.3	*Yr. 13-46	—	3.00	4.00	6.00	8.00

NOTE: It is believed that this type was struck in the 1860's. Numerous minor varieties exist.

3.6000-5.2000 gm.
MINT: GIAMDA

Y#	Date	Year	Good	VG	Fine	VF
A13	Yr. 15-24	(1890)	3.00	4.00	5.00	7.00
	Yr. 15-25	(1891)	3.50	5.00	8.00	12.50

Miscellaneous TANGKAS
(Size of Kong-par Tangka)

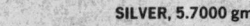

SILVER, 5.7000 gm.

C#	Date	Good	VG	Fine	VF
—	(ca.1795)	—	—	Rare	—

ca. 5.4000 gm.

—	(ca.1840)	—	—	Rare	—

ca. 5.0000 gm.

—	(ca.1850)	—	—	Rare	—

4.6000-4.8000 gm.

C#	Date	Year	Good	VG	Fine	VF
27	(1894)	15-28	3.50	6.50	10.00	15.00
	(1896)	15-30	10.00	15.00	20.00	30.00
	(1906)	15-40	3.50	6.50	10.00	15.00
	(1912)	15-46	15.00	25.00	35.00	45.00

NOTE: In addition to the above meaningful (probably) dates, the following meaningless ones exist: 13-16, 13-31, 13-92, 16-16, 16-61, 16-69, 16-92, 16-93, 92-39, 96-61 (sixes may be reversed threes and nines reversed ones). These are of billon, varying from 3.9 to 4.7 gm.

NOTE: The legend appears to be in ornamental Lansa script and has yet to be deciphered. The type is a copy of the Nepalese issue: 'Cho-tang'. Although struck unofficially, it was legal tender, due to an edict issued in 1881 ordering that no distinction be made between false and genuine coins!

NOTE: This type was cut to make change and the resulting fractions are occasionally encountered.

'Ga-den' TANGKA

SILVER, 5.0000-5.5000 gm.
Five petals around lotus center.

Y#	Date	Mintage	Good	VG	Fine	VF
13	ca.1850	—	5.00	10.00	15.00	25.00

NOTE: Many die varieties exist.

MINT: DODPAL
4.0000-5.2000 gm.
Five dots around lotus center, North symbol:

Y#	Date	Mintage	VG	Fine	VF	XF
13.1	ca1875-95	—	BV	BV	3.00	4.00

NOTE: Five major varieties exist.

MINT: TIP ARSENAL
3.9000-5.2000 gm.
Three elongated dots on either side of lotus center and new arrangement of 8 symbols.

13.2	ca.1895-1901	—	BV	BV	3.50	4.50

NOTE: Five major varieties exist.

BILLON, 4.7000-5.3000 gm.
Seven dots around lotus center, uniform edge and thickness.

Y#	Date	Mintage	VG	Fine	VF	XF
13.3	(ca.1900)	—	15.00	22.50	32.50	45.00

3.8000-5.7000 gm.
Similar to Y#13.2, but not uniform.

Y#	Date	Mintage	VG	Fine	VF	XF
13.4	ca.1901-06	—	BV	BV	3.00	4.00

NOTE: Eight major varieties exist, including an error having the eight symbols rotated one position clockwise.

SILVER, 3.8000 gm.
8mm circle around lotus, North and West symbols are similar.

Y#	Date	Mintage	VG	Fine	VF	XF
13.5	ca.1905	—	15.00	22.50	32.50	45.00

BILLON, 3.0000-5.6000 gm.

MINT: DODE

Nine dots within lotus circle.

Y#	Date	Mintage	VG	Fine	VF	XF
13.6	ca.1906-12	—	BV	BV	3.00	4.00

NOTE: Eight major varieties exist. See Y#13.9, 13.10 and 13.11 for other types, having nine dots within lotus circle.

SILVER, 2.7000-5.0000 gm.

Y#	Date	Mintage	VG	Fine	VF	XF
14	ca.1909	—	3.00	4.50	6.00	8.00

NOTE: This Tangka was struck for presentation to monks.

BILLON, 3.3000-4.5000 gm.
Eleven dots within lotus circle.

Y#	Date	Mintage	VG	Fine	VF	XF
13.7	ca.1912-23	—	BV	BV	3.00	4.00

NOTE: Four major varieties and numerous minor ones exist (40 to 78 dots compose outer circles).

3.0000-5.0000 gm.

Nine dots within lotus circle, northwest symbol.

Y#	Date	Mintage	VG	Fine	VF	XF
13.8	ca.1914-23	—	.80	2.00	2.75	3.00

NOTE: Five major and numerous minor varieties exist (35 to 68 dots compose outer circles).

MINT: SER-KHANG

3.3000-4.6000 gm.
Northwest symbol

Y#	Date	Mintage	VG	Fine	VF	XF
13.9	ca.1920	—	2.75	7.00	10.00	15.00

NOTE: Several other features are unique to this type.

MINT: DODE

3.8000-4.3000 gm.
Nine dots within lotus circle, uniform thickness (1.mm).

Y#	Date	Mintage	VG	Fine	VF	XF
13.10	1929-30	—	7.00	10.00	12.50	15.00

NOTE: Two minor die varieties exist.

SILVER, 3.1000-5.3000 gm.

MINT: TAPCHI

Y#	Date	Mintage	VG	Fine	VF	XF
31	1946-48	—	3.00	4.00	5.00	7.00

NOTE: This type was struck for presentation to monks.

2 TANGKA

BILLON, 9.3000 gm.

MINT: DODE

Y#	Date	Mintage	VG	Fine	VF	XF
15	ca.1912	—	75.00	125.00	175.00	250.00

NOTE: Counterfeits exist. This type is similar to Y#13 except for its uniform edge and its weight.

SHO-SRANG ISSUES

Size same as 'Kong-par' Tangka

1/8 SHO

COPPER

MINT: DODE

Y#	Date	Mintage	Good	VG	Fine	VF
A7	(1909)	—	25.00	50.00	80.00	125.00

NOTE: A silver striking of this type exists (rare).

1/4 SHO

COPPER

Y#	Date	Mintage	Good	VG	Fine	VF
B7	(1909)	—	25.00	50.00	80.00	125.00

NOTE: The above coin struck in silver is a forgery.

2 1/2 SKAR

COPPER

MINT: DODE

Y#	Date	Year	Good	VG	Fine	VF
10	15-43	(1909)	—	—	Rare	—

23.5mm, 3.6900-6.0900 gm.
Lion looking upwards

Y#	Date	Year	Good	VG	Fine	VF
16	15-47	(1913)	3.25	8.00	12.00	20.00
	15-48	(1914)	3.25	8.00	12.00	20.00
	15-49	(1915)	8.00	20.00	25.00	35.00
	15-50	(1916)	6.00	15.00	20.00	30.00
	15-51	(1917)	5.00	12.00	17.50	25.00
	15-52	(1918)	3.25	8.00	12.50	20.00

MINT: MEKYI

Lion looking backwards

Y#	Date	Year	Good	VG	Fine	VF
16.1	15-48	(1914)	4.00	10.00	15.00	22.50

MINT: DODE

Y#	Date	Year	Good	VG	Fine	VF
A19	15-52	(1918)	20.00	50.00	65.00	80.00
	15-53	(1919)	25.00	60.00	75.00	90.00
	15-55	(1920)	25.00	60.00	75.00	90.00

NOTE: Counterfeits dated 15-55 exist.

5 SKAR

COPPER

MINT: DODE

Y#	Date	Year	Good	VG	Fine	VF
A10	15-43	(1909)	—	—	Rare	—

27mm
Lion looking upwards

17	15-47	(1913)	.80	2.00	5.00	9.00
	15-48	(1914)	.50	1.25	3.50	7.00
	15-49	(1915)	.50	1.25	3.50	7.00
	15-50	(1916)	.50	1.25	3.50	7.00
	15-51	(1917)	.50	1.25	3.50	7.00
	15-52	(1918)	.80	2.00	5.00	9.00

MINT: MEKYI

Lion looking backwards.

17.1	15-48	(1914)	.60	1.50	3.50	7.50
	15-49	(1915)	.40	1.00	2.50	6.00
	15-50	(1916)	.40	1.00	2.50	6.00
	15-51	(1917)	.40	1.00	2.50	6.00
	15-52	(1918)	.40	1.00	2.50	6.00

NOTE: The appearance of the lion on all 15-48 specimens and on a few 15-49 specimens varies from those on all others.

21mm

MINT: LOWER DODE

19	15-52	(1918)	.80	2.00	3.00	4.50
	15-53	(1919)	.60	1.50	2.50	4.00
	15-54	(1920)	.50	1.25	2.00	3.50
	15-55	(1921)	.50	1.25	2.00	3.50
	15-56	(1922)	.50	1.25	2.00	3.50
	56-15	(1922) (error)	6.00	15.00	20.00	30.00

MINT: UPPER DODE

Dot added above center on reverse

19.1	15-55	(1921)	4.00	7.00	10.00	15.00
	15-56	(1922)	2.00	3.50	5.00	8.00

7 1/2 SKAR

COPPER

MINT: DODE

11	15-43	(1909)	—	—	Rare	—

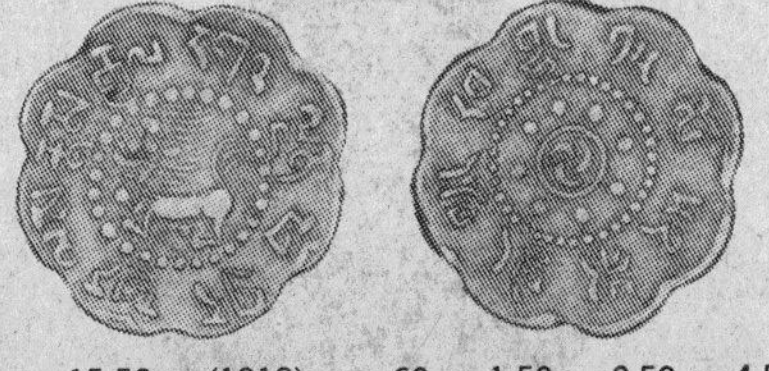

Y#	Date	Year	Good	VG	Fine	VF
20	15-52	(1918)	.60	1.50	2.50	4.50
	15-53	(1919)	.50	1.25	2.00	3.50
	15-54	(1920)	.50	1.25	2.00	3.50
	15-55	(1921)	.50	1.25	2.00	3.50
	15-56	(1922)	.50	1.25	2.00	3.50
	15-60	(1926)	10.00	15.00	20.00	30.00

NOTE: Some 15-52 and 15-53 specimens have the reverse central 'whirlwind' in a counterclockwise direction.

SHO

COPPER, 25.6mm

MINT: DODE

Rev: Central legend horizontal

21	15-52	(1918)	10.00	15.00	25.00	40.00

NOTE: Two varieties exist (lion's head).

MINT: MEKYI

24mm, 3.9500-7.1300 gm.
Lion looking up, no dot.

21.1	15-52	(1918)	.50	1.25	1.75	3.50
	15-53	(1919)	.30	.75	1.25	2.75
	15-54	(1920)	.30	.75	1.25	2.75
	15-55	(1921)	.30	.75	1.25	2.75
	15-56	(1922)	.30	.75	1.25	2.75
	15-57	(1923)	.50	1.25	1.75	3.50
	15-58	(1924)	.30	.75	1.25	2.75
	15-59	(1925)	.30	.75	1.25	2.75
	15-60	(1926)	.30	.75	1.25	2.75
	16-1	(1927)	.30	.75	1.25	2.75
	16-2	(1928)	.30	.75	1.25	2.75

MINT: SER-KHANG

3.0100-7.2700 gm.
Lion looking up, with dot.

21.2	15-54	(1920)	.50	1.25	1.75	3.00
	54-15	(1920) (error)	10.00	15.00	20.00	30.00
	51-54	(1920) (error)	10.00	15.00	20.00	30.00
	15-55	(1921)	.40	1.00	1.50	2.75
	15-55	(1921) (error) 'Year' and '55' transposed	10.00	15.00	20.00	30.00

Lion looking diagonally upwards, with dot.

21.3	15-54	(1920)	2.00	3.00	5.00	8.50
	15-55	(1921)	.30	.75	1.00	2.00
	15-56	(1922)	.30	.75	1.00	2.00
	15-57	(1923)	.40	1.00	1.50	3.00
	15-58	(1924)	.30	.75	1.00	2.00
	15-59	(1925)	.30	.75	1.00	2.00
	15-60	(1926)	.30	.75	1.00	2.00
	16-1/15-60	(1927)	3.00	5.00	8.00	13.50
	16-1	(1927)	.30	.75	1.00	2.00
	16-2	(1928)	.30	.75	1.00	2.00

NOTE: Specimens dated 15-54 may all be contemporary forgeries.

MINT: DODE

24mm, 3.4300-4.7300 gm.
Rev: Central legend vertical

Y#	Date	Year	VG	Fine	VF	XF
21a	15-56	(1922)	5.00	7.00	10.00	17.50
	15-57	(1923)	.60	1.50	2.50	5.00
	15-58	(1924)	.60	1.50	2.50	5.00
	15-59	(1925)	.50	1.25	2.00	4.00
	15-60	(1926)	.50	1.25	2.00	4.00
	16-1	(1927)	.50	1.25	2.00	4.00
	16-1	(1927) dot below O above denomination	.50	1.25	2.00	4.00
	16-2/1	(1927/8)	Reported, not confirmed			
	16-2	(1928)	.60	1.50	2.50	5.00

NOTE: Two varieties (lion) exist for each of the following dates: 15-56, 15-57, 15-58 & 16-2.

MINT: TAPCHI

24mm, 4.0200-6.0900 gm.
The following marks are located in the position indicated by the arrow:

a: ● b: ⬮ c: ✚ d: ↓ e: ⌄ f: ⌄̇ g: ❙

23	16-6 (a)	(1932)	1.00	1.75	3.00	5.00
	16-7 (a)	(1933)	1.25	2.00	3.25	5.50
	16-8 (a)	(1934)	1.50	2.50	4.00	7.00
	16-9 (a)	(1935)	.75	1.50	2.50	4.00
	(b)		.75	1.25	2.00	3.00
	16-10(a)	(1936)	2.00	3.50	6.00	10.00
	(b)		2.00	3.50	6.00	10.00
	(c)		.75	1.25	2.00	3.00
	16-11(a)	(1937)	—	—	—	—
	(b)		2.00	3.50	6.00	10.00
	(c)		1.50	2.50	4.00	7.00
	(d)		1.50	2.50	4.00	7.00
	(e)		.75	1.25	2.00	3.00
	(f)		2.00	3.50	6.00	10.00
	(g)		—	—	—	—
	16-12 (d)	(1938)	—	—	—	—
	(f)		1.50	2.50	4.00	7.00
	(g)		1.50	2.50	4.00	7.00

3 SHO

COPPER
Single cloud line

27	16-20	(1946)	3.00	5.00	9.00	15.00

NOTE: Three varieties of conch-shell on reverse.

Double cloud-line

27.1	16-20	(1946)	6.00	10.00	15.00	25.00

5 SHO

SILVER

Y#	Date	Year	VG	Fine	VF	XF
8	1	(1909)	—	—	Rare	—

MINT: DODE

10.3000 gm.

Lion looking upwards

Y#	Date	Year	VG	Fine	VF	XF
18	15-47	(1913)	20.00	30.00	40.00	60.00
	15-48	(1914)	15.00	25.00	35.00	50.00
	15-49	(1915)	15.00	25.00	35.00	50.00
	15-50	(1916)	15.00	25.00	35.00	50.00
	15-58	(1924)	30.00	50.00	80.00	110.00
	15-59	(1925)	30.00	50.00	80.00	110.00
	15-60	(1926)	30.00	50.00	80.00	110.00

NOTE: Two 15-50 varieties exist: small and large lions, or 14mm vs. 15mm lion-circle.

MINT: MEKYI

Lion looking backwards.

Y#	Date	Year	VG	Fine	VF	XF
18.1	15-49	(1915)	15.00	22.50	30.00	45.00
	15-50	(1916)	15.00	25.00	35.00	50.00
	15-51	(1917)	15.00	25.00	35.00	50.00
	15-52	(1918)	15.00	25.00	35.00	50.00
	15-53	(1919)	30.00	50.00	80.00	110.00
	15-56	(1922)	30.00	50.00	80.00	110.00
	15-59	(1925)	30.00	50.00	80.00	110.00
	15-60	(1926)	30.00	50.00	80.00	110.00
	16-1	(1927)	30.00	50.00	80.00	110.00

MINT: DODE

Y#	Date	Year	VG	Fine	VF	XF
18.2	15-52	(1918)	30.00	50.00	80.00	110.00

NOTE: The reverse of 18.3 varies from those of 18.1 and 18.2.

Y#	Date	Year	VG	Fine	VF	XF
32	—	(1928-29)	—	—	Rare	—

24mm, 5.0000 gm.

Y#	Date	Year	VG	Fine	VF	XF
32a	16-4	(1930)	—	—	Rare	—

COPPER, 29mm

MINT: TAPCHI

Obv: Two mountains with two suns.

Y#	Date	Year	VG	Fine	VF	XF
28	16-21	(1947)	1.40	3.50	6.00	10.00

Obv: Three mountains with two suns.

Y#	Date	Year	VG	Fine	VF	XF
28.1	16-21	(1947)	.80	2.00	2.75	4.00
	16-22	(1948)	.40	1.00	1.75	3.00
	16-22	(1948)	dot after 16			
			1.00	2.50	3.50	5.00
	16-23	(1949)	.40	1.00	1.75	3.00
	16-23	(1949)	dot after 16			
			1.00	2.50	3.50	5.00
	16-24	(1950)	3.25	8.00	13.00	20.00
	16-24/23	(1950)	3.25	8.00	13.00	20.00

Obv: Cloud over middle mountain missing.

Y#	Date	Year	VG	Fine	VF	XF
28.2	16-22	(1948)	4.00	10.00	15.00	25.00

Obv: Moon and sun over mountains.

Y#	Date	Year	VG	Fine	VF	XF
28a	16-23	(1949)	2.50	6.00	10.00	17.50
	16-24		3.25	8.00	13.00	20.00
	16-24	(1950)	.40	1.00	2.25	4.00
	16-24		moon cut over sun			
			2.00	5.00	8.00	14.00
	16-25	(1951)	.40	1.00	2.25	4.00
	16-25/24		.80	2.00	4.00	7.00
	16-26	(1952)	1.20	3.00	5.00	9.00
	Dot before 26		.70	1.75	3.50	6.00
	16-27	(1953)	.90	2.25	4.25	7.50
	Dot before 27		1.10	2.75	4.75	8.50

SRANG

SILVER, 18.5000 gm.

MINT: DODE

Y#	Date	Year	VG	Fine	VF	XF
9	1	(1909)	100.00	165.00	200.00	250.00

With plain edge

Y#	Date	Year	VG	Fine	VF	XF
12	15-43	(1909)	70.00	125.00	150.00	190.00

With reeded edge, lion looking upwards.

Y#	Date	Year	VG	Fine	VF	XF
A18	15-48	(1914)	100.00	200.00	250.00	300.00

Lion looking backwards

Y#	Date	Year	VG	Fine	VF	XF
A18.1	15-52	(1918)	100.00	165.00	200.00	250.00
	15-53	(1919)	110.00	185.00	225.00	275.00

Type similar to Y#32.

—	—	(1928-29)	—	Reported, not confirmed

1 1/2 SRANG

SILVER, 5.0000 gm.

MINT: TAPCHI

Y#	Date	Year	VG	Fine	VF	XF
24	16-10	(1936)	BV	4.00	6.00	9.00
	16-11	(1937)	BV	4.00	6.00	9.00
	16-12	(1938)	BV	4.00	6.00	9.00
	16-20	(1946)	6.00	10.00	13.00	18.00

3 SRANG

SILVER, 11.3000 gm.

MINT: TAPCHI

Y#	Date	Year	VG	Fine	VF	XF
25	16-7	(1933)	BV	8.50	11.50	15.00
	16-8	(1934)	BV	8.50	11.50	15.00

Y#	Date	Year	VG	Fine	VF	XF
26	16-9	(1935)	BV	BV	10.00	13.50
	16-10	(1936)	BV	BV	9.00	12.00
	16-11	(1937)	BV	BV	9.00	12.00
	16-12	(1938)	BV	BV	9.00	12.00
	16-20	(1946)	BV	10.00	12.50	15.00

5 SRANG

NOTE: No coins of this denomination are known to have been struck. Two Tanka types (ty#14 & 31, see under 'Ga-den' Tangkas) circulated briefly with this value and later with a value of 10 Srang.

10 SRANG

BILLON

MINT: TAPCHI

Obv: Two suns. Rev: Numerals for denomination.

Y#	Date	Year	VG	Fine	VF	XF
29	16-22	(1948)	3.00	4.50	7.00	11.00

Rev: Word for denomination.

Y#	Date	Year	VG	Fine	VF	XF
29.1	16-23	(1949)	3.50	6.00	8.50	12.50

Obv: Moon and sun.

Y#	Date	Year	VG	Fine	VF	XF
29a	16-23	(1949)	12.00	20.00	30.00	40.00
	16-24/23		4.00	8.00	11.00	18.00
	16-24/22	(1950)	3.00	6.00	9.00	15.00
	16-24	(1950) moon cut over sun	5.00	10.00	15.00	25.00
	16-25	(1951) w/o dot	3.00	6.00	9.00	15.00
	16-25	w/dot	4.00	8.00	11.00	18.00
	16-26	(1952) w/o dot	4.00	8.00	11.00	18.00
	16-26	w/dot	4.00	8.00	11.00	18.00

***NOTE:** The 'dot' is after the denomination.

COPPER-NICKEL

Obv: Moon and sun.

Y#	Date	Year				
29b	—	(1950)	restrike		—	—

MINT: DOGU

Y#	Date	Year	VG	Fine	VF	XF
30	16-24	(1950)	2.50	5.00	8.50	14.00
	16-25	(1951)	2.50	5.00	8.50	14.00

20 SRANG

GOLD

MINT: SER-KHANG

Y#	Date	Year	Fine	VF	XF	Unc
22	15-52	(1918)	300.00	500.00	650.00	850.00
	15-53	(1919)	300.00	500.00	650.00	850.00
	15-54	(1920)	300.00	500.00	650.00	850.00
	15-55	(1921)	400.00	700.00	1000.	1500.

TRADE COINAGE

MONETARY SYSTEM

1 Rupee = 3 Tangka

1/4 RUPEE

.935 SILVER, 2.8000 gm.

MINT: SZECHUAN (China)

Y#	Date	Mintage	Fine	VF	XF	Unc
1	(1905-09)	*.823	35.00	50.00	75.00	150.00

NOTE: Varieties exist.

GOLD

Y#	Date	Mintage	Fine	VF	XF	Unc
1a	(1905)	—	—	—	Rare	—

1/2 RUPEE

.935 SILVER, 5.6000 gm.

Y#	Date	Mintage	Fine	VF	XF	Unc
2	(1905-09)	*.136	40.00	60.00	85.00	175.00

NOTE: Varieties exist.

GOLD

Y#	Date	Mintage	Fine	VF	XF	Unc
2a	(1905)	—	—	—	Rare	—

RUPEE

SILVER, 11.4000 gm.

Obv: Small bust without collar.

Y#	Date	Mintage	Fine	VF	XF	Unc
3	(1903-05)	*14.127	18.50	25.00	35.00	75.00

Rev: Rosette is horizontal.

Y#	Date	Mintage	Fine	VF	XF	Unc
3.1	(1903-05)	—	25.00	35.00	50.00	100.00

Obv: Small bust with collar. Rev: Similar to Y#3.

Y#	Date	Mintage	Fine	VF	XF	Unc
3.2	(1905-12)					
		*14.127	15.00	20.00	25.00	50.00
		BILLON				
3a	(1912-38)	—	8.00	13.00	20.00	40.00
		GOLD				
3b	(1905)	—	—	—	Rare	—

SILVER
Large bust

Y#	Date	Mintage	Fine	VF	XF	Unc
3.3	(1910)	—	25.00	35.00	50.00	100.00

***NOTE:** Mintage figures are for 1900-1928 and do not include pieces struck between 1929-1938. In addition to the types illustrated above, large quantities of the following coins also circulated in Tibet; China Dollar Y#329 and India Rupees, Y#12 and 23.

CHINA/Peoples Republic

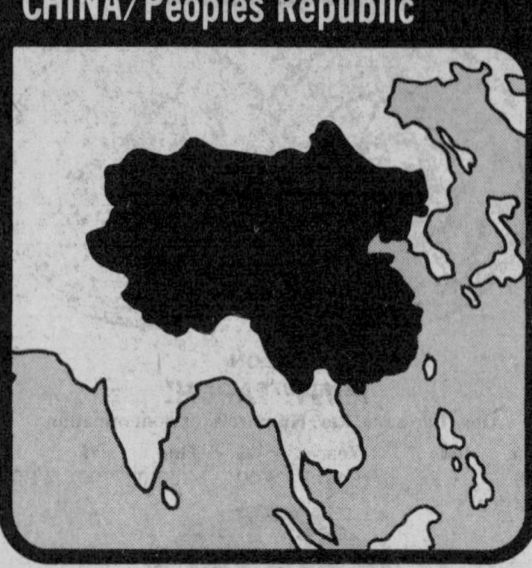

The People's Republic of China, located in eastern Asia, has an area of 3,691,502 sq. mi. (9,560,990 sq. km.) (including Manchuria and Tibet) and a population of 942 million. Capital: Peking. The economy is based on agriculture, mining, and manufacturing. Textiles, clothing, metal ores, tea and rice are exported.

China's ancient civilization began in the Huang Ho basin about 1500 B.C. The warring feudal states comprising early China were first united under Emperor Ch'in Shih Huang Ti (246-210 B.C.) who gave China its name and first central government. Subsequent dynasties alternated brilliant cultural achievements with internal disorder until the Empire was brought down by the revolution of 1911, and the Republic of China installed in its place. Chinese culture attained a pre-eminence in art, literature and philosophy, but a traditional backwardness in industry and administration ill prepared China for the demands of 19th century Western expansionism which exposed it to military and political humiliations, and mandated a drastic revision of political practice in order to secure an accommodation with the modern world.

The Republic of 1911 barely survived the stress of World War I, and was subsequently all but shattered by the rise of nationalism and the emergence of the Chinese Communist movement. Moscow, which practiced a policy of cooperation between Communists and other parties in movements for national liberation, sought to establish an entente between the Chinese Communist Party and the Kuomintang ('National People's Party') of Sun Yat-sen. The ensuing cooperation was based on little more than the hope each had of using the other.

An increasingly uneasy association between the Kuomintang and the Chinese Communist Party developed and continued until April 12, 1927, when Chiang Kai-shek, Sun Yat-sen's political heir, instituted a bloody purge to stamp out the Communists within the Kuomintang and the government and virtually paralyzed their ranks throughout China. Some time after the mid-1927 purges, the Chinese Communist Party turned to armed force to resist Chiang Kai-shek and during the period of 1930-34 acquired control over large parts of Kiangsi, Fukien, Hunan and Hupeh. The Nationalist Nanking government responded with a series of campaigns against the soviet power bases and, by October of 1934, succeeded in driving the remnants of the Communist army to a refuge in Shensi Province. There the Communists reorganized under the leadership of Mao Tse-tung, defeated the Nationalist forces, and on Sept. 21, 1949, established the People's Republic of China. Thereafter relations between Russia and Communist China steadily deteriorated until 1958, when China emerged as an independent center of Communist power.

MONETARY SYSTEM

Before 1949
10 Cash (Wen) = 1 Cent (Fen)
100 Cents (Fen) = 1 Dollar (Yuan)

SOVIET PERIOD

Prior to 1949, the People's Republic of China did not exist as such, but the communists did control areas known as soviets. Most of the soviets were established on the borders of two or more provinces and were named according to the provinces involved. Thus there were such soviets as the Kiangsi- Hunan Soviet, the Hunan-Hupeh-Kiangsi Soviet, the Hupeh-Honan-Anhwei Soviet and others. In 1931 some of the soviets in the southern Kiangsi area were consolidated into the Chinese Soviet Republic, which lasted until the Long March of 1934.

CHINESE SOVIET REPUBLIC

In November, 1931, the first congress of the Chinese Soviet proclaimed and established the "Chinese Soviet Republic" under the Chairmanship of Mao Tse-Tung.

CENT

COPPER
Crude, weak strike.

Y#	Date	Mintage	VG	Fine	VF	XF
506	ND	—	9.00	15.00	25.00	40.00

Well struck; normally found in uncirculated condition.

Y#	Date	Mintage	Fine	VF	XF	Unc
506	ND	Restrike	—	—	7.50	12.50

5 CENTS

COPPER
Crude, weak strike.

Y#	Date	Mintage	VG	Fine	VF	XF
507	ND	—	11.50	18.50	30.00	50.00

Well struck; normally found in uncirculated condition.

Y#	Date	Mintage	Fine	VF	XF	Unc
507	ND	Restrike	—	—	7.50	12.50

20 CENTS

SILVER, 5.5000 gm.

Y#	Date	Mintage	VG	Fine	VF	XF
508	1932	—	30.00	60.00	100.00	165.00
	1933	—	16.50	27.50	45.00	75.00

NOTE: Many minor varieties exist.

HUPEH-HONAN-ANHWEI SOVIET

The Hupeh-Honan Anhwei Soviet District was a large

revolutionary base. It was formerly made up of three separate special districts: East Hupeh, South Honan and West Anhwei which united until after 1930. Between 1931 and 1932 this Bank has issued a quantity of copper and silver coins as well as banknotes.

DOLLAR

SILVER, 26.8000 gm.

Y#	Date	Mintage	VG	Fine	VF	XF
503	1932	—	250.00	400.00	550.00	800.00

27.2000 gm.

Y#	Date	Mintage	VG	Fine	VF	XF
504	1932	—	45.00	75.00	125.00	200.00

NOTE: Attribution of Y#503 to the Hupeh Honan-Anhwei Soviet is not definite.

SZECHUAN-SHENSI SOVIET

The Szechuan-Shensi Soviet District was founded in 1933. Within two years and three months from January, 1933 to March, 1935, this Soviet District had issued quite a quantity of banknotes, copper and silver coins. These issues circulated rather popularly throughout the central district.

200 CASH

COPPER, 37mm
Crude, weak strike.

Y#	Date	Mintage	Good	VG	Fine	VF
510	1932	—	—	—	—	—

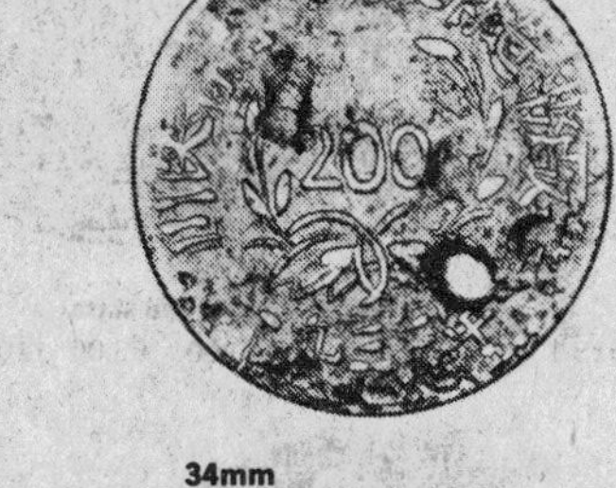

34mm
Rev: Small 200 center.

Y#	Date	Mintage	Good	VG	Fine	VF
510.1	1933	—	18.50	30.00	50.00	80.00

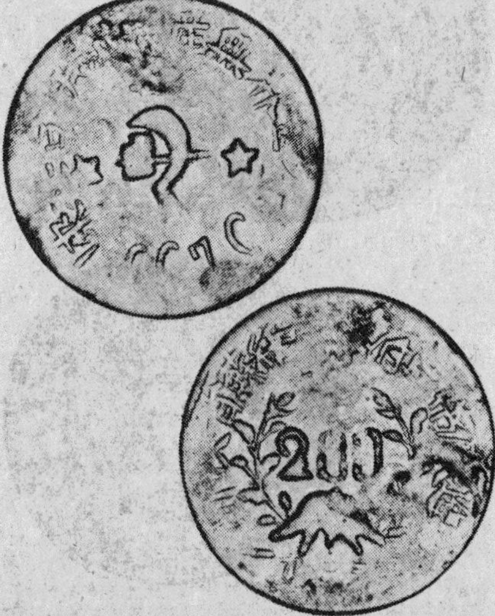

Rev: Large 200 center.

Y#	Date	Mintage	Good	VG	Fine	VF
510.2	1933	—	18.50	30.00	50.00	80.00

Rev: Square O's in 200.

Y#	Date	Mintage	Good	VG	Fine	VF
510.3	1933	—	20.00	35.00	60.00	100.00

Obv: Date with closed 3, digit 4 backwards.

Y#	Date	Mintage	VG	Fine	VF	XF
511	1934	—	18.50	30.00	50.00	85.00

Obv: Date with open 3, 4 backwards.

Y#	Date	Mintage	VG	Fine	VF	XF
511.1	1934	—	18.50	30.00	50.00	85.00

Obv: Date with 4 corrected.

Y#	Date	Mintage	VG	Fine	VF	XF
511.2	1934	—	18.50	30.00	50.00	85.00

Obv: Digit 4 Corrected.
Well struck; usually found in uncirculated condition.

Y#	Date	Mintage	Fine	VF	XF	Unc
511a	1934	(restrike)	—	—	15.00	25.00

500 CASH

COPPER, 35mm.
Obv: Small stars flanking date.

Y#	Date	Mintage	VG	Fine	VF	XF
512	1934	—	27.50	45.00	75.00	125.00

32.5mm
Obv: Large stars flanking date, hammer handle across lower leg of star.

512.1	1934	—	20.00	35.00	60.00	100.00

33-34mm
Obv: Hammer handle extends between right legs of star.

512.2	1934	—	20.00	35.00	60.00	100.00

DOLLAR

SILVER, 26.3000 gm.
Obv: Similar to Y#513.1.
Rev: Large solid stars.

Y#	Date	Mintage	VG	Fine	VF	XF
513	1934	—	45.00	75.00	125.00	200.00

Rev: Medium solid stars.

513.1	1934	—	40.00	65.00	110.00	185.00

Rev: Small solid stars.

513.2	1934	—	40.00	65.00	110.00	185.00

Rev: Outlined stars.

Y#	Date	Mintage	VG	Fine	VF	XF
513.3	1934	—	90.00	150.00	275.00	450.00

Obv: Similar to Y#513.1.
Rev: Pentagram stars

513.4	1934	—	45.00	75.00	125.00	200.00

NOTE: Many minor varieties exist.

Coins Of Uncertain Origin

DOLLAR

SILVER, 26.4000 gm.
c/s: Three Chinese characters in rectangular box, meaning SOVIET on obv. Y#329.

K#	Date	Mintage	VG	Fine	VF	XF
650k	ND	—	125.00	200.00	325.00	550.00

Obverse: Profile of Lenin. Legend translates

Issued by the Chinese Soviets.

Y#	Date	Mintage	VG	Fine	VF	XF
501	ND	—	60.00	120.00	200.00	350.00

Obverse: Hammer and sickle in circled star.
Legend translates: Soviet Government of Hunan Province.

Y#	Date	Mintage	VG	Fine	VF	XF
502	1931	—	75.00	150.00	250.00	400.00

NOTE: Y#501 and Y#502 are considered by some authorities to be fantasies.

PEOPLE'S REPUBLIC

MONETARY SYSTEM

100 Cents = 1 Renminbi (Yuan)

CENT

ALUMINUM

Y#	Date	Mintage	Fine	VF	XF	Unc
1	1955	—	.20	.50	1.50	5.00
	1956	—	.40	1.00	2.50	7.50
	1957	—	.60	1.50	3.50	10.00
	1958	—	.10	.25	.75	2.50
	1959	—	.10	.25	.75	2.50
	1961	—	.10	.25	.75	2.50
	1963	—	.10	.25	.50	1.50
	1964	—	.10	.25	.50	1.00
	1972	—	.10	.25	.50	1.00
	1973	—	.10	.25	.50	1.50
	1974	—	.10	.25	.50	1.00
	1975	—	.10	.25	.50	1.00
	1976	—	.10	.25	.50	1.00

2 CENTS

ALUMINUM

Y#	Date	Mintage	Fine	VF	XF	Unc
2	1956	—	.10	.25	.75	1.50
	1959	—	.20	.50	1.00	4.00
	1960	—	.20	.50	1.00	4.00
	1961	—	.10	.25	.75	1.50
	1962	—	.10	.25	.75	1.50
	1963	—	.10	.25	.75	1.50
	1964	—	.10	.25	.50	1.25
	1974	—	.10	.25	.50	1.50
	1975	—	.10	.25	.50	1.00

5 CENTS

ALUMINUM

Y#	Date	Mintage	Fine	VF	XF	Unc
3	1955	—	.30	.75	2.00	10.00
	1956	—	.15	.35	.75	2.00
	1957	—	.15	.35	.75	2.50
	1974	—	.15	.25	.50	1.50
	1975	—	.15	.25	.50	1.00
	1976	—	.15	.25	.50	1.00

YUAN

COPPER
Alpine Skiing

Y#	Date	Mintage	VF	XF	Unc
—	1980	.070	—	Proof	12.50

Speed Skating

Y#	Date	Mintage	VF	XF	Unc
—	1980	.070	—	Proof	12.50

Biathlon

Y#	Date	Mintage	VF	XF	Unc
—	1980	.070	—	Proof	12.50

Figure Skating

Y#	Date	Mintage	VF	XF	Unc
—	1980	.070	—	Proof	12.50

30 YUAN

15.000 gm., .800 SILVER, .3900 oz ASW
Speed Skating

Y#	Date	Mintage	VF	XF	Unc
—	1980	.020	—	Proof	60.00

250 YUAN

8.0000 gm., .916 GOLD, .2358 oz AGW
Alpine Skiing

Y#	Date	Mintage	VF	XF	Unc
—	1980	.020	—	Proof	650.00

400 YUAN

.917 GOLD
30th Anniversary of Peoples' Republic
Tian An Men

Y#	Date	Mintage	VF	XF	Unc
4	1979	.070	—	Proof only	550.00

30th Anniversary of Peoples' Republic
People's Heroes Monument

Y#	Date	Mintage	VF	XF	Unc
5	1979	.070	—	Proof only	550.00

30th Anniversary of Peoples' Republic
Chairman Mao Memorial Hall

Y#	Date	Mintage	VF	XF	Unc
6	1979	.070	—	Proof only	550.00

30th Anniversary of Peoples' Republic
Great Hall of the People

Y#	Date	Mintage	VF	XF	Unc
7	1979	.070	—	Proof only	550.00

450 YUAN

.900 GOLD, 17.1700 gm.

International Year of the Child

Y#	Date	Mintage	VF	XF	Unc
8	1979	.050	—	Proof only	950.00

NCLT ISSUES

PIEFORTS (P)

KM#	Date	Mintage	Identification	Issue Price	Mkt. Val.
P8	1979	500	450 Yuan, Y8	—	—
—	1980	1,000	30 Yuan, .800 Silver, Alpine Skiing	248.75	275.00
—	1980	1,000	30 Yuan, .800 Silver, Speed Skating	248.75	275.00
—	1980	1,000	30 Yuan, .800 Silver, Biathlon	248.75	275.00
—	1980	1,000	30 Yuan, .800 Silver, Figure Skating	248.75	275.00
—	1980	500	250 Yuan, .916 Gold, Alpine Skiing	1750.	1850.

PROOF SETS

KM#	Date	Mintage	Identification	Issue Price	Mkt. Val.
101	1979(4)	70,000	Y4-7	1695.	2100.
102	1980(4)	70,000	1 Yuan Winter Olympics	48.00	55.00

REPUBLIC OF CHINA

The Republic of China, comprising Taiwan (an island located 90 miles (145 km.) off the southeastern coast of mainland China), the offshore islands of Quemoy and Matsu and nearby islets of the Pescadores chain, has an area of 14,000 sq. mi. (35,981 sq. km.) and a population of 17 million. Capital: Taipei. During the past decade, manufacturing has replaced agriculture in importance. Fruits, vegetables, plywood, textile yarns and fabrics and clothing are exported.

Chinese migration to Taiwan began as early as the sixth century. The Dutch established a base on the island in 1624 and held it until 1661, when they were driven out by supporters of the Ming dynasty who used it as a base for their unsuccessful attempt to displace the ruling Manchu dynasty of mainland China. After being occupied by Manchu forces in 1683; Taiwan remained under the suzerainty of China until its cession to Japan in 1895. It was returned to China following World War II. On Dec. 8, 1949, Taiwan became the last remnant of Sun Yat-sen's Republic of China when Chiang Kai-Shek moved his army and government from mainland China to the island following his defeat by the Communist forces of Mao'Tse-tung, and with American support proceeded to make it the showcase of democracy in Asia.

The coins of Nationalist China do not carry A.D. dating, but are dated according to the year of the republic, which was established in 1911. Thus the year date 38 on a coin indicates it was issued in 1949, or 49 would be 1960, and so on.

10 CENTS

BRONZE

Y#	Date	Mintage	Fine	VF	XF	Unc
531	Yr.38 (1949)	157.600	.10	.25	.75	1.50

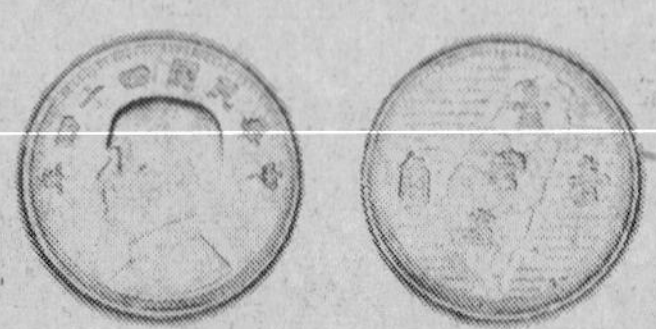

ALUMINUM

Y#	Date	Mintage	Fine	VF	XF	Unc
533	Yr.44 (1955)	583.980	—	—	—	.10

Y#	Date	Mintage	Fine	VF	XF	Unc
545	Yr.56 (1967)	89.999	—	—	.15	.25
	Yr.59 (1970)	30.000	—	.10	.25	.35
	Yr.60 (1971)	19.925	—	.20	.40	1.00
	Yr.61 (1972)	11.141	—	.20	.35	.60
	Yr.62 (1973)	111.400	—	—	.10	.25
	Yr.63 (1974)	71.930	—	.10	.25	.35

20 CENTS

ALUMINUM

Y#	Date	Mintage	Fine	VF	XF	Unc
534	Yr.39 (1950)	327.495	—	—	.15	.25

50 CENTS

5.0000 gm., .720 SILVER, .1157 oz ASW

Y#	Date	Mintage	Fine	VF	XF	Unc
532	Yr.38 (1949)	—	BV	BV	3.50	5.00

BRASS

Y#	Date	Mintage	Fine	VF	XF	Unc
535	Yr.43 (1954)	279.624	—	.10	.20	.40

Y#	Date	Mintage	Fine	VF	XF	Unc
546	Yr.56 (1967)	109.999	—	.10	.15	.25
	Yr.59 (1970)	6.010	—	.15	.25	.50
	Yr.60 (1971)	4.434	—	.25	.50	.75
	Yr.61 (1972)	21.171	—	.20	.40	.60
	Yr.62 (1973)	88.840	—	.20	.35	.50
	Yr.63 (1974)	43.424	—	.20	.35	.50

DOLLAR (YUAN)

COPPER-NICKEL-ZINC

Y#	Date	Mintage	Fine	VF	XF	Unc
536	Yr.49 (1960)	321.717	—	.20	.30	.40
	Yr.59 (1970)	48.800	—	.15	.25	.50
	Yr.60 (1971)	41.532	—	.15	.25	.50
	Yr.61 (1972)	105.309	—	.10	.20	.35
	Yr.62 (1973)	353.924	—	.10	.20	.40
	Yr.63 (1974)	535.605	—	.10	.20	.35
	Yr.64 (1975)	456.874	—	.10	.20	.35
	Yr.65 (1976)	634.497	—	.10	.20	.35

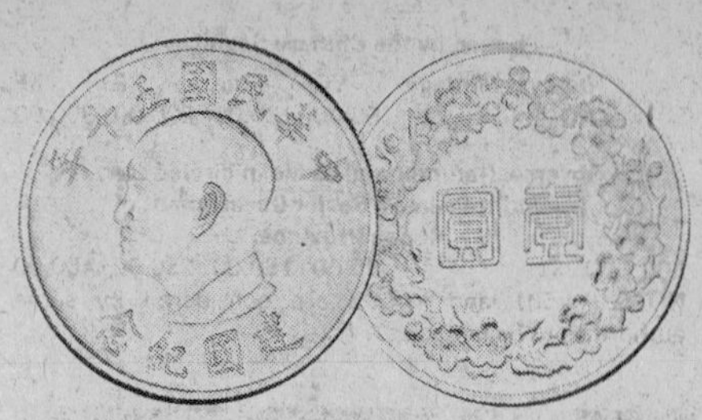

SILVER

Y#	Date	Mintage	Fine	VF	XF	Unc
—	Yr.50 (1961)	—	—	—	50.00	75.00

NOTE: This coin was struck to commemorate the 50th anniversary of the Republic. It was either released accidentally or was released and quickly withdrawn and is scarce today.

COPPER-NICKEL
80th Birthday of Chiang Kai-Shek

Y#	Date	Mintage	Fine	VF	XF	Unc
543	Yr.55 (1966)	—	—	.20	.35	.50

F.A.O. Issue

Y#	Date	Mintage	Fine	VF	XF	Unc
547	Yr.58 (1969)	10.000	—	.15	.40	.75

5 DOLLARS

COPPER-NICKEL
Sun Yat-Sen

Y#	Date	Mintage	Fine	VF	XF	Unc
537	Yr.54 (1965)	—	—	.50	.75	2.00

Y#	Date	Mintage	Fine	VF	XF	Unc
548	Yr.59 (1970)	12.360	—	.40	.50	.75
	Yr.60 (1971)	20.575	—	.35	.50	.75
	Yr.61 (1972)	27.998	—	.40	.50	.65
	Yr.62 (1973)	50.122	—	.35	.50	.75
	Yr.63 (1974)	418.068	—	.35	.50	.75
	Yr.64 (1975)	39.520	—	.35	.50	.75
	Yr.65 (1976)	140.000	—	.20	.35	.50

10 DOLLARS

COPPER-NICKEL
Sun Yat-Sen

Y#	Date	Mintage	Fine	VF	XF	Unc
538	Yr.54 (1965)	—	—	1.00	1.50	3.00

50 DOLLARS

17.5300 gm., .750 SILVER, .4227 oz ASW
Sun Yat-Sen

539	Yr.54 (1965)	—	BV	BV	15.00	18.50

100 DOLLARS

22.5000 gm., .750 SILVER, .5426 oz ASW
Sun Yat-Sen

540	Yr.54 (1965)	—	BV	BV	17.50	21.50

1000 DOLLARS

15.0000 gm., .900 GOLD, .4340 oz AGW
Sun Yat-Sen

541	Yr.54 (1965)	—	BV	BV	500.00	650.00

2000 DOLLARS

30.0000 gm., .900 GOLD, .8681 oz AGW
Sun Yat-Sen

Y#	Date	Mintage	Fine	VF	XF	Unc
542	Yr.54 (1965)	—	BV	BV	600.00	675.00

31.0600 gm., .900 GOLD, .8988 oz AGW
80th Birthday of Chiang Kai-Shek

544	Yr.55 (1966)	—	BV	BV	600.00	700.00

NCLT ISSUES

PATTERNS

KM#	Date	Mintage	Identification	Mkt.Val.
1	(1949)	—	10 Cents, Bronze, K12a	75.00
2	(1949)	—	10 Cents, Aluminum, K12b	75.00
3	(1949)	—	10 Cents, Copper, K12c	75.00
4	(1949)	—	10 Cents, Copper, K12d	75.00
5	(1949)	—	10 Cents, Aluminum, w/o reeded edge, K12e	75.00

6	(1949)	—	10 Cents, Copper, K13	75.00

7	(1949)	—	10 Cents, Copper, K14	75.00

8	(1949)	—	50 Cents, Aluminum-Bronze, K15a	75.00
9	(1949)	—	50 Cents, Aluminum, K15b	75.00

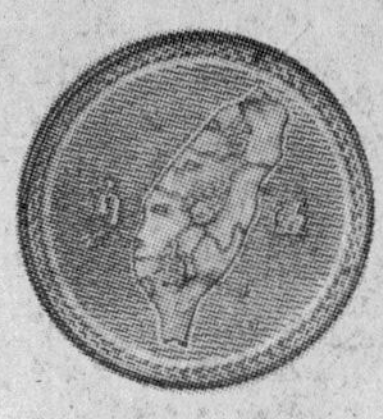

KM#	Date	Mintage	Identification	Mkt.Val.
10	(1949)	—	50 Cents, Silver, K16	200.00
11	(1949)	—	50 Cents, Copper, K16a	75.00

12	(1949)	—	50 Cents, Silver, K17	200.00

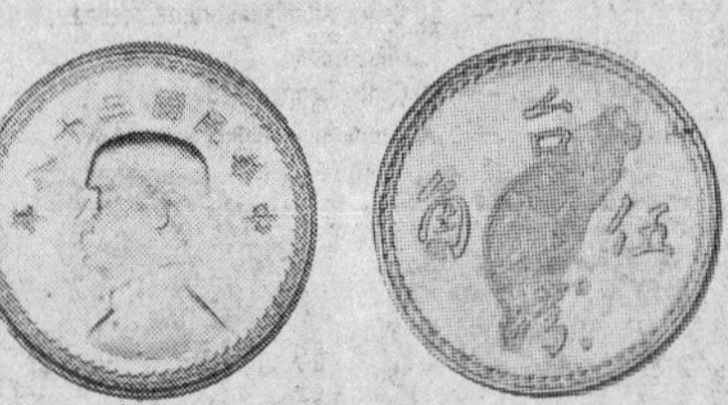

13	(1949)	—	50 Cents, Silver, K18	200.00

14	(1949)	—	50 Cents, Silver, K19	200.00

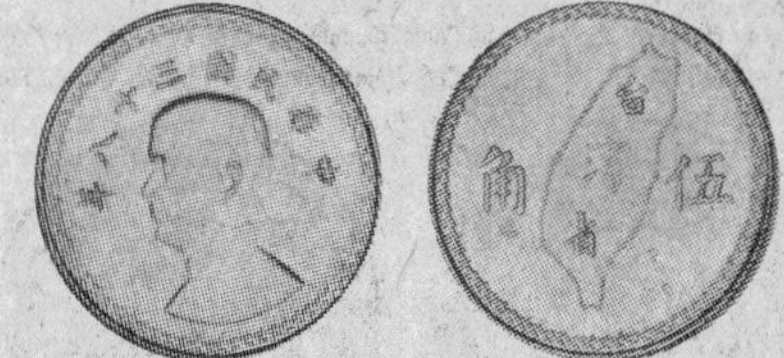

15	(1949)	—	50 Cents, Silver, K20	200.00

16	(1949)	—	1 Dollar, Silver, K21i	200.00

17	(1950)	—	20 Cents, Aluminum, reeded edge, K21a	75.00
18	(1950)	—	20 Cents, Aluminum-Bronze, K21b	75.00
19	(1950)	—	20 Cents, Aluminum-Bronze, w/o reeded edge, K21c	75.00
20	(1950)	—	20 Cents, Copper, K21d	75.00
21	(1950)	—	1 Dollar, Silver	200.00
22	(1950)	—	1 Dollar, Copper-Nickel, 28mm	75.00
23	(1950)	—	1 Dollar, Copper-Nickel, 29mm	75.00

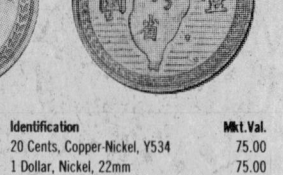

KM#	Date	Mintage	Identification	Mkt.Val.
24	(1950)	—	1 Dollar, Aluminum-Bronze, K22a	75.00
25	(1950)	—	1 Dollar, Aluminum, K22b	75.00

KM#	Date	Mintage	Identification	Mkt.Val.
26	(1954)	—	50 Cents, Aluminum-Bronze, K23	75.00
27	(1954)	—	50 Cents, Aluminum-Bronze, reeded	75.00
			edge, K23a	75.00
28	(1954)	—	50 Cents, Copper, K23b	75.00
29	(1954)	—	50 Cents, Aluminum-Bronze, K23c	75.00

KM#	Date	Mintage	Identification	Mkt.Val.
30	(1954)	—	50 Cents, Aluminum-Bronze, K24	75.00
31	(1954)	—	50 Cents, Aluminum-Bronze, K25	75.00
32	(1954)	—	50 Cents, Aluminum-Bronze, K25a	75.00

KM#	Date	Mintage	Identification	Mkt.Val.
33	(1954)	—	50 Cents, Bronze, K26a	75.00
34	(1955)	—	10 Cents, Aluminum, K27	75.00
35	(1955)	—	10 Cents, Aluminum, simplified	75.00
			"TAI", K27a	75.00
36	(1955)	—	10 Cents, Bronze, K27b	75.00

KM#	Date	Mintage	Identification	Mkt.Val.
37	(1956)	—	20 Cents, Copper-Nickel, Y534	75.00
38	(1959)	—	1 Dollar, Nickel, 22mm	75.00
39	(1959)	—	1 Dollar, Nickel-Silver, 22mm	75.00

KM#	Date	Mintage	Identification	Mkt.Val.
40	(1960)	—	1 Dollar, Nickel-Silver, 24.5mm, y536	100.00
41	(1961)	—	1 Dollar, Nickel-Silver, 25mm	100.00
42	(1961)	—	1 Dollar, Nickel-Aluminum, 25mm	100.00
43	(1961)	—	1 Dollar, Nickel-Silver, 26.5mm	100.00
44	(1962)	—	5 Dollars, Nickel, 28mm	100.00
45	(1964)	—	5 Dollars, Copper-Nickel, 28mm	100.00
46	(1965)	—	10 Dollars, Copper-Nickel, 30mm, rev: clouds replace mountains, Y538	100.00
47	(1965)	—	10 Dollars, Copper-Nickel, 30mm rev: w/o clouds, Y538	100.00

TAEL SYSTEM

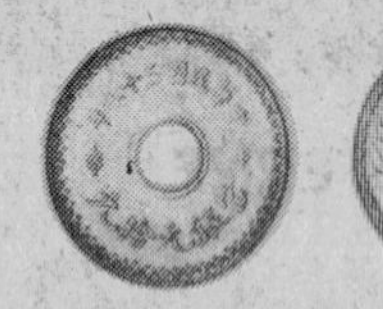

KM#	Date	Mintage	Identification	Mkt.Val.
K7b	(1949)	—	1 Chien, Aluminum-Bronze	250.00

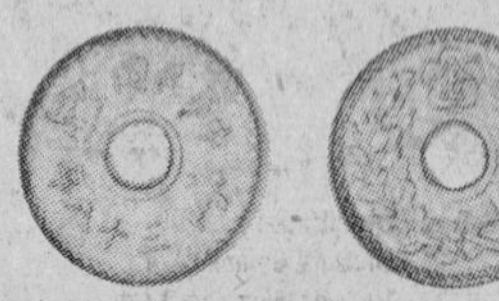

KM#	Date	Mintage	Identification	Mkt.Val.
K6a	(1949)	—	1 Chien, Silver	400.00
K6b	(1949)	—	1 Chien, Aluminum-Bronze	250.00

KM#	Date	Mintage	Identification	Mkt.Val.
K4b	(1949)	—	2 Chien, Aluminum-Bronze	250.00

KM#	Date	Mintage	Identification	Mkt.Val.
K3b	(1949)	—	2-1/2 Chien, Aluminum-Bronze	250.00

KM#	Date	Mintage	Identification	Mkt.Val.
K2b	(1949)	—	5 Chien, Aluminum-Bronze	250.00

KM#	Date	Mintage	Identification	Mkt.Val.
—	(1956)	—	2-1/2 Chien, Copper-Nickel	150.00
—	(1956)	—	2-1/2 Chien, Aluminum-Bronze	150.00
—	(1956)	—	2-1/2 Chien, Aluminum	150.00

MINT SETS

STANDARD METALS

S1	1965(4)	—	Y537-540	22.50

Listings For

CHINESE TURKESTAN: refer to China/Sinkiang

FOREIGN ENCLAVES

The Age of Exploration brought European traders to China as early as the 16th century. By 1560, the Portuguese were firmly in control of Macao. British, French and Dutch traders soon followed, and in 1784 the first clipper ship of the United States arrived.

Commerce, however, was severely limited by the refusal of the Chinese ruling class to treat the representatives of foreign powers as equals. By the end of the 18th century, only the port of Canton had been opened to European merchants, who were forbidden to enter Canton proper or travel inland.

The need for raw materials and expanded markets created by the Industrial Revolution brought increased pressure on China to open its doors to foreign traders. The resultant warfare procured from China extensive trade concessions, the cession of Hong Kong to Great Britain, and the establishment of foreign enclaves at Kiau Chau (Germany), Kwang Chowan (France), Kuantung (Russia), Shanghai and elsewhere that were virtually sovereign empires within the Chinese Empire.

Military defeats, territorial and trade concessions, and the interference by Christian missionaries in local Chinese governments and customs created mass antagonism toward foreigners, and increased the activities of secret societies who became dedicated to ousting the foreigner from China. Chief among the xenophobic organizations was the I Ho Ch'uan "Righteous Harmony Fists", a society known as the 'Boxers' because its members practiced ritual shadow-boxing to make themselves invulnerable to bullets. In the autumn of 1899, they began to murder Chinese Christians and foreigners. The Empress Dowager T'zu Hsi abetted their work by procrastination and allowing many foreigners in China to be killed. The resulting 'Boxer Uprising' was a fiasco, albeit a bloody one.

Massacring Christians and foreigners as they moved north, the Boxers entered Peking in June 1900. There they beseiged some 1,000 foreigners and 3,000 Chinese Christians in the Legation Quarters until a seven—nation expeditionary force drove them off 55 days later. Although the nations had not declared war on China, they exacted additional concessions and heavy indemnities from the Manchu Government.

The free port of Hong Kong, a British-controlled commercial center and entrepot, is located 90 miles (145 km.) southeast of Canton. For historical background and coin listings, refer to Hong Kong.

Listings For

HONG KONG: refer to Hong Kong

KIAU CHAU

Kia Chau (Kiao Chau, Kiaochow, Kiautscho), a former German trading enclave, was located on the Shantung Peninsula of eastern China. Following the murder of two missionaries in Shantung in 1897, Germany occupied Kiaochow Bay, and during subsequent negotiations with the Chinese government obtained a 99-year lease on 177 sq. mi. of land. The enclave was established as a free port in 1899, and a customs house set up to collect tariffs on goods moving to and from the Chinese interior. The Japanese took the port as their first action in World War I to deprive German sea marauders of their east Asian supply and refitting base and retained possession until 1922, when it was restored to China by the Washington Conference on China and naval armaments. It fell again to Japan in 1938, but not until the Chinese had destroyed its manufacturing facilities. It is presently a part of the People's Republic of China.

MONETARY SYSTEM

100 Cents = 1 DOLLAR

5 CENTS

COPPER-NICKEL

Y#	Date	Mintage	Fine	VF	XF	Unc
1	1909	.610	11.50	17.50	25.00	60.00
	1909	—		—	Proof	250.00

10 CENTS

COPPER-NICKEL

Y#	Date	Mintage	Fine	VF	XF	Unc
2	1909	.670	12.50	18.50	27.50	65.00
	1909	—	—	—	Proof	250.00

KWANG CHOWAN

Kwangchowan (Kuang-Chou Wan), a former French commercial center and free port, was located on the Luichow Peninsula which projects southward from China toward the island of Hainan. France acquired a 99-year lease to the 309 sq. mi. (800 sq. km.) enclave, with full territorial jurisdiction, in 1898. It was occupied by Japan during 1943-1945 as a consequence of the Vichy-Tokyo agreement of 1941 which gave control of French Indochina to Japan. Upon relinquishment of all French claims in 1945, it became the Chinese municipality of Chankiang (Ch'ang Chiang). In 1949 it was incorporated in the People's Republic of China. There are no known coins issued specifically for Kwangchowan.

KWANTUNG

Kwantung (Kuan-Tung), a name applied in the late 19th century to the southern tip of the Liaotung peninsula which projects southward into the Gulf of Chihli from present Liaoning province. The British captured Lu-shun on the southeast tip of the peninsula in 1860 and renamed it Port Arthur. In 1898, Russia forced a 25-year lease to the 925 sq. mi. enclave from the Ch'ing dynasty, but lost it to Japan as a result of the Russo-Japanese War. Japan controlled the area until defeated in World War II. From 1945 to 1955, Port Arthur was under joint Russian-Chinese administration, following which it passed to Chinese control. During the Russian occupation, Russian copper and silver coins circulated in the area. Under the Japanese, silver yen counterstamped GIN in Japanese also circulated.

Listings For

MACAO: refer to Macao

Macao, the oldest European settlement in the Far East, is located 35 miles (56 km.) southwest of Hong Kong. For historical background and coin listings, refer to Macao.

SHANGHAI

The port of Shanghai was opened to foreign trade in 1842 as a result of the Opium War, and quickly grew to become the most important port in China. Several countries acquired control over certain sections of the city, and beginning in 1854 organized themselves into what was to become the International Settlement. This confederation remained virtually autonomous until the Second World War when Shanghai was occupied by the Japanese. A number of different tokens and encased postage stamps were issued for use in Shanghai.

NCLT ISSUES

PATTERNS

Kwanping Series

Until recently these coins were a mystery, attributed by some to Taiwan and by others to Korea. Both attributions were wrong. The dies and presumably the coins, were made at the Royal Mint, London about 1858 to facilitate trade and customs payments at Shanghai and elsewhere. Apparently the coins were not accepted in China and remained Essays only.

KM#	Date	Mintage	Identification	Mkt.Val.
K926II	c.1858	—	5 Fen, Silver	500.00

KM#	Date	Mintage	Identification	Mkt.Val.
K926II	c.1858	—	1 Ch'ien, Silver	800.00

KM#	Date	Mintage	Identification	Mkt.Val.
K926I	c.1858	—	2 Ch'ien, Silver	1000.

KM#	Date	Mintage	Identification	Mkt.Val.
K926	c.1858	—	5 Ch'ien, Silver	1500.

KM#	Date	Mintage	Identification	Mkt.Val.
K925	c.1858	—	1 Liang, Silver	1800.

Shanghai Tael Series

The 1867 Tael and two Mace coins of Shanghai were minted at the Hong Kong Mint as proposed trade coins. The designs were unacceptable to the Chinese as they contained the British coat of arms and crown and even a Latin legend. The designs were rejected, the coinage never came about and the patterns which were struck were ordered destroyed.

X913	1867	—	2 Ch'ien, Silver	3500.

X911a	1867	—	1 Liang, Silver, w/o rays from ring	4000.

KM#	Date	Mintage	Identification	Mkt.Val.
X912	1867	—	1 Liang, Silver, w/rays from ring	4000.

TAIWAN

The island of Taiwan (Formosa) had been a part of the Chinese empire since the 17th century. In 1895, however, the island was ceded to Japan as a result of the Sino-Japanese War. Japan held the island until 1945 when it was returned to China.

Prior to 1895, Chinese cash coins and dragon silver coins were issued for the island (see Taiwan Province), but under the Japanese no coins were minted specifically for Taiwan. Japanese silver yen coins, counterstamped GIN in Japanese, were placed in circulation there following the occupation.

COLOMBIA

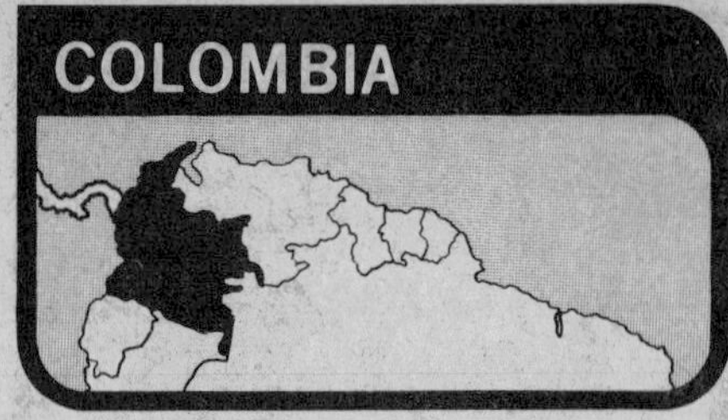

The Republic of Colombia, located in the northwestern corner of South America has an area of 440,000 sq. mi. (1,139,594 sq. km.) and a population of 24.5 million. Capital: Bogota. The economy is primarily agricultural with a mild, rich coffee the chief crop. Colombia has the world's largest platinum deposits and important reserves of coal, iron ore, petroleum and limestone; precious metals and emeralds are also mined. Coffee, crude oil, bananas and sugar are exported.

The northern coast of present Colombia was one of the first parts of the American continent to be visited by Spanish navigators, and the site, at Darien in Panama, of the first permanent European settlement on the American mainland in 1510. New Grenada, as Colombia was known until 1861, stemmed from the settlement of Santa Maria in 1525. New Grenada was established as a Spanish Colony in 1549. Independence was declared in 1813, and secured in 1824. In 1819, Simon Bolivar united Colombia, Venezuela, Panama and Ecuador as the Republic of Greater Colombia. Venezuela withdrew from the Republic in 1829; Ecuador in 1830; Panama in 1903.

COLONIAL COINAGE

RULERS

Spanish

MINTMARKS

NR, Noro - Nuevo Reino (Bogota)
P, PN, Pn - Popayan

MONETARY SYSTEM

8 Reales = 1 Peso or Colombiano
2 Pesos = 1 Escudo
8 Escudos = 1 Onza

1/4 REAL

.903 SILVER

MINTMARK: NR

Obv: Castle. Rev: Lion.

C#	Date	Mintage	Fine	VF	XF
41	1785	—	—	—	—
	1796	—	17.50	35.00	50.00
	1797	—	12.00	20.00	50.00
	1798/5	—	35.00	45.00	65.00
	1798/7	—	20.00	35.00	50.00
	1798	—	10.00	15.00	50.00
	1799	—	10.00	15.00	50.00
	1800	—	10.00	15.00	50.00
	1801	—	10.00	15.00	50.00
	1802	—	10.00	15.00	50.00
	1803/2	—	12.00	20.00	50.00
	1803	—	15.00	25.00	50.00
	1804	—	10.00	15.00	50.00
	1805	—	12.00	20.00	50.00
	1806	—	15.00	25.00	50.00
	1807	—	25.00	40.00	65.00
	1808/6	—	40.00	65.00	100.00
	1808	—	10.00	15.00	50.00
	Similar to C#41				
61	1809	—	35.00	55.00	65.00
	1810/09	—	—	—	—
	1810/1	—	—	—	—
	1810	—	15.00	25.00	40.00
	1811	—	25.00	45.00	60.00
	1812	—	15.00	30.00	45.00
	1813	—	25.00	45.00	65.00
	1814	—	10.00	20.00	35.00
	1815	—	20.00	40.00	60.00
	1816	—	12.00	25.00	35.00
	1817	—	10.00	15.00	30.00
	1818/7	—	10.00	15.00	30.00
	1818	—	10.00	15.00	30.00
	1819	—	45.00	65.00	80.00

MINTMARK: PN

Similar to C#41.

C#	Date	Mintage	Fine	VF	XF
61a	1816	—	25.00	50.00	75.00

1/2 REAL

.903 SILVER

MINTMARK: NR

Obv: Bust of Charles III. Rev: Arms, pillars.

C#	Date	Mintage	Fine	VF	XF
14	1772 VJ	—	150.00	250.00	400.00
	1773 VJ	—	200.00	400.00	750.00
	1777 JJ	—	135.00	225.00	325.00
	1784 JJ	—	275.00	550.00	850.00

MINTMARK: P

C#	Date	Mintage	Fine	VF	XF
14a	1772 JS	—	—	—	—
	1774 JS	—	275.00	500.00	900.00

MINTMARK: NR

Obv: Bust of Charles IV.

C#	Date	Mintage	Fine	VF	XF
42	1792 JJ	—	35.00	60.00	100.00
	1794 JJ	—	65.00	90.00	155.00
	1795 JJ	—	35.00	60.00	100.00
	1796 JJ	—	60.00	85.00	130.00
	1799 JJ	—	35.00	60.00	100.00

Obv. leg: FERND. VII...., bust of Charles IV.

C#	Date	Mintage	Fine	VF	XF
62	1810 JJ	—	55.00	80.00	140.00
	1812 JF(error)	—	—	Rare	—
	1816 FJ	—	55.00	80.00	140.00
	1818 FJ	—	55.00	80.00	140.00
	1819 FJ	—	55.00	80.00	140.00

MINTMARK: P

C#	Date	Mintage	Fine	VF	XF
62a	1810 JF	—	25.00	45.00	115.00
	1816 FJ	—	50.00	70.00	115.00
	1819 MF	—	15.00	30.00	60.00

REAL

.917 SILVER

MINTMARK: NR

Obv. leg: CRS. III.

Rev: Two crowned hemispheres between pillars.

C#	Date	Mintage	Fine	VF	XF
11	1760 JV	—	1300.	2500.	3800.

.903 SILVER

Obv: Bust of Charles III. Rev: Arms, pillars.

C#	Date	Mintage	Fine	VF	XF
15	1772 VJ	—	60.00	85.00	150.00
	1773 VJ	—	40.00	55.00	100.00
	1775 JJ	—	55.00	65.00	125.00
	1776 JJ	—	55.00	65.00	125.00
	1777 JJ	—	55.00	65.00	125.00
	1781 JJ	—	55.00	65.00	125.00
	1784 JJ	—	55.00	65.00	125.00

MINTMARK: P

C#	Date	Mintage	Fine	VF	XF
15a	1772 JS	—	100.00	180.00	275.00

MINTMARK: NR

Obv: Bust of Charles IIII.

C#	Date	Mintage	Fine	VF	XF
43	1792 JJ	—	25.00	45.00	75.00
	1793 JJ	—	50.00	80.00	125.00
	1795 JJ	—	25.00	45.00	75.00
	1796 JJ	—	25.00	45.00	75.00
	1797 JJ	—	25.00	45.00	75.00
	1798 JJ	—	25.00	45.00	75.00
	1799 JJ	—	30.00	50.00	80.00
	1800 JJ	—	20.00	40.00	70.00
	1801 JJ	—	12.50	30.00	60.00
	1802 JJ	—	10.00	27.50	55.00
	1804 JJ	—	25.00	45.00	75.00

Obv. leg: FERDND VII...., bust of Charles IV.

Rev: Arms, pillars.

C#	Date	Mintage	Fine	VF	XF
63	1810 JF	—	12.50	25.00	45.00
	1810 JJ	—	30.00	45.00	75.00
	1812 FJ	—	10.00	20.00	45.00
	1812 JF	—	15.00	27.50	45.00
	1816 FJ	—	7.50	12.50	20.00
	1817 FJ	—	10.00	20.00	45.00
	1818 FJ	—	17.50	32.50	60.00
	1819 FJ	—	12.50	22.50	45.00
	1819 J	—	12.50	22.50	45.00
	1820 FJ	—	55.00	70.00	100.00

MINTMARK: P

C#	Date	Mintage	Fine	VF	XF
63a	1810 JF	—	25.00	40.00	80.00
	1813 JF	—	55.00	75.00	110.00
	1820 FM	—	35.00	50.00	85.00
	1822 FM	—	—	—	—

MINTMARK: NR

Obv: Bust of Ferdinand VII.

C#	Date	Mintage	Fine	VF	XF
A63	1821 FJ	—	55.00	70.00	110.00

2 REALES

.903 SILVER

MINTMARK: NR

Obv: Bust of Charles III. Rev: Arms, pillars.

C#	Date	Mintage	Fine	VF	XF
16	1772 VI	—	150.00	225.00	400.00
	1773 VJ	—	150.00	225.00	400.00
	1775 VJ	—	500.00	850.00	1500.
	1777 JJ	—	400.00	650.00	1250.
	1780 JJ	—	350.00	600.00	1000.
	1784 JJ	—	400.00	600.00	1000.
	1788 JJ	—	1000.	1500.	2000.

Obv: Bust of Charles IV.

C#	Date	Mintage	Fine	VF	XF
44	1792 JJ	—	275.00	425.00	850.00
	1793 JJ	—	150.00	300.00	625.00
	1794 JJ	—	275.00	500.00	1000.
	1795 JJ	—	350.00	600.00	1350.
	1796 JJ	—	400.00	650.00	1400.
	1798 JJ	—	275.00	450.00	775.00
	1800 JJ	—	150.00	350.00	600.00

Obv. leg: FERDND VII...., bust of Charles IV.

C#	Date	Mintage	Fine	VF	XF
64	1811 JF	—	27.50	45.00	75.00
	1816 FJ	—	27.50	45.00	75.00
	1816 JJ/FJ	—	27.50	45.00	75.00
	1817 FJ	—	27.50	45.00	75.00
	1818/7 FJ	—	110.00	120.00	140.00
	1818 FJ	—	27.50	45.00	75.00
	1819 FJ	—	27.50	45.00	75.00

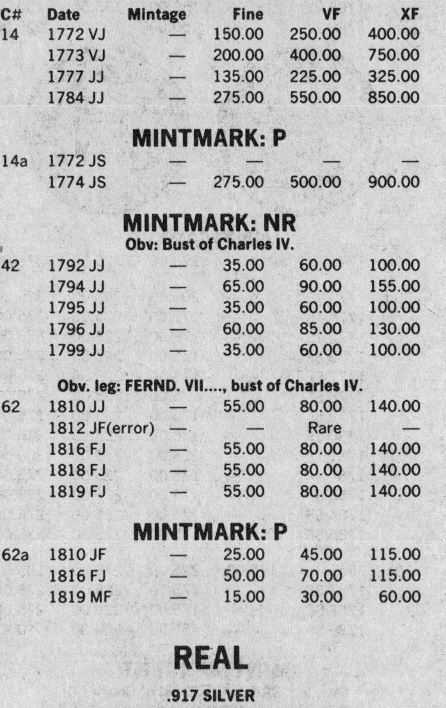

MINTMARK: P

C#	Date	Mintage	Fine	VF	XF
64a	1810 JF	—	20.00	40.00	65.00
	1811/0 JF	—	20.00	40.00	65.00
	1811 JF	—	35.00	50.00	80.00
	1813 JF	—	35.00	50.00	80.00
	1814/3 JF	—	—	—	—
	1814 JF	—	130.00	200.00	400.00
	1818 MF	—	45.00	60.00	80.00
	1819 MF	—	20.00	40.00	65.00
	1820/10 MF	—	175.00	275.00	450.00
	1820 MF	—	35.00	50.00	75.00
	1820 FM	—	35.00	50.00	75.00

Obv. leg: FERDND. 7.D.G.ET. CONST.

C#	Date	Mintage	Fine	VF	XF
65	1822 O	—	25.00	40.00	70.00

8 REALES

.917 SILVER

MINTMARK: NR

Obv. leg: CAROLUS III...., arms.

Rev: Two crowned hemispheres between pillars.

C#	Date	Mintage	Fine	VF	XF
13	1760 JV	—	—	Rare	—
	1761 JV	—	—	Rare	—
	1762 JV	—	—	Rare	—
	1763 JV	—	—	Rare	—

MINTMARK:PN

C#	Date	Mintage	Fine	VF	XF
13a	1769 J	—	5000.	8000.	12,500.

.903 SILVER

MINTMARK: P

Obv. leg: FERDND VII...., bust of Charles IV.

Rev: Arms, pillars.

C#	Date	Mintage	Fine	VF	XF
66	1810 JF	—	600.00	725.00	1500.
	1811 JF	—	500.00	650.00	1500.
	1812 JF	—	500.00	650.00	1500.
	1813/2 JF	—	500.00	650.00	1500.
	1813 JF	—	500.00	650.00	1500.
	1813 F	—	1050.	1650.	2800.
	1814/3 JF	—	525.00	850.00	1500.
	1814 JF	—	500.00	650.00	1500.
	1815 JF	—	700.00	1000.	1650.
	1816 F	—	500.00	650.00	1500.
	1820 FM	—	900.00	1100.	1650.
	1820 MF	—	900.00	1100.	1650.

ESCUDO

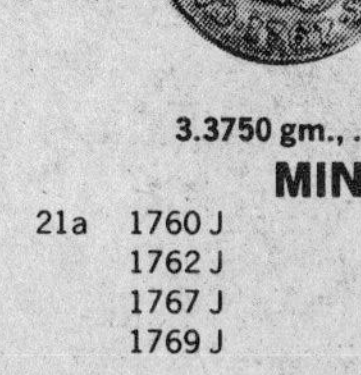

3.3750 gm., .875 GOLD, .0949 oz AGW

MINTMARK: PN

C#	Date	Mintage	Fine	VF	XF
21a	1760 J	—	125.00	175.00	250.00
	1762 J	—	125.00	175.00	250.00
	1767 J	—	125.00	175.00	250.00
	1769 J	—	125.00	175.00	250.00

MINTMARK: NR

C#	Date	Mintage	Fine	VF	XF
25	1763 JV	—	125.00	200.00	350.00
	1767 JV	—	125.00	200.00	350.00
	1771 VJ	—	100.00	150.00	225.00

MINTMARK: P

Obv: Bust of Charles III. Rev: Arms, order chain.

C#	Date	Mintage	Fine	VF	XF
29	1772 VJ	—	75.00	100.00	150.00
	1773 VJ	—	75.00	100.00	150.00
	1774 VJ	—	75.00	100.00	150.00
	1774 JJ	—	75.00	100.00	150.00
	1775 JJ	—	75.00	100.00	150.00
	1776 JJ	—	75.00	100.00	150.00
	1777 JJ	—	75.00	100.00	150.00
	1778 JJ	—	75.00	100.00	150.00
	1779 JJ	—	75.00	100.00	150.00
	1780 JJ	—	125.00	200.00	400.00
	1781 JJ	—	75.00	100.00	150.00
	1782 JJ	—	100.00	150.00	200.00
	1783 JJ	—	100.00	150.00	200.00
	1784 JJ	—	100.00	150.00	200.00
	1785 JJ	—	100.00	150.00	200.00
29b	1786 JJ	—	100.00	150.00	200.00
	1787 JJ	—	100.00	150.00	200.00
	1788 JJ	—	100.00	150.00	200.00
	1789 JJ	—	100.00	150.00	200.00

MINTMARK: P

C#	Date	Mintage	Fine	VF	XF
29a	1772 JS	—	85.00	135.00	175.00
	1772 SF	—	100.00	150.00	225.00
29c	1773 JS	—	100.00	150.00	225.00
	1774 JS	—	75.00	100.00	150.00
	1774 SF	—	100.00	150.00	225.00
	1775 SF	—	100.00	150.00	225.00
	1776 SF	—	75.00	100.00	150.00
	1777 SF	—	75.00	100.00	150.00
	1778 SF	—	75.00	100.00	150.00
	1779 SF	—	75.00	100.00	150.00
	1780 SF	—	75.00	100.00	150.00
	1781 SF	—	75.00	100.00	150.00
	1782 SF	—	75.00	100.00	150.00
	1783 SF	—	75.00	100.00	150.00
	1784 SF	—	75.00	100.00	150.00
	1785 SF	—	75.00	100.00	150.00
29d	1786 SF	—	75.00	100.00	150.00
	1787 SF	—	60.00	85.00	130.00
	1788 SF	—	75.00	100.00	150.00
	1789 SF	—	100.00	150.00	225.00

MINTMARK: NR

Obv. leg: CAROL IV...., bust of Charles III.
Rev: Arms, order chain.

C#	Date	Mintage	Fine	VF	XF
51	1790 JJ	—	100.00	140.00	200.00

MINTMARK: P

C#	Date	Mintage	Fine	VF	XF
51a	1789 SF	—	100.00	150.00	200.00
	1790 SF	—	100.00	150.00	200.00

Obv: Bust of Charles IIII.

C#	Date	Mintage	Fine	VF	XF
55	1791 JJ	—	75.00	120.00	180.00
	1792 JJ	—	100.00	150.00	200.00
	1793 JJ	—	100.00	150.00	200.00
	1794 JJ	—	125.00	175.00	225.00
	1795 JJ	—	75.00	120.00	180.00
	1796 JJ	—	75.00	120.00	180.00
	1797 JJ	—	75.00	120.00	180.00
	1798 JJ	—	75.00	120.00	180.00
	1799 JJ	—	75.00	120.00	180.00
	1800 JJ	—	100.00	150.00	200.00
	1801 JJ	—	100.00	150.00	200.00
	1802 JJ	—	75.00	120.00	180.00
	1803 JJ	—	75.00	120.00	180.00
	1804 JJ	—	75.00	120.00	180.00
	1805 JJ	—	75.00	120.00	180.00
	1806 JJ	—	90.00	125.00	200.00
	1807 JJ	—	125.00	175.00	250.00
	1808 JJ	—	75.00	120.00	180.00

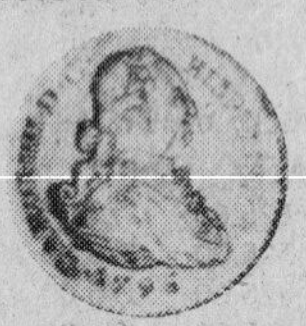

MINTMARK: P

C#	Date	Mintage	Fine	VF	XF
55a	1792 JF	—	75.00	120.00	180.00
	1793 JF	—	75.00	120.00	180.00
	1794 JF	—	75.00	120.00	180.00
	1795 JF	—	75.00	120.00	180.00
	1796 JF	—	75.00	120.00	180.00
	1797 JJ	—	75.00	120.00	180.00
	1798 JF	—	75.00	120.00	180.00
	1799 JF	—	75.00	120.00	180.00
	1800 JF	—	75.00	120.00	180.00
	1801 JF	—	75.00	120.00	180.00
	1802 JF	—	75.00	120.00	180.00
	1803 JF	—	90.00	125.00	200.00
	1804 JF	—	90.00	125.00	200.00
	1804 JT	—	125.00	175.00	275.00
	1805 JT	—	90.00	125.00	200.00
	1805 JF	—	125.00	175.00	275.00
	1806 JT	—	150.00	225.00	400.00
	1806 JF	—	90.00	125.00	200.00
	1807 JF	—	90.00	125.00	200.00
	1808 JF	—	90.00	125.00	200.00

MINTMARK: NR

Obv. leg: FERDND VII...., bust of Charles IV.
Rev: Arms, order chain.

C#	Date	Mintage	Fine	VF	XF
81	1808 JF	—	125.00	175.00	300.00
	1809 JF	—	90.00	125.00	225.00
	1810 JF	—	75.00	120.00	200.00
	1811 JJ	—	125.00	175.00	300.00
	1812 JF	—	75.00	120.00	180.00
	1813 JF	—	75.00	120.00	180.00
	1814 JF	—	75.00	120.00	180.00
	1815 JF	—	75.00	120.00	180.00
	1816 JF	—	75.00	120.00	180.00
	1817 JF	—	75.00	120.00	180.00
	1818 JF	—	75.00	120.00	180.00
	1819 JF	—	75.00	120.00	180.00
	1820 JF	—	90.00	125.00	200.00

MINTMARK: P

C#	Date	Mintage	Fine	VF	XF
81a	1808 JF	—	75.00	120.00	180.00
	1809 JF	—	75.00	120.00	180.00
	1810 JF	—	75.00	120.00	180.00
	1812 JF	—	75.00	120.00	180.00
	1813 JF	—	75.00	120.00	180.00
	1814 JF	—	75.00	120.00	180.00
	1816 FM	—	75.00	120.00	180.00
	1816 FR	—	75.00	120.00	180.00
	1816 F	—	75.00	120.00	180.00
	1817 FM	—	75.00	120.00	180.00
	1818 FM	—	75.00	120.00	180.00
	1819 FM	—	75.00	120.00	180.00

2 ESCUDOS

6.7500 gm., .875 GOLD, .1899 oz AGW

MINTMARK: NR

Obv. leg: CAROLS III...., bust of Ferdinand VI.
Rev: Arms, order chain.

C#	Date	Mintage	Fine	VF	XF
22	1760 J	—	225.00	375.00	725.00
	1760 JV	—	200.00	275.00	550.00
	1761 JV	—	150.00	225.00	400.00
	1762 JV	—	150.00	225.00	400.00

MINTMARK: PN

C#	Date	Mintage	Fine	VF	XF
22a	1760 J	—	175.00	225.00	275.00
	1761 J	—	175.00	225.00	275.00
	1762 J	—	200.00	250.00	350.00
	1763 J	—	200.00	250.00	350.00
	1767 J	—	150.00	175.00	225.00
	1768 J	—	150.00	175.00	225.00
	1769 J	—	150.00	175.00	225.00
	1770 J	—	150.00	175.00	225.00
	1771 J	—	175.00	200.00	250.00

MINTMARK: NR

Obv. leg: CAROLUS III...., bust of Charles III. Rev: Arms.

C#	Date	Mintage	Fine	VF	XF
26	1762 JV	—	225.00	325.00	625.00
	1763 JV	—	175.00	250.00	350.00
	1764 JV	—	150.00	200.00	300.00
	1765 JV	—	150.00	200.00	275.00
	1766/65 JV	—	200.00	275.00	475.00
	1766 JV	—	175.00	250.00	350.00
	1767 JV	—	200.00	275.00	525.00
	1768 JV	—	200.00	275.00	475.00
	1769 V	—	250.00	400.00	725.00
	1770 VJ	—	300.00	450.00	750.00
	1771 VJ	—	300.00	450.00	750.00

Obv. leg: CAROL. III...., bust of Charles III.
Rev: Arms, IN UTROQ...AD, order chain.

C#	Date	Mintage	Fine	VF	XF
30	1772 VJ	—	150.00	175.00	225.00
30a	1773 VJ	—	150.00	175.00	225.00
	1774 VJ	—	150.00	175.00	225.00
	1774 JJ	—	175.00	225.00	275.00
	1775 JJ	—	150.00	175.00	225.00
	1776 JJ	—	150.00	175.00	225.00
	1777 JJ	—	150.00	175.00	225.00
	1778 JJ	—	150.00	175.00	225.00
	1779 JJ	—	150.00	175.00	225.00
	1780/79 JJ	—	175.00	225.00	275.00
	1780 JJ	—	150.00	175.00	225.00
	1781 JJ	—	150.00	175.00	225.00
	1782 JJ	—	150.00	175.00	225.00
	1783 JJ	—	150.00	175.00	225.00
	1784 JJ	—	150.00	175.00	225.00
30a	1785 JJ	—	150.00	175.00	225.00
30b	1786 JJ	—	150.00	200.00	225.00
	1787/86 JJ	—	175.00	250.00	350.00
	1787 JJ	—	150.00	175.00	200.00
	1788 JJ	—	150.00	175.00	200.00
	1789 JJ	—	150.00	200.00	225.00

MINTMARK: P

C#	Date	Mintage	Fine	VF	XF
30c	1772 JS	—	175.00	225.00	275.00
30d	1773 JS	—	200.00	250.00	325.00
	1774 JS	—	175.00	225.00	275.00
	1775 JS	—	175.00	225.00	275.00
	1776 SF	—	175.00	225.00	275.00
	1777 SF	—	175.00	225.00	275.00
	1778 SF	—	175.00	225.00	275.00
	1779 SF	—	175.00	225.00	275.00
	1780 SF	—	175.00	225.00	275.00
	1781 SF	—	225.00	250.00	300.00
	1782 SF	—	175.00	225.00	275.00
	1783 SF	—	175.00	225.00	275.00
	1784 SF	—	175.00	225.00	275.00
	1785 SF	—	175.00	225.00	275.00
30c	30e	175.00	225.00	275.00	185.00
	1787 SF	—	175.00	225.00	275.00
	1788 SF	—	175.00	225.00	275.00
	1789 SF	—	450.00	600.00	1000.

MINTMARK: NR

Obv. leg: CAROL IV...., bust of Charles III.
Rev: Arms, IN UTROQ...AD, order chain.

C#	Date	Mintage	Fine	VF	XF
52	1789 JJ	—	200.00	250.00	300.00
	1790 JJ	—	200.00	275.00	350.00
	1791 JJ	—	200.00	275.00	350.00

MINTMARK: P

C#	Date	Mintage	Fine	VF	XF
52a	1789 SF	—	225.00	275.00	350.00
	1790 SF	—	175.00	225.00	275.00
	1791 SF	—	225.00	275.00	350.00

MINTMARK: NR

Obv. leg: CAROL IIII...., bust of Charles III.

C#	Date	Mintage	Fine	VF	XF
A52	1790 JJ	—	225.00	275.00	350.00
	1791 JJ	—	175.00	225.00	275.00

MINTMARK: P

Similar to C#52a.

C#	Date	Mintage	Fine	VF	XF
A52a	1791 SF	—	225.00	275.00	350.00

MINTMARK: NR

Similar to C#A52.

C#	Date	Mintage	Fine	VF	XF
56	1792 JJ	—	150.00	175.00	235.00
	1793 JJ	—	225.00	275.00	375.00
	1794 JJ	—	175.00	200.00	250.00
	1795 JJ	—	150.00	175.00	225.00
	1796 JJ	—	275.00	325.00	450.00
	1797 JJ	—	175.00	200.00	250.00
	1798 JJ	—	175.00	200.00	250.00
	1799 JJ	—	150.00	175.00	225.00
	1800 JJ	—	225.00	275.00	375.00
	1801 JJ	—	175.00	200.00	250.00
	1803 JJ	—	200.00	225.00	250.00
	1804 JJ	—	225.00	250.00	350.00
	1805 JJ	—	150.00	175.00	225.00
	1806 JJ	—	325.00	375.00	550.00
	1807 JJ	—	150.00	175.00	225.00
	1808 JJ	—	175.00	200.00	250.00

MINTMARK: P

C#	Date	Mintage	Fine	VF	XF
56a	1793 JF	—	150.00	175.00	225.00
	1795 JF	—	350.00	475.00	625.00
	1796 JF	—	150.00	175.00	225.00
	1796 SF	—	150.00	175.00	225.00
	1797 SF	—	150.00	175.00	225.00
	1798 JF	—	175.00	200.00	300.00
	1799 JF	—	150.00	175.00	225.00
	1802 JF	—	150.00	175.00	225.00

C#	Date	Mintage	Fine	VF	XF
56a	1804 JF	—	175.00	200.00	250.00
	1804 SF	—	225.00	275.00	375.00
	1805 JT	—	325.00	400.00	650.00

MINTMARK: NR

Obv. leg: FERDND VII...., bust of Charles IV.
Rev: Arms, order chain.

C#	Date	Mintage	Fine	VF	XF
82	1808 JF	—	225.00	275.00	400.00
	1809 JJ	—	175.00	200.00	350.00
	1810 JF	—	275.00	325.00	550.00
	1811 JF	—	250.00	300.00	525.00

4 ESCUDOS

13.5000 gm., .875 GOLD, .3798 oz AGW

MINTMARK: NR

Obv. leg: CAROLS III...., bust of Ferdinand VI.

C#	Date	Mintage	Fine	VF	XF
23	1760	—	1500.	2500.	3500.

MINTMARK: PN

C#	Date	Mintage	Fine	VF	XF
23a	1760 J	—	500.00	850.00	1500.
	1761 J	—	400.00	700.00	1250.
	1762 J	—	350.00	650.00	1250.

MINTMARK: NR

Obv. leg: CAROLS III...., bust of Charles III.
Rev: Arms, order chain.

C#	Date	Mintage	Fine	VF	XF
27	1769 VJ	—	400.00	700.00	1200.
	1770 VJ	—	500.00	850.00	1500.
	1771 VJ	—	500.00	850.00	1500.

Obv. leg: CAROL III...., bust of Charles III.
Rev: IN UTROQ...DEO., arms, order chain.

C#	Date	Mintage	Fine	VF	XF
31	1775 JJ	—	375.00	575.00	1100.
	1776 JJ	—	350.00	500.00	1000.
	1777 JJ	—	375.00	575.00	1100.
	1778 JJ	—	375.00	575.00	1100.
	1779 JJ	—	375.00	575.00	1100.
	1787 JJ	—	450.00	650.00	1250.

MINTMARK: P

Rev. leg: IN UTROQ...A.D.

C#	Date	Mintage	Fine	VF	XF
31a	1769 J	—	275.00	425.00	850.00
31b	1773 JS	—	300.00	425.00	850.00
	1776 SF	—	350.00	500.00	1000.
	1777 SF	—	300.00	425.00	850.00
	1778 SF	—	350.00	500.00	1000.
	1779 SF	—	350.00	500.00	1000.
	1780 SF	—	350.00	500.00	1000.
	1782 SF	—	300.00	375.00	700.00
	1783 SF	—	350.00	500.00	1000.
31c	1786 SF	—	350.00	500.00	1000.
	1788 SF	—	525.00	850.00	1500.

MINTMARK: NR

Obv. leg: CAROL IV...., bust of Charles III.
Rev: Arms, order chain.

C#	Date	Mintage	Fine	VF	XF
53	1789 JJ	—	450.00	650.00	1200.
	1790 JJ	—	875.00	1200.	1500.

MINTMARK: P

C#	Date	Mintage	Fine	VF	XF
53a	1790 SF	—	350.00	500.00	1000.

MINTMARK: NR

Obv. leg: CAROL IIII...., bust of Charles IV.

C#	Date	Mintage	Fine	VF	XF
57	1792 JJ	—	350.00	450.00	900.00
	1793 JJ	—	350.00	450.00	900.00
	1794 JJ	—	425.00	500.00	1000.
	1797 JJ	—	350.00	425.00	850.00
	1798 JJ	—	425.00	525.00	1050.
	1799 JJ	—	350.00	450.00	900.00
	1801 JJ	—	350.00	425.00	850.00
	1803 JJ	—	350.00	425.00	850.00
	1804 JJ	—	350.00	500.00	1000.
	1805 JJ	—	350.00	450.00	900.00
	1806 JJ	—	350.00	450.00	900.00
	1807 JJ	—	500.00	750.00	1250.

MINTMARK: P

Obv. leg: CAROL IIII...., bust of Charles IV.
Rev: Crowned arms in order chain.

C#	Date	Mintage	Fine	VF	XF
57a	1792 JF	—	300.00	350.00	700.00
	1793 JF	—	300.00	350.00	700.00
	1796 JF	—	300.00	500.00	1000.
	1797 JF	—	375.00	500.00	1000.
	1798 JF	—	375.00	500.00	1000.
	1801 JF	—	450.00	525.00	1050.
	1802 JF	—	375.00	500.00	1000.
	1807 SF	—	800.00	1100.	1600.
	1808 JF	—	1000.	1400.	2000.

MINTMARK: NR

Obv. leg: FERDND VII...., bust of Charles IV.
Rev: Arms, order chain.

C#	Date	Mintage	Fine	VF	XF
83	1818 JF	—	450.00	650.00	1200.
	1819 JF	—	450.00	650.00	1200.

8 ESCUDOS

27.0000 gm., .875 GOLD, .7596 oz AGW

MINTMARK: NR

Obv. leg: CAROLS III...., bust of Ferdinand VI.
Rev: Arms, order chain.

C#	Date	Mintage	Fine	VF	XF
24	1760 JV	—	750.00	1250.	2750.
	1761 JV	—	750.00	1250.	2750.
	1762 JV	—	600.00	1000.	2250.

MINTMARK: PN

C#	Date	Mintage	Fine	VF	XF
24a	1760 J	—	600.00	1000.	2250.
	1761 J	—	750.00	1250.	2750.
	1762 J	—	750.00	1250.	2750.
	1763 J	—	750.00	1250.	2750.
	1767 J	—	750.00	1250.	2750.
	1768 J	—	600.00	1000.	2250.
	1769 J	—	600.00	1000.	2250.
	1770 J	—	600.00	1000.	2250.
	1771 J	—	600.00	1000.	2250.

MINTMARK: NR

Obv. leg: CAROLUS III...., bust of Charles III.
Rev: IN UTROQ. Felix arms, order chain.

C#	Date	Mintage	Fine	VF	XF
28	1762 JV	—	800.00	1200.	2500.
	1763 JV	—	750.00	1000.	2250.
	1764 JV	—	750.00	1100.	2250.
	1765 JV	—	800.00	1500.	2500.
	1766 JV	—	1000.	1600.	2800.
	1767 JV	—	750.00	1000.	2250.
	1768 JV	—	800.00	1200.	2500.
	1769 JV	—	900.00	1300.	2700.
	1769 V	—	1000.	2000.	3400.
	1770 VJ	—	750.00	1000.	2250.
	1771 VJ	—	750.00	1000.	2250.

Obv. leg: CAROL III...., bust of Charles III.

C#	Date	Mintage	Fine	VF	XF
32	1772 VJ	—	550.00	750.00	1250.
	1773 VJ	—	550.00	750.00	1250.
	1774 VJ	—	550.00	750.00	1250.
	1774 JJ	—	1500.	3500.	5000.
	1775 JJ	—	550.00	750.00	1250.
	1776 JJ	—	550.00	750.00	1250.
	1777 JJ	—	550.00	750.00	1250.
	1778 JJ	—	550.00	750.00	1250.
	1779 JJ	—	550.00	750.00	1250.
	1780 JJ	—	550.00	750.00	1250.
	1781 JJ	—	550.00	750.00	1250.
	1782 JJ	—	550.00	750.00	1250.
	1783 JJ	—	550.00	750.00	1250.
	1784 JJ	—	550.00	750.00	1250.
	1785 JJ	—	550.00	750.00	1250.
32a	1786 JJ	—	550.00	750.00	1250.
	1787 JJ	—	550.00	750.00	1250.
	1788 JJ	—	550.00	750.00	1250.
	1789 JJ	—	550.00	750.00	1250.

.900 GOLD

MINTMARK: P

C#	Date	Mintage	Fine	VF	XF
32b	1772 JS	—	550.00	750.00	1250.
	1773 JS	—	550.00	750.00	1250.
	1774 JS	—	550.00	750.00	1250.

C#	Date	Mintage	Fine	VF	XF
32b	1775 JS	—	550.00	750.00	1250.
	1776 JS	—	550.00	750.00	1250.
	1776 SF	—	625.00	850.00	1500.
	1777 SF	—	575.00	750.00	1250.
	1778 SF	—	575.00	750.00	1250.
	1779 SF	—	575.00	750.00	1250.
	1780 SF	—	575.00	750.00	1250.
	1781 SF	—	575.00	750.00	1250.
	1782 SF	—	575.00	750.00	1250.
	1783 SF	—	575.00	750.00	1250.
	1784 SF	—	575.00	750.00	1250.
	1785 SF	—	575.00	750.00	1250.
32c	1786 SF	—	575.00	750.00	1250.
	1787 SF	—	575.00	750.00	1250.
	1788 SF	—	575.00	750.00	1250.
	1789 SF	—	625.00	1000.	1750.

MINTMARK: NR

Obv. leg: CAROL IV...., bust of Charles III.
Rev: Similar to C#32.

C#	Date	Mintage	Fine	VF	XF
54	1789 JJ	—	525.00	650.00	1000.
	1790 JJ	—	525.00	650.00	1000.
	1791 JJ	—	525.00	650.00	1000.

MINTMARK: P

C#	Date	Mintage	Fine	VF	XF
54a	1789 SF	—	525.00	650.00	1000.
	1790 SF	—	525.00	650.00	1000.
	1791 SF	—	675.00	800.00	1200.

MINTMARK: NR

Obv. leg: CAROL IIII...., bust of Charles IV.
Rev: Similar to C#32.

C#	Date	Mintage	Fine	VF	XF
58	1792 JJ	—	525.00	650.00	1000.
	1793 JJ	—	525.00	650.00	1000.
	1794 JJ	—	525.00	650.00	1000.
	1795 JJ	—	525.00	650.00	1000.
	1796 JJ	—	525.00	650.00	1000.
	1797 JJ	—	525.00	650.00	1000.
	1798 JJ	—	525.00	650.00	1000.
	1799 JJ	—	525.00	650.00	1000.
	1800 JJ	—	525.00	650.00	1000.
	1801 JJ	—	525.00	650.00	1000.
	1802 JJ	—	525.00	650.00	1000.
	1803 JJ	—	525.00	650.00	1000.
	1804 JJ	—	525.00	650.00	1000.
	1805 JJ	—	525.00	650.00	1000.
	1806 JJ	—	525.00	650.00	1000.
	1807 JJ	—	525.00	650.00	1000.
	1808 JJ	—	525.00	650.00	1000.
	1808 JF	—	3000.	5500.	8000.

MINTMARK: P

Rev: Similar to C#32.

C#	Date	Mintage	Fine	VF	XF
58a	1791 SF	—	675.00	850.00	1300.
	1792 JF	—	550.00	750.00	1200.
	1793 JF	—	550.00	750.00	1200.
	1794 JF	—	550.00	750.00	1200.
	1795 JF	—	550.00	750.00	1200.
	1796 JF	—	550.00	750.00	1200.
	1797 JF	—	550.00	750.00	1200.
	1798 JF	—	550.00	750.00	1200.
	1799 JF	—	550.00	750.00	1200.
	1800 JF	—	550.00	750.00	1200.
	1801 JF	—	550.00	750.00	1200.
	1802 JF	—	550.00	750.00	1200.
	1803 JF	—	550.00	750.00	1200.
	1804 JJ	—	2250.	3250.	4250.

C#	Date	Mintage	Fine	VF	XF
58a	1804 JF	—	550.00	750.00	1200.
	1805 JF	—	1250.	1750.	2750.
	1805 PJ	—	675.00	1000.	1800.
	1806 JF	—	550.00	750.00	1200.
	1807 JF	—	550.00	750.00	1200.
	1808 JF	—	750.00	900.00	1400.

MINTMARK: NR

Obv. leg: FERDND. VII...., bust of Charles IV.

C#	Date	Mintage	Fine	VF	XF
84	1808 JJ	—	850.00	1250.	2250.
	1808 JF	—	900.00	1400.	2000.
	1809 JF	—	550.00	675.00	1100.
	1810 JF	—	550.00	675.00	1100.
	1811 JF	—	550.00	675.00	1100.
	1812 JF	—	550.00	675.00	1100.
	1813/2 JF	—	550.00	675.00	1100.
	1813 JF	—	550.00	675.00	1100.
	1814 JF	—	550.00	675.00	1100.
	1815 JF	—	550.00	675.00	1100.
	1816 JF	—	550.00	675.00	1100.
	1817 JF	—	550.00	675.00	1100.
	1818 JF	—	550.00	675.00	1100.
	1819 JF	—	550.00	675.00	1100.
	1820 JF	—	550.00	675.00	1100.

MINTMARK: P

C#	Date	Mintage	Fine	VF	XF
84a	1808 JF	—	525.00	650.00	1000.
	1809 JF	—	550.00	675.00	1100.
	1810 JF	—	525.00	650.00	1000.
	1811 JF	—	525.00	650.00	1000.
	1812 JF	—	525.00	650.00	1000.
	1813 JF	—	525.00	650.00	1000.
	1814 JF	—	525.00	650.00	1000.
	1815 JF	—	525.00	650.00	1000.
	1815 FR	—	525.00	650.00	1000.
	1816 FM	—	550.00	675.00	1100.
	1816 JF	—	575.00	750.00	1250.
	1816 FR	—	675.00	800.00	1400.
	1816 F	—	550.00	675.00	1100.
	1817 FM	—	525.00	650.00	1000.
	1818 FM	—	525.00	650.00	1000.
	1819 FM	—	525.00	650.00	1000.
84a	1820 FM	—	525.00	650.00	1000.

REPUBLICAN ISSUES

CARTAGENA

A port city on the northern coast of Colombia. It was a very important city in the Spanish colonies and was heavily fortified to ward off British and French privateers. Cartagena was the first major city in Colombia to declare independence from Spain -- November 11, 1811. In 1815, after a four month siege, it again fell to the Spaniards. In the intervening time coins were made at Cartagena for local use.

1/2 REAL

COPPER

C#	Date	Mintage	Good	VG	Fine	VF
91	1812	—	8.50	12.50	20.00	30.00
	1813	—	8.50	12.50	20.00	30.00
	ND	—	6.50	11.00	17.50	26.50

DOS (2) REALES

COPPER

C#	Date	Mintage	Good	VG	Fine	VF
93	1811	—	12.50	22.50	30.00	50.00
	1812	—	9.00	17.50	25.00	40.00
	1813	—	8.50	15.00	20.00	35.00
	1814	—	8.50	15.00	20.00	35.00

CUNDINAMARCA

A province in central Colombia that includes Bogota. The first province to declare independence - July 16, 1813. The province fell to the Spaniards again from 1816 to 1819. After the battle of Boyaca the province was again freed. Coins were made before and after the Spanish occupation and through 1821 when the Great Colombia plan was put into effect.

1/4 REAL

SILVER
Obv: Liberty cap, date. Rev: Pomegranate.

C#	Date	Mintage	Good	VG	Fine	VF
101	1814	—	10.00	25.00	32.50	60.00
	1815	—	12.50	27.50	35.00	70.00

1/2 REAL

SILVER
State of Cundinamarca

C#	Date	Mintage	Good	VG	Fine	VF
102	1814	—	40.00	100.00	150.00	225.00

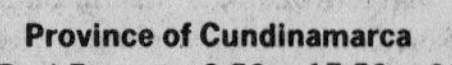

Province of Cundinamarca

C#	Date	Mintage	Good	VG	Fine	VF
111	1821 Ba J.F.	—	8.50	17.50	30.00	55.00

REAL

SILVER
State of Cundinamarca

C#	Date	Mintage	Good	VG	Fine	VF
103	1813 J.F.	—	11.00	20.00	30.00	50.00
	1814 J.F.	—	15.00	27.50	45.00	60.00
	1815 J.F.	—	12.50	25.00	40.00	55.00
	1816 J.F.	—	12.50	25.00	40.00	55.00

Province of Cundinamarca

112	1821 Ba J.F.	—	8.00	15.00	22.50	40.00

2 REALES

SILVER
State of Cundinamarca

104	1815	—	12.50	22.50	35.00	55.00
	1816/15	—	—	—	—	—
	1816	—	12.50	22.50	35.00	55.00

Province of Cundinamarca

113	1820 J.F.	—	12.50	20.00	30.00	45.00
	1821 Ba J.F	—	7.50	12.00	17.50	35.00
	1821 J.F.	—	—	—	Rare	—

8 REALES

SILVER
Province of Cundinamarca

115	1820 J.F.	—	BV	27.50	40.00	75.00
	1820 Ba J.F.	—	BV	30.00	45.00	85.00
	1821 J.F	—	BV	27.50	40.00	75.00
	1821 Ba J.F.	—	BV	30.00	45.00	85.00

Mule, obv. as above C#115. Rev: Like C#108.

A115	1820 J.F.	—	50.00	100.00	200.00	325.00

POPAYAN

MEDIO (1/2) REAL

COPPER
Obv: P/ANO/1813. Rev: Value.

C#	Date	Mintage	VG	Fine	VF	XF
74	1813	—	175.00	275.00	425.00	625.00

2 REALES

COPPER
Obv: NUEVO REYNO DE GRANADA, ANO/1813
Rev: PROVINCIA DE POPAYAN, value.

76	1813	—	30.00	45.00	65.00	100.00

8 REALES

COPPER

77	1813	—	70.00	100.00	150.00	225.00

SANTA MARTA

A city in Colombia on the shores of the Caribbean Sea. Founded in 1525 it is the oldest city in Colombia. Santa Marta was one of the many areas in Colombia that declared independence and practiced the isolation that they interpreted that to mean. The coins made here were made before and after a Spanish occupation of the late teens and copied the Spanish coin types.

1/4 REAL

COPPER

C#	Date	Mintage	Good	VG	Fine	VF
71	1813	—	14.00	17.50	35.00	50.00

72	1820	—	4.50	6.00	10.00	17.50
	1821	—	— Reported, Not Confirmed			

1/2 REAL

COPPER

69	ND (1812-13)	—	—	—	Rare	—

C#	Date	Mintage	Good	VG	Fine	VF
70	1813	—	—	—	Rare	—

2 REALES

SILVER

73	1820	—	—	—	Rare	—

NATIONAL COINAGE

MINTMARKS

A - Paris
B, BA - Santa Fe de Bogota
H - Birmingham
M - Medellin
P, PN - Popayan

REPUBLIC OF NUEVA GRANADA

1813-1821

1/4 REAL

SILVER
Similar to 1/4 Real, C#101

C#	Date	Mintage	VG	Fine	VF
105	1820	—	20.00	40.00	60.00
	1821	—	15.00	35.00	45.00

MINTMARK: BA

105a	1821	—	20.00	40.00	60.00

REAL

SILVER

106	1819 JF	—	20.00	35.00	70.00

2 REALES

SILVER

107	1819 JF	—	17.50	27.50	40.00

Pomegranate divides values

107a	1819 JF	—	50.00	75.00	115.00
	1820 JF	—	55.00	90.00	125.00

8 REALES

SILVER

108	1819 JF	—	50.00	75.00	125.00
	1819/20 JF	—	50.00	75.00	125.00
	1820 JF	—	60.00	100.00	150.00

REPUBLIC OF COLOMBIA

1822-1837

1/4 REAL

SILVER
MINTMARK: BA

121.1	1825 RS	—	—	—	—
	1826 RS	—	45.00	60.00	75.00

The above coin has mintmark below the fraction to the above left of assayer's initials, B.T.S. All following dates have mintmarks above the fraction.

C#	Date	Mintage	VG	Fine	VF
121.3	1827 RS	—	5.00	7.50	15.00
	1828 RS	—	6.00	9.00	17.50
	1829	—	5.50	8.00	15.00
	1833 RS	—	8.00	11.00	20.00
	1834 RS	—	5.50	8.00	11.50
	1836 RS	—	7.50	11.00	14.00

MINTMARK: P

C#	Date	Mintage	VG	Fine	VF
121.2	1826 RU	—	7.50	15.00	25.00
	1833	—	13.50	20.00	30.00
	1834 RU	—	6.00	9.00	13.00
	1836	—	8.00	11.00	15.00

1/2 REAL

SILVER

MINTMARK: BA

Obv: Fasces between crossed cornucopias
Rev: Value in branches

C#	Date	Mintage	VG	Fine	VF
122.1	1833 RS	—	11.00	16.00	25.00
	1834 RS	—	7.50	10.00	30.00
	1835	—	7.50	11.00	20.00

MINTMARK: PN

C#	Date	Mintage	VG	Fine	VF
122.2	1834	—	11.00	16.00	25.00
	1835 RU	—	—	—	—
	1836 RU	—	11.00	16.00	25.00

REAL

SILVER

MINTMARK: BA

C#	Date	Mintage	VG	Fine	VF
123.1	1827 RR	—	4.75	7.00	10.00
	1828 RR	—	4.75	7.00	10.00
	1828 RS	—	4.75	7.00	10.00
	1829 RS	—	—	Rare	—
	1833/29 RS	—	7.00	10.00	17.50
	1833 RS	—	4.00	7.00	10.00
	1834 RS	—	—	—	—
	1835 RS	—	4.00	7.00	10.00
	1836 RS	—	4.00	7.00	10.00

MINTMARK: PN

C#	Date	Mintage	VG	Fine	VF
123.2	1827 RU	—	—	Rare	—
	1828/7 RU	—	4.50	7.50	12.50
	1828 MF	—	4.75	7.00	10.00
	1828 RU	—	4.75	7.00	10.00
	1828 RU/MF	—	—	—	—
	1829 MF	—	4.75	7.00	10.00
	1829 RU	—	4.75	7.00	10.00
	1830 RU	—	4.75	7.00	10.00
	1831 RU	—	4.75	7.00	10.00
	1832 RU	—	4.75	7.00	10.00
	1833 RU	—	4.00	7.00	10.00
	1834	—	7.00	10.00	15.00
	1835	—	Reported, Not Confirmed		

8 REALES

SILVER

C#	Date	Mintage	VG	Fine	VF
126	1834 RS	—	35.00	50.00	110.00
	1835/4 RS	—	—	—	—
	1835 RS	—	35.00	50.00	110.00
	1836 RS	—	30.00	45.00	100.00

PESO

3.3750 gm., .875 GOLD, .0949 oz AGW

BOGOTA MINT

C#	Date	Mintage	Fine	VF	XF
131	1825 JF	—	65.00	100.00	175.00
	1826 JF	—	65.00	100.00	175.00
	1826 PJ	—	75.00	100.00	175.00
	1827 JF	—	75.00	100.00	175.00
	1829 RS	—	75.00	100.00	175.00
	1830 RS	—	75.00	125.00	200.00
	1833 RS	—	75.00	125.00	200.00
	1834 RS	—	75.00	125.00	200.00
	1835 RS	—	75.00	125.00	200.00
	1836 RS	—	75.00	125.00	200.00

ESCUDO

BOGOTA MINT

C#	Date	Mintage	Fine	VF	XF
132	1822 MF	—	—	—	—
	1823 JF	—	75.00	125.00	200.00
	1824 JF	—	75.00	125.00	200.00
	1825 JF	—	75.00	125.00	200.00
	1826 JF	—	75.00	125.00	200.00
	1832 PR	—	75.00	125.00	200.00
	1832 EM	—	—	Rare	—

POPAYAN MINT

C#	Date	Mintage	Fine	VF	XF
132a	1823 FM	—	75.00	125.00	200.00
	1824 FM	—	75.00	125.00	200.00
	1825 FM	—	75.00	125.00	200.00
	1826/5 FM	—	—	—	—
	1826 FM	—	75.00	125.00	200.00
	1826 RU	—	75.00	125.00	200.00
	1827 FM	—	75.00	125.00	200.00
	1827 RU	—	—	Rare	—
	1828 RU	—	75.00	125.00	200.00
	1829 RU	—	75.00	125.00	200.00
	1830 RU	—	75.00	125.00	200.00
	1831 RU	—	75.00	125.00	200.00
	1832 RU	—	75.00	125.00	200.00
	1833/2 RU	—	75.00	125.00	200.00
	1834 RU	—	75.00	125.00	200.00
	1835 RU	—	—	—	—
	1836/4 RU	—	75.00	125.00	200.00
132a	1836 RU	—	75.00	125.00	200.00

2 ESCUDOS

6.7500 gm., .875 GOLD, .1899 oz AGW

BOGOTA MINT

C#	Date	Mintage	Fine	VF	XF
133	1823 JF	—	200.00	250.00	325.00
	1824 JF	—	175.00	225.00	275.00
	1825 JF	—	175.00	225.00	275.00
	1826 JF	—	—	—	—
	1829 RS	—	200.00	250.00	325.00
	1836 RS	—	200.00	250.00	325.00

4 ESCUDOS

13.5000 gm., .875 GOLD, .3798 oz AGW

BOGOTA MINT

C#	Date	Mintage	Fine	VF	XF
134	1826 EJ	—	1200.	1750.	2500.
	1826 JF	—	1000.	1500.	2250.

8 ESCUDOS

27.0000 gm., .875 GOLD, .7596 oz AGW

BOGOTA MINT

C#	Date	Mintage	Fine	VF	XF
135	1822 JF	—	750.00	1200.	1750.
	1823 JF	—	600.00	1000.	1500.
	1824 JF	—	600.00	1000.	1500.
	1825 JF	—	600.00	1000.	1500.
	1826 JF	—	600.00	1000.	1500.
	1827 JF	—	750.00	1200.	1750.
	1827 RR	—	750.00	1200.	1750.
	1828 RR	—	600.00	1000.	1500.
	1829 RS	—	600.00	1000.	1500.
	1830 RS	—	600.00	1000.	1500.
	1831 RS	—	600.00	1000.	1500.
	1832 RS	—	600.00	1000.	1500.
	1833 RS	—	600.00	1000.	1500.
	1834 RS	—	600.00	1000.	1500.
	1835 RS	—	600.00	1000.	1500.
	1836 RS	—	600.00	1000.	1500.
	1837 RS	—	600.00	1000.	1500.

POPAYAN MINT

C#	Date	Mintage	Fine	VF	XF
136	1822 FM	—	750.00	1200.	1750.
	1823 FM	—	600.00	1000.	1500.
	1824 FM	—	600.00	1000.	1500.
	1825 FM	—	600.00	1000.	1500.
	1826 FM	—	600.00	1000.	1500.
	1827 FM	—	750.00	1200.	1750.
	1827 UR	—	750.00	1200.	1750.
	1828 FM	—	750.00	1200.	1750.
	1828 UR	—	600.00	1000.	1500.
	1829 FM	—	—	—	—
	1829 UR	—	600.00	1000.	1500.
	1830 FW	M inverted	—	Rare	—
	1830 UR	—	600.00	1000.	1500.
	1831 UR	—	750.00	1200.	1750.
	1832 UR	—	600.00	1000.	1500.
	1833 UR	—	600.00	1000.	1500.
	1834 UR	—	600.00	1000.	1500.
	1835 UR	—	600.00	1000.	1500.
	1836 UR	—	600.00	1000.	1500.
	1837 UR	—	750.00	1200.	1750.

REPUBLIC OF NUEVA GRANADA

1837-1859

1/4 REAL

SILVER

MINT: BOGOTA

C#	Date	Mintage	VG	Fine	VF
141.1	1837	—	5.50	8.50	11.50
	1838	—	5.50	8.50	11.50
	1839	—	5.00	7.00	10.00
	1840	—	5.50	8.50	11.50
	1841	—	5.00	7.00	10.00
	1842	—	5.00	7.75	11.00
	1843	—	5.00	7.00	10.00
	1844	—	5.00	7.75	11.00
	1845	—	5.00	7.75	11.00
	1846	—	5.00	7.00	10.00
	1847	—	5.50	8.50	11.50
	1848	—	30.00	50.00	100.00

MINT: POPAYAN

C#	Date	Mintage	VG	Fine	VF
141.2	1838	—	8.50	13.50	18.50
	1841	—	5.00	7.00	10.00
	1842	—	5.00	7.00	10.00
	1843	—	5.00	7.00	10.00
	1844	—	5.00	7.00	12.50
	1845	—	5.00	7.00	10.00
	1846	—	5.00	7.75	11.00

1/2 REAL

SILVER

MINT: BOGOTA

C#	Date	Mintage	VG	Fine	VF
142.1	1839 RS	—	4.00	6.00	10.00
	1840 RS	—	5.25	7.50	12.50
	1841	—	Reported, Not Confirmed		
	1842 RS	—	5.00	7.00	10.00
	1843 RS	—	5.00	7.00	10.00
	1844 RS	—	5.00	7.00	10.00
	1845 RS	—	4.00	6.00	10.00
	1846 RS	—	6.00	9.00	13.50
	1847/6 RS	—	4.50	7.00	12.50
	1847 RS	—	4.00	6.00	10.00

MINT: POPAYAN

C#	Date	Mintage	VG	Fine	VF
142.2	1838 RU	—	5.25	7.50	12.50
	1839 RU	—	4.00	6.00	10.00
	1840	—	6.50	9.00	13.50
	1841 RU	—	5.25	7.50	12.50
	1841 VU	—	—	—	—
	1842 UM	—	6.50	9.00	15.00
	1843 UM	—	9.00	13.00	22.50
	1844 UE	—	5.00	7.00	10.00
	1844 UM	—	—	Rare	—
	1845 UE	—	6.00	9.00	15.00
	1846 UE	—	4.00	6.00	10.00
	1846 UM	—	4.00	6.00	10.00
	1848 UE	—	—	Rare	—

REAL

SILVER

MINT: BOGOTA

C#	Date	Mintage	VG	Fine	VF
143.1	1837 RS	—	3.50	5.00	8.00
	1838 RS	—	3.50	5.00	8.00
	1839 RS	—	3.50	5.00	8.00
	1840/39 RS	—	5.00	8.00	13.50
	1841	—	Reported, Not Confirmed		
	1842	—	Reported, Not Confirmed		
	1843 RS	—	3.50	5.00	8.00
	1844 RS	—	3.50	5.00	8.00
	1845 RS	—	3.50	5.00	8.00
	1846 RS	—	5.00	8.00	11.00
	1847	—	Reported, not confirmed		

MINT: POPAYAN

C#	Date	Mintage	VG	Fine	VF
143.2	1839	—	Reported, Not Confirmed		
	1840	—	Reported, Not Confirmed		
	1841	—	Reported, Not Confirmed		
	1844 UM	—	5.00	8.00	11.00
	1845 UM	—	5.00	8.00	11.00
	1846/4	—	5.00	8.00	11.00
	1846	—	5.00	8.00	11.00

2 REALES

SILVER

MINT: BOGOTA

Republica de Nueva Granada

C#	Date	Mintage	VG	Fine	VF
144.1	1839	—	25.00	40.00	60.00
	1840 RS	—	7.00	9.00	17.50
	1841 RS	—	8.50	11.50	22.50
	1842	—	Reported, not confirmed		
	1843 RS	—	8.50	11.00	20.00
	1844 RS	—	6.00	8.50	16.50
	1845 RS	—	12.50	17.50	37.50
	1846 BS	—	35.00	55.00	95.00

MINT: POPAYAN

C#	Date	Mintage	VG	Fine	VF
144.2	1840	—	8.50	11.50	22.50
	1841 VU	—	6.50	9.00	16.50
	1842 VU	—	—	—	—
	1842 UM	—	6.50	9.00	16.50
	1843/2 UM	—	8.50	11.00	20.00
	1843 UM	—	8.50	11.00	20.00
	1844 UM	—	7.00	10.00	18.50

8 REALES

SILVER

C#	Date	Mintage	VG	Fine	VF
145	1837 RS	—	150.00	200.00	275.00
	1838 RS	—	775.00	1000.	1500.

C#	Date	Mintage	VG	Fine	VF
147	1839 RS	—	25.00	30.00	40.00
	1840 RS	—	25.00	30.00	40.00
	1841 RS	—	27.50	32.50	45.00
	1842 RS	—	25.00	30.00	40.00
	1843 RS	—	25.00	30.00	40.00
	1844 RS	—	25.00	30.00	40.00
	1845 RS	—	30.00	35.00	50.00
	1846/4 RS	—	27.50	32.50	45.00
	1846/5 RS	—	27.50	32.50	45.00
	1846 RS	—	25.00	30.00	40.00

FIRST DECIMAL COINAGES

MONETARY SYSTEM

10 Reales = 1 Peso (1847-53)

10 Decimos = 1 Peso (1853-72)

1/2 DECIMO DE REAL

(= 1/20 Real)

COPPER

MINT: HEATON

C#	Date	Mintage	VG	Fine	VF
151	1847	—	3.50	5.25	8.00
	1848	—	7.00	8.50	13.50

DECIMO DE REAL

(= 1/10 Real)

COPPER

MINT: HEATON

C#	Date	Mintage	VG	Fine	VF
152	1847	—	3.00	4.75	7.50
	1847	—	—	Proof	85.00
	1848	—	5.00	7.50	11.50

1/4 REAL

SILVER

BOGOTA MINT

C#	Date	Mintage	VG	Fine	VF
153.1	1850	—	3.00	5.00	7.50
	1851	—	4.50	8.00	11.00

POPAYAN MINT

C#	Date	Mintage	VG	Fine	VF
153.2	1849	—	3.00	5.00	7.50
	1850	—	3.00	5.00	7.50
	1851	—	3.00	5.00	7.50
	1852	—	3.00	5.00	7.50
	1853	—	3.00	5.00	7.50
	1855	—	4.50	6.50	8.50
	1856	—	6.50	9.00	13.00
	1858	—	10.00	20.00	30.00

BOGOTA MINT

Obv: Like C#153. Rev: Caduceus each side '1/4' instead of 3 stars below.

C#	Date	Mintage	VG	Fine	VF
153a	1852	—	15.00	25.00	45.00

MEDIO (1/2) REAL

BOGOTA MINT

C#	Date	Mintage	VG	Fine	VF
154	1850	5.000	10.00	15.00	25.00
	1851	2.500	5.00	7.50	12.50
	1852/1	—	6.50	8.50	15.00
	1852	2.500	5.00	7.50	12.50
	1853	2.500	5.00	7.50	12.50
	1854	—	Reported, Not Confirmed		

MEDIO (1/2) DECIMO

.900 SILVER

C#	Date	Mintage	VG	Fine	VF
161	1853	—	8.50	12.00	17.50
	1854	—	5.00	7.50	12.00
	1855	—	5.00	7.50	12.00
	1856	—	7.50	10.00	15.00
	1857	—	7.50	10.00	15.00
	1858	—	7.50	10.00	15.00

UN (1) REAL

.900 SILVER

BOGOTA MINT

C#	Date	Mintage	Fine	VF	XF
155	1847	—	8.50	12.00	17.50

C#	Date	Mintage	Fine	VF	XF
155a	1851	—	5.00	7.50	12.00
	1852	—	5.00	7.50	12.00
	1853	—	5.00	7.50	12.00

UN (1) DECIMO

.900 SILVER

BOGOTA MINT

C#	Date	Mintage	Fine	VF	XF
162	1853	—	6.00	8.50	15.00
	1854	—	5.00	7.50	12.00
	1855	—	5.00	7.50	12.00
	1856	—	4.50	6.50	10.00
	1857	—	4.50	6.50	10.00
	1858	—	4.50	6.50	10.00

DOS (2) REALES

.900 SILVER

BOGOTA MINT

Obv: Date above shield.

C#	Date	Mintage	VG	Fine	VF
156	1847	—	35.00	65.00	100.00

Obv: Date below shield

C#	Date	Mintage	Fine	VF	XF
156a	1847	—	6.00	8.00	12.00
	1848	—	6.00	8.00	12.00
	1849	—	6.00	8.00	12.00

C#	Date	Mintage	Fine	VF	XF
156b	1850	—	7.50	12.00	15.00
	1851	—	7.50	12.00	15.00
	1852	—	8.50	13.00	18.00
	1853	—	8.50	13.00	18.00

DOS (2) DECIMOS

.900 SILVER

BOGOTA MINT

C#	Date	Mintage	Fine	VF	XF
163	1854	—	10.00	15.00	20.00
	1855	—	5.00	7.50	12.00
	1856/5	—	15.00	25.00	50.00
	1857	—	7.50	12.00	15.00
	1858	—	20.00	25.00	35.00

OCHO (8) REALES

.900 SILVER

C#	Date	Mintage	Fine	VF	XF
158	1847Ba	—	27.50	40.00	75.00

10 REALES

.900 SILVER

C#	Date	Mintage	Fine	VF	XF
159	1847	—	35.00	50.00	75.00
	1848	—	40.00	60.00	80.00
	1849	—	50.00	65.00	85.00

C#	Date	Mintage	Fine	VF	XF
160	1850Ba	—	35.00	50.00	75.00
	1851Ba	—	30.00	45.00	70.00

PESO

1.6875 gm., .875 GOLD, .0474 oz AGW

BOGOTA MINT

C#	Date	Mintage	Fine	VF	XF
148	1837 RS	—	60.00	85.00	135.00
(166)	1838 RS	—	60.00	85.00	135.00
	1839 RS	—	60.00	85.00	135.00
	1840/39 RS	—	60.00	85.00	135.00

C#	Date	Mintage	Fine	VF	XF
(166)	1841 RS	—	75.00	125.00	175.00
	1842 RS	—	60.00	85.00	135.00
	1844 RS	—	50.00	75.00	125.00
	1846 RS	—	50.00	75.00	125.00

.900 SILVER

C#	Date	Mintage	Fine	VF	XF
165	1855	—	27.50	35.00	50.00
	1855/1	—	35.00	45.00	60.00
	1856/5	—	35.00	45.00	60.00
	1856	—	27.50	35.00	50.00
	1857/6	—	35.00	45.00	60.00
	1857	—	27.50	35.00	50.00
	1858/7	—	35.00	45.00	60.00
	1858	—	27.50	35.00	50.00
	1859/6	—	35.00	60.00	85.00

1.6875 gm., .875 GOLD, .0474 oz AGW
Value in wreath

C#	Date	Mintage	Fine	VF	XF
173	1856	—	175.00	275.00	400.00
	1857	—	Reported, not confirmed		
	1858	—	175.00	275.00	400.00

2 PESOS

3.3750 gm., .900 GOLD, .0976 oz AGW

POPAYAN MINT

C#	Date	Mintage	Fine	VF	XF
149	1838 RU	—	75.00	100.00	140.00
(167)	1842 VU	—	75.00	100.00	140.00
	1843 UM	—	75.00	100.00	140.00
	1844 UM	—	75.00	100.00	140.00
	1845 UM	—	75.00	100.00	140.00
	1845 UE	—	75.00	100.00	140.00
	1846 UE	—	75.00	100.00	140.00
	1846 UM	—	75.00	100.00	140.00

BOGOTA MINT

3.2258 gm., .900 GOLD, .0933 oz AGW

C#	Date	Mintage	Fine	VF	XF
170	1848	—	—	Rare	—
	1849	—	200.00	300.00	450.00
	1851	—	200.00	300.00	450.00

MINTMARK: P

Value in wreath

C#	Date	Mintage	Fine	VF	XF
174	1857	—	150.00	225.00	325.00
	1858/4	—	175.00	275.00	375.00
	1858	—	150.00	225.00	325.00

5 PESOS

8.0648 gm., .900 GOLD, .2333 oz AGW

MINTMARK: B

C#	Date	Mintage	Fine	VF	XF
175	1856	—	—	Rare	—
	1857	—	250.00	400.00	650.00
	1858	—	—	Rare	—

10 PESOS

16.4000 gm., .900 GOLD, .4745 oz AGW

BOGOTA MINT

C#	Date	Mintage	Fine	VF	XF
171	1853	—	—	Rare	—
	1854	—	400.00	600.00	800.00
	1855	—	375.00	500.00	700.00
	1856	—	400.00	600.00	800.00
	1857	—	350.00	500.00	700.00

POPAYAN MINT

C#	Date	Mintage	Fine	VF	XF
171.1	1853	—	350.00	500.00	700.00

16.1290 gm., .900 GOLD, .4667 oz AGW

BOGOTA MINT

Rev. leg: DIEZ PESOS

C#	Date	Mintage	Fine	VF	XF
176	1857	—	600.00	800.00	1100.
	1858	—	600.00	800.00	1100.

POPAYAN MINT

C#	Date	Mintage	Fine	VF	XF
176.1	1856	—	350.00	450.00	600.00
	1857	—	350.00	450.00	600.00
	1858	—	350.00	450.00	600.00

16 PESOS

27.0000 gm., .900 GOLD, .7813 oz AGW

BOGOTA MINT

C#	Date	Mintage	Fine	VF	XF
150	1837 RS	—	575.00	700.00	800.00
(168)	1838 RS	—	550.00	650.00	750.00
	1839/8 RS	—	575.00	700.00	800.00
	1839 RS	—	550.00	650.00	750.00
	1840 RS	—	550.00	650.00	750.00
	1841 RS	—	550.00	650.00	750.00
	1842 RS	—	550.00	650.00	750.00
	1843 RS	—	550.00	650.00	750.00
	1844 RS	—	550.00	650.00	750.00
	1845 RS	—	550.00	650.00	750.00
	1846 RS	—	650.00	850.00	1200.
	1847 RS	—	550.00	650.00	750.00
	1848 RS	—	650.00	850.00	1200.
	1849 RS	—	650.00	850.00	1200.

POPAYAN MINT

Obv: Similar to C#150.

C#	Date	Mintage	Fine	VF	XF
150.1	1837 RU	—	550.00	650.00	750.00
(168)	1838 RU	—	550.00	650.00	750.00
	1839 RU	—	550.00	650.00	750.00
	1840 RU	—	650.00	850.00	1200.
	1841 VU	—	550.00	650.00	750.00
	1842 VU	—	550.00	650.00	750.00
	1842 UM	—	550.00	650.00	750.00
	1843 UM	—	550.00	650.00	750.00
	1844 UM	—	550.00	650.00	750.00
	1845 UM	—	550.00	650.00	750.00
	1846 UM	—	650.00	850.00	1200.
	1846 UE	—	650.00	850.00	1200.

BOGOTA MINT

25.8064 gm., .900 GOLD, .7468 oz AGW

C#	Date	Mintage	Fine	VF	XF
172	1848	—	650.00	850.00	1200.
	1849	—	650.00	850.00	1200.
	1850	—	650.00	850.00	1200.
	1851	—	Reported, Not Confirmed		
	1852	—	650.00	850.00	1200.
	1853	—	750.00	1000.	1400.

GRANADINE CONFEDERATION

1859-1862

MONETARY SYSTEM

10 Reales = 1 Peso (1847-86)
10 Decimos = 1 Peso (1847-86)

1/4 REAL

.900 SILVER

POPAYAN MINT

C#	Date	Mintage	VG	Fine	VF
154a	1862	—	15.00	25.00	35.00

SILVER

POPAYAN MINT

C#	Date	Mintage	VG	Fine	VF
180	1859	—	8.50	12.50	17.00
	1860	—	7.00	10.00	15.00
	1861	—	7.00	10.00	15.00
	1862	—	8.00	12.50	17.50

1/4 DECIMO

SILVER

BOGOTA MINT

Rev: Caducei

C#	Date	Mintage	VG	Fine	VF
181	1860	—	20.00	35.00	60.00

Rev: Nine stars

C#	Date	Mintage	VG	Fine	VF
181a	1861	—	8.00	11.50	16.50
	1862	—	8.00	11.50	16.50

POPAYAN MINT

C#	Date	Mintage	VG	Fine	VF
181a.1	1860	—	25.00	45.00	75.00

MEDIO (1/2) DECIMO

.900 SILVER

C#	Date	Mintage	VG	Fine	VF
182	1859	—	22.50	32.50	45.00
	1860	—	20.00	27.50	42.50
	1861	—	20.00	27.50	42.50

UN (1) DECIMO

.900 SILVER

C#	Date	Mintage	Fine	VF	XF
183	1859	—	7.00	11.00	16.00
	1860	—	23.50	32.50	45.00

DOS (2) REALES

.900 SILVER

POPAYAN MINT

C#	Date	Mintage	Fine	VF	XF
184	1862/48	—	12.50	17.50	30.00
	1862	—	12.50	17.50	30.00

NOTE: These are struck from reworked dies of C#156b.

PESO

.900 SILVER

BOGOTA MINT

C#	Date	Mintage	Fine	VF	XF
186	1859	—	25.00	45.00	75.00
	1860	—	25.00	45.00	75.00
	1861	—	45.00	65.00	125.00

POPAYAN MINT

C#	Date	Mintage	Fine	VF	XF
	1862	—	Reported, Not Confirmed		

1.6129 gm., .900 GOLD, .0466 oz AGW

MINTMARK: M

C#	Date	Mintage	Fine	VF	XF
187	1862	—	175.00	250.00	350.00

2 PESOS

3.2258 gm., .900 GOLD, .0933 oz AGW

MINTMARK: P

C#	Date	Mintage	Fine	VF	XF
188	1859	—	150.00	250.00	350.00
	1860	—	175.00	300.00	450.00

5 PESOS

8.0645 gm., .900 GOLD, .2333 oz AGW

MINTMARK: P

C#	Date	Mintage	Fine	VF	XF
190	1859	—	600.00	750.00	1200.

MEDELLIN MINT

C#	Date	Mintage	Fine	VF	XF
189	1862	—	—	—	—

10 PESOS

16.1290 gm., .900 GOLD, .4667 oz AGW

BOGOTA MINT

C#	Date	Mintage	Fine	VF	XF
191	1859	3,481	375.00	525.00	650.00
	1860	9,687	350.00	450.00	550.00
	1861	834 pcs.	400.00	550.00	650.00

POPAYAN MINT

C#	Date	Mintage	Fine	VF	XF
191.1	1858	—	350.00	500.00	600.00
	1859	—	325.00	450.00	550.00
	1860	—	325.00	500.00	600.00
	1861	—	325.00	500.00	600.00
	1862	—	325.00	500.00	600.00

20 PESOS

32.2580 gm., .900 GOLD, .9335 oz AGW

BOGOTA MINT

C#	Date	Mintage	Fine	VF	XF
192	1859	2,002	—	Rare	—

ESTADOS UNIDOS DE NUEVA GRANADA

1861-1862

UN (1) DECIMO

SILVER

C#	Date	Mintage	Fine	VF	XF
195	1861	—	45.00	60.00	90.00

PESO

.900 SILVER

BOGOTA MINT

C#	Date	Mintage	Fine	VF	XF
197	1861	—	170.00	275.00	375.00

ESTADOS UNIDOS DE COLOMBIA

1862-1886

SILVER

1/4 DECIMO

BOGOTA MINT

Y#	Date	Mintage	Fine	VF	XF
1	1863	.048	5.50	7.50	12.50
	1864	.435	4.50	6.50	10.00
	1865	.206	5.00	7.00	10.00
	1866	.267	5.00	7.00	10.00
	1867	.208	5.00	7.00	10.00
	1868	.023	—	Rare	—
	1869	.183	4.50	6.50	10.00
	1870	.092	6.00	8.00	13.50
	1871	.413	4.75	7.00	10.00
	1873 inc w/Y#12		—	Rare	—
	1881 inc w/Y#12		15.00	22.50	42.50

POPAYAN MINT

Y#	Date	Mintage	Fine	VF	XF
1.1	1863	—	4.25	5.50	9.00
	1864	.504	4.25	5.50	9.00
	1865	.291	4.25	5.50	9.00
	1866	.157	4.50	6.50	12.50
	1867	.055	8.00	11.50	17.50
	1868	—	—	—	—
	1869	—	4.25	5.50	9.00
	1870	—	7.00	10.00	15.00
	1871	.155	5.00	6.50	10.00
	1872	.041	5.00	7.00	10.00
	1873	—	4.50	6.50	10.00
	1874	—	6.25	8.00	12.50
	1875	—	4.25	5.50	9.00
	1876	—	7.00	10.00	16.50
	1877	.025	5.00	7.00	10.00
	1878	.025	7.00	10.00	16.50
	1879?	—	—	—	—
	1880	—	4.50	5.00	7.50
	1881	—	4.50	6.50	10.00
	1883?	—	—	—	—

MEDELLIN MINT

Y#	Date	Mintage	Fine	VF	XF
1.2	1874	—	13.50	18.50	27.50

MEDIO (1/2) DECIMO

.900 SILVER

Y#	Date	Mintage	Fine	VF	XF
2	1863	.028	6.00	10.00	15.00
	1864	Inc. Ab.	20.00	40.00	75.00
	1865	.029	6.00	10.00	15.00

.666 SILVER

BOGOTA MINT

Y#	Date	Mintage	Fine	VF	XF
2a	1867	.363	12.00	17.50	35.00

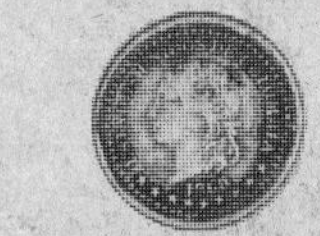

Y#	Date	Mintage	Fine	VF	XF
6	1868	Inc. w/Y#2a	7.50	10.00	15.00
	1869?	.173	—	Rare	—
	1870	.140	12.00	15.00	25.00
	1871	.100	20.00	25.00	35.00
	1872	.119	Reported, Not Confirmed		

MEDELLIN MINT

Y#	Date	Mintage	Fine	VF	XF
6.1	1868	.062	10.00	15.00	25.00
	1869	.026	15.00	25.00	35.00
	1870?	.014	12.00	20.00	30.00
	1873	—	Reported, Not Confirmed		
6.1	1874?	—	10.00	30.00	50.00
	1876	—	—	—	—

POPAYAN MINT

Y#	Date	Mintage	Fine	VF	XF
6.2	1869	—	12.00	17.50	25.00
	1870	.382	12.00	17.50	25.00
	1873	—	Reported, Not Confirmed		
	1874	—	12.00	17.50	25.00
	1875	.573	12.00	17.50	25.00

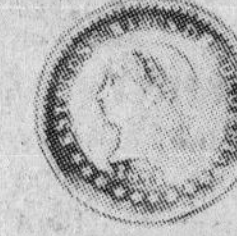

.835 SILVER

MEDELLIN MINT

Y#	Date	Mintage	Fine	VF	XF
6a	1870	Inc. Ab.	20.00	25.00	35.00
	1871	.061	6.00	12.50	17.50
	1872/1	—	17.50	20.00	27.50
	1872	Inc. Ab.	7.50	17.50	22.50
	1873	—	10.00	22.50	30.00
	1874	—	10.00	22.50	30.00

POPAYAN MINT

Y#	Date	Mintage	Fine	VF	XF
6a.1	1875	Inc. Ab.	8.00	12.00	20.00

UN (1) REAL

.900 SILVER

BOGOTA MINT

Y#	Date	Mintage	Fine	VF	XF
3	1863	.096	7.50	10.00	15.00
	1864	.039	10.00	15.00	25.00
	1866	.112	7.50	10.00	15.00

POPAYAN MINT

Y#	Date	Mintage	Fine	VF	XF
3.1	1863	—	7.50	15.00	20.00
	1864	.028	6.50	16.00	22.50

.835 SILVER

BOGOTA MINT

Y#	Date	Mintage	Fine	VF	XF
3a	1866	.606	6.50	10.00	15.00

POPAYAN MINT

Y#	Date	Mintage	Fine	VF	XF
3a.1	1866	.034	25.00	37.50	50.00

BOGOTA MINT

Y#	Date	Mintage	Fine	VF	XF
7	1868	.146	10.00	15.00	20.00
	1869	.082	10.00	15.00	20.00
	1871	.144	8.00	10.00	15.00
	1872	.133	9.00	12.50	17.50

MEDELLIN MINT

AB below bust.

Y#	Date	Mintage	Fine	VF	XF
7.1	1874	—	17.50	27.50	37.50
	1874/3	—	50.00	60.00	75.00

DOS (2) REALES

.835 SILVER

POPAYAN MINT

Y#	Date	Mintage	Fine	VF	XF
A4	1880	3,000	100.00	135.00	200.00

DOS (2) DECIMOS

.900 SILVER

BOGOTA MINT

Y#	Date	Mintage	Fine	VF	XF
4	1865	—	60.00	85.00	125.00

.835 SILVER

Y#	Date	Mintage	Fine	VF	XF
4a	1866	—	10.00	15.00	25.00
	1867	—	10.00	15.00	25.00

POPAYAN MINT

Y#	Date	Mintage	Fine	VF	XF
4a.1	1867	—	20.00	30.00	40.00

0.666/0.835 SILVER

Y#	Date	Mintage	Fine	VF	XF
4b	1867	—	30.00	45.00	75.00

.835 SILVER

BOGOTA MINT

Y#	Date	Mintage	Fine	VF	XF
8	1872	.024	20.00	35.00	65.00

MEDELLIN MINT

Y#	Date	Mintage	Fine	VF	XF
8.1	1870	.015	12.50	17.50	25.00
	1871	.036	15.00	20.00	27.50

Different bust

Y#	Date	Mintage	Fine	VF	XF
8.2	1872	.045	12.50	20.00	30.00
	1873	800 pcs.	—	Rare	—
	1874	—	8.00	15.00	25.00

UN MEDIO (1/2) PESO

.835 SILVER

MEDELLIN MINT

Y#	Date	Mintage	Fine	VF	XF
A9	1868	—	—	Rare	—

CINCO (5) DECIMOS

.835 SILVER

BOGOTA MINT

Y#	Date	Mintage	Fine	VF	XF
9	1868	9,161	60.00	100.00	200.00
	1869	.187	20.00	50.00	100.00
	1870	.206	20.00	45.00	90.00
	1871	.273	25.00	60.00	125.00

MEDELLIN MINT

Y#	Date	Mintage	Fine	VF	XF
9.1	1869	1,054	700.00	1000.	1500.
	1870	Inc. Ab.	Reported, not confirmed		
	1872	.030	75.00	125.00	175.00
	1873	.090	20.00	40.00	80.00

Larger lettering and dates.

Y#	Date	Mintage	Fine	VF	XF
9.2	1873	Inc. Ab.	100.00	150.00	200.00
	1874	.185	10.00	15.00	35.00
	1875/4	.197	15.00	30.00	40.00
	1875	—	Reported, not confirmed		
	1876/5	—	30.00	50.00	90.00
	1876	—	25.00	40.00	60.00

Obv: Modified female head.

Y#	Date	Mintage	Fine	VF	XF
9.3 (11)	1877/4	.168	25.00	50.00	90.00
	1878/4	.318	15.00	30.00	60.00
	1878/5	—	Reported, not confirmed		
	1879/4 pointed tail 9	.379	10.00	25.00	50.00
	1879/4 ball tailed 9	Inc. Ab.	8.00	15.00	30.00
	1880/79/4	.411	80.00	150.00	300.00
	1880	Inc. Ab.	5.00	10.00	20.00
	1881	.379	12.00	20.00	40.00
	1882	—	8.00	15.00	30.00
	1883	1.096	5.00	10.00	20.00
	1884/3	1.429	—	Rare	—
	1884	Inc. Ab.	5.00	10.00	20.00
	1885	—	5.00	10.00	20.00
	1886	—	55.00	90.00	125.00

POPAYAN MINT

Y#	Date	Mintage	Fine	VF	XF
9.4	1869	3,586	250.00	350.00	500.00
	1870/69	1 known	—	Rare	—
	1870	7,774	250.00	350.00	500.00
	1871	—	500.00	750.00	1000.
	1873/69	—	—	Rare	—
	1873	7,743	250.00	350.00	500.00
	1874	.011	300.00	500.00	750.00
	1878	3,158	250.00	350.00	500.00
	1880	.015	Reported, not confirmed		

0.500/0.835 SILVER

MEDELLIN MINT

Y#	Date	Mintage	Fine	VF	XF
9a	1886	—	150.00	200.00	250.00

.500 SILVER
Modified head

Y#	Date	Mintage	Fine	VF	XF
9a.1	1886	—	—	Rare	—

Y#	Date	Mintage	Fine	VF	XF
26	1887	.084	55.00	100.00	150.00
	1888	—	200.00	350.00	450.00
26.1	1888	—	55.00	100.00	150.00
	1889	—	—	Rare	—

PESO

.900 SILVER

BOGOTA MINT

Y#	Date	Mintage	Fine	VF	XF
5	1862	.055	30.00	40.00	60.00
	1863	.018	45.00	55.00	100.00
	1864	.104	25.00	35.00	50.00
	1865	.122	25.00	35.00	50.00
5	1866	.091	25.00	35.00	50.00
	1867	.044	35.00	45.00	65.00
	1868	.017	40.00	50.00	75.00

POPAYAN MINT

Y#	Date	Mintage	Fine	VF	XF
5.1	1863	—	450.00	600.00	750.00

1.6129 gm., .900 GOLD, .0466 oz AGW

MEDELLIN MINT

Y#	Date	Mintage	Fine	VF	XF
A37	1863	.011	500.00	750.00	1000.
	1864	1,072	500.00	750.00	1000.

.900 SILVER

BOGOTA MINT

Y#	Date	Mintage	Fine	VF	XF
10	1868	—	500.00	750.00	1000.
	1869	—	—	Rare	—
	1870	.046	55.00	110.00	135.00
	1871	.040	55.00	110.00	135.00

MEDELLIN MINT

Y#	Date	Mintage	Fine	VF	XF
10.1	1869	3,598	75.00	110.00	135.00
	1870/69	.048	—	—	150.00
	1870	Inc. Ab.	60.00	100.00	125.00
	1871	.055	60.00	100.00	125.00

1.6129 gm., .900 GOLD, .0466 oz AGW
Rev: Condor on shield.

Y#	Date	Mintage	Fine	VF	XF
37	1872/1	.062	55.00	75.00	100.00
	1872	Inc. Ab.	50.00	65.00	85.00
	1873	.018	55.00	75.00	100.00

Rev: Condor

Y#	Date	Mintage	Fine	VF	XF
32	1872	Inc. Ab.	65.00	100.00	125.00
	1873/2	—	—	Rare	—

BOGOTA MINT

Y#	Date	Mintage	Fine	VF	XF
32.1	1872	—	50.00	65.00	100.00
	1873	3,374	50.00	65.00	100.00
	1874	.014	45.00	60.00	85.00
	1875	7,002	45.00	65.00	100.00

2 PESOS

3.2258 gm., .900 GOLD, .0933 oz AGW

MINTMARK: M

Y#	Date	Mintage	Fine	VF	XF
B37	1863	2,996	150.00	225.00	350.00

MEDELLIN MINT

Shield & condor

Y#	Date	Mintage	Fine	VF	XF
38	1871	.066	75.00	100.00	125.00
	1872	.030	75.00	100.00	125.00
	1876	—	85.00	120.00	150.00

5 PESOS

8.0645 gm., .900 GOLD, .2333 oz AGW

MEDELLIN MINT

Colombia & Liberty head

Y#	Date	Mintage	Fine	VF	XF
C37	1862	—	600.00	900.00	1350.
	1863	.029	600.00	900.00	1350.
	1864	8,035	600.00	900.00	1350.
	Estados Unidos de Colombia				
	1863	Inc. Ab.	—	Rare	—

8.0645 gm., .666 GOLD, .1728 oz AGW

Y#	Date	Mintage	Fine	VF	XF
39	1885/inverted 5		550.00	850.00	1250.
	1885/74	—	—	Rare	—

10 PESOS

16.1290 gm., .900 GOLD, .4667 oz AGW

BOGOTA MINT

Y#	Date	Mintage	Fine	VF	XF
40	1862	.011	325.00	375.00	450.00
(33)	1863	.017	325.00	375.00	450.00

MEDELLIN MINT

Y#	Date	Mintage	Fine	VF	XF
40.1	1863	—	—	—	—
(40)	1864	—	—	—	—
	1867	.014	—	—	—

Y#	Date	Mintage	Fine	VF	XF
(40)	1868	.018	325.00	375.00	450.00
	1869	.018	350.00	400.00	500.00
	1870	7,786	350.00	400.00	500.00
	1871	6,018	350.00	400.00	500.00
	1872	.014	—	—	—
	1873	8,623	325.00	375.00	450.00
	1875	—	375.00	425.00	500.00
	1876/5	—	350.00	400.00	500.00
	1876	—	325.00	375.00	450.00
	1886	—	—	Rare	—

POPAYAN MINT

Y#	Date	Mintage	Fine	VF	XF
40.2	1863	—	350.00	400.00	500.00
(35)	1864	.010	325.00	375.00	450.00
	1865	8,727	325.00	375.00	450.00
	1866	.013	325.00	375.00	450.00
	1867	—	—	—	—
	1869	—	350.00	400.00	500.00
	1871	2,617	350.00	400.00	500.00
	1874	—	—	—	—

20 PESOS

32.2580 gm., .900 GOLD, .9335 oz AGW

BOGOTA MINT

Y#	Date	Mintage	Fine	VF	XF
41	1862	—	650.00	750.00	900.00
(34)	1863	—	675.00	800.00	1000.
	1868	—	650.00	750.00	900.00
	1869	—	650.00	750.00	900.00
	1870	.017	650.00	750.00	900.00
	1871	1,641	Reported, Not Confirmed		
	1872	1,471	700.00	800.00	1000.
	1873	2,731	700.00	800.00	1000.
	1874	1,656	700.00	800.00	1000.
	1875	1,696	700.00	800.00	1000.
	1876	2,299	—	—	—

MEDELLIN MINT

NOTE: On 1868, arrows in shield on reverse point between zeros in 0.900. On 1869, arrows point at zeros in 0.900.

Y#	Date	Mintage	Fine	VF	XF
41	1863	—	625.00	725.00	850.00
	1868	7,984	625.00	725.00	850.00
	1869	7,313	625.00	725.00	850.00
	1870	.012	—	—	—
	1871	5,996	—	—	—

Altered design

Y#	Date	Mintage	Fine	VF	XF
41,1	1872	.017	625.00	725.00	850.00
	1873	Inc. Ab.	650.00	750.00	900.00

POPAYAN MINT

Y#	Date	Mintage	Fine	VF	XF
41.2	1862	—	Reported, Not Confirmed		
(36)	1863	—	625.00	725.00	900.00
	1868	—	625.00	725.00	900.00
	1869	—	650.00	750.00	1000.
	1870	8,247	625.00	725.00	900.00
	1871	5,885	—	—	—
	1872	—	625.00	725.00	900.00
	1873	—	625.00	725.00	900.00
	1874/3	5,352	—	—	—
	1874	Inc. Ab.	625.00	725.00	900.00
	1875	5,240	625.00	725.00	900.00
	1877	1,219	—	—	—
	1878	2,873	650.00	750.00	1000.

MODERN DECIMAL SYSTEM

100 Centavos = 1 Peso

1-1/4 CENTAVOS

COPPER-NICKEL

Y#	Date	Mintage	Fine	VF	XF
18	1874	2.400	3.50	5.00	10.00

2-1/2 CENTAVOS

SILVER

Y#	Date	Mintage	Fine	VF	XF
12	1872	.328	6.00	8.00	12.00
	1873	.302	6.00	8.00	12.00
	1874	.075	7.00	10.00	15.00
	1875	.056	7.00	10.00	15.00
	1876	.071	10.00	15.00	25.00

Y#	Date	Mintage	Fine	VF	XF
12	1877	.078	7.00	10.00	15.00
	1878	.347	4.00	6.00	10.00
	1879	.402	4.00	6.00	10.00
	1880	.123	4.00	6.00	10.00
	1881	.123	4.00	6.00	10.00

COPPER-NICKEL, 14mm

Y#	Date	Mintage	VF	XF	Unc
19	1881	24.000	.30	.50	2.00

18mm

Y#	Date	Mintage	VF	XF	Unc
20	1881	4.000	.50	.60	.80

COPPER

Y#	Date	Mintage	VF	XF	Unc
22	1885	—	8.50	15.00	30.00

COPPER-NICKEL

Y#	Date	Mintage	VF	XF	Unc
21	1886	12.000	.40	.50	.80

CINCO (5) CENTAVOS

1.2500 gm., .666 SILVER, .0268 oz ASW

BOGOTA MINT

Y#	Date	Mintage	Fine	VF	XF
A12	1872	—	12.00	20.00	30.00
	1873	.089	8.00	12.00	20.00
	1874	.276	5.00	10.00	15.00

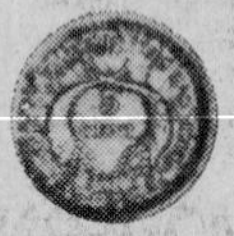

1.2300 gm., .835 SILVER, .0330 oz ASW

MEDELLIN MINT

Y#	Date	Mintage	Fine	VF	XF
13	1874	—	40.00	55.00	75.00

1.2500 gm., .666 SILVER, .0268 oz ASW

BOGOTA MINT

Y#	Date	Mintage	Fine	VF	XF
13a	1875	.077	3.50	6.00	10.00
	1876	.019	10.00	17.50	25.00
	1877	.094	6.00	8.50	12.00
	1878	.190	3.50	6.00	10.00
	1879/8	.177	—	—	—
	1879	Inc. Ab.	3.50	6.00	10.00
	1880	.044	10.00	17.50	25.00
	1881	.219	—	—	—
	1882	—	3.50	6.00	10.00
	1883/2	.412	3.50	6.00	10.00
	1883	Inc. Ab.	3.50	6.00	10.00
	1884	.220	6.00	8.50	12.00
	1885	—	6.00	8.50	12.00

MEDELLIN MINT

Y#	Date	Mintage	Fine	VF	XF
13a.1	1875	—	6.00	8.50	12.00
	1884	—	Reported, Not Confirmed		

10 CENTAVOS

2.5000 gm., .835 SILVER, .0671 oz ASW

BOGOTA MINT

Y#	Date	Mintage	Fine	VF	XF
B12	1872	Inc. Ab.	10.00	15.00	25.00
	1873	.043	7.50	12.50	17.50
	1874	Inc. Bl.	6.00	10.00	15.00

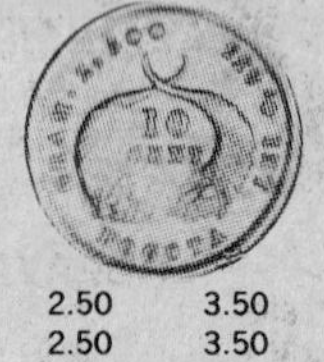

Y#	Date	Mintage	Fine	VF	XF
14	1874	.179	2.50	3.50	5.00
	1875	.265	2.50	3.50	5.00
	1878	.419	2.50	3.50	5.00
	1879	Inc. Ab.	2.50	3.50	5.00
	1880/79	.134	10.00	15.00	25.00
	1880	Inc. Ab.	10.00	15.00	25.00
	1881	.020	3.00	4.00	6.00
	1882	—	4.00	6.00	10.00
	1883	.202	2.50	3.50	5.00
	1884/3	—	3.50	6.00	15.00
	1884	—	2.50	3.50	5.00
	1885	—	7.50	12.00	20.00

MEDELLIN MINT

Y#	Date	Mintage	Fine	VF	XF
14.1	1885	—	10.00	15.00	25.00

0.835/0.500 SILVER

Y#	Date	Mintage	Fine	VF	XF
—	1885	—	10.00	15.00	25.00

0.500/0.835 SILVER

Y#	Date	Mintage	Fine	VF	XF
—	1885	—	22.50	30.00	42.50

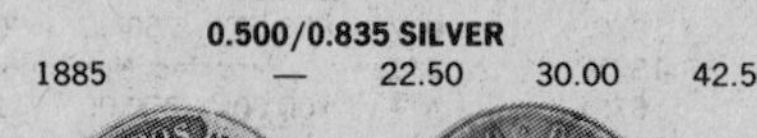

2.5000 gm., .500 SILVER, .0402 oz ASW

Y#	Date	Mintage	Fine	VF	XF
14a	1885	—	22.50	30.00	40.00
	1886	—	22.50	30.00	40.00

20 CENTAVOS

5.0000 gm., .835 SILVER, .1342 oz ASW

MEDELLIN MINT

GRAM 5

Y#	Date	Mintage	Fine	VF	XF
15	1874	—	5.00	7.50	12.50
	1875	—	4.50	6.00	12.00
	1876	—	7.50	12.00	20.00
	1877	—	4.50	6.00	12.00
	1882	—	7.50	12.00	20.00

GRAMOS 5

Y#	Date	Mintage	Fine	VF	XF
15b	1874	—	22.50	32.50	42.50
	1875	—	30.00	37.50	45.00
	1882	—	4.50	6.00	10.00
	1884	—	11.00	16.00	22.50
	1885	—	—	—	—

BOGOTA MINT

Different bust

Y#	Date	Mintage	Fine	VF	XF
15b.1	1882	—	13.50	22.50	32.50
	1882/1	—	7.50	15.00	25.00

Y#	Date	Mintage	Fine	VF	XF
15b.2	1884	—	55.00	70.00	100.00

0.835/0.500 SILVER

MEDELLIN MINT

Y#	Date	Mintage	Fine	VF	XF
15c	1885	—	—	—	—

0.500/0.835 SILVER

Y#	Date	Mintage	Fine	VF	XF
15a	1886Mn	—	50.00	70.00	100.00

50 CENTAVOS

12.5000 gm., .835 SILVER, .3356 oz ASW

BOGOTA MINT

'50' in numerals

Obv. and rev: Small letters.

Y#	Date	Mintage	Fine	VF	XF
16	1872	.027	40.00	75.00	125.00
	1873	.101	20.00	40.00	75.00

Obv. and rev: Large letters.

Y#	Date	Mintage	Fine	VF	XF
16.1	1874	.280	11.00	15.00	35.00
	1875	—	—	Rare	—

CINCUENTA for 50

Y#	Date	Mintage	Fine	VF	XF
17	1874	Inc. Ab.	12.00	15.00	20.00
	1875	.621	11.00	20.00	40.00
	1876	.259	12.50	25.00	50.00
	1877	.133	12.50	20.00	40.00
	1878	.264	11.00	15.00	25.00
	1879	.307	11.00	15.00	20.00
	1880	1.249	11.00	15.00	18.00
	1881	1.086	11.00	15.00	18.00
	1882/1	—	—	Rare	—
	1882	—	11.00	15.00	20.00
	1883	.221	11.00	15.00	20.00
	1884	.993	11.00	15.00	20.00
	1885	—	25.00	50.00	85.00
	1886	—	Reported, not confirmed		

MEDELLIN MINT

Y#	Date	Mintage	Fine	VF	XF
17.1	1886 N	—	Reported, not confirmed		

POPAYAN MINT

Y#	Date	Mintage	VG	Fine	VF
17.2	1880	—	250.00	400.00	600.00

12.5000 gm., .500 SILVER, .2009 oz asw

BOGOTA MINT

Y#	Date	Mintage	Fine	VF	XF
17a	1885	—	10.00	15.00	25.00
	1886	—	15.00	25.00	50.00

MEDELLIN MINT

Y#	Date	Mintage	Fine	VF	XF
17a.1	1886	—	—	Rare	—

REPUBLIC

CENTAVO

COPPER-NICKEL

Y#	Date	Mintage	VF	XF	Unc
57	1918	.430	12.00	20.00	30.00
	1919	Inc. Ab.	25.00	35.00	45.00
	1920	7.540	.30	.50	.85
	1921	12.460	.30	.50	.85
	1933	3.000	.40	.70	1.10
	1935	5.000	.30	.50	.85
	1936	1.540	.40	.70	1.10
	1938	7.920	.30	.40	.60
	1941B	—	.55	.75	1.10
	1946B	—	.55	.75	1.10
	1947B	1.835	.55	.75	1.10
	1948B	1.139	.55	.75	1.10

NICKEL-CLAD STEEL

Y#	Date	Mintage	VF	XF	Unc
57a	1952	8.697	.30	.40	.55
(58)	1952B	Inc. Ab.	.10	.15	.25
	1954B	5.080	.10	.15	.25
	1956	1.315	.10	.15	.30
	1957	.900	.10	.15	.30
	1958	1.596	.10	.15	.25

BRONZE

Y#	Date	Mintage	VF	XF	Unc
61	1942	—	.15	.40	.85
	1942B	—	.15	.40	.85
	1943B	—	.15	.40	.85
	1944B	—	.15	.25	.50
	1945B?	—	.15	.40	.85
	1948B	.585	.30	.90	1.60
	1949B	4.255	.15	.60	1.10
	1950B	5.827	.15	.60	1.10
	1951B	Inc. Ab.	.30	.90	1.60
	1957	2.500	.10	.20	.40
	1958	.590	.25	.50	.85
	1959	2.677	.10	.15	.25
	1960	2.500	.10	.15	.25
	1961	3.673	.10	.15	.25
	1962	4.065	.10	.20	.35
61	1963	1.845	.10	.20	.35
	1964	3.165	.10	.20	.30
	1965 lg. dt.	5.510	.10	.15	.25
	1965 sm. dt	Inc. Ab.	.10	.15	.25
	1966	3.910	.10	.20	.30

COPPER-CLAD STEEL

Y#	Date	Mintage	VF	XF	Unc
61a	1967	5.730	.10	.15	.25
	1968	7.390	.10	.15	.25
	1969	6.870	.10	.15	.25
	1970	3.839	.10	.15	.25
	1971	3.020	.10	.15	.25
	1972	3.100	.10	.15	.25
	1977	—	—	.10	.20
	1974	2.000	—	.10	.20
	1975	1.000	—	.10	.20
	1976	1.000	—	.10	.20
	1977	—	—	.10	.20
	1978	—	—	.10	.20

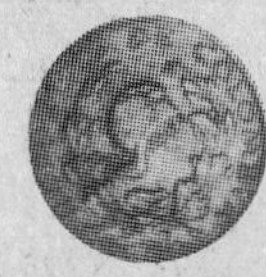

BRONZE
Uprising Sesquicentennial Commemorative

Y#	Date	Mintage	VF	XF	Unc
73	1960	.500	1.75	4.25	8.00

NOTE: This and the other issues in the uprising commemorative series offer the usual design of the period with the dates 1810-1960 added at the bottom of the obverse.

DOS, II (2) CENTAVOS

COPPER-NICKEL
Republica De Colombia

Y#	Date	Mintage	VF	XF	Unc
59	1918	.930	2.75	8.50	30.00
	1919	Inc. Ab.	10.00	20.00	60.00
	1920	3.855	2.25	7.50	13.50
	1921	11.145	.65	1.35	2.25
	1933	3.500	.85	2.00	2.75
	1935	2.500	.85	1.50	2.50
	1938	3.872	.60	.80	1.10
	1941B	—	.70	1.35	2.00
	1942B	—	.70	1.35	2.00
	1946B	—	.70	.85	1.10
	1947B	59.455	.60	.80	1.10

BRONZE

Y#	Date	Mintage	VF	XF	Unc
62	1948B	2.648	1.00	4.25	7.50
	1949B	1.278	1.00	4.25	7.50
	1950B	2.285	1.00	4.25	7.50

ALUMINUM-BRONZE
Divided legend

Y#	Date	Mintage	VF	XF	Unc
67	1952B	5.038	.10	.15	.25
	1965	1.830	.10	.15	.25

Continuous legend

Y#	Date	Mintage	VF	XF	Unc
67.1	1955	2.513	.10	.15	.30
	1955B	Inc. Ab.	.10	.15	.30
	1959	4.609	.10	.15	.25
	1961	—	.10	.15	.30
	1963	.520	.15	.25	.35
	1964	3.350	.10	.15	.30
67.1	1965	—	.10	.15	.30

Uprising Sesquicentennial Commemorative

Y#	Date	Mintage	VF	XF	Unc
74	1960	.250	1.50	2.00	2.75

2-1/2 CENTAVOS

COPPER-NICKEL

Y#	Date	Mintage	VF	XF	Unc
23	1900	.400	85.00	120.00	150.00
	1902	.400	85.00	120.00	150.00

CINCO (5) CENTAVOS

COPPER-NICKEL

Y#	Date	Mintage	VF	XF	Unc
24	1886	1.000	.35	.65	1.00
	1888	—	.35	.65	1.00

Rev: Larger 5

Y#	Date	Mintage	VF	XF	Unc
25	1886	Inc. Ab.	.40	.50	.75
	1902	.400	60.00	100.00	135.00

1.2500 gm., .666 SILVER, .0286 oz ASW

Y#	Date	Mintage	VF	XF	Unc
45	1902	.400	2.00	3.00	6.00

COPPER-NICKEL

Y#	Date	Mintage	VF	XF	Unc
60	1918	—	2.75	4.50	6.50
	1919	1.926	1.75	3.25	5.00
	1920	2.062	1.50	2.25	4.50
	1921	—	2.75	4.50	6.50
	1922	—	2.75	4.50	6.50
	1924	.120	8.50	11.50	15.00
	1933P	2.000	1.50	2.50	3.50
	1933B	—	1.50	2.50	3.50
	1935	11.616	1.50	2.00	3.00
	1936	—	3.50	6.50	8.50
	1938B	2.000	1.35	2.00	3.00
	1938	3.867	1.35	2.00	3.00
	1939/5	—	1.50	2.25	3.50
	1939	—	1.35	2.00	3.00
	1941 lg. date	—	6.50	9.00	12.50
	1941B	—	2.50	3.50	5.00
	1946 sm. date	40.000	.60	.85	1.25
	1946 lg. date	3.330	6.50	9.00	12.50
	1949B	2.750	.60	.80	1.25
	1949	—	.60	.80	1.25
	1950B	3.611	.60	.80	1.25

BRONZE

Y#	Date	Mintage	VF	XF	Unc
63	1942	—	.75	2.00	3.50
	1942B	—	.60	.85	1.25
	1943	—	.35	.60	1.00
	1943B	—	.60	.85	1.50
	1944	—	.60	.85	1.50
	1944B	—	.60	.85	1.50
	1945/4	—	.75	1.25	2.00
	1945B	—	.60	1.00	1.75
	1946/5	—	1.35	1.75	2.50
	1946	—	1.25	1.50	2.00
	1952	—	1.00	2.25	3.50
	1952B	3.985	.40	.50	.75
	1953B	5.180	.25	.40	.80
	1954	—	.25	.40	.80
	1954B	1.159	.10	.20	.40
	1955?	—	.25	.40	.80
	1955B	6.819	.25	.40	.80
	1956	8.772	.25	.40	.80
	1956B	—	.25	.40	.80
	1957	8.912	.25	.40	.80
	1958	15.016	.25	.40	.80
	1959	14.271	.25	.40	.80
	1960	11.716	.10	.20	.40
	1960/1660	Inc. Ab.	.50	.80	1.35
	1961	11.200	.25	.40	.65
	1962	10.928	.10	.20	.35
	1963	15.113	.10	.20	.40
	1964	9.336	.10	.20	.35
	1965	6.460	.10	.20	.40
	1966	7.170	.10	.20	.40

COPPER-CLAD STEEL

Y#	Date	Mintage	VF	XF	Unc
63a	1967	10.280	—	.10	.25
	1968	8.900	—	.10	.25
	1969	17.800	—	.10	.25
	1970	14.842	—	.10	.25
	1971	10.730	—	.10	.25
	1972	10.170	—	.10	.25
	1973	10.525	—	.10	.25
	1974	5.310	—	.10	.20
	1975	5.631	—	.10	.20
	1976	3.009	—	.10	.20
	1978	—	—	.10	.20

BRONZE
Uprising Sesquicentennial Commemorative

Y#	Date	Mintage	VF	XF	Unc
A74	1960	.400	3.00	4.50	6.00

10 CENTAVOS

2.5000 gm., .666 SILVER, .0536 oz ASW

Y#	Date	Mintage	VF	XF	Unc
30	1897 (Brussels)	2.642	4.50	5.50	7.50

2.5000 gm., .900 SILVER, .0723 oz ASW

Y#	Date	Mintage	VF	XF	Unc
47	1911	6.065	2.25	3.00	6.00
	1913	8.305	2.25	3.00	6.00
	1914	3.840	2.25	3.00	6.00
	1920	2.149	5.50	7.50	11.00
	1934B	.140	4.00	6.00	8.50
	1934	Inc. Ab.	25.00	35.00	55.00
	1937	—	5.50	10.00	15.00
	1938	2.055	3.00	4.00	5.00
	1940	—	3.50	4.50	6.50
	1941	—	2.25	3.00	5.00
47	1942	—	12.00	20.00	30.00
	1942B	—	3.00	4.00	5.00

2.5000 gm., .500 SILVER, .0401 oz ASW

Y#	Date	Mintage	VF	XF	Unc
64	1945B	—	1.25	2.00	4.00
	1946/5B	—	—	—	—
	1946B	—	1.75	2.75	4.00
	1947/5B at bottom	7.366	1.75	2.75	4.00
	1947/6B at bottom	Inc. Ab.	1.75	2.75	4.00
	1947B at bottom	Inc. Ab.	1.75	2.75	4.00
	1947B at top	Inc. Ab.	1.75	2.75	4.00
	1948B	3.629	1.75	2.75	4.00
	1949B	5.923	1.75	2.75	4.00
	1950B	6.783	1.75	2.75	4.00
	1951B	5.185	1.75	2.75	4.00
	1952B	1.060	2.00	3.50	12.50

COPPER-NICKEL 18mm

Y#	Date	Mintage	VF	XF	Unc
68	1952B	6.035	.25	.60	1.75
	1953B	6.985	.25	.60	1.75

18.5mm

Y#	Date	Mintage	VF	XF	Unc
68.1	1954B	13.006	.20	.30	1.00
	1955B	9.968	.20	.30	1.00
	1956 small date	36.010	.20	.30	.50
	1958	41.695	.20	.30	1.00
	1959	36.653	.20	.30	.50
	1960	32.290	.20	.30	1.00
	1961	17.780	.20	.30	1.00
	1962	8.930	.20	.30	1.00
	1963	37.540	.20	.30	.60
	1964 large date	61.672	.20	.30	.50
	1965	12.800	.20	.30	.50
	1966 large date	23.540	.20	.30	.50
	1967	6.390	.15	.25	.50

Uprising Sesquicentennial Commemorative

Y#	Date	Mintage	VF	XF	Unc
75	1960	1.000	1.50	2.50	4.50

NICKEL-CLAD STEEL

Y#	Date	Mintage	VF	XF	Unc
64a	1967	26.980	.10	.15	.25
	1968	23.670	.10	.15	.25
	1969	29.450	.10	.15	.25

Obv. leg: Divided after REPUBLICA DE

Y#	Date	Mintage	VF	XF	Unc
82	1969	Inc. Ab.	—	.10	.15
	1970	—	—	.10	.15
	1971	—	.10	.15	.20

Obv. leg: Divided after REPUBLICA

Y#	Date	Mintage	VF	XF	Unc
82.1	1970	38.935	.10	.15	.20
	1971	53.314	.10	.15	.20
	Obv. leg: Continuous				
82.2	1972	58.000	.10	.15	.20
	1973	46.549	.10	.15	.20
	1974	49.740	.10	.15	.20
	1975	46.037	.10	.15	.20
	1976	46.084	.10	.15	.20
	1977	—	.10	.15	.20
	1978	—	.10	.15	.20

20 CENTAVOS

5.0000 gm., .666 SILVER, .1072 oz ASW
Republica de Colombia

Y#	Date	Mintage	VF	XF	Unc
31	1897 (Brussels)	1.441	3.50	5.00	8.50

5.0000 gm., .900 SILVER, .1446 oz ASW

Y#	Date	Mintage	VF	XF	Unc
48	1911	1.206	5.00	6.00	8.50
	1913	1.630	5.00	6.00	8.50
	1914	2.560	5.00	6.00	8.50
	1920	1.242	8.50	12.50	32.50
	1921	.372	8.50	12.50	32.50
	1922	—	12.50	20.00	45.00
	1933B on obv.		5.00	7.50	
		.330	5.00	7.50	11.00
	1933B on rev.	Inc. Ab.	5.00	7.50	11.00
	1933B both sides	Inc. Ab.	5.00	7.50	11.00
	1938	1.410	4.50	6.00	7.50
	1941	—	4.50	6.00	7.50
	1942	—	8.00	12.50	32.50
	1942B	—	4.50	6.00	7.50

5.0000 gm., .500 SILVER, .0803 oz ASW

Y#	Date	Mintage	VF	XF	Unc
65	1945B	—	3.00	3.50	5.00
	1945BB	—	—	—	—
	1946/5B	—	—	—	—
	1946	—	4.00	5.00	6.00
	1946B	—	4.00	5.00	6.00
	1947/5B on wreath	9.708	—	—	—
	1947/5 B in field	9.708	1.75	2.50	4.00
	1947/5B at top	I.A.	2.50	3.50	5.00
	1947B at top	I.A.	2.50	3.50	5.00
	1948/5	1.748	—	Rare	—
	1948/5B	Inc. Ab.	—	—	—
	1948B	Inc. Ab.	2.50	3.50	5.00
	1949B	.403	4.50	13.00	35.00
	1950B	1.899	4.00	13.00	35.00
	1951B	7.498	2.50	3.50	5.00
	1952B	3,887	—	Rare	—

NICKEL-CLAD STEEL

Y#	Date	Mintage	VF	XF	Unc
65a	1967	15.720	.10	.20	.45
	1968	26.680	.10	.20	.45
	1969	22.470	.10	.20	.45

5.0000 gm., .300 SILVER, .0482 oz ASW

Y#	Date	Mintage	VF	XF	Unc
69	1953B	17.819	BV	1.50	3.00

COPPER-NICKEL

Y#	Date	Mintage	VF	XF	Unc
70	1956 small date				
		39.778	.15	.20	.30
	1959	44.779	.15	.20	.30
	1961	10.740	.20	.25	.40
	1963 large date				
		12.035	.10	.20	.40
	1964	29.075	.10	.20	.30
	1965	19.180	.10	.20	.40
	1966	23.060	.10	.20	.30

Uprising Sesquicentennial Commemorative

Y#	Date	Mintage	VF	XF	Unc
76	1960	.500	3.25	5.50	8.00

Gaitan Commemorative

Y#	Date	Mintage	VF	XF	Unc
78	1965	1.000	.10	.20	.45

NICKEL-CLAD STEEL

Obv. leg: Divided after REPUBLICA

Y#	Date	Mintage	VF	XF	Unc
83	1969	Inc/Y#65a	—	.20	.30
	1970	44.358	—	.10	.20

Obv. leg: Divided after REPUBLICA DE

Y#	Date	Mintage	VF	XF	Unc
83.1	1971	77.526	—	.10	.20

Obv. leg: Continuous

Y#	Date	Mintage	VF	XF	Unc
83.2	1971	Inc. Ab.	—	.10	.20
	1971 w/dot between 20 and Centavos				
		Inc. Ab.	—	.10	.20
	1972	41.891	—	.10	.20
	1973	41.440	—	.10	.25
	1974	45.941	—	.10	.20

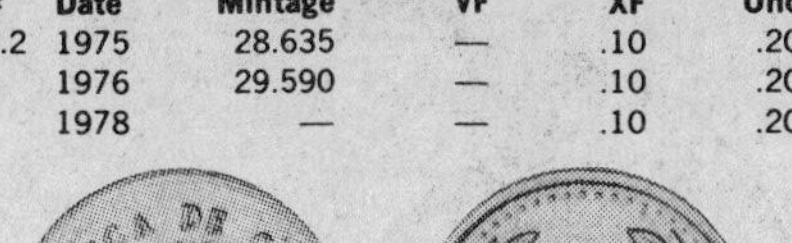

Y#	Date	Mintage	VF	XF	Unc
83.2	1975	28.635	—	.10	.20
	1976	29.590	—	.10	.20
	1978	—	—	.10	.20

Obv: Smaller letters in legend.
Rev: Wreath with larger 20 and CENTAVOS smaller.

Y#	Date	Mintage	VF	XF	Unc
83.3	1979	—	—	.10	.20

25 CENTAVOS

ALUMINUM-BRONZE

Y#	Date	Mintage	VF	XF	Unc
104	1979	—	—	.15	.25

50 CENTAVOS

BOGOTA MINT

Y#	Date	Mintage	Fine	VF	XF
27	1887	1.764	40.00	60.00	90.00
	1888	—	300.00	500.00	750.00
28	1888	—	75.00	150.00	300.00

12.5000 gm., .835 SILVER, .3356 oz ASW

Y#	Date	Mintage	Fine	VF	XF
28a	1889	.130	30.00	60.00	90.00
	1898	—	25.00	40.00	75.00
	1899	—	100.00	200.00	400.00

Incuse lettering on head band

Y#	Date	Mintage	Fine	VF	XF
28a.1	1906	.446	12.00	17.50	22.50
	1907	1.126	15.00	20.00	30.00
	1908	.871	20.00	30.00	40.00
	1908/7	Inc. Ab.	50.00	75.00	125.00

30.4mm

400th Anniversary of Columbus' Discovery of America

Y#	Date	Mintage	VF	XF	Unc
29	1891	25 pcs.	—	Rare	—
	1892	4.826	12.00	17.50	30.00

Reduced size, 29.6mm.

Y#	Date	Mintage	VF	XF	Unc
29.1	1892	Inc. Ab.	12.00	17.50	30.00

Y#	Date	Mintage	VF	XF	Unc
46	1902	.960	15.00	20.00	25.00

12.5000 gm., .900 SILVER, .3617 oz ASW

Sharper featured bust

Y#	Date	Mintage	VF	XF	Unc
49	1912	1.027	12.50	17.50	40.00
	1913	.417	12.50	18.50	50.00
	1914 open top 4				
		.769	12.50	20.00	75.00
	1914 closed top 4				
		Inc. Ab.	12.50	20.00	75.00
	1915	2.232	12.50	17.50	35.00
	1916	1.060	12.50	17.50	40.00
	1917	.099	12.50	17.50	50.00
	1918	.400	12.50	17.50	40.00
	1919	Inc. Ab.	12.50	17.50	40.00
	1921	.300	12.50	17.50	40.00
	1922	—	15.00	25.00	70.00
	1923	.759	20.00	35.00	90.00
	1931	—	75.00	150.00	500.00
	1931B	—	12.50	17.50	25.00
	1932	—	20.00	50.00	100.00
	1932B	1.200	12.50	17.50	25.00
	1932M	1.200	12.50	17.50	25.00
	1933/23B	—	30.00	50.00	100.00
	1933	—	15.00	25.00	100.00
	1933B	.800	12.50	17.50	25.00
	1933M	.800	15.00	25.00	40.00

Rounded feature bust

Y#	Date	Mintage	VF	XF	Unc
49.1	1916	1.300	12.50	17.50	30.00
	1917	.142	15.00	25.00	75.00
	1921	1.000	12.50	17.50	25.00
	1922	3.000	12.50	17.50	30.00
	1934	10.000	12.50	15.00	22.50

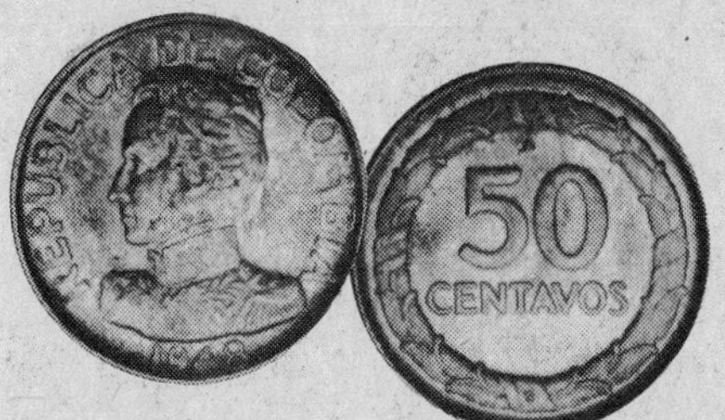

12.5000 gm., .500 SILVER, .2009 oz ASW

Y#	Date	Mintage	VF	XF	Unc
66	1947/3B	1.240	Reported, not confirmed		
	1947/6B	Inc. Ab.	7.50	15.00	50.00
	1947B	Inc. Ab.	15.00	30.00	150.00
	1948/6B	.707	7.50	15.00	50.00
	1948B	Inc. Ab.	15.00	30.00	150.00

COPPER-NICKEL

Y#	Date	Mintage	VF	XF	Unc
71	1958	3.596	.50	.75	1.00
	1959	13.466	.50	.75	1.00
	1960	4.360	.60	.80	1.25
	1961	3.260	.60	.80	1.25
	1962	2.336	.30	.50	.75
	1963	4.098	.30	.50	.75
	1964	9.274	.20	.40	.75
	1965	5.800	.20	.40	.75
	1966	2.820	.30	.50	.75

Uprising Sequicentennial Commemorative

Y#	Date	Mintage	VF	XF	Unc
77	1960	.200	5.00	7.50	15.00

Gaitan Commemorative

Y#	Date	Mintage	VF	XF	Unc
79	1965	.600	.45	.60	.90

NICKEL-CLAD STEEL

Y#	Date	Mintage	VF	XF	Unc
A65	1967	3.460	.25	.40	.65
	1968	5.460	.25	.40	.65
	1969	1.590	.25	.40	.65

Y#	Date	Mintage	VF	XF	Unc
84.1	1970	30.906	.10	.15	.35
	1971	32.650	.10	.15	.30
	1972	25.290	.10	.15	.30
	1973	8.060	.10	.15	.30
	1974	19.541	.10	.15	.25
	1975	4.325	.10	.15	.30
	1976	13.181	.10	.15	.25
	1977	—	.10	.15	.25
	1978	—	.10	.15	.25

NOTE: Various sizes of dates exist.

PESO

25.0000 gm., .900 SILVER, .7234 oz ASW
Bogota Mint Commemorative

Y#	Date	Mintage	VF	XF	Unc
72	1956	.012	22.50	25.00	30.00

COPPER-NICKEL

Y#	Date	Mintage	VF	XF	Unc
80	1967	4.000	.30	.50	1.00

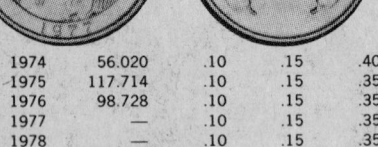

Y#	Date	Mintage	VF	XF	Unc
95	1974	56.020	.10	.15	.40
	1975	117.714	.10	.15	.35
	1976	98.728	.10	.15	.35
	1977	—	.10	.15	.35
	1978	—	.10	.15	.35

2 PESOS

COPPER-NICKEL

Y#	Date	Mintage	VF	XF	Unc
100	1977	—	.15	.25	.40

BRONZE

Y#	Date	Mintage	VF	XF	Unc
100a	1977	—	.15	.25	.40
	1978	—	.15	.25	.40
	1979	—	.15	.25	.40

2-1/2 PESOS

3.9940 gm., .917 GOLD, .1177 oz AGW

Y#	Date	Mintage	VF	XF	Unc
50	1913	.018	100.00	120.00	135.00

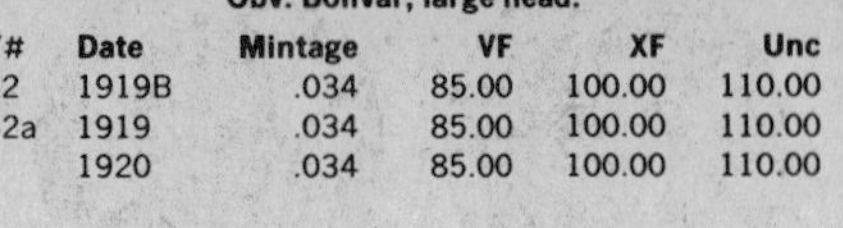

Obv: Bolivar, large head.

Y#	Date	Mintage	VF	XF	Unc
52	1919B	.034	85.00	100.00	110.00
52a	1919	.034	85.00	100.00	110.00
	1920	.034	85.00	100.00	110.00

Obv: Bolivar, small head, Medellin under bust.

Y#	Date	Mintage	VF	XF	Unc
55	1924	—	100.00	120.00	135.00
	1925	—	100.00	120.00	135.00
	1927	—	100.00	120.00	135.00
	1928	.014	100.00	120.00	135.00
	1929	—	100.00	120.00	135.00

5 PESOS

7.9881 gm., .917 GOLD, .2355 oz AGW

Y#	Date	Mintage	VF	XF	Unc
51	1913	—	185.00	200.00	225.00
	1917	.043	185.00	200.00	225.00
	1918	.423	175.00	185.00	200.00
	1919	2.976	175.00	185.00	200.00

Obv: Bolivar, large head.

Y#	Date	Mintage	VF	XF	Unc
53	1919A	Inc/Y#51	175.00	185.00	200.00
	1919	Inc/Y#51	175.00	185.00	200.00
	1920A	.978	175.00	185.00	200.00
	1920	Inc. Ab.	175.00	185.00	200.00
	1919B	.371	175.00	185.00	200.00
	1920B	.108	175.00	185.00	200.00
	1921B	—	—	Rare	—
	1922B	.029	185.00	200.00	215.00
	1923B	.074	185.00	200.00	215.00
	1924	—	175.00	185.00	200.00
	1924B	.705	175.00	185.00	200.00

Y#	Date	Mintage	VF	XF	Unc
56	1924	.825	175.00	185.00	200.00
	1925/4	—	175.00	185.00	200.00
	1925	—	175.00	185.00	200.00
	1926	—	175.00	185.00	200.00
	1927	—	175.00	185.00	200.00
	1928	.384	175.00	185.00	200.00
	1929	.321	175.00	185.00	200.00
	1930	.502	175.00	185.00	200.00

COPPER-NICKEL
Eucharistic Congress Commemorative

Y#	Date	Mintage	VF	XF	Unc
81	1968B	.660	.75	1.25	1.75

6th Pan-American Games Commemorative

Y#	Date	Mintage	VF	XF	Unc
85	1971	2.000	.50	1.00	1.50

10 PESOS

15.9761 gm., .917 GOLD, .4710 oz AGW

Y#	Date	Mintage	VF	XF	Unc
54	1919	.101	325.00	350.00	400.00
	1924B	.055	325.00	350.00	400.00

100 PESOS

4.3000 gm., .900 GOLD, .1244 oz AGW
Eucharistic Congress Commemorative

H#	Date	Mintage	VF	XF	Unc
1	1968	.108	BV	BV	100.00
	1968	8,000	—	Proof	125.00

Battle Of Boyaca Commemorative
Obv: Bust of Bolivar. Rev: Bust of Paris.

H#	Date	Mintage	VF	XF	Unc
7	1969	6,000	—	Proof	140.00

Pan American Games Commemorative
Obv: Javelin thrower Rev: Emblem

Y#	Date	Mintage	VF	XF	Unc
86	1971	6,000	—	Proof	140.00

200 PESOS

8.6000 gm., .900 GOLD, .2488 oz AGW
Eucharistic Congress Commemorative
Obv: Head of Pope Paul VI. Rev: Arms and value.

H#	Date	Mintage	VF	XF	Unc
2	1968	.108	BV	BV	175.00
	1968	8,000	—	Proof	200.00

Battle Of Boyaca Commemorative
Obv: Bust of Bolivar. Rev: Bust of Soublette.

H#	Date	Mintage	VF	XF	Unc
8	1969	6,000	—	Proof	200.00

Pan American Games Commemorative
Obv: Runner. Rev: Emblem.

Y#	Date	Mintage	VF	XF	Unc
87	1971	6,000	—	Proof	200.00

300 PESOS

12.9000 gm., .900 GOLD, .3733 oz AGW
Eucharistic Congress Commemorative
Obv: Head of Pope Paul VI. Rev: Arms and value.

H#	Date	Mintage	VF	XF	Unc
3	1968	.062	—	—	275.00
	1968	8,000	—	Proof	275.00

Battle Of Boyaca Commemorative
Obv: Bust of Bolivar. Rev: Bust of Anzoatequi.

H#	Date	Mintage	VF	XF	Unc
9	1969	6,000	—	Proof	275.00

Pan American Games Commemorative
Obv: Indian prophet and teacher. Rev: Emblem.

Y#	Date	Mintage	VF	XF	Unc
88	1971	6,000	—	Proof	275.00

28.2800 gm., .925 SILVER, .8411 oz ASW
Conservation Series
Obv: Portrait of Bolivar in center.

Y#	Date	Mintage	VF	XF	Unc
101	1979	—	—	—	25.00
	1979	.010	—	Proof	30.00

500 PESOS

21.5000 gm., .900 GOLD, .6221 oz AGW
Eucharistic Congress Commemorative
Obv: Bust of Pope Paul VI. Rev: Arms and value.

H#	Date	Mintage	VF	XF	Unc
4	1968	.014	BV	BV	450.00
	1968	8,000	—	Proof	500.00

Battle Of Boyáca Commemorative
Obv: Bust of Bolivar. Rev: Bust of Rondon.

H#	Date	Mintage	VF	XF	Unc
10	1969	6,000	—	Proof	500.00

Pan American Games Commemorative
Obv: Woman and child. Rev: Emblem.

Y#	Date	Mintage	VF	XF	Unc
89	1971	6,000	—	Proof	500.00

35.0000 gm., .925 SILVER, 1.0409 oz ASW
Conservation Series
Obv: Portrait of Bolivar in center.

Y#	Date	Mintage	VF	XF	Unc
102	1979	—	—	—	40.00
	1979	.010	—	Proof	50.00

1000 PESOS

4.3000 gm., .900 GOLD, .1244 oz AGW
Guillermo Valencia Commemorative

Y#	Date	Mintage	VF	XF	Unc
92	1973	10,003	—	Proof	100.00

Santa Marta Commemorative

Y#	Date	Mintage	VF	XF	Unc
96	1975	2,500	—	Proof	100.00

Tricentennial Of Medellin

Y#	Date	Mintage	VF	XF	Unc
98	1975	4,000	—	Proof	100.00

1500 PESOS

68.5000 gm., .900 GOLD, 1.9823 oz AGW
Eucharistic Congress Commemorative

H#	Date	Mintage	VF	XF	Unc
5	1968	5,722	BV	BV	1350.
	1968	8,000	—	Proof	1400.

Battle Of Boyaca Commemorative

H#	Date	Mintage	VF	XF	Unc
11	1969	6,000	—	Proof	1400.

Pan American Games Commemorative

Y#	Date	Mintage	VF	XF	Unc
90	1971	6,000	—	Proof	1400.

19.1000 gm., .900 GOLD, .5527 oz AGW

Bank Of Republic Museum Commemorative

Y#	Date	Mintage	VF	XF	Unc
91	1973	4,911	—	Proof	375.00

8.6000 gm., .900 GOLD, .2488 OZ AGW

Guillermo Valencia Commemorative

Y#	Date	Mintage	VF	XF	Unc
93	1973	5,003	—	Proof	175.00

2000 PESOS

12.9000 gm., .900 GOLD, .3733 oz AGW

Guillermo Valencia Commemorative

Y#	Date	Mintage	VF	XF	Unc
94	1973	5,003	—	Proof	275.00

8.6000 gm., .900 GOLD, .2488 oz AGW

Santa Marta Commemorative

Y#	Date	Mintage	VF	XF	Unc
97	1975	2,500	—	Proof	225.00

Tricentennial Of Medellin

Y#	Date	Mintage	VF	XF	Unc
99	1975	4,000	—	Proof	200.00

10,000 PESOS

33.4300 gm., .900 GOLD, .9674 oz AGW

Conservation Series

Obv: Portrait of Bolivar in center.

Y#	Date	Mintage	VF	XF	Unc
103	1979	—	BV	BV	650.00
	1979	1,000	—	Proof	750.00

INFLATIONARY COINAGE

P/M - PAPEL MONEDA

1 Peso equaled in value to 1 Centavo of the old silver currency. It later circulated at par with the newer 1 Centavo coins.

1 PESO P/M

COPPER-NICKEL

Y#	Date	Mintage	VF	XF	Unc
42	1907 AM	2.860	1.25	1.75	4.50
	1907 AM	—	—	Proof	50.00
	1910 AM	1.205	1.50	2.00	8.50
	1911 AM	2.816	1.25	1.75	8.50
	1912 AM	6.094	1.25	1.75	8.50
	1912 H	2.000	1.25	1.75	6.50
	1913 AM	.306	3.50	5.50	11.00
	1914 AM	.552	4.50	5.50	11.00
	1916 AM	.234	4.50	6.50	13.00

2 PESOS P/M

COPPER-NICKEL

Y#	Date	Mintage	VF	XF	Unc
43	1907 AM	4.161	2.25	3.75	6.50
	1907 AM	—	—	Proof	60.00
	1910 AM	.649	2.75	4.50	8.50
	1911	.458	2.75	4.50	8.50
	1913	.082 Reported, Not Confirmed			
	1914 AM	1.000	3.00	5.00	10.00

5 PESOS P/M

COPPER-NICKEL

Y#	Date	Mintage	VF	XF	Unc
44	1907 AM	6.143	1.50	2.75	5.50
	1907 AM	—	—	Proof	75.00
	1909	4.000	1.50	2.75	10.00
	1912 H	2.000	1.50	2.75	11.00
	1912 AM	1.897	2.75	6.50	11.00
	1913 AM	Inc. Ab.	2.75	6.50	11.00
	1914	Inc. Ab.	4.50	8.00	12.00

CIVIL WAR ISSUES

Province Of Santander

General Ramon Gonzales Valencia

These coins were struck during 1902 in Santander by General Valencia. They were struck to pay his troops after the Battle of Palonegro. Legend has it that they were struck using the brass of cartridges. The coins were struck uniface.

10 CENTAVOS

UNIFACE THIN BRASS

Similar to Y#S3, 50 Centavos

Y#	Date	Mintage	Fine	VF	XF
S1	ND(1902)	—	13.50	20.00	30.00

20 CENTAVOS

UNIFACE THIN BRASS

Similar to Y#S3, 50 Centavos

Y#	Date	Mintage	Fine	VF	XF
S2	1902	—	11.50	16.50	25.00

50 CENTAVOS

UNIFACE THIN BRASS

Y#	Date	Mintage	Fine	VF	XF
S3	1902	—	3.50	5.00	7.00

NCLT ISSUES

PATTERNS

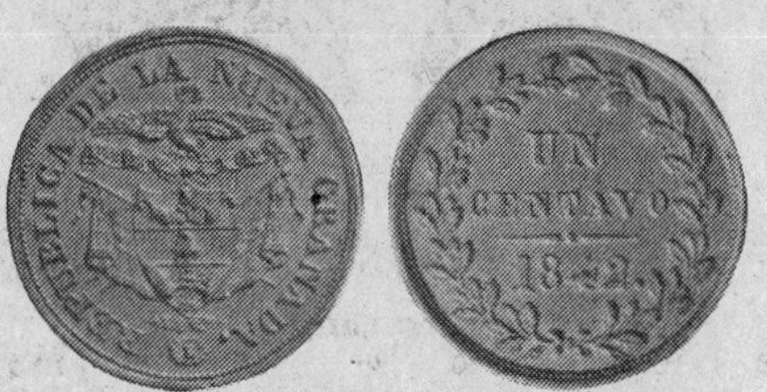

KM#	Date	Mintage	Identification	Mkt.Val.
1	1842	—	1 Centavo, Copper, REPUBLICA DE LA NUEVA GRANADA	—
2	1848	—	1/2 Real, Bogota, .900 Silver, C#154	—
3	1848	—	1 Real, Popayan, .900 Silver, C#155a	—
4	1858	—	20 Pesos, Bronze, REPUBLICA DE LA NUEVA GRANADA	—

KM#	Date	Mintage	Identification	Mkt.Val.
5	1873	—	10 Pesos, Gold, ESSAI	—

KM#	Date	Mintage	Identification	Mkt.Val.
6	1873	—	20 Pesos, Gold, ESSAI	—
7	1881	—	2-1/2 Centavos, Copper-Nickel	—
8	1881	—	2-1/2 Centavos, Copper-Nickel	—
9	1890	—	2 Centavos, Copper	—

KM#	Date	Mintage	Identification	Mkt.Val.
10	1900	—	5 Centavos, Copper-Nickel	—
11	1900	—	10 Centavos, Copper-Nickel	—
12	1952	—	20 Centavos, Silver	—

PIEFORTS (P)

KM#	Date	Mintage	Identification	Mkt.Val.
P1	1848	—	1/2 Real, Bogota, .900 Silver, C#154	—
P2	1848	—	1 Real, Popayan, .900 Silver, C#155a	—

PROOF SETS
STANDARD METALS

KM#	Date	Mintage	Identification	Issue Price	Mkt. Val.
101	1968(5)	8,000	H1-5	340.00	2500.
102	1969(5)	6,000	H7-11	—	2500.
103	1971(5)	6,000	Y86-90	—	2500.
104	1973(3)	—	Y92-94	—	550.00
105	1975(2)	2,500	Y98,99	195.00	300.00
106	1975(2)	4,000	Y96,97	195.00	325.00
107	1979(2)	—	Y101,102	—	80.00

LAZARETO

Leprosarium Coinage
MINT: BOGOTA

Special coinage for use in the three government colonies of Agua de Dios, Cano de Lord, and Contratacion. The hospitals were closed in the late 1950's and patients were allowed to exchange these special coins for regular currency at any bank.

CENTAVO

COPPER-NICKEL

KM#	Date	Mintage	Good	VG	Fine	VF
1	1921	.300	.50	1.00	2.75	5.50

2 CENTAVOS

COPPER-NICKEL

KM#	Date	Mintage	Good	VG	Fine	VF
2	1921	.350	.50	1.00	3.00	6.00

2-1/2 CENTAVOS

BRASS

KM#	Date	Mintage	Good	VG	Fine	VF
3	1901	—	6.00	10.00	15.00	30.00

5 CENTAVOS

BRASS

KM#	Date	Mintage	Good	VG	Fine	VF
4	1901	—	6.00	10.00	15.00	30.00

COPPER-NICKEL

KM#	Date	Mintage	Good	VG	Fine	VF
5	1921	.200	.75	1.50	3.25	6.50

10 CENTAVOS

BRASS

KM#	Date	Mintage	Good	VG	Fine	VF
6	1901	—	10.00	12.50	17.50	35.00

COPPER-NICKEL

KM#	Date	Mintage	Good	VG	Fine	VF
7	1921	.200	.75	1.50	3.25	6.50

20 CENTAVOS

BRASS

KM#	Date	Mintage	Good	VG	Fine	VF
8	1901	—	10.00	12.50	16.00	32.00

50 CENTAVOS

BRASS

KM#	Date	Mintage	Good	VG	Fine	VF
9	1901	—	13.50	17.50	25.00	45.00

COPPER-NICKEL

KM#	Date	Mintage	Good	VG	Fine	VF
10	1921	.120	1.75	3.25	5.50	11.00

BRASS

KM#	Date	Mintage	Good	VG	Fine	VF
11	1928	.050	1.50	4.25	7.50	15.00

COPPER

KM#	Date	Mintage	Good	VG	Fine	VF
11a	1928	Inc. Ab.	—	Rare	—	—

PESO P/M

COPPER-NICKEL

KM#	Date	Mintage	Good	VG	Fine	VF
12	1907	.792	3.75	5.00	9.00	18.00

5 PESOS P/M

COPPER-NICKEL

KM#	Date	Mintage	Good	VG	Fine	VF
13	1907	.159	5.00	8.50	15.00	25.00

10 PESOS P/M

COPPER-NICKEL

KM#	Date	Mintage	Good	VG	Fine	VF
14	1907	.129	6.00	10.00	17.50	27.50

COMOROS/Republic

The Comoros Federal Islamic Republic, a volcanic archipelago located in the Mozambique Channel of the Indian Ocean 300 miles (483 km.) northwest of Madagascar, has an area of 863 sq. mi. (2,166 sq. km.) and a population of 370,000. Capital: Moroni. The economy of the islands is based on agriculture. There are practically no mineral resources. Vanilla, essence for perfumes, copra, and sisal are exported.

Ancient Phoenician traders were probably the first visitors to the Comoro Islands, but the first detailed knowledge of the area was gathered by Arab sailors. Arab dominion and culture were firmly established when the Portuguese, Dutch, and French arrived in the 16th century. In 1843 a Malagasy ruler ceded the island of Mayotte to France; the other three principal islands of the archipelago--Anjouan, Moheli, and Grand Comore-- came under French protection in 1886. The islands were joined administratively with Madagascar in 1912. The Comoros became partially autonomous, with the status of a French overseas territory, in 1946, and achieved complete internal autonomy in 1961. On Dec. 31, 1975, after 133 years of French association, the Comoro Islands became the independent Republic of the Comoros.

Mayotte retained the option of determining its future ties and in 1976 voted to remain French. Its present status is that of a French Territorial Collectivity. French currency now circulates there.

RULERS

Sultan Said Ali
French, 1886-1975

MINTMARKS

(a) - Paris, privy marks only
A - Paris

MONETARY SYSTEM

100 Centimes = 1 Franc

5 CENTIMES

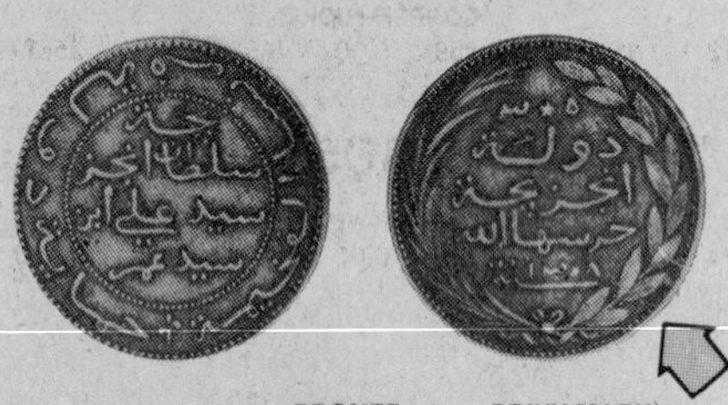

BRONZE — PRIVY MARK

Rev. privy mark: fasces

Y#	Date	Mintage	Fine	VF	XF	Unc
1.1	AH1308A	.100	5.00	10.00	15.00	75.00
	Rev. privy mark: torch					
1.2	AH1308A	.200	5.00	10.00	15.00	75.00

10 CENTIMES

BRONZE — PRIVY MARK

Rev. privy mark: fasces

Y#	Date	Mintage	Fine	VF	XF	Unc
2.1	AH1308A	.050	5.00	10.00	20.00	125.00
	Rev. privy mark: torch					
2.2	AH1308A	.100	5.00	10.00	20.00	125.00

5 FRANCS

.900 SILVER

Y#	Date	Mintage	Fine	VF	XF	Unc
3	AH1308A	2,050	225.00	400.00	750.00	1200.

MODERN COINAGE

FRANC

ALUMINUM

Y#	Date	Mintage	Fine	VF	XF	Unc
4	1964(a)	.500	.10	.15	.20	.30

2 FRANCS

ALUMINUM

Y#	Date	Mintage	Fine	VF	XF	Unc
5	1964(a)	.600	.10	.15	.25	.50

5 FRANCS

ALUMINUM

Y#	Date	Mintage	Fine	VF	XF	Unc
6	1964(a)	1.000	.10	.25	.50	.75

10 FRANCS

NICKEL-BRASS

Y#	Date	Mintage	Fine	VF	XF	Unc
7	1964(a)	.600	.15	.25	.50	1.00

20 FRANCS

NICKEL-BRASS

Y#	Date	Mintage	Fine	VF	XF	Unc
8	1964(a)	.500	.25	.35	.75	1.50

50 FRANCS

NICKEL
F.A.O. Issue

Y#	Date	Mintage	Fine	VF	XF	Unc
9	1975(a)	—	.35	.50	.75	1.00

100 FRANCS

NICKEL
F.A.O. Issue

Y#	Date	Mintage	Fine	VF	XF	Unc
10	1977	.500	.50	.75	1.50	2.50

5000 FRANCS

44.8300 gm., .925 SILVER, 1.2973 oz ASW
Obv: Similar to 20,000 Francs, KM#3.
Rev: Cluster of flowers.

KM#	Date	Mintage	XF	Unc	Proof
1	1976	—	—	45.00	60.00

10,000 FRANCS

3.0700 gm., .900 GOLD, .0888 oz AGW
Obv: Similar to 20,000 Francs, KM#3.

KM#	Date	Mintage	XF	Unc	Proof
2	1976	—	—	65.00	100.00

20,000 FRANCS

6.1400 gm., .900 GOLD, .1776 oz AGW

KM#	Date	Mintage	XF	Unc	Proof
3	1976	—	—	125.00	200.00

NCLT ISSUES

ESSAIS (E)

Standard metals unless otherwise noted

KM#	Date	Mintage	Identification	Issue Price	Mkt. Val.
E4	1964(a)	1,700	1 Franc	—	13.50
E5	1964(a)	1,700	2 Francs	—	14.50
E6	1964(a)	1,700	5 Francs	—	15.50
E7	1964(a)	1,700	10 Francs	—	16.50
E8	1964(a)	1,700	20 Francs	—	17.50

FLEUR DE COIN SETS

1	1964(a)	—	Y4-8	—	12.50

NOTE: This set issued with Reunion set.

PROOF SETS

STANDARD METALS

101	1976(3)	—	KM1-3	229.00	350.00

Listings For

CONGO-BELGE: refer to Zaire

CONGO DEMOCRATIC REPUBLIC: refer to Zaire

CONGO/People's Republic

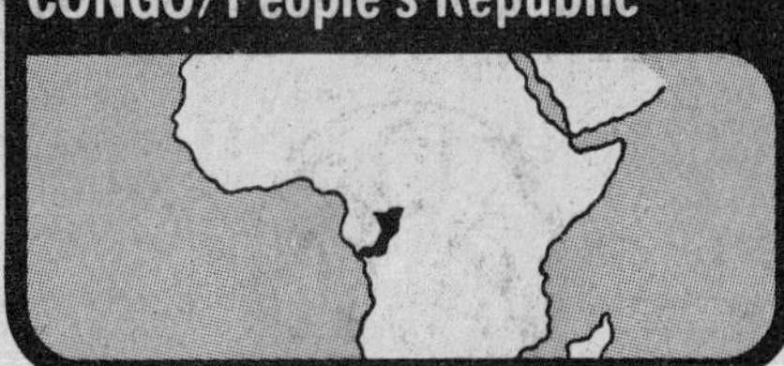

The People's Republic of the Congo (formerly the French Middle Congo overseas territory), located on the equator in west-central Africa, has an area of 132,046 sq. mi. (341,999 sq. km.) and a population of 1.3 million. Capital: Brazzaville. Agriculture, forestry, mining, and food processing are the principal industries. Timber, industrial diamonds, potash, peanuts, and cocoa beans are exported.

The Portuguese were the first Europeans to explore the Congo (Brazzaville) area, 14th century. They conducted a slave trade with the tribal kingdoms of Teke, Loango, and Kongo without attempting developmental colonization. French influence was established in 1883 when the king of Teke signed a treaty with Savorgnan de Brazza, thereby placing his kingdom under the protection of France. While a French protectorate, the area was known as Middle Congo. In 1910 Middle Congo became a part of French Equatorial Africa, which also included Gabon, Ubangi-Shari (now the Central African Republic), and Chad. Following World War II, during which it was an important center of Free French activities, the Middle Congo was given a large measure of internal autonomy, and its inhabitants were made French citizens. Upon approval of the constitution of the Fifth French Republic, 1958, it became a member of the new French Community. On Aug. 15, 1960, Middle Congo became the independent Republic of the Congo-Brazzaville. In Jan. 1970 the country's name was changed to People's Republic of the Congo. A new constitution which asserts the government's advocacy of socialism was adopted in 1973.

NOTE: For earlier and related coinage see French Equatorial Africa and the Equatorial African States.

RULERS

French

MINTMARKS

(a) - Paris, privy marks only

MONETARY SYSTEM

100 Centimes = 1 Franc

100 FRANCS

NICKEL

Y#	Date	Mintage	Fine	VF	XF	Unc
1	1971(a)	2.500	.75	1.25	2.50	4.00
	1972(a)	—	.75	1.25	2.50	4.00

Y#	Date	Mintage	Fine	VF	XF	Unc
2	1975(a)	—	.75	1.00	1.50	2.50

NCLT ISSUES

ESSAIS (E)

Standard metals unless otherwise noted

KM#	Date	Mintage	Identification	Issue Price	Mkt. Val.
E1	1971(a)	—	100 Francs	—	27.50
E2	1975(a)	—	100 Francs	—	25.00

COOK ISLANDS

Cook Islands, a political dependency of New Zealand consisting of 15 islands located in the South Pacific Ocean about 2,000 miles (3,218 km.) northeast of New Zealand, has an area of 93 sq. mi. (241 sq. km.) and a population of 19,000. Capital: Avarua. The United States claims the islands of Danger, Manahiki, Penrhyn, and Rakahanga atolls. Citrus and canned fruits and juices, copra, clothing, jewelry, and mother-of-pearl shell are exported.

The islands were first sighted by Spanish navigator Alvaro de Mendada in 1595. Portuguese navigator Pedro Fernandes de Quieros landed on Rakahanga in 1606. English navigator Capt. James Cook sailed to the islands on three occasions: 1773, 1774 and 1777. He named them Hervey Islands, in honor of Augustus John Hervey, a lord of the Admiralty. The islands were declared a British protectorate in 1888, and were annexed to New Zealand in 1901. They were granted internal self-government in 1965. New Zealand provides an annual subsidy and retains responsibility for defense and foreign affairs.

As a territory of New Zealand, Cook Islands are considered to be within the Commonwealth of Nations.

RULERS

Great Britain, 1888-1901

New Zealand, 1901-

MINTMARKS

FM - Franklin Mint, U.S.A. *

***NOTE:** During 1975-77 the Franklin Mint produced coinage in up to three different qualities. Qualities of issue are designated in () after each date and are defined as follows:

(M) MATTE - Normal circulation strike or a dull finish produced by sandblasting special uncirculated (polish finish) or proof quality dies.

(U) SPECIAL UNCIRCULATED - Polished or proof-like in appearance without any frosted features.

(P) PROOF - The highest quality obtainable having mirror-like fields and frosted features.

MONETARY SYSTEM

(Until 1967)

12 Pence = 1 Shilling

20 Shillings = 1 Pound

(Commencing 1967)

100 Cents = 1 Dollar

CENT

BRONZE

Y#	Date	Mintage	VF	XF	Unc
1	1972	.117	.10	.20	.35
	1972	.017	—	Proof	.50
	1973	8,500	.10	.25	.50
	1973	.013	—	Proof	.50
	1974	.300	.10	.20	.35
	1974	7,300	—	Proof	.50
	1975	.429	—	—	.35
	1975FM(M)	1,000	.45	.90	1.50
	1975FM(U)	2,251	—	.25	.50
	1975FM(P)	.021	—	Proof	1.00
	1976FM(M)	1,001	.45	.90	1.50
	1976FM(U)	1,066	—	.25	.50
	1976FM(P)	.018	—	Proof	1.00
	1977FM(M)	1,171	—	—	.50
	1977FM(U)	1,002	—	.25	.50
	1977FM(P)	5,986	—	Proof	1.00
	1978FM(M)	1,000	—	—	—
	1978FM(U)	767 pcs.	—	—	.50
	1978FM(P)	6,287	—	Proof	1.00
	1979FM(P)	—	—	Proof	—

2 CENTS

BRONZE

Y#	Date	Mintage	VF	XF	Unc
2	1972	.063	.15	.25	.50
	1972	.017	—	Proof	.75
	1973	8,500	.20	.35	.75
	1973	.013	—	Proof	.75
	1974	.120	—	.25	.50
	1974	7,300	—	Proof	.75
	1975	.129	—	—	.50
	1975FM(M)	1,000	.65	1.25	2.00
	1975FM(U)	2,251	—	.50	1.00
	1975FM(P)	.021	—	Proof	1.25
	1976FM(M)	1,001	.65	1.25	2.00
	1976FM(U)	1,066	—	.40	.85
	1976FM(P)	.018	—	Proof	1.25
	1977FM(M)	1,171	—	—	.85
	1977FM(U)	1,002	—	.40	.85
	1977FM(P)	5,986	—	Proof	1.25
	1978FM(M)	1,000	—	—	—
	1978FM(U)	767 pcs.	—	—	.85
	1978FM(P)	6,287	—	Proof	1.25
	1979FM(P)	—	—	Proof	—

5 CENTS

COPPER-NICKEL

Y#	Date	Mintage	VF	XF	Unc
3	1972	.032	.15	.25	.65
	1972	.017	—	Proof	1.00
	1973	8,500	.25	.50	1.00
	1973	.013	—	Proof	1.00
	1974	.080	.15	.20	.50
	1974	7,300	—	Proof	1.00
	1975	.089	—	—	.50
	1975FM(M)	1,000	.85	1.75	3.00
	1975FM(U)	2,251	—	.65	1.25
	1975FM(P)	.021	—	Proof	1.50
	1976FM(M)	1,001	.85	1.75	3.00
	1976FM(U)	1,066	—	.65	1.25
	1976FM(P)	.018	—	Proof	1.50
	1977FM(M)	1,171	—	—	1.25
	1977FM(U)	1,002	—	.65	1.25
	1977FM(P)	5,986	—	Proof	1.50
	1978FM(M)	1,000	—	—	—
	1978FM(U)	767 pcs.	—	—	1.25
	1978FM(P)	6,287	—	Proof	1.50
	1979FM(P)	—	—	Proof	—

10 CENTS

COPPER-NICKEL

Y#	Date	Mintage	VF	XF	Unc
4	1972	.035	.15	.30	.75
	1972	.017	—	Proof	1.75
	1973	.059	.15	.25	.60
	1973	.013	—	Proof	2.00
	1974	.050	.15	.25	.60
	1974	7,300	—	Proof	2.50
	1975	.059	—	.15	.60
	1975FM(M)	1,000	1.50	3.00	5.00
	1975FM(U)	2,251	—	1.00	2.00
	1975FM(P)	.021	—	Proof	2.50
	1976FM(M)	1,001	1.50	3.00	5.00
	1976FM(U)	1,066	—	1.00	2.00
	1976FM(P)	.018	—	Proof	2.50
	1977FM(M)	1,171	—	—	2.00
	1977FM(U)	1,002	—	1.00	2.00
	1977FM(P)	5,986	—	Proof	2.50
	1978FM(M)	1,000	—	—	—
	1978FM(U)	767 pcs.	—	—	2.00
4	1978FM(P)	6,287	—	Proof	2.50
	1979FM(P)	—	—	Proof	—

F.A.O. Issue

Y#	Date	Mintage	VF	XF	Unc
4a	1979FM	—	—	—	—

20 CENTS

COPPER-NICKEL

Y#	Date	Mintage	VF	XF	Unc
5	1972	.031	.25	.50	1.00
	1972	.017	—	Proof	2.50
	1973	.049	.25	.40	1.00
	1973	.013	—	Proof	3.50
	1974	5,500	.75	1.50	3.00
	1974	7,300	—	Proof	5.00
	1975	.060	—	—	1.00
	1975FM(M)	1,000	2.25	4.50	7.50
	1975FM(U)	2,251	—	1.50	3.00
	1975FM(P)	.021	—	Proof	3.50

Y#	Date	Mintage	VF	XF	Unc
15	1976FM(M)	1,001	2.75	4.50	7.50
	1976FM(U)	1,066	—	1.50	3.00
	1976FM(P)	.018	—	Proof	3.50
	1977FM(M)	1,171	—	—	3.00
	1977FM(U)	1,002	—	1.50	3.00
	1977FM(P)	5,986	—	Proof	3.50
	1978FM(M)	1,000	—	—	—
	1978FM(U)	767 pcs.	—	—	3.00
	1978FM(P)	6,287	—	Proof	3.50
	1979FM(P)	—	—	Proof	—

50 CENTS

COPPER-NICKEL

Y#	Date	Mintage	VF	XF	Unc
6	1972	.031	.75	1.00	2.00
	1972	.017	—	Proof	6.00
	1973	.019	.75	1.25	2.50
	1973	.013	—	Proof	6.00
	1974	.010	1.00	2.00	4.00
	1974	7,300	—	Proof	6.00
	1975	.019	—	1.25	2.00
	1975FM(M)	1,000	4.50	9.00	15.00
	1975FM(U)	2,251	—	3.25	6.50
	1975FM(P)	.021	—	Proof	6.00
	1976FM(M)	1,001	4.50	9.00	15.00
	1976FM(U)	1,066	—	3.25	6.50
	1976FM(P)	.018	—	Proof	6.00
	1977FM(M)	1,171	—	—	6.50
	1977FM(U)	1,002	—	3.25	6.50
	1977FM(P)	5,986	—	Proof	7.50
	1978FM(M)	1,000	—	—	—
6	1978FM(U)	767 pcs.	—	—	6.50
	1978FM(P)	6,287	—	Proof	7.50

F.A.O. Issue

Y#	Date	Mintage	VF	XF	Unc
6a	1979FM(P)	—	—	Proof	—

DOLLAR

COPPER-NICKEL

Y#	Date	Mintage	VF	XF	Unc
7	1972	.031	2.25	4.50	12.00
	1972	.027	—	Proof	18.00
	1973	.049	1.75	3.50	12.00
	1973	.013	—	Proof	18.00
	1974	.020	2.25	4.50	10.00
	1974	7,300	—	Proof	18.00
	1975	.029	—	4.50	10.00
	1975FM(M)	1,000	7.50	15.00	25.00
	1975FM(U)	2,251	—	6.50	12.50
	1975FM(P)	.021	—	Proof	15.00
	1976FM(M)	1,001	7.50	15.00	25.00
	1976FM(U)	1,066	—	6.50	12.50
	1976FM(P)	.018	—	Proof	15.00
	1977FM(M)	1,171	—	—	12.50
	1977FM(U)	1,002	—	6.50	12.50
	1977FM(P)	5,986	—	Proof	20.00
	1978FM(M)	1,000	—	—	—
	1978FM(U)	767 pcs.	—	—	12.50
	1978FM(P)	6,287	—	Proof	20.00
	1979FM(P)	—	—	Proof	—

2 DOLLARS

25.7000 gm., .925 SILVER, .7643 oz ASW
20th Anniversary of Coronation
Obv: Similar to 1 Dollar, Y#7.

Y#	Date	Mintage	VF	XF	Unc
8	1973	.016	BV	25.00	30.00
	1973	.046	—	Proof	35.00

2-1/2 DOLLARS

27.1000 gm., .925 SILVER, .8060 oz ASW
Cook 2nd Voyage Commemorative
Obv: Similar to 1 Dollar, Y#7.

Y#	Date	Mintage	VF	XF	Unc
9	1973	6,000	BV	25.00	35.00
	1973	.012	—	Proof	40.00
	1974	2,000	25.00	30.00	40.00
	1974	.012	—	Proof	40.00

5 DOLLARS

27.3200 gm., .500 SILVER, .4392 oz ASW
Obv: Similar to 1 Dollar, Y#7.

Y#	Date	Mintage	VF	XF	Unc
16	1976FM(M)	251 pcs.	65.00	100.00	150.00
	1976FM(U)	2,192	30.00	40.00	80.00
	1976FM(P)	.028	—	Proof	30.00

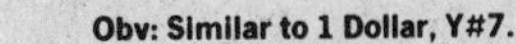

Obv: Similar to 1 Dollar, Y#7.

Y#	Date	Mintage	VF	XF	Unc
19	1977FM(M)	252 pcs.	15.00	25.00	35.00
	1977FM(U)	4,032	BV	15.00	20.00
	1977FM(P)	.011	—	Proof	35.00

Wildlife Conservation

Y#	Date	Mintage	VF	XF	Unc
20	1978FM(M)	250 pcs.	—	—	—
	1978FM(U)	3,659	—	—	—
	1978FM(P)	.011	—	Proof	30.00

Cook Island Conservation Day

Y#	Date	Mintage	VF	XF	Unc
25	1979FM(P)	—	—	Proof	30.00

7-1/2 DOLLARS

34.5500 gm., .925 SILVER, 1.0276 oz ASW
Cook 2nd Voyage Commemorative
Obv: Similar to 1 Dollar, Y#7.

Y#	Date	Mintage	VF	XF	Unc
10	1973	6,000	35.00	45.00	60.00
	1973	.012	—	Proof	50.00
	1974	2,000	37.50	40.00	55.00
	1974	.013	—	Proof	50.00

10 DOLLARS

27.2800 gm., .925 SILVER, .8113 oz ASW
25th Anniversary of Coronation

Y#	Date	Mintage	VF	XF	Unc
21	1978FM(U)	5,350	—	—	50.00
	1978FM(P)	.011	—	Proof	35.00

25 DOLLARS

48.6000 gm., .925 SILVER, 1.4454 oz ASW
Queen's Silver Jubilee
Obv: Similar to 1 Dollar, Y#7.

Y#	Date	Mintage	VF	XF	Unc
17	1977FM(M)	100 pcs.	—	—	—
	1977FM(U)	4,068	—	50.00	75.00
	1977FM(P)	.017	—	Proof	100.00

50 DOLLARS

97.2000 gm., .925 SILVER, 2.8909 oz ASW
Churchill Commemorative

Y#	Date	Mintage	VF	XF	Unc
11	1974	1,202	85.00	125.00	150.00
	1974	2,502	—	Proof	125.00

.925 SILVER, GILT

Y#	Date	Mintage	VF	XF	Unc
11a	1974	2,002	—	Proof	275.00

100 DOLLARS

16.7185 gm., .917 GOLD, .4929 oz AGW
Churchill Commemorative

Y#	Date	Mintage	VF	XF	Unc
12	1974	368 pcs.	400.00	500.00	1250.
	1974	1,453	—	Proof	500.00

9.6000 gm., .900 GOLD, .2778 oz AGW
Cook 2nd Voyage Commemorative

Y#	Date	Mintage	VF	XF	Unc
13	1975FM(M)	100 pcs.	500.00	750.00	1000.
	1975FM(U)	7,447	—	225.00	250.00
	1975FM(P)	.017	—	Proof	200.00

U.S. Bicentennial Commemorative

Y#	Date	Mintage	VF	XF	Unc
14	1976FM(M)	50 pcs.	500.00	750.00	1000.
	1976FM(U)	852 pcs.	—	275.00	400.00
	1976FM(P)	9,373	—	Proof	200.00

Queen's Silver Jubilee

Y#	Date	Mintage	VF	XF	Unc
18	1977FM(M)	50 pcs.	—	—	1000.
	1977FM(U)	562 pcs.	—	275.00	325.00
	1977FM(P)	9,364	—	Proof	200.00

Membership in Commonwealth of Nations

Y#	Date	Mintage	VF	XF	Unc
26	1979FM(P)	—	—	Proof	250.00

200 DOLLARS

16.6000 gm., .900 GOLD, .4803 oz AGW
Discovery of Hawaii by Capt. Cook

Y#	Date	Mintage	VF	XF	Unc
22	1978FM(M)	26 pcs.	—	—	700.00
	1978FM(U)	621 pcs.	—	400.00	450.00
	1978FM(P)	3,216	—	Proof	400.00

Legacy of Captain James Cook

Y#	Date	Mintage	VF	XF	Unc
24	1979FM(U)	271 pcs.	—	—	450.00
	1979FM(P)	1,939	—	Proof	400.00

250 DOLLARS

17.9000 gm., .900 GOLD, .5180 oz AGW
250th Anniversary Birth of James Cook

Y#	Date	Mintage	VF	XF	Unc
23	1978FM(M)	25 pcs.	—	—	—
	1978FM(U)	200 pcs.	—	—	450.00
	1978FM(P)	1,757	—	Proof	400.00

NCLT ISSUES

MINT SETS
STANDARD METALS

KM#	Date	Mintage	Identification	Issue Price	Mkt. Val.
S1	1972(7)	11,045	Y1-7	7.50	10.00
S2	1973(9)	3,652	Y1-7,9,10	52.50	100.00
S3	1973(7)	3,023	Y1-7	10.00	10.00
S4	1973(2)	2,348	Y9, 10	45.00	90.00
S5	1974(9)	913	Y1-7, 9, 10	52.50	110.00
S6	1974(7)	2,087	Y1-7	10.00	12.00
S7	1974(2)	587	Y9, 10	45.00	95.00
S8	1975(7)	2,251	Y1-7	10.00	25.00
S9	1976(8)	1,066	Y1-4,6,7,15,16	20.00	100.00
S10	1977(8)	1,171	Y1-4,6,7,15,19	20.00	40.00
S11	1978(8)	767	Y1-4,6,7,15,20	20.00	—

PROOF SETS
STANDARD METALS

KM#	Date	Mintage	Identification	Issue Price	Mkt. Val.
101	1972(7)	17,101	Y1-7	20.00	25.00
102	1973(9)	7,395	Y1-7,9,10	89.50	100.00
103	1973(7)	5,136	Y1-7	29.50	25.00
104	1973(2)	4,754	Y9,10	60.00	80.00
105	1974(9)	4,444	Y1-7,9,10	95.00	100.00
106	1974(7)	5,300	Y1-7	32.50	30.00
107	1974(2)	2,856	Y9,10	65.00	80.00
108	1975(7)	21,290	Y1-7	31.50	25.00
109	1976(8)	17,658	Y1-4,6,7,15,16	40.00	55.00
110	1977(8)	5,986	Y1-4,6,7,15,19	42.00	60.00
111	1978(8)	6,287	Y1-4,6,7,15,20	42.00	60.00
112	1979(8)	—	Y1-4,6,7,15	44.00	—

COSTA RICA

The Republic of Costa Rica, located in southern Central America between Nicaragua and Panama, has an area of 19,700 sq. mi. (51,022 sq. km.) and a population of 2 million. Capital: San Jose. Agriculture predominates; coffee, bananas, beef and sugar contribute heavily to the country's export earnings.

Costa Rica was discovered by Christopher Columbus in 1502, during his last voyage to the new world, and was a colony of Spain from 1522 until independence in 1821. Columbus named the territory Nueva Cartago; the name Costa Rica wasn't generally employed until 1540. Bartholomew Columbus attempted to found the first settlement but was driven off by Indian attacks and the country wasn't pacified until 1530. Costa Rica was absorbed for two years (1821-23) in the Mexican Empire of Agustin de Iturbide. It was established as a republic in 1848. Today, Costa Rica remains a model of orderly democracy in Latin America.

MINTMARKS

CR - San Jose 1825-1850

NOTE: Also see Central American Republic.

HEATON - Heaton

BIRMM - Birmingham 1889-1893

ISSUING BANK INITIALS - MINT

BCCR - Philadelphia 1951-1958,1961

BICR - Philadelphia 1935

BNCR - London 1937,1948

BNCR - San Jose 1942-1947

GCR - Philadelphia 1905-1914,1929

GCR - San Jose 1917-1941

ASSAYER'S INITIALS

MM - 1842

JB - 1847-1864

GW - 1850-1890

CY - 1902

JCV - 1903

MONETARY SYSTEM

8 Reales = 1 Peso

16 Pesos = 8 Escudos = 1 Onza

1/2 REAL

.750 SILVER
MINTMARK: CR
Obv: Radiant 6 pointed star in circle over branches.
Rev: Tobacco plant and value in circle, date below.

C#	Date	Mintage	VG	Fine	VF
11	1842M.M.	—	25.00	40.00	60.00

REAL

.750 SILVER
MINTMARK: CR

C#	Date	Mintage	Fine	VF	XF
22	1847 JB	—	10.00	15.00	30.00
	1847 JB (error) backwards B	—	12.50	17.50	35.00

C#	Date	Mintage	Fine	VF	XF
23	1849 JB	—	7.50	10.00	25.00
	1850 JB	—	10.00	15.00	40.00

1/2 ESCUDO

1.7000 gm., .875 GOLD, .0478 oz AGW

MINTMARK: CR

Y#	Date	Mintage	Fine	VF	XF
22	1850 JB	3,388	50.00	75.00	100.00
	1851 JB	6,565	50.00	75.00	100.00
	1853 JB	8,491	50.00	75.00	100.00
	1854 JB	4,663	50.00	75.00	100.00
	1855 JB	8,822	50.00	75.00	100.00
	1855 GW	Inc. Ab.	50.00	75.00	100.00
	1864 JB	9,018	50.00	75.00	100.00

ESCUDO

3.3000 gm., .875 GOLD, .0928 oz AGW

MINTMARK: CR

C#	Date	Mintage	Fine	VF	XF
16	1842 MM	.010	275.00	400.00	650.00

Similar to 1/2 Escudo, Y#22.

Y#	Date	Mintage	Fine	VF	XF
23	1850 JB	6,167	75.00	100.00	135.00
	1851 JB	4,388	75.00	100.00	135.00
	1853 JB	2,979	75.00	100.00	135.00
	1855 JB	4,095	75.00	100.00	135.00

2 ESCUDOS

6.7500 gm., .875 GOLD, .1899 oz AGW

MINTMARK: CR

Similar to 1/2 Escudo, Y#22.

Y#	Date	Mintage	Fine	VF	XF
24	1850 JB	3,641	175.00	225.00	375.00
	1854 JB	Inc. Ab.	150.00	200.00	300.00
	1854 GW	Inc. Ab.	175.00	225.00	325.00
	1855 JB	.060	150.00	200.00	300.00
	1855 GW	Inc. Ab.	175.00	225.00	325.00
	1858 GW	.017	150.00	200.00	300.00
	1862 GW	5,896	150.00	200.00	300.00
	1863 GW	5,632	150.00	200.00	300.00

1/2 ONZA

12.6000 gm., .875 GOLD, .3545 oz AGW

MINTMARK: CR

Similar to 1/2 Escudo, Y#22.

C#	Date	Mintage	Fine	VF	XF
25	1850 JB	.018	350.00	500.00	800.00

COUNTERSTAMP ISSUES

1841-1842

Type I

c/s: Radiant 6-pointed star in 7mm circle.

NOTE: An additional plug cut from coin to 'pay for the work'.

1/2 REAL

SILVER

c/s: Type I on Mexico 1/2 Real, KM#72 (C#77).

C#	Date	Mintage	VG	Fine	VF
10.1	ND(1792-1808)	—	—	Rare	—

REAL

SILVER

c/s: Type I on Spanish American 1 Real.

C#	Date	Mintage	VG	Fine	VF
10.2	ND	—	40.00	75.00	125.00

2 REALES

SILVER

c/s: Type I on Bolivia (Potosi) 2 Reales, C#16.

C#	Date	Mintage	VG	Fine	VF
10.3a	ND(1773-89)	—	30.00	60.00	90.00

c/s: Type I on Guatemala 2 Reales, C#26.

C#	Date	Mintage	VG	Fine	VF
10.3b	ND(1772-76)	—	30.00	60.00	90.00

c/s: Type I on Mexico 2 Reales, KM#92 (C#109).

C#	Date	Mintage	VG	Fine	VF
10.3c	ND(1809-12)	—	30.00	60.00	90.00

c/s: Type I on Mexico 2 Reales, KM#372.8 (C#S23).

C#	Date	Mintage	VG	Fine	VF
10.3d	ND(1825-41)	—	30.00	60.00	90.00

c/s: Type I on Peru 2 Reales, C#130-1.

C#	Date	Mintage	VG	Fine	VF
10.3e	ND(1825-40)	—	30.00	60.00	90.00

4 REALES

SILVER

c/s: Type I on Bolivia (Potosi) 4 Reales, C#17.

C#	Date	Mintage	VG	Fine	VF
10.4a	ND(1773-89)	—	125.00	200.00	300.00

c/s Type I on Bolivia (Potosi) 4 Reales, C#35.

C#	Date	Mintage	VG	Fine	VF
10.4b	ND(1791-1808)	—	125.00	200.00	300.00

8 REALES

SILVER

c/s: Type I on Mexico 8 Reales, KM#106 (C#40).

C#	Date	Mintage	VG	Fine	VF
10.5a	ND(1772-89)	—	100.00	150.00	225.00

c/s: Type I on Mexico 8 Reales, KM#376 (Y#S19).

C#	Date	Mintage	VG	Fine	VF
10.5b	ND(1824)	—	150.00	225.00	300.00

c/s: Type I on Mexico 8 Reales, KM#377.10 (Y#S25).

C#	Date	Mintage	VG	Fine	VF
10.5c	ND(1824-41)	—	75.00	125.00	200.00

c/s: Type I on Peru 8 Reales, C#45.

C#	Date	Mintage	VG	Fine	VF
10.5d	ND(1772-89)	—	100.00	150.00	225.00

c/s: Type I on Peru 8 Reales, C#132-1.

C#	Date	Mintage	VG	Fine	VF
10.5e	ND(1825-28)	—	75.00	125.00	200.00

c/s: Type I on Peru 8 Reales, C#132-1a.

C#	Date	Mintage	VG	Fine	VF
10.5f	ND(1828-40)	—	75.00	125.00	200.00

c/s: Type I on North Peru 8 Reales, C#151.

C#	Date	Mintage	VG	Fine	VF
10.5g	ND(1836-39)	—	100.00	150.00	225.00

c/s: Type I on Spanish 8 Reales, C#136.

C#	Date	Mintage	VG	Fine	VF
10.5h	ND(1809-30)	—	100.00	150.00	225.00

(1841-1842)

Type II

c/s: Radiant 6-pointed star in 4mm circle.

4 ESCUDOS

GOLD

c/s: Type II on Costa Rica 4 Escudos (C#9).

C#	Date	Mintage	VG	Fine	VF
10.6	ND(1828-41)	—	—	Rare	—

(1845)

Type III

Obv. c/s: COSTA RICA and 2 R. around female head.
Rev. c/s: HABILITADA POR EL GOB. around tree.

2 REALES

SILVER

c/s: Type III on Spanish 2 Reales, C#38.

C#	Date	Mintage	VG	Fine	VF
14.1	ND(1772-88)	—	15.00	27.50	50.00

c/s: Type III on Spanish (Madrid) 2 Reales, C#69.

C#	Date	Mintage	VG	Fine	VF
14.2	ND(1788-1808)	—	15.00	27.50	50.00

c/s: Type III on Spanish (Seville) 2 Reales, C#69.

C#	Date	Mintage	VG	Fine	VF
14.3	ND(1788-1808)	—	15.00	27.50	50.00

c/s: Type III on Spanish 2 Reales, C#89.

C#	Date	Mintage	VG	Fine	VF
14.4	ND(1811-12)	—	25.00	40.00	65.00

c/s: Type III on Spanish 4 Reales, C#90.

C#	Date	Mintage	VG	Fine	VF
14.5	ND(1808-13)	—	60.00	110.00	165.00

c/s: Type III on Spanish (Madrid) 2 Reales, C#134.

C#	Date	Mintage	VG	Fine	VF
14.6	ND(1810-33)	—	17.50	30.00	55.00

c/s: Type III on Spanish (Seville) 2 Reales, C#134.

C#	Date	Mintage	VG	Fine	VF
14.7	ND(1810-33)	—	17.50	30.00	55.00

c/s: Type III on Spanish 4 Reales, C#135.

C#	Date	Mintage	VG	Fine	VF
14.8	ND(1811-33)	—	50.00	95.00	150.00

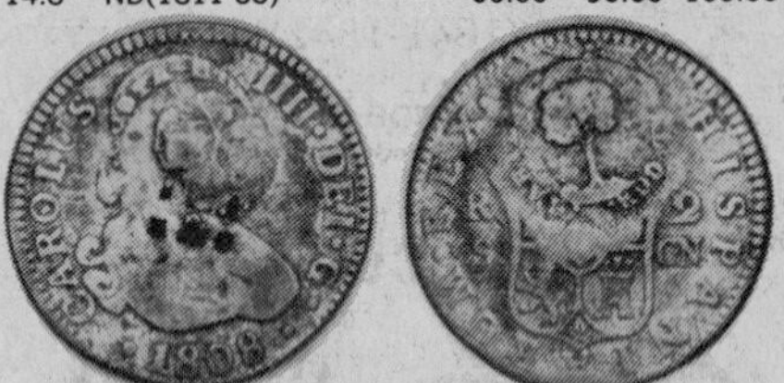

c/s: Type III on Trinidad, Cuba c/s on Spanish (Seville) 2 Reales, KM#12.

C#	Date	Mintage	VG	Fine	VF
14.9	ND(1788-1808)	—	22.50	35.00	60.00

1846

Type IV

Obv. c/s: REPUB. DE CENT. DE AMER. 1846 around sun over mountains in a 14mm circle.
Rev. c/s: HABILITADA EN COSTA RICA J.B... around tree, 1-R.

REAL

SILVER

c/s: Type IV on Spanish American 'cob' 1 Real.

C#	Date	Mintage	VG	Fine	VF
12.1	1846	—	15.00	25.00	45.00

1846

Type V

Obv. c/s: REPUB. DE CENT. DE AMER. 1846 around sun over mountains in a 14mm circle.
Rev. c/s: HABILITADA EN COSTA RICA J-B around tree, 2-R.

2 REALES

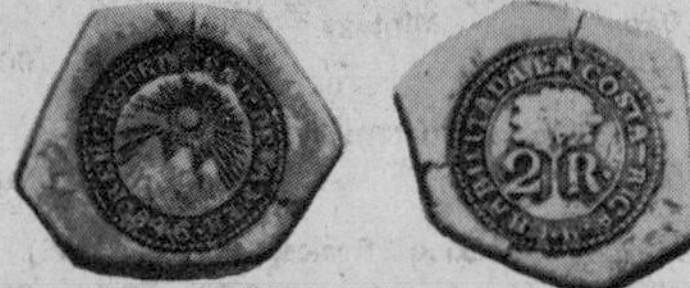

SILVER

c/s: Type V on Bolivia (Potosi) 'cob' 2 Reales of Philip V.

C#	Date	Year	Mintage	Good	VG	Fine
13.1	1846	(1700-46)	—	20.00	35.00	60.00

c/s: Type V on Peru (Lima) 'cob' 2 Reales of Philip V.

C#	Date	Year	Mintage	Good	VG	Fine
13.2	1846	(1700-46)	—	20.00	35.00	60.00

4 REALES

SILVER

c/s: Type IV with additional '4' in square on Guatemala 'cob' 4 Reales.

C#	Date	Year	Mintage	Good	VG	Fine
13.5	1846	—	—	250.00	400.00	600.00

c/s: Type IV with additional '4' in square on United States 50 Cents, C#32a.

C#	Date	Year	Mintage	Good	VG	Fine
13.6	1837	—	—	—	—	—

8 REALES

SILVER

c/s: Type V with additional 8 in circle on Bolivia (Potosi) 'cob' 8 Reales of Philip V.

C#	Date	Year	Mintage	Good	VG	Fine
15.1	1846	(1700-46)	—	400.00	550.00	800.00

c/s: Type V on Guatemala 'cob' 8 Reales, C#8.

C#	Date	Year	Mintage	Good	VG	Fine
15.2	1846	(1747-53)	—	400.00	550.00	800.00

c/s: Type V on Peru (Lima) 'cob' 8 Reales of Charles II.

C#	Date	Year	Mintage	Good	VG	Fine
15.3	1846	(1665-1700)	—	400.00	550.00	800.00

c/s: Type V on Peru (Lima) 'cob' 8 Reales of Philip V.

C#	Date	Year	Mintage	Good	VG	Fine
15.4	1846	(1700-46)	—	400.00	550.00	800.00

1849-1850

c/s: Type V on Mexico City 'Cob' 8 Reales, KM#48.

C#	Date	Year	Mintage	Good	VG	Fine
15.5	1846	(1733-34)	—	400.00	550.00	800.00

Type VI

c/s: HABILITADA POR EL GOBIERNO around lion in 5mm circle.

Latin Types

1/2 REAL

.750 SILVER

c/s: Type VI on Costa Rica 1/2 Real, C#2.

C#	Date	Year	Mintage	VG	Fine	VF
17	(1849)	1831 E	—	9.00	12.50	16.50

C#	Date	Year	Mintage	VG	Fine	VF
17		1831 F	—	9.00	12.50	16.50
		1843 M	—	8.00	11.50	15.00
		1845 B	—	8.00	11.50	15.00
		1846 JB	'CRESCA'			
			—	8.00	11.50	15.00
		1846 JB	'CREZCA'			
			—	8.00	11.50	15.00
		1847 JB	—	8.00	11.50	15.00
		1848 JB	—	8.00	11.50	15.00
		1849 JB	—	8.00	11.50	15.00

c/s: Type VI on Costa Rica 1/2 Real, C#11.

C#	Date	Year	Mintage	VG	Fine	VF
17a	(1848)	1842 MM	—	15.00	25.00	40.00

REAL

.750 SILVER

c/s: Type VI on Costa Rica 1 Real, C#3.

C#	Date	Year	Mintage	VG	Fine	VF
18	(1849)	1831 F	—	10.00	25.00	40.00
		1848 JB	—	17.50	30.00	45.00
		1849 JB	—	10.00	25.00	40.00

c/s: Type VI on Costa Rica 1 Real, C#22.

C#	Date	Year	Mintage	VG	Fine	VF
18a	(1849)	1847 JB	—	25.00	35.00	50.00
		1849 JB	(error) backwards B			
			—	—	—	50.00

c/s: Type VI on Costa Rica 1 Real, C#23.

C#	Date	Year	Mintage	VG	Fine	VF
18b	(1849)	1849 JB	—	20.00	30.00	50.00
		1850 JB	—	20.00	30.00	50.00

2 REALES

.750 SILVER

c/s: Type VI on Costa Rica 2 Reales, C#4.

C#	Date	Year	Mintage	VG	Fine	VF
19	(1849)	1849 JB	—	9.00	14.00	25.00

8 REALES

NOTE: Silver dollar size coins with the lion c/s are modern fabrications.

1/2 ESCUDO

1.7000 gm., .875 GOLD, .0478 oz AGW

c/s: Type VI on Costa Rica 1/2 Escudo, C#6.

C#	Date	Year	Mintage	Fine	VF	XF
20	(1857)	1828 F	Inc. Ab.	100.00	125.00	175.00
		1843 M	Inc. Ab.	100.00	125.00	175.00
		1846 JB	Inc. Ab.	50.00	75.00	100.00
		1847 JB	Inc. Ab.	50.00	75.00	100.00
		1848 JB	Inc. Ab.	50.00	75.00	100.00
		1849 JB	Inc. Ab.	75.00	100.00	125.00

ESCUDO

3.3000 gm., .875 GOLD, .0928 oz AGW

c/s: Type VI on Costa Rica 1 Escudo, C#7.

C#	Date	Year	Mintage	Fine	VF	XF
21	(1857)	1833 E	Inc. Ab.	100.00	125.00	175.00
		1833 F	Inc. Ab.	100.00	125.00	175.00
		1844 M	Inc. Ab.	75.00	100.00	135.00
		1845 JB	Inc. Ab.	100.00	150.00	250.00
		1846 JB	Inc. Ab.	75.00	100.00	135.00
		1847 JB	Inc. Ab.	75.00	100.00	135.00
		1848 JB	Inc. Ab.	75.00	100.00	135.00
		1849 JB	Inc. Ab.	75.00	100.00	135.00

c/s: Type VI on Costa Rica 1 Escudo, C#16.

C#	Date	Mintage	Fine	VF	XF
21a	1842 MM	Inc. Ab.	325.00	400.00	500.00

English Types

6 PENCE

.925 SILVER

c/s: Type VI on Great Britain 6 Pence, C#29.

C#	Date	Year	Mintage	VG	Fine	VF
18a.1	ND (1816-1820)		—	10.00	20.00	35.00

c/s: Type VI on Great Britain 6 Pence, C#60.

C#	Date	Year	Mintage	VG	Fine	VF
18a.2	ND (1826-1829)		—	15.00	27.50	45.00

c/s: Type VI on Great Britain 6 Pence, Y#5.

C#	Date	Year	Mintage	VG	Fine	VF
18a.3	ND (1838-1849)		—	10.00	20.00	35.00

SHILLING

.925 SILVER

c/s: Type VI on Great Britain Shilling, C#32.

C#	Date	Year	Mintage	VG	Fine	VF
19a.2	ND	(1816-20)	—	12.50	22.50	40.00

c/s: Type VI on Great Britain Shilling, Y#6.

C#	Date	Year	Mintage	VG	Fine	VF
19a.1	ND (1838-1849)		—	10.00	20.00	35.00

DECIMAL COINAGE

100 Centavos = 1 Peso (1865-1896)

1/4 CENTAVO

COPPER-NICKEL

Y#	Date	Mintage	VG	Fine	VF	XF
32	ND(1865)	.020	25.00	50.00	80.00	125.00

CENTAVO

COPPER-NICKEL

Y#	Date	Mintage	VG	Fine	VF	XF
30	1865	.033	4.50	10.00	14.00	22.50
	1866	.038	6.00	12.50	18.50	30.00
	1867	.044	10.00	17.50	25.00	40.00
	1868	.020	3.00	7.50	10.00	16.50

Y#	Date	Mintage	VG	Fine	VF	XF
31	1874	.031	2.50	4.00	6.50	10.00

5 CENTAVOS

1.2680 gm., .750 SILVER, .0305 oz ASW

Y#	Date	Mintage	VG	Fine	VF	XF
9	1865 GW	.200	2.50	4.00	9.00	20.00
	1869 GW	—	3.50	7.50	17.50	30.00
	1870 GW	.027	6.00	15.00	35.00	40.00
	1871 GW	—	6.00	15.00	30.00	40.00
	1872 GW	.328	6.00	15.00	30.00	40.00
	1875/1 GW	—	—	—	—	—
	1875 GW	—	2.50	4.00	9.00	20.00

Y#	Date	Mintage	Fine	VF	XF	Unc
13	1885 GW	.180	1.50	3.00	6.00	15.00
	1886/5 GW	.251	1.50	3.50	7.00	17.50
	1886 GW	Inc. Ab.	1.50	3.00	6.00	15.00
	1887 GW	.491	1.50	3.00	6.00	15.00

MINTMARK: HEATON BIRMM

Y#	Date	Mintage	Fine	VF	XF	Unc
17	1889	.541	1.50	2.00	3.00	12.50
	1890	.431	1.50	2.00	3.00	12.50
	1892	.280	1.50	2.00	3.00	12.50

1/16 PESO

.750 SILVER

Y#	Date	Mintage	VG	Fine	VF	XF
5	1850 JB	—	10.00	17.50	30.00	45.00
	1855/0 JB	—	—	—	—	100.00
	1855 JB	—	10.00	17.50	30.00	55.00
	1862 JB	—	30.00	50.00	85.00	125.00

10 CENTAVOS

2.5361 gm., .750 SILVER, .0611 oz ASW

Y#	Date	Mintage	VG	Fine	VF	XF
10	1865 GW	.185	3.00	5.00	12.50	25.00
	1868 GW	.010	35.00	65.00	125.00	200.00
	1870 GW	.048	8.00	12.00	25.00	40.00
	1872 GW	.018	32.50	65.00	125.00	200.00

Y#	Date	Mintage	VG	Fine	VF	XF
10a	1875/1 GW	.286	4.00	6.00	12.50	25.00
	1875 GW	Inc. Ab.	3.00	5.00	10.00	20.00

Y#	Date	Mintage	Fine	VF	XF	Unc
14	1886 GW	.120	2.00	3.50	8.50	20.00
	1887 GW	.245	2.00	3.00	7.50	17.50

MINTMARK: HEATON BIRMM

Y#	Date	Mintage	Fine	VF	XF	Unc
18	1889	.260	2.00	3.00	7.00	12.00
	1890	.220	2.50	4.00	7.00	12.00
	1892	.140	2.50	4.00	7.00	12.00

1/8 PESO

.750 SILVER

Y#	Date	Mintage	VG	Fine	VF	XF
6	1850 JB	—	6.00	10.00	20.00	40.00
	1853 JB	—	6.00	10.00	25.00	50.00
	1855 JB	—	6.00	10.00	20.00	40.00

1/4 PESO

.750 SILVER

Y#	Date	Mintage	VG	Fine	VF	XF
7	1850 JB	—	7.50	12.50	17.50	40.00
	1853 JB	—	10.00	17.50	30.00	50.00
	1855 JB	—	12.50	25.00	40.00	60.00

25 CENTAVOS

6.3402 gm., .750 SILVER, .1528 oz ASW

Y#	Date	Mintage	VG	Fine	VF	XF
11	1864 GW	.223	7.50	15.00	35.00	75.00

Y#	Date	Mintage	VG	Fine	VF	XF
11a	1864 GW	Inc. Ab.	12.50	25.00	40.00	65.00
	1865 GW	.042	5.00	7.50	15.00	35.00
	1875 GW	.121	5.00	7.50	15.00	35.00

GW 9Ds　　9Ds GW

Rev: GW 9Ds

Y#	Date	Mintage	Fine	VF	XF	Unc
15.1	1886 GW	.100	5.00	6.50	13.50	32.50
	1887 GW	.200	BV	5.00	8.50	15.00

Rev: 9Ds GW

Y#	Date	Mintage	Fine	VF	XF	Unc
15.2	1886 GW	Inc. Ab.	5.00	7.00	13.00	37.50
	1887 GW	Inc. Ab.	BV	5.00	7.50	12.50

MINTMARK: HEATON BIRMM.

Y#	Date	Mintage	Fine	VF	XF	Unc
19	1889	.404	BV	5.00	10.00	20.00
	1890/80	.395	BV	6.00	12.50	25.00
	1890	Inc. Ab.	BV	5.00	10.00	20.00
	1892	.440	BV	5.00	10.00	20.00
	1893	.670	BV	BV	6.00	12.50

50 CENTAVOS

12.6804 gm., .750 SILVER, .3058 oz ASW

Y#	Date	Mintage	VG	Fine	VF	XF
12	1865 GW	.029	BV	15.00	25.00	65.00
	1866/5 GW	.117	BV	15.00	25.00	65.00
	1866 GW	I.A.	BV	15.00	25.00	65.00
	1867 GW	.005	50.00	100.00	200.00	275.00
	1870 GW	.006	50.00	100.00	200.00	275.00
	1872 GW	I.A.	50.00	100.00	200.00	275.00
	1875 GW	.069	BV	15.00	25.00	65.00

Y#	Date	Mintage	Fine	VF	XF	Unc
16	1880 GW	.389	BV	12.50	20.00	45.00
	1885 GW	.152	BV	12.50	20.00	45.00
	1886 GW	.097	BV	12.50	20.00	45.00
	1887 GW	.208	BV	12.50	20.00	45.00
	1890 GW	.058	BV	12.50	20.00	45.00

PESO

1.5253 gm., .875 GOLD, .0429 oz AGW

Y#	Date	Mintage	VG	Fine	VF	XF
26	1864 GW	6,383	40.00	50.00	75.00	100.00
	1866 GW	.035	35.00	45.00	70.00	90.00
	1868 GW	—	50.00	60.00	85.00	125.00

NOTE: Several varieties exist of the 1866.

Design modified

Y#	Date	Mintage	VG	Fine	VF	XF
26a	1871 GW	.011	40.00	50.00	65.00	90.00
26a	1872 GW	.037	40.00	50.00	65.00	90.00

2 PESOS

2.9355 gm., .875 GOLD, .0825 oz AGW

Y#	Date	Mintage	VG	Fine	VF	XF
27	1866 GW	.013	65.00	85.00	100.00	150.00
	1867 GW	—	75.00	100.00	125.00	200.00
	1868 GW	—	65.00	85.00	100.00	150.00

Design modified (19mm)

Y#	Date	Mintage	VG	Fine	VF	XF
27a	1876 GW	2,161	125.00	200.00	350.00	500.00

5 PESOS

7.3387 gm., .875 GOLD, 22mm, .2064 oz AGW

Y#	Date	Mintage	VG	Fine	VF	XF
28	1867 GW	.039	BV	150.00	175.00	250.00
	1868 GW	6,752	BV	150.00	175.00	250.00
	1869 GW	.011	BV	150.00	175.00	250.00
	1870 GW	.015	BV	150.00	175.00	250.00

21mm

Y#	Date	Mintage	VG	Fine	VF	XF
28a	1873 GW	5,167	BV	150.00	250.00	350.00
	1875 GW	I.A.	BV	150.00	250.00	350.00

8.0645 gm., .900 GOLD, .2333 oz AGW

Y#	Date	Mintage	VG	Fine	VF	XF
33	1873 GW	I.A.	300.00	500.00	750.00	1000.

10 PESOS

14.6774 gm., .875 GOLD, .4129 oz AGW

Y#	Date	Mintage	VG	Fine	VF	XF
29	1870 GW	.020	BV	275.00	350.00	500.00
	1871 GW	.030	BV	325.00	400.00	550.00
	1872 GW	4,555	BV	275.00	350.00	500.00

Design modified

Y#	Date	Mintage	VG	Fine	VF	XF
29a	1876 GW	3,389	200.00	350.00	500.00	700.00

20 PESOS

32.2580 gm., .900 GOLD, .9334 oz AGW

Y#	Date	Mintage	Fine	VF	XF	Unc
34	1873 GW	—	—	—	7500.	10,000.

COUNTERSTAMP ISSUES

1889

Type VII

Obv. c/s: COSTA RICA above national arms.
Rev: HABILITADA POR EL GOBIERNO around lion/CR in circle.

50 CENTAVOS

12.6804 gm., .750 SILVER, .3058 oz ASW
c/s: Type VII on Colombia (Bogota) 50 Centavos, Y#16.

Y#	Date	Year	Mintage	VG	Fine	VF
20.1	(1889)	1872	—	35.00	75.00	100.00
		1873	—	25.00	50.00	75.00
		1874	—	20.00	40.00	60.00

c/s: Type VII on Colombia (Bogota) Cincuenta Centavos, Y#17.

Y#	Date	Year	Mintage	VG	Fine	VF
20.2	(1889)	1874	—	30.00	45.00	65.00
		1875	—	30.00	45.00	65.00
		1876	—	30.00	45.00	65.00
		1877	—	30.00	45.00	65.00
		1878	—	30.00	45.00	65.00
		1879	—	25.00	40.00	60.00
		1880	—	25.00	40.00	60.00
		1881	—	25.00	40.00	60.00
		1882	—	25.00	40.00	60.00
		1883	—	25.00	40.00	60.00
		1884	—	25.00	40.00	60.00
		1885	—	50.00	80.00	125.00

c/s: Type VII on Colombia (Medellin) Cinco Decimos, Y#9.

Y#	Date	Year	Mintage	VG	Fine	VF
20.3	(1889)	1875	—	35.00	50.00	75.00
		1876	—	35.00	50.00	75.00
		1877	—	35.00	50.00	75.00
		1878	—	35.00	50.00	75.00
		1879	—	35.00	50.00	75.00
		1880	—	35.00	50.00	75.00
		1881	—	30.00	45.00	65.00
		1882	—	30.00	45.00	65.00
		1883	—	30.00	45.00	65.00
		1884	—	25.00	40.00	60.00
		1885	—	25.00	40.00	60.00
		1886	—	75.00	100.00	150.00

MONETARY REFORM

100 Centimos = 1 Colon

2 CENTIMOS

COPPER-NICKEL

Y#	Date	Mintage	VF	XF	Unc
46	1903	.360	1.25	2.25	5.00

5 CENTIMOS

1.0000 gm., .900 SILVER, .0289 oz ASW

Y#	Date	Mintage	VF	XF	Unc
39	1905	.500	1.25	1.75	5.00
	1910	.400	1.25	1.75	5.00
	1912	.540	1.25	1.75	5.00
	1914	.510	1.25	1.75	5.00

5 CENTAVOS

BRASS

Y#	Date	Mintage	VF	XF	Unc
47	1917	.400	2.50	6.00	15.00
	1918	1.000	2.50	6.00	15.00
	1919	.500	2.50	6.00	15.00

5 CENTIMOS

BRASS

Y#	Date	Mintage	VF	XF	Unc
49	1920	.500	2.50	6.00	15.00
	1921	.500	2.50	6.00	15.00
	1922	.500	2.50	6.00	15.00
	1936	1.500	.60	.90	5.00
	1938	1.000	.60	.90	5.00
	1940	1.300	.60	.90	5.00
	1941	1.000	1.75	2.75	5.00

BRONZE

Y#	Date	Mintage	VF	XF	Unc
51	1929	1.500	.60	1.25	6.00

COPPER-NICKEL

Y#	Date	Mintage	VF	XF	Unc
58	1942	.270	1.50	2.00	4.00

NOTE: The above issue was struck over 2 Centimos, Y#46.

BRASS

Y#	Date	Mintage	VF	XF	Unc
A58	1942	1.730	.25	.60	3.50
	1943	1.000	.25	.60	3.50
	1946	1.000	.75	1.35	3.50
	1947	3.000	.25	.60	3.50

COPPER-NICKEL
Large lettering: B.C. - C.R. divided.

Y#	Date	Mintage	VF	XF	Unc
A64	1951	3.000	.50	.75	1.25

Small lettering, Obv: Small ships, 5 stars in shield.
Rev: B.C.C.R. not divided.

Y#	Date	Mintage	VF	XF	Unc
64.1	1951	7.000	.15	.40	.65

STAINLESS-STEEL

Y#	Date	Mintage	VF	XF	Unc
66	1953	9.040	—	.10	.25
	1958	19.940	—	—	.10
	1967	6.020	—	.10	.20

COPPER-NICKEL
Obv: Small ships, 7 stars in shield.

Y#	Date	Mintage	VF	XF	Unc
64.2	1969	20.000	—	.10	.15

Obv: Large ships, 7 stars in shield.

Y#	Date	Mintage	VF	XF	Unc
64.3	1972	12.550	—	.10	.15
	1973	20.000	—	.10	.15
	1976	30.000	—	—	.10

10 CENTIMOS

2.0000 gm., .900 SILVER, .0578 oz ASW

Y#	Date	Mintage	VF	XF	Unc
40	1905	.400	1.75	3.00	4.50
	1910	.400	1.75	3.00	4.50
	1912	.270	2.00	3.50	5.50
	1914	.150	2.25	4.00	7.00

10 CENTAVOS

2.0000 gm., .500 SILVER, .0321 oz ASW

Y#	Date	Mintage	VF	XF	Unc
42	1917	.100	2.50	5.00	7.50

BRASS

Y#	Date	Mintage	VF	XF	Unc
48	1917	.500	1.00	2.00	4.00
	1918	.900	1.00	2.00	4.00
	1919	.250	1.00	3.00	5.50

10 CENTIMOS

BRASS

Y#	Date	Mintage	VF	XF	Unc
50	1920	.850	.60	1.75	3.00
	1921	.750	.60	1.75	3.00
	1922	.750	.60	1.75	3.00

BRONZE

Y#	Date	Mintage	VF	XF	Unc
52	1929	.500	.75	1.75	3.50

BRASS

Y#	Date	Mintage	VF	XF	Unc
54	1936	.750	.50	.60	1.50
	1941	.500	.45	.60	2.00

Y#	Date	Mintage	VF	XF	Unc
B58	1942	1.000	.25	.50	1.00
	1943	.500	.35	.75	2.00
	1946	.500	.35	.75	2.00
	1947	1.500	.25	.50	1.00

COPPER-NICKEL
Obv: Small ships, 5 stars in shield.

Y#	Date	Mintage	VF	XF	Unc
65	1951	2.500	.20	.70	1.00

STAINLESS-STEEL

Y#	Date	Mintage	VF	XF	Unc
67	1953	5.290	—	.10	.25
	1958	10.470	—	—	.15
	1967	5.500	—	.10	.20

COPPER-NICKEL
Obv: Small ships, 7 stars in field.

Y#	Date	Mintage	VF	XF	Unc
65.1	1969	10.000	—	—	.15
	1975	5.000	—	—	.15
	1976	40.000	—	—	.15

Obv: Large ships, 7 stars in field

Y#	Date	Mintage	VF	XF	Unc
65.2	1972	20.000	—	—	.15
	1975	Inc. Ab.	—	—	.15
	1976	Inc. Ab.	—	—	.15

25 CENTIMOS

3.4500 gm., .650 SILVER, .0721 oz ASW

Y#	Date	Mintage	VF	XF	Unc
45	1924	1.340	2.50	3.50	6.00

COPPER-NICKEL

Y#	Date	Mintage	VF	XF	Unc
55	1935	1.200	.50	1.35	2.25

Y#	Date	Mintage	VF	XF	Unc
59	1937	1.600	.60	1.35	2.25
	1937	—	—	Proof	100.00
	1948	9.200	.25	.50	.75

BRASS

Y#	Date	Mintage	VF	XF	Unc
63	1944	.800	.50	.75	1.25
	1945	1.200	.45	.60	1.00
	1946	1.200	.45	.60	1.00

BRONZE

Y#	Date	Mintage	VF	XF	Unc
63a	1945	Inc. Ab.	.90	1.25	2.00

COPPER-NICKEL
Obv: Small ships, 7 stars in shield.

Y#	Date	Mintage	VF	XF	Unc
70.1	1967	4.000	—	—	.20
	1969	4.000	—	—	.20
	1974	—	—	—	.20

Obv: Large ships, 7 stars in shield.

Y#	Date	Mintage	VF	XF	Unc
70.2	1972	8.000	—	—	.20
	1974	—	—	—	—
	1976	12.000	—	—	.20

50 CENTIMOS

10.0000 gm., .900 SILVER, .2893 oz ASW

Y#	Date	Mintage	VF	XF	Unc
41	1902CY	.120	25.00	35.00	50.00
	1903JCV	.380	20.00	30.00	45.00
	1914GCR	.200	500.00	850.00	1200.

10.0000 gm., .500 SILVER, .1607 oz ASW

Y#	Date	Mintage	VF	XF	Unc
A42	1917GCR	9,400	500.00	800.00	1000.
	1918GCR	*.030	550.00	900.00	1250.

NOTE: All but 10 examples of the 1917 issue and most of the 1918 mintage were counterstamped Un Colon, Y#44.

COPPER-NICKEL

Y#	Date	Mintage	VF	XF	Unc
56	1935	.700	1.00	1.75	2.50

Y#	Date	Mintage	VF	XF	Unc
60	1937	.600	.60	1.25	2.00
	1937	—	—	Proof	125.00

Y#	Date	Mintage	VF	XF	Unc
60a	1948	4.000	.30	.50	.90

Obv: Small ships, 7 stars in shield.

Y#	Date	Mintage	VF	XF	Unc
71.1	1965	1.000	.15	.25	1.00
	1968	2.000	.10	.15	.50
	1970	4.000	.10	.15	.30

Obv: Large ships, 7 stars in shield.

Y#	Date	Mintage	VF	XF	Unc
71.2	1972	4.000	.10	.15	.30
	1975	.524	.10	.15	.30
	1976	6.000	.10	.15	.30

UN (1) COLON

COPPER-NICKEL

Y#	Date	Mintage	VF	XF	Unc
57	1935	.350	1.25	2.25	4.00

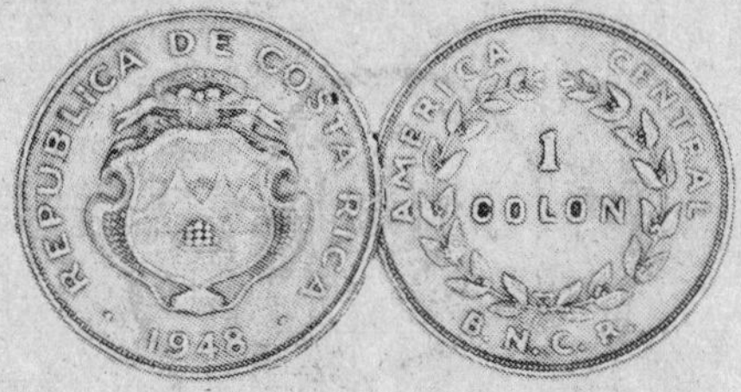

Y#	Date	Mintage	VF	XF	Unc
61	1937	.300	1.25	2.25	3.75
	1937	—	—	Proof	150.00
	1948	1.350	.40	.60	1.00

STAINLESS-STEEL

Y#	Date	Mintage	VF	XF	Unc
68	1954	.990	.20	.40	.75

COPPER-NICKEL
Obv: Small ships, 5 stars in shield.

Y#	Date	Mintage	VF	XF	Unc
68a	1961	1.000	.20	.35	1.00

Obv: Small ships, 7 stars in shield.

Y#	Date	Mintage	VF	XF	Unc
68a.1	1965	1.000	.20	.35	1.00
	1968	2.000	.20	.25	.50
	1970	2.000	.20	.25	.50
	1974	—	—	—	—

Obv: Large ships, 7 stars in shield.

Y#	Date	Mintage	VF	XF	Unc
68a.2	1972	2.000	.20	.25	.50
	1975	1.000	.20	.25	.50
	1976	12.000	.20	.25	.50

DOS (2) COLONES

1.5560 gm., .900 GOLD, .0450 oz AGW

Y#	Date	Mintage	VF	XF	Unc
35	1897	500 pcs.	—Proof Only		500.00
	1900	.045	60.00	80.00	100.00
	1915	5,000	75.00	100.00	125.00
	1916	5,000	75.00	100.00	125.00
	1921	3,000	100.00	125.00	175.00
	1922	.013	60.00	80.00	100.00
	1926	.015	60.00	80.00	100.00
	1928	.025	50.00	75.00	100.00

COPPER-NICKEL

Y#	Date	Mintage	VF	XF	Unc
62	1948	1.380	1.00	1.50	2.00

STAINLESS-STEEL
Obv: Small ships, 5 stars in shield.

Y#	Date	Mintage	VF	XF	Unc
69	1954	1.030	.30	.50	1.25

COPPER-NICKEL

Y#	Date	Mintage	VF	XF	Unc
69a	1961	—	.30	.50	1.25

Obv: Large ships, 7 stars in shield.

Y#	Date	Mintage	VF	XF	Unc
69a.1	1961	1.000	.30	.50	1.00

Obv: Small ships, 7 stars in shield.

Y#	Date	Mintage	VF	XF	Unc
69a.2	1968	2.000	.30	.40	.75
	1970	1.000	.30	.50	.90
	1972	2.000	.30	.40	.75

4.3000 gm., 1.000 SILVER, .1382 oz ASW
20th Anniversary of the Central Bank

H#	Date	Mintage	XF	Unc	Proof
1	1970	2,000	—	5.00	—
	1970	1,800	—	—	12.50

CINCO (5) COLONES

3.8900 gm., .900 GOLD, .1125 oz AGW

Y#	Date	Mintage	VF	XF	Unc
36	1899	.100	75.00	100.00	125.00
	1900	.100	75.00	100.00	125.00

10.7800 gm., 1.000 SILVER, .3466 oz ASW
400th Year of the Founding of New Carthage

H#	Date	Mintage	XF	Unc	Proof
2	1970	500 pcs.	—	12.50	—
	1970	1,800	—	—	25.00

NICKEL
25th Anniversary of the Central Bank

Y#	Date	Mintage	VF	XF	Unc
85	1975	2.000	.75	.90	1.25
	1975	5,000	—	Proof	3.00

DIEZ (10) COLONES

7.7800 gm., .900 GOLD, .2251 oz AGW

Y#	Date	Mintage	VF	XF	Unc
37	1897	.060	BV	175.00	250.00
	1899	.050	BV	175.00	250.00
	1900	.140	BV	160.00	200.00

21.5600 gm., 1.000 SILVER, .6932 oz ASW
Obv: Similar to 5 Colones, H#2.

H#	Date	Mintage	XF	Unc	Proof
3	1970	500 pcs.	—	25.00	—
	1970	1,800	—	—	35.00

NICKEL
25th Anniversary of the Central Bank

Y#	Date	Mintage	VF	XF	Unc
86	1975	.500	1.50	1.75	2.00
	1975	5,000	—	Proof	5.00

VIENTE (20) COLONES

15.5600 gm., .900 GOLD, .4502 oz AGW

38	1897	.020	300.00	350.00	500.00
	1899	.025	300.00	350.00	500.00
	1900	5,000	350.00	450.00	600.00

43.1200 gm., 1.000 SILVER, 1.3864 oz ASW
Obv: Similar to 5 Colones, H#2.

H#	Date	Mintage	XF	Unc	Proof
4	1970	2,800	BV	45.00	—
	1970	1,800	—	—	65.00

NICKEL
25th Anniversary of the Central Bank

Y#	Date	Mintage	VF	XF	Unc
87	1975	.250	3.00	3.50	4.50
	1975	5,000	—	Proof	10.00

25 COLONES

53.9000 gm., 1.000 SILVER, 1.7331 oz ASW
25 Years of Social Legislation
Obv: Similar to 5 Colones, H#2.

H#	Date	Mintage	XF	Unc	Proof
5	1970	700	60.00	75.00	—
	1970	1,800	—	—	60.00

50 COLONES

7.4500 gm., .900 GOLD, .2155 oz AGW

Fr#	Date	Mintage	XF	Unc	Proof
27	1970	3,000	—	—	150.00

25.3100 gm., .500 SILVER, .4069 oz ASW
Conservation Commemorative

Y#	Date	Mintage	VF	XF	Unc
82	1974	5,438	—	—	25.00

28.2800 gm., .925 SILVER, .8411 oz ASW

82a	1974	.011	—	Proof	30.00

100 COLONES

14.9000 gm., .900 GOLD, .4311 oz AGW

Fr#	Date	Mintage	XF	Unc	Proof
26	1970	3,000	—	—	300.00

31.6500 gm., .500 SILVER, .5088 oz ASW
Conservation Commemorative
Obv: Similar to 50 Colones, Y#82.

Y#	Date	Mintage	VF	XF	Unc
83	1974	5,438	—	—	40.00

35.0000 gm., .925 SILVER, 1.0409 oz ASW

83a	1974	.011	—	Proof	50.00

International Year of the Child

88	1979	.095	—	—	—
	1979	5,000	—	Proof	50.00

200 COLONES

29.8000 gm., .900 GOLD, .8623 oz AGW

Obv: Similar to 100 Colones, Fr#26.

Fr#	Date	Mintage	XF	Unc	Proof
25	1970	3,000	—	—	600.00

500 COLONES

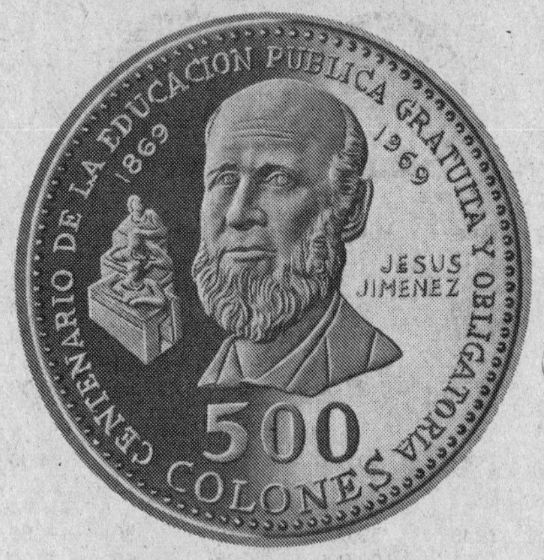

74.5200 gm., .900 GOLD, 2.1565 oz AGW
Obv: Similar to 100 Colones, Fr#26.

Fr#	Date	Mintage	XF	Unc	Proof
24	1970	3,000	—	—	1500.

1000 COLONES

194.0400 gm., .900 GOLD, 5.6153 oz AGW
Obv: Similar to 100 Colones, Fr#26.

Fr#	Date	Mintage	XF	Unc	Proof
23	1970	3,000	—	—	4000.

1500 COLONES

33.4370 gm., .900 GOLD, .9676 oz AGW
Conservation Commemorative
Obv: Similar to 50 Colones, Y#82.

Y#	Date	Mintage	VF	XF	Unc
84	1974	3,348	—	—	700.00
	1974	3,000	—	Proof	800.00

COUNTERSTAMP ISSUES

50 CENTIMOS

1923

Type VIII

Obv. c/s: 1923 in 11mm circle.
Rev. c/s: 50 CENTIMOS in 11mm circle.

.900 SILVER

c/s: 1923/50 CENTIMOS on 25 Centavos, Y#11.

Y#	Date	Year	Mintage	Fine	VF	XF
43.1	1923	1864 GW	—	—	Rare	—

c/s: 1923/50 CENTIMOS on 25 Centavos, Y#11a.

Y#	Date	Year	Mintage	Fine	VF	XF
43.2	1923	1864 GW	—	—	Rare	—
		1865 GW	—	25.00	35.00	50.00
		1875 GW	—	25.00	35.00	50.00

c/s: 1923/50 CENTIMOS on 25 Centavos, Y#15.
Rev: GW 9Ds

Y#	Date	Year	Mintage	Fine	VF	XF
43.3	1923	1886 GW	—	6.00	8.00	12.00
		1887 GW	—	6.00	8.00	12.00

Rev: 9Ds GW

Y#	Date	Year	Mintage	Fine	VF	XF
43.4	1923	1886 GW	—	8.00	12.00	20.00
		1887 GW	—	6.00	8.00	12.00

c/s: 1923/50 CENTIMOS on 25 Centavos, Y#19.

Y#	Date	Year	Mintage	Fine	VF	XF
43.5	1923	1889	—	6.00	8.00	12.00
		1890	—	6.00	8.00	12.00
		1892	—	6.00	8.00	12.00
		1893	—	6.00	8.00	12.00

NOTE: A total mintage of 1,866,000 was created by counterstamping the above coins.

UN (1) COLON

1923

Type IX

Obv. c/s: 1923 in 14mm circle.
Rev. c/s: UN COLON in 14mm circle.

.900 SILVER
1923/UN COLON on 50 Centavos, Y#12.

C#	Date	Year	Mintage	VF	XF	Unc
44.1	1923	1865 GW	—	25.00	35.00	50.00
		1866/5 GW	—	30.00	40.00	60.00
		1867 GW	—	35.00	50.00	75.00
		1870 GW	—	—	Rare	—
		1872 GW	—	—	Rare	—
		1875 GW	—	25.00	35.00	50.00

1923/UN COLON on 50 Centavos, Y#16.

Y#	Date	Year	Mintage	Fine	VF	XF
44.2	1923	1880 GW	—	10.00	12.50	17.50
		1885 GW	—	10.00	12.50	17.50
		1886 GW	—	10.00	12.50	17.50
		1887 GW	—	12.00	15.00	20.00
		1890 GW	—	10.00	12.50	17.50

1923/UN COLON on 50 Centimos, Y#41.

Y#	Date	Year	Mintage	Fine	VF	XF
44.3	1923	1902 CY	—	10.00	15.00	20.00
		1903 JCV	—	10.00	12.50	17.50
		1914 GCR	—	15.00	20.00	25.00

1923/UN COLON on 50 Centimos, Y#A42.

Y#	Date	Year	Mintage	Fine	VF	XF
44.4	1923	1917GCR	9,390	15.00	20.00	30.00
		1918GCR	.030	20.00	30.00	50.00

NOTE: A total mintage of 460,000 was created by counterstamping the above coins.

NCLT ISSUES

PATTERNS

KM#	Date	Mintage	Identification	Mkt.Val.
1	1850	—	Onza, Gold, C#A25	—

PROOF SETS

STANDARD METALS

KM#	Date	Mintage	Identification	Issue Price	Mkt. Val.
101	1937(3)	—	Y59-61	—	350.00
102	1970(5)	2,300	H1-5	52.00	135.00
103	1970(5)	3,000	F23-27	832.00	6500.
104	1974(2)	30,000	Y82a,83a	50.00	75.00
105	1975(3)	—	Y85-87	—	17.50
106	1976(5)	5,000	Y66a,67b,70a,71a,68b	—	—

Listings For

CRETE: refer to Greece

CROATIA: refer to Yugoslavia

CUBA

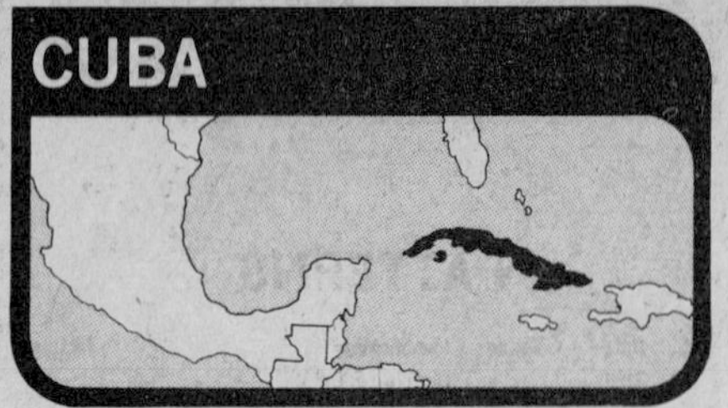

The Republic of Cuba, situated at the northern edge of the Caribbean Sea about 90 miles (145 km.) south of Florida, has an area of 44,200 sq. mi. (114,477 sq. km.) and a population of 9.5 million. Capital: Havana. The Cuban economy is based on the cultivation and refining of sugar, which provides 80 percent of export earnings.

Discovered by Columbus in 1492 and settled by Diego Velasquez in the early 1500s, Cuba remained a Spanish possession until 1898, except for a brief British occupancy in 1762-63. Cuban attempts to gain freedom were crushed, even while Spain was granting independence to its other American possessions. Ten years of warfare, 1868-78, between Spanish troops and Cuban rebels exacted guarantees of rights which were never implemented. The final revolt, begun in 1895, evoked American sympathy, and with the aid of U.S. troops independence was proclaimed on May 20, 1902. Fulgencio Batista seized the government in 1952 and established a dictatorship. Opposition to Batista, led by Fidel Castro, drove him into exile on Jan 1, 1959. A communist-type, 25-member collective leadership headed by Castro was inaugurated in March, 1962.

RULERS

Spanish, until 1898

MONETARY SYSTEM

100 Centavos = 1 Peso

PROVINCE OF TRINIDAD

2 REALES

.903 SILVER

c/s: Lattice on Spanish (Seville) 2 Reales, C#38.

KM#	Date	Mintage	Good	VG	Fine
10	ND(1772-78)	—	8.50	17.50	25.00

c/s: Lattice on Spanish (Madrid) 2 Reales, C#69.

KM#	Date	Mintage	Good	VG	Fine
11	ND(1788-1808)	—	7.50	15.00	22.50

c/s: Lattice on Spanish (Seville) 2 Reales, C#69.

KM#	Date	Mintage	Good	VG	Fine
12	ND(1788-1808)	—	7.50	15.00	22.50

c/s: Lattice on Spanish (Catalonia) 2 Reales, C#134.

KM#	Date	Mintage	Good	VG	Fine
13	ND(1810-33)	—	7.50	15.00	22.50

c/s: Lattice on Spanish (Madrid) 2 Reales, C#134.

KM#	Date	Mintage	Good	VG	Fine
14	ND(1810-33)	—	7.50	15.00	22.50

c/s: Lattice on Spanish (Seville) 2 Reales, C#134.

KM#	Date	Mintage	Good	VG	Fine
15	ND(1810-33)	—	7.50	15.00	22.50

c/s: Lattice on Spanish (Madrid) 4 Reales, C#90.

KM#	Date	Mintage	Good	VG	Fine
16	ND(1808-13)	—	12.50	15.00	20.00

c/s: Lattice on Spanish (Seville) 4 Reales, C#90.

KM#	Date	Mintage	Good	VG	Fine
17	ND(1808-13)	—	12.50	15.00	20.00

CUBA

'KEY' COUNTERSTAMPS

Key counterstamps are found in two varieties:

A - Short & fat

B - Long & thin

It is thought that these c/s were used 1872-1877 by the Cuban revolutionary troops as a fund raising device. Most are struck on Mexican coins.

Values for these pieces vary according to the rarity of the date and type of coin on which the c/s is found. Prices listed here are for the most common.

2 REALES

.903 SILVER

c/s: Key on Mexican 2 Reales, KM#374 (Y#S23).

KM#	Date	Mintage	VG	Fine	VF
1	ND	—	15.00	20.00	25.00

4 REALES

.903 SILVER

c/s: Key on Mexican 4 Reales, KM#375 (Y#S24).

KM#	Date	Mintage	VG	Fine	VF
2	ND	—	20.00	25.00	32.00

8 REALES

.903 SILVER

c/s: Key on Mexican 8 Reales, KM#377 (Y#S25).

KM#	Date	Mintage	VG	Fine	VF
3	ND(1824-97)	—	30.00	45.00	60.00

PESO

.903 SILVER

c/s: Key on Mexican Peso, KM#388.1 (Y#S36).

KM#	Date	Mintage	VG	Fine	VF
4.1	ND(1866-67)	—	40.00	75.00	125.00

c/s: Key on Mexican Peso, KM#408 (Y#15).

KM#	Date	Mintage	VG	Fine	VF
4.2	ND(1869-1909)	—	30.00	45.00	60.00

REGULAR COINAGE

CENTAVO

COPPER-NICKEL

Y#	Date	Mintage	VF	XF	Unc
3	1915	9.390	1.00	2.00	5.00
	1915	—	—	Proof	60.00
	1916	9.310	2.25	3.50	5.50
	1916	—	—	Proof	200.00
	1920	19.300	.40	1.50	2.50
	1938	2.000	8.00	12.50	20.00

BRASS

Y#	Date	Mintage	VF	XF	Unc
3a	1943	20.000	.50	.75	4.00

COPPER-NICKEL

Y#	Date	Mintage	VF	XF	Unc
3b	1946	50.000	.10	.30	.50
	1961	100.000	.35	.60	1.00

BRASS

Marti Centennial

Y#	Date	Mintage	VF	XF	Unc
20	1953	50.000	.15	.45	.75
	1953	—	—	Proof	7.50

COPPER-NICKEL

Y#	Date	Mintage	VF	XF	Unc
24	1958	50.000	.10	.40	.75

ALUMINUM

Y#	Date	Mintage	VF	XF	Unc
27	1963	—	.10	.30	.50
	1966	—	.10	.50	.80
	1969	—	.10	.50	.80
	1970	—	.10	.50	.80
	1971	—	.45	.90	1.50
	1972	—	.10	.50	.80

2 CENTAVOS

COPPER-NICKEL

Y#	Date	Mintage	VF	XF	Unc
4	1915	6.090	1.20	1.60	10.00
	1915	—	—	Proof	80.00
	1916	5.320	1.50	2.50	12.00
	1916	—	—	Proof	125.00

5 CENTAVOS

COPPER-NICKEL

Y#	Date	Mintage	VF	XF	Unc
5	1915	5.090	.50	4.00	10.00
	1915	—	—	Proof	80.00
	1916	1.710	1.00	5.00	12.00
	1916	—	—	Proof	165.00
	1920	10.000	.50	1.00	5.00

Y#	Date	Mintage	VF	XF	Unc
		BRASS			
5a	1943	6.000	2.50	5.00	15.00
		COPPER-NICKEL			
5b	1946	40.000	.15	.35	.60
	1960	20.000	.15	.35	.60
	1961	60.000	.15	.40	.70

ALUMINUM

Y#	Date	Mintage	VF	XF	Unc
28	1963	—	.25	.60	1.50
	1966	—	.25	.60	1.50
	1968	—	.25	.60	1.50
	1969	—	.25	.60	1.50
	1971	—	.25	.60	2.00
	1972	—	.25	.60	1.50

10 CENTAVOS

2.5000 gm., .900 SILVER, .0723 oz ASW

Y#	Date	Mintage	VF	XF	Unc
6	1915	5.690	BV	5.00	10.00
	1915	—	—	Proof	100.00
	1916	.560	6.50	10.00	35.00
	1916	—	—	Proof	200.00
	1920	3.090	BV	2.50	5.00
	1948	5.120	BV	2.50	4.00
	1949	9.980	BV	2.50	4.00

50th Year of Republic

Y#	Date	Mintage	VF	XF	Unc
17	1952	10.000	BV	2.50	4.00

20 CENTAVOS

5.0000 gm., .900 SILVER, .1446 oz ASW

Y#	Date	Mintage	VF	XF	Unc
7	1915	7.910	BV	4.75	12.00
	1915	—	—	Proof	150.00
	1916	2.530	7.50	15.00	25.00
	1916	—	—	Proof	250.00
	1920	6.130	BV	4.75	12.00
	1932	.180	35.00	80.00	200.00
	1948	6.830	BV	4.75	6.00
	1949	13.100	BV	4.75	6.00

50th Year of Republic

Y#	Date	Mintage	VF	XF	Unc
18	1952	8.700	BV	4.75	6.00

COPPER-NICKEL

Y#	Date	Mintage	VF	XF	Unc
25	1962	—	1.00	1.50	3.50
	1968	—	1.00	1.50	3.50

ALUMINUM

Y#	Date	Mintage	VF	XF	Unc
29	1969	—	1.00	1.50	2.50
	1970	—	1.00	1.50	2.50
	1971	—	1.00	1.50	2.50
	1972	—	1.00	1.50	2.50

25 CENTAVOS

6.6800 gm., .900 SILVER, .1933 oz ASW
Marti Centennial

Y#	Date	Mintage	VF	XF	Unc
21	1953	19.000	BV	6.50	7.50
	1953	—	—	Proof	Rare

40 CENTAVOS

10.0000 gm., .900 SILVER, .2893 oz ASW

Y#	Date	Mintage	VF	XF	Unc
8	1915	2.630	BV	25.00	50.00
	1915	—	—	Proof	500.00
	1916	.180	50.00	175.00	400.00
	1916	—	—	Proof	875.00
	1920	.540	10.00	15.00	50.00
	1920	—	—	Proof	Rare

50th Year of Republic

Y#	Date	Mintage	VF	XF	Unc
19	1952	1.250	10.00	12.50	15.00

COPPER-NICKEL

Y#	Date	Mintage	VF	XF	Unc
26	1962	—	BV	9.00	10.00

50 CENTAVOS

13.3600 gm., .900 SILVER, .3866 oz ASW
Marti Centennial

Y#	Date	Mintage	VF	XF	Unc
22	1953	2.000	BV	BV	12.50
	1953	—	—	Proof	Rare

SOUVENIR PESO

26.7300 gm., .900 SILVER, .7735 oz ASW
PAT. 97 on truncation, date widely spaced.

Y#	Date	Mintage	VF	XF	Unc
1	1897	828 pcs.	325.00	450.00	600.00

Date closely spaced, star below 97 baseline.

Y#	Date	Mintage	VF	XF	Unc
1.1	1897	4,286	60.00	80.00	125.00

Date closely spaced, star above 97 baseline.

Y#	Date	Mintage	VF	XF	Unc
1.2	1897	4,856	60.00	80.00	125.00

PESO

.900 SILVER

Y#	Date	Mintage	VF	XF	Unc
2	1898	1,000	350.00	500.00	800.00

Y#	Date	Mintage	VF	XF	Unc
9	1915	1.970	25.00	50.00	75.00
	1915	—	—	Proof	675.00
	1916	.840	30.00	60.00	190.00
	1916	—	—	Proof	900.00
	1932	3.550	25.00	30.00	40.00
	1933	6.000	BV	25.00	40.00
	1934	3.000	BV	25.00	40.00

1.6718 gm., .900 GOLD, .0483 oz AGW

Y#	Date	Mintage	VF	XF	Unc
10	1915	6,850	200.00	300.00	450.00
	1915	—	—	Proof	1000.
	1916	.011	200.00	300.00	500.00
	1916	—	—	Proof	1000.

26.7300 gm., .900 SILVER, .7735 oz ASW
'ABC'

Y#	Date	Mintage	VF	XF	Unc
16	1934	7.000	35.00	50.00	90.00
	1935	12.500	35.00	50.00	90.00
	1936	16.000	35.00	50.00	90.00
	1937	11.500	275.00	425.00	700.00
	1938	10.800	35.00	50.00	90.00
	1939	9.200	35.00	50.00	90.00

Marti Centennial

Y#	Date	Mintage	VF	XF	Unc
23	1953	1.000	BV	25.00	30.00
	1953	—	—	Proof	Rare

2 PESOS

3.3436 gm., .900 GOLD, .0967 oz AGW

Y#	Date	Mintage	VF	XF	Unc
11	1915	.010	100.00	125.00	150.00
	1915	—	—	Proof	1200.
	1916	.150	100.00	125.00	150.00
	1916	—	—	Proof	1200.

4 PESOS

6.6872 gm., .900 GOLD, .1935 oz AGW

Y#	Date	Mintage	VF	XF	Unc
12	1915	6,300	400.00	450.00	600.00
	1915	—	—	Proof	2000.
	1916	.129	175.00	200.00	250.00
	1916	—	—	Proof	2000.

5 PESOS

8.3592 gm., .900 GOLD, .2419 oz AGW

Y#	Date	Mintage	VF	XF	Unc
13	1915	.696	175.00	200.00	225.00
	1915	—	—	Proof	1750.
	1916	1.133	175.00	200.00	225.00
	1916	—	—	Proof	2250.

13.3300 gm., .900 SILVER, .3857 oz ASW
25th Anniversary National Bank of Cuba

Y#	Date	Mintage	VF	XF	Unc
30	1975	.050	—	Proof	40.00

10 PESOS

16.7185 gm., .900 GOLD, .4838 oz AGW

Y#	Date	Mintage	VF	XF	Unc
14	1915	.096	350.00	375.00	400.00
	1915	—	—	Proof	5000.
	1916	1.168	350.00	375.00	400.00
	1916	—	—	Proof	Rare

26.6600 gm., .900 SILVER, .7715 oz ASW
25th Anniversary National Bank of Cuba

Y#	Date	Mintage	VF	XF	Unc
31	1975	.050	—	Proof	45.00

20 PESOS

33.4370 gm., .900 GOLD, .9676 oz AGW

Y#	Date	Mintage	VF	XF	Unc
15	1915	.057	650.00	700.00	850.00
	1915	—	—	Proof	13,000.
	1916	—	—	Proof	*40,000.

***NOTE:** Christensen auction.

26.6680 gm., .925 SILVER, .7931 oz ASW
Agramonte Commemorative

32	1977	.025	—Proof Only	40.00

Gomez Commemorative
Obv: Similar to Y#32.

33	1977	.025	—Proof Only	40.00

Maceo Commemorative
Obv: Similar to Y#32.

Y#	Date	Mintage	VF	XF	Unc
34	1977	.025	—Proof Only		40.00

Nonaligned Nations Conference

36	1979	.020	—	—	40.00

100 PESOS

12.0000 gm., .917 GOLD, .3538 oz AGW
Cespedes Commemorative

35	1977	.025	BV	250.00	275.00

Nonaligned Nations Conference

37	1979	.020	BV	250.00	275.00

NCLT ISSUES

PATTERNS

KM#	Date	Mintage	Identification	Mkt.Val.
1	1870	—	5 Centavos, Copper	—
2	1870	—	10 Centavos, Copper	—
3	1870	—	20 Centavos, Copper	—
4	1870	—	20 Centavos, Silver	—

KM#	Date	Mintage	Identification	Mkt.Val.
5	1870	—	1/2 Peso, Copper	—

6	1870	—	1 Peso, Copper	—
7	1870	—	1 Peso, Silver	—
8	1870	—	1 Peso, Silver, Piefort	—
9	1898	—	20 Centavos, Silver	—

PROOF SETS

STANDARD METALS

KM#	Date	Mintage	Identification	Issue Price	Mkt. Val.
101	1915(7)	20	Y3-9	—	1500.
102	1915(6)	—	Y10-15	—	23,000.
103	1916(7)	20	Y3-9	—	2700.
104	1916(6)	—	Y10-15	—	55,000.
105	1953(4)	—	*Y20-23	—	Rare

NOTE: Spanish or English legends on holders.

Listings For

CURACAO: refer to Netherlands Antilles

CYPRUS

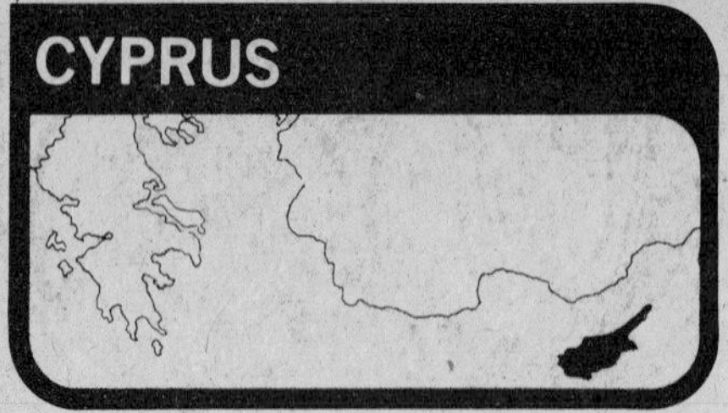

The Republic of Cyprus, a member of the British Commonwealth, lies in the eastern Mediterranean Sea 44 miles (71 km.) south of Turkey and 60 miles (97 km.) west of Syria. It is the third largest island in the Mediterranean Sea, having an area of 3,572 sq. mi. (9,247 sq. km.) and a population of 671,000. Capital: Nicosia. Agriculture and mining are the chief industries. Asbestos, copper, citrus fruit, iron pyrites and potatoes are exported.

The importance of Cyprus dates from the Bronze Age when it was desired as a principal source of copper (from which the island derived its name) and as a strategic trading center. Its role as an international marketplace made it a prime disseminator of the ten prevalent cultures, a role that still influences the civilization of Western man. Because of its fortuitous position and influential role, Cyprus was conquered by a succession of empires: the Assyrian, Egyptian, Persian, Macedonian, Ptolemaic, Roman and Byzantine. It was taken from Isaac Comnenus by Richard the Lion-Hearted in 1191, sold to the Knights Templars, conquered by Venice and Turkey, and made a crown colony of Britain in 1925. Finally, on Aug. 16, 1960, it became an independent republic.

In 1964, the ethnic Turks, who favor partition of Cyprus into seperate Greek and Turkish states, withdrew from active participation in the government. Turkish forces invaded Cyprus in 1974 and gained control of 40 percent of the island. In 1975, Turkish Cypriots proclaimed their own state in northern Cyprus.

Cyprus is a member of the Commonwealth of Nations. The president is Chief of State and Head of Government.

RULERS

British, until 1960

MINTMARKS

H - Birmingham, England

MONETARY SYSTEM

9 Piastres = 1 Shilling
20 Shillings = 1 Pound

1/4 PIASTRE

BRONZE

Y#	Date	Mintage	VF	XF	Unc
1	1879	.150	15.00	30.00	100.00
	1879	—	—	Proof	300.00
	1880	.072	30.00	60.00	110.00
	1880	—	—	Proof	250.00
	1881	.072	30.00	55.00	110.00
	1881	—	—	Proof	300.00
	1881H	.108	15.00	45.00	120.00
	1881H	—	—	Proof	300.00
	1882H	.036	17.50	60.00	125.00
	1884	.072	22.50	55.00	120.00
	1885	.036	20.00	55.00	125.00
	1887	.060	17.50	40.00	150.00
	1887	—	—	Proof	250.00
	1895	.072	17.50	80.00	150.00
	1898	.072	15.00	45.00	125.00
	1900	.036	25.00	55.00	135.00
	1900	—	—	Proof	300.00
	1901	.072	17.50	37.50	100.00

Y#	Date	Mintage	VF	XF	Unc
8	1902	.072	12.50	25.00	80.00
	1905	.422	12.50	35.00	90.00
8	1908	.036	70.00	90.00	350.00

Y#	Date	Mintage	VF	XF	Unc
13	1922	.072	20.00	35.00	60.00
	1926	.360	7.50	20.00	55.00
	1926	—	—	Proof	200.00

1/2 PIASTRE

BRONZE

Y#	Date	Mintage	VF	XF	Unc
2	1879	.250	15.00	35.00	125.00
	1879	—	—	Proof	275.00
	1881	.054	30.00	55.00	125.00
	1881H	.072	25.00	60.00	125.00
	1882H	.054	17.50	65.00	150.00
	1882H	—	—	Proof	250.00
	1884	.036	27.50	75.00	225.00
	1884	—	—	Proof	350.00
	1885	.054	27.50	75.00	225.00
	1886	.122	13.50	40.00	120.00
	1887	.060	32.50	70.00	150.00
	1887	—	—	Proof	275.00
	1889	.054	70.00	100.00	150.00
	1890	.180	15.00	45.00	120.00
	1890	—	—	Proof	250.00
	1891	.108	15.00	45.00	120.00
	1896	.036	70.00	115.00	350.00
	1900	.036	27.50	65.00	150.00
	1900	—	—	Proof	300.00

Y#	Date	Mintage	VF	XF	Unc
9	1908	.036	80.00	175.00	375.00

Y#	Date	Mintage	VF	XF	Unc
14	1922	.036	40.00	115.00	175.00
	1927	.108	10.00	22.50	65.00
	1927	—	—	Proof	225.00
	1930	.180	11.50	22.50	60.00
	1931	.090	17.50	30.00	100.00
	1931	—	—	Proof	—

COPPER-NICKEL

Y#	Date	Mintage	VF	XF	Unc
16	1934	1.440	1.20	5.25	16.50
	1934	—	—	Proof	200.00

Y#	Date	Mintage	VF	XF	Unc
22	1938	1.080	1.75	5.00	7.50
	1938	—	—	Proof	200.00

BRONZE

Y#	Date	Mintage	VF	XF	Unc
22a	1942	1.080	.80	5.00	15.00
	1942	—	—	Proof	200.00
	1943	1.620	.50	5.00	15.00
	1944	2.160	.80	7.50	15.00
	1945	1.080	.80	5.00	15.00

Y#	Date	Mintage	VF	XF	Unc
31	1949	1.080	.40	1.50	5.00
	1949	—	—	Proof	150.00

PIASTRE

BRONZE

Rev: Thin '1'

Y#	Date	Mintage	VF	XF	Unc
3.1	1879	.250	13.50	37.50	100.00
	1879	—	—	Proof	250.00
	1881	.036	25.00	60.00	135.00
	1881	—	—	Proof	300.00
	1881H	.036	30.00	75.00	180.00
	1881H	—	—	Proof	325.00

Rev: Thick '1'

Y#	Date	Mintage	VF	XF	Unc
3.2	1881	Inc. Ab.	—	Proof Only	750.00
	1881H	Inc. Ab.	35.00	200.00	190.00
	1881H	—	—	Proof	375.00
	1882H	.018	80.00	160.00	900.00
	1882H	—	—	Proof	550.00
	1884	.018	80.00	160.00	375.00
	1884	—	—	Proof	500.00
	1885	.054	17.50	50.00	90.00
	1886	.227	25.00	45.00	90.00
	1887	.045	10.00	60.00	150.00
	1889	.027	22.50	70.00	150.00
	1890	.090	25.00	55.00	150.00
	1891	.054	22.50	60.00	150.00
	1895	.054	15.00	50.00	125.00
	1896	.054	90.00	125.00	200.00
	1900	.027	30.00	80.00	160.00
	1900	—	—	Proof	1100.

Y#	Date	Mintage	VF	XF	Unc
10	1908	.027	150.00	250.00	400.00

Y#	Date	Mintage	VF	XF	Unc
15	1922	.054	25.00	55.00	120.00
	1927	.127	30.00	50.00	90.00
	1930	.096	35.00	50.00	100.00
	1931	.045	20.00	50.00	100.00
	1931	—	—	Proof	—

COPPER-NICKEL

Y#	Date	Mintage	VF	XF	Unc
17	1934	1.440	2.50	7.50	15.00
	1934	—	—	Proof	225.00

Y#	Date	Mintage	VF	XF	Unc
23	1938	2.700	1.75	6.00	15.00
	1938	—	—	Proof	250.00

BRONZE

Y#	Date	Mintage	VF	XF	Unc
23a	1942	1.260	1.00	3.50	12.50
	1942	—	—	Proof	250.00
	1943	2.520	1.00	4.50	12.50
	1944	3.240	1.00	4.00	18.50
	1945	1.080	1.00	4.00	12.50
	1946	1.080	1.00	5.00	9.00

Obv: DEI GRATIA REX for REX IMPERATOR

Y#	Date	Mintage	VF	XF	Unc
32	1949	1.080	1.00	2.25	5.00
	1949	—	—	Proof	150.00

3 PIASTRES

1.8851 gm., .925 SILVER, .0561 oz ASW

Y#	Date	Mintage	VF	XF	Unc
4	1901	.300	15.00	25.00	65.00
	1901	—	—	Proof	300.00

4-1/2 PIASTRES

2.8276 gm., .925 SILVER, .0841 oz ASW

Y#	Date	Mintage	VF	XF	Unc
5	1901	.400	20.00	45.00	75.00
	1901	—	—	Proof	600.00

Y#	Date	Mintage	VF	XF	Unc
18	1921	.600	15.00	30.00	55.00

Y#	Date	Mintage	VF	XF	Unc
28	1938	.192	4.00	7.50	15.00
	1938	—	—	Proof	275.00

9 PIASTRES

5.6552 gm., .925 SILVER, .1682 oz ASW

Y#	Date	Mintage	VF	XF	Unc
6	1901	.600	25.00	50.00	100.00
	1901	—	—	Proof	600.00

Y#	Date	Mintage	VF	XF	Unc
11	1907	.060	80.00	250.00	350.00

Y#	Date	Mintage	VF	XF	Unc
19	1913	.050	25.00	100.00	150.00
	1919	.400	15.00	30.00	65.00
	1921	.490	15.00	32.50	55.00

Y#	Date	Mintage	VF	XF	Unc
29	1938	.504	6.00	8.50	15.00
	1938	—	—	Proof	225.00
	1940	.800	6.00	8.50	12.00
	1940	—	—	Proof	225.00

SHILLING

COPPER-NICKEL

Y#	Date	Mintage	VF	XF	Unc
26	1947	1.440	3.00	5.00	10.00
	1947	—	—	Proof	—

Obv. leg: ET IND IMP dropped

Y#	Date	Mintage	VF	XF	Unc
33	1949	1.440	3.50	6.00	8.50
	1949	—	—	Proof	225.00

18 PIASTRES

11.3104 gm., .925 SILVER, .3364 oz ASW

Y#	Date	Mintage	VF	XF	Unc
7	1901	.200	40.00	125.00	300.00
	1901	—	—	Proof	1100.

Y#	Date	Mintage	VF	XF	Unc
12	1907	.020	100.00	250.00	Rare

Y#	Date	Mintage	VF	XF	Unc
20	1913	.025	50.00	200.00	325.00
	1921	.155	15.00	60.00	110.00

Y#	Date	Mintage	VF	XF	Unc
30	1938	.200	12.00	15.00	20.00
	1938	—	—	Proof	250.00
	1940	.100	12.00	17.50	25.00

2 SHILLINGS

COPPER-NICKEL

Y#	Date	Mintage	VF	XF	Unc
27	1947	.720	2.00	3.75	12.50
	1947	—	—	Proof	250.00

Obv. leg: ET IND. IMP. dropped

Y#	Date	Mintage	VF	XF	Unc
34	1949	.720	2.00	3.75	15.00
	1949	—	—	Proof	250.00

45 PIASTRES

28.2759 gm., .925 SILVER, .8409 oz ASW
50th Anniversary of British Rule

Y#	Date	Mintage	VF	XF	Unc
21	1928	.080	27.50	40.00	75.00
	1928	525 pcs.	—	Proof	650.00

DECIMAL CURRENCY

50 Mils = 1 Shilling
20 Shillings = 1 Pound
1000 Mils = 1 Pound

MIL

ALUMINUM

Y#	Date	Mintage	VF	XF	Unc
41	1963	5.000	—	—	.10
	1963	.025	—	Proof	1.25
	1971	.500	—	—	.10
	1972	.500	—	—	.15

3 MILS

BRONZE

Y#	Date	Mintage	VF	XF	Unc
35	1955	6.250	—	—	.25
	1955	2,000	—	Proof	5.00

5 MILS

BRONZE

Y#	Date	Mintage	VF	XF	Unc
36	1955	10.000	.15	.25	.40
	1955	2,000	—	Proof	7.00
	1956	2.950	.15	.30	.45
	1956	—	—	Proof	175.00

Y#	Date	Mintage	VF	XF	Unc
42	1963	12.000	—	—	.25
	1963	.025	—	Proof	3.00
	1970	2.500	—	—	.20
	1971	2.500	—	—	.20
	1972	2.500	—	—	.20
	1973	5.000	—	—	.20
	1974	2.500	—	—	.25
	1977	2.000	—	—	.20
	1978	—	—	—	—

25 MILS

COPPER-NICKEL

Y#	Date	Mintage	VF	XF	Unc
37	1955	2.500	.25	.35	.50
	1955	2,000	—	Proof	8.00

Y#	Date	Mintage	VF	XF	Unc
43	1963	2.500	—	.15	.30
	1963	.025	—	Proof	1.75
	1968	1.500	—	.15	.30
	1971	1.000	—	.15	.30
	1972	.500	—	.15	.35
	1973	1.000	—	.15	.30
	1974	1.000	—	.15	.30
	1976	1.000	—	.15	.30
	1977	1.000	—	.15	.30
	1978	—	—	—	—

50 MILS

COPPER-NICKEL

Y#	Date	Mintage	VF	XF	Unc
38	1955	4.000	.35	.50	1.00
	1955	2,000	—	Proof	10.00

Y#	Date	Mintage	VF	XF	Unc
44	1963	2.800	.20	.30	.75
	1963	.025	—	Proof	2.00
	1970	.500	.20	.35	.75
	1971	.500	.20	.35	.65
	1972	.750	.20	.30	.50
	1973	.750	.20	.30	.50
	1974	1.500	.20	.30	.50
	1976	.500	.20	.30	.50
	1977	.500	.20	.30	.50
	1978	—	—	—	—

100 MILS

COPPER-NICKEL

Y#	Date	Mintage	VF	XF	Unc
39	1955	2.500	.50	.75	1.50
	1955	2,000	—	Proof	12.75
	1957	*.500	2.00	3.00	5.00
	1957	—	—	Proof	200.00

NOTE: All but 10,000 of 1957 issue melted down.

Y#	Date	Mintage	VF	XF	Unc
45	1963	1.750	.40	.60	1.25
	1963	.025	—	Proof	3.25
	1971	.500	.50	.75	1.25
	1973	.750	.40	.60	1.00
	1974	1.000	.50	.75	1.50
	1976	.500	.40	.60	1.00
	1977	.500	.40	.60	1.00
	1978	—	—	—	—

500 MILS

COPPER-NICKEL
F.A.O. Issue

Y#	Date	Mintage	VF	XF	Unc
46	1970	.080	1.50	2.00	4.00
	1970	5,000	—	Proof	20.00
	22.6200 gm., .800 SILVER, .5818 oz ASW				
46a	1970	5,000	—	Proof	125.00

COPPER-NICKEL

Y#	Date	Mintage	VF	XF	Unc
47	1975	.500	1.50	2.00	3.00
	1977	.200	1.50	2.00	3.00
	14.1400 gm., .800 SILVER, .3637 oz ASW				
47a	1975	.010	—	Proof	25.00

COPPER-NICKEL
Refugee Commemorative

Y#	Date	Mintage	VF	XF	Unc
48	1976	.025	2.00	2.50	4.00
	14.1400 gm., .925 SILVER, .4205 oz ASW				
48a	1976	.025	—	Proof	30.00

COPPER-NICKEL
Human Rights Commemorative

Y#	Date	Mintage	VF	XF	Unc
51	1978	.050	—	—	4.00
	14.1400 gm., .925 SILVER, .4205 oz ASW				
51a	1978	5,000	—	Proof	175.00

POUND

COPPER-NICKEL
Refugee Commemorative

Y#	Date	Mintage	VF	XF	Unc
49	1976	.025	2.50	3.00	5.00
	28.2800 gm., .925 SILVER, .8411 oz ASW				
49a	1976	.025	—	Proof	40.00

50 POUNDS

15.9800 gm., .966 GOLD, .4963 oz AGW
Archbishop Makarios Commemorative

Y#	Date	Mintage	VF	XF	Unc
50	1977	.040	BV	325.00	350.00
	1977	5,000	—	Proof	400.00

NCLT ISSUES

MINT SETS

KM#	Date	Mintage	Identification	Issue Price	Mkt. Val.
S1	1955(5)	2,550	Y35-39*	2.20	13.00
S3	1963(5)	8,050	Y41-45	1.95	15.00
S4	1971(5)	3,000	Y41-45	1.65	—
S5	1972(4)	3,000	Y42-45	2.35	—
S6	1973(4)	5,000	Y42-45	2.75	—
S7	1974(4)	5,000	Y42-45	3.25	3.50
S7	1976(3)	5,000	—	1.25	—
S8	1976(2)	25,000	Y48-49	6.50	—
S9	1977(5)	—	Y42-45,47	—	5.50
S10	1978(5)	—	Y42-45,51	5.50	—

***NOTE:** This set consists of 3 uncirculated and 2 circulated coins.

PATTERNS

KM#	Date	Mintage	Identification	Mkt.Val.
1	1879	—	1 Piastre, Uniface	2500.
2	1928	—	1 Crown, Uniface	5500.

PROOF SETS
STANDARD METALS

KM#	Date	Mintage	Identification	Issue Price	Mkt. Val.
101	1901(4)	—	Y4-7	—	2500.
102	1938(3)	—	Y22,23,28	—	700.00
103	1955(5)	2,000	Y35-39	5.50	40.00
104	1963(5)	25,001	Y41-45 with case	9.00	12.50
105	1963(5)	25,001	Y41-45 sealed	8.70	15.00
106	1976(2)	25,000	Y48a,49a	50.00	70.00
107	1977(4)	—	Y42-45	—	5.50

CZECHOSLOVAKIA

The Czechoslovak Socialist Republic, located in central Europe, has an area of 49,371 sq. mi. (127,870 sq. km.) and a population of 15 million. Capital: Prague. Machinery is the chief export of the highly industrialized economy.

Czechoslovakia proclaimed itself a republic on Oct. 28, 1918. When Adolf Hitler became dictator of Nazi Germany he provoked Czechoslovakia's German minority in the Sudetenland to agitate for autonomy. At Munich in Sept. of 1938, France and Britain, vainly seeking to avoid World War II, forced the cession of the Sudetenland to Germany. In March, 1939, Germany invaded Czechoslovakia and established a protectorate over the provinces of Bohemia and Moravia. Bohemia is a historic province in northwest Czechoslovakia that includes the city of Prague, one of the oldest continuously occupied sites in Europe; and Moravia is an area of considerable mineral wealth in central Czechoslovakia. Slovakia, a province in southeastern Czechoslovakia that was once a separate country bounded by Poland, Hungary and Austria, was constituted as a puppet republic. World War II defeat of the Axis powers re-established the physical integrity and independence of Czechoslovakia, while bringing it within the Russian sphere of influence. On Feb. 23-25, 1948, the Communists seized control of the government in a coup d'etat, and adopted a constitution making the country a 'people's republic'. A new constitution adopted June 11, 1960, converted the country into a 'socialist republic'.

MONETARY SYSTEM

100 Haleru = 1 Koruna

HALER

ALUMINUM

Y#	Date	Mintage	Fine	VF	XF	Unc
48	1953	—	—	—	.10	.20
	1954	—	—	—	.10	.20
	1955	—	—	—	.10	.20
	1956	—	—	—	.10	.20
	1957	—	—	—	.10	.15
	1958	—	—	.25	.35	.60
	1959	—	—	—	.10	.15
	1960	—	—	—	.10	.20

Y#	Date	Mintage	Fine	VF	XF	Unc
62	1962	—	—	—	.10	.15
	1963	—	—	—	.10	.15

2 HALERE

ZINC

Y#	Date	Mintage	Fine	VF	XF	Unc
1	1923	2.700	3.00	5.00	7.75	13.00
	1924	17.300	2.25	3.50	5.00	9.00
	1925	2.000	3.00	5.00	7.50	15.00

3 HALERE

ALUMINUM

Y#	Date	Mintage	Fine	VF	XF	Unc
49	1953	—	—	—	.15	.25
	1954	—	—	—	.15	.25

Y#	Date	Mintage	Fine	VF	XF	Unc
63	1962	—	—	—	—	300.00
	1963	—	—	—	.10	.15

NOTE: 3 Halere ceased to be legal tender November 30, 1976.

5 HALERU

BRONZE

Y#	Date	Mintage	Fine	VF	XF	Unc
2	1923	37.800	.20	.30	.50	1.25
	1924	—	17.50	30.00	40.00	50.00
	1925	12.000	.20	.30	.50	2.00
	1926	1.084	1.50	3.25	6.00	10.00
	1927	8.916	.25	.35	.75	1.50
	1928	5.320	.30	.45	.75	1.50
	1929	12.680	.25	.35	.75	1.50
	1930	5.000	.25	.35	.75	2.00
	1931	7.448	.25	.35	.75	1.50
	1932	3.556	.60	1.00	2.00	3.50
	1938	14.244	.25	.35	.75	1.00

ALUMINUM

Y#	Date	Mintage	Fine	VF	XF	Unc
50	1953	—	—	—	.25	.40
	1954	—	—	—	.25	.40
	1955	—	.30	.50	.75	2.00

Y#	Date	Mintage	Fine	VF	XF	Unc
64	1962	—	—	.10	.15	.25
	1963	—	—	.10	.15	.25
	1966	—	—	.10	.15	.25
	1966	—	—	—	Proof	Rare
	1967	—	—	.10	.15	.25
	1968	—	—	.10	.15	.20
	1970	—	—	.10	.15	.20
	1972	—	—	.10	.15	.20
	1973	—	—	.10	.15	.20
	1974	—	—	.10	.15	.20
	1975	—	—	.10	.15	.20
	1976	—	—	.10	.15	.20

Y#	Date	Mintage	Fine	VF	XF	Unc
89	1977	—	—	—	.10	.25

10 HALERU

BRONZE

Y#	Date	Mintage	Fine	VF	XF	Unc
3	1922	6.000	.30	.45	1.00	1.75
	1923	24.000	.25	.35	.75	1.25
	1924	5.320	.30	.45	1.00	2.00
	1925	24.680	.25	.35	.60	1.50
	1926	10.000	.25	.35	.75	1.50
	1927	10.000	.25	.35	.75	1.25
	1928	14.290	.25	.35	.75	1.50
	1929	5.710	1.25	2.00	3.50	5.00
	1930	6.980	.30	.45	1.00	1.75
	1931	6.740	.30	.45	1.00	1.75
	1932	11.280	.25	.35	.75	1.25
	1933	4.190	.35	.60	1.25	4.00
	1934	13.200	.25	.35	.75	1.25
	1935	3.420	.50	.75	1.50	3.75
	1936	8.560	.25	.35	.75	1.25
	1937	20.200	.25	.35	.75	1.25
	1938	15.400	.25	.35	.75	1.10

ALUMINUM

Y#	Date	Mintage	Fine	VF	XF	Unc
51	1953K	—	—	.10	.20	.25
	1953L	—	—	.15	.30	.75
	1954	—	—	.10	.20	.25
	1955	—	.50	.75	1.25	2.00
	1956	—	—	.10	.20	.25
	1958	—	—	.10	.20	.25

Kremnica-130 notches in milled edge.
Leningrad-133 notches in milled edge.

Y#	Date	Mintage	Fine	VF	XF	Unc
65	1961	—	—	.10	.20	.25
	1962	—	—	.10	.20	.25
	1963	—	—	.10	.20	.25
	1964	—	—	.10	.20	.25
	1965	—	—	.10	.20	.25
	1966	—	—	.10	.20	.25
	1966	—	—	—	Proof	Rare
	1967	—	—	.10	.20	.25
	1968	—	—	.10	.20	.25
	1969	—	—	.10	.15	.25
	1970	—	—	.10	.20	.25
	1971	—	—	.10	.20	.25
	1974	—	—	.10	.20	.25

With flat top 3 in date

Y#	Date	Mintage	Fine	VF	XF	Unc
A65	1963	3,600 est.	12.50	25.00	35.00	60.00

Y#	Date	Mintage	Fine	VF	XF	Unc
90	1974	—	—	—	—	.25
90	1975	—	—	—	—	.25
	1976	—	—	—	—	.25
	1977	—	—	—	—	.25
	1978	—	—	—	—	.50

20 HALERU

COPPER-NICKEL

Y#	Date	Mintage	Fine	VF	XF	Unc
4	1921	40.000	—	.25	.45	1.50
	1922	10.000	—	.25	.50	1.50
	1924	20.930	—	.25	.45	1.50
	1925	4.244	.60	1.00	2.00	5.00
	1926	14.825	—	.25	.50	1.50
	1927	11.757	—	.25	.50	1.50
	1928	14.018	—	.25	.50	1.50
	1929	4.225	.30	.50	1.25	2.50
	1930	—	.25	.35	.60	2.00
	1931	5.000	.25	.35	.60	2.00
	1933	Inc. Ab.	2.50	3.50	7.00	12.50
	1937	8.208	.20	.30	.55	1.50
	1938	6.815	.20	.30	.55	1.50

BRONZE

Y#	Date	Mintage	Fine	VF	XF	Unc
33	1947	—	100.00	150.00	185.00	250.00
	1948	24.340	—	.15	.25	.50
	1949	—	—	.15	.25	.50
	1950	—	—	.15	.25	.50

ALUMINUM

Y#	Date	Mintage	Fine	VF	XF	Unc
34	1951	—	—	.15	.25	.40
	1952	—	—	.15	.25	.50

BRASS

Y#	Date	Mintage	Fine	VF	XF	Unc
91	1972	—	—	.15	.25	.50
	1973	—	—	.15	.25	.50
	1974	—	—	.15	.25	.40
	1975	—	—	—	.25	.40
	1976	—	—	—	.25	.40
	1977	—	—	—	—	.30
	1978	—	—	—	—	.30

25 HALERU

COPPER-NICKEL

Y#	Date	Mintage	Fine	VF	XF	Unc
5	1933	22.711	.75	1.25	2.00	3.50

ALUMINUM

Y#	Date	Mintage	Fine	VF	XF	Unc
52	1953(K)	—	—	.20	.30	.45
	1953(L)	—	.30	.50	.60	.85

Y#	Date	Mintage	Fine	VF	XF	Unc
52	1954	—	—	.20	.30	.45

(K) - Kremnica-134 notches in milled edge.
(L) - Leningrad-145 notches in milled edge.

Y#	Date	Mintage	Fine	VF	XF	Unc
66	1962	—	—	.15	.20	.35
	1963	—	—	.15	.20	.35
	1964	—	—	.15	.20	.35

NOTE: 25 Haleru ceased to be legal tender Dec. 31, 1972.

50 HALERU

COPPER-NICKEL

Y#	Date	Mintage	Fine	VF	XF	Unc
6	1921	3.000	.25	.45	.75	1.50
	1922	37.000	.20	.30	.50	1.50
	1924	10.000	.20	.30	.50	1.50
	1925	1.415	.45	.75	1.50	4.00
	1926	1.585	1.25	2.00	4.00	8.00
	1927	2.000	.45	.75	1.50	4.00
	1931	5.000	.25	.45	.75	1.50

BRONZE

Y#	Date	Mintage	Fine	VF	XF	Unc
35	1947	50.000	—	.20	.25	.50
	1948	20.000	—	.25	.35	1.00
	1949	—	—	.20	.25	.50
	1950	—	—	.20	.25	.50

ALUMINUM

Y#	Date	Mintage	Fine	VF	XF	Unc
36	1951	—	.25	.45	.60	1.00
	1952	—	.25	.45	.60	1.00
	1953	—	.60	1.00	2.00	5.00

BRONZE

Y#	Date	Mintage	Fine	VF	XF	Unc
67	1963	—	—	.25	.35	.45
	1964	—	—	.25	.35	.45
	1965	—	—	.25	.35	.45
	1969	—	—	.25	.35	.45
	1970	—	—	.20	.30	.40
	1971	—	—	.20	.30	.40
	1974	—	—	.20	.30	.40
A67	1969 Small date, w/o dots					
		—	13.50	22.50	35.00	55.00

COPPER-NICKEL

Y#	Date	Mintage	Fine	VF	XF	Unc
92	1978	—	—	—	—	.50
	1979	—	—	—	—	.50

KORUNA

COPPER-NICKEL

Y#	Date	Mintage	Fine	VF	XF	Unc
7	1922	50.000	.30	.50	.75	1.75
	1923	13.385	.30	.50	.75	1.75
	1924	21.071	.30	.50	.75	1.75
	1925	8.574	.30	.50	.75	1.75
	1929	5.000	.45	.75	1.25	2.25
	1930	5.000	.90	1.50	3.00	6.50
	1937	3.806	.60	1.00	1.75	3.00
	1938	8.582	.30	.50	.75	1.75

Y#	Date	Mintage	Fine	VF	XF	Unc
37	1946	—	.25	.40	.45	.95
	1947	12.650	1.50	2.50	3.75	6.50

ALUMINUM

Y#	Date	Mintage	Fine	VF	XF	Unc
38	1947	—	25.00	65.00	100.00	150.00
	1950	—	—	.25	.45	.75
	1951	—	.20	.35	.45	.65
	1952	—	.20	.30	.40	.65
	1953	—	.45	.75	1.75	3.25

ALUMINUM-BRONZE

Y#	Date	Mintage	Fine	VF	XF	Unc
61	1957	—	.20	.30	.45	1.00
	1958	—	.20	.30	.45	1.00
	1959	—	.20	.30	.45	1.00
	1960	—	.20	.30	.45	1.00

Y#	Date	Mintage	Fine	VF	XF	Unc
68	1961	—	—	.20	.30	.60
	1962	—	—	.20	.30	.60
	1963	—	—	.20	.30	.60
	1964	—	—	.20	.30	.60
	1965	—	—	.20	.30	.60
	1966	—	.40	.65	.90	1.25
	1966	—	—	—	Proof	Rare
	1967	—	—	.20	.30	.60
	1968	—	—	.20	.30	.60
	1969	—	—	.20	.30	.60
	1970	—	—	.20	.30	.65
	1971	—	—	.20	.30	.50
	1975	—	—	—	.30	.50
	1976	—	—	—	.30	.50
	1977	—	—	—	—	.75
	1980	—	—	—	—	.75

2 KORUNY

COPPER-NICKEL

Y#	Date	Mintage	Fine	VF	XF	Unc
39	1947	20.000	.25	.40	.60	1.25
	1948	20.000	.25	.40	.60	1.25

Y#	Date	Mintage	Fine	VF	XF	Unc
94	1972	—	—	.25	.35	1.00
	1973	—	—	.25	.35	1.00
	1974	—	—	.25	.35	.60
	1975	—	—	.25	.35	.60
	1976	—	—	.25	.35	.60
	1977	—	—	.25	.35	.60

3 KORUNY

COPPER-NICKEL

Y#	Date	Mintage	Fine	VF	XF	Unc
72	1965	—	—	.25	.40	.75
	1966	—	—	.35	.40	.75
	1966	—	—	—	Proof	Rare
	1968	—	—	.35	.40	.75
	1969	—	—	.35	.40	.75

NOTE: 3 Koruny ceased to be legal tender Dec. 31, 1972.

5 KORUN

COPPER-NICKEL

Y#	Date	Mintage	Fine	VF	XF	Unc
8	1925	16.505	2.25	3.50	4.50	6.50
	1926	8.569	2.25	3.75	4.50	6.50
	1927	4.925	3.00	5.00	7.00	10.00

7.0000 gm., .500 SILVER, .1125 oz ASW

Y#	Date	Mintage	Fine	VF	XF	Unc
8a	1928	1.710	BV	3.75	7.50	10.00
(9)	1929	12.860	BV	3.75	4.50	7.50
	1930	10.430	BV	4.00	4,50	7.50
	1931	2.000	BV	5.00	7.50	10.00
	1932	1.000	4.50	7.00	10.00	20.00

NICKEL

Y#	Date	Mintage	Fine	VF	XF	Unc
8b	1937	—	60.00	100.00	150.00	250.00
(10)	1938	12.230	2.25	3.50	5.50	6.50

ALUMINUM

A39	1952	—	20.00	30.00	40.00	55.00

Not released for circulation.

COPPER-NICKEL

73	1966	—	—	.60	.90	2.00
	1966	—	—	—	Proof	Rare

1966 Varieties on obverse of coin

Large Date: No space between letter B in REPUBLIC and coat of arms.

Small Date: Space between letter B in REPUBLIC and coat of arms.

Plain Edge: No ornamental inscription on edge.

So far there has been no indication of any of the varieties as being scarce.

	1967	—	—	.60	.90	1.50
	1968	—	—	.60	.90	1.50
	1969Ty.1, straight date—					
		—	—	.60	.90	1.50
	1969Ty.2, date in semi-circle					
		—	.70	1.20	1.80	3.00
	1970	—	—	.60	.90	1.50
	1973	—	—	.60	.75	1.25
	1974 (3 vars.)	—	—	.60	.75	1.25
	1975	—	—	.60	.75	1.25
	1978	—	—	.50	.75	1.25

10 KORUN

10.0000 gm., .700 SILVER, .2250 oz ASW

10th Anniversary of Independence

11	1928	1.000	BV	BV	7.50	10.00

12	1930	4.948	BV	BV	7.50	12.00
	1931	6.689	BV	BV	7.50	10.00
	1932	11.447	BV	BV	7.50	10.00
	1933	.915	7.50	10.00	15.00	30.00

12.0000 gm., .500 SILVER, .1929 oz ASW

10th Anniversary Slovak Uprising

Y#	Date	Mintage	Fine	VF	XF	Unc
53	1954	.295	BV	BV	6.50	10.00
	1954	5,000	—	—	Proof	15.00

10th Anniversary Nazi Liberation

55	1955	.295	BV	BV	6.50	10.00
	1955	5,000	—	—	Proof	15.00

250th Anniversary Technical College

59	1957	.075	BV	7.50	12.00	17.50
	1957	5,000	—	—	Proof	17.50

J. A. Komensky

60	1957	.150	BV	BV	7.50	12.50
	1957	5,000	—	—	Proof	15.00

20th Anniversary 1944 Slovak Uprising

69	1964	.120	BV	BV	6.50	10.00

Jan Hus Commemorative

71	1965	.055	BV	6.50	10.00	22.50
	1965	5,000	—	—	Proof	35.00

1100th Anniversary of Great Moravia

Y#	Date	Mintage	Fine	VF	XF	Unc
74	1966	.115	BV	BV	7.50	12.00
	1966	5,000	—	—	Proof	15.00

500th Anniversary Bratislava University

75	1967	.055	BV	7.50	12.50	25.00
	1967	5,000	—	—	Proof	50.00

Prague National Theater Centennial

76	1968	.055	BV	7.50	12.50	20.00
	1968	5,000	—	—	Proof	60.00

20 KORUN

12.0000 gm., .700 SILVER, .2700 oz ASW

13	1933	2.280	BV	BV	8.50	10.00
	1934	3.280	BV	BV	10.00	12.50

Death of President Masaryk

Y#	Date	Mintage	Fine	VF	XF	Unc
14	1937	1.000	BV	BV	10.00	12.50

12.0000 gm., .500 SILVER, .1929 oz ASW
Centennial Death of Andrej Sladkovic

Y#	Date	Mintage	Fine	VF	XF	Unc
87	1972	.055	BV	BV	6.50	10.00
	1972	5,000	—	—	Proof	20.00

25 KORUN

16.0000 gm., .500 SILVER, .2572 oz ASW
10th Anniversary Slovak Uprising

Y#	Date	Mintage	Fine	VF	XF	Unc
54	1954	.245	BV	BV	8.50	10.00
	1954	5,000	—	—	Proof	20.00

10th Anniversary Nazi Liberation

Y#	Date	Mintage	Fine	VF	XF	Unc
56	1955	.195	BV	BV	8.50	10.00
	1955	5,000	—	—	Proof	20.00

20th Anniversary Czechoslovakian Liberation

Y#	Date	Mintage	Fine	VF	XF	Unc
70	1965	.145	BV	BV	8.50	10.00
	1965	5,000	—	—	Proof	20.00

Sesquicentennial Prague National Museum Comm.

Y#	Date	Mintage	Fine	VF	XF	Unc
77	1968	.055	BV	8.50	10.00	18.50
	1968	5,000	—	—	Proof	75.00

100th Anniversary Death of J. E. Purkyne

Y#	Date	Mintage	Fine	VF	XF	Unc
79	1969	.045	BV	8.50	10.00	12.50
	1969	5,000	—	—	Proof	20.00

25th Anniversary 1944 Slovak Uprising

Y#	Date	Mintage	Fine	VF	XF	Unc
80	1969	.030	BV	10.00	20.00	35.00
	1969	5,000	—	—	Proof	45.00

50th Anniversary Slovak National Theater

Y#	Date	Mintage	Fine	VF	XF	Unc
81	1970	.045	BV	8.50	10.00	12.50
	1970	5,000	—	—	Proof	40.00

12.0000 gm., .500 SILVER, .1929 oz ASW
25th Anniversary of Liberation

Y#	Date	Mintage	Fine	VF	XF	Unc
82	1970	.095	BV	BV	6.50	10.00
	1970	5,000	—	—	Proof	20.00

50 KORUN

10.0000 gm., .500 SILVER, .1607 oz ASW
1944 Slovak Uprising

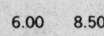

Y#	Date	Mintage	Fine	VF	XF	Unc
40	1947	1.000	BV	BV	5.50	7.50

3rd Anniversary Prague Uprising

Y#	Date	Mintage	Fine	VF	XF	Unc
41	1948	1.000	BV	BV	5.50	7.50

Stalin 70th Birthday

Y#	Date	Mintage	Fine	VF	XF	Unc
45	1949	1.000	BV	BV	6.00	8.50

20.0000 gm., .900 SILVER, .5787 oz ASW
10th Anniversary Nazi Liberation

Y#	Date	Mintage	Fine	VF	XF	Unc
57	1955	.120	BV	BV	18.50	22.50

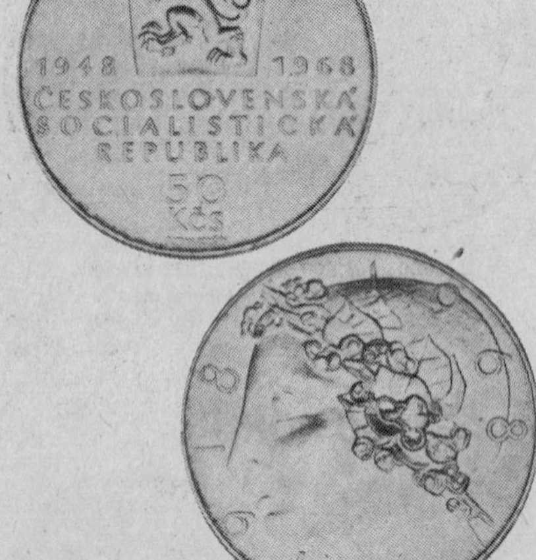

50th Anniversary of Czechoslovakia
20th Anniversary People's Republic

Y#	Date	Mintage	Fine	VF	XF	Unc
78	1968	.058	BV	BV	25.00	50.00
	1968	2,000	—	—	Proof	125.00

13.0000 gm., .700 SILVER, .2926 oz ASW
Lenin Birth Centennial

Y#	Date	Mintage	Fine	VF	XF	Unc
83	1970	.044	BV	BV	10.00	12.00
	1970	6,200	—	—	Proof	50.00

50th Anniversary Czechoslovak Communist Party

Y#	Date	Mintage	Fine	VF	XF	Unc
84	1971	.045	BV	BV	10.00	17.50
	1971	5,000	—	—	Proof	50.00

50th Anniv. Death of Pavol Orsagh-Hviez Doslav

Y#	Date	Mintage	Fine	VF	XF	Unc
85	1971	.045	BV	BV	10.00	12.00
	1971	5,000	—	—	Proof	50.00

50th Anniversary Death of Myslbek

Y#	Date	Mintage	Fine	VF	XF	Unc
88	1972	.045	BV	BV	10.00	12.00
	1972	5,000	—	—	Proof	50.00

25th Anniversary Victory of Communist Party

Y#	Date	Mintage	Fine	VF	XF	Unc
96	1973	.055	BV	BV	10.00	12.00
	1973	5,000	—	—	Proof	55.00

200th Anniversary Birth of Josef Jungmann

Y#	Date	Mintage	Fine	VF	XF	Unc
97	1973	.045	BV	BV	10.00	12.00
	1973	5,000	—	—	Proof	25.00

Janko Jesensky Birth Centennial

Y#	Date	Mintage	Fine	VF	XF	Unc
98	1974	.055	BV	BV	10.00	12.00
	1974	5,000	—	—	Proof	17.50

S. K. Neumann Birth Centennial

Y#	Date	Mintage	Fine	VF	XF	Unc
100	1975	.055	BV	BV	10.00	12.00
	1975	5,000	—	—	Proof	17.50

Jan Kollar

Y#	Date	Mintage	Fine	VF	XF	Unc
103	1977	.075	BV	BV	10.00	12.00
	1977	5,000	—	—	Proof	17.50

Zdenek Nejedly

Y#	Date	Mintage	Fine	VF	XF	Unc
105	1978	.080	BV	BV	10.00	12.00
	1978	—	—	—	Proof	17.50

650th Anniversary of Kremnica Mint

Y#	Date	Mintage	Fine	VF	XF	Unc
106	1978	—	BV	BV	10.00	12.00
	1978	—	—	—	Proof	17.50

30th Anniversary of 9th Congress

Y#	Date	Mintage	Fine	VF	XF	Unc
114	1979	—	BV	BV	15.00	20.00

100 KORUN

14.0000 gm., .500 SILVER, .2250 oz ASW
600th Anniversary Charles University

Y#	Date	Mintage	Fine	VF	XF	Unc
42	1948	1.000	BV	BV	7.50	10.00

30th Anniversary of Independence

Y#	Date	Mintage	Fine	VF	XF	Unc
43	1948	1.000	BV	BV	7.50	10.00

7th Centennial Jihlava Mining Privileges

Y#	Date	Mintage	Fine	VF	XF	Unc
44	1949	1.000	BV	BV	7.50	10.00

Stalin 70th Birthday

Y#	Date	Mintage	Fine	VF	XF	Unc
46	1949	1.000	BV	BV	7.50	10.00

30th Anniversary Communist Party

Y#	Date	Mintage	Fine	VF	XF	Unc
47	1951	1.000	BV	BV	7.50	10.00

24.0000 GM., .900 SILVER, .6945 oz ASW
10th Anniversary Nazi Liberation

Y#	Date	Mintage	Fine	VF	XF	Unc
58	1955	.075	BV	BV	22.50	35.00

15.0000 gm., .700 SILVER, .3376 oz ASW
Centennial Death of Josef Manes

Y#	Date	Mintage	Fine	VF	XF	Unc
86	1971	.045	BV	BV	12.00	15.00
	1971	5,000	—	—	Proof	45.00

Bedrich Smetana Birth Sesquicentennial

Y#	Date	Mintage	Fine	VF	XF	Unc
99	1974	.075	BV	BV	12.00	15.00
	1974	5,000	—	—	Proof	35.00

Janko Kral Death Centennial
Obv: Similar to Y#99.

Y#	Date	Mintage	Fine	VF	XF	Unc
101	1976	.075	BV	BV	12.00	15.00
	1976	5,000	—	—	Proof	25.00

Viktor Kaplan Birth Centennial
Obv: Similar to Y#99.

Y#	Date	Mintage	Fine	VF	XF	Unc
102	1976	.075	BV	BV	12.00	15.00
	1976	5,000	—	—	Proof	25.00

Vaclav Hollar

Y#	Date	Mintage	Fine	VF	XF	Unc
104	1977	.095	BV	BV	12.00	15.00
	1977	5,000	—	—	Proof	25.00

Julio Fucik
Obv: Similar to Y#104.

Y#	Date	Mintage	Fine	VF	XF	Unc
107	1978	.080	BV	BV	12.00	15.00
	1978	—	—	—	Proof	25.00

King Karel IV

Y#	Date	Mintage	Fine	VF	XF	Unc
108	1978	.075	BV	BV	12.00	17.50
	1978	5,000	—	—	Proof	27.50

650th Anniversary of Kremnica Mint

Y#	Date	Mintage	Fine	VF	XF	Unc
—	1978	—	BV	BV	12.00	15.00
	1978	—	—	—	Proof	20.00

Jan Botto

Y#	Date	Mintage	Fine	VF	XF	Unc
109	1979	.080	BV	BV	BV	15.00
	1979	—	—	—	Proof	25.00

650th Anniversary Birth of Peter Parler

Y#	Date	Mintage	Fine	VF	XF	Unc
115	1980	—	—	—	—	30.00
	1980	—	—	—	Proof	40.00

TRADE COINS

NOTE: Of the following issues those listed by other than Yeoman numbers were private issues which did not enjoy legal tender status, although they were struck at the Kremnica Mint. They are hallmarked. St. Wenceslas issues are legal tender (Y#A15 thru #18).

Silver Medallic Issues

(Denominations unknown)

All are hallmarked circled K and 987 in a rectangle.

SILVER, 34mm
10th Anniversary of Republic

KM#	Date	Mintage	VF	XF	Unc
M1	1928	—	40.00	60.00	75.00
	40mm				
M1a	1928	.032	40.00	60.00	75.00
	100th Anniversary of Christianity in Bohemia 28mm Obv: Standing figure with banner. Rev: Arms.				
M2	1929	—	75.00	100.00	150.00
	40mm Similar to KM#M2.				
M3	1929	—	85.00	125.00	175.00
	Tyrs - Sokol Movement 42mm, similar to Dukat, FR#11.				
M4	1932	—	40.00	60.00	75.00
	Homage Commemorative 31mm, similar to Dukat, FR#12.				
M5	1932	—	—	—	—
	30mm, without cross, Svehla				
M6	1933	—	35.00	50.00	65.00
	40mm, Kremnica				
M7	1934	—	40.00	60.00	75.00
	41.5mm, Wallenstein				
M8	1934	—	85.00	125.00	175.00

Gold Ducat Issues

DUKAT

3.4900 gm., .986 GOLD, .1106 oz AGW
Rev: St. Vaclav (Wenceslas).

Y#	Date	Mintage	VF	XF	Unc
A15	1923	1,000	250.00	500.00	750.00

NOTE: The above coins are serially numbered next to date.

Similar to Y#A15.

Y#	Date	Mintage	VF	XF	Unc
15	1923	.062	BV	100.00	125.00
	1924	.033	BV	100.00	125.00
	1925	.066	BV	75.00	100.00
	1926	.059	BV	75.00	100.00
	1927	.026	BV	100.00	125.00
	1928	.019	BV	100.00	135.00
	1929	.010	BV	100.00	200.00
	1930	.011	BV	100.00	175.00
	1931	.043	BV	75.00	100.00
	1932	.027	BV	100.00	125.00
	1933	.058	BV	75.00	100.00
	1934	9,729	BV	125.00	200.00
	1935	.013	BV	100.00	150.00
	1936	.015	BV	100.00	150.00
	1937	324 pcs.	200.00	400.00	600.00
	1938	56 pcs.	500.00	900.00	1200.
	1939	*276 pcs.	175.00	350.00	500.00
	1951	500 pcs.	150.00	300.00	500.00

***NOTE:** Czech reports show mintage of 20 for Czechoslovakia and 256 for state of Slovakia.

1000th Anniversary Christianity in Bohemia
Obv: Standing figure with banner. Rev: Arms.

Fr#	Date	Mintage	VF	XF	Unc
10	1929	—	150.00	225.00	400.00

Sokol Movement Commemorative
Obv: Head of Dr. Tyrs.

Fr#	Date	Mintage	VF	XF	Unc
11	1932	2,209	125.00	200.00	400.00

Homage Commemorative
Obv: Head of Dr. Svehla.

Fr#	Date	Mintage	VF	XF	Unc
12	1933	2,000	125.00	225.00	450.00
	Cross above date.				
12a	1933	1,000	150.00	250.00	500.00

Reopening Of Kremnica Mines
Obv: St. Catherine praying.

Fr#	Date	Mintage	VF	XF	Unc
16	1934	1,379	300.00	450.00	750.00

Obv: Crowned portrait of Charles IV

Fr#	Date	Mintage	VF	XF	Unc
110	1978	.020	—	—	200.00

2 DUKATY

6.9800 gm., .986 GOLD, .2212 oz ASW
Rev: St. Vaclav (Wenceslas).

Y#	Date	Mintage	VF	XF	Unc
16	1923	4,000	BV	275.00	400.00
	1929	3,262	BV	275.00	400.00
	1930	Inc. Ab.	200.00	500.00	750.00
	1931	2,994	BV	275.00	400.00
	1932	5,496	BV	275.00	400.00
	1933	4,671	BV	275.00	400.00
	1934	2,403	BV	325.00	475.00
	1935	2,577	BV	275.00	400.00
	1936	819 pcs.	300.00	600.00	900.00
	1937	8 pcs.	850.00	1500.	2000.
	1938	*186 pcs.	350.00	750.00	1200.
	1951	200 Pcs.	250.00	500.00	750.00

***NOTE:** Czech reports show mintage of 14 for Czechoslavakia and 172 for state of Slovakia.

10th Anniversary of Republic
Rev: St. Prokop.

Fr#	Date	Mintage	VF	XF	Unc
7	1928	—	175.00	250.00	350.00

Reopening Of Kremnica Mines
Obv: St. Catherine praying.

Fr#	Date	Mintage	VF	XF	Unc
15	1934	518 pcs.	600.00	900.00	1500.

Obv: Seated figure of Charles IV.

Fr#	Date	Mintage	VF	XF	Unc
111	1978	.010	175.00	250.00	325.00

3 DUKATY

12.0000 gm., .986 GOLD, .3804 oz AGW
1000th Anniversary Christianity In Bohemia
Obv: Standing figure. Rev: Knight on horse

Fr#	Date	Mintage	VF	XF	Unc
9	1929	—	275.00	550.00	850.00

4 DUKATY

13.9600 gm., .986 GOLD, .4425 oz AGW
10th Anniversary of Republic
Rev: St. Prokop.

Fr#	Date	Mintage	VF	XF	Unc
6	1928	—	325.00	450.00	600.00

5 DUKATY

17.4500 gm., .986 GOLD, .5532 oz AGW
Rev: St. Vaclav (Wenceslas) on horse back.

Y#	Date	Mintage	VF	XF	Unc
17	1929	1,827	375.00	500.00	900.00

Y#	Date	Mintage	VF	XF	Unc
17	1930	543 Pcs.	450.00	700.00	1100.
	1931	1,528	375.00	500.00	900.00
	1932	1,827	375.00	500.00	900.00
	1933	1,752	375.00	500.00	900.00
	1934	1,101	375.00	500.00	900.00
	1935	1,037	375.00	500.00	900.00
	1936	728 pcs.	400.00	650.00	1000.
	1937	4 pcs.	—	Rare	—
	1938	*56 pcs.	1000.	2000.	3000.
	1951	100 pcs.	500.00	850.00	1275.

***NOTE:** Czech reports show mintage of 12 for Czechoslovakia and 44 for state of Slovakia.

1000th Year of Christianity in Bohemia
Obv: Standing figure with banner. Rev: Knight on horse.

Fr#	Date	Mintage	VF	XF	Unc
8	1929	—	400.00	750.00	1000.

Reopening Of Kremnica Mine
Obv: St. Catherine praying.

14	1934	304 pcs.	1500.	2500.	4000.

Wallenstein Coinage Commemorative
Obv: Bust of Wallenstein. Rev: Crowned shield.

18	1934	—	375.00	500.00	850.00

Obv: Standing figure of Charles IV with Duke Wensesias kneeling.

112	1978	.010	—	—	600.00

10 DUKATU

34.9000 gm., .986 GOLD, 1.1064 oz AGW
St. Vaclav Wenceslas on horseback.

Y#	Date	Mintage	VF	XF	Unc
18	1929	1,564	750.00	1250.	2000.
	1930	394 pcs.	1000.	2000.	3000.
	1931	1,239	750.00	1250.	2000.
	1932	1,035	750.00	1250.	2000.
	1933	1,780	750.00	1250.	2000.
	1934	1,298	750.00	1250.	2000.
	1935	600 pcs.	1000.	1500.	2250.
	1936	633 pcs.	1000.	1500.	2250.
	1937	34 pcs.	—	—	—
	1938	*192 pcs.	—	—	—
	1951	100 pcs.	1200.	1750.	2500.

***NOTE:** Czech reports show mintage of 20 for Czechoslovakia and 172 for state of Slovakia.

Reopening Of Kremnica Mines
Obv: St. Catherine praying.

Fr#	Date	Mintage	VF	XF	Unc
13	1934	317 pcs.	2000.	4000.	6000.

Wallenstein Coinage Commemorative
Obv: Bust of Wallenstein. Rev: Crowned shield.

17	1934	—	750.00	1250.	2000.

Obv: City view of Prague behind coat of arms.

Fr#	Date	Mintage	VF	XF	Unc
113	1978	.010	—	—	1500.

BOHEMIA

A region in western Czechoslovakia. Formerly a kingdom it was of considerable importance in the medieval period. Bohemia came under Austrian rule in 1526. Coins were produced for the area until the death of Maria Theresa in 1780 and the land remained an Austrian possession until 1918.

RULERS

Maria Theresa, 1740-1780
Widow, 1765-1780
Joseph II, 1765-1790

MINTMARKS

A - Vienna
C - Prague

MINTMASTER'S INITIALS

AS - A. Stehr
E.v.S.,EVS,PS,VS - P. Erdmann von Schwingerschuh
IK,K - J.W. Kendler

GROESCHL

COPPER
Obv: Crowned arms.
Rev: Value and date in wreath.

C#	Date	Mintage	VG	Fine	VF
25	1781A	—	8.50	12.50	18.50
	1782A	—	8.50	12.50	18.50

3 KREUZER

BILLON
Obv: Veiled head right.
Rev: Crowned imperial eagle; value below.

6c	1776VS-K	—	7.50	10.00	15.00
	1777VS-K	—	7.50	10.00	15.00
	1778VS-K	—	7.50	10.00	15.00
	1779VS-K	—	7.50	10.00	15.00

10 KREUZER

SILVER
Obv: Veiled head right in branches.
Rev: Crowned imperial eagle; value below; sprays to sides.

C#	Date	Mintage	Fine	VF	XF
9b	1777VS-K	—	4.00	6.50	12.50
	1778VS-K	—	4.00	6.50	12.50
	1779VS-K	—	4.00	6.50	12.50

C#	Date	Mintage	Fine	VF	XF
	1780VS-K	—	4.00	6.50	12.50

20 KREUZER

SILVER
Obv: Veiled head right in branches.
Rev: Crowned imperial eagle; value below; sprays to sides.

C#	Date	Mintage	Fine	VF	XF
12b	1768EvS-AS	—	5.00	8.50	15.00
	1769EvS-AS	—	5.00	8.50	15.00
	1770EvS-AS	—	5.00	8.50	15.00
	1771EvS-AS	—	5.00	8.50	15.00
	1772EvS-AS	—	5.00	8.50	15.00
	1773EvS-AS	—	5.00	8.50	15.00
	1774EvS-IK	—	5.00	8.50	15.00
	1775EvS-IK	—	5.00	8.50	15.00
	1776EvS-IK	—	5.00	8.50	15.00
	1777EvS-IK	—	5.00	8.50	15.00
	1778EvS-IK	—	5.00	8.50	15.00
	1779EvS-IK	—	5.00	8.50	15.00
	1780EvS-IK	—	5.00	8.50	15.00

CONVENTION THALER

SILVER
Obv: Veiled head right.
Rev: Crowned imperial eagle; arms on breast.

C#	Date	Mintage	Fine	VF	XF
21	1771EvS-AS	—	75.00	100.00	150.00
	Obv: Head right with smaller veil.				
21.1	1773EvS-AS	—	75.00	100.00	150.00
	1774EvS-IK	—	75.00	100.00	150.00
	1775EvS-IK	—	75.00	100.00	150.00
	Obv: Large veiled head right.				
21.2	1780EvS-IK	—	75.00	100.00	150.00
	1780PS-Ik	—	75.00	100.00	150.00

TRADE COINS

DUCAT

.986 GOLD
Obv: Veiled head right.
Rev: Crowned arms.

C#	Date	Mintage	Fine	VF	XF
23a	1769vS-S	—	350.00	500.00	750.00
	1771	—	350.00	500.00	750.00
	1773vS-S	—	350.00	500.00	750.00
	1773vS-K	—	350.00	500.00	750.00
	1774vS-K	—	350.00	500.00	750.00
	1776vS-K	—	350.00	500.00	750.00
	1779vS-K	—	350.00	500.00	750.00
	1780vS-K	—	350.00	500.00	750.00

BOHEMIA & MORAVIA

Bohemia, a province in north—west Czechoslovakia, was combined with the majority of Moravia in central Czechoslovakia (excluding parts of north and south Moravia which were joined with Silesia in 1938) to form the German protectorate in March, 1939, after the German invasion. Toward the end of war in 1945 the protectorate was dissolved and Bohemia and Moravia once again became part of Czechoslovakia.

10 HALERU

ZINC

Y#	Date	Mintage	Fine	VF	XF	Unc
B29	1940	—	.25	.50	.75	2.50
	1941	—	.25	.50	.75	3.50
	1942	—	.25	.50	.75	3.50
	1943	—	.40	.75	1.50	4.50
	1944	—	.75	1.50	2.50	5.50

20 HALERU

ZINC

Y#	Date	Mintage	Fine	VF	XF	Unc
B30	1940	—	.25	.50	1.00	3.50
	1941	—	.25	.50	1.00	3.50
	1942	—	.25	.50	1.00	3.50
	1943	—	.40	.75	1.50	4.50
	1944	—	.50	1.00	1.75	4.00

50 HALERU

ZINC

Y#	Date	Mintage	Fine	VF	XF	Unc
B31	1940	—	.35	.75	1.25	5.00
	1941	—	.35	.75	1.25	5.00
	1942	—	.35	.75	1.25	5.00
	1943	—	.75	1.50	3.00	7.00
	1944	—	.35	.75	1.25	5.00

KORUNA

ZINC

Y#	Date	Mintage	Fine	VF	XF	Unc
B32	1941	—	.50	1.00	1.75	5.00
	1942	—	.50	1.00	1.75	5.00
	1943	—	.50	1.00	1.75	5.00
	1944	—	.50	1.00	1.75	5.00

OLMUTZ

IN MORAVIA

Olmutz (Olomouc), a town in north-central Czechoslovakia which was, until 1640, the recognized capital of Moravia, obtained the right to mint a coinage in 1141, but exercised it sparingly until the 17th century.

RULERS

Anton Theodor 1777-1811
Rudolph Johann, Archduke of Austria, 1819-1831

10 KREUZER

SILVER
Obv: Bust right, Rev: Arms

C#	Date	Mintage	Fine	VF	XF
5	1779	—	25.00	45.00	75.00

20 KREUZER

SILVER
Obv. and rev. similar to 10 Kreuzer, C#5.

C#	Date	Mintage	Fine	VF	XF
6	1779	—	25.00	45.00	75.00

C#	Date	Mintage	Fine	VF	XF
10	1820	—	17.50	30.00	50.00

1/2 CONVENTION THALER

SILVER
Obv: Bust right, Rev: Arms

C#	Date	Mintage	Fine	VF	XF
7	1779	—	60.00	125.00	300.00

C#	Date	Mintage	Fine	VF	XF
11	1820	—	40.00	75.00	110.00

CONVENTION THALER

SILVER
Obv: Bust right, Rev: Arms

C#	Date	Mintage	Fine	VF	XF
8	1779	—	175.00	275.00	475.00

C#	Date	Mintage	Fine	VF	XF
12	1820	—	175.00	275.00	400.00

TRADE COINS

DUCAT

.986 GOLD

Obv: Bust right, Rev: Arms

C#	Date	Mintage	Fine	VF	XF
9	1779	—	350.00	450.00	600.00
	Similar to Convention Thaler, C#12.				
13	1820	—	375.00	475.00	650.00

ORSINI-ROSENBERG

The Princes of Orsini-Rosenberg were members of the Carinthian family who, in 1648, were given the rank of counts of the Austro-Hungarian Empire. Count Wolfgang Franz Xaver, who was made a prince in 1790, exercised his minting privilege to prepare a convention thaler in 1793 that was not actually struck until 1853.

RULERS

Prince Franz 1739-1796

CONVENTION TALER

SILVER
Obv: Bust right, Rev: Arms

C#	Date	Mintage	Fine	VF	XF
1	1793 (Struck 1853)	—	350.00	450.00	550.00

PAAR

The Princes of Paar were members of an Italian family that for nearly three centuries held office as hereditary Austrian postmaster general. They attained the rank of counts in 1629, and of princes, with the minting privilege, in 1769.

RULERS

Johann Wenzel
as Count, 1741-1769
as Prince, 1769-1792
Prince Wenzel 1792-1812

1/2 CONVENTION THALER

SILVER, 14 gm.
Similar to Thaler, C#2.

C#	Date	Mintage	Fine	VF	XF
1	1771	—	85.00	125.00	175.00

C#	Date	Mintage	Fine	VF	XF
4	1794	—	50.00	100.00	200.00

CONVENTION THALER

SILVER

C#	Date	Mintage	Fine	VF	XF
2	1771	—	225.00	300.00	400.00
	Similar to 1/2 Thaler, C#4.				
5	1794	—	160.00	300.00	500.00

TRADE COINS

DUCAT

.986 GOLD
Similar to Thaler, C#2.

C#	Date	Mintage	Fine	VF	XF
3	1771	—	700.00	1000.	1250.

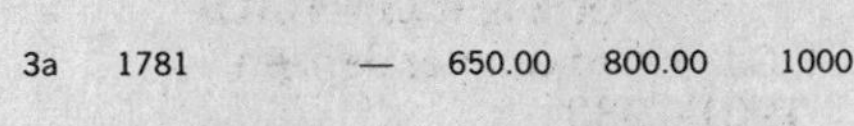

C#	Date	Mintage	Fine	VF	XF
3a	1781	—	650.00	800.00	1000.

C#	Date	Mintage	Fine	VF	XF
6	1794	—	300.00	500.00	800.00

5 DUCATS

.986 GOLD
Similar to 1/2 Thaler, C#4.

C#	Date	Mintage	Fine	VF	XF
7	1794	—	600.00	750.00	1000.

10 DUCATS

.986 GOLD
Similar To 1/2 Thaler, C#4.

C#	Date	Mintage	Fine	VF	XF
8	1794	—	1000.	1200.	2000.

SLOVAKIA

Slovakia (Slovak Socialist Republic), a constituent republic of Czechoslovakia, has an area of 18,923 sq. mi. (49,011 sq. km.) and a population of 4.9 million. Capital: Bratislava. Textiles, steel, and wood products are exported.

In 1938, the Slovaks declared themselves an autonomous state within a federal Czecho-Slovak state. After the German occupation, Slovakia became nominally independent under the protection of the German-Reich, March 16, 1939. Andrej Hlinka, a priest, was appointed Fuhrer or chief of state. Slovakia was liberated from German control in Oct. 1944, but in May 1945 ceased to be an independent Slovak state. In 1968 it became a constituent state of Czechoslovakia.

MONETARY SYSTEM

100 Halierov = 1 Koruna

5 HALIEROV

ZINC

Y#	Date	Mintage	Fine	VF	XF	Unc
S19b	1942	1.000	3.00	5.00	10.00	15.00

10 HALIEROV

BRONZE

Y#	Date	Mintage	Fine	VF	XF	Unc
S20	1939	—	1.50	2.00	4.00	8.00
	1942	—	1.50	2.00	4.00	8.00

20 HALIEROV

BRONZE

Y#	Date	Mintage	Fine	VF	XF	Unc
S21	1940	15.000	1.25	2.00	3.00	5.00
	1941	Inc. Ab.	1.25	2.00	3.00	5.00
	1942	Inc. Ab.	1.25	3.00	5.00	8.00

ALUMINUM

Y#	Date	Mintage	Fine	VF	XF	Unc
S21a	1942	—	1.00	1.50	2.00	3.50
	1943	—	1.00	1.50	2.00	3.50

50 HALIEROV

COPPER-NICKEL

Y#	Date	Mintage	Fine	VF	XF	Unc
S22	1940	—	35.00	60.00	85.00	125.00
	1941	8.000	1.00	2.00	3.00	6.00

ALUMINUM

Y#	Date	Mintage	Fine	VF	XF	Unc
S22b	1943	—	1.00	1.50	2.50	4.00
	1944	—	1.25	2.00	4.00	6.00

KORUNA

COPPER-NICKEL

Y#	Date	Mintage	Fine	VF	XF	Unc
S23	1940	—	1.00	1.50	2.25	6.00
	1941	—	1.00	1.50	2.25	6.00
	1942	10.000	1.00	1.50	2.25	6.00
	1944	—	1.50	2.50	4.50	9.00
	1945	—	1.00	1.50	2.25	6.00

5 KORUN

NICKEL

Y#	Date	Mintage	Fine	VF	XF	Unc
S24	1939	5.000	2.00	3.00	4.00	7.50

Approximately 2,000,000 pieces were melted down by the Czechoslovak National Bank in 1947.

10 KORUN

10.0000 gm., .500 SILVER, .1607 oz ASW
Variety 1-Cross atop church held by left figure.

Y#	Date	Mintage	Fine	VF	XF	Unc
S25	1944	1.38	BV	BV	6.50	10.00
	Variety 2-No cross.					
	1944	Inc. Ab.	BV	BV	7.00	11.00

20 KORUN

12.0000 gm., .500 SILVER, .1929 oz ASW

S26	1939	.200	7.50	12.00	17.50	35.00

Variety 1-Single bar cross in church at lower right.

S27	1941	2.500	BV	BV	7.50	10.00
	Variety 2-Double bar cross.					
	1941	Inc. Ab.	BV	BV	10.00	12.50

50 KORUN

13.0000 gm., .700 SILVER, .2926 oz ASW

S28	1944	2.000	BV	BV	10.00	12.50

Listings for:

DAHOMEY: refer to Benin

DANISH WEST INDIES

The Danish West Indies (now the U.S. organized unincorporated territory of the Virgin Islands of the United States) consist of the islands of St. Thomas, St. John, St. Croix, and 62 islets located in the Caribbean Sea 40 miles (64 km.) east of Puerto Rico. The islands have a combined area of 133 sq. mi. (344 sq. km.) and a population of 110,000. Capital: Charlotte Amalie. Tourism is the principal industry. Watch movements, costume jewelry, pharmaceuticals, and rum are exported.

The Virgin Islands were discovered by Columbus in 1493, during his second voyage to America. During the 17th century the islands, actually the peaks of a submerged mountain range, were held at various times by Spain, Holland, England, France and Denmark, and during the same period were favorite resorts of the buccaneers operating in the Caribbean and the coastal waters of eastern North America. Control of the 100-island chain finally passed to Denmark and England. The Danish islands were purchased by the United States in 1917 for $25 million, mainly because they command the Anegada Passage into the Caribbean Sea, a strategic point on the defense perimeter of the Panama Canal.

RULERS

Danish, until 1917

MINTMARKS

Crown (c) - Copenhagen
Heart (h) - Copenhagen
Orb (o) - Altona

MINTMASTERS INITIALS

P, VBP - Vilhelm Burchard Poulsen

MONEYERS INITIALS

GI, GJ - Knud Gunner Jensen, 1901-1933

MONETARY SYSTEM

(Until 1849)
96 Skilling = 1 Daler

II SKILLING

SILVER
Obv: Crowned arms. Rev: Value and date.

C#	Date	Mintage	VG	Fine	VF	XF
12	1816	—	10.00	17.50	30.00	50.00
	1837 flat top 3	—	10.00	17.50	30.00	45.00
	1837 round top 3	—	12.50	20.00	33.50	50.00
15	1847	—	10.00	17.50	30.00	45.00
18	1848	—	6.50	12.50	20.00	35.00

VI SKILLING

SILVER
Obv: Crowned C7 monogram.
Rev: Similar to XII Skilling, C#10.

9	1767 Danske	—	75.00	125.00	225.00	300.00
	1767 Daske	—	75.00	125.00	225.00	300.00

X SKILLING

SILVER

13	1816	—	12.50	25.00	40.00	60.00
16	1840	—	12.50	20.00	35.00	50.00
	1845	—	12.50	20.00	35.00	50.00
	1845	—	—	—	Proof	300.00
	1847	—	15.00	25.00	40.00	75.00

C#	Date	Mintage	VG	Fine	VF	XF
19	1848	—	15.00	25.00	37.50	55.00
	1848	—	—	—	Proof	200.00
	1848 Plain edge	—	15.00	27.50	40.00	60.00

XII SKILLING

SILVER

10	1767	—	12.50	27.50	45.00	85.00

XX SKILLING

SILVER
Obv: Crowned arms. Rev: Value and date.

14	1816	—	20.00	40.00	75.00	125.00
17	1840	—	20.00	35.00	65.00	110.00
	1845	—	20.00	35.00	65.00	110.00
	1847	—	20.00	35.00	65.00	110.00
20	1848 Incuse edge		20.00	35.00	65.00	110.00
	1848	—	—	—	Proof	350.00
	1848 Plain edge		20.00	40.00	75.00	125.00

XXIIII SKILLING

SILVER

11	1766	—	30.00	50.00	80.00	125.00
	1767	—	30.00	50.00	80.00	125.00

COUNTERSTAMP ISSUES

1849-1859

The only counterstamp authorized for the Danish West Indies was the crowned F R VII monogram, which was used between 1849 through 1859. Although the majority of the coins counterstamped in those years were of United States origin, numerous pieces from European and Latin American countries were also employed for this purpose.

COUNTERFEITS: This series has been counterfeited extensively. A common counterfeit countermark lacks the small cross on top of the crown and small shallow striking of c/s especially in beads of crown.

U. S. Series

1/2 CENT

COPPER
c/s: Crowned FRVII on U.S. 1/2 Cent.

C#	Date	Mintage	Fine	VF	XF
21	—	—	150.00	190.00	250.00

CENT

COPPER
c/s: Crowned FRVII on U.S. large Cent.

C#	Date	Mintage	Fine	VF	XF
22	—	—	100.00	150.00	225.00

10 CENTS

SILVER
c/s: Crowned FRVII on U.S. 10 Cent.

C#	Date	Mintage	Fine	VF	XF
23	—	—	225.00	300.00	375.00

25 CENTS

SILVER
c/s: Crowned FRVII on U.S. 25 Cent.

C#	Date	Mintage	Fine	VF	XF
24	—	—	275.00	375.00	525.00

50 CENTS

SILVER
c/s: Crowned FRVII on U.S. 50 Cent.

C#	Date	Mintage	Fine	VF	XF
25	—	—	275.00	400.00	550.00

DOLLAR

SILVER
c/s: Crowned FRVII on U.S. Dollar.

C#	Date	Mintage	Fine	VF	XF
26	—	—	325.00	500.00	700.00

Brazil Series

40 REIS

COPPER
c/s: Crowned FRVII on Brazil 40 Reis.

C#	Date	Mintage	Fine	VF	XF
32	—	—	30.00	40.00	60.00

960 REIS

SILVER
c/s: Crowned FRVII on Brazil 960 Reis.

C#	Date	Mintage	Fine	VF	XF
33	—	—	300.00	425.00	550.00

British West Indies Series

1/8 DOLLAR

SILVER
c/s: Crowned FRVII on 'Anchor' 1/8 Dollar.

C#	Date	Mintage	Fine	VF	XF
34	—	—	125.00	185.00	250.00

1/4 DOLLAR

SILVER
c/s: Crowned FRVII on 'Anchor' 1/4 Dollar.

C#	Date	Mintage	Fine	VF	XF
35	—	—	225.00	285.00	375.00

English Series

FARTHING

COPPER
c/s: Crowned FRVII on English Farthing.

C#	Date	Mintage	Fine	VF	XF
36	—	—	25.00	32.50	50.00

1/2 PENNY

COPPER
c/s: Crowned FRVII on English 1/2 Penny.

C#	Date	Mintage	Fine	VF	XF
37	—	—	30.00	45.00	65.00

c/s: Crowned FRVII on English Condor 1/2 Penny token.

C#	Date	Mintage	Fine	VF	XF
37a	—	—	40.00	50.00	65.00

6 PENCE

SILVER
c/s: Crowned FRVII on English 6 Pence.

C#	Date	Mintage	Fine	VF	XF
38	—	—	50.00	85.00	125.00

SHILLING

SILVER
c/s: Crowned FRVII on English Shilling.

C#	Date	Mintage	Fine	VF	XF
39	—	—	70.00	95.00	125.00

1/2 CROWN

SILVER
c/s: Crowned FRVII on English 1/2 Crown.

C#	Date	Mintage	Fine	VF	XF
40	—	—	150.00	225.00	325.00

CROWN

SILVER
c/s: Crowned FRVII on English Bank Dollar.

C#	Date	Mintage	Fine	VF	XF
41	—	—	250.00	375.00	500.00

French Series

5 SOLS

SILVER
c/s: Crowned FRVII on French 5 Sols.

C#	Date	Mintage	Fine	VF	XF
42	—	—	30.00	50.00	80.00

1/2 FRANC

SILVER
c/s: Crowned FRVII on French 1/2 Franc.

C#	Date	Mintage	Fine	VF	XF
43	—	—	30.00	50.00	80.00

Mexican Series

8 REALES

SILVER
c/s: Crowned FRVII on Mexican 8 Reales.

C#	Date	Mintage	Fine	VF	XF
44	—	—	110.00	190.00	275.00

Netherlands Series

25 CENTS

SILVER
c/s: Crowned FRVII on Netherlands 25 Cents.

C#	Date	Mintage	Fine	VF	XF
45	—	—	75.00	125.00	200.00

Spanish Series

4 MARAVEDI

COPPER
c/s: Crowned FRVII on Spanish 4 Maravedi.

C#	Date	Mintage	Fine	VF	XF
46	—	—	30.00	50.00	100.00

REAL

SILVER
c/s: Crowned FRVII on Spanish or Spanish Colonial 1 Real.

C#	Date	Mintage	Fine	VF	XF
47	—	—	35.00	60.00	125.00

2 REALES

SILVER
c/s: Crowned FRVII on Spanish or Spanish Colonial 2 Reales.

C#	Date	Mintage	Fine	VF	XF
48	—	—	50.00	75.00	150.00

4 REALES

SILVER
c/s: Crowned FRVII on Spanish or Spanish Colonial 4 Reales.

C#	Date	Mintage	Fine	VF	XF
49	—	—	350.00	550.00	775.00

DECIMAL COINAGE

5 Bit = 1 Cent
20 Cents = 1 Franc
5 Francs = 1 Daler

1/2 CENT - 2 1/2 BIT

BRONZE

Y#	Date	Mintage	Fine	VF	XF	Unc
5	1905-P(h)GJ	.190	5.50	9.00	15.00	25.00
	1905-P(h)GJ	—	—	—	Proof	Rare

CENT

BRONZE

C#	Date	Mintage	Fine	VF	XF	Unc
27	1859(o)	.216	4.00	7.50	12.50	25.00
	1859(o)	10 pcs.	—	—	Proof	Rare
	1860(o)	.250	4.00	7.50	12.50	25.00

Y#	Date	Mintage	Fine	VF	XF	Unc
1	1868(c)	.240	4.00	7.50	12.50	25.00
	1868(c)	—	—	—	Proof	125.00
	1878(h)	.020	6.00	10.00	20.00	50.00
	1879(h)	.040	15.00	22.50	35.00	75.00
	1883(h)	.210	4.00	7.50	12.50	25.00

CENT - 5 BIT

BRONZE

Y#	Date	Mintage	Fine	VF	XF	Unc
6	1905-P(h)GJ	.500	3.50	6.00	9.00	20.00

Y#	Date	Mintage	Fine	VF	XF	Unc
16	1913-VBP(h)AH-GJ	.200	7.50	12.50	20.00	35.00

2 CENTS - 10 BIT

BRONZE

Y#	Date	Mintage	Fine	VF	XF	Unc
7	1905-P(h)GJ	.150	8.50	15.00	25.00	30.00
	1905-P(h)GJ	20 pcs.	—	—	Proof	Rare

3 CENTS

.625 SILVER

C#	Date	Mintage	Fine	VF	XF	Unc
28	1859(c)	.291	6.00	10.00	17.50	40.00
	1859(c)	10 pcs.	—	—	Proof	Rare

5 CENTS

.625 SILVER

C#	Date	Mintage	Fine	VF	XF	Unc
29	1859(c)	.150	5.00	9.00	17.50	40.00
	1859(c)	10 pcs.	—	—	Proof	Rare

Y#	Date	Mintage	Fine	VF	XF	Unc
2	1878(h)	.500	12.50	20.00	35.00	75.00
	1878(h)	—	—	—	Proof	325.00
	1879(h)	Inc. Ab.	15.00	25.00	40.00	80.00

5 CENTS - 25 BIT

NICKEL

	Date	Mintage	Fine	VF	XF	Unc
8	1905-P(h)GJ	.199	4.00	6.00	10.00	20.00
	1905-P(h)GJ	20 pcs.	—	—	Proof	Rare

10 CENTS

.625 SILVER

C#	Date	Mintage	Fine	VF	XF	Unc
30	1859(c)	.250	8.00	15.00	20.00	35.00
	1859(c)	10 pcs.	—	—	Proof	Rare
	1862/1(c)	.140	—	—	—	—
	1862(c)	Inc. Ab.	12.50	17.50	25.00	40.00
	1862(c)	—	—	—	Proof	225.00

Y#	Date	Mintage	Fine	VF	XF	Unc
3	1878(h)	.080	12.50	20.00	35.00	50.00
	1878(h)	—	—	—	Proof	225.00
	1879(h)	.120	20.00	35.00	60.00	75.00
	1879(h)	—	—	—	Proof	275.00

10 CENTS - 50 BIT

.800 SILVER

	Date	Mintage	Fine	VF	XF	Unc
9	1905-P(h)GJ	.175	5.00	8.50	15.00	25.00
	1905-P(h)GJ	20 pcs.	—	—	Proof	Rare

20 CENTS

.625 SILVER

C#	Date	Mintage	Fine	VF	XF	Unc
31	1859(c)	.430	17.50	30.00	55.00	100.00
	1859(c)	10 pcs.	—	—	Proof	Rare
	1862(c)	.560	17.50	30.00	55.00	100.00
	1862(c)	—	—	—	Proof	300.00

Y#	Date	Mintage	Fine	VF	XF	Unc
4	1878(h)	.200	22.50	40.00	75.00	150.00
	1878(h)	—	—	—	Proof	350.00
	1879(h)	.300	75.00	125.00	200.00	350.00

20 CENTS - 1 FRANC

.800 SILVER

	Date	Mintage	Fine	VF	XF	Unc
10	1905-P(h)GJ	.150	12.50	20.00	35.00	60.00
	1905-P(h)GJ	20 pcs.	—	—	Proof	Rare

	Date	Mintage	Fine	VF	XF	Unc
14	1907-P(h)GJ	.101	17.50	30.00	50.00	75.00
	1907-P(h)GJ	10 pcs.	—	—	Proof	Rare

40 CENTS - 2 FRANÇS

.800 SILVER

	Date	Mintage	Fine	VF	XF	Unc
11	1905-P(h)GJ	.038	45.00	75.00	125.00	200.00
	1905-P(h)GJ	20 pcs.	—	—	Proof	Rare

	Date	Mintage	Fine	VF	XF	Unc
15	1907-P(h)GJ	.025	65.00	115.00	175.00	300.00
	1907-P(h)GJ	10 pcs.	—	—	Proof	Rare

4 DALER - 20 FRANCS

.900 GOLD

Y#	Date	Mintage	Fine	VF	XF	Unc
12	1904-P(h)GJ	.121	200.00	350.00	425.00	550.00
	1905-P(h)GJ	I.A.	210.00	375.00	450.00	575.00

10 DALER - 50 FRANCS

.900 GOLD

	Date	Mintage	Fine	VF	XF	Unc
13	1904-P(h)GJ	2,005	1250.	2500.	3500.	4500.

NCLT ISSUES

PROOF SETS
STANDARD METALS

KM#	Date	Mintage	Identification	Issue Price	Mkt. Val.
101	1859(5)	10	C27-31	—	Rare
102	1905(5)	20	Y7-11	—	Rare
103	1907(2)	10	Y14-15	—	Rare

Listings For

DANZIG: refer to Poland

DENMARK

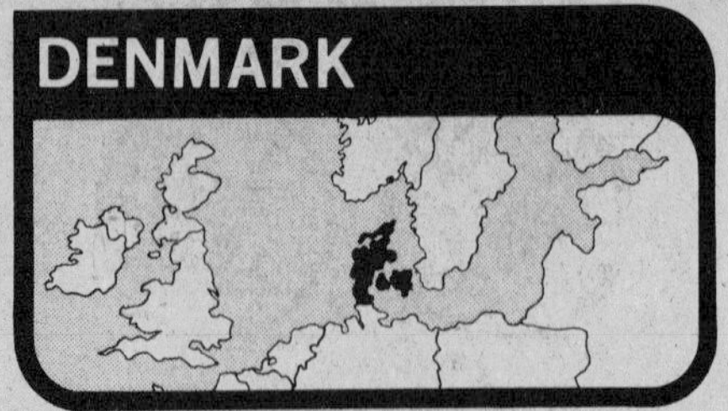

The Kingdom of Denmark, a constitutional monarchy located at the mouth of the Baltic sea, has an area of 16,169 sq. mi. (48,177 sq. km.) and a population of 5 million. Capital: Copenhagen. Most of the country is arable. Agriculture, which employs the majority of the people, is conducted by small farmers served by cooperatives. The largest industries are food processing, iron and metal, and fishing. Machinery, meats (chiefly bacon), dairy products and chemicals are exported.

Denmark, a great power during the Viking period of the 9th-11th centuries, conducted raids on western Europe and England, and in the 11th century united England, Denmark and Norway under the rule of King Canute. Despite a struggle between the crown and the nobility (13th-14th centuries) which forced the King to grant a written constitution, Queen Margaret (1353- 1412) succeeded in uniting Denmark, Norway, Sweden, Finland and Greenland under the Danish crown, placing all of Scandinavia under the rule of Denmark. An unwise alliance with Napoleon contributed to the dismembering of the empire and fostered a liberal movement which succeeded in making Denmark a constitutional monarchy in 1849.

The present decimal system of coinage was introduced in 1874.

RULERS

Christian VII, 1766-1808
Frederik VI, 1808-1839
Christian VIII, 1839-1848
Frederik VII, 1848-1863
Christian IX, 1863-1906
Frederik VIII, 1906-1912
Christian X, 1912-1947
Frederik IX, 1947-1972
Margrethe II, 1972-

MINTMARKS

(c) - Copenhagen, crown
FF - Altona (1842 issues)
(h) - Copenhagen, heart
(o) - Altona, orb
KM - Copenhagen

MINTMASTERS INITIALS

Altona

CHL - C.H. Lyng, 1771-1784
DCL - Didrik Christian Liebst, 1784-1786
MF - Michael Flor, 1786-1816
CB - Cajus Branth, 1817-1819
FF, IFF - Johan Friedrich Freund, 1819-1856
TA - Theodor Andersen, 1848-1851
FA - Hans Frederik Alsing, 1856-1863

Copenhagen

K, HSK - Hans Schierven Knoph, 1761-1784
CHL - Caspar Henrik Lyng, 1784-1797
HIAB - Hans Jacob Arnold Branth, 1797-1810
- Ole Varberg, 1810-1821
CFG - Conrad Frederik Gerlach, 1821-1831
VS, WS - Georg Wilhelm Svendsen, 1831-1861
RH - Rasmus Hinnerup, 1861-1869
CS - Diderik Christian Andreas Svendsen, 1869-1893
P, VBP - Vilhelm Buchard Poulsen, 1893-1918
HCN - Hans Christian Nielsen, 1919-1927
N - Niels Peter Nielsen, 1927-1955
C - Alfred Frederik Christiansen, 1956-1971
S - Vagn Sorensen, 1971-1978
B - Peter M. Bjarno, 1978 -

MONEYERS INITIALS

Altona

FA - Hans Frederik Alsing, 1825-1855
FK - Frederik Christopher Krohn, 1841-1863
HL - Carl Heinrich Lorenz, 1848-1851
PP - Peter Petersen, 1852-1863

Copenhagen

B - Johan Ephraim Bauert, 1763-1799
W - Johan Henrik Wolff, 1771-1788
PG - Peter Leonard Gianelli, 1800-1807
IC, ICF - Johannes Conradsen, 1810-1841
M - Christian Andreas Muller, 1813
CC - Christen Christensen, 1836
FK - Frederik Christopher Krohn, 1841-1873
HC - Harald Conradsen, 1873-1901
GI, GJ - Knud Gunner Jensen, 1901-1933
AH - Andreas Frederik Vilhelm Hansen, 1908-1924
HS, S - Harald Salomon, 1933-1968
B - Frode Bahnsen, 1968 -

MONETARY SYSTEM

(Until 1813)

64 Skilling Danske = 4 Mark = 1 Krone
96 Skilling Danske = 16 Mark = 1 Speciedaler
12 Marks = 1 Ducat

(Commencing 1813)

96 Rigsbank Skilling = 1 Rigs(bank)daler
30 Schilling Courant = 1 Rigs(bank)daler
2 Rigsbankdaler = 1 Rigsdaler Species
2 Rigsbankdaler = 1 Specie(daler)
5 Species(daler) = 1 D'or

1/5 RIGSBANKSKILLING

COPPER

C#	Date	Mintage	Fine	VF	XF
118	1842FF	—	7.50	12.50	22.50

Rev. denomination: 1/5 R.B.S.

C#	Date	Mintage	Fine	VF	XF
118a	1842FF	—	3.00	6.50	10.00

1/2 SKILLING

COPPER, 25mm
Obv: Crowned C7 monogram. Rev: Value, DANSKE K.M, date.

C#	Date	Mintage	VG	Fine	VF
46	1771	—	3.25	5.00	7.50

1/2 RIGSBANKSKILLING

COPPER

C#	Date	Mintage	Fine	VF	XF
100	1838	—	2.50	5.00	12.50
119	1842VS	—	5.00	11.00	17.50

C#	Date	Mintage	Fine	VF	XF
131	1852VS	—	3.50	7.50	15.00

1/2 SKILLINGRIGSMONT

COPPER

C#	Date	Mintage	Fine	VF	XF
—	1854	Pattern	—	Rare	—

BRONZE

C#	Date	Mintage	Fine	VF	XF
134	1857(o)	—	1.50	3.00	6.00
	1857(c)	—	—	—	250.00

Y#	Date	Mintage	Fine	VF	XF
1	1868	—	2.50	4.50	10.00

SKILLING

COPPER, 29mm
Obv: Crowned double C7 monogram. Rev: Value, DANSKE K.M, date.

C#	Date	Mintage	VG	Fine	VF
47	1771	—	1.60	3.30	5.75
	1779	—	100.00	135.00	200.00
	Rev: DANKSE instead of DANSKE.				
47a.1	1771	—	60.00	75.00	110.00
	Rev: DANAKE instead of DANSKE.				
47a.2	1771	—	70.00	100.00	150.00
	Rev: DANASKE instead of DANSKE.				
42a.3	1771	—	85.00	125.00	165.00
	Rev: SKILLIING DANSKE M.K. instead of SKILLING K.M.				
47a.4	1771	—	50.00	65.00	90.00

NOTE: These coins were struck in great numbers for many years at Copenhagen and Altona, the only copper coins minted up to 1809. Many die varieties are known, especially the 1 skilling, with or without periods after "DANSKE" and date, large and small monograms, crowns, rosettes, lettering, etc. A scarce variety shows nothing below the date, and a rare one has no curls on the upper strokes of the C's in the monogram.

BILLON 16mm
Obv: Crowned C7 monogram. Rev: Value, DANSKE H.S.K., date.

C#	Date	Mintage	Fine	VF	XF
49	1779HSK	—	3.00	5.00	10.00

C#	Date	Mintage	Fine	VF	XF
49	1782HSK	—	3.50	6.00	12.50

Obv: Crowned FR VI monogram. Rev: Value, DANSK, date.

C#	Date	Mintage	Fine	VF	XF
104	1808MF	—	6.00	10.00	17.50
	1809MF	—	4.00	7.50	12.50
	1810MF	—	—	Unique	—

15mm

C#	Date	Mintage	Fine	VF	XF
87.1	1812MF	—	2.50	5.00	8.00

13mm

C#	Date	Mintage	Fine	VF	XF
87.2	1812	—	50.00	75.00	125.00

RIGSBANK SKILLING

COPPER

C#	Date	Mintage	Fine	VF	XF
93	1813	—	3.00	6.00	17.50

Obv: Crowned oval arms
Rev: Value and date

C#	Date	Mintage	Fine	VF	XF
101	1818	—	3.00	7.50	22.50

C#	Date	Mintage	Fine	VF	XF
120	1842FF(o)	—	5.00	10.00	21.00
	1842VS(c)	—	5.00	10.00	21.00

Large bust

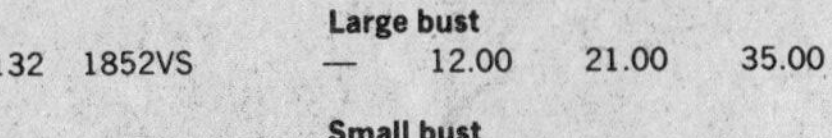

C#	Date	Mintage	Fine	VF	XF
132	1852VS	—	12.00	21.00	35.00

Small bust

C#	Date	Mintage	Fine	VF	XF
132a	1852VS	—	—	Rare	—

Medium bust

C#	Date	Mintage	Fine	VF	XF
132b	1853VS	—	5.00	10.00	20.00

RIGSMONTSKILLING

BRONZE

C#	Date	Mintage	Fine	VF	XF
135	1856(o)	—	1.75	3.50	6.00
	1856(c)	—	—	150.00	200.00
	1860(o)	—	1.75	4.00	7.50
	1863(c)	—	2.00	5.00	9.00

Y#	Date	Mintage	Fine	VF	XF
2	1867	—	2.00	3.50	7.50
	1869	—	2.00	4.00	9.00
	1870	—	2.50	6.00	12.50
	1871	—	3.00	7.50	15.00
	1872	—	2.00	4.00	9.00

2 SKILLING

BILLON, 18mm
Obv: Crowned C7 monogram within legend.

Rev: Crowned arms dividing date, value as legend.

C#	Date	Mintage	VG	Fine	VF
51	1776	—	—	—	—
	1778HSK	—	3.00	4.25	9.25
	1778CHL	—	2.50	3.75	8.00
	1779CHL	—	2.50	3.75	6.50
	1781CHL	—	2.50	3.75	8.00
	1782HSK	—	2.50	3.75	6.50
	1782CHL	—	2.50	3.75	6.50
	1783CHL	—	2.00	3.25	6.00
	1784CHL	—	—	—	—
	1784DCL	—	2.00	3.50	6.00
	1785DCL	—	2.50	3.50	6.50

C#	Date	Mintage	VG	Fine	VF
53	1801HIAB	—	2.00	3.25	5.75
	1801MF	—	3.50	4.75	9.50
	1805MF	—	2.00	3.25	5.75

COPPER
Obv: Truncation in a curved line

C#	Date	Mintage	Fine	VF	XF
88a	1809	—	3.00	6.00	12.50
	1810	—	3.00	6.00	12.50

Obv: Truncation in a broken curved line.

C#	Date	Mintage	Fine	VF	XF
88b	1810	—	3.00	7.00	15.00
	1811	—	3.50	8.00	17.00

C#	Date	Mintage	Fine	VF	XF
94	1815	—	3.00	6.50	15.00

2 RIGSBANKSKILLING

COPPER

C#	Date	Mintage	Fine	VF	XF
102	1818	—	10.00	20.00	45.00

SILVER

C#	Date	Mintage	Fine	VF	XF
106	1836IFF	—	7.00	11.00	15.00

COPPER

C#	Date	Mintage	Fine	VF	XF
121	1842VS	—	50.00	100.00	200.00

3 SKILLING

COPPER

C#	Date	Mintage	Fine	VF	XF
89	1812	—	2.50	6.00	11.00

C#	Date	Mintage	Fine	VF	XF
95	1815	—	5.00	10.00	21.50

3 RIGSBANKSKILLING

SILVER

C#	Date	Mintage	Fine	VF	XF
107	1836IFF	—	15.00	30.00	50.00

C#	Date	Mintage	Fine	VF	XF
122	1842FF	—	3.50	10.00	20.00

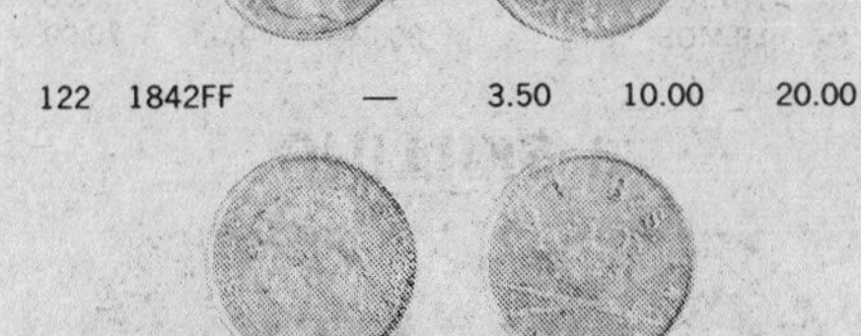

Rev. denomination: 3 R.B.S.

C#	Date	Mintage	Fine	VF	XF
122a	1842FF	—	3.50	7.50	15.00

4 SKILLING

BILLON
Obv: Crowned C VII monogran. Rev: IIII SKILLING, date.

C#	Date	Mintage	VG	Fine	VF
55	1783HSK	—	5.75	8.50	14.00

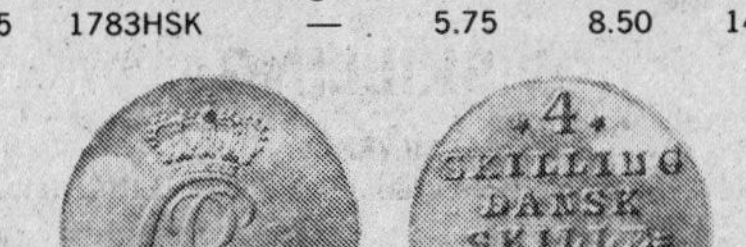

C#	Date	Mintage	VG	Fine	VF
56	1807M.F.	—	5.00	7.50	13.50

COPPER

C#	Date	Mintage	Fine	VF	XF
96	1815	—	7.50	17.50	35.00

4 RIGSBANKSKILLING

SILVER

C#	Date	Mintage	Fine	VF	XF
108	1836IFF	—	17.50	35.00	60.00

With 1-1/4 SCH., for use in Schleswig-Holstein.

C#	Date	Mintage	Fine	VF	XF
123	1841(h)	—	5.50	10.00	20.00
	1842VS(c)	—	4.50	8.00	14.50
	1842FF(o)	—	45.00	75.00	150.00

4 RIGSMONTSKILLING

SILVER

136	1854FF(o)	—	2.50	8.50	25.00
	1856VS(c)	—	2.50	7.50	17.50

Y#	Date	Mintage	Fine	VF	XF
4	1867RH	—	3.00	10.00	20.00
	1869CS	—	4.50	12.50	25.00
	1870CS	—	4.50	12.50	25.00
	1871CS	—	4.00	10.00	22.50
	1872CS	—	4.50	12.50	25.00
	1873CS	—	6.00	17.50	30.00
	1874CS	—	20.00	40.00	70.00

6 SKILLING

COPPER

C#	Date	Mintage	Fine	VF	XF
97	1813	—	8.00	17.50	45.00

8 SKILLING

SILVER

Obv: Crowned C7 monogram. Rev: VIII SKILLING, date.

C#	Date	Mintage	VG	Fine	VF
57	1773HSK	—	12.50	17.50	30.00
	1783HSK	—	11.50	16.00	25.00

Rev: Crowned oval arms.

58	1782HSK	—	135.00	175.00	225.00

8 RIGSBANKSKILLING

SILVER

With 2-1/2 SCHILL.COUR., for use in Schleswig-Holstein.

C#	Date	Mintage	Fine	VF	XF
124	1843FF	—	25.00	50.00	100.00

NOTE: For 8 Reichsbank Schillinge dated 1816-1819 see Schleswig-Holstein in German States listings.

12 SKILLING

COPPER

Struck over 1 Skilling, C#47.

C#	Date	Mintage	Fine	VF	XF
90	1812	—	15.00	30.00	55.00

98	1813	—	7.50	18.50	35.00

1/6 RIGSDALER

SILVER

Offering for fatherland

105	1808MF	—	15.00	25.00	50.00

NOTE: Varieties exist.

16 SKILLING

COPPER

99	1814	—	10.00	25.00	50.00

16 RIGSBANKSKILLING

SILVER

With 5 SCHILL.COURANT for use in Schleswig-Holstein

125	1842VS	—	35.00	60.00	125.00
	1844VS	—	200.00	400.00	750.00

16 RIGSMONTSKILLING

SILVER

137	1854VS(c)	—	—	Rare	—
	1856VS(c)	—	4.00	9.00	20.00
	1857VS(c)	—	4.50	10.00	22.50
	1858VS(c)	—	6.00	15.00	27.50

1/15 SPECIE DALER

SILVER

Obv: Crowned arms. Rev: Value.

C#	Date	Mintage	VG	Fine	VF
59	1796MF	—	12.00	17.50	25.00
	1797MF	—	12.00	17.50	25.00
	1799MF	—	12.00	17.50	25.00

24 SKILLING

SILVER

Obv: Crowned C VII monogram. Rev: Crowned, round draped arms.

C#	Date	Mintage	VG	Fine	VF
62	1767HSK	—	225.00	300.00	450.00

Rev: Crowned oval arms, no drape.

62a	1782HSK	—	225.00	300.00	450.00

Obv: Crowned C7 monogram.

66	1778CHL	—	225.00	300.00	450.00
	1779HSK	—	175.00	250.00	375.00
	1782CHL	—	165.00	225.00	350.00
	1783CHL	—	125.00	175.00	250.00

1/4 SPECIE DALER

RETHWISCH

SILVER

Obv: Crowned double C7 monogram. Rev: Crowned round arms within ribbon.

64	1769HSK	—	225.00	275.00	400.00

32 SKILLING

SILVER

Obv: Bust right. Rev: Arms.

70	1775HSK	—	—	—	—

Obv: Bust left.

70	1775HSK	—	600.00	750.00	1000.

32 RIGSBANKSKILLING

SILVER

C#	Date	Mintage	Fine	VF	XF
109	1818CB	—	—	Rare	—
	1820IFF	—	50.00	90.00	175.00

With 10 SCHILL.COURANT for use in Schleswig-Holstein

126	1842FF	—	35.00	60.00	125.00
	1843FF	—	35.00	60.00	125.00
	1843FF/FK	—	125.00	250.00	350.00

1/3 SPECIE DALER

SILVER

—	1798HIAB	—	—	Rare	—

1/2 KRONE

SILVER

Obv: Bust right. Rev: DEN 29 JANUARII within wreath.

C#	Date	Mintage	VG	Fine	VF
68	1771K	—	400.00	475.00	625.00

1/2 SPECIE DALER

RETHWISCH

SILVER, 30mm

Obv: Crowned double C7 monogram. Rev: Crowned round arms within ribbons.

74	1769HSK	—	275.00	350.00	500.00

Obv: Crowned double C7 monogram dividing value.

74a	1769HSK	—	225.00	275.00	375.00

35mm

Rev: Crowned oval arms between branches.

C#	Date	Mintage	VG	Fine	VF
74b	1777CHL	—	—	—	—
	1786DCL	—	275.00	375.00	525.00

1/2 RIGSDALER

SILVER

C#	Date	Mintage	Fine	VF	XF
138	1854VS(c)	—	25.00	40.00	60.00
	1855VS(c)	—	25.00	40.00	60.00

KRONE

SILVER

Obv: Bust right. Rev: DEN 29 JANUARII.

C#	Date	Mintage	VG	Fine	VF
76	1771K	—	500.00	600.00	750.00

RIGSBANKDALER

SILVER

C#	Date	Mintage	Fine	VF	XF
110	1813M	—	110.00	175.00	275.00
	1813IC	—	65.00	90.00	140.00
	1813IC-MF	—	70.00	100.00	160.00
	1818IC-CB	—	60.00	90.00	140.00
	1819IC-FF	—	70.00	100.00	160.00

RIGSB'KDALER 1/2 SP.

SILVER

Obv: Small head.

C#	Date	Mintage	Fine	VF	XF
110a	1826FF	—	90.00	150.00	250.00
	1827FF	—	90.00	150.00	250.00
	1828FF	—	90.00	150.00	250.00
	1833FF	—	90.00	150.00	250.00
	1833KM	—	110.00	175.00	300.00
	1834KM	—	110.00	175.00	300.00

Obv: Large head.

C#	Date	Mintage	Fine	VF	XF
110b	1833FF	—	90.00	150.00	250.00
	1834FF	—	150.00	250.00	375.00
	1834KM	—	100.00	175.00	275.00
	1835FF	—	150.00	250.00	375.00
	1835WS	—	200.00	300.00	500.00
	1836FF	—	90.00	150.00	250.00
	1838WS	—	90.00	150.00	250.00
	1839FF	—	90.00	150.00	250.00

RIGSBANKDALER

SILVER

With 30 SCHILL.COURANT for use in Schleswig-Holstein

C#	Date	Mintage	Fine	VF	XF
127	1842VS(c)	—	50.00	75.00	110.00
	1843VS(c)	—	55.00	85.00	125.00
	1844FF(o)	—	55.00	85.00	125.00
	1845FF(o)	—	55.00	85.00	125.00
	1846VS(c)	—	55.00	85.00	125.00
	1847FF(o)	—	55.00	85.00	125.00
	1847VS(c)	—	55.00	85.00	100.00
	1848VS(c)	—	50.00	75.00	110.00

Obv: Head of Frederik VII right
Rev: Crowned arms

C#	Date	Mintage	Fine	VF	XF
139	1849VS	—	150.00	225.00	350.00
	1851VS	—	125.00	200.00	325.00

RIGSDALER

SILVER

C#	Date	Mintage	Fine	VF	XF
140	1854VS(c)	—	30.00	50.00	80.00
	1855FF(o)	—	30.00	50.00	80.00
	1855VS(c)	—	35.00	55.00	85.00

ALBERTUS DALER

SILVER

Obv: Wildman with shield; club in right hand.
Rev: Lion shield.

C#	Date	Mintage	VG	Fine	VF
—	1781	—	400.00	550.00	700.00
	1784	—	450.00	600.00	800.00
	1786	—	450.00	600.00	800.00
	1796	—	375.00	500.00	650.00

Obv: Wildman with club in left hand.

C#	Date	Mintage	VG	Fine	VF
—	1781	—	—	Unique	—

REISE DALER

COURANT DALER

SILVER

C#	Date	Mintage	VG	Fine	VF
—	1788	—	600.00	950.00	1400.

RIGSDALER SPECIES

SILVER

C#	Date	Mintage	Fine	VF	XF
82	1795MF-B	—	125.00	150.00	225.00
	1796CHL-B	—	110.00	150.00	225.00
	1797MF-B	—	100.00	150.00	225.00
	1797CHL-B	—	325.00	400.00	575.00
	1798HIAB-B	—	135.00	175.00	250.00
	1799HIAB-B	—	130.00	175.00	250.00
	1799HIAB-PG	—	150.00	190.00	275.00
	1801MF-B	—	275.00	400.00	550.00

Obv: Smaller head.

C#	Date	Mintage	Fine	VF	XF
82a	1799	—	—	—	—

Obv: Head of Frederik VI right
Rev: Crowned oval arms

C#	Date	Mintage	Fine	VF	XF
111	1819IFF	—	500.00	750.00	1250.

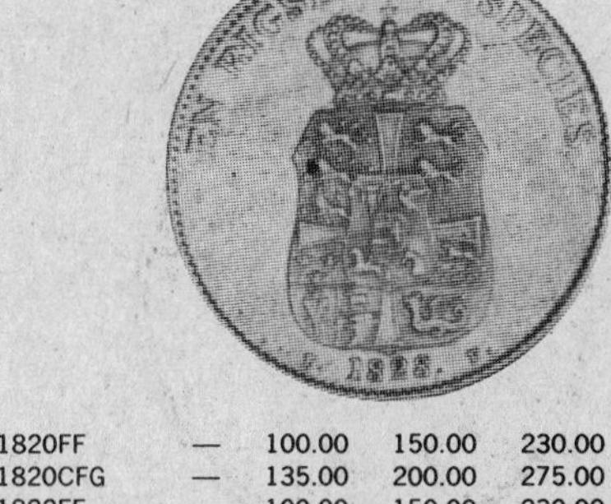

C#	Date	Mintage	Fine	VF	XF
112	1820FF	—	100.00	150.00	230.00
	1820CFG	—	135.00	200.00	275.00
	1822FF	—	100.00	150.00	230.00
	1822CFG	—	135.00	200.00	275.00
	1824FF	—	100.00	150.00	240.00
	1824CFG	—	100.00	150.00	240.00
	1825FF	—	100.00	150.00	240.00
	1825CFG	—	100.00	150.00	240.00
	1826FF	—	100.00	150.00	240.00
	1827FF	—	120.00	185.00	250.00
	1828FF	—	100.00	150.00	240.00
	1829FF	—	100.00	150.00	240.00
	1833FF	—	100.00	150.00	240.00
	1833KM	—	135.00	200.00	275.00
	1834FF	—	100.00	150.00	240.00
	1834KM	—	135.00	200.00	275.00
	1835FF	—	120.00	185.00	250.00
	1835WS	—	100.00	150.00	240.00
	1837WS	—	100.00	150.00	240.00
	1838FF	—	100.00	150.00	240.00
	1838WS	—	100.00	150.00	240.00
	1838SW	Error	—	—	—
	1839FF	—	100.00	150.00	240.00
	1839WS	—	100.00	150.00	240.00

SPECIE DALER

SILVER

Obv: Crowned arms. Rev: Crown above circle containing rampant lion, all above cross.

C#	Date	Mintage	VG	Fine	VF
—	1768HSK	—	500.00	700.00	1200.
	1769HSK	—	125.00	150.00	225.00

Obv: Bust right. Rev: Crowned round arms within ribbon.

C#	Date	Mintage	VG	Fine	VF
80	1769HSK	—	1000.	1250.	1900.

Obv: Crowned double C7 monogram.

C#	Date	Mintage	VG	Fine	VF
81	1769HSK	—	450.00	600.00	900.00

Obv: Smaller crown, taller monogram. Rev: Crowned oval arms between branches.

C#	Date	Mintage	VG	Fine	VF
81a	1771HSK	—	150.00	225.00	300.00
	1776HSK	—	175.00	250.00	350.00
	1776CHL	—	175.00	300.00	435.00
	1780HSK	—	225.00	300.00	400.00

C#	Date	Mintage	VG	Fine	VF
81b	1777CHL	—	130.00	165.00	225.00

SILVER
Small letters

C#	Date	Mintage	Fine	VF	XF
128	1840FF	w/o mm	100.00	170.00	250.00
	1840(h)	—	100.00	170.00	250.00
	1841(h)	—	250.00	325.00	425.00
	1843VS(h)	—	325.00	425.00	500.00
	1843VS(c)	—	130.00	185.00	275.00
	1844FF(o)	—	130.00	185.00	275.00
	1845FF(o)	—	100.00	170.00	250.00
	1845FF(h)	—	—	Rare	—
	1845VS(c)	—	100.00	170.00	250.00
	1846VS(c)	—	100.00	170.00	250.00
	1847FF(o)	—	100.00	170.00	250.00

Large letters

C#	Date	Mintage	Fine	VF	XF
128a	1846VS	—	110.00	170.00	250.00
	1847VS	—	110.00	170.00	250.00
	1848VS	—	110.00	170.00	250.00

Christian VIII Death
And Accession Of Frederik VII

C#	Date	Mintage	Fine	VF	XF
141	1848VS	—	175.00	250.00	350.00

C#	Date	Mintage	Fine	VF	XF
142	1849VS(c)	—	125.00	175.00	275.00
	1851FF(o)	—	275.00	350.00	475.00
	1853FF(o)	—	125.00	175.00	275.00
142	1853VS(c)	—	125.00	175.00	275.00
	1854VS(c)	—	250.00	350.00	425.00

2 RIGSDALER

SILVER

C#	Date	Mintage	Fine	VF	XF
143	1854FF(o)	—	100.00	150.00	250.00
	1854VS(c)	—	100.00	185.00	300.00
	1855FF(o)	—	100.00	185.00	300.00
	1855VS(c)	—	100.00	185.00	300.00
	1856FF(o)	—	200.00	325.00	500.00
	1863RH(c)	—	125.00	225.00	350.00

Frederik VII Death
and Accession of Christian IX

Y#	Date	Mintage	Fine	VF	XF
3	1863RH	.101	175.00	250.00	350.00

Rev: Similar to C#143.

Y#	Date	Mintage	Fine	VF	XF
5	1864RH	—	200.00	325.00	500.00
	1868RH	—	200.00	325.00	500.00
	1871CS	—	200.00	325.00	500.00
	1872CS	—	200.00	325.00	500.00

TRADE COINS

PIASTRE

SILVER
Obv: Crowned arms. Rev: Crown above two circles between two crowned columns.

C#	Date	Mintage	VG	Fine	VF
78	1771	—	2000.	3650.	5500.

XII MARKS

Curant Ducat

.986 GOLD

C#	Date	Mintage	Fine	VF	XF
84	1781CHL W	—	325.00	450.00	650.00
	1782CHL W	—	325.00	450.00	650.00
	1783CHL W	—	300.00	400.00	600.00
	1783CHL B	—	375.00	500.00	750.00
	1783HSK B	—	400.00	525.00	800.00
	1785DCL W	—	325.00	450.00	650.00

DUCAT

.986 GOLD
Obv: Bust right. Rev: DEN 29 JANUARII within wreath.

C#	Date	Mintage	Fine	VF	XF
83	1771K	—	1100.	1250.	1650.

SPECIES DUCAT

.986 GOLD

C#	Date	Mintage	VF	XF	Unc
85	1791	—	600.00	725.00	950.00
	1792	—	700.00	800.00	1100.
	1794	—	800.00	1000.	1300.
	1802	—	750.00	925.00	1250.

CHRISTIAN D'OR

6.6500 gm., .903 GOLD, .1913 oz AGW
Obv: Head right, date below.
Rev: Crowned double C7 monograms.

C#	Date	Mintage	Fine	VF	XF
86	1775	—	2150.	2750.	3250.

Obv: W below head, no date.

Fr#	Date	Mintage	Fine	VF	XF
279	ND W	—	2000.	2650.	3150.

FR(EDERIK) D'OR

.903 GOLD

C#	Date	Mintage	Fine	VF	XF
113	1827IFF	—	850.00	1350.	2150.
114	1828FF	—	850.00	1350.	2150.

C#	Date	Mintage	Fine	VF	XF
114a	1829FF	—	500.00	900.00	1400.
	1830FF	—	—	Rare	—
	1831FF	—	500.00	900.00	1400.
	1833FF	—	500.00	900.00	1400.
	1834FF	—	—	Rare	—
	1835FF	—	500.00	900.00	1400.
	1837FF	—	500.00	900.00	1400.
	1838FF	—	500.00	900.00	1400.

CHR(ISTIAN) D'OR

.903 GOLD

C#	Date	Mintage	Fine	VF	XF
129	1843FF(o)	.038	450.00	700.00	1000.
	1844FF(o)	Inc. Ab.	500.00	800.00	1200.
	1845FF(o)	Inc. Ab.	500.00	800.00	1200.
	1847FF(o)	Inc. Ab.	500.00	800.00	1200.

FR(EDERIK) D'OR

.903 GOLD
Obv: Head of Frederik VII right
Rev: Crowned and supported arms

C#	Date	Mintage	Fine	VF	XF
144	1853FF	678 pcs.	850.00	1350.	2150.

CHR(ISTIAN) D'OR

.903 GOLD
Obv: Head of Christian IX right
Rev: Crowned and supported arms

Y#	Date	Mintage	Fine	VF	XF
6	1869CS	539 pcs.	1500.	2000.	2500.

2 FR(EDERIK) D'OR

13.3000 gm., .903 GOLD, .3827 oz AGW

C#	Date	Mintage	Fine	VF	XF
115	1826IFF	Unique	—	—	—
	1827IFF	—	850.00	1350.	2150.

C#	Date	Mintage	Fine	VF	XF
116	1828FF	—	650.00	1150.	1800.
	1829FF	—	650.00	1150.	1800.
	1830FF	—	650.00	1150.	1800.
	1833FF	—	650.00	1150.	1800.
	1834FF	—	650.00	1150.	1800.
	1835FF	—	650.00	1150.	1800.
	1836FF	—	—	Rare	—

C#	Date	Mintage	Fine	VF	XF
117	1836FF	—	650.00	1150.	1800.
	1837FF	—	650.00	1150.	1800.
	1838FF	—	650.00	1150.	1800.
	1838WS	—	650.00	1150.	1800.
	1839FF	—	650.00	1150.	1800.

2 CHR(ISTIAN) D'OR

.903 GOLD

C#	Date	Mintage	Fine	VF	XF
130	1841(h)	—	550.00	800.00	1200.
	1842FF(o)	—	550.00	800.00	1200.
	1844FF(o)	—	675.00	975.00	1600.
	1844VS(c)	—	675.00	975.00	1600.
	1845FF(o)	—	550.00	800.00	1200.
	1847FF(o)	—	500.00	750.00	1050.

Total mintage 1841(h) and 1844VS(c) 9,222 pcs.
Total mintage 1842-47FF 551 pcs.

2 FR(EDERIK) D'OR

.903 GOLD

C#	Date	Mintage	Fine	VF	XF
145	1850VS(c)	*	700.00	1000.	1500.
	1851FF(o)	1.205	800.00	1150.	1600.
	1852FF(o)	Inc. Ab.	800.00	1150.	1600.
	1853FF(o)	Inc. Ab.	700.00	1000.	1500.
	1854FF(o)	Inc. Ab.	800.00	1150.	1600.
	1855FF(o)	Inc. Ab.	800.00	1150.	1600.
	1856FA(o)	Inc. Ab.	800.00	1150.	1600.
	1857FA(o)	Inc. Ab.	700.00	1000.	1500.
	1859FA(o)	Inc. Ab.	700.00	1000.	1500.
	1863RH(c)	*	1000.	1500.	2000.

*Total mintage 1850VS and 1863 RH .031.

2 CHR(ISTIAN) D'OR

.903 GOLD
Obv: Head of Christian IX right
Rev: Crowned and supported arms

Y#	Date	Mintage	Fine	VF	XF
7	1866RH	.042	1275.	2000.	2500.
	1867RH	Inc. Ab.	—	Rare	—
	1869CS	Inc. Ab.	1275.	2000.	2500.
	1870CS	Inc. Ab.	—	Rare	—

DECIMAL COINAGE

100 Ore = 1 Krone

ORE

BRONZE

Y#	Date	Mintage	VF	XF	Unc
8	1874CS(h)	5.540	7.50	15.00	30.00
	1875CS(h)	2.631	9.00	17.50	35.00
	1876CS(h)	1.483	450.00	600.00	1000.
	1878CS(h)	1.016	60.00	100.00	175.00
	1879CS(h)	1.491	40.00	60.00	90.00
	1880CS(h)	1.989	13.50	27.50	45.00
	1881CS(h)	.260	600.00	900.00	1500.
	1882CS(h)	1.782	12.50	25.00	42.50
	1883CS(h)	2.989	7.00	12.50	25.00
	1886CS(h)	.997	60.00	90.00	125.00
	1887CS(h)	3.007	10.00	20.00	35.00
	1888CS(h)	1.505	15.00	25.00	45.00
	1889CS(h)	2.999	5.50	9.00	18.00
	1891CS(h)	4.982	3.00	6.00	10.00
	1892CS(h)	.494	80.00	130.00	200.00
	1894VBP(h)	4.982	2.00	4.00	10.00
	1897/4VBP(h)	2.988	4.00	7.50	14.00
	1897VBP(h)	Inc. Ab.	4.00	7.50	14.00
	1899/7VBP(h)	5.012	1.75	3.50	7.50
	1899VBP(h)	Inc. Ab.	1.75	3.50	7.50
	1902/802VBP(h)	2.977	2.50	4.00	10.00
	1902VBP(h)	Inc. Ab.	2.50	4.00	10.00
	1904/804VBP(h)	4.962	1.50	2.50	6.00
	1904VBP(h)	Inc. Ab.	1.50	2.50	6.00

Y#	Date	Mintage	VF	XF	Unc
20	1907VBP(h)	5.975	1.25	2.50	5.00
	1909VBP(h)	2.985	1.50	3.00	5.00
	1910VBP(h)	2.994	2.00	4.00	10.00
	1912VBP(h)	3.006	1.75	3.50	7.50

Y#	Date	Mintage	VF	XF	Unc
28	1913VBP(h)GJ	5.011	.65	1.25	4.00
	1915VBP(h)GJ	4.940	1.10	2.00	6.00
	1916VBP(h)GJ	2.439	1.60	3.00	6.50
	1917VBP(h)GJ	2.528	15.00	25.00	50.00
	1919HCN(h)GJ	6.343	.75	1.50	5.00
	1920HCN(h)GJ	Inc. Ab.	8.00	13.00	25.00
	1921HCN(h)GJ	3.731	1.10	2.00	5.00
	1922HCN(h)GJ	1.130	1.10	2.00	5.00
	1923HCN(h)GJ	5.035	1.50	2.50	5.50

IRON

Y#	Date	Mintage	VF	XF	Unc
28a	1918VBP(h)GJ	5.726	2.50	5.00	12.50
	1919HCN(h)GJ	4.017	10.00	17.50	35.00

BRONZE

Y#	Date	Mintage	VF	XF	Unc
46	1926HCN(h)GJ	11.009	6.00	12.50	30.00
	1927HCN(h)GJ	Inc. Ab.	.20	1.00	10.00
	1927N(h)GJ	Inc. Ab.	7.50	15.00	35.00
	1928N(h)GJ	16.780	.20	.50	5.00
	1929N(h)GJ	4.639	.20	.50	5.00
	1930N(h)GJ	9.312	.20	.50	5.00
	1932N(h)GJ	5.089	.20	.50	4.00
	1933N(h)GJ	1.153	1.00	2.50	10.00
	1934N(h)GJ	3.682	.20	.25	3.00
	1935N(h)GJ	5.086	.15	.20	2.00
	1936N(h)GJ	5.445	.15	.20	2.00
	1937N(h)GJ	6.070	.15	.20	2.00
	1938N(h)GJ	4.826	.15	.20	2.00
	1939N(h)GJ	5.662	.15	.20	2.00
	1940N(h)GJ	1.965	.15	.20	2.00

NOTE: For coins dated 1941 refer to Faeroe Islands.

ZINC

Y#	Date	Mintage	VF	XF	Unc
51	1941N(h)S	21.570	.10	.50	10.00
	1942N(h)S	6.997	.10	.50	9.00
51	1943N(h)S	15.082	.10	.50	9.00
	1944N(h)S	11.981	.10	.50	9.00
	1945N(h)S	.916	1.25	3.50	15.00
	1946N(h)S	.100	3.00	7.50	25.00

Y#	Date	Mintage	VF	XF	Unc
56	1948N(h)S	.300	1.00	2.00	7.50
	1949N(h)S	1.271	.10	.20	5.00
	1950N(h)S	9.340	.10	.20	5.00
	1951N(h)S	3.238	.10	.50	1.50
	1952N(h)S	6.139	.10	.15	3.00
	1953N(h)S	11.994	.10	.15	2.50
	1954N(h)S	11.440	.10	.15	2.00
	1955N(h)S	14.155	.10	.15	1.50
	1956C(h)S	17.413	—	.10	1.00
	1957C(h)S	21.928	—	.10	1.00
	1958C(h)S	15.985	—	.10	1.00
	1959C(h)S	18.318	—	.10	.75
	1960C(h)S	18.626	—	—	.50
	1961C(h)S	20.984	—	—	.25
	1962C(h)S	19.994	—	—	.10
	1963C(h)S	14.320	—	—	.10
	1964C(h)S	16.700	—	—	.10
	1965C(h)S	16.520	—	—	.10
	1966C(h)S	33.000	—	—	.10
	1967C(h)S	32.970	—	—	.10
	1968C(h)S	23.900	—	—	.10
	1969C(h)S	26.190	—	—	.10
	1970C(h)S	27.000	—	—	.10
	1971C(h)S	19.000	—	—	.10
	1972S(h)B	13.000	—	—	.10

BRONZE

Y#	Date	Mintage	VF	XF	Unc
66	1960C(h)S	8.990	—	1.50	2.50
	1962C(h)S	Inc. Ab.	—	1.50	2.50
	1963C(h)S	9.980	—	1.50	2.50
	1964C(h)S	2.990	—	1.50	2.50

NOTE: Only an estimated 99,000 of each date of Y#66 were sold, the balance being remelted.

2 ORE

BRONZE

Y#	Date	Mintage	VF	XF	Unc
9	1874CS(h)	7.690	3.00	6.00	20.00
	1875CS(h)	2.817	5.00	8.00	35.00
	1876CS(h)	.231	150.00	250.00	425.00
	1880CS(h)	1.012	15.00	25.00	50.00
	1881CS(h)	1.484	12.50	20.00	40.00
	1883CS(h)	1.375	4.00	7.50	20.00
	1886CS(h)	1.493	5.00	9.00	25.50
	1887CS(h)	Inc. Ab.	65.00	100.00	160.00
	1889CS(h)	1.993	3.00	6.00	15.00
	1891CS(h)	1.903	2.50	5.50	12.50
	1892CS(h)	.573	45.00	70.00	125.00
	1894VBP(h)	2.486	2.50	5.50	12.50
	1897/4VBP(h)	2.479	2.50	5.00	12.50
	1897VBP(h)	Inc. Ab.	2.50	5.00	12.50
	1899/7VBP(h)	2.504	1.50	4.00	10.00
	1899VBP(h)	Inc. Ab.	1.50	4.00	10.00
	1902VBP(h)	3.502	1.25	2.50	7.50
	1906VBP(h)	1.904	3.00	6.00	15.00

Y#	Date	Mintage	VF	XF	Unc
21	1907VBP(h)	3.496	1.50	3.00	10.00
	1909VBP(h)	2.485	2.00	4.00	17.50
	1912VBP(h)	2.480	2.00	4.00	10.00

Y#	Date	Mintage	VF	XF	Unc
29	1913VBP(h)GJ	.373	37.50	55.00	90.00
29	1914VBP(h)GJ	2.126	2.25	4.00	10.00
	1915VBP(h)GJ	2.485	2.25	4.00	10.00
	1916VBP(h)GJ	1.383	3.00	5.00	11.00
	1917VBP(h)GJ	1.117	17.50	30.00	50.00
	1919HCN(h)GJ	.883	6.00	10.00	20.00
	1920HCN(h)GJ	6.761	1.00	2.50	6.00
	1921HCN(h)GJ	2.545	3.00	5.00	10.00
	1923HCN(h)GJ	3.058	3.00	5.00	10.00

IRON

Y#	Date	Mintage	VF	XF	Unc
29a	1918VBP(h)GJ	2.937	3.00	6.00	17.50
	1919HCN(h)GJ	1.944	20.00	40.00	75.00

BRONZE

Y#	Date	Mintage	VF	XF	Unc
47	1926HCN(h)GJ	10.554	50.00	75.00	115.00
	1927HCN(h)GJ	Inc. Ab.	.10	1.00	10.00
	1927N(h)GJ	Inc. Ab.	1.00	2.50	15.00
	1928N(h)GJ	9.506	.10	1.00	7.50
	1929N(h)GJ	2.966	.10	1.00	7.50
	1930N(h)GJ	4.734	1.00	2.00	10.00
	1931N(h)GJ	3.409	.10	.50	6.00
	1932N(h)GJ	Inc. Ab.	1.00	2.00	9.00
	1934N(h)GJ	.756	.25	1.00	7.00
	1935N(h)GJ	1.391	—	.30	4.00
	1936N(h)GJ	2.973	—	.30	3.50
	1937N(h)GJ	3.437	—	.20	3.00
	1938N(h)GJ	2.177	—	.20	2.00
	1939N(h)GJ	3.165	—	.20	1.50
	1940N(h)GJ	1.582	—	.20	1.00

NOTE: For coins dated 1941 refer to Faeroe Islands.

ALUMINUM

Y#	Date	Mintage	VF	XF	Unc
52	1941N(h)S	26.205	.50	1.00	7.50

ZINC

Y#	Date	Mintage	VF	XF	Unc
52a	1942N(h)S	12.934	.10	.60	2.50
	1943N(h)S	9.603	.10	.60	2.50
	1944N(h)S	6.069	.10	.60	2.50
	1945N(h)S	.329	3.00	6.00	10.00
	1947N(h)S	.586	1.00	3.50	8.00

Y#	Date	Mintage	VF	XF	Unc
57	1948N(h)S	1.927	.50	1.00	6.50
	1949N(h)S	1.603	3.00	6.00	17.50
	1950N(h)S	4.544	.50	1.00	6.00
	1951N(h)S	3.766	.75	2.00	7.50
	1952N(h)S	4.874	.15	.50	4.00
	1953N(h)S	8.112	.10	.20	3.50
	1954N(h)S	6.497	.10	.20	3.00
	1955N(h)S	6.968	—	.10	2.00
	1956C(h)S	10.004	—	.10	1.00
	1957C(h)S	15.329	—	.10	.75
	1958C(h)S	8.120	—	.10	.50
	1959C(h)S	10.462	—	.10	.50
	1960C(h)S	16.504	—	.10	.50
	1961C(h)S	15.459	—	.10	.50
	1962C(h)S	10.980	—	.10	.50
	1963C(h)S	19.470	—	.10	.15
	1964C(h)S	15.411	—	.10	.15

Y#	Date	Mintage	VF	XF	Unc
57	1965C(h)S	20.173	—	.10	.15
	1966C(h)S	21.949	—	—	.15
	1967C(h)S	22.439	—	—	.15
	1968C(h)S	17.632	—	—	.15
	1969C(h)S	29.276	—	—	.15
	1970C(h)S	23.864	—	—	.15
	1971C(h)S	35.811	—	—	.10
	1972S(h)B	6.496	—	—	.10
		BRONZE			
67	1960C(h)S	6.190	—	1.25	2.00
	1962C(h)S	Inc. Ab.	—	1.25	2.00
	1963C(h)S	.990	—	1.25	2.00
	1964C(h)S	3.990	—	1.25	2.00
	1965C(h)S	11.980	—	1.25	2.00
	1966C(h)S	12.000	—	1.25	2.00

NOTE: Only an estimated 99,000 of each date of Y#67 were sold, the balance being remelted.

5 ORE

BRONZE

Y#	Date	Mintage	VF	XF	Unc
10	1874CS(h)	2.762	6.50	20.00	60.00
	1875CS(h)	.207	40.00	65.00	125.00
	1882CS(h)	.076	40.00	65.00	125.00
	1884CS(h)	.321	22.50	40.00	90.00
	1890CS(h)	.172	65.00	100.00	175.00
	1891CS(h)	.615	20.00	35.00	75.00
	1894VBP(h)	.595	15.00	25.00	50.00
	1898VBP(h)	.397	22.50	50.00	100.00
	1899VBP(h)	.601	14.00	22.50	45.00
	1902VBP(h)	.601	14.00	22.50	45.00
	1904VBP(h)	.397	20.00	30.00	60.00
	1906VBP(h)	.600	14.00	22.50	45.00

Y#	Date	Mintage	VF	XF	Unc
22	1907VBP(h)	1.399	6.50	17.50	35.00
	1908VBP(h)	1.198	6.50	17.50	35.00
	1912VBP(h)	.999	6.50	17.50	35.00

Y#	Date	Mintage	VF	XF	Unc
30	1913VBP(h)GJ	.216	80.00	110.00	175.00
	1914VBP(h)GJ	.785	11.00	17.00	30.00
	1916VBP(h)GJ	.990	12.50	18.50	35.00
	1917VBP(h)GJ	1.015	12.50	18.50	35.00
	1919HCN(h)GJ	.994	4.50	7.00	17.00
	1920HCN(h)GJ	2.618	5.50	8.00	18.50
	1921HCN(h)GJ	3.248	4.50	7.00	17.00
	1923HCN(h)GJ	.369	100.00	175.00	250.00

IRON

Y#	Date	Mintage	VF	XF	Unc
30a	1918VBP(h)GJ	1.733	7.50	10.00	35.00
	1919HCN(h)GJ	1.035	15.00	20.00	50.00

BRONZE

Y#	Date	Mintage	VF	XF	Unc
48	1926HCN(h)GJ	—	—	Unique	—
	1927HCN(h)GJ	4.564	.15	3.00	12.50
	1927N(h)GJ	Inc. Ab.	4.00	7.00	40.00
	1928N(h)GJ	6.704	.15	.30	12.50
	1929N(h)GJ	1.116	.30	3.75	12.50
	1930N(h)GJ	2.153	.30	3.25	12.50
	1932N(h)GJ	1.011	.30	3.75	12.50
	1934N(h)GJ	.524	.30	3.00	12.50
	1935N(h)GJ	1.123	1.60	4.00	15.00
	1936N(h)GJ	1.091	.15	2.50	5.00
	1937N(h)GJ	1.209	.15	2.50	4.00
	1938N(h)GJ	1.093	.15	2.25	4.00
	1939N(h)GJ	1.402	.15	2.25	3.00
	1940N(h)GJ	2.735	.15	2.00	3.00

NOTE: For coins dated 1941 refer to Faeroe Islands.

ALUMINUM

Y#	Date	Mintage	VF	XF	Unc
53	1941N(h)S	16.984	.15	1.50	15.00

ZINC

Y#	Date	Mintage	VF	XF	Unc
53a	1942N(h)S	2.963	1.00	3.00	12.50
	1943N(h)S	4.522	.30	1.50	12.50
	1944N(h)S	2.800	.30	1.50	12.50
	1945N(h)S	1.700	2.50	5.00	20.00

Y#	Date	Mintage	VF	XF	Unc
58	1950N(h)S	.657	5.00	8.00	20.00
	1951N(h)S	1.858	1.00	2.00	12.50
	1952N(h)S	3.562	.25	1.00	7.50
	1953N(h)S	5.944	.25	1.00	7.50
	1954N(h)S	3.060	.25	.75	6.00
	1955N(h)S	2.314	.50	1.25	7.00
	1956C(h)S	5.888	.15	.50	5.00
	1957C(h)S	8.606	.10	.25	4.00
	1958C(h)S	9.598	.10	.25	3.00
	1959C(h)S	6.110	.10	.25	2.50
	1960C(h)S	11.800	.10	.25	1.50
	1961C(h)S	8.995	.10	.25	1.50
	1962C(h)S	9.729	.10	.25	1.00
	1963C(h)S	8.980	.10	.25	1.00
	1964C(h)S	6.738	.25	.50	2.50

BRONZE

Y#	Date	Mintage	VF	XF	Unc
68	1960C(h)S	3.760	.10	.20	1.50
	1962C(h)S	5.873	.25	.50	2.50
	1963C(h)S	23.287	—	.10	.50

Y#	Date	Mintage	VF	XF	Unc
68	1964C(h)S	41.521	—	.10	.50
	1965C(h)S	14.229	—	.10	.50
	1966C(h)S	23.410	—	.10	.50
	1967C(h)S	15.094	—	.10	.50
	1968C(h)S	16.105	—	.10	.50
	1969C(h)S	23.594	—	.10	.50
	1970C(h)S	26.176	—	.10	.50
	1971C(h)S	10.076	—	.10	.50
	1972S(h)B	27.938	—	.10	.50

COPPER CLAD IRON

Y#	Date	Mintage	VF	XF	Unc
78	1973S(h)B	—	—	—	.15
	1974S(h)B	71.796	—	—	.15
	1975S(h)B	45.004	—	—	.15
	1976S(h)B	73.296	—	—	.15
	1977S(h)B	—	—	—	.10
	1979B H B	—	—	—	.10

10 ORE

1.4500 gm., .400 SILVER, .0186 oz ASW

Y#	Date	Mintage	VF	XF	Unc
11	1874CS(h)	8.974	12.50	25.00	60.00
	1875CS(h)	1.387	15.00	28.00	60.00
	1882CS(h)	1.057	40.00	70.00	110.00
	1884CS(h)	1.019	40.00	70.00	110.00
	1886CS(h)	.508	75.00	100.00	150.00
	1888CS(h)	.306	100.00	150.00	200.00
	1889CS(h)	1.030	14.00	24.00	47.50
	1891CS(h)	1.507	10.00	17.50	40.00
	1894VBP(h)	1.521	9.00	15.00	35.00
	1897VBP(h)	2.044	5.00	9.00	25.00
	1899VBP(h)	2.049	6.00	10.00	25.00
	1903VBP(h)	3.007	4.00	7.00	17.50
	1904VBP(h)	2.449	22.50	32.50	55.00
	1905VBP(h)	1.571	4.00	7.00	12.50

Y#	Date	Mintage	VF	XF	Unc
23	1907VBP(h)	3.068	3.50	6.00	12.50
	1910VBP(h)	2.530	3.50	6.00	12.50
	1911VBP(h)	.579	35.00	50.00	75.00
	1912VBP(h)	1.951	4.00	6.50	13.00

Y#	Date	Mintage	VF	XF	Unc
36	1914VBP(h)GJ	2.128	3.00	5.00	10.00
	1915VBP(h)GJ	.915	6.00	10.00	17.50
	1916VBP(h)GJ	2.699	3.00	5.00	8.00
	1917VBP(h)GJ	4.014	3.00	5.00	8.00
	1918VBP(h)GJ	5.042	1.50	3.00	6.00
	1919HCN(h)GJ	10.184	1.50	2.50	4.00

COPPER-NICKEL

Y#	Date	Mintage	VF	XF	Unc
31	1920HCN(h)GJ	10.233	4.00	5.50	12.50
	1921HCN(h)GJ	8.064	4.00	5.50	11.50
	1922HCN(h)GJ	3.065	22.50	32.50	45.00
	1923HCN(h)GJ	1.790	250.00	325.00	450.00

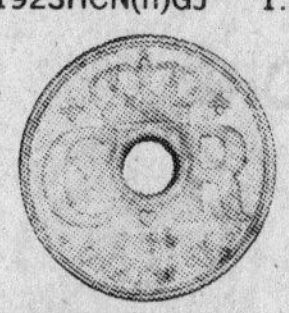

Y#	Date	Mintage	VF	XF	Unc
49	1924HCN(h)GJ	14.661	.15	1.00	8.00
	1925HCN(h)GJ	8.678	.15	1.00	10.00
	1926HCN(h)GJ	4.107	.15	1.00	10.00
	1929N(h)GJ	5.036	.35	1.00	10.00
	1931N(h)GJ	3.054	1.50	3.00	15.00
	1933N(h)GJ	1.274	6.00	10.00	25.00
	1934N(h)GJ	2.013	1.00	2.50	10.00
	1935N(h)GJ	2.848	.35	1.00	7.00

Y#	Date	Mintage	VF	XF	Unc
49	1936N(h)GJ	3.319	.50	1.50	7.50
	1937N(h)GJ	2.233	.35	1.00	7.00
	1938N(h)GJ	2.990	.35	1.00	7.00
	1939N(h)GJ	2.973	.50	1.50	9.00
	1940N(h)GJ	2.998	.35	1.00	5.00
	1941N(h)GJ	.748	2.00	4.00	10.00
	1946N(h)GJ	.459	1.50	2.00	6.00
	1947N(h)GJ	1.292	130.00	160.00	220.00

NOTE: For coins dated 1941 without mintmarks refer to Faeroe Islands.

ZINC

Y#	Date	Mintage	VF	XF	Unc
49a	1941N(h)GJ	7.706	.50	2.25	15.50
	1942N(h)GJ	8.676	.50	2.00	13.50
	1943N(h)GJ	2.181	1.50	3.50	20.00
	1944N(h)GJ	7.994	1.25	3.00	18.00
	1945N(h)GJ	1.280	40.00	55.00	100.00

COPPER-NICKEL

Y#	Date	Mintage	VF	XF	Unc
59	1948N(hS	5.317	.10	.50	4.00
	1949N(hS	7.595	—	.15	3.00
	1950N(hS	6.886	—	.15	2.50
	1951N(hS	8.763	—	.15	2.50
	1952N(hS	6.810	—	.15	1.75
	1953N(hS	11.945	—	.15	1.75
	1954N(hS	19.739	—	.10	1.25
	1955N(hS	17.623	—	.10	1.25
	1956C(h)S	12.323	—	.10	1.25
	1957C(h)S	13.227	—	.10	1.00
	1958C(h)S	10.869	—	.10	1.00
	1959C(h)S	1.254	30.00	40.00	70.00
	1960C(h)S	5.107	—	.10	.60

Y#	Date	Mintage	VF	XF	Unc
69	1960C(h)S	Inc. Ab.	—	.75	1.60
	1961C(h)S	20.258	—	.10	.25
	1962C(h)S	12.785	—	.10	.25
	1963C(h)S	17.171	—	.10	.20
	1964C(h)S	14.282	—	.10	.25
	1965C(h)S	21.857	—	.10	.25
	1966C(h)S	24.160	—	.10	.20
	1967C(h)S	21.544	—	.10	.20
	1968C(h)S	7.585	—	.10	.20
	1969C(h)S	31.534	—	.10	.20
	1970C(h)S	37.813	—	.10	.25
	1971C(h)S	17.719	—	.10	.20
	1972S(h)B	46.959	—	.10	.20

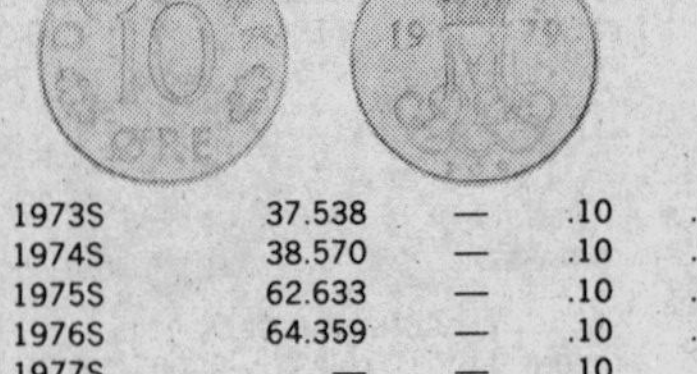

Y#	Date	Mintage	VF	XF	Unc
79	1973S	37.538	—	.10	.20
	1974S	38.570	—	.10	.20
	1975S	62.633	—	.10	.20
	1976S	64.359	—	.10	.20
	1977S	—	—	.10	.15
	1978S	—	—	—	—
	1979S	—	—	.10	.15

25 ORE

2.4200 gm., .600 SILVER, .0467 oz ASW

Y#	Date	Mintage	VF	XF	Unc
12	1874CS(h)	8.139	12.50	25.00	50.00
	1891CS(h)	1.214	15.00	30.00	50.00
	1894VBP(h)	1.206	12.50	22.50	42.50
	1900VBP(h)	1.206	12.50	20.00	40.00
	1904VBP(h)	1.922	15.00	25.00	50.00
12	1905VBP(h)	1.722	8.00	15.00	25.00

Y#	Date	Mintage	VF	XF	Unc
24	1907VBP(h)	2.009	6.00	12.50	22.50
	1911VBP(h)	2.015	6.00	12.50	22.50

Y#	Date	Mintage	VF	XF	Unc
37	1913VBP(h)GJ	2.016	6.00	10.00	17.50
	1914VBP(h)GJ	.347	100.00	150.00	200.00
	1915VBP(h)GJ	2.862	5.00	8.50	15.00
	1916VBP(h)GJ	.938	7.50	12.50	20.00
	1917VBP(h)GJ	1.354	35.00	50.00	80.00
	1918VBP(h)GJ	2.090	5.00	8.50	13.50
	1919HCN(h)GJ	9.295	1.50	2.50	5.00

COPPER-NICKEL

Y#	Date	Mintage	VF	XF	Unc
32	1920HCN(h)GJ	12.288	4.00	7.00	16.50
	1921HCN(h)GJ	9.443	3.50	6.00	15.00
	1922HCN(h)GJ	5.700	25.00	32.50	50.00

Y#	Date	Mintage	VF	XF	Unc
50	1924HCN(h)GJ	8.035	.50	1.50	10.00
	1925HCN(h)GJ	1.905	8.00	15.00	37.50
	1926HCN(h)GJ	2.659	1.25	3.50	20.00
	1929N(h)GJ	.886	1.50	4.00	25.00
	1930N(h)GJ	3.423	1.75	5.00	25.00
	1932N(h)GJ	.846	8.00	15.00	35.00
	1933N(h)GJ	.479	40.00	47.50	75.00
	1934N(h)GJ	1.660	1.50	4.00	20.00
	1935N(h)GJ	1.032	15.00	25.00	45.00
	1936N(h)GJ	1.453	1.50	3.50	15.00
	1937N(h)GJ	1.612	4.00	7.50	20.00
	1938N(h)GJ	1.794	1.75	4.00	12.50
	1939N(h)GJ	1.972	15.00	22.50	45.00
	1940N(h)GJ	1.356	1.00	3.25	9.00
	1946N(h)GJ	2.323	1.25	3.50	6.50
	1947N(h)GJ	1.751	5.00	7.50	12.50

NOTE: For coins dated 1941 refer to Faeroe Islands.

ZINC

Y#	Date	Mintage	VF	XF	Unc
50a	1941N(h)GJ	15.332	1.50	4.00	17.50
	1942N(h)GJ	.997	.50	2.00	12.50
	1943N(h)GJ	5.784	1.50	3.50	17.50
	1944N(h)GJ	10.665	.75	2.00	12.50
	1945N(h)GJ	4.543	1.50	3.00	15.00

COPPER-NICKEL

Y#	Date	Mintage	VF	XF	Unc
60	1948N(h)S	1.852	2.50	3.50	20.00
	1949N(h)S	15.000	—	.15	7.50
	1950N(h)S	13.771	—	.15	7.50
	1951N(h)S	5.045	—	.15	10.00
	1952N(h)S	2.018	.50	1.00	12.50
	1953N(h)S	9.553	—	.15	5.00
	1954N(h)S	11.337	—	.15	4.00
	1955N(h)S	6.385	—	.15	3.00
60	1956C(h)S	10.228	—	.15	2.00
	1957C(h)S	7.421	—	.15	1.50
	1958C(h)S	3.600	—	.15	1.50
	1959C(h)S	2.210	1.50	3.00	7.50
	1960C(h)S	3.452	—	.15	1.00

Y#	Date	Mintage	VF	XF	Unc
70	1960C(h)S	Inc. Ab.	7.50	10.00	18.00
	1961C(h)S	20.860	—	.50	.75
	1962C(h)S	12.560	—	.50	.75
	1964C(h)S	6.175	—	.40	.75
	1965C(h)S	13.492	—	.35	.75
	1966C(h)S	50.220	—	.35	.75
	1967C(h)S	87.468	12.50	17.50	22.50

Y#	Date	Mintage	VF	XF	Unc
76	1966C	Inc. Ab.	—	.10	.30
	1967C	Inc. Ab.	—	.10	.25
	1968C	39.142	—	.10	.25
	1969C(h)	16.974	—	.10	.25
	1970C	5.392	—	.10	.20
	1971C	12.724	—	.10	.20
	1972S	31.422	—	.10	.20

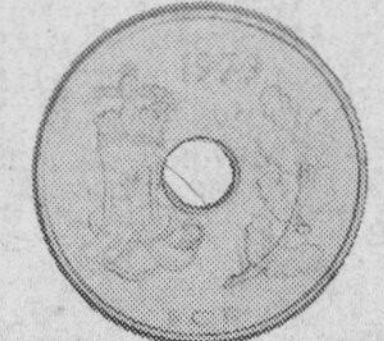

Y#	Date	Mintage	VF	XF	Unc
80	1973S	30.834	—	.10	.20
	1974S	22.178	—	.10	.20
	1975S	28.798	—	.10	.20
	1976S	48.388	—	.10	.20
	1977S	—	—	.10	.20
	1978S	—	—	—	—
	1979B	—	—	.10	.20

1/2 KRONE

ALUMINUM-BRONZE

Y#	Date	Mintage	VF	XF	Unc
33	1924HCN(h)GJ	2.150	5.00	10.00	30.00
	1925HCN(h)GJ	3.432	5.00	10.00	30.00
	1926HCN(h)GJ	.716	17.50	30.00	50.00
	1939N(h)GJ	.226	75.00	100.00	135.00
	1940N(h)GJ	1.871	4.00	7.00	12.50

KRONE

7.5000 gm., .800 SILVER, .1929 oz ASW

Y#	Date	Mintage	VF	XF	Unc
13	1875CS(h)	4.040	20.00	60.00	125.00
	1876CS(h)	1.284	27.50	75.00	150.00
	1892CS(h)	.701	25.00	40.00	60.00
	1898VBP(h)	.201	60.00	85.00	100.00

Y#	Date	Mintage	VF	XF	Unc
38	1915VBP(h)	1.410	6.50	10.00	17.50
	1916VBP(h)	.992	7.50	12.50	22.50

ALUMINUM-BRONZE

Y#	Date	Mintage	VF	XF	Unc
34	1924HCN(h)GJ	.999	200.00	350.00	1000.
	1925HCN(h)GJ	6.314	1.00	10.00	75.00
	1926HCN(h)GJ	2.706	1.00	10.00	90.00
	1929N(h)GJ	.501	9.00	22.50	90.00
	1930N(h)GJ	.540	25.00	45.00	110.00
	1931N(h)GJ	.540	9.00	22.50	65.00
	1934N(h)GJ	.529	7.50	17.50	50.00
	1935N(h)GJ	.504	25.00	50.00	100.00
	1936N(h)GJ	.559	7.50	15.00	50.00
	1938N(h)GJ	.401	25.00	40.00	80.00
	1939N(h)GJ	1.517	1.50	3.50	20.00
	1940N(h)GJ	1.496	1.75	3.50	17.50
	1941N(h)GJ	.661	4.00	6.00	30.00

Y#	Date	Mintage	VF	XF	Unc
54	1942N(h)S	3.952	.50	2.00	17.50
	1943N(h)S	.798	7.50	20.00	50.00
	1944N(h)S	1.760	.50	2.00	15.00
	1945N(h)S	2.581	.50	2.00	15.00
	1946N(h)S	4.321	.50	1.00	8.00
	1947N(h)S	5.060	.50	1.00	7.00

Y#	Date	Mintage	VF	XF	Unc
61	1947N(h)S	Inc. Ab.	1.00	2.50	12.50
	1948N(h)S	4.248	.50	1.00	7.50
	1949N(h)S	1.300	1.50	6.00	17.50
	1952N(h)S	2.124	.75	1.50	10.00
	1953N(h)S	.573	1.50	6.00	17.50
	1954N(h)S	.584	17.50	22.50	37.50
	1955N(h)S	1.359	4.00	7.00	17.50
	1956C(h)S	2.858	.75	1.50	6.00
	1957C(h)S	10.896	.40	1.00	2.50
	1958C(h)S	1.507	.60	1.50	3.00
	1959C(h)S	.242	10.00	15.00	27.50
	1960C(h)S	1.000	—	700.00	900.00

COPPER-NICKEL

Y#	Date	Mintage	VF	XF	Unc
71	1960C(h)S	Inc. Ab.	.40	1.00	3.00
	1961C(h)S	10.348	.20	.40	2.00
	1962C(h)S	27.068	.20	.40	1.50
	1963C(h)S	32.083	.20	.35	1.50
	1964C(h)S	5.984	.20	.35	1.50
	1965C(h)S	13.799	.20	.35	1.00
	1966C(h)S	10.890	.20	.35	.75
	1967C(h)S	18.304	.20	.35	.75
	1968C(h)S	8.213	.20	.35	.75
	1969C(h)S	9.597	—	.20	.40

Y#	Date	Mintage	VF	XF	Unc
71	1970C(h)S	9.460	—	.20	.35
	1971C(h)S	13.985	—	.20	.35
	1972S(h)B	21.019	—	.20	.35

Y#	Date	Mintage	VF	XF	Unc
81	1973S	18.268	—	.20	.30
	1974S	17.742	—	.20	.30
	1975S	20.136	—	.20	.30
	1976S	28.049	—	.20	.30
	1977S	—	—	.20	.30
	1979S	—	—	.20	.30

2 KRONER

15.0000 gm., .800 SILVER, .3858 oz ASW

Y#	Date	Mintage	VF	XF	Unc
14	1875CS(h)	3.396	20.00	70.00	150.00
	1876CS(h)	1.381	22.50	65.00	150.00
	1897VBP(h)	.151	80.00	125.00	175.00
	1899VBP(h)	.152	60.00	90.00	145.00

25th Anniversary of Reign

Y#	Date	Mintage	VF	XF	Unc
15	1888	.101	25.00	40.00	65.00

Golden Wedding Anniversary

Y#	Date	Mintage	VF	XF	Unc
16	1892CS(c)	.101	25.00	40.00	65.00

40th Anniversary of Reign

Y#	Date	Mintage	VF	XF	Unc
17	1903P(h)	.103	20.00	30.00	50.00

Christian IX Death

and Accession of Frederik VIII

Y#	Date	Mintage	VF	XF	Unc
25	1906VBP(h)	.151	12.50	20.00	35.00

Frederik VIII Death
and Accession of Christian X

Y#	Date	Mintage	VF	XF	Unc
40	1912VBP(h)	.102	20.00	30.00	50.00

Y#	Date	Mintage	VF	XF	Unc
39	1915VBP(h)	.657	25.00	35.00	60.00
	1916VBP(h)	.402	15.00	25.00	35.00

Silver Wedding Anniversary

Y#	Date	Mintage	VF	XF	Unc
41	1923HCN(h)	.203	12.50	17.50	25.00

ALUMINUM-BRONZE

Y#	Date	Mintage	VF	XF	Unc
35	1924HCN(h)GJ	1.128	45.00	125.00	450.00
	1925HCN(h)GJ	3.247	1.00	17.50	80.00
	1926HCN(h)GJ	1.125	1.00	17.50	95.00
	1936N(h)GJ	.400	6.00	15.00	50.00
	1938N(h)GJ	.191	25.00	37.50	80.00
	1939N(h)GJ	.723	1.50	6.00	35.00
	1940N(h)GJ	.742	6.00	12.50	37.50
	1941N(h)GJ	.128	45.00	70.00	150.00

15.0000 gm., .800 SILVER, .3858 oz ASW
King's 60th Birthday

Y#	Date	Mintage	VF	XF	Unc
42	1930N(h)	.303	12.50	17.50	25.00

25th Anniversary of Reign

Y#	Date	Mintage	VF	XF	Unc
43	1937N(h)S	.209	12.50	17.50	25.00

King's 75th Birthday

Y#	Date	Mintage	VF	XF	Unc
55	1945N(hS	.157	12.50	20.00	30.00

ALUMINUM-BRONZE

Y#	Date	Mintage	VF	XF	Unc
62	1947N(h)S	1.151	2.00	6.00	17.50
	1948N(h)S	.857	1.00	2.00	10.00
	1949N(h)S	.272	3.50	7.00	20.00
	1951N(h)S	1.576	1.00	2.00	10.00
	1952N(h)S	1.958	.75	1.50	7.50
	1953N(h)S	.431	3.50	6.00	15.00
	1954N(h)S	.715	3.50	6.00	15.00
	1955N(h)S	.456	3.50	6.00	15.00
	1956C(h)S	1.443	1.00	2.00	7.50
	1957C(h)S	2.610	.75	1.00	4.00
	1958C(h)S	2.605	.75	1.00	5.00
	1959C(h)S	.192	12.50	20.00	35.00

15.0000 gm., .800 SILVER, .3858 oz ASW
Greenland Commemorative

Y#	Date	Mintage	VF	XF	Unc
63	1953N(h)S	.152	20.00	27.50	45.00

Princess Margrethe's 18th Birthday

Y#	Date	Mintage	VF	XF	Unc
64	1958C(h)S	.301	7.50	10.00	15.00

5 KRONER

17.0000 gm., .800 SILVER, .4372 oz ASW
Silver Wedding Commemorative

Y#	Date	Mintage	VF	XF	Unc
65	1960C(h)S	.410	BV	15.00	20.00

COPPER-NICKEL

Y#	Date	Mintage	VF	XF	Unc
72	1960C(h)S	6.418	.85	1.00	3.00
	1961C(h)S	9.744	.85	1.00	2.50
	1962C(h)S	2.074	.85	1.00	3.00
	1963C(h)S	0.709	1.00	1.50	5.00
	1964C(h)S	1.443	.85	1.00	3.00
	1965C(h)S	2.574	.85	1.00	2.00
	1966C(h)S	4.370	.85	1.00	2.00
	1967C(h)S	1.864	.85	1.00	2.00
	1968C(h)S	4.132	.85	1.25	2.00
	1969C(h)S	.780	4.50	7.50	11.50
	1970C(h)S	2.246	.85	1.00	1.25
	1971C(h)S	4.767	.85	1.00	1.25
	1972S(h)B	2.599	.85	1.00	1.50

17.0000 gm., .800 SILVER, .4372 oz ASW
Wedding Of Princess Anne Marie

Y#	Date	Mintage	VF	XF	Unc
73	1964(h)-C	.350	BV	15.00	20.00

COPPER-NICKEL

Y#	Date	Mintage	VF	XF	Unc
82	1973S with narrow rim				
		3.774	.85	1.00	1.50
	1973S with wide rim				
		Inc. Ab.	.85	1.00	1.25
	1974S	5.239	.85	1.00	1.25
	1975S	5.810	.85	1.00	1.25
	1976S	7.651	.85	1.00	1.25
	1977S	—	.85	1.00	1.25
	1979S	—	—	1.00	1.25

10 KRONER

4.4803 gm., .900 GOLD, .1296 oz AGW

Y#	Date	Mintage	VF	XF	Unc
18	1873CS(h)	.369	100.00	125.00	175.00
	1874CS(h)	Inc. Ab.	120.00	160.00	200.00
	1877CS(h)	.098	120.00	160.00	200.00
	1890CS(h)	.151	100.00	125.00	175.00
	1898VBP(h)	.100	110.00	150.00	190.00
	1900VBP(h)	.204	100.00	125.00	175.00

Y#	Date	Mintage	VF	XF	Unc
26	1908VBP(h)	.461	95.00	125.00	150.00
	1909VBP(h)	Inc. Ab.	95.00	125.00	150.00

Y#	Date	Mintage	VF	XF	Unc
44	1913VBP(h)	.312	95.00	115.00	135.00
	1917VBP(h)	.132	100.00	125.00	160.00

20.4000 gm., .800 SILVER, .5247 oz ASW
Wedding Of Princess Margrethe

Y#	Date	Mintage	VF	XF	Unc
74	1967	498*	BV	17.50	22.50

NOTE: 78,383 of these coins were remelted.

Wedding Of Princess Benedikte

Y#	Date	Mintage	VF	XF	Unc
75	1968	*.300	BV	17.50	22.50
	1968	100 pcs.	—	Proof	225.00

***NOTE:** 42,923 of these coins were remelted.

Death of Frederik IX and Accession of Margrethe II

77	1972	.400	BV	17.50	22.50

COPPER-NICKEL

83	1979	100.000	—	1.75	2.50

20 KRONOR

8.9606 gm., .900 GOLD, .2592 oz AGW

19	1873CS(h)	1.153	BV	175.00	225.00
	1874CS(h)	Inc. Ab.	700.00	1000.	1500.
	1876CS(h)	0.351	BV	175.00	200.00
	1877CS(h)	Inc. Ab.	175.00	200.00	225.00
	1890CS(h)	.102	BV	175.00	200.00
	1900VBP(h)	.100	BV	175.00	200.00

Y#	Date	Mintage	VF	XF	Unc
27	1908VBP(h)	1.360	BV	175.00	200.00
	1909VBP(h)	Inc. Ab.	BV	175.00	200.00
	1910VBP(h)	Inc. Ab.	BV	175.00	200.00
	1911VBP(h)	Inc. Ab.	BV	175.00	200.00
	1912VBP(h)	Inc. Ab.	BV	175.00	200.00

45	1913VBP(h)	3.482	BV	175.00	200.00
	1914VBP(h)	Inc. Ab.	BV	175.00	200.00
	1915VBP(h)	Inc. Ab.	BV	175.00	200.00
	1916VBP(h)	Inc. Ab.	BV	175.00	200.00
	1917VBP(h)	Inc. Ab.	BV	175.00	200.00
	1926HCN(h)	.358	650.00	900.00	1250.
	1927HCN(h)	Inc. Ab.	650.00	900.00	1250.
	1930N(h)	1.285	650.00	900.00	1250.
	1931N(h)	Inc. Ab.	650.00	900.00	1250.

NCLT ISSUES

MEDALLIC ISSUES

The Medallic Issues are similar to circulation coinage except they are without a denomination. They are all of proof quality.

KM#	Date	Mintage	Identification	Mkt.Val.
M1	1903	—	(2 Kroner), Silver	—
M2	1923	—	(2 Kroner), Silver	—
M3	1930	—	(2 Kroner), Silver	—
M4	1937	—	(2 Kroner), Silver	—
M5	1945	—	(2 Kroner), Silver	—
M6	1953	—	(2 Kroner), Silver	—
M7	1958	110 pcs.	(2 Kroner), Silver	225.00

M8	1960	250 pcs.	(5 Kroner), Silver	175.00
M9	1964	100 pcs.	(5 Kroner), Silver	200.00
M10	1967	100 pcs.	(10 Kroner), Silver	225.00
M11	1968	100 pcs.	(10 Kroner), Silver	225.00
M12	1972	100 pcs.	(10 Kroner), Silver	225.00

PATTERNS

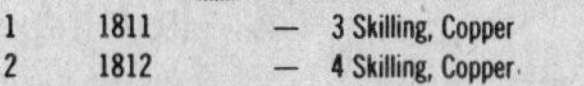

1	1811	—	3 Skilling, Copper	—
2	1812	—	4 Skilling, Copper	—

KM#	Date	Mintage	Identification	Mkt.Val.
3	1812	—	6 Skilling, Copper	—
4	1818	—	2 Rigsbankskilling, Copper	—
5	1833	—	1/2 Rigsbankdaler, Silver	—
6	1842	—	1 Rigsbankskilling, Copper	—

7	1854	—	1 Rigsmontskilling, Copper	—

8	1857	—	2 Rigsdaler, Silver	Rare
9	1857	—	2 Rigsdaler, Copper	—
10	1857	—	2 Rigsdaler	—
11	1948N	—	5 Ore, Zinc, Y#58	—

MINT SETS

STANDARD METALS

KM#	Date	Mintage	Identification	Issue Price	Mkt. Val.
S1	1956(7)	—	Y56-62	—	50.00
S2	1957(7)	—	Y56-62	—	45.00
S3	1958(7)	—	Y56-62	—	45.00
S4	1959(7)	—	Y56-62	—	200.00
S5	1960(10)	—	Y56-60,68-72	—	55.00
S6	1961(7)	—	Y56-58,69-72	—	30.00
S7	1962(8)	—	Y56-58,68-72	—	35.00
S8	1963(7)	—	Y56-58,68,69,71,72	—	25.00
S9	1964(8)	—	Y56-58,68-72	—	25.00
S10	1965(7)	—	Y56,57,68-72	—	15.00
S11	1966(8)	—	Y56,57,68-72,76	—	15.00
S12	1967(8)	—	Y56,57,68-72,76	—	35.00
S13	1968(7)	—	Y56,57,68,69,71,72,76	—	10.00
S14	1969(7)	—	Y56,57,68,69,71,72,76	—	17.50
S15	1970(7)	—	Y56,57,68,69,71,72,76	—	6.00
S16	1971(7)	—	Y56,57,68,69,71,72,76	—	6.00
S17	1972(7)	—	Y56,57,68,69,71,72,76	—	6.00
S18	1973(5)	—	Y78-82	—	6.00
S19	1974(5)	—	Y78-82	6.00	6.00
S20	1975(5)	—	Y78-82	6.00	6.00
S21	1976(5)	—	Y78-82	3.55	4.50
	1979S	—	Y78-83	—	7.50

DJIBOUTI

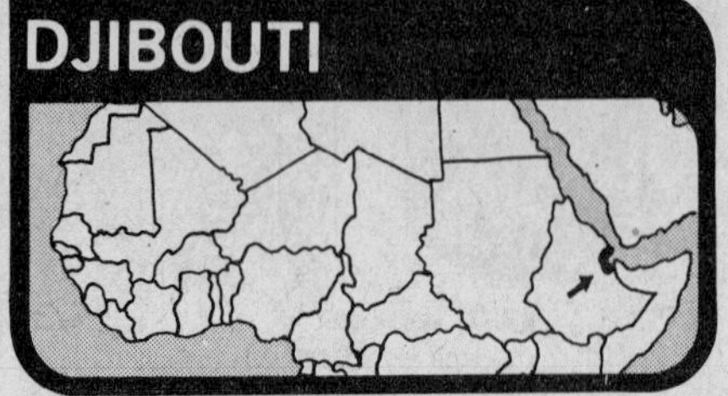

The Republic of Djibouti (formerly French Somaliland and the French Overseas Territory of Afars and Issas), located in northeast Africa at the Bab el Mandeb Strait connecting the Suez Canal and the Red Sea with the Gulf of Aden and the Indian Ocean, has an area of 8,880 sq. mi. (23,000 sq. km.) and a population of 180,000. Capital: Djibouti. The tiny nation has less than one sq. mi. of arable land, and no natural resources except salt, sand, and camels. The commercial activities of the transshipment port of Djibouti and the Addis Ababa-Djibouti railroad are the basis of the economy. Salt, fish and hides are exported.

French interest in former French Somaliland began in 1839 with concessions obtained by a French naval lieutenant from the provincial sultans. French Somaliland was made a protectorate in 1884 and its boundaries were delimited by the Franco-British and Ethiopian accords of 1887 and 1897. It became a colony in 1896 and a territory within the French Union in 1946. In 1958 it voted to join the new French Community as an overseas territory, and reaffirmed that choice by a referendum in March, 1967. Its name was changed from French Somaliland to the French Territory of Afars and Issas on July 5, 1967.

The French Tricolor, which had flown over the strategically important territory for 115 years, was lowered for the last time on June 27, 1977, when French Afars and Issas became Africa's 49th independent state, under the name of the Republic of Djibouti.

Djibouti, a seaport and capital city of the Republic of Djibouti (and formerly of French Somaliland and French Afars and Issas) is located on the east coast of Africa at the southernmost entrance to the Red Sea. The capital was moved from Obok to Djibouti in 1892 and established as the transshipment point for Ethiopia's foreign trade via the Franco-Ethiopian railway linking Djibouti and Addis Ababa.

COUNTERSTAMP ISSUES

RUPEE-TALER (RYAL) CURRENCY SYSTEM

Coins counterstamped (c/s) with 12 scalloped square with Arabic inscription. Sometimes coins have additional c/s's on the coin showing silver fineness.

1/2 RUPEE SIZE

.917 SILVER
c/s: On India 1/2 Rupee

KM#	Date	Mintage	Fine	VF	XF
1	ND	—	17.50	22.50	30.00

RUPEE SIZE

.917 SILVER
c/s: On India Rupee

KM#	Date	Mintage	Fine	VF	XF
2	ND	—	20.00	35.00	45.00

RYAL SIZE (CROWN TALER)

.833 SILVER
c/s: On Austria Thaler

KM#	Date	Mintage	Fine	VF	XF
3	ND	—	40.00	55.00	65.00

Maria Theresa talers and a few other foreign crown size coins were counterstamped. These exist with and without the additional Arabic counterstamp of "830".

TOKEN ISSUES

CHAMBER OF COMMERCE

5 CENTIMES

KM#	Date	Mintage	VG	Fine	VF	XF
		ZINC				
T1	1920	—	1.00	2.00	4.00	8.00
		ALUMINUM				
T5	1921	—	.75	1.50	3.00	6.00

10 CENTIMES

KM#	Date	Mintage	VG	Fine	VF	XF
		ZINC				
T2	1920	—	1.25	2.50	5.00	10.00
		ALUMINUM				
T6	1921	—	1.00	2.00	4.00	8.00

25 CENTIMES

ALUMINUM

KM#	Date	Mintage	VG	Fine	VF	XF
T7	1921	—	1.50	3.00	6.00	12.00

50 CENTIMES

KM#	Date	Mintage	VG	Fine	VF	XF
		ZINC				
T3	1920	—	1.25	2.50	5.00	10.00
		BRASS				
T8	1921	—	1.50	3.00	6.00	12.00
		BRONZE				
T9	1921	—	1.50	3.00	6.00	12.00
T10	1922	—	1.50	3.00	6.00	12.00

FRANC

ALUMINUM

KM#	Date	Mintage	VG	Fine	VF	XF
T4	1920	—	2.00	4.00	8.00	16.00

FRENCH SOMALILAND

MINTMARKS

(a) - Paris (privy marks only)

NOTE: Refer to France for privy marks.

MONETARY SYSTEM

100 Centimes = 1 Franc

FRANC

ALUMINUM

Y#	Date	Mintage	Fine	VF	XF	Unc
1	1948(a)	.200	.35	.75	2.75	6.00
	1949(a)	Inc. Ab.	.35	.75	2.75	6.00

Y#	Date	Mintage	Fine	VF	XF	Unc
5	1959(a)	.500	.25	.35	1.25	2.00
	1965(a)	.200	.35	.75	2.75	4.00

2 FRANCS

ALUMINUM

Y#	Date	Mintage	Fine	VF	XF	Unc
2	1948(a)	.200	.50	1.00	3.00	5.00
	1949(a)	Inc. Ab.	.50	1.00	3.00	5.00

Y#	Date	Mintage	Fine	VF	XF	Unc
6	1959(a)	.200	.40	.75	1.50	2.50
	1965(a)	.240	.25	.40	1.00	1.75

5 FRANCS

ALUMINUM

Y#	Date	Mintage	Fine	VF	XF	Unc
3	1948(a)	.500	.40	.80	2.50	6.00

Y#	Date	Mintage	Fine	VF	XF	Unc
7	1959(a)	.500	.25	.35	1.25	4.00
	1965(a)	.200	.25	.35	1.00	2.25

10 FRANCS

ALUMINUM-BRONZE

Y#	Date	Mintage	Fine	VF	XF	Unc
8	1965(a)	.250	.35	.80	1.50	3.50

20 FRANCS

ALUMINUM-BRONZE

Y#	Date	Mintage	Fine	VF	XF	Unc
4	1952(a)	.500	.50	1.00	2.00	7.50

Y#	Date	Mintage	Fine	VF	XF	Unc
9	1965(a)	.200	.35	.75	1.50	3.00

NOTE: For later coinage see French Afars & Issas.

NCLT ISSUES

ESSAIS

Standard metals unless otherwise noted.

Y#	Date	Mintage	Identification	Issue Price	Mkt Val.
E1	1948(a)	2,000	1 Franc, Copper-Nickel	—	15.00
E2	1948(a)	2,000	2 Francs, Copper-Nickel	—	15.00
E3	1948(a)	2,000	5 Francs, Copper-Nickel	—	20.00
E4	1952(a)	1,200	20 Francs	—	20.00
E8	1965(a)	2,000	10 Francs	—	17.50

PIEFORTS (P)

PIEFORTS WITH ESSAI (PE)

DOUBLE THICKNESS

Standard metals unless otherwise noted.

Y#	Date	Mintage	Identification	Issue Price	Mkt Val.
PE1	1948(a)	104	1 Franc	—	100.00
PE2	1948(a)	104	2 Francs	—	110.00
PE3	1948(a)	104	5 Francs	—	115.00
PE4	1952(a)	104	20 Francs	—	110.00

FLEUR DE COIN SETS

STANDARD METALS

KM#	Date	Mintage	Identification	Issue Price	Mkt. Val.
1	1965(5)	1,898	Y5-9	—	15.00

FRENCH AFARS & ISSAS

MINTMARKS

(a) - Paris (privy marks only)

NOTE: Refer to France for privy marks.

MONETARY SYSTEM

100 Centimes = 1 Franc

FRANC

ALUMINUM

Y#	Date	Mintage	VF	XF	Unc
1	1969(a)	.100	.10	.25	.50
	1971(a)	.100	.10	.25	.50
	1975(a)	.300	—	.10	.25

2 FRANCS

ALUMINUM

Y#	Date	Mintage	VF	XF	Unc
2	1968(a)	.100	.10	.25	.50
	1975(a)	.180	—	.10	.25

5 FRANCS

ALUMINUM

Y#	Date	Mintage	VF	XF	Unc
3	1968(a)	.100	.15	.50	.75
	1975(a)	.300	—	.10	.25

10 FRANCS

ALUMINUM-BRONZE

Y#	Date	Mintage	VF	XF	Unc
4	1969(a)	.100	.25	.50	1.00
	1970(a)	.300	.25	.50	1.00
	1975(a)	.360	.10	.25	.50

20 FRANCS

ALUMINUM-BRONZE

Y#	Date	Mintage	VF	XF	Unc
5	1968(a)	.300	.25	.75	1.25
	1975(a)	.300	.15	.25	.50

50 FRANCS

COPPER-NICKEL

Y#	Date	Mintage	VF	XF	Unc
6	1970(a)	.300	.50	.75	1.25
	1975(a)	.180	.25	.35	.75

100 FRANCS

COPPER-NICKEL

Y#	Date	Mintage	VF	XF	Unc
7	1970(a)	.600	.50	.75	1.50
	1975(a)	.400	.50	.75	1.00

NCLT ISSUES

ESSAIS

Standard metals unless otherwise noted.

Y#	Date	Mintage	Identification	Issue Price	Mkt Val.
E2	1968(a)	1700	2 Francs	—	13.50
E3	1968(a)	1700	5 Francs	—	15.00
E5	1968(a)	1700	20 Francs	—	20.00
E1	1969(a)	1700	1 Franc	—	13.50
E4	1969(a)	1700	10 Francs	—	15.00
E6	1970(a)	1700	50 Francs	—	21.50
E7	1970(a)	1700	100 Francs	—	25.00

DOMINICA

The Commonwealth of Dominica, situated in the Lesser Antilles midway between Guadeloupe to the north and Martinique to the south, has an area of 305 sq. mi. (790 sq. km.) and a population of 80,000. Capital: Roseau. Agriculture is the chief economic activity of the mountainous island. Bananas are the chief export.

Columbus discovered and named the island on Nov. 3, 1493. Spain neglected it and it was finally colonized by the French in 1632. The British drove the French from the island in 1756. Thereafter it changed hands between the French and British a dozen or more times before becoming permanently British in 1805. Throughout the greater part of its British history, Dominica was a presidency of the Leeward Islands. In 1940 its administration was transferred to the Windward Islands and it was established as a separate colony with considerable local autonomy. Dominica became a West Indies associated state with a built in option for independence in 1967. Full independence was attained on Nov. 3, 1978. Dominica, which has a republican form of government, is a member of the Commonwealth of Nations. The Queen of England is recognized as the head of the Commonwealth, but not as the Chief of State of Dominica.

RULERS

British, until 1978

MONETARY SYSTEM

(Until 1798)

10 Bits = 7 Shillings 6 Pence =
= 1 Dollar

(From 1798 until 1813)

11 Bits = 8 Shillings 3 Pence =
= 1 Dollar

(Commemcing 1813)

12 Bits = 10 Shillings = 1 Dollar

1-1/2 BITS (MOCO)

SILVER
c/s: Script 'D' with rays overstruck on center plug of Spanish or Spanish Colonial 8 Reales.

C#	Date	Mintage	VG	Fine	VF
21	ND(1798)	—	50.00	75.00	100.00

2 BITS

SILVER
Holed Spanish or Spanish Colonial 2 Reales.

C#	Date	Mintage	VG	Fine	VF
24	ND(1816)	—	60.00	75.00	100.00

3 BITS

SILVER
Crowned 3 on 1/2 of 23mm center plug cut from Spanish or Spanish Colonial 8 Reales.

C#	Date	Mintage	VG	Fine	VF
25	ND(1813)	—	90.00	150.00	225.00

2 SHILLINGS 6 PENCE

SILVER
c/s: '2.6' on 1/4 segment of Spanish or Spanish Colonial 8 Reales.

C#	Date	Mintage	VG	Fine	VF
26	ND(1816-18)	—	175.00	250.00	400.00

4 BITS

SILVER
c/s: Crowned '4' on center ring segment of Spanish or Spanish Colonial 8 Reales.

C#	Date	Mintage	VG	Fine	VF
27	ND(1813)	—	300.00	450.00	625.00

5-1/2 BITS

4 Shilling 1-1/2 Pence

SILVER
Spanish or Spanish Colonial 4 Reales with crenalated center hole

C#	Date	Mintage	VG	Fine	VF
A27	ND(1798)	—	1000.	1500.	2150.

6 BITS

SILVER
c/s: Crowned 'G' on obv. or rev. of center plug cut from Spanish or Spanish Colonial 8 Reales.

C#	Date	Mintage	VG	Fine	VF
28	ND(1813)	—	75.00	125.00	200.00

11 BITS

SILVER
Spanish or Spanish Colonial 8 Reales with crenalated center hole

C#	Date	Mintage	VG	Fine	VF
22	ND(1798)	—	100.00	175.00	275.00

NOTE: The center plug was used for the 1-1/2 Bits, C#21.

12 BITS

SILVER
c/s: Four crowned '12s' on Spanish or Spanish Colonial 8 Reales with crenalated center hole.

C#	Date	Mintage	VG	Fine	VF
29	ND(1813)	—	300.00	500.00	775.00

16 BITS

SILVER
c/s: Crowned '16' on obv. and rev. of Spanish or Spanish Colonial 8 Reales, C#22.

C#	Date	Mintage	VG	Fine	VF
23	ND(1813)	—	150.00	250.00	350.00

MODERN COINAGE

4 DOLLARS

COPPER-NICKEL
F.A.O. Issue

Y#	Date	Mintage	VF	XF	Unc
4*	1970	.020	3.50	4.50	7.00
	1970	2,000	—	Proof	50.00

*This number refers to Yeoman's East Caribbean Territories listings, where seven companion 4-dollar issues are listed.

10 DOLLARS

20.5000 gm., .925 SILVER, .6097 oz ASW
History of Carnival

Y#	Date	Mintage	VF	XF	Unc
—	1978	—	—	—	20.00
	1978	—	—	Proof	25.00

Visit of Pope John Paul II
Obv: Portrait of Queen Elizabeth

Y#	Date	Mintage	VF	XF	Unc
—	1979	.025	—	—	20.00
	1979	Inc. Ab.	—	Proof	25.00

20 DOLLARS

41.0000 gm., .925 SILVER, 1.2194 oz ASW
50th Anniversary of Graf Zeppelin
Obv: Similar to 10 Dollars, Y#

Y#	Date	Mintage	VF	XF	Unc
—	1978	—	—	—	40.00
	1978	—	—	Proof	50.00

150 DOLLARS

9.6000 gm., .900 GOLD, .2778 oz AGW
Obv: Similar to 10 Dollars, Y#

Y#	Date	Mintage	VF	XF	Unc
—	1978	—	—	—	200.00
	1978	—	—	Proof	250.00

300 DOLLARS

19.2000 gm., .900 GOLD, .5556 oz AGW

Obv: Similar to 10 Dollars, Y#

Y#	Date	Mintage	VF	XF	Unc
—	1978	—	—	—	375.00
	1978	—	—	Proof	425.00

Visit of Pope John Paul II
Obv: Portrait of Queen Elizabeth II.
Rev: Portrait of Pope above denomination.

Y#	Date	Mintage	VF	XF	Unc
—	1979	5,000	—	—	375.00
	1979	Inc. Ab.	—	—	425.00

DOMINICAN REP.

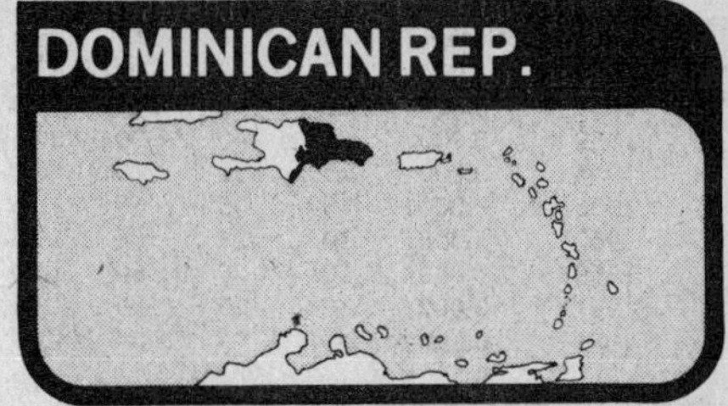

The Dominican Republic, which occupies the eastern two- thirds of the island of Hispaniola, has an area of 18,712 sq. mi. (48,464 sq. km.) and a population of 5.1 million. Capital: Santo Domingo. The agricultural economy produces sugar, coffee, tobacco and cocoa.

Columbus discovered Hispaniola in 1492, and named it La Isla Espanola - 'the Spanish Island'. Santo Domingo, the oldest white settlement in the Western Hemisphere, was the base from which Spain conducted its exploration of the New World. Later, French buccaneers settled the western third of Hispaniola, a colony named St. Dominique, which in 1697 was ceded to France by Spain. In 1804, following a bloody revolt by former slaves, the French colony became the Republic of Haiti - 'mountainous country'. The Spanish called their part of Hispaniola Santo Domingo. In 1822, the Haitians conquered the entire island and held it until 1844, when Juan Pablo Duarte, the national hero of the Dominican Republic, drove them out of eastern Hispaniola and established an independent Dominican republic. The republic returned voluntarily to Spanish dominion - after being rejected by France, Britain and the United States - from 1861 to 1865, when independence was restored.

MINTMARKS

A - Paris
H - Birmingham, England
No mm - Berlin

1/4 REAL

COPPER

Y#	Date	Mintage	Fine	VF	XF	Unc
A1	1844	1.600	5.00	15.00	32.00	90.00

BRASS

Y#	Date	Mintage	Fine	VF	XF	Unc
A1a	1844	—	5.00	10.00	19.00	70.00
	1848 plain 4	—	5.00	10.00	19.00	70.00
	1848 crosslet 4	—	3.50	6.00	15.00	50.00

NOTE: Many varieties exist.

DECIMAL COINAGE

100 Centavos = 1 Peso

CENTAVO

BRASS

Y#	Date	Mintage	Fine	VF	XF	Unc
1	1877	1.000	2.00	3.50	6.00	15.00

BRONZE

Y#	Date	Mintage	Fine	VF	XF	Unc
15	1937	1.000	.50	1.50	6.00	30.00
	1937	—	—	—	Proof	150.00
	1939	2.000	.50	1.25	5.00	25.00
	1941	2.000	.20	.50	2.15	6.00
	1942	2.000	.20	.40	1.20	7.50
	1944	5.000	.20	.50	1.05	6.00
	1947	3.000	.20	.50	1.05	5.00

Y#	Date	Mintage	Fine	VF	XF	Unc
15	1949	3.000	.20	.40	1.00	5.00
	1951	3.000	.20	.40	1.00	4.00
	1952	3.000	.20	.40	1.00	3.00
	1955	3.000	.15	.35	.75	2.00
	1956	3.000	.15	.35	.65	1.25
	1957	5.000	.10	.25	.65	1.25
	1959	5.000	.10	.25	.60	1.00
	1961	5.000	.10	.20	.50	.85
	1961	10 pcs.	—	—	Proof	300.00

100th Anniversary Restoration of the Republic

Y#	Date	Mintage	Fine	VF	XF	Unc
23	1963	13.000	—	—	.20	.50

Y#	Date	Mintage	Fine	VF	XF	Unc
A16	1968	5.000	—	—	.10	.25
	1971	6.000	—	—	—	.20
	1972	3.000	—	—	—	.20
	1972	500 pcs.	—	—	Proof	20.00
	1975	.500	—	—	—	.20

F.A.O. Issue

Y#	Date	Mintage	Fine	VF	XF	Unc
29	1969	5.000	—	.10	.20	.50

Duarte Commemorative

Y#	Date	Mintage	Fine	VF	XF	Unc
37	1976	4.000	—	—	—	.40
	1976	5,000	—	—	Proof	1.00

Y#	Date	Mintage	Fine	VF	XF	Unc
45	1978	3.000	—	—	—	.20
	1978	5,000	—	—	Proof	1.00
	1979	2.985	—	—	—	.20

1-1/4 CENTAVOS

COPPER-NICKEL

Y#	Date	Mintage	Fine	VF	XF	Unc
6	1882	.400	5.00	10.00	30.00	100.00
	1888A	.500	1.75	4.25	10.00	30.00
	1888A	—	—	—	Proof	250.00

2-1/2 CENTAVOS

COPPER-NICKEL

Y#	Date	Mintage	Fine	VF	XF	Unc
4	1877	.021	12.50	17.50	35.00	55.00

Y#	Date	Mintage	Fine	VF	XF	Unc
7	1882	—	4.00	7.50	20.00	90.00
	1888A lg. date					
		4.000	1.00	2.00	7.50	50.00
	1888A lg. date	—	—	—	Proof	250.00
	1888A sm. date					
		.950	1.00	3.00	7.50	50.00
	1888H	4.000	1.00	2.00	7.50	50.00

5 CENTAVOS

COPPER-NICKEL

Y#	Date	Mintage	Fine	VF	XF	Unc
5	1877	.130	8.00	15.00	25.00	65.00

Y#	Date	Mintage	Fine	VF	XF	Unc
16	1937	2.000	1.25	2.00	5.00	25.00
	1937	—	—	—	Proof	175.00
	1939	.200	7.50	15.00	50.00	250.00
	1951	2.000	1.00	1.50	2.00	10.00
	1956	1.000	.20	.30	.85	3.00
	1959	1.000	.20	.50	.60	2.00
	1961	4.000	.10	.20	.35	.75
	1961	10 pcs.	—	—	Proof	300.00
	1971	.440	.10	.15	.20	.35
	1972	2.000	.10	.15	.20	.30
	1972	500 pcs.	—	—	Proof	25.00
	1974	5.000	—	—	.10	.30
	1974	500 pcs.	—	—	Proof	25.00

5.0000 gm., .350 SILVER, .0563 oz ASW

Y#	Date	Mintage	Fine	VF	XF	Unc
16a	1944	2.000	2.00	4.00	10.00	20.00

COPPER-NICKEL
100th Anniversary Restoration of the Republic

Y#	Date	Mintage	Fine	VF	XF	Unc
24	1963	4.000	—	—	.15	.50

COPPER-NICKEL
Duarte Commemorative

Y#	Date	Mintage	Fine	VF	XF	Unc
38	1976	6.000	—	—	.15	.50
	1976	5,000	—	—	Proof	2.00

Y#	Date	Mintage	Fine	VF	XF	Unc
46	1978	2.000	—	—	—	.50
	1978	5,000	—	—	Proof	2.00
	1979	2.985	—	—	—	.50

10 CENTAVOS

2.5000 gm., .350 SILVER, .0281 oz ASW

Y#	Date	Mintage	Fine	VF	XF	Unc
11	1897A	.764	3.75	6.00	14.00	70.00

2.5000 gm., .900 SILVER, .0723 oz ASW

Y#	Date	Mintage	Fine	VF	XF	Unc
17	1937	1.000	BV	2.25	5.00	17.50
	1937	—	—	—	Proof	175.00
	1939	.150	3.00	5.50	11.50	40.00
	1942	2.000	BV	2.50	3.00	7.50
	1944	1.000	BV	2.50	4.00	12.50
	1951	.500	BV	2.50	3.00	7.50
	1952	.500	BV	2.50	3.00	7.50
	1953	.750	BV	2.25	2.75	4.50
	1956	1.000	BV	2.25	2.75	4.50
	1959	2.000	BV	2.25	2.75	4.50
	1961	2.000	BV	2.25	2.75	4.50

2.5000 gm., .650 SILVER, .0522 oz ASW
100th Anniversary Restoration of the Republic

Y#	Date	Mintage	Fine	VF	XF	Unc
25	1963	4.000	BV	BV	1.75	2.25

COPPER-NICKEL
Plain edge

Y#	Date	Mintage	Fine	VF	XF	Unc
17a	1967	10.000	—	.15	.30	1.00
	1973	8.000	—	.15	.30	.85
	1973	500 pcs.	—	—	Proof	30.00
	1975	8.000	—	.15	.25	.75

Duarte Commemorative

Y#	Date	Mintage	Fine	VF	XF	Unc
39	1976	.600	—	.20	.35	.75
	1976	5,000	—	—	Proof	1.50

Y#	Date	Mintage	Fine	VF	XF	Unc
47	1978	—	—	—	—	.75
	1978	—	—	—	Proof	1.50

20 CENTAVOS

5.0000 gm., .350 SILVER, .0563 oz ASW

Y#	Date	Mintage	Fine	VF	XF	Unc
12	1897A	1.395	5.00	7.50	20.00	90.00

25 CENTAVOS

6.2500 gm., .900 SILVER, .1808 oz ASW

Y#	Date	Mintage	Fine	VF	XF	Unc
18	1937	.560	BV	BV	7.50	40.00
	1937	—	—	—	Proof	225.00
	1939	.160	BV	6.50	15.00	75.00
	1942	.560	BV	BV	6.00	25.00
	1944	.400	BV	BV	6.00	25.00
	1947	.400	BV	BV	6.00	25.00
	1951	.400	BV	BV	6.00	25.00
	1952	.400	BV	BV	6.00	7.50
	1956	.400	BV	BV	6.00	7.50
	1960	.600	BV	BV	6.00	7.50
	1961	.800	BV	BV	6.00	7.50

6.2500 gm., .650 SILVER, .1306 oz ASW
100th Anniversary Restoration of the Republic

Y#	Date	Mintage	Fine	VF	XF	Unc
26	1963	2.400	BV	BV	4.00	5.00

COPPER-NICKEL
Plain edge

Y#	Date	Mintage	Fine	VF	XF	Unc
18a	1967	5.000	—	.50	1.00	1.75
	1972	.800	—	.60	1.25	2.00
	1972	500 pcs.	—	—	Proof	27.50

Reeded edge

Y#	Date	Mintage	Fine	VF	XF	Unc
18b	1974	2.000	—	.50	.75	1.50
	1974	500 pcs.	—	—	Proof	27.50

Duarte Commemorative

Y#	Date	Mintage	Fine	VF	XF	Unc
40	1976	3.200	—	.40	.65	1.25
	1976	5,000	—	—	Proof	2.50

Y#	Date	Mintage	Fine	VF	XF	Unc
48	1978	1.000	—	—	—	1.25
	1978	5,000	—	—	Proof	2.50
	1979	1.585	—	—	—	1.25

1/2 PESO

12.5000 gm., .350 SILVER, .1407 oz ASW

Y#	Date	Mintage	Fine	VF	XF	Unc
13	1897A	.917	6.50	20.00	50.00	150.00

12.5000 gm., .900 SILVER, .3617 oz ASW

Y#	Date	Mintage	Fine	VF	XF	Unc
19	1937	.500	BV	BV	15.00	90.00
	1937	—	—	—	Proof	225.00
	1944	.100	BV	BV	15.00	75.00
	1947	.200	BV	BV	15.00	75.00
	1951	.200	BV	BV	15.00	50.00
	1952	.140	BV	BV	12.00	20.00
	1959	.100	BV	BV	12.00	20.00
	1960	.100	BV	BV	12.00	20.00
	1961	.400	BV	BV	12.00	17.50

12.5000 gm., ,650 SILVER, .2612 oz ASW
100th Anniversary Restoration of the Republic

Y#	Date	Mintage	Fine	VF	XF	Unc
27	1963	.300	BV	BV	8.25	10.00

COPPER-NICKEL
Plain edge

Y#	Date	Mintage	Fine	VF	XF	Unc
19a	1967	1.500	—	1.00	1.50	2.50
	1968	.600	—	1.00	1.50	10.00

Reeded edge

Y#	Date	Mintage	Fine	VF	XF	Unc
19b	1973	.600	—	.75	1.25	2.00
	1973	500 pcs.	—	—	Proof	35.00
	1975	.600	—	.75	1.25	2.00

Duarte Commemorative

Y#	Date	Mintage	Fine	VF	XF	Unc
41	1976	.200	—	1.00	1.50	2.50
	1976	5,000	—	—	Proof	3.00

Y#	Date	Mintage	Fine	VF	XF	Unc
49	1978	1.000	—	—	—	2.50
	1978	5,000	—	—	Proof	3.00
	1979	1.585	—	—	—	2.50

PESO

25.0000 gm., .350 SILVER, .2813 oz ASW

Y#	Date	Mintage	Fine	VF	XF	Unc
14	1897A	1.455	15.00	40.00	115.00	325.00

26.7296 gm., .900 SILVER, .7735 oz ASW

Y#	Date	Mintage	Fine	VF	XF	Unc
20	1939	.015	BV	25.00	35.00	200.00
	1939	—	—	—	Proof	1500.
	1952	.020	BV	BV	25.00	40.00

25th Anniversary of Trujillo Regime

Y#	Date	Mintage	Fine	VF	XF	Unc
21	1955	.050*	BV	25.00	35.00	60.00

*30,550 officially melted following Trujillo's assassination in 1961.

26.7296 gm., .650 SILVER, .5586 oz ASW
100th Anniversary Restoration of the Republic

Y#	Date	Mintage	Fine	VF	XF	Unc
28	1963	.020	BV	BV	17.50	25.00

COPPER-NICKEL
125th Anniversary of the Republic

Y#	Date	Mintage	Fine	VF	XF	Unc
30	1969	.030	2.00	5.00	7.50	10.00

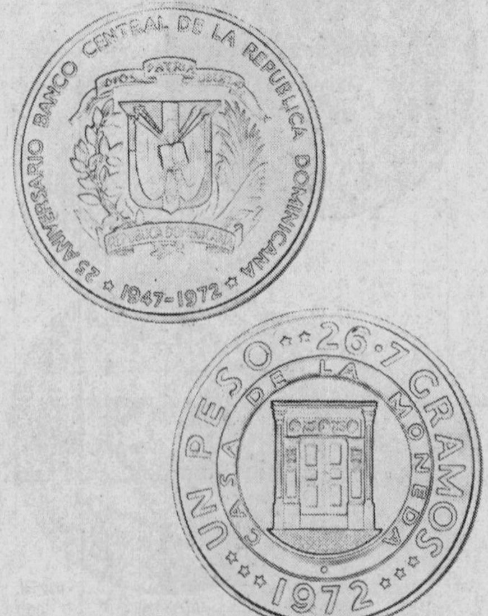

26.7296 gm., .900 SILVER, .5586 oz ASW
25th Anniversary Central Bank

Y#	Date	Mintage	Fine	VF	XF	Unc
31	1972	.027	BV	BV	17.50	25.00

Y#	Date	Mintage	Fine	VF	XF	Unc
31	1972	3,000	—	—	Proof	50.00

12th Central American and Caribbean Games

Y#	Date	Mintage	Fine	VF	XF	Unc
32	1974	.050	BV	BV	17.50	25.00
	1974	5,000	—	—	Proof	50.00

COPPER-NICKEL
Duarte Commemorative

Y#	Date	Mintage	Fine	VF	XF	Unc
42	1976	.030	2.00	2.50	3.00	6.00
	1976	5,000	—	—	Proof	30.00

Y#	Date	Mintage	Fine	VF	XF	Unc
50	1978	.040	—	—	—	3.00
	1978	5,000	—	—	Proof	35.00

Y#	Date	Mintage	Fine	VF	XF	Unc
50	1979	.045	—	—	—	3.00

NOTE: The above coin was counterstamped 10th ANIV.S.N.D. 1969 1979 by the Dominican Republic's National Numismatic Society.

10 PESOS

28.0000 gm., .900 SILVER, .8102 oz ASW
International Banker's Conference

Y#	Date	Mintage	Fine	VF	XF	Unc
34	1975	.026	BV	BV	25.00	30.00
	1975	4,000	—	—	Proof	40.00

30.0000 gm., .900 SILVER, .8681 oz ASW
Pueblo Viejo Mine Commemorative

Y#	Date	Mintage	Fine	VF	XF	Unc
35	1975	.045	BV	BV	27.50	32.50
	1975	5,000	—	—	Proof	45.00

25 PESOS

65.0000 gm., .925 SILVER, 1.9332 oz ASW
Pope John Paul II's Visit
Similar to 100 Pesos, Y#

Y#	Date	Mintage	Fine	VF	XF	Unc
51	1979	3,000	—	—	—	65.00
	1979	6,000	—	—	Proof	75.00

30 PESOS

29.6220 gm., .900 GOLD, .8572 oz AGW
25th Anniversary of Trujillo Regime

Y#	Date	Mintage	Fine	VF	XF	Unc
22	1955	.033	BV	BV	575.00	625.00

11.7000 gm., .900 GOLD, .3385 oz AGW
12th Central American and Caribbean Games

Y#	Date	Mintage	Fine	VF	XF	Unc
33	1974	.025	BV	BV	235.00	250.00
	1974	5,000	—	—	Proof	300.00

78.0000 gm., .925 SILVER, 2.3199 oz ASW
30th Anniversary of Central Bank

Y#	Date	Mintage	Fine	VF	XF	Unc
43	1977	5,000	BV	BV	75.00	85.00
	1977	2,000	—	—	Proof	100.00

100 PESOS

10.0000 gm., .900 GOLD, .2893 oz AGW
Pueblo Viejo Mine Commemorative

Y#	Date	Mintage	Fine	VF	XF	Unc
36	1975	.018	BV	BV	225.00	275.00
	1975	2,000	—	—	Proof	325.00

12.0000 gm., .900 GOLD, .3472 oz AGW
Pope John Paul II's Visit

Y#	Date	Mintage	Fine	VF	XF	Unc
52	1979	1,000	BV	BV	250.00	275.00
52	1979	3,000	—	—	Proof	300.00

200 PESOS

31.0000 gm., .800 GOLD, .7974 oz AGW
Duarte Commemorative

Y#	Date	Mintage	Fine	VF	XF	Unc
44	1977	2,000	BV	BV	525.00	550.00
	1977	1,000	—	—	Proof	600.00

250 PESOS

31.1000 gm., .900 GOLD, .9000 oz AGW
Pope John Paul II's Visit

Y#	Date	Mintage	Fine	VF	XF	Unc
53	1979	1,000	BV	BV	600.00	625.00
	1979	3,000	—	—	Proof	675.00

MONETARY REFORM

(of 1891)

100 Centesimos = 1 Franco

5 CENTESIMOS

BRONZE

Y#	Date	Mintage	Fine	VF	XF	Unc
2	1891A	.400	1.75	2.75	8.00	30.00
	1891A	—	—	—	Proof	200.00

10 CENTESIMOS

BRONZE

Y#	Date	Mintage	Fine	VF	XF	Unc
3	1891A	.300	2.00	3.50	9.50	40.00
	1891A	—	—	—	Proof	250.00

50 CENTESIMOS

.835 SILVER

Y#	Date	Mintage	Fine	VF	XF	Unc
8	1891A	.150	7.50	12.50	35.00	100.00
	1891A	—	—	—	Proof	300.00

UN (1) FRANCO

.835 SILVER

Y#	Date	Mintage	Fine	VF	XF	Unc
9	1891A	.125	10.00	17.50	50.00	200.00
	1891A	—	—	—	Proof	450.00

CINCO (5) FRANCOS

.900 SILVER

Y#	Date	Mintage	Fine	VF	XF	Unc
10	1891A	.150	50.00	125.00	200.00	600.00
	1891A	—	—	—	Proof	3000.

NCLT ISSUES

PATTERNS

KM#	Date	Mintage	Identification	Mkt.Val.
1	1855	—	10 Reales, Silver Plated Copper	3000.
2	1855	—	10 Reales, Copper	2500.
3	1874	—	2 Centavos, Bronze, E (for Essai)	100.00
4	1877	—	1 Centavo, Brass, small date	Rare
5	1877	—	1 Centavo, Bronze, Libertat, E (for Essai)	70.00

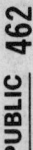

KM#	Date	Mintage	Identification	Mkt.Val.
6	1877	—	2 Centavos, Bronze, Libertat, E (for Essai)	70.00

KM#	Date	Mintage	Identification	Mkt.Val.
7	1878	—	1 Centavo, Bronze, sprays below value, E (for Essai)	60.00
8	1878	—	1 Centavo, Bronze, crossed branches around value, E (for Essai)	60.00

KM#	Date	Mintage	Identification	Mkt.Val.
9	1878	—	2 Centavos, Bronze, sprays below value, E (for Essai)	60.00

KM#	Date	Mintage	Identification	Mkt.Val.
10	1878	—	2 Centavos, Bronze, crossed branches around value, E (for Essai)	60.00

PROOF SETS
STANDARD METALS

KM#	Date	Mintage	Identification	Issue Price	Mkt. Val.
101	1937(5)	10	Y15-19	—	1500.
102	1972(4)	500	YA16,16,18a,31	20.00	120.00
103	1973(2)	500	Y17a,19b	5.00	65.00
104	1974(2)	500	Y16,18b	5.00	50.00
105	1974(2)	500	Y32,33	120.00	350.00
106	1975(2)	500	Y35,36	200.00	350.00
107	1976(6)	5,000	Y37-42	10.00	40.00
108	1978(6)	5,000	Y45-50	—	18.50

EAST AFRICA

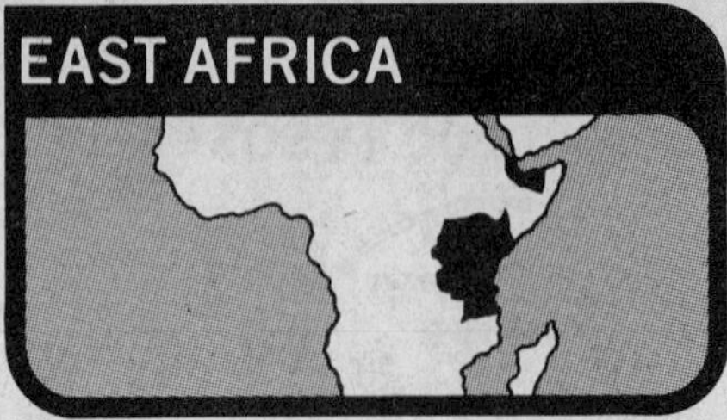

East Africa was an administrative grouping of five separate British territories: Kenya, Tanganyika, the Sultanate of Zanzibar and Pemba (now Tanzania), Uganda and British Somaliland (now Somalia).See individual entries for specific statistics and history.

The common interest of these regions, which comprised a continuous area reaching from the Upper Nile to the Zambezi, invited cooperation in economic matters and consideration of political union. The territorial governors, organized as the East Africa High Commission, met periodically to administer such common activities as taxation, industrial development and education. The authority of the Commission did not infringe upon the constitution and internal autonomy of the individual colonies. A common coinage and banknotes, which were also legal tender in Ethiopia and Aden, was provided for use of the member colonies by the East Africa Currency Board. The coinage through 1919 had the legend "East Africa and Uganda Protectorate".

The East African coinage includes two coins of 1936 which bear the name of Edward VIII.

NOTE: For earlier related coinage see Mombasa.

RULERS
British

MINTMARKS
A - Ackroyd & Best, Morley
I - Bombay Mint
H - Birmingham, England
K,KN - King's Norton
SA - Pretoria Mint

MONETARY SYSTEM
64 Pice = 1 Rupee

PICE

BRONZE

Y#	Date	Mintage	Fine	VF	XF
1	1897	.640	3.00	6.00	15.00
	1897	—	—	Proof	175.00
	1898	6.400	3.00	4.50	10.00
	1898	—	—	Proof	175.00
	1899	3.200	3.00	4.50	10.00
	1899	—	—	Proof	175.00

SILVER

Y#	Date	Mintage	VF	XF	Unc
1a	1897	—	—	Proof Only	650.00
	1898	—	—	Proof Only	650.00
	1899	—	—	Proof Only	650.00

GOLD

Y#	Date	Mintage	VF	XF	Unc
1b	1897	—	—	Proof Only	750.00

DECIMAL CURRENCY
100 Cents = 1 Rupee (to 1920)
100 Cents = 1 Florin (1920-21)
Commencing May 1921
100 Cents = 1 Shilling

1/2 CENT

ALUMINUM

Y#	Date	Mintage	VF	XF	Unc
2	1908	.900	15.00	30.00	100.00

COPPER-NICKEL

Y#	Date	Mintage	VF	XF	Unc
2a (4)	1909	.900	10.00	20.00	65.00

CENT

ALUMINUM

Y#	Date	Mintage	VF	XF	Unc
3	1907	6.948	3.00	8.00	25.00
	1907	—	—	Proof	200.00
	1908	2.871	3.50	12.00	35.00

COPPER-NICKEL

Y#	Date	Mintage	VF	XF	Unc
3a	1908	Inc. Ab.	—	—	—
(5)	1909	25.000	1.25	3.25	8.00
	1910	6.000	1.50	4.00	9.00

Y#	Date	Mintage	VF	XF	Unc
9	1911H	25.000	1.50	2.50	12.50
	1912H	20.000	1.50	2.50	12.50
	1913	4.529	1.75	3.75	15.00
	1914	6.000	2.00	5.00	17.50
	1914H	2.500	3.00	6.00	20.00
	1916H	1.824	2.50	5.00	15.00
	1917H	3.176	3.00	6.00	20.00
	1918H	10.000	1.25	3.25	12.50

Y#	Date	Mintage	VF	XF	Unc
14	1920H	2.908	40.00	60.00	300.00
	1921	*	—	Rare	—

***NOTE:** Not released for circulation.

BRONZE

Y#	Date	Mintage	VF	XF	Unc
20	1922	8.250	.55	2.50	4.00
	1922H	42.750	.45	2.35	3.50
	1923	50.000	.40	2.35	3.50

Y#	Date	Mintage	VF	XF	Unc
20	1924	Inc. Ab.	.40	2.35	5.00
	1924H	18.500	.40	2.35	5.00
	1924KN	10.720	.40	2.35	5.00
	1924KN	—	—	Proof	50.00
	1925	6.000	35.00	60.00	100.00
	1925KN	6.780	.75	3.00	6.50
	1927	10.000	.75	3.00	6.00
	1927	—	—	Proof	175.00
	1928H	12.000	.65	2.50	4.00
	1928KN	11.764	.65	2.50	6.00
	1928KN	—	—	Proof	175.00
	1930	15.000	.65	2.50	4.00
	1930	—	—	Proof	175.00
	1935	10.000	.65	2.00	4.00

Y#	Date	Mintage	VF	XF	Unc
27	1942	25.000	.25	.50	.75
	1942I	15.000	.30	1.15	1.75

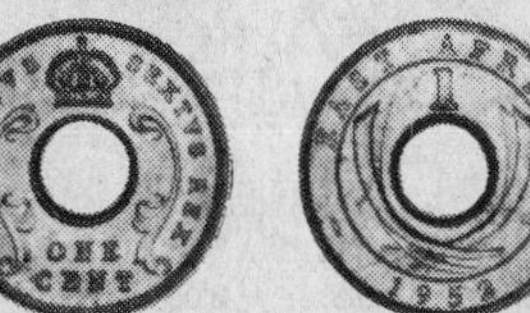

Obv. leg: ET IND.IMP. dropped

Y#	Date	Mintage	VF	XF	Unc
32	1949	4.000	.20	.65	1.00
	1949	—	—	Proof	50.00
	1950	16.000	.20	.65	2.00
	1950	—	—	Proof	175.00
	1951H	16.400	.20	.65	1.00
	1951KN	11.140	.20	.65	2.00
	1951KN	—	—	Proof	175.00
	1952	7.000	.20	.65	1.00
	1952H	5.560	.20	.65	.75
	1952KN	5.230	.20	.75	2.00

Y#	Date	Mintage	VF	XF	Unc
37	1954	8.000	.20	.65	1.00
	1954	—	—	Proof	175.00
	1955	5.000	.20	.45	.75
	1955H	6.380	.20	.65	1.00
	1955KN	4.000	.20	.65	1.00
	1956H	14.940	.15	.30	1.00
	1956KN	9.680	.20	.45	.75
	1957	20.000	.20	.65	1.00
	1957H	Inc. Ab.	1.00	3.50	7.50
	1957KN	Inc. Ab.	.20	.65	1.00
	1959H	20.000	.20	.45	.75
	1959KN	Inc. Ab.	.20	.45	.75
	1961	3.600	.20	.45	.75
	1961H	Inc. Ab.	.20	2.00	3.00
	1962H	10.320	.15	.40	.75

5 CENTS

COPPER-NICKEL

Y#	Date	Mintage	VF	XF	Unc
10	1913H	.300	2.25	7.50	25.00
	1914K	1.240	1.00	7.50	20.00
	1919H	.200	7.50	15.00	40.00

Y#	Date	Mintage	Fine	VF	XF
15	1920H	.550	40.00	85.00	150.00

BRONZE

Y#	Date	Mintage	VF	XF	Unc
21	1921	1.000	3.50	8.50	30.00
	1922	2.500	1.00	3.25	8.00
	1923	2.400	1.00	3.25	8.00
	1923	—	—	Proof	60.00
	1924	4.800	1.00	3.25	8.00
	1925	6.600	1.00	3.25	8.00
	1928	1.200	1.00	3.25	10.00
	1933	5.000	1.00	3.25	7.50
	1934	3.910	1.00	3.25	8.00
	1934	—	—	Proof	175.00
	1935	5.800	1.00	3.25	5.00
	1935	—	—	Proof	175.00
	1936	1.000	2.75	6.50	10.00

Y#	Date	Mintage	VF	XF	Unc
25	1936H	3.500	.75	2.00	3.00
	1936H	—	—	Proof	175.00
	1936KN	2.150	1.75	2.25	3.00

Thick flan

Y#	Date	Mintage	VF	XF	Unc
28	1937	2.000	1.00	2.00	3.00
	1937H	3.000	1.00	2.00	3.00
	1937KN	3.000	1.00	2.00	5.00
	1939H	2.000	1.00	2.00	5.00
	1939KN	2.000	1.00	2.00	5.00
	1941	Inc. Be.	5.00	13.50	20.00
	1941I	20.000	1.00	2.00	3.00

Thin flan

Y#	Date	Mintage	VF	XF	Unc
28.1	1942	16.000	1.00	2.00	3.00
	1942SA	4.120	2.00	3.50	7.50
	1943SA	17.880	1.00	1.70	2.50

Obv. leg: ET IND.IMP. dropped

Y#	Date	Mintage	VF	XF	Unc
33	1949	4.000	.50	3.25	5.00
	1949	—	—	Proof	175.00
	1951H	6.000	.50	2.00	5.00
	1952	11.200	.40	1.00	1.50
	1952	—	—	Proof	175.00

Y#	Date	Mintage	VF	XF	Unc
38	1955	2.000	.25	.65	1.00
	1955	—	—	Proof	175.00
	1955H	4.000	.25	.75	2.00
	1955KN	2.000	1.35	2.00	3.00
	1956H	3.000	.10	2.00	3.00
	1956KN	3.000	.20	.50	1.50
	1957H	4.000	.25	.75	2.00
	1957KN	5.000	.40	.65	1.00
	1961H	4.000	1.35	2.00	3.00
	1963	12.600	—	—	.25

Post-Independence Issue

Y#	Date	Mintage	VF	XF	Unc
41	1964	7.600	—	—	.25

10 CENTS

COPPER-NICKEL

Y#	Date	Mintage	VF	XF	Unc
6	1906	—	—	Rare	—
	1907	1.000	2.75	7.50	27.50
	1910	.500	5.00	10.00	40.00
11	1911H	1.250	2.75	7.50	25.00
	1912H	1.050	3.00	6.50	25.00
	1913	.050	10.00	22.50	60.00
	1918H	.400	5.00	10.00	35.00

Y#	Date	Mintage	VF	XF	Unc
16	1920H	.700	100.00	175.00	350.00

BRONZE

Y#	Date	Mintage	VF	XF	Unc
22	1921	.130	4.00	15.00	30.00

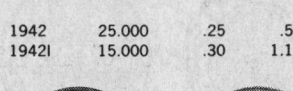

Y#	Date	Mintage	VF	XF	Unc
	1922	7.120	1.00	5.00	10.00
	1923	1.200	2.00	6.50	15.00
	1924	4.900	1.00	5.00	10.00
	1925	4.800	1.00	5.00	10.00
	1927	2.000	1.25	5.50	12.00
	1928	3.800	1.00	5.00	10.00
	1928	—	—	Proof	175.00
	1933	6.260	1.00	5.00	7.50
	1934	3.649	1.00	5.00	10.00
	1935	7.300	1.00	5.00	8.50
	1936	.500	2.75	6.50	12.50

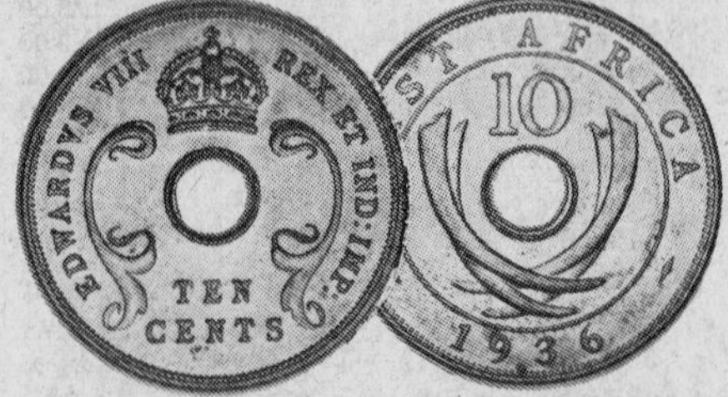

Y#	Date	Mintage	VF	XF	Unc
26	1936	2.000	1.50	2.00	3.00
	1936	—	—	Proof	200.00
	1936H	4.330	1.50	2.00	3.00
	1936KN	4.142	1.50	2.00	3.00

1936 Mule, normal obv. with rev. of Br. West Africa, 1936 Penny, Y#20. (Refer to B.W.A. listings).

Thick flan

Y#	Date	Mintage	VF	XF	Unc
29	1937	2.000	.70	2.35	3.50
	1937	—	—	Proof	175.00
	1937H	2.500	.70	2.35	3.50
	1937KN	2.500	.70	2.35	5.00
	1937KN	—	—	Proof	175.00
	1939H	2.000	.70	2.35	4.50
	1939KN	2.030	.70	2.35	4.50
	1941	15.682	3.00	10.00	15.00
	1941I	Inc. Ab.	.50	1.85	2.75
	1941I	—	—	Proof	175.00

Thin flan

Y#	Date	Mintage	VF	XF	Unc
29.1	1942	12.000	.50	1.85	3.50
	1942	—	—	Proof	175.00
	1942I	4.317	3.00	6.50	10.00
	1943	14.093	3.00	6.50	10.00
	1943SA	Inc. Ab.	.50	1.70	6.00
	1945SA	5.000	.50	1.70	5.00

Obv. leg: ET IND.IMP. dropped

Y#	Date	Mintage	VF	XF	Unc
34	1949	4.000	.40	1.70	3.50
	1949	—	—	Proof	175.00
	1950	8.000	.40	1.70	2.50
	1950	—	—	Proof	175.00
	1951	14.500	.40	1.70	2.00
	1951	—	—	Proof	175.00
	1952	15.800	.40	1.70	2.00
	1952H	2.000	.40	1.70	3.00

Y#	Date	Mintage	VF	XF	Unc
39	1956	6.001	.75	2.00	5.00
39	1956	—	—	Proof	175.00

Post-Independence Issue

Y#	Date	Mintage	VF	XF	Unc
42	1964H	10.002	.10	.20	.40

25 CENTS

2.9160 gm., .800 SILVER, .0750 oz ASW

Y#	Date	Mintage	VF	XF	Unc
7	1906	.400	5.00	15.00	40.00
	1910H	.200	7.50	27.50	55.00

Y#	Date	Mintage	VF	XF	Unc
12	1912	.180	8.00	15.00	40.00
	1913	.300	8.00	15.00	35.00
	1914H	.080	12.50	25.00	50.00
	1914H	—	—	Proof	175.00
	1918H	.040	50.00	85.00	225.00

2.9160 gm., .500 SILVER, .0469 oz ASW

Y#	Date	Mintage	VF	XF	Unc
17	1920H	.748	35.00	55.00	110.00

50 CENTS

5.8319 gm., .800 SILVER, .1500 oz ASW

Y#	Date	Mintage	VF	XF	Unc
8	1906	.200	10.00	30.00	60.00
	1909	.100	15.00	40.00	125.00
	1910	.100	15.00	35.00	75.00

Y#	Date	Mintage	VF	XF	Unc
13	1911	.150	15.00	30.00	85.00
	1911	—	—	Proof	200.00
	1912	.100	15.00	35.00	95.00
	1913	.200	10.00	22.50	70.00
	1914H	.180	10.00	25.00	60.00
	1918H	.060	50.00	100.00	200.00
	1919	.100	25.00	50.00	150.00

5.8319 gm., .500 SILVER, .0937 oz ASW
Fifty Cents-One Shilling

Y#	Date	Mintage	VF	XF	Unc
18	1920A	*.012	1500.	2000.	3000.
	1920H	*.062	500.00	750.00	1200.

***NOTE:** Not released for circulation.

3.8879 gm., .250 SILVER, .0312 oz ASW
Fifty Cents-Half Shilling

Y#	Date	Mintage	VF	XF	Unc
23	1921	6.200	2.00	5.00	25.00
	1922	Inc. Ab.	2.00	5.00	25.00
	1923	.396	5.00	15.00	40.00
	1924	1.000	2.00	5.50	25.00

Y#	Date	Mintage	VF	XF	Unc
30	1937H	4.000	1.25	2.75	12.00
	1937H	—	—	Proof	150.00
	1942H	5.000	1.00	2.50	15.00
	1943I	2.000	2.00	5.00	20.00
	1944SA	1.000	2.00	5.00	20.00

COPPER-NICKEL
Obv. leg: ET INDIA IMPERATOR dropped

Y#	Date	Mintage	VF	XF	Unc
35	1948	7.290	.40	1.70	4.00
	1948	—	—	Proof	175.00
	1949	12.960	.30	1.15	3.50
	1952KN	2.000	.40	1.70	4.00

Y#	Date	Mintage	VF	XF	Unc
40	1954	3.700	.30	1.15	1.75
	1954	—	—	Proof	175.00
	1955H	1.600	.30	1.25	3.00
	1955KHN	—	—	—	—
	1956H	2.000	.25	.85	1.25
	1956KN	2.000	.25	1.00	2.50
	1958H	2.600	.25	.75	2.00
	1960	4.000	.15	.25	1.00
	1962KN	4.000	.15	.25	.85
	1963	6.000	—	.20	.75

FLORIN

11.6638 gm., .500 SILVER, .1875 oz ASW

Y#	Date	Mintage	VF	XF	Unc
19	1920	1.479	25.00	45.00	125.00
	1920A	.542	175.00	250.00	600.00
	1920H	9.689	20.00	30.00	125.00

NOTE: For later coinage see Kenya, Tanzania and Uganda.

SHILLING

7.7759 gm., .250 SILVER, .0625 oz ASW

Y#	Date	Mintage	VF	XF	Unc
24	1921	6.141	2.75	5.50	15.00
	1921H	4.240	2.75	5.50	15.00
	1922	18.858	2.25	5.00	10.00
	1922H	20.052	2.25	5.00	10.00
	1923	4.000	2.50	5.50	12.50
	1924	44.604	2.00	3.50	7.50
	1925	28.405	2.25	3.00	7.50

Y#	Date	Mintage	VF	XF	Unc
31	1937H	8.000	2.00	2.50	17.50
	1937H	—	—	Proof	175.00
	1941I	7.000	2.00	2.50	17.50
	1942H	4.430	2.00	2.50	17.50
	1942I	3.9000	2.00	2.50	17.50
	1943I	8 known			
		—	400.00	600.00	1000.
	1944H	10.000	2.00	2.50	15.00
	1944SA	5.820	2.00	2.50	15.00
	1945SA	10.080	2.00	2.50	20.00
	1946SA	18.260	2.00	2.50	15.00

COPPER-NICKEL
Obv. leg: ET INDIA IMPERATOR dropped

Y#	Date	Mintage	VF	XF	Unc
36	1948	19.704	.90	1.50	4.00
	1949	38.318	.90	1.50	4.00
	1949	—	—	Proof	175.00
	1949H	12.584	.90	1.50	5.00
	1949KN	15.060	.90	1.50	5.00
	1950	56.362	.90	1.50	2.50
	1950	—	—	Proof	175.00
	1950H	11.410	.90	2.25	6.00
	1950KN	10.040	.70	2.00	5.00
	1952	55.605	.50	.75	1.75
	1952	—	—	Proof	175.00
	1952H	8.024	.50	1.25	2.00
	1952KN	9.360	.50	1.25	2.00

NCLT ISSUES

PATTERNS

KM#	Date	Mintage	Identification	Mkt.Val.
1	1906	—	1 Cent, Aluminum, Y#3	1500.
2	1907	—	1/2 Cent, Aluminum, Y#2	2000.
3	1907	—	5 Cents, Copper-Nickel, Y#10	2000.
4	1920(a)	—	50 Cents, Aluminum, Y#18	3000.
5	1920(a)	—	1 Florin, Copper-Nickel	2000.

EAST CARIBBEAN TERR.

The British Caribbean Territories (Eastern group), formed a currency board in 1950 to provide the constituent territories of Trinidad & Tobago, Barbados, British Guiana (now Guyana), British Virgin Islands, Anguilla, Saba, St. Kitts, Nevis, Antigua, Dominica, St. Lucia, St. Vincent and Grenada with a common currency, thereby permitting withdrawal of the regular British Pound currency. This was dissolved in 1965 and after the breakup, the East Caribbean Territories, a grouping including Barbados, the Leeward and Windward Islands, came into being. Coinage of the dissolved 'Eastern Group' continues to circulate although paper currency of the East Caribbean Authority was first issued in 1965.

A series of 4-dollar coins tied to the FAO coinage program were released in 1970 under the name of the Caribbean Development Bank by eight loosely federated island groupings in the eastern Caribbean. These issues are listed individually in this volume under Antigua, Barbados, Dominica, Grenada, Montserrat, St. Kitts, St. Lucia and St. Vincent.

NCLT ISSUES

PROOF SETS

STANDARD METALS

KM#	Date	Mintage	Identification	Issue Price	Mkt. Val.
1	1970(8)	2,000	Y1-8	57.60	350.00

NOTE: These are listed individually under their respective country names.

LISTINGS FOR

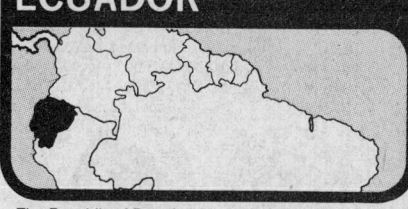

EAST GERMANY: refer to Germany/East

ECUADOR

The Republic of Ecuador, located astride the equator on the Pacific Coast of South America, has an area of 104,506 sq. mi. (270,699 sq. km.) and a population of 6.9 million. Capital: Quito. Agriculture is the mainstay of the economy but there are appreciable deposits of minerals and petroleum. It is the world's largest exporter of bananas and balsa wood. Coffee, cacao and sugar are also valuable exports.

Ecuador was first sighted, 1526, by Francisco Pizarro. Conquest was undertaken by Sebastian de Benalcazar, who founded Quito in 1534. Ecuador was incorporated in the Viceroyalty of New Granada through the 16th and 17th centuries. After two attempts to attain independence were crushed, 1810 and 1812, Antonio Sucre, the able lieutenant of Bolivar, won Ecuador's freedom on May 24, 1822. It then joined Venezuela, Colombia and Panama in a confederacy known as Greater Colombia, and became an independent republic when the confederacy was dissolved, 1830.

MINTMARKS

D - Denver
H - Heaton, Birmingham
HF - LeLocle (Swiss)
LIMA - Lima
Mo - Mexico
PHILA.U.S.A. - Philadelphia

MONETARY SYSTEM

16 Reales = 1 Escudo

UN QUARTO (1/4 REAL)

SILVER, 16mm
Obv: Fortress and bird.

C#	Date	Mintage	VG	Fine	VF	XF
	1842 MV	—	50.00	85.00	125.00	175.00
	14mm					
6	1842 MVS	—	75.00	125.00	200.00	300.00
(Y1)	1842 MV	—	45.00	70.00	120.00	165.00
	1843 MVA	—	—	—	—	—

NOTE: The A and S above are found on the mountain below the castle.

Y#	Date	Mintage	VG	Fine	VF	XF
8	1849 GJ	—	12.50	20.00	30.00	45.00
	1850 GJ	—	15.00	25.00	37.50	50.00
	1851 GJ	—	25.00	40.00	60.00	85.00
	1852 GJ	—	9.00	15.00	25.00	35.00
	1855 GJ	—	9.00	15.00	25.00	35.00
	1856 GJ	—	9.00	15.00	25.00	40.00
	1862 GJ	—	75.00	125.00	150.00	250.00

1/2 REAL

SILVER
Obv. leg: EL ECUADOR EN COLOMBIA, MoR (Medio Real).

C#	Date	Mintage	VG	Fine	VF	XF
1	1833 GJ	—	12.50	17.50	40.00	70.00
	1835 GJ	—	12.50	20.00	45.00	75.00
	Rev: Denomination 1/2 R					
	1833 GJ	—	20.00	35.00	60.00	75.00
	1835 GJ	—	12.50	17.50	25.00	45.00

Obv. leg: REPUBLICA DEL ECUADOR.

C#	Date	Mintage	VG	Fine	VF	XF
7	1838 ST	—	10.00	25.00	45.00	65.00
(Y2)	1838	—	Reported, not confirmed			
	1840 MV	—	10.00	25.00	45.00	65.00
	1840 WV	—	12.50	25.00	45.00	65.00
	1843	—	Reported, not confirmed			

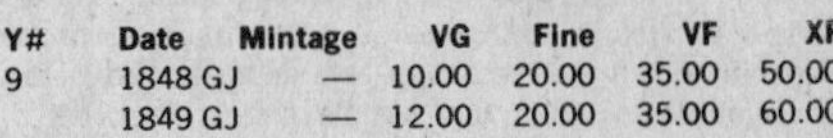

Y#	Date	Mintage	VG	Fine	VF	XF
9	1848 GJ	—	10.00	20.00	35.00	50.00
	1849 GJ	—	12.00	20.00	35.00	60.00

REAL

SILVER
Obv. leg: EL ECUADOR EN COLOMBIA.

C#	Date	Mintage	VG	Fine	VF	XF
2	1833 GJ	—	15.00	25.00	40.00	75.00
	1834 GJ	—	15.00	25.00	40.00	75.00
	1835 GJ	—	15.00	25.00	40.00	75.00
	1836 GJ	—	—	—	—	—

Obv. leg: REPUBLICA DEL ECUADOR.

C#	Date	Mintage	VG	Fine	VF	XF
8	1836 GJ	—	9.00	17.50	35.00	60.00
(Y3)	1836 FP	—	15.00	25.00	50.00	85.00
	1837FP	—	—	—	Rare	—
	1838 ST	—	9.00	17.50	35.00	60.00
	1838 MV	—	Reported, not confirmed			
	1839 MV	—	9.00	17.50	35.00	60.00
	1840 MV	—	9.00	17.50	35.00	60.00
	1841 MV	—	—	—	Rare	—

Obv. and rev. legends transposed.

C#	Date	Mintage	VG	Fine	VF	XF
8a	1837FP	—	—	—	Rare	—
	1838ST	—	50.00	100.00	150.00	250.00

2 REALES

SILVER
Obv. leg: EL ECUADOR EN COLOMBIA.

C#	Date	Mintage	VG	Fine	VF	XF
3	1833 GJ	—	12.00	25.00	40.00	75.00
	1834 GJ	—	12.00	25.00	40.00	75.00
	1835 GJ	—	12.00	25.00	40.00	75.00
	1836 GJ	—	100.00	150.00	250.00	300.00

C#	Date	Mintage	VG	Fine	VF	XF
9	1836 GJ	—	7.50	20.00	30.00	60.00
(Y4)	1836 FP	—	7.50	20.00	30.00	60.00
	1837 FP	—	7.50	20.00	30.00	60.00
	1838 ST	—	8.50	22.00	32.50	65.00
	1838 MV	—	8.50	22.00	32.50	65.00
	1839 MVLA	—	10.00	22.00	32.50	65.00
	1839 MVLA V is inverted A					
		—	10.00	22.00	32.50	65.00
	1840 MV	—	7.50	20.00	30.00	60.00
	1840 MVLAV V is inverted A					
		—	7.50	20.00	30.00	60.00
	1841 MV	—	10.00	22.00	32.50	65.00

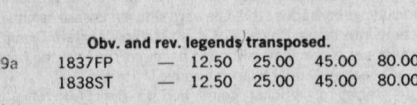

Obv. and rev. legends transposed.

C#	Date	Mintage	VG	Fine	VF	XF
9a	1837FP	—	12.50	25.00	45.00	80.00
	1838ST	—	12.50	25.00	45.00	80.00

Y#	Date	Mintage	VG	Fine	VF	XF
10	1847 GJ	—	7.50	15.00	30.00	55.00
	1848/7 GJ	—	7.50	15.00	30.00	55.00
	1849 GJ	—	7.50	15.00	30.00	55.00
	1850 GJ	—	7.50	15.00	30.00	55.00
	1851 GJ	—	7.50	15.00	30.00	55.00
	1852 GJ	—	7.50	15.00	30.00	55.00

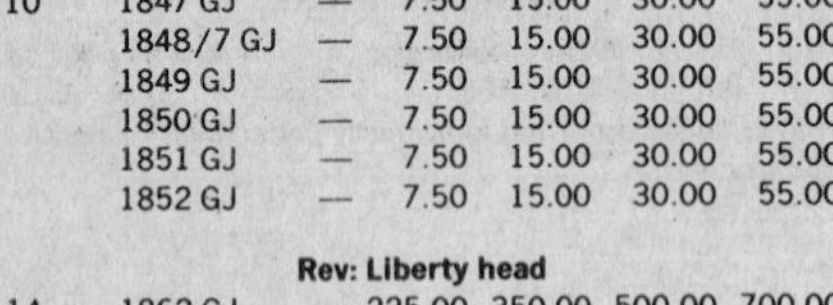

Rev: Liberty head

Y#	Date	Mintage	VG	Fine	VF	XF
14	1862 GJ	—	225.00	350.00	500.00	700.00

4 REALES

SILVER

C#	Date	Mintage	VG	Fine	VF	XF
10	1841 MV	—	12.00	25.00	40.00	85.00
(Y5)	1842 MV	—	12.00	25.00	40.00	85.00
	1843 MV	—	12.00	25.00	40.00	85.00

C#	Date	Mintage	VG	Fine	VF	XF
11	1844 MVA	—	60.00	125.00	175.00	225.00
(Y6)						

NOTE: The A above is found on the breast of the condor.

Similar to 8 Escudos, C#14.

C#	Date	Mintage	VG	Fine	VF	XF
11a	1845 MVA	—	50.00	85.00	110.00	175.00
(Y7)						

NOTE: The A above is found on the breast of the condor.

Y#	Date	Mintage	VG	Fine	VF	XF
11	1855 GJ	—	17.50	25.00	40.00	75.00
	1857 GJ	—	15.00	25.00	35.00	70.00
11a	1862 GJ	—	80.00	125.00	200.00	250.00

Rev: Liberty head

Y#	Date	Mintage	VG	Fine	VF	XF
15	1862	—	65.00	125.00	200.00	250.00

8 REALES

.903 SILVER

Y#	Date	Mintage	VG	Fine	VF	XF
12	1846 GJ	—	375.00	600.00	850.00	1250.

5 FRANCS

.900 SILVER

Y#	Date	Mintage	VG	Fine	VF	XF
13	1858 GJ	—	175.00	250.00	400.00	700.00

ESCUDO

3.3000 gm., .875 GOLD, .0928 oz AGW

C#	Date	Mintage	Fine	VF	XF
4	1833 GJ	—	175.00	210.00	275.00
	1834 GJ	—	175.00	210.00	275.00
	1835 GJ	—	200.00	225.00	300.00

DOUBLE ESCUDO

6.7666 gm., .875 GOLD, .1903 oz AGW

C#	Date	Mintage	Fine	VF	XF
5	1833 GJ	—	250.00	325.00	400.00
	1834 GJ	—	275.00	350.00	450.00
	1835 GJ	—	275.00	350.00	450.00

4 ESCUDOS

13.5000 gm., .875 GOLD, .3798 oz AGW

C#	Date	Mintage	Fine	VF	XF
12	1836 FPA	—	600.00	675.00	800.00
(Y16)	1837 FPA	—	600.00	675.00	800.00
	1838 FPA	—	—	—	—
	1838 STA	—	650.00	700.00	825.00
	1838 MVA	—	675.00	750.00	900.00
	1839 MVA	—	600.00	675.00	800.00
	1841 MVA	—	750.00	800.00	1000.

NOTE: Engraver's initial A near front of bust.

8 ESCUDOS

27.0640 gm., .875 GOLD, .7614 oz AGW

C#	Date	Mintage	Fine	VF	XF
13	1838 STA	—	800.00	1000.	1350.
(Y17)	1838 MVA	—	1400.	1750.	2500.
	1839 MVA	—	800.00	900.00	1100.
	1840 MVA	—	700.00	800.00	1000.
	1841 MVS	—	800.00	900.00	1100.
	1842 MVS	—	800.00	900.00	1100.
	1843 MVS	—	700.00	800.00	1000.

NOTE: Engraver's initial A near front of bust, S toward back.

C#	Date	Mintage	Fine	VF	XF
14	1845 MVA	—	—	Rare	—

Obv: Flagpoles extend below arms.

C#	Date	Mintage	Fine	VF	XF
15 (Y18)	1845 MV	—	1000.	1200.	1500.

No flagpoles below arms
Rev: Similar to Y#15.

C#	Date	Mintage	Fine	VF	XF
15a (Y18)	1845 MV	—	550.00	800.00	1200.

Y#	Date	Mintage	Fine	VF	XF
19	1847 GJ	—	750.00	850.00	1100.
	1848 GJ	—	700.00	800.00	1000.
	1849/7 GJ	—	—	—	2500.
	1849 GJ	—	—	—	—
	1850 GJ	—	650.00	725.00	900.00
	1852/0 GJ	—	650.00	725.00	900.00
	1854 GJ	—	700.00	800.00	950.00
	1855/2 GJ	—	600.00	700.00	850.00
	1856 GJ	—	600.00	700.00	850.00

50 FRANCOS

GOLD
Obv: Similar to 8 Escudos, Y#19. Rev: Head right.

Fr#	Date	Mintage	Fine	VF	XF
9	1862 GJ	—	—	Unique	—

DECIMAL COINAGE

10 Centavos = 1 Decimo
10 Decimos = 1 Sucre
25 Sucres = 1 Condor

MEDIO (1/2) CENTAVO

COPPER-NICKEL

Y#	Date	Mintage	Fine	VF	XF	Unc
24	1884H	1.000	5.00	12.00	25.00	45.00
	1886H	Inc. Ab.	—	—	Rare	—

COPPER

Y#	Date	Mintage	Fine	VF	XF	Unc
20	1890H	2.000	4.00	6.50	11.50	20.00

COPPER-NICKEL

Y#	Date	Mintage	Fine	VF	XF	Unc
33	1909H	4.000	3.00	5.00	8.00	15.00

UN (1) CENTAVO

COPPER

Y#	Date	Mintage	Fine	VF	XF	Unc
21	1872 Heaton	—	15.00	22.50	37.50	65.00
	1890H	2.000	5.00	8.50	16.00	35.00

COPPER-NICKEL

Y#	Date	Mintage	Fine	VF	XF	Unc
25	1884	.500	5.00	12.50	25.00	50.00
	1886	1.000	5.00	12.50	25.00	50.00

Y#	Date	Mintage	Fine	VF	XF	Unc
34	1909H	3.000	3.00	6.00	10.00	17.50

BRONZE

Y#	Date	Mintage	Fine	VF	XF	Unc
44	1928	2.016	.50	1.00	1.25	2.00

DOS (2) CENTAVOS

COPPER

Y#	Date	Mintage	Fine	VF	XF	Unc
23	1872 Heaton	—	11.00	15.00	25.00	40.00

COPPER-NICKEL

Y#	Date	Mintage	Fine	VF	XF	Unc
35	1909H	2.500	2.50	5.00	9.00	18.00

DOS Y MEDIO (2-1/2) CENTAVOS

COPPER-NICKEL

Y#	Date	Mintage	Fine	VF	XF	Unc
36	1917	1.600	6.00	12.00	17.50	32.00

NICKEL

Y#	Date	Mintage	Fine	VF	XF	Unc
45	1928	4.000	1.00	2.00	3.50	6.00

MEDIO (1/2) DECIMO

COPPER-NICKEL

Y#	Date	Mintage	VG	Fine	VF	XF
26	1884Heaton	.600	2.50	6.00	15.00	25.00
	1886Heaton	.600	2.50	6.00	15.00	25.00

1.2500 gm., .900 SILVER, .0361 oz ASW

Y#	Date	Mintage	VG	Fine	VF	XF
27	1893Lima rev: "G.1.250"	1.718	BV	BV	1.25	3.00
	1893Lima rev: "G.1:250"	Inc. Ab.	BV	BV	1.25	3.00
	1894/3Lima	.243	1.25	2.00	4.00	7.50
	1897Lima	.800	BV	1.25	2.00	4.00
	1899/7Lima	.560	BV	1.50	3.00	6.00
	1899Lima	I.A.	BV	1.50	3.00	6.00
	1899Lima obv: ECUADO.R	Inc. Ab.	BV	1.50	3.00	6.00
	1902/802Lima	1.000	BV	BV	1.25	3.00
	1902Lima	I.A.	BV	BV	1.25	3.00
	1905/6Lima	.500	BV	BV	1.25	3.50
	1905Lima	I.A.	BV	BV	1.25	3.50
	1912Lima	.020	BV	BV	1.25	2.00
	1915B'ham	2.000	BV	BV	1.25	2.50

CINCO (5) CENTAVOS

COPPER-NICKEL

Y#	Date	Mintage	VG	Fine	VF	XF
37	1909H	2.000	1.25	2.50	5.00	9.00
37a	1917(Phila.)	1.200	1.00	2.00	3.75	7.50
	1918(Phila.)	7.980	.50	1.00	1.50	3.50

Y#	Date	Mintage	VG	Fine	VF	XF
38	1919	12.000	.50	1.00	1.75	3.00

NOTE: Three varieties exist.

Y#	Date	Mintage	VG	Fine	VF	XF
41	1924H	10.000	.50	1.00	2.00	7.50

NICKEL

Y#	Date	Mintage	VG	Fine	VF	XF
46	1928	16.000	.50	1.00	1.25	1.75

Y#	Date	Mintage	VG	Fine	VF	XF
51	1937HF	15.000	—	—	.50	1.00

BRASS

Y#	Date	Mintage	Fine	VF	XF	Unc
51a	1942(P)	2.000	.75	1.50	2.00	3.00
	1944D	3.000	.75	1.50	2.00	3.00

COPPER-NICKEL

Y#	Date	Mintage	Fine	VF	XF	Unc
51b	1946	40.000	—	—	.15	.25

NICKEL-CLAD STEEL

Y#	Date	Mintage	Fine	VF	XF	Unc
51c	1970	—	—	—	.10	.25

UN (1) DECIMO

2.5000 gm., .900 SILVER, .0723 oz ASW

Y#	Date	Mintage	VG	Fine	VF	XF
28	1884Heaton	.050	2.25	3.00	10.00	17.50
	1889Heaton	.100	BV	2.50	6.00	12.00
	1889/789Santiago	1.000	BV	2.25	2.75	5.00
	1889Santiago	I.A.	BV	2.25	2.75	5.00
	1890Heaton	.150	BV	2.50	5.00	10.00
	1892Lima	.350	BV	BV	2.50	6.00
	1893Lima	.848	BV	BV	2.50	6.00
	1894Lima	.206	BV	BV	2.50	7.00
	1899/4Lima	.220	BV	BV	2.50	6.00
	1899Lima	I.A.	BV	BV	2.50	7.00
	1900Lima JR	.480	BV	BV	2.50	7.00
	1900Lima	I.A.	BV	BV	2.50	6.00
	1902Lima JR	.519	BV	BV	2.50	7.00
	1902Lima	I.A.	BV	BV	2.50	5.00
	1905Lima	.250	BV	BV	2.50	5.00
	1912Lima	.030	2.25	3.00	4.00	10.00
	1915B'ham	1.200	BV	BV	2.50	5.00
	1916Phila	2.000	BV	BV	2.50	5.00

DIEZ (10) CENTAVOS

COPPER-NICKEL

Y#	Date	Mintage	VG	Fine	VF	XF
39	1918	1.000	3.00	6.00	12.00	18.00

Y#	Date	Mintage	VG	Fine	VF	XF
40	1919	2.000	.50	1.00	1.75	3.50

Y#	Date	Mintage	VG	Fine	VF	XF
42	1924H	5.000	.40	.75	1.50	3.00

NICKEL

Y#	Date	Mintage	Fine	VF	XF	Unc
47	1928	16.000	.50	1.00	1.50	2.00

Y#	Date	Mintage	Fine	VF	XF	Unc
52	1937HF	7.500	.50	1.00	1.50	2.00
	BRASS					
52a	1942	5.000	.60	1.25	1.75	2.50
	COPPER-NICKEL					
52b	1946	40.000	—	.25	.50	.75
	NICKEL-CLAD STEEL					
52c	1964	20.000	—	—	—	.25
	1968	15.000	—	—	—	.25
	1972	20.000	—	—	—	.10
	1976	10.000	—	—	—	.10

NOTE: Lettering and date varieties exist.

DOS (2) DECIMOS

5.0000 gm., .900 SILVER, .1446 oz ASW

Y#	Date	Mintage	VG	Fine	VF	XF
29	1884Heaton	.025	5.00	7.50	10.00	17.50
	1889Heaton	.050	5.00	7.50	10.00	17.50
	1889Lima	.075	BV	5.00	7.50	10.00
	1889Santiago	1.000	BV	BV	5.00	7.50
	1890Heaton	.075	BV	5.00	7.50	10.00
	1891Santiago	.230	BV	5.00	7.50	10.00
	1891/89Lima	.025	BV	5.00	7.50	12.00
	1892/89Lima	1.138	BV	BV	5.00	7.50
	1893/89Lima	.390	BV	BV	5.00	7.50
	1894/89Lima	.409	BV	BV	5.00	7.50
	1895/89Lima	.160	BV	BV	5.00	8.50
	1895Phila.	5.000	BV	BV	5.00	7.50
	1896/89Lima	.109	BV	5.00	7.50	12.00
	1912Lima	.050	5.00	7.50	10.00	15.00
	1914Lima	.110	BV	BV	5.00	7.50
	1914Lima.	I.A.	BV	BV	5.00	7.50
	1914Phila.	2.500	BV	BV	5.00	7.50
	1915Lima	.157	5.00	7.50	12.00	17.50
	1916Phila.	1.000	BV	BV	5.00	7.50

20 CENTAVOS

NICKEL

Y#	Date	Mintage	Fine	VF	XF	Unc
53	1937HF	7.500	.40	.75	1.00	1.50
	BRASS					
53a	1942(P)	5.000	.60	1.25	1.75	2.50
	1944D	15.000	.40	.75	1.50	2.00
	COPPER-NICKEL					
53b	1946	30.000	.10	.20	.35	.50
	NICKEL-CLAD STEEL					
53c	1959	14.400	—	—	.10	.25
	1962	14.400	—	—	.15	.25
	1966	24.000	—	—	.10	.25
	1969	24.000	—	—	.10	.25
	1971	12.000	—	—	.10	.25
	1972	48.432	—	—	.10	.25
	1975	—	—	—	.10	.25
	1978	—	—	—	—	—
	1980	—	—	—	—	—
	COPPER-NICKEL					
53d	1974	72.000	—	—	.10	.25
	1975	—	—	—	.10	.25

MEDIO (1/2) SUCRE

12.5000 gm., .900 SILVER, .3617 oz ASW

Y#	Date	Mintage	VG	Fine	VF	XF
30	1884B'ham	.020	12.00	17.50	30.00	60.00
	1899/87	—	—	Reported, not confirmed		

CINQUENTA (50) CENTAVOS

2.5000 gm., .720 SILVER, .0579 oz ASW

Y#	Date	Mintage	VG	Fine	VF	XF
48	1928Phila	1.000	BV	BV	2.00	5.00
	1930Phila	.155	BV	2.00	4.00	7.50

NICKEL-CLAD STEEL

Y#	Date	Mintage	Fine	VF	XF	Unc
57	1963	20.000	—	—	.25	.50
	1971	5.000	—	—	.15	.40
	1974	—	—	—	.15	.50
	1975	—	—	—	—	—
	1977	—	—	—	—	—

UN (1) SUCRE

25.0000 gm., .900 SILVER, .7234 oz ASW

Y#	Date	Mintage	VG	Fine	VF	XF
31	1884Heaton	.250	BV	BV	22.50	30.00
	1888Heaton	.100	BV	BV	27.50	35.00
	1888Santiago	.373	BV	BV	22.50	30.00
	1889Heaton	.150	BV	BV	25.00	35.00
	1889Santiago	.327	BV	BV	25.00	35.00
	1890Heaton	.012	25.00	40.00	65.00	125.00
	1890Lima	.287	BV	BV	22.50	30.00
	1891Lima	.143	BV	BV	25.00	30.00
	1892Heaton	.060	BV	25.00	35.00	45.00
	1892Lima	.058	BV	25.00	40.00	60.00
	1893Lima	—	Reported, not confirmed			
	1895Heaton	.102	BV	BV	22.50	32.50
	1895Lima	.174	BV	BV	22.50	32.50
	1896T.F.Lima	.148	22.50	30.00	45.00	75.00
	1896F.Lima	I.A.	BV	BV	22.50	32.50
	1897Lima	.462	BV	BV	22.50	27.50

5.0000 gm., .720 SILVER, .1157 oz ASW

Y#	Date	Mintage	VG	Fine	VF	XF
49	1928Phila	3.000	BV	BV	4.00	6.00
	1930Phila	.400	BV	BV	5.00	10.00
	1934Phila	2.000	BV	BV	4.00	6.00

NICKEL

Y#	Date	Mintage	Fine	VF	XF	Unc
54	1937HF	9.000	.50	1.00	1.50	2.50
54a	1946	18.000	.40	.75	1.00	1.25
	COPPER-NICKEL					
54b	1959	8.400	.25	.50	.65	1.00
	NICKEL-CLAD STEEL					
54c	1964	20.000	.20	.40	.50	.75
	1970	24.000	.15	.30	.40	.50
	1971	8.092	.20	.40	.50	.75
	1974	40.308	.20	.40	.50	.75
	1978	—	.20	.40	.50	.75

Obv: Modified coat of arms

Y#	Date	Mintage	Fine	VF	XF	Unc
54d	1974	23.100	—	.10	.20	.35
	1975	.592	—	.10	.20	.50
	1977	—	—	.10	.20	.35

DOS (2) SUCRES

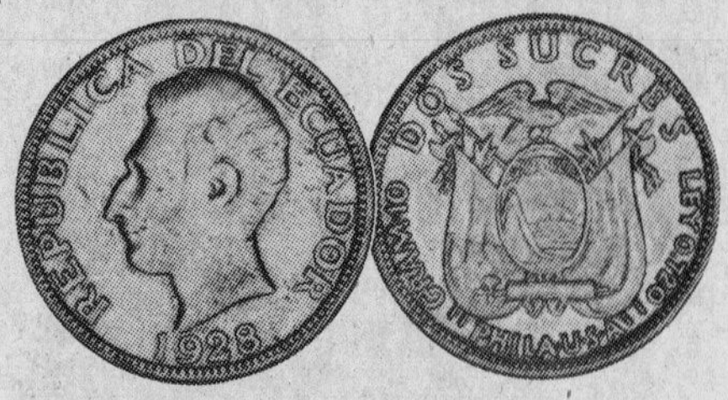

10.0000 gm., .720 SILVER, .2315 oz ASW

Y#	Date	Mintage	Fine	VF	XF	Unc
50	1928Phila	.500	BV	BV	7.50	10.00
	1930Phila	.100	BV	BV	8.50	17.50

Y#	Date	Mintage	Fine	VF	XF	Unc
55	1944Mo	1.000	—	BV	7.50	10.00

COPPER-NICKEL

Y#	Date	Mintage	Fine	VF	XF	Unc
58	1973	—	Reported, not confirmed			
	1974	4.600	Reported, not confirmed			
	1975	5.240	—	—	—	—

CINCO (5) SUCRES

25.0000 gm., .720 SILVER, .5787 oz ASW

Y#	Date	Mintage	Fine	VF	XF	Unc
56	1943Mo	1.000	BV	BV	17.50	20.00
	1944Mo	2.600	BV	BV	17.50	20.00

DIEZ (10) SUCRES

8.1360 gm., .900 GOLD, .2354 oz ASW

Y#	Date	Mintage	Fine	VF	XF	Unc
32	1899B'ham	.100	BV	170.00	180.00	200.00
	1900B'ham	.050	BV	175.00	185.00	225.00

UN (1) CONDOR

8.3592 gm., .900 GOLD, .2419 oz AGW

Y#	Date	Mintage	Fine	VF	XF	Unc
43	1928B'ham	.020	BV	200.00	225.00	275.00

NCLT ISSUES

PATTERNS

KM#	Date	Mintage	Identification	Mkt.Val.
1	1862	—	8 Reales, Silver, plain edge	1750.
2	1862	—	8 Reales, Silver, reeded edge	1750.
3	1928	—	25 Sucres, Copper-Nickel	—

GALAPAGOS ISLANDS

The Galapagos Islands, a territory of Ecuador situated in the Pacific Ocean 650 miles west of Ecuador, have an area of 3,029 sq. mi. and a population of about 3,000. Capital: San Cristobal, on the island of that name. The archipelago of more than 60 islands scattered over 23,000 sq. mi. of the Pacific was discovered by the Spaniards early in the 16th century, and became part of Ecuador in 1832. The islands are notable for their unique plant and animal life, including 15 species of giant tortoise which are the longest-lived animals on earth, with life spans of more than 200 years.

1/2 DECIMO

.900 SILVER
c/s: Script RA on 1/2 Decimo, Y#27.

KM#	Date	Mintage	Good	VG	Fine	VF
1	ND(1893-?)	—	15.00	30.00	40.00	60.00

UN (1) DECIMO

.900 SILVER
c/s: Script RA on Un Decimo, Y#28.

KM#	Date	Mintage	Good	VG	Fine	VF
2	ND(1884-?)	—	10.00	17.50	25.00	40.00

DOS (2) DECIMOS

.900 SILVER

c/s: Script RA on Dos Decimos, Y#29.

KM#	Date	Mintage	Good	VG	Fine	VF
3	ND(1884-?)	—	15.00	30.00	40.00	60.00

1/2 SUCRE

.900 SILVER
c/s: Script RA on 1/2 Sucre, Y#30.

KM#	Date	Mintage	Good	VG	Fine	VF
4	ND(1884-?)	—	20.00	35.00	50.00	75.00

UN (1) SUCRE

.900 SILVER
c/s: Script RA on Un Sucre, Y#31.

KM#	Date	Mintage	Good	VG	Fine	VF
5	ND(1884-?)	—	30.00	55.00	75.00	100.00

NOTE: Both the R and script RA counterstamps, initials of a well known merchant, Rogelio Alvanado, are attributed to the Galapagos Islands where it is believed the coins were used to pay prisoners in a penal colony.

The R counterstamp, 'R' within a beaded circle is found on Guatemalan silver of Carrera and are attributed to Salvador circa 1868-70.

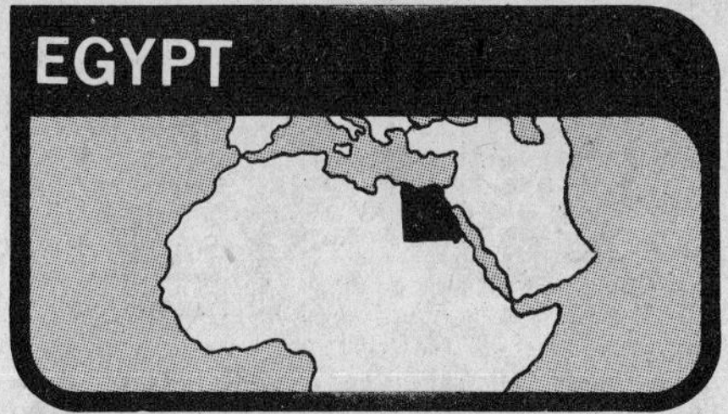

The Arab Republic of Egypt, located on the northeastern corner of Africa, has an area of 386,000 sq. mi. 999,730 sq. km. and a population of 41 million. Capital: Cairo. Although Egypt is an almost rainless expanse of desert, its economy is predominantly agricultural. Cotton, rice and petroleum are exported.

Egyptian history dates back to about 4000 B.C. when the empire was established by uniting the upper and lower kingdoms. Following its 'Golden Age' (16th to 13th centuries B.C.), Egypt was conquered by Persia (525 B.C.) and Alexander the Great (332 B.C.). The Ptolemies ruled until the suicide of Cleopatra (30 B.C.) when Egypt became a Roman colony. Arab caliphs ruled Egypt from 641 to 1516, when the Turks took it for their Ottoman Empire. Turkish rule, interrupted by the occupation of Napoleon (1798-1801), became increasingly casual, permitting Great Britain to inject its influence by purchasing shares in the Suez Canal. British troops occupied Egypt in 1882, becoming the de facto rulers. On Dec. 14, 1914, Egypt was made a protectorate of Britain. British occupation ended on Feb. 28, 1922, when Egypt became a sovereign, independent kingdom. The monarchy was abolished and a republic proclaimed on July 23, 1952.

On Feb. 1, 1958, Egypt and Syria formed the United Arab Republic. Yemen joined on March 8 in an association known as the United Arab States. Syria withdrew from the United Arab Republic on Sept. 29, 1961, and on Dec. 26 Egypt dissolved its ties with Yemen in the United Arab States. On Sept. 2, 1971, Egypt finally shed the name United Arab Republic in favor of the Arab Republic of Egypt.

RULERS

Abdul Hamid I,
AH1187-1203, AD1774-1789
Selim III,
AH1203-1222, AD1789-1807
Mustafa IV,
AH1222-1223, AD1807-1808
Mahmud II,
AH1223-1255, AD1808-1839
Abdul Mejid,
AH1255-1277, AD1839-1861
Abdul Aziz
AH1277-1293, AD1861-1876
Murad V, AH1293, AD1876
Abdul Hamid II,
AH1293-1327, AD1876-1909
Muhammad V
AH1327-1332, AD1909-1914
Hussein Kamil, AD1915-1917
Fuad I (Sultan), AD1917-1922
Fuad I (King), AD1922-1936
Farouk I, AD1936-1952

MONETARY SYSTEM

(Unitl 1834)
40 Para = 1 Guerche (Piastre)
(1834-1885)
40 Paras = 1 Guerche (Piastre)
100 Guerches (Piastres) = 1 Pound
(1885-1916)
10 Ochr-El-Guerches = 1 Piastre
100 Piastres = 1 Pound
(Commencing 1916)
10 Milliemes = 1 Piastre (Guerche)
100 Piastres = 1 Pound (Gunayh)

MINTMARKS

Egyptian coins issued prior to the advent of the British Protectorate series of Sultan Hussein Kamil introduced in 1916 were very similar to Turkish coins of the same period. They can best be distinguished by the presence of the Arabic word 'Misr' (Egypt) on the reverse, which generally appears immediately above the Mohammedan Era accession date of the ruler, which is presented in Arabic numerals. Each coin is individually dated according to the regnal years.

REGNAL YEAR

'MISR' ACCESSION DATE

BP - Budapest, Hungary
H - Birmingham, England
KN - King's Norton, England

DENOMINATIONS

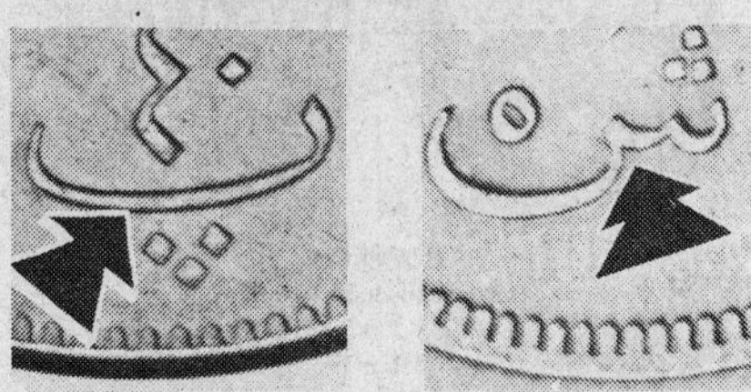

PARA GUERCHE

NOTE: The unit of value on coins of this period is generally presented on the obverse immediately below the toughra, as shown in the illustrations above.

MILLIEMES

PIASTRES

U.A.R. EGYPT

The legend illustrated is Gumhouriyya Misr Al-'Arabiyya which translates to 'The Arab Republic of Egypt'. Similar legends are found on the modern issues of Syria.

OTTOMAN ISSUES

PARA

BILLON, 12-13mm.
Accession Date: AH1223

C#	Year	Mintage	Good	VG	Fine	VF
111	1	—	.75	1.50	2.50	5.00
	2	—	.75	1.50	2.50	5.00
	3	—	.75	1.50	2.50	5.00
	4	—	1.00	2.00	3.50	6.50
	5	—	.75	1.50	2.50	5.00
	6	—	.75	1.50	2.50	5.00
	7	—	.75	1.50	2.50	5.00
	8	—	.75	1.50	2.50	5.00
	9	—	.75	1.50	2.50	5.00
	10	—	.75	1.50	2.50	5.00
	11	—	.75	1.50	2.50	5.00
	12	—	.75	1.50	2.50	5.00
	13	—	.75	1.50	2.50	5.00
	14	—	.75	1.50	2.50	5.00
	15	—	.75	1.50	2.50	5.00
	16	—	.75	1.50	2.50	5.00
	17	—	.75	1.50	2.50	5.00
	18	—	.75	1.50	2.50	5.00
	19	—	.75	1.50	2.50	5.00
	21	—	1.25	2.50	5.00	10.00

COPPER, 17mm.

C#	Year	Mintage	Good	VG	Fine	VF
141	28	—	10.00	25.00	50.00	75.00
	29	—	10.00	25.00	50.00	75.00

15mm.

C#	Year	Mintage	Good	VG	Fine	VF
161	29	—	10.00	22.50	45.00	70.00

NOTE: #161 does not bear any denomination.

15-17mm.

C#	Year	Mintage	Good	VG	Fine	VF
161a	29	—	7.00	17.50	40.00	65.00
	30	—	7.00	17.50	40.00	65.00
	31	—	7.00	17.50	40.00	65.00
	32	—	7.00	17.50	40.00	65.00

Accession Date: AH1255

C#	Year	Mintage	Good	VG	Fine	VF
193	1	—	10.00	25.00	45.00	75.00
	2	—	7.00	17.50	35.00	60.00
	4	—	10.00	25.00	45.00	75.00
	5	—	7.00	17.50	35.00	60.00
	6	—	7.00	17.50	35.00	60.00

Similar to 5 Para, C#197

C#	Year	Mintage	Good	VG	Fine	VF
196	8	—	10.00	25.00	50.00	85.00

1/40 GUERCHE

BRONZE
Accession Date: AH1293

Y#	Year	Mintage	Fine	VF	XF	Unc
12	10	1.669	.50	1.00	2.00	5.00
	12	2.476	.40	.75	1.50	4.00
	19	—	.75	1.50	2.50	5.00
	20	—	4.00	6.00	10.00	20.00
	24	1.601	.75	1.50	2.50	5.50
	26	1.999	.50	1.00	1.50	4.00
	27	1.200	1.25	2.50	3.50	7.00
	29	2.000	.50	1.00	1.50	4.00
	31H	*2.400	.50	1.00	2.00	5.00
	32H	Inc. Ab.	.50	1.00	2.00	5.00
	33H	*1.200	.50	1.00	1.50	3.50
	35H	1.200	1.10	2.25	4.50	8.50

*Estimated.

Accession Date: AH1327

Y#	Year	Mintage	Fine	VF	XF	Unc
23	2H	*2.000	1.25	2.50	8.00	15.00
	3H	*2.000	.75	1.50	5.00	10.00
	4H	*1.200	1.00	2.00	7.50	11.50

Y#	Year	Mintage	Fine	VF	XF	Unc
23	6H	1.200	.75	1.50	4.00	8.50

*Estimated.

1/20 GUERCHE

BRONZE
Accession Date: AH1293

Y#	Year	Mintage	Fine	VF	XF	Unc
13	10	4.105	.50	1.00	2.00	5.50
	12	4.457	.65	1.25	2.50	6.50
	18	—	7.50	15.00	25.00	50.00
	19	—	1.50	3.00	6.00	15.00
	20	—	2.50	5.00	10.00	20.00
	21	—	2.00	3.50	7.50	15.00
	24	.801	1.00	2.00	4.50	9.00
	26	1.405	.75	1.50	2.25	5.50
	27	1.402	.90	1.75	3.00	7.00
	29	3.200	.50	1.00	2.00	6.00
	31H	(?)3.000	.50	1.00	1.75	6.00
	32H	Inc. Ab.	.65	1.25	2.50	5.50
	33H	(?)1.400	.75	1.50	3.00	8.00
	35H	1.400	1.50	3.00	5.50	10.00

Accession Date: AH1327

Y#	Year	Mintage	Fine	VF	XF	Unc
24	2H	*2.000	.75	1.50	3.00	10.00
	3H	*2.000	1.00	2.00	5.00	10.00
	4H	*2.400	.50	1.00	3.50	8.50
	6H	1.400	.50	1.00	2.50	6.50

*Estimated.

4 PARA

BRONZE
Accession Date: AH1277

Y#	Year	Mintage	Fine	VF	XF	Unc
1	4	—	6.50	12.50	22.50	40.00

1/10 GUERCHE

COPPER-NICKEL
Accession Date: AH1293

Y#	Year	Mintage	Fine	VF	XF	Unc
14	10	2.307	.40	.75	1.75	5.50
	12	3.435	.45	.85	2.00	6.50
	18	—	5.00	10.00	17.50	30.00
	19	—	.75	1.50	3.00	8.50
	20	—	.65	1.25	2.50	7.50
	21	—	.65	1.25	2.50	7.50
	22	—	1.50	3.00	6.00	18.00
	23	—	.75	1.50	2.50	8.50
	24	1.005	.40	.75	1.50	5.50
	25	2.000	.40	.75	1.50	5.50
	27	3.010	.25	.50	1.25	4.50
	28	6.000	.40	.75	1.75	4.50
	29	1.500	.75	1.50	3.50	12.50
	30	1.000	.50	1.00	2.00	6.50
	31H	*3.000	.75	1.50	3.50	10.00
	32H	Inc. Ab.	.25	.50	1.25	4.50
	33H	2.000	.25	.50	1.25	4.50
	35H	2.000	1.00	2.00	4.00	10.00

*Estimated.

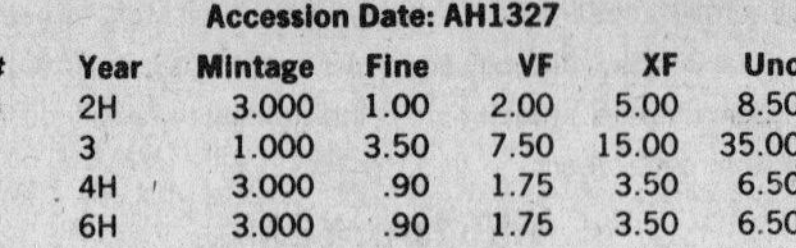

Accession Date: AH1327

Y#	Year	Mintage	Fine	VF	XF	Unc
25	2H	3.000	1.00	2.00	5.00	8.50
	3	1.000	3.50	7.50	15.00	35.00
	4H	3.000	.90	1.75	3.50	6.50
	6H	3.000	.90	1.75	3.50	6.50

5 PARA

BILLON, 15-16mm., 0.5-0.7 gm.
Accession Date: AH1223

C#	Year	Mintage	Good	VG	Fine	VF
112	7	—	2.75	7.00	15.00	27.50
	9	—	2.75	7.00	15.00	27.50
	10	—	2.75	7.00	15.00	27.50
	12	—	2.75	7.00	15.00	27.50
	13	—	2.75	7.00	15.00	27.50
	14	—	2.75	7.00	15.00	27.50
	15	—	2.75	7.00	15.00	27.50
	16	—	2.75	7.00	15.00	27.50
	17	—	2.75	7.00	15.00	27.50
	18	—	2.75	7.00	15.00	27.50
	19	—	2.75	7.00	15.00	27.50
	20	—	2.75	7.00	15.00	27.50
	21	—	2.75	7.00	15.00	27.50

14mm., 0.4 gm.
Obv: Rose added to right of toughra.

C#	Year	Mintage	Good	VG	Fine	VF
130	21	—	4.00	10.00	20.00	35.00
	22	—	4.00	10.00	20.00	35.00
	23	—	4.00	10.00	20.00	35.00
	24	—	4.00	10.00	20.00	35.00
	25	—	5.00	15.00	25.00	45.00
	26	—	5.00	15.00	30.00	50.00
	28	—	5.00	15.00	30.00	50.00

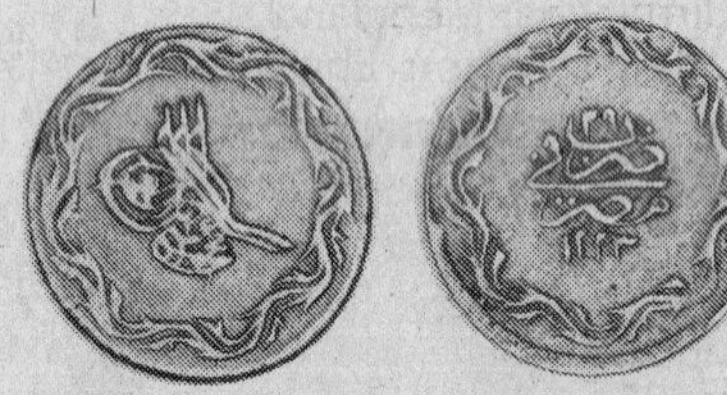

COPPER
Floral designs in wreath

C#	Year	Mintage	Good	VG	Fine	VF
142	28	—	1.50	3.50	10.00	17.50
	29	—	1.50	3.50	10.00	17.50

Without wreath, denomination not shown on coin.

C#	Year	Mintage	Good	VG	Fine	VF
162	29	—	2.00	5.00	9.00	15.00

Obv: Denomination added below toughra.

C#	Year	Mintage	Good	VG	Fine	VF
162a	29	—	1.00	2.50	5.00	9.00
	30	—	1.00	2.50	5.00	9.00
	31	—	1.00	2.50	5.00	9.00
	32	—	1.00	2.50	5.00	9.00

Accession Date: AH1255

C#	Year	Mintage	Good	VG	Fine	VF
194	1	—	.40	1.00	2.00	4.00
	2	—	.40	1.00	2.00	4.00
	3	—	.40	1.00	2.00	4.00
	4	—	.40	1.00	2.00	4.00
	5	—	.40	1.00	2.00	4.00
	6	—	.70	1.75	3.50	6.00

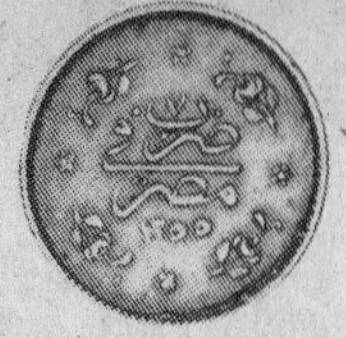

C#	Year	Mintage	Good	VG	Fine	VF
191	6	—	1.00	2.50	5.00	10.00
	7	—	.60	1.50	3.50	7.00
	8	—	.80	2.00	4.50	8.50

C#	Year	Mintage	Good	VG	Fine	VF
197	8	—	2.50	6.00	11.50	20.00
	12	—	2.00	5.00	10.00	17.50
	13	—	2.00	5.00	10.50	17.50
	14	—	1.00	2.50	5.00	10.00
	15	—	.60	1.50	3.50	7.50
	16	—	.60	1.50	3.50	7.50

2/10 GUERCHE

COPPER-NICKEL
Accession Date: AH1293

Y#	Year	Mintage	Fine	VF	XF	Unc
15	10	3.201	.65	1.25	2.50	10.00
	12	2.009	.65	1.25	2.75	12.00
	20	—	2.25	4.50	9.00	20.00
	21	.500	1.00	2.00	4.50	12.50
	24	.500	1.00	2.00	4.50	12.50
	25	.250	1.25	2.50	6.00	16.50
	27	1.002	.75	1.50	3.00	12.00
	28	2.000	.65	1.25	2.50	7.50
	29	1.500	.75	1.50	3.00	12.00
	30	—	2.50	5.00	10.00	22.50
	31H	*1.000	.65	1.25	3.50	10.00
	33H	*1.500	.65	1.25	3.50	10.00
	35H	.750	1.75	3.50	7.50	17.50

*Estimated.

Accession Date: AH1327

Y#	Year	Mintage	Fine	VF	XF	Unc
26	2H	1.000	1.25	2.50	5.00	12.50
	3	.500	3.50	7.00	14.00	30.00
	4H	1.000	1.25	2.50	5.00	12.50
	6H	1.000	1.25	2.50	5.00	12.50

10 PARA

BILLON, 17-18mm., 1.1-1.4 gm.
Accession Date: AH1223

C#	Year	Mintage	Good	VG	Fine	VF
113	8	—	5.00	12.50	22.50	40.00
	9	—	3.50	9.00	17.50	30.00
	15	—	3.50	9.00	17.50	30.00
	18	—	3.50	9.00	17.50	30.00
	19	—	3.50	9.00	17.50	30.00
	20	—	3.50	9.00	17.50	30.00
	21	—	5.00	12.50	22.50	40.00

Weight reduced to ca. 0.8 gm.
Wavy borders around obv. & rev.

C#	Year	Mintage	Good	VG	Fine	VF
131	21	—	3.25	8.00	14.00	28.00
	22	—	3.25	8.00	14.00	28.00
	23	—	3.25	8.00	14.00	28.00
	24	—	5.00	12.50	20.00	35.00
	25	—	3.25	8.00	14.00	28.00

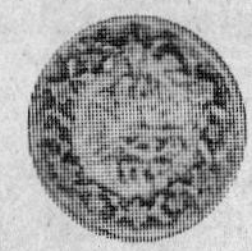

Wreath borders, 12mm, 0.3 gm.

C#	Year	Mintage	Good	VG	Fine	VF
144	28	—	15.00	30.00	70.00	125.00
	29	—	10.00	25.00	60.00	100.00

.900 SILVER, 14mm
Obv: Denomination beneath toughra.

C#	Year	Mintage	VG	Fine	VF	XF
163	29	—	25.00	55.00	100.00	200.00
	30	—	25.00	55.00	100.00	200.00
	31	—	25.00	55.00	100.00	200.00
	32	—	25.00	55.00	100.00	200.00

Accession Date: AH1255

C#	Year	Mintage	VG	Fine	VF	XF
205	1	—	8.50	20.00	35.00	60.00
	2	—	7.50	15.00	22.50	45.00
	3	—	7.50	15.00	22.50	45.00
	4	—	7.50	14.00	22.50	45.00
	5	—	7.50	14.00	22.50	45.00
	6	—	7.50	14.00	22.50	45.00
	7	—	7.50	14.00	22.50	45.00
	8	—	7.50	14.00	22.50	45.00
	9	—	7.50	14.00	22.50	45.00
	10	—	7.50	14.00	22.50	45.00
	11	—	7.50	14.00	22.50	45.00
	12	—	7.50	14.00	22.50	45.00
	14	—	7.50	14.00	22.50	45.00
	15	—	7.50	14.00	22.50	45.00
	18	—	7.50	14.00	22.50	45.00
	19	—	7.50	14.00	22.50	45.00
	20	—	7.50	14.00	22.50	45.00
	21	—	—	Reported, not confirmed		
	22	—	5.50	14.00	22.50	45.00
	23	—	5.50	14.00	22.50	40.00

COPPER, 29mm.

C#	Year	Mintage	VG	Fine	VF	XF
198	15	—	2.00	5.00	10.00	20.00
	16	—	2.50	6.50	13.50	27.50

BRONZE
Accession Date: AH1277
Obv: W/o flower to right of toughra.

Y#	Year	Mintage	Fine	VF	XF	Unc
2	4	—	.75	1.50	4.50	20.00
	5	—	.75	1.50	4.50	20.00
	6	—	1.00	2.00	5.00	25.00
	7	—	1.00	2.00	5.00	25.00
	9	—	.75	1.50	4.50	20.00
	10	—	1.25	2.50	5.50	25.00

COPPER
Obv: Flower added to right of toughra.

Y#	Year	Mintage	VG	Fine	VF	XF
2a	8	—	150.00	300.00	500.00	750.00
	9	—	150.00	300.00	500.00	750.00
	11	—	150.00	300.00	500.00	750.00

.900 SILVER

Y#	Year	Mintage	Fine	VF	XF	Unc
5	2	—	3.00	6.00	10.00	45.00
	3	—	3.00	6.00	10.00	45.00
	4	—	3.00	5.00	7.50	40.00
	5	—	3.00	6.00	10.00	45.00
	6	—	3.00	5.00	7.50	40.00
	7	—	3.00	5.00	7.50	30.00
	8	—	3.00	5.00	7.50	35.00
	9	—	3.00	5.00	7.50	40.00
	10	—	3.00	5.00	7.50	40.00
	11	—	3.00	5.00	7.50	40.00
	12	—	3.00	6.00	10.00	45.00
	13	—	3.00	6.00	10.00	45.00
	14	—	3.00	5.00	7.50	40.00
	15	—	6.00	12.50	25.00	75.00
	16	—	3.00	6.00	10.00	45.00

Accession Date: AH1293

Y#	Year	Mintage	Fine	VF	XF	Unc
A17	1	—	55.00	80.00	110.00	225.00
	2	—	60.00	100.00	140.00	275.00
	3	—	55.00	80.00	110.00	225.00

20 PARA

BILLON, 22-24mm.
Accession Date: AH1223
Rev: Date

C#	Year	Mintage	Good	VG	Fine	VF
114	5	—	6.00	15.00	27.50	50.00
	6	—	6.00	15.00	27.50	50.00
	7	—	6.00	15.00	27.50	50.00
	8	—	6.00	15.00	27.50	50.00
	9	—	6.00	15.00	27.50	50.00
	10	—	6.00	15.00	35.00	70.00
	11	—	6.00	15.00	35.00	70.00

Obv: Date beneath toughra.

C#	Year	Mintage	Good	VG	Fine	VF
115	5	—	20.00	45.00	100.00	175.00

C#	Year	Mintage	Good	VG	Fine	VF
132	21	—	3.50	7.50	15.00	27.50
	22	—	3.00	7.00	12.50	25.00
	23	—	2.50	6.00	10.00	17.50
	24	—	2.50	6.00	10.00	17.50
	25	—	2.50	6.00	10.00	17.50

15mm., 0.6 gm.

C#	Year	Mintage	Good	VG	Fine	VF
145	28	—	4.00	10.00	20.00	35.00
	29	—	4.00	10.00	20.00	35.00

.900 SILVER, 15-16mm
Obv: Denomination below toughra.

C#	Year	Mintage	VG	Fine	VF	XF
164	29	—	15.00	32.50	65.00	100.00
	30	—	15.00	32.50	65.00	100.00
	31	—	15.00	32.50	65.00	100.00
	32	—	15.00	32.50	65.00	100.00

Accession Date: AH1255

C#	Year	Mintage	VG	Fine	VF	XF
206	1	—	8.50	16.50	30.00	50.00
	2	—	—	—	—	—
	3	—	8.50	16.50	30.00	50.00
	4/3	—	10.00	20.00	40.00	60.00
	4	—	8.50	16.50	30.00	50.00
	5	—	6.50	12.50	22.50	40.00
	6	—	6.50	12.50	22.50	40.00
	7	—	6.50	12.50	22.50	40.00
	8	—	6.50	12.50	22.50	40.00
	9	—	6.50	12.50	22.50	40.00
	10	—	6.50	12.50	22.50	40.00
	11	—	10.00	20.00	40.00	60.00
	12	—	8.50	16.50	30.00	50.00
	13	—	8.50	16.50	30.00	50.00
	15	—	9.00	18.50	32.50	55.00
	18	—	8.50	16.50	30.00	50.00
	19	—	10.00	20.00	40.00	60.00
	20	—	8.50	16.50	30.00	50.00
	21	—	8.50	16.50	30.00	50.00
	22	—	8.50	16.50	30.00	50.00
	23	—	8.50	16.50	30.00	50.00

BRONZE
Accession Date: AH1277
Obv: W/o flower to right of toughra.

Y#	Year	Mintage	Fine	VF	XF	Unc
3	3	—	—	2.00	4.00	25.00
	4	—	—	2.00	4.00	20.00
	5	—	—	2.00	4.00	20.00
	6	—	—	2.00	4.00	20.00
	8	—	—	2.00	4.00	25.00
	9	—	—	2.00	4.00	20.00
	10	—	—	2.00	4.00	25.00

Similar, but crude & thick.

Y#	Year	Mintage	VG	Fine	VF	XF
3b	7	—	55.00	100.00	175.00	250.00
	8	—	50.00	90.00	150.00	225.00

COPPER
Obv: Flower to right of toughra.

Y#	Year	Mintage	VG	Fine	VF	XF
3a	8	—	9.00	17.50	27.50	50.00
	9	—	6.50	12.50	22.50	40.00
	10	—	9.00	17.50	27.50	50.00
	11	—	50.00	100.00	200.00	350.00

.900 SILVER

Y#	Year	Mintage	Fine	VF	XF	Unc
6	1	—	—	Reported, not confirmed		
	2	—	7.50	17.50	35.00	75.00
	3	—	6.50	12.50	20.00	60.00
	4	—	5.00	10.00	17.50	50.00
	5	—	5.00	10.00	17.50	50.00
	6	—	5.00	10.00	17.50	50.00
	7	—	5.00	10.00	17.50	50.00
	8	—	5.00	10.00	17.50	50.00
	9	—	5.00	10.00	17.50	50.00
	10	—	5.00	10.00	17.50	50.00
	11	—	5.00	10.00	17.50	50.00
	12	—	5.00	10.00	17.50	50.00
	13	—	6.50	12.50	20.00	45.00

Y#	Year	Mintage	Fine	VF	XF	Unc
6	14	—	6.50	12.50	20.00	55.00
	15	—	7.50	17.50	27.50	75.00

.55 gm.
Accession Date: AH1293

B17	1	—	75.00	110.00	160.00	400.00
	2	—	70.00	100.00	140.00	375.00
	3	—	75.00	110.00	160.00	400.00

5/10 GUERCHE

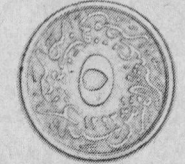

COPPER-NICKEL
Accession Date: AH1293

16	10	7.003	.50	1.00	3.00	8.00
	11	10.005	.50	1.00	3.00	8.00
	13	5.003	.50	1.00	3.00	10.00
	20	1.002	1.10	2.25	5.00	15.00
	21	3.404	.65	1.25	3.00	10.00
	23	1.000	2.50	5.00	8.50	22.50
	24	3.605	.45	.85	2.50	8.50
	25	1.998	.45	.85	2.50	8.50
	27	4.999	.30	.60	2.00	8.00
	29	12.000	.30	.60	2.00	8.00
	30	2.000	.30	.60	2.00	8.00
	33H	1.000	1.00	2.00	5.50	17.50

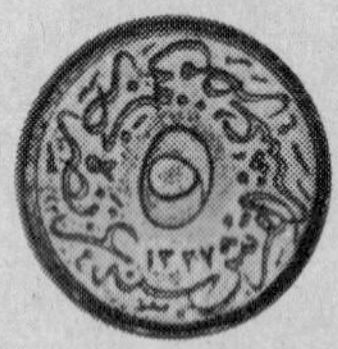

Accession Date: AH1327

27	2H	2.131	1.25	2.50	4.50	15.00
	3	1.000	2.50	5.00	15.00	45.00
	4H	3.327	.75	1.50	3.50	15.00
	6H	3.000	.75	1.50	3.50	15.00

GUERCHE

BILLON, 27-32mm
Accession Date: AH1223

C#	Year	Mintage	Good	VG	Fine	VF
116	1	—	20.00	40.00	60.00	100.00
	3	—	12.50	25.00	40.00	70.00
	5	—	12.50	25.00	40.00	70.00
	6	—	12.50	25.00	40.00	70.00
	7	—	12.50	25.00	40.00	70.00
	8	—	15.00	30.00	50.00	85.00

Obv: Date beneath toughra.

117	5	—	35.00	60.00	125.00	200.00

Wavy borders, 26-28mm.

C#	Year	Mintage	Good	VG	Fine	VF
133	21	—	2.50	6.00	11.00	20.00
	22	—	2.00	5.00	9.50	18.00
	23	—	2.00	5.00	9.50	18.00
	24	—	2.00	5.00	9.50	18.00
	25	—	2.00	5.00	9.50	18.00
	26	—	3.00	7.50	13.50	25.00
	27	—	3.00	7.50	13.50	25.00

Wreath borders

146	28	—	2.50	6.00	11.50	17.50
	29	—	2.75	7.00	13.50	22.50

SILVER, 19-20mm
Obv: Denomination below toughra.

C#	Year	Mintage	VG	Fine	VF	XF
165	29	—	10.00	20.00	35.00	55.00
	30	—	10.00	20.00	35.00	55.00
	31	—	10.00	20.00	35.00	55.00
	32	—	10.00	20.00	35.00	55.00

Accession Date: AH1255

207	1	—	10.00	20.00	35.00	60.00
	2	—	10.00	20.00	35.00	60.00
	3	—	10.00	20.00	35.00	60.00
	4	—	12.50	25.00	40.00	70.00
	5	—	10.00	20.00	35.00	60.00
	6	—	10.00	20.00	35.00	60.00
	8/7	—	12.50	25.00	40.00	70.00
	8	—	10.00	20.00	35.00	60.00
	9	—	10.00	20.00	35.00	60.00
	10	—	10.00	20.00	35.00	60.00
	11	—	5.00	10.00	22.50	37.50
	12	—	10.00	20.00	35.00	60.00
	13	—	12.50	25.00	45.00	75.00
	15	—	10.00	20.00	37.50	65.00
	16	—	—	Reported, not confirmed		
	17	—	—	Reported, not confirmed		
	18	—	10.00	20.00	37.50	65.00
	19	—	10.00	20.00	37.50	65.00
	20	—	—	Reported, not confirmed		
	21	—	—	Reported, not confirmed		
	22	—	12.50	25.00	40.00	70.00
	23	—	11.50	22.50	40.00	70.00

40 PARA (=1 GUERCHE)

BRONZE
Accession Date: AH1277

2 Vars: Large or small toughra.

Y#	Year	Mintage	Fine	VF	XF	Unc
4	10	—	2.00	7.50	15.00	50.00

COPPER
Obv: Flower added to right of toughra.

4a	10	—	600.00	1000.	1500.	2500.

GUERCHE

.900 SILVER

7	1	—	15.00	25.00	50.00	85.00
	2	—	5.00	10.00	20.00	50.00
	3	—	5.00	8.00	15.00	40.00
	4	—	5.00	8.00	15.00	40.00
	5	—	7.50	12.50	25.00	60.00
	6	—	4.00	7.00	10.00	35.00
	7	—	4.00	7.00	10.00	35.00
	8	—	4.00	7.00	10.00	35.00
	9	—	4.00	7.00	10.00	35.00
	10	—	4.00	7.00	10.00	35.00
	11/10	—	4.00	7.00	10.00	35.00
	11	—	4.00	7.00	10.00	35.00
	12	—	4.00	7.00	10.00	35.00
	13	—	7.50	12.50	25.00	50.00
	14	—	5.00	8.00	15.00	45.00
	15	—	4.00	6.00	10.00	35.00
	16	—	4.00	6.00	10.00	35.00

Accession Date: AH1293
Obv: With toughra of Murad V.

G11	1	—	85.00	130.00	200.00	300.00

18a	1	—	3.00	7.50	15.00	45.00
	2	—	3.00	7.50	12.50	40.00
	3	—	3.00	7.50	12.50	40.00
	4	—	2.50	5.00	8.50	35.00
	5	—	5.00	10.00	17.50	45.00

1.35 gm.

18	10	8.192	1.25	1.75	3.00	10.00
	17	.546	1.00	2.00	5.00	15.00
	23	—	6.50	12.50	22.50	45.00
	27	.200	1.25	1.75	4.00	12.50
	29	.100	1.50	2.00	5.00	15.00
	29H	(?).100	1.25	1.75	4.00	15.00
	33H	*.100	1.25	2.00	5.00	15.00
	33H	—	—	—	Proof	60.00

*Estimated.

COPPER-NICKEL

Y#	Year	Mintage	Fine	VF	XF	Unc
17	22	.200	10.00	17.50	30.00	60.00
	23	1.500	1.00	2.00	5.00	22.50
	25	.751	1.50	3.00	10.00	35.00
	27	.999	1.00	2.00	8.50	30.00
	29	3.500	.90	1.75	5.00	25.00
	30	.500	.90	1.75	5.00	20.00
	33H	1.000	1.25	2.50	6.00	30.00

.900 SILVER
Accession Date: AH1327

Y#	Year	Mintage	Fine	VF	XF	Unc
29	2H	.251	1.75	3.50	6.50	15.00
	3H	.171	2.00	4.00	7.50	20.00

COPPER-NICKEL

Y#	Year	Mintage	Fine	VF	XF	Unc
28	2H	1.000	1.75	3.50	10.00	25.00
	3	.300	15.00	25.00	55.00	100.00
	4H	.500	2.25	4.50	12.50	35.00
	6H	2.500	1.25	2.50	5.00	20.00

2 GUERCHE

.900 SILVER, 2.75 gm.
Accession Date: AH1293

Y#	Year	Mintage	Fine	VF	XF	Unc
19	10	4.011	2.50	3.00	3.50	12.50
	11	.989	3.00	4.00	8.00	20.00
	17	.540	2.75	3.25	5.00	15.00
	20	1.113	2.75	3.50	6.00	17.50
	23	—	—	Reported, not confirmed		
	24	.500	3.00	4.00	7.50	22.50
	27	1.000	2.50	3.00	4.00	15.00
	29	.450	2.75	3.50	6.50	20.00
	29H	*1.250	2.75	3.50	5.00	20.00
	30H	Inc. Ab.	2.75	3.50	5.00	20.00
	33H	*.450	2.75	3.50	5.00	20.00

*Estimated.

NOTE: An additional 250,000 specimens are reported minted in 1905, but it is not known whether these were dated Yr. 30 or Yr. 31, the last being yet unreported.

Accession Date: AH1327

Y#	Year	Mintage	Fine	VF	XF	Unc
30	2H	.250	9.00	17.50	27.50	60.00
	3H	.300	9.00	17.50	27.50	60.00

2-1/2 GUERCHE

.900 SILVER
Accession Date: AH1277
Obv: W/o flower to right of toughra.

Y#	Year	Mintage	Fine	VF	XF	Unc
8	4	3.803	22.50	40.00	60.00	225.00

Obv: With flower to right of toughra.

Y#	Year	Mintage	Fine	VF	XF	Unc
8a	8	—	100.00	200.00	300.00	450.00
	9	—	100.00	200.00	250.00	350.00
	10	—	100.00	200.00	250.00	350.00
	11	—	—	—	Rare	—
	12	—	100.00	225.00	300.00	450.00
	13	—	100.00	225.00	300.00	450.00
	15	—	100.00	225.00	300.00	450.00

5 GUERCHE

.900 SILVER
Accession Date: AH1223

C#	Year	Mintage	VG	Fine	VF	XF
166	29	—	85.00	150.00	225.00	350.00
	30	—	85.00	150.00	225.00	350.00
	31	—	85.00	150.00	225.00	350.00

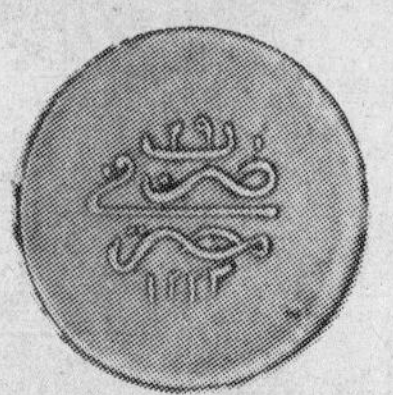

Smooth rim, modified Arabic legends.

C#	Year	Mintage	VG	Fine	VF	XF
166.1	29	—	100.00	200.00	300.00	400.00

Accession Date: AH1255

C#	Year	Mintage	VG	Fine	VF	XF
208	1	—	85.00	150.00	225.00	350.00
	2	—	100.00	200.00	325.00	450.00
	3	—	85.00	150.00	250.00	400.00
	4	—	85.00	150.00	250.00	400.00
	5	—	85.00	150.00	250.00	400.00
	6	—	85.00	150.00	250.00	400.00
	16	—	100.00	200.00	300.00	450.00

Accession Date: AH1277
Obv: W/o flower to right of toughra.

Y#	Year	Mintage	Fine	VF	XF	Unc
9	4	4.108	25.00	45.00	70.00	200.00

Rev: With regnal year retrograde

Y#	Year	Mintage	Fine	VF	XF	Unc
9.1	4	—	35.00	90.00	150.00	300.00

Obv: With flower to right of toughra.

Y#	Year	Mintage	Fine	VF	XF	Unc
9a	1	—	150.00	250.00	325.00	—
	2	—	100.00	225.00	275.00	400.00
	3	—	100.00	225.00	275.00	400.00
	4	—	110.00	225.00	275.00	400.00
	5	—	100.00	225.00	275.00	400.00
	6	—	100.00	225.00	275.00	400.00
	7	—	110.00	225.00	275.00	400.00
	8	—	100.00	225.00	275.00	400.00
	9	—	100.00	225.00	275.00	400.00
	10	—	100.00	225.00	275.00	400.00
	11	—	125.00	225.00	275.00	400.00
	12	—	150.00	275.00	350.00	500.00
	13	—	125.00	225.00	300.00	425.00
	15	—	125.00	225.00	300.00	425.00

6.92 gm.
Accession Date: AH1293

Y#	Year	Mintage	Fine	VF	XF	Unc
20	10	4.195	6.50	7.50	9.00	30.00
	11	Inc. Ab.	7.00	10.00	12.50	35.00
	15	.600	7.00	10.00	20.00	50.00
	16	1.205	6.50	7.50	9.00	30.00
	17	.872	6.50	7.50	12.50	35.00
	20	.464	8.50	17.50	35.00	80.00
	21	.633	7.00	8.00	18.50	50.00
	22	1.118	6.50	7.50	12.50	40.00
	24	1.050	6.50	7.50	12.50	40.00
	27	.448	6.50	7.50	15.00	45.00
	29	.600	6.50	7.50	12.50	30.00
	29H	*3.461	6.50	7.50	10.00	30.00
	30H	Inc. Ab.	6.50	7.50	9.00	30.00
	31H	*1.213	6.50	7.50	25.00	40.00
	32H	*1.959	6.50	7.50	9.00	30.00
	33H	*2.800	6.50	7.50	9.00	30.00

*Estimated.

Accession Date: AH1327

Y#	Year	Mintage	Fine	VF	XF	Unc
31	2H	.574	8.50	17.50	35.00	70.00
	3H	2.400	6.50	7.50	10.00	30.00
	4H	(?)1.351	6.50	8.50	13.50	40.00
	6H	7.400	6.50	7.50	10.00	28.50

10 GUERCHE

.900 SILVER
Accession Date: AH1223

C#	Year	Mintage	VG	Fine	VF	XF
167	29	—	150.00	250.00	500.00	850.00

Accession Date: AH1255

C#	Year	Mintage	Fine	VF	XF	Unc
209	1	—	125.00	200.00	300.00	600.00
	2	—	125.00	200.00	300.00	600.00
	3	—	125.00	200.00	300.00	600.00
	4	—	125.00	200.00	300.00	600.00
	5	—	125.00	200.00	300.00	600.00
	6	—	150.00	275.00	375.00	700.00
	10	—	—	Reported, not confirmed		

NOTE: Has oblique milled and straight milled edges.

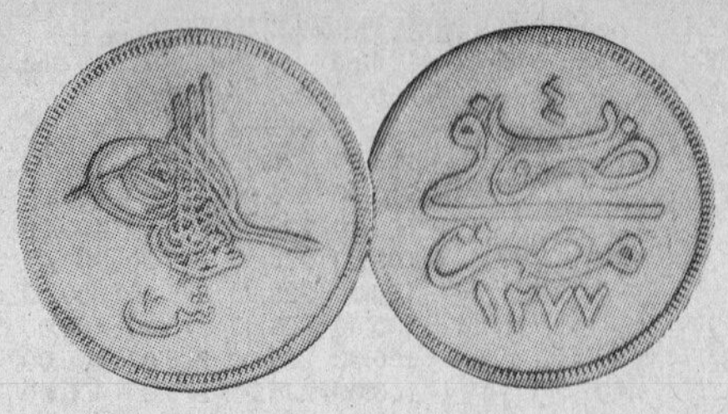

Accession Date: AH1277
Obv: W/o flower to right of toughra.

Y#	Year	Mintage	Fine	VF	XF	Unc
10	4	3.803	45.00	75.00	125.00	375.00

Y#	Year	Mintage	VG	Fine	VF	XF
10a	2	—	85.00	150.00	275.00	500.00
	3	—	100.00	250.00	375.00	600.00
	4	—	85.00	150.00	275.00	500.00
	10	—	100.00	250.00	375.00	600.00

15.27 gm.
Accession Date: AH1293

Y#	Year	Mintage	Fine	VF	XF	Unc
21	10	—	13.50	15.00	20.00	60.00
	11	—	13.50	15.00	20.00	60.00
	12	—	25.00	50.00	100.00	150.00
	15	.300	13.50	20.00	35.00	70.00
	16	.602	13.50	15.00	25.00	70.00
	17	.380	13.50	15.00	27.50	70.00
	20	.340	13.50	20.00	35.00	100.00
	21	.420	13.50	15.00	25.00	80.00
	22	.600	13.50	15.00	22.50	70.00
	24	.500	13.50	15.00	22.50	75.00
	27	.250	13.50	20.00	40.00	90.00
	29	*2.450	13.50	15.00	22.50	70.00
	29H	(?)2.450	13.50	17.50	30.00	80.00
	30H	*1.000	13.50	15.00	22.50	50.00
	31H	*1.250	13.50	18.50	35.00	75.00
	32H	(?)1.250	13.50	15.00	22.50	50.00
	33H	*2.400	13.50	15.00	20.00	50.00

NOTE: Combined mintage of years 10, 11 & 15 - 4,934,565.

*Estimated.

Accession Date: AH1327

Y#	Year	Mintage	Fine	VF	XF	Unc
32	2H	.300	13.50	20.00	35.00	100.00
	3H	1.300	13.50	13.50	22.50	50.00
	4H	.300	13.50	17.50	25.00	70.00
	6H	4.212	13.50	16.50	22.50	45.00

20 GUERCHE

.900 SILVER
Accession Date: AH1223

C#	Year	Mintage	VG	Fine	VF	XF
168	29	—	275.00	550.00	900.00	135.00
	30	—	300.00	600.00	1100.	1500.
	31	—	275.00	525.00	800.00	1150.
	32	—	300.00	600.00	1100.	1500.

Accession Date: AH1255

C#	Year	Mintage	VG	Fine	VF	XF
210	1	—	225.00	400.00	700.00	1000.
	2	—	200.00	375.00	675.00	950.00
	3	—	250.00	475.00	850.00	1100.
	4	—	200.00	375.00	675.00	950.00

Accession Date: AH1277

Y#	Year	Mintage	VG	Fine	VF	XF
11	1	—	170.00	325.00	525.00	825.00
	2	—	170.00	325.00	525.00	825.00
	4	—	225.00	425.00	625.00	1000.

Accession Date: AH1293

Y#	Year	Mintage	VG	Fine	VF	XF
22a	1	—	300.00	600.00	950.00	1600.
	5	—	275.00	550.00	900.00	1350.

27.25 gm.

Y#	Year	Mintage	Fine	VF	XF	Unc
22	10	.874	22.50	25.00	35.00	175.00
	11	.126	22.50	25.00	45.00	175.00
	15	.029	22.50	30.00	55.00	200.00
	16	.055	22.50	25.00	50.00	200.00
	17	.054	22.50	25.00	55.00	200.00
	20	.172	22.50	25.00	40.00	175.00
	21	.158	22.50	25.00	40.00	175.00
	22	.287	22.50	25.00	37.50	175.00
	24	.500	22.50	25.00	40.00	200.00
	27	.250	22.50	30.00	60.00	200.00
	29	.500	22.50	25.00	40.00	175.00
	29H	*.425	22.50	25.00	50.00	175.00
	30H	Inc. Ab.	22.50	25.00	40.00	175.00
	31H	*.200	22.50	25.00	45.00	175.00
	32H	*.250	22.50	25.00	40.00	175.00
	33H	*.300	22.50	25.00	35.00	150.00

*Estimated.

Accession Date: AH1327

Y#	Year	Mintage	Fine	VF	XF	Unc
33	2H	.075	22.50	30.00	50.00	175.00
	3H	.600	22.50	25.00	35.00	125.00
	4H	.100	22.50	25.00	40.00	175.00
	6H	.875	22.50	25.00	30.00	100.00

GOLD COINS

NOTE: The following listings are incomplete, and information, additional dates & types would be appreciated.

Pre-reform issues of Mahmud II

Prior to AH1251 (1834AD)

The basic unit was the 'Mahbub' or 'Zer Mahbub' (Zer - Gold), which weighed approximately 2.35 gr. from AH 1223 until 1247 (Yr. 15), when it was reduced to about 1.6 gr. Fractional denominations were Halves (Nisfiya) and Quaters (Rubiya). The value of the Mahbub in terms of silver Piastres fluctuated according to the relative values of gold and silver, and the price of debased Egyptian silver coin.

1/4 MAHBUB (RUBIYA)

.875 GOLD, 14mm, 0.58gm.
Accession Date: AH1223
Plain borders of dots

C#	Year	Mintage	VG	Fine	VF	XF
118	8	—	20.00	30.00	40.00	55.00
	10	—	20.00	30.00	40.00	55.00
	13	—	20.00	30.00	40.00	55.00
	14	—	20.00	30.00	40.00	55.00

12-13mm, 0.35-0.40gm.

Plain borders of dots.

C#	Year	Mintage	VG	Fine	VF	XF
128	15	—	20.00	30.00	40.00	55.00
	16	—	20.00	30.00	40.00	55.00
	17	—	20.00	30.00	40.00	55.00
	18	—	20.00	30.00	40.00	55.00

Ornamental borders

C#	Year	Mintage	VG	Fine	VF	XF
129	19	—	30.00	40.00	55.00	70.00
	20	—	30.00	40.00	55.00	70.00
	21	—	30.00	40.00	55.00	70.00

Vinelike borders

C#	Year	Mintage	VG	Fine	VF	XF
137	21	—	25.00	35.00	50.00	70.00
	22	—	25.00	35.00	50.00	70.00
	23	—	25.00	35.00	50.00	70.00
	24	—	25.00	35.00	50.00	70.00
	25	—	25.00	35.00	50.00	70.00
	26	—	25.00	35.00	50.00	70.00
	27	—	25.00	35.00	50.00	70.00

1/2 MAHBUB (NISFIYA)

.875 GOLD, 19-20mm., 1.15-1.2gm.
Accession Date: AH1223

C#	Year	Mintage	VG	Fine	VF	XF
119	1	—	32.50	40.00	60.00	80.00
	5	—	32.50	40.00	60.00	80.00
	8	—	32.50	40.00	60.00	80.00

1/2 KHAYRIYA

(=1/2 MAHBUB)

.875 GOLD, 16mm., 0.76-0.80gm.
Accession Date: AH1223

C#	Year	Mintage	VG	Fine	VF	XF
138	21	—	20.00	30.00	45.00	60.00
	22	—	20.00	30.00	45.00	60.00
	23	—	20.00	30.00	45.00	60.00
	24	—	20.00	30.00	45.00	60.00
	25	—	20.00	30.00	45.00	60.00
	26	—	20.00	30.00	45.00	60.00
	27	—	20.00	30.00	45.00	60.00
	28	—	20.00	30.00	45.00	60.00

MAHBUB (ALTIN)

.875 GOLD, 25-26mm., 2.35gm., crude flan
Accession Date: AH1223

C#	Year	Mintage	VG	Fine	VF	XF
120	1	—	55.00	65.00	80.00	100.00
	3	—	55.00	65.00	80.00	100.00
	5	—	55.00	65.00	80.00	100.00
	11	—	55.00	65.00	80.00	100.00
	14	—	55.00	65.00	80.00	100.00

23mm., 2.35gm., thicker & well-shaped flan

C#	Year	Mintage	VG	Fine	VF	XF
120a	15	—	60.00	80.00	100.00	125.00

Without "AZZA NASHRUHU"

C#	Year	Mintage	VG	Fine	VF	XF
120.1	5	—	70.00	100.00	150.00	200.00

2 MAHBUB

.875 GOLD, 28mm., 3.60gm.
Accession Date: AH1223

C#	Year	Mintage	VG	Fine	VF	XF
126	5	—	—	—	—	—

NOTE: The above piece may be a medal or token.

REFORMED COINAGE

AH1251-1326/1834-1908AD

5 GUERCHE (PIASTRES)

Rubiya, or 1/4 Mastriya

.875 GOLD, 0.42 gm.
Accession Date: AH1223

C#	Year	Mintage	VG	Fine	VF	XF
151	29	—	60.00	100.00	125.00	160.00

Obv: Without value below toughra.

C#	Year	Mintage	VG	Fine	VF	XF
169	29	—	60.00	100.00	125.00	160.00

Obv: Denomination added beneath toughra.

C#	Year	Mintage	VG	Fine	VF	XF
169a	30	—	40.00	60.00	80.00	100.00
	32	—	40.00	60.00	80.00	100.00

Accession Date: AH1255

C#	Year	Mintage	VG	Fine	VF	XF
211	1	—	18.50	30.00	40.00	50.00
	2	—	18.50	30.00	40.00	50.00
	3	—	18.50	30.00	40.00	50.00
	4	—	18.50	30.00	40.00	50.00
	5	—	18.50	30.00	40.00	50.00
	6	—	18.50	30.00	40.00	50.00
	7	—	18.50	30.00	40.00	50.00
	8	—	18.50	30.00	40.00	50.00
	9	—	18.50	30.00	40.00	50.00
	10	—	18.50	30.00	40.00	50.00
	11	—	18.50	30.00	40.00	50.00
	12	—	18.50	30.00	40.00	50.00
	13	—	18.50	30.00	40.00	50.00
	14	—	18.50	30.00	40.00	50.00
	15	—	18.50	30.00	40.00	50.00
	16	—	18.50	30.00	40.00	50.00
	18	—	18.50	30.00	40.00	50.00
	19	—	18.50	30.00	40.00	50.00
	20	—	18.50	30.00	40.00	50.00
	22	—	18.50	30.00	40.00	50.00
	23	—	18.50	30.00	40.00	50.00

Accession Date: AH1277

Y#	Year	Mintage	VG	Fine	VF	XF
A11	3	—	16.50	25.00	35.00	45.00
	4	—	16.50	25.00	35.00	45.00
	5	—	16.50	25.00	35.00	45.00
	6	—	16.50	25.00	35.00	45.00
	7	—	16.50	25.00	35.00	45.00
	8	—	16.50	25.00	35.00	45.00
	9	—	16.50	25.00	35.00	45.00
	10	—	16.50	25.00	35.00	45.00
	11	—	—	—	—	—
	12	—	16.50	25.00	35.00	45.00
	13	—	16.50	25.00	35.00	45.00
	14	—	16.50	25.00	35.00	45.00
	15	—	16.50	25.00	35.00	45.00

Accession Date: AH1293
Obv: Flower to right of toughra.

Y#	Year	Mintage	VG	Fine	VF	XF
A22	2	—	—	Reported, not confirmed		
	3	—	—	—	—	—
	5	—	30.00	60.00	100.00	150.00
	7	—	—	—	—	—

Obv: AL-GHAZI to right of toughra.

Y#	Year	Mintage	VG	Fine	VF	XF
A22a	6	—	—	—	—	—
	16	—	—	—	—	—
	18	—	16.50	22.50	30.00	40.00
	24	—	20.00	30.00	40.00	60.00
	34	.008	20.00	30.00	40.00	60.00

10 GUERCHE (PIASTRES)

(= Nousf, or 1/2 masriya)

.875 GOLD, .85 gm.
Accession Date: AH1223

C#	Year	Mintage	VG	Fine	VF	XF
152	28	—	30.00	50.00	70.00	100.00
	29	—	30.00	50.00	70.00	100.00

Obv: Denomination added beneath toughra.

C#	Year	Mintage	VG	Fine	VF	XF
170	29	—	50.00	100.00	130.00	175.00
	30	—	50.00	100.00	130.00	175.00

Accession Date: AH1277

Y#	Year	Mintage	VG	Fine	VF	XF
B11	10	—	25.00	40.00	55.00	75.00
	11	—	25.00	40.00	55.00	75.00
	12	—	25.00	40.00	55.00	75.00
	14	—	25.00	40.00	55.00	75.00

Accession Date: AH1293
Obv: AL-GHAZI to right of toughra.

Y#	Year	Mintage	VG	Fine	VF	XF
B22	17	—	—	—	—	—
	18	—	16.50	22.50	30.00	40.00
	23	—	—	—	—	—
	34	.005	17.50	30.00	40.00	55.00

20 GUERCHE
(= Masriya)

.875 GOLD, 1.70 gm.
Accession Date: AH1223

C#	Year	Mintage	VG	Fine	VF	XF
171	30	—	50.00	75.00	110.00	150.00
171a	32	—	—	—	—	—
	31	—	50.00	75.00	110.00	150.00
	32	—	50.00	75.00	110.00	150.00

Obv and rev: 4 flowers around edge.

Accession Date: AH1255

C#	Year	Mintage	VG	Fine	VF	XF
213	1	—	45.00	85.00	125.00	175.00

25 GUERCHE
(= 1/4 Egyptian Pound)

.875 GOLD, 2.10 gm.
Accession Date: AH1277

Y#	Year	Mintage	VG	Fine	VF	XF
C11	8	—	45.00	55.00	70.00	85.00
	10	—	45.00	55.00	70.00	85.00
	11	—	45.00	55.00	70.00	85.00
	12	—	45.00	55.00	70.00	85.00
	13	—	45.00	55.00	70.00	85.00
	15	—	45.00	55.00	70.00	85.00

NOTE: Yr. 4 is believed to be a pattern.

50 GUERCHE
(= 1/2 Egyptian Pound)

.875 GOLD, 4.20 gm.
Accession Date: AH1255

C#	Year	Mintage	VG	Fine	VF	XF
214	4	—	Reported, not confirmed			
	5	—	85.00	100.00	130.00	160.00
	11	—	85.00	100.00	130.00	160.00
	15	—	85.00	100.00	130.00	160.00
	16	—	85.00	100.00	130.00	160.00

Accession Date: AH1277

Y#	Year	Mintage	VG	Fine	VF	XF
D11	11	—	85.00	100.00	120.00	150.00
	13	—	—	—	—	—
	14	—	—	Reported, not confirmed		
	15	—	85.00	100.00	120.00	150.00
	16	—	85.00	100.00	120.00	150.00

NOTE: Yr. 4 is believed to be a pattern.

Accession Date: AH1277
Obv: Toughra of Murad V without flower

Y#	Year	Mintage	VG	Fine	VF	XF
H11	1	—	—	—	Rare	—

Accession Date: AH1293

Y#	Year	Mintage	VG	Fine	VF	XF
C22	1	—	85.00	110.00	150.00	200.00
	2	—	—	Reported, not confirmed		

100 GUERCHE
(= 1 Egyptian Pound)

.875 GOLD, 8.40 gm.

Accession Date: AH1223

C#	Year	Mintage	VG	Fine	VF	XF
172	30	—	—	—	Rare	—
	31	—	—	—	Rare	—

Accession Date: AH1255

C#	Year	Mintage	VG	Fine	VF	XF
215	1	—	150.00	165.00	185.00	225.00
	3	—	150.00	165.00	185.00	225.00
	4	—	150.00	165.00	185.00	225.00
	5	—	150.00	165.00	185.00	225.00
	6	—	150.00	165.00	185.00	225.00
	7	—	150.00	165.00	185.00	225.00
	8	—	150.00	165.00	185.00	225.00
	9	—	150.00	165.00	185.00	225.00
	10	—	150.00	165.00	185.00	225.00
	12	—	150.00	165.00	185.00	225.00
	13	—	150.00	165.00	185.00	225.00
	14	—	150.00	165.00	185.00	225.00
	15	—	150.00	165.00	185.00	225.00
	16	—	150.00	165.00	185.00	225.00
	17	—	150.00	165.00	185.00	225.00
	18	—	150.00	165.00	185.00	225.00

NOTE: For year 2 see Sudan Y#3.

Accession Date: AH1277

Y#	Year	Mintage	VG	Fine	VF	XF
E11	1	—	150.00	165.00	185.00	225.00
	5	—	150.00	165.00	185.00	225.00
	6	—	150.00	165.00	185.00	225.00
	7	—	150.00	165.00	185.00	225.00
	8	—	150.00	165.00	185.00	225.00
	9	—	150.00	165.00	185.00	225.00
	10	—	150.00	165.00	185.00	225.00
	11	—	150.00	165.00	185.00	225.00
	12	—	150.00	165.00	185.00	225.00
	13	—	150.00	165.00	185.00	225.00
	14	—	150.00	165.00	185.00	225.00
	15	—	150.00	165.00	185.00	225.00
	16	—	150.00	165.00	185.00	225.00

Obv: W/o flower to right of toughra.

Y#	Year	Mintage	VG	Fine	VF	XF
A10	4	—	—	—	Rare	—

Accession Date: AH1293
Obv: Toughra of Murad V.

Y#	Year	Mintage	VG	Fine	VF	XF
J11	1	—	165.00	225.00	300.00	400.00

Obv: Toughra of Abdul Hamid II.

Y#	Year	Mintage	Fine	VF	XF	Unc
D22	1	—	150.00	165.00	185.00	250.00
	8	—	150.00	165.00	185.00	250.00

With floral border

Y#	Year	Mintage	Fine	VF	XF	Unc
F22	12	.052	150.00	160.00	180.00	200.00

500 GUERCHE
(= 5 Egyptian Pounds)

.875 GOLD, 42 gm.
Accession Date: AH1277

Y#	Year	Mintage	Fine	VF	XF	Unc
F11	8	—	4250.	4850.	5500.	6500.
	9	—	4250.	4850.	5500.	6500.
	11	—	4250.	4850.	5500.	6500.
	13	—	4250.	4850.	5500.	6500.
	15	—	4250.	4850.	5500.	6500.

Accession Date: AH1293

Y#	Year	Mintage	Fine	VF	XF	Unc
E22	1	—	4350.	5000.	6000.	7500.
	6	—	4350.	5000.	6000.	7500.

MONETARY REFORM

1/2 MILLIEME

BRONZE

Y#	Date	Year	Mintage	VF	XF	Unc
34	AH 1335	1917	4.000	5.00	7.50	15.00

Y#	Date	Year	Mintage	VF	XF	Unc
47	AH 1342	1924H	3.000	5.00	7.50	15.00

Y#	Date	Year	Mintage	VF	XF	Unc
60	AH 1348	1929BP	1.000	10.00	15.00	30.00
	1351	1932H	2.000	5.00	10.00	20.00

Y#	Date	Year	Mintage	VF	XF	Unc
74	AH 1357	1938	4.000	2.50	5.00	10.00

MILLIEME

COPPER-NICKEL

Y#	Date	Year	Mintage	VF	XF	Unc
35	AH 1335	1917	4.000	1.00	3.00	12.50
	1335	1917H	12.000	1.00	2.50	8.50

BRONZE

Y#	Date	Year	Mintage	VF	XF	Unc
48	AH 1342	1924H	3.000	1.00	2.50	15.00

Y#	Date	Year	Mintage	VF	XF	Unc
61	AH 1348	1929BP	4.500	5.00	8.50	20.00
	1351	1932H	5.000	1.25	2.25	6.50
	1352	1933H	5.110	2.00	4.00	8.50
	1354	1935H	18.000	.50	1.00	4.50

Y#	Date	Year	Mintage	VF	XF	Unc
75	AH 1357	1938	9.180	.30	.50	1.00
	1357	1938	—	—	Proof	45.00
	1364	1945	10.000	.45	1.20	2.00
	1366	1947	—	.60	1.20	2.00
	1369	1950	5.000	.40	1.00	1.50

COPPER-NICKEL

Y#	Date	Year	Mintage	VF	XF	Unc
79	AH 1357	1938	1.520	2.00	4.00	10.00

ALUMINUM-BRONZE

Obv: Small sphinx with outlined base.

Y#	Date	Year	Mintage	VF	XF	Unc
92	AH 1373	1954	—	—	.50	1.25
	1374	1954	—	—	.50	1.00
	1374	1955	—	—	—	—
	1375	1955	—	—	—	—
	1375	1956	—	—	—	—

Obv: Small sphinx without base outlined.

Y#	Date	Year	Mintage	VF	XF	Unc
92.1	AH 1374	1955	—	—	.40	.90
	1375	1955	—	—	.25	.65
	1375	1956	—	—	.20	1.25

Obv: Large sphinx.

Y#	Date	Year	Mintage	VF	XF	Unc
92a	AH 1375	1956	—	—	.30	.65
	1376	1957	—	—	.30	.65
	1377	1958	—	—	.25	.65

Y#	Date	Year	Mintage	VF	XF	Unc
111	AH 1380	1960	—	—	—	.25
	1386	1966	—	—	Proof	2.00

ALUMINUM

Y#	Date	Year	Mintage	VF	XF	Unc
157	AH 1392	1972	—	—	.30	.50

2 MILLIEMES

COPPER-NICKEL

Y#	Date	Year	Mintage	VF	XF	Unc
36	AH 1335	1916H	3.300	2.00	5.00	15.00
	1335	1917	2.706	1.00	2.50	12.00
	1335	1917H	6.000	.75	2.50	12.00

Y#	Date	Year	Mintage	VF	XF	Unc
49	AH 1342	1924H	4.500	1.00	3.00	15.00
	1342	1924H	—	—	Proof	60.00

Y#	Date	Year	Mintage	VF	XF	Unc
62	AH1348	1929BP	3.500?	.50	1.50	7.50

Y#	Date	Year	Mintage	VF	XF	Unc
80	AH 1357	1938	2.500	1.00	2.50	10.00

ALUMINUM-BRONZE

Y#	Date	Year	Mintage	VF	XF	Unc
112	AH 1381	1962	—	.10	.30	.50
	1386	1966	—	—	Proof	2.00

2-1/2 MILLIEMES

COPPER-NICKEL

Y#	Date	Year	Mintage	VF	XF	Unc
63	AH 1352	1933	4.000	1.25	2.25	12.50

5 MILLIEMES

COPPER-NICKEL

Y#	Date	Year	Mintage	VF	XF	Unc
37	AH 1335	1916	3.000	1.50	3.00	15.00
	1335	1916H	3.000	1.50	3.00	15.00
	1335	1917	6.776	.75	2.00	10.00
	1335	1917H	37.000	.75	1.75	8.00

Y#	Date	Year	Mintage	VF	XF	Unc
50	AH 1342	1924	6.000	1.00	3.00	15.00

Y#	Date	Year	Mintage	VF	XF	Unc
64	AH 1348	1929BP	4.000	.75	3.00	12.50
	1352	1933H	3.000	1.00	3.00	12.50
	1354	1935H	8.000	.60	1.50	6.00

BRONZE

Y#	Date	Year	Mintage	VF	XF	Unc
77	AH 1357	1938	—	.40	.75	1.50
	1357	1938	—	—	Proof	35.00
	1362	1943	—	.40	.75	1.50

COPPER-NICKEL

Y#	Date	Year	Mintage	VF	XF	Unc
81	AH 1357	1938	5.400	—	.50	1.50
	1360	1941	—	—	.50	1.50

ALUMINUM-BRONZE

Obv: Small sphinx

Y#	Date	Year	Mintage	VF	XF	Unc
93	AH 1373	1954	—	.75	2.00	7.00
	1374	1954	—	.60	1.25	5.00
	1374	1955	—	.25	1.00	5.00
	1375	1956	—	.25	1.00	5.00

Obv: Large sphinx

Y#	Date	Year	Mintage	VF	XF	Unc
93a	AH 1376	1957	—	.25	.50	4.50
	1377	1957	—	.25	.50	4.50
	1377	1958	—	.25	.50	4.50

Y#	Date	Year	Mintage	VF	XF	Unc
113	AH 1380	1960	—	.10	.30	.60
	1386	1966	—	—	Proof	2.00

ALUMINUM

Y#	Date	Year	Mintage	VF	XF	Unc
113a	AH 1386	1967	—	.10	.30	.50

F.A.O. Issue

Y#	Date	Year	Mintage	VF	XF	Unc
144	AH 1393	1973	10.000	.10	.30	.50

BRASS, 18mm

Y#	Date	Year	Mintage	VF	XF	Unc
141	AH 1393	1973	—	—	.15	.35

Mule: Y#153 and 141

Y#	Date	Year	Mintage	VF	XF	Unc
141.1	AH 1393	1973	—	—	—	—

ALUMINUM, 21mm

Y#	Date	Year	Mintage	VF	XF	Unc
141a	AH 1392	1972	(Issued 1975)		.25	.75

Mule: Y#144 and 141a

Y#	Date	Year	Mintage	VF	XF	Unc
141a.1	AH 1392	1972	—	—	—	—

BRASS, 18mm
I.W.Y. Commemorative

Y#	Date	Year	Mintage	VF	XF	Unc
153	AH 1395	1975	10.000	—	.15	.35

F.A.O. Issue

Y#	Date	Year	Mintage	VF	XF	Unc
179	AH 1397	1977	10.000	.10	.20	.40

1971 Corrective Revolution

Y#	Date	Year	Mintage	VF	XF	Unc
172	AH 1397	1977	—	.10	.20	.40

10 MILLIEMES

COPPER-NICKEL

Y#	Date	Year	Mintage	VF	XF	Unc
38	AH 1335	1916	1.007	2.00	4.50	17.50
	1335	1916H	1.000	2.00	4.50	20.00
	1335	1917	1.011	7.50	12.50	25.00
	1335	1917H	11.000	1.00	2.00	10.00
	1335	1917KN	4.000	1.00	2.50	15.00

Y#	Date	Year	Mintage	VF	XF	Unc
51	AH 1342	1924	2.000	2.00	5.00	25.00

Y#	Date	Year	Mintage	VF	XF	Unc
65	AH 1348	1929BP	1.500	1.00	3.00	20.00
	1352	1933H	1.500	1.00	2.00	15.00
	1354	1935H	4.000	.40	.75	7.50

BRONZE

Y#	Date	Year	Mintage	VF	XF	Unc
78	AH 1357	1938	—	.25	.50	1.00
	1357	1938	—	—	Proof	35.00
	1362	1943	—	.40	.50	1.00

COPPER-NICKEL

Y#	Date	Year	Mintage	VF	XF	Unc
82	AH 1357	1938	3.248	—	.35	1.00
	1360	1941	—	—	.35	1.00

ALUMINUM-BRONZE
Obv: Small sphinx

Y#	Date	Year	Mintage	VF	XF	Unc
94	AH 1373	1954	—	—	1.50	7.50
	1374	1954	—	—	1.50	7.50
	1374	1955	—	—	1.00	7.50

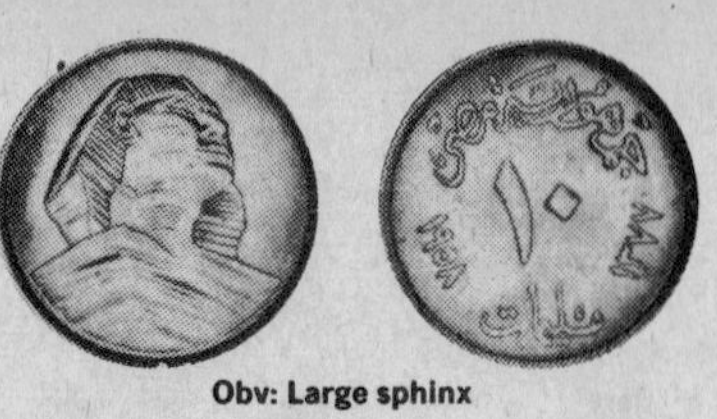

Obv: Large sphinx

Y#	Date	Year	Mintage	VF	XF	Unc
94a	AH 1374	1955	—	—	.80	5.00
	1375	1956	—	—	.60	5.00
	1376	1957	—	—	.50	4.50
	1377	1958	—	—	.50	4.00

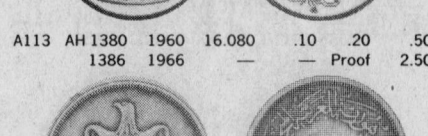

Y#	Date	Year	Mintage	VF	XF	Unc
A113	AH 1380	1960	16.080	.10	.20	.50
	1386	1966	—	—	Proof	2.50

Without "Misr" above denomination

Y#	Date	Year	Mintage	VF	XF	Unc
A113.1	AH 1377	1958	—	20.00	—	—

With "Misr" above denomination

Y#	Date	Year	Mintage	VF	XF	Unc
A113.2	AH 1377	1958	—	20.00	—	—
	1380	1960	—	20.00	—	—

ALUMINUM

Y#	Date	Year	Mintage	VF	XF	Unc
A113a	AH 1386	1967	—	—	.15	.45

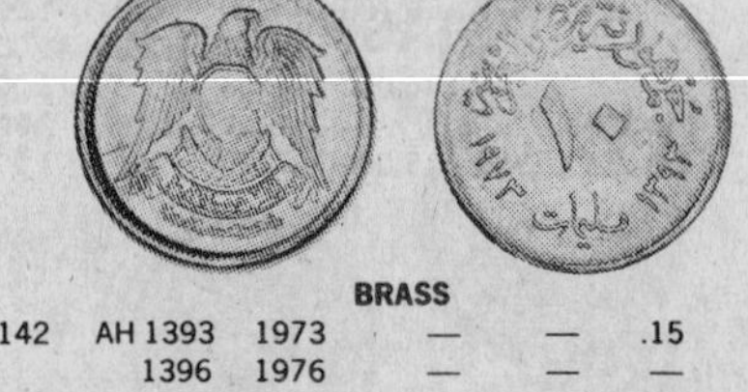

BRASS

Y#	Date	Year	Mintage	VF	XF	Unc
142	AH 1393	1973	—	—	.15	.35
	1396	1976	—	—	—	—

ALUMINUM, 23mm

Y#	Date	Year	Mintage	VF	XF	Unc
142a	AH1392	1972	(Issued 1975)		.25	.60

NOTE: Edge varieties exist.

BRASS, 21mm
F.A.O. Issue

Y#	Date	Year	Mintage	VF	XF	Unc
154	AH1395	1975	10.000	.10	.20	.30

F.A.O. Issue

Y#	Date	Year	Mintage	VF	XF	Unc
160	AH1396	1976	10.000	.10	.20	.30

F.A.O. Issue

Y#	Date	Year	Mintage	VF	XF	Unc
180	AH1397	1977	10.000	.10	.20	.80

1971 Corrective Revolution

Y#	Date	Year	Mintage	VF	XF	Unc
173	AH 1397	1977	—	.10	.20	.50
	1399	1979	—	—	—	1.00

F.A.O. Issue

Y#	Date	Year	Mintage	VF	XF	Unc
189	AH 1398	1978	2.000	.10	.20	.90

International Year of the Child

Y#	Date	Year	Mintage	VF	XF	Unc
194	AH1399	1979	2,000	—	.25	.60

2 PIASTRES

2.8000 gm., .833 SILVER, .0749 oz ASW

Y#	Date	Year	Mintage	VF	XF	Unc
39	AH 1335	1916	2.505	2.50	4.00	17.50
	1335	1917	4.461	2.50	4.00	15.00
	1335	1917H	2.180	2.50	4.00	17.50

Y#	Date	Year	Mintage	VF	XF	Unc
44	AH 1338	1920H	2.820	65.00	90.00	300.00

Y#	Date	Year	Mintage	VF	XF	Unc
52	AH 1342	1923H	2.500	2.50	5.00	10.00

Y#	Date	Year	Mintage	VF	XF	Unc
66	AH 1348	1929BP	.500	2.50	4.00	10.00

NOTE: Edge varieties exist.

Y#	Date	Year	Mintage	VF	XF	Unc
83	AH 1356	1937	.500	2.50	3.50	6.00
	1358	1939	.500	3.00	5.00	10.00
	1361	1942	10.000	2.50	3.50	6.00
	?	1948	Reported, Not Confirmed			

2.8000 gm., .500 SILVER, .0450 oz ASW

Y#	Date	Year	Mintage	VF	XF	Unc
87	AH 1363	1944	31,586	BV	1.50	3.00

20 MILLIEMES

ALUMINUM-BRONZE
Agriculture and Industrial Fair

Y#	Date	Year	Mintage	VF	XF	Unc
105	AH 1378	1958	—	.70	1.50	6.00

5 PIASTRES

7.0000 gm., .833 SILVER, .1874 oz ASW

Y#	Date	Year	Mintage	VF	XF	Unc
40	AH 1335	1916	6.000	BV	10.00	30.00
	1335	1917	8.518	BV	7.50	25.00
	1335	1917H	5.000	BV	12.50	30.00

Y#	Date	Year	Mintage	VF	XF	Unc
45	AH 1338	1920H	1.000	40.00	70.00	175.00

Y#	Date	Year	Mintage	VF	XF	Unc
53	AH 1341	1923	.800	7.50	10.00	32.50
	1341	1923H	1.800	BV	7.50	30.00

Y#	Date	Year	Mintage	VF	XF	Unc
67	AH 1348	1929BP	.800	BV	10.00	22.50
	1352	1933	1.300	BV	7.50	20.00

Y#	Date	Year	Mintage	VF	XF	Unc
84	AH 1356	1937	—	BV	6.50	10.00
	1358	1939	8.000	BV	6.50	10.00

3.5000 gm., .720 SILVER, .0810 oz ASW

Y#	Date	Year	Mintage	VF	XF	Unc
95	1375	1956	—	BV	2.75	4.00
	1376	1956	—	BV	2.75	4.00
	1376	1957	—	BV	2.75	4.00

Y#	Date	Year	Mintage	VF	XF	Unc
114	AH 1380	1960	—	BV	2.75	3.50
	1386	1966	—	—	Proof	5.00

2.5000 gm., .720 SILVER, .0578 oz ASW
Diversion of the Nile

Y#	Date	Year	Mintage	VF	XF	Unc
117	AH 1384	1964	.500	BV	2.00	2.75
	1384	1964	2,000	—	Proof	4.50

COPPER-NICKEL

Y#	Date	Year	Mintage	VF	XF	Unc
123	AH 1387	1967	—	.75	1.00	1.50

International Fair

Y#	Date	Year	Mintage	VF	XF	Unc
125	AH 1388	1968	.500	.70	.90	2.25

Handicraft Fair

Y#	Date	Year	Mintage	VF	XF	Unc
131	AH 1389	1969	.500	.70	.90	2.25

UNICEF 25th Anniversary

Y#	Date	Year	Mintage	VF	XF	Unc
139	AH 1392	1972	.500	.60	.80	2.25

NOTE: Error in spelling "UNICFE"

Obv: Islamic falcon

Y#	Date	Year	Mintage	VF	XF	Unc
158	AH 1392	1972	—	.60	.75	2.00
	1396	1976	—	—	—	—

Cairo State Fair

Y#	Date	Year	Mintage	VF	XF	Unc
143	AH 1393	1973	.500	.60	.75	2.25

National Bank of Egypt 75th Anniversary

Y#	Date	Year	Mintage	VF	XF	Unc
146	AH 1393	1973	1.000	.60	.75	2.00

1st Anniversary October War

Y#	Date	Year	Mintage	VF	XF	Unc
150	AH 1394	1974	2.000	.60	.75	2.00

International Woman's Year

Y#	Date	Year	Mintage	VF	XF	Unc
155	AH 1395	1975	2.000	.50	.65	1.75

1976 Cairo Trade Fair

Y#	Date	Year	Mintage	VF	XF	Unc
162	AH 1396	1976	.500	.60	.75	2.00

1971 Corrective Revolution

Y#	Date	Year	Mintage	VF	XF	Unc
174	AH 1397	1977	—	—	—	1.50
	1399	1979	—	—	—	1.25

50th Anniversary of Textile Industry

Y#	Date	Year	Mintage	VF	XF	Unc
184	AH 1397	1977	1.000	.75	1.00	1.75

F.A.O. Issue

Y#	Date	Year	Mintage	VF	XF	Unc
181	AH 1397	1977	—	.75	1.00	1.75

Portland Cement

Y#	Date	Year	Mintage	VF	XF	Unc
187	AH1398	1978	—	.75	1.00	1.75

F.A.O. Issue

Y#	Date	Year	Mintage	VF	XF	Unc
190	AH1398	1978	1.000	.75	1.00	1.75

International Year of the Child

Y#	Date	Year	Mintage	VF	XF	Unc
195	AH1399	1979	1.000	—	—	—

10 PIASTRES

14.0000 gm., .833 SILVER, .3749 oz ASW

Y#	Date	Year	Mintage	VF	XF	Unc
41	AH 1335	1916	2.900	12.00	17.50	55.00
	1335	1917	4.859	12.00	17.50	45.00
	1335	1917H	2.000	15.00	22.50	85.00

Y#	Date	Year	Mintage	VF	XF	Unc
46	AH 1338	1920H	.500	32.50	70.00	150.00

Y#	Date	Year	Mintage	VF	XF	Unc
54	AH 1341	1923	.400	12.50	17.50	55.00
	1341	1923H	1.000	12.50	17.50	55.00

Rev: Similar to Y#54

Y#	Date	Year	Mintage	VF	XF	Unc
68	AH 1348	1929BP	.400	12.50	17.50	55.00
	1352	1933	.350(?)	12.50	17.50	35.00

Y#	Date	Year	Mintage	VF	XF	Unc
85	AH 1356	1937	2.800	BV	12.00	15.00
	1358	1939	2.850	BV	12.00	15.00

7.0000 gm., .625 SILVER, .1406 oz ASW

Y#	Date	Year	Mintage	VF	XF	Unc
96	AH 1374	1955	1.408	BV	4.50	7.50

NOTE: Varieties in date sizes exist.

7.000 gm., .720 SILVER, .1620 oz ASW

96a	1375	1956	—	BV	5.25	7.00
	1376	1957	—	BV	5.00	6.00

U.A.R. Founding

107	AH 1378	1959	—	BV	5.50	12.00

115	AH 1380	1960	.500	BV	5.00	7.50
	1386	1966	—	—	Proof	10.00

5.0000 gm., .720 SILVER, .1157 oz ASW
Diversion Of The Nile

118	AH 1384	1964	.500	BV	4.00	6.00
	1384	1964	2,000	—	Proof	7.50

COPPER-NICKEL

124	AH 1387	1967	—	.60	.90	3.50

F.A.O. Issue

128	AH 1390	1970	.500	.75	1.25	3.50

Cairo International Fair

129	AH 1389	1969	1.000	.75	1.25	3.00

Banque Misr 50 Years

Y#	Date	Year	Mintage	VF	XF	Unc
132	AH 1390	1970	.500	.75	1.25	3.00

Workers' Congress

133	AH 1390	1970	.500	.75	1.25	3.00

New shorter Arabic inscriptions

133a	AH 1391	1971	.500	.75	1.25	2.75

Cairo State Fair

140	AH 1392	1972	.500	.75	1.25	2.75

Obv: Islamic falcon

159	AH 1392	1972	—	.75	1.00	2.25

Mule: Y#159 and 163

159.1	AH 1392	1972	—	1.50	2.50	7.50

First Anniversary October War

151	AH 1394	1974	2.000	.75	1.00	2.50

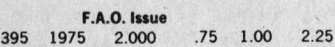

F.A.O. Issue

156	AH 1395	1975	2.000	.75	1.00	2.25

Reopening of the Suez Canal

Y#	Date	Year	Mintage	VF	XF	Unc
163	AH1396	1976	.500	.75	1.00	3.25

F.A.O. Issue

182	AH1397	1977	1.000	.75	1.00	2.25

1971 Corrective Revolution

175	AH1397	1977	—	.75	1.00	2.25
	1399	1979	—	—	—	1.75

20th Anniversary Economic Union

177	AH1397	1977	—	—	—	2.50

Cairo Fair

185	AH1398	1978	—	—	—	2.50

25th Anniversary of Abbasia Mint

192	AH1399	1979	—	—	—	2.50

National Education Day

197	AH1399	1979	—	—	—	2.00

20 PIASTRES

28.0000 gm., .833 SILVER, .7499 oz ASW

Y#	Date	Year	Mintage	VF	XF	Unc
42	AH 1335	1916	1.500	25.00	35.00	100.00
	1335	1917	.840	25.00	40.00	100.00
	1335	1917	—	—	Proof	675.00
	1335	1917H	.250	40.00	65.00	175.00

NOTE: Restrikes exist.

Y#	Date	Year	Mintage	VF	XF	Unc
55	AH 1341	1923	.100	25.00	40.00	125.00
	1341	1923H	.050	25.00	40.00	125.00

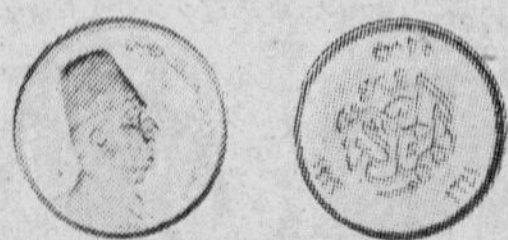

1.7000 gm., .875 GOLD, .0478 oz AGW

Y#	Date	Year	Mintage	VF	XF	Unc
56	AH 1341	1923	.065	40.00	65.00	90.00

Obv: Bust left.

Y#	Date	Year	Mintage	VF	XF	Unc
70	AH 1348	1929	—	40.00	65.00	90.00
	1349	1930	—	40.00	65.00	90.00

28.0000 gm., .833 SILVER, .7499 oz ASW
Rev: Similar to Y#55

Y#	Date	Year	Mintage	VF	XF	Unc
69	AH 1348	1929BP	.050	25.00	35.00	95.00
	1352	1933	.025	25.00	30.00	85.00

Y#	Date	Year	Mintage	VF	XF	Unc
86	AH 1356	1937	—	25.00	30.00	55.00
	1358	1939	—	25.00	30.00	55.00

1.7000 gm., .875 GOLD, .0478 oz AGW
Royal Wedding

Y#	Date	Year	Mintage	VF	XF	Unc
88	AH 1357	1938	.020	40.00	65.00	90.00
	1357	1938	—	—	Proof	120.00

14.0000 gm., .720 SILVER, .3241 oz ASW

Y#	Date	Year	Mintage	VF	XF	Unc
97	AH 1375	1956	—	BV	11.00	12.50

Y#	Date	Year	Mintage	VF	XF	Unc
116	AH 1380	1960	.400	BV	12.50	17.50
	1386	1966	—	—	Proof	17.50

25 PIASTRES

17.5000 gm., .720 SILVER, .4051 oz ASW
Suez Canal Nationalization

Y#	Date	Year	Mintage	VF	XF	Unc
98	AH 1375	1956	.258	BV	15.00	20.00

National Assembly Inauguration
Rev: Similar to Y#98

Y#	Date	Year	Mintage	VF	XF	Unc
102	AH 1376	1957	.246	BV	12.50	17.50

National Assembly

Y#	Date	Year	Mintage	VF	XF	Unc
110	AH 1380	1960	.250	BV	12.50	17.50

10.0000 gm., .720 SILVER, .2315 oz ASW
Diversion of the Nile

Y#	Date	Year	Mintage	VF	XF	Unc
119	AH 1384	1964	.250	BV	7.50	10.00
	1384	1964	2,000	—	Proof	12.00

6.2500 gm., .720 SILVER, .1446 oz ASW
Nasser

Y#	Date	Year	Mintage	VF	XF	Unc
134	AH 1390	1970	.700	BV	5.00	7.50

National Bank of Egypt 75th Anniversary

Y#	Date	Year	Mintage	VF	XF	Unc
147	AH 1393	1973	.100	BV	5.00	8.50

50 PIASTRES

4.2500 gm., .875 GOLD, .1195 oz AGW

Y#	Date	Year	Mintage	VF	XF	Unc
57	AH 1341	1923	.018	90.00	120.00	140.00

Y#	Date	Year	Mintage	VF	XF	Unc
71	AH 1348	1929	—	90.00	120.00	140.00
	1349	1930	—	90.00	120.00	140.00

King Farouk I
Royal Wedding

Y#	Date	Year	Mintage	VF	XF	Unc
89	AH 1357	1938	.010	90.00	120.00	140.00
	1357	1938	—	—	Proof	175.00

28.0000 gm., .900 SILVER, .8102 oz ASW
Evacuation of the British

Y#	Date	Year	Mintage	VF	XF	Unc
99	AH 1375	1956	.250	BV	27.50	35.00

20.0000 gm., .720 SILVER, .4630 oz ASW
Diversion of the Nile

Y#	Date	Year	Mintage	VF	XF	Unc
120	AH 1384	1964	.250	BV	15.00	17.50
	1384	1964	2,000	—	Proof	25.00

12.5000 gm., .720 SILVER, .2893 oz ASW
Nasser

Y#	Date	Year	Mintage	VF	XF	Unc
135	AH 1390	1970	.400	BV	10.00	12.00

1/2 POUND

4.2500 gm., .875 GOLD, .1195 oz AGW
U.A.R. Founding

Y#	Date	Year	Mintage	VF	XF	Unc
106	AH 1377	1958	.030	85.00	100.00	125.00
	1377	1958	Inc. Ab.	—	Proof	150.00

100 PIASTRES

8.5000 gm., .875 GOLD, .2391 oz AGW

Y#	Date	Year	Mintage	VF	XF	Unc
43	AH 1335	1916	.010	175.00	200.00	225.00

NOTE: Restrikes may exist.

Y#	Date	Year	Mintage	VF	XF	Unc
58	AH 1340	1922	.025	175.00	200.00	225.00

Obv: Bust left

Y#	Date	Year	Mintage	VF	XF	Unc
72	AH 1348	1929	—	175.00	200.00	225.00
	1349	1930	—	175.00	200.00	225.00

King Farouk I
Royal Wedding

Y#	Date	Year	Mintage	VF	XF	Unc
90	AH 1357	1938	.005	200.00	225.00	250.00
	1357	1938	—	—	Proof	300.00

POUND

8.5000 gm., .875 GOLD, .2391 oz AGW
3rd and 5th Anniversaries of Revolution

Y#	Date	Year	Mintage	VF	XF	Unc
103	AH 1374	1955	.016	BV	175.00	200.00
	1374	1955	Inc. Ab.	—	Proof	250.00
	1377	1957	.010	BV	175.00	200.00
	1377	1957	Inc. Ab.	—	Proof	250.00

Aswan Dam

Y#	Date	Year	Mintage	VF	XF	Unc
108	AH 1379	1960	.252	BV	175.00	200.00
	1379	1960	5,000	—	Proof	250.00

SILVER
Aswan High Dam

Y#	Date	Year	Mintage	VF	XF	Unc
126	AH 1387	1968	.100	BV	18.00	20.00

Al-Azhar Mosque 1000th Anniversary

Y#	Date	Year	Mintage	VF	XF	Unc
130	AH 1359/1361	1970/1972	.100	BV	18.00	20.00

24.6000 gm., .720 SILVER, .5695 oz ASW
Nasser

136	AH 1390	1970	.400	BV	18.00	20.00

8.0000 gm., .875 GOLD, .2250 oz AGW
Nasser

137	AH 1390	1970	.010	BV	165.00	200.00

25.0000 gm., .720 SILVER, .5787 oz ASW
F A O: Aswan Dam

Y#	Date	Year	Mintage	VF	XF	Unc
145	AH 1393	1973	.050	BV	20.00	22.50

8.0000 gm., .875 GOLD, .2250 oz AGW
National Bank of Egypt 75th Anniversary

148	AH 1393	1973	7,000	BV	175.00	225.00

14.9700 gm., .720 SILVER, .3465 oz ASW
First Anniversary October War

152	AH 1394	1974	.050	12.00	15.00	17.50

F.A.O. Issue

161	AH 1396	1976	.050	12.00	15.00	17.50

Reopening of Suez Canal
Rev: Similar to Y#161

Y#	Date	Year	Mintage	VF	XF	Unc
164	AH 1396	1976	.250	12.00	15.00	17.50

Om Kalsoum

169	AH 1396	1976	.250	12.00	15.00	17.50

8.0000 gm., GOLD, .2250 oz AGW

170	AH 1396	1976	—	BV	175.00	225.00

14.9700 gm., .720 SILVER, .3465 oz ASW
King Faisal

166	AH1396	1976	.100	12.00	15.00	17.50

8.0000 gm., .875 GOLD, .2250 oz AGW

167	AH1396	1976	8,000	BV	175.00	225.00

14.9700 gm., .720 SILVER, .3465 oz ASW
F.A.O. Issue

Y#	Date	Year	Mintage	VF	XF	Unc
183	AH 1397	1977	.050	12.00	15.00	17.50

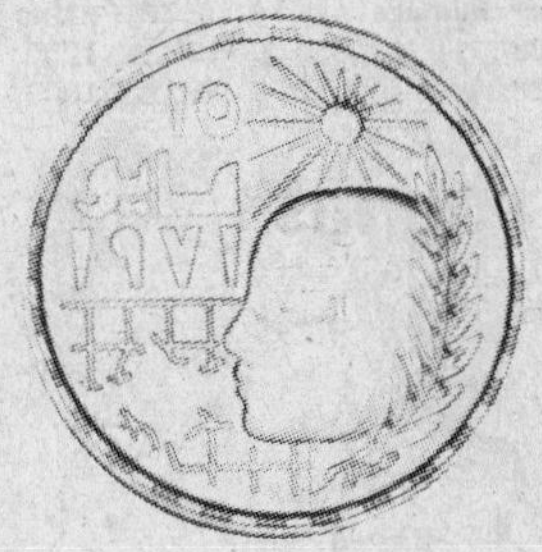

1971 Corrective Revolution

Y#	Date	Year	Mintage	VF	XF	Unc
176	AH 1397	1977	.050	12.00	15.00	17.50
	1399	1979	—	—	—	—

20th Anniversary of Economic Union

Y#	Date	Year	Mintage	VF	XF	Unc
178	AH1397	1977	.250	12.00	15.00	17.50

8.0000 gm., .875 GOLD, .2250 oz AGW

Y#	Date	Year	Mintage	VF	XF	Unc
178a	AH1397	1977	5,000		BV 175.00	225.00

14.9700 gm., .720 SILVER, .3465 oz ASW
Portland Cement

Y#	Date	Year	Mintage	VF	XF	Unc
188	AH1398	1978	.050	12.00	15.00	17.50

25th Anniversary of Ain Shams University

Y#	Date	Year	Mintage	VF	XF	Unc
186	AH1398	1978	.050	12.00	15.00	17.50

F.A.O. Issue

Y#	Date	Year	Mintage	VF	XF	Unc
191	AH1398	1978	.050	12.00	15.00	17.50

14.9700 gm., .720 SILVER, .3465 oz ASW
25th Anniversary of Abbasia Mint

Y#	Date	Year	Mintage	VF	XF	Unc
193	AH1399	1979	2,000	—	Proof	55.00

F.A.O. Issue and I.Y.C.

Y#	Date	Year	Mintage	VF	XF	Unc
196	AH1399	1979	—	12.00	15.00	17.50
	1399	1979	—	—	Proof	50.00

Mule, Obv: Y# (I.Y.C.), Rev: Y#173.

Y#	Date	Year	Mintage	VF	XF	Unc
—	AH1399	1979	—	—	—	—

National Education Day

Y#	Date	Year	Mintage	VF	XF	Unc
198	AH1399	1979	—	—	—	17.50
	1399	1979	2,000	—	Proof	50.00

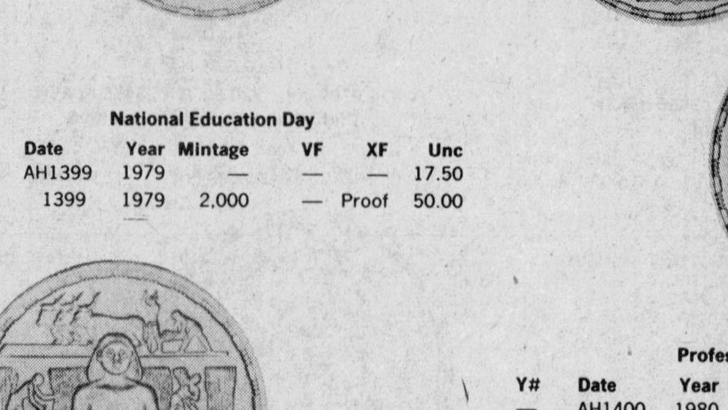

Bank of Land Reform

Y#	Date	Year	Mintage	VF	XF	Unc
—	AH1399	1979	—	—	—	17.50
	1399	1979	2,000	—	Proof	50.00

.875 GOLD

Y#	Date	Year	Mintage	VF	XF	Unc
—	AH1399	1979	800 pcs.	—	Proof	—

14.9700 gm., .720 SILVER, .3465 oz ASW
14th Centennial of Mohamed's Flight to Medina

Y#	Date	Year	Mintage	VF	XF	Unc
—	AH1400	1979	.100	—	—	17.50

.875 GOLD

Y#	Date	Year	Mintage	VF	XF	Unc
—	AH1400	1979	—	—	Proof	—

.720 SILVER
Egyptian - Israeli Peace Treaty

Y#	Date	Year	Mintage	VF	XF	Unc
—	AH1400	1980	—	—	—	—

Professions In Egypt

Y#	Date	Year	Mintage	VF	XF	Unc
—	AH1400	1980	—	—	—	—

500 PIASTRES

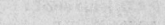

42.5000 gm., .875 GOLD, 1.1957 oz AGW

Y#	Date	Year	Mintage	VF	XF	Unc
59	AH 1340	1922	1,800	825.00	900.00	1250.
	1340	1922	—	—	Proof	1750.

Rev: Similar to Y#59

Y#	Date	Year	Mintage	VF	XF	Unc
73	AH 1348	1929	—	850.00	1000.	1250.
	1349	1930	—	850.00	1000.	1250.
	1351	1932	—	850.00	1000.	1250.

King Farouk I
Royal Wedding

Y#	Date	Year	Mintage	VF	XF	Unc
91	AH 1357	1938	—	850.00	1000.	1250.
	1357	1938	—	—	Proof	1500.

5 POUNDS

42.5000 gm., .875 GOLD, 1.1957 oz AGW
3rd and 5th Anniversaries of Revolution

Y#	Date	Year	Mintage	VF	XF	Unc
104	AH 1374	1955	—	BV 825.00	900.00	
	1374	1955	1,000	—	Proof	1100.
	1377	1957	—	BV 825.00	900.00	
	1377	1957	1,000	—	Proof	1000.

Aswan Dam

Y#	Date	Year	Mintage	VF	XF	Unc
109	AH1379	1960	5,000	BV 550.00	650.00	
	1379	1960	1,000	—	Proof	800.00

Diversion of the Nile

Y#	Date	Year	Mintage	VF	XF	Unc
121	AH 1384	1964	—	BV 500.00	550.00	
	1384	1964	4,000	—	Proof	650.00

1400th Anniversary of the Koran

Y#	Date	Year	Mintage	VF	XF	Unc
127	AH 1388	1968	.010	BV	500.00	550.00

Al-Azhar Mosque 1000th Anniversary

Y#	Date	Year	Mintage	VF	XF	Unc
—	AH 1390	1970	—	BV	500.00	550.00

Nasser

Y#	Date	Year	Mintage	VF	XF	Unc
138	AH 1390	1970	3,000	BV	500.00	550.00

National Bank of Egypt 75th Anniversary

Y#	Date	Year	Mintage	VF	XF	Unc
149	AH 1393	1973	1,000	BV	500.00	550.00

1973 October War

Y#	Date	Year	Mintage	VF	XF	Unc
A152	AH 1394	1974	1,000	BV	500.00	550.00

King Faisal Of Saudi Arabia

Y#	Date	Year	Mintage	VF	XF	Unc
168	AH 1396	1976	2,500	BV	500.00	550.00

Suez Canal

Y#	Date	Year	Mintage	VF	XF	Unc
165	AH 1396	1976	2,000	BV	500.00	550.00

Om Kalsoum

Y#	Date	Year	Mintage	VF	XF	Unc
171	AH 1396	1976	1,000	BV	500.00	550.00

25.0000 gm., .925 SILVER, .7435 oz ASW
President Sadat
Obv: Similar to 10 Pounds, Y#

Y#	Date	Year	Mintage	VF	XF	Unc
—	AH1397	1977	.120	—	Proof	—

26.0000 gm., .875 GOLD, .7315 oz AGW
Bank of Land Reform

Y#	Date	Year	Mintage	VF	XF	Unc
—	AH1399	1979	250 pcs.	—	Proof	—

14th Centennial of Mohamed's Flight to Medina

Y#	Date	Year	Mintage	VF	XF	Unc
—	AH1400	1979	—	—	Proof	750.00

10 POUNDS

52.0000 gm., .875 GOLD, 1.4630 oz AGW
Diversion of the Nile

Y#	Date	Year	Mintage	VF	XF	Unc
122	AH 1384	1964	—	BV	1000.	1100.
	1384	1964	2,000	—	Proof	1250.

50.0000 gm., .925 SILVER, 1.4871 oz ASW
President Sadat

Y#	Date	Year	Mintage	VF	XF	Unc
—	AH 1397	1977	.120	—	Proof	60.00

50 POUNDS

15.0000 gm., .917 GOLD, .4422 oz AGW
President Sadat
Obv: Similar to 10 Pounds, Y#

Y#	Date	Year	Mintage	VF	XF	Unc
—	AH 1397	1977	.120	—	Proof	300.00

100 POUNDS

30.0000 gm., .917 GOLD, .8845 oz AGW
President Sadat
Obv: Similar to 10 Pounds, Y#

Y#	Date	Year	Mintage	VF	XF	Unc
—	AH 1397	1977	.120	—	Proof	600.00

TOKEN ISSUES

The following token issues were struck for firms participating in the construction of the Suez Canal, and were used as currency by the company employees.

Issues Of Ch. & A. Bazin

20 CENTIMES

COPPER

KM#	Date	Mintage	VG	Fine	VF	XF
1	1865	—	50.00	75.00	100.00	135.00

50 CENTIMES

COPPER

KM#	Date	Mintage	VG	Fine	VF	XF
2	1865	—	125.00	150.00	175.00	225.00

FRANC

COPPER

KM#	Date	Mintage	VG	Fine	VF	XF
3	1865	—	125.00	150.00	175.00	225.00

5 FRANCS

COPPER

KM#	Date	Mintage	VG	Fine	VF	XF
4	1865	—	250.00	350.00	500.00	700.00

Issues Of Borel Lavalley et Cie

20 CENTIMES

COPPER

KM#	Date	Mintage	VG	Fine	VF	XF
5	1865	—	40.00	65.00	90.00	120.00

50 CENTIMES

COPPER

KM#	Date	Mintage	VG	Fine	VF	XF
6	1865	—	35.00	60.00	85.00	110.00

FRANC

COPPER

KM#	Date	Mintage	VG	Fine	VF	XF
7	1865	—	65.00	100.00	135.00	185.00

5 FRANCS

COPPER

KM#	Date	Mintage	VG	Fine	VF	XF
8	1865	—	—	—	Rare	—

NOTE: The only known example of KM#8 was illustrated in Wayte Raymond's "Coins of the World" nineteenth century issues and is not to be confused with the modern fantasies encountered in today's market.

NCLT ISSUES

PATTERNS

KM#	Date	Mintage	Identification	Mkt.Val.
1	AH 1277	—	200 Guerche, 2 Egyptian Pounds, .875 Gold, plain edge.	—
2	AH 1277	—	400 Guerche, 4 Egyptian Pounds, .875 Gold, plain edge.	—

SPECIMEN SETS

KM#	Date	Mintage	Identification	Issue Price	Mkt. Val.
S1	1916/7(10)	—	Y34-43	—	1500.

PROOF SETS

STANDARD METALS

KM#	Date	Mintage	Identification	Issue Price	Mkt. Val.
101	1917(9)	—	Y34-42	—	3500.
102	1938(4)	—	Y88-91	—	1750.
103	1955(2)	1,000	Y103,104	—	1350.
104	1957(2)	1,000	Y103,104	—	1250.
105	1960(2)	1,000	Y108,109	—	1000.
106	1964(2)	2,000	Y121,122	—	1900.
107	1964(4)	2,000	Y117-120	18.00	45.00
108	1966(7)	2,500	Y111-A113,114-116	9.00	35.00

EL SALVADOR

The Republic of El Salvador, a Central American country bordered by Guatemala, Honduras and the Pacific Ocean, has an area of 8,260 sq. mi. (21,393 sq. km.) and a population of 4.5 million. Capital: San Salvador. This most intensely cultivated country of Latin America produces coffee (the major crop), cotton, sugar and balsam for export. Gold, silver and other metals are largely unexploited.

The first Spanish attempt to subjugate the area was undertaken in 1523 by Pedro de Alvarado, Cortes' lieutenant. He was forced to retreat by superior Indian forces, but returned in 1525 and succeeded in bringing the region under control of the captain generalcy of Guatemala, where it remained until 1821. In 1821, El Salvador and the other Central American provinces, declared their independence from Spain. In 1823 the Federal Republic of Central America was formed by the five Central American States. When this federation was dissolved in 1839, El Salvador became an independent republic.

MINTMARKS

C.A.M. - Central American Mint, San Salvador
H - Birmingham
S - San Francisco
Mo - Mexico

PROVISIONAL ISSUES

MONETARY SYSTEM

16 Reales = 1 Escudo

1/4 REAL

SILVER

C#	Date	Mintage	Good	VG	Fine	VF
—	—	(3 known)	—	—	Rare	—

1/2 REAL

SILVER

Obv. leg: POR LA LIVERTAD DEL SAL, star above volcano within branches. Rev. leg: MONEDA PROVISIONAL, halo above column within branches.

C#	Date	Mintage	Good	VG	Fine	VF
11	1833	—	75.00	150.00	225.00	350.00

Obv. leg: POR LA LIBERTAD DEL SAL. S-volcano-S over water within circle. Rev: Liberty cap over 1. - column - 1/2 over water.

C#	Date	Mintage	Good	VG	Fine	VF
12.1	1835	—	75.00	150.00	225.00	350.00

Obv. leg: POR LA LIBERTAD DEL SAL, star above S - volcano - S over water.

C#	Date	Mintage	Good	VG	Fine	VF
12.2	1835	—	85.00	175.00	250.00	375.00

Obv. Leg: POR LA LIBERTAD DEL SALVA, Star above S - volcano - S over water. Rev. leg: MONEDA PROVISIONAL. Liberty cap over column: 1 - column - M

C#	Date	Mintage	Good	VG	Fine	VF
12.3	1835	—	75.00	150.00	225.00	325.00

REAL

SILVER
Obv. leg: ESTADO DEL SALVADOR, star above volcano within branches.
Rev. leg: MONEDA PROVISIONAL IND*, star in wreath above 1. - column - R. within branches.

C#	Date	Mintage	Good	VG	Fine	VF
15	1833	—	65.00	125.00	200.00	300.00

Obv. leg: POR LA LIVERTAD DEL SALVADOR.
Rev: 1. - (thin) column - R. within branches.

14.1 1833 — 45.00 90.00 150.00 225.00

Obv: Similar to C#14.1.
Rev: 1. - (thick) column - R. within branches.

14.2 1833 — 45.00 90.00 150.00 225.00

Obv. leg: POR LA LIVERTAD DEL SALVADOR*
Rev: Similar to C#14.2.

14.3 1833 — 60.00 90.00 150.00 225.00

Obv: Star over volcano over water in half circle of stars.

14.4 1833 — 65.00 125.00 200.00 300.00

Obv. leg: POR LA LIVERTAD DE SAL.
Volcano within branches.
Rev. leg: MONEDA PROVISIONAL IND.
Column within branches.

14.5 1834 — — — Rare —

Obv. leg: POR LA LIVERTAD DEL SAL.
Star over S. - volcano - S. within circle.
Rev. leg: MONEDA PROVISIONAL, Liberty cap over I. - column - R., water below within circle.

14.6 1835 — 45.00 90.00 150.00 225.00

Obv. leg: POR LA LIVERTAD DEL SAL.

14.7 1835 NA — 45.00 90.00 150.00 225.00

Obv. leg: POR LA LIBERTAD DEL SAL.
Star over S - volcano - S over water within circle.

14.8 1835 — 45.00 90.00 150.00 225.00

NOTE: Varieties also exist with 2 or 3 dots after SAL.

Obv. leg: POR LA LIBERTAD DEL SAL.
Star over S - volcano - S over water within circle of dots.

C#	Date	Mintage	Good	VG	Fine	VF
14.9	1835	—	45.00	90.00	150.00	225.00

Obv. leg: POR LA LIBERTAD DEL SA:

14.10 1835 — 50.00 100.00 165.00 250.00

Obv. leg: POR LA LIBERTAD DE SALV.

14.11 1835 — 45.00 90.00 150.00 225.00

2 REALES

SILVER
Obv. leg: POR LA LIVERTAD. SALV,
Liberty cap over 2. - column - R. over water.
Rev. leg: MONEDA PROVISIONAL, volcano.

16.1 1828 FP — 50.00 75.00 100.00 150.00

Obv: Inner circle added.

16.2 1828 FP — 50.00 75.00 100.00 150.00
1828 F — 60.00 90.00 125.00 175.00

Obv. leg: POR LA LIBERTAD. SALB.

16.3 1828 FP — 50.00 75.00 100.00 150.00

Obv. leg: POR LA LIBERTAD SALVAD.
Rev. leg: MONEDA PROBISIONAL.

16.4 1829 RL — 55.00 80.00 110.00 165.00

Obv. leg: POR LA LIBERTAD SALVAD.

C#	Date	Mintage	Good	VG	Fine	VF
16.5	1829 RL	—	55.00	80.00	110.00	165.00

Obv. leg: POR LA LIBERTAD SALVADOR.

16.6 1829 — 55.00 80.00 110.00 165.00

Obv. leg: POR LA LIBERTAD DEL SALVADR.
Star over S - volcano - S. over water.
Rev: Liberty cap over 2 - column - R.

17.1 1832 — 55.00 80.00 110.00 165.00

Obv. leg: POR LA LIBERTAD DEL SALVADOR
Rev: Liberty cap over 2 - column - R between sprays within dotted circle.

17.2 1832 RL — 55.00 80.00 110.00 165.00

Rev: 2 - column - R within solid circle.

17.3 1832 RL — 55.00 80.00 110.00 165.00

Obv. leg: POR LA LIBERTAD SALVADORE

17.4 1832 — 55.00 80.00 110.00 165.00

Obv. leg: POR LA LIVERTAD DEL SALV,
Star above retrograde S - volcano - S over water.
Rev: Liberty cap over 2. - column - R within branches.

17.5 1833 — 55.00 80.00 110.00 165.00
1834/3T — 55.00 80.00 110.00 165.00

Obv: Regular S' recut over retrograde S'.

17.6 1834/3 — 55.00 80.00 110.00 165.00

Obv. leg: POR LA LIBERTAD DEL SALVA.
Star over S - volcano - S over water.

17.7 1833 RL — 55.00 80.00 110.00 165.00

NOTE: Varieties exist with 2 or 3 dots after SALVA.

Obv. leg: POR LA LIBERTAD DEL SALVAD

C#	Date	Mintage	Good	VG	Fine	VF
17.8	1833/2 RL	—	65.00	90.00	120.00	175.00
	1833 RL	—	55.00	80.00	110.00	165.00

Obv. leg: POR LA LIBERTAD DEL SALV

17.9	1833 L	—	55.00	80.00	110.00	165.00

Obv. leg: LIBERTAD SALVO DORENO

17.10	1833	—	55.00	80.00	110.00	165.00

Obv. leg: POR LA LIBERTAD DEL SALVADOR.

17.11	1833 RL	—	55.00	80.00	110.00	165.00

Obv. leg: POR LA LIVERTAD DEL SALV.
Rev. leg: MONEDA PROVISIONAL
with retrograde 'S'.

—	1834	—	55.00	80.00	110.00	165.00

4 REALES

SILVER
Obv. leg: POR LA LIBERTAD SALV,
Liberty cap over column between retrograde R. - 4.

18.1	1828 F	—	3000.	4000.	5000.	7000.

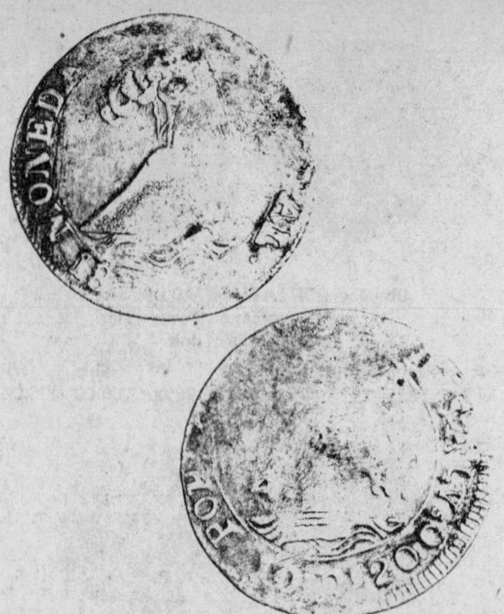

Obv. leg: POR LA LIBERTAD DEL SALV, corrected 4. - R.
Rev. leg: MONEDA PROVISIONAL.

C#	Date	Mintage	Good	VG	Fine	VF
18.2	1828 F	—	3000.	4000.	5000.	7000.

COUNTERSTAMP ISSUES

2 REALES

SILVER
c/s: SA monogram on 2 Reales.

20	1828 FP	—	—	—	—	—
	1829 RL	—	—	—	—	—

NOTE: This counterstamp, illustrated above, appearing to be a SA monogram has previously been attributed to El Salvador and also to various Caribbean Islands. No one is sure so it is included here for easy reference.

REPUBLIC

COUNTERSTAMP ISSUES

1830

Type I
Volcano, 'S' on either side, '1830' below, in rectangle.

4 REALES

SILVER

c/s: Type I on Mexico 4 Reales, KM#97 (C#39).

C#	Date	Year	Mintage	Good	VG	Fine
20	1830	(1772-89)	—	—	Rare	—

1839

Type II
Volcano, '1839' below, in rectangle.
Exists with normal 3 and retrograde 3 in date.

1/2 REAL

SILVER
c/s: Type II on Chile 1/2 Real, C#83.

21	1839	(1833-4)	—	—	Rare	—

REAL

SILVER
c/s: Type II on Peru 1 Real, C#129.1.

22	1839	(1826-36)	—	—	Rare	—

2 REALES

SILVER
c/s: Type II on Peru (Lima) 2 Reales, C#130.1.

23.1	1839	(1828-39)	—	—	Rare	—

c/s: Type II on South Peru 2 Reales, C#178.

23.2	1839	(1837)	—	—	Rare	—

8 REALES

SILVER
c/s: Type II on South Peru 8 Reales, C#180a.

25	1839	(1837-39)	—	—	Rare	—

TYPE III-A
Plain Liberty cap over shield
on draped flags within 10mm circle.

TYPE III-B
Radiant Liberty cap over shield
on draped flags within 12mm circle.

TYPE III-C
Liberty cap over shield
within branches in 12mm circle.

NOTE: Other counterstamp varieties are known to exist.

Spanish 'Real' Series

1/2 REAL

SILVER

c/s: Type III on Guatemala 1/2 Real, C#1.

C#	Date	Year	Mintage	Good	VG	Fine
41	ND	—	—	25.00	50.00	75.00

REAL

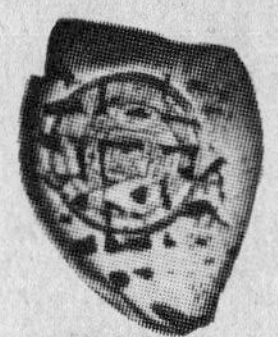
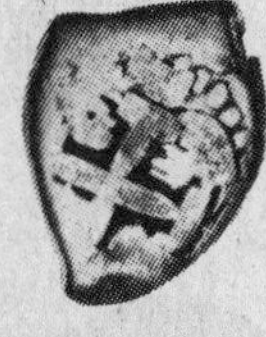

SILVER

c/s: Type III on Bolivia (Potosi) 'cob' 1 Real.

C#	Date	Year	Mintage	Good	VG	Fine
42.1	ND	—	—	12.50	22.50	40.00

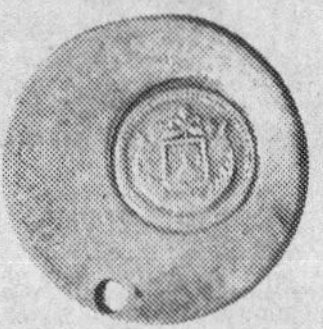

c/s: Type III on Bolivia (Potosi) 1 Real, C#15.

C#	Date	Year	Mintage	Good	VG	Fine
42.2	ND	(1773-89)	—	7.50	12.50	18.50

c/s: Type III on Chile 1 Real, C#66.

C#	Date	Year	Mintage	Good	VG	Fine
42.3	ND	(1808-17)	—	12.50	22.50	40.00

c/s: Type III on Colombia 1 Real, C#143.

C#	Date	Year	Mintage	Good	VG	Fine
42.4	ND	(1837-46)	—	10.00	17.50	25.00

c/s: Type III on Mexico Charles and Johanna 1 Real, KM#9.

C#	Date	Year	Mintage	Good	VG	Fine
42.5	ND	(1536-72)	—	17.50	27.50	40.00

c/s: Type III on Mexico City Philip II Real, KM#27.

C#	Date	Year	Mintage	Good	VG	Fine
42.6	ND	(1556-98)	—	20.00	35.00	50.00

c/s: Type III on Spain 1 Real, C#37.

C#	Date	Year	Mintage	Good	VG	Fine
42.7	ND	(1772-88)	—	10.00	15.00	25.00

2 REALES

SILVER

c/s: Type III on Bolivia (Potosi) 2 Reales, C#16.

C#	Date	Year	Mintage	Good	VG	Fine
43.1	ND	(1773-89)	—	10.00	17.50	25.00

c/s: Type III on Colombia 2 Reales, C#144.

C#	Date	Year	Mintage	Good	VG	Fine
43.2	ND	(1837-46)	—	10.00	17.50	25.00

c/s: Type II on Mexico 2 Reales, KM#86 (C#15).

C#	Date	Year	Mintage	Good	VG	Fine
43.3	ND	(1747-60)	—	30.00	60.00	100.00

c/s: Type II on Mexico 2 Reales, KM#89 (C#71).

C#	Date	Year	Mintage	Good	VG	Fine
43.4	ND	(1789-90)	—	15.00	25.00	40.00

c/s: Type II on Mexico 2 Reales, KM#90 (C#73.7).

C#	Date	Year	Mintage	Good	VG	Fine
43.5	ND	(1790)	—	15.00	25.00	40.00

c/s: Type III on Mexico 2 Reales, KM#91 (C#79).

C#	Date	Year	Mintage	Good	VG	Fine
43.6	ND	(1792-1808)	—	10.00	17.50	30.00

c/s: Type III on Mexico 2 Reales, KM#93 (C#119).

C#	Date	Year	Mintage	Good	VG	Fine
43.7	ND	(1812-21)	—	10.00	17.50	30.00

c/s: Type III on Peru 2 Reales, C#10.

C#	Date	Year	Mintage	Good	VG	Fine
43.8	ND	(1752-59)	—	10.00	17.50	30.00

c/s: Type III on Peru (Lima) 2 Reales, C#74.

C#	Date	Year	Mintage	Good	VG	Fine
43.9	ND	(1791-1808)	—	10.00	17.50	30.00

c/s: Type III on Spanish 2 Reales, C#134.

C#	Date	Year	Mintage	Good	VG	Fine
43.10	ND	(1810-33)	—	10.00	17.50	30.00

4 REALES

SILVER

c/s: Type III on Guatemala 4 Reales, C#123.

C#	Date	Year	Mintage	Good	VG	Fine
44.1	ND	(1747-53)	—	—	Rare	—

c/s: Type III on Mexico Sombrerte 4 Reales, KM#175 (C#L134).

C#	Date	Year	Mintage	Good	VG	Fine
44.2	ND	(1812)	—	—	Rare	—

8 REALES

SILVER

c/s: Type III on Chile 8 Reales, C#24.

C#	Date	Year	Mintage	Good	VG	Fine
45	ND	(1773-89)	—	—	Rare	—

English 'Sterling' Series

6 PENCE

SILVER

c/s: Type III on Great Britain 6 Pence, C#29.

C#	Date	Year	Mintage	Good	VG	Fine
47.1	ND	(1816-20)	—	15.00	25.00	40.00

c/s: Type III on Great Britain 6 Pence, C#79.

C#	Date	Year	Mintage	Good	VG	Fine
47.2	ND	(1831-37)	—	15.00	25.00	40.00

SHILLING

SILVER

c/s: Type III on Great Britain Shilling, C#32.

C#	Date	Year	Mintage	Good	VG	Fine
48.1	ND	(1816-20)	—	17.50	28.50	50.00

c/s: Type III on Great Britain Shilling, C#61a.

C#	Date	Year	Mintage	Good	VG	Fine
48.2	ND	(1823-25)	—	17.50	28.50	50.00

c/s: Type III on Great Britain Shilling, C#62.

C#	Date	Year	Mintage	Good	VG	Fine
48.3	ND	(1825-29)	—	17.50	28.50	50.00

Type IV

R in beaded 5mm circle.

1/2 REAL

SILVER

c/s: Type IV on Guatemala 1/2 Real, Y#2.

KM#	Date	Year	Mintage	Good	VG	Fine
1.1	ND	(1859-61)	—	200.00	275.00	350.00

c/s: Type IV on Guatemala 1/2 Real, Y#8.

KM#	Date	Year	Mintage	Good	VG	Fine
1.2	ND	(1862-65)	—	200.00	275.00	350.00

REAL

SILVER

c/s: Type IV on Colombia 1 Real, C#123.

KM#	Date	Year	Mintage	Good	VG	Fine
2.1	ND	(1827-36)	—	10.00	20.00	35.00

c/s: Type IV on Guatemala 1 Real, Y#3.

KM#	Date	Year	Mintage	Good	VG	Fine
2.2	ND	(1859-60)	—	8.50	15.00	25.00

c/s: Type IV on Guatemala 1 Real, Y#10.

KM#	Date	Year	Mintage	Good	VG	Fine
2.3	ND	(1862-65)	—	8.50	15.00	25.00

2 REALES

SILVER

c/s: Type IV on Guatemala 2 Reales, Y#5.

KM#	Date	Year	Mintage	Good	VG	Fine
3.1	ND	(1860-61)	—	10.00	18.50	30.00

c/s: Type IV on Guatemala 2 Reales, Y#9.

KM#	Date	Year	Mintage	Good	VG	Fine
3.2	ND	(1861-65)	—	10.00	18.50	30.00

4 REALES

SILVER

c/s: Type IV on Guatemala 4 Reales, Y#6.

KM#	Date	Year	Mintage	Good	VG	Fine
4	ND	(1860-61)	—	25.00	40.00	75.00

8 REALES

SILVER
c/s: Type IV on Guatemala 1 Peso, Y#7.

KM#	Date	Year	Mintage	Good	VG	Fine
5	ND	(1859)	—	—	Rare	—

NOTE: Two copper coins of Brazil have also been reported with the Type IV c/s. A 20 Reis dated 1827 and a 80 Reis of the 1820's c/s: '40'.

TYPE V
Zig-Zag Test Mark

2 REALES

SILVER
c/s: Type V on Guatemala 2 Reales, C#122.2
(Peru 2 Reales).

KM#	Date	Year	Mintage	Good	VG	Fine
10	ND	(1825-40)	—	50.00	100.00	150.00

DECIMAL COINAGE

100 Centavos = 1 Peso
(Commencing 1919)
100 Centavos = 1 Colon

CENTAVO

COPPER-NICKEL

Y#	Date	Mintage	Fine	VF	XF	Unc
1	1889H	1.500	2.50	5.00	9.00	15.00
	1913H	2.500	1.25	2.50	4.50	8.00

COPPER

Y#	Date	Mintage	Fine	VF	XF	Unc
3	1892	.180	125.00	250.00	400.00	600.00
	1892	—	—	—	Proof	700.00
	1893	5 known		—	Rare	—

COPPER-NICKEL

Y#	Date	Mintage	Fine	VF	XF	Unc
16	1915	5.000	.35	.75	1.50	4.50
	1919	1.000	.50	1.00	2.00	5.50
	1920	1.490	.50	1.00	2.00	5.00
	1925	.200	2.50	5.00	8.00	15.00
	1926	.400	1.50	3.00	5.00	9.00
	1928S	5.000	.50	1.00	2.00	6.00
	1936	2.500	.50	1.00	2.00	6.00

Y#	Date	Mintage	Fine	VF	XF	Unc
19	1940	1.000	.75	2.00	4.50	10.00

BRONZE

Y#	Date	Mintage	Fine	VF	XF	Unc
19a	1942	5.000	.20	.50	1.00	2.00
	1943	5.000	.20	.50	1.00	2.00
	1945	5.000	.20	.50	1.00	2.00
	1947	5.000	.20	.50	1.00	2.00
	1951	10.000	.10	.20	.40	1.00
	1952	10.000	.10	.20	.40	1.00
	1956	10.000	.10	.20	.40	1.00
	1966	5.000	.20	.30	.50	.75
	1968	5.000	.20	.30	.50	.75
	1969	5.000	.20	.30	.50	.75
	1972	20.000	.10	.15	.25	.50

BRASS

Y#	Date	Mintage	Fine	VF	XF	Unc
19b	1976	20.000	—	.10	.15	.20
	1977	20.000	—	.10	.15	.20

2 CENTAVOS

NICKEL-BRASS

Y#	Date	Mintage	Fine	VF	XF	Unc
A20	1974	10.002	.10	.15	.20	.30

3 CENTAVOS

COPPER-NICKEL

Y#	Date	Mintage	Fine	VF	XF	Unc
2	1889H	.330	1.25	2.50	5.00	10.00
	1913H	1.000	1.75	3.50	6.00	12.00

Y#	Date	Mintage	Fine	VF	XF	Unc
17	1915	2.700	—	2.50	5.50	12.50

NICKEL-BRASS

Y#	Date	Mintage	Fine	VF	XF	Unc
B20	1974	10.002	.10	.15	.20	.30

1/4 REAL

BRONZE

Y#	Date	Mintage	Fine	VF	XF	Unc
15	1909	—	30.00	50.00	80.00	125.00

The decimal value of the above coin was about 3 Centavos. It was apparently struck in response to the continuing use of the real monetary system in local market places and rural areas.

5 CENTAVOS

1.2500 gm., .835 SILVER, .0336 oz ASW

Y#	Date	Mintage	Fine	VF	XF	Unc
8	1892CAM	.800	4.00	10.00	20.00	45.00
	1892CAM	—	—	—	Proof	75.00
	1893CAM	.800	4.00	10.00	20.00	45.00

Y#	Date	Mintage	Fine	VF	XF	Unc
22	1911	1.000	1.50	3.00	5.00	10.00

Y#	Date	Mintage	Fine	VF	XF	Unc
25	1914	2.000	1.25	2.00	3.50	6.00
	1914	*20 pcs.	—	—	Proof	250.00

COPPER-NICKEL

Y#	Date	Mintage	Fine	VF	XF	Unc
18	1915	2.500	.50	1.00	3.00	6.50
	1916	1.500	.50	1.00	3.00	6.50
	1917	1.000	1.00	2.00	4.00	10.00
	1918/7	1.000	1.50	3.00	6.00	15.00
	1918	Inc. Ab.	1.00	2.00	4.00	10.00
	1919	2.000	1.00	2.00	4.00	7.50
	1920	2.000	.25	.50	2.00	6.50
	1921	1.780	.50	1.00	3.00	6.50
	1925	4.000	.50	1.00	3.00	6.00

Y#	Date	Mintage	Fine	VF	XF	Unc
20	1940	.800	.50	1.00	2.00	4.00
	1951	2.000	.25	.50	1.00	2.00
	1956	8.000	.15	.30	.50	.75
	1959	6.000	.15	.30	.50	.75
	1963	10.000	.10	.15	.20	.30
	1966	6.000	.10	.15	.20	.30
	1967	10.000	.10	.15	.20	.30
	1972	10.000	.10	.15	.20	.25
	1974	10.002	.10	.15	.20	.25

COPPER-NICKEL-ZINC

Y#	Date	Mintage	Fine	VF	XF	Unc
20a	1944	5.000	.25	.50	1.00	2.50
	1948	3.000	.65	1.25	2.00	3.00
	1950	2.000	.25	.50	1.00	1.50
	1952	4.000	.20	.35	.50	1.00

NICKEL-CLAD-STEEL

Y#	Date	Mintage	Fine	VF	XF	Unc
20b	1975	15.000	.10	.15	.20	.30

STEEL CLAD NICKEL

Y#	Date	Mintage	Fine	VF	XF	Unc
20c	1976	15.000	.10	.15	.20	.30

COPPER-NICKEL

Y#	Date	Mintage	Fine	VF	XF	Unc
20d	1977	15.000	.10	.15	.20	.30

10 CENTAVOS

2.5000 gm., .835 SILVER, .0671 oz ASW

Y#	Date	Mintage	Fine	VF	XF	Unc
9	1892CAM	.120	80.00	125.00	175.00	350.00
	1892CAM	—	—	—	Proof	300.00

Y#	Date	Mintage	Fine	VF	XF	Unc
23	1911	1.000	2.25	3.50	6.00	12.50

Y#	Date	Mintage	Fine	VF	XF	Unc
26	1914	1.500	2.25	3.50	5.00	9.00
	1914	*20 pcs.	—	—	Proof	350.00

COPPER-NICKEL

Y#	Date	Mintage	Fine	VF	XF	Unc
21	1921	2.000	.50	1.00	3.00	7.50
	1925	2.000	.50	1.00	3.00	7.50
	1940	.500	.50	1.00	2.50	7.00
	1951	1.000	.25	.50	1.00	2.50
	1967	2.000	.15	.25	.75	2.00
	1968	3.000	.10	.15	.40	.75
	1969	3.000	.10	.15	.40	1.00
	1972	7.000	.10	.15	.20	.35

COPPER-NICKEL-ZINC

Y#	Date	Mintage	Fine	VF	XF	Unc
21a	1952	2.000	.20	.50	.75	1.25

NICKEL-CLAD-STEEL

Y#	Date	Mintage	Fine	VF	XF	Unc
21b	1975	15.000	.10	.15	.20	.30

COPPER-NICKEL

Y#	Date	Mintage	Fine	VF	XF	Unc
21c	1977	24.000	.10	.15	.20	.30

20 CENTAVOS

5.000 gm., .835 SILVER, .1342 oz ASW

Y#	Date	Mintage	Fine	VF	XF	Unc
10	1892CAM	.150	15.00	35.00	60.00	150.00
	1892CAM	—	—	—	Proof	175.00

25 CENTAVOS

6.2500 gm., .835 SILVER, .1678 oz ASW

Y#	Date	Mintage	Fine	VF	XF	Unc
—	1893	3 known		—	Rare	—

Y#	Date	Mintage	Fine	VF	XF	Unc
24	1911	.600	6.00	7.50	10.00	17.50

Y#	Date	Mintage	Fine	VF	XF	Unc
27	1914	1.400	5.50	6.50	9.00	14.00
	1914	*20 pcs.	—	—	Proof	500.00

7.5000 gm., .900 SILVER, .2170 oz ASW

Y#	Date	Mintage	Fine	VF	XF	Unc
28	1943	1.000	BV	BV	7.00	8.00
	1944	1.000	BV	BV	7.00	8.00

2.5000 gm., .900 SILVER, .0723 oz ASW

Y#	Date	Mintage	Fine	VF	XF	Unc
31	1953	14.000	BV	BV	2.50	3.50

NICKEL

Y#	Date	Mintage	Fine	VF	XF	Unc
33	1970	14.000	.15	.20	.25	.40
	1973	28.000	.15	.20	.25	.40
	1975	20.000	.15	.20	.25	.40
	1977	22.400	.15	.20	.25	.40

50 CENTAVOS

12.5000 gm., .900 SILVER, .3617 oz ASW

Y#	Date	Mintage	Fine	VF	XF	Unc
4	1892CAM	.430	30.00	65.00	150.00	250.00
	1892CAM	—	—	—	Proof	275.00

Y#	Date	Mintage	Fine	VF	XF	Unc
6	1892CAM	.340	12.00	20.00	50.00	100.00
	1893CAM	Inc. Ab.	12.00	20.00	50.00	100.00
	1894CAM	Inc. Ab.	12.00	20.00	50.00	100.00

5.000 gm., .900 SILVER, .1446 oz ASW

Y#	Date	Mintage	Fine	VF	XF	Unc
32	1953	3.000	BV	BV	6.00	7.50

NICKEL, 1.65 mm thick

Y#	Date	Mintage	Fine	VF	XF	Unc
34	1970	3.000	—	.15	.25	.50

2 mm thick

Y#	Date	Mintage	Fine	VF	XF	Unc
34a	1977	1.500	—	—	—	.75

UN (1) PESO

25.0000 gm., .900 SILVER, .7234 oz ASW

Y#	Date	Mintage	Fine	VF	XF	Unc
5	1892CAM	.041	75.00	150.00	250.00	350.00
	1892CAM	—	—	—	Proof	425.00

Y#	Date	Mintage	Fine	VF	XF	Unc
7	1892CAM	.950	35.00	70.00	125.00	200.00
	1893CAM	Inc. Ab.	BV	22.50	35.00	60.00
	1894CAM	Inc. Ab.	BV	22.50	35.00	60.00
	1895CAM	Inc. Ab.	BV	22.50	35.00	60.00
	1896CAM	Inc. Ab.	100.00	175.00	350.00	—
	1904CAM	.600	BV	22.50	30.00	55.00
	1908CAM	1.600	BV	22.50	30.00	55.00
	1911CAM	.500	BV	22.50	30.00	55.00

Obv: Heavier portrait (wider right shoulder).

Y#	Date	Mintage	Fine	VF	XF	Unc
7a	1904CAM	.400	BV	22.50	30.00	55.00
	1909CAM	.690	BV	22.50	30.00	55.00
	1911CAM	1.020	BV	22.50	30.00	55.00
	1914CAM	2.100	BV	22.50	30.00	55.00
	1914CAM	*20pcs.	—	—	Proof	1000.

UN (1) COLON

SILVER

Y#	Date	Mintage	Fine	VF	XF	Unc
30	1925Mo	2,000	75.00	125.00	200.00	300.00

2.3000 gm., .999 SILVER, .0320 oz ASW

KM#	Date	Mintage	VF	XF	Unc
2	1971	.018	—	Proof	10.00

2-1/2 PESOS

4.0323 gm., .900 GOLD, .1167 oz AGW

Y#	Date	Mintage	Fine	VF	XF	Unc
11	1892CAM					
		597 pcs.	300.00	500.00	800.00	1200.
	1892CAM	—	—	—	Proof	1400.

5 PESOS

8.0645 gm., .900 GOLD, .2334 oz AGW

Y#	Date	Mintage	Fine	VF	XF	Unc
12	1892CAM					
		558 pcs.	450.00	700.00	1200.	1750.
	1892CAM	—	—	—	Proof	2200.

5 COLONES

11.5000 gm., .999 SILVER, .3694 oz ASW

KM#	Date	Mintage	VF	XF	Unc
3	1971	.018	—	Proof	15.00

10 PESOS

16.1290 gm., .900 GOLD, .4667 oz AGW

Y#	Date	Mintage	Fine	VF	XF	Unc
13	1892CAM					
		321 pcs.	700.00	1200.	1750.	2750.
	1892CAM	—	—	—	Proof	2750.

20 PESOS

32.2580 gm., .900 GOLD, .9334 oz AGW

Y#	Date	Mintage	Fine	VF	XF	Unc
14	1892CAM					
		200 pcs.	1250.	2000.	3000.	4000.
	1892CAM	—	—	—	Proof	4250.

20 COLONES

15.5600 gm., .900 GOLD, .4502 oz AGW

Y#	Date	Mintage	Fine	VF	XF	Unc
29	1925	200 pcs.	1250.	2000.	3000.	4000.

25 COLONES

2.9500 gm., .900 GOLD, .0853 oz AGW

KM#	Date	Mintage	VF	XF	Unc
5	1971	4,500	—	Proof	70.00

25.1000 gm., .900 SILVER, .7263 oz ASW
18th Annual Governors' Assembly

Y#	Date	Mintage	Fine	VF	XF	Unc
35	1977	2,000	—	—	—	45.00
	1977	.020	—	—	Proof	60.00

50 COLONES

5.9000 gm., .900 GOLD, .1707 oz AGW

KM#	Date	Mintage	VF	XF	Unc
6	1971	3,400	—	Proof	125.00

100 COLONES

11.8000 gm., .900 GOLD, .3414 oz AGW

KM#	Date	Mintage	VF	XF	Unc
7	1971	2,650	—	Proof	250.00

200 COLONES

23.6000 gm., .900 GOLD, .6829 oz AGW

KM#	Date	Mintage	VF	XF	Unc
8	1971	2,200	—	Proof	500.00

250 COLONES

16.0000 gm., .917 GOLD, .4717 oz AGW
18th Annual Governors' Assembly

Y#	Date	Mintage	Fine	VF	XF	Unc
36	1977	4,000	—	—	—	325.00
	1977	400 pcs.	—	—	Proof	—

NCLT ISSUES

PATTERNS

KM#	Date	Mintage	Identification	Mkt.Val.
1	1892	3 Known	2-1/2 Pesos, .900 Gold, Y#11	—

PROOF SETS
STANDARD METALS

KM#	Date	Mintage	Identification	Issue Price	Mkt. Val.
101	1892(10)	—	Y3-5,8-14	—	10,000.
102	1914(4)	20 Est.	Y7a,25-27	—	2000.
103	1971(6)	—	KM2,3,5-8	—	875.00
104	1971(4)	—	KM5-8	250.00	850.00
105	1971(2)	—	KM2,3	6.00	25.00

Listings For
EQUATORIAL AFRICAN STATES: refer to Central African Empire

EQUATORIAL GUINEA

The Republic of Equatorial Guinea (formerly Spanish Guinea) consists of Rio Muni, located on the coast of west-Central Africa between Cameroon and Gabon, and the off-shore islands of Fernando Po, Annobon, Corisco, Elobey Grande and Elobey Chico. The equatorial country has an area of 10,820 sq. mi. (28,023 sq. km.) and a population of 310,000. Capital: Malabo. The economy is based on agriculture and forestry. Cacao, wood and coffee are exported.

Fernando Po was discovered between 1474 and 1496 by Portuguese navigators charting a route to the spice islands of the Far East. Portugal retained control of it and the adjacent islands until 1778 when they, together with trading rights to the African coast between the Ogooue and Niger rivers, were ceded to Spain. Fernando Po was administered, with Spanish consent, by the British from 1827 to 1844 when it was reclaimed by Spain. Mainland Rio Muni was granted to Spain by the Berlin Conference of 1885. The name of the colony was changed from Spanish Guinea to Equatorial Guinea in Dec. of 1963. Independence was attained on Oct. 12, 1968.

NOTE: The 1969 coinage carries the actual minting date in the stars at the sides of the large date.

PESETA

ALUMINUM-BRONZE

Y#	Date	Mintage	Fine	VF	XF	Unc
1	1969(69)	—	.35	.75	1.00	1.50

5 PESETAS

COPPER-NICKEL

Y#	Date	Mintage	Fine	VF	XF	Unc
2	1969(69)	—	.75	1.50	3.00	7.00

25 PESETAS

COPPER-NICKEL

Y#	Date	Mintage	Fine	VF	XF	Unc
3	1969(69)	—	1.25	2.50	4.00	8.00

5.0000 gm., .999 SILVER, .1606 oz ASW

KM#	Date	Mintage	VF	XF	Unc
1	1970	—	—	Proof	10.00

KM#	Date	Mintage	VF	XF
2	1970	—	—	Proof

50 PESETAS

COPPER-NICKEL

Y#	Date	Mintage	Fine	VF	XF	Unc
4	1969(69)	—	2.00	4.00	6.00	10.00

10.0000 gm., .999 SILVER, .3212 oz ASW

KM#	Date	Mintage	VF	XF	Unc
3	1970	—	—	Proof	15.00

75 PESETAS

15.0000 gm., .999 SILVER, .4818 oz ASW
Obv: Similar to KM#6.

KM#	Date	Mintage	VF	XF	Unc
4	1970	—	—	Proof	20.00

Obv: Similar to KM#6.

KM#	Date	Mintage	VF	XF	Unc
5	1970	—	—	Proof	20.00

KM#	Date	Mintage	VF	XF	Unc
6	1970	—	—	Proof	20.00

Obv: Similar to KM#6.

KM#	Date	Mintage	VF	XF	Unc
7	1970	—	—	Proof	20.00

100 PESETAS

20.0000 gm., .999 SILVER, .6424 oz ASW
Obv: Similar to KM#9.

8	1970	—	—	Proof	25.00

9	1970	—	—	Proof	27.50

150 PESETAS

30.0000 gm., .999 SILVER, .9636 oz ASW

10	1970	—	—	Proof	35.00

KM#	Date	Mintage	VF	XF	Unc
11	1970	—	—	Proof	35.00

12	1970	—	—	Proof	35.00

CENTENARIO ROMA CAPITAL 1870 1970 G.M. MONASSI

13	1970	—	—	Proof	35.00

200 PESETAS

40.0000 gm., .999 SILVER 1.2848 oz ASW

14	1970	—	—	Proof	50.00

KM#	Date	Mintage	VF	XF	Unc
15	1970	—	—	Proof	50.00

250 PESETAS

3.5200 gm., .900 GOLD, .1018 oz AGW
Obv: Naked Maja

Fr#	Date	Mintage	VF	XF	Unc
7	1970	3,000	—	Proof	75.00
	Obv: Praying hands				
8	1970	3,000	—	Proof	75.00

500 PESETAS

7.0500 gm., .900 GOLD, .2040 oz AGW
Obv: Bust of Pope John XXIII

3	1970	3,000	—	Proof	150.00
	Obv: Bust of Lenin				
4	1970	3,000	—	Proof	150.00
	Obv: Facing bust of Lincoln				
5	1970	3,000	—	Proof	150.00
	Obv: Bust of Mahatma Gandhi				
6	1970	3,000	—	Proof	150.00

750 PESETAS

10.5700 gm., .900 GOLD, .3058 oz AGW
Obv: City scene of Rome

11	1970	3,000	—	Proof	225.00
	Obv: Forum and Coliseum.				
10	1970	3,000	—	Proof	225.00
	Obv: Goddess of Rome				
9	1970	3,000	—	Proof	225.00
	Obv: Head of Freedom				
12	1970	3,000	—	Proof	225.00

1000 PESETAS

14.1000 gm., .900 GOLD, .4080 oz AGW
Obv: Rimet cup

2	1970	3,000	—	Proof	300.00

5000 PESETAS

70.5200 gm., .900 GOLD, 2.0407 oz AGW
Obv: Bust of President Macias

1	1970	3,000	—	Proof	1400.

MONETARY REFORM

EKUELE

BRASS

Y#	Date	Mintage	Fine	VF	XF	Unc
5	1975	3.000	.10	.25	.50	1.00

5 EKUELE

COPPER-NICKEL

Y#	Date	Mintage	Fine	VF	XF	Unc
6	1975	2.800	.15	.35	.75	1.50

10 EKUELE

COPPER-NICKEL

Y#	Date	Mintage	Fine	VF	XF	Unc
7	1975	1.300	.30	.65	1.25	2.00

1000 EKUELE

21.4300 gm., .925 SILVER, .6373 oz ASW
President Masie Nguema Biyogo
Obv: Similar to 2000 Ekuele, Y#

Y#	Date	Mintage	Fine	VF	XF	Unc
—	1978	.031	—	—	Proof	—

2000 EKUELE

42.8800 gm., .925 SILVER, 1.2753 oz ASW
President Masie Nguema Biyogo

Y#	Date	Mintage	Fine	VF	XF	Unc
—	1978	.031	—	—	Proof	75.00

31.1000 gm., .927 SILVER, .9270 oz ASW
XXII Olympics

Y#	Date	Mintage	Fine	VF	XF	Unc
—	ND(1979)	.010	—	—	Proof	50.00

5000 EKUELE

6.9600 gm., .917 GOLD, .2052 oz AGW
President Masie Nguema Biyogo
Obv: Similar to 2000 Ekuele, Y#

Y#	Date	Mintage	Fine	VF	XF	Unc
—	1978	.031	—	—	Proof	—

10,000 EKUELE

13.9200 gm., .917 GOLD, .4104 oz AGW
President Masie Nguema Biyogo
Obv: Similar to 2000 Ekuele, Y#

Y#	Date	Mintage	Fine	VF	XF	Unc
—	1978	.031	—	—	Proof	—

NCLT ISSUES

MINT SETS

KM#	Date	Mintage	Identification	Issue Price	Mkt. Val.
S1	1975(3)	—	Y5-7	—	4.00

PROOF SETS
STANDARD METALS

KM#	Date	Mintage	Identification	Issue Price	Mkt. Val.
101	1970(15)	—	KM1-15	126.50	375.00
102	1970(12)	—	Fr17-28	—	3450.

Listings For

ERITREA: refer to Ethiopia

ESSEQUIBO & DEMERARY: refer to Guyana

ESTONIA

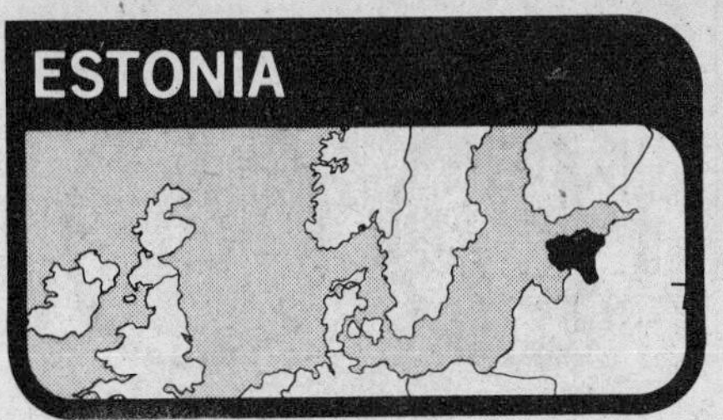

The former free state of Estonia (now the Estonian Soviet Socialist Republic of the U.S.S.R.) is the northernmost of the three Baltic states in eastern Europe. It has an area of 17,400 sq. mi. (45,100 sq. km.) and a population of 1.4 million. Capital: Tallinn. Agriculture and dairy farming are the principal industries. Butter, eggs, bacon, timber and petroleum are exported.

This small and ancient Baltic state has enjoyed but two decades of independence since the 13th century. After having been conquered by the Danes, the Livonian Knights, the Teutonic Knights of Germany (who reduced the people to serfdom), the Swedes, the Poles and Russia, Estonia declared itself an independent republic on Nov. 15, 1917 but was not freed until Feb. 1919. The peace treaty was signed Feb. 2, 1920. Shortly after the start of World War II, it was again occupied by Russia and incorporated as the 16th state of the U.S.S.R. Germany occupied the tiny state from 1941 to 1944, after which it was retaken by Russia. Most of the nations of the world, including the United States and Great Britain, have not recognized Estonia's incorporation into the Soviet Union.

The coinage, issued during the country's brief independence, is obsolete.

MONETARY SYSTEM

100 Marka = 1 Kroon

MARK

Y#	Date	Mintage	Fine	VF	XF	Unc
	COPPER-NICKEL					
4	1922	5.025	2.00	3.50	4.50	8.00
	NICKEL-BRONZE					
4a	1924	1.985	2.50	4.50	6.50	12.00

Y#	Date	Mintage	Fine	VF	XF	Unc
8	1926	3.979	4.00	6.00	8.00	15.00

3 MARKA

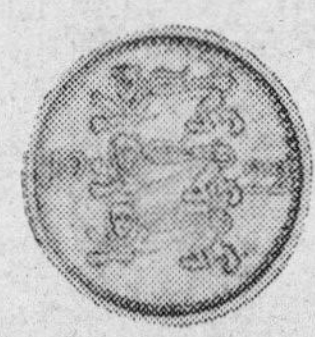

Y#	Date	Mintage	Fine	VF	XF	Unc
	COPPER-NICKEL					
5	1922	2.089	2.50	4.00	5.50	10.00
	NICKEL-BRONZE					
5a	1925	1.134	4.00	5.00	7.50	12.50

Y#	Date	Mintage	Fine	VF	XF	Unc
9	1926	.903	8.00	12.00	20.00	30.00

5 MARKA

COPPER-NICKEL

Y#	Date	Mintage	Fine	VF	XF	Unc
6	1922	3.983	2.50	3.50	6.00	12.00
		NICKEL-BRONZE				
6a	1924	1.335	4.00	6.00	8.50	17.50

Y#	Date	Mintage	Fine	VF	XF	Unc
10	1926	1.038	75.00	150.00	225.00	325.00

10 MARKA

NICKEL-BRONZE

Y#	Date	Mintage	Fine	VF	XF	Unc
7	1925	2.200	4.50	7.50	12.50	22.50
A10	1926	*2.789	—	700.00	900.00	1000.

***NOTE:** Some of this issue were melted down. Not issued to circulation.

20 MARKA

NICKEL-BRONZE

Y#	Date	Mintage	Fine	VF	XF	Unc
B10	1926	—	—	—	—	—

NOTE: Not issued to circulation.

NEW STANDARD

100 Senti = 1 Kroon

SENT

BRONZE

Y#	Date	Mintage	Fine	VF	XF	Unc
1	1929	23.553	1.00	1.75	2.75	5.00

1mm planchet

Y#	Date	Mintage	Fine	VF	XF	Unc
1a	1939	5.000	6.00	10.00	15.00	25.00

0.9mm planchet

Y#	Date	Mintage	Fine	VF	XF	Unc
1.1	1939	Inc. Ab.	6.00	10.00	15.00	25.00

2 SENTI

BRONZE

Y#	Date	Mintage	Fine	VF	XF	Unc
2	1934	5.838	1.50	2.50	3.75	8.50

5 SENTI

BRONZE

Y#	Date	Mintage	Fine	VF	XF	Unc
3	1931	11.000	2.00	2.50	3.75	8.50

10 SENTI

NICKEL-BRONZE

Y#	Date	Mintage	Fine	VF	XF	Unc
11	1931	4.089	2.00	3.50	6.00	11.00

20 SENTI

NICKEL-BRONZE

Y#	Date	Mintage	Fine	VF	XF	Unc
12	1935	4.250	2.00	3.50	5.00	14.00

25 SENTI

NICKEL-BRONZE

Y#	Date	Mintage	Fine	VF	XF	Unc
13	1928	2.025	5.00	7.00	12.50	27.50

50 SENTI

NICKEL-BRONZE

Y#	Date	Mintage	Fine	VF	XF	Unc
14	1936	1.256	5.00	9.00	15.00	30.00

KROON

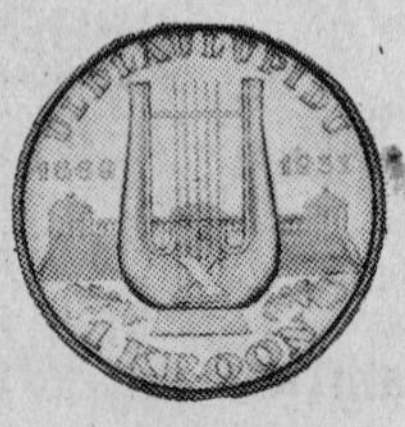

6.0000 gm., .500 SILVER, .0965 oz ASW
Tenth Singing Festival Commemorative

Y#	Date	Mintage	Fine	VF	XF	Unc
18	1933	.350	15.00	22.50	40.00	65.00

ALUMINUM-BRONZE

Y#	Date	Mintage	Fine	VF	XF	Unc
15	1934	3.304	5.00	9.00	15.00	30.00

2 KROONI

12.0000 gm., .500 SILVER, .1929 oz ASW
Tallinn Castle Commemorative

Y#	Date	Mintage	Fine	VF	XF	Unc
16	1930	1.276	8.00	12.00	17.50	30.00

University Of Tartu Tercentenary

Y#	Date	Mintage	Fine	VF	XF	Unc
17	1932	.100	12.00	17.50	35.00	70.00

ETHIOPIA

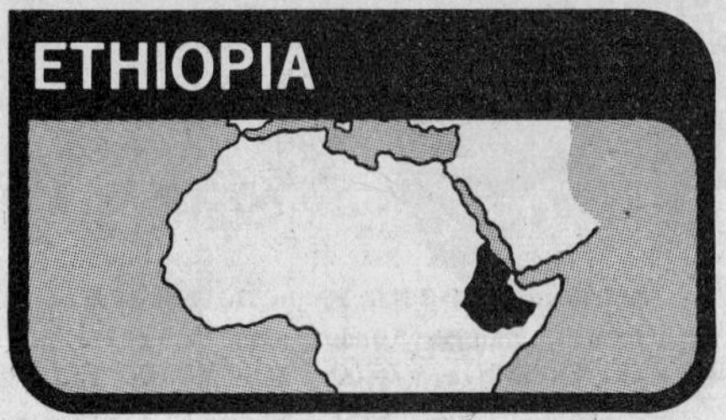

Ethiopia, Africa's oldest independent nation, faces on the Red Sea in east-central Africa. The country has an area of 471,800 sq. mi. (1,221,900 sq. km.) and a population of 27.8 million people who are divided among 40 tribes and speak 270 languages and dialects. Capital: Addis Ababa. The economy is predominantly agricultural and pastoral. Gold and platinum are mined and petroleum fields are being developed. Coffee, oilseeds, hides and cereals are exported.

Ethiopia was supposedly founded by Menelik I, son of Solomon and the Queen of Sheba in the 4th century B.C. Modern Ethiopian history began with the reign of Emperor Menelik II (1889-1913) under whose guidance the country emerged from medieval isolation. Ethiopia was invaded by Mussolini in 1935, and together with Italian Somaliland and Eritrea became part of Italian East Africa until liberated by British and Ethiopian troops in 1941. Haile Selassie I, 225th consecutive Solomonic ruler was deposed by a military committee on Sept. 12, 1974. As of July 1976, Ethiopia's present rule is by a military provisional government which refers to the country as Socialist Ethiopia.

RULERS

Menelik II, 1889-1913
Lij Yasu, 1913-1916
Zauditu, Empress, 1916-1930
Haile Selassie I
1930-36, 1941-1974

MINTMARKS

A - Paris
(a) - Paris, privy marks only

Coinage of Menelik II, 1889-1913

NOTE: The first national issue coinage, dated 1887 and 1888 E.E., carried a cornucopia, a, and fasces on the reverse. Subsequent dates have a torch substituted for the fasces, the a being dropped. All issues bearing these marks were struck at the Paris Mint. Coins without mintmarks were struck in Addis Ababa.

MONETARY SYSTEM

(Until about 1903)
40 Besa = 20 Gersh = 1 Bir
(After 1903)
32 Besa = 16 Gersh = 1 Bir

DATING

Ethiopian coinage is dated by the Ethiopian Era calendar (E.E.) which commenced 7 years and 8 months after the advent of A.D. dating.

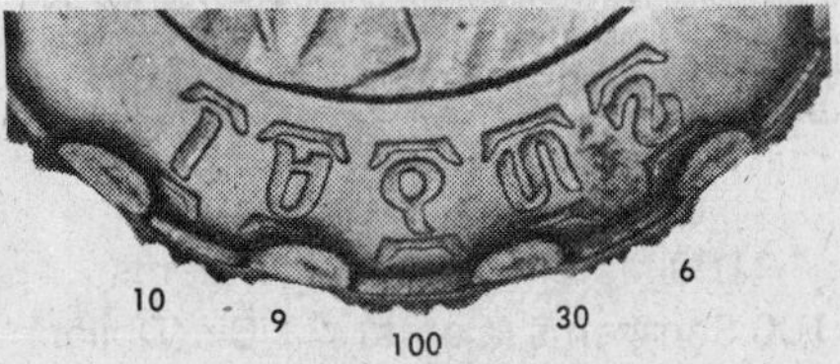

EXAMPLE

1900 (10 and 9 = 19 X 100)
36 (Add 30 and 6)
1936 E.E.
8 (Add)
1943/4 AD

MAHALEKI

SILVER, 15mm
Obv: Crown. Rev: Date, denomination and script of Ethiopia.

Y#	Date	Mintage	Good	VG	Fine	VF
A1	EE1885 (1892)		100.00	150.00	225.00	275.00

NOTE: The above issue has been reported to be the last issue of the Harrar Mint following the capture of that city in 1887 by Menelik's forces.

MONETARY REFORM

1/100 BIR

Yaber Matawasho 'Matonya'

COPPER, 25mm

Y#	Date	Mintage	Fine	VF	XF	Unc
1	EE1889A (1897)	.500	3.00	7.50	12.50	35.00

1/4 GERSH

Ya Gersh Rub

COPPER, 26mm

Y#	Date	Mintage	Fine	VF	XF	Unc
2	EE1888A (1896)	200 pcs.	—	—	—	—

1/2 GERSH

Ya Gersh Alad

COPPER, 30mm

Y#	Date	Mintage	Fine	VF	XF	Unc
3	EE1888A (1896)	200 pcs.	—	—	—	—

1/32 BIR

Ya Bir 32nd

First Issue:

COPPER or BRASS
Enlargement (below lion)

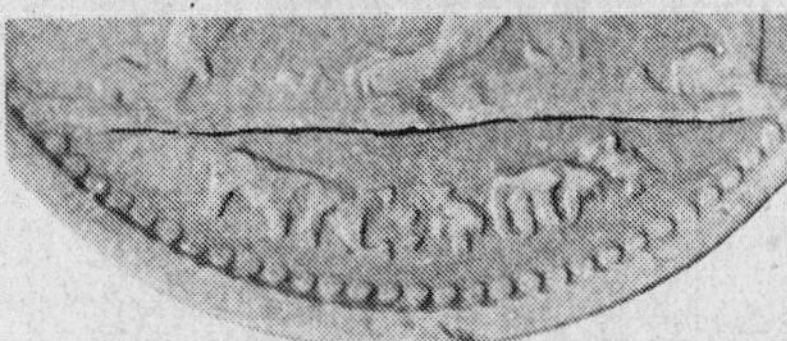

Defaced, with plain and rough edge.

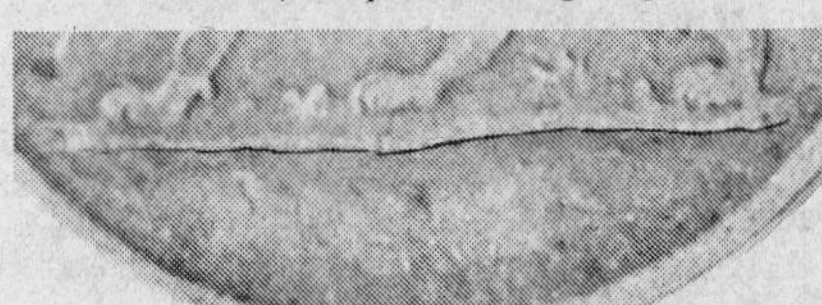

Obliterated, plain and reeded edge.

Y#	Date	Mintage	Fine	VF	XF	Unc
17	EE1889 (1897)		3.00	6.00	12.50	30.00

NOTE: This issue was struck from dies intended for a silver 1/8 Bir of the die series that included Y#19 and 20. These are found with the denomination partially to almost totally effaced from beneath the lion. First struck at the Addis Ababa Mint about 1903 from dies prepared at Paris.

Second Issue

Enlargement (below lion)

Y#	Date	Mintage	Fine	VF	XF	Unc
17a	EE1889 (1897)	3.353	5.00	12.00	25.00	50.00

NOTE: Struck at the Addis Ababa Mint in 1922, 1931 and 1933 from newly prepared dies having corrected denominations.

GERSH

1/20 BIR

COPPER, 38mm

Y#	Date	Mintage	Fine	VF	XF	Unc
4	EE1888A (1896)	200 pcs.	—	—	—	—

1.4038 gm., .835 SILVER, 16mm, .0377 oz ASW
Rev: Lion's left leg raised.

Y#	Date	Mintage	Fine	VF	XF	Unc
5	EE1889A (1897)	1.000	3.50	6.00	12.50	25.00
	1891A (1898)	4.000	2.50	4.50	8.00	17.50
	1895A (1903)	*44.789	1.25	2.00	4.00	8.50

***NOTE:** Struck between 1903-1928.

Rev: Lion's right leg raised, 17mm.

Y#	Date	Mintage	VG	Fine	VF	XF
18	EE1889 (1897)	—	55.00	90.00	125.00	175.00

1/8 BIR

(Ya Bir Tamun of Bir Eighth)

3.5094 gm., .835 SILVER, 20mm, .0942 oz ASW
Rev: Lion's left leg raised.

Y#	Date	Mintage	Fine	VF	XF	Unc
6	EE1887A (1894)	.025	30.00	55.00	85.00	150.00
	1888A (1896)	200 pcs.	—	—	—	—

1/4 BIR
(Ya Bir Rub of Bir Fourth)

7.0188 gm., .835 SILVER, 24mm, .1884 oz ASW
Rev: Lion's left leg raised.

Y#	Date	Mintage	Fine	VF	XF	Unc
7	EE1887A (1894)	.015	15.00	25.00	35.00	90.00
	1888A (1896)	200 pcs.	—	—	—	—
	1889A (1897)	.400	6.00	8.00	12.00	50.00
	1895A (1903)	*.821	6.00	8.00	12.00	45.00

***NOTE:** Struck between 1903 and 1925.

Rev: Lion's right leg raised, 25.5mm.

Y#	Date	Mintage	Fine	VF	XF	Unc
19	EE1889 (1897)	—	15.00	30.00	60.00	—

1/2 BIR
(Ya Bir Alad of Bir Half)

14.0375 gm., .835 SILVER, .3768 oz ASW
Rev: Lion's left leg raised.

Y#	Date	Mintage	Fine	VF	XF	Unc
8	EE1887A (1894)	.010	22.00	35.00	60.00	120.00
	1888A (1896)	200 pcs.	—	—	—	—
	1889A (1897)	*.420	12.00	17.50	35.00	75.00

***NOTE:** Struck between 1897 and 1925.

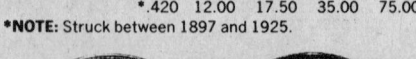

Rev: Lion's right leg raised.

Y#	Date	Mintage	Fine	VF	XF	Unc
20	EE1889 (1897)	—	50.00	85.00	125.00	—

GOLD

Y#	Date	Mintage	Fine	VF	XF	Unc
20a	EE1889 (1897)	—	—	—	1000.	1500.

BIR

28.0750 gm., .835 SILVER, 40mm, .7537 oz ASW
Rev: Lion's left leg raised.

Y#	Date	Mintage	Fine	VF	XF	Unc
9	EE1887A (1894)	.020	30.00	50.00	100.00	275.00
	1888A (1896)	200 pcs.	—	—	—	—
	1889A (1897)	.418	25.00	35.00	60.00	200.00

Rev: Lion's right leg raised.

Y#	Date	Mintage	Fine	VF	XF	Unc
10	EE1892 (1899)	.401	25.00	35.00	60.00	250.00
	1895 (1903)	*.459	25.00	35.00	60.00	250.00
	1895 (1903)	—	—	—	Proof	500.00

***NOTE:** Struck in 1901, 1903 and 1904.

1/4 WERK
(Ya Werk Rub of Werk Fourth)

1.7500 gm., .900 GOLD, 16mm, .0506 oz AGW
Similar to Y#13, 1 Wark.

Y#	Date	Mintage	Fine	VF	XF	Unc
11	EE1889 (1897)	—	50.00	65.00	85.00	100.00

1/2 WERK
(Ya Werk Alad of Werk Half)

3.5000 gm., .900 GOLD, 18mm, .1012 oz AGW

Y#	Date	Mintage	Fine	VF	XF	Unc
12	EE1889 (1897)	—	75.00	100.00	125.00	150.00

Obv: Crowned head of Haile Selassie left.
Rev: St. George slaying dragon.

Y#	Date	Mintage	Fine	VF	XF	Unc
28	EE1923 (1931)	—	100.00	150.00	200.00	300.00

WERK

7.0000 gm., .900 GOLD, 20mm, .2025 oz AGW

Y#	Date	Mintage	Fine	VF	XF	Unc
13	EE1889 (1897)	—	150.00	175.00	225.00	350.00

Y#	Date	Mintage	Fine	VF	XF	Unc
29	EE1923 (1931)	—	175.00	250.00	350.00	500.00

EMPEROR LIJ YASU

No coins, patterns or presentation pieces are known bearing his likeness or titles. Coins of Menelik II were struck during this period with dates frozen.

EMPRESS ZAUDITU

While silver dies for 1/8, 1/4, 1/2 and 1 Bir were prepared for the empress' use bearing the date 1917EE (1925AD) and a few of the silver 1/2 Bir exist, the few pieces that were struck were done in gold or gilt and used as presentation pieces. All have the date but the denominations were mutilated. To find which die was used compare the diameters with the silver equivaletns issued by Menelik II, which were struck during this period with dates frozen.

DECIMAL COINAGE

100 Matonas = 100 Santeems

100 Santeems (Cents) = 1 Bir (Dollar)

MATONA

COPPER

Y#	Date	Mintage	Fine	VF	XF	Unc
23	EE1923 (1931)	*5.000	2.00	3.50	4.50	10.00

***NOTE:** Struck by ICI in Birmingham, England. Other denominations in the Matona series were struck in Addis Ababa.

CENT
(Ano Santeem)

COPPER

Y#	Date	Mintage	Fine	VF	XF	Unc
30	EE1936 (1944)					
		20.000	—	—	.10	.25

NOTE: Coins in the one cent to fifty cent denominations were struck at Philadelphia and the Royal Mint, London between 1944 and 1975 with the date EE1936 frozen.

ALUMINUM
F.A.O. Issue

36	EE1969FM (1977)					
		.035	—	—	—	—
	1969FM (1977)					
		.012	—	—	Proof	3.00
	1970 (1978)	—	—	—	—	2.00

5 MATONAS

COPPER
Plain edge

24	EE1923 (1931)					
		1.363	2.75	4.50	7.50	17.50

Reeded edge

24	EE1923 (1931)					
		Inc. Ab.	2.75	4.50	7.50	17.50

5 CENTS
(Ammist Santeem)

COPPER

31	EE1936 (1944)					
		*219.000	—	—	.10	.25

***NOTE:** Struck between 1944-1966.

COPPER-ZINC

37	EE1969FM (1977)					
		.012	—	—	Proof	4.00

10 MATONAS

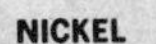

NICKEL

25	EE1923 (1931)					
		.936	1.25	2.00	3.00	4.00

10 CENTS
(Assir Santeem)

COPPER

Y#	Date	Mintage	Fine	VF	XF	Unc
32	EE1936 (1944)					
		*348.998	—	.15	.25	.50

***NOTE:** Struck between 1945-1975.

COPPER-ZINC

38	EE1969FM (1977)					
		.012	—	—	Proof	5.00

25 MATONAS

NICKEL

26	EE1923 (1931)					
		2.742	1.25	2.00	2.75	5.00

25 CENTS
(Haya: Ammist Santeem)

COPPER

33	EE1936 (1944)					
		10.000	15.00	25.00	32.00	45.00

35	EE1936 (1944)					
		*30.000	—	—	—	1.00

***NOTE:** Issued in 1952 and 1953. Crude and refined edges.

COPPER-NICKEL

39	EE1969FM (1977)					
		.012	—	—	Proof	6.00

50 MATONAS

NICKEL

Y#	Date	Mintage	Fine	VF	XF	Unc
27	EE1923 (1931)					
		1.621	1.50	2.50	3.50	6.00

50 CENTS
(Amsa Santeem)

7.0307 gm., .800 SILVER, .1808 oz ASW

34	EE1936 (1944)					
		*30.000	BV	BV	6.00	8.00

***NOTE:** Struck in 1944-1945.

7.0307 gm., .700 SILVER, .1582 oz ASW

34a	EE1936 (1944)					
		*20.434	BV	BV	5.50	8.00

***NOTE:** Struck in 1947.

COPPER-NICKEL

40	EE1969FM (1977)					
		.012	—	—	Proof	12.50

5 DOLLARS

25.0000 gm., .925 SILVER, .7435 oz ASW
Theodros II

H#	Date	Mintage	VF	XF	Unc
7	1972	—	—	Proof	25.00

Yohannes IV

8	1972	—	—	Proof	25.00

Menelik II

H#	Date	Mintage	VF	XF	Unc
9	1972	—	—	Proof	25.00

Zauditu

H#	Date	Mintage	VF	XF	Unc
10	1972	—	—	Proof	25.00

25.0000 gm., .999 SILVER, .8030 oz ASW
Haile Selassie

Y#	Date	Mintage	VF	XF	Unc
10	1972HF	.100	—	—	—
	1972HF	*3,000	—	Proof	35.00

10 DOLLARS

4.0000 gm., .900 GOLD, .1157 oz AGW
Obv: Bust of Haile Selassie. Rev: Arms.

Fr#	Date	Mintage	VF	XF	Unc
34	1966	.028	—	Proof	85.00

.925 SILVER

H#	Date	Mintage	VF	XF	Unc
11	1972	—	—	Proof	30.00

10 BIRR

28.3000 gm., .925 SILVER, .8417 oz ASW
Conservation Series
Obv: Similar to 25 Birr, Y#43.

Y#	Date	Mintage	VF	XF	Unc
42	1979	—	—	—	—
	1979	.010	—	Proof	30.00

20 DOLLARS

8.0000 gm., .900 GOLD, .2315 oz AGW
Obv: Bust of Selassie. Rev: Arms.

Fr#	Date	Mintage	VF	XF	Unc
33	1966	.025	—	Proof	175.00

25 BIRR

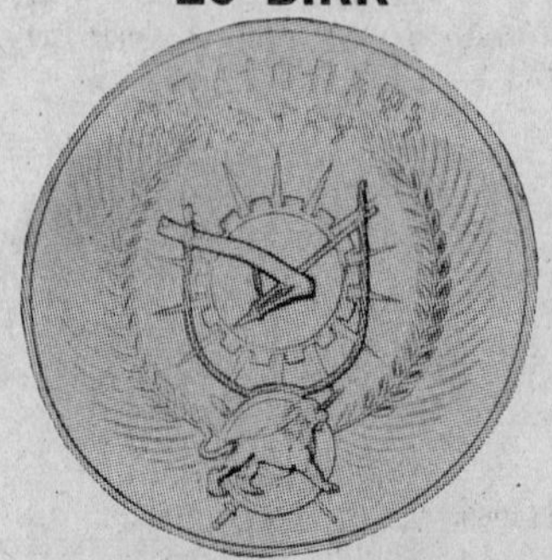

35.0000 gm., .925 SILVER, 1.0409 oz ASW
Conservation Series

Y#	Date	Mintage	VF	XF	Unc
43	1979	—	—	—	—
	1979	.010	—	Proof	50.00

50 DOLLARS

20.0000 gm., .900 GOLD, .5787 oz AGW
Obv: Bust of Selassie. Rev: Arms.

Fr#	Date	Mintage	VF	XF	Unc
32	1966	.015	—	Proof	400.00
	Obv: Bust of Theodoro II. Rev: Lion.				
36	1972	—	—	Proof	400.00
	Obv: Bust of Yohannes IV.				
37	1972	—	—	Proof	400.00
	Obv: Bust of Menelik II.				
38	1972	—	—	Proof	400.00
	Obv: Bust of Zewdith.				
39	1972	—	—	Proof	400.00

100 DOLLARS

40.0000 gm., .900 GOLD, 1.1575 oz AGW
Obv: Bust of Selassie. Rev: Arms.

Fr#	Date	Mintage	VF	XF	Unc
31	1966	.011	—	Proof	800.00
	Obv: Bust of Selassie. Rev: Lion.				
35	1972	—	—	Proof	800.00

200 DOLLARS

80.0000 gm., .900 GOLD, 2.3151 oz AGW

Fr#	Date	Mintage	VF	XF	Unc
30	1966	8,823	—	Proof	1550.

500 BIRR

33.4000 gm., .900 GOLD, .9665 oz ASW
Conservation Series
Obv: Similar to 25 Birr, Y#43.

Y#	Date	Mintage	VF	XF	Unc
44	1979	—	—	—	—
	1979	1,000	—	Proof	800.00

TOKEN ISSUES

PIASTRE
1/16 THALER

ALUMINUM

KM#	Date	Mintage	VG	Fine	VF
1	1922	—	27.50	35.00	75.00

NOTE: Issued by a commercial syndicate in Dire Dawa.

KM#	Date	Mintage	VG	Fine	VF
2	ND	—	7.50	12.50	20.00

NOTE: Issued by P. P. Trohalis in Addis Ababa.

COPPER-NICKEL-ZINC

KM#	Date	Mintage	VG	Fine	VF
3	ND	—	—	—	—

NOTE: Issued by Magdalinos Frere in Addis Ababa.

ALUMINUM

KM#	Date	Mintage	VG	Fine	VF
4	ND	—	7.50	10.00	15.00

NOTE: Issued by Prasso Concessions En Abyssinie.

NCLT ISSUES

PROOF SETS
STANDARD METALS

KM#	Date	Mintage	Identification	Issue Price	Mkt. Val.
101	1894(4)	—	Y6-9	—	1400.
102	1966(5)	8,823	F30-34	—	2200.
103	1972(5)	10,000	H7-11	46.00	150.00
104	1972(5)	10,000	F35-39	—	2400.
105	1977(5)	11,724	Y36-40	25.00	20.00
106	1979(2)	—	Y42,43	—	75.00

ERITREA

Eritrea, an Ethiopian province fronting on the Red Sea, was an Italian colony from 1890 until its incorporation into Italian East Africa in 1936. It was under British military administration from 1941 to Sept. 15, 1952, when the United Nations designated it an autonomous unit within the federation of Ethiopia and Eritrea. On Nov. 14, 1962, it was fully integrated with Ethiopia.

RULERS

Umberto I, 1889-1900
Vittorio Emanuele III, 1900-1945

MINT MARKS

M - Milan
R - Rome

MONETARY SYSTEM

100 Centesimi = 1 Lira
5 Lire = 1 Tallero

50 CENTESIMI

2.5000 gm., .835 SILVER, .0671 oz ASW

Y#	Date	Mintage	Fine	VF	XF	Unc
1	1890M	1.800	20.00	35.00	60.00	125.00

LIRA

5.0000 gm., .835 SILVER, .1342 oz ASW

Y#	Date	Mintage	Fine	VF	XF	Unc
2	1890R	.598	10.00	15.00	30.00	125.00
	1891R	2.401	10.00	15.00	30.00	125.00
	1896R	1.500	40.00	65.00	125.00	250.00

2 LIRE

10.0000 gm., .835 SILVER, .2685 oz ASW

Y#	Date	Mintage	Fine	VF	XF	Unc
3	1890R	1.000	25.00	40.00	65.00	175.00
	1896R	.750	27.50	45.00	70.00	200.00

5 LIRE/TALLERO

28.1250 gm., .900 SILVER, .8139 oz ASW

Y#	Date	Mintage	Fine	VF	XF	Unc
4	1891	.196	125.00	200.00	275.00	800.00
	1896	.200	150.00	250.00	300.00	1000.

TALLERO

28.0668 gm., .835 SILVER, .7535 oz ASW

Y#	Date	Mintage	Fine	VF	XF	Unc
5	1918R	.510	30.00	40.00	75.00	250.00

NCLT ISSUES

PROVAS (Pr)

KM#	Date	Mintage	Identification	Mkt.Val.
Pr5	1918R	—	1 Tallero	500.00

HARAR

Harar, a province and city located in eastern Ethiopia, was founded by Arab immigrants from Yemen in the 7th century. The sultanate conquered Ethiopia in the mid-16th century, and was in turn conquered by Egypt in 1875 and by Ethiopia in 1887.

RULERS

'Abd Al-Shakur,
AH1197-1209/AD1783-1794

Ahmad II,
AH1209-1236/AD1794-1821
'Abd Al-Rahman,
AH1236-1240/AD1821-1825
'Abd Al-Karim,
AH1240-1250/AD1825-1834
Abu Baker II,
AH1250-1268/AD1834-1852
Muhammad II,
AH1272-1292/AD1856-1875
'Abdallah,
AH1303-1304/AD1885-1887

MONETARY SYSTEM

Not known; 22 mahallak were said to be equal to one ashrafi, but it is probable that the 'ashrafi' was a foreign coin of some sort.

The brass coins are of various sizes, but were probably all called 'Mahallak'. The denominations of the billon and silver are unknown.

MAHALLAK

BRASS, 7-9mm, 0.2 gm.
Anonymous, without name of ruler.

C#	Date	Mintage	Good	VG	Fine	VF
10	AH1222	—	10.00	15.00	25.00	40.00
	1227	—	10.00	15.00	25.00	40.00

Other dates reported to exist.

5-7mm, 0.13 gm.

C#	Date	Mintage	Good	VG	Fine	VF
10a	ND	—	4.00	7.50	12.50	18.50

Said to be an issue of 'Abd al-Karim.

About 10 mm, 1/2 gm. Anonymous.

C#	Date	Mintage	Good	VG	Fine	VF
14a	AH1257	—	10.00	17.50	30.00	45.00
	1258	—	10.00	17.50	30.00	45.00

In the name of Muhammad II.
9-12mm.

C#	Date	Mintage	Good	VG	Fine	VF
21	AH1274	—	6.00	11.50	17.50	27.50

Different reverse inscription

C#	Date	Mintage	Good	VG	Fine	VF
24	AH1276	—	Reported, not confirmed			
	1279	—	7.00	11.50	17.50	25.00

1276 is probably a misreading for 1279.

10-14mm.

C#	Date	Mintage	Good	VG	Fine	VF
24a	AH1284	—	3.00	6.00	11.50	17.50

15-19mm.
Anonymous, in name of 'THE WEAK SLAVE'.

C#	Date	Mintage	Good	VG	Fine	VF
35	AH1303	—	3.00	6.00	11.00	16.00
	1304	—	5.00	10.00	17.50	25.00

BILLON COINS
(Mahallak?)

11-12mm, about 1/3 gm.
Anonymous

C#	Date	Mintage	Good	VG	Fine	VF
6	AH1197	—	20.00	30.00	50.00	80.00
	1202	—	18.50	27.50	50.00	80.00

12-14mm, 1.4-2.3 gm.

C#	Date	Mintage	Good	VG	Fine	VF
14	AH1203	—	14.00	20.00	37.50	65.00
	1204	—	10.00	15.00	30.00	50.00
	1205	—	11.50	17.50	34.00	55.00

There is considerable doubt concerning the interpretation of these dates.

SILVER COINS

17mm, 2.7 gm.

C#	Date	Mintage	Good	VG	Fine	VF
18	AH1205	—	—	—	—	—

This piece may be a silver copy of C#14 of the same year.

10mm

C#	Date	Mintage	Good	VG	Fine	VF
30	AH1288	—	20.00	30.00	55.00	85.00

FAEROE ISLANDS

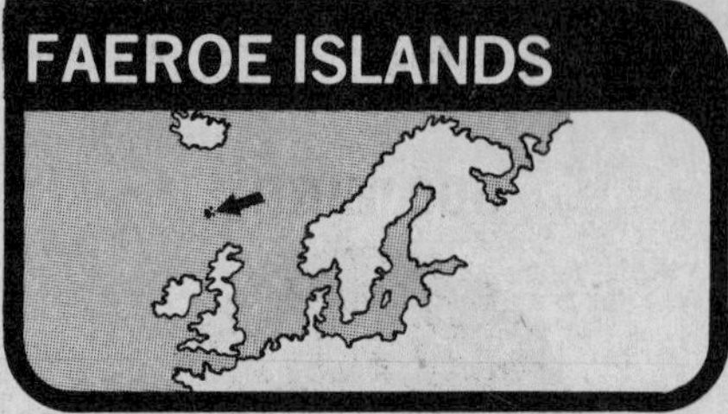

The Faeroe Islands, a self-governing community within the kingdom of Denmark, are situated in the North Atlantic between Iceland and the Shetland Islands. The 17 inhabited islands and numerous islets and reefs have an area of 540 sq. mi. (1,399 sq. km.) and a population of 40,000. Capital: Thorshavn. The principal industries are fishing and grazing. Fish and fish products are exported.

While it is thought that Irish hermits lived on the islands in the 7th and 8th centuries, the present inhabitants are descended from 6th century Norse settlers. The Faeroe Islands became a Norwegian fief in 1035 and became Danish in 1380 when Norway and Denmark were united. They have ever since remained in Danish possession and were granted self-government (except for an appointed governor-general) with their own legislature, executive and flag in 1948.

The islands were occupied by British troops during World War II, after the German occupation of Denmark. The Faeroe Island coinage was struck in London during World War II.

RULERS

Danish

MONETARY SYSTEM

100 Ore = 1 Krone

ORE

BRONZE

Y#	Date	Mintage	Fine	VF	XF	Unc
1	1941	.100	15.00	20.00	30.00	50.00

2 ORE

BRONZE

Y#	Date	Mintage	Fine	VF	XF	Unc
2	1941	.100	5.00	7.50	12.00	25.00

5 ORE

BRONZE

Y#	Date	Mintage	Fine	VF	XF	Unc
3	1941	.100	5.00	7.50	12.50	30.00

10 ORE

COPPER-NICKEL

Y#	Date	Mintage	Fine	VF	XF	Unc
4	1941	.100	5.00	7.50	12.50	35.00

25 ORE

COPPER-NICKEL

Y#	Date	Mintage	Fine	VF	XF	Unc
5	1941	.100	5.00	7.50	12.50	35.00

FALKLAND ISLANDS

The Colony of the Falkland Islands and Dependencies, a British colony located in the South Atlantic about 500 miles northeast of Cape Horn, has an area of 4,700 sq. mi. (12,173 sq. km.) and a population of 2,000. East Falkland, West Falkland, South Georgia, and South Sandwich are the largest of the 200 islands. Capital: Stanley. Sheep grazing is the main industry. Wool, whale oil, and seal oil are exported.

The Falklands were discovered by British navigator John Davis (Davys) in 1592, and named by Capt. John Strong - for Viscount Falkland, treasurer of the British navy - in 1690. French navigator Louis De Bougainville established the first settlement, at Port Louis, in 1764. The following year Capt. John Byron claimed the islands for Britain and left a small party at Saunders Island. Spain later forced the French and British to abandon their settlements but did not implement its claim to the islands. In 1829 the Republic of Buenos Aires, which claimed to have inherited the Spanish rights, sent Louis Vernet to develop a colony on the islands. In 1831 he seized three American sealing vessels, whereupon the men of the corvette, the U.S.S. Lexington, destroyed his settlement and proclaimed the Falklands to be 'free of all governance.' Britain, which had never renounced its claim, then re-established its settlement in 1833.

RULERS

British

MONETARY SYSTEM

100 Pence = 1 Pound

1/2 PENNY

BRONZE

Y#	Date	Mintage	VF	XF	Unc
1	1974	.140	—	.10	.15
	1974	.016	—	Proof	1.50

PENNY

BRONZE

Y#	Date	Mintage	VF	XF	Unc
2	1974	.096	—	.15	.25
	1974	.016	—	Proof	2.00

2 PENCE

BRONZE

Y#	Date	Mintage	VF	XF	Unc
3	1974	.072	.10	.15	.35
	1974	.016	—	Proof	2.50

5 PENCE

COPPER-NICKEL

Y#	Date	Mintage	VF	XF	Unc
4	1974	.062	.20	.30	.60
	1974	.016	—	Proof	3.50

10 PENCE

COPPER-NICKEL

Y#	Date	Mintage	VF	XF	Unc
5	1974	.082	.30	.45	1.00
	1974	.016	—	Proof	4.50

50 PENCE

COPPER-NICKEL
Queen's Silver Jubilee

Y#	Date	Mintage	VF	XF	Unc
10	1977	.100	1.00	1.35	2.00

.925 SILVER

Y#	Date	Mintage	VF	XF	Unc
10a	1977	.025	—	Proof	25.00

1/2 SOVEREIGN

3.9900 gm., .917 GOLD, .1176 oz AGW

Y#	Date	Mintage	XF	Unc	Proof
6	1974	2,500	—	—	125.00

SOVEREIGN (POUND)

7.9900 gm., .917 GOLD, .2356 oz AGW

Y#	Date	Mintage	XF	Unc	Proof
7	1974	2,500	—	—	200.00

2 POUNDS

15.9800 gm., .917 GOLD, .4712 oz AGW

Y#	Date	Mintage	XF	Unc	Proof
8	1974	2,000	—	—	325.00

5 POUNDS

39.9400 gm., .917 GOLD, 1.1776 oz AGW
Obv: Similar to 2 Pounds, Y#8.

Y#	Date	Mintage	XF	Unc	Proof
9	1974	2,000	—	—	800.00

28.2800 gm., .925 SILVER, .8411 oz ASW
Conservation Series
Obv: Portrait of Queen Elizabeth II.

Y#	Date	Mintage	VF	XF	Unc
11	1979	—	BV	BV	35.00
	1979	.010	—	Proof	45.00

10 POUNDS

35.0000 gm., .925 SILVER, 1.0410 oz AGW
Conservation Series
Obv: Portrait of Queen Elizabeth II.

Y#	Date	Mintage	VF	XF	Unc
12	1979	—	BV	BV	50.00
	1979	.010	—	Proof	60.00

150 POUNDS

33.4300 gm., .900 GOLD, .9674 oz AGW
Conservation Series
Obv: Portrait of Queen Elizabeth II.

Y#	Date	Mintage	VF	XF	Unc
13	1979	—	BV	BV	650.00
	1979	1,000	—	Proof	800.00

NCLT ISSUES

PROOF SETS
STANDARD METALS

KM#	Date	Mintage	Identification	Issue Price	Mkt. Val.
101	1974(5)	20,000	Y1-5	12.00	18.00
102	1974(4)	2,000	Y6-9	1100.	1450.
103	1979(2)	10,000	Y11-12	—	100.00

FIJI ISLANDS

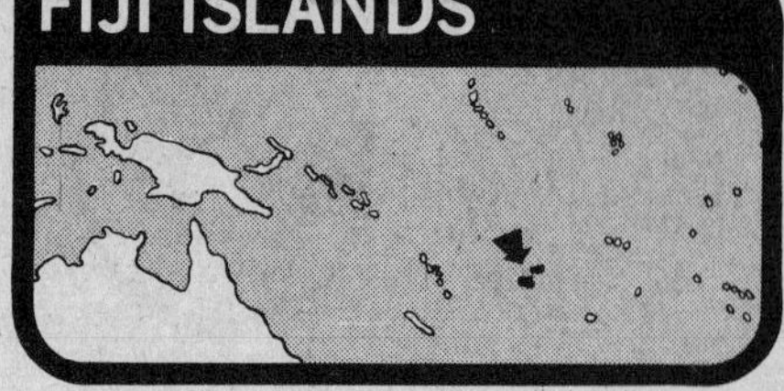

The Dominion of Fiji, an independent member of the British Commonwealth, consists of about 320 islands located in the southwestern Pacific 1,100 miles (1,770 km.) north of New Zealand. The islands have a combined area of 7,073 sq. mi. (18,319 sq. km.) and a population of 588,000. Capital: Suva. Fiji's economy is based on agriculture and mining. Sugar, coconut products, manganese, and gold are exported.

The Fiji Islands were discovered by Dutch navigator Abel Tasman in 1643 and visited by British naval captain James Cook in 1774. The first complete survey of the island was conducted by the United States in 1840. Settlement by missionaries from Tonga and traders attracted by the sandalwood trade began in 1835. Following a lengthy period of intertribal warfare, the islands were unconditionally and voluntarily ceded to Great Britain in 1874 by King Thakombau. Fiji became a sovereign and independent nation on Oct. 10, 1970, the 96th anniversary of the cession of the islands to Queen Victoria. It is a member of the Commonwealth of Nations. The Queen of England is Chief of State.

RULERS

British

MINTMARKS

S - San Francisco, U.S.A.
No mm - Royal Mint

MONETARY SYSTEM

12 Pence = 1 Shilling
2 Shillings = 1 Florin
20 Shillings = 1 Pound

1/2 PENNY

COPPER-NICKEL

Y#	Date	Mintage	Fine	VF	XF	Unc
1	1934	.096	2.50	5.00	7.50	20.00

Y#	Date	Mintage	Fine	VF	XF	Unc
7	1940	.024	12.50	25.00	35.00	55.00
	1940	—	—	—	Proof	275.00
	1941	.096	1.50	3.50	6.00	10.00
	BRASS					
7a	1942S	.250	.75	1.50	5.00	16.50
	1943S	.250	.75	1.50	5.00	16.50

COPPER-NICKEL
Obv. leg: EMPEROR dropped.

Y#	Date	Mintage	Fine	VF	XF	Unc
18	1949	.096	.75	1.50	2.75	6.00
	1949	—	—	—	Proof	200.00
	1950	.115	.35	1.00	1.75	4.00
	1951	.115	.35	1.00	1.75	4.00
	1951	—	—	—	Proof	175.00
	1952	.228	.25	.75	1.25	3.00

Y#	Date	Mintage	Fine	VF	XF	Unc
21	1954	.228	.25	.50	1.00	2.50
	1954	—	—	—	Proof	175.00

PENNY

COPPER-NICKEL

Y#	Date	Mintage	Fine	VF	XF	Unc
2	1934	.480	.75	1.75	4.25	20.00
	1935	.240	.85	2.00	5.50	30.00
	1936	.240	1.50	5.00	8.00	50.00

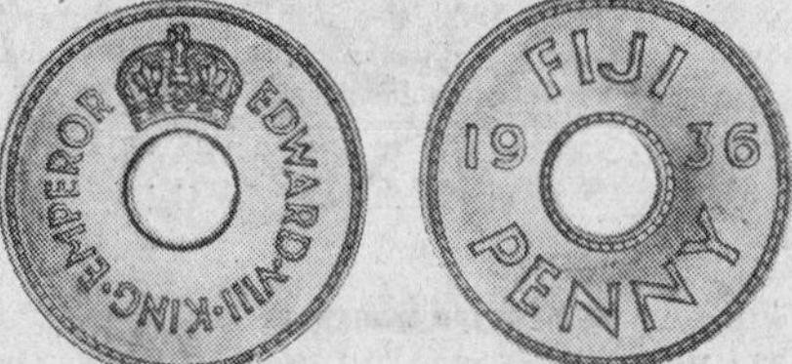

Y#	Date	Mintage	Fine	VF	XF	Unc
6	1936	.120	.75	1.75	4.25	10.00

Y#	Date	Mintage	Fine	VF	XF	Unc
8	1937	.360	.75	1.75	4.25	12.50
	1940	.144	1.75	4.00	7.00	30.00
	1941	.228	.75	2.00	4.00	8.50
	1945	.240	—	5.00	10.00	27.50

BRASS

Y#	Date	Mintage	Fine	VF	XF	Unc
8a	1942S	1.000	1.50	2.50	4.25	15.00
	1943S	1.000	1.50	2.50	4.25	15.00

COPPER-NICKEL
Obv. leg: EMPEROR dropped.

Y#	Date	Mintage	Fine	VF	XF	Unc
19	1949	.120	.35	1.00	1.75	6.50
	1949	—	—	—	Proof	200.00
	1950	.058	3.50	10.00	20.00	65.00
	1950	—	—	—	Proof	225.00
	1952	.230	.25	.75	1.25	4.50
	1952	—	—	—	Proof	200.00

Y#	Date	Mintage	Fine	VF	XF	Unc
22	1954	.511	.20	.50	1.00	2.00
	1954	—	—	—	Proof	185.00
	1955	.230	.25	.60	1.00	3.50
	1956	.230	.25	.60	1.00	3.50
	1957	.360	.15	.45	.80	3.00
	1959	.864	.15	.35	.50	1.00
	1961	.432	.20	.45	.65	1.25
	1963	.432	.20	.45	.65	1.25
	1964	.864	.15	.35	.50	1.00
	1965	1.440	.10	.30	.45	.85

Y#	Date	Mintage	Fine	VF	XF	Unc
22	1966	.720	.15	.30	.45	.85
	1967	.720	.15	.30	.45	.85
	1968	.720	.15	.30	.45	.85

THREEPENCE

NICKEL-BRASS

Y#	Date	Mintage	Fine	VF	XF	Unc
17	1947	.450	1.00	2.00	5.00	15.00
	1947	—	—	—	Proof	225.00

Obv. leg: EMPEROR dropped.

Y#	Date	Mintage	Fine	VF	XF	Unc
20	1950	.450	1.00	1.75	4.25	12.50
	1950	—	—	—	Proof	225.00
	1952	.400	.50	1.00	3.00	9.00

Y#	Date	Mintage	Fine	VF	XF	Unc
23	1955	.400	.50	1.00	2.00	5.00
	1955	—	—	—	Proof	200.00
	1956	.200	.50	1.00	3.00	6.00
	1956	—	—	—	Proof	200.00
	1958	.200	.40	.90	2.50	5.50
	1958	—	—	—	Proof	200.00
	1960	.240	.20	.65	1.00	4.00
	1960	—	—	—	Proof	150.00
	1961	.240	.20	.65	1.00	4.00
	1961	—	—	—	Proof	150.00
	1963	.240	.20	.65	.90	3.50
	1963	—	—	—	Proof	150.00
	1964	.240	.15	.35	.65	2.25
	1965	.800	.15	.30	.45	1.25
	1967	.800	.15	.30	.45	1.25

SIXPENCE

2.8276 gm., .500 SILVER, .0455 oz ASW

Y#	Date	Mintage	Fine	VF	XF	Unc
3	1934	.160	1.75	3.00	15.00	50.00
	1935	.120	3.00	6.00	17.50	65.00
	1936	.040	8.50	17.50	30.00	90.00

Y#	Date	Mintage	Fine	VF	XF	Unc
11	1937	.040	7.50	15.00	25.00	75.00
	1937	—	—	—	Proof	250.00

Obv: Smaller head

Y#	Date	Mintage	Fine	VF	XF	Unc
11a	1938	.040	7.50	15.00	27.50	80.00
	1940	.040	7.50	15.00	27.50	85.00
	1941	.040	7.50	15.00	27.50	85.00

2.8276 gm., .900 SILVER, .0818 oz ASW

Y#	Date	Mintage	Fine	VF	XF	Unc
11b	1942S	.400	BV	BV	3.00	7.00
	1943S	.400	BV	BV	3.00	7.00

COPPER-NICKEL

Y#	Date	Mintage	Fine	VF	XF	Unc
24	1953	.800	.25	.50	1.00	2.00
	1953	—	—	—	Proof	200.00
	1958	.400	.25	.60	1.75	4.00
	1961	.400	.25	.60	1.25	3.00
	1962	.400	.25	.60	1.25	3.00
	1965	.800	.15	.30	.65	1.75
	1967	.800	.15	.30	.65	1.50

SHILLING

5.6552 gm., .500 SILVER, .0909 oz ASW

Y#	Date	Mintage	Fine	VF	XF	Unc
4	1934	.360	4.00	7.00	25.00	90.00
	1935	.180	4.50	8.00	27.50	110.00
	1936	.140	5.50	9.00	30.00	125.00

Y#	Date	Mintage	Fine	VF	XF	Unc
12	1937	.040	6.50	11.00	40.00	135.00
	1937	—	—	—	Proof	300.00

Obv: Smaller head

Y#	Date	Mintage	Fine	VF	XF	Unc
12a	1938	.040	6.00	10.00	35.00	130.00
	1941	.040	6.00	10.00	35.00	130.00

5.6552 gm., .900 SILVER, .1636 oz ASW

Y#	Date	Mintage	Fine	VF	XF	Unc
12b	1942S	.500	BV	BV	5.50	8.50
	1943S	.500	BV	BV	5.50	8.50

COPPER-NICKEL

Y#	Date	Mintage	Fine	VF	XF	Unc
25	1957	.400	.50	1.25	2.50	9.00
	1958	.400	.50	1.25	2.50	9.00
	1961	.200	.75	2.00	5.00	12.00
	1962	.400	.35	1.00	2.00	5.75
	1965	.800	.25	.60	1.25	2.75

FLORIN

11.3104 gm., .500 SILVER, .1818 oz ASW

Y#	Date	Mintage	Fine	VF	XF	Unc
5	1934	.200	BV	7.00	30.00	150.00
	1935	.050	7.50	15.00	50.00	200.00
	1936	.065	6.50	12.50	40.00	175.00

Y#	Date	Mintage	Fine	VF	XF	Unc
13	1937	.030	10.00	18.00	50.00	200.00
	1937	—	—	—	Proof	400.00

Obv: Smaller head

Y#	Date	Mintage	Fine	VF	XF	Unc
13a	1938	.020	15.00	30.00	75.00	225.00
	1941	.020	15.00	30.00	75.00	225.00
	1945	*.100	12.00	30.00	70.00	200.00

***NOTE:** Quantity believed sunk during World War II.

11.3104 gm., .900 SILVER, .3273 oz ASW

Y#	Date	Mintage	Fine	VF	XF	Unc
13b	1942S	.250	BV	BV	11.00	15.00
	1943S	.250	BV	BV	11.00	15.00

COPPER-NICKEL

Y#	Date	Mintage	Fine	VF	XF	Unc
26	1957	.300	.75	1.75	3.25	10.00
	1958	.220	.75	1.75	3.25	10.00
	1962	.200	.35	.75	1.50	4.00
	1964	.200	.35	.75	1.50	4.00
	1965	.400	.25	.65	1.50	3.75

DECIMAL COINAGE

100 Cents = 1 Dollar

CENT

BRONZE

Y#	Date	Mintage	VF	XF	Unc
27	1969	11.000	—	.15	.30
	1969	.010	—	Proof	2.00
	1973	3.000	—	.15	.30
	1975	2.000	—	.15	.30
	1976	2.000	—	.15	.30

2.2600 gm., .925 SILVER, .0672 oz ASW

Y#	Date	Mintage	VF	XF	Unc
27a	1976	3,012	—	Proof	6.00

BRONZE
F.A.O. Coinage

Y#	Date	Mintage	VF	XF	Unc
38	1977	3.000	—	—	.25
	1978	3.028	—	—	—
	1978	2,000	—	Proof	3.00
	1980	2,500	—	Proof	4.00

2 CENTS

BRONZE

Y#	Date	Mintage	VF	XF	Unc
28	1969	8.000	—	.15	.35
	1969	.010	—	Proof	2.75
	1973	2.110	—	.15	.35
	1974	—	—	.15	.35
	1975	1.500	—	.15	.35
	1976	1.000	—	.15	.35
	1977	1.250	—	.10	.25
	1978	1.502	—	.10	.25
	1978	2,000	—	Proof	4.50
	1980	2,500	—	Proof	5.00

4.5300 gm., .925 SILVER, .1347 oz ASW

Y#	Date	Mintage	VF	XF	Unc
28a	1976	3,012	—	Proof	8.00

5 CENTS

COPPER-NICKEL

Y#	Date	Mintage	VF	XF	Unc
29	1969	9.200	.10	.20	.40
	1969	.010	—	Proof	3.25
	1973	.600	.10	.30	.75
	1974	.608	.10	.30	.75
	1975	1.008	.10	.20	.45
	1976	1.200	.10	.20	.45
	1977	.960	.10	.20	.50
	1978	.880	.10	.20	.50
	1978	2,000	—	Proof	5.25
	1980	2,500	—	Proof	6.00

3.2800 gm., .925 SILVER, .0975 oz ASW

Y#	Date	Mintage	VF	XF	Unc
29a	1976	3,012	—	Proof	10.00

10 CENTS

COPPER-NICKEL

Y#	Date	Mintage	VF	XF	Unc
30	1969	3.500	.20	.40	.75
	1969	.010	—	Proof	3.50
	1973	.750	.20	.50	.90
	1975	—	.20	.50	.90
	1976	.800	.20	.50	.90
	1977	.240	.25	.65	1.10
	1978	.660	.20	.45	.85
	1978	2,000	—	Proof	7.50
	1980	2,500	—	Proof	8.00

6.5500 gm., .925 SILVER, .1948 oz ASW

Y#	Date	Mintage	VF	XF	Unc
30a	1976	3,012	—	Proof	13.00

20 CENTS

COPPER-NICKEL

Y#	Date	Mintage	VF	XF	Unc
31	1969	2.000	.35	.80	1.00
	1969	.010	—	Proof	4.25
	1973	.250	.35	1.00	1.50
	1974	.252	.35	1.00	1.50
	1975	—	—	1.00	1.50
	1976	.400	—	.65	.90
	1977	.200	—	.65	.90
	1978	.420	—	.50	.85
	1978	2,000	—	Proof	10.00
	1980	2,500	—	Proof	11.00

13.0900 gm., .925 SILVER, .3893 oz ASW

Y#	Date	Mintage	VF	XF	Unc
31a	1976	3,012	—	Proof	17.50

50 CENTS

COPPER-NICKEL

Y#	Date	Mintage	VF	XF	Unc
A32	1975	—	1.50	3.00	4.00
	1976	.800	1.25	2.25	3.50
	1977	—	1.25	2.25	3.50
	1978	2,000	—	Proof	16.50
	1980	2,500	—	Proof	20.00

18.0000 gm., .925 SILVER, .5353 oz ASW

Y#	Date	Mintage	VF	XF	Unc
A32a	1976	3,012	—	Proof	25.00

COPPER-NICKEL
First Indians in Fiji Centennial

Y#	Date	Mintage	VF	XF	Unc
43	1979	.277	—	—	—
	1979	6,000	—	Proof	—

DOLLAR

COPPER-NICKEL

Y#	Date	Mintage	VF	XF	Unc
32	1969	.070	2.00	4.00	5.75
	1969	.010	—	Proof	10.00
	1976	5,001	1.25	2.25	3.25

28.2800 gm., .925 SILVER, .8411 oz ASW

32a	1976	3,012	—	Proof	40.00

COPPER-NICKEL
Independence Commemorative
Obv: Similar to Dollar, Y#32.

33	1970	.015	—	Proof	35.00

28.2800 gm., .925 SILVER, .8411 oz ASW

33a	1970	1,000	—	Proof	180.00

10 DOLLARS

30.3000 gm., .925 SILVER, .9012 oz ASW
Queen's Silver Jubilee
Obv: Similar to Dollar, Y#32.

39	1977	3,010	—	Proof Only	55.00

28.4500 gm., .925 SILVER, .8462 oz ASW
Conservation Series
Obv: Similar to Dollar, Y#32.

40	1978	—	BV	22.50	25.00
	1978	—	—	Proof	30.00

20 DOLLARS

35.3500 gm., .925 SILVER, 1.0514 oz ASW
Conservation Series
Obv: Similar to Dollar, Y#32.

Y#	Date	Mintage	VF	XF	Unc
41	1978	—	BV	35.00	40.00
	1978	—	—	Proof	50.00

25 DOLLARS

48.6000 gm., .925 SILVER, 1.4455 oz ASW
100th Anniversary of Cession to Great Britain
Obv: Similar to Dollar, Y#32.

34	1974	2,400	—	—	60.00
	1974	8,299	—	Proof	50.00

King Cakobau
Obv: Similar to Dollar, Y#32.

36	1975	836 pcs.	—	—	125.00
	1975	5,157	—	Proof	60.00

100 DOLLARS

31.3600 gm., .500 GOLD, .5042 oz AGW
100th Anniversary of Cession to Great Britain
Obv: Similar to Dollar, Y#32.

Y#	Date	Mintage	VF	XF	Unc
35	1974	1,109	BV	BV	350.00
	1974	2,321	—	Proof	350.00

31.3000 gm., .500 GOLD, .5032 oz AGW
King Cakobau
Obv: Similar to Dollar, Y#32.

37	1975	593 pcs.	BV	BV	350.00
	1975	3,197	—	Proof	350.00

250 DOLLARS

33.4000 gm., .900 GOLD, .9666 oz AGW
Conservation Series

42	1978	—	BV	BV	650.00
	1978	1,000	—	Proof	800.00

NCLT ISSUES

MINT SETS

KM#	Date	Mintage	Identification	Issue Price	Mkt. Val.
S1	1976(7)	5,007	Y27-32	9.00	12.00

PROOF SETS

STANDARD METALS

101	1969(6)	10,000	Y27-32	7.20	16.00
102	1976(7)	3,023	Y27a-32a	87.50	85.00
103	1978(6)	2,000	Y28-31,A32,38	31.00	35.00
104	1980(6)	2,500	Y28-31,A32,38	45.00	50.00

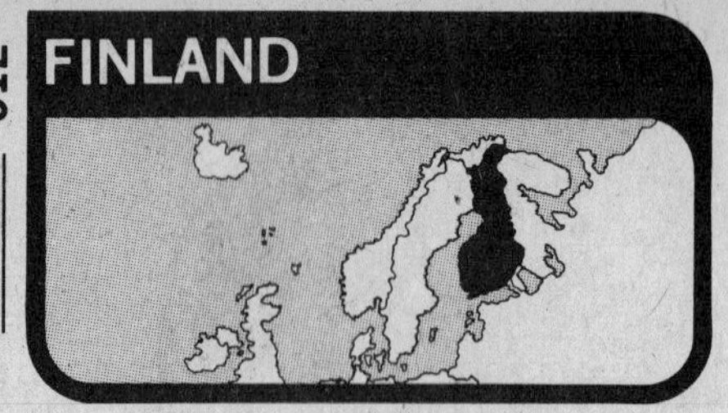

FINLAND

The Republic of Finland, the second most northerly state of the European continent, has an area of 130,160 sq. mi. (337,113 sq. km.) and a population of 4.7 million. Capital: Helsinki. Lumbering and woodworking are the leading industries. Paper, timber, woodpulp and plywood are exported.

The Finns, who probably originated in the Volga region of Russia, took Finland from the Lapps late in the 7th century. They were conquered in the 12th century by Eric IX of Sweden, and brought into contact with Western Christendom. In 1809, Finland was conquered by Alexander I of Russia, and remained an autonomous grand duchy within the Russian Empire until Dec. 6, 1917, when, shortly after the Bolshevik revolution, it declared its independence. After a brief but bitter civil war between the Russian sympathizers and Finnish nationalists in which the Whites (nationalists) were victorious, a new constitution was adopted, and in 1919 Finland was established as a republic.

RULERS

Alexander II, 1855-1881
Alexander III, 1881-1894
Nicholas II, 1894-1917

MONETARY SYSTEM

100 Pennia = 1 Markka

MINTMARKS

H - Birmingham 1921
Heart - Copenhagen 1922
No mm - Helsinki

MINTMASTER AND DESIGNER PRIVY MARKS

Date	Privy Mark
1864-1885	S - Aug. F. Soldan
1885-1912	L - Johan Conrad Lihr
1915-1947	S - Isac Sundell
1948	L - V. U. Liuhto
1948-1958	H - Uolevi Helle
1958-1975	S - Allan Soiniemi
1967-1971	S-H - Allan Soiniemi & Heikki Halvaoja
1976-	K - Timo Koivuranta
1978	K-N - Timo Koivuranta & Antti Neuvonen
1979	K-H - Timo Koivuranta & Heikki Halvaoja

PENNI

COPPER
Coarse lettering

Y#	Date	Mintage	Fine	VF	XF	Unc
7	1864	.030	600.00	1000.	1250.	2000.
(1.1)	1865	.515	6.00	15.00	25.00	75.00
	1866/5	3.673	12.00	25.00	45.00	100.00
	1866	Inc. Ab.	4.00	7.50	15.00	50.00
	1867	3.843	4.00	7.50	15.00	50.00
	1869	1.575	5.00	9.00	25.00	70.00
	1870	.500	20.00	35.00	65.00	120.00
	1871	1.500	4.00	8.00	15.00	35.00

Fine lettering

Y#	Date	Mintage	Fine	VF	XF	Unc
7a	1872	1.000	7.50	15.00	22.50	45.00
(1.2)	1873	2.000	2.00	5.00	10.00	35.00
	1874	1.450	2.00	5.00	10.00	35.00
	1875	1.550	2.00	5.00	10.00	35.00
	1876	2.005	3.50	7.50	10.00	35.00

Y#	Date	Mintage	Fine	VF	XF	Unc
10	1881	.600	4.00	8.00	20.00	55.00
	1882	.100	30.00	45.00	75.00	125.00
10	1883	3.900	.75	1.00	2.00	7.50
	1884	.404	22.50	35.00	65.00	110.00
	1888	2.290	.75	1.50	6.00	10.00
	1891	1.008	2.00	4.00	7.00	15.00
	1892	1.510	.75	1.50	4.00	10.00
	1893	2.290	.75	1.50	3.00	10.00
	1893 with dot after date					
		Inc. Ab.	30.00	60.00	100.00	150.00
	1894	1.810	.75	1.50	4.00	10.00

Y#	Date	Mintage	Fine	VF	XF	Unc
13	1895	.880	2.00	4.00	8.00	20.00
(18)	1898	1.430	.50	1.00	1.50	5.00
	1899	1.540	.50	1.00	1.50	3.00
	1900	3.550	.25	.50	.75	2.00
	1901	1.520	.35	.75	1.00	2.00
	1902	1.000	.50	1.00	1.50	4.00
	1903 sm.3	1.145	.50	1.00	1.50	4.00
	1903 lg.3	I.A.	3.00	6.00	17.50	20.00
	1904	.500	1.75	3.50	6.50	10.00
	1905	1.390	.25	.50	.75	3.00
	1906	1.020	.25	.50	1.00	4.00
	1907 normal 7					
		2.490	.50	.75	1.25	3.00
	1907 no serif on 7 arm					
		Inc. Ab.	.10	.25	.40	1.00
	1908	.950	.25	.50	.75	2.50
	1909	3.060	.10	.25	.40	1.00
	1911	2.550	.10	.20	.30	1.00
	1912	2.450	.10	.20	.30	1.00
	1913	1.650	.10	.20	.30	1.00
	1914	1.900	.10	.20	.30	1.00
	1915	2.250	.10	.20	.65	1.00
	1916	3.040	.10	.20	.30	1.00

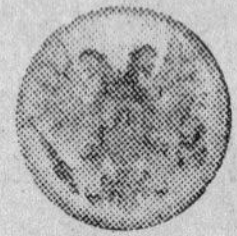

White Government Civil War Issue

Y#	Date	Mintage	Fine	VF	XF	Unc
16	1917	1.650	.10	.20	1.00	2.50
(27)						

BRONZE
Republic Issues

Y#	Date	Mintage	Fine	VF	XF	Unc
22	1919	1.200	.10	.25	.50	1.25
(33)	1920	.720	.25	.50	.65	1.25
	1921	.510	.30	.65	.75	1.25
	1922	1.060	.30	.65	.75	1.35
	1923	.990	.30	.65	.75	1.75
	1924	2.180		.10	.15	1.00

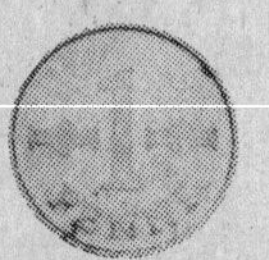

Y#	Date	Mintage	Fine	VF	XF	Unc
44	1963 square edge					
(56)		62.460	—	—	—	1.25
	1963 round edge					
		118.870	—	—	—	.75
	1964	49.300	—	—	—	.75
	1965	43.110	—	—	—	.75
	1966	36.880	—	—	—	.50
	1967	62.790	—	—	—	.25
	1968	73.400	—	—	—	.30
	1969	51.700	—	—	—	.30

ALUMINUM

Y#	Date	Mintage	Fine	VF	XF	Unc
44a	1969	28.500	—	—	.10	.25
(56a)	1970	85.100	—	—	—	.20
	1971	70.240	—	—	—	.20
	1972	95.100	—	—	—	.20
	1973	115.500	—	—	—	.20
	1974	100.132	—	—	—	.10
	1975	111.960	—	—	—	.10
	1976	34.965	—	—	—	.10
	1977	—	—	—	—	.10
	1978	—	—	—	—	.10

5 PENNIA

COPPER
Coarse lettering

Y#	Date	Mintage	Fine	VF	XF	Unc
8	1865	.480	3.00	7.00	35.00	175.00
(2.1)	1866	2.490	2.00	4.00	20.00	100.00
	1867	1.660	2.00	4.00	20.00	100.00
	1870	.300	4.00	8.00	35.00	175.00

Fine lettering

Y#	Date	Mintage	Fine	VF	XF	Unc
8a	1872	.500	3.00	6.00	27.00	130.00
(2.2)	1873	1.000	2.00	4.00	20.00	100.00
	1875	1.000	2.00	4.00	20.00	90.00

Y#	Date	Mintage	Fine	VF	XF	Unc
11	1888	.600	2.50	6.00	25.00	90.00
	1889	1.070	2.50	5.00	20.00	80.00
	1892	.330	3.00	8.00	30.00	100.00

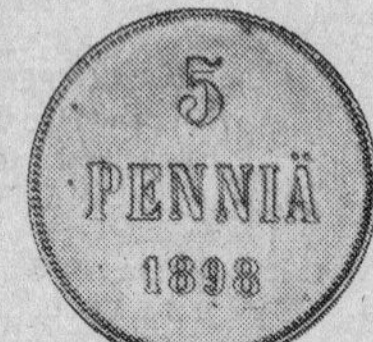

Y#	Date	Mintage	Fine	VF	XF	Unc
14	1896	.410	2.00	5.00	25.00	90.00
(19)	1897	.590	2.00	4.00	20.00	90.00
	1898	1.150	2.00	3.00	15.00	90.00
	1899	.860	2.00	3.00	15.00	90.00
	1901	.990	2.00	3.00	15.00	60.00
	1905	.620	2.00	3.00	15.00	70.00
	1906	.960	2.00	3.00	15.00	70.00
	1907	.770	2.00	3.00	15.00	85.00
	1908	1.660	1.00	2.00	5.00	40.00
	1910	.060	25.00	60.00	80.00	150.00
	1911	1.050	.50	1.00	3.00	30.00
	1912	.460	2.00	5.00	25.00	60.00
	1913	1.060	.50	2.00	3.00	10.00
	1914	.820	.50	2.00	3.00	10.00
	1915	2.080	.25	1.00	1.50	3.00
	1916	4.470	.25	1.00	1.50	3.00
	1917	4.070	.50	2.00	3.00	8.00

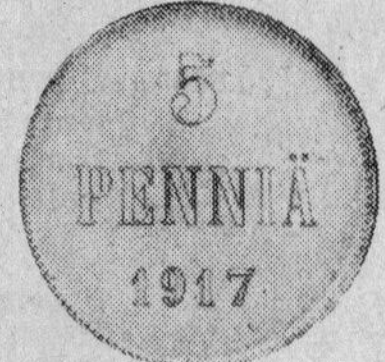

White Government Civil War Issue

Y#	Date	Mintage	Fine	VF	XF	Unc
17	1917	Inc. Ab.	1.10	2.25	3.00	5.00
(28)						

Red Government Civil War Issue
Wreath knot centered between 9 and 1 of date.

Y#	Date	Mintage	Fine	VF	XF	Unc
21.1	1918	.030	15.00	30.00	40.00	60.00
(32)						

Wreath knot above second 1 in 1918

Y#	Date	Mintage	Fine	VF	XF	Unc
21.2	1918	Inc. Ab.	25.00	45.00	75.00	120.00

IRON

Y#	Date	Mintage	Fine	VF	XF	Unc
23a	1918	.090	500.00	1000.	1200.	2000.

BRONZE

Y#	Date	Mintage	Fine	VF	XF	Unc
23	1918	4.270	—	.25	.50	2.00
(34)	1919	4.640	—	.25	.75	2.50
	1920	7.710	—	.25	.50	1.50
	1921	5.910	—	.25	.50	1.50
	1922	8.540	—	.25	.50	1.00
	1927	1.520	.75	1.50	3.00	10.00
	1928	2.110	.50	1.00	2.00	8.00
	1929	1.500	.75	1.50	3.00	8.00
	1930	2.140	.50	1.00	2.00	7.00
	1932	2.130	—	—	.25	3.00
	1934	2.180	—	—	.25	3.00
	1935	1.610	—	—	.25	2.00
	1936	2.610	—	—	.25	2.00
	1937	3.830	—	—	.25	1.00
	1938	4.300	—	—	.25	1.00
	1939	2.270	—	—	.25	1.00
	1940	1.610	—	—	.25	1.50

With punched center hole

Y#	Date	Mintage	Fine	VF	XF	Unc
33	1941	5.950	.50	1.00	1.25	1.75
(40)	1942	4.280	.50	1.00	1.25	1.75
	1943	1.530	.70	2.00	3.00	5.00

Without punched center hole

Y#	Date	Mintage	Fine	VF	XF	Unc
33.1	1941	Inc. Ab.	10.00	15.00	30.00	50.00
(40)	1942	Inc. Ab.	10.00	15.00	30.00	50.00
	1943	Inc. Ab.	20.00	30.00	50.00	70.00

NOTE: The above issues were not authorized by the government and any that exist were smuggled out of the mint by workmen.

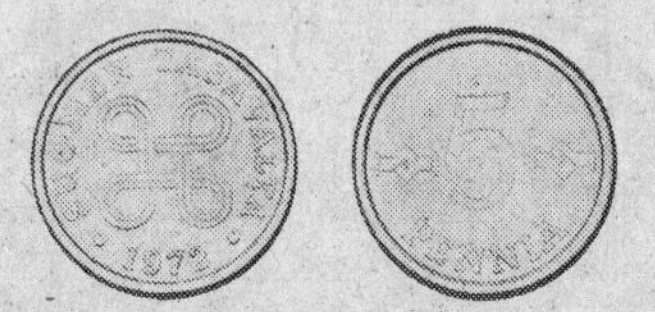

BRONZE

Y#	Date	Mintage	Fine	VF	XF	Unc
45	1963	60.820	—	.10	.20	.50
(57)	1964	4.634	.20	.50	1.25	3.00
	1965	10.264	—	.10	.20	.50
	1966	8.064	—	.10	.35	.80
	1967	9.968	—	.10	.15	.40
	1968	6.144	—	.10	.15	.40
	1969	3.598	—	.10	.20	.50
	1970	13.772	—	.10	.15	.30
	1971	20.010	—	.10	.15	.30
	1972	24.122	—	.10	.15	.25
	1973	25.644	—	.10	.15	.25
	1974	21.530	—	—	.10	.20
	1975	25.010	—	—	.10	.20
	1976	25.551	—	—	.10	.20
	1977	1.449	—	—	.10	.20

ALUMINUM

Y#	Date	Mintage	Fine	VF	XF	Unc
45a	1977	—	—	—	.10	.25
(57a)	1980	—	—	—	—	.25

10 PENNIA

COPPER
Coarse lettering

Y#	Date	Mintage	Fine	VF	XF	Unc
9	1865	.250	4.00	10.00	35.00	175.00
(3.1)	1866/5	.850	4.00	10.00	35.00	175.00
	1866	Inc. Ab.	3.00	10.00	30.00	150.00
	1867	1.440	2.00	8.00	25.00	150.00

Fine lettering

Y#	Date	Mintage	Fine	VF	XF	Unc
9a	1875	.100	40.00	75.00	150.00	400.00
(3.2)	1876 normal 6					
		.300	4.00	12.00	35.00	150.00
	1876 sm.6	I.A.	30.00	75.00	150.00	400.00

Y#	Date	Mintage	Fine	VF	XF	Unc
12	1889	.100	15.00	35.00	100.00	300.00
	1890	.106	12.00	30.00	80.00	250.00
	1891	.300	5.00	12.00	35.00	150.00

Y#	Date	Mintage	Fine	VF	XF	Unc
15	1895	.210	3.00	7.00	25.00	120.00
(20)	1896	.300	2.00	6.00	20.00	150.00
	1897	.502	2.00	5.00	15.00	100.00
	1898	.040	40.00	75.00	125.00	300.00
	1899	.440	2.00	5.00	15.00	90.00
	1900	.520	2.00	5.00	15.00	90.00
	1905	.500	1.00	2.00	12.50	45.00
	1907	.503	1.00	2.00	12.50	45.00
	1908	.320	1.50	3.00	15.00	50.00
	1909	.180	1.50	3.00	15.00	50.00
	1910	.241	1.50	3.00	15.00	50.00
	1911	.370	1.25	3.50	8.00	25.00
	1912	.191	1.75	3.50	8.00	25.00
	1913	.150	3.00	6.00	10.00	30.00
	1914	.605	.75	1.00	2.00	7.50
	1915	.420	.75	1.00	2.00	5.00
	1916	1.952	.50	1.00	2.00	5.00
	1917	1.600	.50	1.00	2.00	5.00

White Government Civil War Issue

Y#	Date	Mintage	Fine	VF	XF	Unc
18	1917	Inc. Ab.	2.50	5.00	7.50	10.00
(29)						

BRONZE
Republic Issues

Y#	Date	Mintage	Fine	VF	XF	Unc
24	1919	3.670	.10	.20	.50	2.00
(35)	1920	2.380	.10	.20	.50	3.50
	1921	3.970	.10	.20	.50	2.00
	1922	2.180	.10	.20	.50	2.00
	1923	.910	.50	1.00	2.00	5.00
	1924	1.350	.15	.30	1.00	4.00
	1926	1.690	.15	.30	1.00	4.00
	1927	1.330	.50	1.00	1.50	6.00
	1928	1.006	.50	1.00	1.50	6.00
	1929	1.560	.25	.50	1.00	5.00
	1930	.650	.50	1.00	1.50	6.50
	1931	1.040	1.00	2.00	2.50	8.50
	1934	1.680	.10	.20	.75	3.00
	1935	1.690	.10	.20	.50	2.00
	1936	2.010	.10	.20	.50	2.00
	1937	2.420	.10	.20	.35	1.00
	1938	2.940	.10	.20	.35	1.00
	1939	2.100	.10	.20	.35	1.00
	1940	2.010	.10	.20	.50	2.00

Y#	Date	Mintage	Fine	VF	XF	Unc
34	1941	3.610	.50	1.00	1.25	1.50
(41)	1942	4.970	.50	1.00	1.25	1.50
	1943	1.860	.75	1.25	2.00	2.50

Without punched center hole

Y#	Date	Mintage	Fine	VF	XF	Unc
34.1	1941	Inc. Ab.	7.50	15.00	25.00	50.00
(41)	1942	Inc. Ab.	7.50	15.00	25.00	50.00
	1943	Inc. Ab.	7.50	15.00	25.00	50.00

IRON
Reduced planchet size

Y#	Date	Mintage	Fine	VF	XF	Unc
34b	1943	1.430	.10	.50	1.00	2.50
(41a)	1944	3.040	.10	.20	.50	2.00
	1945	1.810	.50	1.00	1.50	3.00

Without punched center hole

Y#	Date	Mintage	Fine	VF	XF	Unc
34b.1	1943	Inc. Ab.	6.75	13.50	20.00	25.00
(41a)	1944	Inc. Ab.	5.00	10.00	13.50	16.50
	1945	Inc. Ab.	12.50	25.00	35.00	45.00

NOTE: The above issues were not authorized by the government and any that exist were smuggled out of the mint by workmen.

ALUMINUM-BRONZE

Y#	Date	Mintage	Fine	VF	XF	Unc
46	1963	38.420	—	.10	.20	.50
(58)						1.00
	1965	4.524	—	.10	.20	.50
	1966	3.100	—	.10	.20	.50
	1967	1.050	.15	.25	.60	1.50
	1968	3.004	—	.10	.30	.75
	1969	5.046	—	.10	.15	.40
	1970	4.000	—	.10	.15	.30
	1971	15.026	—	.10	.15	.30
	1972	19.900	—	—	.10	.25
	1973	9.200	—	—	.10	.25
	1974	8.930	—	—	.10	.20
	1975	15.064	—	—	.10	.20
	1976	10.063	—	—	.10	.20
	1977	—	—	—	.10	.20

20 PENNIA

ALUMINUM-BRONZE

Y#	Date	Mintage	Fine	VF	XF	Unc
47	1963	39.970	—	.10	.15	.40
(59)						1.00
	1965	5.704	—	.10	.20	.50
	1966	4.085	—	.10	.20	.50
	1967	1.716	—	.10	.20	.50
	1968	1.330	—	.10	.25	.60
	1969	.201	—	.25	.50	1.00
	1970	.230	—	.25	.50	1.00
	1971	5.150	—	.10	.15	.30
	1972	10.001	—	.10	.20	.50
	1973	9.462	—	—	.10	.20
	1974	12.705	—	—	.10	.20
	1975	12.068	—	—	.10	.20
	1976	20.058	—	—	.10	.20
	1977	—	—	—	.10	.20
	1980	—	—	—	—	.20

NOTE: Some 1971 issues are magnetic and command a higher premium.

25 PENNIA

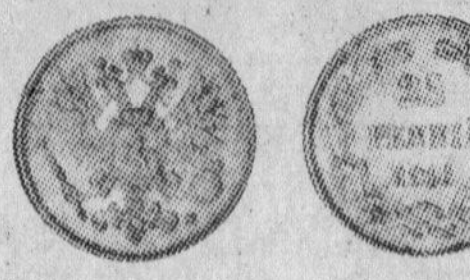

1.2747 gm., .750 SILVER, .0307 oz ASW

Coarse lettering

Y#	Date	Mintage	Fine	VF	XF	Unc
1	1865S	.705	7.00	15.00	50.00	120.00
(4.1)	1866S	.810	7.00	15.00	50.00	120.00
	1867S	.400	150.00	250.00	450.00	700.00
	1868S	.136	125.00	225.00	450.00	700.00
	1869S	.264	25.00	60.00	125.00	250.00
	1871S	.150	45.00	85.00	225.00	450.00

Fine lettering

Y#	Date	Mintage	Fine	VF	XF	Unc
1a	1872S	.400	7.00	12.50	70.00	125.00
(4.2)	1873S	.800	3.00	10.00	25.00	60.00
	1875S	.810	3.00	10.00	25.00	60.00
	1876S	.120	625.00	1250.	1500.	2000.
	1889L	.404	5.00	8.00	25.00	45.00
	1890L	.800	1.25	3.00	10.00	35.00
	1891L	.280	3.00	7.00	15.00	45.00
	1894L	.820	1.25	3.00	10.00	30.00
	1897L	.450	1.25	3.00	10.00	35.00
	1898L	.444	1.25	3.00	10.00	30.00
	1899L	.312	1.25	3.00	10.00	30.00
	1901L	.993	1.25	2.00	5.00	15.00
	1902L	.210	4.00	10.00	30.00	50.00
	1906L	.281	3.00	8.00	25.00	40.00
	1907L	.590	1.25	2.00	5.00	15.00
	1908L	.340	1.25	2.00	5.00	15.00
	1909L	1.099	1.25	2.00	5.00	8.00
	1910L	.392	2.50	4.00	15.00	20.00
	1913S	.832	BV	BV	1.25	2.00
	1915S	2.400	BV	BV	1.25	2.00
	1916S	6.392	BV	BV	1.25	2.00
	1917S	5.820	BV	BV	1.50	2.50

White Government Civil War Issue
Crown over eagle removed

Y#	Date	Mintage	Fine	VF	XF	Unc
19	1917S	2.310	BV	BV	1.25	2.00
(30)						

COPPER-NICKEL
Republic Issues

Y#	Date	Mintage	Fine	VF	XF	Unc
25	1921H	20.100	.15	.20	.30	1.50
(36)	1925S	1.250	.50	1.00	1.50	5.00
	1926S	2.820	.50	1.00	1.50	5.00
	1927S	1.120	.50	1.00	2.00	6.00
	1928S	2.920	.25	.50	1.00	4.00
	1929S	.200	2.00	4.00	10.00	20.00
	1930S	1.090	.60	1.25	1.50	5.00
	1934S	1.260	.15	.30	.65	6.00
	1935S	2.190	.10	.20	.50	5.00
	1936S	2.300	.10	.20	.50	2.50
	1937S	4.020	.10	.20	.40	2.50
	1938S	4.500	.10	.20	.40	2.00
	1939S	2.712	.10	.20	.40	2.00
	1940S	4.840	.10	.20	.40	2.00

BRONZE

Y#	Date	Mintage	Fine	VF	XF	Unc
25a	1940S	.072	1.50	3.00	6.00	12.00
(36a)	1941S	5.980	.10	.20	.40	1.00
	1942S	6.464	.10	.20	.40	1.00
	1943S	4.912	.25	.50	1.00	2.00

IRON

Y#	Date	Mintage	Fine	VF	XF	Unc
25b	1943S	2.700	.10	.20	.50	3.00
(36b)	1944S small closed 4's	5.480	.10	.20	.50	3.00
	1944S large open 4's	Inc. Ab.	.10	.20	.50	3.00
	1945S	6.810	.10	.20	.50	3.00

50 PENNIA

2.5494 gm., .750 SILVER, .0615 oz ASW

Coarse lettering

Y#	Date	Mintage	Fine	VF	XF	Unc
2	1864S	.104	7.00	20.00	60.00	125.00
(5.1)	1865S	1.184	3.00	10.00	30.00	75.00
	1866S	.363	12.00	30.00	100.00	175.00
	1868S	.140	40.00	100.00	350.00	500.00
	1869S	.144	30.00	60.00	125.00	250.00
	1869S slanted 9	Inc. Ab.	—	—	—	—
	1871S	.320	3.00	7.00	30.00	85.00

Fine lettering

Y#	Date	Mintage	Fine	VF	XF	Unc
2a	1872S	.200	4.00	8.00	40.00	75.00
(5.2)	1874S	.402	2.00	5.00	25.00	50.00
	1876S	600 pcs.	1150.	2300.	2500.	3000.
	1889L	.312	2.00	5.00	50.00	70.00
	1890L	.693	1.50	4.00	20.00	30.00
	1891L	.282	2.50	6.00	25.00	35.00
	1892L	.344	1.50	4.00	20.00	30.00
	1893L	.400	2.00	4.00	12.00	30.00
	1907L	.260	2.00	3.00	8.00	15.00
	1908L	.353	2.00	3.00	10.00	15.00
	1911L	.616	2.00	2.50	3.50	5.00
	1914S	.600	2.00	2.50	3.00	5.00
	1915S	1.000	2.00	2.50	3.00	5.00
	1916S	4.752	2.00	2.50	3.00	5.00
	1917S	3.972	2.00	2.50	3.25	5.00

White Government Civil War Issue
Crown over eagle removed

Y#	Date	Mintage	Fine	VF	XF	Unc
20	1917S	.570	3.00	4.00	5.00	6.00
(31)						

COPPER-NICKEL
Republic Issues

Y#	Date	Mintage	Fine	VF	XF	Unc
26	1921H	10.072	—	.10	.30	1.00
(37)	1923S	6.000	—	.20	.50	6.50
	1929S	.984	.50	1.00	8.00	12.00
	1934S	.612	.50	2.00	10.00	12.00
	1935S	.610	.50	2.00	10.00	14.00
	1936S	1.520	—	.20	.50	3.00
	1937S	2.350	—	.20	.30	2.00
	1938S	2.330	—	.20	.30	1.50
	1939S	1.280	—	.20	.30	1.50
	1940S	3.152	—	.20	.30	1.50

BRONZE

Y#	Date	Mintage	Fine	VF	XF	Unc
26a	1940S	.480	.75	2.00	4.00	7.00
(37a)	1941S	3.860	—	.20	.50	1.00
	1942S S close to sword handle	5.900	—	.20	.50	1.00
	1942S S close to edge of coin	Inc. Ab.	—	.50	1.00	1.50
	1943S	3.140	—	.20	.50	1.50

IRON

Y#	Date	Mintage	Fine	VF	XF	Unc
26b	1943S	1.580	.50	1.00	2.00	4.00
(37b)	1944S	7.600	.15	.30	.50	3.00
	1945S	4.700	.15	.30	1.00	5.00
	1946S	2.632	.20	.40	1.00	4.00
	1947S	1.748	.25	.50	1.25	4.00
	1948L	1.112	2.00	3.00	5.00	7.00

ALUMINUM-BRONZE

Y#	Date	Mintage	Fine	VF	XF	Unc
48	1963S	17.311	—	.15	.30	1.00
(60)	1964S	3.101	—	.15	.50	1.50
	1965S	1.667	—	.15	.30	1.00
	1966S	1.051	—	.15	.40	.75
	1967S	.400	.20	.50	1.00	1.50
	1968S	.820	.20	.30	.60	1.00
	1969S	1.341	—	—	.25	.40
	1970S	2.250	—	—	.25	.40
	1971S	10.003	—	—	.20	.30
	1972S	7.892	—	—	.20	.30
	1973S	5.430	—	—	.15	.25
	1974S	5.050	—	—	.15	.25
	1975S	4.305	—	—	.15	.25
	1976K	7.022	—	—	.15	.25
	1977K	—	—	—	.15	.25
	1980	—	—	—	—	.25

NOTE: Some 1971 issues are magnetic and command a premium.

MARKKA

5.1828 gm., .868 SILVER, .1446 oz ASW

Coarse lettering

Y#	Date	Mintage	Fine	VF	XF	Unc
3	1864S	.075	15.00	30.00	60.00	140.00
(6.1)	1865S	1.673	BV	5.00	22.00	60.00
	1866S	1.990	BV	5.00	22.00	60.00
	1867S	.852	10.00	20.00	60.00	120.00

Fine lettering

Y#	Date	Mintage	Fine	VF	XF	Unc
3a	1872S	.538	6.00	12.00	45.00	85.00
(6.2)	1874S	1.002	BV	5.00	12.00	25.00
	1890L	.841	BV	5.00	12.00	22.00
	1892L	.484	BV	5.00	12.00	25.00
	1893L	.254	BV	6.00	15.00	35.00
	1907L	.350	BV	5.00	8.00	20.00
	1908L	.153	5.00	10.00	15.00	30.00
	1915S	1.212	BV	5.00	7.00	10.00

COPPER-NICKEL
Republic Issues

Y#	Date	Mintage	Fine	VF	XF	Unc
27	1921H	10.050	.50	1.00	2.00	4.00
(38)	1922 heart	10.000	.50	2.00	4.00	7.00
	1923S	1.780	10.00	15.00	20.00	35.00
	1924S	3.270	4.00	8.00	12.00	25.00

Reduced size

Y#	Date	Mintage	Fine	VF	XF	Unc
27a	1928S	3.000	—	1.00	8.00	10.00
(39)	1929S	3.862	—	1.00	8.00	10.00
	1930S	10.284	—	.60	6.00	8.00
	1931S	2.830	—	.50	4.00	6.00
	1932S	4.140	—	.50	3.00	5.00
	1933S	4.032	—	.50	3.00	5.00
	1936S	.562	1.00	4.00	12.00	15.00
	1937S	4.930	—	.60	4.00	5.00
	1938S	4.410	—	.50	3.00	4.00
	1939S	3.070	—	.50	3.00	4.00
	1940S	3.372	—	.50	3.00	4.00

COPPER

Y#	Date	Mintage	Fine	VF	XF	Unc
27b	1940S	.084	—	2.00	5.00	10.00
(39a)	1941S	8.970	—	.25	.75	2.00
	1942S	11.200	—	.25	.75	2.00
	1943S	7.460	—	.25	.75	2.50
	1949H	250 pcs.	250.00	500.00	600.00	800.00
	1950H	.320	1.00	2.00	3.00	7.00
	1951H	4.630	.25	.50	1.00	3.00

IRON

Y#	Date	Mintage	Fine	VF	XF	Unc
27c	1943S	7.460	—	.25	1.00	4.00
(39b)	1944S	12.830	—	.25	.80	4.00

Y#	Date	Mintage	Fine	VF	XF	Unc
(39b)	1945S	21.950	—	.25	.80	4.00
	1946S	2.630	.25	.50	1.25	4.00
	1947S	1.750	.25	.50	1.25	4.00
	1948L	20.500	—	.25	.80	4.00
	1949H	17.358	—	.50	2.00	4.00
	1950H	14.654	—	.50	1.00	2.00
	1951H	21.414	—	.50	1.00	2.00
	1952H	5.410	—	1.00	2.00	4.00

Y#	Date	Mintage	Fine	VF	XF	Unc
36	1952	22.050	—	.25	.50	2.00
(47)	1953	28.618	—	.25	.50	2.00

NICKEL-PLATED IRON

Y#	Date	Mintage	Fine	VF	XF	Unc
36a	1953	6.000	1.50	3.00	6.50	10.00
(47a)	1954	36.400	—	.10	.20	.50
	1955	38.100	—	.10	.20	.50
	1956	35.600	—	.10	.20	.50
	1957	29.100	—	.10	.20	.50
	1958	19.940	—	.10	.20	.50
	1959	23.920	—	.10	.20	.50
	1960	22.020	—	.10	.20	.40
	1961	32.220	—	.10	.20	.40
	1962	29.040	—	.10	.20	.50

6.4000 gm., .350 SILVER, .0720 oz ASW

Y#	Date	Mintage	Fine	VF	XF	Unc
49	1964S	10.000	BV	BV	2.50	4.00
(61)	1965S	15.107	BV	BV	2.50	4.00
	1966S	15.200	BV	BV	2.50	4.00
	1967S	6.249	BV	BV	2.50	4.00
	1968S	3.063	BV	BV	2.50	4.00

COPPER-NICKEL

Y#	Date	Mintage	Fine	VF	XF	Unc
49a	1969S	1.300	.40	.50	.75	1.00
(61a)	1970S	12.260	.30	.35	.40	.75
	1971S	19.680	.30	.35	.40	.75
	1972S	19.890	.30	.35	.40	.75
	1973S	17.060	.30	.35	.40	.75
	1974S	18.065	.30	.35	.40	.75
	1975S	11.523	.30	.35	.40	.75
	1976K	12.048	.30	.35	.40	.75
	1977K	—	.30	.35	.40	.75
	1980	—	—	—	—	.75

2 MARKKAA

10.3657 gm., .868 SILVER, .2893 oz ASW

Coarse lettering

Y#	Date	Mintage	Fine	VF	XF	Unc
4	1865S	.203	BV	10.00	30.00	125.00
(7.1)	1866/5S	.820	BV	15.00	40.00	145.00
	1866S	Inc. Ab.	BV	15.00	40.00	125.00
	1867S	5 pieces known				
			—	—	5000.	8500.
	1870S	.500	BV	10.00	25.00	125.00

Fine lettering

Y#	Date	Mintage	Fine	VF	XF	Unc
4a	1872S	.250	BV	10.00	35.00	125.00
(7.2)	1874S	.502	BV	10.00	35.00	125.00
	1905L	.024	75.00	125.00	200.00	550.00
	1906L	.225	BV	10.00	15.00	35.00
	1907L	.125	BV	12.00	30.00	65.00
	1908L	.124	BV	10.00	15.00	25.00

5 MARKKAA

ALUMINUM-BRONZE

Y#	Date	Mintage	Fine	VF	XF	Unc
28	1928S	.580	30.00	50.00	75.00	175.00
(42)	1929S	Inc. Ab.	25.00	45.00	60.00	150.00
	1930S	.592	1.00	2.00	8.00	20.00
	1931S	3.090	.75	1.00	3.00	12.00
	1932S	.964	10.00	17.50	22.50	35.00
	1933S	1.050	.75	1.00	6.00	15.00
	1935S	.440	1.00	3.00	15.00	25.00
	1936S	.470	1.00	3.00	15.00	25.00
	1937S	1.032	.75	1.00	4.00	8.00
	1938S	.912	.75	1.00	4.00	8.00
	1939S	.752	.75	1.00	3.00	8.00
	1940S	.820	1.25	2.50	5.00	10.00
	1941S	1.452	.50	1.00	2.00	5.00
	1942S	1.390	.50	1.00	3.00	10.00
	1946S	6.160	.75	1.50	2.00	4.00

BRASS

Y#	Date	Mintage	Fine	VF	XF	Unc
28a	1946S	Inc. Ab.	.20	.40	.60	1.00
(42a)	1947S	6.550	.20	.40	.50	2.00
	1948L	8.210	.20	.40	.50	2.00
	1949H	11.014	.20	.40	.50	2.00
	1950H lg.0	4.760	.20	.40	.50	2.00
	1950H sm.0	I.A.	.20	.40	.50	2.00
	1951H	7.8000	.20	.40	.50	2.00
	1952H	1.210	1.50	3.00	6.00	15.00

IRON

Y#	Date	Mintage	Fine	VF	XF	Unc
37	1952	10.820	.25	.50	1.00	4.00
(48)	1953	9.772	.25	.50	1.00	4.00

NICKEL-PLATED IRON

Y#	Date	Mintage	Fine	VF	XF	Unc
37a	1953	Inc. Ab.	15.00	30.00	40.00	60.00
(48a)	1954	6.700	—	.25	.75	1.50
	1955	9.900	—	.25	.75	1.50
	1956	8.220	—	.25	.50	1.00
	1957	4.280	—	.25	.50	1.00
	1958	3.300	—	.25	.50	1.00
	1959	5.870	—	.25	.50	1.00
	1960	3.070	—	.50	.75	1.50
	1961	7.254	—	.25	.50	1.00
	1962	4.542	—	.50	1.00	3.00

ALUMINUM-BRONZE

Y#	Date	Mintage	Fine	VF	XF	Unc
50	1972S	.400	1.75	2.00	3.50	5.00
(A62)	1973S	2.188	1.50	1.75	2.00	2.50
	1974S	.300	1.75	2.00	2.25	2.50
	1975S	.300	1.75	2.00	2.25	2.50
	1976K	.400	1.75	2.00	2.25	2.50
	1978K	—	1.50	2.00	2.25	2.50

Y#	Date	Mintage	Fine	VF	XF	Unc
57	1979K	—	1.50	1.75	2.00	3.00
(68)	1980	—	—	—	1.00	2.00

10 MARKKAA

3.2258 gm., .900 GOLD, .0933 oz AGW

Regal Issues

Y#	Date	Mintage	Fine	VF	XF	Unc
5	1878S	.254	120.00	180.00	275.00	375.00
(8)	1879/0S	.200	120.00	180.00	275.00	400.00
	1879S	Inc. Ab.	110.00	170.00	250.00	375.00
	1881S	.100	250.00	325.00	400.00	525.00
	1882S	.386	100.00	160.00	225.00	360.00
	1904L	.102	550.00	700.00	800.00	1000.
	1905L	.043	2800.	3200.	3600.	4250.
	1913L	.396	110.00	170.00	250.00	350.00

ALUMINUM-BRONZE

Y#	Date	Mintage	Fine	VF	XF	Unc
29	1928S	.730	4.00	7.00	25.00	45.00
(43)	1929S	Inc. Ab.	4.00	7.00	20.00	40.00
	1930S	.260	2.00	5.00	20.00	35.00
	1931S	1.530	2.00	4.00	10.00	35.00
	1932S	1.010	2.00	4.00	20.00	35.00
	1934S	.154	3.00	7.00	25.00	40.00
	1935S	.081	4.00	10.00	35.00	65.00
	1936S	.304	3.50	8.00	20.00	40.00
	1937S	.181	3.00	6.00	20.00	35.00
	1938S	.631	1.00	3.00	15.00	35.00
	1939S	.133	4.50	8.00	25.00	40.00

Short roots

Y#	Date	Mintage	Fine	VF	XF	Unc
38	1952H	6.390	.25	.75	2.50	4.00
(49)	1953H	22.650	.25	.50	.75	2.50
	1954H	2.452	.50	1.00	3.00	4.00
	1955H	2.342	.50	.75	1.50	3.00
	1956H	4.240	.50	.75	1.50	3.00
	1958H	3.292	1.00	2.50	4.00	10.00
	1961S	3.580	1.00	1.75	2.50	4.00
	1962S	1.850	1.00	1.75	2.50	4.00

Long roots

Y#	Date	Mintage	Fine	VF	XF	Unc
38a	1958H	Inc. Ab.	.50	.75	2.00	4.00
(49a)	1960S	.740	1.00	1.75	3.00	6.00
	1961S	Inc. Ab.	.50	.75	2.00	4.00
	1962S	—	—	—	—	—

24.0000 gm., .900 SILVER, .6945 oz ASW
50th Anniversary of Independence

Y#	Date	Mintage	Fine	VF	XF	Unc
51	1967SH	1.000	BV	BV	22.50	25.00
(62)						

22.7500 gm., .500 SILVER, .3657 oz ASW
Paasikivi Birth Centennial

Y#	Date	Mintage	Fine	VF	XF	Unc
52	1970SH	.600	BV	BV	12.00	15.00
(63)						

24.2000 gm., .500 SILVER, .3890 oz ASW
10th European Athletic Championships

Y#	Date	Mintage	Fine	VF	XF	Unc
53	1971SH	1.000	BV	BV	12.50	15.00
(64)	1971S(H)	Inc. Ab.	12.50	15.00	17.50	20.00

NOTE: The 1971S(H) variety was the result of a worn die.

23.5000 gm., .500 SILVER, .3778 oz ASW
75th Birthday of President Kekkonen

Y#	Date	Mintage	Fine	VF	XF	Unc
54	1971SH	1.000	BV	BV	12.50	15.00
(65)						

21.7800 gm., .500 SILVER, .3501 oz ASW
60th Anniversary of Independence

Y#	Date	Mintage	Fine	VF	XF	Unc
55	1971SH	.400	BV	BV	11.50	14.00
(66)						

20 MARKKAA

6.4516 gm., .900 GOLD, .1867 oz AGW
Regal Issues

Y#	Date	Mintage	Fine	VF	XF	Unc
6	1878S	.235	325.00	475.00	575.00	650.00
(9)	1879S	.300	175.00	325.00	340.00	390.00
	1880S	.090	600.00	1150.	1250.	1500.
	1891L	.091	175.00	325.00	350.00	425.00
	1903L	.112	175.00	325.00	340.00	400.00
	1904L	.188	175.00	300.00	325.00	375.00
	1910L	.201	175.00	325.00	340.00	390.00
	1911L	.161	175.00	325.00	340.00	390.00
	1912L	.881	175.00	275.00	300.00	375.00
	1913S	.214	175.00	275.00	300.00	375.00

ALUMINUM-BRONZE

Y#	Date	Mintage	Fine	VF	XF	Unc
30	1931S	.016	20.00	30.00	50.00	85.00
(44)	1932S	.014	35.00	55.00	75.00	100.00
	1934S	.390	2.00	4.00	20.00	35.00
	1935S	.250	2.00	4.00	25.00	40.00
	1936S	.110	4.00	8.00	30.00	45.00
	1937S	.510	2.00	3.00	10.00	15.00
	1938S	.360	2.00	3.00	8.00	12.00
	1939S	.960	2.00	3.00	4.00	8.00

Y#	Date	Mintage	Fine	VF	XF	Unc
39	1952H	.083	2.50	5.00	10.00	20.00
(50)	1953H	2.880	.75	1.00	2.00	5.00
	1954H	17.030	.75	1.00	2.00	3.00
	1955H	2.800	.75	1.25	2.50	5.00
	1956H	2.540	.75	1.25	2.50	5.00
	1957H	1.050	1.00	2.00	4.00	5.00
	1958H	.510	2.00	4.00	6.00	10.00
	1959S	1.580	1.00	2.00	4.00	5.00
	1960S	3.850	.75	1.25	2.00	3.00
	1961S	4.430	.75	1.25	2.00	3.00
	1962S	2.280	1.00	2.00	2.50	4.00

25 MARKKAA

26.3000 gm., .500 SILVER, .4228 oz ASW
Winter Games in Lahti

Y#	Date	Mintage	Fine	VF	XF	Unc
56	1978KN	.500	BV	BV	13.50	16.00
(67)						

750th Anniversary of Turku

Y#	Date	Mintage	Fine	VF	XF	Unc
58	1979KH	.300	BV	BV	13.50	16.00

50 MARKKAA

ALUMINUM-BRONZE

Y#	Date	Mintage	Fine	VF	XF	Unc
40	1952H	.991	1.00	2.00	5.00	10.00
(51)	1953H	10.300	.30	1.00	2.50	5.00
	1954H	1.170	.75	2.00	4.00	10.00
	1955H	.583	1.50	3.00	5.00	12.50
	1956H	.792	1.25	2.50	5.00	12.50
	1958H	.242	5.00	10.00	15.00	25.00
	1960S	.110	25.00	35.00	50.00	75.00
	1961S	1.811	.65	1.25	2.00	6.00
	1962S	.405	1.75	3.50	4.00	8.00

100 MARKKAA

4.2105 gm., .900 GOLD, .1218 oz AGW

Y#	Date	Mintage	Fine	VF	XF	Unc
31 (45)	1926S	.050	700.00	900.00	1200.	1500.

5.2000 gm., .500 SILVER, .0836 oz ASW

Y#	Date	Mintage	Fine	VF	XF	Unc
41	1956H	3.012	BV	2.75	3.50	5.00
(53)	1957H	3.012	BV	2.75	3.50	5.00
	1958H	1.704	BV	2.75	3.50	8.00
	1959S	1.270	BV	3.00	5.00	10.00
	1960S	.290	5.00	7.50	10.00	15.00

200 MARKKAA

8.4210 gm., .900 GOLD, .2436 oz AGW

Y#	Date	Mintage	Fine	VF	XF	Unc
32 (46)	1926S	.050	800.00	1000.	1400.	1650.

8.3000 gm., .500 SILVER, .1334 oz ASW

Y#	Date	Mintage	Fine	VF	XF	Unc
42	1956H	1.552	BV	4.50	5.00	7.00
(54)	1957H normal date 7mm wide					
		2.157	BV	4.50	5.00	7.00
	1957H narrow date 6.4mm wide					
		Inc. Ab.	BV	4.50	7.00	12.50
	1958H	1.477	BV	4.50	5.00	8.00
	1958S	.034	125.00	200.00	225.00	350.00
	1959S	.070	25.00	35.00	50.00	70.00

500 MARKKAA

12.0000 gm., .500 SILVER, .1929 oz ASW
1952 Olympic Games Commemoratives

Y#	Date	Mintage	Fine	VF	XF	Unc
35	1951H	.019	75.00	150.00	300.00	575.00
(52)	1952H	.586	15.00	25.00	35.00	45.00

1000 MARKKAA

14.0000 gm., .875 SILVER, .3938 oz ASW
Markka Currency System Centennial

Y#	Date	Mintage	Fine	VF	XF	Unc
43 (55)	1960S	.201	BV	12.50	17.50	30.00

NCLT ISSUES

MINT SETS
STANDARD METALS

KM#	Date	Mintage	Identification	Issue Price	Mkt. Val.
S1	1973(7)	20,000	Y56a,57-60,61a,A62	2.75	4.00
S2	1974(7)	80,000	As above	3.75	4.00
S3	1975(7)	60,000	Y56a,57,58,59 60,61a,A62	3.75	5.00
S4	1976(7)	—	Y56a,57-60,61a,A62	3.75	6.00
S5	1977(7)	—	Y56a,57-60,61a,A62	3.75	5.00
S6	1978(7)	—	Y56a,57-60,61a,A62	4.45	5.50
S7	1979(7)	—	Y56a,57a,58-60,61a,68	4.85	6.00
S8	1980(6)	—	Y45a,46,47,48,49a,57	—	7.00

Listings For

FORMOSA: refer to China

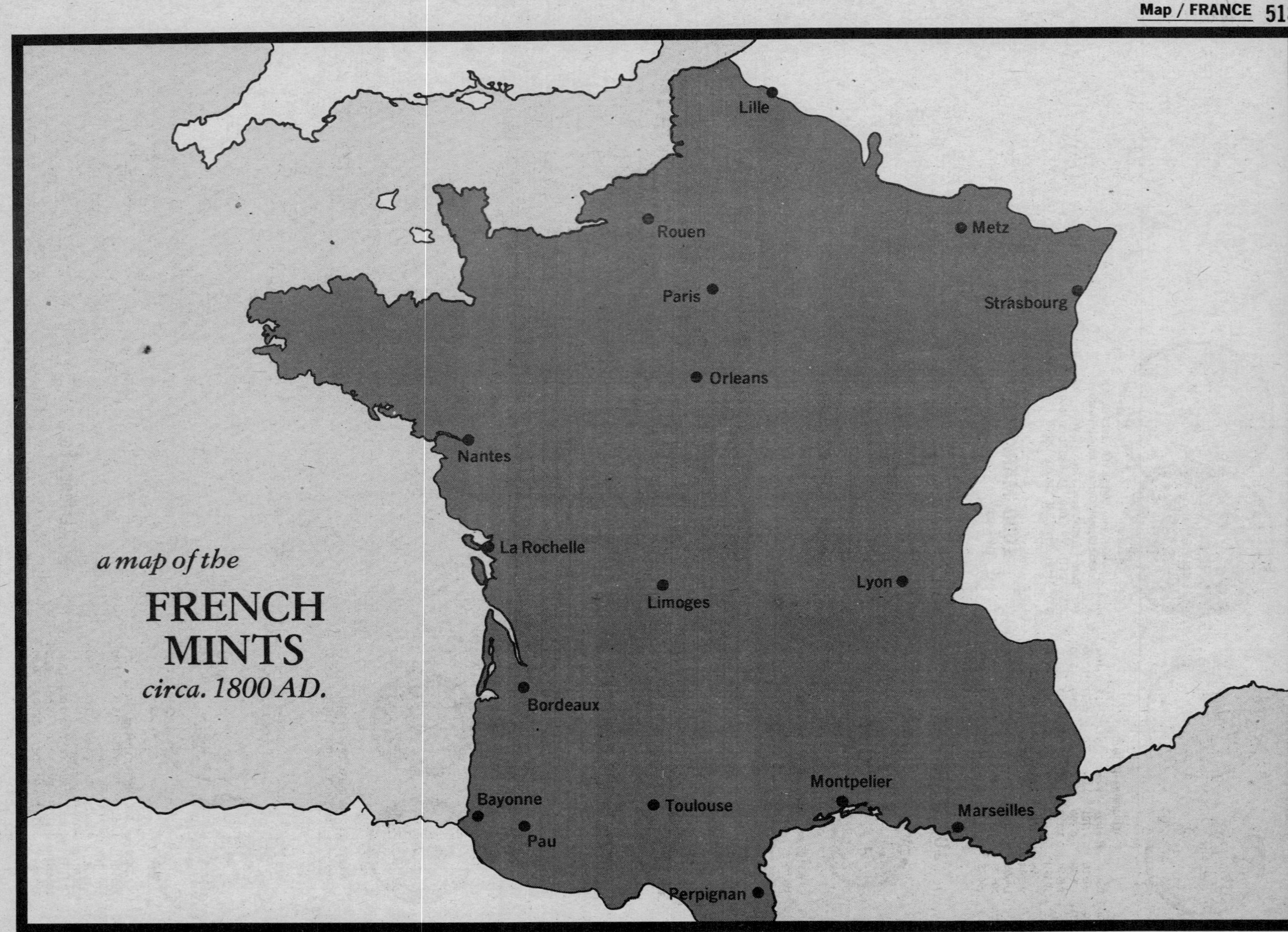
a map of the
FRENCH
MINTS
circa. 1800 AD.
Lille
Rouen
Metz
Paris
Strasbourg
Orleans
Nantes
La Rochelle
Limoges
Lyon
Bordeaux
Montpelier
Bayonne
Toulouse
Marseilles
Pau
Perpignan

FRANCE

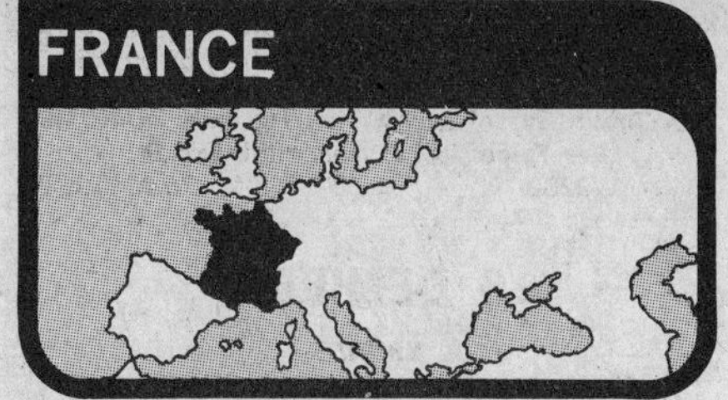

The French Republic, largest of the West European nations, has an area of 212,650 sq. mi. (550,761 sq. km.) and a population of 53 million. Capital: Paris. Agriculture, mining and manufacturing are the most important elements of France's diversified economy. Textiles and clothing, iron and steel products, machinery and transportation equipment, agricultural products and wine are exported.

France, the Gaul of ancient times, emerged from the Renaissance as a modern centralized national state which reached its zenith during the reign of Louis XIV (1643-1715) when it became an absolute monarchy and the foremost power in Europe. Although his reign marks the golden age of French culture, the domestic abuses and extravagance of Louis XIV plunged France into a series of costly wars. This, along with a system of special privileges granted the nobility and other favored groups, weakened the monarchy, brought France to bankruptcy -- and laid the way for the French Revolution of 1789-94 that shook Europe and affected the whole world.

The monarchy was abolished and the First Republic formed in 1793. The new government fell in 1799 to a coup led by Napoleon Bonaparte who, after declaring himself First Consul for life, had himself proclaimed emperor of France and king of Italy. Napoleon's military victories made him master of much of Europe, but his disastrous Russian campaign of 1812 initiated a series of defeats that led to his abdication in 1814 and exile to the island of Elba. The monarchy was briefly restored under Louis XVIII. Napoleon returned to France in March 1815, but his efforts to regain power were totally crushed at the Battle of Waterloo. He was exiled to the island of St. Helena where he died in 1821.

The monarchy under Louis XVIII was again restored in 1815, but the ultrareactionary regime of Charles X (1824-30) was overthrown by a liberal revolution and Louis Philippe of Orleans replaced him as monarch. The monarchy was ousted by the Revolution of 1848 and the Second Republic proclaimed. Louis Napoleon Bonaparte (nephew of Napoleon I) was elected president of the Second Republic. He was proclaimed emperor in 1852. As Napoleon III, he gave France two decades of prosperity under a stable, autocratic regime, but led it to defeat in the Franco-Prussian War of 1870, after which the Third Republic was established.

The Third Republic endured until 1940 and the capitulation of France to the swiftly maneuvering German forces. Marshal Henri Petain formed a puppet government that sued for peace and ruled unoccupied France from Vichy. Meanwhile, General Charles de Gaulle escaped to London where he formed a wartime government in exile and the Free French army. De Gaulle's provisional exile government was officially recognized by the Allies after the liberation of Paris in 1944, and De Gaulle, who had been serving as head of the provisional government, was formally elected to that position. In October 1945, the people overwhelmingly rejected a return to the prewar government, thus paving the way for the formation of the Fourth Republic.

De Gaulle was unanimously elected president of the Fourth Republic, but resigned in January 1946 when leftists withdrew their support. In actual operation, the Fourth Republic was remarkably like the Third, with the National Assembly the focus of power. The later years of the Fourth Republic were marked by a burst of industrial expansion unmatched in modern French history. The growth rate, however, was marred by a nagging inflationary trend that weakened the franc and undermined the competitive posture of France's export trade. This and the Algerian conflict led to the recall of De Gaulle to power, the adoption of a new constitution vesting strong powers in the executive, and the establishment in 1958 of the current Fifth Republic.

RULERS

Louis XVI, 1774-1793
First Republic, 1793-1794, L'An 2
Directory, 1795-1799, L'An 4-7
Consulate, 1799-1803, L'An 8-11
Napoleon as Consul, 1799-1804
Napoleon I as Emperor, 1804-1814
(First Restoration)
Louis XVIII, 1814-1815
Napoleon I, 1815
(Second Restoration)
Louis XVIII, 1815-1824
Charles X, 1824-1830
Louis Philippe, 1830-1848
Second Republic, 1848-1852
Napoleon III, 1852-1870
Third Republic, 1870-1940
Vichy State, 1940-1944
De Gaulle's Provisional Govt., 1944-1945

Fourth Republic, 1944-1958
Fifth Republic, 1958-----

MINTMARKS AND PRIVY MARKS

In addition to the date and mintmark which are customary on western civilization coinage, most coins manufactured by the French Mints contain two small 'Marques et Differents' as the French call them. These privy marks represent the men responsible for the dies which struck the coins. One privy mark is for the Engraver General (since 1880 the title is Chief Engraver.) The other privy mark is the signature of the Mint Director of each Mint. Since 1880 this privy mark has represented the office rather than the personage of the Mint Director, and a standard privy mark has been used (cornucopia).

For most dates these privy marks are unimportant minor features. During some issue dates, however, the marks changed. To be even more accurate sometimes the marks changed when the date didn't, even though it should have. These coins can be attributed to the proper mintage report only by considering the privy marks. Previous references have by and large ignored these privy marks. It is entirely possible that unattributed varieties may exist for any privy mark transition. All transition years which may have two varieties of privy marks have the known attribution indicated after the date (if it has been confirmed).

MINTMARKS
ENGRAVER'S GENERAL

Engraver General privy marks may appear on coins of all mints which are dated as follows:

Date	Privy Mark
1726	Rowel
1740-1786	Tower
1740-1793	Scallop
1742-1788	Lion's head
1750	Ermine
1754-1781	Cross
1759-1791	Wheel
1760-1793	Sheaf of grain
1769-1775	Tree
1769-1793	Eagle's head
1771-1793	Rose
1773-1781	Heart
1774-1792	Lyre
1775	Disk
1775-1792	Half Fleur de lis
1776-1793	Bomb
1779-1793	Tree
1781-1785	Mortar
1782	Cross
1785-1787	Bomb
1786-1792	Pitcher
1786-1793	Lamb with flag
1787	Ball
1788-1793	Star
1792	Mirror
1792-1793	Diamond
L'An 4-L'An 11	Lady Archer
An XI-1816	Tiolier (in script) Alternate
An 13-1815	Tr (in script) Signatures
1817-1824	T (in script) on Louis XVIII 1/4 F. only
1816-1824	Horse Head on other Louis XVIII (h)
1824-1830	T (in script) (t)
1830-1842	Star (s)
1843-1855	Dog Head (d)
1855-1879	Anchor (a)
1870-1871	M on Star (s)
1879	Anchor with Bar (ab)
1880-1896	Fasces (f)
1896-1930	Torch (t)
1931-1958	Wing (w)
1958-1974	Owl (o)
1974—	Fish

MINT DIRECTOR PRIVY MARKS

Not all mints used mintmarks for all periods. In the absence of a mintmark, the cornucopia privy mark serves to attribute a coin to Paris.

A - PARIS

Date	Privy Mark
1768-91	Heron (he)
1791 - L'an 2	Lioness (l)
L'An 4-5	Cornucopia
L'An 6-1821	Cock
1822-42	Anchor
1843-45	Prow of ship
1846-60	Hand (ha)
1860-79	Bee (b)
1871	(Commune), Trident (t)
1880-98	Cornucopia
1897-1920	None (n)
1901—	Cornucopia (c)

AA - METZ

1775-83	Crescent
1783-93	Grenade
1783 - L'an 2	Flask
L'An 5-9	Helmet

B - ROUEN

1786 - L'an 2	Lamb with flag
L'An 5-7	Vase
L'an 12-1844	Sheep
1845-46	Hand
1853-57	Pick & shovel

(b) - BRUSSELS

1939	None

B - BEAUMONT-LE-ROGER

1943-58	Cornucopia

BB - STRASBOURG

1743-1793	Heart
1792 - L'an 2	Heart
L'An 5-1825	Sheaf
1826-34	Beaver
1835-60	Bee (b)
1860-70	Cross (c)

C - CASTELSARRASIN

1914, 42-46	Cornucopia

CC, CL - GENOA

1805, 13-14	Prow of ship

D - LYON

1771-84	Kite hawk
1785-93	Bee
L'AN 2	Sheaf
L'An 4-7	Dog
L'An 8-XI	Monogram
L'An XI-1823	Bee
1823-39	Arc
1839-42	Tower
1848-57	Lion

G - GENEVE

L'An 7-12	Cat
L'An 12 - 1805	Fish

H - LA ROCHELLE

1770-84	Acorn
1785 - L'An 2	Anchor
L'An 11-1817	Monogram
1817-23	Lyre (l)
1824-37	Trident

I - LIMOGES

1766-91	3 Roses
1791 - L'An 2	5 Arrows
L'An 4-10	Flower
L'An XI-1822	Horizontal clasped hands
1823-37	Vertical clasped hands

K - BORDEAUX

1759-80	Clasped Hands
1781-89	Temple
1790 - L'An 2	Cadeuces
L'An 4-13	Oil Lamp (l)
L'An 13-1809	Fish (f)
1809-57	Leaf (l)
1861-68	Pick and hammer
1870-78	Cross

L - BAYONNE

1761-79	Twin tulips, stems down

Date	Privy Mark
1780 - L'An 2	2 Flowers
L'An 4-An XI	Lion head (l)
An XI-1828	Tulip (t)
1810	Tulip to right of date (tr)
1829-35	Rose
1836-37	Monogram

M - TOULOUSE

1766-92	Crown
1792 - L'An 2	Dog's head
An 5-14	Cow (c)
An 14-1811	Hammer (h)
1811-37	Monogram (m)

MA - MARSEILLES

1787-1809	Star
1809-23	Monogram
1824-38	Palm tree
1853-57	Shell

N - MONTPELLIER

1766-91	Bow
1791-93, L'An 2	Bird

Q - PERPIGNAN

1777-81	Bomb
1781-86	Cannon
1787-91	Crown
1792	Anchor
1793 - L'an 2	Angle
L'An 4-1837	Grapes

R - LONDON

1815	Lis (No engraver signature)

R - ORLEANS

1780-88	Walking dog
1788-91	Triangle
1792 - L'an 5	Compass
L'an 5	Cock

T - NANTES

1739-81	Tower
1782 - L'an 2	Cat
L'An 4-1818	Anchor
1818-20	Key
1826-35	Olive branch

U - TURIN

U, L'An 11 - 1814	Heart

W - LILLE

1759-84	Chevron
1785-93	Star
1793 - L'An 2	Level
L'An 4-1840	Caduceus
1841-46	Retort
1853-57	Lamp

& - AIX

1775	Bow

Cow (p) - PAU

1746-77	Tulip
1778-88	Scepter
1789-93	Star

Flag (u)- UTRECHT

1811-14	Fish

Crowned R (R) - ROME

1811-14	Wolf

Thunderbolt (T) - POISSY

1922-24	Cornucopia

Star (S) - Various European Mints

1916	Cornucopia

MONETARY SYSTEM

(Until 1794)

3 Deniers = 1 Liard
4 Liards = 1 Sol
20 Sols = 1 Livre
6 Livres = 1 Ecu
4 Ecus = 1 Louis D'or

EARLY COINAGE

LIARD

COPPER

C#	Date	Mintage	VG	Fine	VF	XF
71	1777H	1.407	1.50	3.00	15.00	60.00
	1777W	1.501	2.00	4.00	17.00	65.00
	1778W	1.557	1.50	3.00	15.00	60.50
	1778&	2.678	1.00	2.00	13.00	55.00
	1779H	.655	2.00	4.00	15.00	60.00
	1779W	1.803	1.00	1.75	13.00	50.00
	1780A	.164	2.50	6.00	20.00	75.00
	1780&	2.765		—	—	—
	1781H	.819	2.00	4.00	15.00	60.00
	1781W	3.191	.75	1.50	10.00	50.00
	1782AA	1.317	2.00	4.00	15.00	60.00
	1782H	.899	2.00	4.00	15.00	60.00
	1782W	2.555	1.00	2.00	13.00	55.00
	1782&	.567	1.50	2.50	15.00	60.00
	1783W	2.802	.75	1.50	10.00	50.00
	1784BB	1.333	Reported, not confirmed			
	1784D	.133	Reported, not confirmed			
	1784I	.781	2.50	6.50	20.00	75.00
	17.84L	8.614	1.00	2.00	13.00	55.00
	1784N	.955	2.50	6.00	20.00	75.00
	1784T	1.427	2.00	4.00	15.00	60.00
	1784&	.566	2.00	4.00	16.00	65.00
	1785AA	1.000	Reported, not confirmed			
	1785B	1.333	Reported, not confirmed			
	1785BB	.096	4.00	10.00	30.00	95.00
	1785L	1.244	.75	1.50	10.00	50.00
	1785N	.280	2.00	4.00	16.00	65.00
	1785T	.592	2.00	4.00	16.00	65.00
	1785W	2.115	.75	1.50	10.00	50.00
	1786AA	—	.75	1.50	10.00	50.00
	1786D	2.000	Reported, not confirmed			
	1786T	—	2.00	4.00	16.00	65.00
	1786W	—	1.50	2.50	15.00	60.00
	1786&	.200	Reported, not confirmed			
	1787T	—	2.00	4.00	16.00	65.00
	1788B	—	1.50	2.50	15.00	60.00
	1788D	.666	2.00	4.00	16.00	65.00
	1788W	.202	2.00	5.00	18.00	70.00
	1789AA	—	2.00	4.00	16.00	65.00
	1789M	2.667	.75	1.50	10.00	50.00
	1789N	2.667	.75	1.50	10.00	50.00
	1789R	—	1.50	2.50	15.00	60.00
	1789T	1.000	1.50	2.50	15.00	60.00
	1789W	—	1.50	2.50	15.00	60.00
	1790B	2.000	—	—	—	—
	1790D	2.000	.75	1.50	10.00	50.00
	1790M	—	2.00	4.00	16.00	65.00
	1790N	—	1.50	2.50	15.00	60.00
	1790T	—	.75	1.50	10.00	50.00
	1790W	—	.75	1.50	10.00	50.00
	1791B	—	.75	1.50	10.00	50.00
	1791D	16.995	.75	1.50	8.50	45.00
	1791H*	.615	2.00	4.00	16.00	65.00
	1791I	1.202	1.50	2.50	15.00	60.00
	1791K	3.683	1.50	2.50	15.00	60.00
	1791N	—	2.00	4.00	16.00	65.00
	1791T	.579	2.00	4.00	16.00	65.00

***NOTE:** The dot appears below the third letter of the monarch's name and denotes second semester coinage.

Province of Bearn Issue
Rev. leg. ends: ....RE.BD (BD LIGATE)

C#	Date	Mintage	VG	Fine	VF	XF
71a	1785(p)	.193	2.50	6.50	18.00	75.00

3 DENIERS

BRONZE
Obv. leg. ends: FRANCOIS.

C#	Date	Mintage	VG	Fine	VF	XF
86	1792D	—	9.00	20.00	60.00	150.00
	1792I	—	10.00	25.00	75.00	190.00
	1792I bell metal					
86		—	10.00	25.00	65.00	150.00

Obv: Draped bust of Louis XVI left, leg. ends: FRANCAIS.
Rev: Fasces divides value within wreath.

C#	Date	Mintage	VG	Fine	VF	XF
86a	1792BB	—	13.00	28.00	75.00	195.00

6 DENIERS

BRONZE
Similar to C#87a, obv. leg. ends: FRANCOIS.

C#	Date	Mintage	VG	Fine	VF	XF
87	1792D	—	12.00	25.00	75.00	175.00
	1792I	—	8.00	19.00	55.00	125.00
	1792MA	—	18.00	40.00	95.00	225.00
	1792T	—	12.00	25.00	75.00	175.00
	1793K	—	18.50	40.00	95.00	225.00
	1793T	—	10.00	23.00	70.00	150.00

Obv. leg. ends: FRANCAIS.

C#	Date	Mintage	VG	Fine	VF	XF
87a	1792BB	—	8.00	20.00	60.00	150.00
	1793BB	—	16.00	40.00	100.00	200.00

1/2 SOL

COPPER

C#	Date	Mintage	VG	Fine	VF	XF
72	1777W	Inc. C#71	2.00	4.00	20.00	100.00
	1778H	—	2.00	4.00	20.00	100.00
	1778I	—	2.00	4.00	20.00	100.00
	1778W	Inc. C#71	2.00	4.00	20.00	100.00
	1778&	Inc. C#71	2.00	4.00	20.00	100.00
	1779D	4.196	—	—	—	—
	1779N	1.232	2.00	4.00	20.00	100.00
	1779&	1.271	1.50	3.00	18.00	90.00
	1780A	Inc. C#71	2.50	5.00	21.00	115.00
	1780H	.773	2.00	4.00	20.00	100.00
	1780/79N	I.A.	3.00	6.00	27.00	125.00
	1780N	.187	2.50	5.00	21.00	115.00
	1780&	Inc. C#71	1.50	3.00	18.00	90.00
	1781A	.164	2.50	5.00	21.00	115.00
	1781AA	1.042	2.00	4.00	20.00	100.00
	1781&	.636	2.50	5.00	21.00	115.00
	1782A	.168	2.50	5.00	23.00	120.00
	1782AA	Inc. C#71	2.00	4.00	20.00	100.00
	1782H	—	2.50	5.00	21.00	115.00
	1782N	—	2.50	5.00	21.00	115.00
	1782&	Inc. C#71	2.50	5.00	21.00	115.00
	1783A*	.124	3.00	8.00	28.00	140.00
	1783M	1.175	2.00	4.00	20.00	100.00
	1783&	.052	5.00	11.00	48.00	140.00
	1784A	.097	4.00	9.00	38.00	125.00
	1784BB	.667	2.50	5.00	21.00	115.00
	1784D	.667	Reported, not confirmed			
	1784M	.799	2.50	5.00	21.00	115.00
	1784&	.500	Reported, not confirmed			
	1785A	.328	3.00	5.50	23.00	120.00
	1785AA	1.000	Reported, not confirmed			
	1785B	.673	2.50	5.00	21.00	115.00
	1785BB	.480	3.00	5.50	23.00	120.00
	1785L	Inc. C#71	1.50	3.00	18.00	90.00
	1785T	Inc. C#71	2.50	5.00	21.00	115.00
	1785&	.320	3.00	5.50	23.00	120.00
	1786AA	—	2.00	4.00	20.00	100.00
	1786D	.500	Reported, not confirmed			
	1786T	—	2.00	4.00	20.00	100.00
	1786&	.500	2.50	5.00	21.00	115.00
	1787AA	—	2.00	4.00	20.00	100.00
	1787T	—	2.00	4.00	20.00	100.00
	1788AA	.291	3.00	6.00	25.00	125.00
	1788B	.800	Reported, not confirmed			
	1788D	Inc. C#71	2.50	5.00	21.00	115.00
	1788MA	1.375	1.50	3.00	18.00	90.00
	1788T	.460	2.50	5.00	21.00	115.00
	1788W					

C#	Date	Mintage	VG	Fine	VF	XF
72		Inc. C#71	2.50	5.00	21.00	115.00
	1789A	—	1.50	3.00	18.00	90.00
	1789M	1.333	1.50	3.00	18.00	90.00
	1789MA	—	2.00	4.00	20.00	100.00
	1789N	1.333	2.00	4.00	20.00	100.00
	1789R	—	2.00	4.00	20.00	100.00
	1789T	.500	2.50	5.00	21.00	115.00
	1789W	—	1.50	3.00	18.00	90.00
	1790B	1.000	Reported, not confirmed			
	1790D	1.000	Reported, not confirmed			
	1790N	—	2.50	5.00	21.00	115.00
	1790T	—	2.50	5.00	21.00	115.00
	1790W	—	2.50	5.00	21.00	115.00
	1791AA	4.105	1.50	3.00	18.00	90.00
	1791B	16.995	1.00	2.00	9.00	60.00
	1791H	Inc. C#71	2.50	5.00	21.00	115.00
	1791I	Inc. C#71	1.50	3.00	18.00	90.00
	1791K	Inc. C#71	1.50	3.00	18.00	90.00
	1791MA	2.121	1.50	3.00	18.00	90.00
	1791T	Inc. C#71	2.50	5.00	21.00	115.00
	1791W	.176	3.00	6.50	25.00	120.00

***NOTE:** The "dot" appears below the third letter of the monarch's name and denotes second semester coinage.

Province of Bearn Issue

Rev. leg. ends: ....RE. BD (LIGATE BD)

C#	Date	Mintage	VG	Fine	VF	XF
72a	1785(p)	—	2.50	5.00	21.00	110.00
	1786(p)	—	2.50	5.00	21.00	110.00

BRONZE

Obv. dated: L'AN II

C#	Date	Mintage	VG	Fine	VF	XF
121	1793H	—	32.00	110.00	275.00	650.00
	1793H (restrike)		35.00	130.00	325.00	700.00
	1793I	1 known	—	—	Rare	—

12 DENIERS

BRONZE

Obv. leg. ends: FRANCOIS.

C#	Date	Mintage	VG	Fine	VF	XF
88	1791A	—	2.50	5.00	20.00	85.00
	1791AA	—	4.50	9.00	30.00	100.00
	1791B	—	3.50	6.50	25.00	90.00
	1791BB	—	6.00	15.00	50.00	160.00
	1791D	—	5.00	10.50	33.00	110.00
	1791I	—	5.00	10.50	33.00	110.00
	1791K	—	4.50	9.00	30.00	100.00
	1791L	—	5.00	10.50	33.00	110.00
	1791M	—	5.00	10.50	33.00	110.00
	1791MA	—	5.00	10.50	33.00	110.00
	1791N	—	5.00	10.50	33.00	110.00
	1791Q	—	5.00	10.50	33.00	110.00
	1791R	—	4.50	9.00	30.00	110.00
	1791T	—	5.00	10.50	33.00	110.00
	1792A	—	2.50	5.00	20.00	85.00
	1792AA	—	5.00	10.50	33.00	110.00
	1792B	—	4.50	9.00	30.00	100.00
	1792BB	—	3.00	6.00	22.00	85.00
	1792D	—	4.50	9.00	30.00	100.00
	1792D.	—	4.50	9.00	30.00	100.00
	1792H	—	8.00	15.00	50.00	115.00
	1792I	—	4.50	9.00	30.00	100.00
	1792K	—	4.50	9.00	30.00	100.00
	1792L	—	4.50	9.00	30.00	100.00
	1792M	—	4.50	9.00	30.00	100.00
	1792MA	—	4.50	9.00	30.00	100.00
	1792N	—	6.00	12.00	35.00	105.00
	1792Q	—	6.00	12.00	35.00	105.00
	1792R	—	4.50	9.00	30.00	100.00
	1792T	—	4.50	9.00	30.00	100.00
	1792W	—	4.50	9.00	30.00	100.00
	1792(p)	—	8.00	17.00	65.00	120.00
	1793A	—	4.50	9.00	30.00	100.00
	1793D	—	4.50	9.00	30.00	100.00
	1793D	—	4.50	9.00	30.00	100.00
	1793K	—	4.50	9.00	30.00	100.00
88	1793L	—	5.00	11.00	40.00	110.00
	1793M	—	5.00	11.00	40.00	110.00
	1793MA	—	8.00	17.00	60.00	150.00
	1793N	—	5.00	11.00	40.00	110.00
	1793T	—	4.50	9.00	30.00	100.00
	1793W	—	4.00	8.00	25.00	95.00
	1793(p)	—	9.00	20.00	75.00	185.00

Obv. leg. ends: FRANCAIS.

C#	Date	Mintage	VG	Fine	VF	XF
88a	1791A	—	Reported not confirmed			
	1792BB	—	4.00	8.00	30.00	110.00
	1793BB	—	8.00	19.00	45.00	125.00

SOL

COPPER

C#	Date	Mintage	VG	Fine	VF	XF
73	1777H	Inc. C#71	2.50	5.00	16.00	90.00
	1777N	.127	—	—	—	—
	1777R	.400	Reported, not confirmed			
	1777W	Inc. C#71	1.50	3.00	10.00	65.00
	1778H	.089	—	—	—	—
	1778I	Inc. C#72	—	—	—	—
	1778N	—	2.50	5.00	16.00	90.00
	1778W	Inc. C#71	1.50	3.00	10.00	65.00
	1778&	Inc. C#71	1.25	3.00	10.00	65.00
	1779A	.051	—	—	—	—
	1779D	Inc. C#72	1.25	3.00	10.00	65.00
	1779H	Inc. C#71	2.50	5.00	16.00	90.00
	1779I	.764	2.50	5.00	16.00	90.00
	1779N	Inc. C#72	2.00	4.00	13.00	80.00
	1779W	Inc. C#71	1.50	3.00	10.00	65.00
	1779&	Inc. C#72	2.00	4.00	13.00	80.00
	1780AA	.497	2.50	5.00	16.00	90.00
	1780H	Inc. C#72	2.00	4.00	13.00	80.00
	1780I	1.024	2.00	4.00	13.00	80.00
	1780N	Inc. C#72	3.00	6.00	18.00	95.00
	1780W	1.426	2.00	4.00	13.00	80.00
	1780&	Inc. C#71	1.25	3.00	10.00	65.00
	1781A	Inc. C#72	3.00	6.00	18.00	95.00
	1781H	Inc. C#71	2.50	5.00	16.00	90.00
	1781W	Inc. C#71	1.25	3.00	10.00	65.00
	1781&	Inc. C#72	2.50	5.00	16.00	90.00
	1782AA	Inc. C#71	2.00	4.00	13.00	80.00
	1782R	.181	3.00	6.00	18.00	95.00
	1782W	Inc. C#71	1.50	3.00	10.00	65.00
	1782&	Inc. C#71	2.50	5.00	16.00	90.00
	1783A	Inc. C#72	3.00	6.00	18.00	95.00
	1783AA	.165	3.00	6.00	18.00	95.00
	1783BB	—	2.00	4.00	13.00	80.00
	1783H	.084	4.50	7.50	20.00	100.00
	1783I	.205	3.00	6.00	18.00	95.00
	1783K	.396	2.50	5.00	16.00	90.00
	1783L	1.000	Reported, not confirmed			
	1783M	Inc. C#71	2.00	4.00	13.00	80.00
	1783N	.855	2.50	5.00	16.00	90.00
	1783R	.061	4.75	8.00	21.00	105.00
	1783W	Inc. C#71	1.50	3.00	10.00	65.00
	1783&	Inc. C#72	—	—	—	—
	1784A	Inc. C#72	4.50	7.50	20.00	100.00
	1784AA	1.252	2.00	4.00	13.00	80.00
	1784BB	Inc. C#72	2.00	4.00	13.00	80.00
	1784D	1.712	1.50	3.00	10.00	65.00
	1784H	.533	2.50	5.00	16.00	90.00
	1784I	Inc. C#71	2.00	4.00	13.00	80.00
73	1784K	1.108	2.00	4.00	13.00	80.00
	1784L	1.000	Reported, not confirmed			
	1784M	Inc. C#72	2.00	4.00	13.00	80.00
	1784N	Inc. C#71	2.00	4.00	13.00	80.00
	1784R	.155	3.00	6.00	18.00	95.00
	1784T	2.000	Reported, not confirmed			
	1784W	2.424	1.50	3.00	9.00	55.00
	1784&	Inc. C#71	2.50	5.00	16.00	80.00
	1785A	Inc. C#72	2.50	5.00	16.00	90.00
	1785AA	.892	2.00	4.00	13.00	80.00
	1785B	Inc. C#72	2.00	4.00	13.00	80.00
	1785BB	.720	2.00	4.00	13.00	80.00
	1785D	—	1.50	3.00	9.00	55.00
	1785H	—	2.00	4.00	13.00	80.00
	1785I	.757	2.00	4.00	13.00	80.00
	1785K	.079	4.50	7.50	20.00	100.00
	1785L	—	2.50	5.00	16.00	90.00
	1785N	Inc. C#71	2.50	5.00	16.00	90.00
	1785R	.073	4.50	7.50	20.00	100.00
	1785T	Inc. C#71	2.00	4.00	13.00	80.00
	1785W	Inc. C#71	1.50	3.00	9.00	55.00
	1785&	Inc. C#72	2.50	5.00	16.00	90.00
	1786A	—	1.35	2.75	8.50	55.00
	1786AA	—	1.50	3.00	9.00	55.00
	1786D	.250	1.50	3.00	9.00	55.00
	1786H	—	2.00	4.00	13.00	80.00
	1786K	—	2.00	4.00	13.00	80.00
	1786R	—	1.25	2.50	7.50	50.00
	1786T	—	1.50	3.00	9.00	55.00
	1786W	—	1.50	3.00	9.00	55.00
	1786&	.250	1.50	3.00	9.00	55.00
	1787B	1.600	Reported, not confirmed			
	1787D	—	1.50	3.00	9.00	55.00
	1787H	—	1.50	3.00	9.00	55.00
	1787I	—	2.00	4.00	13.00	80.00
	1787K	—	1.50	3.00	9.00	55.00
	1787MA	—	2.00	4.00	13.00	80.00
	1787R	—	1.55	3.00	9.00	55.00
	1787T	—	2.00	4.00	13.00	80.00
	1787W	—	1.55	3.00	9.00	55.00
	1788A	.349	—	—	—	—
	1788AA	Inc. C#72	2.50	5.00	16.00	90.00
	1788B	—	1.50	3.00	9.00	55.00
	1788D	Inc. C#71	2.00	4.00	13.00	80.00
	1788H	.042	—	—	—	—
	1788K	—	1.50	3.00	9.00	55.00
	1788MA	Inc. C#72	1.50	3.00	9.00	55.00
	1788R	9,480	12.00	30.00	65.00	155.00
	1788T	Inc. C#72	2.50	5.00	16.00	90.00
	1788W	—	2.50	5.00	16.00	90.00
	1789A*	—	1.35	2.75	8.50	55.00
	1789B	—	1.50	3.00	9.00	55.00
	1789H	—	1.50	3.00	9.00	55.00
	1789K	—	1.50	3.00	9.00	55.00
	1789M	.667	1.50	3.00	9.00	55.00
	1789MA	—	2.00	4.00	13.00	80.00
	1789N	.667	2.00	4.00	13.00	80.00
	1789R	—	1.00	1.75	7.00	40.00
	1789T	.500	Reported, not confirmed			
	1789W	—	1.50	3.00	9.00	55.00
	1790AA	—	1.50	3.00	9.00	55.00
	1790B	3.000	1.50	3.00	9.00	55.00
	1790D	3.000	1.25	2.50	7.00	48.00
	1790K	.120	3.00	6.00	18.00	95.00
	1790M	—	1.25	2.50	7.00	48.00
	1790N	—	2.00	4.00	13.00	80.00
	1790R	—	1.50	3.00	9.00	55.00
	1790W	—	1.25	2.50	7.00	48.00
	1791A(he)	—	1.25	2.50	7.00	48.00
	1791A(he)*	—	1.25	2.50	7.00	48.00
	1791A(l)	—	1.50	3.00	9.00	55.00
	1791A(L)*	—	1.50	3.00	9.00	55.00
	1791A (error: GRTIA)	—	6.00	15.00	33.00	100.00
	1791AA*	Inc. C#72	1.00	1.75	6.50	45.00
	1791B	Inc. C#71	1.00	1.75	6.50	45.00
	1791B*	Inc. C#71	1.00	1.75	6.50	45.00
	1791BB	—	1.25	2.50	7.00	48.00
	1791BB*	—	1.25	2.50	7.00	48.00
	1791D	—	1.25	2.50	7.00	48.00
	1791D*	—	1.25	2.50	7.00	48.00
	1791H*	Inc. C#71	2.00	4.00	13.00	80.00
	1791I*	Inc. C#71	1.50	3.00	9.00	55.00
	1791K	Inc. C#71	1.25	2.50	7.00	48.00
	1791K*	Inc. C#71	1.25	2.50	7.00	48.00
	1791M*	2.192	1.25	2.50	7.00	48.00
	1791MA	Inc. C#72	1.50	3.00	9.00	55.00
	1791N*	1.101	1.50	3.00	9.00	55.00

C#	Date	Mintage	VG	Fine	VF	XF
73	1791Q*	I.A.	1.50	3.00	9.00	55.00
	1791R	5.039	1.00	1.75	6.50	45.00
	1791R*	Inc. Ab	1.00	1.75	6.50	45.00
	1791R (error: LUDOV XIV)	—	6.00	15.50	33.00	100.00
	1791T*	Inc. C#71	1.50	3.00	9.00	55.00
	1791W	.451	2.00	4.00	13.00	80.00
	1791W*	Inc. Ab.	2.00	4.00	13.00	80.00

Province of Bearn Issues
Rev. leg. ends: ......RE:BD (LIGATE BD)

C#	Date	Mintage	VG	Fine	VF	XF
73b	1779(p)	3.214	1.50	3.00	9.00	55.00
	1780(p)	2.923	1.50	3.00	9.00	55.00
	1783(p)	.162	4.50	7.50	20.00	100.00
	1784(p)	.412	2.50	5.00	16.00	90.00
	1785(p)	.573	2.50	5.00	16.00	90.00
	1788(p)	.817	2.50	5.00	16.00	90.00

BELL METAL

C#	Date	Mintage	VG	Fine	VF	XF
73a	1791AA*	Inc. C#72	1.25	2.50	7.00	48.00
	1791D	—	1.50	3.00	9.00	55.00
	1791I*	Inc. C#71	1.50	3.00	9.00	55.00
	1791Q*	Inc. C#73	1.50	3.00	9.00	55.00

***NOTE:** The "dot" appears below the third letter of the monarch's name and denotes second semester coinage.

BRONZE
Obv. date: L'AN II

C#	Date	Mintage	VG	Fine	VF	XF
122	1793A	—	18.00	85.00	225.00	800.00
	1793AA	—	9.00	33.00	100.00	200.00
	1793AA	Restrike		—	Unc.	350.00
	1793B	—	12.00	50.00	130.00	300.00
	1793BB	—	9.00	33.00	100.00	200.00
	1793D	—	9.00	33.00	100.00	200.00
	1793D with eagle's head left	—	6.00	12.50	28.50	65.00
	1793H	—	20.00	80.00	225.00	550.00
	1793I	—	16.00	65.00	165.00	300.00
	1793L	—	20.00	80.00	225.00	550.00
	1793MA	—	16.00	65.00	165.00	300.00
	1793N	—	20.00	80.00	225.00	550.00
	1793T	—	9.00	33.00	100.00	200.00
	1793W	—	12.00	50.00	130.00	300.00

Without A.D. date

C#	Date	Mintage	VG	Fine	VF	XF
122a	L'An					
	II-AA	—	16.00	65.00	165.00	400.00
	II-B	—	Reported, not confirmed			
	II-BB	—	16.00	65.00	165.00	400.00
	II-D	2 known	—	—	Rare	—
	II-I	—	19.00	90.00	225.00	450.00
	II-MA	1 known	—	—	Rare	—
	II-N	1 known	—	—	Rare	—
	II-(p)	—	20.00	85.00	235.00	550.00

2 SOLS

BRONZE
Obv. leg. ends: FRANCOIS.

C#	Date	Mintage	VG	Fine	VF	XF
89	1791A	—	5.00	10.00	35.00	125.00
	1791AA	—	8.00	15.00	50.00	160.00
	1791B	—	8.00	15.00	50.00	160.00
	1791BB	—	9.00	19.00	55.00	250.00
	1791H	—	9.00	19.00	55.00	250.00
	1791K	—	8.50	16.00	55.00	175.00
	1791L	—	8.50	16.00	55.00	175.00
	1791M	—	8.50	16.00	55.00	175.00
	1791R	—	9.00	19.00	58.00	250.00
	1791W	—	8.00	15.00	50.00	160.00
	1792A	—	4.50	8.50	25.00	95.00
	1792AA	—	8.50	16.00	55.00	175.00
	1792B	—	8.50	16.00	55.00	175.00
	1792BB	—	8.50	16.00	55.00	175.00
	1792D	—	8.50	16.00	55.00	175.00
	1792H	—	8.50	16.00	55.00	175.00
	1792I	—	8.50	16.00	55.00	175.00
	1792K	—	8.50	16.00	55.00	175.00
	1792L	—	8.50	16.00	55.00	175.00
	1792M	—	8.50	16.00	55.00	175.00
	1792MA	—	9.00	19.00	58.00	250.00
	1792N	—	8.50	16.00	55.00	175.00
	1792Q	—	8.50	16.00	55.00	175.00
	1792R	—	8.50	16.00	55.00	175.00
	1792T	—	8.50	16.00	55.00	175.00
	1792W	—	6.50	13.00	38.00	160.00
	1792(p)	—	15.00	33.50	100.00	275.00
	1793A	—	8.50	16.00	55.00	175.00
	1793AA	—	9.00	19.00	58.00	250.00
	1793B	—	8.50	16.00	55.00	175.00
	1793BB	—	9.00	19.00	58.00	250.00
	1793D	—	9.00	19.00	58.00	250.00
	1793L	—	9.00	19.00	58.00	250.00
	1793MA	—	15.00	33.00	100.00	275.00
	1793N	—	9.00	19.00	58.00	250.00
	1793Q	—	15.00	33.50	100.00	275.00
	1793R	—	9.00	19.00	58.00	250.00
	1793T	—	9.00	19.00	58.00	250.00
	1793W	—	8.50	16.00	55.00	175.00
	1793(p)	—	17.00	35.00	110.00	300.00

Obv. leg. ends: FRANCAIS.
Rev: Similar to C#89.

C#	Date	Mintage	VG	Fine	VF	XF
89a	1792BB	—	9.00	19.00	58.00	250.00
	1793BB	—	16.00	35.00	100.00	300.00

BRONZE
Obv: Similar to 1 Sol, C#122, dated: L'AN II.

C#	Date	Mintage	VG	Fine	VF	XF
123	1793A	—	Reported, not confirmed			
	1793AA	—	12.00	65.00	175.00	350.00
	1793B	—	10.00	60.00	165.00	325.00
	1793B	Restrike		—	Unc.	400.00
	1793BB	—	14.00	70.00	180.00	375.00
	1793D	1 known	—	—	Rare	—
	1793H	—	12.00	65.00	175.00	350.00
	1793I	—	18.00	90.00	225.00	425.00
	1793L	—	—	—	Rare	—
	1793MA	—	—	—	Rare	—
	1793N	—	20.00	95.00	250.00	500.00
	1793R	—	20.00	95.00	250.00	500.00
	1793T	—	20.00	95.00	250.00	500.00
	1793W	—	20.00	85.00	250.00	500.00
	1793(p)	—	13.00	70.00	200.00	375.00

Without A.D. date

C#	Date	Mintage	VG	Fine	VF	XF
123a	L'An					
	II-AA		20.00	100.00	275.00	700.00
	II-BB	—	20.00	100.00	275.00	700.00
	II-I	—	30.00	150.00	300.00	850.00
	II-R	—	25.00	125.00	290.00	800.00
	II-N	—	Reported, not confirmed			
	II-W	—	—	—	—	—

6 SOLS (1/20 ECU)

1.4740 gm., .917 SILVER, .0435 oz ASW
Posthumous Issue
Obv: Old head of Louis XV left.
Rev: Crowned arms in branches.

C#	Date	Mintage	VG	Fine	VF	XF
—	1779A	.176	7.00	16.00	40.00	100.00

C#	Date	Mintage	VG	Fine	VF	XF
74	1782A*	.022	13.00	50.00	125.00	250.00
	1783A	.053	10.00	35.00	85.00	150.00

***NOTE:** The "dot" appears below the third letter of the monarch's name and denotes second semester coinage.

12 SOLS (1/10 ECU)

2.9480 gm., .917 SILVER, .0869 oz ASW

C#	Date	Mintage	VG	Fine	VF	XF
75	1775A	.016	4.00	20.00	50.00	150.00
	1775I	.042	3.00	16.00	45.00	110.00
	1775N	.019	—	—	—	—
	1775&	.014	—	—	—	—
	1776A	.035	3.50	17.00	45.00	115.00
	1776&	7,934	—	—	—	—
	1777A	.012	4.00	20.00	50.00	150.00
	1777L	.029	—	—	—	—
	1777N	.036	3.00	16.00	45.00	110.00
	1777Q	.022	—	—	—	—
	1778A	.111	2.50	10.00	30.00	85.00
	1778A*	Inc. Ab.	2.50	10.00	30.00	85.00
	1778I	.124	2.50	10.00	30.00	85.00
	1778M	.025	4.00	20.00	50.00	150.00
	1779A*	.111	2.50	10.00	30.00	85.00
	1779AA	.040	3.00	16.00	45.00	110.00
	1779I	.057	—	—	—	—
	1779M	.051	3.00	14.00	37.00	90.00
	1779Q	.035	—	—	—	—
	1780A	.033	3.00	16.00	45.00	110.00
	1780A*	Inc. Ab.	3.00	16.00	45.00	110.00
	1780D	.038	3.00	16.00	45.00	110.00
	1780I	.115	—	—	—	—
	1780L	.014	—	—	—	—
	1780Q	.028	—	—	—	—

C#	Date	Mintage	VG	Fine	VF	XF
75	1781A	.033	3.00	16.00	45.00	110.00
	1781I	.032	—	—	—	—
	1782A	.117	2.50	10.00	30.00	85.00
	1782AA	.015	4.00	20.00	50.00	150.00
	1782N	.016	—	—	—	—
	1783A	.070	3.00	14.00	37.50	90.00
	1783L	.016	4.00	20.00	50.00	150.00
	1784A	.047	3.00	14.00	37.50	90.00
	1784A (error: LVD.XV)					
		—	11.00	32.00	75.00	215.00
	1784AA	.038	3.00	16.00	45.00	110.00
	1784I	.070	3.00	14.00	37.50	90.00
	1784R	.013	4.00	22.00	55.00	160.00
	1785A	.090	2.50	10.50	30.00	85.00
	1785A4A (error: LVD.XV)					
		—	11.00	32.00	75.00	215.00
	1785I	.050	3.00	14.00	37.50	90.00
	1785Q	.020	4.00	22.00	55.00	160.00
	1786A*	—	3.00	14.00	37.50	90.00
	1786A (error: LVD.XV)					
		—	11.00	32.00	75.00	215.00
	1786Q	.026	4.00	20.00	50.00	150.00
	1786R	.021	4.00	20.00	50.00	150.00
	1787A	—	Reported, not confirmed			
	1787D	.017	4.00	22.50	55.00	160.00
	1787R	.375	1.75	7.50	25.00	65.00
	1788A	—	Reported, not confirmed			
	1788D	—	4.00	22.50	55.00	160.00
	1788H	.011	5.00	23.00	57.50	175.00
	1788I	.032	3.00	16.00	45.00	110.00
	1788MA	.092	2.75	14.00	37.50	90.00
	1788N	.013	5.00	23.00	57.50	175.00
	1789A	—	2.50	10.00	30.00	85.00
	1789M*	.200	1.75	7.00	25.00	65.00
	1789N	—	5.00	23.00	57.50	160.00
	1790A	—	Reported, not confirmed			
	1790L	—	3.00	16.00	45.00	110.00

***NOTE:** The "dot" appears below the third letters of the monarch's name and denotes second semester coinage.

Province of Bearn Issue
Obv. leg. ends: ....RE.BD (BD LIGATE)

C#	Date	Mintage	VG	Fine	VF	XF
75a	1777(p)	.012	8.50	28.00	62.50	185.00

15 SOLS

5.0000 gm., .666 SILVER, .1071 oz ASW
Obv: Head of Louis XVI, leg. ends: FRANCOIS.
Rev: Standing angel right inscribing tablet.

C#	Date	Mintage	VG	Fine	VF	XF
90	1791A	.494	5.00	25.00	60.00	200.00
	1791B	.023	9.00	50.00	95.00	330.00
	1791D	.272	6.00	27.50	62.50	245.00
	1791H	.090	7.00	30.00	65.00	270.00
	1791I	4.000	3.00	12.00	42.50	180.00
	1791K	.029	9.00	50.00	95.00	330.00
	1791M	.193	6.00	27.50	62.50	250.00
	1791MA	.063	16.00	37.50	92.50	300.00
	1791N	.157	6.50	30.00	67.50	285.00
	1791Q	—	6.50	30.00	67.50	285.00
	1791R	.157	6.50	30.00	67.50	285.00
	1791T	.025	9.00	50.00	95.00	330.00
	1791W	.169	6.00	27.50	62.50	250.00
	1791(p)	.024	9.00	50.00	95.00	330.00
	1792A	—	4.00	22.50	55.00	170.00
	1792B	—	7.00	30.00	65.00	270.00
	1792H	—	6.00	27.50	62.50	250.00
	1792I	—	4.00	22.50	55.00	170.00
	1792K	—	9.00	50.00	95.00	330.00
	1792L	—	10.00	50.00	100.00	350.00
	1792M	—	7.00	30.00	65.00	270.00
	1792MA	—	7.00	30.00	65.00	270.00
	1792N	—	7.00	30.00	65.00	270.00
	1792Q	—	7.00	30.00	65.00	270.00
	1792R	—	7.00	30.00	65.00	270.00
	1792T	—	9.00	50.00	95.00	230.00
	1792W	—	4.00	22.50	55.00	185.00
	1792(p)	—	11.00	65.00	100.00	400.00
	1793(p)	—	14.00	75.00	130.00	450.00

Obv. leg. ends: FRANCAIS.

C#	Date	Mintage	VG	Fine	VF	XF
90a	1791AA	.206	9.00	50.00	95.00	330.00
	1791BB	.088	7.00	30.00	65.00	270.00
	1791D	—	7.00	30.00	65.00	270.00
	1791K	—	11.00	65.00	100.00	400.00
	1791MA	—	10.00	50.00	90.00	325.00
	1792BB	—	7.00	30.00	65.00	260.00
	1792D	—	7.00	30.00	65.00	260.00
	1792MA	—	7.00	30.00	65.00	260.00

24 SOLS (1/5 ECU)

5.8350 gm., .917 SILVER, .1720 oz ASW

C#	Date	Mintage	VG	Fine	VF	XF
76	1775A	.011	8.00	37.50	100.00	230.00
	1775L	.017	6.00	30.00	90.00	180.00
	1775&	.024	5.00	25.00	75.00	180.00
	1776A	7,515	10.00	45.00	110.00	245.00
	1776I	.016	6.00	30.00	90.00	180.00
	1776N	.025	5.00	25.00	75.00	180.00
	1776&	7,119	13.00	50.00	130.00	300.00
	1777A	5,010	—	—	—	—
	1777L	.021	5.00	25.00	75.00	180.00
	1778A	.036	5.00	25.00	75.00	180.00
	1778A*	Inc. Ab.	5.00	25.00	75.00	180.00
	1778M	.046	5.00	25.00	75.00	180.00
	1779A	—	Reported, not confirmed			
	1779AA	—	6.00	30.00	90.00	180.00
	1780A	8,270	—	—	—	—
	1780I	.020	—	—	—	—
	1780L	.013	6.00	30.00	95.00	190.00
	1780Q	8,800	—	—	—	—
	1781A	8,880	10.00	45.00	110.00	245.00
	1781I	.015	—	—	—	—
	1781K	4,600	15.00	60.00	150.00	300.00
	1782A*	.060	5.00	25.00	75.00	180.00
	1782N	4,790	—	—	—	—
	1782&	6,609	14.00	55.00	135.00	280.00
	1783A	.028	5.00	25.00	75.00	180.00
	1783L	7,645	—	—	—	—
	1784A	.013	6.00	30.00	95.00	190.00
	1784I	.036	—	—	—	—
	1784R	.030	5.00	25.00	75.00	180.00
	1785A	.026	5.00	25.00	75.00	180.00
	1785I	.029	5.00	25.00	75.00	180.00
	1785Q	.032	5.00	25.00	75.00	180.00
	1786A	—	5.00	25.00	75.00	180.00
	1786H	—	Reported, not confirmed			
	1786N	.015	—	—	—	—
	1786Q	.029	5.00	25.00	75.00	180.00
	1786R	.087	4.00	19.00	42.50	110.00
	1787D	7,398	10.00	45.00	110.00	245.00
	1787N	—	5.00	25.00	75.00	180.00
	1787R	.026	5.00	25.00	75.00	180.00
	1788H	.021	5.00	25.00	75.00	180.00
	1788I	.018	6.00	30.00	95.00	190.00
	1788M	.013	6.00	30.00	95.00	190.00
	1788MA	.032	5.00	25.00	75.00	180.00
	1788W	.027	5.00	25.00	75.00	180.00
	1789A	—	4.00	18.00	42.50	110.00
	1789W	—	5.00	25.00	75.00	180.00
	1790A	—	6.00	30.00	85.00	175.00
	1790L	—	6.00	30.00	85.00	175.00

***NOTE:** The "dot" appears below the third letter of the monarch's name and denotes second semester coinage.

Province of Bearn Issues
Obv. leg. ends: ......RE.BD (BD LIGATE)

C#	Date	Mintage	VG	Fine	VF	XF
76a	1775(p)	.014	14.00	55.00	135.00	280.00
	1777(p)	.032	10.00	45.00	110.00	245.00

30 SOLS

10.0000 gm., .666 SILVER, .2141 oz ASW
Obv. leg. ends: FRANCOIS.
Rev: Standing angel right, inscribing tablet.

C#	Date	Mintage	VG	Fine	VF	XF
91	1791A	1.125	12.00	45.00	85.00	250.00
	1791BB	.018	22.50	85.00	210.00	450.00
	1791D	—	16.00	60.00	155.00	330.00
	1791H	—	19.00	75.00	185.00	425.00
	1791I	1.711	10.00	37.50	85.00	245.00
	1791K	.019	21.00	85.00	210.00	450.00
	1791N	1,253	35.00	150.00	350.00	700.00
	1791T	.029	19.00	75.00	185.00	425.00
	1791W	.117	13.00	50.00	125.00	300.00
91	1792A	—	9.00	35.00	85.00	245.00
	1792AA	—	13.00	50.00	125.00	300.00
	1792B	—	13.00	50.00	125.00	300.00
	1792BB	—	16.00	62.50	155.00	330.00
	1792D	—	16.00	62.50	155.00	330.00
	1792H	—	16.00	62.50	155.00	330.00
	1792I	—	9.00	37.50	85.00	245.00
	1792K	—	19.00	75.00	185.00	425.00
	1792MA	—	19.00	75.00	185.00	425.00
	1792N	—	19.00	75.00	185.00	425.00
	1792Q	—	16.00	62.50	155.00	330.00
	1792T	—	19.00	75.00	185.00	425.00
	1792W	—	13.00	50.00	125.00	300.00
	1792(p)	—	21.00	85.00	210.00	460.00
	1793D	—	16.00	62.50	155.00	330.00
	1793K	—	21.00	85.00	210.00	460.00
	1793MA	—	19.00	75.00	185.00	425.00
	1793N	—	30.00	125.00	295.00	625.00
	1793Q	—	16.00	62.50	155.00	330.00
	1793W	—	16.00	62.50	155.00	330.00
	1793(p)	—	21.00	85.00	210.00	460.00

Obv. leg. ends: FRANCAIS.

C#	Date	Mintage	VG	Fine	VF	XF
91a	1791BB	.018	25.00	95.00	215.00	455.00
	1792BB	—	19.00	75.00	185.00	400.00
	1792MA	—	25.00	95.00	215.00	455.00
	1793BB	—	25.00	95.00	215.00	455.00

1/2 ECU DE 3 LIVRES

14.7440 gm., .917 SILVER, .4347 oz ASW

C#	Date	Mintage	VG	Fine	VF	XF
77	1774A	5,102	75.00	190.00	375.00	950.00
	1775A	.018	25.00	85.00	190.00	425.00
	1775BB	7,018	—	—	—	—
	1775H	1,922	50.00	165.00	330.00	750.00
	1775I	.020	25.00	85.00	190.00	425.00
	1775L	7,415	—	—	—	—
	1775N	6,512	30.00	100.00	235.00	550.00
	1775Q	.010	—	—	—	—
	1775T	1,644	—	—	—	—
	1775&	.018	25.00	85.00	190.00	425.00
	1776A	.010	30.00	90.00	210.00	465.00
	1776H	780 pcs.	100.00	325.00	500.00	1500
	1776L	6,782	—	—	—	—
	1776Q	.013	30.00	90.00	210.00	465.00
	1776&	.019	—	—	—	—
	1777A	2,970	—	—	—	—
	1777H	834 pcs.	100.00	325.00	500.00	1500
	1777L	.020	—	—	—	—
	1777T	9,145	32.50	100.00	225.00	495.00
	1777&	.035	19.00	50.00	105.00	335.00
	1778A	2,724	—	—	—	—
	1778H	1,940	50.00	165.00	330.00	750.00
	1778L	4,799	35.00	115.00	255.00	600.00
	1778Q	.021	—	—	—	—
	1778T	3,189	—	—	—	—
	1778&	3,993	—	—	—	—
	1779A	.010	—	—	—	—
	1779BB	4,783	—	—	—	—
	1779H	2,632	45.00	135.00	250.00	525.00
	1779L	2,927	—	—	—	—
	1779Q	.021	—	—	—	—
	1779T	1,688	—	—	—	—
	1779W	.155	10.00	37.50	90.00	185.00
	1780A	8,202	32.50	100.00	225.00	490.00
	1780BB	3,789	35.00	120.00	260.00	650.00
	1780H	2,370	50.00	175.00	315.00	700.00
	1780I	.012	32.50	100.00	225.00	495.00
	1780L	7,280	32.50	100.00	225.00	495.00
	1780R	548 pcs.	—	—	—	—
	1780T	1,637	—	—	—	—
	1780W	.147	10.00	37.50	90.00	185.00
	1781A	.010	32.50	100.00	225.00	495.00

C#	Date	Mintage	VG	Fine	VF	XF
77	1781BB	4,706	—	—	—	—
	1781H	1,952	50.00	165.00	330.00	750.00
	1781I	8,430	—	—	—	—
	1781K	1,952	—	—	—	—
	1781L	9,433	—	—	—	—
	1781Q	.010	—	—	—	—
	1781R	484 pcs.	—	—	—	—
	1781T	1,363	—	—	—	—
	1782A	.015	25.00	85.00	190.00	425.00
	1782H	3,164	35.00	120.00	260.00	650.00
	1782L	.050	15.00	50.00	95.00	310.00
	1782Q	.011	—	—	—	—
	1782T	2,237	—	—	—	—
	1783A*	.123	10.00	37.50	95.00	185.00
	1783H	724 pcs.	100.00	325.00	500.00	1500
	1783L	.034	18.00	50.00	105.00	335.00
	1783R	5,212	—	—	—	—
	1783T	1,641	50.00	165.00	330.00	750.00
	1784A	.402	8.00	25.00	90.00	185.00
	1784A*	Inc. Ab.	8.00	25.00	90.00	185.00
	1784H	—	100.00	330.00	525.00	1500
	1784Q	.017	—	—	—	—
	1784R	.020	—	—	—	—
	1784T	5,037	35.00	105.00	240.00	525.00
	1785A	.029	18.00	50.00	105.00	335.00
	1785Q	.020	25.00	85.00	190.00	425.00
	1785T	2,194	—	—	—	—
	1786L	5,395	—	—	—	—
	1786Q	.041	15.00	50.00	95.00	310.00
	1787Q	.016	25.00	85.00	190.00	425.00
	1787T	1,924	50.00	165.00	330.00	750.00
	1787W	2,822	—	—	—	—
	1788A*	—	15.00	50.00	95.00	310.00
	1788L	7,789	—	—	—	—
	1789A*	7,789	13.00	45.00	90.00	300.00
	1789L	—	35.00	105.00	240.00	525.00
	1789T	—	35.00	105.00	240.00	525.00
	1790A	—	7.00	21.00	80.00	185.00
	1790A*	—	7.00	21.00	80.00	185.00
	1790AA	—	25.00	85.00	190.00	425.00
	1790BB	—	35.00	105.00	240.00	525.00
	1790H	—	45.00	135.00	250.00	525.00
	1790MA	—	50.00	165.00	330.00	750.00
	1790Q	5,050	—	—	—	—
	1790T	—	35.00	105.00	240.00	525.00
	1791A(he)	.778	7.00	21.00	80.00	185.00
	1791A(he)*	I.A.	7.00	21.00	80.00	185.00
	1791A(l)	I.A.	8.00	25.00	90.00	185.00
	1791(.L)*	I.A.	8.00	25.00	90.00	185.00
	1791T	4,217	35.00	105.00	240.00	525.00
	1791W	.117	—	—	—	—
	1792A	—	25.00	85.00	190.00	425.00

***NOTE:** The "dot" appears below the third letter of the monarch's name and denotes second semester coinage.

Province of Bearn Issues
Obv. leg. ends: ......RE.BD (BD LIGATE)

C#	Date	Mintage	VG	Fine	VF	XF
77a	1775(p)	4,681	—	—	—	—
	1785(p)	5,436	—	—	—	—

Obv. leg. ends: FRANCOIS.

C#	Date	Mintage	VG	Fine	VF	XF
92	1792A	—	85.00	290.00	650.00	1400
	1792K	—	175.00	575.00	950.00	2000
	1792N	—	145.00	475.00	825.00	1800
	1792T	—	175.00	575.00	950.00	2000
	1793A	—	115.00	340.00	675.00	1500

Obv. leg. ends: FRANCAIS.

C#	Date	Mintage	VG	Fine	VF	XF
92a	1792BB	—	200.00	900.00	1500	4500

ECU DE 6 LIVRES

29.4880 gm., .917 SILVER, .8695 oz ASW
Posthumous Issue
Rev: Similar to C#78.

C#	Date	Mintage	VG	Fine	VF	XF
A78	1774A	—	40.00	85.00	140.00	300.00

NOTE: Louis XV died on May 10, 1774, consequently any second semester issues are posthumous.

C#	Date	Mintage	VG	Fine	VF	XF
78	1774A	—	—	Proof only		5000
	1775A	.365	25.00	30.00	50.00	150.00
	1775A*	Inc. Ab.	25.00	30.00	50.00	150.00
	1775AA	.010	50.00	95.00	200.00	400.00
	1775B	.016	—	—	—	—
	1775BB	.003	60.00	100.00	200.00	550.00
	1775D	.171	25.00	30.00	75.00	250.00
	1775H	7,261	50.00	95.00	200.00	400.00
	1775I	.265	25.00	30.00	70.00	225.00
	1775K	.613	25.00	30.00	60.00	185.00
	1775L	.833	25.00	30.00	50.00	155.00
	1775M	.132	25.00	30.00	75.00	250.00
	1775N	.190	25.00	30.00	75.00	250.00
	1775N inverted N					
		Inc. Ab.	25.00	30.00	75.00	250.00
	1775Q	.429	25.00	30.00	50.00	150.00
	1775R	1,301	—	—	—	—
	1775T	.015	40.00	85.00	175.00	375.00
	1775W	1.336	25.00	30.00	50.00	150.00
	1775W inverted W					
		Inc. Ab.	25.00	30.00	50.00	150.00
	1775&	.480	25.00	30.00	50.00	150.00
	1776A	.513	25.00	30.00	50.00	150.00
	1776A*	Inc. Ab.	25.00	30.00	50.00	150.00
	1776AA	7,246	50.00	95.00	200.00	400.00
	1776B	8,602	50.00	95.00	200.00	400.00
	1776D	5,165	60.00	100.00	200.00	550.00
	1776H	6,763	55.00	95.00	200.00	475.00
	1776I	.109	25.00	30.00	75.00	250.00
	1776K	.692	25.00	30.50	60.00	185.00
	1776L	1.039	25.00	30.00	50.00	150.00
	1776M	.088	30.00	35.00	80.00	250.00
	1776N	.042	35.00	45.00	90.00	350.00
	1776Q	.533	25.00	30.50	60.00	185.00
	1776R	2,086	—	—	—	—
	1776T	.012	—	—	—	—
	1776W	.450	30.00	40.00	70.00	215.00
	1776&	5,951	—	—	—	—
	1777A	.239	25.00	30.00	70.00	250.00
	1777AA	3,118	—	—	—	—
78	1777B	8,525	50.00	95.00	200.00	400.00
	1777D	.033	35.00	45.00	95.00	350.00
	1777H	5,627	—	—	—	—
	1777I	.089	30.00	35.00	80.00	250.00
	1777K	.447	30.00	40.00	70.00	215.00
	1777L	.944	25.00	30.50	50.00	175.00
	1777M	.355	30.00	35.50	70.00	215.00
	1777N	.020	—	—	—	—
	1777Q	.262	25.00	30.00	70.00	250.00
	1777R	789 pcs.	—	—	—	—
	1777T	.018	45.00	85.00	175.00	375.00
	1777W	.261	25.00	30.00	70.00	250.00
	1777&	.137	25.00	30.00	70.00	250.00
	1778A	4,464	—	—	—	—
	1778AA	3,652	60.00	100.00	200.00	550.00
	1778B	7,135	—	—	—	—
	1778BB	3,009	60.00	100.00	200.00	550.00
	1778D	.063	30.00	35.00	80.00	250.00
	1778H	3,950	60.00	100.00	200.00	550.00
	1778I	.018	45.00	85.00	175.00	375.00
	1778K	.059	30.00	35.00	80.00	250.00
	1778L	.287	25.00	30.00	75.00	250.00
	1778M	.289	25.00	30.00	75.00	250.00
	1778N	.025	—	—	—	—
	1778Q	.346	30.00	35.00	70.00	215.00
	1778T	.010	—	—	—	—
	1778W	.060	30.00	35.00	80.00	250.00
	1778&	5,685	—	—	—	—
	1779A	.030	35.00	45.00	95.00	350.00
	1779B	4,532	60.00	100.00	200.00	550.00
	1779BB	4,783	60.00	100.00	200.00	550.00
	1779H	5,172	60.00	100.00	200.00	550.00
	1779I	.172	25.00	30.00	75.00	250.00
	1779K	8,064	50.00	100.00	200.00	400.00
	1779L	.760	25.00	30.00	55.00	200.00
	1779M	.334	30.00	45.00	70.00	215.00
	1779N	.030	35.00	45.00	95.00	350.00
	1779Q	.108	25.00	30.00	75.00	250.00
	1779T	.010	45.00	85.00	175.00	375.00
	1779W	.040	35.00	45.00	95.00	350.00
	1779&	6,018	—	—	—	—
	1780A	.015	40.00	80.00	160.00	360.00
	1780AA	2,501	65.00	110.00	215.00	600.00
	1780B	.010	45.00	85.50	175.00	375.00
	1780H	4,659	—	—	—	—
	1780I	.081	30.00	35.00	80.00	250.00
	1780K	5,315	60.00	100.00	200.00	550.00
	1780L	.368	30.00	40.00	70.00	215.00
	1780M	.326	30.00	40.00	70.00	215.00
	1780N	.081	30.00	35.00	80.00	250.00
	1780Q	6,244	50.00	95.00	200.00	400.00
	1780R	3,564	60.00	100.00	200.00	550.00
	1780T	7,752	50.00	95.00	200.00	400.00
	1780W	8,715	—	—	—	—
	1780&	5,327	—	—	—	—
	1781A	.200	25.00	30.00	75.00	250.00
	1781A*	Inc. Ab.	25.00	30.00	75.00	250.00
	1781AA	4,639	55.00	100.00	225.00	475.00
	1781B	2,680	—	—	—	—
	1781H	4,206	55.00	100.00	225.00	475.00
	1781I	.054	30.00	35.00	80.00	250.00
	1781K	.034	35.00	45.00	95.00	350.00
	1781L	.178	25.00	30.00	75.00	250.00
	1781M	.264	25.00	30.00	75.00	250.00
	1781N	.020	—	—	—	—
	1781Q	1.007	25.00	30.00	50.00	150.00
	1781R	2,322	—	—	—	—
	1781T	.011	45.00	85.00	175.00	375.00
	1781W	.012	45.00	85.00	175.00	375.00
	1782A	.369	30.00	40.00	70.00	215.00
	1782A*	Inc. Ab.	30.00	40.00	70.00	215.00
	1782AA	3,142	—	—	—	—
	1782D	.036	35.00	45.00	95.00	350.00
	1782H	7,936	50.00	95.00	200.00	400.00
	1782I	.149	25.00	30.00	75.00	250.00
	1782K	.016	45.00	85.00	175.00	375.00
	1782L	.419	25.00	30.00	70.00	215.00
	1782M	.203	25.00	30.00	75.00	250.00
	1782N	2,362	65.00	110.00	215.00	600.00
	1782Q	.843	25.00	30.50	55.00	165.00
	1782R	2,693	—	—	—	—
	1782T	.016	45.00	85.00	175.00	375.00
	1782W	2,822	—	—	—	—
	1783A	2.889	25.00	30.00	45.00	160.00
	1783A*	Inc. Ab.	25.00	30.00	45.00	160.00
	1783B	.055	30.00	35.00	80.00	250.00
	1783H	3,481	—	—	—	—
	1783I	.257	25.00	30.00	75.00	250.00
	1783K	.099	30.00	35.00	80.00	265.00
	1783L	.963	25.00	30.50	55.00	165.00
	1783M	.260	25.00	30.00	75.00	250.00
	1783N	3,996	60.00	100.00	200.00	550.00
	1783Q	.495	25.00	30.00	70.00	215.00
	1783R	.212	25.00	30.00	75.00	250.00
	1783T	.015	45.00	85.00	175.00	375.00
	1783W	.114	30.00	35.00	80.00	265.00
	1783&	5,128	—	—	—	—

C#	Date	Mintage	VG	Fine	VF	XF
78	1784/74	A4.791	235.00	425.00	550.00	750.00
	1784A	Inc. Ab.	25.00	30.00	35.00	150.00
	1784A*	Inc. Ab.	25.00	30.00	35.00	150.00
	1784B	.013	—	—	—	—
	1784BB	—	Reported, not confirmed			
	1784H	.013	45.00	85.00	175.00	375.00
	1784I	3.012	25.00	30.00	35.00	150.00
	1784K	.304	30.00	40.00	70.00	215.00
	1784K reversed K'					
		Inc. Ab.	60.00	100.00	200.00	550.00
	1784L	1.906	25.00	30.00	35.00	150.00
	1784M	.614	25.00	30.00	55.00	165.00
	1784N	.062	30.00	35.00	80.00	250.00
	1784Q	.748	25.00	30.00	55.00	165.00
	1784R	.478	25.00	30.00	55.00	175.00
	1784T	.020	—	—	—	—
	1784W	8,051	50.00	95.00	200.00	400.00
	1784&	3,181	—	—	—	—
	1785A	.571	25.00	30.00	55.00	175.00
	1785AA	5,491	55.00	100.00	225.00	475.00
	1785B	9,379	50.00	95.50	200.00	400.00
	1785H	4,969	55.00	100.00	225.00	475.00
	1785I	1.255	25.00	30.00	35.00	150.00
	1785K	.185	30.00	35.00	80.00	265.00
	1785L	2.005	25.00	30.00	35.00	150.00
	1785M	1.205	25.00	30.00	40.00	150.00
	1785N	7,231	—	—	—	—
	1785Q	.963	25.00	30.00	50.00	165.00
	1785R	1.742	25.00	30.00	35.00	150.00
	1785T	7,992	50.00	95.00	200.00	400.00
	1785W	2,739	65.00	110.00	215.00	600.00
	1786A	5,797	—	—	—	—
	1786B	3,823	60.00	100.00	200.00	550.00
	1786H	2,148	65.00	110.00	215.00	600.00
	1786I	.124	30.00	35.00	80.00	265.00
	1786L	2.314	25.00	30.00	35.00	150.00
	1786M	1.715	25.00	30.00	35.00	150.00
	1786Q	.779	25.50	30.00	55.00	165.00
	1786Q (error: LUD.XI.)					
		—	70.00	160.00	275.00	750.00
	1786R	.306	25.00	30.00	65.00	195.00
	1786W	—	45.00	25.00	175.00	375.00
	1787A*	.011	45.00	85.00	175.00	375.00
	1787B	7,821	50.00	95.00	200.00	400.00
	1787H	5,562	55.00	100.00	225.00	475.00
	1787I	.123	30.00	35.00	80.00	265.00
	1787K	4,195	55.00	100.00	225.00	475.00
	1787L	1.211	25.00	30.00	35.00	150.00
	1787M	.539	25.00	30.00	55.00	175.00
	1787MA	—	Reported, not confirmed			
	1787N	3,739	—	—	—	—
	1787Q	.415	25.00	30.00	55.00	180.00
	1787R	.842	25.00	30.00	35.00	150.00
	1787T	.018	45.00	75.00	160.00	360.00
	1787W	2,822	65.00	110.00	215.00	600.00
	1788A*	.439	25.50	30.00	35.00	150.00
	1788B	.073	30.00	35.00	80.00	250.00
	1788H	1,411	70.00	165.00	300.00	675.00
	1788I	.499	25.00	30.00	35.00	150.00
	1788K	—	45.00	85.00	175.00	375.00
	1788L	2.038	25.00	30.00	32.50	150.00
	1788M	1.343	25.00	30.00	35.00	150.00
	1788MA	.030	—	—	—	—
	1788Q	.672	25.00	30.00	35.00	150.00
	1788R	7,715	—	—	—	—
	1788T	5,729	—	—	—	—
	1788W	.203	30.00	35.00	80.00	265.00
	1789A	—	25.00	30.00	65.00	165.00
	1789A*	Inc. Ab.	25.00	30.00	65.00	165.00
	1789AA	.083	30.00	35.00	80.00	250.00
	1789B	.235	30.00	35.00	80.00	265.00
	1789D	.040	35.00	45.00	95.00	350.00
	1789H	.015	45.00	75.00	160.00	360.00
	1789I	.015	45.00	75.00	160.00	360.00
	1789K	.042	35.00	45.00	95.00	350.00
	1789L	—	25.00	30.00	65.00	165.00
	1789M	1.200	25.00	30.00	35.00	150.00
	1789MA	—	55.00	100.00	225.00	475.00
	1789N	—	55.00	100.00	225.00	475.00
	1789Q	.905	25.00	30.00	35.00	150.00
	1789R	.596	25.00	30.00	35.00	150.00
	1789T	—	45.00	75.00	160.00	360.00
	1789W	—	30.00	35.00	80.00	250.00
	1790A	3.086	25.00	30.00	32.50	150.00
	1790A*	Inc. Ab.	25.00	30.00	32.50	150.00
	1790AA					
		Inc. C#77	30.00	35.00	80.00	265.00
	1790B	.139	30.00	35.00	80.00	265.00
	1790BB	.065	30.00	35.00	90.00	270.00
	1790D	.096	30.00	35.00	90.00	275.00
	1790H	Inc. C#77	45.00	75.50	160.00	360.00
	1790I	2.430	25.00	30.00	32.50	150.00
	1790K	.105	30.00	35.00	80.00	265.00
	1790L	.500	25.00	30.00	55.00	180.00
	1790M	.147	30.00	35.00	80.00	265.00
	1790MA	.243	30.00	35.00	80.00	265.00
	1790N	.223	30.00	35.00	80.00	265.00
78	1790Q	.166	30.00	35.00	80.00	265.00
	1790R	.058	30.00	35.00	90.00	270.00
	1790T	Inc. C#77	30.00	35.00	90.00	270.00
	1790W	.104	30.00	35.00	85.00	265.00
	1791A(he)	1.756	25.50	30.00	55.00	180.00
	1791A(he)*	I.A.	25.00	30.00	55.00	180.00
	1791A(I)	I.A.	95.00	250.00	390.00	1000
	1791AA	.039	30.00	35.00	90.00	275.00
	1791B	1,736	70.00	165.00	300.00	975.00
	1791BB	.023	45.00	85.00	175.00	375.00
	1791D	3,208	60.00	100.00	200.00	550.00
	1791H	.012	50.00	95.00	200.00	425.00
	1791I	1.629	25.00	30.00	35.00	150.00
	1791K	3,652	60.00	100.00	200.00	550.00
	1791L	.011	50.00	95.00	200.00	425.00
	1791M	.035	45.00	85.00	175.00	375.00
	1791MA	.040	45.00	85.00	175.00	400.00
	1791N	.027	45.00	85.00	175.00	375.00
	1791Q	5,050	55.00	100.00	225.00	475.00
	1791R	8,740	55.00	100.00	225.00	475.00
	1791T	.019	45.00	85.00	175.00	375.00
	1791W	.026	45.00	85.00	175.00	375.00
	1792A	—	150.00	325.00	550.00	1500
	1792M	—	200.00	475.00	800.00	2100

***NOTE:** The "dot" appears below the third letter of the monarch's name and denotes second semester coinage.

Province of Bearn Issues

Obv. leg. ends: ...... RE.BD (BD LIGATE)

C#	Date	Mintage	VG	Fine	VF	XF
78a	1775(p)	.184	30.00	35.00	85.00	265.00
	1776(p)	.136	35.00	40.00	90.00	275.00
	1777(p)	.241	30.00	35.00	85.00	265.00
	1778(p)	.708	25.00	30.00	65.00	165.00
	1779(p)	1.948	25.00	30.00	40.00	155.00
	1780(p)	1.557	25.00	30.00	40.00	150.00
	1781(p)	1.141	25.00	30.00	40.00	150.00
	1782(p)	.694	25.00	30.00	45.00	165.00
	1783(p)	.811	25.00	30.00	45.00	165.00
	1784(p)	1.530	25.00	30.00	40.00	150.00
	1785(p)	1.857	25.00	30.00	40.00	150.00
	1786(p)	2.254	25.00	30.00	36.50	130.00
	1787(p)	.646	25.50	30.00	45.00	165.00
	1788(p)	.682	25.50	30.00	45.00	165.00
	1789(p)	3,122	60.00	100.00	200.00	550.00
	1790(p)	5,339	60.00	100.00	200.00	550.00
	1791(p)	1,690	70.00	165.00	300.00	975.00

Obv. legend ends FRANCOIS.

C#	Date	Mintage	VG	Fine	VF	XF
93	1792A	—	60.00	125.00	215.00	600.00
	1792AA	—	90.00	300.00	450.00	900.00
	1792B	—	65.00	130.00	225.00	650.00
	1792D	—	80.00	250.00	350.00	750.00
	1792H	—	80.00	250.00	350.00	750.00
	1792I	—	60.00	125.00	215.00	600.00
	1792I (error: FARNCOIS)					
		—	65.00	130.00	225.00	650.00
	1792K	—	75.00	230.00	325.00	700.00
	1792L	—	135.00	400.00	600.00	1200.
	1792M	—	75.00	230.00	325.00	700.00
	1792MA	—	80.00	250.00	350.00	750.00
	1792N	—	80.00	250.00	350.00	750.00
	1792R	—	75.00	230.00	325.00	700.00
	1792T	—	80.00	250.00	350.00	750.00
	1792W	—	75.00	230.00	325.00	700.00
	1793A	—	60.00	125.00	215.00	600.00
	1793AA	—	80.00	250.00	350.00	750.00
	1793B	—	80.00	250.00	350.00	750.00
93	1793D	—	80.00	250.00	350.00	750.00
	1793I	—	80.00	250.00	350.00	750.00
	1793K	—	80.00	250.00	350.00	750.00
	1793L	—	80.00	250.00	350.00	750.00
	1793M	—	80.00	250.00	350.00	750.00
	1793MA	—	80.00	250.00	350.00	750.00
	1793N	—	80.00	250.00	350.00	750.00
	1793R	—	80.00	250.00	350.00	750.00
	1793T	—	90.00	300.00	450.00	850.00
	1793W	—	80.00	255.00	350.00	750.00

30.0000 gm., .916 SILVER, .8836 oz ASW

Obv. leg. ends: FRANCAIS.

C#	Date	Mintage	VG	Fine	VF	XF
93a	1792BB	—	135.00	400.00	600.00	1300.
	1793BB	—	200.00	600.00	700.00	1800.

6 LIVRES

30.0000 gm., .916 SILVER, .8836 oz ASW

Obv: With A.D. date.

Rev: Similar to C#124a, dated: L'AN II.

C#	Date	Mintage	VG	Fine	VF	XF
124	1793A	—	90.00	250.00	400.00	900.00
	1793AA	—	135.00	350.00	650.00	1300.
	1793B	—	160.00	390.00	750.00	2000.
	1793BB	—	180.00	450.00	850.00	2300.
	1793D	—	135.00	350.00	650.00	1300.
	1793L	—	175.00	375.00	675.00	1375.
	1793MA	—	185.00	400.00	700.00	1450.
	1793N	—	180.00	450.00	850.00	2300.
	1793W	—	175.00	375.00	675.00	1375.

Obv: Without A.D. date.

C#	Date	Mintage	VG	Fine	VF	XF
124a	L'AN					
	II-B	—	300.00	650.00	1200.	3000.
	II-BB	—	400.00	800.00	1700.	4000.
	II-MA	2 known	—	—	Rare	—
	II-W	—	300.00	650.00	1200.	3000.

1/2 LOUIS D'OR

4.0790 gm., .917 GOLD, .1203 oz AGW

Obv: Uniformed bust of Louis XVI left.

Rev: Crowned arms of France and Navarre in ovals.

C#	Date	Mintage	VG	Fine	VF	XF
79	1775A	585 pcs.	900.00	1500.	3500.	5000.
	1776L	683 pcs.	900.00	1500.	3500.	5000.
	1777A	—	950.00	1750.	3750.	5500.
	1777I	2,241	600.00	1000.	2500.	4000.
	1784A	766 pcs.	900.00	1500.	3500.	5000.

LOUIS D'OR

8.1580 gm., .917 GOLD, .2405 oz AGW
Obv: Uniformed bust of Louis XVI left.
Rev: Crowned arms in branches, date at upper left.

C#	Date	Mintage	VG	Fine	VF	XF
80	1774A	—	400.00	800.00	1800.	3000.

Rev: Date over crown.

C#	Date	Mintage	VG	Fine	VF	XF
80a	1774A	—	—	—	2500.	5000.

C#	Date	Mintage	VG	Fine	VF	XF
81	1774A	.490	175.00	325.00	800.00	1650.
	1775A	.221	200.00	400.00	875.00	1800.
	1775BB	604 pcs.	—	—	—	—
	1775D	.013	300.00	575.00	1200.	2500.
	1775H	5,315	325.00	625.00	1350.	3000.
	1775I	2,397	—	—	—	—
	1775K	934 pcs.	—	—	—	—
	1775L	.024	—	—	—	—
	1775M	8,491	300.00	600.00	1200.	2875.
	1775N	.019	—	—	—	—
	1775Q	1,220	—	—	—	—
	1775W	.091	250.00	475.00	1000.	2200.
	1775&	.037	250.00	500.00	1050.	2350.
	1776A	.133	225.00	425.00	925.00	2000.
	1776H	2,443	325.00	625.00	1350.	3000.
	1776L	.011	—	—	—	—
	1776N	.013	300.00	575.00	1200.	2650.
	1776R	431 pcs.	—	—	—	—
	1776&	.019	275.00	525.00	1125.	2500.
	1777A	.104	225.00	425.00	925.00	2000.
	1777H	3,156	325.00	625.00	1350.	3000.
	1777L	813 pcs.	—	—	—	—
	1777&	.013	300.00	575.00	1200.	2650.
	1778A	.048	250.00	500.00	1050.	2350.
	1778H	2,680	325.00	625.00	1350.	3000.
	1778N	2,664	325.00	625.00	1350.	3000.
	1778&	8,255	—	—	—	—
	1779A	6,899	300.00	600.00	1200.	2875.
	1779H	4,880	325.00	625.00	1350.	3000.
	1779N	2,208	325.00	625.00	1350.	3000.
	1779T	—	325.00	625.00	1350.	3000.
	1779&	3,352	—	—	—	—
	1780A	2,895	325.00	625.00	1350.	3000.
	1780BB	391 pcs.	—	—	—	—
	1780H	2,779	325.00	625.00	1350.	3000.
	1780K	—	325.00	625.00	1350.	3000.
	1780N	340 pcs.	—	—	—	—
	1780R	—	Reported, not confirmed			
	1780&	1,266	—	—	—	—
	1781A	6,333	300.00	600.00	1200.	2875.
	1781BB	394 pcs.	—	—	—	—
	1781H	2,325	—	—	—	—
	1781N	1,116	—	—	—	—
	1781&	517 pcs.	—	—	—	—
	1782A*	.255	200.00	400.00	875.00	1850.
	1782H	3,863	325.00	625.00	1350.	3000.
	1782N	1,897	—	—	—	—
	1782R	226 pcs.	—	—	—	—
	1782&	1,272	—	—	—	—
	1783A	.090	250.00	475.00	1000.	2200.
	1783A*	Inc. Ab.	250.00	475.00	1000.	2200.
	1783H	3,061	325.00	625.00	1350.	3000.
	1783M	1,173	—	—	—	—
	1783N	1,746	—	—	—	—
	1783&	2,802	—	—	—	—
	1784A	.016	275.00	525.00	1125.	2500.
	1784H	1,166	—	—	—	—
	1784M	1,525	—	—	—	—
	1784N	354 pcs.	—	—	—	—
	1784&	274 pcs.	—	—	—	—
	1785B	.013	—	—	—	—
	1785BB	541 pcs.	—	—	—	—
	1785H	747 pcs.	—	—	—	—
	1785N	414 pcs.	—	—	—	—

Province of Bearn Issues
Obv. leg. ends: .....RE.BD (BD LIGATE)

C#	Date	Mintage	VG	Fine	VF	XF
81a	1775(p)	.015	300.00	600.00	1200.	2875.
	1776(p)	.013	300.00	600.00	1200.	2875.
	1777(p)	.011	300.00	600.00	1200.	2875.

7.6490 gm., .917 SILVER, .2255 oz AGW
Obv: Head of Louis XVI left.

C#	Date	Mintage	VG	Fine	VF	XF
82	1785A	7 pcs.	—	—	Rare.	—

C#	Date	Mintage	VG	Fine	VF	XF
83	1785A	.050	185.00	265.00	325.00	800.00
	1785AA	.597	240.00	375.00	425.00	1000.
	1785D	.058	185.00	265.00	325.00	800.00
	1785I	.751	240.00	375.00	425.00	1000.
	1785K	.038	200.00	300.00	375.00	875.00
	1785T	—	240.00	375.00	425.00	1000.
	1785W	1.299	215.00	325.00	400.00	925.00
	1786A	5.370	175.00	280.00	325.00	500.00
	1786A*	Inc. Ab.	175.00	280.00	325.00	500.00
	1786AA					
		Inc. 1785AA	175.00	285.00	335.00	500.00
	1786B	.419	175.00	285.00	335.00	500.00
	1786BB	.248	200.00	300.00	375.00	875.00
	1786BB with horn on head					
		—	375.00	625.00	1350.	2350.
	1786D	.899	175.00	185.00	235.00	375.00
	1786D*	Inc. Ab.	175.00	185.00	235.00	375.00
	1786H	.367	175.00	185.00	240.00	325.00
	1786H*	Inc. Ab.	175.00	185.00	240.00	325.00
	1786I	Inc. 1785I	175.00	180.00	225.00	300.00
	1786I*	Inc. Ab.	175.00	180.00	225.00	300.00
	1786K	.504	175.00	180.00	230.00	325.00
	1786N	.284	175.00	215.00	250.00	425.00
	1786N*	Inc. Ab.	175.00	215.00	250.00	425.00
	1786T	.830	175.00	180.00	225.00	325.00
	1786T*	Inc. Ab.	175.00	180.00	225.00	325.00
	1786W					
		Inc. 1785W	175.00	180.00	275.00	350.00
	1786W*	Inc. Ab.	175.00	180.00	225.00	350.00
	1787A	1.927	175.00	180.00	225.00	350.00
	1787A*	Inc. Ab.	175.00	180.00	225.00	350.00
	1787AA*	.193	175.00	220.00	375.00	475.00
	1787B	.099	175.00	230.00	375.00	500.00
	1787D	.424	175.00	180.00	230.00	325.00
	1787D*	Inc. Ab.	175.00	180.00	230.00	325.00
	1787H	.065	175.00	250.00	400.00	525.00
	1787I	.109	170.00	230.00	375.00	500.00
	1787K	.019	—	—	—	—
	1787MA	—	200.00	300.00	475.00	800.00
	1787N	.044	185.00	265.00	425.00	600.00
	1787R	—	200.00	300.00	475.00	800.00
	1787T	.221	175.00	215.00	350.00	525.00
	1787W	.304	175.00	200.00	325.00	500.00
	1788A*	.837	175.00	220.00	325.00	475.00
	1788AA	.073	175.00	230.00	375.00	500.00
	1788B	.030	190.00	280.00	325.00	625.00
	1788D	.256	175.00	215.00	250.00	425.00
	1788H	.023	200.00	300.00	375.00	675.00
	1788I	.036	190.00	280.00	325.00	625.00
	1788I*	Inc. Ab.	190.00	280.00	325.00	625.00
	1788N	.029	200.00	300.00	375.00	675.00
	1788T	.050	175.00	245.00	300.00	525.00
	1788W*	.174	175.00	220.00	275.00	425.00
	1789A	—	175.00	200.00	325.00	400.00
	1789AA	—		Reported, not confirmed		
	1789B	—	200.00	300.00	375.00	675.00
	1789D	.089	175.00	230.00	325.00	500.00
	1789H	.017	215.00	325.00	400.00	725.00
	1789I	.022	200.00	300.00	375.00	675.00
	1789K	—	175.00	245.00	300.00	525.00
	1789M	.019	215.00	325.00	400.00	725.00
	1789MA	—	240.00	375.00	425.00	800.00
	1789N	.017	215.00	325.00	400.00	725.00
	1789Q	.020	—	—	—	—
	1789R	.010	240.00	375.00	425.00	800.00
	1789T	.059	—	—	—	—
	1789W	.104	175.00	230.00	375.00	500.00
	1790A	.164	175.00	230.00	375.00	500.00
	1790AA	.013	240.00	375.00	425.00	800.00
	1790B	.024	215.00	325.00	400.00	725.00
	1790D	.041	190.00	280.00	365.00	625.00
	1790H	7,530	250.00	400.00	475.00	875.00
	1790I	7,622	250.00	400.00	475.00	875.00
	1790MA	.013	—	—	—	—
	1790N	9,683	—	—	—	—
	1790R	6,819	250.00	400.00	475.00	875.00
	1790T	.022	—	—	—	—
	1790W	.133	—	—	—	—
	1791D	—	275.00	425.00	525.00	1000.
	1791H	3,113	275.00	425.00	525.00	1000.
	1791I	—	275.00	425.00	525.00	1000.
	1791MA	2,073	300.00	475.00	600.00	1125.
	1791N	1,852	300.00	475.00	600.00	1125.
	1791R	4,359	—	—	—	—
	1791W	2,562	300.00	475.00	600.00	1125.
	1792A	—	275.00	425.00	525.00	1000.
	1792D	—	300.00	500.00	675.00	1200.

C#	Date	Mintage	VG	Fine	VF	XF
83	1792M	—	300.00	500.00	675.00	1200.
	1792W	1,983	—	—	—	—

***NOTE:** The "dot" appears below the third letter of the monarch's name and denotes second semester coinage.

7.6000 gm., .900 GOLD, .2199 oz AGW
Obv: Head of Louis XVI, leg. ends FRANCOIS.

C#	Date	Mintage	VG	Fine	VF	XF
94	1792A	—	1250.	2500.	5500.	9500.
	1793A	—	1500.	3000.	6500.	10,500.
	1793M	—	2000.	4000.	7000.	11,000.

24 LIVRES

7.6000 gm., .900 GOLD, .2199 oz AGW

C#	Date	Mintage	VG	Fine	VF	XF
125	1793A	—	600.00	1200.	3500.	5500.
	1793BB	—	1250.	2500.	5500.	8000.
	1793D	—	1250.	2250.	4000.	6500.
	1793W	—	1000.	2000.	4000.	6000.

2 LOUIS D'OR

16.3160 gm., .917 GOLD, .4811 oz AGW

C#	Date	Mintage	VG	Fine	VF	XF
84	1775A	.010	550.00	975.00	1475.	2475.
	1775AA	678 pcs.	—	—	—	—
	1775B	4,853	575.00	925.00	1650.	2500.
	1775BB	5,378	—	—	—	—
	1775D	.064	425.00	725.00	1000.	1850.
	1775I	.039	450.00	775.00	1125.	2000.
	1775K	.038	—	—	—	—
	1775L	.018	500.00	900.00	1350.	2350.
	1775M	1,328	650.00	1050.	1850.	3150.
	1775Q	1,220	—	—	—	—
	1775T	.012	500.00	900.00	1350.	2350.
	1775W	.068	425.00	725.00	1000.	1850.
	1775&	.067	425.00	725.00	1000.	1850.
	1776A	9,662	550.00	975.00	1475.	2475.
	1776AA	269 pcs.	—	—	—	—
	1776B	5,724	—	—	—	—
	1776BB	4,423	—	—	—	—
	1776D	.079	425.00	725.00	1000.	1850.
	1776I	.035	450.00	775.00	1125.	2000.
	1776K	.073	425.00	725.00	1000.	1850.
	1776L	.015	500.00	900.00	1350.	2350.
	1776M	4,332	—	—	—	—
	1776N	5,027	575.00	925.00	1650.	2500.
	1776Q	.014	—	—	—	—
	1776T	7,737	550.00	975.00	1475.	2475.
	1776W	.049	450.00	775.00	1125.	2000.
	1776&	.029	—	—	—	—
	1777A	275 pcs.	—	—	—	—
	1777AA	525 pcs.	—	—	—	—
	1777B	6,828	575.00	925.00	1650.	2500.
	1777BB	2,498	—	—	—	—
	1777D	.053	450.00	775.00	1125.	2000.
	1777I	.032	475.00	825.00	1200.	2125.
	1777K	.039	450.00	775.00	1125.	2000.
	1777M	4,560	—	—	—	—
	1777N	5,347	—	—	—	—
	1777Q	3,586	—	—	—	—
	1777T	9,890	550.00	975.00	1475.	2475.
	1777W	.096	425.00	725.00	1000.	1850.
	1777&	.014	550.00	975.00	1475.	2475.
	1778AA	259 pcs.	—	—	—	—
	1778B	2,902	—	—	—	—

C#	Date	Mintage	VG	Fine	VF	XF
84	1778D	.019	500.00	900.00	1350.	2350.
	1778H	4,154	—	—	—	—
	1778I	1,960	650.00	1050.	1850.	3150.
	1778K	1,850	—	—	—	—
	1778M	6,273	575.00	925.00	1650.	2500.
	1778Q	1,074	—	—	—	—
	1778T	8,749	—	—	—	—
	1778W	.042	450.00	775.00	1125.	2000.
	1778&	5,905	—	—	—	—
	1779AA	307 pcs.	—	—	—	—
	1779B	682 pcs.	—	—	—	—
	1779BB	179 pcs.	—	—	—	—
	1779I	—	600.00	1200.	1800.	3000.
	1779K	779 pcs.	—	—	—	—
	1779M	3,225	600.00	1000.	1800.	3000.
	1779T	2,849	600.00	1000.	1800.	3000.
	1779W	.013	550.00	975.00	1475.	2475.
	1780B	443 pcs.	—	—	—	—
	1780I	841 pcs.	675.00	1125.	2000.	3350.
	1780M	233 pcs.	—	—	—	—
	1780T	2,660	—	—	—	—
	1780W	9,240	500.00	975.00	1475.	2475.
	1781AA	487 pcs.	—	—	—	—
	1781B	130 pcs.	—	—	—	—
	1781I	261 pcs.	—	—	—	—
	1781K	404 pcs.	—	—	—	—
	1781M	770 pcs.	—	—	—	—
	1781T	1,637	—	—	—	—
	1781W	8,100	500.00	975.00	1475.	2475.
	1782AA	123 pcs.	—	—	—	—
	1782K	910 pcs.	675.00	1125.	2000.	3350.
	1782M	499 pcs.	—	—	—	—
	1782T	5,644	—	—	—	—
	1782W	.024	—	—	—	—
	1783A	1,870	—	—	—	—
	1783AA	279 pcs.	—	—	—	—
	1783B	1,956	—	—	—	—
	1783K	1,006	650.00	1050.	1850.	3150.
	1783T	5,683	—	—	—	—
	1783W	.027	475.00	825.00	1200.	2125.
	1784A	623 pcs.	—	—	—	—
	1784AA	324 pcs.	—	—	—	—
	1784B	1,444	—	—	—	—
	1784K	234 pcs.	—	—	—	—
	1784Q	368 pcs.	—	—	—	—
	1784T	4,536	—	—	—	—
	1784W	.013	550.00	975.00	1475.	2475.
	1785B	280 pcs.	—	—	—	—

Province of Bearn Issues
Obv. leg. ends: ....RE.BD (BD LIGATE)

C#	Date	Mintage	VG	Fine	VF	XF
84a	1777 (p)	.021	500.00	900.00	1500.	2500.
	1778 (p)	.025	500.00	900.00	1500.	2500.
	1781 (p)	1,054	—	—	—	—
	1782 (p) 544 pcs.		—	—	Rare	—

15.2970 gm., .917 GOLD, .4510 oz AGW

C#	Date	Mintage	VG	Fine	VF	XF
85	1785A	.027	375.00	425.00	725.00	2000.
	1785D	—	375.00	525.00	1000.	2500.
	1785I	—	375.00	525.00	1000.	2500.
	1785T	650 pcs.	450.00	675.00	1200.	2500.
	1785W	3,960	450.00	475.00	875.00	2000.
	1786A	2.420	350.00	450.00	600.00	850.00
	1786AA	.307	350.00	475.00	675.00	975.00
	1786AA*	I.A.	350.00	475.00	675.00	975.00
	1786B	.251	350.00	475.00	675.00	900.00
	1786BB	.139	350.00	500.00	675.00	1350.
	1786D	1.072	350.00	475.00	575.00	725.00
	1786D*	Inc. Ab.	350.00	475.00	575.00	725.00
	1786H	.043	350.00	475.00	675.00	1000.
	1786I	.208	350.00	475.00	575.00	800.00
	1786K	.492	350.00	475.00	575.00	775.00
	1786K*	Inc. Ab.	350.00	475.00	575.00	775.00
	1786N	.217	350.00	475.00	575.00	800.00
	1786T	.396	350.00	475.00	575.00	775.00
	1786T*	Inc. Ab.	350.00	475.00	575.00	775.00
	1786W	.239	350.00	475.00	575.00	800.00
	1786W*	Inc. Ab.	350.00	475.00	575.00	800.00
	1787A	—	350.00	500.00	675.00	925.00
	1787AA*	.155	350.00	500.00	700.00	975.00
	1787B	.087	350.00	475.00	625.00	925.00
	1787D	.109	350.00	475.00	625.00	875.00
	1787H	.012	365.00	475.00	725.00	1525.
	1787I	.010	365.00	475.00	725.00	1525.
85	1787K	.042	350.00	475.00	625.00	875.00
	1787N	.027	350.00	500.00	775.00	1000.
	1787R	—	365.00	475.00	725.00	1525.
	1787T	3,073	425.00	475.00	800.00	1650.
	1787W	—	350.00	475.00	625.00	875.00
	1788A	—	350.00	475.00	625.00	875.00
	1788AA	.153	350.00	500.00	700.00	975.00
	1788B	.019	—	—	—	—
	1788D	—	350.00	475.00	625.00	975.00
	1788K	.018	350.00	500.00	675.00	975.00
	1788T	7,233	365.00	475.00	625.00	1350.
	1788W	—	350.00	475.00	625.00	975.00
	1789AA	—	350.00	475.00	625.00	975.00
	1789B	—	350.00	500.00	675.00	1000.
	1789K	.023	350.00	500.00	675.00	1000.
	1789MA	—	425.00	625.00	875.00	1650.
	1789Q	—	350.00	500.00	675.00	1000.
	1789T	—	Reported, not confirmed			
	1789W	—	350.00	475.00	625.00	975.00
	1790A	—	350.00	475.00	625.00	925.00
	1790AA	—	350.00	475.00	625.00	975.00
	1790B	—	365.00	475.00	625.00	1350.
	1790BB	—	365.00	475.00	625.00	1350.
	1790K	7,381	365.00	475.00	625.00	1350.
	1790M	—	350.00	500.00	675.00	1000.
	1790MA	—	425.00	625.00	875.00	1650.
	1790Q	2,944	—	—	—	—
	1790T	667 pcs.	450.00	675.00	1200.	2000.
	1790W	—	425.00	625.00	875.00	1650.
	1791A	.034	350.00	500.00	675.00	1000.
	1791A*	Inc. Ab.	350.00	500.00	675.00	1000.
	1791AA	1,150	—	—	—	—
	1791B	1,072	—	—	—	—
	1791BB	4,230	425.00	625.00	875.00	1650.
	1791K	903 pcs.	400.00	600.00	1000.	1800.
	1791M	8,921	365.00	475.00	625.00	1350.
	1791M*	Inc. Ab.	365.00	475.00	625.00	1350.
	1791T	667 pcs.	—	—	—	—
	1791W	7,959	365.00	475.00	625.00	1350.
	1792A	—	400.00	600.00	1000.	1800.
	1792A*	—	400.00	600.00	1000.	1800.
	1792BB	—	500.00	800.00	1350.	2350.

***NOTE:** The "dot" appears below the third letter of the monarch's name and denotes second semester coinage.

DECIMAL COINAGE

(Commencing 1794)
10 Centimes = 1 Decime
10 Decimes = 1 Franc

UN (1) CENTIME

BRONZE
First Republic

C#	Date	Mintage	VG	Fine	VF	XF
134	L'AN6A	100.083	.75	1.50	3.75	12.00
	7A	Inc. Ab.	1.25	2.00	5.00	14.00
	8A	Inc. Ab.	5.00	10.00	27.50	75.00

Second Republic

Y#	Date	Mintage	VG	Fine	VF	XF
1	1848A	8.615	.25	1.00	2.50	8.00
	1849A	8.664	.25	1.00	2.50	8.00
	1850A	2.721	1.75	3.50	9.00	18.00
	1851A	2.712	.75	1.50	4.00	9.00

Second Empire

Y#	Date	Mintage	VG	Fine	VF	XF
14	1853A	4.076	.75	2.00	4.00	10.00
	1853B	.824	1.00	4.00	8.00	10.00
	1853BB	2.558	.90	2.00	5.00	12.00
	1853D	.964	1.00	4.00	8.00	10.00
	1853K	.405	4.00	6.00	14.00	35.00
	1853MA	.225	5.50	12.00	18.00	45.00
14	1853W	1.634	1.00	2.50	6.00	13.00
	1854A	2.750	.90	1.50	5.00	12.00
	1854B	1.709	4.00	6.00	14.00	32.00
	1854BB	1.447	1.00	4.00	8.00	18.00
	1854D	1.546	1.00	4.00	8.00	18.00
	1854K	1.150	1.25	5.00	9.00	20.00
	1854MA	1.976	1.00	2.50	6.00	13.00
	1854W	1.399	Reported, Not Confirmed			
	1855A(d)	6.034	.90	1.50	5.00	12.00
	1855A(a)	I.A.	4.50	10.00	15.00	40.00
	1855B(d)	1.971	1.00	4.00	8.00	18.00
	1855BB(a)	.248	6.50	15.00	23.00	60.00
	1855D(a)	2.466	1.00	4.00	8.00	18.00
	1855D(d)	I.A.	1.00	4.00	8.00	18.00
	1855K A	Inc. Ab.	4.00	6.00	13.00	42.00
	1855K(d)	1.455	1.00	2.50	6.00	13.00
	1855MA(a)	I.A.	1.00	4.00	8.00	18.00
	1855MA(d)	2.839	.75	2.50	4.50	10.00
	1855W(d)	3.102	1.00	4.00	8.00	18.00
	1855W(a)	I.A.	.90	3.00	6.00	15.00
	1856A	2.878	.75	2.50	4.50	10.00
	1856B	4.373	.50	2.00	4.00	8.00
	1856BB	1.874	1.00	4.00	8.00	18.00
	1856D	.880	5.50	12.00	18.00	45.00
	1856K	2.062	.75	2.50	4.50	10.00
	1856MA	.305	6.50	15.00	35.00	75.00
	1856W	2.707	.75	2.50	4.50	10.00
	1857A	2.000	1.00	4.00	8.00	18.00
	1857B	3.000	.75	2.50	4.50	10.00
	1857BB	1 piece	—	—	—	—
	1857D	1.000	4.00	6.00	13.00	32.00
	1857K	1.000	1.25	5.00	9.00	20.00
	1857MA	1.500	1.00	4.00	8.00	18.00
	1857W	2.500	.75	2.50	4.50	10.00

Y#	Date	Mintage	VG	Fine	VF	XF
18	1861A	7.398	.25	.35	2.00	5.00
	1861BB	3.012	.30	.50	2.50	6.00
	1861K	1.999	.45	.60	3.00	7.50
	1862A	15.561	.10	.20	.75	1.50
	1862BB	4.493	.30	.50	2.50	6.00
	1862K	7.431	.10	.20	.75	1.50
	1870A	1.000	2.00	5.00	9.00	25.00

Third Republic

Y#	Date	Mintage	Fine	VF	XF	Unc
41	1872A	1.250	.60	1.50	3.00	12.00
	1872K	.750	1.25	3.50	7.00	25.00
	1874A	1.000	.75	2.00	3.50	13.00
	1875A	1.000	.75	2.00	3.50	13.00
	1875K	2.000	.90	2.25	4.00	15.00
	1877A	1.000	.75	2.00	3.50	13.00
	1878A	1.500	.60	1.50	3.00	12.00
	1878K	.289	15.00	30.00	50.00	100.00
	1879A(ab)	.800	2.00	4.00	7.00	15.00
	1882A	.419	3.00	6.50	13.00	37.50
	1884A	.400	7.00	13.00	32.50	70.00
	1885A	.400	2.50	5.00	9.00	22.50
	1886A	.400	2.50	5.00	9.00	22.50
	1887A	.400	2.50	5.00	9.00	22.50
	1888A	.400	2.50	5.00	9.00	22.50
	1889A	.400	2.00	4.00	8.00	20.00
	1890A	.400	2.00	4.00	8.00	20.00
	1891A	1.400	.90	1.75	3.75	13.00
	1892A	.800	1.25	2.50	4.00	14.00
	1893A	.300	3.50	8.00	15.00	37.50
	1894A	.500	1.75	3.25	6.50	18.00
	1895A	3.000	.90	2.00	4.00	10.00
	1896A(f)	3.000	.90	2.00	4.00	10.00
	1897A	2.000	1.15	2.75	5.50	11.50

Y#	Date	Mintage	Fine	VF	XF	Unc
58	1898	.250	2.50	5.50	10.00	20.00
	1899	1.500	1.25	2.75	4.50	12.00
	1900	.221	13.00	27.50	50.00	95.00
	1901	1.000	.90	2.00	4.00	9.00
	1902	1.000	.90	2.00	4.00	9.00
	1903	2.000	.60	1.25	2.75	6.00
	1904	1.000	.90	2.00	4.00	9.00
	1908	4.500	.60	1.25	2.25	5.00
	1909	1.500	1.25	2.50	3.75	8.00

Y#	Date	Mintage	Fine	VF	XF	Unc
58	1910	1.500	11.00	23.00	40.00	75.00
	1911	5.000	.25	1.00	1.50	3.00
	1912	2.000	.60	1.25	2.50	5.50
	1913	1.500	.60	1.25	3.00	6.00
	1914	1.000	.60	1.25	3.00	6.00
	1916	1.996	.50	.90	2.00	3.50
	1919	2.407	.50	.90	2.00	3.50
	1920	2.594	.50	.90	2.00	3.50

NOTE: No privy marks on Y#58 of any date.

CHROME-STEEL
1 New Centime - 1 Old Franc
Fifth Republic

Y#	Date	Mintage	Fine	VF	XF	Unc
102	1962	34.200	—	—	—	.25
	1963	16.811	—	.40	.60	1.20
	1964	22.654	—	—	.10	.20
	1965	47.799	—	—	—	.25
	1966	19.688	—	—	.20	.25
	1967	52.308	—	—	—	.10
	1968	40.890	—	—	—	.15
	1969	35.430	—	—	—	.10
	1970	29.600	—	—	—	.10
	1971	3.070	—	—	—	.10
	1972	1.000	—	—	—	.40
	1973	1.727	—	—	—	.10
	1974	7.850	—	—	—	.10
	1975	.720	—	—	—	.10
	1976	4.450	—	—	—	—
	1977	*.100	—	—	—	—
	1978	—	—	—	—	—
	1979	—	—	—	—	—

DEUX (2) CENTIMES

Small D Large D

BRONZE
Second Empire

Y#	Date	Mintage	VG	Fine	VF	XF
15	1853A	.610	1.25	4.00	7.50	16.00
	1853B	.539	1.25	4.00	8.00	18.00
	1853BB	.168	2.50	7.00	10.00	28.00
	1853D sm.D	—	5.00	13.00	27.50	50.00
	1853D lg.D	—	5.00	13.00	27.50	50.00
	1853K	.117	6.00	17.00	32.50	75.00
	1853MA	.163	3.50	10.00	21.00	40.00
	1853W	.070	6.00	17.00	35.00	80.00
	1854A	3.118	.50	1.25	2.50	6.00
	1854B	1.995	.50	1.50	2.75	6.50
	1854BB	2.003	.50	1.25	2.50	6.00
	1854D with small D					
		2.524	2.50	7.00	10.00	22.50
	1854D lg.D	I.A.	.50	1.25	2.50	6.00
	1854K	1.545	.65	1.50	3.50	8.00
	1854MA	1.312	.65	1.50	3.50	8.00
	1854W	3.402	.20	.75	1.25	5.00
	1855A(d)	5.417	.20	.75	1.25	4.00
	1855A(a)	I.A.	.20	.75	1.25	4.00
	1855B(d)	1.754	.50	1.25	2.50	6.00
	1855B(a)	I.A.	.50	1.25	2.50	6.00
	1855BB(d)					
		2.135	.50	1.25	2.50	6.00
	1855BB(a)	I.A.	.50	1.25	2.50	6.00
	1855D(d) with small D					
		2.554	.50	1.25	2.50	6.00
	1855D(d) with large D					
		Inc. Ab.	.50	1.25	2.50	6.00
	1855D(a) with small D					
		Inc. Ab.	.50	1.25	2.50	6.00
	1855D(a) with large D					
		Inc. Ab.	.50	1.25	2.50	6.00
	1855K(d)	1.068	.50	1.50	2.75	12.00
	1855K a	Inc. Ab.	.50	1.50	3.00	15.00
	1855MA(a)					
		2.438	.65	1.50	3.50	8.00
	1855MA(d)	I.A.	1.00	3.75	7.00	11.00

Y#	Date	Mintage	VG	Fine	VF	XF
15	1855W(a)	.939	.75	2.50	5.00	10.00
	1856A	1.738	.50	1.25	2.50	6.00
	1856B	4.324	.25	1.00	2.00	5.00
	1856BB	1.282	.50	1.75	3.75	7.00
	1856D	.774	Reported, Not Confirmed			
	1856K	2.281	.50	1.50	3.00	6.00
	1856MA	2.781	.50	1.50	3.00	6.00
	1856W	2.581	.50	1.50	3.00	6.00
	1857A	1.250	.60	1.75	3.50	7.00
	1857B	2.000	.50	1.50	3.00	6.00
	1857D with small D					
		1.000	2.50	9.00	18.00	40.00
	1857D lg.D	I.A.	.60	2.00	5.00	6.00
	1857K	.750	1.75	5.00	9.00	14.00
	1857MA	1.250	.50	3.00	5.00	8.00
	1857W	2.250	.50	1.50	3.00	6.00

Obv: Bust points to 1 in date.

Y#	Date	Mintage	VG	Fine	VF	XF
19.1	1861A	4.054	.50	1.00	2.00	4.00
	1861BB	2.440	.50	1.00	2.00	4.00
	1861K	3.291	.50	1.00	2.00	4.00

Obv: Recut die (r), bust points to 8 in date.

Y#	Date	Mintage	VG	Fine	VF	XF
19.2	1861A(r)	I.A.	.50	1.00	2.00	4.00
	1861BB(r)	I.A.	.50	1.00	2.00	4.00
	1861K(r)	I.A.	.50	1.00	2.00	4.00
	1862/1A	7.515	3.00	10.00	21.00	27.50
	1862A	Inc. Ab.	.25	1.00	1.75	4.00
	1862BB	2.807	.50	1.50	3.00	5.00
	1862K	13.692	.15	.65	1.25	3.00

Third Republic

Y#	Date	Mintage	Fine	VF	XF	Unc
42	1877A	.500	2.00	4.00	10.00	25.00
	1878A	.750	1.25	2.50	6.50	19.00
	1878K	.363	5.00	10.00	27.50	55.00
	1879A(ab)	.600	1.25	2.50	6.50	17.00
	1882A	.290	3.75	8.00	15.00	40.00
	1883A	.500	2.00	4.00	8.00	20.00
	1884A	.300	2.00	4.50	12.00	30.00
	1885A	.300	2.00	4.50	12.00	30.00
	1886A	.300	2.00	4.50	12.00	30.00
	1887A	.300	2.00	4.50	12.00	30.00
	1888A	.400	1.75	3.00	10.00	27.50
	1889A	.600	1.75	3.00	9.00	19.00
	1890A	.300	2.00	4.50	12.00	30.00
	1891A	.300	2.00	4.50	12.00	30.00
	1892A	.500	1.50	3.50	8.00	20.00
	1893A	.250	4.00	10.00	17.50	40.00
	1894A	.150	5.00	10.00	20.00	60.00
	1895A	1.000	1.00	2.00	5.50	11.00
	1896A(f)	1.000	1.00	2.00	5.50	11.00
	1897A	1.250	1.00	2.00	5.00	10.00

Y#	Date	Mintage	Fine	VF	XF	Unc
59	1898	.125	5.00	10.00	21.00	50.00
	1899	.750	2.00	4.00	8.00	25.00
	1900	.101	20.00	40.00	75.00	325.00
	1901	1.000	1.00	2.00	6.00	15.00
	1902	.750	1.25	2.50	9.00	22.50
	1903	.750	1.25	2.50	9.00	22.50
	1904	.500	2.00	4.00	11.00	20.00
	1907	.250	6.50	13.00	25.00	70.00
	1908	3.500	.90	1.75	3.50	6.00
	1909	1.750	6.00	12.00	25.00	55.00
	1910	1.750	1.25	2.50	5.00	10.00
	1911	5.000	.60	1.25	2.00	5.00
	1912	1.500	.90	1.75	3.75	8.00
	1913	1.750	.90	1.75	3.75	8.00
	1914	2.000	.60	1.25	2.75	6.00
	1916	.500	1.25	2.50	5.00	11.00
	1919	.902	.60	1.25	3.00	9.00
	1920	.598	1.25	2.50	5.00	11.00

NOTE: No privy marks appeared on Y#59 of any date.

CINQ (5) CENTIMES

BRONZE
First Republic

C#	Date	Mintage	VG	Fine	VF	XF
131	L'AN4A	12.308	2.50	6.00	15.00	65.00
	L'AN4I	.780	7.50	18.00	37.50	115.00
	L'AN4T	—	20.00	55.00	75.00	275.00
	L'AN4W	—	20.00	55.00	75.00	275.00
	L'AN5A	Inc. Ab.	10.00	25.00	60.00	150.00
	L'AN5I	Inc. Ab.	37.50	90.00	200.00	400.00
	L'AN5T	Inc. Ab.	Reported, Not Confirmed			
	L'AN5W	Inc. Ab.	Reported, Not Confirmed			

C#	Date	Mintage	VG	Fine	VF	XF
135	L'AN5A	26.880	1.00	2.50	10.00	65.00
	L'AN5AA	2.230	1.50	4.50	13.00	95.00
	L'AN5B	3.026	1.50	4.50	13.00	95.00
	L'AN5BB	3.660	1.50	4.50	13.00	95.00
	L'AN5D	1.475	5.00	15.00	40.00	200.00
	L'AN5I	9.608	1.50	4.00	12.00	85.00
	L'AN5K	1.997	Reported, Not Confirmed			
	L'AN5R	5.667	2.00	5.00	15.00	95.00
	L'AN5T	.018	Reported, Not Confirmed			
	L'AN5W	2.743	2.00	5.00	16.00	100.00
	L'AN6A	Inc. Ab.	5.00	15.00	30.00	70.00
	L'AN6AA	I.A.	8.00	22.50	45.00	100.00
	L'AN6B	Inc. Ab.	10.00	30.00	55.00	135.00
	L'AN6BB	I.A.	10.00	30.00	55.00	135.00
	L'AN6D	Inc. Ab.	13.00	35.00	75.00	250.00
	L'AN6I	Inc. Ab.	10.00	30.00	55.00	135.00
	L'AN6K	Inc. Ab.	10.00	30.00	55.00	135.00
	L'AN6W	Inc. Ab.	10.00	30.00	55.00	135.00
	L'AN7/5A	I.A.	2.50	6.00	16.50	100.00
	L'AN7/5A/RI.	A.	2.75	7.00	18.00	125.00
	L'AN7/6A	I.A.	3.25	8.00	18.00	120.00
	L'AN7A	Inc. Ab.	2.00	4.50	13.00	85.00
	L'AN7BB	I.A.	5.00	12.00	27.50	75.00
	L'AN7D	Inc. Ab.	10.00	25.00	50.00	135.00
	L'AN7K	Inc. Ab.	5.00	12.00	27.50	75.00
	L'AN7/5W	I.A.	2.50	6.00	18.00	120.00
	L'AN7W	Inc. Ab.	2.00	4.50	13.00	90.00
	L'AN8/7A	I.A.	2.00	4.50	13.00	90.00
	L'AN8/7A/RI.	A.	3.00	7.00	20.00	140.00
	L'AN8A	37.323	1.25	3.00	10.00	75.00
	L'AN8/6AA	I.A.	1.75	4.00	12.00	110.00
	L'AN8AA	20.002	1.25	3.00	10.00	80.00
	L'AN8/7BB	I.A.	2.50	6.00	18.00	120.00
	L'AN8BB	7.984	1.75	4.00	14.00	95.00
	L'AN8D	.691	15.00	40.00	90.00	225.00
	L'AN8G	2.005	7.00	17.00	50.00	140.00
	L'AN8I	4.582	2.00	4.50	14.00	90.00
	L'AN8K	4.639	2.00	4.50	14.00	90.00
	L'AN8W	12.738	1.50	3.75	13.00	85.00
	L'AN9A	Inc. Ab.	5.00	13.00	30.00	200.00
	L'AN9AA	I.A.	8.00	20.00	45.00	300.00
	L'AN9BB	I.A.	3.00	8.00	21.00	100.00
	L'AN9D	Inc. Ab.	9.00	22.50	55.00	275.00
	L'AN9G	Inc. Ab.	7.00	19.00	50.00	165.00
	L'AN9I	Inc. Ab.	2.00	5.50	16.00	95.00
	L'AN9K	Inc. Ab.	2.00	5.50	16.00	95.00
	L'AN9W	Inc. Ab.	2.00	5.50	16.00	95.00

Rev: Value as CNIQ

C#	Date	Mintage	VG	Fine	VF	XF
135a	L'AN5A	—	5.00	14.00	40.00	165.00
	L'AN5I	—	—	—	—	—

C#135 struck over Un Decime, C#132.

KM#	Date	Mintage	VG	Fine	VF	XF
135b	L'AN5A	—	Reported, Not Confirmed			
	L'AN5AA	—	Reported, Not Confirmed			
	L'AN5B	—	Reported, Not Confirmed			
	L'AN5BB	—	Reported, Not Confirmed			
	L'AN5D	—	10.00	25.00	50.00	135.00
	L'AN5I	—	—	—	—	—
	L'AN5R	—	Reported, not confirmed			
	L'AN5T	—	Reported, not confirmed			
	L'AN5W	—	Reported, not confirmed			
	L'AN6A	—	15.00	35.00	85.00	300.00
	L'AN6AA	—	Reported, not confirmed			
	L'AN6B	—	Reported, not confirmed			
	L'AN6D	—	Reported, not confirmed			
	L'AN6I	—	Reported, not confirmed			
	L'AN6W	—	Reported, not confirmed			
	L'AN7A	—	10.00	18.00	50.00	175.00
	L'AN8A	—	Reported, not confirmed			
	L'AN8I	—	Reported, not confirmed			

C#	Date	Mintage	VG	Fine	VF	XF
149	1808BB	—	25.00	65.00	150.00	400.00

Second Empire

Y#	Date	Mintage	VG	Fine	VF	XF
16	1853A	13.928	.50	1.25	2.50	8.00
	1853B	4.424	.75	2.00	4.00	11.00
	1853BB	4.148	.75	2.00	4.00	11.00
	1853D	5.013	.75	2.00	4.00	11.00
	1853K	1.652	1.50	6.00	12.00	25.00
	1853MA	1.654	1.50	6.00	12.00	25.00
	1853W	5.398	.75	2.00	4.00	11.00
	1854A	28.767	.25	1.00	2.00	6.00
	1854B	16.354	.50	1.25	2.50	7.50
	1854BB	20.380	.50	1.25	2.50	7.50
	1854D	18.597	.50	1.25	2.50	7.50
	1854K	13.608	.50	1.25	2.50	7.50
	1854MA	14.835	.50	1.25	2.50	7.50
	1854W	14.957	.50	1.25	2.50	7.50
	1855A(d)	26.932	.25	1.00	2.00	6.00
	1855A(a)	Inc Ab	.25	1.00	2.00	6.00
	1855B(d)	18.290	.50	1.25	2.50	7.50
	1855B(a)	Inc Ab	.50	1.25	2.50	7.50
	1855BB(d)	17.108	.50	1.25	2.50	7.50
	1855BB(a)	I.A.	.50	1.25	2.50	7.50
	1855D	14.250	.50	1.25	2.50	7.50

Y#	Date	Mintage	VG	Fine	VF	XF
16	1855K(d)	15.761	.50	1.25	2.50	7.50
	1855K(a)	I.A.	.50	1.25	2.50	7.50
	1855MA	15.417	.50	1.75	3.50	8.00
	1855W	17.473	.50	1.25	2.50	7.50
	1856A	25.799	.50	1.25	2.50	7.50
	1856B	14.813	.50	1.25	2.50	7.50
	1856BB	10.372	.75	2.00	4.00	10.00
	1856D	7.669	.75	2.00	4.00	10.00
	1856K	14.775	.50	1.25	2.50	7.00
	1856MA	16.997	.50	1.25	2.50	7.00
	1856W	15.472	.50	25	3.00	8.50
	1857A	5.729	.75	2.00	4.00	12.00
	1857B	1.843	1.00	5.00	10.00	20.00
	1857BB	1.662	1.00	5.00	10.00	20.00
	1857D	1.531	1.00	5.00	10.00	20.00
	1857K	2.417	.75	2.50	6.00	13.00
	1857MA	4.188	.75	2.25	6.00	11.00
	1857W	1.842	1.00	7.00	14.00	30.00

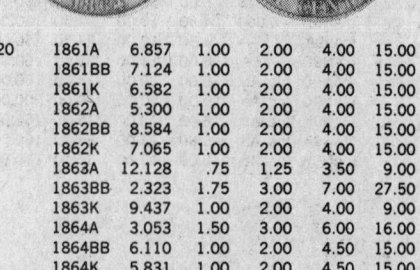

Y#	Date	Mintage	VG	Fine	VF	XF
20	1861A	6.857	1.00	2.00	4.00	15.00
	1861BB	7.124	1.00	2.00	4.00	15.00
	1861K	6.582	1.00	2.00	4.00	15.00
	1862A	5.300	1.00	2.00	4.00	15.00
	1862BB	8.584	1.00	2.00	4.00	15.00
	1862K	7.065	1.00	2.00	4.00	15.00
	1863A	12.128	.75	1.25	3.50	9.00
	1863BB	2.323	1.75	3.00	7.00	27.50
	1863K	9.437	1.00	2.00	4.00	9.00
	1864A	3.053	1.50	3.00	6.00	16.00
	1864BB	6.110	1.00	2.00	4.50	15.00
	1864K	5.831	1.00	2.00	4.50	15.00
	1865A	2.619	1.75	3.00	7.50	20.00
	1865BB	7.226	1.00	2.00	4.00	9.00

Third Republic

Y#	Date	Mintage	VG	Fine	VF	XF
43	1871A	2.238	1.00	2.00	4.00	10.00
	1871K	.016	40.00	100.00	250.00	650.00
	1872A	4.263	.50	1.75	3.00	8.00
	1872K	4.064	.75	3.50	7.00	15.00
	1873A	1.492	1.00	2.50	5.00	8.00
	1873K	1.997	1.00	3.50	7.00	15.00
	1874A	1.730	.75	2.50	5.00	8.00
	1874K	1.326	1.00	3.50	7.00	15.00
	1875A	1.193	.75	2.50	5.00	8.00
	1875K	.760	2.50	14.00	27.50	55.00
	1876A	2.481	.50	1.75	3.00	8.00
	1876K	1.597	2.00	8.00	17.00	45.00
	1877A	.766	2.00	7.00	14.00	35.00
	1877K	1.193	1.00	3.50	7.00	15.00
	1878A	.300	2.50	11.00	20.00	50.00
	1878K	.166	6.00	30.00	75.00	275.00
	1879A(a)	1.955	1.00	2.00	4.00	10.00
	1879A anchor with bar	Inc. Ab.	2.00	6.00	12.50	25.00
	1880A	1.172	1.00	2.50	5.00	9.00
	1881A	2.502	.50	1.75	3.00	8.00
	1882A	1.600	.75	2.00	3.75	8.00
	1883A	2.400	.50	1.75	3.00	8.00
	1884A	1.680	.75	2.00	3.75	8.00
	1885A	2.000	.50	1.75	3.00	7.00
	1886A	1.680	.75	2.00	3.75	8.00
	1887A	1.008	1.00	3.50	7.00	15.00
	1888A	1.660	.75	2.00	3.75	8.00
	1889A	1.660	.75	2.00	3.75	8.00
	1890A	1.680	.75	2.00	3.75	8.00
	1891A	1.600	.50	1.75	3.50	7.00
	1892A	1.600	.50	1.75	3.50	7.00
	1893A	1.600	.50	1.75	3.50	7.00
	1894A	2.240	.35	1.25	2.25	5.50
	1896A(f)	6.695	.25	1.00	2.50	5.00
	1896A(t)	Inc. Ab.	1.00	2.50	7.00	15.00
	1897A	12.600	.25	1.00	2.50	5.00
	1898A	1.200	1.00	3.50	7.00	15.00

Y#	Date	Mintage	Fine	VF	XF	Unc
60	1898	7.900	.75	1.25	3.00	7.00
	1899	7.400	.75	1.25	3.00	7.00
	1900(n)	7.400	.75	1.25	3.00	7.00
	(1)900 (error - 1900)	Inc. Ab.		—	Rare	—
	1901(c)	6.000	.75	1.50	5.00	18.00
	1902	7.900	.75	1.50	4.00	8.00
	1903	2.879	1.50	3.50	6.00	22.00
	1904	8.000	.75	1.50	4.00	8.00
	1905	2.100	1.50	3.50	6.50	20.00
	1906	8.394	.40	1.00	2.50	8.00
	1907	7.900	.40	1.00	2.50	8.00
	1908	6.090	.75	1.75	3.00	9.00
	1909	8.000	.40	1.00	2.50	8.00
	1910	4.000	.75	1.75	3.00	9.00
	1911	15.386	.40	1.00	2.50	8.00
	1912	20.000	.40	1.00	2.50	8.00
	1913	12.603	.40	1.00	2.50	8.00
	1914	7.000	.40	1.00	2.50	8.00
	1915	6.032	.40	1.00	2.50	8.00
	1916	41.531	.40	1.00	2.50	8.00
	1916(s)	Inc. Ab.	.40	1.00	2.50	8.00
	1917	16.963	.40	1.00	2.50	8.00
	1920	8.152	3.00	7.50	15.00	35.00
	1921	.142	35.00	75.00	125.00	300.00

COPPER-NICKEL

Y#	Date	Mintage	Fine	VF	XF	Unc
71	1914	2 Known	—	—	Rare	—
	1917	10.458	.50	1.25	3.00	10.00
	1918	35.592	.25	1.00	2.00	4.00
	1919	43.848	.25	1.00	2.00	4.00
	1920	51.321	.25	1.00	2.00	4.00

Y#	Date	Mintage	Fine	VF	XF	Unc
72	1920	Inc. Ab.	3.00	7.00	12.00	30.00
	1921	32.908	.25	.50	1.00	2.50
	1922	31.700	.25	.50	1.00	2.50
	1922(t)	17.717	.25	.50	1.25	3.00
	1923	23.322	.25	.50	1.00	2.50
	1923(t)	45.097	.25	.50	1.00	2.50
	1924	47.018	.25	.50	1.00	2.50
	1924(t)	21.210	.25	.50	1.00	2.50
	1925	66.838	.25	.50	1.00	2.50
	1926	19.820	.25	.50	1.00	2.50
	1927	6.044	1.00	2.50	4.00	10.00
	1929	.022	Reported, Not Confirmed			
	1930	31.902	.25	.50	1.00	2.50
	1931	34.711	.25	.50	1.00	2.50
	1932	31.112	.15	.25	.75	2.00
	1933	12.970	.25	.50	1.25	4.00
	1934	27.144	.25	.50	1.00	3.00
	1935	57.221	.25	.50	1.00	2.50
	1936	64.341	.15	.25	.75	2.50
	1937	26.329	.15	.25	.75	2.50
	1938	21.614	.25	.50	1.00	2.50

NICKEL-BRONZE

Y#	Date	Mintage	Fine	VF	XF	Unc
72a	.1938.	26.330	.10	.50	1.00	3.00
	.1939.	52.673	.10	.50	.75	2.00

CHROME-STEEL
5 New Centimes - 5 Old Francs
Fifth Republic

Y#	Date	Mintage	Fine	VF	XF	Unc
103	1961	39.000	.20	.40	1.00	3.00
	1962	166.000	—	—	.10	.25
	1963	71.900	.15	.25	.60	1.50
	1964	126.480	—	.15	.30	.50

ALUMINUM-BRONZE

Y#	Date	Mintage	Fine	VF	XF	Unc
A104	1966	502.512	—	—	—	.10
	1967	11.745	—	—	.10	.25
	1968	110.395	—	—	—	.10
	1969	94.955	—	—	—	.10
	1970	58.900	—	—	—	.10
	1971	93.190	—	—	—	.10
	1972	100.515	—	—	—	.10
	1973	100.344	—	—	—	.10
	1974	103.890	—	—	—	.10
	1975	95.835	—	—	—	.10
	1976	148.395	—	—	—	.10
	1977	*110.000	—	—	—	.10
	1978	—	—	—	—	.10
	1979	—	—	—	—	.10

(UN) (1) DECIME

BRONZE
First Republic
Rev: Denomination: DECIME

C#	Date	Mintage	VG	Fine	VF	XF
132	L'AN4A	3.606	12.00	35.00	90.00	250.00
	L'AN4D	.255	20.00	75.00	150.00	450.00
	L'AN4I	.694	14.00	45.00	125.00	325.00
	L'AN5A	Inc. Ab.	20.00	75.00	150.00	400.00
	L'AN5D	Inc. Ab.	Reported, Not Confirmed			
	L'AN5I	Inc. Ab.	50.00	125.00	200.00	600.00

UN countermarked over obliterated 2 and S obliterated from 2 Decimes, C#133.

C#	Date	Mintage	VG	Fine	VF	XF
136	L'AN4A	—	12.00	35.00	90.00	275.00
	L'AN4D	—	Reported, Not Confirmed			
	L'AN4I	—	14.00	45.00	140.00	325.00
	L'AN5A	—	14.50	45.00	140.00	300.00

Rev: Denomination: UN DECIME

C#	Date	Mintage	VG	Fine	VF	XF
	L'AN5D	—	Reported, Not Confirmed			
	L'AN5I	—	—	—	Rare	—

C#	Date	Mintage	VG	Fine	VF	XF
137	L'AN5A	46.581	2.50	7.00	20.00	125.00
	L'AN5AA	.224	11.00	30.00	75.00	300.00
137	L'AN5B	2.041	6.00	12.00	27.50	135.00
	L'AN5BB	.418	7.00	16.00	60.00	175.00
	L'AN5D	4.826	4.00	9.00	20.00	150.00
	L'AN5I	3.800	4.50	10.00	20.00	150.00
	L'AN5R	1.980	6.00	13.00	27.50	150.00
	L'AN5T	.084	Reported, Not Confirmed			
	L'AN5W	3.948	7.00	16.00	60.00	175.00
	L'AN6A	Inc. Ab.	9.00	20.00	65.00	175.00
	L'AN6AA	I.A.	13.00	35.00	110.00	275.00
	L'AN6B	.567	11.00	30.00	75.00	300.00
	L'AN6BB	I.A.	13.00	35.00	110.00	275.00
	L'AN6D	.255	Reported, Not Confirmed			
	L'AN6I	Inc. Ab.	11.00	30.00	75.00	300.00
	L'AN6W	Inc. Ab.	35.00	100.00	200.00	500.00
	L'AN7/5A	I.B.	—	—	—	—
	L'AN7A	Inc. Bl.	2.00	6.00	18.00	100.00
	L'An7AA	—	5.00	12.00	40.00	175.00
	L'AN7BB	Inc. Bl.	7.00	16.00	50.00	175.00
	L'AN7D	Inc. Bl.	9.00	20.00	60.00	175.00
	L'AN7K	Inc. Bl.	7.00	16.00	50.00	175.00
	L'AN7W	Inc. Bl.	5.00	12.00	30.00	150.00
	L'AN8A	22.951	3.00	7.00	20.00	150.00
	L'AN8AA	9.996	4.50	10.00	20.00	150.00
	L'AN8BB	3.786	6.00	13.00	30.00	175.00
	L'AN8D	1.676	7.00	16.00	50.00	175.00
	L'AN8G	1.000	10.00	25.00	70.00	200.00
	L'AN8I	3.424	6.00	13.00	30.00	175.00
	L'AN8K	3.816	6.00	13.00	28.50	160.00
	L'AN8W	6.004	4.50	10.00	27.50	150.00
	L'An9A	—	4.50	10.00	27.50	150.00
	L'AN9BB	I.A.	6.00	13.00	35.00	160.00
	L'AN9D	Inc. Ab.	6.00	13.00	35.00	160.00
	L'AN9G	Inc. Ab.	9.00	20.00	70.00	200.00
	L'AN9I	Inc. Ab.	6.00	13.00	35.00	160.00
	L'AN9K	Inc. Ab.	6.00	13.00	35.00	160.00
	L'AN9W	Inc. Ab.	6.00	13.00	35.00	160.00

C#137 overstruck on 2 Decimes, C#133 and 133a.

C#	Date	Mintage	VG	Fine	VF	XF
137a	L'AN5A	—	15.00	37.50	65.00	150.00
	L'AN5AA	—	—	—	Unique	—
	L'AN5B	—	13.00	32.50	62.50	150.00
	L'AN5BB	—	Reported, Not Confirmed			
	L'AN5D	—	Reported, Not Confirmed			
	L'AN5I	—	7.00	16.00	30.00	100.00
	L'AN5R	—	7.00	16.00	30.00	100.00
	L'AN5T	—	6.00	15.00	30.00	100.00
	L'AN5W	—	Reported, Not Confirmed			
	L'AN6A	—	6.00	15.00	30.00	100.00
	L'AN6AA	—	Reported, Not Confirmed			
	L'AN6B	—	Reported, Not Confirmed			
	L'AN6D	—	Reported, Not Confirmed			
	L'AN6I	—	Reported, Not Confirmed			
	L'AN6W	—	Reported, Not Confirmed			
	L'AN8A	—	Reported, Not Confirmed			
	L'AN8I	—	Reported, Not Confirmed			

STRASBOURG PROVISIONAL ISSUES

C#	Date	Mintage	VG	Fine	VF	XF
174	1814BB	.544	7.00	15.00	35.00	100.00
	1814.BB w/o dot after DECIME					
		Inc. Ab.	8.00	20.00	50.00	125.00
	1814.BB w/dot after DECIME.					
		Inc. Ab.	8.00	20.00	50.00	125.00
	1815.BB	Inc. Ab.	10.00	25.00	55.00	165.00

C#	Date	Mintage	VG	Fine	VF	XF
175	1814.BB	1.208	8.00	20.00	50.00	125.00
	1815BB	I.A.	7.00	15.00	45.00	100.00
	1815.BB	I.A.	8.00	20.00	50.00	125.00

DIX (10) CENTIMES

BILLON SILVER

C#	Date	Mintage	VG	Fine	VF	XF
150	1807A	—	—	—	Rare	—
	1808A	6.269	1.00	3.00	10.00	30.00
	1808B	.163	8.00	20.00	55.00	125.00
	1808BB	1.425	1.50	4.50	12.00	40.00
	1808H	.129	8.00	20.00	55.00	125.00
	1808I	1.062	1.50	4.50	12.00	40.00
	1808M	.860	2.50	7.00	18.00	55.00
	1808Q	—	Reported, Not Confirmed			
	1808T	.054	12.00	35.00	70.00	200.00
	1808W	1.576	1.50	4.50	12.00	40.00
	1809A	7.529	1.00	3.00	7.00	25.00
	1809B	.831	2.50	7.00	18.00	55.00
	1809BB	.695	2.50	7.50	18.50	57.50
	1809H	.631	2.50	7.50	18.50	57.50
	1809I	3.473	1.00	3.00	8.00	25.00
	1809M	1.070	1.50	4.50	12.00	40.00
	1809Q	.555	4.00	8.50	20.00	70.00
	1809T	.134	8.00	20.00	50.00	115.00
	1809W	1.160	1.50	4.50	12.00	40.00
	1810A	—	—	—	Unique	—
	1810B	1.231	1.50	4.50	12.00	40.00
	1810BB	—	—	—	Unique	—
	1810D	—	Reported, Not Confirmed			
	1810H	.673	2.50	7.00	18.00	60.00
	1810I	3.066	1.00	3.00	7.00	25.00
	1810Q	.130	8.00	20.00	50.00	115.00
	1810T	.103	Reported, Not Confirmed			

BRONZE
Second Empire

Y#	Date	Mintage	VG	Fine	VF	XF
17	1852A	.577	8.00	16.00	50.00	95.00
	1853A	12.256	1.00	2.00	5.00	15.00
	1853B	3.546	1.50	3.00	6.50	19.00
	1853BB	4.582	1.50	3.00	6.50	19.00
	1853D	3.709	1.50	3.00	6.50	19.00
	1853K	1.203	2.00	7.00	13.00	27.50
	1853MA	.889	3.00	13.00	19.00	40.00

Y#	Date	Mintage	VG	Fine	VF	XF
17	1853W	3.107	1.50	3.00	6.50	19.00
	1854A	13.327	.50	2.00	5.00	15.00
	1854B	8.065	.75	2.50	5.00	17.00
	1854BB	8.433	.75	2.50	5.00	17.00
	1854D	8.487	.75	2.50	5.00	17.00
	1854K	7.083	.75	2.50	5.00	17.00
	1854MA	7.995	.75	2.50	5.00	17.00
	1854W	8.242	.75	2.50	5.00	17.00
	1855A(d)	14.816	.50	2.00	5.00	15.00
	1855A(a)	I.A.	.50	2.00	5.00	15.00
	1855B(d)	9.960	.75	2.50	5.00	17.00
	1855B(a)	I.A.	.75	2.50	5.00	17.00
	1855BB(d)	11.953	.75	2.50	5.00	17.00
	1855BB(a)	I.A.	.75	2.50	5.00	17.00
	1855D(d)	12.099	.75	2.50	5.00	17.00
	1855D(a)	I.A.	.75	2.50	5.00	17.00
	1855K(d)	11.797	.75	2.50	5.00	17.00
	1855K(a)	I.A.	.75	2.50	5.00	17.00
	1855MA(d)	11.309	.75	2.50	5.00	17.50
	1855MA(a)	I.A.	.75	2.50	5.00	17.50
	1855W(d)	9.837	.75	2.50	5.00	17.50
	1855W(a)	I.A.	.75	2.50	5.00	17.50
	1856A	19.149	.75	2.50	5.00	17.50
	1856B	11.637	.75	2.50	5.00	17.50
	1856BB	7.781	.75	2.50	5.00	17.50
	1856D	4.419	.75	2.50	5.00	17.50
	1856K	8.871	.75	2.50	5.00	17.50
	1856MA	10.937	.75	2.50	5.00	17.50
	1856W	11.402	.75	2.50	5.00	17.50
	1857A	3.096	1.50	3.00	6.50	19.00
	1857B	1.620	2.00	7.00	13.00	27.50
	1857BB	1.685	2.00	7.00	13.00	27.50
	1857D	.699	Reported, Not Confirmed			
	1857K	1.179	2.50	10.00	19.00	35.00
	1857MA	2.052	2.00	7.00	15.00	30.00
	1857W	1.858	2.50	10.00	18.50	33.00

Y#	Date	Mintage	VG	Fine	VF	XF
21	1861A	3.638	2.00	4.50	10.00	22.50
	1861BB	4.625	2.00	4.50	10.00	22.50
	1861K	4.363	1.25	3.50	9.00	20.00
	1862A	4.736	1.25	3.50	9.00	20.00
	1862BB	4.702	1.25	3.50	9.00	20.00
	1862K	5.244	1.25	3.50	9.00	20.00
	1863A	4.873	1.25	3.50	9.00	20.00
	1863BB	1.340	2.50	8.00	20.00	40.00
	1863K	4.521	1.25	3.50	9.00	20.00
	1864A	1.556	3.00	14.00	32.50	45.00
	1864BB	3.053	1.25	3.75	10.00	22.50
	1864K	3.075	1.25	3.75	10.00	22.50
	1865A	1.608	2.50	8.00	20.00	40.00
	1865BB	4.797	1.25	3.50	9.00	20.00

Third Republic

Y#	Date	Mintage	Fine	VF	XF	Unc
44	1870A	.889	4.00	9.00	20.00	45.00
	1871A	1.840	2.50	4.50	12.00	40.00
	1871K	.027	110.00	185.00	425.00	Rare
	1872A	4.399	1.50	3.00	8.00	25.00
	1872K	4.359	3.25	6.00	16.00	55.00
	1873A	2.096	1.50	3.00	10.00	30.00
	1873K	2.001	3.50	7.00	18.00	60.00
	1874A	1.194	2.50	4.50	12.00	40.00
	1874K	1.337	4.00	8.00	20.00	65.00
	1875A	1.434	20.00	40.00	75.00	175.00
	1875K	.430	10.00	25.00	50.00	110.00
	1876A	.458	5.00	10.00	30.00	70.00
	1876K	.601	10.00	25.00	50.00	110.00
	1877A	.392	8.00	16.00	35.00	75.00
	1877K	.403	15.00	35.00	80.00	150.00
	1878A	.150	12.00	32.50	65.00	125.00
	1878K	.100	40.50	85.00	150.00	450.00
	1879A	.823	6.00	13.00	20.00	45.00
44	1880A	1.414	2.50	4.50	12.00	40.00
	1881A	.749	8.00	15.00	25.00	60.00
	1882A	1.100	2.50	5.50	12.00	40.00
	1883A	.700	8.00	15.00	25.00	60.00
	1884A	1.060	4.00	7.00	15.00	40.00
	1885A	.900	6.00	12.00	20.00	42.50
	1886A	1.060	4.00	8.00	18.00	35.00
	1887A	.874	7.00	13.00	25.00	42.50
	1888A	1.050	3.50	7.00	15.00	32.50
	1889A	1.010	3.50	7.00	15.00	32.50
	1890A	1.060	3.50	7.00	15.00	32.50
	1891A	1.000	3.50	7.00	15.00	32.50
	1892A	1.020	3.50	7.00	15.00	32.50
	1893A	1.120	3.50	7.00	15.00	32.50
	1894A	.800	5.00	11.00	22.50	35.00
	1895A	.600	4.50	11.00	25.00	42.50
	1896A(f)	4.447	2.00	4.00	9.00	27.50
	1896A(t)	Inc. Ab.	3.00	6.00	16.00	45.00
	1897A	7.250	1.25	2.75	8.00	25.00
	1898A	1.400	3.00	7.00	18.00	45.00

Y#	Date	Mintage	Fine	VF	XF	Unc
61	1898	4.000	1.50	3.00	7.00	25.00
	1899	4.000	1.50	3.00	7.00	30.00
	1900(n)	5.000	1.00	2.50	4.00	25.00
	1901(c)	2.700	2.00	4.00	9.00	30.00
	1902	3.800	1.50	3.00	7.00	25.00
	1903	3.650	3.00	7.00	15.00	35.00
	1904	3.800	1.50	3.00	7.00	25.00
	1905	.950	9.00	20.00	50.00	110.00
	1906	3.000	3.00	7.00	15.00	35.00
	1907	4.000	1.00	2.50	4.00	25.00
	1908	3.500	1.50	3.00	7.00	25.00
	1909	2.933	3.50	7.00	15.00	35.00
	1910	3.567	1.50	3.00	4.50	20.00
	1911	7.903	1.00	2.50	4.00	18.00
	1912	9.500	.75	1.75	3.00	12.00
	1913	9.000	.75	1.75	3.00	12.00
	1914	6.000	1.00	2.00	3.50	14.00
	1915	4.362	1.00	2.00	3.50	15.00
	1916	22.477	.75	1.50	2.50	10.00
	1916(s)	Inc. Ab.	.75	1.50	3.00	11.00
	1917	11.914	1.00	2.00	4.50	11.00
	1920	4.119	2.50	5.00	15.00	40.00
	1921	1.896	7.50	16.00	37.50	75.00

NICKEL

Y#	Date	Mintage	Fine	VF	XF	Unc
73	1914 dash	3,972	400.00	800.00	1200.	2000.

COPPER-NICKEL

Y#	Date	Mintage	Fine	VF	XF	Unc
73a	1917	8.171	.75	1.50	3.00	6.00
	1918	30.605	.10	.20	.65	3.00
	1919	33.489	.10	.20	.75	3.00
	1920	38.845	.10	.20	1.00	3.00
	1921	42.768	.10	.20	.50	3.00
	1922	23.033	.10	.20	1.00	3.50
	1922(t)	12.412	.40	.75	1.75	4.00
	1923	18.701	.25	.50	1.00	3.50
	1923(t)	30.016	.10	.20	.75	3.00
	1924	43.949	.10	.20	.75	3.00
	1924(t)	13.591	.40	.75	1.75	4.00
	1925	46.266	.10	.20	.50	3.00
	1926	25.660	.10	.20	1.00	3.50
	1927	16.203	.25	.50	1.50	3.75
	1928	6.967	1.00	2.00	3.50	8.00
	1929	24.531	.10	.20	1.00	3.50
	1930	22.146	.10	.20	1.00	3.50
	1931	49.107	.15	.25	1.00	3.00
	1932	30.317	.10	.20	.50	3.00
	1933	13.042	.10	.20	1.25	4.00
	1934	24.067	.10	.20	.75	3.00
	1935	47.487	.10	.20	.50	2.50
	1936	57.738	.15	.25	.50	1.50
	1937	25.308	.10	.20	.40	2.00
	1938	17.063	.10	.20	.40	2.00

NICKEL-BRONZE

Y#	Date	Mintage	Fine	VF	XF	Unc
73c	.1938.	24.151	.25	.50	.75	3.00
	.1939.	62.269	.10	.20	.40	2.00

Thin flan

Y#	Date	Mintage	Fine	VF	XF	Unc
	.1939.	Inc. Ab.	.25	.50	.75	4.50

ZINC

No dash under MES in C MES

Y#	Date	Mintage	Fine	VF	XF	Unc
73b.1	1941	235.9	2.00	3.50	6.00	15.00

With dash under MES in C MES

Y#	Date	Mintage	Fine	VF	XF	Unc
73b.2	1941	Inc. Ab.	1.00	2.00	3.75	10.00

With dot before and after date.

Y#	Date	Mintage	Fine	VF	XF	Unc
73b.3	.1941.	Inc. Ab.	.75	1.25	2.75	5.00

Vichy French State Issues

Y#	Date	Mintage	Fine	VF	XF	Unc
V91	1941	70.860	.25	.50	1.25	6.00
	1942	139.598	.25	.50	1.00	4.00
	1942B	—	—	—	—	—
	1943	21.520	.40	.75	1.50	8.00
	1944B	—	—	—	—	—

Y#	Date	Mintage	Fine	VF	XF	Unc
V93	1943	22.008	.50	1.00	2.50	8.00
	1944	58.463	.50	1.00	2.00	6.00

Fourth Republic Issues

Y#	Date	Mintage	Fine	VF	XF	Unc
74	1945	38.174	.75	1.50	2.00	8.00
	1945B	7.246	1.75	4.00	7.00	20.00
	1945C	8.379	2.50	5.00	8.50	22.00
	1946	—	—	—	Rare	—
	1946B	10.566	1.25	2.50	5.00	12.00

ALUMINUM-BRONZE

10 New Centimes - 10 Old Francs

Fifth Republic

Y#	Date	Mintage	Fine	VF	XF	Unc
104	1962	29.100	—	—	.10	.40
	1963	217.601	—	—	—	.10
	1964	93.409	—	—	.10	.20
	1965	41.220	—	—	—	.30
	1966	16.422	—	.10	.20	.40
	1967	196.728	—	—	—	.10

Y#	Date	Mintage	Fine	VF	XF	Unc
104	1968	111.700	—	—	—	.10
	1969	129.530	—	—	—	.10
	1970	77.020	—	—	—	.10
	1971	26.280	—	—	—	.10
	1972	45.700	—	—	—	.10
	1973	58.000	—	—	—	.10
	1974	91.990	—	—	—	.10
	1975	74.450	—	—	—	.10
	1976	137.320	—	—	—	.10
	1977	*140.000	—	—	—	.10
	1978	—	—	—	—	.10
	1979	—	—	—	—	.10

2 DECIMES

BRONZE
First Republic

C#	Date	Mintage	VG	Fine	VF	XF
133	L'AN4A	151.655	17.00	42.50	95.00	235.00
	L'AN4D	—	—	—	Unique	—
	L'AN4I	12.092	30.00	80.00	185.00	330.00
	L'AN5A	Inc. Ab.	25.00	60.00	125.00	275.00
	L'AN5D	.024		Reported, Not Confirmed		
	L'AN5I	Inc. Ab.	40.00	100.00	250.00	500.00
	Rev. value: 2 DECIME					
133a	L'AN4A	—	6.00	15.00	35.00	75.00
	L'AN5A	—	10.00	25.00	50.00	100.00

VINGT (20) CENTIMES

1.0000 gm., .900 SILVER, .0289 oz ASW
Second Republic

Y#	Date	Mintage	VG	Fine	VF	XF
2	1849A	4,877	100.00	225.00	450.00	900.00
	1850A	6.157	2.00	7.00	13.00	35.00
	1850BB	.048	30.00	65.00	150.00	400.00
	1850K	.344	15.00	35.00	95.00	175.00
	1851A	3.309	2.50	9.00	18.00	50.00

Second Empire - Napoleon III

Y#	Date	Mintage	VG	Fine	VF	XF
22	1853A	.680	4.00	15.00	30.00	70.00
	1854A	1.683	2.50	7.00	15.00	35.00
	1855A(d)	.362	8.00	18.00	40.00	95.00
	1856A	.603	6.00	17.00	35.00	80.00
	1856BB	.013	30.00	90.00	250.00	650.00
	1856D	.396	8.00	18.00	40.00	95.00
	1857A	.840	3.00	11.00	25.00	42.50
	1858A	.704	4.00	15.00	32.00	75.00
	1859A	3.620	1.00	4.00	10.00	25.00
	1860/50A	—	—	—	—	—
	1860A(h)	6.536	1.00	3.00	5.00	15.00
	1860BB(b)	2.986	2.00	4.00	7.00	20.00
	1862A	.054	20.00	45.00	100.00	220.00
	1863BB	.398	15.00	35.00	75.00	125.00

.835 SILVER

Y#	Date	Mintage	VG	Fine	VF	XF
27	1864A	.268	5.00	20.00	40.00	95.00
	1864BB	.112	10.00	30.00	60.00	125.00
	1864K	.058	20.00	45.00	100.00	225.00
	1865A	—		Reported, Not Confirmed		
	1866A	1.460	1.00	5.00	10.00	25.00
	1866BB	.843	3.00	11.00	25.00	40.00
	1866K	.413	8.00	18.00	40.00	95.00
28	1867A	5.611	1.00	2.00	5.00	10.00
	1867BB	3.114	1.00	2.00	5.50	12.00
	1867K	.091	10.00	30.00	75.00	150.00
	1868A	.353	4.00	10.00	25.00	60.00
	1868BB	Inc. Bl.	10.00	25.00	75.00	125.00
	1869BB	.200		Reported, Not Confirmed		

1.0000 gm., .900 SILVER, 15mm, .0289 oz ASW

Y#	Date	Mintage	Fine	VF	XF	Unc
47	1878A	30 pcs.	—	—	—	2200.
	16mm					
—	1889A	100 pcs.	—	—	900.00	1900.

NOTE: Considered an Essai.

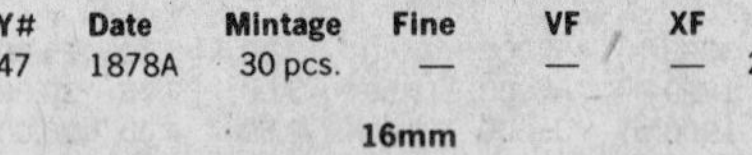

ZINC
Vichy French State Issues

Y#	Date	Mintage	VG	Fine	VF	XF
V90	1941	54.044	1.25	2.50	6.50	15.00

Y#	Date	Mintage	VG	Fine	VF	XF
V92	1941	31.397	.65	1.25	3.00	12.00
	1942	112.868	.50	1.00	2.00	6.00
	1942B	—	—	—	—	—
	1943	64.138	.65	1.25	3.00	8.00
	1943B	—	—	—	—	—
	Thin flan					
	1943	Inc. Ab.	.65	1.25	3.00	8.00
	1944	5.250	3.00	6.00	19.00	45.00
	IRON					
V92a	1944	.695	20.00	45.00	95.00	210.00

ZINC
Fourth Republic Issues

Y#	Date	Mintage	VG	Fine	VF	XF
75	1945	6.003	2.50	5.00	9.50	23.00
	1945B	.100	37.50	75.00	110.00	200.00
	1945C	.299	14.00	30.00	50.00	90.00
	1946	2.662	4.00	9.00	16.00	35.00
	1946B	5.525	37.50	75.00	110.00	190.00

ALUMINUM-BRONZE
Fifth Republic
20 New Centimes - 20 Old Francs

Y#	Date	Mintage	Fine	VF	XF	Unc
105	1962	48.200	—	.15	.20	.50
	1963	190.330	—	—	.10	.30
	1964	127.521	—	—	.10	.30
	1965	27.024	—	—	.25	.40
	1966	21.755	—	—	.20	.40
	1967	138.780	—	—	—	.10
	1968	77.408	—	—	.10	.20
	1969	50.570	—	—	.10	.20
	1970	70.040	—	—	—	.10
	1971	31.080	—	—	—	.10
	1972	39.740	—	—	—	.10
	1973	45.240	—	—	—	.10
	1974	54.250	—	—	—	.10
	1975	40.570	—	—	—	.10
	1976	117.610	—	—	—	.10
	1977	*100.000	—	—	—	—
	1978	—	—	—	—	—
	1979	—	—	—	—	—

QUART (1/4) FRANC

1.2500 gm., .900 SILVER, .0362 oz ASW
Obv: BONAPARTE PREMIER CONSUL

C#	Date	Mintage	VG	Fine	VF	XF
141	AN12A	.171	10.00	30.00	70.00	160.00
	AN12BB	1,565	—	—	Rare	—
	AN12D	—	35.00	85.00	190.00	400.00
	AN12I	.041	15.00	35.00	75.00	200.00
	AN12L	.019	20.00	60.00	115.00	235.00
	AN12M	.039	15.00	35.00	75.00	200.00
	AN12MA	9,080	35.00	95.00	200.00	425.00
	AN12Q	.028	15.00	40.00	80.00	210.00
	AN12T	.010	35.00	95.00	200.00	425.00

Obv: NAPOLEON EMPEREUR

C#	Date	Mintage	VG	Fine	VF	XF
151	AN12A	.019	20.00	60.00	110.00	230.00
	AN12D	5,156	40.00	100.00	200.00	400.00
	AN12H	.012	22.50	65.00	120.00	240.00
	AN12I	.032	15.00	40.00	90.00	190.00
	AN12K	8,122	35.00	90.00	145.00	270.00
	AN12M	.016	22.50	65.00	120.00	240.00
	AN12T	3,606	50.00	125.00	275.00	800.00
	AN13A	.128	11.00	30.00	65.00	140.00
	AN13BB	2,194	70.00	150.00	325.00	900.00
	AN13H	2,744	70.00	150.00	325.00	900.00
	AN13I	.118	11.00	30.00	65.00	140.00
	AN13K	.018	20.00	60.00	110.00	230.00
	AN13L	.025	18.00	60.00	100.00	230.00
	AN13M	.039	15.00	45.00	90.00	190.00
	AN13MA	8,114	35.00	90.00	145.00	270.00
	AN13T	6,801	40.00	100.00	160.00	300.00
	AN13U	.014	45.00	125.00	250.00	500.00
	AN14A	—		Reported, Not Confirmed		
	AN14K	1,757		Reported, Not Confirmed		
	AN14L	—	—	—	Rare	—
	AN14U	—	60.00	200.00	375.00	875.00
151.2	1806A	.031	17.50	50.00	100.00	225.00
	1806I	4,583	45.00	125.00	250.00	500.00
	1806K	4,359	45.00	125.00	250.00	500.00
	1806L	.018	20.00	60.00	110.00	230.00
	1806Q	8,948	35.00	90.00	145.00	270.00
	1806U	1,361		Reported, Not Confirmed		
	1807I	8,356	35.00	90.00	145.00	270.00
	1807K	5,538	45.00	125.00	250.00	500.00
	1807L	7,618	35.00	90.00	145.00	270.00
	1807M	1,626	60.00	135.00	325.00	750.00
	1807Q	9,713	35.00	90.00	145.00	270.00
	1807U	.013	40.00	100.00	165.00	310.00

Negro head

C#	Date	Mintage	VG	Fine	VF	XF
151a	1807A	.041	40.00	100.00	275.00	675.00

Laureate head

C#	Date	Mintage	VG	Fine	VF	XF
151b	1807A	.017	55.00	150.00	375.00	850.00
	1808A	—	40.00	100.00	275.00	500.00
	1808I	1,466	75.00	200.00	400.00	900.00
	1808L	4,393	40.00	110.00	290.00	550.00

C#	Date	Mintage	VG	Fine	VF	XF
161	1809A	.034	50.00	175.00	425.00	900.00

C#	Date	Mintage	VG	Fine	VF	XF
177	1817A	.100	8.00	20.00	70.00	150.00
	1817B	.021	14.00	35.00	95.00	180.00
	1817BB	3,772	Reported, Not Confirmed			
	1817D	.012	16.00	40.00	100.00	195.00
	1817I	.016	16.00	40.00	100.00	195.00
	1817L	.014	16.00	40.00	100.00	195.00
	1817M	4,314	25.00	55.00	125.00	275.00
	1817MA	2,132	Reported, Not Confirmed			
	1817Q	.013	16.00	40.00	100.00	195.00
	1817T	7,606	17.00	45.00	115.00	210.00
	1817W	.014	16.00	40.00	100.00	195.00
	1818A	.028	14.00	35.00	95.00	180.00
	1818B	.016	16.00	40.00	100.00	195.00
	1818W	3,294	25.00	55.00	125.00	275.00
	1819A	.011	16.00	40.00	100.00	195.00
	1819B	.015	16.00	40.00	100.00	195.00
	1819W	3,170	25.00	55.00	125.00	275.00
	1820A	.012	16.00	40.00	100.00	195.00
	1820W	5,894	17.00	45.00	115.00	210.00
	1821A	.022	14.00	35.00	95.00	180.00
	1822A	.036	14.00	35.00	95.00	180.00
	1822B	.030	14.00	35.00	95.00	180.00
	1822W	4,486	25.00	55.00	125.00	275.00
	1823A	.044	14.00	35.00	95.00	180.00
	1823B	.013	16.00	40.00	100.00	195.00
	1823I	1,870	Reported, Not Confirmed			
	1823L	.012	16.00	40.00	100.00	195.00
	1823M	3,994	25.00	55.00	125.00	275.00
	1823Q	.011	16.00	40.00	100.00	195.00
	1823W	.016	16.00	40.00	100.00	195.00
	1824A	.083	8.00	20.00	70.00	150.00
	1824B	.018	16.00	40.00	100.00	195.00
	1824L	.031	14.00	35.00	95.00	180.00
	1824M	7,774	17.00	45.00	115.00	210.00
	1824W	.011	16.00	40.00	100.00	195.00

C#	Date	Mintage	VG	Fine	VF	XF
185	1825A	9,448	17.50	45.00	115.00	210.00
	1826A	.083	8.50	20.00	70.00	150.00
	1826B	.023	14.00	35.00	95.00	180.00
	1826D	.013	16.00	40.00	100.00	195.00
	1826L	.011	16.00	40.00	100.00	195.00
	1826M	4,861	17.00	45.00	115.00	210.00
	1826Q	7,534	17.00	45.00	115.00	210.00
	1826T	1,753	Reported, Not Confirmed			
	1826W	.015	16.00	40.00	100.00	195.00
	1827A	.322	3.00	10.00	20.00	50.00
	1827B	.017	16.00	40.00	100.00	195.00
	1827BB	1,567	25.00	100.00	210.00	400.00
	1827D	7,820	17.00	45.00	115.00	210.00
	1827I	828	Reported, Not Confirmed			
	1827L	7,582	17.00	45.00	115.00	210.00
	1827M	4,292	17.00	45.00	115.00	210.00
	1827W	.022	12.00	30.00	75.00	150.00
	1828A	.446	2.50	10.00	20.00	50.00
	1828B	.023	12.00	30.00	75.00	150.00
	1828BB	.013	16.00	40.00	100.00	195.00
	1828D	.013	16.00	40.00	100.00	195.00
	1828H	.016	16.00	40.00	100.00	195.00
185	1828I	2,226	25.50	55.00	125.00	275.00
	1828L	.015	16.00	40.00	100.00	195.00
	1828M	.048	12.00	30.00	60.00	125.00
	1828Q	.013	16.00	40.00	100.00	195.00
	1828T	6,316	17.00	45.00	115.00	210.00
	1828W	.047	12.00	30.00	60.00	125.00
	1829A	.154	3.00	10.00	25.00	60.00
	1829B	.032	12.00	30.00	60.00	125.00
	1829BB	.014	16.00	40.00	100.00	195.00
	1829D	.052	12.00	30.00	60.00	125.00
	1829I	.010	16.00	40.00	100.00	195.00
	1829K	.027	12.50	30.00	60.00	125.00
	1829L	6,486	17.00	45.00	115.00	210.00
	1829M	.014	16.00	40.00	100.00	195.00
	1829T	6,481	17.00	45.00	115.00	210.00
	1829W	.108	3.00	10.00	25.00	60.00
	1830A	.659	2.00	6.00	18.00	40.00
	1830A T	—	27.50	90.00	200.00	500.00
	1830K	.021	12.00	30.00	60.00	125.00
	1830L	.015	16.00	40.00	100.00	195.00
	1830W	.074	10.00	20.00	45.00	95.00

C#	Date	Mintage	VG	Fine	VF	XF
196	1831A	.075	BV	3.50	12.50	50.00
	1831B	.052	2.00	6.00	16.00	50.00
	1831BB	3,629	Reported, Not Confirmed			
	1831D	.034	2.00	6.00	18.00	55.00
	1831H	.026	2.00	7.00	20.00	55.00
	1831I	967 pcs.	Reported, Not Confirmed			
	1831K	.036	2.00	6.00	18.00	55.00
	1831L	6,182	6.00	15.00	35.00	150.00
	1831M	6,831	Reported, Not Confirmed			
	1831Q	.011	3.50	10.00	25.00	65.00
	1831W	.160	BV	3.00	12.50	50.00
	1832A	.286	BV	2.00	10.00	45.50
	1832B	.135	BV	3.00	12.50	50.00
	1832BB	.011	3.50	10.00	25.00	65.00
	1832D	.141	BV	3.00	12.50	50.00
	1832H	.040	2.00	6.00	18.00	55.00
	1832I	.034	2.00	6.00	18.00	55.00
	1832K	.020	2.00	7.00	20.00	55.00
	1832L	.022	2.00	7.00	20.00	55.00
	1832M	.035	2.00	6.00	18.00	55.00
	1832Q	.018	3.00	10.00	25.00	65.00
	1832T	8,486	6.00	15.00	35.00	150.00
	1832W	.218	BV	3.00	12.50	50.00
	1833A	.155	BV	3.00	12.00	50.00
	1833B	.080	BV	3.00	12.00	50.00
	1833BB	7,890	6.00	15.00	35.00	150.00
	1833D	.016	3.00	10.00	25.00	65.00
	1833H	.014	3.00	10.00	25.00	65.00
	1833I	.024	3.00	10.00	25.00	65.00
	1833K	.022	3.00	10.00	25.00	65.00
	1833L	8,927	6.00	15.00	35.00	150.00
	1833M	.017	3.00	10.00	25.00	65.00
	1833MA	3,452	Reported, Not Confirmed			
	1833T	.018	3.00	10.00	25.00	65.00
	1833W	.141	BV	3.00	12.50	50.00
	1834A	.770	BV	3.00	12.50	50.00
	1834B	.070	BV	3.00	12.50	50.00
	1834BB	6,063	8.00	20.00	50.00	175.00
	1834D	.030	2.00	6.00	18.00	55.00
	1834H	.046	2.00	6.00	18.00	55.00
	1834I	.040	2.00	6.00	18.00	55.00
	1834K	.036	2.00	6.00	18.00	55.00
	1834L	8,789	6.00	15.00	35.00	150.00
	1834M	8,218	6.00	15.00	35.00	150.00
	1834Q	.014	3.25	10.00	25.00	65.00
	1834T	.034	2.00	6.00	18.00	55.00
	1834W	.404	BV	3.00	12.50	50.00
	1835A	.801	BV	3.00	12.50	50.00
	1835B	—	—	—	Rare	—
	1835B (error: PRANCAIS)					
		Inc. Ab.	—	—	Rare	—
	1835BB	.010	4.25	10.00	30.00	70.00
	1835D	.028	2.50	6.00	20.00	55.00
	1835H	9,989	6.00	15.00	35.00	150.00
	1835I	.044	2.00	6.00	18.00	55.00
	1835K	.041	2.00	6.00	18.00	55.00
	1835M	.011	4.00	10.00	30.00	95.00
	1835W	.133	BV	3.00	12.50	50.00
	1836A	.898	BV	3.00	12.50	50.00
	1836B	8,413	6.00	15.00	35.00	150.00
	1836BB	.011	6.00	10.00	30.00	95.00
	1836K	9,500	6.00	15.00	35.00	150.00
	1836W	.089	BV	3.00	12.00	50.00
	1837A	.830	BV	3.00	10.00	45.00
	1837B	.094	BV	3.00	12.00	50.00
	1837BB	9,762	6.00	15.00	35.00	150.00
	1837D	8,352	6.00	15.00	35.00	150.00
	1837K	.011	6.00	10.00	30.00	95.00
	1837W	.168	BV	3.00	12.00	50.00
196	1838A	.922	BV	3.00	9.00	45.00
	1838B	.049	2.00	6.00	18.00	55.00
	1838BB	6,561	35.00	80.00	225.00	500.00
	1838D	6,199	Reported, Not Confirmed			
	1838K	.016	3.50	7.00	30.00	75.00
	1838W	.100	BV	3.00	9.00	45.00
	1839A	1.180	BV	2.00	8.00	40.00
	1839B	.053	BV	3.00	12.00	50.00
	1839BB	.013	4.00	10.00	30.00	95.00
	1839D	5,163	Reported, Not Confirmed			
	1839K	.016	3.50	7.00	30.00	75.00
	1839W	.114	BV	2.00	8.00	40.00
	1840A	1.246	BV	2.00	7.00	35.00
	1840B	.053	BV	3.00	12.00	50.00
	1840D	.015	3.00	7.00	30.00	75.00
	1840K	.030	2.00	6.00	18.00	55.00
	1840W	.042	2.00	6.00	18.00	55.00
	1841A	1.303	BV	2.00	7.00	35.00
	1841B	.289	BV	2.00	8.00	40.00
	1841K	.092	BV	3.00	12.00	50.00
	1841W	.168	BV	2.50	12.00	50.00
	1842A	.647	BV	2.00	9.00	40.00
	1842B	.642	BV	2.00	9.00	40.00
	1842K	.023	3.00	7.00	30.00	75.00
	1842W	.091	BV	3.00	12.00	50.00
	1843A	.478	BV	2.00	9.00	40.00
	1843B	.762	BV	2.00	9.00	40.00
	1843K	.027	3.00	7.00	30.00	75.00
	1843W	.073	BV	3.00	12.00	50.00
	1844A	.816	BV	2.00	9.00	40.00
	1844B	.018	3.00	7.00	30.00	75.00
	1844BB	.036	2.00	6.00	18.00	55.00
	1844K	.023	3.00	7.00	30.00	75.00
	1844W	.367	BV	2.00	10.00	40.00
	1845A	.396	BV	2.00	10.00	40.00
	1845B	4.603	BV	1.25	6.00	25.00
	1845BB	.051	BV	3.00	12.00	50.00
	1845K	.016	Reported, Not Confirmed			
	1845W	.330	BV	2.00	10.00	40.00

25 CENTIMES

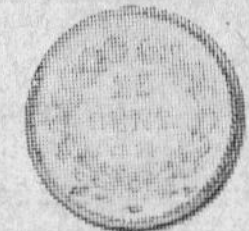

1.2500 gm., .900 SILVER, .0362 oz ASW

C#	Date	Mintage	VG	Fine	VF	XF
197	1845A	Inc. Ab.	Reported, Not Confirmed			
	1845B	Inc. Ab.	BV	2.00	8.00	35.00
	1845BB	Inc. Ab.	1.50	3.00	15.00	55.00
	1845K	Inc. Ab.	3.00	6.50	30.00	125.00
	1845W	Inc. Ab.	BV	2.00	8.00	50.00
	1846A	1.748	BV	2.00	8.00	40.00
	1846BB	7,922	6.00	15.00	40.00	150.00
	1846K	.012	5.25	11.00	35.00	125.00
	1846W	.039	1.25	3.00	12.00	50.00
	1847A	3.000	BV	1.50	5.00	17.00
	1847BB	9,939	6.00	15.00	40.00	150.00
	1847K	3,905	8.00	22.00	75.00	200.00
	1848A	.142	BV	2.00	8.00	50.00
	1848BB	5,886	7.00	20.00	50.00	125.00

NICKEL
Third Republic

Y#	Date	Mintage	Fine	VF	XF	Unc
69	1903	16.000	.65	1.50	3.00	9.00

Y#	Date	Mintage	Fine	VF	XF	Unc
70	1904	16.000	.65	1.50	3.00	9.00
	1905	8.000	1.00	1.75	5.00	14.00

Y#	Date	Mintage	Fine	VF	XF	Unc
76	1914(-)	.941	2.50	5.00	11.00	22.00
	1915(-)	.535	4.00	7.50	16.00	30.00
	1916(-)	.100	12.00	22.50	45.00	90.00
	1917(-)	.065	20.00	40.00	100.00	200.00

COPPER-NICKEL

Y#	Date	Mintage	Fine	VF	XF	Unc
76a	1917	3.085	.75	2.00	3.50	11.50
	1918	18.330	.20	.50	.75	4.00
	1919	5.106	.50	1.25	2.50	10.00
	1920	18.108	.25	.75	1.00	4.00
	1921	18.531	.25	.75	1.00	4.00
	1922	17.766	.25	.75	1.00	4.00
	1923	19.718	.25	.75	1.00	4.00
	1924	24.535	.20	.75	1.00	4.00
	1925	17.807	.25	.75	1.00	4.00
	1926	13.226	.25	.75	1.00	5.00
	1927	13.465	.25	.75	1.00	5.00
	1928	9.960	.50	1.00	2.00	6.00
	1929	12.887	.25	1.00	2.00	6.00
	1930	28.363	.25	.75	1.00	3.00
	1931	22.121	.25	.75	1.00	3.00
	1932	30.364	.25	.75	1.00	3.00
	1933	28.562	.25	.75	1.00	3.00
	1936	4.657	.75	1.50	3.00	9.00
	1937	7.780	.25	1.00	1.75	7.00

NICKEL-BRONZE

Y#	Date	Mintage	Fine	VF	XF	Unc
76b	1938	5.170	.75	1.50	2.50	6.00
	1939 thick flan (1.55mm)					
		42.964	.15	.25	.75	3.50
	1939 thin flan (1.35mm)					
		Inc. Ab.	.75	1.50	3.50	9.00
	1940	3.446	8.00	16.00	30.00	65.00

DEMI (1/2) FRANC

2.5000 gm., .900 SILVER, .0723 oz ASW
Obv: BONAPARTE PREMIER CONSUL

C#	Date	Mintage	VG	Fine	VF	XF
142	ANXIA	.031	35.00	85.00	200.00	500.00
	AN12A	.280	10.00	25.00	75.00	200.00
	AN12BB	2,125	Reported, Not Confirmed			
	AN12D	.015	27.50	65.00	160.00	375.00
	AN12G	7,407	50.00	125.00	275.00	550.00
	AN12H	1,988	Reported, Not Confirmed			
	AN12I	.416	8.00	18.00	60.00	175.00
	AN12K	.012	30.00	75.00	160.00	400.00
	AN12L	.067	16.00	40.00	100.00	330.00
	AN12M	.136	14.00	32.50	75.00	260.00
	AN12MA	.026	25.00	60.00	135.00	360.00
	AN12Q	.054	16.00	40.00	100.00	330.00
	AN12T	.017	27.50	65.00	160.00	375.00
	AN12U	3,150	100.00	275.00	650.00	1250.

Obv: NAPOLEON EMPEREUR

C#	Date	Mintage	VG	Fine	VF	XF
152	AN12A	.039	30.00	75.00	190.00	350.00
	AN12BB	1,825	Reported, Not Confirmed			
	AN12H	7,286	50.00	195.00	300.00	550.00
	AN12I	.022	40.00	110.00	225.00	400.00
	AN12K	.019	40.00	110.00	225.00	400.00
	AN12M	.099	20.00	60.00	110.00	275.00
152	AN12T	3,735	Reported, Not Confirmed			
	AN13A	.427	10.00	30.00	50.00	140.00
	AN13BB	895 pcs.	Reported, not confirmed			
	AN13D	2,402	Reported, Not Confirmed			
	AN13G	1,181	Reported, Not Confirmed			
	AN13H	5,036	45.00	125.00	260.00	450.00
	AN13I	.206	10.00	30.00	55.00	160.00
	AN13K	.037	20.00	60.00	110.00	275.00
	AN13L	.046	20.00	60.00	110.00	275.00
	AN13M	.212	10.00	30.00	55.00	160.00
	AN13MA	6,103	45.00	125.00	260.00	450.00
	AN13Q	.034	20.00	60.00	110.00	275.00
	AN13T	6,140	45.00	125.00	260.00	450.00
	AN13U	1,662	75.00	225.00	450.00	1000.
	AN14A	.020	Reported, Not Confirmed			
	AN14L	3,889	65.00	190.00	400.00	700.00
	AN14U	—	75.00	225.00	400.00	850.00
152.2	1806A	.156	18.00	45.00	100.00	300.00
	1806I	7,027	40.00	110.00	225.00	400.00
	1806K	1,673	Reported, Not Confirmed			
	1806L	.042	20.00	60.00	125.00	300.00
	1806Q	.015	25.00	60.00	160.00	330.00
	1806U	9,592	40.00	110.00	225.00	400.00
	1807I	3,848	50.00	125.00	275.00	500.00
	1807K	2,983	Reported, not confirmed			
	1807L	.017	25.00	60.00	160.00	330.00
	1807M	1,791	Reported, not confirmed			
	1807Q	.014	25.00	60.00	160.00	330.00
	1807U	4,448	85.00	225.00	450.00	1200.

Older head

C#	Date	Mintage	VG	Fine	VF	XF
152a	1807A	.058	100.00	300.00	500.00	1500.

Laureate head

C#	Date	Mintage	VG	Fine	VF	XF
152b	1807A	.105	175.00	500.00	1200.	3000.
	1808A	6.606	2.00	7.00	20.00	60.00
	1808B	.559	6.00	16.00	35.00	95.00
	1808BB	1.596	4.00	10.00	20.00	55.00
	1808D	.871	6.00	16.00	35.00	95.00
	1808H	.336	6.00	17.00	40.00	110.00
	1808I	.298	6.00	17.00	40.00	110.00
	1808K	.363	6.00	17.00	40.00	110.00
	1808L	3,394	40.00	20.00	225.00	375.00
	1808M	.054	12.00	35.00	75.00	200.00
	1808MA	.028	15.00	45.00	90.00	250.00
	1808Q	.289	6.00	17.00	40.00	110.00
	1808T	.128	9.00	22.50	55.00	135.00
	1808U	3,339	60.00	150.00	300.00	600.00
	1808W	1.069	4.00	10.00	20.00	55.00

C#	Date	Mintage	VG	Fine	VF	XF
162	1809A	1.680	3.00	7.00	15.00	50.00
	1809B	.014	12.00	35.00	75.00	190.00
	1809D	.043	9.00	22.50	55.00	135.00
	1809K	.043	9.00	22.50	55.00	135.00
	1809M	.021	10.00	30.00	65.00	145.00
	1809MA	3,176	40.00	110.00	225.00	385.00
	1809Q	.070	8.00	20.00	50.00	125.00
	1809U	5,853	60.00	155.00	300.00	700.00
	1809W	.314	5.00	13.00	30.00	75.00
	1810A	1.362	3.00	7.00	15.00	50.00
	1810B	.285	5.00	13.00	30.00	75.00
	1810BB	.011	25.00	65.00	160.00	450.00
	1810D	.071	8.00	20.00	50.00	125.00
	1810H	3,563	50.00	110.00	225.00	385.00
	1810K	.041	8.50	22.50	55.00	135.00
	1810L	.055	8.50	22.50	55.00	135.00
	1810L(TR)	I.A.	Reported, Not Confirmed			
	1810M	.033	9.00	25.00	60.00	150.00
	1810MA	.011	22.50	60.00	155.00	435.00
	1810W	.240	5.00	13.00	30.00	75.00
	1811A	1.860	3.00	7.00	15.00	50.00
	1811B	.252	5.00	13.00	30.00	75.00
	1811BB	.037	9.50	25.00	60.00	150.00
	1811D	.221	5.00	13.00	30.00	75.00
162	1811H	.120	6.00	17.50	40.00	100.00
	1811I	.134	6.00	17.50	40.00	100.00
	1811K	.016	15.00	45.00	90.00	250.00
	1811L	.095	8.50	22.50	55.00	135.00
	1811M	.049	9.00	25.00	60.00	150.00
	1811MA	.069	9.00	25.00	60.00	150.00
	1811Q	.126	8.50	22.50	55.00	135.00
	1811T	.114	8.50	22.50	55.00	135.00
	1811U	.039	20.00	55.00	120.00	375.00
	1811W	.246	5.00	13.00	30.00	75.00
	1812A	1.720	3.00	7.00	16.00	50.00
	1812B	.192	5.00	13.00	30.00	75.00
	1812D	.155	8.50	22.50	55.00	135.00
	1812H	.270	5.00	13.00	30.00	75.00
	1812I	.137	8.50	22.50	55.00	135.00
	1812K	.034	9.00	25.00	60.00	150.00
	1812L	.052	9.00	25.00	60.00	150.00
	1812M	.105	8.50	22.50	55.00	135.00
	1812MA	.052	9.00	25.00	60.00	150.00
	1812Q	.106	8.50	22.50	55.00	135.00
	1812T	.081	9.00	25.00	60.00	150.00
	1812W	.337	5.00	13.00	30.00	75.00
	1812(u)	5,084	350.00	900.00	1600.	2000.
	1813A	.627	3.50	8.00	18.00	55.00
	1813CL	8,385	75.00	200.00	500.00	1200.
	1813D	.110	8.50	22.50	55.00	135.00
	1813H	.138	8.50	22.50	55.00	135.00
	1813I	.097	8.50	22.50	55.00	135.00
	1813K	.058	9.00	25.00	60.00	150.00
	1813L	.044	9.00	25.00	60.00	150.00
	1813M	.159	8.50	22.50	55.00	135.00
	1813MA	.070	9.00	25.00	60.00	150.00
	1813Q	.044	9.00	25.00	60.00	150.00
	1813T	.053	9.00	25.00	60.00	150.00
	1813W	.058	9.00	25.00	60.00	150.00
	1813(u)	6,894	350.00	900.00	1500.	1900.
	1814A	.107	10.00	30.00	65.00	165.00
	1814M	.036	15.00	35.00	85.00	210.00
	1814Q	—	50.00	130.00	325.00	700.00

C#	Date	Mintage	VG	Fine	VF	XF
178	1816A	.261	7.00	20.00	50.00	125.00
	1816B	.019	15.00	40.00	75.00	135.00
	1816I	2,692	Reported, Not Confirmed			
	1816L	3,273	Reported, Not Confirmed			
	1816M	4,682	25.00	65.00	125.00	280.00
	1816Q	.012	16.00	45.00	90.00	210.00
	1816T	5,964	25.00	65.00	125.00	280.00
	1816W	8,728	20.00	50.00	100.00	225.00
	1817A	.236	7.00	20.00	50.00	125.00
	1817B	8,759	20.00	50.00	100.00	225.00
	1817H	.086	10.00	30.00	65.00	165.00
	1817K	.213	7.00	20.00	50.00	125.00
	1817L	8,767	20.00	50.00	100.00	225.00
	1817W	.025	14.00	35.00	85.00	200.00
	1818A	.050	14.00	35.00	85.00	200.00
	1818B	7,803	20.00	50.00	100.00	225.00
	1818H	.014	16.00	45.00	90.00	210.00
	1818L	2,816	Reported, Not Confirmed			
	1818W	7,811	20.00	50.00	100.00	225.00
	1819A	.047	14.00	35.00	85.00	200.00
	1819H	2,463	Reported, Not Confirmed			
	1819Q	4,488	25.00	65.00	125.00	280.00
	1819T	1,741	Reported, Not Confirmed			
	1819W	5,166	25.00	65.00	125.00	280.00
	1820A	.043	14.00	35.00	85.00	200.00
	1820K	7,794	20.00	50.00	100.00	225.00
	1820Q	.017	16.00	45.00	90.00	210.00
	1821A	.082	10.00	30.00	65.00	165.00
	1821W	.037	14.00	35.00	85.00	200.00
	1822A	.584	7.00	20.00	50.00	125.00
	1822B	.034	14.00	35.00	85.00	200.00
	1822H	1,332	Reported, Not Confirmed			
	1822W	.015	20.00	50.00	100.00	225.00
	1823A	.500	4.00	12.00	25.00	90.00
	1823B	.018	20.00	50.00	100.00	225.00
	1823H	3,558	32.50	85.00	185.00	400.00
	1823I	3,113	32.50	85.00	185.00	400.00
	1823K	8,136	25.00	50.00	100.00	225.00
	1823L	.036	15.00	35.00	85.00	200.00
	1823M	8,632	20.00	50.00	100.00	225.00
	1823Q	.101	10.00	30.00	65.00	165.00
	1823W	.070	14.00	35.00	85.00	200.00
	1824A	.613	4.00	12.00	25.00	90.00
	1824B	.042	14.00	35.00	85.00	200.00
	1824D	.018	20.00	50.00	100.00	225.00
	1824H	.020	20.00	50.00	100.00	225.00
	1824I	.011	20.00	50.00	100.00	225.00
	1824K	.053	14.00	35.00	85.00	200.00
	1824L	.056	14.00	35.00	85.00	200.00
	1824M	.011	20.00	50.00	100.00	225.00

C#	Date	Mintage	VG	Fine	VF	XF
178	1824Q	.170	9.00	25.00	60.00	150.00
	1824W	.102	10.00	30.00	65.00	165.00
186	1825A	.011	15.00	35.00	90.00	210.00
	1826A	.361	5.00	14.00	30.00	85.00
	1826B	6,019	16.00	40.00	110.00	260.00
	1826BB	.011	15.00	35.00	95.00	210.00
	1826D	.020	10.00	30.00	70.00	165.00
	1826H	.023	10.00	30.00	70.00	165.00
	1826I	1,435	Reported, Not Confirmed			
	1826K	.017	10.00	30.00	70.00	165.00
	1826L	.036	10.00	25.00	65.00	155.00
	1826M	9,192	15.00	35.00	90.00	210.00
	1826Q	.063	9.00	25.00	60.00	150.00
	1826W	.038	10.00	25.00	65.00	155.00
	1827A	.786	5.00	14.00	30.00	85.00
	1827B	.019	10.00	25.00	65.00	155.00
	1827BB	2,476	20.00	50.00	175.00	500.00
	1827D	5,629	16.00	40.00	110.00	275.00
	1827H	.014	15.00	35.00	90.00	210.00
	1827I	1,520	Reported, Not Confirmed			
	1827K	9,597	15.00	35.00	90.00	210.00
	1827L	.031	10.00	25.00	65.00	155.00
	1827M	7,288	16.00	40.00	110.00	275.00
	1827Q	.011	4.50	35.00	90.00	210.00
	1827T	8,815	16.00	40.00	110.00	275.00
	1827W	.030	10.00	25.00	65.00	155.00
	1828A	.508	5.00	14.00	30.00	85.00
	1828B	.056	9.00	25.00	60.00	150.00
	1828BB	.023	10.00	25.00	65.00	155.00
	1828D	.083	9.00	25.00	60.00	150.00
	1828H	.026	10.00	25.00	65.00	155.00
	1828I	2,526	20.00	50.00	175.00	500.00
	1828K	.027	10.00	25.00	65.00	155.00
	1828L	.027	10.00	25.00	65.00	155.00
	1828M	.072	9.00	25.00	60.00	150.00
	1828Q	.030	10.00	25.00	65.00	155.00
	1828T	.018	10.00	25.00	65.00	155.00
	1828W	.170	6.00	16.00	40.00	90.00
	1829A	.538	5.00	15.00	30.00	85.00
	1829B	.116	6.00	16.00	40.00	90.00
	1829BB	.022	10.00	25.00	65.00	155.00
	1829D	.028	10.00	25.00	65.00	155.00
	1829H	.058	9.00	25.00	60.00	150.00
	1829I	.015	10.00	25.00	65.00	155.00
	1829K	.037	10.00	25.00	65.00	155.00
	1829L	.016	10.00	25.00	65.00	155.00
	1829M	.016	10.00	25.00	65.00	155.00
	1829MA	.032	10.00	25.00	65.00	155.00
	1829Q	.019	10.00	25.00	65.00	155.00
	1829T	3,609	20.00	50.00	175.00	425.00
	1829W	.126	6.00	16.00	40.00	90.00
	1830A	.377	5.00	15.00	30.00	65.00
	1830K	.022	10.00	25.00	65.00	155.00
	1830L	.018	10.00	25.00	65.00	155.00
	1830M	7,826	16.00	40.00	110.00	275.00
	1830W	.131	6.00	16.00	40.00	90.00
198	1831A	.110	1.50	5.00	15.00	50.00
	1831B	.136	1.50	5.00	15.00	50.00
	1831BB	2,767	Reported, Not Confirmed			
	1831D	.016	3.00	9.00	25.00	60.00
	1831H	.018	3.00	9.00	25.00	60.00
	1831I	.013	4.00	10.00	30.00	75.00
	1831K	.035	2.50	8.00	25.00	55.00
	1831L	4,723	6.00	22.50	65.00	225.00
	1831M	8,289	5.00	17.00	50.00	150.00
	1831MA	—	Reported, Not Confirmed			
	1831Q	.012	3.00	9.00	25.00	60.00
	1831T	5,573	6.00	22.50	65.00	225.00
	1831W	.125	1.50	5.00	15.00	50.00
	1832A	.345	BV	3.00	10.00	30.00
	1832B	.256	BV	3.00	10.00	30.00
	1832BB	.010	5.00	12.00	32.50	90.00
	1832D	.206	BV	3.00	10.00	30.00
	1832H	.077	2.00	6.00	18.00	70.00
	1832I	.026	2.50	8.00	22.50	55.00
	1832K	.040	2.50	8.00	22.50	55.00
	1832L	.034	2.50	8.00	22.50	55.00
	1832M	.092	1.50	5.00	15.00	50.00
	1832MA	.052	2.50	8.00	22.50	55.00
	1832Q	.021	3.00	9.00	25.00	60.00
	1832T	.033	2.50	8.50	22.50	55.00

C#	Date	Mintage	VG	Fine	VF	XF
198	1832W	.427	BV	3.00	10.00	30.00
	1833A	.272	BV	3.00	10.00	35.00
	1833B	.093	1.50	5.00	15.00	50.00
	1833BB	.029	2.50	8.00	22.50	55.00
	1833D	.032	2.50	8.00	22.50	55.00
	1833H	.043	2.50	8.00	22.50	55.00
	1833I	.049	2.50	8.00	22.50	55.00
	1833K	.029	2.50	8.00	22.50	55.00
	1833L	.016	3.00	9.00	25.00	60.00
	1833M	.026	2.50	8.00	22.50	55.00
	1833Q	.055	2.50	8.00	22.50	55.00
	1833T	.014	3.00	9.50	25.00	60.00
	1833W	.151	1.50	5.00	15.00	50.00
	1834A	.419	BV	3.00	10.00	30.00
	1834B	.086	2.00	6.00	18.00	60.00
	1834BB	.020	3.00	9.00	25.00	75.00
	1834D	.064	2.50	8.00	22.50	55.00
	1834H	.086	2.00	6.00	18.00	60.00
	1834I	.025	2.50	8.00	22.50	55.00
	1834K	.069	2.50	8.00	22.50	55.00
	1834L	.010	5.00	12.00	35.00	90.00
	1834M	.019	3.00	9.00	25.00	70.00
	1834Q	1,824	Reported, Not Confirmed			
	1834T	.055	2.50	8.00	22.50	55.00
	1834W	.683	BV	3.00	10.00	30.00
	1835A	.831	BV	3.00	10.00	30.00
	1835B	.054	2.50	8.00	22.50	55.00
	1835BB	5,346	Reported, Not Confirmed			
	1835D	.015	5.00	12.00	35.00	90.00
	1835I	.045	2.50	8.00	22.50	55.00
	1835K	.050	2.50	8.00	22.50	55.00
	1835M	.023	2.50	8.00	22.50	55.00
	1835MA	.029	2.50	8.00	22.50	55.00
	1835W	.183	1.50	5.00	15.00	50.00
	1836A	.432	BV	3.00	10.00	30.00
	1836B	.043	2.50	8.00	22.50	55.00
	1836BB	.022	3.00	9.00	25.00	70.00
	1836D	8,706	5.00	17.00	50.00	150.00
	1836K	.015	5.00	12.50	35.00	90.00
	1836M	6,173	Reported, Not Confirmed			
	1836W	.087	2.00	6.00	18.00	60.00
	1837A	.137	1.50	5.00	15.00	50.00
	1837B	.158	1.50	5.00	15.00	50.00
	1837BB	5,952	6.00	22.50	65.00	200.00
	1837D	7,556	5.00	20.00	60.00	150.00
	1837K	.026	3.00	10.00	25.00	70.00
	1837W	.267	BV	3.00	10.00	30.00
	1838A	.385	BV	3.00	10.00	30.00
	1838B	.084	2.00	6.00	18.00	60.00
	1838BB	5,820	Reported, Not Confirmed			
	1838D	2,432	Reported, Not Confirmed			
	1838K	.017	5.00	12.50	35.00	90.00
	1838W	.132	1.50	5.00	15.00	50.00
	1839A	.636	BV	3.00	8.00	25.00
	1839B	.116	2.00	6.00	18.00	60.00
	1839BB	6,896	6.00	22.50	65.00	200.00
	1839K	.018	5.00	12.50	35.00	90.00
	1839W	.119	2.00	6.00	18.00	60.00
	1840A	1.107	BV	2.50	7.00	22.50
	1840B	.117	2.00	6.00	18.00	60,00
	1840BB	770 pcs.	Reported, Not Confirmed			
	1840D	.019	5.00	12.50	35.00	90.00
	1840K	.043	2.50	8.00	22.50	55.00
	1840W	.079	2.00	6.00	18.00	60.00
	1841A	1.119	BV	2.50	7.00	22.50
	1841B	.831	BV	2.50	7.00	25.00
	1841BB	.010	4.00	18.00	55.00	130.00
	1841K	.026	2.50	8.50	22.50	55.00
	1841W	.234	BV	3.00	10.00	30.00
	1842A	.338	BV	3.00	10.00	30.00
	1842B	.250	BV	3.00	10.00	30.00
	1842BB	.308	BV	3.00	10.00	30.00
	1842K	.035	2.50	8.00	22.50	60.00
	1842W	.215	BV	3.00	10.00	30.00
	1843A	.152	1.50	5.00	15.00	50.00
	1843B	.213	BV	3.00	10.00	30.00
	1843K	.034	2.50	8.00	22.50	60.00
	1843W	.233	BV	3.00	10.00	30.00
	1844A	.196	2.00	4.00	13.00	35.00
	1844B	.046	2.50	8.00	22.50	60.00
	1844BB	.025	2.50	8.00	22.50	60.00
	1844K	.023	2.50	8.00	22.50	60.00
	1844W	.408	BV	3.00	10.00	30.00
	1845A	.494	BV	3.00	10.00	30.00
	1845B	2.501	BV	1.50	7.00	20.00
	1845BB	.044	Reported, Not Confirmed			
	1845K	.022	Reported, Not Confirmed			
	1845W	.525	BV	3.00	10.00	30.00

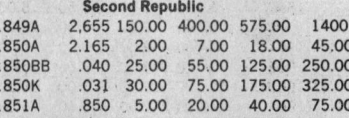

50 CENTIMES

2.5000 gm., .900 SILVER, .0723 oz ASW

C#	Date	Mintage	VG	Fine	VF	XF
199	1845A	.494	2.00	5.00	15.00	40.00
	1845B	Inc. C#198	BV	2.50	7.00	20.00
	1845BB	Inc. C#198	3.00	8.00	25.00	65.00
	1845K	Inc. C#198	Reported, not confirmed			
	1845W	Inc. C#198	Reported, not confirmed			
	1846A	3.165	BV	2.50	7.00	20.00
	1846B	1.000	BV	3.00	9.00	30.00
	1846BB	.017	4.00	16.00	50.00	125.00
	1846K	.022	3.00	9.00	25.00	65.00
	1846W	.070	3.00	9.00	25.00	60.00
	1847A	3.437	BV	2.50	7.00	20.00
	1847BB	.044	2.50	8.00	22.50	60.00
	1847K	8,915	6.00	22.50	65.00	200.00
	1848A	.218	BV	4.00	15.00	40.00
	1848BB	.018	4.00	16.00	50.00	125.00

Second Republic

C#	Date	Mintage	VG	Fine	VF	XF
3	1849A	2,655	150.00	400.00	575.00	1400.
	1850A	2.165	2.00	7.00	18.00	45.00
	1850BB	.040	25.00	55.00	125.00	250.00
	1850K	.031	30.00	75.00	175.00	325.00
	1851A	.850	5.00	20.00	40.00	75.00

President Louis-Napoleon

C#	Date	Mintage	VG	Fine	VF	XF
11	1852A	1.010	40.00	90.00	250.00	375.00

Second Empire

C#	Date	Mintage	VG	Fine	VF	XF
23	1853A	.154	20.00	45.00	100.00	250.00
	1854A	1.080	3.00	15.00	40.00	75.00
	1855A(d)	.400	12.00	35.00	85.00	200.00
	1856A	1.436	3.00	15.00	40.00	75.00
	1856BB	1.196	3.00	15.00	40.00	75.00
	1856D	1.246	3.00	15.00	40.00	75.00
	1857A	1.632	3.00	15.00	40.00	75.00
	1858A	5.559	BV	10.00	22.50	45.00
	1859A	3.880	BV	10.00	22.50	50.00
	1859BB	1.112	3.00	15.00	40.00	75.00
	1860A(h)	2.657	BV	10.00	22.50	50.00
	1860BB(c)	1.555	3.00	15.00	40.00	75.00
	1861BB(c)	.355	20.00	50.00	110.00	250.00
	1862A	1.549	3.00	15.00	40.00	75.00
	1862BB	1.007	4.00	18.00	40.00	80.00
	1863BB	.137	25.00	75.00	200.00	375.00

2.5000 gm., .835 SILVER, .0671 oz ASW

C#	Date	Mintage	VG	Fine	VF	XF
29	1864A	7.598	BV	3.00	8.00	25.00
	1864BB	4.626	BV	3.50	10.00	30.00
	1864K	1.828	2.50	6.00	17.00	45.00
	1865A	7.398	BV	3.00	8.00	25.00
	1865BB	5.175	BV	3.00	8.00	25.00
	1865K	4.901	BV	3.50	10.00	30.00
	1866A	5.921	BV	3.00	8.00	25.00
	1866BB	5.256	BV	3.00	8.00	25.00
	1866K	3.500	BV	3.50	12.00	35.00
	1867A	14.528	BV	2.50	6.00	20.00

C#	Date	Mintage	VG	Fine	VF	XF
29	1867BB	9.992	BV	2.50	7.00	20.00
	1867K	4.692	BV	3.50	10.00	30.00
	1868A	2.789	BV	5.00	16.00	40.00
	1868BB	Inc. 69	45.00	100.00	250.00	500.00
	1869BB	1.800	3.50	10.00	30.00	65.00

Third Republic

Y#	Date	Mintage	Fine	VF	XF	Unc
48	1871A	.236	15.00	40.00	95.00	200.00
	1871K	.723	9.00	25.00	60.00	95.00
	1872A	4.243	3.00	8.00	18.00	50.00
	1872K	1.643	3.50	10.00	30.00	65.00
	1873A	.926	7.00	20.00	50.00	95.00
	1873K	.166	20.00	55.00	135.00	325.00
	1874A	1.228	5.00	15.00	30.00	65.00
	1881A	5.391	2.50	6.00	16.00	32.50
	1882A	2.320	3.50	10.00	30.00	60.00
	1886A	.309	13.00	35.00	80.00	200.00
	1887A	1.866	3.50	10.00	32.50	65.00
	1888A	4.517	3.00	8.00	18.00	50.00
	1894A	3.600	3.00	8.00	18.00	50.00
	1895A	7.200	2.50	4.50	10.00	30.00

Y#	Date	Mintage	Fine	VF	XF	Unc
62	1897	.088	32.50	80.00	190.00	400.00
	1898	30.000	2.00	2.50	5.00	15.00
	1899	18.000	2.00	2.50	6.00	18.00
	1900	9.195	2.00	5.50	13.00	40.00
	1901	4.960	2.00	3.00	5.00	12.00
	1902	3.778	2.00	3.00	5.00	12.00
	1903	2.222	2.00	3.00	6.00	13.00
	1904	4.000	2.00	3.00	5.00	9.00
	1905	2.381	2.00	4.00	8.00	15.00
	1906	2.679	2.00	3.00	7.00	14.00
	1907	7.332	2.00	2.50	3.00	8.00
	1908	14.304	2.00	2.50	3.00	7.00
	1909	9.900	2.00	2.50	3.00	8.00
	1910	15.923	2.00	2.50	3.00	7.00
	1911	1.330	2.00	8.00	15.00	100.00
	1912	16.000	2.00	2.50	3.00	5.00
	1913	14.000	2.00	2.50	3.00	5.00
	1914	9.657	2.00	2.50	3.00	5.00
	1915	40.893	BV	BV	2.50	4.00
	1916	52.963	BV	BV	2.50	4.00
	1917	48.629	BV	BV	2.50	4.00
	1918	36.492	BV	BV	2.50	4.00
	1919	24.299	BV	BV	2.50	4.00
	1920	8.509	BV	BV	2.50	5.00

ALUMINUM-BRONZE

Y#	Date	Mintage	Fine	VF	XF	Unc
77	1921	8.692	.65	1.25	6.00	12.00
	1922	86.226	.25	.50	1.00	5.00
	1923	119.584	.15	.25	.50	4.00
	1924	97.036	.25	.50	1.00	5.00
	1925	48.017	.25	.50	1.25	6.00
	1926	46.447	.25	.50	1.25	6.00
	1927	23.703	.40	.75	1.75	6.50
	1928	10.329	.50	1.00	4.00	8.00
	1929	6.669	1.00	2.00	6.00	12.00

Y#	Date	Mintage	Fine	VF	XF	Unc
80	1931	62.775	.25	.50	1.00	5.00
	1931 R	Inc. Ab.	.15	.25	.75	3.50
	1932	108.839	.25	.50	1.00	4.00
	1933	41.937	.35	.75	1.25	6.00
	1936	16.602	.25	.50	1.00	6.50
	1937	43.950	.25	.50	.75	5.00
	1938	55.707	.25	.50	.75	5.00
	1939	96.594	.15	.25	.50	4.00
	1939B	6.200	1.00	2.00	6.50	15.00
	1940	10.854	.25	.50	1.25	6.50
	1941	82.958	.25	.50	.75	4.00

Y#	Date	Mintage	Fine	VF	XF	Unc
80	1947	*2.170	100.00	200.00	350.00	600.00

***NOTE**: Struck for Colonial use in Africa.

ALUMINUM

Y#	Date	Mintage	Fine	VF	XF	Unc
80a	1941	129.758	.15	.25	.50	2.50
	1944	9.898	.15	.25	.50	3.00
	1944B	.020	Reported, Not Confirmed			
	1944C	17.220	15.00	35.00	75.00	225.00
	1945	26.224	.15	.25	.75	2.50
	1945B	6.357	.50	1.50	3.00	5.50
	1945C	2.968	2.00	4.00	11.00	20.00
	1946	21.764	—	.10	.55	2.00
	1946B	29.344	—	.10	.75	3.50
	1946C	2.841	Reported, Not Confirmed			
	1947	51.744	—	.10	.50	2.50
	1947B	18.504	.25	.50	1.00	3.00

Vichy French State Issues

Y#	Date	Mintage	Fine	VF	XF	Unc
V94	1942	50.134	.15	.25	.50	3.00
	1943	84.462	.10	.15	.60	3.50
	1943B	31.916	7.00	14.00	30.00	75.00
	1943C	.040	Reported, Not Confirmed			
	1944	47.672	.15	.25	.75	5.00
	1944B	27.334	.25	.50	1.00	7.50
	1944C small C					
		27.173	4.00	15.00	35.00	65.00
	1944C large C					
		Inc. Ab.	6.00	20.00	45.00	80.00

ALUMINUM-BRONZE
50 New Centimes - 50 Old Francs

Y#	Date	Mintage	Fine	VF	XF	Unc
106	1962	37.560	.25	.50	.90	2.50
	1963	62.482	.25	.50	.75	2.00
	1964	41.446	.50	1.00	2.00	5.00

1/2 FRANC

NICKEL

Y#	Date	Mintage	Fine	VF	XF	Unc
107	1965 small legends					
		184.834	.15	.20	.25	.50
	1965 large legends					
		Inc. Ab.	.15	.20	.25	.50
	1966	88.890	.15	.20	.25	.50
	1967	28.392	.15	.20	.25	.40
	1968	57.548	.15	.20	.25	.35
	1969	47.144	.15	.20	.25	.40
	1970	42.298	.15	.20	.25	.35
	1971	36.068	.15	.20	.25	.35
	1972	42.302	.15	.20	.25	.35
	1973	48.372	.15	.20	.25	.35
	1974	37.072	.15	.20	.25	.35
	1975	22.752	.15	.20	.25	.40
	1976	115.314	.15	.20	.25	.30
	1977	*130.000	.15	.20	.25	.30
	1978	—	.15	.20	.25	.30
	1979	—	—	—	—	—

FRANC

5.0000 gm., .900 SILVER, .1446 oz ASW
Obv: BONAPARTE PREMIER CONSUL

C#	Date	Mintage	VG	Fine	VF	XF
143	ANXIA	.232	25.00	60.00	125.00	375.00
143	Anxid	.012	50.00	125.00	300.00	625.00
	ANXIG	.013	75.00	175.00	450.00	900.00
	ANXIL	.022	40.00	100.00	130.00	525.00
	ANXIMA	.012	50.00	125.00	300.00	625.00
	ANXIQ	.034	35.00	95.00	200.00	475.00
	ANXIW	5,756	Reported, Not Confirmed			
	AN12A	1.311	10.00	25.00	50.00	200.00
	AN12BB	5,737		2 known	Rare	—
	AN12D	.053	30.00	65.00	110.00	425.00
	AN12G	7,397	100.00	260.00	550.00	1050.
	AN12H	.057	30.00	65.00	140.00	425.00
	AN12I	.279	20.00	50.00	100.00	265.00
	AN12K	.102	25.00	60.00	125.00	375.00
	AN12L	.125	25.00	60.00	125.00	375.00
	AN12M	.285	20.00	50.00	100.00	265.00
	AN12MA	.141	25.00	60.00	125.00	375.00
	AN12Q	.140	25.00	60.00	125.00	375.00
	AN12T	.046	30.00	70.00	150.00	435.00
	AN12U	5,580	100.00	260.00	550.00	1050.
	AN12W	.028	35.00	95.00	200.00	475.00

Obv: NAPOLEON EMPEREUR

C#	Date	Mintage	VG	Fine	VF	XF
153.1	AN12A	.326	20.00	50.00	100.00	275.00
	AN12B	.030	25.00	60.00	125.00	375.00
	AN12D	3,968	Reported, Not Confirmed			
	AN12H	4,398	Reported, Not Confirmed			
	AN12I	.043	25.00	60.00	125.00	375.00
	AN12K	.024	32.50	75.00	155.00	435.00
	AN12L	4,253	Reported, Not Confirmed			
	AN12M	.300	20.00	50.00	100.00	275.00
	AN12MA	5,582	Reported, Not Confirmed			
	AN12Q	.025	32.50	75.00	155.00	435.00
	AN12T	3,462	Reported, Not Confirmed			
	AN12U	1,166	—	—	Rare	—
	AN13A	2.454	9.00	19.00	50.00	150.00
	AN13B	2,906	—	—	—	—
	AN13BB	3,410	Reported, Not Confirmed			
	AN13D	.010	35.00	100.00	210.00	550.00
	AN13G	.011	100.00	260.00	550.00	1050.
	AN13H	.043	32.50	75.00	160.00	450.00
	AN13I	.390	20.00	50.00	100.00	275.00
	AN13K	.061	32.50	75.00	160.00	450.00
	AN13L	.073	25.00	60.00	125.00	375.00
	AN13M	.651	20.00	50.00	100.00	275.00
	AN13MA	.028	32.50	75.00	160.00	450.00
	AN13Q	.117	20.00	50.00	100.00	275.00
	AN13T	.013	35.00	100.00	210.00	550.00
	AN13U	.015	90.00	240.00	500.00	900.00
	AN13W	.017	32.50	95.00	200.00	500.00
	AN14A	.298	25.00	60.00	125.00	375.00
	AN14BB					
		491 pcs.	Reported, not confirmed			
	AN14D	2,450	Reported, Not Confirmed			
	AN14H	7,164	75.00	200.00	375.00	750.00
	AN14I	2,847	Reported, Not Confirmed			
	AN14K	1,526	Reported, Not Confirmed			
	AN14L	4,107	—	—	—	—
	AN14M	1,096	Reported, Not Confirmed			
	AN14MA	6,910	75.00	200.00	400.00	800.00
	AN14U	—	100.00	260.00	550.00	1100.
	AN14W	4,667		3 known	—	Rare
153.2	1806A	.828	10.00	25.00	65.00	150.00
	1806H	8,472	75.00	200.00	425.00	850.00
	1806I	.034	30.00	75.00	160.00	450.00
	1806K	3,173	Reported, Not Confirmed			
	1806L	.253	15.00	40.00	95.00	200.00
	1806M	1,066	Reported, Not Confirmed			
	1806MA	1,010	Reported, Not Confirmed			
	1806Q	.016	40.00	100.00	225.00	500.00
	1806U	.015	75.00	200.00	425.00	850.00
	1806W	.028	30.00	75.00	160.00	475.00
	1807B	3,465	Reported, Not Confirmed			
	1807H	4,728	Reported, Not Confirmed			
	1807I	.011	40.00	110.00	240.00	550.00
	1807K	2,362	Reported, Not Confirmed			
	1807L	.177	20.00	45.00	110.00	225.00
	1807M	.023	32.50	80.00	175.00	500.00
	1807MA	1,493	Reported, Not Confirmed			
	1807Q	9,659	75.00	200.00	425.00	850.00
	1807U	.011	95.00	250.00	535.00	1050.
	1807W	.015	35.00	95.00	215.00	450.00

Negro head

C#	Date	Mintage	VG	Fine	VF	XF
153a	1807A	.100	175.00	400.00	950.00	2000.

Laureate head

C#	Date	Mintage	VG	Fine	VF	XF
153b	1807A	.050	—	—	Rare	—
	1808A	4.599	6.00	12.00	35.00	100.00
	1808B	.765	7.00	17.50	50.00	135.00
	1808BB	2.126	6.00	13.00	37.50	120.00
	1808D	.752	7.00	17.50	50.00	135.00
	1808H	.316	10.00	20.00	60.00	160.00
	1808I	.256	10.00	20.00	60.00	160.00
	1808K	.228	10.00	20.00	60.00	160.00
	1808L	.016	25.00	60.00	135.00	300.00
	1808M	.130	15.00	40.00	80.00	175.00
	1808MA	.029	20.00	55.00	120.00	275.00
	1808Q	.064	15.00	40.00	85.00	185.00
	1808T	.106	15.00	40.00	80.00	175.00
	1808U	.013	50.00	130.00	325.00	700.00
	1808W	2.422	6.00	12.50	35.00	110.00

C#	Date	Mintage	VG	Fine	VF	XF
163	1809A	.980	8.00	18.00	50.00	125.00
	1809B	.202	10.00	22.50	60.00	165.00
	1809D	.047	11.00	30.00	70.00	200.00
	1809H	.034	12.50	30.00	75.00	220.00
	1809K	.074	10.00	22.50	70.00	175.00
	1809L	.028	12.50	30.00	75.00	220.00
	1809M	8,855	30.00	90.00	200.00	450.00
	1809MA	.020	20.00	75.00	175.00	400.00
	1809Q	.163	10.00	22.50	60.00	165.00
	1809U	5,549	50.00	125.00	300.00	750.00
	1809W	.196	10.00	22.50	60.00	165.00
	1810A	1.676	7.00	17.50	50.00	135.00
	1810B	.167	10.00	22.50	60.00	165.00
	1810BB	4,336	35.00	100.00	225.00	650.00
	1810D	.039	12.50	30.00	75.00	220.00
	1810H	.016	20.00	75.00	175.00	400.00
	1810I	.018	20.00	75.00	175.00	400.00
	1810K	.093	10.00	22.50	70.00	175.00
	1810L	.047	11.00	30.00	70.00	200.00
	1810L(TR)	I.A.	—	—	Unique	—
	1810M	.035	12.50	30.00	75.00	220.00
	1810MA	.028	20.00	55.00	120.00	275.00
	1810Q	.073	11.00	30.00	70.00	200.00
	1810U	10,200	50.00	135.00	275.00	700.00
	1810W	.187	10.00	22.50	70.00	175.00
	1811A	1.347	7.00	17.50	50.00	135.00
	1811B	.253	10.00	22.50	70.00	75.00
	1811BB	.012	30.00	90.00	200.00	400.00
	1811D	.242	10.00	22.50	70.00	175.00
	1811H	.105	10.00	22.50	75.00	185.00
	1811I	.085	11.00	25.50	75.00	190.00
	1811K	.048	11.00	30.00	75.00	200.00
	1811L	.188	10.00	22.50	70.00	175.00
	1811M	.081	11.00	25.50	75.00	190.00
	1811MA	.044	11.00	30.00	75.00	200.00
	1811Q	.161	10.00	22.50	70.00	175.00
	1811T	.042	11.00	30.00	75.00	200.00
	1811W	.265	10.00	22.50	70.00	175.00
	1812A	.563	8.00	18.00	50.00	125.00
	1812B	.118	10.00	22.50	70.00	175.00
	1812BB	5,571	35.00	100.00	225.00	600.00
	1812D	.147	10.00	22.50	70.00	175.00
	1812H	.165	10.00	22.50	70.00	175.00
	1812I	.091	11.00	25.00	75.00	190.00
	1812K	.041	11.00	30.00	75.00	200.00
	1812L	.047	11.00	30.00	75.00	200.00
	1812M	.125	10.00	22.50	70.00	175.00
	1812MA	.036	12.50	30.00	75.00	220.00
	1812Q	.034	12.50	30.00	75.00	220.00
	1812R	.012	90.00	250.00	500.00	900.00
163	1812T	.041	12.50	30.00	75.00	220.00
	1812U	.021	45.00	125.00	290.00	750.00
	1812W	.143	10.00	22.50	70.00	175.00
	1812(u)	.012	350.00	925.00	1800.	2000.
	1813A	.446	8.00	18.00	50.00	125.00
	1813B	.061	11.00	30.00	75.00	200.00
	1813CL	7,229	85.00	225.00	500.00	1000.
	1813D	.078	11.00	30.00	75.00	200.00
	1813H	.096	10.00	22.50	70.00	175.00
	1813I	.076	11.00	30.00	75.00	200.00
	1813K	.068	11.00	30.00	75.00	200.00
	1813L	.033	12.50	30.00	75.00	220.00
	1813M	.181	10.00	22.50	70.00	175.00
	1813MA	.044	12.50	30.00	75.00	220.00
	1813Q	.075	11.00	30.00	75.00	200.00
	1813R	779 pcs.	—	—	Rare	—
	1813T	.020	20.00	75.00	175.00	400.00
	1813U	6,065	90.00	235.00	525.00	1050.
	1813W	.093	11.00	30.00	75.00	200.00
	1813(u)	.069	200.00	500.00	900.00	1300.
	1814A	.042	32.50	90.00	225.00	450.00
	1814L	—	—	—	—	—
	1814M	.029	40.00	105.00	265.00	500.00
	1814W	—	—	—	—	—

C#	Date	Mintage	VG	Fine	VF	XF
179	1816A	.253	8.00	18.00	45.00	115.00
	1816B	.016	25.00	60.00	125.00	250.00
	1816I	5,041	35.00	90.00	180.00	325.00
	1816L	5,770	35.00	90.00	180.00	325.00
	1816M	.070	15.00	35.00	75.00	165.00
	1816Q	.025	20.00	50.00	115.00	220.00
	1816T	2,240	Reported, Not Confirmed			
	1816W	.015	25.00	60.00	125.00	250.00
	1817A	.178	10.00	25.00	65.00	125.00
	1817B	.031	20.00	50.00	115.00	220.00
	1817D	5,362	35.00	90.00	180.00	325.00
	1817H	.048	20.00	50.00	115.00	220.00
	1817K	.307	8.00	18.00	45.00	115.00
	1817L	5,059	35.00	90.00	180.00	325.00
	1817M	.021	25.00	60.00	125.00	250.00
	1817Q	5,045	35.00	90.00	180.00	325.00
	1817W	.019	25.00	60.00	125.00	250.00
	1818A	.060	15.00	35.00	75.00	165.00
	1818B	3,866	Reported, Not Confirmed			
	1818H	8,477	30.00	75.00	155.00	310.00
	1818L	1,450	Reported, Not Confirmed			
	1818T	1,728	Reported, Not Confirmed			
	1818W	.016	25.00	60.00	125.00	250.00
	1819A	.027	20.00	50.00	120.00	225.00
	1819B	.010	27.50	70.00	140.00	285.00
	1819H	8,141	30.00	75.00	155.00	310.00
	1819Q	.013	27.50	70.00	140.00	285.00
	1819T	4,094	40.00	95.00	190.00	340.00
	1819W	.024	25.00	60.00	125.00	250.00
	1820A	.028	20.00	50.00	120.00	225.00
	1820B	.016	25.00	65.00	135.00	265.00
	1820H	6,709	32.50	80.00	160.00	320.00
	1820K	.020	25.00	60.00	125.00	250.00
	1820Q	.022	25.00	60.00	125.00	250.00
	1820W	.013	27.50	70.00	140.00	285.00
	1821A	.100	12.50	32.50	70.00	140.00
	1821H	5,083	40.00	95.00	190.00	340.00
	1821Q	4,942	40.00	95.00	190.00	340.00
	1821W	.200	10.00	25.00	65.00	125.00
	1822A	.635	7.00	16.00	40.00	95.00
	1822B	.031	20.00	50.00	120.00	225.00
	1822H	.016	25.00	65.00	130.00	265.00
	1822Q	3,838	Reported, Not Confirmed			
	1822W	.061	13.00	35.00	70.00	145.00
	1823A	.360	7.00	16.00	40.00	100.00
	1823B	7,577	32.50	80.00	160.00	320.00
	1823D	3,485	Reported, Not Confirmed			
	1823H	.014	27.50	70.00	140.00	285.00
	1823I	5,273	40.00	95.00	190.00	340.00
	1823K	5,173	40.00	95.00	190.00	340.00
	1823L	.036	20.00	50.00	120.00	225.00
	1823M	.036	20.00	50.00	120.00	225.00
	1823Q	.033	20.00	55.00	125.00	230.00
	1823W	.277	7.00	16.00	40.00	100.00
	1824A	.417	7.00	16.00	40.00	95.00
	1824B	.066	13.00	35.00	70.00	145.00
	1824D	.030	20.00	50.00	120.00	225.00
	1824H	.033	20.00	50.00	120.00	225.00
	1824I	.033	20.00	50.00	120.00	225.00
	1824K	.123	7.00	16.00	40.00	100.00
	1824L	.054	13.00	35.00	70.00	145.00
	1824M	.059	13.00	35.00	70.00	145.00
	1824MA	7,209	32.50	80.00	160.00	320.00
179	1824Q	.052	13.00	35.00	70.00	145.00
	1824W	.388	7.00	16.00	40.00	95.00

C#	Date	Mintage	VG	Fine	VF	XF
187	1825A	.335	7.00	16.00	40.00	100.00
	1825B	.017	25.00	65.00	130.00	260.00
	1825BB	9,256	40.00	95.00	190.00	345.00
	1825D	.040	20.00	50.00	120.00	225.00
	1825H	.023	25.00	65.00	130.00	260.00
	1825I	6,663	40.00	95.00	190.00	340.00
	1825K	.024	25.00	65.00	130.00	260.00
	1825L	3,830	42.50	110.00	215.00	375.00
	1825M	6,069	40.00	95.00	190.00	340.00
	1825Q	5,653	40.00	95.00	190.00	340.00
	1825W	.078	20.00	50.00	95.00	190.00
	1826A	.326	7.00	16.00	40.00	100.00
	1826B	.020	25.00	65.00	130.00	260.00
	1826BB	.012	35.00	90.00	185.00	330.00
	1826D	.028	25.00	65.00	130.00	260.00
	1826H	.028	25.00	65.00	130.00	260.00
	1826I	4,206	42.50	110.00	215.00	375.00
	1826K	.038	25.00	65.00	130.00	260.00
	1826L	.028	25.00	65.00	130.00	260.00
	1826M	.031	25.00	65.00	130.00	260.00
	1826Q	.025	25.00	65.00	130.00	260.00
	1826T	5,930	40.00	95.00	190.00	340.00
	1826W	.130	8.00	17.50	40.00	110.00
	1827A	.431	6.00	16.00	40.00	100.00
	1827B	.096	20.00	50.00	95.00	190.00
	1827BB	.013	35.00	95.00	190.00	330.00
	1827D	.036	25.00	65.00	130.00	260.00
	1827H	5,444	40.00	95.00	190.00	340.00
	1827I	6,850	40.00	95.00	190.00	340.00
	1827K	.044	20.00	50.00	120.00	225.00
	1827L	.047	20.00	50.00	120.00	225.00
	1827M	.024	25.00	65.00	130.00	260.00
	1827Q	.020	25.00	65.00	130.00	200.00
	1827T	.014	35.00	95.00	190.00	330.00
	1827W	.519	6.00	16.00	40.00	100.00
	1828A	.517	6.00	16.00	40.00	100.00
	1828B	.070	20.00	50.00	95.00	190.00
	1828BB	.024	25.00	65.00	130.00	260.00
	1828D	.076	20.50	50.00	95.00	190.00
	1828H	.027	25.00	65.00	130.00	260.00
	1828I	5,236	40.00	95.00	190.00	340.00
	1828K	.132	8.00	17.50	40.00	110.00
	1828L	.044	20.00	50.00	120.00	225.00
	1828M	.072	20.00	50.00	95.00	190.00
	1828Q	.018	25.00	75.00	160.00	290.00
	1828T	.036	25.00	65.00	130.00	260.00
	1828W	.418	4.00	16.00	40.00	100.00
	1829A	.290	6.00	16.00	40.00	105.00
	1829B	.124	8.00	17.50	40.00	110.00
	1829BB	.021	25.00	75.00	160.00	290.00
	1829D	.031	20.00	50.00	120.00	225.00
	1829H	.051	20.00	50.00	120.00	225.00
	1829I	.020	25.00	75.00	160.00	290.00
	1829K	.050	20.00	50.00	120.00	225.00
	1829L	.033	20.00	50.00	120.00	225.00
	1829M	.046	20.00	50.00	120.00	225.00
	1829MA	.066	17.50	42.50	90.00	185.00
	1829Q	.013	35.00	95.00	190.00	330.00
	1829T	.014	35.00	95.00	190.00	330.00
	1829W	.149	8.00	17.50	40.00	110.00
	1830A	.234	6.00	16.00	40.00	115.00
	1830A reeded edge	—	—	—	Rare	—
	1830B	.075	17.50	42.50	90.00	185.00
	1830I	1,025	Reported, Not Confirmed			
	1830K	.021	25.00	75.00	160.00	290.00
	1830L	.013	35.00	95.00	190.00	330.00
	1830M	.021	25.00	75.00	160.00	290.00
	1830T	8,871	40.00	85.00	190.00	340.00
	1830W	.078	17.50	42.50	90.00	185.00

C#	Date	Mintage	Good	VG	Fine	VF
200	1831A	.202	20.00	40.00	100.00	200.00
	1831B	.400	20.00	40.00	100.00	200.00
	1831BB	.018	35.00	80.00	175.00	290.00
	1831D	.127	25.00	50.00	150.00	235.00

C#	Date	Mintage	Good	VG	Fine	VF
200	1831H	.027	30.00	75.00	160.00	275.00
	1831I	.021	35.00	80.00	175.00	290.00
	1831K	.053	30.00	75.00	160.00	275.00
	1831L	2,406		Reported, Not Confirmed		
	1831M	.038	30.00	75.00	160.00	275.00
	1831Q	.018	35.00	80.00	175.00	290.00
	1831T	.043	30.00	75.50	160.00	275.00
	1831W	.453	20.00	40.00	100.00	200.00

Laureate head

C#	Date	Mintage	VG	Fine	VF	XF
201	1832A	.379	4.00	8.00	15.00	45.00
	1832B	.197	5.00	13.00	30.00	70.00
	1832BB	.042	9.00	27.50	42.50	125.00
	1832D	.127	5.00	12.50	30.00	70.00
	1832H	.080	8.00	20.00	40.00	115.00
	1832I	.037	10.00	30.00	50.00	140.00
	1832K	.035	10.00	30.00	50.00	140.00
	1832L	.031	10.00	30.00	50.00	140.00
	1832M	.051	8.00	20.00	40.00	115.00
	1832MA	.078	8.00	20.00	40.00	115.00
	1832Q	1 Known	—	—	—	—
	1832T	.034	10.00	30.00	50.00	140.00
	1832W	.155	5.00	12.50	30.00	70.00
	1833A	.114	5.00	12.50	30.00	70.00
	1833B	.098	8.00	20.00	40.00	115.00
	1833BB	.079	8.00	20.00	40.00	115.00
	1833D	.024	10.00	30.00	50.00	140.00
	1833H	.026	10.00	30.00	50.00	140.00
	1833I	.034	20.00	40.00	110.00	275.00
	1833K	.030	10.00	30.00	50.00	140.00
	1833L	.018	11.00	30.00	60.00	160.00
	1833M	.049	8.00	20.00	37.50	115.00
	1833MA	.057	8.00	20.00	37.50	115.00
	1833Q	.019	11.00	30.00	60.00	160.00
	1833T	.031	10.00	30.00	50.00	140.00
	1833W	.213	5.00	12.50	27.50	70.00
	1834A	.330	4.00	8.00	15.00	45.00
	1834B	.146	5.00	12.50	27.50	70.00
	1834BB	.068	8.00	20.00	37.50	115.00
	1834D	.059	8.00	20.00	37.50	115.00
	1834H	.079	8.00	20.00	37.50	115.00
	1834I	.045	8.00	20.00	37.50	115.00
	1834K	.070	8.00	20.00	37.50	115.00
	1834L	.012	13.00	35.00	65.00	195.00
	1834M	.037	10.00	30.00	50.00	140.00
	1834MA	.018	11.00	30.00	60.00	160.00
	1834Q	.057	8.00	20.00	37.50	115.00
	1834T	.102	6.00	15.00	30.00	85.00
	1834W	.608	6.00	8.00	15.00	45.00
	1835A	.483	6.00	8.00	15.00	45.00
	1835B	.103	6.00	8.00	30.00	85.00
	1835BB	.046	8.00	20.00	37.50	115.00
	1835D	.052	8.00	20.00	37.50	115.00
	1835H	.017	11.00	30.00	60.00	160.00
	1835I	.048	8.00	20.00	37.50	115.00
	1835K	.058	8.00	19.00	37.50	115.00
	1835L	3,647		Reported, Not Confirmed		
	1835M	.025	10.00	30.00	50.00	140.00
	1835MA	.012	13.00	35.00	65.00	195.00
	1835T	.051	8.00	20.00	37.50	115.00
	1835W	.206	6.00	14.00	30.00	90.00
	1836A	.138	6.00	14.00	30.00	90.00
	1836B	.093	8.00	20.00	37.50	115.00
	1836BB	.050	8.00	20.00	37.50	115.00
	1836D	.019	11.00	30.00	60.00	160.00
	1836K	.040	8.00	20.00	37.50	115.00
	1836W	.049	8.00	20.00	37.50	115.00
	1837A	.241	6.00	12.50	27.50	70.00
	1837B	.212	6.00	12.50	27.50	70.00
	1837BB	.013	13.00	35.00	65.00	195.00
	1837D	2,531		Reported, Not Confirmed		
	1837K	.034	10.00	30.00	50.00	140.00
	1837W	.266	6.00	12.50	27.50	70.00
	1838A	.183	6.00	15.00	30.00	90.00
	1838B	.145	6.00	15.00	30.00	90.00
	1838BB	.024	10.00	30.00	50.00	140.00
	1838D	.012	13.00	35.00	65.00	195.00
	1838K	.017	11.00	30.00	60.00	160.00
	1838MA	.020	11.00	30.00	60.00	160.00
	1838W	.162	6.00	15.00	30.00	90.00
	1839A	.243	6.00	12.50	27.50	70.00
	1839B	.184	6.00	15.00	30.00	90.00
	1839BB	.043	8.00	20.00	37.50	115.00
	1839D	.011	13.00	35.00	65.00	195.00
	1839K	.048	8.00	20.00	37.50	115.00
	1839W	.120	6.00	15.00	30.00	90.00
	1840A	.481	6.00	8.00	15.00	45.00

C#	Date	Mintage	VG	Fine	VF	XF
201	1840B	.148	6.00	15.00	30.00	90.00
	1840BB	.017	11.00	30.00	60.00	160.00
	1840D	7,130	20.00	40.00	110.00	275.00
	1840K	.048	8.00	20.00	37.50	115.00
	1840W	.079	8.00	20.00	37.50	115.00
	1841A	.623	6.00	8.00	15.00	45.00
	1841B	.663	6.00	8.00	15.00	45.00
	1841BB	.053	8.00	20.00	37.50	115.00
	1841K	.042	8.00	20.00	37.50	115.00
	1841W	.321	6.00	12.50	27.50	70.00
	1842A	.130	6.00	15.00	30.00	90.00
	1842B	.158	6.00	15.00	30.00	90.00
	1842BB	.244	6.00	12.50	27.50	70.00
	1842K	.032	10.00	30.00	50.00	140.00
	1842W	.195	6.00	15.00	30.00	90.00
	1843A	.074	8.00	20.00	37.50	115.00
	1843B	.130	6.00	15.00	30.00	90.00
	1843BB	.072	8.00	20.00	37.50	115.00
	1843K	.039	10.00	30.00	50.00	140.00
	1843W	.271	6.00	15.00	30.00	90.00
	1844A	.072	8.00	20.00	37.50	115.00
	1844B	.045	10.00	30.00	50.00	140.00
	1844BB	.076	8.00	20.00	37.50	115.00
	1844K	.023	10.00	30.00	50.00	140.00
	1844W	.381	6.00	12.50	27.50	70.00
	1845A	.215	6.00	15.00	30.00	90.00
	1845B	.882	6.00	8.00	15.00	45.00
	1845BB	.083	8.00	20.00	27.50	115.00
	1845K	.023	10.00	30.00	50.00	140.00
	1845W	.478	6.00	8.00	15.00	45.00
	1846A	1.225	6.00	8.00	13.00	40.00
	1846B	.818	6.00	8.00	15.00	45.00
	1846BB	.024	10.00	30.00	50.00	140.00
	1846K	.023	10.00	30.00	50.00	140.00
	1846W	.074	8.00	20.00	37.50	115.00
	1847A	2.401	6.00	8.00	15.00	40.00
	1847BB	.068	8.00	20.00	37.50	115.00
	1847K	6,787		Reported, Not Confirmed		
	1848A	.228	6.00	15.00	30.00	90.00
	1848BB	.021	10.00	30.00	50.00	140.00

Second Republic

Y#	Date	Mintage	VG	Fine	VF	XF
4	1849A	1.289	8.00	25.00	50.00	100.00
	1849BB	.015	35.00	110.00	215.00	475.00
	1849K	.019	35.00	110.00	215.00	475.00
	1850A	1.041	10.00	30.00	65.00	165.00
	1850BB	.213	25.00	65.00	135.00	265.00
	1850K	.035	30.00	90.00	200.00	375.00
	1851A	.638	12.00	50.00	90.00	150.00

President Louis-Napoleon

Y#	Date	Mintage	VG	Fine	VF	XF
12	1852A	1.015	25.00	75.00	150.00	275.00

Second Empire - Napoleon III

Y#	Date	Mintage	VG	Fine	VF	XF
24	1853A	.183	40.00	90.00	75.00	450.00
	1854A	.764	20.00	55.00	100.00	275.00
	1855A(d)	.757	20.00	55.00	100.00	275.00
	1855A(a)	I.A.	20.00	55.00	100.00	275.00
	1856A	1.196	10.00	30.00	65.00	175.00
	1856BB	1.635	10.00	30.00	65.00	175.00
	1856D	1.227	10.00	30.00	65.00	175.00
	1857A	1.681	10.00	30.00	65.00	175.00
	1858A	5.607	6.00	12.00	27.50	100.00
	1859A	3.830	7.50	18.00	35.00	125.00
	1859BB	1.333	10.00	30.00	65.00	175.00
	1860A(h)	2.740	8.00	25.00	60.00	150.00
	1860A(b)	I.A.	8.00	25.00	60.00	150.00
	1860BB	I.A.	10.00	30.00	65.00	175.00
	1861A	2.012	40.00	90.00	175.00	400.00
	1861BB	.218	55.00	140.00	290.00	500.00

Y#	Date	Mintage	VG	Fine	VF	XF
24	1862BB	1.124	45.00	100.00	190.00	425.00
	1863A	.019		Reported, Not Confirmed		
	1863BB	.054	60.00	175.00	330.00	575.00
	1864A	.022		Reported, Not Confirmed		

5.0000 gm., .835 SILVER, .1342 oz ASW
Laureate head

Y#	Date	Mintage	VG	Fine	VF	XF
30	1866A	14.638	4.00	5.00	10.00	30.00
	1866BB	7.204	4.00	5.50	12.00	30.00
	1866K	1.402	5.00	9.00	20.00	60.00
	1867A	12.131	4.00	5.00	10.00	30.00
	1867BB	7.295	4.00	5.00	12.00	32.50
	1867K	6.092	4.00	5.00	12.00	32.50
	1868A	14.942	4.00	5.00	10.00	30.00
	1868BB	10.230	4.00	5.25	10.00	30.00
	1868K	.022	60.00	140.00	250.00	500.00
	1869A	2.935	5.00	9.00	20.00	60.00
	1869BB	3.094	5.00	9.25	20.00	60.00
	1870A	.788		Reported, Not Confirmed		
	1870BB	1.992	7.00	12.00	30.00	80.00

Third Republic

Y#	Date	Mintage	Fine	VF	XF	Unc
49	1871A small A					
		2.980	5.00	8.00	25.00	75.00
	1871A large A					
		Inc. Ab.	5.00	8.00	25.00	75.00
	1871K small K					
		1.252	6.00	12.00	40.00	95.00
	1871K large K					
		Inc. Ab.	6.00	12.00	40.00	95.00
	1872A small A					
		10.129	5.00	7.50	15.00	50.00
	1872A large A					
		Inc. Ab.	5.00	7.50	15.00	50.00
	1872K large K					
		5.779	5.00	9.00	25.00	65.00
	1872K small K					
		Inc. Ab.	BV	5.00	15.00	45.00
	1873K	.019	75.00	175.00	375.00	Rare
	1878A	30 pcs.	—	—	Proof	20.00
	1881A	2.010	5.00	9.00	25.00	65.00
	1887A	3.292	5.00	7.50	15.00	50.00
	1888A	3.244	5.00	7.50	15.00	50.00
	1889A	100 pcs.	—	—	Proof	1600.
	1894A	1.600	5.00	12.00	35.00	70.00
	1895A	3.200	5.00	7.50	15.00	50.00

Y#	Date	Mintage	Fine	VF	XF	Unc
63	1898	15.000	BV	5.00	6.00	15.00
	1899	11.000	BV	5.00	8.00	22.50
	1900	.099	100.00	225.00	450.00	850.00
	1901	6.200	BV	5.00	8.00	35.00
	1902	6.000	BV	5.00	8.00	35.00
	1903	.472	25.00	50.00	125.00	300.00
	1904	7.000	BV	5.00	8.00	35.00
	1905	6.004	BV	5.00	8.00	35.00
	1906	1.908	BV	5.00	20.00	75.00
	1907	2.563	BV	5.00	16.00	55.00
	1908	3.961	BV	5.00	11.00	40.00
	1909	10.924	BV	5.00	8.00	20.00
	1910	7.725	BV	5.00	8.00	20.00
	1911	5.542	BV	5.00	10.00	30.00
	1912	10.001	BV	5.00	8.00	20.00
	1913	18.654	BV	5.00	7.00	12.00
	1914	14.361	BV	5.00	7.00	10.00
	1914C	.043	110.00	275.00	425.00	775.00
	1915	47.955	BV	BV	BV	6.00
	1916	92.029	BV	BV	BV	6.00
	1917	57.153	BV	BV	BV	6.00
	1918	50.112	BV	BV	BV	6.00
	1919	46.112	BV	BV	BV	6.00

Y#	Date	Mintage	Fine	VF	XF	Unc
	1920	19.322	BV	BV	BV	7.00

ALUMINUM-BRONZE
French Chamber Of Commerce Series

Y#	Date	Mintage	Fine	VF	XF	Unc
78	1920	.590	3.00	6.50	14.00	27.50
	1921	54.572	.25	.40	1.00	8.00
	1922	111.343	.25	.40	1.00	7.00
	1923	140.138	.25	.40	1.00	7.00
	1924	87.715	.25	.50	1.00	7.00
	1925	36.523	.25	.50	1.00	9.00
	1926	1.580	3.00	6.50	14.00	27.50
	1927	11.330	.50	1.00	3.00	12.00
	1928	.405	Reported, Not Confirmed			
81	1931	15.504	.50	1.00	2.00	8.00
	1932	29.768	.50	1.00	2.00	6.50
	1933	15.356	.50	1.00	2.00	8.00
	1934	17.286	.50	1.00	2.00	8.00
	1935	1.166	7.00	15.00	27.50	50.00
	1936	23.817	.50	.75	1.00	5.50
	1937	30.940	.50	.75	1.00	5.50
	1938	66.165	.50	.75	1.00	5.50
	1939	48.434	.50	.75	1.00	5.00
	1940	25.525	.50	.75	1.00	5.50
	1941	34.705	.50	.75	1.00	5.50

ALUMINUM

Y#	Date	Mintage	Fine	VF	XF	Unc
81a	1941	60.877	.15	.25	1.50	5.00
	1943	4,400	—	—	Rare	—
	1944	22.608	.15	.25	1.50	4.00
	1944B	1.725	Reported, Not Confirmed			
	1944C	33.600	.25	.50	1.50	4.00
	1945	61.780	—	.10	1.00	3.50
	1945B	4.251	.25	.75	2.50	12.00
	1945C	5.220	.25	.75	2.50	12.00
	1946	52.516	—	.10	1.00	4.50
	1946B	26.493	—	.10	1.00	4.50
	1946C	9.669	— Reported, Not Confirmed			
	1947	110.448	—	.10	1.00	4.50
	1947B	51.562	.15	.25	1.00	4.50
	1948	96.092	—	.10	1.00	4.00
	1948B	45.481	—	.10	1.00	4.00
	1949	41.090	—	.10	1.00	4.00
	1949B	35.840	—	.10	1.00	4.00
	1950	27.882	.15	.25	1.00	4.00
	1950B	18.800	.15	.25	1.25	5.00
	1957	16.497	—	.10	1.50	3.50
	1957B	63.976	—	.10	.75	3.00
	1958	21.197	—	.10	1900	3.50
	1958B	13.412	—	.10	1.50	3.50
	1959	41.985	—	.10	.75	2.50

ZINC

Y#	Date	Mintage	Fine	VF	XF	Unc
81b	1943A	*.017	—	—	Rare	—

***NOTE:** Struck for Colonial use in Africa.

ALUMINUM
Vichy French State Issues

Y#	Date	Mintage	Fine	VF	XF	Unc
V95	1942	102.972	.15	.25	1.50	6.50
	1943	175.886	.15	.25	1.25	5.00
	1943B	68.082	10.00	17.00	37.50	75.00
	1943C	29.678	Reported, Not Confirmed			
	1944	50.605	.15	.25	1.50	7.00
	1944B	13.622	.75	1.50	5.00	15.00
	1944C	74.859	.25	.75	2.00	6.50

NICKEL
1 New Franc - 100 Old Francs
Fifth Republic

Y#	Date	Mintage	Fine	VF	XF	Unc
108	1960	344.055	.30	.35	.40	.50
	1961	119.611	.30	.35	.40	.50
	1962	14.015	.30	.35	.75	2.00
	1964	77.425	.30	.35	.40	.50
	1965	44.252	.30	.35	.40	.75
	1966	38.038	.30	.35	.40	.75
	1967	11.320	.30	.35	.75	2.00
	1968	51.550	.30	.35	.40	.75
	1969	70.595	.30	.35	.40	.50
	1970	42.560	.30	.35	.40	.75
	1971	42.475	.30	.35	.40	.75
	1972	48.250	.30	.35	.40	.75
	1973	70.000	.30	.35	.40	.50
	1974	82.235	.30	.35	.40	.50
	1975	101.685	.30	.35	.40	.50
	1976	192.520	.30	.35	.40	.50
	1977	*230.000	.30	.35	.40	.50
	1978	—	.30	.35	.40	.50
	1979	—	—	—	—	—

2 FRANCS

10.0000 gm., .900 SILVER, .2893 oz ASW
Obv: BONAPARTE PREMIER CONSUL

C#	Date	Mintage	VG	Fine	VF	XF
144	AN12A	.187	32.50	80.00	300.00	800.00
	AN12BB	1,965	—	—	Rare	—
	AN12D	2,672	Reported, Not Confirmed			
	AN12G	2,859	65.00	175.00	500.00	1700.
	AN12H	.012	60.00	160.00	375.00	1000.
	AN12I	.102	35.00	95.00	325.00	825.00
	AN12K	.026	55.00	150.00	300.00	925.00
	AN12L	.015	60.00	160.00	375.00	1000.
	AN12M	.066	50.00	130.00	350.00	850.00
	AN12MA	6,804	70.00	190.00	475.00	1100.
	AN12Q	.021	55.00	140.00	360.00	925.00
	AN12T	4,484	Reported, Not Confirmed			
	AN12U	—	—	—	Unique	—
	AN12W	5,850	Reported, Not Confirmed			

Obv: NAPOLEON EMPEREUR

C#	Date	Mintage	VG	Fine	VF	XF
154	AN12A	.060	32.50	75.00	375.00	850.00
	AN12B	.014	50.00	130.00	475.00	925.00
	AN12BB	1,798	Reported, Not Confirmed			
	AN12H	2,800	Reported, Not Confirmed			
	AN12I	3,561	Reported, Not Confirmed			
	AN12K	.010	55.00	140.00	390.00	1000.
	AN12L	1,247	Reported, not confirmed			
	AN12M	.016	55.00	140.00	390.00	1000.
	AN12MA	5,249	Reported, Not Confirmed			
	AN12T	1,444	—	—	—	—
	AN13/2A	—	60.00	155.00	525.00	1150.
	AN13A	.742	20.00	50.00	200.00	500.00
	AN13BB	4,341	Reported, Not Confirmed			
	AN13D	2,560	Reported, Not Confirmed			
	AN13G	.013	65.00	175.00	450.00	1000.
	AN13H	3,727	Reported, Not Confirmed			
	AN13I	.124	40.00	90.00	250.00	625.00
	AN13K	.036	42.50	105.00	310.00	750.00
	AN13L	.022	50.00	130.00	375.00	800.00
	AN13M	.334	30.00	75.00	275.00	675.00
	AN13MA	.011	70.00	170.00	435.00	1000.
154	AN13Q	.052	40.00	105.00	300.00	725.00
	AN13T	4,600	Reported, Not Confirmed			
	AN13U	7,221	65.00	185.00	475.00	1100.00
	AN13W	.011	70.00	170.00	435.00	1000.
	AN14A	.232	32.50	80.00	300.00	700.00
	AN14D	204	Reported, Not Confirmed			
	AN14H	1,063	—	—	—	—
	AN14I	6,299	Reported, Not Confirmed			
	AN14K	1,210	—	—	—	—
	AN14L	5,183	Reported, Not Confirmed			
	AN14MA	2 known		—	Rare	—
	AN14U	—	125.00	300.00	625.00	1500.
	AN14W	—	100.00	250.00	550.00	1300.
154	1806A	.169	45.00	115.00	255.00	700.00
	1806BB	1,477	Reported, Not Confirmed			
	1806D	530	Reported, Not Confirmed			
	1806I	.021	60.00	155.00	380.00	800.00
	1806K	754	Reported, Not Confirmed			
	1806L	.072	50.00	130.00	325.00	775.00
	1806MA	2,289	Reported, Not Confirmed			
	1806Q	.042	55.00	150.00	360.00	700.00
	1806U	.010	90.00	240.00	625.00	1400.
	1806W	.010	80.00	180.00	410.00	900.00
	1807B	563	Reported, Not Confirmed			
	1807I	.082	50.00	130.00	325.00	775.00
	1807K	3,665	80.00	225.00	600.00	1400.
	1807L	.054	50.00	130.00	325.00	775.00
	1807M	8,878	85.00	190.00	410.00	900.00
	1807Q	.033	60.00	135.00	340.00	800.00
	1807U	.010	90.00	225.00	500.00	1300.
	1807W	4,114	80.00	225.00	600.00	1400.

With edge having floral design

C#	Date	Mintage	VG	Fine	VF	XF
154a	1807A	.024	325.00	675.00	1300.	3750.

Laureate head

C#	Date	Mintage	VG	Fine	VF	XF
154b	1807A	.043	—	—	—	—
	1808A	1.100	30.00	65.00	160.00	500.00
	1808B	.161	42.50	110.00	250.00	565.00
	1808I	.106	50.00	125.00	325.00	675.00
	1808K	.038	65.00	170.00	360.00	800.00
	1808L	.019	75.00	200.00	425.00	900.00
	1808M	.028	65.00	170.00	360.00	800.00
	1808MA	7,676	85.00	225.00	500.00	1000.
	1808Q	4,965	90.00	245.00	550.00	1150.
	1808U	2,297	—	—	Rare	—
	1808W	.040	65.00	170.00	360.00	800.00

C#	Date	Mintage	VG	Fine	VF	XF
164	1809A	.469	25.00	60.00	155.00	475.00
	1809B	.136	35.00	90.00	190.00	575.00
	1809H	4,534	55.00	165.00	325.00	900.00
	1809K	3,451	60.00	170.00	335.00	950.00
	1809L	.027	40.00	100.00	300.00	700.00
	1809MA	.027	40.00	100.00	300.00	700.00
	1809Q	.020	40.00	100.00	300.00	700.00
	1809U	3,149	75.00	225.00	425.00	1000.
	1809W	.062	37.50	95.00	275.00	650.00
	1810A	.771	25.00	60.00	155.00	475.00
	1810B	.072	37.50	95.00	275.00	650.00
	1810BB	1,389	Reported, Not Confirmed			
	1810D	.018	40.00	100.00	300.00	700.00
	1810H	5,710	65.00	200.00	400.00	900.00
	1810I	.029	40.00	100.00	300.00	700.00
	1810K	3,518	60.00	170.00	335.00	950.00
	1810L	.032	40.00	100.00	300.00	700.00

C#	Date	Mintage	VG	Fine	VF	XF
164	1810M	.011	45.00	100.00	320.00	750.00
	1810MA	8,843	65.00	200.00	400.00	900.00
	1810Q	4,857	60.00	170.00	335.00	950.00
	1810U	3,077	95.00	265.00	550.00	1200.
	1810W	.048	40.00	100.00	300.00	700.00
	1811A	2.509	20.00	50.00	125.00	300.00
	1811B	.290	30.00	75.00	190.00	500.00
	1811BB	.012	45.00	110.00	320.00	750.00
	1811D	.037	40.00	100.00	300.00	700.00
	1811H	.044	40.00	100.00	300.00	700.00
	1811I·	.137	37.50	95.00	275.00	600.00
	1811K	.028	40.00	100.00	300.00	700.00
	1811L	.099	37.50	95.00	275.00	600.00
	1811M	.124	37.50	95.00	275.00	600.00
	1811MA	.039	40.00	100.00	300.00	700.00
	1811Q	.075	37.50	95.00	275.00	600.00
	1811T	.035	40.00	100.00	300.00	700.00
	1811U	3,893	95.00	265.00	550.00	1200.
	1811W	.118	37.50	95.00	275.00	600.00
	1812A	.308	30.00	75.00	190.00	500.00
	1812B	.057	40.00	100.00	300.00	700.00
	1812BB	2,835	Reported, not confirmed			
	1812D	.061	40.00	100.00	300.00	700.00
	1812H	.081	40.00	100.00	300.00	700.00
	1812I	.209	30.00	75.00	190.00	500.00
	1812K	.021	40.00	100.00	300.00	700.00
	1812L	.042	40.00	100.00	300.00	700.00
	1812M	.145	37.50	95.00	275.00	600.00
	1812MA	.016	40.00	100.00	300.00	700.00
	1812Q	.086	37.50	95.00	275.00	600.00
	1812T	.019	40.00	100.00	300.00	700.00
	1812W	.108	37.50	95.00	275.00	600.00
	1812(u)	9,493	90.00	250.00	500.00	1100.
	1813A	.442	25.00	60.00	155.00	475.00
	1813B	.031	40.00	100.00	300.00	700.00
	1813CL	906	—	—	Rare	—
	1813D	.033	40.00	100.00	300.00	700.00
	1813H	.080	37.50	95.00	275.00	600.00
	1813I	.098	37.50	95.00	275.00	600.00
	1813K	.027	40.00	100.00	300.00	700.00
	1813L	.033	40.00	100.00	300.00	700.00
	1813M	.221	30.00	75.00	190.00	500.00
	1813MA	.018	40.00	100.00	300.00	700.00
	1813Q	.253	30.00	75.00	190.00	500.00
	1813T	.011	50.00	125.00	335.00	800.00
	1813W	.088	37.50	95.00	275.00	600.00
	1813/2 (u)	.041	Reported, not confirmed			
	1813(u)	Inc. Ab.	75.00	175.00	400.00	950.00
	1814A	.095	40.00	110.00	325.00	775.00
	1814M	.046	45.00	125.00	365.00	850.00
	1814Q	.016	50.00	140.00	400.00	900.00
171	1815A	6,783	135.00	350.00	700.00	3500.
180	1816A	.061	35.00	90.00	275.00	500.00
	1816B	4,398	65.00	185.00	425.00	725.00
	1816H	7,037	55.00	155.00	375.00	665.00
	1816I	3,956	65.00	185.00	425.00	725.00
	1816L	1,068	Reported, Not Confirmed			
	1816M	1,699	Reported, Not Confirmed			
	1816Q	.013	50.00	140.00	310.00	595.00
	1817A	.214	30.00	75.00	190.00	450.00
	1817B	.015	50.00	140.00	310.00	595.00
	1817H	.037	40.00	95.00	280.00	550.00
	1817K	.213	30.00	75.00	190.00	450.00
	1817L	3,026	Reported, Not Confirmed			
	1817M	.030	40.00	95.00	280.00	550.00
	1817Q	.047	40.00	95.00	280.00	550.00
	1817T	1,456	Reported, Not Confirmed			
	1817W	8,504	55.00	155.00	375.00	665.00
	1818A	.013	50.00	140.00	310.00	595.00
	1818B	3,039	65.00	185.00	425.00	725.00
	1818H	8,530	55.00	155.00	375.00	665.00
	1818L	444 pcs.	Reported, Not Confirmed			
	1818Q	.052	35.00	90.00	275.00	500.00
	1818W	3,208	Reported, Not Confirmed			
180	1819A	2,334	Reported, Not Confirmed			
	1819B	.012	50.00	140.00	310.00	595.00
	1819H	5,309	65.00	185.00	425.00	725.00
	1819Q	.064	35.00	90.00	275.00	500.00
	1820A	.053	35.00	90.00	275.00	500.00
	1820D	2,282	Reported, Not Confirmed			
	1820H	2,801	Reported, Not Confirmed			
	1820K	.011	50.00	140.00	310.00	595.00
	1820Q	.047	35.00	90.00	275.00	500.00
	1821A	.139	30.00	85.00	250.00	475.00
	1821H	2,897	Reported, Not Confirmed			
	1821Q	.028	40.00	95.00	280.00	550.00
	1821W	.022	40.00	95.00	280.00	550.00
	1822A	.421	25.00	60.00	140.00	375.00
	1822B	.030	40.00	95.00	280.00	550.00
	1822D	2,181	Reported, Not Confirmed			
	1822H	9,806	55.00	155.00	375.00	665.00
	1822M	1,496	Reported, Not Confirmed			
	1822Q	.011	50.00	140.00	310.00	595.00
	1822W	.102	32.50	90.00	275.00	500.00
	1823A	.268	30.00	75.00	190.00	450.00
	1823D	7,251	55.00	155.00	375.00	665.00
	1823H	.020	40.00	95.00	280.00	550.00
	1823I	.010	50.00	140.00	310.00	595.00
	1823K	2,545	Reported, Not Confirmed			
	1823L	.027	40.00	95.00	280.00	550.00
	1823M	.094	32.50	90.00	275.00	500.00
	1823Q	3,399	Reported, Not Confirmed			
	1823W	.265	30.00	75.00	190.00	450.00
	1824A	.284	30.00	75.00	190.00	450.00
	1824B	.071	32.50	90.00	275.00	500.00
	1824D	.108	30.00	75.00	200.00	460.00
	1824H	.027	40.00	95.00	280.00	550.00
	1824I	.053	32.50	90.00	275.00	500.00
	1824K	.038	40.00	95.00	280.00	550.00
	1824L	.048	32.50	90.00	275.00	500.00
	1824M	.132	30.00	75.00	200.00	450.00
	1824MA	7,455	55.00	155.00	375.00	665.00
	1824Q	.053	32.50	90.00	275.00	500.00
	1824W	.460	22.50	60.00	135.00	375.00
188	1825A	.034	40.50	95.00	280.00	550.00
	1825B	.017	50.00	140.00	310.00	595.00
	1825BB	5,856	65.00	185.00	725.00	725.00
	1825D	.027	40.00	95.00	280.00	550.00
	1825H	3,215	Reported, Not Confirmed			
	1825I	6,239	65.00	185.00	425.00	725.00
	1825K	.011	55.00	155.00	375.00	650.00
	1825L	4,397	70.00	200.00	450.00	750.00
	1825M	6,770	65.00	185.00	425.00	725.00
	1825Q	4,956	70.00	200.00	450.00	750.00
	1825W	.015	50.00	140.00	310.00	595.00
	1826A	.122	30.00	75900	200.00	450.00
	1826B	.024	40.00	95.00	280.00	550.00
	1826BB	.019	40.00	95.00	280.00	550.00
	1826D	.072	32.50	90.00	275.00	500.00
	1826H	.019	40.00	95.00	280.00	550.00
	1826I	.032	40.00	95.00	280.00	550.00
	1826K	.011	50.00	140.00	310.00	595.00
	1826L	.025	40.00	95.00	280.00	550.00
	1826M	.040	40.00	95.00	280.00	550.00
	1826Q	.021	40.00	95.00	280.00	550.00
	1826T	9,189	55.00	155.00	375.00	650.00
	1826W	.155	30.00	75.00	200.00	450.00
	1827A	.268	30.00	75.00	190.00	400.00
	1827B	.138	30.00	75.00	200.00	450.00
	1827BB	.019	37.50	95.00	280.00	550.00
	1827D	.116	30.00	75.00	200.00	450.00
	1827H	.019	40.00	95.00	280.00	550.00
	1827I	.022	40.00	95.00	280.00	550.00
	1827K	.033	40.00	95.00	280.00	550.00
	1827L	.052	32.50	90.00	275.00	500.00
	1827M	.031	40.00	95.00	280.00	550.00
	1827Q	.014	40.00	100.00	290.00	570.00
	1827T	.043	40.00	95.00	280.00	550.00
	1827W	.481	20.00	50.00	110.00	300.00
	1828A	.235	25.00	65.00	155.00	350.00
	1828B	.059	32.50	90.00	275.00	500.00
	1828BB	.025	40.00	100.00	290.00	570.00
	1828D	.108	27.50	65.00	155.00	375.00
	1828H	.016	40.00	100.00	290.00	570.00
	1828I	4,863	70.00	200.00	450.00	750.00
	1828K	.081	32.50	90.00	275.00	500.00
	1828L	.046	32.50	90.00	275.00	500.00
	1828M	.120	27.50	65.00	155.00	350.00
	1828Q	.024	40.00	100.00	290.00	550.00
188	1828T	.031	40.00	100.00	290.00	550.00
	1828W	.358	20.00	50.00	110.00	300.00
	1829A	.145	25.00	65.00	155.00	350.00
	1829B	.102	25.00	65.00	155.00	350.00
	1829BB	.018	40.00	100.00	290.00	550.00
	1829D	.096	30.00	75.00	200.00	450.00
	1829H	.049	32.50	90.00	275.00	500.00
	1829I	.016	40.00	110.00	300.00	550.00
	1829K	.033	40.00	100.00	290.00	550.00
	1829L	.021	40.00	100.00	290.00	550.00
	1829M	.049	32.50	90.00	275.00	500.00
	1829MA	.041	40.00	100.00	290.00	550.00
	1829Q	.011	45.00	115.00	325.00	625.00
	1829T	.050	32.50	90.00	275.00	500.00
	1829W	.105	30.00	75.00	200.00	450.00
	1830A	.044	40.00	100.00	290.00	550.00
	1830A reeded edge	Inc. Ab.	—	—	Rare	—
	1830B	.064	32.50	90.00	275.00	500.00
	1830I	5,635	65.00	190.00	425.00	725.00
	1830K	.014	42.50	115.00	325.00	600.00
	1830L	.013	42.50	115.00	325.00	600.00
	1830M	.016	40.00	110.00	300.00	595.00
	1830Q	6,688	65.00	190.00	425.00	725.00
	1830T	.012	42.50	115.00	325.00	600.00
	1830W	.109	30.50	75.00	200.00	450.00
202	1831A	.010	15.00	55.00	115.00	300.00
	1831B	.049	12.00	40.00	95.00	220.00
	1831I	.038	12.00	40.00	95.00	220.00
	1831W	.033	12.00	40.00	95.00	220.00
	1832A	.688	10.00	30.00	60.00	175.00
	1832B	.384	10.00	35.00	65.00	190.00
	1832BB	.055	12.00	40.00	95.00	220.00
	1832D	.239	10.00	25.00	65.00	190.00
	1832H	.186	11.00	35.00	90.00	210.00
	1832I	.034	12.00	40.00	95.00	220.00
	1832K	.076	12.00	40.00	95.00	220.00
	1832L	.024	13.00	45.00	105.00	255.00
	1832M	.069	12.00	40.00	95.00	220.00
	1832MA	.064	12.00	40.00	95.00	220.00
	1832Q	.022	13.00	45.00	105.00	255.00
	1832T	.104	11.00	35.00	90.00	210.00
	1832W	.427	10.00	30.00	60.00	135.00
	1833A	.194	11.00	35.00	90.00	210.00
	1833B	.105	11.00	35.00	90.00	210.00
	1833BB	.074	12.00	40.00	95.00	220.00
	1833D	.098	12.00	40.00	95.00	220.00
	1833H	.022	13.00	45.00	105.00	255.00
	1833I	.034	12.00	40.00	95.00	220.00
	1833K	.023	13.00	45.00	105.00	255.00
	1833L	.014	15.00	55.00	115.00	300.00
	1833M	.050	12.00	40.00	95.00	220.00
	1833MA	.021	13.00	45.00	105.00	255.00
	1833Q	.037	12.00	40.00	95.00	220.00
	1833T	.028	12.00	40.00	95.00	220.00
	1833W	.168	11.00	35.00	90.00	210.00
	1834A	.493	10.00	30.00	60.00	175.00
	1834B	.296	10.00	25.00	65.00	190.00
	1834BB	.077	12.00	40.00	95.00	220.00
	1834BB(b)	I.A.	12.00	40.00	95.00	220.00
	1834D	.098	12.00	40.00	95.00	220.00
	1834H	.072	12.00	40.00	95.00	220.00
	1834I	.048	12.00	40.00	95.00	220.00
	1834K	.057	12.00	40.00	95.00	220.00
	1834L	.015	15.00	55.00	115.00	300.00
	1834M	.078	12.00	40.00	95.00	220.00
	1834MA	.019	15.00	55.00	110.00	285.00
	1834Q	.069	12.00	40.00	95.00	220.00
	1834T	.104	11.00	35.50	90.00	210.00
	1834W	.583	10.00	30.00	60.00	175.00
	1835A	.452	11.00	30.00	60.00	175.00
	1835B	.066	12.00	40.00	95.00	220.00
	1835BB	.038	13.00	45.00	105.00	255.00
	1835D	.040	13.00	45.00	105.00	255.00
	1835H	.023	15.00	50.00	110.00	285.00
	1835I	.048	15.00	55.00	115.00	300.00
	1835K	.042	11.00	40.00	95.00	220.00
	1835L	2,669	Reported, Not Confirmed			
	1835M	.041	12.00	75.00	95.00	220.00
	1835MA	.015	15.00	50.00	110.00	285.00
	1835T	.017	15.00	50.00	110.00	285.00
	1835W	.147	11.00	35.00	90.00	210.00
	1836A	.112	11.00	35.00	90.00	210.00
	1836B	.113	11.00	35.00	90.00	210.00
	1836BB	.073	12.00	40.00	95.00	220.00

C#	Date	Mintage	VG	Fine	VF	XF
202	1836D	5,519	25.00	75.00	175.00	475.00
	1836K	.020	14.00	55.00	110.00	285.00
	1836M	6,733	25.00	75.00	175.00	475.00
	1836W	.060	12.00	40.00	95.00	220.00
	1837A	.104	11.00	35.00	90.00	210.00
	1837B	.256	10.00	30.00	60.00	185.00
	1837BB	.022	15.00	55.00	110.00	285.00
	1837D	6,306	25.00	75.00	175.00	475.00
	1837K	.036	15.00	55.00	110.00	285.00
	1837MA	—	—	—	Rare	—
	1837W	.230	10.00	32.50	60.00	185.00
	1838A	.093	11.00	35.00	90.00	210.00
	1838B	.156	11.00	35.00	90.00	210.00
	1838BB	.082	12.00	40.00	95.00	220.00
	1838D	3,478		Reported, Not Confirmed		
	1838K	.019	15.00	55.00	110.00	285.00
	1838MA	.025	15.00	55.00	110.00	285.00
	1838W	.170	11.00	35.00	90.00	210.00
	1839A	.036	12.00	40.00	95.00	220.00
	1839B	.102	11.00	35.00	90.00	210.00
	1839BB	.047	12.00	40.00	95.00	220.00
	1839D(arc)	7,299	25.00	70.00	165.00	435.00
	1839D Tower	I.A.	25.00	70.00	165.00	435.00
	1839K	.031	12.00	40.00	95.00	220.00
	1839W	.105	11.00	35.00	90.00	210.00
	1840A	.042	12.00	40.00	95.00	220.00
	1840B	.121	11.00	35.00	90.00	210.00
	1840BB	.064	12.00	40.00	95.00	220.00
	1840D	.010	15.00	55.00	115.00	300.00
	1840K	.039	12.00	40.00	95.00	220.00
	1840W(c)	.063	12.00	40.00	95.00	220.00
	1840W(r)	I.A.	12.00	40.00	95.00	220.00
	1841A	.068	12.00	40.00	95.00	220.00
	1841B	.022	15.00	55.00	110.00	285.00
	1841BB	.061	12.00	40.00	95.00	220.00
	1841K	.029	15.00	55.00	110.00	285.00
	1841W	.290	10.00	32.50	60.00	185.00
	1842A	.017	15.00	55.00	110.00	285.00
	1842B	.147	11.00	35.00	90.00	210.00
	1842BB	.026	11.00	50.00	110.00	285.00
	1842K	.033	15.00	55.00	110.00	285.00
	1842W	.190	10.00	32.50	60.00	185.00
	1843A	.068	12.00	40.00	95.00	220.00
	1843B	.067	12.00	40.00	95.00	220.00
	1843BB	.059	12.00	40.00	95.00	220.00
	1843K	.037	15.00	55.00	110.00	285.00
	1843W	.296	10.00	32.50	60.00	185.00
	1844A	.030	15.00	55.00	110.00	285.00
	1844B	.013	15.00	55.00	115.00	300.00
	1844BB	.086	11.00	35.00	90.00	210.00
	1844K	.031	15.00	55.00	110.00	285.00
	1844W	.290	10.00	32.50	60.00	185.00
	1845A prow	.019	15.00	55.00	110.00	285.00
	1845A hand	I.A.	15.00	55.00	110.00	285.00
	1845B	.155	11.00	35.00	90.00	210.00
	1845BB	.076	12.00	40.00	95.00	220.00
	1845K	.018	15.00	55.00	110.00	285.00
	1845W	.353	10.00	30.00	60.00	185.00
	1846A	.305	10.00	30.00	60.00	185.00
	1846B	.046	12.00	40.00	95.00	220.00
	1846BB	.044	12.00	40.00	95.00	220.00
	1846K	.018	15.00	55.00	110.00	285.00
	1846W	.049	12.00	40.00	95.00	220.00
	1847A	.784	10.00	30.00	60.00	185.00
	1847BB	.060	12.00	40.00	95.00	220.00
	1847K	6,504	25.00	75.00	175.00	475.00
	1848A	.098	10.00	30.00	60.00	210.00
	1848BB	.027	12.00	40.00	95.00	220.00
	1848D	.012	15.00	55.00	115.00	300.00

Second Republic

Y#	Date	Mintage	VG	Fine	VF	XF
5	1849A	.665	35.00	90.00	275.00	550.00
	1849BB	.014	75.00	225.00	400.00	900.00
	1849K	.017	75.00	225.00	400.00	900.00
	1850A	.857	30.00	85.00	260.00	525.00
	1850BB	.202	45.00	120.00	325.00	600.00
	1850K	9,914	100.00	275.00	500.00	1000.
	1851A	.351	45.00	120.00	325.00	600.00

Second Empire

Y#	Date	Mintage	VG	Fine	VF	XF
25	1853A	.049	100.00	250.00	500.00	1000.
	1854A	.215	80.00	225.00	450.00	900.00
	1855A D	.082	90.00	235.00	475.00	950.00
	1856A	.241	80.00	225.00	450.00	900.00
	1856BB	.693	60.00	175.00	350.00	800.00
	1856D	.289	80.00	225.00	450.00	900.00
	1857A	.389	75.00	200.00	400.00	850.00
	1858A	1,288	—	—	Rare	—
	1859A	894 pcs.		Reported, Not Confirmed		

10.0000 gm., .835 SILVER, .2684 oz ASW

Y#	Date	Mintage	VG	Fine	VF	XF
31	1866A	3.226	10.00	12.50	25.00	75.00
	1866BB	3.090	10.00	12.50	25.00	75.00
	1866K	.437	15.00	35.00	80.00	175.00
	1867A	3.695	10.00	12.50	25.00	75.00
	1867BB	3.471	12.50	17.50	40.00	90.00
	1867K	1.744	15.00	20.00	45.00	100.00
	1868A	3.762	10.00	12.50	25.00	75.00
	1868BB	.733	12.00	20.00	50.00	125.00
	1868K	.087	25.00	55.00	150.00	350.00
	1869A	1.104	12.00	20.00	45.00	100.00
	1869BB	.367	12.00	25.00	60.00	125.00
	1870A	3.187	10.00	12.50	25.00	75.00
	1870BB	1.001		Reported, Not Confirmed		

Third Republic

Y#	Date	Mintage	VG	Fine	VF	XF
45	1870A	.239	15.00	55.00	125.00	300.00
	1870K(a)	.560	10.00	40.00	100.00	225.00
	1870K(s)	I.A.	10.00	40.00	100.00	225.00
	1871K	1.256	10.00	35.00	75.00	175.00

Y#	Date	Mintage	Fine	VF	XF	Unc
50	1870A	1.324	12.50	25.00	75.00	225.00
	1871A	4.757	10.00	15.00	55.00	150.00
	1871K	1.215	13.00	25.00	80.00	235.00
	1872A	2.306	10.00	25.00	75.00	225.00
	1872K	1.467	10.00	30.00	80.00	235.00
	1873A	.528	25.00	75.00	110.00	350.00
	1878A	30 pcs.	—	—	Proof	1800.
	1881A	1.014	15.00	30.00	95.00	265.00
	1887A	2.343	10.00	25.00	75.00	225.00
	1888A	.131	40.00	125.00	200.00	500.00
	1889A	100 pcs.	—	—	Proof	1500.
	1894A	.300	20.00	65.00	110.00	325.00
	1895A	.600	15.00	35.00	105.00	280.00

Y#	Date	Mintage	Fine	VF	XF	Unc
64	1898	5.000	10.00	12.50	15.00	30.00
64	1899	3.500	10.00	12.50	25.00	60.00
	1900	.500	35.00	80.00	250.00	500.00
	1901	1.860	10.00	12.50	32.50	80.00
	1902	2.000	10.00	12.50	25.00	70.00
	1904	1.500	10.00	12.50	35.00	75.00
	1905	2.000	10.00	12.50	25.00	70.00
	1908	2.502	10.00	12.50	25.00	70.00
	1909	1.000	10.00	12.50	35.00	75.00
	1910	2.190	10.00	12.50	15.00	35.00
	1912	1.000	10.00	12.50	20.00	45.00
	1913	.500	20.00	40.00	65.00	250.00
	1914	5.719	10.00	12.50	15.00	20.00
	1914C	.462	10.00	15.00	25.00	45.00
	1915	13.963	10.00	12.50	15.00	20.00
	1916	17.887	10.00	12.50	15.00	20.00
	1917	16.555	10.00	12.50	15.00	20.00
	1918	12.026	10.00	12.50	15.00	20.00
	1919	9.261	10.00	12.50	15.00	20.00
	1920	3.014	10.00	12.50	15.00	20.00

ALUMINUM-BRONZE
French Chamber Of Commerce Series

Y#	Date	Mintage	Fine	VF	XF	Unc
79	1920	14.363	4.00	7.50	18.00	50.00
	1921	Inc. Ab.	1.00	2.00	3.00	14.00
	1922	29.463	.75	1.25	2.50	10.00
	1923	43.960	.75	1.25	2.50	10.00
	1924	29.631	.75	1.25	2.50	10.00
	1925	31.607	.75	1.25	2.50	10.00
	1926	2.962	3.00	6.00	16.00	40.00
	1927	1.678	60.00	190.00	400.00	750.00

Y#	Date	Mintage	Fine	VF	XF	Unc
82	1931	1.717	2.00	4.50	15.00	35.00
	1932	8.943	.50	1.00	2.00	12.50
	1933	8.413	.50	1.00	2.00	12.50
	1934	6.896	.50	1.00	2.00	12.50
	1935	.298	9.00	20.00	65.00	175.00
	1936	12.394	.25	.50	1.00	10.00
	1937	11.055	.25	.50	1.00	10.00
	1938	28.072	.15	.25	.75	9.00
	1939	25.403	.15	.25	.75	9.00
	1940	9.716	.25	.50	1.00	10.00
	1941	16.684	.15	.25	.75	8.00

ALUMINUM

Y#	Date	Mintage	Fine	VF	XF	Unc
82a	1941	—	.25	.50	1.50	12.00
	1944	7.224	.15	.25	.75	12.00
	1944B	.170		Reported, Not Confirmed		
	1944C	9.828		Reported, Not Confirmed		
	1945	16.636	.15	.25	.35	11.00
	1945B	1.726	1.00	3.00	10.00	30.00
	1945C	1.165	1.25	3.75	11.00	32.50
	1946	34.930	.15	.25	1.00	11.00
	1946B	6.018	.15	.25	1.00	12.00
	1946C	1.533		Reported, Not Confirmed		
	1947	78.984	.15	.25	.50	50.00
	1947B	26.220	.15	.25	.50	50.00
	1948	32.354	.15	.25	.50	50.00
	1948B	39.090	.15	.25	.50	50.00
	1949	13.683	.15	.25	.75	6.50
	1949B	23.955	.15	.25	.75	5.00
	1950	12.178	.15	.25	.75	6.50
	1950B	18.185	.15	.25	.75	5.00
	1951	.012	—	Dated 1950		—
	1958 (o)	9.906	—	—	.50	5.00
	1959	17.774	—	—	.25	3.50

Vichy French State Issues

Y#	Date	Mintage	Fine	VF	XF	Unc
V96	1943	106.997	.40	.50	2.00	8.00
	1943B	34.131	7.00	14.00	35.00	70.00
	1943C	7.575	Reported, Not Confirmed			
	1944	25.546	.35	1.00	3.50	15.00
	1944B	10.298	1.25	2.50	6.00	25.00
	1944C	19.470	1.25	2.50	5.50	22.50

BRASS

Allied Occupation Issue

89	1944	50.000	1.50	3.50	6.00	15.00

NICKEL

109	1979	—	.60	.70	.80	1.25

5 FRANCS

25.000 gm., .900 SILVER, .7234 oz ASW

C#	Date	Mintage	VG	Fine	VF	XF
138	L'AN4A	7.471	30.00	80.00	225.00	600.00
	L'AN5/4A	I.A.	35.00	90.00	235.00	650.00
	L'AN5A	Inc. Ab.	BV	40.00	130.00	450.00
	L'AN5BB	.025	50.00	125.00	375.00	900.00
	L'AN5K	.228	35.00	95.00	260.00	675.00
	L'AN5L	2 known	—	—	Rare	—
	L'AN5Q	.537	32.50	75.00	190.00	500.00
	L'AN5T	.019	50.00	125.00	375.00	900.00
	L'AN6A	1.452	BV	40.00	130.00	450.00
	L'AN6BB	.065	40.00	100.00	335.00	800.00
	L'AN6K	.089	40.00	100.00	335.00	800.00
	L'AN6L	.181	35.00	95.00	260.00	675.00
	L'AN6Q	.478	32.50	75.00	190.00	500.00
	L'AN6T	.049	42.50	110.00	350.00	850.00
	L'AN6W	.070	40.00	100.00	335.00	800.00
	L'AN7A	2.656	BV	40.00	140.00	450.00
	L'AN7BB	7,306	Reported, Not Confirmed			
	L'AN7K	.064	40.00	100.00	335.00	800.00
	L'AN7L	.419	32.50	75.00	190.00	500.00
	L'AN7Q	.616	25.00	62.50	180.00	450.00
	L'AN7T	.035	50.00	125.00	375.00	900.00
	L'AN8A	1.079	BV	40.00	130.00	450.00
	L'AN8BB	3,603	Reported, Not Confirmed			
	L'AN8D	3,049	Reported, Not Confirmed			
	L'AN8K	.074	40.00	100.00	335.00	800.00
	L'AN8L	.395	32.50	75.00	190.00	500.00
	L'AN8Q	1.160	BV	40.00	130.00	450.00
	L'AN8T	.047	45.00	110.00	350.00	850.00

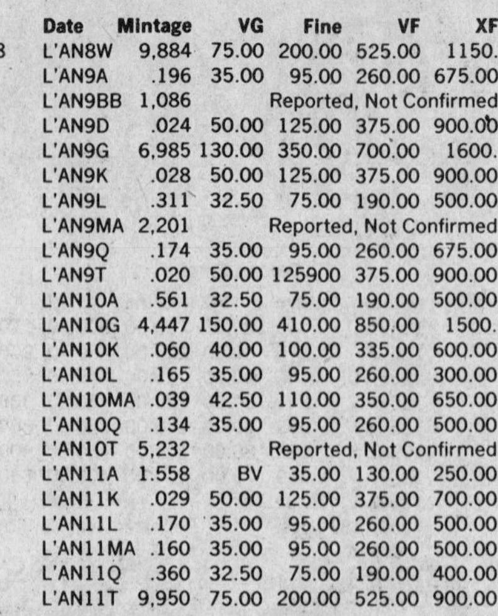

C#	Date	Mintage	VG	Fine	VF	XF
138	L'AN8W	9,884	75.00	200.00	525.00	1150.
	L'AN9A	.196	35.00	95.00	260.00	675.00
	L'AN9BB	1,086	Reported, Not Confirmed			
	L'AN9D	.024	50.00	125.00	375.00	900.00
	L'AN9G	6,985	130.00	350.00	700.00	1600.
	L'AN9K	.028	50.00	125.00	375.00	900.00
	L'AN9L	.311	32.50	75.00	190.00	500.00
	L'AN9MA	2,201	Reported, Not Confirmed			
	L'AN9Q	.174	35.00	95.00	260.00	675.00
	L'AN9T	.020	50.00	125900	375.00	900.00
	L'AN10A	.561	32.50	75.00	190.00	500.00
	L'AN10G	4,447	150.00	410.00	850.00	1500.
	L'AN10K	.060	40.00	100.00	335.00	600.00
	L'AN10L	.165	35.00	95.00	260.00	300.00
	L'AN10MA	.039	42.50	110.00	350.00	650.00
	L'AN10Q	.134	35.00	95.00	260.00	500.00
	L'AN10T	5,232	Reported, Not Confirmed			
	L'AN11A	1.558	BV	35.00	130.00	250.00
	L'AN11K	.029	50.00	125.00	375.00	700.00
	L'AN11L	.170	35.00	95.00	260.00	500.00
	L'AN11MA	.160	35.00	95.00	260.00	500.00
	L'AN11Q	.360	32.50	75.00	190.00	400.00
	L'AN11T	9,950	75.00	200.00	525.00	900.00

Obv. leg: BONAPARTE PREMIER CONSUL

C#	Date	Mintage	VG	Fine	VF	XF
145.1	ANXIA	3.878	BV	40.00	150.00	300.00
	ANXIA no dots flanking privy mark					
		Inc. Ab.	—	—1 Known		—
	ANXID	5,547	—	(1 known)		—
	ANXIK	.031	42.50	110.00	350.00	800.00
	ANXIL	.119	35.00	95.00	260.00	675.00
	ANXIMA	.206	35.00	95.00	260.00	675.00
	ANXIQ	.309	35.00	85.00	210.00	650.00
	ANXIT	.018	50.00	125.00	375.00	900.00

Obv: Similar to C#145.1.

C#	Date	Mintage	VG	Fine	VF	XF
145.2	AN12A	3.454	BV	40.00	150.00	450.00
	AN12B	.035	42.50	110.00	350.00	850.00
	AN12BB	.018	50.00	125.00	375.00	900.00
	AN12D	.116	35.00	95.00	260.00	675.00
	AN12G	.014	125.00	315.00	425.00	1500.
	AN12H	.070	35.00	95.00	260.00	675.00
	AN12I	.422	35.00	85.00	210.00	650.00
	AN12K	.462	35.00	85.00	210.00	650.00
	AN12L	.311	35.00	85.00	210.00	650.00
	AN12M	1.199	BV	45.00	180.00	500.00
	AN12MA	.148	35.00	95.00	260.00	675.00
	AN12Q	.578	30.00	85.00	210.00	650.00
	AN12T	.113	35.00	95.00	260.00	675.00
	AN12U	9,953	125.00	315.00	425.00	1500.
	AN12W	.028	42.50	110.00	350.00	850.00

Obv. leg: NAPOLEON EMPEREUR

Rev: Similar to C#155a.

C#	Date	Mintage	VG	Fine	VF	XF
155	AN12A	.767	35.00	95.00	260.00	675.00
	AN12B	.010	55.00	140.00	400.00	1000.
	AN12D	.014	55.00	140.00	400.00	1000.
	AN12H	.015	55.00	140.00	400.00	1000.
	AN12I	.090	42.50	110.00	350.00	850.00
	AN12K	.071	42.50	110.00	350.00	850.00
	AN12L	.016	55.00	140.00	400.00	1000.
	AN12M	.427	35.50	95.00	260.00	675.00
	AN12MA	2,030	Reported, Not Confirmed			
	AN12Q	.055	45.50	125.00	375.00	900.00
	AN12T	.011	55.00	140.00	400.00	1000.
	AN12W	4,366	125.00	315.00	500.00	1500.

Obv: Monogram below bust.

C#	Date	Mintage	VG	Fine	VF	XF
155a.1	AN13A	5.121	BV	30.00	125.00	350.00
	AN13B	4,901	Reported, Not Confirmed			
	AN13BB	7,510	—	—	—	—
	AN13D	.024	45.00	120.00	400.00	900.00
	AN13G	6,487	125.00	315.00	500.00	1500.
	AN13H	.035	42.50	110.00	350.00	800.00
	AN13I	.333	35.00	95.00	260.00	675.00
	AN13K	.161	42.50	110.00	350.00	850.00
	AN13L	.207	35.00	95.00	260.00	675.00
	AN13M	1.547	BV	40.00	165.00	400.00
	AN13MA	.064	42.50	110.00	350.00	850.00
	AN13Q	.245	35.00	95.00	260.00	675.00
	AN13T	.025	45.00	120.00	400.00	900.00
	AN13U	.021	60.00	175.00	525.00	1100.
	AN13W	.034	42.50	110.00	350.00	850.00
	AN14A	1.855	BV	40.00	165.00	400.00
	AN14BB	831	Reported, Not Confirmed			
	AN14D	3,890	80.00	225.00	500.00	1200.
	AN14H	3,780	80.00	225.00	500.00	1200.
	AN14I	.012	Reported, Not Confirmed			
	AN14K	2,113	90.00	230.00	600.00	1350.
	AN14L	.015	50.00	130.00	375.00	900.00
	AN14M	.040	42.50	110.00	350.00	850.00
	AN14T	632	Reported, Not Confirmed			
	AN14U	.014	100.00	275.00	450.00	1300.
	AN14W	.014	50.00	130.00	375.00	900.00

Obv: Similar to C#155a.1.

C#	Date	Mintage	VG	Fine	VF	XF
155a.2	1806A	.826	BV	40.00	165.00	400.00
	1806B	.025	45.00	110.00	350.00	850.00
	1806BB	.660	BV	40.00	175.00	425.00
	1806D	2,771		Reported, Not Confirmed		
	1806H	.028		Reported, Not Confirmed		
	1806I	.239	35.00	95.00	260.00	675.00
	1806K	.029	42.50	110.00	350.00	850.00
	1806L	.551	BV	40.00	175.00	450.00
	1806M	.022	42.50	110.00	350.00	850.00
	1806Q	.078	42.50	110.00	350.00	850.00
	1806T	.706		Reported, Not Confirmed		
	1806U	.031	90.00	230.00	600.00	1350.
	1806W	.032		Reported, Not Confirmed		
	1807B	.044	42.50	110.00	350.00	850.00
	1807BB	1,296		Reported, Not Confirmed		
	1807D	2,423		Reported, Not Confirmed		
	1807H	4,847	80.00	225.00	500.00	1200.
	1807I	.091	42.50	110.00	350.00	850.00
	1807K	.010	50.00	125.00	325.00	1000.
	1807L	.375	35.00	95.00	260.00	675.00
	1807M	.101	42.50	110.00	350.00	850.00
	1807Q	.025	45.00	120.00	400.00	850.00
	1807T	—	—	—	Unique	—
	1807U	.030	90.00	230.00	600.00	1350.
	1807W	.029	45.00	120.00	400.00	950.00

Obv: As C#155a. Rev: As C#155c.

C#	Date	Mintage	VG	Fine	VF	XF
155b	1807A	.049	310.00	750.00	1450.	2500.

Obv: Laureate head.
Rev. leg: REPUBLIQUE FRANCAISE.

C#	Date	Mintage	VG	Fine	VF	XF
155c	1807A	.041	325.00	800.00	1600.	2600.
	1808A	6.462	BV	BV	50.00	200.00
	1808B	1.542	BV	BV	65.00	300.00
	1808BB	.068	BV	50.00	200.00	500.00
	1808D	.065	BV	50.00	200.00	500.00
	1808H	7,204		Reported, Not Confirmed		
	1808I	.107	BV	40.00	150.00	400.00
	1808K	.054		Reported, Not Confirmed		
	1808L	.144	BV	40.00	150.00	400.00
	1808M	.351	BV	30.00	125.00	375.00
	1808MA	2,681	100.00	200.00	450.00	1200.
	1808Q	.012	50.00	125.00	325.00	900.00
	1808T	2,682		Reported, Not Confirmed		
	1808U	.014	50.00	165.00	475.00	1000.
	1808W	.550	BV	35.00	125.00	375.00

Obv: Similar to C#155c.
Rev. leg: EMPIRE FRANCAIS

C#	Date	Mintage	VG	Fine	VF	XF
165	1809A	3.254	BV	BV	50.00	225.00
	1809B	3.036	BV	BV	50.00	225.00
	1809BB	2,856		Reported, Not Confirmed		
	1809D	.011	40.00	100.00	275.00	800.00
	1809H	9,006	40.00	100.00	275.00	800.00
	1809I	.065	BV	50.00	200.00	500.00
	1809K	.105	BV	25.00	75.00	250.00
	1809L	.217	BV	25.00	75.00	250.00
	1809M	.034	30.00	70.00	200.00	600.00
	1809MA	.012	40.00	100.00	275.00	800.00
	1809T	2,218		Reported, Not Confirmed		
	1809U	.016	65.00	165.00	475.00	1000.
	1809W	1.221	BV	BV	50.00	200.00
	1810A	8.797	BV	BV	35.00	160.00
	1810B	.632	BV	BV	40.00	175.00
	1810BB	.028	30.00	75.00	200.00	600.00
	1810D	.043	25.00	60.00	175.00	550.00
	1810I	.026	30.00	75.00	200.00	600.00
	1810K	.120	BV	25.00	75.00	250.00
	1810L	.185	BV	25.00	70.00	235.00
	1810L	I.A.	BV	40.00	125.00	500.00
	1810M	.072	BV	50.00	150.00	475.00
	1810MA	.012	40.00	100.00	275.00	800.00
	1810Q	.118	BV	25.00	75.00	250.00
	1810U	.014	65.00	165.00	475.00	1000.
	1810W	.297	BV	BV	55.00	225.00
	1811A	31.050	—	BV	30.00	100.00
	1811B	3.772	BV	BV	45.00	200.00
	1811BB	.327	BV	BV	55.00	225.00
	1811D	1.568	BV	BV	50.00	190.00
	1811H	1.029	BV	BV	50.00	190.00
	1811I	1.830	BV	BV	50.00	190.00
	1811K	1.081	BV	BV	50.00	190.00
	1811L	1.123	BV	BV	50.00	190.00
	1811M	1.101	BV	BV	50.00	190.00
	1811MA	.671	BV	BV	50.00	190.00
	1811WA	Inc. Ab.	—	2 Pcs. Known		—
	1811Q	1.213	BV	BV	50.00	190.00
	1811T	.724	BV	BV	50.00	190.00
	1811U	.169	40.00	90.00	300.00	400.00
	1811W	3.290	BV	BV	25.00	80.00
	1812A	9.311	BV	BV	25.00	75.00
	1812B	3.039	BV	BV	25.00	80.00
	1812BB	.139	BV	30.00	60.00	350.00
	1812D	2.295	BV	BV	25.00	80.00
	1812H	1.824	BV	BV	25.00	80.00
	1812I	2.672	BV	BV	25.00	80.00
	1812K	1.664	BV	BV	25.00	80.00
	1812L	.936	BV	BV	25.00	90.00
	1812M	1.617	BV	BV	25.00	80.00
	1812MA	.612	BV	BV	45.00	275.00
	1812Q	1.460	BV	BV	25.00	80.00
	1812R/cr	.049	100.00	275.00	600.00	1250.
	1812T	.926	BV	BV	25.00	80.00
	1812U	.105	70.00	200.00	400.00	850.00
	1812W	4.342	BV	BV	25.00	80.00
	1812(u)	.055	100.00	275.00	600.00	1250.
	1813A	9.757	BV	BV	25.00	75.00
	1813B	.728	BV	BV	30.00	200.00
	1813BB	.025	30.00	75.00	200.00	600.00
	1813CL	.014	165.00	400.00	850.00	1900.
	1813D	.917	BV	BV	35.00	100.00
	1813H	1.795	BV	BV	25.00	80.00
	1813I	2.555	BV	BV	25.00	80.00
	1813K	1.281	BV	BV	25.00	80.00
	1813L	1.161	BV	BV	25.00	80.00
	1813M	2.213	BV	BV	25.00	80.00
	1813MA	.834	BV	BV	35.00	100.00
	1813Q	1.826	BV	BV	25.00	80.00
	1813R/cr	.017	125.00	375.00	750.00	1600.
	1813T	.564	BV	BV	40.00	125.00
	1813U	.060	100.00	275.00	600.00	125.00
	1813W	1.824	BV	BV	25.00	80.00
	1813(u)	.362	100.00	275.00	600.00	1250.
	1814A	1.329	BV	BV	25.00	80.00
	1814B	.020	30.00	75.00	200.00	600.00
	1814BB	5,382		Reported, Not Confirmed		
	1814CL	1,191		Reported, not confirmed		
	1814H	.169	BV	30.00	60.00	150.00

C#	Date	Mintage	VG	Fine	VF	XF
165	1814I	.027	30.00	75.00	200.00	600.00
	1814M	.369	BV	BV	40.00	125.00
	1814MA	.016	30.00	75.00	200.00	600.00
	1814Q	.367	BV	BV	40.00	125.00
	1814T	8,745	60.00	150.00	350.00	750.00
	1814W	.033	30.00	75.00	200.00	600.00

First Restoration

C#	Date	Mintage	VG	Fine	VF	XF
168	1814A	1.466	BV	40.00	110.00	250.00
	1814B	.634	BV	45.00	125.00	300.00
	1814BB	4,913		Reported, Not Confirmed		
	1814D	.082	25.00	60.00	160.00	350.00
	1814H	.046	30.00	70.00	175.00	375.00
	1814I	1.554	BV	40.00	110.00	250.00
	1814K	.355	25.00	50.00	150.00	325.00
	1814L	1.902	BV	40.00	110.00	250.00
	1814M	2.377	BV	32.50	95.00	200.00
	1814MA	.099	25.00	60.00	160.00	350.00
	1814Q	1.182	BV	40.00	110.00	250.00
	1814T	5,235	40.00	100.00	250.00	525.00
	1814W	.104	25.00	60.00	160.00	350.00
	1815A	.413	25.00	50.00	150.00	325.00
	1815B	.254	25.00	50.00	150.00	325.00
	1815BB	1,551		Reported, Not Confirmed		
	1815D	7,482	40.00	100.00	250.00	525.00
	1815H	.034	35.00	100.00	200.00	400.00
	1815I	1.739	BV	40.00	110.00	250.00
	1815K	.108	30.00	70.00	175.00	350.00
	1815L	1.130	BV	40.00	110.00	250.00
	1815M	1.406	BV	40.00	110.00	250.00
	1815MA	7,461		Reported, Not Confirmed		
	1815/4Q	.925	25.00	45.00	110.00	400.00
	1815Q	Inc. Ab.	BV	45.00	125.00	300.00
	1815T	8,006		Reported, Not Confirmed		
	1815W	.114	30.00	70.00	175.00	350.00

"The Hundred Days"

C#	Date	Mintage	VG	Fine	VF	XF
172	1815A	.473	75.00	175.00	450.00	1000.
	1815B	.093	80.00	190.00	500.00	1100.
	1815BB	3,723		Reported, Not Confirmed		
	1815I	.596	75.00	175.00	450.00	1000.
	1815L	.097	80.00	190.00	500.00	1100.
	1815M	.080	80.00	190.00	500.00	1100.

C#	Date	Mintage	VG	Fine	VF	XF
172	1815Q	.021	90.00	210.00	550.00	1350.
	1815W	.021	90.00	210.00	550.00	1350.

Second Restoration

C#	Date	Mintage	VG	Fine	VF	XF
181	1816A	3.210	BV	BV	50.00	150.00
	1816B	.922	BV	BV	90.00	225.00
	1816BB	8,115	Reported, Not Confirmed			
	1816D	6,446	Reported, Not Confirmed			
	1816H	6,575	Reported, Not Confirmed			
	1816I	.306	BV	40.00	110.00	250.00
	1816K	.034	30.00	100.00	225.00	400.00
	1816L	1.001	BV	BV	90.00	225.00
	1816M	.651	BV	BV	100.00	250.00
	1816MA	.018	Reported, Not Confirmed			
	1816Q	.591	BV	32.50	100.00	250.00
	1816T	.011	35.00	95.00	225.00	450.00
	1816W	.072	BV	45.00	120.00	290.00
	1817A	3.778	BV	BV	32.50	150.00
	1817B	1.580	BV	BV	50.00	175.00
	1817BB	3,510	Reported, Not Confirmed			
	1817D	3,605	Reported, Not Confirmed			
	1817H	.110	BV	45.00	120.00	290.00
	1817I	4,204	Reported, Not Confirmed			
	1817K	.386	BV	40.00	110.00	250.00
	1817L	.377	BV	40.00	110.00	250.00
	1817M	.188	BV	45.00	125.00	300.00
	1817MA	.010	Reported, Not Confirmed			
	1817Q	.105	BV	45.00	125.00	300.00
	1817T	.025	Reported, Not Confirmed			
	1817W	.438	BV	40.00	105.00	250.00
	1818A	.086	BV	45.00	125.00	300.00
	1818B	2.190	BV	45.00	40.00	175.00
	1818BB	1,119	Reported, Not Confirmed			
	1818H	.012	Reported, Not Confirmed			
	1818I	1,568	Reported, Not Confirmed			
	1818K	.017	Reported, Not Confirmed			
	1818L	.010	Reported, Not Confirmed			
	1818M	2,920	Reported, Not Confirmed			
	1818MA	7,805	Reported, Not Confirmed			
	1818T	.024	Reported, Not Confirmed			
	1818W	.066	BV	45.00	125.00	300.00
	1819A	.658	BV	32.50	110.00	250.00
	1819B	3.437	BV	BV	40.00	175.00
	1819BB	2,469	Reported, Not Confirmed			
	1819H	.033	30.00	100.00	225.00	400.00
	1819I	1,104	Reported, Not Confirmed			
	1819MA	1,186	Reported, Not Confirmed			
	1819Q	1,618	Reported, Not Confirmed			
	1819T	.020	—	—	—	—
	1819W	.034	30.00	100.00	225.00	400.00
	1820A	3.226	BV	BV	40.00	175.00
	1820B	.210	BV	45.00	125.00	300.00
	1820BB	1,976	Reported, Not Confirmed			
	1820D	.017	Reported, Not Confirmed			
	1820H	.018	Reported, Not Confirmed			
	1820I	639	Reported, Not Confirmed			
	1820K	.018	Reported, Not Confirmed			
	1820MA					
		440 pcs.	Reported, not confirmed			
	1820Q	2,770	Reported, Not Confirmed			
	1820T	.011	35.00	95.00	225.00	450.00
	1820W	.106	BV	45.00	125.00	300.00
	1821A	9.526	BV	BV	35.00	150.00
	1821B	.123	BV	45.00	75.00	300.00
	1821BB	1,527	Reported, Not Confirmed			
	1821H	.018	Reported, Not Confirmed			
	1821I	6,320	Reported, Not Confirmed			
	1821MA	198	Reported, Not Confirmed			
	1821Q	5,626	Reported, Not Confirmed			

C#	Date	Mintage	VG	Fine	VF	XF
181	1821W	3.674	BV	BV	45.00	105.00
	1822A	13.453	BV	BV	30.00	90.00
	1822B	.897	BV	30.00	65.00	175.00
	1822H	.077	BV	45.00	90.00	300.00
	1822I	8,712	Reported, Not Confirmed			
	1822K	.393	BV	40.00	110.00	250.00
	1822Q	.020	Reported, Not Confirmed			
	1822W	4.839	BV	BV	30.00	150.00
	1823A	6.536	BV	BV	30.00	150.00
	1823B	.393	BV	40.00	110.00	275.00
	1823BB	3,712	Reported, Not Confirmed			
	1823D	.994	BV	30.00	65.00	175.00
	1823H	.329	BV	40.00	110.00	275.00
	1823I	.269	BV	45.00	90.00	300.00
	1823K	.800	BV	30.00	65.00	175.00
	1823L	.898	BV	30.00	65.00	175.00
	1823M	.958	BV	30.00	65.00	175.00
	1823MA	3,847	Reported, Not Confirmed			
	1823Q	.715	BV	30.00	65.00	175.00
	1823W	4.168	BV	BV	30.00	150.00
	1824A	9.066	BV	BV	25.00	110.00
	1824B	1.246	BV	30.00	65.00	175.00
	1824D	2.448	BV	30.00	60.00	150.00
	1824H	.771	BV	30.00	65.00	175.00
	1824I	1.039	BV	30.00	65.00	175.00
	1824K	1.010	BV	30.00	65.00	175.00
	1824L	1.068	BV	30.00	65.00	175.00
	1824M	1.589	BV	30.00	65.00	175.00
	1824MA	1.422	BV	30.00	65.00	175.00
	1824Q	1.006	BV	30.00	65.00	175.00
	1824W	9.807	BV	BV	25.00	105.00

Rev: Similar to C#181.

C#	Date	Mintage	VG	Fine	VF	XF
189	1824A	.408	40.00	95.00	200.00	500.00
	1825A	2.492	BV	BV	50.00	150.00
	1825B	.113	BV	40.00	125.00	400.00
	1825BB	.157	BV	40.00	125.00	400.00
	1825D	.185	BV	40.00	125.00	400.00
	1825H	.157	BV	40.00	125.00	400.00
	1825I	.155	BV	40.00	125.00	400.00
	1825K	.326	BV	35.00	110.00	325.00
	1825L	.227	BV	35.00	110.00	325.00
	1825M	.154	BV	40.00	125.00	400.00
	1825MA	.176	BV	40.00	125.00	400.00
	1825Q	.163	BV	40.00	125.00	400.00
	1825W	1.104	BV	BV	55.00	165.00
	1826A	7.171	BV	BV	30.00	100.00
	1826B	.595	BV	32.50	100.00	300.00
	1826BB	.411	BV	32.50	100.00	300.00
	1826D	1.437	BV	BV	30.00	70.00
	1826H	.573	BV	32.50	100.00	300.00
	1826I	.536	BV	32.50	100.00	300.00
	1826K	.429	BV	32.50	100.00	300.00
	1826L	.720	BV	30.00	90.00	250.00
	1826M	.670	BV	30.00	90.00	250.00
	1826MA	1.072	BV	BV	55.00	165.00
	1826Q	.346	BV	32.50	100.00	300.00
	1826T	.203	BV	32.50	100.00	300.00
	1826W	3.583	BV	BV	45.00	140.00
	1827A	6.822	BV	BV	30.00	100.00
	1827A edge in relief					
		Inc. Ab.	40.00	100.00	200.00	500.00
	1827B	2.792	BV	BV	45.00	140.00
	1827BB	.393	BV	32.50	100.00	300.00
	1827D	1.651	BV	BV	55.00	165.00
	1827H	.419	BV	32.50	100.00	300.00
	1827I	.335	BV	32.50	100.00	300.00
	1827K	1.147	BV	BV	55.00	165.00
	1827L	1.144	BV	BV	55.00	165.00
	1827M	.806	BV	25.00	90.00	250.00
	1827MA	1.531	BV	BV	55.00	165.00
	1827Q	.484	BV	32.50	100.00	300.00
	1827T	.865	BV	32.50	90.00	250.00
	1827W	11.525	BV	BV	30.00	100.00
	1828A	8.803	BV	BV	30.00	100.00
	1828B	1.898	BV	BV	55.00	165.00
	1828BB	.699	BV	32.50	100.00	300.00
	1828D	2.743	BV	BV	55.00	165.00
	1828H	.490	BV	32.50	100.00	300.00
	1828I	.124	BV	40.00	115.00	325.00
	1828K	1.632	BV	BV	55.00	165.00
	1828L	1.083	BV	BV	55.00	165.00
	1828M	1.818	BV	BV	55.00	165.00

C#	Date	Mintage	VG	Fine	VF	XF
189	1828MA	1.201	BV	BV	55.00	165.00
	1828Q	.394	BV	32.50	100.00	300.00
	1828T	.933	BV	BV	55.00	165.00
	1828W	9.610	BV	BV	30.00	100.00
	1829A	4.827	BV	BV	30.00	100.00
	1829B	2.834	BV	BV	55.00	165.00
	1829BB	.548	BV	32.50	100.00	300.00
	1829D	1.608	BV	BV	55.00	165.00
	1829H	1.155	BV	BV	55.00	165.00
	1829I	.475	BV	32.50	100.00	300.00
	1829K	1.011	BV	BV	55.00	165.00
	1829L	.857	BV	BV	60.00	175.00
	1829M	.873	BV	BV	60.00	175.00
	1829MA	1.258	BV	BV	55.00	165.00
	1829Q	.360	BV	40.00	115.00	275.00
	1829T	.888	BV	BV	60.00	175.00
	1829W	3.235	BV	BV	30.00	100.00
	1830A	6.333	BV	BV	30.00	100.00
	1830A edge in relief					
		Inc. Ab.	40.00	100.00	200.00	500.00
	1830B	2.910	BV	BV	30.00	100.00
	1830BB	.112	BV	40.00	115.00	325.00
	1830D	.631	BV	BV	60.00	175.00
	1830H	.574	BV	BV	60.00	175.00
	1830I	.067	30.00	80.00	250.00	400.00
	1830K	.713	BV	BV	65.00	175.00
	1830L	.399	BV	40.00	115.00	275.00
	1830M	.496	BV	32.50	100.00	300.00
	1830MA	1.803	BV	BV	55.00	165.00
	1830Q	.151	BV	40.00	115.00	325.00
	1830T	.137	BV	40.00	115.00	325.00
	1830W	4.134	BV	BV	30.00	100.00

Incused edge lettering
Obv. leg: LOUIS PHILIPPE ROI....
Rev: Similar to C#203.1.

C#	Date	Mintage	VG	Fine	VF	XF
203a.1	1830A	Inc. Bl.	30.00	60.00	150.00	500.00
	1830B	Inc. Bl.	30.00	60.00	150.00	500.00
	1830D	Inc. Bl.	35.00	75.00	225.00	650.00
	1830W	Inc. Bl.	35.00	70.00	200.00	575.00

Raised edge lettering

C#	Date	Mintage	VG	Fine	VF	XF
203a.2	1830A	Inc. Bl.	50.00	125.00	275.00	750.00

Incused edge lettering
Obv. leg: LOUIS PHILIPPE I ROI....

C#	Date	Mintage	VG	Fine	VF	XF
203.1	1830A	2.421	BV	BV	40.00	100.00
	1830B	1.025	BV	BV	50.00	125.00
	1830BB	5,125	45.00	125.00	275.00	750.00
	1830D	.368	BV	35.00	80.00	200.00
	1830H	.030	30.00	55.00	150.00	350.00
	1830I	.028	30.00	55.00	150.00	350.00
	1830K	.123	BV	40.50	100.00	225.00
	1830L	8,931	40.00	115.00	250.00	600.00
	1830M	.050	30.00	60.00	125.00	300.00
	1830MA	.065	30.00	60.00	125.00	300.00
	1830Q	.012	40.00	115.00	250.00	550.00

C#	Date	Mintage	VG	Fine	VF	XF
203.1	1830T	.125	BV	40.50	100.00	225.00
	1830W	1.020	BV	BV	55.00	125.00
	1831A	11.785	BV	BV	35.00	100.00
	1831B	7.889	BV	BV	35.00	100.00
	1831BB	.983	BV	BV	50.00	125.00
	1831D	3.460	BV	BV	35.00	250.00
	1831H	.843	BV	BV	50.00	125.00
	1831I	.502	BV	35.00	85.00	200.00
	1831K	1.523	BV	BV	40.00	125.00
	1831L	.430	BV	35.00	85.00	200.00
	1831M	1.337	BV	BV	40.00	125.00
	1831MA	2.062	BV	BV	35.00	115.00
	1831Q	.357	BV	35.00	85.00	200.00
	1831T	1.261	BV	BV	40.00	125.00
	1831W	8.226	BV	BV	35.00	100.00

Raised edge lettering

C#	Date	Mintage	VG	Fine	VF	XF
203.2	1830A	Inc. Ab.	BV	30.00	65.00	200.00
	1831A	Inc. Ab.	BV	30.00	65.00	175.00
	1831B	Inc. Ab.	BV	35.00	70.00	225.00
	1831W	Inc. Ab.	BV	30.00	65.00	200.00

Incused edge lettering
Obv: Similar to C#204a.
Rev: Similar to C#203.

C#	Date	Mintage	VG	Fine	VF	XF
204.1	1831A	Inc. Ab.	30.00	65.00	150.00	350.00
	1831B	Inc. Ab.	BV	40.00	110.00	250.00
	1831BB	Inc. Ab.	BV	BV	35.00	200.00
	1831D	Inc. Ab.	30.00	60.00	115.00	275.00
	1831I	Inc. Ab.	30.00	65.00	150.00	350.00
	1831M	Inc. Ab.	BV	40.00	110.00	250.00
	1831Q	Inc. Ab.	30.00	65.00	150.00	350.00

Raised edge lettering

C#	Date	Mintage	VG	Fine	VF	XF
204.2	1831A	Inc. Ab.	BV	BV	35.00	100.00
	1831B	Inc. Ab.	BV	BV	45.00	125.00
	1831BB	Inc. Ab.	BV	35.00	90.00	200.00
	1831D	Inc. Ab.	BV	BV	55.00	150.00
	1831H	Inc. Ab.	BV	35.00	90.00	200.00
	1831K	Inc. Ab.	BV	35.00	90.00	200.00
	1831L	Inc. Ab.	30.00	60.00	150.00	300.00
	1831M	Inc. Ab.	BV	35.00	90.00	200.00
	1831MA	Inc. Ab.	BV	35.00	90.00	200.00
	1831T	Inc. Ab.	BV	35.00	90.00	200.00
	1831W	Inc. Ab.	BV	BV	45.00	125.00

Rev: Mintmarks at edge outside wreath.

C#	Date	Mintage	Fine	VF	XF	Unc
204	1832A	7.800	BV	BV	40.00	250.00
	1832B	2.852	BV	BV	50.00	275.00
	1832BB	1.725	BV	BV	55.00	300.00
	1832D	3.007	BV	BV	45.00	250.00
	1832H	.900	BV	BV	65.00	330.00
	1832I	.703	BV	BV	65.00	330.00
	1832K	.602	BV	BV	75.00	350.00
	1832L	.567	BV	BV	75.00	350.00
	1832M	.729	BV	BV	65.00	330.00
	1832MA	1.184	BV	BV	55.00	300.00
	1832Q	.716	BV	BV	65.00	330.00
	1832T	1.592	BV	BV	55.00	300.00
	1832W	4.483	BV	BV	45.00	230.00
	1833A	8.211	BV	BV	30.00	250.00
	1833B	3.791	BV	BV	45.00	230.00
	1833BB	1.799	BV	BV	55.00	300.00
	1833D	1.487	BV	BV	55.00	300.00
	1833/2H	.844	BV	BV	55.00	300.00
	1833H	Inc. Ab.	BV	BV	65.00	330.00
	1833I	1.014	BV	BV	65.00	330.00
	1833K	.749	BV	BV	65.00	330.00
	1833L	.378	BV	BV	85.00	375.00

C#	Date	Mintage	Fine	VF	XF	Unc
204	1833M	.669	BV	BV	60.00	350.00
	1833MA	.872	BV	BV	65.00	330.00
	1833Q	.663	BV	BV	60.00	350.00
	1833T	1.437	BV	BV	55.00	300.00
	1833W	9.270	BV	BV	30.00	250.00
	1834A	11.307	BV	BV	30.00	225.00
	1834B	4.453	BV	BV	45.00	230.00
	1834BB(b)	1.621	BV	BV	55.00	300.00
	1834BB	Inc. Ab.	BV	BV	55.00	300.00
	1834D	2.119	BV	BV	50.00	275.00
	1834H	2.184	BV	BV	50.00	275.00
	1834I	1.933	BV	BV	50.00	275.00
	1834K	2.157	BV	BV	50.00	275.00
	1834L	.359	BV	BV	80.00	375.00
	1834M	.889	BV	BV	65.00	330.00
	1834MA	.489	BV	BV	80.00	375.00
	1834Q	.942	BV	BV	55.00	300.00
	1834T	2.119	BV	BV	50.00	275.00
	1834W	11.733	BV	BV	30.00	225.00
	1835A	5.807	BV	BV	30.00	250.00
	1835B	2.793	BV	BV	50.00	275.00
	1835BB	1.286	BV	BV	55.00	300.00
	1835D	1.084	BV	BV	55.00	300.00
	1835H	.467	BV	BV	80.00	375.00
	1835I	.598	BV	BV	60.00	350.00
	1835K	.928	BV	BV	55.00	300.00
	1835L	.064	40.00	90.00	250.00	650.00
	1835M	.412	BV	BV	80.00	375.00
	1835MA	.373	BV	BV	80.	200.00
	1835Q	.040	45.00	100.00	275.00	700.00
	1835T	.294	BV	30.00	85.00	400.00
	1835W	5.016	BV	BV	30.00	250.00
	1836A	1.940	BV	BV	55.00	300.00
	1836B	2.631	BV	BV	55.00	300.00
	1836BB	1.188	BV	BV	55.00	300.00
	1836D	.200	BV	32.50	90.00	425.00
	1836K	.296	BV	30.00	85.00	400.00
	1836M	.072	40.00	90.00	250.00	650.00
	1836MA	.362	BV	BV	85.00	395.00
	1836W	1.614	BV	BV	55.00	300.00
	1837A	6.884	BV	BV	30.00	250.00
	1837B	6.075	BV	BV	30.00	250.00
	1837BB	.600	BV	BV	60.00	350.00
	1837D	.093	35.00	80.00	225.00	600.00
	1837K	.813	BV	BV	65.00	330.00
	1837MA	.724	BV	BV	65.00	330.00
	1837W	6.652	BV	BV	30.00	250.00
	1838A	4.805	BV	BV	30.00	250.00
	1838B	4.002	BV	BV	30.00	250.00
	1838BB	1.535	BV	BV	55.00	300.00
	1838D	.149	BV	40.00	95.00	450.00
	1838K	.450	BV	BV	65.00	330.00
	1838MA	2.116	BV	BV	55.00	300.00
	1838W	4.190	BV	BV	30.00	250.00
	1839A	5.071	BV	BV	30.00	250.00
	1839B	3.467	BV	BV	30.00	250.00
	1839BB	1.064	BV	BV	55.00	300.00
	1839D(b)	.519	BV	BV	65.00	330.00
	1839D	Inc. Ab.	BV	BV	65.00	330.00
	1839K	.897	BV	BV	60.00	300.00
	1839MA	.020	70.00	175.00	375.00	950.00
	1839W	3.269	BV	BV	30.00	250.00
	1840A	4.769	BV	BV	30.00	250.00
	1840B	3.337	BV	BV	30.00	250.00
	1840BB	1.186	BV	BV	55.00	300.00
	1840D	.070	35.00	80.00	225.00	600.00
	1840K	1.186	BV	BV	55.00	300.00
	1840Wc	1.714	BV	BV	55.00	300.00
	1840W	Inc. Ab.	BV	BV	55.00	300.00
	1841A	1.005	BV	BV	55.00	300.00
	1841B	1.652	BV	BV	55.00	300.00
	1841BB	2.082	BV	BV	55.00	300.00
	1841K	.995	BV	BV	65.00	330.00
	1841W	8.926	BV	BV	30.00	250.00
	1842A	.755	BV	BV	60.00	300.00
	1842B	3.489	BV	BV	30.00	250.00
	1842BB	2.471	BV	BV	30.00	250.00
	1842K	1.026	BV	BV	55.00	300.00
	1842W	5.436	BV	BV	30.00	250.00
	1843A	1.838	BV	BV	50.00	290.00
	1843B	2.472	BV	BV	30.00	250.00
	1843BB	1.422	BV	BV	50.00	290.00
	1843K	.794	BV	BV	60.00	300.00
	1843W	7.846	BV	BV	30.00	250.00
	1844A	1.971	BV	BV	50.00	290.00
	1844B	.361	BV	35.00	75.00	375.00
	1844BB	1.890	BV	BV	50.00	290.00
	1844K	.398	BV	35.00	75.00	375.00
	1844W	8.775	BV	BV	30.00	250.00
	1845A D	3.096	BV	BV	30.00	250.00
	1845A	Inc. Ab.	BV	BV	30.00	250.00
	1845BB	2.041	BV	BV	30.00	260.00
	1845K	.537	BV	BV	65.00	330.00
	1845W	11.107	BV	BV	30.00	230.00
	1846A	5.434	BV	BV	30.00	250.00
	1846BB	.840	BV	BV	65.00	330.00
	1846K	.511	BV	BV	65.00	330.00

C#	Date	Mintage	Fine	VF	XF	Unc
204	1846W	1.658	BV	BV	50.00	290.00
	1847A	12.578	BV	BV	30.00	230.00
	1847BB	1.577	BV	BV	50.00	290.00
	1847K	.167	BV	50.00	110.00	450.00
	1848A	3.196	BV	BV	30.00	250.00
	1848BB	.935	BV	BV	65.00	330.00
	1848K	.166	25.00	65.00	150.00	500.00

Second Republic

Y#	Date	Mintage	VG	Fine	VF	XF
7	1848A	16.648	BV	BV	BV	75.00
	1848BB	2.300	BV	BV	BV	90.00
	1848D	.136	30.00	80.00	150.00	300.00
	1848K	.428	BV	40.00	90.00	225.00
	1849A	29.338	BV	BV	BV	65.00
	1849BB	2.594	BV	BV	BV	90.00
	1849D	9,711	75.00	150.00	400.00	800.00
	1849K	.471	BV	40.00	90.00	225.00

Y#	Date	Mintage	VG	Fine	VF	XF
6	1849A	7.437	BV	BV	BV	100.00
	1849BB	.916	BV	40.00	90.00	225.00
	1850A	14.619	BV	BV	BV	75.00
	1850BB	1.169	BV	40.00	90.00	225.00
	1850K	.332	30.00	80.00	150.00	300.00
	1851A	13.223	BV	BV	BV	75.00

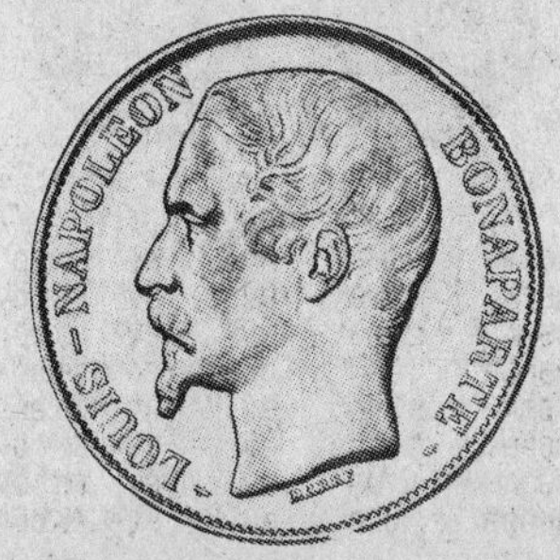

Y#	Date	Mintage	VG	Fine	VF	XF
13	1852A	16.117	BV	30.00	65.00	175.00
	1852A w/sign. J.J.Barre					
		Inc. Ab.	60.00	200.00	350.00	900.00
	1852BB	.041	60.00	200.00	350.00	900.00

Second Empire

Y#	Date	Mintage	Fine	VF	XF	Unc
26	1854A	.011	100.00	275.00	900.00	2500.
	1855A	4.075	30.00	50.00	110.00	300.00
	1855BB	.786	40.00	65.00	150.00	400.00
	1855D	—	45.00	110.00	250.00	600.00
	1856A	4.683	30.00	50.00	110.00	300.00
	1856BB	2.223	35.00	60.00	125.00	350.00
	1856D	2.249	35.00	60.00	125.00	350.00
	1857A	.093	55.00	150.00	400.00	1100.
	1858A	.027	60.00	165.00	450.00	1250.
	1859A	3,365	100.00	275.00	900.00	2500.

1.6129 gm., .900 GOLD, .0467 oz AGW
Bare head, 14.4mm.

Y#	Date	Mintage	Fine	VF	XF	Unc
33	1854A	3.562	50.00	95.00	140.00	225.00
	1854A with plain edge					
		Inc. Ab.	50.00	100.00	160.00	250.00
	1855A	.938	55.00	120.00	175.00	275.00

16.7mm.

Y#	Date	Mintage	Fine	VF	XF	Unc
33a	1856A	2.960	BV	BV	60.00	140.00
	1857A	3.479	BV	BV	50.00	120.00
	1858A	2.983	BV	BV	60.00	130.00
	1858BB	—	70.00	80.00	125.00	250.00
	1859A	5.660	BV	BV	50.00	100.00
	1859BB	2.279	BV	BV	65.00	135.00
	1860A	4.798	BV	BV	50.00	100.00
	1860BB	2.022	BV	BV	60.00	150.00

25.0000 gm., .900 SILVER, .7234 oz ASW

Y#	Date	Mintage	Fine	VF	XF	Unc
32	1861A	.022	50.00	175.00	375.00	1000.
	1862A	.021	50.00	175.00	375.00	1000.
	1863A	.022	50.00	175.00	375.00	1000.
	1864A	.032	50.00	175.00	375.00	1000.
	1865A	.025	50.00	175.00	375.00	1000.
	1865BB	.073	50.00	175.00	375.00	1000.
	1866A	.038	50.00	175.00	375.00	1000.
	1867A	6.586	BV	BV	25.00	75.00
	1867BB	4.224	BV	BV	BV	75.00
	1868A	6.634	BV	BV	BV	75.00
	1868BB	12.090	BV	BV	BV	75.00
	1869A	2.056	BV	BV	BV	75.00
	1869BB	9.597	BV	BV	BV	75.00
	1870A	6.620	BV	BV	BV	75.00
	1870BB	2.055	BV	BV	BV	90.00

1.6129 gm., .900 GOLD, .0467 oz AGW
Laureate head

Y#	Date	Mintage	Fine	VF	XF	Unc
38	1862A	1.101	BV	35.00	55.00	125.00
	1862BB	.882	BV	35.00	65.00	150.00
	1863A	1.591	BV	35.00	55.00	125.00
	1863BB	1.104	BV	35.00	55.00	125.00
	1864A	2.240	BV	35.00	55.00	125.00
	1864BB	1.000	BV	35.00	60.00	130.00
	1865A	.824	BV	35.00	65.00	130.00
	1865BB	.828	BV	35.00	65.00	130.00
	1866A	1.949	BV	35.00	55.00	125.00
	1866BB	1.388	BV	35.00	55.00	125.00
	1867A	1.006	BV	35.00	55.00	125.00
	1867BB	1.504	BV	35.00	55.00	125.00
	1868A	1.864	BV	35.00	55.00	125.00
	1868BB	.439	BV	45.00	95.00	180.00
	1869BB	.288	BV	45.00	95.00	180.00

25.0000 gm., .900 SILVER, .7234 oz ASW
Third Republic

Y#	Date	Mintage	Fine	VF	XF	Unc
51	1870A	1.185	BV	40.00	80.00	200.00

Obv: A.E.OUDINE below head.

Y#	Date	Mintage	Fine	VF	XF	Unc
46.1	1870K		50.00	125.00	300.00	1000.

Obv: E.A.OUDINE below head.

Y#	Date	Mintage	Fine	VF	XF	Unc
46.2	1870A	Inc. Ab.	40.00	110.00	200.00	600.00
	1870K(a)	.544	30.00	90.00	150.00	500.00
	1870K(s)	Inc. Ab.	30.00	90.00	150.00	500.00
	1871K	.630	30.00	90.00	150.00	450.00

Trident

Edge inscription DIEU PROTEGE LA FRANCE
trident symbol-issued by Commune.

Y#	Date	Mintage	Fine	VF	XF	Unc
52a (53)	1871A	.256	125.00	350.00	650.00	1500.

Edge inscription TRAVAIL-GARANTIE-NATIONALE.

Y#	Date	Mintage	Fine	VF	XF	Unc
52b (53a)	1871A	.010	— Reported, Not Confirmed			

Obv: Similar to Y#52a.

Y#	Date	Mintage	Fine	VF	XF	Unc
52	1870A	.261	30.00	70.00	135.00	400.00
	1871A	.238	30.00	70.00	135.00	400.00
	1871K	.075	60.00	150.00	275.00	500.00
	1872A	.057	65.00	160.00	300.00	550.00
	1872K	.021	125.00	325.00	800.00	1400.
	1873A	27.077	BV	BV	BV	40.00

Y#	Date	Mintage	Fine	VF	XF	Unc
52	1873K	3.853	BV	BV	BV	65.00
	1874A	7.999	BV	BV	BV	50.00
	1874K	4.000	BV	BV	BV	65.00
	1875A	13.339	BV	BV	BV	50.00
	1875K	1.661	BV	30.00	50.00	110.00
	1876A	8.800	BV	BV	BV	55.00
	1876K	1.732	BV	30.00	50.00	115.00
	1877A	2.632	BV	BV	30.00	65.00
	1877K	.661	BV	35.00	90.00	200.00
	1878A	1.154	500.00	950.00	1500.	3200.
	1878K	.263	50.00	115.00	200.00	500.00

1.6129 gm., .900 GOLD, .0467 oz AGW
Similar to 10 Francs, Y#9.

Y#	Date	Mintage	Fine	VF	XF	Unc
A54	1878A	30 pcs.	—	—	1850.	3000.
	1889A	40 pcs.	—	—	1750.	2750.

NICKEL

Y#	Date	Mintage	Fine	VF	XF	Unc
83	1933	160.078	2.00	3.50	8.00	25.00

Y#	Date	Mintage	Fine	VF	XF	Unc
84	1933	.406	.75	1.50	4.00	10.00
	1934	56.280	—	Dated 1933		—
	1935	54.164	.75	1.50	5.00	13.00
	1936	.117	250.00	500.00	900.00	3000.
	1937	.157	40.00	75.00	115.00	250.00
	1938	4.977	12.00	25.00	50.00	120.00

ALUMINUM-BRONZE
For Colonial use in Algeria.

Y#	Date	Mintage	Fine	VF	XF	Unc
84a	1938	10.144	30.00	60.00	125.00	275.00
	1939	Inc. Ab.	6.50	13.00	32.50	65.00
	1940	38.758	1.50	3.00	6.00	15.00

For colonial use in Africa.

Y#	Date	Mintage	Fine	VF	XF	Unc
	1945	1.406	.65	1.20	4.00	12.00
	1945C	Inc. Ab.	2.00	4.00	12.00	35.00
	1946	21.790	.50	1.00	3.00	10.00
	1946C	Inc. Ab.	3.50	7.00	12.50	37.50
	1947	2.662	125.00	275.00	575.00	1200.

ALUMINUM

Y#	Date	Mintage	Fine	VF	XF	Unc
84b	1945	95.399	.20	.50	1.00	6.00
	1945B	6.043	1.00	2.00	3.00	12.00
	1945C	2.208	3.50	8.00	20.00	40.00
	1946	61.332	.40	.75	1.00	4.00
	1946B	13.360	.80	1.75	2.75	12.00
	1946C	1.269	5.00	12.00	30.00	55.00
	1947	46.576	.35	.65	1.25	8.00
	1947B	30.839	.35	.65	1.25	8.00
	1948	104.473	.20	.40	.75	5.00
	1948B	28.047	2.00	4.00	12.00	30.00
	1949	203.252	.15	.25	.50	2.00
	1949B	48.414	.35	.65	1.25	8.00
	1950	128.372	.15	.25	.50	3.00
	1950B	28.952	.40	.75	1.50	9.00
	1952	4.000	7.00	15.00	30.00	65.00

COPPER-NICKEL

Y#	Date	Mintage	Fine	VF	XF	Unc
V97	1941	13.782	40.00	85.00	135.00	275.00

This issue was never released for circulation.

12.0000 gm., .835 SILVER, .3221 oz ASW
5 New Francs - 500 Old Francs
Fifth Republic

Y#	Date	Mintage	Fine	VF	XF	Unc
110	1960	55.182	BV	BV	10.00	12.00
	1961	15.630	BV	BV	10.00	12.00
	1962	42.500	BV	BV	10.00	12.00
	1963	37.936	BV	BV	10.00	12.00
	1964	32.378	BV	BV	10.00	12.00
	1965	5.121	BV	BV	10.00	12.00
	1966	5.010	BV	BV	10.00	12.00
	1967	.700	BV	BV	12.00	15.00
	1968	.354	BV	BV	12.00	15.00
	1969	.498	BV	BV	12.00	15.00

NICKEL-CLAD COPPER-NICKEL

Y#	Date	Mintage	Fine	VF	XF	Unc
110a	1970	57.890	1.50	1.75	2.00	2.50
	1971	142.204	1.50	1.75	2.00	2.50
	1972	45.492	1.50	1.75	2.00	2.50
	1973	45.000	1.50	1.75	2.00	2.50
	1974	36.974	1.50	1.75	2.00	2.50
	1975	16.712	1.50	1.75	2.00	2.50
	1976	1.630	1.50	1.75	2.00	2.50
	1977	*.100	—	—	—	—
	1978	—	—	—	—	—
	1979	—	—	—	—	—

10 FRANCS

3.2258 gm., .900 GOLD, .0933 oz AGW

Y#	Date	Mintage	Fine	VF	XF	Unc
9	1850A	.592	BV	BV	160.00	750.00
	1851A	3.115	BV	BV	150.00	600.00

Bare head, 17.2mm

Y#	Date	Mintage	Fine	VF	XF	Unc
34.1	1854A	3.900	75.00	150.00	300.00	875.00
	1855A	6.117	75.00	125.00	275.00	850.00

Plain edge

Y#	Date	Mintage	Fine	VF	XF	Unc
34.2	1854A	Inc. Ab.	85.00	160.00	450.00	925.00

19mm

Y#	Date	Mintage	Fine	VF	XF	Unc
34.3	1855A	.032	BV	BV	80.00	180.00
	1855BB	Inc. Ab.	BV	125.00	180.00	475.00
	1856A	10.778	BV	BV	75.00	150.00
	1857A	14.498	BV	BV	75.00	150.00
	1858A	7.534	BV	BV	75.00	150.00
	1858BB	.677	BV	BV	75.00	220.00
	1859A	10.111	BV	BV	BV	180.00
	1859BB	3.215	BV	BV	BV	160.00
	1860A	6.000	BV	BV	BV	150.00
	1860BB	3.104	BV	BV	BV	160.00

Laureate head

Y#	Date	Mintage	Fine	VF	XF	Unc
39	1861A	.363	BV	75.00	125.00	275.00
	1861BB	.044	BV	100.00	180.00	375.00
	1862A	2.844	BV	BV	75.00	120.00
	1862BB	1.462	BV	BV	75.00	125.00
	1863A	2.346	BV	BV	75.00	120.00
	1863BB	1.905	BV	BV	75.00	125.00
	1864A	3.339	BV	BV	75.00	120.00
	1864BB	1.449	BV	BV	75.00	125.00
	1865A	1.673	BV	BV	75.00	125.00
	1865BB	1.576	BV	BV	75.00	125.00
	1866A	3.720	BV	BV	75.00	120.00

Y#	Date	Mintage	Fine	VF	XF	Unc
39	1866BB	2.776	BV	BV	75.00	120.00
	1867A	1.205	BV	BV	75.00	125.00
	1867BB	2.346	BV	BV	75.00	120.00
	1868A	3.416	BV	BV	75.00	120.00
	1868BB	1.117	BV	BV	75.00	125.00
	1869BB	.109	BV	80.00	160.00	350.00

Y#	Date	Mintage	Fine	VF	XF	Unc
54	1895A	.214	BV	75.00	100.00	150.00
	1896A	.585	BV	BV	75.00	100.00
	1899A	1.600	BV	BV	75.00	100.00

Y#	Date	Mintage	Fine	VF	XF	Unc
65	1899A	.699	BV	BV	75.00	100.00
	1900A	1.570	BV	BV	75.00	90.00
	1901A	2.100	BV	BV	75.00	90.00
	1905A	1.426	BV	BV	75.00	90.00
	1906A	3.665	BV	BV	75.00	90.00
	1907A	3.364	BV	BV	75.00	90.00
	1908A	1.650	BV	BV	75.00	90.00
	1909A	.599	BV	BV	75.00	90.00
	1910A	2.110	BV	BV	75.00	90.00
	1911A	1.881	BV	BV	75.00	90.00
	1912A	1.756	BV	BV	75.00	90.00
	1914A	3.041	BV	BV	75.00	90.00

10.0000 gm., .680 SILVER, .2186 oz ASW

Y#	Date	Mintage	Fine	VF	XF	Unc
86	1929	16.292	BV	BV	7.00	20.00
	1930	36.986	BV	BV	7.00	10.00
	1931	35.468	BV	BV	7.00	10.00
	1932	40.288	BV	BV	7.00	10.00
	1933	31.146	BV	BV	7.00	10.00
	1934	52.001	BV	BV	7.00	10.00
	1937	.052	45.00	100.00	185.00	350.00
	1938	14.090	BV	BV	7.00	12.00
	1939	8.299	BV	BV	7.00	25.00

Long Leaves

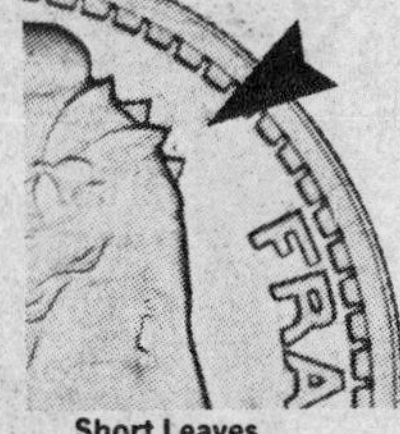
Short Leaves

COPPER-NICKEL

Y#	Date	Mintage	Fine	VF	XF	Unc
86a	(1945(LL)	6.557	1.00	2.00	3.50	9.00
	1945(SI)	Inc. Ab.	6.00	12.00	25.00	50.00
	1946(LL)	24.409	25.00	45.00	100.00	300.00
	1946(SI)	Inc. Ab.	.50	1.00	2.50	6.00
	1946B(LL)	8.452	8.50	18.00	40.00	75.00
	1946B(SL)	I.A.	1.00	2.00	3.50	8.00
	1947	41.627	.50	1.00	2.50	6.00
	1947B	17.188	1.00	2.00	3.50	8.00

Obv: Small head.

Y#	Date	Mintage	Fine	VF	XF	Unc
86b	1947	Inc. Ab.	.40	.65	1.50	6.00
	1947B	Inc. Ab.	3.00	7.00	20.00	45.00
	1948	155.945	.15	.30	.75	3.00
	1948B	40.500	.40	.75	1.00	3.50
	1949	118.149	.20	.30	.50	3.00
	1949B	29.518	.30	1.00	2.00	5.00

ALUMINUM-BRONZE

Y#	Date	Mintage	Fine	VF	XF	Unc
98	1950	13.534	.15	.25	.75	5.00
	1950B	4.808	1.00	2.50	8.00	18.00
	1951	153.689	.15	.25	.50	3.50
	1951B	106.866	—	—	.50	3.75
	1952	76.810	.15	.25	.50	3.75
	1952B	72.346	.15	.25	.50	3.75
	1953	46.272	.15	.25	.75	4.00
	1953B	36.466	.25	.50	1.00	4.50
	1954	2.207	2.00	4.50	11.00	25.00
	1954B	21.634	.75	1.50	3.00	10.00
	1955	47.466	—	—	.50	3.50
	1956	2.570	Reported, Not Confirmed			
	1957	26.351	—	—	.75	3.75
	1958(w)	27.213	—	—	.75	3.75
	1958B	1.500	Reported, Not Confirmed			
	1959	.125	Reported, Not Confirmed			

25.0000 gm., .900 SILVER, .7234 oz ASW
10 New Francs - 1000 Old Francs
Fifth Republic

Y#	Date	Mintage	Fine	VF	XF	Unc
111	1964	131 pcs.	(pattern)		500.00	800.00
	1965	8.051	BV	BV	25.00	35.00
	1966	9.800	BV	BV	25.00	35.00
	1967	10.100	BV	BV	25.00	35.00
	1968	3.884	BV	BV	25.00	35.00
	1969	.551	BV	BV	30.00	40.00
	1970	4.799	BV	BV	25.00	35.00
	1971	.501	BV	BV	25.00	35.00
	1972	1.000	BV	BV	25.00	35.00
	1973	.128	BV	BV	35.00	50.00

NICKEL-BRASS

Y#	Date	Mintage	Fine	VF	XF	Unc
A112	1974	22.348	2.50	2.75	3.00	5.00
	1975	59.013	2.50	2.75	3.00	4.00
	1976	104.093	2.50	2.75	3.00	4.00
	1977	*100.000	2.50	2.75	3.00	4.00
	1978	—	—	—	—	—
	1979	—	—	—	—	—

20 FRANCS

6.4516 gm., .900 GOLD, .1867 oz AGW
Bare head

C#	Date	Mintage	Fine	VF	XF	Unc
146	ANXIA	.058	150.00	200.00	325.00	900.00
	AN12A	.988	BV	130.00	275.00	650.00
	Obv. leg: NAPOLEON EMPEREUR.					
156	AN12A	.428	BV	150.00	275.00	625.00
	Redesigned head.					
156a	AN13A	.519	BV	150.00	200.00	500.00
	AN13I	—	175.00	350.00	450.00	1000.
	AN13Q	522 pcs.	400.00	650.00	950.00	1800.
	AN13T	918 pcs.	350.00	700.00	950.00	1750.
	AN14A	.148	BV	175.00	300.00	6.00
	AN14I	1,646	225.00	350.00	450.00	900.00
	AN14Q	2,710	200.00	300.00	450.00	825.00
	AN14U	1,755	210.00	325.00	450.00	900.00
	AN14W	—	235.00	375.00	550.00	1000.

C#	Date	Mintage	Fine	VF	XF	Unc
	1806A	.964	125.00	150.00	220.00	425.00
	1806I	8,143	125.00	180.00	375.00	600.00
	1806Q	3,973	130.00	210.00	400.00	700.00
	1806U	.017	125.00	180.00	325.00	550.00
	1806W	4,242	150.00	200.00	400.00	700.00
	1807A	14.826	125.00	200.00	250.00	450.00
	1807M	5,296	135.00	180.00	400.00	650.00
	1807U	2,557	145.00	225.00	425.00	725.00
	1807W	5,181	135.00	180.00	400.00	600.00
	Laureate head					
156b	1807A	Inc. Ab.	150.00	210.00	325.00	525.00
	1808A	1.450	150.00	210.00	325.00	475.00
	1808K	281	500.00	900.00	1200.	1800.
	1808M	.022	150.00	245.00	375.00	525.00
	1808Q	646	400.00	700.00	1000.	1600.
	1808U	1,505	150.00	250.00	475.00	875.00
	1808W	8,489	150.00	235.00	350.00	600.00

C#	Date	Mintage	Fine	VF	XF	Unc
166	1809A	.688	120.00	175.00	225.00	350.00
	1809H	501 pcs.	225.00	450.00	650.00	1300.
	1809K	3,614	135.00	210.00	350.00	575.00
	1809L	2,383	140.00	225.00	325.00	575.00
	1809M	5,007	125.00	195.00	300.00	475.00
	1809U	3,400	140.00	220.00	350.00	500.00
	1809W	.017	125.00	150.00	250.00	475.00
	1810A	1.936	125.00	150.00	200.00	350.00
	1810H	2,454	140.00	195.00	275.00	575.00
	1810K	.015	125.00	150.00	250.00	475.00
	1810M	1,983	245.00	375.00	475.00	800.00
	1810Q	2,343	225.00	350.00	450900	825.00

C#	Date	Mintage	Fine	VF	XF	Unc
166	1810U	5,891	135.00	190.00	300.00	500.00
	1810W	.223	125.00	190.00	280.00	375.00
	1811A	3.705	125.00	180.00	300.00	450.00
	1811H	1,278	225.00	350.00	475.00	725.00
	1811K	.011	125.00	210.00	375.00	525.00
	1811M	4,971	140.00	245.00	325.00	475.00
	1811U	.020	135.00	195.00	300.00	450.00
	1811W	.328	125.00	190.00	300.00	275.00
	1812A	3.072	125.00	180.00	250.00	325.00
	1812K	2,650	135.00	275.00	375.00	600.00
	1812L	.018	125.00	190.00	265.00	375.00
	1812M	6,498	135.00	250.00	400.00	675.00
	1812Q	5,470	135.00	195.00	300.00	475.00
	1812R(c)	.014	225.00	375.00	550.00	975.00
	1812U	7,339	145.00	250.00	375.00	625.00
	1812W	.346	125.00	200.00	325.00	475.00
	1813A	2.798	125.00	200.00	275.00	450.00
	1813CL	4,380	300.00	400.00	600.00	900.00
	1813K	869	350.00	500.00	700.00	1100.
	1813L	.019	125.00	195.00	265.00	375.00
	1813Q	.013	125.00	195.00	265.00	375.00
	1813(R)	5,532	220.00	325.00	475.00	850.00
	1813U	925	295.00	450.00	700.00	950.00
	1813W	.104	125.00	200.00	275.00	325.00
	1813(u)	.090	225.00	450.00	625.00	750.00
	1814A	.328	200.00	275.00	375.00	475.00
	1814CL	887	350.00	500.00	700.00	1200.
	1814Q	3,289	145.00	250.00	350.00	550.00
	1814W	.016	125.00	200.00	300.00	475.00
	1815A	.436	125.00	200.00	275.00	375.00
	1815L	.018	135.00	210.00	295.00	450.00
	1815W	9,369	155.00	225.00	350.00	475.00

Engraver: Tiolier

C#	Date	Mintage	Fine	VF	XF	Unc
170	1814A	2.684	BV	140.00	150.00	275.00
	1814K	.063	BV	150.00	225.00	375.00
	1814L	.045	BV	160.00	235.00	375.00
	1814Q	.029	BV	175.00	250.00	450.00
	1814W	.060	BV	150.00	225.00	375.00
	1815A	2.113	BV	70.00	150.00	275.00
	1815B	1,539	150.00	225.00	450.00	775.00
	1815K	.030	BV	175.00	250.00	450.00
	1815L	.034	BV	160.00	250.00	450.00
	1815Q	.039	BV	160.00	250.00	425.00
	1815W	.088	BV	125.00	180.00	350.00

Engraver: T. Wyon, Jr.

C#	Date	Mintage	Fine	VF	XF	Unc
182	1815R	.872	BV	250.00	325.00	450.00

C#	Date	Mintage	Fine	VF	XF	Unc
183	1816A	.522	BV	125.00	195.00	300.00
	1816B	.022	BV	135.00	195.00	275.00
	1816K	4,947	145.00	240.00	350.00	550.00
	1816L	.022	150.00	250.00	350.00	475.00
	1816Q	.016	125.00	200.00	300.00	450.00
	1816W	.054	BV	170.00	270.00	375.00
	1817A	2.135	BV	135.00	150.00	225.00
	1817K	4,803	150.00	250.00	350.00	550.00
	1817L	.036	BV	195.00	300.00	425.00
	1817Q	.097	BV	160.00	265.00	400.00
	1817W	.156	BV	150.00	250.00	375.00
	1818A	2.681	BV	135.00	200.00	300.00
	1818L	5,394	145.00	240.00	350.00	550.00
	1818Q	.025	125.00	200.00	300.00	350.00
	1818T	.016	140.00	225.00	325.00	375.00
	1818W	1.315	BV	125.00	200.00	250.00
	1819A	2.350	BV	135.00	195.00	250.00
	1819Q	.034	BV	200.00	295.00	395.00
	1819T	8,734	140.00	225.00	325.00	475.00
	1819W	.219	BV	120.00	225.00	295.00
	1820A	1.317	BV	125.00	200.00	300.00
	1820Q	.060	BV	190.00	275.00	375.00
	1820T	5,749	150.00	250.00	350.00	550.00
	1820W	.044	BV	195.00	295.00	425.00

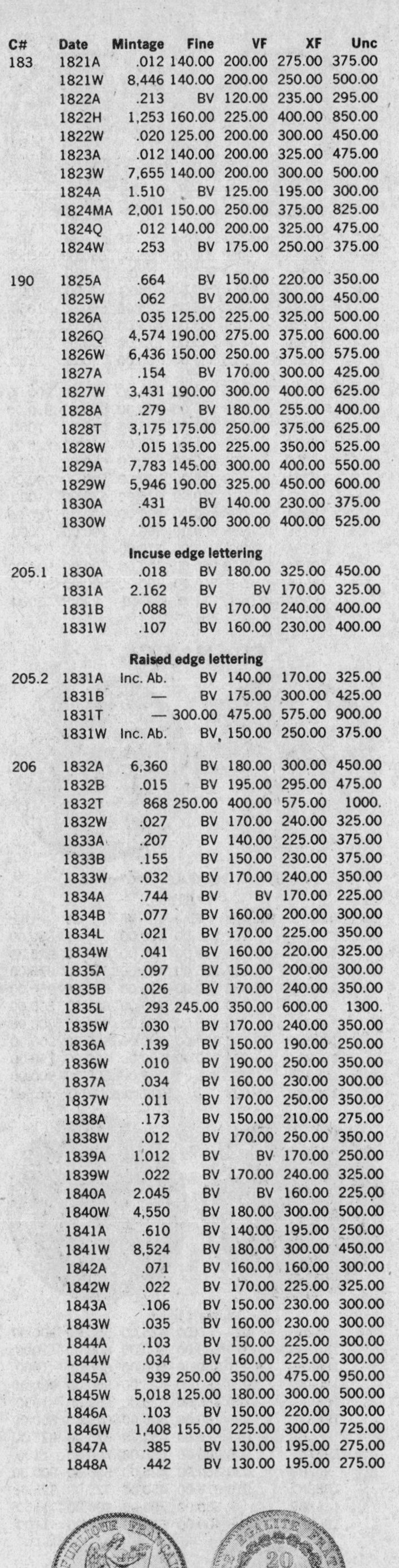

C#	Date	Mintage	Fine	VF	XF	Unc
183	1821A	.012	140.00	200.00	275.00	375.00
	1821W	8,446	140.00	200.00	250.00	500.00
	1822A	.213	BV	120.00	235.00	295.00
	1822H	1,253	160.00	225.00	400.00	850.00
	1822W	.020	125.00	200.00	300.00	450.00
	1823A	.012	140.00	200.00	325.00	475.00
	1823W	7,655	140.00	200.00	300.00	500.00
	1824A	1.510	BV	125.00	195.00	300.00
	1824MA	2,001	150.00	250.00	375.00	825.00
	1824Q	.012	140.00	200.00	325.00	475.00
	1824W	.253	BV	175.00	250.00	375.00
190	1825A	.664	BV	150.00	220.00	350.00
	1825W	.062	BV	200.00	300.00	450.00
	1826A	.035	125.00	225.00	325.00	500.00
	1826Q	4,574	190.00	275.00	375.00	600.00
	1826W	6,436	150.00	250.00	375.00	575.00
	1827A	.154	BV	170.00	300.00	425.00
	1827W	3,431	190.00	300.00	400.00	625.00
	1828A	.279	BV	180.00	255.00	400.00
	1828T	3,175	175.00	250.00	375.00	625.00
	1828W	.015	135.00	225.00	350.00	525.00
	1829A	7,783	145.00	300.00	400.00	550.00
	1829W	5,946	190.00	325.00	450.00	600.00
	1830A	.431	BV	140.00	230.00	375.00
	1830W	.015	145.00	300.00	400.00	525.00
	Incuse edge lettering					
205.1	1830A	.018	BV	180.00	325.00	450.00
	1831A	2.162	BV	BV	170.00	325.00
	1831B	.088	BV	170.00	240.00	400.00
	1831W	.107	BV	160.00	230.00	400.00
	Raised edge lettering					
205.2	1831A	Inc. Ab.	BV	140.00	170.00	325.00
	1831B	—	BV	175.00	300.00	425.00
	1831T	—	300.00	475.00	575.00	900.00
	1831W	Inc. Ab.	BV	150.00	250.00	375.00
206	1832A	6,360	BV	180.00	300.00	450.00
	1832B	.015	BV	195.00	295.00	475.00
	1832T	868	250.00	400.00	575.00	1000.
	1832W	.027	BV	170.00	240.00	325.00
	1833A	.207	BV	140.00	225.00	375.00
	1833B	.155	BV	150.00	230.00	375.00
	1833W	.032	BV	170.00	240.00	350.00
	1834A	.744	BV	BV	170.00	225.00
	1834B	.077	BV	160.00	200.00	300.00
	1834L	.021	BV	170.00	225.00	350.00
	1834W	.041	BV	160.00	220.00	325.00
	1835A	.097	BV	150.00	200.00	300.00
	1835B	.026	BV	170.00	240.00	350.00
	1835L	293	245.00	350.00	600.00	1300.
	1835W	.030	BV	170.00	240.00	350.00
	1836A	.139	BV	150.00	190.00	250.00
	1836W	.010	BV	190.00	250.00	350.00
	1837A	.034	BV	160.00	230.00	300.00
	1837W	.011	BV	170.00	250.00	350.00
	1838A	.173	BV	150.00	210.00	275.00
	1838W	.012	BV	170.00	250.00	350.00
	1839A	1.012	BV	BV	170.00	250.00
	1839W	.022	BV	170.00	240.00	325.00
	1840A	2.045	BV	BV	160.00	225.00
	1840W	4,550	BV	180.00	300.00	500.00
	1841A	.610	BV	140.00	195.00	250.00
	1841W	8,524	BV	180.00	300.00	450.00
	1842A	.071	BV	160.00	160.00	300.00
	1842W	.022	BV	170.00	225.00	325.00
	1843A	.106	BV	150.00	230.00	300.00
	1843W	.035	BV	160.00	230.00	300.00
	1844A	.103	BV	150.00	225.00	300.00
	1844W	.034	BV	160.00	225.00	300.00
	1845A	939	250.00	350.00	475.00	950.00
	1845W	5,018	125.00	180.00	300.00	500.00
	1846A	.103	BV	150.00	220.00	300.00
	1846W	1,408	155.00	225.00	300.00	725.00
	1847A	.385	BV	130.00	195.00	275.00
	1848A	.442	BV	130.00	195.00	275.00

Y#	Date	Mintage	Fine	VF	XF	Unc
8	1848A	1.543	BV	BV	125.00	175.00
	1849A	1.303	BV	BV	125.00	175.00

Y#	Date	Mintage	Fine	VF	XF	Unc
10	1849A	.053	BV	130.00	160.00	240.00
	1850A	3.964	BV	BV	125.00	175.00
	1851A	12.704	BV	BV	125.00	190.00

Y#	Date	Mintage	Fine	VF	XF	Unc
A13	1852A	10.494	BV	BV	125.00	200.00

Y#	Date	Mintage	Fine	VF	XF	Unc
35	1853A	5.729	BV	BV	125.00	180.00
	1854A	23.486	BV	BV	125.00	175.00
	1855A D	16.595	BV	BV	125.00	175.00
	1855A A	Inc. Ab.	BV	BV	125.00	175.00
	1855BB	1.760	BV	BV	125.00	195.00
	1855D	.045	BV	200.00	250.00	300.00
	1856A	17.303	BV	BV	125.00	175.00
	1856BB	1.125	BV	BV	125.00	195.00
	1856D	.318	BV	BV	125.00	175.00
	1857A	19.193	BV	BV	125.00	175.00
	1858A	16.861	BV	BV	125.00	180.00
	1858BB	2.017	BV	BV	125.00	175.00
	1859A	20.295	BV	BV	125.00	175.00
	1859BB	5.871	BV	BV	125.00	175.00
	1860A	10.220	BV	BV	125.00	175.00
	1860BB	5.727	BV	BV	125.00	175.00

Y#	Date	Mintage	Fine	VF	XF	Unc
40	1861A	2.607	BV	BV	125.00	170.00
	1861BB	1.423	BV	BV	125.00	170.00
	1862A	4.826	BV	BV	125.00	160.00
	1862BB	2.907	BV	BV	125.00	170.00
	1863A	3.920	BV	BV	125.00	155.00
	1863BB	4.753	BV	BV	125.00	160.00
	1864A	7.059	BV	BV	125.00	160.00
	1864BB	3.323	BV	BV	125.00	155.00
	1865A	2.951	BV	BV	125.00	170.00
	1865BB	3.088	BV	BV	125.00	165.00
	1866A	6.992	BV	BV	125.00	160.00
	1866BB	6.979	BV	BV	125.00	160.00
	1867A	2.923	BV	BV	125.00	170.00
	1867BB	4.516	BV	BV	125.00	160.00
	1868A	9.281	BV	BV	125.00	160.00
	1868BB	4.829	BV	BV	125.00	160.00
	1869A	4.046	BV	BV	125.00	160.00
	1869BB	7.317	BV	BV	125.00	160.00
	1870A	.865	BV	BV	150.00	175.00
	1870BB	1.853	BV	BV	125.00	170.00

Y#	Date	Mintage	Fine	VF	XF	Unc
55	1871A	2.508	BV	130.00	160.00	225.00
	1874A	1.216	BV	BV	125.00	170.00
	1875A	11.746	BV	BV	125.00	160.00
	1876A	8.825	BV	BV	125.00	160.00
	1877A	12.759	BV	BV	125.00	160.00
	1878A	9.189	BV	BV	125.00	160.00
	1879A	1.038	BV	BV	125.00	170.00
	1886A	.985	BV	BV	125.00	160.00
	1887A	1.231	BV	BV	125.00	170.00
	1888A	.028	BV	200.00	250.00	350.00
	1889A	.873	BV	BV	150.00	280.00

Y#	Date	Mintage	Fine	VF	XF	Unc
55	1890A	1.030	BV	BV	125.00	225.00
	1891A	.871	BV	BV	125.00	225.00
	1892A	.226	BV	BV	140.00	190.00
	1893A	2.517	BV	BV	125.00	160.00
	1894A	.491	BV	BV	125.00	175.00
	1895A	5.293	BV	BV	125.00	160.00
	1896A	5.330	BV	BV	125.00	160.00
	1897A	11.069	BV	BV	125.00	160.00
	1898A	8.866	BV	BV	125.00	160.00
	Edge inscription DIEU PROTEGE LA FRANCE					
66	1899	1.500	BV	BV	125.00	150.00
	1900	.615	BV	BV	140.00	160.00
	1901	2.643	BV	BV	125.00	150.00
	1902	2.394	BV	BV	125.00	150.00
	1903	4.405	BV	BV	125.00	150.00
	1904	7.706	BV	BV	125.00	150.00
	1905	9.158	BV	BV	125.00	150.00
	1906	14.613	BV	BV	125.00	150.00

Edge inscription LIBERTE EGALITE FRATERNITY

Y#	Date	Mintage	Fine	VF	XF	Unc
66a	1907	17.716	BV	BV	125.00	150.00
	1908	6.721	BV	BV	125.00	150.00
	1909	9.637	BV	BV	125.00	150.00
	1910	5.779	BV	BV	125.00	150.00
	1911	5.346	BV	BV	125.00	150.00
	1912	10.332	BV	BV	125.00	150.00
	1913	12.163	BV	BV	125.00	150.00
	1914	6.518	BV	BV	125.00	150.00

NOTE: Some dates from 1907-1914 have been officially restruck.

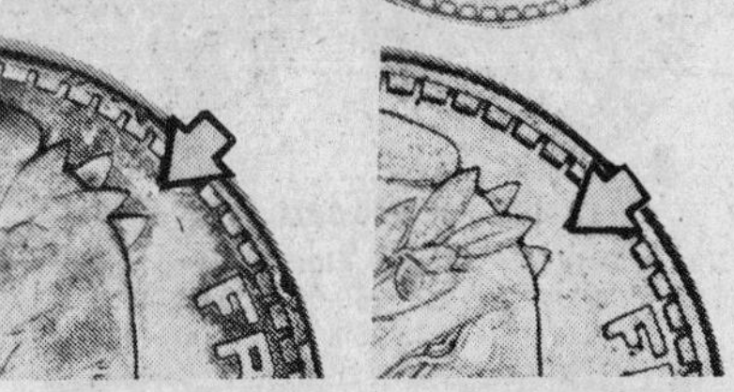

20.0000 gm., .680 SILVER, .4372 oz ASW

Short leaves — **Long leaves**

Y#	Date	Mintage	Fine	VF	XF	Unc
87	1929(SI)	3.234	BV	BV	20.00	45.00
	1933(SI)	24.447*	BV	BV	15.00	25.00
	1933(LL)	Inc. Ab.	BV	BV	15.00	25.00
	1934(SI)	11.785	BV	BV	15.00	30.00
	1936(SI)	.048	150.00	325.00	550.00	950.00
	1937(SI)	1.189	BV	16.00	35.00	65.00
	1938(SI)	10.910	BV	BV	15.00	30.00
	1939(SI)	3,918	300.00	600.00	1300.	3000.

***NOTE:** Counterfeits exist in bronze-aluminum with thin silver sheath.

3 Feathers 4 Feathers

ALUMINUM-BRONZE

Obv: GEORGES GUIRAUD behind head.

Y#	Date	Mintage	Fine	VF	XF	Unc
99	1950 (3 plumes)	5.779	1.00	2.00	5.00	11.00
	1950 (4 plumes)	—	35.00	65.00	95.00	150.00
	1950B (3 plumes)	—	2.50	6.00	25.00	70.00
	1950B (4 plumes)	—	55.00	90.00	130.00	250.00

Obv: G. GUIRAUD behind head.

Y#	Date	Mintage	Fine	VF	XF	Unc
99a	1950 (3 plumes)	120.656	6.00	14.00	28.00	50.00
	1950 (4 plumes)	Inc. Ab.	.25	.40	1.25	5.00
	1950B (3 plumes)	43.355	55.00	90.00	130.00	250.00
	1950B (4 plumes)	Inc. Ab.	.35	.65	1.75	5.00
	1951 (4 plumes)	97.922	.15	.25	1.50	6.00
	1951B (4 plumes)	46.815	.25	.50	2.00	7.00
	1952 (4 plumes)	130.281	.15	.25	1.00	5.00
	1952B (4 plumes)	54.381	.25	.50	1.50	6.50
	1953 (4 plumes)	58.522	.15	.25	1.00	5.50
	1953B (4 plumes)	42.410	.25	.50	2.00	7.00
	1954 (4 plumes)	1.573	Reported, not confirmed			
	1954B (4 plumes)	1.573	100.00	200.00	325.00	500.00
	1957 (4 plumes)	.063	Reported, not confirmed			

40 FRANCS

12.9039 gm., .900 GOLD, .3734 oz AGW

C#	Date	Mintage	Fine	VF	XF	Unc
147	ANXIA	.226	250.00	350.00	450.00	775.00
	AN12A	.253	250.00	350.00	450.00	775.00

C#	Date	Mintage	Fine	VF	XF	Unc
157.1	AN13A	.252	250.00	325.00	425.00	825.00
	AN14A	.121	250.00	300.00	425.00	1000.
157.1	AN14U	—	500.00	1000.	1500.	4000.
	AN14W	—	500.00	1000.	1500.	4000.

C#	Date	Mintage	Fine	VF	XF	Unc
157.2	1806A	.196	240.00	325.00	425.00	750.00
	1806CL	—	850.00	1700.	2900.	5500.
	1806I	7,103	275.00	350.00	525.00	850.00
	1806M	—	275.00	550.00	1400.	2500.
	1806U	.059	260.00	375.00	475.00	800.00
	1806W	4,336	285.00	375.00	600.00	950.00
	1807A	.017	275.00	350.00	500.00	825.00
	1807I	1,859	275.00	450.00	625.00	1190.
	1807M	4,994	285.00	375.00	575.00	950.00
	1807U	619 pcs.	600.00	1200.	1500.	2900.
	1807W	6,043	275.00	350.00	550.00	900.00

Laureate head

C#	Date	Mintage	Fine	VF	XF	Unc
157a	1807A	*.253	295.00	525.00	900.00	1600.
	1808A	.044	275.00	350.00	500.00	1200.
	1808CL	—	600.00	1200.	2100.	3500.
	1808H	.012	285.00	375.00	525.00	1200.
	1808M	4,226	300.00	425.00	600.00	1000.
	1808U	346 pcs.	700.00	1400.	2000.	3500.
	1808W	6,356	300.00	400.00	900.00	1350.

C#	Date	Mintage	Fine	VF	XF	Unc
167	1809A	.013	295.00	425.00	550.00	1200.
	1809M	1,402	300.00	425.00	650.00	1450.
	1809U	—	725.00	1450.	1750.	2900.
	1809W	5,925	285.00	475.00	600.00	1350.
	1810K	886 pcs.	375.00	750.00	1200.	1950.
	1810W	.057	245.00	375.00	525.00	1150.
	1811A	1.262	245.00	375.00	500.00	950.00
	1811K	6,333	285.00	375.00	600.00	1350.
	1812A	.693	245.00	325.00	500.00	1050.
	1812W	.014	260.00	325.00	550.00	1200.
	1813A	.045	260.00	400.00	525.00	1150.
	1813CL	3,070	300.00	500.00	700.00	1450.

C#	Date	Mintage	Fine	VF	XF	Unc
184	1816A	.041	260.00	400.00	625.00	950.00
	1816B	767 pcs.	450.00	900.00	1200.	1950.
	1816L	2,923	300.00	400.00	575.00	1250.
	1816Q	.011	275.00	350.00	500.00	1000.
	1816W	3,210	300.00	400.00	550.00	1250.
	1817A	.090	260.00	300.00	400.00	950.00
	1817L	377 pcs.	500.00	1000.	1400.	2350.
	1818A	.011	275.00	350.00	500.00	1150.
	1818W	.353	275.00	450.00	650.00	900.00
	1819W	4,610	285.00	375.00	525.00	1150.
	1820A	5,480	285.00	375.00	525.00	1150.
	1822A	373 pcs.	500.00	1000.	1400.	2350.
	1822H	611 pcs.	450.00	900.00	1200.	2150.
	1823A	161 pcs.	625.00	1250.	2000.	3000.
	1824A	.015	265.00	425.00	650.00	1050.

C#	Date	Mintage	Fine	VF	XF	Unc
191	1824A	.050	265.00	425.00	650.00	1050.
	1826A	62 pcs.	850.00	1700.	2600.	3550.
	1827A	106 pcs.	750.00	1500.	2000.	3000.
	1828A	.052	265.00	425.00	650.00	1050.
	1829A	.021	285.00	475.00	700.00	1150.
	1830A	.354	245.00	375.00	500.00	900.00
	1830MA	1,026	350.00	700.00	1000.	1550.
207	1831A	.063	245.00	375.00	550.00	900.00
	1832A	.022	260.00	400.00	600.00	950.00
	1832B	3,947	260.00	425.00	575.00	1050.
	1833A	.221	245.00	350.00	525.00	825.00
	1833B	1,392	295.00	500.00	650.00	1200.
	1834A	.303	245.00	350.00	500.00	800.00
	1834L	.012	280.00	375.00	675.00	1000.
	1835A	.036	260.00	400.00	600.00	750.00
	1835L	856	300.00	600.00	900.00	2000.
	1836A	.053	245.00	375.00	475.00	900.00
	1837A	.028	260.00	400.00	500.00	900.00
	1838A	.031	260.00	400.00	500.00	900.00
	1839A	23 pcs.	1150.	2300.	3300.	5000.

50 FRANCS

16.1290 gm., .900 GOLD, .4667 oz AGW

Bare head

Y#	Date	Mintage	Fine	VF	XF	Unc
36	1855A	.152	365.00	500.00	650.00	850.00
	1855BB	3,051	360.00	425.00	600.00	925.00
	1856A	.097	365.00	425.00	550.00	675.00
	1856BB	3,803	360.00	425.00	600.00	950.00
	1857A	.320	365.00	450.00	600.00	800.00
	1858A	.085	365.00	450.00	600.00	800.00
	1858BB	9,135	360.00	500.00	650.00	900.00
	1859A	.034	380.00	500.00	600.00	750.00
	1859BB	.032	365.00	475.00	600.00	800.00
	1860BB	.029	Reported, Not Confirmed			

Laureate head

Y#	Date	Mintage	Fine	VF	XF	Unc
A40	1862A	.024	360.00	425.00	550.00	900.00
	1862BB	7,310	360.00	500.00	600.00	1000.
	1863BB	8,251	360.00	500.00	600.00	1000.
	1864A	.029	360.00	425.00	550.00	900.00
	1865A	3,740	360.00	525.00	650.00	1050.
	1866A	.039	360.00	500.00	625.00	850.00
	1866BB	.017	375.00	450.00	575.00	925.00
	1867A	2,000	300.00	600.00	700.00	1100.
	1867BB	.020	360.00	425.00	550.00	900.00
	1868A	.016	375.00	450.00	575.00	925.00
	1868BB	—	350.00	700.00	800.00	1150.
	1869BB	1,795	400.00	600.00	700.00	1100.

Y#	Date	Mintage	Fine	VF	XF	Unc
56	1878A	5,294	650.00	1300.	2150.	3000.

Y#	Date	Mintage	Fine	VF	XF	Unc
56	1887A	301 pcs.	1100.	2150.	2750.	3600.
	1889A	100 pcs.	1200.	2350.	3100.	5000.
	1896A	800 pcs.	1000.	2000.	2550.	3650.
	1900A	200 pcs.	1150.	2250.	3000.	4350.
	1904A	.020	600.00	1200.	1950.	2650.

ALUMINUM-BRONZE

Y#	Date	Mintage	Fine	VF	XF	Unc
100	1950	.600	50.00	100.00	250.00	500.00
	1951	68.630	.15	.25	1.00	3.00
	1951B	11.829	.50	1.00	3.00	10.00
	1952	74.212	.15	.30	2.00	5.00
	1952B	13.432	—	.75	2.50	9.00
	1953	63.172	—	—	2.00	5.00
	1953B	23.376	—	—	2.50	7.00
	1954	.997	11.00	24.00	50.00	125.00
	1954B	6.531	2.00	5.00	12.00	45.00
	1957	.086	Reported, Not Confirmed			
	1957B	.036	Reported, Not Confirmed			
	1958(w)	.501	20.00	40.00	110.00	155.00

30.0000 gm., .900 SILVER, .8682 oz ASW
5000 Old Francs - 50 New Francs

Y#	Date	Mintage	Fine	VF	XF	Unc
112	1974	4.200	BV	BV	BV	30.00
	1975	6.055	BV	BV	BV	30.00
	1976	7.707	BV	BV	BV	30.00
	1977	*10.000	BV	BV	BV	30.00
	1978	—	BV	BV	BV	30.00
	1979	—	BV	BV	BV	30.00

100 FRANCS

32.2581 gm., .900 GOLD, .9335 oz AGW
Obv: Bare head. Rev: Similar to Y#B40.

Y#	Date	Mintage	Fine	VF	XF	Unc
37	1855A	.051	650.00	725.00	850.00	1000.
	1855BB	4.173	725.00	750.00	950.00	1150.
	1856A	.057	650.00	725.00	900.00	1200.
	1856BB	876 pcs.	700.00	1000.	1300.	2450.
	1857A	.103	650.00	800.00	1150.	1500.
	1858A	.092	650.00	800.00	1150.	1500.
	1858BB	1,928	750.00	900.00	1000.	1250.

Y#	Date	Mintage	Fine	VF	XF	Unc
37	1859A	.022	650.00	800.00	1000.	1250.
	1859BB	9,305	700.00	800.00	900.00	1175.
	1860BB	5,405	700.00	825.00	950.00	1250.

Laureate head

Y#	Date	Mintage	Fine	VF	XF	Unc
B40	1862A	6,650	800.00	1000.	1200.	1500.
	1962BB	3,078	825.00	1050.	1250.	1650.
	1863BB	3,745	825.00	1050.	1250.	1650.
	1864A	5,536	800.00	1000.	1200.	1500.
	1864BB	1,333	900.00	1200.	1400.	1800.
	1865A	1,517	900.00	1200.	1400.	1800.
	1866A	9.041	775.00	950.00	1050.	1400.
	1866BB	3,075	825.00	1050.	1250.	1600.
	1867A	4,309	850.00	1100.	1300.	1600.
	1867BB	2,807	875.00	1150.	1350.	1700.
	1868A	2,315	850.00	1100.	1350.	1700.
	1868BB	—	950.00	1300.	1600.	2550.
	1869A	.029	725.00	850.00	950.00	1250.
	1869BB	.014	750.00	900.00	1000.	1350.
	1870A	.010	3500.	7000.	9000.	11500.

Edge inscription: DIEU PROTEGE LA FRANCE

Y#	Date	Mintage	Fine	VF	XF	Unc
57.1	1878A	.013	650.00	800.00	900.00	1100.
	1879A	.039	650.00	800.00	925.00	1150.
	1881A	.022	650.00	800.00	975.00	1200.
	1882A	.037	650.00	800.00	925.00	1150.
	1885A	2,894	700.00	900.00	1100.	1550.
	1886A	.039	650.00	800.00	925.00	1150.
	1887A	234 pcs.	775.00	1550.	3000.	4750.
	1889A	100 pcs.	1375.	2750.	4000.	6000.
	1894A	143 pcs.	1175.	2350.	3550.	5550.
	1896A	400 pcs.	650.00	1250.	1950.	3550.
	1899A	.010	650.00	800.00	1000.	1250.
	1900A	.020	650.00	875.00	975.00	1200.
	1901A	.010	650.00	800.00	1000.	1250.
	1902A	.010	650.00	800.00	1000.	1250.
	1903A	.010	650.00	800.00	1000.	1250.
	1904A	.020	650.00	875.00	975.00	1200.
	1905A	.010	650.00	800.00	1000.	1250.
	1906A	.030	650.00	825.00	925.00	1250.

Edge inscription: LIBERTE EGALITE FRATERNITY

Y#	Date	Mintage	Fine	VF	XF	Unc
57.2	1907A	.020	650.00	750.00	900.00	1100.
	1908A	.023	650.00	750.00	900.00	1100.
	1909A	.020	650.00	750.00	900.00	1100.
	1910A	.020	650.00	750.00	900.00	1100.
	1911A	.030	650.00	750.00	900.00	1100.
	1912A	.020	650.00	750.00	900.00	1100.

Y#	Date	Mintage	Fine	VF	XF	Unc
57.2	1913A	.030	650.00	750.00	900.00	1100.
	1914A	1,281	2000.	4000.	6000.	8000.

69.5500 gm., .900 GOLD, .1895 oz AGW

Y#	Date	Mintage	Fine	VF	XF	Unc
88	1929	15 pcs.	—	—	3000.	3500.
	1932	50 pcs.	—	—	3500.	4500.
	1933	300 pcs.	—	—	2000.	3000.
	1934	10 pcs.	—	—	4000.	5000.
	1935	6.102	350.00	600.00	750.00	1000.
	1936	7.689	350.00	600.00	750.00	1000.

COPPER-NICKEL

Y#	Date	Mintage	Fine	VF	XF	Unc
101	1954	97.285	.35	.75	2.00	5.00
	1954B	86.261	.35	.50	1.00	4.00
	1955	152.517	.35	.50	1.00	3.50
	1955B	136.585	.35	.50	1.00	3.50
	1956	7.578	2.00	4.00	8.00	25.00
	1956B	19.154	.50	.75	1.50	7.00
	1957	11.312	.60	1.00	1.75	8.00
	1957B	25.702	.50	.75	1.50	7.00
	1958(w)	3.256	2.50	5.00	7.50	16.00
	1958(o)	Inc. Ab.	20.00	37.50	65.00	120.00
	1958B	54.072	.75	1.50	2.50	10.00

MEDALLIC ISSUES

"Mint Visit"

(5 CENTIMES)

BRONZE

LILLE MINT

Emperor and Empress to the Bourse.

Y#	Date	Mintage	Fine	VF	XF	Unc
A16	1853(w)	2,000	12.00	27.50	55.00	125.00
	SILVER					
A16a	1853(w)	—	50.00	110.00	175.00	325.00
	GOLD					
A16b	1853(w)	—	400.00	700.00	1200.	2000.

(10 CENTIMES)

BRONZE

LILLE MINT

Emperor and Empress to the Bourse.

Y#	Date	Mintage	Fine	VF	XF	Unc
A17	1853(w)	—	12.00	25.00	55.00	110.00
	SILVER					
A17a	1853(w)	—	50.00	110.00	175.00	325.00
	GOLD					
A17b	1853(w)	l pcs.	—	—	Rare	—

BRONZE
Monument of Napoleon I Erected.

Y#	Date	Mintage	Fine	VF	XF	Unc
C17	1854(w)	—	16.50	35.00	75.00	175.00
			SILVER			
C17a	1854(w)	—	50.00	110.00	175.00	325.00
			GOLD			
C17b	1854(w)	—	400.00	700.00	1200.	2000.

BRONZE

PARIS MINT
Napoleon III to the Bourse.

Y#	Date	Mintage	Fine	VF	XF	Unc
B17	1854(a)	—	12.00	25.00	55.00	110.00
			SILVER			
B17a	1854(a)	—	50.00	110.00	175.00	325.00
			GOLD			
B17b	1854(a)	—	400.00	700.00	1200.	2000.

PRETENDER ISSUES

Louis XVII

30 SOLS

BRONZE
Obv: Bust left; ESSAI below.
Rev: Value in wreath.

KM#	Date	Fine	VF	XF	Unc
PTE1	ND	90.00	200.00	500.00	900.00

6 DENIERS

BRONZE
Obv: FLEUR DELYS; L above, Roman numeral XVII below.
Rev: Shield divides value.

KM#	Date	Fine	VF	XF	Unc
PT2	ND	75.00	165.00	325.00	700.00

BRONZE (BRASS?)

KM#	Date	Fine	VF	XF	Unc
PT3	ND	90.00	175.00	500.00	900.00

BRONZE
Obv: Bust left; ESSAI below

KM#	Date	Fine	VF	XF	Unc
PTE4	ND	90.00	175.00	500.00	900.00

Rev: PIECE D'ESSAI and date in wreath.

KM#	Date	Fine	VF	XF	Unc
PTE5	1792	90.00	175.00	500.00	900.00

NOTE: These pieces are considered souvenir issues made by Royalist Partisans (Patterns).

Napoleon II

CENTIME

BRONZE, 2.85gm.
Rev: Value and "ESSAI" in wreath.

KM#	Date	Fine	VF	XF	Unc
PTE6	1816	30.00	60.00	115.00	150.00

3 CENTIMES

BRONZE, 7.07gm.
Rev: Value and "ESSAI" in wreath.

KM#	Date	Fine	VF	XF	Unc
PTE7	1816	35.00	70.00	125.00	180.00

5 CENTIMES

BRONZE, 10.67gm.
Rev: Value and "ESSAI" in wreath.

KM#	Date	Fine	VF	XF	Unc
PTE8	1816	37.50	75.00	140.00	200.00

10 CENTIMES

BRONZE
Rev: Value and "ESSAI" in wreath.

KM#	Date	Fine	VF	XF	Unc
PTE9	1816	47.50	85.00	165.00	230.00

1/4 FRANC

SILVER, 1.24gm.
Obv: Young head left.
Rev: Value and "ESSAI" in wreath; date below.

KM#	Date	Fine	VF	XF	Unc
PTE10	1816	60.00	105.00	215.00	300.00
		BRONZE			
PTE10a	1816	35.00	65.00	110.00	180.00

1/2 FRANC

SILVER, 2.35gm.
Obv: Young head left.
Rev: Value and "ESSAI" in wreath; date below.

KM#	Date	Fine	VF	XF	Unc
PTE11	1816	60.00	120.00	235.00	330.00
		BRONZE			
PTE11a	1816	45.00	75.00	115.00	200.00

FRANC

SILVER
Obv: Young head left.
Rev: Value and "ESSAI" in wreath; date below.

KM#	Date	Fine	VF	XF	Unc
PTE12	1816	90.00	170.00	335.00	500.00
		BRONZE			
PTE12a	1816	60.00	120.00	235.00	300.00

2 FRANCS

SILVER
Obv: Young head left.
Rev: Value and "ESSAI" in wreath; date below.

KM#	Date	Fine	VF	XF	Unc
PTE13	1816	140.00	290.00	410.00	750.00
		BRONZE			
PTE13a	1816	70.00	155.00	250.00	400.00

5 FRANCS

SILVER

KM#	Date	Fine	VF	XF	Unc
PTE14	1816	250.00	600.00	1250.	1600.
		BRONZE			
PTE14a	1816	95.00	170.00	335.00	500.00
		GOLD			
PTE14b	1816	1000.	1700.	2200.	3500.

NOTE: Unofficial pieces (Patterns?) struck during the reign of Napoleon III, possibly to give continuity to the dynasty.

Henry V

5 CENTIMES

SILVER
Obv: Small uniformed bust left.
Rev: Value in wreath; date below.

KM#	Date	Fine	VF	XF	Unc
PT15	1832	30.00	55.00	85.00	300.00
		Obv: Head right.			
PT16	1832	35.00	65.00	105.00	350.00
		Smaller size Rev: Value; date below divided by lys.			
PT17	1832	35.00	65.00	105.00	350.00

10 CENTIMES

SILVER
Obv: Small uniformed bust left.
Rev: Value in wreath; date below.

KM#	Date	Fine	VF	XF	Unc
PT18	1832	35.00	65.00	105.00	350.00
		Obv: Larger uniformed bust left.			
PT19	1832	35.00	65.00	105.00	350.00
		Obv: Head left			
PT20	1832	35.00	65.00	105.00	0
		Smaller size Rev: Value; date below divided by lys.			
PT21	1832	40.00	75.00	120.00	375.00

1/4 FRANC

SILVER
Obv: Young head left.
Rev: Crowned arms divides value; date below.
Plain edge.

KM#	Date	Fine	VF	XF	Unc
PT22	1832	40.00	95.00	12K.00	300.00
	1833	40.00	95.00	12K.00	300.00

BRONZE

KM#	Date	Fine	VF	XF	Unc
PT22a	1833	25.00	50.00	100.00	135.00

GILT BRONZE
Piedfort

KM#	Date	Fine	VF	XF	Unc
PTP22b	1833	60.00	135.00	210.00	300.00

1/2 FRANC

SILVER

KM#	Date	Fine	VF	XF	Unc
PT23	1832	40.00	75.00	100.00	200.00
	1833	40.00	75.00	100.00	200.00

BRONZE

KM#	Date	Fine	VF	XF	Unc
PT23a	1833	27.50	55.00	80.00	140.00

Obv: Uniformed bust left, child's head.

KM#	Date	Fine	VF	XF	Unc
PT24	1833	60.00	130.00	200.00	300.00

Obv: Small uniformed bust left.

KM#	Date	Fine	VF	XF	Unc
PT25	1833	45.00	85.00	125.00	240.00

KM#	Date	Fine	VF	XF	Unc
PT26	1858A	75.00	150.00	300.00	500.00

FRANC

SILVER

KM#	Date	Fine	VF	XF	Unc
PT27	1831	15.00	35.00	100.00	250.00

Plain edge

KM#	Date	Fine	VF	XF	Unc
PT28.1	1831	18.00	40.00	125.00	400.00

Reeded edge

KM#	Date	Fine	VF	XF	Unc
PT28.2	1831	18.00	40.00	125.00	400.00
	1832	25.00	55.00	135.00	475.00

Piedfort, plain edge.

KM#	Date	Fine	VF	XF	Unc
PTP28.1	1832	150.00	275.00	375.00	600.00

GOLD

KM#	Date	Fine	VF	XF	Unc
PTP28.1a	1832	600.00	700.00	800.00	1000.00

BRONZE

KM#	Date	Fine	VF	XF	Unc
PTP28.1b	1832	75.00	100.00	150.00	250.00

SILVER
Double piedfort, plain edge.

KM#	Date	Fine	VF	XF	Unc
PTP28.2	1832	225.00	350.00	400.00	600.00

T.W.I. under bust, plain edge.

KM#	Date	Fine	VF	XF	Unc
P29	1832	25.00	50.00	135.00	475.00

2 FRANCS

SILVER
Rev: Crowned arms in wreath; "ESSAI" below.

KM#	Date	Fine	VF	XF	Unc
PTE30	ND	100.00	160.00	250.00	450.00

BRONZE (BRASS?)

KM#	Date	Fine	VF	XF	Unc
PTE30a	ND	55.00	150.00	200.00	300.00

SILVER
Rev: Crowned arms and value in wreath; date below.
Reeded edge

KM#	Date	Fine	VF	XF	Unc
PT31.1	1831	100.00	200.00	400.00	600.00
	1832	115.00	220.00	425.00	650.00
	1833	125.00	235.00	460.00	725.00

Lettered edge

KM#	Date	Fine	VF	XF	Unc
PT31.2	1833	125.00	235.00	460.00	725.00

BRONZE
Plain edge

KM#	Date	Fine	VF	XF	Unc
PT31.3	1833	25.00	55.00	100.00	200.00

SILVER
Piedfort.

KM#	Date	Fine	VF	XF	Unc
PTP31.4	1832	150.00	200.00	350.00	800.00

GOLD

KM#	Date	Fine	VF	XF	Unc
PTP31.4a	1832	300.00	400.00	550.00	1200.

SILVER
Double piedfort.

KM#	Date	Fine	VF	XF	Unc
PTP31.5	1832	175.00	235.00	390.00	950.00

5 FRANCS

SILVER

KM#	Date	Fine	VF	XF	Unc
PT32	1830	200.00	350.00	450.00	800.00

BRONZE

KM#	Date	Fine	VF	XF	Unc
PT32a	1830	80.00	150.00	250.00	400.00

PEWTER

KM#	Date	Fine	VF	XF	Unc
PT32b	1830	40.00	80.00	135.00	200.00

BRONZE, 17.19 gm.
Obv: Head left.
Rev: Crowned arms in wreath; date below.

KM#	Date	Fine	VF	XF	Unc
PT33	1831	60.00	125.00	225.00	350.00

PEWTER

KM#	Date	Fine	VF	XF	Unc
PT33a	1831	40.00	80.00	135.00	200.00

33.3500 SGM., SILVER
Rev: Crowned arms in wreath; date below, value at sides of arms.

KM#	Date	Fine	VF	XF	Unc
PT35.1	1831	200.00	375.00	475.00	600.00
	1832	200.00	375.00	475.00	600.00

Piedfort (double thickness) - plain edge.

KM#	Date	Fine	VF	XF	Unc
PTP35.2	1832	350.00	450.00	600.00	1000.

Double piedfort (quadruple thickness).

KM#	Date	Fine	VF	XF	Unc
PTP35.3	1832	450.00	550.00	700.00	1200.

Quadruple piedfort (octuple thickness).

KM#	Date	Fine	VF	XF	Unc
PTP35.4	1832	—	—	—	—

BRONZE

KM#	Date	Fine	VF	XF	Unc
PT35.5	1831	50.00	75.00	125.00	275.00
	1832	—	—	—	—

GOLD

KM#	Date	Fine	VF	XF	Unc
PT35.5a	1832	750.00	850.00	1000.	2000.

BRONZE
Visit of Henry V to England Commemorative
Rev: 3 line inscription within outer legend; date below.

KM#	Date	Fine	VF	XF	Unc
PT36	1843	100.00	165.00	300.00	500.00

SILVER

KM#	Date	Fine	VF	XF	Unc
PT36a	1843	—	—	—	—

GOLD

KM#	Date	Fine	VF	XF	Unc
PT36b	1843	1000.	1150.	1350.	2100.

SILVER
Plain edge

KM#	Date	Fine	VF	XF	Unc
PT37.1	1871	250.00	375.00	560.00	1200.

Reeded edge

KM#	Date	Fine	VF	XF	Unc
PT37.2	1871	250.00	375.00	560.00	1200.
		BRONZE			
PT37.2a	1871	100.00	160.00	275.00	500.00
		GOLD			
PT37.2b	1871	1000.	1150.	1350.	2100.

SILVER
Plain edge

KM#	Date	Fine	VF	XF	Unc
PT38.1	1873	400.00	800.00	1200.	Rare
		Piedfort (double thickness).			
PTP38.2	1873	600.00	725.00	900.00	1300.
		BRONZE			
PT38.1a	1873	100.00	160.00	275.00	500.00

Napoleon IV

10 CENTIMES

BRONZE, 9.61gm.

KM#	Date	Fine	VF	XF	Unc
PT39	1874	60.00	125.00	250.00	375.00

20 CENTIMES

SILVER
Obv: Head left.
Rev: Crown above value and date.

KM#	Date	Fine	VF	XF	Unc
PT40	1874	65.00	125.00	250.00	375.00

50 CENTIMES

SILVER
Obv: Head left.
Rev: Crown over value and date.

KM#	Date	Fine	VF	XF	Unc
PT41	1874	90.00	185.00	375.00	700.00

FRANC

SILVER

KM#	Date	Fine	VF	XF	Unc
PT42	1874	125.00	250.00	500.00	750.00

2 FRANCS

SILVER
Obv: Head left.
Rev: Crowned and mantled arms divide value; date below.

KM#	Date	Fine	VF	XF	Unc
PT43	1874	190.00	375.00	750.00	1150.

5 FRANCS

SILVER, 25.62gm.
Plain edge.

KM#	Date	Fine	VF	XF	Unc
PT45.1	1870	375.00	750.00	1500.	2000.
		Reeded edge.			
PT45.2	1874	300.00	600.00	1300.	1800.

TOKEN ISSUES

MONNAIES DE CONFIANCE

Boyere

1 SOL 6 DENIERS

BILLON
Obv: Liberty cap on pole above crossed fasces.
Rev: 6 line inscription; date in outside legend.

KM#	Date	Mintage	VG	Fine	VF	XF
T1	1792	—	—	—	—	—

Brun

1 SOL 6 DENIERS

BILLON
Obv: Rooster left below banner.
Rev: 7 line inscription in outside legend.

KM#	Date	Mintage	VG	Fine	VF	XF
T2	ND	—	—	—	—	—

1 SOL 3 DENIERS

COPPER
Obv: 4 line inscription over branches.
Rev: 3 line inscription in outside legend.

KM#	Date	Mintage	VG	Fine	VF	XF
T3	AN 4 (1792)	—	—	—	—	—

Caisse Metallique

18 DENIERS

BILLON
Obv: Liberty cap on pole above crossed fasces.
Rev: 4 line inscription; date in exergue.

KM#	Date	Mintage	VG	Fine	VF	XF
T4	1792	—	—	—	—	—
		COPPER				
T4a	1792	—	—	—	—	—

BILLON
Obv: Epee and branch replace crossed fasces.

KM#	Date	Mintage	VG	Fine	VF	XF
T5	1792	—	—	—	—	—
		SILVER				
T5a	1792	—	—	—	—	—

Caisse Populaire

18 DENIERS

BILLON
Obv: Liberty cap on pole above crossed fasces in outside legend.
Rev: 5 line inscription in circle; legend around border.

KM#	Date	Mintage	VG	Fine	VF	XF
T6	1792	—	—	—	—	—

Clemanson

2 SOLS

COPPER
Obv: Fasces topped by liberty cap in circle; legend around border.
Rev: 9 line inscription in circle; legend around border.

KM#	Date	Mintage	VG	Fine	VF	XF
T7	1792	—	—	—	—	—
		BRASS				
T7a	1792	—	—	—	—	—

COPPER
Obv: Trophy of arms added behind fasces.

KM#	Date	Mintage	VG	Fine	VF	XF
T8	1792	—	—	—	—	—
		BELL METAL				
T8a	1792	—	—	—	—	—

Dayrolant

10 SOLS

COPPER
Obv: Bust of Mirabeau.
Rev: 8 line inscription in circle; legend around border.

KM#	Date	Mintage	VG	Fine	VF	XF
T9	1792	—	—	—	—	—

Fabrique Du Vast

10 CENTIMES

COPPER
Obv: Value in outer legend. Uniface.

KM#	Date	Mintage	VG	Fine	VF	XF
T10	ND	—	—	—	—	—

5 CENTIMES

COPPER
Obv: Value in outer legend.

KM#	Date	Mintage	VG	Fine	VF	XF
T11	ND	—	—	—	—	—

Givry

5 SOLS

COPPER
Obv: Lis in circle; outer legend.
Rev: 4 Line inscription.

KM#	Date	Mintage	VG	Fine	VF	XF
T12	ND	—	—	—	—	—

Leclech et Comp. Clermont

10 SOLS

SILVER
Obv: 5 line inscription in wreath; legend around border.
Rev: 6 line inscription; legend around border.

KM#	Date	Mintage	VG	Fine	VF	XF
T13	1792	—	—	—	—	—

Rev: Value in center of outside legend.

KM#	Date	Mintage	VG	Fine	VF	XF
T14	L'AN4 (1792)	—	—	—	850.00	—

Lefevre, Lesage et Comp.

5 SOLS

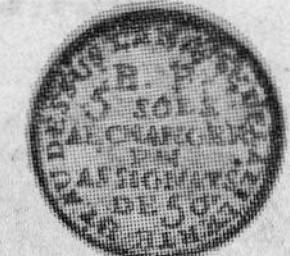

SILVER

KM#	Date	Mintage	VG	Fine	VF	XF
T15	1792	—	—	—	—	—

KM#	Date	Mintage	VG	Fine	VF	XF
T16	1792	—	—	—	—	—

Rev: L after 50.

KM#	Date	Mintage	VG	Fine	VF	XF
T17	1792	—	—	—	—	—

10 SOLS

SILVER

KM#	Date	Mintage	VG	Fine	VF	XF
T18	1792	—	—	—	—	—

KM#	Date	Mintage	VG	Fine	VF	XF
T19	1792	—	—	—	—	—

20 SOLS

SILVER

KM#	Date	Mintage	VG	Fine	VF	XF
T20	1792	—	—	—	—	—

KM#	Date	Mintage	VG	Fine	VF	XF
T21	1792	—	—	—	—	—

Monneron

1 SOL

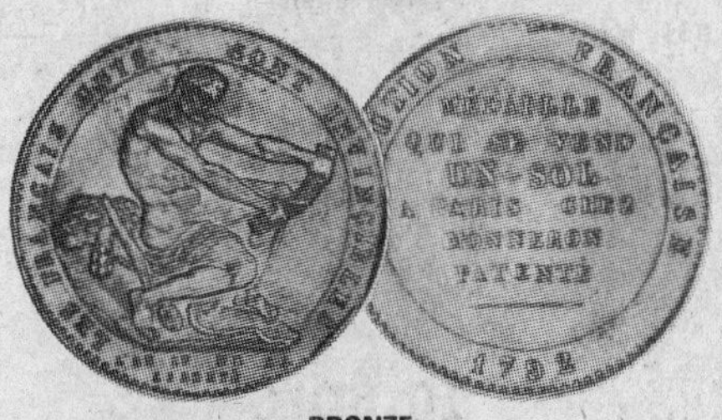

BRONZE

KM#	Date	Mintage	VG	Fine	VF	XF
T22	1792	—	—	—	—	—

2 SOLS

BRONZE

KM#	Date	Mintage	VG	Fine	VF	XF
T23	1791	—	3.00	5.00	8.50	15.00

SILVER

KM#	Date	Mintage	VG	Fine	VF	XF
T23a	1791	—	—	—	—	—

BRONZE
Obv: M.R. at base of column.

KM#	Date	Mintage	VG	Fine	VF	XF
T24	1791	—	—	—	—	—

KM#	Date	Mintage	VG	Fine	VF	XF
T25	1792	—	—	—	8.50	15.00

SILVER

KM#	Date	Mintage	VG	Fine	VF	XF
T25a	1792	—	—	—	—	—

BRONZE
Rev: No brackets on "PATENTE".

KM#	Date	Mintage	VG	Fine	VF	XF
T26	1792	—	—	—	8.50	15.00

KM#	Date	Mintage	VG	Fine	VF	XF
T27	1792	—	—	—	—	—

5 SOLS

BRONZE
Obv: Alleginace scene; Roman numeral date in exergue.
Rev: 6 line legend and date in exergue; legend around border.

KM#	Date	Mintage	VG	Fine	VF	XF
T28	1791	—	—	—	—	—

Rev: 6 line inscription in circle; no date in outer legend.

KM#	Date	Mintage	VG	Fine	VF	XF
T29	1791	—	—	—	—	—

Obv: Allegiance scene; Arabic date in exergue.
Rev: 7 line inscription; "L'AN III" in inner circle; legend around border.

KM#	Date	Mintage	VG	Fine	VF	XF
T30	1792	—	—	—	—	—

SILVER

KM#	Date	Mintage	VG	Fine	VF	XF
T30a	1792	—	—	—	—	—

BRONZE
Rev: "L'AN IV" is date in inner circle.

KM#	Date	Mintage	VG	Fine	VF	XF
T31	1792	—	9.50	15.00	20.00	35.00

Rev: No ornament after 50.

KM#	Date	Mintage	VG	Fine	VF	XF
T32	1792	—	9.50	15.00	20.00	35.00

KM#	Date	Mintage	VG	Fine	VF	XF
T33	1792	—	—	—	—	—

KM#	Date	Mintage	VG	Fine	VF	XF
T34	1792	—	—	—	—	—

KM#	Date	Mintage	VG	Fine	VF	XF
T35	1792	—	20.00	35.00	55.00	85.00
		SILVER				
T35a	1792	—	—	—	—	—

Monnoye D'urgence

2 SOLS

SILVER
Obv: 7 line inscription.
Rev: Outer legend around circle.

KM#	Date	Mintage	VG	Fine	VF	XF
T36	1792	—	—	—	—	—

Montagny

2 SOLS 6 DENIERS

COPPER

KM#	Date	Mintage	VG	Fine	VF	XF
T37	1791	—	7.50	15.00	30.00	50.00

Potter

5 SOLS

SILVER

KM#	Date	Mintage	VG	Fine	VF	XF
T38	1792	—	—	—	—	—
		Larger letters.				
T39	1792	—	—	—	—	—

7 SOLS

SILVER
Obv: 8 line inscription.
Rev: 6 line inscription.

KM#	Date	Mintage	VG	Fine	VF	XF
T40	1792	—	—	—	—	—

10 SOLS

SILVER
Obv: 8 line inscription.
Rev: 6 line inscription.

KM#	Date	Mintage	VG	Fine	VF	XF
41	1792	—	—	—	—	—
		Rev: Value as "10 SOUS".				
42	1792	—	—	—	—	—

20 SOLS

SILVER

KM#	Date	Mintage	VG	Fine	VF	XF
43	1792	—	—	—	—	—

Thevenon

3 SOLS

BRONZE

KM#	Date	Mintage	VG	Fine	VF	XF
44	L'AN III	—	30.00	50.00	75.00	125.00
		SILVER				
44a	L'AN III	—	—	—	—	—

French 'Notgeld' was issued 1915-1932 throughout France and the empire by local government units, chambers of commerce, private merchants and organizations. Most are low denomination from 5 Centimes - 1 Franc, and are struck in aluminum and other base metals.

CHAMBER OF COMMERCE

1 Franc, 1922, Evruex Chamber of Commerce

PROVINCIAL

25 Centimes, 1927, Department De La H'Garonne (Toulouse)

PRIVATE SOCIETY

10 Centimes, 1921, Herault Society of Food Wholesalers

MERCHANT

10 Centimes, ND, Georges Malgrain of Melun, (contractor)

MILITARY

25 Centimes, ND, Girard NCO mess hall of the 77th Infantry

For detailed listings of token issues refer to A CATALOGUE of FRENCH EMERGENCY TOKENS of 1914-1922 by Robert Lamb and MONNAIES et BILLETS de NECESSITE 1914-1931 by Argus Thimonier.

NCLT ISSUES

ESSAIS

Standard metals unless otherwise noted

KM#	Date	Mintage	Identification	Issue Price	Mkt. Val.
E32	1861(a)	—	5 Francs	—	2000.
E56	1878(a)	—	50 Francs	—	1800.
E57	1878(a)	—	100 Francs	—	3500.
E69	1903(a)	—	25 Centimes	—	45.00
E70	1904(a)	—	25 Centimes	—	45.00
E61a	1908(a)	—	10 Centimes, Aluminum	—	25.00
E60	1910(a)	—	5 Centimes	—	25.00
E88	1929(a)	—	100 Francs	—	925.00
E88	1929(a)	—	100 Francs	—	925.00
E88a	1929(a)	—	100 Francs, Gilt Bronze	—	125.00
E84	1933(a)	—	5 Francs	—	45.00
E84	1934(a)	—	5 Francs	—	45.00
E86a	1938(a)	—	10 Francs, Nickel	—	75.00
E87a	1938(a)	—	20 Francs, Nickel	—	75.00
EV91	1941(a)	—	10 Centimes	—	25.00
EV90	1941(a)	—	20 Centimes	—	25.00
EV92	1941(a)	—	20 Centimes	—	25.00
EV93	1943(a)	300	10 Centimes	—	25.00
EV96	1943(a)	300	2 Francs	—	35.00
E74	1944(a)	300	10 Centimes	—	25.00
E75	1945(a)	40	20 Centimes	—	75.00
E84b	1945(a)	1100	5 Francs	—	45.00

KM#	Date	Mintage	Identification	Issue Price	Mkt. Val.
E86b	1945(a)	1100	10 Francs	—	55.00
E98	1950(g)	1700	10 Francs	—	25.00
E99a	1950(a)	1700	20 Francs	—	30.00
E100	1950(a)	1700	50 Francs	—	35.00
E99a	1951(a)	28	20 Francs	—	380.00
E101	1954(a)	1200	100 Francs	—	45.00
E108	1959(a)	4000	1 Franc	—	22.50
E110	1959(a)	4000	5 Francs	—	27.50
E110	1959(a)	Inc. Ab.	5 Francs, small 5 in date	—	27.50
E102	1961(a)	3500	1 Centime	—	20.00
E103	1961(a)	3500	5 Centimes	—	20.00
E104	1962(a)	3500	10 Centimes	—	20.00
E105	1962(a)	3500	20 Centimes	—	20.00
E106	1962(a)	3500	50 Centimes	—	20.00
E111	1964(a)	3500	10 Francs	—	350.00
E109	1965(a)	4700	1/2 Franc	—	20.00
EA104	1966(a)	4128	5 Centimes	—	20.00
E110a	1970(a)	5000	5 Francs	—	20.00

PIEFORTS (P)

With ESSAI (PE)

(Double Thickness)

Standard metals unless otherwise noted

KM#	Date	Mintage	Identification	Issue Price	Mkt. Val.
PE86	1929	—	10 Francs	—	—
PE87	1929	—	20 Francs	—	—
P73b	1941	—	10 Centimes	—	—
PEV96	1943	—	2 Francs	—	85.00
PE75	1945	104	20 Centimes	—	85.00
PE84	1945	104	5 Francs	—	100.00
PE87a	1945	104	20 Francs, Copper-Nickel	—	125.00
PE80a	1946	104	50 Centimes	—	75.00
PE81a	1946	104	1 Franc	—	85.00
PE82a	1946	104	2 Francs	—	100.00
PE86b	1946	104	10 Francs	—	125.00
PE98	1952	104	10 Francs	—	85.00
PE99a	1952	104	20 Francs	—	95.00
PE100	1952	104	50 Francs	—	100.00
PE101	1954	104	100 Francs	—	125.00
PE101a	1958	65	100 Francs, Silver	—	200.00
PE108	1959	104	1 Franc	—	85.00
PE110	1959	100	5 Francs	—	125.00
P108a	1960	50	1 Franc, Silver	—	—
P108b	1960	20	1 Franc, Gold	—	—
P108	1960	500	1 Franc	—	—
P110b	1960	500	5 Francs, Silver	—	—
P110c	1960	50	5 Francs, Gold	—	—
PE102	1961	104	1 Centime	—	65.00
PE103	1961	104	5 Centimes	—	65.00
P103	1961	500	5 Centimes	—	65.00
P103a	1961	50	5 Centimes, Silver	—	125.00
P103b	1961	20	5 Centimes, Gold	—	—
PE104	1962	104	10 Centimes	—	75.00
PE105	1962	104	20 Centimes	—	85.00
PE106	1962	104	50 Centimes	—	85.00
P102	1962	500	1 Centime	—	65.00
P102a	1962	50	1 Centime, Silver	—	100.00
P102b	1962	20	1 Centime, Gold	—	—
P104	1962	500	10 Centimes	—	75.00
P104a	1962	50	10 Centimes, Silver	—	110.00
P104b	1962	20	10 Centimes, Gold	—	—
P105	1962	500	20 Centimes	—	85.00
P105a	1962	50	20 Centimes, Silver	—	135.00
P105b	1962	20	20 Centimes, Gold	—	—
P106	1962	500	50 Centimes	—	85.00
P106a	1962	50	50 Centimes, Silver	—	135.00
P106b	1962	20	50 Centimes, Gold	—	—
P107	1965	500	1/2 Franc	—	60.00
P107a	1965	50	1/2 Franc, Silver	—	100.00
P107b	1965	20	1/2 Franc, Gold	—	—
P111	1965	500	10 Francs	—	250.00
P111a	1965	50	10 Francs, Gold	—	—
PA104	1966	500	5 Centimes	—	65.00
PA104a	1966	50	5 Centimes, Silver	—	125.00
PA104b	1966	20	5 Centimes, Gold	—	—
P102	1967	500	1 Centime	3.00	35.00
P102a	1967	50	1 Centime, Silver	15.00	100.00
P102b	1967	20	1 Centime, Gold	35.00	—
PA104	1967	500	5 Centimes	3.00	40.00
PA104a	1967	50	5 Centimes, Silver	15.00	100.00
PA104b	1967	20	5 Centimes, Gold	40.00	—
P104	1967	500	10 Centimes	3.00	45.00
P104a	1967	50	10 Centimes, Silver	15.00	110.00
P104b	1967	20	10 Centimes, Gold	60.00	—
P105	1967	500	20 Centimes	3.00	45.00
P105a	1967	50	20 Centimes, Silver	15.00	110.00
P105b	1967	20	20 Centimes, Gold	80.00	—
P106	1967	500	50 Centimes	4.00	50.00
P106a	1967	50	50 Centimes, Silver	24.00	115.00
P106b	1967	20	50 Centimes, Gold	140.00	—
P107	1967	500	1/2 Franc	4.00	50.00
P107a	1967	50	1/2 Franc, Silver	15.00	110.00
P107b	1967	20	1/2 Franc, Gold	90.00	—
P108	1967	500	1 Franc	4.00	50.00
P108a	1967	50	1 Franc, Silver	18.00	120.00
P108b	1967	20	1 Franc, Gold	110.00	—
P110	1967	500	5 Francs	24.00	75.00
P110a	1967	50	5 Francs, Gold	180.00	—
P111	1967	500	10 Francs	60.00	250.00
P111a	1967	50	10 Francs, Gold	400.00	—
P102	1968	500	1 Centime	3.00	35.00
P102a	1968	50	1 Centime, Silver	15.00	100.00
P102b	1968	20	1 Centime, Gold	35.00	—
PA104	1968	500	5 Centimes	3.00	40.00
PA104a	1968	50	5 Centimes, Silver	15.00	100.00
PA104b	1968	20	5 Centimes, Gold	40.00	—
P104	1968	500	10 Centimes	3.00	45.00
P104a	1968	50	10 Centimes, Silver	15.00	110.00
P104b	1968	20	10 Centimes, Gold	60.00	—
P105	1968	500	20 Centimes	3.00	45.00
P105a	1968	50	20 Centimes, Silver	15.00	110.00
P105b	1968	20	20 Centimes, Gold	80.00	—
P107	1968	500	1/2 Franc	4.00	50.00
P107a	1968	50	1/2 Franc, Silver	15.00	110.00
P107b	1968	20	1/2 Franc, Gold	90.00	
P108	1968	500	1 Franc	4.00	50.00
P108a	1968	50	1 Franc, Silver	18.00	120.00
P108b	1968	20	1 Franc, Gold	110.00	—
P110	1968	500	5 Francs	24.00	75.00
P110c	1968	50	5 Francs, Gold	180.00	—
P111	1968	500	10 Francs	60.00	250.00
P111a	1968	50	10 Francs, Gold	400.00	—
P110a	1970	500	5 Francs	9.00	35.00
P110b	1970	200	5 Francs, Silver	24.00	75.00
P110c	1970	100	5 Francs, Gold	180.00	—
P110d	1970	100	5 Francs, Platinum	909.00	—
P102	1971	500	1 Centime	9.00	35.00
P102a	1971	100	1 Centime, Silver	15.00	70.00
P102b	1971	100	1 Centime, Gold	42.00	175.00
PA104	1971	500	5 Centimes	9.00	40.00
PA104a	1971	100	5 Centimes, Silver	15.00	75.00
PA104b	1971	100	5 Centimes, Gold	49.00	200.00
P104	1971	500	10 Centimes	9.00	45.00
P104a	1971	100	10 Centimes, Silver	15.00	70.00
P104b	1971	100	10 Centimes, Gold	73.00	300.00
P105	1971	500	20 Centimes	9.00	45.00
P105a	1971	100	20 Centimes, Silver	15.00	70.00
P105b	1971	100	20 Centimes, Gold	98.00	400.00
P107	1971	500	1/2 Franc	9.00	50.00
P107a	1971	100	1/2 Franc, Silver	15.00	80.00
P107b	1971	100	1/2 Franc, Gold	102.00	450.00
P108	1971	500	1 Franc	9.00	50.00
P108a	1971	100	1 Franc, Silver	18.00	80.00
P108b	1971	250	1 Franc, Gold	132.00	550.00
P110a	1971	1000	5 Francs	9.00	20.00
P110b	1971	250	5 Francs, Silver	36.00	50.00
P110c	1971	250	5 Francs, Gold	218.00	900.00
P110d	1971	100	5 Francs, Platinum	909.00	—
P111	1971	250	10 Francs, Silver	60.00	250.00
P102	1972	250	1 Centime	11.00	45.00
P102a	1972	150	1 Centime, Silver	17.00	65.00
P102b	1972	75	1 Centime, Gold	55.00	225.00
PA104	1972	250	5 Centimes	11.00	45.00
PA104a	1972	150	5 Centimes, Silver	17.00	65.00
PA104b	1972	75	5 Centimes, Gold	60.00	250.00
P104	1972	250	10 Centimes	11.00	45.00
P104a	1972	150	10 Centimes, Silver	17.00	65.00
P104b	1972	75	10 Centimes, Gold	86.00	350.00
P105	1972	250	20 Centimes	11.00	50.00
P105a	1972	150	20 Centimes, Silver	17.00	65.00
P105b	1972	75	20 Centimes, Gold	116.00	450.00
P107	1972	250	1/2 Franc	11.00	55.00
P107a	1972	150	1/2 Franc, Silver	17.00	80.00
P107b	1972	75	1/2 Franc, Gold	120.00	500.00
P108	1972	250	1 Franc	11.00	60.00
P108a	1972	150	1 Franc, Silver	20.00	80.00
P108b	1972	75	1 Franc, Gold	156.00	600.00
P110a	1972	500	5 Francs	11.00	25.00
P110b	1972	250	5 Francs, Silver	40.00	85.00
P110c	1972	200	5 Francs, Gold	260.00	900.00
P111	1972	500	10 Francs	66.00	250.00
P111a	1972	200	10 Francs, Gold	560.00	900.00
P111b	1972	20	10 Francs, Platinum	2000.	—
P102	1973	250	1 Centime	—	45.00
P102a	1973	150	1 Centime, Silver	—	65.00
P102b	1973	75	1 Centime, Gold	—	225.00
PA104	1973	250	5 Centimes	—	45.00
PA104a	1973	150	5 Centimes, Silver	—	65.00
PA104b	1973	75	5 Centimes, Gold	—	250.00
P104	1973	250	10 Centimes	—	45.00
P104a	1973	150	10 Centimes, Silver	—	65.00
P104b	1973	75	10 Centimes, Gold	—	350.00
P105	1973	250	20 Centimes	—	50.00
P105a	1973	150	20 Centimes, Silver	—	65.00
P105b	1973	75	20 Centimes, Gold	—	450.00
P107	1973	250	1/2 Franc	—	55.00
P107a	1973	150	1/2 Franc, Silver	—	80.00
P107b	1973	75	1/2 Franc, Gold	—	500.00
P108	1973	250	1 Franc	—	60.00
P108a	1973	150	1 Franc, Silver	—	80.00
P108b	1973	75	1 Franc, Gold	—	600.00
P110a	1973	500	5 Francs	12.50	25.00
P110b	1973	250	5 Francs, Silver	46.00	85.00
P110c	1973	200	5 Francs, Gold	—	900.00
P111	1973	500	10 Francs	75.00	250.00
P111a	1973	200	10 Francs, Gold	—	900.00
P111b	1973	20	10 Francs, Platinum	2300.	—
P102	1974	250	1 Centime	11.00	35.00
P102a	1974	250	1 Centime, Silver	17.00	40.00
P102b	1974	100	1 Centime, Gold	90.00	175.00
PA104	1974	250	5 Centimes	12.00	35.00
PA104a	1974	250	5 Centimes, Silver	18.00	45.00
PA104b	1974	100	5 Centimes, Gold	104.00	200.00
P104	1974	250	10 Centimes	12.50	35.00
P104a	1974	250	10 Centimes, Silver	18.50	50.00
P104b	1974	100	10 Centimes, Gold	156.00	300.00
P105	1974	250	20 Centimes	13.00	40.00
P105a	1974	250	20 Centimes, Silver	19.00	55.00
P105b	1974	100	20 Centimes, Gold	210.00	400.00
P107	1974	250	1/2 Franc	13.00	40.00
P107a	1974	250	1/2 Franc, Silver	20.00	60.00
P107b	1974	100	1/2 Franc, Gold	220.00	475.00
P108	1974	250	1 Franc	14.00	40.00
P108a	1974	250	1 Franc, Silver	24.00	70.00
P108b	1974	100	1 Franc, Gold	280.00	550.00
P110a	1974	500	5 Francs	15.00	35.00
P110b	1974	250	5 Francs, Silver	48.00	90.00
P110c	1974	200	5 Francs, Gold	460.00	900.00
PA112	1974	500	10 Francs	15.00	40.00
PA112a	1974	500	10 Francs, Silver	48.00	90.00
PA112b	1974	250	10 Francs, Gold	460.00	850.00
P112	1974	1,000	50 Francs	100.00	250.00
P112a	1974	250	50 Francs, Gold	1220.	2600.
P112b	1974	50	50 Francs, Platinum	2400.	—
P102	1975	150	1 Centime	—	40.00
P102a	1975	250	1 Centime, Silver	—	40.00
P102b	1975	100	1 Centime, Gold	—	175.00
PA104	1975	150	5 Centimes	—	40.00
PA104a	1975	250	5 Centimes, Silver	—	45.00
PA104b	1975	100	5 Centimes, Gold	—	200.00
P104	1975	150	10 Centimes	—	40.00
P104a	1975	250	10 Centimes, Silver	—	50.00
P104b	1975	100	10 Centimes, Gold	—	300.00
P105	1975	150	20 Centimes	—	40.00
P105a	1975	250	20 Centimes, Silver	—	55.00
P105b	1975	100	20 Centimes, Gold	—	400.00
P107	1975	150	1/2 Franc	—	40.00
P107a	1975	250	1/2 Franc, Silver	—	60.00
P107b	1975	100	1/2 Franc, Gold	—	475.00
P108	1975	150	1 Franc	—	40.00
P108a	1975	250	1 Franc, Silver	—	70.00
P108b	1975	100	1 Franc, Gold	—	550.00
P110a	1975	500	5 Francs	—	35.00
P110b	1975	250	5 Francs, Silver	—	90.00
P110c	1975	100	5 Francs, Gold	—	1000.
PA112	1975	500	10 Francs	—	40.00
PA112a	1975	500	10 Francs, Silver	55.00	90.00
PA112b	1975	200	10 Francs, Gold	527.00	900.00
P112	1975	1,000	50 Francs	114.50	250.00
P112a	1975	250	50 Francs, Gold	1399.	2600.
P112b	1975	25	50 Francs, Platinum	2178.	—
P102	1976	200	1 Centime	13.00	35.00
P102a	1976	300	1 Centime, Silver	19.00	40.00
P102b	1976	100	1 Centime, Gold	90.00	175.00
PA104	1976	200	5 Centimes	14.00	35.00
PA104a	1976	300	5 Centimes, Silver	20.00	45.00
PA104b	1976	100	5 Centimes, Gold	104.00	200.00
P104	1976	200	10 Centimes	14.50	35.00
P104a	1976	300	10 Centimes, Silver	20.00	50.00
P104b	1976	100	10 Centimes, Gold	156.00	300.00
P105	1976	200	20 Centimes	15.00	35.00
P105a	1976	300	20 Centimes, Silver	21.00	55.00
P105b	1976	100	20 Centimes, Gold	210.00	400.00
P107	1976	200	1/2 Franc	15.00	35.00
P107a	1976	250	1/2 Franc, Silver	22.00	60.00
P107b	1976	100	1/2 Franc, Gold	220.00	450.00
P108	1976	200	1 Franc	16.00	40.00
P108a	1976	250	1 Franc, Silver	26.50	70.00
P108b	1976	100	1 Franc, Gold	280.00	550.00
P110a	1976	200	5 Francs	17.50	40.00
P110b	1976	250	5 Francs, Silver	53.00	90.00
P110c	1976	100	5 Francs, Gold	460.00	1000.
PA112	1976	500	10 Francs	17.50	40.00
PA112a	1976	500	10 Francs, Silver	53.00	90.00
PA112b	1976	100	10 Francs, Gold	460.00	1000.
P112	1976	1,000	50 Francs	110.00	150.00
P112a	1976	100	50 Francs, Gold	1220.	3000.
P112b	1976	25	50 Francs, Platinum	2000.	—
P102	1977	200	1 Centime	13.50	25.00
P102a	1977	300	1 Centime, Silver	20.00	40.00
P102b	1977	100	1 Centime, Gold	95.00	175.00
PA104	1977	200	5 Centimes	14.50	25.00
PA104a	1977	300	5 Centimes, Silver	21.00	45.00
PA104b	1977	100	5 Centimes, Gold	110.00	200.00
P104	1977	200	10 Centimes	15.00	25.00
P104a	1977	300	10 Centimes, Silver	22.00	50.00
P104b	1977	100	10 Centimes, Gold	165.00	300.00
P105	1977	200	20 Centimes	16.00	25.00

KM#	Date	Mintage	Identification	Issue Price	Mkt. Val.
P105a	1977	300	20 Centimes, Silver	23.00	55.00
P105b	1977	100	20 Centimes, Gold	222.00	400.00
P107	1977	200	1/2 Franc	16.00	30.00
P107a	1977	300	1/2 Franc, Silver	24.00	60.00
P107b	1977	100	1/2 Franc, Gold	234.00	450.00
P108	1977	200	1 Franc	17.00	30.00
P108a	1977	300	1 Franc, Silver	28.00	70.00
P108b	1977	100	1 Franc, Gold	300.00	550.00
P110a	1977	200	5 Francs	18.50	35.00
P110b	1977	300	5 Francs, Silver	56.00	90.00
P110c	1977	100	5 Francs, Gold	492.00	1000.
PA112	1977	200	10 Francs	18.50	40.00
PA112a	1977	300	10 Francs, Silver	56.00	90.00
PA112b	1977	100	10 Francs, Gold	492.00	1000.
P112	1977	1,000	50 Francs	116.00	120.00
P112a	1977	100	50 Francs, Gold	1290.	2700.
P112b	1977	20	50 Francs, Platinum	2110.	3000.
P102	1978	150	1 Centime	—	—
P102a	1978	350	1 Centime, Silver	—	40.00
P102b	1978	150	1 Centime, Gold	—	125.00
PA104	1978	150	5 Centimes	—	—
PA104a	1978	350	5 Centimes, Silver	—	45.00
PA104b	1978	150	5 Centimes, Gold	—	150.00
P104	1978	150	10 Centimes	—	—
P104a	1978	350	10 Centimes, Silver	—	50.00
P104b	1978	150	10 Centimes, Gold	—	200.00
P105	1978	150	20 Centimes	—	—
P105a	1978	350	20 Centimes, Silver	—	55.00
P105b	1978	150	20 Centimes, Gold	—	275.00
P107	1978	150	1/2 Franc	—	—
P107a	1978	350	1/2 Franc, Silver	—	60.00
P107b	1978	150	1/2 Franc, Gold	—	300.00
P108	1978	150	1 Franc	—	—
P108a	1978	350	1 Franc, Silver	—	70.00
P108b	1978	150	1 Franc, Gold	—	375.00
P109a	1978	350	2 Francs, Silver	—	—
P110a	1978	150	5 Francs	—	—
P110b	1978	350	5 Francs, Silver	—	90.00
P110c	1978	150	5 Francs, Gold	—	900.00
PA112	1978	175	10 Francs	—	—
PA112a	1978	350	10 Francs, Silver	—	90.00
PA112b	1978	150	10 Francs, Gold	—	900.00
P112	1978	600	50 Francs	129.00	—
P112a	1978	150	50 Francs, Gold	—	2700.
P112b	1978	25	50 Francs, Platinum	2208.	3000.
P102	1979	300	1 Centime	21.00	—
P102a	1979	600	1 Centime, Silver	28.00	40.00
P102b	1979	300	1 Centime, Gold	145.00	125.00
PA104	1979	300	5 Centimes	22.50	—
PA104a	1979	600	5 Centimes, Silver	30.00	45.00
PA104b	1979	300	5 Centimes, Gold	167.00	200.00
P104	1979	300	10 Centimes	23.00	—
P104a	1979	600	10 Centimes, Silver	31.50	50.00
P104b	1979	300	10 Centimes, Gold	250.00	300.00
P105	1979	300	20 Centimes	24.50	—
P105a	1979	600	20 Centimes, Silver	33.00	55.00
P105b	1979	300	20 Centimes, Gold	337.00	400.00
P107	1979	300	1/2 Franc	24.50	—
P107a	1979	600	1/2 Franc, Silver	35.00	60.00
P107b	1979	300	1/2 Franc, Gold	356.00	475.00
P108	1979	300	1 Franc	26.50	—
P108a	1979	600	1 Franc, Silver	40.00	70.00
P108b	1979	300	1 Franc, Gold	453.00	550.00
P109	1979	500	2 Francs	27.00	—
P109a	1979	1,250	2 Francs, Silver	52.50	80.00
P109b	1979	600	2 Francs, Gold	596.00	700.00
P109c	1979	40	2 Francs, Platinum	1015.	—
P110a	1979	300	5 Francs	28.00	—
P110b	1979	600	5 Francs, Silver	91.00	90.00
P110c	1979	300	5 Francs, Gold	750.00	900.00
PA112	1979	350	10 Francs	28.00	—
PA112a	1979	700	10 Francs, Silver	91.00	90.00
PA112b	1979	300	10 Francs, Gold	750.00	900.00
P112	1979	2,250	50 Francs	190.00	225.00
P112a	1979	400	50 Francs, Gold	1965.	2500.
P112b	1979	30	50 Francs, Platinum	3475.	—
P102	1979	300	1 Centime	35.00	—
P102a	1979	600	1 Centime, Silver	48.00	—
P102b	1979	300	1 Centime, Gold	149.00	—
PA104	1979	300	5 Centime	35.00	—
PA104a	1979	600	5 Centimes, Silver	49.00	—
PA104b	1979	300	5 Centimes, Gold	177.00	—
P104	1979	300	10 Centimes	35.00	—
P104a	1979	600	10 Centimes, Silver	50.00	—
P104b	1979	300	10 Centimes, Gold	275.00	—
P105	1979	300	20 Centimes	35.00	—
P105a	1979	600	20 Centimes, Silver	53.00	—
P105b	1979	300	20 Centimes, Gold	363.00	—
P107	1979	300	1/2 Franc	35.00	—
P107a	1979	600	1/2 Franc, Silver	54.00	—
P107b	1979	300	1/2 Franc, Gold	386.00	—
P108	1979	300	1 Franc	35.00	—
P108a	1979	600	1 Franc, Silver	64.00	—
P108b	1979	300	1 Franc, Gold	494.00	—
P109	1979	500	2 Francs	45.00	—
P109a	1979	800	2 Francs, Silver	75.00	—
P109b	1979	400	2 Francs, Gold	700.00	—
P110a	1979	300	5 Francs	70.00	—
P110b	1979	600	5 Francs, Silver	80.00	—
P110c	1979	300	5 Francs, Gold	903.00	—
PA112	1979	300	10 Francs	70.00	—
PA112a	1979	700	10 Francs, Silver	77.00	—
PA112b	1979	300	10 Francs, Gold	903.00	—
P112	1979	2,250	50 Francs	225.00	200.00
P112a	1979	400	50 Francs, Gold	2400.	2250.
P112b	1979	—	50 Francs, Platinum	—	3350.

SPECIMEN 'FDC' SETS

(Fleur de Coin)

KM#	Date	Mintage	Identification	Issue Price	Mkt. Val.
S1	1964(7)	25,000	Y102-108,110	4.00	7.50
S2	1965(7)	35,000	Y102,104,105, 107,108,110,111	7.60	20.00
S3	1966(8)	7,071	Y102,A104,104,105, 107,108,110a,111	9.00	125.00
S4	1967(8)	2,387	Same as S3	10.00	300.00
S5	1968(8)	2,998	Same as S3	10.00	375.00
S6	1969(8)	6,050	Same as S3	10.10	140.00
S7	1970(8)	10,000	Same as S3	9.00	50.00
S8	1971(8)	12,500	Same as S3	9.00	50.00
S9	1972(8)	15,000	Same as S3	9.00	90.00
S10	1973(8)	79,000	Same as S3	12.20	35.00
S11	1974(9)	100,300	Y102,A104,104,105,107, 108,110a,A112,113	31.20	35.00
S12	1975(9)	51,000	Same as S11	35.00	35.00
S13	1976(9)	*40,000	Same as S11	35.00	50.00
S14	1977(9)	25,000	Same as S11	36.00	52.50
S15	1978(9)	—	Same as S11	39.00	42.50
S16	1979(10)	—	Y102,A104,104,105,107-109, 110a,A112,112	55.00	60.00

PROOF SETS

STANDARD METALS

KM#	Date	Mintage	Identification	Issue Price	Mkt. Val.
101	1830(7)	—	C185-191	—	—
102	1878(5)	30	Y41-44,48	—	330.00
103	1889(4)	100	Y41-44	—	600.00
104	1897(5)	—	Y41-44,62	—	230.00

Listings For

FRENCH AFARS & ISSAS: refer to Djibouti

FRENCH COLONIES

The coins catalogued under this heading were not issued for use in any particular colony but were intended for general use in the West Indies, particularly Martinique, Guadeloupe, and Saint-Dominique (western Hispaniola) until it attained independence as Haiti in 1804.

RULERS

Louis XVI, 1774-1793
Charles X, 1824-1830
Louis-Philippe I, 1830-1848

MINTMARKS

A - Paris
H - LaRochelle

MONETARY SYSTEM

100 Centimes = 1 Franc

COUNTERSTAMP ISSUE

STAMPEE

BILLON

Uniface, c/s: crowned 'C'.

C#	Date	Mintage	VG	Fine	VF	XF
10	ND(1779)	—	3.00	7.50	15.00	40.00

NOTE: The crowned 'C' was counterstamped on old 2 Sol coins of France and later on specially prepared blank planchets.

STRUCK COINAGE

3 SOUS

BILLON

Obv: Crown above 3 lis. Rev: Value.

C#	Date	Mintage	VG	Fine	VF	XF
9	1781	—	9.00	18.00	35.00	70.00

5 CENTIMES

BRASS

C#	Date	Mintage	Fine	VF	XF	Unc
11	1825A	.607	3.50	8.00	18.00	40.00
	1827H	.600	3.50	8.00	18.00	40.00
	1828A	.501	4.00	9.00	18.00	40.00
	1829A	.299	5.50	15.00	35.00	60.00
	1830A	.402	4.00	9.00	18.00	40.00

BRONZE

C#	Date	Mintage	Fine	VF	XF	Unc
13	1839A	.300	4.50	8.50	15.00	45.00
	1841A	.607	3.50	7.50	16.00	40.00
	1843A	.202	6.00	12.00	30.00	50.00
	1844A	.201	6.00	12.00	30.00	50.00

10 CENTIMES

BRASS

C#	Date	Mintage	Fine	VF	XF	Unc
12	1825A	.301	5.00	13.00	27.50	45.00
	1827H	.300	5.00	13.00	27.50	45.00
	1828A	.235	6.00	15.00	30.00	60.00
	1829A	.152	9.00	20.00	50.00	70.00

BRONZE

C#	Date	Mintage	Fine	VF	XF	Unc
14	1839A	.300	5.00	12.00	27.50	50.00
	1841A	.301	5.00	12.00	27.50	50.00
	1843A	.100	9.00	20.00	55.00	75.00
	1844A	.100	9.00	20.00	55.00	80.00

NCLT ISSUES

ESSAIS (E)

Standard metals unless otherwise noted.

KM#	Date	Mintage	Identification	Issue Price	Mkt. Val.
E1	1824A	—	5 Centimes	—	125.00
E2	1824A	—	5 Centimes, Silver	—	350.00
E3	1824A	—	10 Centimes	—	125.00
E4	1824A	—	10 Centimes, Silver	—	350.00

PIEFORTS (P)

Standard metals unless otherwise noted.

KM#	Date	Mintage	Identification	Issue Price	Mkt. Val.
P1	1839A	—	10 Centimes	—	225.00

Listings For

FRENCH COCHIN CHINA: refer to Vietnam

FRENCH EQUATORIAL AFRICA

French Equatorial Africa, an area consisting of four self governing dependencies (Middle Congo, Ubangi-Shari, Chad and Gabon) in west-central Africa, had an area of 969,111 sq. mi. (2,509,987 sq. km.) and a population of 3.5 million. Capital: Brazzaville. The area, rich in natural resources, exported cotton, timber, coffee, cacao, diamonds and gold.

Little is known of the history of these parts of Africa prior to French occupation - which began with no thought of territorial acquisition. France's initial intent was simply to establish a few supply stations along the west coast of Africa to service the warships assigned to combat the slave trade in the early part of the 19th century. French settlement began in 1839. Gabon (then Gabun) and the Middle Congo were secured between 1885 and 1891; Chad and Ubangi-Shari between 1894 and 1897. The four colonies were joined to form French Equatorial Africa in 1910. The dependencies were changed from colonies to territories within the French Union in 1946, and all the inhabitants were made French citizens. In 1958 they voted to become autonomous republics within the new French Community, and attained full independence in 1960.

RULERS

French, until 1960

MINTMARKS

(a) - Paris, privy marks only
SA - Pretoria (1942-1943)

MONETARY SYSTEM

100 Centimes = 1 Franc

5 CENTIMES

ALUMINUM-BRONZE
Obv: Center hole dividing RF, Phrygian cap above.
Rev: Center hole dividing denomination.

KM#	Date	Mintage	VF	XF	Unc
1	1943	*44.000	—	Rare	—

10 CENTIMES

ALUMINUM-BRONZE

KM#	Date	Mintage	VF	XF	Unc
2	1943	*13.000	300.00	400.00	600.00

25 CENTIMES

ALUMINUM-BRONZE
Similar to 5 Centimes, KM#1.

KM#	Date	Mintage	VF	XF	Unc
3	1943	*4.160	—	Rare	—

***NOTE:** KM#1-3 were not released for circulation.

50 CENTIMES

BRASS

Y#	Date	Mintage	Fine	VF	XF	Unc
1	1942 SA	8.000	2.00	3.50	6.00	10.00

BRONZE

Y#	Date	Mintage	Fine	VF	XF	Unc
1a	1943 SA	16.000	1.50	3.00	4.50	7.00

FRANC

BRASS

Y#	Date	Mintage	Fine	VF	XF	Unc
2	1942 SA	3.000	2.50	5.00	7.00	12.00

BRONZE

Y#	Date	Mintage	Fine	VF	XF	Unc
2a	1943 SA	6.000	2.50	5.00	7.00	12.00

ALUMINUM

Y#	Date	Mintage	VF	XF	Unc
3	1948(a)	15.000	.10	.15	.50	.75

2 FRANCS

ALUMINUM

Y#	Date	Mintage				
4	1948 A	5.040	.30	.65	1.50	4.00

5 FRANCS

ALUMINUM-BRONZE

Y#	Date	Mintage				
5	1958(a)	30.000	.10	.15	.30	.65

10 FRANCS

ALUMINUM-BRONZE

Y#	Date	Mintage				
6	1958(a)	25.000	.15	.20	.50	.75

25 FRANCS

ALUMINUM-BRONZE

Y#	Date	Mintage				
7	1958(a)	12.000	.25	.50	.75	1.75

NOTE: For later coinage see the Equatorial African States plus the Central African Republic, Congo People's Republic, Gabon and Tchad.

NCLT ISSUES

ESSAIS (E)

Standard metals unless otherwise noted

Y#	Date	Mintage	Identification	Issue Price	Mkt Val.
E3	1948(a)	2,000	1 Franc, Copper-Nickel	—	15.00
E4	1948(a)	2,000	2 Francs, Copper-Nickel	—	17.50
E5	1958(a)	2,030	5 Francs	—	12.50
E6	1958(a)	2,030	10 Francs	—	15.00
E7	1958(a)	2,030	25 Francs	—	20.00

PIEFORTS WITH ESSAI (PE)

(DOUBLE THICKNESS)

Standard metals unless otherwise noted

Y#	Date	Mintage	Identification	Issue Price	Mkt Val.
PE3	1948(a)	104	1 Franc	—	100.00
PE4	1948(a)	104	2 Francs	—	110.00

FRENCH GUIANA

The French Overseas Department of French Guiana, located on the northeast coast of South America, bordered by Surinam and Brazil, has an area of 34,740 sq. mi. (89,941 sq. km.) and a population of 58,000. Capital: Cayenne. Placer gold mining and shrimp processing are the chief industries. Shrimp, lumber, gold, cocoa, and bananas are exported.

The coast of Guiana was sighted by Columbus in 1498 and explored by Amerigo Vespucci in 1499. The French established the first successful trading stations and settlements, and placed the area under direct control of the French Crown in 1674. Portuguese and British forces occupied French Guiana for five years during the Napoleonic Wars. Devil's Island, the notorious penal colony in French Guiana where Capt. Alfred Dreyfus was imprisoned, was established in 1852 - and finally closed in 1947. When France adopted a new constitution in 1946, French Guiana voted to remain within the French Union as an Overseas Department.

RULERS

French

MINTMARKS

A - Paris

MONETARY SYSTEM

100 Centimes = 10 Decimes = 1 Franc

COLONIE DE CAYENNE

2 SOUS

BILLON, COPPER or BRONZE

C#	Date	Mintage	VG	Fine	VF	XF
1	1780A	—	6.00	15.00	30.00	70.00
	1781A	—	7.00	20.00	35.00	85.00
	1782A	—	4.00	8.00	20.00	50.00
	1783A	—	7.00	20.00	35.00	85.00
	1786A	—	7.00	20.00	35.00	85.00
	1787A	—	7.00	20.00	35.00	85.00
	1788A	—	7.00	20.00	35.00	85.00
	1789A	—	2.00	4.00	6.00	17.50

NOTE: Many die varieties exist.

BILLON

C#	Date	Mintage	VG	Fine	VF	XF
3	1816A	2.000	—	—	Rare	—

3 SOUS

BILLON

Similar to 2 sous, C#1.

C#	Date	Mintage	VG	Fine	VF	XF
2	1781A	—	12.50	25.00	45.00	65.00

COPPER

C#	Date	Mintage	VG	Fine	VF	XF
2a	1781A	—	15.00	30.00	50.00	75.00

NCLT ISSUES

PATTERNS

KM#	Date	Mintage	Identification	Mkt.Val.
1	1816A	3-4	2 Sous, White Metal, C3a	350.00

GUYANE FRANCAISE

10 CENTIMES

BILLON

C#	Date	Mintage	VG	Fine	VF	XF
4	1818A	2.000	4.00	10.00	25.00	60.00

C#	Date	Mintage	VG	Fine	VF	XF
5	1846A	1.400	8.00	20.00	45.00	75.00

NCLT ISSUES

PATTERNS

KM#	Date	Mintage	Identification	Mkt.Val.
1	ND	—	10 Centimes, white metal, Y4a	225.00

REP. of INDEPENDENT GUIANA

PATTERNS

KM#	Date	Mintage	Identification	Mkt.Val.
1	1887	—	10 Centimes, Bronze, "E" below value	200.00

KM#	Date	Mintage	Identification	Mkt.Val.
2	1887	—	20 Centimes, white metal	250.00

KM#	Date	Mintage	Identification	Mkt.Val.
3	1887	—	5 Francs, white metal, "ESSAI"	500.00
4	1887	—	5 Francs,Silver	4000
5				200.00

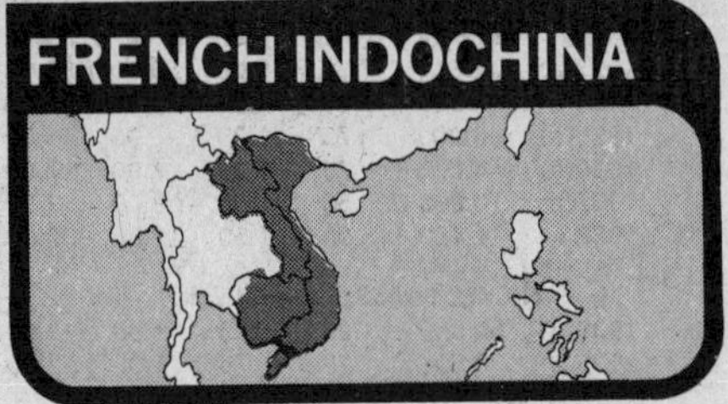

French Indo-China, made up of the protectorates of Annam, Tonkin, Cambodia and Laos and the colony of Cochin-China was located on the Indo-Chinese peninsula of Southeast Asia. The colony had an area of 286,194 sq. mi. (741,242 sq. km.) and a population of 24 million. Principal cities: Saigon, Haiphong, Vientiane, Pnom-Penh and Hanoi.

The history of the states of Indo-China is rooted in the dusty civilizations of antiquity. The forebears of the modern Indo-Chinese peoples originated in the Yellow River Valley of northern China, from whence they were driven into the Indo-Chinese peninsula by the Han Chinese. The Chinese followed southward in the second century B.C., conquering the peninsula and ruling it until 938, leaving a lingering heritage of Chinese learning and culture. Indo-Chinese independence was basically maintained until the arrival of the French in the mid-19th century who established control over all of Vietnam, Laos and Cambodia and administered it as Indo-China. Activities directed toward obtaining Indo- Chinese self-determination, begun in the early 20th century, accelerated during the Japanese occupation of World War II.

In Aug. of 1945, an uprising erupted involving the French and Vietnamese Nationalists, culminated in the French military disaster at Dien Bien Phu (May, 1954) and the subsequent Geneva Conference that brought an end to French colonial rule in Indo-China.

RULERS

French, until 1954

MINTMARKS

A - Paris
(a) - Paris, privy marks only
B - Beaumont le Roger
C - Castle Sarrasin
H - Heaton, Birmingham
(p) - Thunderbolt - Poissy
S - San Francisco, U.S.A.
(s) - San Francisco, privy marks only
None - Osaka, Japan
None - Hanoi, Tonkin

MONETARY SYSTEM

5 Sapeques (Cash) = 1 Cent
100 Cents = 1 Piastre

SAPEQUE

BRONZE

Y#	Date	Mintage	Fine	VF	XF	Unc
1	1887A	5.000	2.50	5.00	10.00	30.00
	1888A	5.000	2.50	5.00	10.00	30.00
	1889A	100 pcs.	—	Proof Only		250.00
	1892A	1.636	6.00	12.00	35.00	65.00
	1893A	.864	15.00	30.00	60.00	150.00
	1894A	2.500	10.00	17.50	45.00	100.00
	1897A	2.829	10.00	17.50	45.00	100.00
	1898A	2.171	6.00	12.00	30.00	55.00
	1899A	5.000	1.75	5.00	10.00	25.00
	1900A	2.657	10.00	17.50	45.00	100.00
	1900A	100 pcs.	—	—	Proof	250.00
	1901A	4.843	2.50	5.00	15.00	50.00
	1902A	2.500	2.00	4.00	11.00	25.00

1/4 CENT

ZINC

Y#	Date	Mintage	Fine	VF	XF	Unc
V31	1941	1 Known	—	—	Rare	—
	1942	221.800	4.00	8.50	15.00	50.00
	1943	279.450	20.00	35.00	75.00	175.00
	1944	46.122	250.00	300.00	350.00	650.00

NOTE: Lead counterfeits dated 1941 and 1942 are known.

1/2 CENT

BRONZE

Y#	Date	Mintage	Fine	VF	XF	Unc
20	1935(a)	26.365	.25	.75	2.00	3.50
	1936(a)	23.635	.25	.75	2.00	3.50
	1937(a)	10.244	.40	1.00	3.00	5.00
	1938(a)	16.665	.25	.75	2.00	3.50
	1939(a)	17.305	.25	.75	2.00	3.50
	1940(a)	11.218	3.00	6.00	12.50	25.00
		ZINC				
20a	1939(a)	.185	100.00	150.00	200.00	250.00
	1940(a)	—	225.00	250.00	300.00	350.00

CENT

BRONZE

Y#	Date	Mintage	Fine	VF	XF	Unc
2	1885A	3.673	2.00	4.00	7.00	20.00
	1885A	—	—	—	Proof	—
	1886A	1.883	3.00	5.00	9.00	25.00
	1887A	2.362	2.00	4.00	8.00	20.00
	1888A	2.564	2.00	4.00	8.00	20.00
	1889A	1.573	3.00	5.00	9.00	25.00
	1889A	100 pcs.	—	—	Proof	350.00
	1892A	2.648	2.00	4.00	8.00	20.00
	1893A	1.852	6.50	17.50	30.00	60.00
	1894A	.465	15.00	30.00	75.00	175.00
		Obv. leg: UN CENTIEME DE PIASTRE				
2a	1895A	.290	85.00	150.00	250.00	500.00

Y#	Date	Mintage	Fine	VF	XF	Unc
3	1896A	5.690	2.00	4.00	8.00	17.50
	1897A	11.055	.75	3.00	6.00	15.00
	1898A	5.000	6.00	17.50	40.00	125.00
	1899A	8.000	.75	2.50	6.00	10.00
	1900A	3.000	3.00	6.00	12.50	30.00
	1900A	100 pcs.	—	—	Proof	350.00
	1901A	9.750	3.00	6.00	10.00	20.00
	1902A	5.050	3.50	7.00	15.00	30.00
	1903A	8.000	3.00	6.00	10.00	20.00
	1906A	2.000	6.00	15.00	25.00	50.00

Y#	Date	Mintage	Fine	VF	XF	Unc
4	1908A	3.000	15.00	30.00	60.00	150.00
	1909A	5.000	10.00	25.00	40.00	85.00
	1910A	7.703	.75	3.00	10.00	20.00
	1911A	15.234	.75	3.00	10.00	15.00
	1912A	17.027	.75	3.00	12.50	25.00
	1913A	3.945	1.50	5.00	14.00	20.00
	1914A	11.027	.75	3.00	12.50	25.00
	1916A	1.312	5.00	10.00	20.00	35.00
	1917A	9.762	.75	3.00	6.00	12.50
	1918A	2.372	4.50	10.00	20.00	35.00
	1919A	9.148	.75	3.00	6.00	12.50
	1920A	18.305	.75	3.00	6.00	12.50
	1920(s)	13.290	.75	3.00	5.00	10.00
	1921(s)	1.710	12.50	15.00	20.00	35.00
	1921A	14.722	.75	1.50	2.50	5.00
	1922A	8.850	.75	1.50	2.50	5.00
	1922(p)	Inc. Ab.	.75	1.50	2.50	5.00
	1923A	1.079	15.00	25.00	50.00	90.00
	1923(p)	27.891	.75	1.50	2.50	5.00
	1926A	11.672	.75	1.50	3.00	6.00
	1927A	3.328	3.00	6.00	15.00	30.00
	1930A	4.682	1.00	2.00	3.50	6.00
	1931A torch privy mark					
		5.318	25.00	30.00	37.50	50.00
	1931A wing privy mark					
		Inc. Ab.	25.00	30.00	37.50	50.00
	1937A	8.902	.50	1.00	1.75	3.50
	1938A	15.499	.50	.75	1.00	3.00
	1939A	17.589	.50	.75	1.00	3.00

ZINC
Vichy Government Issues

Circles **Rosette**
Type 1 with circles on Phrygian cap.
Type 2 with rosette on phrygian cap.
Variety 1, 12 petals - Variety 2, 11 petals.

Y#	Date	Mintage	Fine	VF	XF	Unc
V30	1940 T1	1.990	6.00	12.50	25.00	45.00
	1941 T2 V1	—	5.00	10.00	17.50	30.00

Type 2 with rosette on Phrygian cap.

Y#	Date	Mintage	Fine	VF	XF	Unc
	1940 T2 V2	—	4.00	10.00	25.00	40.00
	1941 T2 V2	—	1.00	3.00	6.00	10.00

NOTE: There are also subvarieties of Type 2, some with 11 large petals and some with 12 small petals.

ALUMINUM

Y#	Date	Mintage	Fine	VF	XF	Unc
V32	1943	—	.25	.50	.75	1.50

5 CENTS

COPPER-NICKEL, 1.8mm thick

Y#	Date	Mintage	Fine	VF	XF	Unc
5	1923(a)	1.611	2.50	5.00	10.00	30.00
	1924(a)	3.389	1.25	2.50	8.00	20.00
	1925(a)	6.000	.75	1.25	6.00	15.00
	1930(a)	4.000	.75	1.25	7.00	17.50
	1937(a)	10.000	.50	1.00	3.00	7.50
	1938 A	1.480	5.00	7.50	12.50	35.00

NICKEL-BRASS, 1.5mm thick

Y#	Date	Mintage	Fine	VF	XF	Unc
5a	1938(a)	50.569	.25	.75	1.00	3.00
	1939(a)	38.501	.25	.75	1.00	3.00

ALUMINUM
Vichy Government Issue

Y#	Date	Mintage	Fine	VF	XF	Unc
V33	1943	—	.25	.75	1.00	2.00

Postwar Issues

Y#	Date	Mintage	Fine	VF	XF	Unc
26	1946(a)	28.000	.15	.40	.50	2.00
	1946B	22.000	.15	.40	.50	2.00

10 CENTS

2.7210 gm., .900 SILVER, .0787 oz ASW
Rev. leg: TITRE 0.900. POIDS 2.721

Y#	Date	Mintage	Fine	VF	XF	Unc
6	1885A	2.040	5.00	12.00	25.00	60.00
	1888A	1.000	6.50	12.50	27.50	65.00
	1889A	100 pcs.	—	Proof Only		500.00
	1892A	.200	—	—	Rare	—
	1893A	.600	9.00	25.00	50.00	125.00
	1894A	.500	12.50	30.00	60.00	150.00
	1895A	.600	9.00	25.00	50.00	125.00

2.7000 gm., .900 SILVER, .0781 oz ASW
Rev. leg: TITRE 0.900. POIDS 2 GR. 7

Y#	Date	Mintage	Fine	VF	XF	Unc
6a	1895A	.300	—	—	Rare	—
	1896A fasces different					
		.650	15.00	25.00	60.00	150.00
	1896A torch different					
		Inc. Ab.	20.00	45.00	90.00	200.00
	1897A	.900	20.00	40.00	85.00	175.00

2.7000 gm., .835 SILVER, .0725 oz ASW
Rev. leg: TITRE 0.835. POIDS 2 GR. 7

Y#	Date	Mintage	Fine	VF	XF	Unc
14	1898A	.500	30.00	120.00	250.00	575.00
	1899A	4.100	12.00	45.00	75.00	150.00
	1900A	3.600	4.00	12.00	22.00	35.00
	1900A	100 pcs.	—	—	Proof	350.00
	1901A	2.950	7.00	25.00	50.00	100.00
	1902A	7.050	3.50	20.00	35.00	75.00
	1903A	1.300	7.00	40.00	70.00	150.00
	1908A	1.000	25.00	70.00	115.00	250.00
	1909A	1.000	20.00	55.00	100.00	225.00
	1910A	2.689	8.00	55.00	100.00	225.00
	1911A	2.311	25.00	65.00	100.00	225.00
	1912A	2.500	15.00	55.00	100.00	225.00
	1913A	4.847	4.00	30.00	60.00	125.00
	1914A	2.667	7.00	40.00	90.00	175.00
	1916A	2.000	8.00	45.00	80.00	175.00
	1917A	1.500	12.00	55.00	100.00	225.00
	1919A	1.500	22.00	65.00	125.00	275.00

3.0000 gm., .400 SILVER, .0386 oz ASW
Rev: No fineness indicated

Y#	Date	Mintage	Fine	VF	XF	Unc
14a	1920(s)	10.000	7.50	15.00	30.00	65.00

2.7000 gm., .680 SILVER, .0590 oz ASW
Rev. leg: TITRE 0.680 POIDS 2 GR. 7

Y#	Date	Mintage	Fine	VF	XF	Unc
16	1921A	12.516	BV	2.00	9.00	17.50
	1922A	22.381	BV	2.00	8.00	15.00
	1923A	21.755	BV	2.00	8.00	15.00
	1924A	2.816	BV	4.00	10.00	20.00
	1925A	4.909	BV	2.00	8.00	17.50
	1927A	6.471	BV	5.00	15.00	30.00
	1928A	1.593	200.00	275.00	350.00	750.00
	1929A	5.831	BV	2.00	8.00	17.50
	1930A	6.608	BV	2.00	8.00	15.00
	1937(a)	25.000	BV	2.00	2.50	4.00

NICKEL

Y#	Date	Mintage	Fine	VF	XF	Unc
21	1939(a) thick planchet					
		16.841	.25	.75	1.25	2.75
	1940(a) thin planchet					
		25.505	.25	1.00	3.00	5.00

COPPER-NICKEL

Y#	Date	Mintage	Fine	VF	XF	Unc
21a	1939(a)	2.237	7.50	15.00	25.00	75.00
	1941S	50.000	.15	.50	1.75	3.50

ALUMINUM

Y#	Date	Mintage	Fine	VF	XF	Unc
27	1945(a)	40.170	.30	1.25	2.00	3.50
	1945B	9.830	.40	2.00	3.50	8.00

20 CENTS

5.4430 gm., .900 SILVER, .1575 oz ASW
Rev. leg: TITRE 0.900. POIDS 5.443

Y#	Date	Mintage	Fine	VF	XF	Unc
7	1885A	1.280	9.00	20.00	60.00	110.00
	1887A	.250	25.00	75.00	150.00	300.00
	1889A	100 pcs.	—	Proof Only		600.00
	1892A	.200	35.00	90.00	200.00	450.00
	1893A	.200	25.00	75.00	150.00	300.00
	1894A	.250	25.00	65.00	125.00	275.00
	1895A	.300	22.00	60.00	110.00	250.00

5.4000 gm., .900 SILVER, .1562 oz ASW
Rev. leg: TITRE 0.900. POIDS 5 GR. 4

Y#	Date	Mintage	Fine	VF	XF	Unc
7a	1895A	.250	65.00	125.00	275.00	600.00
(11)	1896A(torch)	.300	50.00	90.00	165.00	325.00
	1896A (Fasces)	I.A.	40.00	80.00	150.00	300.00
	1897A	.300	65.00	125.00	350.00	600.00

5.4000 gm., .835 SILVER, .1450 oz SAW

Y#	Date	Mintage	Fine	VF	XF	Unc
15	1898A	.250	35.00	75.00	175.00	350.00
	1899A	2.050	7.50	17.50	50.00	150.00
	1900A	1.750	12.00	30.00	75.00	175.00
	1900A	100 pcs.	—	—	Proof	600.00
	1901A	1.375	15.00	45.00	90.00	200.00
	1902A	3.525	7.50	30.00	75.00	175.00
	1903A	.675	35.00	150.00	250.00	600.00
	1908A	.500	40.00	150.00	250.00	400.00
	1909A	.500	50.00	175.00	275.00	500.00
	1911A	2.340	7.50	17.50	50.00	150.00
	1912A	.160	175.00	350.00	600.00	1750.
	1913A	1.252	30.00	75.00	175.00	350.00
	1914A	2.500	4.00	10.00	35.00	100.00
	1916A	1.000	6.00	15.00	45.00	150.00

.900 SILVER
Mule: Obv. of Y#7a and rev. of Y#15.

Y#	Date	Mintage	Fine	VF	XF	Unc
15.1	1909A	Inc. Y15	20.00	50.00	100.00	225.00

6.0000 gm., .400 silver, .0772 oz ASW
Rev: No fineness indicated

Y#	Date	Mintage	Fine	VF	XF	Unc
15a	1920(s)	4.000	15.00	30.00	95.00	150.00

5.4000 gm., .680 SILVER, .1181 oz ASW
Rev. leg: TITRE 0.680 POIDS 5 GR. 4

Y#	Date	Mintage	Fine	VF	XF	Unc
17	1921A	3.763	BV	3.50	6.00	12.50
	1922A	5.812	BV	BV	4.00	9.00
	1923A	7.109	BV	BV	4.00	9.00
	1924A	1.400	3.50	6.00	15.00	30.00
	1925A	2.556	3.50	7.00	15.00	30.00
	1927A	3.245	BV	6.00	15.00	25.00
	1928A	.794	7.50	17.50	40.00	100.00
	1929A	.644	7.50	17.50	40.00	110.00
	1930A	5.576	BV	BV	4.00	9.00
	1937(a)	17.500	BV	BV	4.00	5.00

NICKEL
Security edge

Y#	Date	Mintage	Fine	VF	XF	Unc
22	1939(a)	.345	7.00	12.50	30.00	65.00

COPPER-NICKEL
Reeded edge

Y#	Date	Mintage	Fine	VF	XF	Unc
22a	1939(a)	14.677	.25	1.00	1.50	3.00
	1941S	25.000	.25	.75	1.25	2.50

ALUMINUM

Y#	Date	Mintage	Fine	VF	XF	Unc
28	1945(a)	15.412	.20	.75	2.00	4.00
	1945B	6.665	1.50	3.00	8.00	15.00
	1945C	22.423	.20	.75	2.00	4.00

50 CENTS

13.6070 gm., .900 SILVER, .3937 oz ASW
Rev. leg: TITRE 0.900. POIDS 13.607 GR.

Y#	Date	Mintage	Fine	VF	XF	Unc
8	1885A	.040	75.00	125.00	250.00	750.00
	1889A	100 pcs.	—	Proof Only		1000.
	1894A	.100	25.00	75.00	150.00	275.00
	1895A	.100	35.00	100.00	250.00	550.00

13.5000 gm., .900 SILVER, .3906 oz ASW
Rev. leg: TITRE 0.900. POIDS 13 GR. 5

Y#	Date	Mintage	Fine	VF	XF	Unc
8a	1896A	.110	25.00	65.00	125.00	275.00
(12)	1900A	100 pcs.	—	Proof Only		1000.
	1936(a)	4.000	2.00	4.00	7.50	17.50

COPPER-NICKEL
Rev. leg: BRONZE DE NICKEL

Y#	Date	Mintage	Fine	VF	XF	Unc
23	1946(a)	32.292	1.00	3.00	6.00	12.00

PIASTRE

27.2150 gm., .900 SILVER, .7875 oz ASW
Rev. leg: TITRE 0.900 POIDS 27.215 GR.

Y#	Date	Mintage	Fine	VF	XF	Unc
9	1885A	.800	25.00	40.00	100.00	225.00
	1886A	3.216	BV	BV	25.00	40.00
	1887A	3.076	BV	BV	25.00	40.00
	1888A	.948	25.00	40.00	70.00	125.00
	1889A	1.240	25.00	30.00	50.00	100.00
	1889A	100 pcs.	—	—	Proof	1000.
	1890A	6,108	1000.	1900.	4500.	—
	1893A	.795	25.00	30.00	60.00	115.00
	1894A	1.308	25.00	40.00	80.00	150.00
	1895A	1.782	BV	25.00	40.00	85.00

27.0000 gm., .900 SILVER, .7812 oz ASW
Rev. leg: TITRE 0.900. POIDS 27 GR.

Y#	Date	Mintage	Fine	VF	XF	Unc
9a	1895A	3.798	BV	BV	25.00	35.00
(13)	1896A	11.858	BV	BV	25.00	35.00
	1897A	2.511	BV	25.00	30.00	75.00
	1898A	4.304	BV	BV	25.00	35.00
	1899A	4.681	BV	BV	25.00	35.00
	1900A	13.319	BV	BV	25.00	35.00
	1900A	100 pcs.	—	—	Proof	1000.
	1901A	3.150	BV	BV	35.00	60.00
	1902A	3.327	BV	BV	45.00	75.00
	1903A	10.077	BV	BV	25.00	35.00
	1904A	5.751	BV	BV	25.00	35.00
	1905A	3.561	BV	BV	25.00	40.00
	1906A	10.194	BV	BV	25.00	35.00
	1907A	14.062	BV	BV	25.00	35.00
	1908A	13.986	BV	BV	25.00	35.00
	1909A	9.201	BV	BV	25.00	35.00
	1910A	.761	25.00	40.00	60.00	150.00
	1913A	3.244	BV	BV	25.00	50.00
	1921(s)	4.850	BV	BV	25.00	35.00
	1921H	3.580	BV	BV	25.00	35.00
	1922(s)	1.150	25.00	30.00	55.00	125.00
	1922H	7.420	BV	BV	25.00	35.00
	1924A	2.831	BV	BV	35.00	60.00
	1925A	2.882	BV	BV	25.00	35.00
	1926A	6.383	BV	BV	25.00	35.00
	1927A	8.184	BV	BV	25.00	35.00
	1928A	5.290	BV	BV	30.00	50.00

20.0000 gm., .900 SILVER, .5787 oz ASW

Y#	Date	Mintage	Fine	VF	XF	Unc
18	1931(a)	16.000	BV	BV	17.50	22.50

COPPER-NICKEL
Security edge

Y#	Date	Mintage	Fine	VF	XF	Unc
24	1946(a)	2.520	5.00	12.50	35.00	65.00
	1947(a)	42.219	10.00	35.00	70.00	125.00

Similar to Y#24, reeded edge.

Y#	Date	Mintage	Fine	VF	XF	Unc
24a (25)	1947(a)	Inc. Ab.	1.00	1.50	2.00	5.00

NOTE: For later coinage see Cambodia, Laos and Vietnam.

NCLT ISSUES

ESSAIS (E)

Standard metals unless otherwise noted

Y#	Date	Mintage	Identification	Issue Price	Mkt Val.
E1	1887(a)	—	2 Sapeque, w/o a mm, 16 sided	—	175.00
E3	1897A	—	1 Cent, Copper-Nickel, w/o Essai	—	125.00
E4	1923(p)	—	1 Cent, Essai in field	40.00	100.00
E4	1923(p)	—	1 Cent, Essai at rim	40.00	100.00
E5	1923	—	5 Cents	—	60.00
E17a	1928(a)	—	20 Cents, Bronze	100.00	100.00
—	19(30a)	—	1 Cent, Silver	100.00	200.00
—	19(30a)	—	1 Cent, Al.-Bronze	100.00	75.00
E16a	19(31a)	—	10 Cents, Silver/Bronze	75.00	200.00
E17a	19(31a)	—	20 Cents, Silver/Bronze	100.00	100.00
E12a	1(931a)	—	50 Cents, Silver/Bronze	100.00	125.00
E13	19(31a)	—	1 Piastre, Silver	500.00	750.00
E13a	19(31a)	—	1 Piastre, Silver/Bronze	300.00	250.00
E18	1931(a)	—	1 Piastre, Silver	175.00	300.00
E20	1935(a)	—	1/2 Cent	35.00	55.00
E12a	1936(a)	—	50 Cents, Aluminum	100.00	175.00
E16a	1937(a)	—	10 Cents, Nickel	50.00	90.00
E17	1937(a)	—	20 Cents, Silver	50.00	125.00
E17a	1937(a)	—	20 Cents, Nickel	75.00	100.00
E21	1939(a)	—	10 Cents	35.00	90.00
E22	1939(a)	—	20 Cents, Plain Edge	75.00	125.00
E22	1939(a)	—	20 Cents, Security Edge	75.00	200.00
E22a	1939(a)	—	20 Cents, Reeded Edge	40.00	100.00
EV30	1940(a)	—	1 Cent, Zinc	30.00	40.00
EV30a	1940(a)	—	1 Cent, Aluminum Bronze	50.00	60.00
E27	1945(a)	1,100	10 Cents	27.50	30.00
E28	1945(a)	1,100	20 Cents	—	50.00
E26	1946(a)	1,100	5 Cents	—	30.00
E23	1946(a)	1,100	50 Cents	—	80.00
E24	1946(a)	1,100	1 Piastre, 2 branched palm	—	125.00

Y#	Date	Mintage	Identification	Issue Price	Mkt Val.
—	1946(a)	1,100	1 Piastre, 1 branch palm	—	300.00
E24	1947(a)	—	1 Piastre	—	100.00

PIEFORTS with ESSAI (PE)

(Double Thickness)

Standard metals unless otherwise noted

	Date	Mintage	Identification	Issue Price	Mkt Val.
PE5	1923	—	5 Cents	—	90.00
PE18	1931(a)	—	1 Piastre	—	450.00
PE27	1945(a)	104	10 Cents	—	85.00
PE28	1945(a)	104	20 Cents	—	100.00
PE26	1946(a)	104	5 Cents	—	75.00
PE23	1946(a)	104	50 Cents	—	175.00
PE24	1947(a)	104	1 Piastre	—	225.00

PROOF SETS

STANDARD METALS

KM#	Date	Mintage	Identification	Issue Price	Mkt. Val.
101	1889(6)	100	Y1,2,6-9	—	3500.
102	1900(6)	100	Y1,3,8a,9a,14,15	—	3350.

FRENCH OCEANIA

The Colony of French Oceania (now the Territory of French Polynesia), comprising 130 basalt and coral islands scattered among five archipelagoes in the South Pacific, had an area of 1,544 sq. mi. (3,999 sq. km.) and a population of about 100,000, mostly Polynesians. Capital: Papeete. The colony produced phosphates, copra and vanilla.

Tahiti of the Society Islands, the hub of French Oceania, was visited by Capt. Cook in 1769 and by Capt. Bligh in the Bounty 1788-89. The Society Islands were claimed by France in 1768, and in 1903 grouped with the Marquesas Islands, the Tuamotu Archipelago, the Gambier Islands and the Austral Islands under a single administrative head located at Papeete, Tahiti, to form the colony of French Oceania.

RULERS

French

MINTMARKS

(a) - Paris, privy marks only

MONETARY SYSTEM

100 Centimes = 1 Franc

50 CENTIMES

ALUMINUM

Y#	Date	Mintage	Fine	VF	XF	Unc
1	1949(a)	.795	.35	.70	1.50	3.50

FRANC

ALUMINUM

Y#	Date	Mintage	Fine	VF	XF	Unc
2	1949(a)	2.000	.15	.30	.75	2.25

2 FRANCS

ALUMINUM

Y#	Date	Mintage	Fine	VF	XF	Unc
3	1949(a)	1.000	.30	.70	1.75	4.50

5 FRANCS

ALUMINUM

Y#	Date	Mintage	Fine	VF	XF	Unc
4	1952(a)	2.000	.60	1.25	3.00	5.50

NCLT ISSUES

ESSAIS (E)

Standard metals unless otherwise noted

Y#	Date	Mintage	Identification	Issue Price	Mkt Val.
—	1948(a)	1,100	50 Centimes, incuse design	—	20.00
—	1948(a)	1,100	50 Centimes, raised design	—	20.00
—	1948(a)	1,100	1 Franc, incuse design	—	22.50
—	1948(a)	1,100	1 Franc, raised design	—	22.50
—	1948(a)	1,100	2 Francs, incuse design	—	25.00
—	1948(a)	1,100	2 Francs, raised design	—	25.00
E1a	1949(a)	2,000	50 Centimes, copper-nickel	—	15.00
E2a	1949(a)	2,000	1 Franc, copper-nickel	—	17.50
E3a	1949(a)	2,000	2 Francs, copper-nickel	—	20.00
E4	1952(a)	1,200	5 Francs	—	25.00

PIEFORTS with ESSAI (PE)

(Double Thickness)

Standard metals unless otherwise noted

Y#	Date	Mintage	Identification	Issue Price	Mkt Val.
PE1	1949(a)	104	50 Centimes	—	100.00
PE2	1949(a)	104	1 Franc	—	110.00
PE3	1949(a)	104	2 Francs	—	120.00
PE4	1952(a)	104	5 Francs	—	130.00

FRENCH POLYNESIA

The Territory of French Polynesia (formerly French Oceania has an area of 1,544 sq. mi. (3,999 sq. km.) and a population of 138,000. It is comprised of the same five archipelagoes that were grouped administratively to form French Oceania.

The colony of French Oceania became the Territory of French Polynesia by act of the French National Assembly in March, 1957. In Sept. of 1958 it voted in favor of the new constitution of the Fifth Republic, thereby electing to remain within the new French Community.

Picturesque, mountainous Tahiti, the setting of many tales of adventure and romance, is one of the most inspiringly beautiful islands in the world. Robert Louis Stevenson called it 'God's sweetest works'. It was there that Paul Gaugin, one of the pioneers of the Impressionist movement, painted the brilliant, exotic pictures that later made him famous. The arid coral atolls of Tuamotu comprise the most economically valuable area of French Polynesia. Pearl oysters thrive in the warm, limpid lagoons, and extensive portions of the atolls are valuable phosphate rock.

MINTMARKS

(a) - Paris, privy marks only

MONETARY SYSTEM

100 Centimes = 1 Franc

50 CENTIMES

ALUMINUM

Y#	Date	Mintage	Fine	VF	XF	Unc
1	1965(a)	.500	.15	.25	.75	2.00

FRANC

ALUMINUM

Y#	Date	Mintage	Fine	VF	XF	Unc
2	1965(a)	4.300	.10	.15	.30	.75

Obv. leg: I.E.O.M. added

Y#	Date	Mintage	Fine	VF	XF	Unc
2a	1975(a)	2.000	.10	.15	.30	.75
	1979(a)	—	.10	.15	.30	.75

2 FRANCS

ALUMINUM

Y#	Date	Mintage	Fine	VF	XF	Unc
3	1965(a)	1.750	.15	.25	.40	.75

Obv. leg: I.E.O.M. added

Y#	Date	Mintage	Fine	VF	XF	Unc
3a	1973(a)	—	.10	.15	.35	.85
	1975(a)	1.000	.10	.15	.35	.85
	1979(a)	—	.10	.15	.35	.85

5 FRANCS

ALUMINUM

Y#	Date	Mintage	Fine	VF	XF	Unc
4	1965(a)	1.520	.15	.35	.75	1.75

Obv. leg: I.E.O.M. added
Rev: Similar to 5 Francs, Y#4.

Y#	Date	Mintage	Fine	VF	XF	Unc
4a	1975(a)	.500	.15	.25	.75	1.50
	1979(a)	—	.15	.25	.75	1.50

10 FRANCS

NICKEL

Y#	Date	Mintage	Fine	VF	XF	Unc
5	1967(a)	1.000	.25	.40	1.00	2.50

Obv: I.E.O.M. below head

Y#	Date	Mintage	Fine	VF	XF	Unc
5a	1972(a)	.300	.15	.25	1.00	2.00
	1973(a)	.400	.15	.25	1.00	2.00
	1975(a)	1.000	.15	.20	.60	1.25
	1979(a)	—	.15	.20	.60	1.25

20 FRANCS

NICKEL

Y#	Date	Mintage	Fine	VF	XF	Unc
6	1967(a)	.750	.20	.50	1.25	2.50

Y#	Date	Mintage	Fine	VF	XF	Unc
6	1969(a)	.250	.50	1.00	2.00	4.00
	1970(a)	.500	.50	1.00	1.75	2.75

Obv: I.E.O.M. below head

Y#	Date	Mintage	Fine	VF	XF	Unc
6a	1972(a)	.300	.20	.40	1.25	2.50
	1973(a)	.300	.20	.40	1.25	2.50
	1975(a)	.700	.15	.30	.80	2.00
	1979(a)	—	.15	.30	.80	2.00

50 FRANCS

NICKEL

Y#	Date	Mintage	Fine	VF	XF	Unc
7	1967(a)	.600	.75	1.25	2.50	5.00

Obv: I.E.O.M. below head. Rev: Similar to Y#7.

Y#	Date	Mintage	Fine	VF	XF	Unc
7a	1975(a)	.500	.50	1.00	2.00	4.00
	1979(a)	—	.50	1.00	2.00	4.00

100 FRANCS

NICKEL-BRONZE

Y#	Date	Mintage	Fine	VF	XF	Unc
8	1976	2.000	.75	1.50	2.75	6.00
	1979	—	.75	1.50	2.75	6.00

NCLT ISSUES

ESSAIS (E)

Standard metals unless otherwise noted

Y#	Date	Mintage	Identification	Issue Price	Mkt Val.
E5	1967(a)	1,700	10 Francs	—	15.00
E6	1967(a)	1,700	20 Francs	—	18.50
E7	1967(a)	1,700	50 Francs	—	21.50

PIEFORTS (P)

(Double Thickness)

Standard metals unless otherwise noted

Y#	Date	Mintage	Identification	Issue Price	Mkt Val.
P2a	1979(a)	—	1 Franc	—	20.00
P2b	1979(a)	250	1 Franc, .925 Silver	—	50.00
P2c	1979(a)	200	1 Franc, .920 Gold	—	700.00
P3a	1979(a)	—	2 Francs	—	25.00
P3b	1979(a)	250	2 Francs, .925 Silver	—	65.00
P3c	1979(a)	200	2 Francs, .920 Gold	—	1200.
P4a	1979(a)	—	5 Francs	—	35.00
P4b	1979(a)	250	5 Francs, .925 Silver	—	75.00
P4c	1979(a)	200	5 Francs, .920 Gold	—	1800.
P5a	1979(a)	—	10 Francs	—	45.00
P5b	1979(a)	250	10 Francs, .925 Silver	—	80.00
P5c	1979(a)	200	10 Francs, .920 Gold	—	1000.
P6a	1979(a)	—	20 Francs	—	65.00
P6b	1979(a)	250	20 Francs, .925 Silver	—	90.00
P6c	1979(a)	200	20 Francs, .920 Gold	—	1600.
P7a	1979(a)	—	50 Francs	—	75.00
P7b	1979(a)	250	50 Francs, .925 Silver	—	125.00
P7c	1979(a)	200	50 Francs, .920 Gold	—	2300.
P8	1979(a)	—	100 Francs	—	80.00
P8a	1979(a)	350	100 Francs, .925 Silver	—	300.00
P8b	1979(a)	250	100 Francs, .920 Gold	—	1600.

PIEFORTS with ESSAI (PE)

(DOUBLE THICKNESS)

Standard metals unless otherwise noted

Y#	Date	Mintage	Identification	Issue Price	Mkt Val.
PE5	1967(a)	500	10 Francs	—	30.00
PE5a	1967(a)	50	10 Francs, .950 Silver	—	110.00
PE5b	1967(a)	20	10 Francs, .920 Gold	—	600.00
PE6	1967(a)	500	20 Francs	—	35.00
PE6a	1967(a)	50	20 Francs, .950 Silver	—	130.00
PE6b	1967(a)	20	20 Francs, .920 Gold	—	800.00
PE7	1967(a)	500	50 Francs	—	40.00
PE7a	1967(a)	50	50 Francs, .950 Silver	—	150.00
PE7b	1967(a)	20	50 Francs, .920 Gold	—	1,000.

FLEUR DE COIN SETS

KM#	Date	Mintage	Identification	Issue Price	Mkt. Val.
1	1965(a) (4)	2,200	Y1-4	—	10.00
2	1967(3)	2,200	Y5-7	10.00	—

NOTE: KM#1 was issued with French Somaliland. H#1: refer to French Afars and Issas.

NOTE: KM#2 was issued with New Caledonia and New Hebrides.

Listings For

FRENCH SOMALILAND: refer to Djibouti

FR. WEST AFRICA

French West Africa (Afrique Occidentale Francaise), a former federation of French colonial territories on the northwest coast of Africa, has an area of 1,831,079 sq. mi. (4,742,495 sq. km.) and a population of about 17 million. Capital: Dakar. The constituent territories were Mauritania, Senegal, Dahomey, French Sudan, Ivory Coast, Upper Volta, Niger, French Guinea, and later on the mandated area of Togo. Peanuts, palm kernels, cacao, coffee and bananas were exported.

Prior to the mid-19th century, France, as the other European states, maintained establishments on the west coast of Africa for the purpose of trading in slaves and gum, but made no serious attempt at colonization. From 1854 onward, the coastal settlements were gradually extended into the interior until, by the opening of the 20th century, acquisition ended and organization and development began. French West Africa was formed in 1895 by grouping the several colonies under one administration (at Dakar) while retaining a large measure of autonomy to each of the constituent territories. The inhabitants of French West Africa were made French citizens in 1946. With the exception of French Guinea, all of the colonies voted in 1958 to become autonomous members of the new French Community. French Guinea voted to become the fully independent Republic of Guinea. The present-day independent states are members of the "Union Monetaire Ouest-Africaine."

Also see West African States.

MINTMARKS

(a) - Paris, privy marks only

MONETARY SYSTEM

100 Centimes = 1 Franc
5 Francs = 1 Unit

TOKEN ISSUES

(GABON, MIDDLE CONGO, EQUATORIAL AFRICA)

In 1883, Savorgnan de Brazza replaced existing paper currencies with a series of eight metal tokens. The five lower denominations, cut from sheet zinc, stamped with an "F", lacked denominations but were identifiable to value by the shape in which they were cut. The three high values were struck on brass planchets. This issue was made legal tender in 1887 and circulated until September 19, 1888, the day of the fire at the station at Franceville. Rather than scrap all the damaged tokens, the zinc pieces were counterstamped with an additional "P". A new issue of the regular zinc tokens was made in 1893.

0.10 FRANC

ZINC, Uniface
Countermarked F

KM#	Date	Mintage	VG	Fine	VF
1	ND (1883,93)	—	15.00	22.50	35.00

With additional mark "P"

KM#	Date	Mintage	VG	Fine	VF
1a	ND (1888)	—	25.00	37.50	60.00

0.20 FRANC

ZINC, Uniface
Countermarked "F"

KM#	Date	Mintage	VG	Fine	VF
2	ND (1883,93)	—	15.00	22.50	35.00

With additional mark "P"

KM#	Date	Mintage	VG	Fine	VF
2a	ND (1888)	—	25.00	37.50	60.00

0.50 FRANC

ZINC Uniface
Countermarked "F"

KM#	Date	Mintage	VG	Fine	VF
3	ND (1883,93)	—	15.00	22.50	35.00

With additional mark "P"

KM#	Date	Mintage	VG	Fine	VF
3a	ND (1888)	—	25.00	37.50	60.00

FRANC

ZINC, Uniface
Countermarked "F"

KM#	Date	Mintage	VG	Fine	VF
4	ND (1883,93)	—	15.00	22.50	35.00

With additional mark "P"

KM#	Date	Mintage	VG	Fine	VF
4a	ND (1888)	—	25.00	37.50	60.00

1.50 FRANCS

ZINC, Uniface
Countermarked "F"

KM#	Date	Mintage	Good	VG	Fine
5	ND (1883,93)	—	15.00	22.50	35.00

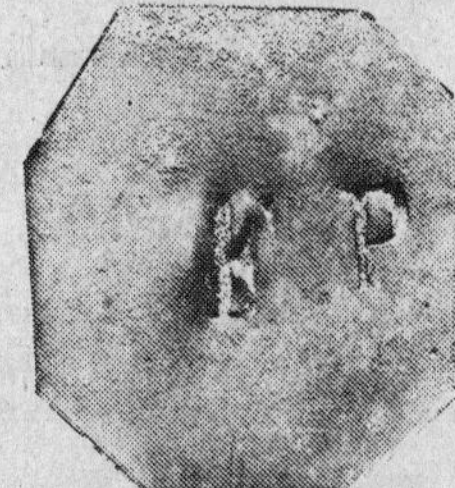

With additional mark "P"

KM#	Date	Mintage	Good	VG	Fine
5a	ND (1888)	—	25.00	37.50	60.00

1 UNIT (=5 FRANCS)

BRASS

Y#	Date	Mintage	Fine	VF	XF
A6	1883	—	50.00	65.00	150.00

5 UNITS (=25 FRANCS)

BRASS

Y#	Date	Mintage	Fine	VF	XF
A7	1883	—	50.00	65.00	150.00

10 UNITS (=50 FRANCS)

BRASS

Y#	Date	Mintage	Fine	VF	XF
A8	1883	—	50.00	65.00	150.00

COLONIAL ISSUES

50 CENTIMES

ALUMINUM-BRONZE

Y#	Date	Mintage	Fine	VF	XF	Unc
1	1944	10.000	.75	1.75	5.00	10.00

FRANC

ALUMINUM-BRONZE

Y#	Date	Mintage	Fine	VF	XF	Unc
2	1944	15.000	1.50	2.50	3.50	5.00

ALUMINUM

Y#	Date	Mintage	Fine	VF	XF	Unc
3	1948(a)	30.110	.10	.15	.20	.50
	1955(a)	5.200	.25	.35	.50	.75

2 FRANCS

ALUMINUM

Y#	Date	Mintage	Fine	VF	XF	Unc
4	1948(a)	12.665	.10	.15	.25	.75
	1955(a)	1.400	.15	.25	.50	1.00

5 FRANCS

ALUMINUM-BRONZE

Y#	Date	Mintage	Fine	VF	XF	Unc
5	1956(a)	85.000	.15	.30	.45	.75

10 FRANCS

ALUMINUM-BRONZE

Y#	Date	Mintage	Fine	VF	XF	Unc
6	1956(a)	64.133	.25	.50	.75	1.25

For French West Africa and Togo

Y#	Date	Mintage	Fine	VF	XF	Unc
8	1957(a)	30.000	.25	.50	.75	3.00

25 FRANCS

ALUMINUM-BRONZE

Y#	Date	Mintage	Fine	VF	XF	Unc
7	1956(a)	20.000	.25	.50	.75	2.00

For French West Africa and Togo

Y#	Date	Mintage	Fine	VF	XF	Unc
9	1957(a)	30.000	.30	.60	1.00	1.50

NCLT ISSUES

ESSAIS (E)

Standard metals unless otherwise noted

Y#	Date	Mintage	Identification	Issue Price	Mkt Val.
E3a	1948(a)	2,000	1 Franc, Copper-Nickel	—	15.00
E4a	1948(a)	2,000	2 Francs, Copper-Nickel	—	17.50
E5	1956(a)	2,300	5 Francs	—	15.00
E6	1956(a)	2,300	10 Francs	—	17.50
E7	1956(a)	2,300	25 Francs	—	20.00
E8	1957(a)	2,300	10 Francs	—	15.00
E9	1957(a)	2,300	25 Francs	—	20.00

PIEFORTS with ESSAIS (PE)

(Double Thickness)

Standard metals unless otherwise noted

Y#	Date	Mintage	Identification	Issue Price	Mkt Val.
PE3	1948(a)	104	1 Franc	—	100.00
PE4	1948(a)	104	2 Francs	—	110.00

Listings For

FUJAIRAH: refer to United Arab Emirates

GABON

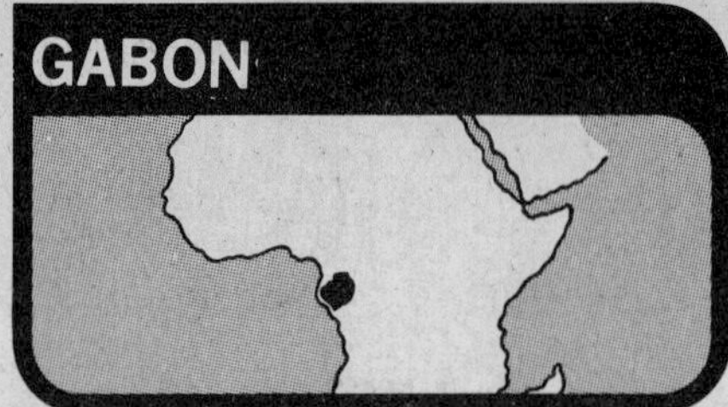

The Gabonese Republic, a member of the French Community, straddles the equator on the west coast of Africa. The hot and humid rain forest country has an area of 103,347 sq. mi. (267,667 sq. km.) and a population of 950,000, almost all of Bantu origin. Capital: Libreville. Extravagantly rich in resources, Gabon exports crude oil, manganese ore, gold and timbers.

Gabon was first visited by Portuguese navigator Diego Cam in the 15th century. Dutch, French and British traders, lured by the rich stands of hard woods and oil palms, quickly followed. The French founded their first settlement on the left bank of the Gabon River in 1839 and established their presence by signing treaties with the tribal chiefs. After gradually extending their influence into the interior during the last half of the 19th century, France occupied Gabon in 1885 and, in 1910, organized it as one of the four territories of French Equatorial Africa. It became an autonomous republic within the French Union in 1946, and on Aug. 17, 1960, became a completely independent republic within the new French Community.

NOTE: For earlier and related coinage see French Equatorial Africa, Central African States and the Equatorial African States.

MINTMARKS

(a) - Paris, privy marks only

10 FRANCS

3.2000 gm., .900 GOLD, .0926 oz AGW
Similar to 25 Francs, KM#2.

KM#	Date	Mintage	XF	Unc	Proof
1	1960	500 pcs.	—	—	100.00

25 FRANCS

8.0000 gm., .900 GOLD, .2315 oz AGW

KM#	Date	Mintage	XF	Unc	Proof
2	1960	.010	BV	165.00	175.00
	1960	500 pcs.	—	—	200.00

50 FRANCS

16.0000 gm., .900 GOLD, .4630 oz AGW
Similar to 25 Francs, KM#2.

KM#	Date	Mintage	XF	Unc	Proof
3	1960	500 pcs.	—	—	325.00

100 FRANCS

32.0000 gm., .900 GOLD, .9260 oz AGW
Similar to 25 Francs, KM#2.

KM#	Date	Mintage	XF	Unc	Proof
4	1960	500 pcs.	—	—	650.00

NICKEL

Y#	Date	Mintage	Fine	VF	XF	Unc
1	1971(a)	1.300	.50	1.00	2.50	4.00
	1972(a)	2.000	.50	1.00	1.25	2.50
2	1975(a)	—	.50	1.00	1.25	2.50

1000 FRANCS

3.5000 gm., .900 GOLD, .1012 oz AGW

KM#	Date	Mintage	XF	Unc	Proof
6	1969	4,000	—	—	125.00

3000 FRANCS

10.5000 gm., .900 GOLD, .3038 oz AGW

KM#	Date	Mintage	XF	Unc	Proof
7	1969	4,000	—	—	250.00

5000 FRANCS

17.5000 gm., .900 GOLD, .5064 oz AGW

KM#	Date	Mintage	XF	Unc	Proof
8	1969	4,000	—	—	375.00

10,000 FRANCS

35.0000 gm., .900 GOLD, 1.0128 oz AGW

KM#	Date	Mintage	XF	Unc	Proof
9	1969	4,000	—	—	700.00

20,000 FRANCS

70.0000 gm., .900 GOLD, 2.0257 oz AGW
Rev: Apollo XI at launching pad.

KM#	Date	Mintage	XF	Unc	Proof
10	1969	4,000	—	—	1500.

NCLT ISSUES

ESSAIS (E)

Standard metals unless otherwise noted

Y#	Date	Mintage	Identification	Issue Price	Mkt Val.
—	1960	10	25 Francs	—	—
E1	1971(a)	—	100 Francs	—	25.00
—	1971(a)	—	5000 Francs, Copper-Aluminum-Nickel		125.00
E2	1975(a)	—	100 Francs	—	20.00

PROOF SETS

STANDARD METALS

KM#	Date	Mintage	Identification	Issue Price	Mkt. Val.
101	1960(4)	500	KM1-4	—	1250.
102	1969(5)	4,000	KM6-10	—	2950.

GAMBIA, THE

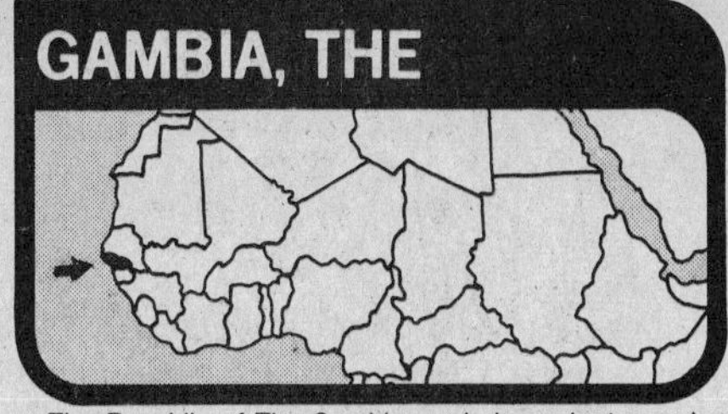

The Republic of The Gambia, an independent member of the British Commonwealth, occupies a strip of land 7 miles (11 km.) to 20 miles (32 km.) wide and 200 miles (322 km.) long encompassing both sides of West Africa's Gambia River, and completely surrounded by Senegal. The republic, one of Africa's smallest countries, has an area of 4,003 sq. mi. (10,367 sq. km.) and a population of 525,000. Capital: Banjul. Agriculture and tourism are the principal industries. Peanuts constitute 95 per cent of export earnings.

The Gambia was once part of the great empires of Ghana and Songhay. When Portuguese gold seekers and slave traders visited The Gambia in the 15th century, it was part of the Kingdom of Mali. In 1588 the territory became, through purchase, the first British colony in Africa. English slavers established Fort James, the first settlement, on a small island a dozen miles up the Gambia River in 1664. After alternate periods of union with Sierra Leone and existence as a seperate colony The Gambia became a British colony in 1888. On Feb. 18, 1965, The Gambia achieved independence as a constitutional monarchy within the Commonwealth of Nations, with the Queen of England as Chief of State. It became a republic on April 24, 1970, remaining a member of the Commonwealth, but with the president as Chief of State and Head of Government.

Gambia's 8 Shillings coin is a unique denomination in world coinage.

NOTE: For earlier coinage see British West Africa.

RULERS

Elizabeth II, 1952-1970

MONETARY SYSTEM

12 Pence = 1 Shilling
4 Shillings = 1 Dirham
20 Shillings = 1 Pound

PENNY

BRONZE

Y#	Date	Mintage	VF	XF	Unc
1	1966	3.600	.10	.20	.35
	1966	6,600	—	Proof	1.75

3 PENCE

NICKEL-BRASS

Y#	Date	Mintage	VF	XF	Unc
2	1966	2.000	.10	.15	.30
	1966	6,600	—	Proof	2.00

6 PENCE

COPPER-NICKEL

Y#	Date	Mintage	VF	XF	Unc
3	1966	1.500	.15	.25	.50
	1966	6,600	—	Proof	2.25

SHILLING

COPPER-NICKEL

Y#	Date	Mintage	VF	XF	Unc
4	1966	2.500	.30	.50	.75
	1966	6,600	—	Proof	2.75

2 SHILLINGS

COPPER-NICKEL

Y#	Date	Mintage	VF	XF	Unc
5	1966	1.600	.35	.75	1.50
	1966	6,600	—	Proof	3.50

4 SHILLINGS

COPPER-NICKEL
Obv: Similar to 2 Shillings, Y#5.

Y#	Date	Mintage	VF	XF	Unc
6	1966	.800	1.00	1.75	3.50
	1966	6,600	—	Proof	6.00

8 SHILLINGS

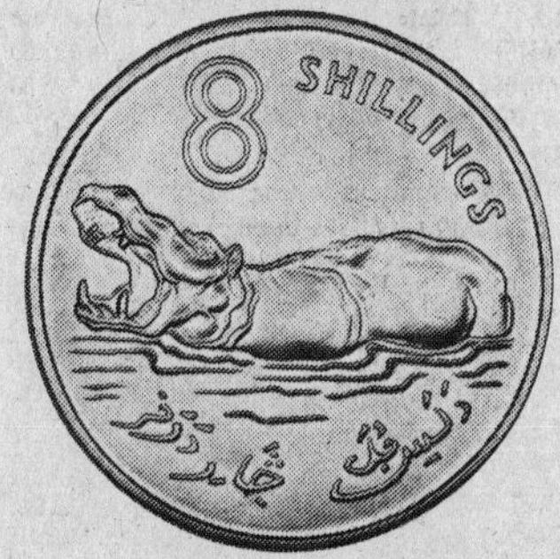

COPPER-NICKEL
Obv: Similar to 2 Shillings, Y#5.

Y#	Date	Mintage	VF	XF	Unc
7	1970	.025	2.25	4.25	8.50

33.7000 gm., .925 SILVER, 1.0023 oz ASW

Y#	Date	Mintage	VF	XF	Unc
7a	1970	4,500	—	Proof	60.00

DECIMAL COINAGE

100 Bututs = 1 Dalasi

BUTUT

BRONZE

Y#	Date	Mintage	VF	XF	Unc
8	1971	7.500	—	.10	.20
8	1971	.020	—	Proof	1.50
	1973	3.000	—	.10	.25
	1974	2.000	—	—	—
	1974	6,285	—	Proof	—
	1975	—	—	—	—

F.A.O. Issue

Y#	Date	Mintage	VF	XF	Unc
14	1974	11.500	—	.10	.20

5 BUTUTS

BRONZE

Y#	Date	Mintage	VF	XF	Unc
9	1971	3.900	.05	.10	.20
	1971	.026	—	Proof	2.00

10 BUTUTS

NICKEL-BRASS

Y#	Date	Mintage	VF	XF	Unc
10	1971	2.250	.10	.15	.30
	1971	.026	—	Proof	2.50

25 BUTUTS

COPPER-NICKEL

Y#	Date	Mintage	VF	XF	Unc
11	1971	2.400	.25	.40	.65
	1971	.026	—	Proof	3.00

50 BUTUTS

COPPER-NICKEL

Y#	Date	Mintage	VF	XF	Unc
12	1971	1.300	.50	.75	1.00
	1971	.026	—	Proof	3.50

DALASI

COPPER-NICKEL
Obv: Similar to 50 Bututs, Y#12.

Y#	Date	Mintage	VF	XF	Unc
13	1971	1.300	1.00	1.50	3.00
	1971	.026	—	Proof	8.50

10 DALASIS

28.2800 gm., .500 SILVER, .4546 oz ASW
Jawara Commemorative

Y#	Date	Mintage	VF	XF	Unc
—	1974	.030	—	—	—

Independence Commemorative
Obv: Similar to 50 Bututs, Y#12.

Y#	Date	Mintage	VF	XF	Unc
15	1975	*.050	BV	BV	16.50

28.2800 gm., .925 SILVER, .8411 oz ASW

Y#	Date	Mintage	VF	XF	Unc
15a	1975	*.020	—	Proof	20.00

*Estimated mintages.

20 DALASIS

35.0000 gm., .900 SILVER, 1.0128 oz ASW
Conservation Series

Y#	Date	Mintage	VF	XF	Unc
16	1977	—	BV	BV	25.00
	1977	—	—	Proof	30.00

40 DALASIS

41.8800 gm., .900 SILVER, 1.2119 oz ASW
Conservation Series

Y#	Date	Mintage	VF	XF	Unc
17	1977	—	BV	BV	40.00
	1977	—	—	Proof	50.00

500 DALASIS

GOLD
Conservation Series
Obv: Similar to 20 Dalasis, Y#16.

Y#	Date	Mintage	VF	XF	Unc
18	1977	—	BV	BV	650.00
	1977	—	—	Proof	750.00

NCLT ISSUES

PROOF SETS

STANDARD METALS

KM#	Date	Mintage	Identification	Issue Price	Mkt. Val.
101	1966(6)	5,100	Y1-6	13.00	17.50
102	1970/66(7)	1,500	Y1-6,7a	25.00	70.00
103	1971(6)	20,050	Y8-13	—	18.00
104	1977	—	Y16-17	60.00	75.00

NOTE: The original issue for 1971 was 50 sets. An additional 20,000 sets have been produced.

Listings For

GERMAN EAST AFRICA: refer to Tanzania

GERMAN NEW GUINEA: refer to Papua-New Guinea

1 Aachen
2 Anhalt-Bernburg
3 Anhalt-Dessau
4 Baden
5 Bavaria
6 Berg
7 Birkenfeld
8 Brandenburg-Ansbach-Bayreuth
9 Brunswick-Luneburg & Wolfenbuttel
10 Corvey
11 East Friesland
12 Eichstadt
13 Erfurt
14 Freising
15 Friedberg
16 Fulda
17 Furstenberg
18 Halle
19 Hannover
20 Hesse-Cassel
21 Hesse-Darmstadt
22 Hildesheim
23 Hohenzollern
24 Jever
25 Julich
26 Knyphausen
27 Lauenburg
28 Lippe-Detmold
29 Mainz
30 Mansfeld
31 Mecklenburg-Schwerin
32 Mecklenburg-Strelitz
33 Muhlhausen
34 Munster
35 Nassau
36 Oldenburg
37 Osnabruck
38 Paderborn
39 Passau
40 Prussia
41 Pyrmont
42 Reuss-Greiz
43 Reuss-Schleiz
44 Rhein Pfalz
45 Saxe-Altenburg
46 Saxe-Coburg-Gotha
47 Saxe-Meiningen
48 Saxe-Weimar-Eisenach
49 Saxony
50 Schaumburg-Hessen & Lippe
51 Schleswig-Holstein
52 Schwarzburg-Rudolstadt
53 Schwarzburg-Sonderhausen
54 Stolberg-Wernigerode
55 Trier
56 Waldeck-Pyrmont
57 Wallmoden-Gimborn
58 Wurttemberg
59 Wurzburg

GERMAN EMPIRE

Although the origin of the German Empire can be traced to the Treaty of Verdun, 843, that ceded Charlemagne's lands east of the Rhine to German Prince Louis, it was for centuries little more than a geographic expression, consisting of hundreds of effectively autonomous big and little states. Nominally the states owed their allegiance to the Holy Roman Emperor, who was also a German king, but as the Emperors exhibited less and less concern for Germany the actual power devolved on the lords of the individual states. The fragmentation of the empire climaxed with the tragic denouement of the Thirty Years War, 1618-48, which devastated much of Germany, destroyed its agriculture and medieval commercial eminence and ended the attempt of the Hapsburgs to unify Germany. Deprived of admin- istrative capacity by a lack of resources, the imperial au- thority became utterly powerless. At this time Germany contained an estimated 1,800 individual states, some with a population of as little as 300. The German Empire of recent history (the creation of Bismarck) was formed on April 14, 1871, when the king of Prussia became Emperor William I of Germany. The new empire comprised 4 kingdoms, 5 grand duchies, 13 duchies and principalities, 3 free cities and the nonautonomous province of Alsace- Lorraine. The states had the right to issue gold and silver coins of higher value than 1 mark; coins of 1 mark and under were general issues of the empire.

MINTMARKS

A - Berlin, 1850-date
A - Clausthal (Hannover) 1832-1849
B - Bayreuth, Franconia (Prussia) 1796-1804
B - Breslau (Prussia, Silesia) 1750-1826
B - Brunswick (Brunswick) 1850-1860
B - Brunswick (Westphalia) 1809-1813
B - Dresden (Saxony) 1861-1872
B - Hannover (Brunswick) 1860-1871
B - Hannover (East Friesland) 1823-1825
B - Hannover (Germany) 1866-1878
B - Hannover (Hannover) 1821-1866
B - Regensburg (Regensburg) 1809
B.H. Frankfurt (Free City of Frankfurt) 1808
B (rosette) H - Regensburg (Prince Primate of Germany) 1802-1812
C - Cassel (Westphalia) 1810-1813
C - Clausthal (Brunswick)
C - Clausthal (Hannover) 1813-1834
C - Clausthal (Westphalia) 1810-1811
C - Dresden (Saxony) 1779-1804
C - Frankfurt (Germany) 1866-1879
C - Ober Hessen (Ober-Hessen) 1807, 1814-1821
D - Aurich (East Friesland under Prussia) 1750-1806
D - Dusseldorf, Rhineland (Prussia) 1816-1848
D - Munich (Germany) 1872-date
E - Dresden (Germany) 1872-1887
E - Muldenhutte (Germany) 1887-1953
F - Dresden (Saxony) 1845-1858
F- Magdeburg (Prussia) 1750-1806
F - Ober-Hessen (Ober-Hessen) 1803-1807
F - Stuttgart (Germany) 1872-date
G - Dresden (Saxony) 1833-1844, 1850-1854
G - Glatz (Prussian Silesia) 1807-1809
G - Karlsruhe (Germany) 1872-date
G - Stettin In Pomerania (Prussia) 1750-1806
GN-BW - Bamberg (Bamberg)
H - Darmstadt (Germany) 1872-1882
H - Dresden (Saxony) 1804-1812
H.K. - Rostock (Rostock) 1862-1864
I - Hamburg (Germany)
J - Hamburg (Germany) 1873-date
J - Paris (Westphalia) 1808-1809
M.C. - Brunswick (brunswick) 1813-14, 1820
P.R. - Dusseldorf (Julich-Berg) 1783-1804
S - Dresden (Saxony) 1813-1832
S - Hannover (Hannover) 1839-1844
ST - Strickling (Blomberg) 1820-1840
T - Trebbe (Lemgo) 1812-1820

MONETARY SYSTEM

Until 1871 the Mark (Marck) was a measure of weight.

North German States until 1837
2 Heller = 1 Pfennig
8 Pfennige = 1 Mariengroschen
12 Pfennige = 1 Groschen
24 Groschen = 1 Thaler
2 Gulden = 1-1/3 Reichsthaler
1 Speciesthaler (Before 1753)
1 Convention Thaler (After 1753)

North German States after 1837
12 Pfennige = 1 Groschen
30 Groschen = 1 Thaler
Vereinsthaler After 1857

South German States until 1837
8 Heller = 4 Pfennige = 1 Kreuzer
24 Kreuzer Landmunze = 20 Kreuzer Convention Munze
120 Convention Kreuzer = 2 Convention Gulden = 1 Convention Thaler

South German States after 1837
8 Heller = 4 Pfennige = 1 Kreuzer

German States 1857-1871

As a result of the Monetary Convention of 1857, all the German States adopted a Vereinsthaler of uniform weight being 1/30 fine pound silver. They did continue to use their regional minor coin units to divide the Vereinsthaler for small change purposes.

After the German unification in 1871 when the old Thaler system was abandoned in favor of the mark system (100 pfennig = 1 mark) the Vereinsthaler continued to circulate as a legal tender 3 Mark coin, and the double Thaler as a 6 Mark coin until 1908. In 1908 the Vereinsthalers were officially demonetized and the Thaler coinage was replaced by the new 3 Mark coin which had the same specifications as the old Vereinsthaler. The double Thaler coinage was not replaced as there was no great demand for a 6 Mark coin. Until the 1930's the German public continued to refer to the 3 Mark piece as a 'Thaler'.

MONETARY SYSTEM

Commencing 1871
100 Pfennig = 1 Mark

AACHEN

(Achen, Urbs, Aquensis, Aquis Grani)

Located in the Rhineland on the Belgian-Dutch border. It was the reputed birthplace of Charlemagne and the Imperial Coronation City for 700 years. The Mint was established in 1166. City coinage began in the 14th century. Made a part of France in 1801 and went to Prussia in 1815.

FREE CITY

MONETARY SYSTEM

24 Heller = 1 Marck
48 Marck = 1 Reichsthaler

4 HELLER

COPPER
Obv: Eagle dividing date.
Rev: IIII REICHS STAT ACH.

C#	Date	Mintage	VG	Fine	VF	XF
1a	1758	—	.75	1.50	4.00	15.00
	1759	—	.75	1.50	4.00	15.00
	1763	—	.75	1.50	4.00	15.00
	1767	—	.75	1.50	4.00	15.00

12 HELLER

COPPER

C#	Date	Mintage	VG	Fine	VF	XF
2	1758	—	.75	2.00	5.00	15.00
	1759	—	.75	2.00	5.00	15.00
	1760	—	.75	2.00	5.00	15.00
	1761	—	.75	2.00	5.00	15.00
	1764	—	.75	2.00	5.00	15.00
	1765	—	.75	2.00	5.00	15.00
	1767	—	.75	2.00	5.00	15.00
	1791	—	.75	2.00	5.00	15.00
	1792	—	.75	2.00	5.00	15.00
	1793	—	.75	2.00	5.00	15.00
	1794	—	.75	2.00	5.00	15.00
	1797	—	.75	2.00	5.00	15.00

NOTE: Many varieties exist.

ANHALT — BERNBURG

Located in north-central Germany. Appeared as part of the patrimony of Albrecht the Bear of Brandenburg in 1170. Bracteates Were First Made In The 12th century. It was originally in the inheritance of Heinrich the Fat in 1252 and became extinct in 1468. The division of 1603, among the sons of Joachim Ernst revitalized Anhalt-Bernburg. Bernburg passed to Dessau after the death of Alexander Carl in 1863.

RULERS

Friedrich Albrecht, 1765-1796
Alexius Friedrich Christian, 1796-1834
Alexander Carl, 1834-1863

MINTMASTER'S INITIALS

H.C.A.S., S. - Heinrich Christian Andreas Siegel (1767-1795)
H.S. - Hans Schielder (1795-1821)
Z - Johann Carl Ludwig Zincken (1821-1831)

PFENNIG

COPPER
Obv: Bear on wall.
Rev: Value and date, S under date.

C#	Date	Mintage	VG	Fine	VF	XF
40	1776S	—	2.00	3.00	6.00	15.00
	1777S	—	2.00	3.00	6.00	15.00
	1793S	—	2.00	3.00	6.00	15.00
	1794S	—	2.00	3.00	6.00	15.00
	1795S	—	2.00	3.00	6.00	15.00

NOTE: Varieties exist.

Obv: Crowned AFC monogram.
Rev: Value and date in 5 lines.

C#	Date	Mintage	Fine	VF	XF	Unc
—	1796	—	3.00	8.00	20.00	50.00
	1797	—	3.00	8.00	20.00	50.00

Obv: Crowned bear walking on wall.
Rev: Value PFENN. and date.

C#	Date	Mintage	Fine	VF	XF	Unc
50.1	1796	—	3.00	8.00	20.00	50.00

Rev: Value PFENNIG, SCHEIDE MUNZE with umlaut (..) over U.

C#	Date	Mintage	Fine	VF	XF	Unc
50.2	1796	—	2.50	5.00	15.00	45.00
	1797	—	2.50	5.00	15.00	45.00
	1799	—	2.50	5.00	15.00	45.00

SCHEIDE MUNTZ, no umlaut.

C#	Date	Mintage	Fine	VF	XF	Unc
50.3	1797	—	2.50	5.00	15.00	45.00

C#	Date	Mintage	Fine	VF	XF	Unc
57	1807	—	2.00	3.00	10.00	40.00

Rev. legend: SCHEIDE MUNTZ

C#	Date	Mintage	Fine	VF	XF	Unc
57a	1808	—	2.00	3.00	15.00	45.00

Rev. legend: SCHEIDEMUNZE

C#	Date	Mintage	Fine	VF	XF	Unc
58	1822	—	1.00	2.50	12.00	35.00
	1823	—	1.00	2.50	12.00	35.00
	1827	—	1.00	2.50	12.00	35.00

Rev. legend: SCHEIDEMUNZE HZL ANHALT

C#	Date	Mintage	Fine	VF	XF	Unc
58a	1831Z	—	2.00	4.00	15.00	35.00

1-1/2 PFENNIG

COPPER
Obv: Bear on wall.
Rev: Value and date.

C#	Date	Mintage	VG	Fine	VF	XF
41	1776S	—	2.00	12.00	25.00	50.00

4 PFENNIGE

COPPER

C#	Date	Mintage	Fine	VF	XF	Unc
59	1822	—	2.25	4.50	20.00	45.00
	1823	—	2.25	4.50	20.00	45.00

4 PFENNINGE value

C#	Date	Mintage	Fine	VF	XF	Unc
59a	1831Z	—	3.00	6.50	20.00	45.00

1/48 THALER

BILLON
Obv: Crowned monogram. Rev: Value and date.

C#	Date	Mintage	VG	Fine	VF	XF
42	1793	—	2.00	3.00	5.00	15.00
	1794	—	2.00	3.00	5.00	15.00
	1795	—	2.00	3.00	5.00	15.00
	1796	—	2.00	3.00	5.00	15.00

NOTE: Varieties exist.

Obv: Crowned arms in branches.

C#	Date	Mintage	Fine	VF	XF	Unc
60	1807	—	4.00	8.00	20.00	50.00

1/24 THALER

BILLON
Rev. legend: H:ANH:BERNB:.....

C#	Date	Mintage	Fine	VF	XF	Unc
61	1822	—	2.00	4.00	20.00	45.00
	1823	—	2.00	4.00	20.00	45.00
	1827	—	2.00	4.00	20.00	45.00

Rev. legend: HZL. ANHALT......

C#	Date	Mintage	Fine	VF	XF	Unc
61a	1831Z	—	3.00	6.50	20.00	45.00

1/12 THALER

BILLON
Obv: Crowned bear walking on wall. Rev: Value and date.

C#	Date	Mintage	Fine	VF	XF	Unc
51	1799 HS	—	4.00	10.00	30.00	75.00

1/6 THALER

SILVER

C#	Date	Mintage	Fine	VF	XF	Unc
52	1799 HS	—	8.00	18.00	30.00	75.00

C#	Date	Mintage	Fine	VF	XF	Unc
73	1856A	.060	5.00	9.00	20.00	50.00

C#	Date	Mintage	Fine	VF	XF	Unc
74	1861A	.062	5.00	8.00	18.00	45.00
	1862A	.060	5.00	8.00	18.00	45.00

1/3 THALER

SILVER

C#	Date	Mintage	Fine	VF	XF	Unc
53	1799	—	15.00	25.00	40.00	90.00
	1799 HS	—	15.00	25.00	40.00	90.00

2/3 THALER

SILVER

C#	Date	Mintage	VG	Fine	VF	XF
44	1793	—	30.00	60.00	75.00	100.00

C#	Date	Mintage	Fine	VF	XF	Unc
55	1799 HS	—	17.50	35.00	55.00	100.00

Legend: HERZOG ZU ANHALT.....
Value: XX EINE FEINE MARK

C#	Date	Mintage	Fine	VF	XF	Unc
62	1806 HS	—	12.00	25.00	40.00	90.00
	1808 HS	—	12.00	25.00	40.00	90.00
	1809 HS	—	12.00	25.00	40.00	90.00

24 MARIENGROSCHEN

(= 2/3 Thaler)

SILVER
Obv: Crowned bear walking on wall.
Rev: Value 24 MARIENGROSCHEN and date.

C#	Date	Mintage	Fine	VF	XF	Unc
54	1796 HS	—	25.00	40.00	60.00	125.00
	1797 HS	—	25.00	40.00	60.00	125.00

Rev: Value XXIV MARIENGROSCHEN

C#	Date	Mintage	Fine	VF	XF	Unc
54a	1796 HS	—	25.00	40.00	70.00	140.00

Rev: Value XXIIII MARIENGROSCHEN

C#	Date	Mintage	Fine	VF	XF	Unc
54b	1796 HS	—	25.00	40.00	60.00	125.00

Obv: 2/3 in oval within gate of wall.

C#	Date	Mintage	Fine	VF	XF	Unc
54c	1796 HS	—	25.00	45.00	75.00	150.00

THALER

(Convention)

SILVER

C#	Date	Mintage	VG	Fine	VF	XF
46	1793	—	200.00	400.00	500.00	650.00
	1794	—	200.00	400.00	500.00	650.00

C#	Date	Mintage	VG	Fine	VF	XF
46a	1795 HS	—	110.00	275.00	350.00	475.00
	1796 HS	—	110.00	275.00	350.00	475.00

28.0600 gm., .833 SILVER, .7518 oz ASW
Crowned draped arms.

Rev. value: X/EINE within laurel wreath.

C#	Date	Mintage	Fine	VF	XF	Unc
63	1806 HS	—	250.00	500.00	1000.	1500.
	1809 HS	—	250.00	500.00	1000.	1500.

(Mining)

22.2700 gm., .750 SILVER, .5370 oz ASW

C#	Date	Mintage	Fine	VF	XF	Unc
75	1834	.015	35.00	50.00	100.00	300.00

C#	Date	Mintage	Fine	VF	XF	Unc
76	1846A	.010	25.00	45.00	90.00	150.00
	1852A	.010	25.00	45.00	90.00	150.00
	1855A	.020	25.00	45.00	90.00	150.00

(Vereins)

18.5200 gm., .900 SILVER, .4823 oz ASW

C#	Date	Mintage	Fine	VF	XF	Unc
77	1859A	.024	25.00	50.00	100.00	225.00

(Mining)

C#	Date	Mintage	Fine	VF	XF	Unc
78	1861A	.010	20.00	35.00	75.00	150.00
	1862A	.020	20.00	35.00	75.00	150.00

2 THALER

37.1200 gm., .900 SILVER, 1.0743 oz ASW

C#	Date	Mintage	Fine	VF	XF	Unc
79	1840A	3,600	250.00	500.00	1000.	1500.
	1845A	7,200	200.00	400.00	800.00	1500.
	1855A	5,000	200.00	400.00	800.00	1500.

5 THALER

6.6500 gm., .900 GOLD, .1924 oz AGW

C#	Date	Mintage	Fine	VF	XF	Unc
56	1796 HS	—	300.00	600.00	1100.	1900.

TRADE COINS

DUCAT

3.5000 gm., .986 GOLD, .1109 oz AGW
Obv. leg: EX AURO ANHALTINO, bear walking on wall.
Rev. leg: ALEXIUS FRIED CHRIST....., value.

C#	Date	Mintage	Fine	VF	XF	Unc
64	1825Z	116 pcs.		1000.	2000.	3000.

JOINT COINAGE
UNDER ALEXANDER CARL FOR ANHALT-COTHEN AND ANHALT-DESSAU

PFENNIG

COPPER
Obv: Crowned shield. Rev. legend: 288 EINEN THALER

C#	Date	Mintage	Fine	VF	XF	Unc
65	1839	.589	2.00	4.50	10.00	30.00
	1840	.654	2.00	4.50	10.00	30.00

C#	Date	Mintage	Fine	VF	XF	Unc
66	1856A	.360	1.50	3.00	8.00	25.00
	1862A	.360	1.50	3.00	8.00	25.00
	1864A	.300	1.50	3.00	8.00	25.00
	1867B	.180	1.75	3.50	9.00	30.00

3 PFENNIGE

COPPER

C#	Date	Mintage	Fine	VF	XF	Unc
67	1839	.386	2.50	5.00	10.00	35.00
	1840	.292	2.50	5.00	10.00	35.00

C#	Date	Mintage	Fine	VF	XF	Unc
68	1861A	.240	2.50	5.00	10.00	35.00
	1864A	.200	2.50	5.00	10.00	35.00
	1867B	.240	2.50	5.00	10.00	35.00

6 PFENNIGE

BILLON

C#	Date	Mintage	Fine	VF	XF	Unc
69	1840	.322	3.50	7.50	20.00	40.00

GROSCHEN

BILLON
Obv: Crowned shield. Rev. legend: 24 EINEN THALER

C#	Date	Mintage	Fine	VF	XF	Unc
70	1839	.319	3.50	7.50	20.00	40.00
	1840	Inc. Ab.	3.50	7.50	20.00	40.00

SILBERGROSCHEN

BILLON

C#	Date	Mintage	Fine	VF	XF	Unc
71	1851A	.176	1.75	3.50	8.00	30.00
	1852A	.197	1.75	3.50	8.00	30.00
	1855A	.303	1.75	3.50	8.00	30.00
	1859A	.150	1.75	3.50	8.00	30.00
	1862A	.300	1.75	3.50	8.00	30.00

2-1/2 SILBERGROSCHEN

BILLON

C#	Date	Mintage	Fine	VF	XF	Unc
72	1856A	.120	3.00	6.00	12.00	40.00
	1859A	.060	3.50	7.00	15.00	40.00
	1861A	.120	3.00	6.00	12.00	40.00
	1862A	.240	3.00	6.00	12.00	40.00
	1864A	.120	3.00	6.00	12.00	40.00

ANHALT — COTHEN

Cothen has a checkered history after the patrimony of Heinrich the Fat in 1252. It was often ruled with other segments of the House of Anhalt. Although not involved in the division of 1603, Cothen surfaced through Ploetzkau in 1665. It passed to Dessau after the death of Heinrich in 1847.

RULER

Heinrich, 1830-1847

2 THALER

37.1200 gm., .900 SILVER, 1.0743 oz ASW

C#	Date	Mintage	Fine	VF	XF	Unc
115	1840A	3,100	400.00	800.00	1500.	2500.

ANHALT — DESSAU

Dessau was part of the 1252 division that included Zerbst and Cothen. In 1396 Zerbst divided into Zerbst and Dessau. In 1508 Zerbst was absorbed into Dessau. Dessau was given to the eldest son of Joachim Ernst in the division of 1603. It was the longest surviving branch of Anhalt.

RULERS

Leopold Friedrich, 1817-1871
Friedrich I, 1871-1904
Friedrich II, 1904-1918

PFENNIG

COPPER

C#	Date	Mintage	Fine	VF	XF	Unc
120	1864A	.300	1.50	3.00	7.50	25.00
	1867B	.300	1.50	3.00	7.50	25.00

3 PFENNIGE

COPPER

C#	Date	Mintage	Fine	VF	XF	Unc
121	1864A	.200	1.75	3.50	8.00	25.00
	1867B	.200	1.75	3.50	8.00	25.00

2 1/2 SILBERGROSCHEN

BILLON

C#	Date	Mintage	Fine	VF	XF	Unc
122	1864A	—	2.50	5.00	8.00	25.00

VI EINEN (1/6) THALER

SILVER

C#	Date	Mintage	Fine	VF	XF	Unc
123	1865A	.120	5.00	10.00	20.00	35.00

EIN (1) THALER

(Vereins)

18.5200 gm., .900 SILVER, .5360 oz ASW

C#	Date	Mintage	Fine	VF	XF	Unc
124	1858A	.027*	25.00	50.00	100.00	225.00

Separation Of Anhalt Duchies - 1603
Reunion Of Anhalt Duchies - 1863

C#	Date	Mintage	Fine	VF	XF	Unc
125	1863A	.050	25.00	50.00	100.00	200.00

C#	Date	Mintage	Fine	VF	XF	Unc
126	1866A	.031	25.00	50.00	100.00	200.00
	1869A	.032	25.00	50.00	100.00	200.00

2 THALER

(= 3-1/2 Gulden)

37.1200 gm., .900 SILVER, 1.0743 oz ASW

C#	Date	Mintage	Fine	VF	XF	Unc
127	1839A	4,700	250.00	500.00	900.00	1500.
	1843A	4,700	250.00	500.00	900.00	1500.
	1846A	4,700	250.00	500.00	900.00	1500.

MONETARY REFORM

2 MARK

11.1110 gm., .900 SILVER, .3215 oz ASW

Y#	Date	Mintage	Fine	VF	XF	Unc
1	1876A	.200	100.00	200.00	900.00	1400.

Y#	Date	Mintage	Fine	VF	XF	Unc
3	1896A	.050	75.00	200.00	400.00	600.00
	1896A	—	—	—	Proof	900.00

Y#	Date	Mintage	Fine	VF	XF	Unc
7	1904A	.050	60.00	200.00	400.00	600.00
	1904A	150 pcs.	—	—	Proof	700.00

3 MARK

16.6670 gm., .900 SILVER, .4823 oz ASW

Y#	Date	Mintage	Fine	VF	XF	Unc
8	1909A	.100	15.00	50.00	80.00	150.00
	1911A	.100	15.00	50.00	75.00	125.00
	Common type	—	—	—	Proof	250.00

Silver Wedding Anniversary Commemorative

Y#	Date	Mintage	Fine	VF	XF	Unc
10	1914A	.200	15.00	30.00	50.00	70.00
	1914A	1,000	—	—	Proof	140.00

5 MARK

27.7770 gm., .900 SILVER, .8038 oz ASW

Y#	Date	Mintage	Fine	VF	XF	Unc
4	1896A	.010	300.00	600.00	1200.	1900.
	1896A	—	—	—	Proof	1300.

Silver Wedding Anniversary Commemorative
Rev: Similar to Y#4.

Y#	Date	Mintage	Fine	VF	XF	Unc
11	1914A	.030	80.00	175.00	250.00	300.00
	1914A	1,000	—	—	Proof	400.00

10 MARK

3.9820 gm., .900 GOLD, .1152 oz AGW

Y#	Date	Mintage	Fine	VF	XF	Unc
5	1896A	.020	450.00	800.00	1400.	2000.
	1901A	.020	450.00	800.00	1400.	2000.

20 MARK

7.9650 gm., .900 GOLD, .2304 oz AGW

Y#	Date	Mintage	Fine	VF	XF	Unc
2	1875A	.025	450.00	800.00	1500.	2000.

Y#	Date	Mintage	Fine	VF	XF	Unc
6	1896A	.015	350.00	750.00	1200.	1750.
	1901A	.015	350.00	750.00	1200.	1750.

Y#	Date	Mintage	Fine	VF	XF	Unc
9	1904A	.025	350.00	700.00	1100.	1600.

NCLT ISSUES

PATTERNS

KM#	Date	Mintage	Identification	Mkt.Val.
1	1914	—	3 Marks, Silver	—

KM#	Date	Mintage	Identification	Mkt.Val.
2	1914	—	5 Marks, Silver	Rare

ANHALT-ZERBST

Zerbst was one of the major parts of the division of 1252. It was divided into Zerbst and Dessau in 1396 and absorbed Bernburg in 1486. Zerbst ceded to Dessau in 1508 and was given to the 4th son of Joachim Ernst in the division of 1603. It became extinct in 1793 and was divided between Dessau, Bernburg and Cothen.

RULERS

Friedrich August, 1747-1793

HELLER

COPPER
Obv: Bust of Friedrich August right.
Rev: Arms separate date; value below.

C#	Date	Mintage	Good	VG	Fine	VF
145	1766	—	7.50	12.50	20.00	35.00

PFENNING

COPPER, 24mm

C#	Date	Mintage	Good	VG	Fine	VF
146.1	1766	—	4.50	7.50	12.50	25.00

20mm

C#	Date	Mintage	Good	VG	Fine	VF
146.2	1766	—	4.50	7.50	12.50	25.00

4 PFENNIG

BILLON
Obv: Arms.
Rev: Value and date in circle; F.A.Z.L.M A cross center.

C#	Date	Mintage	Good	VG	Fine	VF
147.1	1767	—	22.50	35.00	50.00	75.00

Rev: Without F.A.Z.L.M.

C#	Date	Mintage	Good	VG	Fine	VF
147.2	1767	—	22.50	35.00	50.00	75.00

16 PFENNIGE

(= 4 Groschen = 5 Kreuzer)

BILLON

C#	Date	Mintage	Good	VG	Fine	VF
148	1764	—	32.50	50.00	75.00	110.00

Obv: Arms.
Rev: Value and date in circle; value in Roman numerals.

C#	Date	Mintage	Good	VG	Fine	VF
149	1767	—	32.50	50.00	75.00	110.00

4 GROSCHEN

SILVER

C#	Date	Mintage	Fine	VF	XF	Unc
152	1767	—	10.00	15.00	30.00	60.00

32 PFENNIGE

(= 10 Kreuzer)

BILLON
Obv: Bust of Friedrich August right; date below.
Rev: Arms and value.

C#	Date	Mintage	Good	VG	Fine	VF
150	1764	—	12.50	20.00	32.50	50.00

1/6 THALER

SILVER

C#	Date	Mintage	Fine	VF	XF	Unc
151	1766	—	25.00	40.00	65.00	125.00

2/3 THALER

SILVER
Obv: Bust of Friedrich August right.
Rev: Helmed and supported arms; date in Roman numerals.

C#	Date	Mintage	Fine	VF	XF	Unc
154.1	1763	—	27.50	42.50	65.00	125.00

Rev: Date in Arabic numerals.

C#	Date	Mintage	Fine	VF	XF	Unc
154.2	1767	—	27.50	42.50	65.00	125.00

NOTE: Varieties exist.

THALER

SILVER
Obv: Bust of Friedrich August right.
Rev: Helmed and supported arms.

C#	Date	Mintage	Fine	VF	XF	Unc
155	1767	—	950.00	1250.	1650.	2500.

TRADE COINS

DUCAT

3.5000 gm., .986 GOLD, .1109 oz AGW
Obv: Bust of Friedrich August right.
Rev: Arms and date.

C#	Date	Mintage	Fine	VF	XF	Unc
157	1764	—	1350.	1750.	2250.	3000.

ARENBERG

Located on the Dutch border in Northwest Germany. The first coins were made c.1550. It was occupied by France in 1801 and was mediatized in 1815.

RULERS

Ludwig Engelbert, 1778-1803

THALER

(Convention)

SILVER
Obv: Large head right.
Rev: Crowned, mantled and supported arms, date below.

C#	Date	Mintage	VG	Fine	VF	XF
1	1783	—	350.00	750.00	1000.	1350.

C#	Date	Mintage	VG	Fine	VF	XF
1a	1785	—	300.00	650.00	900.00	1200.

TRADE COINS

DUCAT

3.5000 gm., .986 GOLD, .1109 oz AGW
Rev: Crowned and mantled arms.

C#	Date	Mintage	Fine	VF	XF
2	1783	—	1500.	2000.	2500.

AUGSBURG

(Bishopric)

A Bishopric located in Bavaria. See was founded in 887. The first coinage was struck in the 10th century. It was a continuous line of 980 years before being secularized in 1803.

RULERS

Clemens Wenzel, Prince of Poland and Saxony,
Bishop, 1768-1803

HELLER

COPPER
Obv: Crowned arms.
Rev: Value and date.

C#	Date	Mintage	VG	Fine	VF	XF
10	1773	—	2.50	3.50	5.00	15.00

1/4 KREUTZER

COPPER
Obv: Crowned arms; legend around border.
Rev: Value and date.

C#	Date	Mintage	VG	Fine	VF	XF
11	1773	—	2.50	3.50	5.00	15.00

1/2 KREUTZER

COPPER
Obv: Crowned arms; legend around border.
Rev: Value and date.

C#	Date	Mintage	VG	Fine	VF	XF
12	1773	—	2.50	3.50	5.00	15.00

KREUTZER

COPPER

C#	Date	Mintage	VG	Fine	VF	XF
13	1773	—	2.50	3.50	5.00	15.00
	1774	—	2.50	3.50	5.00	15.00
	1775	—	2.50	3.50	5.00	15.00

10 KREUTZER

SILVER
Obv: Bust of Clemens Wenzel right.
Rev: Crowned arms.

C#	Date	Mintage	VG	Fine	VF	XF
16	1773	—	5.00	8.50	12.50	20.00
	1774	—	5.00	8.50	12.50	20.00
	1775	—	5.00	8.50	12.50	20.00

20 KREUTZER

SILVER

C#	Date	Mintage	VG	Fine	VF	XF
17	1773	—	12.50	20.00	32.50	50.00

1/48 THALER

(2-1/2 Kreutzer)

SILVER
Obv: Crowned arms. Legend around border.
Rev: Value and date.

C#	Date	Mintage	VG	Fine	VF	XF
14	1773	—	4.50	7.50	10.00	15.00

1/24 THALER

(5 Kreutzer)

SILVER
Obv: Crowned arms; legend around border.
Rev: Value and date.

C#	Date	Mintage	VG	Fine	VF	XF
15	1773	—	4.50	7.50	10.00	15.00

(Free City)

Founded as a Roman colony in the reign of Augustus it was declared a Free City in 1276. The mint rights were granted in 1521 but the first coins are dated somewhat earlier. Augsburg was given to Bavaria in 1806.

HELLER

COPPER
Obv: Pine cone in cartouche.
Rev: Date.

C#	Date	Mintage	VG	Fine	VF	XF
1b	1766	—	3.00	4.50	6.00	20.00
	1769	—	3.00	4.50	6.00	20.00
	1770	—	3.00	4.50	6.00	20.00
	1772	—	3.00	4.50	6.00	20.00
	1773	—	3.00	4.50	6.00	20.00
	1774	—	3.00	4.50	6.00	20.00
	1775	—	3.00	4.50	6.00	20.00

Rev: Value and date.

C#	Date	Mintage	VG	Fine	VF	XF
4a	1759-1780	—	3.00	4.50	6.00	20.00

Rev: Without STADTMYNZ in legend.

C#	Date	Mintage	VG	Fine	VF	XF
4c	1764	—	2.00	3.50	5.00	18.50
	1766	—	2.00	3.50	5.00	18.50
	1769	—	2.00	3.50	5.00	18.50

Obv: Pine cone in cartouche topped by mural crown.
Rev: Value with date beneath.

C#	Date	Mintage	VG	Fine	VF	XF
2	1780	—	3.00	4.50	6.00	20.00
	1782	—	3.00	4.50	6.00	20.00
	1786	—	3.00	4.50	6.00	20.00
	1787	—	3.00	4.50	6.00	20.00
	1793	—	3.00	4.50	6.00	20.00
	1796	—	3.00	4.50	6.00	20.00
	1797	—	3.00	4.50	6.00	20.00
	1798	—	3.00	4.50	6.00	20.00
	1799	—	3.00	4.50	6.00	20.00
	1801	—	3.00	4.50	6.00	20.00

Obv: State arms in oval shield. Rev: Value and date.

C#	Date	Mintage	Fine	VF	XF	Unc
2a	1801	—	1.00	2.00	15.00	40.00
	1802	—	1.00	2.00	15.00	40.00
	1803	—	1.00	2.00	15.00	40.00
	1804	—	1.00	2.00	15.00	40.00
	1805	—	1.00	2.00	15.00	40.00

PFENNING

COPPER
Obv: Pine cone in wreath.
Rev: Value over date.

C#	Date	Mintage	VG	Fine	VF	XF
3a	1759	—	2.00	3.50	5.00	15.00
	1760	—	2.00	3.50	5.00	15.00

C#	Date	Mintage	VG	Fine	VF	XF
	1760	—	2.00	3.50	5.00	15.00
	1761	—	2.00	3.50	5.00	15.00
	1762	—	2.00	3.50	5.00	15.00
	1763	—	2.00	3.50	5.00	15.00
	1764	—	2.00	3.50	5.00	15.00
	1765	—	2.00	3.50	5.00	15.00
	1766	—	2.00	3.50	5.00	15.00
	1769	—	2.00	3.50	5.00	15.00
	1770	—	2.00	3.50	5.00	15.00
	1771	—	2.00	3.50	5.00	15.00
	1772	—	2.00	3.50	5.00	15.00
	1780	—	2.00	3.50	5.00	15.00

C#	Date	Mintage	VG	Fine	VF	XF
3b	1780	—	2.00	3.50	5.00	15.00
	1781	—	2.00	3.50	5.00	15.00
	1782	—	2.00	3.50	5.00	15.00
	1785	—	2.00	3.50	5.00	15.00
	1786	—	2.00	3.50	5.00	15.00
	1789	—	2.00	3.50	5.00	15.00
	1790	—	2.00	3.50	5.00	15.00
	1796	—	2.00	3.50	5.00	15.00
	1797	—	2.00	3.50	5.00	15.00
	1798	—	2.00	3.50	5.00	15.00
	1799	—	2.00	3.50	5.00	15.00
	1800	—	2.00	3.50	5.00	15.00

Rev: Without STADTMYNZ in legend.

C#	Date	Mintage	VG	Fine	VF	XF
3c	1764	—	2.00	3.50	5.00	15.00
	1765	—	2.00	3.50	5.00	15.00
	1766	—	2.00	3.50	5.00	15.00
	1769	—	2.00	3.50	5.00	15.00

Obv: State arms in oval shield.
Rev: Value and date, legend: STADT MUNZE.

C#	Date	Mintage	Fine	VF	XF	Unc
3d	1801	—	2.50	5.00	12.00	30.00
	1802	—	2.50	5.00	12.00	30.00
	1803	—	2.50	5.00	12.00	30.00
	1804	—	2.50	5.00	12.00	30.00
	1805	—	2.50	5.00	12.00	30.00

KREUTZER

BILLON
Obv: Pine cone. Rev: Value.

C#	Date	Mintage	VG	Fine	VF	XF
7	1766	—	10.00	15.00	25.00	50.00

5 KREUTZER

BILLON

C#	Date	Mintage	VG	Fine	VF	XF
12	1766	—	4.50	7.50	12.50	35.00

TRADE COINS

DUCAT

3.5000 gm., .986 GOLD, .1109 oz AGW

C#	Date	Mintage	Fine	VF	XF	Unc
37	1767	—	950.00	1200.	1800.	2750.

BADEN

Located in southwest Germany. The ruling house of Baden began in 1112. Various branches developed and religious wars between the branches were settled in 1648. The branches unified under Baden—Durlach after the extinction of the Baden-Baden line in 1771. The last ruler abdicated at the end of World War I. The first coins were issued in the late 1300s.

RULERS

Carl Friedrich, Margrave in all Baden, 1771-1803
As Elector, 1803-1806
As Grand Duke, 1806-1811
Carl Ludwig Friedrich, 1811-1818
Ludwig I, 1818-1830
Leopold I, 1830-1852
Ludwig II, 1852-1856, Insane and deposed
Friedrich I As Prince Regent, 1852-1856
As Grand Duke, 1856-1907
Friedrich II, 1907-1918

1/4 KREUZER

COPPER

C#	Date	Mintage	Fine	VF	XF	Unc
40	1802	.024	7.50	15.00	30.00	60.00

Obv: Crowned shield. Rev: Value, date within wreath.

C#	Date	Mintage	Fine	VF	XF	Unc
49	1810	—	—	—	—	—

C#	Date	Mintage	Fine	VF	XF	Unc
76	1824	.128	5.00	10.00	20.00	35.00

1/2 KREUZER

COPPER

C#	Date	Mintage	Fine	VF	XF	Unc
41	1803	.027	5.00	10.00	25.00	50.00
	1804	.104	4.50	9.00	15.00	30.00
	1805	.157	4.50	9.00	15.00	30.00

Obv: Crowned shield. Rev: Value, date within wreath.

C#	Date	Mintage	Fine	VF	XF	Unc
50	1809	.877	2.50	5.00	10.00	25.00
	1810	.129	3.50	7.50	15.00	30.00

Obv: Crowned shield. Rev: Value, date within wreath.

C#	Date	Mintage	Fine	VF	XF	Unc
64	1812	.105	3.00	6.00	15.00	30.00

C#	Date	Mintage	Fine	VF	XF	Unc
67	1814	.078	5.00	10.00	20.00	40.00
	1815	.062	5.00	10.00	20.00	40.00
	1816	.039	5.00	10.00	20.00	40.00
	1817	.102	5.00	10.00	20.00	40.00

Obv: Smaller crowned draped arms.

C#	Date	Mintage	Fine	VF	XF	Unc
67b	1814	Inc. Ab.	3.50	7.50	20.00	40.00

Rev: 1/2 KREU/ZER

C#	Date	Mintage	Fine	VF	XF	Unc
67a	1817	—	3.50	7.50	20.00	40.00

C#	Date	Mintage	Fine	VF	XF	Unc
74	1821	.127	3.50	7.00	15.00	30.00

C#	Date	Mintage	Fine	VF	XF	Unc
77	1822	.109	3.50	7.00	15.00	30.00
	1823	.035	3.50	7.00	15.00	35.00
	1824	.066	3.50	7.00	15.00	35.00
	1825	.053	3.50	7.00	15.00	30.00
	1826	.191	3.50	7.00	15.00	30.00

C#	Date	Mintage	Fine	VF	XF	Unc
79	1828	.137	4.00	8.00	18.00	35.00
	1829	.204	4.00	8.00	18.00	35.00
	1830	Inc. Ab.	4.00	8.00	18.00	35.00

Obv: D on truncation

C#	Date	Mintage	Fine	VF	XF	Unc
100	1830	.024	3.50	7.00	15.00	40.00
	1834	.076	3.50	7.00	15.00	30.00
	1835	.028	3.50	7.00	15.00	40.00

C#	Date	Mintage	Fine	VF	XF	Unc
100a	1842	.101	3.00	6.00	15.00	25.00
	1844	.052	3.00	6.00	15.00	35.00
	1845	.074	3.00	6.00	15.00	35.00
	1846	.090	3.00	6.00	15.00	30.00
	1847	.256	3.00	6.00	15.00	25.00
	1848	.089	3.00	6.00	15.00	30.00
	1849	.102	3.00	6.00	15.00	25.00
	1850	.074	3.00	6.00	15.00	35.00
	1851	.087	3.00	6.00	15.00	30.00
	1852	.227	3.00	6.00	15.00	25.00

C#	Date	Mintage	Fine	VF	XF	Unc
138	1856	.195	5.00	10.00	15.00	25.00

C#	Date	Mintage	Fine	VF	XF	Unc
141	1859	.219	1.50	3.00	7.50	20.00
	1860	.120	1.50	3.00	7.50	20.00
	1861	.109	1.50	3.00	7.50	20.00
	1862	.117	1.50	3.00	7.50	20.00
	1863	.298	1.50	3.00	7.50	20.00
	1864	.094	1.50	3.00	7.50	20.00
	1865	.349	1.50	3.00	7.50	20.00
	1866	.239	1.50	3.00	7.50	20.00
	1867	—	1.50	3.00	7.50	20.00
	1870	.038	1.50	3.00	7.50	20.00
	1871	—	1.50	3.00	7.50	20.00

EIN (1) KREUZER

COPPER

C#	Date	Mintage	Fine	VF	XF	Unc
42	1803	.146	5.00	10.00	25.00	55.00
	1805	.096	5.00	10.00	25.00	55.00

C#	Date	Mintage	Fine	VF	XF	Unc
51	1807	.096	3.50	7.00	15.00	30.00
	1808	1.704	3.50	7.00	15.00	25.00

C#	Date	Mintage	Fine	VF	XF	Unc
52	1809	1.263	3.50	7.00	15.00	25.00
	1810	.639	3.50	7.00	15.00	25.00
	1811	.125	3.50	7.00	15.00	25.00

Obv: Crowned arms. Rev: Value, date within wreath.

C#	Date	Mintage	Fine	VF	XF	Unc
65	1812	.285	5.00	10.00	25.00	45.00

Obv: Leg., crowned arms. Rev: Value: 1 KREUZ/ER, date.

C#	Date	Mintage	Fine	VF	XF	Unc
66	1813	—	3.00	6.00	15.00	30.00

Obv: Legend, crowned arms. Rev: 1/KREUZER/1813 circle of dots.

C#	Date	Mintage	Fine	VF	XF	Unc
66a	1813	.320	3.50	7.00	20.00	40.00

C#	Date	Mintage	Fine	VF	XF	Unc
66b	1813	—	3.50	7.00	20.00	40.00

C#	Date	Mintage	Fine	VF	XF	Unc
68	1813	—	5.00	10.00	25.00	45.00
	1814	.489	5.00	10.00	25.00	45.00

Obv: Date between dots.

C#	Date	Mintage	Fine	VF	XF	Unc
68a	1814	Inc. Ab.	3.50	7.00	15.00	25.00
	1815	.490	3.50	7.00	15.00	25.00
	1816	.464	3.50	7.00	15.00	25.00
	1817	.327	3.50	7.00	15.00	25.00

Rev: 1 KREU-/zer

C#	Date	Mintage	Fine	VF	XF	Unc
68b	1814	—	3.50	7.00	15.00	25.00
	1815	.490	3.50	7.00	15.00	25.00
	1816	.464	3.50	7.00	15.00	25.00
	1817	Inc. Ab.	3.50	7.00	15.00	25.00

C#	Date	Mintage	Fine	VF	XF	Unc
75	1820	—	2.50	5.00	12.00	24.00

Obv: Legend, crowned arms. Rev: Value within wreath.

C#	Date	Mintage	Fine	VF	XF	Unc
78	1821	.055	3.50	7.00	15.00	25.00
	1822	.197	3.50	7.00	15.00	25.00
	1823	.205	3.50	7.00	15.00	25.00
	1824	.253	3.50	7.00	15.00	25.00
	1825	.335	3.50	7.00	15.00	25.00
	1826	—	3.50	7.00	15.00	25.00

C#	Date	Mintage	Fine	VF	XF	Unc
80	1827	.515	3.00	6.00	12.00	25.00
	1828	1.206	3.00	6.00	12.00	20.00
	1829	.603	3.00	6.00	12.00	25.00
	1830	.149	3.00	6.00	12.00	25.00

Recovery of Grand Duchess Sophie

C#	Date	Mintage	Fine	VF	XF	Unc
103	1832	—	7.50	15.00	25.00	40.00

Obv. leg: With period after BADEN.

C#	Date	Mintage	Fine	VF	XF	Unc
102.1	1831	.227	2.50	5.00	10.00	25.00

Obv. leg: Without period after BADEN.

C#	Date	Mintage	Fine	VF	XF	Unc
102.2	1831	Inc. Ab.	1.50	3.00	8.00	20.00
	1832	.172	1.50	3.00	8.00	20.00
	1833	.181	1.50	3.00	8.00	20.00
	1834	.250	1.50	3.00	8.00	20.00
	1835	.294	1.50	3.00	8.00	20.00
	1836	.163	1.50	3.00	8.00	20.00

Obv: Without D on truncation.

C#	Date	Mintage	Fine	VF	XF	Unc
	1836	.321	2.50	5.00	8.00	20.00
	1837	Inc. Ab.	2.50	5.00	8.00	20.00
	1838	.642	2.50	5.00	8.00	20.00
	1839	.254	2.50	5.00	8.00	20.00
	1840	.573	2.50	5.00	8.00	20.00
	1841	.423	2.50	5.00	8.00	20.00
	1842	.865	2.50	5.00	8.00	20.00
	1843	.527	2.50	5.00	8.00	20.00
	1844	.663	2.50	5.00	8.00	20.00
	1845	1.442	2.50	5.00	8.00	20.00

C#	Date	Mintage	Fine	VF	XF	Unc
102a	1845	Inc. Ab.	2.50	5.00	10.00	20.00
	1846	.452	2.50	5.00	10.00	20.00
	1847	.639	2.50	5.00	10.00	20.00
	1848	.232	2.50	5.00	10.00	20.00
	1849	.872	2.50	5.00	10.00	20.00
	1850	.238	2.50	5.00	10.00	20.00
	1851	1.208	2.50	5.00	10.00	20.00

C#	Date	Mintage	Fine	VF	XF	Unc
102.2	1852	.821	2.50	5.00	10.00	20.00

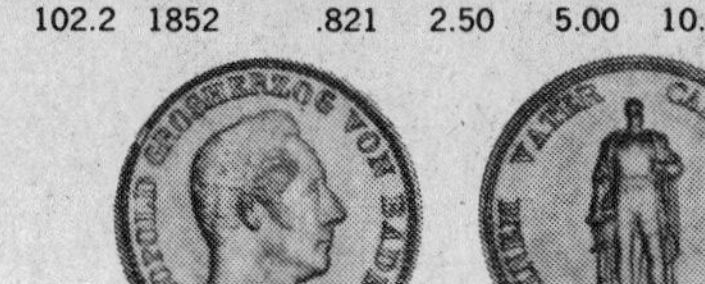

Erection of Carl Friedrich's Statue

C#	Date	Mintage	Fine	VF	XF	Unc
104	1844	.054	5.00	10.00	20.00	50.00

Titles as Prince Regent

C#	Date	Mintage	Fine	VF	XF	Unc
130	1856	.707	3.00	6.00	25.00	40.00

Titles as Grand Duke

C#	Date	Mintage	Fine	VF	XF	Unc
139	1856	.660	5.00	10.00	25.00	40.00

Birth Of Heir
Obv: Head. Rev: CARLSRUHE/DER IUGEND....

C#	Date	Mintage	Fine	VF	XF	Unc
140	1857	—	4.00	10.00	20.00	30.00

C#	Date	Mintage	Fine	VF	XF	Unc
142	1859	.898	1.25	3.00	6.00	20.00
	1860	.655	1.25	3.00	6.00	20.00
	1861	.726	1.25	3.00	6.00	20.00
	1862	.623	1.25	3.00	6.00	20.00
	1863	.765	1.25	3.00	6.00	20.00
	1864	.724	1.25	3.00	6.00	20.00
	1865	.778	1.25	3.00	6.00	20.00
	1866	.732	1.25	3.00	6.00	20.00
	1867	.698	1.25	3.00	6.00	20.00
	1868	.885	1.25	3.00	6.00	20.00
	1869	.858	1.25	3.00	6.00	20.00
	1870	.918	1.25	3.00	6.00	20.00
	1871	—	1.25	3.00	6.00	20.00

Leopold Memorial

C#	Date	Mintage	Fine	VF	XF	Unc
143	1861	—	4.00	10.00	25.00	50.00

50th Anniversary Baden's Constitution

C#	Date	Mintage	Fine	VF	XF	Unc
144	1868	.025	6.00	15.00	25.00	50.00

Church at Seckenheim
Obv: Arms. Rev: Legend.

C#	Date	Mintage	Fine	VF	XF	Unc
146	1869	—	8.00	20.00	40.00	75.00

Victory over France in Franco-Prussian War

C#	Date	Mintage	Fine	VF	XF	Unc
145	1871	—	8.00	20.00	30.00	50.00

Obv: SCHEIDE MUNZE under shield.

C#	Date	Mintage	Fine	VF	XF	Unc
145a	1871	—	2.50	6.00	15.00	35.00

Buehl, Victory Commemorative

C#	Date	Mintage	Fine	VF	XF	Unc
147	1871	—	5.00	15.00	30.00	65.00

Karlsruhe, Victory Commemorative
Obv: Arms. Rev: Legend.

C#	Date	Mintage	Fine	VF	XF	Unc
148	1871	—	5.00	12.50	25.00	60.00

Offenburg, Victory Commemorative
Obv: Arms. Rev: Legend.

C#	Date	Mintage	Fine	VF	XF	Unc
149	1871	—	6.00	15.00	45.00	100.00

DREI (3) KREUZER

.313 BILLON
Obv: Crowned heart-shaped arms with garland.
Rev: Value above two laurel branches.

C#	Date	Mintage	Fine	VF	XF	Unc
43	1803	.189	5.00	12.00	25.00	60.00
	1805	.445	5.00	12.00	25.00	60.00
	1806	.126	5.00	12.00	25.00	60.00

Obv: Lion in shield faces left.

C#	Date	Mintage	Fine	VF	XF	Unc
53	1808	.410	6.00	15.00	25.00	60.00

Obv: Lion in shield faces right.

C#	Date	Mintage	Fine	VF	XF	Unc
54	1809	.208	6.00	15.00	25.00	60.00
	1810	.262	6.00	15.00	25.00	60.00
	1811	.316	6.00	15.00	25.00	60.00

Rev. value: III KREUZER above olive branches

C#	Date	Mintage	Fine	VF	XF	Unc
69	1812	.734	2.50	6.00	20.00	40.00
	1813	.273	2.50	6.00	20.00	40.00
69a	1812 with Z backwards in KREUZER	Inc. Ab.	2.50	6.00	20.00	40.00

Rev. value: 3 KREUTZER within branches

C#	Date	Mintage	Fine	VF	XF	Unc
71	1813	—	3.50	7.50	20.00	40.00
	1814	.280	3.50	7.50	20.00	40.00
	1815	.214	3.50	7.50	20.00	40.00
	1816	.243	3.50	7.50	20.00	40.00

Rev. value: 3 KREUZER

C#	Date	Mintage	Fine	VF	XF	Unc
71a	1817	.371	3.50	7.50	20.00	40.00
	1818	.593	3.50	7.50	20.00	40.00

Obv: Crowned draped shield.

C#	Date	Mintage	Fine	VF	XF	Unc
81	1819	.815	4.00	10.00	20.00	40.00
	1820	Inc. Ab.	4.00	10.00	20.00	40.00

Obv: Larger shield, no drape.

C#	Date	Mintage	Fine	VF	XF	Unc
82	1820	Inc. Ab.	4.00	10.00	20.00	50.00
	1821	.065	4.00	10.00	20.00	50.00
	1824	.096	4.00	10.00	20.00	50.00
	1825	.073	4.00	10.00	20.00	50.00

.375 BILLON
Rev. value: DREI KREUZER

C#	Date	Mintage	Fine	VF	XF	Unc
83	1829	1.277	3.00	7.00	14.00	30.00
	1830	1.009	3.00	7.00	14.00	30.00

Rev. value: 3 KREUZER

C#	Date	Mintage	Fine	VF	XF	Unc
106	1832	.729	2.00	5.00	10.00	30.00
	1833	.846	2.00	5.00	10.00	30.00
	1834	.549	2.00	5.00	10.00	30.00
	1835	.476	2.00	5.00	10.00	30.00
	1836	.723	2.00	5.00	10.00	30.00
	1837	—	2.00	5.00	10.00	30.00

.333 BILLON
Obv: Crowned shield between two crowned griffins.

C#	Date	Mintage	Fine	VF	XF	Unc
107	1841	.328	2.00	4.50	10.00	30.00
	1842	.420	2.00	4.50	10.00	30.00
	1843	.168	2.00	4.50	10.00	30.00
	1844	.361	2.00	4.50	10.00	30.00
	1845	.385	2.00	4.50	10.00	30.00
	1846	.219	2.00	4.50	10.00	30.00
	1847	.392	2.00	4.50	10.00	30.00
	1848	.195	2.00	4.50	10.00	30.00
	1849	.397	2.00	4.50	10.00	30.00
	1850	.212	2.00	4.50	10.00	30.00
	1851	.196	2.00	4.50	10.00	30.00
	1852	.192	2.00	4.50	10.00	30.00

C#	Date	Mintage	Fine	VF	XF	Unc
131	1853	—	6.00	15.00	30.00	45.00
	1854	—	6.00	15.00	30.00	45.00
	1855	—	6.00	15.00	30.00	45.00
	1856	—	6.00	15.00	30.00	45.00

.350 BILLON
Obv: SCHEIDE/MUNZE under arms.

C#	Date	Mintage	Fine	VF	XF	Unc
150	1866	.240	2.00	4.50	7.50	30.00
	1867	.389	2.00	4.50	7.50	30.00
	1868	.315	2.00	4.50	7.50	30.00
	1869	.285	2.00	4.50	7.50	30.00
	1870	.259	2.00	4.50	7.50	30.00
	1871	—	2.00	4.50	7.50	30.00

6 KREUZER

.375 BILLON
Obv: Crowned spade-shaped arms with garland.

C#	Date	Mintage	Fine	VF	XF	Unc
45	1804	—	8.00	20.00	50.00	80.00

Obv: Crowned many-quartered arms with mantle.

C#	Date	Mintage	Fine	VF	XF	Unc
46	1804	—	8.00	20.00	50.00	80.00
	1805	—	8.00	20.00	50.00	80.00

Obv: Lion in arms facing left.

C#	Date	Mintage	Fine	VF	XF	Unc
55	1807	.371	4.00	10.00	20.00	60.00
	1808	1.118	4.00	10.00	15.00	40.00

Obv: Lion in arms facing right.

C#	Date	Mintage	Fine	VF	XF	Unc
56	1809	.539	6.00	15.00	25.00	55.00

Obv. leg: G.H.BADEN....

C#	Date	Mintage	Fine	VF	XF	Unc
70	1812	.339	2.50	6.00	20.00	50.00
	1813	.559	2.50	6.00	20.00	50.00

Obv. leg: G H BADEN..... Rev: VI KREUTZER, date. within wreath

C#	Date	Mintage	Fine	VF	XF	Unc
70a	1813	Inc. Ab.	3.00	7.50	20.00	50.00

Rev. value: 6 KREUTZER within olive wreath

C#	Date	Mintage	Fine	VF	XF	Unc
72	1814	.115	3.00	7.50	20.00	50.00
	1815	.244	3.00	7.50	20.00	50.00
	1816	1.603	1.75	4.00	10.00	35.00
	1817	.563	3.00	7.50	20.00	50.00

Rev. value: 6 KREUZER within olive wreath

C#	Date	Mintage	Fine	VF	XF	Unc
72a	1816	Inc. Ab.	3.00	7.50	20.00	50.00
	1817	Inc. Ab.	3.00	7.50	20.00	50.00
	1818	.112	3.00	7.50	20.00	50.00

Obv: Legend, head right, Rev: Crowned draped arms

C#	Date	Mintage	Fine	VF	XF	Unc
84	1819	.390	12.50	30.00	45.00	65.00

Obv: Larger head right, hair combed forward.
Rev: Crowned shield

C#	Date	Mintage	Fine	VF	XF	Unc
85	1820	.095	12.50	30.00	45.00	65.00

Rev: Crowned shield within wreath

C#	Date	Mintage	Fine	VF	XF	Unc
86	1820	Inc. Ab.	6.00	15.00	25.00	50.00
	1821	.186	6.00	15.00	25.00	50.00

Obv: With D on truncation.

C#	Date	Mintage	Fine	VF	XF	Unc
108.1	1831	.862	2.75	7.00	15.00	35.00
	1832	.929	2.75	7.00	15.00	35.00
	1833	1.003	2.75	7.00	15.00	30.00
	1834	.898	2.75	7.00	15.00	35.00
	1835	1.025	2.75	7.00	15.00	30.00
	1836	.917	2.75	7.00	15.00	35.00

Obv: Without D on truncation.

C#	Date	Mintage	Fine	VF	XF	Unc
108.2	1835	Inc. Ab.	3.00	7.50	20.00	40.00
	1837	.415	3.00	7.50	20.00	40.00

.333 BILLON

C#	Date	Mintage	Fine	VF	XF	Unc
109	1840	1.317	2.00	5.00	11.00	30.00
	1841	.168	2.00	5.00	11.00	30.00
	1842	.612	2.00	5.00	11.00	30.00
	1843	.615	2.00	5.00	11.00	30.00
	1844	.757	2.00	5.00	11.00	30.00
	1845	.262	2.00	5.00	11.00	30.00
	1846	.368	2.00	5.00	11.00	30.00
	1847	.857	2.00	5.00	11.00	30.00
	1848	.377	2.00	5.00	11.00	30.00
	1849	.371	2.00	5.00	11.00	30.00
	1850	.200	2.00	5.00	11.00	30.00
132	1855	—	15.00	35.00	50.00	75.00
	1856	—	15.00	35.00	50.00	75.00

ZEHN (10) KREUZER

.500 SILVER
Obv: Bust with long hair

C#	Date	Mintage	Fine	VF	XF	Unc
57	1808	.068	12.50	30.00	50.00	125.00

Obv: Bust with short hair

C#	Date	Mintage	Fine	VF	XF	Unc
58	1809	Inc. Ab.	10.00	25.00	45.00	100.00

C#	Date	Mintage	Fine	VF	XF	Unc
87	1829	.527	7.50	15.00	20.00	50.00
	1830	.510	7.50	15.00	20.00	50.00

20 KREUZER

SILVER
Obv: Head right. Rev: 3-fold arms.

C#	Date	Mintage	VG	Fine	VF	XF
14b	1779	—	35.00	50.00	75.00	150.00

.583 SILVER
Obv: Bust with long hair, Rev: Lion in shield facing left.

C#	Date	Mintage	Fine	VF	XF	Unc
59	1807	.015	20.00	50.00	75.00	150.00

Obv: Bust with long hair, Rev: Lion in shield facing right

C#	Date	Mintage	Fine	VF	XF	Unc
60	1808	—	12.50	30.00	50.00	125.00

Obv: Bust with short hair

C#	Date	Mintage	Fine	VF	XF	Unc
61	1809	—	10.00	25.00	40.00	100.00
	1810	.170	10.00	25.00	40.00	100.00

1/2 GULDEN

.900 SILVER

C#	Date	Mintage	Fine	VF	XF	Unc
110	1838	1.044	8.00	20.00	30.00	70.00
	1839	.500	8.00	20.00	30.00	70.00
	1840	.511	8.00	20.00	30.00	70.00
	1841	.417	8.00	20.00	30.00	70.00
	1842	.362	8.00	20.00	30.00	70.00
	1843	.469	8.00	20.00	30.00	70.00
	1844	.274	8.00	20.00	30.00	70.00
	1845	.322	8.00	20.00	30.00	70.00
	1846	.118	8.00	20.00	30.00	70.00

Obv: Without D on truncation, larger head.

C#	Date	Mintage	Fine	VF	XF	Unc
110a	1846	Inc. Ab.	10.00	25.00	35.00	75.00
	1847	.537	10.00	25.00	35.00	75.00
	1848	.332	10.00	25.00	35.00	75.00
	1849	.069	10.00	25.00	35.00	75.00
	1850	—	10.00	25.00	35.00	75.00
	1851	.122	10.00	25.00	35.00	75.00
	1852	.026	10.00	25.00	35.00	75.00

Obv: With VOIGT below head.

C#	Date	Mintage	Fine	VF	XF	Unc
133	1856	.150	17.50	40.00	65.00	90.00
	1860	.342	8.00	20.00	30.00	70.00

C#	Date	Mintage	Fine	VF	XF	Unc
151	1860	Inc. Ab.	8.00	20.00	30.00	50.00
	1861	.264	8.00	20.00	30.00	50.00
	1862	.233	8.00	20.00	30.00	50.00
	1863	.227	8.00	20.00	30.00	50.00
	1864	.117	8.00	20.00	30.00	50.00
	1865	.184	8.00	20.00	30.00	50.00

C#	Date	Mintage	Fine	VF	XF	Unc
152	1867	.155	12.50	30.00	40.00	65.00
	1868	.070	12.50	30.00	40.00	65.00
	1869	.073	12.50	30.00	40.00	65.00

EIN (1) GULDEN

.750 SILVER
Obv: Bust with short hair

C#	Date	Mintage	Fine	VF	XF	Unc
88	1821	.090	30.00	75.00	140.00	200.00
	1822	.045	30.00	75.00	140.00	200.00
	1823	.039	30.00	75.00	140.00	200.00
	1824	.050	30.00	75.00	140.00	200.00
	1825	.022	30.00	75.00	140.00	200.00

Obv: Curly hair.

C#	Date	Mintage	Fine	VF	XF	Unc
88a	1826	.094	80.00	200.00	300.00	500.00

.900 SILVER
Obv: No period after BADEN. Rev: Value within oak wreath.

C#	Date	Mintage	Fine	VF	XF	Unc
112	1837	.629	15.00	35.00	60.00	100.00
	1838	.210	15.00	35.00	60.00	100.00
	1839	.485	15.00	35.00	60.00	100.00
	1840	.468	15.00	35.00	60.00	100.00
	1841	.387	15.00	35.00	60.00	100.00

Obv: With period after BADEN.

C#	Date	Mintage	Fine	VF	XF	Unc
112a	1842	.390	15.00	35.00	60.00	100.00
	1843	.444	15.00	35.00	60.00	100.00
	1844	.585	15.00	35.00	60.00	100.00
	1845	.439	15.00	35.00	60.00	100.00

C#	Date	Mintage	Fine	VF	XF	Unc
112b	1845	Inc. Ab.	15.00	25.00	40.00	75.00
	1846	—	15.00	25.00	40.00	75.00
	1847	.397	15.00	25.00	40.00	75.00
	1848	.116	15.00	25.00	40.00	75.00
	1849	.021	15.00	25.00	40.00	75.00
	1850	8,652	15.00	35.00	50.00	85.00
	1851	.089	15.00	25.00	40.00	75.00
	1852	.033	15.00	25.00	40.00	75.00

C#	Date	Mintage	Fine	VF	XF	Unc
114	1852	Inc. Ab.	35.00	90.00	150.00	225.00

C#	Date	Mintage	Fine	VF	XF	Unc
134	1856	.149	30.00	75.00	150.00	200.00

Obv: With VOIGT below head.

C#	Date	Mintage	Fine	VF	XF	Unc
153	1856	.342	15.00	35.00	65.00	100.00
	1859	.195	15.00	35.00	65.00	100.00
	1860	.044	15.00	35.00	65.00	100.00

Mint Visit Commemorative

C#	Date	Mintage	Fine	VF	XF	Unc
154	1857	776 pcs.	90.00	225.00	400.00	600.00

First Shooting Festival At Mannheim

C#	Date	Mintage	Fine	VF	XF	Unc
155	1863	.012	25.00	60.00	90.00	175.00

Second Shooting Festival at Karlsruhe

C#	Date	Mintage	Fine	VF	XF	Unc
156	1867	.014	25.00	60.00	90.00	175.00

ZWEI (2) GULDEN

25.450 gm., .750 SILVER, .6138 oz ASW

C#	Date	Mintage	Fine	VF	XF	Unc
90	1821	.030	65.00	130.00	250.00	525.00
	1822	.020	65.00	130.00	250.00	550.00
	1823	7,040	100.00	200.00	350.00	625.00
	1824	.017	75.00	150.00	275.00	600.00
	1825	6,642	100.00	200.00	350.00	625.00

21.2100 gm., .900 SILVER, .6138 oz ASW

C#	Date	Mintage	Fine	VF	XF	Unc
120	1846	.592	30.00	65.00	130.00	250.00
	1847	.232	30.00	65.00	130.00	250.00
	1848	.273	30.00	65.00	130.00	250.00
	1849	.014	30.00	65.00	130.00	350.00
	1850	.140	30.00	65.00	130.00	250.00
	1851	.124	30.00	65.00	130.00	250.00
	1852	.142	30.00	65.00	130.00	250.00

Rev: Similar to C#120.

C#	Date	Mintage	Fine	VF	XF	Unc
135	1856	.084	175.00	350.00	650.00	1125.

5 GULDEN

3.4250 gm., .904 GOLD, .0995 oz AGW

Obv: With designer's initials PH below head.

C#	Date	Mintage	Fine	VF	XF	Unc
94.1	1819	3,695	400.00	650.00	1000.	2250.

Obv: Without designer's initials below head.

C#	Date	Mintage	Fine	VF	XF	Unc
94.2	1819	Inc. Ab.	450.00	750.00	1250.	2000.
	1821	465 pcs.	800.00	1325.	2000.	3000.
	1822	1,718	450.00	750.00	1250.	2000.
	1823	1,854	450.00	750.00	1250.	2000.
	1824	2,763	450.00	750.00	1250.	2000.
	1825	1,508	450.00	750.00	1250.	2000.
	1826	887 pcs.	700.00	1150.	1750.	2500.

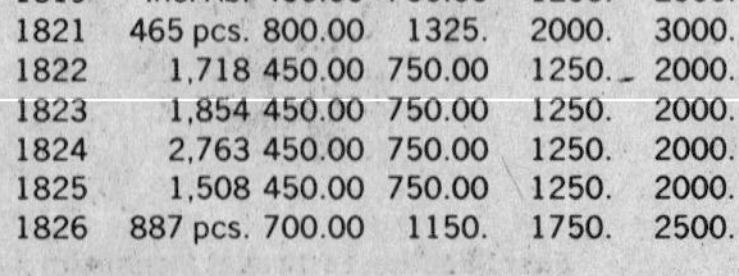

Obv: Curly hair.

C#	Date	Mintage	Fine	VF	XF	Unc
94a	1827	2,877	500.00	800.00	1000.	2000.
	1828	2,317	500.00	800.00	1000.	2000.

10 GULDEN

6.8500 gm., .904 GOLD, .1991 oz AGW

Obv: With designer's initials below head.

C#	Date	Mintage	Fine	VF	XF	Unc
95.1	1819	4,332	600.00	800.00	1300.	2000.

Obv: Without designer's initials below head.

C#	Date	Mintage	Fine	VF	XF	Unc
95.2	1821	812 pcs.	750.00	1200.	1800.	2500.
	1823	373 pcs.	800.00	1350.	2000.	2750.
	1824	328 pcs.	800.00	1350.	2000.	2750.
	1825	Inc. Ab.		1850.	2800.	3500.

EIN (1) THALER

(Convention)

SILVER

C#	Date	Mintage	VG	Fine	VF	XF
21	1778W	—	125.00	250.00	400.00	800.00
	1779 S	—	125.00	250.00	400.00	800.00

28.0600 gm., .833 SILVER, .7521 oz ASW

C#	Date	Mintage	Fine	VF	XF	Unc
48	1803FE	675 pcs.	400.00	825.00	1600.	2250.

Obv: Short hair. Rev: Crowned shield

C#	Date	Mintage	Fine	VF	XF	Unc
62	1809E	6,219	200.00	400.00	650.00	1150.
	1810	2,815	200.00	400.00	650.00	1150.
	1811E	3,885	200.00	400.00	650.00	1150.

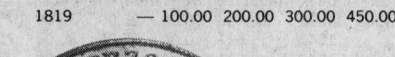

(Krone)

29.5200 gm., .871 SILVER, .8270 oz ASW

C#	Date	Mintage	Fine	VF	XF	Unc
73	1813D	—	100.00	200.00	350.00	650.00
	1814D	.036	100.00	200.00	350.00	650.00

C#	Date	Mintage	Fine	VF	XF	Unc
73a	1814	Inc. Ab.	75.00	150.00	250.00	400.00
	1815	.038	75.00	150.00	250.00	400.00
	1816	.036	75.00	150.00	250.00	400.00
	1817	.052	75.00	150.00	250.00	400.00
	1818	.039	75.00	150.00	250.00	400.00
91	1819	—	100.00	200.00	300.00	450.00

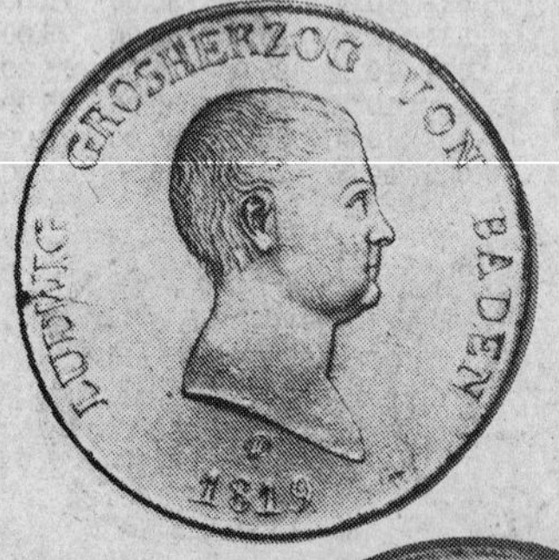

C#	Date	Mintage	Fine	VF	XF	Unc
92	1819WD	—	115.00	225.00	400.00	750.00

Obv: DOELL on truncation.

C#	Date	Mintage	Fine	VF	XF	Unc
92a	1819	—	115.00	225.00	325.00	650.00
	1820	.038	115.00	225.00	325.00	650.00
	1821	.019	115.00	225.00	325.00	650.00

18.1500 gm., .875 SILVER, .5106 oz ASW

C#	Date	Mintage	Fine	VF	XF	Unc
93	1829	.168	45.00	90.00	200.00	375.00
	1830	.101	45.00	90.00	200.00	375.00

C#	Date	Mintage	Fine	VF	XF	Unc
115	1830	.238	45.00	90.00	185.00	325.00
	1831	.168	45.00	90.00	185.00	325.00
	1832	.176	45.00	90.00	185.00	325.00

Rev: With star under date.

C#	Date	Mintage	Fine	VF	XF	Unc
115a	1832	Inc. Ab.	50.00	100.00	180.00	325.00

Obv: With period after BADEN. Rev: Star under date.

C#	Date	Mintage	Fine	VF	XF	Unc
115b	1832	Inc. Ab.	50.00	100.00	180.00	325.00
	1833	.115	50.00	100.00	180.00	325.00

Rev: Without star under date.

C#	Date	Mintage	Fine	VF	XF	Unc
115c	1833	Inc. Ab.	45.00	90.00	180.00	325.00
	1834	.036	45.00	90.00	180.00	325.00
	1835	.075	45.00	90.00	180.00	325.00
	1836	.085	45.00	90.00	180.00	325.00
	1837	—	45.00	90.00	180.00	325.00

Rev: With oversize 6 in date.

C#	Date	Mintage	Fine	VF	XF	Unc
115e	1836	—	45.00	90.00	180.00	325.00

Mint Visit Commemorative

C#	Date	Mintage	Fine	VF	XF	Unc
116	1832	—	400.00	800.00	1200.	1600.

C#	Date	Mintage	Fine	VF	XF	Unc
117	1834	6,517	125.00	250.00	500.00	850.00

Rev: Eagle holds shield, value KRONEN-THALER.

C#	Date	Mintage	Fine	VF	XF	Unc
118	1836	8,250	115.00	225.00	450.00	750.00

Mule: Obv. C#115 with Rev. C#118.

C#	Date	Mintage	Fine	VF	XF	Unc
115/8	1836	—	—	—	Rare	—

Rev: Arms of Ten Customs Union States.

C#	Date	Mintage	Fine	VF	XF	Unc
119	1836	.018	40.00	80.00	165.00	265.00

(Vereins)

18.5200 gm., .900 SILVER, .5360 oz ASW

C#	Date	Mintage	Fine	VF	XF	Unc
157	1857	.019	25.00	45.00	100.00	250.00
	1858	.232	25.00	45.00	100.00	225.00
	1859	.289	25.00	45.00	100.00	225.00
	1860	.174	25.00	45.00	100.00	225.00
	1861	.358	25.00	45.00	100.00	225.00
	1862	.400	25.00	45.00	100.00	225.00
	1863	.326	25.00	45.00	100.00	225.00
	1864	.322	25.00	45.00	100.00	225.00
	1865	.265	25.00	45.00	100.00	225.00

Rev: Similar to C#157.

C#	Date	Mintage	Fine	VF	XF	Unc
158	1865	Inc. Ab.	25.00	45.00	100.00	225.00
	1866	.149	25.00	45.00	100.00	225.00
	1867	.096	25.00	45.00	100.00	225.00

C#	Date	Mintage	Fine	VF	XF	Unc
158	1868	.102	25.00	45.00	100.00	225.00
	1869	.062	25.00	45.00	100.00	225.00
	1870	.022	25.00	45.00	100.00	250.00
	1871	—	25.00	45.00	100.00	225.00

2 THALER

(= 3-1/2 Gulden)

37.1200 gm., .900 SILVER, 1.0743 oz ASW

C#	Date	Mintage	Fine	VF	XF	Unc
121	1841	.231	75.00	150.00	350.00	650.00
	1842	.033	75.00	150.00	350.00	650.00
	1843	.035	100.00	200.00	350.00	650.00

Carl Friedrich Commemorative

C#	Date	Mintage	Fine	VF	XF	Unc
122	1844	4,323	90.00	185.00	350.00	500.00

C#	Date	Mintage	Fine	VF	XF	Unc
123	1845	.057	100.00	200.00	400.00	600.00
	1846	1,130	200.00	425.00	800.00	1250.
	1847	.031	100.00	200.00	350.00	550.00
	1852	.060	100.00	200.00	350.00	550.00

Obv: BALBACH below truncation.

C#	Date	Mintage	Fine	VF	XF	Unc
136	1852	9 pcs.	—	—	Rare	—
	1854	.085	375.00	750.00	1500.	2800.

Obv: Different head, no engraver's name.

C#	Date	Mintage	Fine	VF	XF	Unc
136a	1855	2 pcs.	—	—	Rare	—

FUNF (5) THALER

(= 500 Kreuzer)

6.6500 gm., .900 GOLD

C#	Date	Mintage	Fine	VF	XF	Unc
97	1830	1,788	550.00	750.00	1200.	2000.

TRADE COINS

EIN (1) DUCAT

3.5000 gm., .986 GOLD, .1109 oz AGW
Birth of twin Princesses Commemorative
Obv: Bust of Amalie Frederika of Hesse.
Rev: 2 shields, crowned.

C#	Date	Mintage	Fine	VF	XF
30	1776	—	1350.	1750.	2250.

Birth of twin Princesses Commemorative
Obv: Facing heads of twin Princesses.
Rev: 9 line inscription.

C#	Date	Mintage	Fine	VF	XF
31	1776	—	750.00	1500.	2000.

Birth Of Prince Charles Commemorative

C#	Date	Mintage	Fine	VF	XF
32	1786	—	1000.	1500.	1950.

C#	Date	Mintage	Fine	VF	XF	Unc
63	1807	972 pcs.	—	1000.	2000.	3500.

C#	Date	Mintage	Fine	VF	XF	Unc
124	1832	6,631	—	900.00	1100.	2000.
	1833	2,496	—	900.00	1100.	2000.
	1834	1,992	—	900.00	1100.	2000.
	1835	2,470	—	900.00	1100.	2000.
	1836	1,777	—	900.00	1100.	2000.

Obv: Without designer's initial or star below head.

C#	Date	Mintage	Fine	VF	XF	Unc
	1837	1,467	—	900.00	1100.	2000.
	1838	2,095	—	900.00	1100.	2000.
	1839	2,448	—	900.00	1100.	2000.
	1840	2,044	—	900.00	1100.	2000.
	1841	2,145	—	900.00	1100.	2000.
	1842	2,130	—	900.00	1100.	2000.

C#	Date	Mintage	Fine	VF	XF	Unc
124a	1843	1,350	—	1000.	1350.	2200.
	1844	850 pcs.	—	800.00	1500.	2200.
	1845	2,097	—	750.00	1350.	2000.
	1846	1,950	—	750.00	1350.	2000.

Obv: Larger head

C#	Date	Mintage	Fine	VF	XF	Unc
124b	1847	1,870	—	900.00	1100.	1800.
	1848	1,590	—	900.00	1100.	1800.
	1849	1,420	—	900.00	1100.	1800.
	1850	1,390	—	900.00	1100.	1800.
	1851	1,280	—	900.00	1100.	1800.
	1852	1,450	—	900.00	1100.	1800.

Obv: With star under head.

C#	Date	Mintage	Fine	VF	XF	Unc
124 c	1852	Inc. Ab.	—	1000.	1500.	2000.

NOTE: Struck posthumously.

C#	Date	Mintage	Fine	VF	XF	Unc
137	1854	1,820	—	1200.	2500.	3500.

MONETARY REFORM

2 MARK

11.1110 gm., .900 SILVER, .3215 oz ASW

Y#	Date	Mintage	Fine	VF	XF	Unc
12	1876G	1.740	40.00	100.00	500.00	1500.
	1877G	.760	45.00	100.00	500.00	1700.
	1880G	.070	75.00	175.00	700.00	1800.
	1883G	.050	125.00	200.00	900.00	2000.
	1888G	.080	75.00	150.00	800.00	1800.

Y#	Date	Mintage	Fine	VF	XF	Unc
12a	1892G	.110	40.00	100.00	300.00	600.00
	1894G	.110	40.00	90.00	275.00	500.00
	1896G	.210	30.00	70.00	250.00	400.00
	1898G	.090	45.00	125.00	400.00	900.00
	1899G	.330	27.50	60.00	250.00	450.00
	1900G	.220	27.50	60.00	275.00	500.00
	1901G	.400	25.00	60.00	225.00	450.00
	1902G	5,368	300.00	800.00	1500.	3200.

50th Year of Reign Commemorative

Y#	Date	Mintage	Fine	VF	XF	Unc
20	1902G	.380	4.00	10.00	17.50	30.00

Y#	Date	Mintage	Fine	VF	XF	Unc
17	1902G	.200	30.00	75.00	150.00	350.00
	1903G	.490	10.00	20.00	60.00	125.00
	1904G	1.120	10.00	18.00	50.00	115.00
	1905G	.610	10.00	18.00	50.00	115.00
	1906G	.110	30.00	90.00	175.00	325.00
	1907G	.910	10.00	15.00	50.00	100.00

Golden Wedding Anniversary Commemorative

Y#	Date	Mintage	Fine	VF	XF	Unc
22	1906	.350	10.00	18.00	25.00	35.00

Friedrich Death Commemorative

Y#	Date	Mintage	Fine	VF	XF	Unc
24	1907	.350	10.00	16.50	27.50	50.00
	1907	—	—	—	Proof	75.00

Y#	Date	Mintage	Fine	VF	XF	Unc
26	1911G	.080	70.00	225.00	350.00	750.00
	1913G	.140	60.00	200.00	300.00	700.00
	Common type	—	—	—	Proof	1000.

3 MARK

16.6670 gm., .900 SILVER, .4823 oz ASW

Y#	Date	Mintage	Fine	VF	XF	Unc
27	1908G	.300	15.00	18.00	25.00	80.00
	1909G	.760	15.00	18.00	20.00	60.00
	1910G	.670	15.00	18.00	20.00	40.00
	1911G	.380	15.00	18.00	20.00	40.00
	1912G	.840	15.00	18.00	20.00	40.00
	1914G	.410	15.00	18.00	20.00	45.00
	1915G	.170	20.00	45.00	90.00	125.00
	Common type	—	—	—	Proof	150.00

5 MARK

27.7770 gm., .900 SILVER, .8038 oz ASW

Y#	Date	Mintage	Fine	VF	XF	Unc
13.1	1875G	.310	40.00	65.00	150.00	650.00
	1876G	.470	35.00	60.00	125.00	650.00
	1888G	.030	400.00	700.00	1200.	2200.

Obv: Without cross bar in 'A' of BADEN.

Y#	Date	Mintage	Fine	VF	XF	Unc
13.2	1875G	Inc. Ab.	40.00	65.00	400.00	1600.
	1876G	Inc. Ab.	30.00	50.00	400.00	1600.
	1888G	Inc. Ab.	50.00	85.00	300.00	1400.
	Common Type	—	—	—	Proof	1750.

1.9910 gm., .900 GOLD, .0576 oz AGW

Y#	Date	Mintage	Fine	VF	XF	Unc
14	1877G	.350	75.00	250.00	350.00	600.00

27.7770 gm., .900 SILVER, .8038 oz ASW
Obv: Without crossbar in 'A' in BADEN.

Y#	Date	Mintage	Fine	VF	XF	Unc
13a.1	1891	.040	200.00	450.00	700.00	1400.

Obv: Normal 'A' in BADEN.

Y#	Date	Mintage	Fine	VF	XF	Unc
13a.2	1891	Inc. Ab.	40.00	90.00	350.00	1300.
	1893	.040	40.00	90.00	350.00	1300.
	1894	.060	30.00	80.00	300.00	1300.
	1895	.070	30.00	70.00	275.00	1200.
	1898	.130	25.00	60.00	200.00	900.00
	1899	.060	25.00	60.00	225.00	950.00
	1900	.130	25.00	50.00	175.00	800.00
	1901	.130	25.00	50.00	175.00	800.00
	1902	.040	30.00	90.00	350.00	1300.
	Common Type	—	—	—	Proof	800.00

50th Year of Reign Commemorative
Rev: Similar to Y#13a.

Y#	Date	Mintage	Fine	VF	XF	Unc
21	1902G	.050	55.00	90.00	150.00	225.00

Rev: Similar to Y#13a.

Y#	Date	Mintage	Fine	VF	XF	Unc
18	1902G	.130	25.00	50.00	140.00	300.00
	1903G	.440	25.00	40.00	150.00	300.00
	1904G	.240	30.00	50.00	150.00	325.00
	1907G	.240	25.00	40.00	125.00	300.00
	Common type	—	—	—	Proof	400.00

Golden Wedding Anniversary Commemorative
Rev: Similar to Y#13a.

Y#	Date	Mintage	Fine	VF	XF	Unc
23	1906	.060	45.00	100.00	140.00	200.00
	1906	—	—	—	Proof	250.00

Death Of Friedrich Commemorative
Rev: Similar to Y#13a.

Y#	Date	Mintage	Fine	VF	XF	Unc
25	1907	.060	50.00	160.00	200.00	250.00

Rev: Similar to Y#13a.

Y#	Date	Mintage	Fine	VF	XF	Unc
28	1908G	.180	25.00	60.00	160.00	475.00
	1913G	.240	25.00	50.00	115.00	225.00
	Common type	—	—	—	Proof	400.00

10 MARK

3.9820 gm., .900 GOLD, .1152 oz AGW
Rev: Type 1 eagle.

Y#	Date	Mintage	Fine	VF	XF	Unc
15	1872G	.270	90.00	125.00	200.00	400.00
	1873G	.470	85.00	110.00	200.00	400.00

Rev: Type II eagle

Y#	Date	Mintage	Fine	VF	XF	Unc
15a	1875G	.340	90.00	150.00	225.00	400.00
	1876G	1.390	90.00	150.00	225.00	375.00
	1877G	.160	90.00	150.00	225.00	375.00
	1878G	.240	90.00	150.00	225.00	375.00
	1879G	.098	110.00	225.00	325.00	475.00
	1880G	1,169	1850.	4000.	10,000.	15,000.
	1881G	.190	110.00	200.00	300.00	450.00
	1888G	.120	90.00	150.00	225.00	400.00

Rev: Type III eagle

Y#	Date	Mintage	Fine	VF	XF	Unc
15b	1890G	.073	120.00	200.00	275.00	600.00
	1891G	.110	100.00	165.00	225.00	475.00
	1893G	.180	90.00	110.00	160.00	300.00
	1896G	.052	90.00	150.00	225.00	450.00
	1897G	.070	90.00	150.00	225.00	450.00
	1898G	.260	90.00	110.00	160.00	300.00

Y#	Date	Mintage	Fine	VF	XF	Unc
	1900G	.031	90.00	150.00	225.00	450.00
	1901G	.091	90.00	135.00	200.00	400.00

Y#	Date	Mintage	Fine	VF	XF	Unc
19	1902G	.030	140.00	225.00	325.00	675.00
	1903G	.110	90.00	130.00	180.00	300.00
	1904G	.150	90.00	130.00	180.00	300.00
	1905G	.096	90.00	150.00	200.00	375.00
	1906G	.120	90.00	130.00	180.00	300.00
	1907G	.120	90.00	130.00	180.00	300.00

Y#	Date	Mintage	Fine	VF	XF	Unc
29	1909G	.086	110.00	180.00	275.00	500.00
	1910G	.061	110.00	180.00	275.00	500.00
	1911G	.029	325.00	550.00	900.00	1700.
	1912G	.026	350.00	600.00	1000.	1800.
	1913G	.042	125.00	200.00	325.00	600.00

20 MARK

7.9650 gm., .900 GOLD, .2304 oz AGW
Rev: Type I eagle

Y#	Date	Mintage	Fine	VF	XF	Unc
16	1872G	.400	90.00	100.00	150.00	400.00
	1873G	.520	90.00	100.00	150.00	400.00

Rev: Type II eagle

Y#	Date	Mintage	Fine	VF	XF	Unc
16a	1874G	.150	200.00	400.00	500.00	800.00

Rev: Type III eagle

Y#	Date	Mintage	Fine	VF	XF	Unc
16b	1894G	.400	90.00	180.00	275.00	425.00
	1895G	.100	150.00	300.00	400.00	600.00

Y#	Date	Mintage	Fine	VF	XF	Unc
30	1911G	.190	90.00	120.00	175.00	300.00
	1912G	.310	90.00	120.00	175.00	300.00
	1913G	.085	90.00	140.00	200.00	310.00
	1914G	.280	90.00	120.00	175.00	200.00

NCLT ISSUES

PATTERNS

KM#	Date	Mintage	Identification	Mkt.Val.
1	1839	—	6 Kreuzer, .333 Billon, C109	—

BAMBERG

Bishopric in northern Bavaria. The see was founded in 1007 and the first coinage appeared soon after. The bishops were made princes of the empire in the mid-1200s. It was annexed to Bavaria in 1802.

RULERS

Adam Friedrich, Bishop, 1757-1779
Franz Ludwig, Bishop of Bamberg and Wurzburg, 1779-1795
Christoph Franz, Bishop, 1795-1801
Georg Karl, 1801-1803

HELLER

COPPER
Obv: Lion rampant behind diagonal.
Rev: Value "I GUTTER HELLER" and date.

C#	Date	Mintage	VG	Fine	VF	XF
15	1761	—	5.00	7.50	12.50	20.00

Rev: Value "I HELLER" and date.

C#	Date	Mintage	VG	Fine	VF	XF
16	1772	—	5.00	7.50	12.50	20.00

Obv: Arms. Rev: Value over date.

C#	Date	Mintage	VG	Fine	VF	XF
36	1780	—	3.00	4.00	6.00	15.00
	1786	—	3.00	4.00	6.00	15.00

PFENNIG

COPPER
Obv: Lion rampant behind diagonal.
Rev: Value "I LEICHTER PFENNIG" and date.

C#	Date	Mintage	VG	Fine	VF	XF
17	1761	—	4.50	6.50	10.00	15.00

1/2 KREUZER

COPPER
Obv: Lion rampant behind diagonal.
Rev: Value "1/2 LEICHTER KREUZER" and date.

C#	Date	Mintage	VG	Fine	VF	XF
18	1762	—	5.00	7.50	12.50	20.00
	1763	—	5.00	7.50	12.50	20.00

KREUZER

BILLON
Obv: Lion rampant behind diagonal.
Rev: Value and date.

C#	Date	Mintage	VG	Fine	VF	XF
19	1765	—	5.00	7.50	12.50	20.00
	1766	—	5.00	7.50	12.50	20.00

BILLON
Obv: Arms. Rev: Value over date.

C#	Date	Mintage	VG	Fine	VF	XF
37	1786	—	3.50	4.50	6.00	15.00

2-1/2 KREUZER

BILLON
Obv: Facing bust of St. Heinrich holding sword and orb.
Rev: Value and date.

C#	Date	Mintage	VG	Fine	VF	XF
20	1766	—	5.00	7.50	12.50	20.00

5 KREUZER

BILLON
Obv: Facing bust of St. Heinrich holding sword and orb.
Rev: Value and date in cartouche.

C#	Date	Mintage	VG	Fine	VF	XF
25	1766	—	7.50	12.50	20.00	35.00

20 KREUZER
(Convention)

SILVER

C#	Date	Mintage	Fine	VF	XF	Unc
55	1800	—	15.00	25.00	40.00	95.00

GROSCHEN

BILLON
Death of the Bishop Commemorative
Obv: 5 helmed arms.
Rev: 9 line inscription and date.

C#	Date	Mintage	VG	Fine	VF	XF
23	1779	—	8.50	12.50	20.00	35.00

SILVER
Death of the Bishop Commemorative
Obv: Arms. Rev: 9 line inscription.

C#	Date	Mintage	VG	Fine	VF	XF
39	1795	—	6.00	10.00	15.00	25.00

1/2 THALER
(Convention)

SILVER

C#	Date	Mintage	Fine	VF	XF	Unc
56	1800	—	60.00	100.00	175.00	300.00

Obv: Fuller bust

C#	Date	Mintage	Fine	VF	XF	Unc
56a	1800	—	45.00	75.00	125.00	300.00

THALER
(Convention)

SILVER
Obv: Bust of Adam Friedrich right.
Rev: Crowned arms with lion supporters.

C#	Date	Mintage	VG	Fine	VF	XF
31	1760	—	250.00	450.00	600.00	950.00

Contribution Thaler

C#	Date	Mintage	VG	Fine	VF	XF
47	1795	—	75.00	150.00	200.00	300.00

NOTE: Made from the silver service of the Bishop.

C#	Date	Mintage	Fine	VF	XF	Unc
57	1800	—	60.00	100.00	175.00	400.00

Obv: Crowned arms with small mantle, date in upper field.

C#	Date	Mintage	Fine	VF	XF	Unc
57a	1800	—	50.00	85.00	150.00	300.00

Rev: BAMBERG in frame below city view.

C#	Date	Mintage	Fine	VF	XF	Unc
57b	1800	—	75.00	150.00	250.00	400.00

TRADE COINS

DUCAT

3.5000 gm., .986 GOLD, .1109 oz AGW
Homage of Bamberg Commemorative
Obv: Bust of Adam Friedrich right.
Rev: Standing knight; lance in right hand, left hand on shield.

C#	Date	Mintage	VG	Fine	VF	XF
33	1757	—	650.00	1000.	1500.	2500.

Homage of Bamberg Commemorative
Obv: Bust of Bishop.
Rev: Pyramid at left and seated female at right.

C#	Date	Mintage	Fine	VF	XF	Unc
50	1779	—	800.00	1350.	1750.	2250.

Homage of Bamberg Commemorative

C#	Date	Mintage	Fine	VF	XF	Unc
59	1795	—	300.00	500.00	1000.	1500.

Obv: Two female figures holding coats-of-arms of Bavaria and Bamberg. Rev: Inscription.

C#	Date	Mintage	Fine	VF	XF	Unc
60	1802	—	350.00	600.00	1200.	2000.

BAVARIA

Located in South Germany. In 1180 the duchy of Bavaria was given to the count of Wittelsbach by the emperor. He is the ancestor of all who ruled in Bavaria until 1918. Primogeniture was proclaimed in 1506 and in 1623 the dukes of Bavaria were given the electoral right. Bavaria, which had been divided for the various heirs, was reunited in 1799. The title of king was granted to Bavaria in 1805.

RULERS

Carl Theodor, 1777-1799
Maximilian IV, Joseph as Elector, 1799-1805
As King Maximilian I, Joseph, 1806-1825
Ludwig I, 1825-1848
Maximilian II, 1848-1864
Ludwig II, 1864-1886
Otto, 1886-1913
Prince Regent Luitpold, 1886-1912
Ludwig III, 1913-1918

HELLER

COPPER
Obv: Shield dividing date within diamond.
Rev: Value in diamond.

C#	Date	Mintage	VG	Fine	VF	XF
50	1780	—	1.50	2.50	5.00	10.00
	1781	—	1.50	2.50	5.00	10.00
	1782	—	1.50	2.50	5.00	10.00
	1783	—	1.50	2.50	5.00	10.00
	1785	—	1.50	2.50	5.00	10.00
	1787	—	1.50	2.50	5.00	10.00
	1788	—	1.50	2.50	5.00	10.00
	1790	—	1.50	2.50	5.00	10.00
	1791	—	1.50	2.50	5.00	10.00
	1792	—	1.50	2.50	5.00	10.00
	1793	—	1.50	2.50	5.00	10.00
	1795	—	1.50	2.50	5.00	10.00
	1796	—	1.50	2.50	5.00	10.00
	1799	—	1.50	2.50	5.00	10.00

Obv: Diamond shield dividing date. Rev: Value.

C#	Date	Mintage	VG	Fine	VF	XF
50a	1780	—	2.00	3.00	5.00	10.00
	1783	—	2.00	3.00	5.00	10.00

Obv: Crowned 3-fold arms in spray dividing date at top. Rev: Value in diamond.

C#	Date	Mintage	VG	Fine	VF	XF
51	1793	—	5.00	7.50	9.50	18.00
	1794	—	5.00	7.50	9.50	18.00

Obv: Lozenge shield divides date. Rev: Value.

C#	Date	Mintage	Fine	VF	XF	Unc
100	1799	—	3.00	5.00	10.00	40.00
	1800	—	3.00	5.00	10.00	35.00
	1801	—	3.00	5.00	10.00	35.00
	1802	—	3.00	5.00	10.00	35.00
	1803	—	3.00	5.00	10.00	35.00
	1804	—	3.00	5.00	10.00	35.00
	1805	—	3.00	5.00	10.00	35.00

C#	Date	Mintage	Fine	VF	XF	Unc
134	1806	—	3.00	5.00	10.00	35.00
	1807	—	3.00	5.00	10.00	35.00
	1808	—	3.00	5.00	10.00	35.00
	1809	—	3.00	5.00	10.00	35.00
	1810	—	3.00	5.00	10.00	35.00
	1811	—	3.00	5.00	10.00	35.00
	1812	—	3.00	5.00	10.00	35.00
	1813	—	3.00	5.00	10.00	35.00
	1814	—	3.00	5.00	10.00	35.00
	1815	—	3.00	5.00	10.00	35.00
	1817	—	3.00	5.00	10.00	35.00
	1818	—	3.00	5.00	10.00	35.00
	1819	—	3.00	5.00	10.00	35.00
	1820	—	3.00	5.00	10.00	35.00
	1821	—	3.00	5.00	10.00	35.00
	1822	—	3.00	5.00	10.00	35.00
	1823	—	3.00	5.00	10.00	35.00
	1824	—	3.00	5.00	10.00	35.00
	1825	—	3.00	5.00	10.00	35.00

C#	Date	Mintage	Fine	VF	XF	Unc
155	1828	—	2.00	4.00	8.00	30.00
	1829	—	2.00	4.00	8.00	30.00
	1830	—	2.00	4.00	8.00	30.00
	1831	—	2.00	4.00	8.00	30.00
	1832	—	2.00	4.00	8.00	30.00
	1833	—	2.00	4.00	8.00	30.00
	1834	—	2.00	4.00	8.00	30.00
	1835	—	2.00	4.00	8.00	30.00

C#	Date	Mintage	Fine	VF	XF	Unc
158	1839	.256	2.00	4.00	8.00	30.00
	1840	.169	2.00	4.00	8.00	30.00
	1841	—	2.00	4.00	8.00	30.00
	1842	—	2.00	4.00	8.00	30.00
	1843	—	2.00	4.00	8.00	30.00
	1844	.190	2.00	4.00	8.00	30.00
	1845	.434	2.00	4.00	8.00	30.00
	1846	—	2.00	4.00	8.00	30.00
	1847	.074	2.00	4.00	8.00	30.00
	1848	.514	2.00	4.00	8.00	30.00

C#	Date	Mintage	Fine	VF	XF	Unc
220	1849	.346	2.00	3.00	6.00	25.00
	1850	.306	2.00	3.00	6.00	25.00
	1851	.437	2.00	3.00	6.00	25.00
	1852	.206	2.00	3.00	6.00	25.00
	1853	.279	2.00	3.00	6.00	25.00
	1854	.193	2.00	3.00	6.00	25.00
	1855	.132	2.00	3.00	6.00	25.00
	1856	.034	2.00	3.00	6.00	25.00

PFENNIG

COPPER
Obv: Diamond shield of arms.
Rev: Value over date.

C#	Date	Mintage	VG	Fine	VF	XF
52	1782	—	1.50	2.50	4.50	10.00
	1783	—	1.50	2.50	4.50	10.00
	1784	—	1.50	2.50	4.50	10.00
	1785	—	1.50	2.50	4.50	10.00
	1786	—	1.50	2.50	4.50	10.00
	1787	—	1.50	2.50	4.50	10.00
	1788	—	1.50	2.50	4.50	10.00
	1789	—	1.50	2.50	4.50	10.00
	1790	—	1.50	2.50	4.50	10.00
	1792	—	1.50	2.50	4.50	10.00
	1793	—	1.50	2.50	4.50	10.00
	1794	—	1.50	2.50	4.50	10.00
	1795	—	1.50	2.50	4.50	10.00
	1796	—	1.50	2.50	4.50	10.00
	1797	—	1.50	2.50	4.50	10.00
	1798	—	1.50	2.50	4.50	10.00
	1799	—	1.50	2.50	4.50	10.00

Obv: Crowned 3-fold arms in spray.

C#	Date	Mintage	VG	Fine	VF	XF
53	1793	—	2.00	4.00	7.00	12.00
	1794	—	2.00	4.00	7.00	12.00

Obv: Arms in order chain.

C#	Date	Mintage	VG	Fine	VF	XF
53a	1793	—	2.00	3.00	6.00	12.00
	1794	—	2.00	3.00	6.00	12.00

Obv: Bavaria shield in ornamental cartouche.

C#	Date	Mintage	Fine	VF	XF	Unc
101	1799	—	3.00	5.00	10.00	40.00
	1800	—	3.00	5.00	10.00	35.00
	1801	—	3.00	5.00	10.00	35.00
	1802	—	3.00	5.00	10.00	35.00
	1803	—	3.00	5.00	10.00	35.00
	1804	—	3.00	5.00	10.00	35.00
	1805	—	3.00	5.00	10.00	35.00

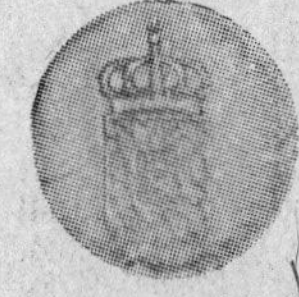

C#	Date	Mintage	Fine	VF	XF	Unc
135	1806	—	2.00	4.00	9.00	35.00
	1807	—	2.00	4.00	9.00	35.00
	1808	—	2.00	4.00	9.00	35.00
	1809	—	2.00	4.00	9.00	35.00
	1810	—	2.00	4.00	9.00	35.00
	1811	—	2.00	4.00	9.00	35.00

C#	Date	Mintage	Fine	VF	XF	Unc
135	1812	—	2.00	4.00	9.00	35.00
	1813	—	2.00	4.00	9.00	35.00
	1814	—	2.00	4.00	9.00	35.00
	1815	—	2.00	4.00	9.00	35.00
	1816	—	2.00	4.00	9.00	35.00
	1817	—	2.00	4.00	9.00	35.00
	1818	—	2.00	4.00	9.00	35.00
	1819	—	2.00	4.00	9.00	35.00
	1820	—	2.00	4.00	9.00	35.00
	1821	—	2.00	4.00	9.00	35.00
	1822	—	2.00	4.00	9.00	35.00
	1823	—	2.00	4.00	9.00	35.00
	1824	—	2.00	4.00	9.00	35.00
	1825	—	2.00	4.00	9.00	35.00
156	1828	—	2.00	3.00	7.50	30.00
	1829	—	2.00	3.00	7.50	30.00
	1830	—	2.00	3.00	7.50	30.00
	1831	—	2.00	3.00	7.50	30.00
	1832	—	2.00	3.00	7.50	30.00
	1833	—	2.00	3.00	7.50	30.00
	1834	—	2.00	3.00	7.50	30.00
	1835	—	2.00	3.00	7.50	30.00
159	1839	.801	2.00	3.00	6.00	25.00
	1840	.732	2.00	3.00	6.00	25.00
	1841	.970	2.00	3.00	6.00	25.00
	1842	.817	2.00	3.00	6.00	25.00
	1843	.892	2.00	3.00	6.00	25.00
	1844	.645	2.00	3.00	6.00	25.00
	1845	1.037	2.00	3.00	6.00	25.00
	1846	1.487	2.00	3.00	6.00	25.00
	1847	1.808	2.00	3.00	6.00	25.00
	1848	1.815	2.00	3.00	6.00	25.00
221	1849	2.120	1.00	2.00	5.00	20.00
	1850	2.494	1.00	2.00	5.00	20.00
	1851	2.162	1.00	2.00	5.00	20.00
	1852	2.634	1.00	2.00	5.00	20.00
	1853	1.950	1.00	2.00	5.00	20.00
	1854	1.842	1.00	2.00	5.00	20.00
	1855	1.576	1.00	2.00	5.00	20.00
	1856	1.530	1.00	2.00	5.00	20.00
224	1858	—	1.00	2.25	3.50	15.00
	1859	—	1.00	2.25	3.50	15.00
	1860	—	1.00	2.25	3.50	15.00
	1861	—	1.00	2.25	3.50	15.00
	1862	—	1.00	2.25	3.50	15.00
	1863	2.284	1.00	2.25	3.50	15.00
	1864	2.304	1.00	2.25	3.50	15.00
250	1865	1.401	1.00	2.50	5.00	16.00
	1866	1.485	1.00	2.50	5.00	16.00
	1867	1.633	1.00	2.50	5.00	16.00
	1868	1.394	1.00	2.50	5.00	16.00
	1869	1.474	1.00	2.50	5.00	16.00
	1870	1.608	1.00	2.50	5.00	16.00
	1871	1.534	1.00	2.50	5.00	16.00

2 PFENNIG

COPPER

Obv: Diamond shield of arms.

Rev: Value over date.

C#	Date	Mintage	VG	Fine	VF	XF
54	1782	—	1.00	2.50	4.50	10.00
	1786	—	1.00	2.50	4.50	10.00
	1790	—	1.00	2.50	4.50	10.00
	1793	—	1.00	2.50	4.50	10.00
	1795	—	1.00	2.50	4.50	10.00
	1796	—	1.00	2.50	4.50	10.00
	1799	—	1.00	2.50	4.50	10.00

Obv: Crowned 3-fold arms in spray.

C#	Date	Mintage	VG	Fine	VF	XF
55	1793	—	2.00	3.50	5.00	10.00

Obv: Bavaria shield.

C#	Date	Mintage	Fine	VF	XF	Unc
102	1799	—	3.00	6.00	12.00	35.00
	1800	—	3.00	6.00	12.00	35.00
	1801	—	3.00	6.00	12.00	35.00
	1802	—	3.00	6.00	12.00	35.00
	1803	—	3.00	6.00	12.00	35.00
	1804	—	3.00	6.00	12.00	35.00
	1805	—	3.00	6.00	12.00	35.00

Obv: Crowned arms on plain field.

C#	Date	Mintage	Fine	VF	XF	Unc
136	1806	—	3.00	5.00	10.00	30.00
	1807	—	3.00	5.00	10.00	30.00
	1808	—	3.00	5.00	10.00	30.00
	1809	—	3.00	5.00	10.00	30.00
	1810	—	3.00	5.00	10.00	30.00
	1811	—	3.00	5.00	10.00	30.00
	1812	—	3.00	5.00	10.00	30.00
	1813	—	3.00	5.00	10.00	30.00
	1814	—	3.00	5.00	10.00	30.00
	1815	—	3.00	5.00	10.00	30.00
	1816	—	3.00	5.00	10.00	30.00
	1817	—	3.00	5.00	10.00	30.00
	1818	—	3.00	5.00	10.00	30.00
	1819	—	3.00	5.00	10.00	30.00
	1820	—	3.00	5.00	10.00	30.00
	1821	—	3.00	5.00	10.00	30.00
	1822	—	3.00	5.00	10.00	30.00
	1823	—	3.00	5.00	10.00	30.00
	1824	—	3.00	5.00	10.00	30.00
	1825	—	3.00	5.00	10.00	30.00
157	1828	—	3.00	5.00	10.00	30.00
	1829	—	3.00	5.00	10.00	30.00
	1830	—	2.00	4.00	10.00	30.00
	1831	—	2.00	4.00	10.00	30.00
	1832	—	2.00	4.00	10.00	30.00
	1833	—	2.00	4.00	10.00	30.00
	1834	—	2.00	4.00	10.00	30.00
	1835	—	2.00	4.00	10.00	30.00
160	1839	.320	2.00	3.00	8.00	30.00
	1840	.320	2.00	3.00	8.00	30.00
	1841	.442	2.00	3.00	8.00	30.00
	1842	.353	2.00	3.00	8.00	30.00
	1843	.203	2.00	3.00	8.00	30.00
	1844	.226	2.00	3.00	8.00	30.00
	1845	.242	2.00	3.00	8.00	30.00
	1846	.232	2.00	3.00	8.00	30.00
	1847	.663	2.00	3.00	8.00	30.00
	1848	.776	—	2.00	5.00	20.00

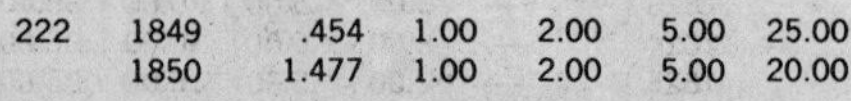

C#	Date	Mintage	Fine	VF	XF	Unc
222	1849	.454	1.00	2.00	5.00	25.00
	1850	1.477	1.00	2.00	5.00	20.00

C#	Date	Mintage	Fine	VF	XF	Unc
225	1858	—	1.00	2.00	4.00	15.00
	1859	—	1.00	2.00	4.00	15.00
	1860	—	1.00	2.00	4.00	15.00
	1861	—	1.00	2.00	4.00	15.00
	1862	—	1.00	2.00	4.00	15.00
	1863	.228	1.00	2.00	4.00	15.00

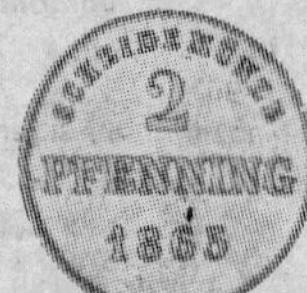

C#	Date	Mintage	Fine	VF	XF	Unc
251	1864	.589	1.00	1.50	3.00	15.00
	1865	.358	1.00	1.50	3.00	15.00
	1866	.234	1.00	1.50	3.00	15.00
	1867	.481	1.00	1.50	3.00	15.00
	1868	.208	1.00	1.50	3.00	15.00
	1869	.466	1.00	1.50	3.00	15.00
	1870	.476	1.00	1.50	3.00	15.00
	1871	.466	1.00	1.50	3.00	15.00

1/2 KREUZER

COPPER

C#	Date	Mintage	Fine	VF	XF	Unc
223	1851	.796	1.00	2.00	4.00	15.00
	1852	.981	1.00	2.00	4.00	15.00
	1853	.797	1.00	2.00	4.00	15.00
	1854	.528	1.00	2.00	4.00	15.00
	1855	.641	1.00	2.00	4.00	15.00
	1856	.462	1.00	2.00	4.00	15.00

KREUZER

BILLON

Obv: Head right. Rev: Crowned round arms, value numeral divides date.

C#	Date	Mintage	VG	Fine	VF	XF
57	1794	—	2.00	3.50	5.00	10.00
	1795	—	2.00	3.50	5.00	10.00
	1796	—	2.00	3.50	5.00	10.00
	1797	—	2.00	3.50	5.00	10.00
	1798	—	2.00	3.50	5.00	10.00

Rev: Arms, value and date.

C#	Date	Mintage	VG	Fine	VF	XF
57a	1795	—	2.00	3.50	5.00	10.00
	1796	—	2.00	3.50	5.00	10.00
	1797	—	2.00	3.50	5.00	10.00

Obv: Head right, MAX. IOS.
Rev: Crowned shield within palm branches.

C#	Date	Mintage	Fine	VF	XF	Unc
103a	1799	—	3.00	6.00	12.00	35.00
	1800	—	3.00	6.00	12.00	35.00
	1803	—	3.00	6.00	12.00	35.00

Rev: With numeral value separating date.

C#	Date	Mintage	Fine	VF	XF	Unc
103	1801	—	3.00	6.00	12.00	35.00
	1802	—	3.00	6.00	12.00	35.00

Obv. leg: MAX. IOS. H.I.B.C. Rev: No numeric value.

C#	Date	Mintage	Fine	VF	XF	Unc
103.1	1800	—	3.00	6.00	12.00	35.00
	1801	—	3.00	6.00	12.00	35.00
	1802	—	3.00	6.00	12.00	35.00
	1803	—	3.00	6.00	12.00	35.00
	1806/0	—	3.50	7.50	15.00	45.00

Rev: Numeral value separating date.

C#	Date	Mintage	Fine	VF	XF	Unc
103.1a	1804	—	3.00	6.00	12.00	35.00

Obv. leg: MAX. IOS. C.Z.
Rev: LAND MUNZ, oval arms separating value.

C#	Date	Mintage	Fine	VF	XF	Unc
103.2	1804	—	3.00	6.00	12.00	35.00
	1805	—	3.00	6.00	12.00	35.00

COPPER

C#	Date	Mintage	Fine	VF	XF	Unc
130	1806	.145	4.00	8.00	18.00	45.00

BILLON
Obv: Head right. Rev: Crowned arms above crossed sword and scepter.

C#	Date	Mintage	Fine	VF	XF	Unc
137	1806	—	3.00	5.00	10.00	35.00
	1807	—	3.00	5.00	10.00	35.00
	1808	—	3.00	5.00	10.00	35.00
	1809	—	3.00	5.00	10.00	35.00
	1810	—	3.00	5.00	10.00	35.00
	1811	—	3.00	5.00	10.00	35.00
	1812	—	3.00	5.00	10.00	35.00
	1813	—	3.00	5.00	10.00	35.00
	1814	—	3.00	5.00	10.00	35.00
	1815	—	3.00	5.00	10.00	35.00
	1816	—	3.00	5.00	10.00	35.00
	1817	—	3.00	5.00	10.00	35.00
	1818	—	3.00	5.00	10.00	35.00
	1819	—	3.00	5.00	10.00	35.00
	1820	—	3.00	5.00	10.00	35.00
	1821	—	3.00	5.00	10.00	35.00
	1822	—	3.00	5.00	10.00	35.00
	1823	—	3.00	5.00	10.00	35.00
	1824	—	3.00	5.00	10.00	35.00
	1825	—	3.00	5.00	10.00	35.00

Obv. leg: LUDWIG

C#	Date	Mintage	Fine	VF	XF	Unc
161	1827	—	3.00	5.00	10.00	30.00
	1828	—	3.00	5.00	10.00	30.00
	1829	—	3.00	5.00	10.00	30.00
	1830	—	3.00	5.00	10.00	30.00

C#	Date	Mintage	Fine	VF	XF	Unc
161a	1830	—	3.00	5.00	10.00	30.00
	1831	—	3.00	5.00	10.00	30.00
	1832	—	3.00	5.00	10.00	30.00
	1833	—	3.00	5.00	10.00	30.00
	1834	—	3.00	5.00	10.00	30.00
	1835	—	3.00	5.00	10.00	30.00

C#	Date	Mintage	Fine	VF	XF	Unc
189	1839	1.474	1.00	2.00	6.00	25.00
	1840	1.769	1.00	2.00	6.00	25.00
	1841	1.591	1.00	2.00	6.00	25.00
	1842	1.855	1.00	2.00	6.00	25.00
	1843	1.373	1.00	2.00	6.00	25.00
	1844	1.324	1.00	2.00	6.00	25.00
	1845	1.660	1.00	2.00	6.00	25.00
	1846	1.849	1.00	2.00	6.00	25.00
	1847	1.519	1.00	2.00	6.00	25.00
	1848	1.746	1.00	2.00	6.00	25.00

C#	Date	Mintage	Fine	VF	XF	Unc
226	1849	1.971	1.00	2.00	5.00	20.00
	1850	3.135	1.00	2.00	5.00	20.00
	1851	2.084	1.00	2.00	5.00	20.00
	1852	1.915	1.00	2.00	5.00	20.00
	1853	1.528	1.00	2.00	5.00	20.00
	1854	1.650	1.00	2.00	5.00	20.00
	1855	1.510	1.00	2.00	5.00	20.00
	1856	1.335	1.00	2.00	5.00	20.00

C#	Date	Mintage	Fine	VF	XF	Unc
229	1858	2.400	.50	1.00	4.00	15.00
	1859	—	.50	1.00	4.00	15.00
	1860	.231	2.00	3.00	5.00	20.00
	1861	3.276	.50	1.00	2.50	15.00
	1862	3.358	.50	1.00	2.50	15.00
	1863	3.356	.50	1.00	2.50	15.00
	1864	3.293	.50	1.00	2.50	15.00

C#	Date	Mintage	Fine	VF	XF	Unc
252	1865	1.837	.50	1.00	2.50	15.00
	1866	2.542	.50	1.00	2.50	15.00
	1867	2.305	.50	1.00	2.50	15.00
	1868	2.526	.50	1.00	2.50	15.00
	1869	2.774	.50	1.00	2.50	15.00
	1870	2.199	.50	1.00	2.50	15.00
	1871	2.634	.50	1.00	2.50	15.00

3 KREUZER

BILLON
Obv: Head right.
Rev: Crowned arms, date below.

C#	Date	Mintage	VG	Fine	VF	XF
59	1794	—	3.00	4.50	6.00	20.00
	1795	—	3.00	4.50	6.00	20.00
	1796	—	3.00	4.50	6.00	20.00
	1797	—	3.00	4.50	6.00	20.00
	1798	—	3.00	4.50	6.00	20.00

Obv: Head right, MAX. IOS. P. B.
Rev: Crowned oval arms separating value.

C#	Date	Mintage	Fine	VF	XF	Unc
104	1799	—	3.00	5.00	10.00	30.00
	1800	—	3.00	5.00	10.00	30.00
	1801	—	3.00	5.00	10.00	30.00
	1802	—	3.00	5.00	10.00	30.00

Obv. leg: MAX. IOS. H.I.B.C. &

C#	Date	Mintage	Fine	VF	XF	Unc
104a	1803	—	3.00	5.00	10.00	30.00
	1804	—	3.00	5.00	10.00	30.00

Obv. leg: MAX. IOS. C.Z.P.B.

C#	Date	Mintage	Fine	VF	XF	Unc
104b	1804	—	3.00	5.00	10.00	30.00
	1805	—	3.00	5.00	10.00	30.00

1.2500 gm., .667 SILVER, .0268 oz ASW
Obv: Head right. Rev: Shield with crown above crossed scepter and sword.

C#	Date	Mintage	Fine	VF	XF	Unc
138	1807	—	4.00	10.00	15.00	35.00
	1808	—	4.00	10.00	15.00	35.00
	1809	—	4.00	10.00	15.00	35.00
	1810	—	4.00	10.00	15.00	35.00
	1811	—	4.00	10.00	15.00	35.00
	1812	—	4.00	10.00	15.00	35.00
	1813	—	4.00	10.00	15.00	35.00
	1814	—	4.00	10.00	15.00	35.00
	1815	—	4.00	10.00	15.00	35.00
	1816	—	4.00	10.00	15.00	35.00
	1817	—	4.00	10.00	15.00	35.00
	1818	—	4.00	10.00	15.00	35.00
	1819	—	4.00	10.00	15.00	35.00
	1820	—	4.00	10.00	15.00	35.00
	1821	—	4.00	10.00	15.00	35.00
	1822	—	4.00	10.00	15.00	35.00
	1823	—	4.00	10.00	15.00	35.00
	1824	—	4.00	10.00	15.00	35.00
	1825	—	4.00	10.00	15.00	35.00

Obv. leg: LUDWIG

C#	Date	Mintage	Fine	VF	XF	Unc
162	1827	—	4.00	10.00	15.00	35.00
	1828	—	4.00	10.00	15.00	35.00
	1829	—	4.00	10.00	15.00	35.00
	1830	—	4.00	10.00	15.00	35.00

C#	Date	Mintage	Fine	VF	XF	Unc
162a	1830	—	4.00	8.00	15.00	35.00
	1831	—	4.00	8.00	15.00	35.00
	1832	—	4.00	8.00	15.00	35.00
	1833	—	4.00	8.00	15.00	35.00
	1834	—	4.00	8.00	15.00	35.00
	1835	—	4.00	8.00	15.00	35.00
	1836	—	4.00	8.00	15.00	35.00

C#	Date	Mintage	Fine	VF	XF	Unc
190	1839	.456	2.00	3.00	5.00	25.00
	1840	.235	2.00	3.00	5.00	25.00
	1841	.337	2.00	3.00	5.00	25.00
	1842	.370	2.00	3.00	5.00	25.00
	1843	.337	2.00	3.00	5.00	25.00
	1844	.269	2.00	3.00	5.00	25.00
	1845	.361	2.00	3.00	5.00	25.00
	1846	.463	2.00	3.00	5.00	25.00
	1847	.563	2.00	3.00	5.00	25.00
	1848	.447	2.00	3.00	5.00	25.00

C#	Date	Mintage	Fine	VF	XF	Unc
227	1849	.373	1.00	2.50	5.00	25.00
	1850	.615	1.00	2.50	5.00	25.00
	1851	.582	1.00	2.50	5.00	25.00
	1852	.282	1.00	2.50	5.00	25.00
	1853	.280	1.00	2.50	5.00	25.00
	1854	.388	1.00	2.50	5.00	25.00
	1855	.285	1.00	2.50	5.00	25.00
	1856	.091	1.00	2.50	5.00	35.00

C#	Date	Mintage	Fine	VF	XF	Unc
253	1865	.832	1.00	3.00	5.00	25.00
	1866	.566	1.00	3.00	5.00	25.00
	1867	.099	2.00	5.00	8.00	35.00
	1868	.065	2.00	5.00	8.00	35.00

6 KREUZER

BILLON
Obv: Head right.
Rev: Crowned arms, date below.

C#	Date	Mintage	VG	Fine	VF	XF
61	1794	—	4.00	7.00	9.50	20.00
	1795	—	4.00	7.00	9.50	20.00
	1796	—	4.00	7.00	9.50	20.00
	1797	—	4.00	7.00	9.50	20.00
	1798	—	4.00	7.00	9.50	20.00

Obv: Head right, MAX. IOS. P.B.
Rev: Crowned oval arms separating value.

C#	Date	Mintage	Fine	VF	XF	Unc
105	1799	—	3.00	6.00	10.00	50.00
	1800	—	3.00	6.00	10.00	50.00
	1802	—	3.00	6.00	10.00	50.00
	1803	—	3.00	6.00	10.00	50.00

Obv. leg: MAX. IOS. H.I.B.C. &

C#	Date	Mintage	Fine	VF	XF	Unc
105a	1801	—	3.00	6.00	10.00	50.00
	1803	—	3.00	6.00	10.00	50.00
	1804	—	3.00	6.00	10.00	50.00

Obv. leg: MAX. IOS. C.Z.P.B.

C#	Date	Mintage	Fine	VF	XF	Unc
105b	1804	—	3.00	6.00	10.00	50.00
	1805	—	3.00	6.00	10.00	50.00

2.5000 gm., .667 SILVER, .0536 oz ASW
Obv: Head Right.
Rev: Crowned arms with shield divided.

C#	Date	Mintage	Fine	VF	XF	Unc
131	1806	—	6.00	15.00	30.00	60.00

C#	Date	Mintage	Fine	VF	XF	Unc
139	1806	—	3.00	6.00	12.50	50.00
	1807	—	3.00	6.00	12.50	50.00
	1808	—	3.00	6.00	12.50	50.00
	1809	—	3.00	6.00	12.50	50.00
	1810	—	3.00	6.00	12.50	50.00
	1811	—	3.00	6.00	12.50	50.00
	1812	—	3.00	6.00	12.50	50.00
	1813	—	3.00	6.00	12.50	50.00
	1814	—	3.00	6.00	12.50	50.00
	1815	—	3.00	6.00	12.50	50.00
	1816	—	3.00	6.00	12.50	50.00
	1817	—	3.00	6.00	12.50	50.00
	1818	—	3.00	6.00	12.50	50.00
	1819	—	3.00	6.00	12.50	50.00
	1820	—	3.00	6.00	12.50	50.00
	1821	—	3.00	6.00	12.50	50.00
	1822	—	3.00	6.00	12.50	50.00
	1823	—	3.00	6.00	12.50	50.00
	1824	—	3.00	6.00	12.50	50.00
	1825	—	3.00	6.00	12.50	50.00

C#	Date	Mintage	Fine	VF	XF	Unc
163	1827	—	3.00	6.00	12.50	50.00
	1828	—	3.00	6.00	12.50	50.00
	1829	—	3.00	6.00	12.50	50.00

C#	Date	Mintage	Fine	VF	XF	Unc
163a	1830	—	3.00	6.00	12.00	50.00
	1831	—	3.00	6.00	12.00	50.00
	1832	—	3.00	6.00	12.00	50.00
	1833	—	3.00	6.00	12.00	50.00
	1834	—	3.00	6.00	12.00	50.00
	1835	—	3.00	6.00	12.00	50.00

C#	Date	Mintage	Fine	VF	XF	Unc
191	1839	.800	2.00	3.00	6.00	40.00
	1840	—	2.00	3.00	6.00	40.00
	1841	—	2.00	3.00	6.00	40.00
	1842	—	2.00	3.00	6.00	40.00
	1843	—	2.00	3.00	6.00	40.00
	1844	—	2.00	3.00	6.00	40.00
	1845	—	2.00	3.00	6.00	40.00
	1846	—	2.00	3.00	6.00	40.00
	1847	—	2.00	3.00	6.00	40.00
	1848	—	2.00	3.00	6.00	40.00

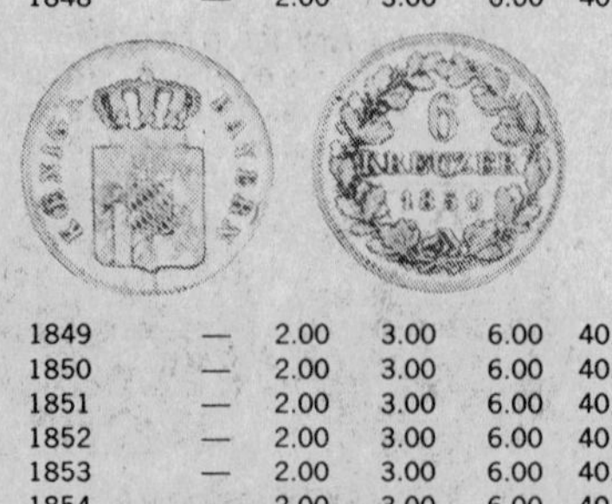

C#	Date	Mintage	Fine	VF	XF	Unc
228	1849	—	2.00	3.00	6.00	40.00
	1850	—	2.00	3.00	6.00	40.00
	1851	—	2.00	3.00	6.00	40.00
	1852	—	2.00	3.00	6.00	40.00
	1853	—	2.00	3.00	6.00	40.00
	1854	—	2.00	3.00	6.00	40.00
	1855	—	2.00	3.00	6.00	40.00
	1856	—	2.00	3.00	6.00	40.00

Obv. leg: SCHEIDE MUNZE added.

C#	Date	Mintage	Fine	VF	XF	Unc
254	1866	.087	4.00	8.00	12.00	40.00
	1867	.024	4.00	10.00	15.00	45.00

10 KREUZER

(Convention)

SILVER

C#	Date	Mintage	VG	Fine	VF	XF
69	1778-98	—	5.00	8.00	11.00	15.00

Vicariat Issue

C#	Date	Mintage	VG	Fine	VF	XF
65a	1790	—	5.00	10.00	15.00	20.00

Vicariat Issue

C#	Date	Mintage	VG	Fine	VF	XF
67a	1792	—	5.00	10.00	15.00	20.00

Obv: Head right in wreath. Rev: Crowned 3 fold oval arms.

C#	Date	Mintage	Fine	VF	XF	Unc
108	1800	—	15.00	30.00	50.00	100.00
	1801	—	15.00	30.00	50.00	100.00

20 KREUZER

(Convention)

SILVER

C#	Date	Mintage	VG	Fine	VF	XF
71	1778-99	—	5.00	8.00	12.00	20.00

Vicariat Issue

C#	Date	Mintage	VG	Fine	VF	XF
72a	1790	—	7.00	12.00	17.50	25.00

Vicariat Issue
Obv: Bust right.
Rev: Eagle with arms on breast.

C#	Date	Mintage	VG	Fine	VF	XF
72b	1792	—	7.00	12.00	17.50	25.00

Obv: Bust in wreath.
Rev: 3-fold oval arms.

C#	Date	Mintage	VG	Fine	VF	XF
74	1793	—	5.00	8.00	12.50	18.00
	1794	—	5.00	8.00	12.50	18.00

Obv: Head right in wreath. Rev: Crowned 3-fold oval arms.

C#	Date	Mintage	Fine	VF	XF	Unc
112	1799	—	20.00	40.00	65.00	100.00
	1800	—	20.00	40.00	65.00	100.00
	1801	—	20.00	40.00	65.00	100.00
	1802	—	20.00	40.00	65.00	100.00
	1803	—	20.00	40.00	65.00	100.00

Obv: Uniformed bust right.

C#	Date	Mintage	Fine	VF	XF	Unc
114	1804	—	15.00	35.00	50.00	100.00
	1805	—	15.00	35.00	50.00	100.00

.583 SILVER
Obv: Head right.
Rev: Crowned arms within branches.

C#	Date	Mintage	Fine	VF	XF	Unc
140	1806	—	10.00	25.00	40.00	85.00
	1807	—	10.00	25.00	40.00	85.00
	1808	—	10.00	25.00	40.00	85.00
	1809	—	10.00	25.00	40.00	85.00
	1810	—	10.00	25.00	40.00	85.00
	1811	—	10.00	25.00	40.00	85.00
	1812	—	10.00	25.00	40.00	85.00
	1813	—	10.00	25.00	40.00	85.00
	1814	—	10.00	25.00	40.00	85.00
	1815	—	10.00	25.00	40.00	85.00
	1816	—	10.00	25.00	40.00	85.00
	1817	—	10.00	25.00	40.00	85.00
	1818	—	10.00	25.00	40.00	85.00
	1819	—	10.00	25.00	40.00	85.00
	1820	—	10.00	25.00	40.00	85.00
	1821	—	10.00	25.00	40.00	85.00
	1822	—	10.00	25.00	40.00	85.00
	1823	—	10.00	25.00	40.00	85.00
	1824	—	10.00	25.00	40.00	85.00
	1825	—	10.00	25.00	40.00	85.00

1/2 GULDEN

.900 SILVER

C#	Date	Mintage	Fine	VF	XF	Unc
192	1838	1.750	10.00	22.50	35.00	70.00
	1839	.474	10.00	22.50	35.00	70.00
	1840	.233	10.00	22.50	35.00	70.00
	1841	.243	10.00	22.50	35.00	70.00
	1842	.508	10.00	22.50	35.00	70.00
	1843	.337	10.00	22.50	35.00	70.00
	1844	1.452	10.00	22.50	35.00	70.00
	1845	1.869	10.00	22.50	35.00	70.00
	1846	1.181	10.00	22.50	35.00	70.00
	1847	.241	10.00	22.50	35.00	70.00
	1848	.407	10.00	22.50	35.00	70.00

C#	Date	Mintage	Fine	VF	XF	Unc
230	1848	Inc. Ab.	10.00	25.00	40.00	75.00
	1849	.218	10.00	25.00	40.00	75.00
	1850	.189	10.00	25.00	40.00	75.00
	1851	.171	10.00	25.00	40.00	75.00
	1852	.120	10.00	25.00	40.00	75.00
	1853	.206	10.00	25.00	40.00	75.00
	1854	.146	10.00	25.00	40.00	75.00
	1855	.060	10.00	25.00	40.00	75.00

C#	Date	Mintage	Fine	VF	XF	Unc
230	1856	.074	10.00	25.00	40.00	75.00
	1857	.020	10.00	25.00	40.00	75.00
	1858	.183	10.00	25.00	40.00	75.00
	1859	.405	10.00	25.00	40.00	75.00
	1860	.292	10.00	25.00	40.00	75.00
	1861	.254	10.00	25.00	40.00	75.00
	1862	.141	10.00	25.00	40.00	75.00
	1863	.190	10.00	25.00	40.00	75.00
	1864	.160	10.00	25.00	40.00	75.00

Obv: Head with part in hair.

C#	Date	Mintage	Fine	VF	XF	Unc
255a	1864	Inc. Ab.	15.00	36.00	75.00	150.00
	1865	.227	15.00	36.00	75.00	150.00
	1866	.101	15.00	36.00	75.00	150.00

Obv: Head without part in hair.

C#	Date	Mintage	Fine	VF	XF	Unc
255b	1866	Inc. Ab.	15.00	35.00	65.00	90.00
	1867	.100	15.00	35.00	65.00	90.00
	1868	.121	15.00	35.00	65.00	90.00
	1869	.133	15.00	35.00	65.00	90.00
	1870	.111	15.00	35.00	65.00	90.00
	1871	.051	15.00	35.00	65.00	90.00

EIN (1) GOLDGULDEN

.986 GOLD

C#	Date	Mintage	Fine	VF	XF	Unc
126	1803S.P.Q.W.	—	—	1500.	2000.	3000.
150	1815	—	—	800.00	1200.	1650.
150a	N.D.	—	—	1250.	1750.	2750.
	1817	—	—	1250.	1750.	2750.

Date in chronogram.

C#	Date	Mintage	Fine	VF	XF	Unc
216	ND 1826	—	—	1000.	1500.	1850.
217	ND(1827-36)	—	—	1100.	1600.	2150.

Obv: Head right. Rev: Wurzburg city view.

C#	Date	Mintage	Fine	VF	XF	Unc
218	ND(1843)	—	—	1100.	1600.	2150.

Rev: Wurzburg shield.

C#	Date	Mintage	Fine	VF	XF	Unc
219	ND(1843)	—	—	1100.	1600.	2150.

Rev: Wurzburg city view.

C#	Date	Mintage	Fine	VF	XF	Unc
244	ND(1850)	—	—	1500.	2000.	3000.

Rev: Wurzburg shield.

C#	Date	Mintage	Fine	VF	XF	Unc
245	ND(1850)	—	—	1500.	2000.	3000.

Mule. Obv: Head left of DUCAT.

Rev: Wurzburg city view.

C#	Date	Mintage	Fine	VF	XF	Unc
245a	ND	—	—	—	—	—

Rev: Wurzburg city view.

C#	Date	Mintage	Fine	VF	XF	Unc
263	ND	1864	—	800.00	1200.	1650.

Rev: Wurzburg shield.

C#	Date	Mintage	Fine	VF	XF	Unc
264	ND 1864	—	—	800.00	1200.	1650.

GULDEN

.900 SILVER

C#	Date	Mintage	Fine	VF	XF	Unc
193	1837	2.057	15.00	30.00	45.00	80.00
	1838	2.045	15.00	30.00	45.00	80.00
	1839	2.320	15.00	30.00	45.00	80.00
	1840	3.591	15.00	30.00	45.00	80.00
	1841	4.362	15.00	30.00	45.00	80.00
	1842	1.449	15.00	30.00	45.00	80.00
	1843	4.832	15.00	30.00	45.00	80.00
	1844	3.491	15.00	30.00	45.00	80.00
	1845	1.115	15.00	30.00	45.00	80.00
	1846	.686	15.00	30.00	45.00	80.00
	1847	.387	15.00	30.00	45.00	80.00
	1848	.437	15.00	30.00	45.00	80.00

C#	Date	Mintage	Fine	VF	XF	Unc
231	1848	Inc. Ab.	15.00	30.00	45.00	80.00
	1849	.366	15.00	30.00	45.00	80.00
	1850	.343	15.00	30.00	45.00	80.00
	1851	.224	15.00	30.00	45.00	80.00
	1852	.453	15.00	30.00	45.00	80.00
	1853	.257	15.00	30.00	45.00	80.00
	1854	.513	15.00	30.00	45.00	80.00
	1855	1.076	15.00	30.00	45.00	80.00
	1856	.455	15.00	30.00	45.00	80.00
	1857	.032	15.00	30.00	45.00	80.00
	1858	.144	15.00	30.00	45.00	80.00
	1859	.529	15.00	30.00	45.00	80.00
	1860	.452	15.00	30.00	45.00	80.00
	1861	.358	15.00	30.00	45.00	80.00
	1862	.266	15.00	30.00	45.00	80.00
	1863	.234	15.00	30.00	45.00	80.00
	1864	.414	15.00	30.00	45.00	80.00

Obv: Part in hair.

C#	Date	Mintage	Fine	VF	XF	Unc
256	1864	Inc. Ab.	20.00	40.00	65.00	100.00
	1865	.167	20.00	40.00	65.00	100.00
	1866	.122	20.00	40.00	65.00	100.00

Obv: No part in hair.

C#	Date	Mintage	Fine	VF	XF	Unc
256a	1866	Inc. Ab.	20.00	40.00	65.00	100.00
	1867	.086	20.00	40.00	65.00	100.00
256a	1868	.122	20.00	40.00	65.00	100.00
	1869	.122	20.00	40.00	65.00	100.00
	1870	.072	20.00	40.00	65.00	100.00
	1871	.035	20.00	40.00	65.00	100.00

ZWEY (2) GULDEN

21.2100 gm., .900 SILVER, .6138 oz ASW
Obv. leg: LUDWIG I KOENIG V. BAYERN.

C#	Date	Mintage	Fine	VF	XF	Unc
194	1845	.883	25.00	45.00	85.00	175.00
	1846	1.523	25.00	45.00	85.00	175.00
	1847	1.491	25.00	45.00	85.00	175.00
	1848	.950	25.00	45.00	85.00	175.00

Obv. leg: MAXIMILIAN II KOENIG V. BAYERN.
Rev: Similar to C#194.

C#	Date	Mintage	Fine	VF	XF	Unc
232	1848	Inc. Ab.	25.00	35.00	75.00	150.00
	1849	.741	25.00	35.00	75.00	150.00
	1850	.915	25.00	35.00	75.00	150.00
	1851	1.157	25.00	35.00	75.00	150.00
	1852	1.356	25.00	35.00	75.00	150.00
	1853	.634	25.00	35.00	75.00	150.00
	1854	.430	25.00	35.00	75.00	150.00
	1855	.585	25.00	35.00	75.00	150.00
	1856	.510	25.00	35.00	75.00	150.00

Restoration of Madonna Column in Munich
Obv: Similar to C#232.

C#	Date	Mintage	Fine	VF	XF	Unc
233	1855	1.000	25.00	35.00	45.00	100.00

1/2 THALER
(Convention)

SILVER

C#	Date	Mintage	VG	Fine	VF	XF
75	1778-98	—	30.00	60.00	85.00	110.00

Rev: Madonna.

C#	Date	Mintage	VG	Fine	VF	XF
76	1779	—	12.50	15.00	25.00	50.00
	1782	—	12.50	15.00	25.00	50.00

Vicariat Issue
Obv: Clothed bust right.
Rev: Eagle with 3-fold arms on breast.

C#	Date	Mintage	VG	Fine	VF	XF
77	1790	—	75.00	175.00	250.00	300.00

Vicariat Issue
Obv: Head right.

C#	Date	Mintage	VG	Fine	VF	XF
78a	1792	—	75.00	175.00	250.00	300.00

C#	Date	Mintage	Fine	VF	XF	Unc
115	1799	—	50.00	125.00	200.00	450.00
	1800	—	50.00	125.00	200.00	400.00
	1801	—	50.00	125.00	200.00	400.00
	1802	—	50.00	125.00	200.00	400.00
	1803	—	50.00	125.00	200.00	400.00

C#	Date	Mintage	Fine	VF	XF	Unc
116	1803	—	40.00	90.00	160.00	260.00
	1804	—	40.00	90.00	160.00	260.00
	1805	—	40.00	90.00	160.00	260.00

(Without Denomination)

.833 SILVER

C#	Date	Mintage	Fine	VF	XF	Unc
123	ND (1799-1805)	—	65.00	165.00	250.00	450.00
146	ND (1806-8)	Abt. 1500	100.00	250.00	400.00	750.00

Obv: Head, script legends.

C#	Date	Mintage	Fine	VF	XF	Unc
147	ND (1807-8)	—	100.00	250.00	400.00	750.00

Obv: Legends in block letters.

C#	Date	Mintage	Fine	VF	XF	Unc
148	ND (1808-37)	.025	95.00	200.00	300.00	625.00

THALER

(Convention)

SILVER
Obv: Head right with bound hair, H.S. on neck.
Rev: Crowned 3-fold arms in laurel branches, date below.

C#	Date	Mintage	VG	Fine	VF	XF
79	1778	—	25.00	35.00	50.00	75.00
	1779	—	25.00	35.00	50.00	75.00
	1780	—	25.00	35.00	50.00	75.00
	1781	—	25.00	35.00	50.00	75.00

NOTE: Varieties exist.

C#	Date	Mintage	VG	Fine	VF	XF
79a	1778	—	25.00	30.00	40.00	75.00
	1779	—	25.00	30.00	40.00	75.00
	1780	—	25.00	30.00	40.00	75.00
	1781	—	25.00	30.00	40.00	75.00

Obv: Head right with bound hair; S T below head.
Rev: Crowned 3-fold arms in laurel branches, date below.

C#	Date	Mintage	VG	Fine	VF	XF
79b	1780	—	25.00	30.00	45.00	75.00
	1781	—	25.00	30.00	45.00	75.00

NOTE: Varieties exist.

Obv: Bust right with bound hair; H.S.T. on arm.
Rev: Madonna and child.

C#	Date	Mintage	VG	Fine	VF	XF
80	1778	—	25.00	30.00	40.00	65.00
	1779	—	25.00	30.00	40.00	65.00
	1780	—	25.00	30.00	40.00	65.00
	1781	—	25.00	30.00	40.00	65.00
	1782	—	25.00	30.00	40.00	65.00
	1783	—	25.00	30.00	40.00	65.00

Obv: Bust right with unbound hair, I.S.(CH) on shoulder.

C#	Date	Mintage	Fine	VF	XF	Unc
80a	1778	—	25.00	45.00	75.00	150.00
	1779	—	25.00	45.00	75.00	150.00
	1780	—	25.00	45.00	75.00	150.00
	1781	—	25.00	45.00	75.00	150.00
	1782	—	25.00	45.00	75.00	150.00
	1783	—	25.00	45.00	75.00	150.00
	1784	—	25.00	45.00	75.00	150.00
	1786	—	25.00	45.00	75.00	150.00
	1789	—	25.00	45.00	75.00	150.00
	1792	—	25.00	45.00	75.00	150.00

NOTE: Varieties exist.

Obv: Bust right with A under bust for Amberg Mint.

C#	Date	Mintage	VG	Fine	VF	XF
80c	1778A	—	25.00	30.00	50.00	75.00
	1779A	—	25.00	30.00	50.00	75.00

Vicariat Issue
Obv: Clothed bust right with R.C.D. beneath.
Rev: Eagle with 3-fold arms on breast.

C#	Date	Mintage	VG	Fine	VF	XF
84	1790	—	125.00	275.00	350.00	500.00

Vicariat Issue

C#	Date	Mintage	VG	Fine	VF	XF
84a	1790	—	100.00	225.00	300.00	450.00

Obv: Clothed bust left.

C#	Date	Mintage	VG	Fine	VF	XF
84b	1790	—	—	—	Rare	—

Obv: Head right with loose hair.
Rev: Crowned 3-fold arms in spray, date below divided by A.S.

C#	Date	Mintage	VG	Fine	VF	XF
81	1790	—	25.00	40.00	60.00	100.00
	1791	—	25.00	40.00	60.00	100.00
	1792	—	25.00	40.00	60.00	100.00
	1793	—	25.00	40.00	60.00	100.00

Rev: Ligate AE in BAYARIAE.

C#	Date	Mintage	Fine	VF	XF	Unc
80b	1795	—	25.00	50.00	75.00	125.00
	1796	—	25.00	50.00	75.00	125.00
	1797	—	25.00	50.00	75.00	125.00
	1798	—	25.00	50.00	75.00	125.00
	1799	—	25.00	50.00	75.00	125.00

NOTE: Varieties exist.

Vicariat Issue

C#	Date	Mintage	VG	Fine	VF	XF
87	1792	—	150.00	350.00	400.00	550.00

Obv: Armored bust right with A beneath.
Rev: Crowned 3-fold arms in spray; date below.

C#	Date	Mintage	VG	Fine	VF	XF
83	1794A	—	100.00	250.00	350.00	500.00

Issued by the Abbott of St. Emmeram Monastery
Obv: Bust right; 3 line inscription around border.
Rev: Madonna and child.

C#	Date	Mintage	VG	Fine	VF	XF
82	1796	—	—	—	Rare	—

C#	Date	Mintage	Fine	VF	XF	Unc
118	1799	—	60.00	130.00	300.00	525.00
	1800	—	60.00	130.00	300.00	525.00
	1801	—	60.00	130.00	300.00	525.00
	1802	—	60.00	130.00	300.00	525.00

Obv. leg: D.G. MAXIM. IOSEPH

C#	Date	Mintage	Fine	VF	XF	Unc
118a	1802	—	95.00	200.00	350.00	650.00

Obv. leg: D.G. MAX. IOSEPH

C#	Date	Mintage	Fine	VF	XF	Unc
118c	1802	—	95.00	200.00	350.00	650.00
	1803	—	95.00	200.00	350.00	650.00

Obv: Uniformed bust right, MAXIMILIAN

C#	Date	Mintage	Fine	VF	XF	Unc
118b	1802	—	100.00	250.00	500.00	825.00

C#	Date	Mintage	Fine	VF	XF	Unc
120	1803	—	75.00	180.00	325.00	600.00

Obv. leg. ends: ....ZU PFALZBAIERN.

C#	Date	Mintage	Fine	VF	XF	Unc
121	1803	—	100.00	250.00	500.00	825.00
	1804	—	100.00	250.00	500.00	825.00
	1805	—	100.00	250.00	500.00	825.00

C#	Date	Mintage	Fine	VF	XF	Unc
122	1805	—	75.00	175.00	300.00	600.00

28.0000 gm., .833 SILVER, .7500 oz ASW

C#	Date	Mintage	Fine	VF	XF	Unc
132	1806	—	80.00	180.00	325.00	600.00

Rev: Crowned lions facing outward.

C#	Date	Mintage	Fine	VF	XF	Unc
132a	1806	—	125.00	300.00	500.00	825.00

Obv: Bust with pigtail.

C#	Date	Mintage	Fine	VF	XF	Unc
141	1807	.100	100.00	250.00	500.00	825.00

C#	Date	Mintage	Fine	VF	XF	Unc
142	1807	Inc. Ab.	50.00	115.00	225.00	400.00
	1808	.055	50.00	115.00	225.00	400.00
	1809	8,932	50.00	115.00	225.00	400.00
	1810	6,721	50.00	115.00	225.00	400.00
	1811	.011	50.00	115.00	225.00	400.00
	1812	8,432	50.00	115.00	225.00	400.00
	1813	5,888	50.00	115.00	225.00	400.00
	1814	4,579	50.00	115.00	225.00	400.00
	1815	6,913	50.00	115.00	225.00	400.00
	1816	.011	50.00	115.00	225.00	400.00
	1817	4,638	50.00	115.00	225.00	400.00
	1818	—	50.00	115.00	225.00	400.00
	1819	—	50.00	115.00	225.00	400.00
	1820	3,974	50.00	115.00	225.00	400.00
	1821	3,826	50.00	115.00	225.00	400.00
	1822	—	50.00	115.00	225.00	400.00

(Krone)

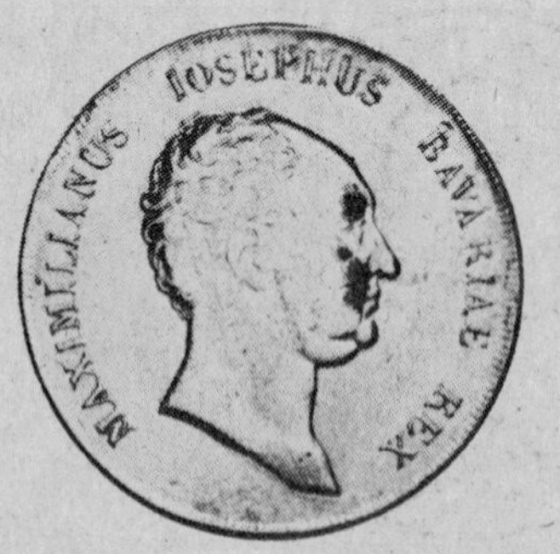

29.3400 gm., .872 SILVER, .8190 oz ASW

C#	Date	Mintage	Fine	VF	XF	Unc
143	1809	.063	30.00	65.00	150.00	250.00
	1810	.924	30.00	65.00	150.00	250.00
	1811	.196	30.00	65.00	150.00	250.00
	1812	.618	30.00	65.00	150.00	250.00
	1813	.656	30.00	65.00	150.00	250.00
	1814	.975	30.00	65.00	150.00	250.00
	1815	.769	30.00	65.00	150.00	250.00
	1816	2.453	30.00	65.00	150.00	250.00
	1817	.399	30.00	65.00	150.00	250.00
	1818	.119	30.00	65.00	150.00	250.00
	1819	.292	30.00	65.00	150.00	250.00
	1820	.132	30.00	65.00	150.00	250.00
	1821	.260	30.00	65.00	150.00	250.00
	1822	.052	30.00	65.00	150.00	250.00
	1823	.016	30.00	65.00	150.00	250.00
	1824	.031	30.00	65.00	150.00	250.00
	1825	.081	30.00	65.00	150.00	250.00

Obv: Error: JOEPHUS in legend.

C#	Date	Mintage	Fine	VF	XF	Unc
143a	1813	Inc. Ab.	30.00	65.00	150.00	250.00

(Convention)

28.0000 gm., .833 SILVER, .7500 oz ASW
Granting of Bavarian Constitution

C#	Date	Mintage	Fine	VF	XF	Unc
144	1818	.040	30.00	65.00	115.00	165.00

C#	Date	Mintage	Fine	VF	XF	Unc
145	1822	.051	50.00	100.00	200.00	400.00
	1823	.047	50.00	100.00	200.00	400.00
	1824	3,907	150.00	250.00	450.00	800.00
	1825	1,932	150.00	250.00	500.00	850.00

Coronation of Ludwig I Commemorative

C#	Date	Mintage	Fine	VF	XF	Unc
165	1825	—	125.00	225.00	375.00	500.00

Death of Reichenbach and Fraunhofer
Obv: Similar to C#165.

C#	Date	Mintage	Fine	VF	XF	Unc
166	1826	—	100.00	200.00	325.00	450.00

Removal of University From Landshut to Munich
Obv: Similar to C#165.

C#	Date	Mintage	Fine	VF	XF	Unc
167	1826	—	100.00	200.00	325.00	450.00

(Krone)

29.5400 gm., .872 SILVER, .8276 oz ASW
Obv. leg: LUDWIG KOENIG

C#	Date	Mintage	Fine	VF	XF	Unc
164	1826	.051	50.00	115.00	225.00	400.00
	1827	.066	50.00	115.00	225.00	400.00
	1828	.079	50.00	115.00	225.00	400.00
	1829	.094	50.00	115.00	225.00	400.00

(Convention)

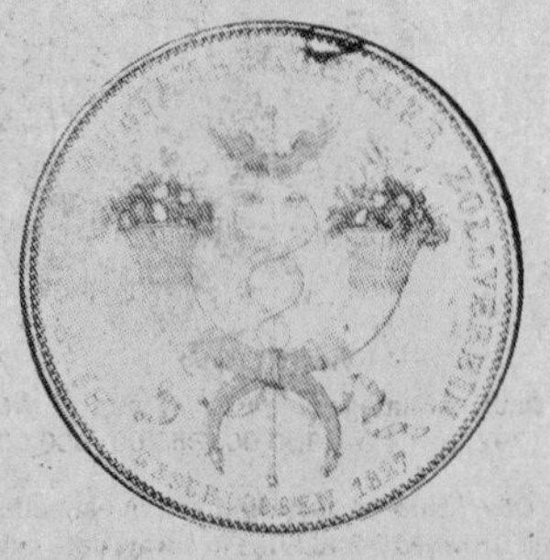

28.0000 gm., .833 SILVER, .7500 oz ASW
Bavaria-Wurttemberg Customs Treaty Signing
Obv: Similar to C#165.

C#	Date	Mintage	Fine	VF	XF	Unc
168	1827	—	100.00	200.00	325.00	450.00

Founding of Order of Ludwig Commemorative
Obv: Similar to C#165.

C#	Date	Mintage	Fine	VF	XF	Unc
169	1827	—	100.00	200.00	325.00	450.00

Founding of Theresien Order Commemorative
Obv: Similar to C#165.

C#	Date	Mintage	Fine	VF	XF	Unc
170	1827	—	100.00	200.00	325.00	450.00

Blessings of Heaven On Royal Family
Obv: Similar to C#165.

C#	Date	Mintage	Fine	VF	XF	Unc
171	1828	—	60.00	130.00	200.00	300.00

Constitution Monument Erection
Obv: Similar to C#165.

C#	Date	Mintage	Fine	VF	XF	Unc
172	1828	—	100.00	200.00	325.00	450.00

Commercial Treaty Between Bavaria
Prussia, Hesse and Wurttemberg
Obv: Similar to C#165.

C#	Date	Mintage	Fine	VF	XF	Unc
173	1829	—	100.00	200.00	325.00	450.00

Loyalty of Bavarians to Royal Family
Obv: Similar to C#165.

C#	Date	Mintage	Fine	VF	XF	Unc
174	1830	—	100.00	200.00	325.00	450.00

(Krone)

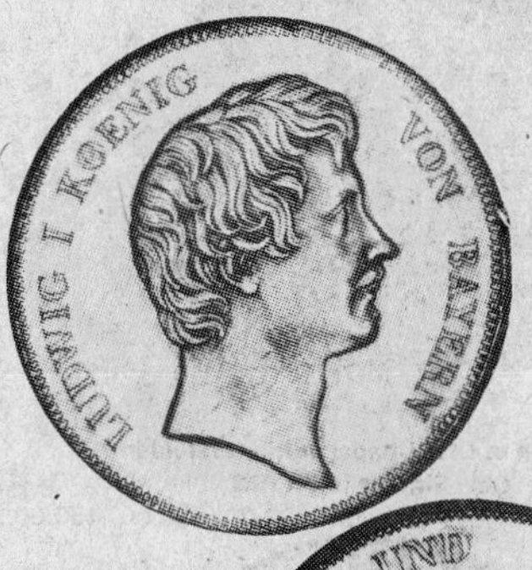

C#	Date	Mintage	Fine	VF	XF	Unc
164a	1830	.061	50.00	110.00	225.00	400.00
	1831	.064	50.00	110.00	225.00	400.00
	1832	.070	50.00	110.00	225.00	400.00
	1833	.040	50.00	110.00	225.00	400.00
	1834	.017	60.00	130.00	250.00	450.00
	1835	7,502	65.00	150.00	250.00	525.00
	1836	7,816	65.00	150.00	250.00	525.00
	1837	.212	50.00	100.00	225.00	350.00

(Convention)

28.0600 gm., .833 SILVER, .7500 oz ASW
Opening of the Legislature
Similar to C#165.

C#	Date	Mintage	Fine	VF	XF	Unc
175	1831	—	150.00	300.00	400.00	525.00

Prince Otto of Bavaria First King of Greece

Obv: Similar to C#165.

C#	Date	Mintage	Fine	VF	XF	Unc
176	1832	—	100.00	200.00	325.00	450.00

Formation of Customs Union With Prussia,
Saxony, Hesse and Thuringia
Obv: Similar to C#165.

C#	Date	Mintage	Fine	VF	XF	Unc
177	1833	—	100.00	200.00	325.00	450.00

Monument For Bavarians Who Fell In Russia
Obv: Similar to C#165.

C#	Date	Mintage	Fine	VF	XF	Unc
178	1833	—	100.00	200.00	325.00	450.00

Provincial Legislature Commemorative
Obv: Similar to C#165.

C#	Date	Mintage	Fine	VF	XF	Unc
179	1834	—	100.00	225.00	375.00	500.00

Erection of Monument at Oberwittelsbach
Obv: Similar to C#165.

C#	Date	Mintage	Fine	VF	XF	Unc
180	1834	—	100.00	225.00	375.00	500.00

Entry of Baden to German Customs Union
Obv: Similar to C#165.

C#	Date	Mintage	Fine	VF	XF	Unc
181	1835	—	100.00	225.00	375.00	500.00

Establishment of Bavarian Mortgage Bank
Obv: Similar to C#165.

C#	Date	Mintage	Fine	VF	XF	Unc
182	1835	—	125.00	275.00	400.00	525.00

Monument for King Otto Leaving His Mother
Obv: Similar to C#165.

C#	Date	Mintage	Fine	VF	XF	Unc
183	1835	—	100.00	200.00	325.00	450.00

Construction of First Steam Railway
Obv: Similar to C#165.

C#	Date	Mintage	Fine	VF	XF	Unc
184	1835	—	150.00	325.00	450.00	600.00

Monument in Munich to King Maximilian Joseph
Obv: Similar to C#165.

C#	Date	Mintage	Fine	VF	XF	Unc
185	1835	—	100.00	200.00	325.00	450.00

28.0600 gm., .833 SILVER, .7500 oz ASW
Sceptre not beyond shoulder

C#	Date	Mintage	Fine	VF	XF	Unc
185a	1835	—	100.00	200.00	325.00	450.00

School Given To Benedictine Order
Obv: Similar to C#165.

C#	Date	Mintage	Fine	VF	XF	Unc
186	1835	—	140.00	275.00	400.00	500.00

Erection of Otto Chapel at Kieffersfelden
Obv: Similar to C#165.

C#	Date	Mintage	Fine	VF	XF	Unc
187	1836	—	100.00	200.00	325.00	450.00

Order of St. Michael as Order of Merit
Obv: Similar to C#165.

C#	Date	Mintage	Fine	VF	XF	Unc
188	1837	—	140.00	275.00	400.00	525.00

(Vereins)

18.5200 gm., .900 SILVER, .5360 oz ASW

C#	Date	Mintage	Fine	VF	XF	Unc
234	1857	1.560	15.00	30.00	60.00	100.00
	1858	2.283	15.00	30.00	60.00	100.00
	1859	2.661	15.00	30.00	60.00	100.00
	1860	2.471	15.00	30.00	60.00	100.00
	1861	2.682	15.00	30.00	60.00	100.00
	1862	2.587	15.00	30.00	60.00	100.00
	1863	2.587	15.00	30.00	60.00	100.00
	1864	1.458	15.00	30.00	60.00	100.00

Obv: Part in hair.

C#	Date	Mintage	Fine	VF	XF	Unc
257.1	1864	Inc. Ab.	20.00	45.00	90.00	160.00
	1865	1.144	20.00	40.00	90.00	160.00
	1866	1.075	20.00	40.00	90.00	160.00

Obv: No part in hair.

C#	Date	Mintage	Fine	VF	XF	Unc
257.2	1866	Inc. Ab.	20.00	40.00	80.00	145.00
	1867	.595	20.00	40.00	80.00	145.00
	1868	.312	20.00	40.00	80.00	145.00
	1869	.277	20.00	40.00	80.00	145.00
	1870	.264	20.00	40.00	80.00	145.00
	1871	.718	20.00	40.00	80.00	145.00

Obv: J. REIS below truncation.

C#	Date	Mintage	Fine	VF	XF	Unc
257.3	1871	Inc. Ab.	100.00	225.00	300.00	500.00

C#	Date	Mintage	Fine	VF	XF	Unc
258	ND(1865)	.110	15.00	25.00	50.00	100.00
	1866	Inc. Ab.	15.00	25.00	45.00	100.00
	1867	Inc. Ab.	15.00	25.00	45.00	100.00
	1868	Inc. Ab.	15.00	25.00	45.00	100.00
	1869	Inc. Ab.	15.00	25.00	45.00	100.00
	1870	Inc. Ab.	15.00	25.00	45.00	100.00
	1871	Inc. Ab.	15.00	25.00	45.00	100.00

German Victory In Franco-Prussian War

C#	Date	Mintage	Fine	VF	XF	Unc
259	1871	.150	20.00	30.00	60.00	125.00

ZWEI (2) THALERS
(= 3-1/2 Gulden)

37.1200 gm., .900 SILVER, 1.0743 oz ASW
Monetary Union of Six South German States

C#	Date	Mintage	Fine	VF	XF	Unc
197	1837	—	130.00	250.00	375.00	500.00

Reapportionment of Bavaria
Obv: Similar to C#197.

C#	Date	Mintage	Fine	VF	XF	Unc
198	1838	—	130.00	250.00	375.00	500.00

Maximillian I, Elector of Bavaria Commemorative
Obv: Similar to C#197.

C#	Date	Mintage	Fine	VF	XF	Unc
199	1839	—	135.00	275.00	375.00	500.00

C#	Date	Mintage	Fine	VF	XF	Unc
195	1839	.113	75.00	150.00	250.00	500.00
	1840	.193	75.00	150.00	250.00	500.00
	1841	.450	75.00	150.00	250.00	500.00

Albrecht Durer Commemorative
Obv: Similar to C#197.

C#	Date	Mintage	Fine	VF	XF	Unc
200	1840	—	135.00	275.00	400.00	500.00

Jean Paul Friedrich Richter Commemorative
Obv: Similar to C#197.

C#	Date	Mintage	Fine	VF	XF	Unc
201	1841	—	140.00	275.00	400.00	600.00

Walhalla Commemorative
Obv: Similar to C#197.

C#	Date	Mintage	Fine	VF	XF	Unc
202	1842	—	125.00	250.00	325.00	450.00

Marriage of Crown Prince of Bavaria and Marie, Crown Princess of Prussia
Obv: Similar to C#197.

C#	Date	Mintage	Fine	VF	XF	Unc
203	1842	—	125.00	250.00	325.00	450.00

Obv: (Error date) 1 OCTB. 1842

C#	Date	Mintage	Fine	VF	XF	Unc
203a	1842	—	135.00	275.00	400.00	550.00

Obv: Similar to C#195.

C#	Date	Mintage	Fine	VF	XF	Unc
196	1842	.085	—	125.00	230.00	400.00
	1843	.277	60.00	125.00	225.00	400.00
	1844	.122	60.00	125.00	225.00	400.00
	1845	.167	60.00	125.00	225.00	400.00
	1846	.132	60.00	125.00	225.00	400.00
196	1847	.012	60.00	125.00	225.00	400.00
	1848	.192	60.00	125.00	225.00	400.00

100th Anniversary Academy of Erlangen
Obv: Similar to C#197.

C#	Date	Mintage	Fine	VF	XF	Unc
204	1843	—	130.00	250.00	400.00	525.00

Completion of Temple of Heroes Hall in Munich
Obv: Similar to C#197.

C#	Date	Mintage	Fine	VF	XF	Unc
205	1844	—	135.00	275.00	400.00	600.00

Chancellor Baron Von Kreittmayr
Obv: Similar to C#197.

C#	Date	Mintage	Fine	VF	XF	Unc
206	1845	—	225.00	450.00	725.00	1000.

Birth of Two Grandsons Commemorative
Obv: Similar to C#197.

C#	Date	Mintage	Fine	VF	XF	Unc
207	1845	—	200.00	375.00	525.00	725.00

Completion of Canal Between Danube and Main Rivers
Obv: Similar to C#197.

C#	Date	Mintage	Fine	VF	XF	Unc
208	1846	—	200.00	400.00	600.00	900.00

Bishop Julius Echter Von Mespelbrunn Commemorative
Obv: Similar to C#197.

C#	Date	Mintage	Fine	VF	XF	Unc
209	1847	—	250.00	500.00	225.00	1200.

Abdication of Ludwig I for Maximilian
Obv: Similar to C#197.

C#	Date	Mintage	Fine	VF	XF	Unc
210	1848	—	500.00	1000.	1600.	2300.

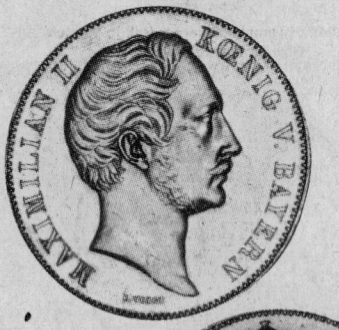

New Constitution Commemorative
Edge: VEREINSMUNZE

C#	Date	Mintage	Fine	VF	XF	Unc
237	1848	—	150.00	300.00	525.00	800.00

Edge: CONVENTION-VOM

C#	Date	Mintage	Fine	VF	XF	Unc
237a	1848	—	175.00	350.00	450.00	600.00
	Restrike Post 1857	—				

Edge: DREY EIN HALB GULDEN

C#	Date	Mintage	Fine	VF	XF	Unc
237b	1848	—	175.00	350.00	450.00	600.00
	(restrike post 1857)	—				

Johann Christoph von Gluck
Obv: Similar to C#237. Edge: VEREINSMUNZE.

C#	Date	Mintage	Fine	VF	XF	Unc
238	1848	—	350.00	725.00	1375.	2000.

Edge: CONVENTION-VOM

C#	Date	Mintage	Fine	VF	XF	Unc
238a	1848	—	350.00	725.00	1375.	2000.

Orlando Di Lasso
Obv: Similar to C#237. Edge: VEREINSMUNZE.

C#	Date	Mintage	Fine	VF	XF	Unc
239	1849	—	600.00	1150.	1950.	2650.

Rev: Similar to C#196.

C#	Date	Mintage	Fine	VF	XF	Unc
235	1849	—	60.00	130.00	225.00	400.00
	1850	—	60.00	130.00	225.00	400.00
	1851	—	60.00	130.00	225.00	400.00
	1852	—	60.00	130.00	225.00	400.00
	1853	—	60.00	130.00	225.00	400.00
	1854	—	60.00	130.00	225.00	400.00
	1855	.417	60.00	130.00	225.00	400.00
	1856	.142	60.00	130.00	225.00	400.00

Exhibition of German Products in Crystal Palace
Obv: Similar to C#237. Edge: VEREINS MUNZE.

C#	Date	Mintage	Fine	VF	XF	Unc
240	1854	—	150.00	300.00	425.00	600.00

Edge CONVENTION-VOM

C#	Date	Mintage	Fine	VF	XF	Unc
240a	1854	—	150.00	300.00	425.00	600.00

Erection of Monument to King Maximilian II
Obv: Similar to C#237.

C#	Date	Mintage	Fine	VF	XF	Unc
241	1856	1,152	250.00	500.00	850.00	1250.

37.0400 gm., .900 SILVER, 1.0717 oz ASW

C#	Date	Mintage	Fine	VF	XF	Unc
236	1859	.029	150.00	325.00	525.00	850.00
	1860	.069	140.00	275.00	450.00	800.00

Obv: Different hair style. Rev: Similar to C#236.

C#	Date	Mintage	Fine	VF	XF	Unc
236.1	1861	.029	200.00	400.00	600.00	1000.
	1862	8,727	200.00	400.00	600.00	1000.
	1863	.011	200.00	400.00	600.00	1000.
	1864	8,201	200.00	400.00	600.00	1000.

Rev: Similar to C#236.

C#	Date	Mintage	Fine	VF	XF	Unc
260	1865	2,490	2500.	5000.	6500.	8500.
	1867	1,760	2500.	5000.	6500.	8500.
	1869	—	2500.	5000.	6500.	8500.

1/2 KRONE

5.5550 gm., .900 GOLD, .1608 oz AGW

C#	Date	Mintage	Fine	VF	XF	Unc
248	1857	1,749	—	3000.	3750.	4500.
	1858	1,020	—	3000.	3750.	4500.
	1859	1,200	—	3000.	3750.	4500.
	1860	—	—	3000.	3750.	4500.
	1861	32 pcs.	—	4000.	6500.	10,000.
	1863	—	—	3000.	3850.	4850.
	1864	—	—	3000.	3850.	4850.

C#	Date	Mintage	Fine	VF	XF	Unc
261	1864	—	—	3500.	4000.	5000.
	1865	—	—	3500.	4000.	5000.
	1866	—	—	3500.	4000.	5000.
	1867	12 pcs.	—	3500.	4000.	5000.
	1868	—	—	3500.	4000.	5000.
	1869	—	—	3500.	4000.	5000.

KRONE

11.1110 gm., .900 GOLD, .3215 oz AGW

C#	Date	Mintage	Fine	VF	XF	Unc
249	1857	771 pcs.	—	3600.	4500.	5600.
	1858	753 pcs.	—	3600.	4500.	5600.
	1859	200 pcs.	—	4100.	5100.	6400.
	1860	45 pcs.	—	4350.	5500.	6800.
	1861	65 pcs.	—	4350.	5500.	6800.
	1863	—	—	4350.	5500.	6800.
	1864	—	—	4350.	5500.	6800.

C#	Date	Mintage	Fine	VF	XF	Unc
262	1864	—	—	3850.	4800.	6000.
	1865	—	—	3850.	4800.	6000.
	1866	—	—	3850.	4800.	6000.
	1867	12 pcs.	—	3850.	4800.	6000.
	1868	—	—	3850.	4800.	6000.
	1869	—	—	3850.	4800.	6000.

TRADE COINS

DUCAT

3.5000 gm., .986 GOLD, .1109 oz AGW

C#	Date	Mintage	Fine	VF	XF
90	1778-93	—	1250.	1750.	2250.

C#	Date	Mintage	Fine	VF	XF
90a	1794	—	1250.	1750.	2250.
	1795	—	1250.	1750.	2250.
	1796	—	1250.	1750.	2250.
	1797	—	1250.	1750.	2250.
	1798	—	1250.	1750.	2250.

3.4900 gm., .937 GOLD, .1051 oz AGW
Danube-Gold Ducat

C#	Date	Mintage	Fine	VF	XF
91	1779	—	1500.	2000.	2750.
	1780	—	1500.	2000.	2750.
91	1793	—	1500.	2000.	2750.

Inn-Gold Ducat
Rev: River God at left, date in Roman Numerals in exergue.

C#	Date	Mintage	Fine	VF	XF
92	1779	—	1500.	2000.	2750.
	1780	—	1500.	2000.	2750.
	1793	—	1500.	2000.	2750.
	1798	—	1500.	2000.	2750.

Isar-Gold Ducat

C#	Date	Mintage	Fine	VF	XF
93	1779	—	1700.	2100.	3000.
	1780	—	1700.	2100.	3000.
	1793	—	1700.	2100.	3000.
	1798	—	1700.	2100.	3000.

3.5000 gm., .986 GOLD, .1109 oz AGW
Vicariat Issues

C#	Date	Mintage	Fine	VF	XF
94	1790	—	1000.	1500.	2000.
	1792	—	1000.	1500.	2000.

Obv. leg: D.G. MAX. IOS....

C#	Date	Mintage	Fine	VF	XF	Unc
124	1799	—	—	800.00	1250.	1800.
	1800	—	—	800.00	1250.	1800.
	1801	—	—	800.00	1250.	1800.
	1802	—	—	800.00	1250.	1800.

Obv. leg: D.G. MAXIM. IOSEPH

C#	Date	Mintage	Fine	VF	XF	Unc
124a	1799	—	—	600.00	1750.	2400.
	1800	—	—	600.00	1750.	2400.
	1801	—	—	600.00	1750.	2400.
	1802	—	—	600.00	1750.	2400.
	1803	—	—	600.00	1750.	2400.

Obv. leg: MAXIMILIAN IOSEPH....

C#	Date	Mintage	Fine	VF	XF	Unc
128	1804	—	—	1500.	2000.	3000.
	1805	—	—	1500.	2000.	3000.

C#	Date	Mintage	Fine	VF	XF	Unc
133	1806	2,900	—	1500.	2000.	2650.

C#	Date	Mintage	Fine	VF	XF	Unc
149	1807	2,260	—	1000.	1250.	1600.
	1808	—	—	1000.	1250.	1600.
	1809	—	—	1000.	1250.	1600.
	1810	—	—	1000.	1250.	1600.
	1811	—	—	1000.	1250.	1600.
	1812	—	—	1000.	1250.	1600.
	1813	—	—	1000.	1250.	1600.
	1814	—	—	1000.	1250.	1600.
149	1815	—	—	1000.	1250.	1600.
	1816	—	—	1000.	1250.	1600.
	1817	—	—	1000.	1250.	1600.
	1818	—	—	1000.	1250.	1600.
	1819	—	—	1000.	1250.	1600.
	1820	—	—	1000.	1250.	1600.
	1821	—	—	1000.	1250.	1600.
	1822	—	—	1000.	1250.	1600.
149a	1821	—	—	1200.	1500.	2000.
	1822	—	—	1200.	1500.	2000.

Obv: Older head

C#	Date	Mintage	Fine	VF	XF	Unc
149b	1823	4,400	—	825.00	1000.	1300.
	1824	.019	—	775.00	950.00	1200.
	1825	3,000	—	850.00	1050.	1325.

Rev. leg: EX AURO DANUBII around River God.

C#	Date	Mintage	Fine	VF	XF	Unc
151	1821	—	—	3250.	4000.	5500.

Rev. leg: EX AURO OENI around River God.

C#	Date	Mintage	Fine	VF	XF	Unc
152	1821	—	—	3125.	3750.	4500.

C#	Date	Mintage	Fine	VF	XF	Unc
153	1821	—	—	2500.	3000.	4000.
154	1821	—	—	1750.	2750.	3200.
211	1826	696 pcs.	—	1400.	1750.	2200.
	1827	4,200	—	750.00	1000.	1400.
	1828	3,090	—	750.00	1000.	1400.

Obv. leg: LUDWIG I

C#	Date	Mintage	Fine	VF	XF	Unc
211a	1828	1,351	—	1500.	2000.	2400.
	1829	1,143	—	1500.	2000.	2400.
	1830	1,731	—	1500.	2000.	2400.
	1831	3,907	—	1500.	2000.	2400.
	1832	1,884	—	1500.	2000.	2400.
	1833	1,230	—	1500.	2000.	2400.
	1834	1,711	—	1500.	2000.	2400.

Struck in collared dies

C#	Date	Mintage	Fine	VF	XF	Unc
211b	1835	2,048	—	1500.	2000.	2400.

C#	Date	Mintage	Fine	VF	XF	Unc
211c	1840	5,000	—	1000.	1250.	1500.
	1841	2,309	—	1000.	1250.	1500.
	1842	810 pcs.	—	1000.	1250.	1500.
	1843	2,358	—	1000.	1250.	1500.
	1844	4,259	—	1000.	1250.	1500.
	1845	2,470	—	1000.	1250.	1500.
	1846	3,642	—	1000.	1250.	1500.
	1847	5,122	—	1000.	1250.	1500.

C#	Date	Mintage	Fine	VF	XF	Unc
211c	1848	1,470	—	1000.	1250.	1500.

Rev. leg: EX AURO DANUBII around River God.

C#	Date	Mintage	Fine	VF	XF	Unc
212	1830	—	—	2250.	2750.	3600.

Obv. legend in German

C#	Date	Mintage	Fine	VF	XF	Unc
212a	1830	—	—	2300.	2900.	3600.
213	1830	—	—	3000.	3750.	4500.
214	1830	—	—	1500.	2000.	3600.
215	1830	—	—	1500.	2000.	3600.

Obv. legend in German.
Rev. leg: AUGUSTA NEMETUM, EX AURO RHENI.

C#	Date	Mintage	Fine	VF	XF	Unc
215a	1830	—	—	2300.	2900.	3600.
215b	1842	—	—	1500.	1750.	2500.
	1846	—	—	1500.	1750.	2500.

Obv. leg: .....KOENIG V BAYERN

C#	Date	Mintage	Fine	VF	XF	Unc
242	1849	1,470	—	700.00	900.00	1450.
	1850	1,519	—	700.00	900.00	1450.
	1851	3,815	—	700.00	900.00	1350.
	1852	4,396	—	700.00	900.00	1350.
	1853	5,603	—	700.00	900.00	1350.
	1854	5,707	—	700.00	900.00	1350.
	1855	1,540	—	700.00	900.00	1450.
	1856	3,782	—	700.00	900.00	1350.

Obv. leg: .....BAVARIAE REX

C#	Date	Mintage	Fine	VF	XF	Unc
242a	1850	100 pcs.	—	3850.	4800.	6000.

Rev. leg: AUS DEM BERGBAU BEI GOLDKRONACH

C#	Date	Mintage	Fine	VF	XF	Unc
243	1855	—	—	5150.	6400.	8000.
246	1850	—	—	1500.	2000.	2500.
	1851	—	—	1500.	2000.	2500.
	1852	—	—	1500.	2000.	2500.
	1853	—	—	1500.	2000.	2500.
	1854	—	—	1500.	2000.	2500.
	1855	—	—	1500.	2000.	2500.
	1856	—	—	1500.	2000.	2500.

Reduced size

C#	Date	Mintage	Fine	VF	XF	Unc
246a	1863	—	—	3850.	4800.	6000.

2 DUCATS

7.0000 gm., .986 GOLD, .2219 oz AGW

Obv: Head right.
Rev: Crowned 3-fold arms in spray; date below.

C#	Date	Mintage	Fine	VF	XF
95	1787	—	2750.	3250.	3750.

Vicariat Issues
Rev: Eagle with 3-fold arms on breast, value below.

C#	Date	Mintage	Fine	VF	XF
96	1790	—	1750.	2250.	2750.
	1792	—	1750.	2250.	2750.

3 DUCATS

10.5000 gm., .986 GOLD, .3329 oz AGW

C#	Date	Mintage	Fine	VF	XF
97	1787	—	—	Rare	—

Vicariat Issues

C#	Date	Mintage	Fine	VF	XF
98	1790	—	—	Rare	—
	1792	—	—	Rare	—

MONETARY REFORM

2 MARK

11.1110 gm., .900 SILVER, .3215 oz ASW

Y#	Date	Mintage	VF	XF	Unc
31	1876D	5.37	50.00	300.00	800.00
	1877D	1.512	60.00	320.00	800.00
	1880D	.169	125.00	450.00	1000.
	1883D	.104	100.00	400.00	900.00
36	1888D	.172	165.00	330.00	1000.
36a	1891D	.246	30.00	80.00	225.00
	1893D	.246	30.00	80.00	225.00
	1896D	.492	16.00	60.00	150.00
	1898D	.201	30.00	80.00	225.00
	1899D	.753	15.00	40.00	125.00
	1900D	.722	15.00	40.00	125.00
	1901D	.829	15.00	40.00	125.00
	1902D	1.341	10.00	45.00	100.00
	1903D	1.406	10.00	40.00	100.00
	1904D	2.320	10.00	40.00	100.00
	1905D	1.406	10.00	25.00	80.00
	1906D	1.055	10.00	25.00	80.00
	1907D	2.106	10.00	20.00	80.00
	1908D	.633	10.00	25.00	80.00
	1912D	.214	15.00	40.00	100.00
	1913D	.098	60.00	150.00	225.00

90th Birthday Commemorative

Y#	Date	Mintage	VF	XF	Unc
41	1911D	.640	10.00	15.00	25.00
	1911D	—	—	Proof	100.00
44	1914D	.574	40.00	90.00	125.00

3 MARK

16.6670 gm., .900 SILVER, .4823 oz ASW

Y#	Date	Mintage	VF	XF	Unc
37	1908D	.681	15.00	20.00	40.00
	1909D	.827	15.00	20.00	40.00
	1910D	1.497	15.00	16.00	30.00
	1911D	.843	15.00	16.00	30.00
	1912D	1.014	15.00	16.00	30.00
	1913D	.713	15.00	16.00	30.00

90th Birthday Commemorative

Y#	Date	Mintage	VF	XF	Unc
42	1911D	.640	15.00	18.00	25.00
	1911D	—	—	Proof	60.00
45	1914D	.717	15.00	25.00	50.00
	1914D	—	—	Proof	90.00

Golden Wedding Anniversary Commemorative

Y#	Date	Mintage	VF	XF	Unc
48	1918D	130 pcs.	—	Proof Only	10,000.

5 MARK

27.7770 gm., .900 SILVER, .8038 oz ASW
Rev: Similar to Y#38.

Y#	Date	Mintage	VF	XF	Unc
32	1874D	.085	40.00	300.00	1100.
	1875D	.657	30.00	225.00	700.00
	1876D	1.130	30.00	225.00	700.00

1.9910 gm., .900 GOLD, .0576 oz AGW

Y#	Date	Mintage	VF	XF	Unc
33	1877D	.635	180.00	400.00	500.00
	1878D	.128	900.00	1200.	1700.

27.7770 gm., .900 SILVER, .8038 oz ASW

Y#	Date	Mintage	VF	XF	Unc
38	1888D	.069	300.00	800.00	1100.

Obv: Similar to Y#38.

Y#	Date	Mintage	VF	XF	Unc
38a	1891D	.098	25.00	80.00	200.00
	1893D	.098	25.00	80.00	225.00
	1894D	.141	25.00	70.00	180.00
	1895D	.141	25.00	90.00	250.00
	1896D	.028	130.00	300.00	450.00
	1898D	.303	25.00	55.00	125.00
	1899D	.141	25.00	70.00	150.00
	1900D	.295	25.00	60.00	125.00
	1901D	.295	25.00	60.00	125.00
	1902D	.506	25.00	40.00	100.00
	1903D	1.012	25.00	40.00	100.00
	1904D	.548	25.00	40.00	100.00
	1906D	.070	100.00	180.00	250.00
	1907D	.753	25.00	40.00	100.00
	1908D	.577	25.00	45.00	110.00
	1913D	.520	25.00	45.00	110.00

Regents 90th Birthday Commemorative
Rev: Similar to Y#38a.

Y#	Date	Mintage	VF	XF	Unc
43	1911D	.160	51.00	100.00	170.00

Rev: Similar to Y#38a.

Y#	Date	Mintage	VF	XF	Unc
46	1914D	.142	110.00	160.00	200.00

10 MARK

3.9820 gm., .900 GOLD, .1152 oz AGW
Obv: J. REIS under truncation. Rev: Type I eagle.

Y#	Date	Mintage	VF	XF	Unc
34	1872D	.626	100.00	140.00	475.00
	1873D	1.198	100.00	130.00	300.00

Obv: Continuous legend.

Y#	Date	Mintage	VF	XF	Unc
34a	1874D	.407	100.00	225.00	325.00
	1875D	.816	100.00	200.00	300.00
	1876D	.684	100.00	200.00	300.00
	1877D	.283	125.00	250.00	350.00
	1878D	.638	100.00	200.00	300.00
	1879D	.224	125.00	250.00	350.00
	1880D	.229	115.00	250.00	350.00
	1881D	.157	100.00	250.00	350.00

Obv. leg: ....VON BAYERN. Rev: Type II eagle.

Y#	Date	Mintage	VF	XF	Unc
39	1888D	.281	200.00	300.00	425.00

Rev: Type III eagle

Y#	Date	Mintage	VF	XF	Unc
39a	1890D	.422	150.00	200.00	225.00
	1893D	.422	150.00	200.00	225.00
	1896D	.281	150.00	200.00	225.00
	1898D	.590	150.00	200.00	225.00
	1900D	.141	210.00	250.00	325.00

Obv. leg:....V. BAYERN

Y#	Date	Mintage	VF	XF	Unc
39b	1900D	Inc. Ab.	200.00	325.00	425.00
	1901D	.141	100.00	300.00	400.00
	1902D	.070	100.00	300.00	400.00
	1903D	.534	100.00	225.00	300.00
	1904D	.210	100.00	225.00	300.00
	1905D	.281	100.00	225.00	275.00
	1906D	.141	100.00	200.00	300.00
	1907D	.211	90.00	200.00	300.00
	1909D	.209	90.00	200.00	300.00
	1910D	.141	110.00	200.00	300.00
	1911D	.072	100.00	200.00	250.00
	1912D	.141	100.00	200.00	250.00

20 MARK

7.9650 gm., .900 GOLD, .2304 oz AGW
Rev: Type I eagle.

Y#	Date	Mintage	VF	XF	Unc
35	1872D	1.554	175.00	300.00	450.00
	1873D	2.770	150.00	225.00	300.00

Rev: Type II eagle

Y#	Date	Mintage	VF	XF	Unc
35a	1874D	.615	150.00	250.00	300.00
	1875D	—	1500.	2000.	2500.
	1876D	.482	175.00	275.00	425.00
	1878D	.050	600.00	1000.	1600.

Rev: Type III eagle

Y#	Date	Mintage	VF	XF	Unc
40	1895D	.501	125.00	175.00	225.00
	1900D	.502	125.00	175.00	225.00
	1905D	.501	125.00	175.00	225.00
	1913D	*.311	2000.	2200.	2800.

Y#	Date	Mintage	VF	XF	Unc
47	1914D	*.533	1650.	2000.	2400.

***NOTE:** Never officially released.

NCLT ISSUES

PATTERNS

KM#	Date	Mintage	Identification	Mkt.Val.
1	1904	—	5 Marks, Silver, eagle in ring	—
2	1904	—	5 Marks, Silver, w/o ring	—
3	1911	—	3 Marks, Silver, Birthday of Prince Regent	—

KM#	Date	Mintage	Identification	Mkt.Val.
4	1913	—	2 Marks, Copper	40.00
5	1913	—	2 Marks, Silver	—
6	1913	—	2 Marks, Gold	—

KM#	Date	Mintage	Identification	Mkt.Val.
7	1913	—	3 Marks, Copper	40.00
8	1913	—	3 Marks, Silver	—
9	1913	—	3 Marks, Gold	—

KM#	Date	Mintage	Identification	Mkt.Val.
10	1913	—	5 Marks, Copper	40.00
11	1913	—	5 Marks, Silver	—
12	1913	—	5 Marks, Gold	—

KM#	Date	Mintage	Identification	Mkt.Val.
13	1913	—	10 Marks, Copper	40.00
14	1913	—	10 Marks, Silver	—
15	1913	—	10 Marks, Gold	—

KM#	Date	Mintage	Identification	Mkt.Val.
16	1913G	—	20 Marks, Copper	40.00
17	1913G	—	20 Marks, Silver	—
18	1913G	—	20 Marks, Gold	—

BERG

Located in western Germany. The first count of Berg took his title in 1101 and the first coins appeared c. 1135. Not until 1380, did a duke rule in Berg. In 1801 Berg was absorbed by France but in 1806, along with Cleves and Julich, became the grand duchy of Berg. It was transferred to Westphalia in 1808 and given to Prussia in 1814.

RULERS

Maximilian IV, Joseph (of Bavaria) 1799-1806
Joachim Murat, 1806-1808

MINTMASTER'S INITIALS

P.R., R., .R. - Peter Rudesheim
T.S., S, S., T:S, Sr - Theodor Stockmar

1/2 STUBER

COPPER

C#	Date	Mintage	Fine	VF	XF	Unc
1	1802.R.	—	2.00	6.00	18.00	45.00
	1803.R.	—	2.00	6.00	18.00	45.00
	1804.R.	—	2.00	6.00	18.00	45.00
1a	1805 S	—	2.00	6.00	18.00	45.00
	Obv: Monogram without rosettes					
1b	1805 S	—	2.00	6.00	18.00	45.00

3 STUBER

BILLON

C#	Date	Mintage	Fine	VF	XF	Unc
2	1801.R.	—	3.00	6.50	20.00	60.00
	1802.R.	—	3.00	6.50	20.00	60.00
	1803.R.	—	3.00	6.50	20.00	60.00
	1804.R.	—	3.00	6.50	20.00	60.00
	1805.R.	—	3.00	6.50	20.00	60.00
	1806.R.	—	3.00	6.50	20.00	60.00
2b	1805 S	—	3.00	6.50	20.00	60.00
	1806 S	—	3.00	6.50	20.00	60.00
	Obv: Royal crown					
2a	1806 S	—	3.00	6.50	20.00	60.00

C#	Date	Mintage	Fine	VF	XF	Unc
5	1806 S	—	2.50	6.00	20.00	60.00
	1806 Sr	—	2.50	6.00	20.00	60.00
	1807 S	—	2.50	6.00	20.00	60.00
	1807 Sr	—	2.50	6.00	20.00	60.00

NOTE: C#2, 2a, and 5 were restruck officially in 1808-1809 for circulation and were equal to 10 Centimes.

1/2 THALER

(Reichs)

9.6300-9.7100 gm., .750 SILVER, .2347 oz ASW

C#	Date	Mintage	Fine	VF	XF	Unc
3	1803 PR	—	120.00	200.00	400.00	750.00
	1804 PR	—	120.00	200.00	400.00	750.00

THALER

(Reichs)

19.4000 gm., .750 SILVER, .4678 oz ASW

C#	Date	Mintage	Fine	VF	XF	Unc
4	1802 PR	—	200.00	325.00	600.00	1000.
	1803 PR	—	200.00	325.00	600.00	1000.
	1804 PR	—	200.00	325.00	600.00	1000.
	1805 PR	—	200.00	325.00	600.00	1000.

C#	Date	Mintage	Fine	VF	XF	Unc
	Obv: T. S. below larger head					
4a	1805 TS	9,396	275.00	450.00	650.00	1200.
	1806 TS	7,044	275.00	450.00	650.00	1200.

C#	Date	Mintage	Fine	VF	XF	Unc
6	1806 TS	8,356	425.00	725.00	1250.	1600.

(Cassa)

17.3000 gm., .751 SILVER, .4080 oz ASW

C#	Date	Mintage	Fine	VF	XF	Unc
7	1807 TS	—	775.00	1300.	2000.	3000.

Obv: Similar to C#7.

C#	Date	Mintage	Fine	VF	XF	Unc
7a	1807 TS	—	1200.	2000.	3000.	4000.

BIRKENFELD

Located in southwest Germany. For most of the time prior to 1801, Birkenfeld was in the possession of the counts palatine. It was a part of France from 1801-1814, Prussia from 1814-1817 and was made a principality in 1817.

RULERS

Paul Friedrich August (of Oldenburg), 1829-1853

Nikolaus Friedrich Peter (of Oldenburg), 1853-1900

PFENNIG

COPPER

C#	Date	Mintage	Fine	VF	XF	Unc
1	1848	.158	3.00	8.00	20.00	50.00

C#	Date	Mintage	Fine	VF	XF	Unc
6	1859	.072	5.00	10.00	25.00	60.00

2 PFENNIGE

COPPER

Obv: Crowned PFA monogram.

C#	Date	Mintage	Fine	VF	XF	Unc
2	1848	.117	3.00	5.00	20.00	40.00

Obv: Crowned NFP monogram.

C#	Date	Mintage	Fine	VF	XF	Unc
7	1858	.072	4.00	8.00	25.00	50.00

3 PFENNIGE

COPPER

Obv: Crowned PFA monogram.

C#	Date	Mintage	Fine	VF	XF	Unc
3	1848	.121	4.00	8.00	20.00	40.00

Obv: Crowned NFP monogram.

C#	Date	Mintage	Fine	VF	XF	Unc
8	1858B	.072	4.00	8.00	25.00	50.00

1/2 SILBER GROSCHEN

BILLON

C#	Date	Mintage	Fine	VF	XF	Unc
9	1858B	.060	5.00	10.00	25.00	50.00

SILBER GROSCHEN

BILLON

Obv: Crowned arms. Rev: Value.

C#	Date	Mintage	Fine	VF	XF	Unc
4	1848	.063	4.50	9.00	25.00	50.00

Obv: Different arms

C#	Date	Mintage	Fine	VF	XF	Unc
10	1858B	.060	5.00	10.00	25.00	50.00

2-1/2 SILBER GROSCHEN

(= 1/12 Thaler)

BILLON

Obv: Crowned arms. Rev: Value.

C#	Date	Mintage	Fine	VF	XF	Unc
5	1848	.023	10.00	20.00	32.50	60.00

Obv: Different arms.

C#	Date	Mintage	Fine	VF	XF	Unc
11	1858B	.036	7.50	15.00	25.00	50.00

BRANDENBURG—ANSBACH

Located in western Bavaria. The first coins appeared c. 1150. This area was given and sold to many individuals, usually with some relationship to the elector of Brandenburg. It was sold to Prussia in 1791 and was ceded to Bavaria in 1806.

RULERS

Alexander, 1757-1791

MINTMASTERS INITIALS

G - Johann Samuel Gotzinger, 1750-1795

K-E - Johann Bernhard Keen & Johann Jacob Ebenauer, 1758-1765

W-K - Westphal & Kern, 1768-1781

W-E - Westphal & Ebsnauer, 1769-1781

I.C.E. - Johann Christian E. Berhard, 1765-1768

PFENNIG

COPPER

Obv: Crowned arms.
Rev: Value in cartouche.

C#	Date	Mintage	VG	Fine	VF	XF
60	1757	—	3.00	5.00	7.50	18.00

Obv: Arms over branches; S below.
Rev: Value and date.

C#	Date	Mintage	VG	Fine	VF	XF
63	1766	—	3.00	5.00	7.50	18.00

BILLON

Obv: 2 shields of arms; date above.
Rev: Blank.

C#	Date	Mintage	VG	Fine	VF	XF
66	1763	—	3.00	5.00	7.50	18.00

Obv: Arms. Rev: Value over date.

C#	Date	Mintage	VG	Fine	VF	XF
65	1770-91, ND	—	3.00	4.50	8.00	18.00

Obv: Hohenzollern arms.
Rev: Eagle dividing value.

C#	Date	Mintage	VG	Fine	VF	XF
68	1781	—	3.00	4.50	8.00	18.00

Rev: Value on eagle's breast.

C#	Date	Mintage	VG	Fine	VF	XF
69	1791	—	3.00	4.50	8.00	18.00

2 PFENNIG

COPPER

Obv: Crowned arms.
Rev: Value in cartouche.

C#	Date	Mintage	VG	Fine	VF	XF
61	1757	—	3.00	5.00	7.50	12.50

4 PFENNING

BILLON

Obv: Arms. Rev: Value and date.

C#	Date	Mintage	VG	Fine	VF	XF
70	1766-1789	—	3.00	5.00	7.50	12.50

KREUZER

BILLON

Obv: Head of Alexander right.
Rev: Crowned eagle divides date; value on breast.

C#	Date	Mintage	VG	Fine	VF	XF
72	1761	—	4.50	6.50	10.00	25.00

Obv: Eagle in diamond.
Rev: Value and date in diamond.

C#	Date	Mintage	VG	Fine	VF	XF
72.5	1765S	—	3.00	5.00	7.50	25.00

Obv: Crowned arms. Rev: Value over date.

C#	Date	Mintage	VG	Fine	VF	XF
72.7	1780	—	2.50	3.50	8.00	20.00
	1784	—	2.50	3.50	8.00	20.00

C#	Date	Mintage	VG	Fine	VF	XF
73	1785-90	—	2.50	3.50	8.00	20.00

2 KREUZER

BILLON

Obv: Arms. Rev: Eagle.

C#	Date	Mintage	VG	Fine	VF	XF
75	1760	—	5.00	7.50	12.50	30.00

2-1/2 KREUZER

(Convention)

BILLON

Obv: Arms. Rev: Value and date.

C#	Date	Mintage	VG	Fine	VF	XF
76	1767-1779	—	3.00	5.00	7.50	20.00

Obv: Bust right. Rev: Eagle; date below.

C#	Date	Mintage	VG	Fine	VF	XF
77	1779	—	3.50	5.00	9.00	25.00
	1785	—	3.50	5.00	9.00	25.00

Similar to C#77.

C#	Date	Mintage	VG	Fine	VF	XF
78	1786	—	4.50	6.00	10.00	25.00

4 KREUZER

BILLON

Obv: Arms. Rev: Hohenzollern arms.

C#	Date	Mintage	VG	Fine	VF	XF
81	1760	—	7.50	12.50	20.00	40.00

5 KREUZER
(Convention)

BILLON

Obv: Shield on pedestal. Rev: Value and date.

C#	Date	Mintage	VG	Fine	VF	XF
83	1766	—	4.50	6.00	10.00	25.00
	1784	—	4.50	6.00	10.00	25.00

Obv: Bust in wreath.
Rev: Crowned arms on pedestal, value below.

C#	Date	Mintage	VG	Fine	VF	XF
84	1781	—	6.50	9.50	14.00	30.00

10 KREUZER
(Convention)

SILVER

Obv: Head right in sprays.
Rev: Crowned arms on pedestal, date below.

C#	Date	Mintage	VG	Fine	VF	XF
92	1765	—	4.00	8.50	12.50	25.00
	1780	—	4.00	8.50	12.50	25.00

20 KREUZER
(Convention)

SILVER

Obv: Head right in sprays.
Rev: Crowned arms in oval on pedestal, date below.

C#	Date	Mintage	VG	Fine	VF	XF
95	1761-87	—	3.00	6.00	8.50	30.00

Rev: Arms on pedestal, value and date below.

C#	Date	Mintage	VG	Fine	VF	XF
95a	1785	—	3.00	6.00	8.50	30.00

Obv: Bust right. Rev: Quartered arms supported.

C#	Date	Mintage	VG	Fine	VF	XF
96	1779	—	3.00	7.50	10.00	30.00

C#	Date	Mintage	VG	Fine	VF	XF
96a	1779	—	3.00	7.50	10.00	30.00

1/4 THALER
(Convention)

SILVER

C#	Date	Mintage	Fine	VF	XF	Unc
98	1760	—	20.00	35.00	55.00	100.00
	1763	—	20.00	35.00	55.00	100.00

Obv: Margrave on horseback.
Rev: Eagle with lion shield.

C#	Date	Mintage	Fine	VF	XF	Unc
100	1765	—	100.00	125.00	175.00	250.00

Obv: Bust of Alexander right.
Rev: Porcelain factory at Bruckberg.

C#	Date	Mintage	Fine	VF	XF	Unc
101	1767	—	75.00	125.00	200.00	275.00

Acquisition of Bayreuth Commemorative
Obv: Head of Alexander right.
Rev: Eagle holding ribbon with 2 shields; date within.

C#	Date	Mintage	Fine	VF	XF	Unc
102	1769	—	125.00	175.00	250.00	350.00

Obv: Head right. Rev: Arms.

C#	Date	Mintage	VG	Fine	VF	XF
103	1775	—	10.00	20.00	27.50	45.00

Peace of Teschen Commemorative
Obv: Female standing by shield and altar.
Rev: 3 line legend in wreath.

C#	Date	Mintage	VG	Fine	VF	XF
104	1779	—	25.00	60.00	75.00	100.00

1/2 THALER
(Convention)

SILVER

C#	Date	Mintage	Fine	VF	XF	Unc
111	1760	—	65.00	100.00	150.00	200.00
112	1764	—	32.50	50.00	75.00	150.00

Obv: Bust of Alexander right.
Rev: 3 shields of arms.

C#	Date	Mintage	Fine	VF	XF	Unc
113	1765	—	100.00	140.00	175.00	225.00

Obv: Margrave on horseback.
Rev: Eagle with lion shield.

C#	Date	Mintage	Fine	VF	XF	Unc
114	1765	—	100.00	125.00	175.00	250.00

Obv: Bust of Alexander right.
Rev: Porcelain factory at Bruckberg.

C#	Date	Mintage	Fine	VF	XF	Unc
115	1767	—	100.00	125.00	175.00	250.00

C#	Date	Mintage	Fine	VF	XF	Unc
116	1775	—	75.00	100.00	125.00	200.00

THALER
(Convention)

SILVER

Obv: Bust of Alexander right.
Rev: Crowned and supported arms.

C#	Date	Mintage	Fine	VF	XF	Unc
118b	1764 KE	—	100.00	125.00	175.00	250.00

Rev: 3 crowned shields of arms, supported.

C#	Date	Mintage	Fine	VF	XF	Unc
119	1765 KE	—	100.00	135.00	175.00	250.00
	1766 KK	—	100.00	135.00	175.00	250.00

Obv: Margrave on horse back.
Rev: Crowned eagle over draped arms.

C#	Date	Mintage	Fine	VF	XF	Unc
120	1765 KK	—	375.00	500.00	700.00	1000.

Obv: Bare head right.
Rev: 3 crowned shields of arms, supported.

C#	Date	Mintage	Fine	VF	XF	Unc
121	1767 KK	—	100.00	150.00	200.00	300.00
	1768 KK	—	100.00	150.00	200.00	300.00

Acquisition of Bayreuth Commemorative
Obv: Facing busts of Georg Friedrich and Alexander.
Rev: Altar with book on top and crowned shield on each side.

C#	Date	Mintage	Fine	VF	XF	Unc
122	1769	—	100.00	135.00	175.00	250.00

Acquisition of Bayreuth Commemorative
Obv: Head of Alexander right.
Rev: Eagle holding ribbon with 2 shields; date within.

C#	Date	Mintage	Fine	VF	XF	Unc
123	1769	—	200.00	275.00	425.00	975.00

Obv: Head of Alexander right, leg: ..MARCH BRAND....
Rev: Crowned and supported arms on military trophies.

C#	Date	Mintage	Fine	VF	XF	Unc
124	1769	—	75.00	100.00	150.00	275.00
	1771	—	100.00	125.00	175.00	300.00

Obv. leg: .....MARCH. BR.....

C#	Date	Mintage	Fine	VF	XF	Unc
124a	1771	—	100.00	125.00	175.00	300.00

Obv: Head of Alexander right.
Rev: Lion holds crowned shield in cartouche.

C#	Date	Mintage	Fine	VF	XF	Unc
125	1773 WK	—	100.00	125.00	175.00	300.00

Obv: Head of Alexander right.
Rev: Eagle holding crowned arms.

C#	Date	Mintage	Fine	VF	XF	Unc
125a	1773 WK	—	275.00	400.00	650.00	950.00

Obv: Bust of Alexander right.

C#	Date	Mintage	Fine	VF	XF	Unc
125e	1773 WK	—	110.00	150.00	225.00	350.00

Rev: Lion holds crowned Hohenzollern arms on military trophies.

C#	Date	Mintage	Fine	VF	XF	Unc
125b	1774 WK	—	100.00	135.00	200.00	275.00

Rev: Lion holds crowned shield of 4 arms on military trophies.

C#	Date	Mintage	Fine	VF	XF	Unc
125c	1774 WK	—	110.00	150.00	225.00	350.00

C#	Date	Mintage	Fine	VF	XF	Unc
125d	1774 WK	—	100.00	125.00	175.00	200.00

Forestry Prize Thaler

Rev: Large tree surrounded by smaller trees; date in exergue.

C#	Date	Mintage	Fine	VF	XF	Unc
126	1774	—	225.00	300.00	450.00	650.00

Obv: Bust right.
Rev: 4 line inscription, date below.

C#	Date	Mintage	Fine	VF	XF	Unc
127	1775	—	450.00	600.00	750.00	900.00

C#	Date	Mintage	Fine	VF	XF	Unc
—	1775	—	110.00	125.00	150.00	250.00

NOTE: Varieties exist.

Obv: Head right.

C#	Date	Mintage	Fine	VF	XF	Unc
128a	1775	—	110.00	125.00	150.00	250.00

Obv: Bust right. Rev: Crowned arms with eagle supporters; S below, divided date at sides.

C#	Date	Mintage	Fine	VF	XF	Unc
128	1775	—	110.00	125.00	150.00	250.00
	1776	—	110.00	125.00	150.00	250.00

NOTE: Varieties exist.

C#	Date	Mintage	Fine	VF	XF	Unc
129	1777	—	110.00	125.00	150.00	250.00

Obv: Bust right.
Rev: Crowned shield of arms in double order chain.

C#	Date	Mintage	Fine	VF	XF	Unc
130	1778	—	125.00	165.00	200.00	300.00

Rev: Crowned arms between eagles; crown separates date; W K and X.E.-F.M. below.

C#	Date	Mintage	Fine	VF	XF	Unc
131	1778	—	110.00	125.00	150.00	250.00

C#	Date	Mintage	Fine	VF	XF	Unc
132	1778	—	135.00	165.00	200.00	300.00

Revival of the Order of the Red Eagle
Rev: Crowned order star in collar of the order, date below.

C#	Date	Mintage	Fine	VF	XF	Unc
133	1779	—	1000.	1250.	1650.	2000.

Rev: Crowned eagle with arms divides date within 2 concentric circles of 16 shields each.

C#	Date	Mintage	Fine	VF	XF	Unc
134	1779	—	125.00	150.00	200.00	300.00

Rev: Lion holding crowned arms; second lion below arms; SCHWABACH and date in exergue.

C#	Date	Mintage	Fine	VF	XF	Unc
135	1779	—	165.00	200.00	250.00	350.00

Peace of Teschen Commemorative

C#	Date	Mintage	Fine	VF	XF	Unc
136	1779	—	125.00	150.00	200.00	300.00

Peace of Teschen Commemorative

C#	Date	Mintage	Fine	VF	XF	Unc
137	1779	—	125.00	150.00	200.00	300.00

Obv: Armored bust right.
Rev: Crowned and mantled arms; S below, date at sides.

C#	Date	Mintage	Fine	VF	XF	Unc
138	1780	—	125.00	150.00	200.00	300.00

Obv: Head right with G below.

C#	Date	Mintage	Fine	VF	XF	Unc
138a	1784	—	225.00	300.00	400.00	600.00

Obv: Larger head with G below.

C#	Date	Mintage	Fine	VF	XF	Unc
138a	1785	—	125.00	150.00	200.00	300.00

Rev: Crowned and mantled arms divide date.

C#	Date	Mintage	Fine	VF	XF	Unc
139	1786 EB	—	100.00	125.00	175.00	200.00

TRADE COINS

CAROLIN

9.7000 gm., .770 GOLD, .2401 oz AGW
Obv: Bust of Alexander right.
Rev: Arms in order chain.

C#	Date	Mintage	Fine	VF	XF	Unc
150	1766	—	1350.	1750.	2000.	2750.

DUCAT

3.5000 gm., .986 GOLD, .1109 oz AGW
Obv: Bust of Alexander right.
Rev: Arms.

C#	Date	Mintage	Fine	VF	XF	Unc
142	1762	—	650.00	1000.	1500.	2500.

Rev: 3 shields of arms.

C#	Date	Mintage	Fine	VF	XF	Unc
143	1763	—	650.00	1000.	1500.	2500.

Obv: Margrave on horseback.
Rev: Crowned eagle over draped arms.

C#	Date	Mintage	Fine	VF	XF	Unc
144	1765	—	1000.	1500.	2250.	3250.

Acquisition of Bayreuth Commemorative
Obv: Head of Alexander right.
Rev: Eagle holding ribbon with 2 shields; date within.

C#	Date	Mintage	Fine	VF	XF	Unc
145	1769	—	1000.	1500.	2250.	3250.

Acquisition of Bayreuth Commemorative
Obv: Facing busts of Georg Friedrich and Alexander.

Rev: Altar with book on top and crowned shield on each side.

146 1769 — 750.00 1000. 1650. 2750.

Obv: Knight at altar. Rev: Legend.

147 1769 — 600.00 950.00 1350. 2250.

Obv: Bust right. Rev: Crown above 3 shields of arms; value below, date at sides.

143a 1777 — 1000. 1250. 2000. 3000.

Revival of the Order of the Red Eagle
Rev: Crowned order star in collar of the order; date below.

148 1779 — 1000. 1500. 2250. 3000.

BRANDENBURG — BAYREUTH

Located in northern Bavaria. Became the property of the first Hohenzollern elector of Brandenburg, Friedrich I. Bayreuth passed to several individuals and became extinct in 1769 with the lands passing to Ansbach.

RULERS

Friedrich Christian, 1763-69
Alexander, 1769-1791

MINTMASTERS INITIALS

C.L.R. - Christopher Lorenz Ruckdeschel, 1747-1768
E.S. - Eberhard & Schmiedhammer, 1765-1766
R.E. - Ruckdeschel & Eberhard, 1766-1768
G - Johann Samuel Gotzinger (Ansbach), 1750-1795

HELLER

COPPER
Obv: FC script monogram.
Rev: 3 line value and date.

C#	Date	Mintage	VG	Fine	VF	XF
50	1767	—	5.00	7.50	11.50	25.00

50a 1767 — 7.50 12.50 20.00 45.00

PFENNIG

BILLON
Uniface
Obv: 2 shields and date.

51 1763 — 5.00 7.50 11.50 25.00
1764 — 5.00 7.50 11.50 25.00
1765 — 5.00 7.50 11.50 25.00
1766 — 5.00 7.50 11.50 25.00
1767 — 5.00 7.50 11.50 25.00

Obv: Crowned eagle.
Rev: Crowned and mantled arms.

52 1764 — 5.00 7.50 11.50 25.00

Obv: Hohenzollern arms.
Rev: Value with B and date below.

75 1780 — 3.00 4.50 8.00 20.00
1781 — 3.00 4.50 8.00 20.00
1782 — 3.00 4.50 8.00 20.00
1783 — 3.00 4.50 8.00 20.00

4 PFENNIG

BILLON
Obv: Eagle and B. Rev: Value and date.

78 1779 — 5.00 6.50 8.50 20.00

Obv: Hohenzollern arms.
Rev: Value with B and date below.

80 1780 — 5.00 6.50 8.50 20.00

KREUZER

BILLON
Obv: Bust of Friedrich Christian right.
Rev: Value on eagle.

C#	Date	Mintage	VG	Fine	VF	XF
53	1764	—	5.00	7.50	11.50	25.00
	1765	—	5.00	7.50	11.50	25.00
	1766	—	5.00	7.50	11.50	25.00
	1767	—	5.00	7.50	11.50	25.00

Obv: Hohenzollern arms.
Rev: Value with B and date below.

82 1785 — 3.50 4.50 8.00 20.00
1786 — 3.50 4.50 8.00 20.00

Obv: Crowned and mantled arms.
Rev: Value and date in cartouche; S below date.

83 1789 — 5.00 7.50 9.50 20.00

2-1/2 KREUZER

(Convention)

BILLON
Obv: FC monogram.
Rev: Crowned arms.

55 1765 — 5.00 7.50 11.50 25.00
1766 — 5.00 7.50 11.50 25.00
1767 — 5.00 7.50 11.50 25.00
1768 — 5.00 7.50 11.50 25.00

Obv: Bust right. Rev: Eagle.

84 1779 — 6.00 7.50 9.50 20.00

Obv: Arms.
Rev: 3 line inscription with date below.

85 1780-86 — 3.50 5.00 8.50 20.00

4 KREUZER

BILLON
Obv: Crowned eagle shield on pedestal.
Rev: Value and date.

57 1763 — 7.50 10.00 15.00 35.00

5 KREUZER

(Convention)

BILLON

58 1763 — 10.00 15.00 25.00 50.00
1764 — 10.00 15.00 25.00 50.00
1765 — 10.00 15.00 25.00 50.00
1766 — 10.00 15.00 25.00 50.00
1767 — 10.00 15.00 25.00 50.00
1768 — 10.00 15.00 25.00 50.00

10 KREUZER

(Convention)

SILVER
Obv: Bust of Friedrich Christian right in wreath.
Rev: Crowned eagle on pedestal showing value.

60 1763 — 10.00 15.00 25.00 50.00
1765 — 10.00 15.00 25.00 50.00

Obv: Bust of Friedrich Christian right in wreath.
Rev: Eagle arms on pedestal showing value.

60a 1766 — 10.00 15.00 25.00 50.00
1768 — 10.00 15.00 25.00 50.00

Obv: Bust right. Rev: Eagle shield on pedestal.

C#	Date	Mintage	Fine	VF	XF	Unc
90	1780	—	10.00	20.00	35.00	60.00

15 KREUZER

(Convention)

SILVER

C#	Date	Mintage	VG	Fine	VF	XF
62	1763	—	15.00	25.00	40.00	75.00

20 KREUZER

(Convention)

SILVER
Obv: Bust of Friedrich Christian right in wreath.
Rev: Crowned eagle on pedestal; value in pedestal.

63 1763 CLR — 9.50 15.00 25.00 50.00
1764 CLR — 9.50 15.00 25.00 50.00

C#	Date	Mintage	VG	Fine	VF	XF
63	1765 CLR	—	9.50	15.00	25.00	50.00

Rev: Eagle arms on pedestal showing value.

63a 1766 CLR — 9.50 15.00 25.00 50.00
1768 CLR — 9.50 15.00 25.00 50.00

Obv: Bust right. Rev: Eagle shield on pedestal.

C#	Date	Mintage	Fine	VF	XF	Unc
92	1780	—	8.00	12.00	30.00	75.00
	1782	—	10.00	15.00	30.00	75.00

Similar to C#92.

92a 1785 — 10.00 15.00 30.00 75.00

Rev: Arms on pedestal, value and date beneath.

92b 1787 — 12.50 15.00 30.00 75.00

30 KREUZER

(Convention)

SILVER

64 1767 — 17.50 30.00 45.00 85.00

GROSCHEN

BILLON
Obv: Bust of Friedrich Christian right.
Rev: Legend.

C#	Date	Mintage	VG	Fine	VF	XF
56	1765	—	10.00	15.00	25.00	50.00

1/12 THALER

(Reichs)

SILVER

59 1763 — 10.00 15.00 25.00 50.00

1/6 THALER

(Reichs)

SILVER
Obv: Bust of Friedrich Christian right.
Rev: Value and date.

61 1763 — 12.50 20.00 32.50 60.00

1/2 THALER

(Convention)

SILVER

C#	Date	Mintage	Fine	VF	XF	Unc
66	1763	—	150.00	225.00	300.00	450.00
	1766	—	150.00	225.00	300.00	450.00
	1767	—	150.00	225.00	300.00	450.00

THALER

(Convention)

SILVER
Obv: Armored bust of Friedrich Christian right.
Rev: Crowned arms divide date.

68 1763 CLR — 125.00 175.00 250.00 350.00

Rev: Crowned arms divide date; small letters in legend.

68a 1766 ES — 100.00 150.00 225.00 325.00

Rev: Crowned arms with lion supporters; date below.

69 1766 ES — 65.00 100.00 150.00 300.00
1768 RE — 200.00 275.00 400.00 650.00

Friedrich Christian Commemorative
Obv: Armored bust of Friedrich Christian right.
Rev: 8 line inscription.

70 1769 G — 175.00 250.00 325.00 500.00

Obv: Bust right with W on arm.
Rev: Lion holding crowned arms; BAYREUTH and date in exergue.

95 1779 — 165.00 200.00 250.00 500.00

C#	Date	Mintage	Fine	VF	XF	Unc
95	1782	—	125.00	150.00	200.00	400.00
	1783	—	125.00	150.00	200.00	400.00

Obv: Bust right. Rev: Crowned and mantled arms, with supporters; divided date with B in circle and E-B below.

C#	Date	Mintage	Fine	VF	XF	Unc
96	1786	—	225.00	300.00	400.00	750.00

TRADE COINS

DUCAT

3.5000 gm., .986 GOLD, .1109 oz AGW
Obv: Bust of Friedrich Christian right.
Rev: Crowned arms.

C#	Date	Mintage	Fine	VF	XF	Unc
71	1763	—	500.00	850.00	1250.	2000.

Birthday of Friedrich Christian Commemorative
Rev: Crowned bible, sword and scales.

C#	Date	Mintage	Fine	VF	XF	Unc
72	1764	—	650.00	1000.	1500.	2500.

C#	Date	Mintage	Fine	VF	XF	Unc
73	1767	—	500.00	850.00	1250.	2000.

BRANDENBURG-ANSBACH-BAYREUTH

Held by Prussia from 1791 to 1805 and then given to Bavaria.

RULERS

Friedrich Wilhelm II
of Prussia, 1791-1797
Friedrich Wilhelm III
of Prussia, 1797-1805

PFENNIG

BILLON
Obv: Crowned FWR monogram divides date above.
Rev: Value and B.

C#	Date	Mintage	VG	Fine	VF	XF
1	1792B	—	3.00	5.00	7.50	15.00
	1793B	—	3.00	5.00	7.50	15.00
	1794B	—	3.00	5.00	7.50	15.00
	1795B	—	3.00	5.00	7.50	15.00
	1796B	—	3.00	5.00	7.50	15.00

Similar to C#1.

C#	Date	Mintage	VG	Fine	VF	XF
2	1796B	—	7.50	12.50	17.50	25.00
	1797B	—	7.50	12.50	17.50	25.00

Obv: Crowned FWR monogram. Rev: Value.

C#	Date	Mintage	Fine	VF	XF	Unc
9	1799B	.534	2.50	5.00	10.00	40.00
	1801B	.616	2.50	5.00	10.00	40.00
	1803B	.984	2.50	5.00	10.00	40.00

KREUZER

BILLON
Obv: Crowned eagle with monogram on breast.
Rev: Value and date in cartouche; S beneath.

C#	Date	Mintage	VG	Fine	VF	XF
3	1792S	—	3.00	5.00	7.50	15.00
	1793S	—	3.00	5.00	7.50	15.00
	1794S	—	3.00	5.00	7.50	15.00
	1795S	—	3.00	5.00	7.50	15.00
	1796S	—	3.00	5.00	7.50	15.00
	1797S	—	3.00	5.00	7.50	15.00

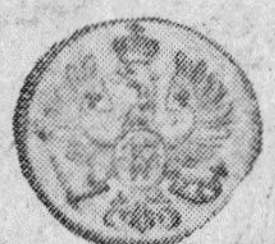

C#	Date	Mintage	Fine	VF	XF	Unc
11	1798B	.310	2.50	5.00	10.00	40.00
	1799B	.415	2.50	5.00	10.00	40.00
	1800B	.533	2.50	5.00	10.00	40.00

Rev: Value within garlands

C#	Date	Mintage	Fine	VF	XF	Unc
12	1802B	.324	2.50	5.00	10.00	40.00
	1803B	.533	2.50	5.00	10.00	40.00
	1804B	1.243	2.50	5.00	10.00	40.00

3 KREUZER

BILLON
Obv: Eagle on trophies, date below.
Rev: Value over spray and B or S.

C#	Date	Mintage	VG	Fine	VF	XF
5	1794	—	3.50	5.00	10.00	15.00
	1795	—	3.50	5.00	10.00	15.00
	1796	—	3.50	5.00	10.00	15.00
	1797	—	3.50	5.00	10.00	15.00

NOTE: Varieties exist.

Obv: Crowned eagle, FWR monogram on breast.
Rev: Value above branches.

C#	Date	Mintage	Fine	VF	XF	Unc
13	1798B	.559	3.00	6.00	10.00	40.00
	1799B	1.114	3.00	6.00	10.00	40.00
	1800B	1.076	3.00	6.00	10.00	40.00
	1801B	1.335	3.00	6.00	10.00	40.00
	1802B	1.330	3.00	6.00	10.00	40.00

6 KREUZER

BILLON
Similar to C#14.

C#	Date	Mintage	VG	Fine	VF	XF
6	1797	—	7.50	11.50	15.00	25.00

C#	Date	Mintage	Fine	VF	XF	Unc
14	1798B	.759	4.00	7.50	11.00	40.00
	1799B	.537	4.00	7.50	11.00	40.00
	1800B	.383	4.00	7.50	11.00	40.00
	1801B	.340	4.00	7.50	11.00	40.00
	1802B	.249	4.00	7.50	11.00	40.00

GULDEN

SILVER
Obv: Bust right. Rev: Crowned arms with wildman supporters, date in exergue.

C#	Date	Mintage	VG	Fine	VF	XF
7	1792	—	15.00	40.00	75.00	125.00
	1794	—	15.00	40.00	75.00	125.00

THALER

(Convention)

SILVER
Obv: Bust right.
Rev: Crowned oval arms in sprays.

C#	Date	Mintage	VG	Fine	VF	XF
8	1794	—	50.00	120.00	200.00	300.00
	1795	—	50.00	120.00	200.00	300.00
	1796	—	50.00	120.00	200.00	300.00

TRADE COINS

DUCAT

.3500 gm., .986 GOLD, .1109 oz AGW
Obv: Arms within branches.
Rev: AUS DER FURSTENZECHE above branches.

C#	Date	Mintage	Fine	VF	XF	Unc
15	1803	—	—	—	Rare	—

BREMEN

Located in northwest Germany. The city was founded c. 787 but was ruled by the archbishops until 1646 when it became a free city. Bremen was granted the mint right in 1369 and there was practically continuous coinage until 1907.

SCHWAREN

COPPER

C#	Date	Mintage	VG	Fine	VF	XF
1	1781	.219	1.00	2.50	4.00	12.00
	1797	.220	1.00	2.50	4.00	12.00
	1859	.069	2.00	4.00	6.00	15.00

NOTE: Varieties exist.

2-1/2 SCHWAREN

COPPER
Obv: Key divides date.
Rev: Value; P.B. in exergue.

C#	Date	Mintage	Fine	VF	XF	Unc
2.1	1797	.123	2.50	5.00	12.00	30.00
	1802	.157	2.00	3.00	10.00	30.00

Rev: Value between flowers.

C#	Date	Mintage	Fine	VF	XF	Unc
2.2	1820	.147	2.00	3.00	10.00	30.00

C#	Date	Mintage	Fine	VF	XF	Unc
2a	1841	.105	2.00	3.00	10.00	30.00
	1853	.142	2.00	3.00	10.00	30.00
	1861	*.101	2.00	3.00	10.00	30.00
	1866	.072	2.00	3.00	10.00	30.00

***NOTE:** 157,600 additional pieces were struck in 1865, dated 1861.

1/2 GROTEN

BILLON
Obv: Crowned key. Rev: Value and date.

C#	Date	Mintage	VG	Fine	VF	XF
6	1781	.230	2.00	3.50	5.00	15.00

C#	Date	Mintage	VG	Fine	VF	XF
6	1787	—	2.00	3.50	5.00	15.00

Obv: Key divides date. Rev: Value.

C#	Date	Mintage	VG	Fine	VF	XF
6a	1789	.145	2.00	3.50	5.00	15.00

COPPER

C#	Date	Mintage	Fine	VF	XF	Unc
3	1841	Inc. Ab.	4.00	9.00	18.00	35.00

GROTEN

BILLON

C#	Date	Mintage	Fine	VF	XF	Unc
11	1840	.262	2.00	4.00	10.00	30.00

6 GROTE

1.9500 gm., .740 SILVER, .0463 oz ASW

C#	Date	Mintage	Fine	VF	XF	Unc
15	1840	.079	2.50	5.00	10.00	40.00

2.9200 gm., .494 SILVER, .0463 oz ASW

C#	Date	Mintage	Fine	VF	XF	Unc
15a	1857	.311	2.50	5.00	10.00	40.00

C#	Date	Mintage	Fine	VF	XF	Unc
15b	1861	.127	2.50	5.00	10.00	40.00

12 GROTE

3.9000 gm., .740 SILVER, .0927 oz ASW

C#	Date	Mintage	Fine	VF	XF	Unc
19	1840	.193	4.00	8.00	12.00	35.00
	1841	.112	4.00	8.00	12.00	35.00
	1845	.063	4.00	8.00	12.00	35.00
	1846	.056	4.00	8.00	12.00	35.00

Obv: Crowned cornered arms.

C#	Date	Mintage	Fine	VF	XF	Unc
19a	1859	.450	3.00	8.00	12.00	35.00
	1860	.150	4.00	8.00	12.00	35.00

36 GROTE

8.7700 gm., .986 SILVER, .2780 oz ASW

C#	Date	Mintage	Fine	VF	XF	Unc
21	1840	.170	15.00	25.00	40.00	75.00
	1841	.044	15.00	25.00	40.00	75.00
	1845	.084	15.00	25.00	40.00	75.00
	1846	.085	15.00	25.00	40.00	75.00
	1859	.121	15.00	25.00	40.00	75.00

C#	Date	Mintage	Fine	VF	XF	Unc
22	1859	.050	15.00	30.00	45.00	80.00
	1864	.100	15.00	30.00	45.00	80.00

EIN (1) THALER

17.5400 gm., .986 SILVER, .5560 oz ASW
50th Anniversary of Liberation of Germany

C#	Date	Mintage	Fine	VF	XF	Unc
26	1863	.020	20.00	50.00	85.00	150.00

Opening Of New Business Exchange

C#	Date	Mintage	Fine	VF	XF	Unc
27	1864	5,000	40.00	115.00	160.00	200.00

2nd German Shooting Festival

C#	Date	Mintage	Fine	VF	XF	Unc
28	1865	.050	18.00	40.00	65.00	100.00

Victory Over French

C#	Date	Mintage	Fine	VF	XF	Unc
29	1871B	.061	20.00	50.00	90.00	140.00

MONETARY REFORM

2 MARK

11.1110 gm., .900 SILVER, .3215 oz ASW

Y#	Date	Mintage	Fine	VF	XF	Unc
49	1904J	.100	15.00	40.00	75.00	110.00
	1904J	200 pcs.	—	—	Proof	400.00

5 MARK

27.7770 gm., .900 SILVER, .8038 oz ASW

Y#	Date	Mintage	Fine	VF	XF	Unc
50	1904	—	1500.	3000.	4000.	8000.
	1906J	.041	50.00	125.00	250.00	325.00
	1906J	—	—	—	Proof	700.00

10 MARK

3.9820 gm., .900 GOLD, .1152 oz AGW

Y#	Date	Mintage	Fine	VF	XF	Unc
51	1907J	.020	400.00	600.00	800.00	1100.

20 MARK

7.9650 gm., .900 GOLD, .2304 oz AGW

Y#	Date	Mintage	Fine	VF	XF	Unc
52	1906J	.020	400.00	800.00	1000.	1200.

BRESLAU

Located in Silesia. The bishopric was founded c. 1000. In 1290 the bishops were made princes of the Empire and granted the mint right. Coins were first issued in quantity c. 1510. The bishopric was secularized in 1810-11 with most of it going to Prussia. The balance of the lands are in modern Poland or Czechoslovakia.

RULERS

Philipp Gotthard, 1747-1795
Joseph, 1795-1823

1/2 TALER
(Convention)

SILVER

C#	Date	Mintage	VG	Fine	VF	XF
5	1796	—	100.00	275.00	400.00	600.00

TALER
(Convention)

SILVER
Obv: Clerical bust right.
Rev: Crowned and mantled arms.

C#	Date	Mintage	VG	Fine	VF	XF
2	1753	—	300.00	600.00	750.00	1000.
	1770	—	200.00	450.00	600.00	850.00
	1773	—	200.00	450.00	600.00	850.00
	1777	—	200.00	450.00	600.00	850.00

TRADE COINS

DUCAT

3.5000 gm., .986 GOLD, .1109 oz AGW
Obv: Bust right. Rev: Arms.

C#	Date	Mintage	Fine	VF	XF	Unc
3	1770-77	—	—	750.00	1000.	2000.

Similar to C#3.

C#	Date	Mintage	Fine	VF	XF	Unc
6	1796	—	—	1000.	1350.	2500.

BRETZENHEIM

Located in the Rhineland. Purchased by Carl Theodor of Pfalz-Sulzbach in 1790. The principality was mediatized in 1803. Karl August was the only one to issue coins for Bretzenheim.

RULERS

Carl August, 1790-1803

10 KREUZER
(Convention)

SILVER
Obv: Bust right.
Rev: 5-fold arms with 3-fold center shield.

C#	Date	Mintage	VG	Fine	VF	XF
1	1790	—	25.00	50.00	75.00	110.00

20 KREUZER
(Convention)

SILVER
Obv: Bust right. Rev: Arms.

C#	Date	Mintage	VG	Fine	VF	XF
2	1790	—	15.00	25.00	40.00	60.00

1/2 THALER
(Convention)

SILVER
Obv: Bust right.
Rev: Arms with ostrich supporters.

C#	Date	Mintage	VG	Fine	VF	XF
3	1790A.S.	—	200.00	400.00	600.00	800.00

THALER
(Convention)

SILVER
Obv: Bust right; A.S. below.
Rev: Crowned arms with ostrich supporters.

C#	Date	Mintage	VG	Fine	VF	XF
4	1790A.S.	—	250.00	500.00	650.00	800.00

TRADE COINS

DUCAT

3.5000 gm., .986 GOLD, .1109 oz AGW
Obv: Bust right. Rev: Crowned arms on cross.

C#	Date	Mintage	Fine	VF	XF	Unc
5	1790	—	1250.	1500.	2200.	3000.

BRUNSWICK-LUNEBURG

Located in north-central Germany. The first duke began his rule in 1235. The first coinage appeared c. 1175. There was considerable shuffling of territory until 1692 when Ernst August became the elector of Hannover. George Ludwig became George I of England in 1714. There was separate coinage for Luneburg until the reign of George III. They changed the name to Hannover in 1814.

RULERS

Georg III, (King of Great Britain)
1760-1814
After 1814 See Kingdom Of Hannover

PFENNIG

COPPER
Rev: Denomination: PFENNING

C#	Date	Mintage	Fine	VF	XF	Unc
100.1	1761 I.W.S.	—	2.00	4.00	8.00	30.00
	1762 I.W.S.	—	2.00	4.00	8.00	30.00
	1763 I.W.S.	—	2.00	4.00	8.00	30.00
	1764 I.W.S.	—	2.00	4.00	8.00	30.00
	1765 I.W.S.	—	2.00	4.00	8.00	30.00
	1767 I.W.S.	—	2.00	4.00	8.00	30.00
	1768 I.W.S.	—	2.00	4.00	8.00	30.00

Rev: Denomination: PFENN

C#	Date	Mintage	Fine	VF	XF	Unc
100.2	1769 I.W.S.	—	2.00	4.00	8.00	30.00
	1770 I.W.S.	—	2.00	4.00	8.00	30.00
	1771 I.W.S.	—	2.00	4.00	8.00	30.00
	1772 I.W.S.	—	2.00	4.00	8.00	30.00
	1773 I.W.S.	—	2.00	4.00	8.00	30.00
	1774 I.W.S.	—	2.00	4.00	8.00	30.00
	1775 I.W.S.	—	2.00	4.00	8.00	30.00
	1776 I.W.S.	—	2.00	4.00	8.00	30.00
	1777 I.W.S.	—	2.00	4.00	8.00	30.00
	1778 I.W.S.	—	2.00	4.00	8.00	30.00
	1779 I.W.S.	—	2.00	4.00	8.00	30.00
	1780 I.W.S.	—	2.00	4.00	8.00	30.00
	1781 I.W.S.	—	2.00	4.00	8.00	30.00
	1782 I.W.S.	—	2.00	4.00	8.00	30.00
	1783 I.W.S.	—	2.00	4.00	8.00	30.00
	1784 I.W.S.	—	2.00	4.00	8.00	30.00
	1785 I.W.S.	—	2.00	4.00	8.00	30.00
	1786 I.W.S.	—	2.00	4.00	8.00	30.00
	1787 I.W.S.	—	2.00	4.00	8.00	30.00
	1788 I.W.S.	—	2.00	4.00	8.00	30.00
	1789 I.W.S.	—	2.00	4.00	8.00	30.00
	1790 I.W.S.	—	2.00	4.00	8.00	30.00
	1790 .C.	—	2.00	4.00	8.00	30.00
	1791 .C.	—	2.00	4.00	8.00	30.00
	1792 .C.	—	2.00	4.00	8.00	30.00
	1793 P.L.M	—	2.00	4.00	8.00	30.00
	1794 P.L.M	—	2.00	4.00	8.00	30.00
	1795 P.L.M	—	2.00	4.00	8.00	30.00
	1796 P.L.M	—	2.00	4.00	8.00	30.00
	1797 P.L.M	—	2.00	4.00	8.00	30.00
	1798 P.L.M	—	2.00	4.00	8.00	30.00
	1799 P.L.M	—	2.00	4.00	8.00	30.00
	1800/700 P.L.M		2.00	4.00	8.00	30.00
	1800 P.L.M	—	2.00	4.00	8.00	30.00
	1801 .C.	—	2.00	4.00	8.00	30.00
	1802 .C.	—	2.00	4.00	8.00	30.00
	1802 G.F.M	—	2.00	4.00	8.00	30.00
	1803 G.F.M.	—	2.00	4.00	8.00	30.00
	1804 G.F.M	—	2.00	4.00	8.00	30.00
	1806 G.F.M	—	2.00	4.00	8.00	30.00

Obv: St. Andrew. Rev: Value.

C#	Date	Mintage	Fine	VF	XF	Unc
104.1	1780 I.W.S.	—	2.00	4.00	8.00	30.00
	1781 I.W.S.	—	2.00	4.00	8.00	30.00
	1782 I.W.S.	—	2.00	4.00	8.00	30.00
	1783 I.W.S.	—	2.00	4.00	8.00	30.00
	1784 I.W.S.	—	2.00	4.00	8.00	30.00
	1785 I.W.S.	—	2.00	4.00	8.00	30.00
	1786 I.W.S.	—	2.00	4.00	8.00	30.00
104.1	1787 I.W.S.	—	2.00	4.00	8.00	30.00
	1788 I.W.S.	—	2.00	4.00	8.00	30.00
	1789 I.W.S.	—	2.00	4.00	8.00	30.00
	1793 P.L.M.	—	2.00	4.00	8.00	30.00

Obv: Cross under St. Andrew's right arm.

C#	Date	Mintage	Fine	VF	XF	Unc
104.2	1782 S	—	2.50	5.00	10.00	35.00

C#	Date	Mintage	Fine	VF	XF	Unc
106	1760 I.B.H.	—	2.00	4.00	8.00	30.00
	1762 I.B.H.	—	2.00	4.00	8.00	30.00
	1763 I.A.P.	—	2.00	4.00	8.00	30.00
	1764 I.A.P.	—	2.00	4.00	8.00	30.00
	1765 I.A.P.	—	2.00	4.00	8.00	30.00
	1766 I.A.P.	—	2.00	4.00	8.00	30.00
	1768 I.A.P.	—	2.00	4.00	8.00	30.00
	1769 I.A.P.	—	2.00	4.00	8.00	30.00
	1770 I.A.P.	—	2.00	4.00	8.00	30.00
	1772 I.A.P.	—	2.00	4.00	8.00	30.00
	1774 L.C.R	—	2.00	4.00	8.00	30.00
	1776 L.C.R	—	2.00	4.00	8.00	30.00
	1777 L.C.R	—	2.00	4.00	8.00	30.00
	1778 L.C.R	—	2.00	4.00	8.00	30.00
	1780 C.E.S	—	2.00	4.00	8.00	30.00
	1781 C.E.S	—	2.00	4.00	8.00	30.00
	1783 C.E.S	—	2.00	4.00	8.00	30.00
	1784 C.E.S	—	2.00	4.00	8.00	30.00
	1785 C.E.S	—	2.00	4.00	8.00	30.00
	1788 .C.	—	2.00	4.00	8.00	30.00
	1794 P.L.M	—	2.00	4.00	8.00	30.00
	1795 P.L.M	—	2.00	4.00	8.00	30.00
	1796 P.L.M	—	2.00	4.00	8.00	30.00
	1803 G.F.M	—	2.00	4.00	8.00	30.00
	1804 G.F.M	—	2.00	4.00	8.00	30.00

BILLON, 11mm
Obv: Crowned GR monogram. Rev: Blank.

C#	Date	Mintage	Fine	VF	XF	Unc
	1764	—	8.00	17.00	22.00	40.00

1-1/2 PFENNIG

COPPER

C#	Date	Mintage	Fine	VF	XF	Unc
101	1792 .C.	—	3.00	6.00	8.50	30.00
	1792 P.L.M.	—	3.00	6.00	8.50	30.00

2 PFENNIG

COPPER

C#	Date	Mintage	Fine	VF	XF	Unc
102	1794 P.L.M	—	2.50	5.00	8.00	30.00
	1795 P.L.M	—	2.50	5.00	8.00	30.00
	1796 P.L.M	—	2.50	5.00	8.00	30.00
	1797 P.L.M	—	2.50	5.00	8.00	30.00
	1798 P.L.M	—	2.50	5.00	8.00	30.00
	1799 P.L.M	—	2.50	5.00	8.00	30.00
	1800 P.L.M	—	2.50	5.00	8.00	30.00
	1801 .C.	—	2.50	5.00	8.00	30.00
	1802 G.F.M	—	2.50	5.00	8.00	30.00
	1803 G.F.M	—	2.50	5.00	8.00	30.00
	1804 G.F.M	—	2.50	5.00	8.00	30.00
	1807 G.F.M	—	2.50	5.00	8.00	30.00

4 PFENNIG

COPPER

C#	Date	Mintage	Fine	VF	XF	Unc
103	1794 P.L.M.	—	5.00	10.00	15.00	40.00
	1795 P.L.M.	—	5.00	10.00	15.00	40.00
	1796 P.L.M.	—	5.00	10.00	15.00	40.00

Obv: St. Andrew. Rev: Value.

C#	Date	Mintage	Fine	VF	XF	Unc
105	1792 .C.	—	6.00	12.00	20.00	40.00
	1794 P.L.M.	—	6.00	12.00	20.00	40.00

BILLON
Obv: Crowned GR monogram.
Rev: Value, NACH DEM LEIPZIGER FUS

C#	Date	Mintage	Fine	VF	XF	Unc
109	1761 I.W.S.	—	3.00	6.00	12.00	35.00

Rev: K. GR. BR...., value.

C#	Date	Mintage	Fine	VF	XF	Unc
109a	1762 I.B.H.	—	3.00	7.00	12.00	35.00
	1763 I.A.P.	—	3.00	7.00	12.00	35.00
	1765 I.A.P.	—	3.00	6.00	12.00	35.00
	1766 I.A.P.	—	3.00	6.00	12.00	35.00
	1768 I.A.P.	—	3.00	7.00	12.00	35.00
	1770 I.A.P.	—	3.00	6.00	12.00	35.00
	1771 I.A.P.	—	3.00	7.00	12.00	35.00
	1772 I.A.P.	—	3.00	7.00	12.00	35.00
	1775 L.C.R.	—	3.00	6.00	12.00	35.00
	1777 L.C.R.	—	3.00	6.00	12.00	35.00
	1779 .C.	—	3.00	6.00	12.00	35.00

Rev: NACH DEM REICHS FUS

C#	Date	Mintage	Fine	VF	XF	Unc
109b	1762 I.W.S	—	3.00	6.00	12.00	35.00
	1763 I.W.S	—	3.00	6.00	12.00	35.00
	1764 I.W.S	—	3.00	6.00	12.00	35.00
	1765 I.W.S	—	3.00	6.00	12.00	35.00
	1767 I.W.S	—	3.00	7.00	12.00	35.00
	1769 I.W.S	—	3.00	7.00	12.00	35.00
	1771 I.W.S.	—	3.00	9.00	14.00	35.00
	1772 I.W.S	—	3.00	6.00	12.00	35.00
	1774 I.W.S	—	3.00	6.00	12.00	35.00
	1776 I.W.S	—	3.00	6.00	12.00	35.00
	1777 I.W.S	—	3.00	6.00	12.00	35.00
	1779 I.W.S	—	3.00	6.00	12.00	35.00
	1780 I.W.S	—	3.00	6.00	12.00	35.00
	1781 I.W.S	—	3.00	6.00	12.00	35.00
	1782 I.W.S	—	3.00	6.00	12.00	35.00
	1783 I.W.S.	—	4.00	9.00	14.00	35.00
	1784 I.W.S	—	3.00	7.00	12.00	35.00
	1785 I.W.S	—	3.00	7.00	12.00	35.00
	1787 I.W.S	—	3.00	6.00	12.00	35.00
	1788 I.W.S	—	3.00	7.00	12.00	35.00
	1791 .C.	—	3.00	6.00	12.00	35.00
	1792 .C.	—	3.00	6.00	12.00	35.00
	1793 P.L.M	—	3.00	6.00	12.00	35.00
	1795 P.L.M	—	3.00	6.00	12.00	35.00
	1797 P.L.M	—	3.00	6.00	12.00	35.00
	1799 P.L.M	—	3.00	6.00	12.00	35.00
	1802 .C.	—	3.00	6.00	12.00	35.00
	1804 G.F.M	—	3.00	6.00	12.00	35.00

6 PFENNIG

BILLON
Obv: Crowned GR monogram. Rev: VI in orb.

C#	Date	Mintage	Fine	VF	XF	Unc
112	1763 I.W.S.	—	5.00	10.00	16.00	40.00
	1764 I.W.S.	—	3.50	7.00	12.00	35.00

MARIEN GROSCHEN

BILLON
Obv: Crowned GR monogram.
Rev: Value, NACH DEM LEIPZIGER FUS

C#	Date	Mintage	Fine	VF	XF	Unc
117	1761 I.W.S.	—	3.50	7.00	15.00	40.00

Rev: Value, K. GR. BR.....

C#	Date	Mintage	Fine	VF	XF	Unc
117a	1763 I.A.P.	—	3.00	6.00	12.00	35.00
	1764 I.A.P.	—	3.00	6.00	12.00	35.00
	1765 I.A.P.	—	3.00	6.00	12.00	35.00

C#	Date	Mintage	Fine	VF	XF	Unc
117a	1766 I.A.P.	—	4.00	8.00	13.00	35.00
	1768 I.A.P.	—	4.00	8.00	13.00	35.00
	1769 I.W.S.	—	4.00	8.00	13.00	35.00
	1770 I.A.P.	—	3.00	6.00	12.00	35.00
	1771 I.A.P.	—	4.00	8.00	13.00	35.00
	1775 L.C.R.	—	5.00	10.00	16.00	35.00
	1776 L.C.R.	—	5.00	10.00	16.00	35.00

C#	Date	Mintage	Fine	VF	XF	Unc
117b	1762 I.W.S.	—	4.00	8.00	13.00	35.00
	1763 I.W.S.	—	4.00	8.00	13.00	35.00
	1765 I.W.S.	—	4.00	8.00	13.00	35.00
	1766 I.W.S	—	4.00	8.00	13.00	35.00
	1767 I.W.S	—	4.00	8.00	13.00	35.00
	1768 I.W.S.	—	4.00	8.00	13.00	35.00
	1769 I.W.S	—	3.00	6.00	12.00	35.00
	1770 I.W.S	—	3.00	6.00	12.00	35.00
	1771 I.W.S	—	3.00	6.00	12.00	35.00
	1773 I.W.S	—	4.00	8.00	13.00	35.00
	1774 I.W.S.	—	4.00	8.00	13.00	35.00
	1775 I.W.S	—	3.00	6.00	12.00	35.00
	1776 I.W.S.	—	5.00	10.00	16.00	35.00
	1777 I.W.S	—	4.00	8.00	13.00	35.00
	1778 I.W.S	—	4.00	8.00	13.00	35.00
	1779 I.W.S	—	4.00	8.00	13.00	35.00
	1781 I.W.S	—	4.00	8.00	13.00	35.00
	1782 I.W.S	—	3.00	6.00	12.00	35.00
	1783 I.W.S	—	3.00	6.00	12.00	35.00
	1784 I.W.S	—	3.00	6.00	12.00	35.00
	1785 I.W.S	—	3.00	6.00	12.00	35.00
	1787 I.W.S	—	4.00	8.00	13.00	35.00
	1790 .C.	—	3.00	6.00	12.00	35.00
	1791 .C.	—	3.00	6.00	12.00	35.00
	1793 P.L.M	—	3.00	6.00	12.00	35.00
	1797 P.L.M	—	3.00	6.00	12.00	35.00
	1799 P.L.M	—	3.00	6.00	12.00	35.00
	1802 .C.	—	3.00	6.00	12.00	35.00
	1803 G.F.M	—	3.00	6.00	12.00	35.00
	1804 G.F.M	—	3.00	6.00	12.00	35.00

2 MARIEN GROSCHEN

BILLON

Obv: Crowned GR monogram. Rev: Value.

C#	Date	Mintage	Fine	VF	XF	Unc
123	1760 I.W.S.	—	3.00	7.00	12.00	35.00
	1762 I.W.S.	—	5.00	10.00	15.00	35.00

.993 SILVER

Obv: Value. Rev: Wildman.

C#	Date	Mintage	Fine	VF	XF	Unc
124.1	1763 I.A.P.	—	5.00	9.00	14.00	40.00
	1766 I.A.P.	—	5.00	9.00	14.00	40.00
	1768 I.A.P.	—	5.00	9.00	14.00	40.00
	1770 I.A.P.	—	5.00	10.00	15.00	40.00
	1771 I.A.P.	—	5.00	9.00	14.00	40.00
	1772 I.A.P.	—	5.00	10.00	15.00	40.00
	1773 I.A.P.	—	5.00	9.00	14.00	40.00
	1774 L.C.R.	—	5.00	9.00	14.00	40.00
	1775 L.C.R.	—	5.00	10.00	15.00	40.00
	1776 L.C.R.	—	5.00	10.00	15.00	40.00
	1778 L.C.R.	—	5.00	9.00	14.00	40.00
	1779 .C.	—	5.00	9.00	14.00	40.00
	1780 C.E.S.	—	5.00	9.00	14.00	40.00
	1781 C.E.S.	—	5.00	9.00	14.00	40.00
	1782 C.E.S.	—	5.00	9.00	14.00	40.00
	1783 C.E.S.	—	5.00	9.00	14.00	40.00
	1785 C.E.S.	—	5.00	9.00	14.00	40.00

Rev: Date in center legend.

C#	Date	Mintage	Fine	VF	XF	Unc
124.2	1785 C.E.S.	—	5.00	10.00	15.00	40.00

4 MARIEN GROSCHEN

SILVER

Obv: Value. Rev: Wildman.

C#	Date	Mintage	Fine	VF	XF	Unc
128.1	1762 I.B.H.	—	4.00	7.50	15.00	50.00
	1763 I.A.P.	—	4.00	7.50	15.00	50.00
	1764 I.A.P.	—	4.00	7.50	15.00	50.00
	1766I.A.P.	—	4.00	7.50	15.00	50.00
	1767I.A.P.	—	4.00	7.50	15.00	50.00
	1768I.A.P.	—	4.00	7.50	15.00	50.00
	1769I.A.P.	—	4.00	7.50	15.00	50.00
	1770I.A.P.	—	4.00	7.50	15.00	50.00
	1771I.A.P.	—	4.00	7.50	15.00	50.00
	1772I.A.P.	—	5.00	10.00	15.00	50.00
	1773L.C.R.	—	4.00	7.50	15.00	50.00
	1774L.C.R.	—	4.00	7.50	15.00	50.00
	1775L.C.R.	—	4.00	7.50	15.00	50.00
	1776L.C.R.	—	4.00	7.50	15.00	50.00
	1777L.C.R.	—	4.00	7.50	15.00	50.00
	1778L.C.R.	—	4.00	7.50	15.00	50.00
128.1	1779 .C.	—	4.00	7.50	15.00	50.00
	1780C.E.S.	—	4.00	7.50	15.00	50.00
	1781C.E.S.	—	4.00	7.50	15.00	50.00
	1782C.E.S.	—	4.00	9.00	15.00	50.00
	1783C.E.S.	—	4.00	9.00	15.00	50.00
	1784C.E.S.	—	4.00	7.50	15.00	50.00
	1785C.E.S.	—	4.00	7.50	15.00	50.00
	1786.C.	—	4.00	7.50	15.00	50.00

Rev: Date in center legend.

C#	Date	Mintage	Fine	VF	XF	Unc
128.2	1787.C.	—	4.00	8.00	15.00	50.00
	1788.C.	—	4.00	8.00	15.00	50.00

16 GUTE GROSCHEN

SILVER

Obv: arms. Rev: Value.

C#	Date	Mintage	Fine	VF	XF	Unc
—	1761I.W.S.	—	—	—	Rare	—
	1763I.W.S.	—	—	—	Rare	—

24 MARIEN GROSCHEN

SILVER

C#	Date	Mintage	Fine	VF	XF	Unc
152	1761 I.W.S	—	10.00	20.00	32.50	60.00
	1762 I.W.S	—	10.00	20.00	32.50	60.00
	1763 I.W.S	—	10.00	20.00	32.50	60.00
	1764 I.W.S	—	10.00	20.00	32.50	60.00
	1765 I.W.S	—	10.00	20.00	32.50	60.00
	1766 I.W.S.	—	10.00	20.00	32.50	60.00
	1767 I.W.S	—	10.00	20.00	32.50	60.00
	1768 I.W.S	—	10.00	20.00	32.50	60.00
	1769 I.W.S	—	10.00	20.00	32.50	60.00
	1770 I.W.S	—	10.00	20.00	32.50	60.00
	1771 I.W.S	—	10.00	20.00	32.50	60.00
	1772 I.W.S	—	10.00	20.00	32.50	60.00
	1773 I.W.S	—	10.00	20.00	32.50	60.00
	1774 I.W.S	—	10.00	20.00	32.50	60.00
	1775 I.W.S	—	10.00	20.00	32.50	60.00
	1776 I.W.S	—	10.00	20.00	32.50	60.00
	1777 I.W.S	—	10.00	20.00	32.50	60.00
	1778 I.W.S	—	10.00	20.00	32.50	60.00
	1779 I.W.S	—	10.00	20.00	32.50	60.00
	1780 I.W.S	—	10.00	20.00	32.50	60.00
	1781 I.W.S	—	10.00	20.00	32.50	60.00
	1782 I.W.S	—	10.00	20.00	32.50	60.00
	1783 I.W.S	—	10.00	20.00	32.50	60.00
	1784 I.W.S	—	10.00	20.00	32.50	60.00
	1785 I.W.S	—	10.00	20.00	32.50	60.00
	1786 I.W.S	—	10.00	20.00	32.50	60.00
	1787 I.W.S	—	10.00	20.00	32.50	60.00
	1788 I.W.S	—	10.00	20.00	32.50	60.00
	1789 I.W.S	—	10.00	20.00	32.50	60.00
	1790 I.W.S	—	10.00	20.00	32.50	60.00
	1790 .C.	—	10.00	20.00	32.50	60.00
	1791 .C.	—	10.00	20.00	32.50	60.00
	1792 .C.	—	10.00	20.00	32.50	60.00
	1792 P.L.M	—	10.00	20.00	32.50	60.00
	1793 P.L.M	—	10.00	20.00	32.50	60.00
	1794P.L.M.	—	10.00	20.00	32.50	60.00
	1795P.L.M.	—	10.00	20.00	32.50	60.00
	1796P.L.M.	—	10.00	20.00	32.50	60.00
	1797P.L.M.	—	10.00	20.00	32.50	60.00
	1798P.L.M.	—	10.00	20.00	32.50	60.00
	1799P.L.M.	—	10.00	20.00	32.50	60.00
	1800 P.L.M	—	10.00	20.00	32.50	60.00
	1800 .C.	—	10.00	20.00	32.50	60.00
	1800 E.C.	—	10.00	20.00	32.50	60.00
	1801P.L.M.	—	10.00	20.00	32.50	60.00

Obv: Baroque arms. Rev: Wildman

C#	Date	Mintage	Fine	VF	XF	Unc
154	1762I.B.H.	—	12.00	25.00	40.00	75.00
	1763I.A.P.	—	12.00	25.00	40.00	75.00
	1764I.A.P.	—	12.00	25.00	40.00	75.00
	1765I.A.P.	—	12.00	25.00	40.00	75.00
	1766I.A.P.	—	12.00	25.00	40.00	75.00
	1767I.A.P.	—	12.00	25.00	40.00	75.00
	1768I.A.P.	—	12.00	25.00	40.00	75.00
	1769I.A.P.	—	12.00	25.00	40.00	75.00
	1770I.A.P.	—	12.00	25.00	40.00	75.00
	1771I.A.P.	—	12.00	25.00	40.00	75.00
	1772I.A.P.	—	12.00	25.00	40.00	75.00
	1773I.A.P.	—	12.00	25.00	40.00	75.00
154	1774L.C.R.	—	12.00	25.00	40.00	75.00
	1775L.C.R.	—	12.00	25.00	40.00	75.00
	1776L.C.R.	—	12.00	25.00	40.00	75.00
	1777L.C.R.	—	12.00	25.00	40.00	75.00
	1778L.C.R.	—	12.00	25.00	40.00	75.00
	1779.C.	—	12.00	25.00	40.00	75.00
	1780C.E.S.	—	12.00	25.00	40.00	75.00
	1781C.E.S.	—	12.00	25.00	40.00	75.00
	1782C.E.S.	—	12.00	25.00	40.00	75.00
	1783C.E.S.	—	12.00	25.00	40.00	75.00
	1784C.E.S.	—	12.00	25.00	40.00	75.00

Obv: Plain arms

C#	Date	Mintage	Fine	VF	XF	Unc
154a	1785C.E.S.	—	12.00	25.00	40.00	75.00
	1786.C.	—	12.00	25.00	40.00	75.00
	1787.C.	—	12.00	25.00	40.00	75.00
	1788.C.	—	12.00	25.00	40.00	75.00
	1789.C.	—	12.00	25.00	40.00	75.00

24 EINEN (1/24)THALER

BILLON

Obv: Horse. Rev: Value, NACH DEM REICHS FUS.

C#	Date	Mintage	Fine	VF	XF	Unc
121	1760 I.W.S.	—	5.00	10.00	15.00	40.00
	1760 I.A.S.	—	3.00	7.00	12.00	40.00
	1761 I.A.S.	—	3.00	7.00	12.00	40.00
	1762 I.A.S.	—	3.00	7.00	12.00	40.00
	1762 I.W.S.	—	6.00	12.00	17.00	40.00
	1764 I.W.S.	—	5.00	10.00	16.00	40.00
	1764 .C.	—	5.00	10.00	16.00	40.00
	1768 .C.	—	5.00	10.00	16.00	40.00
	1769 I.H.Z.	—	5.00	10.00	16.00	40.00

Rev: Value, NACH DEM LEIPZIGER FUS

C#	Date	Mintage	Fine	VF	XF	Unc
121a	1760 I.W.S.	—	5.00	10.00	16.00	50.00

12 EINEN (1/12)THALER

BILLON

Obv: Horse. Rev: Value, NACH DEM LEIPZIGER FUS

C#	Date	Mintage	Fine	VF	XF	Unc
126	1760 I.W.S.	—	5.00	10.00	15.00	50.00

SILVER

C#	Date	Mintage	Fine	VF	XF	Unc
126a	1760 I.A.S.	—	4.00	7.00	12.00	50.00
	1760 I.W.S	—	4.00	8.00	12.00	50.00
	1761 I.A.S.	—	4.00	8.00	12.00	50.00
	1761 I.W.S	—	4.00	7.00	12.00	50.00
	1762 I.A.S.	—	4.00	7.00	12.00	50.00
	1762 I.W.S	—	4.00	7.00	12.00	50.00
	1763 I.A.S.	—	4.00	7.00	12.00	50.00
	1763 I.W.S.	—	4.00	7.00	12.00	50.00
	1763 .C.	—	4.00	7.00	12.00	50.00
	1764 I.W.S.	—	4.00	7.00	12.00	50.00
	1764 .C.	—	4.00	8.00	12.00	50.00
	1765 .C.	—	4.00	7.00	12.00	50.00
	1767 .C.	—	4.00	8.00	12.00	50.00
	1768 I.W.S	—	4.00	8.00	12.00	50.00
	1768 .C.	—	4.00	7.00	12.00	50.00
	1769 I.W.S.	—	5.00	10.00	15.00	50.00
	1769 I.H.Z.	—	4.00	8.00	12.00	50.00
	1770 I.W.S	—	4.00	8.00	12.00	50.00
	1771 I.W.S	—	4.00	7.00	12.00	50.00
	1772 I.W.S	—	4.00	8.00	12.00	50.00
	1772 I.H.Z.	—	4.00	8.00	12.00	50.00
	1773 I.W.S	—	4.00	7.00	12.00	50.00
	1774 I.W.S	—	3.00	7.00	12.00	40.00
	1775 I.W.S	—	3.00	7.00	12.00	40.00
	1776 I.W.S	—	4.00	8.00	12.00	40.00
	1777 I.W.S	—	3.00	7.00	12.00	40.00
	1778 I.W.S	—	3.00	7.00	12.00	40.00
	1779 I.W.S	—	4.00	8.00	12.00	40.00
	1780 I.W.S	—	3.00	7.00	12.00	40.00
	1781 I.W.S	—	3.00	7.00	12.00	40.00
	1782 I.W.S	—	4.00	8.00	12.00	40.00
	1783 I.W.S	—	4.00	8.00	12.00	40.00
	1784 I.W.S	—	3.00	7.00	12.00	40.00
	1785 I.W.S	—	5.00	10.00	15.00	40.00
	1786 I.W.S	—	4.00	8.00	12.00	40.00
	1787 I.W.S	—	4.00	8.00	12.00	40.00
	1788 I.W.S	—	4.00	8.00	12.00	40.00
	1789 I.W.S	—	3.00	7.00	12.00	40.00
	1790 .C.	—	4.00	8.00	12.00	40.00
	1791 .C.	—	3.00	7.00	12.00	40.00
	1792 .C.	—	3.00	7.00	12.00	40.00
	1792 P.L.M.	—	4.00	8.00	12.00	40.00
	1793 P.L.M	—	3.00	7.00	12.00	40.00
	1794 P.L.M	—	4.00	8.00	12.00	40.00
	1795 P.L.M	—	3.00	7.00	12.00	40.00

C#	Date	Mintage	Fine	VF	XF	Unc
126a	1796 P.L.M	—	3.00	7.00	12.00	40.00
	1797 P.L.M	—	3.00	7.00	12.00	40.00
	1798 P.L.M	—	3.00	7.00	12.00	40.00
	1799 P.L.M	—	3.00	7.00	12.00	40.00
	1800 P.L.M	—	3.00	7.00	12.00	40.00
	1801 P.L.M	—	3.00	7.00	12.00	40.00
	1801 E.C	—	4.00	8.00	12.00	40.00
	1801 .C.	8,780	4.00	8.00	12.00	40.00
	1801G.F.M.	—		A Counterfeit		
	1802 .C.	—	3.00	7.00	12.00	40.00
	1802 G.F.M	—	3.00	7.00	12.00	40.00
	1803 G.F.M	—	3.00	7.00	12.00	40.00
	1804 G.F.M	—	3.00	7.00	12.00	40.00
	1805 G.F.M	—	3.00	7.00	12.00	40.00
	1806 G.F.M	—	3.00	7.00	12.00	40.00
	1807 G.F.M	—	3.00	7.00	12.00	40.00

1/6 THALER

SILVER

Obv: Arms. Rev: St. Andrew.

C#	Date	Mintage	Fine	VF	XF	Unc
130	1761I.W.S.	—	7.00	15.00	25.00	50.00
	1762I.W.S.	—	7.00	15.00	25.00	50.00
	1764I.W.S.	—	7.00	15.00	25.00	50.00
	1768I.W.S.	—	7.00	15.00	25.00	50.00
	1769I.W.S.	—	7.00	15.00	25.00	50.00
	1771I.W.S.	—	7.00	15.00	25.00	50.00
	1780I.W.S.	—	7.00	15.00	25.00	50.00
	1782I.W.S.	—	7.00	15.00	25.00	50.00
	1785I.W.S.	—	7.00	15.00	25.00	50.00
	1786I.W.S.	—	7.00	15.00	25.00	50.00
	1789I.W.S.	—	7.00	15.00	25.00	50.00
	1790I.W.S.	—	7.00	15.00	25.00	50.00
	1790.C.	—	7.00	15.00	25.00	50.00

C#	Date	Mintage	Fine	VF	XF	Unc
132	1762 I.B.H	—	7.00	15.00	25.00	50.00
	1763 I.A.P	—	7.00	15.00	25.00	50.00
	1764 I.A.P	—	7.00	15.00	25.00	50.00
	1765 I.A.P	—	7.00	15.00	25.00	50.00
	1766 I.A.P	—	7.00	15.00	25.00	50.00
	1767 I.A.P	—	7.00	15.00	25.00	50.00
	1768 I.A.P	—	7.00	15.00	25.00	50.00
	1769 I.A.P	—	7.00	15.00	25.00	50.00
	1770 I.A.P	—	7.00	15.00	25.00	50.00
	1771 I.A.P	—	7.00	15.00	25.00	50.00
	1772 I.A.P	—	7.00	15.00	25.00	50.00
	1773 I.A.P	—	7.00	15.00	25.00	50.00
	1773 L.C.R	—	7.00	15.00	25.00	50.00
	1774 L.C.R	—	7.00	15.00	25.00	50.00
	1775 L.C.R	—	7.00	15.00	25.00	50.00
	1776 L.C.R	—	7.00	15.00	25.00	50.00
	1778 L.C.R	—	7.00	15.00	25.00	50.00
	1779 .C.	—	7.00	15.00	25.00	50.00
	1780 C.E.S	—	7.00	15.00	25.00	50.00
	1781 C.E.S	—	7.00	15.00	25.00	50.00
	1782 C.E.S	—	7.00	15.00	25.00	50.00
	1783 C.E.S	—	7.00	15.00	25.00	50.00
	1784 C.E.S	—	7.00	15.00	25.00	50.00

Obv: Arms divide date.

C#	Date	Mintage	Fine	VF	XF	Unc
132a	1785 C.E.S	—	7.00	15.00	25.00	50.00
	1786 .C.	—	7.00	15.00	25.00	50.00
	1787 .C.	—	7.00	15.00	25.00	50.00
	1788 .C.	—	7.00	15.00	25.00	50.00
	1789 .C.	—	7.00	15.00	25.00	50.00

Rev. leg: N.D.R.F. added.

C#	Date	Mintage	Fine	VF	XF	Unc
132d	1790 C.	—	7.00	15.00	25.00	50.00
	1791 C.	—	7.00	15.00	25.00	50.00

Rev: Date in circular legend.

C#	Date	Mintage	Fine	VF	XF	Unc
132b	1793 P.L.M.	—	7.00	15.00	25.00	50.00
	1794 P.L.M.	—	7.00	15.00	25.00	50.00
	1795 P.L.M.	—	7.00	15.00	25.00	50.00
	1797 P.L.M.	—	7.00	15.00	25.00	50.00
	1798 P.L.M.	—	7.00	15.00	25.00	50.00
	1799 P.L.M.	—	7.00	15.00	25.00	50.00
	1800 P.L.M.	—	7.00	15.00	25.00	50.00

C#	Date	Mintage	Fine	VF	XF	Unc
130a	1804 G.F.M.	—	7.00	15.00	25.00	50.00

C#	Date	Mintage	Fine	VF	XF	Unc
132c	1804 G.F.M.	—	7.00	15.00	25.00	50.00

Obv: Head. Rev: Baroque arms

C#	Date	Mintage	Fine	VF	XF	Unc
134	1773 I.W.S.	—	7.00	15.00	25.00	50.00
	1780 I.W.S.	—	7.00	15.00	25.00	50.00
	1782 I.W.S.	—	7.00	15.00	25.00	50.00

Obv: Mailed bust.

C#	Date	Mintage	Fine	VF	XF	Unc
134a	1776 I.W.S.	—	7.00	15.00	25.00	50.00
	1778 I.W.S.	—	7.00	15.00	25.00	50.00
	1779 I.W.S.	—	7.00	15.00	25.00	50.00

Obv: Head. Rev: Plain arms.

C#	Date	Mintage	Fine	VF	XF	Unc
134b	1783 I.W.S.	—	8.00	17.50	27.50	50.00
	1784 I.W.S.	—	8.00	17.50	27.50	50.00

C#	Date	Mintage	Fine	VF	XF	Unc
137	1786 I.W.S.	—	7.00	15.00	25.00	50.00
	1787 I.W.S.	—	7.00	15.00	25.00	50.00
	1789 I.W.S.	—	7.00	15.00	25.00	50.00

C#	Date	Mintage	Fine	VF	XF	Unc
134c	1792 .C.	—	7.00	15.00	25.00	50.00
	1794 P.L.M	—	7.00	15.00	25.00	50.00
	1795/94 P.L.M.		7.00	15.00	25.00	50.00
	1795 P.L.M	—	7.00	15.00	25.00	50.00
	1796 P.L.M	—	7.00	15.00	25.00	50.00
	1797 P.L.M	—	7.00	15.00	25.00	50.00

Obv: Small head.

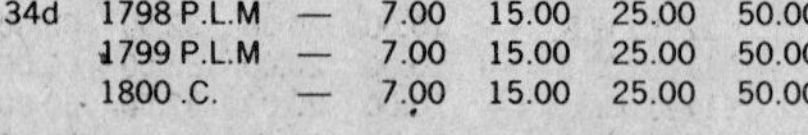

C#	Date	Mintage	Fine	VF	XF	Unc
134d	1798 P.L.M	—	7.00	15.00	25.00	50.00
	1799 P.L.M	—	7.00	15.00	25.00	50.00
	1800 .C.	—	7.00	15.00	25.00	50.00

W/o French arms or titles

C#	Date	Mintage	Fine	VF	XF	Unc
138a	1802 G.	—	7.00	15.00	25.00	50.00
	1802 G.F.M.	—	7.00	15.00	25.00	50.00
	1803 G.F.M	—	7.00	15.00	25.00	50.00
	1804/3 G.F.M		7.00	15.00	25.00	50.00

C#	Date	Mintage	Fine	VF	XF	Unc
138b	1807 G.M.	—	7.00	15.00	25.00	50.00

1/3 THALER

SILVER

Obv: Plain arms. Rev: St. Andrew.

C#	Date	Mintage	Fine	VF	XF	Unc
143	1764I.W.S.	—	10.00	20.00	35.00	75.00
	1766I.W.S.	—	10.00	20.00	35.00	75.00
	1770I.W.S.	—	10.00	20.00	35.00	75.00

Obv: Baroque arms.

C#	Date	Mintage	Fine	VF	XF	Unc
143a	1779I.W.S.	—	10.00	20.00	35.00	75.00
	1781I.W.S.	—	10.00	20.00	35.00	75.00
	1783I.W.S.	—	10.00	20.00	35.00	75.00
	1784I.W.S.	—	10.00	20.00	35.00	75.00
	1788I.W.S.	—	10.00	27.50	40.00	75.00
	1790.C.	—	10.00	20.00	35.00	75.00
	1793P.L.M.	—	10.00	20.00	35.00	75.00

C#	Date	Mintage	Fine	VF	XF	Unc
145	1762I.B.H.	—	10.00	20.00	35.00	75.00
	1764I.A.P.	—	10.00	20.00	35.00	75.00
	1765I.A.P.	—	10.00	20.00	35.00	75.00
	1766I.A.P.	—	10.00	20.00	35.00	75.00
	1767I.A.P.	—	10.00	20.00	35.00	75.00
	1768I.A.P.	—	10.00	20.00	35.00	75.00
	1769I.A.P.	—	10.00	20.00	35.00	75.00
	1770I.A.P.	—	10.00	20.00	35.00	75.00
	1771I.A.P.	—	10.00	20.00	35.00	75.00
	1772I.A.P.	—	10.00	25.00	35.00	75.00
	1772L.C.R.	—	10.00	20.00	35.00	75.00
	1773L.C.R.	—	10.00	20.00	35.00	75.00
	1774L.C.R.	—	10.00	20.00	35.00	75.00
	1775L.C.R.	—	10.00	20.00	35.00	75.00
	1776L.C.R.	—	10.00	20.00	35.00	75.00
	1777L.C.R.	—	10.00	20.00	35.00	75.00
	1778L.C.R.	—	10.00	20.00	35.00	75.00
	1779.C.	—	10.00	20.00	35.00	75.00
	1780C.E.S.	—	10.00	20.00	35.00	75.00
	1781C.E.S.	—	10.00	20.00	35.00	75.00
	1782C.E.S.	—	10.00	20.00	35.00	75.00
	1783C.E.S.	—	10.00	20.00	35.00	75.00
	1784C.E.S.	—	10.00	20.00	35.00	75.00

C#	Date	Mintage	Fine	VF	XF	Unc
145a	1785C.E.S.	—	10.00	20.00	35.00	75.00
	1786.C.	—	10.00	20.00	35.00	75.00
	1787.C.	—	10.00	20.00	35.00	75.00
	1788.C.	—	10.00	20.00	35.00	75.00
	1789.C.	—	10.00	20.00	35.00	75.00

Obv: Arms. Rev: Horse.

C#	Date	Mintage	Fine	VF	XF	Unc
146	1767.C.	—	25.00	50.00	75.00	75.00

C#	Date	Mintage	Fine	VF	XF	Unc
147	1774I.W.S.	—	12.00	25.00	35.00	75.00
	1777I.W.S.	—	14.00	27.50	45.00	75.00

C#	Date	Mintage	Fine	VF	XF	Unc
147a	1778I.W.S.	—	12.00	25.00	40.00	75.00

C#	Date	Mintage	Fine	VF	XF	Unc
147a	1779I.W.S.	—	12.00	25.00	40.00	75.00

C#	Date	Mintage	Fine	VF	XF	Unc
147b	1785I.W.S.	—	12.00	25.00	40.00	75.00
	1786I.W.S.	—	12.00	25.00	40.00	75.00
	1787I.W.S.	—	12.00	25.00	40.00	75.00
	1788I.W.S.	—	15.00	30.00	50.00	75.00

C#	Date	Mintage	Fine	VF	XF	Unc
147c	1789 I.W.S.	—	12.00	25.00	40.00	75.00
	1790 .C.	—	12.00	25.00	40.00	75.00
	1791 .C.	—	12.00	25.00	40.00	75.00
	1793 P.L.M	—	12.00	25.00	40.00	75.00
	1794 P.L.M	—	12.00	25.00	40.00	75.00
	1795 P.L.M	—	12.00	25.00	40.00	75.00
	1796 P.L.M	—	12.00	25.00	40.00	75.00
	1797 P.L.M	—	12.00	25.00	40.00	75.00
	1798 P.L.M	—	12.00	25.00	40.00	75.00
	1799 P.L.M	—	12.00	25.00	40.00	75.00
	1800 P.L.M	—	12.00	25.00	40.00	75.00
	1800 .C.	—	12.00	25.00	40.00	75.00

C#	Date	Mintage	Fine	VF	XF	Unc
147d	1803G.F.M.	—	12.00	25.00	40.00	75.00
	1804G.F.M.	—	12.00	25.00	40.00	75.00

C#	Date	Mintage	Fine	VF	XF	Unc
143a	1804G.F.M.	—	12.00	25.00	40.00	75.00

1/2 THALER

(Cassen)

SILVER

Obv: Similar to C#150a.

Rev. value: CASSEN GELD

C#	Date	Mintage	Fine	VF	XF	Unc
150	1801 C	372 pcs.	150.00	350.00	450.00	600.00

Rev. value: CASSEN GELD

C#	Date	Mintage	Fine	VF	XF	Unc
150a	1801 C	—	150.00	350.00	450.00	600.00

2/3 THALER

SILVER

Obv: Head. Rev: Supported arms.

C#	Date	Mintage	Fine	VF	XF	Unc
156	1776I.W.S.	—	40.00	80.00	120.00	160.00
	1778I.W.S.	—	40.00	80.00	120.00	160.00
	1781I.W.S.	—	40.00	80.00	120.00	160.00

Obv: Head. Rev: Arms with no supports

C#	Date	Mintage	Fine	VF	XF	Unc
158	1772 I.W.S.	—	25.00	50.00	80.00	110.00
	1773 I.W.S.	—	25.00	50.00	80.00	110.00
	1774 I.W.S.	—	25.00	50.00	80.00	110.00
	1775 I.W.S.	—	25.00	50.00	80.00	110.00
	1776 I.W.S	—	25.00	55.00	80.00	125.00
	1777 I.W.S	—	25.00	55.00	80.00	125.00
	1779 I.W.S	—	25.00	50.00	80.00	110.00
	1780 I.W.S	—	25.00	55.00	80.00	125.00
	1781 I.W.S	—	25.00	50.00	80.00	110.00
	1782 I.W.S	—	25.00	50.00	80.00	110.00
	1783 I.W.S	—	25.00	50.00	80.00	110.00
	1784 I.W.S	—	25.00	55.00	80.00	125.00
	1785 I.W.S	—	25.00	55.00	80.00	125.00
	1786 I.W.S	—	25.00	50.00	80.00	110.00
	1787 I.W.S	—	25.00	55.00	80.00	125.00
	1788 I.W.S	—	25.00	50.00	80.00	110.00
	1789 I.W.S	—	25.00	50.00	80.00	110.00
	1790 .C.	—	25.00	50.00	80.00	110.00
	1791/0	—	—	—	—	—
	1791 .C.	—	25.00	50.00	80.00	110.00
	1792 P.L.M	—	25.00	50.00	80.00	110.00
	1793P.L.M.	—	25.00	50.00	80.00	110.00
	1794P.L.M.	—	25.00	50.00	80.00	110.00
	1795P.L.M.	—	25.00	50.00	80.00	110.00
	1796P.L.M.	—	25.00	50.00	80.00	110.00
	1797P.L.M.	—	25.00	50.00	80.00	110.00
	1798P.L.M.	—	25.00	50.00	80.00	110.00
	1799P.L.M.	—	25.00	50.00	80.00	110.00
	1800P.L.M.	—	25.00	50.00	80.00	110.00
	1800.C.	—	25.00	50.00	80.00	110.00

Rev: 2/3 value

C#	Date	Mintage	Fine	VF	XF	Unc
160	1801.C.	—	22.00	45.00	65.00	100.00
	1802.C.	—	22.00	45.00	65.00	100.00

C#	Date	Mintage	Fine	VF	XF	Unc
162	1801 .C.	—	17.00	35.00	55.00	90.00
	1802	—	17.00	35.00	55.00	90.00
	1802 .C.	—	17.00	35.00	55.00	90.00
	1802 G.F.M	—	17.00	35.00	55.00	90.00
	1803G.F.M	—	17.00	35.00	55.00	90.00
	1804G.F.M	—	17.00	35.00	55.00	90.00
	1805G.F.M.	—	17.00	35.00	55.00	90.00

Obv: Round arms

C#	Date	Mintage	Fine	VF	XF	Unc
162a	1805 G.F.M	—	17.00	35.00	70.00	100.00
	1806G.F.M.	—	17.00	35.00	70.00	100.00
	1807G.F.M.	—	17.00	35.00	70.00	100.00

THALER

SILVER

C#	Date	Mintage	Fine	VF	XF	Unc
164	1761I.W.S.	—	40.00	75.00	140.00	250.00
	1762I.W.S.	—	40.00	75.00	140.00	250.00
	1763I.W.S.	—	50.00	100.00	150.00	250.00
	1764I.W.S.	—	40.00	75.00	140.00	250.00
	1765I.W.S.	—	40.00	75.00	140.00	250.00
	1766I.W.S.	—	40.00	75.00	140.00	250.00
	1767I.W.S.	—	40.00	75.00	140.00	250.00
	1768I.W.S.	—	40.00	75.00	140.00	250.00
	1769I.W.S.	—	40.00	75.00	140.00	250.00
	1770I.W.S.	—	40.00	75.00	140.00	250.00
	1771I.W.S.	—	40.00	75.00	140.00	250.00
	1772I.W.S.	—	40.00	75.00	140.00	250.00
	1773I.W.S.	—	40.00	75.00	140.00	250.00

Obv: Crowned shield. Rev: LAUTENTHAL MINE.

C#	Date	Mintage	Fine	VF	XF	Unc
165	1763I.A.P.	—	150.00	300.00	500.00	800.00

Rev: Wildman and tree

C#	Date	Mintage	Fine	VF	XF	Unc
166	1763I.A.P.	—	75.00	150.00	200.00	300.00
	1764I.A.P.	—	75.00	150.00	200.00	300.00
	1765I.A.P.	—	75.00	150.00	200.00	300.00
	1770I.A.P.	—	75.00	150.00	200.00	300.00
	1774L.C.R.	—	75.00	150.00	200.00	300.00
	1775L.C.R.	—	75.00	150.00	200.00	300.00
	1776L.C.R.	—	75.00	150.00	200.00	300.00
	1784C.E.S.	—	75.00	150.00	200.00	300.00

Rev: SEGEN GOTTS MINE

C#	Date	Mintage	Fine	VF	XF	Unc
167	1765I.A.P.	—	200.00	400.00	600.00	900.00

Obv: Bust. Rev: Crowned shield.

C#	Date	Mintage	Fine	VF	XF	Unc
168	1773I.W.S.	—	75.00	150.00	200.00	300.00
	1774I.W.S.	—	75.00	150.00	200.00	300.00
	1776I.W.S.	—	75.00	150.00	200.00	300.00
	1779I.W.S.	—	75.00	150.00	200.00	300.00
	1780I.W.S.	—	75.00	150.00	200.00	300.00
	1782I.W.S.	—	75.00	150.00	200.00	300.00
	1784I.W.S.	—	75.00	150.00	200.00	300.00
	1786I.W.S.	—	75.00	150.00	200.00	300.00
	1791.C.	—	75.00	150.00	200.00	300.00
	1792P.L.M.	—	75.00	150.00	200.00	300.00
	1794P.L.M.	—	75.00	150.00	200.00	300.00
	1797P.L.M.	—	125.00	250.00	400.00	550.00

Obv: Supported arms. Rev: GUTE DES HERRN MINE.

C#	Date	Mintage	Fine	VF	XF	Unc
169	1774L.C.R.	—	200.00	400.00	600.00	1000.

C#	Date	Mintage	Fine	VF	XF	Unc
170	1777I.W.S.	—	75.00	150.00	200.00	300.00
	1778I.W.S.	—	75.00	150.00	200.00	300.00

(Cassengeld)

C#	Date	Mintage	Fine	VF	XF	Unc
171	1801C	126 pcs.	375.00	750.00	1150.	2000.

5 THALER

6.6500 gm., .900 GOLD, .1924 oz AGW
Obv: Bust. Rev: Arms.

C#	Date	Mintage	Fine	VF	XF	Unc
173	1768.C.	—	400.00	800.00	1200.	1700.
173a	1783	—	400.00	800.00	1200.	1700.

TRADE COINS

DUCAT

3.5000 gm., .986 GOLD, .1109 oz AGW

C#	Date	Mintage	Fine	VF	XF	Unc
172	1767I.A.P.	—	400.00	800.00	1000.	1500.
	1774L.C.R.	—	400.00	800.00	1000.	1500.
	1776L.C.R.	—	400.00	800.00	1000.	1500.
	1780C.E.S.	—	400.00	800.00	1000.	1500.

C#	Date	Mintage	Fine	VF	XF	Unc
172	1783C.E.S.	—	400.00	800.00	1000.	1500.
	1785C.E.S.	—	400.00	800.00	1000.	1500.
	1789.C.	—	400.00	800.00	1000.	1500.

C#	Date	Mintage	Fine	VF	XF	Unc
172a	1791.C.	—	400.00	800.00	1000.	1500.
	1793P.L.M.	—	400.00	800.00	1000.	1500.
	1795P.L.M.	—	400.00	800.00	1000.	1500.
	1796P.L.M.	—	400.00	800.00	1000.	1500.
	1797P.L.M.	—	400.00	800.00	1000.	1500.
	1798P.L.M.	—	400.00	800.00	1000.	1500.
	1799P.L.M.	—	400.00	800.00	1000.	1500.
	1800P.L.M.	—	400.00	800.00	1000.	1500.

Obv: Square arms

C#	Date	Mintage	Fine	VF	XF	Unc
172b	1802.C.	—	400.00	800.00	1000.	1500.
	1802G.F.M.	—	400.00	800.00	1000.	1500.
	1804G.F.M	—	400.00	800.00	1000.	1500.

PISTOLE

6.6500 gm., .900 GOLD, .1924 oz AGW

C#	Date	Mintage	Fine	VF	XF	Unc
174	1803 C	—	400.00	800.00	1000.	1400.

BRUNSWICK — WOLFENBUTTEL

Located in north-central Germany. Wolfenbuttel was annexed to Brunswick in 1257. The Wolfenbuttel line of the Brunswick house was founded in 1318 and was a fairly constant line until 1884 when Prussia began a government that lasted until 1913. Brunswick was given to the Kaiser's son-in-law in 1913 and he was forced to abdicate in 1918.

RULERS

Carl I, 1735-1780
Carl Wilhelm Ferdinand, 1780-1806
Friedrich Wilhelm, 1806-1815
Carl II (under regency of George III of Great Britain), 1815-1820
Carl II (under regency of George IV of Great Britain), 1820-1823
Carl II, 1823-1830
Wilhelm, 1831-1884
Prussian rule, 1884-1913
Ernst August, 1913-1918

MINTMASTER'S INITIALS

B - Johann W. Chr. Bramleu

PFENNIG

COPPER

C#	Date	Mintage	Fine	VF	XF	Unc
113	1780M.C.	—	2.00	4.00	8.00	30.00
	1781M.C.	—	2.00	4.00	8.00	30.00
	1782M.C.	—	2.00	4.00	8.00	30.00
	1783M.C.	—	2.00	4.00	8.00	30.00
	1784M.C.	—	2.00	4.00	8.00	30.00
	1785M.C.	—	2.00	4.00	8.00	30.00

C#	Date	Mintage	Fine	VF	XF	Unc
113	1786M.C.	—	2.00	4.00	8.00	30.00
	1787M.C.	—	2.00	4.00	8.00	30.00
	1788M.C.	—	2.00	4.00	8.00	30.00
	1789M.C.	—	2.00	4.00	8.00	30.00
	1790M.C.	—	2.00	4.00	8.00	30.00
	1791M.C.	—	2.00	4.00	8.00	30.00
	1792M.C.	—	2.00	4.00	8.00	30.00
	1793M.C.	—	2.00	4.00	8.00	30.00
	1794M.C.	—	2.00	4.00	8.00	30.00
	1795M.C.	—	2.00	4.00	8.00	30.00
	1796M.C.	—	2.00	4.00	8.00	30.00
	1797M.C.	—	2.00	4.00	8.00	30.00
	1798M.C.	—	2.00	4.00	8.00	30.00
	1799M.C.	—	2.00	4.00	8.00	30.00
	1800M.C.	—	2.00	4.00	8.00	30.00
	1801M.C.	—	2.00	4.00	8.00	30.00
	1802M.C.	—	2.00	4.00	8.00	30.00
	1803M.C.	—	2.00	4.00	8.00	30.00
	1804M.C.	—	2.00	4.00	8.00	30.00
	1805M.C.	—	2.00	4.00	8.00	30.00
	1806M.C.	—	2.00	4.00	8.00	30.00

Obv: Wildman. Rev: Value.

C#	Date	Mintage	Fine	VF	XF	Unc
114	1780C.E.S.	—	2.00	4.00	8.00	30.00
	1781C.E.S.	—	2.00	4.00	8.00	30.00
	1783C.E.S.	—	2.00	4.00	8.00	30.00
	1784C.E.S.	—	2.00	4.00	8.00	30.00
	1785C.E.S.	—	2.00	4.00	8.00	30.00
	1788.C.S.	—	2.00	4.00	8.00	30.00

Obv: M.C. below horse.

C#	Date	Mintage	Fine	VF	XF	Unc
164.1	1813 M.C.	—	2.00	4.00	8.00	30.00
	1814 M.C.	—	2.00	4.00	8.00	30.00

Obv: F.R. below horse.

C#	Date	Mintage	Fine	VF	XF	Unc
164.2	1814 F.R.	—	2.00	4.00	8.00	30.00
	1815	—	2.00	4.00	8.00	30.00

Obv. leg: FRIEDRICH WILHELM.....

C#	Date	Mintage	Fine	VF	XF	Unc
164a	1818	—	2.00	4.00	8.00	30.00

Obv: F.R. below horse, GEORG P.R.T.N.

C#	Date	Mintage	Fine	VF	XF	Unc
175	1816 F.R.	—	2.00	4.00	8.00	30.00
	1818 F.R.	—	2.00	4.00	8.00	30.00

C#	Date	Mintage	Fine	VF	XF	Unc
175a	1816 F.R.	—	2.00	4.00	8.00	30.00
	1817 F.R.	—	2.00	4.00	8.00	30.00
	1818 F.R.	—	2.00	4.00	8.00	30.00
	1819 F.R.	—	2.00	4.00	8.00	30.00
	1820 F.R.	—	2.00	4.00	8.00	30.00

Obv. legend: GEORG D.G.

C#	Date	Mintage	Fine	VF	XF	Unc
175b	1818 F.R.	—	2.00	4.00	8.00	30.00

Obv. legend: GEORG T.N. begins at lower left.

C#	Date	Mintage	Fine	VF	XF	Unc
175c	1818 F.R.	—	2.00	4.00	8.00	30.00
	1819 F.R.	—	2.00	4.00	8.00	30.00

Legend begins at upper left.

C#	Date	Mintage	Fine	VF	XF	Unc
175d	1818 F.R.	—	2.00	4.00	8.00	30.00
	1819 F.R.	—	2.00	4.00	8.00	30.00
	1820 F.R.	—	2.00	4.00	8.00	30.00

Obv: No F.R., leg: GEORG IV. T.N....
Rev: 'M.C.' below date.

C#	Date	Mintage	Fine	VF	XF	Unc
184	1819 M.C.	—	2.00	4.00	8.00	30.00
	1820 M.C.	—	2.00	4.00	8.00	30.00

Obv. legend: GEORGE IV D.G.R.T.N.....

C#	Date	Mintage	Fine	VF	XF	Unc
184a	1820 M.C.	—	2.00	4.00	8.00	30.00
	1822 M.C.	—	2.00	4.00	8.00	30.00
	1823 M.C.	—	2.00	4.00	8.00	30.00

Obv. legend ends: BR. U.LUEN., Rev: Value.

C#	Date	Mintage	Fine	VF	XF	Unc
194	1822 CvC	—	1.50	4.00	8.00	30.00
	1823 CvC	—	1.50	4.00	8.00	30.00
	1824 CvC	—	1.50	4.00	8.00	30.00
	1825 CvC	—	1.50	4.00	8.00	30.00
	1826 CvC	—	1.50	4.00	8.00	30.00
	1828 CvC	—	1.50	4.00	8.00	30.00
	1829/8 CvC	—	1.50	4.00	8.00	30.00
	1829 CvC	—	1.50	4.00	8.00	30.00
	1830 CvC	—	1.50	4.00	8.00	30.00

Obv. legend ends: BRAUNSCHW. UL.

C#	Date	Mintage	Fine	VF	XF	Unc
194a	1824 Cvc	—	2.00	4.00	8.00	30.00

Obv. legend ends: BR. U. LUEN. Rev. value: PFENNING

C#	Date	Mintage	Fine	VF	XF	Unc
206	1831 CvC	—	1.00	3.00	6.00	30.00
	1832 CvC	—	1.00	3.00	6.00	30.00
	1833 CvC	—	1.00	3.00	6.00	30.00
	1834 CvC	—	1.00	3.00	6.00	30.00

Rev. value: PFENNIG

C#	Date	Mintage	Fine	VF	XF	Unc
206a	1834 Cvc	—	2.00	4.00	8.00	25.00

C#	Date	Mintage	Fine	VF	XF	Unc
207	1851 B	—	1.00	3.00	6.00	30.00
	1852 B	.270	1.00	3.00	6.00	30.00
	1853 B	.139	1.00	3.00	6.00	30.00
	1855 B	.079	1.00	3.00	6.00	30.00
	1856 B	.514	1.00	3.00	6.00	30.00

Rev: No B under date.

C#	Date	Mintage	Fine	VF	XF	Unc
207a	1854	.126	1.50	3.50	8.00	30.00
	1856	Inc.Ab.	1.50	3.50	8.00	30.00

Obv. legend: HERZOGTH.BRAUNSCHWEIG.

C#	Date	Mintage	Fine	VF	XF	Unc
208	1859	.103	.75	1.50	5.00	25.00
	1860	.307	.75	1.50	5.00	25.00

2 PFENNIGE

COPPER

C#	Date	Mintage	Fine	VF	XF	Unc
165.1	1814 F.R.	—	1.00	3.00	8.00	30.00
	1815 F.R.	—	1.00	3.00	8.00	30.00

Obv: No F.R. below monogram.

C#	Date	Mintage	Fine	VF	XF	Unc
165.2	1815	—	1.00	3.00	8.00	30.00

Rev: M.C. below date.

C#	Date	Mintage	Fine	VF	XF	Unc
185.1	1820 M.C.	—	1.00	3.00	8.00	30.00

Rev: C.V.C. below date

C#	Date	Mintage	Fine	VF	XF	Unc
185.2	1823 Cvc	—	1.00	3.00	8.00	30.00

C#	Date	Mintage	Fine	VF	XF	Unc
195	1824 Cvc	—	1.00	3.00	8.00	30.00
	1826 Cvc	—	1.00	3.00	8.00	30.00
	1827 Cvc	—	1.00	3.00	8.00	30.00
	1828 Cvc	—	1.00	3.00	8.00	30.00
	1829 Cvc	—	1.00	3.00	8.00	30.00
	1830 Cvc	—	1.00	3.00	8.00	30.00

Obv. legend ends: BRAUNSCHW.U.L.

C#	Date	Mintage	Fine	VF	XF	Unc
209	1832 Cvc	—	1.00	3.00	8.00	30.00
	1833 Cvc	—	1.00	3.00	8.00	30.00
	1834 Cvc	—	1.00	3.00	8.00	30.00

DEN: PFENNIG

C#	Date	Mintage	Fine	VF	XF	Unc
209a	1834 CvC	—	2.50	5.00	10.00	35.00

C#	Date	Mintage	Fine	VF	XF	Unc
210	1851 B	—	.75	2.00	5.00	25.00
	1852 B	.135	.75	2.00	5.00	25.00
	1853 B	.124	.75	2.00	5.00	25.00
	1854 B	.063	.75	2.00	5.00	25.00
	1855 B	.189	.75	2.00	5.00	25.00
	1855	—	—	—	—	—
	1856 B	.253	.75	2.00	5.00	25.00

C#	Date	Mintage	Fine	VF	XF	Unc
211	1859	.062	.75	2.00	5.00	25.00
	1860	.147	.75	2.00	5.00	25.00

2-1/2 PFENNIGE

COPPER
Obv: Prancing horse. Rev: Value.

C#	Date	Mintage	Fine	VF	XF	Unc
115	1792M.C.	—	3.00	7.50	15.00	35.00

4 PFENNIGE

BILLON
Obv: Horse. Rev: Value

C#	Date	Mintage	Fine	VF	XF	Unc
117	1780M.C.	—	3.00	7.00	15.00	40.00
	1787M.C.	—	3.00	6.00	15.00	40.00
	1788M.C.	—	3.00	6.00	15.00	40.00
	1790M.C.	—	3.00	6.00	15.00	40.00
	1792M.C.	—	3.00	5.00	15.00	40.00
	1793M.C.	—	3.00	5.00	15.00	40.00
	1795M.C.	—	3.00	6.00	15.00	40.00
	1796M.C.	—	3.00	6.00	15.00	40.00
	1797M.C.	—	3.00	9.00	20.00	50.00
	1798M.C.	—	3.00	6.00	15.00	40.00
	1799M.C.	—	3.00	6.00	15.00	40.00
	1800M.C.	—	3.00	5.00	15.00	40.00
	1801M.C.	—	3.00	5.00	15.00	40.00
	1802M.C.	—	3.00	5.00	15.00	40.00
	1803M.C.	—	3.00	5.00	15.00	40.00
	1804M.C.	—	3.00	5.00	15.00	40.00

Obv: Prancing horse left, 'F.R.' below, legend ends: BRIETL. Rev: Value.

C#	Date	Mintage	Fine	VF	XF	Unc
176	1820 F.R.	.035	4.00	9.00	20.00	60.00

Obv: No F.R. Rev: C.V.C. below date.

C#	Date	Mintage	Fine	VF	XF	Unc
186	1823 CvC	.063	3.00	5.00	20.00	50.00

6 PFENNIGE

BILLON
Obv: Horse. Rev: Value

C#	Date	Mintage	Fine	VF	XF	Unc
119	1784M.C.	—	3.00	6.00	15.00	50.00
119	1787M.C.	—	3.00	6.00	15.00	50.00
	1788M.C.	—	3.00	6.00	15.00	50.00
	1791M.C.	—	3.00	6.00	15.00	50.00
	1793M.C.	—	3.00	6.00	15.00	50.00
	1800M.C.	—	3.00	6.00	15.00	50.00
	1802M.C.	—	3.00	6.00	15.00	50.00
	1804M.C.	—	3.00	6.00	15.00	50.00

Obv: M.C. below horse.

C#	Date	Mintage	Fine	VF	XF	Unc
166	1814 M.C.	—	3.00	6.00	15.00	50.00

Obv: B. instead of BR in legend.

C#	Date	Mintage	Fine	VF	XF	Unc
166a.1	1814 M.C.	—	3.00	6.00	15.00	50.00

Obv: F.R. below mound.

C#	Date	Mintage	Fine	VF	XF	Unc
166a.2	1814 F.R.	—	3.00	6.00	15.00	50.00
	1815 F.R.	.133	3.00	6.00	15.00	50.00

Obv. legend: GEORG T.N. CAROLI D. BR

C#	Date	Mintage	Fine	VF	XF	Unc
177	1816 F.R.	.036	3.00	6.00	15.00	50.00
	1819 F.R.	.030	3.00	6.00	15.00	50.00

Obv. legend: GEORG IV. Rev: C.V.C. below date.

C#	Date	Mintage	Fine	VF	XF	Unc
187	1823 CvC	.060	3.00	5.00	15.00	50.00

Obv. legend ends: BR U L

C#	Date	Mintage	Fine	VF	XF	Unc
196	1828 CvC	—	3.00	5.00	15.00	50.00

1/2 GROSCHEN

(= 1/16 Thaler)

(Vereins)

BILLON

C#	Date	Mintage	Fine	VF	XF	Unc
212	1858	.576	1.00	2.00	10.00	40.00
	1859	.131	1.00	2.00	10.00	40.00
	1860	.313	1.00	2.00	10.00	40.00

MARIEN GROSCHEN

BILLON

C#	Date	Mintage	Fine	VF	XF	Unc
121	1788M.C.	—	3.00	6.00	10.00	40.00
	1789M.C.	—	3.00	6.00	10.00	40.00
	1790M.C.	—	3.00	6.00	10.00	40.00
	1791M.C.	—	3.00	6.00	10.00	40.00
	1792M.C.	—	3.00	6.00	10.00	40.00
	1793M.C.	—	3.00	6.00	10.00	40.00
	1799M.C.	—	3.00	6.00	10.00	40.00
	1800M.C.	—	3.00	6.00	10.00	40.00
	1802M.C.	—	3.00	6.00	10.00	40.00
	1803M.C.	—	3.00	6.00	10.00	40.00
	1804M.C.	—	3.00	6.00	10.00	40.00
	1805M.C.	—	3.00	6.00	10.00	40.00
	1806M.C.	—	3.00	6.00	10.00	40.00

GROSCHEN

(= 1/30 Thaler)

(Vereins)

BILLON

C#	Date	Mintage	Fine	VF	XF	Unc
213	1857	.039	1.00	2.50	6.00	30.00
	1858	.713	.75	2.50	6.00	30.00
	1859	.594	.75	2.50	6.00	30.00
	1860	.095	1.00	2.50	6.00	30.00

2 MARIEN GROSCHEN

SILVER

Obv: Crowned monogram. Rev: Horse.

C#	Date	Mintage	Fine	VF	XF	Unc
125	1781C.E.S.	—	5.00	9.00	15.00	50.00
	1783C.E.S.	—	5.00	9.00	15.00	50.00
	1784C.E.S.	—	5.00	9.00	15.00	50.00
	1787.C.	—	5.00	9.00	15.00	50.00

Obv: Value. Rev: Wildman.

C#	Date	Mintage	Fine	VF	XF	Unc
129	1781C.E.S.	—	5.00	9.00	15.00	50.00
	1782C.E.S.	—	5.00	9.00	15.00	50.00
	1783C.E.S.	—	5.00	9.00	15.00	50.00
	1784C.E.S.	—	5.00	9.00	15.00	50.00
	1786.C.	—	5.00	9.00	15.00	50.00
	1789.C.	—	5.00	9.00	15.00	50.00

BILLON

C#	Date	Mintage	Fine	VF	XF	Unc
127	1804M.C.	—	5.00	9.00	20.00	60.00

4 MARIEN GROSCHEN

SILVER

Obv: Crowned monogram. Rev: Horse.

C#	Date	Mintage	Fine	VF	XF	Unc
133	1781C.E.S.	—	5.00	10.00	20.00	60.00
	1782C.E.S.	—	5.00	10.00	20.00	60.00
	1783C.E.S.	—	5.00	10.00	20.00	60.00
	1784C.E.S.	—	5.00	10.00	20.00	60.00

Obv: Value, date in circular legend. Rev: Wildman.

C#	Date	Mintage	Fine	VF	XF	Unc
137	1781C.E.S.	—	5.00	10.00	20.00	60.00
	1782C.E.S.	—	5.00	10.00	20.00	60.00
	1783C.E.S.	—	5.00	10.00	20.00	60.00
	1784C.E.S.	—	5.00	10.00	20.00	60.00
	1785C.E.S.	—	5.00	10.00	20.00	60.00
	1786.C.	—	5.00	10.00	20.00	60.00

Obv: Date in center legend.

C#	Date	Mintage	Fine	VF	XF	Unc
137a	1787.C.	—	5.00	10.00	20.00	60.00
	1788.C.	—	5.00	10.00	20.00	60.00
	1789.C.	—	5.00	10.00	20.00	60.00

6 MARIEN GROSCHEN

SILVER

Obv: Value, mintmark. Rev: Wildman.

C#	Date	Mintage	Fine	VF	XF	Unc
141.1	1781C.E.S.	—	7.00	15.00	25.00	75.00
	1782C.E.S.	—	7.00	15.00	25.00	75.00
	1783C.E.S.	—	7.00	15.00	25.00	75.00
	1784C.E.S.	—	7.00	15.00	25.00	75.00

Rev: Wildman, mintmark.

C#	Date	Mintage	Fine	VF	XF	Unc
141.2	1785C.E.S.	—	7.00	15.00	25.00	75.00
	1785.C.	—	7.00	15.00	25.00	75.00
	1786.C.	—	7.00	15.00	25.00	75.00
	1787.C.	—	7.00	15.00	25.00	75.00
	1788.C.	—	7.00	15.00	25.00	75.00

8 GUTE GROSCHEN

SILVER

Obv: Arms. Rev: Value.

C#	Date	Mintage	Fine	VF	XF	Unc
145	1783M.C.	—	7.00	14.00	20.00	60.00
	1784M.C.	—	7.00	14.00	20.00	60.00

Obv: Revised arms

C#	Date	Mintage	Fine	VF	XF	Unc
145a	1786M.C.	—	7.00	14.00	20.00	60.00
	1787M.C.	—	7.00	14.00	20.00	60.00
	1788M.C.	—	7.00	14.00	20.00	60.00
	1791M.C.	—	7.00	14.00	20.00	60.00
145a	1793M.C.	—	7.00	14.00	20.00	60.00
	1794M.C.	—	7.00	14.00	20.00	60.00
	1796M.C.	—	7.00	14.00	20.00	60.00
	1797M.C.	—	7.00	14.00	20.00	60.00
	1798M.C.	—	7.00	14.00	20.00	60.00
	1799M.C.	—	7.00	14.00	20.00	60.00
	1801M.C.	—	7.00	14.00	20.00	60.00
	1803M.C.	—	7.00	14.00	20.00	60.00
	1804M.C.	—	7.00	14.00	20.00	60.00
	1805M.C.	—	7.00	14.00	20.00	60.00

12 MARIEN GROSCHEN

SILVER

Obv: Value, date in circular legend. Rev: Wildman.

C#	Date	Mintage	Fine	VF	XF	Unc
143	1781C.E.S.	—	10.00	20.00	35.00	75.00
	1782C.E.S.	—	10.00	20.00	35.00	75.00
	1783C.E.S.	—	10.00	20.00	35.00	75.00
	1784C.E.S.	—	10.00	20.00	35.00	75.00
	1785C.E.S.	—	10.00	20.00	35.00	75.00

Obv: Date and mintmark in center inscription.

C#	Date	Mintage	Fine	VF	XF	Unc
143a	1786.C.	—	10.00	20.00	35.00	75.00

Rev: Mintmark in exerque.

C#	Date	Mintage	Fine	VF	XF	Unc
143b	1787.C.	—	10.00	20.00	35.00	75.00
	1788.C.	—	10.00	20.00	35.00	75.00
	1789.C.	—	10.00	20.00	35.00	75.00

16 GUTE GROSCHEN

SILVER

Obv: Arms. Rev: Value.

C#	Date	Mintage	Fine	VF	XF	Unc
149	1780M.C.	—	15.00	30.00	45.00	75.00
	1781M.C.	—	20.00	40.00	55.00	75.00
	1782M.C.	—	15.00	30.00	45.00	75.00
	1783M.C.	—	15.00	30.00	45.00	75.00
	1784M.C.	—	15.00	30.00	45.00	75.00

Obv: Changed arms.

C#	Date	Mintage	Fine	VF	XF	Unc
149a	1784M.C.	—	12.00	25.00	40.00	75.00
	1785M.C.	—	12.00	25.00	40.00	75.00
	1786M.C.	—	12.00	25.00	40.00	75.00
	1787M.C.	—	12.00	25.00	40.00	75.00
	1788M.C.	—	12.00	25.00	40.00	75.00
	1789M.C.	—	12.00	25.00	40.00	75.00
	1790M.C.	—	12.00	25.00	40.00	75.00
	1791M.C.	—	12.00	25.00	40.00	75.00
	1792M.C.	—	12.00	25.00	40.00	75.00
	1793M.C.	—	12.00	25.00	40.00	75.00
	1794M.C.	—	12.00	25.00	40.00	75.00
	1795M.C.	—	12.00	25.00	40.00	75.00
	1796M.C.	—	12.00	25.00	40.00	75.00
	1797M.C.	—	12.00	25.00	40.00	75.00
	1798M.C.	—	12.00	25.00	40.00	75.00
	1799M.C.	—	12.00	25.00	40.00	75.00
	1801M.C.	—	12.00	25.00	40.00	75.00
	1802M.C.	—	12.00	25.00	40.00	75.00
	1803M.C.	—	12.00	25.00	40.00	75.00
	1804M.C.	—	12.00	25.00	40.00	75.00
	1805M.C.	—	12.00	25.00	40.00	75.00

24 MARIEN GROSCHEN

(= 2/3 Thaler)

SILVER

Obv: Baroque arms. Rev: Wildman.

C#	Date	Mintage	Fine	VF	XF	Unc
151	1781 C.E.S.	—	25.00	50.00	70.00	125.00
	1782 C.E.S.	—	25.00	50.00	70.00	125.00
	1783 C.E.S.	—	25.00	50.00	70.00	125.00

Obv: Plain arms

C#	Date	Mintage	Fine	VF	XF	Unc
151a	1784 C.E.S.	—	25.00	50.00	70.00	125.00
	1786 .C.	—	25.00	50.00	70.00	125.00

Obv: Value, date in circular legend.

C#	Date	Mintage	Fine	VF	XF	Unc
147	1781 C.E.S.	—	20.00	45.00	65.00	125.00
	1782 C.E.S.	—	20.00	45.00	65.00	125.00
	1783 C.E.S.	—	20.00	45.00	65.00	125.00
	1784 C.E.S.	—	20.00	45.00	65.00	125.00

Obv: Date in center legend.

C#	Date	Mintage	Fine	VF	XF	Unc
147a	1784 C.E.S.	—	15.00	30.00	50.00	125.00
	1785 C.E.S.	—	15.00	30.00	50.00	125.00
	1786 C.E.S.	—	15.00	30.00	50.00	125.00
	1786 .C.	—	15.00	30.00	50.00	125.00
	1787 .C.	—	15.00	30.00	50.00	125.00
	1788 .C.	—	15.00	30.00	50.00	125.00
	1789 .C.	—	15.00	30.00	50.00	125.00

Obv: Value. Rev: Horse.

C#	Date	Mintage	Fine	VF	XF	Unc
152	1781 C.E.S.	—	25.00	50.00	100.00	150.00

Obv: Horse. Rev: Value XXIIII

C#	Date	Mintage	Fine	VF	XF	Unc
153	1789 M.C.	—	15.00	30.00	50.00	125.00
	1790 M.C.	—	15.00	30.00	50.00	125.00
	1795 M.C.	—	15.00	30.00	50.00	125.00
	1796 M.C.	—	15.00	30.00	50.00	125.00
	1797 M.C.	—	15.00	30.00	50.00	125.00
	1798 M.C.	—	15.00	30.00	50.00	125.00
	1799 M.C.	—	15.00	30.00	50.00	125.00
	1800 M.C.	—	15.00	30.00	50.00	125.00

NOTE: Varieties exist.

Obv: Arms. Rev: Value 24.

C#	Date	Mintage	Fine	VF	XF	Unc
155	1789 M.C.	—	15.00	30.00	45.00	100.00
	1790 M.C.	—	15.00	30.00	45.00	100.00
	1791 M.C.	—	15.00	30.00	45.00	100.00
	1792 M.C.	—	15.00	30.00	45.00	100.00
	1793 M.C.	—	15.00	30.00	45.00	100.00
	1794 M.C.	—	—	30.00	45.00	100.00
	1795 M.C.	—	15.00	30.00	45.00	100.00
	1796 M.C.	—	15.00	30.00	45.00	100.00
	1797 M.C.	—	15.00	30.00	45.00	100.00
	1798 M.C.	—	15.00	30.00	45.00	100.00
	1799 M.C.	—	15.00	30.00	45.00	100.00
	1800 M.C.	—	15.00	30.00	45.00	100.00
	1801 M.C.	—	15.00	30.00	45.00	100.00
	1802 M.C.	—	15.00	30.00	45.00	100.00
	1803 M.C.	—	15.00	30.00	45.00	100.00
	1804 M.C.	—	15.00	30.00	45.00	100.00
	1805 M.C.	—	15.00	30.00	45.00	100.00
	1806 M.C.	—	15.00	30.00	45.00	100.00

13.0800 gm., .993 SILVER, .4176 oz ASW

Obv: Crowned arms with small garlands.

Rev: 24 between stars.

C#	Date	Mintage	Fine	VF	XF	Unc
170	1814 F.R.	—	15.00	30.00	45.00	100.00
	1815 F.R.	.036	15.00	30.00	45.00	100.00

C#	Date	Mintage	Fine	VF	XF	Unc
180	1815 F.R.	—	15.00	30.00	45.00	100.00
	1816 F.R.	.027	15.00	30.00	45.00	100.00
	1817 F.R.	.019	15.00	30.00	45.00	100.00
	1818 F.R.	.017	15.00	30.00	45.00	100.00

Obv. leg: REX BRITANNIAR.

C#	Date	Mintage	Fine	VF	XF	Unc
190	1820 M.C.	.024	15.00	30.00	45.00	100.00

Rev: C.V.C. below date

C#	Date	Mintage	Fine	VF	XF	Unc
	1821 CvC	.029	15.00	30.00	45.00	100.00

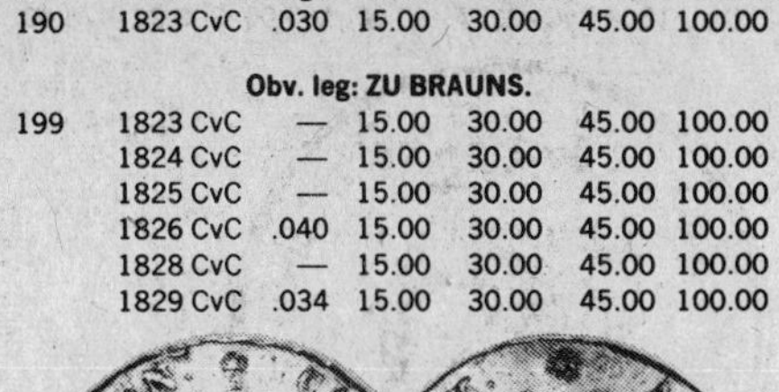

C#	Date	Mintage	Fine	VF	XF	Unc
190	1823 CvC	.030	15.00	30.00	45.00	100.00

Obv. leg: ZU BRAUNS.

C#	Date	Mintage	Fine	VF	XF	Unc
199	1823 CvC	—	15.00	30.00	45.00	100.00
	1824 CvC	—	15.00	30.00	45.00	100.00
	1825 CvC	—	15.00	30.00	45.00	100.00
	1826 CvC	.040	15.00	30.00	45.00	100.00
	1828 CvC	—	15.00	30.00	45.00	100.00
	1829 CvC	.034	15.00	30.00	45.00	100.00

Obv. leg: ZU BRAUNSCHW.

C#	Date	Mintage	Fine	VF	XF	Unc
199a	1824 CvC	.032	15.00	30.00	45.00	100.00
	1825 CvC	.032	15.00	30.00	45.00	100.00
	1826 CvC	—	15.00	30.00	45.00	100.00
	1828 CvC	—	15.00	30.00	45.00	100.00
	1829 CvC	—	15.00	30.00	45.00	100.00

C#	Date	Mintage	Fine	VF	XF	Unc
215	1832 CvC	.032	15.00	30.00	45.00	100.00
	1833 CvC	.027	15.00	30.00	45.00	100.00
	1834 CvC	.030	15.00	30.00	45.00	100.00

24 EINEN (1/24)THALER

BILLON

Obv: Horse. Rev: Value

C#	Date	Mintage	Fine	VF	XF	Unc
123	1780M.C.	—	3.00	6.00	15.00	50.00
	1781M.C.	—	3.00	6.00	15.00	50.00
	1786M.C.	—	3.00	6.00	15.00	50.00
	1787M.C.	—	3.00	6.00	15.00	50.00
	1788M.C.	—	3.00	6.00	15.00	50.00
	1790M.C.	—	3.00	6.00	15.00	50.00
	1797 M.C.	—	3.00	10.00	15.00	50.00
	1798M.C.	—	3.00	6.00	15.00	50.00
	1802M.C.	—	3.00	6.00	15.00	50.00

Rev: F.R. under date.

C#	Date	Mintage	Fine	VF	XF	Unc
167	1814 F.R.	—	3.00	6.00	15.00	50.00
	1815 F.R.	.066	3.00	6.00	15.00	50.00

Obv. leg: GEORG T.N.CAROLI D.BR:. Rev: Value.

C#	Date	Mintage	Fine	VF	XF	Unc
178	1819 F.R.	.058	4.00	8.00	15.00	50.00

Obv. leg: GEORG IV. Rev: Value, M.C. below date.

C#	Date	Mintage	Fine	VF	XF	Unc
188.1	1820 M.C.	—	3.00	6.00	15.00	50.00

Rev: C.V.C. below date

C#	Date	Mintage	Fine	VF	XF	Unc
188.2	1823 CvC	—	3.00	6.00	15.00	50.00

Obv. leg: BRAUNSCHW. U. LUEN.

C#	Date	Mintage	Fine	VF	XF	Unc
197	1825 C.V.C.	—	30.00	60.00	90.00	150.00

12 EINEN (1/12)THALER

BILLON

C#	Date	Mintage	Fine	VF	XF	Unc
131	1780M.C.	—	5.00	10.00	15.00	50.00
131	1781M.C.	—	5.00	10.00	15.00	50.00
	1782M.C.	—	5.00	10.00	15.00	50.00
	1783M.C.	—	5.00	10.00	15.00	50.00
	1784M.C.	—	5.00	10.00	15.00	50.00
	1787M.C.	—	5.00	10.00	15.00	50.00
	1788M.C.	—	5.00	10.00	15.00	50.00
	1789M.C.	—	5.00	10.00	15.00	50.00
	1790M.C.	—	5.00	10.00	15.00	50.00
	1791M.C.	—	5.00	10.00	15.00	50.00
	1792M.C.	—	5.00	10.00	15.00	50.00
	1793M.C.	—	5.00	10.00	15.00	50.00
	1794M.C.	—	5.00	10.00	15.00	50.00
	1795M.C.	—	5.00	10.00	15.00	50.00
	1796M.C.	—	5.00	10.00	15.00	50.00
	1797M.C.	—	5.00	10.00	15.00	50.00
	1798M.C.	—	5.00	10.00	15.00	50.00
	1799M.C.	—	5.00	10.00	15.00	50.00
	1800M.C.	—	5.00	10.00	15.00	50.00
	1801M.C.	—	5.00	10.00	15.00	50.00
	1802M.C.	—	5.00	10.00	15.00	50.00
	1803M.C.	—	5.00	10.00	15.00	50.00
	1804M.C.	—	5.00	10.00	15.00	50.00
	1805M.C.	—	5.00	10.00	15.00	50.00
	1806M.C.	—	5.00	10.00	15.00	50.00

Obv: Prancing horse left, M.C. below. Rev: Value.

C#	Date	Mintage	Fine	VF	XF	Unc
168	1814 M.C.	—	3.00	7.00	15.00	50.00
	1815 M.C.	—	3.00	7.00	15.00	50.00

Obv: F.R. below horse.

C#	Date	Mintage	Fine	VF	XF	Unc
168a	1815 F.R.	—	3.00	7.00	15.00	50.00

Obv: No initials below horse. Rev: F.R. below date.

C#	Date	Mintage	Fine	VF	XF	Unc
168c	1815 F.R.	—	3.00	7.00	15.00	50.00

Obv: F.R below horse. Rev: Nothing below date.

C#	Date	Mintage	Fine	VF	XF	Unc
168b	1815 F.R.	—	3.00	6.00	15.00	50.00

Obv. leg: GEORG D.

C#	Date	Mintage	Fine	VF	XF	Unc
179	1816 F.R.	—	5.00	10.00	20.00	50.00
	1817 F.R.	—	5.00	10.00	20.00	50.00
	1818 F.R.	—	5.00	10.00	20.00	50.00
	1819 F.R.	—	5.00	10.00	20.00	50.00

Obv. leg: GEORG IV.

C#	Date	Mintage	Fine	VF	XF	Unc
189.1	1820 M.C.	—	5.00	10.00	20.00	50.00

Rev: C.V.C. below date

C#	Date	Mintage	Fine	VF	XF	Unc
189.2	1821 CvC	—	5.00	10.00	20.00	50.00
	1822 CvC	—	5.00	10.00	20.00	50.00
	1823 CvC	—	5.00	10.00	20.00	50.00

Obv. leg: BRAUNSCHW. U. LUEN.

C#	Date	Mintage	Fine	VF	XF	Unc
198	1823 CvC	—	2.00	5.00	10.00	35.00
	1824 CvC	—	2.00	5.00	10.00	35.00
	1825 CvC	—	2.00	5.00	10.00	35.00
	1826 CvC	—	2.00	5.00	10.00	35.00
	1827 CvC	—	2.00	5.00	10.00	35.00
	1828 CvC	—	2.00	5.00	10.00	35.00
	1829 CvC	—	2.00	5.00	10.00	35.00
	1830 CvC	—	2.00	5.00	10.00	35.00

Obv. leg: BRAUNSCHW. U.L.

C#	Date	Mintage	Fine	VF	XF	Unc
198a	1823 CvC	—	2.00	5.00	10.00	35.00
	1824 CvC	—	2.00	5.00	10.00	35.00
	1825 CvC	—	2.00	5.00	10.00	35.00
	1826 CvC	—	2.00	5.00	10.00	35.00

Obv. leg: BRAUNS. U. LUEN.

C#	Date	Mintage	Fine	VF	XF	Unc
198b	1823 CvC	—	2.00	5.00	10.00	35.00
	1824 CvC	—	2.00	5.00	10.00	35.00
	1828 CvC	—	2.00	5.00	10.00	35.00
	1829 CvC	—	2.00	5.00	10.00	35.00

VI EINEN (1/6) THALER

SILVER

C#	Date	Mintage	Fine	VF	XF	Unc
139	1780M.C.	—	7.00	15.00	25.00	60.00
	1781M.C.	—	7.00	15.00	25.00	60.00
	1782M.C.	—	7.00	15.00	25.00	60.00
	1783M.C.	—	7.00	15.00	25.00	60.00
	1784M.C.	—	7.00	15.00	25.00	60.00
	1785M.C.	—	7.00	15.00	25.00	60.00
	1786M.C.	—	7.00	15.00	25.00	60.00
	1787M.C.	—	7.00	15.00	25.00	60.00
	1788M.C.	—	7.00	15.00	25.00	60.00
	1789M.C.	—	7.00	15.00	25.00	60.00
	1790M.C.	—	7.00	15.00	25.00	60.00
	1791M.C.	—	7.00	15.00	25.00	60.00
	1792M.C.	—	7.00	15.00	25.00	60.00
	1793M.C.	—	7.00	15.00	25.00	60.00
	1794M.C.	—	7.00	15.00	25.00	60.00
	1797M.C.	—	7.00	15.00	25.00	60.00
	1798M.C.	—	7.00	15.00	25.00	60.00
	1799M.C.	—	7.00	15.00	25.00	60.00
	1801M.C.	—	7.00	15.00	25.00	60.00
	1802M.C.	—	7.00	15.00	25.00	60.00
	1803M.C.	—	7.00	15.00	25.00	60.00
	1804M.C.	—	7.00	15.00	25.00	60.00

5.2000 gm., .563 SILVER, .0941 oz ASW

Obv: Prancing horse left, M.C. below. Rev: Value.

C#	Date	Mintage	Fine	VF	XF	Unc
169	1813 M.C.	—	15.00	30.00	60.00	125.00
169a	1814 M.C.	—	20.00	40.00	75.00	150.00

5.3500 gm., .521 FINE SILVER, .0896 oz ASW

Obv: Head right.

C#	Date	Mintage	Fine	VF	XF	Unc
214	1840 CvC	.060	7.00	15.00	30.00	60.00

THALER

(Species)

SILVER

C#	Date	Mintage	Fine	VF	XF	Unc
157	1783M.C.	—	250.00	550.00	800.00	1000.

Obv: Arms. Rev: Value.

C#	Date	Mintage	Fine	VF	XF	Unc
156	1782M.C.	—	45.00	90.00	150.00	225.00
	1783M.C.	—	45.00	90.00	150.00	225.00

Obv: Smaller arms.

C#	Date	Mintage	Fine	VF	XF	Unc
156a	1787M.C.	—	45.00	90.00	150.00	225.00
	1788M.C.	—	45.00	90.00	150.00	225.00
	1789M.C.	—	45.00	90.00	150.00	225.00
	1790M.C.	—	45.00	90.00	150.00	225.00
	1792M.C.	—	45.00	90.00	150.00	225.00
	1794M.C.	—	45.00	90.00	150.00	225.00
	1795M.C.	—	45.00	90.00	150.00	225.00
	1796M.C.	—	45.00	90.00	150.00	225.00
	1801M.C.	—	45.00	90.00	150.00	225.00

28.0600 gm., .833 SILVER, .7516 oz ASW
Obv: Crowned arms with garlands. Rev: Value.

C#	Date	Mintage	Fine	VF	XF	Unc
190.5	1821 CvC	1,480	400.00	850.00	1200.	2000.

(Convention)

22.2700 gm., .750 SILVER, .5371 oz ASW
Obv: FRITZ.F. at truncation.

C#	Date	Mintage	Fine	VF	XF	Unc
216	1837 CvC	2,788	80.00	160.00	275.00	400.00
	1838 CvC	.033	40.00	65.00	150.00	300.00
	1839 CvC	.041	40.00	65.00	150.00	300.00

Obv: Smaller head, no name at truncation.
Rev: Similar to C#216.

C#	Date	Mintage	Fine	VF	XF	Unc
216a	1839 CvC	I.A.	25.00	40.00	100.00	200.00
	1840 CvC	.086	25.00	40.00	100.00	200.00
	1841 CvC	.304	25.00	40.00	100.00	200.00
	1842 CvC	.117	25.00	40.00	100.00	200.00
	1848 CvC	.011	45.00	90.00	180.00	300.00
	1850 CvC	5,671	50.00	105.00	200.00	325.00

Obv. legend ends: U.L.
Rev: Similar to C#216.

C#	Date	Mintage	Fine	VF	XF	Unc
216b	1851 B	5,742	60.00	115.00	225.00	325.00

Obv. legend ends: LUN.
Rev: Similar to C#216.

C#	Date	Mintage	Fine	VF	XF	Unc
217	1853 B	.024	25.00	50.00	100.00	200.00
	1854 B	.097	20.00	30.00	80.00	165.00
	1855 B	.010	30.00	60.00	125.00	225.00

(Vereins)

18.5200 gm., .900 SILVER, .5360 oz ASW

C#	Date	Mintage	Fine	VF	XF	Unc
219	1858 B	.049	25.00	50.00	100.00	200.00
	1859 B	.030	25.00	50.00	100.00	200.00
	1865 B	.020	25.00	50.00	100.00	200.00
	1866 B	.010	25.00	50.00	100.00	200.00
	1867 B	.010	25.00	50.00	100.00	200.00
	1870 B	.107	25.00	50.00	100.00	200.00
	1871 B	.048	25.00	50.00	100.00	200.00

2 THALER

(= 3-1/2 Gulden)

37.1200 GM., .900 SILVER, 1.0743 oz ASW
Obv: FRITZ F. at truncation, CVC below.
Rev: Crowned draped arms.

C#	Date	Mintage	Fine	VF	XF	Unc
220	1842 CvC	.052	75.00	150.00	250.00	400.00
	1843 CvC	.068	75.00	150.00	250.00	400.00
	1844 CvC	.015	75.00	150.00	250.00	400.00
	1845 CvC	.011	80.00	165.00	300.00	475.00
	1846 CvC	.015	80.00	165.00	300.00	475.00
	1847 CvC	.015	80.00	165.00	300.00	475.00
	1848 CvC	.011	80.00	165.00	300.00	475.00
	1849 CvC	.013	80.00	165.00	300.00	475.00
	1850 CvC	.077	80.00	165.00	300.00	475.00

C#	Date	Mintage	Fine	VF	XF	Unc
220a	1850	—	—	—	—	—
	1850 B	Inc.Ab.	75.00	150.00	275.00	400.00
	1851 B	.010	75.00	150.00	275.00	400.00
	1852 B	.011	75.00	150.00	275.00	400.00
	1854 B	.253	50.00	115.00	225.00	325.00
	1855 B	.620	50.00	115.00	225.00	325.00

25th Anniversary of Reign

C#	Date	Mintage	Fine	VF	XF	Unc
221	1856 B	.017	50.00	115.00	180.00	300.00

2 1/2 THALER

3.3200 gm., .900 GOLD, .0961 oz AGW
Obv: Bust right. Rev: Running horse left.

C#	Date	Mintage	Fine	VF	XF	Unc
109	1777	—	200.00	300.00	500.00	800.00

3.3200 gm., .900 GOLD, .0961 oz AGW
Obv: Arms. Rev: Value.

C#	Date	Mintage	Fine	VF	XF	Unc
160	1781 M.C.	—	200.00	400.00	600.00	900.00
	1782 M.C.	—	200.00	400.00	600.00	900.00

Obv: Arms change.

C#	Date	Mintage	Fine	VF	XF	Unc
160a	1788 M.C.	—	200.00	400.00	600.00	900.00
	1789 M.C.	—	200.00	400.00	600.00	900.00
	1791 M.C.	—	200.00	400.00	600.00	900.00
	1793 M.C.	—	200.00	400.00	600.00	900.00
	1794 M.C.	—	200.00	400.00	600.00	900.00
	1796 M.C.	—	200.00	400.00	600.00	900.00
	1800 M.C.	—	200.00	400.00	600.00	900.00
	1802 M.C.	—	200.00	400.00	600.00	900.00
	1806 M.C.	—	200.00	400.00	600.00	900.00

3.3200 gm., .900 SILVER, .0961 oz ASW
Obv: Crowned many quartered arms with garlands.
Rev: Value, F.R. below.

C#	Date	Mintage	Fine	VF	XF	Unc
172	1815 F.R.	—	400.00	800.00	1250.	1750.

Rev. leg: BR.....

C#	Date	Mintage	Fine	VF	XF	Unc
181	1816 F.R.	—	400.00	800.00	1250.	1750.
	1818 F.R.	—	400.00	800.00	1250.	1750.
	1819 F.R.	—	400.00	800.00	1250.	1750.

3.3200 gm., .900 GOLD, .0961 oz AGW

C#	Date	Mintage	Fine	VF	XF	Unc
191	1822 CvC	—	450.00	900.00	1250.	1750.

Rev: No legend around border.

C#	Date	Mintage	Fine	VF	XF	Unc
201	1825 CvC	—	500.00	1000.	1500.	2200.
	1828 CvC	—	500.00	1000.	1500.	2200.

C#	Date	Mintage	Fine	VF	XF	Unc
204	1829 CvC	—	600.00	1200.	1750.	2500.

Obv: Crowned arms between two wildmen. Rev: Value.

C#	Date	Mintage	Fine	VF	XF	Unc
223	1832 CvC	—	450.00	900.00	1250.	1800.

C#	Date	Mintage	Fine	VF	XF	Unc
226	1851B	4,138	450.00	900.00	1250.	1800.

V (5) THALER

6.6500 gm., .900 GOLD, .1924 oz AGW

Obv: Head right. Rev: Running horse left.

C#	Date	Mintage	Fine	VF	XF	Unc
110	1776	—	500.00	800.00	1500.	2000.
	1777	—	500.00	800.00	1500.	2000.
	1778	—	500.00	800.00	1500.	2000.

Obv: Arms. Rev: Value.

C#	Date	Mintage	Fine	VF	XF	Unc
161	1780 M.C.	—	250.00	500.00	800.00	1400.
	1781 M.C.	—	250.00	500.00	800.00	1400.
	1782 M.C.	—	250.00	500.00	800.00	1400.
	1783 M.C.	—	250.00	500.00	800.00	1400.

Obv: Change in arms.

C#	Date	Mintage	Fine	VF	XF	Unc
161a	1785 M.C.	—	250.00	500.00	800.00	1400.
	1786 M.C.	—	250.00	500.00	800.00	1400.
	1790 M.C.	—	250.00	500.00	800.00	1400.
	1795 M.C.	—	250.00	500.00	800.00	1400.
	1796 M.C.	—	250.00	500.00	800.00	1400.
	1797 M.C.	—	250.00	500.00	800.00	1400.
	1798 M.C.	—	250.00	500.00	800.00	1400.
	1799 M.C.	—	250.00	500.00	800.00	1400.
	1800 M.C.	—	250.00	500.00	800.00	1400.
	1801 M.C.	—	250.00	500.00	800.00	1400.
	1802 M.C.	—	250.00	500.00	800.00	1400.
	1804 M.C.	—	250.00	500.00	800.00	1400.
	1805 M.C.	—	250.00	500.00	800.00	1400.
	1806 M.C.	—	250.00	500.00	800.00	1400.

C#	Date	Mintage	Fine	VF	XF	Unc
173	1814 F.R.	—	350.00	700.00	1000.	1500.
	1815 F.R.	—	350.00	700.00	1000.	1500.

Rev. leg: BR. ET LUN.

C#	Date	Mintage	Fine	VF	XF	Unc
182	1816 F.R.	—	250.00	500.00	750.00	1000.
	1817 F.R.	—	250.00	500.00	750.00	1000.
	1818 F.R.	—	250.00	500.00	750.00	1000.
	1819 F.R.	—	250.00	500.00	750.00	1000.
192	1822 CvC	—	250.00	525.00	800.00	1000.
	1823 CvC	—	250.00	525.00	800.00	1000.

C#	Date	Mintage	Fine	VF	XF	Unc
202	1824 CvC	—	400.00	800.00	1200.	1500.
	1825 CvC	—	400.00	800.00	1200.	1500.
	1828 CvC	—	400.00	800.00	1200.	1500.
	1830.CvC	—	400.00	800.00	1200.	1500.

C#	Date	Mintage	Fine	VF	XF	Unc
224	1832 CvC	—	400.00	800.00	1200.	1500.
	1834 CvC	—	400.00	800.00	1200.	1500.

X (10) THALER

13.3000 gm., .900 GOLD, .3848 oz AGW

C#	Date	Mintage	Fine	VF	XF	Unc
111	1777	—	1200.	1500.	2000.	2500.
162	1781 M.C.	—	300.00	600.00	1000.	1400.
	1782 M.C.	—	300.00	600.00	1000.	1400.
	1783 M.C.	—	300.00	600.00	1000.	1400.
	1784 M.C.	—	300.00	600.00	1000.	1400.

Obv: Change in arms.

C#	Date	Mintage	Fine	VF	XF	Unc
162a	1794 M.C.	—	300.00	600.00	1000.	1400.
	1795 M.C.	—	300.00	600.00	1000.	1400.
	1796 M.C.	—	300.00	600.00	1000.	1400.
	1797 M.C.	—	300.00	600.00	1000.	1400.
	1799 M.C.	—	300.00	600.00	1000.	1400.
	1800 M.C.	—	300.00	600.00	1000.	1400.
	1801 M.C.	—	300.00	600.00	1000.	1400.
	1804 M.C.	—	300.00	600.00	1000.	1400.
	1805 M.C.	—	300.00	600.00	1000.	1400.
	1806 M.C.	—	300.00	600.00	1000.	1400.

C#	Date	Mintage	Fine	VF	XF	Unc
174	1813 M.C.	—	300.00	600.00	1000.	1400.
	1814 M.C.	—	300.00	600.00	1000.	1400.
174a	1814 F.R.	—	500.00	1000.	1500.	3000.

C#	Date	Mintage	Fine	VF	XF	Unc
183	1817 F.R.	—	400.00	800.00	1200.	1500.
	1818 F.R.	—	400.00	800.00	1200.	1500.
	1819 F.R.	—	450.00	925.00	1400.	1750.
193	1822 CvC	—	600.00	1150.	1700.	1900.

C#	Date	Mintage	Fine	VF	XF	Unc
203	1824 CvC	—	450.00	925.00	1400.	1750.
	1825 CvC	—	450.00	925.00	1400.	1750.
	1829 CvC	—	450.00	925.00	1400.	1750.
	1830 CvC	—	450.00	925.00	1400.	1750.

C#	Date	Mintage	Fine	VF	XF	Unc
205	1827 CvC	—	450.00	925.00	1400.	1750.
	1828 CvC	—	450.00	925.00	1400.	1750.
	1829 CvC	—	450.00	925.00	1400.	1750.

C#	Date	Mintage	Fine	VF	XF	Unc
222	1831 CvC	—	600.00	1150.	1600.	2000.

C#	Date	Mintage	Fine	VF	XF	Unc
225	1831 CvC	—	600.00	1150.	1600.	2000.
	1832 CvC	—	600.00	1150.	1600.	2000.
	1833 CvC	—	450.00	925.00	1400.	1750.
	1834 CvC	—	450.00	925.00	1400.	1750.

Obv. legend ends: U.L.

C#	Date	Mintage	Fine	VF	XF	Unc
227	1850 B	9,763	300.00	600.00	1000.	1800.

Obv. legend ends: LUN.

C#	Date	Mintage	Fine	VF	XF	Unc
227a	1853 B	.150	300.00	600.00	1000.	1600.
	1854 B	.163	300.00	600.00	1000.	1600.
	1855 B	.020	300.00	600.00	1000.	1600.
	1856 B	.057	300.00	600.00	1000.	1600.
	1857 B	.054	300.00	600.00	1000.	1600.

KRONE

11.1110 gm., .900 GOLD, .3215 oz AGW
Obv: B below head.

C#	Date	Mintage	Fine	VF	XF	Unc
228	1857 B	—	500.00	1000.	2000.	3000.
	1858 B	.032	500.00	1000.	2000.	3000.
	1859 B	.013	500.00	1000.	2000.	3000.

TRADE COINS

DUCAT

3.5000 gm., .986 GOLD, .1109 oz AGW

C#	Date	Mintage	Fine	VF	XF	Unc
158	1780 MC	—	300.00	600.00	1000.	1500.
159	1781 MC	—	300.00	600.00	1000.	1500.
	1782 MC	—	300.00	600.00	1000.	1500.
	1783 MC	—	300.00	600.00	1000.	1500.
	1784 MC	—	300.00	600.00	1000.	1500.

Obv: Change in arms.

C#	Date	Mintage	Fine	VF	XF	Unc
159a	1784 MC	—	300.00	600.00	1000.	1500.
	1785 MC	—	300.00	600.00	1000.	1500.
	1786 MC	—	300.00	600.00	1000.	1500.
	1787 MC	—	300.00	600.00	1000.	1500.
	1788 MC	—	300.00	600.00	1000.	1500.
	1789 MC	—	300.00	600.00	1000.	1500.
	1792 MC	—	300.00	600.00	1000.	1500.
	1794 MC	—	—	—	—	—
	1797 MC	—	300.00	600.00	1000.	1500.
	1798 MC	—	300.00	600.00	1000.	1500.
	1800 MC	—	300.00	600.00	1000.	1500.
	1801 MC	—	300.00	600.00	1000.	1500.

Obv: Crowned many quartered arms with garlands.
Rev: Value, EX AVRO HERCINIA.

C#	Date	Mintage	Fine	VF	XF	Unc
171.1	1814 HC	376 pcs.	700.00	1350.	2000.	2500.

Rev: F.R. below value

C#	Date	Mintage	Fine	VF	XF	Unc
171.2	1815 F.R.	220 pcs.	800.00	1700.	2500.	3000.
200	1825 CvC	530 pcs.	700.00	1500.	2000.	2500.

MONETARY REFORM

3 MARK

16.6670 gm., .900 SILVER, .4823 oz ASW
Ernst August Wedding And Accession

Y#	Date	Mintage	Fine	VF	XF	Unc
54	1915A	1,700	350.00	800.00	1300.	1800.
	1915A	—	—	—	Proof	1600.

Obv. leg: U.LUNEB added.
Rev: Similar to Y#54.

Y#	Date	Mintage	Fine	VF	XF	Unc
54a	1915A	.032	45.00	100.00	140.00	200.00
	1915A	—	—	—	Proof	225.00

5 MARK

27.7770 gm., .900 SILVER, .8038 oz ASW
Ernst August Wedding And Accession

Y#	Date	Mintage	Fine	VF	XF	Unc
55	1915A	1,400	500.00	1200.	2000.	2500.
	1915A	—	—	—	Proof	2700.

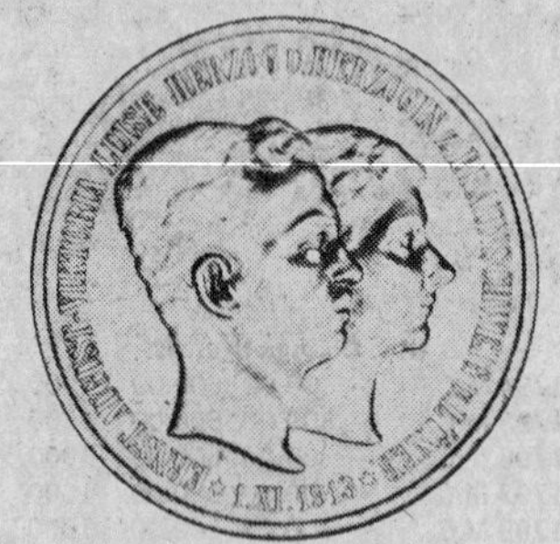

Obv. leg: U.LUNEB added.
Rev: Similar to Y#55.

Y#	Date	Mintage	Fine	VF	XF	Unc
55a	1915A	8,600	150.00	300.00	550.00	750.00
	1915A	—	—	—	Proof	600.00

20 MARK

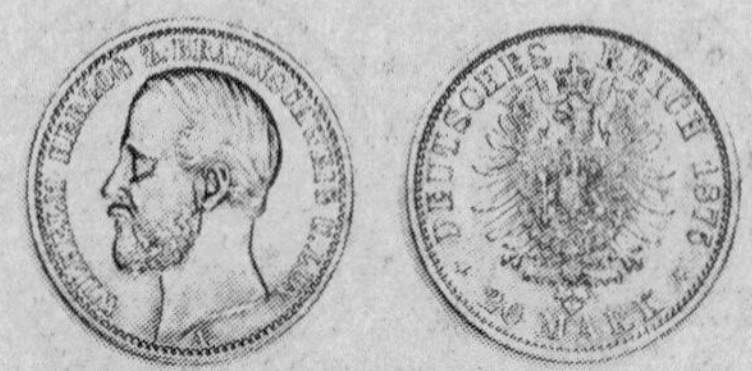

7.9650 gm., .900 GOLD, .2304 oz AGW
Rev: Type 2 eagle

Y#	Date	Mintage	Fine	VF	XF	Unc
53	1875A	.100	300.00	600.00	900.00	1200.
	1876A	—	—	—	Rare	—

NCLT ISSUES

PATTERNS

KM#	Date	Mintage	Identification	Mkt.Val.
1	1913	—	3 Marks, Silver	—
2	1913	—	5 Marks, Silver	—

COLOGNE

Archbishopric

The See of Cologne was founded in 313 and raised in rank to an archbishopric in 785. The first coins were minted in c. 960. It was awarded the electorate in 1356. Cologne was secularized in 1801.

RULERS

Sede Vacante, 1761
Maximilian Friedrich, Graf von Konigsegg-Rothenfels, 1761-1784
Maximilian Franz von Oesterreich, 1784-1801
Anton Victor von Oesterreich, 1801

1/4 STUBER

COPPER
Obv: MFF monogram.
Rev: Value and date in cartouche.

C#	Date	Mintage	VG	Fine	VF	XF
42	1763	—	5.00	7.50	12.50	25.00
	1764	—	5.00	7.50	12.50	25.00
	1765	—	5.00	7.50	12.50	25.00
	1766	—	5.00	7.50	12.50	25.00
	1767	—	5.00	7.50	12.50	25.00

BILLON
Obv: Bust of Maximilian Friedrich right.
Rev: Value and date.

C#	Date	Mintage	VG	Fine	VF	XF
44	1776	—	7.50	12.50	20.00	40.00

STUBER

BILLON
Obv: Bust of Maximilian Friedrich right.
Rev: Value and date.

C#	Date	Mintage	VG	Fine	VF	XF
46	1776	—	5.00	7.50	12.50	25.00
	1777	—	5.00	7.50	12.50	25.00

2-1/2 STUBER

BILLON
Obv: Cologne cross with Konigsegg arms in center.
Rev: Value and date.

C#	Date	Mintage	VG	Fine	VF	XF
48	1765	—	7.50	12.50	20.00	40.00

5 STUBER

BILLON
Obv: Cologne cross with Konigsegg arms in center.
Rev: Value and date.

C#	Date	Mintage	VG	Fine	VF	XF
50	1764	—	10.00	15.00	25.00	50.00
	1765	—	10.00	15.00	25.00	50.00

Obv: Crowned arms with crozier and sword behind.
Rev: Value and date in branches.

C#	Date	Mintage	VG	Fine	VF	XF
50a	1765	—	12.50	20.00	32.50	50.00
	1766	—	12.50	20.00	32.50	50.00

1/8 THALER

(= 10 Stuber)

SILVER
Sede Vacante Issue
Obv: St. Peter over shield.
Rev: 4 line inscription and date.

C#	Date	Mintage	VG	Fine	VF	XF
38	1761	—	40.00	55.00	75.00	110.00

Obv: Complex coat of arms.
Rev: Value and date.

C#	Date	Mintage	VG	Fine	VF	XF
52	1764	—	12.50	20.00	32.50	50.00
	1765	—	12.50	20.00	32.50	50.00
	1766	—	12.50	20.00	32.50	50.00

1/4 THALER
(= 20 Stuber)

SILVER
Sede Vacante Issue
Obv: St. Peter over shield.
Rev: Madonna, child and wise men.

C#	Date	Mintage	Fine	VF	XF	Unc
39	1761	—	60.00	100.00	150.00	300.00

Obv: Bust of Maximilian Friedrich right.
Rev: Arms.

C#	Date	Mintage	Fine	VF	XF	Unc
54	1766	—	15.00	27.50	42.50	75.00

1/2 THALER

SILVER
Obv: Bust of Maximilian Friedrich right.
Rev: Arms.

C#	Date	Mintage	Fine	VF	XF	Unc
58	1765	—	35.00	55.00	95.00	250.00

THALER

SILVER
Sede Vacante Issue
Obv: St. Peter over shield.
Rev: Madonna, child and wise men.

C#	Date	Mintage	Fine	VF	XF	Unc
40	1761	—	750.00	1000.	1500.	2250.

Obv: Bust of Maximilian Friedrich left, date below.
Rev: Crowned and supported arms; value below.

C#	Date	Mintage	Fine	VF	XF	Unc
60	1762 F.G.	—	150.00	195.00	275.00	550.00

Obv: Bust of Maximilian Friedrich right; date below.

C#	Date	Mintage	Fine	VF	XF	Unc
61	1764 I.K.	—	150.00	195.00	275.00	550.00
	1765 I.K.	—	150.00	195.00	275.00	550.00

Rev: Crowned and supported oval arms; value below.

C#	Date	Mintage	Fine	VF	XF	Unc
62	1766 I.K.	—	1000.	1350.	2000.	3000.

Obv: Larger bust of Maximilian Friedrich right, date below.

C#	Date	Mintage	Fine	VF	XF	Unc
62a	1777 I.G.S.	—	300.00	450.00	750.00	1150.

Free City

Founded in 50 A.D. as a Roman colony. Beginning c. 940 an imperial mint was located in the city. In 1288 the city became self-governing. They joined the Hanseatic League in 1201. The mint right was obtained in 1474 and the first dated coins c. 1511. Cologne was formally absorbed by France in 1797 and was given to Prussia in 1815.

4 HELLER

COPPER
Obv: Crowned arms and eagle.
Rev: Value over date.

C#	Date	Mintage	VG	Fine	VF	XF
1	1770-92	—	1.50	4.00	7.50	15.00

Ration Token
Rev: Value divides date vertically.

C#	Date	Mintage	VG	Fine	VF	XF
1a	1789	—	4.00	7.00	10.00	20.00

Ration Token
Rev: Value.

C#	Date	Mintage	VG	Fine	VF	XF
1b	ND(1789)	—	2.00	4.50	7.50	15.00

8 HELLER

COPPER
Obv: Crowned arms and eagle.
Rev: Value over date.

C#	Date	Mintage	VG	Fine	VF	XF
2	1793	—	3.00	6.00	12.00	24.00

CORVEY

ABBEY

The Benedictine Abbey was founded in 820. The right to mint imperial coins was granted in 833. The first coins with the abbot's name were struck in 1046. In 1793 Corvey was made a bishopric and was secularized to Nassau-Dietz in 1803. From 1807 to 1813 it was part of Westphalia and became part of Prussia in 1813.

RULERS

Theodor, Abbott, 1776-1793
Bishop, 1793-1794
Ferdinand, Freiheir von Luenig, 1794-1803

2 PFENNIG

COPPER
Obv: Crowned arms. Rev: Value over date.

C#	Date	Mintage	VG	Fine	VF	XF
14	1787	—	10.00	15.00	20.00	40.00

4 PFENNIG

COPPER
Obv: Crowned arms. Rev: Value over date.

C#	Date	Mintage	VG	Fine	VF	XF
15	1787	—	12.50	16.50	20.00	40.00

EAST FRIESLAND

Located on the North Sea coast in North Germany. At the death of the last prince in 1744, East Friesland passed to Prussia. From 1815 to 1866 East Friesland was part of Hannover until Hannover was absorbed by Prussia in 1866.

RULERS

Friedrich Wilhelm II (of Prussia), 1786-1797
Friedrich Wilhelm (Of Prussia), 1797-1807
George IV (of Great Britain), 1815-1820

4 GUTE PFENNIG

BILLON
Obv: Crowned script FR monogram.
Rev: Value, D divides date.

C#	Date	Mintage	VG	Fine	VF	XF
12	1764 D	1.482	4.50	7.00	11.50	17.50
	1765 D	.335	4.50	7.00	11.50	17.50
	1766 D	.539	4.50	7.00	11.50	17.50
	1767 D	1.227	4.50	7.00	11.50	17.50
	1768 D	.022	4.50	7.00	11.50	17.50

Rev: F below date.

C#	Date	Mintage	VG	Fine	VF	XF
12a	1764 F	—	4.50	7.00	11.50	17.50

Obv: Crowned block FR monogram divides date.
Rev: Value with Arabic 4, A below.

C#	Date	Mintage	VG	Fine	VF	XF
12b	1764 A	—	4.50	7.00	11.50	17.50
	1766 A	—	4.50	7.00	11.50	17.50

Obv: Crowned block FR monogram in cartouche.
Rev: Value with Roman 4, date and A below.

C#	Date	Mintage	VG	Fine	VF	XF
12c	1774 A	—	4.50	7.00	11.50	17.50

1/4 STUBER

COPPER
Obv: Crowned script FR monogram.
Rev: Value and date, D below.

C#	Date	Mintage	VG	Fine	VF	XF
2	1764 D	—	5.00	7.50	12.50	20.00
	1765 D	—	5.00	7.50	12.50	20.00
	1767 D	.233	5.00	7.50	12.50	20.00

Rev: A below date.

C#	Date	Mintage	VG	Fine	VF	XF
2a	1777 A	—	5.00	7.50	12.50	20.00
	1778 A	—	5.00	7.50	12.50	20.00
	1779 A	—	5.00	7.50	12.50	20.00
	1781 A	—	5.00	7.50	12.50	20.00
	1784 A	.108	5.00	7.50	12.50	20.00

Obv: Crowned FWR monogram. Rev: Value over date.

C#	Date	Mintage	VG	Fine	VF	XF
32	1787	.086	3.50	7.50	10.00	20.00

Similar to C#32. Mintmark between asterisks.

C#	Date	Mintage	VG	Fine	VF	XF
33.1	1792A	.120	3.00	6.00	9.00	20.00

Similar to C#35.

C#	Date	Mintage	VG	Fine	VF	XF
33.2	1794	—	3.00	6.00	9.00	20.00

C#	Date	Mintage	Fine	VF	XF	Unc
35	1799 A	.216	2.00	4.00	10.00	30.00
	1802 A	1.296	2.00	4.00	10.00	30.00
	1803 A	Inc. Ab.	2.00	4.00	10.00	30.00
	1804 A	.216	2.00	4.00	10.00	30.00

C#	Date	Mintage	Fine	VF	XF	Unc
40	1823	.710	2.50	5.00	10.00	30.00
	1824	Inc. Ab.	2.50	5.00	10.00	30.00
	1825	Inc. Ab.	2.50	5.00	10.00	30.00

1/2 STUBER

BILLON
Obv: Crowned script FR monogram, A below.
Rev: Value and date.

C#	Date	Mintage	VG	Fine	VF	XF
5	1772 A	—	6.50	10.00	15.00	25.00
	1781 A	.108	6.50	10.00	15.00	25.00

Obv: Crowned arms divide date, in inner circle.
Rev: Floreated cross with O F H S in angels.

C#	Date	Mintage	VG	Fine	VF	XF
6	1781 A	—	17.50	30.00	45.00	65.00
	1782 A	—	17.50	30.00	45.00	65.00

STUBER

BILLON
Obv: Head of Friedrich right.
Rev: Crowned flying eagle over value and date.

C#	Date	Mintage	VG	Fine	VF	XF
7	1771 A	3.697	5.00	7.50	12.50	20.00
	1772 A	.199	5.00	7.50	12.50	20.00
	1775 A	—	5.00	7.50	12.50	20.00
	1776 A	—	5.00	7.50	12.50	20.00
	1777 A	—	5.00	7.50	12.50	20.00
	1781 A	—	5.00	7.50	12.50	20.00

Obv: Bust. Rev: Value.

C#	Date	Mintage	Fine	VF	XF	Unc
37	1804 A	.378	6.00	13.50	20.00	50.00

C#	Date	Mintage	Fine	VF	XF	Unc
41	1823 B	.161	6.00	11.50	17.00	50.00

2 STUBER

BILLON
Obv: Head of Friedrich right.
Rev: Crowned flying eagle over value, A divides date.

C#	Date	Mintage	VG	Fine	VF	XF
8	1773 A	—	8.50	12.50	20.00	35.00
	1775 A	—	8.50	12.50	20.00	35.00

Obv: Bust. Rev: Value.

C#	Date	Mintage	Fine	VF	XF	Unc
38	1804 A	.216	10.00	20.00	40.00	75.00

Obv: Crowned monogram GR. Rev: Value.

C#	Date	Mintage	Fine	VF	XF	Unc
42	1823 B	.081	10.00	20.00	40.00	75.00

MARIENGROSCHEN

BILLON
Obv: Crowned script FR monogram in cartouche.
Rev: Value over date, D below.

C#	Date	Mintage	VG	Fine	VF	XF
15	1767 D	1.221	5.00	7.50	12.50	20.00
	1768 D	Inc. Ab.	5.00	7.50	12.50	20.00

Rev: F below date.

C#	Date	Mintage	VG	Fine	VF	XF
16	1764 F	—	5.00	7.50	12.50	20.00

Obv: Crowned block FR monogram in branches.
Rev: A below date.

C#	Date	Mintage	VG	Fine	VF	XF
17a	1771 A	—	6.00	10.00	15.00	25.00

Obv: Crowned block FR monogram in cartouche.
Rev: Crowned flying eagle over value and date, A below.

C#	Date	Mintage	VG	Fine	VF	XF
17b	1771 A	—	6.00	10.00	15.00	25.00

Rev: Value and date, A below.

C#	Date	Mintage	VG	Fine	VF	XF
17	1774 A	—	6.00	10.00	15.00	25.00
	1775 A	—	6.00	10.00	15.00	25.00

2 MARIENGROSCHEN

BILLON
Obv: Crowned script FR monogram in cartouche.
Rev: Value and date, F below.

C#	Date	Mintage	VG	Fine	VF	XF
21	1764 F	—	8.50	12.50	20.00	35.00

EICHSTADT

A bishopric in central Bavaria which was founded in 745. The Imperial Mint was founded c. 908 and Episcopal coinage began in the 11th century. Eichstadt was secularized in 1803 and given to Salzburg. It passed to Bavaria in 1805.

RULERS

Raimund Anton Graf von Strasoldo, 1757-1781
Sede Vacante, 1781
Johann Anton III, 1781-1790
Sede Vacante, 1790
Joseph, 1790-1803

MINTMASTERS INITIALS

F - Johann Martin Forster, 1763-1764
R - Georg Nikolaus Riedner, 1764-1765, 1781
S - Suegmund Scholz, 1763-1765
IOS. SCH. - Joseph Schuffel, 1783
W - Johann Peter Werner, 1790
C.D. - Cajetan Destouches, 1796

KREUZER

BILLON
Obv: Crowned arms.

C#	Date	Mintage	VG	Fine	VF	XF
17	1763	—	—	—	Rare	—

2-1/2 KREUZER

BILLON
Obv: 2 shields of arms.
Rev: Value and date.

C#	Date	Mintage	VG	Fine	VF	XF
18	1764 NSR	—	5.00	8.50	12.50	20.00

5 KREUZER

SILVER
Obv: Crowned arms, date below.
Rev: Value.

C#	Date	Mintage	VG	Fine	VF	XF
19	1763 FSN	—	6.50	10.00	15.00	25.00
	1765 SRN	—	—	—	Rare	—

10 KREUZER

SILVER
Obv: Crowned arms, date below.
Rev: Value.

C#	Date	Mintage	VG	Fine	VF	XF
20	1763 FSN	—	8.50	12.50	20.00	35.00
	1765 Srn	—	8.50	12.50	20.00	35.00

20 KREUZER

SILVER
Obv: Crowned arms, date below.
Rev: Value.

C#	Date	Mintage	VG	Fine	VF	XF
21	1763 FSN	—	10.00	15.00	25.00	40.00
	1765 SRN	—	10.00	15.00	25.00	40.00

30 KREUZER

SILVER
Obv: Bust of Raimund Anton right.
Rev: Crowned arms, value below; Roman numeral date to right.

C#	Date	Mintage	VG	Fine	VF	XF
22	1764 NSR	—	35.00	75.00	125.00	200.00

1/2 THALER

SILVER
Obv: Bust of Raimund Anton right.
Rev: Crowned arms; Roman numeral date to right.

C#	Date	Mintage	VG	Fine	VF	XF
23	1764 NSR	—	100.00	175.00	275.00	500.00

(Convention)

SILVER

C#	Date	Mintage	VG	Fine	VF	XF
26	1783	—	25.00	50.00	80.00	125.00

Rev: Date in chronogram.

C#	Date	Mintage	VG	Fine	VF	XF
29	1796	—	40.00	85.00	110.00	150.00

EIN (1) TALER

SILVER
Obv: Bust of Raimond Anton right.
Rev: Crowned arms; Roman numeral date to right.

C#	Date	Mintage	VG	Fine	VF	XF
24	1764 NSF	—	70.00	125.00	175.00	350.00

(Convention)

SILVER
Sede Vacante Issue

C#	Date	Mintage	VG	Fine	VF	XF
25	1781	—	75.00	175.00	225.00	300.00

C#	Date	Mintage	VG	Fine	VF	XF
27	1783	—	75.00	150.00	200.00	300.00

C#	Date	Mintage	Fine	VF	XF	Unc
6	1794	—	1.50	3.00	9.00	45.00
	1795	—	1.50	3.00	9.00	45.00
	1796	—	1.50	3.00	9.00	45.00
	1797	—	1.50	3.00	9.00	45.00
	1798	—	1.50	3.00	9.00	45.00
	1799	—	1.50	3.00	9.00	45.00
	1800	—	1.50	3.00	9.00	45.00
	1801	—	1.50	3.00	9.00	45.00
	1802	—	1.50	3.00	9.00	45.00
	1803	—	1.50	3.00	9.00	45.00
	1804	—	1.50	3.00	9.00	45.00
	1805	—	1.50	3.00	9.00	45.00
	1806	—	1.50	3.00	9.00	45.00

KREUZER

BILLON

Obv: Similar to C#15. Rev: Value.

C#	Date	Mintage	VG	Fine	VF	XF
13a	1780-89	—	2.00	3.50	6.00	12.00

C#	Date	Mintage	VG	Fine	VF	XF
15	1773	—	2.00	3.50	6.00	12.00
	1774	—	2.00	3.50	6.00	12.00

Obv: 3 line inscription. Rev: Value and date.

C#	Date	Mintage	VG	Fine	VF	XF
17	1778	—	4.00	6.50	8.50	17.00

Obv: FRANKFURT on 1 line.

C#	Date	Mintage	VG	Fine	VF	XF
19	1778	—	3.00	5.00	6.50	12.00
	1779	—	3.00	5.00	6.50	12.00
	1780	—	3.00	5.00	6.50	12.00
	1781	—	3.00	5.00	6.50	12.00
	1782	—	3.00	5.00	6.50	12.00
	1783	—	3.00	5.00	6.50	12.00

C#	Date	Mintage	VG	Fine	VF	XF
19a	1784	—	4.00	6.50	8.50	17.00
	1787	—	4.00	6.50	8.50	17.00
	1788	—	—	—	—	—

(Convention)

C#	Date	Mintage	Fine	VF	XF	Unc
21	1803	—	1.50	4.00	10.00	40.00
	1805	—	1.50	4.00	10.00	40.00
	1806	—	1.50	4.00	10.00	40.00
	1807	—	1.50	4.00	10.00	40.00

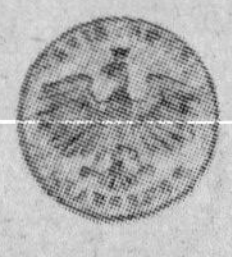

C#	Date	Mintage	Fine	VF	XF	Unc
24	1838	.078	1.50	3.00	8.00	40.00
	1841	.123	1.50	3.00	8.00	40.00
	1842	.402	1.50	3.00	8.00	40.00
	1843	.169	1.50	3.00	8.00	40.00
	1844	.215	1.50	3.00	8.00	40.00
	1845	.205	1.50	3.00	8.00	40.00
	1846	.101	1.50	3.00	8.00	40.00
	1847	.553	1.50	3.00	8.00	40.00
	1848	.482	1.50	3.00	8.00	40.00
	1849	.627	1.50	3.00	8.00	40.00
	1850	.612	1.50	3.00	8.00	40.00
	1851	.543	1.50	3.00	8.00	40.00
	1852	.889	1.50	3.00	8.00	40.00
	1853	.526	1.50	3.00	8.00	40.00
	1854	.589	1.50	3.00	8.00	40.00
	1855	.677	1.50	3.00	8.00	40.00
	1856	1.227	1.50	3.00	8.00	40.00
	1857	.774	1.50	3.00	8.00	40.00

C#	Date	Mintage	Fine	VF	XF	Unc
25	1859	.358	1.50	3.00	8.00	40.00
	1860	.640	1.50	3.00	8.00	40.00
	1861	.313	1.50	3.00	8.00	40.00
	1862	—	25.00	52.50	80.00	125.00

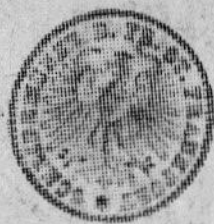

C#	Date	Mintage	Fine	VF	XF	Unc
25.1	1862	.645	1.50	3.00	6.00	35.00
	1863	.611	1.50	3.00	6.00	35.00
	1864	.344	1.50	3.00	6.00	35.00
	1865	.366	1.50	3.00	6.00	35.00
	1866	.151	1.50	3.00	6.00	35.00

3 KREUZER

BILLON

Obv: Crowned eagle. Rev: Value in wreath.

C#	Date	Mintage	Fine	VF	XF	Unc
29	1838	.080	2.00	4.00	10.00	40.00
	1841	.085	2.00	4.00	10.00	40.00
	1842	.109	2.00	4.00	10.00	40.00
	1843	.089	2.00	4.00	10.00	40.00
	1846	.154	2.00	4.00	10.00	40.00

C#	Date	Mintage	Fine	VF	XF	Unc
29a	1846	Inc. Ab.	2.00	4.00	10.00	40.00
	1848	.038	2.00	4.00	10.00	40.00
	1849	.950	2.00	4.00	10.00	40.00
	1850	.182	2.00	4.00	10.00	40.00
	1851	.158	2.00	4.00	10.00	40.00
	1852	.129	2.00	4.00	10.00	40.00
	1853	.069	2.00	4.00	10.00	40.00
	1854	.154	2.00	4.00	10.00	40.00
	1855	.148	2.00	4.00	10.00	40.00
	1856	.084	2.00	4.00	10.00	40.00

C#	Date	Mintage	Fine	VF	XF	Unc
30	1866	.096	3.00	6.00	15.00	50.00

5 KREUZER

SILVER

Obv: Eagle divides S-F. Rev: 5 in wreath.

C#	Date	Mintage	VG	Fine	VF	XF
34	1778	—	6.00	10.00	50.00	100.00
	1779	—	6.00	10.00	50.00	100.00
	1785	—	6.00	10.00	50.00	100.00

6 KREUZER

.333 SILVER

C#	Date	Mintage	Fine	VF	XF	Unc
37	1838	.110	2.50	5.00	15.00	50.00
	1841	.123	2.50	5.00	15.00	50.00
	1842	.161	2.50	5.00	15.00	50.00
	1843	.260	2.50	5.00	15.00	50.00
	1844	.370	2.50	5.00	15.00	50.00
	1845	.105	2.50	5.00	15.00	50.00
	1846	.211	2.50	5.00	15.00	50.00

Obv: Legend at sides.

C#	Date	Mintage	Fine	VF	XF	Unc
37a	1846	Inc. Ab.	2.50	5.00	10.00	50.00
	1848	.291	2.50	5.00	10.00	50.00
	1849	.171	2.50	5.00	10.00	50.00
	1850	.152	2.50	5.00	10.00	50.00
	1851	.159	2.50	5.00	10.00	50.00
	1852	.221	2.50	5.00	10.00	50.00
	1853	.106	2.50	5.00	10.00	50.00
	1855	.181	2.50	5.00	10.00	50.00
	1856	.166	2.50	5.00	10.00	50.00

C#	Date	Mintage	Fine	VF	XF	Unc
38	1853	Inc. Ab.	2.50	5.00	15.00	50.00
	1854	.212	2.50	5.00	15.00	50.00
	1856	Inc. Ab.	2.50	5.00	15.00	50.00

.350 SILVER

C#	Date	Mintage	Fine	VF	XF	Unc
39	1866	.038	5.00	10.00	20.00	50.00

10 KREUZER

SILVER

Obv: Eagle. Rev: 10 in wreath.

C#	Date	Mintage	VG	Fine	VF	XF
44	1776	—	—	10.00	60.00	125.00
	1778	—	3.00	10.00	60.00	125.00

Rev: Value and date

C#	Date	Mintage	VG	Fine	VF	XF
46	1788	—	3.00	10.00	60.00	125.00

20 KREUZER

SILVER

Rev: 20 in wreath

C#	Date	Mintage	VG	Fine	VF	XF
56	1776	—	3.00	7.50	15.00	50.00

Obv: Crowned eagle arms in cartouche.
Rev: Value equivalent with date, 20 below.

C#	Date	Mintage	VG	Fine	VF	XF
58	1781	—	3.00	7.50	15.00	50.00
	1782	—	3.00	7.50	15.00	50.00
	1783	—	3.00	7.50	15.00	50.00
	1784	—	3.00	7.50	15.00	50.00

Obv: Eagle. Rev: Value and date.

C#	Date	Mintage	VG	Fine	VF	XF
60	1790	—	3.00	7.50	15.00	50.00

1/2 GULDEN

.900 SILVER

C#	Date	Mintage	Fine	VF	XF	Unc
64	1838	.120	10.00	20.00	40.00	125.00
	1840	.096	10.00	20.00	40.00	125.00
	1841	.161	10.00	20.00	40.00	125.00

C#	Date	Mintage	Fine	VF	XF	Unc
64a	1842	.075	12.00	25.00	45.00	125.00
	1843	.056	12.00	25.00	45.00	125.00
	1844	.049	12.00	25.00	45.00	125.00
	1845	.072	12.00	25.00	45.00	125.00
	1846	.047	12.00	25.00	45.00	125.00
	1847	.051	12.00	25.00	45.00	125.00
	1849	.055	12.00	25.00	45.00	125.00

C#	Date	Mintage	Fine	VF	XF	Unc
64b	1862	.014	30.00	65.00	110.00	250.00

GULDEN

.900 SILVER

C#	Date	Mintage	Fine	VF	XF	Unc
70	1838	.120	15.00	35.00	80.00	200.00
	1839	—	—	—	—	2500.
	1840	.391	12.00	25.00	45.00	150.00
	1841	.161	12.00	25.00	45.00	150.00

Obv: Eagle with large arabesques.

C#	Date	Mintage	Fine	VF	XF	Unc
70a	1842	.123	15.00	30.00	50.00	150.00
	1843	.172	15.00	30.00	50.00	150.00
	1844	.122	15.00	30.00	50.00	150.00
	1845	.101	15.00	30.00	50.00	200.00
	1846	.120	15.00	30.00	50.00	200.00
	1847	.121	15.00	30.00	50.00	200.00
	1848	.078	15.00	30.00	50.00	200.00
	1849	.090	15.00	30.00	50.00	200.00
	1850	.030	15.00	30.00	50.00	200.00
	1851	.064	15.00	30.00	50.00	200.00
	1852	.064	15.00	30.00	50.00	200.00
	1853	.029	15.00	30.00	50.00	200.00
	1854	.034	15.00	30.00	50.00	200.00
	1855	.038	15.00	30.00	50.00	200.00

Obv: Eagle with small arabesques.

C#	Date	Mintage	Fine	VF	XF	Unc
70b	1859	.059	25.00	50.00	85.00	200.00
	1861	.211	12.00	25.00	50.00	200.00

Obv: Eagle w/o arabesques.

C#	Date	Mintage	Fine	VF	XF	Unc
70c	1862	.011	25.00	50.00	85.00	200.00
	1863	.056	25.00	50.00	85.00	200.00

ZWEY (2) GULDEN

21.2200 gm., .900 SILVER, .6138 oz ASW

C#	Date	Mintage	Fine	VF	XF	Unc
82	1845	.114	40.00	90.00	175.00	400.00
	1846	.281	40.00	90.00	175.00	400.00
	1847	.215	40.00	90.00	175.00	400.00
	1848	.147	40.00	90.00	175.00	400.00
	1849	.023	50.00	100.00	200.00	400.00
	1850	.031	50.00	100.00	200.00	400.00
	1851	.032	50.00	100.00	200.00	400.00
	1852	.026	50.00	100.00	200.00	400.00
	1853	.056	50.00	100.00	200.00	400.00
	1854	6,028	75.00	165.00	300.00	650.00
	1856	.036	50.00	100.00	200.00	400.00

Establishment of German Parliament

C#	Date	Mintage	Fine	VF	XF	Unc
83	1848	8,600	50.00	100.00	150.00	275.00

Archduke Johann of Austria elected as Vicar
Obv: Similar to C#83.

C#	Date	Mintage	Fine	VF	XF	Unc
84	1848	.036	30.00	60.00	90.00	200.00

Opening of German Parliament

C#	Date	Mintage	Fine	VF	XF	Unc
A84	1848	—	—	—	—	10,000.

Friedrich Wilhelm IV of Prussia elected as Emperor of Germany
Obv: Similar to C#83.

C#	Date	Mintage	Fine	VF	XF	Unc
85	1849	200 pcs.	1500.	3250.	4500.	6000.

Plain edge.

C#	Date	Mintage	Fine	VF	XF	Unc
85a	1849 (1890) (restrike)	–	—	—	—	—

Centenary of Goethe's Birth

C#	Date	Mintage	Fine	VF	XF	Unc
86	1849	8,500	50.00	100.00	150.00	225.00

300th Anniversary of Religious Freedom

C#	Date	Mintage	Fine	VF	XF	Unc
87	1855	.032	40.00	80.00	125.00	200.00

1/2 TALER
(Convention)

SILVER
Obv: Eagle. Rev: Value and date.

C#	Date	Mintage	VG	Fine	VF	XF
68	1791	—	10.00	25.00	80.00	200.00

EIN (1) THALER

(Convention)

SILVER

C#	Date	Mintage	VG	Fine	VF	XF
73	1772	—	50.00	150.00	225.00	400.00

Opening of the Bridge at Hausen

C#	Date	Mintage	VG	Fine	VF	XF
74	1776	—	50.00	150.00	400.00	800.00

Obv: Crowned eagle; H.G.B.H. below.
Rev: Value and date in wreath.

C#	Date	Mintage	VG	Fine	VF	XF
75	1793	—	50.00	150.00	200.00	325.00
	1796	—	50.00	150.00	200.00	350.00

NOTE: Varieties exist.

(Contribution)

C#	Date	Mintage	VG	Fine	VF	XF
76	1796	—	60.00	175.00	250.00	300.00

(Vereins)

18.5000 gm., .900 SILVER, .5360 oz ASW

C#	Date	Mintage	Fine	VF	XF	Unc
77	1857	1,350	300.00	1000.	3000.	8500.

Obv: With house roofs visible around tower at left.

C#	Date	Mintage	Fine	VF	XF	Unc
77	1857	—	150.00	325.00	650.00	1000.
	1858	.012	50.00	110.00	250.00	550.00

(Gedenk)

Schiller Commemorative

C#	Date	Mintage	Fine	VF	XF	Unc
79	1859	.025	30.00	65.00	85.00	150.00

(Vereins)

C#	Date	Mintage	Fine	VF	XF	Unc
78	1859	.283	12.00	25.00	60.00	125.00
	1860	1.700	12.00	25.00	60.00	100.00

Obv: Different hair-knot.

C#	Date	Mintage	Fine	VF	XF	Unc
78a	1861	.016	50.00	200.00	400.00	800.00

Obv: Different dress.

C#	Date	Mintage	Fine	VF	XF	Unc
78b	1862	.312	12.00	25.00	60.00	100.00
	1863	.021	30.00	60.00	150.00	300.00
	1864	.105	12.00	25.00	60.00	100.00
	1865	.207	12.00	25.00	60.00	100.00

(Gedenk)

German Shooting Festival Commemorative

C#	Date	Mintage	Fine	VF	XF	Unc
80	1862	.044	25.00	50.00	80.00	125.00

Assembly of Princes Commemorative

C#	Date	Mintage	Fine	VF	XF	Unc
81	1863	.020	40.00	85.00	125.00	200.00

ZWEI (2) THALER

(= 3-1/2 Gulden)

37.1000 gm., .900 SILVER, 1.0743 oz ASW
New Mint Opening In 1840 Commemorative

C#	Date	Mintage	Fine	VF	XF	Unc
88	1840	649 pcs.	350.00	725.00	1250.	3000.

Obv: City view

C#	Date	Mintage	Fine	VF	XF	Unc
89	1840	Inc. C#90	75.00	150.00	275.00	600.00
	1841	Inc. C#90	75.00	150.00	275.00	600.00
	1842	Inc. C#90	75.00	150.00	275.00	600.00
	1843	Inc. C#90	75.00	150.00	275.00	600.00
	1844	Inc. C#90	75.00	150.00	275.00	600.00

Obv: City arms

C#	Date	Mintage	Fine	VF	XF	Unc
90	1841	.121	60.00	130.00	250.00	500.00
	1842	.287	60.00	130.00	250.00	500.00
	1843	.123	60.00	130.00	250.00	500.00
	1844	.196	60.00	130.00	250.00	500.00
	1845	.036	60.00	130.00	250.00	500.00
	1846	.072	60.00	130.00	250.00	500.00
	1847	.071	60.00	130.00	250.00	500.00
	1851	8,354	90.00	180.00	300.00	600.00
	1854	.107	60.00	130.00	250.00	500.00
	1855	.072	60.00	130.00	250.00	500.00

37.0000 gm., .900 SILVER, 1.0717 oz ASW

C#	Date	Mintage	Fine	VF	XF	Unc
91	1860	.341	30.00	65.00	90.00	150.00
	1861	1.787	30.00	65.00	90.00	125.00
	1862	.344	30.00	65.00	90.00	150.00
	1866	.637	30.00	65.00	90.00	150.00

TRADE COINS

DUCAT

3.5000 gm., .986 GOLD, .1109 oz AGW
Contribution Ducat

C#	Date	Mintage	Fine	VF	XF	Unc
94	1796	—	200.00	350.00	450.00	800.00

C#	Date	Mintage	Fine	VF	XF	Unc
95	1853	1,121	500.00	1100.	1850.	2500.
	1856	665 pcs.	550.00	1200.	2200.	2900.

MEDALLIC ISSUES

KREUZER

BILLON

KM#	Date	Mintage	Fine	VF	XF	Unc
M1	ND (1839)	—	2.50	5.00	15.00	50.00

3 KREUZER

BILLON
Rev: View of city.

KM#	Date	Mintage	Fine	VF	XF	Unc
M2	ND (1839)	—	—	—	—	—

6 KREUZER

.333 SILVER
Rev: View of city.

KM#	Date	Mintage	Fine	VF	XF	Unc
M3	ND (1839)	—	—	—	—	—

3/4 DUCAT

2.6250 gm., .986 GOLD, .0832 oz AGW
Coronation of Joseph II
Obv: Globe, Rev: Legend.

KM#	Date	Mintage	Fine	VF	XF	Unc
M4	1764	—	—	—	—	—

SILVER

KM#	Date	Mintage	Fine	VF	XF	Unc
M4a	1764	—	—	—	—	55.00

Coronation of Leopold II
Obv: Crossed insignia. Rev: Legend.

KM#	Date	Mintage	Fine	VF	XF	Unc
M5	1790	—	—	—	—	—

SILVER

KM#	Date	Mintage	Fine	VF	XF	Unc
M5a	1790	—	—	—	—	—

2.6250 gm., .986 GOLD, .0832 oz AGW
Coronation of Francis II
Obv: Crossed insignia. Rev: Legend.

KM#	Date	Mintage	Fine	VF	XF	Unc
M6	1792	—	—	—	—	—

DUCAT

.981 GOLD
Coronation of Joseph II
Obv: Bust of Joseph II.
Rev: Peace standing over fallen knight (War).

KM#	Date	Mintage	Fine	VF	XF	Unc
M7	1764	—	—	—	—	—

SILVER

KM#	Date	Mintage	Fine	VF	XF	Unc
M7a	1764	—	—	—	—	—

3.5000 gm., .986 GOLD, .1109 oz AGW
Coronation of Leopold II
Obv: Head of Leopold II. Rev: Altar.

KM#	Date	Mintage	Fine	VF	XF	Unc
M8	1790	—	—	—	—	—

SILVER

KM#	Date	Mintage	Fine	VF	XF	Unc
M8a	1790	—	—	—	—	50.00

3.5000 gm., .986 GOLD, .1109 oz AGW
Coronation of Francis II

KM#	Date	Mintage	Fine	VF	XF	Unc
M9	1792	—	800.00	1200.	1600.	2000.

SILVER

KM#	Date	Mintage	Fine	VF	XF	Unc
M9a	1792	—	—	—	—	52.50

3.5000 gm., .986 GOLD, .1109 oz AGW
Obv: Bust of Francis II.

Rev: 2 standing figures.

KM#	Date	Mintage	Fine	VF	XF	Unc
M10	ND (1792)	—	—	—	—	—

1-1/2 DUCATS

5.2500 gm., .986 GOLD, .1664 oz AGW
Coronation of Joseph II
Obv: Globe. Rev: Line inscription.

KM#	Date	Mintage	Fine	VF	XF	Unc
M11	1764	—	—	—	—	—

SILVER

KM#	Date	Mintage	Fine	VF	XF	Unc
M11a	1764	—	—	—	—	55.00

5.2500 gm., .986 GOLD, .1664 oz AGW
Coronation of Leopold II
Obv: Regal insignia.
Rev: Line inscription.

KM#	Date	Mintage	Fine	VF	XF	Unc
M12	1790	—	—	—	—	—

SILVER

KM#	Date	Mintage	Fine	VF	XF	Unc
M12a	1790	—	—	—	—	—

5.2500 gm., .986 GOLD, .1664 oz AGW
Coronation of Francis II.
Obv: Regal insignia.
Rev: Line inscription.

KM#	Date	Mintage	Fine	VF	XF	Unc
M13	1792	—	—	—	—	—

SILVER

KM#	Date	Mintage	Fine	VF	XF	Unc
M13a	1792	—	—	—	—	—

2 DUCATS

7.0000 gm., .986 GOLD, .2219 oz AGW
Coronation of Joseph II
Obv: Bust of Joseph II.
Rev: Peace standing over fallen knight (War).

KM#	Date	Mintage	Fine	VF	XF	Unc
M14	1764	—	—	—	—	—

SILVER

KM#	Date	Mintage	Fine	VF	XF	Unc
M14a	1764	—	—	—	—	—

7.0000 gm., .986 GOLD, .2219 oz AGW
Coronation of Leopold II
Obv: Head of Leopold II.
Rev: Altar.

KM#	Date	Mintage	Fine	VF	XF	Unc
M15	1790	—	—	—	—	—

SILVER

KM#	Date	Mintage	Fine	VF	XF	Unc
M15a	1790	—	—	—	55.00	65.00

7.0000 gm., .986 GOLD, .2219 oz AGW
Coronation of Francis II
Obv: Head of Francis II.
Rev: Figure at altar.

KM#	Date	Mintage	Fine	VF	XF	Unc
M16	1792	—	1000.	1300.	1800.	2500.

SILVER
300th Anniversary of the Reformation

KM#	Date	Mintage	Fine	VF	XF	Unc
M17	1817	—	—	—	—	70.00

PATTERNS

KM#	Date	Mintage	Identification	Mkt.Val.
1	1852	—	1 Heller, Copper, C4	—
2	1852	—	6 Kreuzer, Silver, C38	—

JEWISH PFENNIGS

JUDEN PFENNIGE –
'JEW PENNIES'

THELER

COPPER

C#	Date	Mintage	Fine	VF	XF	Unc
T1	1807	—	1.50	3.00	6.00	20.00

ATRIBUO

COPPER
Obv: Hand holding branch in shield. Rev: Value.

C#	Date	Mintage	Fine	VF	XF	Unc
T2	1809	—	1.00	2.50	5.00	25.00

1/4 HALBAG

COPPER

C#	Date	Mintage	Fine	VF	XF	Unc
T3	1818	—	1.50	3.00	6.00	25.00

HELLER

COPPER
Obv: Griffin. Rev: Value.

C#	Date	Mintage	Fine	VF	XF	Unc
T8	1819	—	5.00	13.50	20.00	40.00

C#	Date	Mintage	Fine	VF	XF	Unc
T9	1820	—	1.00	2.00	4.00	25.00

Without asterisks on sides of "1".

C#	Date	Mintage	Fine	VF	XF	Unc
T9a	1820	—	1.00	2.00	4.00	25.00

C#	Date	Mintage	Fine	VF	XF	Unc
T6a	1821	—	1.00	2.00	4.00	25.00

PFENNIG

COPPER

C#	Date	Mintage	Fine	VF	XF	Unc
T4	1819	—	.75	1.50	3.00	25.00

Rev: 1 PFENNIG

C#	Date	Mintage	Fine	VF	XF	Unc
T4a	1819	—	.75	1.50	3.00	25.00

C#	Date	Mintage	Fine	VF	XF	Unc
T5	1819	—	.75	1.50	3.00	25.00

Obv: Lion

C#	Date	Mintage	Fine	VF	XF	Unc
T6	1819	—	1.50	3.00	6.00	25.00

Obv: Rose branch

C#	Date	Mintage	Fine	VF	XF	Unc
T7	1819	—	5.00	13.50	20.00	45.00

C#	Date	Mintage	Fine	VF	XF	Unc
T10	1822	—	1.00	2.00	4.00	25.00

FREISING

Bishopric

A bishopric located in central Bavaria, was founded in 724. It became the site of an imperial mint in the 11th century. Bracteates of the bishops appeared c. 1150. The bishops were made princes of the empire in the 17th century. It became secularized in 1802 with part of the territories going to Bavaria and the rest to Salzburg.

RULERS
Joseph Conrad, 1790-1803

EIN (1) THALER
(Convention)

SILVER

C#	Date	Mintage	VG	Fine	VF	XF
2	1790	—	250.00	500.00	850.00	1000.

Obv: Smaller bust with KORNLEIN below.
Rev: Crowned and mantled arms.

C#	Date	Mintage	VG	Fine	VF	XF
2a	ND	—	100.00	225.00	300.00	400.00

FRIEDBERG

A city in Hesse-Darmstadt which was first settled by the Romans. It became a free city in 1211. A site of an Imperial Mint and obtained the mint right in 1541. In 1802 Friedberg passed to Hesse-Darmstadt and was mediatized in 1818.

RULERS
Franz Heinrich, 1755-1776
Johann Maria Rudolph, 1777-1805

20 KREUZER

SILVER
Obv: Arms. Rev: Crowned imperial eagle.

C#	Date	Mintage	Fine	VF	XF	Unc
1	1766	—	55.00	75.00	100.00	200.00

1/2 THALER

SILVER

C#	Date	Mintage	Fine	VF	XF	Unc
2	1766	—	125.00	175.00	250.00	400.00

EIN (1) THALER

SILVER

Obv: St. George on horse slaying dragon.
Rev: Crowned imperial eagle.

C#	Date	Mintage	Fine	VF	XF	Unc
3	1766	—	650.00	1000.	1500.	2500.

(Convention)

C#	Date	Mintage	Fine	VF	XF	Unc
4	1804	—	200.00	400.00	600.00	925.00

FUGGER

A wealthy banking and commercial family of Augsberg which began banking c. 1370 and became the bankers of the Hapsburgs by 1475. In 1500 they were given the county of Kirchberg and the lordship of Weissenborn (in Swabia) as security for a loan. The emperor made them hereditary counts of these areas and gave them the mint right in 1534. There was a complicated succession with many lines and few coin issuers. The land was divided by Bavaria and Wurttemberg in 1806.

RULERS

Cajetan zu Zinnenberg, (Elder line) 1751-1791
and Carl zu Norndorf, (Younger line, 1710-1784

THALER

SILVER

C#	Date	Mintage	VG	Fine	VF	XF
1	1781	—	300.00	600.00	850.00	1150.

FULDA

Located in central Germany, the abbey was founded in 744. The abbot became prince of the empire in the late 10th century. The first coins were struck in the 11th century. In 1803, Fulda was secularized and passed successively to Orange-Nassau, Westphalia, Hesse-Cassel and Prussia.

RULERS

Heinrich VIII, 1759-1788
Sede Vacante, 1788
Adalbert III, 1788-1802

1/2 THALER

(Contribution)

SILVER

C#	Date	Mintage	VG	Fine	VF	XF
53	1796	—	30.00	70.00	100.00	150.00

C#	Date	Mintage	VG	Fine	VF	XF
54	1796	—	50.00	125.00	225.00	300.00

THALER

SILVER
Sede Vacante Issue

C#	Date	Mintage	VG	Fine	VF	XF
52	1788	—	50.00	125.00	175.00	300.00

(Contribution)

C#	Date	Mintage	VG	Fine	VF	XF
55	1795	—	30.00	70.00	100.00	250.00
	1796	—	30.00	70.00	100.00	250.00

C#	Date	Mintage	VG	Fine	VF	XF
56	1795	—	50.00	100.00	175.00	300.00

Obv: Bust right.

57	1795	—	50.00	100.00	175.00	300.00

TRADE COINS

DUCAT

3.5000 gm., .986 GOLD, .1109 oz AGW

51	1779	—	500.00	1250.	1750.	2500.

Obv: 3 helmeted arms. Rev: 9 line inscription.

51a	1779	—	600.00	1500.	2250.	2750.

Obv: Bust right.

51b	1779	—	500.00	1250.	1750.	2500.

FURSTENBERG

A noble family with holdings in Baden and Wurttenberg. The lord of Furstenberg assumed the title of Count in the 13th century which was raised to the rank of prince in 1664. The Furstenberg possessions were mediatized in 1806.

RULERS

Joseph Wenzel, 1762-1783
Joseph Maria Benedict, 1783-1796
Karl Joachim, 1796-1804

1/2 KREUZER

COPPER
Obv: Crowned arms.
Rev: Value and date.

4	1772	—	7.50	12.50	20.00	35.00

EIN (1) KREUZER

COPPER
Obv: Crowned arms. Rev: Value and date.

5	1772 G	—	7.50	12.50	20.00	35.00
	1773 G	—	7.50	12.50	20.00	35.00

C#	Date	Mintage	Fine	VF	XF	Unc
13	1804 W.	.040	5.00	10.00	25.00	50.00

3 KREUZER

BILLON
Obv: Monogram of CJ. Rev: Crowned arms dividing date.

14	1804 W.	.012	10.00	20.00	32.50	75.00

6 KREUZER

BILLON
Obv: Monogram of CJ. Rev: Crowned arms dividing date.

C#	Date	Mintage	Fine	VF	XF	Unc
15	1804 W.	6,720	45.00	75.00	200.00	300.00

10 KREUZER

.500 SILVER

16	1804 W.	6,075	60.00	100.00	200.00	300.00

20 KREUZER

.583 SILVER
Obv: Bust right, legend ends: PRINC. IN FURSTENBERG.
Rev: Crowned arms.

17	1804 W.	3,010	75.00	125.00	200.00	300.00

Obv legend ends: PRINC FURSTENBERG.

17a	1804	Inc. Ab.	75.00	125.00	200.00	300.00

1/48 THALER

BILLON
Obv: Crowned arms. Rev: Value and date.

C#	Date	Mintage	VG	Fine	VF	XF
6	1772 G	—	12.50	20.00	35.00	55.00

1/24 THALER

BILLON
Obv: Crowned Arms. Rev: Value and date.

7	1772 G	—	10.00	15.00	25.00	40.00

EIN (1) THALER
(Mining)

SILVER
Obv: Armored bust of Joseph Wenzel right.
Rev: Mining scene with St. Wenzel to right, legend and date in exergue.

8	1767	500 pcs.	500.00	750.00	1000.	1500.

C#	Date	Mintage	Fine	VF	XF	Unc
11	1790	806 pcs.	300.00	500.00	1000.	2000.

(Convention)

28.1000 gm., .832 SILVER, .7521 OZ ASW
Obv: Bust right, I.L.W. below truncation.

18	1804 C.H.	388 pcs.	600.00	950.00	1350.	2000.

3 THALER

SILVER
Obv: Armored bust of Joseph Wenzel right.
Rev: Mining scene with St. Wenzel to right, legend and date in exergue.

C#	Date	Mintage	VG	Fine	VF	XF
9	1767	—	2500.	3500.	5000.	6500.

4 THALER

SILVER
Obv: Armored bust of Joseph Wenzel right.
Rev: Mining scene with St. Wenzel to right, legend and date in exergue.

9a	1767	—	—	—	Rare	—

9 THALER

SILVER
Obv: Armored bust of Joseph Wenzel right.
Rev: Mining scene with St. Wenzel to right, legend and date in exergue.

9b	1767	—	—	—	Rare	—

FURTHER AUSTRIA

(Vorderoesterreich)

Name given to imperial lands in South Swabia in the 18th century. In 1805 it was divided by Baden and Bavaria.

RULERS

Joseph II, 1780-1790
Leopold II, 1790-1792
Franz II (Austria), 1792-1805

MINTMARKS

A - Wien
F - Hall
G - Baia Mare (Nagybanya)
H - Gunzburg

HELLER

COPPER

Obv: Crowned arms. Rev: Value and date.

C#	Date	Mintage	Fine	VF	XF	Unc
1	1783H	—	8.50	17.50	35.00	75.00
	1784H	—	8.50	17.50	35.00	75.00
	1785H	—	8.50	17.50	35.00	75.00
	1787H	—	15.00	30.00	50.00	100.00
	1788H	—	8.50	17.50	35.00	75.00
	1789H	—	8.50	17.50	35.00	75.00
	1790H	—	8.50	17.50	35.00	75.00
	1791H	—	8.50	17.50	35.00	75.00
	1792H	—	8.50	17.50	35.00	75.00

Obv: Crowned shield.

C#	Date	Mintage	Fine	VF	XF	Unc
12	1792H	—	10.00	20.00	40.00	100.00
	1793H	—	17.50	35.00	70.00	100.00
	1797H	—	20.00	40.00	65.00	110.00
	1798H	—	—	—	Rare	—
	1799H	—	22.50	50.00	85.00	125.00
	1801H	—	17.50	35.00	70.00	100.00
	1803H	—	17.50	35.00	70.00	100.00

1/4 KREUTZER

COPPER
Obv: Crowned arms. Rev: Value and date.

C#	Date	Mintage	VG	Fine	VF	XF
2	1783H	—	2.50	5.00	10.00	25.00
	1784H	—	2.50	5.00	10.00	25.00
	1789H	—	2.50	5.00	10.00	25.00
	1790H	—	2.50	5.00	10.00	25.00

1.99 gm.

C#	Date	Mintage	Fine	VF	XF	Unc
13	1792H	—	—	—	Rare	—
	1793H	—	8.50	22.50	45.00	100.00
	1797H	—	8.50	22.50	45.00	100.00
	1798H	—	—	—	Rare	—
	1799H	—	—	—	Rare	—
	1800H	—	—	—	Rare	—

Reduced weight, 1.4 gm. Rev: Smaller lettering.

C#	Date	Mintage	Fine	VF	XF	Unc
13a	1801H	—	—	—	Rare	—
	1802H	—	10.00	25.00	50.00	100.00
	1803H	—	6.50	20.00	40.00	80.00

1/2 KREUTZER

COPPER
Obv: Crowned arms; legend of Joseph II.
Rev: Value and date in cartouche.

C#	Date	Mintage	VG	Fine	VF	XF
3	1783H	—	5.00	10.00	20.00	40.00
	1784H	—	5.00	10.00	20.00	40.00
	1789H	—	5.00	10.00	20.00	40.00

Obv: Crowned arms; legend of Leopold II.

C#	Date	Mintage	VG	Fine	VF	XF
8	1791H	—	—	—	Rare	—
	1792H	—	—	—	Rare	—

3.88 gm.

C#	Date	Mintage	Fine	VF	XF	Unc
14	1792H	—	—	—	Rare	—
	1793H	—	22.50	100.00	135.00	225.00
	1797H	—	—	—	Rare	—
	1798H	—	—	—	Rare	—
	1799H	—	—	—	Rare	—
	1800H	—	—	—	Rare	—

Reduced weight, 2.8 gm.

C#	Date	Mintage	Fine	VF	XF	Unc
14b	1801H	—	—	—	Rare	—
	1802H	—	15.00	85.00	125.00	185.00
	1803H	—	8.50	20.00	40.00	75.00
	1804H	—	—	—	Rare	—
14a	1805H	—	—	—	Rare	—

EIN (1) KREUTZER

COPPER
Obv: Crowned arms; legend of Joseph II.
Rev: Value and date in cartouche.

C#	Date	Mintage	VG	Fine	VF	XF
4	1783	—	4.00	7.50	15.00	50.00
	1784	—	4.00	7.50	15.00	50.00
	1788	—	4.00	7.50	15.00	50.00
	1789	—	4.00	7.50	15.00	50.00

Obv: Crowned arms; legend of Leopold II.

C#	Date	Mintage	VG	Fine	VF	XF
9	1791H	—	—	—	Rare	—
	1792H	—	15.00	30.00	60.00	100.00

7.77 gm.

C#	Date	Mintage	Fine	VF	XF	Unc
15	1792H	—	3.75	8.50	15.00	50.00
	1793H	—	3.75	8.50	15.00	50.00
	1794H	—	3.75	8.50	15.00	50.00
	1795H	—	3.75	8.50	15.00	50.00

Rev: Smaller lettering; reduced weight, 5.7 gm.

C#	Date	Mintage	Fine	VF	XF	Unc
15b	1801H	—	3.50	8.50	13.50	50.00
	1802H	—	3.50	8.50	13.50	50.00
	1803H	—	3.50	8.50	13.50	50.00
	1804H	—	3.50	8.50	13.50	50.00

C#	Date	Mintage	Fine	VF	XF	Unc
15a	1804H	—	—	—	Rare	—
	1805H	—	3.75	7.50	15.00	50.00

3 KREUTZER

BILLON
Obv: 3 shields and date.
Rev: Value over sprays.

C#	Date	Mintage	Fine	VF	XF	Unc
5	1786H	—	15.00	35.00	75.00	150.00
	1787H	—	15.00	35.00	75.00	150.00
	1791H	—	15.00	35.00	75.00	150.00
	1792H	—	15.00	35.00	75.00	150.00

.312 SILVER
Obv: Value. Rev: 3 shields, 1.46 gm.

C#	Date	Mintage	Fine	VF	XF	Unc
16	1793A	—	15.00	30.00	62.50	185.00
	1793H	—	15.00	30.00	62.50	185.00
	1794A	—	—	—	Rare	—
	1794H	—	10.00	25.00	50.00	150.00
	1795H	—	10.00	25.00	50.00	150.00
	1796H	—	15.00	30.00	62.50	185.00
	1797H	—	10.00	25.00	50.00	150.00
	1799H	—	—	—	Rare	—
	1800H	—	—	—	Rare	—

Reduced weight, 1.41 gm.

C#	Date	Mintage	Fine	VF	XF	Unc
16a	1802A	—	—	—	Rare	—
	1802G	—	—	—	Rare	—
	1802H	—	—	—	Rare	—
	1803H	—	—	—	Rare	—
	1804H	—	—	—	Rare	—
	1805H	—	—	—	Rare	—

6 KREUTZER

BILLON
Similar to C#17.

C#	Date	Mintage	VG	Fine	VF	XF
6	1786H	—	10.00	15.00	22.50	45.00
	1787H	—	10.00	15.00	22.50	45.00
	1792H	—	10.00	15.00	22.50	45.00

.375 SILVER, 2.45 gm.

C#	Date	Mintage	Fine	VF	XF	Unc
17	1792H	—	11.50	22.50	45.00	65.00
	1793A	—	15.00	30.00	55.00	80.00
	1793H	—	7.50	15.00	30.00	50.00
	1794A	—	—	—	Rare	—
	1794H V	—	7.50	15.00	30.00	50.00
	1795H	—	10.00	20.00	40.00	60.00
	1796H	—	7.50	17.50	35.00	55.00
	1797H	—	6.50	15.00	30.00	50.00
	1798H	—	15.00	30.00	55.00	80.00
	1799H V	—	7.50	17.50	37.50	55.00

C#	Date	Mintage	Fine	VF	XF	Unc
17	1800H	—	10.00	22.50	45.00	65.00

Reduced weight, 2.35 gm.

C#	Date	Mintage	Fine	VF	XF	Unc
17a	1802A	—	—	—	Rare	—
	1802G	—	—	—	Rare	—
	1802H	—	8.50	17.50	35.00	60.00
	1803H	—	6.50	12.50	25.00	45.00
	1804H V	—	5.00	10.00	20.00	40.00
	1805A	—	10.00	20.00	40.00	65.00
	1805H V	—	7.50	15.00	30.00	50.00

HALL in SWABIA

(Schwabisch Halle)

A city in southern Germany. The first hellers were minted here in the 12th century. Hall became a free city in 1276 and obtained the mint right in 1396. Annexed to Wurttemberg in 1803.

Free City

PFENNIG

BILLON
Uniface, shields on Imperial eagle.

C#	Date	Mintage	Fine	VF	XF	Unc
3	1751-1784	—	5.00	10.00	17.50	50.00

1/2 THALER

(Convention)

SILVER
Similar to 1 Convention Thaler, C#7.

C#	Date	Mintage	Fine	VF	XF	Unc
5	1777	—	125.00	175.00	275.00	350.00

EIN (1) THALER

(Convention)

SILVER

C#	Date	Mintage	Fine	VF	XF	Unc
7	1777	—	350.00	550.00	750.00	1000.

TRADE COINS

DUCAT

3.5000 gm., .986 GOLD, .1109 oz AGW
Similar to 1 Convention Thaler, C#7.

C#	Date	Mintage	Fine	VF	XF	Unc
10	1777	—	700.00	1000.	1250.	1500.
	ND	—	700.00	1000.	1250.	1500.

HAMBURG

The city of Hamburg is located on the Elbe River about 75 miles from the North Sea. It was founded by Charlemagne in the 9th century. In 1241 it joined Lubeck to form the Hanseatic League. The mint right was leased to the citizens in 1292, however the first local hohlpfennigs had been struck almost 50 years earlier. In 1510 Hamburg was formally made a free city, though in fact it had been free for about 250 years. It was occupied by the French during the Napoleonic period. In 1866 it joined the North German Confederation and became a part of the German Empire in 1871. The Hamburg coinage is almost continuous up to the time of World War I.

RULERS

Joseph II, 1765-1790
Leopold II, 1790-1792
Francis II, 1792-1806

MINTMASTER'S INITIALS

O.H.K. - Otto Hinrich Knorre (1761-1805)

H.S.K. - Hans Schierven Knoph (1805-1809)

C.A.I.G. - Ginquembre (1809)

DREILING

BILLON

Obv: Castle w/O.H.K. below. Rev: 'I' between rosettes.

C#	Date	Mintage	Fine	VF	XF	Unc
1a.1	1783 OHK	.272	1.75	4.00	8.00	30.00
	1786 OHK	.393	1.75	4.00	8.00	30.00
	1793 OHK	.768	1.75	4.00	8.00	30.00
	1794 OHK	I.A.	1.75	4.00	8.00	30.00
	1796 OHK	.172	1.75	4.00	8.00	30.00
	1797 OHK	.529	1.75	4.00	8.00	30.00
	1798 OHK	—	1.75	4.00	8.00	30.00
	1800 OHK	.656	1.75	4.00	8.00	30.00
	1803 OHK	.355	1.75	4.00	8.00	30.00

Obv: Castle w/H.S.K. below.

C#	Date	Mintage	Fine	VF	XF	Unc
1a.2	1807 HSK	.384	1.50	4.00	8.00	30.00
	1809 HSK	.768	1.50	4.00	8.00	30.00

Rev: 'I' between dots.

C#	Date	Mintage	Fine	VF	XF	Unc
1a.3	1823 HSK	.021	3.00	5.00	10.00	30.00
	1832 HSK	.036	2.50	4.50	8.50	30.00
	1833 HSK	.303	1.50	4.00	8.00	30.00
	1836 HSK	.293	1.50	4.00	8.00	30.00
	1839 HSK	.299	1.50	4.00	8.00	30.00

Obv: Redesigned castle. Rev: 'I' between rosettes.

C#	Date	Mintage	Fine	VF	XF	Unc
1a.4	1841 HSK	.554	1.50	4.00	8.00	30.00

Obv: W/o initials below castle.
Rev: "I" between 5-pointed stars.

C#	Date	Mintage	Fine	VF	XF	Unc
1a.5	1846	.574	1.25	3.00	8.00	30.00

Rev: 'I' between 6-pointed stars.

C#	Date	Mintage	Fine	VF	XF	Unc
1a.6	1851	.578	1.25	3.00	8.00	30.00

Beaded borders.

C#	Date	Mintage	Fine	VF	XF	Unc
1a.7	1855A	.320	1.25	3.00	10.00	25.00
	1855	2.613	1.25	2.00	5.00	25.00

SECHSLING

BILLON

Obv: Castle w/O.H.K. below. Rev: 'I' between rosettes.

C#	Date	Mintage	Fine	VF	XF	Unc
3a.1	1778 OHK	.259	2.00	5.00	10.00	35.00
	1783 OHK	.182	2.00	5.00	10.00	35.00
	1794 OHK	.256	2.00	5.00	10.00	35.00
	1797 OHK	.163	2.00	5.00	10.00	35.00
	1800 OHK	.227	2.00	5.00	10.00	35.00
	1803 OHK	.182	2.00	5.00	10.00	35.00

Obv: Castle w/H.S.K. below.

C#	Date	Mintage	Fine	VF	XF	Unc
3a.2	1807 HSK	.096	1.75	5.00	10.00	35.00
	1809 HSK	.192	1.75	5.00	10.00	35.00
	1817 HSK	.048	2.00	5.00	10.00	35.00
	1823 HSK	.030	2.50	5.00	10.00	35.00
	1833 HSK	.135	1.75	5.00	10.00	35.00
	1836 HSK	.155	1.75	5.00	10.00	35.00
	1839 HSK	.354	1.25	5.00	10.00	35.00

Rev: 'I' between dots.

C#	Date	Mintage	Fine	VF	XF	Unc
3a.3	1832 HSK	.066	2.00	5.00	10.00	35.00

Obv: Redesigned castle. Rev: 'I' between rosettes.

C#	Date	Mintage	Fine	VF	XF	Unc
3a.4	1841 HSK	.293	1.25	5.00	10.00	35.00

Obv: W/o initials below castle.
Rev: "I" between 5-pointed stars.

C#	Date	Mintage	Fine	VF	XF	Unc
3a.5	1846	.480	1.25	5.00	10.00	35.00

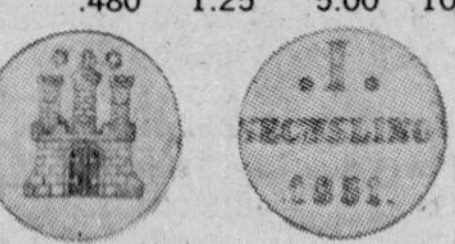

Rev: 'I' between 6-pointed stars.

C#	Date	Mintage	Fine	VF	XF	Unc
3a.6	1851	.480	1.25	5.00	10.00	35.00

Beaded borders.

C#	Date	Mintage	Fine	VF	XF	Unc
3a.7	1855A	.098	2.00	5.00	10.00	35.00
	1855	1.841	1.00	2.00	5.00	25.00

SCHILLING

BILLON

Obv: Castle w/O.H.K. below. Rev: 'I' between rosettes.

C#	Date	Mintage	Fine	VF	XF	Unc
6.1	1778 OHK	2.320	2.00	4.00	10.00	35.00
	1790 OHK	.570	2.50	5.00	10.00	35.00
	1794 OHK	1.200	2.00	4.00	10.00	35.00
	1795 OHK	.664	2.50	5.00	10.00	35.00

Obv: Castle w/H.S.K. below.

C#	Date	Mintage	Fine	VF	XF	Unc
6.2	1817 HSK	.019	3.50	5.50	10.00	35.00
	1818 HSK	.029	3.00	5.00	10.00	35.00
	1819 HSK	.149	2.00	5.00	10.00	35.00

Rev. leg: HAMB. COVR., 'I' between dots.

C#	Date	Mintage	Fine	VF	XF	Unc
6a.1	1823 HSK	.138	1.50	5.00	10.00	35.00
	1828 HSK	.142	1.50	5.00	10.00	35.00
	1832 HSK	.142	1.50	5.00	10.00	35.00

Rev: 'I' between rosettes.

C#	Date	Mintage	Fine	VF	XF	Unc
6a.2	1837 HSK	.153	1.50	5.00	10.00	35.00
	1840 HSK	.144	1.50	5.00	10.00	35.00

Obv: Redesigned castle.

C#	Date	Mintage	Fine	VF	XF	Unc
6a.3	1841 HSK	.149	2.00	5.00	10.00	35.00

Rev: 'I' between 5-pointed stars.

C#	Date	Mintage	Fine	VF	XF	Unc
6a.4	1846	.240	1.50	5.00	10.00	35.00

Rev: 'I' between 6-pointed stars.

C#	Date	Mintage	Fine	VF	XF	Unc
6a.5	1851	.240	1.50	5.00	10.00	35.00

Beaded borders.

C#	Date	Mintage	Fine	VF	XF	Unc
6a.6	1855A	.112	1.25	5.00	8.00	35.00
	1855	1.841	1.00	1.75	5.00	30.00

4 SCHILLING

3.0500 gm., .562 SILVER, .0551 oz ASW

C#	Date	Mintage	Fine	VF	XF	Unc
15	1797 OHK	.236	10.00	20.00	40.00	100.00

8 SCHILLING

5.5000 gm., .625 SILVER, .1105 oz ASW

C#	Date	Mintage	Fine	VF	XF	Unc
21	1797 OHK	.206	15.00	30.00	50.00	125.00

Obv: 3 small towers; O.H.K. below.

C#	Date	Mintage	Fine	VF	XF	Unc
21a	1797 OHK	I.A.	15.00	30.00	50.00	125.00

16 SCHILLING

9.1600 gm., .750 SILVER, .2209 oz ASW

C#	Date	Mintage	Fine	VF	XF	Unc
27	1789 OHK	.080	25.00	65.00	100.00	175.00

32 SCHILLING

18.3200 gm., .750 SILVER, .4418 oz ASW
Similar to C#35. Obv. leg: JOSEPHVS.II.D.G....

C#	Date	Mintage	Fine	VF	XF	Unc
30a	1766 OHK	.018	50.00	100.00	200.00	300.00
	1767 OHK	—	50.00	100.00	200.00	300.00

Similar to C#35.

C#	Date	Mintage	Fine	VF	XF	Unc
33	1788 OHK	.060	25.00	50.00	100.00	175.00
	1789 OHK	.315	22.50	45.00	90.00	150.00

C#	Date	Mintage	Fine	VF	XF	Unc
35	1794 OHK	.130	30.00	65.00	90.00	165.00
	1795 OHK	.951	25.00	50.00	75.00	125.00
	1796 OHK	1.138	25.00	50.00	75.00	125.00
	1797 OHK	.180	30.00	65.00	90.00	165.00

14.1700 gm., .969 SILVER, .4415 oz ASW

C#	Date	Mintage	Fine	VF	XF	Unc
39	1808 HSK	.210	20.00	35.00	50.00	110.00

C#	Date	Mintage	Fine	VF	XF	Unc
39a	1809 HSK	.880	15.00	35.00	50.00	100.00
39b	1809 AIG	3.058	17.50	35.00	50.00	100.00

TRADE COINS

DUCAT

3.4900 gm., .989 GOLD, .1110 oz AGW

C#	Date	Mintage	Fine	VF	XF	Unc
43	1766 OHK	2,904	250.00	350.00	550.00	750.00
	1767 OHK	3,640	250.00	350.00	550.00	750.00
	1768 OHK	—	250.00	350.00	550.00	750.00
	1769 OHK	—	250.00	350.00	550.00	750.00
	1770 OHK	3,192	250.00	350.00	550.00	750.00
	1771 OHK	—	250.00	350.00	550.00	750.00
	1772 OHK	—	250.00	350.00	550.00	750.00

3.4900 gm., .979 GOLD, .1099 oz AGW

C#	Date	Mintage	Fine	VF	XF	Unc
45	1773	—	250.00	350.00	500.00	750.00
	1774	—	250.00	350.00	500.00	750.00
	1775	—	250.00	350.00	500.00	750.00
	1776	—	250.00	350.00	500.00	750.00
	1777	—	250.00	350.00	500.00	750.00
	1778	—	250.00	350.00	500.00	750.00
	1779	3,192	250.00	350.00	500.00	750.00
	1780	4,471	250.00	350.00	500.00	750.00
	1781	4,414	250.00	350.00	500.00	750.00
	1782	4,500	250.00	350.00	500.00	750.00
	1783	4,500	250.00	350.00	500.00	750.00
	1784	3,231	250.00	350.00	500.00	750.00
	1785	3,714	250.00	350.00	500.00	750.00
	1786	4,500	250.00	350.00	500.00	750.00
	1787	4,689	250.00	350.00	500.00	750.00
	1788	4,500	250.00	350.00	500.00	750.00

Rev: Crowned eagle, titles of Leopold II.

C#	Date	Mintage	Fine	VF	XF	Unc
47	1791	5,633	400.00	500.00	750.00	1000.
	1792	5,054	400.00	500.00	750.00	1000.

Obv: Oblong tablet, MON. AVR.
Rev: Double eagle, leg: ...D. G. ROM....

C#	Date	Mintage	Fine	VF	XF	Unc
49	1800	3,370	300.00	450.00	600.00	800.00
	1801	7,236	250.00	450.00	600.00	800.00
	1802	9,199	250.00	450.00	600.00	800.00
	1803	6,365	250.00	450.00	600.00	800.00
	1804	7,284	250.00	450.00	600.00	800.00
	1805	—	250.00	450.00	600.00	800.00
	1806	7,521	250.00	450.00	600.00	800.00

C#	Date	Mintage	Fine	VF	XF	Unc
52	1807	6,000	250.00	450.00	600.00	800.00

C#	Date	Mintage	Fine	VF	XF	Unc
53	1808	7,500	200.00	300.00	450.00	650.00
	1809	7,500	200.00	300.00	450.00	650.00
	1810	7,407	200.00	300.00	450.00	650.00

C#	Date	Mintage	Fine	VF	XF	Unc
55	1811	.011	150.00	250.00	350.00	550.00
	1815	9,965	150.00	250.00	350.00	550.00
	1817	5,000	150.00	250.00	350.00	550.00
	1818	7,000	150.00	250.00	350.00	550.00
	1819	8,901	150.00	250.00	350.00	550.00
	1820	7,000	150.00	250.00	350.00	550.00
	1821	9,900	150.00	250.00	350.00	550.00
	1822	.013	150.00	250.00	350.00	550.00
	1823	8,700	150.00	250.00	350.00	550.00
	1824	6,970	150.00	250.00	350.00	550.00
	1825	.010	150.00	250.00	350.00	550.00
	1826	.012	150.00	250.00	350.00	550.00
	1827	.011	150.00	250.00	350.00	550.00
	1828	8,601	150.00	250.00	350.00	550.00
	1829	9,606	150.00	250.00	350.00	550.00
	1830	.012	150.00	250.00	350.00	550.00
	1831	9,200	150.00	250.00	350.00	550.00
	1832	9,500	150.00	250.00	350.00	550.00
	1833	9,440	150.00	250.00	350.00	550.00
	1834	.010	150.00	250.00	350.00	550.00

C#	Date	Mintage	Fine	VF	XF	Unc
56.1	1835	.010	150.00	250.00	350.00	550.00
	1836	8,067	150.00	250.00	350.00	550.00
	1837	8,156	150.00	250.00	350.00	550.00
	1838	9,000	150.00	250.00	350.00	550.00
	1839	9,045	150.00	250.00	350.00	550.00
	1840	9,882	150.00	250.00	350.00	550.00
	1841	.010	150.00	250.00	350.00	550.00
	1842	.012	150.00	250.00	350.00	550.00

Struck in a collar.

C#	Date	Mintage	Fine	VF	XF	Unc
56.2	1843	.012	150.00	250.00	350.00	550.00
	1844	9,768	150.00	250.00	350.00	550.00
	1845	.012	150.00	250.00	350.00	550.00
	1846	.010	150.00	250.00	350.00	550.00
	1847	.011	150.00	250.00	350.00	550.00
	1848	.010	150.00	250.00	350.00	550.00
	1849	.013	150.00	250.00	350.00	550.00
	1850	.010	150.00	250.00	350.00	550.00

Obv: Knights shield redesigned.
Rev. leg: AEQV. POND.MARC.COL.

C#	Date	Mintage	Fine	VF	XF	Unc
56.3	1851	.011	150.00	250.00	300.00	500.00
	1852	8,498	150.00	250.00	300.00	500.00
	1853	9,477	150.00	250.00	300.00	500.00

C#	Date	Mintage	Fine	VF	XF	Unc
56a.1	1854	.010	125.00	250.00	300.00	500.00
	1855	.012	125.00	250.00	300.00	500.00
	1856	.011	125.00	250.00	300.00	500.00
	1857	.011	125.00	250.00	300.00	500.00
	1858	.012	125.00	250.00	300.00	500.00
	1859	.010	125.00	250.00	300.00	500.00
	1860	.014	125.00	250.00	300.00	500.00
	1861	.015	125.00	250.00	300.00	500.00
	1862	.015	125.00	250.00	300.00	500.00
	1863	.017	125.00	250.00	300.00	500.00
	1864	.020	100.00	250.00	300.00	500.00
	1865	.024	100.00	250.00	300.00	500.00
	1866	.017	125.00	250.00	300.00	500.00
	1867	.024	100.00	250.00	300.00	500.00

Rev: Mintmark B below shell.

C#	Date	Mintage	Fine	VF	XF	Unc
56a.2	1868B	.026	100.00	200.00	250.00	500.00
	1869B	.025	100.00	200.00	250.00	500.00
	1870B	.026	100.00	200.00	250.00	500.00
	1871B	.030	100.00	200.00	250.00	500.00
	1872B	.030	100.00	200.00	250.00	500.00

2 DUCATS

6.9800 gm., .989 GOLD, .2220 oz AGW

C#	Date	Mintage	Fine	VF	XF	Unc
44	1766 OHK	613 pcs.	850.00	1250.	1750.	2500.
	1767 OHK	584 pcs.	850.00	1250.	1750.	2500.
	1768 OHK	—	850.00	1250.	1750.	2500.
	1769 OHK	—	850.00	1250.	1750.	2500.
	1770 OHK	536 pcs.	850.00	1250.	1750.	2500.
	1771 OHK	—	850.00	1250.	1750.	2500.

Rev: No frame for O.H.K.

C#	Date	Mintage	Fine	VF	XF	Unc
44a	1772 OHK	—	1000.	1500.	1950.	2750.

6.9800 gm., .979 GOLD, .2197 oz AGW

C#	Date	Mintage	Fine	VF	XF	Unc
46b	1773	—	850.00	1000.	1500.	2500.
	1774	—	800.00	1000.	1500.	2500.
	1775	—	800.00	1000.	1500.	2500.
	1776	—	800.00	1000.	1500.	2500.
	1777	—	800.00	1000.	1500.	2500.
	1778	—	950.00	1350.	1850.	2500.
	1779	479 pcs.	850.00	1100.	1650.	2500.
	1780	875 pcs.	750.00	950.00	1250.	2500.
	1781	231 pcs.	950.00	1350.	1950.	2500.
	1782	450 pcs.	850.00	1100.	1650.	2500.
	1783	450 pcs.	850.00	1100.	1650.	2500.
	1784	455 pcs.	850.00	1100.	1650.	2500.
	1785	879 pcs.	750.00	950.00	1250.	2500.
	1786	400 pcs.	950.00	1250.	1750.	2500.
	1787	320 pcs.	950.00	1350.	1850.	2500.
	1788	400 pcs.	950.00	1250.	1750.	2500.

NOTE: Varieties exist.

Obv: Tablet, arms above.
Rev: Crowned small imperial eagle, date above.

C#	Date	Mintage	Fine	VF	XF	Unc
46c	1789	402 pcs.	800.00	1100.	1500.	2500.
	1790	500 pcs.	800.00	1100.	1500.	2500.

Obv: 3 towers over tablet.
Rev: Crowned eagle, titles of Leopold II.

C#	Date	Mintage	Fine	VF	XF	Unc
48	1791	502 pcs.	800.00	1100.	1500.	2500.
	1792	701 pcs.	800.00	1100.	1500.	2500.

Rev. leg: ...D.G.ROM.IMP...

C#	Date	Mintage	Fine	VF	XF	Unc
50	1800	811 pcs.	500.00	825.00	1225.	2000.
	1801	1,273	400.00	700.00	1050.	2000.
	1802	1,256	400.00	700.00	1050.	2000.
	1803	837 pcs.	500.00	700.00	1200.	2000.
	1805	—	450.00	700.00	1050.	2000.

Rev. leg: ....D.G.R.IMP...

C#	Date	Mintage	Fine	VF	XF	Unc
50a	1806	1,201	400.00	700.00	1050.	2000.

C#	Date	Mintage	Fine	VF	XF	Unc
54	1808	1,250	400.00	800.00	1250.	2000.
	1809	1,250	400.00	800.00	1250.	2000.
	1810	1,050	400.00	800.00	1250.	2000.
	1814	1,072	400.00	800.00	1225.	2000.

4 DUCATS

13.9600 gm., .979 GOLD, .4394 oz AGW
Obv: 3 towers. Rev: Crowned eagle.

C#	Date	Mintage	Fine	VF	XF	Unc
51	1797	—	2500.	3250.	4000.	6000.

MONETARY REFORM

2 MARK

11.1110 gm., .900 SILVER, .3215 oz ASW

Y#	Date	Mintage	Fine	VF	XF	Unc
57	1876J	2.325	15.00	35.00	250.00	600.00
	1877J	.500	20.00	45.00	400.00	700.00
	1878J	.350	20.00	50.00	300.00	650.00
	1880J	.099	50.00	90.00	400.00	950.00
	1883J	.060	40.00	80.00	450.00	1000.
	1888J	.100	20.00	50.00	300.00	600.00

Y#	Date	Mintage	Fine	VF	XF	Unc
57a	1892J	.141	15.00	25.00	75.00	275.00
	1893J	.146	15.00	25.00	70.00	250.00
	1896J	.286	12.50	20.00	60.00	185.00
	1898J	.118	15.00	25.00	70.00	250.00
	1899J	.286	12.50	20.00	65.00	165.00
	1900J	.577	9.00	15.00	50.00	125.00
	1901J	.482	9.00	15.00	50.00	125.00
	1902J	.779	9.00	15.00	50.00	125.00
	1903J	.817	9.00	15.00	50.00	125.00
	1904J	1.248	9.00	15.00	50.00	125.00
	1905J	.204	12.50	20.00	70.00	175.00
	1906J	1.225	9.00	15.00	45.00	90.00
	1907J	1.226	9.00	15.00	40.00	75.00
	1908J	.368	9.00	15.00	40.00	85.00
	1911J	.204	9.00	15.00	45.00	85.00
	1912J	.079	15.00	25.00	100.00	175.00
	1913J	.105	9.00	15.00	45.00	90.00
	1914J	.328	9.00	15.00	45.00	90.00
	Common Type	—	—	—	Proof	125.00

3 MARK

16.6670 gm., .900 SILVER, .4823 oz ASW

Y#	Date	Mintage	Fine	VF	XF	Unc
58	1908J	.408	12.50	15.00	20.00	45.00
	1909J	1.389	12.50	15.00	20.00	45.00
	1910J	.526	12.50	15.00	20.00	45.00
	1911J	.922	12.50	15.00	20.00	45.00
	1912J	.491	12.50	15.00	20.00	45.00
	1913J	.344	12.50	15.00	20.00	45.00
	1914J	.575	12.50	15.00	20.00	45.00
	Common Type	—	—	—	Proof	160.00

5 MARK

27.7770 gm., .900 SILVER, .8038 oz ASW

Y#	Date	Mintage	Fine	VF	XF	Unc
59	1875J	.286	25.00	45.00	375.00	650.00
	1876J	.930	21.00	27.50	325.00	500.00
	1888J	.040	55.00	85.00	400.00	700.00

1.9910 gm., .900 GOLD, .0576 oz AGW

Y#	Date	Mintage	Fine	VF	XF	Unc
60	1877J	.441	100.00	140.00	200.00	350.00

27.7770 gm., .900 SILVER, .8038 oz ASW

Y#	Date	Mintage	Fine	VF	XF	Unc
59a	1891J	.059	21.00	30.00	90.00	200.00
	1893J	.055	21.00	27.50	80.00	175.00
	1894J	.082	21.00	22.50	70.00	160.00
	1895J	.082	21.00	22.50	70.00	160.00
	1896J	.016	110.00	225.00	400.00	800.00
	1898J	.176	21.00	22.50	55.00	120.00
	1899J	.082	21.00	22.50	60.00	135.00
	1900J	.172	21.00	22.50	55.00	110.00
	1901J	.172	21.00	22.50	55.00	110.00
	1902J	.294	21.00	22.50	45.00	85.00
	1903J	.588	21.00	22.50	45.00	85.00
	1904J	.319	21.00	22.50	45.00	85.00
	1907J	.326	21.00	22.50	45.00	85.00
	1908J	.458	21.00	22.00	40.00	75.00
	1913J	.327	21.00	22.00	40.00	75.00

10 MARK

3.9820 gm., .900 GOLD, .1152 oz AGW
Obv: Helmeted, rounded arms. Rev: Type 1 eagle.

Y#	Date	Mintage	Fine	VF	XF	Unc
56	1873B	.025	500.00	750.00	1100.	1400.

Rev: Type 2 eagle.

Y#	Date	Mintage	Fine	VF	XF	Unc
56a	1874B	.050	350.00	500.00	725.00	900.00

Y#	Date	Mintage	Fine	VF	XF	Unc
61	1875J	.565	75.00	110.00	125.00	150.00
	1876J	—	650.00	800.00	1300.	1750.
	1877J	.220	75.00	110.00	125.00	150.00
	1878J	.316	75.00	110.00	125.00	150.00
	1879J	.255	75.00	110.00	125.00	150.00
	1880J	.139	110.00	140.00	160.00	175.00
	1888J	.163	110.00	140.00	160.00	175.00

Y#	Date	Mintage	Fine	VF	XF	Unc
61a	1890J	.245	75.00	110.00	125.00	150.00
	1893J	.246	75.00	110.00	125.00	150.00
	1896J	.164	75.00	110.00	125.00	150.00
	1898J	.344	75.00	110.00	125.00	150.00
	1900J	.082	100.00	150.00	175.00	225.00
	1901J	.082	100.00	150.00	165.00	190.00
	1902J	.041	250.00	300.00	400.00	500.00
	1903J	.230	75.00	110.00	125.00	150.00
	1905J	.164	75.00	110.00	125.00	150.00
	1906J	.163	75.00	110.00	125.00	150.00
	1907J	.111	75.00	110.00	125.00	150.00
	1908J	.032	250.00	400.00	550.00	750.00
	1909J	.122	75.00	110.00	125.00	150.00
	1910J	.041	175.00	250.00	400.00	500.00
	1911J	.075	100.00	125.00	225.00	350.00
	1912J	.048	200.00	300.00	450.00	550.00
	1913J	.041	200.00	300.00	450.00	550.00

20 MARK

7.9650 gm., .900 GOLD, .2304 oz AGW
Rev: Type 2 eagle

Y#	Date	Mintage	Fine	VF	XF	Unc
62	1875J	.313	150.00	160.00	175.00	200.00
	1876J	1.723	BV	150.00	175.00	185.00
	1877J	1.324	BV	150.00	175.00	185.00
	1878J	2.080	BV	150.00	175.00	185.00
	1879J	.104	350.00	600.00	800.00	1200.
	1880J	.120	150.00	160.00	175.00	225.00
	1881J	500 pcs.	4500.	6000.	8000.	10,000.
	1883J	.125	150.00	160.00	200.00	225.00
	1884J	.639	150.00	160.00	175.00	185.00
	1887J	.251	150.00	160.00	175.00	190.00
	1889J	.014	500.00	750.00	850.00	1250.

Rev: Type 3 eagle.

Y#	Date	Mintage	Fine	VF	XF	Unc
62a	1893J	.815	BV	150.00	160.00	175.00
	1894J	.501	BV	150.00	160.00	175.00
	1895J	.501	BV	150.00	160.00	175.00
	1897J	.500	BV	150.00	160.00	175.00
	1899J	1.002	BV	150.00	160.00	175.00
	1900J	.501	BV	150.00	160.00	175.00
	1913J	.491	BV	150.00	160.00	175.00

HANAU — MUNZENBERG

Hanau, in West Germany was founded by the Romans. In 1368 they were granted the right to mint hellers. They were given municipal rights in 1393 and were raised to princely rank in 1696. Hanau was passed to Hesse-Cassel in 1815.

RULERS

Wilhelm, Count (under regency of Mother, Mary of England) 1760-1765
Wilhelm, Count, 1765-1785

MINTMASTER'S INITIALS

I.I.E. - Johan Jacob Encke, 1740-1770
C.L.R. - Christian Ludwig Ruden, 1771-1784

HELLER

COPPER

C#	Date	Mintage	VG	Fine	VF	XF
20	1768	—	3.00	5.00	10.00	20.00
	1769	—	3.00	5.00	10.00	20.00
	1770	—	3.00	5.00	10.00	20.00
	1771	—	3.00	5.00	10.00	20.00
	1772	—	3.00	5.00	10.00	20.00
	1773	—	3.00	5.00	10.00	20.00

KREUZER

COPPER
Obv: Crowned arms.
Rev: Value and date in ornate circle.

C#	Date	Mintage	VG	Fine	VF	XF
21	1773	—	5.00	7.50	11.50	20.00

BILLON
Obv: Arms. Rev: Value and date.

C#	Date	Mintage	VG	Fine	VF	XF
23	1765	—	5.00	7.50	11.50	20.00

Obv: Crowned arms.
Rev: Value and date in ornate circle.

C#	Date	Mintage	VG	Fine	VF	XF
24	1773	—	5.00	7.50	11.50	20.00

5 KREUZER

BILLON
Obv: Arms. Rev: Value and date.

C#	Date	Mintage	VG	Fine	VF	XF
27	1765	—	5.00	7.50	11.50	20.00
	1766	—	5.00	7.50	11.50	20.00

SILVER
Obv: Bust of Wilhelm left.
Rev: Crowned arms.

C#	Date	Mintage	Fine	VF	XF	Unc
29	1775	—	7.50	11.50	25.00	75.00

10 KREUZER

SILVER
Obv: MLH monogram.
Rev: Dual arms and pillar.

C#	Date	Mintage	Fine	VF	XF	Unc
10	1763	—	17.50	25.00	35.00	90.00

Obv: Bust of Wilhelm. Rev: Arms.

C#	Date	Mintage	Fine	VF	XF	Unc
31	1766	—	7.50	11.50	25.00	65.00

20 KREUZER

SILVER
Obv: Dual arms and pillar.
Rev: Value and date.

C#	Date	Mintage	Fine	VF	XF	Unc
12	1764	—	25.00	35.00	50.00	125.00

Obv: Bust of Wilhelm right.
Rev: Arms and date.

C#	Date	Mintage	Fine	VF	XF	Unc
33	1765	—	12.50	20.00	40.00	100.00
	1766	—	12.50	20.00	40.00	100.00

1/2 THALER

SILVER
Obv: Bust of Mary right.

C#	Date	Mintage	Fine	VF	XF	Unc
14	1763 IIE	—	150.00	225.00	300.00	550.00

Obv: Head of Wilhelm right.
Rev: Arms and date.

C#	Date	Mintage	Fine	VF	XF	Unc
35	1765	—	50.00	75.00	100.00	175.00

Mining 1/2 Thaler - Bieber Mines
Obv: Armored bust of Wilhelm right.
Rev: Arms and date.

C#	Date	Mintage	Fine	VF	XF	Unc
37	1770	—	50.00	75.00	100.00	180.00

THALER

SILVER
Obv: Bust of Mary right.
Rev: Crowned dual arms; divided date above.

C#	Date	Mintage	Fine	VF	XF	Unc
15	1764 IIE	—	500.00	750.00	950.00	1150.

Obv: Bust of Wilhelm right.
Rev: Crowned arms, date below.

C#	Date	Mintage	Fine	VF	XF	Unc
39	1765 IE	—	150.00	250.00	375.00	550.00
	1765 IR	—	—	—	—	—

Mining Thaler - Bieber Mines
Obv: Bust of Wilhelm right w/o mantle.
Rev: Similar to C#40.2.

C#	Date	Mintage	Fine	VF	XF	Unc
40.1	1769 IIE	—	125.00	175.00	300.00	750.00
	1770 IIE	—	125.00	175.00	300.00	750.00
	1771 CLR	—	125.00	175.00	300.00	750.00

Obv: Bust w/mantle.

C#	Date	Mintage	Fine	VF	XF	Unc
40.2	1771 CLR	—	125.00	175.00	300.00	750.00

Mining Thaler - Bieber Mines
Obv. leg: WILH.D.G.LANDG...., head right.

Rev: Similar to C#41.3.

C#	Date	Mintage	Fine	VF	XF	Unc
41.1	1774 CLR	—	125.00	175.00	300.00	500.00

Obv. leg: WILHELMUS D.G ..., small head right.

C#	Date	Mintage	Fine	VF	XF	Unc
41.2	1774 CLR	—	125.00	175.00	300.00	500.00
	1777 CLR	—	125.00	175.00	300.00	500.00
	1778 CLR	—	125.00	175.00	300.00	500.00

Obv: Large head right.

C#	Date	Mintage	Fine	VF	XF	Unc
41.3	1774 CLR	—	125.00	175.00	300.00	500.00
	1775 CLR	—	125.00	175.00	300.00	500.00
	1775 CLK (error)					
		—	125.00	175.00	300.00	500.00
	1777 CLR	—	125.00	175.00	300.00	500.00
	1778 CLR	—	125.00	175.00	300.00	500.00

Mining Thaler - Bieber Mines
Obv: Larger head of Wilhelm right.
Rev: Arms, date below.

C#	Date	Mintage	Fine	VF	XF	Unc
41a	1784 CLR	—	175.00	250.00	350.00	600.00

TRADE COINS

DUCAT

3.5000 gm., .986 GOLD, .1109 oz AGW
Marriage Commemorative
Wilhelm to Wilhelmine Caroline of Denmark
Obv: Bust of Wilhelmine Caroline of Denmark right.
Rev: 7 line inscription; date below.

C#	Date	Mintage	Fine	VF	XF	Unc
42	1764	—	1000.	1400.	2000.	3500.

Obv: Bust of Wilhelm right.
Rev: Arms and date.

C#	Date	Mintage	Fine	VF	XF	Unc
43	1768	—	850.00	1250.	1750.	2500.

HANNOVER

A state located in northwest Germany which became Hannover when Ernst August of Brunswick-Luneberg chose the title of Elector of Hannover after his capital city. During the Napoleonic wars it was first occupied by Prussia and then incorporated into the Kingdom of Westphalia. In 1814 it was raised to the status of a Kingdom. Hannover was absorbed by Prussia in 1866.

RULERS

George III, 1760-1820
Georg IV, 1820-1830
Wilhelm IV, 1830-1837
Ernst August, 1837-1851
Georg V, 1851-1866

MINTMASTER'S INITIALS

B - Ludwig August Bruel, 1802-1817
B - Theodor Wilhelm Bruel, 1844-1868
C.H.H. - Christian Heinrich Haase
H. - Christian Heinrich Haase
L.B. - Ludwig August Bruel
L.A.B. - Ludwig August Bruel
S - Carl Schulter

PFENNIG

COPPER
Obv: H below crowned GR monogram. Rev: value, date.

C#	Date	Mintage	Fine	VF	XF	Unc
1	1814H	—	2.50	5.00	12.50	40.00

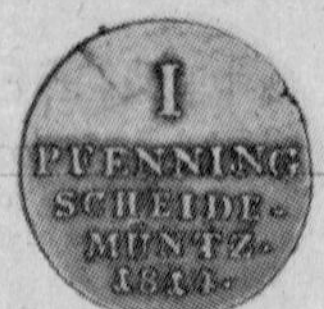

Obv: C below crowned monogram.

C#	Date	Mintage	Fine	VF	XF	Unc
	1814C	—	2.00	4.00	10.00	40.00
1a	1814C	—	2.00	4.00	10.00	40.00
	1817C	—	2.00	4.00	10.00	40.00
	1818C	—	2.00	4.00	10.00	40.00
	1819C	—	2.00	4.00	10.00	40.00
	1820C	—	2.00	4.00	10.00	40.00
17	1821C	—	2.00	4.00	10.00	40.00
	1822C	—	2.00	4.00	10.00	40.00
	1823C	—	2.00	4.00	10.00	40.00
	1824C	—	2.00	4.00	10.00	40.00
	1825C	—	2.00	4.00	10.00	40.00
	1826C	—	2.00	4.00	10.00	40.00
	1827 without mintmark					
		—	2.00	4.00	10.00	40.00
	1827C	—	2.00	4.00	10.00	40.00
	1828C	—	2.00	4.00	10.00	40.00
	1829C	—	2.00	4.00	10.00	40.00
	1830C	—	2.00	4.00	10.00	40.00

Rev: B below value.

C#	Date	Mintage	Fine	VF	XF	Unc
17a	1826B	—	2.00	4.00	10.00	40.00
	1828B	—	2.00	4.00	10.00	40.00
	1829B	—	2.00	4.00	10.00	40.00
	1830B	—	2.00	4.00	10.00	40.00

Obv: Date below crowned WR monogram.
Rev: A below value.

C#	Date	Mintage	Fine	VF	XF	Unc
35.1	1832A	—	2.00	4.00	10.00	40.00
	1833A	—	2.00	4.00	10.00	40.00
	1834A	—	2.00	4.00	10.00	40.00

Rev: B below value.

C#	Date	Mintage	Fine	VF	XF	Unc
35.2	1832B	—	2.00	4.00	10.00	40.00
	1833B	—	2.00	4.00	10.00	40.00
	1834B	—	2.00	4.00	10.00	40.00
	1835B	—	2.00	4.00	10.00	40.00

Rev: C below value.

C#	Date	Mintage	Fine	VF	XF	Unc
35.3	1831/30C	—	2.50	5.00	10.00	40.00
	1831C	—	2.00	4.00	10.00	40.00
	1832C	—	2.00	4.00	10.00	40.00
	1833C	—	2.00	4.00	10.00	40.00

Obv: IV below WR monogram.

C#	Date	Mintage	Fine	VF	XF	Unc
35a	1834A	—	4.00	8.00	15.00	45.00

Obv: Crowned shield with prancing horse.
Rev: A below value.

C#	Date	Mintage	Fine	VF	XF	Unc
36.1	1835A	—	2.00	4.50	10.00	40.00
	1836A	—	2.00	4.50	10.00	40.00
	1837A	—	2.00	4.50	10.00	40.00

Rev: B below value.

C#	Date	Mintage	Fine	VF	XF	Unc
36.2	1835B	—	2.00	4.00	7.50	30.00
	1836B	—	2.00	4.00	7.50	30.00
	1837B	—	2.00	4.00	7.50	30.00

Obv: Crowned EAR monogram. Rev: A below value.

C#	Date	Mintage	Fine	VF	XF	Unc
56.1	1837A	—	2.00	4.00	8.00	30.00
	1838A	—	2.00	4.00	8.00	30.00
	1839A	—	2.00	4.00	8.00	30.00
	1840A	—	2.00	4.00	8.00	30.00
	1841A	—	2.00	4.00	8.00	30.00
	1842A	—	2.00	4.00	8.00	30.00
	1843A	—	2.00	4.00	8.00	30.00
	1844A	—	2.00	4.00	8.00	30.00
	1845A	—	2.00	4.00	8.00	30.00
	1846A	—	2.00	4.00	8.00	30.00

Rev: B below value.

C#	Date	Mintage	Fine	VF	XF	Unc
56.2	1838B	—	5.00	10.00	20.00	50.00

Rev: S below value.

C#	Date	Mintage	Fine	VF	XF	Unc
56.3	1839S	—	5.00	10.00	20.00	50.00
	1841S	—	5.00	10.00	20.00	50.00
	1842S	—	5.00	10.00	20.00	50.00

Obv: Date below monogram. Rev: SCHEIDEMUNZE below value, B mintmark.

C#	Date	Mintage	Fine	VF	XF	Unc
56a	1838B	—	10.00	20.00	37.00	75.00

King's Visit to Clausthal Mint
Rev. leg: GLUCK AUF

C#	Date	Mintage	Fine	VF	XF	Unc
58	1839	—	15.00	30.00	65.00	100.00

Rev: B below value.

C#	Date	Mintage	Fine	VF	XF	Unc
59.1	1845B	—	2.00	4.00	7.50	30.00
	1846B	—	2.00	4.00	7.50	30.00
	1847B	—	2.00	4.00	7.50	30.00
	1848B	—	2.00	4.00	7.50	30.00
	1849B	—	2.00	4.00	7.50	30.00
	1850B	—	2.00	4.00	7.50	30.00
	1851B	—	2.00	4.00	7.50	30.00

Rev: A below value.

C#	Date	Mintage	Fine	VF	XF	Unc
59.2	1846A	—	1.00	2.50	5.00	30.00
	1847A	—	1.00	2:50	5.00	30.00
	1848A	—	1.00	2.50	5.00	30.00
	1849A	—	1.00	2.50	5.00	30.00

Obv: V below monogram.

C#	Date	Mintage	Fine	VF	XF	Unc
83	1852B	—	10.00	21.00	45.00	75.00

C#	Date	Mintage	Fine	VF	XF	Unc
84	1853B	—	1.00	2.50	5.00	30.00
	1854B	—	1.00	2.50	5.00	30.00
	1855B	—	1.00	2.50	5.00	30.00
	1856B	—	1.00	2.50	5.00	30.00

C#	Date	Mintage	Fine	VF	XF	Unc
85	1858B	—	1.00	2.50	5.00	30.00
	1859B	—	1.00	2.50	5.00	30.00
	1860B	—	1.00	2.50	5.00	30.00
	1861B	—	1.00	2.50	5.00	30.00
	1862B	—	1.00	2.50	5.00	30.00
	1863B	2.324	1.00	2.50	5.00	30.00
	1864B	—	1.00	2.50	5.00	30.00

2 PFENNIG

COPPER

Obv: Crowned GR monogram, date below. Rev: Value.

C#	Date	Mintage	Fine	VF	XF	Unc
2	1817C	—	3.00	7.50	20.00	50.00
	1818C	—	3.00	7.50	20.00	50.00

C#	Date	Mintage	Fine	VF	XF	Unc
18	1821C	—	2.00	4.00	7.50	35.00
	1822C	—	2.00	4.00	7.50	35.00
	1823C	—	2.00	4.00	7.50	35.00
	1824C	—	2.00	4.00	7.50	35.00
	1825C	—	2.00	4.00	7.50	35.00
	1826C	—	2.00	4.00	7.50	35.00
	1827C	—	2.00	4.00	7.50	35.00
	1828C	—	2.00	4.00	7.50	35.00
	1829C	—	2.00	4.00	7.50	35.00
	1830C	—	2.00	4.00	7.50	35.00

Rev: B below value.

C#	Date	Mintage	Fine	VF	XF	Unc
18a	1826B	.154	2.50	5.00	10.00	40.00

Obv: Crowned WR monogram above date.
Rev: C below value

C#	Date	Mintage	Fine	VF	XF	Unc
37.1	1831C	—	2.50	5.00	12.50	40.00
	1833C	—	2.50	5.00	12.50	40.00
	1834C	—	2.50	5.00	12.50	40.00

Rev: A below value.

C#	Date	Mintage	Fine	VF	XF	Unc
37.2	1834A	—	5.00	10.00	20.00	50.00

Obv: IV below monogram. Rev: Date.

C#	Date	Mintage	Fine	VF	XF	Unc
37a	1834A	—	5.00	10.00	20.00	50.00

Obv: Crowned shield with prancing horse.

C#	Date	Mintage	Fine	VF	XF	Unc
38	1835A	—	2.50	5.00	12.50	40.00
	1836A	—	2.50	5.00	12.50	40.00
	1837A	—	2.50	5.00	12.50	40.00

Pearl circle around coin

C#	Date	Mintage	Fine	VF	XF	Unc
38a	1837A	—	6.00	12.50	25.00	50.00

Obv: Crowned EAR monogram. Rev: Value, A below date.

C#	Date	Mintage	Fine	VF	XF	Unc
60.1	1837A	—	2.50	5.00	10.00	35.00
	1838A	—	2.50	5.00	10.00	35.00
	1839A	—	2.50	5.00	10.00	35.00
	1840A	—	2.50	5.00	10.00	35.00
	1841A	—	2.50	5.00	10.00	35.00
	1842A	—	2.50	5.00	10.00	35.00
	1843A	—	2.50	5.00	10.00	35.00
	1844A	—	2.50	5.00	10.00	35.00
	1845A	—	2.50	5.00	10.00	35.00
	1846A	—	2.50	5.00	10.00	35.00

Rev: S below date.

C#	Date	Mintage	Fine	VF	XF	Unc
60.2	1842S	—	3.00	7.50	17.00	35.00
	1844S	—	3.00	7.50	17.00	35.00

Rev: B below date, struck in a ring.

C#	Date	Mintage	Fine	VF	XF	Unc
61.1	1845B	—	1.50	3.00	6.00	30.00
	1846B	—	1.50	3.00	6.00	30.00
	1847B	—	1.50	3.00	6.00	30.00
	1848B	—	1.50	3.00	6.00	30.00
	1849B	—	1.50	3.00	6.00	30.00
	1850B	—	1.50	3.00	6.00	30.00
	1851B	—	1.50	3.00	6.00	30.00

Rev: A below date.

C#	Date	Mintage	Fine	VF	XF	Unc
61.2	1846A	—	1.50	3.00	6.00	30.00
	1847A	—	1.50	3.00	6.00	30.00
	1848A	—	1.50	3.00	6.00	30.00
	1849A	—	1.50	3.00	6.00	30.00

Rev: B below date.

C#	Date	Mintage	Fine	VF	XF	Unc
86	1852B	—	2.00	4.00	7.50	30.00
	1853B	—	2.00	4.00	7.50	30.00
	1854B	—	2.00	4.00	7.50	30.00
	1855B	—	2.00	4.00	7.50	30.00
	1856B	—	2.00	4.00	7.50	30.00

C#	Date	Mintage	Fine	VF	XF	Unc
87	1858B	—	1.50	3.00	6.00	30.00
	1859B	—	1.50	3.00	6.00	30.00
	1860B	—	1.50	3.00	6.00	30.00
	1861B	—	1.50	3.00	6.00	30.00
	1862B	—	1.50	3.00	6.00	30.00
	1863B	.607	1.50	3.00	6.00	30.00
	1864B	—	1.50	3.00	6.00	30.00

4 PFENNIG

(= 1/2 Marien Groschen)

BILLON

Obv. C below crowned GR monogram
Rev. legend: NACH DEM REICHS FUSS

C#	Date	Mintage	Fine	VF	XF	Unc
3.1	1814C	—	3.00	6.25	12.50	40.00
	1815C	—	3.00	6.25	12.50	40.00

H below monogram

C#	Date	Mintage	Fine	VF	XF	Unc
3.2	1815H.	—	3.00	6.00	12.50	40.00
	1816H.	—	3.00	6.00	12.50	40.00

Obv. legend: CONVENT MUNZE

C#	Date	Mintage	Fine	VF	XF	Unc
3a	1816H.	.071	3.50	7.50	20.00	50.00
	1817H.	Inc. Ab.	3.50	7.50	20.00	50.00

Obv: IV below monogram,
leg: CONVENTIONS MUNZE.

C#	Date	Mintage	Fine	VF	XF	Unc
20	1822B	—	2.50	5.00	10.00	40.00
	1826B	—	2.50	5.00	10.00	40.00
	1828B	—	2.50	5.00	10.00	40.00
	1830B	—	2.50	5.00	10.00	40.00

COPPER

Obv: Date below monogram.

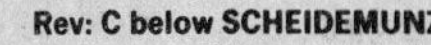
Rev: C below SCHEIDEMUNZE

C#	Date	Mintage	Fine	VF	XF	Unc
19	1827C	—	15.00	35.00	62.50	125.00

C#	Date	Mintage	Fine	VF	XF	Unc
39	1831C	—	15.00	35.00	62.50	125.00

Rev: B below date.

C#	Date	Mintage	Fine	VF	XF	Unc
40	1835B	—	2.50	5.00	10.00	30.00
	1836B	—	2.50	5.00	10.00	30.00
	1837B	—	2.50	5.00	10.00	30.00
62.1	1838B	—	2.00	4.00	7.50	30.00

Rev: S below date.

C#	Date	Mintage	Fine	VF	XF	Unc
62.2	1840S	—	2.00	4.00	7.50	30.00
	1841S	—	2.00	4.00	7.50	30.00
	1842S	—	2.00	4.00	7.50	30.00

6 PFENNIG

BILLON

Obv: Crowned shield with prancing horse.
Rev: S below value.

C#	Date	Mintage	Fine	VF	XF	Unc
63.1	1843S	—	3.00	6.00	12.50	40.00
	1844S	—	3.00	6.00	12.50	40.00

Rev: B below shield.

C#	Date	Mintage	Fine	VF	XF	Unc
63.2	1844B	—	3.00	6.00	12.50	40.00
	1845B	—	3.00	6.00	12.50	40.00
	1846B	—	3.00	6.00	12.50	40.00

C#	Date	Mintage	Fine	VF	XF	Unc
64	1846B	—	2.00	4.00	7.50	30.00
	1847B	—	2.00	4.00	7.50	30.00
	1848B	—	2.00	4.00	7.50	30.00
	1849B	—	2.00	4.00	7.50	30.00
	1850B	—	2.00	4.00	7.50	30.00
	1851B	—	2.00	4.00	7.50	30.00

C#	Date	Mintage	Fine	VF	XF	Unc
88	1852B	—	2.00	4.00	7.50	30.00
	1853B	—	2.00	4.00	7.50	30.00
	1854B	—	2.00	4.00	7.50	30.00
	1855B	—	2.00	4.00	7.50	30.00

1/2 GROSCHEN

BILLON

C#	Date	Mintage	Fine	VF	XF	Unc
89	1858B	—	2.00	4.00	7.50	30.00
	1859B	—	2.00	4.00	7.50	30.00
	1861B	—	2.00	4.00	7.50	30.00
	1862B	—	2.00	4.00	7.50	30.00
	1863B	.047	2.00	4.00	7.50	30.00

C#	Date	Mintage	Fine	VF	XF	Unc
	1864B	—	2.00	4.00	7.50	30.00
	1865B	—	2.00	4.00	7.50	30.00

MARIEN GROSCHEN

(= 1/36 Thaler)

BILLON

Obv: C below crowned GR monogram.
Rev: Value, leg: NACH DEM REICHFUSS.

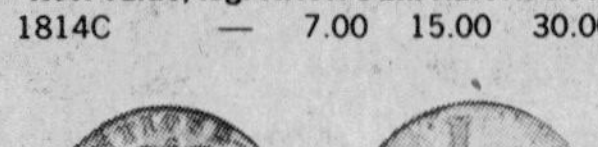

C#	Date	Mintage	Fine	VF	XF	Unc
4	1814C	—	7.00	15.00	30.00	60.00

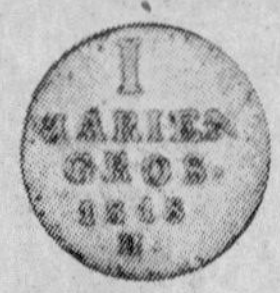

Obv: H below monogram.

C#	Date	Mintage	Fine	VF	XF	Unc
4a	1816H.	.443	6.00	12.50	25.00	50.00
	1817H.	Inc. Ab.	6.00	12.50	25.00	50.00
	1818H.	Inc. Ab.	6.00	12.50	25.00	50.00

GROSCHEN

BILLON

C#	Date	Mintage	Fine	VF	XF	Unc
91	1858B	—	2.00	4.00	7.50	30.00
	1859B	—	2.00	4.00	7.50	30.00
	1860B	—	2.00	4.00	7.50	30.00
	1861B	—	2.00	4.00	7.50	30.00
	1862B	—	2.00	4.00	7.50	30.00
	1863B	.069	2.00	4.00	7.50	30.00
	1864B	—	2.00	4.00	7.50	30.00
	1865B	—	2.00	4.00	7.50	30.00
	1866B	.076	2.00	4.00	7.50	30.00

16 GUTE GROSCHEN

11.7700 gm., .993 SILVER, .3758 oz ASW
Obv: Prancing horse with M on ledge, leg: GEORGIUS.III.D.G.BRITAN.&.HANNOV.REX.

C#	Date	Mintage	Fine	VF	XF	Unc
11	1820	—	50.00	100.00	150.00	250.00

Obv. leg: GEORGIUS.III.D.G.BRITANNIARUM.

C#	Date	Mintage	Fine	VF	XF	Unc
11a	1820	—	50.00	100.00	150.00	250.00

Obv: Prancing horse, M on ledge XX.EINE.F.MARK. below, leg: GEORGIUS.IV.D.G.BRITAN.& HANNOV.REX.
Rev: Value, CONVENTIONS-MUNZE. below.

C#	Date	Mintage	Fine	VF	XF	Unc
25	1820	—	12.00	25.00	50.00	75.00

Obv: XX.E.F. MARK below ledge.
Rev. leg: CONV-MUNZE FEIN SILBER.

C#	Date	Mintage	Fine	VF	XF	Unc
25b	1820	—	12.00	25.00	50.00	75.00

Obv: XX.EINE.F.MARK. below ledge.

C#	Date	Mintage	Fine	VF	XF	Unc
25g	1820	—	12.00	25.00	50.00	75.00

Obv: XX.E.F.MARK. below ledge.
Rev: FEIN SILB.

C#	Date	Mintage	Fine	VF	XF	Unc
25c	1821	—	15.00	30.00	40.00	60.00

Rev: CONV MUNZE FEIN SILB around bottom.

C#	Date	Mintage	Fine	VF	XF	Unc
25d	1821	—	15.00	30.00	40.00	60.00

NOTE: Seven obverse legend varieties exist.

Rev: FEINES SILB under GROSCHEN.

C#	Date	Mintage	Fine	VF	XF	Unc
25a	1822	—	15.00	30.00	40.00	75.00

NOTE: Two obverse legend varieties exist.

C#	Date	Mintage	Fine	VF	XF	Unc
25e	1822	—	15.00	30.00	40.00	75.00

NOTE: Two obverse legend varieties exist.

C#	Date	Mintage	Fine	VF	XF	Unc
25f	1822	—	15.00	30.00	40.00	75.00
	1823	—	15.00	30.00	40.00	75.00
	1824	—	15.00	30.00	40.00	75.00
	1825	—	15.00	30.00	40.00	75.00
	1826	—	15.00	30.00	40.00	75.00
	1827	—	15.00	30.00	40.00	75.00
	1828	—	15.00	30.00	40.00	75.00
	1829	—	15.00	30.00	40.00	75.00
	1830	—	15.00	30.00	40.00	75.00

NOTE: Two obverse legend varieties exist for 1822, 1823 and 1825.

C#	Date	Mintage	Fine	VF	XF	Unc
45	1830	—	15.00	30.00	50.00	90.00
	1831	—	15.00	30.00	50.00	90.00
	1832	—	15.00	30.00	50.00	90.00
	1832A	—	15.00	30.00	50.00	90.00

Obv: With 'L' on ledge.

C#	Date	Mintage	Fine	VF	XF	Unc
45a	1832A	—	15.00	30.00	50.00	90.00
	1833A	—	15.00	30.00	50.00	90.00
	1834A	—	15.00	30.00	50.00	90.00

Obv: With 'M' on ledge.

C#	Date	Mintage	Fine	VF	XF	Unc
45b	1832A	—	15.00	30.00	50.00	90.00

Obv: With 'W' on ledge.

C#	Date	Mintage	Fine	VF	XF	Unc
45c	1834A	—	15.00	30.00	50.00	90.00

1/24 THALER

BILLON

Obv: Date below prancing horse.
Rev. value, legend: NACH DEM REICHFUSS

C#	Date	Mintage	Fine	VF	XF	Unc
5	1814C	—	6.00	12.50	25.00	50.00

Obv: IV below crowned GR monogram, leg: CONVENTIONSMUNZE. Rev: Value.

C#	Date	Mintage	Fine	VF	XF	Unc
6	1817H.	.946	5.00	10.00	25.00	50.00
	1818	—	5.00	10.00	25.00	50.00

Obv: IV below monogram.

C#	Date	Mintage	Fine	VF	XF	Unc
21	1826B	.139	3.00	6.00	12.00	40.00
	1827B	.328	3.00	6.00	12.00	40.00
	1828B	.904	3.00	6.00	12.00	40.00

Rev: B below date.

C#	Date	Mintage	Fine	VF	XF	Unc
41	1834B	—	2.00	4.00	10.00	40.00
	1834.B.	—	—	—	—	—
	1835B	—	2.00	4.00	10.00	35.00
	1836B	—	2.00	4.00	10.00	35.00
	1837B	—	2.00	4.00	10.00	35.00

Rev: A below date.

C#	Date	Mintage	Fine	VF	XF	Unc
41a	1835A	—	2.00	4.00	10.00	35.00
	1836A	—	2.00	4.00	10.00	35.00

Rev: B below date.

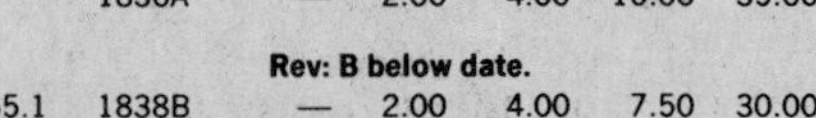

C#	Date	Mintage	Fine	VF	XF	Unc
65.1	1838B	—	2.00	4.00	7.50	30.00

Rev: S below date.

C#	Date	Mintage	Fine	VF	XF	Unc
65.2	1839S	—	2.00	4.00	7.50	30.00
	1841S	—	2.00	4.00	7.50	30.00
	1842S	—	2.00	4.00	7.50	30.00

Rev: A below date.

C#	Date	Mintage	Fine	VF	XF	Unc
65.3	1839A	—	2.00	4.00	7.50	30.00
	1840A	—	2.00	4.00	7.50	30.00
	1841A	—	2.00	4.00	7.50	30.00
	1842A	—	2.00	4.00	7.50	30.00
	1843A	—	2.00	4.00	7.50	30.00
	1844A	—	2.00	4.00	7.50	30.00
	1845A	—	2.00	4.00	7.50	30.00
	1846A	—	2.00	4.00	7.50	30.00

Obv: B below prancing horse. Rev: Value, SCHEIDEMUNZE.

C#	Date	Mintage	Fine	VF	XF	Unc
	1845B	—	2.00	4.00	7.50	30.00
	1846B	—	2.00	4.00	7.50	30.00

Obv. leg: NEC ASPERA TERRENT.

C#	Date	Mintage	Fine	VF	XF	Unc
90	1854B	—	2.00	4.00	7.50	30.00
	1855B	—	2.00	4.00	7.50	30.00
	1856B	—	2.00	4.00	7.50	30.00

1/12 THALER

(= 3 Mariengroschen)

BILLON

Obv: Prancing horse, S on ledge.
Rev: Value, leg: NACHDEM REICHS FUSS.

C#	Date	Mintage	Fine	VF	XF	Unc
7	1814C	—	6.00	12.50	20.00	50.00
	1815C	—	6.00	12.50	20.00	50.00
	1816C	—	6.00	12.50	20.00	50.00

Obv: C.H.H. below ledge.
Rev. leg: CONVENTIONSMUNZE

C#	Date	Mintage	Fine	VF	XF	Unc
8.1	1816C.H.H.	—	2.50	5.00	12.50	40.00
	1817C.H.H.	—	2.50	5.00	12.50	40.00
	1818C.H.H.	2.000	2.50	5.00	12.50	40.00

Obv: L.A.B. below ledge.

C#	Date	Mintage	Fine	VF	XF	Unc
8.2	1819L.A.B.	—	2.50	5.00	12.50	40.00
	1820L.A.B.	Inc. Ab.	2.50	5.00	12.50	40.00

Obv: L.B. below ledge

C#	Date	Mintage	Fine	VF	XF	Unc
8.3	1819L.B.	Inc. Ab.	2.50	5.00	12.50	40.00
22	1820L.B.	—	2.50	5.00	10.00	40.00
	1821L.B.	Inc. Ab.	2.50	5.00	10.00	40.00
23	1822L.B.	1.908	3.00	6.00	12.00	40.00
	1823L.B.	1.900	3.00	6.00	12.00	40.00
	1824L.B.	.502	3.00	6.00	12.00	40.00

Obv: B below head.

C#	Date	Mintage	Fine	VF	XF	Unc
43	1834B	—	3.00	6.00	12.00	40.00
	1835B	—	3.00	6.00	12.00	40.00
	1836B	—	3.00	6.00	12.00	40.00
	1837B	—	3.00	6.00	12.00	40.00

2.6700 gm., .521 SILVER, .0447 oz ASW

C#	Date	Mintage	Fine	VF	XF	Unc
66.1	1838B	—	3.50	7.50	15.00	40.00

Obv: S below head.

C#	Date	Mintage	Fine	VF	XF	Unc
66.2	1839S	—	3.50	7.50	15.00	40.00
	1840S	—	3.50	7.50	15.00	40.00
66a	1841S	—	3.00	6.00	12.00	40.00
	1842S	—	3.00	6.00	12.00	40.00
	1843S	—	3.00	6.00	12.00	40.00
	1844S	—	3.00	6.00	12.00	40.00

Obv: B below head.

C#	Date	Mintage	Fine	VF	XF	Unc
66b	1844B	—	3.00	6.00	12.00	35.00
	1845B	—	3.00	6.00	12.00	35.00
	1846B	—	3.00	6.00	12.00	35.00
	1847B	—	3.00	6.00	12.00	35.00

Obv: Larger head.

C#	Date	Mintage	Fine	VF	XF	Unc
66c	1848B	—	4.50	9.00	17.00	45.00
	1849B	—	4.50	9.00	17.00	45.00
	1850B	—	4.50	9.00	17.00	45.00
	1851B	—	4.50	9.00	17.00	45.00

Obv: BREHMER F at truncation.

C#	Date	Mintage	Fine	VF	XF	Unc
92	1852B	—	2.00	4.00	7.50	30.00
	1853B	—	2.00	4.00	7.50	30.00

Obv: Without name at truncation.
Rev. value: SCHEIDEMUNZE.

C#	Date	Mintage	Fine	VF	XF	Unc
93	1859B	—	3.00	6.00	12.00	35.00
	1860B	—	3.00	6.00	12.00	35.00
	1862B	—	3.00	6.00	12.00	35.00

1/6 THALER

5.8500 gm., .500 SILVER, .0940 oz ASW
Obv: B below ledge.

C#	Date	Mintage	Fine	VF	XF	Unc
24	1821B	.150	7.50	15.00	30.00	60.00

5.3500 gm., .521 SILVER, .0896 oz ASW

C#	Date	Mintage	Fine	VF	XF	Unc
44	1834	.360	6.00	12.00	25.00	50.00

Obv: S below larger head.
Rev: Crowned arms on cartouche.

C#	Date	Mintage	Fine	VF	XF	Unc
67	1840S	.457	8.00	17.00	30.00	60.00

Rev: Shield with square corners.

C#	Date	Mintage	Fine	VF	XF	Unc
67a	1841S	Inc. Ab.	7.00	15.00	25.00	50.00

C#	Date	Mintage	Fine	VF	XF	Unc
67b	1844B	Inc. Ab.	7.00	15.00	25.00	50.00
	1845B	Inc. Ab.	7.00	15.00	25.00	50.00
	1847B	Inc. Ab.	7.00	15.00	25.00	50.00

5.3400 gm., .520 SILVER, .0893 oz ASW

C#	Date	Mintage	Fine	VF	XF	Unc
94	1859B	—	6.00	12.00	30.00	60.00
	1860B	—	6.00	12.00	30.00	60.00
	1862B	—	6.00	12.00	30.00	60.00
	1863B	.087	6.00	12.00	30.00	60.00
	1866B	5,904	6.00	12.00	30.00	60.00

2/3 THALER

13.0800 gm., .993 SILVER, .4176 oz ASW

C#	Date	Mintage	Fine	VF	XF	Unc
10	1813C	—	30.00	65.00	95.00	150.00
	1814C	—	30.00	65.00	95.00	150.00

Obv: M below truncation.

C#	Date	Mintage	Fine	VF	XF	Unc
10a	1814	—	25.00	55.00	80.00	140.00

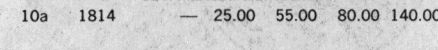

C#	Date	Mintage	Fine	VF	XF	Unc
26	1822C	—	15.00	32.50	50.00	80.00
	1823C	—	15.00	32.50	50.00	80.00
	1824C	—	15.00	32.50	50.00	80.00
	1825C	—	15.00	32.50	50.00	80.00
	1826C	—	15.00	32.50	50.00	80.00
	1827C	—	15.00	32.50	50.00	80.00
	1828C	—	15.00	32.50	50.00	80.00
	1829C	—	15.00	32.50	50.00	80.00

NOTE: Several varieties exist.

17.3200 gm., .750 SILVER, .4177 oz ASW
Rev: Value, 18 STUCK EINE MARK FEIN.

C#	Date	Mintage	Fine	VF	XF	Unc
26a	1826B	—	35.00	70.00	90.00	125.00
	1827B	—	35.00	70.00	90.00	125.00
	1828B	—	35.00	70.00	90.00	125.00

13.0800 gm., .993 SILVER, .4176 oz ASW
Obv: Ribbon inscribed
HONI SOIT QUI MAL Y PENSE.

C#	Date	Mintage	Fine	VF	XF	Unc
46	1832	—	25.00	50.00	65.00	100.00
	1833	—	25.00	50.00	65.00	100.00

C#	Date	Mintage	Fine	VF	XF	Unc
46.5	1833A	.050	45.00	90.00	145.00	200.00

Obv: Head right, W at truncation.

C#	Date	Mintage	Fine	VF	XF	Unc
47	1834A	Inc. Ab.	45.00	90.00	150.00	200.00

Struck in collar

C#	Date	Mintage	Fine	VF	XF	Unc
47a	1834A	Inc. Ab.	45.00	90.00	150.00	200.00

Rev: 2/3 divides date

C#	Date	Mintage	Fine	VF	XF	Unc
47b	1834A	Inc. Ab.	35.00	75.00	125.00	200.00

Rev: AUSBEUTE DER GRUBE

C#	Date	Mintage	Fine	VF	XF	Unc
48	1834A	Inc. Ab.	85.00	175.00	250.00	350.00

Obv: Different head right, A below. Rev: Value.

C#	Date	Mintage	Fine	VF	XF	Unc
68a	1838A	—	30.00	60.00	90.00	140.00
	1839A	—	30.00	60.00	90.00	140.00

THALER

23.5400 gm., .993 SILVER, .7516 oz ASW
Silver Mines of Clausthal Commemorative

C#	Date	Mintage	Fine	VF	XF	Unc
27	1830	—	400.00	1000.	1500.	2500.

22.2700 gm., .750 SILVER, .5371 oz ASW

C#	Date	Mintage	Fine	VF	XF	Unc
49	1834B	.044	40.00	100.00	300.00	750.00

Obv: Similar to C#49, A below head.

C#	Date	Mintage	Fine	VF	XF	Unc
50	1834A	—	40.00	100.00	250.00	500.00
	1835A	—	40.00	100.00	250.00	500.00

Obv: Similar to C#49.

C#	Date	Mintage	Fine	VF	XF	Unc
49a	1835A	—	40.00	100.00	200.00	400.00
	1836A	—	40.00	100.00	200.00	400.00
	1837A	—	40.00	100.00	200.00	400.00

Rev: Similar to C#49a.

C#	Date	Mintage	Fine	VF	XF	Unc
49b	1836B	—	60.00	150.00	300.00	600.00

C#	Date	Mintage	Fine	VF	XF	Unc
69	1838A	—	30.00	80.00	175.00	450.00

C#	Date	Mintage	Fine	VF	XF	Unc
69a	1838A	—	25.00	80.00	175.00	450.00
	1839A	—	25.00	80.00	175.00	450.00
	1840A	—	25.00	80.00	175.00	450.00

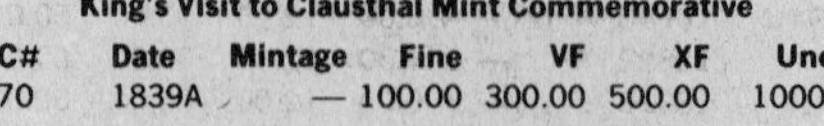

22.2700 gm., .750 SILVER, .5371 oz ASW
King's Visit to Clausthal Mint Commemorative

C#	Date	Mintage	Fine	VF	XF	Unc
70	1839A	—	100.00	300.00	500.00	1000.

C#	Date	Mintage	Fine	VF	XF	Unc
71a	1840A	—	40.00	90.00	200.00	450.00
	1841A	—	40.00	90.00	200.00	450.00

Obv: S below truncation.

C#	Date	Mintage	Fine	VF	XF	Unc
71b	1840S	—	80.00	200.00	500.00	900.00

Obv: BRANDT F. at truncation.

C#	Date	Mintage	Fine	VF	XF	Unc
71c	1841S	—	40.00	75.00	175.00	350.00

Obv: A below head.

C#	Date	Mintage	Fine	VF	XF	Unc
71d	1842A	.620	15.00	40.00	125.00	325.00
	1843A	.638	15.00	40.00	125.00	325.00
	1844A	.622	15.00	40.00	125.00	325.00
	1845A	.656	15.00	40.00	125.00	325.00
	1846A	.650	15.00	40.00	125.00	325.00
	1847A	.625	15.00	40.00	125.00	325.00
	1848A	.661	15.00	40.00	125.00	325.00
	1849A	.357	15.00	40.00	125.00	325.00

Obv: B below head.

C#	Date	Mintage	Fine	VF	XF	Unc
71e	1844B	—	20.00	50.00	150.00	350.00
	1845B	—	20.00	50.00	150.00	350.00
	1846B	—	20.00	50.00	150.00	350.00
	1847B	—	20.00	50.00	150.00	350.00

Obv: BREHMER F. at truncation.

C#	Date	Mintage	Fine	VF	XF	Unc
71f	1848B	—	15.00	50.00	150.00	325.00
	1849B	—	15.00	50.00	150.00	325.00

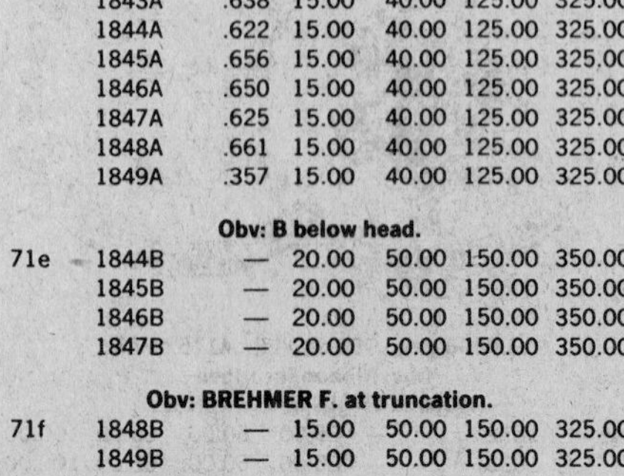

Wedding of Crown Prince Georg of Hannover and Duchess Marie of Sachsen-Altenburg

C#	Date	Mintage	Fine	VF	XF	Unc
73	1843S	1,010	200.00	500.00	800.00	1400.

C#	Date	Mintage	Fine	VF	XF	Unc
74	1848B	—	15.00	50.00	150.00	325.00
	1849B	—	15.00	50.00	150.00	325.00

Rev: HARZ SEGEN over crown

C#	Date	Mintage	Fine	VF	XF	Unc
74b	1849	—	60.00	150.00	300.00	600.00

Rev: BERGSEGEN DES HARZES over crown

C#	Date	Mintage	Fine	VF	XF	Unc
74a	1850B	.712	15.00	50.00	100.00	250.00
	1851B	.453	15.00	50.00	100.00	250.00

Rev: BERGSEGEN DES HARZES over crown.

C#	Date	Mintage	Fine	VF	XF	Unc
95	1852B	.170	15.00	50.00	100.00	250.00
	1853B	.180	15.00	50.00	100.00	250.00
	1854B	.951	15.00	50.00	100.00	250.00
	1855B	.974	15.00	50.00	100.00	250.00
	1856B	.077	15.00	50.00	100.00	250.00

Rev: Date in chronogram.

C#	Date	Mintage	VG	Fine	VF	XF
30	1796	—	80.00	165.00	225.00	350.00

2 THALERS
(Convention)

SILVER
Sede Vacante Issue

C#	Date	Mintage	Fine	VF	XF	Unc
28	1790	—	200.00	400.00	650.00	950.00

ERFURT

A city in central Germany. It was a mint for the archbishops of Mainz in the 11th, 12th and 13th centuries. It also served as an imperial mint in the 12th century. Independence was granted in 1255 and the mint right was obtained in 1341 and 1354. Coins were made until 1802 when Erfurt fell to Prussia.

RULERS
Friedrich Carl Joseph
Archbishop, 1774-1802

6 PFENNIG
BILLON
Obv: Wheel in crowned shield. Rev: Value.

C#	Date	Mintage	Fine	VF	XF	Unc
7	1801 S	—	4.00	8.50	15.00	50.00

GROSCHEN

BILLON

C#	Date	Mintage	Fine	VF	XF	Unc
9	1801 S	—	4.00	8.00	15.00	50.00
	Obv: Shield within branches.					
9a	1802 S	—	4.00	8.00	15.00	50.00

1/48 THALER
BILLON
Obv: Crowned wheel in oval within branches.
Rev: Value, date in cartouche.

C#	Date	Mintage	Fine	VF	XF	Unc
3	1781 E	—	3.50	7.50	15.50	50.00

C#	Date	Mintage	Fine	VF	XF	Unc
4	1784 C	—	3.00	6.00	15.00	50.00
	Similar to C#4. Rev: Value in cartouche.					
4a	1788 E	—	3.00	6.00	15.00	50.00
	1789 E	—	3.00	6.00	15.00	50.00
	1790 E	—	3.00	6.00	15.00	50.00
	1791 E	—	3.00	6.00	15.00	50.00
	1793 E	—	3.00	6.00	15.00	50.00
	1794 E	—	3.00	6.00	15.00	50.00
4b	1798 E	—	3.00	6.00	15.00	50.00
	Obv: Arms in long shield					
6	1800 C	—	3.00	6.00	15.00	50.00

1/24 THALER
BILLON
Obv: Arms in long shield.

C#	Date	Mintage	Fine	VF	XF	Unc
8	1800 C	—	3.00	6.00	15.00	45.00

FRANKFURT

(Free City)

A city in West-central Germany was founded as a Roman settlement in the 1st century and for several centuries was the site of the election of the Holy Roman Emperors. It housed the Imperial Mint from early times and obtained the mint right in 1428 with almost continuous coinage until 1866. Frankfurt am Main was merged into the Confederation of the Rhine in 1806 and was made the Grand Duchy of Frankfurt in 1810. The 1815 Congress of Vienna restored its freedom in 1815 but when they sided with the Austrians, the victorious Prussians absorbed them into Prussia in 1866.

MINTMASTER'S INITIALS
C - Conrad
G.B. - Johann Georg Bunsen
S.T. - Samuel Tomschutz
Z - Christian Zollmann

HELLER

COPPER

C#	Date	Mintage	Fine	VF	XF	Unc
2	1814 G.B.	.332	3.00	7.00	20.00	50.00

C#	Date	Mintage	Fine	VF	XF	Unc
2a	1814 G(F)B	—	2.00	4.00	10.00	40.00
	1815 G(F)B	.166	2.00	4.00	10.00	40.00
	1816 G(F)B	—	2.00	4.00	10.00	40.00
	1817 G(F)B	—	2.00	4.00	10.00	40.00
	1818 G(F)B	—	2.00	4.00	10.00	40.00
	1819 G(F)B	—	2.00	4.00	10.00	40.00
	1820 G(F)B	—	2.00	4.00	10.00	40.00
	1821 G(F)B	—	2.00	4.00	10.00	40.00
	1822 G(F)B	—	2.00	4.00	10.00	40.00
	1824 G(F)B	—	2.00	4.00	10.00	40.00
	1825 G(F)B	—	2.00	4.00	10.00	40.00
2b	1836 S(F)T	.120	2.00	4.50	20.00	50.00
	1837 S(F)T	.144	2.00	4.50	20.00	50.00

C#	Date	Mintage	Fine	VF	XF	Unc
3	1838	—	2.50	5.00	20.00	50.00

C#	Date	Mintage	Fine	VF	XF	Unc
3a	1841	.173	1.50	3.00	10.00	40.00
	1842	.328	1.50	3.00	10.00	40.00
	1844	.162	1.50	3.00	10.00	40.00
	1845	.169	1.50	3.00	10.00	40.00
	1846	.205	1.50	3.00	10.00	40.00
	1847	.453	1.50	3.00	10.00	40.00
	1849	.396	1.50	3.00	10.00	40.00
	1850	.669	1.50	3.00	10.00	40.00
	1851	.275	1.50	3.00	10.00	40.00
	1852	.325	1.50	3.00	10.00	40.00
	Obv. leg: FREIE STADT.					
3b	1843	.038	1.50	3.00	6.00	30.00

C#	Date	Mintage	Fine	VF	XF	Unc
4	1853	.411	1.50	3.00	6.00	30.00
	1854	.271	1.50	3.00	6.00	30.00
	1855	.430	1.50	3.00	6.00	30.00
	1856	.484	1.50	3.00	6.00	30.00
	1857	.723	1.50	3.00	6.00	30.00
	1858	.377	1.50	3.00	6.00	30.00

C#	Date	Mintage	Fine	VF	XF	Unc
5	1859	.377	1.50	3.00	6.00	30.00
	1860	.353	1.50	3.00	6.00	30.00
	1861	.378	1.50	3.00	6.00	30.00
	1862	.391	1.50	3.00	6.00	30.00
	1863	.370	1.50	3.00	6.00	30.00
	1864	.390	1.50	3.00	6.00	30.00
	1865	.384	1.50	3.00	6.00	30.00

PFENNIG

COPPER

C#	Date	Mintage	Fine	VF	XF	Unc
6	1786	—	1.50	3.00	9.00	45.00
	1787	—	1.50	3.00	9.00	45.00
	1788	—	1.50	3.00	9.00	45.00
	1789	—	1.50	3.00	9.00	45.00
	1790	—	1.50	3.00	9.00	45.00
	1791	—	1.50	3.00	9.00	45.00
	1792	—	1.50	3.00	9.00	45.00
	1793	—	1.50	3.00	9.00	45.00

Visit of Royal Family to Mint Commemorative
Obv: Similar to C#95.

C#	Date	Mintage	Fine	VF	XF	Unc
96	1853B	—	1000.	2500.	4000.	7000.

18.5200 gm., .900 SILVER, .5360 oz ASW
Obv: Similar to C#95.

C#	Date	Mintage	Fine	VF	XF	Unc
97	1857B	.274	15.00	30.00	75.00	150.00
	1858B	.432	15.00	30.00	75.00	150.00
	1859B	.554	15.00	30.00	75.00	150.00
	1860B	.790	15.00	30.00	75.00	150.00
	1861B	.736	15.00	30.00	75.00	150.00
	1862B	.133	15.00	30.00	75.00	150.00
	1863B	.233	15.00	30.00	75.00	150.00
	1864B	.158	15.00	30.00	75.00	150.00
	1865B	—	15.00	30.00	75.00	150.00
	1866B	.159	15.00	30.00	75.00	150.00

50th Anniversary of Battle of Waterloo
Obv: Similar to C#95.

C#	Date	Mintage	Fine	VF	XF	Unc
98	1865B	.015	25.00	75.00	125.00	200.00

50th Anniversary of Union of East Friesia and Hannover
Obv: Similar to C#95.

C#	Date	Mintage	Fine	VF	XF	Unc
99	1865B	1,000	150.00	400.00	600.00	900.00

50th Anniversary of Union of East Friesia and Hannover
Obv: Similar to C#95.

C#	Date	Mintage	Fine	VF	XF	Unc
100	1865B	2,000	140.00	350.00	550.00	900.00

2 THALER
(= 3-1/2 Gulden)

37.1200 gm., .900 SILVER, 1.0742 oz ASW
Visit Of Royal Family To Mint Commemorative

C#	Date	Mintage	Fine	VF	XF	Unc
101	1854B	—	1000.	2000.	3000.	6000.
	1854B	—	—	—	Proof	7500.

Obv: Similar to C#101.

C#	Date	Mintage	Fine	VF	XF	Unc
102	1854B	.102	60.00	150.00	250.00	400.00
	1855B	.842	50.00	150.00	250.00	400.00

37.0400 gm., .900 SILVER, 1.0719 oz ASW
Obv: Similar to C#101.

C#	Date	Mintage	Fine	VF	XF	Unc
103	1862B	.133	50.00	150.00	250.00	400.00
	1866B	.038	50.00	150.00	250.00	400.00

2-1/2 THALER

3.3400 gm., .903 GOLD, .0970 oz AGW

C#	Date	Mintage	Fine	VF	XF	Unc
13	1814C.H.H.	—	400.00	850.00	1250.	2500.

C#	Date	Mintage	Fine	VF	XF	Unc
29	1821B	—	200.00	400.00	600.00	1000.
	1827B	—	200.00	400.00	600.00	1000.
	1830B	—	200.00	400.00	600.00	1000.

C#	Date	Mintage	Fine	VF	XF	Unc
52	1832B	—	200.00	450.00	650.00	1500.
	1833B	—	200.00	450.00	650.00	1500.
	1835B	—	200.00	450.00	650.00	1500.

3.3200 gm., .896 GOLD, .0956 oz AGW

C#	Date	Mintage	Fine	VF	XF	Unc
52a	1836B	—	200.00	450.00	650.00	1500.
	1837B	—	200.00	450.00	650.00	1500.

C#	Date	Mintage	Fine	VF	XF	Unc
76.1	1839S	—	200.00	450.00	650.00	1500.
	1840S	—	200.00	450.00	650.00	1500.
	1843S	—	200.00	450.00	650.00	1500.

C#	Date	Mintage	Fine	VF	XF	Unc
76.2	1845B	—	200.00	400.00	550.00	750.00
	1846B	—	200.00	400.00	550.00	750.00
	1847B	—	200.00	400.00	550.00	750.00
	1848B	—	200.00	400.00	550.00	750.00

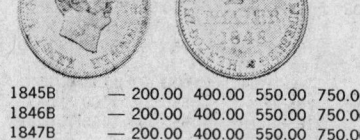

Rev: Crowned arms, date divided above, value below.

C#	Date	Mintage	Fine	VF	XF	Unc
77	1850B	—	200.00	400.00	600.00	800.00

Obv: Head left, BREHMER F. at truncation, B below.

C#	Date	Mintage	Fine	VF	XF	Unc
104	1853B	—	250.00	525.00	650.00	800.00
	1855B	—	250.00	525.00	650.00	800.00

5 THALER

6.6500 gm., .896 GOLD, .1916 oz AGW
Rev: T.W. below date, reeded edge.

C#	Date	Mintage	Fine	VF	XF	Unc
14	1813TW	—	250.00	525.00	700.00	900.00
	1814TW	—	250.00	525.00	700.00	900.00
	1815TW	—	250.00	525.00	700.00	900.00

6.6800 gm., .903 GOLD, .1940 oz AGW
Obv: Prancing horse, EX AURO HERCINIAE below.
Rev: C below date.

C#	Date	Mintage	Fine	VF	XF	Unc
15	1814C	—	1000.	2000.	2500.	4000.
	1815C	—	1000.	2000.	2500.	4000.
30	1821C	185 pcs.	1500.	3200.	4000.	6000.

C#	Date	Mintage	Fine	VF	XF	Unc
31	1821B	—	250.00	475.00	700.00	1000.
	1825B	—	250.00	475.00	700.00	1250.
	1828B	—	250.00	475.00	700.00	1250.
	1829B	—	250.00	475.00	700.00	1250.
	1830B	—	250.00	475.00	700.00	1250.

6.6500 gm., .896 GOLD, .1916 oz AGW

C#	Date	Mintage	Fine	VF	XF	Unc
53	1835B	—	350.00	700.00	1000.	2000.

C#	Date	Mintage	Fine	VF	XF	Unc
78	1839B	—	275.00	550.00	750.00	1500.

Obv: B below head.

C#	Date	Mintage	Fine	VF	XF	Unc
79	1845B	—	275.00	575.00	725.00	1200.
	1846B	—	275.00	575.00	725.00	1200.
	1848B	—	275.00	575.00	725.00	1200.

C#	Date	Mintage	Fine	VF	XF	Unc
—	1849B	—	275.00	575.00	725.00	1200.
	1851B	—	275.00	575.00	725.00	1200.

Rev. leg: HARZ GOLD added.

C#	Date	Mintage	Fine	VF	XF	Unc
80	1849B	—	500.00	1000.	1200.	1500.
	1850B	—	500.00	1000.	1200.	1500.

Obv: BREHMER F. at truncation, B below.

C#	Date	Mintage	Fine	VF	XF	Unc
105	1853B	—	250.00	550.00	700.00	1200.
	1855B	—	250.00	550.00	700.00	1200.
	1856B	—	250.00	550.00	700.00	1200.

Rev. leg: HARZ GOLD added.

C#	Date	Mintage	Fine	VF	XF	Unc
106	1853B	—	550.00	1100.	1400.	2000.
	1856B	—	550.00	1100.	1400.	2000.

10 THALER

13.3600 gm., .903 GOLD, .3879 oz AGW

C#	Date	Mintage	Fine	VF	XF	Unc
16	1813C.H.H.	—	750.00	1500.	2000.	3000.
	1814C.H.H.	—	750.00	1500.	2000.	3000.

C#	Date	Mintage	Fine	VF	XF	Unc
32	1821B	—	350.00	750.00	1000.	1500.
	1822B	—	350.00	750.00	1000.	1500.
	1823B	—	350.00	750.00	1000.	1500.
	1824B	—	350.00	750.00	1000.	1500.
	1825B	—	350.00	750.00	1000.	1500.
	1827B	—	350.00	750.00	1000.	1500.
	1828B	—	350.00	750.00	1000.	1500.
	1829B	—	350.00	750.00	1000.	1500.
	1830B	—	350.00	750.00	1000.	1500.

C#	Date	Mintage	Fine	VF	XF	Unc
54	1832	—	450.00	900.00	1500.	2500.

C#	Date	Mintage	Fine	VF	XF	Unc
55	1833	—	450.00	900.00	1500.	2500.

13.3000 gm., .896 GOLD, .3832 oz AGW
Obv: B under head.
Rev: Different shape of crown and shield.

C#	Date	Mintage	Fine	VF	XF	Unc
55a	1835B	—	450.00	900.00	1300.	2000.
	1836B	—	450.00	900.00	1300.	2000.
55a	1837B	—	450.00	900,00	1300.	2000.

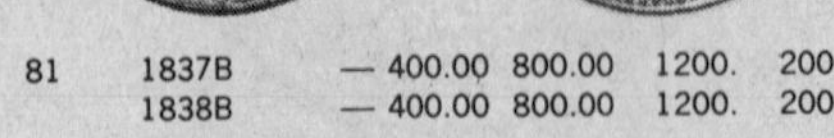

C#	Date	Mintage	Fine	VF	XF	Unc
81	1837B	—	400.00	800.00	1200.	2000.
	1838B	—	400.00	800.00	1200.	2000.

Obv: S below head.

C#	Date	Mintage	Fine	VF	XF	Unc
81a	1839S	—	400.00	800.00	1200.	2000.

Obv: BRANDT F. on truncation.
Rev: Crowned arms on cartouche.

C#	Date	Mintage	Fine	VF	XF	Unc
82	1844S	—	350.00	700.00	900.00	1700.

Obv: B below head.

C#	Date	Mintage	Fine	VF	XF	Unc
82a	1844B	—	350.00	700.00	900.00	1700.

Obv: No markings on truncation, leg: V. HANNOVER

C#	Date	Mintage	Fine	VF	XF	Unc
82b	1846B	—	350.00	700.00	900.00	1700.
	1847B	—	350.00	700.00	900.00	1700.
	1848B	—	350.00	700.00	900.00	1700.

Obv. leg: VON HANNOVER

C#	Date	Mintage	Fine	VF	XF	Unc
82c	1849B	—	350.00	700.00	900.00	1700.
	1850B	—	350.00	700.00	900.00	1700.
	1851B	—	350.00	700.00	900.00	1700.

C#	Date	Mintage	Fine	VF	XF	Unc
107	1853B	—	350.00	750.00	1000.	1700.
	1854B	—	350.00	750.00	1000.	1700.
	1855B	—	350.00	750.00	1000.	1700.
	1856B	—	350.00	750.00	1000.	1700.

TRADE COINS

DUCAT

3.5000 gm., .986 GOLD, .1109 oz AGW
Obv: Prancing horse.
Rev: Value, leg: EX AURO HERCINIAE.

C#	Date	Mintage	Fine	VF	XF	Unc
12	1815C	—	1000.	2000.	3000.	4000.
	1818C	—	1000.	2000.	3000.	4000.
28	1821C	252 pcs.	1250.	2550.	3200.	4000.
	1824C	749 pcs.	1200.	2250.	2800.	4000.
	1827C	1,300	900.00	1750.	2200.	4000.

C#	Date	Mintage	Fine	VF	XF	Unc
51	1831C	1,550	600.00	1200.	2000.	3500.

1/2 KRONE

5.5500 gm., .900 GOLD, .1606 oz AGW

C#	Date	Mintage	Fine	VF	XF	Unc
108	1857B	4,105	480.00	960.00	1200.	1500.
	1858B	116 pcs.	750.00	1500.	1900.	2400.
	1859B	790 pcs.	600.00	1275.	1600.	2000.
	1862B	96 pcs.	750.00	1500.	1900.	2400.
	1864B	.013	480.00	960.00	1200.	1500.
	1866B	2,909	480.00	960.00	1200.	1500.

KRONE

11.1100 gm., .900 GOLD, .3215 oz AGW

C#	Date	Mintage	Fine	VF	XF	Unc
109	1857B	.145	375.00	750.00	1000.	1500.
	1858B	.047	375.00	750.00	1000.	1500.
	1859B	.020	375.00	750.00	1000.	1500.
	1860B	.015	375.00	750.00	1000.	1500.
	1861B	780 pcs.	750.00	1550.	1925.	2400.
	1862B	.020	375.00	750.00	1000.	1500.
	1863B	.126	375.00	750.00	1000.	1500.
	1864B	.014	375.00	750.00	1000.	1500.
	1866B	.383	375.00	750.00	1000.	1500.

NCLT ISSUES

MEDALLIC ISSUE

KM#	Date	Mintage	Identification	Mkt.Val.
M1	1872	6,317	1 Thaler, Silver	100.00

PATTERNS

KM#	Date	Mintage	Identification	Mkt.Val.
1	1813	—	5 Thaler, Gold, plain edge, C14	1125.

KM#	Date	Mintage	Identification	Mkt.Val.
2	1834A	—	16 Gute Groschen, Silver, plain edge, C25	—
3	1834.B	—	1/24 Thaler, Billon, C41b	—
4	1840A	—	1 Thaler, Silver, C71	9000.

HESSE — CASSEL

A state located in southwest Germany was ruled by Landgraves until 1292 when they became Prince of the Empire. The Hesse-Cassel line was founded in 1567 and was given the title of Elector in 1803. Hesse-Cassel was merged into Westphalia from 1807-1813 and was absorbed by Prussia in 1866.

RULERS

Friedrich II, 1760-1785
Count Wilhelm IX, 1785-1803
Wilhelm I, As Elector, 1803-1821
Wilhelm II, 1821-1847
Friedrich Wilhelm I, 1847-1866

MINTMASTER'S INITIALS

BR - Balthasar Reinhard, 1765-1783
CP - Christoph Pfeuffer
F., D.F. - Dietrich Flalda, 1774-1831
FH - Friedrich Heenwagen, (Hanau), 1786-1821
FU - Friedrich Ulrich, 1764-1773
FH - Friedrich Henglin (Stuttgart), 1760-1794
H - Holzheimer (Hanau)
K - Wilhelm Korner, 1804-1833

HELLER

COPPER

Obv: Crowned double FL monogram.
Rev: Value and date, leg: SCHEIDE MUNTZ.

C#	Date	Mintage	VG	Fine		XF
20	1760	—	1.00	2.50	4.00	10.00
	1761	—	1.00	2.50	4.00	10.00

Similar to C#20 w/o SCHEIDE MUNTZ.

C#	Date	Mintage	VG	Fine		XF
23	1772	—	1.00	2.00	4.00	10.00

Obv: Crowned lion left on pedestal.
Rev: Value over date.

C#	Date	Mintage	VG	Fine		XF
33	1774	—	1.00	2.00	4.00	10.00
	1775	—	1.00	2.00	4.00	10.00

Similar to C#33.

C#	Date	Mintage	VG	Fine		XF
88	1790	—	1.00	2.50	5.00	12.50

Obv: Crowned monogram. Rev: Value and date.

C#	Date	Mintage	Fine	VF	XF	Unc
89	1791	—	2.00	5.00	10.00	40.00
	1792	—	2.00	5.00	10.00	40.00
	1793	—	2.00	5.00	10.00	40.00
	1794	—	2.00	5.00	10.00	40.00
	1795	—	2.00	5.00	10.00	40.00
	1796	—	2.00	5.00	10.00	40.00
	1797	—	2.00	5.00	10.00	40.00
	1798	—	2.00	5.00	10.00	40.00
	1799	—	2.00	5.00	10.00	40.00
	1800	—	2.00	5.00	10.00	40.00
	1801	—	2.00	5.00	10.00	40.00
	1802	—	2.00	5.00	10.00	40.00
	1803	—	2.00	5.00	10.00	40.00

C#	Date	Mintage	Fine	VF	XF	Unc
111	1803	—	2.00	5.00	10.00	40.00
	1805	—	2.00	5.00	10.00	40.00
	1806	—	2.00	5.00	10.00	40.00
	1814	—	2.00	5.00	10.00	40.00

Obv: Crowned WK monogram.

C#	Date	Mintage	Fine	VF	XF	Unc
	1817	—	2.00	5.00	10.00	40.00
	1818	—	2.00	5.00	10.00	40.00
	1819	—	2.00	5.00	10.00	40.00
	1820	—	2.00	5.00	10.00	40.00
121	1822	—	2.00	5.00	10.00	40.00
	1823	—	2.00	5.00	10.00	40.00
	1824	—	2.00	5.00	10.00	40.00
	1825	—	2.00	5.00	10.00	40.00
	1827	—	2.00	5.00	10.00	40.00

C#	Date	Mintage	Fine	VF	XF	Unc
121a	1822	—	2.00	4.00	7.50	40.00
	1825	—	2.00	4.00	7.50	40.00
	1827	—	2.00	4.00	7.50	40.00
	1828	—	2.00	4.00	7.50	40.00
	1829	—	2.00	4.00	7.50	40.00
	1831	—	2.00	4.00	7.50	40.00

Obv: Crowned arms, leg: KURHESSEN.
Rev. value: SCHEIDE MUNZE.

C#	Date	Mintage	Fine	VF	XF	Unc
135	1842	.037	5.00	15.00	25.00	50.00

Obv. leg: 360 EINEN THALER.

C#	Date	Mintage	Fine	VF	XF	Unc
138	1843	—	1.50	3.50	6.00	30.00
	1845	—	1.50	3.50	6.00	30.00
	1847	—	1.50	3.50	6.00	30.00

C#	Date	Mintage	Fine	VF	XF	Unc
153	1849	—	1.00	2.50	5.00	30.00
	1852	—	1.00	2.50	5.00	30.00
	1854	—	1.00	2.50	5.00	30.00
	1856	—	1.00	2.50	5.00	30.00
	1858	—	1.00	2.50	5.00	30.00
	1859	—	1.00	2.50	5.00	30.00
	1860	—	1.00	2.50	5.00	30.00
	1861	—	1.00	2.50	5.00	30.00
	1862	—	1.00	2.50	5.00	30.00
	1863	—	1.00	2.50	5.00	30.00
	1864	—	1.00	2.50	5.00	30.00
	1865	—	1.00	2.50	5.00	30.00
	1866	—	1.00	2.50	5.00	30.00

2 HELLER

COPPER

Obv: Crowned script FL monogram.
Rev: Value and date, leg: SCHEIDE MUNTZ.

C#	Date	Mintage	VG	Fine	VF	XF
29	1765	—	1.00	2.00	4.00	10.00

Obv: Crowned double FL monogram.
Rev: W/o leg: SCHEIDE MUNTZ.

C#	Date	Mintage	VG	Fine	VF	XF
24	1772	—	1.00	2.50	5.00	12.00

Obv: Lion holding shield with FL monogram.
Rev: Value over date.

C#	Date	Mintage	VG	Fine	VF	XF
34	1774	—	1.00	2.00	4.00	10.00
	1775	—	1.00	2.00	4.00	10.00
	1776	—	1.00	2.00	4.00	10.00
	1777	—	1.00	2.00	4.00	10.00

C#	Date	Mintage	VG	Fine	VF	XF
90	1790	—	1.00	2.50	5.00	12.00
	1791	—	1.00	2.50	5.00	12.00
	1792	—	1.00	2.50	5.00	12.00
	1793	—	1.00	2.50	5.00	12.00
	1794	—	1.00	2.50	5.00	12.00
	1795	—	1.00	2.50	5.00	12.00

Obv: WK monogram with elector's cap. Rev: Value.

C#	Date	Mintage	Fine	VF	XF	Unc
112	1814	—	3.00	7.50	15.00	45.00

Obv: Crowned WK monogram.

C#	Date	Mintage	Fine	VF	XF	Unc
	1816	—	2.00	5.00	10.00	40.00
	1818	—	2.00	5.00	10.00	40.00
	1820	—	2.00	5.00	10.00	40.00

C#	Date	Mintage	Fine	VF	XF	Unc
122	1831	—	2.00	5.00	10.00	40.00
134	1833	—	2.00	5.00	10.00	40.00
136	1842	—	—	—	Rare	—

C#	Date	Mintage	Fine	VF	XF	Unc
139	1843	—	3.00	7.00	15.00	40.00

3 HELLER

COPPER

Obv: Crowned double FL monogram.
Rev: Value and date, leg: SCHEIDE MUNTZ.

C#	Date	Mintage	VG	Fine	VF	XF
21	1760	—	1.00	2.50	5.00	15.00
	1761	—	1.00	2.50	5.00	15.00

Rev: Value and date.

C#	Date	Mintage	VG	Fine	VF	XF
25	1772	—	1.00	3.00	6.00	15.00

Obv: Crowned script FL monogram.
Rev: Value and date.

C#	Date	Mintage	VG	Fine	VF	XF
31	1774	—	1.00	2.00	4.00	15.00

Obv: Crowned WL monogram. Rev: Value over date.

C#	Date	Mintage	VG	Fine	VF	XF
91	1791	—	2.00	5.00	6.50	15.00

C#	Date	Mintage	Fine	VF	XF	Unc
137	1842	—	—	—	Rare	—

C#	Date	Mintage	Fine	VF	XF	Unc
140	1843	—	1.50	4.00	7.50	30.00
	1844	—	1.50	4.00	7.50	30.00
	1845	—	1.50	4.00	7.50	30.00
	1846	—	1.50	4.00	7.50	30.00

C#	Date	Mintage	Fine	VF	XF	Unc
154	1848	—	1.00	3.00	6.00	30.00
	1849	—	1.00	3.00	6.00	30.00
	1850	—	1.00	3.00	6.00	30.00
	1851	—	1.00	3.00	6.00	30.00
	1852	—	1.00	3.00	6.00	30.00
	1853	—	1.00	3.00	6.00	30.00
	1854	—	1.00	3.00	6.00	30.00
	1856	—	1.00	3.00	6.00	30.00
	1858	—	1.00	3.00	6.00	30.00
	1859	—	1.00	3.00	6.00	30.00
	1860	—	1.00	3.00	6.00	30.00
	1861	—	1.00	3.00	6.00	30.00
	1862	—	1.00	3.00	6.00	30.00
	1863	—	1.00	3.00	6.00	30.00
	1864	—	1.00	3.00	6.00	30.00
	1865	—	1.00	3.00	6.00	30.00
	1866	—	1.00	3.00	6.00	30.00

4 HELLER

COPPER

Obv: Crowned script FL monogram.
Rev: Value and date, leg: SCHEIDE MUNTZ.

C#	Date	Mintage	VG	Fine	VF	XF
30	1765	—	1.00	3.00	7.50	15.00

Obv: Crowned double FL monogram.

C#	Date	Mintage	VG	Fine	VF	XF
22	1760	—	1.25	3.50	7.00	15.00
	1761	—	1.25	3.50	7.00	15.00
	1762	—	1.25	3.50	7.00	15.00

Rev: Value and date.

C#	Date	Mintage	VG	Fine	VF	XF
26	1773	—	1.50	4.00	8.00	16.00

Obv: Crowned lion left on pedestal.
Rev: Value over date.

C#	Date	Mintage	VG	Fine	VF	XF
35	1774	—	3.00	5.00	6.50	15.00
	1775	—	3.00	5.00	6.50	15.00
	1776	—	3.00	5.00	6.50	15.00
	1777	—	3.00	5.00	6.50	15.00
	1778	—	3.00	5.00	6.50	15.00
	1779	—	3.00	5.00	6.50	15.00
	1780	—	3.00	5.00	6.50	15.00
	1781	—	3.00	5.00	6.50	15.00
	1782	—	3.00	5.00	6.50	15.00

Obv: Lion holding shield which has FL monogram.

C#	Date	Mintage	VG	Fine	VF	XF
92	1788	—	4.00	6.00	8.50	16.00
	1789	—	4.00	6.00	8.50	16.00
	1790	—	4.00	6.00	8.50	16.00
	1791	—	4.00	6.00	8.50	16.00
	1792	—	4.00	6.00	8.50	16.00
	1793	—	4.00	6.00	8.50	16.00

C#	Date	Mintage	VG	Fine	VF	XF
35	1778	—	3.00	5.00	6.50	15.00
	1779	—	3.00	5.00	6.50	15.00
	1780	—	3.00	5.00	6.50	15.00
	1781	—	3.00	5.00	6.50	15.00
	1782	—	3.00	5.00	6.50	15.00

Obv: Lion holding shield which has FL monogram.

C#	Date	Mintage	VG	Fine	VF	XF
92	1788	—	4.00	6.00	8.50	16.00
	1789	—	4.00	6.00	8.50	16.00
	1790	—	4.00	6.00	8.50	16.00
	1791	—	4.00	6.00	8.50	16.00
	1792	—	4.00	6.00	8.50	16.00
	1793	—	4.00	6.00	8.50	16.00
	1794	—	4.00	6.00	8.50	16.00

Obv: Crowned WK monogram. Rev: Value.

C#	Date	Mintage	Fine	VF	XF	Unc
113	1815	—	2.00	5.00	10.00	35.00
	1816	—	2.00	5.00	10.00	35.00
	1817	—	2.00	5.00	10.00	35.00
	1818	—	2.00	5.00	10.00	35.00
	1819	—	2.00	5.00	10.00	35.00
	1820	—	2.00	5.00	10.00	35.00
	1821	—	2.00	5.00	10.00	35.00

C#	Date	Mintage	Fine	VF	XF	Unc
123	1821	—	1.50	4.00	9.00	30.00
	1822	—	1.50	4.00	9.00	30.00
	1824	—	1.50	4.00	9.00	30.00
	1826	—	1.50	4.00	9.00	30.00
	1827	—	1.50	4.00	9.00	30.00
	1828	—	1.50	4.00	9.00	30.00
	1829	—	1.50	4.00	9.00	30.00
	1830	—	1.50	4.00	9.00	30.00
	1831	—	1.50	4.00	9.00	30.00

6 HELLER

BILLON
Obv: Arms. Rev: Value and date.

C#	Date	Mintage	VG	Fine	VF	XF
41	1770	—	1.50	4.00	8.00	20.00

COPPER
Obv: Crowned double FL monogram.

C#	Date	Mintage	VG	Fine	VF	XF
27	1772	—	2.25	6.00	12.00	24.00

Obv: Crowned FL monogram.

C#	Date	Mintage	VG	Fine	VF	XF
32	1775	—	2.00	5.00	10.00	20.00

8 HELLER

BILLON
Obv: Crowned lion. Rev: Value and date.

C#	Date	Mintage	VG	Fine	VF	XF
43	1769	—	1.50	5.00	10.00	25.00

COPPER

C#	Date	Mintage	VG	Fine	VF	XF
28	1772	—	2.50	8.00	15.00	25.00

C#	Date	Mintage	VG	Fine	VF	XF
36	1774	—	3.00	7.00	11.50	20.00
	1775	—	3.00	7.00	11.50	20.00
	1776	—	3.00	7.00	11.50	20.00
	1777	—	3.00	7.00	11.50	20.00
	1778	—	3.00	7.00	11.50	20.00
	1779	—	3.00	7.00	11.50	20.00
	1780	—	3.00	7.00	11.50	20.00
	1781	—	3.00	7.00	11.50	20.00
	1782	—	3.00	7.00	11.50	20.00

ALBUS

BILLON
Obv: Crowned FL monogram. Rev: Value and date.

C#	Date	Mintage	VG	Fine	VF	XF
45	1768 FU	—	1.50	4.00	7.50	20.00
	1769	—	1.50	4.00	7.50	20.00
	1770	—	1.50	4.00	7.50	20.00

2 ALBUS

BILLON

C#	Date	Mintage	VG	Fine	VF	XF
50	1775	—	1.50	3.00	6.00	12.00
	1776	—	1.50	3.00	6.00	12.00
	1777	—	1.50	3.00	6.00	12.00
	1778	—	1.50	3.00	6.00	12.00
	1779 BR	—	1.50	3.00	6.00	12.00
	1780 BR	—	1.50	3.00	6.00	12.00
	1781 BR	—	1.50	3.00	6.00	12.00
	1782 BR	—	1.50	3.00	6.00	12.00

4 ALBUS

SILVER
Obv: Arms in crowned cartouche.
Rev: Value and date in circle.

C#	Date	Mintage	VG	Fine	VF	XF
56	1762	—	2.00	4.50	8.00	20.00
	1763	—	2.00	4.50	8.00	20.00
	1764	—	2.00	4.50	8.00	20.00

1/2 SILVER GROSCHEN

BILLON
Obv: Crowned arms. Rev. value: SCHEIDE MUNZE

C#	Date	Mintage	Fine	VF	XF	Unc
141	1842	1.491	2.50	6.00	10.00	35.00

SILVER GROSCHEN

BILLON

C#	Date	Mintage	Fine	VF	XF	Unc
142	1841	5.925	2.00	5.00	10.00	30.00
	1845	.062	2.00	5.00	10.00	40.00
	1847	.456	2.00	5.00	10.00	40.00

C#	Date	Mintage	Fine	VF	XF	Unc
155	1851	.262	2.00	5.00	10.00	40.00
	1852	.147	2.00	5.00	10.00	40.00
	1853	.125	2.00	5.00	10.00	40.00
	1854	.098	2.00	5.00	10.00	40.00
	1855	.054	2.00	5.00	10.00	40.00
	1856	.234	2.00	5.00	10.00	40.00
	1857	.119	2.00	5.00	10.00	40.00
	1858	.058	2.00	5.00	10.00	40.00
	1859	.235	2.00	5.00	10.00	40.00
	1860	.156	2.00	5.00	10.00	40.00
	1861	.165	2.00	5.00	10.00	40.00
	1862	—	2.00	5.00	10.00	40.00
	1863	—	2.00	5.00	10.00	40.00
	1864	.122	2.00	5.00	10.00	40.00
	1865	.192	2.00	5.00	10.00	40.00
	1866	.182	2.00	5.00	10.00	40.00

2 SILVER GROSCHEN

BILLON
Obv: Crowned arms. Rev. value: SCHEIDE MUNZE

C#	Date	Mintage	Fine	VF	XF	Unc
143	1842	2.414	3.00	7.00	15.00	40.00

2 1/2 SILVER GROSCHEN

BILLON

C#	Date	Mintage	Fine	VF	XF	Unc
156	1852 CP	.034	4.00	10.00	15.00	40.00
	1853 CP	.049	4.00	10.00	15.00	40.00
	1856 CP	.039	4.00	10.00	15.00	40.00
	1859 CP	.069	4.00	10.00	15.00	40.00
	1860 CP	.042	4.00	10.00	15.00	40.00
	1861 CP	.034	4.00	10.00	15.00	40.00
	1862 CP	.031	4.00	10.00	15.00	40.00
	1865 CP	.023	4.00	10.00	15.00	40.00

24 EINEN (1/24)THALER

BILLON
Obv: Rampant lion left; B.R. in exergue.
Rev: Value over date.

C#	Date	Mintage	VG	Fine	VF	XF
47	1780 BR	—	3.00	6.00	10.00	25.00

Obv: Rampant lion left.
Rev: Value over date; D.F. in exergue.

C#	Date	Mintage	VG	Fine	VF	XF
48	1783 DF	—	3.00	6.00	10.00	25.00
	1784 DF	—	3.00	6.00	10.00	25.00
	1785 DF	—	3.00	6.00	10.00	25.00

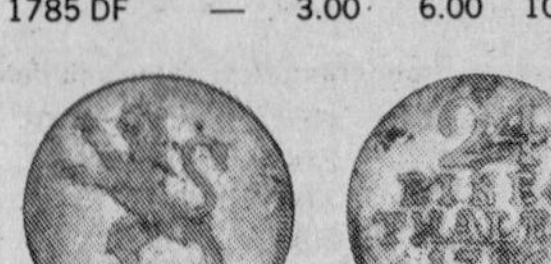

C#	Date	Mintage	Fine	VF	XF	Unc
96	1786 DF	—	3.00	7.00	15.00	50.00
	1787	—	3.00	7.00	15.00	50.00
	1788	—	3.00	7.00	15.00	50.00
	1789	—	3.00	7.00	15.00	50.00
	1790	—	3.00	7.00	15.00	50.00
	1791	—	3.00	7.00	15.00	50.00
	1792	—	3.00	7.00	15.00	50.00
	1793	—	3.00	7.00	15.00	50.00
	1794	—	3.00	7.00	15.00	50.00
	1795	—	3.00	7.00	15.00	50.00
	1796	—	3.00	7.00	15.00	50.00
	1797	—	3.00	7.00	15.00	50.00
	1798	—	3.00	7.00	15.00	50.00
	1799	—	3.00	7.00	15.00	50.00
	1800	—	3.00	7.00	15.00	50.00
	1801	—	3.00	7.00	15.00	50.00
	1802	—	3.00	7.00	15.00	50.00

C#	Date	Mintage	Fine	VF	XF	Unc
115.1	1803 F	.526	3.00	7.00	15.00	50.00
	1804 F	—	3.00	7.00	15.00	50.00
	1805 F	—	3.00	7.00	15.00	50.00
	1806 F	—	3.00	7.00	15.00	50.00
	1807 F	.997	3.00	7.00	15.00	50.00

Rev: No mintmark below date.

C#	Date	Mintage	Fine	VF	XF	Unc
115.2	1814	—	2.00	5.00	10.00	40.00
	1815	—	2.00	5.00	10.00	40.00
	1816	—	2.00	5.00	10.00	40.00
	1817	—	2.00	5.00	10.00	40.00
	1818	—	2.00	5.00	10.00	40.00
	1819	—	2.00	5.00	10.00	40.00
	1820	—	2.00	5.00	10.00	40.00
	1821	—	2.00	5.00	10.00	40.00
124	1822	—	2.50	6.00	12.00	40.00

1/12 THALER

SILVER

Obv: Arms. Rev: Value and date.

C#	Date	Mintage	VG	Fine	VF	XF
52	1764 FU	—	2.50	5.00	10.00	20.00

Obv: Crowned lion on pedestal.

C#	Date	Mintage	VG	Fine	VF	XF
54	1765 FU	—	2.00	4.00	8.00	20.00
	1766 FU	—	2.00	4.00	8.00	20.00
	1767 FU	—	2.00	4.00	8.00	20.00
	1768 FU	—	2.00	4.00	8.00	20.00
	1769 FU	—	2.00	4.00	8.00	20.00

VIII EINEN (1/8) THALER

SILVER

C#	Date	Mintage	VG	Fine	VF	XF
58	1766 FU	—	2.00	4.00	8.00	20.00
	1767 FU	—	2.00	4.00	8.00	20.00
	1768 FU	—	2.00	4.00	8.00	20.00
	1769 FU	—	2.00	4.00	8.00	20.00

Obv: Lion in crowned cartouche.
Rev: Value over wreath.

C#	Date	Mintage	VG	Fine	VF	XF
60	1776	—	3.00	7.00	9.50	20.00

VI EINEN (1/6) THALER

SILVER

C#	Date	Mintage	VG	Fine	VF	XF
62	1766 FU	—	2.00	4.00	9.00	20.00

C#	Date	Mintage	VG	Fine	VF	XF
62a	1766	—	2.00	4.00	9.00	20.00

Rev. leg. around circular cord.

C#	Date	Mintage	VG	Fine	VF	XF
62b	1767 FU	—	2.00	4.00	9.00	20.00

Rev. leg. around circle.

C#	Date	Mintage	VG	Fine	VF	XF
62c	1768 FU	—	2.00	4.00	9.00	20.00
	1769 FU	—	2.00	4.00	9.00	20.00
	1770	—	2.00	4.00	9.00	20.00
	1771	—	2.00	4.00	9.00	20.00
	1772	—	2.00	4.00	9.00	20.00

Similar to C#62.
Rev. leg: 6 EINEN......

C#	Date	Mintage	VG	Fine	VF	XF
66	1773	—	2.00	4.00	9.00	20.00

Obv: Arms. Rev: Value over date.

C#	Date	Mintage	VG	Fine	VF	XF
98	1790	—	3.00	7.00	10.00	20.00
	1791	—	3.00	7.00	10.00	20.00
98	1792	—	3.00	7.00	10.00	20.00
	1793	—	3.00	7.00	10.00	20.00
	1794	—	3.00	7.00	10.00	20.00
	1795	—	3.00	7.00	10.00	20.00
	1796	—	3.00	7.00	10.00	20.00

Obv: Lion shield. Rev: Value, date.

C#	Date	Mintage	Fine	VF	XF	Unc
99	1798 E	—	10.00	25.00	45.00	75.00
	1799 F	—	10.00	25.00	45.00	75.00
	1800 F	—	10.00	25.00	45.00	75.00
	1801 F	—	10.00	25.00	45.00	75.00
	1802 F	—	10.00	25.00	45.00	75.00

.625 SILVER

Obv: Crowned arms within laurel branches. Rev: Value.

C#	Date	Mintage	Fine	VF	XF	Unc
116	1803 F	—	10.00	25.00	45.00	75.00

C#	Date	Mintage	Fine	VF	XF	Unc
116a	1803 F	—	10.00	25.00	45.00	75.00
	1804 F	—	10.00	25.00	45.00	75.00
	1805 F	—	10.00	25.00	45.00	75.00
	1806 F	—	10.00	25.00	45.00	75.00
	1807 F	.040	10.00	25.00	45.00	75.00
125	1821	.038	10.00	25.00	45.00	75.00
	1822	.056	10.00	25.00	45.00	75.00

Obv. leg: KURF S.L.V. HESSEN.

C#	Date	Mintage	Fine	VF	XF	Unc
126	1823	.182	7.00	15.00	30.00	60.00
	1824	.276	7.00	15.00	30.00	60.00
	1825	.306	7.00	15.00	30.00	60.00
	1826	.147	7.00	15.00	30.00	60.00
	1827	.280	7.00	15.00	30.00	60.00
	1828	.395	7.00	15.00	30.00	60.00
	1829	.590	7.00	15.00	30.00	60.00
	1830	.524	7.00	15.00	30.00	60.00
	1831	.201	7.00	15.00	30.00	60.00

Obv. leg: KURF. V. HESSEN

C#	Date	Mintage	Fine	VF	XF	Unc
126a	1831	.022	20.00	45.00	75.00	150.00

Rev: THAELR (error)

C#	Date	Mintage	Fine	VF	XF	Unc
126b	1828	—	50.00	115.00	200.00	325.00

C#	Date	Mintage	Fine	VF	XF	Unc
144	1833	.046	3.00	7.00	20.00	40.00
	1834	.599	3.00	7.00	20.00	40.00
	1835	.810	3.00	7.00	20.00	40.00
	1836	.528	3.00	7.00	20.00	40.00
	1837	.624	3.00	7.00	20.00	40.00
	1838	.558	3.00	7.00	20.00	40.00
	1839	.228	3.00	7.00	20.00	40.00
	1840	6,000	5.00	10.00	25.00	55.00
	1841	.192	3.00	7.00	20.00	40.00
	1842	1.404	3.00	7.00	20.00	40.00
	1843	.138	3.00	7.00	20.00	40.00
	1844	6,132	5.00	10.00	25.00	55.00
	1845	.095	3.00	7.00	20.00	40.00
	1846	.045	3.00	7.00	20.00	40.00

Obv: Legend on chain: KURPR.-MITREG

C#	Date	Mintage	Fine	VF	XF	Unc
144a	1846	Inc.Ab.	10.00	25.00	45.00	80.00
	1847	.103	10.00	25.00	45.00	80.00

.500 SILVER

Obv: C.P. at truncation.

C#	Date	Mintage	Fine	VF	XF	Unc
157	1851 CP	.030	10.00	20.00	35.00	60.00
	1852 CP	.033	10.00	20.00	35.00	60.00
	1854 CP	.013	10.00	20.00	35.00	60.00
	1855 CP	.022	10.00	20.00	35.00	60.00
	1856 CP	—	10.00	20.00	35.00	60.00

IV EINEN (1/4) THALER

SILVER

C#	Date	Mintage	VG	Fine	VF	XF
67	1763	—	2.50	6.00	10.00	20.00
	1764	—	2.50	6.00	10.00	20.00
	1765	—	2.50	6.00	10.00	20.00
	1766	—	2.50	6.00	10.00	20.00
	1767 FU	—	2.50	6.00	10.00	20.00

C#	Date	Mintage	VG	Fine	VF	XF
68	1768 FU	—	2.50	6.00	10.00	20.00
	1769 FU	—	2.50	6.00	10.00	20.00
	1770 FU	—	2.50	6.00	10.00	20.00
	1771 FU	—	2.50	6.00	10.00	20.00
	1772 FU	—	2.50	6.00	10.00	20.00

1/3 THALER

SILVER

Obv: Bust of Friedrich II right. Rev: Arms.

C#	Date	Mintage	VG	Fine	VF	XF
70	1766	—	7.00	15.00	25.00	50.00

Obv: Head of Friedrich II right.

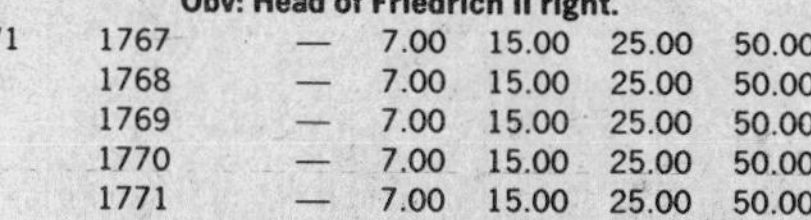

C#	Date	Mintage	VG	Fine	VF	XF
71	1767	—	7.00	15.00	25.00	50.00
	1768	—	7.00	15.00	25.00	50.00
	1769	—	7.00	15.00	25.00	50.00
	1770	—	7.00	15.00	25.00	50.00
	1771	—	7.00	15.00	25.00	50.00

.625 SILVER

C#	Date	Mintage	Fine	VF	XF	Unc
127	1822	.105	8.00	20.00	35.00	75.00
	1823	.125	8.00	20.00	35.00	75.00
	1824	.099	8.00	20.00	35.00	75.00
	1825	.162	8.00	20.00	35.00	75.00
	1826	.280	8.00	20.00	35.00	75.00
	1827	.278	8.00	20.00	35.00	75.00
	1828	—	8.00	20.00	35.00	75.00
	1829	.219	8.00	20.00	35.00	75.00

1/2 THALER

(Reichs)

SILVER

C#	Date	Mintage	VG	Fine	VF	XF
73	1776 BR	—	20.00	35.00	60.00	85.00

(Convention)

Bieber Mines Commemorative

C#	Date	Mintage	VG	Fine	VF	XF
103	1786	—	9.00	25.00	50.00	75.00

(Reichs)

C#	Date	Mintage	VG	Fine	VF	XF
101	1789 F	—	8.00	20.00	35.00	60.00

.750 SILVER

C#	Date	Mintage	Fine	VF	XF	Unc
117	1819	—	8.00	20.00	35.00	75.00
	1820	—	8.00	20.00	35.00	75.00

2/3 THALER

(Reichs)

SILVER

Obv: Bust of Friedrich II right. Rev: Arms.

C#	Date	Mintage	VG	Fine	VF	XF
75	1766	—	10.00	20.00	30.00	50.00

Obv: Head of Friedrich II right.

C#	Date	Mintage	VG	Fine	VF	XF
76	1767	—	10.00	20.00	30.00	50.00

C#	Date	Mintage	VG	Fine	VF	XF
78	1785	—	10.00	25.00	45.00	75.00

THALER

(Convention)

SILVER

Obv: Bust left. Rev: Crowned arms.

C#	Date	Mintage	VG	Fine	VF	XF
80	1763 U	—	50.00	150.00	275.00	400.00

C#	Date	Mintage	VG	Fine	VF	XF
81	1765 FU	—	40.00	100.00	180.00	300.00

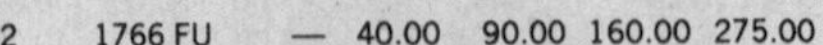

C#	Date	Mintage	VG	Fine	VF	XF
82	1766 FU	—	40.00	90.00	160.00	275.00

C#	Date	Mintage	VG	Fine	VF	XF
83	1766 FU	—	30.00	75.00	140.00	250.00

(Reichs)

C#	Date	Mintage	VG	Fine	VF	XF
84	1776 BR	—	60.00	100.00	165.00	225.00
	1778 BR	—	50.00	85.00	150.00	200.00
	1779 BR	—	50.00	85.00	150.00	200.00

NOTE: Varieties exist.

MINING

Rev: BIBERER SILBER on pedestal below arms.

C#	Date	Mintage	VG	Fine	VF	XF
106	1785 IFH	—	50.00	100.00	175.00	300.00

C#	Date	Mintage	Fine	VF	XF	Unc
106a	1787 FH	—	60.00	150.00	250.00	500.00
	1789 FH	—	60.00	150.00	250.00	500.00
	1791 FH	—	60.00	150.00	250.00	500.00
	1793 FH	—	60.00	150.00	250.00	500.00
	1794 FH	—	60.00	150.00	250.00	500.00
	1796 FH	—	60.00	150.00	250.00	500.00
	1798 FH	—	60.00	150.00	250.00	500.00
	1800 FH	—	60.00	150.00	250.00	500.00

NOTE: Many varieties exist.

Obv: Smaller head.

C#	Date	Mintage	Fine	VF	XF	Unc
106b	1802 FH	—	800.00	3000.	6000.	9000.
—	1813 K	—	500.00	1500.	2500.	5500.

NOTE: Possibly a pattern.

(Reichs)

Rev: Crowned multiple arms in sprays.

C#	Date	Mintage	Fine	VF	XF	Unc
105	1789 F	—	65.00	100.00	165.00	300.00

22.2700 gm., .750 SILVER, .5371 oz ASW
Obv: Head right, KURF. SOUV. Rev: Value within wreath.

C#	Date	Mintage	Fine	VF	XF	Unc
118	1819	—	100.00	200.00	600.00	1200.
	1820	—	100.00	200.00	600.00	1200.

Obv: Military bust right, SOUV.LANDGR.Z.HESSEN.

C#	Date	Mintage	Fine	VF	XF	Unc
128.1	1821	2,385	150.00	300.00	600.00	1200.
	1822	3,456	150.00	300.00	600.00	1200.

Obv: No period after HESSEN.

C#	Date	Mintage	Fine	VF	XF	Unc
128.2	1821	Inc. Ab.	150.00	300.00	600.00	1200.

C#	Date	Mintage	Fine	VF	XF	Unc
145	1832	.020	20.00	50.00	250.00	500.00
	1833	.017	20.00	50.00	250.00	500.00
	1834	.037	20.00	50.00	250.00	500.00
	1835	.014	20.00	50.00	250.00	500.00
	1836	.040	20.00	50.00	250.00	500.00
	1837	.026	20.00	50.00	250.00	500.00
	1838	4,041	40.00	65.00	300.00	600.00
	1839	2,574	40.00	65.00	300.00	600.00
	1841	.025	20.00	50.00	250.00	500.00
	1842	.031	20.00	50.00	250.00	500.00

Obv: C.PFEUFFER F. at truncation.

C#	Date	Mintage	Fine	VF	XF	Unc
158	1851	3,963	75.00	125.00	250.00	400.00
	1854	7,338	60.00	100.00	225.00	375.00
	1855	.028	50.00	100.00	225.00	375.00

18.5200 gm., .900 SILVER, .5360 oz ASW
Obv: C.P. at truncation

C#	Date	Mintage	Fine	VF	XF	Unc
159	1858 CP	.062	35.00	60.00	150.00	300.00
	1859 CP	.037	35.00	60.00	150.00	300.00
	1860 CP	.031	35.00	60.00	150.00	300.00
	1862 CP	.032	35.00	60.00	150.00	300.00
	1864 CP	.032	35.00	60.00	150.00	300.00
	1865 CP	.031	35.00	60.00	150.00	300.00

Obv: Without C.P. at truncation.

C#	Date	Mintage	Fine	VF	XF	Unc
159a	1858	Inc. Ab.	35.00	60.00	150.00	300.00
	1859	Inc. Ab.	35.00	60.00	150.00	300.00
	1860	Inc. Ab.	35.00	60.00	150.00	300.00
	1861	.032	35.00	60.00	150.00	300.00
	1862	—	35.00	60.00	150.00	300.00
	1863	.032	35.00	60.00	150.00	300.00
	1864	Inc. Ab.	35.00	60.00	150.00	300.00
	1865	Inc. Ab.	35.00	60.00	150.00	300.00

2 THALER

(Reichs)

(= 3-1/2 Gulden)

SILVER
Obv: Head right; K on neck.
Rev: Crowned multiple arms hung with garlands
D. F separates date.

C#	Date	Mintage	VG	Fine	VF	XF
108	1789	250 pcs.	300.00	600.00	850.00	1500.

37.1200 gm., .900 SILVER, 1.0742 oz ASW

C#	Date	Mintage	Fine	VF	XF	Unc
146	1840	.019	110.00	200.00	400.00	1000.
	1841	.019	110.00	200.00	400.00	1000.
	1842	.019	110.00	200.00	400.00	1000.
	1843	.018	110.00	200.00	400.00	1000.
	1844	.059	110.00	200.00	400.00	1000.
	1845	—	110.00	200.00	400.00	1000.

Obv: Larger letters.

C#	Date	Mintage	Fine	VF	XF	Unc
146b	1844	Inc. Ab.	165.00	275.00	550.00	1200.
	1845	—	165.00	275.00	550.00	1200.

Obv. leg: KURPRINZ-MITREGENT.

C#	Date	Mintage	Fine	VF	XF	Unc
146a	1847	.010	475.00	800.00	1500.	2500.

Obv: CP on truncation.

C#	Date	Mintage	Fine	VF	XF	Unc
160	1851 CP	3,996	175.00	300.00	500.00	900.00
	1854 CP	.141	100.00	200.00	325.00	550.00
	1855 CP	.357	85.00	140.00	250.00	450.00

5 THALER

(= 1 Pistole)

6.6500 gm., .900 GOLD, .1924 oz AGW

C#	Date	Mintage	Fine	VF	XF	Unc
86	1771 BR	—	1200.	1800.	2500.	4000.
	1777 BR	—	1200.	1800.	2500.	4000.
	1778 BR	—	1200.	1800.	2500.	4000.

C#	Date	Mintage	Fine	VF	XF	Unc
86a	1783 DF	—	600.00	1200.	1800.	2500.
	1784 DF	—	600.00	1200.	1800.	2500.
	1785 DF	—	600.00	1200.	1800.	2500.

Obv: Wilhelm IX; head right.

C#	Date	Mintage	Fine	VF	XF	Unc
109	1786	—	300.00	650.00	900.00	1400.
	1787	—	300.00	650.00	900.00	1400.
	1788	—	300.00	650.00	900.00	1400.
	1790	—	300.00	650.00	900.00	1400.
110	1791 F	—	300.00	650.00	1000.	1500.
	1792 F	—	300.00	650.00	1000.	1500.
	1793 F	—	300.00	650.00	1000.	1500.
	1794 F	—	300.00	650.00	1000.	1500.
	1795 F	—	300.00	650.00	1000.	1500.
	1796 F	—	300.00	650.00	1000.	1500.
	1797 F	—	300.00	650.00	1000.	1500.
	1798 F	—	300.00	650.00	1000.	1500.
	1799 F	—	300.00	650.00	1000.	1500.
	1800 F	—	300.00	650.00	1000.	1500.
	1801 F	—	300.00	650.00	1000.	1500.

Obv: Head right. Rev: Column with electoral cap, flags and reclining lion in front.

C#	Date	Mintage	Fine	VF	XF	Unc
119	1803 F	1,659	600.00	1200.	1800.	2500.
	1805 F	1,941	600.00	1200.	1800.	2500.
	1806 F	875 pcs.	700.00	1400.	2000.	2700.

C#	Date	Mintage	Fine	VF	XF	Unc
—	1815	2,226	600.00	1200.	2000.	2500.

Obv. leg: WILHELMUS I.ELECT.HASS. LANDGR.M.D.FULD.

C#	Date	Mintage	Fine	VF	XF	Unc
—	1817	2,352	600.00	1200.	2000.	2500.
	1819	1,548	600.00	1200.	2000.	2500.
—	1820	534 pcs.	850.00	1700.	2500.	5000.

C#	Date	Mintage	Fine	VF	XF	Unc
129	1821	1,142	600.00	1200.	2000.	3500.
	1823	1,140	600.00	1200.	2000.	3500.

Obv. leg: S.L.V.HESSEN

C#	Date	Mintage	Fine	VF	XF	Unc
129a	1823	518 pcs.	600.00	1200.	2000.	3500.
	1825	409 pcs.	600.00	1200.	2000.	3500.
	1828	952 pcs.	600.00	1200.	2000.	3500.
	1829	502 pcs.	600.00	1200.	2000.	3500.

C#	Date	Mintage	Fine	VF	XF	Unc
147	1834	1,025	400.00	800.00	1200.	2000.
	1836	2,002	400.00	800.00	1200.	2000.
	1837	256 pcs.	500.00	1000.	1500.	2500.
	1839	1,996	400.00	800.00	1200.	2000.
	1840	.017	400.00	800.00	1200.	2000.
	1841	.016	400.00	800.00	1200.	2000.
	1842	6,909	400.00	800.00	1200.	2000.
	1843	1,657	400.00	800.00	1200.	2000.
147	1844	1,495	400.00	800.00	1200.	2000.
	1845	1,364	400.00	800.00	1200.	2000.

Obv. leg: KURPR.-MITREG

C#	Date	Mintage	Fine	VF	XF	Unc
147a	1847	1,438	500.00	1000.	1750.	2250.

Obv: CP at truncation.

C#	Date	Mintage	Fine	VF	XF	Unc
161	1851 CP	—	500.00	1000.	1750.	2250.

10 THALER

(= 2 Pistole)

13.3000 gm., .900 GOLD, .3848 oz AGW

C#	Date	Mintage	Fine	VF	XF	Unc
87	1773 FU	—	1950.	2750.	3500.	5000.

C#	Date	Mintage	Fine	VF	XF	Unc
87a	1775 BR	—	2000.	2750.	3500.	5000.
	1776 BR	—	2000.	2750.	3500.	5000.
	1777 BR	—	2000.	2750.	3500.	5000.

C#	Date	Mintage	Fine	VF	XF	Unc
87b	1780 DF	—	2000.	2750.	3500.	5000.
	1785 DF	—	2000.	2750.	3500.	5000.

C#	Date	Mintage	Fine	VF	XF	Unc
148	1838	126 pcs.	1400.	2000.	3000.	4000.
	1840	Inc. C#147	1000.	1500.	2500.	3500.
	1841	Inc. C#147	1000.	1500.	2500.	3500.

TRADE COINS

DUCAT

3.5000 gm., .986 GOLD, .1109 oz AGW

C#	Date	Mintage	Fine	VF	XF	Unc
85	1775 R.N.	—	1500.	2500.	3500.	5000.

OBER-HESSEN

1/4 KREUZER

COPPER

Obv: Crowned arms. Rev: Value over date.

C#	Date	Mintage	VG	Fine	VF	XF
37	1783	—	3.50	6.00	9.50	15.00

Obv: Arms, HESSEN CASSEL. Rev: Value.

C#	Date	Mintage	Fine	VF	XF	Unc
93	1801	—	2.50	5.00	10.00	40.00
	1802	—	2.50	5.00	10.00	40.00

Obv: Crowned arms. Rev: Value within rosettes.

C#	Date	Mintage	Fine	VF	XF	Unc
130	1824	—	2.50	5.00	10.00	40.00
	1825	—	2.50	5.00	10.00	40.00
	1827	—	2.50	5.00	10.00	40.00
	1829	—	2.50	5.00	10.00	40.00
	1830	—	2.50	5.00	10.00	40.00

Similar to C#130

C#	Date	Mintage	Fine	VF	XF	Unc
149	1834	—	2.50	5.00	10.00	40.00
	1835	—	2.50	5.00	10.00	40.00

1/2 KREUZER

COPPER

Obv: Crowned arms. Rev: Value over date.

C#	Date	Mintage	VG	Fine	VF	XF
38	1783	—	3.00	6.00	9.50	15.00

Obv: Arms, HESSEN CASSEL. Rev: Value.

C#	Date	Mintage	Fine	VF	XF	Unc
94	1801	—	2.50	5.00	10.00	40.00
	1802	—	2.50	5.00	10.00	40.00
	1803	—	2.50	5.00	10.00	40.00

Obv: Elector's cap over arms. Rev: Value.

C#	Date	Mintage	Fine	VF	XF	Unc
114	1803F	—	2.50	5.00	10.00	40.00
	1804F	—	2.50	5.00	10.00	40.00

C#	Date	Mintage	Fine	VF	XF	Unc
131	1824	—	2.50	5.00	10.00	40.00
	1825	—	2.50	5.00	10.00	40.00
	1826	—	2.50	5.00	10.00	40.00
	1827	—	2.50	5.00	10.00	40.00
	1828	—	2.50	5.00	10.00	40.00
	1829	—	2.50	5.00	10.00	40.00
	1830	—	2.50	5.00	10.00	40.00

Similar to C#131

C#	Date	Mintage	Fine	VF	XF	Unc
150	1834	—	2.50	5.00	10.00	40.00
	1835	—	—	—	Pattern	—

KREUZER

COPPER

Obv: Crowned arms. Rev: Value over date.

C#	Date	Mintage	VG	Fine	VF	XF
39	1783	—	3.00	6.00	9.50	15.00

Obv: Crowned arms. Rev: Value within rosettes.

C#	Date	Mintage	Fine	VF	XF	Unc
132	1825	—	2.50	5.00	10.00	40.00
	1828	—	2.50	5.00	10.00	40.00
	1829	—	2.50	5.00	10.00	40.00

Similar to C#132

C#	Date	Mintage	Fine	VF	XF	Unc
151	1832	—	2.50	5.00	10.00	40.00
	1833	—	2.50	5.00	10.00	40.00
	1835	—	2.50	5.00	10.00	40.00

6 KREUZER

BILLON

Obv: Crowned arms. Rev: Value within rosettes.

C#	Date	Mintage	Fine	VF	XF	Unc
133	1826	—	2.50	5.00	10.00	40.00
	1827	—	2.50	5.00	10.00	40.00
	1828	—	2.50	5.00	10.00	40.00

Rev: No rosettes.

C#	Date	Mintage	Fine	VF	XF	Unc
152	1831	—	2.50	5.00	10.00	40.00
	1832	—	2.50	5.00	10.00	40.00

C#	Date	Mintage	Fine	VF	XF	Unc
152	1833	—	2.50	5.00	10.00	40.00
	1834	—	2.50	5.00	10.00	40.00

HESSE-DARMSTADT

A state located in southwest Germany was founded in 1567. The Landgrave was elevated to the status of grand duke in 1806. In 1815 the Congress of Vienna awarded them the cities of Mainz and Worms which they relinguished along with the newly acquired Hesse—Homburg, to the Prussians in 1866. They joined the German Empire in 1871 and endured until the abdication of the Grand Duke in 1918.

RULERS

Ludwig IX, 1768-1790
Ludwig X, 1790-1806
As Grand Duke Ludwig I, 1806-1830
Ludwig II, 1830-1848
Ludwig III, 1848-1877
Ludwig IV, 1877-1892
Ernst Ludwig, 1892-1918

MINTMASTER'S INITIALS

R.F. - Remigius Fehr
H.R. - Hector Roessler

HELLER

COPPER
Obv: Crowned pointed arms, G.H.-K.M. Rev: Value.

C#	Date	Mintage	Fine	VF	XF	Unc
108	1824	—	2.00	4.00	7.50	40.00

Similar to C#108

C#	Date	Mintage	Fine	VF	XF	Unc
127	1837	—	2.00	4.00	7.50	35.00
	1840	—	2.00	4.00	7.50	35.00
	1841	—	2.00	4.00	7.50	35.00
	1842	.103	2.00	4.00	7.50	35.00
	1843	.175	2.00	4.00	7.50	35.00
	1844	.241	2.00	4.00	7.50	35.00
	1845	—	2.00	4.00	7.50	35.00
	1846	—	2.00	4.00	7.50	35.00
	1847	—	2.00	4.00	7.50	35.00

Obv: Crowned squared arms

C#	Date	Mintage	Fine	VF	XF	Unc
128	1847	—	1.50	3.00	6.00	35.00

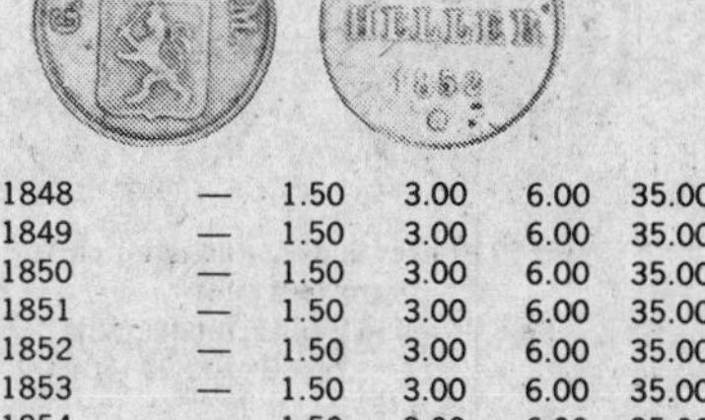

C#	Date	Mintage	Fine	VF	XF	Unc
150	1848	—	1.50	3.00	6.00	35.00
	1849	—	1.50	3.00	6.00	35.00
	1850	—	1.50	3.00	6.00	35.00
	1851	—	1.50	3.00	6.00	35.00
	1852	—	1.50	3.00	6.00	35.00
	1853	—	1.50	3.00	6.00	35.00
	1854	—	1.50	3.00	6.00	35.00
	1855	—	1.50	3.00	6.00	35.00

PFENNIG

COPPER
Obv: Lion in cartouche; H.D. above; flags and cannons at sides. Rev: Value over date.

C#	Date	Mintage	VG	Fine	VF	XF
65	1773	—	2.00	4.00	6.00	18.00

Obv: Lion in oval; H.D. above, only one cannon.

C#	Date	Mintage	VG	Fine	VF	XF
66	1774	—	2.00	4.00	6.00	18.00

Obv: Lion in crowned oval.
Rev: Value over date (Zoll - Toll).

C#	Date	Mintage	VG	Fine	VF	XF
68	1777	—	3.00	5.00	7.50	22.00

Obv: Lion in crowned oval; HESSEN DARMST.
Rev: Value over date.

C#	Date	Mintage	VG	Fine	VF	XF
69	1784	—	1.00	3.00	5.00	15.00
	1785	—	1.00	3.00	5.00	15.00
	1786	—	1.00	3.00	5.00	15.00
	1787	—	1.00	3.00	5.00	15.00
69	1788	—	1.00	3.00	5.00	15.00
	1789	—	1.00	3.00	5.00	15.00
	1790	—	1.00	3.00	5.00	15.00
	1791	—	1.00	3.00	5.00	15.00
	1792	—	1.00	3.00	5.00	15.00
	1793	—	1.00	3.00	5.00	15.00
	1794	—	1.00	3.00	5.00	15.00
	1795	—	1.00	3.00	5.00	15.00
	1796	—	1.00	3.00	5.00	15.00
	1797	—	1.00	3.00	5.00	15.00

Obv: Lion in crowned oval; H.D. above.

C#	Date	Mintage	VG	Fine	VF	XF
70	1789	—	2.00	4.00	6.00	—

C#	Date	Mintage	Fine	VF	XF	Unc
86	1797	—	2.00	3.00	10.00	40.00
	1798	—	2.00	3.00	10.00	40.00
	1799	—	2.00	3.00	10.00	40.00
	1800	—	2.00	3.00	10.00	40.00
	1801	—	2.00	3.00	10.00	40.00
	1802	—	2.00	3.00	10.00	40.00
	1803	—	2.00	3.00	10.00	40.00
	1804	—	2.00	3.00	10.00	40.00
	1805	—	2.00	3.00	10.00	40.00
	1806	—	2.00	3.00	10.00	40.00

C#	Date	Mintage	Fine	VF	XF	Unc
107	1811	—	2.00	3.00	10.00	40.00
	1819	—	2.00	3.00	8.00	40.00

Obv: With GH-KM.

C#	Date	Mintage	Fine	VF	XF	Unc
107.1	1819	—	2.00	3.00	8.00	40.00

C#	Date	Mintage	VG	Fine	XF	Unc
151	1857	.140	1.00	2.50	8.00	40.00
	1858	.202	1.00	2.50	8.00	40.00
	1859	.257	1.00	2.50	8.00	40.00
	1860	.268	1.00	2.50	8.00	40.00
	1861	.311	1.00	2.50	8.00	40.00
	1862	.324	1.00	2.50	8.00	40.00
	1863	.190	1.00	2.50	8.00	40.00
	1864	—	1.00	2.50	8.00	40.00
	1865	.279	1.00	2.50	8.00	40.00
	1866	.317	1.00	2.50	8.00	40.00
	1867	.296	1.00	2.50	8.00	40.00
	1868	.332	1.00	2.50	8.00	40.00
	1869	.322	1.00	2.50	8.00	40.00
	1870	.526	1.00	2.50	8.00	40.00
	1871	.322	1.00	2.50	8.00	40.00
	1872	.338	1.00	2.50	8.00	40.00

2 PFENNIG

COPPER
Obv: Crowned arms; H.D. above; flags and cannons at sides. Rev: Value over date.

C#	Date	Mintage	VG	Fine	VF	XF
67	1776	—	2.00	4.50	6.00	16.00

1/4 STUBER

COPPER

C#	Date	Mintage	Fine	VF	XF	Unc
87	1805	—	6.00	10.00	20.00	40.00

1/2 STUBER

COPPER
Obv: Crowned LLX monogram. Rev: Value.

C#	Date	Mintage	Fine	VF	XF	Unc
88	1805	—	3.00	6.00	12.00	40.00

1/4 KREUZER

COPPER
Obv: Crowned arms. Rev: Value.

C#	Date	Mintage	Fine	VF	XF	Unc
106	1809	—	2.50	5.00	10.00	40.00
	1816	—	2.50	5.00	10.00	40.00

Obv. legend: G.H.-S.M.

C#	Date	Mintage	Fine	VF	XF	Unc
106a	1809	—	2.50	5.00	10.00	40.00
	1816	—	2.50	5.00	10.00	40.00
	1817	—	2.50	5.00	10.00	40.00

1/2 KREUZER

COPPER

C#	Date	Mintage	Fine	VF	XF	Unc
109	1809	—	2.00	4.00	8.00	40.00
	1817	—	2.00	4.00	8.00	40.00

Obv. leg: G.H.-S.M.

C#	Date	Mintage	Fine	VF	XF	Unc
109a	1817	—	2.00	4.00	7.00	40.00

KREUZER

BILLON
Obv: Crowned arms. Rev: Value over date.

C#	Date	Mintage	VG	Fine	VF	XF
71	1771	—	2.00	4.00	6.00	16.00

Obv: Crowned arms; H.D. above.

C#	Date	Mintage	VG	Fine	VF	XF
74	1784	—	2.00	4.00	6.00	16.00

Obv: Lion on pedestal, H.D. within. Rev: Value.

C#	Date	Mintage	Fine	VF	XF	Unc
90	1800	—	2.00	4.00	10.00	40.00

Obv: Lion divides H.D. Rev: LAND MUNZE, value.

C#	Date	Mintage	Fine	VF	XF	Unc
92	1801	—	2.00	4.00	10.00	40.00
	1802	—	2.00	4.00	10.00	40.00
	1803	—	2.00	4.00	10.00	40.00
	1804	—	2.00	4.00	10.00	40.00
	1805	—	2.00	4.00	10.00	40.00

Obv: Crowned lion between H.D.
Rev: Value, LAND MUNZ.

C#	Date	Mintage	Fine	VF	XF	Unc
110	1806	—	2.50	5.00	10.00	50.00

Obv: Crowned lion with sword between H.D.

C#	Date	Mintage	Fine	VF	XF	Unc
110a	1806	—	3.00	6.00	12.50	50.00

Obv: Crowned lion between H.D.-L.M. Rev: Value.

C#	Date	Mintage	Fine	VF	XF	Unc
111	1806	—	3.00	7.00	15.00	50.00
	1807	—	3.00	7.00	15.00	50.00

Obv: Crowned lion with sword between H.D.-L.M.

C#	Date	Mintage	Fine	VF	XF	Unc
111a	1807	—	3.00	6.00	12.50	50.00

Obv: Crowned lion with sword between G.H.-L.M.

C#	Date	Mintage	Fine	VF	XF	Unc
112	1807	—	3.00	6.00	12.50	50.00
	1808	—	3.00	6.00	12.50	50.00
	1809	—	3.00	6.00	12.50	50.00

Obv: Crowned arms between G.H.-L.M.

C#	Date	Mintage	Fine	VF	XF	Unc
113	1809	—	3.00	6.00	12.50	50.00
	1810	—	3.00	6.00	12.50	50.00
	1817	—	3.00	6.00	12.50	50.00

Obv: Crowned arms between G.H.-S.M.

C#	Date	Mintage	Fine	VF	XF	Unc
114	1819	—	3.00	6.00	12.50	50.00

C#	Date	Mintage	Fine	VF	XF	Unc
129	1834	—	1.50	3.00	6.00	40.00
	1835	—	1.50	3.00	6.00	40.00
	1836	—	1.50	3.00	6.00	40.00
	1837	—	1.50	3.00	6.00	40.00
	1838	—	1.50	3.00	6.00	40.00

C#	Date	Mintage	Fine	VF	XF	Unc
130	1837	—	2.00	3.50	6.00	40.00
	1838	—	2.00	3.50	6.00	40.00
	1839	—	2.00	3.50	6.00	40.00
	1840	—	2.00	3.50	6.00	40.00
	1841	—	2.00	3.50	6.00	40.00
	1842	.438	2.00	3.50	6.00	40.00

C#	Date	Mintage	Fine	VF	XF	Unc
131	1843	.129	2.00	3.50	6.00	40.00
	1844	—	2.00	3.50	6.00	40.00
	1845	.516	2.00	3.50	6.00	40.00
	1847	—	2.00	3.50	6.00	40.00

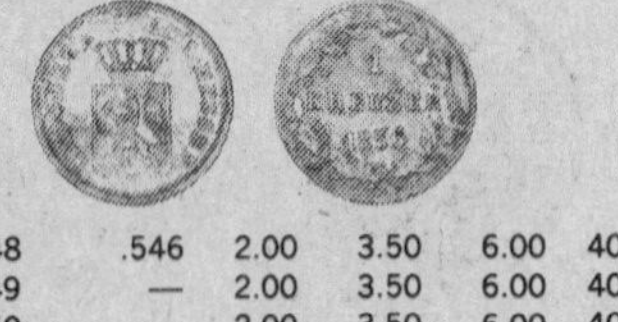

C#	Date	Mintage	Fine	VF	XF	Unc
152	1848	.546	2.00	3.50	6.00	40.00
	1849	—	2.00	3.50	6.00	40.00
	1850	—	2.00	3.50	6.00	40.00
	1852	—	2.00	3.50	6.00	40.00
	1854	.236	2.00	3.50	6.00	40.00
	1855	.162	2.00	3.50	6.00	40.00
	1856	.334	2.00	3.50	6.00	40.00

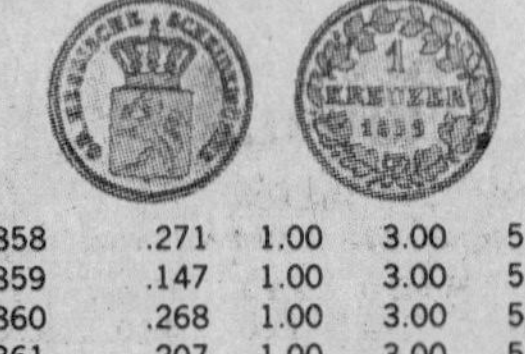

C#	Date	Mintage	Fine	VF	XF	Unc
153	1858	.271	1.00	3.00	5.00	35.00
	1859	.147	1.00	3.00	5.00	35.00
	1860	.268	1.00	3.00	5.00	35.00
	1861	.207	1.00	3.00	5.00	35.00
	1862	.211	1.00	3.00	5.00	35.00
	1863	.190	1.00	3.00	5.00	35.00
	1864	.376	1.00	3.00	5.00	35.00
	1865	.181	1.00	3.00	5.00	35.00
	1866	.247	1.00	3.00	5.00	35.00
	1867	.273	1.00	3.00	5.00	35.00
	1868	.199	1.00	3.00	5.00	35.00
	1869	.249	1.00	3.00	5.00	35.00
	1870	.349	1.00	3.00	5.00	35.00
	1871	.366	1.00	3.00	5.00	35.00
	1872	.128	1.00	3.00	5.00	35.00

3 KREUZER

BILLON
Obv: Lion on pedestal divides H.D.
Rev: LAND MUNZE, value.

C#	Date	Mintage	Fine	VF	XF	Unc
94	1800	—	3.50	7.25	12.00	50.00
	1801	—	3.50	7.25	12.00	50.00
	1802	—	3.50	7.25	12.00	50.00
	1803	—	3.50	7.25	12.00	50.00
	1804	—	3.50	7.25	12.00	50.00
	1805	—	3.50	7.25	12.00	50.00

Obv: Crowned arms G.H.-L.M. Rev. value: III KREUZER

C#	Date	Mintage	Fine	VF	XF	Unc
115	1808	—	3.50	7.25	12.00	50.00
	1809	—	3.50	7.25	12.00	50.00
	1810	—	3.50	7.25	12.00	50.00

Rev. value: 3 KREUZER

C#	Date	Mintage	Fine	VF	XF	Unc
116	1817	—	3.50	7.25	12.00	50.00
117	1819	—	2.00	4.50	9.00	50.00
	1822	—	2.00	4.50	9.00	50.00

Obv: Crowned arms, GR HERZOGTH.
Rev: Value, SCHEIDEMUNZE.

C#	Date	Mintage	Fine	VF	XF	Unc
132	1833	—	2.50	5.50	12.00	45.00

Obv: Crowned pointed arms

C#	Date	Mintage	Fine	VF	XF	Unc
132a	1833	—	2.00	4.50	12.00	45.00
	1834	—	2.00	4.50	12.00	45.00
	1835	—	2.00	4.50	12.00	45.00
	1836	—	2.00	4.50	12.00	45.00

Rev: Value within wreath.

C#	Date	Mintage	Fine	VF	XF	Unc
134	1838	—	2.50	5.00	15.00	50.00
	1839	—	2.50	5.00	15.00	50.00
	1840	—	2.50	5.00	15.00	50.00
	1841	—	2.50	5.00	15.00	50.00
	1842	.280	2.50	5.00	15.00	50.00

Obv: Crowned squared arms, GROSHERZOGTHUM HESSEN.

C#	Date	Mintage	Fine	VF	XF	Unc
135	1843	.288	2.00	4.00	10.00	45.00
	1844	—	2.00	4.00	10.00	45.00
	1845	.245	2.00	4.00	10.00	45.00
	1846	—	2.00	4.00	10.00	45.00
	1847	—	2.00	4.00	10.00	45.00

C#	Date	Mintage	Fine	VF	XF	Unc
154	1848	.082	2.00	4.00	10.00	40.00
	1850	—	2.00	4.00	10.00	40.00
	1851	—	2.00	4.00	10.00	40.00
	1852	—	2.00	4.00	10.00	40.00
	1853	—	2.00	4.00	10.00	40.00
	1854	.076	2.00	4.00	10.00	40.00
	1855	.148	2.00	4.00	10.00	40.00
	1856	.062	2.00	4.00	10.00	40.00

C#	Date	Mintage	Fine	VF	XF	Unc
155	1864	.095	2.00	4.00	10.00	40.00
	1865	.087	2.00	4.00	10.00	40.00
	1866	.090	2.00	4.00	10.00	40.00
	1867	.077	2.00	4.00	10.00	40.00

5 KREUZER

BILLON
Obv: Crowned L. Rev: Value.

C#	Date	Mintage	Fine	VF	XF	Unc
118	1807	—	10.00	20.00	35.00	75.00

Obv: Curled edges on L

C#	Date	Mintage	Fine	VF	XF	Unc
118a	1807	—	10.00	20.00	35.00	75.00

Obv: Head right, L at truncation. Rev: Crowned arms dividing date, R.IUSTIRT F. below.

C#	Date	Mintage	Fine	VF	XF	Unc
119	1808	—	7.50	15.00	30.00	60.00

6 KREUZER

.500 SILVER
Obv: Crowned arms, GR:HERZOGTH. Rev: Value.

C#	Date	Mintage	Fine	VF	XF	Unc
120	1819	—	3.50	7.50	15.00	40.00
	1820	—	3.50	7.50	15.00	40.00

C#	Date	Mintage	Fine	VF	XF	Unc
120a	1821	—	2.50	5.00	10.00	40.00
	1824	—	2.50	5.00	10.00	40.00
	1826	—	2.50	5.00	10.00	40.00
	1827	—	2.50	5.00	10.00	40.00
	1828	—	2.50	5.00	10.00	40.00
	1833	—	2.50	5.00	10.00	40.00

C#	Date	Mintage	Fine	VF	XF	Unc
136	1833	—	3.00	7.50	12.50	40.00
	1834	—	3.00	7.50	12.50	40.00
	1835	—	3.00	7.50	12.50	40.00
	1836	—	3.00	7.50	12.50	40.00
	1837	—	3.00	7.50	12.50	40.00

BILLON

C#	Date	Mintage	Fine	VF	XF	Unc
137	1838	—	2.00	4.00	8.00	40.00
	1839	—	2.00	4.00	8.00	40.00
	1840	—	2.00	4.00	8.00	40.00
	1841	—	2.00	4.00	8.00	40.00
	1842	.816	2.00	4.00	8.00	40.00

C#	Date	Mintage	Fine	VF	XF	Unc
138	1843	.775	1.50	3.00	6.50	35.00
	1844	.331	1.50	3.00	6.50	35.00
	1845	.235	1.50	3.00	6.50	35.00
	1846	.897	1.50	3.00	6.50	35.00
	1847	—	1.50	3.00	6.50	35.00
156	1848	.243	1.50	3.00	6.50	35.00
	1850	—	1.50	3.00	6.50	35.00
	1851	—	1.50	3.00	6.50	35.00
	1852	—	1.50	3.00	6.50	35.00
	1853	—	1.50	3.00	6.50	35.00
	1854	.033	1.50	3.00	6.50	35.00
	1855	.072	1.50	3.00	6.50	35.00
	1856	.044	1.50	3.00	6.50	35.00

Visit Of Princes Ludwig And Heinrich To Darmstadt Mint
Rev: Crowned L and H monograms

C#	Date	Mintage	Fine	VF	XF	Unc
—	1848	—	50.00	100.00	200.00	400.00

C#	Date	Mintage	Fine	VF	XF	Unc
157	1864	.052	2.00	4.50	7.50	40.00
	1865	.039	2.00	4.50	7.50	40.00
	1866	.043	2.00	4.50	7.50	40.00
	1867	.060	2.00	4.50	7.50	40.00

Visit of Prince Wilhelm and Princess Anna to Darmstadt Mint
Rev: Crowned A and W monograms.

C#	Date	Mintage	Fine	VF	XF	Unc
—	1859	—	50.00	100.00	200.00	400.00

10 KREUZER

.500 SILVER
Obv: Head right.
Rev: Crowned arms dividing date, R.F. below.

C#	Date	Mintage	Fine	VF	XF	Unc
121	1808R.F.	—	12.00	25.00	50.00	75.00

20 KREUZER

SILVER
Obv: Head right.
Rev: Crowned arms and trophies.

C#	Date	Mintage	VG	Fine	VF	XF
78	1772	—	11.00	22.50	35.00	65.00

.584 SILVER
Obv: Head right, FRISCH F. at truncation.
Rev: Crowned arms dividing date, R.F. below.

C#	Date	Mintage	Fine	VF	XF	Unc
122.1	1807	—	4.50	9.00	20.00	50.00

C#	Date	Mintage	Fine	VF	XF	Unc
122.2	1807R.F.	—	4.50	9.00	20.00	50.00
	1808R.F.	—	4.50	9.00	20.00	50.00
	1809R.F.	—	4.50	9.00	20.00	50.00

Obv. leg: LUDWIG.....

C#	Date	Mintage	Fine	VF	XF	Unc
122.2a	1809R.F.	—	4.50	9.00	20.00	50.00

1/2 GULDEN

.900 SILVER

C#	Date	Mintage	Fine	VF	XF	Unc
139	1838	1.080	6.00	12.50	25.00	65.00
	1839	Inc. Ab.	6.00	12.50	25.00	65.00
	1840	Inc. Ab.	6.00	12.50	25.00	65.00
	1841	Inc. Ab.	6.00	12.50	25.00	65.00
	1843	.151	10.00	20.00	40.00	75.00
	1844	.081	10.00	20.00	40.00	75.00
	1845	.167	10.00	20.00	40.00	75.00
	1846	.033	6.00	12.50	25.00	65.00

C#	Date	Mintage	Fine	VF	XF	Unc
158	1855	.047	15.00	30.00	50.00	100.00

GULDEN

.900 SILVER
Obv: Small head left. Rev: Value within wreath.

C#	Date	Mintage	Fine	VF	XF	Unc
140	1837	1.122	12.00	25.00	40.00	100.00

C#	Date	Mintage	Fine	VF	XF	Unc
140a	1838	Inc. Ab.	12.00	25.00	50.00	100.00

Obv: VOIGHT below head.

C#	Date	Mintage	Fine	VF	XF	Unc
140b	1839	Inc. Ab.	10.00	20.00	40.00	100.00
	1840	Inc. Ab.	10.00	20.00	40.00	100.00
	1841	Inc. Ab.	10.00	20.00	40.00	100.00
	1842	.605	10.00	20.00	40.00	100.00
	1843	.314	10.00	20.00	40.00	100.00
	1844	.191	10.00	20.00	40.00	100.00
	1845	.176	10.00	20.00	40.00	100.00
	1846	.144	12.00	25.00	50.00	110.00
	1847	.251	10.00	20.00	40.00	100.00

Visit of Crown Prince of Russia

C#	Date	Mintage	Fine	VF	XF	Unc
141	1843	—	100.00	200.00	400.00	650.00

Public Freedom Through German Parliament

C#	Date	Mintage	Fine	VF	XF	Unc
142	1848	—	60.00	125.00	200.00	300.00

Rev: Value within wreath

C#	Date	Mintage	Fine	VF	XF	Unc
159	1848	.090	25.00	50.00	100.00	150.00
	1854	.044	11.00	22.50	60.00	115.00
	1855	.090	11.00	22.50	60.00	115.00
	1856	.153	11.00	22.50	60.00	115.00

ZWEY (2) GULDEN

21.2100 gm., .900 SILVER, .6138 oz ASW

C#	Date	Mintage	Fine	VF	XF	Unc
144	1845	.044	30.00	75.00	150.00	300.00
	1846	.270	30.00	75.00	150.00	300.00
	1847	.030	30.00	75.00	150.00	300.00

Rev: Similar to C#144.

C#	Date	Mintage	Fine	VF	XF	Unc
161	1848	.252	35.00	75.00	150.00	300.00
	1849	Inc. Ab.	35.00	75.00	150.00	300.00
	1853	Inc. Ab.	35.00	75.00	150.00	300.00
	1854	.127	35.00	75.00	150.00	300.00
	1855	.149	35.00	75.00	150.00	300.00
	1856	.064	35.00	75.00	150.00	300.00

1/2 THALER
(Convention)

SILVER
Obv: Bust right.
Rev: Crowned arms and trophies.

C#	Date	Mintage	VG	Fine	VF	XF
80	1771	—	18.00	35.00	60.00	125.00

C#	Date	Mintage	VG	Fine	VF	XF
96	1793	—	20.00	40.00	65.00	125.00

Obv: Armored bust right.
Rev: Crowned multiple arms flanked by trophies.

C#	Date	Mintage	VG	Fine	VF	XF
96a	1793	—	25.00	50.00	85.00	140.00

EIN (1) THALER
(Convention)

SILVER

C#	Date	Mintage	VG	Fine	VF	XF
82	1770 AK	—	300.00	600.00	750.00	1000.

NOTE: Varieties exist.

C#	Date	Mintage	VG	Fine	VF	XF
83	1770 AK	—	50.00	100.00	200.00	300.00
	1772 RF	—	50.00	100.00	200.00	300.00

NOTE: Varieties exist.

Obv: Head right.
Rev: Crowned arms with lion supporters.

C#	Date	Mintage	VG	Fine	VF	XF
93	1793 RF	—	300.00	600.00	850.00	1250.

Obv: Civilian bust right.

C#	Date	Mintage	VG	Fine	VF	XF
101	1793 RF	—	250.00	500.00	750.00	1150.

Obv: Armored bust right.

C#	Date	Mintage	VG	Fine	VF	XF
102	1793	—	375.00	750.00	1150.	1650.

Rev: Crowned arms backed by flags and cannon.

C#	Date	Mintage	VG	Fine	VF	XF
103	1793	—	300.00	600.00	850.00	1250.

28.0600 gm., .833 SILVER, .7516 oz ASW

C#	Date	Mintage	Fine	VF	XF	Unc
123	1809 L	—	150.00	400.00	800.00	1600.

(Krone)

29.5100 gm., .872 SILVER, .8274 oz ASW

C#	Date	Mintage	Fine	VF	XF	Unc
124	1819 HR	.019	125.00	400.00	800.00	1600.

Rev: Similar to C#124.

C#	Date	Mintage	Fine	VF	XF	Unc
125	1825 HR	.171	60.00	200.00	400.00	800.00

Rev: Similar to C#124.

C#	Date	Mintage	Fine	VF	XF	Unc
143	1833 HR	.124	50.00	125.00	250.00	500.00
	1835 HR	.558	50.00	125.00	250.00	500.00
	1836 HR	Inc. Ab.	50.00	125.00	250.00	500.00
	1837 HR	Inc. Ab.	50.00	125.00	250.00	500.00

(Vereins)

18.5200 gm., .900 SILVER, .5360 oz ASW

C#	Date	Mintage	Fine	VF	XF	Unc
160	1857	.091	20.00	40.00	100.00	250.00
	1858	.537	20.00	40.00	100.00	250.00
	1859	.594	20.00	40.00	100.00	250.00
	1860	.608	20.00	40.00	100.00	250.00
	1861	.414	20.00	40.00	100.00	250.00
	1862	.242	20.00	40.00	100.00	250.00
160	1863	.215	20.00	40.00	100.00	250.00
	1864	.073	20.00	40.00	100.00	250.00
	1865	.078	20.00	40.00	100.00	250.00
	1866	.059	20.00	40.00	100.00	250.00
	1867	.024	20.00	40.00	100.00	250.00
	1868	.048	20.00	40.00	100.00	250.00
	1869	.034	20.00	40.00	100.00	250.00
	1870	.039	20.00	40.00	100.00	250.00
	1871	.033	20.00	40.00	100.00	250.00

2 THALER

(= 3-1/2 Gulden)

37.1200 gm., .900 SILVER, 1.0742 oz ASW

C#	Date	Mintage	Fine	VF	XF	Unc
145	1839	.024	60.00	125.00	250.00	500.00
	1840	.368	50.00	125.00	250.00	500.00
	1841	.688	50.00	125.00	250.00	500.00
	1842	.286	50.00	125.00	250.00	500.00

Obv: Similar to C#145.

C#	Date	Mintage	Fine	VF	XF	Unc
146	1844	.377	50.00	125.00	250.00	500.00

Rev: Similar to C#146.

C#	Date	Mintage	Fine	VF	XF	Unc
162	1854	.043	300.00	750.00	1500.	3000.

5 GULDEN

3.4250 gm., .904 GOLD, .0995 oz AGW
Obv: Head left, C.V. below. Rev: Crowned draped arms, value 5G, legend AUS HESS. RHEINGOLD.

C#	Date	Mintage	Fine	VF	XF	Unc
147	1835 HR	60 pcs.	1500.	3000.	5000.	7000.

C#	Date	Mintage	Fine	VF	XF	Unc
148	1835 HR	.022	350.00	700.00	1000.	1500.
	1840 HR	Inc. Ab.	350.00	700.00	1000.	1500.
	1841 HR	Inc. Ab.	350.00	700.00	1000.	1500.

10 GULDEN

6.8500 gm., .904 GOLD, .1991 oz AGW
Obv: Head left. Rev: Crowned draped arms, HR around date

C#	Date	Mintage	Fine	VF	XF	Unc
126	1826 HR	1,700	500.00	1000.	1500.	3000.
	1827 HR	1,705	500.00	1000.	1500.	3000.

C#	Date	Mintage	Fine	VF	XF	Unc
149	1840 HR	.017	500.00	1000.	1250.	2000.
	1841 HR	Inc. Ab.	500.00	1000.	1250.	2000.
	1842 HR	Inc. Ab.	500.00	1000.	1250.	2000.

MONETARY REFORM

2 MARK

11.1110 gm., .900 SILVER, .3215 oz ASW

Y#	Date	Mintage	VF	XF	Unc
63	1876H	.202	150.00	825.00	2000.
	1877H	.338	115.00	500.00	1500.
68	1888A	.022	550.00	1300.	2800.
	1888A	500 pcs.	—	Proof	4000.

Rev: Type 3 eagle.

Y#	Date	Mintage	VF	XF	Unc
68a	1891A	.063	400.00	650.00	900.00
	1891A	—	—	Proof	1500.

Y#	Date	Mintage	VF	XF	Unc
75	1895A	.054	165.00	325.00	500.00
	1896A	8,950	425.00	725.00	1000.
	1896A	200 pcs.	—	Proof	1100.
	1898A	.034	200.00	400.00	600.00
	1898A	360 pcs.	—	Proof	1200.
	1899A	.053	165.00	325.00	500.00
	1899A	128 pcs.	—	Proof	1200.
	1900A	8,950	350.00	650.00	900.00
	1900A	200 pcs.	—	Proof	1200.

400th Birthday of Philipp The Magnanimous

Y#	Date	Mintage	VF	XF	Unc
80	1904	.100	22.50	35.00	75.00
	1904	2,250	—	Proof	150.00

3 MARK

16.6670 gm., .900 SILVER, .4823 oz ASW

Y#	Date	Mintage	VF	XF	Unc
79	1910A	.200	40.00	60.00	125.00
	1910A	—	—	Proof	250.00

25 Year Jubilee
Rev: Similar to Y#79.

Y#	Date	Mintage	VF	XF	Unc
82	1917A	1,333	—	1000.	1500.
	1917A	Inc. Ab.	—	Proof	2000.

5 MARK

27.7770 gm., .900 SILVER, .8038 oz ASW
Rev: Type 2 eagle.

Y#	Date	Mintage	VF	XF	Unc
64	1875H	.148	75.00	1000.	2000.
	1875H	—	—	Proof	850.00
	1876H	.290	55.00	500.00	1300.
	1876H	—	—	Proof	850.00

1.9910 gm., .900 GOLD, .0576 oz AGW

Y#	Date	Mintage	VF	XF	Unc
65	1877H	.103	350.00	500.00	750.00

Rev: Type 2 eagle.

Y#	Date	Mintage	VF	XF	Unc
70	1877H	.079	400.00	625.00	825.00

27.7770 gm., .900 SILVER, .8038 oz ASW
Rev: Type 2 eagle.

Y#	Date	Mintage	VF	XF	Unc
69	1888A	8,940	1000.	1650.	2300.
	1888A	500 pcs.	—	Proof	2500.

Rev: Type 3 eagle.

Y#	Date	Mintage	VF	XF	Unc
69a	1891A	.025	350.00	800.00	1200.
	1891A	—	—	Proof	1300.

Rev: Similar to Y#81.

Y#	Date	Mintage	VF	XF	Unc
76	1895A	.039	130.00	250.00	500.00
	1898A	.037	130.00	250.00	500.00
	1899A	4,475	425.00	725.00	1000.
	1900A	.018	275.00	425.00	650.00
	1900A	*200 pcs.	—	Proof	1000.

400th Birthday of Philipp The Magnanimous

Y#	Date	Mintage	VF	XF	Unc
81	1904	.040	80.00	110.00	200.00
	1904	700 pcs.	—	Proof	500.00

10 MARK

3.9820 gm., .900 GOLD, .1152 oz AGW

Y#	Date	Mintage	VF	XF	Unc
66	1872H	.030	250.00	500.00	650.00
	1873H	.423	150.00	170.00	190.00

Rev: Type 2 eagle.

Y#	Date	Mintage	VF	XF	Unc
66a	1875H	.191	165.00	200.00	225.00
	1876H	.513	100.00	180.00	200.00
	1877H	.094	225.00	275.00	325.00

Y#	Date	Mintage	VF	XF	Unc
71	1878H	.132	200.00	250.00	325.00
	1879H	.056	250.00	325.00	400.00
	1880H	.109	200.00	250.00	275.00
	1888A	.036	575.00	750.00	950.00

Edge: Vines and stars

Y#	Date	Mintage	VF	XF	Unc
71a	1890A	.054	500.00	625.00	850.00

Rev: Type 3 eagle.

Y#	Date	Mintage	VF	XF	Unc
73	1893A	.054	450.00	575.00	750.00

Y#	Date	Mintage	VF	XF	Unc
77	1896A	.036	325.00	650.00	1000.
	1898A	.075	300.00	400.00	525.00

20 MARK

7.9650 gm., .900 GOLD, .2304 oz AGW
Rev: Type 1 eagle.

Y#	Date	Mintage	VF	XF	Unc
67	1872H	.183	190.00	225.00	300.00
	1873H	.521	145.00	190.00	225.00

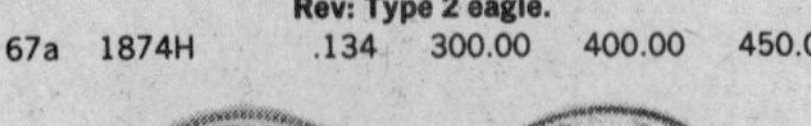

Rev: Type 2 eagle.

Y#	Date	Mintage	VF	XF	Unc
67a	1874H	.134	300.00	400.00	450.00

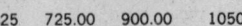

Y#	Date	Mintage	VF	XF	Unc
72	1892A	.025	725.00	900.00	1050.

Rev: Type 3 eagle.

Y#	Date	Mintage	VF	XF	Unc
74	1893A	.025	475.00	625.00	825.00
	1893A	—	—	Proof	950.00

Y#	Date	Mintage	VF	XF	Unc
78	1896A	.015	500.00	1000.	1500.
	1897A	.045	165.00	225.00	275.00
	1898A	.070	150.00	200.00	275.00
	1899A	.040	180.00	225.00	275.00
	1900A	.040	165.00	225.00	275.00
	1901A	.080	150.00	200.00	275.00
	1903A	.040	165.00	200.00	275.00
78a	1905A	.045	200.00	225.00	400.00
	1906A	.085	140.00	200.00	325.00
	1908A	.040	200.00	225.00	300.00
	1911A	.150	135.00	190.00	250.00

NCLT ISSUES

PATTERNS

KM#	Date	Mintage	Identification	Mkt.Val.
1	1910	—	3 Marks, Silver	—

HESSE — HOMBURG

Hesse-Homburg, located in southwest Germany was created from part of Hesse-Darmstadt in 1622 and was made subordinate to Darmstadt in 1806. In 1815 it was restored to independence and added the lordships of Meisenheim and Kreuznach. The Homburg line which was founded in 1596 became extinct in 1866. The property passed to Darmstadt and was almost immediately annexed to Prussia.

RULERS

Ludwig, 1829-1839
Philipp, 1839-1846
Gustav, 1846-1848
Ferdinand, 1848-1866

KREUZER

BILLON

C#	Date	Mintage	Fine	VF	XF	Unc
3	1840	.048	20.00	45.00	75.00	110.00

3 KREUZER

BILLON

C#	Date	Mintage	Fine	VF	XF	Unc
4	1840	.015	20.00	45.00	70.00	115.00

6 KREUZER

BILLON
Obv: Crowned arms. Rev: Value within wreath.

C#	Date	Mintage	Fine	VF	XF	Unc
5	1840	.057	15.00	35.00	50.00	100.00

1/2 GULDEN

.900 SILVER

C#	Date	Mintage	Fine	VF	XF	Unc
1	1838	.011	25.00	50.00	90.00	200.00
	1839	—	—	—	Proof	250.00

Obv: RS at truncation.

C#	Date	Mintage	Fine	VF	XF	Unc
6	1840	.010	25.00	50.00	100.00	250.00
	1841	6,560	25.00	50.00	100.00	250.00
	1843	6,900	25.00	50.00	100.00	250.00
	1844	.018	25.00	50.00	100.00	250.00
	1845	Inc. Ab.	25.00	50.00	100.00	250.00
	1846	4,300	25.00	50.00	100.00	250.00

GULDEN

.900 SILVER

C#	Date	Mintage	Fine	VF	XF	Unc
2	1838	.011	35.00	75.00	115.00	250.00
	1839	—	—	—	Proof	300.00

C#	Date	Mintage	Fine	VF	XF	Unc
7	1841	.014	35.00	75.00	115.00	200.00
	1843	6,800	35.00	75.00	115.00	250.00
	1844	.014	35.00	75.00	115.00	200.00
	1845	.081	35.00	75.00	115.00	200.00
	1846	8,100	35.00	75.00	115.00	250.00

ZWEY (2) GULDEN

.900 SILVER

C#	Date	Mintage	Fine	VF	XF	Unc
8	1846	.011	300.00	600.00	1000.	1500.

EIN (1) THALER
(Vereins)

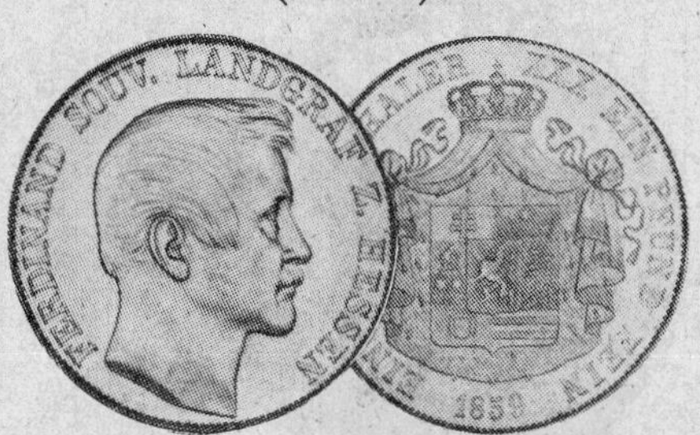

.900 SILVER

C#	Date	Mintage	Fine	VF	XF	Unc
9	1858	5,000	40.00	100.00	200.00	400.00
	1859	6,579	40.00	100.00	200.00	400.00
	1860	6,593	40.00	100.00	200.00	400.00
	1861	6,588	40.00	100.00	200.00	400.00
	1862	6,592	40.00	100.00	200.00	400.00
	1863	6,575	40.00	100.00	200.00	400.00

HILDESHEIM

Bishopric

A bishopric located in western Germany was established in 822. The first mint was installed in the Mundburg Castle c. 977. Hildescheim coins were minted there although the bishopric didn't legally receive the mint right until 1054. In 1803 it was secularized and assigned to Prussia. From 1807-1813 it formed part of Westphalia and in the latter part of 1813 was given to Hanover.

RULERS

Sede Vacante, 1761-1763
Friedrich Wilhelm, Bishop, 1763-1789

MARIEN GROSCHEN

BILLON
Obv: Crowned arms.
Rev: Value and date.

C#	Date	Mintage	VG	Fine	VF	XF
1	1762	—	3.00	5.00	9.00	20.00
	1763	—	3.00	5.00	9.00	20.00

2 MARIEN GROSCHEN

BILLON
Obv: Crowned arms.
Rev: Value and date.

C#	Date	Mintage	VG	Fine	VF	XF
3.5	1763	—	5.00	8.50	12.50	25.00

Obv: Crowned arms; crozier and sword behind.

C#	Date	Mintage	VG	Fine	VF	XF
15	1763	—	5.00	8.50	12.50	25.00

4 MARIEN GROSCHEN

BILLON
Obv: Crowned arms; crozier and sword behind.
Rev: Value and date.

C#	Date	Mintage	VG	Fine	VF	XF
18	1763	—	5.00	8.50	12.50	25.00

SCHILLING
(= 1/28 Thaler)

BILLON
Obv: Crowned arms.
Rev: Value and date.

C#	Date	Mintage	VG	Fine	VF	XF
2	1763	—	3.00	5.00	8.50	20.00

1/24 THALER

BILLON
Obv: Crowned arms.
Rev: Value and date.

C#	Date	Mintage	VG	Fine	VF	XF
3	1762	—	5.00	8.50	12.50	25.00
	1763	—	5.00	8.50	12.50	25.00

Obv: Crowned arms; crozier and sword behind.

C#	Date	Mintage	VG	Fine	VF	XF
13	1763	—	4.00	6.50	10.00	20.00

1/12 THALER

BILLON
Obv: Crowned arms.
Rev: Value and date.

C#	Date	Mintage	VG	Fine	VF	XF
4	1762	—	35.00	50.00	75.00	120.00
	1763	—	35.00	50.00	75.00	120.00

Obv: Crowned arms; crozier and sword behind.

C#	Date	Mintage	VG	Fine	VF	XF
17	1763	—	20.00	37.50	50.00	85.00
	1764	—	20.00	37.50	50.00	85.00
	1765	—	20.00	37.50	50.00	85.00

1/6 THALER

SILVER
Obv: Crowned arms.
Rev: Value and date.

C#	Date	Mintage	VG	Fine	VF	XF
6	1763	—	42.50	60.00	85.00	120.00

C#	Date	Mintage	VG	Fine	VF	XF
19	1763	—	40.00	55.00	75.00	100.00
	1764	—	40.00	55.00	75.00	100.00

1/3 THALER

SILVER
Obv: Bust of Friedrich Wilhelm right.
Rev: Crowned arms and date.

C#	Date	Mintage	VG	Fine	VF	XF
20	1764	—	50.00	65.00	100.00	150.00

Obv: Crowned arms; crozier and sword behind.
Rev: Value and date.

C#	Date	Mintage	VG	Fine	VF	XF
21	1764	—	50.00	65.00	100.00	150.00

2/3 THALER

SILVER

C#	Date	Mintage	Fine	VF	XF	Unc
8	1761	—	75.00	125.00	175.00	250.00

Obv: Bust of Friedrich Wilhelm.
Rev: Crowned arms.

C#	Date	Mintage	Fine	VF	XF	Unc
22	1764	—	150.00	200.00	275.00	450.00

THALER

SILVER
Obv: Bust of Friedrich Wilhelm right.
Rev: Crowned and mantled arms; crozier and sword behind; value and date below.

C#	Date	Mintage	Fine	VF	XF	Unc
—	1766 I.H-V.U.	—	450.00	650.00	1000.	2000.

Obv: Larger bust of Friedrich Wilhelm right.
Rev: Larger crown on mantled arms; crozier and sword behind.

C#	Date	Mintage	Fine	VF	XF	Unc
—	1766	—	750.00	1000.	1500.	2500.
	1768	—	450.00	600.00	950.00	1350.

5 THALER

6.6500 gm., .900 GOLD, .1924 oz AGW
Obv: Bust of Friedrich Wilhelm left.
Rev: Crowned and mantled arms; value and date below.

C#	Date	Mintage	Fine	VF	XF	Unc
27	1764 I.H-V.U.	—	750.00	1000.	1500.	2500.
	1765 I.H-V.U.	—	750.00	1000.	1500.	2500.

Obv: Bust right.

C#	Date	Mintage	Fine	VF	XF	Unc
27a	1765	—	750.00	1000.	1500.	2500.

10 THALER

13.3000 gm., .900 GOLD, .3848 oz AGW
Obv: Bust of Friedrich Wilhelm left.
Rev: Crowned and mantled arms; value and date below.

C#	Date	Mintage	Fine	VF	XF	Unc
28	1766	—	1250.	1750.	2500.	4000.

1/2 PISTOLE

6.6500 gm., .900 GOLD, .1924 oz AGW
Sede Vacante Issue

C#	Date	Mintage	Fine	VF	XF	Unc
10	1763	—	500.00	750.00	1000.	1750.

Obv: Crowned and mantled arms.

C#	Date	Mintage	Fine	VF	XF	Unc
26	1763	—	500.00	750.00	1000.	1750.

TRADE COINS

DUCAT

3.5000 gm., .986 GOLD, .1109 oz AGW
Obv: Bust of Friedrich Wilhelm left.
Rev: Crowned and mantled arms; date above, value below.

C#	Date	Mintage	Fine	VF	XF	Unc
25	1778	—	500.00	750.00	1250.	2000.

HOHENLOHE — INGELFINGEN

Principality

This principality was located in southern Germany. The Hohenlohe house started in the 10th century and the Ingelfingen line was founded in 1701. The first ruler to be made prince of the empire was in 1764 and the last prince abdicated in 1806.

RULERS

Phillip Heinrich, 1743-1781
as Prince, 1764-1781
with Heinrich August, 1765-1796
Friedrich Ludwig, 1796-1806

10 KREUZER
(Convention)

SILVER

Obv: Arms on crowned mantle. Rev: Value.

C#	Date	Mintage	VG	Fine	VF	XF
2	1770	—	9.00	20.00	35.00	75.00

20 KREUZER
(Convention)

SILVER

Obv: Arms on crowned mantle. Rev: Value.

C#	Date	Mintage	VG	Fine	VF	XF
3	1770	—	15.00	35.00	60.00	100.00

THALER
(Convention)

SILVER

C#	Date	Mintage	VG	Fine	VF	XF
5	1796	—	225.00	375.00	750.00	1250.

TRADE COINS

DUCAT

3.5000 gm., .986 GOLD, .1109 oz AGW

Obv: Bust right. Rev: Value over date.

C#	Date	Mintage	VG	Fine	VF	XF
7	1796	—	600.00	1000.	1500.	2250.

HOHENLOHE-KIRCHBERG

This principality was located in southern Germany. The Kirchberg line was founded in 1701. The first ruler to be made prince of the empire was in 1764 and the last prince died in 1819.

RULERS

Christian Friedrich Carl, 1767-1806

1/2 THALER
(Convention)

SILVER

Obv: Bust. Rev: Arms, leg: ZWANZIG EINE.....

C#	Date	Mintage	Fine	VF	XF	Unc
13	1781	—	30.00	65.00	100.00	200.00
	1804	—	30.00	65.00	100.00	200.00
13a	1786	—	50.00	100.00	150.00	250.00

EIN (1) THALER
(Convention)

SILVER

Obv: Bust. Rev: Arms, leg: ZEHEN EINE.....

C#	Date	Mintage	Fine	VF	XF	Unc
15	1781 WK	—	300.00	650.00	1000.	1750.

HOHENLOHE — NEUENSTEIN — OEHRINGEN

Principality

This principality was located in southern Germany. The Neuenstein-Oehringen line was founded in 1610 and the first prince of the empire from this line was proclaimed in 1764. The line became extinct in 1805 and the lands passed to Ingelfingen.

RULERS

Ludwig Friedrich Carl, 1765-1805

EIN (1) KREUZER
(Convention)

BILLON

Obv: Crowned arms in sprays.
Rev: LFC monogram, value and date.

C#	Date	Mintage	VG	Fine	VF	XF
48	1774	—	6.00	13.00	19.50	30.00

2 1/2 KREUZER
(Convention)

BILLON

Obv: Crowned arms in sprays.
Rev: LFC monogram, value and date.

C#	Date	Mintage	VG	Fine	VF	XF
49	1774	—	8.00	17.50	25.00	45.00

10 KREUZER
(Convention)

SILVER

Obv: Crowned arms. Rev: Value over date.

C#	Date	Mintage	VG	Fine	VF	XF
51	1770	—	10.00	25.00	35.00	50.00
	1785	—	10.00	25.00	35.00	50.00
	Rev: 10 line inscription.					
53	1803	—	15.00	35.00	60.00	95.00

20 KREUZER
(Convention)

SILVER

Obv: Crowned arms. Rev: Value over date.

C#	Date	Mintage	VG	Fine	VF	XF
57	1770	—	10.00	25.00	45.00	85.00
	1785	—	10.00	25.00	45.00	85.00

EIN (1) THALER
(Convention)

SILVER

C#	Date	Mintage	VG	Fine	VF	XF
59	1770 SR	—	125.00	300.00	500.00	850.00

C#	Date	Mintage	VG	Fine	VF	XF
60	1785 KR	—	125.00	300.00	500.00	850.00
	Obv: Bust left.					
61	1797	—	100.00	250.00	450.00	750.00

TRADE COINS

DUCAT

3.5000 gm., .986 GOLD, .1109 oz AGW

Obv: Bust right. Rev: Crowned arms.

C#	Date	Mintage	Fine	VF	XF	Unc
62	1770	—	1000.	1500.	2250.	3000.
	Similar to C#62.					
63	1785	—	1000.	1500.	2250.	3000.
	81st Birthday Commemorative Similar to C#62.					
65	1804	—	1250.	2000.	2750.	3500.

NOTE: Also comes in silver.

2 DUCATS

7.0000 gm., .986 GOLD, .2219 oz AGW

81st Birthday Commemorative

Obv: Bust right. Rev: Crowned arms.

C#	Date	Mintage	Fine	VF	XF	Unc
66	1804	—	1750.	2500.	3250.	4000.

HOHENZOLLERN — HECHINGEN

Located in southern Germany, the Hechingen line was founded in 1576. They obtained the mint right c. 1622 and were named prince of the empire in 1623. As a result of the 1848 revolutions the princes abdicated in favor of Prussia in 1849.

RULERS

Joseph Wilhelm, 1750-1798
Hermann Friedrich Otto, 1798 - 1810
Friedrich Hermann Otto, 1810 - 1838
Friedrich Wilhelm Constantin, 1838 - 1849

MINTMASTER'S INITIALS

C.H. - Johann Christian Heuglin

3 KREUZER

BILLON
Obv: Crowned arms. Rev: Value within wreath.

C#	Date	Mintage	Fine	VF	XF	Unc
3	1845	.030	7.50	15.00	25.00	50.00
	1846	.030	7.50	15.00	25.00	50.00
	1847	8,000	10.00	20.00	35.00	70.00

6 KREUZER

BILLON
Obv: Crowned arms. Rev: Value within wreath.

C#	Date	Mintage	Fine	VF	XF	Unc
4	1841	.024	10.00	20.00	45.00	75.00
	1842	.026	10.00	20.00	45.00	75.00
	1845	.025	10.00	20.00	45.00	75.00
	1846	.025	10.00	20.00	45.00	75.00
	1847	.026	10.00	20.00	45.00	75.00

1/2 GULDEN

.900 SILVER
Obv: Head right, VOIGT below. Rev: Value within wreath.

C#	Date	Mintage	Fine	VF	XF	Unc
5	1839	.015	25.00	50.00	100.00	150.00
	1841	6,000	25.00	50.00	100.00	200.00
	1842	5,540	25.00	50.00	100.00	200.00
	1843	6,000	25.00	50.00	100.00	200.00
	1844	6,000	25.00	50.00	100.00	200.00
	1845	6,000	25.00	50.00	100.00	200.00
	1846	6,000	25.00	50.00	100.00	200.00
	1847	6,000	25.00	50.00	100.00	200.00

GULDEN

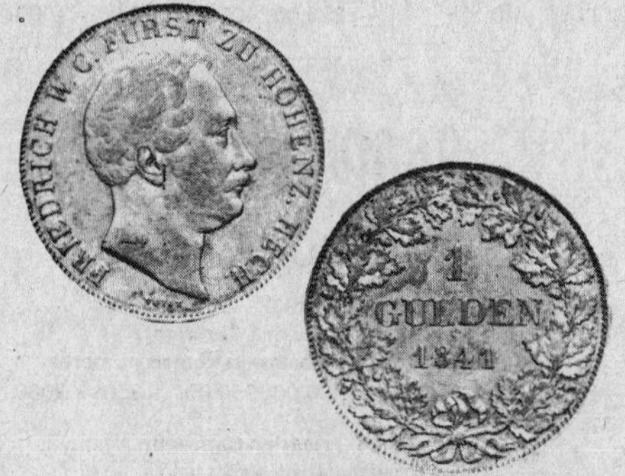

.900 SILVER

C#	Date	Mintage	Fine	VF	XF	Unc
6	1839	.015	30.00	65.00	125.00	200.00
	1841	6,000	30.00	65.00	125.00	250.00
	1842	6,000	30.00	65.00	125.00	250.00
	1843	8,280	30.00	65.00	125.00	250.00
	1844	6,000	30.00	65.00	125.00	250.00
	1845	5,465	30.00	65.00	125.00	250.00
	1846	5,718	30.00	65.00	125.00	250.00
	1847	6,324	30.00	65.00	125.00	250.00

ZWEY (2) GULDEN

21.2100 gm., .900 SILVER, .6138 oz ASW

C#	Date	Mintage	Fine	VF	XF	Unc
7	1846	4,300	200.00	400.00	600.00	1100.
	1847	4,300	200.00	400.00	600.00	1100.

EIN (1) TALER

(Convention)

SILVER
Obv: Bust right; star below.
Rev: Crowned arms in sprays.

C#	Date	Mintage	VG	Fine	VF	XF
1	1783 ARW	—	100.00	225.00	300.00	500.00

28.0600 gm., .833 SILVER, .7516 oz ASW
Obv: Bust left. Rev: Crowned arms within branches.

C#	Date	Mintage	Fine	VF	XF	Unc
2	1804 C.H.	2,000	325.00	650.00	1050.	1500.

2 THALER

(= 3-1/2 Gulden)

37.1200 gm., .900 SILVER, 1.0742 oz ASW

C#	Date	Mintage	Fine	VF	XF	Unc
8	1844	2,346	400.00	1250.	2500.	5000.
	1845	1,000	400.00	1250.	2500.	5000.
	1846	570 pcs.	500.00	1500.	3000.	5000.

HOHENZOLLERN — SIGMARINGEN

Located in southern Germany, the Sigmaringen line was founded in 1576. They obtained the mint right c. 1622 and were named prince of the empire in 1623. As a result of the 1848 revolutions the princes abdicated in favor of Prussia in 1849.

RULERS

Carl, 1831-1848
Carl Anton, 1848-1849

EIN (1) KREUZER

COPPER
Obv: Crowned arms. Rev: EIN KREUZER within wreath.

C#	Date	Mintage	Fine	VF	XF	Unc
1	1842	.180	5.00	10.00	20.00	40.00
	1846	.055	5.00	10.00	20.00	40.00

BILLON
Rev: 1 KREUZER within wreath

C#	Date	Mintage	Fine	VF	XF	Unc
2	1842	.120	5.00	10.00	20.00	40.00
	1846	.060	5.00	10.00	20.00	40.00

3 KREUZER

BILLON

C#	Date	Mintage	Fine	VF	XF	Unc
3	1839	.052	6.00	12.00	20.00	50.00
	1841	.068	6.00	12.00	20.00	50.00
	1842	.072	6.00	12.00	20.00	50.00
	1844	.170	6.00	12.00	20.00	50.00
	1845	.126	6.00	12.00	20.00	50.00
	1846	.126	6.00	12.00	20.00	50.00
	1847	.060	6.00	12.00	20.00	50.00

6 KREUZER

BILLON
Obv: Crowned arms. Rev: Value within wreath.

C#	Date	Mintage	Fine	VF	XF	Unc
4	1839	.075	6.00	12.00	25.00	50.00
	1840	.075	6.00	12.00	25.00	50.00
	1841	.075	6.00	12.00	25.00	50.00
	1842	.074	6.00	12.00	25.00	50.00
	1844	.140	6.00	12.00	25.00	50.00
	1845	.208	6.00	12.00	25.00	50.00
	1846	.208	6.00	12.00	25.00	50.00
	1847	—	6.00	12.00	25.00	50.00

1/2 GULDEN

.900 SILVER

C#	Date	Mintage	Fine	VF	XF	Unc
5	1838	.012	20.00	40.00	70.00	150.00
	1839	.012	20.00	40.00	70.00	150.00
	1840	.012	20.00	40.00	70.00	150.00
	1841	.012	20.00	40.00	70.00	150.00
	1842	.012	20.00	40.00	70.00	150.00
	1843	.012	20.00	40.00	70.00	150.00
	1844	.012	20.00	40.00	70.00	150.00
	1845	.012	20.00	40.00	70.00	150.00
	1846	.012	20.00	40.00	70.00	150.00
	1847	3,068	20.00	40.00	70.00	150.00
	1848	—	20.00	40.00	70.00	150.00

GULDEN

.900 SILVER
Obv: Head left, D below. Rev: Value within wreath.

C#	Date	Mintage	Fine	VF	XF	Unc
6	1838 D	—	35.00	70.00	110.00	200.00

Obv: DOELL below head.

C#	Date	Mintage	Fine	VF	XF	Unc
6a	1838	.018	35.00	70.00	100.00	200.00
	1839	.012	35.00	70.00	100.00	200.00
	1840	.012	35.00	70.00	100.00	200.00
	1841	.012	35.00	70.00	100.00	200.00
	1842	.012	35.00	70.00	100.00	200.00
	1843	.012	35.00	70.00	100.00	200.00
	1844	.012	35.00	70.00	100.00	200.00
	1845	.012	35.00	70.00	100.00	200.00
	1846	.012	35.00	70.00	100.00	200.00
	1847	.012	35.00	70.00	100.00	200.00
	1848	3,068	35.00	70.00	100.00	250.00

Obv: BALBACH below head

C#	Date	Mintage	Fine	VF	XF	Unc
10a	1849	5,000	35.00	75.00	125.00	175.00

ZWEI (2) GULDEN

21.2100 gm., .900 SILVER, .6138 oz ASW

C#	Date	Mintage	Fine	VF	XF	Unc
7	1845 D	9,206	150.00	400.00	750.00	1500.
	1846 D	9,206	150.00	400.00	750.00	1500.
	1847 D	9,206	150.00	400.00	750.00	1500.
	1848 D	6,905	150.00	400.00	750.00	1500.

BALBACH below bust

C#	Date	Mintage	Fine	VF	XF	Unc
11a	1849	1,213	400.00	800.00	1400.	2500.

2 THALER

(= 3-1/2 Gulden)

37.1200 gm., .900 SILVER, 1.0742 oz ASW

C#	Date	Mintage	Fine	VF	XF	Unc
8	1841	2,857	350.00	900.00	2200.	3000.
	1842	2,857	350.00	900.00	2200.	3000.
	1843	2,877	350.00	900.00	2200.	3000.

Obv: Similar to C#8

C#	Date	Mintage	Fine	VF	XF	Unc
9	1844	3,300	300.00	800.00	1500.	2600.
	1846	6,600	300.00	800.00	1500.	2600.
	1847	2,000	300.00	800.00	1500.	2600.

HOHENZOLLERN UNDER PRUSSIA

In 1849, Prussia obtained the Hohenzollern lands due to the 1848 revolutions and political unrest. One series of coins was issued by Prussia for their Hohenzollern holdings.

RULERS

Friedrich Wilhelm IV (of Prussia), 1849-1861

KREUZER

COPPER

C#	Date	Mintage	Fine	VF	XF	Unc
1	1852A	.030	5.00	11.00	20.00	40.00

3 KREUZER

BILLON

Obv: Eagle with shield. Rev: Value within wreath.

C#	Date	Mintage	Fine	VF	XF	Unc
2	1852A	.022	12.00	25.00	40.00	80.00

6 KREUZER

BILLON

Obv: Eagle with shield. Rev: Value within wreath.

C#	Date	Mintage	Fine	VF	XF	Unc
3	1852A	.027	10.00	20.00	35.00	70.00

1/2 GULDEN

.900 SILVER

Obv: Head right, A below. Rev: Value within wreath.

C#	Date	Mintage	Fine	VF	XF	Unc
4	1852A	.053	20.00	40.00	55.00	125.00

GULDEN

.900 SILVER

C#	Date	Mintage	Fine	VF	XF	Unc
5	1852A	.050	30.00	60.00	90.00	200.00

HOLSTEIN

Located between Germany and Denmark, Holstein was originally a part of the duchy of Saxony. It is often associated with Schleswig. The first coinage appeared in the 14th century. The present house was founded in 1679 and passed to Denmark in 1761. The Danes struck coins for their lands in Holstein during the 18th and 19th centuries. They were ceded to the Germans in 1864.

RULERS

Friedrich Carl of Holstein Ploen, 1729-61

THALER

SILVER

Obv: Bust of Friedrich Carl right.
Rev: Crowned arms in sprays divide date.

C#	Date	Mintage	VG	Fine	VF	XF
11	1761	—	450.00	750.00	1000.	1500.

Obv: Bust of Friedrich Carl right.
Rev: Crowned arms in sprays.

C#	Date	Mintage	VG	Fine	VF	XF
11a	ND	—	225.00	400.00	600.00	1000.

TRADE COINS

DUCAT

3.5000 gm., .986 GOLD, .1109 oz AGW
Obv: Bust of Friedrich Carl right.
Rev: Crowned arms, date below in Roman numerals.

C#	Date	Mintage	VG	Fine	VF	XF
13	1760	—	600.00	950.00	1350.	2000.

Obv: Bust of Friedrich Carl right.
Rev: Crowned arms, value below.

C#	Date	Mintage	VG	Fine	VF	XF
13a	1760	—	600.00	950.00	1350.	2000.

ISENBURG

Located in western Germany. The first coins for the Isenburg line appeared c. 1600. The territories of the Isenburg family were consolidated in 1806 and the ruler was made a sovereign prince of the Rhine Confederation. The 1815 Congress of Vienna placed the principality under Austrian rule. It was mediatized to Hess-Darmstadt in 1815 and eventually went to Prussia.

RULERS

Carl, 1806-1813

6 KREUZER

BILLON

Obv: Crowned C. Rev: Value within wreath.

C#	Date	Mintage	Fine	VF	XF	Unc
1	1811	1.000	75.00	150.00	200.00	300.00

12 KREUZER

SILVER
Obv: Head left, J. LAROQUE F. at truncation.
Rev: Value within wreath.

C#	Date	Mintage	Fine	VF	XF	Unc
2	1811	.500	75.00	150.00	250.00	350.00

EIN (1) THALER

(Reichs)

SILVER

C#	Date	Mintage	Fine	VF	XF	Unc
3	1811	—	600.00	1200.	2000.	3000.

TRADE COINS

DUCAT

3.5000 gm., .986 GOLD, .1109 oz AGW

C#	Date	Mintage	Fine	VF	XF	Unc
4	1811	—	2250.	4500.	6000.	7500.

JEVER

Located in northwestern Germany on the North Sea. Early coins were struck c. 1000. The line ended in 1575 and Jever passed to Oldenburg in 1575, Anhalt-Zerbst in 1667 and Russia In 1793. The area was administered by the widow of the last duke of Anhalt-Zerbst for Catherine II of Russia. It finally passed to Oldenburg again in 1818.

RULERS

Friedrich August of Anhalt-Zerbst, 1753-1793
Friederike Auguste Sophie, 1793-1807

HELLER

COPPER
Obv: Bust of Friedrich August right.
Rev: Arms divide date; "JEVER" above; value below.

C#	Date	Mintage	VG	Fine	VF	XF
1	1764	—	4.50	7.50	10.00	20.00

PFENNIG

COPPER
Obv: Bust of Friedrich August right.
Rev: Arms divide date; "JEVER" above; value below.

C#	Date	Mintage	VG	Fine	VF	XF
2	1764	—	4.50	7.50	10.00	20.00

1/4 STUBER

COPPER
Obv: Arms. Rev: Value over date.

C#	Date	Mintage	VG	Fine	VF	XF
10	1799	—	5.00	10.00	15.00	30.00

STUBER

BILLON
Obv: Arms. Rev: Value over date.

C#	Date	Mintage	VG	Fine	VF	XF
11	1798	—	5.00	10.00	15.00	30.00

2 STUBER

BILLON
Obv: Arms. Rev: Value over date.

C#	Date	Mintage	VG	Fine	VF	XF
12	1798	—	7.00	15.00	20.00	35.00

GROTE

BILLON
Obv: Bust of Friedrich August right.
Rev: Arms divide date; value below.

C#	Date	Mintage	VG	Fine	VF	XF
3	1764	—	5.00	8.50	12.50	30.00

Obv: Arms. Rev: Value over date.

C#	Date	Mintage	VG	Fine	VF	XF
13	1798	—	7.00	15.00	20.00	35.00

3 GROTE

BILLON
Obv: Arms. Rev: Value over date.

C#	Date	Mintage	VG	Fine	VF	XF
14	1798	—	10.00	20.00	27.50	40.00

4 GROTE

BILLON
Obv: Bust of Friedrich August right.
Rev: Arms divide date; value below.

C#	Date	Mintage	VG	Fine	VF	XF
4	1764	—	6.00	10.00	15.00	30.00

Rev: Arms divide 16-P, date, 5-K; "JEVER" above, value below.

C#	Date	Mintage	VG	Fine	VF	XF
4a	1764	—	6.00	10.00	15.00	30.00

12 GROTE

SILVER
Obv: Bust of Friedrich August right.
Rev: Arms divide date; value below.

C#	Date	Mintage	VG	Fine	VF	XF
5	1764	—	12.50	25.00	35.00	50.00

Rev: Arms divide 48-P, date, 15-K; "JEVER" above, value below.

C#	Date	Mintage	VG	Fine	VF	XF
5a	1764	—	15.00	27.50	40.00	55.00

1/2 THALER

(Reichs)

11.1400 gm., .750 SILVER, .2686 oz ASW

C#	Date	Mintage	VG	Fine	VF	XF
15	1798	—	30.00	100.00	200.00	350.00

2/3 THALER

SILVER
Obv: Bust of Friedrich August right.
Rev: Helmed arms over date in Roman numerals.

C#	Date	Mintage	VG	Fine	VF	XF
7	1763	—	225.00	500.00	850.00	1250.

EIN (1) THALER

(Reichs)

22.2700 gm., .750 SILVER, .5371 oz ASW

C#	Date	Mintage	VG	Fine	VF	XF
16	1798	—	150.00	200.00	350.00	650.00

JULICH — BERG

The duchy of Julich-Berg was located in northwestern Germany. Julich was founded c. 847 and the mint right was acquired in 1237. It was united sporadically with Berg from 1348 and permanently from 1423. Between 1609 and 1624 it was held jointly by Pfalz-Neuburg and Brandenburg. It was given to Pfalz-Neuburg until 1801 when France gained possession. In 1815 the lands went to Prussia.

RULERS

Carl Theodor, 1742-1799

1/4 STUBER

COPPER
Obv: C T monogram. Rev: Value over date.

C#	Date	Mintage	VG	Fine	VF	XF
2	1765-94	—	2.50	4.00	6.00	12.00

NOTE: Varieties exist.

1/2 STUBER

COPPER
Obv: C T monogram. Rev: Value over date.

C#	Date	Mintage	VG	Fine	VF	XF
3	1765-94	—	2.50	4.00	6.00	12.00

2 STUBER

BILLON
Obv: Crowned arms. Rev: Value over date.

C#	Date	Mintage	VG	Fine	VF	XF
5	1792	—	4.00	7.00	12.50	25.00
	1793	—	4.00	7.00	12.50	25.00
	1794	—	4.00	7.00	12.50	25.00

3 STUBER

BILLON
Obv: Crowned arms. Rev: Value over date.

C#	Date	Mintage	VG	Fine	VF	XF
7	1792	—	4.00	7.00	12.50	25.00
	1793	—	4.00	7.00	12.50	25.00
	1794	—	4.00	7.00	12.50	25.00

EIN (1) THALER

(Convention)

SILVER

C#	Date	Mintage	VG	Fine	VF	XF
17	1772 PM	—	100.00	200.00	275.00	450.00
	1774 PM	—	100.00	200.00	275.00	450.00

NOTE: Varieties exist.

KNYPHAUSEN

The district of Knyphausen was located in northwestern Germany in East Friesland. Local nobility ruled from the 14th century and until 1623 when it was sold to Oldenburg. It became autonomous in 1653 and was acquired through marriage to the Bentinck family in 1733. Coins were struck c. 1800. It was claimed by both Anhalt and Oldenburg and the arms of Knyphausen appear on coins of both places.

RULERS

Wilhelm Gustav Friedrich, 1774-1835

1/8 THALER

(= 9 Grote)

SILVER
Obv: Arms.
Rev: Crowned double-headed eagle dividing value.

C#	Date	Mintage	Fine	VF	XF	Unc
2	1807	—	75.00	150.00	200.00	275.00
	Obv: Crowned arms **Rev: Crowned lion.**					
1	1807	.016	40.00	85.00	150.00	225.00

NCLT ISSUES

PATTERNS

KM#	Date	Mintage	Identification	Mkt.Val.
1	1806	10 pcs.	2-1/2 Thaler, Gold	—
2	1806	—	5 Thaler, Gold	—
3	1806	—	10 Thaler, Gold	—

LAUENBURG

The duchy, located in northern Germany was established in 1260. The ruling line became extinct in 1689 and the lands were inherited by Hannover in 1705. After the Napoleonic Wars, the 1815 Congress of Vienna assigned the property to Prussia who traded it to Denmark for Swedish Pomerania. Prussia regained Lauenburg in 1864.

RULERS

Frederick VI (of Denmark), 1816-1839

MINTMASTER'S INITIALS

F.F. - Johann Friedrich Freund

2/3 THALER

17.3200 gm., .750 SILVER, .4177 oz ASW
Obv: Head left, F.A. at truncation.
Rev: Value within wreath.

C#	Date	Mintage	Fine	VF	XF	Unc
1	1830 F.F.	—	75.00	150.00	250.00	350.00

LEININGEN

Scattered lands located in southwestern Germany. It was founded c. 1110. First coins were struck in the 13th century. Leiningen was annexed to France in 1801. The lands were mediatized in 1806 and were absorbed by Baden, Bavaria, Hesse and Nassau.

RULERS

Karl Friedrich Wilhelm, 1756-1807

PFENNIG

BILLON
Obv: Eagles below crown within branches. Rev: Value.

C#	Date	Mintage				
1	1805	—	7.50	15.00	25.00	50.00

2 PFENNIG

BILLON
Obv: Crowned arms. Rev: Value, branch below.

C#	Date	Mintage				
2	1805	—	7.50	15.00	25.00	50.00

3 KREUZER

BILLON
Obv: Crowned arms within branches.
Rev: Value, branch below.

C#	Date	Mintage				
3	1804	—	7.50	15.00	25.00	50.00

C#	Date	Mintage				
3a	1805	—	7.50	15.00	25.00	50.00

6 KREUZER

BILLON
Obv: Crowned arms within branches.
Rev: Value, branch below.

C#	Date	Mintage				
5	1804	—	7.50	15.00	30.00	65.00

Obv: Eagles below crown within branches.

C#	Date	Mintage				
5a	1805	—	7.50	15.00	30.00	65.00

LIPPE — DETMOLD

A state located in northwestern Germany was founded c. 1120. The first coinage was struck c. 1225. The rulers were elevated to the rank of count in 1528 and given the title of prince in 1720, but it wasn't confirmed until 1789. The principality joined the German Empire 1871 and remained until abdicated in 1918.

RULERS

Friedrich Wilhelm Leopold
under Regency of Ludwig Heinrich Adolf, 1782-1789
Alone, 1789-1802
Paul Alexander Leopold II
under Regency of Pauline of Anhalt-Bernburg, 1802-1820
As Independent Prince, 1820-1851
Paul Friedrich Emil Leopold III, 1851-1875
Woldemar, 1875 - 1895
Alexander, 1895 - 1905
Leopold IV, 1905-1918

HELLER

COPPER
Obv: Rose displayed.
Rev: Value stated in 5 lines; date below.

C#	Date	Mintage	VG	Fine	VF	XF
40	1783	—	5.00	10.00	13.50	25.00
	Rev: Value over date.					
51	1791	—	3.00	5.00	7.50	20.00
	1798	—	3.00	5.00	7.50	20.00

C#	Date	Mintage	Fine	VF	XF	Unc
70	1802 T	.166	2.00	3.50	8.00	35.00
	1802	Inc. Ab.	2.00	3.50	8.00	35.00
	1809 T	.108	2.00	3.50	8.00	35.00
	1812 T	—	2.00	3.50	8.00	35.00
	1814 T	—	2.00	3.50	8.00	35.00
	1816 T	—	2.00	3.50	8.00	35.00
	1816	—	2.00	3.50	8.00	35.00
	Obv: Blooming rose. Rev. value: I HELLER, date.					
74	1821ST	—	2.00	3.50	8.00	35.00
	1822ST	—	2.00	3.50	8.00	35.00
	1825ST	—	2.00	3.50	8.00	35.00
	1826ST	—	2.00	3.50	8.00	35.00
	1828ST	—	2.00	3.50	8.00	35.00
	1835ST	—	2.00	3.50	8.00	35.00
	1836ST	—	2.00	3.50	8.00	35.00
	1840ST	—	2.00	3.50	8.00	35.00
	Rev. value: 1 HELLER, date.					
74a	1826 ST	—	2.00	3.50	8.00	35.00

PFENNING

COPPER
Obv: Rose displayed. Rev: Value over date.

C#	Date	Mintage	VG	Fine	VF	XF
52	1791	—	3.00	5.00	7.50	15.00

Obv: Blooming rose. Rev: Value, rosette under date.

C#	Date	Mintage	Fine	VF	XF	Unc
71.1	1802	.120	2.00	4.50	8.00	35.00
	Rev: T under date.					
71.2	1818 T	—	2.00	4.50	8.00	35.00
	Rev: Without T.					
71.3	1818	—	2.00	4.50	8.00	35.00

Rev: ST below date.

C#	Date	Mintage	Fine	VF	XF	Unc
75	1820ST	—	2.00	3.50	8.00	35.00
	1821ST	—	2.00	3.50	8.00	35.00
	1824ST	—	2.00	3.50	8.00	35.00
	1825ST	—	2.00	3.50	8.00	35.00

Rev. Value: PFENNING

C#	Date	Mintage	Fine	VF	XF	Unc
75a	1824ST	—	3.00	6.00	15.00	40.00

C#	Date	Mintage	Fine	VF	XF	Unc
75b	1828ST	—	2.00	3.50	8.00	35.00
	1829ST	—	2.00	3.50	8.00	35.00
	1830ST	—	2.00	3.50	8.00	35.00
	1836ST	—	2.00	3.50	8.00	35.00
	1840ST	—	2.00	3.50	8.00	35.00

C#	Date	Mintage	Fine	VF	XF	Unc
77	1847 A	.972	2.00	3.25	8.00	35.00

C#	Date	Mintage	Fine	VF	XF	Unc
83	1851 A	1.080	1.00	2.75	8.00	35.00
	1858 A	.900	1.00	2.75	8.00	35.00

1-1/2 PFENNING

COPPER

C#	Date	Mintage	Fine	VF	XF	Unc
76	1821 T	—	3.00	7.25	16.00	45.00
	1823 T	—	3.00	7.25	16.00	45.00
	1824 T	—	3.00	7.25	16.00	45.00
	1825 T	—	3.00	7.25	16.00	45.00

2 PFENNING

BILLON
Obv: Rose. Rev: Value over date.

C#	Date	Mintage	VG	Fine	VF	XF
42	1785	—	5.00	10.00	15.00	25.00

COPPER
Obv: Blooming rose.
Rev: Value, rosette under date.

C#	Date	Mintage	Fine	VF	XF	Unc
72	1802	.127	2.00	4.50	9.00	35.00

3 PFENNINGE

COPPER
Obv: Crowned shield with blooming rose. Rev: Value.

C#	Date	Mintage	Fine	VF	XF	Unc
78	1847A	1.020	1.50	3.00	6.00	25.00

C#	Date	Mintage	Fine	VF	XF	Unc
84	1858A	.060	2.00	4.00	8.00	35.00

4 PFENNING

BILLON
Obv: Rose. Rev: Value over date.

C#	Date	Mintage	VG	Fine	VF	XF
44	1784	—	5.00	10.00	15.00	25.00

MATTIER

BILLON
Obv: L H A C monogram in rose.
Rev: Value over date.

C#	Date	Mintage	VG	Fine	VF	XF
46	1785	—	5.00	10.00	15.00	25.00

Obv: Rose displayed.

C#	Date	Mintage	VG	Fine	VF	XF
54	1789	—	5.00	10.00	15.00	25.00

Similar to C#54.

C#	Date	Mintage	VG	Fine	VF	XF
60	1791	—	5.00	9.00	12.50	25.00
	1792	—	5.00	9.00	12.50	25.00
	1793	—	5.00	9.00	12.50	25.00
	1794	—	5.00	9.00	12.50	25.00
	1795	—	5.00	9.00	12.50	25.00
	1796	—	5.00	9.00	12.50	25.00
	1797	—	5.00	9.00	12.50	25.00
	1798	—	5.00	9.00	12.50	25.00
	1799	—	5.00	9.00	12.50	25.00

1/2 SILBER GROSCHEN

BILLON
Obv: Head right. Rev: Value.

C#	Date	Mintage	Fine	VF	XF	Unc
79	1847A	.321	7.50	15.00	25.00	50.00

MARIEN GROSCHEN

BILLON
Obv: L H A C monogram in rose.
Rev: Value over date.

C#	Date	Mintage	VG	Fine	VF	XF
48	1784	—	5.00	10.00	15.00	25.00
	1786	—	5.00	10.00	15.00	25.00

Obv: Rose displayed.

C#	Date	Mintage	VG	Fine	VF	XF
56	1789	—	5.00	10.00	15.00	25.00

Similar to C#56.

C#	Date	Mintage	VG	Fine	VF	XF
62	1790	—	5.00	10.00	13.50	25.00
	1791	—	5.00	10.00	13.50	25.00
	1792	—	5.00	10.00	13.50	25.00
	1793	—	5.00	10.00	13.50	25.00
	1794	—	5.00	10.00	13.50	25.00
	1795	—	5.00	10.00	13.50	25.00

SILBER GROSCHEN

BILLON

C#	Date	Mintage	Fine	VF	XF	Unc
80	1847A	.750	7.50	15.00	25.00	50.00

C#	Date	Mintage	Fine	VF	XF	Unc
85	1860A	.432	5.00	10.00	20.00	40.00

2-1/2 SILBER GROSCHEN

BILLON
Obv: Head right. Rev: Value.

C#	Date	Mintage	Fine	VF	XF	Unc
81	1847A	.363	7.50	15.00	30.00	50.00

C#	Date	Mintage	Fine	VF	XF	Unc
86	1860A	.120	7.50	15.00	30.00	50.00

GULDEN

(Prize)

SILVER

C#	Date	Mintage	VG	Fine	VF	XF
68	1793	—	50.00	110.00	165.00	250.00

1/12 THALER

BILLON
Obv: Rose. Rev: Value over date.

C#	Date	Mintage	VG	Fine	VF	XF
65	1789	—	6.00	12.50	19.50	30.00
	1790	—	6.00	12.50	19.50	30.00

EIN (1) THALER

(Vereins)

18.5200 gm., .900 SILVER, .5360 oz ASW

C#	Date	Mintage	Fine	VF	XF	Unc
87	1860A	.026	35.00	100.00	200.00	400.00
	1866A	.018	35.00	100.00	200.00	400.00

2 THALER

(= 3-1/2 Gulden)

37.1200 gm., .900 SILVER, 1.0742 oz ASW

C#	Date	Mintage	Fine	VF	XF	Unc
82	1843A	.017	200.00	500.00	1000.	1500.

MONETARY REFORM

2 MARK

11.1110 gm., .900 SILVER, .3215 oz ASW

Y#	Date	Mintage	VF	XF	Unc
83	1906A	.020	145.00	230.00	350.00
	1906A	1,100	—	Proof	500.00

3 MARK

16.6670 gm., .900 SILVER, .4823 oz ASW

Y#	Date	Mintage	VF	XF	Unc
84	1913A	.015	150.00	230.00	300.00
	1913A	—	—	Proof	350.00

LOWENSTEIN — WERTHEIM

Virneburg

The county of Loewenstein, in Wurttemberg, was founded c. 1100. Wertheim, in Bavaria, was obtained by marriage in 1600 along with the mint right. The Protestant line of Virneburg was founded in 1635. Loewenstein—Wertheim was mediatized in 1806.

RULERS

Johann Ludwig Vollrath, 1721-1790
Friedrich Ludwig, 1721-1796
Carl Ludwig, 1721-1799
Friedrich Carl, 1799-1806

MINTMASTER'S INITIALS

W.E. - Weber & Eberhard, 1765-1777

KREUZER

BILLON
Obv: JLVGIL monogram. Rev: Arms.

C#	Date	Mintage	VG	Fine	VF	XF
20	1772	—	8.00	12.50	20.00	35.00
	Obv: Crowned 3-fold arms. Rev: Value over date.					
9	1798	—	5.00	11.50	15.00	30.00

3 KREUZER

BILLON
Obv: Bust of Johann Ludwig Vollrath right.
Rev: Arms.

C#	Date	Mintage	VG	Fine	VF	XF
22	1772	—	10.00	15.00	22.50	40.00

10 KREUZER

SILVER
Obv: 3 shields of arms.
Rev: Arms.

C#	Date	Mintage	Fine	VF	XF	Unc
14	1767	—	15.00	22.50	37.50	55.00
	Obv: Bust of Johann Ludwig Vollrath right.					
27	1767	—	20.00	35.00	52.50	70.00

20 KREUZER

SILVER
Obv: Bust of Johann Ludwig Vollrath right.
Rev: Arms.

C#	Date	Mintage	Fine	VF	XF	Unc
28	1767	—	17.50	27.50	42.50	65.00
66	1770	—	65.00	100.00	125.00	200.00

1/2 THALER

SILVER
Obv: Bust of Friedrich Ludwig right.
Rev: 6 shields of arms, crowned.

C#	Date	Mintage	Fine	VF	XF	Unc
45	1770 WE	—	1000.	1500.	2000.	2750.
	Obv: Bust of Carl Ludwig right. Rev: 5 shields of arms, crowned.					
68	1770 WE	—	500.00	700.00	950.00	1500.

THALER

SILVER
Obv: Head of Johann Ludwig Vollrath right.
Rev: Crowned and supported arms; date below.

C#	Date	Mintage	Fine	VF	XF	Unc
33	1766 WE	—	250.00	350.00	500.00	900.00
	1767 WE	—	250.00	350.00	500.00	900.00
	Obv: Bust of Johann Ludwig Vollrath right, leg:...IN LOW WERTH. Rev: "SUUM CUIQUE" in crowned cartouche; lion below.					
34	1768 WE	—	250.00	350.00	500.00	900.00
	1776 WE	—	250.00	350.00	500.00	900.00
	Obv. leg: ....IN LOEW WERTH.					
34a	1769 WE	—	200.00	250.00	400.00	700.00
	Obv: Bust of Friedrich Ludwig right. Rev: 6 shields of arms, crowned.					
47	1768 WE	—	300.00	450.00	600.00	1000.
	Obv: Bust of Carl Ludwig right. Rev: 5 shields of arms, crowned.					
70	1770 WE	—	600.00	950.00	1350.	1850.

TRADE COINS

1/4 DUCAT

.8750 gm., .986 GOLD, .0277 oz AGW
Obv: Arms. Rev: Crouching lion.

C#	Date	Mintage	VG	Fine	VF	XF
35	ND (1765-84)	—	150.00	350.00	500.00	850.00

DUCAT

3.5000 gm., .986 GOLD, .1109 oz AGW
Obv: Bust of Carl Ludwig right.
Rev: 5 shields of arms, crowned.

C#	Date	Mintage	Fine	VF	XF	Unc
71	1767 WE	—	1250.	1750.	2500.	3500.
	Obv: Bust of Johann Ludwig Vollrath right. Rev: Arms.					
37	1768 WE	—	1000.	1500.	2250.	3000.
	1769 WE	—	1000.	1500.	2250.	3000.
	1771 WE	—	1000.	1500.	2250.	3000.
	Rev: Lion					
36	ND WE	—	1000.	1500.	2250.	3000.
	50th Year of Reign Commemorative. Obv: Bust. Rev: Kneeling figure.					
38	1780	—	1500.	2250.	3250.	4000.
	Obv: Bust right. Rev: Crowned arms.					
72	1799	—	1750.	2500.	3500.	4000.

2 DUCATS

7.0000 gm., .986 GOLD, .2219 oz AGW
Obv: Bust right. Rev: Crowned arms.
Thick planchet.

C#	Date	Mintage	Fine	VF	XF	Unc
73	1799	—	2250.	3000.	3950.	4750.

Rochefort

The Catholic line of Rochefort was founded in 1635. Rochefort counts were made princes of the empire in 1711. Lowenstein-Wertheim was mediatized in 1806 after which other counts were made Bavarian princes in 1812.

RULERS

Carl Thomas, 1735-1789
Constantin, 1789-1806

MINTMASTER'S INITIALS

W.E. - Weber & Eberhard, 1765-1777
E(W)W - Eberhard (Wertheim) Weber, 1765-1777

PFENNING

COPPER
Obv: CFZL monogram.
Rev: Value over date.

C#	Date	Mintage	VG	Fine	VF	XF
80	1781	—	5.00	9.50	13.50	25.00

C#	Date	Mintage	Fine	VF	XF	Unc
115	1790	—	2.50	5.00	10.00	40.00
	1791	—	2.50	5.00	10.00	40.00
	1792	—	2.50	5.00	10.00	40.00
	1793	—	2.50	5.00	10.00	40.00
	1794	—	2.50	5.00	10.00	40.00
	1795	—	2.50	5.00	10.00	40.00
	1796	—	2.50	5.00	10.00	40.00
	1797	—	2.50	5.00	10.00	40.00
	1798	—	2.50	5.00	10.00	40.00
	1799	—	2.50	5.00	10.00	40.00
	1800	—	2.50	5.00	10.00	40.00
	Obv: Crowned CF monogram.					
—	1790	—	2.50	5.00	10.00	40.00

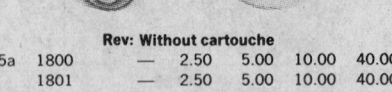

Rev: Without cartouche

C#	Date	Mintage	Fine	VF	XF	Unc
115a	1800	—	2.50	5.00	10.00	40.00
	1801	—	2.50	5.00	10.00	40.00
	1802	—	2.50	5.00	10.00	40.00

KREUZER

COPPER
Obv: CFZL monogram. Rev: Value and date.

C#	Date	Mintage	VG	Fine	VF	XF
81	1767	—	7.00	15.00	25.00	40.00
	Obv: Bust of Carl Thomas right.					
82	1767	—	7.00	15.00	25.00	40.00
	1768	—	7.00	15.00	25.00	40.00
	1769	—	15.00	35.00	50.00	90.00
	BILLON. Obv: Arms. Rev: Value and date.					
87	1765	—	5.00	10.00	15.00	25.00

Obv: Arms. Rev: Ceres.

C#	Date	Mintage	Fine	VF	XF	Unc
118	ND	—	3.00	7.00	14.00	40.00
	1790	—	3.00	7.00	14.00	40.00
118a	1798	—	3.00	7.00	14.00	40.00
	ND	—	3.00	7.00	14.00	40.00
	Obv: Prince's crown over arms.					
119	1798	—	3.00	7.00	14.00	40.00

2 KREUZER

BILLON
Obv: Arms. Rev: Value and date.

C#	Date	Mintage	VG	Fine	VF	XF
89	1767	—	16.00	35.00	50.00	75.00

2-1/2 KREUZER

BILLON

Obv: Bust of Carl Thomas right.
Rev: Value and date.

C#	Date	Mintage	VG	Fine	VF	XF
91	1769	—	7.00	15.00	25.00	40.00

3 KREUZER

BILLON
Obv: Crowned arms. Rev: Seated lion with 'C' shield.

C#	Date	Mintage	Fine	VF	XF	Unc
122	1790	—	5.00	10.00	15.00	45.00

5 KREUZER

BILLON
Obv: Head of Carl Thomas right.
Rev: Arms.

C#	Date	Mintage	VG	Fine	VF	XF
93	1767	—	7.00	15.00	25.00	40.00
	1769	—	7.00	15.00	25.00	40.00

10 KREUZER

SILVER
Obv: Head of Carl Thomas right.
Rev: Arms.

C#	Date	Mintage	Fine	VF	XF	Unc
96	1767	—	10.00	17.50	30.00	45.00

Obv: Arms. Rev: Value and date.

97	1767	—	7.50	15.00	25.00	45.00

20 KREUZER

SILVER
Obv: Head of Carl Thomas right.
Rev: Arms.

99	1762	—	70.00	95.00	125.00	150.00
	1763	—	15.00	22.50	30.00	50.00
	1764	—	15.00	22.50	30.00	50.00
	1765	—	15.00	22.50	30.00	50.00
	1766	—	15.00	22.50	30.00	50.00
	1767	—	15.00	22.50	30.00	50.00
	1768	—	15.00	22.50	30.00	50.00
	1769	—	15.00	22.50	30.00	50.00

Obv: Arms. Rev: Value and date.

100	1767	—	15.00	22.50	30.00	50.00

30 KREUZER

SILVER
Obv: Bust of Carl Thomas right.
Rev: Arms in diamond.

102	1767	—	50.00	85.00	125.00	175.00

1/2 THALER

SILVER
Obv: Head of Carl Thomas right.
Rev: Arms.

104	1768 WE	—	125.00	200.00	325.00	450.00

106	1769 WE	—	45.00	75.00	100.00	200.00

(Convention)

Obv: Head. Rev: Arms.

124	1789	—	60.00	100.00	150.00	300.00

THALER

SILVER
Obv: Armored bust of Carl Thomas right.
Rev: Crowned and supported arms; date below.

C#	Date	Mintage	Fine	VF	XF	Unc
108	1754	—	225.00	350.00	500.00	1000.

Obv: Older armored bust of Carl Thomas right.
Rev: Crowned and supported arms; date in legend.

110	1766	—	150.00	200.00	275.00	600.00

Obv: Larger bust of Carl Thomas right.

110a	1767 EW	—	150.00	200.00	275.00	600.00

110b	1767 WE	—	145.00	200.00	275.00	600.00
	1768 WE	—	145.00	200.00	275.00	600.00
	1769 WE	—	150.00	225.00	300.00	600.00
	1769 WE 1 tail on left lion					
		—	150.00	225.00	300.00	600.00
	1769 WE left lion looks up, not down					
		—	100.00	175.00	225.00	550.00
	1769 WE & omitted from obv. leg.					
		—	145.00	200.00	275.00	600.00

Obv: Head of Carl Thomas right.

111	1767 WE	—	200.00	250.00	350.00	700.00
	1769 WE	—	150.00	225.00	300.00	600.00
	1769 WE	—	125.00	175.00	250.00	500.00
	1769 WE	—	125.00	175.00	250.00	500.00

2 THALERS

(Thick)

SILVER
Obv: Armored bust of Carl Thomas right.
Rev: Crowned and supported arms; date below.

109	1754	—	950.00	1250.	2000.	4500.

TRADE COINS

DUCAT

3.5000 gm., .986 GOLD, .1109 oz AGW
Obv: Armored bust of Carl Thomas left.
Rev: Crowned and supported arms.

112	1754	—	950.00	1250.	1750.	2750.

Obv: Bust. Rev: Allegory.

126	1791	—	800.00	1650.	2000.	2750.

JOINT COINAGE

Virneburg & Rochefort

PFENNING

COPPER

Obv: L.W. with arms of Werthem below.
Rev: Value and date.

C#	Date	Mintage	VG	Fine	VF	XF
129	1765	—	3.00	7.50	12.50	20.00

Obv: L.W. over 3 shields of arms.
Rev: Value and date in branches.

130	1766	—	3.00	6.50	10.00	15.00

Obv: Arms on cartouche.

130a	1766	—	3.00	6.50	10.00	15.00

Rev: Value in cartouche.

130b	1769-81	—	3.00	6.50	9.50	15.00

Obv: 3-fold arms below L W.
Rev: Value over date in ornamental border.

132	1791	—	2.00	4.00	6.00	10.00

BILLON
Obv: Arms. Rev: Value over date.

136	1794	—	2.00	5.00	8.50	15.00
	1795	—	2.00	5.00	8.50	15.00

COPPER

C#	Date	Mintage	Fine	VF	XF	Unc
133	1802	—	2.50	5.00	10.00	35.00
	1804	—	2.50	5.00	10.00	35.00

Obv: Spade shield

133a	1804	—	2.50	5.00	10.00	35.00

Obv: (error) L.M. above shield.

133b	1804	—	3.50	7.00	12.00	35.00

Rev: Eagle over 3 roses. Rev: 1 PF value.

138	1798	—	2.50	5.00	10.00	35.00
	1799	—	2.50	5.00	10.00	35.00
	1800	—	2.50	5.00	10.00	35.00
	1801	—	2.50	5.00	10.00	35.00
	1802	—	2.50	5.00	10.00	35.00
	1803	—	2.50	5.00	10.00	35.00
	1804	—	2.50	5.00	10.00	35.00

2 PFENNING

COPPER

C#	Date	Mintage	VG	Fine	VF	XF
134	1766	—	2.00	5.00	7.50	15.00

Obv: Arms on cartouche. Rev: Value in cartouche.

134a	1776	—	2.00	5.00	8.50	15.00
	1777	—	2.00	5.00	8.50	15.00
	1778	—	2.00	5.00	8.50	15.00
	1779	—	2.00	5.00	8.50	15.00
	1780	—	2.00	5.00	8.50	15.00
	1781	—	2.00	5.00	8.50	15.00

KREUZER

BILLON
Obv: Arms. Rev: Value over date.

139	1776	—	2.00	4.00	6.50	15.00

C#	Date	Mintage	Fine	VF	XF	Unc
140	1800	—	3.50	7.25	15.00	40.00
	1801	—	3.50	7.25	15.00	40.00
	1802	—	3.50	7.25	15.00	40.00
	1803	—	3.50	7.25	15.00	40.00
	1804	—	3.50	7.25	15.00	40.00
	1805	—	3.50	7.25	15.00	40.00
	1806	—	3.50	7.25	15.00	40.00

NOTE: Varieties exist.

2-1/2 KREUZER
(Convention)

(= 3 Kreuzer Land Munze)

BILLON
Obv: 3-fold arms.
Rev: 3 line inscription above date.

C#	Date	Mintage	VG	Fine	VF	XF
141	1776	—	2.00	5.00	7.50	15.00

3 KREUZER

Obv: Arms. Rev: Value

C#	Date	Mintage	Fine	VF	XF	Unc
142	1800	—	8.00	17.00	25.00	45.00
	1801	—	8.00	17.00	25.00	45.00
	1802	—	8.00	17.00	25.00	45.00
	1803	—	8.00	17.00	25.00	45.00
	1804	—	8.00	17.00	25.00	45.00
	1805	—	8.00	17.00	25.00	45.00

5 KREUZER

BILLON
Obv: Arms. Rev: Value and date.

C#	Date	Mintage	VG	Fine	VF	XF
145	1767	—	4.50	10.00	15.00	25.00

LUBECK

Bishopric

The bishopric was established at Lubeck c. 1160. The first coins were struck c. 1190. The bishops became Protestant during the Reformation. Territories were absorbed into Oldenburg during the reign of the last bishop.

RULERS
Friedrich August, 1750-1785

THALER

SILVER

C#	Date	Mintage	VG	Fine	VF	XF
1	1775	1,000	150.00	375.00	500.00	1000.
	Obv: Bust left.					
2	1775	10 pcs.	375.00	850.00	1250.	2500.

5 THALERS

6.6500 gm., .900 GOLD, .1924 oz AGW

C#	Date	Mintage	VG	Fine	VF	XF
3	1776	—	500.00	1250.	1650.	2250.

Free City

Lubeck became a free city of the empire in 1188 and from c. 1190 into the 13th century an imperial mint existed in the town. It was granted the mint right in 1188, 1226 and 1340, but actually began its first civic coinage c 1350. Occupied by the French during the Napoleonic Wars, it was restored as a free city in 1813 and became part of the German Empire in 1871.

SCHILLING

BILLON
Obv: Crowned eagle. Rev: Value over date.

C#	Date	Mintage	VG	Fine	VF	XF
5	1789 HDF	.554	3.00	7.00	10.00	20.00

32 SCHILLINGE

18.3200 gm., .750 SILVER, .4418 oz ASW

C#	Date	Mintage	Fine	VF	XF	Unc
16	1796 HDF	—	35.00	50.00	85.00	160.00
	1797 HDF	—	35.00	50.00	85.00	160.00

1/2 THALER
(Specie)

SILVER, 14.4 gm.
Obv: Crowned eagle. Rev: St. John and lamb.

C#	Date	Mintage	VG	Fine	VF	XF
14	1776	—	25.00	50.00	70.00	110.00

EIN (1) THALER
(Specie)

SILVER, 18.8 gm.

C#	Date	Mintage	VG	Fine	VF	XF
19	1776 HDF	—	100.00	275.00	400.00	650.00

2 THALERS
(Specie)

SILVER, 37.6 gm.
Obv: Crowned eagle. Rev: St. John and lamb.

C#	Date	Mintage	VG	Fine	VF	XF
20	1776 HDF	—	—	—	Rare	—

TRADE COINS

DUCAT

3.5000 gm., .986 GOLD, .1109 oz AGW
Obv: Crowned eagle, leg: LEOPOLDVS II.
Rev: 4 line inscription and date in tablet.

C#	Date	Mintage	Fine	VF	XF	Unc
22	1790	—	850.00	1250.	1750.	2500.
	Similar to C#22. Obv: Eagle. Rev: MON AVR LVBECENS					
22a	1791	1,800	225.00	475.00	800.00	1355.
	1792	—	225.00	475.00	800.00	1355.
	Obv. leg. ends: AVG.					
23	1792	—	—	475.00	800.00	1350.
	Obv. leg. ends: AVGVST.					
23a	1792	—	225.00	475.00	800.00	1350.

C#	Date	Mintage	Fine	VF	XF	Unc
23b	1793 HDF	1,200	250.00	500.00	850.00	1400.
	1794 HDF	1,953	225.00	475.00	800.00	1325.
	1797 HDF	1,490	250.00	500.00	850.00	1400.

C#	Date	Mintage	Fine	VF	XF	Unc
24	1801 HDF	—	250.00	500.00	850.00	1400.

10 DUCATS

35.0000 gm., .986 GOLD, 1.1095 oz AGW
Obv: Crowned eagle. Rev: St. John and lamb.

C#	Date	Mintage	Fine	VF	XF	Unc
—	1776	—	—	—	Rare	—

MONETARY REFORM

2 MARK

11.1110 gm., .900 SILVER, .3215 oz ASW

Y#	Date	Mintage	VF	XF	Unc
85	1901A	.025	100.00	140.00	250.00
	1901A	—	—	Proof	375.00

Y#	Date	Mintage	VF	XF	Unc
85a	1904A	.025	50.00	90.00	150.00
	1905A	.025	50.00	90.00	150.00
	1906A	.025	50.00	90.00	150.00
	1907A	.025	50.00	75.00	150.00
	1911A	.025	50.00	75.00	150.00
	1912A	.025	50.00	75.00	150.00
	Common Type	—	—	Proof	300.00

3 MARK

16.6670 gm., .900 SILVER, .4823 oz ASW

Y#	Date	Mintage	VF	XF	Unc
86	1908A	.033	40.00	70.00	125.00
	1909A	.033	40.00	70.00	125.00
	1910A	.033	40.00	70.00	125.00
	1911A	.033	30.00	65.00	125.00
	1912A	.034	30.00	65.00	125.00
	1913A	.015	30.00	65.00	125.00
	1914A	.010	50.00	80.00	150.00
	Common Type	—	—	Proof	250.00

5 MARK

27.7770 gm., .900 SILVER, .8038 oz ASW

Y#	Date	Mintage	VF	XF	Unc
87	1904A	.010	200.00	300.00	500.00
	1907A	.010	180.00	300.00	500.00
	1908A	.010	165.00	275.00	500.00
	1913A	6,000	180.00	275.00	500.00
	Common Type	—	—	Proof	600.00

10 MARK

3.9820 gm., .900 GOLD, .1152 oz AGW

Y#	Date	Mintage	VF	XF	Unc
88	1901A	.010	400.00	500.00	600.00
	1904A	.010	400.00	500.00	600.00
	Common Type	—	—	Proof	1200.

Y#	Date	Mintage	VF	XF	Unc
88a	1905A	.010	500.00	625.00	825.00
	1906A	.010	500.00	625.00	825.00
	1909A	.010	500.00	625.00	825.00
	1910A	.010	500.00	625.00	825.00

NCLT ISSUES

PATTERNS

KM#	Date	Mintage	Identification	Mkt.Val.
1	ND	—	2 Marks, Silver, uniface	—

MAINZ

Archbishopric

Mainz, located on the Rhine 25 miles west of Frankfurt, became an archbishopric in 747. It was a residence and mint of Charlemagne, and the imperial mint established then functioned into the 11th century. The archbishops were recognized as presidents of the electoral college and arch-chancellors of the Empire by the Golden Bull of 1356. In 1797, Mainz was ceded to France and in 1801 the French annexed all of the territories on the left bank of the Rhine. The remaining lands were secularized in 1803 and portions were divided between Hesse-Darmstadt, Nassau and Prussia.

Mainz became a free city of the Empire in 1118 but lost the title in 1163 through an unsuccessful revolt against ecclesiastical authority. They obtained the mint right in 1420 but rarely availed itself of the privilege. Siege coins were struck in 1793 when the French garrison was beseiged by the Prussians.

RULERS

Emeric Joseph, 1763-1774
Friedrich Carl Joseph, 1774-1802

HELLER

COPPER
Obv: Arms in sprays.
Rev: Value and date.

C#	Date	Mintage	VG	Fine	VF	XF
35	1769	—	3.50	5.00	7.50	20.00

Obv: EJ monogram above wheel.

C#	Date	Mintage	VG	Fine	VF	XF
36	1769	—	3.50	5.00	7.50	20.00

PFENNIG

COPPER
Obv: Large wheel over sword and crozier, elector's cap above. Rev: Value, C.M.L.M. and date.

C#	Date	Mintage	VG	Fine	VF	XF
37	1766	—	3.50	5.00	7.50	20.00

C#	Date	Mintage	VG	Fine	VF	XF
38	1768	—	3.50	5.00	7.50	20.00
	1769	—	3.50	5.00	7.50	20.00
	1770	—	3.50	5.00	7.50	20.00

Obv: No legend.

C#	Date	Mintage	VG	Fine	VF	XF
38a	1769	—	3.50	5.00	7.50	20.00
	1770	—	3.50	5.00	7.50	20.00

Obv: Arms within cartouche, leg: EM.10.D.G.EL.M.E.W.

C#	Date	Mintage	VG	Fine	VF	XF
38b	1771	—	3.50	5.00	7.50	20.00

Obv: Crowned arms. Rev: Value over date.

C#	Date	Mintage	VG	Fine	VF	XF
75	1779	—	4.50	7.50	11.50	20.00
	1781	—	4.50	7.50	11.50	20.00

Obv: F C I K monogram.

C#	Date	Mintage	VG	Fine	VF	XF
76	1781	—	7.50	10.00	13.50	20.00

2 PFENNIGE

COPPER
Obv: Large wheel over sword and crozier, elector's cap above. Rev: Value, C.M.L.M. and date.

C#	Date	Mintage	VG	Fine	VF	XF
39	1766	—	3.50	5.00	7.50	20.00

Obv: Quartered arms with dragon supporters, elector's cap above. Rev: Value, SCHEIDE MUNZ and date.

C#	Date	Mintage	VG	Fine	VF	XF
40	1768	—	3.50	5.00	7.50	20.00

3 PFENNIG

COPPER
Obv: Quartered arms with dragon supporters, elector's cap above. Rev: Value, SCHEIDE MUNZ and date.

C#	Date	Mintage	VG	Fine	VF	XF
41	1768	—	5.00	7.50	12.50	20.00

4 PFENNIGE

COPPER
Obv: Large wheel and sword and crozier, elector's cap above. Rev: Value, C.M.L.M. and date.

C#	Date	Mintage	VG	Fine	VF	XF
42	1766	—	5.00	7.50	12.50	20.00

1/4 KREUTZER

COPPER
Obv: Bust right. Rev: Value over date.

C#	Date	Mintage	VG	Fine	VF	XF
77	1795	—	3.00	5.00	7.50	20.00

1/2 KREUTZER

COPPER
Obv: Bust right. Rev: Value over date.

C#	Date	Mintage	VG	Fine	VF	XF
78	1795	—	3.75	6.50	9.50	20.00
	1796	—	3.75	6.50	9.50	20.00

KREUZER

BILLON
Obv: Arms. Rev: Value and date.

C#	Date	Mintage	VG	Fine	VF	XF
46	1765	—	3.00	4.50	6.50	25.00

Obv: Bust right. Rev: Crowned arms in sprays on pedestal divides date.

C#	Date	Mintage	VG	Fine	VF	XF
80	1795	—	4.00	6.50	9.50	25.00

3 KREUZER

BILLON
Obv: Bust right. Rev: Crowned arms in sprays on pedestal divides date.

C#	Date	Mintage	VG	Fine	VF	XF
87	1796	—	5.00	7.50	12.50	25.00

5 KREUZER
(Convention)

SILVER
Obv: Arms supported by dragon.
Rev: EJC monogram on pedestal.

C#	Date	Mintage	Fine	VF	XF	Unc
50	1763	—	8.50	13.50	25.00	50.00

Obv: Arms on pedestal.
Rev: Value and date.

C#	Date	Mintage	Fine	VF	XF	Unc
52	1765	—	7.50	12.50	20.00	50.00

Obv: 2-fold arms.

C#	Date	Mintage	Fine	VF	XF	Unc
53	1767	—	8.50	13.50	25.00	50.00

Obv: Bust right. Rev: Crowned 3-fold arms.

C#	Date	Mintage	VG	Fine	VF	XF
91	1795	—	6.00	12.50	16.50	25.00

Obv: Arms. Rev: Inscription.

C#	Date	Mintage	VG	Fine	VF	XF
92	1795	—	6.00	12.50	16.50	25.00

10 KREUZER
(Convention)

SILVER
Obv: Bust of Emeric Joseph right.
Rev: Quartered arms and date.

C#	Date	Mintage	Fine	VF	XF	Unc
56	1764	—	8.50	13.50	25.00	50.00

Rev: 2-fold arms.

C#	Date	Mintage	Fine	VF	XF	Unc
56a	1765	—	8.50	13.50	25.00	50.00
	1766	—	8.50	13.50	25.00	50.00

Rev: 3-fold arms.

C#	Date	Mintage	Fine	VF	XF	Unc
56b	1773	—	7.50	12.50	20.00	50.00
	1774	—	7.50	12.50	20.00	50.00

Obv: Bust right. Rev: Arms.

C#	Date	Mintage	VG	Fine	VF	XF
94	1795	—	5.00	12.00	17.50	25.00

NOTE: Varieties exist.

20 KREUZER

SILVER
Obv: Bust of Emeric Joseph right.
Rev: Quartered arms and date.

C#	Date	Mintage	Fine	VF	XF	Unc
58	1765	—	12.50	20.00	35.00	55.00

Rev: 2-fold arms.

C#	Date	Mintage	Fine	VF	XF	Unc
58a	1766	—	15.00	22.50	40.00	65.00

Rev: 3-fold arms.

C#	Date	Mintage	Fine	VF	XF	Unc
58b	1768	—	10.00	15.00	22.50	50.00
	1772	—	10.00	15.00	22.50	50.00

30 KREUZER

SILVER
Obv: Bust of Emeric Joseph right.
Rev: Quartered arms and date.

C#	Date	Mintage	Fine	VF	XF	Unc
62	1765	—	17.50	30.00	50.00	75.00

Rev: 2 shields of arms.

C#	Date	Mintage	Fine	VF	XF	Unc
62a	1766	—	17.50	30.00	50.00	75.00

1/12 THALER

SILVER
Death of the Archbishop Commemorative
Obv: Arms.
Rev: 10 line inscription.

C#	Date	Mintage	Fine	VF	XF	Unc
54	1774	—	8.50	13.50	25.00	60.00

1/6 THALER

SILVER
Obv: Arms. Rev: 10 line inscription.

C#	Date	Mintage	Fine	VF	XF	Unc
60	1774	—	15.00	25.00	45.00	90.00

1/3 THALER

SILVER
Obv: Arms. Rev: 10 line inscription.

C#	Date	Mintage	Fine	VF	XF	Unc
63	1774	—	16.50	27.50	45.00	90.00

1/2 THALER
(Convention)

SILVER
Obv: Bust of Emeric Joseph right.
Rev: Arms.

C#	Date	Mintage	Fine	VF	XF	Unc
64	1765	—	75.00	100.00	135.00	250.00

Rev: 2-fold arms.

C#	Date	Mintage	Fine	VF	XF	Unc
65	1766	—	85.00	110.00	150.00	300.00

Rev: Arms with dragon supporters.

C#	Date	Mintage	Fine	VF	XF	Unc
65.5	1769	—	75.00	100.00	135.00	250.00

C#	Date	Mintage	Fine	VF	XF	Unc
97	1795	—	120.00	175.00	225.00	400.00

EIN (1) THALER
(Convention)

SILVER
Obv: Bust of Emeric Joseph right.
Rev: Arms with dragon supporters, date below.

C#	Date	Mintage	Fine	VF	XF	Unc
66	1764 EG	—	150.00	200.00	275.00	600.00
	1765 EG	—	150.00	200.00	275.00	600.00

Rev: 2-fold arms, no supporters, date to right.

C#	Date	Mintage	Fine	VF	XF	Unc
67	1766 FB	—	185.00	275.00	350.00	700.00
	1767 FB	—	185.00	275.00	350.00	700.00
	1768 FB	—	185.00	275.00	350.00	700.00

Rev: Arms with supporters, date at top.

C#	Date	Mintage	Fine	VF	XF	Unc
68	1768 DF	—	185.00	275.00	350.00	700.00
	1769 DF	—	185.00	275.00	350.00	700.00

Rev: Oval arms.

C#	Date	Mintage	Fine	VF	XF	Unc
69	1770 DF	—	100.00	125.00	165.00	300.00
	1771 DF	—	100.00	125.00	165.00	300.00

C#	Date	Mintage	Fine	VF	XF	Unc
99	1794 IA	—	200.00	375.00	500.00	900.00

C#	Date	Mintage	Fine	VF	XF	Unc
99a	1794 IL	—	250.00	450.00	650.00	1100.

(Contribution)

Rev: 4 line inscription over Roman numeral date in sprays; I. L. below.

C#	Date	Mintage	Fine	VF	XF	Unc
100	1794 IL	—	350.00	500.00	750.00	1400.

(Convention)

Obv: Capped arms.
Rev: Value, date and I. A. in sprays.

C#	Date	Mintage	Fine	VF	XF	Unc
101	1794 IA	—	350.00	500.00	750.00	1400.

C#	Date	Mintage	Fine	VF	XF	Unc
101a	1794 IA	—	225.00	325.00	500.00	900.00

Obv: Capped arms in pointed shield; I. L. below.
Rev: Value in smaller letters; date and I. A. in wreath; I. L. below.

C#	Date	Mintage	Fine	VF	XF	Unc
101b	1794 IA	—	200.00	300.00	450.00	800.00

C#	Date	Mintage	Fine	VF	XF	Unc
102	1795 IA	—	450.00	850.00	1250.	2000.

Rev: Capped arms in sprays; date and I. A. below.

C#	Date	Mintage	Fine	VF	XF	Unc
102a	1796 IA	—	400.00	750.00	1150.	2000.

Obv: Bust right; F.S. below.
Rev: Monument with I. A. below.

C#	Date	Mintage	Fine	VF	XF	Unc
102b	1796 IA	—	400.00	750.00	1150.	2000.

C#	Date	Mintage	Fine	VF	XF	Unc
103	1796 IA	—	250.00	450.00	600.00	1100.

TRADE COINS

DUCAT

3.5000 gm., .986 GOLD, .1109 oz AGW
Obv: Bust of Emeric Joseph right.
Rev: 3-fold arms.

C#	Date	Mintage	Fine	VF	XF	Unc
70	1768	—	750.00	1000.	1500.	2250.
	1769	—	750.00	1000.	1500.	2250.
	1771	—	750.00	1000.	1500.	2250.

Rev: 2-line inscription and date in Roman numerals (CDDCCLXXII).

C#	Date	Mintage	Fine	VF	XF	Unc
71	1772 RN	—	1500.	2000.	2750.	3750.

C#	Date	Mintage	Fine	VF	XF	Unc
104	1795	—	700.00	1000.	1500.	2500.

Rev: City view; Roman numeral date in exergue.

C#	Date	Mintage	Fine	VF	XF	Unc
105	1795	—	700.00	1000.	1500.	2500.

Contribution Ducat
Rev: Arms.

C#	Date	Mintage	Fine	VF	XF	Unc
106	1795	—	—	—	Rare	—

Siege Coinage

RULERS

General Doyre, French

SOL

COPPER

C#	Date	Mintage	VG	Fine	VF	XF
1	1793	—	6.00	15.00	27.50	40.00

2 SOLS

COPPER
Obv: Liberty cap above fasces within branches.
Rev: Value.

C#	Date	Mintage	VG	Fine	VF	XF
2	1793	—	10.00	25.00	35.00	50.00

5 SOLS

COPPER
Obv: Liberty cap above fasces within branches.
Rev: Value.

C#	Date	Mintage	VG	Fine	VF	XF
3	1793	—	8.00	20.00	30.00	45.00

MANSFELD

Mansfeld-Bornstadt

A small, silver mining state, located between Anhalt and Thuringia. Bracteats were struck c. 1200. The ruling family of Mansfeld was much divided during the 15th and 16th centuries and there were prolific coin issuers during this period. The county of Mansfeld was annexed to Electoral Saxony and then passed to Prussia in 1815.

RULERS

Heinrich, 1717-1780

1/2 THALER

SILVER
Obv: Crowned and mantled arms.
Rev: St. George and dragon, date in exergue.

C#	Date	Mintage	VG	Fine	VF	XF
5	1774	—	135.00	200.00	275.00	375.00

THALER

SILVER
Obv: Crowned and mantled arms.
Rev: St. George and dragon, date in exergue.

C#	Date	Mintage	VG	Fine	VF	XF
6	1774	—	150.00	275.00	400.00	600.00

TRADE COINS

DUCAT

3.5000 gm., .986 GOLD, .1109 oz AGW
Obv: Crowned and mantled arms.
Rev: St. George and dragon, date in exergue.

C#	Date	Mintage	VG	Fine	VF	XF
9	1774	—	375.00	600.00	850.00	1250.

MECKLENBURG — SCHWERIN

The duchy of Mecklenburg was located along the Baltic Coast between Holstein and Pomerania. Schwerin was annexed to Mecklenburg in 1357. In 1658 the Mecklenburg dynasty was divided into two lines. The 1815 Congress of Vienna elevated the duchy to the status of grand duchy and it became a part of the German Empire in 1871 until 1918 when the last grand duke abdicated.

RULERS

Friedrick II, 1756-1785
Friedrich Franz I, 1785-1837
Paul Friedrich, 1837-1842
Friedrich Franz II, 1842-1883
Friedrich Franz III, 1883-1897
Friedrich Franz IV, 1897-1918

PFENNIG

COPPER

C#	Date	Mintage	Fine	VF	XF	Unc
73	1831	.514	3.00	8.00	13.00	30.00

C#	Date	Mintage	Fine	VF	XF	Unc
102	1872	2.335	1.00	2.00	6.00	25.00

2 PFENNIG

COPPER

C#	Date	Mintage	Fine	VF	XF	Unc
74	1831	.257	2.00	4.00	8.00	30.00

C#	Date	Mintage	Fine	VF	XF	Unc
103	1872	1.155	1.00	2.00	5.00	25.00

3 PFENNIG

(= 1 Dreiling)

BILLON

Obv: Crowned F. Rev: Value over date.

C#	Date	Mintage	VG	Fine	VF	XF
28	1763	.245	3.00	6.50	9.50	20.00
	1764	.572	3.00	6.50	9.50	20.00
	1765	.166	3.00	6.50	9.50	20.00
	1766	.142	3.00	6.50	9.50	20.00
	1767	.163	3.00	6.50	9.50	20.00
	1775	.386	3.00	6.50	9.50	20.00
	1779	.110	3.00	6.50	9.50	20.00
	1780	.131	3.00	6.50	9.50	20.00
	1781	.126	3.00	6.50	9.50	20.00
	1782	.143	3.00	6.50	9.50	20.00
	1783	.113	3.00	6.50	9.50	20.00
	1784	.189	3.00	6.50	9.50	20.00

Obv: Crowned FF monogram. Rev: Value, leg: MECK: SCHW: MUNZE

C#	Date	Mintage	Fine	VF	XF	Unc
56	1787	.156	3.00	7.00	15.00	50.00
	1790	.103	3.00	7.00	15.00	50.00
	1791	.126	3.00	7.00	15.00	50.00
	1793	.078	3.00	7.00	15.00	50.00
	1797	.168	3.00	7.00	15.00	50.00

Rev. leg: MECK. SCHWERIN: SCHEID

C#	Date	Mintage	Fine	VF	XF	Unc
57	1801	.204	3.00	6.00	12.00	50.00
	1803	.117	3.00	6.00	12.00	50.00
	1804	.113	3.00	6.00	12.00	50.00
	1805	.414	3.00	6.00	12.00	50.00
	1810	.117	3.00	6.00	12.00	50.00
	1811	.273	3.00	6.00	12.00	50.00
	1814	.060	3.00	6.00	12.00	50.00
	1815	.081	3.00	6.00	12.00	50.00
75	1816	.199	3.00	6.00	12.00	50.00
	1817	.083	3.00	6.00	12.00	50.00
	1818	.077	3.00	6.00	12.00	50.00
	1819	.251	3.00	6.00	12.00	50.00

Rev. value: I DREILING, date.

C#	Date	Mintage	Fine	VF	XF	Unc
76	1819	.596	2.00	3.50	8.00	50.00
	1820	.845	2.00	3.50	8.00	50.00
	1821	.516	2.00	3.50	8.00	50.00
	1822	1.021	2.00	3.50	8.00	50.00
	1824	.235	2.00	3.50	8.00	50.00

C#	Date	Mintage	Fine	VF	XF	Unc
76.4	1828	.684	2.00	3.50	8.00	40.00
	1829	.207	2.00	3.50	8.00	50.00
	1830	.793	2.00	3.50	8.00	40.00

C#	Date	Mintage	Fine	VF	XF	Unc
76.7	1831	.064	2.00	3.50	8.00	50.00
	1832	.308	2.00	3.50	8.00	50.00
	1833	.048	2.00	3.50	8.00	50.00
	1836	.452	2.00	3.50	8.00	50.00

C#	Date	Mintage	Fine	VF	XF	Unc
94	1838	—	2.00	4.00	8.00	50.00
	1839	.172	2.00	4.00	8.00	50.00
	1840	.112	2.00	4.00	8.00	50.00
	1841	.100	2.00	4.00	8.00	50.00
	1842	.157	2.00	4.00	8.00	50.00

C#	Date	Mintage	Fine	VF	XF	Unc
105	1842	.203	2.00	4.00	8.00	50.00
	1843	.230	2.00	4.00	8.00	50.00
	1844	.125	2.00	4.00	8.00	50.00
	1845	.170	2.00	4.00	8.00	50.00
	1846	.077	2.00	4.00	8.00	50.00

COPPER

C#	Date	Mintage	Fine	VF	XF	Unc
101	1843	.089	2.00	4.00	8.00	40.00
	1845	.151	2.00	4.00	8.00	40.00
	1846	.073	2.00	4.00	8.00	40.00
	1848	—	2.00	4.00	8.00	40.00

C#	Date	Mintage	Fine	VF	XF	Unc
101a	1852A	—	1.00	3.00	7.00	40.00
	1853A	—	1.00	3.00	7.00	40.00
	1854A	—	1.00	3.00	7.00	40.00
	1855A	1.135	1.00	3.00	7.00	40.00
	1858A	—	1.00	3.00	7.00	40.00
	1859A	—	1.00	3.00	7.00	40.00
	1860A	—	1.00	3.00	7.00	40.00
	1861A	—	1.00	3.00	7.00	40.00
	1863A	—	1.00	3.00	7.00	40.00
	1864A	1.076	1.00	3.00	7.00	40.00

5 PFENNIG

COPPER

C#	Date	Mintage	Fine	VF	XF	Unc
104	1872	.459	1.00	3.00	7.00	25.00

6 PFENNIG

BILLON

Obv: Crowned F. Rev: Value over date.

C#	Date	Mintage	VG	Fine	VF	XF
31	1763	.231	3.00	6.00	9.00	25.00
	1764	.674	3.00	6.00	9.00	25.00
	1765	.549	3.00	6.00	9.00	25.00
	1766	.542	3.00	6.00	9.00	25.00
	1767	.294	3.00	6.00	9.00	25.00
	1769	.101	3.00	6.00	9.00	25.00
	1775	.252	3.00	6.00	9.00	25.00
	1778	.230	3.00	6.00	9.00	25.00
	1779	.143	3.00	6.00	9.00	25.00
	1780	.201	3.00	6.00	9.00	25.00
	1783	.154	3.00	6.00	9.00	25.00
	1784	.134	3.00	6.00	9.00	25.00
	1785	.150	3.00	6.00	9.00	25.00

Obv: Crowned FF monogram. Rev: Value.

C#	Date	Mintage	Fine	VF	XF	Unc
58	1786	.147	2.50	5.00	20.00	50.00
	1788	.201	2.50	5.00	20.00	50.00
	1790	.097	2.50	5.00	20.00	50.00
	1792	.058	2.50	5.00	20.00	50.00
	1793	.085	2.50	5.00	20.00	50.00
	1794	.096	2.50	5.00	20.00	50.00
59	1801	.080	2.50	5.00	20.00	50.00
	1802	.141	2.50	5.00	20.00	50.00
	1803	.060	2.50	5.00	20.00	50.00
	1804	.062	2.50	5.00	20.00	50.00
	1805	.321	2.50	5.00	20.00	50.00
	1809	.084	2.50	5.00	20.00	50.00
	1810	.081	2.50	5.00	20.00	50.00
	1811	.222	2.50	5.00	20.00	50.00
	1813	.254	2.50	5.00	20.00	50.00
	1815	.199	2.50	5.00	20.00	50.00
77	1816	.255	2.50	5.00	20.00	50.00
	1817	.300	2.50	5.00	20.00	50.00

No legends

C#	Date	Mintage	Fine	VF	XF	Unc
79	1831	.128	3.00	6.50	20.00	50.00

SECHSLING

BILLON

C#	Date	Mintage	Fine	VF	XF	Unc
78	1820	.150	2.50	5.00	15.00	45.00
	1821	.249	2.50	5.00	15.00	45.00
	1822	.272	2.50	5.00	15.00	45.00
	1823	.320	2.50	5.00	15.00	45.00
	1824	.419	2.50	5.00	15.00	45.00

C#	Date	Mintage	Fine	VF	XF	Unc
78.4	1828	—	3.00	6.00	15.00	45.00
	1829	.190	3.00	6.00	15.00	45.00

SCHILLING

1.0800 gm., .375 SILVER, .0130 oz ASW

Obv: Crowned F. Rev: Value over date.

C#	Date	Mintage	VG	Fine	VF	XF
35	1763	.890	3.00	6.00	9.00	25.00
	1764	.977	3.00	6.00	9.00	25.00
	1765	1.308	3.00	6.00	9.00	25.00
	1766	2.041	3.00	6.00	9.00	25.00
	1767	2.897	3.00	6.00	9.00	25.00
	1768	1.601	3.00	6.00	9.00	25.00
	1769	1.521	3.00	6.00	9.00	25.00
	1770	1.811	3.00	6.00	9.00	25.00
	1771	2.150	3.00	6.00	9.00	25.00
	1772	2.354	3.00	6.00	9.00	25.00
	1773	1.562	3.00	6.00	9.00	25.00
	1774	2.437	3.00	6.00	9.00	25.00
	1775	2.126	3.00	6.00	9.00	25.00
	1778	.759	3.00	6.00	9.00	25.00
	1779	.642	3.00	6.00	9.00	25.00
	1780	.286	3.00	6.00	9.00	25.00
	1781	.526	3.00	6.00	9.00	25.00
	1782	.350	3.00	6.00	9.00	25.00
	1783	.283	3.00	6.00	9.00	25.00
	1784	.379	3.00	6.00	9.00	25.00
	1785	.167	3.00	6.00	9.00	25.00

C#	Date	Mintage	Fine	VF	XF	Unc
61	1785	.074	2.50	5.00	15.00	45.00
	1786	.237	2.50	5.00	15.00	45.00
	1787	.169	2.50	5.00	15.00	45.00
	1788	.167	2.50	5.00	15.00	45.00
	1789	.362	2.50	5.00	15.00	45.00
	1790	1.207	2.50	5.00	15.00	45.00
	1791	.260	2.50	5.00	15.00	45.00
	1792	.821	2.50	5.00	15.00	45.00
	1793	.460	2.50	5.00	15.00	45.00
	1794	1.195	2.50	5.00	15.00	45.00
	1795	1.093	2.50	5.00	15.00	45.00
	1796	.142	2.50	5.00	15.00	45.00
	1797	1.065	2.50	5.00	15.00	45.00
	1798	2.020	2.50	5.00	15.00	45.00
	1799	2.438	2.50	5.00	15.00	45.00
	1800	1.546	2.50	5.00	15.00	45.00
	1801	1.301	2.50	5.00	15.00	45.00
	1802	2.431	2.50	5.00	15.00	45.00
	1803	2.348	2.50	5.00	15.00	45.00
	1804	2.603	2.50	5.00	15.00	45.00
	1805	2.501	2.50	5.00	15.00	45.00
	1806	1.766	2.50	5.00	15.00	45.00
	1807	.585	2.50	5.00	15.00	45.00
	1808	.243	2.50	5.00	15.00	45.00
	1809	.342	2.50	5.00	15.00	45.00
	1810	.250	2.50	5.00	15.00	45.00
80	1817	.031	10.00	20.00	30.00	60.00

1.1100 gm., .312 SILVER, .0111 oz ASW

Obv. leg: GR. HZ. U.M.S.

C#	Date	Mintage	Fine	VF	XF	Unc
81	1826	.159	4.00	8.00	12.00	45.00
	1827	.342	4.00	8.00	12.00	45.00

Obv. leg: GR. HERZOG V. Rev: Value, legend.

C#	Date	Mintage	Fine	VF	XF	Unc
81.4	1829	.054	2.50	5.00	10.00	45.00

C#	Date	Mintage	Fine	VF	XF	Unc
81.4	1830	.501	2.50	5.00	10.00	45.00
	1831	.528	2.50	5.00	10.00	45.00
	1832	.119	2.50	5.00	10.00	45.00
	1833	.091	2.50	5.00	10.00	45.00
	1834	.118	2.50	5.00	10.00	45.00
	1835	.109	2.50	5.00	10.00	45.00
	1836	.163	2.50	5.00	10.00	45.00
	1837	.082	2.50	5.00	10.00	45.00

Obv: Crowned PF monogram

C#	Date	Mintage	Fine	VF	XF	Unc
95	1838	.021	2.50	5.00	10.00	45.00
	1839	.125	2.50	5.00	10.00	45.00
	1840	.052	2.50	5.00	10.00	45.00
	1841	.046	2.50	5.00	10.00	45.00
	1842	.030	2.50	5.00	10.00	45.00

2 SCHILLINGE

1.9700 gm., .437 SILVER, .0277 oz ASW
Obv: Crowned F. Rev: Value over date.

C#	Date	Mintage	VG	Fine	VF	XF
41	1763	.546	5.00	8.50	12.50	25.00
	1764	1.072	5.00	8.50	12.50	25.00
	1765	1.820	5.00	8.50	12.50	25.00
	1766	.695	5.00	8.50	12.50	25.00
	1767	.505	5.00	8.50	12.50	25.00
	1768	.400	5.00	8.50	12.50	25.00
	1769	.195	5.00	8.50	12.50	25.00
	1777	.060	5.00	8.50	12.50	25.00
	1778	.049	5.00	8.50	12.50	25.00

GOLD

C#	Date	Mintage	VG	Fine	VF	XF
41a	1766	—	—	—	Rare	—

1.9700 gm., .437 SILVER, .0277 oz ASW
Obv: Crowned FF monogram on baroque shield.
Rev: Value.

C#	Date	Mintage	Fine	VF	XF	Unc
62	1786	.018	15.00	30.00	50.00	75.00

4 SCHILLINGE

3.0600 gm., .562 SILVER, 1.7197 oz ASW
Obv: Crowned shield with F within.
Rev: Value over date.

C#	Date	Mintage	VG	Fine	VF	XF
43	1763	.169	3.00	6.50	10.00	25.00
	1764	.275	3.00	6.50	10.00	25.00
	1765	.036	3.00	6.50	10.00	25.00
	1766	.115	3.00	6.50	10.00	25.00
	1774	.034	3.00	6.50	10.00	25.00
	1782	.020	3.00	6.50	10.00	25.00
	1783	.029	3.00	6.50	10.00	25.00

.563 SILVER
Obv: Crowned FF monogram on cartouche. Rev: Value.

C#	Date	Mintage	Fine	VF	XF	Unc
63	1785	.012	16.00	35.00	55.00	90.00
	1809	1,408	30.00	60.00	90.00	150.00

3.3000 gm., .437 SILVER, .0464 oz ASW
Obv: Crowned FF monogram.

C#	Date	Mintage	Fine	VF	XF	Unc
82	1826	.621	5.00	10.00	18.00	45.00

3.0600 gm., .500 SILVER, .0492 oz ASW
Obv: Head left, leg: GR. HERZOG....

C#	Date	Mintage	Fine	VF	XF	Unc
83	1828	.070	7.50	15.00	25.00	45.00

Obv. leg: GROSSHERZOG....

C#	Date	Mintage	Fine	VF	XF	Unc
83a	1829	.200	4.00	8.00	20.00	45.00
	1830	1.793	4.00	8.00	20.00	45.00
	1831	.476	4.00	8.00	20.00	45.00
	1832	.121	4.00	8.00	20.00	45.00
	1833	.049	4.00	8.00	15.00	45.00

Obv: Crowned arms within two crossed branches.

C#	Date	Mintage	Fine	VF	XF	Unc
96	1838	.015	5.00	10.00	17.00	45.00
	1839	.039	5.00	10.00	17.00	45.00

8 SCHILLINGE

6.6000 gm., .437 SILVER, .0927 oz ASW

C#	Date	Mintage	Fine	VF	XF	Unc
84	1827	.025	10.00	20.00	35.00	60.00

12 SCHILLINGE

8.8000 gm., .562 SILVER, .1590 oz ASW
Obv: Crowned arms in order collar, date below.
Rev: Value.

C#	Date	Mintage	VG	Fine	VF	XF
47	1774	.074	6.00	12.50	20.00	35.00
	1775	.099	6.00	12.50	20.00	35.00
	1776	.026	6.00	12.50	20.00	35.00
	1777	.032	6.00	12.50	20.00	35.00

Obv: Crowned arms.

C#	Date	Mintage	Fine	VF	XF	Unc
66	1791	.019	16.00	35.00	65.00	110.00
	1792	Inc. Ab.	16.00	35.00	65.00	110.00

32 SCHILLINGE

18.3400 gm., .750 SILVER, .4423 oz ASW
Obv: Crowned arms. Rev: Value.

C#	Date	Mintage	Fine	VF	XF	Unc
69	1797	.059	14.00	25.00	45.00	75.00

1/48 THALER

BILLON

C#	Date	Mintage	VG	Fine	VF	XF
106	1842	.108	2.00	4.00	20.00	45.00
	1843	.139	2.00	4.00	20.00	45.00
	1844	.116	2.00	4.00	20.00	45.00
	1845	.246	2.00	4.00	20.00	45.00
	1846	.154	2.00	4.00	20.00	45.00

C#	Date	Mintage	VG	Fine	VF	XF
107	1848	—	2.50	5.00	20.00	45.00

C#	Date	Mintage	VG	Fine	VF	XF
107a	1852A	—	1.50	3.00	10.00	40.00
	1853A	—	1.50	3.00	10.00	40.00
	1855A	2.819	1.50	3.00	10.00	40.00
	1858A	—	1.50	3.00	10.00	40.00
	1860A	—	1.50	3.00	10.00	40.00
	1851A	—	1.50	3.00	10.00	40.00
	1862A	—	1.50	3.00	10.00	40.00
	1863A	—	1.50	3.00	10.00	40.00
	1864A	—	1.50	3.00	10.00	40.00
	1866A	2.034	1.50	3.00	10.00	40.00

1/12 THALER

2.4400 gm., .500 SILVER, .0392 oz ASW
Head right.

C#	Date	Mintage	VG	Fine	VF	XF
108	1848	2.047	4.00	8.00	15.00	40.00

1/6 THALER

5.3500 gm., .521 SILVER, .0896 oz ASW

C#	Date	Mintage	VG	Fine	VF	XF
109	1848A	.137	6.00	12.00	20.00	40.00

1/3 THALER

8.6600 gm., .750 SILVER, .2088 oz ASW
Obv: Arms. Rev: Value.

C#	Date	Mintage	VG	Fine	VF	XF
68	1790	.021	15.00	30.00	45.00	80.00

2/3 THALER

17.3200 gm., .750 SILVER, .4177 oz ASW

C#	Date	Mintage	Fine	VF	XF	Unc
70	1789	.089	14.00	25.00	45.00	90.00
	1790	.158	14.00	25.00	45.00	90.00
	1791	.014	14.00	25.00	45.00	90.00
	1795	.132	14.00	25.00	45.00	90.00
	1796	.552	14.00	25.00	45.00	90.00
	1797	.060	14.00	25.00	45.00	90.00
	1800	.162	14.00	25.00	45.00	90.00
	1801	.169	14.00	25.00	45.00	90.00
	1808	.655	14.00	25.00	45.00	90.00
	1810	.338	14.00	25.00	45.00	90.00

C#	Date	Mintage	Fine	VF	XF	Unc
71	1813	9,918	50.00	100.00	150.00	300.00

Obv. leg: G.G. HERZOG. Rev: Date below value.

C#	Date	Mintage	Fine	VF	XF	Unc
85	1817	6,783	75.00	150.00	250.00	400.00

Obv: leg: G.G. GR. HERZ.

C#	Date	Mintage	Fine	VF	XF	Unc
85a	1825	.035	32.00	65.00	90.00	180.00

Obv. leg: SCHW.

C#	Date	Mintage	Fine	VF	XF	Unc
86	1825	.043	15.00	32.50	45.00	90.00

Obv. leg: SCHWERIN

C#	Date	Mintage	Fine	VF	XF	Unc
86a	1826	.103	15.00	32.50	45.00	90.00

Obv: Head left. Rev: Crowned draped arms.

C#	Date	Mintage	Fine	VF	XF	Unc
87	1828	.057	16.00	35.00	50.00	100.00
87a	1829	—	—	—	Rare	—

13.1700 gm., .986 SILVER, .4175 oz ASW

C#	Date	Mintage	Fine	VF	XF	Unc
97	1839	.291	15.00	30.00	50.00	100.00
	1840	.856	15.00	30.00	50.00	100.00
	1841	.118	15.00	30.00	50.00	100.00

Obv: Different head. Rev: Larger arms.

C#	Date	Mintage	Fine	VF	XF	Unc
110	1845	1,563	112.00	225.00	325.00	500.00

EIN (1) THALER

22.2700 gm., .750 SILVER, .5370 oz ASW

C#	Date	Mintage	Fine	VF	XF	Unc
111	1848A	.528	25.00	70.00	150.00	300.00

18.5200 gm., .900 SILVER, .5360 oz ASW

C#	Date	Mintage	Fine	VF	XF	Unc
112	1864A	.100	22.00	50.00	125.00	250.00

25th Anniversary of Reign

C#	Date	Mintage	Fine	VF	XF	Unc
113	1867A	.010	35.00	90.00	200.00	400.00

ZWEI (2) THALER

3.1200 gm., .875 GOLD, .0878 oz AGW

C#	Date	Mintage	Fine	VF	XF	Unc
55	1769	1,144	750.00	1250.	1650.	2500.
	1778	2,417	750.00	1250.	1650.	2500.
	1782	1,625	750.00	1250.	1650.	2500.
	1783	441 pcs.	1000.	1750.	2500.	4000.

SILVER

C#	Date	Mintage	Fine	VF	XF	Unc
55a	1769	—	—	—	—	—

3.1200 gm., .875 GOLD, .0878 oz AGW

C#	Date	Mintage	Fine	VF	XF	Unc
72	1792	1,638	400.00	800.00	1200.	1750.

C#	Date	Mintage	Fine	VF	XF	Unc
72a	1797	.012	230.00	460.00	700.00	950.00

Obv: Head left. Rev: Crowned arms within collar.

C#	Date	Mintage	Fine	VF	XF	Unc
89	1830	—	750.00	1500.	2000.	3000.

ZWEI EIN HALB (2-1/2) THALER

3.3300 gm., .896 GOLD, .0959 oz AGW

C#	Date	Mintage	Fine	VF	XF	Unc
90	1831	7,755	250.00	500.00	700.00	1100.
	1833	124 pcs.	500.00	1000.	1500.	2000.
	1835	195 pcs.	500.00	1000.	1500.	2000.

C#	Date	Mintage	Fine	VF	XF	Unc
98	1840	2,910	275.00	550.00	750.00	1100.

FUNF (5) THALER

6.6600 gm., .896 GOLD, .1919 oz AGW

C#	Date	Mintage	Fine	VF	XF	Unc
92	1828	1,753	500.00	1000.	1250.	2000.
	1831	3,878	500.00	1000.	1250.	2000.
	1832	3,334	500.00	1000.	1250.	2000.
	1833	125 pcs.	750.00	1500.	2000.	2500.
	1835	100 pcs.	750.00	1500.	2000.	2500.

Obv: Head right.

C#	Date	Mintage	Fine	VF	XF	Unc
99	1840	1,454	625.00	1250.	1875.	2500.

ZEHN (10) THALER

13.3200 gm., .896 GOLD, .3837 oz AGW

C#	Date	Mintage	Fine	VF	XF	Unc
93	1828	876 pcs.	750.00	1500.	2000.	2500.
	1831	1,938	625.00	1250.	1625.	2300.
	1832	1,667	625.00	1250.	1625.	2300.
	1833	128 pcs.	1000.	2000.	2800.	4000.

C#	Date	Mintage	Fine	VF	XF	Unc
100	1839	.092	550.00	1100.	1500.	2000.

TRADE COINS

DUCAT

3.5000 gm., .986 GOLD, .1109 oz AGW
Obv: Head left. Rev: Crowned arms within collar between bull and griffin.

Y#	Date	Mintage	Fine	VF	XF	Unc
88	1830	—	1000.	2000.	3000.	5000.

MONETARY REFORM

2 MARK

11.1110 gm., .900 SILVER, .3215 OZ ASW

Y#	Date	Mintage	VF	XF	Unc
89	1876A	.300	150.00	450.00	750.00
	1876A	—	—	Proof	1500.

Y#	Date	Mintage	VF	XF	Unc
93	1901A	.050	165.00	300.00	450.00
	1901A	1,000	—	Proof	550.00

Friedrich Franz IV Wedding Commemorative

Y#	Date	Mintage	VF	XF	Unc
96	1904A	.100	30.00	50.00	100.00
	1904A	6,000	—	Proof	250.00

3 MARK

16.6670 gm., .900 SILVER, .4823 oz ASW
100 Years As Grand Duchy

Y#	Date	Mintage	VF	XF	Unc
98	1915A	.033	75.00	125.00	200.00
	1915A	—	—	Proof	400.00

5 MARK

27.7770 gm., .900 SILVER, .8038 oz ASW
Friedrich Franz IV Wedding Commemorative

Y#	Date	Mintage	VF	XF	Unc
97	1904A	.040	75.00	125.00	250.00
	1904A	2,500	—	Proof	500.00

100 Years as Grand Duchy

Y#	Date	Mintage	VF	XF	Unc
99	1915A	.010	225.00	375.00	700.00
	1915A	—	—	Proof	1000.

10 MARK

3.9820 gm., .900 GOLD, .1152 oz AGW
Obv: Head right. Rev: Type 1 eagle.

Y#	Date	Mintage	VF	XF	Unc
90	1872A	.016	850.00	1100.	1400.

Rev: Type 2 eagle

Y#	Date	Mintage	VF	XF	Unc
90a	1878A	.050	600.00	725.00	900.00

Y#	Date	Mintage	VF	XF	Unc
92	1890A	.100	250.00	400.00	550.00

Rev: Type 3 eagle

Y#	Date	Mintage	VF	XF	Unc
94	1901A	.010	900.00	1100.	1325.
	1901A	200 pcs.	—	Proof	—

20 MARK

7.9650 gm., .900 GOLD, .2304 oz AGW
Rev: Type 1 eagle

Y#	Date	Mintage	VF	XF	Unc
91	1872A	.069	550.00	725.00	900.00

Rev: Type 3 eagle

Y#	Date	Mintage	VF	XF	Unc
95	1901A	5,000	1150.	1650.	2300.
	1901A	200 pcs.	—	Proof	—

NCLT ISSUES

PATTERNS

KM#	Date	Mintage	Identification	Mkt.Val.
1	1828	5-6 pcs.	5 Thaler, Gold, C91	6000.

MECKLENBURG — STRELITZ

The duchy of Mecklenburg was located along the Baltic Coast between Holstein and Pomerania. The Strelitz line was founded in 1658 when the Mecklenburg line was divided into two lines. The 1815 Congress of Vienna elevated the duchy to the status of grand duchy. It became a part of the German Empire in 1871 until 1918 when the last grand duke died.

RULERS

Adolf Friedrich, 1752-1794
Karl II, 1794-1816
Georg, 1816-1860
Friedrich Wilhelm, 1860-1904
Adolph Friedrich V, 1904-1914

PFENNIG

COPPER
Obv: Crowned G. Rev: Value.

C#	Date	Mintage	Fine	VF	XF	Unc
40	1838	.058	2.50	5.25	10.00	35.00

C#	Date	Mintage	Fine	VF	XF	Unc
46	1872	.118	1.50	3.00	6.00	30.00

1-1/2 PFENNIG

COPPER

C#	Date	Mintage	Fine	VF	XF	Unc
41	1838	.040	3.00	6.50	15.00	40.00

2 PFENNIG

COPPER

C#	Date	Mintage	Fine	VF	XF	Unc
47	1872	.203	1.50	3.00	6.00	30.00

3 PFENNIG

COPPER
Obv: Crowned AF monogram; date below.
Rev: Value; I.H.L. below.

C#	Date	Mintage	VG	Fine	VF	XF
3	1764 IHL	—	3.00	5.00	10.00	20.00
	1766 IHL	—	3.00	5.00	10.00	20.00
	1785 IHL	—	3.00	5.00	10.00	20.00
	1793 IHL	—	3.00	5.00	10.00	20.00

SILVER

C#	Date	Mintage	VG	Fine	VF	XF
3b	1793 IHL	—	—	—	—	—

COPPER
Rev: Value; S.M. (Scheide Munze) below.

C#	Date	Mintage	VG	Fine	VF	XF
3a	1793	—	5.00	8.50	12.50	25.00

C#	Date	Mintage	Fine	VF	XF	Unc
42	1832	.290	2.00	4.00	8.00	35.00
	1843	.283	2.00	4.00	8.00	35.00
	1845	.193	2.00	4.00	8.00	35.00
	1847	—	2.00	4.00	8.00	35.00

C#	Date	Mintage	Fine	VF	XF	Unc
42a	1855A	1.501	2.00	4.00	8.00	35.00
	1859A	.580	2.00	4.00	8.00	35.00

C#	Date	Mintage	Fine	VF	XF	Unc
45	1862A	Inc. Ab.	2.00	4.00	8.00	35.00
	1864A	Inc. Ab.	2.00	4.00	8.00	35.00

5 PFENNIG

COPPER

C#	Date	Mintage	Fine	VF	XF	Unc
48	1872	.118	3.00	6.00	12.00	35.00

SECHSLING

BILLON
Obv: Crowned AF monogram; date below.
Rev: Value; I.H.L. below.

C#	Date	Mintage	VG	Fine	VF	XF
5	1764 IHL	—	3.00	6.00	11.50	22.50
	1766 IHL	—	3.00	6.00	11.50	22.50

1/48 THALER

BILLON
Obv: Crowned AF monogram; date below.
Rev: Value; I.H.L. below.

C#	Date	Mintage	VG	Fine	VF	XF
9	1764 IHL	—	3.00	6.00	11.50	22.50
	1766 IHL	—	3.00	6.00	11.50	22.50

C#	Date	Mintage	Fine	VF	XF	Unc
43	1838	.145	2.50	5.00	12.00	40.00
	1841	.055	2.50	5.00	12.00	40.00
	1845	.097	2.50	5.00	12.00	40.00
	1847	.231	2.50	5.00	12.00	40.00

C#	Date	Mintage	Fine	VF	XF	Unc
43a	1855A	.634	2.00	4.00	9.00	35.00
	1859A	.720	2.00	4.00	9.00	35.00

C#	Date	Mintage	Fine	VF	XF	Unc
49	1862A	Inc. Ab.	2.00	4.00	9.00	35.00
	1864A	Inc. Ab.	2.00	4.00	9.00	35.00

1/24 THALER

1.6700 gm., .437 SILVER, .0235 oz ASW
Obv: Crowned AF monogram; date below.
Rev: Value; I.H.L. below.

C#	Date	Mintage	VG	Fine	VF	XF
14	1766 IHL	—	6.00	12.50	20.00	35.00

1/12 THALER

3.3400 gm., .437 SILVER, .0469 oz ASW
Obv: Crowned arms; leg. ends: MEG.
Rev: Value; I.H.L. below.

C#	Date	Mintage	VG	Fine	VF	XF
19	1764	—	7.00	15.00	25.00	45.00

Obv. leg. ends: MECKL.

C#	Date	Mintage	VG	Fine	VF	XF
19a	1766	—	7.00	15.00	25.00	45.00
	1768	—	7.00	15.00	25.00	45.00
	1773	—	7.00	15.00	25.00	45.00

4 SCHILLINGE

3.2500 gm., .375 SILVER, .0392 oz ASW

C#	Date	Mintage	Fine	VF	XF	Unc
44	1846	.165	5.00	10.00	25.00	50.00
	1847	.170	5.00	10.00	25.00	50.00
	1849	.135	5.00	10.00	25.00	50.00

1/6 THALER

5.8500 gm., .500 SILVER, .0940 oz ASW
Obv: Head of Adolf Friedrich right; leg. ends: MEGAR. Rev: Crowned arms; value below.

C#	Date	Mintage	VG	Fine	VF	XF
23	1764	—	9.00	20.00	35.00	60.00
	1768	—	9.00	20.00	35.00	60.00

COPPER

C#	Date	Mintage	VG	Fine	VF	XF
23a	1768	—	—	—	—	—

SILVER
Obv. leg. ends: MECKLEN.

C#	Date	Mintage	VG	Fine	VF	XF
25	1773	—	12.00	25.00	42.50	65.00

1/3 THALER

9.3500 gm., .625 SILVER, .1879 oz ASW
Obv: Armored bust of Adolf Friedrich right.
Rev: Crowned arms in Order of the Garter.

C#	Date	Mintage	VG	Fine	VF	XF
33	1773	—	20.00	45.00	65.00	100.00

EIN (1) THALER

18.5200 gm., .900 SILVER, .5360 oz ASW

C#	Date	Mintage	Fine	VF	XF	Unc
50	1870A	.050	20.00	50.00	125.00	250.00

MONETARY REFORM

2 MARK

11.1110 gm., .900 SILVER, .3215 oz ASW

Y#	Date	Mintage	VF	XF	Unc
100	1877A	.100	250.00	900.00	2000.
	1877A	—	—	Proof	1200.

Y#	Date	Mintage	VF	XF	Unc
103	1905A	.010	200.00	325.00	400.00
	1905A	2,500	—	Proof	600.00

3 MARK

16.6670 gm., .900 SILVER, .4823 oz ASW

Y#	Date	Mintage	VF	XF	Unc
106	1913A	7,000	325.00	500.00	725.00
	1913A	—	—	Proof	800.00

10 MARK

3.9820 gm., .900 GOLD, .1152 oz AGW
Rev: Type 1 eagle.

Y#	Date	Mintage	VF	XF	Unc
101	1873A	1,500	4600.	5600.	6600.
	1873A	—	—	Proof	8000.

Y#	Date	Mintage	VF	XF	Unc
101a	1874A	3,000	3100.	4000.	4800.
	1880A	4,000	3100.	4000.	4800.

Y#	Date	Mintage	VF	XF	Unc
104	1905A	1,000	2125.	4300.	5750.
	1905A	150 pcs.	—	Proof	6250.

20 MARK

7.9650 gm., .900 GOLD, .2304 oz AGW

Y#	Date	Mintage	VF	XF	Unc
102	1873A	6,750	3000.	4250.	5500.

Rev: Type 2 eagle

Y#	Date	Mintage	VF	XF	Unc
102a	1874A	6,000	3000.	4250.	5500.

Rev: Type 3 eagle

Y#	Date	Mintage	VF	XF	Unc
105	1905A	1,000	3600.	5300.	6600.
	1905A	160 pcs.	—	Proof	8150.

MUHLHAUSEN

A free city located in Thuringia. During the 12th and 13th centuries it was the site of an imperial mint. In the 16th, 17th and 18th centuries the town had its own local coinage. It was annexed to Prussia in 1802, then passed to Westphalia in 1807 and reverted back to Prussia in 1815.

RULERS

Joseph II, 1765-1790

2 PFENNINGE

COPPER
Obv: 3 line inscription, date below.
Rev: Value.

C#	Date	Mintage	VG	Fine	VF	XF
1a	1767	—	6.00	12.50	20.00	35.00

3 PFENNINGE

BILLON
Obv: Helmed arms.
Rev: Orb divides date, value in orb.

C#	Date	Mintage	VG	Fine	VF	XF
2a	1767	—	15.00	32.50	50.00	65.00

6 PFENNINGE

BILLON
Obv: Helmed arms.
Rev: Orb dividing date, value in orb.

C#	Date	Mintage	VG	Fine	VF	XF
3a	1767	—	15.00	32.50	50.00	65.00

1/24 THALER

BILLON
Obv: Helmed arms.
Rev: Value and date.

C#	Date	Mintage	VG	Fine	VF	XF
4	1767	—	7.00	15.00	25.00	40.00

1/12 THALER

SILVER
Obv: Helmed arms. Rev: Value and date.

C#	Date	Mintage	VG	Fine	VF	XF
5	1767	—	7.00	15.00	25.00	40.00

2/3 THALER

SILVER
Obv: Helmed arms.
Rev: Value, date above.

C#	Date	Mintage	VG	Fine	VF	XF
6a	1767	—	50.00	100.00	200.00	300.00

THALER

SILVER
Obv: Laureated bust of Joseph II.
Rev: Helmed arms.

C#	Date	Mintage	VG	Fine	VF	XF
7	1767	—	500.00	1000.	1500.	2250.

MUNSTER (Bishopric)

Bishopric

A bishopric, located in Westphalia, was established c. 802. The first Munster coinage was struck c. 1228. In 1802 the bishopric was secularized and divided. From 1806-1810 most of Munster belonged to Berg, from 1810-1814 to France and from 1814 onward, to Prussia.

During the 16th and 17th centuries treasury tokens, mostly counterstamped with the arms or initials of the current treasurer were issued. These were replaced in the middle of the 17th century by Cathedral coins, showing St. Paul with a sword. They last appeared at the end of the 18th century.

RULERS

Maximilian Friedrich, Graf von Konigsegg-Rothenees, 1762-1784
Sede Vacante, 1801

SCHILLING

(= 1/28 Thaler)

BILLON
Obv: MF monogram.
Rev: St. Paul, value and date.

C#	Date	Mintage	VG	Fine	VF	XF
28	1764	—	4.50	10.00	17.50	30.00

24 MARIENGROSCHEN

SILVER
Obv: Arms. Rev: Value and date.

C#	Date	Mintage	VG	Fine	VF	XF
36	1763	—	40.00	75.00	110.00	165.00

1/48 THALER

BILLON
Obv: MF monogram.
Rev: Value and date.

C#	Date	Mintage	VG	Fine	VF	XF
26	1766	—	4.00	8.50	12.50	25.00

1/24 THALER

(Reichs)

BILLON
Obv: Value. Rev: Date.

C#	Date	Mintage	Fine	VF	XF	Unc
40	1801	—	10.00	20.00	35.00	55.00

1/12 THALER

BILLON
Obv: MF monogram.
Rev: Value and date.

C#	Date	Mintage	VG	Fine	VF	XF
30	1763	—	6.00	12.50	20.00	35.00
	1764	—	6.00	12.50	20.00	35.00
	1765	—	6.00	12.50	20.00	35.00
	1766	—	6.00	12.50	20.00	35.00
	1767	—	6.00	12.50	20.00	35.00
	1768	—	6.00	12.50	20.00	35.00
	1769	—	6.00	12.50	20.00	35.00

1/6 THALER

SILVER
Sede Vacante Issue
Obv: St. Paul in cartouche.
Rev: Charlemagne over value.

C#	Date	Mintage	VG	Fine	VF	XF
22	1761	—	25.00	50.00	75.00	125.00

Obv: St. Paul in chapter arms.

C#	Date	Mintage	VG	Fine	VF	XF
22.5	1761	—	25.00	50.00	75.00	125.00

Obv: Arms. Rev: Value and date.

C#	Date	Mintage	VG	Fine	VF	XF
32	1763	—	25.00	50.00	75.00	125.00
	1764	—	25.00	50.00	75.00	125.00

1/3 THALER

SILVER
Sede Vacante Issue
Obv: St. Paul in cartouche.
Rev: Charlemagne over value.

C#	Date	Mintage	VG	Fine	VF	XF
23	1761	—	60.00	125.00	150.00	200.00

Obv: St. Paul in chapter arms.

C#	Date	Mintage	VG	Fine	VF	XF
23.5	1761	—	60.00	125.00	150.00	200.00

Obv: Supported arms.
Rev: Value and date.

C#	Date	Mintage	VG	Fine	VF	XF
34	1764	—	40.00	75.00	110.00	165.00
	1765	—	40.00	75.00	110.00	165.00

(Reichs)

Obv: St. Paul. Rev: Charlemagne

C#	Date	Mintage	Fine	VF	XF	Unc
41	1801	—	30.00	60.00	90.00	180.00

2/3 THALER

SILVER

C#	Date	Mintage	VG	Fine	VF	XF
38	1764	—	85.00	175.00	250.00	400.00

(Reichs)

Obv: St. Paul. Rev: Charlemagne

C#	Date	Mintage	Fine	VF	XF	Unc
42	1801	—	35.00	70.00	115.00	250.00

EIN (1) THALER

SILVER
Sede Vacante Issue

C#	Date	Mintage	VG	Fine	VF	XF
24	1761	—	300.00	600.00	850.00	1250.

(Species)

Obv: Arms. Rev: Charlemagne

C#	Date	Mintage	Fine	VF	XF	Unc
43	1801	—	300.00	1000.	2000.	4000.

Cathedral Coinage

PFENNING

COPPPER
Obv: 3 line legend. Rev: Value over date.

C#	Date	Mintage	VG	Fine	VF	XF
1	1790	—	3.00	5.00	8.50	20.00

2 PFENNING

COPPER
Obv: 3 line legend. Rev: Value over date.

C#	Date	Mintage	VG	Fine	VF	XF
2	1790	—	3.00	5.00	8.50	20.00

3 PFENNING

COPPER
Obv: St. Paul. Rev: Value over date.

C#	Date	Mintage	VG	Fine	VF	XF
3a	1787	—	3.00	7.50	10.00	20.00

4 PFENNING

COPPER
Obv: St. Paul. Rev: Value over date.

C#	Date	Mintage	VG	Fine	VF	XF
4a	1787	—	—	—	—	—
	1788	—	Reported, not confirmed			
	1789	—	Reported, not confirmed			
	1790	—	Reported, not confirmed			

6 PFENNING

COPPER
Obv: St. Paul. Rev: Value over date.

C#	Date	Mintage	VG	Fine	VF	XF
5b	1787	—	4.00	8.00	12.50	20.00
	1788	—	4.00	8.00	12.50	20.00
	1789	—	4.00	8.00	12.50	20.00
	1790	—	4.00	8.00	12.50	20.00

NASSAU

The duchy of Nassau, located on both sides of the River Lahn in the Middle Rhineland was established in 1158. The lands were frequently divided and combined. The first coins were struck c. 1260. The Weilburg line was founded in 1355 and the Usingen line in 1642. In 1806 they united under a common administration. The Usingen line became extinct in 1816 leaving a fully united duchy under the Weilburg rulers. The house ended with the ouster of the duke in 1866 by Prussia.

NASSAU-DIETZ

RULERS

Wilhelm V, 1766-1806

HELLER

COPPER
Obv: Crowned ONN monogram. Rev: Value above date.

C#	Date	Mintage	Fine	VF	XF	Unc
1	1791	—	—	—	—	—

2 HELLER

COPPER
Obv: Crowned ONN monogram. Rev: Value above date.

C#	Date	Mintage	Fine	VF	XF	Unc
2	1791	—	—	—	—	—

JOINT COINAGE

NASSAU-USINGEN & NASSAU-WEILBURG

RULERS

Friedrich August, 1803-1816
Friedrich Wilhelm, 1788-1816

MINTMASTER'S INITIALS

C.T. - Christian Teichmann

1/4 KREUZER

COPPER
Obv: Crowned arms, leg: HERZOGL NASS.
Rev: Value, L below date.

C#	Date	Mintage	Fine	VF	XF	Unc
1	1808	.449	2.50	5.00	15.00	40.00

C#	Date	Mintage	Fine	VF	XF	Unc
1a	1808	Inc. Ab.	2.50	5.00	15.00	40.00
	1809	—	2.50	5.00	15.00	40.00
	1810	—	2.50	5.00	15.00	40.00
	1811	—	2.50	5.00	15.00	40.00
	1812	1.470	1.50	3.00	15.00	40.00
	1813	.280	2.50	5.00	15.00	40.00
	1814	.278	2.50	5.00	15.00	40.00

NOTE: Several varieties exist.

1/2 KREUZER

COPPER

C#	Date	Mintage	Fine	VF	XF	Unc
2	1813	.445	2.50	5.00	15.00	40.00

KREUZER

COPPER

C#	Date	Mintage	Fine	VF	XF	Unc
3	1808	.799	3.00	6.50	15.00	40.00
	1809	—	3.00	6.50	15.00	40.00

Rev: L below wreath, 22-24mm.

C#	Date	Mintage	Fine	VF	XF	Unc
3a	1808	Inc. Ab.	5.00	10.00	15.00	40.00

Obv. leg: HERZ:

C#	Date	Mintage	Fine	VF	XF	Unc
3b	1809	—	2.50	5.00	15.00	40.00
	1810	—	2.50	5.00	15.00	40.00
	1813	.131	2.50	5.00	15.00	40.00

3 KREUZER

(= 1 Groschen)

BILLON

Obv. leg: HERZ. NASS. SCHEIDE.M.
Rev: Value.

C#	Date	Mintage	Fine	VF	XF	Unc
4a	1809	.010	7.50	15.00	25.00	50.00

Obv. leg: HERZ. NASSAU. SCHEIDEMUNZ.

C#	Date	Mintage	Fine	VF	XF	Unc
4	1810.	.750	2.50	5.00	15.00	40.00

Obv. leg: HERZ. NASSAU. SCHEIDE. M.

C#	Date	Mintage	Fine	VF	XF	Unc
4b	1811	.270	2.50	5.00	15.00	40.00
	1812	.480	2.50	5.00	15.00	40.00
	1813	.506	2.50	5.00	15.00	40.00
	1814	.844	2.50	5.00	15.00	40.00
	1815	.675	2.50	5.00	15.00	40.00
	1816	.091	2.50	5.00	15.00	40.00
	1817	.259	2.50	5.00	15.00	40.00
	1818	.675	2.50	5.00	15.00	40.00
	1819	.928	2.50	5.00	15.00	40.00

5 KREUZER

BILLON
Obv: Crowned arms, 5 below, leg: HERZ. NASSAU.....
Rev: Value within wreath.

C#	Date	Mintage	Fine	VF	XF	Unc
5	1808	4,000	20.00	40.00	80.00	125.00
	1809	—	20.00	40.00	80.00	125.00

Obv. leg: HERZOGL. NASS....

C#	Date	Mintage	Fine	VF	XF	Unc
5a	1808	Inc. Ab.	25.00	50.00	90.00	140.00

Obv. leg: HERZ. NASSAUISCHE.
Rev: Value, L below.

C#	Date	Mintage	Fine	VF	XF	Unc
5b	1808	—	25.00	50.00	90.00	140.00
	1809	—	25.00	50.00	90.00	140.00

10 KREUZER

.500 SILVER
Obv: Crowned arms, 10 below, HERZ. NASSAUISCHE CONVENTIONS MUNZ. Rev: Value within wreath, L below.

C#	Date	Mintage	Fine	VF	XF	Unc
6	1809	—	25.00	55.00	100.00	175.00

Obv. leg: HERZ. NASSAU. CONVENT. MUNZ

C#	Date	Mintage	Fine	VF	XF	Unc
6a	1809	—	20.00	45.00	90.00	150.00

Obv. leg: HERZ. NASSAUISCHE.....

C#	Date	Mintage	Fine	VF	XF	Unc
6b	1809	—	20.00	45.00	90.00	150.00

Obv. leg: HERZ. NASSAU. Rev: No L.

C#	Date	Mintage	Fine	VF	XF	Unc
6c	1809	—	20.00	45.00	90.00	150.00

20 KREUZER

.583 SILVER
Obv: Crowned shield, leg: HERZ.
NASSAUISCHE CONVENTIONS MUNZ.
Rev: Value within wreath.

C#	Date	Mintage	Fine	VF	XF	Unc
7	1809	—	20.00	40.00	60.00	125.00

Obv. leg: HERZ. NASSAUISCHE CONVENT. MUNZ

C#	Date	Mintage	Fine	VF	XF	Unc
7a	1809	—	20.00	40.00	60.00	125.00

Rev: Wreath without bow, running horse below.

C#	Date	Mintage	Fine	VF	XF	Unc
7b	1809	—	20.00	40.00	60.00	125.00

Rev: 60 between rosettes

C#	Date	Mintage	Fine	VF	XF	Unc
7c	1809	—	20.00	40.00	60.00	125.00

Obv. leg: .....CONVENTIONS. Rev: Value within branches.

C#	Date	Mintage	Fine	VF	XF	Unc
7d	1809	—	20.00	40.00	60.00	125.00

Obv. leg: ......CONVENT. Rev: L below wreath.

C#	Date	Mintage	Fine	VF	XF	Unc
7e	1809	—	20.00	40.00	60.00	125.00

Rev: No bow on wreath, prancing horse below.

C#	Date	Mintage	Fine	VF	XF	Unc
7f	1809	—	20.00	40.00	60.00	125.00

Obv. leg: HERZ: NASS: CONV: MUNZ:

C#	Date	Mintage	Fine	VF	XF	Unc
7g	1809	—	20.00	40.00	60.00	125.00

TRADE COINS

DUCAT

3.5000 gm., .986 GOLD, .1109 oz AGW

C#	Date	Mintage	Fine	VF	XF	Unc
8	1809	3,543	500.00	1000.	1500.	2000.

SEPARATE COINAGE

Nassau-Usingen

RULERS

Friedrich August, 1803-1816

10 KREUZER

.500 SILVER

Obv: Head right. Rev: Crowned arms dividing date.

C#	Date	Mintage	Fine	VF	XF	Unc
9.1	1809	—	35.00	70.00	110.00	160.00

Obv: L at truncation.

C#	Date	Mintage	Fine	VF	XF	Unc
9.2	1809 L	—	—	—	—	—

20 KREUZER

.583 SILVER

Obv: Head right, L at truncation. Rev: Crowned arms.

C#	Date	Mintage	Fine	VF	XF	Unc
10	1809 L	—	20.00	45.00	90.00	150.00

Rev: Crowned arms dividing date

C#	Date	Mintage	Fine	VF	XF	Unc
10a	1809 L	—	20.00	45.00	90.00	150.00

1/2 THALER

(Convention)

SILVER

C#	Date	Mintage	Fine	VF	XF	Unc
11	1809 L	—	50.00	110.00	200.00	400.00

EIN (1) THALER

(Convention)

.833 SILVER

Obv: Head right, L at truncation.

Rev: Crowned arms within wreath.

C#	Date	Mintage	Fine	VF	XF	Unc
12	1809 L	—	200.00	500.00	1000.	2000.

Rev: Crowned arms between branches

C#	Date	Mintage	Fine	VF	XF	Unc
12b	1809 L	—	200.00	500.00	1000.	2000.

C#	Date	Mintage	Fine	VF	XF	Unc
12a	1809 CT	—	100.00	300.00	600.00	900.00
	1810 CT	—	100.00	300.00	600.00	900.00
	1811 CT	—	100.00	300.00	600.00	900.00
	1812 CT	—	100.00	300.00	600.00	900.00

Rev: Date dividing C.T.

C#	Date	Mintage	Fine	VF	XF	Unc
12c	1810 CT	—	100.00	300.00	600.00	900.00
	1811 CT	—	100.00	300.00	600.00	900.00
	1812 CT	—	100.00	300.00	600.00	900.00
	1813 CT	.042	100.00	300.00	600.00	900.00
	1815 CT	—	100.00	300.00	600.00	900.00

SEPARATE COINAGE

Nassau-Weilburg

RULERS

Friedrich Wilhelm II, 1788-1816

10 KREUZER

.500 SILVER

C#	Date	Mintage	Fine	VF	XF	Unc
30	1809	—	30.00	65.00	100.00	150.00

Obv: L at truncation

C#	Date	Mintage	Fine	VF	XF	Unc
30a	1809	—	30.00	65.00	100.00	150.00

20 KREUZER

.583 SILVER

C#	Date	Mintage	Fine	VF	XF	Unc
31	1809	—	30.00	60.00	100.00	150.00
	1810	—	30.00	60.00	100.00	150.00

1/2 THALER

(Convention)

SILVER

Obv: Head right, L on truncation.

Rev: Crowned arms between branches.

C#	Date	Mintage	Fine	VF	XF	Unc
32	1809 L	—	80.00	160.00	250.00	350.00

EIN (1) THALER

(Convention)

28.0600 gm., .833 SILVER, .7516 oz ASW

Obv: Head right, L on truncation.

Rev: Crowned arms between laurel and oak branches.

C#	Date	Mintage	Fine	VF	XF	Unc
33	1809 L	—	200.00	500.00	1000.	2000.

Rev: Arms between laurel and palm branches.

C#	Date	Mintage	Fine	VF	XF	Unc
33a	1809 L	—	200.00	500.00	1000.	2000.

Edge: Leaf ornamentation.

C#	Date	Mintage	Fine	VF	XF	Unc
33b	1809 CT	—	100.00	300.00	600.00	900.00
	1810 CT	—	100.00	300.00	600.00	900.00
	1811 CT	—	100.00	300.00	600.00	900.00
	1812 CT	—	100.00	300.00	600.00	900.00

Rev: Date dividing C.T.

C#	Date	Mintage	Fine	VF	XF	Unc
33c	1810 CT	—	100.00	300.00	600.00	900.00
	1811 CT	—	100.00	300.00	600.00	900.00
	1812 CT	—	100.00	300.00	600.00	900.00

Obv: L on truncation

C#	Date	Mintage	Fine	VF	XF	Unc
33d	1812 CT	—	100.00	300.00	600.00	900.00

Obv: Older portrait

C#	Date	Mintage	Fine	VF	XF	Unc
33e	1813 CT	.042	100.00	300.00	600.00	900.00
	1815 CT	—	100.00	300.00	600.00	900.00

United Nassau

RULERS

Friedrich Wilhelm II, 1816-1839

Duke Adolph, 1839-1866

MINTMASTER'S INITIALS

C.T. - Christian Teichmann

HELLER

COPPER

Obv: Crowned arms. Rev: Value.

C#	Date	Mintage	Fine	VF	XF	Unc
51	1842	.182	2.00	4.00	10.00	35.00

PFENNIG

COPPER

C#	Date	Mintage	Fine	VF	XF	Unc
52	1859	.220	1.00	3.00	8.00	35.00
	1860	.580	1.00	3.00	8.00	35.00
	1862	.490	1.00	3.00	8.00	35.00

1/4 KREUZER

COPPER

C#	Date	Mintage	Fine	VF	XF	Unc
35	1817.	.433	2.00	4.00	7.50	35.00
	1818.	.894	2.00	4.00	7.50	35.00
	1819.	4.932	1.00	3.00	6.00	35.00

Rev: Without period after date.

C#	Date	Mintage	Fine	VF	XF	Unc
35a	1817	Inc. Ab.	2.00	4.00	7.50	35.00
	1819	Inc. Ab.	2.00	4.00	7.50	35.00
	1822	4.210	1.00	3.00	6.00	35.00

NOTE: Several varieties exist.

EIN (1) KREUZER

COPPER, 22-24mm

Obv: Crowned spade-shaped arms. Rev: Value in wreath.

C#	Date	Mintage	Fine	VF	XF	Unc
36	1817	.203	2.50	5.00	10.00	40.00
	1818	.084	2.50	5.00	10.00	40.00

BILLON, 14mm
Rev: Without wreath.

C#	Date	Mintage	Fine	VF	XF	Unc
38	1817	.079	4.00	8.00	12.00	50.00
	1823	.545	2.50	5.00	8.00	40.00
	1824	.564	2.50	5.00	8.00	40.00
	1828	—	2.50	5.00	8.00	40.00

COPPER, 22-24mm

C#	Date	Mintage	Fine	VF	XF	Unc
37	1830	.265	1.50	3.00	6.00	40.00
	1832	.517	1.50	3.00	6.00	40.00
	1834	.326	1.50	3.00	6.00	40.00
	1836	.200	1.50	3.00	6.00	40.00
	1838	.269	1.50	3.00	6.00	40.00

BILLON, 14mm
Obv: Crowned square arms.

C#	Date	Mintage	Fine	VF	XF	Unc
39	1832	.144	2.50	5.00	10.00	50.00
	1833	1.037	2.00	5.00	10.00	40.00
	1835	.408	2.50	5.00	10.00	40.00

COPPER

C#	Date	Mintage	Fine	VF	XF	Unc
53	1842	.480	2.00	4.00	7.50	40.00
	1844	.188	2.00	4.00	7.50	40.00
	1848	.249	2.00	4.00	7.50	40.00
	1854	.274	2.00	4.00	7.50	40.00
	1855	—	2.00	4.00	7.50	40.00
	1856	.357	2.00	4.00	7.50	40.00

C#	Date	Mintage	Fine	VF	XF	Unc
54	1859	.836	1.00	3.00	6.00	35.00
	1860	.610	1.00	3.00	6.00	35.00
	1861	.556	1.00	3.00	6.00	35.00
	1862	.610	1.00	3.00	6.00	35.00
	1863	.576	1.00	3.00	6.00	35.00

BILLON

C#	Date	Mintage	Fine	VF	XF	Unc
55	1861	.664	2.50	5.00	10.00	40.00

3 KREUZER

BILLON
Obv: Crowned spade-shaped arms, NASSAU. Rev: Value.

C#	Date	Mintage	Fine	VF	XF	Unc
40	1817	.259	2.50	5.00	10.00	40.00
	1818	.675	2.50	5.00	10.00	40.00
	1819	.928	2.50	5.00	10.00	40.00

C#	Date	Mintage	Fine	VF	XF	Unc
40a	1822	.671	2.50	5.00	10.00	40.00
	1823	.671	2.50	5.00	10.00	40.00
	1824	—	2.50	5.00	10.00	40.00
	1825	.192	2.50	5.00	10.00	40.00
	1826	.352	2.50	5.00	10.00	40.00
	1827	.308	2.50	5.00	10.00	40.00
	1828	.308	2.50	5.00	10.00	40.00

C#	Date	Mintage	Fine	VF	XF	Unc
41	1831	.509	2.50	5.00	10.00	40.00
	1832	.388	2.50	5.00	10.00	40.00
	1833	.042	2.50	5.00	10.00	40.00
	1834	.292	2.50	5.00	10.00	40.00
	1836	.340	2.50	5.00	10.00	40.00

C#	Date	Mintage	Fine	VF	XF	Unc
56	1841	—	— Reported, Not Confirmed			
	1842	.112	2.50	5.00	8.00	40.00
	1844	.056	2.50	5.00	8.00	40.00
	1845	—	2.50	5.00	8.00	40.00
	1847	.210	2.50	5.00	8.00	40.00
	1848	.541	2.50	5.00	8.00	40.00
	1853	.091	2.50	5.00	8.00	40.00
	1855	.179	2.50	5.00	8.00	40.00

6 KREUZER

BILLON
Obv: Crowned square arms, leg: NASSAUISCHE.
Rev: Value in wreath.

C#	Date	Mintage	Fine	VF	XF	Unc
42	1817	.109	3.00	6.00	10.00	40.00
	1818	.263	3.00	6.00	10.00	40.00
	1819	.378	3.00	6.00	10.00	40.00

Obv. leg: NASSAU.

C#	Date	Mintage	Fine	VF	XF	Unc
42a	1822	.306	3.00	6.00	10.00	40.00
	1823	.306	3.00	6.00	10.00	40.00
	1824	.083	3.00	6.00	12.50	40.00
	1825	.176	3.00	6.00	10.00	40.00
	1826	.314	3.00	6.00	10.00	40.00
	1827	.302	3.00	6.00	10.00	40.00
	1828	.303	3.00	6.00	10.00	40.00

C#	Date	Mintage	Fine	VF	XF	Unc
43	1831	1.100	3.00	6.00	10.00	40.00
	1832	.377	3.00	6.00	10.00	40.00
	1833	.641	3.00	6.00	10.00	40.00
	1834	.565	3.00	6.00	10.00	40.00
	1835	.832	3.00	6.00	10.00	40.00
	1836	.452	3.00	6.00	10.00	40.00
	1837	.314	3.00	6.00	10.00	40.00

C#	Date	Mintage	Fine	VF	XF	Unc
43a	1838	.201	3.00	6.00	10.00	40.00
	1839	.109	3.00	6.00	10.00	40.00

C#	Date	Mintage	Fine	VF	XF	Unc
57	1840	.094	2.00	4.00	9.00	40.00
	1841	.321	2.00	4.00	9.00	40.00
	1844	.073	2.00	4.00	9.00	40.00
	1846	—	2.00	4.00	9.00	40.00
	1847	—	2.00	4.00	9.00	40.00
	1848	.198	2.00	4.00	9.00	40.00
	1855	.190	2.00	4.00	9.00	40.00

1/2 GULDEN

.900 SILVER

C#	Date	Mintage	Fine	VF	XF	Unc
44	1838	.108	12.00	25.00	40.00	100.00
	1839	.108	12.00	25.00	40.00	100.00

C#	Date	Mintage	Fine	VF	XF	Unc
58	1840	.095	12.00	25.00	40.00	100.00
	1841	.125	12.00	25.00	40.00	100.00
	1842	.031	12.00	25.00	40.00	100.00
	1843	.104	12.00	25.00	40.00	100.00
	1844	.117	12.00	25.00	40.00	100.00
	1845	.072	12.00	25.00	40.00	100.00

Obv: Head left

C#	Date	Mintage	Fine	VF	XF	Unc
59	1856	.313	16.00	35.00	60.00	100.00
	1860	.104	22.00	45.00	70.00	130.00

GULDEN

.900 SILVER

C#	Date	Mintage	Fine	VF	XF	Unc
45	1838	.190	25.00	50.00	100.00	150.00
	1839	.108	25.00	50.00	100.00	150.00

Obv: With Zollmann on truncation.

C#	Date	Mintage	Fine	VF	XF	Unc
60	1840	.117	16.00	35.00	55.00	110.00
	1841	.124	16.00	35.00	55.00	110.00
	1842	.020	16.00	35.00	55.00	110.00
	1843	.236	16.00	35.00	55.00	110.00
	1844	.093	16.00	35.00	55.00	110.00
	1845	.138	16.00	35.00	55.00	110.00
	1846	.048	16.00	35.00	55.00	110.00
	1847	.231	16.00	35.00	55.00	110.00
	1855	.188	16.00	35.00	55.00	110.00

Obv: W/o name on truncation.

C#	Date	Mintage	Fine	VF	XF	Unc
61	1855	Inc. Ab.	22.00	45.00	75.00	130.00
	1856	.040	22.00	45.00	75.00	130.00

ZWEY (2) GULDEN

21.2100 gm., .900 SILVER, .6138 oz ASW

C#	Date	Mintage	Fine	VF	XF	Unc
65	1846	.177	50.00	125.00	300.00	600.00
	1847	.088	60.00	150.00	350.00	700.00

EIN (1) THALER

(Krone)

29.5300 gm., .871 SILVER, .8270 oz ASW
Obv: Head right, L below. Rev: Crowned draped arms, date below dividing C.T.

C#	Date	Mintage	Fine	VF	XF	Unc
46	1816 CT	—	175.00	500.00	1000.	2000.

C#	Date	Mintage	Fine	VF	XF	Unc
47	1817 CT	.013	250.00	500.00	1000.	2000.

Obv: Head right, P.Z. at truncation.
Rev: Crowned draped arms.

C#	Date	Mintage	Fine	VF	XF	Unc
48	1818 CT	4,500	200.00	500.00	1000.	2000.
	1825 CT	2,000	200.00	500.00	1000.	2000.

Obv: Deep ZOLLMANN. F at truncation.
Rev: Crowned arms between lions.

C#	Date	Mintage	Fine	VF	XF	Unc
49	1831	—	125.00	300.00	600.00	900.00
	1832	—	125.00	300.00	600.00	900.00
	1833	—	125.00	300.00	600.00	900.00
	1836	—	125.00	300.00	600.00	900.00
	1837	2,683	125.00	300.00	600.00	900.00

Visit of Duke to the Mint
Rev. leg: BESUCHT ZUM.

C#	Date	Mintage	Fine	VF	XF	Unc
49a	1831	—	425.00	1000.	2000.	3000.

(Vereins)

18.5200 gm., .900 SILVER, .5360 oz ASW
Obv: Z on truncation.

C#	Date	Mintage	Fine	VF	XF	Unc
62	1859 Z	.050	35.00	75.00	150.00	300.00
	1860 Z	.030	35.00	75.00	150.00	300.00

Obv: F. KORN at truncation.

C#	Date	Mintage	Fine	VF	XF	Unc
62a	1863	.145	35.00	75.00	150.00	300.00

Visit of Grand Duke to Mint

C#	Date	Mintage	Fine	VF	XF	Unc
63	1861	3 pcs.	—	—		Proof 12,500.

25th Anniversary of Reign

C#	Date	Mintage	Fine	VF	XF	Unc
64	1864	6,162	40.00	100.00	200.00	400.00

ZWEI (2) THALER

(= 3-1/2 Gulden)

37.1200 gm., .900 SILVER, 1.0742 oz ASW
Obv: Similar to C#67a, ZOLLMANN at truncation.

C#	Date	Mintage	Fine	VF	XF	Unc
66	1840	.056	140.00	400.00	800.00	1600.

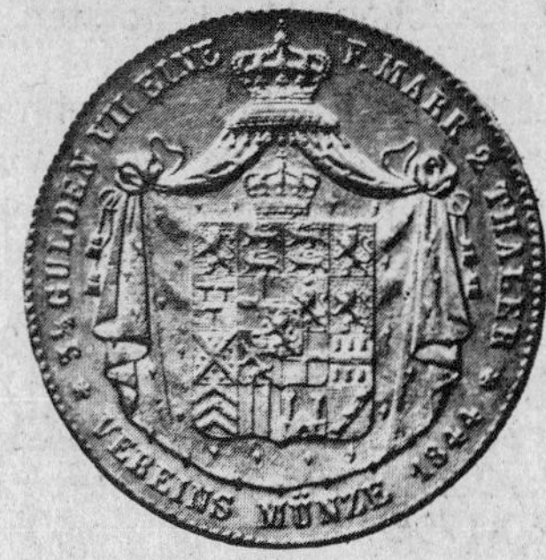

C#	Date	Mintage	Fine	VF	XF	Unc
67a	1844	.021	125.00	400.00	800.00	1600.
	1847	—	350.00	700.00	1500.	2500.

Obv: Truncation bare

C#	Date	Mintage	Fine	VF	XF	Unc
67	1844	Inc. Ab.	125.00	400.00	800.00	1600.
	1854	.072	125.00	400.00	800.00	1600.

37.0400 gm., .900 SILVER, 1.0719 oz ASW
Obv: C ZOLLMANN on truncation.

C#	Date	Mintage	Fine	VF	XF	Unc
68	1860	—	125.00	400.00	800.00	1600.

TRADE COINS

DUCAT

3.5000 gm., .986 GOLD, .1109 oz AGW
Obv: Head right. Rev: Crowned draped arms.

C#	Date	Mintage	Fine	VF	XF	Unc
50	1818 CT	501 pcs.	—	—	—	2500.

NCLT ISSUES

PATTERNS

KM#	Date	Mintage	Identification	Mkt.Val.
1	1839	—	3 Kreuzer, Y56	—

NURNBERG

Nurnberg, in Franconia, was made a free city in 1219. In that same year an imperial mint was established there and continued throughout the rest of the century. The mint right was obtained in 1376 and again in 1422. City coins were struck from c. 1390 to 1806 when the city was made part of Bavaria.

MINTMASTERS INITIALS

F, I.M.F. - Johann Martin Forster, 1755-1764
OEXLEIN, I.L.OE. - Johann Leonhard Oexlein
K.R. - Georg Knoll and Riedner
R, G.N.R. - Georg Nikolaus Riedner, 1764-1793
S.S. - Sigmund Scholz, 1760-1779
S.F. - Scholz and Forster, 1760-1764
S.R. - Scholz and Riedner, 1764-1770
I.P.W. - Johann Peter Werner, 1760-1796

PFENNIG

BILLON
Obv: Arms divide date; value above.
Rev: Blank.

C#	Date	Mintage	VG	Fine	VF	XF
1	1760	—	2.00	3.50	7.00	15.00
	1761	—	2.00	3.50	7.00	15.00
	1762	—	2.00	3.50	7.00	15.00
	1763	—	2.00	3.50	7.00	15.00
	1764	—	2.00	3.50	7.00	15.00
	1765	—	2.00	3.50	7.00	15.00
	1766	—	2.00	3.50	7.00	15.00
	1767	—	2.00	3.50	7.00	15.00
	1768	—	2.00	3.50	7.00	15.00
	1769	—	2.00	3.50	7.00	15.00
	1770	—	2.00	3.50	7.00	15.00
	1771	—	2.00	3.50	7.00	15.00
	1772	—	2.00	3.50	7.00	15.00
	1773	—	2.00	3.50	7.00	15.00
	1775	—	2.00	3.50	7.00	15.00
	1776	—	2.00	3.50	7.00	15.00
	1777	—	2.00	3.50	7.00	15.00
	1778	—	2.00	3.50	7.00	15.00
	1779	—	2.00	3.50	7.00	15.00
	1780	—	2.00	3.50	7.00	15.00
	1781	—	2.00	3.50	7.00	15.00
	1782	—	2.00	3.50	7.00	15.00
	1783	—	2.00	3.50	7.00	15.00
	1784	—	2.00	3.50	7.00	15.00
	1785	—	2.00	3.50	7.00	15.00
	1786	—	2.00	3.50	7.00	15.00
	1787	—	2.00	3.50	7.00	15.00
	1790	—	2.00	3.50	7.00	15.00

Rev: Crowned imperial eagle.

C#	Date	Mintage	VG	Fine	VF	XF
3	1767	—	3.00	4.00	7.50	15.00
	1768	—	3.00	4.00	7.50	15.00
	1769	—	3.00	4.00	7.50	15.00
	1770	—	3.00	4.00	7.50	15.00
	1771	—	3.00	4.00	7.50	15.00
	1772	—	3.00	4.00	7.50	15.00
	1773	—	3.00	4.00	7.50	15.00
	1774	—	3.00	4.00	7.50	15.00
	1775	—	3.00	4.00	7.50	15.00
	1776	—	3.00	4.00	7.50	15.00
	1777	—	3.00	4.00	7.50	15.00
	1778	—	3.00	4.00	7.50	15.00
	1779	—	3.00	4.00	7.50	15.00
	1780	—	3.00	4.00	7.50	15.00

Obv: Arms with value and date above.

C#	Date	Mintage	VG	Fine	VF	XF
3c	1772	—	3.00	4.00	8.00	15.00
	1778	—	3.00	4.00	8.00	15.00
	1779	—	3.00	4.00	8.00	15.00
	1781	—	3.00	4.00	8.00	15.00
	1782	—	3.00	4.00	8.00	15.00
	1784	—	3.00	4.00	8.00	15.00
	1789	—	3.00	4.00	8.00	15.00

Obv: Arms draped with garlands; value and date above.
Rev: Blank.

C#	Date	Mintage	VG	Fine	VF	XF
3a	1788	—	3.00	4.00	8.00	15.00
	1789	—	3.00	4.00	8.00	15.00

Obv: Oval arms with value and date above.

C#	Date	Mintage	VG	Fine	VF	XF
3b	1789	—	3.00	4.00	8.00	15.00
	1790	—	3.00	4.00	8.00	15.00
	1791	—	3.00	4.00	8.00	15.00
	1792	—	3.00	4.00	8.00	15.00
	1793	—	3.00	4.00	8.00	15.00
	1797	—	3.00	4.00	8.00	15.00

Obv: 2 shields of arms; value and date above.

C#	Date	Mintage	VG	Fine	VF	XF
6	1793	—	3.00	4.00	8.00	15.00
	1794	—	3.00	4.00	8.00	15.00

Obv: 2 shields of arms; date above, value below.

C#	Date	Mintage	VG	Fine	VF	XF
6a	1795	—	3.00	4.00	8.00	15.00

Obv: 3 shields of arms divide date.

C#	Date	Mintage	VG	Fine	VF	XF
7	1795	—	3.00	4.00	8.00	15.00
	1796	—	3.00	4.00	8.00	15.00
	1797	—	3.00	4.00	8.00	15.00

Obv: Arms with mural crown above divides date.

C#	Date	Mintage	VG	Fine	VF	XF
8	1796	—	3.00	5.00	8.50	15.00

Obv: Arms with value and date above.

C#	Date	Mintage	VG	Fine	VF	XF
9	1798	—	3.00	4.00	8.00	15.00
	1799	—	3.00	5.00	8.50	15.00

State shield between branches over value and date. Uniface.

C#	Date	Mintage	Fine	VF	XF	Unc
10	1799	—	2.00	5.00	10.00	35.00
	1806	—	2.00	5.00	10.00	35.00

Oval state shield with garland draped over urn, value below date. Uniface.

C#	Date	Mintage	Fine	VF	XF	Unc
10a	1806	—	2.00	5.00	10.00	35.00

Oval state shield, garland with loop over value and date. Uniface.

C#	Date	Mintage	Fine	VF	XF	Unc
10b	1806	—	2.00	5.00	10.00	35.00

Garland hanging from urn on pedestal above state shield. value and date below. Uniface.

C#	Date	Mintage	Fine	VF	XF	Unc
11	1806	—	2.00	5.00	10.00	35.00
	1807	—	2.00	5.00	10.00	35.00

State shield in front of altar, value and date below. Uniface.

C#	Date	Mintage	Fine	VF	XF	Unc
11a	1806	—	2.00	5.00	10.00	35.00
	1807	—	2.00	5.00	10.00	35.00

4 PFENNIG

BILLON
Obv: N over Harpie arms.
Rev: Diamond arms; value at top, date on bottom.

C#	Date	Mintage	VG	Fine	VF	XF
13	1764	—	20.00	45.00	70.00	90.00
	1765	—	20.00	45.00	70.00	90.00
	1766	—	20.00	45.00	70.00	90.00
	1774	—	20.00	45.00	70.00	90.00
	1776	—	20.00	45.00	70.00	90.00
	1783	—	20.00	45.00	70.00	90.00

KREUZER

BILLON
Obv: Mural crown over arms in branches; F in pedestal below. Rev: Value and date in inner circle.

C#	Date	Mintage	VG	Fine	VF	XF
19	1763	—	3.50	6.00	9.50	15.00

Obv: City view; date below.
Rev: 3 shields of arms; 1(N) KR below.

C#	Date	Mintage	VG	Fine	VF	XF
21	1773	—	3.50	6.00	9.50	15.00

Obv: 2 shields. Rev: Value over date.

C#	Date	Mintage	VG	Fine	VF	XF
23	1786	—	3.00	6.00	9.50	15.00

Obv: Arms. Rev: Value.

C#	Date	Mintage	VG	Fine	VF	XF
25	1796	—	3.00	6.00	9.50	15.00
	1797	—	3.00	6.00	9.50	15.00
	1798	—	3.00	6.00	9.50	15.00
	1799	—	3.00	6.00	9.50	15.00

Obv: Arms with mural crown and garlands.
Rev: Garlands surround value; date above.

C#	Date	Mintage	VG	Fine	VF	XF
26	1796	—	3.50	6.00	9.50	15.00

Obv: Seated female with shield.

C#	Date	Mintage	VG	Fine	VF	XF
27	1797	—	3.00	6.00	9.50	15.00

Obv: Oval arms in drapery.

C#	Date	Mintage	VG	Fine	VF	XF
28	1797	—	4.00	6.50	10.00	15.00

Obv: Oval arms in branches.
Rev: Value and date over sprays; N below.

C#	Date	Mintage	VG	Fine	VF	XF
29	1797	—	3.50	6.00	9.50	15.00

Obv: Arms in garlands and sprays.
Rev: Value and date in cartouche.

C#	Date	Mintage	VG	Fine	VF	XF
30	1798	—	3.50	6.00	9.50	15.00

Rev: Garlands over value and date.

C#	Date	Mintage	VG	Fine	VF	XF
31	1798	—	3.50	6.00	9.50	15.00
	1799	—	3.50	6.00	9.50	15.00

Obv: Female figure holding arms at right, beside altar left.

C#	Date	Mintage	VG	Fine	VF	XF
32	1798	—	4.00	6.50	10.00	15.00

Obv: Father Time; date above.
Rev: Value in wreath.

C#	Date	Mintage	VG	Fine	VF	XF
34	1799	—	2.50	4.00	7.50	15.00

Obv: Pyramid with city arms; date below.
Rev: City view.

C#	Date	Mintage	VG	Fine	VF	XF
36	1806	—	2.50	4.00	7.50	15.00

Rev: Rose bush.

C#	Date	Mintage	VG	Fine	VF	XF
36a	1806	—	2.25	3.00	6.00	15.00

Obv: Spade arms with mural crown and garlands.
Rev: Value and date.

C#	Date	Mintage	VG	Fine	VF	XF
37	1806	—	2.25	3.00	6.00	15.00
	1807	—	2.25	3.00	6.00	15.00

Obv: Pyramid with city arms; date below.
Rev: City view.

C#	Date	Mintage	VG	Fine	VF	XF
38	1807	—	4.00	6.50	10.00	15.00

2-1/2 KREUZER
(Convention)

BILLON
Obv: Square arms; date below.
Rev: Crowned imperial eagle, leg: FRANCISCUS.....

C#	Date	Mintage	VG	Fine	VF	XF
40	1760 R	—	3.00	7.50	12.50	20.00
	1763 R	—	3.00	7.50	12.50	20.00
	1764 R	—	3.00	7.50	12.50	20.00

Rev. leg: JOSEPHUS.....

C#	Date	Mintage	VG	Fine	VF	XF
42a	1766 R	—	3.00	7.00	11.50	20.00
	1767 R	—	3.00	7.00	11.50	20.00
	1776 R	—	3.00	7.00	11.50	20.00

Obv: Arms in ornamental shield; date below.
Rev: Crowned imperial eagle.

C#	Date	Mintage	VG	Fine	VF	XF
42	1774 R	—	3.00	7.00	11.50	20.00
	1778 R	—	3.00	7.00	11.50	20.00
	1779 R	—	3.00	7.00	11.50	20.00

3 KREUZER

BILLON
Obv: Crowned shield with garland.
Rev: Value within wreath, date below.

C#	Date	Mintage	Fine	VF	XF	Unc
44	1806	—	2.00	6.00	15.00	50.00

Rev. leg: NURNB: SCHEIDE MUNZ

C#	Date	Mintage	Fine	VF	XF	Unc
44a	1806	—	2.00	6.00	15.00	50.00
	1807	—	2.00	6.00	15.00	50.00

5 KREUZER

BILLON
Obv: Square arms divide date; value above.
Rev: Crowned imperial eagle, leg: FRANCISCUS.....

C#	Date	Mintage	VG	Fine	VF	XF
48	1763 F	—	5.00	10.00	20.00	35.00
	1764 R	—	5.00	10.00	20.00	35.00
	1765 R	—	5.00	10.00	20.00	35.00

Rev. leg: JOSEPHUS.....

C#	Date	Mintage	VG	Fine	VF	XF
49	1766 R	—	15.00	30.00	55.00	75.00

6 KREUZER

BILLON
Obv: Crowned shield with garland.
Rev: Value within wreath, date below.

C#	Date	Mintage	Fine	VF	XF	Unc
51	1806	—	4.00	8.00	15.00	50.00
	1807	—	4.00	8.00	15.00	50.00

10 KREUZER
(Convention)

SILVER
Obv: Crowned arms on pedestal between branches.
Rev: Crowned imperial eagle, leg: FRANCISCUS.....

C#	Date	Mintage	VG	Fine	VF	XF
53	1763 SF	—	65.00	125.00	175.00	300.00
	1764 SF	—	65.00	125.00	175.00	300.00

Rev. leg: JOSEPHUS.....

C#	Date	Mintage	VG	Fine	VF	XF
55	1766 SR	—	65.00	125.00	175.00	300.00

20 KREUZER
(Convention)

SILVER
Obv: Bust of Francis right in wreath.

Rev: Crowned arms on pedestal between branches, value and date below.

C#	Date	Mintage	Fine	VF	XF	Unc
57	1760 SF	—	12.00	25.00	40.00	65.00
	1762 SF	—	12.00	25.00	40.00	65.00
	1763 SF	—	12.00	25.00	40.00	65.00
	1764 SR	—	12.00	25.00	40.00	65.00
	1765 SR	—	12.00	25.00	40.00	65.00

Obv: Crowned arms on pedestal between branches; value and date below.
Rev: Crowned Imperial eagle. Leg: FRANCISCUS.....

C#	Date	Mintage	VG	Fine	VF	XF
58	1764 SR	—	12.00	25.00	40.00	65.00
	1765 SR	—	12.00	25.00	40.00	65.00

Obv: Bust of Joseph right in wreath.
Rev: Crowned arms on pedestal between branches; value and date below.

C#	Date	Mintage	VG	Fine	VF	XF
59	1765 SR	—	12.00	25.00	40.00	65.00

Obv: Crowned arms on pedestal between branches, value and date below.
Rev: Crowned Imperial eagle, leg: JOSEPHUS.....

C#	Date	Mintage	VG	Fine	VF	XF
60	1765 SR	—	12.00	25.00	40.00	65.00
	1766 SR	—	12.00	25.00	40.00	65.00
	1767 SR	—	12.00	25.00	40.00	65.00
	1768 SR	—	12.00	25.00	40.00	65.00

Obv: 3 shields of arms divide date; value below.
Rev: Crowned Imperial eagle.

C#	Date	Mintage	Fine	VF	XF	Unc
61	1769 SR	—	55.00	110.00	140.00	175.00

Obv: Crowned arms, date and value in diamond.
Rev: Crowned Imperial eagle in diamond.

C#	Date	Mintage	Fine	VF	XF	Unc
63	1770 SR	—	100.00	200.00	250.00	375.00
	1772 SR	—	100.00	200.00	250.00	375.00
	1774 SR	—	100.00	200.00	250.00	375.00
	1776 SR	—	100.00	200.00	250.00	375.00

Obv: Crowned arms; value below.
Rev: Crowned Imperial eagle.

C#	Date	Mintage	Fine	VF	XF	Unc
65	1774 SR	—	50.00	100.00	135.00	165.00

30 KREUZER

(Convention)

SILVER
Obv: Crowned arms over value.
Rev: Crowned Imperial eagle.

C#	Date	Mintage	Fine	VF	XF	Unc
67	1765 SR	—	60.00	125.00	175.00	250.00

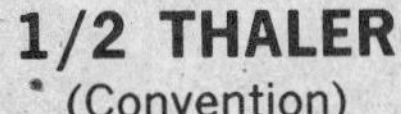

1/2 THALER

(Convention)

SILVER
Obv: River God holding arms.
Rev: Crowned Imperial eagle.

C#	Date	Mintage	Fine	VF	XF	Unc
68	1760 SF	—	85.00	175.00	250.00	375.00

C#	Date	Mintage	Fine	VF	XF	Unc
69	1766 SR	—	65.00	125.00	175.00	300.00
	1768 SR	—	65.00	125.00	175.00	300.00

EIN (1) THALER

(Convention)

SILVER
Obv: Bust of Francis right.
Rev: Crowned Imperial eagle.

C#	Date	Mintage	Fine	VF	XF	Unc
74	1760 SS-IMF	—	100.00	300.00	600.00	900.00
	1762 SS-IMF	—	100.00	300.00	600.00	900.00
	1763 SS-IMF	—	100.00	300.00	600.00	900.00

Obv: Seated figure beside shield of arms.

C#	Date	Mintage	Fine	VF	XF	Unc
75	1761 SF	—	75.00	150.00	200.00	400.00

Peace of Teschen Commemorative
Obv: Female figure standing next to altar; arms at left.

C#	Date	Mintage	Fine	VF	XF	Unc
76	1763 SF-ILOE	—	75.00	150.00	200.00	400.00

Obv: Bust of Franz I. Rev: Imperial eagle.

C#	Date	Mintage	Fine	VF	XF	Unc
77	1764 SS-GNR	—	125.00	250.00	500.00	1000.

Rev: LEGE VINDICE at bottom.

C#	Date	Mintage	Fine	VF	XF	Unc
77a	1765 SR	—	75.00	150.00	225.00	400.00

C#	Date	Mintage	Fine	VF	XF	Unc
78	1765 SSGNR	—	75.00	150.00	225.00	400.00

C#	Date	Mintage	Fine	VF	XF	Unc
79	1765 SR	—	300.00	650.00	1000.	1500.

Rev: City view.

C#	Date	Mintage	Fine	VF	XF	Unc
80	1765 SR	—	150.00	300.00	600.00	1200.

Rev: Crowned Imperial eagle with arms on chest.

C#	Date	Mintage	Fine	VF	XF	Unc
81	1765 SR	—	100.00	200.00	400.00	800.00
	1768 SR	—	100.00	200.00	400.00	800.00
	1780 SR	—	150.00	225.00	350.00	650.00

Obv: City view.
Rev: Crowned Imperial eagle.

C#	Date	Mintage	Fine	VF	XF	Unc
81a	1765 SR	—	100.00	200.00	400.00	800.00
	1768 SR	—	85.00	200.00	400.00	800.00
	1779 KR	—	150.00	250.00	375.00	500.00

Obv: Masonry crown over arms.

C#	Date	Mintage	Fine	VF	XF	Unc
82	1766 SR	—	250.00	500.00	1000.	2000.

C#	Date	Mintage	Fine	VF	XF	Unc
82a	1766 SR	—	125.00	300.00	500.00	1000.
	1767 SR	—	125.00	300.00	500.00	1000.
	Obv: Masonry crown over oval arms.					
82b	1767 SR	—	125.00	200.00	400.00	800.00
	1768 SR	—	125.00	200.00	400.00	800.00
	1776 SR	—	125.00	200.00	400.00	800.00
	Obv: Bust of Francis II right. Rev: Value in cartouche, date above, arms below.					
83	1795	—	900.00	1500.	2200.	2800.

TRADE COINS

1/2 DUCAT

GOLD

C#	Date	Mintage	Fine	VF	XF	Unc
84	1773	—	175.00	300.00	500.00	750.00

DUCAT

3.5000 gm., .986 GOLD, .1109 oz AGW

C#	Date	Mintage	Fine	VF	XF	Unc
86	1766 SR	—	1000.	1500.	2250.	3500.
	Obv: City view. Rev: Bust of Leopold II right.					
87	1790	—	850.00	1350.	1750.	2500.
	Rev: Bust of Francis II right.					
88	ND(1792)	—	750.00	1250.	1650.	2500.

C#	Date	Mintage	Fine	VF	XF	Unc
89	1806	—	250.00	400.00	650.00	1000.

2 DUCATS

7.0000 gm., .986 GOLD, .2219 oz AGW
Obv: City view. Rev: Lamb with flag.

C#	Date	Mintage	Fine	VF	XF	Unc
90	1806	—	500.00	1150.	1925.	3200.

3 DUCATS

10.5000 gm., .986 GOLD, .3329 oz AGW
Obv: City view. Rev: Lamb with flag.

C#	Date	Mintage	Fine	VF	XF	Unc
—	1806	—	1000.	2150.	3600.	6000.

OLDENBURG

The county of Oldenburg, located on the North Sea, near Friesland was established in 1180. The first coins were struck c. 1290. It was ruled by Denmark from 1667 to 1773 and was raised to the status of duchy in 1777. The Bishopric of Lubeck was joined to it in 1803 and the territory was annexed to France in 1810. The 1815 Congress of Vienna elevated Oldenburg to grand duchy. They entered the German Empire in 1871 and remained there until the grand duke abdicated in 1918.

RULERS

Friedrich V of Denmark, 1746-1766
Christian VII of Denmark, 1766-1773
Friedrich August
  As Count, 1773
  As Duke, 1775-1785
Peter Friedrich Wilhelm, 1785-1823
Peter Friedrich Ludwig, 1823-1829
Paul Friedrich August, 1829-1853
Nickolaus Friedrich Peter, 1853-1900
Friedrich August, 1900-1918

MINTMASTER'S INITIALS

I.H.M. - Johann Heinrich Madelung
N - Samuel Mathias Neudorf
B - Johann Ephraim Bauert

2 PFENNIG

BILLON
Obv: Crowned FV monogram.
Rev: Value and date.

C#	Date	Mintage	Good	VG	Fine	VF
2	1764	.014	2.50	5.00	10.00	20.00

4 PFENNIG

BILLON
Obv: Crowned F5R monogram, A.D.M.F. below.
Rev: Value and date, I.H.M. below date.

C#	Date	Mintage	Good	VG	Fine	VF
5	1762	.629	2.00	4.00	8.00	20.00
	1763	.016	3.00	6.00	10.00	20.00

SCHWAREN

COPPER

C#	Date	Mintage	Fine	VF	XF	Unc
43	1846	.126	2.50	5.00	10.00	40.00

Rev: B below date.

C#	Date	Mintage	Fine	VF	XF	Unc
43a	1852 B	.144	2.50	5.00	10.00	40.00

C#	Date	Mintage	Fine	VF	XF	Unc
54	1854 B	.072	2.50	5.00	9.00	40.00
	1856 B	.072	2.50	5.00	9.00	40.00

C#	Date	Mintage	Fine	VF	XF	Unc
55	1858 B	1.084	1.00	3.00	6.00	35.00
	1859 B	.108	1.50	3.00	6.00	40.00
	1860 B	.288	1.50	3.00	6.00	40.00
	1862 B	.180	1.50	3.00	6.00	40.00
	1864 B	.180	1.50	3.00	6.00	40.00
	1865 B	.108	1.50	3.00	6.00	40.00
	1866 B	.144	1.50	3.00	6.00	40.00
	1869 B	.180	1.50	3.00	6.00	40.00

3 SCHWAREN

(= 3 Pfennig)

COPPER

C#	Date	Mintage	Fine	VF	XF	Unc
57	1858 B	.372	1.50	3.00	6.00	40.00
	1859 B	.432	1.50	3.00	6.00	40.00
	1860 B	.060	1.50	3.00	10.00	40.00
	1862 B	.012	1.50	3.00	10.00	40.00
	1864 B	.060	1.50	3.00	10.00	40.00
	1865 B	.060	1.50	3.00	10.00	40.00
	1866 B	.036	1.50	3.00	10.00	40.00
	1869 B	.096	1.50	3.00	10.00	40.00

1/4 GROTE

(= 1 Pfennig)

COPPER

C#	Date	Mintage	Fine	VF	XF	Unc
44	1846	.090	2.50	5.00	10.00	40.00

1/2 GROTE

COPPER

C#	Date	Mintage	Fine	VF	XF	Unc
25	1802	.078	4.50	8.00	15.00	40.00
	1816	.149	4.50	8.00	15.00	40.00

C#	Date	Mintage	Fine	VF	XF	Unc
45	1831	.072	2.50	4.00	9.00	40.00
	1835	.075	2.50	4.00	9.00	40.00

Obv: Crowned square-bottomed shield without garlands.

C#	Date	Mintage	Fine	VF	XF	Unc
45a	1840	.122	2.50	4.00	9.00	40.00

C#	Date	Mintage	Fine	VF	XF	Unc
46	1846	.088	2.50	4.00	9.00	40.00

C#	Date	Mintage	Fine	VF	XF	Unc
56	1853 B	.072	2.00	4.00	9.00	40.00
	1856 B	.072	2.00	4.00	9.00	40.00

GROTE

BILLON

Obv: Crowned F5R monogram; 15TH A.D.M.F. below. Rev: Value and date.

C#	Date	Mintage	Good	VG	Fine	VF
4.1	1761	.181	3.00	6.00	10.00	20.00

Obv: Crowned F5R monogram; 15TH at sides, A.D.M.F. below.

C#	Date	Mintage	Good	VG	Fine	VF
4.2	1761	Inc. Ab.	3.00	6.00	10.00	20.00

Obv: Crowned arms. Rev: Value and date.

C#	Date	Mintage	Good	VG	Fine	VF
27	1792	.072	3.00	6.00	10.00	20.00

Obv: Crowned arms with garland, N.D.C.F. Rev: Value.

C#	Date	Mintage	Fine	VF	XF	Unc
28	1817	.391	5.00	10.00	20.00	40.00

Obv. leg: SCHEIDE-M.

C#	Date	Mintage	Fine	VF	XF	Unc
47	1836 B	.361	4.00	8.00	15.00	40.00

C#	Date	Mintage	Fine	VF	XF	Unc
48	1849 B	.043	3.00	6.00	10.00	40.00
	1850 B	.081	3.00	6.00	10.00	40.00

C#	Date	Mintage	Fine	VF	XF	Unc
58	1853 B	.057	3.00	6.00	10.00	40.00
	1856 B	.072	3.00	6.00	10.00	40.00
	1857 B	.027	3.00	6.00	10.00	40.00

1-1/2 GROTE

BILLON

Obv: Crowned F5R monogram; small letters below monogram. Rev: Value and date.

C#	Date	Mintage	Good	VG	Fine	VF
6.1	1761	.230	3.50	7.00	12.50	20.00

Obv: 15-TH at sides of monogram.

C#	Date	Mintage	Good	VG	Fine	VF
6.2	1761	Inc. Ab.	3.50	7.00	12.50	20.00

Obv: Large letters below monogram.

C#	Date	Mintage	Good	VG	Fine	VF
6.3	1761	Inc. Ab.	3.50	7.00	12.50	20.00

Obv: Crowned arms. Rev: Value and date.

C#	Date	Mintage	Good	VG	Fine	VF
30	1791	.048	2.50	5.00	8.50	15.00

2 GROTE

(= 1/36 Thaler)

BILLON

Obv: Crowned F5R monogram, A.D.M.F. below. Rev: Value and date.

C#	Date	Mintage	Good	VG	Fine	VF
8	1761	.548	3.50	7.00	12.50	20.00

C#	Date	Mintage	Good	VG	Fine	VF
32	1792	.396	2.00	4.00	8.50	15.00

Obv. leg: N.D.C.F.

C#	Date	Mintage	Fine	VF	XF	Unc
33	1815	1.080	5.00	10.00	15.00	40.00

3 GROTE

(= 1/24 Thaler)

BILLON

Obv: Crowned F5R monogram; 14-1/2 TH A.D.M.F. below. Rev: Value and date.

C#	Date	Mintage	Good	VG	Fine	VF
10	1761	.119	5.00	10.00	20.00	35.00

C#	Date	Mintage	Fine	VF	XF	Unc
49	1840 S	.486	4.00	8.00	15.00	40.00

C#	Date	Mintage	Fine	VF	XF	Unc
61	1856 B	.156	4.50	9.00	15.00	40.00

4 GROTE

(= 1/18 Thaler)

BILLON

Obv: Crowned F5R monogram; 14-1/2 TH A.D.M.F. below. Rev: Value and date.

C#	Date	Mintage	Good	VG	Fine	VF
12	1761	.409	5.00	10.00	20.00	32.50

Obv: Crowned arms.

C#	Date	Mintage	Good	VG	Fine	VF
34	1792	.036	4.00	7.50	12.50	25.00

Obv: Crowned arms with garlands, N.D.C.F. Rev: Value.

C#	Date	Mintage	Fine	VF	XF	Unc
35	1816	.393	5.00	10.00	20.00	40.00
	1818	.126	5.00	10.00	20.00	40.00

C#	Date	Mintage	Fine	VF	XF	Unc
50	1840 S	.380	3.00	6.50	10.00	40.00

6 GROTE

(= 1/12 Thaler)

2.9200 gm., .500 SILVER, .0469 oz ASW

Obv: Head of Friedrich right. Rev: Value and date in circle.

C#	Date	Mintage	Good	VG	Fine	VF
14.1	1761	.137	7.00	15.00	25.00	50.00

Obv: N below head.

C#	Date	Mintage	Good	VG	Fine	VF
14.2	1761 N	Inc. Ab.	7.00	15.00	25.00	50.00

Rev: No circle around value and date.

C#	Date	Mintage	Good	VG	Fine	VF
14.3	1763 B	.070	7.00	15.00	25.00	50.00
	1764 N	Inc. Ab.	7.00	15.00	25.00	50.00

Obv: Crowned shield with garlands. Rev: Value.

C#	Date	Mintage	Fine	VF	XF	Unc
37	1816	.309	5.00	10.00	20.00	40.00
	1818	.060	5.00	10.00	20.00	40.00

12 GROTE

(= 1/6 Thaler)

5.8500 gm., .500 SILVER, .0940 oz ASW

Obv: Head of Friedrich right. Rev: Value and date in circle.

C#	Date	Mintage	Fine	VF	XF	Unc
15.1	1761	.145	20.00	35.00	55.00	85.00
	1761 N	Inc. Ab.	20.00	35.00	55.00	85.00
	1761 B	Inc. Ab.	20.00	35.00	55.00	85.00

Rev: I.H.M. at bottom.

C#	Date	Mintage	Fine	VF	XF	Unc
15.2	1763	.232	20.00	35.00	55.00	85.00
	1763 B	Inc. Ab.	20.00	35.00	55.00	85.00
	1763 N	Inc. Ab.	20.00	35.00	55.00	85.00
	1764	Inc. Ab.	20.00	35.00	55.00	85.00
	1764 N	Inc. Ab.	20.00	35.00	55.00	85.00
	1765 N	Inc. Ab.	20.00	35.00	55.00	85.00

4.8700 gm., .520 SILVER, .0783 oz ASW

C#	Date	Mintage	Fine	VF	XF	Unc
39	1816	.036	12.00	25.00	40.00	60.00
	1818	.066	12.00	25.00	40.00	60.00

1/2 GROSCHEN

BILLON

C#	Date	Mintage	Fine	VF	XF	Unc
59	1858 B	1.020	2.00	5.00	9.00	35.00
	1864 B	.060	2.50	5.00	10.00	40.00
	1865 B	.048	2.50	5.00	10.00	40.00
	1866 B	.168	2.50	5.00	10.00	40.00
	1869 B	.120	2.50	5.00	10.00	40.00

MARIENGROSCHEN

BILLON

C#	Date	Mintage	Good	VG	Fine	VF
9.1	1761	—	2.00	4.00	8.50	15.00
	1762	1.967	2.00	4.00	8.50	15.00

Rev: I.H.M. below date.

C#	Date	Mintage	Good	VG	Fine	VF
9.2	1762	—	2.00	4.00	8.50	15.00
	1763	.232	2.00	4.00	8.50	15.00

Rev: Value stated GROSCH.

C#	Date	Mintage	Good	VG	Fine	VF
9.3	1762	—	2.00	4.00	8.50	15.00

GROSCHEN

BILLON

C#	Date	Mintage	Fine	VF	XF	Unc
60	1858 B	.720	2.00	5.00	10.00	35.00

C#	Date	Mintage	Fine	VF	XF	Unc
60a	1858 B	1.080	3.00	7.50	10.00	35.00
	1864 B	.030	3.50	7.50	10.00	50.00
	1865 B	.030	3.50	7.50	10.00	50.00
	1866 B	.120	3.50	7.50	10.00	40.00
	1869 B	.090	3.50	7.50	10.00	40.00

2 MARIENGROSCHEN

BILLON
Obv: Crowned F5R monogram; 14-1/2 TH A.D.M.F. below. Rev: Value and date.

C#	Date	Mintage	Good	VG	Fine	VF
13.1	1761	Inc. Ab.	4.00	7.50	12.50	25.00
	Rev: I.H.M. below date.					
13.2	1762	.874	4.00	7.50	12.50	25.00
	1763	.523	4.00	7.50	12.50	25.00
	Obv: "2" to left of monogram. Rev: No letters below date.					
13.3	1761	Inc. Ab.	4.00	7.50	12.50	25.00
	1762	Inc. Ab.	4.00	7.50	12.50	25.00
	Rev: I.H.M. below date.					
13.4	1762	Inc. Ab.	4.00	7.50	12.50	25.00
	1763	Inc. Ab.	4.00	7.50	12.50	25.00

2-1/2 GROSCHEN

(= 1/12 Thaler)

3.2200 gm., .375 SILVER, .0388 oz ASW

C#	Date	Mintage	Fine	VF	XF	Unc
62	1858 B	.600	3.50	7.00	10.00	35.00

1/48 THALER

BILLON
Obv: Crowned F5R monogram, A.D.M.F. below date at sides. Rev: Value; I.H.M. below value.

C#	Date	Mintage	Good	VG	Fine	VF
7	1762	.412	2.50	5.00	8.50	15.00

1/24 THALER

BILLON
Obv: Crowned F5R monogram; 14-1/2 TH A.D.M.F. below, date at sides. Rev: Value, I.H.M. below value.

C#	Date	Mintage	Good	VG	Fine	VF
11	1762	.277	3.00	6.00	12.50	25.00

1/6 THALER

5.3500 gm., .521 SILVER, .0896 oz ASW

C#	Date	Mintage	Fine	VF	XF	Unc
51	1846 B	.164	15.00	30.00	40.00	65.00

1/3 THALER

8.6600 gm., .750 SILVER, .2088 oz ASW
Obv: Head of Friedrich right.
Rev: Large fraction in center.

C#	Date	Mintage	Fine	VF	XF	Unc
17	1761 B	8,358	50.00	75.00	110.00	165.00
	1762 B	5,538	50.00	75.00	110.00	165.00

.625 SILVER

C#	Date	Mintage	Fine	VF	XF	Unc
41	1816	.018	40.00	65.00	125.00	275.00
	1818	.033	40.00	65.00	125.00	275.00

2/3 THALER

17.3200 gm., .750 SILVER, .4177 oz ASW
Obv: Head of Friedrich right.
Rev: Large fraction in circle.

C#	Date	Mintage	Fine	VF	XF	Unc
18.1	1761 B	.033	45.00	95.00	150.00	225.00
	1761 N	Inc. Ab.	45.00	95.00	150.00	225.00
	Rev: Date at bottom.					
18.2	1761 B	Inc. Ab.	45.00	95.00	150.00	225.00
	1761 N	Inc. Ab.	45.00	95.00	150.00	225.00
	1762 B	.115	45.00	95.00	150.00	225.00
	1762 N	Inc. Ab.	45.00	95.00	150.00	225.00
	1763 N	—	45.00	95.00	150.00	225.00
	1764 N	.034	45.00	95.00	150.00	225.00
	1765 N	—	45.00	95.00	150.00	225.00

EIN (1) THALER

22.2700 gm., .750 SILVER, .5370 oz ASW

C#	Date	Mintage	Fine	VF	XF	Unc
52	1846 B	.042	75.00	125.00	250.00	500.00

18.5200 gm., .900 SILVER, .5360 oz ASW

C#	Date	Mintage	Fine	VF	XF	Unc
63	1858	.017	55.00	90.00	165.00	350.00
	1860	.047	50.00	80.00	150.00	300.00
	1866	.072	45.00	75.00	135.00	275.00

2 THALER

(= 3-1/2 Gulden)

37.1200 gm., .900 SILVER, 1.0742 oz ASW

C#	Date	Mintage	Fine	VF	XF	Unc
53	1840	.019	600.00	1200.	2400.	4500.
	1840	—	—	—	Proof	4000.

MONETARY REFORM

2 MARK

11.1110 gm., .900 SILVER, .3215 oz ASW

Y#	Date	Mintage	VF	XF	Unc
108	1891A	.100	165.00	250.00	400.00
	1891A	—	—	Proof	500.00

Y#	Date	Mintage	VF	XF	Unc
109	1900A	.050	125.00	200.00	350.00
	1901A	.075	125.00	200.00	350.00
	Common Type	—	—	Proof	600.00

5 MARK

27.7770 gm., .900 SILVER, .8038 oz ASW

Y#	Date	Mintage	VF	XF	Unc
110	1900A	.020	300.00	600.00	2000.
	1900A	—	—	Proof	2500.
	1901A	.010	350.00	700.00	2000.
	1901A	—	—	Proof	2500.

10 MARK

3.9820 gm., .900 GOLD, .1152 oz AGW

Y#	Date	Mintage	VF	XF	Unc
107	1874B	.015	2250.	3250.	4300.

OSNABRUCK

The city of Osnabruck is located northeast of Munster. Although the city owed its original growth to the bishopric it achieved considerable independence from the bishops and joined the Hanseatic League. It had its own local coinage from the early 16th century until 1805. It was absorbed by Hannover in 1803.

HELLER

COPPER
Obv: Arms. Rev: Value over date.

C#	Date	Mintage	VG	Fine	VF	XF
1	1790	—	6.00	15.00	25.00	40.00

Obv: Wheel. Rev: Value, date below.

C#	Date	Mintage	Fine	VF	XF	Unc
1a	1791	—	2.50	5.00	9.00	45.00
	1795	—	2.50	5.00	9.00	45.00
	1801	—	2.50	5.00	9.00	45.00

PFENNING

COPPER
Obv: Arms. Rev: Value over date.

C#	Date	Mintage	VG	Fine	VF	XF
2	1790	—	7.50	15.00	25.00	40.00

Obv: Wheel. Rev: Value, date below.

C#	Date	Mintage	Fine	VF	XF	Unc
3	1791	—	2.50	5.00	10.00	45.00

1-1/2 PFENNING

COPPER
Obv: Wheel. Rev: Value, date below.

C#	Date	Mintage	Fine	VF	XF	Unc
5	1791	—	2.50	5.00	10.00	45.00
	1795	—	2.50	5.00	10.00	45.00
	1805	—	2.50	5.00	10.00	45.00

2 PFENNING

COPPER
Obv: Wheel. Rev: Value, date below.

C#	Date	Mintage	Fine	VF	XF	Unc
7	1791	—	2.50	5.00	10.00	45.00
	1792	—	2.50	5.00	10.00	45.00
	1793	—	2.50	5.00	10.00	45.00
	1794	—	2.50	5.00	10.00	45.00
	1795	—	2.50	5.00	10.00	45.00
	1796	—	2.50	5.00	10.00	45.00
	1797	—	2.50	5.00	10.00	45.00
	1798	—	2.50	5.00	10.00	45.00
	1799	—	2.50	5.00	10.00	45.00
	1800	—	2.50	5.00	10.00	45.00
	1801	—	2.50	5.00	10.00	45.00
	1802	—	2.50	5.00	10.00	45.00
	1803	—	2.50	5.00	10.00	45.00
	1804	—	2.50	5.00	10.00	45.00
	1805	—	2.50	5.00	10.00	45.00

3 PFENNING

COPPER
Obv: Wheel between 2 wildmen.
Rev: Value over date.

C#	Date	Mintage	VG	Fine	VF	XF
10	1790	—	20.00	35.00	60.00	95.00

C#	Date	Mintage	Fine	VF	XF	Unc
11	1805	—	4.00	8.00	15.00	45.00

PADERBORN

The city of Paderborn is located in Westphalia. It owed its initial growth to the bishopric which was founded in 795 and obtained the mint right in 1028. As Paderborn's prosperity grew they joined the Hanseatic League, however they did not receive the mint right. In 1605 the Bishop struck copper coins bearing the Greek word "gift." It was secularized and annexed to Prussia in 1803. From 1807 to 1813 the district was joined to Westphalia, but reverted back to Prussia in the latter year.

RULERS
Wilhelm Anton, 1763-1782
Friedrich Wilhelm, 1782-1789

PFENNIG

COPPER
Obv: Arms. Rev: Value.

C#	Date	Mintage	VG	Fine	VF	XF
40	1786	—	2.00	4.00	8.00	20.00

16 GUTE GROSCHEN

SILVER
Obv: Arms. Rev: Value.

C#	Date	Mintage	VG	Fine	VF	XF
44	1785	—	12.00	24.00	35.00	60.00

12 EINEN (1/12)THALER

BILLON
Obv: Arms. Rev: Value.

C#	Date	Mintage	VG	Fine	VF	XF
42	1783	—	2.50	5.00	10.00	25.00

1/2 THALER

(Convention)

SILVER
Obv: Arms. Rev: St. Liborius.

C#	Date	Mintage	VG	Fine	VF	XF
46	1786	—	15.00	35.00	50.00	75.00

TRADE COINS

DUCAT

3.5000 gm., .986 GOLD, .1109 oz AGW
Obv: Bust right. Rev: Crowned and mantled arms.

C#	Date	Mintage	Fine	VF	XF	Unc
38	1776	—	850.00	1250.	1950.	3000.
	1777	—	850.00	1250.	1950.	3000.

Obv: Crowned arms. Rev: Value over date.

C#	Date	Mintage	Fine	VF	XF	Unc
48	1784	—	900.00	1250.	2000.	3000.

PASSAU

The bishopric, in Bavaria near the Austrian border, was established in 738. The bishops obtained the mint right prior to 999 but they originally struck coins jointly at the imperial mint in Passau. Ecclesiastical coinage began in the 12th century. In 1803 they were secularized and divided between Bavaria and Salzburg. In 1805 Bavaria absorbed the Salzburg portion.

RULERS
Leopold Ernst, Bishop, 1763-1783
Joseph, Bishop, 1783-1795

EIN (1) THALER

SILVER
Obv: Bust right; H. ST on arm.
Rev: Capped and mantled arms; date below.

C#	Date	Mintage	VG	Fine	VF	XF
8	1779	—	300.00	500.00	900.00	1800.

C#	Date	Mintage	VG	Fine	VF	XF
10	1792	—	300.00	500.00	900.00	1800.

TRADE COINS

DUCAT

3.5000 gm., .986 GOLD, .1109 oz AGW
Obv: Bust right.
Rev: Capped and mantled arms; date below.

C#	Date	Mintage	Fine	VF	XF	Unc
9	1779	—	850.00	1250.	1750.	2500.

PFALZ

(Rhenish Palatinate, Rheinpfalz)

The office of count palatine of the Rhine is first mentioned in the 10th century and the first coins were struck in the 11th century. There were many divisions. The lines of Neuburg, Sulzbach, Zweibrucken and Birkenfeld were founded in 1569 and were culminated in Maximilian Josef of Zweibrucken who became king and elector of Bavaria by 1805.

Chur Pfalz

RULERS

Carl Theodor, 1742-1799
Elector Paletine, 1742-1799
Elector of Bavaria, 1777-1799

1/4 KREUZER

COPPER
Obv: Crowned arms.
Rev: Value over date in wreath.

C#	Date	Mintage	VG	Fine	VF	XF
2	1773-95	—	2.50	5.00	7.50	15.00

1/2 KREUZER

COPPER
Obv: Crowned arms.
Rev: Value over date in wreath.

C#	Date	Mintage	VG	Fine	VF	XF
3	1773-86	—	3.00	6.00	9.50	20.00

KREUZER
(Convention)

BILLON
Obv: 3-fold arms. Rev: Value and date.

C#	Date	Mintage	VG	Fine	VF	XF
15	1773	—	3.50	7.00	10.00	20.00

C#	Date	Mintage	VG	Fine	VF	XF
17	1773-95	—	3.00	6.00	9.50	20.00

Rev: Value and date.

C#	Date	Mintage	VG	Fine	VF	XF
21	1786	—	3.50	7.00	9.50	20.00

C#	Date	Mintage	VG	Fine	VF	XF
17a	1794	—	3.00	6.00	9.50	20.00

5 KREUZER
(Convention)

BILLON
Obv: Head right. Rev: 3-fold arms and value.

C#	Date	Mintage	VG	Fine	VF	XF
29a	1780-89	—	4.50	9.00	12.50	25.00

10 KREUZER
(Convention)

SILVER
Obv: Head right. Rev: 3-fold arms and value.

C#	Date	Mintage	VG	Fine	VF	XF
31a	1777-94	—	5.00	11.50	15.00	25.00

Vicariat Issue
Rev: Eagle with 3-fold arms on breast.

C#	Date	Mintage	VG	Fine	VF	XF
59.1	1790	—	4.00	8.00	15.00	25.00

Vicariat Issue
Rev: Date in legend.

C#	Date	Mintage	VG	Fine	VF	XF
59.6	1792	—	4.00	8.00	15.00	25.00

20 KREUZER
(Convention)

SILVER
Obv: Head right.
Rev: Eagle with 3-fold arms on breast.

C#	Date	Mintage	VG	Fine	VF	XF
38a	1779-93	—	4.00	8.00	15.00	25.00

Vicariat Issue
Rev: Imperial eagle.

C#	Date	Mintage	VG	Fine	VF	XF
59.2	1790	—	7.00	15.00	25.00	35.00

Vicariat Issue
Rev: Eagle with 3-fold arms on breast; date in legend.

C#	Date	Mintage	VG	Fine	VF	XF
59.7	1792	—	7.00	15.00	25.00	35.00

GULDEN

SILVER

C#	Date	Mintage	VG	Fine	VF	XF
51	1771	—	12.00	25.00	37.50	60.00
	1772	—	12.00	25.00	37.50	60.00
	1773	—	12.00	25.00	37.50	60.00
	1774	—	12.00	25.00	37.50	60.00
	1776	—	12.00	25.00	37.50	60.00

C#	Date	Mintage	VG	Fine	VF	XF
51a	1779-93	—	12.00	27.50	35.00	60.00

Vicariat Issue
Rev: Eagle with multiple arms on breast.

C#	Date	Mintage	VG	Fine	VF	XF
59.3	1790	—	12.00	27.50	40.00	65.00

Vicariat Issue
Obv: Armored bust right.
Rev: Eagle with 3-fold arms on breast.

C#	Date	Mintage	VG	Fine	VF	XF
59.8	1792	—	12.00	27.50	40.00	65.00

EIN (1) THALER
(Convention)

SILVER

C#	Date	Mintage	VG	Fine	VF	XF
59	1773 AS	—	75.00	150.00	300.00	600.00
	1774 AS	—	75.00	150.00	300.00	600.00
	1775 AS	—	75.00	150.00	300.00	600.00
	1776 AS	—	75.00	150.00	300.00	600.00
	1777 AS	—	75.00	150.00	300.00	600.00

NOTE: Varieties exist.

C#	Date	Mintage	VG	Fine	VF	XF
59a	1778-95	—	35.00	75.00	150.00	300.00

Obv: Curaissed bust right.

C#	Date	Mintage	VG	Fine	VF	XF
59b	1781 AS	—	65.00	100.00	150.00	300.00

Vicariat Issue

C#	Date	Mintage	VG	Fine	VF	XF
59.4	1790 AS	—	225.00	400.00	800.00	1500.

Vicariat Issue

C#	Date	Mintage	VG	Fine	VF	XF
59.9	1792 AS	—	300.00	600.00	900.00	1500.

TRADE COINS

DUCAT

3.5000 gm., .986 GOLD, .1109 oz AGW
Obv: Bust right.
Rev: City view of Mannheim.

C#	Date	Mintage	Fine	VF	XF	Unc
63	1778	—	950.00	1500.	2250.	3000.
	50th Year of Reign Commemorative **Obv: Lion holds city arms of Mannheim.** **Rev: 5 line inscription and date.**					
67	1792	—	650.00	950.00	1450.	2000.

Rhein Pfalz

RULERS

Maximilian Joseph,
Elector of Pfalz-Bayern,
1799-1805

1/2 KREUZER

COPPER
Obv: Crowned shield with lion, dividing RP.
Rev: Value and date within wreath.

C#	Date	Mintage	Fine	VF	XF	Unc
1	1802	—	3.50	7.00	14.00	40.00

KREUZER

COPPER
Obv: Crowned shield with lion, dividing RP.
Rev: Value and date within wreath.

C#	Date	Mintage	Fine	VF	XF	Unc
2	1802	—	5.00	10.00	20.00	40.00

EIN (1) THALER

(Convention)

SILVER
Obv: Head right.
Rev: Crowned shield within branches.

C#	Date	Mintage	Fine	VF	XF	Unc
3	1802	—	300.00	600.00	1250.	3000.

Pfalz-Birkenfeld -Zweibrucken

RULERS

Christian IV, 1735-1775
Carl II, 1775-1795

HELLER

COPPER
Obv: Crowned C P monogram.
Rev: Value over date.

C#	Date	Mintage	VG	Fine	VF	XF
34	1788	—	3.00	6.00	9.50	20.00

1/2 KREUZER

COPPER
Obv: Crowned C P monogram.
Rev: Value over date.

C#	Date	Mintage	VG	Fine	VF	XF
35	1788	—	2.50	5.00	8.50	20.00

KREUZER

COPPER

C#	Date	Mintage	VG	Fine	VF	XF
3	1774	—	4.00	8.00	12.50	20.00

C#	Date	Mintage	VG	Fine	VF	XF
36	1788	—	2.50	5.00	7.50	18.00

EIN (1) THALER

(Convention)

SILVER

C#	Date	Mintage	VG	Fine	VF	XF
31	1765 IM	—	100.00	300.00	500.00	1000.
	1775 IM	—	100.00	300.00	500.00	1000.

NOTE: Varieties exist.

TRADE COINS

DUCAT

3.5000 gm., .986 GOLD, .1109 oz AGW

C#	Date	Mintage	Fine	VF	XF	Unc
40	1788 W	—	750.00	1150.	1750.	2500.
	1790 W	—	750.00	1150.	1750.	2500.

2 DUCATS

7.0000 gm., .986 GOLD, .2219 oz AGW
Obv: Head right; numeral 2 below.
Rev: Crowned and mantled arms with supporters divide date.

C#	Date	Mintage	Fine	VF	XF	Unc
41	1788	—	1750.	2250.	3000.	4000.

POMERANIA

A duchy on the Baltic Sea, near modern day Poland, was founded in the late 11th century. After many divisions, Pomerania was annexed to Sweden in 1637. Brandenburg—Prussia had an interest in the area and slowly acquired bits until in 1815 all of Pomerania belonged to Prussia. The arms of Pomerania appear on coins of Brandenburg—Prussia from the 17th century onward.

RULERS

Adolf Fredrik of Sweden, 1751-1771
Gustav III, King of Sweden, 1771-1792
Gustav IV Adolf of Sweden, 1792-1809

3 PFENNINGE

COPPER
Obv: Crowned griffon holding sword, "K.3.P.L.M."
Rev: Value over date.

C#	Date	Mintage	VG	Fine	VF	XF
27	1776	.384	5.00	10.00	15.00	25.00
	1792	.384	5.00	10.00	15.00	25.00
29	1806	.384	5.00	10.00	15.00	25.00
	1808	.258	5.00	10.00	15.00	25.00
	Obv. leg: "K. SCHWED. POM. LANDES M".					
30	1806	—	—	—	Rare	—
	Obv. leg: "K.S.P. LANDESM".					
31	1808	—	—	—	Rare	—

2 GUTE GROSCHEN

(= 1/2 Thaler)

SILVER
Obv: Crowned script AFR monogram; date below.
Rev: Crowned griffon holding sword; value in exergue.

C#	Date	Mintage	VG	Fine	VF	XF
8	1759	—	7.00	15.00	25.00	50.00

4 GUTE GROSCHEN

SILVER
Obv: Crowned AFR monogram; date below.
Rev: Crowned griffon holding sword; value in exergue.

C#	Date	Mintage	VG	Fine	VF	XF
12	1758 OHK	—	30.00	65.00	100.00	150.00
	1759 OHK	—	30.00	65.00	100.00	150.00

8 GUTE GROSCHEN

SILVER
Obv: Crowned AFR monogram; date below.

Rev: Crowned griffon holding sword; value in exergue.

C#	Date	Mintage	VG	Fine	VF	XF
17	1758 OHK	—	15.00	35.00	50.00	85.00
	1759 OHK	—	15.00	35.00	50.00	85.00
	1760 OHK	—	15.00	35.00	50.00	85.00

Obv: Head of Adolf Fredrik right.
Rev: Value and date.

C#	Date	Mintage	VG	Fine	VF	XF
19	1760 OHK	—	35.00	75.00	100.00	150.00
	1761 LFK	—	35.00	75.00	100.00	150.00
	1761 ICS	—	35.00	75.00	100.00	150.00
	1761 IHL	—	35.00	75.00	100.00	150.00

1/48 THALER

BILLON
Obv: Crowned script AFR monogram; date below.
Rev: Value.

C#	Date	Mintage	VG	Fine	VF	XF
2	1760 OHK	—	5.00	10.00	15.00	25.00
	1761 LFK	—	5.00	10.00	15.00	25.00
	1761 IDL	—	5.00	10.00	15.00	25.00
	1761 IHL	—	5.00	10.00	15.00	25.00
	1761 LDS	—	5.00	10.00	15.00	25.00

Obv: Crowned AF monogram; date below.
Rev: Value in inner circle.

C#	Date	Mintage	VG	Fine	VF	XF
3	1763 IDL	—	5.00	10.00	15.00	25.00
	1763 LDS	—	5.00	10.00	15.00	25.00

1/24 THALER

BILLON
Obv: Crowned script AFR monogram; date below.
Rev: Value.

C#	Date	Mintage	VG	Fine	VF	XF
5	1759 OHK	—	6.00	12.50	20.00	35.00
	1760 OHK	—	6.00	12.50	20.00	35.00
	1761 LFK	—	6.00	12.50	20.00	35.00
	1761 ICS	—	6.00	12.50	20.00	35.00
	1761 IHL	—	6.00	12.50	20.00	35.00
	1761 IDL	—	6.00	12.50	20.00	35.00

Obv: Crowned AF monogram; date below "K.S.P.L.M." above.

C#	Date	Mintage	VG	Fine	VF	XF
6	1763 IDL	—	7.00	13.50	22.50	40.00
	1763 IDL no "K.S.P.L.M."	—	7.00	13.50	22.50	40.00

1/12 THALER

SILVER
Obv: Head of Adolf Fredrik right.
Rev: Value and date.

C#	Date	Mintage	VG	Fine	VF	XF
9	1761 IDL	—	7.00	15.00	25.00	50.00

GOLD (weight of 1 Ducat)

C#	Date	Mintage	VG	Fine	VF	XF
—	1761 IDL	—	—	—	Rare	—

SILVER
Obv: Crowned AF monogram.
Rev: Value in inner circle.

C#	Date	Mintage	VG	Fine	VF	XF
10	1763 IDL	—	7.00	15.00	25.00	50.00
	1763 IHL	—	7.00	15.00	25.00	50.00
	1763 LDS	—	7.00	15.00	25.00	50.00
	1767 IHL	—	7.00	15.00	25.00	50.00
	1767 LDS	—	7.00	15.00	25.00	50.00
	1768 LDS	—	7.00	15.00	25.00	50.00

GOLD (weight of 1 Ducat)

C#	Date	Mintage	VG	Fine	VF	XF
—	1763 IDL	—	—	—	Rare	—

1/6 THALER

SILVER
Obv: Head of Adolf Fredrik right.
Rev: Value and date.

C#	Date	Mintage	VG	Fine	VF	XF
15	1760 OHK	—	15.00	35.00	55.00	95.00
	1761 LFK	—	15.00	35.00	55.00	95.00
	1761 ICS	—	15.00	35.00	55.00	95.00
	1761 IHL	—	15.00	35.00	55.00	95.00
	1761 DL	—	15.00	35.00	55.00	95.00
	1761 F	—	15.00	35.00	55.00	95.00

1/3 THALER

SILVER
Rev: Value and date in branches.

C#	Date	Mintage	VG	Fine	VF	XF
20	1760	—	45.00	100.00	125.00	165.00

Rev: Crowned and supported arms; date and value in exergue.

C#	Date	Mintage	VG	Fine	VF	XF
21	1763 IHL	—	50.00	100.00	150.00	200.00

2/3 THALER

SILVER
Obv: Head of Adolf Fredrik right.
Rev: Crowned and supported arms; date and value in exergue.

C#	Date	Mintage	VG	Fine	VF	XF
23	1763 IHL	—	75.00	150.00	200.00	300.00

5 THALER

6.6500 gm., .900 GOLD, .1924 oz AGW
Obv: Head of Adolf Fredrik right.
Rev: Crowned griffon holding sword; date above, value in exergue.

C#	Date	Mintage	VG	Fine	VF	XF
25	1759 OHK	—	700.00	1250.	1850.	2750.

10 THALER

13.3000 gm., .900 GOLD, .3848 oz AGW
Obv: Head of Adolf Fredrik right.
Rev: Crowned griffon holding sword; date above, value in exergue.

C#	Date	Mintage	VG	Fine	VF	XF
26	1759 OHK	—	1500.	2250.	3500.	4750.

PRINCE PRIMATE

OF THE RHENISH CONFEDERATION

Issues For Carl Von Dalberg, 1804-1817

HELLER

COPPER
Obv. leg: FURST PRIM SCHEIDE MUNZ.
Rev: Value between stars.

C#	Date	Mintage	Fine	VF	XF	Unc
1	1808	.033	4.00	8.00	15.00	40.00
	1810	—	4.00	8.00	15.00	40.00
	1812	—	4.00	8.00	15.00	40.00

Obv. leg: GROSH FRANKF SCHEIDE MUNZ.

C#	Date	Mintage	Fine	VF	XF	Unc
2	1810	—	4.00	8.00	15.00	40.00
	1812	—	4.00	8.00	15.00	40.00

KREUZER

BILLON
Obv. leg: SCHEID.MUNZ.

C#	Date	Mintage	Fine	VF	XF	Unc
3	1808 BH	—	5.00	10.00	20.00	50.00
	1809 BH	—	5.00	10.00	20.00	50.00
	1810 BH	—	5.00	10.00	20.00	50.00

Obv. leg: SCHEIDMUNZ.

C#	Date	Mintage	Fine	VF	XF	Unc
	1809 BH	—	5.00	10.00	20.00	50.00

1/2 THALER

(Convention)

.833 SILVER

C#	Date	Mintage	Fine	VF	XF	Unc
5	1809 B	—	75.00	150.00	225.00	400.00

EIN (1) THALER

(Convention)

28.0600 gm., .833 SILVER, .7516 oz ASW

C#	Date	Mintage	Fine	VF	XF	Unc
4	1808 BH	—	150.00	300.00	600.00	1200.

.833 SILVER

C#	Date	Mintage	Fine	VF	XF	Unc
6	1809 B	—	125.00	250.00	500.00	1000.

C#	Date	Mintage	Fine	VF	XF	Unc
7	1809 CB	—	150.00	300.00	600.00	1200.

TRADE COINS

DUCAT

3.5000 gm., .986 GOLD, .1109 oz AGW

C#	Date	Mintage	Fine	VF	XF	Unc
8	1809 BH	—	700.00	1050.	1800.	3000.

PRUSSIA

The Kingdom of Prussia, Located In north central Germany, came into being in 1701. The ruler received the title of King in Prussia in exchange for his support during the War of the Spanish Succession. During the Napoleonic Wars, Prussia allied itself with Saxony. When they were defeated in 1806 they were forced to cede a large portion of their territory. In 1813 the French were expelled and their territories were returned to them plus additional territories. After defeating Denmark and Austria, in 1864 and 1866 they acquired more territory. Prussia was the pivotal state of unification of Germany in 1871 and their King was proclaimed emperor of all Germany. World War I brought an end to the Empire and the Kingdom of Prussia in 1918.

RULERS

Friedrich II, 1740-1786
Friedrich Wilhelm II, 1786-1797
Friedrich Wilhelm III, 1797-1840
Friedrich Wilhelm IV, 1840-1861
Wilhelm I, 1861-1888
Friedrich III, March 1888-June 1888
Wilhelm II, 1888-1918

MINTMARKS

A - Berlin = Prussia, East Friesland, East Prussia, Posen
B - Bayreuth = Brandenburg-Ausbach-Bayreuth
B - Breslau = Silesia, Posen, South Prussia
C - = Cleve
D - Aurich = East Friesland, Prussia
E - Konigsberg = East Prussia
S - Schwabach = Brandenburg-Ausbach-Bayreuth

PFENNIG

(Guter)

BILLON
Obv: Crowned FR monogram with date below.
Rev: Value with "A" mintmark below.

C#	Date	Mintage	VG	Fine	VF	XF
3a	1768A	—	5.00	10.00	15.00	25.00
	1769A	—	5.00	10.00	15.00	25.00
	1770A	—	5.00	10.00	15.00	25.00

Obv: Crowned FR monogram with "A" mintmark below.
Rev: Value over date

C#	Date	Mintage	VG	Fine	VF	XF
3b	1771A	—	5.00	10.00	15.00	25.00
	1772A	—	5.00	10.00	15.00	25.00
	1773A	—	5.00	10.00	15.00	25.00
	1774A	—	5.00	10.00	15.00	25.00
	1775A	—	5.00	10.00	15.00	25.00
	1776A	—	5.00	10.00	15.00	25.00
	1777A	—	5.00	10.00	15.00	25.00
	1778A	—	5.00	10.00	15.00	25.00
	1779A	—	5.00	10.00	15.00	25.00
	1780A	—	5.00	10.00	15.00	25.00
	1781A	—	5.00	10.00	15.00	25.00
	1782A	—	5.00	10.00	15.00	25.00
	1783A	—	5.00	10.00	15.00	25.00
	1784A	—	5.00	10.00	15.00	25.00
	1785A	—	5.00	10.00	15.00	25.00
	1786A	—	5.00	10.00	15.00	25.00

COPPER
Similar to C#95.

C#	Date	Mintage	VG	Fine	VF	XF
80	1788	—	2.00	4.00	6.00	15.00
	1789	—	2.00	4.00	6.00	15.00
	1790	—	2.00	4.00	6.00	15.00
	1791	—	2.00	4.00	6.00	15.00
	1792	—	2.00	4.00	6.00	15.00
	1793	—	2.00	4.00	6.00	15.00
	1794	—	2.00	4.00	6.00	15.00
	1795	—	2.00	4.00	6.00	15.00
	1796	—	2.00	4.00	6.00	15.00
	1797	—	2.00	4.00	6.00	15.00

C#	Date	Mintage	VG	Fine	VF	XF
95	1799	—	2.00	3.75	5.00	12.00
	1801	—	2.00	3.75	5.00	12.00
	1804	—	2.00	3.75	5.00	12.00
	1806	—	2.00	3.75	5.00	12.00

BILLON
Similar to C#95.

C#	Date	Mintage	VG	Fine	VF	XF
81	1787	—	2.00	3.00	5.00	15.00
	1788	—	2.00	3.00	5.00	15.00
	1789	—	2.00	3.00	5.00	15.00
	1790	—	2.00	3.00	5.00	15.00
	1791	—	2.00	3.00	5.00	15.00
	1792	—	2.00	3.00	5.00	15.00
	1793	—	2.00	3.00	5.00	15.00
	1794	—	2.00	3.00	5.00	15.00
	1795	—	2.00	3.00	5.00	15.00
	1796	—	2.00	3.00	5.00	15.00
	1797	—	2.00	3.00	5.00	15.00

Obv: Crowned FRW monogram.

C#	Date	Mintage	VG	Fine	VF	XF
100	1799A	—	4.00	8.00	16.00	25.00
	1801A	—	4.00	8.00	16.00	25.00
	1802A	—	4.00	8.00	16.00	25.00
	1803A	—	4.00	8.00	16.00	25.00
	1804A	—	4.00	8.00	16.00	25.00

Obv: Smaller W in crowned FRW monogram.

C#	Date	Mintage	VG	Fine	VF	XF
100a	1804A	—	4.00	12.00	18.00	25.00
	1806A	—	4.00	12.00	18.00	25.00

COPPER

C#	Date	Mintage	Fine	VF	XF	Unc
97	1810A	—	2.00	4.00	10.00	50.00
	1811A	—	2.00	4.00	10.00	50.00
	1814A	—	2.00	4.00	10.00	50.00
	1816A	—	2.00	4.00	10.00	50.00

Rev: A below date.

C#	Date	Mintage	Fine	VF	XF	Unc
123	1821A	—	1.50	3.00	8.00	40.00
	1822A	—	1.50	3.00	8.00	40.00
	1825A	—	1.50	3.00	8.00	40.00
	1826A	—	1.50	3.00	8.00	40.00
	1827A	—	1.50	3.00	8.00	40.00
	1828A	—	1.50	3.00	8.00	40.00
	1832A	—	1.50	3.00	8.00	40.00
	1833A	—	1.50	3.00	8.00	40.00
	1835A	—	1.50	3.00	8.00	40.00
	1836A	—	1.50	3.00	8.00	40.00
	1837A	—	1.50	3.00	8.00	40.00
	1838A	—	1.50	3.00	8.00	40.00
	1839A	—	1.50	3.00	8.00	40.00
	1840A	—	1.50	3.00	8.00	40.00

Rev: B below date

C#	Date	Mintage	Fine	VF	XF	Unc
123a	1821B	—	4.00	8.00	14.00	50.00
	1822B	—	4.00	8.00	14.00	50.00
123b	1826B	—	4.00	8.00	14.00	50.00

Rev: D below date

C#	Date	Mintage	Fine	VF	XF	Unc
123c	1821D	—	1.50	3.00	8.00	40.00
	1822D	—	1.50	3.00	8.00	40.00
	1823D	—	1.50	3.00	8.00	40.00
	1824D	—	1.50	3.00	8.00	40.00
	1825D	—	1.50	3.00	8.00	40.00
	1826D	—	1.50	3.00	8.00	40.00
	1827D	—	1.50	3.00	8.00	40.00
	1828D	—	1.50	3.00	8.00	40.00
	1829D	—	1.50	3.00	8.00	40.00
	1830D	—	1.50	3.00	8.00	40.00
	1831D	—	1.50	3.00	8.00	40.00
	1832D	—	1.50	3.00	8.00	40.00
	1833D	—	1.50	3.00	8.00	40.00
	1834D	—	1.50	3.00	8.00	40.00
	1835D	—	1.50	3.00	8.00	40.00
	1836D	—	1.50	3.00	8.00	40.00
	1837D	—	1.50	3.00	8.00	40.00
	1838D	—	1.50	3.00	8.00	40.00
	1839D	—	1.50	3.00	8.00	40.00
	1840D	—	1.50	3.00	8.00	40.00

Rev: A below date

C#	Date	Mintage	Fine	VF	XF	Unc
136	1841A	—	1.00	2.00	5.00	40.00
	1842A	—	1.00	2.00	5.00	40.00

Rev: D below date

C#	Date	Mintage	Fine	VF	XF	Unc
136a	1841D	—	1.00	2.00	5.00	40.00
	1842D	—	1.00	2.00	5.00	40.00

Rev: A below date

C#	Date	Mintage	Fine	VF	XF	Unc
140	1843A	—	1.00	2.00	5.00	40.00
	1844A	—	1.00	2.00	5.00	40.00
	1845A	—	1.00	2.00	5.00	40.00

Rev: D below date

C#	Date	Mintage	Fine	VF	XF	Unc
140a	1844D	—	1.00	2.00	5.00	40.00
	1845D	—	1.00	2.00	5.00	40.00

Rev: A below date

C#	Date	Mintage	Fine	VF	XF	Unc
140b	1846A	—	1.00	2.00	4.00	30.00
	1847A	—	1.00	2.00	4.00	30.00
	1848A	—	1.00	2.00	4.00	30.00
	1849A	—	1.00	2.00	4.00	30.00
	1850A	—	1.00	2.00	4.00	30.00
	1851A	—	1.00	2.00	4.00	30.00
	1852A	—	1.00	2.00	4.00	30.00
	1853A	—	1.00	2.00	4.00	30.00
	1854A	—	1.00	2.00	4.00	30.00
	1855A	—	1.00	2.00	4.00	30.00
	1856A	—	1.00	2.00	4.00	30.00
	1857A	—	1.00	2.00	4.00	30.00

C#	Date	Mintage	Fine	VF	XF	Unc
140b	1858A	—	1.00	2.00	4.00	30.00
	1859A	—	1.00	2.00	4.00	30.00
	1860A	—	1.00	2.00	4.00	30.00

Rev: D below date

C#	Date	Mintage	Fine	VF	XF	Unc
140c	1846D	—	1.00	2.00	4.00	30.00
	1847D	—	1.00	2.00	4.00	30.00
	1848D	—	1.00	2.00	4.00	30.00

Rev: A below date

C#	Date	Mintage	Fine	VF	XF	Unc
161	1861A	—	.50	1.00	3.00	25.00
	1862A	—	.50	1.00	3.00	25.00
	1863A	—	.50	1.00	3.00	25.00
	1864A	—	.50	1.00	3.00	25.00
	1865A	—	.50	1.00	3.00	25.00
	1866A	—	.50	1.00	3.00	25.00
	1867A	—	.50	1.00	3.00	25.00
	1868A	—	.50	1.00	3.00	25.00
	1869A	—	.50	1.00	3.00	25.00
	1870A	—	.50	1.00	3.00	25.00
	1871A	—	.50	1.00	3.00	25.00
	1872A	—	.50	1.00	3.00	25.00
	1873A	—	.50	1.00	3.00	25.00

Rev: B below date

C#	Date	Mintage	Fine	VF	XF	Unc
161a	1867B	—	.50	1.00	3.00	25.00
	1868B	—	.50	1.00	3.00	25.00
	1869B	—	.50	1.00	3.00	25.00
	1870B	—	.50	1.00	3.00	25.00
	1871B	—	.50	1.00	3.00	25.00
	1872B	—	.50	1.00	3.00	25.00
	1873B	—	.50	1.00	3.00	25.00

Rev: C below date

C#	Date	Mintage	Fine	VF	XF	Unc
161b	1867C	—	.50	1.00	3.00	25.00
	1868C	—	.50	1.00	3.00	25.00
	1870C	—	.50	1.00	3.00	25.00
	1871C	—	.50	1.00	3.00	25.00
	1872C	—	.50	1.00	3.00	25.00
	1873C	—	.50	1.00	3.00	25.00

2 PFENNIG

COPPER

C#	Date	Mintage	Fine	VF	XF	Unc
98	1810A	—	2.00	4.00	10.00	40.00
	1814A	—	2.00	4.00	10.00	40.00
	1816A	—	2.00	4.00	10.00	40.00

Rev: A below date

C#	Date	Mintage	Fine	VF	XF	Unc
124	1821A	—	1.00	2.00	6.00	40.00
	1822A	—	1.00	2.00	6.00	40.00
	1825A	—	1.00	2.00	6.00	40.00
	1826A	—	1.00	2.00	6.00	40.00
	1827A	—	1.00	2.00	6.00	40.00
	1828A	—	1.00	2.00	6.00	40.00
	1830A	—	1.00	2.00	6.00	40.00
	1833A	—	1.00	2.00	6.00	40.00
	1835A	—	1.00	2.00	6.00	40.00
	1836A	—	1.00	2.00	6.00	40.00
	1837A	—	1.00	2.00	6.00	40.00
	1838A	—	1.00	2.00	6.00	40.00
	1839A	—	1.00	2.00	6.00	40.00
	1840A	—	1.00	2.00	6.00	40.00

Rev: B below date

C#	Date	Mintage	Fine	VF	XF	Unc
124a	1821B	—	3.00	6.50	12.50	50.00
	1822B	—	3.00	6.50	12.50	50.00
	1823B	—	3.00	6.50	12.50	50.00

Rev: D below date

C#	Date	Mintage	Fine	VF	XF	Unc
124b	1823D	—	1.00	2.50	6.00	40.00
	1824D	—	—	2.50	6.00	40.00
	1825D	—	1.00	2.50	6.00	40.00
	1826D	—	1.00	2.50	6.00	40.00
	1827D	—	1.00	2.50	6.00	40.00

C#	Date	Mintage	Fine	VF	XF	Unc
124b	1828D	—	1.00	2.50	6.00	40.00
	1829D	—	1.00	2.50	6.00	40.00
	1830D	—	1.00	2.50	6.00	40.00
	1831D	—	1.00	2.50	6.00	40.00
	1833D	—	1.00	2.50	6.00	40.00
	1834D	—	1.00	2.50	6.00	40.00
	1835D	—	1.00	2.50	6.00	40.00
	1836D	—	1.00	2.50	6.00	40.00
	1837D	—	1.00	2.50	6.00	40.00
	1838D	—	1.00	2.50	6.00	40.00
	1839D	—	1.00	2.50	6.00	40.00

Rev: D below date, pattern struck in collar.

C#	Date	Mintage	Fine	VF	XF	Unc
124c	1833D	—	10.00	23.00	35.00	70.00

Rev: A below date

C#	Date	Mintage	Fine	VF	XF	Unc
137	1841A	—	1.00	2.25	5.00	40.00
	1842A	—	1.00	2.25	5.00	40.00

Rev: D below date

C#	Date	Mintage	Fine	VF	XF	Unc
137a	1841D	—	1.00	2.25	5.00	40.00
	1842D	—	1.00	2.25	5.00	40.00

Rev: A below date

C#	Date	Mintage	Fine	VF	XF	Unc
141	1843A	—	.50	1.00	3.00	40.00
	1844A	—	.50	1.00	3.00	40.00
	1845A	—	.50	1.00	3.00	40.00

Rev: D below date

C#	Date	Mintage	Fine	VF	XF	Unc
141a	1844D	—	1.00	2.00	5.00	40.00
	1845D	—	1.00	2.00	5.00	40.00

Rev: A below date

C#	Date	Mintage	Fine	VF	XF	Unc
141b	1846A	—	.50	1.00	3.00	30.00
	1847A	—	.50	1.00	3.00	30.00
	1848A	—	.50	1.00	3.00	30.00
	1849A	—	.50	1.00	3.00	30.00
	1850A	—	.50	1.00	3.00	30.00
	1851A	—	.50	1.00	3.00	30.00
	1852A	—	.50	1.00	3.00	30.00
	1853A	—	.50	1.00	3.00	30.00
	1854A	—	.50	1.00	3.00	30.00
	1855A	—	.50	1.00	3.00	30.00
	1856A	—	.50	1.00	3.00	30.00
	1857A	—	.50	1.00	3.00	30.00
	1858A	—	.50	1.00	3.00	30.00
	1859A	—	.50	1.00	3.00	30.00
	1860A	—	.50	1.00	3.00	30.00

Rev: D below date

C#	Date	Mintage	Fine	VF	XF	Unc
141c	1846D	—	.50	1.50	5.00	30.00
	1847D	—	.50	1.50	5.00	30.00
	1848D	—	.50	1.50	5.00	30.00

Rev: A below date

C#	Date	Mintage	Fine	VF	XF	Unc
162	1861A	—	.50	1.00	3.00	30.00
	1862A	—	.50	1.00	3.00	30.00
	1863A	—	.50	1.00	3.00	30.00
	1864A	—	.50	1.00	3.00	30.00
	1865A	—	.50	1.00	3.00	30.00
	1866A	—	.50	1.00	3.00	30.00
	1867A	—	.50	1.00	3.00	30.00
	1868A	—	.50	1.00	3.00	30.00
	1869A	—	.50	1.00	3.00	30.00
	1870A	—	.50	1.00	3.00	30.00
	1871A	—	.50	1.00	3.00	30.00

Rev: B below date

C#	Date	Mintage	Fine	VF	XF	Unc
162a	1867B	—	.50	1.00	3.00	30.00
	1868B	—	.50	1.00	3.00	30.00
	1869B	—	.50	1.00	3.00	30.00
	1870B	—	.50	1.00	3.00	30.00
	1871B	—	.50	1.00	3.00	30.00
	1873B	—	.50	1.00	3.00	30.00

Rev: C below date

C#	Date	Mintage	Fine	VF	XF	Unc
	1867C	—	.50	1.00	3.00	30.00
	1868C	—	.50	1.00	3.00	30.00
	1871C	—	.50	1.00	3.00	30.00
	1872C	—	.50	1.00	3.00	30.00

3 PFENNIG
(Gute)

BILLON
Obv: Crowned FR monogram divides date.
Rev: Value over A mintmark.

C#	Date	Mintage	VG	Fine	VF	XF
4a	1764A	—	3.50	6.00	10.00	20.00
	1765A	—	3.50	6.00	10.00	20.00
	1767A	—	3.50	6.00	10.00	20.00
	1769A	—	3.50	6.00	10.00	20.00
	1770A	—	3.50	6.00	10.00	20.00

Rev: F under value.

C#	Date	Mintage	VG	Fine	VF	XF
4b	1764F	—	7.50	12.50	20.00	35.00
	1765F	—	7.50	12.50	20.00	35.00

COPPER
Rev: Value.

C#	Date	Mintage	VG	Fine	VF	XF
—	1770	—	4.50	7.50	12.50	20.00

BILLON
Obv: Crowned FR monogram over A mintmark.
Rev: Value over date.

C#	Date	Mintage	VG	Fine	VF	XF
4c	1772A	—	3.50	6.00	10.00	20.00
	1774A	—	3.50	6.00	10.00	20.00
	1775A	—	3.50	6.00	10.00	20.00
	1776A	—	3.50	6.00	10.00	20.00
	1777A	—	3.50	6.00	10.00	20.00
	1778A	—	3.50	6.00	10.00	20.00
	1779A	—	3.50	6.00	10.00	20.00
	1780A	—	3.50	6.00	10.00	20.00
	1781A	—	3.50	6.00	10.00	20.00
	1782A	—	3.50	6.00	10.00	20.00
	1783A	—	3.50	6.00	10.00	20.00
	1784A	—	3.50	6.00	10.00	20.00
	1786A	—	3.50	6.00	10.00	20.00

C#	Date	Mintage	VG	Fine	VF	XF
82	1787A	—	2.00	5.00	8.00	20.00
	1788A	—	2.00	5.00	8.00	20.00
	1789A	—	2.00	5.00	8.00	20.00
	1790A	—	2.00	5.00	8.00	20.00
	1791A	—	2.00	5.00	8.00	20.00
	1792A	—	2.00	5.00	8.00	20.00
	1793A	—	2.00	5.00	8.00	20.00
	1794A	—	2.00	5.00	8.00	20.00
	1795A	—	2.00	5.00	8.00	20.00
	1797A	—	2.00	5.00	8.00	20.00
102	1799A	—	3.00	6.00	10.00	20.00
	1801A	—	3.00	6.00	10.00	20.00
	1802A	—	3.00	6.00	10.00	20.00
	1803A	—	3.00	6.00	10.00	20.00
	1804A	—	3.00	6.00	10.00	20.00
	1806A	—	3.00	6.00	10.00	20.00

Obv: Smaller W in crowned F R W monogram.

C#	Date	Mintage	VG	Fine	VF	XF
102a	1804	—	2.50	5.00	10.00	20.00
	1806	—	2.50	5.00	10.00	20.00

COPPER
Rev: A below date

C#	Date	Mintage	Fine	VF	XF	Unc
125	1821A	—	2.00	4.00	8.00	40.00
	1822A	—	2.00	4.00	8.00	40.00
	1823A	—	2.00	4.00	8.00	40.00
	1824A	—	2.00	4.00	8.00	40.00

C#	Date	Mintage	Fine	VF	XF	Unc
125	1825A	—	2.00	4.00	8.00	40.00
	1826A	—	2.00	4.00	8.00	40.00
	1827A	—	2.00	4.00	8.00	40.00
	1828A	—	2.00	4.00	8.00	40.00
	1829A	—	2.00	4.00	8.00	40.00
	1830A	—	2.00	4.00	8.00	40.00
	1831A	—	2.00	4.00	8.00	40.00
	1832A	—	2.00	4.00	8.00	40.00
	1833A	—	2.00	4.00	8.00	40.00
	1835A	—	2.00	4.00	8.00	40.00
	1836A	—	2.00	4.00	8.00	40.00
	1837A	—	2.00	4.00	8.00	40.00
	1838A	—	2.00	4.00	8.00	40.00
	1839A	—	2.00	4.00	8.00	40.00
	1840A	—	2.00	4.00	8.00	40.00

Rev: B below date

C#	Date	Mintage	Fine	VF	XF	Unc
125a	1821B	—	5.00	10.00	15.00	45.00
	1822B	—	5.00	10.00	15.00	45.00

Rev: D below date

C#	Date	Mintage	Fine	VF	XF	Unc
125b	1823D	—	2.00	4.00	8.00	40.00
	1824D	—	2.00	4.00	8.00	40.00
	1825D	—	2.00	4.00	8.00	40.00
	1826D	—	2.00	4.00	8.00	40.00
	1827D	—	2.00	4.00	8.00	40.00
	1828D	—	2.00	4.00	8.00	40.00
	1829D	—	2.00	4.00	8.00	40.00
	1830D	—	2.00	4.00	8.00	40.00
	1831D	—	2.00	4.00	8.00	40.00
	1832D	—	2.00	4.00	8.00	40.00
	1833D	—	2.00	4.00	8.00	40.00
	1834D	—	2.00	4.00	8.00	40.00
	1835D	—	2.00	4.00	8.00	40.00
	1836D	—	2.00	4.00	8.00	40.00
	1837D	—	2.00	4.00	8.00	40.00
	1838D	—	2.00	4.00	8.00	40.00
	1839D	—	2.00	4.00	8.00	40.00
	1840D	—	2.00	4.00	8.00	40.00

Rev: A below date

C#	Date	Mintage	Fine	VF	XF	Unc
138	1841A	—	1.00	2.00	5.00	40.00
	1842A	—	1.00	2.00	5.00	40.00

Rev: D below date

C#	Date	Mintage	Fine	VF	XF	Unc
138a	1841D	—	1.00	2.00	5.00	40.00
	1842D	—	1.00	2.00	5.00	40.00

Rev: A below date

C#	Date	Mintage	Fine	VF	XF	Unc
143	1843A	—	1.00	2.00	5.00	40.00
	1844A	—	1.00	2.00	5.00	40.00
	1845A	—	1.00	2.00	5.00	40.00

Rev: D below date

C#	Date	Mintage	Fine	VF	XF	Unc
143a	1843D	—	1.00	2.00	5.00	40.00
	1844D	—	1.00	2.00	5.00	40.00

Struck in collared dies. Rev: A below date

C#	Date	Mintage	Fine	VF	XF	Unc
143b	1846A	—	1.00	2.00	4.00	30.00
	1847A	—	1.00	2.00	4.00	30.00
	1848A	—	1.00	2.00	4.00	30.00
	1849A	—	1.00	2.00	4.00	30.00
	1850A	—	1.00	2.00	4.00	30.00
	1851A	—	1.00	2.00	4.00	30.00
	1852A	—	1.00	2.00	4.00	30.00
	1853A	—	1.00	2.00	4.00	30.00
	1854A	—	1.00	2.00	4.00	30.00
	1855A	—	1.00	2.00	4.00	30.00
	1856A	—	1.00	2.00	4.00	30.00
	1857A	—	1.00	2.00	4.00	30.00

C#	Date	Mintage	Fine	VF	XF	Unc
143b	1858A	—	1.00	2.00	4.00	30.00
	1859A	—	1.00	2.00	4.00	30.00
	1860A	—	1.00	2.00	4.00	30.00

Struck in collared dies. Rev: D below date

C#	Date	Mintage	Fine	VF	XF	Unc
143c	1846D	—	1.00	2.00	4.00	30.00
	1847D	—	1.00	2.00	4.00	30.00
	1848D	—	1.00	2.00	4.00	30.00

Mule. Rev: Reuss-Schleis 3 PFENNIGE.

C#	Date	Mintage	Fine	VF	XF	Unc
143d	1850A	—	15.00	40.00	75.00	150.00

Rev: A below date

C#	Date	Mintage	Fine	VF	XF	Unc
163	1861A	—	.50	1.00	3.00	30.00
	1862A	—	.50	1.00	3.00	30.00
	1863A	—	.50	1.00	3.00	30.00
	1864A	—	.50	1.00	3.00	30.00
	1865A	—	.50	1.00	3.00	30.00
	1866A	—	.50	1.00	3.00	30.00
	1867A	—	.50	1.00	3.00	30.00
	1868A	—	.50	1.00	3.00	30.00
	1869A	—	.50	1.00	3.00	30.00
	1870A	—	.50	1.00	3.00	30.00
	1871A	—	.50	1.00	3.00	30.00
	1872A	—	.50	1.00	3.00	30.00
	1873A	—	.50	1.00	3.00	30.00

Rev: B below date

C#	Date	Mintage	Fine	VF	XF	Unc
163a	1867B	—	.50	1.00	3.00	30.00
	1868B	—	.50	1.00	3.00	30.00
	1869B	—	.50	1.00	3.00	30.00
	1870B	—	.50	1.00	3.00	30.00
	1871B	—	.50	1.00	3.00	30.00
	1872B	—	.50	1.00	3.00	30.00
	1873B	—	.50	1.00	3.00	30.00

Rev: C below date

C#	Date	Mintage	Fine	VF	XF	Unc
	1867C	—	.50	1.00	3.00	30.00
	1868C	—	.50	1.00	3.00	30.00
	1869C	—	.50	1.00	3.00	30.00
	1870C	—	.50	1.00	3.00	30.00
	1871C	—	.50	1.00	3.00	30.00
	1872C	—	.50	1.00	3.00	30.00
	1873C	—	.50	1.00	3.00	30.00

4 PFENNIG

COPPER

Rev: A below date

C#	Date	Mintage	Fine	VF	XF	Unc
126	1821A	—	2.50	5.00	10.00	45.00
	1822A	—	2.50	5.00	10.00	45.00
	1825A	—	2.50	5.00	10.00	45.00
	1826A	—	2.50	5.00	10.00	45.00
	1827A	—	2.50	5.00	10.00	45.00
	1829A	—	2.50	5.00	10.00	45.00
	1830A	—	2.50	5.00	10.00	45.00
	1832A	—	2.50	5.00	10.00	45.00
	1834A	—	2.50	5.00	10.00	45.00
	1836A	—	2.50	5.00	10.00	45.00
	1837A	—	2.50	5.00	10.00	45.00
	1838A	—	2.50	5.00	10.00	45.00
	1839A	—	2.50	5.00	10.00	45.00
	1840A	—	2.50	5.00	10.00	45.00

Rev: B below date

C#	Date	Mintage	Fine	VF	XF	Unc
126a	1821B	—	5.00	10.00	25.00	50.00
	1822B	—	5.00	10.00	25.00	50.00
	1825B	—	5.00	10.00	25.00	50.00

Rev: D below date

C#	Date	Mintage	Fine	VF	XF	Unc
126b	1823D	—	2.50	5.00	10.00	45.00
	1824D	—	2.50	5.00	10.00	45.00
	1825D	—	2.50	5.00	10.00	45.00
	1826D	—	2.50	5.00	10.00	45.00
	1828D	—	2.50	5.00	10.00	45.00
	1829D	—	2.50	5.00	10.00	45.00
	1831D	—	2.50	5.00	10.00	45.00
	1832D	—	2.50	5.00	10.00	45.00
	1833D	—	2.50	5.00	10.00	45.00
	1834D	—	2.50	5.00	10.00	45.00
	1836D	—	2.50	5.00	10.00	45.00
	1837D	—	2.50	5.00	10.00	45.00
	1838D	—	2.50	5.00	10.00	45.00
	1839D	—	2.50	5.00	10.00	45.00
	1840D	—	2.50	5.00	10.00	45.00

Rev: A below date

C#	Date	Mintage	Fine	VF	XF	Unc
139	1841A	—	2.50	5.00	7.50	40.00
	1842A	—	2.50	5.00	7.50	40.00

Rev: D below date

C#	Date	Mintage	Fine	VF	XF	Unc
139a	1841D	—	2.50	5.00	7.50	40.00
	1842D	—	2.50	5.00	7.50	40.00

Rev: A below date

C#	Date	Mintage	Fine	VF	XF	Unc
144	1843A	—	2.50	5.00	7.50	40.00
	1844A	—	2.50	5.00	7.50	40.00
	1845A	—	2.50	5.00	7.50	40.00

Rev: D below date

C#	Date	Mintage	Fine	VF	XF	Unc
144a	1844D	—	4.00	8.00	12.00	45.00

Struck in collared dies. Rev: A below date

C#	Date	Mintage	Fine	VF	XF	Unc
144b	1846A	—	2.00	5.00	7.50	30.00
	1847A	—	2.00	5.00	7.50	30.00
	1848A	—	2.00	5.00	7.50	30.00
	1849A	—	2.00	5.00	7.50	30.00
	1850A	—	2.00	5.00	7.50	30.00
	1851A	—	2.00	5.00	7.50	30.00
	1852A	—	2.00	5.00	7.50	30.00
	1853A	—	2.00	5.00	7.50	30.00
	1854A	—	2.00	5.00	7.50	30.00
	1855A	—	2.00	5.00	7.50	30.00
	1856A	—	2.00	5.00	7.50	30.00
	1857A	—	2.00	5.00	7.50	30.00
	1858A	—	2.00	5.00	7.50	30.00
	1860A	—	2.00	5.00	7.50	30.00

Struck in collared dies. Rev: D below date

C#	Date	Mintage	Fine	VF	XF	Unc
144c	1846D	—	2.00	5.00	7.50	35.00
	1847D	—	2.00	5.00	7.50	35.00
	1848D	—	2.00	5.00	7.50	35.00

Rev: A below date

C#	Date	Mintage	Fine	VF	XF	Unc
164	1861A	—	2.00	4.00	6.00	30.00
	1862A	—	2.00	4.00	6.00	30.00
	1863A	—	2.00	4.00	6.00	30.00
	1864A	—	2.00	4.00	6.00	30.00
	1865A	—	2.00	4.00	6.00	30.00
	1866A	—	2.00	4.00	6.00	30.00
	1867A	—	2.00	4.00	6.00	30.00
	1868A	—	2.00	4.00	6.00	30.00
	1869A	—	2.00	4.00	6.00	30.00
	1870A	—	2.00	4.00	6.00	30.00
	1871A	—	2.00	4.00	6.00	30.00

Rev: C below date

C#	Date	Mintage	Fine	VF	XF	Unc
164a	1867C	—	2.00	4.00	6.00	35.00
	1868C	—	2.00	4.00	6.00	35.00
	1871C	—	2.00	4.00	6.00	35.00

1/2 SILBER GROSCHEN

BILLON

Rev: A below date

C#	Date	Mintage	Fine	VF	XF	Unc
127	1821A	—	2.50	5.00	8.00	45.00
	1822A	—	2.50	5.00	8.00	45.00
	1823A	—	2.50	5.00	8.00	45.00
	1824A	—	2.50	5.00	8.00	45.00
	1825A	—	2.50	5.00	8.00	45.00
	1826A	—	2.50	5.00	8.00	45.00
	1827A	—	2.50	5.00	8.00	45.00
	1828A	—	2.50	5.00	8.00	45.00
	1829A	—	2.50	5.00	8.00	45.00
	1830A	—	2.50	5.00	8.00	45.00
	1831A	—	2.50	5.00	8.00	45.00
	1832A	—	2.50	5.00	8.00	45.00
	1833A	—	2.50	5.00	8.00	45.00
	1834A	—	2.50	5.00	8.00	45.00
	1835A	—	2.50	5.00	8.00	45.00
	1836A	—	2.50	5.00	8.00	45.00
	1837A	—	2.50	5.00	8.00	45.00
	1838A	—	2.50	5.00	8.00	45.00
	1839A	—	2.50	5.00	8.00	45.00
	1840A	—	2.50	5.00	8.00	45.00

Rev: D below date

C#	Date	Mintage	Fine	VF	XF	Unc
127a	1824D	—	3.00	6.00	10.00	50.00
	1825D	—	3.00	6.00	10.00	50.00
	1826D	—	3.00	6.00	10.00	50.00
	1828D	—	3.00	6.00	10.00	50.00

Rev: A below date

C#	Date	Mintage	Fine	VF	XF	Unc
145	1841A	—	2.00	4.00	7.00	40.00
	1842A	—	2.00	4.00	7.00	40.00
	1843A	—	2.00	4.00	7.00	40.00
	1844A	—	2.00	4.00	7.00	40.00
	1845A	—	2.00	4.00	7.00	40.00
	1846A	—	2.00	4.00	7.00	40.00
	1847A	—	2.00	4.00	7.00	40.00
	1848A	—	2.00	4.00	7.00	40.00
	1849A	—	2.00	4.00	7.00	40.00

C#	Date	Mintage	Fine	VF	XF	Unc
145	1850A	—	2.00	4.00	7.00	40.00
	1851A	—	2.00	4.00	7.00	40.00
	1852A	—	2.00	4.00	7.00	40.00

Obv: Older head. Rev: A below date

C#	Date	Mintage	Fine	VF	XF	Unc
145a	1853A	—	2.00	4.00	7.00	40.00
	1854A	—	2.00	4.00	7.00	40.00
	1855A	—	2.00	4.00	7.00	40.00
	1856A	—	2.00	4.00	7.00	40.00
	1857A	—	2.00	4.00	7.00	40.00
	1858A	—	2.00	4.00	7.00	40.00
	1859A	—	2.00	4.00	7.00	40.00
	1860A	—	2.00	4.00	7.00	40.00

Rev: A below date

C#	Date	Mintage	Fine	VF	XF	Unc
165	1861A	—	1.00	3.00	5.00	35.00
	1862A	—	1.00	3.00	5.00	35.00
	1863A	—	1.00	3.00	5.00	35.00
	1864A	—	1.00	3.00	5.00	35.00
	1865A	—	1.00	3.00	5.00	35.00
	1866A	—	1.00	3.00	5.00	35.00
	1867A	—	1.00	3.00	5.00	35.00
	1868A	—	1.00	3.00	5.00	35.00
	1869A	—	1.00	3.00	5.00	35.00
	1870A	—	1.00	3.00	5.00	35.00
	1871A	—	1.00	3.00	5.00	35.00
	1872A	—	1.00	3.00	5.00	35.00

Rev: B below date

C#	Date	Mintage	Fine	VF	XF	Unc
165a	1866B	—	1.00	3.00	5.00	35.00
	1867B	—	1.00	3.00	5.00	35.00
	1868B	—	1.00	3.00	5.00	35.00
	1869B	—	1.00	3.00	5.00	35.00
	1870B	—	1.00	3.00	5.00	35.00
	1871B	—	1.00	3.00	5.00	35.00
	1872B	—	1.00	3.00	5.00	35.00
	1873B	—	1.00	3.00	5.00	35.00

Rev: C below date

C#	Date	Mintage	Fine	VF	XF	Unc
165b	1867C	—	1.00	3.00	5.00	35.00
	1868C	—	1.00	3.00	5.00	35.00
	1872C	—	1.00	3.00	5.00	35.00

SILBER GROSCHEN

BILLON

Rev: A below date

C#	Date	Mintage	Fine	VF	XF	Unc
128	1821A	—	2.50	5.00	9.00	40.00
	1822A	—	2.50	5.00	9.00	40.00
	1823A	—	2.50	5.00	9.00	40.00
	1824A	—	2.50	5.00	9.00	40.00
	1825A	—	2.50	5.00	9.00	40.00
	1826A	—	2.50	5.00	9.00	40.00
	1827A	—	2.50	5.00	9.00	40.00
	1828A	—	2.50	5.00	9.00	40.00
	1829A	—	2.50	5.00	9.00	40.00
	1830A	—	2.50	5.00	9.00	40.00
	1831A	—	2.50	5.00	9.00	40.00
	1832A	—	2.50	5.00	9.00	40.00
	1833A	—	2.50	5.00	9.00	40.00
	1834A	—	2.50	5.00	9.00	40.00
	1835A	—	2.50	5.00	9.00	40.00
	1836A	—	2.50	5.00	9.00	40.00
	1837A	—	2.50	5.00	9.00	40.00
	1838A	—	2.50	5.00	9.00	40.00
	1839A	—	2.50	5.00	9.00	40.00
	1840A	—	2.50	5.00	9.00	40.00

Rev: D below date

C#	Date	Mintage	Fine	VF	XF	Unc
128a	1821D	—	3.50	7.00	12.00	40.00
	1822D	—	3.50	7.00	12.00	40.00
	1823D	—	3.50	7.00	12.00	40.00
	1824D	—	3.50	7.00	12.00	40.00
	1825D	—	3.50	7.00	12.00	40.00
	1826D	—	3.50	7.00	12.00	40.00
	1827D	—	3.50	7.00	12.00	40.00
	1828D	—	3.50	7.00	12.00	40.00
	1830D	—	3.50	7.00	12.00	40.00
	1832D	—	3.50	7.00	12.00	40.00
	1833D	—	3.50	7.00	12.00	40.00
	1834D	—	3.50	7.00	12.00	40.00
	1837D	—	3.50	7.00	12.00	40.00
	1839D	—	3.50	7.00	12.00	40.00
	1840D	—	3.50	7.00	12.00	40.00

Rev: A below date

C#	Date	Mintage	Fine	VF	XF	Unc
146	1841A	—	2.00	4.00	7.00	35.00
	1842A	—	2.00	4.00	7.00	35.00
	1843A	—	2.00	4.00	7.00	35.00
	1844A	—	2.00	4.00	7.00	35.00
	1845A	—	2.00	4.00	7.00	35.00
	1846A	—	2.00	4.00	7.00	35.00
	1847A	—	2.00	4.00	7.00	35.00
	1848A	—	2.00	4.00	7.00	35.00
	1849A	—	2.00	4.00	7.00	35.00
	1850A	—	2.00	4.00	7.00	35.00
	1851A	—	2.00	4.00	7.00	35.00
	1852A	—	2.00	4.00	7.00	35.00

Rev: D below date

C#	Date	Mintage	Fine	VF	XF	Unc
146a	1841D	—	2.00	5.00	8.00	35.00
	1842D	—	2.00	5.00	8.00	35.00
	1843D	—	2.00	5.00	8.00	35.00
	1844D	—	2.00	5.00	8.00	35.00
	1845D	—	2.00	5.00	8.00	35.00
	1847D	—	2.00	5.00	8.00	35.00
	1848D	—	2.00	5.00	8.00	35.00

Obv: Older head. Rev: A below date.

C#	Date	Mintage	Fine	VF	XF	Unc
146b	1853A	—	2.00	4.00	7.00	35.00
	1854A	—	2.00	4.00	7.00	35.00
	1855A	—	2.00	4.00	7.00	35.00
	1856A	—	2.00	4.00	7.00	35.00
	1857A	—	2.00	4.00	7.00	35.00
	1858A	—	2.00	4.00	7.00	35.00
	1859A	—	2.00	4.00	7.00	35.00
	1860A	—	2.00	4.00	7.00	35.00

Rev: A below date

C#	Date	Mintage	Fine	VF	XF	Unc
166	1861A	—	1.00	3.00	5.00	30.00
	1862A	—	1.00	3.00	5.00	30.00
	1863A	—	1.00	3.00	5.00	30.00
	1864A	—	1.00	3.00	5.00	30.00
	1865A	—	1.00	3.00	5.00	30.00
	1866A	—	1.00	3.00	5.00	30.00
	1867A	—	1.00	3.00	5.00	30.00
	1868A	—	1.00	3.00	5.00	30.00
	1869A	—	1.00	3.00	5.00	30.00
	1870A	—	1.00	3.00	5.00	30.00
	1871A	—	1.00	3.00	5.00	30.00
	1872A	—	1.00	3.00	5.00	30.00
	1873A	—	1.00	3.00	5.00	30.00

Rev: B below date

C#	Date	Mintage	Fine	VF	XF	Unc
166a	1866B	—	1.00	3.00	5.00	30.00
	1867B	—	1.00	3.00	5.00	30.00
	1868B	—	1.00	3.00	5.00	30.00
	1869B	—	1.00	3.00	5.00	30.00
	1870B	—	1.00	3.00	5.00	30.00
	1871B	—	1.00	3.00	5.00	30.00
	1872B	—	1.00	3.00	5.00	30.00
	1873B	—	1.00	3.00	5.00	30.00

Rev: C below head

C#	Date	Mintage	Fine	VF	XF	Unc
166b	1867C	—	1.00	3.00	5.00	30.00
	1868C	—	1.00	3.00	5.00	30.00
	1869C	—	1.00	3.00	5.00	30.00
	1870C	—	1.00	3.00	5.00	30.00
	1871C	—	1.00	3.00	5.00	30.00
	1872C	—	1.00	3.00	5.00	30.00
	1873C	—	1.00	3.00	5.00	30.00

2-1/2 SILBER GROSCHEN

BILLON
Rev: A below date

C#	Date	Mintage	Fine	VF	XF	Unc
147	1842A	—	2.50	5.00	9.00	40.00
	1843A	—	2.50	5.00	9.00	40.00
	1844A	—	2.50	5.00	9.00	40.00
	1848A	—	2.50	5.00	9.00	40.00
	1849A	—	2.50	5.00	9.00	40.00
	1850A	—	2.50	5.00	9.00	40.00
	1851A	—	2.50	5.00	9.00	40.00
	1852A	—	2.50	5.00	9.00	40.00

Rev: A below date

C#	Date	Mintage	Fine	VF	XF	Unc
147a	1853A	—	2.50	5.00	9.00	40.00
	1854A	—	2.50	5.00	9.00	40.00
	1855A	—	2.50	5.00	9.00	40.00
	1856A	—	2.50	5.00	9.00	40.00
	1857A	—	2.50	5.00	9.00	40.00
	1858A	—	2.50	5.00	9.00	40.00
	1859A	—	2.50	5.00	9.00	40.00
	1860A	—	2.50	5.00	9.00	40.00

Rev: A below date

C#	Date	Mintage	Fine	VF	XF	Unc
167	1861A	—	2.00	4.00	7.50	35.00
	1862A	—	2.00	4.00	7.50	35.00
	1863A	—	2.00	4.00	7.50	35.00
	1864A	—	2.00	4.00	7.50	35.00
	1865A	—	2.00	4.00	7.50	35.00
	1866A	—	2.00	4.00	7.50	35.00
	1867A	—	2.00	4.00	7.50	35.00
	1868A	—	2.00	4.00	7.50	35.00
	1869A	—	2.00	4.00	7.50	35.00
	1870A	—	2.00	4.00	7.50	35.00
	1871A	—	2.00	4.00	7.50	35.00
	1872A	—	2.00	4.00	7.50	35.00
	1873A	—	2.00	4.00	7.50	35.00

Rev: B below date

C#	Date	Mintage	Fine	VF	XF	Unc
167a	1869B	—	2.00	4.00	7.50	35.00
	1870B	—	2.00	4.00	7.50	35.00
	1871B	—	2.00	4.00	7.50	35.00
	1872B	—	2.00	4.00	7.50	35.00
	1873B	—	2.00	4.00	7.50	35.00

Rev: C below date

C#	Date	Mintage	Fine	VF	XF	Unc
167b	1867C	—	2.00	4.00	7.50	35.00
	1868C	—	2.00	4.00	7.50	35.00
	1869C	—	2.00	4.00	7.50	35.00
	1870C	—	2.00	4.00	7.50	35.00
	1871C	—	2.00	4.00	7.50	35.00
	1872C	—	2.00	4.00	7.50	35.00
	1873C	—	2.00	4.00	7.50	35.00

4 GROSCHEN

5.3450 gm., .521 SILVER, .0895 oz ASW
Rev: A below value.

C#	Date	Mintage	VG	Fine	VF	XF
84	1796A	—	12.50	20.00	35.00	60.00
	1797A	—	12.50	20.00	35.00	60.00

Rev: B below value.

C#	Date	Mintage	VG	Fine	VF	XF
84a	1796B	—	12.50	20.00	35.00	60.00

Rev: E below value.

C#	Date	Mintage	VG	Fine	VF	XF
84b	1796E	—	12.50	20.00	35.00	60.00
	1797E	—	12.50	20.00	35.00	60.00
	1798E	—	12.50	20.00	35.00	60.00

5.3450 gm., .521 SILVER, .0895 oz ASW
Rev: A below value.

C#	Date	Mintage	Fine	VF	XF	Unc
104	1798A	—	8.00	11.00	40.00	75.00
	1799A	—	8.00	16.00	40.00	75.00
	1800A	—	8.00	16.00	40.00	75.00
	1801A	—	8.00	16.00	40.00	75.00
	1802A	—	8.00	16.00	40.00	75.00
	1803A	—	8.00	16.00	40.00	75.00
	1804A	—	8.00	16.00	40.00	75.00
	1805A	—	8.00	16.00	40.00	75.00
	1806A	—	8.00	16.00	40.00	75.00
	1807A	—	8.00	16.00	40.00	75.00
	1808A	—	8.00	16.00	40.00	75.00
	1809A	—	8.00	16.00	40.00	75.00

Rev: B below date.

C#	Date	Mintage	Fine	VF	XF	Unc
104b	1802B	—	10.00	23.00	55.00	100.00
	1803B	—	10.00	23.00	55.00	100.00
	1804B	—	10.00	23.00	55.00	100.00
	1805B	—	10.00	23.00	55.00	100.00

Rev: G below value.

C#	Date	Mintage	Fine	VF	XF	Unc
104a	1808G	—	20.00	40.00	65.00	100.00
	1809G	—	20.00	40.00	65.00	100.00

Rev: A below date.

C#	Date	Mintage	Fine	VF	XF	Unc
106	1816A	11.652	10.00	25.00	50.00	90.00
	1817A	14.484	10.00	25.00	50.00	90.00
	1818A	—	10.00	25.00	50.00	90.00
106.1	1818D	—	15.00	35.00	60.00	100.00

48 EINEN (1/48)THALER

BILLON
Rev: A below value.

C#	Date	Mintage	VG	Fine	VF	XF
12	1764A	—	3.50	6.00	10.00	20.00
	1765A	—	3.50	6.00	10.00	20.00
	1766A	—	3.50	6.00	10.00	20.00
	1767A	—	3.50	6.00	10.00	20.00
	1768A	—	3.50	6.00	10.00	20.00
	1769A	—	3.50	6.00	10.00	20.00
	1770A	—	3.50	6.00	10.00	20.00

Rev: F below value.

C#	Date	Mintage	VG	Fine	VF	XF
12b	1764F	—	5.00	8.50	12.50	25.00
	1765F	—	5.00	8.50	12.50	25.00
	1766F	—	5.00	8.50	12.50	25.00

Obv: Crowned FR monogram; A below.
Rev: Value and date.

C#	Date	Mintage	VG	Fine	VF	XF
12a	1771A	—	3.50	6.00	10.00	20.00
	1772A	—	3.50	6.00	10.00	20.00
	1773A	—	3.50	6.00	10.00	20.00
	1774A	—	3.50	6.00	10.00	20.00
	1775A	—	3.50	6.00	10.00	20.00
	1776A	—	3.50	6.00	10.00	20.00
	1777A	—	3.50	6.00	10.00	20.00
	1778A	—	3.50	6.00	10.00	20.00
	1779A	—	3.50	6.00	10.00	20.00
12a	1780A	—	3.50	6.00	10.00	20.00

24 EINEN (1/24)THALER

BILLON
Obv: Crowned FR monogram divides date.
Rev: Value above sprays. A mintmark.

C#	Date	Mintage	VG	Fine	VF	XF
15	1764A	—	3.00	5.00	10.00	20.00
	1769A	—	3.00	5.00	10.00	20.00
	1781A	—	3.00	5.00	10.00	20.00
	1782A	—	3.00	5.00	10.00	20.00
	1783A	—	3.00	5.00	10.00	20.00
	1784A	—	3.00	5.00	10.00	20.00
	1785A	—	3.00	5.00	10.00	20.00
	1786A	—	3.00	5.00	10.00	20.00

Rev: B mintmark.

C#	Date	Mintage	VG	Fine	VF	XF
15a	1781B	—	3.00	5.00	10.00	20.00

Rev: E mintmark.

C#	Date	Mintage	VG	Fine	VF	XF
15b	1782E	—	3.00	5.00	10.00	20.00

Rev: F mintmark.

C#	Date	Mintage	VG	Fine	VF	XF
15c	1764F	—	3.00	5.00	10.00	20.00
	1765F	—	3.00	5.00	10.00	20.00
	1766F	—	3.00	5.00	10.00	20.00

12 EINEN (1/12) THALER

BILLON
Obv: Head of Friedrick right.
Rev: Value over date; A below.

C#	Date	Mintage	VG	Fine	VF	XF
18	1764A	—	3.50	6.00	10.00	20.00

Obv: Larger head.

C#	Date	Mintage	VG	Fine	VF	XF
18a	1764A	—	3.50	6.00	10.00	20.00
	1765A	—	3.50	6.00	10.00	20.00
	1766A	—	3.50	6.00	10.00	20.00
	1767A	—	3.50	6.00	10.00	20.00
	1770A	—	3.50	6.00	10.00	20.00
	1771A	—	3.50	6.00	10.00	20.00

Rev: B below date.

C#	Date	Mintage	VG	Fine	VF	XF
18b	1764B	—	5.00	7.50	12.50	25.00
	1765B	—	5.00	7.50	12.50	25.00
	1766B	—	5.00	7.50	12.50	25.00
	1767B	—	5.00	7.50	12.50	25.00
	1768B	—	5.00	7.50	12.50	25.00
	1769B	—	5.00	7.50	12.50	25.00

Rev: C below date.

C#	Date	Mintage	VG	Fine	VF	XF
18c	1764C	—	7.50	12.50	20.00	40.00

Rev: D below date.

C#	Date	Mintage	VG	Fine	VF	XF
18d	1764D	—	5.00	7.50	12.50	25.00

Obv: Berlin type head.

C#	Date	Mintage	VG	Fine	VF	XF
18e	1765D	—	5.00	7.50	12.50	25.00
	1766D	—	5.00	7.50	12.50	25.00
	1767D	—	5.00	7.50	12.50	25.00
	1768D	—	5.00	7.50	12.50	25.00

Rev: E below date.

C#	Date	Mintage	VG	Fine	VF	XF
18f	1764E	—	5.00	7.50	12.50	25.00
	1765E	—	5.00	7.50	12.50	25.00
	1766E	—	5.00	7.50	12.50	25.00
	1767E	—	5.00	7.50	12.50	25.00
	1768E	—	5.00	7.50	12.50	25.00
	1769E	—	5.00	7.50	12.50	25.00
	1770E	—	5.00	7.50	12.50	25.00
	1771E	—	5.00	7.50	12.50	25.00
	1772E	—	5.00	7.50	12.50	25.00

Rev: F under date.

C#	Date	Mintage	VG	Fine	VF	XF
18g	1764F	—	5.00	7.50	12.50	25.00
	1765F	—	5.00	7.50	12.50	25.00
	1766F	—	5.00	7.50	12.50	25.00
	1767F	—	5.00	7.50	12.50	25.00

Obv: Old head.

C#	Date	Mintage	VG	Fine	VF	XF
18h	1786A	—	5.00	7.50	12.50	25.00

1/6 THALER

5.3450 gm., .521 SILVER, .0895 oz ASW
Obv: Head of Friedrich right.
Rev: Value over date; A below date.

C#	Date	Mintage	VG	Fine	VF	XF
21	1764A	—	10.00	15.00	25.00	40.00
	1765A	—	10.00	15.00	25.00	40.00
	1766A	—	10.00	15.00	25.00	40.00
	1768A	—	10.00	15.00	25.00	40.00
	1780A	—	10.00	15.00	25.00	40.00
	1786A	—	10.00	15.00	25.00	40.00

Rev: B below date.

C#	Date	Mintage	VG	Fine	VF	XF
21a	1764B	—	10.00	15.00	25.00	40.00

C#	Date	Mintage	VG	Fine	VF	XF
21a	1765B	—	10.00	15.00	25.00	40.00
	1766B	—	10.00	15.00	25.00	40.00
	1767B	—	10.00	15.00	25.00	40.00
	1768B	—	10.00	15.00	25.00	40.00
	1770B	—	10.00	15.00	25.00	40.00
	Rev: C below date.					
21b	1764C	—	15.00	25.00	40.00	60.00
	1765C	—	15.00	25.00	40.00	60.00
	Rev: D under date.					
21c	1764D	—	10.00	15.00	25.00	40.00
	1765D	—	10.00	15.00	25.00	40.00
	1767D	—	10.00	15.00	25.00	40.00
	Rev: E under date.					
21d	1764E	—	15.00	25.00	40.00	60.00
	Obv: Berlin type head.					
21e	1764E	—	10.00	15.00	25.00	40.00
	1767E	—	10.00	15.00	25.00	40.00
	1768E	—	10.00	15.00	25.00	40.00
	1769E	—	10.00	15.00	25.00	40.00
	1770E	—	10.00	15.00	25.00	40.00
	1771E	—	10.00	15.00	25.00	40.00
	1772E	—	10.00	15.00	25.00	40.00
	1773E	—	10.00	15.00	25.00	40.00
	1775E	—	10.00	15.00	25.00	40.00
	1776E	—	10.00	15.00	25.00	40.00
	1777E	—	10.00	15.00	25.00	40.00
	1778E	—	10.00	15.00	25.00	40.00
	Rev: F below date.					
21f	1764F	—	10.00	15.00	25.00	40.00
	Obv: Smaller head.					
21g	1765F	—	10.00	15.00	25.00	40.00
	1766F	—	10.00	15.00	25.00	40.00

Rev: A below date

C#	Date	Mintage	Fine	VF	XF	Unc
105	1809A	—	6.00	14.00	30.00	60.00
	1810A	—	6.00	14.00	30.00	60.00
	1811A	—	6.00	14.00	30.00	60.00
	1812A	—	6.00	14.00	30.00	60.00
	1813A	—	6.00	14.00	30.00	60.00
	1814A	—	6.00	14.00	30.00	60.00
	1815A	—	6.00	14.00	30.00	60.00
	1816A	—	6.00	14.00	30.00	60.00
	Rev: B below date					
105a	1812B	—	10.00	23.00	45.00	75.00
	1813B	—	10.00	23.00	45.00	75.00
	1814B	—	10.00	23.00	45.00	75.00
	1815B	—	10.00	23.00	45.00	75.00
	1816B	—	10.00	23.00	45.00	75.00
	1817B	—	10.00	23.00	45.00	75.00
	Rev: D below date					
105b	1817D	—	10.00	25.00	50.00	100.00
	1818D	—	10.00	25.00	50.00	100.00
	Obv: A below head					
129	1822A	3.264	6.00	12.00	35.00	75.00
	1823A	8.550	6.00	12.00	35.00	75.00
	1824A	3.504	6.00	12.00	35.00	75.00
	1825A	4.662	6.00	12.00	35.00	75.00
	1826A	3.300	6.00	12.00	35.00	75.00
	1827A	.972	6.00	12.00	35.00	75.00
	1835A	.060	7.00	18.00	35.00	75.00
	1837A	.042	7.00	18.00	35.00	75.00
	1838A	.048	7.00	18.00	35.00	75.00
	1839A	.576	5.00	10.00	35.00	75.00
	1840A	.954	5.00	10.00	35.00	75.00
	Obv: D below head					
129a	1823D	.066	15.00	35.00	60.00	100.00
	1826D	.636	7.00	17.00	35.00	75.00
	1827D	.924	7.00	17.00	35.00	75.00
	1828D	—	7.00	17.00	35.00	75.00
129a	1835D	—	15.00	35.00	60.00	100.00
	1840D	.762	7.00	17.00	35.00	75.00

Obv: A below head

C#	Date	Mintage	Fine	VF	XF	Unc
148	1841A	.786	4.00	8.00	30.00	60.00
	1842A	3.046	4.00	8.00	30.00	60.00
	1843A	1.566	4.00	8.00	30.00	60.00
	1844A	.948	4.00	8.00	30.00	60.00
	1845A	.312	6.00	13.00	40.00	80.00
	1846A	.270	6.00	13.00	40.00	80.00
	1847A	.240	6.00	13.00	40.00	80.00
	1848A	.912	4.00	8.00	30.00	60.00
	1849A	2.556	4.00	8.00	30.00	60.00
	1850A	.078	7.00	15.00	45.00	90.00
	1851A	—	4.00	8.00	30.00	60.00
	1852A	.372	6.00	13.00	40.00	80.00
	Obv: D below head					
148a	1841D	.678	7.00	17.00	35.00	80.00
	1842D	.576	7.00	17.00	35.00	80.00
	1843D	.426	7.00	17.00	35.00	80.00
	1844D	.270	7.00	17.00	35.00	80.00
	1845D	.096	10.00	20.00	55.00	105.00
	Obv: A below older head					
148b	1853A	.216	20.00	40.00	80.00	130.00
	1854A	.116	20.00	40.00	80.00	130.00
	1855A	.030	20.00	40.00	80.00	130.00
	1856A	.051	20.00	40.00	80.00	130.00
	Rev: Crowned eagle with sceptor and orb.					
149	1858A	.096	20.00	40.00	78.00	130.00
	1859A	.032	20.00	45.00	80.00	140.00
	1860A	.128	20.00	40.00	78.00	130.00

C#	Date	Mintage	Fine	VF	XF	Unc
168	1861A	.249	15.00	30.00	45.00	75.00
	1862A	1.180	10.00	30.00	45.00	75.00
	1863A	.413	15.00	30.00	45.00	75.00
	1864A	.441	15.00	30.00	45.00	75.00
	Rev: Eagle with larger head.					
168a	1865A	.194	15.00	35.00	55.00	100.00
	1867A	.148	15.00	35.00	55.00	100.00
	1868A	.128	15.00	35.00	55.00	100.00

4 EINEN (1/4) THALER

(Reichs)

SILVER
Obv: Head of Friedrich right. Rev: Crowned eagle; value above; A divides date in exergue.

C#	Date	Mintage	VG	Fine	VF	XF
23	1764A	—	15.00	25.00	40.00	60.00
	1765A	—	15.00	25.00	40.00	60.00
	1766A	—	15.00	25.00	40.00	60.00
	Rev: B divides date in exergue.					
23c	1768B	—	15.00	25.00	40.00	60.00
	Rev: E divides date in exergue.					
23d	1764E	—	15.00	25.00	40.00	60.00
	Rev: F divides date in exergue.					
23a	1764F	—	30.00	50.00	75.00	100.00
	Obv: Berlin head.					
23e	1764F	—	35.00	60.00	95.00	145.00
	Rev: A divides date.					
23f	1786A	—	20.00	35.00	55.00	85.00
	Cornerstone Laying At Bellevue Castle					
	Obv: Old head right. Rev: Castle.					
23b	1786	—	50.00	100.00	150.00	225.00

1/3 THALER

(Reichs)

8.3520 gm., .666 SILVER, .1788 oz ASW

C#	Date	Mintage	VG	Fine	VF	XF
27a	1764A	—	15.00	25.00	40.00	75.00
	1770A	—	15.00	25.00	40.00	75.00
	1771A	—	15.00	25.00	40.00	75.00
	1772A	—	15.00	25.00	40.00	75.00
	1773A	—	15.00	25.00	40.00	75.00
	1774A	—	15.00	25.00	40.00	75.00
	Obv: Old head.					
27b	1774A	—	12.50	20.00	35.00	65.00
	1775A	—	12.50	20.00	35.00	65.00
	1786A	—	12.50	20.00	35.00	65.00

Rev: B under date.

C#	Date	Mintage	VG	Fine	VF	XF
27c	1765B	—	15.00	25.00	40.00	75.00
	1767B	—	15.00	25.00	40.00	75.00
	1768B	—	15.00	25.00	40.00	75.00
	1769B	—	15.00	25.00	40.00	75.00
	1770B	—	15.00	25.00	40.00	75.00
	1771B	—	15.00	25.00	40.00	75.00
	1772B	—	15.00	25.00	40.00	75.00
	1773B	—	15.00	25.00	40.00	75.00
	1774B	—	15.00	25.00	40.00	75.00
	Rev: E under date.					
27d	1768E	—	15.00	25.00	40.00	75.00
	1769E	—	15.00	25.00	40.00	75.00
	1773E	—	15.00	25.00	40.00	75.00
	1774E	—	15.00	25.00	40.00	75.00
	Obv: Old head.					
27e	1774E	—	15.00	25.00	40.00	75.00
	1775E	—	15.00	25.00	40.00	75.00
	1776E	—	15.00	25.00	40.00	75.00
	1779E	—	15.00	25.00	40.00	75.00
	1780E	—	15.00	25.00	40.00	75.00
	1781E	—	15.00	25.00	40.00	75.00
	1786E	—	15.00	25.00	40.00	75.00
	Rev: F under date.					
27f	1764F	—	15.00	25.00	40.00	75.00
	1765F	—	15.00	25.00	40.00	75.00

Rev: B under date.

C#	Date	Mintage	VG	Fine	VF	XF
27g	1774B	—	15.00	25.00	40.00	75.00
	1775B	—	15.00	25.00	40.00	75.00
	1776B	—	15.00	25.00	40.00	75.00
	1777B	—	15.00	25.00	40.00	75.00
	1778B	—	15.00	25.00	40.00	75.00
	1779B	—	15.00	25.00	40.00	75.00
	1780B	—	15.00	25.00	40.00	75.00
	1783B	—	15.00	25.00	40.00	75.00
	1784B	—	15.00	25.00	40.00	75.00
	1786B	—	15.00	25.00	40.00	75.00

Obv: Armored bust right.
Rev: Crowned arms divide date; A below arms.

C#	Date	Mintage	VG	Fine	VF	XF
86	1786A	—	25.00	40.00	60.00	95.00
	1787A	—	25.00	40.00	60.00	95.00
	1788A	—	25.00	40.00	60.00	95.00
	1789A	—	25.00	40.00	60.00	95.00
	1790A	—	25.00	40.00	60.00	95.00
	1791A	—	25.00	40.00	60.00	95.00
	1792A	—	25.00	40.00	60.00	95.00
	1793A	—	25.00	40.00	60.00	95.00
	1796A	—	25.00	40.00	60.00	95.00

Rev: B below arms.

C#	Date	Mintage	VG	Fine	VF	XF
86a	1787B	—	25.00	40.00	60.00	95.00
	1788B	—	25.00	40.00	60.00	95.00
	1789B	—	25.00	40.00	60.00	95.00
	1790B	—	25.00	40.00	60.00	95.00
	1793B	—	25.00	40.00	60.00	95.00
	1796B	—	25.00	40.00	60.00	95.00
	1797B	—	25.00	40.00	60.00	95.00

Rev: E below arms.

C#	Date	Mintage	VG	Fine	VF	XF
86b	1787E	—	25.00	40.00	60.00	95.00
	1788E	—	25.00	40.00	60.00	95.00
	1789E	—	25.00	40.00	60.00	95.00
	1790E	—	25.00	40.00	60.00	95.00
	1791E	—	25.00	40.00	60.00	95.00
	1792E	—	25.00	40.00	60.00	95.00
	1793E	—	25.00	40.00	60.00	95.00
	1794E	—	25.00	40.00	60.00	95.00
	1795E	—	25.00	40.00	60.00	95.00
	1796E	—	25.00	40.00	60.00	95.00
	1797E	—	25.00	40.00	60.00	95.00
	1798E	—	25.00	40.00	60.00	95.00

8.3520 gm., .666 SILVER, .1788 oz ASW
Rev: A below bow on branches.

C#	Date	Mintage	Fine	VF	XF	Unc
108	1800A	—	20.00	40.00	65.00	120.00
	1801A	—	20.00	40.00	65.00	120.00
	1802A	—	20.00	40.00	65.00	120.00
	1804A	—	20.00	40.00	65.00	120.00
	1807A	—	20.00	40.00	65.00	120.00

Rev: G below bow on branches

C#	Date	Mintage	Fine	VF	XF	Unc
108a	1809G	—	50.00	130.00	275.00	450.00

C#	Date	Mintage	Fine	VF	XF	Unc
109	1809A	—	40.00	85.00	175.00	350.00

Rev: G below date

C#	Date	Mintage	Fine	VF	XF	Unc
109a	1809G	—	50.00	125.00	275.00	450.00

2 EINEN (1/2) THALER

(Reichs)

SILVER
Rev: A divides date.

C#	Date	Mintage	VG	Fine	VF	XF
28.5	1764A	—	25.00	40.00	60.00	95.00
	1764*A*	—	25.00	40.00	60.00	95.00
	1765A	—	25.00	40.00	60.00	95.00
	1765*A*	—	25.00	40.00	60.00	95.00
	1766A	—	25.00	40.00	60.00	95.00
	1767A	—	25.00	40.00	60.00	95.00

Rev: B divides date.

C#	Date	Mintage	VG	Fine	VF	XF
28.5b	1767B	—	30.00	50.00	75.00	100.00

Rev: E divides date.

C#	Date	Mintage	VG	Fine	VF	XF
28.5c	1764E	—	30.00	50.00	75.00	100.00

Rev: F divides date.

C#	Date	Mintage	VG	Fine	VF	XF
28.5d	1764F	—	30.00	50.00	75.00	100.00
	1765F	—	30.00	50.00	75.00	100.00

King's Death Commemorative
Obv: Old head.

C#	Date	Mintage	VG	Fine	VF	XF
—	1786A	—	30.00	50.00	75.00	100.00

Cornerstone Laying At Bellevue Castle
Obv: Old head. Rev: Castle.

C#	Date	Mintage	VG	Fine	VF	XF
28.5a	1786A	—	75.00	165.00	225.00	300.00

2/3 THALER

(= 1 Gulden)

17.3230 gm., .750 SILVER, .4177 oz ASW
Obv: Crowned arms in laurel sprays.
Rev: Large value fraction over date.

C#	Date	Mintage	VG	Fine	VF	XF
87	1796	—	25.00	50.00	75.00	125.00
	1797	—	25.00	50.00	75.00	125.00
	1801	—	25.00	50.00	75.00	125.00

Obv: Crowned arms in palm branches.

C#	Date	Mintage	VG	Fine	VF	XF
87a	1797	—	30.00	60.00	100.00	150.00

Obv. leg: FR. WILH. II.....

C#	Date	Mintage	VG	Fine	VF	XF
87b	1797	—	30.00	60.00	100.00	150.00

17.3230 gm., .750 SILVER, .4177 oz ASW
Similar to C#87, leg. ends: VON PREUSSEN

C#	Date	Mintage	Fine	VF	XF	Unc
111	1810A	—	50.00	100.00	175.00	250.00

THALER

(Reichs)

22.2720 gm., .750 SILVER, .5371 oz ASW
Obv: Head of Friedrich right.
Rev: Crowned eagle on military trophies; value above
A divides date.

C#	Date	Mintage	VG	Fine	VF	XF
32a	1764A	—	40.00	75.00	150.00	250.00
	1765A	—	40.00	75.00	150.00	250.00
	1766A	—	40.00	75.00	150.00	250.00
	1767A	—	40.00	75.00	150.00	250.00
	1768A	—	40.00	75.00	150.00	250.00
	1769A	—	40.00	75.00	150.00	250.00
	1770A	—	40.00	75.00	150.00	250.00
	1771A	—	40.00	75.00	150.00	250.00
	1772A	—	40.00	75.00	150.00	250.00
	1773A	—	40.00	75.00	150.00	250.00
	1774A	—	40.00	75.00	150.00	250.00

Rev: B divides date.

C#	Date	Mintage	VG	Fine	VF	XF
32b	1764.B.	—	50.00	100.00	200.00	400.00
	1765.B.	—	50.00	100.00	200.00	400.00
	1766.B.	—	50.00	100.00	200.00	400.00
	1767.B.	—	50.00	100.00	200.00	400.00
	1768.B.	—	50.00	100.00	200.00	400.00
	1770.B.	—	50.00	100.00	200.00	400.00
	1770B	—	50.00	100.00	200.00	400.00
	1771.B.	—	50.00	100.00	200.00	400.00
	1771B	—	50.00	100.00	200.00	400.00
	1772.B.	—	50.00	100.00	200.00	400.00

Rev: D divides date.

C#	Date	Mintage	VG	Fine	VF	XF
32e	1765D	—	50.00	100.00	150.00	300.00

Rev: E divides date.

C#	Date	Mintage	VG	Fine	VF	XF
32f	1764E	—	60.00	120.00	250.00	450.00
	1772E	—	60.00	120.00	250.00	450.00

Rev: F divides date.

C#	Date	Mintage	VG	Fine	VF	XF
32g	1764F	—	50.00	100.00	150.00	300.00
	1765F	—	50.00	100.00	150.00	300.00
	1766F	—	50.00	100.00	150.00	300.00
	1767F	—	50.00	100.00	150.00	300.00

(Albertus)

C#	Date	Mintage	Fine	VF	XF	Unc
35	1766(F)	—	1500.	2500.	3150.	4000.
	1767(A)	—	1500.	2500.	3150.	4000.

(Levant)

Levant Trade Commemorative
Obv: Laureate, armored bust of Friedrich right.
Rev: Crowned eagle with crowned arms on breast.

C#	Date	Mintage	Fine	VF	XF	Unc
36	1766(A)	—	1950.	2750.	3500.	4500.
	1767(A)	—	1950.	2750.	3500.	4500.

Levant Trade Commemorative

Obv: Laureate bust of Friedrich right.

C#	Date	Mintage	Fine	VF	XF	Unc
36a	1767(A)	—	1950.	2750.	3500.	4500.

(Reichs)

22.2720 gm., .750 SILVER, .5371 oz ASW
Rev: A divides date.

C#	Date	Mintage	VG	Fine	VF	XF
32c	1775A	—	40.00	75.00	150.00	300.00
	1776A	—	40.00	75.00	150.00	300.00
	1777A	—	40.00	75.00	150.00	300.00
	1778A	—	40.00	75.00	150.00	300.00
	1779A	—	40.00	75.00	150.00	300.00
	1780A	—	40.00	75.00	150.00	300.00
	1781A	—	40.00	75.00	150.00	300.00
	1782A	—	40.00	75.00	150.00	300.00
	1783A	—	40.00	75.00	150.00	300.00
	1784A	—	40.00	85.00	150.00	300.00
	1785A	—	40.00	75.00	150.00	300.00
	1786A	—	40.00	125.00	250.00	350.00

Rev: B divides date.

C#	Date	Mintage	VG	Fine	VF	XF
32h	1780B	—	40.00	115.00	175.00	300.00
	1781B	—	40.00	75.00	150.00	300.00
	1782B	—	40.00	75.00	150.00	300.00
	1783B	—	40.00	115.00	175.00	300.00
	1784B	—	40.00	100.00	150.00	300.00
	1785B	—	40.00	75.00	150.00	300.00
	1786B	—	40.00	75.00	150.00	300.00

Rev: E divides date.

C#	Date	Mintage	VG	Fine	VF	XF
32i	1781E	—	40.00	75.00	150.00	300.00
	1782E	—	40.00	75.00	150.00	300.00
	1783E	—	40.00	100.00	150.00	300.00
	1784E	—	40.00	100.00	150.00	300.00
	1785E	—	40.00	125.00	250.00	400.00
	1786E	—	40.00	75.00	150.00	300.00

Death Thaler
Obv: Similar to C#32c.
Rev: With period stops at sides of "A" mintmark.

C#	Date	Mintage	VG	Fine	VF	XF
32d	1786.A.	—	50.00	100.00	150.00	300.00

Rev: A divides date.

C#	Date	Mintage	VG	Fine	VF	XF
88	1786A	—	50.00	100.00	150.00	300.00
	1787A	—	50.00	100.00	150.00	300.00
	1788A	—	50.00	100.00	150.00	300.00
	1789A	—	50.00	100.00	150.00	300.00
	1790A	—	50.00	100.00	150.00	300.00

Rev: B divides date.

C#	Date	Mintage	VG	Fine	VF	XF
88a	1788B	—	75.00	150.00	200.00	400.00
	1789B	—	75.00	150.00	200.00	400.00
	1790B	—	75.00	150.00	200.00	400.00
	1791B	—	75.00	150.00	200.00	400.00

Rev: A below date.

C#	Date	Mintage	VG	Fine	VF	XF
90	1790A	—	40.00	75.00	150.00	300.00
	1791A	—	40.00	75.00	150.00	300.00
	1792A	—	40.00	75.00	150.00	300.00
	1793A	—	40.00	75.00	150.00	300.00
	1794A open 4	—	40.00	75.00	150.00	300.00
	1794A closed 4		40.00	75.00	150.00	300.00
	1795A	—	40.00	75.00	150.00	300.00
	1796A	—	40.00	75.00	150.00	300.00
	1797A	—	40.00	75.00	150.00	300.00

Rev: B below date.

C#	Date	Mintage	VG	Fine	VF	XF
90a	1791B	—	50.00	75.00	150.00	300.00
	1792B	—	50.00	75.00	150.00	300.00
	1793B	—	50.00	75.00	150.00	300.00
	1794B	—	50.00	75.00	150.00	300.00
	1795B	—	50.00	75.00	150.00	300.00
	1796B	—	50.00	75.00	150.00	300.00
	1797B	—	50.00	75.00	150.00	300.00

Rev: E below date.

C#	Date	Mintage	VG	Fine	VF	XF
90b	1791E	—	50.00	75.00	150.00	300.00
	1792E	—	50.00	75.00	150.00	300.00
	1793E	—	50.00	75.00	150.00	300.00
	1794E	—	50.00	75.00	150.00	300.00
	1795E	—	50.00	75.00	150.00	300.00

(Albertus)

Obv: Crowned arms dividing date.
Rev: Wildman standing with crowned arms to right.

C#	Date	Mintage	Fine	VF	XF	Unc
91	1797	—	1500.	2500.	4000.	8000.

(Reichs)

22.2720 gm., .750 SILVER, .5371 oz ASW
Rev: Similar to C#90, A below date.

C#	Date	Mintage	Fine	VF	XF	Unc
113	1797A	—	25.00	50.00	125.00	250.00
	1798A	—	25.00	50.00	125.00	250.00
	1799A	—	25.00	50.00	125.00	250.00
	1800A	—	25.00	50.00	125.00	250.00
	1801A	—	25.00	50.00	125.00	250.00
	1802A	—	25.00	50.00	125.00	250.00
	1803A	—	25.00	50.00	125.00	250.00
	1804A	—	25.00	50.00	125.00	250.00
	1805A	—	25.00	50.00	125.00	250.00
	1806A	—	25.00	50.00	125.00	250.00
	1807A	—	25.00	50.00	125.00	250.00
	1809A	—	25.00	50.00	125.00	250.00

Rev: B below date

C#	Date	Mintage	Fine	VF	XF	Unc
113b	1799B	—	40.00	75.00	180.00	350.00
	1800B	—	40.00	75.00	180.00	350.00
	1801B	—	35.00	75.00	180.00	360.00
	1802B	—	35.00	75.00	180.00	360.00
	1803B	—	35.00	75.00	180.00	360.00

Rev: G below date

C#	Date	Mintage	Fine	VF	XF	Unc
113a	1808G	.033	50.00	115.00	215.00	430.00
	1809G	—	75.00	180.00	325.00	600.00

Rev: A below date

C#	Date	Mintage	Fine	VF	XF	Unc
114	1809A	—	20.00	50.00	150.00	300.00
	1810A	—	20.00	50.00	150.00	300.00
	1811A	—	20.00	50.00	150.00	300.00
	1812A	—	20.00	50.00	150.00	300.00
	1813A	—	20.00	50.00	150.00	300.00
	1814A	—	20.00	50.00	150.00	300.00
	1815A	—	20.00	50.00	150.00	300.00
	1816A	—	20.00	50.00	150.00	300.00

Rev: B below date

C#	Date	Mintage	Fine	VF	XF	Unc
114a	1812B	—	30.00	60.00	175.00	350.00
	1813B	—	30.00	60.00	175.00	350.00
	1815B	—	30.00	60.00	175.00	350.00
	1816B	—	30.00	60.00	175.00	350.00

Visit Of Friedrich Wilhelm IV To Berlin Mint
Rev: GOTT SCHUTZE IHN within wreath.

C#	Date	Mintage	Fine	VF	XF	Unc
115	1812A	—	800.00	1500.	3000.	5000.

Obv: Uniformed bust left, legend FR. WILH....
Rev: Crowned eagle on cannon, flags and drums, A below date.

C#	Date	Mintage	Fine	VF	XF	Unc
116	1816A	—	200.00	400.00	1000.	2000.

C#	Date	Mintage	Fine	VF	XF	Unc
116	1817A	—	200.00	400.00	1000.	2000.

Obv. leg: FRIEDR. WILHELM ...., Rev: A below date.

C#	Date	Mintage	Fine	VF	XF	Unc
116a	1816A	—	20.00	50.00	150.00	300.00
	1817A	—	20.00	50.00	150.00	300.00
	1818A	—	20.00	50.00	150.00	300.00
	1819A	—	20.00	50.00	150.00	300.00
	1820A	—	20.00	50.00	150.00	300.00
	1821A	—	20.00	50.00	150.00	300.00
	1822A	—	20.00	50.00	150.00	300.00

Rev: D below date

C#	Date	Mintage	Fine	VF	XF	Unc
116b	1818D	—	30.00	60.00	200.00	325.00
	1819D	—	30.00	60.00	200.00	325.00
	1820D	—	30.00	60.00	200.00	325.00
	1821D	—	30.00	60.00	200.00	325.00
	1822D	—	30.00	60.00	200.00	325.00

Obv: A below head right

C#	Date	Mintage	Fine	VF	XF	Unc
130	1823A	.761	20.00	50.00	150.00	300.00
	1824A	1.144	20.00	50.00	150.00	300.00
	1825A	.405	20.00	50.00	150.00	300.00
	1826A	.687	20.00	50.00	150.00	300.00

Obv: D below head

C#	Date	Mintage	Fine	VF	XF	Unc
130a	1823D	.013	30.00	80.00	175.00	350.00
	1824D	.016	30.00	80.00	175.00	350.00
	1825D	.036	30.00	80.00	175.00	350.00

Obv: A below head. Rev: Arms of different design.

C#	Date	Mintage	Fine	VF	XF	Unc
130b	1827A	.078	30.00	80.00	150.00	300.00
	1828A	1.578	40.00	100.00	225.00	425.00

Obv: D below head. Rev: Arms of different design.

C#	Date	Mintage	Fine	VF	XF	Unc
130c	1828D	.012	75.00	120.00	200.00	400.00

Obv: A below older head. Rev: Similar to C#130.

C#	Date	Mintage	Fine	VF	XF	Unc
130d	1828A	1.578	20.00	40.00	80.00	200.00
	1829A	4.002	20.00	40.00	80.00	200.00
	1830A	6.888	20.00	40.00	80.00	200.00
	1831A	4.595	20.00	40.00	80.00	200.00
	1832A	.267	20.00	40.00	80.00	200.00
	1833A	.448	20.00	40.00	80.00	200.00
	1834A	1.299	20.00	40.00	80.00	200.00
	1835A	.449	20.00	40.00	80.00	200.00
	1836A	.526	20.00	40.00	80.00	200.00
	1837A	.466	20.00	40.00	80.00	200.00
	1838A	.314	20.00	40.00	80.00	200.00
	1839A	.247	20.00	40.00	80.00	200.00
	1840A	1.630	20.00	40.00	80.00	200.00

Obv: D below older head

C#	Date	Mintage	Fine	VF	XF	Unc
130e	1829D	.277	20.00	40.00	100.00	200.00
	1830D	.651	20.00	40.00	100.00	200.00
	1831D	.045	25.00	40.00	100.00	200.00
	1832D	.029	25.00	40.00	100.00	200.00
	1833D	.019	25.00	40.00	100.00	200.00
	1834D	.021	25.00	40.00	100.00	200.00
	1835D	.016	25.00	40.00	100.00	200.00
	1836D	.021	25.00	40.00	100.00	200.00
	1837D	.015	25.00	40.00	100.00	200.00
	1838D	.025	25.00	40.00	100.00	200.00
	1839D	.012	25.00	40.00	100.00	200.00
	1840D	.011	25.00	40.00	100.00	200.00

(Mining)

Obv: A below head

C#	Date	Mintage	Fine	VF	XF	Unc
131	1826A	.050	40.00	80.00	200.00	400.00
	1827A	.050	40.00	80.00	200.00	400.00
	1828A	.050	40.00	80.00	200.00	400.00

Obv: A below older head
Rev: Similar to C#131.

C#	Date	Mintage	Fine	VF	XF	Unc
131a	1829A	—	25.00	60.00	150.00	300.00
	1830A	—	25.00	60.00	150.00	300.00
	1831A	—	25.00	60.00	150.00	300.00
	1832A	—	25.00	60.00	150.00	300.00
	1833A	—	25.00	60.00	150.00	300.00
	1834A	—	25.00	60.00	150.00	300.00
	1835A	—	25.00	60.00	150.00	300.00
	1836A	—	25.00	60.00	150.00	300.00
	1837A	—	25.00	60.00	150.00	300.00
	1838A	—	25.00	60.00	150.00	300.00
	1839A	—	25.00	60.00	150.00	300.00
	1840A	—	25.00	60.00	150.00	300.00

Rev: Similar to C#130.

C#	Date	Mintage	Fine	VF	XF	Unc
150	1841A	2.280	30.00	75.00	150.00	350.00

(Reichs)

Obv: A below head. Rev: Different crown on shield.

C#	Date	Mintage	Fine	VF	XF	Unc
150b	1842A	.518	20.00	40.00	100.00	200.00
	1843A	.600	20.00	40.00	100.00	200.00
	1844A	.918	20.00	40.00	100.00	200.00
	1845A	.720	20.00	40.00	100.00	200.00
	1846A	1.115	20.00	40.00	100.00	200.00
	1847A	1.283	20.00	40.00	100.00	200.00
	1848A	3.743	20.00	40.00	100.00	200.00
	1849A	.892	20.00	40.00	100.00	200.00
	1850A	.350	20.00	40.00	100.00	200.00
	1851A	.731	20.00	40.00	100.00	200.00
	1852A	.329	20.00	40.00	100.00	200.00

Obv: A below older head. Rev: Similar to C#150b.

C#	Date	Mintage	Fine	VF	XF	Unc
150a	1853A	.300	20.00	50.00	100.00	200.00
	1854A	3.500	17.50	40.00	100.00	200.00
	1855A	7.300	17.50	40.00	100.00	200.00
	1856A	.940	20.00	40.00	100.00	200.00

(Mining)

Obv: A below head

C#	Date	Mintage	Fine	VF	XF	Unc
151	1841A	.050	45.00	100.00	200.00	400.00

Obv: A below larger head. Rev: Dot after THALER.

C#	Date	Mintage	Fine	VF	XF	Unc
151b	1842A	.050	25.00	50.00	125.00	250.00
	1843A	.050	25.00	50.00	125.00	250.00
	1844A	.050	25.00	50.00	125.00	250.00
	1845A	.050	25.00	50.00	125.00	250.00
	1846A	.050	25.00	50.00	125.00	250.00

Rev: Without dot after THALER.

C#	Date	Mintage	Fine	VF	XF	Unc
151c	1847A	.050	25.00	50.00	125.00	250.00
	1848A	.050	25.00	50.00	125.00	250.00
	1849A	.050	25.00	50.00	125.00	250.00
	1850A	.050	25.00	50.00	125.00	250.00
	1851A	.050	25.00	50.00	125.00	250.00
	1852A	.050	25.00	50.00	125.00	250.00

Obv: A below older head

C#	Date	Mintage	Fine	VF	XF	Unc
151a	1853A	.050	25.00	50.00	125.00	250.00
	1854A	.050	25.00	50.00	125.00	250.00
	1855A	.050	25.00	50.00	125.00	250.00
	1856A	.050	25.00	50.00	125.00	250.00

(Vereins)

18.5200 gm., .900 SILVER, .5360 oz ASW

Obv: A below head.

C#	Date	Mintage	Fine	VF	XF	Unc
152	1857A	.836	20.00	35.00	200.00	350.00
	1858A	1.120	20.00	35.00	200.00	350.00
	1859A	17.600	18.00	30.00	175.00	350.00
	1860A	17.429	18.00	30.00	175.00	350.00
	1861A	.010	50.00	100.00	250.00	400.00

(Mining)

Obv: Similar to C#152.

C#	Date	Mintage	Fine	VF	XF	Unc
153	1857A	.047	25.00	60.00	150.00	300.00
	1858A	.095	25.00	60.00	150.00	300.00
	1859A	.094	25.00	60.00	150.00	300.00
	1860A	.298	25.00	60.00	150.00	300.00

(Vereins)

Coronation of Wilhelm and Augusta

C#	Date	Mintage	Fine	VF	XF	Unc
169	1861A	1.000	17.00	22.00	35.00	60.00

Obv: A below head right. Rev: Eagle.

C#	Date	Mintage	Fine	VF	XF	Unc
170	1861A	13.716	17.00	25.00	50.00	100.00
	1862A	6.057	17.00	30.00	60.00	120.00
	1863A	1.668	17.00	30.00	60.00	120.00

Obv: Larger head, A under bust

C#	Date	Mintage	Fine	VF	XF	Unc
170a	1864A	1.379	17.00	25.00	50.00	100.00
	1865A	2.584	17.00	25.00	50.00	100.00
	1866A	24.409	16.00	25.00	50.00	100.00
	1867A	31.390	16.00	25.00	50.00	100.00
	1868A	6.286	17.00	25.00	50.00	100.00
	1869A	3.630	17.00	25.00	50.00	100.00
	1870A	3.140	17.00	25.00	50.00	100.00
	1871A	7.600	17.00	25.00	50.00	100.00

Obv: B under bust

C#	Date	Mintage	Fine	VF	XF	Unc
170b	1866B	.034	35.00	75.00	150.00	250.00
	1867B	.593	35.00	70.00	145.00	225.00
	1868B	.048	35.00	75.00	150.00	250.00
	1869B	.370	35.00	70.00	145.00	225.00
	1870B	.611	35.00	70.00	145.00	225.00
	1871B	.245	35.00	70.00	145.00	225.00

Obv: C under bust

C#	Date	Mintage	Fine	VF	XF	Unc
170c	1867C	.179	50.00	100.00	200.00	400.00
	1868C	5,139	80.00	150.00	300.00	500.00
	1869C	.044	50.00	110.00	225.00	450.00
	1870C	.190	50.00	100.00	200.00	400.00
	1871C	.028	50.00	110.00	225.00	450.00

(Mining)

C#	Date	Mintage	Fine	VF	XF	Unc
171	1861A	.070	25.00	50.00	100.00	250.00
	1862A	.145	25.00	50.00	100.00	250.00

(Vereins)

Victory over Austria

C#	Date	Mintage	Fine	VF	XF	Unc
172	1866A	.500	20.00	30.00	100.00	150.00

Victory over France

C#	Date	Mintage	Fine	VF	XF	Unc
173	1871A	.880	20.00	30.00	50.00	75.00

2 THALER

(= 3-1/2 Gulden)

37.1190 gm., .900 SILVER, 1.0742 oz ASW
Rev: Similar to C#154.

C#	Date	Mintage	Fine	VF	XF	Unc
132	1839A	.172	70.00	140.00	300.00	500.00
	1840A	.789	50.00	100.00	200.00	400.00
132a	1841A	—	—	—	Rare	—

C#	Date	Mintage	Fine	VF	XF	Unc
154	1841A	4.307	50.00	100.00	200.00	400.00
	1842A	1.249	50.00	100.00	200.00	400.00
	1843A	.193	50.00	100.00	200.00	400.00
	1844A	1.069	50.00	100.00	200.00	400.00
	1845A	.961	50.00	100.00	200.00	400.00
	1846A	1.472	50.00	100.00	200.00	400.00
	1847A	.232	50.00	100.00	200.00	400.00
	1848A	4,147	200.00	350.00	700.00	1200.
	1850A	.221	50.00	100.00	200.00	400.00
	1851A	.379	50.00	100.00	200.00	400.00

Rev: Similar to C#154.

C#	Date	Mintage	Fine	VF	XF	Unc
154a	1853A	2,500	300.00	450.00	1000.	1600.
	1854A	.147	50.00	100.00	200.00	400.00
	1855A	.100	50.00	100.00	200.00	400.00
	1856A	.627	40.00	80.00	150.00	300.00

37.0370 gm., .900 SILVER, 1.0718 oz ASW
Obv: Similar to C#154a.

C#	Date	Mintage	Fine	VF	XF	Unc
155	1858A	.017	150.00	400.00	800.00	1400.
	1859A	.174	110.00	300.00	750.00	1200.

Rev: Similar to C#155.

C#	Date	Mintage	Fine	VF	XF	Unc
174	1861A	9,490	300.00	700.00	1400.	2250.
	1862A	.058	150.00	300.00	600.00	1000.
	1863A	337 pcs.	1500.	2000.	3000.	4000.
	1863A	—	—	—	Proof	3000.

Rev: FR monogram on eagle's breast.

C#	Date	Mintage	Fine	VF	XF	Unc
174a	1865A	.023	150.00	300.00	600.00	1000.
	1866A	5,110	200.00	400.00	800.00	1500.
	1867A	1,195	350.00	700.00	1400.	2800.
	1868A	1,584	350.00	700.00	1400.	2800.
	1869A	1,901	350.00	700.00	1400.	2800.
	1870A	3,155	250.00	500.00	1000.	2000.
	1871A	1,134	350.00	700.00	1400.	2800.

Obv: C below head

C#	Date	Mintage	Fine	VF	XF	Unc
174b	1866C	.226	75.00	150.00	300.00	600.00
	1867C	1.049	50.00	125.00	250.00	500.00

1/2 FREDERICK D'OR

3.3410 gm., .903 GOLD, .0970 oz AGW

Rev: A in exergue below eagle.

C#	Date	Mintage	VG	Fine	VF	XF
48	1765A	—	200.00	275.00	450.00	600.00
	1769A	—	200.00	275.00	450.00	600.00
	1770A	—	200.00	275.00	450.00	600.00
	1772A	—	200.00	275.00	450.00	600.00
	1773A	—	200.00	275.00	450.00	600.00
	1774A	—	200.00	275.00	450.00	600.00

Rev: B in exergue.

C#	Date	Mintage	VG	Fine	VF	XF
	1765B	—	200.00	275.00	450.00	600.00
	1766B	—	200.00	275.00	450.00	600.00
	1767B	—	200.00	275.00	450.00	600.00
	1768B	—	200.00	275.00	450.00	600.00
	1769B	—	200.00	275.00	450.00	600.00
	1770B	—	200.00	275.00	450.00	600.00
	1771B	—	200.00	275.00	450.00	600.00
	1772B	—	200.00	275.00	450.00	600.00
	1773B	—	200.00	275.00	450.00	600.00
	1774B	—	200.00	275.00	450.00	600.00
	1775B	—	200.00	275.00	450.00	600.00

Obv: Old head right.

C#	Date	Mintage	VG	Fine	VF	XF
48c	1776B	—	275.00	350.00	500.00	750.00
	1777B	—	275.00	350.00	500.00	750.00

Obv: Old head right.
Rev: Crowned eagle on military trophies; date below.

C#	Date	Mintage	VG	Fine	VF	XF
48a	1784A	—	275.00	350.00	500.00	750.00
	1786A	—	275.00	350.00	500.00	750.00

Obv: L at truncation

C#	Date	Mintage	Fine	VF	XF	Unc
118	1802A	—	200.00	450.00	575.00	725.00
	1803A	—	200.00	450.00	575.00	725.00
	1804A	—	200.00	450.00	575.00	725.00
	1806A	—	200.00	450.00	575.00	725.00
	1814A	—	200.00	450.00	575.00	725.00
	1816A	—	250.00	500.00	650.00	800.00

C#	Date	Mintage	Fine	VF	XF	Unc
121	1817A	—	250.00	500.00	650.00	800.00

C#	Date	Mintage	Fine	VF	XF	Unc
133	1825A	—	200.00	425.00	525.00	650.00
	1827A	—	225.00	450.00	550.00	700.00
	1828A	—	200.00	425.00	550.00	675.00
	1829A	—	200.00	425.00	550.00	675.00
	1832A	—	225.00	475.00	600.00	750.00
	1833A	—	225.00	475.00	575.00	725.00
	1834A	—	225.00	450.00	550.00	700.00
	1838A	—	200.00	425.00	550.00	675.00
	1839A	—	200.00	425.00	525.00	650.00
	1840A	—	200.00	425.00	525.00	650.00

C#	Date	Mintage	Fine	VF	XF	Unc
156	1841A	—	200.00	425.00	550.00	675.00
	1842A	—	200.00	425.00	550.00	675.00
	1843A	—	225.00	450.00	575.00	725.00
	1844A	—	225.00	450.00	550.00	700.00
	1845A	—	200.00	425.00	550.00	675.00
	1846A	—	225.00	450.00	550.00	700.00
	1849A	—	200.00	425.00	550.00	675.00

Obv: Older head

C#	Date	Mintage	Fine	VF	XF	Unc
156a	1853A	—	250.00	500.00	650.00	800.00

FREDERICK D'OR

6.6820 gm., .903 GOLD, .1940 oz AGW
Rev: A below date.

C#	Date	Mintage	VG	Fine	VF	XF
53	1764A	—	225.00	300.00	475.00	650.00
	1765A	—	225.00	300.00	475.00	650.00
	1766A	—	225.00	300.00	475.00	650.00
	1767A	—	225.00	300.00	475.00	650.00
	1768A	—	225.00	300.00	475.00	650.00
	1769A	—	225.00	300.00	475.00	650.00
	1770A	—	225.00	300.00	475.00	650.00
	1771A	—	225.00	300.00	475.00	650.00
	1772A	—	225.00	300.00	475.00	650.00
	1773A	—	225.00	300.00	475.00	650.00
	1774A	—	225.00	300.00	475.00	650.00
	1775A	—	225.00	300.00	475.00	650.00

Rev: B below eagle.

C#	Date	Mintage	VG	Fine	VF	XF
53b	1764B	—	225.00	300.00	475.00	650.00
	1765B	—	225.00	300.00	475.00	650.00
	1766B	—	225.00	300.00	475.00	650.00
	1767B	—	225.00	300.00	475.00	650.00
	1768B	—	225.00	300.00	475.00	650.00
	1769B	—	225.00	300.00	475.00	650.00
	1770B	—	225.00	300.00	475.00	650.00
	1771B	—	225.00	300.00	475.00	650.00
	1772B	—	225.00	300.00	475.00	650.00
	1773B	—	225.00	300.00	475.00	650.00
	1774B	—	225.00	300.00	475.00	650.00
	1775B	—	225.00	300.00	475.00	650.00

Rev: A below eagle.

C#	Date	Mintage	VG	Fine	VF	XF
53a	1775A	—	500.00	750.00	1000.	1500.
	1776A	—	500.00	750.00	1000.	1500.
	1777A	—	500.00	750.00	1000.	1500.
	1778A	—	500.00	750.00	1000.	1500.
	1779A	—	500.00	750.00	1000.	1500.
	1780A	—	500.00	750.00	1000.	1500.
	1781A	—	500.00	750.00	1000.	1500.
	1782A	—	500.00	750.00	1000.	1500.
	1783A	—	500.00	750.00	1000.	1500.
	1784A	—	500.00	750.00	1000.	1500.
	1786A	—	500.00	750.00	1000.	1500.

Rev: B below eagle.

C#	Date	Mintage	VG	Fine	VF	XF
53c	1776B	—	500.00	750.00	1000.	1500.
	1777B	—	500.00	750.00	1000.	1500.
	1780B	—	500.00	750.00	1000.	1500.
	1781B	—	500.00	750.00	1000.	1500.
	1781B with "D.20AUGUST"	—		Rare		—
	1782B	—	500.00	750.00	1000.	1500.
	1783B	—	500.00	750.00	1000.	1500.
	1784B	—	500.00	750.00	1000.	1500.
	1785B	—	500.00	750.00	1000.	1500.
	1786B	—	500.00	750.00	1000.	1500.

Rev: A below date.

C#	Date	Mintage	VG	Fine	VF	XF
93	1786A	—	300.00	375.00	650.00	900.00
	1788A	—	300.00	375.00	650.00	900.00
	1789A	—	300.00	375.00	650.00	900.00
	1790A	—	300.00	375.00	650.00	900.00
	1791A	—	300.00	375.00	650.00	900.00
	1792A	—	300.00	375.00	650.00	900.00
	1793A	—	300.00	375.00	650.00	900.00
	1794A	—	300.00	375.00	650.00	900.00
	1795A	—	300.00	375.00	650.00	900.00
	1796A	—	300.00	375.00	650.00	900.00
	1797A	—	300.00	375.00	650.00	900.00

Rev: B below date.

C#	Date	Mintage	VG	Fine	VF	XF
93a	1787B	—	300.00	375.00	650.00	900.00
	1788B	—	300.00	375.00	650.00	900.00
	1789B	—	300.00	375.00	650.00	900.00
	1790B	—	300.00	375.00	650.00	900.00
	1791B	—	300.00	375.00	650.00	900.00
	1792B	—	300.00	375.00	650.00	900.00
	1793B	—	300.00	375.00	650.00	900.00
	1794B	—	300.00	375.00	650.00	900.00
	1795B	—	300.00	375.00	650.00	900.00
	1796B	—	300.00	375.00	650.00	900.00
	1797B	—	300.00	375.00	650.00	900.00

C#	Date	Mintage	VG	Fine	VF	XF
117	1797A	—	250.00	500.00	700.00	900.00
	1798A	—	250.00	500.00	700.00	900.00

C#	Date	Mintage	Fine	VF	XF	Unc
119	1798A	—	225.00	450.00	575.00	725.00
	1799A	—	225.00	450.00	575.00	725.00
	1800A	—	225.00	450.00	575.00	725.00
	1801A	—	225.00	450.00	575.00	725.00
	1802A	—	225.00	450.00	575.00	725.00
	1803A	—	225.00	450.00	575.00	725.00
	1804A	—	225.00	450.00	575.00	725.00
	1805A	—	225.00	450.00	575.00	725.00
	1806A	—	225.00	450.00	575.00	725.00
	1807A	—	225.00	450.00	575.00	725.00
	1808A	—	225.00	450.00	575.00	725.00
	1809A	—	225.00	450.00	575.00	725.00
	1810A	—	225.00	450.00	575.00	725.00
	1811A	—	225.00	450.00	575.00	725.00
	1812A	—	225.00	450.00	575.00	725.00
	1813A	—	225.00	450.00	575.00	725.00
	1816A	—	325.00	650.00	800.00	1000.

Rev: B below date.

C#	Date	Mintage	Fine	VF	XF	Unc
119a	1800B	—	400.00	700.00	950.00	1200.
	1801B	—	400.00	700.00	950.00	1200.
	1802B	—	400.00	700.00	950.00	1200.
	1803B	—	400.00	700.00	950.00	1200.
	1804B	—	400.00	700.00	950.00	1200.
	1805B	—	400.00	700.00	950.00	1200.

C#	Date	Mintage	Fine	VF	XF	Unc
122	1817A	—	250.00	500.00	650.00	800.00
	1818A	—	250.00	500.00	650.00	800.00
	1819A	—	250.00	500.00	650.00	800.00
	1822A	—	250.00	500.00	650.00	800.00

C#	Date	Mintage	Fine	VF	XF	Unc
134	1825A	—	225.00	450.00	575.00	725.00
	1827A	—	250.00	500.00	625.00	775.00
	1828A	—	225.00	475.00	600.00	750.00
	1829A	—	225.00	475.00	600.00	750.00
	1830A	—	225.00	475.00	600.00	750.00
	1831A	—	225.00	450.00	575.00	725.00
	1832A	—	250.00	525.00	650.00	825.00
	1833A	—	250.00	500.00	650.00	800.00
	1834A	—	300.00	625.00	775.00	950.00
	1836A	—	225.00	475.00	600.00	750.00
	1837A	—	225.00	475.00	600.00	750.00
	1838A	—	225.00	475.00	600.00	750.00
	1839A	—	225.00	475.00	600.00	750.00
	1840A	—	225.00	450.00	575.00	725.00

C#	Date	Mintage	Fine	VF	XF	Unc
157	1841A	—	225.00	450.00	550.00	700.00
	1842A	—	225.00	450.00	550.00	700.00
	1843A	—	250.00	500.00	650.00	800.00
	1844A	—	250.00	500.00	625.00	775.00
	1845A	—	250.00	500.00	625.00	775.00
	1846A	—	225.00	475.00	600.00	750.00
	1847A	—	250.00	500.00	625.00	775.00
	1848A	—	225.00	450.00	550.00	700.00
	1849A	—	225.00	450.00	575.00	725.00
	1850A	—	325.00	650.00	825.00	1025.
	1851A	—	300.00	600.00	750.00	950.00
	1852A	—	225.00	475.00	575.00	725.00

C#	Date	Mintage	Fine	VF	XF	Unc
157a	1853A	—	225.00	450.00	575.00	725.00
	1854A	—	225.00	475.00	575.00	725.00
	1855A	—	225.00	475.00	600.00	750.00

2 FREDERICK D'OR

13.3630 gm., .903 GOLD, .3880 oz AGW

C#	Date	Mintage	Fine	VF	XF	Unc
56	1764A	—	1000.	1500.	2250.	3000.
	1765A	—	1000.	1500.	2250.	3000.
	1766A	—	1000.	1500.	2250.	3000.
	1767A	—	1000.	1500.	2250.	3000.
	1768A	—	1000.	1500.	2250.	3000.
	1769A	—	1000.	1500.	2250.	3000.
	1770A	—	1000.	1500.	2250.	3000.
	1771A	—	1000.	1500.	2250.	3000.
	1775A	—	1000.	1500.	2250.	3000.

Obv: Old head of Friedrich right.

C#	Date	Mintage	Fine	VF	XF	Unc
56a	1776A	—	1250.	1750.	2500.	3500.

Obv: L at truncation

C#	Date	Mintage	Fine	VF	XF	Unc
120	1800A	—	450.00	900.00	1120.	1400.
	1801A	—	450.00	900.00	1120.	1400.
	1802A	—	450.00	900.00	1120.	1400.
	1806A	—	450.00	900.00	1120.	1400.
	1811A	—	450.00	900.00	1120.	1400.
	1813A	—	450.00	900.00	1120.	1400.
	1814A	—	450.00	900.00	1120.	1400.

C#	Date	Mintage	Fine	VF	XF	Unc
135	1825A	—	425.00	850.00	1050.	1325.
	1826A	—	475.00	950.00	1175.	1500.
	1827A	—	450.00	900.00	1125.	1400.
	1828A	—	425.00	850.00	1050.	1325.
	1829A	—	425.00	850.00	1075.	1350.
	1830A	—	420.00	850.00	1055.	1320.
	1831A	—	425.00	850.00	1050.	1325.
	1832A	—	450.00	925.00	1150.	1450.
	1836A	—	425.00	850.00	1075.	1350.
	1837A	—	425.00	850.00	1075.	1350.
	1838A	—	425.00	850.00	1075.	1350.
	1839A	—	425.00	850.00	1075.	1350.
	1840A	—	425.00	850.00	1050.	1325.

C#	Date	Mintage	Fine	VF	XF	Unc
158	1841A	—	425.00	850.00	1050.	1325.
	1842A	—	425.00	850.00	1075.	1350.
	1843A	—	450.00	925.00	1150.	1450.
	1844A	—	450.00	925.00	1155.	1425.
	1845A	—	450.00	900.00	1125.	1425.
	1846A	—	435.00	875.00	1100.	1350.
	1848A	—	425.00	850.00	1050.	1325.
	1849A	—	425.00	850.00	1050.	1325.
	1852A	—	435.00	875.00	1100.	1350.

C#	Date	Mintage	Fine	VF	XF	Unc
158a	1853A	—	450.00	900.00	1125.	1400.
	1854A	—	450.00	925.00	1150.	1425.
	1855A	—	450.00	900.00	1125.	1425.

1/2 KRONE

5.5550 gm., .900 GOLD, .1607 oz AGW

C#	Date	Mintage	Fine	VF	XF	Unc
159	1858A	2,036	700.00	1125.	2000.	2400.

C#	Date	Mintage	Fine	VF	XF	Unc
175	1862A	6,365	700.00	1100.	1200.	1400.
	1863A	3,642	700.00	1100.	1200.	1400.
	1864A	4,840	700.00	1100.	1200.	1400.
	1866A	.014	600.00	1000.	1100.	1300.
	1867A	5,711	700.00	1100.	1200.	1400.
	1868A	.092	500.00	900.00	1000.	1200.
	1869A	—	700.00	1100.	1200.	1450.

Obv: B below head

C#	Date	Mintage	Fine	VF	XF	Unc
175a	1868B	3,718	600.00	1025.	1275.	1600.

KRONE

11.1110 gm., .916 GOLD, .3272 oz ASW

C#	Date	Mintage	Fine	VF	XF	Unc
160	1858A	6,320	600.00	1150.	1450.	1800.
	1859A	.034	500.00	900.00	1125.	1400.
	1860A	.016	500.00	900.00	1125.	1400.

Obv: A below head

C#	Date	Mintage	Fine	VF	XF	Unc
176	1861A	2,488	600.00	1150.	1450.	1800.
	1862A	5,558	600.00	1075.	1350.	1675.
	1863A	2,653	600.00	1150.	1440.	1800.
	1864A	792 pcs.	1000.	1525.	1925.	2400.
	1866A	720 pcs.	1000.	1525.	1925.	2400.
	1867A	4,087	600.00	1075.	1350.	1675.
	1868A	.097	500.00	1025.	1275.	1600.
	1869A	—	600.00	1150.	1450.	1800.
	1870A	1,764	600.00	1175.	1475.	1850.

Obv: B below head

C#	Date	Mintage	Fine	VF	XF	Unc
176a	1867B	.015	500.00	1025.	1275.	1600.
	1868B	.040	500.00	1100.	1350.	1700.

TRADE COINS

DUCAT

3.5000 gm., .986 GOLD, .1109 oz AGW

C#	Date	Mintage	Fine	VF	XF	Unc
92	1787	—	275.00	400.00	850.00	1200.
	1790	—	275.00	400.00	850.00	1200.

MONETARY REFORM

2 MARK

11.1110 gm., .900 SILVER, .3215 oz ASW

Y#	Date	Mintage	VF	XF	Unc
111	1876-A	13.370	35.00	215.00	500.00
	1876-B	3.985	35.00	200.00	500.00
	1876-C	5.233	35.00	200.00	500.00
	1877-A	3.634	35.00	200.00	400.00
	1877-B	1.301	35.00	200.00	400.00
	1877-C	1.307	35.00	200.00	400.00
	1879A	.029	200.00	425.00	800.00
	1880A	.665	60.00	200.00	500.00
	1883A	.164	115.00	260.00	500.00
	1884A	.140	115.00	260.00	500.00

Y#	Date	Mintage	VF	XF	Unc
116	1888A	.500	25.00	75.00	125.00

Rev: Small eagle

Y#	Date	Mintage	VF	XF	Unc
120	1888A	.141	250.00	400.00	600.00
	1888A	—	—	Proof	750.00

Rev: Larger eagle

Y#	Date	Mintage	VF	XF	Unc
120a	1891A	.544	20.00	40.00	150.00
	1892A	.182	40.00	150.00	250.00
	1893A	.948	16.00	40.00	150.00
	1896A	1.772	15.00	40.00	150.00
	1898A	1.042	15.00	40.00	150.00
	1899A	2.351	15.00	40.00	100.00
	1900A	2.682	15.00	40.00	100.00
	1901A	.398	60.00	150.00	250.00
	1902A	3.948	12.00	40.00	75.00
	1903A	4.079	12.00	40.00	75.00
	1904A	9.981	12.00	25.00	40.00
	1905A	6.423	12.00	25.00	40.00
	1906A	4.000	12.00	25.00	40.00
	1907A	8.085	12.00	25.00	40.00
	1908A	2.389	12.00	25.00	70.00
	1911A	1.181	12.00	30.00	70.00
	1912A	.733	15.00	40.00	75.00
	Common type	—	—	Proof	150.00

200 Years Kingdom of Prussia

Y#	Date	Mintage	VF	XF	Unc
128	1901A	2.600	9.00	14.00	20.00
	1901A	—	—	Proof	55.00

100 Years Defeat of Napoleon

Y#	Date	Mintage	VF	XF	Unc
132	1913A	1.500	9.00	14.00	20.00
	1913A	—	—	Proof	40.00

25th Year of Reign

Y#	Date	Mintage	VF	XF	Unc
134	1913A	1.500	9.00	15.00	25.00
	1913A	—	—	Proof	60.00

3 MARK

16.6670 gm., .900 SILVER, .4823 oz ASW

Y#	Date	Mintage	VF	XF	Unc
121	1908A	2.859	12.00	13.00	25.00
	1909A	6.344	12.00	13.00	25.00
	1910A	5.791	12.00	13.00	25.00
	1911A	3.242	12.00	13.00	25.00
	1912A	4.626	12.00	13.00	25.00
	Common type	—	—	Proof	100.00

Berlin University Commemorative
Rev: Similar to Y#131.

Y#	Date	Mintage	VF	XF	Unc
130	1910A	.200	25.00	50.00	70.00
	1910A	—	—	Proof	180.00

Breslau University Commemorative

Y#	Date	Mintage	VF	XF	Unc
131	1911A	.400	30.00	50.00	75.00
	1911A	—	—	Proof	150.00

100 Years Defeat of Napoleon

Y#	Date	Mintage	VF	XF	Unc
133	1913A	1.000	15.00	20.00	25.00
	1913A	—	—	Proof	50.00

25th Year of Reign

Y#	Date	Mintage	VF	XF	Unc
135	1913A	1.000	15.00	20.00	25.00
	1913A	—	—	Proof	100.00

Rev: Similar to Y#135.

Y#	Date	Mintage	VF	XF	Unc
125	1914A	2.020	15.00	20.00	30.00
	1914A	—	—	Proof	85.00

Centenary Absorption of Mansfeld
Rev: Similar to Y#131.

Y#	Date	Mintage	VF	XF	Unc
136	1915A	.030	100.00	225.00	400.00
	1915A	—	—	Proof	600.00

5 MARK

27.7770 gm., .900 SILVER, .8038 oz ASW

Y#	Date	Mintage	VF	XF	Unc
112	1874 A	.838	30.00	300.00	600.00
	1875 A	.853	30.00	300.00	600.00
	1875 B	.919	30.00	300.00	600.00
	1876 A	2.041	30.00	250.00	500.00
	1876 B	2.098	30.00	250.00	500.00
	1876 C	.812	30.00	300.00	600.00

1.9910 gm., .900 GOLD, .0576 oz AGW

Y#	Date	Mintage	VF	XF	Unc
113	1877 A	1.217	150.00	250.00	350.00
	1877 B	.517	175.00	250.00	400.00
	1877 C	.688	175.00	250.00	400.00
	1878 A	.502	250.00	325.00	400.00

27.7770 gm., .900 SILVER, .8038 oz ASW
Rev: Similar to Y#122.

Y#	Date	Mintage	VF	XF	Unc
117	1888A	.200	50.00	100.00	175.00
	1888A	—	—	Proof	250.00

Rev: Type 2 eagle.

Y#	Date	Mintage	VF	XF	Unc
122	1888A	.056	350.00	650.00	1000.
	1888A	—	—	Proof	1200.

Obv: Similar to Y#122.

Y#	Date	Mintage	VF	XF	Unc
122a	1891A	.130	30.00	75.00	300.00
	1892A	.224	30.00	75.00	450.00
	1893A	.215	30.00	75.00	350.00
	1894A	.440	25.00	45.00	300.00
	1895A	.831	25.00	40.00	250.00
	1896A	.046	100.00	165.00	600.00
	1898A	1.134	20.00	30.00	250.00
	1899A	.529	20.00	30.00	300.00
	1900A	1.080	20.00	30.00	200.00
	1901A	.668	20.00	30.00	300.00
	1902A	1.951	20.00	25.00	200.00
	1903A	3.856	20.00	25.00	100.00
	1904A	2.060	20.00	25.00	100.00
	1906A	.231	30.00	50.00	200.00
	1907A	2.102	20.00	25.00	100.00
	1908A	2.231	20.00	25.00	100.00

200 Years Kingdom of Prussia
Rev: Similar to Y#122a.

Y#	Date	Mintage	VF	XF	Unc
129	1901A	.460	35.00	65.00	90.00
	1901A	—	—	Proof	200.00

Rev: Similar to Y#122a.

Y#	Date	Mintage	VF	XF	Unc
126	1913A	1.962	21.00	30.00	50.00
	1914A	1.587	21.00	30.00	50.00
	Common type	—	—	Proof	200.00

10 MARK

3.9820 gm., .900 GOLD, .1152 oz AGW

Y#	Date	Mintage	VF	XF	Unc
114	1872A	3.123	70.00	90.00	115.00
	1873A	3.016	70.00	90.00	115.00

Obv: B below head

Y#	Date	Mintage	VF	XF	Unc
114b	1872B	1.418	70.00	90.00	115.00
	1873B	2.273	70.00	90.00	105.00

Obv: C below head.

Y#	Date	Mintage	VF	XF	Unc
114c	1872C	1.747	70.00	90.00	105.00
	1873C	2.295	70.00	90.00	105.00

Obv: A below head. Rev: Type 2 eagle.

Y#	Date	Mintage	VF	XF	Unc
114a	1874A	.833	70.00	90.00	140.00
	1875A	2.430	70.00	90.00	140.00
	1877A	.851	70.00	90.00	140.00
	1878A	1.126	70.00	90.00	115.00
	1879A	1.012	70.00	90.00	115.00
	1880A	1.762	70.00	90.00	115.00
	1882A	8,382	650.00	1300.	2000.
	1883A	.013	650.00	950.00	1300.
	1886A	.014	650.00	950.00	1300.
	1888A	.189	80.00	115.00	180.00

Obv: B below head

Y#	Date	Mintage	VF	XF	Unc
114d	1874B	1.028	70.00	90.00	105.00
	1875B	.456	70.00	90.00	105.00
	1876B	2,800	2225.	3250.	4300.
	1877B	.247	70.00	90.00	130.00
	1878B	.015	650.00	950.00	1300.

Obv: C below head

Y#	Date	Mintage	VF	XF	Unc
114e	1874C	.321	70.00	90.00	105.00
	1875C	1.532	70.00	90.00	105.00
	1876C	.027	525.00	1000.	1325.
	1877C	.328	70.00	90.00	105.00
	1878C	.516	70.00	90.00	105.00
	1879C	.282	70.00	90.00	105.00

Y#	Date	Mintage	VF	XF	Unc
118	1888A	.876	80.00	100.00	125.00

Rev: Type 2 eagle

Y#	Date	Mintage	VF	XF	Unc
123	1889A	.024	1250.	2250.	3250.

Rev: Type 3 eagle

Y#	Date	Mintage	VF	XF	Unc
123a	1890A	1.512	70.00	80.00	100.00
	1892A	.035	650.00	900.00	1150.
	1893A	.368	70.00	80.00	100.00
	1894A	.018	800.00	1150.	1650.
	1895A	.029	750.00	1100.	1500.
	1896A	1.081	70.00	80.00	100.00
	1897A	.114	70.00	80.00	100.00
	1898A	2.280	70.00	80.00	100.00
	1899A	.300	70.00	80.00	100.00
	1900A	.742	70.00	80.00	100.00
	1901A	.702	70.00	80.00	100.00
	1902A	.271	70.00	80.00	100.00
	1903A	1.685	70.00	80.00	100.00
	1904A	1.178	70.00	80.00	100.00
	1905A	1.073	70.00	80.00	100.00
	1906A	.542	70.00	80.00	100.00
	1907A	.813	70.00	80.00	100.00
	1909A	.532	70.00	80.00	100.00
	1910A	.803	70.00	80.00	100.00
	1911A	.271	70.00	80.00	100.00
	1912A	.542	70.00	80.00	100.00

20 MARK

7.9650 gm., .900 GOLD, .2304 oz AGW
Obv: A below head

Y#	Date	Mintage	VF	XF	Unc
115	1871A	.502	140.00	200.00	300.00
	1872A	7.717	140.00	145.00	200.00
	1873A	9.063	140.00	145.00	200.00

Obv: B below head

Y#	Date	Mintage	VF	XF	Unc
115b	1872B	1.918	140.00	150.00	200.00
	1873B	3.441	140.00	150.00	200.00

Obv: C below head

Y#	Date	Mintage	VF	XF	Unc
115c	1872C	3.056	140.00	150.00	200.00
	1873C	5.228	140.00	150.00	200.00

Obv: A below head. Rev: Type 2 eagle

Y#	Date	Mintage	VF	XF	Unc
115a	1874A	.762	140.00	150.00	200.00
	1875A	4.203	140.00	150.00	200.00
	1876A	2.673	140.00	150.00	200.00
	1877A	1.250	140.00	150.00	200.00
	1878A	2.175	140.00	150.00	200.00
	1879A	1.023	140.00	150.00	200.00
	1881A	.428	140.00	150.00	200.00
	1882A	.655	140.00	150.00	200.00
	1883A	4.283	140.00	150.00	200.00
	1884A	.224	140.00	150.00	200.00
	1885A	.407	140.00	150.00	200.00
	1886A	.176	140.00	150.00	200.00
	1887A	5.645	140.00	150.00	200.00
	1888A	.534	140.00	150.00	200.00

Obv: B below head

Y#	Date	Mintage	VF	XF	Unc
115d	1874B	.824	140.00	150.00	200.00
	1875B	—	165.00	250.00	600.00
	1877B	.501	165.00	225.00	280.00

Obv: C below head

Y#	Date	Mintage	VF	XF	Unc
115e	1874C	.088	140.00	155.00	200.00
	1876C	.423	165.00	230.00	500.00
	1877C	6,384	1000.	1350.	2000.
	1878C	.082	140.00	230.00	600.00

Obv: A below head

Y#	Date	Mintage	VF	XF	Unc
119	1888A	5.364	140.00	150.00	200.00

Y#	Date	Mintage	VF	XF	Unc
124	1888A	.756	100.00	175.00	200.00
	1889A	10.885	140.00	150.00	200.00

Rev: Type 3 eagle

Y#	Date	Mintage	VF	XF	Unc
124a	1890A	3.695	140.00	150.00	200.00
	1891A	2.752	140.00	150.00	200.00
	1892A	1.815	140.00	150.00	200.00
	1893A	3.172	140.00	150.00	200.00
	1894A	5.815	140.00	150.00	200.00
	1895A	4.135	140.00	150.00	200.00
	1896A	4.239	140.00	150.00	200.00
	1897A	5.394	140.00	150.00	200.00
	1898A	6.592	140.00	150.00	200.00
	1899A	5.873	140.00	150.00	200.00
	1900A	5.163	140.00	150.00	200.00
	1901A	5.188	140.00	150.00	200.00
	1902A	4.138	140.00	150.00	200.00
	1903A	2.870	140.00	150.00	200.00
	1904A	3.453	140.00	150.00	200.00
	1905A	4.221	140.00	150.00	200.00
	1906A	7.788	140.00	150.00	200.00
	1907A	2.576	140.00	150.00	200.00
	1908A	3.274	140.00	150.00	200.00
	1909A	5.213	140.00	150.00	200.00
	1910A	8.646	140.00	150.00	200.00
	1911A	4.746	140.00	150.00	200.00
	1912A	5.569	140.00	150.00	200.00
	1913A	6.102	140.00	150.00	200.00

Obv: J below head

Y#	Date	Mintage	VF	XF	Unc
124b	1905J	.921	140.00	150.00	200.00
	1906J	.102	165.00	230.00	300.00
	1909J	.350	140.00	150.00	200.00
	1910J	.753	140.00	150.00	200.00
	1912J	.503	140.00	150.00	200.00

Obv: A below bust

Y#	Date	Mintage	VF	XF	Unc
127	1913A	6.102	140.00	150.00	200.00
	1914A	2.137	140.00	150.00	200.00
	1915A	1.268	1200.	1750.	2250.

NCLT ISSUES

PATTERNS

KM#	Date	Mintage	Identification	Mkt.Val.
1	1788	—	1 Thaler, Silver, C89	—

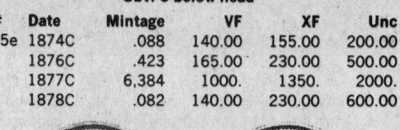

PYRMONT

A county, southwest of Hannover, was established c. 1160. Their first coins were struck in the 13th century. In 1625 Pyrmont was incorporated with Waldeck. Occasional issues of special coins for Pyrmont were struck in the 18th and 19th centuries.

RULERS

Georg, Prince, 1805-1812

24 EINEN (1/24) THALER

BILLON
Obv: Crowned and mantled 2 shields of arms.
Rev: Value over date.

C#	Date	Mintage	VG	Fine	VF	XF
6	1806	—	30.00	55.00	100.00	150.00
	1807	—	30.00	55.00	100.00	150.00

EIN (1) THALER
(Convention)

28.0600 gm., .833 SILVER, .7516 oz ASW

C#	Date	Mintage	Fine	VF	XF	Unc
7	1811	—	850.00	1250.	2000.	2750.

REGENSBURG (RATISBON)

The bishopric, located in central Bavaria, was established in 470. Regular episcopal coins appeared in the 11th century. Regensburg became a free city in 1180 and in 1230 received the right to mint its own coins. The dated city coinage extends from c. 1511 to 1802. In 1803 the city was given to the bishop and the city and bishopric were united with Bavaria.

Bishopric

RULERS

Anton Ignaz, Bishop, 1769-1787

EIN (1) THALER
(Convention)

SILVER

C#	Date	Mintage	Fine	VF	XF	Unc
3	1786	—	300.00	475.00	750.00	1100.

Sede Vacante Issue

C#	Date	Mintage	Fine	VF	XF	Unc
9	1787	—	150.00	275.00	450.00	800.00

TRADE COINS

DUCAT

3.5000 gm., .986 GOLD, .1109 oz AGW
Obv: Bust right.
Rev: Crowned and mantled arms.

C#	Date	Mintage	VG	Fine	VF	XF
4	1770	—	500.00	950.00	1500.	2250.

Free City

MINTMASTERS INITIALS

I.C.B., B. - Johann Christoph Busch, 1741-1766
R. - George Nikolaus Riedner, 1766-1767
G.C.B., BF - Georg Christoph Busch, 1773-1803
K, Kornlein - Johann Nikolaus Kornlein, 1773-1802
Z, GZ - Johann Leonhard Zollner, 1791-1802

HELLER

COPPER
Obv: Crossed keys.
Rev: Blank.

C#	Date	Mintage	VG	Fine	VF	XF
1	1754	—	2.00	3.75	6.00	15.00
	1755	—	2.00	3.75	6.00	15.00
	1756	—	2.00	3.75	6.00	15.00
	1757	—	2.00	3.75	6.00	15.00
	1758	—	2.00	3.75	6.00	15.00
	1759	—	2.00	3.75	6.00	15.00
	1760	—	2.00	3.75	6.00	15.00
	1761	—	2.00	3.75	6.00	15.00
	1762	—	2.00	3.75	6.00	15.00
	1763	—	2.00	3.75	6.00	15.00
	1764	—	2.00	3.75	6.00	15.00
	1765	—	2.00	3.75	6.00	15.00
	1766	—	2.00	3.75	6.00	15.00
	1767	—	2.00	3.75	6.00	15.00
	1768	—	2.00	3.75	6.00	15.00
	1769	—	2.00	3.75	6.00	15.00
	1770	—	2.00	3.75	6.00	15.00
	1771	—	2.00	3.75	6.00	15.00
	1772	—	2.00	3.75	6.00	15.00
	1773	—	2.00	3.75	6.00	15.00
	1774	—	2.00	3.75	6.00	15.00
	1775	—	2.00	3.75	6.00	15.00
	1776	—	2.00	3.75	6.00	15.00
	1777	—	2.00	3.75	6.00	15.00
	1778	—	2.00	3.75	6.00	15.00
	1779	—	2.00	3.75	6.00	15.00
	1780	—	2.00	3.75	6.00	15.00
	1781	—	2.00	3.75	6.00	15.00
	1782	—	2.00	3.75	6.00	15.00
	1783	—	2.00	3.75	6.00	15.00
	1784	—	2.00	3.75	6.00	15.00
	(This date struck also in 1785).					
	1786	—	2.00	3.75	6.00	15.00
	1787	—	2.00	3.75	6.00	15.00
	1788	—	2.00	3.75	6.00	15.00
	(This date struck also in 1789 & 1790).					
	1791	—	2.00	3.75	6.00	15.00
	1792	—	2.00	3.75	6.00	15.00
	1793	—	2.00	3.75	6.00	15.00

NOTE: Varieties exist.

Uniface

C#	Date	Mintage	VG	Fine	VF	XF
2	1794	—	2.00	3.75	6.00	15.00
	1795	—	2.00	3.75	6.00	15.00
	1796	—	2.00	3.75	6.00	15.00
	1797	—	2.00	3.75	6.00	15.00
	(This date struck also in 1798).					
	1799	—	2.00	3.75	6.00	15.00
	1801	—	2.00	3.75	6.00	15.00
	1802	—	2.00	3.75	6.00	15.00
	1803	—	2.00	3.75	6.00	15.00

PFENNING

BILLON
Obv: Crossed keys in cartouche; date above.
Rev: Value in wreath.

C#	Date	Mintage	VG	Fine	VF	XF
3	1754	—	2.00	4.00	6.50	20.00
	1755	—	2.00	4.00	6.50	20.00
	1756	—	2.00	4.00	6.50	20.00
	1758	—	2.00	4.00	6.50	20.00
	1759	—	2.00	4.00	6.50	20.00
	(This date struck also in 1760).					
	1761	—	2.00	4.00	6.50	20.00
	(This date struck also in 1762).					
	1763	—	2.00	4.00	6.50	20.00
	1764	—	2.00	4.00	6.50	20.00
	1765	—	2.00	4.00	6.50	20.00
	1766	—	2.00	4.00	6.50	20.00
3a	1767	—	2.00	4.00	6.50	20.00
	1774	—	2.00	4.00	6.50	20.00
	1776	—	2.00	4.00	6.50	20.00
	1778	—	2.00	4.00	6.50	20.00
	1779	—	2.00	4.00	6.50	20.00
3b	1780	—	2.00	4.00	6.50	20.00
	1781	—	2.00	4.00	6.50	20.00
	1783	—	2.00	4.00	6.50	20.00
	(This date struck also in 1784).					
3c	1785	—	2.00	4.00	6.50	20.00
	(This date struck also in 1787, 1788 & 1789).					
	1790	—	2.00	4.00	6.50	20.00
3d	1791	—	2.00	4.00	6.50	20.00
	1792	—	2.00	4.00	6.50	20.00

C#	Date	Mintage	VG	Fine	VF	XF
3d	1793	—	2.00	4.00	6.50	20.00
	(This date struck also in 1794, 1795 & 1796).					
	1797	—	2.00	4.00	6.50	20.00
	(This date struck also in 1798 & 1803).					
		—	2.00	4.00	6.50	20.00

KREUZER

BILLON

Obv: Crossed keys divide date.
Rev: Crowned imperial eagle.

C#	Date	Mintage	VG	Fine	VF	XF
5	1754-85	—	3.00	5.00	7.00	20.00
	1754	—	3.00	5.00	7.00	20.00

C#	Date	Mintage	VG	Fine	VF	XF
5a	1754	—	3.00	5.00	7.00	20.00
	(This date struck also in 1755 & 1757).					
	1758	—	3.00	5.00	7.00	20.00
	(This date struck also in 1759, 1762 & 1763.)					
	1764	—	3.00	5.00	7.00	20.00
	(This date struck also in 1765 & 1766).					
5b	1767	—	3.00	5.00	7.00	20.00
	1774	—	3.00	5.00	7.00	20.00
5c	1776	—	3.00	5.00	7.00	20.00
	1781	—	3.00	5.00	7.00	20.00
5d	1785	—	3.00	5.00	7.00	20.00
	(This date struck also in 1787, 1788, 1789, 1790, 1791, 1792, 1794, 1796, 1797, 1798, & 1803).					

Obv: Crossed keys.
Rev: Imperial eagle.

C#	Date	Mintage	VG	Fine	VF	XF
7	1787	—	3.00	5.00	7.50	20.00

2 KREUZER

SILVER

C#	Date	Mintage	VG	Fine	VF	XF
9	1754	—	5.00	7.50	12.50	25.00

Obv: B under keys

C#	Date	Mintage	VG	Fine	VF	XF
9a	1754	—	5.00	7.50	12.50	25.00
	(This date struck also in 1760 & 1763).					

BILLON

Obv: Arms in cartouche; date below.
Rev: Imperial eagle; value on chest.

C#	Date	Mintage	VG	Fine	VF	XF
10	1767	—	3.75	5.00	7.50	20.00

Obv: Crossed keys in cartouche over date.
Rev: Crowned imperial eagle with value on breast.

C#	Date	Mintage	VG	Fine	VF	XF
11	1775	—	4.00	6.50	10.00	20.00
11a	1787	—	4.00	6.50	10.00	20.00
	(This date struck also in 1792).					

10 KREUZER

SILVER

C#	Date	Mintage	VG	Fine	VF	XF
15	1754	—	7.50	12.50	20.00	40.00
15a	1776	—	7.50	12.50	20.00	40.00

Obv: Arms.
Rev: Crowned imperial eagle.

C#	Date	Mintage	VG	Fine	VF	XF
17	1781	—	7.50	12.50	20.00	40.00

Rev: Eagle holds sword and orb.

C#	Date	Mintage	VG	Fine	VF	XF
17a	1781	—	7.50	12.50	20.00	40.00

Obv: Date moved to above pedestal.

C#	Date	Mintage	VG	Fine	VF	XF
17b	1781	—	7.50	12.50	20.00	40.00

Rev: No sword or orb held by eagle.

C#	Date	Mintage	VG	Fine	VF	XF
17c	1781	—	7.50	12.50	20.00	40.00
	(This date struck also in 1783).					

20 KREUZER

SILVER

C#	Date	Mintage	Fine	VF	XF	Unc
21	1754	—	10.00	15.00	25.00	50.00
21a	1774	—	8.50	13.50	22.50	50.00

Rev: No branches around eagle.

C#	Date	Mintage	Fine	VF	XF	Unc
21b	1774	—	8.50	13.50	22.50	50.00

Obv: Date at bottom.

C#	Date	Mintage	Fine	VF	XF	Unc
21c	1774	—	8.50	13.50	22.50	50.00

(Convention)

Obv: Arms. Rev: Imperial eagle with branches around.

C#	Date	Mintage	Fine	VF	XF	Unc
23	1774	—	7.50	12.50	20.00	50.00
	1775	—	7.50	12.50	20.00	50.00

NOTE: Varieties exist.

1/4 THALER

SILVER

C#	Date	Mintage	Fine	VF	XF	Unc
26	1754 ICB	—	100.00	175.00	250.00	450.00

(Convention)

Archery Contest
Obv: 8 line inscription.
Rev: Target and cross bows.

C#	Date	Mintage	VG	Fine	VF	XF
28	1788	—	30.00	60.00	75.00	125.00

1/2 THALER

SILVER

C#	Date	Mintage	Fine	VF	XF	Unc
31	1754 ICB	—	125.00	200.00	275.00	400.00
	(This date also struck in 1759).					

(Convention)

Peace Of Hubertusburg Commemorative
Obv: 8 line inscription. Rev: Globe.

C#	Date	Mintage	Fine	VF	XF	Unc
33	1763	—	175.00	225.00	300.00	450.00

Obv: Crossed key arms, leg: NON DORMIT CUSTOS.
Rev: Bust of Joseph II right.

C#	Date	Mintage	Fine	VF	XF	Unc
35	1774 GCB	—	25.00	50.00	70.00	150.00

Obv: Different portrait

C#	Date	Mintage	Fine	VF	XF	Unc
35a	1774 GCB	—	25.00	50.00	70.00	150.00
36	1775 GCB	—	35.00	70.00	100.00	150.00

C#	Date	Mintage	Fine	VF	XF	Unc
37	1781 GCB	—	35.00	70.00	100.00	150.00

C#	Date	Mintage	Fine	VF	XF	Unc
36a	1782 GCB	—	35.00	70.00	100.00	150.00
35b	1782 GCB	—	65.00	100.00	150.00	200.00

C#	Date	Mintage	Fine	VF	XF	Unc
38	1784 KB	1,280	125.00	225.00	300.00	500.00

Archery Contest
Obv: 8 line legend.
Rev: Target and crossbows.

C#	Date	Mintage	Fine	VF	XF	Unc
40	1788	—	50.00	100.00	125.00	250.00

C#	Date	Mintage	Fine	VF	XF	Unc
42	1791 GCB	—	40.00	85.00	150.00	300.00
	(This date struck also in 1792, 1794, 1795, 1796, 1797, 1798 & 1802).					

EIN (1) THALER

SILVER

C#	Date	Mintage	Fine	VF	XF	Unc
45	1754 ICB	—	100.00	200.00	400.00	800.00
45a	1756 ICB	—	100.00	200.00	400.00	800.00
45b	1756 ICB	—	100.00	200.00	400.00	800.00
	(This date also struck in 1757).					
46	1759 ICB	—	150.00	250.00	500.00	1000.
45b	1762 ICB	—	100.00	200.00	400.00	800.00
	(This date also struck in 1764).					

(Convention)

SILVER

Peace Of Hubertusburg Commemorative
Obv: Peace crowning column.

Rev: 8 line inscription.

C#	Date	Mintage	Fine	VF	XF	Unc
47	1763	—	250.00	375.00	600.00	1000.

Obv: Eagle over arms; date below.
Rev: Bust of Joseph II right.

C#	Date	Mintage	Fine	VF	XF	Unc
48	1766	—	500.00	750.00	1000.	2000.
49	1766	—	100.00	200.00	400.00	800.00

Obv: Different portrait

C#	Date	Mintage	Fine	VF	XF	Unc
48a	1766 BF	—	200.00	300.00	600.00	1200.
50	1773 GCB	—	150.00	300.00	600.00	1200.
50a	1774 GCB	—	150.00	250.00	500.00	1200.

Obv: Different portrait

C#	Date	Mintage	Fine	VF	XF	Unc
50b	1774 GCB	—	150.00	250.00	500.00	1000.

Different portrait

C#	Date	Mintage	Fine	VF	XF	Unc
50c	1774 GCB	—	150.00	250.00	500.00	1000.
49a	1775	—	75.00	150.00	300.00	600.00

C#	Date	Mintage	Fine	VF	XF	Unc
50d	1775 GCB	—	200.00	400.00	800.00	1600.

Rev: Similar to C#53.

C#	Date	Mintage	Fine	VF	XF	Unc
49b	1780 BF	—	50.00	150.00	300.00	600.00

(This date also struck in 1783, 1784, 1785, 1787, 1788, 1789, 1790 & 1791.)

Obv: Crowned imperial eagle.
Rev: City view with city arms of crossed keys in exergue.

C#	Date	Mintage	Fine	VF	XF	Unc
51	(1780-90)	—	125.00	300.00	500.00	800.00

Archery Contest

C#	Date	Mintage	Fine	VF	XF	Unc
52	1788	—	200.00	500.00	850.00	1600.

Obv: Arms in wreath; date in exergue.

C#	Date	Mintage	Fine	VF	XF	Unc
54	1791 GCB	—	200.00	350.00	700.00	1400.

C#	Date	Mintage	Fine	VF	XF	Unc
53	1791	—	150.00	300.00	600.00	1200.

(This date also struck in 1792).

Obv: Laureate head of Francis II right; KORNLEIN below.
Rev: Sunrise over city view; date in exergue.

C#	Date	Mintage	Fine	VF	XF	Unc
55	1792	—	350.00	800.00	1500.	3000.

C#	Date	Mintage	Fine	VF	XF	Unc
56	1793 GCB	—	150.00	300.00	600.00	1200.

(This date also struck in 1794, 1795, 1796, 1797, & 1798.)

Obv: Laureate head of Francis II right; KORNLEIN below.
Rev: Crowned imperial eagle over city arms; dates at sides.

C#	Date	Mintage	Fine	VF	XF	Unc
57	1801-1802 Z	—	1500.	2500.	3500.	6000.

TRADE COINS

1/4 DUCAT

.8750 gm., .986 GOLD, .0277 oz AGW
Obv: Imperial eagle.
Rev: City view of Regensburg.

C#	Date	Mintage	Fine	VF	XF	Unc
87	ND	—	150.00	300.00	450.00	650.00

1/2 DUCAT

1.7500 gm., .986 GOLD, .0555 oz AGW

C#	Date	Mintage	Fine	VF	XF	Unc
89	ND	—	300.00	600.00	950.00	1250.

DUCAT

3.5000 gm., .986 GOLD, .1109 oz AGW

C#	Date	Mintage	Fine	VF	XF	Unc
91	ND	—	425.00	850.00	1150.	1500.

C#	Date	Mintage	Fine	VF	XF	Unc
93	ND	—	475.00	950.00	1250.	1750.

Rev: Imperial eagle.

C#	Date	Mintage	Fine	VF	XF	Unc
95	ND	—	475.00	950.00	1250.	1750.

Obv: City view.
Rev: Head of Leopold II right.

C#	Date	Mintage	VG	Fine	VF	XF
101	ND (1790-1792)		300.00	600.00	1000.	1500.

Obv: Crowned imperial eagle.

C#	Date	Mintage	VG	Fine	VF	XF
103	ND (1792-1803)		300.00	650.00	1150.	1650.

2 DUCATS

7.0000 gm., .986 GOLD, .2219 oz AGW
Obv: Imperial eagle.
Rev: City view of Regensburg.

C#	Date	Mintage	Fine	VF	XF	Unc
97	ND	—	1000.	1500.	2500.	3500.

3 DUCATS

10.5000 gm., .986 GOLD, .3329 oz AGW
Obv: Bust of Joseph II, right.
Rev: Imperial eagle.

C#	Date	Mintage	Fine	VF	XF	Unc
99	ND	—	1500.	2500.	3500.	5000.

REUSS — GREIZ

The Reuss family, whose lands were located in Thuringia, was founded c. 1035. Greiz was founded in 1303. Upper and Lower Greiz lines were founded in 1535 and the territories were divided until 1768. In 1778 the ruler was made a prince of the Holy Roman Empire. The principality endured until 1918.

SOLEMNIVM
A·MDLXXXVI·
PER ACTORVM
MEMORIAM
PATRVM PATRIAE
INDVLGENTIA
CELEBRANT
SAGITTARII RATISB
A·MDCCLXXXVIII·

Untergreiz

RULER

Heinrich III, 1733-1768

MINTMASTER'S INITIALS

I.E.C. - Johann Christian Eberhard, 1755-1764
I.C.K. - Johann Christian Knaust
L. - Georg Christoph Lowell

1/48 THALER

(= 6 Pfennig)

BILLON
Obv: Crowned lion rampant left.
Rev: Value and date.

C#	Date	Mintage	VG	Fine	VF	XF
12	1763 E.	—	6.00	12.00	20.00	40.00

1/24 THALER

(= 1 GROSCHEN)

BILLON
Obv: Crowned arms.
Rev: Value in center; date in outer legend.

C#	Date	Mintage	VG	Fine	VF	XF
18	1763 I.C.E.	—	5.00	10.00	20.00	40.00
	1764 I.C.E.	—	5.00	10.00	20.00	40.00

NOTE: Varieties exist.

1/12 THALER

BILLON
Obv: Crowned arms.
Rev: Value in center; date in outer legend.

C#	Date	Mintage	VG	Fine	VF	XF
22	1763 I.C.E.	—	6.00	10.00	20.00	40.00

NOTE: Varieties exist.

Rev: Value and date in center.

C#	Date	Mintage	VG	Fine	VF	XF
22a	1763 I.C.E.	—	6.00	10.00	20.00	40.00

1/6 THALER

SILVER
Obv: Helmed arms.
Rev: Value in center; date in outer legend.

C#	Date	Mintage	VG	Fine	VF	XF
26	1763 I.C.E.	—	10.00	20.00	35.00	60.00

THALER

SILVER
Obv: Armored bust of Heinrich right.
Rev: Helmed arms divide arms.

C#	Date	Mintage	Fine	VF	XF	Unc
32	1763	—	225.00	350.00	750.00	1500.
	1764	—	225.00	350.00	750.00	1500.

TRADE COINS

DUCAT

3.5000 gm., .986 GOLD, .1109 oz AGW
Obv: Armored bust of Heinrich right.
Rev: Helmed arms; date below.

C#	Date	Mintage	VG	Fine	VF	XF
34	1764	—	500.00	1000.	1500.	2250.

NOTE: Became extinct in 1768. Lands passed to Obergreiz.

Obergreiz

RULERS

Heinrich XI, 1723-1800
Heinrich XIII, 1800-1817
Heinrich XIX, 1817-1836
Heinrich XX, 1836-1859
Heinrich XXII, 1859-1902
Heinrich XXIV, 1902-1918

HELLER

COPPER
Obv: Crowned lion rampant left.
Rev: Value and date.

C#	Date	Mintage	VG	Fine	VF	XF
1	1769	—	6.00	12.00	20.00	35.00
	1770	—	6.00	12.00	20.00	35.00

Obv: Crowned lion on crowned oval shield. Rev: Value.

C#	Date	Mintage	Fine	VF	XF	Unc
37	1812	—	3.50	7.00	15.00	50.00
	1815	—	3.50	7.00	15.00	50.00
52	1817	—	3.50	7.00	15.00	50.00
	1819	—	3.50	7.00	15.00	50.00

1/2 PFENNIG

COPPER
Obv: Crowned Reuss lion left.
Rev: Value over date, G.R.P. in value.

C#	Date	Mintage	VG	Fine	VF	XF
2	1775	—	6.00	12.50	17.50	25.00

Rev: Value over date, F.R.P. in value.

C#	Date	Mintage	VG	Fine	VF	XF
2a	1787	—	3.50	7.50	11.50	20.00
	1789	—	3.50	7.50	11.50	20.00

PFENNIG

COPPER
Obv: Crowned Reuss lion left.
Rev: Value over date, G.R.P. in value.

C#	Date	Mintage	VG	Fine	VF	XF
3	1775	—	2.50	5.00	7.00	15.00

SILVER
Rev: Value over date.

C#	Date	Mintage	VG	Fine	VF	XF
3b	1775	—	—	Rare	—	—

COPPER
Rev: Value over date; F.R.P. in value.

C#	Date	Mintage	VG	Fine	VF	XF
3a	1787	—	2.50	5.00	7.50	15.00
	1789	—	2.50	5.00	7.50	15.00

C#	Date	Mintage	Fine	VF	XF	Unc
38	1806	—	3.50	7.00	15.00	50.00
	1808	—	3.50	7.00	15.00	50.00

Obv: Crowned lion on crowned oval shield

C#	Date	Mintage	Fine	VF	XF	Unc
39	1808	—	3.50	7.00	15.00	50.00
	1810	—	3.50	7.00	15.00	50.00
	1812	—	3.50	7.00	15.00	50.00
	1813	—	3.50	7.00	15.00	50.00
	1814	—	3.50	7.00	15.00	50.00
	1815	—	3.50	7.00	15.00	50.00
	1816	—	3.50	7.00	15.00	50.00

C#	Date	Mintage	Fine	VF	XF	Unc
53	1817	—	3.00	5.00	10.00	40.00
	1819	—	3.00	5.00	10.00	40.00
	1820	—	3.00	5.00	10.00	40.00
	1821	—	3.00	5.00	10.00	40.00
	1822	—	3.00	5.00	10.00	40.00
	1823	—	3.00	5.00	10.00	40.00
	1824	—	3.00	5.00	10.00	40.00
	1825	—	3.00	5.00	10.00	40.00
	1826	—	3.00	5.00	10.00	40.00
	1827	—	3.00	5.00	10.00	40.00
	1828	—	3.00	5.00	10.00	40.00
	1829	—	3.00	5.00	10.00	40.00
	1830	—	3.00	5.00	10.00	40.00
	1831	—	3.00	5.00	10.00	40.00
	1832	—	3.00	5.00	10.00	40.00

King's crown

C#	Date	Mintage	Fine	VF	XF	Unc
57	1864 A	.360	2.00	3.50	8.00	35.00

Prince's crown

C#	Date	Mintage	Fine	VF	XF	Unc
57a	1868 A	.360	2.00	3.50	8.00	35.00

2 PFENNIG

COPPER
Obv: Crowned lion rampant left.
Rev: Value and date.

C#	Date	Mintage	VG	Fine	VF	XF
4	1760	—	6.00	12.50	20.00	35.00
	1761	—	6.00	12.50	20.00	35.00

3 PFENNIG

BILLON
Obv: Hxler monogram in cartouche.
Rev: Value in orb on shield divides date.

C#	Date	Mintage	VG	Fine	VF	XF
9	1763 I.C.E.	—	6.00	12.50	20.00	35.00

Obv: Crowned arms.

C#	Date	Mintage	VG	Fine	VF	XF
10	1764	—	5.00	10.00	15.00	30.00
	1769	—	5.00	10.00	15.00	30.00

NOTE: Varieties exist.

Obv: Crowned Reuss lion left.

C#	Date	Mintage	VG	Fine	VF	XF
10.5	1787	—	6.00	12.00	20.00	35.00

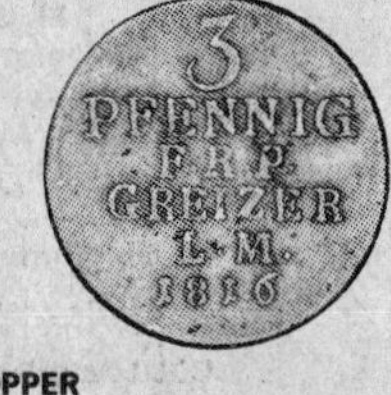

COPPER

C#	Date	Mintage	Fine	VF	XF	Unc
40	1805	—	3.00	6.00	10.00	50.00
	1808	—	3.00	6.00	10.00	50.00
	1810	—	3.00	6.00	10.00	50.00
	1812	—	3.00	6.00	10.00	50.00
	1813	—	3.00	6.00	10.00	50.00
	1814	—	3.00	6.00	10.00	50.00
	1815	—	3.00	6.00	10.00	50.00
	1816	—	3.00	6.00	10.00	50.00

C#	Date	Mintage	Fine	VF	XF	Unc
54	1817	—	3.00	6.00	10.00	50.00
	1819	—	3.00	6.00	10.00	50.00
	1820	—	3.00	6.00	10.00	50.00
	1821	—	3.00	6.00	10.00	50.00
	1822	—	3.00	6.00	10.00	50.00
	1823	—	3.00	6.00	10.00	50.00
	1824	—	3.00	6.00	10.00	50.00
	1825	—	3.00	6.00	10.00	50.00
	1826	—	3.00	6.00	10.00	50.00
	1827	—	3.00	6.00	10.00	50.00
	1828	—	3.00	6.00	10.00	50.00
	1829	—	3.00	6.00	10.00	50.00
	1830	—	3.00	6.00	10.00	50.00
	1831	—	3.00	6.00	10.00	50.00
	1832	—	3.00	6.00	10.00	50.00
	1833	—	3.00	6.00	10.00	50.00

King's crown

C#	Date	Mintage	Fine	VF	XF	Unc
58	1864 A	.360	1.25	3.00	6.00	40.00

Prince's crown

C#	Date	Mintage	Fine	VF	XF	Unc
58a	1868 A	.240	1.25	3.00	6.00	40.00

SILBER GROSCHEN

BILLON
Obv: Crowned arms; cornucopia on left.
Rev: Value in center; date in outer legend.

C#	Date	Mintage	VG	Fine	VF	XF
18	1763 I.C.E.	—	6.50	13.50	22.50	40.00

Obv: Crowned arms; cornucopia on right.

C#	Date	Mintage	VG	Fine	VF	XF
18a	1763 I.C.E.	—	6.50	13.50	22.50	40.00

Obv: Crowned lion on pointed shield. Rev: Value.

C#	Date	Mintage	Fine	VF	XF	Unc
42	1805	.361	5.00	11.00	25.00	50.00
	1812	—	5.00	11.00	25.00	50.00

C#	Date	Mintage	Fine	VF	XF	Unc
59	1868 A	.090	4.00	8.00	14.00	40.00

48 EINEN (1/48) THALER

BILLON
Obv: Hxler monogram in cartouche.
Rev: Value and year.

C#	Date	Mintage	VG	Fine	VF	XF
11	1763 I.C.E.	—	7.00	15.00	25.00	40.00
	Obv: Crowned arms.					
12	1769	—	5.00	10.00	15.00	30.00
	GOLD (weight of 1/2 Ducat)					
12a	1769	—	—	—	Rare	—
	Obv: Crowned Reuss lion left. Rev: Value and date in cartouche.					
12.5	1787	—	5.00	10.00	15.00	30.00
	1789	—	5.00	10.00	15.00	30.00

12 EINEN (1/12) THALER

SILVER
Obv: Helmed arms.
Rev: Value and year.

C#	Date	Mintage	VG	Fine	VF	XF
20	1763 I.C.E.	—	6.50	13.50	22.50	40.00
	Rev: Value in field; date in outer legend.					
20a	1763 I.C.E.	—	6.50	13.50	22.50	40.00
	Obv: Crowned and mantled arms. Rev: Value and date.					
22	1789	—	6.00	13.00	22.00	40.00

1/6 THALER

SILVER
Obv: Helmed arms.
Rev: Value in field; date in outer legend.

C#	Date	Mintage	VG	Fine	VF	XF
26	1763 I.C.E.	—	12.00	25.00	40.00	60.00

.542 SILVER
Obv: Crowned draped heart shaped arms.
Rev: Value within crossed branches.

C#	Date	Mintage	Fine	VF	XF	Unc
45	1808 L	9,000	55.00	115.00	200.00	325.00

1/3 THALER

.833 SILVER
Obv: Crowned draped heart shaped arms.
Rev: Value within tied branches.

C#	Date	Mintage	Fine	VF	XF	Unc
47	1809 L	1,500	110.00	225.00	350.00	550.00

1/2 THALER
(Convention)

SILVER
Obv: Head right.
Rev: Crowned and mantled arms; date divided below.

C#	Date	Mintage	Fine	VF	XF	Unc
30	1786	—	60.00	100.00	175.00	400.00

EIN (1) THALER
(Convention)

SILVER
Obv: Head of Heinrich right; S.T. below.
Rev: Helmed arms; date divided below.

C#	Date	Mintage	Fine	VF	XF	Unc
32	1769 ICK	—	200.00	400.00	600.00	1200.

Mining Thaler From Neue Hoffnung Mine

C#	Date	Mintage	Fine	VF	XF	Unc
33	1775 ICK	—	250.00	500.00	1000.	2000.
	Rev: Crowned and mantled arms, date below divided by ICK.					
34	1778 ICK	—	150.00	300.00	600.00	1200.

Obv: Head right.

C#	Date	Mintage	VG	Fine	VF	XF
35	1790 ICK	—	500.00	1000.	2000.	3500.

28.0600 gm., .833 SILVER, .7516 oz ASW
Obv. leg: D.G. HENR. XIII .....

C#	Date	Mintage	Fine	VF	XF	Unc
49	1806 L	345 pcs.	500.00	1000.	2000.	4000.
	1807 L	200 pcs.	500.00	1000.	2000.	4000.

Obv. leg: V.G.G. HEINRICH .....
Rev: Similar to C#49.

C#	Date	Mintage	Fine	VF	XF	Unc
50	1807 L	300 pcs.	500.00	1000.	2000.	4000.
	1812 L	2,275	400.00	800.00	1600.	3200.
	No D. F. Rev: Value within tied branches.					
51	1812 L	—	200.00	500.00	1000.	2000.

18.5200 gm., .900 SILVER, .5360 oz ASW

C#	Date	Mintage	Fine	VF	XF	Unc
55	1858 A	9,500	50.00	100.00	200.00	400.00

C#	Date	Mintage	Fine	VF	XF	Unc
60	1868 A	7,100	50.00	100.00	200.00	400.00

2 THALER
(= 3-1/2 Gulden)

37.1200 gm., .900 SILVER, 1.0742 oz ASW

C#	Date	Mintage	Fine	VF	XF	Unc
56	1841 A	2,400	250.00	500.00	1000.	2000.
	1844 A	2,400	250.00	500.00	1000.	2000.
	1848 A	2,400	250.00	500.00	1000.	2000.
	1851 A	2,400	250.00	500.00	1000.	2000.

MONETARY REFORM

2 MARK

11.1110 gm., .900 SILVER, .3215 oz ASW
Obv: Head right. Rev: Type 2 eagle.

Y#	Date	Mintage	VF	XF	Unc
137	1877B	.020	200.00	750.00	2000.

Rev: Type 3 eagle.

Y#	Date	Mintage	VF	XF	Unc
137a	1892A	.010	300.00	450.00	850.00
	1892A	—	—	Proof	950.00

Y#	Date	Mintage	VF	XF	Unc
139	1899A	.010	150.00	250.00	500.00
	1899A	120 pcs.	—	Proof	700.00
	1901A	.010	150.00	250.00	450.00
	1901A	—	—	Proof	550.00

3 MARK

16.6670 gm., .900 SILVER, .4823 oz ASW

Y#	Date	Mintage	VF	XF	Unc
140	1909A	.010	200.00	300.00	400.00
	1909A	—	—	Proof	700.00

20 MARK

7.9650 gm., .900 GOLD, .2304 oz AGW
Rev: Type 2 eagle.

Y#	Date	Mintage	VF	XF	Unc
138	1875B	1,510	10,000.	14,000.	20,000.

REUSS — EBERSDORF

The Reuss family, whose lands were located in Thuringia, was founded c. 1035. The Ebersdorf line was founded in 1671 from the Lobenstein branch. The county became a principality in 1806. They inherited Lobenstein in 1824 and were forced to abdicate in 1849 and Lobenstein-Ebersdorf went to Schleiz.

RULERS

Heinrich XXIV, 1747-1779
Heinrich LI, 1779-1822

PFENNIG

BILLON
Obv: Crowned arms.
Rev: Value and date in cartouche.

C#	Date	Mintage	VG	Fine	VF	XF
1	1765	.016	6.00	12.50	20.00	35.00

COPPER
Obv: Crowned shield with hound's head. Rev: Value.

C#	Date	Mintage	Fine	VF	XF	Unc
20	1812	—	5.00	10.00	15.00	40.00

2 PFENNIG

COPPER
Obv: Crowned shield with hound's head. Rev: Value.

C#	Date	Mintage	Fine	VF	XF	Unc
21	1812	—	6.00	12.00	16.00	40.00

3 PFENNIG

BILLON
Obv: Crowned arms.
Rev: Value and date in cartouche.

C#	Date	Mintage	VG	Fine	VF	XF
3	1765 ICK	.010	5.00	10.00	17.50	30.00

COPPER
Obv: Crowned shield with hound's head. Rev: Value.

C#	Date	Mintage	Fine	VF	XF	Unc
22	1812	—	6.00	12.00	18.00	40.00

4 PFENNIG

COPPER
Obv: Crowned shield with hound's head. Rev: Value.

C#	Date	Mintage	Fine	VF	XF	Unc
23	1812	—	7.50	15.00	25.00	50.00

6 PFENNIG

BILLON
Obv: Crowned shield with hound's head. Rev: Value.

C#	Date	Mintage	Fine	VF	XF	Unc
27	1812	—	6.00	12.00	18.00	40.00

8 PFENNIG

BILLON
Obv: Crowned shield with hound's head. Rev: Value.

C#	Date	Mintage	Fine	VF	XF	Unc
29	1812	—	7.50	15.00	25.00	50.00

GROSCHEN

BILLON
Obv: Crowned spade-shaped arms. Rev: Value.

C#	Date	Mintage	Fine	VF	XF	Unc
31	1812	—	7.50	15.00	25.00	50.00
	1814	.087	7.50	15.00	25.00	50.00

1/48 THALER

BILLON
Obv: Crowned arms.
Rev: Value and date in cartouche.

C#	Date	Mintage	VG	Fine	VF	XF
5	1765 ICK	.008	10.00	20.00	35.00	50.00

1/24 THALER

BILLON
Obv: Crowned arms.
Rev: Value in center; date in legend.

C#	Date	Mintage	VG	Fine	VF	XF
7	1763 ICK	.044	5.00	10.00	17.50	30.00

1/12 THALER

BILLON
Obv: Crowned arms; leg: HEINRICH XXIV.
Rev: Value and date in center.

C#	Date	Mintage	VG	Fine	VF	XF
9	1763 ICE	.031	6.00	12.50	20.00	32.50
	1764 ICE	Inc. Ab.	6.00	12.50	20.00	32.50

Obv. leg: HEINRICH D XXIV.

C#	Date	Mintage	VG	Fine	VF	XF
9a	1764	Inc. Ab.	6.00	12.50	20.00	32.50

Obv: I.C.E. under arms.

C#	Date	Mintage	VG	Fine	VF	XF
9b	1764	Inc. Ab.	6.00	12.50	20.00	32.50

1/6 THALER

SILVER
Obv: Crowned arms.
Rev: Value and date in center.

C#	Date	Mintage	VG	Fine	VF	XF
11	1763 ICE	.009	6.00	12.50	20.00	45.00
	1764 ICE	Inc. Ab.	6.00	12.50	20.00	45.00

1/3 THALER

SILVER
Obv: Crowned arms.
Rev: Value and date in center; I.C.E. below date.

C#	Date	Mintage	VG	Fine	VF	XF
13	1763	.005	50.00	100.00	150.00	200.00

Obv: Crowned arms; I.C.E. below.
Rev: Value and date in center.

C#	Date	Mintage	VG	Fine	VF	XF
13a	1764	Inc. Ab.	50.00	100.00	150.00	200.00

2/3 THALER

SILVER
Obv: Bust of Heinrich right.
Rev: Crowned arms; value below.

C#	Date	Mintage	VG	Fine	VF	XF
15	1765 ICE	.002	60.00	125.00	175.00	250.00

EIN (1) THALER

(Convention)

SILVER
Obv: Bust of Heinrich right.
Rev: Helmed arms.

C#	Date	Mintage	Fine	VF	XF	Unc
17	1765 ICE	.005	200.00	400.00	600.00	1000.
	1766 ICK	I.A.	200.00	400.00	600.00	1000.

(Species)

28.0600 gm., .833 SILVER, .7516 oz ASW
Obv: Crowned draped heart shaped arms. Rev: Value.

C#	Date	Mintage	Fine	VF	XF	Unc
33	1812	1,575	400.00	800.00	1600.	3200.

REUSS-GERA

The Reuss family, whose lands were located in Thuringia, was founded c. 1035. The Gera line was founded in 1635 and went to Schleiz in 1802.

RULER

Heinrich XXX, 1748-1802

PFENNIG

COPPER
Obv: Hound's head.
Rev: Value and date.

C#	Date	Mintage	VG	Fine	VF	XF
1	1761	—	5.00	10.00	15.00	25.00

2 PFENNIG

COPPER
Obv: Hound's head.
Rev: Value and date.

C#	Date	Mintage	VG	Fine	VF	XF
2	1761	—	6.00	12.50	20.00	35.00

1/24 THALER

BILLON
Obv: Helmed arms.
Rev: Value in center; date in legend.

C#	Date	Mintage	VG	Fine	VF	XF
6	1763 ICE	—	7.00	15.00	25.00	40.00
	1764 ICE	—	7.00	15.00	25.00	40.00

1/12 THALER

BILLON
Obv: Helmed arms.
Rev: Value in center; date in legend.

C#	Date	Mintage	VG	Fine	VF	XF
8	1763 ICE	—	6.00	13.50	22.50	37.50
	1764 ICE	—	6.00	13.50	22.50	37.50

Rev: Value and date in center.

C#	Date	Mintage	VG	Fine	VF	XF
8a	1763 ICE	—	6.00	13.50	22.50	37.50

1/6 THALER

SILVER
Obv: Helmed arms.
Rev: Value in center; date in legend.

C#	Date	Mintage	VG	Fine	VF	XF
10	1763 ICE	—	15.00	30.00	50.00	75.00

2/3 THALER

SILVER
Peace of Hubertusburg Commemorative
Obv: Helmed arms.
Rev: Figure of Freedom handing scepter to Virtue.

C#	Date	Mintage	VG	Fine	VF	XF
11	1763	—	70.00	150.00	200.00	325.00

THALER

SILVER
Peace of Hubertusburg Commemorative
Obv: Helmed arms.
Rev: Figure of Freedom handing scepter to Virtue.

C#	Date	Mintage	Fine	VF	XF	Unc
12	1763	—	500.00	1000.	2000.	3000.

REUSS — LOBENSTEIN

The Reuss family, whose lands were located in Thuringia, was founded c. 1035. The Lobenstein line was founded in 1635. The county became a principality in 1790. In 1824 Lobenstein was given to Ebersdorf.

RULERS

Heinrich XXXV, 1782-1805
Heinrich LIV, 1805-1824

3 PFENNIG

BILLON
Obv: Crowned lion

C#	Date	Mintage	Fine	VF	XF	Unc
10	1804	.110	5.00	10.00	15.00	50.00
	1807	—	5.00	10.00	15.00	50.00
	Obv: Uncrowned lion					
15	1807	—	5.00	10.00	15.00	50.00

1/48 THALER

BILLON
Obv: Crowned lion. Rev: Value.

C#	Date	Mintage	Fine	VF	XF	Unc
12	1805	.033	8.00	15.00	25.00	50.00

REUSS — LOBENSTEIN — EBERSDORF

This line was formed by the merger between Ebersdorf and Lobenstein in 1824. The prince abdicated during political troubles in 1848 and the lands went to Schleiz in 1849.

RULERS

Heinrich LXXII (As Prince of Reuss-Ebersdorf) 1822-1824
(As Prince of Reuss-Lobenstein-Ebersdorf), 1824-1849

PFENNIG

COPPER
Obv: Crowned shield with crowned lion. Rev: Value.

C#	Date	Mintage	Fine	VF	XF	Unc
1	1841A	.316	2.50	5.00	10.00	35.00
	1844A	.381	2.50	5.00	10.00	35.00

3 PFENNIG

COPPER
Obv: Crowned shield with crowned lion. Rev: Value.

C#	Date	Mintage	Fine	VF	XF	Unc
2	1841A	.107	2.50	5.00	10.00	35.00
	1844A	.180	2.50	5.00	10.00	35.00

1/2 SILBER GROSCHEN

BILLON
Obv: Crowned shield with crowned lion. Rev: Value.

C#	Date	Mintage	Fine	VF	XF	Unc
3	1841A	.070	7.50	15.00	25.00	50.00

SILBER GROSCHEN

BILLON
Obv: Crowned shield with crowned lion. Rev: Value.

C#	Date	Mintage	Fine	VF	XF	Unc
4	1841A	.059	5.00	10.00	18.00	50.00
	1844A	.087	5.00	10.00	18.00	50.00

2 THALER

(= 3-1/2 Gulden)

37.1200 gm., .900 SILVER, 1.0742 oz ASW

C#	Date	Mintage	Fine	VF	XF	Unc
5	1840A	2,750	300.00	500.00	1000.	2000.
	1847A	5,500	300.00	500.00	1000.	2000.

25th Anniversary of Reign

C#	Date	Mintage	Fine	VF	XF	Unc
6	1847A	500 pcs.	500.00	1000.	2000.	4000.

REUSS — SCHLEIZ

The Reuss family, whose lands were located in Thuringia, was founded c. 1035. The Schliez line originated as Saalburg in 1635 until 1666. The county of Schleiz became a principality in 1806 and lasted until 1918 when the last prince abdicated.

RULERS

Heinrich XII, 1744-1784
Heinrich XLII, 1784-1818
Heinrich LXII, 1818-1854
Heinrich LXVII, 1854-1867
Heinrich XIV, 1867-1913

1/2 PFENNIG

(= 1 Heller)

COPPER

C#	Date	Mintage	Fine	VF	XF	Unc
25	1841A	—	7.50	15.00	35.00	65.00

PFENNIG

COPPER

C#	Date	Mintage	Fine	VF	XF	Unc
26	1841A	—	2.50	5.00	9.00	30.00
	1847A	—	2.50	5.00	9.00	30.00

C#	Date	Mintage	Fine	VF	XF	Unc
27	1850A	.362	1.50	5.00	8.00	30.00

C#	Date	Mintage	Fine	VF	XF	Unc
35	1855A	.360	1.00	5.00	8.00	30.00
	1858A	.360	1.00	5.00	8.00	30.00
	1862A	.202	1.00	5.00	8.00	30.00
	1864A	.360	1.00	5.00	8.00	30.00

C#	Date	Mintage	Fine	VF	XF	Unc
40	1868A	.360	1.00	5.00	8.00	30.00

3 PFENNIG

COPPER
Obv: Oval crowned shield with crowned lion. Rev: Value.

C#	Date	Mintage	Fine	VF	XF	Unc
20	1815	—	3.00	7.25	15.00	40.00
	1816	—	3.00	7.25	15.00	40.00

C#	Date	Mintage	Fine	VF	XF	Unc
28	1841A	—	3.00	7.00	12.00	35.00
	1844A	.070	3.00	7.00	12.00	35.00

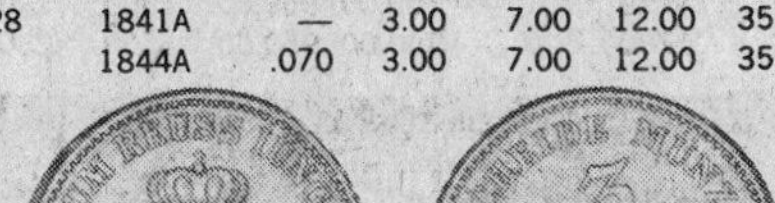

C#	Date	Mintage	Fine	VF	XF	Unc
29	1850A	.242	2.00	4.00	6.00	30.00

C#	Date	Mintage	Fine	VF	XF	Unc
36	1855A	—	1.00	4.00	6.00	30.00
	1858A	.360	1.00	4.00	6.00	30.00
	1862A	.125	1.00	4.00	6.00	30.00
	1864A	.120	1.00	4.00	6.00	30.00

C#	Date	Mintage	Fine	VF	XF	Unc
41	1868A	.120	1.00	4.00	6.00	30.00

SILBER GROSCHEN

BILLON
Obv: Oval crowned arms, crowned lion with 1 tail.
Rev: Value.

C#	Date	Mintage	Fine	VF	XF	Unc
22	1815	—	8.00	16.00	30.00	55.00

Obv: Uncrowned lion with 1 tail.

C#	Date	Mintage	Fine	VF	XF	Unc
22a	1816S	—	8.00	16.00	30.00	55.00

Obv: Crowned lion with 2 tails.

C#	Date	Mintage	Fine	VF	XF	Unc
22b	1816S	—	8.00	16.00	30.00	55.00

C#	Date	Mintage	Fine	VF	XF	Unc
30	1841A	.064	3.00	7.00	20.00	40.00
	1844A	.092	3.00	7.00	20.00	40.00
	1846A	.062	3.00	7.00	20.00	40.00

Obv. leg: JUNGERER LINIE

C#	Date	Mintage	Fine	VF	XF	Unc
31	1850A	.062	4.00	8.00	15.00	40.00
37	1855A	.034	5.00	10.00	18.00	50.00

2 SILBER GROSCHEN

BILLON
Obv: Crowned shield with crowned lion. Rev: Value.

C#	Date	Mintage	Fine	VF	XF	Unc
32	1850A	.064	15.00	30.00	55.00	75.00
38	1855A	.031	15.00	30.00	55.00	75.00

1/24 THALER

BILLON
Obv: Helmed arms; name abbreviated.
Rev: Value and date in circle.

C#	Date	Mintage	VG	Fine	VF	XF
5	1763 ICE	.139	6.00	12.50	20.00	40.00
	1764 ICE	Inc. Ab.	6.00	12.50	20.00	40.00

1/12 THALER

BILLON
Obv: Helmed arms; name complete.
Rev: Value and date in field (no circle).

C#	Date	Mintage	VG	Fine	VF	XF
7	1763 ICE	.054	7.00	15.00	25.00	50.00

1/6 THALER
(Reichs)

SILVER
Obv: Helmed arms.
Rev: Value; date in outer legend.

C#	Date	Mintage	VG	Fine	VF	XF
9	1763 ICE	.007	15.00	30.00	50.00	75.00

1/3 THALER
(Reichs)

SILVER
Obv: Helmed arms.
Rev: Value divide date at top.

C#	Date	Mintage	VG	Fine	VF	XF
11	1763 ICE	560 pcs.	200.00	350.00	500.00	850.00

2/3 THALER
(Reichs)

SILVER
Peace of Hubertusburg Commemorative
Obv: Bust of Heinrich left.
Rev: Helmed arms; value below.

C#	Date	Mintage	VG	Fine	VF	XF
13	1763 ICE	—	75.00	125.00	175.00	350.00

Rev: Different helmed arms; value below.

C#	Date	Mintage	VG	Fine	VF	XF
14	1764 ICE	—	75.00	125.00	175.00	350.00

EIN (1) THALER
(Convention)

SILVER
Peace of Hubertusburg Commemorative
Obv: Bust of Heinrich left.
Rev: Helmed arms; date below.

C#	Date	Mintage	Fine	VF	XF	Unc
15	1763 ICE	—	300.00	600.00	1000.	2000.

Rev: Different helmed arms; date in legend.

C#	Date	Mintage	Fine	VF	XF	Unc
16	1764 ICE	—	250.00	325.00	500.00	1000.

(Vereins)

18.5200 gm., .900 SILVER, .5360 oz ASW

C#	Date	Mintage	Fine	VF	XF	Unc
39	1858A	10,000	40.00	100.00	200.00	400.00
	1862A	10,000	40.00	100.00	200.00	400.00

Rev: Similar to C#39.

C#	Date	Mintage	Fine	VF	XF	Unc
42	1868A	.014	35.00	100.00	200.00	400.00

2 THALER
(= 3-1/2 Gulden)

37.1200 gm., .900 SILVER, 1.0742 oz ASW

C#	Date	Mintage	Fine	VF	XF	Unc
33	1840A	2,650	250.00	500.00	1000.	2000.
	1844A	3,000	250.00	500.00	1000.	2000.
	1846A	2,650	250.00	500.00	1000.	2000.
	1853A	2,700	250.00	500.00	1000.	2000.
	1854A	2,700	250.00	500.00	1000.	2000.

25th Anniversary of Reign
Obv: Similar to C#33

C#	Date	Mintage	Fine	VF	XF	Unc
34	1843A	500 pcs.	400.00	1000.	2000.	4000.

TRADE COINS

DUCAT

3.5000 gm., .986 GOLD, .1109 oz AGW
Peace of Hubertusburg Commemorative
Obv: Crowned GR monogram divides date.
Rev: Helmed arms.

C#	Date	Mintage	Fine	VF	XF	Unc
17	1763 ICE	885 pcs.	300.00	450.00	850.00	1500.

Obv: Bust of Heinrich left.
Rev: Helmed arms; date in legend.

C#	Date	Mintage	Fine	VF	XF	Unc
18	1764	224 pcs.	500.00	950.00	1750.	2750.

MONETARY REFORM

2 MARK

11.1110 gm., .900 SILVER, .3215 oz ASW

Y#	Date	Mintage	VF	XF	Unc
141	1884A	.100	200.00	500.00	1200.
	1884A	—	—	Proof	2200.

10 MARK

3.9820 gm., .900 GOLD, .1152 oz AGW

Y#	Date	Mintage	VF	XF	Unc
142	1882A	5,000	4000.	7000.	8500.
	1882A	—	—	Proof	5000.

20 MARK

7.9650 gm., .900 GOLD, .2304 oz AGW

Y#	Date	Mintage	VF	XF	Unc
143	1881A	.013	2000.	3000.	4000.

ROSTOCK

A city, near the Baltic Sea in Mecklenburg, has a history from the 12th century. The first municipal charter dates from 1218. In 1325 Rostock obtained the mint right and not long after, joined the Hanseatic League. The city coinage extends to 1864.

PFENNIG

COPPER
Obv: Griffon in circle; ROSTOCKER in outer circle.
Rev: Value over date.

C#	Date	Mintage	VG	Fine	VF	XF
1	1782	—	3.00	6.00	10.00	20.00

NOTE: Varieties exist.

Obv: ROSTOCKER MUNZE in outer circle.

C#	Date	Mintage	VG	Fine	VF	XF
1a	1793	—	3.00	7.00	11.50	20.00
	1794	—	3.00	7.00	11.50	20.00
	1795	—	3.00	7.00	11.50	20.00
	1796	—	3.00	7.00	11.50	20.00
	1797	—	3.00	7.00	11.50	20.00

NOTE: Varieties exist.

Rev: Value on tablet.

C#	Date	Mintage	VG	Fine	VF	XF
2	1798	—	4.00	8.00	12.50	20.00

NOTE: Varieties exist.

Obv: Griffin shield within ring. Rev: Value.

C#	Date	Mintage	Fine	VF	XF	Unc
2a	1796	—	2.00	6.00	12.00	50.00
	1797	—	2.00	6.00	12.00	50.00
	1800	—	2.00	6.00	12.00	50.00
	1801	—	2.00	6.00	12.00	50.00
	1802	—	2.00	6.00	12.00	50.00

Obv. leg: ROSTOCKER begins at 8 o'clock.

C#	Date	Mintage	Fine	VF	XF	Unc
4	1802	—	2.00	6.00	12.00	50.00
	1805	—	2.00	6.00	12.00	50.00

Obv: No circle between griffin and legend

C#	Date	Mintage	Fine	VF	XF	Unc
4a	1815	—	2.00	6.00	12.00	50.00
	1824	—	2.00	5.00	10.00	50.00

Obv: Without legend

C#	Date	Mintage	Fine	VF	XF	Unc
5	1848	—	2.50	5.00	10.00	40.00

3 PFENNIG

COPPER

C#	Date	Mintage	Fine	VF	XF	Unc
10	1815A.S.	—	2.00	6.00	12.00	50.00
	1824A.S.	—	2.00	6.00	12.00	50.00
10a	1843B.S.	.192	2.00	5.00	10.00	45.00

C#	Date	Mintage	Fine	VF	XF	Unc
11	1855	—	2.00	5.00	10.00	45.00

C#	Date	Mintage	Fine	VF	XF	Unc
12	1859	—	2.00	5.00	10.00	45.00

C#	Date	Mintage	Fine	VF	XF	Unc
12a	1862H.K.	—	2.00	5.00	10.00	45.00
	1864H.K.	—	2.00	5.00	10.00	45.00

TRADE COINS

DUCAT

3.5000 gm., .986 GOLD, .1109 oz AGW
Obv: Oval arms in sprays.
Rev: Crowned imperial eagle.

C#	Date	Mintage	Fine	VF	XF	Unc
17	1783	—	600.00	950.00	1500.	2300.

C#	Date	Mintage	Fine	VF	XF	Unc
18	1796	—	650.00	1000.	1350.	2000.

SAINT ALBAN

A priory, near Mainz, received the mint right in 1518, however, only coins of the 18th century are known.

TRADE COINS

DUCAT

3.5000 GM., .986 GOLD, .1109 oz AGW

C#	Date	Mintage	Fine	VF	XF	Unc
1	1778	—	700.00	950.00	1500.	2300.
	1779	—	700.00	950.00	1500.	2300.
	1780	—	700.00	950.00	1500.	2300.

SALM

A county, on the Belgian border, is first recorded in 1019. There were many divisions throughout the centuries. The lands were mediatized in 1806.

RULERS
Friedrich III, 1779-1794

10 KREUZER
(Convention)

SILVER
Obv: Head right.
Rev: Crowned and mantled arms.

C#	Date	Mintage	VG	Fine	VF	XF
2	1780	—	20.00	40.00	65.00	100.00

EIN (1) THALER
(Convention)

SILVER
Obv: Head right.
Rev: Crowned and mantled arms; B F N below.

C#	Date	Mintage	Fine	VF	XF	Unc
5	1780	—	400.00	850.00	1500.	2500.

Rev: Crowned arms in sprays, R.F. and date below.

C#	Date	Mintage	Fine	VF	XF	Unc
6	1782	—	300.00	600.00	950.00	1250.

TRADE COINS

DUCAT

3.5000 gm., .986 GOLD, .1109 oz AGW
Obv: Head right.
Rev: Crowned and mantled arms.

C#	Date	Mintage	Fine	VF	XF	Unc
8	1780	—	1250.	1750.	2500.	3200.
	1782	—	1250.	1750.	2500.	3200.

CAROLIN

9.7000 gm., .770 GOLD, .2401 oz AGW
Obv: Head right. Rev: Arms.

C#	Date	Mintage	Fine	VF	XF	Unc
10	1782	—	1650.	2250.	3250.	4000.

SAXE — ALTENBURG

A duchy, located in Thuringia in northwest Germany. It came into being in 1826 when Saxe-Gotha-Altenburg became extinct. The duke of Saxe-Hildburghausen ceded Hildburghausen to Meiningen in exchange for Saxe-Altenburg. The last duke abdicated in 1918.

RULERS
Joseph, 1834-1848
Georg, 1848-1853
Ernst I, 1853-1908

MINTMASTER'S INITIALS
B - Gustav Julius Buschick
F - Gustav Theodor Fischer
G - Johann Georg Grohmann

PFENNIG

COPPER
Obv: Crowned arms. Rev: Value.

C#	Date	Mintage	Fine	VF	XF	Unc
1	1841 G	.220	2.50	5.00	9.00	35.00
	Obv: Crowned heart shaped arms					
2	1843 G	.089	5.00	10.00	15.00	40.00
	Rev: F below date					
11	1852 F	.120	2.50	5.00	10.00	35.00

C#	Date	Mintage	Fine	VF	XF	Unc
	Rev: F below date.					
14	1856 F	.041	2.50	5.00	10.00	40.00
	1858 F	.129	2.00	4.00	8.00	35.00
	Rev: Without mintmark					
14a	1857	—	2.00	4.00	8.00	35.00
	Rev: B below date					
14b	1861 B	.163	2.00	4.00	8.00	35.00
	1863 B	.302	2.00	4.00	8.00	35.00
	1865 B	.150	2.00	4.00	8.00	35.00

2 PFENNIG

COPPER
Obv: Crowned arms. Rev: Value.

C#	Date	Mintage	Fine	VF	XF	Unc
3	1841 G	.150	2.50	5.00	10.00	40.00
	Obv: Crowned heart shaped arms					
4	1843 G	.046	5.00	10.00	15.00	50.00

C#	Date	Mintage	Fine	VF	XF	Unc
12	1852 F	.060	4.00	6.00	12.00	40.00
15	1856 F	.029	4.00	8.00	15.00	50.00

5 PFENNIG

(= 1/2 Neugroschen)

BILLON
Obv: Crowned arms. Rev: Value.

C#	Date	Mintage	Fine	VF	XF	Unc
5	1841 G	.097	4.50	9.00	18.00	50.00
	1842 G	.130	4.50	9.00	18.00	50.00

10 PFENNIG

(= 1 Neugroschen)

BILLON
Obv: Crowned arms. Rev: Value.

C#	Date	Mintage	Fine	VF	XF	Unc
6	1841 G	.146	4.50	9.00	18.00	50.00
	1842 G	.065	4.50	9.00	18.00	50.00

20 PFENNIG

(= 2 Neugroschen)

BILLON

C#	Date	Mintage	Fine	VF	XF	Unc
7	ND	—	11.00	22.00	35.00	60.00
7a	1841 G	.231	7.00	14.00	20.00	50.00

1/6 THALER

5.3450 gm., .521 SILVER, .0895 oz ASW

C#	Date	Mintage	Fine	VF	XF	Unc
8	1841 G	.060	10.00	20.00	35.00	60.00
	1842 G	.060	10.00	20.00	35.00	60.00

EIN (1) THALER

22.2720 gm., .750 SILVER, .5371 oz ASW

C#	Date	Mintage	Fine	VF	XF	Unc
9	1841 G	.020	50.00	150.00	300.00	600.00

(Vereins)

18.5200 gm., .900 SILVER, .5360 oz ASW

C#	Date	Mintage	Fine	VF	XF	Unc
16	1858 F	.032	40.00	100.00	200.00	400.00
	1864 B	.022	40.00	100.00	200.00	400.00
	1869 B	.023	40.00	100.00	200.00	400.00

2 THALER

(= 3-1/2 Gulden)

37.1190 gm., .900 SILVER, 1.0742 oz ASW

C#	Date	Mintage	Fine	VF	XF	Unc
10	1841 G	9,400	250.00	500.00	1000.	2000.
	1842 G	4,700	250.00	500.00	1000.	2000.
	1843 G	4,700	250.00	500.00	1000.	2000.
	1847 F	9,400	250.00	500.00	1000.	2000.

C#	Date	Mintage	Fine	VF	XF	Unc
	Rev: Similar to Thaler, C#16.					
13	1852 F	9,400	250.00	500.00	1000.	2000.

MONETARY REFORM

2 MARK

11.1110 gm., .900 SILVER, .3215 oz ASW
Ernst 75th Birthday

Y#	Date	Mintage	VF	XF	Unc
144	1901A	.050	200.00	300.00	600.00
	1901A	500 pcs.	—	Proof	1200.

5 MARK

27.7770 gm., .900 SILVER, .8038 oz ASW

Ernst 75th Birthday

Y#	Date	Mintage	VF	XF	Unc
145	1901A	.020	325.00	600.00	1200.
	1901A	500 pcs.	—	Proof	1500.

Ernst 50th Year of Reign
Rev: Similar to 2 Mark, Y#144.

Y#	Date	Mintage	VF	XF	Unc
147	1903A	.020	175.00	250.00	400.00
	1903A	300 pcs.	—	Proof	600.00

20 MARK

7.9650 gm., .900 GOLD, .2304 oz AGW

Y#	Date	Mintage	VF	XF	Unc
146	1887A	.015	1000.	1500.	2000.

SAXE — COBURG — SAALFELD

A duchy, located in northwest Germany, was founded in 1680 as Saxe-Saalfeld. They obtained Coburg in 1735. In 1826, Saalfeld was given to Meiningen and the ruler became the first duke of Saxe-Coburg-Gotha.

RULERS

Ernst Friedrich, 1764-1800
Franz, 1800-1806
Ernst I, 1806-1826

MINTMASTER'S INITIALS

G - Bergrichter Graupner
L - Georg Christoph Loewel
S - Laurentius Theodor Sommer

HELLER

COPPER
Obv: Crowned arms with garlands.
Rev: Value.

C#	Date	Mintage	Fine	VF	XF	Unc
63	1808	—	2.50	5.00	10.00	40.00
	1809	.112	2.50	5.00	10.00	40.00
	1810	.071	2.50	5.00	10.00	40.00
	1814	.050	2.50	5.00	10.00	40.00
	1815	Inc. Ab.	2.50	5.00	10.00	40.00
	1817	—	2.50	5.00	10.00	40.00
	1818	—	2.50	5.00	10.00	40.00
	1819	—	2.50	5.00	10.00	40.00
	1824	—	2.50	5.00	10.00	40.00

Obv: Crowned E within two crossed branches.

C#	Date	Mintage	Fine	VF	XF	Unc
68	1809	—	2.50	5.00	10.00	40.00

1/2 PFENNIG

COPPER
Obv: Crowned arms.
Rev: Value, SCHIEDE MUNZE over date.

C#	Date	Mintage	VG	Fine	VF	XF
24	1772	—	3.00	6.00	9.00	18.00

Rev: Value over date.

C#	Date	Mintage	VG	Fine	VF	XF
24a	1798	—	3.00	6.00	9.00	18.00
	1799	—	3.00	6.00	9.00	18.00
	1800	—	3.00	6.00	9.00	18.00

PFENNIG

COPPER
Obv: Crowned arms.
Rev: Value over date.

C#	Date	Mintage	VG	Fine	VF	XF
25	1770	—	3.00	6.00	9.00	15.00
	1771	—	3.00	6.00	9.00	15.00
	1772	—	3.00	6.00	9.00	15.00
	1798	—	3.00	6.00	9.00	15.00

C#	Date	Mintage	Fine	VF	XF	Unc
47	1804	—	3.00	6.00	10.00	40.00
	1805	—	3.00	6.00	10.00	40.00

Rev: No rosettes on sides of 'I'

C#	Date	Mintage	Fine	VF	XF	Unc
47a	1805	—	3.00	6.00	10.00	40.00

BILLON
Obv: Crowned heart shaped arms. Rev. value: 1 PFENNIG.

C#	Date	Mintage	Fine	VF	XF	Unc
56	1805	—	3.00	6.00	12.00	50.00
73	1808	.962	3.00	6.00	12.00	50.00

COPPER

C#	Date	Mintage	Fine	VF	XF	Unc
64	1808	.083	2.00	5.00	10.00	40.00
	1809	.055	2.00	5.00	10.00	40.00
	1814	.043	2.00	5.00	10.00	40.00
	1815	Inc. Ab.	2.00	5.00	10.00	40.00
	1817	—	2.00	5.00	10.00	40.00
	1819	—	2.00	5.00	10.00	40.00
	1820	—	2.00	5.00	10.00	40.00
	1821	—	2.00	5.00	10.00	40.00
	1822	—	2.00	5.00	10.00	40.00
	1823	—	2.00	5.00	10.00	40.00
	1824	—	2.00	5.00	10.00	40.00
	1826	—	2.00	5.00	10.00	40.00

Obv: Crowned E within two crossed branches.

C#	Date	Mintage	Fine	VF	XF	Unc
69	1809	—	2.00	5.00	10.00	40.00

1-1/2 PFENNIG

COPPER
Obv: Crowned arms.
Rev: Value, SCHIEDE MUNZE over date.

C#	Date	Mintage	VG	Fine	VF	XF
26	1772	—	3.00	6.00	9.00	15.00

Rev: Value over date.

C#	Date	Mintage	VG	Fine	VF	XF
26a	1799	—	3.00	6.00	9.00	15.00

2 PFENNIG

COPPER
Obv: Crowned E within two crossed branches.
Rev: Value, leg: H.S.C.S.S.M.

C#	Date	Mintage	Fine	VF	XF	Unc
70	1810	.124	2.00	5.00	10.00	40.00
	1817	—	2.00	5.00	10.00	40.00
	1818	—	2.00	5.00	10.00	40.00

Rev: Without rosettes on both sides of '2'.

C#	Date	Mintage	Fine	VF	XF	Unc
70a	1810	Inc. Ab.	2.00	5.00	10.00	40.00

3 PFENNIG

BILLON
Obv: Crowned shield. Rev: Value.

C#	Date	Mintage	Fine	VF	XF	Unc
49	1804	—	3.50	7.50	15.00	50.00
	1805	—	3.50	7.50	15.00	50.00
	1806	—	3.50	7.50	15.00	50.00

COPPER
Obv: Arms on crowned cartouche with festoons.

C#	Date	Mintage	Fine	VF	XF	Unc
48	1806	—	3.00	6.00	10.00	40.00

Rev. value: III PFENNIG

C#	Date	Mintage	Fine	VF	XF	Unc
65	1807	—	3.00	6.00	10.00	40.00
	1808	.063	3.00	6.00	10.00	40.00

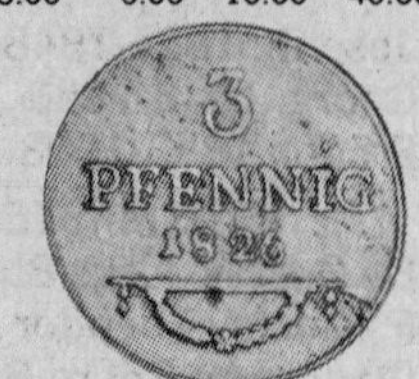

C#	Date	Mintage	Fine	VF	XF	Unc
65a	1821	—	3.00	6.00	10.00	40.00
	1822	—	3.00	6.00	10.00	40.00
	1823	—	3.00	6.00	10.00	40.00
	1824	—	3.00	6.00	10.00	40.00
	1825	—	3.00	6.00	10.00	40.00
	1826	—	3.00	6.00	10.00	40.00

4 PFENNIG

COPPER
Obv: Crowned E within two crossed branches. Rev: Value.

C#	Date	Mintage	Fine	VF	XF	Unc
71	1809	.027	5.00	11.00	22.00	50.00
	1810	8,106	8.00	17.00	25.00	50.00
	1818	—	8.00	17.00	25.00	50.00
	1820	—	8.00	17.00	25.00	50.00

KREUZER

BILLON
Obv: Crowned shield. Rev: Value.

C#	Date	Mintage	Fine	VF	XF	Unc
57	1805	—	5.00	10.00	15.00	50.00

Obv: Crowned E within two crossed branches.
Rev: Value, leg: H.S.C.

C#	Date	Mintage	Fine	VF	XF	Unc
74	1808	.058	5.00	10.00	15.00	50.00
	1812	.018	5.00	10.00	15.00	50.00
	1813	.018	5.00	10.00	15.00	50.00
	1815	.021	5.00	10.00	15.00	50.00
	1817	—	5.00	10.00	15.00	50.00
	1818	—	5.00	10.00	15.00	50.00
	1820	—	5.00	10.00	15.00	50.00

Rev: Value, leg: H.S.C.S.

C#	Date	Mintage	Fine	VF	XF	Unc
74a	1824 S	—	4.00	8.00	12.50	50.00
	1825 S	—	4.00	8.00	12.50	50.00
	1826 S	—	4.00	8.00	12.50	50.00

6 PFENNIG

BILLON
Obv: Crowned E within two crossed branches. Rev: Value.

C#	Date	Mintage	Fine	VF	XF	Unc
66	1808	.047	5.00	11.00	20.00	50.00
	1810	—	5.00	11.00	20.00	50.00
	1818 S	—	5.00	11.00	20.00	50.00
	1820 S	—	5.00	11.00	20.00	50.00

3 KREUZER

BILLON
Obv: Crowned oval arms. Rev: Value.

C#	Date	Mintage	Fine	VF	XF	Unc
58	1804	—	3.00	6.50	11.00	50.00

Obv: Pointed arms.

C#	Date	Mintage	Fine	VF	XF	Unc
58a	1804	—	3.00	6.00	11.00	50.00
	1805	—	3.00	6.00	11.00	50.00

Rev. leg: H.S. COBURG. L.M.

C#	Date	Mintage	Fine	VF	XF	Unc
59	1805	—	3.00	6.00	11.00	50.00

Rev. leg: H.S. COBURG LAND. M.

C#	Date	Mintage	Fine	VF	XF	Unc
59a	1805	—	3.00	6.00	11.00	50.00

Obv: Crowned E within, L below crossed branches.
Rev: Value, leg: H.S.C.

C#	Date	Mintage	Fine	VF	XF	Unc
75b	1808	—	4.00	8.00	12.50	50.00

C#	Date	Mintage	Fine	VF	XF	Unc
75	1808 L	.137	4.00	8.00	12.50	50.00
	1810 L	.151	4.00	8.00	12.50	50.00
	1812 L	.196	4.00	8.00	12.50	50.00
	1813 L	.143	4.00	8.00	12.50	50.00
	1814 L	.116	4.00	8.00	12.50	50.00
	1815 L	.026	4.00	8.00	12.50	50.00

Obv: S below crossed branches.

C#	Date	Mintage	Fine	VF	XF	Unc
75c	1816 S	—	4.00	8.00	12.50	50.00
	1817 S	—	4.00	8.00	12.50	50.00
	1818 S	—	4.00	8.00	12.50	50.00
	1819 S	—	4.00	8.00	12.50	50.00

Rev. leg: H.S.C.S.

C#	Date	Mintage	Fine	VF	XF	Unc
75a	1818 S	—	4.00	9.00	14.00	50.00
	1820 S	—	4.00	9.00	14.00	50.00
	1821 S	—	4.00	9.00	14.00	50.00
	1822 S	—	4.00	9.00	14.00	50.00
	1823 S	—	4.00	9.00	14.00	50.00
	1824 S	—	4.00	9.00	14.00	50.00
	1825 S	—	4.00	9.00	14.00	50.00
	1826 S	—	4.00	9.00	14.00	50.00

Obv: G below crossed branches.

C#	Date	Mintage	Fine	VF	XF	Unc
75d	1826 G	—	4.00	9.00	14.00	50.00

6 KREUZER

BILLON
Obv: Crowned shield. Rev: Value.

C#	Date	Mintage	Fine	VF	XF	Unc
60	1804	—	3.00	5.25	12.00	50.00
	1805	—	3.00	5.25	12.00	50.00

Rev. leg: H.S. COBURG. LAND. M.

C#	Date	Mintage	Fine	VF	XF	Unc
61	1805	—	3.00	5.25	12.00	50.00

Obv: Crowned E within, L below crossed branches.
Rev. leg: H.S.C.

C#	Date	Mintage	Fine	VF	XF	Unc
76	1808 L	.075	4.00	9.00	15.00	50.00
	1810 L	.056	4.00	9.00	15.00	50.00
	1812 L	.090	4.00	9.00	15.00	50.00
	1813 L	.042	4.00	9.00	15.00	50.00
	1814 L	.050	4.00	9.00	15.00	50.00
	1815 L	.011	4.00	9.00	15.00	50.00

Obv: S below crossed branches.

C#	Date	Mintage	Fine	VF	XF	Unc
76b	1816 S	—	4.00	9.00	15.00	50.00
	1817 S	—	4.00	9.00	15.00	50.00
	1818 S	—	4.00	9.00	15.00	50.00
	1819 S	—	4.00	9.00	15.00	50.00
	1820 S	—	4.00	9.00	15.00	50.00

Rev. leg: H.S.C.S.

C#	Date	Mintage	Fine	VF	XF	Unc
76a	1821 S	—	4.00	9.00	15.00	50.00
	1822 S	—	4.00	9.00	15.00	50.00
	1823 S	—	4.00	9.00	15.00	50.00
	1824 S	—	4.00	9.00	15.00	50.00
	1825 S	—	4.00	9.00	15.00	50.00
	1826 S	—	4.00	9.00	15.00	50.00

10 KREUZER

.500 SILVER
Obv: Crowned arms, leg: SACHS. SOUV.
Rev: Value within bound branches.

C#	Date	Mintage	Fine	VF	XF	Unc
77	1820 S	—	15.00	25.00	50.00	100.00

Obv. leg: SACHS. COBURG.

C#	Date	Mintage	Fine	VF	XF	Unc
70a	1824 S	—	15.00	25.00	50.00	100.00

20 KREUZER

.583 SILVER
Obv: Crowned pointed arms.
Rev: Value and date within wreath.

C#	Date	Mintage	Fine	VF	XF	Unc
79	1807L	—	15.00	35.00	65.00	120.00

Rev: Date below wreath.

C#	Date	Mintage	Fine	VF	XF	Unc
79a	1807	—	15.00	35.00	65.00	120.00

C#	Date	Mintage	Fine	VF	XF	Unc
80	1812 L	.030	12.00	25.00	50.00	100.00
	1813 L	.046	12.00	25.00	50.00	100.00
	1819 S	—	12.00	25.00	50.00	100.00
	1820 S	—	12.00	25.00	50.00	100.00

C#	Date	Mintage	Fine	VF	XF	Unc
80a	1823 S	—	15.00	30.00	45.00	90.00
	1824 S	—	15.00	30.00	45.00	90.00
	1825 S	—	15.00	30.00	45.00	90.00
	1826 S	—	15.00	30.00	45.00	90.00

48 EINEN (1/48) THALER

BILLON
Obv: 4-fold arms with Saxon center shield.
Rev: Value over date.

C#	Date	Mintage	VG	Fine	VF	XF
29	1765-91	—	4.00	8.00	12.50	20.00

Obv: Crowned shield with four sections.
Rev: Value within branches around rim.

C#	Date	Mintage	Fine	VF	XF	Unc
52	1804	—	3.00	6.50	15.00	50.00

Obv: Arms on crowned cartouche with festoons.
Rev: Plain.

C#	Date	Mintage	Fine	VF	XF	Unc
52a	1805	—	3.00	6.50	15.00	50.00

24 EINEN (1/24) THALER

BILLON
Obv: 4-fold arms with Saxon center shield.
Rev: Value over date.

C#	Date	Mintage	VG	Fine	VF	XF
30b	1774	—	6.00	12.00	19.00	30.00

Obv: Crowned shield with festoons. Rev: Value.

C#	Date	Mintage	Fine	VF	XF	Unc
54	1805	—	4.00	8.00	15.00	50.00

Obv: Crowned E within two crossed branches.

C#	Date	Mintage	Fine	VF	XF	Unc
67	1808	.026	5.00	10.00	20.00	50.00
	1810	—	5.00	10.00	20.00	50.00
	1818 S	—	5.00	10.00	20.00	50.00

12 EINEN (1/12) THALER

BILLON
Obv: 4-fold arms with Saxon center shield.
Rev: Value over date.

C#	Date	Mintage	VG	Fine	VF	XF
33a	1774	—	6.00	12.00	20.00	30.00

Obv: Crowned arms.

C#	Date	Mintage	VG	Fine	VF	XF
35	1775-85	—	6.00	12.00	20.00	30.00

EIN (1) THALER

(Convention)

28.0600 gm., .833 SILVER, .7521 oz ASW

C#	Date	Mintage	Fine	VF	XF	Unc
62	1805 L	600 pcs.	300.00	600.00	1200.	2400.

C#	Date	Mintage	Fine	VF	XF	Unc
81	1817	—	200.00	400.00	800.00	1600.

Edge: E IN SPECIESTHALER

C#	Date	Mintage	Fine	VF	XF	Unc
81a	1817	—	175.00	325.00	600.00	1000.

(Krone)

29.3800 gm., .871 SILVER, .8228 oz ASW
Obv: Bust in armor left, ermine cape. Rev: Crown, sceptor, sword and date within bound branches.

C#	Date	Mintage	Fine	VF	XF	Unc
82	1825	—	500.00	1000.	2000.	4000.
	1825	—	—	—	Proof	5000.

SAXE — COBURG — GOTHA

Located in northwest Germany, Saxe-Coburg-Gotha was created for the duke of Saxe-Coburg-Saalfeld after the dispersal of Saalfeld and the acquisition of Gotha in 1826. The last duke abdicated in 1918.

RULERS

Ernst I, 1826-1844
Ernst II, 1844-1893
Alfred, 1893-1900
Carl Edward, 1900-1918

MINTMASTER'S INITIALS

B - Gustav Julius Buschick, 1860-
E.K. - Ernst Kleinsteuber, 1828-38
F - Gustav Theodor Fischer, 1845-60
G - Bergrichter Graupner, 1826-28
G - Johann Georg Grohmann, 1833-44
ST - Strebel

PFENNIG

COPPER

Obv: Crowned arms. Rev: Value.

C#	Date	Mintage	Fine	VF	XF	Unc
83	1833	—	2.00	4.00	7.50	40.00
	1834	—	2.00	4.00	7.50	40.00
	1835	—	2.00	4.00	7.50	40.00
	1836	—	2.00	4.00	7.50	40.00
	1837	—	2.00	4.00	7.50	40.00

Obv: Crowned arms within branches.

C#	Date	Mintage	Fine	VF	XF	Unc
100	1841 G	.333	1.50	3.00	6.00	40.00

Obv: F above crowned arms

C#	Date	Mintage	Fine	VF	XF	Unc
109	1847 F	.207	1.50	3.00	6.00	40.00
	1851 F	.059	1.50	3.00	6.00	40.00
	1852 F	.201	1.50	3.00	6.00	40.00
	1856 F	.600	1.50	3.00	6.00	40.00

Obv: B above arms

C#	Date	Mintage	Fine	VF	XF	Unc
109a	1865 B	.150	1.50	3.00	6.00	40.00

C#	Date	Mintage	Fine	VF	XF	Unc
109b	1868 B	.200	1.50	3.00	6.00	40.00
	1870 B	.096	1.50	3.00	6.00	40.00

1-1/2 PFENNIG

COPPER

Obv: Crowned arms. Rev: Value.

C#	Date	Mintage	Fine	VF	XF	Unc
84	1834	—	2.00	4.00	8.00	40.00
	1835	—	2.00	4.00	8.00	40.00

2 PFENNIG

COPPER

Obv: Crowned arms. Rev: Value.

C#	Date	Mintage	Fine	VF	XF	Unc
85	1834	—	2.00	4.00	8.00	40.00
	1835	—	2.00	4.00	8.00	40.00

C#	Date	Mintage	Fine	VF	XF	Unc
101	1841 G	.333	2.00	4.00	8.00	40.00

Obv: F and date below bow

C#	Date	Mintage	Fine	VF	XF	Unc
110	1847 F	.130	1.00	4.00	8.00	40.00
	1851 F	.125	1.00	4.00	8.00	40.00
	1852 F	.146	1.00	4.00	8.00	40.00
	1856 F	.600	1.00	4.00	8.00	40.00

C#	Date	Mintage	Fine	VF	XF	Unc
110a	1868 B	.134	1.00	4.00	8.00	40.00
	1870 B	.118	1.00	4.00	8.00	40.00

3 PFENNIG

COPPER

C#	Date	Mintage	Fine	VF	XF	Unc
86	1834	—	1.50	5.00	10.00	40.00

KREUZER

BILLON

Obv: ST below crowned E. Rev: Value in script.

C#	Date	Mintage	Fine	VF	XF	Unc
86.5	1827 ST	—	5.00	10.00	15.00	50.00

Rev: Value across center

C#	Date	Mintage	Fine	VF	XF	Unc
87	1827 ST	—	5.00	10.00	15.00	50.00
	1828 ST	—	5.00	10.00	15.00	50.00

Obv: EK below crowned E

C#	Date	Mintage	Fine	VF	XF	Unc
87a	1828 EK	—	5.00	10.00	15.00	50.00
	1829 EK	—	5.00	10.00	15.00	50.00
	1830 EK	—	5.00	10.00	15.00	50.00

Rev: KREUZER around bottom rim

C#	Date	Mintage	Fine	VF	XF	Unc
88	1831	—	5.00	10.00	15.00	50.00
	1832	—	5.00	10.00	15.00	50.00
	1833	—	5.00	10.00	15.00	50.00
	1834	—	5.00	10.00	15.00	50.00
	1836	—	5.00	10.00	15.00	50.00
	1837	—	5.00	10.00	15.00	50.00

3 KREUZER

BILLON

Obv: Crowned E within branches, ST below.
Rev: Value in script.

C#	Date	Mintage	Fine	VF	XF	Unc
89.5	1827 ST	—	7.00	15.00	28.00	50.00

Rev: Value across center

C#	Date	Mintage	Fine	VF	XF	Unc
90	1827	—	3.00	6.00	10.00	50.00
	1828 ST	—	3.00	6.00	10.00	50.00
	1829 S	—	3.00	6.00	10.00	50.00
	1829 ST	—	3.00	6.00	10.00	50.00

Obv: EK below crowned E

C#	Date	Mintage	Fine	VF	XF	Unc
90a	1828 EK	—	3.00	6.00	10.00	50.00
	1830 EK	—	3.00	6.00	10.00	50.00
	1831 EK	—	3.00	6.00	10.00	50.00

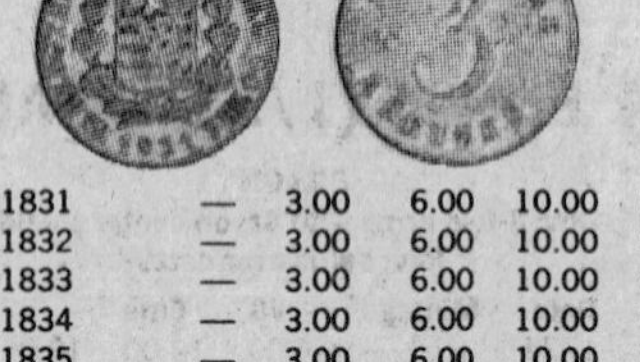

C#	Date	Mintage	Fine	VF	XF	Unc
91	1831	—	3.00	6.00	10.00	50.00
	1832	—	3.00	6.00	10.00	50.00
	1833	—	3.00	6.00	10.00	50.00
	1834	—	3.00	6.00	10.00	50.00
	1835	—	3.00	6.00	10.00	50.00
	1836	—	3.00	6.00	10.00	50.00
	1837	—	3.00	6.00	10.00	50.00
	1838	.358	3.00	6.00	10.00	50.00

Obv: Crowned arms. Rev: Value within branches.

C#	Date	Mintage	Fine	VF	XF	Unc
101.3	1838	.358	3.00	6.00	12.00	50.00

6 KREUZER

BILLON

Obv: G below crowned E within branches.

C#	Date	Mintage	Fine	VF	XF	Unc
92	1827 G	—	5.00	10.00	15.00	50.00

Obv: ST below crowned E

C#	Date	Mintage	Fine	VF	XF	Unc
92a	1827 ST	—	5.00	10.00	15.00	50.00
	1828 ST	—	5.00	10.00	15.00	50.00

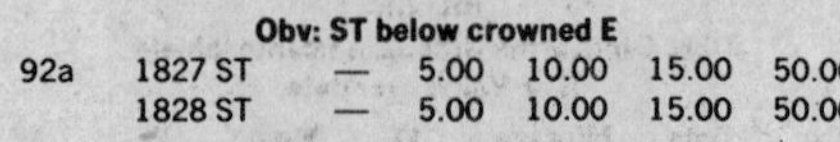

Obv: EK below crowned E

C#	Date	Mintage	Fine	VF	XF	Unc
92b	1828 EK	—	5.00	10.00	15.00	50.00
	1830 EK	—	5.00	10.00	15.00	50.00

C#	Date	Mintage	Fine	VF	XF	Unc
93	1831	—	3.00	6.00	12.00	50.00
	1832	—	3.00	6.00	12.00	50.00
	1833	—	3.00	6.00	12.00	50.00
	1834	—	3.00	6.00	12.00	50.00
93	1835	—	3.00	6.00	12.00	50.00
	1836	—	3.00	6.00	12.00	50.00
	1837	—	3.00	6.00	12.00	50.00
	1838	.209	3.00	6.00	12.00	50.00

C#	Date	Mintage	Fine	VF	XF	Unc
101.6	1838	—	3.00	6.00	12.00	50.00

10 KREUZER

.500 SILVER

Obv: Head left.
Rev: Crowned arms within crossed branches.

C#	Date	Mintage	Fine	VF	XF	Unc
94	1831	—	15.00	30.00	45.00	75.00
	1832	—	15.00	30.00	45.00	75.00
	1833	—	15.00	30.00	45.00	75.00
	1834	—	15.00	30.00	45.00	75.00

C#	Date	Mintage	Fine	VF	XF	Unc
94b	1835	—	15.00	30.00	45.00	75.00
	1836	—	15.00	30.00	45.00	75.00
	1837	—	15.00	30.00	45.00	75.00

20 KREUZER

.583 SILVER

Obv. leg: COBURG & GOTHA, crowned arms.
Rev: ST below value.

C#	Date	Mintage	Fine	VF	XF	Unc
95	1827 ST	—	15.00	30.00	50.00	80.00

Obv. leg: COBURG UND GOTHA

C#	Date	Mintage	Fine	VF	XF	Unc
95a	1827 ST	—	15.00	30.00	50.00	80.00
	1828 ST	—	15.00	30.00	50.00	80.00

Rev: E.K. below branches

C#	Date	Mintage	Fine	VF	XF	Unc
95b	1828 EK	—	15.00	30.00	50.00	80.00
	1830 EK	—	15.00	30.00	50.00	80.00

Obv: Head left.
Rev: Crowned arms within crossed branches.

C#	Date	Mintage	Fine	VF	XF	Unc
96	1831	—	15.00	30.00	45.00	75.00
	1834	—	15.00	30.00	45.00	75.00

Obv. leg: ZU SACHSEN COBURG-GOTHA

C#	Date	Mintage	Fine	VF	XF	Unc
96a	1835	—	14.00	28.00	43.00	75.00
	1836	—	14.00	28.00	43.00	75.00

1/2 GROSCHEN

BILLON

Obv: Crowned arms within branches. Rev: Value.

C#	Date	Mintage	Fine	VF	XF	Unc
102	1841 G	.247	5.00	10.00	15.00	45.00
	1844 G	.065	5.00	10.00	15.00	50.00

C#	Date	Mintage	Fine	VF	XF	Unc
111	1851 F	.032	3.00	6.00	10.00	50.00
	1855 F	.130	3.00	6.00	10.00	50.00
	1858 F	.060	3.00	6.00	10.00	50.00

Obv: B below arms

C#	Date	Mintage	Fine	VF	XF	Unc
114	1868 B	.032	3.00	6.00	10.00	50.00

C#	Date	Mintage	Fine	VF	XF	Unc
114	1870 B	.052	3.00	6.00	10.00	50.00

GROSCHEN

BILLON
Obv: Crowned arms within branches.
Rev: Value, LAND MUNZE

C#	Date	Mintage	Fine	VF	XF	Unc
89	1837	—	7.00	15.00	20.00	50.00
	Rev: Date below value					
103	1841 G	.355	8.00	18.00	28.00	50.00
	Obv: No branches around arms					
112	1847 F	.130	3.00	6.00	15.00	50.00
	1851 F	.049	3.00	6.00	15.00	50.00
	1855 F	.130	3.00	6.00	15.00	50.00
	1858 F	.033	3.00	6.00	15.00	50.00
	Obv: Head left					
115	1865 B	.070	3.00	6.00	15.00	50.00
	1868 B	.031	3.00	6.00	15.00	50.00
	1870 B	.030	3.00	6.00	15.00	50.00

2 GROSCHEN

BILLON
Obv: Crowned arms within branches. Rev: Value.

C#	Date	Mintage	Fine	VF	XF	Unc
104	1841 G	.215	8.00	16.00	25.00	45.00
	1844 G	.032	9.00	18.00	30.00	60.00
113	1847 F	.097	3.00	6.00	15.00	50.00
	1851 F	.032	3.00	6.00	15.00	50.00
	1855 F	.081	3.00	6.00	15.00	50.00
	1858 F	.055	3.00	6.00	15.00	50.00
	Obv: Head left					
116	1865 B	.070	4.00	8.00	15.00	50.00
	1868 B	.030	4.00	8.00	15.00	50.00
	1870 B	.031	4.00	8.00	15.00	50.00

1/6 THALER

5.3450 gm., .521 SILVER, .0895 oz ASW
Obv: Head left. Rev: Crowned arms within wreath.

C#	Date	Mintage	Fine	VF	XF	Unc
105	1841 G	.048	16.00	32.00	50.00	80.00
	1842 G	.048	16.00	32.00	50.00	80.00
	1843 G	.048	16.00	32.00	50.00	80.00
	Obv: Different head					
117	1845 F	.123	15.00	30.00	45.00	60.00

C#	Date	Mintage	Fine	VF	XF	Unc
117a	1848 F	.130	12.00	25.00	35.00	55.00
	Obv: Head with beard					
117b	1852 F	.048	15.00	30.00	45.00	60.00
	1855 F	.060	15.00	30.00	45.00	60.00

.520 SILVER

C#	Date	Mintage	Fine	VF	XF	Unc
118	1864 B	.060	12.00	25.00	35.00	55.00

25th Anniversary of Reign

C#	Date	Mintage	Fine	VF	XF	Unc
119	1869 B	.012	15.00	30.00	45.00	75.00

1/2 THALER

(Convention)

(= 1 Gulden)

.833 SILVER

C#	Date	Mintage	Fine	VF	XF	Unc
97	1830 EK	—	25.00	55.00	85.00	150.00
	1831	—	25.00	55.00	85.00	150.00
	1832	—	25.00	55.00	85.00	150.00
	1834	—	25.00	55.00	85.00	150.00
	1835	—	25.00	55.00	85.00	150.00
97a	1834 HF	—	25.00	55.00	85.00	150.00

EIN (1) THALER

(Krone)

29.3800 gm., .871 SILVER, .8228 oz ASW

C#	Date	Mintage	Fine	VF	XF	Unc
98	1827	—	400.00	1000.	2000.	3000.

(Convention)

28.0600 gm., .833 SILVER, .7521 oz ASW

C#	Date	Mintage	Fine	VF	XF	Unc
99	1828	31 pcs.	4000.	5000.	6000.	8000.
	1828	—	—	—	Proof	10,000.

C#	Date	Mintage	Fine	VF	XF	Unc
99a	1829 EK	1,095	400.00	1000.	2000.	3000.
	Rev: Without mintmaster's initials.					
99b	1832	304 pcs.	3000.	4000.	5000.	6500.
	1833	Inc. Ab.	3000.	4000.	5000.	6500.
99c	1835	—	800.00	1500.	2150.	3200.

22.2700 gm., .750 SILVER, .5371 oz ASW
Rev: Crowned draped arms within wreath

C#	Date	Mintage	Fine	VF	XF	Unc
106	1841 G	.016	50.00	100.00	200.00	400.00
	1842 G	.016	50.00	100.00	200.00	400.00

C#	Date	Mintage	Fine	VF	XF	Unc
120	1846 F	.032	50.00	100.00	200.00	400.00

C#	Date	Mintage	Fine	VF	XF	Unc
120a	1848 F	.016	60.00	150.00	300.00	600.00

Rev: Similar to C#120a.

C#	Date	Mintage	Fine	VF	XF	Unc
120b	1851 F	8,000	60.00	150.00	300.00	600.00
	1852 F	8,000	60.00	150.00	300.00	600.00

(Vereins)

18.5000 gm., .900 SILVER, .5360 oz ASW

C#	Date	Mintage	Fine	VF	XF	Unc
121	1862 B	.040	35.00	75.00	150.00	300.00
	1864 B	.040	35.00	75.00	150.00	300.00
	1870 B	.022	35.00	75.00	150.00	300.00

25th Anniversary of Reign

C#	Date	Mintage	Fine	VF	XF	Unc
122	1869 B	6,000	50.00	100.00	200.00	400.00

2 THALER

(= 3-1/2 Gulden)

37.1200 gm., .900 SILVER, 1.0743 oz ASW

C#	Date	Mintage	Fine	VF	XF	Unc
107	1841 G	.011	250.00	600.00	1200.	2400.
	1842 G	5,350	300.00	600.00	1200.	2400.
	1843 G	5,350	300.00	600.00	1200.	2400.

Rev: Similar to C#107.

C#	Date	Mintage	Fine	VF	XF	Unc
123	1847 F	.011	400.00	800.00	1600.	3200.

C#	Date	Mintage	Fine	VF	XF	Unc
123a	1854 F	.016	250.00	500.00	1000.	2000.

TRADE COINS

DUCAT

3.5000 gm., .986 GOLD, .1109 oz AGW
Obv: Head left, Z.S. Rev: Crowned arms within bound branches.

C#	Date	Mintage	Fine	VF	XF	Unc
108	1831 EK	600 pcs.	900.00	1500.	2000.	3000.

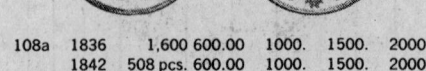

C#	Date	Mintage	Fine	VF	XF	Unc
108a	1836	1,600	600.00	1000.	1500.	2000.
	1842	508 pcs.	600.00	1000.	1500.	2000.

MONETARY REFORM

2 MARK

11.1110 gm., .900 SILVER, .3215 oz ASW

Y#	Date	Mintage	VF	XF	Unc
149	1895A	.020	300.00	900.00	1200.

Y#	Date	Mintage	VF	XF	Unc
152	1905A	.010	250.00	450.00	800.00
	1905A	—	—	Proof	675.00
	1911A	100 pcs.	4000.	6000.	8000.

5 MARK

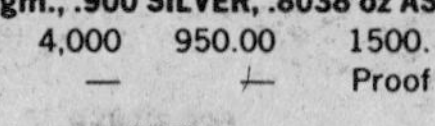

27.7770 gm., .900 SILVER, .8038 oz ASW

Y#	Date	Mintage	VF	XF	Unc
150	1895A	4,000	950.00	1500.	2500.
	1895A	—	—	Proof	3000.

Rev: Similar to Y#150.

Y#	Date	Mintage	VF	XF	Unc
153	1907A	.010	500.00	1000.	1800.
	1907A	—	—	Proof	2200.

10 MARK

3.9820 gm., .900 GOLD, .1152 oz AGW

Y#	Date	Mintage	VF	XF	Unc
154	1905A	.010	750.00	1600.	2000.
	1905A	—	—	Proof	2000.

20 MARK

7.9650 gm., .900 GOLD, .2304 oz AGW
Rev: Type 1 eagle.

Y#	Date	Mintage	VF	XF	Unc
148	1872E	1,000	8000.	10,000.	11,500.

Y#	Date	Mintage	VF	XF	Unc
148a	1886A	.020	650.00	1000.	1300.

Y#	Date	Mintage	VF	XF	Unc
151	1895A	.010	1200.	2000.	2800.

Y#	Date	Mintage	VF	XF	Unc
155	1905A	.010	800.00	1200.	1900.
	1905A	—	—	Proof	2200.

SAXE — GOTHA — ALTENBURG

Saxe-Gotha-Altenburg was founded in 1680 and became extinct in 1825 when Gotha went to Coburg and Altenburg went to the duke of Hildburghausen.

RULERS

Ernst Ludwig, 1772-1804

GULDEN

SILVER

C#	Date	Mintage	VG	Fine	VF	XF
37	1774	—	25.00	50.00	75.00	110.00

24 EINEN (1/24) THALER

BILLON
Obv: Crowned arms in sprays.
Rev: Value over date.

C#	Date	Mintage	VG	Fine	VF	XF
36	1773	—	4.00	10.00	15.00	25.00

1/2 THALER
(Convention)

SILVER
Obv: L.C.R. below bust.

C#	Date	Mintage	VG	Fine	VF	XF
38	1774	—	35.00	75.00	125.00	200.00
	1776	—	35.00	75.00	125.00	200.00

Obv: Stork below bust.

C#	Date	Mintage	VG	Fine	VF	XF
38a	1774	—	35.00	75.00	135.00	200.00
	1776	—	35.00	75.00	135.00	200.00

EIN (1) THALER
(Convention)

SILVER
Obv: Armored bust right; L C R below.
Rev: Crowned arms with lion supporters; date below.

C#	Date	Mintage	Fine	VF	XF	Unc
39	1774	—	200.00	400.00	800.00	1200.

NOTE: Called "Light Taler".

Obv: Head right with crane below.
Rev: Crowned arms in sprays; date divided above.

C#	Date	Mintage	Fine	VF	XF	Unc
40	1775	—	50.00	250.00	500.00	1000.
	1776	—	50.00	250.00	500.00	1000.

SAXE — HILDBURGHAUSEN

Saxe-Hildburghausen was founded in 1680. During the 1826 reshuffle, it was exchanged for Altenburg.

RULERS

Ernst Friedrich III Carl, 1745-1780
Joseph Friedrich, Prince Regent, 1780-1784
Joint Regent, 1784-87
Alone, 1786-1826

HELLER

COPPER
Obv: Crowned arms in sprays; date below.
Rev: Value.

C#	Date	Mintage	VG	Fine	VF	XF
55	1781	—	3.00	7.00	11.50	20.00
	1784	—	3.00	7.00	11.50	20.00

C#	Date	Mintage	VG	Fine	VF	XF
65	1787	—	3.00	7.00	11.50	20.00
	1788	—	3.00	7.00	11.50	20.00

C#	Date	Mintage	Fine	VF	XF	Unc
65a	1804	—	3.00	6.00	10.00	40.00
	1805	—	3.00	6.00	10.00	40.00
	1806	—	3.00	6.00	10.00	40.00

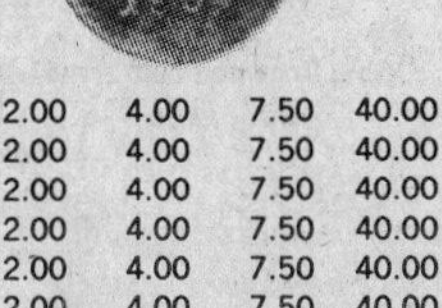

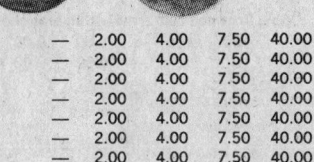

C#	Date	Mintage	Fine	VF	XF	Unc
66	1808	—	2.00	4.00	7.50	40.00
	1809	—	2.00	4.00	7.50	40.00
	1811	—	2.00	4.00	7.50	40.00
	1812	—	2.00	4.00	7.50	40.00
	1816	—	2.00	4.00	7.50	40.00
	1817	—	2.00	4.00	7.50	40.00
	1818	—	2.00	4.00	7.50	40.00

Obv: Crowned F within crossed branches. Rev: Value.

C#	Date	Mintage	Fine	VF	XF	Unc
67	1820	—	2.00	4.00	7.00	40.00
	1821	—	2.00	4.00	7.00	40.00
	1822	—	2.00	4.00	7.00	40.00
	1823	—	2.00	4.00	7.00	40.00
	1824	—	2.00	4.00	7.00	40.00
	1825	—	2.00	4.00	7.00	40.00

PFENNIG

COPPER

C#	Date	Mintage	Fine	VF	XF	Unc
69	1823	—	2.00	4.00	6.00	40.00
	1825	—	2.00	4.00	6.00	40.00
	1826	—	2.00	4.00	6.00	40.00

Obv: Crowned rectangular arms.

C#	Date	Mintage	Fine	VF	XF	Unc
69.5	1826	—	12.00	23.00	35.00	75.00

1/8 KREUZER

COPPER
Obv: Crowned F within crossed branches.
Rev: Value, leg: KREUZER LANDMUNZE.

C#	Date	Mintage	Fine	VF	XF	Unc
67a	1825	—	2.50	5.00	8.00	40.00

1/4 KREUZER

COPPER
Obv: Crowned F within crossed branches.
Rev. value: KREUZER LANDMUNZE.

C#	Date	Mintage	Fine	VF	XF	Unc
70	1825	—	2.50	5.00	10.00	40.00

Obv: Crowned heart shaped arms, H.S.H.H.

C#	Date	Mintage	Fine	VF	XF	Unc
71	1825	—	2.50	5.00	10.00	40.00

1/2 KREUZER

COPPER
Obv: Crowned arms. Rev: Value in script.

C#	Date	Mintage	Fine	VF	XF	Unc
72	1808	—	2.00	4.50	7.00	40.00
	1809	—	2.00	4.50	7.00	40.00

Obv: Crowned heart-shaped arms, leg: HERZ.S.

C#	Date	Mintage	Fine	VF	XF	Unc
73	1823	—	3.00	6.00	10.00	40.00

Obv. leg: HERZOGTHUM

C#	Date	Mintage	Fine	VF	XF	Unc
73b	1823	—	3.00	6.00	10.00	40.00

Rev: Value, leg: KREUZER LANDMUNZE.

C#	Date	Mintage	Fine	VF	XF	Unc
73a	1823	—	3.00	6.00	10.00	40.00

KREUZER
(Convention)

BILLON
Obv: Arms. Rev: Value over date.

C#	Date	Mintage	VG	Fine	VF	XF
12	1774	—	4.00	8.00	11.50	20.00
	1775	—	4.00	8.00	11.50	20.00
	1776	—	4.00	8.00	11.50	20.00
	1777	—	4.00	8.00	11.50	20.00
	1778	—	4.00	8.00	11.50	20.00

Obv: Crowned I F monogram separates H H.

C#	Date	Mintage	VG	Fine	VF	XF
56	1781	—	5.00	10.00	15.00	25.00

Obv: Saxon arms separate H H.

C#	Date	Mintage	VG	Fine	VF	XF
74	1784-99	—	3.00	6.00	9.50	20.00

C#	Date	Mintage	Fine	VF	XF	Unc
74a	1804	—	4.50	9.00	14.00	50.00
	1805	—	4.50	9.25	14.00	50.00

Obv: Crowned oval arms within branches. Rev: Value.

C#	Date	Mintage	Fine	VF	XF	Unc
76	1806	—	4.50	9.00	14.00	50.00
	1811	—	4.50	9.00	14.00	50.00

2-1/2 KREUZER
(Convention)

BILLON
Obv: Crowned I F monogram.
Rev: Value and date.

C#	Date	Mintage	VG	Fine	VF	XF
58	1781	—	10.00	15.00	22.50	30.00

3 KREUZER

BILLON
Obv: Crowned F within wreath.
Rev: Value within ring.

C#	Date	Mintage	Fine	VF	XF	Unc
83	1808	—	7.00	15.00	25.00	50.00
	1810	—	7.00	15.00	25.00	50.00
	1811	—	7.00	15.00	25.00	50.00
	1812	—	7.00	15.00	25.00	50.00
	1815	—	7.00	15.00	25.00	50.00
	1816	—	7.00	15.00	25.00	50.00
	1817	—	7.00	15.00	25.00	50.00
	1818	—	7.00	15.00	25.00	50.00
	1820	—	7.00	15.00	25.00	50.00

6 KREUZER

BILLON
Obv: Crowned F within wreath. Rev: Value within ring.

C#	Date	Mintage	Fine	VF	XF	Unc
86	1808	—	9.00	18.50	28.00	50.00
	1811	—	9.00	18.50	28.00	50.00
	1812	—	9.00	18.50	28.00	50.00
	1815	—	9.00	18.50	28.00	50.00
	1816	—	9.00	18.50	28.00	50.00
	1817	—	9.00	18.50	28.00	50.00
	1818	—	9.00	18.50	28.00	50.00

Obv: Crowned F within crossed branches. Rev: Value.

C#	Date	Mintage	Fine	VF	XF	Unc
88	1820	—	8.00	17.00	25.00	50.00
	1821	—	8.00	17.00	25.00	50.00
	1823	—	8.00	17.00	25.00	50.00
	1824	—	8.00	17.00	25.00	50.00
	1825	—	8.00	17.00	25.00	50.00

20 KREUZER

BILLON
Obv: Bust right.
Rev: Arms over date.

C#	Date	Mintage	VG	Fine	VF	XF
60	1781	—	12.00	25.00	35.00	50.00

Obv: Head right.

C#	Date	Mintage	VG	Fine	VF	XF
93	1796	—	20.00	50.00	75.00	100.00

GROSCHEN

BILLON
Obv: Arms. Rev: Value over date.

C#	Date	Mintage	VG	Fine	VF	XF
81	1788	—	5.00	10.00	12.50	20.00

Obv: Crowned F.

C#	Date	Mintage	VG	Fine	VF	XF
82	1790	—	5.00	10.00	13.50	20.00

48 EINEN (1/48) THALER

BILLON
Obv: Crowned arms.
Rev: Value and date.

C#	Date	Mintage	VG	Fine	VF	XF
79	1788	—	3.00	7.50	11.50	20.00

(Reichs)

Obv: Saxon arms.
Rev: Value over date.

C#	Date	Mintage	VG	Fine	VF	XF
78	1788	—	3.00	7.50	11.50	20.00

EIN (1) THALER
(Convention)

SILVER

C#	Date	Mintage	VG	Fine	VF	XF
62	1781	—	100.00	275.00	450.00	650.00

C#	Date	Mintage	VG	Fine	VF	XF
63	ND	—	100.00	225.00	300.00	450.00

SAXE — MEININGEN

Saxe-Meiningen was founded in 1680. It was called Saxe-Coburg—Meiningen until 1826 when it exchanged Coburg for Hildburghausen.

RULERS

Carl, under Regency, 1763-1775
Alone, 1775-1782
Bernhard II Under Regency of Luise Eleonore, 1803-1821
Alone, 1821-1866
Georg II, 1866-1914
Bernhard III, 1914-1918

MINTMASTER'S INITIALS

K - Georg Krell
L - Georg Christoph Loewel

HELLER

COPPER
Obv: Crowned heart-shaped arms, leg: H. Rev: Value.

C#	Date	Mintage	Fine	VF	XF	Unc
21	1814	—	2.50	5.25	8.00	40.00

Obv. leg: HERZ.

C#	Date	Mintage	Fine	VF	XF	Unc
21a	1814	—	2.25	4.75	7.00	40.00

PFENNIG

COPPER
Obv: Crowned heart shaped arms, leg: HERZ.
Rev: Value.

C#	Date	Mintage	VG	Fine	VF	XF
23	1818	.090	3.50	7.00	15.00	40.00

C#	Date	Mintage	VG	Fine	VF	XF
34	1832	.275	1.50	3.00	6.00	35.00
	1833	.093	1.50	3.00	6.00	40.00
	1835	.034	1.50	3.00	6.00	40.00

Obv: Crowned arms within branches.

C#	Date	Mintage	VG	Fine	VF	XF
35	1839	.079	1.50	3.00	6.00	35.00
	1842	.132	1.50	3.00	6.00	35.00

C#	Date	Mintage	Fine	VF	XF	Unc
37	1860	.240	1.50	2.50	5.00	35.00
	1862	.243	1.50	2.50	5.00	35.00
	1863	.240	1.50	2.50	5.00	35.00
	1865	.240	1.00	2.50	5.00	35.00
	1866	.480	1.00	2.50	5.00	35.00

C#	Date	Mintage	Fine	VF	XF	Unc
65	1867	.240	1.00	2.50	5.00	35.00
	1868	.480	1.00	2.50	5.00	35.00

2 PFENNIG

COPPER

C#	Date	Mintage	Fine	VF	XF	Unc
39	1832	.202	2.00	4.00	7.00	35.00
	1833	.101	2.00	4.00	7.00	35.00
	1835	.036	2.00	4.00	7.00	35.00

C#	Date	Mintage	Fine	VF	XF	Unc
40	1839	.075	1.50	3.00	6.00	35.00
	1842	.184	1.50	3.00	6.00	35.00

C#	Date	Mintage	Fine	VF	XF	Unc
42	1860	.361	1.50	3.00	6.00	30.00
	1862	.357	1.50	3.00	6.00	30.00
	1863	.120	1.50	3.00	6.00	30.00
	1864	.480	1.50	3.00	6.00	30.00
	1865	.240	1.50	3.00	6.00	30.00
	1866	.480	1.00	3.00	6.00	30.00

C#	Date	Mintage	Fine	VF	XF	Unc
66	1867	.480	1.00	3.00	6.00	30.00
	1868	.240	1.00	3.00	6.00	30.00
	1869	.240	1.00	3.00	6.00	30.00
	1870	.720	1.00	3.00	6.00	30.00

1/8 KREUZER

COPPER

C#	Date	Mintage	Fine	VF	XF	Unc
30	1828	—	2.00	4.00	7.00	40.00

1/4 KREUZER

COPPER
Obv: Crowned heart shaped arms, leg: HERZ.
Rev: Value.

C#	Date	Mintage	Fine	VF	XF	Unc
22	1812	—	2.00	4.00	8.00	40.00
	1814	—	2.00	4.00	8.00	40.00
	1818	.066	2.00	4.00	8.00	40.00

Rev: Value, leg: LANDMUNZE.

C#	Date	Mintage	Fine	VF	XF	Unc
31	1823	—	2.00	4.00	8.00	40.00

C#	Date	Mintage	Fine	VF	XF	Unc
33	1828	—	1.50	3.00	7.00	40.00
	1829	.168	1.50	3.00	7.00	35.00
	1830	.161	1.50	3.00	7.00	35.00
	1831	.321	1.50	3.00	7.00	35.00
	1832	.063	1.50	3.00	7.00	35.00

Obv. leg: MEINIGEN

C#	Date	Mintage	Fine	VF	XF	Unc
33a	1829	Inc. Ab.	1.50	3.00	7.00	35.00

Rev: Value: KREUZER.

C#	Date	Mintage	Fine	VF	XF	Unc
36	1854	.240	1.50	3.00	7.00	35.00

1/2 KREUZER

COPPER

C#	Date	Mintage	Fine	VF	XF	Unc
24	1812	—	2.00	4.00	7.00	35.00
	1814	—	2.00	4.00	7.00	35.00
	1818	.102	2.00	4.00	7.00	35.00

C#	Date	Mintage	Fine	VF	XF	Unc
38	1828	—	2.00	4.00	7.00	35.00
	1829	.121	2.00	4.00	7.00	35.00
	1830L	.144	2.00	4.00	7.00	35.00
	1831L	.341	2.00	4.00	7.00	35.00
	1832L	.045	2.00	4.00	7.00	40.00

Obv: Rosette below arms. Rev. value: KREUZER.

C#	Date	Mintage	Fine	VF	XF	Unc
41	1854	.240	2.00	4.00	7.00	35.00

KREUZER
(Convention)

BILLON
Obv: Arms separates SC M.
Rev: Value over date.

C#	Date	Mintage	VG	Fine	VF	XF
15	1781	—	8.00	16.00	22.00	30.00

Obv: Crowned arms in sprays.
Rev: Value over date.

C#	Date	Mintage	VG	Fine	VF	XF
17	1786-1794	—	4.00	8.00	12.50	20.00
18	1794	—	5.00	10.00	13.00	20.00

Obv: Crowned draped arms, H.S.C.M. Rev: Value.

C#	Date	Mintage	Fine	VF	XF	Unc
26	1808	—	4.00	8.00	15.00	50.00

Obv: Drape extends beneath crown.

C#	Date	Mintage	Fine	VF	XF	Unc
26a	1812	—	4.00	8.00	12.00	50.00

COPPER

C#	Date	Mintage	Fine	VF	XF	Unc
25	1814	—	2.50	5.00	8.00	40.00
	1818	.090	2.50	5.00	8.00	40.00

Obv: Crowned rectangular arms, leg: HERZ.

C#	Date	Mintage	Fine	VF	XF	Unc
43	1828	—	2.00	4.00	8.00	35.00
	1829	.144	2.00	4.00	8.00	35.00
	1830	.118	2.00	4.00	8.00	35.00

BILLON
Obv: Crowned arms dividing S.M.

C#	Date	Mintage	Fine	VF	XF	Unc
47	1828	.211	2.00	4.00	8.00	40.00
	1829	—	2.00	4.00	8.00	40.00
	1829 L	.255	2.00	4.00	8.00	40.00
	1830 L	.092	2.00	4.00	8.00	40.00

COPPER

C#	Date	Mintage	Fine	VF	XF	Unc
43a	1831	.166	2.00	4.00	7.00	35.00
	1832	.032	2.00	4.00	7.00	35.00
	1833	.104	2.00	4.00	7.00	35.00
	1834	.177	2.00	4.00	7.00	35.00
	1835	.035	2.00	4.00	7.00	35.00

BILLON
Obv: Crowned arms within bound branches, L initial.

C#	Date	Mintage	Fine	VF	XF	Unc
48	1831 L	.212	2.00	4.00	7.00	50.00
	1832 L	.348	2.00	4.00	7.00	50.00
	1833 L	.272	2.00	4.00	7.00	50.00
	1834 L	.162	2.00	4.00	7.00	50.00

Obv: K mintmaster initial.

C#	Date	Mintage	Fine	VF	XF	Unc
48a	1835 K	.059	2.00	4.00	7.00	50.00
	1836 K	.055	2.00	4.00	7.00	50.00
	1837 K	.049	2.00	4.00	7.00	50.00

C#	Date	Mintage	Fine	VF	XF	Unc
49	1839	.348	2.00	4.00	7.00	45.00

COPPER
Obv: Crowned arms within branches. Rev: Value.

C#	Date	Mintage	Fine	VF	XF	Unc
44	1842	.180	1.50	3.00	6.00	35.00

Obv: Rosette below crowned arms.

C#	Date	Mintage	Fine	VF	XF	Unc
45	1854	.202	1.50	3.00	6.00	35.00

BILLON
Obv: Crowned arms, leg: HERZ.
Rev: Value within branches.

C#	Date	Mintage	Fine	VF	XF	Unc
50	1864	.240	1.00	3.00	7.00	40.00
	1866	.240	1.00	3.00	7.00	40.00

3 KREUZER

BILLON
Obv: Crowned draped arms. Rev: Value within wreath.

C#	Date	Mintage	Fine	VF	XF	Unc
27	1808	—	8.00	16.00	24.00	50.00

Obv: Drape extends beneath crown

C#	Date	Mintage	Fine	VF	XF	Unc
27a	1812	—	6.00	12.00	18.00	50.00
	1813	—	6.00	12.00	18.00	50.00

Obv: Crowned arms dividing S.M. Rev: Value.

C#	Date	Mintage	Fine	VF	XF	Unc
51	1827	.171	2.50	5.00	9.00	45.00
	1828	.077	2.50	5.00	9.00	45.00
	1829	—	2.50	5.00	9.00	45.00

Obv: L mintmaster initial

C#	Date	Mintage	Fine	VF	XF	Unc
51a	1829 L	1.263	2.50	5.00	9.00	45.00
	1830 L	.533	2.50	5.00	9.00	45.00

C#	Date	Mintage	Fine	VF	XF	Unc
52	1831 L	.540	2.50	5.00	9.00	45.00
	1832 L	.918	2.50	5.00	9.00	45.00
	1833 L	1.284	2.50	5.00	9.00	45.00

C#	Date	Mintage	Fine	VF	XF	Unc
52	1834 L	.187	2.50	5.00	9.00	45.00
	1835 L	—	—	—	—	—
52a	1835 K	.800	2.50	5.00	9.00	45.00
	1836 K	.399	2.50	5.00	9.00	45.00
	1837 K	.246	2.50	5.00	9.00	45.00

Obv: Crowned arms, leg: HERZOGTHUM.
Rev: Value within branches.

C#	Date	Mintage	Fine	VF	XF	Unc
53	1840	.207	2.50	5.00	9.00	45.00

6 KREUZER

BILLON
Obv: Crowned, draped arms, leg: S.COB.
Rev: Value within wreath.

C#	Date	Mintage	Fine	VF	XF	Unc
28	1808	—	9.00	19.00	30.00	50.00
	1812	—	9.00	19.00	30.00	50.00
	1813	—	9.00	19.00	30.00	50.00

Obv: Drape extends beneath crown

C#	Date	Mintage	Fine	VF	XF	Unc
28a	1812	—	7.00	15.00	30.00	50.00
	1813	—	7.00	15.00	30.00	50.00
54	1826	—	2.50	5.00	10.00	50.00
	1827	.486	2.50	5.00	10.00	50.00
	1828	.179	2.50	5.00	10.00	50.00
	1829	—	2.50	5.00	10.00	50.00

Obv: With L mintmaster initial.

C#	Date	Mintage	Fine	VF	XF	Unc
54a	1828 L	—	—	—	—	—
	1829 L	1.513	2.00	5.00	10.00	50.00
	1830 L	.747	2.50	5.00	10.00	50.00

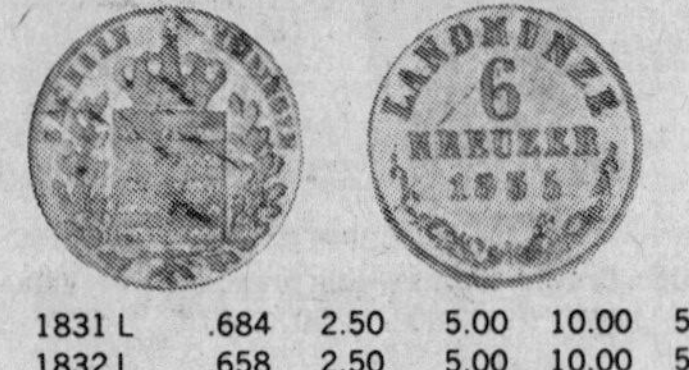

C#	Date	Mintage	Fine	VF	XF	Unc
55	1831 L	.684	2.50	5.00	10.00	50.00
	1832 L	.658	2.50	5.00	10.00	50.00
	1833 L	.723	2.50	5.00	10.00	50.00
	1834 L	.409	2.50	5.00	10.00	50.00
	1835 L	.512	2.50	5.00	10.00	50.00

Obv: With K mintmaster initial

C#	Date	Mintage	Fine	VF	XF	Unc
55a	1836 K	.432	2.50	5.00	10.00	50.00
	1837 K	.253	2.50	5.00	10.00	50.00

Obv: Crowned arms, leg: HERZOGTHUM.
Rev: Value within branches.

C#	Date	Mintage	Fine	VF	XF	Unc
56	1840	.097	2.50	5.00	10.00	50.00

20 KREUZER

.583 SILVER
Obv: Bust right.
Rev: Value within square entwined with flowers.

C#	Date	Mintage	Fine	VF	XF	Unc
29	1812	—	—	—	Unique	—

1/2 GULDEN

.900 SILVER

C#	Date	Mintage	Fine	VF	XF	Unc
57	1838	.071	10.00	20.00	35.00	60.00
	1839	.045	10.00	20.00	35.00	60.00
	1840	.032	10.00	20.00	35.00	60.00
	1841	.057	10.00	20.00	35.00	60.00

Obv: Different head with HELFRICHT below.

C#	Date	Mintage	Fine	VF	XF	Unc
57a	1843	.133	10.00	20.00	30.00	60.00
	1846	.106	10.00	20.00	30.00	60.00

Obv: Bearded head

C#	Date	Mintage	Fine	VF	XF	Unc
57b	1854	.108	10.00	20.00	30.00	60.00

GULDEN

.900 SILVER

C#	Date	Mintage	Fine	VF	XF	Unc
58	1829	2,000	75.00	150.00	200.00	400.00

C#	Date	Mintage	Fine	VF	XF	Unc
59	1830 L	9,118	35.00	75.00	120.00	250.00
	1831 L	5,511	50.00	100.00	150.00	300.00
	1832 L	4,688	50.00	100.00	150.00	300.00
	1833 L	.010	35.00	75.00	120.00	250.00

C#	Date	Mintage	Fine	VF	XF	Unc
59a	1835 K	2,015	75.00	150.00	200.00	400.00
	1836 K	2,028	75.00	150.00	200.00	400.00
	1837 K	2,148	75.00	150.00	200.00	400.00

C#	Date	Mintage	Fine	VF	XF	Unc
60	1838	.071	20.00	40.00	90.00	180.00
	1839	.071	20.00	40.00	90.00	180.00
	1840	.032	20.00	40.00	90.00	180.00
	1841	.031	20.00	40.00	90.00	180.00

Obv: HELFRICHT below head

C#	Date	Mintage	Fine	VF	XF	Unc
60a	1843	.133	20.00	40.00	85.00	150.00
	1846	.149	20.00	40.00	85.00	150.00

Obv: Bearded head

C#	Date	Mintage	Fine	VF	XF	Unc
60b	1854	.108	20.00	40.00	85.00	150.00

2 GULDEN

21.2100 gm., .900 SILVER, .6138 oz ASW

C#	Date	Mintage	Fine	VF	XF	Unc
62	1854	.167	45.00	100.00	200.00	400.00

EIN (1) THALER

(Convention)

28.0600 gm., .833 SILVER, .7521 oz ASW

C#	Date	Mintage	VG	Fine	VF	XF
19	ND	—	80.00	175.00	300.00	525.00

18.5000 gm., .900 SILVER, .5360 oz ASW

C#	Date	Mintage	Fine	VF	XF	Unc
61	1859	.040	35.00	75.00	150.00	300.00
	1860	.040	35.00	75.00	150.00	300.00
	1861	.040	35.00	75.00	150.00	300.00
	1862	.040	35.00	75.00	150.00	300.00
	1863	.040	35.00	75.00	150.00	300.00
	1864	.040	35.00	75.00	150.00	300.00
	1865	.040	35.00	75.00	150.00	300.00
	1866	.040	35.00	75.00	150.00	300.00

C#	Date	Mintage	Fine	VF	XF	Unc
67	1867	6,644	75.00	200.00	400.00	800.00

2 THALER

(= 3-1/2 Gulden)

37.1200 gm., .900 SILVER, 1.0743 oz ASW

C#	Date	Mintage	Fine	VF	XF	Unc
63	1841	.012	350.00	700.00	1400.	2800.

Obv: Similar to C#63.

C#	Date	Mintage	Fine	VF	XF	Unc
64	1843	.011	250.00	500.00	1000.	2000.
	1846	.015	250.00	500.00	1000.	2000.

Rev: Similar to C#64.

C#	Date	Mintage	Fine	VF	XF	Unc
64a	1853	.014	250.00	500.00	1000.	2000.
	1854	.014	250.00	500.00	1000.	2000.

TRADE COINS

DUCAT

3.5000 gm., .986 GOLD, .1109 oz AGW

C#	Date	Mintage	VG	Fine	VF	XF
16	1780	—	700.00	1250.	1650.	2250.

2 DUCATS

7.0000 gm., .986 GOLD, .2219 oz AGW
Obv: 2 shields. Rev: Inscription.

C#	Date	Mintage	VG	Fine	VF	XF
16.5	1780	—	800.00	1500.	2000.	2950.

MONETARY REFORM

2 MARK

11.1110 gm., .900 SILVER, .3215 oz ASW

Y#	Date	Mintage	VF	XF	Unc
159	1901D	.020	200.00	350.00	550.00

Y#	Date	Mintage	VF	XF	Unc
161	1902D with long beard				
		.020	600.00	1000.	1500.
	1902D with short beard				
		.020	200.00	300.00	550.00
	1913D	5,000	250.00	500.00	750.00

Death of Georg II

Y#	Date	Mintage	VF	XF	Unc
166	1915D	.030	100.00	150.00	200.00

3 MARK

16.6670 gm., .900 SILVER, .4823 oz ASW

Y#	Date	Mintage	VF	XF	Unc
162	1908D	.035	75.00	125.00	200.00
	1913D	.030	75.00	125.00	225.00

Death of Georg II

Y#	Date	Mintage	VF	XF	Unc
167	1915D	.030	75.00	150.00	200.00

5 MARK

27.7770 gm., .900 SILVER, .8038 oz ASW

Y#	Date	Mintage	VF	XF	Unc
160	1901D	.020	200.00	350.00	600.00

Rev: Similar to Y#160.

Y#	Date	Mintage	VF	XF	Unc
163	1902D long beard				
		.020	200.00	350.00	700.00
	1902D short beard				
		.020	100.00	200.00	350.00
	1908D	.060	100.00	200.00	300.00

10 MARK

3.9820 gm., .900 GOLD, .1152 oz AGW

C#	Date	Mintage	Fine	VF	XF	Unc
157	1890D	2,000	2000.	3000.	5000.	7200.
	1898D	2,000	2000.	3000.	5000.	7200.

C#	Date	Mintage	Fine	VF	XF	Unc
164	1902D	2,000	1000.	1800.	2500.	4000.
	1909D	2,000	1500.	2000.	3000.	4500.

C#	Date	Mintage	Fine	VF	XF	Unc
	1914D	1,002	1500.	2000.	3000.	4500.

20 MARK

7.9650 gm., .900 GOLD, .2304 oz AGW
Rev: Type 1 eagle.

C#	Date	Mintage	Fine	VF	XF	Unc
156	1872D	3,000	4000.	7500.	9000.	10,000.
	1872D	—	—	—	Proof	11,500.

Rev: Type 2 eagle.

C#	Date	Mintage	Fine	VF	XF	Unc
156a	1882D	3,061	3000.	4000.	8000.	9000.
158	1889D	4,032	3000.	5000.	7300.	8000.

Rev: Type 3 eagle.

C#	Date	Mintage	Fine	VF	XF	Unc
158a	1900D	1,005	3000.	8000.	9000.	11,000.
	1905D	1,000	3000.	8000.	9000.	11,000.

C#	Date	Mintage	Fine	VF	XF	Unc
165	1910D	1,004	3000.	5000.	6000.	7500.
	1914D	1,001	3000.	5000.	6000.	7500.
	Common type	—	—	Proof		6500.

NCLT ISSUES

PATTERNS

KM#	Date	Mintage	Identification	Mkt.Val.
1	1900	—	5 Marks, Silver	—

SAXE — WEIMAR — EISENACH

Saxe-Weimar-Eisenach was founded in 1644. It was raised to the status of a grand duchy in 1814. The last grand duke abdicated in 1918.

RULERS

Anna Amalia of Brunswich, 1758-1775
Regent for Carl August
Carl August, 1775-1828
Carl Friedrich, 1828-1853
Carl Alexander, 1853-1901
Wilhelm Ernst, 1901-1918

MINTMASTER'S INITIALS

F.S. - Friedrich Shafer, 1749-1776
J.L.S.T., L.S., ST - Johann Leonhard Stockmar
KL - Klinghammer, 1760-1765

HELLER

COPPER
Obv: Crowned Saxon arms.
Rev: Value and date.

C#	Date	Mintage	VG	Fine	VF	XF
31	1760	—	3.00	5.00	7.50	15.00

Obv: Similar to C#55b but L. ST. below arms.
Rev: Similar to C#55b.

C#	Date	Mintage	Fine	VF	XF	Unc
55	1790	—	3.00	6.00	12.00	40.00

Obv: Similar to C#55b but lion below arms.

C#	Date	Mintage	Fine	VF	XF	Unc
55a	1791	—	3.00	6.00	12.00	40.00

C#	Date	Mintage	Fine	VF	XF	Unc
55b	1794	—	3.00	6.00	12.00	40.00

C#	Date	Mintage	Fine	VF	XF	Unc
55c	1801	—	3.00	6.00	12.00	40.00
	1813	—	3.00	6.00	12.00	40.00

PFENNIG

COPPER
Obv: Crowned Saxon arms.
Rev: Value and date.

C#	Date	Mintage	VG	Fine	VF	XF
32	1761	—	3.00	5.00	7.50	15.00
	1762	—	3.00	5.00	7.50	15.00

C#	Date	Mintage	Fine	VF	XF	Unc
56	1790	—	3.00	5.00	10.00	40.00

Obv: Similar to C#56 but lion below arms.

C#	Date	Mintage	Fine	VF	XF	Unc
56a	1792	—	3.00	5.00	10.00	40.00

Obv: Similar to C#56 but no symbol below arms.

C#	Date	Mintage	Fine	VF	XF	Unc
56b	1796	—	3.00	5.00	10.00	40.00

Rev: Value and date; line below date.

C#	Date	Mintage	Fine	VF	XF	Unc
56c	1799	—	3.00	5.00	10.00	40.00
	1801	—	3.00	5.00	10.00	40.00
	1803	—	3.00	5.00	10.00	40.00
	1807	.030	3.00	5.00	10.00	40.00

Rev: Value and date; 1's in date reversed; line below date.

C#	Date	Mintage	Fine	VF	XF	Unc
56d	1810	.080	2.50	5.00	10.00	40.00
	1813	—	2.50	5.00	10.00	40.00

Rev: Value and date; line below date.

C#	Date	Mintage	Fine	VF	XF	Unc
61	1821	—	2.00	4.00	8.00	35.00
	1824	—	2.00	4.00	8.00	35.00
	1826	—	2.00	4.00	8.00	35.00
77	1830	—	2.00	4.00	8.00	35.00

C#	Date	Mintage	Fine	VF	XF	Unc
81	1840A	.760	2.00	4.00	8.00	35.00
	1841A	.760	2.00	4.00	8.00	35.00
	1844A	.361	2.00	4.00	8.00	35.00
81	1851A	.360	2.00	4.00	8.00	35.00

Denticled Border

C#	Date	Mintage	Fine	VF	XF	Unc
89	1858A	.720	1.00	3.00	6.00	35.00
	1865A	.720	1.00	3.00	6.00	35.00

1-1/2 PFENNIG

COPPER
Obv: S.W.U.E. above arms

C#	Date	Mintage	Fine	VF	XF	Unc
57	1799	—	3.00	6.00	12.00	40.00
	1807	.034	3.00	6.00	12.00	40.00

Obv: S.W.E. above arms

C#	Date	Mintage	Fine	VF	XF	Unc
62	1824	—	1.50	3.00	7.00	35.00
78	1830	—	1.50	3.00	7.00	35.00

2 PFENNIG

COPPER
Obv: Crowned Saxon arms.
Rev: Value and date.

C#	Date	Mintage	VG	Fine	VF	XF
33	1760	—	3.00	5.00	7.50	15.00

Obv: Similar to C#58c but with L.S.T. below.
Rev: Similar to C#58c but with rosette below date.

C#	Date	Mintage	Fine	VF	XF	Unc
58	1790	—	3.00	6.00	12.00	40.00

Obv: Similar to C#58c but with no symbol below.

C#	Date	Mintage	Fine	VF	XF	Unc
58a	1792	—	3.00	6.00	12.00	40.00
	1796	—	3.00	6.00	12.00	40.00

Obv: Similar to C#58c but small U in S.W.U.E. and no symbol below, leaf edge.

C#	Date	Mintage	Fine	VF	XF	Unc
58b	1799	—	3.00	6.00	12.00	40.00

C#	Date	Mintage	Fine	VF	XF	Unc
58c	1803	—	3.00	6.00	12.00	40.00
	1807	—	3.00	6.00	12.00	40.00

Milled Edge

C#	Date	Mintage	Fine	VF	XF	Unc
58d	1803	—	3.00	6.00	12.00	40.00
	1807	—	3.00	6.00	12.00	40.00

Rev: Similar to C#58c but with rosette below date.

C#	Date	Mintage	Fine	VF	XF	Unc
58e	1813	—	3.00	6.00	12.00	40.00

Obv: Saxon arms; S.W.E. above.
Rev: Value over date; rosette below date.

C#	Date	Mintage	Fine	VF	XF	Unc
63	1821	—	2.00	5.00	10.00	35.00
	1826	—	2.00	5.00	10.00	35.00

Rev: Line below date.

C#	Date	Mintage	Fine	VF	XF	Unc
79	1830	—	1.50	5.00	10.00	35.00

Obv: Crowned Saxon arms in circular legend.
Rev: Value over date, "SCHEIDE MUNZE" above.
Denticled Border

C#	Date	Mintage	Fine	VF	XF	Unc
90	1858A	—	1.00	5.00	10.00	35.00
	1865A	—	1.00	5.00	10.00	35.00

3 PFENNIG

COPPER
Obv: Crowned Saxon arms.
Rev: Value and date.

C#	Date	Mintage	VG	Fine	VF	XF
34	1760 FS	—	3.50	7.50	12.50	20.00
	1761 FS	—	3.50	7.50	12.50	20.00
	1762 FS	—	3.50	7.50	12.50	20.00

BILLON
Rev: Value in orb.

C#	Date	Mintage	VG	Fine	VF	XF
35	1760 FS	—	3.50	7.50	12.50	20.00

Obv: 2 shields of arms.
Rev: Value in orb divides date.

C#	Date	Mintage	VG	Fine	VF	XF
36	1763 FS	—	2.50	5.00	7.50	15.00
	1764 FS	—	2.50	5.00	7.50	15.00

COPPER
Obv: Saxon arms; L.S.T. below; S.W.U.E. above.
Rev: Value over date; rosette below; no final E in value.

C#	Date	Mintage	Fine	VF	XF	Unc
59	1791	—	3.00	6.00	12.00	40.00

Obv: Lion below arms.

C#	Date	Mintage	Fine	VF	XF	Unc
59a	1792	—	3.00	6.00	12.00	40.00

Obv: No symbol below arms.

C#	Date	Mintage	Fine	VF	XF	Unc
59b	1794	—	3.00	6.00	12.00	40.00

Rev: Line under date; E added to value.
Leaf Edge

C#	Date	Mintage	Fine	VF	XF	Unc
59c	1799	—	3.00	6.00	12.00	40.00
	1807	—	3.00	6.00	12.00	40.00

Reeded Edge

C#	Date	Mintage	Fine	VF	XF	Unc
59d	1807	—	3.00	6.00	12.00	40.00

Rev: Rosette under date.

C#	Date	Mintage	Fine	VF	XF	Unc
59e	1804	—	3.00	6.00	12.00	40.00

Obv: S.W.E. above Saxon arms.
Rev: Line below date.
Leaf Edge

C#	Date	Mintage	Fine	VF	XF	Unc
64	1824	—	1.50	5.00	10.00	35.00

Reeded Edge

C#	Date	Mintage	Fine	VF	XF	Unc
64	1824	—	1.50	5.00	10.00	35.00

Arched Date

C#	Date	Mintage	Fine	VF	XF	Unc
80	1830	—	1.50	5.00	10.00	35.00

Straight Date

C#	Date	Mintage	Fine	VF	XF	Unc
—	1830	—	1.50	5.00	10.00	35.00

Obv: Crowned Saxon arms in circular legend.
Rev: Value over date; SCHEIDE MUNZE above.

C#	Date	Mintage	Fine	VF	XF	Unc
82	1840A	—	1.50	5.00	10.00	35.00

4 PFENNIG

COPPER
Obv: Saxon arms; S.W.u.E. above.
Rev: Value over date; no line under date.

C#	Date	Mintage	Fine	VF	XF	Unc
60	1810	.146	3.50	7.25	15.00	40.00

Rev: Line under date.

C#	Date	Mintage	Fine	VF	XF	Unc
60a	1810	Inc. Ab.	3.50	7.25	15.00	40.00
	1812	—	3.50	7.25	15.00	40.00

Rev: Rosette under date.

C#	Date	Mintage	Fine	VF	XF	Unc
60b	1813	—	3.50	7.25	15.00	40.00

Obv: S.W.E. above Saxon arms.
Reeded Edge

C#	Date	Mintage	Fine	VF	XF	Unc
65	1821	.092	3.00	6.00	10.00	40.00
	1826	—	3.00	6.00	10.00	40.00

Leaf Edge

C#	Date	Mintage	Fine	VF	XF	Unc
65a	1821	Inc. Ab.	3.00	6.00	12.00	40.00

6 PFENNIG

BILLON
Obv: ADS monogram.
Rev: Value in orb divides date.

C#	Date	Mintage	VG	Fine	VF	XF
37	1759 FS	—	6.00	12.50	20.00	35.00
	1760 FS	—	6.00	12.50	20.00	35.00

Obv: Crowned Saxon arms.

C#	Date	Mintage	VG	Fine	VF	XF
38	1760 FS	—	6.00	12.50	20.00	35.00

Obv: 2 shields of arms.

C#	Date	Mintage	VG	Fine	VF	XF
39	1763 FS	—	6.00	12.50	20.00	35.00
	1764 FS	—	6.00	12.50	20.00	35.00

1/2 GROSCHEN

BILLON
Obv: Crowned arms. Rev: Value.

C#	Date	Mintage	Fine	VF	XF	Unc
85	1840A	2.400	2.00	6.00	12.00	40.00
91	1858A	.300	2.00	6.00	12.00	40.00

GROSCHEN

BILLON
Obv: Crowned arms. Rev: Value.

C#	Date	Mintage	Fine	VF	XF	Unc
86	1840A	2.408	2.00	6.00	12.00	40.00
92	1858A	.300	2.00	6.00	12.00	40.00

1/48 THALER

BILLON

C#	Date	Mintage	Fine	VF	XF	Unc
67	1794	—	5.00	10.00	20.00	45.00
	1796	—	5.00	10.00	20.00	45.00
	1799	—	5.00	10.00	20.00	45.00
	1801	—	5.00	10.00	20.00	45.00
	1804	—	5.00	10.00	20.00	45.00
	1808	.286	5.00	10.00	20.00	45.00
	1810	.327	5.00	10.00	20.00	45.00
	1813	—	5.00	10.00	20.00	45.00
	1814	—	5.00	10.00	20.00	45.00

Obv: G.H.S.W.E. above arms

C#	Date	Mintage	Fine	VF	XF	Unc
68	1815		5.00	10.00	20.00	45.00

Obv: S.W.E. above arms

C#	Date	Mintage	Fine	VF	XF	Unc
69	1821	.243	3.00	6.00	12.00	40.00
	1824	—	3.00	6.00	12.00	40.00
	1826	—	3.00	6.00	12.00	40.00

Obv: Saxon arms with S.W.E. above.

C#	Date	Mintage	Fine	VF	XF	Unc
83	1831	—	3.00	6.00	12.00	40.00

Rev: Reversed 1's in date.

C#	Date	Mintage	Fine	VF	XF	Unc
83a	1831	—	3.00	6.00	12.00	40.00

1/24 THALER

BILLON
Obv: Script A and Saxon arms.
Rev: Value and date.

C#	Date	Mintage	VG	Fine	VF	XF
40	1763 FS	—	5.00	10.00	25.00	45.00
	1764 FS	—	5.00	10.00	25.00	45.00

Obv: S.W.U.E. above arms. Rev: Value.

C#	Date	Mintage	Fine	VF	XF	Unc
70	1794	—	5.00	10.00	20.00	45.00
	1796	—	5.00	10.00	20.00	45.00
	1799	—	5.00	10.00	20.00	45.00
	1801	—	5.00	10.00	20.00	45.00
	1804	—	5.00	10.00	20.00	45.00
	1808	.199	5.00	10.00	20.00	45.00
	1810	.452	5.00	10.00	20.00	45.00
	1813	—	5.00	10.00	20.00	45.00
	1814	—	5.00	10.00	20.00	45.00

Obv: G.H.S.W.E. above arms

C#	Date	Mintage	Fine	VF	XF	Unc
71	1815	—	7.00	14.00	25.00	50.00

Obv: S.W.E. above arms

C#	Date	Mintage	Fine	VF	XF	Unc
72	1821	.493	3.00	6.00	12.00	40.00
	1824	—	3.00	6.00	12.00	40.00
	1826	—	3.00	6.00	12.00	40.00

Rev. value: ENIEN

C#	Date	Mintage	Fine	VF	XF	Unc
72a	1821	Inc. Ab.	—	—	—	—

Rev. value: EINEN

C#	Date	Mintage	Fine	VF	XF	Unc
84	1830	—	3.00	6.00	12.00	40.00

1/12 THALER

BILLON
Obv: Script A and Saxon arms.
Rev: Value and date.

C#	Date	Mintage	VG	Fine	VF	XF
41	1763 FS	—	6.00	13.00	25.00	45.00
	1764 FS	—	6.00	13.00	25.00	45.00

1/6 THALER

SILVER

C#	Date	Mintage	Fine	VF	XF	Unc
42	1763 FS	—	20.00	32.50	50.00	75.00
42a	1763 FS	—	20.00	32.50	50.00	75.00
	1764 FS	—	20.00	32.50	50.00	75.00

1/3 THALER

SILVER

C#	Date	Mintage	Fine	VF	XF	Unc
43	1763 FS	—	50.00	85.00	135.00	175.00
	1764 FS	—	50.00	85.00	135.00	175.00
	1765 FS	—	50.00	85.00	135.00	175.00

1/2 THALER

.833 SILVER

C#	Date	Mintage	Fine	VF	XF	Unc
74	1813 LS	—	30.00	65.00	140.00	225.00

2/3 THALER

SILVER
Obv: AADS script monogram.
Rev: Crowned arms.

C#	Date	Mintage	Fine	VF	XF	Unc
45	1760 FS	—	65.00	100.00	150.00	225.00

Rev: Saxon arms.

C#	Date	Mintage	Fine	VF	XF	Unc
46	1763 FS	—	65.00	100.00	150.00	225.00

C#	Date	Mintage	Fine	VF	XF	Unc
46a	1763 FS	—	65.00	100.00	150.00	225.00
	1764 FS	—	65.00	100.00	150.00	225.00
	1765 FS	—	65.00	100.00	150.00	225.00

EIN (1) THALER

(Reichs)

SILVER
Obv: Crowned AADS script monogram.
Rev: Crowned Saxon arms over value.

C#	Date	Mintage	Fine	VF	XF	Unc
49	1760 FS	—	500.00	750.00	1150.	1900.

(Convention)

Obv: Large bust of Anna Amalia left.
Rev: Crowned complex arms over value.

C#	Date	Mintage	Fine	VF	XF	Unc
50a	1763 FS	—	350.00	500.00	750.00	1500.

C#	Date	Mintage	Fine	VF	XF	Unc
50	1763 FS	—	175.00	300.00	450.00	900.00
	1764 FS	—	175.00	300.00	450.00	900.00
	1765 FS	—	175.00	300.00	450.00	900.00

28.0600 gm., .833 SILVER, .7516 oz ASW

C#	Date	Mintage	Fine	VF	XF	Unc
75	1813 LS	—	200.00	400.00	800.00	1600.

C#	Date	Mintage	Fine	VF	XF	Unc
76	1815	5,273	300.00	600.00	1200.	2400.

22.2700 gm., .750 SILVER, .5370 oz ASW

C#	Date	Mintage	Fine	VF	XF	Unc
87	1841A	.203	40.00	100.00	200.00	400.00

(Vereins)

18.5200 gm., .900 SILVER, .5360 oz ASW

C#	Date	Mintage	Fine	VF	XF	Unc
93	1858A	.063	30.00	75.00	150.00	300.00
	1866A	.044	30.00	75.00	150.00	300.00
	1870A	.045	30.00	75.00	150.00	300.00

2 THALER

(= 3-1/2 Gulden)

37.1200 gm., .900 SILVER, 1.0742 oz ASW

C#	Date	Mintage	Fine	VF	XF	Unc
88	1840A	.019	250.00	500.00	1000.	2000.
	1842A	.038	250.00	500.00	1000.	2000.
	1843A	Inc. Ab.	250.00	500.00	1000.	2000.
	1848A	.019	250.00	500.00	1000.	2000.

Rev: Similar to C#88.

C#	Date	Mintage	Fine	VF	XF	Unc
94	1855A	.019	180.00	375.00	650.00	1200.

5 THALER

6.6500 gm., .900 GOLD, .1924 oz AGW
Obv: Bust of Anna Amalia left.
Rev: Crowned arms.

C#	Date	Mintage	Fine	VF	XF	Unc
53	1764 FS	—	1450.	2000.	2750.	4000.

TRADE COINS

DUCAT

3.5000 gm., .986 GOLD, .1109 oz AGW
Obv: Bust of Anna Amalia left.
Rev: Crowned arms.

C#	Date	Mintage	Fine	VF	XF	Unc
52	1764 FS	—	1000.	1500.	2250.	3500.

MONETARY REFORM

2 MARK

11.1110 gm., .900 SILVER, .3215 oz ASW
Obv: Head left, A below. Rev: Type 3 eagle.

Y#	Date	Mintage	VF	XF	Unc
168	1892A	.050	175.00	300.00	500.00
	1898A	.100	150.00	250.00	450.00
	1898A	—	—	Proof	600.00

Y#	Date	Mintage	VF	XF	Unc
170	1901A	.100	225.00	400.00	650.00
	1901A	—	—	Proof	600.00

Grand Duke's 1st Marriage

Y#	Date	Mintage	VF	XF	Unc
172	1903A	.040	50.00	75.00	100.00
	1903A	1,000	—	Proof	150.00

Jena University 350th Anniversary

Y#	Date	Mintage	VF	XF	Unc
174	1908A	.050	50.00	75.00	100.00

3 MARK

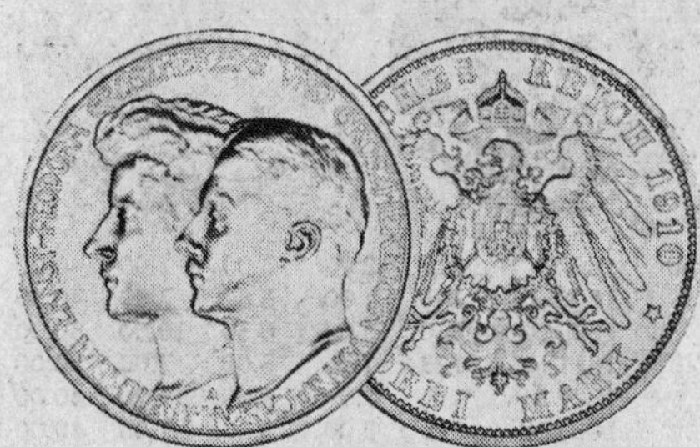

16.6670 gm., .900 SILVER, .4823 oz ASW
Grand Duke's 2nd Marriage

Y#	Date	Mintage	VF	XF	Unc
176	1910A	.133	25.00	45.00	60.00
	1910A	—	—	Proof	100.00

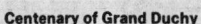

Centenary of Grand Duchy

Y#	Date	Mintage	VF	XF	Unc
177	1915A	.050	80.00	125.00	175.00

5 MARK

27.7770 gm., .900 SILVER, .8038 oz ASW
Grand Duke's 1st Marriage

Y#	Date	Mintage	VF	XF	Unc
173	1903A	.024	100.00	200.00	250.00
	1903A	*1,000	—	Proof	400.00

Jena University 350th Anniversary
Rev: Similar to Y#173.

Y#	Date	Mintage	VF	XF	Unc
175	1908A	.040	90.00	175.00	250.00

20 MARK

7.9650 gm., .900 GOLD, .2304 oz AGW

Y#	Date	Mintage	VF	XF	Unc
169	1892A	5,000	1200.	1500.	2500.
	1896A	.015	900.00	1200.	2000.

Y#	Date	Mintage	VF	XF	Unc
171	1901A	5,000	1700.	2500.	3500.

NCLT ISSUES

PATTERNS

KM#	Date	Mintage	Identification	Mkt.Val.
1	1908	—	5 Marks, Silver	—
2	1910	—	3 Marks, Silver	—

SAXONY

Saxony, located in southeast Germany was founded in 850. The first coinage was struck c. 990. It was divided into two lines in 1464. The Electoral Right was obtained by the elder line in 1547. During the time of the Reformation, Saxony was one of the more powerful states in Central Europe. It became a kingdom in 1806. At the Congress of Vienna in 1815, they were forced to cede half its territories to Prussia.

RULERS

Friedrich Christian, Elector, 1763
Xaver, Prince Regent, 1763-1768
Friedrich August III, 1763-1806
Later Friedrich August I, 1806-1827
Anton, 1827-1836
Friedrich August II, 1836-1854
Johann, 1854-1873
Albert, 1873-1902
Georg, 1902-1904
Friedrich August III, 1904-1918

MINTMASTER'S INITIALS

B - Gustav Julius Buschick
C - Ernst Diettrich Croll
F - Gustav Theodor Fischer
G - Johann Georg Grohmann
IGS, GS, S - Johann Gotthelf Studer, 1814-1832
SGH, H - Samuel Gottlieb Helbig 1804-1813

HELLER

COPPER

C#	Date	Mintage	Fine	VF	XF	Unc
90	1778 C	—	2.00	3.00	6.00	35.00
	1779 C	—	2.00	3.00	6.00	35.00
	1780 C	—	2.00	3.00	6.00	35.00
	1781 C	—	2.00	3.00	6.00	35.00
	1782 C	—	2.00	3.00	6.00	35.00
	1783 C	—	2.00	3.00	6.00	35.00
	1787 C	—	2.00	3.00	6.00	35.00
	1789 C	—	2.00	3.00	6.00	35.00
	1792 C	—	2.00	3.00	6.00	35.00
	1796 C	—	2.00	3.00	6.00	35.00
	1799 C	—	2.00	3.00	6.00	35.00
	1801 C	—	2.00	3.00	6.00	35.00
	1805H	—	2.00	3.00	6.00	35.00

Obv: Crowned arms within branches.
Rev: Value, without legends

C#	Date	Mintage	Fine	VF	XF	Unc
157	1813 H	.562	2.00	3.00	6.00	35.00
	1813 S	Inc. Ab.	2.00	3.00	6.00	35.00

PFENNIG

COPPER

C#	Date	Mintage	Fine	VF	XF	Unc
91	1772 C	—	2.00	3.00	6.00	35.00
	1773 C	—	2.00	3.00	6.00	35.00
	1774 C	—	2.00	3.00	6.00	35.00
	1775 C	—	2.00	3.00	6.00	35.00
	1776 C	—	2.00	3.00	6.00	35.00
	1777 C	—	2.00	3.00	6.00	35.00
	1778 C	—	2.00	3.00	6.00	35.00
	1779 C	—	2.00	3.00	6.00	35.00
	1780 C	—	2.00	3.00	6.00	35.00
	1781 C	—	2.00	3.00	6.00	35.00
	1782/72 C	—	—	—	—	—
	1782 C	—	2.00	3.00	6.00	35.00
	1783 C	—	2.00	3.00	6.00	35.00
	1784 C	—	2.00	3.00	6.00	35.00
	1785 C	—	2.00	3.00	6.00	35.00
	1788 C	—	2.00	3.00	6.00	35.00
	1789 C	—	2.00	3.00	6.00	35.00
	1790/89 C	—	—	Reported, not confirmed		
	1790 C	—	—	Reported, not confirmed		
	1796 C	—	2.00	3.00	6.00	35.00
	1797 C	—	2.00	3.00	6.00	35.00
	1799 C	—	2.00	3.00	6.00	35.00
	1800 C	—	2.00	3.00	6.00	35.00
	1801 C	—	2.00	3.00	6.00	35.00
	1804/799 C	—	2.00	4.00	8.50	35.00
	1804 C	—	2.00	3.00	6.00	35.00
	1805 H	—	2.00	3.00	6.00	35.00
	1806 H/795 C	—	2.00	4.00	8.50	35.00
	1806 H	—	2.00	3.00	6.00	35.00

Obv: Crowned arms within branches.
Rev: Value, without legends, pearl borders both sides.

C#	Date	Mintage	Fine	VF	XF	Unc
158	1807 H	.922	2.00	4.00	8.00	35.00
	1807 H/799 C	—	—	—	—	—
	1807/6 H	—	5.00	10.00	15.00	35.00

Obv: Trefoil border

C#	Date	Mintage	Fine	VF	XF	Unc
158a	1808 H	.014	4.00	7.00	15.00	35.00

C#	Date	Mintage	Fine	VF	XF	Unc
158b	1811 H	1.267	2.00	4.00	8.00	35.00
	1815 S	—	2.00	4.00	8.00	35.00
	1816 S	—	2.00	4.00	8.00	35.00
	1822 S	—	2.00	4.00	8.00	35.00
	1825 S	.230	2.00	4.00	8.00	35.00

C#	Date	Mintage	Fine	VF	XF	Unc
201	1831 S	1.154	1.50	3.00	6.00	35.00
	1832 S	.527	1.50	3.00	6.00	35.00
	1833 G	1.152	1.50	3.00	6.00	35.00

C#	Date	Mintage	Fine	VF	XF	Unc
220	1836 G	.226	1.50	3.00	6.00	35.00
	1837 G	.940	1.50	3.00	6.00	35.00
	1838 G	1.473	1.50	3.00	6.00	35.00

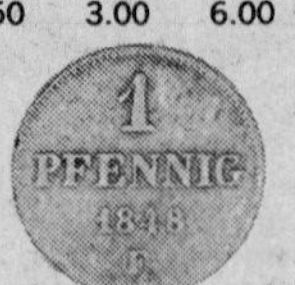

C#	Date	Mintage	Fine	VF	XF	Unc
221	1841 G	.492	1.00	2.50	5.00	35.00
	1842 G	.323	1.00	2.50	5.00	35.00
	1843 G	1.115	1.00	2.50	5.00	35.00
	1846 F	.450	1.00	2.50	5.00	35.00
	1847 F	.546	1.00	2.50	5.00	35.00
	1848 F	1.447	1.00	2.50	5.00	35.00
	1849 F	.783	1.00	2.50	5.00	35.00
	1850 F	.815	1.00	2.50	5.00	35.00
	1851 F	1.556	1.00	2.50	5.00	35.00
	1852 F	.918	1.00	2.50	5.00	35.00
	1853 F	1.164	1.00	2.50	5.00	35.00
	1854 F	.548	1.00	2.50	5.00	35.00

C#	Date	Mintage	Fine	VF	XF	Unc
248	1855 F	.657	1.00	2.50	5.00	35.00
	1856 F	3.457	1.00	2.50	5.00	30.00
	1859 F	2.341	1.00	2.50	5.00	30.00

C#	Date	Mintage	Fine	VF	XF	Unc
248a	1861 B	.338	2.50	5.00	10.00	35.00

C#	Date	Mintage	Fine	VF	XF	Unc
250	1862 B	1.094	1.00	2.50	5.00	30.00
	1863 B	4.484	1.00	2.50	5.00	30.00
	1865 B	3.877	1.00	2.50	5.00	30.00
	1866 B	1.129	1.00	2.50	5.00	30.00
	1868 B	2.084	1.00	2.50	5.00	30.00
	1871 B	.331	1.00	2.50	5.00	35.00
	1872 B	.591	1.00	2.50	5.00	30.00
	1873 B	.549	1.00	2.50	5.00	30.00

2 PFENNIG

COPPER

C#	Date	Mintage	Fine	VF	XF	Unc
222	1841 G	1.263	2.50	5.00	10.00	35.00

C#	Date	Mintage	Fine	VF	XF	Unc
222a	1841 G	Inc. Ab.	1.50	3.50	7.00	35.00
	1843 G	.112	1.50	3.50	7.00	35.00
	1846 F	.090	1.50	3.50	7.00	35.00
	1847 F	.401	1.50	3.50	7.00	35.00
	1848 F	.518	1.50	3.50	7.00	35.00
	1849 F	.365	1.50	3.50	7.00	35.00
	1850 F	.647	1.00	3.50	7.00	35.00
	1851 F	.271	1.00	3.50	7.00	35.00
	1852 F	.361	1.00	3.50	7.00	35.00
	1853 F	.576	1.00	3.50	7.00	35.00
222a	1854 F	.056	2.00	3.50	7.00	35.00

C#	Date	Mintage	Fine	VF	XF	Unc
249	1855 F	.536	1.00	2.50	5.00	30.00
	1856 F	2.182	1.00	2.50	5.00	30.00
	1859 F	1.103	1.00	2.50	5.00	30.00

C#	Date	Mintage	Fine	VF	XF	Unc
249a	1861 B	.163	2.50	5.00	10.00	30.00

C#	Date	Mintage	Fine	VF	XF	Unc
251	1862 B	.739	1.00	2.50	5.00	30.00
	1863 B	.456	1.00	2.50	5.00	30.00
	1864 B	3.139	1.00	2.50	5.00	30.00
	1866 B	.551	1.00	2.50	5.00	30.00
	1869 B	2.220	1.00	2.50	5.00	30.00
	1873 B	.262	1.00	2.50	5.00	30.00

3 PFENNIG

BILLON
Obv: Capped arms in sprays.
Rev: Value over date.

C#	Date	Mintage	VG	Fine	VF	XF
95	1764 C	—	2.00	3.50	6.00	15.00
	1765 C	—	2.00	3.50	6.00	15.00
	1779 C	—	2.00	3.50	6.00	15.00
	1781 C	—	2.00	3.50	6.00	15.00
	1782 C	—	2.00	3.50	6.00	15.00
	1784 C	—	2.00	3.50	6.00	15.00
	1785 C	—	2.00	3.50	6.00	15.00
	1793 C	—	2.00	3.50	6.00	15.00

COPPER

C#	Date	Mintage	Fine	VF	XF	Unc
92	1797 C	—	2.00	3.00	10.00	40.00
	1799 C	—	2.00	3.00	10.00	40.00
	1800 C	—	2.00	3.00	10.00	40.00
	1801 C	—	2.00	3.00	10.00	40.00
	1802 C	—	2.00	3.00	10.00	40.00
	1803 C	—	2.00	3.00	10.00	40.00
	1804 H	—	2.00	3.00	10.00	40.00
	1806 H	—	2.00	3.00	10.00	40.00

C#	Date	Mintage	Fine	VF	XF	Unc
160	1807 H	.317	2.00	3.00	7.00	40.00
	1808 H	.295	2.00	3.00	7.00	40.00
	1809 H	4,800	3.00	6.50	10.00	50.00
	1811 H	.128	2.00	3.00	7.00	40.00
	1822 S	—	2.00	3.00	7.00	40.00
	1823 S	.019	2.00	3.00	7.00	40.00

Obv: Crowned arched arms. Rev: 3 PFENNIGE.

C#	Date	Mintage	Fine	VF	XF	Unc
161	1825 S	.168	1.50	3.00	7.00	40.00
202	1831 S	.077	2.00	4.00	7.00	40.00
	1832 S	.226	1.50	3.00	7.00	40.00

Rev: G below date

C#	Date	Mintage	Fine	VF	XF	Unc
202b	1833 G	.069	2.00	4.00	7.00	40.00

Rev: G below date

C#	Date	Mintage	Fine	VF	XF	Unc
202a	1834 G	.500	1.50	3.00	7.00	40.00

Obv: Crowned rectangular arms

C#	Date	Mintage	Fine	VF	XF	Unc
223	1836 G	.039	2.00	4.00	7.00	40.00
	1837 G	.542	1.50	3.25	7.00	40.00

4 PFENNIG

COPPER

Obv: Crowned arms within branches. Rev: Value.

C#	Date	Mintage	Fine	VF	XF	Unc
162	1808 H	1.548	2.50	5.00	20.00	60.00
	1809 H	1.059	2.50	5.00	20.00	60.00
	1810 H	.886	2.50	5.00	20.00	60.00

5 PFENNIG

COPPER

C#	Date	Mintage	Fine	VF	XF	Unc
252	1862 B	2.468	1.00	3.00	5.00	35.00
	1863 B	.693	1.50	3.00	5.00	35.00
	1864 B	1.090	1.00	3.00	5.00	35.00
	1866 B	.141	1.50	3.00	5.00	35.00
	1867 B	.444	1.50	3.00	5.00	35.00
	1869 B	.860	1.50	3.00	5.00	35.00

8 PFENNIG

BILLON

Obv: Crowned arms within branches. Rev: Value.

C#	Date	Mintage	Fine	VF	XF	Unc
165	1808 H	2.594	4.00	8.00	15.00	45.00
	1809 H	4.722	4.00	8.00	15.00	45.00

KREUZER

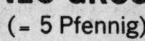

BILLON

(For Duchy of Henneberg)

C#	Date	Mintage	VG	Fine	VF	XF
96	1765	—	5.00	10.00	15.00	30.00
	1780	—	5.00	10.00	15.00	30.00

1/2 NEU-GROSCHEN

(= 5 Pfennig)

BILLON

C#	Date	Mintage	Fine	VF	XF	Unc
224	1841 G	2.248	1.00	3.00	6.00	35.00
	1842 G	2.845	1.00	3.00	6.00	35.00
	1843 G	3.552	1.00	3.00	6.00	35.00
	1844 G	1.354	1.00	3.00	6.00	35.00
	1848 F	.500	1.50	3.00	6.00	35.00
	1849 F	.579	1.50	3.00	6.00	35.00
	1851 F	.506	1.50	3.00	6.00	35.00
	1852 F	.497	1.50	3.00	6.00	35.00
	1853 F	.256	1.50	3.00	6.00	35.00
	1854 F	.107	1.50	3.00	6.00	35.00

C#	Date	Mintage	Fine	VF	XF	Unc
253	1855 F	.444	1.50	3.00	6.00	35.00
	1856 F	.713	1.50	3.00	6.00	35.00

NEU-GROSCHEN

(= 10 Pfennig)

BILLON

C#	Date	Mintage	Fine	VF	XF	Unc
225	1841 G	4.500	1.00	3.25	6.00	35.00
	1842 G	2.463	1.00	3.25	6.00	35.00
	1845 F	.457	1.00	3.25	6.00	35.00
	1846 F	1.656	1.00	3.25	6.00	35.00
	1847 F	1.532	1.00	3.25	6.00	35.00
	1848 F	.105	1.00	3.25	6.00	35.00
	1849 F	1.049	1.00	3.25	6.00	35.00
	1850 F	.505	1.00	3.25	6.00	35.00
	1851 F	.676	1.00	3.25	6.00	35.00
	1852 F	.949	1.00	3.25	6.00	35.00
	1853 F	.798	1.00	3.25	6.00	35.00
	1854 F	.443	1.00	3.00	6.00	35.00

Rev: F below value

C#	Date	Mintage	Fine	VF	XF	Unc
254	1855 F	1.106	1.00	2.50	5.00	35.00
	1856 F	1.188	1.00	2.50	5.00	35.00

Rev: B below value

C#	Date	Mintage	Fine	VF	XF	Unc
254a	1861 B	.395	3.00	6.50	10.00	35.00

C#	Date	Mintage	Fine	VF	XF	Unc
255	1863 B	1.514	1.00	3.00	6.00	35.00
	1865 B	.557	1.00	3.00	6.00	25.00
	1867 B	.296	1.00	3.00	6.00	35.00

C#	Date	Mintage	Fine	VF	XF	Unc
256	1867 B	.897	1.00	3.00	6.00	35.00
	1868 B	.608	1.00	3.00	6.00	35.00
	1870 B	.908	1.00	3.00	6.00	35.00
	1871 B	.293	1.00	3.00	6.00	35.00
	1873 B	.420	1.00	3.00	6.00	35.00

2 GROSCHEN

SILVER

(For Vicariat)

Obv: Head right.

Rev: Imperial eagle.

C#	Date	Mintage	VG	Fine	VF	XF
102	1790	—	6.00	15.00	30.00	50.00

Obv: Bust right.

C#	Date	Mintage	VG	Fine	VF	XF
104	1792	—	6.00	15.00	30.00	50.00

2 NEU-GROSCHEN

(= 20 Pfennig)

BILLON

C#	Date	Mintage	Fine	VF	XF	Unc
226	1841 G	3.125	2.00	4.00	8.00	35.00
	1842 G	1.413	2.00	4.00	8.00	35.00
	1844 G	1.477	2.00	4.00	8.00	35.00
	1846 F	.516	2.00	4.00	8.00	35.00
	1847 F	.425	2.00	4.00	8.00	35.00
	1848 F	1.062	2.00	4.00	8.00	35.00
	1849 F	.656	2.00	4.00	8.00	35.00
	1850 F	.380	2.00	4.00	8.00	35.00
	1851 F	.588	2.00	4.00	8.00	35.00
	1852 F	.974	2.00	4.00	8.00	35.00
	1853 F	.604	2.00	4.00	8.00	35.00
	1854 F	.790	2.00	4.00	8.00	35.00

C#	Date	Mintage	Fine	VF	XF	Unc
257	1855 F	.921	1.50	3.00	6.00	35.00
	1856 F	2.207	1.00	3.00	6.00	35.00

C#	Date	Mintage	Fine	VF	XF	Unc
258	1863 B	.557	2.00	4.00	8.00	35.00
	1864 B	.447	2.00	4.00	8.00	35.00
	1865 B	.371	2.00	4.00	8.00	35.00
	1866 B	.448	2.00	4.00	8.00	35.00

C#	Date	Mintage	Fine	VF	XF	Unc
259	1868 B	.419	1.00	3.00	6.00	35.00
	1869 B	.599	1.00	3.00	6.00	35.00
	1871 B	.245	1.00	3.00	6.00	35.00
	1873 B	.468	1.00	3.00	6.00	35.00

48 EINEN (1/48) THALER

BILLON

Obv: Crowned arms.

Rev: Value; date in outer legend.

C#	Date	Mintage	VG	Fine	VF	XF
74	1763 EDC	—	4.00	8.50	12.50	20.00

Obv: Crowned shield between crossed laurel branches.

Rev: Date below, value.

C#	Date	Mintage	Fine	VF	XF	Unc
97	1764 C	—	3.00	5.00	12.00	50.00
	1765 C	—	3.00	5.00	12.00	50.00
	1771 C	—	3.00	5.00	12.00	50.00
	1779 C	—	3.00	5.00	12.00	50.00
	1781 C	—	3.00	5.00	12.00	50.00
	1785 C	—	3.00	5.00	12.00	50.00
	1793 C	—	3.00	5.00	12.00	50.00
	1799 C	—	3.00	5.00	12.00	50.00
	1802 C	—	2.50	5.00	12.00	50.00
	1803 C	—	2.50	5.00	12.00	50.00
	1805 H	—	2.50	5.00	12.00	50.00
	1806 H	—	2.50	5.00	12.00	50.00

C#	Date	Mintage	Fine	VF	XF	Unc
163	1806 H	—	2.50	5.00	10.00	40.00
	1806/797 H	—	—	—	—	—
	1807 H	2.990	2.50	5.00	10.00	30.00
	1808 H	1.816	2.50	5.00	10.00	30.00
	1811/01 H	—	—	—	—	—
	1811 H	4.242	2.50	5.00	10.00	40.00
	1812 H	5.382	2.50	5.00	10.00	40.00
	1812 S	Inc. Ab.	2.50	5.00	10.00	40.00
	1813 H	.730	2.50	5.00	10.00	40.00
	1813 S	Inc. Ab.	2.50	5.00	10.00	40.00
	1814 S	2.871	2.50	5.00	10.00	40.00
	1815 S	1.059	2.50	5.00	10.00	40.00

24 EINEN (1/24) THALER

BILLON

Obv: Crowned arms.
Rev: Value; date in outer legend.

C#	Date	Mintage	VG	Fine	VF	XF
75	1763 FWoF	—	3.00	7.50	15.00	25.00
	1763 EDC	—	3.00	7.50	15.00	25.00
	1763 JFoF	—	3.00	7.50	15.00	25.00

Obv. leg: XAVERIVS ....

C#	Date	Mintage	VG	Fine	VF	XF
80	1764 EDC	—	3.00	7.50	15.00	25.00
	1765 EDC	—	3.00	7.50	15.00	25.00
	1766 EDC	—	3.00	7.50	15.00	25.00
	1767 EDC	—	3.00	7.50	15.00	25.00
	1768 EDC	—	3.00	7.50	15.00	25.00

Obv: Crowned shield between crossed laurel branches.
Rev: Value, date below.

C#	Date	Mintage	Fine	VF	XF	Unc
98	1764 EDC	—	3.00	6.00	15.00	40.00
	1798 EDC	—	3.00	6.00	12.00	40.00
	1800 EDC	—	3.00	6.00	12.00	40.00
	1801 EDC	—	3.00	6.00	12.00	40.00
	1802 EDC	—	3.00	6.00	12.00	40.00

C#	Date	Mintage	Fine	VF	XF	Unc
166	1816 IGS	.146	3.00	6.00	12.00	40.00
	1817 IGS	.252	3.00	6.00	12.00	40.00
	1817 IGS	.166	3.00	6.00	12.00	40.00

Obv. leg: FRIED......

C#	Date	Mintage	Fine	VF	XF	Unc
167	1819 IGS	.337	3.00	6.00	12.00	40.00
	1820 IGS	.268	3.00	6.00	12.00	40.00
	1821 IGS	.321	3.00	6.00	12.00	40.00
	1822 IGS	.439	3.00	6.00	12.00	40.00

Obv. leg: FRIEDR.....

C#	Date	Mintage	Fine	VF	XF	Unc
167a	1823 IGS	.368	5.00	10.00	15.00	40.00

Obv: Crowned arched arms

C#	Date	Mintage	Fine	VF	XF	Unc
168	1824 S	.332	3.00	6.00	10.00	40.00
	1825 S	.262	3.00	6.00	10.00	40.00
	1826 S	.311	3.00	6.00	10.00	40.00
	1827 S	.067	3.00	6.00	10.00	40.00

Obv: Crowned arched arms within crossed branches.

C#	Date	Mintage	Fine	VF	XF	Unc
203	1827 S	.066	10.00	20.00	30.00	55.00
	1828 S	.100	10.00	20.00	30.00	55.00

12 EINEN (1/12) THALER

BILLON

C#	Date	Mintage	VG	Fine	VF	XF
76	1763 FWoF	—	5.00	10.00	17.50	30.00
	1763 EDC	—	5.00	10.00	17.50	30.00
	1763 JFoF	—	5.00	10.00	17.50	30.00

Obv: Different crowned arms, leg: XAVERIVS ....

C#	Date	Mintage	VG	Fine	VF	XF
81	1764 EDC	—	5.00	12.50	20.00	35.00
	1765 EDC	—	5.00	12.50	20.00	35.00
	1766 EDC	—	5.00	12.50	20.00	35.00
	1767 EDC	—	5.00	12.50	20.00	35.00
	1768 EDC	—	5.00	12.50	20.00	35.00

C#	Date	Mintage	Fine	VF	XF	Unc
100	1763 EDC	—	3.00	5.00	10.00	35.00
	1764 FWoF	—	3.00	6.00	15.00	45.00
	1764 EDC	—	3.00	6.00	15.00	45.00
	1765 EDC	—	3.00	6.00	15.00	45.00
	1797 EDC	—	3.00	6.00	15.00	45.00
	1798 EDC	—	3.00	6.00	15.00	45.00
	1799 EDC	—	3.00	6.00	15.00	45.00
	1800 EDC	—	3.00	6.00	15.00	45.00
	1801 EDC	—	3.00	6.00	15.00	45.00
	1802 EDC	—	3.00	6.00	15.00	45.00

C#	Date	Mintage	Fine	VF	XF	Unc
169	1806 SGH	.037	3.00	6.00	12.50	40.00
	1808 SGH	.140	3.00	6.00	12.50	40.00
	1809 SGH	1.071	3.00	6.00	12.50	40.00
	1810 SGH	.515	3.00	6.00	12.50	40.00
	1811 SGH	—	3.00	6.00	12.50	40.00
	1812 IGS	5.172	3.00	6.00	12.50	40.00
	1812 SGH	I.A.	3.00	6.00	12.50	40.00
	1813 IGS	2.055	3.00	6.00	12.50	40.00
	1813 SGH	I.A.	3.00	6.00	12.50	40.00
	1816 IGS	—	3.00	6.00	12.50	40.00
	1817 IGS	—	3.00	6.00	12.50	40.00
	1818 IGS	—	3.00	6.00	12.50	40.00

Obv. leg: VGVST....

C#	Date	Mintage	Fine	VF	XF	Unc
169a	1809 SGH	I.A.	3.00	6.00	12.50	40.00

Obv. leg: FRIED....

C#	Date	Mintage	Fine	VF	XF	Unc
170	1819 IGS	—	6.00	12.00	18.00	45.00
	1820 IGS	—	6.00	12.00	18.00	45.00
	1821 IGS	—	6.00	12.00	18.00	45.00
	1822 IGS	—	6.00	12.00	18.00	45.00
	1823 IGS	1.624	6.00	12.00	18.00	45.00

Obv. leg: FRIEDR.....

C#	Date	Mintage	Fine	VF	XF	Unc
170a	1823 IGS	I.A.	7.00	15.00	23.00	50.00

Obv: Crowned arched arms

C#	Date	Mintage	Fine	VF	XF	Unc
171	1824 S	2.470	6.00	12.00	18.00	45.00
	1825 S	1.721	6.00	12.00	18.00	45.00
	1826 S	.763	6.00	12.00	18.00	45.00
	1827 S	.564	6.00	12.00	18.00	45.00

Obv: Crowned arched arms within crossed branches.

C#	Date	Mintage	Fine	VF	XF	Unc
204	1827 S	.060	6.00	12.00	20.00	45.00
	1828 S	.256	5.00	10.00	18.00	45.00
204a	1829 S	1.431	3.00	6.00	12.00	40.00
	1830 S	1.684	3.00	6.00	12.00	40.00
	1831 S	.206	3.00	6.00	12.00	40.00
	1832 S	.882	3.00	6.00	12.00	40.00

C#	Date	Mintage	Fine	VF	XF	Unc
227	1836 G	.690	6.00	12.00	18.00	45.00

1/6 THALER

(Reichs)

SILVER

C#	Date	Mintage	Fine	VF	XF	Unc
A77	1763 EDC	—	12.50	20.00	35.00	60.00

Obv: Bust of Xaver right.
Rev: Crowned arms; value below.

C#	Date	Mintage	Fine	VF	XF	Unc
82	1764 EDC	—	10.00	15.00	25.00	50.00
	1765 EDC	—	10.00	15.00	25.00	50.00
	1766 EDC	—	10.00	15.00	25.00	50.00
	1767 EDC	—	10.00	15.00	25.00	50.00

Obv: Young head right.
Rev: Electors cap over arms in branches; date in exergue.

C#	Date	Mintage	Fine	VF	XF	Unc
106	1764 FWoF	—	10.00	20.00	35.00	60.00
	1764 EDC	—	10.00	20.00	35.00	60.00
	1766 EDC	—	10.00	20.00	35.00	60.00
	1767 EDC	—	10.00	20.00	35.00	60.00
	1768 EDC	—	10.00	20.00	35.00	60.00

C#	Date	Mintage	Fine	VF	XF	Unc
108	1803 IEC	—	5.00	10.00	25.00	50.00
	1804 IEC	—	5.00	10.00	25.00	50.00
	1804 SGH	—	5.00	10.00	25.00	50.00
	1805 SGH	—	5.00	10.00	25.00	50.00
	1806 SGH	—	5.00	10.00	25.00	50.00

5.3970 gm., .542 SILVER, .0940 oz ASW

C#	Date	Mintage	Fine	VF	XF	Unc
172	1806 SGH	.018	12.00	25.00	45.00	75.00
	1807 SGH	.317	6.00	12.00	25.00	50.00
	1808 SGH	2.421	6.00	12.00	25.00	50.00
	1809 SGH	3.608	6.00	12.00	25.00	50.00
	1810 SGH	2.405	6.00	12.00	25.00	50.00
	1813 SGH	.229	6.00	12.00	25.00	50.00
172a	1813IGS	—	15.00	30.00	50.00	110.00
	1817IGS	.119	15.00	30.00	50.00	110.00

C#	Date	Mintage	Fine	VF	XF	Unc
173	1825 GS	.068	15.00	30.00	50.00	110.00

Death Of King Friedrich August

C#	Date	Mintage	Fine	VF	XF	Unc
174	1827 S	.048	14.00	27.00	40.00	60.00

Rev: Crowned arched arms within crossed branches.

C#	Date	Mintage	Fine	VF	XF	Unc
205	1827 S	.019	25.00	45.00	80.00	150.00
	1828 S	.018	25.00	45.00	80.00	150.00

Obv: Older head

C#	Date	Mintage	Fine	VF	XF	Unc
205a	1829 S	.124	20.00	35.00	60.00	120.00

Death Of King Anton

C#	Date	Mintage	Fine	VF	XF	Unc
206	1836 G	.046	12.00	25.00	40.00	75.00

5.3450 gm., .521 SILVER, .0895 oz ASW

C#	Date	Mintage	Fine	VF	XF	Unc
228	1841 G	.450	5.00	10.00	20.00	40.00
	1842 G	1.322	5.00	10.00	20.00	40.00
	1843 G	.655	5.00	10.00	20.00	40.00
	1846 F	.601	5.00	10.00	20.00	40.00
	1847 F	.366	5.00	10.00	20.00	40.00
	1848 F	.270	5.00	10.00	20.00	40.00
	1849 F	.449	5.00	10.00	20.00	40.00
	1850 F	.134	5.00	10.00	20.00	40.00

Value as 6 EINEN THALER

C#	Date	Mintage	Fine	VF	XF	Unc
228a	1851 F	.228	7.00	15.00	35.00	60.00
	1852 F	.340	7.00	15.00	35.00	60.00

Death Of King Friedrich August II
Obv: Head right, D.9.AUG. 1854 below.
Rev. leg: ER SAEETE.

C#	Date	Mintage	Fine	VF	XF	Unc
229	40.00	75.00	10.00	20.00	40.00	75.00

C#	Date	Mintage	Fine	VF	XF	Unc
260	1855 F	.476	5.00	10.00	18.00	35.00
	1856 F	1.529	5.00	10.00	18.00	35.00

5.3420 gm., .520 SILVER, .0893 oz ASW

C#	Date	Mintage	Fine	VF	XF	Unc
261	1860 B	.871	5.00	10.00	18.00	35.00
	1860 F	.052	20.00	40.00	55.00	75.00
	1861 B	1.099	5.00	10.00	18.00	35.00
	1863 B	.589	5.00	10.00	18.00	35.00
	1864 B	.161	5.00	10.00	18.00	35.00
	1865 B	.683	5.00	10.00	18.00	35.00
	1866/5 B	I.A.	—	—	—	—
	1866 B	.475	5.00	10.00	18.00	35.00
	1869 B	.626	5.00	10.00	18.00	35.00
	1870 B	.280	5.00	10.00	18.00	35.00
	1871 B	.293	5.00	10.00	18.00	35.00

1/3 THALER

(Reichs)

SILVER
Obv: Bust of Xaver right.
Rev: Capped arms, value below.

C#	Date	Mintage	Fine	VF	XF	Unc
83	1764 EDC	—	15.00	25.00	55.00	100.00
	1765 EDC	—	15.00	25.00	40.00	80.00
	1766 EDC	—	15.00	25.00	40.00	80.00
	1767 EDC	—	15.00	25.00	40.00	80.00
	1768 EDC	—	15.00	25.00	40.00	80.00

Obv: Head right.
Rev: Capped arms in sprays; date in exergue.

C#	Date	Mintage	VG	Fine	VF	XF
111	1780 IEC	—	7.00	15.00	22.50	35.00
	1781 IEC	—	7.00	15.00	22.50	35.00
	1782 IEC	—	7.00	15.00	22.50	35.00
	1783 IEC	—	7.00	15.00	22.50	35.00
	1784 IEC	—	7.00	15.00	22.50	35.00
	1785 IEC	—	7.00	15.00	22.50	35.00
	1786 IEC	—	7.00	15.00	22.50	35.00

C#	Date	Mintage	VG	Fine	VF	XF
111	1787 IEC	—	7.00	15.00	22.50	35.00
	1788 IEC	—	7.00	15.00	22.50	35.00
	1789 IEC	—	7.00	15.00	22.50	35.00
	1790 IEC	—	7.00	15.00	22.50	35.00

Vicariat Issue
Rev: Imperial eagle.

C#	Date	Mintage	VG	Fine	VF	XF
112	1790 IEC	—	12.00	25.00	40.00	65.00

C#	Date	Mintage	VG	Fine	VF	XF
114	1792 IEC	—	12.00	25.00	40.00	65.00

Rev: Crowned shield between crossed laurel branches.

C#	Date	Mintage	Fine	VF	XF	Unc
113	1791 IEC	—	15.00	25.00	45.00	80.00
	1792 IEC	—	7.00	15.00	30.00	60.00
	1793 IEC	—	7.00	15.00	30.00	60.00
	1794 IEC	—	7.00	15.00	30.00	60.00
	1795 IEC	—	7.00	15.00	30.00	60.00
	1796 IEC	—	7.00	15.00	30.00	60.00
	1797 IEC	—	7.00	15.00	30.00	60.00
	1800 IEC	—	7.00	15.00	30.00	60.00
	1801 IEC	—	7.00	15.00	30.00	60.00
	1802 IEC	—	7.00	15.00	30.00	60.00

7.0160 gm., .833 SILVER, .1880 oz ASW
Obv. leg: FEID, head right.
Rev: Crowned oval arms within crossed branches.

C#	Date	Mintage	Fine	VF	XF	Unc
175	1806 SGH	.027	9.00	18.00	40.00	80.00
	1808 SGH	.277	9.00	18.00	30.00	60.00
	1809 SGH	.303	9.00	18.00	30.00	60.00
	1810 SGH	.295	9.00	18.00	30.00	60.00
	1811 SGH	.278	9.00	18.00	30.00	60.00
	1812 SGH	.080	9.00	18.00	35.00	60.00

Obv: I.G.S. mintmasters initial.

C#	Date	Mintage	Fine	VF	XF	Unc
	1815 IGS	5.740	20.00	50.00	90.00	200.00
	1816 IGS	9,049	20.00	50.00	90.00	200.00
	1817 IGS	8,929	20.00	50.00	90.00	200.00

Obv. leg: FEIN.

C#	Date	Mintage	Fine	VF	XF	Unc
175a	1808	Inc. Ab.	20.00	35.00	60.00	125.00

Obv. leg: ACHTZIG

C#	Date	Mintage	Fine	VF	XF	Unc
175b	1808	Inc. Ab.	20.00	35.00	60.00	125.00

Obv: Uniformed bust left.

C#	Date	Mintage	Fine	VF	XF	Unc
176	1818 IGS	.019	25.00	50.00	75.00	150.00
	1821 IGS	—	25.00	50.00	75.00	150.00

8.2540 gm., .708 SILVER, .1880 oz ASW
Obv: Head right.
Rev: Crowned arched arms within crossed branches.

C#	Date	Mintage	Fine	VF	XF	Unc
207	1827 S	8,700	25.00	50.00	75.00	200.00
	1828 S	.010	25.00	50.00	75.00	200.00
	1829 S	.021	20.00	40.00	50.00	130.00
	1830 S	.097	20.00	40.00	50.00	130.00

8.3520 gm., .667 SILVER, .1790 oz ASW

C#	Date	Mintage	Fine	VF	XF	Unc
230	1852 F	.194	10.00	20.00	30.00	60.00
	1853 F	.403	7.00	15.00	25.00	50.00
	1854 F	1.156	7.00	15.00	25.00	50.00

Death Of King Friedrich August II

C#	Date	Mintage	Fine	VF	XF	Unc
231	1854 F	.029	10.00	25.00	35.00	75.00

Obv: Mintmark below head left.

Rev: Crowned draped rectangular arms.

C#	Date	Mintage	Fine	VF	XF	Unc
262	1856 F	.308	8.00	17.00	25.00	50.00
263	1858 F	.326	7.00	15.00	25.00	50.00
	1859 F	.617	7.00	15.00	25.00	50.00

C#	Date	Mintage	Fine	VF	XF	Unc
264	1860 B	.345	8.00	17.00	25.00	50.00

2/3 THALER

SILVER

C#	Date	Mintage	Fine	VF	XF	Unc
77	1763 FWoF	—	35.00	50.00	100.00	200.00
	1763 EDC	—	35.00	50.00	100.00	200.00
	1763 JFoF	—	35.00	50.00	100.00	200.00

Obv: Bust of Xaver right.
Rev: Capped arms; value below.

C#	Date	Mintage	Fine	VF	XF	Unc
84	1764 EDC	—	25.00	40.00	100.00	200.00
	1765 EDC	—	25.00	40.00	100.00	200.00
	1766 EDC	—	25.00	40.00	100.00	200.00
	1767 EDC	—	25.00	40.00	100.00	200.00
	1768 EDC	—	25.00	40.00	100.00	200.00

(Reichs)

Obv: Young bust. Rev: 2 oval shields.

C#	Date	Mintage	Fine	VF	XF	Unc
117	1765	—	10.00	20.00	37.50	75.00
	1766	—	10.00	20.00	37.50	75.00
	1767	—	10.00	20.00	37.50	75.00
	1768	—	10.00	20.00	37.50	75.00

Obv: Head right.
Rev: Electors cap over dual arms in branches, date and value in exergue.

C#	Date	Mintage	VG	Fine	VF	XF
118	1769 EDC	—	10.00	20.00	37.50	60.00
	1770 EDC	—	10.00	20.00	37.50	60.00
	1771 EDC	—	10.00	20.00	37.50	60.00
	1772 EDC	—	10.00	20.00	37.50	60.00
	1773 EDC	—	10.00	20.00	37.50	60.00
	1774 EDC	—	10.00	20.00	37.50	60.00
	1777 EDC	—	10.00	20.00	37.50	60.00
	1779 EDC	—	10.00	20.00	37.50	60.00
	1780 EDC	—	10.00	20.00	37.50	60.00
	1781 EDC	—	10.00	20.00	37.50	60.00
	1782 EDC	—	10.00	20.00	37.50	60.00
	1783 EDC	—	10.00	20.00	37.50	60.00
	1784 EDC	—	10.00	20.00	37.50	60.00
	1785 EDC	—	10.00	20.00	37.50	60.00
	1786 EDC	—	10.00	20.00	37.50	60.00

C#	Date	Mintage	VG	Fine	VF	XF
118	1787 EDC	—	10.00	20.00	37.50	60.00
	1788 EDC	—	10.00	20.00	37.50	60.00

Vicariat Issue

C#	Date	Mintage	VG	Fine	VF	XF
120	1790 IEC	—	17.00	35.00	55.00	75.00

Obv: Bust right.
Rev: Double headed eagle behind crowned shield.

C#	Date	Mintage	VG	Fine	VF	XF
122	1792 IEC	—	17.00	35.00	55.00	75.00

C#	Date	Mintage	Fine	VF	XF	Unc
121	1791 IEC	—	12.00	30.00	50.00	100.00
	1792 IEC	—	12.00	30.00	50.00	100.00
	1793 IEC	—	12.00	25.00	35.00	75.00
	1794 IEC	—	12.00	25.00	35.00	75.00
	1795 IEC	—	12.00	25.00	35.00	75.00
	1796 IEC	—	12.00	25.00	35.00	75.00
	1797 IEC	—	12.00	25.00	35.00	75.00
	1798 IEC	—	12.00	25.00	35.00	75.00
	1799 IEC	—	12.00	25.00	35.00	75.00
	1800 IEC	—	12.00	25.00	35.00	75.00
	1801 IEC	—	12.00	25.00	35.00	75.00
	1802 IEC	—	12.00	25.00	35.00	75.00
	1805 SGH	—	12.00	25.00	35.00	75.00
	1806 SGH	—	12.00	25.00	35.00	75.00

14.0310 gm., .833 SILVER, .3760 oz ASW

C#	Date	Mintage	Fine	VF	XF	Unc
177	1806 SGH	.084	15.00	30.00	50.00	100.00
	1807 SGH	.075	15.00	30.00	50.00	100.00
	1808 SGH	.171	15.00	30.00	50.00	100.00
	1809 SGH	.165	15.00	30.00	50.00	100.00
	1810 SGH	.165	15.00	30.00	50.00	100.00
	1811 SGH	.161	15.00	30.00	50.00	100.00
	1812 SGH	.086	15.00	30.00	50.00	100.00
	1813 IGS	—	15.00	30.00	50.00	150.00
	1814 IGS	.025	15.00	30.00	50.00	150.00
	1815 IGS	.048	15.00	30.00	50.00	150.00

C#	Date	Mintage	Fine	VF	XF	Unc
177	1816 IGS	.055	15.00	30.00	50.00	150.00
	1817 IGS	.060	15.00	30.00	50.00	150.00

Obv: Uniformed bust left.

C#	Date	Mintage	Fine	VF	XF	Unc
178a	1822 IGS	.023	50.00	100.00	200.00	350.00

Obv: Head right.
Rev: Crowned arched arms within branches.

C#	Date	Mintage	Fine	VF	XF	Unc
208	1827 S	.011	30.00	65.00	150.00	250.00
	1828 S	.012	30.00	65.00	150.00	250.00

Obv: Different head right.

C#	Date	Mintage	Fine	VF	XF	Unc
208a	1829 S	.013	30.00	65.00	150.00	250.00

EIN (1) THALER

(Convention)

SILVER

C#	Date	Mintage	Fine	VF	XF	Unc
78	1763 FWoF	—	50.00	100.00	200.00	400.00
	1763 EDC	—	50.00	100.00	200.00	400.00
	1763 JFoF	—	50.00	100.00	200.00	400.00

C#	Date	Mintage	Fine	VF	XF	Unc
85	1764 EDC	—	50.00	100.00	200.00	400.00
	1765 EDC	—	50.00	100.00	200.00	400.00
	1766 EDC	—	50.00	100.00	200.00	400.00
	1767 EDC	—	50.00	100.00	200.00	400.00
	1768 EDC	—	50.00	100.00	200.00	400.00

Freiberg Mining Academy Commemorative

C#	Date	Mintage	Fine	VF	XF	Unc
86	1765	—	500.00	1000.	1500.	3000.

(Prize)

C#	Date	Mintage	Fine	VF	XF	Unc
130	1766	—	500.00	1000.	1500.	3000.

(Convention)

C#	Date	Mintage	Fine	VF	XF	Unc
131	1769 EDC	—	40.00	75.00	125.00	250.00
	1770 EDC	—	40.00	75.00	125.00	250.00
	1771 EDC	—	40.00	75.00	125.00	250.00
	1772 EDC	—	40.00	75.00	125.00	250.00
	1773 EDC	—	40.00	75.00	125.00	250.00
	1774 EDC	—	40.00	75.00	125.00	250.00
	1775 EDC	—	40.00	75.00	125.00	250.00
	1776 EDC	—	40.00	75.00	125.00	250.00
	1777 EDC	—	40.00	75.00	125.00	250.00
	1778 EDC	—	40.00	75.00	125.00	250.00
	1779 IEC	—	40.00	75.00	125.00	250.00
	1780 IEC	—	40.00	75.00	125.00	250.00
	1781 IEC	—	40.00	75.00	125.00	250.00
	1782 IEC	—	40.00	75.00	125.00	250.00
	1783 IEC	—	40.00	75.00	125.00	250.00
	1784 IEC	—	40.00	75.00	125.00	250.00
	1785 IEC	—	40.00	75.00	125.00	250.00
	1786 IEC	—	40.00	75.00	125.00	250.00
	1787 IEC	—	40.00	75.00	125.00	250.00
	1788 IEC	—	40.00	75.00	125.00	250.00
	1789 IEC	—	40.00	75.00	125.00	250.00
	1790 IEC	—	40.00	75.00	125.00	250.00

NOTE: Varieties exist.

(Mining)

C#	Date	Mintage	Fine	VF	XF	Unc
132	1769 EDC	—	40.00	75.00	125.00	250.00
	1770 EDC	—	40.00	75.00	125.00	250.00
	1771 EDC	—	40.00	75.00	125.00	250.00
	1772 EDC	—	40.00	75.00	125.00	250.00
	1773 EDC	—	40.00	75.00	125.00	250.00
	1774 EDC	—	40.00	75.00	125.00	250.00
	1775 EDC	—	40.00	75.00	125.00	250.00
	1776 EDC	—	40.00	75.00	125.00	250.00
	1777 EDC	—	40.00	75.00	125.00	250.00
	1778 EDC	—	40.00	75.00	125.00	250.00
	1779 IEC	—	40.00	75.00	125.00	250.00
	1780 IEC	—	40.00	75.00	125.00	250.00
	1781 IEC	—	40.00	75.00	125.00	250.00
	1782 IEC	—	40.00	75.00	125.00	250.00
	1783 IEC	—	40.00	75.00	125.00	250.00
	1784 IEC	—	40.00	75.00	125.00	250.00
	1785 IEC	—	40.00	75.00	125.00	250.00
	1786 IEC	—	40.00	75.00	125.00	250.00
	1787 IEC	—	40.00	75.00	125.00	250.00
	1788 IEC	—	40.00	75.00	125.00	250.00
	1789 IEC	—	40.00	75.00	125.00	250.00
	1790 IEC	—	40.00	75.00	125.00	250.00

(Convention)

Obv: Similar to C#132.

C#	Date	Mintage	Fine	VF	XF	Unc
133	1780	—	300.00	600.00	1200.	2400.

Vicariat Issue

C#	Date	Mintage	Fine	VF	XF	Unc
134	1790	—	50.00	100.00	200.00	400.00

(Mining)

C#	Date	Mintage	Fine	VF	XF	Unc
136	1791 IEC	—	50.00	100.00	200.00	400.00
	1792 IEC	—	50.00	100.00	200.00	400.00
	1793 IEC	—	50.00	100.00	200.00	400.00
	1794 IEC	—	50.00	100.00	200.00	400.00
	1795 IEC	—	50.00	100.00	200.00	400.00
	1796 IEC	—	50.00	100.00	200.00	400.00
	1797 IEC	—	50.00	100.00	200.00	400.00
136	1798 IEC	—	50.00	100.00	200.00	400.00
	1799 IEC	—	50.00	100.00	200.00	400.00
	1800 IEC	—	50.00	100.00	200.00	400.00
	1801 IEC	—	50.00	100.00	200.00	400.00
	1802 IEC	—	50.00	100.00	200.00	400.00
	1803 IEC	—	50.00	100.00	200.00	400.00
	1804 IEC	—	50.00	100.00	200.00	400.00
	1804 SGH	—	50.00	100.00	200.00	400.00
	1805 SGH	—	50.00	100.00	200.00	400.00
	1806 SGH	—	50.00	100.00	200.00	400.00

(Convention)

C#	Date	Mintage	Fine	VF	XF	Unc
135	1791 IEC	—	30.00	40.00	80.00	160.00
	1792 IEC	—	30.00	40.00	80.00	160.00
	1793 IEC	—	30.00	40.00	80.00	160.00
	1794 IEC	—	30.00	40.00	80.00	160.00
	1795 IEC	—	30.00	40.00	80.00	160.00
	1796 IEC	—	30.00	40.00	80.00	160.00
	1797 IEC	—	30.00	40.00	80.00	160.00
	1798 IEC	—	30.00	40.00	80.00	160.00
	1799 IEC	—	30.00	40.00	80.00	160.00
	1800 IEC	—	30.00	40.00	80.00	160.00
	1801 IEC	—	30.00	40.00	80.00	160.00
	1802 IEC	—	30.00	40.00	80.00	160.00
	1803 IEC	—	30.00	40.00	80.00	160.00
	1804 IEC	—	30.00	40.00	80.00	160.00
	1804 SGH	—	30.00	40.00	80.00	160.00
	1805 SGH	—	30.00	40.00	80.00	160.00
	1806 SGH	—	30.00	40.00	80.00	160.00

Vicariat Issue
Obv: Armored bust right; date below.
Rev: Imperial eagle with capped arms on breast; I.E.C. below.

C#	Date	Mintage	Fine	VF	XF	Unc
137	1792 IEC	—	50.00	100.00	200.00	400.00

28.0630 gm., .833 SILVER, .7520 oz ASW
Obv: Large bust

C#	Date	Mintage	Fine	VF	XF	Unc
180	1806 SGH	.663	200.00	400.00	800.00	1300.

Obv: Small bust. Rev: Similar to C#180.

C#	Date	Mintage	Fine	VF	XF	Unc
180b	1807SGH	.461	40.00	75.00	150.00	300.00
	1808SGH	1.534	40.00	75.00	150.00	300.00
	1809SGH	.563	40.00	75.00	150.00	300.00
	1810SGH	.368	40.00	75.00	150.00	300.00
	1811SGH	.395	40.00	75.00	150.00	300.00
	1812SGH	.134	40.00	75.00	150.00	300.00
	1813IGS	.773	40.00	75.00	150.00	300.00
	1813SGH	I.A.	65.00	100.00	200.00	350.00
	1815IGS	.510	40.00	75.00	150.00	300.00
	1816IGS	—	40.00	75.00	150.00	300.00
	1817IGS	—	225.00	350.00	700.00	1500.

Edge inscription: GOTT SEGNE SACHSEN

C#	Date	Mintage	Fine	VF	XF	Unc
180a	1816 IGS	—	55.00	90.00	150.00	275.00

(Mining)

Obv: Similar to C#180b.

C#	Date	Mintage	Fine	VF	XF	Unc
181	1807SGH	—	40.00	100.00	200.00	400.00
	1808SGH	—	40.00	100.00	200.00	400.00
	1809SGH	—	40.00	100.00	200.00	400.00
	1810SGH	—	40.00	100.00	200.00	400.00
	1811SGH	—	40.00	100.00	200.00	400.00
	1812SGH	—	40.00	100.00	200.00	400.00
	1813SGH	—	40.00	100.00	200.00	400.00
	1813 IGS	—	40.00	100.00	200.00	400.00
	1815 IGS	—	40.00	100.00	200.00	400.00
	1816 IGS	—	40.00	100.00	200.00	400.00

Legend right to left.

C#	Date	Mintage	Fine	VF	XF	Unc
181a	1811SGH	—	60.00	150.00	300.00	600.00
	1813SGH	—	60.00	150.00	300.00	600.00
	1815SGH	—	60.00	150.00	300.00	600.00
	1816SGH	—	60.00	150.00	300.00	600.00
	1811IGS	—	40.00	85.00	300.00	600.00
	1813IGS	—	40.00	85.00	300.00	600.00
	1815IGS	—	40.00	85.00	300.00	600.00
	1816IGS	—	30.00	55.00	300.00	600.00

(Convention)

Mining Academy at Freiberg

C#	Date	Mintage	Fine	VF	XF	Unc
182	1815	—	800.00	1400.	2500.	4000.

Rev: Similar to C#184.

C#	Date	Mintage	Fine	VF	XF	Unc
183	1816IGS	—	400.00	800.00	1600.	3000.

C#	Date	Mintage	Fine	VF	XF	Unc
184	1817IGS	—	40.00	75.00	150.00	300.00
	1818IGS	—	40.00	75.00	150.00	300.00
	1819IGS	—	40.00	75.00	150.00	300.00
	1820IGS	—	40.00	75.00	150.00	300.00
	1821IGS	—	40.00	75.00	150.00	300.00

(Mining)

Rev. leg: DER SEGEN.

C#	Date	Mintage	Fine	VF	XF	Unc
185	1817IGS	—	50.00	100.00	200.00	400.00
	1818IGS	—	50.00	100.00	200.00	400.00
	1819IGS	—	50.00	100.00	200.00	400.00
	1820IGS	—	50.00	100.00	200.00	400.00
	1821IGS	—	50.00	100.00	200.00	400.00

(Convention)

Obv: Different bust. Rev. leg: Without DER SEGEN

C#	Date	Mintage	Fine	VF	XF	Unc
186	1822 IGS	—	40.00	75.00	150.00	300.00
	1823 IGS	.512	40.00	75.00	150.00	300.00

(Mining)

Obv. leg: With DER SEGEN added.

C#	Date	Mintage	Fine	VF	XF	Unc
187	1822IGS	—	45.00	100.00	200.00	400.00
	1823IGS	—	45.00	100.00	200.00	400.00

(Convention)

C#	Date	Mintage	Fine	VF	XF	Unc
188	1824 S	.546	35.00	75.00	165.00	325.00
	1825 S	.546	35.00	75.00	165.00	325.00
	1826 S	.546	35.00	75.00	165.00	325.00
	1827 S	.423	35.00	75.00	165.00	325.00

(Mining)

Rev: Arms dividing date.

C#	Date	Mintage	Fine	VF	XF	Unc
189	1824 S	—	40.00	100.00	250.00	400.00
	1825 S	—	40.00	100.00	250.00	400.00
	1826 S	—	40.00	100.00	250.00	400.00
	1827 S	.018	40.00	100.00	250.00	400.00

Rev: Circle between arms and outer legends.

C#	Date	Mintage	Fine	VF	XF	Unc
189a	1824GS	—	150.00	375.00	750.00	1500.

(Convention)

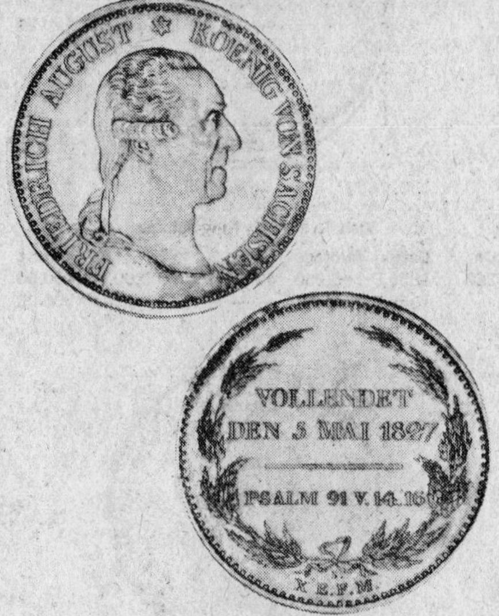

Death Of King Friedrich August

C#	Date	Mintage	Fine	VF	XF	Unc
190	1827 S	.014	45.00	100.00	200.00	400.00

(Mining)

Edge inscription: SEGEN DES BERGBAUS

C#	Date	Mintage	Fine	VF	XF	Unc
190a	1827 S	4,357	100.00	200.00	400.00	800.00

(Convention)

C#	Date	Mintage	Fine	VF	XF	Unc
209	1827 S	.107	35.00	75.00	150.00	300.00
	1828 S	.609	35.00	75.00	150.00	300.00

Rev: Similar to C#209.

C#	Date	Mintage	Fine	VF	XF	Unc
209a	1829 S	.534	30.00	60.00	125.00	250.00
	1830 S	.620	30.00	60.00	125.00	250.00
	1831 S	.697	30.00	60.00	125.00	250.00
	1832 S	.979	30.00	60.00	125.00	250.00
	1833 G	.190	30.00	60.00	125.00	250.00
	1834 G	.486	30.00	60.00	125.00	250.00
	1835 G	.458	30.00	60.00	125.00	250.00
	1836 G	.585	30.00	60.00	125.00	250.00

(Mining)

Rev. leg: SEGEN DES BERGBAUS.

C#	Date	Mintage	Fine	VF	XF	Unc
210	1828 S	.018	75.00	200.00	400.00	800.00

Obv: Older head.

C#	Date	Mintage	Fine	VF	XF	Unc
210a	1829 S	.019	60.00	150.00	300.00	600.00
	1830 S	.019	60.00	150.00	300.00	600.00
	1831 S	.019	60.00	150.00	300.00	600.00
	1832 S	.013	60.00	150.00	300.00	600.00
	1833 G	3,000	75.00	175.00	350.00	700.00
	1834 G	5,500	75.00	175.00	350.00	700.00
	1835 G	4,986	75.00	175.00	350.00	700.00
	1836 G	4,836	75.00	175.00	350.00	700.00

(Convention)

Mining Academy At Freiberg
Obv: Similar to C#210.

C#	Date	Mintage	Fine	VF	XF	Unc
211	1829	200 pcs.	800.00	1600.	2650.	4000.

Forstin University
Rev. leg: FORSTINSTITUT, DEM FLEISSE UND GESITTETEN BETRAGEN within wreath.

C#	Date	Mintage	Fine	VF	XF	Unc
212	1830	25 pcs.	2100.	3250.	5250.	8250.

Agriculture Educational Establishment At Tharant
Rev: LANDWIRTSCHAFTL

C#	Date	Mintage	Fine	VF	XF	Unc
213	1830	25 pcs.	2100.	3250.	5250.	8250.

New Constitution

C#	Date	Mintage	Fine	VF	XF	Unc
214	1831 S	.014	60.00	150.00	300.00	500.00

Death of King Anton

C#	Date	Mintage	Fine	VF	XF	Unc
215	1836 G	.012	60.00	150.00	300.00	500.00

(Mining)

Edge inscription: SEGEN DES BERGBAUS

C#	Date	Mintage	Fine	VF	XF	Unc
215a	1836 G	2,500	150.00	400.00	800.00	1200.

(Convention)

Obv. legend divided.

C#	Date	Mintage	Fine	VF	XF	Unc
232	1836 G	.034	100.00	250.00	500.00	1000.
	1837 G	.031	100.00	250.00	500.00	1000.

Obv. legend continuous.

C#	Date	Mintage	Fine	VF	XF	Unc
232a	1837 G	.094	40.00	100.00	200.00	400.00
	1838 G	.139	40.00	100.00	200.00	400.00

(Mining)

Obv. leg: KOENIG. Rev. leg: SEGEN DES, etc.

C#	Date	Mintage	Fine	VF	XF	Unc
233	1836 G	3,262	600.00	1250.	2500.	4000.
	1837 G	5,770	150.00	250.00	500.00	1000.
	1838 G	.036	80.00	200.00	400.00	800.00

(Convention)

22.2720 gm., .750 SILVER, .5371 oz ASW
Visit To Dresden Mint
Lettered edge

C#	Date	Mintage	Fine	VF	XF	Unc
234	1839 G	—	1000.	1650.	2500.	4000.

Plain edge

C#	Date	Mintage	Fine	VF	XF	Unc
234a	1839	—	2100.	3000.	4000.	6000.

C#	Date	Mintage	Fine	VF	XF	Unc
235	1839 G	.643	30.00	50.00	100.00	200.00
	1840 G	1.406	30.00	50.00	100.00	200.00
	1841 G	2.505	30.00	50.00	100.00	200.00
	1842 G	.974	30.00	50.00	100.00	200.00
	1843 G	1.251	30.00	50.00	100.00	200.00
	1844 G	1.026	30.00	50.00	100.00	200.00

Obv: With F below head.

C#	Date	Mintage	Fine	VF	XF	Unc
235a	1845 F	.973	30.00	50.00	100.00	200.00
	1846 F	.860	30.00	50.00	100.00	200.00
	1847 F	.677	30.00	50.00	100.00	200.00
	1848 F	1.592	30.00	50.00	100.00	200.00
	1849 F	1.368	30.00	50.00	100.00	200.00

C#	Date	Mintage	Fine	VF	XF	Unc
235b	1850 F	1.074	30.00	45.00	100.00	200.00
	1851 F	1.351	30.00	45.00	100.00	200.00
	1852 F	1.105	30.00	45.00	100.00	200.00
	1853 F	1.171	30.00	45.00	100.00	200.00
	1854 F	1.075	30.00	45.00	100.00	200.00

(Mining)

Obv: With G below head.

C#	Date	Mintage	Fine	VF	XF	Unc
236	1841 G	.011	50.00	125.00	250.00	500.00
	1842 G	.017	50.00	125.00	250.00	500.00
	1843 G	.017	50.00	125.00	250.00	500.00
	1844 G	.011	50.00	125.00	250.00	500.00

Obv: With F below head.

C#	Date	Mintage	Fine	VF	XF	Unc
236b	1845 F	.019	50.00	125.00	250.00	500.00
	1846 F	.022	50.00	125.00	250.00	500.00
	1847 F	.040	50.00	125.00	250.00	500.00
	1848 F	.021	50.00	125.00	250.00	500.00
	1849 F	.038	50.00	125.00	250.00	500.00
236a	1850 F	.034	45.00	100.00	225.00	450.00
	1851 F	.033	45.00	100.00	225.00	450.00
	1852 F	.047	45.00	100.00	225.00	450.00
	1853 F	.055	45.00	100.00	225.00	450.00
	1854 F	.037	45.00	100.00	225.00	450.00

Death of King Friedrich August II

C#	Date	Mintage	Fine	VF	XF	Unc
237	1854 F	.016	35.00	70.00	140.00	200.00

(Mining)

Edge: SEGEN DES BERGBAUS and crossed hammers.

C#	Date	Mintage	Fine	VF	XF	Unc
237a	1854 F	8,829	40.00	100.00	200.00	300.00

(Convention)

Obv: Similar to C#267.

C#	Date	Mintage	Fine	VF	XF	Unc
265	1854 F	.525	30.00	70.00	150.00	300.00

(Mining)

Rev: Similar to C#265.

C#	Date	Mintage	Fine	VF	XF	Unc
266	1854 F	.027	60.00	125.00	250.00	500.00

(Convention)

Visit To Mint By King Johann

C#	Date	Mintage	Fine	VF	XF	Unc
267	1855 F	5,250	40.00	100.00	200.00	400.00
	1855 F	—	—	—	Proof	500.00

Rev: Similar to C#269

C#	Date	Mintage	Fine	VF	XF	Unc
268	1855 F	.863	30.00	50.00	125.00	250.00
	1856 F	1.089	30.00	50.00	125.00	250.00

(Mining)

C#	Date	Mintage	Fine	VF	XF	Unc
269	1855F	.056	50.00	100.00	225.00	450.00
	1856F	.056	50.00	100.00	225.00	450.00

(Vereins)

18.5200 gm., .900 SILVER, .5360 oz ASW
Obv: Similar to C#269

C#	Date	Mintage	Fine	VF	XF	Unc
270	1857 F	.969	30.00	40.00	100.00	200.00
	1858 F	.200	30.00	40.00	100.00	200.00
	1859 F	2.490	30.00	40.00	100.00	200.00

(Mining)

Obv: Similar to C#269.

C#	Date	Mintage	Fine	VF	XF	Unc
271	1857 F	.035	40.00	100.00	200.00	400.00
	1858 F	.034	40.00	100.00	200.00	400.00

C#	Date	Mintage	Fine	VF	XF	Unc
272	1858 F	.061	30.00	60.00	125.00	250.00
	1859 F	.094	30.00	60.00	125.00	250.00
	1860 B	.298	30.00	60.00	125.00	250.00
	1861 B large letters					
		.016	35.00	75.00	130.00	275.00
	1861 B small letters					
		.130	30.00	60.00	125.00	250.00

C#	Date	Mintage	Fine	VF	XF	Unc
272a	1861 B	.130	30.00	50.00	100.00	200.00
	1862 B	.145	30.00	50.00	100.00	200.00
	1863 B	.135	30.00	50.00	100.00	200.00
	1864 B	.120	30.00	50.00	100.00	200.00
	1865 B	.221	30.00	50.00	100.00	200.00
	1866 B	.185	30.00	50.00	100.00	200.00
	1867 B	.175	30.00	50.00	100.00	200.00

C#	Date	Mintage	Fine	VF	XF	Unc
272b	1868 B	.181	30.00	50.00	100.00	200.00
	1869 B	.190	30.00	50.00	100.00	200.00
	1870 B	.236	30.00	50.00	100.00	200.00
	1871 B	.203	30.00	50.00	100.00	200.00

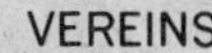

VEREINS

C#	Date	Mintage	Fine	VF	XF	Unc
273	1860 B	2.669	20.00	40.00	100.00	200.00
	1861 B	1.409	20.00	40.00	100.00	200.00

Obv: Similar to C#273

C#	Date	Mintage	Fine	VF	XF	Unc
273a	1861 B	1.070	20.00	35.00	70.00	150.00
	1862 B	2.134	20.00	35.00	70.00	150.00
	1863 B	1.471	20.00	35.00	70.00	150.00
	1864 B	1.904	20.00	35.00	70.00	150.00
	1865 B	1.335	20.00	35.00	70.00	150.00
	1866 B	1.181	20.00	35.00	70.00	150.00
	1867 B	2.020	20.00	35.00	70.00	150.00
	1869 B	1.622	20.00	35.00	70.00	150.00
	1870 B	1.693	20.00	35.00	70.00	150.00
	1871 B	1.687	20.00	35.00	70.00	150.00

Victory Over France Commemorative

C#	Date	Mintage	Fine	VF	XF	Unc
274	1871 B	.045	25.00	50.00	100.00	200.00

2 THALER

(= 3-1/2 Gulden)

SILVER

C#	Date	Mintage	Fine	VF	XF	Unc
140	1780	—	500.00	1000.	1500.	3000.

Obv: Armored bust right; F.H. KRUGER F. below.

C#	Date	Mintage	Fine	VF	XF	Unc
140a	1780	—	500.00	1000.	1500.	3000.

37.1200 gm., .900 SILVER, 1.0742 oz ASW
Obv: with G below head

C#	Date	Mintage	Fine	VF	XF	Unc
238	1839 G	.020	60.00	100.00	200.00	400.00
	1840 G	.068	60.00	100.00	200.00	400.00
	1841 G	.039	60.00	100.00	200.00	400.00
	1842 G	.071	60.00	100.00	200.00	400.00
	1843 G	.059	60.00	100.00	200.00	400.00

Similar to C#238 with F below head.

C#	Date	Mintage	Fine	VF	XF	Unc
238a	1847 F	.147	60.00	100.00	200.00	400.00
	1848 F	.078	60.00	100.00	200.00	400.00
	1849 F	.015	60.00	100.00	200.00	400.00
	1850 F	.113	60.00	100.00	200.00	400.00
	1851 F	.246	60.00	100.00	200.00	400.00
	1852 F	.209	60.00	100.00	200.00	400.00
	1853 F	.303	60.00	100.00	200.00	400.00
	1854 F	.886	50.00	100.00	200.00	400.00

Mining Academy At Freiberg
Obv: Similar to C#238.

C#	Date	Mintage	Fine	VF	XF	Unc
239	1841 G	200 pcs.	1000.	1650.	2650.	4000.

Forest and Agriculture Education Establishment
Obv: Similar to C#238.

C#	Date	Mintage	Fine	VF	XF	Unc
240	1847 F	50 pcs.	3000.	4200.	5500.	8000.

Death Of King Friedrich August II

C#	Date	Mintage	Fine	VF	XF	Unc
241	1854 F	6,148	100.00	200.00	400.00	750.00
	1854 F	—	—	—	Proof	900.00

Rev: Similar to C#238.

C#	Date	Mintage	Fine	VF	XF	Unc
275	1855 F	.462	40.00	100.00	200.00	400.00
	1856 F	.091	50.00	100.00	200.00	400.00

Mining Academy At Freiberg
Obv: Similar to C#275 with F below head.

C#	Date	Mintage	Fine	VF	XF	Unc
276	1857 F	100 pcs.	1200.	1800.	3000.	4000.

Obv: With B below head

C#	Date	Mintage	Fine	VF	XF	Unc
276a	1857 B	206 pcs.	900.00	1650.	2650.	4000.

37.0370 gm., .900 SILVER, 1.0718 oz ASW
Obv: Similar to C#275.

C#	Date	Mintage	Fine	VF	XF	Unc
277	1857 F	.351	40.00	100.00	200.00	400.00
	1858 F	.454	40.00	100.00	200.00	400.00
	1859 F	.323	40.00	100.00	200.00	400.00

Rev. value: VEREINSTHAELR

C#	Date	Mintage	Fine	VF	XF	Unc
277a	1858	Inc. Ab.	40.00	100.00	200.00	400.00

Obv: Similar to C#275.

C#	Date	Mintage	Fine	VF	XF	Unc
278	1861 B	.730	50.00	125.00	250.00	500.00

Golden Wedding Anniversary

C#	Date	Mintage	Fine	VF	XF	Unc
279	1872 B	049	50.00	100.00	200.00	400.00

Without legend on rim

C#	Date	Mintage	Fine	VF	XF	Unc
279a	1872 B	Inc. Ab.	125.00	275.00	375.00	525.00

2-1/2 THALER

3.3410 gm., .902 GOLD, .0970 oz AGW

C#	Date	Mintage	Fine	VF	XF	Unc
245	1842 G	560 pcs.	500.00	875.00	1100.	1350.
	1845 F	420 pcs.	500.00	925.00	1150.	1450.
	1848 F	82 pcs.	600.00	1000.	1400.	2000.
	1854 F	308 pcs.	500.00	975.00	1225.	1525.

5 THALER

.900 GOLD

C#	Date	Mintage	VG	Fine	VF	XF
148	1777 EDC	—	500.00	900.00	1250.	2000.
	1779 IEC	—	500.00	900.00	1250.	2000.
	1781 IEC	—	500.00	900.00	1250.	2000.
	1782 IEC	—	500.00	900.00	1250.	2000.
	1785 IEC	—	500.00	900.00	1250.	2000.

C#	Date	Mintage	Fine	VF	XF	Unc
150	1791IEC	—	200.00	400.00	650.00	1000.
	1792IEC	—	200.00	400.00	650.00	1000.
	1794IEC	—	200.00	400.00	650.00	1000.
	1795IEC	—	200.00	400.00	650.00	1000.
	1797IEC	—	200.00	400.00	650.00	1000.
	1798IEC	—	200.00	400.00	650.00	1000.
	1799IEC	—	200.00	400.00	650.00	1000.
	1800IEC	—	200.00	400.00	650.00	1000.
	1801IEC	—	200.00	400.00	650.00	1000.
150a	1806 SGH	—	200.00	400.00	675.00	1125.

6.6820 gm., .902 GOLD, .1939 oz AGW
Obv: Head right.
Rev: Crowned oval arms within crossed branches.

C#	Date	Mintage	Fine	VF	XF	Unc
195	1806 SGH	.044	300.00	575.00	700.00	875.00
	1807 SGH	.152	300.00	500.00	650.00	800.00
	1808 SGH	.135	300.00	500.00	650.00	800.00
	1809 SGH	.054	300.00	575.00	700.00	875.00
	1810 SGH	.235	300.00	500.00	650.00	800.00
	1812 SGH	.098	300.00	500.00	650.00	800.00
	1813 SGH	.118	300.00	500.00	650.00	800.00

Rev: With IGS below branches.

C#	Date	Mintage	Fine	VF	XF	Unc
195a	1815 IGS	.020	400.00	625.00	775.00	950.00
	1816 IGS	—	400.00	625.00	775.00	950.00
	1817 IGS	—	400.00	625.00	775.00	950.00

Obv: Uniformed bust left

C#	Date	Mintage	Fine	VF	XF	Unc
196	1818 IGS	—	1000.	1800.	2250.	2800.

C#	Date	Mintage	Fine	VF	XF	Unc
197	1825 S	.060	600.00	1025.	1275.	1600.
	1826 S	2,590	600.00	1100.	1350.	1700.
	1827 S	700 pcs.	1000.	1675.	2075.	2600.

C#	Date	Mintage	Fine	VF	XF	Unc
218	1827 S	405 pcs.	1000.	1800.	2250.	2800.
	1828 S	855 pcs.	1000.	1675.	2075.	3250.

Obv: Older head

C#	Date	Mintage	Fine	VF	XF	Unc
218a	1829 S	385 pcs.	800.00	1275.	1600.	2000.
	1830 S	2,800	600.00	1025.	1275.	1600.
	1831 S	245 pcs.	800.00	1275.	1600.	2000.
	1832 S	175 pcs.	800.00	1375.	1725.	2150.
	1834 G	490 pcs.	800.00	1275.	1600.	2000.
	1835 G	380 pcs.	800.00	1275.	1600.	2000.
	1836 G	455 pcs.	800.00	1275.	1600.	2000.

C#	Date	Mintage	Fine	VF	XF	Unc
243	1837 G	490 pcs.	800.00	1275.	1600.	2000.
	1838 G	175 pcs.	1000.	1525.	1925.	2400.
	1839 G	210 pcs.	1000.	1525.	1925.	2400.

C#	Date	Mintage	Fine	VF	XF	Unc
246	1842 G	4,455	450.00	725.00	905.00	1120.
	1845 F	1,483	500.00	925.00	1150.	1450.
	1848 F	1,964	500.00	875.00	1100.	1350.
	1849 F	1,110	500.00	975.00	1225.	1525.
	1853 F	511 pcs.	700.00	1125.	1400.	1750.
	1854 F	4,570	450.00	725.00	900.00	1125.

10 THALER

13.3640 gm., .902 GOLD, .3880 oz AGW

C#	Date	Mintage	VG	Fine	VF	XF
152	1779 IDC	—	500.00	1150.	1650.	2250.

C#	Date	Mintage	VG	Fine	VF	XF
154	1779 IEC	—	500.00	1150.	1650.	2250.
	1780 IEC	—	500.00	1150.	1650.	2250.
	1782 IEC	—	500.00	1150.	1650.	2250.
	1783 IEC	—	500.00	1150.	1650.	2250.
	1784 IEC	—	500.00	1150.	1650.	2250.
	1785 IEC	—	500.00	1150.	1650.	2250.
	1786 IEC	—	500.00	1150.	1650.	2250.
	1787 IEC	—	500.00	1150.	1650.	2250.
	1790 IEC	—	500.00	1150.	1650.	2250.

C#	Date	Mintage	Fine	VF	XF	Unc
156	1791IEC	—	500.00	875.00	1450.	2400.
	1794IEC	—	500.00	875.00	1450.	2400.
	1795IEC	—	500.00	875.00	1450.	2400.
	1796IEC	—	500.00	875.00	1450.	2400.
	1797IEC	—	500.00	875.00	1450.	2400.
	1798IEC	—	500.00	875.00	1450.	2400.
	1799IEC	—	500.00	875.00	1450.	2400.
	1800IEC	—	500.00	875.00	1450.	2400.
	1801IEC	—	500.00	875.00	1450.	2400.
	1802IEC	—	500.00	875.00	1450.	2400.
	1803IEC	—	500.00	875.00	1450.	2400.
	1804IEC	—	500.00	875.00	1450.	2400.
156a	1804SGH	—	250.00	425.00	725.00	1200.
	1806SGH	—	250.00	425.00	725.00	1200.

Rev: S.G.H. below branches.

C#	Date	Mintage	Fine	VF	XF	Unc
198	1806SGH	—	500.00	900.00	1150.	1400.
	1807 SGH	—	450.00	825.00	1000.	1300.
	1808 SGH	—	450.00	825.00	1000.	1300.
	1809 SGH	—	450.00	825.00	1000.	1300.
	1810 SGH	—	450.00	825.00	1000.	1300.
	1811 SGH	—	450.00	825.00	1000.	1300.
	1812 SGH	—	450.00	825.00	1000.	1300.
	1813 SGH	—	—	—	—	—

Rev: I.G.S. below branches.

C#	Date	Mintage	Fine	VF	XF	Unc
198a	1813 IGS	—	500.00	900.00	1125.	1400.
	1816 IGS	—	500.00	900.00	1125.	1400.
	1817 IGS	—	500.00	900.00	1125.	1400.

C#	Date	Mintage	Fine	VF	XF	Unc
199	1818 IGS	—	1200.	2300.	2900.	3600.

C#	Date	Mintage	Fine	VF	XF	Unc
200	1825 S	—	600.00	1100.	1350.	1700.
	1826 S	—	600.00	1100.	1350.	1700.
	1827 S	9,520	600.00	1100.	1350.	1700.

Obv: Head right.
Rev: Crowned arched arms within crossed branches.

C#	Date	Mintage	Fine	VF	XF	Unc
219	1827 S	875 Pcs.	1000.	1800.	2250.	2800.
	1828 S	5,530	600.00	1100.	1350.	1700.

Obv: Older head

C#	Date	Mintage	Fine	VF	XF	Unc
219a	1829 S	3,010	500.00	925.00	1150.	1450.
	1830 S	.018	450.00	875.00	1100.	1350.
	1831 S	3,255	500.00	925.00	1150.	1450.
	1832 S	2,625	500.00	1000.	1250.	1500.
	1834 G	3,080	500.00	925.00	1150.	1450.
	1835 G	2,715	500.00	925.00	1150.	1450.
	1836 G	4,655	500.00	925.00	1150.	1450.

Obv: Different head.
Rev: Crowned rectangular arms within crossed branches.

C#	Date	Mintage	Fine	VF	XF	Unc
244	1836 G	1,110	600.00	1150.	1450.	1800.
	1837 G	2,400	600.00	1000.	1300.	1600.
	1838 G	1,750	600.00	1000.	1300.	1600.
	1839 G	1,855	600.00	1000.	1300.	1600.

Obv: Smaller head. Rev: Crowned draped arms.

C#	Date	Mintage	Fine	VF	XF	Unc
247	1845 F	2,100	600.00	1000.	1300.	1600.
	1848 F	4,761	500.00	1000.	1250.	1500.
	1849 F	1,928	600.00	1000.	1300.	1600.
	1853 F	1,038	600.00	1150.	1400.	1750.
	1854 F	1,620	600.00	1000.	1300.	1600.

1/2 KRONE

5.5560 gm., .900 GOLD, .1608 oz AGW
Obv: F below head.

C#	Date	Mintage	Fine	VF	XF	Unc
280	1857 F	4,831	500.00	1000.	1225.	1525.
	1858 F	2,455	550.00	1100.	1350.	2000.

Obv: B below head

C#	Date	Mintage	Fine	VF	XF	Unc
280a	1862 B	2,177	550.00	1100.	1350.	1700.
	1866 B	1,559	600.00	1200.	1500.	1850.
	1868 B	1,516	600.00	1200.	1500.	1850.
	1870 B	1,740	600.00	1200.	1500.	1850.

KRONE

11.1110 gm., .900 GOLD, .3215 oz AGW
Obv: F below head.

C#	Date	Mintage	Fine	VF	XF	Unc
281	1857 F	3,580	550.00	1000.	1300.	1600.
	1858 F	4,610	550.00	1000.	1300.	1600.
	1859 F	9,040	500.00	1000.	1250.	1500.

Obv: B below head

C#	Date	Mintage	Fine	VF	XF	Unc
	1860 B	5,067	600.00	1000.	1300.	1600.
	1861 B	3,908	600.00	1000.	1300.	1600.
	1862 B	3,229	600.00	1000.	1300.	1600.
	1863 B	3,538	600.00	1000.	1300.	1600.
	1865 B	4,371	600.00	1000.	1300.	1600.
	1867 B	2,155	600.00	1100.	1350.	1700.
	1868 B	5,262	600.00	1000.	1300.	1600.
	1870 B	2,700	600.00	1100.	1350.	1700.
	1871 B	2,140	600.00	1100.	1350.	1700.

TRADE COINS

DUCAT

3.5000 gm., .986 GOLD, .1109 oz AGW

C#	Date	Mintage	Fine	VF	XF	Unc
79	1763 FWoF	—	400.00	700.00	950.00	1350.

C#	Date	Mintage	Fine	VF	XF	Unc
87	1766 EDC	—	375.00	600.00	850.00	1250.
	1767 EDC	—	375.00	600.00	850.00	1250.
	1768 EDC	—	375.00	600.00	850.00	1250.

C#	Date	Mintage	Fine	VF	XF	Unc
142	1764 EDC	—	650.00	950.00	1250.	2000.
	1765 EDC	—	650.00	950.00	1250.	2000.
	1766 EDC	—	650.00	950.00	1250.	2000.
	1767 EDC	—	650.00	950.00	1250.	2000.
	1768 EDC	—	650.00	950.00	1250.	2000.

C#	Date	Mintage	Fine	VF	XF	Unc
142a	1769 EDC	—	650.00	950.00	1250.	2000.
	1770 EDC	—	650.00	950.00	1250.	2000.
	1771 EDC	—	650.00	950.00	1250.	2000.
	1772 EDC	—	650.00	950.00	1250.	2000.
	1773 EDC	—	650.00	950.00	1250.	2000.
	1774 EDC	—	650.00	950.00	1250.	2000.
	1775 EDC	—	650.00	950.00	1250.	2000.
	1776 EDC	—	650.00	950.00	1250.	2000.
	1777 EDC	—	650.00	950.00	1250.	2000.
	1778 EDC	—	650.00	950.00	1250.	2000.

C#	Date	Mintage	Fine	VF	XF	Unc
142c	1779 IEC	—	650.00	950.00	1250.	2000.
	1780 IEC	—	650.00	950.00	1250.	2000.
	1781 IEC	—	650.00	950.00	1250.	2000.
	1782 IEC	—	650.00	950.00	1250.	2000.
	1783 IEC	—	650.00	950.00	1250.	2000.
	1784 IEC	—	650.00	950.00	1250.	2000.
	1785 IEC	—	650.00	950.00	1250.	2000.
	1786 IEC	—	650.00	950.00	1250.	2000.
	1787 IEC	—	650.00	950.00	1250.	2000.
	1788 IEC	—	650.00	950.00	1250.	2000.
	1789 IEC	—	650.00	950.00	1250.	2000.
	1790 IEC	—	650.00	950.00	1250.	2000.

C#	Date	Mintage	Fine	VF	XF	Unc
145	1791 IEC	—	150.00	300.00	475.00	800.00
	1792 IEC	—	150.00	300.00	475.00	800.00
	1793 IEC	—	150.00	300.00	475.00	800.00
	1794 IEC	—	150.00	300.00	475.00	800.00
	1795 IEC	—	150.00	300.00	475.00	800.00
	1796 IEC	—	150.00	300.00	475.00	800.00
	1797 IEC	—	150.00	300.00	475.00	800.00
	1798 IEC	—	150.00	300.00	475.00	800.00
	1799 IEC	—	150.00	300.00	475.00	800.00
	1800 IEC	—	150.00	300.00	475.00	800.00
	1801 IEC	—	150.00	300.00	475.00	800.00
	1802 IEC	—	150.00	300.00	475.00	800.00
	1803 IEC	—	150.00	300.00	475.00	800.00
	1804 IEC	—	150.00	300.00	475.00	800.00
145a	1804 SGH	—	200.00	375.00	625.00	1050.
	1805 SGH	—	200.00	375.00	625.00	1050.
	1806 SGH	—	200.00	375.00	625.00	1050.

Vicariat Issue

C#	Date	Mintage	Fine	VF	XF	Unc
146	1792 IEC	—	750.00	1000.	1500.	2000.

C#	Date	Mintage	Fine	VF	XF	Unc
192	1806 SGH	3,207	200.00	400.00	575.00	875.00
	1807 SGH	2,660	200.00	425.00	650.00	950.00
	1808 SGH	2,010	250.00	475.00	700.00	1050.
	1809 SGH	1,608	250.00	475.00	700.00	1050.
	1810 SGH	1,072	250.00	500.00	750.00	1125.
	1811 SGH	268 pcs.	450.00	900.00	1350.	2000.
	1812 SGH	67 pcs.	500.00	1000.	1500.	2200.
	1813 SGH	—	250.00	475.00	700.00	1000.

C#	Date	Mintage	Fine	VF	XF	Unc
192a	1813 IGS	—	200.00	400.00	625.00	925.00
	1815 IGS	804 pcs.	200.00	400.00	625.00	925.00
	1816 IGS	2,243	200.00	400.00	575.00	875.00
	1817 IGS	1,812	200.00	400.00	575.00	875.00
	1818 IGS	1,466	200.00	400.00	625.00	925.00
	1819 IGS	1,466	200.00	400.00	625.00	925.00
	1820 IGS	2,502	200.00	400.00	575.00	875.00
	1821 IGS	1,948	200.00	400.00	575.00	875.00
	1822 IGS	1,898	200.00	400.00	575.00	875.00

400th Jubilee of Leipzig University
Obv: Bust in coronet and cape right.
Rev. leg: SALVA SIT.

Fr#	Date	Mintage	Fine	VF	XF	Unc
2586	1809	—	500.00	1000.	1500.	2250.

Obv: Uniformed bust left, leg: FRIEDR.AUGUST.....
Rev: Crowned oval arms within crossed branches.

C#	Date	Mintage	Fine	VF	XF	Unc
193	1823 IGS	350 pcs.	500.00	850.00	1300.	1900.

Obv. leg: FRIEDR.AUG.KOEN....

C#	Date	Mintage	Fine	VF	XF	Unc
194	1824 IGS	1,911	250.00	425.00	650.00	1000.

C#	Date	Mintage	Fine	VF	XF	Unc
194a	1825 IGS	740 pcs.	250.00	425.00	650.00	950.00
	1826 IGS	1,425	250.00	400.00	625.00	925.00
	1827 IGS	386 pcs.	500.00	800.00	1200.	1800.

Rev: S below shield.

C#	Date	Mintage	Fine	VF	XF	Unc
217	1827 S	587 pcs.	400.00	700.00	1050.	1600.
	1828 S	771 pcs.	350.00	675.00	1025.	1550.

C#	Date	Mintage	Fine	VF	XF	Unc
217a	1829 S	1,408	300.00	575.00	850.00	1275.
	1830 S	1,274	300.00	600.00	875.00	1325.
	1831 S	470 pcs.	350.00	650.00	950.00	1450.
	1832 S	839 pcs.	—	—	—	1350.

Rev: G below shield.

C#	Date	Mintage	Fine	VF	XF	Unc
217b	1833 G	564 pcs.	350.00	650.00	950.00	1450.
	1834 G	1,582	300.00	575.00	850.00	1275.
	1835 G	119 pcs.	450.00	700.00	1050.	1600.
	1836 G	804 pcs.	350.00	600.00	875.00	1325.

Obv: Different head

C#	Date	Mintage	Fine	VF	XF	Unc
242	1836 G	100 pcs.	600.00	1150.	1750.	2600.
	1837 G	168 pcs.	700.00	1200.	1600.	2400.
	1838 G	637 pcs.	500.00	1000.	1500.	2200.

MONETARY REFORM

2 MARK

11.1110 gm., .900 SILVER, .1321 oz ASW

Y#	Date	Mintage	VF	XF	Unc
180	1876E	1.613	100.00	400.00	800.00
	1877E	.796	100.00	400.00	800.00
	1879E	.036	125.00	500.00	1000.
	1880E	.058	125.00	500.00	1000.
	1883E	.056	125.00	500.00	1000.
	1888E	.091	125.00	500.00	1000.

Y#	Date	Mintage	VF	XF	Unc
180a	1891E	.130	50.00	100.00	200.00
	1893E	.130	50.00	100.00	200.00
	1895E	.117	50.00	100.00	200.00
	1896E	.144	40.00	100.00	200.00
	1898E	.107	40.00	100.00	200.00
	1899E	.401	40.00	100.00	200.00
	1900E	.384	40.00	75.00	150.00
	1901E	.440	30.00	75.00	150.00
	1902E	.543	30.00	75.00	150.00

Death Of Albert

Y#	Date	Mintage	VF	XF	Unc
185	1902E	.168	25.00	50.00	75.00
	1902E	—	—	Proof	125.00

Y#	Date	Mintage	VF	XF	Unc
187	1903E	.746	45.00	100.00	200.00

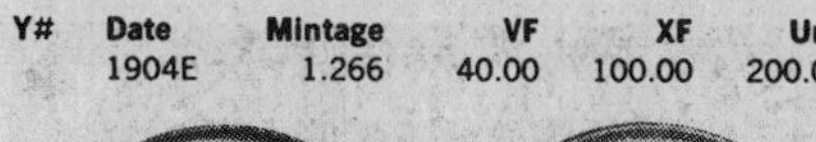

Y#	Date	Mintage	VF	XF	Unc
	1904E	1.266	40.00	100.00	200.00

Death Of Georg

Y#	Date	Mintage	VF	XF	Unc
191	1904E	.150	25.00	45.00	75.00
	1904E	55 pcs.	—	Proof	300.00

Y#	Date	Mintage	VF	XF	Unc
193	1905E	.559	35.00	45.00	100.00
	1905E	100 pcs.	—	Proof	300.00
	1906E	.559	35.00	45.00	100.00
	1907E	1.118	30.00	45.00	100.00
	1908E	.336	30.00	45.00	100.00
	1911E	.186	30.00	45.00	100.00
	1912E	.168	30.00	45.00	100.00
	1914E	.298	30.00	40.00	100.00
	Common type		—	Proof	150.00

500th Anniversary Leipzig University

Y#	Date	Mintage	VF	XF	Unc
198	1909	.125	20.00	35.00	50.00

3 MARK

16.6670 gm., .900 SILVER, .4823 oz ASW

Y#	Date	Mintage	VF	XF	Unc
194	1908E	.276	15.00	20.00	40.00
	1909E	1.197	15.00	20.00	35.00
	1910E	.745	15.00	20.00	30.00
	1911E	.581	15.00	20.00	30.00
	1912E	.379	15.00	20.00	30.00
	1913E	.307	15.00	20.00	30.00
	Common type		—	Proof	150.00

Battle Of Leipzig Centennial

Y#	Date	Mintage	VF	XF	Unc
200	1913E	1.000	15.00	20.00	30.00
	1913E	.017	—	Proof	110.00

Jubilee Of Reformation

Obv: Capped robed bust right in circle. Rev: Type 3 eagle.

Y#	Date	Mintage	VF	XF	Unc
201	1917E	100 pcs.	—	Proof	30,000.

5 MARK

27.7770 gm., .900 SILVER, .8038 oz ASW

Y#	Date	Mintage	VF	XF	Unc
181	1875E	.494	40.00	500.00	1500.
	1876E	.635	40.00	500.00	1500.
	1889E	.036	60.00	600.00	1600.

1.9910 gm., .900 GOLD, .0576 oz AGW

Y#	Date	Mintage	VF	XF	Unc
182	1877E	.402	300.00	400.00	500.00

27.7770 gm., .900 SILVER, .8038 oz ASW

Obv: Similar to Y#181.

Y#	Date	Mintage	VF	XF	Unc
181a	1891E	.052	35.00	250.00	500.00
	1893E	.052	35.00	250.00	500.00
	1894E	.075	35.00	200.00	500.00
	1895E	.089	35.00	200.00	500.00
	1898E	.160	35.00	200.00	450.00
	1899E	.074	35.00	200.00	500.00
	1900E	.157	35.00	150.00	400.00
	1901E	.156	35.00	150.00	400.00
	1902E	.168	35.00	150.00	350.00

Death Of Albert

Rev: Similar to Y#181a.

Y#	Date	Mintage	VF	XF	Unc
186	1902E	.100	65.00	125.00	150.00
	1902E	—	—	Proof	500.00

Rev: Similar to Y#181a.

Y#	Date	Mintage	VF	XF	Unc
188	1903E	.536	50.00	200.00	400.00
	1904E	.291	45.00	225.00	450.00
	Common type		—	Proof	500.00

Death Of Georg

Rev: Similar to Y#181a.

Y#	Date	Mintage	VF	XF	Unc
192	1904E	.037	125.00	225.00	275.00
	1904E	70 pcs.	—	Proof	325.00

Rev: Similar to Y#181a.

Y#	Date	Mintage	VF	XF	Unc
195	1907E	.398	30.00	50.00	150.00
	1908E	.317	30.00	50.00	150.00
	1914E	.298	30.00	50.00	135.00

500th Anniversary Leipzig University

Rev: Similar to Y#181a.

Y#	Date	Mintage	VF	XF	Unc
199	1909	.050	90.00	140.00	200.00
	1909	—	—	Proof	600.00

10 MARK

3.9820 gm., .900 GOLD, .1152 oz AGW
Obv: E below head. Rev: Type 1 eagle.

Y#	Date	Mintage	VF	XF	Unc
178	1872E	.339	150.00	200.00	250.00
	1873E	.715	150.00	200.00	250.00

Rev: Type 2 eagle

Y#	Date	Mintage	VF	XF	Unc
183	1874E	.048	400.00	500.00	600.00
	1875E	.528	100.00	175.00	225.00
	1877E	.201	200.00	300.00	400.00
	1878E	.225	200.00	300.00	400.00
	1879E	.182	200.00	300.00	400.00
	1881E	.240	150.00	200.00	300.00
	1888E	.149	150.00	200.00	300.00

Rev: Type 3 eagle

Y#	Date	Mintage	VF	XF	Unc
183a	1891E	.224	150.00	200.00	300.00
	1893E	.224	150.00	200.00	300.00
	1896E	.150	150.00	200.00	300.00
	1898E	.313	150.00	200.00	300.00
	1900E	.074	150.00	250.00	350.00
	1901E	.075	150.00	250.00	350.00
	1902E	.037	200.00	300.00	400.00

Y#	Date	Mintage	VF	XF	Unc
189	1903E	.284	150.00	200.00	300.00
	1904E	.149	150.00	200.00	300.00

Y#	Date	Mintage	VF	XF	Unc
196	1905E	.112	200.00	225.00	300.00
	1906E	.075	200.00	250.00	350.00
	1907E	.112	200.00	225.00	300.00
	1909E	.112	200.00	225.00	300.00
	1910E	.075	200.00	225.00	300.00
	1911E	.038	225.00	250.00	350.00
	1912E	.075	200.00	225.00	300.00

20 MARK

7.9650 gm., .900 GOLD, .2304 oz AGW
Rev: Type 1 eagle.

Y#	Date	Mintage	VF	XF	Unc
179	1872E	.890	150.00	250.00	300.00
	1873E	.203	150.00	250.00	300.00

Rev: Type 2 eagle.

Y#	Date	Mintage	VF	XF	Unc
184	1874E	.153	200.00	250.00	400.00
	1876E	.482	200.00	250.00	350.00
	1877E	1,181	4000.	7000.	10,000.
	1878E	1,564	3500.	6000.	9000.

Rev: Type 3 eagle

Y#	Date	Mintage	VF	XF	Unc
184a	1894E	.639	150.00	200.00	300.00
	1895E	.113	200.00	300.00	400.00

Y#	Date	Mintage	VF	XF	Unc
190	1903E	.250	200.00	275.00	350.00

Y#	Date	Mintage	VF	XF	Unc
197	1905E	.500	150.00	200.00	260.00
	1913E	.121	250.00	300.00	400.00
	1914E	.325	250.00	300.00	400.00
	Common Type	—	—	Proof	1300.

NCLT ISSUES

PATTERNS

KM#	Date	Mintage	Identification	Mkt.Val.
1	1808 SGH	—	Thaler, Silver	—
2	1814 IGS	134	Ducat, Gold	4000.
3	1913	—	3 Marks, Silver	—

SCHAUMBURG-HESSEN

Located in northwest Germany, Schaumburg—Hessen was founded in 1640 when Schaumburg-Gehmen was divided between Hesse-Cassel and Lippe—Alverdissen. The two became known as Schaumburg-Hessen and Schaumburg—Lippe. Cassel struck coins for its half as late as 1832.

RULERS

Friedrich II (of Hesse-Cassel), 1760-1785
Wilhelm (Of Hesse-Cassel), 1785-1821
Wilhelm II, (Of Hesse-Cassel), 1821-1847

MONETARY SYSTEMS

12 Gute Pfennig = 1 Groschen

PFENNIG

(Guter)

COPPER
Obv: Crowned nettle; flat sides.
Rev. value: GUTER PFENN.

C#	Date	Mintage	VG	Fine	VF	XF
2	1772-85	—	2.00	4.00	6.50	15.00

Rev. value: PFENNIG

C#	Date	Mintage	VG	Fine	VF	XF
2a	1783	—	2.50	5.00	7.50	15.00

Obv: Crowned shield separating WL. Rev: Value.

C#	Date	Mintage	Fine	VF	XF	Unc
3	1787	—	2.00	4.00	8.00	35.00
	1788	—	2.00	4.00	8.00	35.00
	1789	—	2.00	4.00	8.00	35.00
	1790	—	2.00	4.00	8.00	35.00
	1791	—	2.00	4.00	8.00	35.00
	1792	—	2.00	4.00	8.00	35.00
	1793	—	2.00	4.00	8.00	35.00
	1794	—	2.00	4.00	8.00	35.00
	1795	—	2.00	4.00	8.00	35.00
	1796	—	2.00	4.00	8.00	35.00
	1797	—	2.00	4.00	8.00	35.00
	1798	—	2.00	4.00	8.00	35.00
	1799	—	2.00	4.00	8.00	35.00
	1800	—	2.00	4.00	8.00	35.00
	1801	—	2.00	4.00	8.00	35.00
	1802	—	2.00	4.00	8.00	35.00
	1803	—	2.00	4.00	8.00	35.00

Obv: Elector's cap over arms dividing W.K.
Rev: Value, F below.

C#	Date	Mintage	Fine	VF	XF	Unc
4	1804F	—	2.00	4.00	8.00	35.00
	1805F	—	2.00	4.00	8.00	35.00
	1806F	—	2.00	4.00	8.00	35.00
	1807F	—	2.00	4.00	8.00	35.00
	1814F	—	2.00	4.00	8.00	35.00

Rev: Rosette under value and date

C#	Date	Mintage	Fine	VF	XF	Unc
4b	1815	—	1.50	3.00	6.00	30.00

C#	Date	Mintage	Fine	VF	XF	Unc
4a	1816	—	1.00	2.50	5.00	30.00
	1818	—	1.00	2.50	5.00	30.00
	1819	—	1.00	2.50	5.00	30.00
	1820	—	1.00	2.50	5.00	30.00
	1821	—	1.00	2.50	5.00	30.00
5	1824	—	1.00	2.50	5.00	30.00
	1826	—	1.00	2.50	5.00	30.00
	1827	—	1.00	2.50	5.00	30.00
	1828	—	1.00	2.50	5.00	30.00
	1829	—	1.00	2.50	5.00	30.00
	1830	—	1.00	2.50	5.00	30.00
6	1832	—	1.00	2.50	5.00	30.00

SCHAUMBURG — LIPPE

Located in northwest Germany, Schaumburg-Lippe was founded in 1640 when Schaumburg-Gehmen was divided between Hesse-Cassel and Lippe-Alverdissen. The two became known as Schaumburg—Hessen and Schaumburg-Lippe. They were elevated into a county independent of Lippe. Schaumburg-Lippe minted currency into the 20th century. The last prince died in 1911.

RULERS

Philip II Ernst, 1777-1787
Georg Wilhelm, 1787-1860
Adolph Georg, 1860-1893
Albrecht Georg, 1893-1911

PFENNIG

(Guter)

COPPER

Obv: Crowned arms. Rev: Value.

C#	Date	Mintage	Fine	VF	XF	Unc
36	1824	—	1.50	3.00	6.00	30.00
	1826	—	1.50	3.00	6.00	30.00

C#	Date	Mintage	Fine	VF	XF	Unc
37	1858A	1.440	1.00	2.50	5.00	30.00

2 PFENNIG

COPPER

C#	Date	Mintage	Fine	VF	XF	Unc
38	1858A	.360	1.00	2.50	5.00	30.00

3 PFENNIG

COPPER

C#	Date	Mintage	Fine	VF	XF	Unc
39	1858A	.360	1.00	2.50	5.00	30.00

4 PFENNIG

COPPER

Obv: Crowned arms, garlands and roses. Rev: Value.

C#	Date	Mintage	Fine	VF	XF	Unc
30	1802	.288	3.00	6.00	9.00	35.00

BILLON

Obv: Crowned arms.

C#	Date	Mintage	Fine	VF	XF	Unc
41	1821	.491	3.00	6.00	10.00	40.00

C#	Date	Mintage	Fine	VF	XF	Unc
41a	1828	—	3.00	6.00	10.00	40.00

COPPER

C#	Date	Mintage	Fine	VF	XF	Unc
40	1858A	.180	2.00	4.00	8.00	35.00

1/2 SILBERGROSCHEN

BILLON

C#	Date	Mintage	Fine	VF	XF	Unc
45	1858A	.120	2.50	5.00	10.00	40.00

MARIENGROSCHEN

BILLON

Obv: Crowned arms, garlands and roses. Rev: Value.

C#	Date	Mintage	Fine	VF	XF	Unc
32	1802	.144	4.50	9.00	20.00	50.00

Obv: Crowned arms.

C#	Date	Mintage	Fine	VF	XF	Unc
42	1821	.143	3.00	6.00	10.00	35.00
	1828	—	3.00	6.00	10.00	35.00

SILBERGROSCHEN

BILLON

C#	Date	Mintage	Fine	VF	XF	Unc
46	1858A	.210	4.00	8.00	12.00	35.00

2 1/2 SILBERGROSCHEN

BILLON

C#	Date	Mintage	Fine	VF	XF	Unc
47	1858A	.061	7.00	15.00	25.00	50.00

1/24 THALER

BILLON

C#	Date	Mintage	Fine	VF	XF	Unc
43	1821	.195	4.00	8.00	12.00	35.00
	1826	—	4.00	8.00	12.00	35.00

1/2 THALER

14.0310 gm., .833 SILVER, .3760 oz ASW

C#	Date	Mintage	Fine	VF	XF	Unc
44	1821	5,400	30.00	60.00	100.00	225.00

THALER

28.0630 gm., .833 SILVER, .7520 oz ASW

C#	Date	Mintage	Fine	VF	XF	Unc
34	1802	4,000	250.00	500.00	1000.	2000.

18.5200 gm., .900 SILVER, .5360 oz ASW

C#	Date	Mintage	Fine	VF	XF	Unc
48	1860B	8,356	50.00	125.00	250.00	500.00

C#	Date	Mintage	Fine	VF	XF	Unc
51	1865B	7,000	50.00	125.00	250.00	500.00

2 THALER

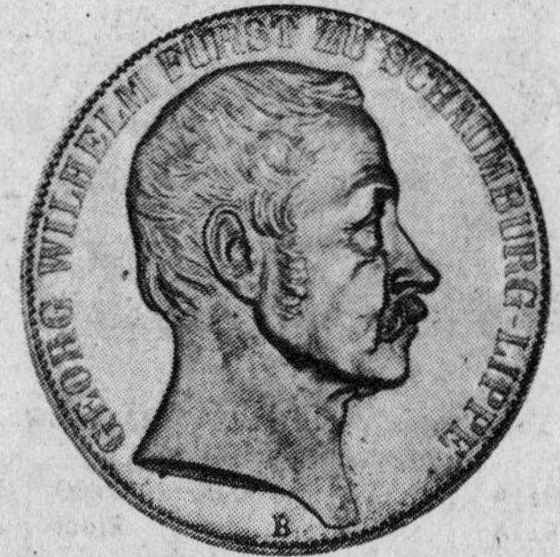

37.0370 gm., .900 SILVER, 1.0718 oz ASW
50th Anniversary of Reign as Prince

C#	Date	Mintage	Fine	VF	XF	Unc
49	1857B	2,000	125.00	250.00	500.00	1000.

10 THALER

13.2840 gm., .900 GOLD, .3826 oz AGW
Obv: Draped bust left, with ALSING at truncation.
Rev: Crowned draped arms.

C#	Date	Mintage	Fine	VF	XF	Unc
50	1829with FF	—				
		1,035	900.00	1700.	2500.	4000.
	1829(w/o FF)	—	1200.	2000.	3000.	4500.

TRADE COINS

DUCAT

3.5000 gm., .986 GOLD, .1109 oz AGW
Obv: Crowned arms in sprays.
Rev: Tablet.

C#	Date	Mintage	VG	Fine	VF	XF
25	1777	—	500.00	950.00	1350.	2000.
	Obv: Bust.					
26	1783	—	600.00	1150.	1500.	2250.

MONETARY REFORM

2 MARK

11.1110 gm., .900 SILVER, .3215 oz ASW

Y#	Date	Mintage	VF	XF	Unc
203	1898A	5,000	400.00	700.00	1000.
	1898A	162 pcs.	—	Proof	1200.
	1904A	5,000	300.00	600.00	1000.
	1904A	200 pcs.	—	—	1150.

3 MARK

16.6670 gm., .900 SILVER, .4823 oz ASW
Death Of Prince George

Y#	Date	Mintage	VF	XF	Unc
206	1911A	.050	60.00	85.00	125.00
	1911A	—	—	Proof	250.00

5 MARK

27.7770 gm., .900 SILVER, .8038 oz ASW

Y#	Date	Mintage	VF	XF	Unc
204	1898A	3,000	1000.	1500.	2000.
	1898A	90 pcs.	—	Proof	2100.
	1904A	3,000	1000.	1400.	1700.
	1904A	250 pcs.	—	Proof	2500.

20 MARK

7.9650 gm., .900 GOLD, .2304 oz AGW

Y#	Date	Mintage	VF	XF	Unc
202	1874B	3,000	7000.	10,000.	13,000.

Y#	Date	Mintage	VF	XF	Unc
205	1898A	5,000	1200.	2000.	2400.
	1904A	5,500	1200.	1900.	2300.
	1904A	—	—	Proof	2400.

SCHLESWIG — HOLSTEIN

Schleswig-Holstein is the border area between Denmark and Germany. The duchy of Schleswig was Danish while Holstein was German. The 1773 Treaty of Zarskoje Selo transferred Holstein to the Danes in exchange for Oldenburg. There was a great deal of trouble in the area during the 19th century. It was settled when Prussia annexed the territory in 1866.

RULERS

Christian VII (of Denmark), 1784-1808
Friedrich VI (of Denmark), 1808-1839
Christian VIII (of Denmark), 1839-1848

PROVISIONAL GOVERNMENT

1848-1851

ALTONA MINTMASTER'S INITIALS

C.B. - Calus Branth
I.F.F., F.F - Johann Friedrich Freund
MF, M.F, M.F. - Michael Flor
T.A. - Theodor C.W. Andersen
V.S. - Georg Vilhelm Svendsen

MONETARY SYSTEM

4 Dreiling = 2 Sechsling = 1 Schilling
60 Schilling = 1 Speciesdaler

DREILING

COPPER

C#	Date	Mintage	Fine	VF	XF	Unc
1	1787	2.400	3.50	7.00	12.00	40.00

C#	Date	Mintage	Fine	VF	XF	Unc
23	1850 TA	.200	2.50	5.00	8.00	35.00

SECHSLING

COPPER

C#	Date	Mintage	Fine	VF	XF	Unc
2	1787	6.000	2.00	4.00	7.00	35.00

C#	Date	Mintage	Fine	VF	XF	Unc
24	1850 TA	.203	2.50	5.00	9.00	35.00
	1851 TA	.163	3.00	6.00	9.00	35.00

2 SECHSLING

BILLON
Obv: Crowned interlaced CR monogram, VIII within.
Rev: Value.

C#	Date	Mintage	Fine	VF	XF	Unc
3	1787 MF	.761	5.00	9.00	13.00	50.00
	1788 MF	—	5.00	9.00	13.00	50.00
	1796 MF	.538	5.00	9.00	13.00	50.00
	1799 MF	.960	5.00	9.00	13.00	50.00
	1800 MF	.480	5.00	9.00	13.00	50.00

SCHILLING

SILVER

C#	Date	Mintage	Fine	VF	XF	Unc
25	1851 TA	—	—	—	Rare	—

2-1/2 SCHILLING

(1/24 Speciesthaler)

BILLON

C#	Date	Mintage	Fine	VF	XF	Unc
4	1787 MF	4.800	2.50	5.00	8.00	40.00
	1796 MF	2.880	2.50	5.00	8.00	40.00
	1799 MF	1.440	2.50	5.00	8.00	40.00
	1800 MF	.096	4.00	8.00	15.00	45.00
	1801 MF	.211	4.00	8.00	15.00	45.00

C#	Date	Mintage	Fine	VF	XF	Unc
20	1809 MF	.960	4.00	8.00	15.00	45.00
	1812 MF	.528	4.00	8.00	15.00	45.00

5 SCHILLING

(1/12 Speciesthaler)

4.2140 gm., .500 SILVER, .0677 oz ASW
Obv: Crowned interlaced CR monogram, VII within.
Rev: Value.

C#	Date	Mintage	Fine	VF	XF	Unc
5	1787 MF	1.800	3.00	6.00	10.00	45.00
	1788 MF	—	4.00	8.00	15.00	45.00
	1797 MF	.527	4.00	8.00	15.00	45.00
	1800 MF	.048	4.00	8.00	15.00	45.00
	1801 MF	.103	4.00	8.00	15.00	45.00

8 SCHILLING

BILLON

C#	Date	Mintage	Fine	VF	XF	Unc
21	1816 MF	.056	7.00	15.00	30.00	60.00
	1818 CB	.243	5.00	10.00	20.00	50.00
	1819 IFF	.925	5.00	10.00	20.00	50.00

10 SCHILLING

(1/6 Speciesthaler)

.875 SILVER

C#	Date	Mintage	Fine	VF	XF	Unc
6	1787 MF	.540	10.00	20.00	40.00	80.00
	1788 MF	.300	12.00	25.00	45.00	90.00
	1789 MF	.183	15.00	35.00	50.00	100.00
	1796 MF	.129	15.00	35.00	50.00	100.00

16 SCHILLING

4.2140 gm., .500 SILVER, .0677 oz ASW

C#	Date	Mintage	Fine	VF	XF	Unc
22	1816 MF	.031	7.00	15.00	30.00	60.00
	1818 CB	.125	7.00	15.00	30.00	60.00

Rev: 1/12 SP added

C#	Date	Mintage	Fine	VF	XF	Unc
22a	1831 IFF	.198	7.00	15.00	30.00	60.00
	1839 IFF	.063	7.00	15.00	30.00	60.00

20 SCHILLING

(1/3 Speciesthaler)

9.6310 gm., .875 SILVER, .2710 oz ASW
Obv: Head right, bow-tied hair, B below.
Rev: Crowned oval arms dividing 1/3 SP.

C#	Date	Mintage	Fine	VF	XF	Unc
7	1787 MF	.300	20.00	40.00	60.00	120.00
	1788 MF	.414	20.00	40.00	60.00	120.00
	1789 MF	—	20.00	40.00	60.00	120.00
	1797 MF	.066	20.00	40.00	60.00	120.00
	1799 MF	—	—	—	Rare	—
	1808 MF	.124	20.00	40.00	60.00	120.00

Obv: With A below head

C#	Date	Mintage	Fine	VF	XF	Unc
	1787 MF	I.A.	20.00	40.00	60.00	120.00

40 SCHILLING

(2/3 Speciesthaler)

9.6310 gm., .875 SILVER, .2710 oz ASW

C#	Date	Mintage	Fine	VF	XF	Unc
8	1787 MF	.333	40.00	80.00	110.00	200.00
	1797 MF	.070	40.00	80.00	110.00	200.00
	1799 MF	—	—	—	Rare	—
	1808 MF	—	40.00	80.00	110.00	200.00

60 SCHILLING

(= Speciesthaler)

28.8930 gm., .875 SILVER, .8129 oz ASW
Obv: B below large head.

C#	Date	Mintage	Fine	VF	XF	Unc
9	1787 MF	.412	50.00	150.00	300.00	500.00
	1788 MF	.644	50.00	150.00	300.00	500.00
	1789 MF	—	50.00	170.00	250.00	400.00
	1790 MF	.402	200.00	600.00	800.00	1200.
	1791 MF	1,000	—	—	Rare	—
	1794 MF	1.106	50.00	160.00	300.00	500.00
	1795 MF	1.774	50.00	160.00	300.00	500.00
	1796 MF	1.086	60.00	200.00	400.00	800.00
	1799 MF	I.A.	230.00	300.00	500.00	1000.
	1800 MF	I.A.	175.00	235.00	400.00	800.00
	1801 MF	.312	50.00	150.00	300.00	500.00
	1804 MF	.106	50.00	150.00	300.00	500.00
	1807 MF	.102	50.00	130.00	300.00	500.00
	1808 MF	1.304	100.00	350.00	600.00	1000.

NOTE: Many die varieties exist.

Obv: DI below head

C#	Date	Mintage	Fine	VF	XF	Unc
9a	1787 MF	—	100.00	200.00	300.00	600.00
	1788 MF	—	50.00	150.00	250.00	500.00

Obv: H below large head.

C#	Date	Mintage	Fine	VF	XF	Unc
9b	1788 MF	I.A.	75.00	150.00	250.00	500.00

Obv: M below head

C#	Date	Mintage	Fine	VF	XF	Unc
9c	1788 MF	I.A.	110.00	225.00	350.00	600.00
	1790 MF	I.A.	50.00	150.00	250.00	500.00
	1799 MF	I.A.	—	—	Rare	—

Obv: PG below head

C#	Date	Mintage	Fine	VF	XF	Unc
9d	1799 MF	.064	—	—	Rare	—
	1800 MF	.146	50.00	150.00	250.00	500.00

SCHWARZBURG — RUDOLSTADT

The Schwarzburg family held territory in central and northern Thuringia. After many divisions, two lines, Sondershausen and Rudolstadt were founded in 1552. The count of Rudolstadt was raised to the rank of prince in 1710. The last prince abdicated in 1918.

RULERS

Johann Friedrich, 1744-1767
Ludwig Gunther IV, 1767-1790
Friedrich Carl, 1790-1793

Ludwig Friedrich II, 1793-1807
Friedrich Gunther, 1807-1867
Albert, 1867-1869
Gunther Viktor, 1890-1918

MINTMASTER'S INITIALS

I.C.E. - Johann Christian Eberhard 1755-1765
I.C.K. - Johann Christian Knaust 1765-1794
L - Georg Christoph Loewel

HELLER

COPPER
Obv: Crowned LG monogram. Rev: Value and date.

C#	Date	Mintage	Good	VG	Fine	VF
30	1769	—	3.00	6.00	10.00	20.00

1/2 PFENNIG

COPPER
Obv: Crowned L G monogram. Rev: Value over date.

C#	Date	Mintage	VG	Fine	VF	XF
31	1783	—	2.50	5.00	7.50	15.00

Obv: Crowned F C monogram.

C#	Date	Mintage	VG	Fine	VF	XF
41	1792	—	3.00	6.00	9.50	15.00

PFENNIG

COPPER
Obv: Crowned LG monogram in branches. Rev: Value and date.

C#	Date	Mintage	Good	VG	Fine	VF
32	1772	—	2.00	4.00	8.50	15.00

Obv: Crowned F C monogram. Rev: Value over date.

C#	Date	Mintage	VG	Fine	VF	XF
42	1792	—	2.50	5.00	10.00	15.00

Obv: SCHWARZB/RUD-LM. Rev: Value: 1 PF in script.

C#	Date	Mintage	Fine	VF	XF	Unc
50	1801	—	2.00	4.00	10.00	40.00
	1802	—	2.00	4.00	10.00	40.00

Obv: Crowned FG monogram within branches. Rev: Value.

C#	Date	Mintage	Fine	VF	XF	Unc
63	1825	—	2.00	5.00	8.00	35.00

Obv: Crowned arms. Rev. value: SCHEIDE MUNZE.

C#	Date	Mintage	Fine	VF	XF	Unc
65	1842A	—	2.00	5.00	8.00	35.00

2 PFENNIG

COPPER
Obv: Crowned JF monogram in branches. Rev: Value and date.

C#	Date	Mintage	Good	VG	Fine	VF
2	1760	—	2.00	4.00	8.50	15.00
	1761	—	2.00	4.00	8.50	15.00

Obv: Crowned FG monogram within crossed branches. Rev: Value.

C#	Date	Mintage	Fine	VF	XF	Unc
57	1812	—	3.00	6.00	10.00	40.00

Obv: Crowned arms

C#	Date	Mintage	Fine	VF	XF	Unc
66	1842A	—	2.00	4.00	8.00	35.00

3 PFENNIG

BILLON
Obv: JF monogram in crowned shield. Rev: Value in orb which separates date.

C#	Date	Mintage	Good	VG	Fine	VF
7	1764 I.C.E.	—	4.00	8.00	15.00	30.00

COPPER
Obv. leg: SCHWARZB/RUD-LM. Rev: Value, 3 PF in script.

C#	Date	Mintage	Fine	VF	XF	Unc
51	1804	—	3.50	7.00	15.00	40.00

Obv: Monogram FG within crossed branches. Rev: Value.

C#	Date	Mintage	Fine	VF	XF	Unc
58	1813	—	3.50	7.00	15.00	40.00

Obv: Crown above monogram

C#	Date	Mintage	Fine	VF	XF	Unc
64	1825	—	2.50	5.00	10.00	35.00

Obv: Crowned arms. Rev. leg: SCHEIDEMUNZE.

C#	Date	Mintage	Fine	VF	XF	Unc
67	1842A	—	2.50	5.00	10.00	35.00

4 PFENNIG

COPPER
Obv: Monogram FG within crossed branches. Rev: Value.

C#	Date	Mintage	Fine	VF	XF	Unc
59	1812	—	3.50	7.00	15.00	35.00
	1813	—	3.50	7.00	15.00	35.00

6 PFENNIG

BILLON
Obv: JF monogram in crowned shield. Rev: Value in orb which separates date.

C#	Date	Mintage	Good	VG	Fine	VF
12.1	1763 I.C.E.	—	9.00	15.00	27.50	45.00

Rev: I.C.K. under orb.

C#	Date	Mintage	Good	VG	Fine	VF
12.2	1766 I.C.K.	—	4.00	8.00	15.00	30.00

Obv: Crowned cartouche with L G monogram. Rev: Value in orb, date above.

C#	Date	Mintage	VG	Fine	VF	XF
34	1779	—	6.00	12.00	24.00	35.00
	1780	—	6.00	12.00	24.00	35.00
	1781	—	6.00	12.00	24.00	35.00
	1782	—	6.00	12.00	24.00	35.00
	1784	—	6.00	12.00	24.00	35.00
	1785	—	6.00	12.00	24.00	35.00
	1786	—	6.00	12.00	24.00	35.00

Obv: Crowned cartouche with F C monogram.

C#	Date	Mintage	VG	Fine	VF	XF
44	1792	—	5.00	7.00	14.50	25.00

Obv. leg: SCHWARZB/RUD-LM. Rev: Value, 6 PF in script.

C#	Date	Mintage	Fine	VF	XF	Unc
53	1800	—	2.50	5.00	10.00	40.00
	1801	—	2.50	5.00	10.00	40.00
60	1808	—	2.50	5.00	10.00	40.00

Obv: Rosette above & ledge below SCHWARZB/RUD-LM.

C#	Date	Mintage	Fine	VF	XF	Unc
60a	1812	—	2.50	5.00	10.00	40.00
	1813	—	2.50	5.00	10.00	40.00

1/8 KREUZER

COPPER
Obv: Crowned arms within branches. Rev: Value.

C#	Date	Mintage	Fine	VF	XF	Unc
73	1840	.024	2.50	5.00	10.00	35.00
	1855	—	2.50	5.00	10.00	35.00

1/4 KREUZER

COPPER

C#	Date	Mintage	Fine	VF	XF	Unc
74	1840	.972	2.00	4.00	8.00	30.00
	1852	—	2.00	4.00	8.00	30.00
	1853	—	2.00	4.00	8.00	30.00
	1855	—	2.00	4.00	8.00	30.00
	1856	—	2.00	4.00	8.00	30.00

C#	Date	Mintage	Fine	VF	XF	Unc
74a	1857	—	1.00	2.00	5.00	30.00
	1859	—	1.00	2.00	5.00	30.00
	1860	—	1.00	2.00	5.00	30.00
	1861	—	1.00	2.00	5.00	30.00
	1863	—	1.00	2.00	5.00	30.00
	1865	—	1.00	2.00	5.00	30.00
	1866	—	1.00	2.00	5.00	30.00

C#	Date	Mintage	Fine	VF	XF	Unc
82	1868	.096	1.00	2.00	5.00	30.00

KREUZER

COPPER

C#	Date	Mintage	Fine	VF	XF	Unc
76	1840	.480	2.00	4.00	7.00	30.00

C#	Date	Mintage	Fine	VF	XF	Unc
76a	1864	—	1.00	3.00	6.00	30.00
	1865	—	1.00	3.00	6.00	30.00
	1866	—	1.00	3.00	6.00	30.00
83	1868	.037	1.00	3.00	6.00	30.00

3 KREUZER

BILLON
Obv: Crowned arms. Rev: Value within wreath.

C#	Date	Mintage	Fine	VF	XF	Unc
77	1839	.155	7.00	15.00	25.00	50.00
	1840	Inc. Ab.	7.00	15.00	25.00	50.00
	1841	Inc. Ab.	7.00	15.00	25.00	50.00
	1842	Inc. Ab.	7.00	15.00	25.00	50.00
	1846	Inc. Ab.	7.00	15.00	25.00	50.00

Obv. leg: SCHEIDE MUNZE added.

C#	Date	Mintage	Fine	VF	XF	Unc
77a	1866	.010	15.00	30.00	50.00	75.00

6 KREUZER

BILLON

C#	Date	Mintage	Fine	VF	XF	Unc
78	1840	.165	6.00	12.00	25.00	50.00
	1842	Inc. Ab.	6.00	12.00	25.00	50.00
	1846	Inc. Ab.	6.00	12.00	25.00	50.00

Obv. leg: SCHEIDE MUNZE added.

C#	Date	Mintage	Fine	VF	XF	Unc
78a	1866	.010	12.00	25.00	45.00	75.00

1/2 GROSCHEN

BILLON
Obv: Crowned arms. Rev: Value.

C#	Date	Mintage	Fine	VF	XF	Unc
68	1841A	—	7.00	15.00	25.00	50.00

GROSCHEN

BILLON
Obv. leg: SCHWARZB. RUD-LM. Rev: Value.

C#	Date	Mintage	Fine	VF	XF	Unc
61	1803	—	5.00	10.00	20.00	40.00
	1808	—	5.00	10.00	20.00	40.00

Obv: Rosette above, legend below. Rev: Value with rosettes.

C#	Date	Mintage	Fine	VF	XF	Unc
61a	1812	—	5.00	10.00	20.00	40.00

Obv: Crowned arms. Rev: Value.

C#	Date	Mintage	Fine	VF	XF	Unc
69	1841A	—	7.00	15.00	25.00	50.00

1/2 GULDEN

5.3030 gm., .900 SILVER, .1535 oz ASW

C#	Date	Mintage	Fine	VF	XF	Unc
79	1841	.157	12.00	25.00	50.00	150.00
	1842	Inc. Ab.	12.00	25.00	50.00	150.00
	1843	Inc. Ab.	12.00	25.00	50.00	150.00
	1846	Inc. Ab.	12.00	25.00	50.00	150.00

GULDEN

10.6060 gm., .900 SILVER, .3069 oz ASW
Obv: Similar to 1/2 Gulden, C#79.

C#	Date	Mintage	Fine	VF	XF	Unc
80	1841	.163	12.00	25.00	50.00	150.00
	1842	Inc. Ab.	12.00	25.00	50.00	150.00
	1843	Inc. Ab.	12.00	25.00	50.00	150.00
	1846	Inc. Ab.	12.00	25.00	50.00	150.00

ZWEY (2) GULDEN

21.2110 gm., .900 SILVER, .6138 oz ASW
Obv: Similar to 1/2 Gulden, C#79.

C#	Date	Mintage	Fine	VF	XF	Unc
81	1846	500 pcs.	300.00	750.00	1250.	2500.

1/48 THALER

BILLON
Obv: JF monogram in crowned shield, I.C.E. under shield.
Rev: Value and date.

C#	Date	Mintage	Good	VG	Fine	VF
15.1	1764 I.C.E.	—	4.00	8.00	12.50	20.00

Obv: I.C.K. under shield.

C#	Date	Mintage	Good	VG	Fine	VF
15.2	1766 I.C.K.	—	4.00	8.00	12.50	20.00

1/24 THALER

BILLON
Obv: Crowned arms.
Rev: Value and date in branches.

C#	Date	Mintage	Good	VG	Fine	VF
19.1	1763 I.C.E.	—	4.00	8.00	15.00	30.00

Rev: Value

C#	Date	Mintage	Good	VG	Fine	VF
19.2	1763 I.C.E.	—	4.00	8.00	15.00	30.00
	1764 I.C.E.	—	4.00	8.00	15.00	30.00

1/12 THALER

BILLON
Obv: Crowned arms. Rev: Value.

C#	Date	Mintage	Good	VG	Fine	VF
22.1	1763 I.C.E.	—	5.00	10.00	20.00	35.00
	1764 I.C.E.	—	5.00	10.00	20.00	35.00

Obv: Larger crowned arms.

C#	Date	Mintage	Good	VG	Fine	VF
22.2	1766 I.C.K.	—	5.00	10.00	20.00	35.00

1/6 THALER

SILVER
Obv: Bust of Johann Friedrich right.
Rev: Value and date below eagle.

C#	Date	Mintage	VG	Fine	VF	XF
24	1764 I.C.E.	—	20.00	40.00	65.00	100.00

1/2 THALER

(Convention)

SILVER
Obv: Bust right. Rev: Crowned arms with wildman and wildwoman supporters; date in exergue.

C#	Date	Mintage	VG	Fine	VF	XF
46	1791 I.C.K.	—	35.00	67.50	100.00	150.00

2/3 THALER

SILVER
Obv: Bust of Johann Friedrich right.
Rev: Crowned oval arms with wildman supporters; date below.

C#	Date	Mintage	Fine	VF	XF	Unc
26	1764 I.C.E.	—	50.00	100.00	150.00	250.00

THALER

(Convention)

SILVER
Obv: Bust of Johann Friedrich right.
Rev: Crowned oval arms with wildman supporters; date below.

C#	Date	Mintage	VG	Fine	VF	XF
28	1764 I.C.E.	—	125.00	200.00	400.00	600.00
	1765 I.C.E.	—	125.00	200.00	400.00	600.00

Obv: Bust of Ludwig Gunther right.
Rev: Crowned ornamental arms; date below.

C#	Date	Mintage	VG	Fine	VF	XF
37	1768 I.C.K.	—	125.00	250.00	375.00	500.00

Marriage of the Crown Prince

C#	Date	Mintage	VG	Fine	VF	XF
38	1780 I.C.K.	—	80.00	145.00	200.00	300.00

C#	Date	Mintage	VG	Fine	VF	XF
39	1786 I.C.K.	—	85.00	150.00	250.00	350.00

C#	Date	Mintage	VG	Fine	VF	XF
48	1791 I.C.K.	—	85.00	150.00	250.00	350.00

(Species)

28.0630 gm., .833 SILVER, .7520 oz ASW

C#	Date	Mintage	Fine	VF	XF	Unc
62	1812 L	—	100.00	275.00	500.00	1000.
	1813 L	—	100.00	275.00	500.00	1000.

(Vereins)

18.5200 gm., .900 SILVER, .5360 oz ASW

C#	Date	Mintage	Fine	VF	XF	Unc
70	1858	.016	30.00	75.00	150.00	300.00
	1859	6,000	40.00	85.00	170.00	350.00

C#	Date	Mintage	Fine	VF	XF	Unc
70a	1862	.048	30.00	75.00	150.00	300.00
	1863	.017	30.00	75.00	150.00	300.00

C#	Date	Mintage	Fine	VF	XF	Unc
70b	1866	.027	30.00	60.00	120.00	300.00

50th Anniversary of Reign
Obv: Similar to C#70.
Rev. leg: ZUR FEIER 50 JAEHRIGER REGIERUNG....

C#	Date	Mintage	Fine	VF	XF	Unc
71	1864	4,500	50.00	125.00	250.00	500.00
	1864	—	—	—	Proof	500.00

C#	Date	Mintage	Fine	VF	XF	Unc
84	1867	.013	30.00	75.00	150.00	300.00

2 THALER

(= 3-1/2 Gulden)

37.1200 gm., .900 SILVER, 1.0742 oz ASW

C#	Date	Mintage	Fine	VF	XF	Unc
72	1841A	.010	150.00	400.00	800.00	1600.
	1845A	5,100	150.00	400.00	800.00	1600.

TRADE COINS

DUCAT

3.5000 gm., .986 GOLD, .1109 oz AGW

C#	Date	Mintage	Fine	VF	XF	Unc
55	1803	—	300.00	550.00	850.00	1250.

MONETARY REFORM

2 MARK

11.1110 gm., .900 SILVER, .3215 oz ASW

Y#	Date	Mintage	VF	XF	Unc
207	1898A	.100	175.00	300.00	500.00
	1898A	375 pcs.	—	Proof	950.00

10 MARK

3.9820 gm., .900 GOLD, .1152 oz AGW

Y#	Date	Mintage	VF	XF	Unc
208	1898A	.010	1500.	2180.	2500.

SCHWARZBURG — SONDERSHAUSEN

The Schwarzburg family held territory in central and northern Thuringia. After many divisions, two lines, Sondershausen and Rudolstadt were founded in 1552. The count of Sondershausen was raised to the rank of prince in 1709. The last prince died in 1909 and the lands passed to Rudolstadt.

RULERS

Christian Gunther III, 1750-1794
Gunther Friedrich Carl I, 1794-1835
Gunther Friedrich Carl II
1835-1880
Karl Gunther, 1880-1909

MINTMASTERS INITIALS

S, H.C.A.S. - Heinrich Christian Andreas Siegel (1763-1764)

PFENNIG

COPPER

C#	Date	Mintage	Fine	VF	XF	Unc
18	1846A	1.613	2.00	4.00	7.00	35.00
	1858A	.360	2.00	4.00	7.00	35.00

3 PFENNIG

BILLON
Obv: CG monogram.
Rev: Value and date.

C#	Date	Mintage	Good	VG	Fine	VF
2	1764 S	—	5.00	10.00	20.00	40.00

COPPER

C#	Date	Mintage	Fine	VF	XF	Unc
19	1846A	.682	2.00	4.00	7.00	30.00
	1858A	.360	2.00	4.00	7.00	35.00
	1870A	.120	2.00	4.00	7.00	35.00

1/2 SILBER GROSCHEN

BILLON

C#	Date	Mintage	Fine	VF	XF	Unc
20	1846A	.657	4.00	8.00	12.00	40.00
	1851A	Inc. Ab.	4.00	8.00	12.00	40.00
	1858A	.180	4.00	8.00	12.00	40.00

SILBER GROSCHEN

BILLON

C#	Date	Mintage	Fine	VF	XF	Unc
21	1846A	.584	5.00	9.00	14.00	40.00
	1851A	Inc. Ab.	5.00	9.00	14.00	40.00

C#	Date	Mintage	Fine	VF	XF	Unc
21	1858A	.150	5.00	9.00	14.00	40.00
	1870A	.120	5.00	9.00	14.00	40.00

1/48 THALER

BILLON
Obv: CG monogram.
Rev: Value and date.

C#	Date	Mintage	Good	VG	Fine	VF
4	1764 S	—	3.00	6.00	10.00	20.00

1/24 THALER

BILLON
Obv: Arms in crowned cartouche.
Rev: Value and date.

6	1763 H.C.A.S.	—	6.00	12.00	20.00	35.00

1/12 THALER

BILLON
Obv: Arms in crowned cartouche.
Rev: Value in circle.

8	1763	—	7.00	12.00	25.00	40.00

Obv: Crowned arms.

9	1763	—	3.00	6.00	12.50	20.00
	1764	—	3.00	6.00	12.50	20.00

1/6 THALER

SILVER
Obv: Bust of Christian Gunther right.
Rev: Crowned Baroque arms.

10	1764 H.C.A.S.	—	15.00	30.00	55.00	85.00

1/3 THALER

SILVER
Obv: Bust of Christian Gunther right.
Rev: Crowned Baroque arms.

12	1763 H.S.	—	25.00	50.00	75.00	110.00
	1764 H.S.	—	25.00	50.00	75.00	110.00

2/3 THALER

SILVER
Obv: Bust of Christian Gunther right.
Rev: Crowned Baroque arms.

14	1764 H.C.A.S.	—	36.00	75.00	110.00	175.00

THALER
(Convention)

SILVER
Obv: Bust of Christian Gunther right.
Rev: Crowned Baroque arms.

16	1764 H.C.A.S.	—	400.00	750.00	1250.	2000.

(Vereins)

18.5200 gm., .900 SILVER, .5360 oz ASW

C#	Date	Mintage	Fine	VF	XF	Unc
22	1859A	.015	30.00	75.00	150.00	300.00
	1865A	.010	30.00	75.00	150.00	300.00
	1870A	.011	30.00	75.00	150.00	300.00

2 THALER
(= 3-1/2 Gulden)

.900 SILVER

C#	Date	Mintage	Fine	VF	XF	Unc
23	1841A	4,300	150.00	300.00	600.00	1200.
	1845A	8,600	150.00	300.00	600.00	1200.
	1854A	8,600	150.00	300.00	600.00	1200.

MONETARY REFORM

2 MARK

11.1110 gm., .900 SILVER, .3215 oz ASW

Y#	Date	Mintage	VF	XF	Unc
209	1896A	.050	200.00	550.00	625.00
	1896A	190 pcs.	—	Proof	750.00

25th Year of Reign
Struck with thick rim

211	1905A	.013	100.00	150.00	200.00
	1905A	5,000	—	Proof	315.00

Struck with thin rim

211a	1905A	.062	40.00	75.00	100.00
	1905A	5,000	—	Proof	150.00

3 MARK

16.6670 gm., .900 SILVER, .4823 oz ASW
Death Of Karl Gunther

212	1909A	.070	50.00	80.00	100.00

Y#	Date	Mintage	VF	XF	Unc
	1909A	—	—	Proof	175.00

20 MARK

7.9650 gm., .900 GOLD, .2304 oz AGW

210	1896A	5,000	1500.	3000.	3500.

SCHWARZENBERG

Located in Franconia, Schwarzenberg was founded in 1420. The rulers were elevated to the rank of prince and were given the mint right in 1670. The lands were mediatized in 1806.

RULERS

Johann (Nepomuk) 1782-1789

20 KREUZER
(Convention)

SILVER
Similar to Thaler, C#7.

C#	Date	Mintage	VG	Fine	VF	XF
6	1783	—	15.00	30.00	50.00	75.00

THALER
(Convention)

SILVER

7	1783	—	80.00	175.00	350.00	700.00

TRADE COINS

DUCAT

3.5000 gm., .986 GOLD, .1109 oz AGW

C#	Date	Mintage	Fine	VF	XF	Unc
8	1783	—	400.00	750.00	1000.	1350.

10 DUCAT

35.0000 gm., .986 GOLD, 1.1095 oz AGW
Thaler, C#7 struck in gold.

C#	Date	Mintage	Fine	VF	XF	Unc
9	1783	—	—	—	Rare	—

SILESIA

A duchy, located in northeastern Germany, was separated into many segments. They were greatly influenced by Bohemia and Austria. The first coins were struck c. 1169. Special coins for Silesian possessions were struck by Bohemia from 1327. From 1526, when Bohemia and its Silesian possessions fell to Austria, a special series of coins were struck by Austria for the area. After the Prussian invasion, in 1740, they also minted coins from 1743 through 1797.

RULERS

Friedrich II, King of Prussia, 1740-1786
Friedrich Wilhelm III, 1797-1840

1/2 KREUZER

COPPER

C#	Date	Mintage	VG	Fine	VF	XF
47	1788B	—	3.00	5.00	7.50	15.00
	1789B	—	3.00	5.00	7.50	15.00
	1794B	—	3.00	5.00	7.50	15.00
	1795B	—	3.00	5.00	7.50	15.00
	1796B	—	3.00	5.00	7.50	15.00
	1797B	—	3.00	5.00	7.50	15.00

SILVER

C#	Date	Mintage	VG	Fine	VF	XF
47a	1787B	—	—	—	Rare	—
	1789B	—	—	—	Rare	—

COPPER
Obv: Crowned FW monogram. Rev: Value.

C#	Date	Mintage	Fine	VF	XF	Unc
53	1806A	—	3.00	5.00	10.00	35.00

KREUZER

BILLON
Obv: Head of Friedrich right.
Rev: Crowned eagle; value above, B divides date.

C#	Date	Mintage	VG	Fine	VF	XF
10	1766B	—	4.00	7.50	12.50	20.00
	1767B	—	4.00	7.50	12.50	20.00

Rev: Crowned flying eagle over value; B divides date.

C#	Date	Mintage	VG	Fine	VF	XF
11	1771B	—	3.00	6.50	10.00	15.00
	1772B	—	3.00	6.50	10.00	15.00
	1773B	—	3.00	6.50	10.00	15.00
	1774B	—	3.00	6.50	10.00	15.00
	1775B	—	3.00	6.50	10.00	15.00
	1776B	—	3.00	6.50	10.00	15.00
	1777B	—	3.00	6.50	10.00	15.00
	1778B	—	3.00	6.50	10.00	15.00
	1779B	—	3.00	6.50	10.00	15.00
	1780B	—	3.00	6.50	10.00	15.00
	1781B	—	3.00	6.50	10.00	15.00
	1782B	—	3.00	6.50	10.00	15.00
	1783B	—	3.00	6.50	10.00	15.00
	1784B	—	3.00	6.50	10.00	15.00
	1785B	—	3.00	6.50	10.00	15.00
	1786B	—	3.00	6.50	10.00	15.00

Obv: Bust of Friedrich Wilhelm right.
Rev: Crowned arms separate value and date.

C#	Date	Mintage	VG	Fine	VF	XF
51	1787B	—	3.00	6.00	10.00	15.00
	1788B	—	3.00	6.00	10.00	15.00
	1789B	—	3.00	6.00	10.00	15.00
	1790B	—	3.00	6.00	10.00	15.00
	1792B	—	3.00	6.00	10.00	15.00
	1793B	—	3.00	6.00	10.00	15.00
	1794B	—	3.00	6.00	10.00	15.00
	1795B	—	3.00	6.00	10.00	15.00
	1796B	—	3.00	6.00	10.00	15.00
	1797B	—	3.00	6.00	10.00	15.00

Obv: Uniformed bust left. Rev: Crowned arms with eagle.

C#	Date	Mintage	Fine	VF	XF	Unc
57	1806A	—	2.00	4.00	10.00	45.00
	1808G	—	2.00	4.00	10.00	45.00

Obv: Crowned arms with eagle within crossed branches.
Rev: Value.

C#	Date	Mintage	Fine	VF	XF	Unc
54	1810A	.055	2.00	4.00	10.00	45.00

3 KREUZER

BILLON
Obv: Crowned head of Friedrich right.
Rev: Crowned eagle divides date at top; value and B below.

C#	Date	Mintage	VG	Fine	VF	XF
23	1764B	—	5.00	10.00	20.00	35.00

Obv: Laureate head of Friedrich right.

C#	Date	Mintage	VG	Fine	VF	XF
23a	1765B	—	5.00	10.00	20.00	35.00

Rev: Crowned flying eagle; value below, B divides date.

C#	Date	Mintage	VG	Fine	VF	XF
24	1771B	—	4.00	7.50	12.50	20.00
	1772B	—	4.00	7.50	12.50	20.00
	1773B	—	4.00	7.50	12.50	20.00
	1774B	—	4.00	7.50	12.50	20.00
	1778B	—	4.00	7.50	12.50	20.00
	1779B	—	4.00	7.50	12.50	20.00
	1780B	—	4.00	7.50	12.50	20.00
	1781B	—	4.00	7.50	12.50	20.00
	1782B	—	4.00	7.50	12.50	20.00
	1783B	—	4.00	7.50	12.50	20.00
	1784B	—	4.00	7.50	12.50	20.00
	1785B	—	4.00	7.50	12.50	20.00
	1786B	—	4.00	7.50	12.50	20.00

Rev: "D. 20 AUGUST" above crowned eagle.

C#	Date	Mintage	VG	Fine	VF	XF
24a	1781B	—	—	—	Rare	—

9 KREUZER

BILLON
Obv: Uniformed bust left.
Rev: Crowned eagle with sceptor and orb.

C#	Date	Mintage	Fine	VF	XF	Unc
60	1808G	—	10.00	20.00	40.00	80.00

18 KREUZER

.563 SILVER
Obv: Uniformed bust left.
Rev: Crowned eagle with sceptor and orb.

C#	Date	Mintage	Fine	VF	XF	Unc
61	1808G	—	20.00	45.00	65.00	100.00

GROSCHEL

BILLON
Obv: Crowned block FR monogram divides date.
Rev: Value over branches.

C#	Date	Mintage	VG	Fine	VF	XF
5	1769B	—	5.00	10.00	20.00	35.00

Obv: Crowned script FR monogram divides date.

C#	Date	Mintage	VG	Fine	VF	XF
5a	1769B	—	5.00	10.00	20.00	35.00
	1770B	—	5.00	10.00	20.00	35.00
	1771B	—	5.00	10.00	20.00	35.00
	1772B	—	5.00	10.00	20.00	35.00
	1773B	—	5.00	10.00	20.00	35.00
	1774B	—	5.00	10.00	20.00	35.00
	1775B	—	5.00	10.00	20.00	35.00
	1776B	—	5.00	10.00	20.00	35.00
	1777B	—	5.00	10.00	20.00	35.00

Obv: Crowned script FR monogram.
Rev: Value over date.

C#	Date	Mintage	VG	Fine	VF	XF
5b	1778B	—	5.00	10.00	20.00	35.00
	1779B	—	5.00	10.00	20.00	35.00
	1780B	—	5.00	10.00	20.00	35.00
	1781B	—	5.00	10.00	20.00	35.00
	1782B	—	5.00	10.00	20.00	35.00
	1783B	—	5.00	10.00	20.00	35.00
	1784B	—	5.00	10.00	20.00	35.00
	1785B	—	5.00	10.00	20.00	35.00
	1786B	—	5.00	10.00	20.00	35.00

Obv: Crowned FW monogram.
Rev: Value and date.

C#	Date	Mintage	VG	Fine	VF	XF
49	1787B	—	3.00	5.00	10.00	15.00
	1788B	—	3.00	5.00	10.00	15.00
	1789B	—	3.00	5.00	10.00	15.00
	1790B	—	3.00	5.00	10.00	15.00
	1791B	—	3.00	5.00	10.00	15.00
	1792B	—	3.00	5.00	10.00	15.00
	1793B	—	3.00	5.00	10.00	15.00
	1794B	—	3.00	5.00	10.00	15.00
	1795B	—	3.00	5.00	10.00	15.00
	1796B	—	3.00	5.00	10.00	15.00
	1797B	—	3.00	5.00	10.00	15.00

Rev: Value spelled "GROSCHEL".

C#	Date	Mintage	VG	Fine	VF	XF
49a	1797B	—	—	—	—	—

Obv: Crowned FWR monogram. Rev: Value.

C#	Date	Mintage	Fine	VF	XF	Unc
56	1797B	—	3.00	6.00	10.00	45.00
	1805A	—	3.00	6.00	10.00	45.00
	1806A	—	3.00	6.00	10.00	45.00
	1808G	—	3.00	6.00	10.00	45.00
	1809G	—	3.00	6.00	10.00	45.00

2 GROSCHEL

BILLON
Obv: Head of Friedrich right.
Rev: Value and date; B below.

C#	Date	Mintage	VG	Fine	VF	XF
15	1771B	—	3.00	5.00	10.00	15.00
	1772B	—	3.00	5.00	10.00	15.00
	1773B	—	3.00	5.00	10.00	15.00
	1774B	—	3.00	5.00	10.00	15.00
	1775B	—	3.00	5.00	10.00	15.00
	1776B	—	3.00	5.00	10.00	15.00
	1777B	—	3.00	5.00	10.00	15.00
	1778B	—	3.00	5.00	10.00	15.00
	1779B	—	3.00	5.00	10.00	15.00
	1780B	—	3.00	5.00	10.00	15.00
	1781B	—	3.00	5.00	10.00	15.00
	1782B	—	3.00	5.00	10.00	15.00
	1783B	—	3.00	5.00	10.00	15.00
	1784B	—	3.00	5.00	10.00	15.00
	1785B	—	3.00	5.00	10.00	15.00
	1786B	—	3.00	5.00	10.00	15.00

1/2 FRIEDRICH D'OR

6.6500 gm., .900 GOLD, .1924 oz AGW
Obv: Head of Friedrich right.
Rev: Crowned eagle on military trophies; date above.

C#	Date	Mintage	Fine	VF	XF	Unc
39	1765B	—	250.00	350.00	600.00	1000.
	1766B	—	250.00	350.00	600.00	1000.
	1767B	—	250.00	350.00	600.00	1000.
	1768B	—	250.00	350.00	600.00	1000.
	1769B	—	250.00	350.00	600.00	1000.
	1770B	—	250.00	350.00	600.00	1000.
	1771B	—	250.00	350.00	600.00	1000.
	1772B	—	250.00	350.00	600.00	1000.
	1773B	—	250.00	350.00	600.00	1000.
	1774B	—	250.00	350.00	600.00	1000.
	1775B	—	250.00	350.00	600.00	1000.

Obv: Old head of Friedrich right.

C#	Date	Mintage	Fine	VF	XF	Unc
39a	1776B	—	750.00	1250.	2000.	3000.
	1777B	—	750.00	1250.	2000.	3000.

FRIEDRICH D'OR

.900 GOLD
Obv: Head of Friedrich right.
Rev: Crowned eagle on military trophies; date above.

C#	Date	Mintage	Fine	VF	XF	Unc
43	1764B	—	500.00	800.00	1400.	2000.
	1765B	—	500.00	800.00	1400.	2000.
	1766B	—	500.00	800.00	1400.	2000.
	1767B	—	500.00	800.00	1400.	2000.
	1768B	—	500.00	800.00	1400.	2000.
	1769B	—	500.00	800.00	1400.	2000.
	1770B	—	500.00	800.00	1400.	2000.
	1771B	—	500.00	800.00	1400.	2000.
	1772B	—	500.00	800.00	1400.	2000.
	1773B	—	500.00	800.00	1400.	2000.
	1774B	—	500.00	800.00	1400.	2000.
	1775B	—	500.00	800.00	1400.	2000.

Obv: Old head of Friedrich right.

C#	Date	Mintage	Fine	VF	XF	Unc
43a	1776B	—	400.00	600.00	1000.	1500.
	1777B	—	400.00	600.00	1000.	1500.
	1780B	—	400.00	600.00	1000.	1500.
	1781B	—	400.00	600.00	1000.	1500.
	1782B	—	400.00	600.00	1000.	1500.
	1783B	—	400.00	600.00	1000.	1500.
	1784B	—	400.00	600.00	1000.	1500.
	1785B	—	400.00	600.00	1000.	1500.
	1786B	—	400.00	600.00	1000.	1500.

Rev: "D. 20 AUGUST" above crowned eagle.

C#	Date	Mintage	Fine	VF	XF	Unc
43b	1781B	—	—	—	Rare	—

SILESIA — WURTTEMBERG — OELS

The duchy of Oels, in Silesia, was acquired by Wurttemberg, through marriage in 1647. In 1792, when the last duke of the line died, Oels went to Brunswick—Wolfenbuttel.

RULERS

Carl Christian Erdmann, 1744-1792

THALER

(Reichs)

SILVER

C#	Date	Mintage	VG	Fine	VF	XF
1	1785B	—	75.00	150.00	300.00	500.00

NOTE: Varieties exist.

STOLBERG-WERNIGERODE

Stolberg, a county located in the Harz mountains of central Germany, had its own coinage from the 11th century. The lines of Wernigerode and Stolberg were established in 1641. A division of the lands occurred in 1645 but only the Wernigerode branch issued coins after 1800. Although administered by Prussia from 1714, the country retained a certain amount of sovereignty until 1876.

RULERS

Heinrich Ernst II, 1771-1778
Christian Friedrich, 1778-1824
Henrich XII, 1824-1854

TRADE COINS

DUCAT

3.5000 gm., .986 GOLD, .1109 oz AGW
Obv: Head right.
Rev: Stag left; date in exergue.

C#	Date	Mintage	Fine	VF	XF	Unc
20	1778	—	1750.	2500.	3250.	4000.
24	1784	—	1950.	2750.	3500.	4500.
	1795	—	1950.	2750.	3500.	4500.

Golden Wedding Anniversary Of The Count

C#	Date	Mintage	Fine	VF	XF	Unc
25	1818	308 pcs.	600.00	900.00	1200.	1700.

SILVER

C#	Date	Mintage	Fine	VF	XF	Unc
25a	1818	—	—	—	Proof	—

.986 GOLD

C#	Date	Mintage	Fine	VF	XF	Unc
26	1824	—	500.00	800.00	1000.	1500.

STOLBERG — ROSSLA

Stolberg, a country located in the Harz mountains of central Germany, had its own coinage from the 11th century. The Rosala line was founded in 1704. The last count abdicated in 1776.

RULERS

Friedrich Botho, 1739-1768
  Jointly with Carl Ludwig of Stolberg-Stolberg, 1761-1768
Heinrich Christian Friedrich, 1768-1810
  Jointly with Carl Ludwig of Stolberg-Stolberg

MINTMASTERS INITIALS

C, I.E.V.C. - Johann Eberhard Volkmar Claus, (1750-1766)
E.F.R. - Ernst Friedrich Rupstein, (1766-1792)
Z, E.H.A.Z. - Ernst Hermann Agathus Ziegler, (1792-1801)

PFENNIG

COPPER
Obv: Stag left before column.
Rev: Value over date.

C#	Date	Mintage	VG	Fine	VF	XF
47	1799	—	3.00	5.00	10.00	20.00
	1801 Z	—	3.00	5.00	10.00	20.00

24 MARIENGROSCHEN

SILVER
Obv: Value and date in inner circle with "I.E.V.C.".
Rev: Stag left before column with "S" in base, in inner circle.

C#	Date	Mintage	VG	Fine	VF	XF
—	1763	—	30.00	60.00	90.00	150.00

Obv: Initials E.F.R.

C#	Date	Mintage	VG	Fine	VF	XF
—	1766	—	30.00	60.00	90.00	150.00

1/48 THALER

SILVER
Obv: Value and date.
Rev: Stag left before column.

C#	Date	Mintage	VG	Fine	VF	XF
—	1767 E.F.R.	—	7.00	14.00	25.00	40.00
	1768 E.F.R.	—	7.00	14.00	25.00	40.00
	1777 E.F.R.	—	7.00	14.00	25.00	40.00
	1791 E.F.R.	—	7.00	14.00	25.00	40.00

24 EINEN (1/24) THALER

SILVER
Obv: Stag left before column with "S" in base in inner circle.

Rev: Value with "C" below in circle.

C#	Date	Mintage	VG	Fine	VF	XF
28	1763	—	5.00	10.00	17.00	25.00
	1764	—	5.00	10.00	17.00	25.00

Rev: Value in circle without "C".

C#	Date	Mintage	VG	Fine	VF	XF
—	1763	—	5.00	10.00	17.00	25.00

Obv: Value and date in center.
Rev: Stag left before column with "S" in base; no inner circle.

C#	Date	Mintage	VG	Fine	VF	XF
29	1766 E.F.R.	—	5.00	10.00	17.00	25.00

Obv: Stag left before column.
Rev: Value over date.

C#	Date	Mintage	VG	Fine	VF	XF
48	1771 E.F.R.	—	5.00	10.00	15.00	25.00

12 EINEN (1/12) THALER

SILVER
Obv: Stag left before column with "S" in base in inner circle.
Rev: Value in center; "C" below.

C#	Date	Mintage	VG	Fine	VF	XF
30	1763	—	5.00	10.00	17.00	25.00
	1764	—	5.00	10.00	17.00	25.00

Rev: Value in cartouche.

C#	Date	Mintage	VG	Fine	VF	XF
—	1763	—	8.50	17.50	37.50	55.00

Obv: Stag left before column.
Rev: Value over date.

C#	Date	Mintage	VG	Fine	VF	XF
49	1768 E.F.R.	—	5.00	11.00	15.00	25.00
	1770 E.F.R.	—	5.00	11.00	15.00	25.00

1/6 THALER

SILVER
Obv: Helmed arms; value below.
Rev: Stag left before column with "S" in base in inner circle.

C#	Date	Mintage	VG	Fine	VF	XF
32	1763	—	12.00	25.00	40.00	60.00

Obv: "C" below arms.
Rev: Value in cartouche below stag in inner circle.

C#	Date	Mintage	VG	Fine	VF	XF
—	1763	—	12.00	25.00	40.00	60.00
	1764	—	12.00	25.00	40.00	60.00

Obv: Crowned arms.
Rev: Stag left before column.

C#	Date	Mintage	VG	Fine	VF	XF
—	1766 E.F.R.	—	12.00	25.00	40.00	60.00

(Reichs)

Obv: Stag left before column.
Rev: Crowned arms divide date, value below.

C#	Date	Mintage	VG	Fine	VF	XF
49a	1768 E.F.R.	—	10.00	20.00	35.00	50.00
	1770 E.F.R.	—	10.00	20.00	35.00	50.00
	1777 E.F.R.	—	10.00	20.00	35.00	50.00
	1790 E.F.R.	—	10.00	20.00	35.00	50.00

1/3 THALER

SILVER
Obv: Crowned arms; value below.
Rev: Stag left before column with "S" in base in inner circle; "C" in exergue.

C#	Date	Mintage	VG	Fine	VF	XF
—	1764	—	20.00	40.00	55.00	85.00

Obv: Crowned arms; "C" below.
Rev: Stag left before column with "S" in base in inner circle; date in exergue.

C#	Date	Mintage	VG	Fine	VF	XF
—	1763	—	20.00	40.00	55.00	85.00

(Reichs)

Obv: Stag left before column.
Rev: Crowned arms divide date, value below.

C#	Date	Mintage	VG	Fine	VF	XF
50	1768 E.F.R.	—	10.00	22.00	30.00	45.00
	1770 E.F.R.	—	10.00	22.00	30.00	45.00
	1777 E.F.R.	—	10.00	22.00	30.00	45.00
	1790 E.F.R.	—	10.00	22.00	30.00	45.00

1/2 THALER

SILVER
Obv: Crowned oval arms; "C" below.
Rev: Stag left before column with "S" in base, in inner circle; date in exergue.

C#	Date	Mintage	VG	Fine	VF	XF
35	1763	—	45.00	100.00	125.00	175.00

2/3 THALER

SILVER
Obv: Crowned oval arms; value below.
Rev: Stag left before column with "S" in base in inner circle; "C" in exergue.

C#	Date	Mintage	VG	Fine	VF	XF
—	1764	—	30.00	60.00	115.00	150.00

Obv: Crowned oval arms; value and "T" below.

C#	Date	Mintage	VG	Fine	VF	XF
—	1764	—	30.00	60.00	115.00	150.00

Obv: Crowned ornamental arms divide date; value below.
Rev: Stag left before column with "S" in base, in inner circle.

C#	Date	Mintage	VG	Fine	VF	XF
37	1765 I.E.V.C.	—	30.00	60.00	115.00	150.00

Obv: Crowned square arms divide date; value below.

C#	Date	Mintage	VG	Fine	VF	XF
—	1766 E.F.R.	—	60.00	125.00	165.00	200.00

(Reichs)

Obv: Stag left before column.
Rev: Crowned arms divide date; value below.

C#	Date	Mintage	VG	Fine	VF	XF
52	1768 E.F.R.	—	20.00	40.00	60.00	95.00
	1770 E.F.R.	—	20.00	40.00	60.00	95.00
	1777 E.F.R.	—	20.00	40.00	60.00	95.00
	1782 E.F.R.	—	20.00	40.00	60.00	95.00
	1788 E.F.R.	—	20.00	40.00	60.00	95.00
	1790 E.F.R.	—	20.00	40.00	60.00	95.00
	1793 E.F.R.	—	20.00	40.00	60.00	95.00

C#	Date	Mintage	VG	Fine	VF	XF
53	1796 E.H.A.Z.	—	20.00	45.00	70.00	100.00

THALER

SILVER
Obv: Crowned oval arms in sprays and garlands; "C" below. Rev: Stag left before column with "S" in base, in inner circle; date below.

C#	Date	Mintage	VG	Fine	VF	XF
39	1763	—	100.00	300.00	400.00	600.00

Obv: Crowned "square" arms in garlands; "C" below.
Rev: Stag left before column with "S" in base, in inner circle.

C#	Date	Mintage	VG	Fine	VF	XF
40	1764	—	100.00	300.00	400.00	600.00

Obv: Crowned ornamental arms in garlands; "C" below.
Rev: Stag left before column with "S" in base; no inner circle.

C#	Date	Mintage	VG	Fine	VF	XF
—	1764	—	100.00	300.00	400.00	600.00

1-1/3 THALER

(Reichs)

SILVER
Obv: Stag left before column.
Rev: Helmeted arms divide date, value below.

C#	Date	Mintage	VG	Fine	VF	XF
54	1796 E.H.A.Z.	—	150.00	400.00	700.00	1200.

TRADE COINS

1/2 DUCAT

1.7500 gm., .986 GOLD, .0832 oz AGW
Obv: Stag left before column with "S" in base; no inner circle. Rev: Helmed arms divide date.

C#	Date	Mintage	VG	Fine	VF	XF
41	1766 E.F.R.	—	375.00	600.00	850.00	1200.

Obv: Stag left before column.
Rev: Helmeted arms divide date.

C#	Date	Mintage	VG	Fine	VF	XF
56a	1770 E.F.R.	—	400.00	750.00	1000.	1350.

DUCAT

3.5000 gm., .986 GOLD, .0832 oz AGW
Obv: Small stag left before column with "S" in base; no inner circle. Rev: Helmed arms; date in outer legend.

C#	Date	Mintage	VG	Fine	VF	XF
42	1764 I.E.V.C.	—	400.00	750.00	1000.	1500.

Obv: Large stag left before column with "S" in base; no inner circle. Rev: Helmed arms divide date.

C#	Date	Mintage	VG	Fine	VF	XF
—	1766 E.F.R.	—	400.00	750.00	1000.	1500.

Obv: Stag left before column.
Rev: Helmeted arms divide date.

C#	Date	Mintage	VG	Fine	VF	XF
57	1768	—	400.00	750.00	1000.	1250.
	1770	—	400.00	750.00	1000.	1250.

Rev: E.F.R. below arms.

C#	Date	Mintage	VG	Fine	VF	XF
57a	1788	—	400.00	750.00	1000.	1250.

Rev: E.H.A.Z below arms.

C#	Date	Mintage	VG	Fine	VF	XF
57b	1793	—	400.00	750.00	1000.	1250.

Rev: Helmeted arms; date in legend; arms divide EH - AZ.

C#	Date	Mintage	VG	Fine	VF	XF
57c	1796	—	400.00	750.00	1000.	1250.

Obv: Bust left; SENIOR DOMUS in field.
Rev: Z below arms.

C#	Date	Mintage	VG	Fine	VF	XF
45	1796	—	500.00	950.00	1350.	1750.

STRALSUND

The town of Stralsund, located on the Baltic Sea, was founded in 1234. They were a leading member of the Hanseatic League. In the 13th century coins were struck there. The town obtained the mint right in 1325 and struck coins as late as 1688. From 1637 to 1815 they belonged to Sweden. In 1815, together with the rest of Swedish Pomerania, they fell to Prussia.

RULERS

Adolf Frederick of Sweden, 1751-1771

WITTEN

BILLON
Obv: Crowned arrowhead, date above.
Rev: Value.

C#	Date	Mintage	VG	Fine	VF	XF
1	1763 LDS	—	5.00	10.00	20.00	40.00

SECHSLING

BILLON
Obv: Crowned arrowhead, date above.
Rev: Value.

C#	Date	Mintage	VG	Fine	VF	XF
2	1763 LDS	—	5.00	10.00	20.00	40.00

STRASBOURG

Strasbourg was established as a bishopric sometime during the 4th century. It was the largest bishopric in the area but was reduced in size when other bishoprics were formed in the area. Strasbourg became a Carolingran Mint in c. 800 and the bishops were given the mint right in 873. From that date until 1773 there were regular issues of coins from the bishopric. It was secularized and annexed to France in 1789.

RULERS

Louis Constantine, 1756-1779

KREUZER

COPPER

C#	Date	Mintage	VG	Fine	VF	XF
1	1773	—	40.00	65.00	100.00	150.00

5 KREUZER

BILLON

C#	Date	Mintage	VG	Fine	VF	XF
4	1773	—	100.00	150.00	200.00	250.00

10 KREUZER

SILVER

C#	Date	Mintage	VG	Fine	VF	XF
8	1773	—	60.00	100.00	150.00	200.00

20 KREUZER

SILVER

C#	Date	Mintage	VG	Fine	VF	XF
12	1773	—	125.00	200.00	350.00	450.00

1/12 THALER

SILVER

C#	Date	Mintage	VG	Fine	VF	XF
6	1759	—	100.00	150.00	225.00	350.00

1/6 THALER

SILVER

C#	Date	Mintage	VG	Fine	VF	XF
10	1759	—	100.00	175.00	300.00	425.00

1/2 THALER

SILVER

C#	Date	Mintage	Fine	VF	XF	Unc
16	1759	—	1250.	2000.	3000.	5000.

THALER

SILVER
Obv: Bust of Louis Constantine right.
Rev: Crowned and mantled arms under bishops hat.

C#	Date	Mintage	Fine	VF	XF	Unc
18	1759	—	900.00	2000.	3500.	7500.
	1760	—	900.00	2000.	3500.	7500.

TEUTONIC ORDER

The Order of Knights was founded during the Third Crusade in 1198. They acquired considerable territory by conquest from the heathen Prussians in the late 13th and early 14th centuries. The seat of the Grand Master moved from Acre to Venice and in 1309 to Marienburg, Prussia. The Teutonic Order began striking coins in the late 13th century. In 1355 permission was granted to strike hellers at Mergentheim. However, the bulk of the Order's coinage until 1525 was schillings and half schoters minted in and for Prussia. In 1809 the Order was suppressed and Mergentheim was annexed to Wurttemberg.

RULERS

Carl Alexander, Grand Master, 1761-1780

KREUZER

BILLON
Obv: Crowned order arms in sprays.
Rev: Value over date which separates W E.

C#	Date	Mintage	VG	Fine	VF	XF
15	1776	—	4.50	9.00	15.00	30.00

2-1/2 KREUZER

BILLON
Obv: Crowned order arms in sprays.
Rev: Value over date which separates W E.

C#	Date	Mintage	VG	Fine	VF	XF
17	1776	—	5.00	10.00	15.00	30.00

5 KREUZER
(Convention)

BILLON
Obv: Crowned order arms in sprays; 5 below.
Rev: Value over date in cartouche.

C#	Date	Mintage	VG	Fine	VF	XF
19	1776	—	6.00	12.00	17.50	35.00

10 KREUZER
(Convention)

SILVER
Death of the Grand Master Commemorative
Obv: Order arms.
Rev: 9 line inscription.

C#	Date	Mintage	VG	Fine	VF	XF
21	1780	—	5.00	10.00	15.00	30.00

20 KREUZER
(Convention)

SILVER
Obv: Bust right.
Rev: Inscription and date.

C#	Date	Mintage	VG	Fine	VF	XF
23	1776	—	5.00	10.00	15.00	30.00

30 KREUZER
(Convention)

SILVER
Death of the Grand Master Commemorative

C#	Date	Mintage	VG	Fine	VF	XF
25	1780	—	15.00	35.00	55.00	85.00

1/2 THALER
(Convention)

SILVER
Obv: Bust right.
Rev: Inscription and date.

C#	Date	Mintage	VG	Fine	VF	XF
27	1776	—	35.00	75.00	125.00	200.00

THALER
(Convention)

SILVER
Obv: Bust right.
Rev: Crowned and supported arms; value in exergue.

C#	Date	Mintage	VG	Fine	VF	XF
29	1776	—	200.00	500.00	1000.	1750.

2 THALER
(Convention)

SILVER
Obv: Bust right.
Rev: Crowned and supported arms; value in exergue.

C#	Date	Mintage	VG	Fine	VF	XF
30	1776	—	500.00	1000.	2000.	4000.

TRIER

Archbishopric

The town of Trier, located near the German-Luxembourg border became the seat of a bishopric early in the Christian era. It gained the status of archbishopric c. 830. They began striking their own coinage c. 990. It became one of the seven imperial electorates of the Empire in 1356. In 1802 Trier was secularized and divided between France and Nassau. Prussia obtained most of the domain in 1814.

RULERS

Clemens Wenzel, Archbishop, 1768-1794

PFENNIG

COPPER
Obv: CWC monogram.
Rev: Value over date; G.M. below.

C#	Date	Mintage	VG	Fine	VF	XF
66	1789	—	2.00	4.00	7.00	15.00

2 PFENNIG

COPPER
Obv: CWC monogram.
Rev: Value over date; G.M. below.

C#	Date	Mintage	VG	Fine	VF	XF
67	1789	—	2.00	5.00	8.00	16.00

4 PFENNIG

COPPER
Obv: CWC monogram.
Rev: Value over date; G.M. below.

C#	Date	Mintage	VG	Fine	VF	XF
68	1789	—	2.00	5.00	8.00	16.00

KREUZER

BILLON
Obv: CWC monogram.
Rev: Value over date.

C#	Date	Mintage	VG	Fine	VF	XF
70	1794	—	2.50	5.00	8.00	16.00

5 KREUZER
(Convention)

BILLON
Obv: Arms. Rev: Value over date.

C#	Date	Mintage	VG	Fine	VF	XF
74	1770	—	3.00	6.00	9.00	18.00
	1771	—	3.00	6.00	9.00	18.00

20 KREUZER
(Convention)

SILVER
Obv: Bust right. Rev: Arms.

C#	Date	Mintage	VG	Fine	VF	XF
78	1769	—	10.00	20.00	30.00	50.00

Obv: Arms. Rev: Value over date.

C#	Date	Mintage	VG	Fine	VF	XF
79	1769	—	10.00	20.00	30.00	50.00
81	1771	—	10.00	20.00	30.00	50.00

ALBUS

BILLON
Obv: CWC monogram.
Rev: Value over date.

C#	Date	Mintage	VG	Fine	VF	XF
72	1789	—	3.00	5.00	8.00	16.00
	1790	—	3.00	5.00	8.00	16.00
	1791	—	3.00	5.00	8.00	16.00

3 ALBUS

BILLON
Obv: Arms. Rev: Value over date.

C#	Date	Mintage	VG	Fine	VF	XF
76	1789	—	3.00	6.00	9.00	18.00
	1790	—	3.00	6.00	9.00	18.00
	1791	—	3.00	6.00	9.00	18.00
	1792	—	3.00	6.00	9.00	18.00
	1793	—	3.00	6.00	9.00	18.00

1/2 THALER
(Convention)

SILVER

C#	Date	Mintage	VG	Fine	VF	XF
83	1770	—	20.00	50.00	95.00	140.00

C#	Date	Mintage	VG	Fine	VF	XF
83a	1773	—	20.00	50.00	95.00	140.00

THALER

(Convention)

SILVER

Obv: Bust right with date and E.G. below.
Rev: Capped arms supported by crowned lions; value below.

C#	Date	Mintage	VG	Fine	VF	XF
85	1768	—	400.00	1000.	2000.	3000.

C#	Date	Mintage	VG	Fine	VF	XF
86	1769	—	50.00	150.00	300.00	600.00

C#	Date	Mintage	VG	Fine	VF	XF
87.1	1771	—	50.00	150.00	300.00	600.00

Rev: Similar to C#87.1.

C#	Date	Mintage	VG	Fine	VF	XF
87.2	1771	—	50.00	150.00	300.00	600.00

Rev: Capped arms with value and S.C. below.

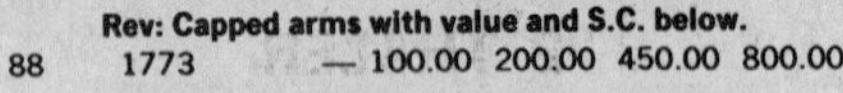

C#	Date	Mintage	VG	Fine	VF	XF
88	1773	—	100.00	200.00	450.00	800.00

C#	Date	Mintage	VG	Fine	VF	XF
88a	1773GM	—	100.00	200.00	450.00	800.00

(Contribution)

Rev: Date in chronogram

C#	Date	Mintage	VG	Fine	VF	XF
89	1794GM	—	50.00	150.00	300.00	600.00

NOTE: Varieties exist.

TRADE COINS

DUCAT

3.5000 gm., .986 GOLD, .1109 oz AGW

C#	Date	Mintage	Fine	VF	XF	Unc
90	1770	—	1750.	2500.	3500.	4500.

WALDECK-PYRMONT

The county of Waldeck was located on the border of Hesse. Their first coinage appeared c. 1250. Pyrmont was united with Waldeck in 1625 but was ruled separately for a while in the 19th century. They were reunited in 1812. The rulers gained the status of prince in 1712. The administration was turned over to Prussia in 1867 but the princes retained some sovereignty until 1918.

RULERS

Carl August Friedrich in Waldeck, 1763-1812
Georg (In Pyrmont), 1805-1812
(Refer to Pyrmont for listings)
(In Waldeck-Pyrmont), 1812-1813
Georg Heinrich, 1813-1845
Emma, As Regent For Georg Victor, 1845-1852
Georg Victor, 1852-1893
Friedrich, 1893-1918

MINTMASTER'S INITIALS

A.W. - Albert Welle
F.W., F*W, W, .W. - Friedrich Welle

PFENNIG

COPPER

Obv: Crowned F.
Rev: Value over date.

C#	Date	Mintage	VG	Fine	VF	XF
42	1773-99	—	1.00	2.50	5.00	10.00

C#	Date	Mintage	VG	Fine	VF	XF
42a	1780-96	—	1.00	2.50	5.00	10.00

Obv: Crowned F monogram. Rev: Value.

C#	Date	Mintage	Fine	VF	XF	Unc
42b	1809 FW	—	2.50	5.00	10.00	40.00
	1810 FW	—	2.50	5.00	10.00	40.00

Obv: Crowned arms.

C#	Date	Mintage	VG	Fine	VF	XF
43	1781-99	—	2.00	4.00	8.00	16.00

Obv: Crowned arms

C#	Date	Mintage	Fine	VF	XF	Unc
43a	1809 FW	—	2.50	5.00	10.00	40.00
	Rev. value: 1 PFENNIG					
43b	1810 FW	—	2.50	5.00	10.00	40.00
	Obv: Crowned GH monogram					
65	1816 FW	—	2.50	5.00	10.00	40.00
	1817 FW	—	2.50	5.00	10.00	40.00
66	1816 FW	—	2.50	5.00	10.00	40.00
	1817 FW	—	2.50	5.00	10.00	40.00
	Obv: Crowned Waldeck-Pyrmont arms					
67	1821 FW	—	2.00	4.00	8.00	35.00
	Obv: Arms in beaded border					
67a	1821 FW	—	2.00	4.00	8.00	35.00
	Obv: Crowned draped arms					
68	1825 FW	—	2.00	4.00	8.00	35.00
69	1842A	.352	2.00	4.00	8.00	35.00
	1843A	.220	2.00	4.00	8.00	35.00
	1845A	.384	2.00	4.00	8.00	35.00

C#	Date	Mintage	Fine	VF	XF	Unc
85	1855A	.366	2.00	4.00	8.00	35.00
85a	1867B	.540	1.00	3.00	6.00	35.00

3 PFENNIG

COPPER

Obv: Crowned F within legend. Rev: Value over date.

C#	Date	Mintage	VG	Fine	VF	XF
44	1781	—	3.50	7.00	11.50	20.00
	Obv: Crowned F, no legend.					
44b	1797	—	3.00	6.00	9.50	20.00
	1798	—	3.00	6.00	9.50	20.00

Obv: Crowned F monogram, leg: FURSTL. WALDECK SCH. MUNZ. Rev. value: III PFENNIGE.

C#	Date	Mintage	Fine	VF	XF	Unc
44a	1781 FW	—	3.50	7.25	15.00	50.00
	1782 FW	—	3.50	7.25	15.00	50.00
	1783 FW	—	3.50	7.25	15.00	50.00
	1784 FW	—	3.50	7.25	15.00	40.00
	1785 FW	—	3.50	7.25	15.00	40.00
	1786 FW	—	3.50	7.25	15.00	40.00
	1787 FW	—	3.50	7.25	15.00	40.00
	1788 FW	—	3.50	7.25	15.00	40.00
	1789 FW	—	3.50	7.25	15.00	40.00
	1790 FW	—	3.50	7.25	15.00	40.00
	1791 FW	—	3.50	7.25	15.00	40.00
	1792 FW	—	3.50	7.25	15.00	40.00
	1793 FW	—	3.50	7.25	15.00	40.00
	1794 FW	—	3.50	7.25	15.00	40.00
	1795 FW	—	3.50	7.25	15.00	40.00

C#	Date	Mintage	Fine	VF	XF	Unc
44a	1796 FW	—	3.50	7.25	15.00	40.00
	1797 FW	—	3.50	7.25	15.00	40.00
	1798 FW	—	3.50	7.25	15.00	40.00
	1799 FW	—	3.50	7.25	15.00	40.00
	1800 FW	—	3.50	7.25	15.00	40.00
	1801 FW	—	3.50	7.25	15.00	40.00
	1803 FW	—	3.50	7.25	15.00	40.00
	1804 FW	—	3.50	7.25	15.00	40.00
	1805 FW	—	3.50	7.25	15.00	40.00
	1806 FW	—	3.50	7.25	15.00	40.00
	1807 FW	—	3.50	7.25	15.00	40.00
	1808 FW	—	3.50	7.25	15.00	40.00
	1809 FW	—	3.50	7.25	15.00	40.00
	1810 FW	—	3.50	7.25	15.00	40.00
	Obv: Crowned star arms					
45	1781 FW	—	3.50	7.25	15.00	40.00
	1782 FW	—	3.50	7.25	15.00	40.00
	1783 FW	—	3.50	7.25	15.00	40.00
	1784 FW	—	3.50	7.25	15.00	40.00
	1785 FW	—	3.50	7.25	15.00	40.00
	1786 FW	—	3.50	7.25	15.00	40.00
	1787 FW	—	3.50	7.25	15.00	40.00
	1788 FW	—	3.50	7.25	15.00	40.00
	1789 FW	—	3.50	7.25	15.00	40.00
	1790 FW	—	3.50	7.25	15.00	40.00
	1791 FW	—	3.50	7.25	15.00	40.00
	1792 FW	—	3.50	7.25	15.00	40.00
	1793 FW	—	3.50	7.25	15.00	40.00
	1794 FW	—	3.50	7.25	15.00	40.00
	1795 FW	—	3.50	7.25	15.00	40.00
	1796 FW	—	3.50	7.25	15.00	40.00
	1797 FW	—	3.50	7.25	15.00	40.00
	1798 FW	—	3.50	7.25	15.00	40.00
	1799 FW	—	3.50	7.25	15.00	40.00
	1800 FW	—	3.50	7.25	15.00	40.00
	1801 FW	—	3.50	7.25	15.00	40.00
	1802 FW	—	3.50	7.25	15.00	40.00
	1803 FW	—	3.50	7.25	15.00	40.00
	1804 FW	—	3.50	7.25	15.00	40.00
	1805 FW	—	3.50	7.25	15.00	40.00
	1806 FW	—	3.50	7.25	15.00	40.00
	1807 FW	—	3.50	7.25	15.00	40.00
	1808 FW	—	3.50	7.25	15.00	40.00
	1809 FW	—	3.50	7.25	15.00	40.00
	Obv: Arms within pearl circle					
45a	1810 FW	—	4.00	8.00	15.00	40.00
	Obv: Crowned draped arms					
70	1819 FW	—	2.50	5.00	10.00	35.00
	Rev. value: PFENNIG					
70b	1819 FW	—	2.50	5.00	10.00	35.00
	Rev. value: PFENNIGE, leg: SCHEIDE MUNZE.					
70a	1819 FW	—	2.50	5.00	10.00	35.00

C#	Date	Mintage	Fine	VF	XF	Unc
71	1824 FW	—	2.50	5.00	10.00	35.00
	1825 FW	—	2.50	5.00	10.00	35.00

C#	Date	Mintage	Fine	VF	XF	Unc
72	1842A	.247	2.50	5.00	8.00	35.00
	1843A	.114	2.50	5.00	8.00	35.00
	1845A	.249	2.50	5.00	8.00	35.00

C#	Date	Mintage	Fine	VF	XF	Unc
86	1855A	.243	2.50	5.00	8.00	35.00

C#	Date	Mintage	Fine	VF	XF	Unc
86	1867B	.420	2.00	4.00	8.00	35.00

10 KREUZER

SILVER

C#	Date	Mintage	VG	Fine	VF	XF
50	1763	—	6.00	15.00	25.00	40.00

1/2 GROSCHEN

COPPER

C#	Date	Mintage	Fine	VF	XF	Unc
46	1809 FW	—	3.50	7.00	15.00	40.00
	Obv: Crowned draped arms.					
73	1825 FW	—	4.00	8.00	15.00	40.00

GROSCHEN

(Marien)

BILLON

C#	Date	Mintage	Fine	VF	XF	Unc
74	1814 FW	—	4.00	8.00	18.00	45.00
	1820 FW	—	4.00	8.00	18.00	45.00
	Obv: Star arms of Waldeck.					
74a	1820 FW	—	4.00	8.00	18.00	45.00
	Obv: Crowned draped arms.					
74b	1820 FW	—	4.00	8.00	18.00	45.00
	1823 FW	—	4.00	8.00	18.00	45.00

(Silber)

Obv: Inscription WALDECK U.P. Rev: Value. 1 SILBER GROSCHEN

C#	Date	Mintage	Fine	VF	XF	Unc
76	1836 AW	.164	3.00	6.00	15.00	45.00
	1839 AW	.046	3.00	6.00	15.00	45.00

Obv: Inscription WALDECK U. PYRMONT

C#	Date	Mintage	Fine	VF	XF	Unc
77	1842A	.310	3.00	6.00	15.00	40.00
	1843A	.191	3.00	6.00	15.00	40.00
	1845A	.182	3.00	6.00	15.00	40.00
	Rev: A below value and date.					
87	1855A	.156	3.00	6.00	15.00	40.00

C#	Date	Mintage	Fine	VF	XF	Unc
87a	1867B	.180	3.00	6.00	15.00	40.00

2 MARIEN GROSCHEN

BILLON

C#	Date	Mintage	Fine	VF	XF	Unc
78	1820 FW	—	4.00	8.00	15.00	45.00
	1822 FW	—	4.00	8.00	15.00	45.00
	1823 FW	—	4.00	8.00	15.00	45.00
	1824 FW	—	4.00	8.00	15.00	45.00
	1825 FW	—	4.00	8.00	15.00	45.00
	Rev: A.W. below value.					
78a	1827 AW	—	3.00	6.50	15.00	45.00
	1828 AW	—	3.00	6.50	15.00	45.00

24 EINEN (1/24) THALER

BILLON

C#	Date	Mintage	Fine	VF	XF	Unc
75	1818 FW	—	5.00	10.00	15.00	45.00
	1819 FW	—	5.00	10.00	15.00	45.00

1/6 THALER

.521 SILVER

C#	Date	Mintage	Fine	VF	XF	Unc
79	1837 AW	.034	5.00	10.00	20.00	50.00

C#	Date	Mintage	Fine	VF	XF	Unc
79a	1843A	.038	5.00	10.00	20.00	50.00
	1845A	.038	5.00	10.00	20.00	50.00

IV EINEN (1/4) THALER

SILVER

C#	Date	Mintage	Fine	VF	XF	Unc
53	1810 FW	—	20.00	40.00	75.00	125.00
	Rev: Date and value in larger letters.					
53a	1810 FW	—	20.00	40.00	75.00	125.00

C#	Date	Mintage	Fine	VF	XF	Unc
	Obv. legend ends: PYRMONT & .					
62	1812 FW	—	150.00	300.00	400.00	600.00
	Obv. legend ends: PYRMONT EC					
62a	1813 FW	—	150.00	300.00	400.00	600.00

3 EINEN (1/3) THALER

.620 SILVER

C#	Date	Mintage	Fine	VF	XF	Unc
80	1824 FW	—	15.00	30.00	50.00	100.00

C#	Date	Mintage	Fine	VF	XF	Unc
80a	1824 FW	—	15.00	30.00	50.00	100.00

C#	Date	Mintage	Fine	VF	XF	Unc
81	1824 FW	—	30.00	65.00	100.00	150.00

THALER

SILVER

C#	Date	Mintage	VG	Fine	VF	XF
57	1781	—	400.00	850.00	1400.	2000.

28.0630 gm., .833 SILVER, .7520 oz ASW

C#	Date	Mintage	Fine	VF	XF	Unc
59	1810 FW	—	350.00	750.00	1500.	3000.

C#	Date	Mintage	Fine	VF	XF	Unc
59a	1810 FW	—	500.00	1000.	2000.	4000.

29.5170 gm., .868 SILVER, .8238 oz ASW

C#	Date	Mintage	Fine	VF	XF	Unc
63	1813 FW	—	600.00	1250.	2500.	5000.
	Similar to C#63. Edge inscription: KRONEN THALER					
64	1813 FW	—	600.00	1250.	2500.	5000.
	Similar to C#63. Edge inscription: WALDECKISCHER					
64a	1813 FW	—	600.00	1250.	2500.	5000.
	Edge: Stars					
64b	1813 FW	—	600.00	1250.	2500.	5000.

C#	Date	Mintage	Fine	VF	XF	Unc
82	1824 FW	—	250.00	500.00	1000.	2000.

C#	Date	Mintage	Fine	VF	XF	Unc
88	1859A	.014	40.00	100.00	200.00	400.00
	1867A	.019	40.00	100.00	200.00	400.00

2 THALER
(= 3-1/2 Gulden)

37.1200 gm., .900 SILVER, 1.0742 oz ASW

C#	Date	Mintage	Fine	VF	XF	Unc
83	1842A	4,500	300.00	600.00	1250.	2500.
	1845A	4,500	300.00	600.00	1250.	2500.

Rev: Similar to C#83.

C#	Date	Mintage	Fine	VF	XF	Unc
84	1847A	1,000	1500.	2000.	3000.	6000.

C#	Date	Mintage	Fine	VF	XF	Unc
89	1856A	.011	250.00	500.00	1000.	2000.

TRADE COINS

DUCAT

3.5000 gm., .986 GOLD, .1109 oz AGW
Obv: Head right.
Rev: Crowned and mantled arms.

C#	Date	Mintage	VG	Fine	VF	XF
61	1781	—	1750.	2500.	3500.	4500.

MONETARY REFORM

5 MARK

27.7770 gm., .900 SILVER, .8038 oz ASW

C#	Date	Mintage	Fine	VF	XF	Unc
213	1903A	2,000	400.00	1000.	2000.	2550.
	1903A	300 pcs.	—	—	Proof	2750.

20 MARK

7.9650 gm., .900 GOLD, .2304 oz AGW

C#	Date	Mintage	VF	XF	Unc
214	1903A	2,000	2000.	3000.	3600.
	1903A	150 pcs.	—	Proof	4000.

WALLMODEN — GIMBORN

The town of Gimborn, located in Westphalia, was purchased from Schwarzenberg in 1782. The following year it was raised to the rank of county. In 1806, Wallmoden-Gimborn was annexed to Berg. In 1815, the land went to Prussia.

RULERS

Johann Ludwig, 1782-1806

1/24 THALER

BILLON

C#	Date	Mintage	Fine	VF	XF	Unc
1	1802	—	15.00	35.00	60.00	80.00

1/2 THALER

SILVER

C#	Date	Mintage	Fine	VF	XF	Unc
2	1802	—	60.00	130.00	225.00	325.00

TRADE COINS

DUCAT

3.5000 gm., .986 GOLD, .1109 oz AGW

C#	Date	Mintage	Fine	VF	XF	Unc
3	1802	—	500.00	1000.	1500.	2000.

WESTPHALIA

A kingdom, located in western Germany, created by Napoleon for his brother. It was comprised of parts of Hesse-Cassel, Brunswick, Hildesheim, Paderborn, Holberstadt, Osnabruck, Minden, etc. In 1813 and 1814, Westphalia was divided and returned to its former owners.

Jerome (Hieronymus) Napoleon, 1807-1813

MINTMASTER'S INITIALS

F - Dietrich Heinrich Fulda

GERMAN STANDARD

PFENNIG

COPPER

Obv: Crowned HN monogram. Rev: Value.

C#	Date	Mintage	Fine	VF	XF	Unc
1	1808C	—	2.50	5.00	10.00	45.00

2 PFENNIG

COPPER

Obv: Crowned HN monogram. Rev: Value.

C#	Date	Mintage	Fine	VF	XF	Unc
2	1808C	—	5.00	10.00	15.00	50.00
	1810C	—	5.00	10.00	15.00	50.00

4 PFENNIG

BILLON SILVER

Obv: Crowned HN monogram. Rev: Value.

C#	Date	Mintage	Fine	VF	XF	Unc
3	1808C	—	5.00	10.00	20.00	50.00
3a	1809C	—	5.00	10.00	20.00	50.00

MARIEN GROSCHEN

BILLON SILVER

Obv: Crowned HN monogram. Rev: Value.

C#	Date	Mintage	Fine	VF	XF	Unc
4	1808C	—	5.00	9.00	15.00	50.00
	1810C	—	5.00	9.00	15.00	50.00

24 MARIEN GROSCHEN

17.3200 gm., .750 SILVER, .4177 oz ASW

C#	Date	Mintage	Fine	VF	XF	Unc
12	1810B	—	30.00	60.00	90.00	180.00

24 EINEN (1/24) THALER

BILLON SILVER

Obv: Crowned HN monogram with ribbons. Rev: Value.

C#	Date	Mintage	Fine	VF	XF	Unc
17	1807 F	—	5.00	11.00	20.00	50.00
	1808/7 F	—	6.00	13.50	25.00	50.00
	1808 F	—	5.00	11.00	20.00	50.00
	1809 F	—	5.00	11.00	20.00	50.00

Obv: Crown without ribbons

C#	Date	Mintage	Fine	VF	XF	Unc
17a	1809C	—	5.00	11.00	20.00	50.00

12 EINEN (1/12) THALER

BILLON SILVER

C#	Date	Mintage	Fine	VF	XF	Unc
5	1808C	—	7.00	14.00	22.00	50.00
	1809C	—	7.00	14.00	22.00	50.00
	1810C	—	7.00	14.00	22.00	50.00

1/6 THALER

(Reichs)

3.1800 gm., .994 SILVER, .1016 oz ASW

C#	Date	Mintage	Fine	VF	XF	Unc
6	1808C	—	10.00	20.00	35.00	75.00
	1812C	—	10.00	20.00	35.00	75.00
6a	1810C	—	10.00	20.00	35.00	75.00

5.8500 gm., .500 SILVER, .0939 oz ASW

C#	Date	Mintage	Fine	VF	XF	Unc
18	1808 F	—	11.00	22.50	40.00	80.00
	1809 C	—	11.00	22.50	40.00	80.00
	1809 F	—	11.00	22.50	40.00	80.00
	1810 C	—	11.00	22.50	40.00	80.00
	1810 F	—	11.00	22.50	40.00	80.00
	1813 C	—	11.00	22.50	40.00	80.00

C#	Date	Mintage	Fine	VF	XF	Unc
11	1808B	—	11.00	22.50	40.00	80.00
	1809B	—	11.00	22.50	40.00	80.00
	1810B	—	11.00	22.50	40.00	80.00
	1812B	—	11.00	22.50	40.00	80.00
	1813B	—	11.00	22.50	40.00	80.00

2/3 THALER

(Reichs)

13.0800 gm., .994 SILVER, .4180 oz ASW

C#	Date	Mintage	Fine	VF	XF	Unc
7	1808C	—	30.00	60.00	100.00	200.00
	1810C	—	30.00	60.00	100.00	200.00

Rev: Similar to C#7.

C#	Date	Mintage	Fine	VF	XF	Unc
7a	1809C	—	25.00	50.00	80.00	160.00
	1810C	—	25.00	50.00	80.00	160.00

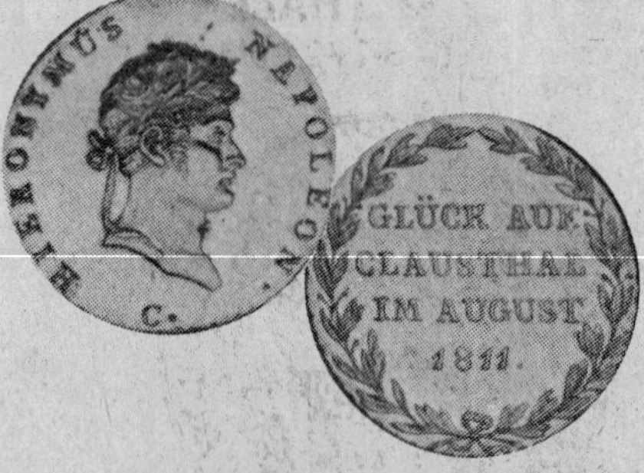

C#	Date	Mintage	Fine	VF	XF	Unc
8	1811C	—	75.00	150.00	275.00	500.00

GOLD

C#	Date	Mintage	Fine	VF	XF	Unc
8a	1811C	22 pcs.	—	—	—	—

.994 SILVER

C#	Date	Mintage	Fine	VF	XF	Unc
9	1811C	—	25.00	50.00	80.00	160.00
	1812C	—	25.00	50.00	80.00	160.00
	1813C	—	25.00	50.00	80.00	160.00

THALER

28.0600 gm., .833 SILVER, .7652 oz ASW

C#	Date	Mintage	Fine	VF	XF	Unc
19	1810C	5 pcs.	3500.	7500.	15,000.	25,000.
	Obv: Similar to C#10. Rev: Similar to C#19.					
20	1810C	—	150.00	375.00	750.00	1500.
	1811C	—	150.00	375.00	750.00	1500.
	1812C	—	150.00	375.00	750.00	1500.

C#	Date	Mintage	Fine	VF	XF	Unc
20a	1811C	—	150.00	375.00	750.00	1500.
	1812C	—	150.00	375.00	750.00	1500.
	1813C	—	150.00	375.00	750.00	1500.

C#	Date	Mintage	Fine	VF	XF	Unc
10	1811C	—	200.00	600.00	1250.	2500.

V (5) THALER

6.6500 gm., .900 GOLD, .1924 oz AGW

C#	Date	Mintage	Fine	VF	XF	Unc
13	1810B	—	400.00	800.00	1200.	2250.
	Obv: Bust left					
14	1811B	—	1000.	2000.	3000.	3500.

C#	Date	Mintage	Fine	VF	XF	Unc
14a	1811B	—	650.00	1300.	2500.	2500.
	1812B	—	425.00	850.00	1300.	2700.
	1813B	—	425.00	850.00	1300.	2700.

X (10) THALER

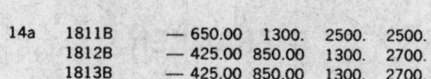

13.3000 gm., .900 GOLD, .3848 oz AGW

C#	Date	Mintage	Fine	VF	XF	Unc
15	1810B	—	500.00	1000.	1500.	2500.
	Obv: Bust left, without laurel wreath.					
16	1811B	—	1000.	2000.	3000.	3500.

C#	Date	Mintage	Fine	VF	XF	Unc
16a	1811B	—	700.00	1400.	2100.	2400.
	1812B	—	700.00	1400.	2100.	2400.
	1813B	—	700.00	1400.	2100.	2400.

PATTERNS

KM#	Date	Mintage	Identification	Mkt.Val.
1	1811C	—	Convention Thaler, Copper	—

KM#	Date	Mintage	Identification	Mkt.Val.
2	1812C	—	Mining Thaler, Copper	—

FRENCH STANDARD

CENTIME

COPPER

C#	Date	Mintage	Fine	VF	XF	Unc
21	1809C	—	2.00	5.00	10.00	40.00
	1812C	—	2.00	5.00	10.00	40.00

2 CENTIMES

COPPER

C#	Date	Mintage	Fine	VF	XF	Unc
22	1808C	—	2.00	5.00	10.00	40.00
	1809C	—	2.00	5.00	10.00	40.00
	1810C	—	2.00	5.00	10.00	40.00
	1812C	—	2.00	5.00	10.00	40.00
22a	1808J	—	2.00	5.00	10.00	40.00

3 CENTIMES

COPPER

C#	Date	Mintage	Fine	VF	XF	Unc
23	1808C	—	2.00	5.00	10.00	40.00
	1809C	—	2.00	5.00	10.00	40.00
	1810C	—	2.00	5.00	10.00	40.00
	1812C	—	2.00	5.00	10.00	40.00
23a	1808J	—	2.00	5.00	10.00	40.00

5 CENTIMES

COPPER

C#	Date	Mintage	Fine	VF	XF	Unc
24	1808C	—	2.00	5.00	10.00	40.00
	1809C	—	2.00	5.00	10.00	40.00
	1812C	—	2.00	5.00	10.00	40.00
24a	1808J	—	2.00	5.00	10.00	40.00
	1809J	—	2.00	5.00	10.00	40.00

10 CENTIMES

BILLON

C#	Date	Mintage	Fine	VF	XF	Unc
25	1808C	—	3.00	6.00	15.00	50.00
	1810C	--	3.00	6.00	15.00	50.00
	1812C	—	3.00	6.00	15.00	50.00

20 CENTIMES

BILLON

C#	Date	Mintage	Fine	VF	XF	Unc
26	1808C	—	3.50	7.00	15.00	50.00
	1810C	—	3.50	7.00	15.00	50.00
	1812C	—	3.50	7.00	15.00	50.00

1/2 FRANK

2.5000 gm., .900 SILVER, .0723 oz ASW

C#	Date	Mintage	Fine	VF	XF	Unc
27a	1808J	—	25.00	50.00	100.00	200.00

FRANK

5.0000 gm., .900 SILVER, .1447 oz ASW

C#	Date	Mintage	Fine	VF	XF	Unc
28	1808J	—	50.00	100.00	200.00	400.00

2 FRANKEN

10.0000 gm., .900 SILVER, .2894 oz ASW

C#	Date	Mintage	Fine	VF	XF	Unc
29	1808J	—	75.00	150.00	200.00	400.00

5 FRANKEN

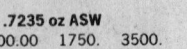

25.0000 gm., .900 SILVER, .7235 oz ASW

C#	Date	Mintage	Fine	VF	XF	Unc
30	1808J	—	400.00	800.00	1750.	3500.
30a	1809J	—	400.00	800.00	1750.	3500.

1.6200 gm., .900 GOLD, .0469 oz AGW

C#	Date	Mintage	Fine	VF	XF	Unc
31	1813C	—	125.00	250.00	400.00	800.00

10 FRANKEN

3.2300 gm., .900 GOLD, .0936 oz AGW

C#	Date	Mintage	Fine	VF	XF	Unc
32	1813C	—	125.00	250.00	400.00	800.00

20 FRANKEN

6.4500 gm., .900 GOLD, .1868 oz AGW

C#	Date	Mintage	Fine	VF	XF	Unc
33	1808J	—	150.00	300.00	500.00	1000.
	1809J	—	150.00	300.00	500.00	1000.
33a	1808C	.013	150.00	300.00	500.00	1000.
	1809C	9,104	150.00	300.00	500.00	1000.
	1811C	.019	150.00	300.00	500.00	1000.
	1813C	—	150.00	300.00	500.00	1000.
	MM: Horse's head					
33b	1809C	—	—	—	—	500.00
	Without edge inscription (restrikes ca. 1867)					
33c	—	—	—	—	—	—

40 FRANKEN

12.9000 gm., .900 GOLD, .3733 oz AGW

C#	Date	Mintage	Fine	VF	XF	Unc
34	1813C	5,465	1175.	2350.	3500.	6000.
	Without edge inscription (restrikes ca. 1867)					
34a	1813C	Inc. Ab.	725.00	1450.	2200.	4000.

NCLT ISSUES

PATTERNS

KM#	Date	Mintage	Identification	Mkt.Val.
1	1808J	—	10 Centimes, Billon, C25a	—
2	1808J	—	20 Centimes, Billon, C26a	—
3	1808C	—	1/2 Frank, Silver, C27	—

WISMAR

A seaport on the Baltic, the city of Wismar is said to have obtained municipal rights from Mecklenburg in 1229. It was an important member of the Hanseatic League in the 13th and 14th centuries. Their coinage began at the end of the 13th century and terminated in 1854. They belonged to Sweden from 1648 to 1803. A special plate money was struck by the Swedes in 1715 when the town was under siege. In 1803, Sweden sold Wismar to Mecklenburg-Schwerin. The transaction was confirmed in 1815.

City

RULERS

Friedrich Franz I, 1785-1837
Paul Friedrich, 1837-1842
Friedrich Franz II, 1842-1883

MINTMASTER'S INITIALS

F.L. - F. Lautersack
F.S. - Friedrich Schmidt
H.M. - Joachim Heinrich Meese
I.C.M - Carl Johann Joachim Mau
I.Z. - Johann Joachim Zeller
S. - Heinrich Schroeder

Under Sweden

3 PFENING

COPPER
Obv: Arms.
Rev: Value over date in cartouche.

C#	Date	Mintage	VG	Fine	VF	XF
1	1761-99	—	3.00	7.00	12.50	20.00

NOTE: Varieties exist.

Under Mecklenburg-Schwerin

3 PFENING

COPPER

C#	Date	Mintage	Fine	VF	XF	Unc
3	1824 FL	—	—	—	—	—
	1824 IZ	—	2.50	5.00	10.00	35.00
	1825 IZ	—	2.50	5.00	10.00	35.00

Obv: MONETA

C#	Date	Mintage	Fine	VF	XF	Unc
3b	1829 HM	—	2.50	5.00	10.00	35.00
	1830 HM	—	2.50	5.00	10.00	35.00
3d	1835 ICM	—	2.50	5.00	10.00	35.00
3e	1840 FS	—	2.50	5.00	10.00	35.00
3f	1845 S	—	2.50	5.00	10.00	35.00

Obv: Special head.

C#	Date	Mintage	Fine	VF	XF	Unc
3a	1835 ICM	—	2.50	5.00	10.00	35.00

C#	Date	Mintage	Fine	VF	XF	Unc
3c	1840 FS	—	2.50	5.00	10.00	35.00

Obv: Crowned arms. Rev. value: 3 PFENNINGE.

C#	Date	Mintage	Fine	VF	XF	Unc
4	1854 S	—	2.50	5.00	10.00	35.00

WURTTEMBERG

Located in South Germany, between Baden and Bavaria, Wurttemberg obtained the mint right in 1374. In 1495 the rulers became dukes. In 1802 the duke exchanged some of his lands on the Rhine with France for territories nearer his capital city. Napoleon elevated the duke to the status of elector in 1803 and made him a king in 1806. The kingdom joined the German Empire in 1871 and endured until the king abdicated in 1918.

RULERS

Carl Eugen, Duke, 1744-1793
Ludwig Eugen, 1793-1795
Friedrich I Eugen, 1795-1797
Friedrich, as Duke Friedrich II, 1797-1803
As Elector Friedrich I, 1803-1806
As King Friedrich I, 1806-1816
Wilhelm I, 1816-1864
Karl I, 1864-1891
Wilhelm II, 1891-1918

MINTMASTER'S INITIALS

A.D. - Gottlob August Doell
C.H. - Johann Christian Heuglin
C.S., C. Sch. F. - Christian Schnitzspahn
W., L.W., I.L.W. - Johann Ludwig Wagner

1/4 KREUZER

COPPER
Obv: Crowned rectangular arms within branches.
Rev: Value

C#	Date	Mintage	Fine	VF	XF	Unc
158	1842	.198	1.00	3.00	6.00	35.00
	1843	.118	1.00	3.00	6.00	35.00
	1852	—	1.00	3.00	6.00	35.00
	1853	—	1.00	3.00	6.00	35.00
	1854	—	1.00	3.00	6.00	35.00
	1855	—	1.00	3.00	6.00	35.00
	1856	—	1.00	3.00	6.00	35.00

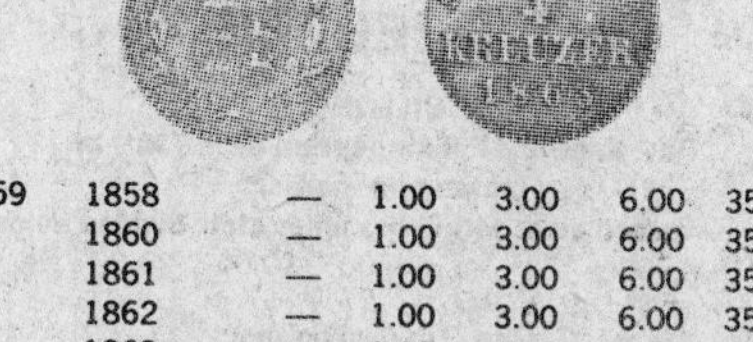

C#	Date	Mintage	Fine	VF	XF	Unc
159	1858	—	1.00	3.00	6.00	35.00
	1860	—	1.00	3.00	6.00	35.00
	1861	—	1.00	3.00	6.00	35.00
	1862	—	1.00	3.00	6.00	35.00
	1863	—	1.00	3.00	6.00	35.00
	1864	—	1.00	3.00	6.00	35.00

C#	Date	Mintage	Fine	VF	XF	Unc
203	1865	—	1.00	3.00	6.00	30.00
	1866	—	1.00	3.00	6.00	30.00
	1867	—	1.00	3.00	6.00	30.00
	1868	—	1.00	3.00	6.00	30.00
	1869	—	1.00	3.00	6.00	30.00
	1871	—	1.00	3.00	6.00	30.00
	1872	—	1.00	3.00	6.00	30.00

1/2 KREUZER

BILLON
Obv: 3 antlers in round shield.
Rev: 1/2 over date.

C#	Date	Mintage	VG	Fine	VF	XF
5	1766	—	2.00	4.00	8.00	16.00

Obv: Crowned round arms. Rev: Blank.

C#	Date	Mintage	VG	Fine	VF	XF
7	1769	—	2.00	4.00	8.00	16.00
	1774	—	2.00	4.00	8.00	16.00
	1775	—	2.00	4.00	8.00	16.00
	1787	—	2.00	4.00	8.00	16.00

Rev: Fraction and date.

C#	Date	Mintage	VG	Fine	VF	XF
9	1791	—	2.50	5.00	8.00	16.00

Obv: Bust right. Rev: Fraction.

C#	Date	Mintage	VG	Fine	VF	XF
82	ND	—	8.00	16.50	22.50	30.00

Obv: Crowned F II, date below. Rev: 1/2.

C#	Date	Mintage	Fine	VF	XF	Unc
106	1798	—	2.50	5.00	10.00	40.00

Obv: Crowned FR monogram.

C#	Date	Mintage	Fine	VF	XF	Unc
138	1812	—	2.50	5.00	10.00	40.00
	1813	.470	2.50	5.00	10.00	40.00
	1816	.126	2.50	5.00	10.00	40.00

Obv: Crowned W.

C#	Date	Mintage	Fine	VF	XF	Unc
162	ND	—	3.00	6.00	10.00	40.00

Obv: Crowned W dividing date.

C#	Date	Mintage	Fine	VF	XF	Unc
—	1818	—	3.00	6.00	10.00	40.00

C#	Date	Mintage	Fine	VF	XF	Unc
163	1824	.840	2.00	5.00	10.00	40.00
	1828	—	2.00	5.00	10.00	40.00
	1829	.780	2.00	5.00	10.00	40.00
	1831	.620	2.00	5.00	10.00	40.00
	1833	Inc. 1831	2.00	5.00	10.00	40.00
	1834	Inc. 1831	2.00	5.00	10.00	40.00
	1835	Inc. 1831	2.00	5.00	10.00	40.00
	1836	Inc. 1831	2.00	5.00	10.00	40.00
	1837	Inc. 1831	2.00	5.00	10.00	40.00

COPPER

C#	Date	Mintage	Fine	VF	XF	Unc
160	1840	—	1.00	3.00	7.00	35.00
	1841	—	1.00	3.00	7.00	35.00
	1842	.452	1.00	3.00	7.00	35.00
	1844	—	1.00	3.00	7.00	35.00
	1845	—	1.00	3.00	7.00	35.00
	1846	—	1.00	3.00	7.00	35.00
	1847	—	1.00	3.00	7.00	35.00
	1848	—	1.00	3.00	7.00	35.00
	1849	—	1.00	3.00	7.00	35.00
	1850	—	1.00	3.00	7.00	35.00
	1851	—	1.00	3.00	7.00	35.00
	1852	—	1.00	3.00	7.00	35.00
	1853	—	1.00	3.00	7.00	35.00
	1854	—	1.00	3.00	7.00	35.00
	1855	—	1.00	3.00	7.00	35.00
	1856	—	1.00	3.00	7.00	35.00

C#	Date	Mintage	Fine	VF	XF	Unc
161	1858	—	1.00	3.00	6.00	30.00
	1859	—	1.00	3.00	6.00	30.00
	1860	—	1.00	3.00	6.00	30.00
	1861	—	1.00	3.00	6.00	30.00
	1862	—	1.00	3.00	6.00	30.00
	1863	—	1.00	3.00	6.00	30.00
	1864	—	1.00	3.00	6.00	30.00

C#	Date	Mintage	Fine	VF	XF	Unc
204	1865	—	1.00	2.50	5.00	30.00
	1866	—	1.00	2.50	5.00	30.00

C#	Date	Mintage	Fine	VF	XF	Unc
204	1867	—	1.00	2.50	5.00	30.00
	1868	—	1.00	2.50	5.00	30.00
	1869	—	1.00	2.50	5.00	30.00
	1870	.147	1.00	2.50	5.00	30.00
	1871	.290	1.00	2.50	5.00	30.00
	1872	.177	1.00	2.50	5.00	30.00

EIN (1) KREUZER

BILLON

Obv: Bust of Carl Eugen right.
Rev: Crowned and mantled/arms; crown divides date; value at bottom.

C#	Date	Mintage	VG	Fine	VF	XF
16	1766	—	4.50	6.50	10.00	15.00
	1767	—	4.50	6.50	10.00	15.00
	1769	—	4.50	6.50	10.00	15.00
	1770	—	4.50	6.50	10.00	15.00
	1772	—	4.50	6.50	10.00	15.00

Obv: Bust right. Rev: Crowned arms in cartouche; date above, value below.

C#	Date	Mintage	VG	Fine	VF	XF
18	1785	—	2.00	4.00	6.50	15.00
	1790	—	2.00	4.00	6.50	15.00
	1791	—	2.00	4.00	6.50	15.00

Rev: Arms.

C#	Date	Mintage	VG	Fine	VF	XF
84	1794	—	3.00	7.00	10.00	20.00

Obv: Arms. Rev: Value over date.

C#	Date	Mintage	VG	Fine	VF	XF
95	1796	—	3.00	9.00	12.50	20.00

Obv: Crowned F II. Rev: Value above branches.

C#	Date	Mintage	Fine	VF	XF	Unc
108	1798	—	2.50	5.00	10.00	45.00

Rev: Branches reach middle of coin

C#	Date	Mintage	Fine	VF	XF	Unc
108a	1799	—	2.50	5.00	10.00	45.00
	1800	—	2.50	5.00	10.00	45.00
	1801	—	2.50	5.00	10.00	45.00
	1802	—	2.50	5.00	10.00	45.00

Obv: With legends. Rev: Crowned arms.

C#	Date	Mintage	Fine	VF	XF	Unc
122	1803	—	2.50	5.00	10.00	45.00
	1804	—	2.50	5.00	10.00	45.00

Obv: Crowned F II monogram, without legends.
Rev: Value above branches.

C#	Date	Mintage	Fine	VF	XF	Unc
122a	1805	—	2.50	5.00	10.00	45.00

Obv: Crowned FR monogram

C#	Date	Mintage	Fine	VF	XF	Unc
139	1807	—	2.50	5.00	10.00	45.00
	1808	—	2.50	5.00	10.00	45.00
	1809	—	2.50	5.00	10.00	45.00
	1810	—	2.50	5.00	10.00	45.00
	1811	—	2.50	5.00	10.00	45.00
	1812	—	2.50	5.00	10.00	45.00
	1813	.530	2.50	5.00	10.00	45.00
	1814	—	2.50	5.00	10.00	45.00
	1816	.630	2.50	5.00	10.00	45.00

Obv: Crowned W within wreath

C#	Date	Mintage	Fine	VF	XF	Unc
164	1818	—	2.50	5.00	10.00	45.00

C#	Date	Mintage	Fine	VF	XF	Unc
165	1824 W	.780	2.00	4.00	8.00	40.00
	1825 W	.300	2.00	4.00	8.00	40.00
	1826 W	—	2.00	4.00	8.00	40.00
	1827 W	—	2.00	4.00	8.00	40.00
	1828 W	—	2.00	4.00	8.00	40.00
	1829 W	—	2.00	4.00	8.00	40.00
	1830 W	—	2.00	4.00	8.00	40.00
	1831 W	—	2.00	4.00	8.00	40.00
	1832 W	—	2.00	4.00	8.00	40.00
	1833 W	—	2.00	4.00	8.00	40.00
	1834 W	—	2.00	4.00	8.00	40.00
	1835 W	—	2.00	4.00	8.00	40.00
	1836 W	—	2.00	4.00	8.00	40.00
	1837 W	—	2.00	4.00	8.00	40.00
	1838 W	—	2.00	4.00	8.00	40.00

Obv: Crowned arms, leg: WURTTEMBERG.
Rev: Value within wreath.

C#	Date	Mintage	Fine	VF	XF	Unc
166	1839	—	1.50	4.00	8.00	40.00
	1840	—	1.50	4.00	8.00	40.00
	1841	—	1.50	4.00	8.00	40.00
	1842	—	1.50	4.00	8.00	40.00

C#	Date	Mintage	Fine	VF	XF	Unc
166a	1842	—	1.00	3.00	6.00	40.00
	1843	—	1.00	3.00	6.00	40.00
	1844	—	1.00	3.00	6.00	40.00
	1845	—	1.00	3.00	6.00	40.00
	1846	—	1.00	3.00	6.00	40.00
	1847	—	1.00	3.00	6.00	40.00
	1848	—	1.00	3.00	6.00	40.00
	1849	—	1.00	3.00	6.00	40.00
	1850	—	1.00	3.00	6.00	40.00
	1851	—	1.00	3.00	6.00	40.00
	1852	—	1.00	3.00	6.00	40.00
	1853	—	1.00	3.00	6.00	40.00
	1854	—	1.00	3.00	6.00	40.00
	1855	—	1.00	3.00	6.00	40.00
	1856	—	1.00	3.00	6.00	40.00
	1857	—	1.00	3.00	6.00	40.00

C#	Date	Mintage	Fine	VF	XF	Unc
166b	1857	.095	1.00	3.00	6.00	35.00
	1858	.072	1.00	3.00	6.00	35.00
	1859	.050	1.00	3.00	6.00	35.00
	1860	.049	1.00	3.00	6.00	35.00
	1861	.097	1.00	3.00	6.00	35.00
	1862	.056	1.00	3.00	6.00	35.00
	1863	.098	1.00	3.00	6.00	35.00
	1864	.151	1.00	3.00	6.00	35.00

C#	Date	Mintage	Fine	VF	XF	Unc
205	1865	.086	1.00	2.00	5.00	35.00
	1866	.078	1.00	2.00	5.00	35.00
	1867	.119	1.00	2.00	5.00	35.00
	1868	.119	1.00	2.00	5.00	35.00
	1869	.120	1.00	2.00	5.00	35.00
	1870	.126	1.00	2.00	5.00	35.00
	1871	—	1.00	2.00	5.00	35.00
	1872	.100	1.00	2.00	5.00	35.00
	1873	.080	1.00	2.00	5.00	35.00

3 KREUZER

BILLON

Obv: Crowned F II monogram over 3 within rectangular border.
Rev: Crowned arms within branches, date divided below.

C#	Date	Mintage	Fine	VF	XF	Unc
110	1798	—	5.00	10.00	20.00	50.00

Obv: 3 in oval border

C#	Date	Mintage	Fine	VF	XF	Unc
110b	1799	—	7.00	15.00	25.00	50.00

Rev: W dividing date

C#	Date	Mintage	Fine	VF	XF	Unc
110a	1800	—	7.00	15.00	25.00	50.00

Obv: 3 between round clasps. Rev: Date not divided.

C#	Date	Mintage	Fine	VF	XF	Unc
110c	1800	—	5.00	10.00	15.00	50.00

Obv: 3 in oval border. Rev: Date divided by W.

C#	Date	Mintage	Fine	VF	XF	Unc
110d	1801	—	7.00	15.00	25.00	50.00
	1802	—	7.00	15.00	25.00	50.00

Obv: F. II. monogram, W below inscription.
Rev: Crowned oval arms.

C#	Date	Mintage	Fine	VF	XF	Unc
124	1803	—	5.00	10.00	15.00	50.00

Rev: Crowned rectangular arms

C#	Date	Mintage	Fine	VF	XF	Unc
124a	1804	—	4.00	8.00	13.00	50.00
	1805	—	6.00	13.00	20.00	50.00
	1806	—	4.00	8.00	13.00	50.00

Obv: FR monogram. Rev: Crowned electoral arms.

C#	Date	Mintage	Fine	VF	XF	Unc
140	1806	—	6.00	12.00	20.00	50.00

C#	Date	Mintage	Fine	VF	XF	Unc
141	1807	—	3.00	6.00	13.00	50.00
141	1808	—	3.00	6.00	13.00	50.00
	1809	—	3.00	6.00	13.00	50.00
	1810	—	5.00	10.00	17.00	50.00
	1811	—	3.00	6.00	13.00	50.00
	1812	—	3.00	6.00	13.00	50.00
	1813	—	3.00	6.00	13.00	50.00
	1814	.160	3.00	6.00	13.00	50.00

Obv: Crowned W within wreath. Rev: Value.

C#	Date	Mintage	Fine	VF	XF	Unc
167	1818	—	4.00	8.25	15.00	50.00

C#	Date	Mintage	Fine	VF	XF	Unc
168	1823	—	7.00	14.00	24.00	50.00

Obv: Date and W below head

C#	Date	Mintage	Fine	VF	XF	Unc
—	1823 W	—	6.00	12.00	20.00	45.00
	1824 W	—	6.00	12.00	20.00	45.00
	1825 W	.380	6.00	12.00	20.00	45.00

Rev: Crowned tapered arms within branches

C#	Date	Mintage	Fine	VF	XF	Unc
168a	1826	—	3.00	6.00	13.00	45.00
	1827	—	3.00	6.00	13.00	45.00
	1828	—	3.00	6.00	13.00	45.00
	1829	—	3.00	6.00	13.00	45.00
	1830	—	3.00	6.00	13.00	45.00
	1831	—	3.00	6.00	13.00	45.00
	1832	—	3.00	6.00	13.00	45.00
	1834	—	3.00	6.00	13.00	45.00
	1835	—	3.00	6.00	13.00	45.00
	1836	—	3.00	6.00	13.00	45.00
	1837	—	3.00	6.00	13.00	45.00

Obv: Crowned rectangular arms, leg: WURTTEMBERG.
Rev: Value within wreath.

C#	Date	Mintage	Fine	VF	XF	Unc
169	1839	—	2.00	5.00	10.00	40.00
	1840	—	2.00	5.00	10.00	40.00
	1841	—	2.00	5.00	10.00	40.00
	1842	—	2.00	5.00	10.00	40.00

C#	Date	Mintage	Fine	VF	XF	Unc
169a	1842	—	1.50	4.00	8.00	40.00
	1843	—	1.50	4.00	8.00	40.00
	1844	—	1.50	4.00	8.00	40.00
	1845	—	1.50	4.00	8.00	40.00
	1846	—	1.50	4.00	8.00	40.00
	1847	—	1.50	4.00	8.00	40.00
	1848	—	1.50	4.00	8.00	40.00
	1849	—	1.50	4.00	8.00	40.00
	1850	—	1.50	4.00	8.00	40.00
	1851	—	1.50	4.00	8.00	40.00
	1852	—	1.50	4.00	8.00	40.00
	1853	—	1.50	4.00	8.00	40.00
	1854	—	1.50	4.00	8.00	40.00
	1855	—	1.50	4.00	8.00	40.00
	1856	—	1.50	4.00	8.00	40.00

4 KREUZER

BILLON

Obv: 3 shields of arms.
Rev: Arms and date.

C#	Date	Mintage	VG	Fine	VF	XF
34	1760	—	50.00	100.00	150.00	200.00

5 KREUZER

(Convention)

BILLON

Obv: Bust right. Rev: Arms.

C#	Date	Mintage	VG	Fine	VF	XF
40a	1790	—	2.00	5.00	10.00	20.00

6 KREUZER

BILLON

Obv: Bust of Carl Eugen right.
Rev: Arms and date.

C#	Date	Mintage	VG	Fine	VF	XF
40	1769	—	6.50	10.00	15.00	25.00

BILLON

Obv: Crowned F-II monogram. Rev: Crowned arms.

C#	Date	Mintage	Fine	VF	XF	Unc
112	1799	—	8.00	16.00	30.00	60.00

Obv: F. II. monogram, legend.
Rev: Crowned arms dividing date.

C#	Date	Mintage	Fine	VF	XF	Unc
126	1803W	—	10.00	20.00	35.00	70.00

Obv: No W below monogram

C#	Date	Mintage	Fine	VF	XF	Unc
126a	1804	—	6.00	13.00	22.00	45.00
	1805	—	6.00	13.00	22.00	45.00

Electoral arms

C#	Date	Mintage	Fine	VF	XF	Unc
142	1806	—	10.00	20.00	32.00	60.00

Rev: Crowned arms with flags in left half of shield

C#	Date	Mintage	Fine	VF	XF	Unc
142a	1806	—	10.00	20.00	32.00	60.00

Rev: Arms dividing date

C#	Date	Mintage	Fine	VF	XF	Unc
142b	1806	—	10.00	20.00	32.00	60.00

C#	Date	Mintage	Fine	VF	XF	Unc
143	1806	—	4.00	8.00	15.00	45.00
	1807	—	4.00	8.00	15.00	45.00
	1808	—	4.00	8.00	15.00	45.00
	1809	—	4.00	8.00	15.00	45.00
	1810	—	4.00	8.00	15.00	45.00
	1811	—	4.00	8.00	15.00	45.00
	1812	—	4.00	8.00	15.00	45.00
	1814	—	4.00	8.00	15.00	45.00

Obv: Crowned W within wreath. Rev: Value.

C#	Date	Mintage	Fine	VF	XF	Unc
170	1817	—	4.00	8.00	15.00	45.00
	1818	—	4.00	8.00	15.00	45.00
170a	1819	—	4.00	8.00	15.00	45.00
	1821	—	4.00	8.00	15.00	45.00

Obv: Head right, date below.
Rev: Crowned circular arms within wreath.

C#	Date	Mintage	Fine	VF	XF	Unc
171.1	1823	—	6.00	12.00	18.00	50.00

Obv: Narrower head

C#	Date	Mintage	Fine	VF	XF	Unc
171.2	1823	—	7.00	15.00	25.00	50.00

Obv: WILHELM KON....

C#	Date	Mintage	Fine	VF	XF	Unc
171.3	1823	—	5.00	10.00	15.00	45.00
	1825	—	5.00	10.00	15.00	45.00

Rev: Crowned tapered arms within branches.

C#	Date	Mintage	Fine	VF	XF	Unc
171a	1825	—	5.00	11.00	20.00	50.00
	1826	—	5.00	11.00	20.00	50.00
	1827	—	5.00	11.00	20.00	50.00
	1828	—	5.00	11.00	20.00	50.00
	1829	—	4.50	9.00	15.00	45.00
	1830	—	4.50	9.00	15.00	45.00
	1831	—	4.50	9.00	15.00	45.00
	1832	—	4.00	8.00	13.00	45.00
	1833	—	4.00	8.00	13.00	45.00
	1834	—	4.00	8.00	13.00	45.00
	1835	—	4.00	8.00	13.00	45.00
	1836	—	4.00	8.00	13.00	45.00
	1837	—	4.00	8.00	13.00	45.00

C#	Date	Mintage	Fine	VF	XF	Unc
172	1838	—	2.00	4.75	8.00	40.00
	1839	—	2.00	4.75	8.00	40.00
	1840	—	2.00	4.75	8.00	40.00
	1841	—	2.00	4.75	8.00	40.00
	1842	—	2.00	4.75	8.00	40.00

C#	Date	Mintage	Fine	VF	XF	Unc
172a	1842	—	2.00	4.00	7.00	40.00
	1843	—	2.00	4.00	7.00	40.00
	1844	—	2.00	4.00	7.00	40.00
172a	1845	—	2.00	4.00	7.00	40.00
	1846	—	2.00	4.00	7.00	40.00
	1847	—	2.00	4.00	7.00	40.00
	1848	—	2.00	4.00	7.00	40.00
	1849	—	2.00	4.00	7.00	40.00
	1850	—	2.00	4.00	7.00	40.00
	1851	—	2.00	4.00	7.00	40.00
	1852	—	2.00	4.00	7.00	40.00
	1853	—	2.00	4.00	7.00	40.00
	1854	—	2.00	4.00	7.00	40.00
	1855	—	2.00	4.00	7.00	40.00
	1856	—	2.00	4.00	7.00	40.00

10 KREUZER

(Convention)

BILLON
Obv: Bust of Carl Eugen right.
Rev: Arms and date.

C#	Date	Mintage	VG	Fine	VF	XF
42	1763	—	6.00	12.50	20.00	35.00
43	1764	—	6.00	12.50	20.00	35.00

Obv: Bust right in wreath.
Rev: Crowned arms; value and date below.

C#	Date	Mintage	VG	Fine	VF	XF
44	1765	—	4.00	8.00	12.00	20.00
	1790	—	4.00	8.00	12.00	20.00

3.900 gm., .500 SILVER, .0627 oz ASW
Obv: Bust left.
Rev: Crowned arms with chain, CUM DEO-ET. IURE

C#	Date	Mintage	Fine	VF	XF	Unc
115	1799	—	11.50	23.00	35.00	70.00

Obv: Bust.
Rev: Crowned round arms within branches dividing date.

C#	Date	Mintage	Fine	VF	XF	Unc
128	1805 ILW	—	20.00	40.00	65.00	125.00

Rev: Crowned oval arm within branches, AD NORMAN.

C#	Date	Mintage	Fine	VF	XF	Unc
144	1808 ILW	.025	13.50	27.00	55.00	100.00
	1809 ILW	.010	17.50	35.00	70.00	140.00

Obv: Head right. NACH DEM Rev: Legend.

C#	Date	Mintage	Fine	VF	XF	Unc
145	1812 ILW	.026	16.50	33.50	80.00	150.00

Obv: Different head right. Rev: Value within wreath.

C#	Date	Mintage	Fine	VF	XF	Unc
173	1818 W	.152	10.00	20.00	40.00	80.00

3.9000 gm., .500 SILVER, .0627 oz ASW
Obv: Larger head right, date below.
Rev: Crowned circular arms.

C#	Date	Mintage	Fine	VF	XF	Unc
174	1823	.011	13.50	27.50	45.00	90.00

12 KREUZER

3.9000 gm., .500 SILVER, .0627 oz ASW

C#	Date	Mintage	Fine	VF	XF	Unc
175	1824 W	.045	13.50	27.50	45.00	90.00

C#	Date	Mintage	Fine	VF	XF	Unc
175a	1825 W	.025	15.00	30.00	50.00	100.00

20 KREUZER

(Convention)

6.6800 gm., .583 SILVER, .1251 oz ASW
Obv: Head of Carl Eugen right in wreath.
Rev: Crowned ornamental arms; value and date below.

C#	Date	Mintage	VG	Fine	VF	XF
56	1763	—	8.50	13.50	22.50	40.00
	1764	—	8.50	13.50	22.50	40.00

C#	Date	Mintage	VG	Fine	VF	XF
57	1765	—	5.00	10.00	15.00	30.00
	1767	—	5.00	10.00	15.00	30.00

Obv: Bust of Carl Eugen right in diamond.
Rev: Crowned and supported arms.

C#	Date	Mintage	VG	Fine	VF	XF
59	1769	—	10.00	15.00	25.00	50.00

C#	Date	Mintage	VG	Fine	VF	XF
61	1770	—	8.50	13.50	22.50	40.00

C#	Date	Mintage	VG	Fine	VF	XF
57a	1775	—	5.00	10.00	15.00	30.00

Rev: Crowned arms.

C#	Date	Mintage	VG	Fine	VF	XF
58	1768	—	5.00	10.00	15.00	30.00
	1774	—	5.00	10.00	15.00	30.00

C#	Date	Mintage	VG	Fine	VF	XF
99	1796	—	35.00	75.00	100.00	150.00

C#	Date	Mintage	Fine	VF	XF	Unc
116	1798 W	—	20.00	40.00	65.00	125.00

Rev: (20) below date, divided legend

C#	Date	Mintage	Fine	VF	XF	Unc
116a	1798	—	20.00	40.00	65.00	125.00
	1799	—	20.00	40.00	65.00	125.00

Obv: Different bust left, leg: ....ELECTOR.
Rev: Crowned oval arms.

C#	Date	Mintage	Fine	VF	XF	Unc
130	1805 ILW	—	17.50	35.00	60.00	125.00

Obv. leg: WURTTEMB

C#	Date	Mintage	Fine	VF	XF	Unc
146	1807 ILW	—	12.50	25.00	40.00	100.00
	1808 ILW	—	12.50	25.00	40.00	100.00
	1809 ILW	—	12.50	25.00	40.00	100.00
	1810 ILW	—	12.50	25.00	40.00	100.00

Obv: Head left.

C#	Date	Mintage	Fine	VF	XF	Unc
147	1810 ILW	—	17.50	35.00	70.00	125.00
	1812 ILW	—	17.50	35.00	70.00	125.00

Obv: Larger head

C#	Date	Mintage	Fine	VF	XF	Unc
147a	1810	—	17.50	35.00	60.00	125.00

Obv: Head right

C#	Date	Mintage	Fine	VF	XF	Unc
148	1812 ILW	.105	12.50	25.00	50.00	100.00

C#	Date	Mintage	Fine	VF	XF	Unc
176	1818 W	.180	15.00	30.00	50.00	100.00

Obv: Larger head right, date below.

C#	Date	Mintage	Fine	VF	XF	Unc
177	1823 W	.033	22.50	45.00	85.00	150.00

24 KREUZER

6.6800 gm., .583 SILVER, .1251 oz ASW

C#	Date	Mintage	Fine	VF	XF	Unc
178	1824 W	—	20.00	40.00	70.00	125.00
	1825 W	—	17.50	35.00	60.00	125.00

1/2 GULDEN

5.2900 gm., .900 SILVER, .1530 oz ASW
Obv: With VOIGT under head.

C#	Date	Mintage	Fine	VF	XF	Unc
179	1838	.824	15.00	50.00	100.00	200.00
	1839	.464	15.00	50.00	100.00	200.00
	1840	.516	15.00	35.00	75.00	150.00
	1841	.412	15.00	35.00	75.00	150.00
	1844	.154	15.00	35.00	75.00	150.00
	1845	.280	15.00	35.00	75.00	150.00
	1846	.338	15.00	35.00	75.00	150.00
	1847	.682	15.00	35.00	70.00	140.00
	1848	.498	15.00	35.00	70.00	140.00
	1849	.312	15.00	35.00	75.00	150.00
	1850	.286	15.00	35.00	75.00	150.00
	1852	.228	15.00	35.00	75.00	150.00
	1853	.192	15.00	35.00	75.00	150.00
	1854	.140	15.00	35.00	75.00	150.00
	1855	.112	15.00	35.00	75.00	150.00
	1856	.108	15.00	35.00	75.00	150.00

Obv: Without VOIGT under head.

C#	Date	Mintage	Fine	VF	XF	Unc
179a	1858	.219	15.00	90.00	150.00	250.00
	1859	.072	15.00	90.00	150.00	250.00
	1860	.299	15.00	40.00	80.00	160.00
	1861	.693	15.00	40.00	80.00	160.00
	1862	.149	15.00	50.00	100.00	200.00
	1863	—	15.00	50.00	100.00	200.00
	1864	.161	15.00	30.00	65.00	140.00

Obv: Head right with C.S. on truncation.

C#	Date	Mintage	Fine	VF	XF	Unc
206	1865 CS	.166	15.00	50.00	100.00	250.00
	1866 CS	.276	15.00	50.00	100.00	250.00
	1867 CS	.071	15.00	50.00	100.00	250.00
	1868 CS	.105	15.00	50.00	100.00	250.00

Obv: Without C.S. on truncation.

C#	Date	Mintage	Fine	VF	XF	Unc
206a	1868	Inc. Ab.	15.00	50.00	100.00	200.00
	1869	.072	15.00	50.00	100.00	200.00
	1870	.044	15.00	60.00	100.00	200.00
	1871	.041	15.00	60.00	100.00	200.00

GULDEN

12.7200 gm., .750 SILVER, .3071 oz ASW
Obv: Head right.
Rev: Crowned round arms within wreath.

C#	Date	Mintage	Fine	VF	XF	Unc
180	1824 W	.021	25.00	100.00	300.00	450.00

Rev: Crowned tapered arms

C#	Date	Mintage	Fine	VF	XF	Unc
181	1825 W	—	25.00	100.00	200.00	300.00

10.6100 gm., .900 SILVER, .3071 oz ASW
Obv: With VOIGT under head.

C#	Date	Mintage	Fine	VF	XF	Unc
182	1838	.712	15.00	50.00	100.00	200.00
	1839	.365	15.00	50.00	100.00	200.00
	1840	2.561	15.00	50.00	100.00	200.00
	1841	—	25.00	100.00	200.00	400.00
	1842	2.493	15.00	50.00	100.00	200.00
	1843	1.983	15.00	50.00	100.00	200.00
	1844	.379	15.00	50.00	100.00	200.00
	1845	.044	15.00	50.00	100.00	200.00
	1846	.042	15.00	50.00	100.00	200.00
	1847	.056	15.00	50.00	100.00	200.00
	1848	.058	15.00	50.00	100.00	200.00
	1849	.129	15.00	50.00	100.00	200.00
	1850	.114	15.00	50.00	100.00	200.00
	1851	.096	15.00	50.00	100.00	200.00
	1852	.032	15.00	50.00	100.00	200.00
	1853	.235	15.00	50.00	100.00	200.00
	1854	.090	15.00	50.00	100.00	200.00
	1855	.223	15.00	50.00	100.00	200.00
	1856	—	15.00	50.00	100.00	125.00

Obv: With A.D. below head

C#	Date	Mintage	Fine	VF	XF	Unc
182a	1837 AD	.443	25.00	100.00	150.00	300.00
	1838 AD	Inc.Ab.	25.00	100.00	150.00	300.00

Obv: Without VOIGT under head.

C#	Date	Mintage	Fine	VF	XF	Unc
182b	1839	—	15.00	35.00	75.00	150.00
	1840	—	15.00	35.00	75.00	150.00
	1841	—	25.00	75.00	125.00	250.00
182c	1848	Inc. Ab.	25.00	75.00	125.00	250.00

25th Anniversary of Reign

C#	Date	Mintage	Fine	VF	XF	Unc
183	1841	—	15.00	30.00	50.00	150.00

Visit Of King To New Mint
Obv: Head left, VOIGT below. Rev: View of Stuttgart Mint.

C#	Date	Mintage	Fine	VF	XF	Unc
184	1844	—	500.00	1000.	1500.	2000.

NOTE: Restrikes exist.

2 GULDEN

25.4500 gm., .750 SILVER, .6138 oz ASW

C#	Date	Mintage	Fine	VF	XF	Unc
187	1824	.015	225.00	450.00	825.00	1500.

Obv: Larger head right.
Rev: Legend ends "SC."

C#	Date	Mintage	Fine	VF	XF	Unc
187a	1824 ILW			—		
		Inc. Ab.	400.00	800.00	1500.	2500.

Obv: WAGNER F at truncation.
Rev: Crowned pointed arms within branches.

C#	Date	Mintage	Fine	VF	XF	Unc
188	1825 W	9,934	300.00	600.00	1250.	2500.

Obv: Without name at bottom.

C#	Date	Mintage	Fine	VF	XF	Unc
188a	1825 W	Inc. Ab	600.00	1250.	2500.	5000.

21.2100 gm., .900 SILVER, .6138 oz ASW

C#	Date	Mintage	Fine	VF	XF	Unc
189	1845	.562	50.00	100.00	225.00	450.00
	1846	.621	50.00	100.00	225.00	450.00
	1847	1.160	50.00	100.00	225.00	450.00
	1848	.336	50.00	100.00	225.00	450.00
	1849	.486	50.00	100.00	225.00	450.00
	1850	.280	50.00	100.00	225.00	450.00
	1851	.140	50.00	100.00	225.00	450.00
	1852	.225	50.00	100.00	225.00	450.00
	1853	.175	50.00	100.00	225.00	450.00
	1854	.074	50.00	100.00	225.00	450.00
	1855	.133	50.00	100.00	225.00	450.00
	1856	.267	50.00	100.00	225.00	450.00

5 GULDEN

.904 GOLD

C#	Date	Mintage	Fine	VF	XF	Unc
198	1825 W	5,956	550.00	1100.	1350.	1700.
198a	1824 W	2,282	550.00	1100.	1350.	1700.
	1835 W	1,443	600.00	1250.	1500.	1900.
198b	1839 W	822 pcs.	800.00	1600.	2000.	2500.

10 GULDEN

3.3400 gm., .896 GOLD, .0961 oz AGW
Obv: Head right, W below.
Rev: Crowned, pointed arms within branches.

C#	Date	Mintage	Fine	VF	XF	Unc
199	1824 W	1,896	1000.	1900.	2400.	3000.
	1825 W	1,240	1000.	1900.	2400.	3000.

Visit Of King To Mint

Rev: IN DES KOENIGS.

C#	Date	Mintage	Fine	VF	XF	Unc
200	1825 W	8 pcs.	—	—	—	25,000.

48 EINEN (1/48) THALER

(Convention)

BILLON
Obv: Crowned antler arms.
Rev: Value in cartouche.

C#	Date	Mintage	VG	Fine	VF	XF
30	1767	—	2.00	4.50	6.50	15.00
	1769	—	2.00	4.50	6.50	15.00
	1770	—	2.00	4.50	6.50	15.00
	1772	—	2.00	4.50	6.50	15.00
	1775	—	2.00	4.50	6.50	15.00
	1776	—	2.00	4.50	6.50	15.00
	1779	—	2.00	4.50	6.50	15.00
	1781	—	2.00	4.50	6.50	15.00
	1782	—	2.00	4.50	6.50	15.00
	1783	—	2.00	4.50	6.50	15.00
	1784	—	2.00	4.50	6.50	15.00
	1785	—	2.00	4.50	6.50	15.00
	1787	—	2.00	4.50	6.50	15.00
	1788	—	2.00	4.50	6.50	15.00
	1789	—	2.00	4.50	6.50	15.00
	1790	—	2.00	4.50	6.50	15.00
	1791	—	2.00	4.50	6.50	15.00
	1792	—	2.00	4.50	6.50	15.00
86	1794	—	4.00	8.00	15.00	30.00
97	1796	—	4.00	8.00	15.00	30.00

1/2 THALER

14.0300 gm., .833 SILVER, .3759 oz ASW
Obv: Bust left.
Rev: Crowned oval arms within branches.

C#	Date	Mintage	Fine	VF	XF	Unc
132	1805 ILW	—	100.00	250.00	500.00	1000.

THALER

(Convention)

SILVER
Obv: Bust of Carl Eugen right.
Rev: Crowned square arms in right branches.

C#	Date	Mintage	Fine	VF	XF	Unc
74	1760	—	200.00	350.00	700.00	1400.

Rev: Crowned oval arms in order chain and branches.

C#	Date	Mintage	Fine	VF	XF	Unc
74a	1760 straight date	—	200.00	300.00	600.00	1200.
	1761 curved date	—	200.00	300.00	600.00	1200.

Rev: Crowned ornamnetal shield in order collar and branches.

C#	Date	Mintage	Fine	VF	XF	Unc
74b	1762	—	200.00	300.00	600.00	1200.
	1763	—	200.00	300.00	600.00	1200.

Rev: Crowned arms in branches.

C#	Date	Mintage	Fine	VF	XF	Unc
74c	1764	—	200.00	375.00	600.00	1200.
	1765	—	200.00	375.00	600.00	1200.
	1766	—	200.00	375.00	600.00	1200.

Rev: Crowned and supported arms; date and value below.

C#	Date	Mintage	Fine	VF	XF	Unc
75	1768	—	250.00	450.00	700.00	1400.

C#	Date	Mintage	VG	Fine	VF	XF
76	1769	—	100.00	200.00	350.00	700.00
	1776	—	100.00	200.00	350.00	700.00

NOTE: Varieties exist.

Obv: Bust right with W on arm. Rev: Crowned round shield in order collar; date and value below.

C#	Date	Mintage	VG	Fine	VF	XF
76a	1777	—	100.00	200.00	350.00	700.00
	1779	—	100.00	200.00	350.00	700.00

C#	Date	Mintage	VG	Fine	VF	XF
76b	1779	—	100.00	200.00	350.00	700.00

Rev: Crowned round arms in sprays; divided date at top; value at bottom.

C#	Date	Mintage	VG	Fine	VF	XF
76c	1780	—	100.00	200.00	350.00	700.00

Rev: Crowned oval arms in sprays on order star; divided date at top; value at bottom.

C#	Date	Mintage	VG	Fine	VF	XF
76d	1781	—	100.00	200.00	350.00	700.00

C#	Date	Mintage	VG	Fine	VF	XF
76e	1784	—	100.00	200.00	400.00	800.00

C#	Date	Mintage	VG	Fine	VF	XF
90	1794	—	150.00	300.00	600.00	1200.

300 Years of Duchy

C#	Date	Mintage	VG	Fine	VF	XF
103	1795	—	150.00	375.00	750.00	1500.

28.0600 gm., .833 SILVER, .7518 oz ASW
Obv: Armored bust left.

C#	Date	Mintage	Fine	VF	XF	Unc
119	1798	—	375.00	750.00	1500.	3000.

Rev: Crown divides legend

C#	Date	Mintage	Fine	VF	XF	Unc
119a	1798 W	—	375.00	750.00	1500.	3000.

C#	Date	Mintage	Fine	VF	XF	Unc
134	1803	—	500.00	1000.	2000.	4000.
	Obv. leg: D G. REX					
149	1806	—	1000.	2000.	4000.	8000.
	Obv. leg: D.G.REX					
149a	1806	—	750.00	1500.	3000.	6000.
	Obv: I.L. WAGNER F. below bust. Rev: Legend with larger letters.					
149b	1806	—	2000.	4250.	8500.	17000.

C#	Date	Mintage	Fine	VF	XF	Unc
150	1809	—	1000.	2000.	4000.	8000.
	Obv: With I.L.W. below bust, leg: WURTTEMBERGIAE.					
150a	1809 ILW	—	1000.	2000.	4000.	8000.

(Kronen)

29.4900 gm., .868 SILVER, .8231 oz ASW
Obv: Military bust; leg:.... .D.G.REX ....
Rev: Crowned arms between lion and stag.

C#	Date	Mintage	Fine	VF	XF	Unc
151	1810 ILW	—	600.00	1250.	2500.	5000.
	Obv: Military bust; leg: .... I KOENIG					
152	1810 ILW	—	600.00	1250.	2500.	5000.
	Obv: Large head.					
A153	1810 ILW	—	400.00	900.00	1750.	3500.

Obv: Small head.

C#	Date	Mintage	Fine	VF	XF	Unc
153	1810 ILW	—	400.00	900.00	1750.	3500.
	Obv: Larger head. Rev: Palm branches in exergue.					
153a	1811 ILW	—	500.00	1000.	2100.	4200.

C#	Date	Mintage	Fine	VF	XF	Unc
154	1812 ILW	.015	225.00	450.00	900.00	1750.

(Convention)

28.0600 gm., .833 SILVER, .7518 oz ASW
Obv: Head left, WAGNER F below.
Rev: Value within wreath.

C#	Date	Mintage	Fine	VF	XF	Unc
190	1817	—	700.00	1500.	2650.	5000.

C#	Date	Mintage	Fine	VF	XF	Unc
190a	1818	—	500.00	1000.	2000.	4000.

(Kronen)

29.4900 gm., .868 SILVER, .8231 oz ASW

C#	Date	Mintage	Fine	VF	XF	Unc
191	1817	.044	500.00	1000.	2000.	4000.

Rev: Similar to C#191.

C#	Date	Mintage	Fine	VF	XF	Unc
191a	1818	Inc. Ab.	450.00	900.00	1750.	3500.

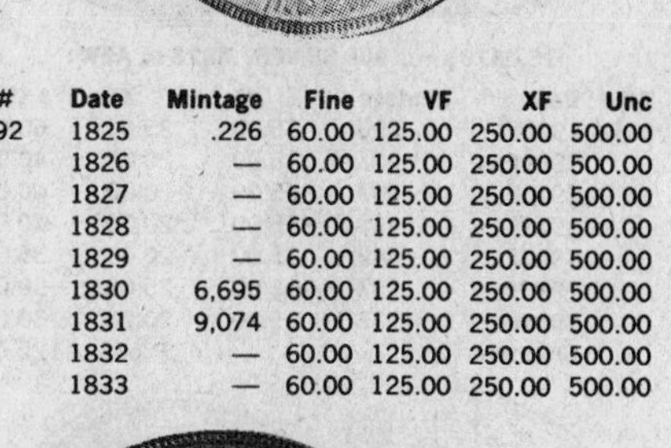

C#	Date	Mintage	Fine	VF	XF	Unc
192	1825	.226	60.00	125.00	250.00	500.00
	1826	—	60.00	125.00	250.00	500.00
	1827	—	60.00	125.00	250.00	500.00
	1828	—	60.00	125.00	250.00	500.00
	1829	—	60.00	125.00	250.00	500.00
	1830	6,695	60.00	125.00	250.00	500.00
	1831	9,074	60.00	125.00	250.00	500.00
	1832	—	60.00	125.00	250.00	500.00
	1833	—	60.00	125.00	250.00	500.00

Obv: With W on truncation

C#	Date	Mintage	Fine	VF	XF	Unc
192a	1834 W	—	60.00	125.00	250.00	500.00
	1835 W	—	60.00	125.00	250.00	500.00
	1837 W	.170	60.00	125.00	250.00	500.00

Free Trade Commemorative

C#	Date	Mintage	Fine	VF	XF	Unc
193	1833 W	—	50.00	100.00	200.00	400.00

(Vereins)

18.5200 gm., .900 SILVER, .5360 oz ASW

C#	Date	Mintage	Fine	VF	XF	Unc
186	1857	.452	25.00	75.00	175.00	350.00
	1858	.644	25.00	75.00	175.00	350.00
	1859	1.333	25.00	75.00	175.00	350.00
	1860	.645	25.00	75.00	175.00	350.00
	1861	.754	25.00	75.00	175.00	350.00
	1862	.648	25.00	75.00	175.00	350.00
	1863	.621	25.00	75.00	175.00	350.00
	1864	.533	25.00	75.00	175.00	350.00

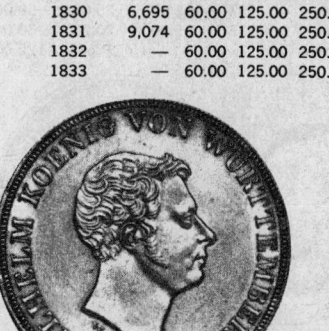

C#	Date	Mintage	Fine	VF	XF	Unc
207	1865	.276	50.00	100.00	200.00	400.00

Rev: Antlers extend into legend

C#	Date	Mintage	Fine	VF	XF	Unc
207a	1865	Inc. Ab.	75.00	150.00	300.00	600.00
	1866	.346	50.00	100.00	200.00	400.00
	1867	.165	50.00	100.00	200.00	400.00
207b	1868	.078	50.00	100.00	200.00	400.00
	1869	.031	50.00	100.00	200.00	400.00
	1870	.044	50.00	100.00	200.00	400.00

Victorious Conclusion Of Franco-Prussian War

C#	Date	Mintage	Fine	VF	XF	Unc
208	1871 C. SCH.F.	.114	20.00	40.00	80.00	175.00

2 THALER

(= 3-1/2 Gulden)

50.0000 gm., .833 SILVER, 1.3399 oz ASW
Obv: Bust left, D.G.DUX.
Rev: Crowned arms with chain.

C#	Date	Mintage	Fine	VF	XF	Unc
120	1798	—	500.00	1000.	2000.	4000.

37.1200 gm., .900 SILVER, 1.0742 oz ASW

C#	Date	Mintage	Fine	VF	XF	Unc
194	1840	.162	100.00	225.00	450.00	900.00
	1842	.051	100.00	225.00	450.00	900.00
	1843	.245	100.00	225.00	450.00	900.00
	1854	.168	100.00	225.00	450.00	900.00
	1855	Inc.Ab.	100.00	225.00	450.00	900.00

Marriage Of Crown Prince Carl To Olga,
Grand Duchess Of Russia
Rev: Similar to C#194.

C#	Date	Mintage	Fine	VF	XF	Unc
195	1846	5,808	100.00	250.00	500.00	1000.

Restoration Of Ulm Cathedral

C#	Date	Mintage	Fine	VF	XF	Unc
209	1869	—	130.00	250.00	500.00	1000.00
	1871	4,031	130.00	250.00	500.00	1000.00

TRADE COINS

DUCAT

3.5000 gm., .986 GOLD, .1109 oz AGW
Obv: Bust of Carl Eugen right.
Rev: Crowned arms and date.

C#	Date	Mintage	Fine	VF	XF	Unc
78	1762	—	1000.	1500.	2250.	4000.
	1790	—	1000.	1500.	2250.	4000.
	1791	—	1000.	1500.	2250.	4000.

C#	Date	Mintage	Fine	VF	XF	Unc
78b	1790	—	1100.	1500.	2250.	4000.

C#	Date	Mintage	Fine	VF	XF	Unc
78c	1791	—	1100.	1500.	2250.	4000.

C#	Date	Mintage	Fine	VF	XF	Unc
92	1794	—	1150.	1600.	2350.	4000.

Visit Of Duke To Mint
Obv: Bust right. Rev: IN HOCHST within wreath.

C#	Date	Mintage	Fine	VF	XF	Unc
136	1803 ILW	—	1000.	1850.	2300.	4000.

Rev. leg: DEN 9. IAN 1804 added.

C#	Date	Mintage	Fine	VF	XF	Unc
136a	1804 ILW	—	1000.	1850.	2300.	4000.

Rev: Crowned circular arms within branches

C#	Date	Mintage	Fine	VF	XF	Unc
137	1804 CH	—	600.00	950.00	1200.	2000.

C#	Date	Mintage	Fine	VF	XF	Unc
155	1808 CH	—	800.00	1400.	1750.	2500.

C#	Date	Mintage	Fine	VF	XF	Unc
156	1813 ILW	—	900.00	1600.	2000.	2750.

C#	Date	Mintage	Fine	VF	XF	Unc
196	1818 W	—	800.00	1400.	1750.	2500.

C#	Date	Mintage	Fine	VF	XF	Unc
197	1840	.081	200.00	350.00	450.00	700.00
	1841	.232	200.00	350.00	450.00	700.00
197	1842	.025	200.00	350.00	450.00	700.00
	1848	.062	200.00	350.00	450.00	700.00

4 DUCATS

14.0000 gm., .986 GOLD, .4438 oz AGW
25th Anniversary of Reign

C#	Date	Mintage	Fine	VF	XF	Unc
201	1841	6,236	600.00	1000.	1250.	2000.

Visit Of King To Mint
Obv: Head left with VOIGT below. Rev: View of mint.

C#	Date	Mintage	Fine	VF	XF	Unc
202	1844	17 pcs.	6000.	10,000.	12,500.	15,000.

FREDERICK D'OR = 1 KAROLIN

.900 GOLD

C#	Date	Mintage	Fine	VF	XF	Unc
157	1810 ILW	—	2000.	3000.	3750.	4500.

MONETARY REFORM

2 MARK

11.1110 gm., .900 SILVER, .3215 oz ASW

Y#	Date	Mintage	VF	XF	Unc
215	1876F	1.550	100.00	750.00	2000.
	1877F	1.107	125.00	800.00	2000.
	1880F	.129	200.00	800.00	2500.
	1883F	.074	200.00	800.00	2300.
	1888F	.123	150.00	600.00	1700.

Y#	Date	Mintage	VF	XF	Unc
220	1892	.177	45.00	75.00	200.00
	1893	.174	45.00	75.00	200.00
	1896	.351	30.00	75.00	180.00
	1898	.144	50.00	100.00	250.00
	1899	.538	25.00	50.00	175.00
	1900	.516	20.00	50.00	100.00
	1901	.592	20.00	60.00	150.00
	1902	.816	20.00	50.00	100.00
	1903	.811	20.00	50.00	100.00
	1904	1.988	20.00	40.00	90.00
	1905	.610	20.00	50.00	100.00
	1906	1.505	20.00	40.00	90.00
	1907	1.504	20.00	40.00	90.00
	1908	.451	20.00	40.00	90.00
	1912	.251	25.00	60.00	125.00
	1913	.226	25.00	60.00	150.00
	1914	.316	20.00	35.00	90.00
	Common Type	—	—	Proof	150.00

3 MARK

16.6670 gm., .900 SILVER, .4823 oz ASW

Y#	Date	Mintage	VF	XF	Unc
221	1908F	.300	15.00	25.00	60.00
	1909F	1.907	15.00	20.00	40.00
	1910F	.837	15.00	20.00	40.00
	1911F	.425	15.00	20.00	40.00
	1912F	.849	15.00	20.00	35.00
	1913F	.267	15.00	25.00	50.00
	1914F	.733	15.00	20.00	30.00
	Common Type	—	—	Proof	125.00

Silver Wedding Anniversary
Obv: With normal bar in H of Charlotte

Y#	Date	Mintage	VF	XF	Unc
225	1911F	.493	20.00	30.00	45.00
	1911F	—	—	Proof	80.00

Obv: With high bar in H of Charlotte

Y#	Date	Mintage	VF	XF	Unc
225a	1911F	7,000	300.00	450.00	600.00

25th Year of Reign

Y#	Date	Mintage	VF	XF	Unc
226	1916F	1,000	—	Proof Only	5000.

NOTE: 650 pieces have been melted.

5 MARK

27.7770 gm., .900 SILVER, .8038 oz ASW

Y#	Date	Mintage	VF	XF	Unc
216	1874F	.113	50.00	1000.	3000.
	1875F	.318	50.00	800.00	2700.
	1876F	.897	50.00	800.00	2500.
	1888F	.049	100.00	800.00	2500.

1.9910 gm., .900 GOLD, .0576 oz AGW

Y#	Date	Mintage	VF	XF	Unc
217	1877F	.488	200.00	300.00	600.00
	1878F	.050	1000.	1800.	2500.

27.7770 gm., .900 SILVER, .8038 oz ASW

Y#	Date	Mintage	VF	XF	Unc
222	1892F	.069	40.00	150.00	300.00
	1893F	.071	75.00	250.00	500.00
	1894F	.020	300.00	600.00	1000.
	1895F	.201	40.00	80.00	150.00
	1898F	.216	30.00	60.00	100.00
	1899F	.112	30.00	60.00	100.00
	1900F	.211	25.00	50.00	100.00
	1901F	.211	25.00	50.00	100.00
	1902F	.361	25.00	60.00	100.00
	1903F	.722	25.00	40.00	100.00
	1904F	.391	40.00	75.00	125.00
	1906F	.045	75.00	150.00	200.00
	1907F	.436	30.00	40.00	125.00
	1908F	.522	25.00	35.00	100.00
	1913F	.341	25.00	35.00	100.00
	Common Type	—	—	Proof	200.00

10 MARK

3.9820 gm., .900 GOLD, .1152 oz AGW

Rev: Type 1 eagle.

Y#	Date	Mintage	VF	XF	Unc
218	1872F	.271	150.00	200.00	600.00
	1873F	.675	150.00	200.00	500.00

Rev: Type 2 eagle.

Y#	Date	Mintage	VF	XF	Unc
218a	1874F	.205	200.00	250.00	500.00
	1875F	.532	150.00	200.00	350.00
	1876F	.933	150.00	200.00	350.00
	1877F	.271	200.00	250.00	400.00
	1878F	.337	200.00	250.00	400.00
	1879F	.211	150.00	200.00	350.00
	1880F	.245	200.00	250.00	400.00
	1881F	.079	200.00	250.00	450.00
	1888F	.200	200.00	250.00	400.00

Rev: Type 3 eagle.

Y#	Date	Mintage	VF	XF	Unc
218b	1890F	.220	200.00	250.00	350.00
	1891F	.080	300.00	400.00	600.00

Y#	Date	Mintage	VF	XF	Unc
223	1893F	.300	150.00	200.00	250.00
	1896F	.200	150.00	200.00	250.00
	1898F	.420	150.00	200.00	250.00
	1900F	.090	200.00	250.00	300.00
	1901F	.110	200.00	250.00	300.00
	1902F	.050	200.00	250.00	300.00
	1903	.180	200.00	250.00	300.00
	1904	.350	150.00	200.00	250.00
	1905	.200	150.00	200.00	250.00
	1906	.100	200.00	250.00	300.00
	1907	.150	150.00	200.00	250.00
	1909	.100	150.00	200.00	250.00
	1910	.150	200.00	250.00	300.00
	1911	.050	300.00	600.00	800.00
	1912	.049	400.00	700.00	1000.
	1913	.050	300.00	700.00	1000.

20 MARK

7.9650 gm., .900 GOLD, .2304 oz AGW

Rev: Type 1 eagle.

Y#	Date	Mintage	VF	XF	Unc
219	1872F	.662	175.00	250.00	350.00
	1873F	1.352	175.00	225.00	300.00

Rev: Type 2 eagle.

Y#	Date	Mintage	VF	XF	Unc
219a	1874F	.322	250.00	300.00	400.00
	1876F	.359	250.00	300.00	400.00

Rev: Type 3 eagle.

Y#	Date	Mintage	VF	XF	Unc
224	1894F	.501	150.00	250.00	300.00
	1897F	.400	150.00	250.00	300.00
	1898F	.106	150.00	250.00	300.00
	1900F	.500	150.00	250.00	300.00
	1905F	.501	150.00	250.00	300.00
	1913F	.043	3500.	5000.	6000.
	1914F	.558	5000.	10,000.	20,000.

NCLT ISSUES

PATTERNS

KM#	Date	Mintage	Identification	Mkt.Val.
1	1904	—	5 Marks, Silver	—
2	1905	—	3 Marks, Silver, uniface	—
3	1905	—	5 Marks, Silver	—
4	1905	—	5 Marks, Silver, beaded rim	—
5	1911	—	3 Marks, Silver	—
6	1911	—	3 Marks, Silver, busts divide dates	—

KM#	Date	Mintage	Identification	Mkt.Val.
7	1911F	—	3 Marks, Silver	—

KM#	Date	Mintage	Identification	Mkt.Val.
8	19xx	—	5 Marks, Silver, uniface	—

WURZBURG

BISHOPRIC

A bishopric, located in Franconia, was established in 741. The mint right was obtained in the 11th century. The first coins were struck c. 1040. In 1441 the bishops were confirmed as dukes. In 1803 the area was secularized and granted to Bavaria. It was made a grand duchy in 1806 but the 1815 Congress of Vienna returned it to Bavaria.

RULERS

Adam Friedrich, Bishop, 1755-1779
Franz Ludwig, Bishop, 1779-1795
Georg Carl, Freiherr von Fechenbach
Bishop, 1795-1803
Ferdinand, Grand Duke, 1806-1814
1806-1814

MINTMASTERS INITIALS

P.B. - Philipp Bischof, 1754-1761
G.N. - Georg Neumeister, 1754-1762
M.P. - Martinengo & Prange, 1762-1794
L - Loos - George Friedrica Loos, 1742-1766
V.Lon - Franz Anton Van Lon, 1727-1764

MONETARY SYSTEM

3 Drier (Kortling) = 1 Shillinger
7 Shillinger = 15 Kreuzer
28 Shillinger = 1 Guter Gulden
44-4/5 Shillinger = 1 Convention Thaler

1/2 PFENNING

COPPER
Obv: AFF monogram
Rev: Value and date

C#	Date	Mintage	VG	Fine	VF	XF
14	1760	—	3.00	5.00	10.00	20.00
	1761	—	3.00	5.00	10.00	20.00

Obv: 2 shields; crown above.

C#	Date	Mintage	VG	Fine	VF	XF
15	1761	—	3.00	5.00	10.00	20.00
	1762	—	3.00	5.00	10.00	20.00
	1763	—	3.00	5.00	10.00	20.00
	1764	—	3.00	5.00	10.00	20.00
	ND	—	3.00	5.00	10.00	20.00

3 PFENNIGE

BILLON
Obv: Value in orb. Rev: blank.

C#	Date	Mintage	VG	Fine	VF	XF
19	1759	—	3.50	7.00	11.50	20.00
	1760	—	3.50	7.00	11.50	20.00
	1761	—	3.50	7.00	11.50	20.00
	1762	—	3.50	7.00	11.50	20.00
	1763	—	3.50	7.00	11.50	20.00

KORTLING

(= 1/84 "Guter" Gulden)

BILLON
Obv: Crown over 3 shields.
Rev: Value in orb.

C#	Date	Mintage	VG	Fine	VF	XF
21	1764	—	4.00	7.50	12.50	20.00
66	1794	—	3.00	5.00	10.00	20.00

C#	Date	Mintage	Fine	VF	XF	Unc
102	1795	—	5.00	10.00	20.00	50.00

Obv: Crowned oval arms. Rev: Date, value.

C#	Date	Mintage	Fine	VF	XF	Unc
102a	1796	—	2.00	5.00	15.00	40.00
	1797	—	2.00	5.00	15.00	40.00
	1798	—	2.00	5.00	15.00	40.00
	1799	—	2.00	5.00	15.00	40.00

SCHILLINGER

BILLON
Obv: Arms. Rev: Madonna.

C#	Date	Mintage	VG	Fine	VF	XF
23	1763	—	6.00	12.50	20.00	35.00

Obv. leg: ...FRANC.LUD.D.G.

C#	Date	Mintage	VG	Fine	VF	XF
72	1794	—	3.00	6.00	10.00	20.00
	1795	—	3.00	6.00	10.00	20.00

Similar to C#72, obv. leg: ...GEORG.CAROL.D.G.

C#	Date	Mintage	VG	Fine	VF	XF
104	1795	—	2.50	5.00	10.00	20.00
	1796	—	2.50	5.00	10.00	20.00

VIERTEL (1/4) KREUZER

COPPER

C#	Date	Mintage	Fine	VF	XF	Unc
151	1811	—	2.50	5.00	10.00	35.00

1/2 KREUZER

COPPER
Obv: Crown over 2 shields, in cartouche
Rev: Value and date in cartouche

C#	Date	Mintage	VG	Fine	VF	XF
16	1762	—	3.00	5.00	10.00	20.00
	ND	—	3.00	5.00	10.00	20.00

C#	Date	Mintage	Fine	VF	XF	Unc
152	1810	—	2.50	5.00	15.00	35.00
	1811	—	2.50	5.00	15.00	35.00

KREUZER

SILVER
Obv: Crowned arms, dividing G.W.L.M. above. Rev: Value.

C#	Date	Mintage	Fine	VF	XF	Unc
153	1808	—	2.50	5.00	15.00	35.00

Obv: Without legend

C#	Date	Mintage	Fine	VF	XF	Unc
153a	1808	—	2.50	5.00	15.00	35.00

Rev: Value and G.W.L.M.

C#	Date	Mintage	Fine	VF	XF	Unc
153b	1808	—	2.50	5.00	15.00	35.00

2 KREUZER

BILLON
Obv: AF monogram. Rev: Arms.

C#	Date	Mintage	VG	Fine	VF	XF
25	1764	—	5.00	10.00	15.00	30.00
	1765	—	5.00	10.00	15.00	30.00

3 KREUZER

SILVER

C#	Date	Mintage	Fine	VF	XF	Unc
154	1807	—	4.00	8.00	14.00	35.00
	1808	—	4.00	8.00	14.00	35.00
	1809	—	4.00	8.00	14.00	35.00

4 KREUZER

BILLON
Obv: Arms. Rev: Madonna.

C#	Date	Mintage	VG	Fine	VF	XF
30	1763	—	5.00	10.00	15.00	30.00

5 KREUZER

(Convention)

BILLON
Obv: AF monogram. Rev: Arms.

C#	Date	Mintage	Fine	VF	XF	Unc
32	1764	—	5.00	7.50	15.00	35.00
	1765	—	5.00	7.50	15.00	35.00

6 KREUZER

SILVER
Obv: Large crown.

C#	Date	Mintage	Fine	VF	XF	Unc
155	1807	—	5.00	10.00	20.00	40.00
	1808	—	5.00	10.00	20.00	40.00

Obv: Small crown.

C#	Date	Mintage	Fine	VF	XF	Unc
155a	1809	—	5.00	10.00	20.00	40.00

10 KREUZER

(Convention)

SILVER
Obv: Bust of Adam Friedrich right.
Rev: Standing Madonna holding child.

C#	Date	Mintage	Fine	VF	XF	Unc
35	1760	—	100.00	175.00	225.00	300.00

Rev: Crowned arms.

C#	Date	Mintage	Fine	VF	XF	Unc
37	1762	—	10.00	15.00	25.00	50.00
	1763	—	10.00	15.00	25.00	50.00
	1764	—	10.00	15.00	25.00	50.00
37	1765	—	10.00	15.00	25.00	50.00
	1766	—	10.00	15.00	25.00	50.00

20 KREUZER

(Convention)

SILVER
Obv: Bust of Adam Friedrich right.
Rev: Standing Madonna holding child.

C#	Date	Mintage	Fine	VF	XF	Unc
39	1760	—	10.00	20.00	35.00	70.00
	1763	—	10.00	20.00	35.00	70.00
	1764	—	10.00	20.00	35.00	70.00

Obv: Crowned arms.
Rev: Value and date.

C#	Date	Mintage	Fine	VF	XF	Unc
41	1761	—	10.00	20.00	35.00	70.00

Obv: Bust of Adam Friedrich right.
Rev: Crowned arms.

C#	Date	Mintage	Fine	VF	XF	Unc
43	1762	—	10.00	20.00	35.00	70.00

C#	Date	Mintage	Fine	VF	XF	Unc
43a	1763-76	—	8.00	16.00	30.00	60.00

C#	Date	Mintage	Fine	VF	XF	Unc
43b	1764	—	10.00	15.00	25.00	50.00
	1765	—	10.00	15.00	25.00	50.00
	1766	—	10.00	15.00	25.00	50.00
	1767	—	10.00	15.00	25.00	50.00
	1768	—	10.00	15.00	25.00	50.00
	1769	—	10.00	15.00	25.00	50.00

Obv: Bust with ermine mantle.
Rev: Crowned and mantled round arms.

C#	Date	Mintage	Fine	VF	XF	Unc
76	1779	—	30.00	50.00	75.00	150.00

NOTE: Supposedly removed from circulation at the insistence of the Bishop's brother, The Elector of Mainz. He contended that ermine mantles were to be worn only by electors.

C#	Date	Mintage	Fine	VF	XF	Unc
78	1785	—	10.00	20.00	55.00	100.00
	1786	—	10.00	20.00	55.00	100.00
	1787	—	10.00	20.00	55.00	100.00

C#	Date	Mintage	Fine	VF	XF	Unc
80	1788	—	15.00	25.00	55.00	100.00
	1789	—	15.00	25.00	55.00	100.00
	1790	—	15.00	25.00	55.00	100.00
	1791	—	15.00	25.00	55.00	100.00

C#	Date	Mintage	Fine	VF	XF	Unc
83	1795	—	17.50	28.50	60.00	100.00

C#	Date	Mintage	Fine	VF	XF	Unc
107	1795	—	8.00	15.00	30.00	60.00

Obv. leg: 60 EINE....
Rev. leg: PRO PATRIA....

C#	Date	Mintage	Fine	VF	XF	Unc
108	1795	—	8.00	15.00	30.00	60.00

Obv: Similar to C#108.
Rev: Similar to C#107.

C#	Date	Mintage	Fine	VF	XF	Unc
110	1795	—	8.00	15.00	30.00	60.00

Obv: Bust. Rev: Madonna.

C#	Date	Mintage	Fine	VF	XF	Unc
111	1795	—	8.00	15.00	30.00	60.00

C#	Date	Mintage	Fine	VF	XF	Unc
112	1795	—	8.00	15.00	30.00	60.00

C#	Date	Mintage	Fine	VF	XF	Unc
114	1796	—	8.00	15.00	30.00	60.00

1/2 GROSCHEN

BILLON
Death of the Bishop Commemorative
Obv: Crowned arms.
Rev: 9 line inscription.

C#	Date	Mintage	VG	Fine	VF	XF
69	1795	—	6.00	14.00	20.00	35.00

GROSCHEN

BILLON
Death of the Bishop Commemorative
Obv: Crowned arms.
Rev: 9 line inscription.

C#	Date	Mintage	VG	Fine	VF	XF
28	1779	—	8.00	17.00	27.50	35.00

Death of the Bishop Commemorative

C#	Date	Mintage	VG	Fine	VF	XF
74	1795	—	8.00	17.00	27.50	35.00

1/2 THALER
(Convention)

SILVER
Obv: Bust of Adam Friedrich right.
Rev: Crowned and mantled arms.

C#	Date	Mintage	Fine	VF	XF	Unc
45	1760	—	50.00	75.00	125.00	250.00

C#	Date	Mintage	Fine	VF	XF	Unc
46	1761	—	50.00	75.00	125.00	250.00

C#	Date	Mintage	Fine	VF	XF	Unc
48	1765	—	50.00	75.00	125.00	250.00

C#	Date	Mintage	Fine	VF	XF	Unc
49	1764	—	50.00	75.00	125.00	250.00
	1765	—	50.00	75.00	125.00	250.00

THALER
(Convention)

SILVER
Obv: Bust of Adam Friedrich right.
Rev: 11 line inscription; date in chronogram.

C#	Date	Mintage	Fine	VF	XF	Unc
50	1760	—	600.00	1250.	2500.	5000.

Rev: Crowned, mantled arms into legend.

C#	Date	Mintage	Fine	VF	XF	Unc
51	1760	—	300.00	600.00	1250.	2500.

Rev: Smaller arms within legend.

C#	Date	Mintage	Fine	VF	XF	Unc
51a	1760 OEXLEIN under bust	—	300.00	600.00	1250.	2500.
	1760 w/o OEXLEIN under bust	—	300.00	600.00	1250.	2500.

C#	Date	Mintage	Fine	VF	XF	Unc
52	1760 AD FRIDER.	—	200.00	350.00	700.00	1400.
	1760 ADAM FRIDERIC	—	200.00	350.00	700.00	1400.
	1760 ADAM FRIDER.	—	200.00	350.00	700.00	1400.

Rev: Seated Madonna holding child.

C#	Date	Mintage	Fine	VF	XF	Unc
53	1763	—	600.00	1250.	2500.	5000.

C#	Date	Mintage	Fine	VF	XF	Unc
53a	1764 G.F. LOOS F. below bust	—	100.00	150.00	375.00	750.00
	1764 LOOS below bust	—	100.00	150.00	375.00	750.00

C#	Date	Mintage	Fine	VF	XF	Unc
53b	1765 L under bust					
		—	100.00	150.00	375.00	750.00
	1765 LOOS under bust					
		—	100.00	150.00	375.00	750.00
	1765 G.F. LOOS under bust					
		—	100.00	150.00	375.00	750.00
	1765 FRANCONIE in rev. leg.					
		—	100.00	150.00	375.00	750.00

C#	Date	Mintage	Fine	VF	XF	Unc
53c	1773	—	110.00	225.00	450.00	900.00
	1775	—	110.00	225.00	450.00	900.00
	1776	—	110.00	225.00	450.00	900.00
	1779	—	110.00	225.00	450.00	900.00

NOTE: Varieties exist.

C#	Date	Mintage	Fine	VF	XF	Unc
55	1763 G.F. LOOS F. below bust					
		—	100.00	150.00	375.00	750.00
	1763 V.LON F. below bust					
		—	100.00	150.00	375.00	750.00
	1763 AD.FRI. in obv. leg.					
		—	100.00	150.00	375.00	750.00
	1764	—	100.00	150.00	375.00	750.00
55a	1765 LOOS under bust					
		—	100.00	150.00	375.00	750.00
	1765 G.F. LOOS F. under bust					
		—	100.00	150.00	375.00	750.00
	1765 L under bust					
		—	100.00	150.00	375.00	750.00
	1766 LOOS under bust					
		—	100.00	150.00	375.00	750.00
	1766 G.F. LOOS F. under bust					
		—	100.00	150.00	375.00	750.00

C#	Date	Mintage	Fine	VF	XF	Unc
55b	1767 L below bust					
		—	100.00	150.00	375.00	750.00
	1769 L below bust					
		—	100.00	150.00	375.00	750.00
	1769R.F below bust					
		—	100.00	150.00	375.00	750.00
	1770 L below bust					
		—	100.00	150.00	375.00	750.00
	1770R.F. below bust					
		—	100.00	150.00	375.00	750.00
	1771R.F. below bust					
		—	100.00	150.00	375.00	750.00
	1772R.F. below bust					
		—	100.00	150.00	375.00	750.00
	1773R.F. below bust					
		—	100.00	150.00	375.00	750.00

C#	Date	Mintage	Fine	VF	XF	Unc
55c	1774R.F. below bust					
		—	100.00	150.00	375.00	750.00
	1777R.F. below bust					
		—	100.00	150.00	375.00	750.00

Rev: Arms at left, Bishop at right; value and date in exergue.

C#	Date	Mintage	Fine	VF	XF	Unc
56	1766	—	1000.	1500.	3000.	6000.

C#	Date	Mintage	Fine	VF	XF	Unc
85	1779	—	100.00	200.00	400.00	800.00

C#	Date	Mintage	Fine	VF	XF	Unc
86	1779	—	90.00	175.00	350.00	700.00
	1781	—	90.00	175.00	350.00	700.00
	1784	—	90.00	175.00	350.00	700.00

Obv: Similar to C#89.

C#	Date	Mintage	Fine	VF	XF	Unc
87	1785	—	100.00	175.00	350.00	700.00

Rev: Madonna with child; value and date below.

C#	Date	Mintage	Fine	VF	XF	Unc
88	1786	—	100.00	200.00	400.00	800.00

C#	Date	Mintage	Fine	VF	XF	Unc
89	1786	—	100.00	200.00	400.00	800.00
	1787	—	100.00	200.00	400.00	800.00
	1791	—	100.00	200.00	400.00	800.00

Obv: Bust right with G.F. below.
Rev: St. Kilianus standing divides date; value in exergue.

C#	Date	Mintage	Fine	VF	XF	Unc
90	1790	—	125.00	250.00	500.00	1000.

Obv: Bust right with R.F. below.
Rev: Cherub placing wreath atop globe on base holding book, etc.

C#	Date	Mintage	Fine	VF	XF	Unc
89a	1794	—	150.00	250.00	500.00	1000.

Contribution Thaler
Rev: Value and date in wreath; PRO PATRIA above.

C#	Date	Mintage	Fine	VF	XF	Unc
91	1794	—	150.00	300.00	600.00	1000.
	1795	—	150.00	300.00	600.00	1000.

Obv: Crowned and mantled arms; W below.

C#	Date	Mintage	Fine	VF	XF	Unc
92	1794	—	250.00	500.00	1000.	2000.
	1795	—	250.00	500.00	1000.	2000.

C#	Date	Mintage	Fine	VF	XF	Unc
117	1795	—	100.00	225.00	450.00	900.00

C#	Date	Mintage	Fine	VF	XF	Unc
118	1795	—	150.00	350.00	700.00	1400.

2 THALER
(Convention)

SILVER
Prize Double Thalers
Obv: Similar to Thaler, C#89.
Rev. leg: V EINE FEINE MARCK.

C#	Date	Mintage	Fine	VF	XF	Unc
93	1786	—	200.00	400.00	750.00	1500.
	1787	—	200.00	400.00	750.00	1500.
	1791	—	200.00	400.00	750.00	1500.

GOLDGULDEN

GOLD
Homage of Wurzburg
Obv: Bust of Adam Friedrich right.
Rev. Arms.

C#	Date	Mintage	Fine	VF	XF	Unc
57	1755	—	500.00	750.00	1000.	1500.

Obv: Fame over arms.
Rev: 3 female figures.

C#	Date	Mintage	Fine	VF	XF	Unc
58	ND	—	650.00	1000.	1500.	2250.

Peace of Hubertusburg
Obv: Bust of Adam Friedrich right.
Rev: Franconia standing.

C#	Date	Mintage	Fine	VF	XF	Unc
59	1764	—	500.00	750.00	1000.	1500.

C#	Date	Mintage	Fine	VF	XF	Unc
60	1773	—	650.00	950.00	1250.	1600.
	1774	—	650.00	950.00	1250.	1600.
	1775	—	650.00	950.00	1250.	1600.
	1776	—	650.00	950.00	1250.	1600.
	1777	—	650.00	950.00	1250.	1600.
	1778	—	650.00	950.00	1250.	1600.

Obv: Bust right, arms at shoulder.
Rev: Palm tree with arms before; date in exergue.

C#	Date	Mintage	Fine	VF	XF	Unc
94	1779	—	500.00	700.00	900.00	1400.

C#	Date	Mintage	Fine	VF	XF	Unc
95	1786	—	750.00	1100.	1500.	2000.

C#	Date	Mintage	Fine	VF	XF	Unc
96	1782	—	750.00	1100.	1500.	2000.
	1786	—	750.00	1100.	1500.	2000.
	1791	—	750.00	1100.	1500.	2000.
	1794	—	750.00	1100.	1500.	2000.

Obv: Bust right; arms at shoulder. Rev: St. Burkhard standing dividing date; value in exergue.

C#	Date	Mintage	Fine	VF	XF	Unc
97	1790	—	700.00	950.00	1250.	2000.

Obv: Arms. Rev: Palm tree.

C#	Date	Mintage	Fine	VF	XF	Unc
119	1795	—	500.00	850.00	1350.	2000.

Obv: Bust to left. Rev: View of city.

C#	Date	Mintage	Fine	VF	XF	Unc
120	1795	—	600.00	1000.	1500.	2250.
	1798	—	600.00	1000.	1500.	2250.

After 1800, except for the period 1806-1814, the Goldgulden struck by the Bavarian kings in the name of Wurzburg were New Years gift items and were not legal tender.

Obv: Head of Ferdinand right.
Rev: Palm tree, arms, value and date.

C#	Date	Mintage	Fine	VF	XF	Unc
159	1807	—	1000.	1500.	2250.	3000.
	1809	—	1000.	1500.	2250.	3000.

C#	Date	Mintage	Fine	VF	XF	Unc
160	1812	—	1250.	1750.	2500.	3250.

Rev: Crowned battle flag; value and date.

C#	Date	Mintage	Fine	VF	XF	Unc
161	1813	—	1000.	1500.	2250.	3000.

Obv: Head of Ferdinand
Rev: Altar, shield of arms; value and date.

C#	Date	Mintage	Fine	VF	XF	Unc
162	1814	—	1000.	1500.	2250.	3000.

2 GOLDGULDEN

GOLD
Obv: Bust right; arms at shoulder.
Rev: St. Kilianus standing; divides date.

C#	Date	Mintage	Fine	VF	XF	Unc
99	1786	—	1350.	2000.	2500.	3500.

EIN (1) CAROLIN

9.7000 gm., .770 GOLD, .2401 oz AGW
Obv: Bust. Rev: Arms.

C#	Date	Mintage	Fine	VF	XF	Unc
121	1795	—	1200.	1750.	2250.	3000.

TRADE COINS

DUCAT

3.5000 gm., .986 GOLD, .1109 oz AGW
Obv: Bust of Adam Friedrich right.
Rev: Crowned arms; no legend.

C#	Date	Mintage	Fine	VF	XF	Unc
61	1755-1770	—	—	—	—	—

Obv: Bust right.
Rev: Palm trees and arms.

C#	Date	Mintage	Fine	VF	XF	Unc
60	1773	—	950.00	1250.	1750.	2250.
	1774	—	950.00	1250.	1750.	2250.
	1777	—	950.00	1250.	1750.	2250.
	1778	—	950.00	1250.	1750.	2250.

Obv: Bust right in diamond.
Rev: Arms in diamond.

C#	Date	Mintage	Fine	VF	XF	Unc
62	1772	—	900.00	1250.	1650.	2000.
63	1773	—	850.00	1150.	1500.	2000.
	1774	—	850.00	1150.	1500.	2000.
	1775	—	850.00	1150.	1500.	2000.
	1776	—	850.00	1150.	1500.	2000.
	1777	—	850.00	1150.	1500.	2000.
	1778	—	850.00	1150.	1500.	2000.
	1779	—	850.00	1150.	1500.	2000.
A98	1780	—	—	—	Rare	—
98	1785	—	700.00	950.00	1250.	1600.

NCLT ISSUES

MEDALLIC ISSUES

GOLDGULDEN

3.2500 gm., .770 GOLD, .0805 oz AGW
Obv: Head of Maximilian Joseph right.
Rev: Palm above Wurzburg coat-of-arms, value and date.

Sch#	Date	Mintage	VF	XF	Unc
928	1803	—	—	950.00	1500.

Rev: Palm above Wurzburg coat-of-arms and S.P.-Q.W.

Sch#	Date	Mintage	VF	XF	Unc
928b	1803	—	—	950.00	1500.

Obv: Head of Maximilian Joseph left.
Rev: City view of Wurzburg.

Sch#	Date	Mintage	VF	XF	Unc
934	1815	—	—	1000.	1750.
935	ND(1815)	—	—	1000.	1750.

Rev: St. Kilian and city view, value, no date.

Sch#	Date	Mintage	VF	XF	Unc
936	ND(1816)	—	—	1000.	1750.

Rev: Coat-of-arms, value.

Sch#	Date	Mintage	VF	XF	Unc
937	1817	—	—	950.00	1500.
938	ND(1817)	—	—	950.00	1500.

Obv: Head of Ludwig left.
Rev: 6 line inscription.

Sch#	Date	Mintage	VF	XF	Unc
939	1826	65 pcs.	—	2500.	4000.

Rev: View of Wurzburg, value and date.

Sch#	Date	Mintage	VF	XF	Unc
940	ND(1827)	—	—	950.00	1500.

Roman I follows king's name.

Sch#	Date	Mintage	VF	XF	Unc
941	ND(1827)	—	—	950.00	1500.

Rev: City view of Wurzburg.

Sch#	Date	Mintage	VF	XF	Unc
941a	ND	—	—	950.00	1500.

Rev: Arms in sprays.

Sch#	Date	Mintage	VF	XF	Unc
941b	ND	—	—	950.00	1500.

Obv: Head of Ludwig right.
Rev: City view of Wurzburg.

Sch#	Date	Mintage	VF	XF	Unc
942	ND	—	—	950.00	1500.

Rev: Arms in sprays.

Sch#	Date	Mintage	VF	XF	Unc
943	ND	—	—	950.00	1500.

Obv: Head of Maximilian right.

Sch#	Date	Mintage	VF	XF	Unc
944	ND(1850)	215	—	1000.	1750.

Rev: City view of Wurzburg.

Sch#	Date	Mintage	VF	XF	Unc
945	ND(1850)	215	—	1000.	1750.

Obv: Head of Ludwig II left.

Sch#	Date	Mintage	VF	XF	Unc
946	ND(1864)	350	—	1000.	1750.

Rev: Wurzburg coat-of-arms.

Sch#	Date	Mintage	VF	XF	Unc
947	ND(1864)	350	—	1000.	1750.

Rev: City view of Wurzburg, St. Kilian and value.

Sch#	Date	Mintage	VF	XF	Unc
947a	ND	—	—	1500.	2750.

Germany, a nation of north-central Europe which from 1871 to 1945 was, successively, an empire, a republic and a totalitarian state, attained its territorial peak as an empire when it comprised a 208,780 sq. mi. (540,740 sq. km.) homeland and an overseas colonial empire.

As the power of the Roman Empire waned, several war like tribes residing in northern Germany moved south and west, invading France, Belgium, England, Italy and Spain. In 800 A.D. the Frankish king Charlemagne, who ruled most of France and Germany, was crowned Emperor of the Holy Roman Empire, a loose federation of an estimated 1,800 German states that lasted until 1806. Modern Germany was formed from the eastern part of Charlemagne's empire.

After 1812, the German States were reduced to a federation of 32, of which Prussia was the strongest. In 1871, Prussian chancellor Otto Von Bismarck united the German states into an empire ruled by William I, the Prussian king. The empire initiated a colonial endeavor and became one of the world's greatest powers. Germany disintegrated as a result of World War I, and was reestablished as the Weimar Republic. The humiliation of defeat, economic depression, poverty and discontent gave rise to Adolf Hitler, 1933, who reconstituted Germany as the Third Reich and after initial diplomatic and military triumphs, led it to disaster in World War II. For subsequent history, see East and West Germany.

RULERS

Wilhem I, 1871-1888
Friedrich III, 1888
Wilhem II, 1888-1918

MINTMARKS

A - Berlin
B - Hannover (1866-1878)
B - Vienna (1938-1944)
C - Frankfurt (1866-1879)
D - Munich
E - Dresden (1872-1887)
E - Muldenhutten (1887-1953)
F - Stuttgart
G - Karlsruhe
H - Darmstadt (1872-1882)
J - Hamburg

MONETARY SYSTEM

(Until 1923)
100 Pfennig = 1 Mark
(During 1923-1924)
100 Rentenpfennig = 1 Rentenmark
(Commencing 1924)
100 Reichspfennig = 1 Reichsmark
(Commencing 1945)
100 Pfennig = 1 Mark

PFENNIG

COPPER

Y#	Date	Mintage	Fine	VF	XF	Unc
1	1873A	.184	75.00	150.00	275.00	475.00

Y#	Date	Mintage	Fine	VF	XF	Unc
1	1873B	.095	125.00	300.00	500.00	800.00
	1873D	.052	100.00	250.00	400.00	700.00
	1874A	26.760	.50	4.00	10.00	35.00
	1874B	8.743	.50	7.00	20.00	65.00
	1874C	15.744	.50	7.00	20.00	65.00
	1874D	7.074	1.00	10.00	20.00	75.00
	1874E	4.522	3.00	15.00	30.00	75.00
	1874F	3.985	.50	9.00	20.00	55.00
	1874G	4.768	5.00	30.00	45.00	90.00
	1874H	2.013	40.00	65.00	100.00	190.00
	1875A	64.669	.25	2.75	10.00	30.00
	1875B	27.618	.50	4.00	15.00	40.00
	1875C	22.654	.50	3.00	10.00	30.00
	1875D	13.342	.50	3.00	10.00	30.00
	1875E	7.779	5.00	18.00	30.00	60.00
	1875F	15.271	.50	4.00	15.00	40.00
	1875G	12.021	2.00	20.00	30.00	60.00
	1875H	3.516	35.00	75.00	125.00	175.00
	1875J	7.242	1.00	8.00	18.00	50.00
	1876A	34.542	.50	3.00	11.00	30.00
	1876B	5.995	.50	2.50	12.00	35.00
	1876C	11.044	.50	2.50	12.00	35.00
	1876D	12.651	.50	2.50	12.00	35.00
	1876E	6.532	1.00	5.00	20.00	50.00
	1876F	11.404	.50	2.50	12.00	35.00
	1876G	3.331	4.00	20.00	35.00	70.00
	1876H	2.998	20.00	50.00	90.00	135.00
	1876J	1.165	90.00	120.00	150.00	210.00
	1877A	.472	100.00	150.00	175.00	250.00
	1877B	.088	400.00	600.00	800.00	1100.
	1885A	5.448	.75	5.00	15.00	25.00
	1885E	.430	60.00	100.00	150.00	200.00
	1885G	1.100	25.00	45.00	65.00	100.00
	1885J	1.696	10.00	25.00	40.00	65.00
	1886A	14.114	.50	2.50	15.00	35.00
	1886D	2.873	.50	2.50	15.00	35.00
	1886E	2.060	4.00	8.00	25.00	60.00
	1886F	1.726	2.00	4.00	15.00	45.00
	1886G	.814	30.00	40.00	60.00	90.00
	1886J	1.593	4.00	8.00	25.00	45.00
	1887A	15.923	.50	1.00	10.00	25.00
	1887D	5.177	.50	2.50	10.00	30.00
	1887E	2.315	2.00	5.00	15.00	35.00
	1887E with dot after PFENNIG					
		25 pcs.	—	—	—	3500.
	1887F	6.345	2.00	4.00	15.00	35.00
	1887G	1.888	2.50	6.00	25.00	40.00
	1887J	2.082	2.00	4.00	18.00	35.00
	1888A	19.936	.50	2.50	10.00	25.00
	1888D	3.277	.50	2.50	12.00	25.00
	1888E	1.310	4.00	8.00	25.00	40.00
	1888F	.584	20.00	30.00	50.00	75.00
	1888G	1.385	5.00	10.00	20.00	30.00
	1888J	2.803	2.00	4.00	12.00	20.00
	1889A	20.750	.50	1.00	12.00	25.00
	1889D	8.454	.50	2.50	15.00	30.00
	1889E	4.330	.50	2.50	15.00	30.00
	1889F	5.010	.50	2.50	15.00	30.00
	1889G	3.411	.50	2.75	15.00	30.00
	1889J	3.308	.50	2.75	15.00	30.00
	Common Date	—	—	—	Proof	175.00

Y#	Date	Mintage	Fine	VF	XF	Unc
3	1890A	17.295	.10	.50	2.00	7.00
	1890D	7.030	.25	.75	2.00	10.00
	1890E	3.730	.25	1.00	5.00	12.00
	1890F	4.189	.25	1.00	5.00	12.00
	1890G	3.050	.25	1.00	5.00	12.00
	1890J	2.247	.25	1.00	5.00	12.00
	1891A	12.040	.10	.50	2.00	7.00
	1891D	.876	8.00	15.00	20.00	40.00
	1891E	.528	20.00	40.00	50.00	90.00
	1891F	1.263	2.00	4.00	8.00	25.00
	1891G	.360	20.00	45.00	80.00	112.00
	1891J	1.837	4.00	12.00	20.00	35.00
	1892A	22.341	.10	.50	2.00	5.00
	1892D	6.139	.25	.60	3.00	7.00
	1892E	3.195	.25	2.00	5.00	15.00
	1892F	5.013	.25	1.00	4.00	10.00
	1892G	2.689	.25	1.50	5.00	12.00
	1892J	3.980	.25	1.00	3.00	7.00
	1893A	18.966	.10	.50	1.50	5.00
	1893D	7.027	.20	.60	3.00	7.00
	1893E	1.218	5.00	10.00	20.00	30.00
	1893F	1.460	.25	1.25	5.00	12.00
	1893G	.700	10.00	20.00	30.00	50.00
	1893J	1.825	.50	1.50	7.00	12.00
	1894A	17.592	.10	.30	2.00	5.00
	1894D	5.530	.20	.60	4.00	7.00
	1894E	5.040	.25	1.00	5.00	12.00
	1894F	4.206	.20	.60	4.00	9.00

Y#	Date	Mintage	Fine	VF	XF	Unc
3	1894G	2.351	.25	1.00	5.00	10.00
	1894J	2.619	.25	1.25	6.00	12.00
	1895A	20.152	.10	.30	1.00	4.00
	1895D	1.496	5.00	15.00	30.00	45.00
	1895E	1.191	4.00	12.00	25.00	40.00
	1895F	4.366	.20	.60	4.00	9.00
	1895G	3.051	.25	1.25	5.00	10.00
	1895J	3.839	.50	4.00	14.00	22.00
	1896A	27.094	.10	.20	1.00	4.00
	1896D	7.025	.10	.20	1.00	4.00
	1896E	3.725	.20	.60	3.00	7.00
	1896F	3.450	.10	.20	1.00	4.00
	1896G	3.028	.20	.60	3.00	7.00
	1897A	8.534	.20	.60	3.00	7.00
	1897D	2.600	.50	1.50	6.00	12.00
	1897E	1.294	2.00	6.00	12.00	17.00
	1897F	2.390	1.00	3.50	10.00	15.00
	1897G	1.122	3.00	10.00	20.00	25.00
	1897J	4.941	.25	1.00	4.00	7.00
	1898A	18.564	.10	.20	1.00	4.00
	1898D	4.430	.10	.30	1.50	4.50
	1898E	2.432	.20	.60	4.00	7.00
	1898F	4.193	.20	.60	2.00	6.00
	1898G	1.951	.20	.60	4.00	7.00
	1898J	3.231	.20	.60	5.00	15.00
	1899A	22.009	.10	.20	2.00	6.00
	1899D	4.590	.10	.20	1.00	3.00
	1899E	3.725	.20	.60	2.00	3.00
	1899F	4.300	.10	.20	3.00	7.00
	1899G	2.550	.20	.60	2.00	3.50
	1899J	2.416	.20	.60	3.00	6.00
	1900A	51.804	.10	.20	3.00	7.00
	1900D	14.635	.10	.20	1.00	3.00
	1900E	7.887	.20	.60	2.00	3.00
	1900F	10.312	.10	.30	3.00	7.00
	1900G	6.138	.20	.60	2.00	5.00
	1900J	9.917	.20	.60	3.00	7.00
	1901A	21.045	.10	.20	3.00	7.00
	1901D	5.337	.20	.60	2.00	7.00
	1901E	1.397	1.00	3.50	5.50	13.00
	1901F	2.925	.20	.60	2.50	8.00
	1901G	1.977	.50	1.20	4.00	12.00
	1901J	2.011	2.00	8.00	15.00	25.00
	1902A	7.474	.10	.30	1.00	5.00
	1902D	2.811	.25	1.00	3.00	10.00
	1902E	1.183	.50	3.00	10.00	25.00
	1902F	1.250	.50	3.00	4.50	12.00
	1902G	.881	.50	4.50	12.00	25.00
	1902J	.012	350.00	600.00	900.00	1200.
	1903A	12.690	.10	.30	2.00	5.00
	1903D	3.140	.20	.60	2.00	6.00
	1903E	1.956	.20	.60	2.50	7.00
	1903F	2.945	.10	.30	2.00	6.00
	1903G	1.377	.50	3.50	7.50	22.00
	1903J	2.832	.10	.30	2.00	6.00
	1904A	28.625	.10	.20	1.00	3.00
	1904D	4.118	.10	.30	1.00	4.00
	1904E	2.778	.20	.60	2.50	7.00
	1904F	4.520	.10	.30	1.00	4.00
	1904G	3.232	.10	.30	2.00	6.00
	1904J	4.467	.10	.30	1.00	4.00
	1905A	19.631	.10	.20	1.00	3.00
	1905D	6.084	.10	.20	1.00	3.00
	1905E	3.564	.10	.30	1.00	4.00
	1905F	4.153	.10	.20	1.00	3.00
	1905G	3.051	.20	.60	1.75	6.00
	1905J	4.085	.10	.20	1.00	3.00
	1906A	46.921	.10	.20	1.00	3.00
	1906D	5.633	.10	.20	1.00	3.00
	1906E	7.278	.10	.30	1.00	4.00
	1906F	7.173	.10	.20	1.00	3.00
	1906G	5.194	.10	.20	1.00	3.00
	1906J	3.622	.10	.20	1.00	3.00
	1907A	33.711	.10	.20	1.00	3.00
	1907D	14.691	.10	.20	1.00	3.00
	1907E	3.719	.10	.20	1.00	3.00
	1907F	7.026	.10	.20	1.00	3.00
	1907G	3.052	.10	.20	1.00	3.00
	1907J	6.722	.10	.20	1.00	3.00
	1908A	21.922	.10	.20	1.00	3.00
	1908D	10.629	.10	.20	1.00	3.00
	1908E	3.400	.10	.30	1.00	4.00
	1908F	6.112	.10	.20	1.00	3.00
	1908G	3.663	.10	.20	1.00	3.00
	1908J	5.581	.10	.20	1.00	3.00
	1909A	21.430	.10	.20	1.00	2.50
	1909D	2.814	.10	.30	1.00	5.00
	1909E	2.562	.25	1.50	3.50	10.00
	1909F	2.425	.25	1.25	3.00	9.00
	1909G	1.220	.25	1.50	3.50	10.00
	1909J	1.634	.25	1.25	3.00	9.00
	1910A	10.761	.10	.20	1.00	2.50
	1910D	4.221	.10	.20	1.00	2.50
	1910E	1.600	.20	.60	2.50	7.00
	1910F	3.009	.10	.30	1.00	3.00
	1910G	1.834	.25	.60	1.75	7.00
	1910J	2.450	.10	.30	1.00	3.00

Y#	Date	Mintage	Fine	VF	XF	Unc
3	1911A	38.172	.10	.20	1.00	2.50
	1911D	8.657	.10	.20	1.00	2.50
	1911E	5.236	.10	.20	1.00	2.50
	1911F	5.780	.10	.20	1.00	2.50
	1911G	2.075	.10	.20	1.00	2.50
	1911J	5.594	.10	.20	1.00	2.50
	1912A	42.693	.10	.20	1.00	2.50
	1912D	10.173	.10	.20	1.00	2.50
	1912E	5.689	.10	.20	1.00	2.50
	1912F	7.441	.10	.20	1.00	2.50
	1912G	5.526	.10	.20	1.00	2.50
	1912J	5.615	.10	.20	1.00	2.50
	1913A	32.671	.10	.20	1.00	2.50
	1913D	8.161	.10	.20	1.00	2.50
	1913E	2.258	.25	2.00	5.00	9.00
	1913F	6.620	.10	.20	1.00	2.50
	1913G	3.209	.10	.20	1.00	2.50
	1913J	1.456	.25	2.00	5.00	9.00
	1914A	9.976	.10	.20	1.00	2.50
	1914D	1.842	.10	.20	1.00	2.50
	1914E	2.926	.20	.60	1.25	5.00
	1914F	3.316	.10	.20	1.00	2.50
	1914G	2.100	.20	.60	1.25	5.00
	1914J	4.368	.10	.20	1.00	2.50
	1915A	14.738	.10	.20	1.00	2.50
	1915D	1.771	.10	.20	1.00	2.50
	1915E	2.779	.20	.60	1.25	5.00
	1915F	1.411	.20	.60	1.25	5.00
	1915G	2.041	.20	.60	1.50	6.00
	1915J	2.981	.20	.60	1.25	5.00
	1916A	5.960	.10	.30	1.00	3.00
	1916D	5.401	.20	.60	1.75	6.00
	1916E	.818	.50	3.00	4.50	10.00
	1916F	1.104	.25	3.50	4.75	9.00
	1916G	.671	1.00	6.00	10.00	12.00
	1916J	.898	.50	3.50	5.50	12.00
	Common Date	—	—	—	Proof	40.00

ALUMINUM

Y#	Date	Mintage	Fine	VF	XF	Unc
19	1916G	—	75.00	140.00	225.00	400.00
	1917A	27.159	.25	.50	1.00	2.00
	1917D	6.940	.25	1.00	2.00	5.00
	1917E	3.862	.25	4.00	6.00	10.00
	1917F	5.125	.25	1.50	3.00	6.00
	1917G	3.139	.25	2.00	4.00	7.00
	1917J	4.182	.25	3.00	6.00	11.00
	1918D	.318	5.00	12.00	25.00	45.00
	1918F	—	—	380.00	—	—
	Common Date	—	—	—	Proof	60.00

NOTE: 1916-A, 1916-F and 1918-A are patterns. The 1918-F is a pattern from ruins of the Stuttgart Mint destroyed in World War II.

RENTENPFENNIG

BRONZE

Y#	Date	Mintage	Fine	VF	XF	Unc
32	1923A	12.629	.10	1.00	2.00	9.00
	1923D	*2.314	.10	1.25	5.00	15.00
	1923E	2.200	.10	1.25	8.00	17.00
	1923F	.160	.10	1.50	10.00	22.00
	1923G	1.004	.10	.50	1.00	12.00
	1923J	1.470	.10	.50	5.00	15.00
	1924A	55.273	.10	.50	1.00	6.00
	1924D	17.540	.10	.50	2.00	9.00
	1924E	6.838	.10	1.00	5.00	12.00
	1924F	10.347	.50	2.00	9.00	8.00
	1924G	7.366	.10	1.00	5.00	12.00
	1924J	11.024	.10	.50	1.00	6.00
	1925A	—	400.00	600.00	700.00	900.00
	1929F	—	140.00	200.00	350.00	550.00
	Common Date	—	—	—	Proof	50.00

REICHSPFENNIG

BRONZE

Y#	Date	Mintage	Fine	VF	XF	Unc
37	1924A	13.496	.10	.25	1.00	5.00

Y#	Date	Mintage	Fine	VF	XF	Unc
37	1924D	6.206	.10	.25	1.00	5.00
	1924E	1.100	45.00	100.00	150.00	250.00
	1924F	2.650	.10	.20	1.00	5.00
	1924G	5.100	.10	.25	1.25	7.00
	1924J	24.400	.10	.25	1.00	5.00
	1925A	40.925	.10	.25	1.00	4.00
	1925D	1.558	1.00	7.50	15.00	35.00
	1925E	10.460	.10	.25	1.00	4.00
	1925F	5.673	.10	.25	1.00	4.00
	1925G	13.502	.10	.25	1.00	4.00
	1925J	30.300	.10	.25	1.00	4.00
	1927A	4.671	.10	.25	1.00	4.00
	1927D	4.203	.10	.50	1.25	5.00
	1927E	8.000	.10	.25	2.00	7.00
	1927F	2.350	.10	.50	1.25	5.00
	1927G	3.236	.10	.25	2.25	7.00
	1928A	19.300	.10	.25	1.00	3.00
	1928D	10.200	.10	.25	1.00	3.00
	1928F	8.672	.10	.25	1.00	3.00
	1928G	3.764	.10	.25	1.25	5.00
	1929A	37.170	.10	.25	1.00	3.00
	1929D	9.337	.10	.25	1.00	3.00
	1929E	6.600	.10	.25	1.00	4.00
	1929F	3.150	.10	.25	1.00	5.00
	1929G	1.986	.10	.50	1.25	5.00
	1930A	40.997	.10	.25	1.00	3.00
	1930D	6.441	.10	.25	1.00	3.00
	1930E	1.412	3.00	20.00	40.00	35.00
	1930F	6.415	.10	.25	1.00	5.00
	1930G	5.017	.10	.25	1.00	3.00
	1931A	38.481	.10	.25	1.00	3.00
	1931D	5.998	.10	.25	1.00	3.00
	1931E	12.800	.10	.25	1.25	5.00
	1931F	12.591	.10	.25	1.00	3.00
	1931G	2.622	.10	.25	1.50	7.00
	1932A	17.096	.10	.25	1.00	3.00
	1933A	37.846	.10	.25	1.00	3.00
	1933E	2.945	.25	1.00	3.00	8.00
	1933F	5.023	.10	.25	1.00	5.00
	1934A	51.214	.10	.25	1.00	3.00
	1934D	7.408	.10	.25	1.00	3.00
	1934E	4.628	.10	1.50	6.00	12.00
	1934F	5.667	.10	.25	1.00	3.00
	1934G	2.450	.10	.25	1.00	4.00
	1934J	4.271	.10	.25	1.50	7.00
	1935A	35.894	.10	.25	1.00	2.50
	1935D	15.489	.10	.25	1.00	2.50
	1935E	8.351	.10	.25	1.50	7.00
	1935F	12.094	.10	.25	1.00	2.50
	1935G	7.454	.10	.25	1.00	2.50
	1935J	8.505	.10	.25	1.00	2.50
	1936A	*50.949	.10	.25	1.00	2.50
	1936D	12.262	.10	.25	1.00	2.50
	1936E	2.576	.50	2.50	8.00	15.00
	1936F	6.915	.10	.25	1.00	2.50
	1936G	*2.940	.10	.25	1.00	4.00
	1936J	*5.421	.10	.25	1.25	5.00
	Common Date	—	—	—	Proof	50.00

*Combined mintage for Y#37 and Y#88.

Nazi State

Y#	Date	Mintage	Fine	VF	XF	Unc
88	1936A	w/Y37	2.50	7.00	12.00	25.00
	1936E	.150	30.00	60.00	100.00	150.00
	1936F	4.600	25.00	50.00	90.00	135.00
	1936G	w/Y37	10.00	30.00	50.00	80.00
	1936J	w/Y37	10.00	30.00	50.00	80.00
	1937A	67.180	.10	.25	.50	3.00
	1937D	14.060	.10	.25	.50	3.00
	1937E	10.700	.10	.25	1.00	5.00
	1937F	11.058	.10	.25	1.00	4.00
	1937G	4.250	.10	.25	1.00	4.00
	1937J	6.714	.10	.25	1.00	4.00
	1938A	75.707	.10	.25	.50	2.50
	1938B	2.378	.25	4.00	6.00	10.00
	1938D	13.930	.10	.25	.50	2.50
	1938E	14.503	.10	.25	.50	2.50
	1938F	11.714	.10	.25	.50	2.50
	1938G	8.390	.10	.25	.50	2.50
	1938J	15.458	.10	.25	.50	2.50
	1939A	97.541	.10	.25	.50	2.50
	1939B	22.732	.10	.25	1.00	2.50
	1939D	20.760	.10	.25	.50	2.50
	1939E	12.478	.10	.25	.50	2.50
	1939F	12.482	.10	.25	.50	2.50
	1939G	12.250	.10	.25	.50	2.50
	1939J	8.368	.10	.25	.50	2.50
	1940A	27.094	.10	.25	.50	3.00
	1940F	7.850	.10	.25	1.00	3.00
	1940G	3.875	.25	8.00	12.00	22.00
	1940J	7.450	.25	3.00	5.00	10.00

Y#	Date	Mintage	Fine	VF	XF	Unc
88	Common Date	—	—	—	Proof	60.00

ZINC

Y#	Date	Mintage	Fine	VF	XF	Unc
A92	1940A	223.948	.10	.20	.60	2.50
	1940B	62.198	.10	.20	.60	2.50
	1940D	43.951	.10	.20	.60	2.50
	1940E	20.749	.10	2.00	4.00	7.50
	1940F	33.854	.10	.25	.75	2.50
	1940G	20.165	.10	.25	.75	2.50
	1940J	24.459	.10	.25	.75	2.50
	1941A	281.618	.10	.15	.50	2.00
	1941B	62.285	.10	.75	1.00	4.00
	1941D	73.745	.10	.15	.50	2.00
	1941E	49.041	.10	.30	.75	4.00
	1941F	51.017	.10	.15	.50	2.00
	1941G	44.810	.10	.30	.75	2.50
	1941J	57.625	.10	.15	.50	2.50
	1942A	558.877	.10	.15	.50	2.50
	1942B	124.740	.10	.60	1.00	4.00
	1942D	134.145	.10	.15	.50	2.50
	1942E	84.674	.10	.60	1.00	5.00
	1942F	90.788	.10	.15	.50	2.50
	1942G	59.858	.10	.15	.50	2.50
	1942J	122.934	.10	.30	.75	2.50
	1943A	372.401	.10	.15	.50	2.50
	1943B	79.315	.10	.30	.75	2.50
	1943D	91.629	.10	.15	.50	2.50
	1943E	34.191	.25	4.50	10.00	20.00
	1943F	70.269	.10	.30	.75	2.50
	1943G	24.688	.10	1.25	4.50	12.00
	1943J	37.695	.10	1.25	1.75	10.00
	1944A	124.421	.10	.30	1.25	4.00
	1944B	87.850	.10	1.25	1.75	7.00
	1944D	56.755	.10	.60	1.25	4.00
	1944E	41.729	.10	1.25	2.50	9.00
	1944F	15.580	.10	2.00	4.50	12.00
	1944G	34.967	.10	.60	1.25	4.00
	1945A	17.145	.25	4.50	8.50	20.00
	1945E	6.800	40.00	75.00	100.00	175.00
	Common Date	—	—	—	Proof	100.00

Allied Occupation
Modified design, swastika and wreath removed.
Eagle missing tail feathers.

Y#	Date	Mintage	Fine	VF	XF	Unc
98	1944D	—	—	2200.	3500.	4500.

Y#	Date	Mintage	Fine	VF	XF	Unc
98a	1945F	2.984	2.50	9.00	20.00	40.00
	1946F	1.633	15.00	30.00	60.00	110.00
	1946G	1.500	40.00	60.00	100.00	140.00
	Common Date	—	—	—	Proof	—

2 PFENNIG

COPPER

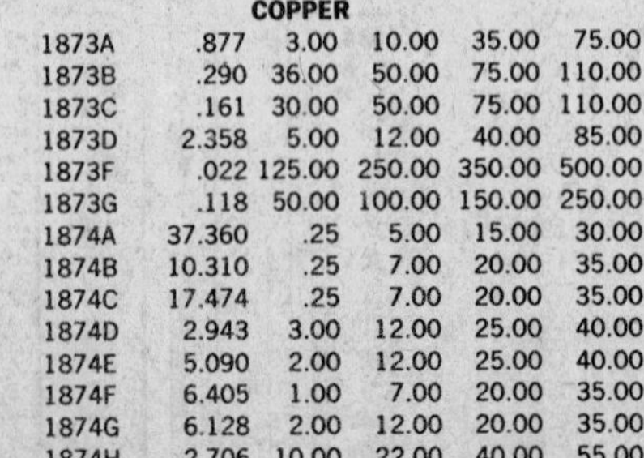

Y#	Date	Mintage	Fine	VF	XF	Unc
2	1873A	.877	3.00	10.00	35.00	75.00
	1873B	.290	36.00	50.00	75.00	110.00
	1873C	.161	30.00	50.00	75.00	110.00
	1873D	2.358	5.00	12.00	40.00	85.00
	1873F	.022	125.00	250.00	350.00	500.00
	1873G	.118	50.00	100.00	150.00	250.00
	1874A	37.360	.25	5.00	15.00	30.00
	1874B	10.310	.25	7.00	20.00	35.00
	1874C	17.474	.25	7.00	20.00	35.00
	1874D	2.943	3.00	12.00	25.00	40.00
	1874E	5.090	2.00	12.00	25.00	40.00
	1874F	6.405	1.00	7.00	20.00	35.00
	1874G	6.128	2.00	12.00	20.00	35.00
	1874H	2.706	10.00	22.00	40.00	55.00

Y#	Date	Mintage	Fine	VF	XF	Unc
2	1875A	28.963	.25	1.00	15.00	30.00
	1875B	15.844	.25	3.00	20.00	35.00
	1875C	35.541	.25	1.00	15.00	30.00
	1875D	11.160	.25	1.00	15.00	30.00
	1875E	7.872	.25	1.00	15.00	30.00
	1875F	9.827	.25	1.00	15.00	30.00
	1875G	11.903	.25	1.00	15.00	30.00
	1875H	3.309	3.00	7.00	20.00	40.00
	1875J	14.210	.25	1.00	15.00	30.00
	1876A	18.906	.25	1.00	15.00	30.00
	1876B	7.097	.25	1.00	15.00	30.00
	1876C	12.280	.25	1.00	15.00	30.00
	1876D	10.296	.25	1.00	15.00	30.00
	1876E	4.988	.25	1.00	15.00	30.00
	1876F	7.207	.25	1.00	15.00	30.00
	1876G	3.502	.25	2.50	15.00	30.00
	1876H	3.630	.25	3.00	20.00	35.00
	1876J	1.995	3.00	7.00	25.00	40.00
	1877A	9.827	.25	1.00	15.00	30.00
	1877B	.060	180.00	250.00	400.00	600.00
	Common Date	—	—	—	Proof	175.00

Y#	Date	Mintage	Fine	VF	XF	Unc
4	1904A	5.414	.10	.20	1.00	5.00
	1904D	1.404	.10	.30	2.00	7.00
	1904E	.744	.50	5.00	12.00	25.00
	1904F	1.002	.10	.60	4.00	10.00
	1904G	.495	.25	3.00	12.00	22.00
	1904J	.044	5.00	12.00	25.00	42.00
	1905A	5.172	.10	.20	1.00	5.00
	1905D	1.570	.10	.30	2.00	7.00
	1905E	.924	.10	.60	3.00	10.00
	1905F	1.115	.10	.60	2.50	7.00
	1905G	1.030	.10	.60	3.00	10.00
	1905J	1.609	.10	.60	3.00	10.00
	1906A	8.459	.10	.25	1.00	4.00
	1906D	3.539	.10	.25	1.00	4.00
	1906E	2.055	.10	.25	1.00	4.00
	1906F	2.840	.10	.25	1.00	4.00
	1906G	1.527	.10	.25	1.00	4.00
	1906J	1.908	.10	.25	1.00	4.00
	1907A	13.468	.10	.25	1.00	4.00
	1907D	1.921	.10	.25	1.00	4.00
	1907E	.744	.25	1.25	5.00	10.00
	1907F	1.059	.10	.30	1.00	5.00
	1907G	.610	.10	.60	3.00	6.00
	1907J	.952	.10	.30	1.00	5.00
	1908A	5.421	.10	.25	1.00	4.00
	1908D	1.407	.10	.30	1.00	5.00
	1908E	.745	.25	4.00	7.00	10.00
	1908F	1.003	.10	.30	2.00	5.00
	1908G	.610	.25	1.00	3.00	6.00
	1908J	.817	.10	.30	2.00	5.00
	1910A	5.421	.10	.25	1.00	4.00
	1910D	1.407	.10	.30	1.00	5.00
	1910E	.745	.10	4.00	6.00	10.00
	1910F	1.003	.10	1.00	3.00	6.00
	1910G	.517	.10	1.00	4.00	7.00
	1910J	.568	.10	.60	3.00	6.00
	1911A	8.187	.10	.25	.60	4.00
	1911D	2.100	.10	.30	2.00	5.00
	1911E	1.133	.10	.30	3.00	5.00
	1911F	1.490	.10	.30	3.00	5.00
	1911G	1.313	.10	.30	3.00	5.00
	1911J	1.883	.10	.30	2.00	5.00
	1912A	13.580	.10	.25	1.00	4.00
	1912D	3.109	.10	.30	1.25	4.00
	1912E	1.808	.10	.60	3.00	5.00
	1912F	2.366	.10	.30	2.00	4.00
	1912G	1.395	.10	.30	1.50	5.00
	1912J	1.605	.10	.30	1.50	5.00
	1913A	4.212	.10	.25	1.00	3.00
	1913D	2.525	.10	.30	1.00	4.00
	1913E	.413	4.00	12.00	18.00	26.00
	1913F	1.602	.10	.30	1.25	4.50
	1913G	.741	.10	1.00	1.75	6.00
	1913J	1.254	.10	.30	1.00	4.00
	1914A	5.350	.10	.25	1.00	2.50
	1914E	1.201	.25	2.00	4.50	12.50
	1914F	.158	30.00	50.00	80.00	125.00
	1914G	.610	1.00	6.00	12.00	25.00
	1914J	.817	.10	1.00	2.50	5.00
	1915A	3.897	.10	.25	1.00	3.00
	1915D	1.407	.10	.60	1.25	4.00
	1915E	.288	6.00	12.00	20.00	30.00
	1915F	.904	.10	.25	1.00	2.50
	1916A	3.524	.10	.30	1.00	3.00
	1916D	.915	.10	1.00	1.25	3.00
	1916E	.484	.10	2.00	6.00	10.00
	1916F	.651	.10	1.00	4.00	7.00

Y#	Date	Mintage	Fine	VF	XF	Unc
4	1916G	.397	.10	2.00	5.00	10.00
	1916J	.531	.10	2.00	5.00	10.00
	Common Date	—	—	—	Proof	60.00

2 RENTENPFENNIG

BRONZE

Y#	Date	Mintage	Fine	VF	XF	Unc
33	1923A	8.587	.10	.40	2.00	6.00
	1923D	1.490	.10	.30	3.00	6.00
	1923F	W	1924	3.00	5.00	15.00
	1923G	w/1924	.10	1.00	6.00	10.00
	1923J	w/1924	.10	5.00	12.00	22.00
	1924A	80.864	.10	.40	2.00	6.00
	1924D	19.899	.10	.50	2.50	6.00
	1924E	6.595	.10	.30	1.75	10.00
	1924E	185 pcs.	—	—	Proof	—
	1924F	14.969	.10	.30	3.00	6.00
	1924G	10.349	.10	.30	3.00	7.00
	1924J	21.196	.10	.30	3.00	6.00
	Common Date	—	—	—	Proof	60.00

2 REICHSPFENNIG

BRONZE

Y#	Date	Mintage	Fine	VF	XF	Unc
38	1923F	—	100.00	250.00	500.00	1000.
	1924A	19.620	.10	.25	1.00	4.00
	1924D	3.482	.10	.30	1.00	10.00
	1924E	4.253	.10	1.00	7.00	15.00
	1924F	4.567	.10	.20	1.00	6.00
	1924G	7.560	.10	.20	1.00	6.00
	1924J	7.489	.10	.20	1.00	6.00
	1925A	22.433	.10	.20	1.00	3.00
	1925D	2.412	.10	.50	2.50	10.00
	1925E	5.414	.10	.30	1.00	5.00
	1925F	4.851	.10	.30	1.00	5.00
	1925G	2.456	.10	1.00	7.00	14.00
	1936A	3.220	.10	1.25	7.00	15.00
	1936D	6.525	.10	.15	.30	2.00
	1936E	.573	10.00	20.00	30.00	55.00
	1936F	3.100	.10	.30	.60	4.00
	Common Date	—	—	—	Proof	60.00

Nazi State

Y#	Date	Mintage	Fine	VF	XF	Unc
89	1936A	W/1937	.25	5.00	10.00	17.00
	1936D	W/1937	.10	5.00	10.00	17.00
	1936F	3.100	.25	15.00	30.00	45.00
	1937A	34.404	.10	.15	.30	3.00
	1937D	9.016	.10	.15	.30	4.00
	1937E	w/1938E	12.00	30.00	50.00	75.00
	1937F	7.487	.10	.30	1.00	4.00
	1937G	.490	2.00	5.00	12.00	20.00
	1937J	.450	1.00	3.00	10.00	17.00
	1938A	27.264	.10	.15	.30	2.00
	1938B	2.714	1.00	5.00	10.00	17.00
	1938D	8.770	.10	.20	.60	3.00
	1938E	5.450	.10	.60	2.00	5.00
	1938F	10.090	.10	.20	.60	3.00
	1938G	3.685	.10	.20	.60	3.00
	1938J	7.243	.10	.20	.60	3.00
	1939A	37.348	.10	.15	.30	2.00
	1939B	9.361	.10	.20	.60	3.00
	1939D	7.555	.10	.20	.60	3.00
	1939E	6.650	.10	1.00	4.00	9.00
	1939F	7.019	.10	.20	.60	3.00
	1939G	4.885	.10	.20	.60	3.00
	1939J	6.996	.10	.20	.60	3.00
	1940A	22.681	.10	.20	.60	3.00
	1940D	3.855	.10	2.00	4.00	9.00
	1940E	3.412	2.00	10.00	15.00	22.00
	1940G	1.161	15.00	60.00	90.00	125.00
	1940J	2.357	1.00	6.00	12.00	20.00

Y#	Date	Mintage	Fine	VF	XF	Unc
89	Common Date	—	—	—	Proof	40.00

4 REICHSPFENNIG

BRONZE

Y#	Date	Mintage	Fine	VF	XF	Unc
39	1932A	27.101	2.00	5.00	7.00	15.00
	1932D	7.055	2.00	7.00	12.00	25.00
	1932E	3.729	2.00	9.00	20.00	40.00
	1932F	5.022	2.00	7.50	15.00	27.00
	1932G	3.050	2.00	12.00	25.00	50.00
	1932J	4.094	2.00	10.00	20.00	40.00
	Common Date	—	—	—	Proof	75.00

5 PFENNIG

COPPER-NICKEL

Y#	Date	Mintage	Fine	VF	XF	Unc
5	1874A	10.003	.30	1.50	12.00	30.00
	1874B	5.054	.20	2.50	15.00	45.00
	1874C	3.707	.20	2.50	15.00	45.00
	1874D	2.447	.20	2.50	15.00	45.00
	1874E	5.465	5.00	10.00	30.00	65.00
	1874F	3.562	.20	2.50	15.00	45.00
	1874G	2.721	.20	3.00	15.00	45.00
	1875A	30.844	.10	1.00	15.00	35.00
	1875B	11.658	.20	2.00	15.00	45.00
	1875C	18.082	.20	2.00	15.00	45.00
	1875D	12.380	.20	2.00	15.00	45.00
	1875E	6.745	.20	2.00	15.00	45.00
	1875F	9.758	.20	2.00	15.00	45.00
	1875G	10.220	.20	2.00	15.00	45.00
	1875H	.703	17.00	40.00	75.00	125.00
	1875J	9.781	.20	2.00	15.00	45.00
	1876A	22.342	.10	1.00	15.00	30.00
	1876B	8.925	.20	2.00	15.00	35.00
	1876C	8.680	.20	2.00	15.00	35.00
	1876D	14.467	.20	2.00	15.00	35.00
	1876E	6.899	.20	2.00	15.00	35.00
	1876F	6.826	.20	2.00	15.00	35.00
	1876G	6.942	.20	2.00	15.00	35.00
	1876H	3.027	1.00	5.00	25.00	55.00
	1876J	11.920	.20	2.00	15.00	35.00
	1888A	7.366	.10	1.00	10.00	25.00
	1888D	1.967	.50	5.00	20.00	45.00
	1888E	1.016	.25	3.00	15.00	40.00
	1888/78D	—	10.00	25.00	40.00	100.00
	1888F	1.412	.20	2.00	12.00	30.00
	1888G	.853	.50	7.00	20.00	45.00
	1888J	1.130	.50	7.00	25.00	50.00
	1889A	10.804	.10	1.00	8.00	20.00
	1889D	2.816	.20	2.00	10.00	30.00
	1889E	1.492	.20	3.00	12.00	30.00
	1889F	2.010	.20	2.00	10.00	30.00
	1889G	1.221	.20	3.00	15.00	35.00
	1889J	1.636	.20	4.00	15.00	35.00
	Common Date	—	—	—	Proof	125.00

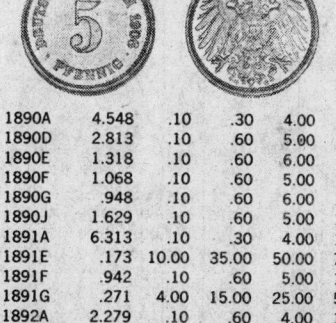

Y#	Date	Mintage	Fine	VF	XF	Unc
8	1890A	4.548	.10	.30	4.00	10.00
	1890D	2.813	.10	.60	5.00	12.00
	1890E	1.318	.10	.60	6.00	15.00
	1890F	1.068	.10	.60	5.00	12.00
	1890G	.948	.10	.60	6.00	15.00
	1890J	1.629	.10	.60	5.00	12.00
	1891A	6.313	.10	.30	4.00	10.00
	1891E	.173	10.00	35.00	50.00	70.00
	1891F	.942	.10	.60	5.00	12.00
	1891G	.271	4.00	15.00	25.00	50.00
	1892A	2.279	.10	.60	4.00	10.00
	1892D	.920	.10	.60	5.00	12.00
	1892E	.346	1.00	7.50	15.00	30.00
	1892F	.464	2.00	10.00	18.00	35.00
	1892G	.800	1.00	9.00	15.00	30.00

Y#	Date	Mintage	Fine	VF	XF	Unc
8	1892J	.093	75.00	120.00	175.00	250.00
	1893A	8.572	.10	.30	4.00	10.00
	1893D	1.892	.10	.60	5.00	12.00
	1893E	1.149	.10	.60	6.00	15.00
	1893F	1.546	.10	.60	5.00	12.00
	1893G	.422	.25	9.00	18.00	35.00
	1893J	1.544	.10	.60	4.00	12.00
	1894A	10.830	.10	.30	4.00	10.00
	1894D	2.812	.10	.60	4.00	12.00
	1894E	.802	.10	1.00	6.00	15.00
	1894F	.300	.25	3.00	10.00	25.00
	1894G	.280	.25	3.50	10.00	30.00
	1894J	1.634	.10	.60	5.00	12.00
	1895E	.686	.10	1.50	5.00	15.00
	1895F	1.705	.10	1.00	4.00	12.00
	1895G	.940	.10	1.25	5.00	15.00
	1896A	1.459	.10	.60	4.00	12.00
	1896E	.658	.10	1.25	5.00	15.00
	1896F	2.009	.10	.60	5.00	15.00
	1896G	w/1897	100.00	250.00	500.00	800.00
	1896J	1.634	.10	.60	4.00	12.00
	1897A	9.390	.10	.30	3.00	7.00
	1897D	2.812	.10	.60	3.00	8.00
	1897E	.833	.10	1.25	4.00	10.00
	1897F	—	—	—	—	—
	1897/1797G	—	—	—	—	—
	1897G	1.221	.10	.60	3.00	8.00
	1898A	10.836	.10	.40	2.00	5.00
	1898D	2.812	.10	.30	3.00	6.00
	1898E	1.492	.10	.60	3.00	7.00
	1898F	2.007	.10	.60	3.00	6.00
	1898G	1.220	.10	1.00	4.00	10.00
	1898J	1.635	.10	.60	2.00	6.00
	1899A	10.884	.15	.30	1.00	4.00
	1899D	2.812	.10	.30	2.00	5.00
	1899E	1.488	.10	.60	2.00	6.00
	1899F	2.006	.10	.30	2.00	5.00
	1899G	1.222	.10	.30	2.00	5.00
	1899J	1.634	.10	.30	2.00	5.00
	1900A	18.941	.10	.30	1.00	4.00
	1900D	4.254	.10	.30	2.00	5.00
	1900E	2.236	.10	.60	2.00	5.00
	1900F	3.209	.10	.30	2.00	5.00
	1900G	2.136	.10	.60	2.00	5.00
	1900J	2.859	.10	.60	2.00	5.00
	1901A	8.155	.10	.30	1.00	4.00
	1901D	2.779	.10	.30	1.00	4.00
	1901E	1.492	.10	.60	2.00	5.00
	1901F	1.810	.10	.30	1.00	4.00
	1901G	.915	.10	.60	2.00	5.00
	1901J	1.226	.10	.30	1.00	4.00
	1902A	8.949	.10	.30	1.00	4.00
	1902D	2.812	.10	.30	1.00	4.00
	1902E	1.120	.10	.60	3.00	7.00
	1902F	1.800	.10	.60	2.00	5.00
	1902G	1.220	.10	.60	2.00	7.00
	1902J	1.636	.10	.30	2.00	4.00
	1903A	5.932	.10	.30	1.00	4.00
	1903D	1.406	.10	.60	2.00	5.00
	1903E	1.114	.10	1.25	3.50	10.00
	1903F	1.209	.10	1.00	3.00	9.00
	1903G	.610	.10	1.50	4.25	10.00
	1903J	.817	.10	1.00	3.00	9.00
	1904A	6.791	.10	.30	2.00	5.00
	1904D	1.408	.10	.60	2.00	5.00
	1904E	.746	.10	1.25	3.00	10.00
	1904F	1.006	.10	.60	2.00	6.00
	1904G	.610	.10	1.00	2.00	7.00
	1904J	.818	.10	.60	2.00	6.00
	1905A	8.129	.10	.30	1.00	4.00
	1905D	2.109	.10	.30	1.00	4.00
	1905E	1.117	.10	.30	1.00	4.00
	1905F	1.505	.10	.30	1.00	4.00
	1905G	.915	.10	.60	2.00	6.00
	1905J	1.226	.10	.30	1.00	4.00
	1906A	18.970	.10	.20	.60	2.00
	1906D	4.922	.10	.20	.60	2.00
	1906E	2.605	.10	.20	.60	2.00
	1906F	3.512	.10	.20	.60	2.00
	1906G	2.136	.10	.60	2.00	4.00
	1906J	2.859	.10	.20	.60	2.50
	1907A	11.930	.10	.20	.60	2.50
	1907D	2.113	.10	.20	.60	2.50
	1907E	1.517	.10	.60	2.00	4.00
	1907F	1.845	.10	.20	.60	2.50
	1907G	.915	.10	.30	1.00	3.00
	1907J	1.636	.10	.20	.60	2.50
	1908A	22.114	.15	.20	.60	2.50
	1908D	4.991	.10	.20	.60	2.50
	1908E	2.919	.10	.20	.60	2.50
	1908/7F	—	40.00	75.00	100.00	175.00
	1908F	5.124	.10	.20	.60	2.50
	1908/1108G	—	—	—	—	—
	1908G	3.357	.10	.20	.60	2.50
	1908J	3.264	.10	.20	.60	2.50
	1909A	5.797	.10	.30	2.00	5.00
	1909D	2.753	.10	.60	2.00	6.00

Y#	Date	Mintage	Fine	VF	XF	Unc
	1909E	.984	.10	2.00	7.00	12.00
	1909F	.252	.50	6.00	10.00	15.00
	1909J	1.632	.10	.60	2.00	6.00
	1910A	7.344	.10	.20	.60	2.50
	1910D	2.814	.10	.20	.60	2.50
	1910E	1.290	.10	.30	1.00	3.00
	1910F	1.721	.10	.20	.60	2.50
	1910G	1.222	.10	.30	1.00	3.00
	1910J	.152	10.00	30.00	50.00	80.00
	1911A	15.660	.10	.15	.30	1.00
	1911D	2.221	.10	.20	.60	2.50
	1911E	1.770	.10	.20	.60	2.50
	1911F	2.714	.10	.20	.60	2.50
	1911G	1.833	.10	.20	.60	2.50
	1911J	3.116	.10	.20	.60	2.50
	1912A	19.320	.10	.15	.30	1.50
	1912D	4.015	.10	.15	.30	1.50
	1912E	2.568	.10	.30	.60	2.00
	1912F	3.679	.10	.15	.30	1.50
	1912G	2.440	.10	.15	.30	1.50
	1912J	3.020	.10	.15	.30	1.50
	1913A	15.506	.10	.15	.30	1.50
	1913D	5.519	.10	.15	.30	1.50
	1913E	2.373	.10	.60	1.00	5.00
	1913F	2.054	.10	.15	.30	1.50
	1913G	1.221	.10	.15	.30	1.50
	1913J	.253	2.00	15.00	20.00	28.00
	1914A	23.605	.10	.15	.30	1.50
	1914D	3.014	.10	.15	.30	1.50
	1914E	1.710	.10	.15	.30	1.50
	1914F	2.206	.10	.15	.30	1.50
	1914G	1.218	.10	.15	.30	1.50
	1914J	3.235	.10	.15	.30	1.50
	1915 w/o mm	—	1.00	5.00	12.00	20.00
	1915D	3.516	.10	.30	2.00	5.00
	1915E	.834	.50	7.00	10.00	15.00
	1915F	1.894	.10	.30	1.25	4.00
	1915G	.894	.50	6.00	10.00	12.00
	1915J	1.669	.10	2.00	5.00	10.00
	Common Date	—	—	—	Proof	50.00

IRON

Y#	Date	Mintage	Fine	VF	XF	Unc
21	1915A	34.631	.10	.20	1.00	4.00
	1915D	2.021	.10	4.00	8.00	15.00
	1915E	4.670	.10	5.00	10.00	20.00
	1915F	3.500	.10	2.00	5.00	12.00
	1915G	3.676	.10	2.00	5.00	12.00
	1915J	2.100	.10	2.00	5.00	12.00
	1916A	51.003	.10	.30	.60	2.50
	1916D	19.590	.10	.30	1.00	4.00
	1916E	2.271	1.00	5.00	10.00	20.00
	1916F	10.479	.10	.30	1.00	4.00
	1916G	5.599	.10	1.00	3.00	7.50
	1916J	10.253	.10	2.00	7.00	15.00
	1917A	87.315	.10	.20	.60	2.00
	1917D	19.581	.10	.30	.60	2.50
	1917E	11.092	.25	5.00	8.00	12.00
	1917F	10.930	.10	.30	.60	2.50
	1917F muling with Polish rev. of Y#5, see Poland					
	1917G	6.720	.10	.30	1.00	3.00
	1917J	11.686	.10	2.00	5.00	10.00
	1918A	223.516	.10	.20	.60	2.00
	1918D	29.130	.10	.30	.60	2.50
	1918E	23.600	.10	2.00	6.00	9.00
	1918E	24 pcs.	—	—	Proof	—
	1918F	24.598	.10	.30	.60	2.00
	1918G	12.697	.10	.30	.60	2.00
	1918J	20.240	.10	.30	.60	2.00
	1919A	112.102	.10	.20	.60	2.00
	1919D	41.163	.10	.20	.60	2.00
	1919E	20.608	.10	2.00	5.00	7.00
	1919E	44 pcs.	—	—	Pcs.	—
	1919F	32.700	.10	.20	.60	2.00
	1919G	13.925	.10	.60	2.00	6.00
	1919J	16.249	.10	.60	2.00	5.00
	1920A	80.300	.10	.20	.60	2.00
	1920D	25.502	.10	.30	.60	2.50
	1920E	11.646	.50	10.00	20.00	30.00
	1920E	55 pcs.	—	—	Proof	—
	1920F	24.300	.10	.20	.60	2.00
	1920G	10.244	.10	1.50	3.00	6.00
	1920J	16.857	.10	.20	.60	2.00
	1921A	143.418	.10	.20	.60	2.00
	1921D	38.133	.10	.20	.60	2.00
	1921E	21.104	.10	5.00	12.00	20.00
	1921E	28 pcs.			Proof	—
	1921F	24.800	.10	.20	.60	2.00
	1921G	21.289	.10	.20	.60	2.00
	1921J	28.928	.15	1.00	3.00	6.00
	1922A	89.062	.10	.20	.60	1.25

Y#	Date	Mintage	Fine	VF	XF	Unc
21	1922D	31.240	.10	.20	.60	2.00
	1922E	19.156	.10	8.00	15.00	20.00
	1922E	25 pcs.			Proof	—
	1922F	16.436	.10	.25	.60	2.00
	1922G	19.708	.10	.25	.60	2.00
	1922J	16.820	.10	7.00	10.00	15.00
	Common Date	—	—	—	Proof	75.00

5 RENTENPFENNIG

ALUMINUM-BRONZE

Y#	Date	Mintage	Fine	VF	XF	Unc
34	1923A	3.083	.15	.60	2.00	12.00
	1923D	W/1924	.15	1.00	3.00	15.00
	1923F	W/1924	20.00	75.00	110.00	150.00
	1923G	w/1924	15.00	40.00	75.00	115.00
	1924A	171.966	.20	.30	.40	4.00
	1924D	31.163	.15	.30	.60	5.00
	1924E	12.206	.15	.30	.60	7.00
	1924E	189 pcs.			Proof	—
	1924F	29.032	.15	.30	.60	6.00
	1924G	19.217	.15	.30	.60	6.00
	1924J	32.332	.15	.30	.60	6.00
	1925F	—	100.00	250.00	500.00	700.00
	Common Date	—	—	—	Proof	60.00

5 REICHSPFENNIG

ALUMINUM-BRONZE

Y#	Date	Mintage	Fine	VF	XF	Unc
40	1924A	14.469	.25	.60	1.50	5.00
	1924D	8.139	.15	.30	2.00	7.00
	1924E	5.976	.15	.55	5.00	12.00
	1924E	166 pcs.			Proof	—
	1924F	3.134	.15	.55	3.00	10.00
	1924G	4.790	.15	.60	5.00	12.00
	1924J	2.200	.15	.60	3.00	10.00
	1925A	85.239	.15	.15	.30	4.00
	1925D	39.750	.15	.15	.30	4.00
	1925E	17.554	.15	.60	3.00	10.00
	1925E	61 pcs.			Proof	—
	1925F lg.5	20.990	.15	.20	.60	5.00
	1925F sm.5	I.A.	.15	.20	.60	4.00
	1925G	10.232	.15	.60	3.00	10.00
	1925J	10.950	.15	.60	5.00	12.00
	1926A	22.377	.15	.15	.60	5.00
	1926E	5.990	7.00	20.00	30.00	40.00
	1926E	33 pcs.	—	—	Proof	—
	1926F	2.871	4.00	10.00	20.00	35.00
	1930A	7.418	.15	.30	3.00	10.00
	1935A	19.178	.15	.15	.30	3.00
	1935D	5.480	.15	.20	.60	5.00
	1935E	2.384	.15	.40	1.25	7.00
	1935F	4.585	.15	.30	.90	6.00
	1935G	2.652	.15	1.00	5.00	12.00
	1935J	2.614	.15	.30	3.00	10.00
	1936A	36.992	.15	.15	.30	3.00
	1936D	8.108	.15	.20	.60	5.00
	1936E	2.981	.15	.60	3.00	10.00
	1936F	6.643	.15	.20	1.00	5.00
	1936G	2.274	.15	.20	1.00	6.00
	1936J	4.470	.15	.60	5.00	12.00
	Common Date	—	—	—	Proof	60.00

Nazi State

Y#	Date	Mintage	Fine	VF	XF	Unc
90	1936A	w/1937	6.00	20.00	40.00	60.00
	1936D	w/1937	7.00	25.00	50.00	75.00
	1936G	w/1937	30.00	60.00	100.00	140.00
	1937A	29.700	.10	.15	.30	2.00
	1937D	4.992	.10	.15	.30	2.50
	1937E	4.474	.10	.60	3.00	7.00
	1937F	2.092	.10	.15	.30	2.50
	1937G	2.749	.25	5.00	10.00	16.00
	1937J	6.991	.10	2.00	5.00	12.00
	1938A	54.012	.10	.15	.30	2.00

Y#	Date	Mintage	Fine	VF	XF	Unc
90	1938B	3.447	.10	.60	2.00	7.00
	1938D	17.708	.10	.15	.30	2.50
	1938E	8.602	.10	.20	.60	3.00
	1938F	8.147	.10	.15	.30	2.50
	1938G	7.323	.10	.20	.60	2.50
	1938J	7.646	.10	.20	.60	2.50
	1939A	35.337	.10	.15	.30	2.00
	1939B	8.313	.10	.20	.60	4.00
	1939D	8.304	.10	.60	3.00	7.00
	1939E	5.138	.10	.60	3.00	7.00
	1939F	10.339	.10	.20	1.00	3.00
	1939G	4.266	.10	2.00	10.00	15.00
	1939J	4.177	.10	1.25	7.00	10.00
	Common Date	—	—	—	Proof	60.00

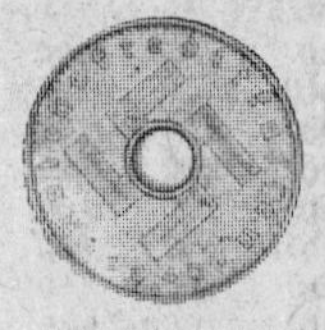

ZINC

Y#	Date	Mintage	Fine	VF	XF	Unc
94	1940A	—	2.00	5.00	10.00	15.00
	1940B	3.020	10.00	30.00	50.00	100.00
	1940D	—	4.00	10.00	15.00	20.00
	1940E	2.445	20.00	50.00	75.00	150.00
	1940F	—	50.00	125.00	175.00	275.00
	1940G	—	40.00	100.00	175.00	250.00
	1940J	—	25.00	65.00	95.00	150.00
	1941A	—	8.00	25.00	35.00	65.00
	1941F	—	20.00	50.00	75.00	150.00
	Common Date	—	—	—	Proof	150.00

Y#	Date	Mintage	Fine	VF	XF	Unc
B92	1940A	174.684	.10	.15	.30	2.50
	1940B	63.469	.10	.25	.75	4.00
	1940D	44.364	.10	.20	.60	3.00
	1940E	25.800	.10	.35	1.00	5.00
	1940F	31.381	.10	.20	.60	3.00
	1940G	24.148	.10	.35	1.00	5.00
	1940J	30.518	.10	.20	.60	3.00
	1941A	246.216	.10	.15	.30	2.50
	1941B	60.297	.10	.30	1.00	4.00
	1941D	51.100	.10	.20	.60	2.50
	1941E	26.354	.10	.20	.60	2.50
	1941F	36.725	.10	.20	.60	2.50
	1941G	21.276	.10	.30	1.00	4.00
	1941J	52.872	.10	.20	.60	3.00
	1942A	161.042	.10	.15	.30	2.00
	1942B	12.405	.10	1.00	2.00	7.00
	1942D	15.486	.10	.15	.30	2.00
	1942E	8.800	2.00	15.00	20.00	30.00
	1942F	24.662	.10	.15	.30	2.00
	1942G	12.749	.10	.15	.30	2.50
	1943A	46.830	.10	1.00	1.75	7.00
	1943B	.833	14.00	40.00	55.00	100.00
	1943D	13.650	.10	2.00	5.00	12.00
	1943E	16.581	.25	5.00	9.00	15.00
	1943F	9.891	.10	.60	2.00	6.00
	1943G	7.237	.10	.30	1.00	4.00
	1944A	23.699	2.00	12.00	20.00	30.00
	1944D	26.340	.10	.60	2.00	5.00
	1944E	19.720	.25	4.00	6.00	10.00
	1944F	6.853	.10	1.00	3.00	7.00
	1944G	3.540	30.00	60.00	100.00	190.00
	Common Date	—	—	—	Proof	60.00

ZINC
Allied Occupation

Y#	Date	Mintage	Fine	VF	XF	Unc
99	1947A	—	2.00	7.00	12.00	18.00
	1947D	16.528	1.50	5.00	8.00	14.00
	1948A	—	4.00	15.00	20.00	30.00
	1948E	7.666	100.00	150.00	225.00	325.00
	Common Date	—	—	—	Proof	—

10 PFENNIG

COPPER-NICKEL

Y#	Date	Mintage	Fine	VF	XF	Unc
6	1873A	.931	3.00	7.00	20.00	90.00
	1873B	.333	15.00	20.00	35.00	125.00
	1873C	.522	15.00	20.00	35.00	125.00
	1873D	.472	5.00	10.00	25.00	80.00
	1873F	.476	15.00	30.00	40.00	135.00
	1873G	.519	10.00	20.00	35.00	125.00
	1873H	.044	85.00	125.00	185.00	275.00
	1874A	7.664	.20	2.00	12.00	35.00
	1874B	2.669	2.00	5.00	15.00	55.00
	1874C	12.029	.20	2.00	10.00	35.00
	1874D	3.586	10.00	25.00	50.00	150.00
	1874E	3.157	5.00	15.00	30.00	60.00
	1874F	7.309	.20	2.00	12.00	45.00
	1874G	5.552	.20	2.00	12.00	45.00
	1874H	3.323	10.00	25.00	55.00	115.00
	1875A	15.523	.20	2.00	10.00	45.00
	1875B	4.120	.20	2.00	12.00	45.00
	1875C	8.304	.20	2.00	10.00	45.00
	1875D	13.365	.20	2.00	10.00	45.00
	1875E	9.833	.20	2.00	12.00	50.00
	1875F	7.975	.20	2.00	12.00	45.00
	1875G	5.390	.20	5.00	15.00	45.00
	1875H	4.268	10.00	20.00	35.00	100.00
	1875J	9.407	.20	2.00	10.00	45.00
	1876A	34.175	.25	2.00	10.00	45.00
	1876B	10.120	.20	2.00	10.00	45.00
	1876C	13.214	.20	2.00	10.00	45.00
	1876D	16.787	.20	2.00	10.00	45.00
	1876E	6.161	.20	4.00	12.00	50.00
	1876F	7.034	.20	2.00	10.00	45.00
	1876G	6.222	.20	3.00	15.00	50.00
	1876H	3.227	15.00	30.00	45.00	135.00
	1876J	11.315	.20	2.00	10.00	95.00
	1888A	8.519	.20	2.00	10.00	30.00
	1888D	2.493	.20	2.00	10.00	30.00
	1888E	1.268	.50	6.00	20.00	40.00
	1888F	1.340	.50	8.00	20.00	40.00
	1888G	1.081	.50	8.00	20.00	40.00
	1888J	1.436	.20	2.00	10.00	30.00
	1889A	11.542	.20	2.00	10.00	30.00
	1889D	2.813	.20	2.00	10.00	30.00
	1889E	1.493	.20	2.00	10.00	30.00
	1889F	2.432	.20	2.00	10.00	30.00
	1889G	1.223	.25	5.00	20.00	40.00
	1889J	1.638	.20	2.00	10.00	30.00
	Common Date	—	—	—	Proof	125.00

Y#	Date	Mintage	Fine	VF	XF	Unc
9	1890A	6.878	.10	.20	.75	6.00
	1890F	.784	.20	1.00	3.00	10.00
	1890G	.976	.20	1.00	4.00	12.00
	1890J	1.637	.10	.60	2.00	7.00
	1891A	4.239	.10	.20	1.00	6.00
	1891D	2.812	.10	.30	2.00	7.00
	1891E	1.489	.10	.60	2.00	10.00
	1891F	1.226	.10	2.00	5.00	12.00
	1891G	.247	.50	15.00	25.00	40.00
	1892A	2.413	.10	.45	1.25	5.00
	1892D	2.812	.10	.45	1.25	5.00
	1892E	.870	.10	1.50	5.00	12.00
	1892F	.663	.10	1.50	5.00	12.00
	1892G	.300	.50	12.00	25.00	40.00
	1892J	—	75.00	300.00	600.00	900.00
	1892J	—	—	—	Proof	750.00
	1893A	8.435	.10	.20	.75	6.00
	1893E	.362	.25	5.00	12.00	35.00
	1893F	1.345	.10	.30	1.00	6.00
	1893G	.921	.10	1.00	3.00	10.00
	1893J	1.636	.10	.30	1.00	6.00
	1894E	.260	.50	15.00	25.00	40.00
	1896A	4.996	.10	.30	1.00	6.00
	1896D	2.812	.10	.30	1.00	6.00
	1896E	1.495	.10	.60	2.00	7.00
	1896F	2.009	.10	.30	1.00	6.00
	1896G	.200	.50	15.00	25.00	40.00
	1896J	1.632	.10	.30	1.00	6.00
	1897A	5.842	.10	.30	1.00	6.00
	1897G	1.020	.10	1.00	2.00	10.00

Y#	Date	Mintage	Fine	VF	XF	Unc
9	1898A	10.833	.10	.20	.75	4.00
	1898D	2.814	.10	.20	.75	4.00
	1898E	.805	.10	.40	2.00	6.00
	1898F	2.007	.10	.40	2.00	6.00
	1898G	.480	.20	3.00	6.00	15.00
	1898J	1.635	.10	.30	1.00	5.00
	1899A	10.838	.10	.20	.75	4.00
	1899D	3.813	.10	.20	.75	4.00
	1899E	2.175	.10	.30	1.00	5.00
	1899F	2.008	.10	.20	.75	4.00
	1899G	1.382	.10	.20	.75	4.00
	1899J	1.635	.10	.20	.75	4.00
	1900A	34.559	.10	.20	.75	3.00
	1900D	8.694	.10	.20	.75	3.00
	1900E	4.490	.10	.30	1.00	5.00
	1900F	5.933	.10	.20	.75	3.00
	1900G	4.239	.10	.30	1.00	5.00
	1900J	5.720	.10	.20	.75	3.00
	1901A	10.200	.10	.20	.75	3.00
	1901D	3.259	.10	.20	.75	3.00
	1901E	1.863	.10	.20	.75	4.00
	1901F	2.594	.10	.20	.75	4.00
	1901G	1.527	.10	.20	.75	4.00
	1901J	1.225	.10	.20	.75	4.00
	1902A	5.878	.10	.20	.75	3.00
	1902D	1.406	.10	.20	.75	3.00
	1902E	.502	.20	3.00	6.00	15.00
	1902F	1.003	.10	.20	.75	4.00
	1902G	.610	.10	1.00	3.00	7.00
	1902J	.815	.10	1.00	3.00	6.00
	1903A	5.131	.10	.20	.75	3.00
	1903D	1.406	.10	.20	.75	3.00
	1903E	.988	.10	.20	.75	3.00
	1903F	1.003	.10	.20	.75	3.00
	1903G	.610	.10	.30	1.00	5.00
	1903J	.816	.10	.30	1.00	5.00
	1904A	5.189	.10	.20	.75	3.00
	1904D	1.056	.10	.30	1.00	5.00
	1904E	.559	.10	.60	2.00	6.00
	1904F	.753	.10	.20	.75	3.00
	1904G	.457	.20	2.00	5.00	10.00
	1904J	.612	.20	1.00	3.00	7.00
	1905A	8.650	.10	.20	.75	3.00
	1905A	250 pcs.			Proof	—
	1905D	1.846	.10	.20	.75	3.00
	1905E	.980	.10	.20	.75	4.00
	1905F	1.310	.10	.20	.75	3.00
	1905G	.642	.10	.60	1.25	5.00
	1905J	1.430	.10	.20	.75	4.00
	1906A	14.470	.10	.20	.75	3.00
	1906A	160 pcs.			Proof	—
	1906D	4.132	.10	.20	.75	3.00
	1906E	2.189	.10	.20	.75	3.00
	1906F	2.953	.10	.20	.75	3.00
	1906F	100 pcs.			Proof	—
	1906G	1.952	.10	.20	.75	3.00
	1906G	10-30 pcs.			Proof	—
	1906J	2.042	.10	.20	.60	3.00
	1907A	17.971	.10	.20	.60	3.00
	1907D	2.813	.10	.20	.60	3.00
	1907E	2.291	.10	.20	.60	3.00
	1907F	3.206	.10	.20	.60	3.00
	1907G	1.889	.10	.20	.60	3.00
	1907J	2.750	.10	.20	.60	3.00
	1908A	20.410	.10	.20	.60	3.00
	1908D	6.773	.10	.20	.60	3.00
	1908E	2.490	.10	.20	.60	3.00
	1908F	3.535	.10	.20	.60	3.00
	1908G	1.708	.10	.20	.60	3.00
	1908J	2.649	.10	.20	.60	3.00
	1909A	2.270	.10	.60	2.00	6.00
	1909D	.966	.10	1.00	3.00	7.00
	1909E	.806	.10	3.00	6.00	15.00
	1909F	.780	.10	3.00	6.00	15.00
	1909G	.980	.10	2.00	5.00	12.00
	1909J	.725	.10	2.00	5.00	12.00
	1910A	3.734	.10	.15	.30	4.00
	1910D	1.406	.10	.15	.30	2.50
	1910E	.300	.25	8.00	12.00	20.00
	1910F	1.003	.10	.15	.30	2.50
	1910G	.610	.10	.20	.60	3.00
	1911A	13.554	.10	.15	.30	2.00
	1911D	2.508	.10	.15	.30	2.00
	1911E	2.246	.10	.15	.30	2.50
	1911F	2.235	.10	.15	.30	2.00
	1911G	1.678	.10	.15	.30	2.50
	1911J	3.062	.10	.15	.30	2.00
	1912A	21.312	.10	.15	.30	2.00
	1912D	6.988	.10	.15	.30	2.00
	1912E	2.649	.10	.15	.30	2.50
	1912F	3.787	.10	.15	.30	2.00
	1912G	2.441	.10	.15	.30	2.50
	1912J	2.730	.10	.15	.30	2.00
	1913A	13.466	.10	.15,	.30	2.00
	1913D	3.164	.10	.15	.30	2.00
	1913E	1.478	.10	.15	.30	2.50
	1913F	1.991	.10	.15	.30	2.00

Y#	Date	Mintage	Fine	VF	XF	Unc
9	1913G	1.373	.10	.15	.30	2.50
	1913J	1.550	.10	.15	.30	2.00
	1914A	18.570	.10	.15	.30	2.00
	1914D	2.301	.10	.15	.30	2.00
	1914E	3.478	.10	.15	.30	2.00
	1914F	4.515	.10	.15	.30	2.00
	1914G	2.689	.10	.15	.30	2.00
	1914J	1.589	.10	.15	.30	2.00
	1915A	10.639	.10	.15	.30	2.00
	1915D	2.277	.10	.15	.30	2.50
	1915E	1.027	.10	.60	2.00	6.00
	1915F	1.508	.10	.15	.30	2.00
	1915G	.363	50.00	85.00	125.00	120.00
	1915J	2.677	.10	.60	2.00	6.00
	1916D	1.128	.10	.60	2.00	7.00
	Common Date	—	—	—	Proof	40.00

IRON

Y#	Date	Mintage	Fine	VF	XF	Unc
22	1915A	—	125.00	275.00	350.00	450.00
	1915A	—	—	—	Proof	—
	1916 no mint mark		—	—	—	—
	1916A	69.143	.10	.30	1.00	4.00
	1916D	11.609	.10	.30	1.00	4.00
	1916E	8.280	.10	.30	3.00	7.00
	1916F	7.473	.10	.30	3.00	6.00
	1916G	5.878	.10	.30	3.00	7.00
	1916J	11.683	.10	.30	3.00	7.00
	1917A	53.198	.10	.25	.60	2.00
	1917D	16.370	.10	.30	1.00	3.00
	1917E	9.182	.10	.30	3.00	6.00
	1917F	11.341	.10	.30	2.00	5.00
	1917F muling with Polish rev. of Y#6, see Poland					
	1917G	7.088	.10	.30	3.00	6.00
	1917J	9.205	.10	.30	3.00	7.00
	1918D	.042	200.00	500.00	800.00	1200.
	1921A	16.265	.20	4.00	6.00	12.00
	1922D	—	.20	7.00	12.00	20.00
	1922E	2.235	20.00	40.00	65.00	90.00
	1922E	26 pcs.			Proof	—
	1922F	1.928	.10	2.00	4.50	10.00
	1922G	1.358	15.00	30.00	55.00	90.00
	1922J	2.420	.10	4.00	6.00	12.00
	Common Date	—	—	—	Proof	75.00

ZINC
Eagle and beaded border as Y#22

Y#	Date	Mintage	Fine	VF	XF	Unc
22a	1916F	—	100.00	300.00	600.00	800.00
	1917	—	75.00	100.00	150.00	250.00
	1917A	—	75.00	130.00	220.00	350.00
	1922J	—	—	—	—	—

Y#	Date	Mintage	Fine	VF	XF	Unc
25.1	1917	75.073	.25	.40	.60	2.00
	1918	202.008	.25	.40	.60	2.00
	1918	28 pcs.	—	—	Proof	—
	1919	147.800	.25	.40	.60	2.00
	1919	50 pcs.	—	—	Proof	—
	1920	223.019	.25	.40	.60	2.00
	1920	40 pcs.	—	—	Proof	—
	1921	319.334	.25	.40	.60	2.00
	1921	24 pcs.	—	—	Proof	—
	1922	274.499	.25	.40	.60	2.00
	1922	12 pcs.	—	—	Proof	—
	Common Date	—	—	—	Proof	100.00

Thinner planchet

Y#	Date	Mintage	Fine	VF	XF	Unc
25.2	1918	Inc. Ab.	—	—	—	—
	1920	Inc. Ab.	—	—	—	—
	1921	Inc. Ab.	—	—	—	—

IRON

Y#	Date	Mintage	Fine	VF	XF	Unc
25a	1922	—	40.00	75.00	125.00	200.00

10 RENTENPFENNIG

ALUMINUM-BRONZE

Y#	Date	Mintage	Fine	VF	XF	Unc
35	1923A	w/1924	.15	2.00	5.00	16.00
	1923D	w/1924	.15	3.00	6.00	20.00
	1923F	w/1924	45.00	85.00	150.00	235.00
	1923G	w/1924	3.00	15.00	30.00	50.00
	1924A	169.956	.20	.30	.60	5.00
	1924D	33.894	.15	.30	.60	6.00
	1924E	18.679	.15	.60	1.00	10.00
	1924E	190 pcs.	—	—	Proof	—
	1924F	42.237	.15	.30	.60	6.00
	1924G	18.758	.15	.30	.60	6.00
	1924J	33.928	.15	.30	.60	6.00
	1925F	.013	250.00	500.00	850.00	1250.
	Common Date	—	—	—	Proof	60.00

*Combined mintage for Y#35 and Y#41.

10 REICHSPFENNIG

ALUMINUM-BRONZE

Y#	Date	Mintage	Fine	VF	XF	Unc
41	1924A	20.883	.15	.25	.60	5.00
	1924D	9.639	.10	.30	1.00	6.00
	1924E	5.185	.10	.60	1.00	7.00
	1924F	2.758	.10	.30	.60	6.00
	1924G	4.363	.10	.60	1.00	7.00
	1924J	3.993	.10	.30	.60	6.00
	1925A	102.319	.10	.15	.30	4.00
	1925D	36.853	.10	.15	.30	4.00
	1925E	18.700	.10	.30	.60	5.00
	1925F	12.516	.10	.15	.30	4.00
	1925G	10.360	.10	.30	.60	5.00
	1925J	8.755	2.00	10.00	20.00	35.00
	1926A	14.390	.10	1.25	4.00	10.00
	1926G	1.481	2.00	11.00	20.00	30.00
	1928A	2.308	1.00	6.00	9.00	15.00
	1928G	w/1929	35.00	90.00	135.00	185.00
	1929A	25.712	.10	.30	1.00	5.00
	1929D	7.049	.10	.30	1.00	5.00
	1929E	3.138	.10	.60	2.00	7.00
	1929F	3.740	.10	.60	2.00	6.00
	1929G	2.729	.10	2.00	6.00	14.00
	1929J	4.086	.10	2.00	5.00	13.00
	1930A	7.540	.10	1.25	3.00	12.00
	1930D	2.148	.10	2.00	6.00	14.00
	1930E	2.090	1.00	10.00	20.00	45.00
	1930F	2.006	1.00	5.00	9.00	20.00
	1930G	1.542	6.00	20.00	30.00	50.00
	1930J	1.637	.50	7.00	10.00	25.00
	1931A	9.661	.10	1.50	5.00	12.00
	1931D	.664	30.00	60.00	90.00	125.00
	1931F	1.482	.50	6.00	10.00	25.00
	1931G	.038	100.00	210.00	350.00	475.00
	1932A	4.528	.10	2.00	6.00	14.00
	1932D	2.812	.10	3.00	7.00	15.00
	1932E	1.491	1.00	12.00	20.00	42.00
	1932F	1.806	.25	5.00	8.00	20.00
	1932G	.137	435.00	700.00	1000.	1375.
	1933A	1.349	15.00	35.00	60.00	85.00
	1933G	1.046	4.00	10.00	15.00	35.00
	1933J	1.634	.50	8.00	13.00	30.00
	1934A	3.200	.10	2.00	6.00	14.00
	1934D	1.252	.25	6.00	10.00	20.00
	1934E	w/1935	20.00	35.00	60.00	75.00
	1934F	.100	15.00	45.00	65.00	90.00
	1934G	.150	20.00	50.00	80.00	115.00
	1935A	35.890	.10	.20	.60	4.00
	1935D	8.960	.10	.60	1.00	5.00
	1935E	5.966	.10	.40	1.25	5.00
	1935F	7.944	.10	.30	1.00	4.00
	1935G	4.847	.10	.60	1.75	6.00
	1935J	8.995	.10	.30	1.00	4.00
	1936A	24.527	.10	.15	.30	2.00
	1936D	8.092	.10	.20	.60	3.00
	1936E	2.441	.10	.50	1.50	7.00
	1936F	4.889	.10	.30	1.00	5.00
	1936G	1.715	.10	.50	1.50	7.00
	1936J	1.632	.10	2.00	4.00	8.50
	Common Date	—	—	—	Proof	60.00

Nazi State

Y#	Date	Mintage	Fine	VF	XF	Unc
91	1936A	w/1937A	2.00	12.00	20.00	35.00
	1936E	.245	75.00	140.00	200.00	300.00
	1936G	.129	75.00	140.00	200.00	300.00
	1937A	36.830	.10	.30	2.00	6.00
	1937D	6.882	.10	.60	3.00	7.00
	1937E	3.786	1.00	12.00	20.00	35.00
	1937F	5.934	.10	2.00	5.00	12.00
	1937G	2.131	.20	5.00	7.00	16.00
	1937J	4.439	.10	2.00	5.00	12.00
	1938A	70.068	.10	.20	.60	4.00
	1938B	7.852	.10	2.00	5.00	12.00
	1938D	16.990	.10	.30	1.25	5.00
	1938E	10.739	.10	.60	1.50	6.00
	1938F	12.307	.10	1.00	1.50	6.00
	1938G	8.584	.10	.60	1.50	6.00
	1938J	10.389	.10	.60	1.50	6.00
	1939A	40.171	.10	.30	.60	4.00
	1939B	7.814	.10	.60	1.25	5.00
	1939D	11.307	.10	.30	1.00	4.00
	1939E	5.079	.25	5.00	8.00	15.00
	1939F	6.993	.10	1.00	2.00	7.00
	1939G	5.532	.25	6.00	10.00	17.00
	1939J	5.557	.10	.60	1.25	5.00
	Common Date	—	—	—	Proof	60.00

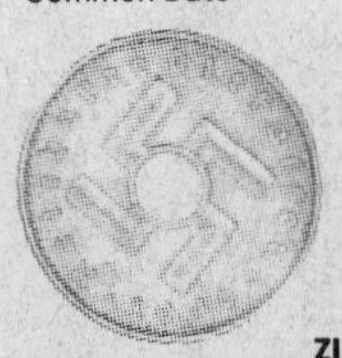
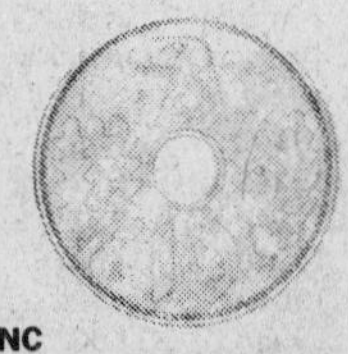

ZINC

Y#	Date	Mintage	Fine	VF	XF	Unc
95	1940A	—	2.00	5.00	10.00	20.00
	1940B	.840	50.00	200.00	325.00	450.00
	1940D	—	10.00	50.00	75.00	150.00
	1940E	5.100	10.00	50.00	75.00	150.00
	1940F	—	30.00	120.00	175.00	250.00
	1940G	.150	10.00	50.00	75.00	120.00
	1940J	—	10.00	50.00	75.00	150.00
	1941A	—	6.00	30.00	55.00	100.00
	1941F	—	10.00	50.00	75.00	150.00
	Common Date	—	—	—	Proof	150.00

Y#	Date	Mintage	Fine	VF	XF	Unc
C92	1940A	212.948	.10	.25	.40	2.00
	1940B	76.274	.10	.30	.60	4.00
	1940D	45.434	.10	.30	.60	4.00
	1940E	34.350	.10	.30	.60	4.00
	1940F	27.603	.10	.30	.60	4.00
	1940G	27.308	.10	.30	.60	4.00
	1940J	41.678	.10	.30	.60	4.00
	1941A	240.284	.10	.30	.40	2.00
	1941B	70.747	.10	.30	.60	4.00
	1941D	77.560	.10	.30	.60	4.00
	1941E	36.548	.10	.30	.60	4.00
	1941F	42.834	.10	.30	.60	4.00
	1941G	28.765	.10	.30	.60	4.00
	1941J	30.525	.10	.30	.60	4.00
	1942A	184.545	.10	.25	.60	2.50
	1942B	16.329	.10	1.50	2.00	9.00
	1942D	40.852	.10	.60	1.00	4.00
	1942E	18.334	.10	1.00	2.00	7.50
	1942F	32.690	.10	.25	.30	2.00
	1942G	20.295	.10	1.00	1.50	6.00
	1942J	29.957	.10	1.00	1.50	7.50
	1943A	157.357	.10	1.00	1.50	5.00
	1943B	11.940	1.00	7.00	15.00	30.00
	1943D	17.304	.10	1.25	2.00	5.00
	1943E	10.445	1.00	12.00	18.00	32.00
	1943F	24.804	.10	1.50	3.00	7.00
	1943G	3.618	.25	4.50	10.00	15.00
	1943J	1.821	20.00	45.00	75.00	110.00
	1944A	84.164	.10	.60	1.25	4.00
	1944B	40.781	.10	2.00	3.25	7.50
	1944D	30.369	.10	1.75	3.00	6.00
	1944E	29.963	.10	2.50	3.50	9.00
	1944F	19.639	.10	2.50	3.50	9.00
	1944G	13.023	.10	2.50	3.50	9.00
	1945A	7.112	.10	6.00	12.00	22.00

Y#	Date	Mintage	Fine	VF	XF	Unc
C92	1945E	4.897	12.00	25.00	40.00	60.00
	Common Date	—	—	—	Proof	60.00

Allied Occupation

Y#	Date	Mintage	Fine	VF	XF	Unc
100	1945F	5.942	1.00	9.00	15.00	25.00
	1946F	3.738	10.00	20.00	40.00	70.00
	1946G	1.600	50.00	125.00	175.00	210.00
	1947A	—	2.00	15.00	20.00	25.00
	1947E	2.612	100.00	175.00	250.00	400.00
	1947F	1.269	1.00	5.00	8.00	15.00
	1948A	—	2.00	15.00	25.00	40.00
	1948F	19.579	1.00	5.00	8.00	15.00
	Common Date	—	—	—	Proof	100.00

20 PFENNIG

1.1110 gms., .900 SILVER, .0321 oz ASW

Y#	Date	Mintage	Fine	VF	XF	Unc
12	1873A	2.159	4.00	10.00	20.00	35.00
	1873B	.664	15.00	25.00	50.00	75.00
	1873C	.904	10.00	15.00	35.00	55.00
	1873D	1.201	10.00	15.00	30.00	45.00
	1873E	100 pcs.	250.00	500.00	750.00	1000.
	1873F	.450	10.00	15.00	35.00	50.00
	1873G	.763	10.00	15.00	35.00	50.00
	1873H	.054	50.00	100.00	160.00	225.00
	1874A	8.830	5.00	8.00	12.00	22.00
	1874B	9.222	5.00	8.00	12.00	22.00
	1874C	1.303	6.00	12.00	20.00	35.00
	1874D	10.087	4.00	6.00	12.00	22.00
	1874E	2.281	2.50	10.00	20.00	35.00
	1874F	7.222	4.00	8.00	12.00	22.00
	1874G	3.281	5.00	10.00	16.00	27.00
	1874H	1.842	10.00	15.00	22.00	40.00
	1875A	9.034	3.00	6.00	10.00	22.00
	1875B	2.768	6.00	12.00	20.00	35.00
	1875C	5.938	4.00	8.00	12.00	22.00
	1875D	15.032	3.00	6.00	10.00	20.00
	1875E	1.486	5.00	10.00	20.00	35.00
	1875F	7.668	4.00	8.00	12.00	22.00
	1875G	3.940	5.00	10.00	16.00	30.00
	1875H	1.340	7.00	15.00	25.00	45.00
	1875J	3.502	7.00	15.00	25.00	45.00
	1876A	6.959	3.00	7.00	12.00	22.00
	1876B	5.089	3.00	7.00	12.00	22.00
	1876C	5.911	3.00	7.00	12.00	22.00
	1876D	14.152	3.00	6.00	10.00	20.00
	1876E	11.648	3.00	6.00	10.00	20.00
	1876F	13.635	3.00	6.00	10.00	20.00
	1876G	7.820	6.00	9.00	15.00	25.00
	1876H	1.433	10.00	20.00	35.00	65.00
	1876J	10.272	5.00	9.00	15.00	25.00
	1877F	.700	85.00	150.00	285.00	500.00
	Common Date	—	—	—	Proof	300.00

COPPER-NICKEL

Y#	Date	Mintage	Fine	VF	XF	Unc
7	1887A	2.712	6.00	17.00	30.00	55.00
	1887D	.704	10.00	32.00	45.00	75.00
	1887E	.373	10.00	37.00	60.00	100.00
	1887E star under value					
		50 pcs.	—	—	—	4000.
	1887F	.503	15.00	35.00	60.00	100.00
	1887G	.306	10.00	35.00	55.00	95.00
	1887J	.408	10.00	30.00	45.00	75.00
	1888A	5.426	4.00	15.00	25.00	50.00
	1888D	1.406	5.00	25.00	40.00	62.00
	1888E	.744	7.00	30.00	45.00	75.00
	1888F	1.005	10.00	35.00	55.00	90.00
	1888G	.611	10.00	35.00	55.00	90.00
	1888J	.818	10.00	35.00	55.00	90.00
	Common Date	—	—	—	Proof	300.00

Y#	Date	Mintage	Fine	VF	XF	Unc
10	1890A	2.716	7.00	30.00	45.00	95.00
	1890/80D	Inc. Ab.	7.50	30.00	60.00	125.00
	1890D	.703	10.00	35.00	55.00	110.00
	1890E	.373	15.00	45.00	75.00	135.00
	1890F	.503	10.00	35.00	55.00	110.00
	1890G	.306	15.00	60.00	100.00	160.00
	1890J	.410	12.00	50.00	85.00	150.00
	1892A	2.712	10.00	35.00	50.00	100.00
	1892D	.703	10.00	45.00	75.00	135.00
	1892E	.372	12.00	50.00	85.00	150.00
	1892F	.502	10.00	45.00	75.00	135.00
	1892G	.304	12.00	50.00	85.00	150.00
	1892J	.409	12.00	50.00	85.00	150.00
	Common Date	—	—	—	Proof	250.00

25 PFENNIG

NICKEL

Y#	Date	Mintage	Fine	VF	XF	Unc
11	1909A	.962	1.00	6.00	10.00	17.00
	1909D	1.406	1.00	6.00	12.00	20.00
	1909E	.250	5.00	12.00	20.00	35.00
	1909F	.400	2.00	10.00	15.00	30.00
	1909G	.610	2.00	10.00	20.00	35.00
	1909J	.010	250.00	450.00	750.00	1100.
	1910A	9.522	2.00	10.00	15.00	30.00
	1910D	1.408	2.00	10.00	20.00	35.00
	1910E	1.242	2.00	10.00	15.00	30.00
	1910F	1.605	3.00	12.00	20.00	40.00
	1910G	.330	3.00	12.00	20.00	40.00
	1910J	1.561	2.00	9.00	15.00	25.00
	1911A	3.179	2.00	9.00	15.00	25.00
	1911D	.506	2.00	10.00	20.00	35.00
	1911E	.747	2.50	10.00	15.00	30.00
	1911G	.892	2.50	10.00	20.00	35.00
	1911J	.516	3.00	15.00	35.00	50.00
	1912A	2.590	2.00	7.00	12.00	20.00
	1912D	.900	2.00	9.00	15.00	25.00
	1912F	1.003	2.00	10.00	20.00	35.00
	1912J	.362	7.00	20.00	45.00	75.00
	Common Date	—	—	—	Proof	75.00

50 PFENNIG

2.7770 gms., .900 SILVER, .0803 oz ASW

Y#	Date	Mintage	Fine	VF	XF	Unc
13	1875A	7.095	7.00	12.00	25.00	45.00
	1875B	2.799	10.00	15.00	35.00	65.00
	1875C	2.047	7.00	15.00	25.00	55.00
	1875D	4.668	10.00	15.00	35.00	75.00
	1875E	.353	100.00	175.00	250.00	375.00
	1875F	.874	25.00	40.00	75.00	125.00
	1875G	2.034	12.00	20.00	45.00	80.00
	1875H	.175	135.00	225.00	375.00	500.00
	1875J	2.411	12.00	20.00	45.00	80.00
	1876A	34.475	12.00	15.00	30.00	50.00
	1876B	11.016	10.00	15.00	35.00	60.00
	1876C	10.945	10.00	15.00	30.00	50.00
	1876D	3.641	15.00	30.00	50.00	85.00
	1876E	4.127	7.00	12.00	25.00	50.00
	1876F	4.448	12.00	20.00	40.00	65.00
	1876G	1.797	12.00	20.00	40.00	65.00
	1876H	1.877	15.00	30.00	50.00	85.00
	1876J	3.589	10.00	15.00	35.00	60.00
	1877A	3.249	12.00	20.00	40.00	65.00
	1877B	3.691	12.00	20.00	40.00	65.00
	1877C	2.388	15.00	30.00	50.00	85.00
	1877D	3.004	12.00	20.00	40.00	65.00
	1877E	1.121	20.00	40.00	80.00	135.00
	1877F	1.311	15.00	20.00	45.00	75.00
	1877H	.622	60.00	80.00	135.00	210.00

Y#	Date	Mintage	Fine	VF	XF	Unc
13	1877J	1.526	40.00	65.00	115.00	175.00
	Common Date	—	—	—	Proof	300.00

Y#	Date	Mintage	Fine	VF	XF	Unc
14	1877A	6.746	25.00	50.00	100.00	150.00
	1877B	3.097	25.00	50.00	100.00	150.00
	1877C	2.820	30.00	60.00	110.00	170.00
	1877D	5.315	25.00	50.00	120.00	180.00
	1877E	2.296	30.00	60.00	110.00	170.00
	1877F	2.145	30.00	60.00	125.00	185.00
	1877G	2.061	30.00	50.00	110.00	170.00
	1877H	1.510	30.00	50.00	110.00	170.00
	1877J	1.337	30.00	55.00	110.00	170.00
	1878E	.364	150.00	300.00	450.00	550.00
	Common Date	—	—	—	Proof	300.00

Y#	Date	Mintage	Fine	VF	XF	Unc
15	1896A	.389	80.00	200.00	300.00	375.00
	1898A	.387	100.00	250.00	350.00	435.00
	1900J	.192	90.00	250.00	350.00	450.00
	1901A	.194	90.00	250.00	350.00	435.00
	1902F	.095	180.00	325.00	500.00	750.00
	1903A	.384	75.00	200.00	300.00	375.00
	Common Date	—	—	—	Proof	500.00

ALUMINUM
Weimar Republic

Y#	Date	Mintage	Fine	VF	XF	Unc
26	1919A	7.173	.10	.30	2.00	6.00
	1919D	.791	.10	.60	3.00	7.00
	1919E	.930	7.00	15.00	25.00	45.00
	1919E	35 pcs.	—	—	Proof	—
	1919F	.160	10.00	20.00	30.00	50.00
	1919G	.660	.10	2.00	4.00	9.00
	1919J	.800	5.00	12.00	20.00	30.00
	1920A	119.793	.05	.15	.30	1.00
	1920D	28.306	.05	.15	.30	1.00
	1920E	14.400	.10	1.00	6.00	10.00
	1920E	226 pcs.	—	—	Proof	—
	1920F	10.932	.10	.15	.30	1.00
	1920G	5.040	.10	.60	2.00	5.00
	1920J	15.423	.10	.30	.60	3.00
	1921A	184.468	.05	.15	.30	1.00
	1921D	48.729	.05	.15	.30	1.00
	1921E	31.210	.10	1.00	2.00	5.00
	1921E	332 pcs.	—	—	Proof	—
	1921F	46.950	.05	.15	.30	1.00
	1921G	19.107	.10	.15	.30	1.00
	1921J	28.013	.10	.30	.60	2.00
	1922A	145.215	.05	.15	.30	1.00
	1922D	58.019	.10	.15	.30	1.00
	1922E	33.930	.10	2.00	6.00	9.00
	1922E	333 pcs.	—	—	Proof	—
	1922F	33.000	.10	.15	.30	1.00
	1922G	36.745	.10	.15	.30	1.00
	1922J	36.202	.10	1.00	2.00	4.50
	Common Date	—	—	—	Proof	40.00

50 RENTENPFENNIG

ALUMINUM-BRONZE

Y#	Date	Mintage	Fine	VF	XF	Unc
36	1923A	.451	5.00	15.00	30.00	50.00
	1923D	.192	12.00	20.00	35.00	55.00
	1923F	.120	50.00	100.00	160.00	235.00
	1923G	.120	20.00	40.00	75.00	110.00

Y#	Date	Mintage	Fine	VF	XF	Unc
36	1923J	4,000	400.00	900.00	1200.	1500.
	1924A	117.365	1.00	7.50	15.00	25.00
	1924D	30.971	1.00	9.00	20.00	45.00
	1924E	14.668	1.00	10.00	15.00	40.00
	1924F	21.968	1.00	7.00	15.00	35.00
	1924G	13.349	1.00	12.00	20.00	40.00
	1924J	17.252	1.00	7.00	15.00	35.00
	Common Date	—	—	—	Proof	100.00

50 REICHSPFENNIG

ALUMINUM-BRONZE

Y#	Date	Mintage	Fine	VF	XF	Unc
42	1924A	.801	350.00	950.00	1300.	1750.
	1924E	w/1925	750.00	2000.	3000.	4500.
	1924F	.055	600.00	1900.	2750.	4000.
	1924G	.011	1000.	2500.	3500.	5000.
	1925E	1.805	350.00	950.00	1300.	1750.
	1925E	196 pcs.	—	—	Proof	—
	Common Date	—	—	—	Proof	5000.

NICKEL

Y#	Date	Mintage	Fine	VF	XF	Unc
43	1927A	16.309	.50	2.00	5.00	10.00
	1927D	2.228	.50	3.00	7.00	12.00
	1927E	1.070	.50	4.50	10.00	15.00
	1927E	23 pcs.	—	—	Proof	—
	1927F	1.940	.50	3.00	7.00	12.00
	1927G	1.756	.50	4.50	10.00	15.00
	1927J	4.056	.50	3.00	7.00	12.00
	1928A	43.864	.25	.90	3.00	7.00
	1928D	14.088	.25	1.50	5.00	10.00
	1928E	8.618	.25	2.00	6.00	12.00
	1928E	93 pcs.	—	—	Proof	—
	1928F	9.954	.25	1.50	5.00	10.00
	1928G	6.177	.25	2.75	7.00	15.00
	1928J	6.565	.25	1.50	5.00	10.00
	1929A	10.298	.25	1.25	4.00	7.00
	1929D	1.965	.25	2.00	6.00	12.00
	1929E	—	—	—	May Not Exist	
	1929F	1.162	3.00	9.00	20.00	30.00
	1930A	4.128	.25	2.75	7.00	10.00
	1930D	1.406	.50	8.00	12.00	20.00
	1930E	.745	2.00	12.00	25.00	35.00
	1930F	.320	10.00	40.00	60.00	80.00
	1930G	.610	3.00	14.00	30.00	40.00
	1930J	.526	2.00	14.00	30.00	40.00
	1931A	5.624	.25	3.00	5.00	7.50
	1931D	1.125	.50	6.00	15.00	25.00
	1931F	1.484	.50	6.00	15.00	20.00
	1931G	.060	60.00	200.00	275.00	350.00
	1931J	.291	10.00	20.00	80.00	125.00
	1932E	.598	35.00	70.00	100.00	200.00
	1932G	.096	750.00	1000.	1500.	1900.
	1933G	.333	35.00	75.00	100.00	160.00
	1933J	.654	25.00	75.00	100.00	150.00
	1935A	6.390	.25	2.00	4.00	8.00
	1935D	2.812	.50	4.50	6.00	12.00
	1935E	.745	7.00	15.00	25.00	45.00
	1935F	2.006	.50	4.50	6.00	12.00
	1935G	.650	10.00	20.00	35.00	65.00
	1935J	1.635	1.00	9.00	15.00	25.00
	1936A	7.696	.25	2.75	5.00	8.00
	1936D	.844	2.00	10.00	15.00	30.00
	1936E	1.190	7.00	17.00	25.00	45.00
	1936F	.602	9.00	25.00	35.00	75.00
	1936G	.936	5.00	15.00	30.00	60.00
	1936J	.490	25.00	50.00	80.00	110.00
	1937A	10.842	.25	1.00	1.50	5.00
	1937D	2.814	.25	1.50	3.00	7.00
	1937F	1.700	.25	3.00	4.50	10.00
	1937J	.300	35.00	75.00	100.00	150.00
	1938E	1.200	1.00	9.00	18.00	25.00
	1938G	1.299	.50	7.50	15.00	20.00
	1938J	1.333	1.00	9.00	18.00	25.00
	Common Date	—	—	—	Proof	60.00

ALUMINUM
Nazi State

Y#	Date	Mintage	Fine	VF	XF	Unc
80	1935A	75.912	.20	.50	1.00	7.00
	1935D	19.688	.25	.75	2.50	10.00
	1935E	10.418	.50	2.00	5.00	12.00
	1935F	14.061	.25	.75	2.50	10.00
	1935G	8.540	.40	4.00	9.00	22.00
	1935J	11.438	.25	3.00	7.00	20.00
	Common Date	—	—	—	Proof	120.00

NICKEL

Y#	Date	Mintage	Fine	VF	XF	Unc
93	1938A	5.051	7.00	15.00	25.00	50.00
	1938B	1.124	10.00	25.00	50.00	90.00
	1938D	1.260	7.00	20.00	40.00	75.00
	1938E	.949	10.00	30.00	50.00	90.00
	1938F	1.210	10.00	25.00	50.00	90.00
	1938G	.460	15.00	40.00	75.00	140.00
	1938J	.730	15.00	40.00	75.00	140.00
	1939A	15.037	6.00	15.00	25.00	50.00
	1939B	2.826	7.00	15.00	35.00	60.00
	1939D	3.648	7.00	15.00	35.00	75.00
	1939E	1.924	7.50	20.00	40.00	70.00
	1939F	2.602	10.00	25.00	50.00	90.00
	1939G	1.565	12.00	35.00	70.00	125.00
	1939J	2.114	10.00	30.00	50.00	90.00
	Common Date	—	—	—	Proof	200.00

ALUMINUM

Y#	Date	Mintage	Fine	VF	XF	Unc
92	1939A	5.000	.10	.75	2.00	10.00
	1939B	5.482	.10	1.00	2.00	10.00
	1939D	.600	2.00	12.00	30.00	50.00
	1939E	2.000	.25	3.00	7.50	20.00
	1939F	3.600	.10	1.75	6.00	15.00
	1939G	.560	5.00	15.00	35.00	50.00
	1939J	1.000	.25	4.50	12.00	23.00
	1940A	56.128	.10	.30	1.50	5.00
	1940B	10.016	.10	1.75	3.00	7.00
	1940D	13.800	.10	.75	2.00	5.00
	1940E	5.618	.50	7.50	15.00	25.00
	1940F	6.663	.10	1.00	1.75	5.00
	1940G	5.616	.50	5.50	7.50	15.00
	1940J	7.335	.50	7.50	15.00	25.00
	1941A	31.263	.10	1.00	1.75	5.00
	1941B	4.291	.25	3.50	6.00	15.00
	1941D	7.200	.10	2.50	4.50	12.00
	1941E	3.806	.10	2.75	4.50	12.00
	1941F	5.128	.10	1.75	3.50	10.00
	1941G	3.091	.25	4.50	7.50	20.00
	1941J	4.165	.25	4.50	7.50	20.00
	1942A	11.580	.10	.30	1.50	5.00
	1942B	2.876	2.50	15.00	25.00	45.00
	1942D	2.247	.10	1.75	4.00	10.00
	1942E	3.810	.25	4.50	7.50	20.00
	1942F	5.133	.25	4.50	7.50	20.00
	1942G	1.400	.25	6.00	10.00	25.00
	1943A	29.325	.10	.30	1.50	10.00
	1943B	8.229	.10	2.75	4.50	12.00
	1943D	5.315	.10	.30	1.50	10.00
	1943G	2.892	.25	4.50	7.50	20.00
	1943J	4.166	1.00	10.00	20.00	30.00
	1944B	5.622	.10	1.75	4.00	10.00
	1944D	4.886	10.00	30.00	45.00	70.00
	1944F	3.739	.10	.60	1.50	7.00
	1944G	1.190	20.00	60.00	100.00	125.00
	Common Date	—	—	—	Proof	40.00

1/2 MARK

2.7770 gms., .900 SILVER, .0803 oz ASW

Y#	Date	Mintage	Fine	VF	XF	Unc
16	1905A	37.766	BV	BV	5.00	12.00
	1905A	920 pcs.	—	—	Proof	—
	1905D	7.636	BV	2.50	5.00	12.00
	1905E	4.908	BV	2.50	5.00	14.00
	1905F	6.310	BV	2.50	5.00	12.00
	1905G	3.886	BV	2.50	5.00	15.00
	1905J	6.316	BV	2.50	5.00	12.00
	1906A	29.754	BV	BV	5.00	12.00
	1906A	583 pcs.	—	—	Proof	—
	1906D	11.977	BV	BV	5.00	12.00
	1906E	5.821	BV	2.50	5.00	14.00
	1906F	8.036	BV	2.50	5.00	12.00
	1906F	200 pcs.	—	—	Proof	—
	1906G	4.273	BV	2.50	5.00	12.00
	1906G	10-30 pcs.	—	—	Proof	—
	1906J	2.179	BV	2.50	5.00	15.00
	1907A	14.168	BV	2.50	3.00	10.00
	1907D	2.884	BV	2.50	3.00	11.00
	1907E	.600	BV	3.50	10.00	22.00
	1907F	1.202	BV	2.50	5.00	12.00
	1907G	.927	BV	3.50	10.00	22.00
	1907J	3.268	BV	2.50	5.00	12.00
	1908A	5.018	BV	2.50	4.00	10.00
	1908D	.400	BV	7.50	20.00	42.00
	1908E	.591	BV	4.50	10.00	22.00
	1908F	1,000	500.00	1000.	1500.	2125.
	1908G	.675	BV	3.00	10.00	20.00
	1908/7J	—	—	—	—	—
	1908J	1.309	BV	3.00	10.00	20.00
	1909A	5.404	BV	2.50	3.00	10.00
	1909/5D	—	BV	—	—	—
	1909D	1.001	BV	2.50	3.00	11.00
	1909E	.745	BV	2.50	5.00	16.00
	1909F	.999	BV	2.50	5.00	12.00
	1909G	.607	BV	3.50	7.00	17.00
	1909J	.816	BV	3.00	5.00	16.00
	1911A	2.710	BV	2.50	5.00	14.00
	1911/05D	—	—	—	—	—
	1911D	.703	BV	2.50	5.00	16.00
	1911E	.376	BV	9.00	20.00	32.00
	1911F	.502	BV	4.50	10.00	25.00
	1911G	.610	BV	3.50	10.00	20.00
	1911J	.418	BV	9.00	20.00	32.00
	1912A	2.709	BV	2.50	5.00	14.00
	1912/5D	—	BV	3.50	10.00	22.00
	1912D	.703	BV	3.50	10.00	20.00
	1912E	.369	BV	7.50	15.00	30.00
	1912F	.501	BV	3.50	10.00	20.00
	1912J	.399	BV	9.00	20.00	32.00
	1913A	5.419	BV	2.50	3.00	9.00
	1913/05D	—	BV	2.50	5.00	10.00
	1913D	1.406	BV	2.50	4.00	10.00
	1913E	.745	BV	2.50	5.00	15.00
	1913F	1.003	BV	2.50	4.00	10.00
	1913G	.610	BV	2.50	5.00	14.00
	1913J	.817	BV	4.50	10.00	22.00
	1914A	13.525	BV	2.50	2.50	8.00
	1914/05D	—	BV	6.50	15.00	30.00
	1914D	.328	BV	6.00	12.00	25.00
	1914J	2.292	BV	2.50	3.00	9.00
	1915A	13.015	BV	BV	3.00	7.00
	1915/05D	—	BV	BV	3.00	7.50
	1915D	5.117	BV	BV	3.00	7.50
	1915E	3.308	BV	BV	3.00	7.50
	1915F	5.309	BV	BV	3.00	7.50
	1915G	2.730	BV	BV	3.00	7.50
	1915J	2.285	BV	BV	3.00	7.50
	1916A	9.750	BV	BV	3.00	7.50
	1916/616D	—	—	—	—	—
	1916/05D	—	—	—	—	—
	1916/06D	—	—	—	—	—
	1916/5D	—	—	—	—	—
	1916D	4.397	BV	BV	3.00	7.50
	1916E	1.640	BV	2.50	6.00	13.00
	1916F	2.410	BV	2.50	4.00	7.50
	1916G	1.779	BV	2.50	6.00	12.00
	1916J	1.464	BV	2.50	4.00	20.00
	1917A	14.692	BV	2.50	4.00	7.00
	1917/05D	Inc. Ab.	BV	2.50	5.00	10.00
	1917D	.979	BV	2.50	3.00	7.00
	1917E	1.561	BV	4.50	5.00	8.00
	1917F	.450	BV	4.50	8.00	17.00
	1917G	.619	BV	3.50	8.00	17.00
	1917J	1.039	BV	4.50	8.00	16.00
	1918A	14.622	BV	2.50	3.00	7.00
	1918/05D	—	—	—	—	—
	1918/15D	—	—	—	—	—
	1918D	3.670	BV	2.50	3.00	11.00
	1918E	2.807	BV	5.00	10.00	20.00
	1918E	19 pcs.	—	—	Proof	—
	1918F	4.010	BV	2.50	3.00	8.00
	1918G	1.032	BV	2.50	6.00	12.00
	1918J	3.452	BV	3.00	5.00	15.00
	1919A	9.124	BV	2.50	4.00	10.00
	1919/1619D	—	—	—	—	—
	1919/05D	—	—	—	—	—
	1919/15D	—	—	—	—	—
	1919D	2.195	BV	3.00	6.00	12.00
	1919E	1.767	BV	7.50	12.00	22.00
	1919E	39 pcs.	—	—	Proof	—
	1919F	1.559	BV	2.50	6.00	12.00
	1919J	1.875	BV	3.50	7.50	15.00
	Common Date	—	—	—	Proof	40.00

MARK

.900 SILVER

Y#	Date	Mintage	Fine	VF	XF	Unc
17	1873A	.930	5.00	12.00	50.00	85.00
	1873B	.089	8.00	25.00	100.00	150.00
	1873C	.018	75.00	150.00	250.00	350.00
	1873D	.244	8.00	15.00	75.00	110.00
	1873F	.109	10.00	25.00	100.00	150.00
	1874A	6.310	BV	12.00	35.00	60.00
	1874B	2.672	5.00	15.00	70.00	100.00
	1874C	.840	8.00	15.00	70.00	100.00
	1874D	7.079	BV	10.00	35.00	55.00
	1874E	3.240	5.00	15.00	70.00	100.00
	1874F	6.155	BV	10.00	35.00	55.00
	1874G	4.210	35.00	80.00	160.00	225.00
	1874H	1.893	5.00	12.00	50.00	75.00
	1875A	30.340	BV	10.00	50.00	75.00
	1875B	7.690	5.00	15.00	70.00	100.00
	1875C	6.209	5.00	12.00	50.00	75.00
	1875D	7.538	5.00	10.00	35.00	55.00
	1875E	4.646	5.00	15.00	70.00	100.00
	1875F	7.074	5.00	10.00	35.00	55.00
	1875G	6.072	5.00	12.00	50.00	75.00
	1875H	2.300	5.00	12.00	50.00	75.00
	1875J	7.728	5.00	8.00	25.00	40.00
	1876A	17.297	BV	7.00	35.00	55.00
	1876C	4.790	5.00	12.00	50.00	85.00
	1876D	2.956	5.00	12.00	50.00	85.00
	1876F	4.161	5.00	12.00	50.00	85.00
	1876G	2.333	5.00	12.00	40.00	75.00
	1876H	2.481	5.00	12.00	40.00	75.00
	1876J	1.109	5.00	12.00	50.00	85.00
	1877A	.697	5.00	12.00	40.00	75.00
	1877B	.048	25.00	40.00	125.00	185.00
	1878A	1.527	5.00	12.00	50.00	85.00
	1878B	.582	5.00	15.00	75.00	125.00
	1878C	.600	5.00	25.00	120.00	175.00
	1878E	.318	5.00	20.00	100.00	150.00
	1878F	1.039	5.00	12.00	50.00	85.00
	1878G	.525	5.00	12.00	50.00	85.00
	1878J	.895	5.00	12.00	50.00	85.00
	1879A	.156	25.00	90.00	150.00	250.00
	1880A	1.071	5.00	12.00	50.00	85.00
	1880D	.338	5.00	12.00	55.00	100.00
	1880E	.173	5.00	20.00	90.00	135.00
	1880F	.223	5.00	20.00	90.00	135.00
	1880G	.146	8.00	25.00	125.00	175.00
	1880H	.164	8.00	30.00	135.00	185.00
	1880J	.197	5.00	20.00	100.00	150.00
	1881A	6.386	5.00	10.00	35.00	75.00
	1881D	2.040	5.00	10.00	35.00	75.00
	1881E	1.081	5.00	15.00	55.00	110.00
	1881F	1.455	5.00	15.00	45.00	90.00
	1881G	.426	5.00	20.00	60.00	125.00
	1881H	.387	5.00	20.00	60.00	125.00
	1881J	.790	5.00	15.00	45.00	90.00
	1882A	1.474	5.00	15.00	40.00	80.00
	1882G	.459	5.00	20.00	60.00	125.00
	1882H	.109	30.00	60.00	175.00	300.00
	1882J	.098	5.00	20.00	60.00	125.00
	1883A	.809	5.00	10.00	35.00	75.00
	1883D	.208	15.00	30.00	75.00	150.00
	1883E	.112	25.00	50.00	150.00	300.00
	1883F	.148	15.00	30.00	90.00	185.00
	1883G	.091	30.00	60.00	175.00	350.00
	1883J	.121	20.00	40.00	110.00	225.00
	1885A	1.467	5.00	10.00	30.00	60.00
	1885G	.468	6.00	15.00	55.00	110.00
	1885J	.413	6.00	15.00	55.00	110.00

Y#	Date	Mintage	Fine	VF	XF	Unc
17	1886A	1.101	5.00	8.00	22.00	45.00
	1886D	1.445	5.00	10.00	30.00	60.00
	1886E	.764	6.00	15.00	55.00	100.00
	1886F	1.031	5.00	10.00	30.00	65.00
	1886G	.161	15.00	30.00	90.00	175.00
	1886J	.427	6.00	20.00	55.00	110.00
	1887A	3.006	5.00	15.00	55.00	90.00
	Common Date	—	—	—	Proof	150.00

Y#	Date	Mintage	Fine	VF	XF	Unc
18	1891A	.711	5.00	10.00	15.00	30.00
		W/1892	175.00	250.00	350.00	500.00
	1892A	.909	BV	5.00	15.00	30.00
	1892D	.418	5.00	10.00	20.00	40.00
	1892E	.223	6.00	15.00	25.00	50.00
	1892F	.302	6.00	7.00	20.00	40.00
	1892G	.183	10.00	20.00	30.00	60.00
	1892J	.237	10.00	25.00	40.00	75.00
	1893A	1.633	BV	5.00	12.00	25.00
	1893D	.425	5.00	7.00	12.00	25.00
	1893E	.224	6.00	15.00	25.00	50.00
	1893F	.300	6.00	15.00	25.00	55.00
	1893J	.254	6.00	12.00	25.00	55.00
	1894G	.184	10.00	35.00	50.00	85.00
	1896A	2.160	BV	5.00	12.00	25.00
	1896D	.562	5.00	8.00	15.00	30.00
	1896E	.297	6.00	15.00	25.00	50.00
	1896F	.401	5.00	7.00	16.00	35.00
	1896G	.243	6.00	15.00	25.00	55.00
	1896J	.326	5.00	10.00	20.00	40.00
	1898A	1.000	5.00	12.00	20.00	40.00
	1899A	1.439	BV	5.00	10.00	20.00
	1899D	.633	5.00	6.00	12.00	25.00
	1899E	.335	6.00	10.00	15.00	35.00
	1899F	.393	5.00	7.00	15.00	35.00
	1899G	.274	6.00	12.00	20.00	40.00
	1899J	.368	5.00	7.00	15.00	35.00
	1900A	1.625	BV	5.00	7.00	15.00
	1900/600D	—	5.00	6.00	10.00	20.00
	1900D	.421	5.00	7.00	15.00	30.00
	1900E	.223	6.00	10.00	20.00	40.00
	1900F	.301	6.00	10.00	15.00	30.00
	1900G	.183	8.00	15.00	25.00	50.00
	1900J	.246	6.00	15.00	25.00	50.00
	1901A	3.821	BV	5.00	7.00	15.00
	1901D	.915	BV	5.00	10.00	20.00
	1901E	.484	5.00	8.00	12.00	25.00
	1901F	.802	BV	5.00	7.00	15.00
	1901G	.579	5.00	6.00	10.00	20.00
	1901J	.531	5.00	6.00	10.00	20.00
	1902A	5.222	BV	BV	5.00	15.00
	1902D	1.546	BV	BV	5.00	15.00
	1902E	.819	BV	5.00	6.00	15.00
	1902F	.953	BV	5.00	6.00	15.00
	1902G	.270	8.00	20.00	30.00	50.00
	1902J	.898	BV	5.00	6.00	15.00
	1903A	3.965	BV	BV	5.00	15.00
	1903D	.914	BV	5.00	6.00	15.00
	1903E	.485	5.00	7.00	12.00	25.00
	1903F	.652	5.00	6.00	10.00	22.00
	1903G	.614	5.00	6.00	10.00	22.00
	1903J	.531	5.00	10.00	15.00	30.00
	1904A	3.243	BV	BV	5.00	15.00
	1904D	1.761	BV	BV	5.00	15.00
	1904E	.931	BV	BV	5.00	15.00
	1904F	1.255	BV	BV	5.00	15.00
	1904G	.664	BV	5.00	6.00	15.00
	1904J	1.021	BV	BV	5.00	15.00
	1905A	10.303	BV	BV	5.00	15.00
	1905A	460 pcs.	—	—	Proof	—
	1905D	1.759	BV	BV	5.00	14.00
	1905E	.931	BV	BV	5.00	15.00
		W/1904	1000.	1800.	2250.	2750.
	1905G	.860	BV	5.00	6.00	15.00
	1905J	1.021	BV	BV	5.00	15.00
	1906A	5.414	BV	BV	5.00	10.00
	1906A	430 pcs.	—	—	Proof	—
	1906D	1.412	BV	BV	7.00	12.00
	1906E	.745	BV	BV	5.00	14.00
	1906F	2.257	BV	BV	5.00	12.00
	1906F	200 pcs.	—	—	Proof	—
	1906G	.609	BV	BV	5.00	15.00
	1906G	10-30 pcs.	—	—	Proof	—
	1906J	.372	BV	BV	5.00	15.00
	1907A	9.201	BV	BV	5.00	10.00
	1907D	2.387	BV	BV	5.00	10.00
	1907E	1.265	BV	BV	5.00	10.00
	1907F	1.704	BV	BV	5.00	10.00
18	1907G	1.035	BV	BV	5.00	10.00
	1907J	1.833	BV	BV	5.00	10.00
	1908A	4.338	BV	BV	5.00	10.00
	1908D	1.126	BV	BV	5.00	10.00
	1908E	.596	BV	5.00	10.00	15.00
	1908F	.802	BV	BV	7.00	10.00
	1908G	.488	BV	5.00	10.00	15.00
	1908J	.653	1.50	1.75	3.50	10.00
	1909A	4.151	BV	BV	5.00	10.00
	1909D	1.968	BV	BV	5.00	10.00
	1909E	W/1910	30.00	90.00	125.00	185.00
	1909G	.854	10.00	25.00	40.00	65.00
	1909J	.053	60.00	150.00	225.00	300.00
	1910A	5.870	BV	BV	5.00	10.00
	1910D	1.406	BV	BV	5.00	10.00
	1910E	1.050	BV	5.00	10.00	16.00
	1910F	1.631	BV	5.00	10.00	16.00
	1910G	.610	BV	5.00	10.00	16.00
	1910J	1.094	BV	5.00	10.00	15.00
	1911A	5.693	BV	BV	5.00	10.00
	1911D	.126	5.00	10.00	30.00	45.00
	1911E	.738	BV	5.00	10.00	16.00
	1911F	.773	BV	5.00	10.00	16.00
	1911G	.305	BV	5.00	10.00	16.00
	1911J	.812	BV	5.00	10.00	16.00
	1912A	2.439	BV	BV	5.00	10.00
	1912D	.632	BV	BV	5.00	12.00
	1912E	.708	BV	5.00	10.00	16.00
	1912F	.502	BV	5.00	10.00	16.00
	1912J	.409	BV	5.00	10.00	20.00
	1913F	.450	10.00	30.00	50.00	65.00
	1913G	.275	25.00	40.00	60.00	95.00
	1913J	.368	10.00	30.00	45.00	60.00
	1914A	11.304	BV	BV	5.00	12.00
	1914/9D	—	—	—	—	—
	1914D	3.515	BV	BV	5.00	10.00
	1914E	2.235	BV	BV	5.00	10.00
	1914F	2.300	BV	BV	5.00	10.00
	1914G	1.911	BV	BV	5.00	10.00
	1914J	2.978	BV	BV	5.00	10.00
	1915A	13.817	BV	BV	5.00	10.00
	1915D	4.218	BV	BV	5.00	10.00
	1915E	2.235	BV	BV	10.00	15.00
	1915F	2.911	BV	BV	5.00	10.00
	1915G	1.749	BV	BV	5.00	10.00
	1915J	1.634	BV	BV	5.00	10.00
	1916F	.306	5.00	20.00	35.00	50.00
	Common Date	—	—	—	Proof	75.00

.500 SILVER

Y#	Date	Mintage	Fine	VF	XF	Unc
44	1924A	75.536	5.00	12.00	25.00	45.00
	1924D	17.099	5.00	20.00	40.00	75.00
	1924E	12.293	5.00	12.00	25.00	45.00
	1924E	115 pcs.	—	—	Proof	—
	1924F	16.550	5.00	12.00	25.00	45.00
	1924G	10.065	5.00	12.00	25.00	45.00
	1924J	13.481	5.00	12.00	25.00	40.00
	1925A	13.878	10.00	30.00	65.00	90.00
	1925D	6.100	5.00	20.00	35.00	55.00
	Common Date	—	—	—	Proof	100.00

REICHSMARK

.500 SILVER

Y#	Date	Mintage	Fine	VF	XF	Unc
45	1925A	34.527	5.00	10.00	20.00	35.00
	1925A	600 pcs.	—	—	Proof	—
	1925D	13.854	5.00	15.00	25.00	40.00
	1925E	6.460	5.00	20.00	35.00	50.00
	1925E	—	—	—	—	—
	1925F	8.035	5.00	20.00	30.00	45.00
	1925G	4.520	5.00	20.00	30.00	45.00
	1925J	6.800	5.00	15.00	25.00	40.00
	1926A	35.555	5.00	12.00	20.00	35.00
	1926D	4.424	5.00	15.00	25.00	35.00
	1926E	3.225	5.00	20.00	40.00	55.00
	1926E	31 pcs.	—	—	Proof	—
	1926F	3.045	5.00	15.00	25.00	40.00
	1926G	3.410	5.00	25.00	40.00	55.00
45	1926J	1.290	30.00	80.00	125.00	175.00
	1927A	.364	75.00	200.00	450.00	600.00
	1927F	1.959	15.00	40.00	60.00	90.00
	1927J	2.451	15.00	40.00	80.00	110.00
	Common Date	—	—	—	Proof	80.00

NICKEL
Nazi State

Y#	Date	Mintage	Fine	VF	XF	Unc
81	1933A	6.030	.50	3.00	6.00	12.00
	1933D	4.562	.50	3.00	6.00	12.00
	1933E	3.500	.50	5.00	11.00	22.00
	1933F	1.400	.50	5.00	11.00	22.00
	1933G	2.000	.50	5.00	11.00	22.00
	1934A	52.345	.50	1.00	2.00	4.00
	1934D	30.597	.50	1.00	2.00	4.00
	1934E	15.135	.50	3.00	6.00	12.00
	1934F	23.672	.50	2.50	5.00	10.00
	1934G	13.252	.50	3.00	7.00	15.00
	1934J	16.820	.50	2.50	5.00	10.00
	1935A	57.896	.50	3.00	6.00	12.00
	1935J	3.621	1.00	7.00	15.00	30.00
	1936A	20.287	.50	3.00	5.50	11.00
	1936D	4.940	.50	5.00	11.00	22.00
	1936E	3.200	.50	7.00	15.00	30.00
	1936F	2.075	.50	5.00	11.00	22.00
	1936G	.620	40.00	90.00	135.00	180.00
	1936J	2.975	.50	5.00	11.00	22.00
	1937A	49.976	.50	1.50	3.00	6.00
	1937D	10.529	.50	2.00	4.50	9.00
	1937E	2.926	1.00	7.00	14.00	27.00
	1937F	6.221	.50	3.00	7.00	15.00
	1937G	2.143	.50	5.00	11.00	22.00
	1937J	4.721	.50	6.00	12.00	25.00
	1938A	9.829	.50	2.50	4.50	9.00
	1938E	2.073	2.00	8.00	16.00	32.00
	1938F	2.739	1.50	7.00	15.00	30.00
	1938G	4.381	1.00	7.00	14.00	27.00
	1938J	1.269	30.00	75.00	100.00	140.00
	1939A	52.150	2.00	8.00	16.00	32.00
	1939B	9.836	60.00	125.00	185.00	235.00
	1939D	12.522	5.00	25.00	50.00	100.00
	1939E	6.570	20.00	65.00	85.00	125.00
	1939F	10.033	10.00	45.00	65.00	100.00
	1939G	5.475	60.00	130.00	175.00	260.00
	1939J	8.478	15.00	60.00	80.00	125.00
	Common Date	—	—	—	Proof	50.00

2 REICHSMARK

10 gm., .500 SILVER, .1608 oz ASW

Y#	Date	Mintage	Fine	VF	XF	Unc
46	1925A	16.145	5.00	10.00	15.00	32.00
	1925A	600 pcs.	—	—	Proof	—
	1925D	2.272	5.00	15.00	40.00	75.00
	1925E	1.971	5.00	15.00	50.00	85.00
	1925E	101 pcs.	—	—	Proof	—
	1925F	2.414	5.00	20.00	45.00	80.00
	1925G	.929	5.00	30.00	50.00	85.00
	1925J	2.326	5.00	25.00	50.00	85.00
	1926A	31.645	5.00	12.00	20.00	45.00
	1926D	11.322	5.00	12.00	25.00	55.00
	1926E	5.107	5.00	15.00	30.00	60.00
	1926E	30 pcs.	—	—	Proof	—
	1926F	7.115	5.00	12.00	25.00	55.00
	1926G	5.171	5.00	15.00	30.00	60.00
	1926J	5.305	5.00	15.00	30.00	60.00
	1927A	6.399	5.00	15.00	30.00	60.00
	1927D	.466	225.00	400.00	700.00	1000.
	1927E	.373	190.00	290.00	475.00	700.00
	1927E	53 pcs.	—	—	Proof	—
	1927F	.502	50.00	100.00	160.00	250.00
	1927J	.540	45.00	100.00	150.00	225.00
	1931D	2.109	20.00	40.00	60.00	90.00
	1931E	1.118	20.00	40.00	60.00	90.00
	1931F	1.505	20.00	50.00	90.00	135.00
	1931G	.915	35.00	80.00	110.00	160.00
	1931J	1.226	25.00	60.00	85.00	135.00
	Common Date	—	—	—	Proof	75.00

8.0000 gm., .625 SILVER, .1607 oz ASW
Martin Luther 450th Anniversary

Y#	Date	Mintage	Fine	VF	XF	Unc
78	1933A	.542	5.00	7.50	25.00	50.00
	1933D	.141	7.00	20.00	25.00	50.00
	1933E	.075	7.00	22.00	40.00	60.00
	1933F	.100	7.00	20.00	35.00	50.00
	1933G	.061	7.00	30.00	40.00	65.00
	1933J	.082	7.00	20.00	35.00	55.00
	Common Type	—	—	—	Proof	115.00

First Anniversary Nazi Rule
Potsdam Garrison Church

Y#	Date	Mintage	Fine	VF	XF	Unc
83	1934A	2.710	5.00	7.00	25.00	75.00
	1934D	.703	5.00	12.00	35.00	100.00
	1934E	.373	5.00	15.00	35.00	100.00
	1934F	.502	5.00	15.00	30.00	85.00
	1934G	.305	5.00	20.00	35.00	110.00
	1934J	.409	5.00	15.00	35.00	110.00
	Common Type	—	—	—	Proof	115.00

175th Anniversary Schiller's Birth

Y#	Date	Mintage	Fine	VF	XF	Unc
86	1934F	.300	7.50	30.00	45.00	85.00
	1934F	—	—	—	Proof	175.00

Nazi-Hindenburg Issue

Y#	Date	Mintage	Fine	VF	XF	Unc
96	1936D	.840	5.00	10.00	15.00	22.00
	1936E	w/1937	20.00	40.00	80.00	120.00
	1936G	w/1937	5.00	15.00	20.00	37.00
	1936J	w/1937	20.00	65.00	90.00	135.00
	1937A	23.425	BV	5.00	10.00	15.00
	1937D	6.190	BV	5.00	10.00	15.00
	1937E	3.725	BV	5.00	10.00	15.00
	1937F	5.015	BV	5.00	10.00	15.00
	1937G	1.913	BV	5.00	10.00	15.00
	1937J	2.756	BV	5.00	10.00	15.00
	1938A	13.201	BV	5.00	8.00	12.00
	1938B	13.163	BV	5.00	8.00	12.00
	1938D	3.711	BV	5.00	8.00	12.00
	1938E	4.731	BV	5.00	8.00	12.00
	1938F	1.882	5.00	10.00	12.00	22.00
	1938G	2.313	BV	5.00	8.00	12.00
	1938J	2.306	BV	5.00	8.00	12.00
	1939A	26.855	BV	5.00	8.00	12.00
	1939B	3.522	BV	5.00	8.00	12.00
	1939D	5.357	BV	5.00	8.00	12.00
	1939E	.251	15.00	35.00	50.00	75.00
	1939F	3.180	BV	5.00	8.00	12.00
	1939G	2.305	BV	6.00	10.00	15.00
	1939J	3.414	BV	5.00	8.00	12.00
	Common Date	—	—	—	Proof	80.00

3 MARK

ALUMINUM
Reeded edge

Y#	Date	Mintage	Fine	VF	XF	Unc
29	1922A	15.497	.25	2.50	5.00	10.00
	1922A	—	—	—	Proof	50.00
	1922E	2,000	80.00	150.00	260.00	425.00
	1922E	1,000	—	—	Proof	400.00

Lettered edge

Y#	Date	Mintage	Fine	VF	XF	Unc
29a	1922F	—	—	300.00	325.00	375.00

NOTE: The market values for Y#29a are for fire damaged coins. Only 1 pc. is known in perfect condition.

3rd Anniversary Weimar Constitution

Y#	Date	Mintage	Fine	VF	XF	Unc
28	1922A	32.514	.20	.60	1.00	2.50
	1922D	8.441	200.00	300.00	400.00	550.00
	1922D	—	—	—	Proof	525.00
	1922E	2.440	.25	2.50	5.00	10.00
	1922E	.022	—	—	Proof	—
	1922F	6.023	1.00	10.00	20.00	25.00
	1922G	3.655	.25	2.50	5.00	10.00
	1922J	4.896	.25	2.50	5.00	10.00
	1923E	2.030	20.00	45.00	60.00	90.00
	1923E	2,291	—	—	Proof	—
	1923F	—	—	150.00	—	—
	Common Date	—	—	—	Proof	25.00

15.0000 gm., .500 SILVER, .2411 oz ASW

Y#	Date	Mintage	Fine	VF	XF	Unc
47	1924A	24.386	15.00	40.00	70.00	100.00
	1924D	3.769	15.00	45.00	60.00	90.00
	1924E	3.353	25.00	65.00	85.00	125.00
	1924E	115 pcs.	—	—	Proof	—
	1924F	4.518	20.00	50.00	80.00	120.00
	1924G	2.745	25.00	70.00	90.00	130.00
	1924J	3.677	20.00	45.00	70.00	100.00
	1925D	2.558	35.00	90.00	130.00	185.00
	Common Date	—	—	—	Proof	150.00

3 REICHSMARK

15.0000 gm., .500 SILVER, .2411 oz ASW
Rhineland - 1000 Years

Y#	Date	Mintage	Fine	VF	XF	Unc
50	1925A	3.052	—	25.00	50.00	60.00
	1925D	1.123	—	30.00	50.00	70.00
	1925E	.441	—	30.00	60.00	100.00
	1925E	229 pcs.	—	—	Proof	—
	1925F	.173	—	40.00	65.00	120.00
	1925G	.300	—	35.00	50.00	100.00
	1925J	.492	—	40.00	75.00	125.00
	Common Date	—	—	—	Proof	160.00

Lubeck - 700 Years

Y#	Date	Mintage	Fine	VF	XF	Unc
52	1926A	.200	—	100.00	185.00	235.00
	1926A	—	—	—	Proof	300.00

100th Year Bremerhaven

Y#	Date	Mintage	Fine	VF	XF	Unc
53	1927A	.150	—	125.00	200.00	240.00
	1927A	—	—	—	Proof	350.00

Nordhausen 1000th Anniversary

Y#	Date	Mintage	Fine	VF	XF	Unc
55	1927A	.100	—	100.00	175.00	225.00
	1927A	—	—	—	Proof	325.00

Marburg University 400th Year

Y#	Date	Mintage	Fine	VF	XF	Unc
56	1927A	.130	—	100.00	175.00	210.00
	1927A	—	—	—	Proof	275.00

Tubingen University 450th Year

Y#	Date	Mintage	Fine	VF	XF	Unc
57	1927F	.050	—	50.00	75.00	100.00
	1927F	—	—	—	Proof	725.00

Founding Of Naumburg

Y#	Date	Mintage	Fine	VF	XF	Unc
60	1928A	.100	—	100.00	200.00	250.00
	1928A	—	—	—	Proof	400.00

400th Year Durer's Death

Y#	Date	Mintage	Fine	VF	XF	Unc
59	1928D	.050	—	350.00	450.00	550.00

Dinkelsbuhl's 1000th Anniversary

Y#	Date	Mintage	Fine	VF	XF	Unc
61	1928D	.040	—	475.00	900.00	1100.
	1928D	—	—	—	Proof	920.00

Lessing's 200th Anniversary

Y#	Date	Mintage	Fine	VF	XF	Unc
62	1929A	.217	—	50.00	70.00	95.00
	1929D	.056	—	50.00	75.00	110.00
	1929E	.030	—	60.00	90.00	135.00
	1929F	.040	—	30.00	80.00	160.00
	1929G	.024	—	50.00	80.00	125.00
	1929J	.033	—	50.00	75.00	130.00
	Common Date	—	—	—	Proof	200.00

Waldeck-Prussia Union

Y#	Date	Mintage	Fine	VF	XF	Unc
64	1929A	.170	—	90.00	160.00	225.00
	1929A	—	—	—	Proof	375.00

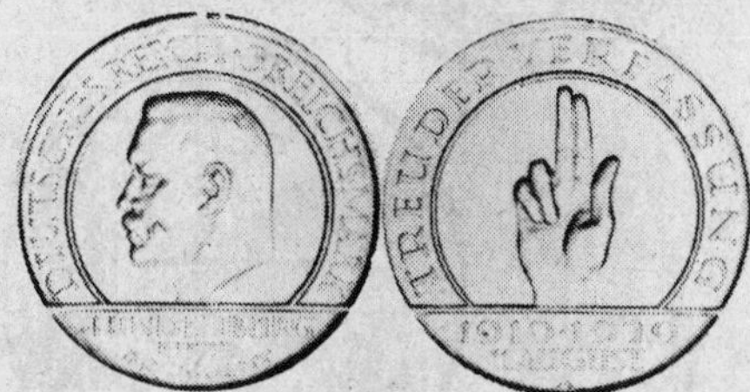

Constitution 10th Year

Y#	Date	Mintage	Fine	VF	XF	Unc
65	1929A	1.421	—	30.00	40.00	60.00
	1929D	.499	—	35.00	45.00	70.00
	1929E	.122	—	40.00	55.00	90.00
	1929F	.370	—	35.00	45.00	65.00
	1929G	.256	—	40.00	50.00	90.00
	1929J	.342	—	38.00	50.00	80.00
	Common Date	—	—	—	Proof	165.00

Meissen 1000th Anniversary

Y#	Date	Mintage	Fine	VF	XF	Unc
67	1929E	.200	—	50.00	70.00	115.00
	1929E	—	—	—	Proof	175.00

Graf Zeppelin Flight

Y#	Date	Mintage	Fine	VF	XF	Unc
69	1930A	.542	—	50.00	90.00	130.00
	1930D	.141	—	60.00	90.00	145.00
	1930E	.075	—	60.00	90.00	150.00
	1930F	.100	—	60.00	90.00	135.00
	1930G	.061	—	60.00	85.00	140.00
	1930J	.082	—	60.00	85.00	140.00
	Common Date	—	—	—	Proof	300.00

700th Year Death of Von Der Vogelweide

Y#	Date	Mintage	Fine	VF	XF	Unc
71	1930A	.163	—	50.00	100.00	160.00
	1930D	.042	—	50.00	90.00	140.00
	1930E	.022	—	50.00	100.00	165.00
	1930F	.030	—	60.00	100.00	150.00
	1930G	.018	—	60.00	100.00	155.00
	1930J	.025	—	60.00	100.00	160.00
	Common Date	—	—	—	Proof	300.00

Rhineland Evacuation

Y#	Date	Mintage	Fine	VF	XF	Unc
72	1930A	1.734	—	35.00	55.00	90.00
	1930D	.450	—	35.00	55.00	95.00
	1930E	.038	—	150.00	250.00	300.00
	1930F	.321	—	35.00	55.00	95.00
	1930G	.195	—	35.00	60.00	110.00
	1930J	.261	—	35.00	60.00	100.00
	Common Date	—	—	—	Proof	200.00

300th Anniversary Magdeburg Rebuilding

Y#	Date	Mintage	Fine	VF	XF	Unc
74	1931A	.100	—	185.00	250.00	325.00
	1931A	—	—	—	Proof	550.00

Centenary Von Stein Death

Y#	Date	Mintage	Fine	VF	XF	Unc
75	1931A	.150	—	125.00	185.00	240.00
	1931A	—	—	—	Proof	425.00

15.0000 gm., .500 SILVER, .2411 oz ASW

Y#	Date	Mintage	Fine	VF	XF	Unc
48	1931A	13.324	125.00	250.00	375.00	500.00
	1931D	2.232	150.00	310.00	450.00	600.00
	1931E	2.235	140.00	300.00	460.00	650.00
	1931F	2.357	125.00	285.00	425.00	600.00
	1931G	1.468	150.00	310.00	500.00	700.00
	1931J	1.115	150.00	310.00	500.00	700.00
	1932A	2.933	140.00	300.00	475.00	675.00
	1932D	1.986	150.00	310.00	500.00	700.00
	1932F	.653	250.00	600.00	1050.	1500.
	1932G	.210	400.00	1000.	1500.	2000.
	1932J	1.336	150.00	310.00	500.00	700.00
	1933G	.152	750.00	1500.	2000.	2500.
	1933G	—	—	—	Proof	2500.
	Common Date	—	—	—	Proof	800.00

Centenary Goethe's Death

Y#	Date	Mintage	Fine	VF	XF	Unc
76	1932A	.217	—	75.00	90.00	125.00
	1932D	.056	—	80.00	100.00	160.00
	1932E	.030	—	90.00	120.00	185.00
	1932F	.040	—	75.00	100.00	160.00
	1932G	.024	—	80.00	110.00	175.00
	1932J	.033	—	80.00	110.00	175.00
	Common Date	—	—	—	Proof	325.00

5 REICHSMARK

25.0000 gm., .500 SILVER, .4019 oz ASW

Rhineland-1000 Years

Y#	Date	Mintage	Fine	VF	XF	Unc
51	1925A	.684	—	70.00	115.00	150.00
	1925D	.452	—	80.00	125.00	160.00
	1925E	.204	—	85.00	125.00	180.00
	1925E	226 pcs.	—	—	Proof	—
	1925F	.212	—	85.00	130.00	180.00
	1925G	.089	—	90.00	135.00	195.00
	1925J	.043	—	100.00	150.00	235.00
	Common Date	—	—	—	Proof	300.00

100th Year Bremerhaven

Y#	Date	Mintage	Fine	VF	XF	Unc
54	1927A	.050	—	450.00	600.00	800.00
	1927A	—	—	—	Proof	900.00

450th Year University of Tubingen

Y#	Date	Mintage	Fine	VF	XF	Unc
58	1927F	.040	—	435.00	600.00	800.00
	1927F	—	—	—	Proof	900.00

Y#	Date	Mintage	Fine	VF	XF	Unc
49	1927A	7.926	20.00	60.00	100.00	210.00
	1927D	1.471	25.00	75.00	110.00	210.00
	1927E	1.100	30.00	80.00	150.00	275.00
	1927E	152 pcs.	—	—	Proof	—
	1927F	.700	25.00	75.00	110.00	210.00
	1927G	.759	25.00	75.00	115.00	210.00
	1927J	1.006	25.00	90.00	140.00	250.00
	1928A	15.466	20.00	60.00	100.00	190.00
	1928D	4.613	20.00	70.00	110.00	200.00
	1928E	2.310	35.00	100.00	175.00	300.00
	1928E	60 pcs.	—	—	Proof	—
	1928F	3.771	20.00	60.00	110.00	200.00
	1928G	1.923	25.00	80.00	125.00	250.00
	1928J	2.450	25.00	80.00	140.00	250.00
	1929A	6.730	20.00	70.00	110.00	200.00
	1929D	2.020	25.00	85.00	150.00	275.00
	1929E	.860	35.00	100.00	175.00	300.00
	1929F	.814	35.00	100.00	175.00	300.00
	1929G	.950	45.00	120.00	150.00	275.00
	1929J	.779	30.00	95.00	150.00	275.00
	1930A	3.790	25.00	80.00	130.00	250.00
	1930D	.606	50.00	230.00	325.00	475.00
	1930E	.354	100.00	350.00	500.00	675.00
	1930F	.630	150.00	400.00	650.00	900.00
	1930G	.367	150.00	400.00	650.00	900.00
	1930J	.740	100.00	350.00	500.00	700.00
	1931A	14.651	20.00	70.00	120.00	180.00
	1931D	3.254	25.00	80.00	130.00	200.00
	1931E	2.245	25.00	85.00	140.00	210.00
	1931F	4.152	25.00	80.00	135.00	200.00
	1931G	1.620	75.00	260.00	350.00	550.00
	1931J	3.092	25.00	85.00	140.00	210.00
	1932A	32.303	20.00	60.00	100.00	150.00
	1932D	8.556	20.00	70.00	110.00	175.00
	1932E	4.013	30.00	100.00	150.00	235.00
	1932F	5.019	25.00	80.00	125.00	200.00
	1932G	3.504	25.00	80.00	125.00	200.00
	1932J	3.752	30.00	100.00	175.00	235.00
	1933J	.423	450.00	800.00	1200.	1800.
	1933J	—	—	—	Proof	1700.
	Common Date	—	—	—	Proof	300.00

Lessing's 200th Anniversary

Y#	Date	Mintage	Fine	VF	XF	Unc
63	1929A	.087	—	80.00	135.00	225.00
	1929D	.022	—	100.00	160.00	250.00
	1929E	.012	—	125.00	210.00	325.00
	1929F	.016	—	110.00	160.00	275.00
	1929G	9,760	—	110.00	160.00	300.00
	1929J	.013	—	110.00	160.00	255.00
	Common Date	—	—	—	Proof	350.00

Constitution 10th Year

Y#	Date	Mintage	Fine	VF	XF	Unc
66	1929A	.325	—	75.00	125.00	185.00
	1929D	.084	—	100.00	180.00	235.00
	1929E	.045	—	100.00	175.00	225.00
	1929F	.060	—	100.00	160.00	215.00
	1929G	.037	—	100.00	180.00	235.00
	1929J	.049	—	100.00	175.00	225.00
	Common Date	—	—	—	Proof	425.00

Meissen 1000th Anniversary

Y#	Date	Mintage	Fine	VF	XF	Unc
68	1929E	.120	—	375.00	550.00	725.00
	1929E	—	—	—	Proof	675.00

Graf Zeppelin Flight

Y#	Date	Mintage	Fine	VF	XF	Unc
70	1930A	.217	—	125.00	180.00	235.00
	1930D	.056	—	160.00	210.00	260.00
	1930E	.030	—	175.00	260.00	335.00
	1930F	.040	—	180.00	260.00	310.00

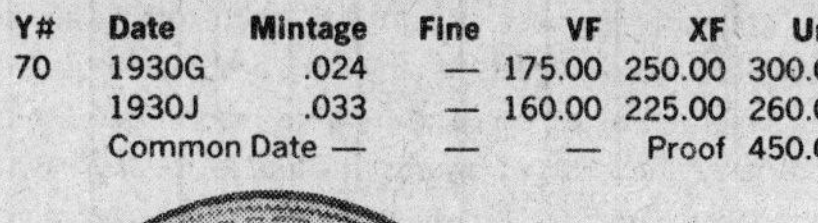

Y#	Date	Mintage	Fine	VF	XF	Unc
70	1930G	.024	—	175.00	250.00	300.00
	1930J	.033	—	160.00	225.00	260.00
	Common Date —		—	—	Proof	450.00

Rhineland Evacuation

Y#	Date	Mintage	Fine	VF	XF	Unc
73	1930A	.325	—	125.00	200.00	235.00
	1930D	.084	—	140.00	215.00	300.00
	1930E	.045	—	150.00	250.00	350.00
	1930F	.060	—	140.00	200.00	300.00
	1930G	.037	—	185.00	285.00	385.00
	1930J	.049	—	150.00	250.00	350.00
	Common Date —		—	—	Proof	450.00

Centenary Goethe's Death

Y#	Date	Mintage	Fine	VF	XF	Unc
77	1932A	.011	500.00	1700.	2500.	3000.
	1932D	2,812	550.00	1800.	2750.	3250.
	1932E	1,490	600.00	2000.	3000.	3750.
	1932F	2,006	550.00	2000.	3000.	3750.
	1932G	1,220	600.00	1800.	2750.	3500.
	1932J	1,634	600.00	2000.	3000.	3750.
	Common Date —		—	—	Proof	3500.

Martin Luther 450th Anniversary

Y#	Date	Mintage	Fine	VF	XF	Unc
79	1933A	.108	25.00	60.00	100.00	190.00
	1933D	.028	25.00	110.00	200.00	325.00
	1933D	—	—	—	Proof	310.00
	1933E	.012	27.50	110.00	200.00	325.00
	1933F	.020	25.00	110.00	200.00	325.00
	1933F	—	—	—	Proof	385.00
	1933G	.012	30.00	150.00	250.00	375.00
	1933J	.016	27.50	110.00	220.00	325.00
	Common Date —		—	—	Proof	325.00

175th Anniversary

Schiller's Birth

Y#	Date	Mintage	Fine	VF	XF	Unc
87	1934F	.100	50.00	170.00	210.00	325.00
	1934F	—	—	—	Proof	600.00

.900 SILVER
First Anniversary Nazi Rule
Potsdam Garrison Church

Y#	Date	Mintage	Fine	VF	XF	Unc
84	1934A	2.168	BV	14.00	35.00	90.00
	1934D	.562	BV	15.00	40.00	110.00
	1934E	.298	BV	20.00	55.00	135.00
	1934F	.401	BV	15.00	40.00	110.00
	1934G	.244	BV	20.00	60.00	135.00
	1934J	.327	BV	22.00	60.00	150.00

Rev: Date 21 MARZ 1933 dropped

Y#	Date	Mintage	Fine	VF	XF	Unc
85	1934A	14.526	BV	14.00	20.00	25.00
	1934D	6.303	BV	14.00	20.00	30.00
	1934E	2.739	BV	14.00	25.00	50.00
	1934F	4.844	BV	14.00	20.00	35.00
	1934G	2.304	BV	14.00	15.00	50.00
	1934J	4.294	BV	14.00	22.00	50.00
	1935A	23.407	BV	14.00	22.00	50.00
	1935D	3.539	BV	14.00	20.00	35.00
	1935E	2.476	BV	14.00	22.00	55.00
	1935F	2.177	BV	14.00	25.00	60.00
	1935G	1.966	BV	14.00	22.00	50.00
	1935J	1.425	BV	14.00	35.00	70.00

Nazi-Hindenburg Issue

Y#	Date	Mintage	Fine	VF	XF	Unc
82	1935A	19.325	BV	BV	15.00	25.00
	1935D	6.596	BV	BV	15.00	25.00
	1935E	3.260	BV	BV	15.00	25.00
	1935F	4.372	BV	BV	15.00	25.00
	1935G	2.371	BV	BV	15.00	25.00
	1935J	2.830	BV	BV	15.00	25.00
	1936A	30.611	BV	BV	15.00	25.00
	1936D	7.032	BV	BV	15.00	25.00
	1936E	3.320	BV	BV	15.00	25.00
	1936F	4.926	BV	BV	15.00	25.00
	1936G	2.734	BV	BV	15.00	35.00
	1936J	3.706	BV	BV	25.00	55.00
	Common Date —		—	—	Proof	75.00

Swastika-Hindenburg

Y#	Date	Mintage	Fine	VF	XF	Unc
97	1936A	8.430	BV	BV	15.00	25.00
	1936D	1.872	BV	BV	15.00	25.00
	1936E	.870	BV	BV	20.00	35.00
	1936F	1.732	BV	BV	15.00	25.00
	1936G	.743	BV	BV	20.00	35.00
	1936J	.640	BV	15.00	50.00	100.00
	1937A	6.662	BV	BV	15.00	25.00
	1937D	2.173	BV	BV	15.00	25.00

Y#	Date	Mintage	Fine	VF	XF	Unc
97	1937E	1.490	BV	BV	20.00	35.00
	1937F	1.578	BV	BV	15.00	30.00
	1937G	1.472	BV	BV	15.00	30.00
	1937J	2.191	BV	BV	15.00	30.00
	1938A	6.789	BV	BV	15.00	25.00
	1938D	1.304	BV	BV	15.00	25.00
	1938E	.425	BV	BV	15.00	30.00
	1938F	.740	BV	BV	15.00	25.00
	1938G	.861	BV	BV	15.00	30.00
	1938J	1.302	BV	BV	15.00	25.00
	1939A	3.428	BV	BV	15.00	30.00
	1939B	1.942	BV	BV	15.00	30.00
	1939D	1.216	BV	BV	15.00	35.00
	1939E	1.320	BV	20.00	50.00	100.00
	1939F	1.060	BV	12.00	30.00	50.00
	1939G	.567	BV	20.00	50.00	85.00
	1939J	1.710	BV	12.00	20.00	45.00
	Common Date —		—	—	Proof	200.00

200 MARK

ALUMINUM

Y#	Date	Mintage	Fine	VF	XF	Unc
30	1923A	174.900	.10	.30	1.00	2.00
	1923D	35.189	.10	.60	1.00	2.00
	1923E	11.250	.20	1.25	2.00	5.00
	1923F	20.090	.10	.60	1.25	2.50
	1923G	24.923	.20	.90	1.00	2.00
	1923J	16.258	.20	1.00	2.00	4.00
	Common Date —		—	—	Proof	40.00

500 MARK

ALUMINUM

Y#	Date	Mintage	Fine	VF	XF	Unc
31	1923A	59.278	.10	.50	1.00	2.00
	1923D	13.683	.10	.50	1.00	2.00
	1923E	2.128	1.00	5.00	10.00	15.00
	1923F	7.963	.10	.75	1.50	2.50
	1923G	4.404	.10	1.50	3.00	7.50
	1923J	1.008	15.00	30.00	50.00	85.00
	Common Date —		—	—	Proof	47.50

NOTE: For later coin issues refer to East Germany and West Germany.

TOKEN COINAGE

WWI Occupation Issues

Issued by authority of the German Military Commander of the East for use in the Baltic states, Poland, and Northwest Russia.

KOPECK

IRON

Y#	Date	Mintage	Fine	VF	XF	Unc
A18	1916A	11.942	1.00	3.00	6.00	12.00
	1916J	8.000	1.00	3.00	6.00	12.00
	Common Date —		—	—	Proof	75.00

2 KOPECKS

IRON

Y#	Date	Mintage	Fine	VF	XF	Unc
B18	1916A	6.973	1.00	3.00	7.00	14.00
	1916J	8.000	1.00	3.00	7.00	14.00
	Common Date —		—	—	Proof	75.00

3 KOPECKS

IRON

C18	1916A	8.670	1.00	4.00	8.00	16.00
	1916J	8.000	1.00	4.00	8.00	16.00
	Common Date —		—	—	Proof	75.00

Token Coinage 1914-1923

German Notgeld coins 1914-1923 were issued mostly by cities and towns, but also by commercial interests, transportation and utility companies, and private organizations. Most were struck to ease the growing coin shortage starting with the First World War and ending in the record inflation of 1923. The majority of these coins are low denominations of 1 pfennig through 1 mark, struck in zinc, iron, steel and aluminum. The two major varieties are Kriegsgeld and Notgeld.

KRIEGSGELD

'War money' struck 1914-1919 during World War I and nearly always carries the term 'Kriegsgeld' in the legend.

NOTGELD

'Emergency money' struck 1918-1921 and following the same format as the earlier Kriegsgeld but dropping the word Kriegs from the legend.

INFLATION NOTGELD

These tokens are usually more elaborate in design and larger in size and denomination. Most are aluminum or bronze and are often plated. The most popular in this catagory are the issues of Westphalia.

Another interesting experiment was the counter stamping of old imperial coinage with inflationary values. Due to the skyrocketing rate of inflation this method was soon abandoned. CAUTION, collectors should be aware that certain counter marks are fantasies struck much later.

PORCELAIN NOTGELD

City of Bitterfeld 1 Mark 1921

Waiblingen 100 Pfennig 1923

Porcelain Notgeld was issued extensively but rarely saw circulation because of its fragile nature plus the fact that most were issued for fund raising purposes and sold at a premium. The best known types are the official state issues of Saxony 1920-1921 which did see limited use in circulation. Most porcelain coins were made in Meissen and carry the crossed swords mintmark. Colors most commonly found are brown, white and black. Gilt and other colors of trim exist.

For further information on Notgeld 1914-1923 refer to EMERGENCY COINS OF GERMANY by Richard Upton & the Emergency Money Society, and CATALOGUE OF GERMAN WAR TOKENS by Robert A. Lamb.

For procelain Notgeld refer to MUNZEN AUS PROZEL-LAN UND TON by Karl Scheuch 1965-1969 and a general reference is DIE DEUTSCHEN MUNZEN SEIT 1871 by Kurt Jaeger.

NCLT ISSUES

MEDALLIC ISSUES

5 MARK SIZE

SILVER
von Hindenburg Commemorative

KM#	Date	Mintage	VF	XF	Unc
M1	1928	—	—	28.50	40.00
		GOLD			
M1a	1928	—	—	400.00	500.00

10 MARK SIZE

GOLD, 19.5mm
von Hindenburg Commemorative

M2	1928	—	—	—	—
		SILVER			
M2a	1928	—	—	—	—

20 MARK SIZE

GOLD, 22.5mm
von Hindenburg Commemorative

M3	1928	—	—	—	—
		SILVER			
M3a	1928	—	—	—	—

PATTERNS

KM#	Date	Mintage	Identification	Mkt.Val.
1	1877A	—	50 Pfennig, Silver	175.00
2	1877A	—	50 Pfennig, Silver	175.00
3	1877D	—	1/2 Mark, Silver	—
4	1877D	—	1/2 Mark, Lead, uniface obverse	150.00
5	1877D	—	1/2 Mark, Silver, uniface obverse	175.00
6	1877D	—	1/2 Mark, Copper, uniface reverse	75.00
7	1877D	—	1/2 Mark, Silver, uniface reverse	125.00

KM#	Date	Mintage	Identification	Mkt.Val.
8	1886A	—	20 Pfennig, Copper-Nickel	—
9	1886A	—	20 Pfenning, Copper-Nickel, plain center background	—
10	1886A	—	20 Pfennig, Copper-Nickel, stars around eagle	—
11	1886A	—	20 Pfennig, Copper-Nickel, rope loop border around eagle	—
12	1886A	—	20 Pfennig, Copper-Nickel, scored center behind '20'	—

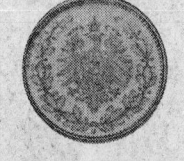

KM#	Date	Mintage	Identification	Mkt.Val.
13	ND	—	2 Pfennig, Copper	—

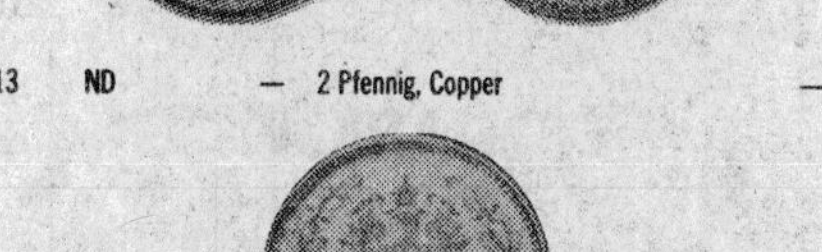

KM#	Date	Mintage	Identification	Mkt.Val.
14	ND D	—	1/2 Mark, Silver, uniface reverse	—
15	19XX	—	1/2 Mark, Silver	75.00
16	1900A	—	1/2 Mark, Silver	—
17	1901D	—	1/2 Mark, Silver, eagle in circle	—
18	1901D	—	1/2 Mark, Silver, eagle in diamond	—
19	1901D	—	1/2 Mark, Silver, mm below eagle	—
20	1901D	—	1/2 Mark, Silver, date on obv.	—
21	1901D	—	1/2 Mark, Silver, date on rev.	—
22	1901D	—	1/2 Mark, Silver, incuse diamond	—
23	1902A	—	50 Pfennig, Silver	—
24	1903A	—	50 Pfennig, Silver	—
25	1903D	—	50 Pfennig, Silver, crown over branch	—

KM#	Date	Mintage	Identification	Mkt.Val.
26	1907	—	25 Pfennig, Nickel	60.00

KM#	Date	Mintage	Identification	Mkt.Val.
27	1908	—	25 Pfennig, Nickel	50.00

KM#	Date	Mintage	Identification	Mkt.Val.
28	1908	—	25 Pfennig, Nickel	65.00

KM#	Date	Mintage	Identification	Mkt.Val.
29	1908	—	25 Pfennig, Copper	—
30	1908	—	25 Pfennig, Bronze	—
31	1908	—	25 Pfennig, Silver-plated	—
32	1908	—	25 Pfennig, Nickel	—
33	1908	—	25 Pfennig, Gold	—

KM#	Date	Mintage	Identification	Mkt.Val.
34	1908	—	25 Pfennig, Copper	—
35	1908	—	25 Pfennig, Nickel	40.00

KM#	Date	Mintage	Identification	Mkt.Val.
36	1908	—	25 Pfennig, Copper	—
37	1908	—	25 Pfennig, Nickel	40.00
38	1908	—	25 Pfennig, Nickel	40.00

KM#	Date	Mintage	Identification	Mkt.Val.
39	1908	—	25 Pfennig, Nickel	65.00

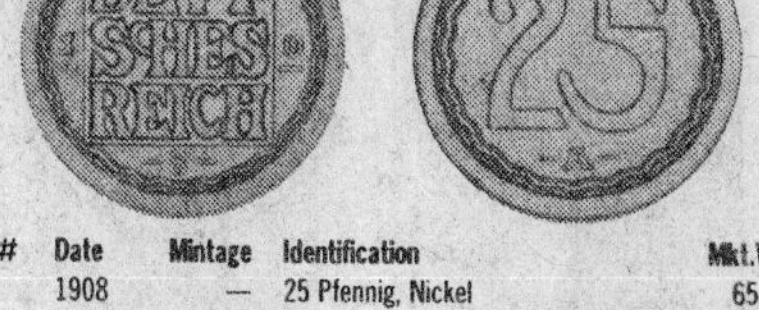

KM#	Date	Mintage	Identification	Mkt.Val.
40	1908	—	25 Pfennig, Nickel	65.00

KM#	Date	Mintage	Identification	Mkt.Val.
41	1908D	—	25 Pfennig, Copper	—
42	1908D	—	25 Pfennig, Nickel	65.00

KM#	Date	Mintage	Identification	Mkt.Val.
43	1908	—	25 Pfennig, Nickel	40.00

KM#	Date	Mintage	Identification	Mkt.Val.
44	1908	—	25 Pfennig, Nickel	50.00

KM#	Date	Mintage	Identification	Mkt.Val.
45	1909	—	25 Pfennig, Nickel	65.00

KM#	Date	Mintage	Identification	Mkt.Val.
46	1909	—	25 Pfennig, Nickel	50.00

KM#	Date	Mintage	Identification	Mkt.Val.
47	1909	—	25 Pfennig, Nickel	65.00

KM#	Date	Mintage	Identification	Mkt.Val.
48	1909	—	25 Pfennig, Nickel	60.00

KM#	Date	Mintage	Identification	Mkt.Val.
49	1909	—	25 Pfennig, Nickel	65.00

KM#	Date	Mintage	Identification	Mkt.Val.
50	1909	—	25 Pfennig, Nickel	50.00
51	1909	—	25 Pfennig, Nickel	65.00
52	1909	—	25 Pfennig, Nickel, screaming eagle	—
53	1909	—	1/2 Mark, Silver	—
54	1909A	—	1/2 Mark, Iron	—
55	19–E	—	1/2 Mark, Iron	—
56	1915	—	1 Pfennig, Iron	Rare
57	1915	—	10 Pfennig, Iron	450.00
58	1916A	—	1 Pfennig, Aluminum	600.00
59	1916F	—	1 Pfennig, Aluminum	—
60	1918A	—	1 Pfennig, Aluminum	200.00
61	1919	—	50 Pfennig, Nickel	65.00
62	1921	—	1 Mark, Iron	—
63	1921	—	1 Mark, Nickel	—
64	1922	—	5 Marks, Aluminum	—
65	1923	—	20 Marks, Aluminum	—
66	1923	—	100 Marks, Aluminum	—
67	1923	—	1000 Marks, Silver	—
68	1924	—	1 Mark, Nickel	—
69	1924	—	3 Marks, Silver	—
70	1925D	—	50 Pfennig, Bronze	—
71	1925D	—	50 Pfennig, Silver	—

KM#	Date	Mintage	Identification	Mkt.Val.
72	1925D	—	50 Pfennig, Bronze	—
73	1925D	—	50 Pfennig, Aluminum-Bronze	—
74	1925D	—	50 Pfennig, Silver	—
75	1925F	—	50 Pfennig, Aluminum-Bronze	4500.
76	1925A	—	1 Mark, Copper	—
77	1925	—	1 Mark, Silver, eagle on each side	—
78	1925	—	3 Marks, Copper, Bavaria	—
79	1925	—	3 Marks, Nickel, Bavaria	—
80	1925	—	3 Marks, Silver, Bavaria	—
81	1925	—	3 Marks, Gold, Bavaria	—
82	1925	—	3 Marks, Brass	—
83	1925	—	3 Marks, Silvered Bronze	—
84	1925	—	3 Marks, Silver	—
85	1925	—	3 Marks, Brass, date in legend	—
86	1925	—	3 Marks, Silvered Bronze, date in legend	—
87	1925	—	3 Marks, Silver, date in legend	—
88	1925	—	3 Marks, Brass, new head	—
89	1925	—	3 Marks, Silvered Bronze, new head	—

KM#	Date	Mintage	Identification	Mkt.Val.
90	1925	—	3 Marks, Silver, new head	—
91	1925	—	3 Marks, Brass, small 3	—
92	1925	—	3 Marks, Silvered Bronze, small 3	—
93	1925	—	3 Marks, Brass	—
94	1925	—	3 Marks, Nickel	—
95	1925	—	3 Marks, Silvered Bronze, new eagle	—
96	1925	—	3 Marks, Nickel, new eagle	—
97	1925	—	3 Marks, Brass	—
98	1925	—	3 Marks, red Bronze	—
99	1925	—	3 Marks, Silvered Bronze	—
100	1925	—	3 Marks, Tin, new eagle	—
101	1925	—	3 Marks, Silvered Bronze, new eagle	—
102	1925D	—	3 Marks, Copper, eagle right	—

KM#	Date	Mintage	Identification	Mkt.Val.
103	1925	—	5 Marks, Brass, Bavaria	—
104	1925	—	5 Marks, Silver, Bavaria	—

KM#	Date	Mintage	Identification	Mkt.Val.
105	1925	—	5 Marks, Silver	—
106	1925D	—	5 Marks, Silver	—

KM#	Date	Mintage	Identification	Mkt.Val.
107	1925	—	5 Marks, Brass, tall head	—
108	1925	—	5 Marks, Silver, tall head	—
109	1925D	—	5 Marks, Brass, tall head	—

KM#	Date	Mintage	Identification	Mkt.Val.
110	1925	—	5 Marks, Brass, date behind head	—
111	1925	—	5 Marks, matte Silver, date behind head	—

KM#	Date	Mintage	Identification	Mkt.Val.
112	1925D	—	5 Marks, red Copper, new eagle	—
113	1925D	—	5 Marks, Silver, new eagle	—

KM#	Date	Mintage	Identification	Mkt.Val.
114	1925	—	5 Marks, Brass, tall head	—
115	1925	—	5 Marks, Silvered Bronze, tall head	—
116	1925	—	5 Marks, Silver, tall head	—

KM#	Date	Mintage	Identification	Mkt.Val.
117	1925	—	5 Marks, Brass, date behind head	—
118	1925	—	5 Marks, Silver, date behind head	—

KM#	Date	Mintage	Identification	Mkt.Val.
119	1925E	—	5 Marks, Silver	

KM#	Date	Mintage	Identification	Mkt.Val.
120	1925E	—	5 Marks, Silver, Saxony	—
121	1925F	—	5 Marks, Silver, Wurttemberg	—
122	1925E	—	20 Marks, Silver	—
123	1925E	—	20 Marks, Gold, Saxony	—

KM#	Date	Mintage	Identification	Mkt.Val.
124	1926E	—	50 Pfennig, Nickel	—
125	1926E	—	50 Pfennig, Nickel, heraldic eagle	—
126	1926E	—	50 Pfennig, Nickel, large eagle head	—
127	1926E	—	50 Pfennig, Nickel, 3 wheat ears	—
128	1926E	—	50 Pfennig, Nickel, 2 arched oak leaves	—
129	1926E	—	50 Pfennig, Nickel, value in ornamented circle	—
130	1926E	—	50 Pfennig, Nickel, value over 2 cornucopiae	—
131	1926E	—	50 Pfennig, Nickel, value over 2 oak leaves	—

KM#	Date	Mintage	Identification	Mkt.Val.
132	1926J	—	50 Pfennig, Nickel	—
133	1926E	—	1 Mark, Silver	—
134	1926	—	3 Marks, Copper	—
135	1926	—	3 Marks, Silver	—
136	1926A	—	5 Marks, Silver	—
137	1926D	—	5 Marks, Silver	—

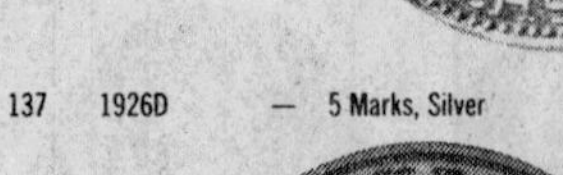

KM#	Date	Mintage	Identification	Mkt.Val.
138	1926E	—	5 Marks, Silver	—
139	1926E	—	5 Marks, Silver	750.00
140	1927F	—	50 Pfennig, Nickel	—
141	1927F	—	1 Mark, Silver	—
142	1927F	—	3 Marks, Silver	—
143	1927A	—	5 Marks, Silver, large stars	—
144	1927A	—	5 Marks, Silver, 50 stars in inner circle	—
145	1927A	—	5 Marks, Silver, 54 stars in inner circle	—
146	1929A	—	5 Marks, Silver, zeppelin right	—
147	1929A	—	5 Marks, Silver, line border on reverse	—
148	1929A	—	5 Marks, Silver, obv. letters incuse	—
149	1929A	—	5 Marks, Silver, zeppelin left	—
150	1930	—	3 Marks, Silver, Vogelweide	—

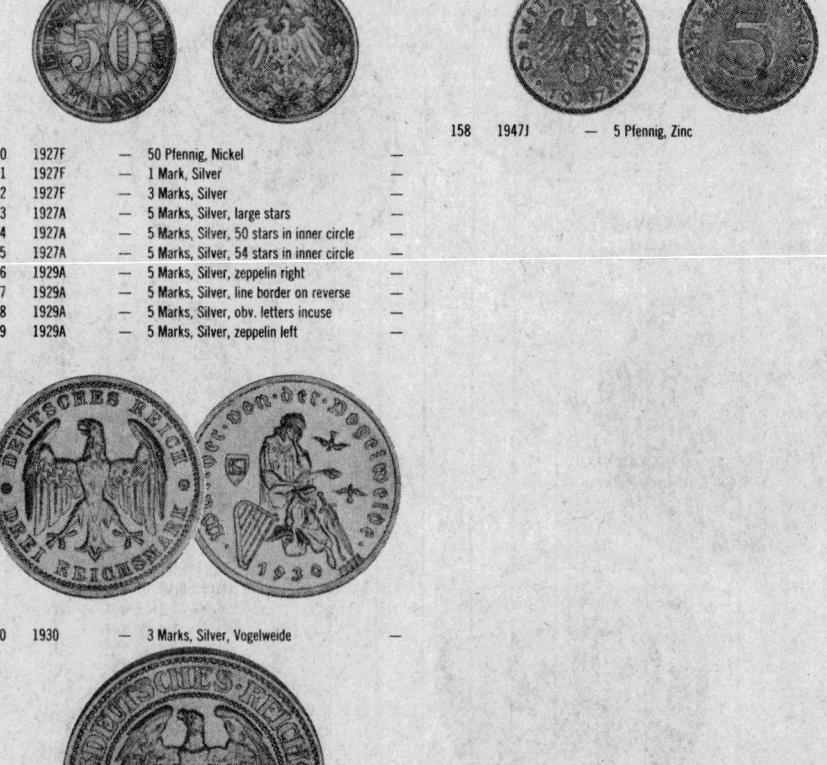

KM#	Date	Mintage	Identification	Mkt.Val.
151	1932A	—	5 Marks, Pewter	—
152	1932A	—	5 Marks, Silver	—
152	1935A	—	50 Pfennig, Nickel	—
154	1935E	—	1 Mark, Nickel	500.00
155	1936A	—	5 Pfennig, Aluminum-Bronze	—
156	1939A	—	1 Mark, Nickel	—
157	1940	—	1 Mark, Nickel	125.00
158	1947J	—	5 Pfennig, Zinc	125.00

W. GERMANY

The Federal Republic of Germany (West Germany), located in north-central Europe, has an area (including West Berlin) of 95,930 sq. mi. (248,457 sq. km.) and a population of 62 million. Capital: Bonn. The economy centers about one of the world's foremost industrial establishments. Machinery, motor vehicles, iron, steel, yarns and fabrics are exported.

During the post-Normandy phase of World War II, Allied troops occupied the western German provinces of Schleswig-Holstein, Hamburg, Lower Saxony, Bremen, North Rhine-Westphalia, Hesse, Rhineland-Palatinate, Baden-Wurttemberg, Bavaria and Saarland. The conquered provinces were divided into American, British and French occupation zones. Five eastern German provinces were occupied and administered by the forces of the Soviet Union.

The western occupation forces restored the civil status of their zones on Sept. 21, 1949, and resumed diplomatic relations with the provinces on July 2, 1951. On May 5, 1955, nine of the ten western provinces, organized as the Federal Republic of Germany, became fully independent. The tenth, Saarland, was restored to the republic on Jan 1, 1957.

From the late 14th century until the fall of Napoleon, the city of Saarbrucken was ruled by the counts of Nassau- Saarbrucken, but the surrounding territory was subject to the political and cultural domination of France. At the close of the Napoleonic era, the Saarland came under the control of Prussia. France was awarded the Saar coal mines following World War I, and the Saarland was made an autonomous territory of the League of Nations, its future political affiliation to be determined by referendum. The plebiscite, 1935, chose reincorporation into Germany. France reoccupied the Saarland, 1945, establishing strong economic ties and assuming the obligation of defense and foreign affairs. After sustained agitation by West Germany, France agreed, 1955, to the return of the Saar to Germany by Jan. 1957.

The Saar, the 10th state of the German Federal Republic, is located in the coal-rich Saar basin on the Franco-German frontier, and has an area of 991 sq. mi. and a population of 1.2 million. Capital: Saarbrucken. It is an important center of mining and heavy industry.

MINTMARKS

D - Munich
F - Stuttgart
G - Karlsruhe
J - Hamburg

MONETARY SYSTEM

100 Pfennig = 1 Deutsche Mark (DM)

PFENNIG

BRONZE-CLAD STEEL
Currency Reform

Y#	Date	Mintage	VF	XF	Unc
101	1948D	46.325	.50	3.00	25.00
	1948F	68.203	.50	3.00	25.00
	1948F	250 pcs	—	Proof	—
	1948G	45.604	.50	4.00	30.00
	1948J	79.304	.50	3.00	25.00
	1949D	99.863	.25	2.00	25.00
	1949F	129.935	.25	2.00	25.00
	1949F	250 pcs	—	Proof	—
	1949G	70.954	.25	2.00	25.00
	1949J	101.932	.25	2.00	25.00

Federal Republic

Y#	Date	Mintage	VF	XF	Unc
105	1950D	772.592	.10	.15	1.00
	1950F	898.277	.10	.15	1.00
	1950F	620 pcs.	—	Proof	60.00
105	1950G	515.673	.10	.15	1.00
	1950G	1,800	—	Proof	4.00
	1950J	784.424	.10	.15	1.00
	1966D	65.063	—	.10	2.00
	1966F	75.031	—	.10	2.00
	1966F	100 pcs.	—	Proof	60.00
	1966G	48.261	—	.10	2.00
	1966G	3,070	—	Proof	15.00
	1966J	66.842	—	.10	2.00
	1966J	1,000	—	Proof	35.00
	1967D	39.082	—	.10	1.00
	1967F	45.003	—	.10	1.00
	1967F	1,500	—	Proof	22.00
	1967G	20.787	—	.10	1.00
	1967G	4,500	—	Proof	12.00
	1967J	42.583	—	.10	1.00
	1967J	1,500	—	Proof	35.00
	1968D	32.797	—	.10	1.00
	1968F	26.338	—	.10	1.00
	1968F	3,000	—	Proof	20.00
	1968G	20.832	—	.10	1.00
	1968G	6,023	—	Proof	10.00
	1968J	23.414	—	.25	1.00
	1968J	2,000	—	Proof	20.00
	1969D	78.178	—	.10	.50
	1969F	90.172	—	.10	.50
	1969F	5,100	—	Proof	6.00
	1969G	61.836	—	.10	.50
	1969G	8,700	—	Proof	6.00
	1969J	80.220	—	.10	.50
	1969J	5,000	—	Proof	6.00
	1970D	91.151	—	.10	.25
	1970F	105.236	—	.10	.25
	1970F	5,240	—	Proof	7.00
	1970G	82.421	—	.10	.25
	1970G	10,200	—	Proof	6.00
	1970J small J mintmark				
		93.455	—	.10	.25
	1970J large J mintmark				
		Inc. Ab.	—	.10	.25
	1970J	5,000	—	Proof	7.00
	1971D	116.612	—	.10	.25
	1971D	8,000	—	Proof	6.00
	1971F	157.393	—	.10	.25
	1971F	8,000	—	Proof	7.00
	1971G	77.674	—	.10	.25
	1971G	10,200	—	Proof	6.00
	1971J	120.218	—	.10	.25
	1971J	8,000	—	Proof	6.00
	1972D	90.696	—	.10	.25
	1972D	8,000	—	Proof	6.00
	1972F	105.006	—	.10	.25
	1972F	8,000	—	Proof	6.00
	1972G	60.660	—	.10	.25
	1972G	10,000	—	Proof	6.00
	1972J	93.492	—	.10	.25
	1972J	8,000	—	Proof	6.00
	1973D	38.976	—	.10	.25
	1973D	9,000	—	Proof	6.00
	1973F	45.006	—	.10	.25
	1973F	9,000	—	Proof	6.00
	1973G	25.811	—	.10	.25
	1973G	9,000	—	Proof	6.00
	1973J	40.057	—	.10	.25
	1973J	9,000	—	Proof	6.00
	1974D	90.951	—	.10	.25
	1974D	.035	—	Proof	4.00
	1974F	105.091	—	.10	.25
	1974F	.035	—	Proof	4.00
	1974G	60.548	—	.10	.25
	1974G	.035	—	Proof	4.00
	1974J	93.527	—	.10	.25
	1974J	.035	—	Proof	4.00
	1975D	91.053	—	.10	.25
	1975D	.043	—	Proof	2.50
	1975F	105.007	—	.10	.25
	1975F	.043	—	Proof	2.50
	1975G	60.704	—	.10	.25
	1975G	.043	—	Proof	2.50
	1975J	93.495	—	.10	.25
	1975J	.043	—	Proof	2.50
	1976D	130.227	—	.10	.25
	1976D	.043	—	Proof	2.00
	1976F	150.037	—	.10	.25
	1976F	.043	—	Proof	2.00
	1976G	86.586	—	.10	.25
	1976G	.043	—	Proof	2.00
	1976J	133.500	—	.10	.25
	1976J	.043	—	Proof	2.00
	1977D	143.000	—	.10	.25
	1977D	164.918	—	Proof	2.00
	1977F	165.000	—	.10	.25
	1977F	.051	—	Proof	2.00
	1977G	95.200	—	.10	.25
	1977G	.051	—	Proof	2.00
	1977J	146.788	—	.10	.25
	1977J	146.788	—	Proof	2.00
	1978D	156.000	—	.10	.25
	1978D	.054	—	Proof	2.00
	1978F	180.000	—	.10	.25
	1978F	.054	—	Proof	2.00
	1978G	103.800	—	.10	.25
	1978G	.054	—	Proof	2.00
	1978J	160.200	—	.10	.25
	1978J	.054	—	Proof	2.00
	1979D	156.000	—	—	.25
	1979D	.089	—	Proof	2.00
	1979F	180.000	—	—	.25
	1979F	.089	—	Proof	2.00
	1979G	103.800	—	—	.25
	1979G	.089	—	Proof	2.00
	1979J	160.200	—	—	.25
	1979J	.089	—	Proof	2.00

2 PFENNIG

BRONZE
Federal Republic

Y#	Date	Mintage	VF	XF	Unc
106	1950D	26.263	—	.25	4.00
	1950F	30.278	—	.25	4.00
	1950F	200 pcs.	—	Proof	—
	1950G	17.151	—	.25	4.50
	1950J	27.216	—	.25	4.00
	1958D	19.440	—	.20	3.00
	1958F	30.000	—	.20	3.00
	1958F	100 pcs.	—	Proof	—
	1958G	100 pcs.	—	.20	4.00
	1958J	21.250	—	.20	3.00
	1959D	19.690	—	.20	1.00
	1959F	19.140	—	.20	1.00
	1959F	75 pcs.	—	Proof	—
	1959G	12.899	—	.20	2.00
	1959J	25.482	—	.20	1.00
	1960D	21.979	—	.20	1.00
	1960F	15.915	—	.20	1.00
	1960F	75 pcs.	—	Proof	—
	1960G	5.657	—	.35	3.00
	1960J	17.799	—	.20	1.00
	1961D	26.662	—	.10	1.00
	1961F	28.714	—	.10	1.00
	1961G	18.060	—	.10	1.00
	1961J	22.147	—	.10	1.00
	1962D	21.297	—	.35	1.00
	1962F	41.316	—	.10	.50
	1962G	17.297	—	.10	.50
	1962J	30.706	—	.10	.50
	1963D	7.648	—	.10	1.00
	1963F	23.857	—	.10	.50
	1963G	35.838	—	.10	.50
	1963G	—	—	Proof	—
	1963J	42.884	—	.10	.50
	1964D	20.336	—	.10	.50
	1964F	28.296	—	.10	.25
	1964G	18.431	—	.10	.25
	1964G	*600	—	Proof	25.00
	1964J	13.370	—	.10	.25
	1965D	48.541	—	.10	.25
	1965F	45.477	—	.10	.25
	1965F	300 pcs.	—	Proof	85.00
	1965G	13.584	—	.10	.25
	1965G	1,200	—	Proof	5.00
	1965J	33.397	—	.10	.25
	1966D	65.077	—	.10	.25
	1966F	52.543	—	.10	.25
	1966F	100 pcs.	—	Proof	85.00
	1966G	40.804	—	.10	.25
	1966G	3,070	—	Proof	20.00
	1966J	46.754	—	.10	.25
	1966J	1,000	—	Proof	40.00
	1967D	25.997	—	.10	.25
	1967F	30.004	—	.10	.25
	1967F	1,500	—	Proof	28.00
	1967G	6.280	—	.10	.25
	1967G	4,500	—	Proof	15.00
	1967J	26.725	—	.10	.25
	1967J	1,500	—	Proof	40.00
	1968D	Inc. Bl.	.35	.75	2.00
	1968G	15.357	—	.10	2.00
	1968G	3,651	—	Proof	6.50
	1968J	3,651	300.00	375.00	450.00
	1969J	—	200.00	300.00	400.00

BRONZE CLAD STEEL

Y#	Date	Mintage	VF	XF	Unc
106a	1967G	520 pcs.	—	Proof	1300.
	1968D	19.523	—	.10	.25
	1968F	22.602	—	.10	.25

Y#	Date	Mintage	VF	XF	Unc
106a	1968F	3,000	—	Proof	25.00
	1968G	13.004	—	.10	.25
	1968G	2,372	—	Proof	12.00
	1968J	20.026	—	.10	.25
	1968J	2,000	—	Proof	25.00
	1969D	39.012	—	.10	.25
	1969F	45.029	—	.10	.25
	1969F	5,100	—	Proof	7.00
	1969G	32.157	—	.10	.25
	1969G	8,700	—	Proof	7.00
	1969J	40.102	—	.10	.25
	1969J	5,000	—	Proof	7.00
	1970D	45.525	—	.10	.25
	1970F	73.851	—	.10	.25
	1970F	5,140	—	Proof	10.00
	1970G	30.330	—	.10	.25
	1970G	10,200	—	Proof	7.00
	1970J small J mintmark				
		46.730	—	.10	.25
	1970J large J mintmark				
		Inc. Ab.	—	.10	.25
	1970J	5,000	—	Proof	7.00
	1971D	71.755	—	.10	.25
	1971D	8,000	—	Proof	7.00
	1971F	82.765	—	.10	.25
	1971F	8,000	—	Proof	8.00
	1971G	47.850	—	.10	.25
	1971G	.010	—	Proof	7.00
	1971J	73.641	—	.10	.25
	1971J	8,000	—	Proof	7.00
	1972D	52.403	—	.10	.25
	1972D	8,000	—	Proof	7.00
	1972F	60.272	—	.10	.25
	1972F	8,000	—	Proof	7.00
	1972G	34.864	—	.10	.25
	1972G	.010	—	Proof	7.00
	1972J	53.673	—	.10	.25
	1972J	8,000	—	Proof	7.00
	1973D	26.190	—	.10	.25
	1973D	9,000	—	Proof	7.00
	1973F	30.160	—	.10	.25
	1973F	9,000	—	Proof	7.00
	1973G	17.379	—	.10	.25
	1973G	9,000	—	Proof	7.00
	1973J	26.830	—	.10	.25
	1973J	9,000	—	Proof	7.00
	1974D	58.667	—	.10	.25
	1974D	.035	—	Proof	5.00
	1974F	67.596	—	.10	.25
	1974F	.035	—	Proof	5.00
	1974G	39.007	—	.10	.25
	1974G	.035	—	Proof	5.00
	1974J	60.195	—	.10	.25
	1974J	.035	—	Proof	5.00
	1975D	58.634	—	.10	.25
	1975D	.043	—	Proof	3.00
	1975F	67.685	—	.10	.25
	1975F	.043	—	Proof	3.00
	1975G	39.391	—	.10	.25
	1975G	.043	—	Proof	3.00
	1975J	60.207	—	.10	.25
	1975J	.043	—	Proof	3.00
	1976D	78.074	—	.10	.25
	1976D	.043	—	Proof	2.50
	1976F	90.130	—	.10	.25
	1976F	.043	—	Proof	2.50
	1976G	51.988	—	.10	.25
	1976G	.043	—	Proof	2.50
	1976J	80.145	—	.10	.25
	1976J	.043	—	Proof	2.50
	1977D	84.516	—	.10	.25
	1977D	.051	—	Proof	2.00
	1977F	97.504	—	.10	.25
	1977F	.051	—	Proof	2.00
	1977G	56.276	—	.10	.25
	1977G	.051	—	Proof	2.00
	1977J	86.888	—	.10	.25
	1977J	.051	—	Proof	2.00
	1978D	84.500	—	.10	.25
	1978D	.054	—	Proof	2.00
	1978F	97.500	—	.10	.25
	1978F	.054	—	Proof	2.00
	1978G	56.225	—	.10	.25
	1978G	.054	—	Proof	2.00
	1978J	86.775	—	.10	.25
	1978J	.054	—	Proof	2.00
	1979D	91.000	—	—	.20
	1979D	.089	—	Proof	2.00
	1979F	105.000	—	—	.20
	1979F	.089	—	Proof	2.00
	1979G	60.550	—	—	.20
	1979G	.089	—	Proof	2.00
	1979J	93.480	—	—	.20
	1979J	.089	—	Proof	2.00

5 PFENNIG

BRASS-CLAD STEEL
Currency Reform

Y#	Date	Mintage	VF	XF	Unc
102	1949D	60.026	.10	1.50	25.00
	1949F	66.082	.10	1.50	30.00
	1949F	250 pcs.	—	Proof	—
	1949G	57.356	.10	1.50	25.00
	1949J	68.977	.10	1.50	25.00

Federal Republic

Y#	Date	Mintage	VF	XF	Unc
107	1950D	271.962	.10	.20	2.00
	1950F	342.284	—	.10	2.00
	1950F	500 pcs.	—	Proof	100.00
	1950G	180.492	—	.10	2.00
	1950G	1,800	—	Proof	6.00
	1950J	285.283	—	.10	2.00
	1966D	26.036	—	.10	2.00
	1966F	30.047	—	.10	2.00
	1966F	100 pcs.	—	Proof	100.00
	1966G	17.333	—	.10	2.00
	1966G	3,070	—	Proof	25.00
	1966J	26.741	—	.10	2.00
	1966J	1,000	—	Proof	45.00
	1967D	10.418	—	.10	1.00
	1967F	12.012	—	.10	1.00
	1967F	1,500	—	Proof	35.00
	1967G	1.736	1.00	2.00	5.00
	1967G	4,500	—	Proof	20.00
	1967J	10.706	—	.10	1.00
	1967J	1,500	—	Proof	45.00
	1968D	13.047	—	.10	.50
	1968F	15.026	—	.10	.50
	1968F	3,000	—	Proof	30.00
	1968G	13.855	—	.10	.50
	1968G	6,023	—	Proof	15.00
	1968J	13.362	—	.10	.50
	1968J	2,000	—	Proof	30.00
	1969D	23.488	—	.10	.25
	1969F	27.046	—	.10	.25
	1969F	5,000	—	Proof	8.00
	1969G	15.631	—	.10	.25
	1969G	8,700	—	Proof	8.00
	1969J	24.120	—	.10	.25
	1969J	5,000	—	Proof	8.00
	1970D	39.940	—	.10	.25
	1970F	45.517	—	.10	.25
	1970F	5,140	—	Proof	12.00
	1970G	27.638	—	.10	.25
	1970G	10,200	—	Proof	8.00
	1970J	40.873	—	.10	.25
	1970J	5,000	—	Proof	8.00
	1971D	57.345	—	.10	.25
	1971D	8,000	—	Proof	8.00
	1971F	66.426	—	.10	.25
	1971F	8,000	—	Proof	12.00
	1971G	38.284	—	.10	.25
	1971G	10,000	—	Proof	8.00
	1971J	58.566	—	.10	.25
	1971J	8,000	—	Proof	8.00
	1972D	52.325	—	.10	.25
	1972D	8,000	—	Proof	7.50
	1972F	60.292	—	.10	.25
	1972F	8,000	—	Proof	7.50
	1972G	34.719	—	.10	.25
	1972G	10,000	—	Proof	7.50
	1972J	54.218	—	.10	.25
	1972J	8,000	—	Proof	7.50
	1973D	15.596	—	.10	.25
	1973D	9,000	—	Proof	7.50
	1973F	18.039	—	.10	.25
	1973F	9,000	—	Proof	7.50
	1973G	10.391	—	.10	.25
	1973G	9,000	—	Proof	7.50
	1973J	16.035	—	.10	.25
	1973J	9,000	—	Proof	7.50
	1974D	15.769	—	.10	.25
	1974D	.035	—	Proof	6.00
	1974F	18.143	—	.10	.25
	1974F	.035	—	Proof	6.00
	1974G	10.508	—	.10	.25
	1974G	.035	—	Proof	6.00
107	1974J	16.055	—	.10	.25
	1974J	.035	—	Proof	6.00
	1975D	15.715	—	—	.25
	1975D	.043	—	Proof	3.50
	1975F	18.013	—	—	.25
	1975F	.043	—	Proof	3.50
	1975G	10.466	—	—	.25
	1975G	.043	—	Proof	3.50
	1975J	16.201	—	—	.25
	1975J	.043	—	Proof	3.50
	1976D	47.091	—	—	.25
	1976D	.043	—	Proof	3.00
	1976F	54.370	—	—	.25
	1976F	.043	—	Proof	3.00
	1976G	31.367	—	—	.25
	1976G	.043	—	Proof	3.00
	1976J	48.321	—	—	.25
	1976J	.043	—	Proof	3.00
	1977D	52.159	—	—	.25
	1977D	.051	—	Proof	3.00
	1977F	60.124	—	—	.25
	1977F	.051	—	Proof	3.00
	1977G	34.600	—	—	.25
	1977G	.051	—	Proof	3.00
	1977J	53.481	—	—	.25
	1977J	.051	—	Proof	3.00
	1978D	41.600	—	—	.25
	1978D	.054	—	Proof	3.00
	1978F	48.000	—	—	.25
	1978F	.054	—	Proof	3.00
	1978G	27.680	—	—	.25
	1978G	.054	—	Proof	3.00
	1978J	42.720	—	—	.25
	1978J	.054	—	Proof	3.00
	1979D	41.600	—	—	.10
	1979D	.089	—	Proof	2.00
	1979F	48.000	—	—	.10
	1979F	.089	—	Proof	2.00
	1979G	27.680	—	—	.10
	1979G	.089	—	Proof	2.00
	1979J	42.711	—	—	.10
	1979J	.089	—	Proof	2.00

10 PFENNIG

BRASS-CLAD STEEL
Currency Reform

Y#	Date	Mintage	VF	XF	Unc
103	1949D	140.558	10.00	25.00	10.00
	1949F	120.932	.25	10.00	30.00
	1949F	250 pcs.	—	Proof	—
	1949G	82.933	.25	10.00	30.00
	1949J large J mintmark				
		154.095	.25	10.00	25.00
	1949J small J mintmark				
		Inc. Ab.	.25	10.00	25.00

Federal Republic

Y#	Date	Mintage	VF	XF	Unc
108	1950D	393.209	—	.10	2.00
	1950F	523.513	—	.10	2.00
	1950F	500 pcs.	—	Proof	125.00
	1950G	309.045	—	.10	2.00
	1950G	1,800	—	Proof	7.00
	1950J	402.452	—	.10	2.00
	1966D	31.220	—	.10	1.00
	1966F	36.097	—	.10	1.00
	1966F	100 pcs.	—	Proof	125.00
	1966G	25.338	—	.10	1.00
	1966G	3,070	—	Proof	30.00
	1966J	32.116	—	.10	1.00
	1966J	1,000	—	Proof	50.00
	1967D	15.632	—	.10	1.00
	1967F	18.049	—	.10	1.00
	1967F	1,500	—	Proof	40.00
	1967G	1.518	1.00	2.00	3.00
	1967G	4,500	—	Proof	25.00
	1967J	16.051	—	.10	1.00
	1967J	1,500	—	Proof	50.00
	1968D	5.207	—	.10	1.00

Y#	Date	Mintage	VF	XF	Unc
108	1968F	6.010	—	.20	1.00
	1968F	3,000	—	Proof	35.00
	1968G	12.384	—	.20	2.00
	1968G	6,023	—	Proof	18.00
	1968J	5.422	—	.20	2.00
	1968J	2,000	—	Proof	35.00
	1969D	41.693	—	.20	2.00
	1969F	48.084	—	.10	.25
	1969F	5,000	—	Proof	9.00
	1969G	48.760	—	.10	.25
	1969G	8,700	—	Proof	9.00
	1969J	42.756	—	.10	.25
	1969J	5,000	—	Proof	9.00
	1970D	54.085	—	.10	.25
	1970F	60.086	—	.10	.25
	1970F	5,140	—	Proof	14.00
	1970G	35.900	—	.10	.25
	1970G	10,200	—	Proof	9.00
	1970J	40.115	—	.10	.25
	1970J	5,000	—	Proof	9.00
	1971D	54.022	—	.10	.25
	1971D	8,000	—	Proof	9.00
	1971F	92.534	—	.10	.25
	1971F	8,000	—	Proof	14.00
	1971G	88.614	—	.10	.25
	1971G	.010	—	Proof	9.00
	1971J small J mintmark				
		65.622	—	.10	.25
	1971J large J mintmark				
		Inc. Ab.	—	.10	.25
	1971J	8,000	—	Proof	9.00
	1972D	104.345	—	.10	.25
	1972D	8,000	—	Proof	8.00
	1972F	110.177	—	.10	.25
	1972F	8,000	—	Proof	8.00
	1972G	71.766	—	.10	.25
	1972G	10,000	—	Proof	8.00
	1972J	96.991	—	.10	.25
	1972J	8,000	—	Proof	8.00
	1973D	26.052	—	.10	.25
	1973D	9,000	—	Proof	8.00
	1973F	30.070	—	.10	.25
	1973F	9,000	—	Proof	8.00
	1973G	17.294	—	.10	.25
	1973G	9,000	—	Proof	8.00
	1973J	26.774	—	.10	.25
	1973J	9,000	—	Proof	8.00
	1974D	15.707	—	.10	.25
	1974D	.035	—	Proof	7.00
	1974F	18.135	—	.10	.25
	1974F	.035	—	Proof	7.00
	1974G	10.450	—	.10	.25
	1974G	.035	—	Proof	7.00
	1974J	16.056	—	.10	.25
	1974J	.035	—	Proof	7.00
	1975D	15.654	—	.10	.25
	1975D	.043	—	Proof	4.00
	1975F	18.043	—	.10	.25
	1975F	.043	—	Proof	4.00
	1975G	10.403	—	.10	.25
	1975G	.043	—	Proof	4.00
	1975J	16.111	—	—	.25
	1975J	.043	—	Proof	4.00
	1976D	65.200	—	—	.25
	1976D	.043	—	Proof	3.50
	1976F	75.282	—	—	.25
	1976F	.043	—	Proof	3.50
	1976G	43.372	—	—	.25
	1976G	.043	—	Proof	3.50
	1976J	66.930	—	—	.25
	1976J	.043	—	Proof	3.50
	1977D	64.989	—	—	.25
	1977D	.051	—	Proof	3.50
	1977F	75.052	—	—	.25
	1977F	.051	—	Proof	3.50
	1977G	43.300	—	—	.25
	1977G	.051	—	Proof	3.50
	1977J	66.800	—	—	.25
	1977J	.051	—	Proof	3.50
	1978D	91.000	—	—	.10
	1978D	.054	—	Proof	3.00
	1978F	105.000	—	—	.10
	1978F	.054	—	Proof	3.00
	1978G	60.590	—	—	.10
	1978G	.054	—	Proof	3.00
	1978J	93.490	—	—	.10
	1978J	.054	—	Proof	3.00
	1979D	104.000	—	—	.10
	1979D	.089	—	Proof	2.00
	1979F	120.000	—	—	.10
	1979F	.089	—	Proof	2.00
	1979G	69.200	—	—	.10
	1979G	.089	—	Proof	2.00
	1979J	106.800	—	—	.10
	1979J	.089	—	Proof	2.00

50 PFENNIG

COPPER-NICKEL
Currency Reform

Y#	Date	Mintage	VF	XF	Unc
104	1949D	39.108	.50	3.00	22.00
	1949F	45.118	.50	3.00	22.00
	1949F	200 pcs.	—	Proof	—
	1949G	25.924	.50	3.00	22.00
	1949J	42.303	.50	3.00	22.00
	1950G	.030	100.00	175.00	250.00

NOTE: This coin was restruck without authorization by a mint official using genuine dies - quantity unknown.

Federal Republic
Reeded edge

Y#	Date	Mintage	VF	XF	Unc
109	1950D	100.735	.35	.50	3.00
	1950F	115.595	.35	.50	3.00
	1950F	450 pcs.	—	Proof	150.00
	1950G	66.421	.35	.50	4.00
	1950G	1,800	—	Proof	9.00
	1950J	102.736	.35	.50	3.00
	1966D	8.328	.35	.50	1.00
	1966F	9.605	.35	.50	1.00
	1966F	100 pcs.	—	Proof	150.00
	1966G	5.543	.35	.50	2.00
	1966G	3,070	—	Proof	35.00
	1966J	8.569	.35	.50	1.00
	1966J	1,000	—	Proof	60.00
	1967D	5.207	.35	.50	1.00
	1967F	6.005	.35	.50	1.00
	1967F	1,500	—	Proof	45.00
	1967G	1.843	.35	.75	2.50
	1967G	4,500	—	Proof	30.00
	1967J	10.684	.35	.50	1.00
	1967J	1,500	—	Proof	60.00
	1968D	7.809	.35	.50	1.00
	1968F	9.004	.35	.50	1.00
	1968F	3,000	—	Proof	40.00
	1968G	6.818	.35	.50	3.50
	1968G	6,023	—	Proof	20.00
	1968J	2.672	.35	.50	2.00
	1968J	2,000	—	Proof	40.00
	1969D	14.561	.35	.50	.50
	1969F	16.804	.35	.50	.50
	1969F	5,000	—	Proof	10.00
	1969G	9.704	.35	.50	.50
	1969G	8,700	—	Proof	10.00
	1969J	14.969	.35	.50	.50
	1969J	5,000	—	Proof	10.00
	1970D	25.294	.35	.50	.50
	1970F	26.455	.35	.50	.50
	1970F	5,140	—	Proof	16.00
	1970G	11.955	.35	.50	.50
	1970G	10,200	—	Proof	10.00
	1970J	10.683	.35	.50	.50
	1970J	5,000	—	Proof	10.00
	1971D	23.393	.35	.50	.50
	1971D	8,000	—	Proof	10.00
	1971F	29.746	.35	.50	.50
	1971F	8,000	—	Proof	16.00
	1971G	15.556	.35	.50	.50
	1971G	.010	—	Proof	10.00
	1971J large J mintmark				
		24.044	.35	.50	.50
	1971J small J mintmark				
		Inc. Ab.	.35	.50	.50
	1971J	8,000	—	Proof	10.00

Plain edge

Y#	Date	Mintage	VF	XF	Unc
109a	1972D	26.008	.35	.50	.50
	1972D	8,000	—	Proof	12.00
	1972F	30.043	.35	.50	.50
	1972F	8,000	—	Proof	12.00
	1972G	17.337	.35	.50	.50
	1972G	10,000	—	Proof	12.00
	1972J	26.707	.35	.50	.50
	1972J	8,000	—	Proof	12.00
	1973D	7.810	.35	.50	.50
	1973D	9,000	—	Proof	12.00
	1973F	8.994	.35	.50	.50
	1973F	9,000	—	Proof	12.00
	1973G	5.201	.35	.50	.50
109a	1973G	9,000	—	Proof	12.00
	1973J	8.011	.35	.50	.50
	1973J	9,000	—	Proof	12.00
	1974D	18.264	.35	.50	.50
	1974D	.035	—	Proof	10.00
	1974F large F mintmark				
		21.036	.35	.50	.50
	1974F small F mintmark				
		Inc. Ab.	.35	.50	.50
	1974F	.035	—	Proof	10.00
	1974G	12.159	.35	.50	.50
	1974G	.035	—	Proof	10.00
	1974J	18.752	.35	.50	.50
	1974J	.035	—	Proof	10.00
	1975D	13.055	.35	.50	.50
	1975D	.043	—	Proof	5.00
	1975F	15.003	.35	.50	.50
	1975F	.043	—	Proof	5.00
	1975G	8.675	.35	.50	.50
	1975G	.043	—	Proof	5.00
	1975J	13.379	.35	.50	.50
	1975J	.043	—	Proof	5.00
	1976D	10.411	.35	.50	.50
	1976D	.043	—	Proof	4.00
	1976F	12.048	.35	.50	.50
	1976F	.043	—	Proof	4.00
	1976G	6.653	.35	.50	.50
	1976G	.043	—	Proof	4.00
	1976J	10.716	.35	.50	.50
	1976J	.043	—	Proof	4.00
	1977D	10.400	.35	.50	.50
	1977D	.051	—	Proof	4.00
	1977F	12.000	.35	.50	.50
	1977F	.051	—	Proof	4.00
	1977G	6.921	.35	.50	.50
	1977G	.051	—	Proof	4.00
	1977J	10.708	.35	.50	.50
	1977J	.051	—	Proof	4.00
	1978D	10.400	—	—	.50
	1978D	.054	—	Proof	3.50
	1978F	12.000	—	—	.50
	1978F	.054	—	Proof	3.50
	1978G	6.640	—	—	.50
	1978G	.054	—	Proof	3.50
	1978J	10.680	—	—	.50
	1978J	.054	—	Proof	3.50
	1979D	10.400	—	—	.50
	1979D	.089	—	Proof	2.00
	1979F	12.000	—	—	.50
	1979F	.089	—	Proof	2.00
	1979G	6.920	—	—	.50
	1979G	.089	—	Proof	2.00
	1979J	10.680	—	—	.50
	1979J	.089	—	Proof	2.00

MARK

COPPER-NICKEL
Federal Republic

Y#	Date	Mintage	VF	XF	Unc
110	1950D	60.467	.65	.85	6.00
	1950F	69.183	.65	.85	6.00
	1950F	150 pcs.	—	Proof	—
	1950G	39.826	.65	.85	8.00
	1950J	61.483	.65	.85	6.00
	1954D	5.202	.65	.85	5.00
	1954F	6.000	.65	.85	5.00
	1954F	175 pcs.	—	Proof	—
	1954G	3.459	.65	.85	5.00
	1954J	5.341	.65	.85	5.00
	1955D	3.093	.65	.85	4.00
	1955F	6.303	.65	.85	4.00
	1955F	100 pcs.	—	Proof	—
	1955G	2.500	.65	1.00	4.00
	1955J	5.294	.65	.85	4.00
	1956D	13.231	.65	.85	3.00
	1956F	14.700	.65	.85	3.00
	1956F	100 pcs.	—	Proof	—
	1956G	8.362	.65	.85	3.00
	1956J	11.478	.65	.85	3.00
	1957D	6.820	.65	.85	3.00
	1957F	6.390	.65	.85	3.00
	1957F	100 pcs.	—	Proof	—
	1957G	3.841	.65	.85	3.00
	1957J	6.632	.65	.85	4.00
	1958D	4.150	.65	.85	3.00
	1958F	4.109	.65	.85	3.00
	1958F	100 pcs.	—	Proof	—

Y#	Date	Mintage	VF	XF	Unc
110	1958G	3.460	.65	.85	3.00
	1958J	4.656	.65	.85	3.00
	1959D	10.409	.65	.75	2.50
	1959F	12.004	.65	.75	2.50
	1959F	100 pcs.	—	Proof	—
	1959G	6.921	.65	.75	2.50
	1959J	10.691	.65	.75	2.50
	1960D	5.453	.65	.75	2.50
	1960F	6.303	.65	.75	2.50
	1960F	100 pcs.	—	Proof	—
	1960G	3.632	.65	.75	2.50
	1960J	5.612	.65	.75	2.50
	1961D	7.536	.65	.75	2.00
	1961F	8.409	.65	.75	2.00
	1961G	4.843	.65	.75	2.00
	1961J	7.483	.65	.75	2.00
	1962D	10.327	.65	.75	2.00
	1962F	10.515	.65	.75	1.50
	1962G	6.054	.65	.75	2.00
	1962J	10.822	.65	.75	2.00
	1963D	12.624	.65	.75	1.50
	1963F	19.617	.65	.75	1.50
	1963G	11.253	.65	.75	1.50
	1963G	*600 pcs.	—	Proof	—
	1963J	15.906	.65	.75	1.50
	1964D	8.048	.65	.75	1.50
	1964F	6.011	.65	.75	1.50
	1964G	3.465	.65	.75	1.50
	1964G	*600 pcs.	—	Proof	75.00
	1964J	6.958	.65	.75	1.50
	1965D	9.388	.65	.75	1.50
	1965F	10.903	.65	.75	1.50
	1965F	300 pcs.	—	Proof	225.00
	1965G	6.232	.65	.75	1.50
	1965G	1,200	—	Proof	14.00
	1965J	8.024	.65	.75	1.50
	1966D	11.717	.65	.75	1.00
	1966F	13.519	.65	.75	1.00
	1966F	100 pcs.	—	Proof	225.00
	1966G	7.799	.65	.75	1.50
	1966G	3,070	—	Proof	40.00
	1966J	12.030	.65	.75	1.00
	1966J	1,000	—	Proof	75.00
	1967D	13.017	.65	.75	1.00
	1967F	3.659	.65	.75	1.00
	1967F	1,500	—	Proof	55.00
	1967G	4.324	.65	.75	1.00
	1967G	4,500	—	Proof	35.00
	1967J	13.357	.65	.75	1.00
	1967J	1,500	—	Proof	75.00
	1968D	1.303	.65	.75	1.00
	1968F	12.859	.65	.75	1.00
	1968F	3,000	—	Proof	45.00
	1968G	5.198	.65	.75	3.00
	1968G	6,023	—	Proof	25.00
	1968J	1.338	.65	1.00	3.00
	1968J	2,000	—	Proof	50.00
	1969D	13.025	.65	.75	1.00
	1969F	15.021	.65	.75	1.00
	1969F	5,000	—	Proof	14.00
	1969G	8.665	.65	.75	1.00
	1969G	8,700	—	Proof	14.00
	1969J	13.370	.65	.75	1.00
	1969J	5,000	—	Proof	14.00
	1970D	17.928	.65	.75	1.00
	1970F	19.408	.65	.75	1.00
	1970F	5,140	—	Proof	18.00
	1970G	20.386	.65	.75	1.00
	1970G	10,200	—	Proof	14.00
	1970J	10.707	.65	.75	1.00
	1970J	5,000	—	Proof	14.00
	1971D	24.513	.65	.75	1.00
	1971D	8,000	—	Proof	14.00
	1971F	28.275	.65	.75	1.00
	1971F	8,000	—	Proof	18.00
	1971G	16.375	.65	.75	1.00
	1971G	.010	—	Proof	14.00
	1971J	25.214	.65	.75	1.00
	1971J	8,000	—	Proof	14.00
	1972D	20.904	.65	.75	1.00
	1972D	8,000	—	Proof	14.00
	1972F	24.086	.65	.75	1.00
	1972F	8,000	—	Proof	14.00
	1972G	18.868	.65	.75	1.00
	1972G	.010	—	Proof	14.00
	1972J	21.360	.65	.75	1.00
	1972J	8,000	—	Proof	14.00
	1973D	14.327	.65	.75	1.00
	1973D	9,000	—	Proof	14.00
	1973F	16.592	.65	.75	1.00
	1973F	9,000	—	Proof	14.00
	1973G	10.409	.65	.75	1.00
	1973G	9,000	—	Proof	14.00
	1973J	14.704	.65	.75	1.00
	1973J	9,000	—	Proof	14.00
	1974D	20.876	.65	.75	1.00
	1974D	.035	—	Proof	12.00
110	1974F	24.057	.65	.75	1.00
	1974F	.035	—	Proof	12.00
	1974G	13.931	.65	.75	1.00
	1974G	.035	—	Proof	12.00
	1974J	21.440	.65	.75	1.00
	1974J	.035	—	Proof	12.00
	1975D	18.241	.65	.75	1.00
	1975D	.043	—	Proof	6.00
	1975F	21.059	.65	.75	1.00
	1975F	.043	—	Proof	6.00
	1975G	12.142	.65	.75	1.00
	1975G	.043	—	Proof	6.00
	1975J	18.770	.65	.75	1.00
	1975J	.043	—	Proof	6.00
	1976D	15.670	.65	.75	1.00
	1976D	.043	—	Proof	6.00
	1976F	18.105	.65	.75	1.00
	1976F	.043	—	Proof	6.00
	1976G	10.382	.65	.75	1.00
	1976G	.043	—	Proof	6.00
	1976J	16.046	.65	.75	1.00
	1976J	.043	—	Proof	6.00
	1977D	20.801	.65	.75	1.00
	1977D	.051	—	Proof	5.00
	1977F	24.026	.65	.75	1.00
	1977F	.051	—	Proof	5.00
	1977G	13.849	.65	.75	1.00
	1977G	.051	—	Proof	5.00
	1977J	21.416	.65	.75	1.00
	1977J	.051	—	Proof	5.00
	1978D	15.600	—	—	.75
	1978D	.054	—	Proof	3.50
	1978F	—	—	—	.75
	1978F	.054	—	Proof	3.50
	1978G	10.380	—	—	.75
	1978G	.054	—	Proof	3.50
	1978J	—	—	—	.75
	1978J	.054	—	Proof	3.50
	1979D	18.200	—	—	1.25
	1979D	.089	—	Proof	2.00
	1979F	21.000	—	—	1.25
	1979F	.089	—	Proof	2.00
	1979G	12.110	—	—	1.25
	1979G	.089	—	Proof	2.00
	1979J	18.690	—	—	1.25
	1979J	.089	—	Proof	2.00

2 MARK

COPPER-NICKEL
Federal Republic

Y#	Date	Mintage	VF	XF	Unc
111	1951D	19.564	20.00	50.00	90.00
	1951F	22.609	20.00	30.00	80.00
	1951F	150 pcs.	—	Proof	—
	1951G	13.012	50.00	75.00	125.00

NOTE: This coin was restruck without authorization by a mint official using genuine dies - quantity unknown.

Y#	Date	Mintage	VF	XF	Unc
	1951J	20.104	20.00	30.00	80.00

Max Planck Issue

Y#	Date	Mintage	VF	XF	Unc
117	1957D	7.452	1.00	2.00	15.00
	1957F	6.337	1.00	2.00	15.00
	1957F	100 pcs.	—	Proof	—
	1957G	2.598	1.00	2.00	20.00
	1957J	11.210	1.00	2.00	15.00
	1958D	12.623	1.00	2.00	9.50
	1958F	16.825	1.00	2.00	9.50
	1958F	300 pcs.	—	Proof	—
	1958G	10.744	1.00	2.00	9.50
	1958J	9.408	1.00	2.00	9.50
	1959D	1.020	4.00	7.50	25.00
	1959F	1.500	10.00	15.00	35.00
	1960D	3.535	1.00	2.00	7.00
	1960F	3.754	1.00	2.00	7.00
	1960F	50 pcs.	—	Proof	—
	1960G	2.695	1.00	3.00	9.50
117	1960J	4.676	1.00	2.00	7.00
	1961D	3.918	1.00	2.00	7.00
	1961F	3.302	1.00	2.00	7.00
	1961G	2.776	1.00	2.00	8.00
	1961J	2.940	1.00	2.00	8.00
	1962D	4.105	1.00	2.00	7.00
	1962F	4.056	1.00	2.00	7.00
	1962G	1.800	1.00	2.00	7.00
	1962J	3.609	1.00	2.00	7.00
	1963D	4.411	1.00	2.00	4.00
	1963F	8.613	1.00	2.00	4.00
	1963G	3.448	1.00	2.00	4.00
	1963G	*600 pcs.	—	Proof	—
	1963J	7.348	1.00	2.00	3.00
	1964D	5.205	1.00	2.00	3.00
	1964F	2.648	1.00	2.00	3.00
	1964G	3.044	1.00	2.00	3.00
	1964G	600 pcs.	—	Proof	100.00
	1964J	2.681	1.00	2.00	3.00
	1965D	3.903	1.00	1.25	2.00
	1965F	4.405	1.00	1.25	2.00
	1965F	300 pcs.	—	Proof	350.00
	1965G	2.599	1.00	1.25	3.00
	1965G	1,200	—	Proof	18.00
	1965J	4.007	1.00	1.25	2.00
	1966D	5.855	1.00	1.25	1.50
	1966F	6.755	1.00	1.25	1.50
	1966F	100 pcs.	—	Proof	350.00
	1966G	3.895	1.00	1.25	1.50
	1966G	3,070	—	Proof	50.00
	1966J	6.014	1.00	1.25	2.00
	1966J	1,000	—	Proof	100.00
	1967D	3.254	1.00	1.25	1.50
	1967F	3.758	1.00	1.25	1.50
	1967F	1,500	—	Proof	80.00
	1967G	1.878	1.00	1.25	1.50
	1967G	4,500	—	Proof	40.00
	1967J	6.684	1.00	1.25	1.50
	1967J	1,500	—	Proof	100.00
	1968D	4.166	1.00	4.00	5.00
	1968F	4.806	1.00	4.00	5.00
	1968F	3,000	—	Proof	60.00
	1968G	3.060	1.00	1.25	1.50
	1968G	6,023	—	Proof	35.00
	1968J	.939	1.00	4.00	5.50
	1968J	2,000	—	Proof	75.00
	1969D	2.602	1.00	1.25	1.50
	1969F	3.005	1.00	1.25	1.50
	1969F	5,100	—	Proof	20.00
	1969G	1.754	1.00	1.25	1.50
	1969G	8,700	—	Proof	20.00
	1969J	2.680	1.00	1.25	1.50
	1969J	5,000	—	Proof	20.00
	1970D	5.203	1.00	1.10	1.25
	1970F	6.018	1.00	1.10	1.25
	1970F	5,140	—	Proof	25.00
	1970G	3.461	1.00	1.10	1.25
	1970G	.010	—	Proof	20.00
	1970J	5.691	1.00	1.10	1.25
	1970J	5,000	—	Proof	20.00
	1971D	8.451	1.00	1.10	1.25
	1971D	8,000	—	Proof	20.00
	1971F	10.017	1.00	1.10	1.25
	1971F	8,000	—	Proof	25.00
	1971G	5.631	1.00	1.10	1.25
	1971G	.010	—	Proof	20.00
	1971J	8.786	1.00	1.10	1.25
	1971J	8,000	—	Proof	20.00

COPPER-NICKEL CLAD NICKEL
Konrad Adenauer Issue

Y#	Date	Mintage	VF	XF	Unc
A117	1969D	7.001	1.25	1.50	1.75
	1969F	7.006	1.25	1.50	1.75
	1969G	7.010	1.25	1.50	1.75
	1969J	7.000	1.25	1.50	1.75
	1970D	7.318	1.25	1.50	1.75
	1970F	8.422	1.25	1.50	1.75
	1970G	4.844	1.25	1.50	2.00
	1970J	7.476	1.25	1.50	1.75
	1971D	7.287	1.25	1.50	1.75
	1971F	8.400	1.25	1.50	1.75
	1971G	4.848	1.25	1.50	1.75
	1971J	7.476	1.25	1.50	1.75
	1972D	7.286	1.25	1.50	1.75
	1972D	8,000	—	Proof	18.00
	1972F	8.392	1.25	1.50	1.75

Y#	Date	Mintage	VF	XF	Unc
	1972F	8,000	—	Proof	18.00
	1972G	4.848	1.25	1.50	1.75
	1972G	.010	—	Proof	18.00
	1972J	7.476	1.25	1.50	1.75
	1972J	8,000	—	Proof	18.00
	1973D	10.393	1.25	1.50	1.75
	1973D	9,000	—	Proof	18.00
	1973F	11.066	1.25	1.50	1.75
	1973F	9,000	—	Proof	18.00
	1973G	9.022	1.25	1.50	1.75
	1973G	9,000	—	Proof	18.00
	1973J	12.272	1.25	1.50	1.75
	1973J	9,000	—	Proof	18.00
	1974D	5.151	1.25	1.50	1.75
	1974D	.035	—	Proof	16.00
	1974F	5.956	1.25	1.50	1.75
	1974F	.035	—	Proof	16.00
	1974G	3.790	1.25	1.50	1.75
	1974G	.035	—	Proof	16.00
	1974J	5.282	1.25	1.50	1.75
	1974J	.035	—	Proof	16.00
	1975D	4.553	1.25	1.50	1.75
	1975D	.043	—	Proof	8.00
	1975F	5.270	1.25	1.50	1.75
	1975F	.043	—	Proof	8.00
	1975G	3.035	1.25	1.50	1.75
	1975G	.043	—	Proof	8.00
	1975J	4.673	1.25	1.50	1.75
	1975J	.043	—	Proof	8.00
	1976D	4.576	1.20	1.35	1.50
	1976D	.043	—	Proof	8.00
	1976F	5.257	1.20	1.35	1.50
	1976F	.043	—	Proof	8.00
	1976G	3.028	1.20	1.35	1.50
	1976G	.043	—	Proof	8.00
	1976J	4.673	1.20	1.35	1.50
	1976J	.043	—	Proof	8.00
	1977D	5.906	1.20	1.35	1.50
	1977D	.051	—	Proof	6.00
	1977F	6.765	1.20	1.35	1.50
	1977F	.051	—	Proof	6.00
	1977G	3.892	1.20	1.35	1.50
	1977G	.051	—	Proof	6.00
	1977J	6.007	1.20	1.35	1.50
	1977J	.051	—	Proof	6.00
	1978D	3.304	—	1.25	1.50
	1978D	—	—	Proof	4.00
	1978F	3,804	—	1.25	1.50
	1978F	—	—	Proof	4.00
	1978G	2.217	—	1.25	1.50
	1978G	—	—	Proof	4.00
	1978J	3.392	—	1.25	1.50
	1978J	—	—	Proof	4.00
	1979D	3.209	—	1.25	1.50
	1979D	—	—	Proof	2.00
	1979F	3.689	—	1.25	1.50
	1979F	—	—	Proof	2.00
	1979G	2.165	—	1.25	1.50
	1979G	—	—	Proof	2.00
	1979J	3.293	—	1.25	1.50
	1979J	—	—	Proof	2.00

Theodor Heuss Issue

Y#	Date	Mintage	VF	XF	Unc
B117	1970D	7.317	1.20	1.35	1.65
	1970F	8.426	1.20	1.35	1.65
	1970G	4.844	1.20	1.35	1.65
	1970J	7.476	1.20	1.35	1.65
	1971D	7.280	1.20	1.35	1.65
	1971F	8.403	1.20	1.35	1.75
	1971G	4.841	1.20	1.35	1.65
	1971J	7.476	1.20	1.35	1.65
	1972D	7.288	1.20	1.35	1.75
	1972D	8,000	—	Proof	18.00
	1972F	8.401	1.20	1.35	1.65
	1972F	8,000	—	Proof	18.00
	1972G	4.859	1.20	1.35	1.65
	1972G	.010	—	Proof	18.00
	1972J	7.476	1.20	1.35	1.65
	1972J	8,000	—	Proof	18.00
	1973D	10.379	1.20	1.35	1.65
	1973D	9,000	—	Proof	18.00
	1973F	11.018	1.20	1.35	1.65
	1973F	9,000	—	Proof	18.00
	1973G	8.975	1.20	1.35	1.65
	1973G	9,000	—	Proof	18.00
	1973J	12.360	1.20	1.35	1.65
B117	1973J	9,000	—	Proof	18.00
	1974D	5.147	1.20	1.35	1.65
	1974D	.035	—	Proof	16.00
	1974F	5.899	1.20	1.35	1.65
	1974F	.035	—	Proof	16.00
	1974G	3.820	1.20	1.35	1.65
	1974G	.035	—	Proof	16.00
	1974J	5.280	1.20	1.35	1.65
	1974J	.035	—	Proof	16.00
	1975D	4.623	1.20	1.35	1.65
	1975D	.043	—	Proof	8.00
	1975F	5.251	1.20	1.35	1.65
	1975F	.043	—	Proof	8.00
	1975G	3.034	1.20	1.35	1.65
	1975G	.043	—	Proof	8.00
	1975J	4.675	1.20	1.35	1.65
	1975J	.043	—	Proof	8.00
	1976D	4.546	1.20	1.35	1.50
	1976D	.043	—	Proof	8.00
	1976F	5.259	1.20	1.35	1.50
	1976F	.043	—	Proof	8.00
	1976G	3.028	1.20	1.35	1.50
	1976G	.043	—	Proof	8.00
	1976J	4.681	1.20	1.35	1.50
	1976J	.043	—	Proof	8.00
	1977D	5.857	1.10	1.25	1.50
	1977D	.051	—	Proof	6.00
	1977F	6.752	1.10	1.25	1.50
	1977F	.051	—	Proof	6.00
	1977G	3.892	1.10	1.25	1.50
	1977G	.051	—	Proof	6.00
	1977J	6.009	1.10	1.25	1.50
	1977J	.051	—	Proof	6.00
	1978D	3.304	—	—	1.50
	1978D	—	—	Proof	4.00
	1978F	3.804	—	1.25	1.50
	1978F	—	—	Proof	4.00
	1978G	2.217	—	1.25	1.50
	1978G	—	—	Proof	4.00
	1978J	3.392	—	—	1.50
	1978J	—	—	Proof	4.00
	1979D	3.209	—	1.25	1.50
	1979D	—	—	Proof	2.00
	1979F	3.689	—	1.25	1.50
	1979F	—	—	Proof	2.00
	1979G	2.165	—	1.25	1.50
	1979G	—	—	Proof	2.00
	1979J	3.293	—	1.25	1.50
	1979J	—	—	Proof	2.00

Dr. Kurt Schumacher

Y#	Date	Mintage	VF	XF	Unc
148	1979D	3.209	—	—	1.75
	1979D	—	—	Proof	2.00
	1979F	3.689	—	—	1.75
	1979F	—	—	Proof	2.00
	1979G	2.165	—	—	1.75
	1979G	—	—	Proof	2.00
	1979J	3.293	—	—	1.75
	1979J	—	—	Proof	2.00

5 MARK

11.2000 gms., .625 SILVER, .2250 oz ASW
Federal Republic

Y#	Date	Mintage	VF	XF	Unc
112	1951D	20.600	7.00	10.00	40.00
	1951F	24.000	7.00	10.00	42.00
	1951F	280 pcs.	—	Proof	—
	1951G	13.840	7.00	10.00	50.00
112	1951J	21.360	7.00	10.00	45.00
	1956D	1.092	10.00	30.00	110.00
	1956F	1.200	10.00	30.00	110.00
	1956F	23 pcs.	—	Proof	—
	1956J	1.068	10.00	30.00	100.00
	1957D	.566	15.00	50.00	150.00
	1957F	2.100	15.00	50.00	115.00
	1957G	.692	15.00	50.00	125.00
	1957J	1.630	15.00	50.00	115.00
	1957-J (error) edge reads "GRUSS DICH DEUTSCHLAND AUS HERZENSGRUND"				
		Inc. Ab.	—	700.00	1000.
	1958D	1.226	BV	25.00	100.00
	1958F	.600	BV	30.00	185.00
	1958F	100 pcs.	—	Proof	—
	1958G	1.557	BV	25.00	100.00
	1958J	.060	200.00	500.00	1000.
	1959D	.496	BV	25.00	125.00
	1959G	.692	20.00	50.00	135.00
	1959J	.713	BV	25.00	125.00
	1960D	1.040	BV	10.00	50.00
	1960F	1.576	BV	10.00	50.00
	1960F	50 pcs.	—	Proof	—
	1960G	.692	BV	15.00	65.00
	1960J	1.618	BV	10.00	50.00
	1961D	1.040	BV	15.00	60.00
	1961F	.824	BV	15.00	60.00
	1961J	.518	BV	20.00	85.00
	1963D	2.080	BV	7.50	40.00
	1963F	1.254	BV	7.50	50.00
	1963G	.600	BV	15.00	65.00
	1963G	—	—	Proof	30.00
	1963J	2.136	BV	7.50	40.00
	1964D	.456	BV	25.00	90.00
	1964F	2.646	BV	7.50	30.00
	1964G	1.649	BV	7.50	30.00
	1964G	*600 pcs.	—	Proof	130.00
	1964J	1.335	BV	7.50	35.00
	1965D	4.354	BV	7.50	15.00
	1965F	4.050	BV	7.50	15.00
	1965F	300 pcs.	—	Proof	500.00
	1965G	2.335	BV	7.50	16.00
	1965G	8,233	—	Proof	25.00
	1965J	3.605	BV	7.00	20.00
	1966D	5.200	BV	7.00	20.00
	1966F	6.000	BV	7.00	20.00
	1966F	100 pcs.	—	Proof	500.00
	1966G	3.460	BV	7.00	22.00
	1966G	3,070	—	Proof	90.00
	1966J	5.340	BV	7.00	22.00
	1966J	1,000	—	Proof	150.00
	1967D	3.120	BV	7.00	25.00
	1967F	3.598	BV	7.00	25.00
	1967F	1,500	—	Proof	130.00
	1967G	1.406	BV	7.00	30.00
	1967G	4,500	—	Proof	65.00
	1967J	3.204	BV	7.00	30.00
	1967J	1,500	—	Proof	150.00
	1968D	1.300	BV	7.00	20.00
	1968F	1.497	BV	7.00	20.00
	1968F	3,000	—	Proof	100.00
	1968G	1.535	BV	7.00	20.00
	1968G	6,023	—	Proof	65.00
	1968J	1.335	BV	7.00	20.00
	1968J	2,000	—	Proof	125.00
	1969D	2.080	BV	7.00	20.00
	1969F	2.395	BV	7.00	20.00
	1969F	5,000	—	Proof	40.00
	1969G	3.484	BV	7.00	20.00
	1969G	8,700	—	Proof	40.00
	1969J	2.136	BV	7.00	20.00
	1969J	5,000	—	Proof	40.00
	1970D	2.000	BV	7.00	15.00
	1970F	1.995	BV	7.00	15.00
	1970F	5,140	—	Proof	40.00
	1970G	6.000	BV	7.00	15.00
	1970G	10,200	—	Proof	40.00
	1970J	4.000	BV	BV	7.50
	1970J	5,000	—	Proof	40.00
	1971D	4.000	BV	BV	7.50
	1971D	8,000	—	Proof	40.00
	1971F	3.993	BV	BV	7.50
	1971F	8,000	—	Proof	40.00
	1971G	6.010	BV	BV	7.50
	1971G	.010	—	Proof	40.00
	1971J	6.000	BV	BV	7.50
	1971J	8,000	—	Proof	40.00
	1972D	3.000	BV	BV	7.50
	1972D	8,000	—	Proof	30.00
	1972F	8.992	BV	BV	7.50
	1972F	8,100	—	Proof	30.00
	1972G	4.999	BV	BV	7.50
	1972G	.010	—	Proof	30.00
	1972J	6.000	BV	BV	7.50
	1972J	8,000	—	Proof	30.00
	1973D	3.380	BV	BV	7.50
	1973D	9,000	—	Proof	30.00

Y#	Date	Mintage	VF	XF	Unc
112	1973F	3.891	BV	BV	7.50
	1973F	9,100	—	Proof	30.00
	1973G	2.240	BV	BV	7.50
	1973G	9,000	—	Proof	30.00
	1973J	5.571	BV	BV	7.50
	1973J	9,000	—	Proof	30.00
	1974D	4.594	BV	BV	7.50
	1974D	.035	—	Proof	28.00
	1974F	6.514	BV	BV	7.50
	1974F	.035	—	Proof	28.00
	1974G	3.708	BV	BV	7.50
	1974G	.035	—	Proof	28.00
	1974J	2.968	BV	BV	7.50
	1974J	.035	—	Proof	28.00

Uninscribed- plain edge errors

Y#	Date	Mintage	VF	XF	Unc
	1959D	Inc. Ab.	200.00	300.00	450.00
	1959J	Inc. Ab.	200.00	300.00	450.00
	1963J	Inc. Ab.	200.00	300.00	450.00
	1964F	Inc. Ab.	200.00	300.00	450.00
	1965F	Inc. Ab.	200.00	300.00	450.00
	1965G	Inc. Ab.	200.00	300.00	450.00
	1966G	Inc. Ab.	200.00	300.00	450.00
	1967G	Inc. Ab.	200.00	300.00	450.00

COPPER-NICKEL, CLAD NICKEL, 10gm.

Y#	Date	Mintage	VF	XF	Unc
139	1975D	65.663	2.60	2.75	3.00
	1975D	.043	—	Proof	14.00
	1975F	75.002	2.60	2.75	3.00
	1975F	.043	—	Proof	14.00
	1975G	43.297	2.60	2.75	3.00
	1975G	.043	—	Proof	14.00
	1975J	67.372	2.60	2.75	3.00
	1975J	.043	—	Proof	14.00
	1976D	7.821	2.60	2.75	3.00
	1976D	.043	—	Proof	12.00
	1976F	9.072	2.60	2.75	3.00
	1976F	.043	—	Proof	12.00
	1976G	5.784	2.60	2.75	3.00
	1976G	.043	—	Proof	12.00
	1976J	8.068	2.60	2.75	3.00
	1976J	.043	—	Proof	12.00
	1977D	8.321	2.60	2.75	3.00
	1977D	.051	—	Proof	12.00
	1977F	9.612	2.60	2.75	3.00
	1977F	.051	—	Proof	12.00
	1977G	5.746	2.60	2.75	3.00
	1977G	.051	—	Proof	12.00
	1977J	8.577	2.60	2.75	3.00
	1977J	.051	—	Proof	12.00
	1978D	7.854	—	—	2.75
	1978D	—	—	Proof	5.00
	1978F	9.054	—	—	2.75
	1978F	—	—	Proof	5.00
	1978G	5.244	—	—	2.75
	1978G	—	—	Proof	5.00
	1978J	8.064	—	—	3.00
	1978J	—	—	Proof	5.00
	1979D	7.889	—	—	2.75
	1979D	—	—	Proof	4.00
	1979F	9.089	—	—	2.75
	1979F	—	—	Proof	4.00
	1979G	5.279	—	—	2.75
	1979G	—	—	Proof	4.00
	1979J	8.099	—	—	2.75
	1979J	—	—	Proof	4.00

5 gm, thin variety

Y#	Date	Mintage	VF	XF	Unc
	1975G	—	—	2.75	3.00

NOTE: Illegally produced by a German Mint official.

5 MARK COMMEMORATIVES

11.2000 gms., .625 SILVER, .2250 oz ASW
Nurnberg Museum

Y#	Date	Mintage	VF	XF	Unc
113	1952D	.200	350.00	600.00	1000.
	1952D	3,000	—	Proof	6000.

Friedrich von Schiller

Y#	Date	Mintage	VF	XF	Unc
114	1955F	.199	200.00	500.00	900.00
	1955F	1,217	—	Proof	3100.

Ludwig von Baden

Y#	Date	Mintage	VF	XF	Unc
115	1955G	.200	200.00	400.00	750.00
	1955G	*2,000	—	Proof	3100.

NOTE: This coin was restruck without authorization by a German mint official using genuine dies. Quantity unknown.

Von Eichendorff

Y#	Date	Mintage	VF	XF	Unc
116	1957J	.200	200.00	400.00	750.00
	1957J	*2,000	—	Proof	3100.

Johann Fichte

Y#	Date	Mintage	VF	XF	Unc
118	1964J	.500	30.00	80.00	225.00
	1964J	5,000	—	Proof	1200.

Gottfried Wilhelm Leibniz

Y#	Date	Mintage	VF	XF	Unc
119	1966D	2.000	BV	20.00	40.00
	1966D	.075	—	Proof	200.00

Wilhelm & Alexander von Humboldt

Y#	Date	Mintage	VF	XF	Unc
120	1967F	1.940	BV	15.00	50.00
	1967F	.060	—	Proof	300.00

Friedrich Raiffeisen

Y#	Date	Mintage	VF	XF	Unc
121	1968J	3.943	BV	7.00	10.00
	1968J	.140	—	Proof	75.00

Johannes Gutenberg

Y#	Date	Mintage	VF	XF	Unc
122	1968G	2.930	BV	7.00	15.00
	1968G	.100	—	Proof	140.00

Max von Pettenkoffer

Y#	Date	Mintage	VF	XF	Unc
123	1968D	2.930	BV	7.00	13.00
	1968D	.100	—	Proof	75.00

Varieties with frosted and unfrosted finishes. Unfrosted variety scarcer.

Theodor Fontane

Y#	Date	Mintage	VF	XF	Unc
124	1969G	2.900	BV	7.00	20.00
	1969G	.170	—	Proof	75.00

Gerhard Mercator

Y#	Date	Mintage	VF	XF	Unc
125	1969F	4.804	BV	7.00	10.00
	1969F	.200	—	Proof	42.00

Ludwig Beethoven

Y#	Date	Mintage	VF	XF	Unc
131	1970F	4.800	BV	7.00	10.00
	1970F	.200	—	Proof	42.00

German Unification

Y#	Date	Mintage	VF	XF	Unc
132	1971G	4.800	BV	7.00	10.00
	1971G	.200	—	Proof	42.00

Albrecht Durer

Y#	Date	Mintage	VF	XF	Unc
133	1971D	7.800	BV	7.00	10.00
	1971D	.200	—	Proof	42.00

Nicholas Copernicus

Y#	Date	Mintage	VF	XF	Unc
134	1973J	7.750	BV	7.00	10.00
	1973J	.250	—	Proof	25.00

125th Anniversary Frankfurt Parliament

Y#	Date	Mintage	VF	XF	Unc
135	1973G	7.750	BV	7.00	10.00
	1973G	.250	—	Proof	25.00

25th Anniversary Constitution

Y#	Date	Mintage	VF	XF	Unc
136	1974F	7.750	BV	7.00	10.00
	1974F	.250	—	Proof	25.00

Immanuel Kant

Y#	Date	Mintage	VF	XF	Unc
137	1974D	7.750	BV	7.00	10.00
	1974D	.250	—	Proof	50.00

Friedrich Ebert

Y#	Date	Mintage	VF	XF	Unc
138	1975J	7.750	BV	7.00	10.00
	1975J	.250	—	Proof	45.00

European Monument Protection Year

11.2 gm., 2.1mm thick

Y#	Date	Mintage	VF	XF	Unc
140	1975F	7.750	BV	7.00	10.00
	1975F	.250	—	Proof	42.00

5.3 gm., 1.4mm thick

Y#	Date	Mintage	VF	XF	Unc
	1975F	Inc. Ab.	BV	7.00	10.00

Albert Schweitzer

Y#	Date	Mintage	VF	XF	Unc
141	1975G	7.750	BV	7.00	10.00
	1975G	.250	—	Proof	45.00

Grimmelshausen

Y#	Date	Mintage	VF	XF	Unc
142	1976D	7.750	BV	7.00	10.00
	1976D	.250	—	Proof	50.00

Carl Friedrich Gauss

Y#	Date	Mintage	VF	XF	Unc
143	1977J	7.750	BV	7.00	10.00
	1977J	.250	—	Proof	50.00

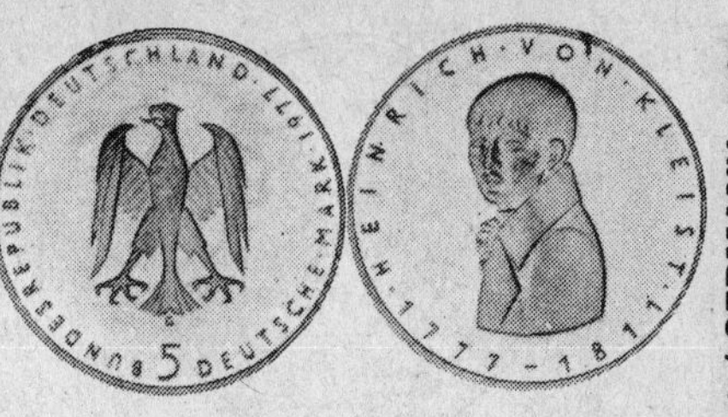

Heinrich von Kleist

Y#	Date	Mintage	VF	XF	Unc
144	1977G	7.750	BV	7.00	10.00
	1977G	.250	—	Proof	45.00

Gustav Stresemann

Y#	Date	Mintage	VF	XF	Unc
145	1978D	7.750	BV	6.75	10.00
	1978D	.250	—	Proof	30.00

Balthasar Neumann

Y#	Date	Mintage	VF	XF	Unc
146	1978F	7.750	BV	6.75	10.00
	1978F	.250	—	Proof	30.00

150th Anniversary of German Archeological Institute

Y#	Date	Mintage	VF	XF	Unc
147	1979J	7.750	BV	BV	7.00
	1979J	.250	—	Proof	50.00

Otto Hahn

Y#	Date	Mintage	VF	XF	Unc
149	1979G	—	—	—	—
	1979G	—	—	Proof	—

10 MARK COMMEMORATIVES

OLYMPIC SERIES

15.5000 gms., .625 SILVER, .3115 oz ASW
Series I, 'In Deutschland'

Y#	Date	Mintage	VF	XF	Unc
126	1972D	2.500	BV	9.50	15.00
	1972D	.125	—	Proof	30.00
	1972F	2.375	BV	9.50	15.00
	1972F	.125	—	Proof	30.00
	1972G	2.500	BV	9.50	20.00
	1972G	.125	—	Proof	30.00
	1972J	2.500	BV	9.50	15.00
	1972J	.125	—	Proof	30.00

Series II, 'Munich Olympics Symbol: 'Schleife' (knot).

Y#	Date	Mintage	VF	XF	Unc
127	1972D	5.000	BV	9.50	11.00
	1972D	.125	—	Proof	14.00
	1972F	4.875	BV	9.50	11.00
	1972F	.125	—	Proof	14.00
	1972G	5.000	BV	9.50	11.00
	1972G	.125	—	Proof	14.00
	1972J	5.000	BV	9.50	11.00
	1972J	.125	—	Proof	14.00

Series III, 'Athletes'

Y#	Date	Mintage	VF	XF	Unc
128	1972D	5.000	BV	9.50	11.00
	1972D	.150	—	Proof	14.00
	1972F	4.850	BV	9.50	11.00
	1972F	.150	—	Proof	14.00
	1972G	5.000	BV	9.50	11.00
	1972G	.150	—	Proof	14.00
	1972J	5.000	BV	9.50	11.00
	1972J	.150	—	Proof	14.00

Series IV, 'Stadium'

Y#	Date	Mintage	VF	XF	Unc
129	1972D	5.000	BV	9.50	11.00
	1972D	.150	—	Proof	14.00
	1972F	4.850	BV	9.50	11.00
	1972F	.150	—	Proof	14.00
	1972G	5.000	BV	9.50	11.00
	1972G	.150	—	Proof	14.00
	1972J	5.000	BV	9.50	11.00
	1972J	.150	—	Proof	14.00

Series V, 'In Munchen'

Y#	Date	Mintage	VF	XF	Unc
126a	1972D	2.500	BV	9.50	12.00
	1972D	.150	—	Proof	15.00
	1972F	2.350	BV	9.50	12.00
	1972F	.150	—	Proof	15.00
	1972G	2.500	BV	9.50	12.00
	1972G	.150	—	Proof	15.00
	1972J	2.500	BV	9.50	12.00
	1972J	.150	—	Proof	15.00

Series VI, 'Olympic Flame'

Y#	Date	Mintage	VF	XF	Unc
130	1972D	5.000	BV	9.50	11.00
	1972D	.150	—	Proof	14.00
	1972F	4.850	BV	9.50	11.00
	1972F	.150	—	Proof	14.00
	1972G	5.000	BV	9.50	11.00
	1972G	.150	—	Proof	14.00
	1972J	5.000	BV	9.50	11.00
	1972J	.150	—	Proof	14.00

NCLT ISSUES

MINT SETS

STANDARD METALS

KM#	Date	Mintage	Identification	Issue Price	Mkt. Val.
S1	1975D(9)	.026	Y105,106a,107-110,A117,B117,139		17.50
S2	1975F(9)	.026	Y105,106a,107-110,A117,B117,139		17.50
S3	1975G(9)	.026	Y105,106a,107-110,A117,B117,139		17.50
S4	1975J(9)	.026	Y105,106a,107-110,A117,B117,139		17.50
S5	1976D(9)	.026	Y105,106a,107-110,A117,B117,139		15.00
S6	1976F(9)	.026	Y105,106a,107-110,A117,B117,139		15.00
S7	1976G(9)	.026	Y105,106a,107-110,A117,B117,139		15.00
S8	1976J(9)	.026	Y105,106a,107-110,A117,B117,139		15.00
S9	1977D(9)	—	Y105,106a,107-110,A117,B117,139		15.00
S10	1977F(9)	—	Y105,106a,107-110,A117,B117,139		15.00
S11	1977G(9)	—	Y105,106a,107-110,A117,B117,139		15.00
S12	1977J(9)	—	Y105,106a,107-110,A117,B117,139		15.00

NOTE: Mint sets are issued in pliable plastic.

PROOF SETS

NOTE: 1964 and 1965 proof sets contained 1 pfennig, 5 pf., 10 pf., 50 pfennig coins dated 1950. The 7 piece 1963G (set) was issued as individual coins. Modern proof sets are issued in stiff plastic cases.

STANDARD METALS

KM#	Date	Mintage	Identification	Issue Price	Mkt. Val.
101	1950-64G(7)	*600	Y105-110,117	—	350.00
102	1950-65F(8)	—	Y105-110,112,117	—	1650.
103	1950-65G(8)	1,200	Y105-110,112,117	—	85.00
104	1966F(8)	100	Y105-110,112,117	—	1650.
105	1966G(8)	3,070	Y105-110,112,117	—	300.00
106	1966J(8)	1,000	Y105-110,112,117	—	550.00
107	1967F(8)	1,500	Y105-110,112,117	—	425.00
108	1967G(8)	4,150	Y105-110,112,117	—	225.00
109	1967G(8)	550	Y105,106a*,107-110,112,117	—	1500.

***NOTE:** This coin was restruck without authorization by a German mint official using genuine dies. Quantity unknown.

KM#	Date	Mintage	Identification	Issue Price	Mkt. Val.
110	1967J(8)	1,500	Y105-110,112,117	—	550.00
111	1968F(8)	3,000	Y105-110,112,117	—	350.00
112	1968G(8)	6,023	Y105-106a,107-110,112,117	—	200.00
113	1968J(8)	2,000	Y105-110,112,117	—	400.00
114	1969F(8)	5,000	Y105,106a,107-110,112,117	—	110.00
115	1969G(8)	8,700	Y105,106a,107-110,112,117	—	110.00
116	1969J(8)	5,000	Y105,106a,107-110,112,117	—	110.00
117	1970F(8)	5,140	Y105,106a,107-110,112,117	—	135.00
118	1970G(8)	10,200	Y105,106a,107-110,112,117	—	110.00
119	1970J(8)	5,000	Y105,106a,107-110,112,117	—	110.00
120	1971d(8)	8,000	Y105,106a,107-110,112,117	—	110.00
121	1971F(8)	8,000	Y105,106a,107-110,112,117	—	135.00
122	1971G(8)	10,200	Y105,106a,107-110,112,117	—	110.00
123	1971J(8)	8,000	Y105,106a,107-110,112,117	—	110.00
124	1972D(8)	8,000	Y105,106a,107-110,112,A117	—	115.00
125	1972F(8)	8,000	Y105,106a,107-110,112,A117	—	115.00
126	1972G(8)	10,000	Y105,106a,107-110,112,A117	—	115.00
127	1972J(8)	8,000	Y105,106a,107-110,112,A117	—	115.00
128	1973D(8)	9,000	Y105,106a,107-110,112,A117	—	115.00
129	1973F(8)	9,000	Y105,106a,107-110,112,A117	—	115.00
130	1973G(8)	9,000	Y105,106a,107-110,112,A117	—	115.00
131	1973J(8)	9,000	Y105,106a,107-110,112,A117	—	115.00
132	1974D(8)	35,000	Y105,106a,107-110,112,A117	12.50	100.00
133	1974F(8)	35,000	Y105,106a,107-110,112,A117	12.50	100.00
134	1974G(8)	35,000	Y105,106a,107-110,112,A117	12.50	100.00
135	1974J(8)	35,000	Y105,106a,107-110,112,A117	12.50	100.00
136	1975D(8)	43,120	Y105,106a,107-110,A117,139	12.50	55.00
137	1975F(8)	43,100	Y105,106a,107-110,A117,139	12.50	55.00
138	1975G(8)	43,100	Y105,106a,107-110,A117,139	12.50	55.00
139	1975J(8)	43,120	50.00	12.50	55.00
140	1976D(9)	43,120	Y105,106a,107-110,A117,B117,139	12.50	50.00
141	1976F(9)	43,100	Y105,106a,107-110,A117,B117,139	12.50	50.00
142	1976G(9)	43,100	Y105,106a,107-110,A117,B117,139	12.50	50.00
143	1976J(9)	43,120	Y105,106a,107-110,A117,B117,139	12.50	50.00
144	1977D(9)	50,620	Y105,106a,107-110,A117,B117,139	12.50	40.00
145	1977F(9)	50,600	Y105,106a,107-110,A117,B117,139	12.50	40.00
146	1977G(9)	50,600	Y105,106a,107-110,A117,B117,139	12.50	40.00
147	1977J(9)	50,620	Y105,106a,107-110,A117,B117,139	12.50	40.00
148	1978D(9)	—	Y105,106a,107-110,A117,B117, 139	—	32.00
149	1978F(9)	—	Y105,106a,107-110,A117,B117, 139	—	32.00
150	1978G(9)	—	Y105,106a,107-110,A117,B117, 139	—	32.00
151	1978J(9)	—	Y105,106a,107-110,A117,B117,		

KM#	Date	Mintage	Identification	Issue Price	Mkt. Val.
151			139	—	32.00
152	1979D(10)	—	Y105,106a,107-110,A117,B117, 139,148	—	20.00
153	1979F(10)	—	Y105,106a,107-110,A117,B117, 139,148	—	20.00
154	1979G(10)	—	Y105,106a,107-110,A117,B117, 139,148	—	20.00
155	1979J(10)	—	Y105,106a,107-110,A117,B117, 139,148	—	20.00

SAARLAND

MINTMARKS

(a) - Paris - privy marks only

10 FRANKEN

ALUMINUM-BRONZE

Y#	Date	Mintage	Fine	VF	XF	Unc
1	1954(a)	11.000	.75	1.50	3.00	6.50

20 FRANKEN

ALUMINUM-BRONZE

Y#	Date	Mintage	Fine	VF	XF	Unc
2	1954(a)	12.950	.75	1.50	3.00	9.00

50 FRANKEN

ALUMINUM-BRONZE

Y#	Date	Mintage	Fine	VF	XF	Unc
3	1954(a)	5.300	2.00	4.00	10.00	25.00

100 FRANKEN

COPPER-NICKEL

Y#	Date	Mintage	Fine	VF	XF	Unc
4	1955(a)	11.000	1.25	2.50	7.50	18.00

NCLT ISSUES

ESSAIS

Standard metals unless otherwise noted

Y#	Date	Mintage	Identification	Issue Price	Mkt Val.
E1	1954(a)	1100	10 Franken	—	60.00
E1a	1954(a)	50	10 Franken, Gold	—	300.00
E2	1954(a)	1100	20 Franken	—	65.00
E2a	1954(a)	50	20 Franken, Gold	—	400.00
E3	1954(a)	1100	50 Franken	—	75.00
E3a	1954(a)	50	50 Franken, Gold	—	500.00
E4a	1955(a)	10	100 Franken, Gold	—	Rare

GERMANY — EAST

The German Democratic Republic (East Germany), located on the great north European plain, has an area of 41,757 sq. mi. (108,150 sq. km.) and a population of 17.2 million. The figures include East Berlin which has been incorporated into the G.D.R. Capital: East Berlin. The economy is highly industrialized. Machinery, transport equipment, chemicals, and lignite are exported.

During the closing days of World War II in Europe, Soviet troops advancing into Germany from the east occupied the German provinces of Mecklenburg, Brandenburg, Lusatia, Saxony and Thuringia. These five provinces comprised the occupation zone administered by the Soviet Union after the cessation of hostilities. The other three zones were administered by the U.S., Great Britain and France. Under the Potsdam agreement, questions affecting Germany as a whole were to be settled by the commanders in chief of the occupation zones acting jointly and by unanimous decision. When Soviet intransigence rendered the quadripartite commission inoperable, the three western zones were united to form the Federal Republic of Germany, May 23, 1949. Thereupon the Soviet Union dissolved its occupation zone and established it as the Democratic Republic of Germany, Oct. 7, 1949.

MINTMARKS

A - Berlin
E - Muldenhutten

MONETARY SYSTEM

100 Pfennig = 1 Mark

PFENNIG

ALUMINUM

Y#	Date	Mintage	VF	XF	Unc
1	1948A	—	.25	.75	5.00
	1949A	—	.25	.75	5.00
	1949E	—	5.00	10.00	20.00
	1950A	—	.25	.75	5.00
	1950E	—	1.00	2.25	5.00

Y#	Date	Mintage	VF	XF	Unc
5	1952A	—	.30	.50	2.00
	1952E	—	.40	1.00	5.00
	1953A	—	.30	.75	2.00
	1953E	—	.40	1.25	5.00

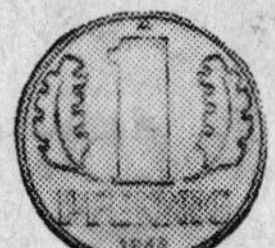

Y#	Date	Mintage	VF	XF	Unc
8	1960A	—	.15	.25	1.00
	1961A	—	.15	.25	1.00
	1962A	—	.10	.25	1.00
	1963A	—	.10	.25	.40
	1964A	—	.10	.25	1.00
	1965A	—	2.50	5.00	10.00
	1968A	—	.10	.25	1.00
	1972A	—	.10	.25	1.00
	1973A	—	.35	.85	1.75
	1975A	—	.35	.50	1.00

5 PFENNIG

ALUMINUM

Y#	Date	Mintage	VF	XF	Unc
2	1948A	—	.50	1.00	2.50
	1949A	—	.50	1.00	2.50
	1950A	—	.50	1.25	2.50

Y#	Date	Mintage	VF	XF	Unc
6	1952A	—	.30	.75	1.00
	1952E	—	.50	1.00	5.00
	1953A	—	.40	.60	1.00
	1953E	—	.50	1.00	5.00

Y#	Date	Mintage	VF	XF	Unc
9	1968A	—	.25	.50	1.00
	1972A	—	.25	.50	1.00
	1975A	—	.25	.50	1.00

10 PFENNIG

ALUMINUM

Y#	Date	Mintage	VF	XF	Unc
3	1948A	—	.50	1.25	5.00
	1949A	—	.50	1.25	5.00
	1950A	—	.50	1.25	5.00
	1950E	—	1.50	5.00	10.00

Y#	Date	Mintage	VF	XF	Unc
7	1952A	—	.25	.50	1.00
	1952E	—	.50	1.50	5.00
	1953A	—	.50	1.00	5.00
	1953E	—	1.00	5.00	10.00

Y#	Date	Mintage	VF	XF	Unc
10	1963A	—	2.00	5.00	10.00
	1965A	—	.15	.25	1.00
	1967A	—	—	.25	1.50
	1968A	—	—	.25	1.00
	1970A	—	.50	1.25	2.00
	1971A	—	—	.25	1.00
	1972A	—	—	.25	1.00
	1973A	—	—	.25	1.00

20 PFENNIG

ALUMINUM-BRONZE

Y#	Date	Mintage	VF	XF	Unc
A11	1969	—	—	.25	1.00
	1971	—	—	.25	1.00
	1972A	—	—	.25	1.00
	1973A	—	—	.25	1.00
	1974A	—	—	.25	1.00

50 PFENNIG

ALUMINUM-BRONZE

Y#	Date	Mintage	VF	XF	Unc
1-4	1949A	Inc.Below	—	Rare	—
	1950A	67.700	2.50	4.00	7.50

ALUMINUM

Y#	Date	Mintage	VF	XF	Unc
11	1958A	—	.35	.75	1.25
	1968A	—	.40	1.00	2.00
	1971A	—	.25	.40	1.00
	1972A	—	.25	.40	1.00
	1973A	—	.25	.40	1.00

MARK

ALUMINUM

Y#	Date	Mintage	VF	XF	Unc
12	1956A	—	.50	1.00	2.00
	1962A	—	.50	1.25	2.50
	1963A	—	.50	1.25	2.50

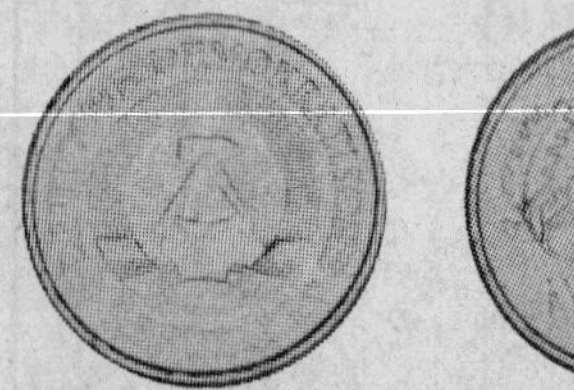
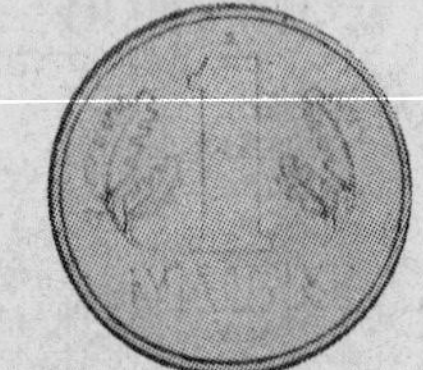

Y#	Date	Mintage	VF	XF	Unc
67	1972A	—	—	.75	1.50
	1973A	—	—	.75	1.50
	1975A	—	—	.75	1.50
	1977A	—	—	.75	1.50
	1978A	—	—	.75	1.50

2 MARK

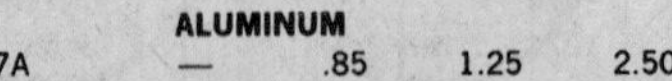

ALUMINUM

Y#	Date	Mintage	VF	XF	Unc
13	1957A	—	.85	1.25	2.50

Y#	Date	Mintage	VF	XF	Unc
68	1974A	—	—	1.00	2.00
	1975	—	—	1.00	2.00
	1977A	—	—	1.00	2.00
	1978A	—	—	1.00	2.00

5 MARK

COPPER-NICKEL

Robert Koch

Y#	Date	Mintage	VF	XF	Unc
18	1968	.100	—	6.00	26.00

20th Anniversary D.D.R.

Y#	Date	Mintage	VF	XF	Unc
21	1969	10.000	—	2.00	4.00
21a	1969	.013	—	—	65.00

NOTE: Y#21 was struck in .900 cu .100 ni and is reddish brown in color. Y#21a was struck in .750 cu .250 ni and is whitish in color.

Heinrich Hertz

Y#	Date	Mintage	VF	XF	Unc
22	1969	.100	—	3.50	9.00

Wilhelm Conrad Rontgen

Y#	Date	Mintage	VF	XF	Unc
25	1970	.100	—	3.50	9.00

Brandenburg Gate

Y#	Date	Mintage	VF	XF	Unc
A29	1971	*.500	—	2.00	3.00

Johannes Kepler

Y#	Date	Mintage	VF	XF	Unc
28	1971	.100	—	3.50	10.00

Johannes Brahms

Y#	Date	Mintage	VF	XF	Unc
33	1972	.055	—	8.50	16.00

City of Meissen

Y#	Date	Mintage	VF	XF	Unc
34	1972	*.500	—	—	3.00

Otto Lilienthal

Y#	Date	Mintage	VF	XF	Unc
40	1973	.100	—	3.50	9.00

Philipp Reis

Y#	Date	Mintage	VF	XF	Unc
45	1974	.100	—	2.50	9.00

Thomas Mann

Y#	Date	Mintage	VF	XF	Unc
50	1975	.100	—	4.50	7.50

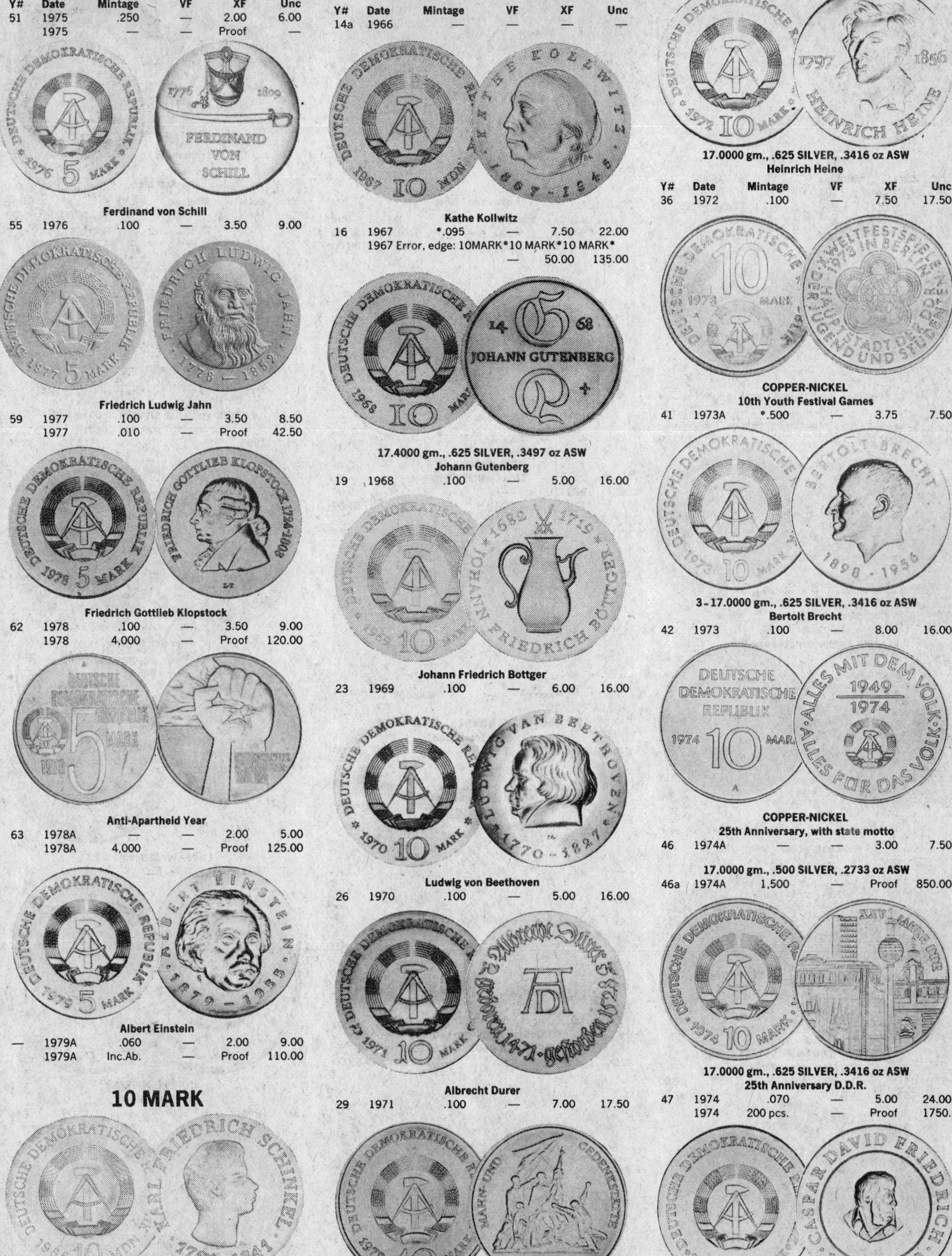

International Women's Year

Y#	Date	Mintage	VF	XF	Unc
51	1975	.250	—	2.00	6.00
	1975	—	—	Proof	—

Ferdinand von Schill

Y#	Date	Mintage	VF	XF	Unc
55	1976	.100	—	3.50	9.00

Friedrich Ludwig Jahn

Y#	Date	Mintage	VF	XF	Unc
59	1977	.100	—	3.50	8.50
	1977	.010	—	Proof	42.50

Friedrich Gottlieb Klopstock

Y#	Date	Mintage	VF	XF	Unc
62	1978	.100	—	3.50	9.00
	1978	4,000	—	Proof	120.00

Anti-Apartheid Year

Y#	Date	Mintage	VF	XF	Unc
63	1978A	—	—	2.00	5.00
	1978A	4,000	—	Proof	125.00

Albert Einstein

Y#	Date	Mintage	VF	XF	Unc
—	1979A	.060	—	2.00	9.00
	1979A	Inc.Ab.	—	Proof	110.00

10 MARK

17.0000 gm., .800 SILVER, .4373 oz ASW
Karl Friedrich Schinkel
Edge: 10 MARK DER DEUTSCHEN NOTEN BANK

Y#	Date	Mintage	VF	XF	Unc
14	1966	.050	—	17.50	65.00

Plain edge

Y#	Date	Mintage	VF	XF	Unc
14a	1966	—	—	—	—

Kathe Kollwitz

Y#	Date	Mintage	VF	XF	Unc
16	1967	*.095	—	7.50	22.00
	1967 Error, edge: 10MARK*10 MARK*10 MARK*		—	50.00	135.00

17.4000 gm., .625 SILVER, .3497 oz ASW
Johann Gutenberg

Y#	Date	Mintage	VF	XF	Unc
19	1968	.100	—	5.00	16.00

Johann Friedrich Bottger

Y#	Date	Mintage	VF	XF	Unc
23	1969	.100	—	6.00	16.00

Ludwig von Beethoven

Y#	Date	Mintage	VF	XF	Unc
26	1970	.100	—	5.00	16.00

Albrecht Durer

Y#	Date	Mintage	VF	XF	Unc
29	1971	.100	—	7.00	17.50

COPPER-NICKEL
Buchenwald Memorial

Y#	Date	Mintage	VF	XF	Unc
35	1972A	*.500	—	3.00	4.00

17.0000 gm., .625 SILVER, .3416 oz ASW
Heinrich Heine

Y#	Date	Mintage	VF	XF	Unc
36	1972	.100	—	7.50	17.50

COPPER-NICKEL
10th Youth Festival Games

Y#	Date	Mintage	VF	XF	Unc
41	1973A	*.500	—	3.75	7.50

3 - 17.0000 gm., .625 SILVER, .3416 oz ASW
Bertolt Brecht

Y#	Date	Mintage	VF	XF	Unc
42	1973	.100	—	8.00	16.00

COPPER-NICKEL
25th Anniversary, with state motto

Y#	Date	Mintage	VF	XF	Unc
46	1974A	—	—	3.00	7.50

17.0000 gm., .500 SILVER, .2733 oz ASW

Y#	Date	Mintage	VF	XF	Unc
46a	1974A	1,500	—	Proof	850.00

17.0000 gm., .625 SILVER, .3416 oz ASW
25th Anniversary D.D.R.

Y#	Date	Mintage	VF	XF	Unc
47	1974	.070	—	5.00	24.00
	1974	200 pcs.	—	Proof	1750.

Caspar David Friedrich

Y#	Date	Mintage	VF	XF	Unc
48	1974	.075	—	5.00	28.00
	1974	400 Pcs.	—	Proof	400.00

Albert Schweitzer

Y#	Date	Mintage	VF	XF	Unc
52	1975	.100	—	5.00	22.00
	1975	1,040	—	Proof	950.00

17.0000 gm., .500 SILVER, .2733 oz ASW
Plain edge
Mule with Warsaw obverse similar to Y#53.

Y#	Date	Mintage	VF	XF	Unc
52a	1975A	6,700	—	10.00	100.00

COPPER-NICKEL
20th Anniversary Warsaw Pact

Y#	Date	Mintage	VF	XF	Unc
53	1975A	—	—	3.50	5.00

National People's Army

Y#	Date	Mintage	VF	XF	Unc
56	1976A	—	—	3.00	10.00

17.0000 gm., .500 SILVER, .2733 oz ASW
Carl Maria von Weber

Y#	Date	Mintage	VF	XF	Unc
57	1976	.100	—	7.50	22.00
	1976	6,000	—	Proof	92.00

Otto von Guericke

Y#	Date	Mintage	VF	XF	Unc
60	1977	.075	—	7.50	22.00
	1977	7,000	—	Proof	95.00

Justus von Liebig

Y#	Date	Mintage	VF	XF	Unc
64	1978	4,000	—	10.00	22.00
	1978	4,500	—	Proof	100.00

COPPER-NICKEL
First Orbital Flight

Y#	Date	Mintage	VF	XF	Unc
65	1978	—	—	2.50	9.00
	1978	2,000	—	Proof	650.00

17.0000 gm., .500 SILVER, .2733 oz ASW
Ludwig Feuerbach

Y#	Date	Mintage	VF	XF	Unc
70	1979	.055	—	5.00	21.00

20 MARK

20.9000 gm., .800 SILVER, .5376 oz ASW
Gottfried Wilhelm Leibniz
Edge: 20 MARK DER DEUTSCHEN NOTEN BANK

Y#	Date	Mintage	VF	XF	Unc
15	1966	.050	—	16.00	65.00

Wilhelm von Humboldt

Y#	Date	Mintage	VF	XF	Unc
17	1967	.100	—	10.00	36.00
	1967 Error, edge: 20 MARK*20 MARK*20 MARK*20 MARK*	Inc. Ab.	—	65.00	170.00

Karl Marx

Y#	Date	Mintage	VF	XF	Unc
20	1968	.100	—	16.00	36.00

20.9000 gm., .625 SILVER, .4200 oz ASW
Johann Wolfgang von Goethe

Y#	Date	Mintage	VF	XF	Unc
24	1969	.100	—	12.50	38.00

Friedrich Engels

Y#	Date	Mintage	VF	XF	Unc
27	1970	.100	—	12.50	27.00

Liebknecht-Luxemburg

Y#	Date	Mintage	VF	XF	Unc
30	1971	.100	—	12.50	26.00
	1971	—	—	Proof	90.00

COPPER-NICKEL
Heinrich Mann

Y#	Date	Mintage	VF	XF	Unc
31	1971	*.500	—	3.00	7.50

Ernst Thalmann

Y#	Date	Mintage	VF	XF	Unc
32	1971A	*.500	—	3.00	7.50

Friedrich von Schiller

Y#	Date	Mintage	VF	XF	Unc
38	1972A	.750	—	3.00	6.00

20.9000 gm., .625 SILVER, .4200 oz ASW
Lucas Cranach

Y#	Date	Mintage	VF	XF	Unc
37	1972	.100	—	12.50	32.00

COPPER-NICKEL
Wilhelm Pieck

Y#	Date	Mintage	VF	XF	Unc
39	1972A	.500	—	5.00	7.50

20.9000 gm., .625 SILVER, .4200 oz ASW
August Bebel

Y#	Date	Mintage	VF	XF	Unc
43	1973	.100	—	12.50	34.00

COPPER-NICKEL
Otto Grotewohl

Y#	Date	Mintage	VF	XF	Unc
44	1973A	—	—	3.00	7.50

20.9000 gm., .625 SILVER, .4200 oz ASW
Immanuel Kant

Y#	Date	Mintage	VF	XF	Unc
49	1974	.100	—	12.50	32.00
	1974	4,000	—	Proof	140.00

Johann Sebastian Bach

Y#	Date	Mintage	VF	XF	Unc
54	1975	.100	—	12.50	30.00
	1975	—	—	Proof	90.00

Wilhelm Liebknecht

Y#	Date	Mintage	VF	XF	Unc
58	1976	.100	—	12.50	32.00
	1976	4,000	—	Proof	160.00

20.9000 gm., .500 SILVER, .3360 oz ASW
Carl Friedrich Gauss

Y#	Date	Mintage	VF	XF	Unc
61	1977	.055	—	10.00	32.00

Johann Gottfried von Herder

Y#	Date	Mintage	VF	XF	Unc
66	1978	.070	—	10.00	35.00
	1978	4,500	—	Proof	135.00

Gotthold Ephraim Lessing

Y#	Date	Mintage	VF	XF	Unc
71	1979	—	—	10.00	37.00
	1979	—	—	Proof	140.00

COPPER-NICKEL
30th Anniversary of East German Regime

Y#	Date	Mintage	VF	XF	Unc
72	1979A	—	—	—	15.00
	1979A	.010	—	Proof	—

20.9200 gm., .500 SILVER, .3360 oz ASW
Ernst Abbe

Y#	Date	Mintage	VF	XF	Unc
	1980A	.040	—	—	32.50
	1980A	5,500	—	Proof	—

NCLT ISSUES

PROVAS

KM#	Date	Mintage	Identification	Mkt.Val.
PR1	ND	—	10 Mark, Silver, Otto von Guericke	—

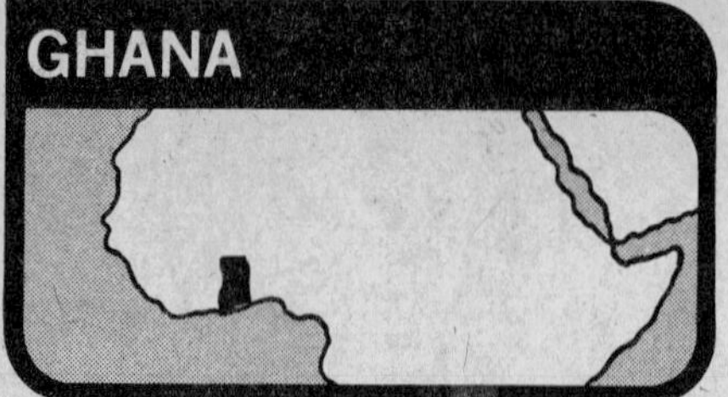

The Republic of Ghana, a member of the British Commonwealth situated on the West Coast of Africa between Ivory Coast and Togo, has an area of 92,100 sq. mi. (238,538 sq. km.) and a population of 10.6 million, almost entirely African. Capital: Accra. Cocoa (the major crop), coconuts, palm kernels and coffee are exported. Mining, second in importance to agriculture, is concentrated on gold, manganese and industrial diamonds.

Ghana was first visited by Portuguese traders in 1470, and through the 17th century was used by various European powers -- England, Denmark, Holland, Germany -- as a center for their slave trade. Britain achieved control of the Gold Coast in 1821, and established the colony of Gold Coast in 1874. In 1901 Britain annexed the neighboring Ashanti Kingdom; in the same year a northern region known as the Northern Territories became a British protectorate. Part of the former German colony of Togoland was mandated to Britain by the League of Nations and administered as part of the Gold Coast. The state of Ghana, comprising the Gold Coast and British Togoland, obtained independence on March 6, 1957, becoming the first Negro African colony to do so. On July 1, 1960, Ghana adopted a republican constitution, changing from a ministerial to a presidential form of Government. The government was overthrown, the constitution suspended and the National Assembly dissolved by the Ghanaian Army and police on Feb. 24, 1966. The government was returned to civilian authority in Oct. 1969, but was again seized by military officers in a bloodless coup on Jan. 13, 1972. Ghana remains a member of the Commonwealth of Nations, with executive authority vested in the Supreme Military council.

Ghana's monetary denomination of 'cedi' is derived from the word 'sedie' meaning cowrie, a shell money commonly employed by coastal tribes.

NOTE: See also British West Africa.

GOLD COAST

RULERS

British, until 1957

MONETARY SYSTEM

8 Tackoe = 1 Ackey

TACKOE

C#	Date	Mintage	VF	XF	Unc
	SILVER				
1	1796	—	125.00	200.00	450.00
	1796	—	—	Proof	625.00
	BRONZED-COPPER				
1a	1796	—		Proof only	300.00
	COPPER-GILT				
1b	1796	—		Proof only	325.00

1/4 ACKEY

C#	Date	Mintage	VF	XF	Unc
	SILVER				
2	1796	—	150.00	225.00	450.00
	1796	—	—	Proof	500.00
	1796 (error) PARLIMENT				
2		—	125.00	200.00	450.00
	1796 (error) PARLIMENT				
		—	—	Proof	600.00
	BRONZED-COPPER				
2a	1796	—		250.00	350.00
	COPPER-GILT				
2b	1796	—		Proof only	500.00

1/2 ACKEY

C#	Date	Mintage	VF	XF	Unc
	SILVER				
3	1796	—	250.00	350.00	800.00
	1796	—	—	Proof	900.00
	1796 (error) PARLIMENT				
		—	200.00	300.00	600.00
	1796 (error) PARLIMENT				
		—	—	Proof	775.00
	BRONZED-COPPER				
3a	1796	—		Proof only	500.00
	COPPER-GILT				
3b	1796	—		Proof only	800.00

C#	Date	Mintage	VF	XF	Unc
5	1818	—		Proof only	450.00
	BRONZED-COPPER				
5a	1818	—		Proof only	Rare
	PEWTER				
5b	1818	—		Proof only	Rare

ACKEY

C#	Date	Mintage	VF	XF	Unc
	SILVER				
4	1796	—	750.00	1000.	1500.
	1796	—	—	Proof	3500.
	1796 (error) PARLIMENT				
		—	675.00	900.00	1350.
	1796 (error) PARLIMENT				
		—	—	Proof	3000.
	BRONZED-COPPER				
4a	1796	—		Proof only	550.00
	COPPER-GILT				
4b	1796	—		Proof only	1250.

C#	Date	Mintage	VF	XF	Unc
	SILVER				
6	1818	—		Proof only	600.00
	BRONZED-COPPER				
6a	1818	—		Proof only	Rare
	PEWTER				
6b	1818	—		Proof only	Rare

NOTE: For later issues see British West Africa.

GHANA

12 Pence = 1 Shilling

1/2 PENNY

Y#	Date	Mintage	VF	XF	Unc
	BRONZE High relief				
1	1958	.020	.10	.15	.20
	1958	Inc. Ab.	—	Proof	1.00
	Low relief				
1.1	1958	31.200	.10	.15	.20

PENNY

Y#	Date	Mintage	VF	XF	Unc
	BRONZE High relief				
2	1958	.020	.15	.20	.30
	1958	Inc. Ab.	—	Proof	4.00
	Low relief				
2.1	1958	60.000	.15	.20	.30

3 PENCE

Y#	Date	Mintage	VF	XF	Unc
	COPPER-NICKEL High relief				
3	1958	.020	.15	.20	.35
	1958	Inc. Ab.	—	Proof	1.75
	Low relief				
3.1	1958	—	.15	.20	.35

6 PENCE

COPPER-NICKEL
High relief

Y#	Date	Mintage	VF	XF	Unc
4	1958	—	.50	1.00	1.50
	1958	—	—	Proof	1.75

Low relief

Y#	Date	Mintage	VF	XF	Unc
4.1	1958	15.200	.20	.30	.50

SHILLING

COPPER-NICKEL
High relief

Y#	Date	Mintage	VF	XF	Unc
5	1958	.020	.25	.35	.75
	1958	Inc. Ab.	—	Proof	2.00

Low relief

Y#	Date	Mintage	VF	XF	Unc
5.1	1958	34.400	.25	.35	.75

2 SHILLINGS

COPPER-NICKEL
High relief

Y#	Date	Mintage	VF	XF	Unc
6	1958	.020	1.00	1.50	2.50
	1958	Inc. Ab.	—	Proof	2.50

Low relief

Y#	Date	Mintage	VF	XF	Unc
6.1	1958	72.700	.60	.80	1.25

10 SHILLINGS

28.2800 gm. .925 SILVER, .8411 oz ASW

Y#	Date	Mintage	XF	Unc	Proof
7	1958	.012	—	—	27.50

DECIMAL COINAGE

100 Pesewas = 1 Cedi

1/2 PESEWA

BRONZE

Y#	Date	Mintage	VF	XF	Unc
12	1967	3.000	—	.10	.15
	1967	2,000	—	Proof	2.00

PESEWA

BRONZE

Y#	Date	Mintage	VF	XF	Unc
13	1967	20.400	—	.10	.15
	1967	2,000	—	Proof	2.50
	1975	50.250	—	.10	.15

2-1/2 PESEWAS

COPPER-NICKEL

Y#	Date	Mintage	VF	XF	Unc
14	1967	6.000	.10	.20	.30
	1967	2,000	—	Proof	3.00

5 PESEWAS

COPPER-NICKEL

Y#	Date	Mintage	VF	XF	Unc
8	1965	30.000	.15	.20	.40

Y#	Date	Mintage	VF	XF	Unc
15	1967	2.400	.15	.20	.35
	1967	2,000	—	Proof	3.50
	1973	8.000	.15	.20	.35
	1975	20.000	.15	.20	.25

10 PESEWAS

COPPER-NICKEL

Y#	Date	Mintage	VF	XF	Unc
9	1965	50.000	.20	.30	.40

Y#	Date	Mintage	VF	XF	Unc
16	1967	13.200	.20	.30	.50
	1967	2,000	—	Proof	4.00
	1975	20.000	.20	.30	.50

20 PESEWAS

COPPER-NICKEL

Y#	Date	Mintage	VF	XF	Unc
17	1967	25.800	.30	.40	.60
	1967	2,000	—	Proof	7.50
	1975	—	.30	.60	1.00

25 PESEWAS

COPPER-NICKEL

Y#	Date	Mintage	VF	XF	Unc
10	1965	60.100	.75	1.00	1.50

50 PESEWAS

COPPER-NICKEL

Y#	Date	Mintage	VF	XF	Unc
11	1965	18.200	1.00	1.25	1.75

12.4500 gm., BRASS

Y#	Date	Mintage	VF	XF	Unc
—	1979	—	—	—	—

CEDI

12.1000 gm., BRASS

Y#	Date	Mintage	VF	XF	Unc
—	1979	—	—	Proof	—

NCLT ISSUES

MEDALLIC ISSUES

(CROWN)

28.2800 gm., .925 SILVER, .8411 oz ASW
OAU Summit Meeting
Obv: Bust of Nkrumah left.
Rev: Africa within geometric design.

KM#	Date	Mintage	XF	Unc	Proof
M1	1965	1000	—	—	65.00
		COPPER-NICKEL			
M2	1965	10,000	—	—	35.00
		28.2800 gm., .917 GOLD, .8338 oz AGW			
M3	1965	50 pcs.	—	—	600.00

(2 POUNDS)

15.9800 gm., .917 GOLD, .4711 oz AGW
Republic Day

KM#	Date	Mintage	XF	Unc	Proof
M5	1960	.015	—	—	350.00
		OAU Summit Meeting Similar to Crown, M1.			
M4	1965	2,020	—	—	400.00

Kotoka Commemorative
Obv: Bust of Kotoka 1/2 left.
Rev: Arms with date below.

KM#	Date	Mintage	XF	Unc	Proof
M6	1968	2,000	—	—	350.00
		Freedom in Unity			
M7	1973	2,000	—	—	400.00
		Operation Feed Yourself Obv: Native planting crops. Rev: Arms and date.			
M8	1975	—	—	—	400.00
		20th Anniversary of Independence			
M9	1977	—	—	—	350.00

PROOF SETS
STANDARD METALS

KM#	Date	Mintage	Identification	Issue Price	Mkt. Val.
101	1958(7)	20,431	Y1-7	—	35.00
102	1967(6)	2,000	Y12-17	8.53	30.00

Listings For

GHURFAH: refer to Yemen Democratic Republic

GIBRALTAR

The British Colony of Gibraltar, located at the southernmost point of the Iberian Peninsula, has an area of 2.25 sq. mi. (5.8 sq. km.) and a population of 27,000. Capital (and only town): Gibraltar. Aside from its strategic importance as guardian of the western entrance to the Mediterranean Sea, Gibraltar is also a free port, British naval base, and coaling station.

Gibraltar, rooted in Greek mythology as one of the Pillars of Hercules, has long been a coveted stronghold. Moslems took it from Spain and fortified it in 711. Spain retook it in 1309, lost it again to the Moors in 1333 and retook it in 1462. After Barbarossa sacked Gibraltar in 1540, Spain strengthened its defenses and held it until the War of the Spanish Succession when it was captured by a combined British and Dutch force, 1704. Britain held it against the Franco-Spanish attacks of 1704-05 and through the historic 'Great Siege' of 1779-83. Recently Spain has attempted to discourage British occupancy by harassment and economic devices. In 1967, Gibraltar's inhabitants voted 12,138 to 44 to remain under British rule.

Gibraltar's celebrated Barbary ape, the last monkey to be found in a wild state in Europe, is featured on the colony's first decimal crown, released in 1972.

RULERS

British

MONETARY SYSTEM

24 Quarts (Quartos) = 1 Real

TOKEN ISSUES

QUART (QUARTO)

COPPER
Robert Keeling

Fr#	Date	Mintage	VG	Fine	VF	XF
5	1802	—	7.50	15.00	25.00	50.00

Fr#	Date	Mintage	VG	Fine	VF	XF
7.1	1810 large date	—	5.00	10.00	25.00	50.00

Fr#	Date	Mintage	VG	Fine	VF	XF
7.2	1810 small date	—	6.50	12.50	27.50	55.00

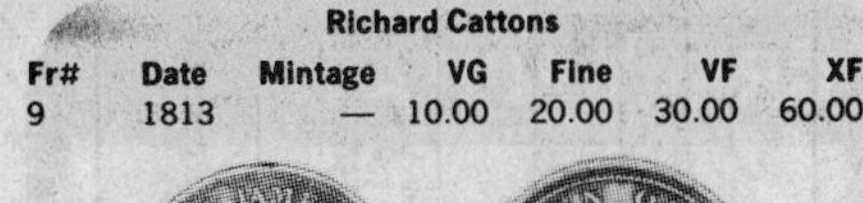

Richard Cattons

Fr#	Date	Mintage	VG	Fine	VF	XF
9	1813	—	10.00	20.00	30.00	60.00

James Spittles

Fr#	Date	Mintage	VG	Fine	VF	XF
12	1820	—	10.00	20.00	30.00	55.00

2 QUARTS (QUARTOS)

COPPER
Robert Keeling

Fr#	Date	Mintage	VG	Fine	VF	XF
4.1	1802 toothed border	—	6.50	12.50	27.50	50.00
4.2	1802 plain border	—	7.50	15.00	30.00	55.00

Large date 5mm tall

Fr#	Date	Mintage	VG	Fine	VF	XF
6	1810	—	7.50	15.00	27.50	45.00

Small date 4mm tall

Fr#	Date	Mintage	VG	Fine	VF	XF
6.2	1810	—	10.00	18.50	32.50	55.00

Richard Cattons

Fr#	Date	Mintage	VG	Fine	VF	XF
8	1813	—	12.50	25.00	40.00	65.00

James Spittles

Fr#	Date	Mintage	VG	Fine	VF	XF
10	1818	—	12.50	25.00	35.00	65.00

Fr#	Date	Mintage	VG	Fine	VF	XF
11	1820	—	13.50	27.50	40.00	70.00

REGULAR COINAGE

1/2 QUART

COPPER

C#	Date	Mintage	Fine	VF	XF	Unc
1	ND(1841)	—	—	Proof Only		Rare
	1842	.390	4.50	9.00	22.50	60.00
	1861	—	—	Proof Only		Rare

QUART

COPPER

C#	Date	Mintage	Fine	VF	XF	Unc
2	1841	—	—	Proof Only		Rare
	1842/0	.100	6.50	12.50	25.00	65.00
	1861	—	—	Proof Only		Rare

2 QUARTS

COPPER

C#	Date	Mintage	Fine	VF	XF	Unc
3	1841	—	—	Proof Only		Rare
	1842/1	.050	8.50	17.50	35.00	80.00
	1861	—	—	Proof Only		Rare

MONETARY REFORM

4 Farthings = 1 Penny
12 Pence = 1 Shilling
2 Shillings = 1 Florin
5 Shillings = 1 Crown
20 Shillings = 1 Pound

CROWN

COPPER-NICKEL

Y#	Date	Mintage	VF	XF	Unc
1	1967	.125	1.00	1.25	4.00
	1968	.040	1.25	1.75	3.00
	1969	.042	1.25	1.75	3.00
	1970	.042	1.25	1.75	3.50

28.2700 gm., .500 SILVER, .4545 oz ASW

Y#	Date	Mintage	VF	XF	Unc
1a	1967	.010	—	Proof	45.00
	1967	50 pcs.	Frosted	Proof	200.00

25 POUNDS

7.7700 gm., .917 GOLD, .2291 oz AGW
250th Anniversary Introduction of British Sterling

Y#	Date	Mintage	VF	XF	Unc
4	1975	2,300	Bv	165.00	175.00
	1975	750 pcs.	—	Proof	200.00

50 POUNDS

15.5500 gm., .917 GOLD, .4585 oz AGW
250th Anniversary Introduction of British Sterling

Y#	Date	Mintage	VF	XF	Unc
5	1975	1,530	Bv	325.00	350.00
	1975	750 pcs.	—	Proof	400.00

100 POUNDS

31.1000 gm., .917 GOLD, .9170 oz AGW

250th Anniversary Introduction of British Sterling

Y#	Date	Mintage	VF	XF	Unc
6	1975	1,530	Bv	625.00	675.00
	1975	750 pcs.	—	Proof	750.00

DECIMAL COINAGE

5 New Pence = 1 Shilling
25 New Pence = 1 Crown
100 New Pence = 1 Pound

25 NEW PENCE

COPPER-NICKEL

2	1971	.080	1.00	1.50	4.00
	28.2700 gm., .500 SILVER, .4545 oz ASW				
2a	1971	.020	—	Proof	40.00

COPPER-NICKEL
25th Wedding Anniversary

3	1972	.070	1.00	1.50	4.00
	28.2700 gm., .500 SILVER, .4545 oz ASW				
3a	1972	.015	—	Proof	35.00
	COPPER-NICKEL Queen's Silver Jubilee				
7	1977	.100	.75	1.25	2.25
	28.2800 gm., .925 SILVER, .8411 oz ASW				
7a	1977	.025	—	Proof	50.00

NCLT ISSUES

MINT SETS

KM#	Date	Mintage	Identification	Issue Price	Mkt. Val.
S1	1975(3)	1,530	Y4-6	—	1200.

PROOF SETS

STANDARD METALS

KM#	Date	Mintage	Identification	Issue Price	Mkt. Val.
101	1975(3)	750	Y4-6	875.00	1350.

Listings For

GOLD COAST: refer to Ghana

GREAT BRITAIN

The United Kingdom of Great Britain and Northern Ireland, located off the northwest coast of the European continent, has an area of 94,200 sq. mi. (243,977 sq. km.) and a population of 55.9 million. Capital: London. The economy is based on industrial activity and trading. Machinery, motor vehicles, chemicals, and textile yarns and fabrics are exported.

After the departure of the Romans, who brought Britain into an active relationship with Europe, Britain fell prey to invaders from Scandinavia and the Low Countries who drove the original Britons into Scotland and Wales, and established a profusion of kingdoms that finally united in the 11th century under the Danish King Canute. Norman rule, following the conquest of 1066, stimulated the development of those institutions which have since distinguished British life. Henry VIII (1509-47) turned Britain from continental adventuring and faced it to the sea - a decision that made Britain a world power during the reign of Elizabeth I (1558-1603). Strengthened by the Industrial Revolution and the defeat of Napoleon, 19th century Britain turned to the remote parts of the world and established a colonial empire of such extent and prosperity that the world has never seen its like. World Wars I and II sealed the fate of the Empire and relegated Britain to a lesser role in world affairs by draining her resources and inaugurating a world-wide movement toward national self-determination in her former colonies.

By the mid-20th century, most of the territories formerly comprising the British Empire had gained independence, and the empire had evolved into the Commonwealth of Nations, an association of equal and autonomous states which enjoy special trade interests. The commonwealth is presently (1980) composed of 42 member nations, including the United Kingdom. All recognize the British monarch as head of the Commonwealth. Fourteen continue to recognize the British monarch as Chief of State. They are: United Kingdom, Australia, New Zealand, Bahamas, Barbados, Canada, Fiji, Jamaica, Mauritius, Papua New Guinea, Solomon Islands, St. Lucia, Kiribati, and Tuvalu.

RULERS

George III, 1760-1820
George IV, 1820-1830
William IV, 1830-1837
Victoria, 1837-1901
Edward VII, 1901-1910
George V, 1910-1936
Edward VIII, 1936
George VI, 1936-1952
Elizabeth II, 1952-

MINTMARKS

H - Heaton
KN - King's Norton

MONETARY SYSTEM

4 Farthings = 1 Penny
12 Pence = 1 Shilling
2 Shillings = 1 Florin
5 Shillings = 1 Crown
20 Shillings = 1 Pound (Sovereign)
21 Shillings = 1 Guinea

TRADESMENS' TOKENS

18th Century English

1/2 PENNY

COPPER

The late 1700's witnessed a severe shortage of small change. Regal coppers were last struck in 1775. Coins in circulation were badly worn and accompanied by many counterfeits. In 1787 Matthew Boulton produced the first token issue for the Parys Mines Co. Gaining popularity these were followed by many issues of merchants, manufacturers, shopkeepers, workhouse officials, etc. along with these tokens were issued for general circulation, often of light weight, mules, without an issuer's name or address, advertising tokens without an expressed value, along with political and collector types circulated. The commonest denomination was the 1/2 penny, with farthings and one penny tokens also being issued. Illustrated is a 1/2 penny token of Coventry of Lady Godiva. These can be found listed in 'British Tokens and Their Values' by P. Seaby and M. Bussell.

18th Century Scottish

1/2 PENNY

COPPER

Various tokens were also issued in Scotland and can be found listed in either Seaby's "Coins and Tokens of Scotland" or "The Provincial Token Coinage of the 18th Century" by Dalton and Hamer.

19th Century English

PENNY

COPPER

SHILLING

SILVER

The early 1800's witnessed a severe shortage of both copper and silver. The last issue of shillings and sixpence was in 1787. The turn of the century brought into circulation the countermarked Spanish dollars and fractions in two issues, both being heavily counterfeited. The Bank of England introduced their dollar or 5 shillings but the rise in value of silver caused many to be melted down. Private trader's and town tokens appeared in 1811 and 1812 along with regular bank tokens of the Bank of England. Private tokens continued to circulate until 1813 when they were finally forbidden by Act of Parliament. Various denominations were produced, the shilling being the commonest of the silver tokens and the penny for the copper tokens. These can be found listed in 'British Tokens and Their Values' by P. Seaby and M. Bussell.

2 SHILLINGS

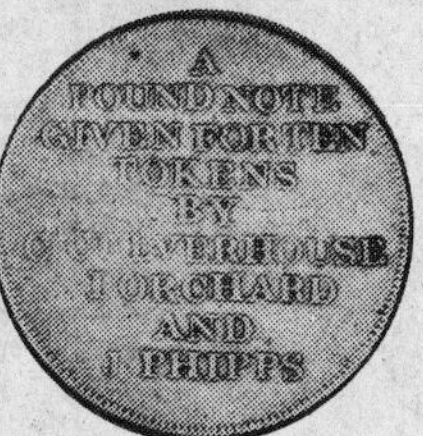

SILVER

4 SHILLINGS

SILVER

REGULAR COINAGE

1/4 FARTHING

COPPER

Y#	Date	Mintage	Fine	VF	XF	Unc
1*	1839	3.840	8.00	16.00	35.00	60.00
	1851	2.215	8.00	16.00	35.00	60.00
	1852	Inc. Ab.	8.00	20.00	35.00	60.00
	1853	Inc. Ab.	8.00	16.00	35.00	60.00

BRONZED COPPER

Y#	Date	Mintage	Fine	VF	XF	Unc
1c*	1852	—	—	—	Proof	200.00
1c*	1853	—	—	—	Proof	200.00
1a*	1853	—	—	—	Proof	200.00
	1868	—	—	Proof Only		325.00

COPPER-NICKEL

Y#	Date	Mintage	Fine	VF	XF	Unc
1b*	1868	—	—	Proof Only		200.00

***NOTE:** Although the design of the above series is of the homeland type, the issues were struck for Ceylon. Catalogue no. is of Ceylon.

1/3 FARTHING

COPPER

C#	Date	Mintage	Fine	VF	XF	Unc
60*	1827	—	2.00	5.00	15.00	40.00
	1827	—	—	—	Proof	90.00

C#	Date	Mintage	Fine	VF	XF	Unc
61*	1835	—	2.75	5.50	12.50	22.50
	1835	—	—	—	Proof	85.00

Y#	Date	Mintage	Fine	VF	XF	Unc
1*	1844	1.301	6.00	25.00	50.00	75.00
	1844 (error, RE for REG.) Inc. Ab.		11.50	35.00	80.00	200.00

BRONZE

Y#	Date	Mintage	Fine	VF	XF	Unc
2*	1866	.576	1.50	4.00	7.50	25.00
	1866	—	—	—	Proof	100.00
	1868	.144	2.00	5.00	10.00	25.00
	1868	—	—	—	Proof	130.00
	1876	.162	2.00	5.00	10.00	22.50
	1878	.288	1.50	4.00	7.50	20.00
	1878	—	—	—	Proof	130.00
	1881	.144	1.50	4.00	10.00	22.50
	1881	—	—	—	Proof	130.00
	1884	.144	1.25	3.50	7.00	20.00
	1885	.288	1.25	3.00	7.00	20.00

COPPER NICKEL

Y#	Date	Mintage	Fine	VF	XF	Unc
2a*	1868	—	—	—	Proof	275.00

ALUMINUM

Y#	Date	Mintage	Fine	VF	XF	Unc
2b*	1868	—	—	—	Proof	—

BRONZE

Y#	Date	Mintage	Fine	VF	XF	Unc
3*	1902	.288	1.00	1.50	4.00	10.00

Y#	Date	Mintage	Fine	VF	XF	Unc
4*	1913	.288	1.00	1.50	4.00	10.00

***NOTE:** Although the designs of the above types are in the homeland style, the issues were struck for Malta. Catalogue nos. are of Malta.

1/2 FARTHING

COPPER

Rev: Britannia's head breaks legend.

C#	Date	Mintage	Fine	VF	XF	Unc
37*	1828	7.680	4.00	15.00	35.00	75.00

C#	Date	Mintage	Fine	VF	XF	Unc
37*	1828	—	—	—	Proof	140.00
	1830	—	—	—	Proof	160.00

Rev: Britannia's head below legend.

C#	Date	Mintage	Fine	VF	XF	Unc
37.1	1828	Inc. Ab.	6.00	20.00	40.00	65.00
	1830 large date					
		8.776	4.00	15.00	30.00	65.00
	1830 small date					
		Inc. Ab.	7.50	20.00	35.00	100.00
	1830	—	—	—	Proof	—

BRONZED COPPER

C#	Date	Mintage	Fine	VF	XF	Unc
37a*	1828	—	—	—	Proof	—

COPPER

C#	Date	Mintage	Fine	VF	XF	Unc
39*	1837	1.935	15.00	40.00	100.00	200.00

Y#	Date	Mintage	Fine	VF	XF	Unc
2*	1839	2.043	2.50	6.00	17.50	35.00
	1842	—	2.00	5.00	12.50	25.00
	1843	3.441	1.50	2.00	4.00	10.00
	1844	6.451	1.50	2.00	4.00	8.00
	1844 w/ E of Regina over N					
		Inc. Ab.	4.00	17.50	35.00	60.00
	1847	3.011	1.75	4.50	10.00	25.00
	1851	—	2.50	6.00	20.00	50.00
	1852	.989	1.50	6.50	17.50	40.00
	1853	.955	3.00	7.50	30.00	60.00
	1853	—	—	—	Proof	80.00
	1854	.677	5.00	10.00	35.00	80.00
	1856 small date					
		.914	5.00	12.00	35.00	90.00
	1856 large date					
		Inc. Ab.	10.00	35.00	75.00	175.00

BRONZED COPPER (OMS)

Y#	Date	Mintage	Fine	VF	XF	Unc
2a*	1839	—	—	—	Proof	100.00
	1853	—	—	—	Proof	80.00

BRONZE (OMS)

Y#	Date	Mintage	Fine	VF	XF	Unc
2b*	1868	—	—	—	Proof	200.00

COPPER-NICKEL (OMS)

Y#	Date	Mintage	Fine	VF	XF	Unc
2c*	1868	—	—	—	Proof	225.00

***NOTE:** Although the design of the above series is of the homeland type, the issues were originally struck for Ceylon. The issue was made current also in the United Kingdom by proclamation in 1842. Catalog nos. are of Ceylon.

FARTHING

COPPER

C#	Date	Mintage	Fine	VF	XF	Unc
15	1771	—	10.00	35.00	75.00	150.00
	1771	—	—	—	Proof	250.00
	1773	—	5.00	10.00	50.00	75.00
	1774	—	5.00	20.00	65.00	85.00
	1775	—	6.00	20.00	70.00	100.00

NOTE: Contemporary counterfeits of C#15 are quite common.

C#	Date	Mintage	Fine	VF	XF	Unc
16	1799	—	2.50	7.50	27.50	45.00
	1799	—	—	—	Proof	100.00

C#	Date	Mintage	Fine	VF	XF	Unc
17	1806	—	2.00	6.50	20.00	35.00
	1806	—	—	—	Proof	75.00
	1807	—	2.50	8.50	30.00	45.00

GILT COPPER (OMS)

C#	Date	Mintage	Fine	VF	XF	Unc
17a	1806	—	—	—	Proof	—

BRONZED COPPER (OMS)

C#	Date	Mintage	Fine	VF	XF	Unc
17b	1806	—	—	—	Proof	—

SILVER (OMS)

C#	Date	Mintage	Fine	VF	XF	Unc
17c	1806	—	—	—	Proof	—

GOLD (OMS)

C#	Date	Mintage	Fine	VF	XF	Unc
17d	1806	—	—	—	Proof	—

COPPER

C#	Date	Mintage	Fine	VF	XF	Unc
52	1821	2.688	1.00	3.00	12.00	25.00
	1822	5.924	1.00	3.00	12.00	25.00
	1823	2.365	1.50	4.00	20.00	35.00
	1823 w/ letter I for 1 in date					
		Inc. Ab.	3.50	20.00	50.00	75.00
	1825	4.300	1.50	3.50	10.00	30.00
	1826	6.666	1.25	6.00	15.00	40.00

C#	Date	Mintage	Fine	VF	XF	Unc
52a	1826	Inc. Ab.	1.00	3.50	10.00	40.00
	1826	—	—	—	Proof	75.00
	1827	2.365	1.50	10.00	30,00	50.00
	1828	2.365	1.50	7.50	20.00	40.00
	1829	1.505	2.50	10.00	35.00	60.00
	1830	2.365	2.00	8.00	25.00	40.00
	1831	—	—	Proof Only		135.00

BRONZED COPPER

C#	Date	Mintage	Fine	VF	XF	Unc
52b	1826	—	—	—	Proof	—

COPPER

C#	Date	Mintage	Fine	VF	XF	Unc
71	1831	2.688	1.50	5.00	20.00	45.00
	1831	—	—	—	Proof	125.00
	1834	1.935	2.00	5.00	20.00	60.00
	1835	1.720	1.50	5.00	35.00	70.00
	1836	1.290	2.00	5.00	35.00	70.00
	1837	3.010	1.50	5.00	20.00	60.00

Y#	Date	Mintage	Fine	VF	XF	Unc
1	1838	.591	2.00	3.50	14.00	25.00
	1839	4.301	1.50	3.00	8.50	20.00
	1839	—	—	—	Proof	85.00
	1840	3.011	1.25	3.00	10.00	22.50
	1841	1.720	1.50	3.50	12.00	30.00
	1841*	—	—	—	Proof	115.00
	1842	1.290	3.50	10.00	30.00	60.00
	1842 4 over inverted 4					
		—	—	—	Rare	—
1	1843	4.086	1.50	3.50	10.00	20.00
	1843 w/ letter I for 1 in date					
		Inc. Ab.	3.50	9.00	25.00	50.00
	1844	.430	20.00	60.00	150.00	300.00
	1845	3.226	1.50	5.00	15.00	25.00
	1846	2.580	3.50	8.50	27.50	55.00
	1847	3.880	1.50	3.50	10.00	35.00
	1848	1.290	1.25	3.50	15.00	45.00
	1849	.645	7.00	15.00	50.00	100.00
	1850	.430	1.50	3.25	15.00	35.00
	1851	1.935	5.00	12.00	35.00	75.00
	1851 D of DEI/tipped D					
		—	8.50	20.00	60.00	100.00
	1852	.823	5.00	12.00	40.00	100.00
	1853/2	1.029	—	60.00	100.00	225.00
	1853 WW designer's initials raised					
		Inc. Ab.	1.00	3.00	7.00	22.50
	1853 WW designer's initials incuse					
		Inc. Ab.	1.50	5.00	12.50	32.50
	1853	—	—	—	Proof	115.00
	1854	6.505	1.25	3.50	12.00	27.50
	1855 WW designer's initials raised					
		3.441	2.00	4.50	15.00	35.00
	1855 WW designer's initials incuse					
		Inc. Ab.	1.25	3.50	12.00	35.00
	1856	1.771	2.50	10.00	30.00	70.00
	1856 w/ R of Victoria over E					
		Inc. Ab.	10.00	25.00	60.00	100.00
	1857	1.075	1.25	3.50	10.00	22.50
	1858	1.720	1.50	3.00	10.00	22.50
	1859	1.290	6.50	20.00	45.00	100.00
	1860	—	250.00	600.00	1200.	2000.
	1864	—	—	—	Rare	—

NOTE: Proofs dated 1841 were probably restruck at a later date.

BRONZE

Y#	Date	Mintage	Fine	VF	XF	Unc
16	1860 w/ beaded border					
		2.867	1.75	4.00	12.00	27.50
	1860	—	—	—	Proof	500.00
	1860 w/ toothed border					
		Inc. Ab.	1.00	3.00	6.00	20.00
	1860 w/ toothed/beaded border					
		Inc. Ab.	50.00	180.00	400.00	1150.
	1861	8.602	1.00	3.00	6.00	20.00
	1861	—	—	—	Proof	450.00
	1862 sm. 8					
		14.336	1.50	4.00	8.00	17.50
	1862 lg.8	—	—	5.00	10.00	27.50
	1862	—	—	—	Proof	450.00
	1863	1.434	25.00	50.00	100.00	225.00
	1863	—	—	—	Proof	500.00
	1864	2.509	1.25	2.75	6.00	20.00
	1865/2	4.659	2.00	5.00	12.00	50.00
	1865/3	Inc. Ab.	—	8.00	20.00	55.00
	1865 lg.8	I.A.	1.00	2.50	6.00	20.00
	1865 sm.8	I.A.	1.00	2.00	5.00	20.00
	1866	3.584	.65	1.50	4.00	17.50
	1866	—	—	—	Proof	450.00
	1867	5.018	1.25	2.00	6.00	20.00
	1867	—	—	—	Proof	450.00
	1868	4.851	1.50	2.50	8.00	25.00
	1868	—	—	—	Proof	275.00
	1869	3.226	3.00	5.00	12.00	35.00
	1872	2.150	2.50	4.50	10.00	27.50
	1873	3.226	1.25	3.00	6.00	20.00
	1874H	3.584	1.25	3.00	8.00	20.00
	1874H (1 Known)		—	—	Proof	—
	1874 w/ normal G's over horizontal G's					
		Inc. Ab.	45.00	100.00	300.00	575.00
	1875 large date, obverse of 1873					
		.713	8.50	20.00	45.00	125.00
	1875 small date, obverse of 1873					
		Inc. Ab.	15.00	30.00	50.00	150.00
	1875 small date, obverse of 1874					
		Inc. Ab.	15.00	25.00	45.00	125.00
	1875H obverse of 1873					
		6.093	100.00	175.00	500.00	1350.
	1875H obverse of 1874					
		Inc. Ab.	1.00	2.50	5.00	17.50
	1875H	—	—	—	Proof	600.00
	1876H	1.175	6.00	17.50	35.00	85.00
	1877	—	—	Proof Only		Rare
	1878	4.009	1.00	2.00	5.00	20.00
	1878	—	—	—	Proof	450.00
	1879	3.977	1.50	3.00	6.00	20.00
	1879 large 9					
		Inc. Ab.	1.25	3.50	8.50	27.50
	1880 w/ 3 berries in wreath					
		1.843	4.00	10.00	20.00	50.00

Y#	Date	Mintage	Fine	VF	XF	Unc
16	1880 w/ 4 berries in wreath					
		Inc. Ab.	1.50	4.00	10.00	22.50
	1881 w/ 3 berries in wreath					
		3.495	1.00	3.00	6.00	13.50
	1881 w/ 4 berries in wreath					
		Inc. Ab.	8.00	20.00	50.00	100.00
	1881 shield heraldically colored					
		—	—	Proof Only		500.00
	1881H	1.792	2.00	4.00	10.00	22.50
	1882H	1.792	1.50	4.00	7.00	20.00
	1882H	—	—	—	Proof	500.00
	1883	1.129	2.00	7.50	15.00	30.00
	1883	—	—	—	Proof	500.00
	1884	5.782	.75	1.50	3.00	10.00
	1884	—	—	—	Proof	500.00
	1885	5.442	1.00	2.00	3.50	10.00
	1885	—	—	—	Proof	500.00
	1886	7.768	1.00	2.00	3.00	10.00
	1886	—	—	—	Proof	500.00
	1887	1.341	2.00	3.50	8.50	20.00
	1888	1.887	1.00	2.00	4.00	13.00
	1890	2.133	1.00	2.00	4.00	13.00
	1890	—	—	—	Proof	500.00
	1891	4.960	.75	1.50	3.00	13.00
	1891	—	—	—	Proof	400.00
	1892	.887	3.50	9.50	26.00	60.00
	1892	—	—	—	Proof	500.00
	1893	3.904	.75	1.50	3.00	12.00
	1894	2.397	1.00	1.50	3.00	13.00
	1895	2.853	10.00	20.00	45.00	100.00

COPPER NICKEL (OMS)

Y#	Date	Mintage	Fine	VF	XF	Unc
16a	1868	—	—	—	Proof	600.00

SILVER (OMS)

Y#	Date	Mintage	Fine	VF	XF	Unc
16b	1861	—	—	—	Proof	1500.

GOLD (OMS)

Y#	Date	Mintage	Fine	VF	XF	Unc
16c	1861	—	—	—	Proof	—

BRONZE

Y#	Date	Mintage	Fine	VF	XF	Unc
32	1895	Inc. Ab.	.75	1.50	3.00	6.00
	1896	3.669	.75	1.50	3.00	6.00
	1896	—	—	—	Proof	400.00
	1897	4.580	.75	1.50	4.00	10.00

Blackened finish

Y#	Date	Mintage	Fine	VF	XF	Unc
	1897	Inc. Ab.	.50	1.00	3.00	7.50
	1898	4.010	.50	1.00	2.50	6.00
	1899	3.865	.50	1.00	2.00	6.00
	1900	5.969	.50	1.00	1.50	5.00
	1901	8.016	.50	1.00	1.50	4.00

Y#	Date	Mintage	Fine	VF	XF	Unc
46	1902	5.125	1.00	1.50	3.00	7.00
	1903	5.331	1.25	1.75	4.00	10.00
	1904	3.629	2.00	4.00	6.00	15.00
	1905	4.080	1.00	1.50	3.50	10.00
	1906	5.340	1.00	1.50	4.00	9.00
	1907	4.399	.75	1.25	3.00	9.00
	1908	4.265	1.00	1.75	2.50	9.00
	1909	8.852	.75	1.00	2.50	7.00
	1910	2.598	3.00	5.00	10.00	20.00

Y#	Date	Mintage	Fine	VF	XF	Unc
60	1911	5.197	.75	1.25	2.50	7.00
	1912	7.670	.35	.75	1.50	5.50
	1913	4.184	.65	1.00	2.00	5.00
	1914	6.127	.35	.75	1.75	5.00
	1915	7.129	.65	1.75	4.00	11.50
	1916	10.993	.35	.75	1.50	4.00
	1917	21.435	.15	.35	1.50	4.00
	1918	19.362	2.00	5.00	10.00	22.50

Bright finish

Y#	Date	Mintage	Fine	VF	XF	Unc
	1918	Inc. Ab.	.15	.35	.60	2.00

Y#	Date	Mintage	Fine	VF	XF	Unc
60	1919	15.089	.15	.35	.60	2.00
	1920	11.481	.15	.35	.75	2.50
	1921	9.469	.15	.35	.75	3.00
	1922	9.957	.35	.50	.75	2.50
	1923	8.034	.50	.65	1.00	3.00
	1924	8.733	.15	.35	.50	3.00
	1925	12.635	.15	.35	.50	3.00
	1926	9.792	.35	.75	1.00	3.50
	1926	—	—	—	Proof	125.00
	1927	7.868	.15	.35	.60	3.00
	1927	—	—	—	Proof	125.00
	1928	11.625	.15	.35	.50	2.50
	1928	—	—	—	Proof	125.00
	1929	8.419	.15	.35	.60	1.50
	1929	—	—	—	Proof	125.00
	1930	4.195	.15	.35	.60	2.50
	1930	—	—	—	Proof	125.00
	1931	6.595	.15	.35	.60	2.50
	1931	—	—	—	Proof	125.00
	1932	9.293	.15	.25	.60	2.00
	1932	—	—	—	Proof	125.00
	1933	4.560	.15	.35	.50	2.00
	1933	—	—	—	Proof	125.00
	1934	3.053	.35	1.00	1.50	4.00
	1934	—	—	—	Proof	125.00
	1935	2.227	1.00	2.00	3.00	7.00
	1935	—	—	—	Proof	180.00
	1936	9.734	.10	.20	.75	2.50
	1936	—	—	—	Proof	180.00

Y#	Date	Mintage	Fine	VF	XF	Unc
82	1937	8.131	.15	.35	.65	2.00
	1937	.026	—	—	Proof	4.00
	1938	7.450	.20	.50	1.00	5.00
	1938	—	—	—	Proof	—
	1939	31.440	—	.25	.50	2.00
	1939	—	—	—	Proof	—
	1940	18.360	—	.15	.50	1.75
	1940	—	—	—	Proof	—
	1941	27.312	—	.25	.50	1.50
	1941	—	—	—	Proof	—
	1942	28.858	—	.25	.40	1.50
	1942	—	—	—	Proof	—
	1943	33.346	—	.25	.35	1.00
	1943	—	—	—	Proof	—
	1944	25.138	—	.25	.35	1.00
	1944	—	—	—	Proof	—
	1945	23.736	—	.25	.35	1.50
	1945	—	—	—	Proof	—
	1946	24.365	—	.25	.35	1.50
	1946	—	—	—	Proof	—
	1947	14.746	—	.25	.35	1.50
	1947	—	—	—	Proof	—
	1948	16.662	—	.15	.35	1.25
	1948	—	—	—	Proof	—

Obv. leg: IND IMP omitted

Y#	Date	Mintage	Fine	VF	XF	Unc
104	1949	8.424	—	.15	.25	1.25
	1949	—	—	—	Proof	—
	1950	10.325	—	.15	.25	1.25
	1950	.018	—	—	Proof	5.00
	1951	14.016	—	.25	.30	1.00
	1951	.020	—	—	Proof	5.00
	1952	5.251	.10	.25	.30	1.25
	1952	—	—	—	Proof	—

Y#	Date	Mintage	Fine	VF	XF	Unc
116	1953	6.109	.25	.50	.75	1.50
	1953	.040	—	—	Proof	3.50

Obv. leg: BRITT OMN omitted

Y#	Date	Mintage	Fine	VF	XF	Unc
127	1954	6.566	.15	.25	.35	1.50
	1954	—	—	—	Proof	—
	1955	5.779	.15	.25	.35	1.50
	1955	—	—	—	Proof	—
	1956	1.997	.50	.75	1.50	4.00
	1956	—	—	—	Proof	—

1/2 PENNY

C#	Date	Mintage	Fine	VF	XF	Unc
18	1770	—	3.50	17.50	45.00	75.00
	1770	—	—	—	Proof	175.00
	1771	*	3.50	15.00	40.00	70.00
	1772 w/o stop on reverse					
		—	4.50	17.50	27.50	80.00
	1772 GEORIVS					
		—	10.00	35.00	60.00	125.00
	1773	—	3.00	15.00	35.00	70.00
	1773 w/o stop after rex					
		—	4.50	17.50	27.50	70.00
	1773 w/o stop on reverse					
		—	4.50	17.50	40.00	75.00
	1774	—	4.50	15.00	40.00	70.00
	1775	—	4.50	17.50	45.00	80.00

NOTE: Contemporary counterfeits of C#18, especially 1770 and 1775, are very common. The counterfeits vary in quality, but most are somewhat smaller, thinner, and more crudely designed than the genuine.

***NOTE:** Die varieties exist.

SILVER

C#	Date	Mintage	Fine	VF	XF	Unc
18a	1770	—	—	—	Proof	—

C#	Date	Mintage	Fine	VF	XF	Unc
19	1799 w/ 5 incuse gunports					
		—	2.00	7.50	15.00	40.00
	1799 w/ 6 relief gunports					
		—	3.00	9.00	17.50	45.00
	1799 w/ 9 relief gunports					
		—	3.75	10.00	25.00	65.00
	1799 plain hull					
		—	3.00	7.50	15.00	30.00
	1799 w/ raised line along hull					
		—	4.50	9.00	20.00	45.00
	1799	—	—	—	Proof	150.00

C#	Date	Mintage	Fine	VF	XF	Unc
20	1806	—	1.50	4.50	15.00	35.00
	1806	—	—	—	Proof	150.00
	1807	—	2.25	6.00	17.50	35.00

C#	Date	Mintage	Fine	VF	XF	Unc
53	1825	.215	8.00	20.00	70.00	100.00
	1825	—	—	—	Proof	300.00
	1826	9.032	3.00	6.00	25.00	65.00
	1826	—	—	—	Proof	175.00
	1827	5.376	3.00	9.00	25.00	60.00

BRONZED COPPER

C#	Date	Mintage	Fine	VF	XF	Unc
53a	1826	—	—	—	Proof	125.00

COPPER

C#	Date	Mintage	Fine	VF	XF	Unc
72	1831	.806	2.50	8.50	30.00	80.00
	1834	.538	2.50	8.50	30.00	80.00
	1837	.349	2.25	7.50	27.50	70.00

BRONZED COPPER

C#	Date	Mintage	Fine	VF	XF	Unc
72a	1831	—	—	—	Proof	125.00

COPPER

Y#	Date	Mintage	Fine	VF	XF	Unc
2	1838	.460	1.00	5.00	12.00	25.00
	1839	—	—	Proof Only		200.00
	1841	1.075	1.00	3.50	10.00	25.00
	1843	.968	5.00	12.00	40.00	90.00
	1844	1.075	2.00	6.00	20.00	50.00
	1845	1.075	35.00	70.00	175.00	400.00
	1846	.860	2.50	7.00	17.50	32.50
	1847	.753	2.50	10.00	25.00	60.00
	1848/7	.323	2.50	7.00	25.00	50.00
	1848	Inc. Ab.	2.50	8.00	30.00	65.00
	1851	.215	2.00	7.00	15.00	40.00
	1851 dots on shield					
		Inc. Ab.	1.50	5.00	15.00	35.00
	1852	.637	2.00	7.00	20.00	40.00
	1852 dots on shield					
		Inc. Ab.	1.25	8.00	20.00	35.00
	1853/2	1.559	4.50	15.00	40.00	90.00
	1853	Inc. Ab.	1.50	3.50	7.50	30.00
	1853	—	—	—	Proof	135.00
	1854	12.354	1.00	2.50	7.00	30.00
	1855	1.456	1.00	3.00	7.00	30.00
	1856	1.942	1.50	5.00	12.00	45.00
	1857	1.183	2.00	5.00	12.00	45.00
	1857 dots on shield					
		Inc. Ab.	1.00	4.00	15.00	35.00
	1858/6	2.473	3.00	15.00	35.00	70.00
	1858/7	Inc. Ab.	2.00	6.00	15.00	35.00
	1858	Inc. Ab.	1.00	4.00	12.00	35.00
	1858 sm.date	—	1.50	6.00	15.00	37.50
	1859/8	1.290	5.00	12.50	27.50	75.00
	1859	Inc. Ab.	2.00	7.00	17.50	40.00
	1860	—	180.00	300.00	900.00	1800.

BRONZED COPPER (OMS)

Y#	Date	Mintage	Fine	VF	XF	Unc
2a	1839	—	—	—	Proof	160.00
	1841	—	—	—	Proof	—
	1853	—	—	—	Proof	—

SILVER (OMS)

Y#	Date	Mintage	Fine	VF	XF	Unc
2b	1841	—	—	—	Proof	—

BRONZE
Beaded border

Y#	Date	Mintage	Fine	VF	XF	Unc
17.1	1860	6.630	1.50	4.00	10.00	35.00
	1860	—	—	—	Proof	500.00
	1860 toothed/beaded border					
		1 Known	—	—	—	—

Toothed border

Y#	Date	Mintage	Fine	VF	XF	Unc
17.2	1860	Inc. Ab.	2.00	7.50	17.50	35.00
	1860 w/ 7 berries in wreath					
		Inc. Ab.	1.75	5.00	12.00	40.00
	1860 w/ 7 berries in wreath					
		—	—	—	Proof	500.00
	1860 w/7 berries in wreath; rd.top lighthouse					
		Inc. Ab.	10.00	25.00	70.00	250.00
	1860 w/5 berries in wreath					
		Inc. Ab.	5.00	12.00	35.00	100.00
	1860 w/4 berries in wreath					
		Inc. Ab.	2.00	5.00	12.00	40.00
	1860 w/4 berries in wreath; rd.top lighthouse					
		Inc. Ab.	5.00	12.00	35.00	100.00
	1861/81	54.118	—	—	Rare	—
	1861	Inc. Ab.	1.25	3.00	10.00	30.00
	1861	—	—	—	Proof	300.00
	1861 w/5 berries in wreath L.C.W. on rock					
		Inc. Ab.	10.00	25.00	70.00	250.00
	1861 w/4 berries in wreath L.C.W. on rock					
		Inc. Ab.	1.25	3.00	12.50	45.00
	1861 w/4 berries in wreath L.C.W. on rock					
		—	—	—	Proof	550.00
	1861 w/4 berries in wreath					
		—	1.00	2.00	6.00	17.50
	1861 w/L.C.W. on rock					
		Inc. Ab.	1.00	2.00	6.00	17.50
	1861 w/HALF over HALP					
		Inc. Ab.	20.00	60.00	150.00	400.00
	1862 w/L.C.W. on rock, B to left of lighthouse					
		—	75.00	150.00	500.00	1250.
	1862 w/C to left of lighthouse					
		—	75.00	150.00	500.00	1250.
	1862 w/A to left of lighthouse					
		—	50.00	100.00	300.00	900.00
	1862	—	—	—	Proof	450.00
	1862	61.107	1.00	2.50	6.00	17.50
	1862L.C.W.	Inc. Ab.	4.00	10.00	20.00	60.00
	1863	15.950	2.00	4.50	12.00	27.50
	1863 sm.3	I.A.	2.00	5.00	12.50	30.00
	1863 sm.3	—	—	—	Proof	450.00
	1863 lg.3	I.A.	1.75	5.00	12.50	30.00
	1864	.538	3.00	10.00	25.00	70.00
	1865/3	8.064	30.00	80.00	200.00	500.00
	1865	Inc. Ab.	3.00	9.00	25.00	70.00
	1866	2.509	2.00	7.50	20.00	45.00
	1866	—	—	—	Proof	450.00
	1867	2.509	3.00	15.00	30.00	90.00
	1867	—	—	—	Proof	500.00
	1868	3.046	2.00	10.00	25.00	75.00
	1868	—	—	—	Proof	250.00
	1869	3.226	6.00	30.00	65.00	180.00
	1870	4.351	3.00	8.50	25.00	75.00
	1871	1.075	20.00	40.00	125.00	300.00
	1872	4.659	2.00	8.00	20.00	45.00
	1873	3.405	2.50	12.00	30.00	80.00
	1874 w/6 berries in wreath; large date					
		1.348	10.00	30.00	60.00	150.00
	1874 w/6 berries in wreath; small date					
		Inc. Ab.	—	18.00	30.00	70.00
	1874 obv. of 1873, wreath w/5 berries					
		Inc. Ab.	3.50	20.00	35.00	85.00
	1874 obv. 1874,wr. w/4 berries;lg.dt.as 1873					
		Inc. Ab.	3.50	20.00	40.00	100.00
	1874H w/6 berries in wreath; sm.dt.					
		5.018	2.00	5.50	10.00	27.50
	1874H	—	—	—	Proof	450.00
	1874H w/6 berries in wr.;sm.dt. hvy.plan.					
		1 known	—	—	—	—
	1875	5.431	1.25	5.00	10.00	30.00
	1875H	1.254	3.25	12.00	27.50	60.00
	1875H	—	—	—	Proof	550.00
	1876H lg.date					
		6.810	3.50	8.00	15.00	40.00
	1876H sm.dt.	I.A.	2.00	5.50	10.00	30.00
	1876H sm.date	—	—	—	Proof	550.00
	1876H sm.date heavy planchet					
		—	25.00	80.00	200.00	550.00
	1877	5.210	2.00	8.50	20.00	35.00

Y#	Date	Mintage	Fine	VF	XF	Unc
17.2	1877	—	—	—	Proof	450.00
	1878 sm.date					
		1.426	3.50	25.00	50.00	100.00
	1878 sm.date	—	—	—	Proof	450.00
	1878 lg.date	I.A.	35.00	100.00	300.00	800.00
	1878 lg.date	—	—	—	Proof	1000.
	1879	3.583	2.00	4.00	12.50	27.50
	1880	2.423	2.00	6.00	17.50	35.00
	1880	—	—	—	Proof	550.00
	1881 similar to 1880					
		2.008	1.75	6.00	14.00	35.00
	1881 shield heraldically colored					
		—	—	Proof Only		750.00
	1881 shield heraldically colored, broach on bust					
		2 known	—	Proof Only		1500.
	1881H	1.792	1.50	5.50	15.00	35.00
	1882H	4.480	1.50	4.50	12.00	30.00
	1882H different dies	—	—	—	Proof	900.00
	1883 rose on front of dress					
		3.001	4.00	12.00	25.00	70.00
	1883 rose on front of dress					
		—	—	—	Proof	550.00
	1883 broach on front of dress					
		Inc. Ab.	1.75	5.50	12.00	37.50
	1884	6.990	1.25	3.50	10.00	30.00
	1884	—	—	—	Proof	500.00
	1885	8.601	1.00	3.50	8.50	30.00
	1885	—	—	—	Proof	500.00
	1886	8.586	1.00	3.00	7.50	35.00
	1886	—	—	—	Proof	110.00
	1887	10.701	1.00	2.50	7.50	30.00
	1888	6.814	1.00	2.50	7.00	30.00
	1889/8	7.748	17.50	65.00	140.00	325.00
	1889/8	1 known			Proof	—
	1889	Inc. Ab.	1.00	2.50	8.00	30.00
	1890	11.254	1.00	2.50	5.00	25.00
	1890	—	—	—	Proof	425.00
	1891	13.192	1.00	2.50	6.00	20.00
	1891	—	—	—	Proof	400.00
	1892	2.478	1.75	5.00	15.00	40.00
	1892	—	—	—	Proof	500.00
	1893	7.229	1.00	3.00	7.00	20.00
	1894	1.768	1.75	5.00	15.00	40.00

SILVER (OMS)

Y#	Date	Mintage	Fine	VF	XF	Unc
17c	1861	—	—	—	Proof	1500.

COPPER NICKEL (OMS)

Y#	Date	Mintage	Fine	VF	XF	Unc
17d	1861	—	—	—	Proof	650.00
	1868	—	—	—	Proof	325.00

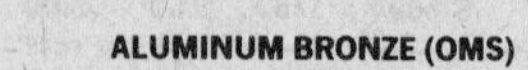

ALUMINUM BRONZE (OMS)

Y#	Date	Mintage	Fine	VF	XF	Unc
17e	1861	—	—	—	Proof	900.00

GOLD (OMS)

Y#	Date	Mintage	Fine	VF	XF	Unc
17f	1861	Unique	—	—	Proof	—

BRASS (OMS)

Y#	Date	Mintage	Fine	VF	XF	Unc
17g	1872	Unique	—	—	Proof	—

Obv. leg: IND IMP omitted
BRONZE

Y#	Date	Mintage	Fine	VF	XF	Unc
33	1895	3.032	1.00	1.75	5.50	11.50
	1895	—	—	—	Proof	500.00
	1896	9.143	1.00	1.50	6.00	10.00
	1896	—	—	—	Proof	500.00
	1897	8.690	1.00	1.75	7.00	15.00
	1897 high sea level					
		Inc. Ab.	—	1.25	4.00	9.00
	1898	8.595	1.00	2.00	7.00	15.00
	1899	12.108	1.00	1.50	5.00	9.00
	1900	13.805	1.00	2.00	4.00	7.00
	1901	11.127	.50	1.50	3.00	6.00
	1901	—	—	—	Proof	500.00

Rev: Low horizon

Y#	Date	Mintage	Fine	VF	XF	Unc
47	1902	13.673	10.00	20.00	45.00	100.00

Rev: High horizon

Y#	Date	Mintage	Fine	VF	XF	Unc
	1902	Inc. Ab.	.75	2.00	5.00	12.00
	1903	11.451	.75	2.00	6.00	17.50
	1904	8.131	1.25	4.00	9.00	22.50
	1905	10.125	.75	2.00	5.00	14.00
	1906	11.101	.75	2.00	5.00	14.00
	1907	16.849	.75	2.00	5.00	14.00
	1908	16.621	.75	2.00	6.00	15.00
	1909	8.279	.75	3.00	7.50	20.00
	1910	10.770	1.00	2.50	5.00	13.50

Y#	Date	Mintage	Fine	VF	XF	Unc
61	1911	12.571	.75	2.00	4.00	10.00
	1912	21.186	.65	1.50	4.00	10.00
	1913	17.476	.75	2.50	6.00	14.50
	1914	20.289	.65	2.00	5.00	10.00
	1915	21.563	1.00	1.75	7.00	13.50
	1916	39.386	.65	1.00	4.50	10.00
	1917	38.245	.75	1.00	4.50	10.00
	1918	22.321	.65	1.25	4.50	10.00
	1919	28.104	.45	1.25	4.50	8.50
	Obv: Modified effigy					
	1920	35.147	.15	1.00	3.00	8.50
	1921	28.027	.35	2.00	3.00	8.50
	1922	10.735	.35	2.75	6.00	12.50
	1923	12.266	.50	1.50	3.00	8.50
	1924	13.971	.35	1.25	3.00	10.00
	1925 obv. of 1924	12.216	.65	2.00	6.00	13.50
	1925 obv. of 1926	Inc. Ab.	.75	3.00	8.50	22.50
	1926	6.712	.65	2.00	6.00	12.50
	1926	—	—	—	Proof	90.00
	1927	15.590	.15	1.50	4.00	10.00
	1927	—	—	—	Proof	80.00

Obv: Smaller head

Y#	Date	Mintage	Fine	VF	XF	Unc
62	1928	20.935	.35	.85	2.50	6.00
	1928	—	—	—	Proof	85.00
	1929	25.680	.35	1.00	3.00	6.00
	1929	—	—	—	Proof	85.00
	1930	12.533	.15	.60	3.00	6.00
	1930	—	—	—	Proof	85.00
	1931	16.138	.15	.50	2.50	6.00
	1931	—	—	—	Proof	85.00
	1932	14.448	.15	.60	3.00	7.00
	1932	—	—	—	Proof	85.00
	1933	10.560	.35	.65	3.00	7.50
	1933	—	—	—	Proof	85.00
	1934	7.704	.15	1.75	6.00	12.00
	1934	—	—	—	Proof	85.00
	1935	12.180	.35	.75	3.50	7.00
	1935	—	—	—	Proof	85.00
	1936	19.807	.35	.60	2.00	5.00
	1936	—	—	—	Proof	100.00

Y#	Date	Mintage	Fine	VF	XF	Unc
83	1937	27.706	.10	.20	1.25	2.75
	1937	.026	—	—	Proof	6.00
	1938	40.320	.10	.25	1.00	3.50
	1938	—	—	—	Proof	—
	1939	28.925	.10	.25	2.00	5.00
	1939	—	—	—	Proof	—
	1940	32.162	.15	.35	2.00	7.00
	1940	—	—	—	Proof	—
	1941	45.120	—	.15	1.00	6.00
	1941	—	—	—	Proof	—
	1942	71.909	—	.10	.75	2.50
	1942	—	—	—	Proof	—
	1943	76.200	—	.10	1.00	2.75
	1943	—	—	—	Proof	—
	1944	81.480	—	.10	.50	3.00
	1944	—	—	—	Proof	—
	1945	57.000	—	.10	.75	2.50
	1945	—	—	—	Proof	—
	1946	22.726	—	.50	4.00	8.00
	1946	—	—	—	Proof	—

Y#	Date	Mintage	Fine	VF	XF	Unc
83	1947	27.266	.10	.25	3.00	7.00
	1947	—	—	—	Proof	—
	1948	26.947	—	.10	.75	2.00
	1948	—	—	—	Proof	—

Obv. leg: IND IMP omitted

Y#	Date	Mintage	Fine	VF	XF	Unc
105	1949	24.744	—	.10	.50	3.50
	1950	24.154	—	.10	1.50	6.00
	1950	.018	—	—	Proof	7.00
	1951	18.869	.15	.35	2.00	8.00
	1951	.020	—	—	Proof	8.00
	1952	33.278	—	.10	.75	3.00
	1952	—	—	—	Proof	—

Y#	Date	Mintage	Fine	VF	XF	Unc
117	1953	8.910	.10	.25	1.50	4.00
	1953	.040	—	—	Proof	6.00

Obv. leg: BRITT OMN omitted

Y#	Date	Mintage	Fine	VF	XF	Unc
128	1954	17.375	.15	.40	1.25	6.00
	1954	—	—	—	Proof	—
	1955	21.799	.15	.40	1.25	5.00
	1955	—	—	—	Proof	—
	1956	21.799	.10	.30	1.25	6.00
	1956	—	—	—	Proof	—
	1957	39.672	—	.10	.35	2.00
	1957	—	—	—	Proof	—
	1958	66.283	—	—	.10	.50
	1958	—	—	—	Proof	—
	1959	79.224	—	—	.10	.50
	1959	—	—	—	Proof	—
	1960	41.340	—	—	.10	.25
	1960	—	—	—	Proof	—
	1962	41.340	—	—	.10	.25
	1962	—	—	—	Proof	—
	1963	44.766	—	—	.10	.25
	1963	—	—	—	Proof	—
	1964	72.134	—	—	.10	.25
	1965	105.965	—	—	.10	.25
	1966	96.082	—	—	.10	.25
	1967	100.000	—	—	.10	.25
	1970	.731	—	Proof Only		2.00

PENNY

.925 SILVER

C#	Date	Mintage	Fine	VF	XF	Unc
24	1763	—	6.50	12.50	17.50	45.00
	1763	—	—	—	Proof	—
	1765	1 Known	—	—	Rare	—
	1766	—	6.50	10.00	20.00	45.00
	1770	—	6.50	10.00	20.00	45.00
	1772	—	6.50	10.00	20.00	45.00
	1776	—	6.50	12.50	22.50	50.00
	1779	—	6.50	10.00	20.00	45.00
	1780	—	6.00	10.00	20.00	45.00
	1781	—	6.00	10.00	17.50	45.00
	1784	—	6.00	10.00	20.00	45.00
	1786	—	6.00	10.00	20.00	45.00
	Obv: Older bust					
24a	1792	—	7.50	12.50	20.00	45.00

C#	Date	Mintage	Fine	VF	XF	Unc
24b	1795	—	5.00	10.00	15.00	30.00
	1800	—	4.00	8.50	12.50	20.00

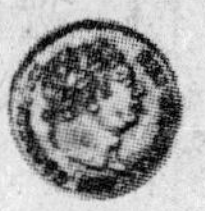

C#	Date	Mintage	Fine	VF	XF	Unc
24c	1817	—	4.00	12.50	17.50	35.00
	1818	—	4.00	12.50	17.50	35.00
	1820	—	4.00	12.50	17.50	35.00

NOTE: Later dates included in Maundy Sets.

COPPER

C#	Date	Mintage	Fine	VF	XF	Unc
21	1797	—	8.00	25.00	85.00	175.00
	1797	—	—	—	Proof	225.00

C#	Date	Mintage	Fine	VF	XF	Unc
22	1806	—	3.50	8.50	30.00	70.00
	1806	—	—	—	Proof	—
	1807	—	4.00	12.50	35.00	75.00
	1808	Unique	—	—	—	—

C#	Date	Mintage	Fine	VF	XF	Unc
54	1825	1.075	4.50	12.00	40.00	85.00
	1825	—	—	—	Proof	300.00
	1826	5.913	3.00	10.00	30.00	75.00
	1826	—	—	—	Proof	250.00
	1827	1.452	40.00	100.00	450.00	750.00

BRONZED COPPER

C#	Date	Mintage	Fine	VF	XF	Unc
54a	1826	—	—	—	Proof	—

COPPER
Rev: Similar to C#54

C#	Date	Mintage	Fine	VF	XF	Unc
73	1831	.806	5.00	22.50	60.00	150.00
	1831 W/ .W.W Incuse On Truncation					
		Inc.Ab.	5.00	22.50	60.00	165.00
	1831 W/ .W.W Incuse On Truncation					
		Inc.Ab.	5.00	25.00	65.00	175.00
	1834	.323	6.00	27.50	80.00	175.00
	1837	.175	10.00	40.00	125.00	225.00

BRONZED COPPER

C#	Date	Mintage	Fine	VF	XF	Unc
73a	1831	—	—	—	Proof	225.00

COPPER
Rev: Similar to C#54

Y#	Date	Mintage	Fine	VF	XF	Unc
3	1839	—	—	Bronzed	Proof	300.00
	1841 REG:	.914	8.00	25.00	50.00	125.00
	1841	—	—	—	Proof	185.00
	1841 w/o colon after REG					
		Inc. Ab.	3.00	7.50	20.00	60.00
	1843 REG:	.484	12.00	55.00	175.00	300.00
	1843 w/o colon after REG					
		Inc. Ab.	20.00	55.00	200.00	375.00
	1844	.215	3.50	10.00	22.50	60.00
	1844	—	—	—	Proof	—
	1845	.323	5.00	15.00	50.00	85.00
	1846	.484	3.50	12.00	35.00	50.00
	1847	.430	3.50	10.00	20.00	50.00
	1848/6	.161	10.00	35.00	90.00	140.00
	1848/7	Inc. Ab.	3.00	10.00	25.00	50.00
	1848	Inc. Ab.	4.25	10.00	22.50	50.00
	1849	.269	40.00	100.00	250.00	400.00
	1851	.432	4.75	12.00	25.00	60.00
	1853	1.021	3.00	5.00	10.00	45.00
	1853	—	—	—	Proof	185.00
	1854/3	6.720	17.50	60.00	125.00	300.00
	1854	Inc. Ab.	3.00	5.00	12.00	40.00
	1855	5.274	3.00	5.00	12.00	40.00
	1856	1.212	8.50	30.00	75.00	200.00
	1856	—	—	—	Proof	250.00
	1857 lg.date					
		.753	3.00	6.00	12.00	55.00
	1857 sm. date					
		Inc.Ab.	2.00	6.00	12.00	30.00
	1858/3	Inc.Ab.	8.00	30.00	60.00	140.00
	1858/6	Inc.Ab.	13.00	45.00	75.00	225.00
	1858/7	Inc.Ab.	3.00	7.25	15.00	50.00
	1858 large date					

Y#	Date	Mintage	Fine	VF	XF	Unc
3		1.559	2.00	5.00	10.00	35.00
	1858 small date					
		Inc. Ab.	3.00	7.50	15.00	50.00
	1859	1.075	3.00	10.00	18.00	45.00
	1859	—	—	—	Proof	—
	1860/59	.032	125.00	250.00	400.00	1000.

NOTE: 1833-1857 occur w/ plain and ornamental trident.

BRONZED COPPER

Y#	Date	Mintage	Fine	VF	XF	Unc
3a	1839	—	—	—	Proof	—
	1841	—	—	—	Proof	—
	1853	—	—	—	Proof	—

SILVER

Y#	Date	Mintage	Fine	VF	XF	Unc
3b	1841	—	—	—	Proof	—

BRONZE

Y#	Date	Mintage	Fine	VF	XF	Unc
18	1860 beaded border; raised lines on shield					
		5.053	3.50	10.00	30.00	80.00
	1860 beaded border; raised lines on shield					
		—	—	—	Proof	400.00
	1860 beaded border; raised lines on shield, extra thick flan			—	Proof	900.00
	1860 beaded border; incuse lines on shield					
		Inc. Ab.	1.50	8.00	20.00	80.00
	1860 beaded border; incuse lines on shield					
		—	—	—	Proof	800.00
	1860 beaded border/toothed border					
		Inc. Ab.	50.00	150.00	300.00	900.00
	1860 toothed border/beaded border					
		Inc. Ab.	50.00	150.00	300.00	900.00
	1860 toothed border, L.C.W. below foot, L.C.WYON on shoulder					
		Inc. Ab.	8.50	40.00	150.00	375.00
	1860 toothed border, L.C.W. below shield, L.C.WYON below shoulder					
		Inc. Ab.	3.50	10.00	25.00	65.00
	1860 toothed border, L.C.WYON on shoulder, L.C.W. below shield					
		Inc. Ab.	2.00	8.00	25.00	80.00
	1860 toothed border, L.C.WYON on shoulder, L.C.W. below shield			—	Proof	400.00
	1860 toothed border, w/o obv. sign., 15 leaves					
		—	2.50	10.00	35.00	85.00
	1860 toothed border, w/o obv. sign., 16 leaves					
		—	—	20.00	65.00	150.00
	1861 L.C.WYON on trunc.; L.C.W. below shield					
		—	6.50	25.00	60.00	200.00
	1861 L.C.WYON on trunc., w/o sign. on rev.					
		—	4.50	18.00	40.00	115.00
	1861 L.C.WYON below trunc. L.C.W. below shield					
		—	1.75	7.00	18.00	50.00
	1861 L.C.WYON below trunc., w/o sign. on rev.					
		—	18.00	40.00	100.00	300.00
	1861 w/o obv. sign., 15 lvs. L.C.W. below shield					
		—	1.75	7.00	18.00	50.00
	1861 w/o obv. sign., 15 leaves w/o rev. sign.					
		—	50.00	150.00	300.00	1000.
	1861 w/o obv. sign., 16 lvs. L.C.W. below shield					
		—	1.25	5.00	12.00	32.50
	1861 w/o obv. sign., 16 lvs. L.C.W. below shield					
		—	—	—	Proof	600.00
	1861/81 w/o obv. sign., 16 lvs. L.C.W. below shield	—	50.00	150.00	300.00	1000.
	1861 w/o obv. sign., 16 leaves, w/o rev. sign.					
		—	1.25	4.50	11.00	30.00
	1861 w/o obv. sign., 16 leaves, w/o rev. sign.					
		—	—	—	Proof	500.00
	1862/1662	—	50.00	150.00	300.00	1000.
	1862	—	—	—	Proof	600.00
	1862 L.C.WYON on shoulder w/o rev. sign.					
		—	350.00	1000.	2500.	6000.
	1862 w/o sign. on obv.					
		—	2.00	5.50	15.00	35.00
	1862 date numerals small, from 1/2 penny die					
		—	15.00	40.00	100.00	200.00
	1863 normal 3		2.00	6.00	17.50	40.00
	1863 normal 3		—	—	Proof	600.00
	1863 normal 3, w/2, 3, or 4 below date					
		—	60.00	100.00	200.00	500.00
	1864 w/plain 4 in date					
		3.441	12.50	30.00	125.00	350.00
	1864 w/crosslet 4 in date					
		Inc. Ab.	15.00	50.00	150.00	400.00
	1865/3	8.602	17.50	75.00	200.00	450.00
	1865	Inc. Ab.	7.50	15.00	30.00	80.00
	1866	9.999	2.00	7.00	25.00	60.00

Y#	Date	Mintage	Fine	VF	XF	Unc
18	1867	5.484	3.50	17.50	35.00	80.00
	1867	—	—	—	Proof	700.00
	1868	1.183	6.00	25.00	75.00	225.00
	1868	Inc. Ab.	—	—	Proof	400.00
	1869	2.580	40.00	125.00	325.00	650.00
	1870	5.695	3.50	17.50	50.00	150.00
	1871	1.290	15.00	60.00	150.00	350.00
	1872	8.495	2.50	8.00	20.00	50.00
	1872 rev. upside down					
		Unique	—	—	Proof	—
	1873	8.494	2.50	7.00	20.00	45.00
	1874 obv. and rev. as on 1873					
		5.622	3.50	10.00	22.50	60.00
	1874 obv. as 1873, 16 lvs.; new rev., sm.dt.					
		—	8.00	20.00	40.00	75.00
	1874 new obv.,17 lvs.,tn ribbs.; rev.as 1873					
		—	2.50	10.00	25.00	60.00
	1874 new obv.,17 lvs.,tn.ribs. new rev.,sm.dt.	—	3.50	13.00	30.00	70.00
	1874 new obv.,17 lvs., tk.ribbs. rev.as 1873					
		—	10.00	40.00	120.00	350.00
	1874 new obv.,17 lvs.,tk. ribbs.,new rev.,sm.dt.		2.50	6.00	30.00	60.00
	1874H obv. and rev. as on 1873					
		5.622	2.50	6.00	30.00	60.00
	1874H obv. as 1873, 16 lvs.; new rev., lg.dt.	—	4.00	10.00	35.00	60.00
	1874H new obv.,17 lvs.,tn.ribbs.; rev. as 1873					
		—	2.50	6.00	30.00	60.00
	1874H new obv.,17 lvs.,tn. ribbs.; new rev. sm. dt.	—	2.50	6.00	15.00	45.00
	1874H new obv.,17 lvs.,tn.ribs.,new rev. sm.dt.		—	—	Proof	500.00
	1874H new obv.,17 lvs.,tn.ribs.,new rev. lg.dt.		20.00	70.00	240.00	800.00
	1875 rev. as 1873					
		10.691	8.50	35.00	140.00	325.00
	1875 new rev. small date					
		Inc. Ab.	2.50	9.00	22.50	55.00
	1875 new rev. large date					
		Inc. Ab.	2.50	8.00	20.00	50.00
	1875 new rev. lg.dt., hvy. planchet					
		Unique	—	—	Proof	—
	1875H new rev. small date					
		.753	150.00	400.00	1000.	2500.
	1875H new rev. large date					
		Inc. Ab.	15.00	60.00	200.00	550.00
	1875H new rev. large date					
		—	—	—	Proof	1000.
	1876H large date					
		11.075	4.00	15.00	35.00	85.00
	1876H large date					
		Inc. Ab.	—	—	Proof	700.00
	1876H small date					
		Inc. Ab.	3.00	8.00	15.00	40.00
	1877 small date					
		9.625	175.00	550.00	1500.	3000.
	1877 large date					
		Inc. Ab.	3.00	8.00	15.00	40.00
	1877 lg. date		—	—	Proof	700.00
	1878	2.764	4.00	17.50	40.00	100.00
	1878	—	—	—	Proof	700.00
	1879 lg.dt.; raised lines on wreath					
		7.666	6.50	25.00	110.00	275.00
	1879 lg.dt.; incuse lines in wreath					
		—	3.00	8.00	15.00	40.00
	1879 lg.dt., incuse lines in wreath					
		Unique	—	—	Proof	—
	1879 sm.dt.		7.50	30.00	135.00	325.00
	1880	3.001	3.00	18.50	40.00	90.00
	1880	—	—	—	Proof	675.00
	1880 rock to left of lighthouse					
		—	5.00	20.00	45.00	100.00
	1880 obv. 15 leaves as 1881					
		1 known	—	—	Proof	Rare
	1881	2.302	3.00	15.00	35.00	100.00
	1881	—	—	—	Proof	225.00
	1881 obv. as 1880; shld. heraldically colored	I.A.	150.00	400.00	1000.	3000.
	1881 obv. as 1880; shld. heraldically colored	I.A.	—	—	Proof	—
	1881 obv. and rev. as 1880					
		Inc. Ab.	5.00	20.00	50.00	115.00
	1881 shield heraldically colored					
		—	—	—	Proof	1400.
	1881	Inc. Ab.	7.00	20.00	45.00	100.00
	1881	—	—	—	Proof	225.00
	1881H obv: 15 leaves in wreath					
		3.763	3.00	8.00	18.00	45.00
	1881H obv: 15 leaves in wreath					
		—	—	—	Proof	1000.
	1882H convex shield					
		7.526	5.00	20.00	45.00	100.00
	1882H flat shield					
		Inc. Ab.	3.00	7.00	17.50	40.00

Y#	Date	Mintage	Fine	VF	XF	Unc
	1882H	—	—	—	Proof	1300.
	1882	Inc. Ab.	30.00	100.00	300.00	550.00
	1883	6.237	2.00	7.00	15.00	40.00
	1883	—	—	—	Proof	700.00
	1884	11.703	1.50	4.00	15.00	35.00
	1884	—	—	—	Proof	700.00
	1885	7.146	1.50	6.00	15.00	35.00
	1885	—	—	—	Proof	700.00
	1886	6.088	1.00	5.00	11.00	30.00
	1886	—	—	—	Proof	900.00
	1887	5.315	1.25	5.00	12.50	30.00
	1888	7.146	1.25	5.00	12.50	27.50
	1889	12.560	1.25	5.00	15.00	32.50
	1889 14 leaves in wreath	—	1.25	4.00	10.00	25.00
	1889 14 leaves in wreath	—	—	—	Proof	900.00
	1890	15.331	1.00	4.00	10.00	22.50
	1890	—	—	—	Proof	650.00
	1891	17.886	2.00	4.00	10.00	22.50
	1891	—	—	—	Proof	650.00
	1892	10.502	1.00	4.00	12.00	27.50
	1892	—	—	—	Proof	650.00
	1893	8.162	1.00	4.00	10.00	27.50
	1893	—	—	—	Proof	900.00
	1894	3.883	3.00	10.00	25.00	45.00

COPPER, heavy planchet

Y#	Date	Mintage	Fine	VF	XF	Unc
18a	1860 toothed border, L.C.W. on truncation	—	—	—	Proof	400.00
	1861 L.C.WYON below truncation, L.C.W. below shield	—	—	—	Proof	500.00

COPPER-NICKEL

Y#	Date	Mintage	Fine	VF	XF	Unc
18b	1868	—	—	—	Proof	800.00
	1875	—	—	—	Proof	2100.
	1877	—	—	—	Proof	2300.

SILVER

Y#	Date	Mintage	Fine	VF	XF	Unc
18c	1860	—	—	—	Proof	4000.
	1861	—	—	—	Proof	4000.

GOLD

Y#	Date	Mintage	Fine	VF	XF	Unc
18d	1860	Unique	—	—	Proof	—
	1861	Unique	—	—	Proof	—

BRONZE

Rev: Without sea behind Britannia

Y#	Date	Mintage	Fine	VF	XF	Unc
34	1895	5.396	8.00	20.00	100.00	275.00
	1895	Inc. Ab.	—	—	Proof	325.00
	1895 P 2mm. from trident	—	6.50	25.00	150.00	275.00
	1895 P 2mm. from trident	—	—	—	Proof	875.00
	1895 P 1mm. from trident	—	.75	3.00	7.00	15.00
	1895 P 1mm. from trident	—	—	—	Proof	675.00
	1896	24.147	.35	1.25	5.00	11.00
	1896	—	—	—	Proof	650.00
	1897 normal sea level	20.757	.35	1.00	4.00	10.00
	1897 normal sea level	—	—	—	Proof	750.00
	1897 high sea level	—	4.00	20.00	75.00	150.00
	1898	14.297	.50	2.50	7.50	15.00
	1899	26.441	.50	1.50	4.00	8.50
	1900	31.778	.75	1.50	3.50	7.50
	1901	22.206	.45	1.00	2.50	7.00
	1901	—	—	—	Proof	500.00

Y#	Date	Mintage	Fine	VF	XF	Unc
48	1902 sea level as 1901	22.977	2.00	10.00	25.00	70.00
48	1902 high sea level	Inc. Ab.	.50	2.00	5.00	11.50
	1903	21.414	.45	3.00	7.50	17.00
	1904	12.913	1.00	5.00	10.00	22.50
	1905	17.784	.75	3.00	12.50	18.50
	1906	37.990	.75	3.00	10.00	17.50
	1907	47.322	.35	3.00	6.00	15.00
	1908	31.506	.75	3.00	7.50	25.00
	1908	—	—	—	Proof	Rare
	1909	19.617	.75	3.00	10.00	20.00
	1910	29.549	.35	2.00	6.00	17.50

Y#	Date	Mintage	Fine	VF	XF	Unc
63	1911	23.079	.50	1.00	5.00	13.50
	1912	48.306	.50	1.00	6.00	13.50
	1912H	16.800	.75	3.00	20.00	45.00
	1913	65.497	.35	1.00	6.50	25.00
	1914	50.821	.35	1.00	6.50	16.50
	1915	47.311	.35	1.25	7.50	18.50
	1916	36.411	.35	1.00	5.00	15.00
	1917	107.905	.35	1.00	4.00	15.00
	1918	84.230	.15	1.00	6.00	15.00
	1918H	3.661	1.25	12.00	75.00	200.00
	1918KN	Inc. Ab.	3.00	17.50	100.00	275.00
	1919	113.761	.35	1.25	4.00	17.50
	1919H	5.210	1.25	10.00	75.00	175.00
	1919KN	Inc. Ab.	5.00	25.00	175.00	450.00
	1920	124.693	.35	.75	4.50	11.50
	1921	129.718	.35	.65	2.25	8.50
	1922	16.347	.60	2.00	8.50	27.50
	1922 rev. as 1927		50.00	100.00	200.00	500.00
	1926	4.499	.50	3.00	15.00	40.00
	1926	—	—	—	Proof	225.00

Obv: Modified head

Y#	Date	Mintage	Fine	VF	XF	Unc
	1926	Inc. Ab.	8.00	40.00	175.00	600.00
	1926	—	—	—	Proof	—
	1927	60.987	.35	.75	3.50	8.50
	1927	—	—	—	Proof	225.00

Obv: Smaller head

Y#	Date	Mintage	Fine	VF	XF	Unc
64	1928	50.178	.10	.50	2.25	6.50
	1928	—	—	—	Proof	200.00
	1929	49.132	.10	.50	2.00	6.00
	1929	—	—	—	Proof	200.00
	1930	29.098	.10	.50	4.00	10.00
	1930	—	—	—	Proof	200.00
	1931	19.843	.35	1.25	5.50	13.50
	1931	—	—	—	Proof	200.00
	1932	8.278	.50	2.50	12.00	40.00
	1932	—	—	—	Proof	200.00
	1933	8 Known	—	—	Rare	—
	1934	13.966	.35	1.50	10.00	17.50
	1934	—	—	—	Proof	200.00
	1935	56.070	.15	.50	1.50	4.50
	1935	—	—	—	Proof	200.00
	1936	134.160	.15	.35	1.00	4.00
	1936	—	—	—	Proof	200.00

Y#	Date	Mintage	Fine	VF	XF	Unc
84	1937	109.032	.10	.25	1.00	3.00
	1937	.026	—	—	Proof	12.00
	1938	121.560	.10	.35	1.50	4.00
	1938	—	—	—	Proof	—
	1939	55.560	.10	.50	2.25	5.50
	1939	—	—	—	Proof	—
	1940	42.284	.15	.85	2.25	15.00
	1940	—	—	—	Proof	—
	1944	42.600	.15	.75	2.00	10.00
	1944	—	—	—	Proof	—
	1945	79.531	.15	.75	1.50	8.00
	1945	—	—	—	Proof	—
	1946	66.856	.10	.50	1.00	3.00
	1946	—	—	—	Proof	—
	1947	52.220	.10	.35	1.00	2.50
	1948	63.961	—	.15	1.00	2.50
	1948	—	—	—	Proof	—

Obv. leg: IND IMP. omitted

Y#	Date	Mintage	Fine	VF	XF	Unc
106	1949	14.324	.15	.50	1.00	3.50
	1949	—	—	—	Proof	—
	1950	.240	6.00	9.00	12.00	30.00
	1950	—	—	—	Proof	30.00
	1951	.120	15.00	17.50	20.00	35.00
	1951	—	—	—	Proof	30.00

Y#	Date	Mintage	Fine	VF	XF	Unc
118	1953	1.308	1.50	2.50	3.50	10.00
	1953	—	—	—	Proof	10.00

Obv. leg: Without BRITT OMN

Y#	Date	Mintage	Fine	VF	XF	Unc
A128	1954	Unique	—	—	Rare	—
	1961	39.703	—	—	—	2.00
	1961	—	—	—	Proof	—
	1962	137.640	—	—	—	.75
	1962	—	—	—	Proof	—
	1963	134.014	—	—	—	.50
	1963	—	—	—	Proof	—
	1964	144.462	—	—	—	.25
	1964	—	—	—	Proof	—
	1965	135.534	—	—	—	.25
	1966	157.430	—	—	—	.25
	1967	164.000	—	—	—	.25
	1970	.731	—		Proof Only	5.00

1-1/2 PENCE

.925 SILVER

C#	Date	Mintage	Fine	VF	XF	Unc
40*	1834	.800	2.50	4.00	12.00	25.00
21	1835/4	.634	5.50	17.50	35.00	75.00
	1835	.160	2.75	4.00	12.00	25.00
	1836	.160	2.75	3.50	12.00	25.00
	1837	.310	6.00	17.50	35.00	70.00

Y#	Date	Mintage	Fine	VF	XF	Unc
3*	1838	.540	1.75	3.50	12.00	25.00
A3	1839	.760	1.50	3.00	10.00	18.50
	1840	.100	3.50	7.50	20.00	45.00
	1841	.160	1.75	3.50	15.00	25.00
	1842	1.870	1.75	3.50	15.00	22.50
	1843/34	.480	5.00	12.50	22.50	60.00
	1843	Inc. Ab.	3.00	6.00	10.00	20.00
	1860	.160	4.00	7.00	15.00	35.00
	1862	.260	4.00	7.00	15.00	35.00
	1870	—	—	—	Proof	400.00

***NOTE:** Although the design of the above series is of the homeland type, the issues were struck for Ceylon and Jamaica. Catalog nos. are of Ceylon and Jamaica.

2 PENCE

194138 gm., .925 SILVER, .0420 oz ASW

C#	Date	Mintage	Fine	VF	XF	Unc
25	1763	—	3.50	12.50	20.00	40.00
	1763	—	—	—	Proof	—
	1765 10-20 Pcs.		—	—	Rare	—
	1766	—	3.50	10.00	15.00	35.00
	1772/62	—	3.50	10.00	15.00	30.00
	1772	—	3.50	10.00	15.00	35.00
	1776	—	4.50	12.50	17.50	40.00
	1780	—	3.50	10.00	15.00	30.00
	1784	—	3.50	10.00	15.00	30.00
	1786	—	3.50	10.00	15.00	30.00
25a	1792	—	10.00	25.00	50.00	75.00
25b	1795	—	3.50	12.50	22.50	40.00
	1800	—	3.50	12.50	20.00	35.00

C#	Date	Mintage	Fine	VF	XF	Unc
25c	1817	—	2.00	8.00	12.50	25.00
	1818	—	2.00	8.00	12.50	25.00
	1820	—	2.00	8.00	12.50	25.00

Later dates included in maundy sets.

COPPER

C#	Date	Mintage	Fine	VF	XF	Unc
23	1797	.722	20.00	40.00	100.00	225.00
	1797	Inc. Ab.	—	—	Proof	275.00

BRONZED COPPER

C#	Date	Mintage	Fine	VF	XF	Unc
23a	1797	—	—	—	Proof	—

GILT COPPER

C#	Date	Mintage	Fine	VF	XF	Unc
23b	1797	—	—	—	Proof	—

SILVER

Y#	Date	Mintage	Fine	VF	XF	Unc
B3	1838	—	2.00	4.00	8.00	12.00
	1848	—	2.00	5.00	9.00	13.00

NOTE: Identical to Maundy Issues, minted for colonial use.

3 PENCE

1.4138 gm., .925 SILVER, .0420 oz ASW

C#	Date	Mintage	Fine	VF	XF	Unc
26	1762	—	3.00	7.50	12.50	25.00
	1763	—	2.50	6.00	12.50	25.00
	1763	—	—	—	Proof	—
	1765 10-20 Pcs.		—	—	Rare	—
	1766	—	3.00	10.00	17.50	42.50
	1770	—	3.00	10.00	17.50	42.50
	1772	—	3.00	10.00	17.50	37.50
	1780	—	3.50	10.00	17.50	37.50
	1784	—	3.50	15.00	25.00	50.00
	1786	—	3.00	10.00	17.50	37.50

C#	Date	Mintage	Fine	VF	XF	Unc
26a	1792	—	12.50	30.00	60.00	135.00

C#	Date	Mintage	Fine	VF	XF	Unc
26b	1795	—	4.50	15.00	22.50	45.00
	1800	—	3.50	12.50	20.00	40.00
26c	1817	—	3.50	12.50	17.50	37.50
	1818	—	3.50	12.50	17.50	37.50
	1820	—	3.50	12.50	17.50	37.50

CURRENCY THREEPENCES

From the reign of William IV until 1944 during the reign of George VI, silver threepences were struck for currency. Until 1927 they were identical indesign to the Maundy threepences. The Maundy coins are sharper strikes and almost prooflike in appearance.

C#	Date	Mintage	Fine	VF	XF	Unc
76	1834	.400	2.25	9.00	25.00	45.00
	1835	.491	2.50	8.00	25.00	40.00
	1836	.411	2.25	8.00	25.00	40.00
	1837	.430	4.00	12.50	32.50	50.00

Y#	Date	Mintage	Fine	VF	XF	Unc
A3	1838	1.200	2.25	7.50	25.00	50.00
	1839	.570	2.50	15.00	37.50	65.00
	1840	.630	2.50	8.00	27.50	45.00
	1841	.440	4.00	10.00	35.00	60.00
	1842	—	4.50	10.00	35.00	60.00
	1843	2.030	3.00	7.50	25.00	55.00
	1844	1.050	5.00	10.00	35.00	75.00
	1845	1.319	2.50	5.00	16.50	40.00
	1846	.052	3.50	15.00	50.00	80.00
	1849	.131	3.50	12.00	40.00	75.00
	1850	.955	2.50	8.00	22.00	50.00
	1851	.484	2.50	7.00	27.50	50.00
	1853	.036	4.00	17.50	45.00	75.00
	1854	1.472	2.50	7.00	25.00	55.00
	1855	.388	3.00	10.00	30.00	50.00
	1856	1.018	2.50	7.00	20.00	45.00
	1857	1.767	2.50	7.50	25.00	50.00
	1858	1.446	2.50	7.00	22.00	45.00
	1859	3.584	2.50	7.00	22.00	40.00
	1860	3.410	2.50	7.00	20.00	40.00
	1861	3.299	2.50	7.00	25.00	40.00
	1862	1.161	2.50	9.00	27.50	45.00
	1863	.954	3.00	10.00	30.00	75.00
	1864	1.335	2.50	7.00	20.00	55.00
	1865	1.747	2.50	8.00	35.00	75.00
	1866	1.905	2.50	7.00	22.00	45.00
	1867	.717	2.50	7.00	25.00	45.00
	1868	1.462	2.50	6.00	20.00	45.00
	1868 Error - 'RRITANIAR'					
		Inc. Ab.	60.00	80.00	120.00	200.00
	1870	1.288	2.00	5.00	20.00	40.00
	1871	1.004	2.00	6.50	20.00	40.00
	1872	1.298	2.00	5.00	18.00	35.00
	1873	4.060	1.50	3.50	15.00	35.00
	1874	4.432	1.50	3.50	15.00	35.00
	1875	3.311	1.50	3.50	15.00	35.00
	1876	1.839	1.50	3.50	15.00	35.00
	1877	2.627	1.50	3.50	15.00	35.00
	1878	2.424	1.50	3.50	15.00	35.00
	1879	3.145	2.50	5.00	15.00	35.00
	1879	—	—	—	Proof	110.00
	1880	1.615	1.25	3.75	15.00	35.00
	1881	3.253	1.25	3.50	27.50	27.50
	1882	.447	4.00	8.00	20.00	45.00
	1883	4.374	1.25	2.50	10.00	25.00
	1884	3.327	1.25	3.00	10.00	25.00
	1885	5.188	1.25	2.50	10.00	25.00
	1886	6.157	1.25	2.50	10.00	25.00
	1887	2.785	3.00	7.50	20.00	45.00
	1887	—	—	—	Proof	90.00

Y#	Date	Mintage	Fine	VF	XF	Unc
A18	1887	Inc. Ab.	1.25	2.50	6.00	11.50
	1887	Inc. Ab.	—	—	Proof	60.00
	1888	.523	3.00	6.00	12.00	22.50
	1889	4.591	1.25	2.50	9.00	20.00
	1890	4.470	1.25	2.50	9.00	20.00
	1891	6.328	1.25	2.50	9.00	20.00
	1892	2.583	1.25	3.75	10.00	22.50
	1893 w/open 3 in date					
		3.076	20.00	40.00	100.00	175.00
	1893 w/closed 3 in date					
		Inc. Ab.	20.00	40.00	100.00	175.00

Y#	Date	Mintage	Fine	VF	XF	Unc
35	1893	Inc. Ab.	BV	2.00	6.00	12.50
	1893	—	—	—	Proof	45.00
	1894	1.618	BV	2.50	6.00	12.50
	1895	4.798	BV	2.50	6.00	12.50
	1896	4.607	BV	2.00	5.00	12.50
	1897	4.550	BV	2.00	4.50	12.50
	1898	4.576	BV	2.00	4.50	12.50
	1899	6.253	BV	2.00	4.50	12.50
	1900	10.661	BV	1.75	4.00	10.00
	1901	6.100	BV	1.50	3.50	10.00

Y#	Date	Mintage	Fine	VF	XF	Unc
49	1902	8.287	BV	1.50	6.00	12.50
	1902	.015	—	—	Proof	25.00
	1903	5.235	BV	1.75	8.00	15.00
	1904 type of 1903 w/small ball on '3'					
		3.630	4.00	12.50	25.00	50.00

Y#	Date	Mintage	Fine	VF	XF	Unc
	1904 type of 1905 w/large ball on '3'					
		Inc. Ab.	3.00	10.00	20.00	40.00
	1905	3.563	3.00	10.00	20.00	40.00
	1906	3.174	4.00	10.00	16.50	35.00
	1907	4.841	BV	2.50	8.00	15.00
	1908	8.176	BV	2.50	8.00	17.50
	1909	4.055	1.50	3.00	10.00	22.50
	1910	4.565	BV	2.25	6.00	15.00

Y#	Date	Mintage	Fine	VF	XF	Unc
65	1911	5.843	BV	1.25	4.00	10.00
	1911	6,007	—	—	Proof	40.00
	1912	8.934	BV	1.25	4.00	10.00
	1913	7.144	BV	1.25	4.00	10.00
	1914	6.735	BV	1.25	3.00	7.50
	1915	5.452	BV	1.25	3.00	7.50
	1916	18.556	BV	1.25	2.00	6.00
	1917	21.664	BV	1.25	2.00	6.00
	1918	20.632	BV	1.25	2.00	6.00
	1919	16.846	BV	1.25	2.00	7.00
	1920	16.705	BV	1.25	2.00	7.00

1.4138 gm., .500 SILVER, .0227 oz ASW

Y#	Date	Mintage	Fine	VF	XF	Unc
65a	1920	Inc. Ab.	BV	.75	2.50	7.00
	1921	8.751	BV	.75	2.50	9.00
	1922	7.981	BV	1.00	3.75	9.00
	1925	3.733	1.50	2.00	8.50	20.00
	1926	4.109	1.50	6.00	15.00	30.00

Obv: Modified effigy

Y#	Date	Mintage	Fine	VF	XF	Unc
65a.1	1926	Inc. Ab.	1.00	2.00	9.00	20.00

Rev: Oak sprigs with acorns

Y#	Date	Mintage	Fine	VF	XF	Unc
70	1927	.015	—	Proof Only		80.00
	1928	1.302	2.00	3.50	8.50	17.50
	1930	1.319	1.50	3.00	7.50	12.50
	1931	6.252	BV	.75	1.25	3.50
	1932	5.887	BV	.75	1.25	3.50
	1933	5.579	BV	.75	1.25	3.50
	1934	7.406	BV	.75	1.25	3.50
	1935	7.028	BV	.75	1.25	3.50
	1936	3.239	BV	.75	1.25	3.50

Y#	Date	Mintage	Fine	VF	XF	Unc
86	1937	8.148	BV	BV	1.00	3.00
	1937	.026	—	—	Proof	10.00
	1938	6.402	BV	BV	1.00	2.00
	1939	1.356	BV	1.75	4.00	10.00
	1940	7.914	BV	BV	1.50	3.50
	1941	7.979	BV	BV	1.50	3.50
	1942	4.144	1.50	3.50	9.00	15.00
	1943	1.379	2.00	5.00	10.00	18.00
	1944	2.006	3.00	8.50	17.50	40.00
	1945	.320	Entire issue melted by mint.			

NICKEL-BRASS

Y#	Date	Mintage	Fine	VF	XF	Unc
85	1937	45.708	—	.35	.75	3.00
	1937	.026	—	—	Proof	7.00
	1938	14.532	—	.50	3.00	10.00
	1939	5.603	—	2.25	8.00	17.50
	1940	12.636	—	.50	2.75	8.00
	1941	60.239	—	.35	.75	3.50
	1942	103.214	—	.25	.75	3.00
	1943	101.702	—	.30	1.00	4.00
	1944	69.760	—	.35	2.00	6.00
	1945	33.942	—	.35	2.00	7.00
	1946	.621	2.00	5.00	40.00	225.00
	1948	4.230	.35	1.00	3.00	20.00

Obv. leg: IND IMP. omitted

Y#	Date	Mintage	Fine	VF	XF	Unc
107	1949	.464	2.75	10.00	100.00	200.00
	1950	1.600	.50	2.00	12.50	35.00
	1950	.018	—	—	Proof	30.00
	1951	1.184	.75	2.50	12.50	35.00
	1951	.020	—	—	Proof	25.00
	1952	25.494	—	.35	1.75	4.00

Y#	Date	Mintage	Fine	VF	XF	Unc
119	1953	30.618	—	—	.75	2.25
	1953	.040	—	—	Proof	5.00

Obv. leg: BRITT OMN omitted

Y#	Date	Mintage	Fine	VF	XF	Unc
129	1954	41.720	—	—	1.50	8.00
	1954	—	—	—	Proof	—
	1955	41.075	—	—	1.75	8.00
	1955	—	—	—	Proof	—
	1956	36.902	—	—	2.00	8.00
	1956	—	—	—	Proof	—
	1957	24.294	—	—	.75	5.00
	1957	—	—	—	Proof	—
	1958	20.504	—	—	2.00	11.00
	1958	—	—	—	Proof	—
	1959	28.499	—	—	.85	4.50
	1959	—	—	—	Proof	—
	1960	83.078	—	—	.50	3.00
	1960	—	—	—	Proof	—
	1961	41.102	—	—	—	1.00
	1961	—	—	—	Proof	—
	1962	47.242	—	—	—	.50
	1962	—	—	—	Proof	—
	1963	35.280	—	—	—	.50
	1963	—	—	—	Proof	—
	1964	47.440	—	—	—	.25
	1965	23.907	—	—	—	.25
	1966	55.320	—	—	—	.25
	1967	49.000	—	—	—	.25
	1970	.731	—	Proof Only		3.00

4 PENCE (GROAT)

1.8851 gm., .925 SILVER, .0561 oz ASW
Obv: Young head of George III right
Rev: Crowned numeral

C#	Date	Mintage	Fine	VF	XF	Unc
27	1763	—	5.00	17.50	27.50	50.00
	1763	—	—	—	Proof	Rare
	1765	10-20 Pcs.	—	—	Rare	—
	1766	—	5.00	20.00	30.00	55.00
27	1770	—	5.00	20.00	32.50	60.00
	1772/0	—	5.00	20.00	30.00	55.00
	1772	—	5.00	20.00	30.00	55.00
	1776	—	5.00	20.00	35.00	60.00
	1778	—	5.00	20.00	30.00	55.00
	1784	—	5.00	20.00	30.00	55.00
	1786	—	5.00	20.00	30.00	55.00

Obv: Larger lettering

C#	Date	Mintage	Fine	VF	XF	Unc
27.1	1786	—	5.00	20.00	32.50	60.00

Obv: Armored bust of George III right
Rev: Small Crown Over Thin Numerals.

C#	Date	Mintage	Fine	VF	XF	Unc
27a	1792	—	4.00	17.50	45.00	75.00

Rev: Crowned numeral

C#	Date	Mintage	Fine	VF	XF	Unc
27b	1795	—	6.00	17.50	25.00	50.00
	1800	—	4.00	15.00	25.00	50.00

Obv: Old head of George III

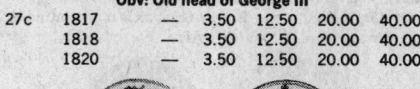

C#	Date	Mintage	Fine	VF	XF	Unc
27c	1817	—	3.50	12.50	20.00	40.00
	1818	—	3.50	12.50	20.00	40.00
	1820	—	3.50	12.50	20.00	40.00

C#	Date	Mintage	Fine	VF	XF	Unc
58	1822	—	3.00	8.00	15.00	32.50
	1823	—	3.00	8.00	15.00	32.50
	1824	—	3.00	9.00	16.50	35.00
	1825	—	3.00	8.00	15.00	32.50
	1826	—	3.00	8.00	15.00	32.50
	1827	—	3.00	8.00	15.00	32.50
	1828	—	3.00	8.00	15.00	32.50
	1829	—	3.00	8.00	15.00	32.50
	1830	—	4.00	8.00	15.00	32.50

C#	Date	Mintage	Fine	VF	XF	Unc
77	1831	—	3.50	10.00	14.00	27.50
	1832	—	3.50	10.00	14.00	27.50
	1833	—	3.50	10.00	14.00	27.50
	1834	—	3.50	10.00	14.00	27.50
	1835	—	3.00	10.00	14.00	27.50
	1836	—	3.00	10.00	14.00	27.50
	1837	—	4.50	10.00	14.00	27.50

C#	Date	Mintage	Fine	VF	XF	Unc
26	1836	4.253	4.00	6.00	10.00	25.00
	1836	—	—	—	Proof	200.00
	1836 with plain edge					
		—	—	—	Proof	—
	1837	.962	5.00	7.00	12.00	35.00
	1837	—	—	—	Proof	225.00

GOLD (OMS)

C#	Date	Mintage	Fine	VF	XF	Unc
26a	1836	—	—	—	Proof	—

NOTE: Although the design of the above coin is of the homeland type,the issues were struck for British Guiana. Catalog nos. are of British Guiana.

1.8851 gm., .925 SILVER, .0561 oz ASW

Y#	Date	Mintage	Fine	VF	XF	Unc
4	1838	2.150	2.00	4.00	12.50	25.00
	1838 w/plain edge					
		—	—	—	Proof	125.00
	1838/8 w/second 8 over horizontal 8					
		Inc. Ab.	2.50	7.50	20.00	50.00
	1839	1.461	2.00	6.00	20.00	45.00
	1839 w/plain edge					
		—	—	—	Proof	175.00

Y#	Date	Mintage	Fine	VF	XF	Unc
4	1840	1.497	2.50	5.00	15.00	25.00
	1841	.345	2.50	7.00	25.00	50.00
	1842/1	.725	5.00	7.50	30.00	60.00
	1842	Inc. Ab.	2.50	6.00	20.00	35.00
	1842	—	—	—	Proof	165.00
	1843	1.818	2.50	6.00	17.50	35.00
	1844	.855	2.50	7.50	20.00	40.00
	1845	.915	2.50	6.00	20.00	35.00
	1846	1.366	2.50	5.50	15.00	30.00
	1847/6	.226	30.00	60.00	125.00	225.00
	1848/6	.713	5.00	12.00	25.00	50.00
	1848/7	Inc. Ab.	5.00	12.00	25.00	50.00
	1848	Inc. Ab.	2.50	5.00	15.00	30.00
	1849/8	.380	3.50	12.00	40.00	70.00
	1849	Inc. Ab.	2.50	7.50	25.00	40.00
	1851	.031	10.00	30.00	100.00	160.00
	1852	—	35.00	60.00	150.00	225.00
	1853	.012	15.00	45.00	150.00	300.00
	1853	—	—	—	Proof	120.00
	1853 W/ Plain Edge					
		Inc. Ab.	—	Proof Only		250.00
	1854	1.097	2.50	4.00	15.00	40.00
	1855	.646	2.50	4.00	15.00	40.00
	1857	—	—	—	Proof	300.00
	1862	—	—	—	Proof	225.00

NOTE: The above issue was produced for circulation in both Great Britain and British Guiana, and the latter is found listed there as Yeoman #A1.

Y#	Date	Mintage	Fine	VF	XF	Unc
B2	1888	.120	3.00	10.00	20.00	40.00

NOTE: The above piece was exclusively for use in British Guiana and the West Indies. Catalog no. is for British Guiana.

MAUNDY SETS

These small silver coins are a special ceremonial issue struck each year for use at the traditional ceremony on Maundy Thursday when the reigning monarch (or a representative) distributes them to a selected group of elderly men and women. The amount distributed to each person (in pence) is equal to the present age of the monarch. The issue has consisted since the reign of Charles II of silver 1,2,3 and 4 penny pieces.

.925 SILVER

C#	Date	Mintage	Fine	VF	XF	Unc
24-27	1763	—	35.00	60.00	80.00	175.00
	1763	—	—	—	Proof	650.00
	1765	—	—	—	Rare	—
	1766	—	35.00	60.00	80.00	175.00
	1772	—	35.00	60.00	80.00	175.00
	1780	—	35.00	60.00	80.00	175.00
	1784	—	35.00	60.00	80.00	175.00
	1786	—	35.00	60.00	80.00	175.00
24-27a	1792	—	50.00	85.00	140.00	250.00

C#	Date	Mintage	Fine	VF	XF	Unc
24-27b	1795	—	35.00	60.00	85.00	200.00
	1800	—	32.50	55.00	75.00	150.00
24-27c	1817	1,584	30.00	40.00	65.00	135.00
	1818	1,188	30.00	40.00	65.00	135.00
	1820	1,584	30.00	40.00	65.00	135.00

C#	Date	Mintage	Fine	VF	XF	Unc
55-58	1822	2,970	30.00	40.00	60.00	125.00
	1822	—	—	—	Proof	350.00
	1823	1,980	30.00	40.00	65.00	125.00
	1824	1,584	40.00	50.00	80.00	175.00

C#	Date	Mintage	Fine	VF	XF	Unc
55-58	1825	2,376	30.00	40.00	60.00	125.00
	1826	2,376	30.00	40.00	60.00	125.00
	1827	2,772	30.00	40.00	60.00	125.00
	1828	2,772	30.00	40.00	60.00	125.00
	1828	—	—	—	Proof	400.00
	1829	2,772	30.00	40.00	60.00	125.00
	1830	2,772	30.00	40.00	60.00	125.00

C#	Date	Mintage	Fine	VF	XF	Unc
74-77	1831	3,564	30.00	50.00	60.00	125.00
	1831	—	—	—	Proof	350.00
	1832	2,574	30.00	50.00	60.00	125.00
	1833	2,574	30.00	50.00	65.00	125.00
	1834	2,574	30.00	50.00	60.00	125.00
	1835	2,574	30.00	50.00	60.00	125.00
	1836	2,574	30.00	50.00	60.00	125.00
	1836	2,574	30.00	50.00	60.00	125.00

Y#	Date	Mintage	Fine	VF	XF	Unc
A-D12	1838	4,158	30.00	35.00	40.00	90.00
	1838	—	—	—	Proof	350.00
	1839	4,125	90.00	35.00	40.00	90.00
	1839	300	—	—	Proof	250.00
	1840	4,125	90.00	35.00	40.00	90.00
	1841	2,574	100.00	40.00	50.00	100.00
	1842	4,125	90.00	35.00	40.00	90.00
	1843	4,158	90.00	35.00	40.00	90.00
	1844	4,158	90.00	35.00	40.00	90.00
	1845	4,158	90.00	35.00	40.00	90.00
	1846	4,158	90.00	35.00	40.00	90.00
	1847	4,158	90.00	35.00	40.00	90.00
	1848	4,158	90.00	35.00	40.00	90.00
	1849	4,158	100.00	40.00	50.00	100.00
	1850	4,158	90.00	35.00	40.00	90.00
	1851	4,158	90.00	35.00	40.00	90.00
	1852	4,158	90.00	35.00	40.00	90.00
	1853	4,158	90.00	35.00	40.00	90.00
	1853	—	—	—	Proof	350.00
	1854	4,158	90.00	35.00	40.00	90.00
	1855	4,158	95.00	35.00	50.00	95.00
	1856	4,158	90.00	35.00	40.00	90.00
	1857	4,158	90.00	35.00	40.00	90.00
	1858	4,158	90.00	35.00	40.00	90.00
	1859	4,158	90.00	35.00	40.00	90.00
	1860	4,158	90.00	35.00	40.00	90.00
	1861	4,158	90.00	35.00	40.00	90.00
	1862	4,158	90.00	35.00	40.00	90.00
	1863	4,158	90.00	35.00	40.00	90.00
	1864	4,158	90.00	35.00	40.00	90.00
	1865	4,158	90.00	35.00	40.00	90.00
	1866	4,158	90.00	35.00	40.00	90.00
	1867	4,158	90.00	35.00	40.00	90.00
	1867	—	—	—	Proof	400.00
	1868	4,158	90.00	35.00	40.00	90.00
	1869	4,158	95.00	40.00	45.00	95.00
	1870	4,488	90.00	35.00	40.00	90.00
	1871	4,488	90.00	35.00	40.00	90.00
	1871	—	—	—	Proof	400.00
	1872	4,328	90.00	35.00	40.00	90.00
	1873	4,162	90.00	35.00	40.00	90.00
	1874	4,488	90.00	35.00	40.00	90.00
	1875	4,154	90.00	35.00	40.00	90.00
	1876	4,488	90.00	35.00	40.00	90.00
	1877	4,488	90.00	35.00	40.00	90.00
	1878	4,488	90.00	35.00	40.00	90.00
	1878	—	—	—	Proof	350.00
	1879	4,488	90.00	35.00	40.00	90.00
	1880	4,488	90.00	35.00	40.00	90.00
	1881	4,488	90.00	35.00	40.00	90.00
	1882	4,488	90.00	35.00	40.00	90.00
	1883	4,488	90.00	35.00	40.00	90.00
	1884	4,488	90.00	35.00	40.00	90.00
	1885	4,488	90.00	35.00	40.00	90.00
	1886	4,488	90.00	35.00	40.00	90.00
	1887	4,488	120.00	40.00	50.00	120.00

Y#	Date	Mintage	Fine	VF	XF	Unc
A-D27	1888	4,488	30.00	40.00	50.00	100.00
	1889	4,488	30.00	40.00	50.00	100.00
	1888	—	—	—	Proof	300.00
	1890	4,488	30.00	40.00	50.00	100.00
	1891	4,488	30.00	40.00	50.00	100.00
	1892	4,488	30.00	40.00	50.00	100.00

Y#	Date	Mintage	Fine	VF	XF	Unc
A-D41	1893	8,976	25.00	27.50	30.00	70.00
	1894	8,976	25.00	27.50	30.00	70.00
	1895	8,877	25.00	27.50	30.00	70.00
	1896	8,476	25.00	27.50	30.00	70.00
	1897	9,388	25.00	27.50	30.00	70.00
	1898	9,147	25.00	27.50	30.00	70.00
	1899	8,976	25.00	27.50	30.00	70.00
	1900	8,976	25.00	27.50	30.00	70.00
	1901	8,976	25.00	27.50	30.00	70.00

Y#	Date	Mintage	Fine	VF	XF	Unc
A-D55	1902	8,976	25.00	27.50	30.00	70.00
	1902	—	—	—	Proof	90.00
	1903	8,976	25.00	27.50	30.00	70.00
	1904	8,976	25.00	27.50	30.00	70.00
	1905	8,976	25.00	27.50	30.00	70.00
	1906	8,800	25.00	27.50	30.00	70.00
	1907	8,760	20.00	25.00	30.00	70.00
	1908	8,760	20.00	25.00	30.00	70.00
	1909	1,983	25.00	30.00	40.00	90.00
	1910	1,440	25.00	30.00	45.00	100.00

Y#	Date	Mintage	Fine	VF	XF	Unc
A-D81	1911	1,768	20.00	30.00	40.00	80.00
	1911	6,007	—	—	Proof	95.00
	1912	1,246	20.00	30.00	40.00	70.00
	1913	1,228	20.00	30.00	40.00	70.00
	1914	982	27.00	45.00	55.00	100.00
	1915	1,293	20.00	30.00	40.00	70.00
	1916	1,128	20.00	30.00	40.00	70.00
	1917	1,237	20.00	30.00	40.00	70.00
	1918	1,375	20.00	30.00	40.00	70.00
	1919	1,258	20.00	30.00	40.00	70.00
	1920	1,399	20.00	30.00	40.00	70.00

.500 SILVER

Y#	Date	Mintage	Fine	VF	XF	Unc
E-H81	1921	1,386	25.00	35.00	40.00	70.00
	1922	1,373	25.00	35.00	40.00	70.00
	1923	1,430	25.00	35.00	40.00	70.00
	1924	1,515	25.00	35.00	40.00	70.00
	1925	1,438	25.00	35.00	40.00	70.00
	1926	1,504	25.00	35.00	40.00	70.00
	1927	1,647	25.00	35.00	40.00	70.00

Obv: Modified effigy

Y#	Date	Mintage	Fine	VF	XF	Unc
I-L81	1928	1,642	20.00	35.00	40.00	70.00
	1929	1,761	20.00	35.00	40.00	70.00
	1930	1,724	20.00	35.00	40.00	70.00
	1931	1,759	20.00	35.00	40.00	70.00
	1932	1,835	20.00	35.00	40.00	70.00
	1933	1,872	20.00	35.00	40.00	70.00
	1934	1,887	20.00	35.00	40.00	75.00
	1935	1,926	25.00	40.00	60.00	90.00
	1936	1,323	45.00	75.00	85.00	135.00

Y#	Date	Mintage	VF	XF	Unc
A-D93	1937	1,325	35.00	45.00	75.00
	1938	1,275	30.00	40.00	75.00
	1939	1,234	30.00	40.00	75.00
	1940	1,277	30.00	40.00	75.00
	1941	1,253	30.00	40.00	75.00
	1942	1,231	30.00	40.00	75.00
	1943	1,239	30.00	40.00	75.00
	1944	1,259	30.00	40.00	75.00
	1945	1,355	30.00	40.00	75.00
	1946	1,365	35.00	45.00	75.00
	.925 SILVER				
E-H93	1947	1,375	30.00	40.00	75.00
	1948	1,385	30.00	40.00	75.00
	Obv. leg: IND IMP. omitted				
A-D113	1949	1,395	30.00	40.00	80.00
	1950	1,405	30.00	40.00	80.00
	1951	1,468	30.00	40.00	80.00
	1952	1,012	45.00	55.00	90.00
	Elizabeth II				
A-D126	1953	1,025	100.00	150.00	225.00
	Obv. leg: BRITT OMN omitted				
A-D135	1954	1,020	30.00	40.00	80.00
	1955	1,036	30.00	40.00	80.00
	1956	1,088	30.00	40.00	80.00
	1957	1,094	30.00	40.00	80.00
	1958	1,100	30.00	40.00	80.00
	1959	1,106	30.00	40.00	80.00
	1960	1,112	30.00	40.00	80.00
	1961	1,118	30.00	40.00	80.00
	1962	1,125	30.00	40.00	80.00
	1963	1,131	30.00	40.00	80.00
	1964	1,137	30.00	40.00	80.00
	1965	1,143	30.00	40.00	80.00
	1966	1,206	30.00	40.00	80.00
	1967	986	30.00	40.00	85.00
	1968	964	40.00	50.00	100.00
	1969	1,002	40.00	50.00	90.00
	1970	980	40.00	50.00	85.00
	1971	1,018	40.00	50.00	80.00
	1972	1,026	40.00	50.00	80.00
	1973	1,004	40.00	55.00	85.00
	1974	4,456	40.00	55.00	85.00
	1975	1,050	40.00	55.00	85.00
	1976	1,158	40.00	55.00	125.00
	1977	—	55.00	75.00	200.00
	1978	1,138	—	—	—

NOTE: The mintage figures above represent the maximum number of complete sets. The following figures represent the actual mintage of each piece.

MAUNDY MINTAGES

*The figures given are the numbers of coins issued by the Mint in a particular year, not the number of coins that bear a particular date.

3D PENCE *These mintage figures are for Maundy coinage only.

Additional coins were struck for normal circulation.

Year	1D	2D	3D	4D
(1816)*	4,752	2,376	1,584	1,584
1817	10,296	2,376	1,584	1,386
1818	9,504	2,376	1,584	1,188
(1819)*	6,336	1,980	1,320	792
1820	7,920	1,584	1,320	990
(1821)*	3,960	1,980	1,320	990
1822	11,880	5,940	3,960	2,970
1823	12,672	3,960	2,640	1,980
1824	9,504	3,168	2,112	1,584
1825	8,712	3,960	3,432	2,376
1826	8,712	3,960	3,432	2,376
1978	—	—	—	—
1827	7,920	3,960	3,168	2,772
1828	7,920	3,960	3,168	2,772
1829	7,920	3,960	3,168	2,772
1830	7,920	3,960	3,168	2,772
1831	10,296	4,752	3,960	3,564
1832	8,712	3,564	2,904	2,574
1833	8,712	3,564	2,904	2,574
1834	8,712	3,564	2,904	2,574
1835	8,712	3,564	2,904	2,574
1836	8,712	3,564	2,904	2,574
1837	8,712	3,564	2,904	2,574
1838	8,976	4,488*	4,312	4,158
1839	8,976	4,488	4,356	4,125
1840	8,976	4,488	4,356	4,125
1841	7,920	3,960	2,904	2,574
1842	8,976	4,488	4,356	4,125
1843	7,920	4,752	4,488	4,158
1844	7,920	4,752	4,488	4,158
1845	7,920	4,752	4,488	4,158
1846	7,920	4,752	4,488	4,158
1847	7,920	4,752	4,488	4,158
1848	7,920	4,752*	4,488	4,158
1849	7,920	4,752	4,488	4,158
1850	7,920	4,752	4,488	4,158
1851	7,128	4,752	4,488	4,158
1852	7,920	4,752	4,488	4,158
1853	7,920	4,752	4,488	4,158
1854	7,920	4,752	4,488	4,158
1855	7,920	4,752	4,488	4,158
1856	7,920	4,752	4,488	4,158
1857	7,920	4,752	4,488	4,158
1858	7,920	4,752	4,488	4,158
1859	7,920	4,752	4,488	4,158
1860	7,920	4,752	4,488	4,158
1861	7,920	4,752	4,488	4,158
1862	7,920	4,752	4,488	4,158
1863	7,920	4,752	4,488	4,158
1864	7,920	4,752	4,488	4,158
1865	7,920	4,752	4,488	4,158
1866	7,920	4,752	4,488	4,158
1867	7,920	4,752	4,488	4,158
1868	7,920	4,752	4,488	4,158
1869	7,920	4,752	4,488	4,158
1870	9,002	5,347	4,488	4,569
1871	9,286	4,753	4,488	4,627
1872	8,956	4,719	4,488	4,328
1873	7,932	4,756	4,488	4,162
1874	8,741	5,578	4,488	5,937
1875	8,459	5,745	4,488	4,154
1876	10,426	6,655	4,488	4,862
1877	8,936	7,189	4,488	4,850
1878	9,903	6,709	4,488	5,735
1879	10,626	6,925	4,488	5,202
1880	11,088	6,247	4,488	5,199
1881	9,017	6,001	4,488	6,203
1882	10,607	7,264	4,488	4,146
1883	11,673	7,232	4,488	5,096
1884	14,109	6,042	4,488	5,353
1885	12,302	5,958	4,488	5,791
1886	15,952	9,167	4,488	6,785
1887	17,506	8,296	4,488	5,292
1888	14,480	9,528	4,488	9,583
1889	14,028	6,727	4,488	6,088
1890	13,115	8,613	4,488	9,087
1891	21,743	10,000	4,488	11,303
1892	15,525	11,583	4,488	8,524
1893	21,593	14,182	8,976	10,832
1894	18,391	12,099	8,976	9,385
1895	17,408	10,766	8,976	8,877
1896	17,380	10,795	8,976	8,476
1897	16,477	11,000	8,976	9,388
1898	16,634	11,945	8,976	9,147
1899	17,402	14,514	8,976	13,561
1900	17,299	10,987	8,976	9,571
1901	17,644	13,539	8,976	11,928
1902	21,278	14,079	8,976	10,117
1903	17,209	13,386	8,976	9,729
1904	18,524	13,827	8,876	11,568
1905	17,504	11,139	8,976	10,998
1906	17,850	11,325	8,800	11,065
1907	18,388	8,760	11,132	—
1908	18,150	14,815	8,760	9,929
1909	2,948	2,695	1,983	2,428
1910	3,392	2,998	1,440	2,755
1911	1,913	1,635	1,991	1,768
1912	1,616	1,678	1,246	1,700
1913	1,590	1,880	1,228	1,798
1914	1,818	1,659	982	1,651
1915	2,072	1,465	1,293	1,441
1916	1,647	1,509	1,128	1,499
1917	1,820	1,506	1,237	1,478
1918	1,911	1,547	1,375	1,479
1919	1,699	1,567	1,258	1,524
1920	1,715	1,630	1,399	1,460
1921	1,847	1,794	1,386	1,542
1922	1,758	3,074	1,373	1,609
1923	1,840	1,527	1,430	1,635
1924	1,619	1,602	1,515	1,665
1925	1,890	1,670	1,438	1,786
1926	2,180	1,902	1,504	1,762
1927	1,647	1,766	1,690	1,681
1928	1,846	1,706	1,835	1,642
1929	1,837	1,862	1,761	1,969
1930	1,724	1,901	1,948	1,744
1931	1,759	1,897	1,818	1,915
1932	1,835	1,960	2,042	1,937
1933	1,872	2,066	1,920	1,931
1934	1,919	1,927	1,887	1,893
1935	1,975	1,928	2,007	1,995
1936	1,329	1,365	1,307	1,323
1937	1,329	1,472	1,351	1,325
1938	1,275	1,374	1,350	1,424
1939	1,253	1,436	1,234	1,332
1940	1,375	1,277	1,290	1,367
1941	1,255	1,345	1,253	1,345
1942	1,243	1,231	1,325	1,325
1943	1,347	1,239	1,335	1,335
1944	1,259	1,345	1,345	1,345
1945	1,367	1,355	1,355	1,355
1946	1,479	1,365	1,365	1,365
1947	1,387	1,479	1,375	1,375
1948	1,397	1,385	1,491	1,385
1949	1,407	1,395	1,395	1,503
1950	1,527	1,405	1,405	1,515
1951	1,480	1,580	1,468	1,580
1952	1,024	1,064	1,012	1,064
1953	1,050	1,025	1,078	1,078
1954	1,088	1,020	1,076	1,076
1955	1,036	1,082	1,082	1,082
1956	1,100	1,088	1,088	1,088
1957	1,168	1,094	1,094	1,094
1958	1,112	1,164	1,100	1,100
1959	1,118	1,106	1,172	1,106
1960	1,124	1,112	1,112	1,180
1961	1,200	1,118	1,118	1,118
1962	1,127	1,197	1,125	1,197
1963	1,133	1,131	1,205	1,205
1964	1,215	1,137	1,213	1,213
1965	1,143	1,221	1,221	1,221
1966	1,206	1,206	1,206	1,206
1967	1,068	986	986	986
1968	964	1,048	964	964
1969	1,002	1,002	1,088	1,002
1970	980	980	980	1,068
1971	1,108	1,018	1,018	1,108
1972	1,026	1,118	1,026	1,118
1973	1,004	1,004	1,098	1,098
1974	—	—	—	—
1975	1,050	1,148	1,148	1,148
1976	1,158	1,158	1,158	1,158
1977	—	—	—	—
1978	—	—	—	—

6 PENCE

2.8276 gm., .925 SILVER, .0841 oz ASW

C#	Date	Mintage	Fine	VF	XF	Unc
28	1787	—	7.50	15.00	25.00	45.00
	1787 W/ Plain Edge					
		—	—	—	Proof	—
	Rev: Hearts in Hanoverian shield					
1-28	1787	—	7.50	17.50	30.00	50.00

C#	Date	Mintage	Fine	VF	XF	Unc
29	1816	—	6.50	12.50	25.00	45.00
	1817	10.922	6.50	12.50	25.00	45.00
	1817	—	—	—	Proof	100.00
	1817 W/ Plain Edge					
		—	—	—	Proof	100.00
	1818	4.285	7.50	17.50	35.00	75.00
	1818	—	—	—	Proof	110.00
	1819/8	—	6.00	12.50	30.00	50.00
	1819	4.712	6.50	15.00	25.00	45.00
	1819	—	—	—	Proof	115.00
	1820	1.489	6.00	12.50	27.50	50.00
	1820	—	—	—	Proof	—

GOLD (OMS)

C#	Date	Mintage	Fine	VF	XF	Unc
29a	1816	—	—	—	Proof	—

2.8276 gm., 925 SILVER, .0841 oz ASW

C#	Date	Mintage	Fine	VF	XF	Unc
1-59	1821	.863	6.00	15.00	35.00	75.00
	1821	—	—	—	Proof	150.00
	1821 (error) BBITANNIAR					
		—	35.00	75.00	125.00	200.00

C#	Date	Mintage	Fine	VF	XF	Unc
59a	1824	.634	6.00	14.00	50.00	120.00
	1824	—	—	—	Proof	175.00
	1825	.483	5.00	12.00	45.00	100.00
	1825	—	—	—	Proof	150.00
	1826	.689	10.00	50.00	150.00	225.00
	1826	—	—	—	Proof	—

C#	Date	Mintage	Fine	VF	XF	Unc
60	1826	Inc. Ab.	5.00	10.00	20.00	50.00
	1826	Inc. Ab.	—	—	Proof	125.00
	1827	.166	15.00	40.00	100.00	250.00
	1828	.016	5.00	17.50	60.00	140.00
	1829	.404	4.00	12.50	50.00	100.00
	1829	—	—	—	Proof	250.00

C#	Date	Mintage	Fine	VF	XF	Unc
79	1831	1.340	4.00	12.50	40.00	60.00
	1831	Inc. Ab.	—	—	Proof	200.00
	1831 w/plain edge					
		—	—	—	Proof	130.00
	1834	5.892	3.25	12.00	30.00	75.00
	1834	—	—	—	Proof	200.00
	1834 w/round-topped 3					
		Inc. Ab.	—	—	Proof	200.00
	1835	1.555	4.00	15.00	40.00	80.00
	1835 w/round-topped 3					
		Inc. Ab.	—	—	Proof	450.00
	1836	1.988	8.00	26.00	60.00	150.00
	1836	—	—	—	Proof	450.00
	1837	.507	5.00	12.50	35.00	90.00
	1837	—	—	—	Proof	450.00

Y#	Date	Mintage	Fine	VF	XF	Unc
5	1838	1.608	3.00	8.00	30.00	60.00
5	1838	—	—	—	Proof	150.00
	1839	3.311	3.00	8.00	30.00	60.00
	1839	Inc. Ab.	—	—	Proof	150.00
	1840	2.099	4.00	12.00	35.00	90.00
	1841	1.386	3.00	12.00	35.00	90.00
	1842	.602	3.00	12.00	35.00	80.00
	1843	3.160	3.00	8.00	30.00	60.00
	1844	3.976	3.00	8.00	30.00	60.00
	1844 large 44					
		Inc. Ab.	3.00	10.00	35.00	80.00
	1845	3.714	3.00	7.00	30.00	80.00
	1846	4.267	3.00	8.00	30.00	70.00
	1848/6	.586	12.50	35.00	80.00	175.00
	1848/7	Inc. Ab.	12.00	35.00	80.00	175.00
	1848	Inc. Ab.	12.00	35.00	80.00	175.00
	1849	.210	—	None Reported		—
	1850/30	.499	—	30.00	60.00	120.00
	1850	Inc. Ab.	4.50	12.00	40.00	80.00
	1851	2.288	3.50	12.00	40.00	80.00
	1852	.905	3.00	10.00	35.00	70.00
	1853	3.838	3.00	10.00	35.00	60.00
	1853	Inc. Ab.	—	—	Proof	150.00
	1854	.840	22.50	75.00	200.00	350.00
	1855	1.129	3.00	8.00	30.00	50.00
	1855	—	—	—	Proof	200.00
	1856	2.780	3.00	8.00	30.00	50.00
	1857	2.233	3.00	12.00	35.00	80.00
	1858	1.932	3.00	12.00	35.00	80.00
	1858	—	—	—	Proof	200.00
	1859/8	4.689	4.00	10.00	35.00	70.00
	1859	Inc. Ab.	3.50	8.50	30.00	60.00
	1860	1.101	3.50	10.00	40.00	80.00
	1861	.600	—	Reported, Not Confirmed		
	1862	.990	7.50	30.00	65.00	150.00
	1863	.491	7.00	30.00	60.00	150.00
	1864	4.253	3.00	8.00	30.00	70.00
	1865	1.632	3.50	12.00	35.00	80.00
	1866	5.140	3.50	10.00	30.00	60.00
	1866 w/o die numbers					
		Inc. Ab.	30.00	60.00	85.00	200.00

New portrait

Y#	Date	Mintage	Fine	VF	XF	Unc
5.1	1867	1.362	6.00	22.50	50.00	150.00
	1867	—	—	—	Proof	250.00
	1868	1.069	6.00	22.50	50.00	150.00
	1869	.388	6.00	22.50	50.00	150.00
	1869	—	—	—	Proof	250.00
	1870	.080	5.00	20.00	40.00	120.00
	1870	—	—	—	Proof	200.00
	1870 w/plain edge					
		—	—	—	Proof	175.00
	1871	3.663	4.00	10.00	25.00	70.00
	1871	—	—	—	Proof	—
	1871 w/plain edge					
		—	—	—	Proof	—
	1871 w/o die numbers					
		Inc. Ab.	4.00	15.00	40.00	100.00
	1872	3.382	3.00	10.00	25.00	70.00
	1873	4.595	3.00	7.50	22.50	50.00
	1874	4.226	4.00	7.50	22.50	50.00
	1875	3.257	3.00	7.50	22.50	50.00
	1876	.841	7.50	20.00	50.00	125.00
	1877	4.066	3.50	7.50	22.50	50.00
	1877 w/o die numbers					
		Inc. Ab.	3.00	7.50	22.50	50.00
	1878/7	2.625	35.00	100.00	150.00	225.00
	1878	Inc. Ab.	3.00	7.50	22.50	50.00
	1878	—	—	—	Proof	200.00
	1878 (error) DRITANNIAR					
		Inc. Ab.	30.00	80.00	150.00	300.00
	1879	3.326	6.00	12.50	40.00	125.00
	1879	—	—	—	Proof	200.00
	1879 w/o die numbers					
		Inc. Ab.	3.00	6.00	15.00	45.00
	1880 obverse of 1879					
		3.892	3.00	7.00	20.00	60.00

Obv: New portrait, longer hair waves

Y#	Date	Mintage	Fine	VF	XF	Unc
5.2	1880	Inc. Ab.	2.75	5.00	15.00	45.00
	1880	—	—	—	Proof	185.00
	1881	6.239	2.75	5.00	15.00	45.00
	1881	—	—	—	Proof	200.00
	1881 w/plain edge					
5.2	—	—	—	—	Proof	200.00
	1882	.760	6.00	17.50	40.00	70.00
	1883	4.987	3.50	5.00	15.00	35.00
	1884	3.423	2.75	5.00	15.00	35.00
	1885	4.653	2.75	5.00	15.00	35.00
	1885	—	—	—	Proof	225.00
	1886	2.728	2.75	4.00	12.50	32.50
	1886	—	—	—	Proof	225.00
	1887	3.676	2.75	4.00	12.50	32.50
	1887	—	—	—	Proof	185.00

Y#	Date	Mintage	Fine	VF	XF	Unc
19	1887	Inc. Ab.	2.75	3.25	5.00	15.00
	1887	—	—	—	Proof	80.00

Y#	Date	Mintage	Fine	VF	XF	Unc
22	1887	Inc. Ab.	2.75	3.25	5.00	15.00
	1887	Inc. Ab.	—	—	Proof	100.00
	1888	4.198	2.75	3.25	6.00	20.00
	1888	—	—	—	Proof	—
	1889	8.739	2.75	3.50	7.00	20.00
	1890	9.387	2.75	3.50	7.00	20.00
	1890	—	—	—	Proof	—
	1891	7.023	2.75	3.50	7.00	20.00
	1892	6.246	2.75	3.50	7.00	20.00
	1893	7.351	100.00	225.00	500.00	950.00

Y#	Date	Mintage	Fine	VF	XF	Unc
36	1893	Inc. Ab.	2.75	3.50	9.00	20.00
	1893	1,312	—	—	Proof	75.00
	1894	3.468	2.75	3.25	10.00	25.00
	1895	7.025	BV	3.50	10.00	25.00
	1896	6.652	BV	3.50	10.00	25.00
	1897	5.031	BV	2.75	8.00	20.00
	1898	5.914	BV	2.75	8.00	20.00
	1899	7.997	BV	2.75	8.00	20.00
	1900	8.980	BV	2.75	8.00	20.00
	1901	5.109	BV	2.75	8.00	20.00

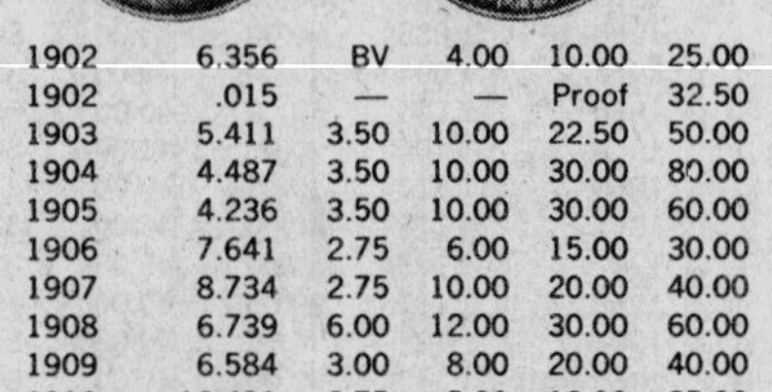

Y#	Date	Mintage	Fine	VF	XF	Unc
50	1902	6.356	BV	4.00	10.00	25.00
	1902	.015	—	—	Proof	32.50
	1903	5.411	3.50	10.00	22.50	50.00
	1904	4.487	3.50	10.00	30.00	80.00
	1905	4.236	3.50	10.00	30.00	60.00
	1906	7.641	2.75	6.00	15.00	30.00
	1907	8.734	2.75	10.00	20.00	40.00
	1908	6.739	6.00	12.00	30.00	60.00
	1909	6.584	3.00	8.00	20.00	40.00
	1910	12.491	2.75	5.00	12.00	25.00

Y#	Date	Mintage	Fine	VF	XF	Unc
66	1911	9.165	BV	2.75	5.00	12.00
	1911	6,007	—	—	Proof	40.00
	1912	10.984	BV	2.75	10.00	40.00
	1913	7.500	BV	3.00	12.00	40.00
	1914	22.715	BV	2.75	5.00	12.00
	1915	15.695	BV	2.75	5.00	12.00
	1916	22.207	BV	2.75	5.00	12.00
	1917	7.725	BV	3.50	12.00	35.00
	1918	27.559	BV	2.75	5.00	17.50
	1919	13.375	BV	2.75	8.00	25.00
	1920	14.136	BV	2.75	10.00	30.00

2.8276 gm., .500 SILVER, .0455 oz ASW

Y#	Date	Mintage	Fine	VF	XF	Unc
66a	1920	Inc. Ab.	BV	1.50	10.00	30.00
	1921	30.340	BV	1.50	9.00	25.00

Y#	Date	Mintage	Fine	VF	XF	Unc
66a	1922	16.879	BV	1.50	9.00	20.00
	1923	6.383	1.75	5.00	10.00	25.00
	1924	17.444	BV	1.50	9.00	25.00
	1925	12.721	BV	1.50	8.00	25.00
	1926	21.810	BV	1.50	8.00	20.00

Obv: Modified effigy, slightly smaller bust

Y#	Date	Mintage	Fine	VF	XF	Unc
66a.1	1926	Inc. Ab.	BV	1.50	7.50	20.00
	1927	8.925	BV	1.50	6.00	15.00

Rev: Oak sprigs with acorns

Y#	Date	Mintage	Fine	VF	XF	Unc
71	1927	.015	—	—	Proof	45.00
	1928	23.123	BV	1.50	2.50	9.00
	1929	28.319	BV	1.50	2.25	9.00
	1930	16.990	BV	1.50	3.50	10.00
	1931	16.873	BV	1.50	4.00	9.00
	1932	9.406	BV	1.50	6.50	12.50
	1933	22.185	BV	1.50	2.75	9.00
	1934	9.304	BV	1.75	6.50	14.00
	1935	13.996	BV	1.50	2.50	9.00
	1936	24.380	BV	1.50	2.00	7.00
87	1937	22.303	BV	1.50	1.75	4.00
	1937	.026	—	—	Proof	10.00
	1938	13.403	1.50	1.75	3.50	10.00
	1939	28.670	BV	1.50	1.75	4.00
	1940	20.875	BV	1.50	1.75	4.50
	1941	23.087	BV	1.50	1.75	4.00
	1942	44.943	BV	1.50	1.75	2.25
	1943	46.927	BV	1.50	1.75	2.25
	1944	37.953	BV	1.50	1.75	2.25
	1945	39.939	BV	1.50	1.75	2.25
	1946	43.466	BV	1.50	1.75	2.25

COPPER-NICKEL

Y#	Date	Mintage	Fine	VF	XF	Unc
95	1947	29.993	.15	.25	.50	2.50
	1948	88.324	.15	.25	.50	1.25

Rev. leg: IND IMP. omitted

Y#	Date	Mintage	Fine	VF	XF	Unc
108	1949	41.336	.15	.35	.75	4.00
	1950	32.742	.25	.50	1.00	5.00
	1950	.018	—	—	Proof	10.00
	1951	40.399	.25	.50	1.00	5.00
	1951	.020	—	—	Proof	10.00
	1952	1.013	1.50	3.00	15.00	40.00

Y#	Date	Mintage	Fine	VF	XF	Unc
120	1953	70.324	.20	.35	1.00	2.00
	1953	.040	—	—	Proof	7.50

Obv. leg: BRITT OMN. omitted

Y#	Date	Mintage	Fine	VF	XF	Unc
130	1954	105.240	.20	.35	.75	6.00
	1955	109.930	.20	.30	.50	1.00
	1956	109.840	.20	.35	.75	2.00
	1957	150.650	.15	.25	.35	.50
	1958	123.520	.20	.35	1.00	5.00
	1959	93.090	.20	.30	.40	.50
	1960	103.290	.20	.35	1.00	5.00
	1961	111.280	.20	.35	.50	5.00
	1962	158.360	.20	.30	.40	.50
	1963	125.860	.20	.30	.40	.50
	1964	137.350	.20	.30	.40	.50
	1965	149.950	.20	.30	.40	.50
130	1966	171.640	.20	.30	.40	.50
	1967	78.000	.20	.30	.40	.50
	1970	.731	—	Proof Only		3.50

SHILLING

5.6552 gm., .925 SILVER, .1682 oz ASW

C#	Date	Mintage	Fine	VF	XF	Unc
30	1763	—	100.00	250.00	400.00	500.00

Rev: No hearts in Hanoverian shield.

C#	Date	Mintage	Fine	VF	XF	Unc
31	1787	—	10.00	20.00	37.50	50.00
	1787 w/o stops at date	—	20.00	35.00	60.00	80.00
	1787 w/o stops on obverse	—	30.00	65.00	125.00	175.00
	1787 w/o stop over head	—	17.50	35.00	50.00	100.00
	1787	—	—	—	Proof	—
	1787 w/plain edge	—	—	—	Proof	—

Rev: Hearts in Hanoverian shield.

C#	Date	Mintage	Fine	VF	XF	Unc
31.1	1787	—	10.00	20.00	35.00	50.00
31a	1798 w/o stop over head*	—	—	1000.	2500.	4000.

*Known as Dorrien and Magens shilling struck for merchants.

C#	Date	Mintage	Fine	VF	XF	Unc
32	1816	—	5.50	7.50	30.00	45.00
	1816	—	—	—	Proof	175.00
	1816 w/plain edge		—	—	Proof	175.00
	1817	23.031	6.00	8.50	30.00	45.00
	1817 w/plain edge		—	—	Proof	175.00
	1818	1.342	10.00	35.00	75.00	125.00
	1819/8	7.595	10.00	25.00	60.00	120.00
	1819	Inc. Ab.	5.50	10.00	30.00	45.00
	1820	7.975	5.50	10.00	30.00	50.00
	1820	—	—	—	Proof	—

GOLD (OMS)

C#	Date	Mintage	Fine	VF	XF	Unc
32a	1816	—	—	—	Proof	—

5.6552 gm., .925 SILVER, .1682 oz ASW

C#	Date	Mintage	Fine	VF	XF	Unc
61	1821	2.463	6.00	12.00	60.00	125.00
	1821	—	—	—	Proof	200.00

C#	Date	Mintage	Fine	VF	XF	Unc
61a	1823	.693	10.00	25.00	75.00	150.00
	—	.993	20.00	50.00	150.00	250.00
	1824	4.158	5.50	7.50	35.00	100.00
61a	1824	—	—	—	Proof	225.00
	1825/3	2.459	8.50	20.00	60.00	150.00
	1825	Inc. Ab.	5.50	10.00	45.00	100.00
	1825	—	—	—	Proof	225.00

C#	Date	Mintage	Fine	VF	XF	Unc
62	1825	Inc. Ab.	5.50	7.50	40.00	100.00
	1825	—	—	—	Proof	200.00
	1825 w/plain edge				Proof	200.00
	1826	6.352	5.50	7.50	35.00	100.00
	1826	—	—	—	Proof	175.00
	1827	.574	6.00	35.00	100.00	175.00
	1829	.879	6.00	35.00	100.00	150.00
	1829	—	—	—	Proof	200.00

C#	Date	Mintage	Fine	VF	XF	Unc
80	1831 w/plain edge	—		Proof only		200.00
	1831 w/milled edge	—		Proof only		Rare
	1834	3.223	6.00	15.00	40.00	90.00
	1834	—	—	—	Proof	325.00
	1835	1.449	6.00	25.00	80.00	150.00
	1835	—	—	—	Proof	325.00
	1836	3.568	5.50	15.00	40.00	80.00
	1836	—	—	—	Proof	375.00
	1837	.479	6.00	25.00	75.00	150.00
	1837	—	—	—	Proof	325.00

COPPER (OMS)

C#	Date	Mintage	Fine	VF	XF	Unc
80a	1837	—	—	—	Proof	—

5.6552 gm., .925 SILVER, .1682 oz ASW

Y#	Date	Mintage	Fine	VF	XF	Unc
6	1838	1.956	6.00	12.50	35.00	85.00
	1838	Inc. Ab.	—	—	Proof	250.00
	1839WW	5.667	5.50	15.00	35.00	85.00
	1839 w/o WW	Inc. Ab.	5.50	15.00	35.00	85.00
	1839	Inc. Ab.	—	—	Proof	180.00
	1840	1.639	10.00	40.00	125.00	250.00
	1840	—	—	—	Proof	180.00
	1841	.875	6.00	25.00	75.00	125.00
	1842	2.095	5.50	15.00	40.00	80.00
	1842	—	—	—	Proof	300.00
	1843	1.465	7.50	25.00	75.00	125.00
	1844	4.467	5.50	15.00	45.00	90.00
	1845	4.083	5.50	20.00	50.00	100.00
	1846	4.031	5.50	20.00	50.00	100.00
	1848/6	1.041	15.00	60.00	175.00	225.00
	1849	.645	5.50	15.00	40.00	80.00
	1850/46	.685	150.00	250.00	500.00	1000.
	1850	Inc. Ab.	100.00	175.00	600.00	800.00
	1851	.470	20.00	80.00	200.00	500.00
	1851	—	—	—	Proof	600.00
	1852	1.307	5.50	15.00	40.00	70.00
	1853	4.256	5.50	15.00	40.00	70.00
	1853	Inc. Ab.	—	—	Proof	250.00
	1854	.552	45.00	125.00	275.00	400.00
	1855	1.368	5.50	17.50	45.00	90.00
	1856	3.168	5.50	17.50	40.00	80.00
	1857	2.562	5.50	17.50	40.00	70.00
	1858	3.109	5.50	17.50	40.00	70.00
	1859	4.562	7.00	17.50	40.00	80.00
	1860	1.671	6.00	20.00	60.00	120.00
	1861	1.382	6.00	20.00	60.00	120.00
	1862	.954	15.00	60.00	120.00	275.00
	1863	.859	15.00	60.00	120.00	250.00
	1864	4.519	5.50	12.50	40.00	70.00
	1865	5.619	5.50	12.50	40.00	70.00
	1866	4.990	5.50	12.50	40.00	70.00
	1867	2.166	6.00	12.50	45.00	90.00
	1867 Error 'BBITANNIAR'	—	—	—	—	—
	1867	—	—	—	Proof	300.00

Y#	Date	Mintage	Fine	VF	XF	Unc
6	1867 w/plain edge					
		—	—	—	Proof	300.00
	1868	3.330	BV	12.50	30.00	80.00
	1869	.737	6.00	15.00	40.00	100.00
	1870	1.467	BV	15.00	40.00	100.00
	1871	4.910	BV	12.50	30.00	80.00
	1871	—	—	—	Proof	300.00
	1871 w/plain edge					
		—	—	—	Proof	300.00
	1872	8.898	BV	6.00	35.00	60.00
	1873	6.590	BV	6.00	30.00	50.00
	1874	5.504	BV	6.00	30.00	60.00
	1875	4.354	BV	6.00	30.00	60.00
	1876	1.057	BV	8.00	40.00	80.00
	1877	2.981	BV	6.00	35.00	70.00
	1878	3.127	BV	6.00	35.00	70.00
	1878	—	—	—	Proof	300.00
	1879 w/die numbers					
		3.611	BV	15.00	40.00	100.00
	1879 w/o die numbers					
		Inc. Ab.	BV	15.00	40.00	100.00
	1880	4.843	BV	6.00	25.00	60.00
	1880	—	—	—	Proof	300.00
	1880 w/plain edge					
		—	—	—	Proof	300.00
	1881	5.255	BV	6.00	25.00	60.00
	1881	—	—	—	Proof	300.00
	1881 w/plain edge					
		—	—	—	Proof	300.00
	1882	1.612	5.50	15.00	40.00	100.00
	1883	7.281	BV	6.00	25.00	60.00
	1884	3.924	BV	6.00	25.00	60.00
	1884	—	—	—	Proof	300.00
	1885	3.337	BV	6.00	25.00	60.00
	1885	—	—	—	Proof	300.00
	1886	2.087	BV	6.00	25.00	60.00
	1886	—	—	—	Proof	310.00
	1887	4.034	BV	9.00	27.50	80.00
	1887	—	—	—	Proof	310.00

Y#	Date	Mintage	Fine	VF	XF	Unc
20	1887	Inc. Ab.	BV	5.50	7.50	15.00
	1887	1,084	—	—	Proof	80.00
	1888	4.527	BV	5.50	15.00	30.00
	1889 small head					
		7.040	20.00	60.00	200.00	400.00
	1889	—	—	—	Proof	400.00

Y#	Date	Mintage	Fine	VF	XF	Unc
21	1889 lg.head	—	BV	7.50	20.00	35.00
	1890	8.794	BV	6.00	20.00	40.00
	1891	5.665	BV	6.00	20.00	40.00
	1891	—	—	—	Proof	450.00
	1892	4.592	BV	6.00	25.00	40.00

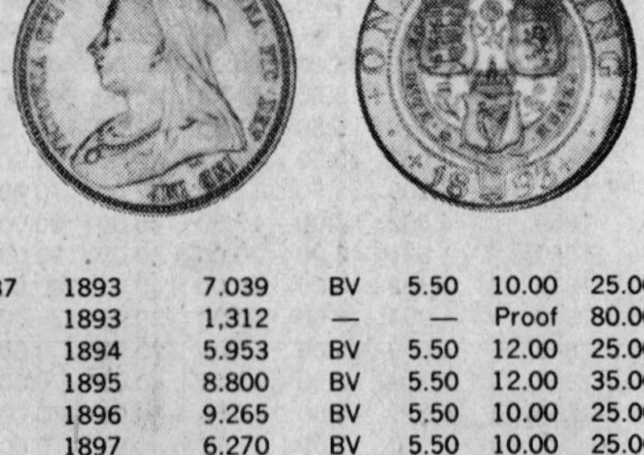

Y#	Date	Mintage	Fine	VF	XF	Unc
37	1893	7.039	BV	5.50	10.00	25.00
	1893	1,312	—	—	Proof	80.00
	1894	5.953	BV	5.50	12.00	25.00
	1895	8.800	BV	5.50	12.00	35.00
	1896	9.265	BV	5.50	10.00	25.00
	1897	6.270	BV	5.50	10.00	25.00
	1898	9.769	BV	5.50	10.00	25.00
	1899	10.965	BV	5.50	10.00	25.00
	1900	10.938	BV	5.50	10.00	25.00
	1901	3.426	BV	5.50	10.00	25.00

Y#	Date	Mintage	Fine	VF	XF	Unc
51	1902	7.890	BV	5.50	12.00	25.00
	1902	.015	—	—	Proof	50.00
	1903	2.062	8.00	15.00	60.00	90.00
	1904	2.040	BV	15.00	50.00	0
	1905	.488	25.00	75.00	200.00	350.00
	1906	10.791	BV	5.50	20.00	40.00
	1907	14.083	BV	6.00	25.00	60.00
	1908	3.807	BV	10.00	60.00	100.00
	1909	5.665	BV	15.00	60.00	100.00
	1910	26.547	BV	7.50	25.00	40.00

Y#	Date	Mintage	Fine	VF	XF	Unc
67	1911	20.066	BV	5.50	7.50	20.00
	1911	6,007	—	—	Proof	70.00
	1912	15.594	BV	5.50	12.50	40.00
	1913	9.002	BV	6.00	22.50	50.00
	1914	23.416	BV	5.50	7.50	17.50
	1915	39.279	BV	5.50	7.50	12.50
	1916	35.862	BV	5.50	7.50	15.00
	1917	22.203	BV	5.50	7.50	20.00
	1918	34.916	BV	5.50	7.50	20.00
	1919	10.824	BV	5.50	7.50	25.00

5.6552 gm., .500 SILVER, .0909 oz ASW

Y#	Date	Mintage	Fine	VF	XF	Unc
67a	1920	22.825	BV	3.00	10.00	30.00
	1921	22.649	BV	3.00	10.00	32.50
	1922	27.216	BV	3.00	10.00	32.50
	1923	14.575	BV	3.00	10.00	30.00
	1924	9.250	BV	4.00	12.00	30.00
	1925	5.419	BV	9.00	27.50	60.00
	1926	22.516	BV	3.00	10.00	30.00

Obv: Modified effigy, slightly smaller bust

Y#	Date	Mintage	Fine	VF	XF	Unc
67a.1	1926	Inc. Ab.	BV	3.00	5.00	17.50
	1927	9.262	BV	3.00	12.00	25.00

Rev: Larger lion and crown

Y#	Date	Mintage	Fine	VF	XF	Unc
72	1927	Inc. Ab.	BV	3.00	8.00	20.00
	1927	.015	—	—	Proof	35.00
	1928	18.137	BV	BV	3.00	10.00
	1929	19.343	BV	BV	3.00	10.00
	1930	3.137	BV	5.00	20.00	40.00
	1931	6.994	BV	BV	7.50	15.00
	1932	12.168	BV	BV	7.50	15.00
	1933	11.512	BV	BV	7.50	15.00
	1934	6.138	BV	3.00	12.00	35.00
	1935	9.183	BV	BV	3.00	10.00
	1936	11.911	BV	BV	3.00	10.00

Rev: English crest.

Y#	Date	Mintage	Fine	VF	XF	Unc
88	1937	8.359	BV	BV	3.00	10.00
	1937	.026	—	—	Proof	15.00
	1938	4.833	BV	BV	3.50	15.00
	1939	11.053	BV	BV	3.00	5.00
	1940	11.099	BV	BV	3.00	7.00
	1941	11.392	BV	BV	3.00	6.00
	1942	17.454	BV	BV	3.00	5.00
	1943	11.404	BV	BV	3.00	4.00
	1944	11.587	BV	BV	3.00	3.75
	1945	15.143	BV	BV	3.00	3.75
	1946	18.664	BV	BV	3.00	3.75

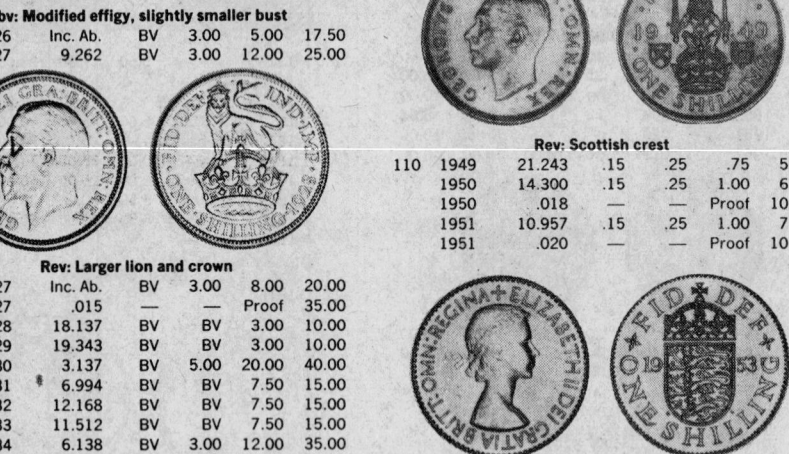

Rev: Scottish crest

Y#	Date	Mintage	Fine	VF	XF	Unc
89	1937	7.749	1.00	1.25	1.75	10.00
	1937	.026	—	—	Proof	15.00
	1938	4.798	1.00	1.25	2.50	12.00
	1939	10.264	1.00	1.25	1.50	5.00
	1940	9.913	1.00	1.25	2.00	6.50
	1941	8.086	1.00	1.25	2.25	7.00
	1942	13.677	1.00	1.25	1.50	5.00
	1943	9.824	1.00	1.25	1.50	5.50
	1944	10.990	1.00	1.25	1.75	4.50
	1945	15.106	1.00	1.25	1.50	3.00
	1946	16.382	1.00	1.25	1.50	3.00

COPPER-NICKEL

Rev: English crest.

Y#	Date	Mintage	Fine	VF	XF	Unc
96	1947	12.121	.25	.50	1.50	4.00
	1948	45.577	.25	.50	1.25	5.00

Rev: Scottish crest

Y#	Date	Mintage	Fine	VF	XF	Unc
97	1947	12.283	.15	.35	1.50	6.00
	1948	45.352	.15	.25	1.25	4.00

Rev: English crest, leg: IND IMP. omitted.

Y#	Date	Mintage	Fine	VF	XF	Unc
109	1949	19.328	.15	.25	.75	4.00
	1950	19.244	.15	.25	1.00	5.00
	1950	.018	—	—	Proof	15.00
	1951	9.957	.15	.25	1.00	5.00
	1951	.020	—	—	Proof	15.00

Rev: Scottish crest

Y#	Date	Mintage	Fine	VF	XF	Unc
110	1949	21.243	.15	.25	.75	5.00
	1950	14.300	.15	.25	1.00	6.00
	1950	.018	—	—	Proof	10.00
	1951	10.957	.15	.25	1.00	7.00
	1951	.020	—	—	Proof	10.00

Rev: English arms

Y#	Date	Mintage	Fine	VF	XF	Unc
121	1953	41.943	.15	.25	.50	1.00
	1953	.040	—	—	Proof	10.00

Rev: Scottish arms

Y#	Date	Mintage	Fine	VF	XF	Unc
122	1953	20.664	—	—	1.00	1.50
	1953	.040	—	—	Proof	10.00

Obv. leg: BRITT OMN omitted. Rev: English arms.

Y#	Date	Mintage	Fine	VF	XF	Unc
131	1954	30.162	.25	.35	.50	3.50
	1955	45.260	.25	.35	.50	3.00
	1956	44.970	.25	.35	.50	5.00
	1957	42.774	.25	.35	.50	1.50
	1958	14.392	.25	.35	1.00	22.00
	1959	19.443	.25	.35	.50	1.50
	1960	27.028	.25	.35	.50	1.50
	1961	39.817	.25	.35	.50	1.50
	1962	36.704	.25	.35	.50	.75
	1963	44.714	.25	.35	.50	.75
	1964	13.617	.25	.35	.50	.75
	1965	11.236	.25	.35	.50	.75
	1966	15.000	.25	.35	.50	.75
	1970	.731	—		Proof Only	2.75

Rev: Scottish arms.

Y#	Date	Mintage	Fine	VF	XF	Unc
132	1954	26.772	.25	.35	.50	2.50
	1955	27.951	.25	.35	.50	3.00
	1956	42.854	.25	.35	.60	5.00
	1957	17.960	.25	.35	1.00	22.00
	1958	40.823	.25	.35	.50	.75
	1959	1.013	.75	2.00	3.50	20.00
	1960	14.376	.25	.35	.50	1.00
	1961	2.763	.25	.35	2.00	8.00
	1962	18.967	.25	.35	.50	.75
	1963	32.300	.25	.35	.50	.75
	1964	5.247	.25	.35	.50	.50
	1965	31.364	.25	.35	.50	.75
	1966	15.600	.25	.35	.50	.75
	1970	.731	—		Proof Only	2.75

18 PENCE

(1 Shilling 6 Pence)

BANK OF ENGLAND

.925 SILVER

C#	Date	Mintage	Fine	VF	XF	Unc
39	1811	—	10.00	12.50	25.00	50.00
	1811	—	—	—	Proof	150.00
	1812	—	10.00	12.50	25.00	50.00
	1812	—	—	—	Proof	150.00

C#	Date	Mintage	Fine	VF	XF	Unc
39a	1812	—	10.00	12.50	22.50	50.00
	1813	—	12.00	15.00	27.50	60.00
	1814	—	10.00	12.50	17.50	40.00
	1815	—	10.00	12.50	17.50	40.00
	1816	—	12.00	15.00	27.50	60.00

FLORIN

(2 Shillings)

11.3104 gm., .925 SILVER, .3364 oz ASW

Y#	Date	Mintage	Fine	VF	XF	Unc
7	1848	—	—	—	Proof	400.00
	1849	.414	12.00	25.00	65.00	125.00

GOLD (OMS)

Y#	Date	Mintage	Fine	VF	XF	Unc
7a	1848	—	—	—	Proof	—

11.3104 gm., .925 SILVER, .3364 oz ASW

Gothic type

Obv: Roman dating in gothic script

Y#	Date	Mintage	Fine	VF	XF	Unc
8	1851	1,540	175.00	500.00	800.00	2000.
	1851	—	—	—	Proof	2000.
	1852	1.015	10.00	25.00	90.00	165.00
	1852	—	—	—	Proof	—
	1853	3.920	10.00	22.50	90.00	175.00
	1853	—	—	—	Proof	—
	1854	.550	150.00	400.00	900.00	2000.
	1855	.831	12.00	30.00	75.00	175.00
	1856	2.202	12.00	35.00	80.00	175.00
	1857	1.671	10.00	27.50	60.00	150.00
	1857	—	—	—	Proof	—
	1858	2.239	10.00	27.50	60.00	150.00
	1858	—	—	—	Proof	—
	1859	2.568	10.00	27.50	60.00	150.00
	1860	1.475	12.00	40.00	100.00	225.00
	1862	.594	20.00	80.00	225.00	400.00
	1862 w/plain edge		—	—	Proof	—
	1863	.939	25.00	120.00	325.00	700.00
	1863 w/plain edge		—	—	Proof	—
	1864	1.861	10.00	25.00	60.00	150.00
	1864	—	—	—	Proof	—
	1865	1.580	12.00	35.00	80.00	175.00
	1866	.915	12.00	37.50	85.00	180.00
	1867	.424	20.00	75.00	250.00	500.00
	1867 w/plain edge		—	—	Proof	—
	1868	.870	10.00	35.00	80.00	175.00
	1869	.297	10.00	27.50	60.00	150.00
	1869	—	—	—	Proof	Rare
	1870	1.081	10.00	27.50	60.00	150.00
	1871	3.426	10.00	27.50	60.00	150.00
	1871	—	—	—	Proof	—
	1871 w/plain edge		—	—	Proof	—
	1872	7.200	10.00	25.00	60.00	150.00
	1873	5.922	10.00	30.00	60.00	150.00
	1873	—	—	—	Proof	—
	1874	1.643	10.00	25.00	60.00	150.00
	1875	1.117	10.00	30.00	75.00	175.00
	1876	.580	10.00	30.00	75.00	175.00
	1877	.682	10.00	30.00	75.00	175.00
	1877 w/o W.W.	Inc. Ab.	20.00	80.00	200.00	400.00
	1878	1.787	10.00	25.00	60.00	150.00
	1878	—	—	—	Proof	—
	1879	1.512	10.00	30.00	60.00	200.00
	1879 W.W. w/die number	Inc. Ab.	12.00	35.00	125.00	300.00
	1879 w/o W.W., no die numbers	Inc. Ab.	10.00	30.00	85.00	200.00
	1880	2.161	10.00	25.00	50.00	150.00
	1880	—	—	—	Proof	—
	1881	2.576	10.00	25.00	55.00	150.00
	1881	—	—	—	Proof	—
	1881 w/plain edge		—	—	Proof	—
	1881 (error) MDCCCLXXRI	Inc. Ab.	12.00	30.00	90.00	175.00
	1883	3.556	10.00	25.00	55.00	150.00
	1884	1.447	10.00	25.00	55.00	150.00
	1885	1.758	10.00	25.00	55.00	150.00
	1885	—	—	—	Proof	—
	1886	.592	10.00	25.00	55.00	150.00
	1887	1.777	12.00	30.00	100.00	200.00
	1887	—	—	—	Proof	—

Y#	Date	Mintage	Fine	VF	XF	Unc
23	1887	Inc. Ab.	BV	10.00	12.00	20.00
	1887	1,084	—	—	Proof	125.00
	1888	1.548	BV	10.00	20.00	40.00
	1889	2.974	BV	10.00	25.00	40.00
	1890	1.685	BV	25.00	70.00	125.00
	1891	.836	15.00	50.00	125.00	275.00
	1892	.283	20.00	60.00	150.00	275.00
	1892	—	—	—	Proof	550.00

Y#	Date	Mintage	Fine	VF	XF	Unc
38	1893	1.666	BV	10.00	20.00	40.00
	1893	1,312	—	—	Proof	90.00
	1894	1.953	BV	11.00	20.00	60.00
	1895	2.183	BV	11.00	20.00	60.00
	1896	2.944	BV	10.00	20.00	60.00
	1897	1.700	BV	10.00	20.00	60.00
	1898	3.061	BV	11.00	20.00	60.00
	1899	3.970	BV	11.00	20.00	60.00
	1900	5.529	BV	10.00	20.00	60.00
	1901	2.649	BV	10.00	20.00	50.00

Y#	Date	Mintage	Fine	VF	XF	Unc
52	1902	2.190	BV	12.00	30.00	60.00
	1902	.015	—	—	Proof	70.00
	1903	.995	12.00	25.00	70.00	125.00
	1904	2.770	17.50	35.00	75.00	225.00
	1905	1.188	30.00	60.00	175.00	325.00
	1906	6.910	10.00	20.00	50.00	100.00
	1907	5.948	10.00	15.00	60.00	120.00
	1908	3.280	10.00	20.00	90.00	150.00
	1909	3.483	10.00	25.00	80.00	175.00
	1910	5.651	10.00	12.00	40.00	80.00

Y#	Date	Mintage	Fine	VF	XF	Unc
68	1911	5.951	BV	10.00	20.00	60.00
	1911	6,007	—	—	Proof	70.00
	1912	8.572	BV	10.00	30.00	80.00
	1913	4.545	BV	12.00	30.00	80.00
	1914	21.253	BV	10.00	15.00	20.00
	1915	12.358	BV	10.00	15.00	20.00
	1916	21.064	BV	10.00	15.00	20.00
	1917	11.182	BV	10.00	15.00	35.00
	1918	29.212	BV	10.00	12.00	30.00
	1919	9.469	BV	10.00	17.50	40.00

11.3104 gm., .500 SILVER, .1818 oz ASW

Y#	Date	Mintage	Fine	VF	XF	Unc
68a	1920	15.388	BV	6.00	15.00	60.00
	1921	34.864	BV	6.00	10.00	40.00
	1922	23.861	BV	6.00	10.00	50.00
	1923	21.547	BV	6.00	10.00	40.00
	1924	4.582	BV	7.00	15.00	60.00
	1925	1.404	7.00	35.00	100.00	200.00
	1926	5.125	BV	10.00	30.00	80.00

Rev: Decorative

Y#	Date	Mintage	Fine	VF	XF	Unc
73	1927	.015	—		Proof Only	75.00
	1928	11.088	BV	BV	6.00	25.00
	1929	16.397	BV	BV	6.00	25.00

Y#	Date	Mintage	Fine	VF	XF	Unc
73	1930	5.734	BV	BV	10.00	35.00
	1931	6.556	BV	BV	6.00	30.00
	1932	.717	7.50	17.50	60.00	200.00
	1933	8.685	BV	BV	6.00	25.00
	1935	7.541	BV	BV	6.00	25.00
	1936	9.897	BV	BV	6.00	12.00

Y#	Date	Mintage	Fine	VF	XF	Unc
90	1937	13.007	BV	BV	6.00	10.00
	1937	.026	—	—	Proof	20.00
	1938	7.910	BV	BV	6.00	20.00
	1939	20.851	BV	BV	6.00	10.00
	1940	18.700	BV	BV	6.00	8.00
	1941	24.451	BV	BV	6.00	8.00
	1942	39.895	BV	BV	6.00	8.00
	1943	26.712	BV	BV	6.00	8.00
	1944	27.560	BV	BV	6.00	8.00
	1945	25.858	BV	BV	6.00	8.00
	1946	2.300	BV	BV	6.00	8.00

COPPER-NICKEL

Y#	Date	Mintage	Fine	VF	XF	Unc
98	1947	22.910	.50	.75	1.25	3.50
	1948	67.554	.50	.65	1.00	3.00

Rev. leg: IND IMP. omitted

Y#	Date	Mintage	Fine	VF	XF	Unc
111	1949	28.615	.50	1.00	1.50	7.50
	1950	24.358	.50	1.00	1.50	9.00
	1950	.018	—	—	Proof	14.00
	1951	27.412	.75	1.00	1.50	7.00
	1951	.020	—	—	Proof	15.00

Y#	Date	Mintage	Fine	VF	XF	Unc
123	1953	11.959	.50	.65	1.00	3.00
	1953	.040	—	—	Proof	12.00

Obv. leg: BRITT OMN omitted

Y#	Date	Mintage	Fine	VF	XF	Unc
133	1954	13.085	.50	1.00	7.00	60.00
	1955	25.887	.50	.65	1.00	4.00
	1956	47.824	.50	.65	1.00	4.00
	1957	33.071	.50	.75	3.50	40.00
	1958	9.565	.50	.75	3.00	15.00
	1959	14.080	.50	.75	3.50	60.00
	1960	13.832	.50	.60	.75	2.25
	1961	37.735	.50	.60	.75	2.00
	1962	35.130	.50	.60	.75	1.75
	1963	25.580	.50	.60	.75	1.00
	1964	16.313	.50	.60	.75	1.00
	1965	48.723	.50	.60	.75	1.00
	1966	84.574	.50	.60	.75	1.00
	1967	22.000	.50	.60	.75	1.75
	1970	.731	—	Proof Only		4.00

1/2 CROWN

14.1380 gm., .925 SILVER, .4204 oz ASW
Obv: Large bust

C#	Date	Mintage	Fine	VF	XF	Unc
33	1816	—	15.00	35.00	90.00	150.00
	1816	—	—	—	Proof	500.00
	1816 w/plain edge		—	—	Proof	500.00
	1817	8.093	15.00	35.00	90.00	150.00
	1817	—	—	—	Proof	500.00
	1817 w/plain edge		—	—	Proof	500.00

Obv: Small head

C#	Date	Mintage	Fine	VF	XF	Unc
33a	1817	Inc. Ab.	15.00	35.00	90.00	150.00
	1817	—	—	—	Proof	500.00
	1817 w/plain edge		—	—	Proof	—
	1818	2.905	15.00	37.50	95.00	150.00
	1818	—	—	—	Proof	500.00
	1819	4.790	15.00	37.50	95.00	150.00
	1819	—	—	—	Proof	500.00
	1820	2.397	15.00	40.00	100.00	200.00
	1820	—	—	—	Proof	500.00
	1820 w/plain edge		—	—	Proof	500.00

C#	Date	Mintage	Fine	VF	XF	Unc
63	1820	Inc. Ab.	15.00	40.00	100.00	200.00
	1820	—	—	—	Proof	500.00
	1820 w/plain edge		—	—	Proof	500.00
	1821	1.435	15.00	50.00	110.00	200.00
	1821	—	—	—	Proof	500.00
	1823	2.004	200.00	500.00	1200.	1800.

C#	Date	Mintage	Fine	VF	XF	Unc
63a	1823	Inc. Ab.	15.00	50.00	125.00	200.00
	1823	—	—	—	Proof	500.00
	1824	.466	15.00	60.00	150.00	250.00
	1824	—	—	—	Proof	500.00

C#	Date	Mintage	Fine	VF	XF	Unc
64	1825	2.259	15.00	40.00	100.00	200.00
	1825	—	—	—	Proof	500.00
	1825 w/plain edge		—	—	Proof	500.00
	1826	2.189	15.00	40.00	120.00	175.00
	1826	—	—	—	Proof	500.00
	1828	.050	17.50	80.00	250.00	350.00
	1829	.508	17.50	70.00	200.00	350.00

C#	Date	Mintage	Fine	VF	XF	Unc
81	1831	—	—	Proof Only		800.00
	1831 w/plain edge		—	—	Proof	800.00
	1834 W.W. in caps					
		.993	20.00	50.00	150.00	250.00
	1834	—	—	—	Proof	—
	1834 W.W. in script					
		Inc. Ab.	15.00	40.00	90.00	150.00
	1834	—	—	—	Proof	—
	1834 w/plain edge		—	—	Proof	—
	1835	.281	25.00	70.00	150.00	325.00
	1836/5	1.589	35.00	80.00	175.00	400.00
	1836	Inc. Ab.	17.50	40.00	100.00	175.00
	1836 w/plain edge		—	—	Proof	—
	1837	.151	17.50	60.00	140.00	225.00

Y#	Date	Mintage	Fine	VF	XF	Unc
9	1839	—	100.00	700.00	1200.	1600.
	1839	—	—	—	Proof	700.00
	1840	.386	20.00	60.00	175.00	275.00
	1841	.043	25.00	100.00	275.00	350.00
	1842	.486	17.50	35.00	120.00	175.00
	1843	.455	25.00	80.00	240.00	325.00
	1844	1.999	15.00	35.00	120.00	200.00
	1845	2.232	15.00	35.00	140.00	200.00
	1846	1.907	15.00	40.00	150.00	200.00
	1848/6	.367	40.00	120.00	200.00	400.00
	1848	Inc. Ab.	50.00	100.00	350.00	500.00
	1849 large date					
		.261	20.00	50.00	175.00	250.00
	1849 small date					
		Inc. Ab.	17.50	50.00	150.00	250.00
	1850	.483	20.00	50.00	150.00	250.00
	1850	—	—	—	Proof	600.00
	1851	—	—	Proof Only		800.00
	1853	—	—	Proof Only		600.00
	1862	—	—	Proof Only		1000.
	1864	—	—	Proof Only		1000.

.925 SILVER

Obv: Second young head

Y#	Date	Mintage	Fine	VF	XF	Unc
9.2	1874	2.189	15.00	25.00	75.00	150.00
	1874	—	—	—	Proof	400.00
	1874 w/plain edge		—	—	Proof	400.00
	1875	1.114	15.00	30.00	80.00	140.00
	1875	—	—	—	Proof	400.00
	1875 w/plain edge		—	—	Proof	400.00
	1876/5	.633	—	100.00	200.00	400.00
	1876	Inc. Ab.	15.00	35.00	85.00	175.00
	1877	.447	15.00	35.00	85.00	175.00
	1878	1.466	15.00	35.00	75.00	150.00
	1878	—	—	—	Proof	500.00
	1879	.901	15.00	50.00	125.00	250.00
	1879	—	—	—	Proof	500.00
	1880	1.346	15.00	35.00	70.00	150.00
	1880	—	—	—	Proof	500.00
	1881	2.301	15.00	20.00	70.00	125.00
	1881	—	—	—	Proof	500.00
	1881 w/plain edge		—	—	Proof	500.00
	1882	.808	15.00	30.00	70.00	125.00
	1883	2.983	15.00	30.00	70.00	125.00
	1884	1.569	15.00	32.50	90.00	150.00
	1885	1.628	15.00	30.00	70.00	150.00
	1885	—	—	—	Proof	500.00
	1886	.892	15.00	25.00	65.00	125.00
	1886	—	—	—	Proof	550.00
	1887	1.438	15.00	40.00	80.00	150.00
	1887	—	—	—	Proof	550.00

.916 GOLD (OMS)

Y#	Date	Mintage	Fine	VF	XF	Unc
9.2a	1874	—	—	—	Proof	Rare

14.1380 gm., .925 SILVER, .4204 oz ASW

Y#	Date	Mintage	Fine	VF	XF	Unc
24	1887	Inc. Ab.	BV	15.00	20.00	40.00
	1887	1,084	—	—	Proof	175.00
	1888	1,429	BV	15.00	25.00	60.00
	1889	4.812	BV	15.00	20.00	50.00
	1890	3.228	BV	15.00	30.00	60.00
	1891	2.285	BV	15.00	30.00	70.00
	1892	1.711	BV	15.00	30.00	70.00

Y#	Date	Mintage	Fine	VF	XF	Unc
39	1893	1.793	BV	15.00	25.00	60.00
	1893	1,312	—	—	Proof	125.00
	1894	1.525	BV	15.00	40.00	70.00
	1895	1.773	BV	15.00	35.00	70.00
	1896	2.149	BV	15.00	35.00	60.00
	1897	1.679	BV	15.00	35.00	60.00
	1898	1.870	BV	15.00	20.00	70.00
	1899	2.864	BV	15.00	20.00	70.00
	1900	4.479	BV	15.00	30.00	60.00
	1901	1.577	BV	15.00	30.00	60.00

Y#	Date	Mintage	Fine	VF	XF	Unc
53	1902	1.316	BV	15.00	40.00	80.00
	1902	.015	—	—	Proof	100.00
	1903	.275	50.00	135.00	425.00	900.00
	1904	.710	20.00	60.00	200.00	450.00
	1905	.166	100.00	275.00	750.00	1750.
	1906	2.886	BV	20.00	60.00	150.00
	1907	3.694	BV	25.00	70.00	160.00
	1908	1.759	BV	30.00	75.00	180.00
53	1909	3.052	BV	20.00	60.00	160.00
	1910	2.558	BV	15.00	45.00	100.00

Y#	Date	Mintage	Fine	VF	XF	Unc
69	1911	2.915	BV	15.00	30.00	100.00
	1911	6,007	—	—	Proof	125.00
	1912	4.701	BV	15.00	25.00	80.00
	1913	4.090	BV	15.00	25.00	100.00
	1914	18.333	BV	BV	15.00	35.00
	1915	32.433	BV	BV	15.00	30.00
	1916	29.530	BV	BV	15.00	30.00
	1917	11.172	BV	BV	15.00	35.00
	1918	29.080	BV	BV	15.00	35.00
	1919	10.267	BV	BV	15.00	40.00

14.1380 gm., .500 SILVER, .2273 oz ASW

Y#	Date	Mintage	Fine	VF	XF	Unc
69a	1920	17.983	BV	7.50	25.00	50.00
	1921	23.678	BV	7.50	25.00	50.00
	1922 crown touches shield	16.397	BV	7.50	20.00	50.00
	1922 groove between crown and shield	16.397	BV	7.50	20.00	50.00
	1923	26.309	BV	7.50	10.00	40.00
	1924	5.866	BV	8.50	25.00	60.00
	1925	1.413	7.50	30.00	125.00	200.00
	1926	4.474	BV	7.50	35.00	70.00

Obv: Modified effigy; larger beads.

Y#	Date	Mintage	Fine	VF	XF	Unc
69a.1	1926	Inc. Ab.	BV	7.50	50.00	100.00
	1927	6.853	BV	BV	10.00	35.00

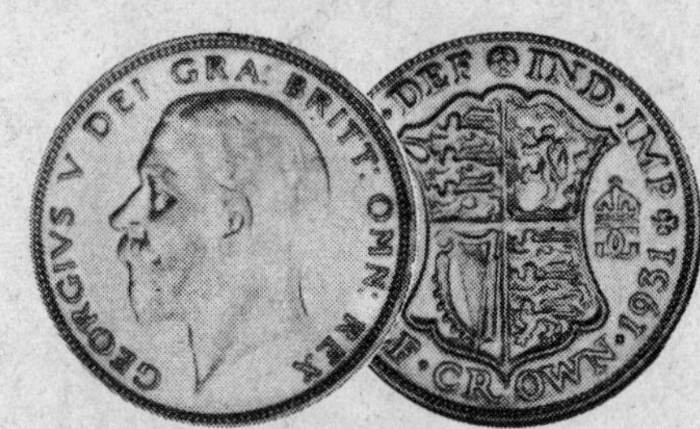

Y#	Date	Mintage	Fine	VF	XF	Unc
74	1927	.015	—		Proof Only	70.00
	1928	18.763	BV	BV	7.50	17.50
	1929	17.633	BV	BV	7.50	17.50
	1930	.810	7.50	25.00	100.00	200.00
	1931	11.264	BV	BV	7.50	20.00
	1932	4.794	BV	7.50	15.00	50.00
	1933	10.311	BV	BV	7.50	20.00
	1934	2.422	BV	7.50	20.00	70.00
	1935	7.022	BV	BV	7.50	17.50
	1936	7.039	BV	BV	7.50	15.00

Y#	Date	Mintage	Fine	VF	XF	Unc
91	1937	9.106	BV	BV	7.50	10.00
	1937	.026	—	—	Proof	20.00
	1938	6.426	BV	BV	7.50	22.50
	1939	15.479	BV	BV	7.50	10.00
	1940	17.948	BV	BV	7.50	10.00
	1941	15.774	BV	BV	7.50	10.00
	1942	31.220	BV	BV	7.50	10.00
	1943	15.463	BV	BV	7.50	10.00
	1944	15.255	BV	BV	7.50	10.00
	1945	19.849	BV	BV	7.50	10.00
	1946	22.725	BV	BV	7.50	10.00

COPPER-NICKEL

Y#	Date	Mintage	Fine	VF	XF	Unc
99	1947	21.910	.35	1.00	2.00	7.00
	1948	71.165	.35	1.00	2.00	6.00

Rev. leg: IND IMP. omitted

Y#	Date	Mintage	Fine	VF	XF	Unc
112	1949	28.273	.35	1.00	2.00	12.00
	1950	28.336	.35	1.00	2.00	12.00
	1950	.018	—	—	Proof	16.00
	1951	9.004	.35	1.00	2.00	12.00
	1951	.020	—	—	Proof	16.00
	1952	1 Known	—	—	Rare	—

Y#	Date	Mintage	Fine	VF	XF	Unc
124	1953	3.883	—	.60	2.00	4.00
	1953	.040	—	—	Proof	15.00

Obv. leg: BRITT OMN omitted.

Y#	Date	Mintage	Fine	VF	XF	Unc
134	1954	11.615	.50	1.00	4.00	45.00
	1955	23.629	.35	.50	1.00	7.00
	1956	33.935	.35	.50	2.00	7.50
	1957	34.201	.35	.50	1.00	4.00
	1958	15.746	.35	.75	5.00	30.00
	1959	9.029	.50	1.00	8.00	40.00
	1960	19.929	.35	.50	.75	5.00
	1961	25.888	.35	.50	.75	1.50
	1962	23.998	.35	.50	.75	1.25
	1963	17.573	.35	.50	.75	1.25
	1964	4.577	.35	.50	.75	5.00
	1965	8.125	.25	.35	.50	1.25
	1966	14.811	.25	.35	.50	1.25
	1967	21.000	.25	.35	.50	2.50
	1970	.731	—		Proof Only	6.00

3 SHILLINGS

BANK OF ENGLAND

.925 SILVER

C#	Date	Mintage	Fine	VF	XF	Unc
40	1811	—	20.00	25.00	40.00	100.00

C#	Date	Mintage	Fine	VF	XF	Unc
40	1811	—	—	—	Proof	—
	1812	—	20.00	25.00	40.00	100.00

C#	Date	Mintage	Fine	VF	XF	Unc
40a	1812	—	20.00	25.00	40.00	100.00
	1812	—	—	—	Proof	—
	1813	—	20.00	25.00	40.00	100.00
	1814	—	20.00	25.00	40.00	100.00
	1815	—	20.00	25.00	40.00	100.00
	1816	—	150.00	275.00	500.00	1000.

DOUBLE FLORIN

22.6207 gm., .925 SILVER, .6727 oz ASW

Y#	Date	Mintage	Fine	VF	XF	Unc
25	1887 Roman I					
		.483	22.00	27.50	35.00	50.00
	1887 Roman I					
		1,084	—	—	Proof	250.00
	1887 Arabic 1					
		Inc. Ab.	22.00	27.50	35.00	50.00
	1887 Arabic 1					
		—	—	—	Proof	250.00
	1888	.243	25.00	32.50	45.00	85.00
	1888 2nd I in VICTORIA, inverted 1					
		Inc. Ab.	25.00	35.00	75.00	200.00
	1889	1.185	22.00	27.50	35.00	80.00
	1889 2nd I in VICTORIA, inverted 1					
		Inc. Ab.	25.00	32.50	60.00	225.00
	1890	.782	25.00	32.50	45.00	80.00

CROWN (5 SHILLINGS)

BANK of ENGLAND

.903 SILVER

C#	Date	Mintage	Fine	VF	XF	Unc
41	1804	—	55.00	100.00	200.00	450.00
	1804	—	—	—	Proof	500.00

NOTE: The silver proofs were struck on specially prepared flans while circulation strikes were struck over Spanish and Spanish Colonial 8 Reales.

COPPER (OMS)

C#	Date	Mintage	Fine	VF	XF	Unc
41a	1804	—	—	Proof	—	Rare

28.2759 gm., .925 SILVER, .8409 oz ASW

C#	Date	Mintage	Fine	VF	XF	Unc
34	1818 LVIII	.155	30.00	75.00	200.00	450.00
	1818 LVIII	—	—		Proof-like	475.00
	1818 LIX	I.A.	35.00	85.00	225.00	450.00
	1819/8 LIX	.683	40.00	100.00	275.00	550.00
	1819 LIX	I.A.	35.00	125.00	275.00	450.00
	1819 LX	I.A.	35.00	80.00	250.00	400.00
	1819 LX	—	—		Proof-like	500.00
	1819 w/plain edge		—	—	Proof	—
	1820/19 LX	—	35.00	80.00	170.00	400.00
	1820 LX	.448	35.00	80.00	170.00	400.00
	1820 LX	—	—		Proof-like	500.00

Secundo on edge

C#	Date	Mintage	Fine	VF	XF	Unc
65	1821	.438	35.00	85.00	300.00	700.00
	1821	—	—	—	Proof	2000.
	1822	.125	40.00	125.00	325.00	750.00
	1822	—	—	—	Proof	2000.

Tertio on edge

C#	Date	Mintage	Fine	VF	XF	Unc
65.1	1821	—	—	—	Proof	2500.
	1822	—	40.00	100.00	300.00	750.00
	1822	—	—	—	Proof	2000.

COPPER (OMS)

C#	Date	Mintage	Fine	VF	XF	Unc
65a	1821	—	—	—	Proof	—
	1821 SECUNDO on edge					
		—	—	—	Proof	—

WHITE METAL (OMS)

C#	Date	Mintage	Fine	VF	XF	Unc
65b	1823	—	—	—	Proof	—

28.2759 gm., .925 SILVER, .8409 oz ASW

C#	Date	Mintage	Fine	VF	XF	Unc
A66	1826 w/unmilled, plain edge					
		—	—		Proof Only	—
	1826 SEPTIMO on edge					
		150 pcs.	—		Proof Only	3000.
	1826LVIII	—	—		Proof Only	—

Obv: Portrait of William IV.

C#	Date	Mintage	Fine	VF	XF	Unc
A82	1831	100 pcs.	—		Proof Only	6000.

Y#	Date	Mintage	Fine	VF	XF	Unc
10	1839	—	—	Proof Only		3500.
	1844	.090	35.00	100.00	250.00	550.00
	1844	—	—	—	Proof	2000.
	1845	.160	35.00	100.00	250.00	600.00
	1845	—	—	—	Proof	2000.
	1847	.140	40.00	125.00	275.00	750.00
	1847	—	—	—	Proof	2250.

GOLD (OMS)

Y#	Date	Mintage	Fine	VF	XF	Unc
10a	1847 w/plain edge	—	—	Proof		—

28.2759 gm., .925 SILVER, .8409 oz ASW

Y#	Date	Mintage	Fine	VF	XF	Unc
11	1847 UNDECIMO on edge					
		8,000	—	Proof Only		1250.
	1847 SEPTIMO on edge					
		—	—	Proof Only		5500.
	1847 plain edge					
		—	—	Proof Only		1750.
	1853 SEPTIMO on edge					
		460 pcs.	—	Proof Only		5500.
	1853 plain edge					
		—	—	Proof Only		Rare

Y#	Date	Mintage	Fine	VF	XF	Unc
26	1887	.274	27.50	35.00	50.00	100.00
	1887	1,084	—	—	Proof	400.00
	1888	.132	27.50	40.00	75.00	125.00
	1889	1.807	27.50	35.00	60.00	120.00
	1890	.998	27.50	35.00	50.00	100.00
	1891	.566	27.50	35.00	60.00	125.00
	1892	.451	27.50	35.00	60.00	135.00

Rev: Similar to Y#26.

Y#	Date	Mintage	Fine	VF	XF	Unc
40	1893LVI	.498	27.50	35.00	90.00	200.00
	1893LVI	1,312	—	—	Proof	550.00
	1893LVII	I.A.	30.00	70.00	175.00	400.00
	1894LVII	.145	27.50	40.00	135.00	200.00
	1894LVIII	I.A.	27.50	50.00	120.00	225.00
	1895LVIII	.253	27.50	40.00	120.00	250.00
	1895LIX	I.A.	30.00	40.00	100.00	200.00
	1896LIX	.318	35.00	60.00	175.00	325.00
	1896LX	I.A.	27.50	35.00	100.00	200.00
	1897LX	.252	27.50	35.00	100.00	200.00
	1897LXI	I.A.	27.50	35.00	90.00	200.00
	1898LXI	.161	35.00	70.00	200.00	400.00
	1898LXII	I.A.	30.00	40.00	120.00	250.00
	1899LXII	.166	30.00	45.00	120.00	225.00
	1899LXIII	I.A.	27.50	45.00	120.00	225.00
	1900LXIII	.353	27.50	35.00	100.00	200.00
	1900LXIV	I.A.	27.50	35.00	100.00	200.00

Rev: Similar to Y#26.

Y#	Date	Mintage	Fine	VF	XF	Unc
54	1902	.256	60.00	80.00	120.00	200.00
	1902	.015	—	—	Proof	250.00

28.2759 gm., .500 SILVER, .4545 oz ASW

Y#	Date	Mintage	Fine	VF	XF	Unc
75	1927	.015	—	Proof Only		175.00
	1928	9,034	60.00	100.00	150.00	250.00
	1929	4,994	65.00	100.00	175.00	275.00
	1930	4,847	65.00	110.00	165.00	275.00
	1931	4,056	70.00	120.00	175.00	275.00
	1932	2,395	80.00	150.00	225.00	375.00
	1932	—	—	—	Proof	—
	1933	7,132	80.00	120.00	160.00	250.00
	1934	932 pcs.	200.00	475.00	900.00	1650.
	1934	—	—	—	Proof	—
	1936	2,473	90.00	125.00	200.00	275.00

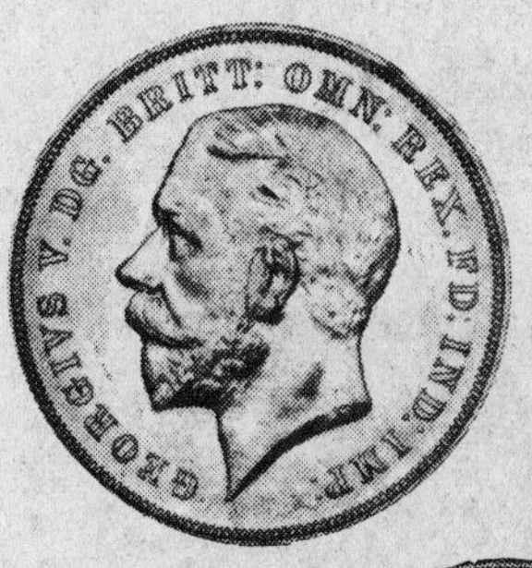

George V Silver Jubilee

Y#	Date	Mintage	Fine	VF	XF	Unc
76	1935 incused edge lettering					
		.715	BV	15.00	20.00	27.50
	1935 specimen in box of issue					
		—	—	—	—	35.00
	1935 error, edge lettering: MEN.ANNO-REGNI					
	XXV.	Inc. Ab.	—	—	Rare	—

.925 SILVER

Y#	Date	Mintage	Fine	VF	XF	Unc
76a	1935 incused edge lettering					
		—	—	—	Proof	60.00
	1935 raised edge lettering					
		2,500	—	Proof Only		350.00

GOLD (OMS)

Y#	Date	Mintage	Fine	VF	XF	Unc
76b	1936	30 pcs.	—	—	Proof	Rare

28.2759 gm., .500 SILVER, .4545 oz ASW

Y#	Date	Mintage	Fine	VF	XF	Unc
92	1937	.419	15.00	20.00	25.00	45.00
	1937	.026	—	—	Proof	70.00

COPPER-NICKEL
Festival Of Britain

Y#	Date	Mintage	Fine	VF	XF	Unc
114	1951	2.003	—		Proof Like	15.00

Coronation

Y#	Date	Mintage	Fine	VF	XF	Unc
125	1953	5.963	3.00	4.00	5.00	10.00
	1953	.040	—	—	Proof	40.00

British Exhibition In New York

Y#	Date	Mintage	Fine	VF	XF	Unc
136	1960	1.024	2.50	5.00	8.50	15.00
	1960	.070	—	—	Proof	20.00

NOTE: Proof crowns are usually bagmarked and scratched. Perfect specimens bring a premium.

Winston Churchill

Y#	Date	Mintage	Fine	VF	XF	Unc
138	1965	9.640	.25	.50	1.00	1.50
	1965	—	—	—	Proof	—

DECIMAL COINAGE

5 New Pence = 1 Shilling
25 New Pence = 1 Crown
100 New Pence = 1 Pound

1/2 NEW PENNY

BRONZE

Y#	Date	Mintage	Fine	VF	XF	Unc
139	1971	1,394.188	—	—	—	.25
	1971	.191	—	—	Proof	2.00
	1972	.062	—		Proof Only	1.50
	1973	104.992	—	—	—	.15
	1973	.060	—	—	Proof	2.00
	1974	333.448	—	—	—	.15
	1974	.063	—	—	Proof	1.50
	1975	209.200	—	—	—	.10
	1975	.063	—	—	Proof	1.50
	1976	221.048	—	—	—	.10
	1976	.061	—	—	Proof	1.50
	1977	—	—	—	—	.10
	1977	—	—	—	Proof	1.50
	1978	—	—	—	—	.10
	1978	—	—	—	Proof	1.50
	1979	—	—	—	—	.10
	1979	—	—	—	Proof	1.50
	1980	—	—	—	—	—
	1980	—	—	—	Proof	—

NEW PENNY

BRONZE

Y#	Date	Mintage	Fine	VF	XF	Unc
140	1971	1,521.666	—	—	—	.40
	1971	.191	—	—	Proof	1.75
	1972	.062	—		Proof Only	1.75
	1973	88.532	—	—	—	.30
	1973	.060	—	—	Proof	2.00
	1974	298.692	—	—	—	.15
	1974	.063	—	—	Proof	1.75
	1975	241.800	—	—	—	.15
	1975	.063	—	—	Proof	1.75
	1976	245.696	—	—	—	.10
	1976	.061	—	—	Proof	1.75
	1977	—	—	—	—	.15
	1977	—	—	—	Proof	1.75
	1978	—	—	—	—	.15
	1978	—	—	—	Proof	1.75
	1979	—	—	—	—	.15
	1979	—	—	—	Proof	1.75
	1980	—	—	—	—	—
	1980	—	—	—	Proof	—

2 NEW PENCE

BRONZE

Y#	Date	Mintage	Fine	VF	XF	Unc
141	1971	1,406.203	—	—	.10	.50
	1971	.191	—	—	Proof	3.00
	1972	.062	—		Proof Only	2.00
	1973	.060	—		Proof Only	3.00
	1974	.063	—		Proof Only	2.00
	1975	111.119	—	—	.10	.25
	1975	.063	—	—	Proof	2.00
	1976	179.532	—	—	.10	.20
	1976	.061	—	—	Proof	2.00
	1977	—	—	—	—	.20
	1977	—	—	—	Proof	2.00
	1978	—	—	—	—	.20
	1978	—	—	—	Proof	2.00
	1979	—	—	—	—	.20
	1979	—	—	—	Proof	2.00
	1980	—	—	—	—	—
	1980	—	—	—	Proof	—

5 NEW PENCE

COPPER-NICKEL

Y#	Date	Mintage	Fine	VF	XF	Unc
142	1968	98.868	—	—	.15	.75
	1969	119.270	—	—	.15	.75
	1970	225.948	—	—	.15	.30
	1971	81.783	—	—	.15	.30
	1971	.191	—	—	Proof	2.50
	1972	.166	—		Proof Only	2.50
	1973	.060	—		Proof Only	2.50
	1974	.063	—		Proof Only	2.50
	1975	86.950	—	—	.15	.30
	1975	.063	—	—	Proof	2.50
	1976	.061	—	—	Proof	2.50
	1977	—	—	—	.10	.30
	1977	—	—	—	Proof	2.50
	1978	—	—	—	—	.25
	1978	—	—	—	Proof	2.50
	1979	—	—	—	—	—
	1979	—	—	—	Proof	2.50

Y#	Date	Mintage	Fine	VF	XF	Unc
142	1980	—	—	—	—	—
	1980	—	—	—	Proof	—

10 NEW PENCE

COPPER-NICKEL

Y#	Date	Mintage	Fine	VF	XF	Unc
143	1968	336.143	—	—	.25	.75
	1969	314.008	—	—	.25	1.00
	1970	133.571	—	—	.25	1.00
	1971	63.205	—	—	.25	1.00
	1971	.191	—	—	Proof	3.00
	1972	—	—		Proof Only	3.00
	1973	152.174	—	—	.35	.75
	1973	—	—	—	Proof	3.00
	1974	92.741	—	—	.25	.50
	1974	—	—	—	Proof	3.00
	1975	181.559	—	—	.20	1.00
	1975	—	—	—	Proof	3.00
	1976	196.745	—	—	.20	.75
	1976	—	—	—	Proof	3.00
	1977	—	—	—	.20	.60
	1977	—	—	—	Proof	3.00
	1978	—	—	—	—	—
	1978	—	—	—	Proof	3.00
	1979	—	—	—	—	—
	1979	—	—	—	Proof	3.00
	1980	—	—	—	—	—
	1980	—	—	—	Proof	—

25 NEW PENCE

COPPER-NICKEL
Royal Silver Wedding Anniversary

Y#	Date	Mintage	Fine	VF	XF	Unc
145	1972	7.452	—	—	—	1.75
	1972	.062	—	—	Proof	7.50

.925 SILVER

Y#	Date	Mintage	Fine	VF	XF	Unc
145a	1972	.165	—	—	—	50.00

COPPER-NICKEL
Silver Jubilee Of Reign

Y#	Date	Mintage	Fine	VF	XF	Unc
147	1977	15.000	—	—	—	1.50
	1977	—	—	—	Proof	25.00
	1977(RMF)*	—	—	—	—	3.00

NOTE: Sealed in Royal Mint Folder.

.925 SILVER

Y#	Date	Mintage	Fine	VF	XF	Unc
147a	1977	.250	—	—	Proof	35.00

COPPER-NICKEL
80th Birthday of Queen Mother

Y#	Date	Mintage	Fine	VF	XF	Unc
148	1980	—	—	—	—	—

.925 SILVER

Y#	Date	Mintage	Fine	VF	XF	Unc
148a	1980	—	—	—	—	—

50 NEW PENCE

COPPER-NICKEL

Y#	Date	Mintage	Fine	VF	XF	Unc
144	1969	188.400	—	1.25	1.50	3.50
	1970	19.461	—	—	—	4.50
	1971	.191	—	—	Proof	6.00
	1972	—	—	—	Proof	6.00
	1974	—	—		Proof Only	6.00
	1975	—	—		Proof Only	6.00
	1976	28.050	—	1.00	1.25	2.75
	1976	—	—	—	Proof	4.00
	1977	—	—	1.00	1.25	2.25
	1977	—	—	—	Proof	4.00
	1978	—	—	—	—	2.00
	1978	—	—	—	Proof	4.00
	1979	—	—	—	—	1.50
	1979	—	—	—	Proof	4.00
	1980	—	—	—	—	—
	1980	—	—	—	Proof	—

Commemorates Entry Into E.E.C.

Y#	Date	Mintage	Fine	VF	XF	Unc
146	1973	37.602	—	—	—	2.50
	1973	.029	—	—	Proof	5.00

COUNTERSTAMP ISSUES

Bank Of England

Emergency Issue: Foreign silver coins, usually Spanish and Spanish Colonial having a bust of George III within an oval (1797) or octagonal (1804) countermark. Marked 8 Reales circulated at 4 Shillings 9 Pence In 1797 And 5 Shillings In 1804.

Type I

1797
Head of George III in oval

NOTE: Coins bearing this cmk. in other positions than center obverse and on smaller coins than 4 Reales are considered spurious by some authorities.

Type II

1804
Head of George III in octagon.

NOTE: Coins other than 8 Reales bearing this cmk. are considered spurious by some authorities.

1/2 DOLLAR

c/s: Type I on Spanish (Madrid) 4 Reales, C#70.

C#	Date	Year	Mintage	VG	Fine	VF
37	ND	(1788-1808)	—	75.00	125.00	175.00

DOLLAR

(4 Shillings 9 Pence - 5 Shillings)

SILVER
c/s: Type I on Bolivia (Potosi) 8 Reales, C#13.

C#	Date	Year	Mintage	Fine	VF	XF
38.1	ND	(1767-70)	—	—	Rare	—

c/s: Type I on Bolivia (Potosi) 8 Reales, C#18.

C#	Date	Year	Mintage	Fine	VF	XF
38.2	ND	(1773-89)	—	100.00	150.00	250.00

c/s: Type I on Bolivia (Potosi) 8 Reales, C#27.

C#	Date	Year	Mintage	Fine	VF	XF
38.3	ND	(1789-91)	—	125.00	175.00	300.00

c/s: Type I on Bolivia (Potosi) 8 Reales, C#37.

C#	Date	Year	Mintage	Fine	VF	XF
38.4	ND	(1791-1808)	—	100.00	150.00	250.00

c/s: Type I on Chile (Santiago) 8 Reales, C#61.

C#	Date	Year	Mintage	Fine	VF	XF
38.5	ND	(1791-1808)	—	150.00	250.00	400.00

c/s: Type I on France 1 Ecu, C#78.

C#	Date	Year	Mintage	Fine	VF	XF
38.6	ND	(1774-92)	—	—	Rare	—

c/s: Type I on Guatemala 8 Reales, C#47.

C#	Date	Year	Mintage	Fine	VF	XF
38.7	ND	(1790-1808)	—	150.00	275.00	450.00

c/s: Type I on Mexico 8 Reales, KM#104 (C#17).

C#	Date	Year	Mintage	Fine	VF	XF
38.8	ND	(1747-60)	—	—	Rare	—

c/s: Type I on Mexico 8 Reales, KM#105 (C#35).

C#	Date	Year	Mintage	Fine	VF	XF
38.9	ND	(1760-71)	—	—	Rare	—

c/s: Type I on Mexico 8 Reales, KM#106 (C#40).

C#	Date	Year	Mintage	Fine	VF	XF
38.10	ND	(1772-89)	—	85.00	125.00	200.00

c/s: Type I on Mexico 8 Reales, KM#107 (C#73).

C#	Date	Year	Mintage	Fine	VF	XF
38.11	ND	(1789-90)	—	100.00	150.00	225.00

c/s: Type I on Mexico 8 Reales, KM#109 (C#81).

C#	Date	Year	Mintage	Fine	VF	XF
38.12	ND	(1791-1808)	—	85.00	125.00	200.00

c/s: Type I on Peru (Lima) 8 Reales, C#35.

C#	Date	Year	Mintage	Fine	VF	XF
38.13	ND	(1760-72)	—	—	Rare	—

c/s: Type I on Peru (Lima) 8 Reales, C#45.

C#	Date	Year	Mintage	Fine	VF	XF
38.14	ND	(1772-89)	—	100.00	150.00	225.00

c/s: Type I on Peru (Lima) 8 Reales, C#69.

C#	Date	Year	Mintage	Fine	VF	XF
38.15	ND	(1789-91)	—	120.00	175.00	300.00

c/s: Type I on Peru (Lima) 8 Reales, C#76.

C#	Date	Year	Mintage	Fine	VF	XF
38.16	ND	(1791-1808)	—	100.00	150.00	225.00

c/s: Type I on Spanish 8 Reales, C#40.

C#	Date	Year	Mintage	Fine	VF	XF
38.17	ND	(1772-88)	—	150.00	250.00	400.00

c/s: Type I on Spanish 8 Reales, C#71.

C#	Date	Year	Mintage	Fine	VF	XF
38.18	ND	(1788-1808)	—	150.00	250.00	400.00

c/s: Type 1 on Austria (Burgau) Thaler C# 14.

C#	Date	Year	Mintage	Fine	VF	XF
38.19	ND	(1780)	—	—	Rare	—

c/s: Type II on Bolivia (Potosi) 8 Reales, C#18.

C#	Date	Year	Mintage	Fine	VF	XF
38a.1	ND	(1773-89)	—	125.00	250.00	400.00

c/s: Type II on Bolivia (Potosi) 8 Reales, C#37.

C#	Date	Year	Mintage	Fine	VF	XF
38a.2	ND	(1791-1808)	—	125.00	250.00	400.00

c/s: Type II on France 1 Ecu, C#78.

C#	Date	Year	Mintage	Fine	VF	XF
38a.3	ND	(1774-92)	—	—	Rare	—

c/s: Type II on Mexico 8 Reales, KM#106 (C#40).

C#	Date	Year	Mintage	Fine	VF	XF
38a.4	ND	(1772-89)	—	100.00	175.00	325.00

c/s: Type II on Mexico 8 Reales, KM#109 (C#81).

C#	Date	Year	Mintage	Fine	VF	XF
38a.5	ND	(1791-1808)	—	100.00	175.00	325.00

c/s: Type II on Peru (Lima) 8 Reales, C#45.

C#	Date	Year	Mintage	Fine	VF	XF
38a.6	ND	(1772-89)	—	—	Rare	—

c/s: Type II on Peru (Lima) 8 Reales, C#76.

C#	Date	Year	Mintage	Fine	VF	XF
38a.7	ND	(1791-1808)	—	—	Rare	—

c/s: Type II on Spanish (Seville) 8 Reales, C#71.

C#	Date	Year	Mintage	Fine	VF	XF
38a.8	ND	(1788-1808)	—	—	Rare	—

c/s: Type II on United States 1 Dollar, C#34.

C#	Date	Year	Mintage	Fine	VF	XF
38a.9	ND	(1795-98)	—	—	Rare	—

c/s: Type II on United States 1 Dollar, C#34a.

C#	Date	Year	Mintage	Fine	VF	XF
38a.10	ND	(1798-1803)	—	—	Rare	—

Glasgow Bank

4 SHILLINGS 9 PENCE

.903 SILVER
c/s: 4/9 GLASGOW BANK on
Spanish or Spanish Colonial 8 Reales.

KM#	Date	Mintage	VG	Fine	VF
SC1	ND	—	—	Rare	—

5 SHILLINGS

.903 SILVER
c/s: 5/. GLASGOW BANK on
Spanish or Spanish Colonial 8 Reales.

KM#	Date	Mintage	VG	Fine	VF
SC2	ND	—	150.00	200.00	300.00

Thistle Bank

4 SHILLINGS 9 PENCE

.903 SILVER
Obv. c/s: 4/9 THISTLE BANK, rev. c/s: Thistle
on Spanish or Spanish Colonial 8 Reales.

KM#	Date	Mintage	VG	Fine	VF
SC3	ND	—	125.00	175.00	250.00

Obv. c/s: 4/9 THISTLE BANK w/o rev. Thistle c/s
on Spanish or Spanish Colonial 8 Reales.

KM#	Date	Mintage	VG	Fine	VF
SC4	ND	—	—	Rare	—

5 SHILLINGS

.903 SILVER
Obv. c/s: 5/.THISTLE BANK, rev. c/s: Thistle
on Spanish or Spanish Colonial 8 Reales.

KM#	Date	Mintage	VG	Fine	VF
SC5	ND	—	125.00	175.00	250.00

Merchant Issues

Obv. c/s: CATRINE.COTTON.WORKS 5/6

During the same period of the Bank of England countermarks of George III, various silver coins, usually Spanish and Spanish Colonial, were countermarked by various merchants throughout Scotland. The new face value varied somewhat around an average of 4 Shillings 9 Pence. Illustrated is a countermark of the Catrine Cotton Works, Ayrshire new value of 5 Shillings 6 Pence on a silver 8 Reales, Charles IIII from the Lima Mint. These issues can be found listed in Seaby's "Coins and Tokens of Scotland."

TRADE COINAGE

TRADE DOLLAR

26.9568 gm., .900 SILVER, .7800 oz ASW

Issued to facilitate British trade in the Orient, the reverse design incorporates the statement of denomination in Chinese characters and Malay script.

NOTE: This issue was struck only at the Bombay (B) and Calcutta (C) mints in India, except for 1925 and 1930 issues which were struck at London, although through error the mintmarks did not appear on some early issues as indicated.

Y#	Date	Mintage	Fine	VF	XF	Unc
T1	1895-B	3.316	40.00	65.00	90.00	120.00
	1895-B	Inc. Ab.	—	—	Proof	300.00
	1895	Inc. Ab.	40.00	70.00	100.00	130.00
	1895	Inc. Ab.	—	—	Proof	300.00
	1896-B	6.136	50.00	85.00	120.00	150.00
	1896-B	Inc. Ab.	—	—	Proof	300.00
	1897/6-B	21.286	60.00	95.00	135.00	175.00
	1897-B	Inc. Ab.	BV	25.00	27.50	35.00
	1897-B	Inc. Ab.	—	—	Proof	275.00
	1897	Inc. Ab.	BV	25.00	30.00	37.50
	1898-B	21.546	BV	25.00	27.50	35.00
	1898B	Inc. Ab.	—	—	Proof	275.00
	1898	Inc. Ab.	BV	25.00	27.50	35.00
	1899-B	30.743	BV	25.00	27.50	35.00
	1899B	Inc. Ab.	—	—	Proof	275.00
	1900/1000B	9.107	—	—	—	—
	1900/890B	I.A.	—	—	—	—
	1900-B	Inc. Ab.	BV	25.00	27.50	35.00
	1900-B	Inc. Ab.	—	—	Proof	250.00
	1900B (restrike)	25 Known	—	—	Proof	250.00
	1900-C	.363	200.00	275.00	350.00	—
	1900	Inc. Ab.	225.00	300.00	375.00	—
	1901/0-B	25.680	125.00	160.00	200.00	250.00
	1901-B	Inc. Ab.	BV	25.00	27.50	35.00
	1901-B	Inc. Ab.	—	—	Proof	275.00
	1901-C	1.514	BV	25.00	35.00	50.00
	1902-B	30.404	BV	25.00	27.50	35.00
	1902-B	Inc. Ab.	—	—	Proof	275.00
	1902-C	1.267	25.00	32.50	40.00	50.00
	1902-C	Inc. Ab.	—	—	Proof	275.00
	1903/2-B	3.956	25.00	35.00	50.00	75.00
	1903-B	Inc. Ab.	BV	25.00	27.50	35.00
	1903-B	Inc. Ab.	—	—	Proof	300.00
	1904/898-B	.649	90.00	140.00	175.00	225.00
	1904/3-B	I.A.	90.00	140.00	175.00	225.00
	1904-B	Inc. Ab.	30.00	45.00	75.00	125.00
	1904-B	Inc. Ab.	—	—	Proof	300.00
	1907-B	1.946	BV	25.00	30.00	37.50
	1908/3-B	6.871	35.00	60.00	85.00	125.00
	1908/7-B	I.A.	35.00	60.00	85.00	125.00
	1908-B	Inc. Ab.	BV	25.00	27.50	35.00
	1908-B	Inc. Ab.	—	—	Proof	275.00
	1909/8-B	5.954	35.00	60.00	85.00	125.00
	1909-B	Inc. Ab.	BV	25.00	27.50	35.00
	1910/00-B	5.553	35.00	60.00	85.00	125.00
	1910-B	Inc. Ab.	BV	25.00	30.00	37.50
	1911-B	37.471	BV	25.00	27.50	35.00
	1912-B	5.672	BV	25.00	27.50	35.00
	1913-B	1.567	60.00	90.00	150.00	200.00
	1921-B	5 Known	—	—	—	2000.
	1921-B	.050		(restrike)	Proof	400.00
	1925	6.870	BV	25.00	27.50	35.00
	1929/1-B	5.100	35.00	60.00	85.00	125.00
	1929-B	Inc. Ab.	BV	25.00	27.50	35.00
	1930-B	10.400	BV	25.00	27.50	35.00
	1930-B	Inc. Ab.	—	—	Proof	250.00
	1930	6.660	BV	25.00	27.50	35.00
	1934-B	17.335	50.00	85.00	125.00	175.00
	1934-B	Inc. Ab.	—	—	Proof	325.00
	1934B (restrike)	20 Known	—	—	Proof	100.00
	1935-B	15 Known	—	—	—	1500.
	1935-B (restrike)	20 Known	—	—	Proof	400.00
			GOLD			
T1a	1895B	—	—		Proof Only	—
	1896B	—	—		Proof Only	—
	1897B	—	—		Proof Only	—
	1898B	—	—		Proof Only	—

Y#	Date	Mintage	Fine	VF	XF	Unc
T1a	1900B	—	—	Proof Only		—
	1901B	—	—	Proof Only		—
	1902B	—	—	Proof Only		—

1/4 GUINEA

2.0875 gm., .917 GOLD, .0615 oz AGW

C#	Date	Mintage	Fine	VF	XF	Unc
42	1762	—	125.00	175.00	250.00	400.00

1/3 GUINEA

2.7834 gm., .917 GOLD, .0820 oz AGW

Fr#	Date	Mintage	Fine	VF	XF	Unc
230	1797	—	125.00	175.00	225.00	350.00
	1798	—	125.00	175.00	225.00	350.00
	1799	—	125.00	175.00	225.00	350.00
	1800	—	125.00	175.00	225.00	350.00

Fr#	Date	Mintage	Fine	VF	XF	Unc
231	1801	—	125.00	175.00	225.00	350.00
	1802	—	125.00	175.00	225.00	350.00
	1803	—	125.00	175.00	225.00	350.00

Fr#	Date	Mintage	Fine	VF	XF	Unc
232	1804	—	100.00	150.00	200.00	275.00
	1806	—	100.00	150.00	200.00	275.00
	1808	—	100.00	150.00	200.00	275.00
	1809	—	100.00	150.00	200.00	275.00
	1810	—	100.00	150.00	200.00	275.00
	1811	—	100.00	150.00	200.00	275.00
	1813	—	100.00	150.00	200.00	275.00
	1813	—	—	—	Proof	1200.

1/2 GUINEA

4.1750 gm., .917 GOLD, .1230 oz AGW
Obv.: Young head. Rev.: Crowned arms.

Fr#	Date	Mintage	Fine	VF	XF	Unc
223	1762	—	250.00	375.00	750.00	1000.
	1763	—	250.00	375.00	750.00	1000.

Obv: Redesigned head.

Fr#	Date	Mintage	Fine	VF	XF	Unc
224	1764	—	225.00	350.00	550.00	750.00
	1764	—	—	—	Proof	1800.
	1765	—	225.00	350.00	550.00	750.00
	1766	—	225.00	350.00	550.00	750.00
	1768	—	225.00	350.00	550.00	750.00
	1769	—	225.00	350.00	550.00	750.00
	1772	—	225.00	350.00	550.00	750.00
	1773	—	225.00	350.00	550.00	750.00
	1774	—	225.00	350.00	550.00	750.00
	1775	—	225.00	350.00	550.00	750.00

Obv: New head, laurel in legend.

Fr#	Date	Mintage	Fine	VF	XF	Unc
225	1774	—	600.00	900.00	1100.	1350.
	.1775	—	500.00	750.00	900.00	1200.

Fr#	Date	Mintage	Fine	VF	XF	Unc
226	1775	—	175.00	250.00	350.00	600.00
	1775	—	—	—	Proof	1750.
	1776	—	175.00	250.00	350.00	600.00
	1777	—	175.00	250.00	350.00	600.00
	1778	—	175.00	250.00	350.00	600.00
	1779	—	175.00	250.00	350.00	600.00
	1781	—	175.00	250.00	350.00	600.00
	1784	—	175.00	250.00	350.00	600.00
	1785	—	175.00	250.00	350.00	600.00
	1786	—	175.00	250.00	350.00	600.00

Rev: Spade type.

Fr#	Date	Mintage	Fine	VF	XF	Unc
227	1787	—	150.00	225.00	300.00	500.00
	1787	—	—	—	Proof	1500.
	1788	—	150.00	225.00	300.00	500.00
	1789	—	150.00	225.00	300.00	500.00
	1790	—	150.00	225.00	300.00	500.00
	1791	—	150.00	225.00	300.00	500.00
	1792	—	150.00	225.00	300.00	500.00
	1793	—	150.00	225.00	300.00	500.00
	1794	—	150.00	225.00	300.00	500.00
	1795	—	150.00	225.00	300.00	500.00
	1796	—	150.00	225.00	300.00	500.00
	1797	—	150.00	225.00	300.00	500.00
	1798	—	150.00	225.00	300.00	500.00
	1800	—	150.00	225.00	300.00	500.00

Rev: Shield in garter type.

Fr#	Date	Mintage	Fine	VF	XF	Unc
228	1801	—	175.00	250.00	350.00	550.00
	1802	—	175.00	250.00	350.00	550.00
	1803	—	175.00	250.00	350.00	550.00

Obv: Old head, short hair.

Fr#	Date	Mintage	Fine	VF	XF	Unc
229	1804	—	150.00	225.00	275.00	375.00
	1806	—	150.00	225.00	275.00	375.00
	1808	—	150.00	225.00	275.00	375.00
	1809	—	150.00	225.00	275.00	375.00
	1810	—	150.00	225.00	275.00	375.00
	1811	—	150.00	225.00	275.00	375.00
	1813	—	150.00	225.00	275.00	375.00

1/2 SOVEREIGN

NOTE: 1/2 Sovereigns were struck at various foreign mints. The mintmark on the St. George/Dragon type is usually found on the base under the right rear hoof of the horse. On shield type reverse the mintmark is found under the shield. Refer to appropriate country listings elsewhere in this catalog for coins having mintmarks.

MINTMARKS

C - Canada
I - Bombay
M - Melbourne
P - Perth
S - Sydney
SA - South Africa

3.9940 gm., .917 GOLD, .1177 oz AGW

C#	Date	Mintage	Fine	VF	XF	Unc
50	1817	2.080	85.00	125.00	200.00	300.00
	1817	—	—	—	Proof	—
	1818/7	1.030	—	—	Rare	—
	1818	Inc. Ab.	85.00	125.00	250.00	350.00
	1818	—	—	—	Proof	—
	1820	.035	100.00	150.00	275.00	425.00

Rev: Ornate shield.

C#	Date	Mintage	Fine	VF	XF	Unc
66	1821	.231	250.00	400.00	800.00	1700.
	1821	—	—	—	Proof	2500.

Rev: Plain shield.

C#	Date	Mintage	Fine	VF	XF	Unc
67	1823	.224	125.00	200.00	375.00	650.00
	1823	—	—	—	Proof	—
	1824	.592	135.00	200.00	375.00	650.00

Rev: Bare head.

C#	Date	Mintage	Fine	VF	XF	Unc
68	1825	.761	125.00	200.00	325.00	625.00
	1825	—	—	—	Proof	1000.
	1826	.345	125.00	200.00	375.00	650.00
	1826	—	—	—	Proof	—
	1827	.492	125.00	200.00	375.00	650.00
	1828	1.245	125.00	200.00	375.00	650.00

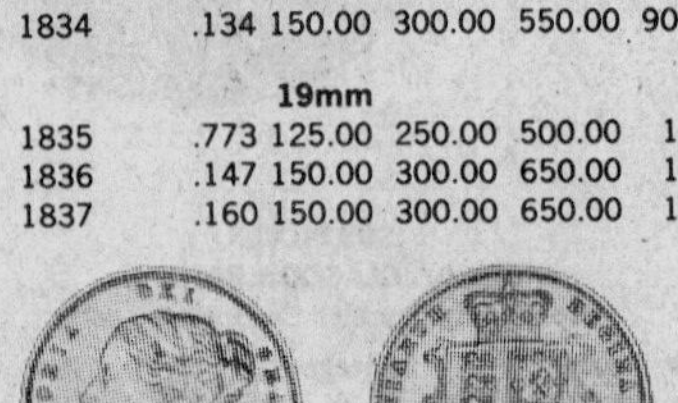

C#	Date	Mintage	Fine	VF	XF	Unc
A82	1831	—	—	Proof Only		1000.

18mm

C#	Date	Mintage	Fine	VF	XF	Unc
82	1834	.134	150.00	300.00	550.00	900.00

19mm

C#	Date	Mintage	Fine	VF	XF	Unc
82a	1835	.773	125.00	250.00	500.00	1200.
	1836	.147	150.00	300.00	650.00	1250.
	1837	.160	150.00	300.00	650.00	1250.

Y#	Date	Mintage	Fine	VF	XF	Unc
13	1838	.273	125.00	175.00	250.00	350.00
	1839	1.230	—	Proof Only		1200.
	1841	.509	85.00	100.00	175.00	275.00
	1842	2.223	85.00	100.00	125.00	200.00
	1843	1.252	85.00	100.00	125.00	200.00
	1844	1.127	85.00	100.00	125.00	200.00
	1845	.888	90.00	110.00	135.00	225.00
	1846	1.064	85.00	100.00	125.00	250.00
	1847	.983	85.00	100.00	125.00	225.00
	1848	.411	85.00	125.00	175.00	275.00
	1849	.845	85.00	100.00	135.00	225.00
	1850	.180	125.00	200.00	400.00	650.00
	1851	.774	85.00	100.00	125.00	225.00
	1852	1.378	85.00	100.00	125.00	225.00
	1853	2.709	85.00	100.00	125.00	225.00
	1853	—	—	—	Proof	—
	1854	1.125	125.00	175.00	300.00	525.00

NOTE: 1854 is much rarer than the mintage figure indicates.

Y#	Date	Mintage	Fine	VF	XF	Unc
	1855	1.120	85.00	100.00	125.00	200.00
	1856	2.392	85.00	100.00	125.00	200.00
	1857	.728	85.00	100.00	125.00	200.00
	1858	.856	85.00	100.00	125.00	200.00
	1859	2.204	85.00	100.00	125.00	200.00
	1860	1.132	85.00	100.00	125.00	200.00
	1861	1.131	85.00	100.00	125.00	200.00
	1862	—	100.00	150.00	250.00	400.00
	1863 w/die number	1.572	85.00	100.00	150.00	200.00
	1863 w/o die number	Inc. Ab.	85.00	100.00	150.00	225.00

With die number

Y#	Date	Mintage	Fine	VF	XF	Unc
13.1	1864	1.758	85.00	100.00	125.00	175.00
	1865	1.835	85.00	100.00	125.00	175.00
	1866	2.059	85.00	100.00	125.00	175.00
	1867	.993	85.00	100.00	125.00	175.00
	1869	1.862	85.00	100.00	125.00	175.00
	1870	.160	85.00	100.00	125.00	175.00
	1871	2.063	85.00	100.00	125.00	175.00
	1872	3.249	85.00	100.00	125.00	175.00
	1873	1.927	85.00	100.00	125.00	175.00
	1874	1.884	85.00	100.00	150.00	200.00
	1875	.516	85.00	100.00	150.00	200.00
	1876	2.785	85.00	100.00	150.00	200.00
	1877	2.197	85.00	100.00	150.00	200.00
	1878	2.082	85.00	100.00	125.00	165.00
	1879	.035	85.00	100.00	175.00	400.00

Y#	Date	Mintage	Fine	VF	XF	Unc
13.1	1880	1.009	85.00	100.00	125.00	165.00
	1883	2.870	85.00	100.00	125.00	165.00
	1884	1.114	85.00	100.00	125.00	165.00
	1885	4.469	85.00	100.00	125.00	165.00

Y#	Date	Mintage	Fine	VF	XF	Unc
28	1887	.872	85.00	100.00	125.00	165.00
	1890	2.266	85.00	100.00	125.00	165.00
	1891	1.079	85.00	100.00	125.00	165.00
	1892	13.680	85.00	100.00	125.00	165.00
	1893	4.427	85.00	125.00	225.00	275.00
42	1893	Inc. Ab.	BV	85.00	100.00	125.00
	1894	3.795	BV	85.00	100.00	125.00
	1895	1.717	BV	85.00	100.00	125.00
	1896	2.947	BV	85.00	100.00	125.00
	1897	3.568	BV	85.00	100.00	125.00
	1898	2.869	BV	85.00	100.00	125.00
	1899	3.362	BV	85.00	100.00	125.00
	1900	4.307	BV	85.00	100.00	125.00
	1901	2.038	BV	85.00	100.00	125.00

Y#	Date	Mintage	Fine	VF	XF	Unc
56	1902	4.244	BV	85.00	100.00	125.00
	1902	.015	—	—	Proof	175.00
	1903	2.522	BV	85.00	100.00	125.00
	1904	1.717	BV	85.00	100.00	125.00
	1905	3.024	BV	85.00	100.00	150.00
	1906	4.245	BV	85.00	100.00	150.00
	1907	4.233	BV	85.00	100.00	125.00
	1908	3.997	BV	85.00	100.00	125.00
	1909	4.011	BV	85.00	100.00	150.00
	1910	5.024	BV	85.00	100.00	125.00

Y#	Date	Mintage	Fine	VF	XF	Unc
77	1911	6.104	BV	85.00	100.00	125.00
	1911	3,764	—	—	Proof	300.00
	1912	6.224	BV	85.00	100.00	125.00
	1913	6.094	BV	85.00	100.00	125.00
	1914	7.251	BV	85.00	100.00	125.00
	1915	2.043	BV	85.00	100.00	125.00
100	1937	5,501	—	—	Proof	350.00

GUINEA

8.3500 gm., 917 GOLD, .2461 oz AGW

First issue

Fr#	Date	Mintage	Fine	VF	XF	Unc
217	1761	—	750.00	1500.	2000.	3250.

Second issue

Fr#	Date	Mintage	Fine	VF	XF	Unc
218	1763	—	500.00	850.00	1200.	2250.
	1764	—	500.00	850.00	1200.	2250.

Third issue

Fr#	Date	Mintage	Fine	VF	XF	Unc
219	1765	—	225.00	275.00	350.00	600.00
	1766	—	225.00	275.00	350.00	600.00
	1767	—	225.00	275.00	350.00	600.00
	1768	—	225.00	275.00	350.00	600.00
	1769	—	225.00	275.00	350.00	600.00
	1770	—	200.00	250.00	325.00	550.00
	1771	—	200.00	250.00	325.00	550.00
	1772	—	200.00	250.00	325.00	550.00
	1773	—	200.00	250.00	325.00	550.00

Fourth issue

Fr#	Date	Mintage	Fine	VF	XF	Unc
220	1774	—	200.00	250.00	300.00	500.00
	1774	—	—	—	Proof	—
	1775	—	200.00	250.00	300.00	500.00
	1776	—	200.00	250.00	300.00	500.00
	1777	—	200.00	250.00	300.00	500.00
	1778	—	200.00	250.00	300.00	500.00
	1779	—	200.00	250.00	300.00	500.00
	1781	—	200.00	250.00	300.00	500.00
	1782	—	200.00	250.00	300.00	500.00
	1783	—	200.00	250.00	300.00	500.00
	1784	—	200.00	250.00	300.00	500.00
	1785	—	200.00	250.00	300.00	500.00
	1786	—	200.00	250.00	300.00	500.00

Rev: Spade type

Fr#	Date	Mintage	Fine	VF	XF	Unc
221	1787	—	175.00	200.00	275.00	450.00
	1788	—	175.00	200.00	275.00	450.00
	1789	—	175.00	200.00	275.00	450.00
	1790	—	175.00	200.00	275.00	450.00
	1791	—	175.00	200.00	275.00	450.00
	1792	—	175.00	200.00	275.00	450.00
	1793	—	175.00	200.00	275.00	450.00
	1794	—	175.00	200.00	275.00	450.00
	1795	—	175.00	200.00	275.00	450.00
	1796	—	175.00	200.00	275.00	450.00
	1797	—	175.00	200.00	275.00	450.00
	1798*	—	175.00	200.00	275.00	450.00
	1799	—	175.00	200.00	275.00	450.00

***NOTE:** Commonly counterfeited

Rev: Shield in garter.

Fr#	Date	Mintage	Fine	VF	XF	Unc
222	1813	—	450.00	650.00	850.00	1500.

SOVEREIGN

NOTE: Sovereigns were struck at various foreign mints. The mintmark on the St. George/Dragon type is usually found on the base under the right rear hoof of the horse. On shield type reverse the mintmark is found under the shield. Refer to appropriate country listings elsewhere in this catalog for coins having mintmarks.

MINTMARKS

C - Canada
I - Bombay
M - Melbourne
P - Perth
S - Sydney
SA - South Africa

7.9881 gm., .917 GOLD, .2354 oz AGW

C#	Date	Mintage	Fine	VF	XF	Unc
51	1817	3.235	165.00	200.00	400.00	650.00
	1817	—	—	—	Proof	—
	1818	2.347	175.00	225.00	500.00	900.00
	1819	3,574	1000.	1800.		Unknown
	1820	.932	165.00	200.00	400.00	650.00
	1820	—	—	—	Proof	—

C#	Date	Mintage	Fine	VF	XF	Unc
69	1821	9.405	175.00	250.00	450.00	750.00
	1821	—	—	—	Proof	—
	1822*	5.357	175.00	250.00	475.00	750.00
	1823	.617	300.00	700.00		Unknown
	1824	3.768	200.00	250.00	400.00	650.00
	1825	4.200	250.00	550.00	875.00	Unkn.

***NOTE:** This coin is commonly counterfeited.

C#	Date	Mintage	Fine	VF	XF	Unc
70	1825	Inc. Ab.	165.00	200.00	400.00	700.00
	1825	—	—	—	Proof	—
	1825 with plain edge		—	—	Proof	—
	1826	5.724	165.00	200.00	400.00	650.00
	1826	—	—	—	Proof	—
	1827	2.267	175.00	225.00	425.00	675.00
	1828 only 6 or 7 known					
		.386	750.00	2500.	4000.	6000.
	1829	2.445	175.00	250.00	400.00	600.00
	1830	2.388	175.00	250.00	400.00	600.00
	1830	—	—	—	Proof	—
	1830 w/plain edge		—	—	Proof	18,000.

C#	Date	Mintage	Fine	VF	XF	Unc
83	1831	.599	200.00	350.00	600.00	900.00
	1831	—	—	—	Proof	—
	1832*	3.737	175.00	250.00	400.00	650.00
	1833	1.225	175.00	300.00	550.00	850.00
	1835	.723	175.00	300.00	550.00	850.00
	1836	1.714	175.00	300.00	550.00	850.00
	1837	1.173	175.00	275.00	475.00	725.00

***NOTE:** This coin is commonly counterfeited.

Rev: Without die number

Y#	Date	Mintage	Fine	VF	XF	Unc
14	1838	2.719	165.00	200.00	375.00	700.00
	1838	—	—	—	Proof	—
	1839	.504	500.00	800.00	1750.	2500.
	1839	—	—	—	Proof	—
	1841	.124	1500.	2000.	4000.	7500.
	1842	4.865	BV	BV	175.00	375.00
	1843 broad shield					
		5.982	BV	BV	165.00	200.00
	1843 narrow shield					
		Inc. Ab.	175.00	250.00	400.00	650.00
	1844	3.000	BV	BV	175.00	350.00
	1845	3.801	BV	BV	175.00	350.00
	1846	3.803	BV	BV	175.00	350.00
	1847	4.667	BV	BV	175.00	325.00
	1848	2.247	BV	BV	175.00	350.00

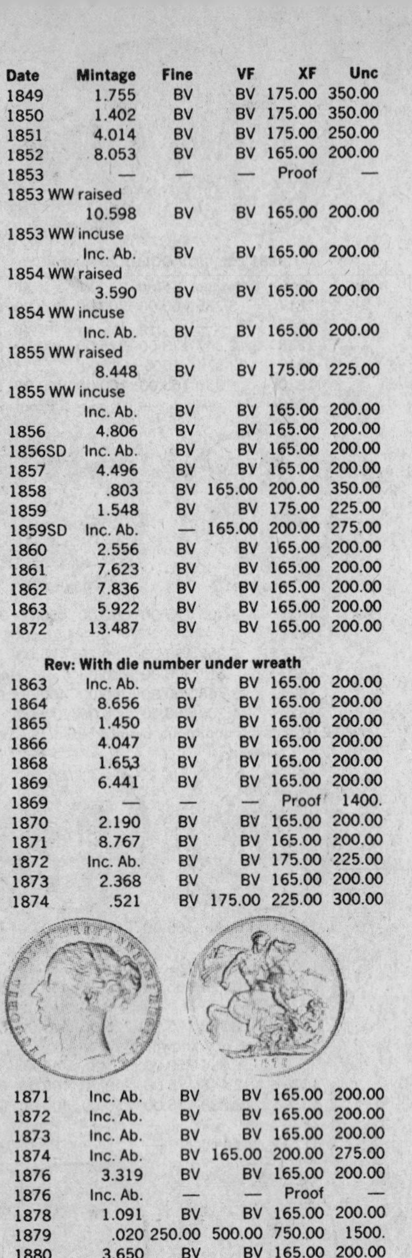

Y#	Date	Mintage	Fine	VF	XF	Unc
14	1849	1.755	BV	BV	175.00	350.00
	1850	1.402	BV	BV	175.00	350.00
	1851	4.014	BV	BV	175.00	250.00
	1852	8.053	BV	BV	165.00	200.00
	1853	—	—	—	Proof	—
	1853 WW raised	10.598	BV	BV	165.00	200.00
	1853 WW incuse	Inc. Ab.	BV	BV	165.00	200.00
	1854 WW raised	3.590	BV	BV	165.00	200.00
	1854 WW incuse	Inc. Ab.	BV	BV	165.00	200.00
	1855 WW raised	8.448	BV	BV	175.00	225.00
	1855 WW incuse	Inc. Ab.	BV	BV	165.00	200.00
	1856	4.806	BV	BV	165.00	200.00
	1856SD	Inc. Ab.	BV	BV	165.00	200.00
	1857	4.496	BV	BV	165.00	200.00
	1858	.803	BV	165.00	200.00	350.00
	1859	1.548	BV	BV	175.00	225.00
	1859SD	Inc. Ab.	—	165.00	200.00	275.00
	1860	2.556	BV	BV	165.00	200.00
	1861	7.623	BV	BV	165.00	200.00
	1862	7.836	BV	BV	165.00	200.00
	1863	5.922	BV	BV	165.00	200.00
	1872	13.487	BV	BV	165.00	200.00

Rev: With die number under wreath

Y#	Date	Mintage	Fine	VF	XF	Unc
14.1	1863	Inc. Ab.	BV	BV	165.00	200.00
	1864	8.656	BV	BV	165.00	200.00
	1865	1.450	BV	BV	165.00	200.00
	1866	4.047	BV	BV	165.00	200.00
	1868	1.653	BV	BV	165.00	200.00
	1869	6.441	BV	BV	165.00	200.00
	1869	—	—	—	Proof	1400.
	1870	2.190	BV	BV	165.00	200.00
	1871	8.767	BV	BV	165.00	200.00
	1872	Inc. Ab.	BV	BV	175.00	225.00
	1873	2.368	BV	BV	165.00	200.00
	1874	.521	BV	175.00	225.00	300.00

Y#	Date	Mintage	Fine	VF	XF	Unc
15	1871	Inc. Ab.	BV	BV	165.00	200.00
	1872	Inc. Ab.	BV	BV	165.00	200.00
	1873	Inc. Ab.	BV	BV	165.00	200.00
	1874	Inc. Ab.	BV	165.00	200.00	275.00
	1876	3.319	BV	BV	165.00	200.00
	1876	Inc. Ab.	—	—	Proof	—
	1878	1.091	BV	BV	165.00	200.00
	1879	.020	250.00	500.00	750.00	1500.
	1880	3.650	BV	BV	165.00	200.00
	1884	1.770	BV	BV	165.00	200.00
	1885	.718	BV	BV	175.00	225.00

Y#	Date	Mintage	Fine	VF	XF	Unc
29	1887	1.111	BV	BV	165.00	200.00
	1887	797 pcs.	—	—	Proof	650.00
	1888	2.777	BV	BV	175.00	225.00
	1889	7.257	BV	BV	175.00	225.00
	1890	6.530	BV	BV	175.00	225.00
	1891	6.329	BV	BV	175.00	225.00
	1892	7.105	BV	BV	175.00	225.00

Y#	Date	Mintage	Fine	VF	XF	Unc
43	1893	6.898	BV	BV	165.00	200.00
	1893	773 pcs.	—	—	Proof	750.00
	1894	3.783	BV	BV	165.00	200.00
	1895	2.285	BV	BV	165.00	200.00
	1896	3.334	BV	BV	165.00	200.00
	1898	4.361	BV	BV	165.00	200.00
	1899	7.520	BV	BV	165.00	200.00
	1900	10.847	BV	BV	165.00	200.00
	1901	1.579	BV	BV	165.00	200.00

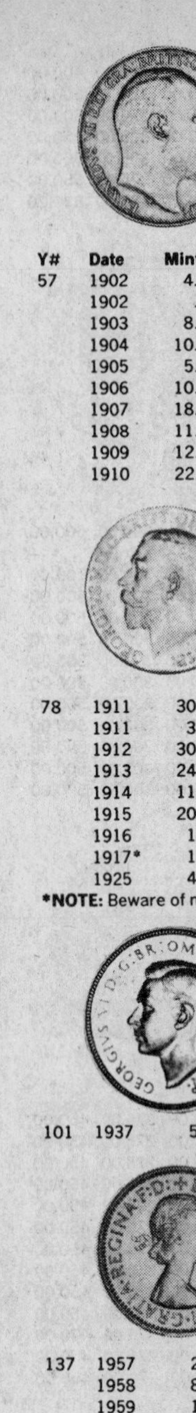

Y#	Date	Mintage	Fine	VF	XF	Unc
57	1902	4.738	BV	BV	165.00	200.00
	1902	.015	BV	BV	Proof	300.00
	1903	8.889	BV	BV	165.00	200.00
	1904	10.041	BV	BV	165.00	200.00
	1905	5.910	BV	BV	165.00	200.00
	1906	10.467	BV	BV	165.00	200.00
	1907	18.459	BV	BV	165.00	200.00
	1908	11.729	BV	BV	165.00	200.00
	1909	12.157	BV	BV	165.00	200.00
	1910	22.380	BV	BV	165.00	200.00

Y#	Date	Mintage	Fine	VF	XF	Unc
78	1911	30.044	BV	BV	165.00	200.00
	1911	3,764	—	—	Proof	600.00
	1912	30.318	BV	BV	165.00	200.00
	1913	24.540	BV	BV	165.00	200.00
	1914	11.501	BV	BV	165.00	200.00
	1915	20.295	BV	BV	165.00	200.00
	1916	1.554	BV	BV	175.00	250.00
	1917*	1.015	—	—	Rare	—
	1925	4.407	BV	BV	165.00	200.00

***NOTE:** Beware of numerous counterfeits.

Y#	Date	Mintage	Fine	VF	XF	Unc
101	1937	5,501	—		Proof Only	750.00

Y#	Date	Mintage	Fine	VF	XF	Unc
137	1957	2.072	BV	BV	165.00	200.00
	1958	8.700	BV	BV	165.00	200.00
	1959	1.358	BV	BV	165.00	200.00
	1962	3.000	BV	BV	165.00	200.00
	1963	7.400	BV	BV	165.00	200.00
	1964	3.000	BV	BV	165.00	200.00
	1965	3.800	BV	BV	165.00	180.00
	1966	7.050	BV	BV	165.00	180.00
	1967	5.000	BV	BV	165.00	180.00
	1968	4.203	BV	BV	165.00	180.00

Y#	Date	Mintage	Fine	VF	XF	Unc
A137	1974	1.000	BV	BV	165.00	180.00
	1976	1.150	BV	BV	165.00	180.00
	1979	.050	—	—	Proof	140.00

2 POUNDS

15.9761 gm., .917 GOLD, .4708 oz AGW

C#	Date	Mintage	Fine	VF	XF	Unc
70.5	1823	—	350.00	600.00	800.00	1250.

C#	Date	Mintage	Fine	VF	XF	Unc
70.6	1826	450 pcs.	—		Proof Only	2500.

C#	Date	Mintage	Fine	VF	XF	Unc
84	1831	225 pcs.	—		Proof Only	4000.

Y#	Date	Mintage	Fine	VF	XF	Unc
30	1887	.091	325.00	400.00	500.00	750.00

NOTE: Proof issues with mintmark S under right rear hoof of horse were struck at Sydney.

Y#	Date	Mintage	Fine	VF	XF	Unc
44	1893	.052	325.00	375.00	500.00	750.00
	1893	—	—	—	Proof	—

Y#	Date	Mintage	Fine	VF	XF	Unc
58	1902	.046	325.00	375.00	450.00	600.00

NOTE: Proof issues with mintmark S under right rear hoof of horse were struck at Sydney. Refer to Australia listings.

Y#	Date	Mintage	Fine	VF	XF	Unc
79	1911	2,812	—		Proof Only	1200.

Y#	Date	Mintage	Fine	VF	XF	Unc
102	1937	5,501	—		Proof Only	750.00

5 POUNDS

39.9403 gm., .917 GOLD, 1.1771 oz AGW

Fr#	Date	Mintage	Fine	VF	XF	Unc
238	1826	150 pcs.	—	Proof Only		10,000.

251	1839	400 pcs.	—	Proof Only		15,000.

Y#	Date	Mintage	Fine	VF	XF	Unc
31	1887	.054	800.00	900.00	1100.	1400.

NOTE: Proof issues with mintmark S under right rear hoof of horse were struck at Sydney.

Y#	Date	Mintage	Fine	VF	XF	Unc
45	1893	.020	850.00	950.00	1250.	1750.
	1893	—	—	—	Proof	—

59	1902	.035	800.00	900.00	1100.	1400.

NOTE: Proof issues with mintmark S under right rear hoof of horse were struck at Sydney.

80	1911	2,812	—	Proof Only		2500.

Y#	Date	Mintage	Fine	VF	XF	Unc
103	1937	5,501	—	Proof Only		2250.

NCLT ISSUES

PATTERNS

KM#	Date	Mintage	Identification	Mkt.Val.
1	1764	—	1 Shilling, Silver, C30	650.00
2	1775	—	1 Shilling, Silver, C30	—
3	1778	—	1 Shilling, Silver, C30	750.00
4	1786	—	6 Pence, Silver, C28	—
5	1786	—	1 Shilling, Silver, C31	—
6	1820	—	6 Pence,Silver,C59	800.00
7	1820	—	1 Shilling, Silver, C61	850.00
8	1820	—	2 Pounds, .916 Gold, C51.5	12,500.

9	1820	—	5 Pounds, .916 Gold, Fr234	—
10	1825	—	2 Pounds, .916 Gold, C70.6	3500.
11	1837	—	4 Pence, .925 Silver, Y4	165.00
12	1846	—	1 Florin, .925 Silver, Y7	350.00
13	1946	—	6 Pence, Copper-Nickel, Y95	—
14	1953	—	1/2 Sovereign, .916 Gold	—
15	1953	—	1 Sovereign, .916 Gold	—
16	1953	—	2 Pounds, .916 Gold	—
17	1953	—	5 Pounds, .916 Gold, Y103	—

MINT SETS

KM#	Date	Mintage	Identification	Issue Price	Mkt. Val.
S101	1953(9)	—	Y116-124	1.25	22.00
S102	1968/71(5)	—	Y139-143. 10p and 5P dated 1968. 2P, 1P, 1/2 P dated 1971. Blue wallet.	.50	1.00

PROOF SETS

STANDARD METALS

101	1826(11)	400*	C52-54,60,62,64, 65,68,70,72,75	—	18,000.
102	1831(14)	150*	C71,72,73,74,75,76,77, 79,80,81,82,83,Crown,L2	—	14,000.
103	1839(15)	400*	Y1-3,A3,4-6,9-14, Plus 3 Maundy coins	—	22,500.
104	1853(16)	460*	Y1-6,A3,8-10,12-14, Plus 3 Maundy coins	—	12,000.
105	1887(12)	797*	YA18,19,20,22-26, 28-31	—	6000.
106	1887(7)	—	YA18,19,20,22-25	—	900.00
107	1893(10)	773*	Y35-40,42-45	—	6000.
108	1893(6)	—	Y35-40	—	800.00

***NOTE:** Estimated mintage figures.

109	1902(13)	8,066	Y50-59	—	2500.
110	1902(11)	7,057	Y50-57	—	600.00
111	1911(12)	2,812	Y66-69,77-81	—	5000.

KM#	Date	Mintage	Identification	Issue Price	Mkt. Val.
112	1911(10)	952	Y66-69,77,78,81	—	900.00
113	1911(8)	2,241	Y66-69,81	—	275.00
114	1927(6)	15,030	Y71-75	—	350.00
115	1937(15)	26,402	Y82-93	—	200.00
116	1937(4)	5,501	Y100-103	—	2750.
117	1950(9)	17,513	Y104-112	2.50	70.00
118	1951(10)	20,000	Y104-112,A114	2.80	75.00
119	1953(10)	40,000	Y116-125	3.50	65.00
120	1970(8)	750,000	Y128-133,A128 Issued 1971/2	8.75	30.00
121	1971(6)	350,000	Y139-144 (Issued 1973)	8.85	24.00
122	1972(7)	150,000	Y139-144,145 (issued 1976)	13.00	20.00
123	1973(6)	100,000	Y139-143,146 (Issued 1976)	13.00	18.00
124	1974(6)	100,000	Y139-144 (Issued 1976)	13.00	15.00
125	1975(6)	100,000	Y139-144 (Issued 1976)	13.00	15.00
126	1976(6)	100,000	Y139-144	13.00	15.00
127	1977(7)	300,000	Y139-144,147	17.00	22.00
128	1978(6)	—	Y139-144	15.00	15.00
129	1979(6)	—	Y139-144	15.00	15.00
130	1980(6)	—	Y139-144	23.00	—

The Hellenic Republic of Greece is situated in southeastern Europe on the southern tip of the Balkan Peninsula. The republic includes many islands, the most important of which are Crete and the Ionian Islands. Greece (including islands) has an area of 51,182 sq. mi. (132,560 sq. km.) and a population of 9.25 million. Capital: Athens. Greece is still largely agricultural. Tobacco, cotton, fruit and wool are exported.

Greece, the Mother of Western civilization, attained the peak of its culture in the 5th century B.C., when it contributed more to government, drama, art and architecture than any other people to this time. Greece fell under Roman domination in the 2nd and 1st centuries B.C., becoming part of the Byzantine Empire until Constantinople fell to the Crusaders in 1202. With the fall of Constantinople to the Turks in 1453, Greece became part of the Ottoman Empire. Independence from Turkey was won with the revolution of 1821-27. In 1833, Greece was established as a monarchy, with sovereignty guaranteed by Britain, France and Russia. After a lengthy power struggle between the monarchist forces and democratic factions, Greece was proclaimed a republic in 1925. The monarchy was restored in 1935 and reconfirmed by a plebiscite in 1946. On April 21, 1967, a military junta took control of the government and suspended the constitution, forcing the King to flee to England. The monarchy was formally abolished by plebiscite, Dec. 8, 1974, and Greece established as the 'Hellenic Republic,' the third republic in Greek history.

RULERS

John Capodistrias, 1827-1831
King Otto, 1832-1862
George I, 1863-1913
Constantine I, 1913-1923
George II, 1922-1923, 1935-1947
Paul I, 1947-1964
Constantine II, 1964-1973

MINTMARKS

(a) - Paris, privy marks only
A - Paris
B - Vienna
BB - Strassburg
H - Heaton, Birmingham
K - Bordeaux
KN - King's Norton
(1) - London
(o) - Aegina (1828-1832), Owl
(o) - Athens (1838-1855), Owl
(p) - Poissy - Thunderbolt
Cornucopia - Paris

MONETARY SYSTEM

UNTIL 1831
100 Lepta = 1 Phoenix
COMMENCING 1831
100 Lepta = 1 Drachma

LEPTON

COPPER, 17mm
Obv: Phoenix in solid circle.

C#	Date	Mintage	VG	Fine	VF	XF
1.1	1828	1.310	15.00	30.00	55.00	125.00
	1830	Inc. Ab.	85.00	125.00	175.00	275.00

Obv: Phoenix in pearl circle, 17mm.

C#	Date	Mintage	VG	Fine	VF	XF
1.2	1830	Inc. Ab.	25.00	45.00	65.00	85.00

Obv: Without circle, 16mm.

C#	Date	Mintage	VG	Fine	VF	XF
1.3	1831	Inc. Ab.	30.00	50.00	75.00	100.00

Type 1 — ΒΑΣΙΛΕΙΑ

C#	Date	Mintage	VG	Fine	VF	XF
6	1832	—	17.50	30.00	55.00	95.00
	1833	—	15.00	25.00	55.00	95.00
	1834	—	100.00	150.00	200.00	300.00
	1837	.160	30.00	50.00	75.00	125.00
	1838	.270	30.00	50.00	75.00	125.00
	1839	.150	25.00	45.00	65.00	100.00
	1840	.700	30.00	50.00	75.00	125.00
	1841	.370	20.00	40.00	60.00	115.00
	1842	.120	17.50	30.00	50.00	85.00
	1843	.630	17.50	30.00	50.00	85.00

Type 2 — ΒΑΣΙΛΕΙΟΝ

C#	Date	Mintage	VG	Fine	VF	XF
6a	1844	.151	27.50	45.00	85.00	175.00
	1845	.160	17.50	40.00	75.00	150.00
	1846	.141	17.50	40.00	75.00	150.00

Obv: Smaller crowned arms
Rev: Redesigned wreath

C#	Date	Mintage	VG	Fine	VF	XF
6a.1	1847	.273	40.00	60.00	85.00	125.00
	1848	.084	20.00	40.00	60.00	115.00
	1849	.090	20.00	40.00	60.00	115.00

Size reduced to 15mm

C#	Date	Mintage	VG	Fine	VF	XF
6b	1851	.400	20.00	35.00	55.00	75.00
	1857	.243	20.00	35.00	60.00	90.00

Y#	Date	Mintage	Fine	VF	XF	Unc
1	1869BB	22.505	3.00	5.00	8.00	15.00
	1870BB	Inc. Ab.	8.50	12.00	20.00	35.00

Y#	Date	Mintage	Fine	VF	XF	Unc
10	1878A	—	— Reported, Not Confirmed			
	1878K	Inc. Ab.	4.00	6.00	10.00	15.00
	1879A	Inc. Ab.	35.00	70.00	100.00	150.00

2 LEPTA

COPPER
Type 1 — ΒΑΣΙΛΕΙΑ

C#	Date	Mintage	VG	Fine	VF	XF
7	1832	—	17.50	35.00	50.00	70.00
	1833	—	15.00	35.00	45.00	60.00
	1834	—	30.00	50.00	70.00	90.00
	1836	.049	75.00	110.00	140.00	200.00
	1837	.222	12.50	20.00	35.00	50.00
	1838	.701	10.00	17.50	30.00	45.00
	1839	.661	10.00	17.50	30.00	55.00
	1840	.520	7.50	12.50	20.00	45.00
	1842	.470	10.00	17.50	30.00	55.00

Type 2 — ΒΑΣΙΛΕΙΟΝ

C#	Date	Mintage	VG	Fine	VF	XF
7a	1844	.206	12.50	20.00	35.00	55.00
	1845	.242	8.50	15.00	25.00	45.00

Obv: Smaller crowned arms
Rev: Redesigned wreath

C#	Date	Mintage	VG	Fine	VF	XF
7a.1	1847	.082	25.00	45.00	65.00	85.00
	1848	.258	15.00	25.00	45.00	70.00
	1849	.146	10.00	17.50	30.00	45.00

Size reduced to 17mm.

C#	Date	Mintage	VG	Fine	VF	XF
7b	1851	.388	15.00	25.00	45.00	60.00
	1857	.544	8.00	13.50	22.00	30.00

Y#	Date	Mintage	Fine	VF	XF	Unc
2	1869BB	11.231	10.00	15.00	22.00	35.00

Y#	Date	Mintage	Fine	VF	XF	Unc
11	1878K large anchor					
		Inc. Ab.	7.50	12.00	20.00	35.00
	1878K small anchor					
		—	25.00	45.00	65.00	150.00

5 LEPTA

COPPER, 28mm
Obv: Phoenix in solid circle.

C#	Date	Mintage	VG	Fine	VF	XF
2.1	1828	.640	17.50	30.00	55.00	90.00
	1830	Inc. Ab.	17.50	30.00	55.00	90.00
	Obv: Phoenix in pearl circle.					
2.2	1830	Inc. Ab.	7.50	12.50	25.00	50.00
	Obv: Phoenix in pearl circle, 26mm.					
2.3	1830	Inc. Ab.	45.00	70.00	95.00	125.00
	Obv: Without circle.					
2.4	1831	Inc. Ab.	17.50	30.00	55.00	100.00

C#	Date	Mintage	VG	Fine	VF	XF
	Type 1 — ΒΑΣΙΛΕΙΑ					
8	1833	—	17.50	30.00	55.00	85.00
	1834	—	20.00	40.00	60.00	90.00
	1836	1,000	100.00	150.00	200.00	300.00
	1837	.116	35.00	55.00	75.00	100.00
	1838	1.472	10.00	17.50	30.00	65.00
	1839	1.186	5.00	8.50	15.00	40.00
	1840	.417	8.50	15.00	25.00	50.00
	1841	.864	8.50	15.00	25.00	50.00
	1842	.682	5.00	8.50	20.00	40.00
	Type 2 — ΒΑΣΙΛΕΙΟΝ					
8a	1844	.089	45.00	70.00	95.00	150.00
	1845	.316	12.50	20.00	35.00	50.00
	1846	.190	15.00	22.50	40.00	55.00

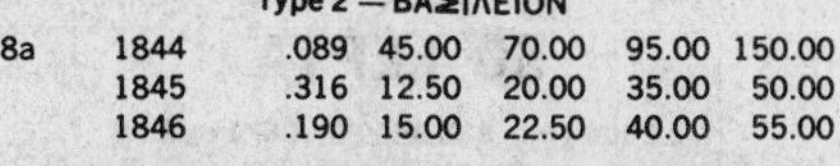

Obv: Smaller crowned arms
Rev: Redesigned wreath

C#	Date	Mintage	VG	Fine	VF	XF
8a.1	1847	.270	40.00	60.00	80.00	125.00
	1848	.394	30.00	40.00	50.00	95.00
	1849	.374	25.00	35.00	45.00	80.00

Size reduced to 23mm.

C#	Date	Mintage	VG	Fine	VF	XF
8b	1851	.620	17.50	30.00	55.00	70.00
	1857	.350	15.00	22.50	40.00	55.00

Y#	Date	Mintage	Fine	VF	XF	Unc
3	1869BB	36.343	1.00	2.00	4.00	15.00
	1870BB	Inc. Ab.	2.50	5.00	15.00	30.00

Y#	Date	Mintage	Fine	VF	XF	Unc
12	1878K	Inc. Ab.	.50	1.00	3.00	10.00
	1879A	Inc. Ab.	25.00	50.00	75.00	125.00
	1882A	14.261	.50	1.00	3.00	5.00

COPPER-NICKEL

Y#	Date	Mintage	Fine	VF	XF	Unc
16	1894A	4.000	.75	2.50	7.50	15.00
	1895A	4.000	.75	2.00	6.00	12.00

NICKEL

Y#	Date	Mintage	Fine	VF	XF	Unc
19	1912(a)	25.053	.25	.75	2.00	5.00

ALUMINUM

Y#	Date	Mintage	Fine	VF	XF	Unc
38	1954	15.000	—	—	.10	.25
	1971	1.002	.25	.40	.75	3.50

10 LEPTA

COPPER, 35mm.
Obv: Phoenix in solid circle.

C#	Date	Mintage	VG	Fine	VF	XF
3.1	1828	2.995	27.50	40.00	65.00	125.00
	1830	Inc. Ab.	30.00	50.00	75.00	150.00
	Obv: Phoenix in pearl circle, 33mm.					
3.2	1830	Inc. Ab.	50.00	70.00	125.00	200.00

Obv: Without circle.

C#	Date	Mintage	VG	Fine	VF	XF
3.3	1831	—	17.50	30.00	75.00	150.00

C#	Date	Mintage	VG	Fine	VF	XF
	Type 1 — ΒΑΣΙΛΕΙΑ					
9	1833	—	15.00	22.50	40.00	75.00
	1836	.919	12.50	20.00	35.00	65.00
	1837	2.660	8.00	13.50	22.50	45.00
	1838	.918	14.50	22.50	40.00	75.00
	1843	.700	15.00	25.00	45.00	85.00
	1844	1.064	120.00	175.00	350.00	500.00
	Type 2 — ΒΑΣΙΛΕΙΟΝ					
9a	1844	Inc. Ab.	9.50	16.50	27.50	45.00
	1845	.985	12.50	20.00	35.00	60.00
	1846/45	1.275	35.00	50.00	75.00	175.00
	1846	Inc. Ab.	8.50	15.00	25.00	45.00

Obv: Smaller crowned arms
Rev: Redesigned wreath

C#	Date	Mintage	VG	Fine	VF	XF
9a.1	1847	.740	12.50	20.00	35.00	55.00
	1848	1.174	7.50	12.50	20.00	45.00
	1849 small crown					
		1.160	11.50	20.00	32.50	50.00
	1849 large crown					
		Inc. Ab.	135.00	200.00	275.00	350.00
	1850	1.282	12.50	20.00	35.00	55.00
	1851	.587	10.00	17.50	30.00	55.00
	1857	.883	10.00	17.50	30.00	40.00

Y#	Date	Mintage	Fine	VF	XF	Unc
4	1869BB	22.491	7.50	11.50	22.50	75.00

Y#	Date	Mintage	Fine	VF	XF	Unc
4	1870BB	Inc. Ab.	3.75	6.50	12.50	35.00
13	1878K	Inc. Ab.	5.00	7.50	12.50	25.00
	1879A	Inc. Ab.	15.00	35.00	60.00	95.00
	1882A	16.000	5.00	7.50	20.00	60.00

COPPER-NICKEL

Y#	Date	Mintage	Fine	VF	XF	Unc
17	1894A	3.000	.75	2.50	7.50	15.00
	1895A	3.000	.75	2.50	7.50	15.00

NICKEL

Y#	Date	Mintage	Fine	VF	XF	Unc
20	1912(a)	28.973	.25	1.75	5.00	15.00
	1912	—	—	—	—	—

1.5200 gm., ALUMINUM
1.7mm thick

Y#	Date	Mintage	Fine	VF	XF	Unc
29	1922	120.00	.25	1.50	5.00	10.00

1.6500 gm., 2.2mm thick

Y#	Date	Mintage	Fine	VF	XF	Unc
29a	1922	—	—	—	—	—
39	1954	48.000	—	.10	.15	.75
	1959	20.000	—	.10	.15	.25
	1964	12.000	—	.10	.15	.25
	1965	*	—	—	—	—
	1966	20.000	—	.10	.15	.25
	1969	20.000	—	.10	.15	.25
	1971	5.922	—	.10	.20	1.50

*Only sold in mint sets.

Obv: Soldier and Phoenix

Y#	Date	Mintage	Fine	VF	XF	Unc
A58	1973	2.742	—	—	—	6.00

Obv: Modified design; soldier omitted.

Y#	Date	Mintage	Fine	VF	XF	Unc
64	1973	4.110	—	—	—	.15
72	1976	.083	—	—	—	.15

20 LEPTA

COPPER

C#	Date	Mintage	VG	Fine	VF	XF
4	1831	1.305	25.00	45.00	100.00	175.00

1.0000 gm., .835 SILVER, .0268 oz ASW

Y#	Date	Mintage	Fine	VF	XF	Unc
5	1874A	.723	3.00	5.00	10.00	35.00
	1883A	1.000	1.25	2.00	5.00	25.00

COPPER-NICKEL

Y#	Date	Mintage	Fine	VF	XF	Unc
18	1893A	.248	8.50	10.00	15.00	35.00
	1894A	4.752	.15	.25	1.00	20.00
	1895A	5.000	.15	.25	1.00	20.00

NICKEL

Y#	Date	Mintage	Fine	VF	XF	Unc
21	1912(a)	10.145	.20	.35	7.50	25.00

COPPER-NICKEL

Y#	Date	Mintage	Fine	VF	XF	Unc
31	1926	20.000	.30	.50	1.00	7.50

ALUMINUM

Y#	Date	Mintage	Fine	VF	XF	Unc
40	1954	24.000	—	.10	.15	.25
	1959	20.000	—	.10	.15	.25
	1964	8.000	—	.10	.15	.20
	1965	*	—	—	—	—
	1966	15.000	—	.10	.15	.25
	1969	20.000	—	.10	.15	.25
	1971	4.108	—	.15	.25	2.00

*Only sold in mint sets.

Y#	Date	Mintage	Fine	VF	XF	Unc
B58	1973	2.718	—	.10	.15	6.00

Y#	Date	Mintage	Fine	VF	XF	Unc
65	1973	5.246	—	—	—	.20

Y#	Date	Mintage	Fine	VF	XF	Unc
73	1976	1.032	—	—	—	.20

1/4 DRACHMA

SILVER, 17mm.
Obv: Young head.

C#	Date	Mintage	VG	Fine	VF	XF
10	1833	—	25.00	45.00	75.00	125.00
	1834A	—	25.00	45.00	75.00	125.00
	1845	—	200.00	300.00	375.00	500.00
	1846	—	250.00	350.00	450.00	750.00

Obv: Old head, 15mm.

C#	Date	Mintage	VG	Fine	VF	XF
14	1851	—	250.00	400.00	600.00	750.00
	1855	—	300.00	500.00	700.00	850.00

1/2 DRACHMA

SILVER

C#	Date	Mintage	VG	Fine	VF	XF
11	1833	—	15.00	25.00	75.00	125.00
	1834A	—	15.00	25.00	75.00	125.00
	1842 Owl	—	350.00	600.00	1000.	1500.
	1843 Owl	—	350.00	550.00	750.00	1250.
	1846	—	350.00	600.00	1000.	1500.
	1847	—	275.00	400.00	850.00	2000.
15	1851	—	350.00	650.00	1000.	1500.
	1855	—	150.00	225.00	450.00	750.00

50 LEPTA

2.5000 gm., .835 SILVER, .0671 oz ASW
Obv: Young head.

Y#	Date	Mintage	Fine	VF	XF	Unc
6	1868A	60 pcs.	—	—	Rare	—

Obv: Old head.

Y#	Date	Mintage	Fine	VF	XF	Unc
6.1	1874A	4.500	8.50	15.00	25.00	40.00
	1883A	.600	17.50	30.00	45.00	65.00

COPPER-NICKEL

Y#	Date	Mintage	Fine	VF	XF	Unc
30	1921H	1.000	650.00	1000.	1750.	3000.
	1921KN	1.524	300.00	500.00	1250.	2500.

Y#	Date	Mintage	Fine	VF	XF	Unc
32	1926	20.000	.20	.35	.75	7.50
	1926B	20.000	.20	.35	.75	7.50

Y#	Date	Mintage	Fine	VF	XF	Unc
41	1954	37.228	.50	.75	3.00	3.75
	1957	5.108	1.75	3.00	5.00	25.00
	1959	10.160	.95	1.50	3.50	6.00
	1962 plain edge					
		20.500	.15	.25	.50	1.00
	1962 serrated edge					
		Inc. Ab.	.15	.25	.50	1.00
	1964	20.000	.15	.25	.50	1.00
	1965	*	—	—	—	—

*Only sold in mint sets.

Y#	Date	Mintage	Fine	VF	XF	Unc
49	1966	30.000	.15	.25	.75	1.00
	1970	10.160	.20	.35	.85	1.50

Y#	Date	Mintage	Fine	VF	XF	Unc
58	1971	10.999	—	.10	.15	.20
	1973	9.342	—	.10	.15	.20

NICKEL-BRASS

Y#	Date	Mintage	Fine	VF	XF	Unc
66	1973	19.512	—	—	—	.25

Y#	Date	Mintage	Fine	VF	XF	Unc
74	1976	15.406	—	—	—	.25
	1978	—	—	—	—	.25

PHOENIX

SILVER

C#	Date	Mintage	VG	Fine	VF	XF
5	1828	.014	250.00	450.00	750.00	1000.

DRACHMA

5.0000 gm., .835 SILVER, .1342 oz ASW
Obv: Young head.

C#	Date	Mintage	VG	Fine	VF	XF
12	1832	—	40.00	60.00	80.00	125.00
	1833	—	35.00	55.00	75.00	100.00
	1833A	—	35.00	55.00	75.00	100.00
	1834A	—	35.00	55.00	75.00	100.00
	1845(o)	—	700.00	1200.	1750.	3000.
	1846	—	350.00	600.00	900.00	1500.
	1847	—	475.00	700.00	1000.	1750.

Obv: Old head.

C#	Date	Mintage	VG	Fine	VF	XF
15	1851	—	150.00	300.00	500.00	1000.

Obv: Young head.

Y#	Date	Mintage	Fine	VF	XF	Unc
7	1868	—	—	—	Pattern	1000.
	1868A	2.200	BV	5.00	50.00	195.00
	1873A	2.331	BV	5.00	30.00	125.00
	1874A	Inc. Ab.	BV	4.50	35.00	125.00
	1883A	.800	5.00	8.00	50.00	150.00

Y#	Date	Mintage	Fine	VF	XF	Unc
22	1910(a)	4.570	BV	4.50	8.50	50.00
	1911(a)	1.881	BV	5.00	10.00	75.00

COPPER-NICKEL

Y#	Date	Mintage	Fine	VF	XF	Unc
33	1926	15.000	.15	.25	1.50	7.50
	1926B	20.000	.15	.25	1.50	7.50

Y#	Date	Mintage	Fine	VF	XF	Unc
42	1954	24.091	.15	.25	.30	.35
	1957	8.151	.75	2.00	6.00	10.00
	1959	10.180	.75	1.75	5.00	8.50
	1962	20.060	.50	.75	1.00	2.00
	1965	*	—	—	—	—

*Only sold in mint sets.

Y#	Date	Mintage	Fine	VF	XF	Unc
50	1966	20.000	—	—	—	.35
	1967	20.000	—	—	—	.25
	1970	7.001	—	.10	.25	1.00

Y#	Date	Mintage	Fine	VF	XF	Unc
59	1971	11.985	.10	.20	.25	.90
	1973	8.196	.10	.20	.25	.90

NICKEL-BRASS

Y#	Date	Mintage	Fine	VF	XF	Unc
67	1973	12.842	.10	.20	.35	.60

Y#	Date	Mintage	Fine	VF	XF	Unc
75	1976	26.450	—	—	—	.40
	1978	—	—	—	—	.40

NOTE: Varieties exist for the 1976 dated coins.

2 DRACHMAI

10.0000 gm., .835 SILVER, .2685 oz ASW

Y#	Date	Mintage	Fine	VF	XF	Unc
8	1868A	.500	40.00	75.00	125.00	750.00
	1873A	.387	20.00	35.00	50.00	500.00
	1883A	.250	25.00	45.00	65.00	500.00

Y#	Date	Mintage	Fine	VF	XF	Unc
23	1911(a)	1.500	BV	10.00	17.50	75.00

COPPER-NICKEL

Y#	Date	Mintage	Fine	VF	XF	Unc
34	1926	22.000	—	1.00	5.00	25.00

Y#	Date	Mintage	Fine	VF	XF	Unc
43	1954	12.609	1.00	1.50	3.35	6.00
	1957	10.171	1.00	2.00	3.35	7.00
	1959	5.000	1.75	3.00	5.00	9.00
	1962	10.096	1.00	1.50	3.35	6.00
	1965	*	—	—	—	—

*Only sold in mint sets.

Y#	Date	Mintage	Fine	VF	XF	Unc
51	1966	10.000	.30	.50	.75	1.00
	1967	10.000	—	—	.50	1.00
	1970	7.000	—	—	.15	2.00

Y#	Date	Mintage	Fine	VF	XF	Unc
60	1971	9.998	—	—	.15	1.50
	1973	7.972	—	—	.15	1.25

NICKEL-BRASS

Y#	Date	Mintage	Fine	VF	XF	Unc
68	1973	10.935	.20	.30	.45	.85

Y#	Date	Mintage	Fine	VF	XF	Unc
76	1976	23.950	—	—	—	.50
	1978	—	—	—	—	—

5 DRACHMAI

25.0000 gm., .900 SILVER, .7234 oz ASW

C#	Date	Mintage	VG	Fine	VF	XF
13	1833	—	50.00	95.00	125.00	350.00
	1833A	—	50.00	95.00	125.00	350.00
	1833(o)	—	475.00	1500.	2500.	4000.
	1844(o)	—	275.00	750.00	1250.	2000.
	1845	—	750.00	2000.	3500.	5000.

Rev: Similar to C#13.

C#	Date	Mintage	VG	Fine	VF	XF
16	1851	—	350.00	600.00	1000.	2000.

Y#	Date	Mintage	Fine	VF	XF	Unc
14	1875A	1.000	25.00	40.00	75.00	350.00
	1875A reversed anchor					
		—	450.00	750.00	1100.	2500.
	1876A	2.092	25.00	40.00	75.00	350.00

1.6129 gm., .900 GOLD, .0467 oz AGW

Y#	Date	Mintage	Fine	VF	XF	Unc
24	1876A	9,294	350.00	600.00	1200.	2000.

NICKEL

LONDON MINT: In second set of berries on left only one berry will have a dot on it.

Y#	Date	Mintage	Fine	VF	XF	Unc
35	1930	23.500	.50	1.00	1.50	20.00

BRUSSELS MINT: Two berries will have dots.

Y#	Date	Mintage	Fine	VF	XF	Unc
35.1	1930	1.500	1.00	1.50	5.00	40.00

COPPER-NICKEL

Y#	Date	Mintage	Fine	VF	XF	Unc
44	1954	21.000	.30	.50	2.50	4.50
	1965	*	—	—	—	—

*Only sold in mint sets.

Y#	Date	Mintage	Fine	VF	XF	Unc
52	1966	12.000	.15	.25	.50	.75
	1970	5.000	.30	.50	2.00	3.75

Y#	Date	Mintage	Fine	VF	XF	Unc
61	1971	4.014	—	—	—	4.00
	1973	3.166	—	—	—	3.00

Denomination spelling ends with I.

Y#	Date	Mintage	Fine	VF	XF	Unc
69	1973	13.931	—	—	—	1.00

Denomination spelling ends with A.

Y#	Date	Mintage	Fine	VF	XF	Unc
69.1	1973	Inc. Ab.	—	—	—	—

Y#	Date	Mintage	Fine	VF	XF	Unc
77	1976	24.350	—	—	—	1.00
	1978	—	—	—	—	—

10 DRACHMAI

3.2258 gm., .900 GOLD, .0933 oz AGW

Y#	Date	Mintage	Fine	VF	XF	Unc
25	1876A	.019	300.00	500.00	850.00	1500.

7.0000 gm., .500 SILVER, .1125 oz ASW

Y#	Date	Mintage	Fine	VF	XF	Unc
36	1930	7.500	BV	5.00	25.00	50.00

NICKEL

Y#	Date	Mintage	Fine	VF	XF	Unc
45	1959	20.000	.30	.50	1.50	2.50
	1965	*	—	—	—	—

*Only sold in mint sets.

COPPER-NICKEL

Y#	Date	Mintage	Fine	VF	XF	Unc
53	1968	40.000	.75	1.25	2.00	3.25
	Rev. Phoenix					
62	1971	.502	.45	.75	1.00	4.00
	1973	.541	.45	.75	1.00	4.00

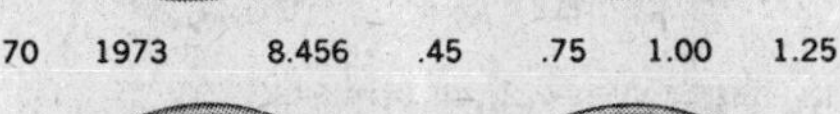

Y#	Date	Mintage	Fine	VF	XF	Unc
70	1973	8.456	.45	.75	1.00	1.25

Y#	Date	Mintage	Fine	VF	XF	Unc
78	1976	22.748	—	—	—	1.50
	1978	—	—	—	—	—

20 DRACHMAI

6.4516 gm., .900 GOLD, .1867 oz AGW

C#	Date	Mintage	VG	Fine	VF	XF
17	1833	958 pcs.	350.00	500.00	1000.	1500.

Y#	Date	Mintage	Fine	VF	XF	Unc
A25	1876A	.037	125.00	200.00	450.00	750.00

Y#	Date	Mintage	Fine	VF	XF	Unc
26	1884A	.550	125.00	150.00	175.00	275.00

11.3333 gm., .500 SILVER, .1822 oz ASW

Y#	Date	Mintage	Fine	VF	XF	Unc
37	1930	11.500	BV	6.50	20.00	35.00

.900 GOLD

Y#	Date	Mintage	Fine	VF	XF	Unc
B37	1935	200 pcs.	—	—	—	7500.

7.5000 gm., .835 SILVER, .2013 oz ASW

Y#	Date	Mintage	Fine	VF	XF	Unc
46	1960	20.000	BV	BV	6.50	10.00
	1965	*	—	—	—	15.00

*Only sold in mint sets.

6.4516 gm., .900 GOLD, .1867 oz AGW
1967 Revolution

Y#	Date	Mintage	Fine	VF	XF	Unc
56	1967	.020	—	—	—	400.00

COPPER-NICKEL

Y#	Date	Mintage	Fine	VF	XF	Unc
63	1973	3.092	.75	1.25	3.00	4.00

Wide rim

Y#	Date	Mintage	Fine	VF	XF	Unc
63.1	1973	Inc. Ab.	.75	1.25	2.00	3.00

Y#	Date	Mintage	Fine	VF	XF	Unc
71	1973	10.079	.75	1.25	2.00	3.00

Y#	Date	Mintage	Fine	VF	XF	Unc
79	1976	17.325	—	—	—	3.00
79	1978	—	—	—	—	—

30 DRACHMAI

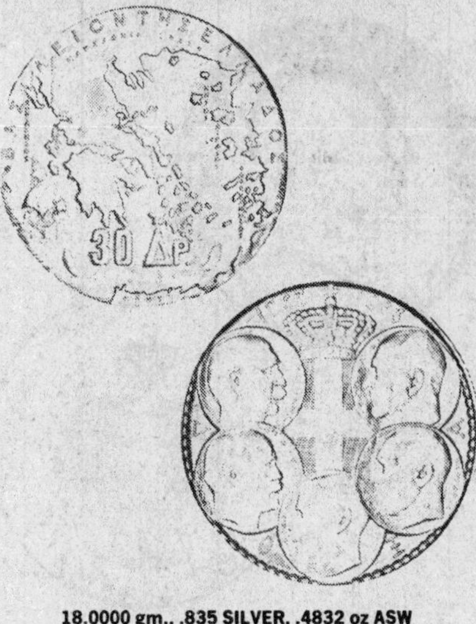

18.0000 gm., .835 SILVER, .4832 oz ASW
Centennial Of Royal Greek Dynasty

Y#	Date	Mintage	Fine	VF	XF	Unc
47	1963	3.000	BV	BV	15.00	17.50

12.0000 gm., .835 SILVER, .3221 oz ASW
Constantine And Anne-Marie
Wedding

Y#	Date	Mintage	Fine	VF	XF	Unc
48	1964 Berne, thin letters on edge					
		1.000	BV	BV	10.00	12.50
	1964 Konigsberg, thick letters on edge					
		1.000	BV	BV	10.00	12.50

50 DRACHMAI

16.1290 gm., .900 GOLD, .4667 oz AGW

Y#	Date	Mintage	Fine	VF	XF	Unc
27	1876A	182 pcs.	—	—	—	8000.

12.0000 gm., .835 SILVER, .3221 oz ASW
1967 Revolution

Y#	Date	Mintage	Fine	VF	XF	Unc
54	1967(1970)	.100	—	—	—	40.00

100 DRACHMAI

32.2580 gm., .900 GOLD, .9335 oz AGW

Y#	Date	Mintage	Fine	VF	XF	Unc
28	1876	76 pcs.	—	—	—	30,000.

SILVER
Restoration Of Monarchy

A37	1935	500 pcs.	—	—	Proof	850.00

.900 GOLD

C37	1935	140 pcs.	—	—	—	7500.

COPPER

C37a	1935	—	—	—	—	—

25.0000 gm., .835 SILVER, .6712 oz ASW
1967 Revolution

55	1967(1970)	.030	—	—	—	75.00

32.2580 gm., .900 GOLD, .9335 oz AGW
1967 Revolution

Y#	Date	Mintage	Fine	VF	XF	Unc
57	1967(1970)	.010	—	—	—	1100.

.650 SILVER
50th Anniversary of Bank of Greece

82	1978	—	—	—	—	—

500 DRACHMAI

SILVER
Common Market Membership

80	1979	—	—	—	—	75.00

10,000 DRACHMAI

GOLD
Common Market Membership

81	1979	—	—	—	—	900.00

NCLT ISSUES

PATTERNS

KM#	Date	Mintage	Identification	Mkt.Val.
1	1828	—	1 Lepton, Copper	—

2	1842	—	1/2 Drachma, Silver	—
3	ND(1845)	—	5 Drachmai, Silver	—

4	1851	—	1 Drachma, Silver	—
5	1852	16	20 Drachmai, Gold	4000.
6	1852	8	40 Drachmai, Gold	3500.
7	ND(1863)	—	20 Drachmai, Copper, uniface-rev.	—
8	1868	—	50 Lepta, Silver, w/o a mm.	—
9	1868	3	50 Lepta, Silver, E to left of date	—
10	1868	2	1 Drachma, Silver, w/o a mm.	—
11	1868	2	1 Drachma, Silver, E to left of date	—

12	1868A	—	2 Drachmai, Silver	—

13	1868	2	2 Drachmai, Silver, w/o a mm.	—

KM#	Date	Mintage	Identification	Mkt.Val.
14	1869	—	1 Lepton, Copper, ESSAI	—

15	1869	—	2 Lepta, Copper, ESSAI	—

16	1869	—	5 Lepta, Copper, Essai	—

17	1869	—	10 Lepta, Copper, ESSAI	—
18	1869	—	20 Lepta, Silver	—

19	1869	4	5 Drachmai, Gold, E (Essai)	—

20	1869	3	10 Drachmai, Gold E (Essai)	—

21	1869	1	20 Drachmai, Gold, E (Essai)	—
22	ND(1873)	—	5 Drachmai, Bronze	—

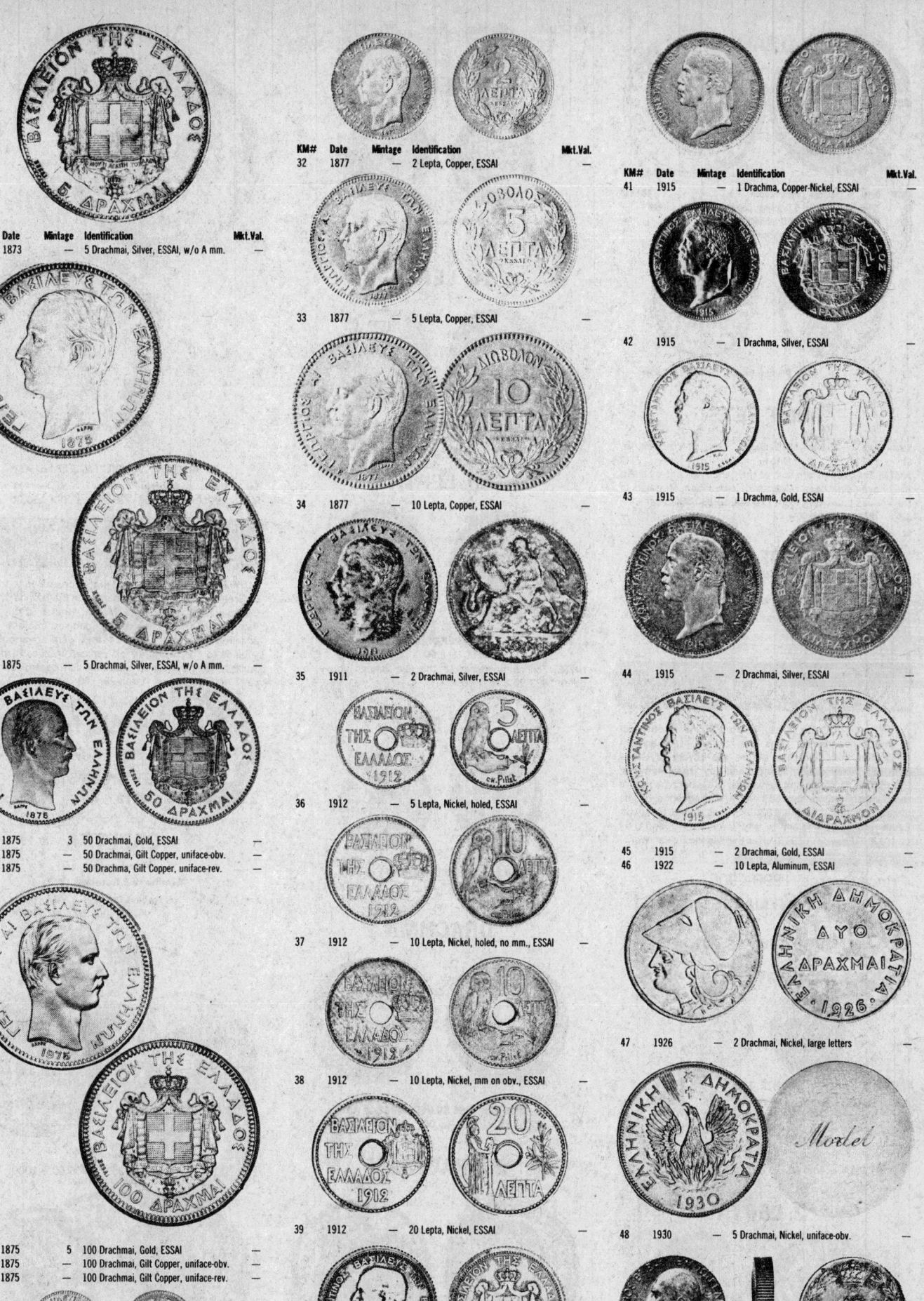

KM#	Date	Mintage	Identification	Mkt.Val.
23	1873	—	5 Drachmai, Silver, ESSAI, w/o A mm.	—
24	1875	—	5 Drachmai, Silver, ESSAI, w/o A mm.	—
25	1875	3	50 Drachmai, Gold, ESSAI	—
26	1875	—	50 Drachmai, Gilt Copper, uniface-obv.	—
27	1875	—	50 Drachma, Gilt Copper, uniface-rev.	—

KM#	Date	Mintage	Identification	Mkt.Val.
28	1875	5	100 Drachmai, Gold, ESSAI	—
29	1875	—	100 Drachmai, Gilt Copper, uniface-obv.	—
30	1875	—	100 Drachmai, Gilt Copper, uniface-rev.	—

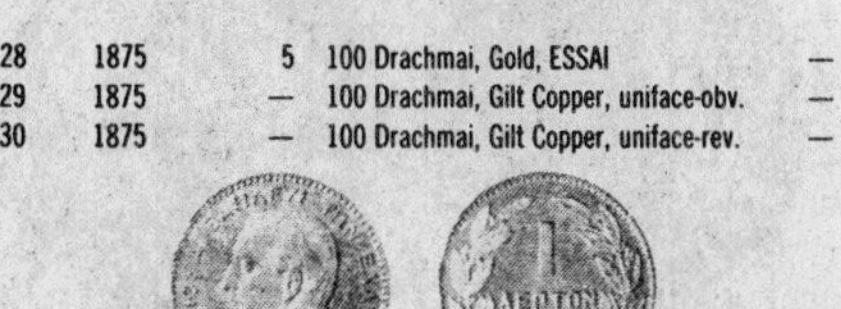

KM#	Date	Mintage	Identification	Mkt.Val.
31	1877	—	1 Lepton, Copper, ESSAI	—

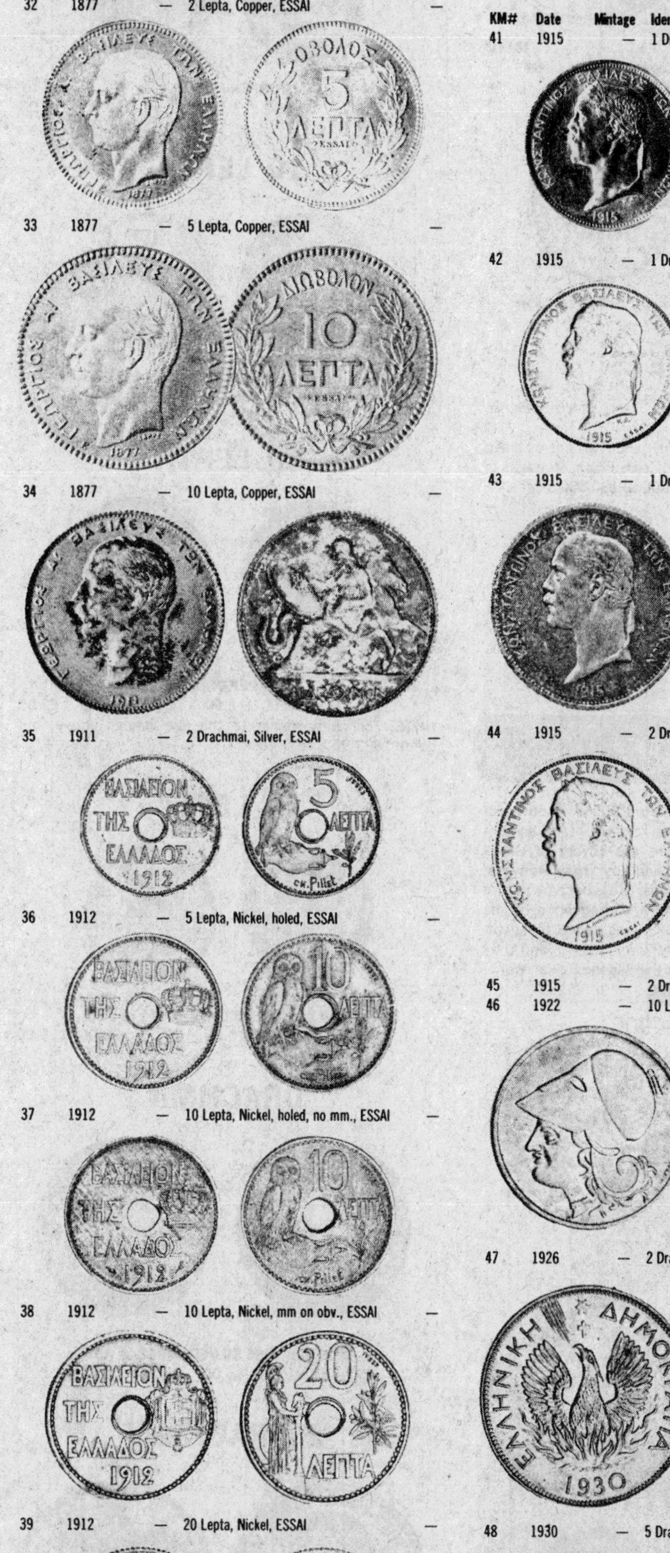

KM#	Date	Mintage	Identification	Mkt.Val.
32	1877	—	2 Lepta, Copper, ESSAI	—
33	1877	—	5 Lepta, Copper, ESSAI	—
34	1877	—	10 Lepta, Copper, ESSAI	—
35	1911	—	2 Drachmai, Silver, ESSAI	—
36	1912	—	5 Lepta, Nickel, holed, ESSAI	—
37	1912	—	10 Lepta, Nickel, holed, no mm., ESSAI	—
38	1912	—	10 Lepta, Nickel, mm on obv., ESSAI	—
39	1912	—	20 Lepta, Nickel, ESSAI	—

KM#	Date	Mintage	Identification	Mkt.Val.
40	1913	—	1 Drachma, Silver, ESSAI	—

KM#	Date	Mintage	Identification	Mkt.Val.
41	1915	—	1 Drachma, Copper-Nickel, ESSAI	—
42	1915	—	1 Drachma, Silver, ESSAI	—
43	1915	—	1 Drachma, Gold, ESSAI	—
44	1915	—	2 Drachmai, Silver, ESSAI	—
45	1915	—	2 Drachmai, Gold, ESSAI	—
46	1922	—	10 Lepta, Aluminum, ESSAI	—
47	1926	—	2 Drachmai, Nickel, large letters	—

KM#	Date	Mintage	Identification	Mkt.Val.
48	1930	—	5 Drachmai, Nickel, uniface-obv.	—
49	1935	—	20 Drachmai, Lead, Piefort	—

KM#	Date	Mintage	Identification	Mkt.Val.
50	1954	—	5 Drachmai, Copper-Nickel "hollow cheek"	—
51	1960	—	20 Drachmai, Silver	—
52	1960	—	20 Drachmai, Gold	—

KM#	Date	Mintage	Identification	Mkt.Val.
53	1976	—	1 Drachma, Nickel, 4 spritsails and 2 waves	—

MINT SETS

KM#	Date	Mintage	Identification	Issue Price	Mkt. Val.
S1	1965(7)	—	Y39,41-46	—	20.00

NOTE: These coins are sold at the mint in Greece as a set; they have never been released for circulation. Mintages of the various coins vary from 170,000 to 190,000 pieces.

KM#	Date	Mintage	Identification	Issue Price	Mkt. Val.
S2	1978	50,000	—	—	—

PROOF SETS

STANDARD METALS

KM#	Date	Mintage	Identification	Issue Price	Mkt. Val.
101	1935(3)	2,000	YA37,B37,C37	—	15,750.
102	1965(7)	4,987	Y39,41-46	10.25	37.50
103	1967(2)	10,000	Y56,57	—	1500.
104	1978	20,000	—	—	—

CRETE

The island of Crete (Kreti), located 60 miles southeast of the Peloponnesus, was the center of a brilliant civilization that flourished before the advent of Greek culture. After being conquered by the Romans, Byzantines, Moslems and Venetians, Crete became part of the Turkish Empire in 1669. As a consequence of the Greek Revolution of the 1820S, it was ceded to Egypt. Egypt returned the island to the Turks in 1840, and they ceded it to Greece in 1913, after the Second Balkan War.

RULERS

Prince George, 1898-1906

MINTMARKS

A - Paris
(a) - Paris (privy marks only)

LEPTON

BRONZE, 15mm

Y#	Date	Mintage	Fine	VF	XF	Unc
1.1	1900A	.289	3.00	6.00	10.00	20.00
	1901A	1.711	1.50	4.00	8.00	17.50
			16mm			
1.2	1901A	Inc. Ab.	1.50	4.00	8.00	17.50

2 LEPTA

BRONZE

Y#	Date	Mintage	Fine	VF	XF	Unc
2	1900A	.793	2.00	3.50	10.00	20.00
2	1901A	.707	5.00	7.50	12.50	30.00

5 LEPTA

COPPER NICKEL

Y#	Date	Mintage	Fine	VF	XF	Unc
3	1900A	4.000	1.50	2.50	10.00	20.00

10 LEPTA

COPPER-NICKEL

Y#	Date	Mintage	Fine	VF	XF	Unc
4	1900A	2.000	.95	1.50	10.00	20.00

20 LEPTA

COPPER-NICKEL

Y#	Date	Mintage	Fine	VF	XF	Unc
5	1900A	1.250	1.50	2.50	10.00	22.50

NOTE: For coins similar to the five listings above, but dated 1893-95, see Greece.

50 LEPTA

2.5000 gm., .835 SILVER, .0671 oz ASW

Y#	Date	Mintage	Fine	VF	XF	Unc
6	1901(a)	.600	10.00	20.00	35.00	125.00

DRACHMA

5.0000 gm., .835 SILVER, .1342 oz ASW

Y#	Date	Mintage	Fine	VF	XF	Unc
7	1901(a)	.500	15.00	25.00	45.00	250.00

2 DRACHMAI

10.0000 gm., .835 SILVER, .2685 oz ASW

Y#	Date	Mintage	Fine	VF	XF	Unc
8	1901(a)	.175	20.00	40.00	75.00	300.00

5 DRACHMAI

25.0000 gm., .900 SILVER, .7234 oz ASW

Y#	Date	Mintage	Fine	VF	XF	Unc
9	1901(a)	.150	20.00	35.00	150.00	400.00

IONIAN ISLANDS

The Ionian Islands, situated in the Ionian Sea to the west of Greece, is the collective name for the islands of Corfu, Cephalonia, Zante, Santa Maura, Ithaca, Cythera and Paxo, with their minor dependencies. Before Britain acquired the islands, 1809-14, they were at various times subject to the authority of Venice, France, Russia and Turkey. They remained under British control until their cession to Greece on March 29, 1864.

Under Russia/Turkey

(1799-1807)

MONETARY SYSTEM

2 Soldi = 1 Gazetta

GAZETTA

COPPER
Similar to 5 Gazettae, C#2.

C#	Date	Mintage	Good	VG	Fine	VF
1	1801	—	125.00	200.00	350.00	550.00

5 GAZETTAE

COPPER

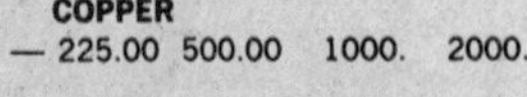

C#	Date	Mintage	Good	VG	Fine	VF
2	1801	—	225.00	500.00	1000.	2000.

Value as 5 GAZZETE.

C#	Date	Mintage	Good	VG	Fine	VF
2a	1801	—	225.00	500.00	1000.	2000.

10 GAZETTAE

COPPER

Obv. leg: set special head

C#	Date	Mintage	Good	VG	Fine	VF
3	1801	—	750.00	1250.	2000.	3000.

Obv. leg: set special head

C#	Date	Mintage	Good	VG	Fine	VF
3a	1801	—	—	—	Rare	—

Under British Rule

(1809-1863)

MONETARY SYSTEM

40 Paras = 1 Piastre

220 Paras = 1 Dollar

25 PARAS

SILVER

Two countermarks, 25 and 25 with poorly drawn portrait of George III, on 3 Tari or 20 Grani coins of Sicily.

C#	Date	Mintage	Good	VG	Fine	VF
16	(1814)	—	125.00	200.00	350.00	550.00

30 PARAS

SILVER

Two countermarks, 30 and 30 with poorly drawn portrait of George III, on 1 Real of Spain.

C#	Date	Mintage	Good	VG	Fine	VF
17	(1814)	—	—	—	Rare	—

NOTE: One piece exists with only reverse countermark on French coin of Louis XIV, but it is considered by some experts a contemporary counterfeit, since the authorization for these coins mentions only Spanish and Sicilian coins. However, it may be that the islanders were permitted to present any silver coins for countermarking.

50 PARAS

SILVER

Two countermarks, 50 and 50 with poorly drawn portrait of George III, on 6 Tari or 30 Grani coins of Sicily.

C#	Date	Mintage	Good	VG	Fine	VF
18	(1814)	—	120.00	165.00	275.00	450.00

NOTE: At least one coin exists with only 50 countermark.

60 PARAS

SILVER

Two countermarks, 60 and 60 with poorly drawn portrait of George III in oval, on 2 Reales of Spain.

C#	Date	Mintage	Good	VG	Fine	VF
19	(1814)	—	275.00	400.00	650.00	1000.

DECIMAL COINAGE

MONETARY SYSTEM

(Until 1835)

4 Lepta = Obol

100 Oboli = 1 Dollar

(Commencing 1835)

5 Lepta = Obol

100 Oboli = 1 Dollar

LEPTON

COPPER

Obv: Winged lion above date.

Rev: Seated Britannia above 4 (= 1/4 obol)

C#	Date	Mintage	Good	VG	Fine	VF
20	1821	—	60.00	100.00	150.00	275.00

NOTE: Most of these coins are overstruck on Turkish coins by native craftsmen, and are very crude.

C#	Date	Mintage	VG	Fine	VF	XF
24	1834.	—	.90	1.50	6.00	15.00
	1834.	—	—	—	Proof	175.00
	1835.	—	.90	1.50	6.00	15.00
	1848.	13.483	.90	1.50	6.00	15.00
	1849.	Inc. Ab.	.90	1.50	6.00	15.00
	1849	—	—	—	Proof	175.00
	1851.	Inc. Ab.	.90	1.50	6.00	15.00
	1851.	—	—	—	Proof	175.00
	1853.	Inc. Ab.	.90	1.50	12.50	30.00
	1853	—	—	—	Proof	175.00
	1857	Inc. Ab.	.90	1.50	6.00	15.00
	1857.	Inc. Ab.	7.50	12.50	25.00	50.00
	1862.	Inc. Ab.	.90	1.50	6.00	15.00
	1862	—	—	—	Proof	175.00

2 LEPTA

COPPER

C#	Date	Mintage	Good	VG	Fine	VF
21	1819.	9.462	2.00	3.50	7.50	15.00
	1819	—	—	—	Proof	200.00
	1820.	Inc. Ab.	2.00	3.50	7.50	15.00
	1820	—	—	—	Proof	200.00

OBOL

COPPER

C#	Date	Mintage	Good	VG	Fine	VF
22	1819.	8.279	9.50	15.00	22.50	45.00
	1819	—	—	—	Proof	250.00

SILVER

C#	Date	Mintage	Good	VG	Fine	VF
22a	1819	—	—		Proof Only	500.00

2 OBOL

COPPER

C#	Date	Mintage	Good	VG	Fine	VF
23	1819	4.140	30.00	50.00	75.00	125.00
	1819	—	—	—	Proof	650.00

30 LEPTA

.925 SILVER

C#	Date	Mintage	VG	Fine	VF	XF
25	1834	—	8.50	15.00	30.00	75.00
	1834	—	—	—	Proof	250.00
	1834.	—	15.00	25.00	50.00	75.00
	1848.	.331	100.00	150.00	250.00	300.00
	1849	Inc. Ab.	8.50	15.00	40.00	75.00
	1849	—	—	—	Proof	250.00
	1849.	Inc. Ab.	20.00	30.00	50.00	80.00
	1851	Inc. Ab.	8.50	15.00	40.00	75.00
	1851	—	—	—	Proof	250.00
	1852	Inc. Ab.	8.50	15.00	40.00	75.00
	1852	—	—	—	Proof	250.00
	1857	Inc. Ab.	25.00	25.00	50.00	75.00
	1857.	Inc. Ab.	15.00	25.00	50.00	80.00
	1862	Inc. Ab.	8.50	15.00	35.00	50.00

GREENLAND

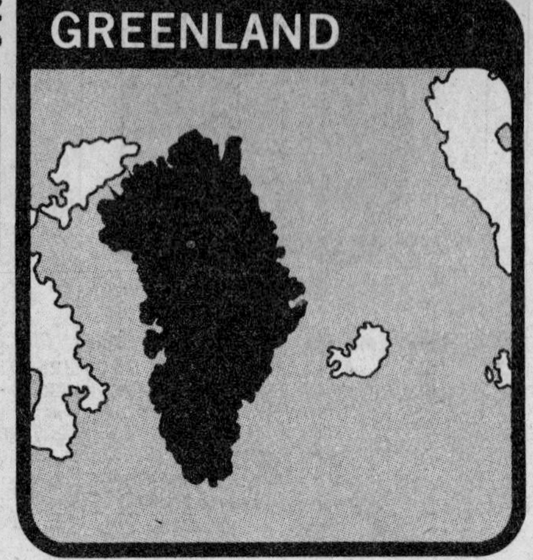

Greenland, an integral part of the Danish realm, is a huge island situated between the North Atlantic Ocean and the Polar Sea, almost entirely within the Arctic Circle. It has an area of 840,000 sq. mi. (2,175,600 sq. km.) and a population of 49,000. Capital: Godthrab. Greenland is the world's only source of natural cryolite, a fluoride of sodium and aluminum important in making aluminum. Fish products and minerals are exported.

Eric the Red discovered Greenland in 982 and established the first settlement in 986. Greenland was a republic until 1261, when the sovereignty of Norway was extended to the island. The original colony was abandoned about 1400 when increasing cold interfered with the breeding of cattle. Successful recolonization was undertaken by Denmark in 1721. In 1921 Denmark extended its claim to include the entire island, and made it a colony of the crown in 1924. The island's colonial status was abolished by amendment to the Danish constitution on June 5, 1953, and Greenland became an integral part of the Kingdom of Denmark. It has been an autonomous state since May 1, 1979.

RULERS

Danish

MINTMARKS

Heart (h) Copenhagen

MINTMASTERS INITIALS

HCN - Hans Christian Nielsen, 1919-1927

C - Alfred Frederik Christiansen, 1956-1971

MONEYERS INITIALS

GI, GJ - Knud Gunnar Jensen, 1901-1933

HS, S - Harald Salomon, 1933-1968

MONETARY SYSTEM

100 Ore = 1 Krone

TOKEN ISSUES

Cryolite Mining & Trading Co.

10 ORE

COPPER-NICKEL

Y#	Date	Mintage	VG	Fine	VF	XF
1	1922	—	5.00	10.00	15.00	25.00

50 ORE

COPPER-NICKEL
Similar to 10 Ore, Y#1.

Y#	Date	Mintage	VG	Fine	VF	XF
2	1922	—	17.50	30.00	40.00	50.00

2 KRONER

COPPER-NICKEL

Y#	Date	Mintage	VG	Fine	VF	XF
3	1922	—	12.00	20.00	30.00	40.00

10 KRONER

COPPER-NICKEL
Similar to 2 Kroner, Y#3.

Y#	Date	Mintage	VG	Fine	VF	XF
4	1922	—	25.00	35.00	45.00	55.00

ALUMINUM-BRONZE

Y#	Date	Mintage	VG	Fine	VF	XF
4a	1922	—	125.00	200.00	300.00	400.00

Greenland Minedrift

10 ORE

COPPER
Similar to 100 Ore, KM#3.

KM#	Date	Mintage	VG	Fine	VF	XF
1	1911	—	15.00	25.00	40.00	70.00

25 ORE

COPPER
Similar to 100 Ore, KM#3.

KM#	Date	Mintage	VG	Fine	VF	XF
2	1911	—	15.00	25.00	40.00	70.00

100 ORE

COPPER

KM#	Date	Mintage	VG	Fine	VF	XF
3	1911	—	15.00	25.00	40.00	70.00

Thule-Kap York

5 ORE

ALUMINUM
Similar to 500 Ore, KM#7.

KM#	Date	Mintage	VG	Fine	VF	XF
4	1910	—	2.00	3.50	5.50	8.00

25 ORE

ALUMINUM
Similar to 500 Ore, KM#7.

KM#	Date	Mintage	VG	Fine	VF	XF
5	1910	—	1.50	2.50	4.00	6.00

100 ORE

ALUMINUM
Similar to 500 Ore, KM#7.

KM#	Date	Mintage	VG	Fine	VF	XF
6	1910	—	4.00	6.50	11.00	16.00

500 ORE

ALUMINUM

KM#	Date	Mintage	VG	Fine	VF	XF
7	1910	—	6.00	10.00	16.00	22.50

5 KRONE

ALUMINUM
Similar to 500 Ore, KM#7.

KM#	Date	Mintage	VG	Fine	VF	XF
8	1910	—	10.00	18.00	30.00	45.00

10 KRONE

ALUMINUM
Similar to 500 Ore, KM#7.

KM#	Date	Mintage	VG	Fine	VF	XF
9	1910	—	30.00	50.00	85.00	125.00

REGULAR COINAGE

25 ORE

COPPER-NICKEL

Y#	Date	Mintage	Fine	VF	XF	Unc
5	1926HCN(h)GJ	.310	1.50	2.50	4.50	8.50

Center hole added to Y#5

Y#	Date	Mintage	Fine	VF	XF	Unc
6	1926HCN(h)GJ	.060	6.00	10.00	20.00	—

NOTE: Y#5 was withdrawn from circulation and hole added in the USA.

50 ORE

ALUMINUM-BRONZE

Y#	Date	Mintage	Fine	VF	XF	Unc
7	1926HCN(h)GJ	.196	1.50	3.00	5.00	12.00

KRONE

ALUMINUM-BRONZE

Y#	Date	Mintage	Fine	VF	XF	Unc
8	1926HCN(h)GJ	.287	2.00	3.00	6.00	20.00

Y#	Date	Mintage	Fine	VF	XF	Unc
10	1957C(h)S	.100	3.50	6.00	8.00	17.50

COPPER-NICKEL

Y#	Date	Mintage	Fine	VF	XF	Unc
10a	1960C(h)S	.108	1.50	3.00	5.00	11.00
	1964C(h)S	.110	1.25	3.00	5.00	10.00

5 KRONER

BRASS

Y#	Date	Mintage	Fine	VF	XF	Unc
9	1944	.100	15.00	30.00	50.00	75.00

GRENADA

Grenada, located in the Windward Islands of the Caribbean Sea 90 miles (145 km.) north of Trinidad, has (with Carriacou and Petit Martinique) an area of 133 sq. mi. (344 sq. km.) and a population of 96,000. Capital: St. George's. Grenada is the smallest independent nation in the Western Hemisphere. The economy is based on agriculture and tourism. Sugar, coconuts, nutmeg, cocoa, and bananas are exported.

Columbus discovered Grenada in 1498 during his third voyage to the Americas. Spain failed to colonize the island, and in 1627 granted it to the British who sold it to the French who colonized it in 1650. Grenada was captured by the British in 1763, retaken by the French in 1779, and finally ceded to the British in 1783. In 1958 Grenada joined the Federation of the West Indies, which was dissolved in 1962. In 1967 it became an internally self-governing British associated state. Full independence was attained on Feb. 4, 1974. Grenada is a member of the Commonwealth of Nations. The prime minister is the Head of Government.

The early coinage of Grenada consists of cut and counterstamped pieces of the Spanish 8 Reales, which were valued at 11 Bits. In 1787 8 Reales coins were cut into 11 triangular pieces and counterstamped with an incuse G. Later in 1814 large denomination cut pieces were issued being 1/2, 1/3 or 1/6 cuts and counterstamped with a 'TR', incuse 'G' and a number 6, 4, 2, or 1 indicating the value in bitts.

RULERS

British

MONETARY SYSTEM

1789-1798

1 Bit = 9 Pence
11 Bits = 8 Shillings 3 Pence
= 1 Dollar

1798-1840

12 Bits = 9 Shillings = 1 Dollar

BIT

SILVER
c/s: Incuse 'G' on 1/11th of Spanish or Spanish Colonial 8 Reales.

C#	Date	Mintage	VG	Fine	VF
1	ND(1787)	—	50.00	75.00	125.00

c/s: 'TR', 'G', '1' on 1/3 cut of Spanish or Spanish Colonial 2 Reales.

C#	Date	Mintage	VG	Fine	VF
1.5	ND(1818)	—	75.00	125.00	150.00

c/s: 'GS', 'G', '1' on 1/3 cut of Spanish or Spanish Colonial 2 Reales.

C#	Date	Mintage	VG	Fine	VF
1.6	ND(1818)	—	75.00	125.00	150.00

2 BITS

SILVER
c/s: 'TR', 'G', '2' on 1/6 cut of Spanish or Spanish Colonial 8 Reales.

C#	Date	Mintage	VG	Fine	VF
2	ND(1814)	—	75.00	125.00	150.00

c/s: 'GS', 'G', '2' on 1/6 cut of Spanish or Spanish Colonial 8 Reales.

C#	Date	Mintage	VG	Fine	VF
2.1	ND(1814)	—	75.00	125.00	150.00

4 BITS

SILVER
c/s: 'TR', 'G', '4' on 1/3 cut of Spanish or Spanish Colonial 8 Reales.

C#	Date	Mintage	VG	Fine	VF
3	ND(1814)	—	125.00	175.00	225.00

c/s: 'GS', 'G', '4' on 1/6 cut of Spanish or Spanish Colonial 8 Reales.

C#	Date	Mintage	VG	Fine	VF
3.1	ND(1814)	—	125.00	175.00	225.00

6 BITS

SILVER
c/s: 'TR', 'G', '6' on 1/2 cut of Spanish or Spanish Colonial 8 Reales.

C#	Date	Mintage	VG	Fine	VF
4	ND(1814)	—	200.00	275.00	375.00

c/s: 'GS', 'G', '6' on 1/2 cut of Spanish or Spanish Colonial 8 Reales.

C#	Date	Mintage	VG	Fine	VF
4.1	ND(1814)	—	200.00	275.00	375.00

66 SHILLINGS

GOLD

C#	Date	Mintage	VG	Fine	VF
10	ND(1798)	—	—	Rare	—

NOTE: Brazilian or Portuguese 6400 Reis plugged with a gold plug to raise the weight to legal specifications. The plug was counterstamped with the script initials IW, WS or JR. Three 'G' counterstamps are also spaced along the edge to prevent clipping.

C#	Date	Mintage	VG	Fine	VF
10.5	ND(1798)	—	—	Rare	—

NOTE: A heavier 6400 Reis coin not needing the center plug to raise the weight but with the three 'G' counterstamps along the edge.

72 SHILLINGS

GOLD

C#	Date	Mintage	VG	Fine	VF
11	ND	—	Reported, Not Confirmed		

NOTE: Full weight 6400 Reis with 'G' counterstamp in center.

MODERN COINAGE

4 DOLLARS

COPPER-NICKEL
F.A.O. Issue

Y#	Date	Mintage	VF	XF	Unc
5*	1970	.020	—	6.00	7.50
	1970	2,000	—	Proof	50.00

***NOTE:** This number refers to Yeoman's East Caribbean Territories listings, where seven companion 4-Dollar issues are listed.

GUADALOUPE

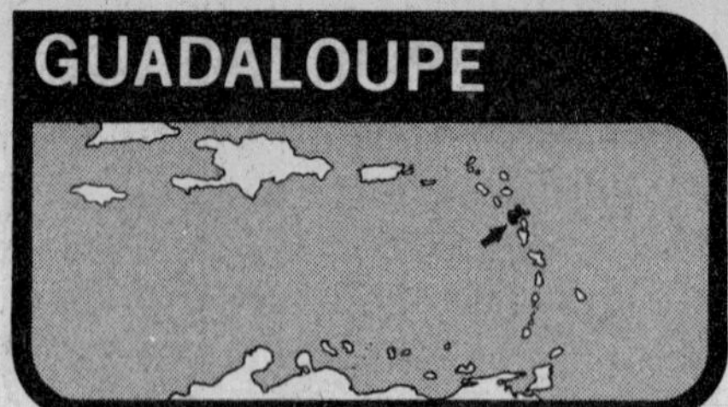

The French Overseas Department of Guadeloupe, located in the Leeward Islands of the West Indies about 300 miles (493 km.) southeast of Puerto Rico, has an area of 687 sq. mi. (1,780 sq. km.) and a population of 330,000. Actually it is two islands separated by a narrow salt water stream: volcanic Basse-Terre to the west and the flatter limestone formation of Grande-Terre to the east. Capital: Basse-Terre, on the island of that name. The principal industries are agriculture, the distillation of liquors, and tourism. Sugar, bananas, and rum are exported.

Guadeloupe was discovered by Columbus in 1493 and settled in 1635 by two Frenchmen, L'Olive and Duplessis, who took possession in the name of the French Company of the Islands of America. When repeated efforts by private companies to colonize the island failed, it was relinquished to the French crown in 1674, and established as a dependency of Martinique. The British occupied the island on two occasions, 1759-63 and 1810-16, before it passed permanently to France. A colony until 1946 Guadeloupe was then made an overseas territory of the French Union. In 1958 it voted to become an Overseas Department within the new French Community.

The well known R.F. in garland oval counterstamp of the French Government is only legitimate if on a French Colonies 12 deniers 1767 C#4. Two other similar but incuse RF counterstamps are on cut pieces in the values of 1 and 4 escalins.

RULERS

French, until 1759, 1763-1810, 1816 -
British, 1759-1763, 1810-1816

FRENCH ISSUES

Until 1810

3 SOUS 9 DENIERS

BRONZE
c/s: 'RF' in garland oval on Fr. Col. 12 Deniers, C#4.

C#	Date	Year	Good	VG	Fine	VF
2	ND(1793)(1767)		13.50	20.00	28.50	40.00

ESCALIN

SILVER
c/s: 'R.F.' on cut from outside ring of a center cut Spanish or Spanish Colonial 8 Reales.

C#	Date	Year	Good	VG	Fine	VF
14	ND(1802)	—	40.00	65.00	100.00	140.00

4 E (ESCALINS)

SILVER
c/s: 4E RF on center plug of Spanish or Spanish Colonial

8 Reales.

C#	Date	Year	Good	VG	Fine	VF
16	ND(1802)	—	500.00	750.00	900.00	1200.

4 ESCUDOS

.917 GOLD
c/s: 'G' in 15 pointed circular indent on Brazil 6400 Reis of John V.

C#	Date	Year	Good	VG	Fine	VF
21.1	ND(1803)	(1727-50)	1000.	1500.	2350.	3000.

c/s: 'G' in 15 pointed circular indent on Brazil 6400 Reis, C#75.

C#	Date	Year	Good	VG	Fine	VF
21.2	ND(1803)	(1789-1805)	1000.	1500.	2350.	3000.

Additional counterstamps used here are GT for Grande Terre and PP for Pointe-A-Pitre. Both of these are found on commonly circulating coins in the first years of the 1800's.

BRITISH OCCUPATION

1810-1816

10 SOUS

SILVER
c/s: Crowned 'G' counterstamp on Spanish or Spanish Colonial 1/2 Real.

C#	Date	Year	Good	VG	Fine	VF
61.1	ND(1811)	—	25.00	45.00	75.00	100.00

c/s: Crowned 'G' on Great Britain 3 Pence

C#	Date	Year	Good	VG	Fine	VF
61.2	ND(1811)	—	25.00	45.00	75.00	100.00

c/s: Crowned 'G' on French 1/20 Ecu, C#38.

C#	Date	Year	Good	VG	Fine	VF
61.3	ND(1811)(1727)		40.00	75.00	100.00	140.00

20 SOUS

SILVER
c/s: Crowned 'G' on Spanish Colonial 1 Real

C#	Date	Year	Good	VG	Fine	VF
62.1	ND(1811)	—	25.00	40.00	65.00	90.00

c/s: Crowned 'G' on French 12 Sous, C#44.

C#	Date	Year	Good	VG	Fine	VF
62.2	ND(1811)	(1743-70)	25.00	40.00	60.00	85.00

c/s: Crowned 'G' on Great Britain 6 Pence

C#	Date	Year	Good	VG	Fine	VF
62.3	ND(1811)	—	25.00	40.00	60.00	85.00

SILVER
c/s: Radiant 'G' on center plug of Spanish or

Spanish Colonial 8 Reales.

C#	Date	Year	Good	VG	Fine	VF
64	ND(1811)	—	65.00	110.00	165.00	225.00

40 SOUS

SILVER
c/s: Crowned 'G' on French 1/3 Ecu, C#30.

C#	Date	Year	Good	VG	Fine	VF
68.1	ND(1811)					
		(1720-23)	55.00	75.00	100.00	150.00

c/s: Crowned 'G' on French 24 Sols, C#76.

C#	Date	Year	Good	VG	Fine	VF
68.2	ND(1811)					
		(1774-90)	30.00	50.00	75.00	100.00

c/s: Crowned 'G' on Great Britain, C#31.

C#	Date	Year	Good	VG	Fine	VF
68.3	ND(1811)	(1787)	30.00	40.00	60.00	85.00

2 LIVRES 5 SOUS

SILVER
c/s: Crowned 'G' on quarter segment of Spanish or Spanish Colonial 8 Reales.

C#	Date	Year	Good	VG	Fine	VF
70	ND(1813)	—	—	30.00	40.00	55.00

9 LIVRES

SILVER
c/s: Crowned 'G' on obv. and rev. on Mexico 8 Reales, KM#106 (C#40) with a crenalated square hole.

C#	Date	Year	Good	VG	Fine	VF
72	ND(1811)					
		(1772-89)	150.00	185.00	235.00	300.00

NOTE: The square plug was used in making 20 Sous, C#64.

82 LIVRES, 10 SOUS

.917 GOLD
c/s: Crowned 'G' and value on Brazil 6400 Reis, C#34.

C#	Date	Year	Good	VG	Fine	VF
75.1	ND(1811)					
		(1751-77)	650.00	1000.	1750.	2750.

c/s: Crowned 'G' and value on Brazil 6400 Reis, C#53.

C#	Date	Year	Good	VG	Fine	VF
75.2	ND(1811)					
		(1777-86)	650.00	1000.	1750.	2750.

c/s: Crowned 'G' and value on Brazil 6400 Reis, C#75.

C#	Date	Year	Good	VG	Fine	VF
75.3	ND(1811)					
		(1789-1805)	650.00	1000.	1750.	2500.

MODERN COINAGE

MONETARY SYSTEM

100 Centimes = 1 Franc

50 CENTIMES

COPPER-NICKEL

Y#	Date	Mintage	Fine	VF	XF	Unc
1	1903	.600	3.00	6.00	12.50	25.00
	1921	.600	3.50	7.50	15.00	30.00

FRANC

COPPER-NICKEL

Y#	Date	Mintage	Fine	VF	XF	Unc
2	1903	.700	6.00	12.50	25.00	50.00
	1921	.700	4.00	10.00	17.50	35.00

GUATEMALA

The Republic of Guatemala, the northernmost of the five Central American republics, has an area of 42,000 sq. mi. (108,780 sq. km.) and a population of 6.5 million. Capital: Guatemala City. The economy of Guatemala is heavily dependent on agriculture. The country is, however, rich in nickel resources which are being developed. Coffee, cotton and bananas are exported.

Guatemala, once the site of the ancient Mayan civilization, was conquered by Pedro de Alvarado, the resourceful lieutenant of Cortes who undertook the conquest from Mexico. Skilled in strategy and cruelty, he progressed rapidly along the Pacific coastal lowlands to the highland plain of Quetzaltenango where the decisive battle for Guatemala was fought. After routing the Indian forces, he established the first capital of Guatemala, 1524 - Guatemala of the colonial period included all of Central America but Panama. Guatemala declared its independence of Spain in 1821 and was absorbed into the short-lived Mexican empire of Agustin Iturbide, 1822-23. From 1823 to 1839 Guatemala was a constituent state of the Central American Republic. Upon dissolution of the federation, Guatemala became an independent republic.

COLONIAL ISSUES

RULERS

Spanish until 1821

MINTMARKS

G or G-G-Guatemala until 1776
NG - Nueva Guatemala - 1777 onward

1/4 REAL

.903 SILVER

MINTMARK: G

Obv: Castle. Rev: Lion.

C#	Date	Mintage	VG	Fine	VF	XF
36	1796G	—	6.00	12.00	22.50	40.00
	1797G	—	8.50	17.50	25.00	50.00
	1798G	—	8.50	17.50	25.00	50.00
	1799G	—	8.50	17.50	25.00	50.00
	1800G	—	8.50	17.50	25.00	50.00
	1801G	—	8.50	17.50	25.00	50.00
	1802G	—	8.50	17.50	25.00	50.00
	1803G	—	8.50	17.50	25.00	50.00
	1804G	—	8.50	17.50	25.00	50.00
	1805G	—	25.00	50.00	70.00	100.00
	1806G	—	20.00	40.00	60.00	90.00
	1807G	—	8.50	17.50	25.00	50.00
	1808G	—	8.50	17.50	25.00	50.00

C#	Date	Mintage	VG	Fine	VF	XF
62	1809G	—	8.50	17.50	45.00	60.00
	1810G	—	8.50	17.50	35.00	50.00
	1811G	—	25.00	50.00	75.00	100.00
	1812G	—	25.00	50.00	75.00	100.00
	1813G	—	8.50	17.50	40.00	60.00
	1814G	—	8.50	17.50	40.00	60.00
	1815G	—	8.50	17.50	40.00	60.00
	1816G	—	8.50	17.50	35.00	50.00
	1817G	—	8.50	17.50	40.00	60.00
	1818G	—	8.50	17.50	40.00	60.00
	1819G	—	8.50	17.50	40.00	60.00
	1820G	—	8.50	17.50	40.00	60.00
	1821G	—	6.00	12.50	17.50	35.00
	1822G	—	375.00	700.00	1200.	2000.

1/2 REAL

.903 SILVER

MINTMARK: G

Obv. leg: CAR. III..., arms. Rev: Pillars.

C#	Date	Mintage	VG	Fine	VF	XF
19	1760 P	—	60.00	120.00	200.00	450.00
	1760	—	60.00	120.00	200.00	450.00
	1761 P	—	60.00	120.00	200.00	450.00
	1761	—	60.00	120.00	200.00	450.00
	1762 P	—	60.00	120.00	200.00	450.00

C#	Date	Mintage	VG	Fine	VF	XF
19	1762	—	60.00	120.00	200.00	450.00
	1763	—	60.00	120.00	200.00	450.00
	1764	—	60.00	120.00	200.00	450.00
	1765	—	60.00	120.00	200.00	450.00
	1766 P	—	60.00	120.00	200.00	450.00
	1767 P	—	60.00	120.00	200.00	450.00
	1768	—	60.00	120.00	200.00	450.00
	1769 P	—	60.00	120.00	200.00	450.00
	1770	—	60.00	120.00	200.00	450.00
	1771	—	60.00	120.00	200.00	450.00

Obv: Bust Charles III. Rev: Arms, pillars.

C#	Date	Mintage	VG	Fine	VF	XF
24	1772 P	—	20.00	40.00	60.00	100.00
	1773 P	—	15.00	25.00	50.00	75.00
	1776 P	—	20.00	35.00	60.00	100.00

MINTMARK: NG

C#	Date	Mintage	VG	Fine	VF	XF
24a	1780 P	—	8.50	17.50	40.00	75.00
	1781 P	—	8.50	17.50	40.00	75.00
	1782 P	—	8.50	17.50	40.00	75.00
	1783 P	—	8.50	17.50	40.00	75.00
	1785 P	—	8.50	17.50	40.00	75.00
	1785M	—	8.50	17.50	40.00	75.00
	1786 M	—	8.50	17.50	40.00	75.00
	1787 M	—	8.50	17.50	40.00	75.00

Obv. leg: CAROLVS IV....., bust of Charles III.

C#	Date	Mintage	VG	Fine	VF	XF
37	1789 M	—	12.00	25.00	50.00	75.00
	1790 M	—	12.00	25.00	50.00	75.00

Obv. leg: CAROLUS IIII....

C#	Date	Mintage	VG	Fine	VF	XF
43	1790 M	—	35.00	65.00	100.00	175.00
	1791 M	—	10.00	20.00	35.00	65.00
	1792 M	—	17.50	35.00	60.00	85.00
	1793 M	—	10.00	20.00	35.00	65.00
	1794 M	—	10.00	20.00	35.00	65.00
	1795 M	—	10.00	20.00	35.00	65.00
	1796 M	—	10.00	20.00	35.00	65.00
	1797 M	—	17.50	35.00	60.00	85.00
	1798 M	—	8.50	17.50	35.00	65.00
	1801 M	—	7.50	12.00	25.00	55.00
	1802 M	—	7.50	12.00	25.00	55.00
	1803 M	—	8.50	17.50	35.00	65.00
	1804 M	—	8.50	17.50	35.00	65.00
	1805 M	—	8.50	17.50	35.00	65.00
	1806 M	—	8.50	17.50	35.00	65.00
	1807 M	—	8.50	17.50	35.00	65.00
	1808 M	—	20.00	40.00	75.00	125.00

Obv. leg: FERDIND VII...., bust of Charles IV.

C#	Date	Mintage	VG	Fine	VF	XF
63	1808 M	—	5.00	10.00	17.50	40.00
	1809 M	—	4.50	9.00	20.00	40.00
	1810 M	—	5.00	10.00	20.00	45.00

Obv: Bust of Ferdinand VII.

C#	Date	Mintage	VG	Fine	VF	XF
68	1808 M	—	27.50	55.00	90.00	125.00
	1811 M	—	—	—	Rare	—
	1812 M	—	12.50	25.00	50.00	90.00
	1813 M	—	12.50	25.00	55.00	100.00
	1814 M	—	6.00	10.00	20.00	40.00
	1815 M	—	5.00	10.00	20.00	40.00
	1816 M	—	4.00	7.50	12.00	25.00
	1817 M	—	7.50	15.00	35.00	65.00
	1818 M	—	8.50	17.50	35.00	65.00
	1819 M	—	7.50	15.00	35.00	65.00
	1820 M	—	4.00	7.50	12.00	20.00
	1821 M	—	7.50	15.00	30.00	60.00

REAL

.903 SILVER

MINTMARK: G

Obv leg: CAROLUS III...., arms. Rev: Pillars.

C#	Date	Mintage	VG	Fine	VF	XF
20	1760 P	—	60.00	120.00	200.00	450.00
	1761 P	—	60.00	120.00	200.00	450.00
	1762 P	—	60.00	120.00	200.00	450.00
	1764 P	—	60.00	120.00	200.00	450.00
	1765 P	—	60.00	120.00	200.00	450.00
	1766 P	—	60.00	120.00	200.00	450.00
	1767 P	—	60.00	120.00	200.00	450.00
	1768 P	—	60.00	120.00	200.00	450.00
	1769 P	—	60.00	120.00	200.00	450.00
	1770 P	—	60.00	120.00	200.00	450.00
	1771 P	—	60.00	120.00	200.00	450.00

Obv: Bust of Charles III. Rev: Arms, pillars.

C#	Date	Mintage	VG	Fine	VF	XF
25	1772 P	—	27.50	55.00	80.00	120.00
	1773 P	—	15.00	30.00	45.00	85.00
	1776 P	—	12.00	25.00	40.00	70.00

MINTMARK: NG

C#	Date	Mintage	VG	Fine	VF	XF
25a	1780 P	—	10.00	20.00	40.00	80.00
	1781 P	—	9.00	17.50	35.00	75.00
	1782 P	—	12.00	25.00	40.00	75.00
	1783 P	—	15.00	30.00	45.00	90.00
	1785 M	—	15.00	30.00	45.00	90.00
	1786 M	—	15.00	30.00	45.00	90.00
	1787 M	—	15.00	30.00	45.00	90.00

Obv. leg: CAROLUS IIII...., bust of Charles III.

C#	Date	Mintage	VG	Fine	VF	XF
38	1789 M	—	15.00	30.00	45.00	90.00
	1790 M	—	10.00	20.00	40.00	80.00

Obv: Bust of Charles IIII.

C#	Date	Mintage	VG	Fine	VF	XF
44	1791 M	—	12.50	25.00	45.00	70.00
	1792 M	—	6.00	12.00	27.50	55.00
	1793 M	—	6.00	12.00	27.50	55.00
	1794 M	—	6.00	12.00	30.00	55.00
	1795 M	—	6.00	12.00	30.00	55.00
	1796 M	—	6.00	12.00	30.00	55.00
	1797 M	—	6.00	12.00	30.00	55.00
	1798 M	—	6.00	12.00	30.00	55.00
	1799 M	—	6.00	12.00	30.00	55.00
	1800 M	—	6.00	12.00	30.00	55.00
	1801 M	—	6.00	12.00	30.00	55.00
	1802 M	—	6.00	12.00	30.00	55.00
	1803 M	—	6.00	12.00	30.00	55.00
	1804 M	—	6.00	12.00	30.00	55.00
	1805 M	—	6.00	12.00	30.00	55.00
	1806 M	—	6.00	12.00	30.00	55.00
	1807 M	—	6.00	12.00	30.00	55.00

Obv. leg: FERDIND VII...., bust of Charles IV.

C#	Date	Mintage	VG	Fine	VF	XF
64	1808 M	—	5.00	9.00	17.50	50.00
	1809 M	—	4.00	8.50	15.00	30.00
	1810 M	—	6.00	12.00	20.00	45.00

Obv: Bust of Ferdinand VII.

C#	Date	Mintage	VG	Fine	VF	XF
69	1808 M	—	—	—	Rare	—
	1811 M	—	4.00	8.00	15.00	30.00
	1812 M	—	4.00	8.00	15.00	30.00
	1813 M	—	10.00	17.50	35.00	60.00
	1814 M	—	4.00	9.00	17.50	35.00
	1815 M	—	3.00	6.00	12.00	25.00
	1816 M	—	4.00	7.50	15.00	27.50
	1817 M	—	3.00	6.00	12.00	25.00
	1818 M	—	3.00	6.00	10.00	22.50
	1819 M	—	4.00	7.50	15.00	35.00
	1820 M	—	3.00	6.00	10.00	22.50
	1821 M	—	3.00	6.00	10.00	22.50

2 REALES

.903 SILVER

MINTMARK: G

Obv. leg: CAROLUS III...

C#	Date	Mintage	VG	Fine	VF	XF
21	1760 P	—	65.00	125.00	225.00	475.00
	1761 P	—	65.00	125.00	225.00	550.00
	1762 P	—	65.00	125.00	225.00	475.00
	1763 P	—	65.00	125.00	225.00	475.00
	1764 P	—	65.00	125.00	250.00	550.00
	1765 P	—	65.00	125.00	225.00	475.00
	1766 P	—	65.00	125.00	250.00	550.00
	1767 P	—	65.00	125.00	225.00	450.00
	1768 P	—	65.00	125.00	225.00	450.00
	1769 P	—	65.00	125.00	225.00	450.00
	1770 P	—	65.00	125.00	225.00	450.00
	1771 P	—	65.00	125.00	225.00	450.00

Obv: Bust of Charles III. Rev: Arms, pillars.

C#	Date	Mintage	VG	Fine	VF	XF
26	1772 P	—	8.50	17.50	40.00	70.00
	1773 P	—	8.50	17.50	45.00	75.00
	1776 P	—	25.00	50.00	70.00	120.00

MINTMARK: NG

C#	Date	Mintage	VG	Fine	VF	XF
26a	1779 P	—	30.00	55.00	80.00	120.00
	1780 P	—	25.00	50.00	75.00	120.00
26a	1781 P	—	35.00	65.00	90.00	170.00
	1782 P	—	30.00	55.00	75.00	110.00
	1783 P	—	35.00	65.00	85.00	170.00
	1785 M	—	30.00	55.00	75.00	110.00
	1786 M	—	30.00	55.00	75.00	110.00
	1787 M	—	30.00	55.00	75.00	110.00

Obv. leg: CAROLUS IV...., bust of Charles III.

C#	Date	Mintage	VG	Fine	VF	XF
39	1789 M	—	30.00	60.00	90.00	175.00
	1790 M	—	25.00	50.00	75.00	100.00

Obv: Bust of Charles IIII.

C#	Date	Mintage	VG	Fine	VF	XF
45	1790 M	—	50.00	100.00	125.00	175.00
	1791 M	—	20.00	40.00	65.00	120.00
	1792 M	—	6.00	10.00	17.50	45.00
	1793 M	—	6.00	10.00	17.50	45.00
	1794 M	—	6.00	10.00	17.50	45.00
	1795/4 M	—	7.50	12.50	22.50	55.00
	1795 M	—	6.00	10.00	17.50	45.00
	1796 M	—	6.00	10.00	17.50	45.00
	1797 M	—	6.00	10.00	20.00	45.00
	1798 M	—	25.00	50.00	70.00	100.00
	1799 M	—	6.00	10.00	17.50	45.00
	1800 M	—	6.00	10.00	17.50	45.00
	1801 M	—	6.00	10.00	17.50	45.00
	1802 M	—	8.50	17.50	35.00	50.00
	1803 M	—	17.50	35.00	60.00	80.00
	1804 M	—	6.00	10.00	17.50	45.00
	1805 M	—	6.00	10.00	17.50	45.00
	1806 M	—	25.00	50.00	70.00	100.00
	1807 M	—	25.00	50.00	70.00	100.00
	1808 M	—	15.00	30.00	45.00	75.00

Obv. leg: FERDIND VII...., bust of Charles IV.

C#	Date	Mintage	VG	Fine	VF	XF
65	1808 M	—	10.00	20.00	35.00	70.00
	1809 M	—	7.50	15.00	30.00	60.00
	1810 M	—	6.50	12.00	25.00	50.00

Obv: Bust Ferdinand VII.

C#	Date	Mintage	VG	Fine	VF	XF
70	1808 M	—	17.50	35.00	90.00	160.00
	1811 M	—	12.50	25.00	35.00	60.00
	1812 M	—	7.50	12.50	25.00	50.00
	1813 M	—	17.50	35.00	90.00	160.00
	1814 M	—	17.50	35.00	90.00	160.00
	1815 M	—	7.50	12.50	25.00	50.00
	1816 M	—	8.50	15.00	30.00	60.00
	1817 M	—	7.50	12.50	25.00	50.00
	1818 M	—	7.50	12.50	25.00	50.00
	1819 M	—	7.50	12.50	25.00	50.00
	1820 M	—	7.50	12.50	25.00	50.00
	1821 M	—	6.50	10.00	22.50	45.00
	1822 M	—	40.00	80.00	125.00	225.00

4 REALES

.903 SILVER

MINTMARK: G

Obv. leg: CAROLUS III...

C#	Date	Mintage	VG	Fine	VF	XF
22	1760 P	—	150.00	275.00	400.00	950.00
	1761 P	—	125.00	200.00	300.00	800.00
	1762 P	—	120.00	200.00	275.00	650.00
	1763 P	—	120.00	200.00	275.00	650.00
	1764 P	—	125.00	250.00	350.00	900.00
	1765 P	—	150.00	275.00	400.00	950.00
	1766 P	—	125.00	200.00	300.00	800.00
	1767 P	—	125.00	200.00	275.00	650.00
	1768 P	—	80.00	150.00	250.00	575.00
	1769 P	—	80.00	150.00	250.00	575.00
	1770 P	—	75.00	125.00	225.00	500.00
	1771 P	—	65.00	120.00	175.00	450.00

Obv: Bust of Charles III. Rev: Arms, pillars.

C#	Date	Mintage	VG	Fine	VF	XF
27	1772 P	—	50.00	100.00	175.00	350.00
	1773 P	—	65.00	125.00	200.00	475.00
	1776 P	—	65.00	125.00	200.00	475.00

MINTMARK NG

C#	Date	Mintage	VG	Fine	VF	XF
27a	1777 P	—	45.00	85.00	165.00	350.00
	1778 P	—	45.00	85.00	165.00	350.00
	1779 P	—	45.00	85.00	165.00	350.00
	1780 P	—	45.00	85.00	165.00	350.00
	1781 P	—	45.00	85.00	165.00	350.00
	1782 P	—	45.00	85.00	165.00	350.00
	1783 P	—	45.00	85.00	165.00	350.00
	1784 M	—	45.00	85.00	165.00	350.00
	1785 M	—	45.00	85.00	165.00	350.00
	1786 M	—	45.00	85.00	165.00	350.00
	1787 M	—	45.00	85.00	165.00	350.00

Obv. leg: CAROLUS IV..., bust of Charles III.

C#	Date	Mintage	VG	Fine	VF	XF
40	1789 M	—	250.00	500.00	775.00	1650.
	1790 M	—	250.00	500.00	775.00	1650.

Obv: Bust of Carolus IIII.

C#	Date	Mintage	VG	Fine	VF	XF
46	1790 M	—	200.00	400.00	500.00	1000.
	1791 M	—	45.00	90.00	135.00	225.00
	1792 M	—	22.50	45.00	80.00	150.00
	1793 M	—	17.50	30.00	60.00	125.00
	1794/3 M	—	17.50	35.00	65.00	135.00
	1794 M	—	22.50	45.00	75.00	150.00
	1795 M	—	35.00	65.00	125.00	200.00
	1796 M	—	17.50	30.00	60.00	125.00
	1797 M	—	20.00	40.00	75.00	135.00
	1798 M	—	20.00	40.00	75.00	135.00
	1799 M	—	20.00	40.00	75.00	135.00
	1800 M	—	22.50	45.00	80.00	150.00
	1801 M	—	17.50	30.00	60.00	125.00
	1802 M	—	20.00	40.00	75.00	135.00
	1803 M	—	22.50	45.00	80.00	150.00
	1804 M	—	27.50	55.00	90.00	165.00
	1805 M	—	20.00	40.00	80.00	135.00
	1806/5 M	—	17.50	35.00	65.00	150.00
	1806 M	—	17.50	30.00	60.00	125.00
	1807 M	—	15.00	27.50	50.00	100.00

Obv. leg: FERDIND VII..., bust of Charles IV.

C#	Date	Mintage	VG	Fine	VF	XF
66	1808 M	—	85.00	165.00	275.00	450.00
	1809 M	—	45.00	90.00	165.00	350.00
	1810 M	—	45.00	90.00	165.00	350.00

Obv: Bust Ferdinand VII.

C#	Date	Mintage	VG	Fine	VF	XF
71	1808 M	—	125.00	250.00	400.00	650.00
	1811 M	—	40.00	80.00	150.00	250.00
	1812 M	—	40.00	80.00	150.00	250.00
	1813 M	—	100.00	175.00	250.00	500.00
	1814 M	—	10.00	15.00	30.00	60.00
	1815/4 M	—	20.00	40.00	80.00	135.00
	1815 M	—	25.00	50.00	75.00	120.00
	1816 M	—	30.00	60.00	110.00	165.00
	1817 M	—	30.00	60.00	110.00	165.00
	1818 M	—	27.50	55.00	110.00	165.00
	1819 M	—	30.00	60.00	100.00	175.00
	1820 M	—	40.00	80.00	125.00	250.00
	1821 M	—	30.00	60.00	100.00	175.00

8 REALES

.903 SILVER

MINTMARK: G

Obv. leg: CAROLUS III, arms. Rev: Pillars.

C#	Date	Mintage	VG	Fine	VF	XF
23	1760 P	—	150.00	250.00	400.00	725.00
	1761 P	—	175.00	275.00	425.00	775.00
	1762 P	—	150.00	250.00	375.00	650.00
	1763 P	—	150.00	250.00	400.00	725.00
	1764 P	—	225.00	350.00	525.00	875.00
	1765 P	—	225.00	350.00	525.00	875.00
	1766 P	—	140.00	200.00	350.00	600.00
	1767 P	—	175.00	275.00	425.00	775.00
	1768 P	—	125.00	175.00	325.00	525.00
	1769 P	—	125.00	175.00	325.00	525.00
	1770 P	—	125.00	175.00	350.00	550.00
	1771 P	—	140.00	200.00	375.00	600.00

Obv: Bust of Charles III. Rev: Arms, pillars.

C#	Date	Mintage	VG	Fine	VF	XF
28	1772 P	—	150.00	275.00	400.00	800.00
	1773 P	—	150.00	275.00	400.00	800.00
	1774 P	—	150.00	275.00	400.00	800.00
	1775 P	—	150.00	275.00	400.00	800.00
	1776 P	—	150.00	275.00	400.00	800.00

MINTMARK: NG

C#	Date	Mintage	VG	Fine	VF	XF
28a	1776 P(NG/GN)	—	—	Rare		—
	1777 P	—	55.00	110.00	200.00	325.00
	1778 P	—	100.00	200.00	300.00	500.00
	1779 P	—	100.00	200.00	300.00	500.00
	1780 P	—	110.00	225.00	325.00	550.00
	1781 P	—	135.00	275.00	375.00	650.00
	1782 P	—	100.00	200.00	300.00	500.00
	1783 P	—	110.00	225.00	325.00	550.00
	1785 M	—	155.00	300.00	400.00	650.00
	1786 M	—	110.00	225.00	325.00	550.00
	1787 M	—	110.00	225.00	325.00	550.00

Obv. leg: CAROLUS IV..... Rev: Similar to C#28a.

C#	Date	Mintage	VG	Fine	VF	XF
41	1789 M	—	80.00	150.00	200.00	250.00
	1790 M	—	100.00	200.00	275.00	375.00

Obv: Bust of Charles IIII. Rev: Similar to C#28a.

C#	Date	Mintage	VG	Fine	VF	XF
47	1790 M	—	125.00	200.00	300.00	600.00
	1791 M	—	75.00	125.00	150.00	225.00
	1792 M	—	30.00	60.00	90.00	125.00
	1793 M	—	35.00	65.00	100.00	135.00
	1794 M	—	30.00	60.00	90.00	125.00
	1795 M	—	30.00	60.00	90.00	125.00
	1796 M	—	30.00	60.00	90.00	125.00
	1797/6 M	—	35.00	75.00	125.00	150.00
	1797 M	—	35.00	65.00	100.00	135.00
	1798 M	—	30.00	60.00	90.00	125.00
	1799 M	—	35.00	65.00	100.00	125.00
	1800 M	—	30.00	60.00	90.00	125.00
	1801 M	—	30.00	60.00	90.00	125.00
	1802 M	—	30.00	60.00	90.00	125.00
	1803 M	—	30.00	60.00	90.00	125.00
	1804 M	—	30.00	60.00	90.00	125.00
	1805 M	—	30.00	60.00	90.00	125.00
	1806/5 M	—	35.00	75.00	125.00	150.00
	1806 M	—	30.00	60.00	90.00	125.00
	1807 M	—	30.00	60.00	90.00	125.00
	1808 M	—	75.00	125.00	200.00	400.00

Obv. leg: FERDIND VII...., bust of Charles IV.
Rev: Similar to C#28a.

C#	Date	Mintage	VG	Fine	VF	XF
67	1808 M	—	45.00	90.00	150.00	250.00
	1809/8 M	—	45.00	90.00	150.00	250.00
	1809 M	—	45.00	90.00	150.00	250.00
	1810 M	—	40.00	80.00	125.00	200.00
	1811 M	—	50.00	100.00	175.00	300.00

Rev: Similar to C#28a.

C#	Date	Mintage	VG	Fine	VF	XF
72	1808 M	—	150.00	300.00	550.00	900.00
	1811 M	—	45.00	80.00	125.00	200.00
	1812 M	—	35.00	70.00	100.00	175.00
	1813 M	—	35.00	70.00	100.00	175.00
	1814 M	—	35.00	70.00	90.00	150.00
	1815 M	—	30.00	60.00	90.00	125.00
	1816 M	—	30.00	60.00	90.00	125.00
	1817 M	—	30.00	60.00	90.00	125.00
	1818 M	—	30.00	60.00	90.00	125.00
	1819 M	—	30.00	60.00	90.00	125.00
	1820 M	—	30.00	60.00	90.00	125.00
	1821 M	—	30.00	60.00	90.00	125.00
	1822 M	—	1250.	2500.	3500.	6000.

ESCUDO

3.3750 gm., .875 GOLD, .0949 oz ASW

MINTMARK: G

Obv: Young bust of Charles III.
Rev: Arms, order chain.

C#	Date	Mintage	VG	Fine	VF	XF
30.1	1765	—	—	—	Rare	—
	1770	—	—	—	Rare	—

MINTMARK: NG

Obv: Bust of Charles III; older, standard bust.

C#	Date	Mintage	VG	Fine	VF	XF
29	1778 M	—	150.00	225.00	325.00	550.00
	1783 D	—	125.00	200.00	300.00	500.00

Obv. leg: CAROL IV...., bust of Charles III.

C#	Date	Mintage	VG	Fine	VF	XF
48	1789 M	—	200.00	325.00	450.00	650.00
	1790 M	—	200.00	325.00	450.00	550.00
	1791 M	—	150.00	225.00	325.00	500.00

Obv: Bust of Charles IIII.

C#	Date	Mintage	VG	Fine	VF	XF
52	1794 M	—	150.00	250.00	300.00	500.00
	1797 M	—	150.00	225.00	275.00	450.00
	1801 M	—	150.00	225.00	275.00	450.00

Obv: Bust of Ferdinand VII.

C#	Date	Mintage	VG	Fine	VF	XF
73	1817 M	—	150.00	225.00	325.00	550.00

2 ESCUDOS

6.7500 gm., .875 GOLD, .1899 oz AGW

MINTMARK: NG

Obv: Bust of Charles III. Rev: Arms, order chain.

C#	Date	Mintage	VG	Fine	VF	XF
30	1778 P	—	275.00	450.00	750.00	1100.
	1783 P	—	275.00	450.00	800.00	1350.
	1785 M	—	300.00	500.00	850.00	1350.

Obv. leg: CAROL IV...., bust of Charles III.

C#	Date	Mintage	VG	Fine	VF	XF
49	1789 M	—	600.00	1000.	1650.	2200.

Obv: Bust of Charles IIII.

C#	Date	Mintage	VG	Fine	VF	XF
53	1794 M	—	400.00	650.00	750.00	900.00

Obv: Bust of Ferdinand VII.

C#	Date	Mintage	VG	Fine	VF	XF
74	1808 M	—	600.00	1000.	1650.	2800.
	1811 M	—	325.00	500.00	650.00	800.00
	1817 M	—	325.00	500.00	650.00	800.00

4 ESCUDOS

13.5000 gm., .875 GOLD, .3798 oz AGW

MINTMARK: G

Obv: Young bust of Charles III.
Rev: Arms, order chain.

C#	Date	Mintage	VG	Fine	VF	XF
30.5	1765 J	—	1300.	2200.	4250.	8000.

MINTMARK: NG

Obv: Older, standard bust of Charles III.

C#	Date	Mintage	VG	Fine	VF	XF
31	1778 P	—	600.00	1000.	1500.	2500.
	1781 P	—	600.00	1000.	1500.	2500.
	1783 P	—	450.00	750.00	1000.	1500.

Obv. leg: CAROL IV...., bust of Charles III.

C#	Date	Mintage	VG	Fine	VF	XF
50	1789 M	—	600.00	1000.	1500.	2250.

Obv: Bust of Charles IIII.

C#	Date	Mintage	VG	Fine	VF	XF
54	1794 M	—	500.00	850.00	1250.	2000.
	1797 M	—	500.00	850.00	1250.	2000.
	1801 M	—	450.00	750.00	1000.	1500.

Obv: Bust of Ferdinand VII.

C#	Date	Mintage	VG	Fine	VF	XF
75	1813 M	—	600.00	1000.	1500.	2250.
	1817 M	—	500.00	900.00	1250.	2000.

8 ESCUDOS

27.0000 gm., .875 GOLD, .7596 oz AGW

Obv: Bust of Charles III.
Rev: Arms, order chain.

C#	Date	Mintage	VG	Fine	VF	XF
32	1761J	—	—	—	Rare	—

Obv: Young bust of Charles III.

C#	Date	Mintage	VG	Fine	VF	XF
32a	1765	—	500.00	750.00	2250.	5500.
	1768	—	650.00	1250.	3750.	7500.
	1770	—	650.00	1250.	3750.	7500.

Obv: Older, standard bust of Charles III.

C#	Date	Mintage	VG	Fine	VF	XF
33	1778 P	—	650.00	1250.	2750.	4000.
	1781 P	—	650.00	1250.	2750.	4000.
	1783 P	—	800.00	1500.	3000.	4250.
	1785 M	—	800.00	1500.	3000.	4250.

Obv. leg: CAROL IV...., bust of Charles III.

C#	Date	Mintage	VG	Fine	VF	XF
51	1789 M	—	800.00	1500.	3000.	3750.
	1790 M	—	1100.	1800.	3250.	4000.

Obv: Bust of Charles IIII.

C#	Date	Mintage	VG	Fine	VF	XF
55	1794 M	—	1200.	1750.	2750.	3500.
	1797 M	—	1200.	1750.	2750.	3500.
	1801 M	—	1200.	1750.	2750.	3500.

Obv: Bust of Ferdinand VII.

C#	Date	Mintage	VG	Fine	VF	XF
76	1808 M	Unique	—	—	Rare	—
	1811 M	—	2000.	3500.	6000.	12,000.
	1817 M	—	700.00	1200.	2500.	3500.

PROVISIONAL ISSUE

REAL

.903 SILVER

MINTMARK: NG

Obv. leg: ESTADO DE GUATEMALA

C#	Date	Mintage	VG	Fine	VF	XF
94	1829 M	—	100.00	175.00	325.00	550.00

COUNTERSTAMP ISSUES

1838-1841

Type I
Sun over a row of volcanos in 6.5mm circle.

NOTE: A c/s of a sun over a volcano has been reported (c.f. C#124a) which has not been confirmed at this writing.

REAL

SILVER
c/s: Type I on Spanish Colonial 'cob' 1 Real.

C#	Date	Mintage	Good	VG	Fine
121	ND	—	—	Rare	—

2 REALES
(Soles, Sueldos)

SILVER
c/s: Type I on Bolivia 2 Soles, C#53.

C#	Date	Mintage	Good	VG	Fine
122.1	ND(1827-30	—	30.00	60.00	85.00

c/s: Type I on Peru 2 Reales, C#130.1.

C#	Date	Mintage	Good	VG	Fine
122.2	ND(1825-40)	—	30.00	60.00	85.00

4 REALES

SILVER
c/s: Type I on Bolivia (Potosi) 'cob' 4 Reales of Ferdinand VI.

C#	Date	Mintage	Good	VG	Fine
123.1	ND(1746-59)	—	70.00	120.00	165.00

c/s: Type I on Bolivia (Potosi) 'cob' 4 Reales of Charles III.

C#	Date	Mintage	Good	VG	Fine
123.2	ND(1759-88)	—	70.00	120.00	165.00

c/s: Type I on Guatemala 'cob' 4 Reales, C#4.

C#	Date	Mintage	Good	VG	Fine
123.3	ND(1700-46)	—	90.00	150.00	225.00

c/s: Type I on Guatemala 'cob' 4 Reales, C#7.5.

C#	Date	Mintage	Good	VG	Fine
123.4	ND(1747-53)	—	90.00	150.00	225.00

c/s: Type I on Mexico 'cob' 4 Reales of Philip II.

C#	Date	Mintage	Good	VG	Fine
123.5	ND(1556-98)	—	90.00	150.00	225.00

c/s: Type I on Peru (Lima) 'cob' 4 Reales of Philip V.

C#	Date	Mintage	Good	VG	Fine
123.6	ND(1700-46)	—	70.00	120.00	165.00

NOTE: Market valuations are for pierced, holed or specimens without a visible date. Undamaged and/or specimens with a visible date command a premium.

8 REALES

SILVER
c/s: Type I on Bolivia (Potosi) 'cob' 8 Reales of Philip II.

C#	Date	Mintage	Good	VG	Fine
124.1	ND(1556-98)	—	40.00	65.00	100.00

c/s: Type I on Bolivia (Potosi) 'cob' 8 Reales of Philip IV.

C#	Date	Mintage	Good	VG	Fine
124.2	ND(1621-65)	—	40.00	65.00	100.00

c/s: Type I on Bolivia (Potosi) 'Royal' 8 Reales of Charles II.

C#	Date	Mintage	Good	VG	Fine
124.3	ND(1665-1700)	—	225.00	350.00	450.00

c/s: Type I on Bolivia (Potosi) 'cob' 8 Reales of Charles II.

C#	Date	Mintage	Good	VG	Fine
124.4	ND(1665-1700)		40.00	65.00	100.00

c/s: Type I on Bolivia (Potosi) 'cob' 8 Reales of Philip V.

C#	Date	Mintage	Good	VG	Fine
124.5	ND(1700-46)		40.00	65.00	100.00

c/s: Type I on Bolivia (Potosi) 'cob' 8 Reales Ferdinand VI.

C#	Date	Mintage	Good	VG	Fine
124.6	ND(1746-59)	—	50.00	90.00	125.00

c/s: Type I on Bolivia (Potosi) 'cob' 8 Reales of Charles III.

C#	Date	Mintage	Good	VG	Fine
124.7	ND(1759-88)	—	40.00	65.00	100.00

c/s: Type I on Guatemala 'cob' 8 Reales, C#5.

C#	Date	Mintage	Good	VG	Fine
124.8	ND(1733-46)	—	125.00	175.00	225.00

c/s: Type I on Guatemala 'cob' 8 Reales, C#8.

C#	Date	Mintage	Good	VG	Fine
124.9	ND(1747-53)	—	125.00	150.00	200.00

c/s: Type I on Mexico 'cob' 8 Reales of Philip II, KM#43.

124.10 ND(1556-98) — Reported, Not Confirmed

c/s: Type I on Mexico 'cob' 8 Reales of Philip IV, KM#45.

124.11 ND(1621-67) — Reported, Not Confirmed

c/s: Type I on Mexico 'Royal' 8 Reales of Philip V, KM#R47.

C#	Date	Mintage	Good	VG	Fine
124.12	ND(1701-28)	—	—	Rare	—

c/s: Type I on Mexico 'cob' 8 Reales of Philip V, KM#47a.

C#	Date	Mintage	Good	VG	Fine
124.13	ND(1729-33)	—	50.00	70.00	100.00

c/s: Type I on Mexico 'Klippe' 8 Reales of Philip V, KM#48.

C#	Date	Mintage	Good	VG	Fine
124.14	ND(1733-34)	—	55.00	75.00	120.00

c/s: Type I on Peru (Lima) 'Royal' 8 Reales of Philip II.

C#	Date	Mintage	Good	VG	Fine
124.15	ND(1556-98)	—	275.00	375.00	550.00

c/s: Type I on Peru (Lima) 'cob' 8 Reales of Philip IV.

C#	Date	Mintage	Good	VG	Fine
124.16	ND(1621-65)	—	75.00	100.00	150.00

c/s: Type I on Peru (Lima) 'cob' 8 Reales of Charles II.

C#	Date	Mintage	Good	VG	Fine
124.17	ND(1665-1700)	—	50.00	75.00	125.00

c/s: Type I on Peru (Lima) 'cob' 8 Reales of Philip V.

C#	Date	Mintage	Good	VG	Fine
124.18	ND(1700-46)	—	50.00	75.00	125.00

NOTE: Market valuations are for pierced, holed or specimens without a visible date. Undamaged and/or specimens with a visible date command a premium.

Type II

Obv: Sun over 3 volcanos in 6.5mm circle.
Rev: Star, bow and arrow in 7mm circle.

8 REALES

(Soles, Sueldos)

.900 SILVER

c/s: Type II on Bolivia 8 Soles, C#55.

C#	Date	Mintage	Good	VG	Fine
134.1	ND(1827-40)	—	100.00	150.00	200.00
	c/s: Type II on Chile 8 Reales, Y#22.				
134.2	ND(1837-40	—	125.00	175.00	225.00
	c/s: Type II on Peru 8 Reales, C#125.				
134.3	ND(1822-23)	—	60.00	85.00	120.00
	c/s: Type II on Peru 8 Reales, C#132.1.				
134.4	ND(1825-28)	—	60.00	85.00	120.00
	c/s: Type II on Peru 8 Reales, C#132.1a.				
134.5	ND(1828-40)	—	60.00	85.00	120.00
	c/s: Type II on Peru (Cuzco) 8 Reales, C#132.3.				
134.6	ND(1826-36)	—	60.00	85.00	120.00
	c/s: Type II on Peru (South) 8 Reales, C#180a.				
134.7	ND(1837-39)	—	75.00	120.00	170.00
	c/s: Type II on Peru (North) 8 Reales, C#151.				
134.8	ND(1836-39)	—	60.00	85.00	120.00

NOTE: Coins dated after 1840 with the Type II c/s are believed to be counterfeit by some authorities.

TYPE III

A sun over a volcano.

4 REALES

SILVER

c/s: Type III on "cob" 4 Reales

C#	Date	Mintage	VG	Fine	VF
123a	ND	—	—	—	—

8 REALES

SILVER

c/s: Type III on "cob" 8 Reales

C#	Date	Mintage	VG	Fine	VF
124a	ND	—	—	—	—

REPUBLIC ISSUES

8 Reales = 1 Peso

1/4 REAL

.903 SILVER

Y#	Date	Mintage	Fine	VF	XF	Unc
1	1859	—	—	—	—	—
	1860	.116	8.00	15.00	25.00	35.00
	1861	—	7.00	12.50	17.50	27.50
	1862	—	6.50	10.00	15.00	25.00
	1863	—	7.00	12.50	20.00	30.00
	1864	—	7.00	12.50	20.00	30.00
	1865	.023	17.50	25.00	35.00	55.00
	1866	.205	5.00	8.50	12.50	20.00
	1867	.169	5.00	8.50	12.50	20.00
	1868	.148	5.00	8.50	12.50	20.00
	1869	.242	5.00	8.50	12.50	20.00

.900 SILVER

Rev: 0.900 below wreath.

Y#	Date	Mintage	Fine	VF	XF	Unc
36	1872P	—	1.50	2.50	3.50	5.50
	1873P	.308	1.00	1.75	3.00	5.00
	1874P	—	8.50	12.50	18.50	27.50
	1875P	—	1.00	1.75	3.00	4.50

Y#	Date	Mintage	Fine	VF	XF	Unc
36	1876P	—	1.00	1.75	3.00	4.50
	1878P	.680	1.00	1.75	3.00	4.50

.835 SILVER
Rev: 0.835 below small wreath.

Y#	Date	Mintage	Fine	VF	XF	Unc
36b (40)	1878	Inc. Ab.	2.00	3.00	5.00	7.50

Rev: 0.835 below large wreath.

Y#	Date	Mintage	Fine	VF	XF	Unc
36c	1878	Inc. Ab.	2.00	3.00	4.50	6.00
(41)	1879	.171	2.00	3.00	4.50	6.00

Obv: Long rayed sun.

Y#	Date	Mintage	Fine	VF	XF	Unc
42	1879	Inc. Ab.	1.50	2.00	3.00	5.00
	1880	.115	1.00	1.75	3.00	5.00
	1881	.073	3.00	4.50	8.00	13.50
	1882	—	1.00	1.50	2.50	4.00
	1883	.195	15.00	25.00	40.00	70.00
	1884	.100	1.00	1.50	2.50	4.00
	1885	—	7.50	12.50	20.00	35.00
	1886	—	1.25	2.00	3.50	5.50

Rev: No fineness indicated,

Y#	Date	Mintage	Fine	VF	XF	Unc
36a	1878 large G					
(44)		Inc. Y36	2.75	4.50	7.00	10.00
	1878 medium G					
		Inc. Ab.	2.25	3.50	6.00	9.00
	1878 small G					
		Inc. Ab.	2.00	3.75	5.50	9.00
	1879 large G					
		Inc. Y42	5.50	9.00	15.00	25.00

Obv: Mountains with short rayed sun.

Y#	Date	Mintage	Fine	VF	XF	Unc
45	1887	—	1.50	2.50	4.00	6.00
	1888	—	1.00	1.50	2.25	3.50

Obv: G below mountains.

Y#	Date	Mintage	Fine	VF	XF	Unc
46	1889	.870	2.75	4.00	7.50	15.00

Rev: Five stars below wreath.

Y#	Date	Mintage	Fine	VF	XF	Unc
47	1889	Inc. Ab.	1.00	1.50	2.00	2.50
	1890	—	1.00	1.50	2.00	2.50
	1891	—	1.50	2.50	4.00	6.50
	1893/1	—	1.00	1.50	2.50	3.50

Obv: Mountains with long rayed sun.

Y#	Date	Mintage	Fine	VF	XF	Unc
48	1892	.512	20.00	35.00	90.00	180.00
	1893	.749	1.00	1.50	2.00	3.00

Rev: Three stars below thin wreath.

Y#	Date	Mintage	Fine	VF	XF	Unc
49	1893	Inc. Ab.	1.00	1.50	2.00	3.50
	1894	.059	6.50	10.00	15.00	25.00

Rev: Five stars below full wreath.

Y#	Date	Mintage	Fine	VF	XF	Unc
74	1893	Inc. Ab.	1.00	1.50	2.00	3.50
	1894	Inc. Ab.	1.00	1.50	2.00	3.50
	1894H	.800	BV	.75	1.50	2.50
	1895	1.482	BV	.75	1.25	2.00

Y#	Date	Mintage	Fine	VF	XF	Unc
	1896	2.071	BV	.75	1.25	2.00
	1897	.989	BV	.75	1.50	2.25
	1898	.384	BV	1.00	1.75	3.00
	1899	.080	1.50	2.50	4.00	6.00

Rev: Four Maltese crosses, different wreath.

Y#	Date	Mintage	Fine	VF	XF	Unc
—	1897	—	—	—	—	—

COPPER-NICKEL

Y#	Date	Mintage	Fine	VF	XF	Unc
85	1900H	2.944	.25	.40	1.00	1.50
	1901H	5.056	.25	.40	.75	1.25

MEDIO 1/2 REAL

.903 SILVER
Rev: MED: REAL

Y#	Date	Mintage	Fine	VF	XF	Unc
2	1859	—	15.00	25.00	40.00	75.00
	1860R	.191	4.00	6.50	11.50	17.50
	1861	—	4.00	6.50	11.50	17.50

Obv. leg: RAFAEL CARRERA PTE.
Rev: MED. RL

Y#	Date	Mintage	Fine	VF	XF	Unc
8	1862R	—	3.50	6.00	10.00	15.00
	1863R	—	6.00	10.00	15.00	22.50
	1865/3R	.057	4.00	7.50	11.50	17.50
	1865	Inc. Ab.	4.00	7.50	11.50	17.50

Obv. leg: R. CARRERA FUNDADOR

Y#	Date	Mintage	Fine	VF	XF	Unc
20	1867R	.092	3.00	5.50	8.50	12.50
	1868R	.102	3.00	5.50	8.50	12.50
	1869	.117	3.00	5.50	8.50	12.50

.900 SILVER

Y#	Date	Mintage	Fine	VF	XF	Unc
37	1872P	—	2.00	3.00	4.00	6.50
	1873P	.035	2.50	4.00	6.50	10.00

.835 SILVER

Y#	Date	Mintage	Fine	VF	XF	Unc
37b	1878	—	2.75	4.50	6.50	10.00
(43)	1879 wide date					
		Inc. Y59	3.00	5.00	8.00	12.50
	1879 narrow date					
		Inc. Y59	3.00	5.00	8.00	12.50

Rev: No fineness

Y#	Date	Mintage	Fine	VF	XF	Unc
37a	1878	—	2.75	4.50	6.50	9.50
(50)	1893	Inc. Y64	4.50	7.50	10.00	15.00

Obv: 1/2 RL.

Y#	Date	Mintage	Fine	VF	XF	Unc
59	1879D	1.683	1.50	2.50	3.50	6.00
	1880/79D	2.715	3.00	6.00	9.00	17.50
	1880D	Inc. Ab.	1.50	2.00	3.00	5.00

Y#	Date	Mintage	Fine	VF	XF	Unc
59	1880E	Inc. Ab.	6.00	10.00	15.00	22.50

Obv: MEDIO REAL

Y#	Date	Mintage	Fine	VF	XF	Unc
60	1880E	Inc. Y59	BV	1.50	2.50	4.00
	1881E	—	BV	2.00	3.00	4.50
	1883E	.046	6.00	10.00	15.00	22.50

Rev: Star replaces assayer's initial.

Y#	Date	Mintage	Fine	VF	XF	Unc
60.1	1889	.481	BV	1.50	2.25	4.00
	1890/89	—	2.00	3.00	7.50	12.50
	1890	—	BV	1.50	2.25	4.00

Rev: No fineness, small wreath.

Y#	Date	Mintage	Fine	VF	XF	Unc
64	1893	.360	20.00	30.00	60.00	100.00

Rev: Large wreath.

Y#	Date	Mintage	Fine	VF	XF	Unc
65	1893 large date					
		Inc. Ab.	6.00	10.00	17.50	30.00
	1893 small date					
		Inc. Ab.	6.00	10.00	17.50	30.00

Y#	Date	Mintage	Fine	VF	XF	Unc
75	1894	.619	BV	1.50	2.25	4.00
	1894H	.900	BV	1.50	2.00	3.00
	1895	.819	BV	1.50	2.00	3.00
	1895H	.300	1.50	2.50	3.75	6.00
	1896	1.062	BV	1.50	2.00	3.00
	1897	.528	BV	1.50	2.00	3.00

.600 SILVER

Y#	Date	Mintage	Fine	VF	XF	Unc
76	1899	.486	1.00	1.50	2.50	3.50

COPPER-NICKEL

Y#	Date	Mintage	Fine	VF	XF	Unc
86	1900	5.348	.30	.50	.60	1.75
	1901	6.652	.30	.50	.60	1.75

UN (1) REAL

.903 SILVER
Rev: UN REAL.

Y#	Date	Mintage	Fine	VF	XF	Unc
3	1859	—	50.00	80.00	Rare	—
	1859R	—	7.50	15.00	22.50	35.00
	1860R	.177	4.00	6.00	10.00	17.50

Obv. leg: RAFAEL CARRERA PTE.
Rev: UN RL.

Y#	Date	Mintage	Fine	VF	XF	Unc
9	1861R	—	3.50	5.00	7.50	12.50
	1862R	—	3.00	3.50	6.00	10.00
	1863R	—	3.50	5.00	7.50	12.50

Y#	Date	Mintage	Fine	VF	XF	Unc
9	1864R	—	3.00	3.50	6.00	10.00
	1865R w/FRENER F below bust	—	3.00	3.50	6.00	10.00
	1865R w/o FRENER F	—	—	—	—	—

Obv. leg: R. CARRERA FUNDADOR

Y#	Date	Mintage	Fine	VF	XF	Unc
21	1866R	.385	3.00	3.50	6.00	10.00
	1867R	.199	3.00	4.00	7.50	12.50

Y#	Date	Mintage	Fine	VF	XF	Unc
22	1868R	.335	3.00	4.00	7.50	12.50
	1869R	.131	3.00	4.00	7.50	12.50

.900 SILVER

Y#	Date	Mintage	Fine	VF	XF	Unc
38	1872P	3,816	9.00	15.00	30.00	50.00
	1874P	—	4.00	6.50	12.50	25.00
	1878F	.159	4.50	7.50	15.00	30.00

Obv: No fineness

Y#	Date	Mintage	Fine	VF	XF	Unc
38.1 (51)	1878	Inc. Ab.	7.50	12.50	25.00	50.00

Y#	Date	Mintage	Fine	VF	XF	Unc
52	1879D	.037	12.50	20.00	30.00	55.00

.835 SILVER

Y#	Date	Mintage	Fine	VF	XF	Unc
52a (61)	1883	.046	3.00	5.00	10.00	15.00

Rev: Star replaces assayer's initial

Y#	Date	Mintage	Fine	VF	XF	Unc
52a.1 (61a)	1889	.332	BV	2.75	3.50	5.00
	1890	—	BV	2.75	3.50	5.00
	1891	—	BV	2.75	3.50	5.00
	1893	.293	2.75	4.00	5.00	7.00

Y#	Date	Mintage	Fine	VF	XF	Unc
77	1894	.326	BV	2.75	3.75	5.50
	1894H	.600	BV	2.75	3.25	4.50
	1895H	.200	3.25	5.00	8.50	12.50
	1896	.203	BV	2.75	3.75	5.50
	1897	.701	BV	2.75	3.25	4.50
	1898	.040	7.50	10.00	17.50	27.50

Rev: No fineness.

Y#	Date	Mintage	Fine	VF	XF	Unc
78	1899	—	7.50	10.00	17.50	27.50

.750 SILVER

Y#	Date	Mintage	Fine	VF	XF	Unc
79	1899	—	65.00	90.00	150.00	—

.600 SILVER

Y#	Date	Mintage	Fine	VF	XF	Unc
80	1899	—	2.00	2.50	5.00	7.50

.500 SILVER

Y#	Date	Mintage	Fine	VF	XF	Unc
81	1899	—	BV	1.50	2.00	3.00
	1900	1.874	BV	1.50	2.00	3.00

COPPER-NICKEL

Y#	Date	Mintage	Fine	VF	XF	Unc
87	1900	4.612	—	.35	.75	1.50
	1901	7.388	—	.30	.75	1.25
	1910	4.000	—	.35	.75	1.50
	1911	2.000	—	.40	1.00	1.75
	1912	8.000	—	.30	.75	1.25

DOS (2) REALES

.903 SILVER

Obv. leg: RAFAEL CARRERA PTE., thick letters.

Y#	Date	Mintage	Fine	VF	XF	Unc
4	1859	—	135.00	225.00	350.00	—

Obv: Thin letters.

Y#	Date	Mintage	Fine	VF	XF	Unc
5	1860R	—	8.50	12.00	17.50	30.00
	1861R	—	10.00	15.00	20.00	35.00

Rev: Narrower shield.

Y#	Date	Mintage	Fine	VF	XF	Unc
10	1862R	—	5.75	6.50	8.50	12.50
	1863R	—	6.50	7.50	10.00	15.00
	1864R	—	5.75	6.50	8.50	12.50
	1865R	.410	5.75	6.50	8.50	12.50
	1865R w/o period after date	—	5.75	6.50	8.50	12.50

Obv. leg: R. CARRERA FUNDADOR

Y#	Date	Mintage	Fine	VF	XF	Unc
23	1866R	.334	5.75	6.50	8.50	12.50
	1867R	.293	5.75	6.50	8.50	12.50
	1868R	.267	6.50	7.50	10.00	15.00
	1869R	.124	8.50	12.00	17.50	30.00

.900 SILVER

Y#	Date	Mintage	Fine	VF	XF	Unc
39	1872P	—	8.50	12.00	17.50	25.00
	1873P	.610	5.75	6.50	8.50	12.00

Y#	Date	Mintage	Fine	VF	XF	Unc
53	1879D	.101	8.50	12.00	17.50	25.00

.835 SILVER

Y#	Date	Mintage	Fine	VF	XF	Unc
53a (62)	1881E	2.975	7.50	10.00	12.50	15.00

Rev: Star between date.

Y#	Date	Mintage	Fine	VF	XF	Unc
53a.1 (62a)	1892	—	180.00	300.00	400.00	—

Rev: Without star.

Y#	Date	Mintage	Fine	VF	XF	Unc
53a.2 (62b)	1892	—	180.00	300.00	400.00	—

Y#	Date	Mintage	Fine	VF	XF	Unc
82	1894	1.094	BV	5.50	7.00	10.00
	1894H	.900	BV	5.50	7.00	10.00

Y#	Date	Mintage	Fine	VF	XF	Unc
82	1895	2.783	BV	5.50	7.00	10.00
	1895H	.300	5.50	6.50	10.00	12.50
	1896	.605	BV	5.50	7.00	10.00
	1897	1.041	BV	5.50	7.00	10.00
	1898	5.172	BV	5.50	7.00	10.00
	1899	.040	10.00	15.00	20.00	35.00

CUATRO (4) REALES

0.8065, .875 GOLD, .0226 oz AGW

Y#	Date	Mintage	Fine	VF	XF	Unc
13	1860R	—	17.50	25.00	35.00	55.00
	1861R	.277	17.50	25.00	35.00	55.00
	1862R	—	17.50	25.00	35.00	55.00
	1863R	—	17.50	25.00	35.00	55.00
	1864R	—	17.50	25.00	35.00	55.00

.903 SILVER
Obv. leg: RAFAEL CARRERA PTE.

Y#	Date	Mintage	Fine	VF	XF	Unc
6	1860R	4,760	25.00	40.00	65.00	100.00
	1861R	—	15.00	20.00	30.00	45.00

Rev: Shield narrowed.

Y#	Date	Mintage	Fine	VF	XF	Unc
11	1863R	—	15.00	17.50	22.50	30.00
	1865R	.082	15.00	17.50	22.50	27.50

Obv. leg: R. CARRERA FUNDADOR

Y#	Date	Mintage	Fine	VF	XF	Unc
24	1867R	.054	15.00	18.00	25.00	35.00
	1868R	.036	15.00	20.00	30.00	40.00
	1869R	—	—	Reported, not confirmed		

.900 SILVER

Y#	Date	Mintage	Fine	VF	XF	Unc
54	1873P	.024	25.00	40.00	70.00	110.00
	1878D	.010	35.00	50.00	80.00	125.00
	1879D	7,664	45.00	60.00	90.00	135.00
	1879P	—	50.00	75.00	125.00	175.00
	1892R.G.	—	75.00	125.00	250.00	500.00
	1893	—	135.00	200.00	500.00	800.00
	1893R.G.	—	135.00	200.00	500.00	800.00

.835 SILVER

Y#	Date	Mintage	Fine	VF	XF	Unc
54a (63)	1892	2,600	150.00	250.00	500.00	800.00

.900 SILVER

Y#	Date	Mintage	Fine	VF	XF	Unc
83	1894H	.500	BV	15.00	17.50	25.00

Obv. and rev: With H

Y#	Date	Mintage	Fine	VF	XF	Unc
83a	1894H	Inc. Ab.	90.00	150.00	250.00	450.00

DECIMAL COINAGE

100 Centavos (Centimos) = 1 Peso

CENTAVO

BRONZE

Y#	Date	Mintage	Fine	VF	XF	Unc
34	1871	—	4.00	6.00	8.00	15.00

Y#	Date	Mintage	Fine	VF	XF	Unc
68	1881	—	4.75	7.50	11.50	17.50

Die breaks in 1881 have the appearance of 1884.

Y#	Date	Mintage	Fine	VF	XF	Unc
68.1	1881	—	5.50	9.00	15.00	30.00

5 CENTAVOS

.835 SILVER

Y#	Date	Mintage	Fine	VF	XF	Unc
70	1881	.118	20.00	30.00	45.00	70.00

10 CENTAVOS

.835 SILVER

Y#	Date	Mintage	Fine	VF	XF	Unc
71	1881	.056	25.00	40.00	55.00	100.00

12-1/2 CENTAVOS

BRONZE
Provisional Issue

Y#	Date	Mintage	Fine	VF	XF	Unc
89	1915	6.000	1.00	1.75	3.50	7.50

25 CENTIMOS

.900 SILVER

Y#	Date	Mintage	Fine	VF	XF	Unc
29	1869R	.181	9.00	15.00	25.00	50.00
	1870R	.180	6.00	10.00	20.00	40.00

25 CENTAVOS

5.0000 gm., .835 SILVER, .1342 oz ASW

Y#	Date	Mintage	Fine	VF	XF	Unc
69	1881E	5.044	BV	4.50	6.00	8.50
	1882E	—	BV	4.50	6.00	8.50
	1885E	—	BV	4.50	6.00	8.50
	1888E	—	4.50	6.00	8.50	12.00
	1888	—	7.50	12.00	20.00	30.00
	1888G	—	BV	4.50	6.00	8.50
	1889G	.496	BV	4.50	6.00	8.50

Star replaces assayer's initial

Y#	Date	Mintage	Fine	VF	XF	Unc
69.1	1889	Inc. Ab.	BV	4.50	6.00	8.50
	1890	—	BV	5.00	7.50	10.00
	1891	—	7.50	12.00	20.00	30.00

Y#	Date	Mintage	Fine	VF	XF	Unc
72	1882	—	200.00	300.00	400.00	—

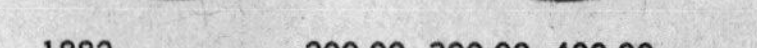

Y#	Date	Mintage	Fine	VF	XF	Unc
69a	1892	—	30.00	50.00	75.00	100.00

Star replaces assayer's initial

Y#	Date	Mintage	Fine	VF	XF	Unc
69a.1	1890	—	7.50	12.00	20.00	30.00
	1892	—	BV	4.50	6.00	8.50
	1893	—	BV	Bv	4.50	6.50

BRONZE
Provisional Issue

Y#	Date	Mintage	Fine	VF	XF	Unc
90	1915	4.000	.60	1.00	1.25	1.50

50 CENTAVOS

10.0000 gm., .835 SILVER, .2684 oz ASW

Y#	Date	Mintage	Fine	VF	XF	Unc
35	1870R	.140	8.50	10.00	20.00	40.00

ALUMINUM-BRONZE
Provisional Issue

Y#	Date	Mintage	Fine	VF	XF	Unc
91	1922	3.803	.90	1.50	5.00	10.00

PESO

.903 SILVER

Y#	Date	Mintage	Fine	VF	XF	Unc
7	1859	—	150.00	200.00	400.00	—
	1859R	—	225.00	375.00	625.00	—

1.6129 gm., .875 GOLD, .0454 oz AGW

Y#	Date	Mintage	VG	Fine	VF	XF
14	1859R	—	35.00	50.00	75.00	125.00
	1860R	.037	35.00	50.00	75.00	125.00

27.0000 .GM., .903 SILVER, .7839 oz ASW
Rev: Similar to Y#25.

Y#	Date	Mintage	VG	Fine	VF	XF
12	1862R	—	40.00	85.00	120.00	165.00
	1863R	—	27.50	35.00	45.00	65.00
	1864R	—	25.00	30.00	35.0	45.00
	1864.R	—	25.00	30.00	35.0	45.00
	1865R	.119	25.00	30.00	35.0	45.00

Rev: L10Ds.20Gs

Y#	Date	Mintage	Fine	VF	XF	Unc
25	1866R	.109	22.50	27.50	35.00	55.00
	1867R	.173	22.50	27.50	35.00	55.00
	1868R	.060	25.00	30.00	40.00	65.00
	Rev: W/o 'L' before 10Ds.20Gs.					
	1869	.186	75.00	125.00	250.00	450.00
	1870	—	60.00	100.00	150.00	250.00

25.0000 gm., .900 SILVER, .7234 oz ASW
Obv: Similar to Y#25.
Rev: L0.900

Y#	Date	Mintage	Fine	VF	XF	Unc
30	1869R	Inc. Ab.	22.50	27.50	32.50	45.00
	1870R	.283	22.50	27.50	32.50	45.00
	1871R	—	22.50	27.50	32.50	45.00
	Rev: W/o 'L' before 0.900.					
30.1	1869	Inc. Ab.	22.50	27.50	32.50	45.00

Rev: Date and fineness at bottom.

Y#	Date	Mintage	Fine	VF	XF	Unc
56	1872P	.014	45.00	70.00	100.00	—
	1872R (2 known)	—	—	Rare	—	
	1873P	.078	45.00	70.00	100.00	—
	1873P (error fineness 0900)					
		—	50.00	80.00	125.00	200.00
	Rev: Quetzal with a short tail.					
56.1	1873P	—	50.00	80.00	125.00	200.00

Obv: Similar to Y#56.
Rev: With date and fineness at top.

Y#	Date	Mintage	Fine	VF	XF	Unc
57	1878D	1,076	475.00	800.00	1500.	—
	1879D	.010	375.00	600.00	1000.	—

Obv: Similar to Y#56.
Rev: Full spray design.

Y#	Date	Mintage	VG	Fine	VF	XF
58	1879D	Inc. Ab.	150.00	275.00	375.00	500.00
	1893G	—	—	—	Rare	—
	1893RG	1,119	—	—	Rare	—

Obv: Modified Liberty design
Rev: Similar to Y#58

Y#	Date	Mintage	Fine	VF	XF	Unc
58a	1882/1E	—	—	—	Rare	—
	1888G	—	325.00	550.00	900.00	1600.
	1889G	—	325.00	550.00	900.00	1600.

Y#	Date	Mintage	VG	Fine	VF	XF
73	1882A.E.	—	25.00	50.00	75.00	125.00
	1889MG	6,794	100.00	200.00	350.00	550.00

Y#	Date	Mintage	Fine	VF	XF	Unc
84	1894	1.696	BV	22.50	27.50	40.00
	1894H	.875	BV	22.50	27.50	40.00
	1895	1.415	BV	22.50	27.50	40.00
	1895H	.375	22.50	27.50	35.00	50.00
	1896/5	1.403	BV	22.50	27.50	40.00
	1896	Inc. Ab.	BV	22.50	27.50	40.00
	1897	—	22.50	27.50	35.00	50.00

ALUMINUM-BRONZE
Provisional Issue

Y#	Date	Mintage	Fine	VF	XF	Unc
92	1923	1.477	1.00	1.75	2.25	3.00

2 PESOS

3.2258 gm., .875 GOLD, .0907 oz AGW

Y#	Date	Mintage	VG	Fine	VF	XF
15	1859R	—	65.00	75.00	125.00	200.00

4 PESOS

6.4516 gm., .875 GOLD, .1815 oz AGW

Y#	Date	Mintage	VG	Fine	VF	XF
16	1861R	—	125.00	150.00	225.00	350.00
	1862R	—	125.00	150.00	225.00	350.00

Y#	Date	Mintage	VG	Fine	VF	XF
26	1866R	561 pcs.	175.00	300.00	400.00	500.00
	1868R	778 pcs.	175.00	300.00	400.00	500.00
	1869R	.020	125.00	175.00	250.00	375.00

5 PESOS

8.0645 gm., .900 GOLD, .2333 oz AGW

Y#	Date	Mintage	VG	Fine	VF	XF
31	1869R	.049	175.00	200.00	250.00	300.00

Y#	Date	Mintage	VG	Fine	VF	XF
66	1872P	—	175.00	225.00	300.00	400.00
	1873P	—	—	—	Rare	—
	1874P	—	175.00	225.00	300.00	400.00
	1875P	—	—	—	Rare	—
	1876F	—	—	—	Rare	—
	1877F	—	175.00	225.00	300.00	400.00
	1878D	—	175.00	225.00	300.00	400.00

ALUMINUM-BRONZE
Provisional Issue

Y#	Date	Mintage	Fine	VF	XF	Unc
93	1923	.440	2.00	3.00	4.00	6.00

8 PESOS

12.9039 gm., .875 GOLD, .3630 oz AGW

Y#	Date	Mintage	VG	Fine	VF	XF
17	1864R	—	250.00	325.00	450.00	700.00

Similar to 4 Pesos, Y#26.

Y#	Date	Mintage	VG	Fine	VF	XF
27	1868R	—	250.00	275.00	400.00	550.00

10 PESOS

16.1290 gm., .900 GOLD, .4667 oz AGW

Y#	Date	Mintage	VG	Fine	VF	XF
32	1869R	.020	325.00	550.00	675.00	975.00

16 PESOS

25.8078 gm., .875 GOLD, .7259 oz AGW
Obv: Similar to 10 Pesos, Y#32.

Y#	Date	Mintage	VG	Fine	VF	XF
18	1863R	—	750.00	1400.	2000.	3000.
	1864R	—	—	—	—	—
	1865R	—	—	—	—	—

Reduced size

Y#	Date	Mintage	VG	Fine	VF	XF
19	1865R	190 pcs.	800.00	1400.	2000.	3000.

Obv: Similar to 10 Pesos, Y#32.

Y#	Date	Mintage	VG	Fine	VF	XF
28	1867R	467 pcs.	—	—	Rare	—
	1869R	3,465	500.00	650.00	1000.	1500.

20 PESOS

32.2580 gm., .900 GOLD, .9334 oz AGW

Y#	Date	Mintage	VG	Fine	VF	XF
33	1869R	.016	625.00	700.00	1000.	1500.

Similar to 5 Pesos, Y#66.

Y#	Date	Mintage	VG	Fine	VF	XF
67	1877F	—	1000.	1750.	2750.	4000.
	1878F	—	1000.	1750.	2750.	4000.

COUNTERSTAMP ISSUES

By 1894 foreign coins had become so prevalent that the government on August 10 granted permission to countermark the foreign 'dollars' with the 1/2 Real dies dated 1894 to nationalize them.

'PESO'

.917 SILVER
c/s: On Brazil 2000 Reis, C#198a.

Y#	Date	Year	Mintage	Fine	VF	XF
A88.1	1894	1875	—	—	Rare	—

25.0000 gm., .900 SILVER, .7234 oz ASW
c/s: On Chile 8 Reales, Y#22a.

Y#	Date	Year	Mintage	Fine	VF	XF
A88.2	1894	1848JM	—	—	Rare	—
	1894	1849ML	—Reported, not confirmed			

c/s: On Chile Peso, Y#A38.

Y#	Date	Year	Mintage	Fine	VF	XF
A88.3	1894	1855	—	—	Rare	—

c/s: On Chile Peso, Y#48.

Y#	Date	Year	Mintage	Fine	VF	XF
88a	1894	1867	—	225.00	350.00	575.00
		1868	—	200.00	325.00	525.00
		1869	—	120.00	225.00	350.00
		1870/69	—	80.00	120.00	175.00
		1870	—	60.00	80.00	120.00
		1871	—	85.00	150.00	200.00
		1872	—	40.00	65.00	100.00
		1873	—	40.00	65.00	100.00
		1874	—	30.00	45.00	65.00
		1875	—	27.50	40.00	55.00
		1876	—	27.50	40.00	55.00
		1877	—	27.50	40.00	55.00
		1878	—	27.50	40.00	55.00
		1879	—	27.50	40.00	55.00
		1880	—	27.50	40.00	55.00
		1881	—	25.00	35.00	50.00
		1882	—	25.00	35.00	50.00
		1883	—	25.00	35.00	50.00
		1884	—	25.00	35.00	50.00
		1885	—	35.00	60.00	85.00
		1886	—	30.00	45.00	75.00
		1887	—Reported, not confirmed			

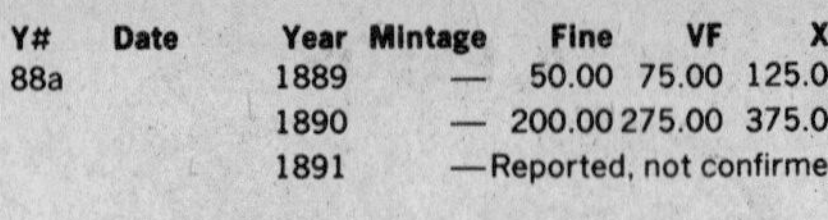

Y#	Date	Year	Mintage	Fine	VF	XF
88a		1889	—	50.00	75.00	125.00
		1890	—	200.00	275.00	375.00
		1891	—Reported, not confirmed			

c/s: Off center

Y#	Date	Year	Mintage	Fine	VF	XF
88a.1	1894	1880	—	—	—	—

.903 SILVER
c/s: On Guatemala Peso, Y#7.

Y#	Date	Year	Mintage	Fine	VF	XF
A88.4	1894	1859	—Reported, not confirmed			

c/s: On Guatemala Peso, Y#30.

Y#	Date	Year	Mintage	Fine	VF	XF
A88.5	1894	1869	—	—	Rare	—

c/s: On Guatemala Peso, Y#73.

Y#	Date	Year	Mintage	Fine	VF	XF
A88.6	1894	1882A.E.	—	—	Rare	—

c/s: On Guatemala Peso, Y#84.

Y#	Date	Year	Mintage	Fine	VF	XF
A88.7	1894	1894	—Reported, not confirmed			
		1894H	—	—	Rare	—

c/s: On Honduras Peso, Y#25.

Y#	Date	Year	Mintage	Fine	VF	XF
A88.8	1894	1882	—	—	Rare	—

c/s: On Honduras Peso, Y#25a.

Y#	Date	Year	Mintage	Fine	VF	XF
A88.9	1894	1890	—	—	Rare	—
		1891	—	—	Rare	—

c/s: On Peru Un Sol, Y#18.

Y#	Date	Year	Mintage	Fine	VF	XF
88	1894	1864Y.B.	—	25.00	35.00	50.00
		1864Y.B. Deteoro	—	125.00	200.00	—
		1865Y.B.	—	85.00	140.00	225.00
		1866Y.B.	—	30.00	45.00	60.00
		1867Y.B.	—	35.00	50.00	65.00
		1868Y.B.	—	35.00	50.00	65.00
		1869Y.B.	—	35.00	50.00	65.00
		1870Y.B.	—Reported, not confirmed			
		1870Y.J.	—	35.00	50.00	65.00
		1871Y.J.	—	35.00	50.00	65.00
		1872Y.J.	—	30.00	45.00	60.00
		1873Y.J.	—	85.00	140.00	225.00
		1873L.D.	—	140.00	225.00	350.00
		1873L.D.	—	70.00	120.00	170.00
		1874Y.J.	—	30.00	45.00	60.00
		1875Y.J.	—	27.50	40.00	42.50
		1879Y.J.	—	27.50	40.00	42.50
		1880Y.J.	—	45.00	60.00	75.00
		1880B.F.	—Reported, not confirmed			
		1881B.F.	—	45.00	60.00	75.00
		1882B.F.	—	55.00	85.00	110.00
		1882F.N.	—	85.00	140.00	200.00
		1883F.N.	—	120.00	200.00	275.00
		1884B.D.	—	55.00	85.00	110.00
		1884R.D.	—	27.50	40.00	50.00
		1885R.D.	—	27.50	40.00	50.00
		1885T.D.	—	27.50	40.00	50.00
		1886R.D.	—Reported, not confirmed			
		1886T.F.	—	35.00	45.00	65.00
		1887T.F.	—	25.00	35.00	45.00
		1888T.F.	—	25.00	35.00	45.00
		1889T.F.	—	25.00	35.00	45.00
		1890T.F.	—	25.00	35.00	45.00
		1891T.F.	—	25.00	35.00	45.00
		1892T.F.	—	25.00	35.00	45.00
		1893T.F.	—	25.00	35.00	45.00
		1393T.F. (error)	—	450.00	600.00	900.00
		1894T.F.	—	25.00	35.00	45.00

c/s: On Peru 5 Pesetas, Y#30.

Y#	Date	Year	Mintage	Fine	VF	XF
88b	1894	1880	B.F. with B under wreath w/o dot			
			—	125.00	175.00	250.00
		1880	B.F. with B. under wreath			
			—	125.00	175.00	250.00

c/s: On Peru 5 Pesetas, Y#30a.

Y#	Date	Year	Mintage	Fine	VF	XF
88b.1	1894	1881B	—Reported, not confirmed			
		1882LM	—	300.00	500.00	800.00

c/s: On Salvador Peso, Y#7.

Y#	Date	Year	Mintage	Fine	VF	XF
A88.10	1894	1892	—	700.00	900.00	1250.
		1893	—	700.00	900.00	1250.
		1894	—Reported, not confirmed			

MONETARY REFORM

100 Centavos = 1 Quetzal

MEDIO (1/2) CENTAVO

BRASS

Y#	Date	Mintage	VF	XF	Unc
94	1932	6.000	.50	.75	1.65
	1946	.640	.75	1.25	3.50

UN (1) CENTAVO

BRONZE

Y#	Date	Mintage	VF	XF	Unc
95	1925	.357	4.00	6.00	25.00

Y#	Date	Mintage	VF	XF	Unc
96	1929	.500	2.00	4.00	25.00

BRASS

Y#	Date	Mintage	VF	XF	Unc
97	1932	3.000	1.50	3.00	7.50
	1933	1.500	2.25	4.50	12.00
	1934	1.000	2.00	4.50	12.00
	1936	1.500	1.75	4.50	12.00
	1938	1.000	1.75	4.50	12.00
	1939	1.500	2.00	4.75	9.50
	1946	.539	.05	.50	6.00
	1947	1.121	.05	.25	2.50
	1948	1.651	.05	.25	3.50
	1949	1.022	.05	.35	3.50

Y#	Date	Mintage	VF	XF	Unc
108	1943	.450	6.50	10.00	20.00
	1944	2.050	1.00	1.75	5.50

Y#	Date	Mintage	VF	XF	Unc
111	1949	1.091	.10	.25	3.50
	1950	3.663	.10	.20	1.75
	1951	3.586	.15	.40	.75
	1952	1.445	.10	.20	1.00
	1953	2.214	.10	.20	1.00
	1954	1.455	.10	.25	2.25

NICKEL-BRASS

Y#	Date	Mintage	VF	XF	Unc
112	1954	10.000	—	.10	.50
	1957	1.600	.10	.15	.75
	1958	2.000	.10	.15	.60

BRASS

Y#	Date	Mintage	VF	XF	Unc
113	1958	10.001	—	—	.20
	1961	1.826	—	—	.15
	1963	4.926	—	—	.15
	1964	4.280	—	—	.15

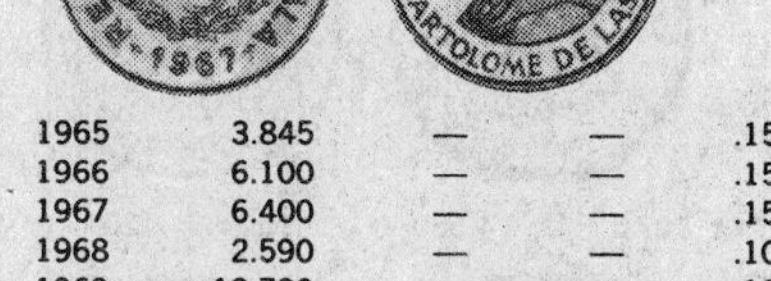

Y#	Date	Mintage	VF	XF	Unc
122	1965	3.845	—	—	.15
	1966	6.100	—	—	.15
	1967	6.400	—	—	.15
	1968	2.590	—	—	.10
	1969	13.780	—	—	.10
	1970	10.511	—	—	.15

Y#	Date	Mintage	VF	XF	Unc
122a	1972	11.500	—	—	.15
	1973	12.000	—	—	.15

Y#	Date	Mintage	VF	XF	Unc
122b	1974	10.000	—	—	.10
	1975	15.000	—	—	.10
	1976	15.230	—	—	.10
	1977	30.000	—	—	.10
	1978	—	—	—	.10
	1979	—	—	—	.10

DOS (2) CENTAVOS

BRASS

Y#	Date	Mintage	VF	XF	Unc
98	1932	3.000	.60	2.50	12.00

Y#	Date	Mintage	VF	XF	Unc
109	1943	.150	7.50	12.00	30.00
	1944	1.100	1.75	3.00	7.50

5 CENTAVOS

1.6667 gm., .720 SILVER, .0386 oz ASW
Obv: Long-tailed quetzal

Y#	Date	Mintage	VF	XF	Unc
99	1925	.573	2.00	5.00	20.00
	1944	1.026	BV	BV	10.00
	1945	4.026	BV	BV	7.50
	1947	1.834	BV	BV	8.50
	1948	1.103	BV	BV	10.00
	1949	.551	BV	2.00	12.00

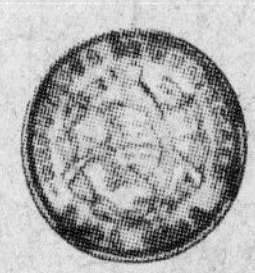

Obv: Short-tailed quetzal

Y#	Date	Mintage	VF	XF	Unc
99a	1928	1.000	BV	3.00	8.50
	1929	1.000	1.25	3.00	8.50
	1932	2.000	BV	1.75	7.50
	1933	.600	1.25	3.50	10.00
	1934	1.200	BV	3.00	8.50
	1937	.400	1.50	3.00	8.50
	1938	.300	2.00	3.00	8.50
	1943	.900	BV	1.25	5.00

Rev: Small tree

Y#	Date	Mintage	VF	XF	Unc
114	1949	.305	1.25	3.00	12.50

Rev: Large tree

Y#	Date	Mintage	VF	XF	Unc
115	1950	.453	BV	1.50	7.00
	1951	1.032	BV	1.25	5.00
	1952	.913	BV	1.25	5.00
	1953	.447	BV	2.50	5.00
	1954	.520	BV	1.25	7.50
	1955	2.062	BV	1.25	4.00
	1956	1.301	BV	1.50	2.50
	1957	2.941	BV	1.25	1.75

Small crude date

Large crude date

Y#	Date	Mintage	VF	XF	Unc
115a	1958 small date				
		3.025	BV	BV	1.50
	1958 large date				
		Inc. Ab.	BV	BV	2.00
	1959	.232	BV	BV	2.00

Rev: Level ground at tree

Y#	Date	Mintage	VF	XF	Unc
116	1960	4.770	BV	BV	1.50
	1961	6.756	BV	BV	1.50
	1964	1.529	BV	BV	1.50

NICKEL-BRASS

Y#	Date	Mintage	VF	XF	Unc
123	1965	1.642	.15	.50	1.00
	1966	3.600	—	.10	.20
	1967	2.800	—	.10	.20
	1968	4.030	—	.10	.20
	1969	7.210	—	.10	.25
	1970	8.121	—	.10	.25

Y#	Date	Mintage	VF	XF	Unc
123a	1971	8.270	—	.10	.25
	1974	10.575	—	.10	.20
	1975	10.000	—	.10	.20
	1976	6.000	—	.10	.20

Y#	Date	Mintage	VF	XF	Unc
123b	1977	20.000	—	.10	.15
	1978	—	—	.10	.15

10 CENTAVOS

3.3333 gm., .720 SILVER, .0772 oz ASW

Obv: Long-tailed quetzal

Y#	Date	Mintage	VF	XF	Unc
100	1925	.573	BV	5.00	25.00
	1944	.155	BV	3.50	8.00
	1945	1.499	BV	2.50	3.50
	1947	.471	BV	2.50	6.00
	1948	.324	BV	2.50	3.50
	1949	.145	BV	3.50	7.50

Obv: Short-tailed quetzal

Y#	Date	Mintage	VF	XF	Unc
100a	1928	.500	2.50	5.00	15.00
	1929	.500	BV	3.50	17.50
	1932	.500	BV	3.50	15.00
	1933	.650	BV	3.00	15.00
	1934	.300	BV	3.00	20.00
	1936	.200	2.50	4.50	25.00
	1938	.150	3.00	5.00	17.50
	1943	.600	BV	2.50	7.50
	1947	Inc. Y100	2.50	3.00	7.50

Rev: Small monolith

Y#	Date	Mintage	VF	XF	Unc
117	1949	.281	2.50	3.50	8.00
	1950	.550	BV	2.50	3.50
	1951	.263	BV	2.50	5.00
	1952	.307	BV	2.50	3.50
	1953	.388	BV	2.50	5.00
	1955	.896	BV	2.50	5.00
	1956	.501	BV	2.50	7.50
	1958	1.528	BV	2.50	6.00

Rev: Larger monolith

Y#	Date	Mintage	VF	XF	Unc
117a	1957	1.123	BV	2.50	3.50
	1958	Inc. Y117	BV	2.50	5.00

Obv: Long-tailed quetzal. Rev: Small monolith.

Y#	Date	Mintage	VF	XF	Unc
117b	1958	Inc. Y117	BV	2.50	4.00
	1959	.461	BV	2.50	4.00

Y#	Date	Mintage	VF	XF	Unc
118	1960	1.743	BV	BV	2.50
	1961	2.647	BV	BV	2.50
	1964	.965	BV	BV	2.50

NICKEL-BRASS

Y#	Date	Mintage	VF	XF	Unc
124	1965	2.227	.15	.25	.75
	1966	1.550	.15	.20	.50
	1967	3.120	.15	.20	.40
	1968	3.220	.15	.20	.40
	1969	3.530	.15	.20	.40
	1970	4.153	.15	.20	.40

Y#	Date	Mintage	VF	XF	Unc
124a	1971	4.580	.15	.20	.40

COPPER-NICKEL

Y#	Date	Mintage	VF	XF	Unc
124b	1973	1.100	.15	.20	.50
	1974	3.500	.15	.20	.40
	1975	6.000	.15	.20	.40
	1976	2.000	.15	.20	.35

Y#	Date	Mintage	VF	XF	Unc
124c	1977	5.000	.15	.20	.25
	1978	—	.15	.20	.25
	1979	—	.15	.20	.25

1/4 QUETZAL

8.3333 gm., .720 SILVER, .1929 oz ASW

Lettered edge

Y#	Date	Mintage	VF	XF	Unc
101	1925	1.160	8.50	20.00	45.00

Rev: Larger design

Y#	Date	Mintage	VF	XF	Unc
102	1926	2.000	6.50	10.00	25.00
	1928	.400	6.50	10.00	27.50
	1929	.400	6.50	10.00	27.50

Reeded edge

Y#	Date	Mintage	VF	XF	Unc
102a	1946	.203	6.50	10.00	17.50
	1947	.134	6.50	10.00	12.50
	1948	.129	6.50	10.00	15.00
	1949	.025	10.00	20.00	35.00

25 CENTAVOS

8.3333 gm., .720 SILVER, .1929 oz ASW

Y#	Date	Mintage	VF	XF	Unc
110	1943	.900	7.00	12.50	25.00

Y#	Date	Mintage	VF	XF	Unc
119	1950	.081	6.50	8.50	22.50
	1951	.011	15.00	25.00	75.00
	1952	.112	BV	7.50	12.00
	1954	.246	BV	6.50	10.00
	1955	.409	BV	6.50	10.00
	1956	.342	BV	6.50	10.00
	1957	.257	BV	6.50	10.00
	1958	.394	BV	6.50	10.00
	1959	.277	BV	6.50	10.00

Y#	Date	Mintage	VF	XF	Unc
120	1960	.560	BV	6.00	8.00
	1961	.750	BV	6.00	8.00
	1963	1.100	BV	6.00	8.00
	1964	.299	BV	6.50	8.00

NICKEL-BRASS

Y#	Date	Mintage	VF	XF	Unc
125	1965	1.178	1.00	1.25	1.75
	1966	.910	1.00	1.25	1.75

Rev: Modified die

Y#	Date	Mintage	VF	XF	Unc
125a	1967	1.140	.75	1.00	1.75
	1968	1.540	.75	1.00	1.50
	1969	2.070	.75	1.00	1.50
	1970	2.501	.75	1.00	1.50

Y#	Date	Mintage	VF	XF	Unc
125b	1971	2.850	.40	.60	1.00
	1975	1.592	.35	.50	.75
	1976	2.000	.35	.50	.75

Y#	Date	Mintage	VF	XF	Unc
125c	1977	2.000	.35	.50	.75
	1978	—	.35	.50	.65

1/2 QUETZAL

16.6667 gm., .720 SILVER, .3858 oz ASW

Y#	Date	Mintage	VF	XF	Unc
103	1925	.400	35.00	50.00	90.00

50 CENTAVOS

11.9444 gm., .720 SILVER,, .2765 oz ASW

Y#	Date	Mintage	VF	XF	Unc
121	1962	1.983	8.50	10.00	15.00
	1963	.350	8.50	10.00	15.00

QUETZAL

33.3333 gm., .720 SILVER, .7716 oz ASW

Y#	Date	Mintage	VF	XF	Unc
104	1925	*.010	750.00	1500.	2500.

***NOTE:** 7,000 pcs. were withdrawn and remelted soon after issue and more met with the same fate in 1932.

5 QUETZALES

8.3592 gm., .900 GOLD, .2419 oz AGW

Y#	Date	Mintage	VF	XF	Unc
105	1926	.048	250.00	300.00	375.00

10 QUETZALES

16.7185 gm., .900 GOLD, .4838 oz AGW

Y#	Date	Mintage	VF	XF	Unc
106	1926	.018	475.00	700.00	925.00

20 QUETZALES

33.4370 gm., .900 GOLD, .9676 oz AGW

Y#	Date	Mintage	VF	XF	Unc
107	1926	.049	650.00	800.00	1200.

NCLT ISSUES

ESSAIS

KM#	Date	Mintage	Identification	Mkt.Val.
E1	1894(a)	—	10 Pesos, Gold	—

PATTERNS

KM#	Date	Mintage	Identification	Mkt.Val.
1	1854AE	—	8 Reales, Silver, Columbus	6000.

GUERNSEY

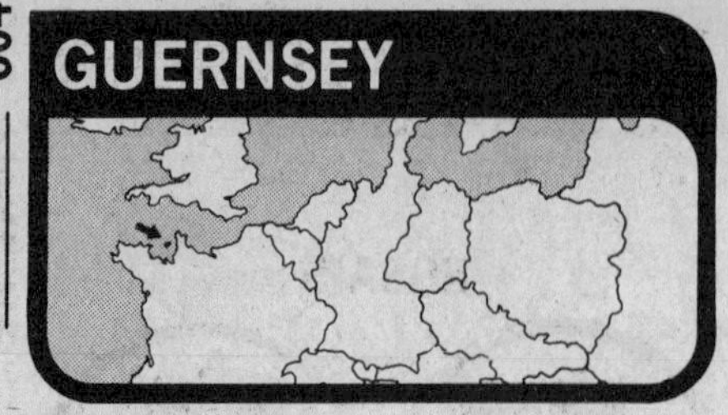

The Bailiwick of Guernsey, a British crown dependency located in the English Channel 30 miles (48 km.) west of Normandy, France, has an area of 30 sq. mi. (78 sq. km.) (including the isles of Alderney, Jethou, Herm, Brechou, and Sark), and a population of 53,794. Capital: St. Peter Port. Agriculture and cattle breeding are the main occupations.

Militant monks from the Duchy of Normandy established the first permanent settlements on Guernsey prior to the Norman invasion of England, but the prevalence of prehistoric monuments suggests an earlier occupancy. The island, the only part of the Duchy of Normandy belonging to the British crown, has been a possession of Britain since the Norman Conquest of 1066. During the Anglo-French wars, the harbors of Guernsey were employed in the building apd outfitting of ships for the English privateers preying on French shipping. Guernsey is administered by its own laws and customs. Acts passed by the British Parliament are not applicable to Guernsey unless the island is specifically mentioned. During World War II, German troops occupied the island from June 30, 1940 till May 9, 1945.

RULERS

British

MINTMARKS

H - Heaton, Birmingham

MONETARY SYSTEM

8 Doubles = 1 Penny
12 Pence = 1 Shilling
5 Shillings = 1 Crown
20 Shillings = 1 Pound

TOKEN ISSUES

Bank Of Guernsey

5 SHILLINGS

.892 SILVER

P#	Date	Mintage	VG	Fine	VF
90	1809	*20 known	2000.	2500.	3500.

NOTE: The above issue was struck over Spanish 8 Reales .They were forbidden by the Guernsey legislation to circulate in 1809.

REGULAR COINAGE

DOUBLE

COPPER

Y#	Date	Mintage	Fine	VF	XF	Unc
A1	1830	1.649	2.00	4.00	12.00	20.00
	1830	—	—	—	Proof	100.00
	1868/30	.064	4.00	8.00	20.00	50.00
	1868	Inc. Ab.	6.00	12.50	25.00	60.00

BRONZE
Obv: Three leaves above shield.

Y#	Date	Mintage	Fine	VF	XF	Unc
1	1885H	.080	1.00	1.50	4.00	7.50
	1885H	—	—	—	Proof	70.00
	1889H	.112	.60	1.50	3.00	6.00
	1889H	—	—	—	Proof	60.00
	1893H	.051	1.00	2.25	4.00	11.00
	1899H	.056	1.00	2.25	3.50	9.00
	1902H	.084	.60	1.50	2.25	4.25
	1903H	.112	.40	1.00	2.00	3.50
	1911H	.067	.80	2.00	5.00	10.00

Obv: Cluster of leaves above shield.

Y#	Date	Mintage	Fine	VF	XF	Unc
1a	1911H	.067	.60	1.50	3.00	7.00
	1914H	.045	1.50	3.50	7.50	15.00
	1929H	.079	.50	1.25	2.00	5.00
	1933H	.096	.50	1.25	2.00	4.00
	1938H	.096	.40	1.00	1.75	3.00

2 DOUBLES

COPPER

Y#	Date	Mintage	Fine	VF	XF	Unc
B1	1858	.056	12.00	25.00	60.00	100.00

BRONZE
Obv: Three leaves above shield.

Y#	Date	Mintage	Fine	VF	XF	Unc
2	1868	.035	7.00	15.00	40.00	120.00
	1874	.045	5.00	10.00	27.50	80.00
	1885H	.077	1.25	3.00	7.50	15.00
	1885H	—	—	—	Proof	70.00
	1889H	.036	2.50	5.00	10.00	17.50
	1889H	—	—	—	Proof	80.00
	1899H	.036	4.00	7.50	15.00	25.00
	1902H	.018	7.00	12.00	25.00	40.00
	1903H	.018	7.00	12.00	25.00	40.00
	1906H	.018	12.00	20.00	30.00	60.00
	1908H	.018	12.00	20.00	30.00	60.00
	1911H	.029	7.00	12.00	20.00	35.00

Obv: Cluster of leaves above shield.

Y#	Date	Mintage	Fine	VF	XF	Unc
2a	1914H	.029	7.00	12.00	20.00	35.00
	1917H	.015	30.00	75.00	125.00	250.00
	1918H	.057	2.00	4.50	7.00	12.50
	1920H	.057	2.00	4.50	7.00	12.00
	1929H	.079	2.00	4.00	6.00	9.00

4 DOUBLES

COPPER

Y#	Date	Mintage	Fine	VF	XF	Unc
C1	1830	.655	3.00	7.00	15.00	35.00
	1830	—	—	—	Proof	150.00
	1858	.114	9.00	15.00	40.00	100.00

NOTE: A rare mule exists of the St. Helena obverse 1/2 Penny 1821 and reverse of Guernsey 4 Doubles dated 1830.

BRONZE
Obv: Three leaves above shield.

Y#	Date	Mintage	Fine	VF	XF	Unc
3	1864/54	.213	9.00	18.00	50.00	100.00
	1864	Inc. Ab.	2.00	4.00	12.00	25.00
	1868	.058	2.50	6.00	15.00	30.00
	1874	.069	2.50	6.00	15.00	30.00
	1885H	.070	2.50	5.00	12.00	25.00
	1885H	—	—	—	Proof	75.00
	1889H	.104	1.50	3.00	6.00	12.00
	1889H	—	—	—	Proof	70.00
	1893H	.052	2.50	5.00	12.00	25.00
	1902H	.105	1.25	2.50	7.00	12.50
	1903H	.052	2.00	4.50	10.00	20.00
	1906H	.052	2.00	4.50	10.00	20.00
	1908H	.026	7.50	15.00	25.00	40.00
	1910H	.052	2.00	4.50	12.00	25.00
	1911H	.052	2.50	6.00	15.00	25.00

NOTE: Varieties exist.

Obv: Cluster of leaves above shield.

Y#	Date	Mintage	Fine	VF	XF	Unc
3a	1914H	.209	.80	2.00	4.50	7.50
	1918H	.157	.70	1.75	4.50	7.50
	1920H	.157	.60	1.50	3.50	7.00
	1945H	.096	.60	1.50	3.00	7.00
	1949H	.019	2.00	4.00	7.00	12.00

Y#	Date	Mintage	Fine	VF	XF	Unc
6	1956	.240	.50	1.00	2.00	6.00
	1956	2,100	—	—	Proof	10.00

Y#	Date	Mintage	Fine	VF	XF	Unc
6	1966	.010	—	Proof Only		4.00

8 DOUBLES

COPPER

Y#	Date	Mintage	Fine	VF	XF	Unc
D1	1834	.222	6.00	12.00	35.00	100.00
	1834	—	—	—	Proof	250.00
	1858	.111	15.00	25.00	50.00	150.00
	1858	—	—	—	Proof	250.00

BRONZE
Obv: Three leaves above shield.

Y#	Date	Mintage	Fine	VF	XF	Unc
4	1864	.280	2.50	5.00	15.00	40.00
	1864	—	—	—	Proof	125.00
	1868	.060	4.00	10.00	30.00	70.00
	1874	.070	3.00	7.50	20.00	50.00
	1885H	.070	3.00	7.50	15.00	32.50
	1885H	—	—	—	Proof	100.00
	1889H	.220	1.00	2.50	5.00	10.00
	1889H	—	—	—	Proof	125.00
	1893H	.118	2.25	4.50	10.00	20.00
	1893H large date and denomination					
		Inc. Ab.	—	—	—	—
	1902H	.240	1.00	2.50	6.00	12.00
	1903H	.120	2.00	4.00	10.00	17.50
	1910H	.090	3.50	7.00	15.00	27.50
	1911H	.080	5.00	10.00	25.00	40.00

Obv: Cluster of leaves above shield.

Y#	Date	Mintage	Fine	VF	XF	Unc
5	1914H	.160	1.25	3.00	6.00	12.00
	1918H	.160	1.25	3.00	6.00	12.00
	1920H	.160	.80	2.00	5.00	10.00
	1934H	.120	1.25	3.00	5.00	10.00
	1934H	500 pcs.	—	—	Proof	75.00
	1938H	.120	.40	1.00	3.00	9.00
	1945H	.190	.50	1.25	2.50	7.00
	1947H	.240	.50	1.25	2.50	5.00
	1949H	.230	.40	1.00	1.50	4.00

Y#	Date	Mintage	Fine	VF	XF	Unc
7	1956	.500	.25	.50	.75	3.00
	1956	2,100	—	—	Proof	12.00
	1959	.500	.10	.20	.50	2.00
	1966	.010	—	Proof Only		4.00

3 PENCE

COPPER-NICKEL
Thin flan

Y#	Date	Mintage	Fine	VF	XF	Unc
8	1956	.500	.15	.35	1.00	4.00
	1956	2,100	—	—	Proof	12.00

Thick flan

Y#	Date	Mintage	Fine	VF	XF	Unc
8a	1959	.500	.15	.20	.50	2.00
	1966	.010	—	Proof Only		4.50

10 SHILLINGS

COPPER-NICKEL
900th Anniversary Norman Conquest

Y#	Date	Mintage	Fine	VF	XF	Unc
9	1966	.300	.50	1.00	1.50	2.00
	1966	.010	—	—	Proof	5.00

DECIMAL COINAGE

100 Pence = 1 Pound

1/2 NEW PENNY

BRONZE

Y#	Date	Mintage	Fine	VF	XF	Unc
10	1971	2.294	—	.10	.15	.20
	1971	.010	—	—	Proof	1.50

1/2 PENNY

BRONZE

Y#	Date	Mintage	Fine	VF	XF	Unc
18	1979	—	—	—	—	—
	1979	.020	—	—	Proof	—

NEW PENNY

BRONZE

Y#	Date	Mintage	Fine	VF	XF	Unc
11	1971	1.386	—	.10	.15	.20
	1971	.010	—	—	Proof	2.00

PENNY

BRONZE

Y#	Date	Mintage	Fine	VF	XF	Unc
19	1977	—	.10	.15	.20	.25
	1979	—	—	—	—	—
	1979	.020	—	—	Proof	—

2 NEW PENCE

BRONZE

Y#	Date	Mintage	Fine	VF	XF	Unc
12	1971	.654	.10	.15	.20	.25
	1971	.010	—	—	Proof	2.50

2 PENCE

BRONZE

Y#	Date	Mintage	Fine	VF	XF	Unc
20	1977	—	.10	.15	.20	.25
	1979	—	—	—	—	—
	1979	.020	—	—	Proof	—

5 NEW PENCE

COPPER-NICKEL

Y#	Date	Mintage	Fine	VF	XF	Unc
13	1968	.800	.15	.20	.30	.50
	1971	.254	.15	.20	.30	.50
	1971	.010	—	—	Proof	3.00

5 PENCE

COPPER-NICKEL

Y#	Date	Mintage	Fine	VF	XF	Unc
21	1977	—	.15	.20	.25	.40

Y#	Date	Mintage	Fine	VF	XF	Unc
21	1979	—	—	—	—	—
	1979	.020	—	—	Proof	—

10 NEW PENCE

COPPER-NICKEL

Y#	Date	Mintage	Fine	VF	XF	Unc
14	1968	.600	.25	.35	.50	1.00
	1970	—	.25	.35	.65	1.75
	1971	.254	.25	.35	.50	1.00
	1971	.010	—	—	Proof	3.50

10 PENCE

COPPER-NICKEL

Y#	Date	Mintage	Fine	VF	XF	Unc
22	1977	—	.25	.35	.50	.75
	1979	—	—	—	—	—
	1979	.020	—	—	Proof	—

25 NEW PENCE

COPPER-NICKEL
25th Wedding Anniversary

Y#	Date	Mintage	Fine	VF	XF	Unc
16	1972	.050	1.00	1.25	2.50	8.00

28.2759 gm., .925 SILVER, .8410 oz ASW

Y#	Date	Mintage	Fine	VF	XF	Unc
16a	1972	.015	—	—	Proof	35.00

COPPER-NICKEL
Queen's Silver Jubilee

Y#	Date	Mintage	Fine	VF	XF	Unc
17	1977	—	.75	1.50	1.75	2.50

28.2759 gm., .925 SILVER, .8410 oz AGW

Y#	Date	Mintage	Fine	VF	XF	Unc
17a	1977	.025	—	—	Proof	35.00

COPPER-NICKEL
Royal Visit Commemorative

Y#	Date	Mintage	Fine	VF	XF	Unc
24	1978	—	.75	1.50	1.75	2.50

28.2759 gm., .925 SILVER, .8410 oz ASW

Y#	Date	Mintage	Fine	VF	XF	Unc
24a	1978	.025	—	—	Proof	35.00

50 NEW PENCE

COPPER-NICKEL

Y#	Date	Mintage	Fine	VF	XF	Unc
15	1969	.200	1.25	1.50	1.75	2.50
	1970	—	1.25	1.50	1.75	2.50
	1971	.254	1.25	1.50	1.75	2.50
	1971	.010	—	—	Proof	9.00

50 PENCE

COPPER-NICKEL

Y#	Date	Mintage	Fine	VF	XF	Unc
23	1979	—	—	—	—	—
	1979	.020	—	—	Proof	—

NCLT ISSUES

PROOF SETS

STANDARD METALS

KM#	Date	Mintage	Identification	Issue Price	Mkt. Val.
101	1956(6)	1,050	Y6-8 (Double Set)	—	60.00
102	1966(4)	10,000	Y6-9	—	17.50
103	1971(6)	10,000	Y10-15	16.00	17.50
104	1979(6)	20,000	Y18-23	25.00	—

GUINEA

The People's Revolutionary Republic of Guinea, situated on the Atlantic Coast of Africa between Sierra Leone and Portuguese Guinea, has an area of 95,000 sq. mi. (246,048 sq. km.) and a population of 4.5 million. Capital: Conakry. Although Guinea contains one-third of the world's reserves of bauxite and significant deposits of iron ore, gold and diamonds, the economy is still dependent on argiculture. Aluminum, bananas, copra and coffee are exported.

The coast of Guinea was known to Portuguese navigators of the 15th century but was seldom visited by European traders of the 16th-18th centuries because of its dangerous coastal waters. French penetration of the area began in the mid-19th century with the entering into of protectorate treaties with several of the coastal chiefs. After a long struggle with Guinea's native leader Samory Toure, France secured the area and until 1890 administered it as a part of Senegal. In 1895 the colony (Guinee Francais) became an autonomous part of the federation of French West Africa. The inhabitants were extended French citizenship in 1946 when the colony became an overseas territory of the French Union. Guinea became an independent republic on Oct. 2, 1958, when it declined to enter the new French Community.

MONETARY SYSTEM

100 Centimes = 1 Franc

FRANC

COPPER-NICKEL

Y#	Date	Mintage	VF	XF	Unc
4	1962	—	—	.75	1.50
	1962	—	—	Proof	50.00

5 FRANCS

ALUMINUM-BRONZE

Y#	Date	Mintage	VF	XF	Unc
1	1959	—	3.50	5.00	10.00

COPPER-NICKEL

Y#	Date	Mintage	VF	XF	Unc
5	1962	—	1.25	2.00	3.50
	1962	—	—	Proof	70.00

10 FRANCS

ALUMINUM-BRONZE

Y#	Date	Mintage	VF	XF	Unc
2	1959	—	5.00	8.00	15.00

COPPER-NICKEL

Y#	Date	Mintage	VF	XF	Unc
6	1962	—	3.00	5.00	7.00
	1962	—	—	Proof	90.00

25 FRANCS

ALUMINUM-BRONZE

Y#	Date	Mintage	VF	XF	Unc
3	1959	—	8.00	12.00	20.00

COPPER-NICKEL

Y#	Date	Mintage	VF	XF	Unc
7	1962	—	3.00	6.00	10.00
	1962	—	—	Proof	125.00

50 FRANCS

COPPER-NICKEL

Y#	Date	Mintage	VF	XF	Unc
8	1969	4.000	—	—	65.00

NOTE: Not released into circulation.

100 FRANCS

5.7800 gm., 1.000 SILVER, .1858 oz ASW
Rev: Arms over value.

KM#	Date	Mintage	XF	Unc	Proof
1	1969	7,400	—	—	15.00
	1970	—	—	—	15.00

COPPER-NICKEL

Y#	Date	Mintage	VF	XF	Unc
9	1971	2.585	—	—	110.00

NOTE: Not released into circulation.

200 FRANCS

11.5600 gm., 1.000 SILVER, .3717 oz ASW

KM#	Date	Mintage	XF	Unc	Proof
2	1969	6,500	—	—	30.00
	1970	—	—	—	20.00

Almany Samory Toure

KM#	Date	Mintage	XF	Unc	Proof
3	1969	5,000	—	—	30.00
	1970	—	—	—	20.00

250 FRANCS

14.4500 gm., 1.000 SILVER, .464 oz ASW

KM#	Date	Mintage	XF	Unc	Proof
4	1969	.024	—	—	30.00
	1970	—	—	—	25.00

Alpha Yaya Diallo

KM#	Date	Mintage	XF	Unc	Proof
5	1969	5,100	—	—	30.00

Obv: Similar to KM#4.

KM#	Date	Mintage	XF	Unc	Proof
6	1970	—	—	—	20.00

Obv: Similar to KM#5.

KM#	Date	Mintage	XF	Unc	Proof
7	1970	—	—	—	22.50

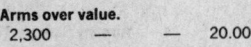

Rev: Arms over value.

KM#	Date	Mintage	XF	Unc	Proof
8	1970	2,300	—	—	20.00

Rev: Arms over value.

KM#	Date	Mintage	XF	Unc	Proof
9	1970	1,600	—	—	20.00

500 FRANCS

28.9100 gm., 1.000 SILVER, .9295 oz ASW

KM#	Date	Mintage	XF	Unc	Proof
10	1969	7,200	—	—	40.00
	1970	1,900	—	—	35.00

Rev: Arms over value.

KM#	Date	Mintage	XF	Unc	Proof
11	1969	5,200	—	—	40.00
	1970	—	—	—	35.00

Akhnaton

KM#	Date	Mintage	XF	Unc	Proof
12	1970	—	—	—	40.00

Chephren
Rev: Arms over value.

KM#	Date	Mintage	XF	Unc	Proof
13	1970	750	—	—	40.00

Cleopatra
Rev: Arms over value.

KM#	Date	Mintage	XF	Unc	Proof
14	1970	750	—	—	40.00

Nefertiti
Rev: Arms over value.

KM#	Date	Mintage	XF	Unc	Proof
15	1970	750	—	—	40.00

Rameses III
Rev: Arms over value.

KM#	Date	Mintage	XF	Unc	Proof
16	1970	750	—	—	40.00

Tutankhamen
Rev: Arms over value.

KM#	Date	Mintage	XF	Unc	Proof
17	1970	750	—	—	40.00

Tiyi
Rev: Arms over value.

KM#	Date	Mintage	XF	Unc	Proof
18	1970	750	—	—	40.00

Gamal Abdel Nasser
Rev: Arms over value.

KM#	Date	Mintage	XF	Unc	Proof
19	1970	950	—	—	40.00

1000 FRANCS

4.0000 gm., .900 GOLD, .1157 oz AGW
Obv: Similar to 200 Francs, KM#2.
Rev: Similar to 250 Francs, KM#6.

KM#	Date	Mintage	XF	Unc	Proof
20	1969	4,000	—	—	100.00

2000 FRANCS

8.0000 gm., .900 GOLD, .2315 oz AGW
Obv: Similar to 250 Francs, KM#4.
Rev: Similar to 250 Francs, KM#6.

KM#	Date	Mintage	XF	Unc	Proof
21	1969	4,000	—	—	175.00
	Obv: Similar to 250 Francs, KM#8.				
22	1970	—	—	—	175.00
	Obv: Similar to 250 Francs, KM#9.				
23	1970	—	—	—	175.00

5000 FRANCS

20.0000 gm., .900 GOLD, .5787 oz AGW

KM#	Date	Mintage	XF	Unc	Proof
24	1969	4,000	—	—	375.00
	Obv: Similar to 500 Francs, KM#10.				
25	1970	—	—	—	400.00
	Obv: Similar to 500 Francs, KM#12.				
26	1970	—	—	—	400.00
	Obv: Similar to 500 Francs, KM#13.				
27	1970	—	—	—	400.00
	Obv: Similar to 500 Francs, KM#14.				
28	1970	—	—	—	400.00
	Obv: Similar to 500 Francs, KM#15.				
29	1970	—	—	—	400.00
	Obv: Similar to 500 Francs, KM#16.				
30	1970	—	—	—	400.00
	Obv: Similar to 500 Francs, KM#17.				
31	1970	—	—	—	400.00
	Obv: Similar to 500 Francs, KM#18.				
32	1970	—	—	—	400.00
	Obv: Similar to 500 Francs, KM#19.				
33	1970	500	—	—	400.00

10,000 FRANCS

40.0000 gm., .900 GOLD, 1.1575 oz AGW
Sekou Toure

KM#	Date	Mintage	XF	Unc	Proof
34	1969	4,000	—	—	800.00

DECIMAL COINAGE

100 Cauris = 1 Syli

50 CAURIS

ALUMINUM

Y#	Date	Mintage	VF	XF	Unc
10	1971	—	1.00	2.00	7.50

SYLI

ALUMINUM

Y#	Date	Mintage	VF	XF	Unc
11	1971	—	1.00	2.00	6.00

2 SYLIS

ALUMINUM

Y#	Date	Mintage	VF	XF	Unc
12	1971	—	1.00	2.00	6.00

5 SYLIS

ALUMINUM

Y#	Date	Mintage	VF	XF	Unc
13	1971	—	1.00	2.00	6.00

500 SYLIS

28.9100 gm., .925 SILVER, .8598 oz ASW
Makeba

KM#	Date	Mintage	VF	XF	Unc
44	1977	—	—	—	35.00
	1977	—	—	Proof	45.00

Lumumba
Rev: Similar to KM#44.

KM#	Date	Mintage	VF	XF	Unc
45	1977	—	—	—	35.00
	1977	—	—	Proof	45.00

1000 SYLIS

2.9300 gm., .900 GOLD, .0847 oz AGW
Makeba

KM#	Date	Mintage	VF	XF	Unc
46	1977	—	—	—	75.00
	1977	—	—	Proof	85.00

Nkrumah

KM#	Date	Mintage	VF	XF	Unc
47	1977	—	—	—	75.00
	1977	—	—	Proof	85.00

2000 SYLIS

5.8700 gm., .900 GOLD, .1698 oz AGW

Mao Tse Tung

KM#	Date	Mintage	VF	XF	Unc
48	1977	—	—	—	125.00
	1977	—	—	Proof	150.00

Sekou Toure

KM#	Date	Mintage	VF	XF	Unc
49	1977	—	—	—	125.00
	1977	—	—	Proof	150.00

NCLT ISSUES

MINT SETS

KM#	Date	Mintage	Identification	Issue Price	Mkt. Val.
S1	1977(6)	—	KM44-49	—	475.00

PROOF SETS
STANDARD METALS

KM#	Date	Mintage	Identification	Issue Price	Mkt. Val.
101	1962(4)	—	Y4-7	—	300.00
102	1969(7)	—	KM1-5,10,11	62.50	175.00
103	1969(4)	—	KM20,21,24,34	236.50	1400.
104	1970(7)	—	KM1-3,6,7,10,11	62.50	135.00
105	1970(7)	—	KM12-18	85.00	275.00
106	1970(7)	—	KM26-32	440.00	2750.
107	1970(3)	—	KM4,8,9	29.95	65.00
108	1977(6)	—	KM44-49	—	550.00

NOTE: Coins were issued in sets made per order containing from 1 to 11 different coins.

GUINEA-BISSAU

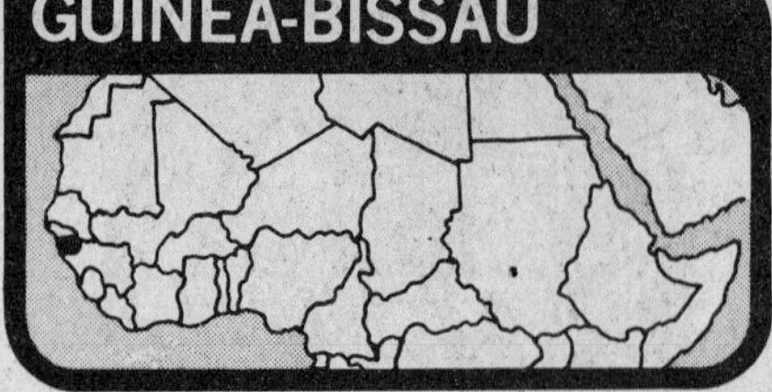

The Republic of Guinea-Bissau, a former Portuguese overseas province on the west coast of Africa between Senegal and Guinea, has an area of 14,000 sq. mi. (32,260 sq. km.) and a population of 700,000. Capital: Bissau. The country has undeveloped deposits of oil and bauxite. Peanuts, oil-palm kernels and hides are exported.

Portuguese Guinea was discovered by Portuguese navigator Nuno Tristao in 1446. Trading rights in the area were granted to Cape Verde islanders but few prominent posts were established before 1851, and they were principally coastal installations. The chief export of this colony's early period was slaves for South America, a practice that adversely affected trade with the native people and retarded subjection of the interior. Territorial disputes with France delayed final demarcation of the colony's frontiers until 1905.

The African Party for the Independence of Guinea-Bissau was founded in 1956, and several years later began a guerrilla warfare that grew in effectiveness until 1974, when the rebels controlled most of the colony. Portugal's costly overseas wars in her African territories resulted in a military coup in Portugal in April 1974, that appreciably brightened the prospects for freedom for Guinea-Bissau. In August, 1974, the Lisbon government signed an agreement granting independence to Portuguese Guinea effective Sept. 10, 1974. The new republic took the name of Guinea—Bissau.

PORTUGUESE GUINEA

MONETARY SYSTEM

100 Centavos = 1 Escudo

5 CENTAVOS

BRONZE

Y#	Date	Mintage	Fine	VF	XF	Unc
1	1933	.100	2.00	3.50	7.50	10.00

10 CENTAVOS

BRONZE

Y#	Date	Mintage	Fine	VF	XF	Unc
2	1933	.250	2.00	3.00	5.00	12.00

ALUMINUM

Y#	Date	Mintage	Fine	VF	XF	Unc
12	1973	.100	.20	.35	.60	1.00

20 CENTAVOS

BRONZE

Y#	Date	Mintage	Fine	VF	XF	Unc
3	1933	.350	1.00	2.00	3.50	5.00

Y#	Date	Mintage	Fine	VF	XF	Unc
13	1973	.100	.45	.75	1.25	2.00

50 CENTAVOS

NICKEL-BRONZE

Y#	Date	Mintage	Fine	VF	XF	Unc
4	1933	.600	1.75	3.50	8.50	20.00

BRONZE
500th Anniversary of Discovery

Y#	Date	Mintage	Fine	VF	XF	Unc
6	1946	2.000	.65	1.25	2.00	4.00

Y#	Date	Mintage	Fine	VF	XF	Unc
8	1952	10.000	.10	.25	.50	1.00

22.5mm

Y#	Date	Mintage	Fine	VF	XF	Unc
8a	1973	—	—	—	—	—

ESCUDO

NICKEL-BRONZE

Y#	Date	Mintage	Fine	VF	XF	Unc
5	1933	.800	2.50	5.00	12.50	25.00

BRONZE
500th Anniversary of Discovery

Y#	Date	Mintage	Fine	VF	XF	Unc
7	1946	2.000	.60	1.00	1.50	3.50

Y#	Date	Mintage	Fine	VF	XF	Unc
14	1973	.250	.60	1.00	1.75	3.00

2-1/2 ESCUDOS

COPPER-NICKEL

Y#	Date	Mintage	Fine	VF	XF	Unc
9	1952	6.000	.40	.70	1.00	1.75

5 ESCUDOS

COPPER-NICKEL

Y#	Date	Mintage	Fine	VF	XF	Unc
15	1973	.800	1.00	1.75	3.00	5.00

10 ESCUDOS

5.0000 gm., .720 SILVER, .1157 oz ASW

Y#	Date	Mintage	Fine	VF	XF	Unc
10	1952	1.200	BV	3.50	4.00	5.00

COPPER-NICKEL

Y#	Date	Mintage	Fine	VF	XF	Unc
10a	1973	1.700	1.75	3.00	5.00	7.50

20 ESCUDOS

10.0000 gm., .720 SILVER, .2315 oz ASW

Y#	Date	Mintage	Fine	VF	XF	Unc
11	1952	.75)	BV	7.00	8.00	10.00

NCLT ISSUES

PROVAS (Pr)

STANDARD METALS

Stamped 'PROVA' in field

Y#	Date	Mintage	Identification	Issue Price	Mkt Val.
Pr1	1933	—	5 Centavos	—	20.00
Pr2	1933	—	10 Centavos	—	20.00
Pr3	1933	—	20 Centavos	—	20.00
Pr4	1933	—	50 Centavos	—	30.00
Pr5	1933	—	1 Escudo	—	35.00
Pr6	1946	—	50 Centavos	—	20.00
Pr7	1946	—	1 Escudo	—	20.00
Pr8	1952	—	50 Centavos	—	20.00
Pr9	1952	—	2-1/2 Escudos	—	30.00
Pr10	1952	—	10 Escudos	—	45.00
Pr11	1952	—	20 Escudos	—	45.00
Pr8a	1973	—	50 Centavos	—	20.00
Pr10a	1973	—	10 Escudos	—	30.00

GUINEA-BISSAU

MONETARY SYSTEM

100 Centavos = 1 Peso

50 CENTAVOS

ALUMINUM
F.A.O. Issue

Y#	Date	Mintage	VF	XF	Unc
1	1977	6.000	—	.10	.20

PESO

ALUMINUM-BRONZE
F.A.O. Issue

Y#	Date	Mintage	VF	XF	Unc
2	1977	7.000	—	.15	.30

2-1/2 PESOS

ALUMINUM-BRONZE
F.A.O. Issue

Y#	Date	Mintage	VF	XF	Unc
3	1977	4.000	.15	.25	.50

5 PESOS

COPPER-NICKEL
F.A.O. Issue

Y#	Date	Mintage	VF	XF	Unc
4	1977	6.000	.25	.50	1.00

20 PESOS

COPPER-NICKEL
F.A.O. Issue

Y#	Date	Mintage	VF	XF	Unc
5	1977	2.500	.50	1.00	2.00

GUYANA

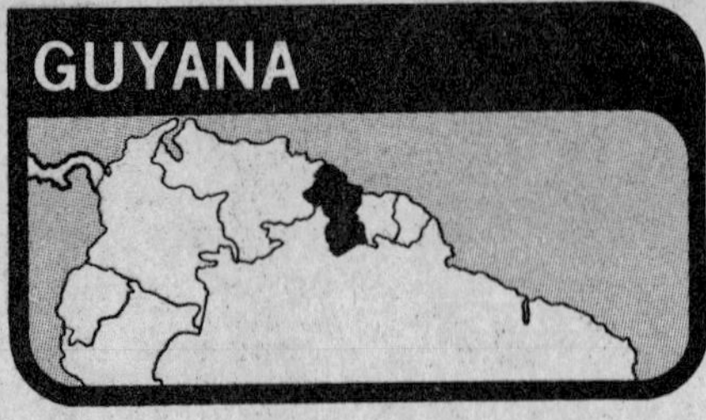

The Cooperative Republic of Guyana, an independent member of the British Commonwealth situated on the northeast coast of South America, has an area of 83,000 sq. mi. (214,970 sq. km.) and a population of 800,000. Capital: Georgetown. The economy is basically agrarian. Sugar, rice and bauxite are exported.

The original area of Guyana, which included present-day Surinam, French Guiana, and parts of Brazil and Venezuela, was sighted by Columbus in 1498. The first European settlement was made late in the 16th century by the Dutch. For the next 150 years, possession alternated between the Dutch and the British, with a short interval of French control. The British exercised de facto control after 1796, although the area, which included the Dutch colonies of Essequibo, Demerara and Berbice, wasn't ceded to them by the Dutch until 1814. From 1803 to 1831, Essequibo and Demerara were administered separately from Berbice. The three colonies were united in the British Crown Colony of British Guiana in 1831. British Guiana won internal self—government in 1952 and full independence, under the traditional name of Guyana, on May 26, 1966. Guyana became a republic on Feb. 23, 1970. It is a member of the Commonwealth of Nations. The president is the Chief of State. The prime minister is the Head of Government.

RULERS

British, until 1966

MONETARY SYSTEM

(Until 1839)

20 Stiver = 1 Guilder (Gulden)

3 Guilders = 12 Bits = 5 Shillings = 1 Dollar

(Commencing 1839)

3-1/8 Guilders = 50 Pence

ESSEQUIBO & DEMERARA

NECESSITY COINAGE

1808 EMERGENCY ISSUES

During the time of the countermarked coins of the Bank of England for George III, silver coins usually 8 Reales of Spain or Spanish Colonial were punched to form two new values. The plug or center was countermarked as 3 Bits while the holed 8 Reales was countermarked 3 Guilders.

3 BITS

.903 SILVER

c/s: E & D 3 Bt on serrated center plug from 8 Reales

C#	Date	Mintage	VG	Fine	VF	XF
1	ND(1808)	—	200.00	375.00	550.00	600.00

3 GUILDERS

.903 SILVER

c/s: E & D 3 G D in dotted oval on Mexico 8 Reales, KM#109 (C#81).

C#	Date	Mintage	VG	Fine	VF	XF
2	ND(1808)	—	1000.	1650.	2250.	—

1798-1799 GOLD CONTROL ISSUES

As a control for gold coins, usually Portuguese or Brazil 6400 Reis, in circulation were countermarked to guarantee proper weight to prevent filing and cutting. All defective coins were withdrawn in 1808.

22 GUILDERS

GOLD

c/s: ED in oval on Brazil 6400 Reis.

C#	Date	Mintage	VG	Fine	VF	XF
3a	ND(1798-99)	—	—	—	Rare	—

COLONIAL ISSUES

1/2 STIVER

COPPER

C#	Date	Mintage	Fine	VF	XF	Unc
4	1813	.215	3.50	7.50	15.00	30.00
	1813	—	—	—	Proof	425.00

GILT

C#	Date	Mintage	Fine	VF	XF	Unc
4a	1813	—	—		Proof Only	650.00

STIVER

COPPER

C#	Date	Mintage	Fine	VF	XF	Unc
5	1813	.215	5.00	10.00	20.00	40.00
	1813	—	—	—	Proof	400.00

GILT

C#	Date	Mintage	Fine	VF	XF	Unc
5a	1813	—	—	—	Proof	650.00

1/8 GUILDER

.816 SILVER

C#	Date	Mintage	Fine	VF	XF	Unc
16	1832	.098	12.50	15.00	45.00	90.00
	1832	—	—	—	Proof	250.00
	1835/3	.071	20.00	30.00	50.00	100.00
	1835	Inc. Ab.	15.00	22.50	40.00	80.00
	1835	—	—	—	Proof	250.00

1/4 GUILDER

.816 SILVER

Similar to 2 Guilders, C#9.

C#	Date	Mintage	Fine	VF	XF	Unc
6	1809	.124	12.50	20.00	35.00	70.00

Similar to 1 Guilder, C#13.

C#	Date	Mintage	Fine	VF	XF	Unc
11	1816	.043	12.50	25.00	50.00	130.00
	1816	—	—	—	Proof	300.00

C#	Date	Mintage	Fine	VF	XF	Unc
17	1832	.039	15.00	25.00	40.00	80.00
	1833	.097	12.50	20.00	35.00	70.00
	1833	—	—	—	Proof	300.00
	1835/3	.073	15.00	25.00	40.00	80.00
	1835	Inc. Ab.	12.50	20.00	35.00	70.00
	1835	—	—	—	Proof	300.00

1/2 GUILDER

.816 SILVER

Similar to 2 Guilders, C#9.

C#	Date	Mintage	Fine	VF	XF	Unc
7	1809	.064	20.00	40.00	80.00	160.00

C#	Date	Mintage	Fine	VF	XF	Unc
12	1816	.034	20.00	40.00	75.00	150.00
	1816	—	—	—	Proof	350.00

C#	Date	Mintage	Fine	VF	XF	Unc
18	1832	.087	20.00	30.00	75.00	150.00
	1832	—	—	—	Proof	350.00
	1835/3	.036	25.00	35.00	65.00	130.00
	1835	Inc. Ab.	25.00	35.00	65.00	130.00
	1835	—	—	—	Proof	350.00

GUILDER

.816 SILVER

C#	Date	Mintage	Fine	VF	XF	Unc
8	1809	.032	25.00	50.00	90.00	300.00

C#	Date	Mintage	Fine	VF	XF	Unc
13	1816	.034	25.00	40.00	155.00	—
	1816	—	—	—	Proof	400.00

C#	Date	Mintage	Fine	VF	XF	Unc
19	1832	.047	20.00	37.50	70.00	160.00
	1832	—	—	—	Proof	400.00
	1835	.022	25.00	45.00	80.00	325.00
	1835	—	—	—	Proof	400.00

2 GUILDERS

.816 SILVER

C#	Date	Mintage	Fine	VF	XF	Unc
9	1809	.016	150.00	225.00	425.00	1700.

C#	Date	Mintage	Fine	VF	XF	Unc
14	1816	.015	125.00	150.00	170.00	350.00
	1816	—	—	—	Proof	800.00

C#	Date	Mintage	Fine	VF	XF	Unc
20	1832	.014	150.00	225.00	200.00	400.00
	1832	—	—	—	Proof	1600.

3 GUILDERS

.816 SILVER

C#	Date	Mintage	Fine	VF	XF	Unc
10	1809	.021	225.00	300.00	400.00	800.00

C#	Date	Mintage	Fine	VF	XF	Unc
15	1816	.010	275.00	425.00	500.00	1000.
	1816	—	—	—	Proof	2000.

Rev: Similar to 3 Guilders C#15.

C#	Date	Mintage	Fine	VF	XF	Unc
21	1832	7,156	325.00	425.00	550.00	1100.
	1832	—	—	—	Proof	2400.

BRITISH GUIANA

1/8 GUILDER

.816 SILVER

C#	Date	Mintage	Fine	VF	XF	Unc
22	1836	.180	3.50	7.50	12.50	37.50
	1836	—	—	—	Proof	170.00

1/4 GUILDER

.816 SILVER
Similar to 1 Guilder, C#25.

C#	Date	Mintage	Fine	VF	XF	Unc
23	1836	.216	5.00	10.00	15.00	45.00
	1836	—	—	—	Proof	250.00

1/2 GUILDER

.816 SILVER
Similar to 1 Guilder, C#25.

C#	Date	Mintage	Fine	VF	XF	Unc
24	1836	.118	9.00	17.50	30.00	100.00
	1836	—	—	—	Proof	225.00

GUILDER

.816 SILVER

C#	Date	Mintage	Fine	VF	XF	Unc
25	1836	.057	10.00	20.00	37.50	125.00
	1836 plain edge		—	—	Proof	350.00
	1836 reeded edge		—	—	Proof	750.00

MONETARY REFORM

4 PENCE

1.8851 gm., .925 SILVER, .0560 oz ASW

From 1836 through 1888 regular issue 4 Pence (Groats) of Great Britain were circulated in British Guiana and the West Indies. These are listed under Great Britain.

Colonial Issues

Rev. leg: BRITISH GUIANA and WEST INDIES

Y#	Date	Mintage	Fine	VF	XF	Unc
1	1891	.336	1.75	3.50	6.00	20.00
	1894	.120	2.00	4.00	7.50	22.50
	1900	.045	4.00	8.50	12.50	30.00
	1901	.060	4.00	8.50	12.50	30.00

Y#	Date	Mintage	Fine	VF	XF	Unc
2	1903	.060	5.00	10.00	17.50	40.00
	1908	.030	5.00	10.00	20.00	50.00
	1909	.036	5.00	10.00	20.00	50.00
	1910	.066	3.50	7.50	17.50	40.00

Y#	Date	Mintage	Fine	VF	XF	Unc
3	1911	.030	5.00	10.00	20.00	50.00
	1913	.030	5.00	10.00	20.00	50.00
	1916	.030	5.00	10.00	20.00	50.00

Rev. leg: BRITISH GUIANA

Y#	Date	Mintage	Fine	VF	XF	Unc
4	1917	.072	2.50	5.00	10.00	25.00
	1918	.210	1.75	3.50	8.50	22.50
	1921	.090	2.50	5.00	12.50	32.50
	1923	.012	6.50	12.50	25.00	60.00
	1925	.030	3.50	7.50	17.50	40.00
	1926	.030	3.50	7.50	17.50	40.00
	1931	.015	5.00	10.00	25.00	60.00
	1931	—	—	—	Proof	150.00
	1935	.036	1.75	2.50	8.50	35.00
	1936	.063	1.75	2.50	5.00	15.00

Y#	Date	Mintage	Fine	VF	XF	Unc
5	1938	.030	1.75	2.25	3.50	8.50
	1938	—	—	—	Proof	100.00
	1939	.048	1.75	2.25	3.50	7.50
	1940	.090	BV	1.75	2.50	6.00
	1941	.120	BV	1.75	2.50	6.00
	1942	.180	BV	1.75	2.50	5.00
	1943	.240	BV	1.75	2.25	4.00

1.8851 gm., .500 SILVER, .0303 oz ASW

Y#	Date	Mintage	Fine	VF	XF	Unc
5a	1944	.090	1.00	1.50	2.25	4.50
	1945	.120	1.00	1.25	1.75	3.50

GUYANA

MONETARY SYSTEM

100 Cents = 1 Dollar

MINTMARKS

FM - Franklin Mint, U.S.A.*

NOTE: During 1975-77 the Franklin Mint produced coinage in up to 3 different qualities. Qualities of issue are designated in ( ) after each date and are defined as follows:

(M) MATTE - Normal circulation strike or a dull finish produced by sandblasting special uncirculated (polish finish) or proof quality dies.

(U) SPECIAL UNCIRCULATED - Polished or proof-like in appearance without any frosted features.

(P) PROOF - The highest quality obtainable having mirror-like fields and frosted features.

CENT

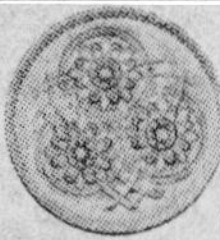

NICKEL-BRASS

Y#	Date	Mintage	VF	XF	Unc
1	1967	6.000	—	.10	.15
	1967	5,100	—	Proof	2.00
	1969	4.000	—	.10	.25
	1970	6.000	—	.10	.25
	1971	4.000	—	.10	.25
	1972	4.000	—	.10	.25
	1973	4.000	—	.10	.25
	1974	11.000	—	.10	.20
	1975	—	—	.10	.25
	1976	—	—	.10	.25
	1977	16.000	—	—	—

BRONZE

Y#	Date	Mintage	VF	XF	Unc
7	1976FM(M)	.015	—	.15	.30
	1976FM(U)	50 pcs.	—	—	—
	1976FM(P)	.028	—	Proof	1.00
	1977FM(U)	.015	—	.15	.30
	1977FM(P)	7,215	—	Proof	1.00
7	1978FM(U)	.015	—	—	.30
	1978FM(P)	5,044	—	Proof	1.00
	1979FM(U)	.015	—	—	—
	1979FM(P)	3,547	—	Proof	1.00
	1980FM(U)	—	—	—	—
	1980FM(P)	—	—	Proof	—

5 CENTS

NICKEL-BRASS

Y#	Date	Mintage	VF	XF	Unc
2	1967	4.600	—	.15	.25
	1967	5,100	—	Proof	2.25
	1972	1.200	—	.15	.30
	1974	3.000	—	.15	.30
	1975	—	—	.15	.30
	1976	—	Reported, not confirmed		
	1977	1.500	—	—	—

BRASS

Y#	Date	Mintage	VF	XF	Unc
8	1976FM(M)	.015	.10	.20	.40
	1976FM(U)	50 pcs.	—	—	—
	1976FM(P)	.028	—	Proof	1.50
	1977FM(U)	.015	.10	.20	.40
	1977FM(P)	7,215	—	Proof	1.25
	1978FM(U)	.015	—	—	.40
	1978FM(P)	5,044	—	Proof	1.50
	1979FM(U)	.015	—	—	—
	1979FM(P)	3,547	—	Proof	1.50
	1980FM(U)	—	—	—	—
	1980FM(P)	—	—	Proof	—

10 CENTS

COPPER-NICKEL

Y#	Date	Mintage	VF	XF	Unc
3	1967	4.000	.10	.20	.40
	1967	5,100	—	Proof	2.50
	1973	1.500	.10	.20	.35
	1974	1.700	—	—	—
	1976	—	—	—	—
	1977	—	—	—	—

Y#	Date	Mintage	VF	XF	Unc
9	1976FM(M)	.010	.15	.30	.60
	1976FM(U)	50 pcs.	—	—	—
	1976FM(P)	.028	—	Proof	1.50
	1977	1.500	.15	.30	.60
	1977FM(U)	.010	.15	.30	.60
	1977FM(P)	7,215	—	Proof	1.50
	1978FM(U)	.010	.15	.30	.60
	1978FM(P)	5,044	—	Proof	2.00
	1979FM(U)	.010	—	—	—
	1979FM(P)	3,547	—	Proof	2.00
	1980FM(U)	—	—	—	—
	1980FM(P)	—	—	Proof	—

25 CENTS

COPPER-NICKEL

Y#	Date	Mintage	VF	XF	Unc
4	1967	3.500	.20	.35	.65
4	1967	5,100	—	Proof	3.00
	1972	1.000	.20	.35	.65
	1974	1.000	.20	.35	.65
	1975	—	.20	.35	.65
	1976	—	—	—	—
	1977	—	—	—	—

Y#	Date	Mintage	VF	XF	Unc
10	1976FM(M)	4,000	.50	1.00	2.00
	1976FM(U)	50 pcs.	—	—	—
	1976FM(P)	.028	—	Proof	2.50
	1977	2.000	.50	1.00	2.00
	1977FM(U)	4,000	1.00	2.00	4.00
	1977FM(P)	7,215	—	Proof	2.50
	1978FM(U)	4,000	1.00	2.00	4.00
	1978FM(P)	5,044	—	Proof	3.00
	1979FM(U)	4,000	—	—	—
	1979FM(P)	3,547	—	Proof	3.00
	1980FM(U)	—	—	—	—
	1980FM(P)	—	—	Proof	—

50 CENTS

COPPER-NICKEL

Y#	Date	Mintage	VF	XF	Unc
5	1967	1.000	.65	.80	1.25
	1967	5,100	—	Proof	3.50

Y#	Date	Mintage	VF	XF	Unc
11	1976FM(M)	2,000	1.25	2.50	5.00
	1976FM(U)	50 pcs.	—	—	—
	1976FM(P)	.028	—	Proof	2.50
	1977FM(U)	2,000	1.25	2.50	5.00
	1977FM(P)	7,215	—	Proof	4.25
	1978FM(U)	2,000	1.25	2.50	5.00
	1978FM(P)	5,044	—	Proof	3.50
	1979FM(U)	2,000	—	—	—
	1979FM(P)	3,547	—	Proof	3.50
	1980FM(U)	—	—	—	—
	1980FM(P)	—	—	Proof	—

DOLLAR

COPPER-NICKEL

F.A.O. Issue

Y#	Date	Mintage	VF	XF	Unc
6	1970	.500	2.00	2.75	4.00
	1970	5,000	—	Proof	8.50

Y#	Date	Mintage	VF	XF	Unc
12	1976FM(M)	600 pcs.	7.50	12.50	15.00
	1976FM(U)	50 pcs.	—	—	—
	1976FM(P)	.028	—	Proof	5.00
	1977FM(U)	500 pcs.	9.00	15.00	20.00
	1977FM(P)	7,215	—	Proof	6.00
	1978FM(U)	500 pcs.	9.00	15.00	20.00
	1978FM(P)	5,044	—	Proof	10.00
	1979FM(U)	500 pcs.	—	—	—
	1979FM(P)	3,547	—	Proof	10.00
	1980FM(U)	—	—	—	—
	1980FM(P)	—	—	Proof	—

5 DOLLARS

COPPER-NICKEL

Y#	Date	Mintage	VF	XF	Unc
13	1976FM(M)	400 pcs.	9.00	17.50	35.00
	1976FM(U)	150 pcs.	50.00	80.00	150.00
	1977FM(U)	100 pcs.	55.00	90.00	150.00
	1978FM(U)	100 pcs.	55.00	90.00	150.00
	1979FM(U)	100 pcs.	—	—	—
	1980FM(U)	—	—	—	—

37.7600 gm., .500 SILVER, .6070 oz ASW

Y#	Date	Mintage	VF	XF	Unc
13a	1976FM(P)	.018	—	Proof	18.50
	1977FM(P)	5,685	—	Proof	20.00
	1978FM(P)	3,825	—	Proof	22.00
	1979FM(P)	2,665	—	Proof	22.00
	1980FM(P)	—	—	—	—

10 DOLLARS

COPPER-NICKEL
Obv: Similar to 5 Dollars Y#13

Y#	Date	Mintage	VF	XF	Unc
14	1976FM(M)	300 pcs.	10.00	20.00	40.00
	1976FM(U)	300 pcs.	60.00	100.00	175.00
	1977FM(U)	100 pcs.	60.00	100.00	175.00
	1978FM(U)	100 pcs.	60.00	100.00	175.00
	1979FM(U)	100 pcs.	—	—	—

43.4000 gm., .925 SILVER, 1.2908 oz ASW

Y#	Date	Mintage	VF	XF	Unc
14a	1976FM(P)	.018	—	Proof	40.00
	1977FM(P)	5,685	—	Proof	42.50
	1978FM(P)	3,825	—	Proof	45.00
	1979FM(P)	2,665	—	Proof	—
	1980FM(P)	—	—	Proof	—

50 DOLLARS

48.3000 gm., .925 SILVER, 1.4365 oz ASW
Enmore Martyrs

Y#	Date	Mintage	VF	XF	Unc
15	1976FM(U)	100 pcs.	—	125.00	200.00
	1976FM(P)	1,001	—	Proof	125.00

100 DOLLARS

5.7400 gm., .500 GOLD, .0923 oz AGW

Y#	Date	Mintage	VF	XF	Unc
16	1976FM(U)	100 pcs.	—	175.00	300.00
	1976FM(P)	.021	—	Proof	75.00

5.5800 gm., .500 GOLD, .0897 oz AGW

Y#	Date	Mintage	VF	XF	Unc
17	1977FM(U)	100 pcs.	—	175.00	300.00
	1977FM(P)	7,635	—	Proof	70.00

NCLT ISSUES

PROOF SETS

STANDARD METALS

KM#	Date	Mintage	Identification	Issue Price	Mkt. Val.
101	1967(5)	5,100	Y1-5	10.50	15.00
102	1976FM(8)	17,536	Y7-12,13A,14A	45.00	65.00
103	1976FM(6)	10,302	Y7-12	15.00	22.50
104	1977FM(8)	5,685	Y7-12,13a,14a	45.00	75.00
105	1977FM(6)	1,530	Y7-12	15.00	35.00
106	1978FM(8)	3,825	Y7-12,13a,14a	47.50	80.00
107	1978FM(6)	1,219	Y7-12	16.00	40.00
108	1979FM(8)	2,665	Y7-12,13a,14a	47.50	75.00
109	1979FM(6)	882	Y7-12	16.00	—
110	1980FM(8)	—	Y7-12,13a,14a	100.00	—
111	1980FM(6)	—	Y7-12	19.00	—

HAITI

The Republic of Haiti, which occupies the western one-third of the island of Hispaniola in the Caribbean Sea between Puerto Rico and Cuba, has an area of 10,714 sq. mi. (27,749 sq. km.) and a population of 5 million. Capital: Port-au-Prince. The economy is based on agriculture; light manufacturing and tourism are becoming increasingly important. Coffee, bauxite, sugar, essential oils and handicrafts are exported.

Columbus discovered Hispaniola in 1492. Spain colonized the island, making Santo Domingo the base for exploration of the Western Hemisphere. The area that is now Haiti was ceded to France by Spain in 1697. Slaves brought over from Africa to work the coffee and sugar cane plantations made it one of the richest colonies of the French Empire. The Republic of Haiti was established in 1804 by the slave revolt of the 1790's, making it the oldest Negro Republic in the world and the second oldest republic (after the United States) in the Western Hemisphere.

Haiti utilizes French legends on its coins although the language is spoken by only about 10 percent of the people.

Two dating systems are observed on the 19th century coins of Haiti. One is Christian, the other is revolutionary and dates from 1803 when the French were ousted from power by a native revolt. Thus, a date of AN30 is the equivalent of 1833 A.D. Some coins carry both date forms, and in the date listing which follows only those coins which are exclusively dated according to the revolutionary period are enumerated by AN dates in the date column.

MINTMARKS

A - Paris
(a) - Paris, privy marks only

MONETARY SYSTEM

12 Deniers = 1 Sol
20 Sols = 1 Livre

7 SOLS, 6 DENIERS

SILVER

C#	Date	Mintage	Good	VG	Fine
15	1807	—	50.00	80.00	125.00
	1808	—	30.00	50.00	75.00
	1809	—	30.00	50.00	75.00

15 SOLS

SILVER

C#	Date	Mintage	Good	VG	Fine
17	1807	—	30.00	50.00	75.00
	1808	—	20.00	35.00	75.00
	1809	—	50.00	80.00	125.00

DECIMAL COINAGE

100 Centimes = 1 Gourde

UNE (1) CENTIME

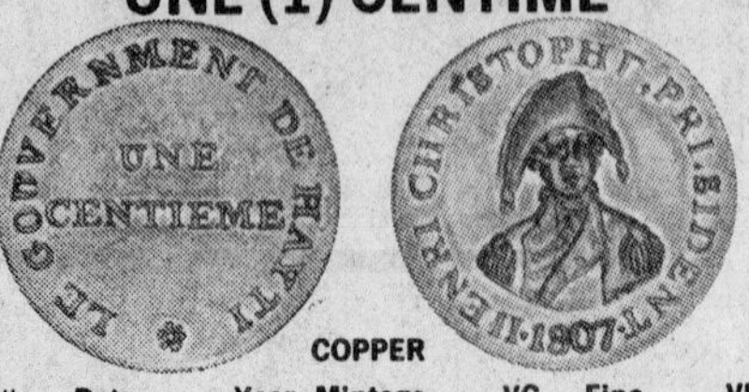

COPPER

C#	Date	Year	Mintage	VG	Fine	VF
11	1807	—	—	—	—	275.00
	1807	—	—	—	Proof	750.00

C#	Date	Year	Mintage	VG	Fine	VF
31	1828	AN 25	—	10.00	25.00	40.00
	1829	AN 26	—	3.50	6.50	15.00
	1830	AN 27	—	3.50	5.00	10.00
	1830	AN 28	—	17.50	30.00	50.00
	1831	AN 28	—	2.50	3.50	5.00
	1832	AN 28	—	20.00	30.00	70.00
	1832	AN 29	—	1.50	2.00	4.00
	1834	AN 31	—	1.75	2.50	4.00
	1840	AN 37	—	1.75	2.75	4.00
	1841	AN 38	—	2.00	5.00	6.00
	1842	AN 39	—	1.50	2.00	4.00

C#	Date	Year	Mintage	VG	Fine	VF
41	1846	AN 43	—	1.50	2.25	4.00

Cruder workmanship

C#	Date	Year	Mintage	VG	Fine	VF
51	1846	AN 43	—	1.00	2.50	4.00
66	1850	AN 47	—	50.00	80.00	120.00

Rev: Arms substituted for fasces.

C#	Date	Mintage	VG	Fine	VF
69	1850	—	3.00	5.00	8.00

BRONZE

Y#	Date	Mintage	VF	XF	Unc
1	1881	.830	3.50	5.50	8.00
	1881	—	—	Proof	200.00

Y#	Date	Mintage	VF	XF	Unc
3	1886A	2.500	3.00	5.00	10.00
	1894A	2.070	3.00	5.00	10.00
	1895A	5.420	3.00	5.00	10.00

DEUX (2) CENTIMES

COPPER

C#	Date	Year	Mintage	VG	Fine	VF
32	1828	AN 25	—	15.00	25.00	40.00
	1828	AN 26	—	12.00	20.00	35.00
	1829	AN 26	—	2.00	3.00	5.00
	1830	AN 26	—	20.00	40.00	80.00
	1830	AN 27	—	3.00	4.00	6.00
	1831	AN 28	—	2.00	3.00	5.00
	1840	AN 37	—	2.00	3.00	4.00
	1840(4 is backwards)		—	4.00	6.00	8.00
	1841	AN 38	—	3.00	4.00	6.00
	1842	AN 39	—	3.00	4.00	6.00

C#	Date	Year	Mintage	VG	Fine	VF
42	1846	AN 43	—	3.00	4.00	5.00
	1846	AN 43/2	—	3.25	4.75	6.00

Cruder workmanship, star after legends.

C#	Date	Year	Mintage	VG	Fine	VF
52	1846	AN 43	—	3.00	4.00	5.00

NOTE: Varieties exist without accents on E's, date as AN.43.

C#	Date	Year	Mintage	VG	Fine	VF
61	1849	AN 46	—	30.00	45.00	80.00
67	1850	AN 47	—	45.00	60.00	90.00

Rev: Arms substituted for fasces.

C#	Date	Mintage	VG	Fine	VF
70	1850	—	3.00	5.00	10.00

Y#	Date	Mintage	VF	XF	Unc
2	1881	.830	3.50	5.00	8.00
2	1881	—	—	Proof	150.00

Y#	Date	Mintage	VF	XF	Unc
4	1886A	1.250	2.00	4.00	10.00
	1894A	3.750	2.00	4.00	12.00

CINQ (5) CENTIMES

COPPER

Y#	Date	Mintage	VF	XF	Unc
A1	1863	—	2.00	5.00	9.00
	1863	—	—	Proof	75.00

COPPER-NICKEL

Y#	Date	Mintage	VF	XF	Unc
A5	1889	.120	25.00	40.00	75.00

Y#	Date	Mintage	VF	XF	Unc
14	1904	—	4.00	8.00	25.00

Y#	Date	Mintage	VF	XF	Unc
10	1904(a)	2.000	.50	3.00	8.00
	1904(a)	—	—	Proof	90.00
	1905(a)	20.000	.50	2.50	7.50
	1906(a)	10.000	Reported, Not Confirmed		

Y#	Date	Mintage	VF	XF	Unc
15	1949	10.000	.20	.40	1.25

NICKEL-SILVER

Y#	Date	Mintage	VF	XF	Unc
17	1953	3.000	.10	.15	.50

COPPER-NICKEL

Y#	Date	Mintage	VF	XF	Unc
20	1958	15.000	—	—	.10
	1970	—	—	—	.10

F.A.O. Issue

Y#	Date	Mintage	VF	XF	Unc
23	1975	16.000	—	—	.15

6 CENTIMES

.835 SILVER
Obv: Arms type.

C#	Date	Year	Mintage	VG	Fine	VF
21	1813	AN 10	—	80.00	120.00	200.00
		Rev: Petion bust.				
24	1818	AN 15	—	100.00	150.00	250.00
		Rev: Boyer bust.				
33	1818	AN 15	—	10.00	15.00	25.00

COPPER

C#	Date	Year	Mintage	Fine	VF	XF
53	1846	AN 43	—	5.00	7.50	10.00

C#	Date	Year	Mintage	Fine	VF	XF
62	1849	AN 46	—	27.50	40.00	50.00
68	1850	AN 47	—	60.00	100.00	200.00

6-1/4 CENTIMES

COPPER

C#	Date	Year	Mintage	Fine	VF	XF
43	1846	AN 43	—	7.00	10.00	12.00

C#	Date	Mintage	Fine	VF	XF
71	1850	—	5.00	6.00	8.00

DIX (10) CENTIMES

BRONZE

Y#	Date	Mintage	VF	XF	Unc
B1	1863	—	2.25	5.00	20.00
	1863	—	—	Proof	80.00

2.5000 gm., .835 SILVER, .0671oz ASW

Y#	Date	Mintage	VF	XF	Unc
6	1881(a)	1.500	2.00	3.00	18.00
	1881(a)	—	—	Proof	150.00
	1882(a)	1.800	2.00	3.00	18.00
	1882(a)	—	—	Proof	150.00
	1886(a)	1.500	3.50	5.00	25.00
	1886(a)	—	—	Proof	175.00
	1887(a)	1.050	2.75	3.75	18.00
	1887(a)	—	—	Proof	150.00
	1890(a)	1.000	3.50	5.00	20.00
	1890(a)	—	—	Proof	175.00
	1894(a)	3.720	2.00	3.00	18.00
	1894(a)	—	—	Proof	150.00

COPPER-NICKEL

Y#	Date	Mintage	VF	XF	Unc
11	1906	10.000	.75	3.00	10.00
	1907	.200	Reported, Not Confirmed		

Y#	Date	Mintage	VF	XF	Unc
16	1949	5.000	.25	.50	1.25

NICKEL-SILVER

Y#	Date	Mintage	VF	XF	Unc
18	1953	1.500	.10	.20	.40

COPPER-NICKEL

Y#	Date	Mintage	VF	XF	Unc
21	1958	7.500	.10	.15	.30
	1970	—	—	—	.20

F.A.O. Issue

Y#	Date	Mintage	VF	XF	Unc
24	1975	12.000	—	—	.25

12 CENTIMES

SILVER
Obv: Arms type.

C#	Date	Year	Mintage	Good	VG	Fine
22	(1813)	AN 10	—	8.00	13.50	25.00
	(1814)	AN XI	—	4.00	10.00	18.00
	(1815)	AN 12	—	10.00	15.00	30.00

C#	Date	Year	Mintage	Good	VG	Fine
		Rev: Petion type, large head.				
25	(1817)	AN 14	—	7.00	12.50	18.00

C#	Date	Year	Mintage	Good	VG	Fine
		Rev: Petion type, small head.				
25a	(1817)	AN 14	—	7.00	12.50	18.00
		Rev: Boyer type.				
34	(1827)	AN 24	—	15.00	21.00	29.00
	(1828)	AN 25	—	20.00	35.00	75.00
	(1829)	AN 26	—	25.00	40.00	100.00

VINGT (20) CENTIMES

BRONZE

Y#	Date	Mintage	VF	XF	Unc
C1	1863	—	2.75	5.00	25.00
	1863	—	—	Proof	80.00

5.000 gm., .835 SILVER, .1342 oz ASW

Y#	Date	Mintage	VF	XF	Unc
7	1881(a)	1.250	4.25	6.50	20.00
	1881(a)	—	—	Proof	175.00
	1882(a)	1.250	4.25	6.50	20.00
	1882(a)	—	—	Proof	175.00
	1887(a)	.350	5.00	7.50	25.00
	1887(a)	—	—	Proof	200.00
	1890(a)	.070	7.50	15.00	40.00
	1890(a)	—	—	Proof	200.00
	1894(a)	1.850	4.25	6.50	20.00
	1894(a)	—	—	Proof	175.00
	1895(a)	1.270	4.25	6.50	20.00
	1895(a)	—	—	Proof	175.00

COPPER-NICKEL

Y#	Date	Mintage	VF	XF	Unc
12	1907	5.000	1.25	4.00	12.50
	1908	5.000	Reported, Not Confirmed		

NICKEL-SILVER

Y#	Date	Mintage	VF	XF	Unc
19	1956	2.500	.35	.50	1.75

Y#	Date	Mintage	VF	XF	Unc
22	1970	—	—	—	.50

COPPER-NICKEL
F.A.O. Issue

Y#	Date	Mintage	VF	XF	Unc
25	1972	1.500	—	—	1.00
	1975	4.000	—	—	.50

25 CENTIMES

SILVER
Arms type
Rev: Solid spear shafts above cannons.

C#	Date	Year	Mintage	Good	VG	Fine
23.1	(1813)	AN 10	—	8.00	12.00	16.00

Rev: Dotted spear shafts above cannons.

C#	Date	Year	Mintage	Good	VG	Fine
23.2	(1814)	AN XI	—	7.00	10.00	15.00
	(1815)	AN 12	—	5.00	7.00	10.00
	(1816)	AN 13	—	6.00	9.00	12.50

Rev: Petion type.

C#	Date	Year	Mintage	Good	VG	Fine
26	(1817)	AN 14	—	6.00	8.00	10.00
	(1817)	AN 14P	—	16.00	28.00	60.00

Rev: Boyer type.

C#	Date	Year	Mintage	Good	VG	Fine
35	(1818)	AN 15	—	10.00	15.00	25.00
	(1827)	AN 24	—	8.00	12.00	15.00
	(1828)	AN 25	—	5.00	8.00	10.00
	(1829)	AN 26	—	8.00	15.00	25.00
	(1831)	AN 28	—	6.00	12.00	15.00
	(1833)	AN 30	—	12.50	17.50	30.00
	(1834)	AN 31	—	10.00	15.00	25.00

50 CENTIMES

SILVER

C#	Date	Year	Mintage	Good	VG	Fine
36	(1827)	AN 24	—	45.00	70.00	100.00
	(1828)	AN 25	—	12.00	13.50	17.50
	(1829)	AN 26	—	12.00	15.00	20.00
	(1830)	AN 27	—	12.00	15.00	25.00
	(1831)	AN 28	—	12.00	13.50	17.50
	(1832)	AN 29	—	12.00	13.50	17.50
	(1833)	AN 30	—	15.00	25.00	50.00

12.5000 gm., .835 SILVER, .3356 oz ASW

Y#	Date	Mintage	VF	XF	Unc
8	1882(a)	.440	12.00	15.00	35.00
	1882(a)	—	—	Proof	250.00
	1883(a)	.400	12.00	15.00	35.00
	1883(a)	—	—	Proof	200.00
	1887(a)	.250	12.00	17.50	50.00
	1887(a)	—	—	Proof	200.00
	1890(a)	.100	12.00	17.50	50.00
	1890(a)	—	—	Proof	200.00
	1895(a)	.900	12.00	15.00	35.00
	1895(a)	—	—	Proof	200.00

COPPER-NICKEL

Y#	Date	Mintage	VF	XF	Unc
13	1907	2.000	1.50	5.00	15.00
	1908	.800	1.75	7.50	18.00

F.A.O. Issue

Y#	Date	Mintage	VF	XF	Unc
26	1972	.600	—	—	1.25
	1975	1.200	—	—	.80
	1979	—	—	—	—

100 CENTIMES

SILVER

C#	Date	Year	Mintage	VG	Fine	VF
37	(1829)	AN 26	—	17.50	20.00	30.00
	(1830)	AN 27	—	20.00	22.50	30.00
	(1833)	AN 30	—	25.00	35.00	50.00

GOURDE

25.0000 gm., .900 SILVER, .7234 oz ASW

Y#	Date	Mintage	VF	XF	Unc
9	1881(a)	.200	35.00	60.00	125.00
	1881(a)	—	—	Proof	1300.
	1882(a)	.500	25.00	50.00	100.00
	1882(a)	—	—	Proof	1250.
	1887(a)	.200	25.00	50.00	125.00

Y#	Date	Mintage	VF	XF	Unc
	1887(a)	—	—	Proof	1250.
	1895(a)	.100	35.00	75.00	150.00
	1895(a)	—	—	Proof	1250.

BRONZE
Insurrection Issue
Blank reverse

5	1889	100.00	125.00	250.00	350.00

5 GOURDES

23.5200 gm., 1.000 SILVER, .7562 oz ASW

KM#	Date	Mintage	VF	XF	Unc
1	1967	4,650	—	Proof	30.00
	1968	5,750	—	Proof	30.00
	1969	1,175	—	Proof	32.50
	1970	2,060	—	Proof	30.00

Rev: Similar to KM#1.

2	1971	8,250	—	Proof	30.00

10 GOURDES

47.0500 gm., 1.000 SILVER 1.5128 oz ASW

3	1967	6,750	—	Proof	60.00
	1968	5,725	—	Proof	60.00
	1969	1,100	—	Proof	65.00
	1970	1,500	—	Proof	65.00

Rev: Similar to KM#3.

KM#	Date	Mintage	VF	XF	Unc
4	1971	—	—	Proof	65.00

Rev: Similar to KM#3.

5	1971	—	—	Proof	65.00

Rev: Similar to KM#3.

6	1971	—	—	Proof	65.00

Rev: Similar to KM#3.

7	1971	—	—	Proof	65.00

Rev: Similar to KM#3.

8	1971	—	—	Proof	65.00

Rev: Similar to KM#3.

KM#	Date	Mintage	VF	XF	Unc
9	1971	—	—	Proof	65.00

Rev: Similar to KM#3.

10	1971	—	—	Proof	65.00

Rev: Similar to KM#3.

11	1971	—	—	Proof	65.00

Rev: Similar to KM#3.

12	1971	—	—	Proof	65.00

20 GOURDES

3.9500 gm., .900 GOLD, .1143 oz AGW

13	1967	6,525	—	Proof	75.00
	1968	—	—	Proof	75.00
	1969	—	—	Proof	75.00
	1970	—	—	Proof	75.00

25 GOURDES

117.6000 gm., 1.000 SILVER, 3.7813 oz ASW
Actual size 60mm.

KM#	Date	Mintage	VF	XF	Unc
14	1967	4,650	—	Proof	150.00
	1968	5,810	—	Proof	150.00
	1969	1,115	—	Proof	150.00
	1970	1,000	—	Proof	165.00

Rev: Similar to KM#14. Actual size 60mm.

15	1971	—	—	—	170.00

8.3800 gm., SILVER, .2492 oz ASW
Rev: Similar to KM#14.

16	1973	6,500	—	Proof	12.00

Rev: Similar to KM#14.

KM#	Date	Mintage	VF	XF	Unc
17	1973	Inc. Ab.	—	Proof	12.00

American Bicentennial Commemorative
Obv: BICENTENAIRE DES U.S.A. above battle scene.
Rev: Similar to KM#14

19	1974	—	—	125.00	150.00

Obv: REPUBLIC D'HAITI above battle scene.

19a	1976	.010	—	Proof	12.00

International Women's Year
Rev: Similar to KM#14.

20	1975	—	—	Proof	12.00

Holy Year Commemorative

21	1975	—	—	Proof	15.00

30 GOURDES

9.1100 gm., .585 GOLD,.1713 oz AGW

22	1969	—	—	Proof	115.00
	1970	—	—	Proof	115.00

40 GOURDES

12.1500 gm., .585 GOLD, .2285 oz AGW

KM#	Date	Mintage	VF	XF	Unc
23	1969	—	—	Proof	150.00
	1970	—	—	Proof	150.00

50 GOURDES

9.8700 gm., .900 GOLD, .2856 oz AGW

24	1967	6,475	—	Proof	200.00
	1968	—	—	Proof	200.00
	1969	—	—	Proof	200.00
	1970	—	—	Proof	200.00

Rev: Similar to KM#24.

25	1971	1,250	—	Proof	200.00

16.7500 gm., .925 SILVER, .4981 oz ASW

26	1973	6,705	—	Proof	22.50

Rev: Similar to KM#26.

27	1973	Inc. Ab.	—	Proof	22.50

1976 Olympiad Commemorative
Rev: Similar to KM#26.

KM#	Date	Mintage	VF	XF	Unc
28	1974	.013	—	—	20.00
	1974	2,238	—	Proof	20.00
	1976	8,000	—	Proof	20.00

Rev: Smaller 4 in date.

KM#	Date	Mintage	VF	XF	Unc
28a	1974	—	—	Proof	17.50

Holy Year Commemorative
Rev: Similar to KM#26.

KM#	Date	Mintage	VF	XF	Unc
29	1974	—	—	Proof	17.50
	1975	—	—	Proof	17.50
	1976	6,000	—	Proof	17.50

Rev: Similar to KM#26.

KM#	Date	Mintage	VF	XF	Unc
30	1977	—	—	—	20.00
	1977	—	—	Proof	25.00

Human Rights
Rev: Similar to KM#26.

KM#	Date	Mintage	VF	XF	Unc
31	1977	—	—	—	20.00
	1977	—	—	Proof	25.00

1980 Moscow Olympics
Rev: Similar to KM#26.

KM#	Date	Mintage	VF	XF	Unc
32	1977	8,000	—	—	20.00
	1977	—	—	Proof	25.00

20th Anniversary of European Market
Rev: Similar to KM#26.

KM#	Date	Mintage	VF	XF	Unc
33	1977	—	—	—	20.00
	1977	—	—	Proof	25.00

Rev: Similar to KM#26.

KM#	Date	Mintage	VF	XF	Unc
34	1977	—	—	—	20.00
	1977	—	—	Proof	25.00

60 GOURDES

18.2200 gm., .585 GOLD,.3427 oz AGW

KM#	Date	Mintage	VF	XF	Unc
35	1969	—	—	Proof	225.00
	1970	—	—	Proof	225.00

100 GOURDES

19.7500 gm., .900 GOLD, .5715 oz AGW

KM#	Date	Mintage	VF	XF	Unc
36	1967	6,925	—	Proof	375.00
	1968	—	—	Proof	375.00
	1969	—	—	Proof	375.00
	1970	—	—	Proof	375.00

Obv: Osceola. Rev: Similar to KM#36.

KM#	Date	Mintage	VF	XF	Unc
37	1971	—	—	Proof	400.00

Obv: Sitting Bull. Rev: Similar to KM#36.

KM#	Date	Mintage	VF	XF	Unc
38	1971	—	—	Proof	400.00

Obv: Playing Fox. Rev: Similar to KM#36.

KM#	Date	Mintage	VF	XF	Unc
39	1971	—	—	Proof	400.00

Obv: Geronimo. Rev: Similar to KM#36.

KM#	Date	Mintage	VF	XF	Unc
40	1971	—	—	Proof	400.00

Obv: Billy Bowlegs. Rev: Similar to KM#36.

KM#	Date	Mintage	VF	XF	Unc
41	1971	—	—	Proof	400.00

Obv: Joseph. Rev: Similar to KM#36.

KM#	Date	Mintage	VF	XF	Unc
42	1971	—	—	Proof	400.00

Obv: War Eagle. Rev: Similar to KM#36.

KM#	Date	Mintage	VF	XF	Unc
43	1971	—	—	Proof	400.00

Obv: Red Cloud. Rev: Similar to KM#36.

KM#	Date	Mintage	VF	XF	Unc
44	1971	—	—	Proof	400.00

Rev: Similar to KM#36.

KM#	Date	Mintage	VF	XF	Unc
45	1971	—	—	Proof	400.00

1.4500 gm., .900 GOLD, .0419 oz AGW
Obv: Same as 25 Gourdes, KM#16.
Rev: Similar to KM#36.

KM#	Date	Mintage	VF	XF	Unc
46	1973	1,757	—	Proof	40.00

43.0000 gm., .925 SILVER, 1.2789 oz ASW
Obv: Facing portraits of Sadat and Begin.
Rev: Similar to KM#36.

KM#	Date	Mintage	VF	XF	Unc
47	1977	—	—	—	45.00
	1977	—	—	Proof	55.00

Rev: Similar to KM#36.

KM#	Date	Mintage	VF	XF	Unc
48	1977	—	—	—	45.00
	1977	—	—	Proof	55.00

Rev: Similar to KM#36.

KM#	Date	Mintage	VF	XF	Unc
49	1977	—	—	—	45.00
	1977	—	—	Proof	55.00

Rev: Similar to KM#36.

KM#	Date	Mintage	VF	XF	Unc
50	1977	—	—	—	45.00
	1977	—	—	Proof	55.00

200 GOURDES

39.4900 gm., .900 GOLD, 1.1427oz AGW
Rev: Similar to 100 Gourdes, KM#36.

KM#	Date	Mintage	VF	XF	Unc
51	1967	3,725	—	Proof	750.00
	1968	—	—	Proof	775.00
	1969	—	—	Proof	775.00
	1970	—	—	Proof	750.00

Rev: Similar to 100 Gourdes, KM#36.

KM#	Date	Mintage	VF	XF	Unc
52	1971	1,330	—	—	775.00

2.9100 gm., .900 GOLD, .0842 oz AGW
Obv: Same as 25 Gourdes, KM#17. Rev: Similar to 100 Gourdes, KM#36.

KM#	Date	Mintage	VF	XF	Unc
53	1973	1,330	—	—	75.00

Holy Year Commemorative
Rev: Fineness stamped on hexagonal mound, spears with spearheads.

KM#	Date	Mintage	VF	XF	Unc
54	1974	—	—	Proof	70.00

Holy Year Commemorative
Rev: Fineness stamped on oval mound, spears with arrowheads.

KM#	Date	Mintage	VF	XF	Unc
54a	1975	—	—	Proof	70.00

International Women's Year Commemorative
Rev: Similar to above.

KM#	Date	Mintage	VF	XF	Unc
55	1975	—	—	Proof	70.00

250 GOURDES

75.9500 gm., .585 GOLD, 1.4286oz AGW
Rev: Similar to 100 Gourdes, KM#36.

KM#	Date	Mintage	VF	XF	Unc
56	1969	—	—	Proof	1000.

4.2500 gm., .900 GOLD, .1229oz AGW
Obv: Kneeling slave in broken chains.
Rev: Similar to 100 Gourdes, KM#36.

KM#	Date	Mintage	VF	XF	Unc
57	1977	—	—	—	85.00
	1977	—	—	Proof	100.00

Rev: Similar to 100 Gourdes, KM#36.

KM#	Date	Mintage	VF	XF	Unc
58	1977	—	—	—	85.00
	1977	—	—	Proof	100.00

Obv: Sailboat with star design in center.
Rev: Similar to 100 Gourdes, KM#36.

KM#	Date	Mintage	VF	XF	Unc
59	1977	—	—	—	85.00
	1977	—	—	Proof	100.00

Obv: Portrait of Lindbergh in flier's cap above Spirit of St. Louis. Rev: Similar to 100 Gourdes, KM#36.

KM#	Date	Mintage	VF	XF	Unc
60	1977	—	—	—	85.00
	1977	—	—	Proof	100.00

500 GOURDES

151.9000 gm., .585 GOLD, 2.8572oz AGW
Rev: Similar to KM#66.

KM#	Date	Mintage	VF	XF	Unc
61	1969	—	—	Proof	2000.

7.2800 gm., .900 GOLD, .2106 oz AGW
Obv: Same as 50 Gourdes, KM#26.
Rev: Similar to KM#66.

KM#	Date	Mintage	VF	XF	Unc
62	1973	2,375	—	—	165.00
	1973	Inc. Ab.	—	Proof	175.00

Obv: Same as 25 Gourdes, KM#19.
Rev: Similar to KM#66.

KM#	Date	Mintage	VF	XF	Unc
63	1974	—	—	Proof	165.00

6.4600 gm., .900 GOLD, .1869oz AGW
1976 Montreal Olympiad Commemorative
Rev: Fineness stamped on hexagonal mound, spears with spearheads.

KM#	Date	Mintage	VF	XF	Unc
64	1974	3,489	—	—	175.00
	1974	1,020	—	Proof	200.00

1976 Montreal Olympiad Commemorative
Rev: Fineness stamped on hexagonal mound, spears with arrowheads.

KM#	Date	Mintage	VF	XF	Unc
64a	1975	120 pcs.	—	—	—

8.5000 gm., .900 GOLD, .2459oz AGW
Obv: Soccer ball in center.
Rev: Similar to KM#66.

KM#	Date	Mintage	VF	XF	Unc
65	1977	—	—	—	175.00
	1977	—	—	Proof	200.00

1980 Moscow Olympics

KM#	Date	Mintage	VF	XF	Unc
66	1977	—	—	—	175.00
	1977	—	—	Proof	200.00

20th Anniversary of European Common Market
Obv: Map of Europe. Rev: Similar to KM#66.

KM#	Date	Mintage	VF	XF	Unc
67	1977	—	—	—	175.00
	1977	—	—	Proof	200.00

Rev: Similar to KM#66.

KM#	Date	Mintage	VF	XF	Unc
68	1977	—	—	—	175.00
	1977	—	—	Proof	200.00

Duvalier Commemorative
Rev: Similar to KM#66.

KM#	Date	Mintage	VF	XF	Unc
69	1977	—	—	—	175.00
	1977	—	—	Proof	200.00

1000 GOURDES

197.4800 gm., .900 GOLD, 5.7148oz AGW
Dr. Francois Du Valier
Rev: Similar to KM#72.

KM#	Date	Mintage	VF	XF	Unc
70	1967	2,525	—	Proof	4750.
	1968	—	—	Proof	4750.
	1969	—	—	Proof	4750.
	1970	—	—	Proof	4750.

14.5600 gm., .900 GOLD, .4213 oz AGW
Obv: Same as 50 Gourdes, KM#26.
Rev: Similar to KM#72.

KM#	Date	Mintage	VF	XF	Unc
71	1973	1,120	—	Proof	300.00

13.1000 gm., .900 GOLD, .3790oz AGW
American Bicentennial Commemorative
Obv: BICENTENAIRE DES U.S.A. above battle scene.

KM#	Date	Mintage	VF	XF	Unc
72	1974	—	—	375.00	400.00

Obv: REPUBLIC D'HAITI above battle scene.

KM#	Date	Mintage	VF	XF	Unc
72a	1974	—	—	—	275.00
	1974	8,000	—	Proof	300.00

NCLT ISSUES

PATTERNS

KM#	Date	Mintage	Identification	Mkt.Val.
1	1807	—	1 Centime, Copper, diagonal milling	—
2	1807	—	1 Centime, Copper, plain edge	—
3	1807	—	1 Centime, Copper, Piefort, diagonal milling	—
4	1807	—	1 Centime, Silver	—

KM#	Date	Mintage	Identification	Mkt.Val.
5	1808	—	7-1/2 Sols, Silver	—

KM#	Date	Mintage	Identification	Mkt.Val.
6	1808	—	15 Sols, Copper	—
7	1808	—	15 Sols, Silver	—

KM#	Date	Mintage	Identification	Mkt.Val.
8	1808	—	30 Sols, Silver	—

KM#	Date	Mintage	Identification	Mkt.Val.
9	1811	—	Crown, Copper	—
10	1811	—	Crown, Silver	—
11	1811	—	Crown, Silver, smaller bust, thin planchet	—

KM#	Date	Mintage	Identification	Mkt.Val.
12	1811	—	Crown, Silver	—
13	1812	—	1/2 Crown, Copper, Essai, diagonal milling	—
14	1812	—	1/2 Crown, Silver, Essai, diagonal milling	—
15	1812	—	1/2 Crown, Silver, Essai, plain edge	—
16	1812	—	Crown, Silver, diagonal milling	—
17	1813	—	Crown, Silver	—

KM#	Date	Mintage	Identification	Mkt.Val.
18	1814	—	1/2 Crown, white metal, diagonal milling	—
19	1814	—	1/2 Crown, Silver, 29mm	—
20	1814	—	1/2 Crown, Silver, 33mm	—
21	1814	—	Crown, Silver	—
22	1814	—	Base metal (for gold?)	—
23	1814	—	Base metal (for gold?)	—
24	AN 12(1815)	—	25 Centimes, Copper	—
25	1815	—	Crown, Copper, milled edge	—
26	1815	—	Crown, Silver, milled edge	—
27	AN 13(1816)	—	1 Centime, Copper, CENTIME is arched	—
28	AN 13(1816)	—	1 Centime, Copper, CENTIME is straight	—
29	AN 13(1816)	—	2 Centimes, Copper	—
30	AN 13(1816)	—	2 Centimes, Copper	—
31	1820	—	Crown, Aluminum	—
32	1820	—	Crown, Copper-Nickel	—
33	1820	—	Crown, Copper	—
34	1820	—	Crown, Silver, plain edge	—
35	1820	—	Crown, Silver, reeded edge	—
36	1820	—	Crown, white metal	—
37	1820	—	Crown, Silver	—
38	AN 27(1830)	—	100 Centimes, Copper	—
39	AN 44(1846)	—	100 Centimes, Brass	—
40	AN 44(1846)	—	100 Centimes, Copper	—
41	AN 44(1846)	—	100 Centimes, Silver	—

KM#	Date	Mintage	Identification	Mkt.Val.
42	1849	—	100 Centimes, Copper	—
43	1849	—	100 Centimes, Silver	—
44	1849	—	100 Centimes, Silver	—
45	1850	—	6 Centimes, Copper	—

KM#	Date	Mintage	Identification	Mkt.Val.
46	1850	—	6 Centimes, Copper	—
47	1850	—	6 Centimes, obv. of KM#46, rev. of KM#48.	—
48	1850	—	100 Centimes, Silver	—
48	1851	—	100 Centimes, Silvered Bronze	—

KM#	Date	Mintage	Identification	Mkt.Val.
49	1852	—	100 Centimes, Silver	—
50	1853	—	10 Centimes, Copper	—
51	1853	—	10 Centimes, Silver	—

KM#	Date	Mintage	Identification	Mkt.Val.
52	1853	—	Gourde, Silver	—
53	1854	—	Gourde, Silver	—
54	1854	—	Gourde, Silver	—
55	1854	—	Gourde, Copper	—
56	1854	—	Gourde, Silver	—
57	ND(1854)	—	Gourde, Copper	—
58	ND(1854)	—	Gourde, Bronze	—
59	ND(1854)	—	Gourde, Silver, plain edge	—
60	ND(1854)	—	Gourde, Silver, milled edge	—
61	ND(1854)	—	Gourde, Bronze, plain edge	—
62	ND(1854)	—	Gourde, Bronze, milled edge	—
63	ND(1854)	—	Gourde, Silver, plain edge	—
64	ND(1854)	—	Gourde, Silver, milled edge	—
65	ND(1854)	—	Gourde, Silver, thick planchet	—
66	1854	—	20 Gourdes, Gold	—
67	1854	—	20 Gourdes, Gold, ESSAI	—
68	1855	—	10 Centimes, Copper	—
69	1856	—	1 Piastre, Silver	—
70	1857	—	1 Piastre, Base Silver, milled edge	—
71	1857	—	1 Piastre, Copper, plain edge	—
72	1857	—	1 Piastre, Silver, milled edge	—
73	1858	—	1 Piastre, Silver	—
74	1877	—	20 Centimes, Copper	—
75	1877	—	20 Centimes, Silver	—
76	1877	—	20 Centimes, Silver, Piefort	—
77	1877	—	20 Centimes, Silver, Piefort, w/o C.T.	—
78	1877	—	20 Centimes, Copper-Nickel	—
79	1877	—	20 Centimes, Copper-Nickel, ESSAI	—
80	1877	—	20 Centimes, Silver	—
81	1877	—	20 Centimes, Silver, Piefort	—
82	1881	—	Gourde, Copper	—
83	1881	—	Gourde, Silver	—
84	1889	—	1 Centime, Copper	—
85	1889	—	2 Centimes, Copper	—

MINT SETS

STANDARD METALS

KM#	Date	Mintage	Identification	Issue Price	Mkt. Val.
S1	1973(9)	8,000	KM16,17,26,27,46,53,62(2),74	190.00	580.00
S2	1973(4)	—	KM16,17,26,27	60.00	48.00
S3	1974(2)	—	KM19,63	122.50	300.00
S4	1975(2)	—	KM20,55	50.25	80.00
94	1975(2)	—	KM21,29	56.50	32.50

PROOF SETS

STANDARD METALS

KM#	Date	Mintage	Identification	Issue Price	Mkt. Val.
101	1967(5)	2,525	KM13,24,36,51,70	722.00	6150.
102	1967(3)	4,650	KM1,3,14	47.00	225.00
103	1968(5)	475	KM13,24,36,51,70	823.00	6175.
104	1968(3)	5,725	KM1,3,14	53.50	225.00
105	1969(5)	20,000	KM22,23,35,56,61	475.00	3400.
106	1969(5)	140	KM13,24,36,51,70	823.00	6175.
107	1969(3)	1,100	KM1,3,14	53.50	240.00
108	1970(5)	—	KM13,24,36,51,70	823.00	6150.
109	1970(3)	1,000	KM1,3,14	53.50	250.00
110	1971(9)	—	KM4-12	135.00	575.00
111	1971(9)	—	KM37-45	—	3500.
112	1973(8)	1,250	KM16,17,26,27,46,53,62,71	830.00	650.00
113	1973(4)	3,500	KM16,17,26,27	60.00	65.00
114	1975(2)	—	KM20,55	67.25	80.00
115	1975(2)	—	KM21,29	75.50	—
116	1976(3)	6,000	KM19a,28,29	—	45.00

Listings For

HARAR: refer to Ethiopia

HAWAII: refer to United States

HEJAZ: refer to Saudi Arabia.

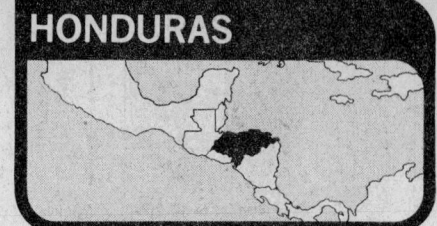

HONDURAS

The Republic of Honduras, situated in Central America between Nicaragua and Guatemala, has an area of 42,300 sq. mi. (109,556 sq. km.) and a population of 2.8 million. Capital: Tegucigalpa. Agriculture, mining (gold and silver), and logging are the chief industries. Bananas, timber and coffee are exported.

Honduras, a site of the ancient Mayan Empire, was claimed for Spain by Columbus in 1502, during his last voyage to the Americas. The first settlement was made by Cristobal de Olid under orders of Hernan Cortes, then in Mexico. The area, regarded as one of the most promising sources of gold and silver in the new world, was a part of the Captaincy General of Guatemala throughout the colonial period. After declaring its independence from Spain, 1821, Honduras fell briefly to the Mexican empire of Agustin de Iturbide, then in the Central American Union (1823-39). Upon dissolution of the federation, Honduras became an independent republic.

Dies for the coinage of 1871 and 1878-80 were made in the United States. Those for 1862 were made in England.

RULERS

Spanish, until 1821

Agustin Iturbide (Emperor of Mexico), 1822-1823

MINTMARKS

A - Paris, 1869-1870

T - Tegucigalpa, 1825-1862

MONETARY SYSTEM

16 Reales = 1 Escudo

COLONIAL ISSUES

8 REALES

SILVER, crude
Obv: Bust of Fernando VII.
Rev: Arms within legends.

C#	Date	Mintage	VG	Fine	VF
7	1813	—	—	Rare	—

EMPIRE OF MEXICO

2 REALES

SILVER
Obv: Bust of Iturbide left.

C#	Date	Mintage	VG	Fine	VF
9	1823	2 known	—	Rare	—

PROVISIONAL GOVERNMENT

(1823)

1/2 REAL

SILVER
Obv: T.L./1823. Rev: Similar to C#12.

C#	Date	Mintage	VG	Fine	VF
11	1823	—	—	Rare	—

C#	Date	Mintage	VG	Fine	VF
12	1823	—	—	Rare	—

2 REALES

SILVER

C#	Date	Mintage	VG	Fine	VF
13	1823	—	—	Rare	—

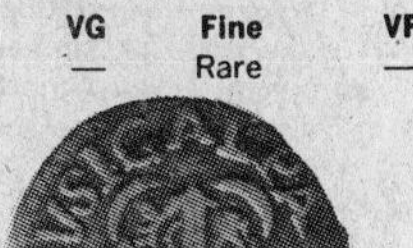

C#	Date	Mintage	VG	Fine	VF
14	1823	—	—	Rare	—

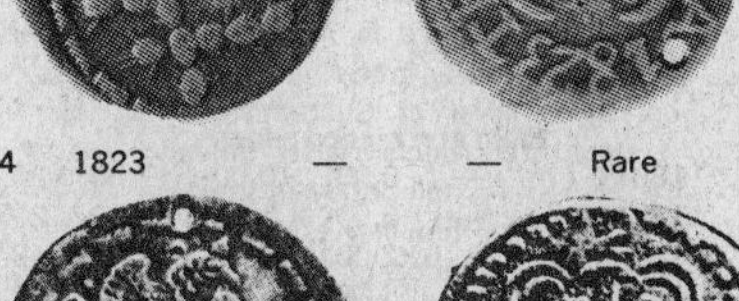

C#	Date	Mintage	VG	Fine	VF
15	1823	—	—	Rare	—

C#	Date	Mintage	VG	Fine	VF
17	1823	—	—	Rare	—

PROVISIONAL ISSUES

2 REALES

C#	Date	Mintage	VG	Fine	VF
	.917 SILVER				
25	1825T NR	—	100.00	160.00	250.00
	.903 SILVER				
23	1825	—	140.00	170.00	275.00

INDEPENDENT STATE OF HONDURAS

1/2 REAL

.333 SILVER

C#	Date	Mintage	Good	VG	Fine	VF
31.1	1832T F	—	3.50	7.00	10.00	17.50
	1833T F	—	3.50	7.00	10.00	17.50
	1837TF	—	Reported, not confirmed			
	.250 SILVER					
31.2	1845T F	—	6.00	12.00	18.00	30.00

REAL

C#	Date	Mintage	Good	VG	Fine	VF
	.333 SILVER					
32.1	1832T F	—	3.00	6.00	9.00	18.00
	1839T F	—	6.00	12.00	18.00	30.00
	.200 SILVER					
32.2	1840T F	—	6.00	12.00	18.00	30.00
32.2	1844T G	—	4.00	8.00	12.00	20.00
	1845T G	—	6.00	12.00	18.00	30.00
	1846	—	6.00	12.00	18.00	30.00
	.172 SILVER					
32.3	1849T G	—	5.00	10.00	15.00	25.00
	.100 SILVER					
32.4	1851T G	—	4.00	8.00	12.00	20.00

2 REALES

C#	Date	Mintage	Good	VG	Fine	VF
	.333 SILVER					
33.1	1832T F	—	3.00	6.00	9.00	15.00
	1833T F	—	2.00	4.00	7.00	11.50
	1839T F	—	2.50	5.00	8.00	12.50
	.200 SILVER					
33.2	1842T G	—	2.50	5.00	8.00	12.50
	1844T G	—	2.50	5.00	8.00	12.50
	1845T G	—	3.50	7.00	10.00	18.00
	1847TG	—	2.50	5.00	8.00	12.50
	.172 SILVER					
33.3	1848T G	—	3.00	6.00	9.00	15.00
	1849	—	3.50	7.00	10.00	18.00
	1850	—	3.50	7.00	10.00	18.00
	.100 SILVER					
33.4	1851T G	—	3.00	6.00	9.00	15.00
	.0625 SILVER					
33.5	1852T G	—	3.50	7.00	10.00	18.00
	.0400 SILVER					
33.6	1853T G	—	2.50	5.00	8.00	12.50
	1855T G	—	6.00	12.00	18.00	30.00

4 REALES

C#	Date	Mintage	Good	VG	Fine	VF
	.172 SILVER					
34.1	1849T G	—	5.00	10.00	15.00	30.00
	1850T G	—	3.00	6.00	11.00	20.00
	.100 SILVER					
34.2	1851T G	—	2.50	5.00	10.00	20.00
	.0625 SILVER					
34.3	1852T G	—	2.50	5.00	10.00	20.00
	.0400 SILVER					
34.4	1853T G	—	2.50	5.00	10.00	20.00
	1854T G	—	2.50	5.00	10.00	20.00
	1855T G	—	3.50	7.50	12.50	22.50
	COPPER					
34.5	1856T G	—	2.50	5.00	10.00	20.00
	COPPER-LEAD ALLOY					
34.6	1857T G	—	3.50	7.50	12.50	22.50

8 REALES

COPPER

C#	Date	Mintage	Good	VG	Fine	VF
35.1	1856T G	—	6.00	12.00	18.00	30.00
	COPPER-LEAD ALLOY					
35.2	1857T FL	—	6.00	12.00	18.00	30.00
	1858T FL	—	6.00	12.00	18.00	30.00
	1859T FI	—	9.00	18.00	30.00	42.00
	1860	—	9.00	18.00	30.00	42.00
	1861T FL	—	7.50	15.00	24.00	36.00

PROVISIONAL ISSUES

PESO

COPPER
Rev: Dots separate legends.

Y#	Date	Mintage	VG	Fine	VF	XF
P1.1	1862T A	—	7.00	12.50	20.00	35.00
	Rev: Rosettes separate legends.					
P1.2	1862T A	—	10.00	17.50	25.00	40.00
	BRONZE					
P1.2a	1862T A	—	—	—	Proof	300.00
	SILVER					
P1.2b	1862T A	—	—	—	Proof	Rare

2 PESOS

COPPER
Rev: Dots separate legends.

Y#	Date	Mintage	VG	Fine	VF	XF
P2.1	1862T A	—	4.00	7.00	12.00	20.00

Y#	Date	Mintage	VG	Fine	VF	XF
	Rev: Rosettes separate legends.					
P2.2	1862T A	—	7.00	12.00	17.00	25.00
	BRONZE					
P2.2a	1862T A	—	—	—	Proof	400.00
	SILVER					
P2.2b	1862T A	—	—	—	Proof	Rare

4 PESOS

COPPER
Rev: Dots separate legends.

Y#	Date	Mintage	VG	Fine	VF	XF
P3.1	1862T A	—	8.00	15.00	25.00	30.00

Rev: Rosettes separate legends.

Y#	Date	Mintage	VG	Fine	VF	XF
P3.2	1862T A	—	10.00	20.00	30.00	35.00

BRONZE

Y#	Date	Mintage	VG	Fine	VF	XF
P3.2a	1862T A	—	—	—	Proof	Rare

SILVER

Y#	Date	Mintage	VG	Fine	VF	XF
P3.2b	1862T A	—	—	—	Proof	Rare

8 PESOS

COPPER
Rev: Dots separate legends; curved base 2 in date.

Y#	Date	Mintage	VG	Fine	VF	XF
P4.1	1862T A	—	12.50	22.50	35.00	60.00

Obv: Similar to P4.1.
Rev: Rosettes separate legends; square base 2 in date.

Y#	Date	Mintage	VG	Fine	VF	XF
P4.2	1862T A	—	16.50	30.00	50.00	80.00

BRONZE

Y#	Date	Mintage	VG	Fine	VF	XF
P4.2a	1862T A	—	—	—	Proof	Rare

SILVER

Y#	Date	Mintage	VG	Fine	VF	XF
P4.2b	1862T A	—	—	—	Proof	Rare

NOTE: A 16 Pesos fantasy issue exists similar to #P4.2b.

REPUBLIC

1/8 REAL

COPPER-NICKEL

Y#	Date	Mintage	VG	Fine	VF	XF
1	1869A	—	2.50	4.00	6.00	10.00
	1870A	—	2.50	4.00	6.00	10.00

1/4 REAL

COPPER-NICKEL

Y#	Date	Mintage	VG	Fine	VF	XF
2	1869A	—	2.50	4.00	7.50	10.00
	1870A	—	2.00	3.50	5.00	8.50

1/2 REAL

COPPER-NICKEL

Y#	Date	Mintage	VG	Fine	VF	XF
3	1869A	—	1.75	2.50	4.50	7.50
	1870A	—	2.00	3.00	5.50	8.50

REAL

COPPER-NICKEL

Y#	Date	Mintage	VG	Fine	VF	XF
4	1869A	—	4.00	8.50	13.50	21.50
	1870A	—	3.75	8.00	12.50	20.00

PESO SYSTEM

100 Centavos = 1 Peso

1/2 CENTAVO

BRONZE

Y#	Date	Mintage	VG	Fine	VF	XF
13	1881	—	15.00	25.00	40.00	65.00
	1883	—	17.50	27.50	45.00	70.00
	1885	—	15.00	25.00	40.00	65.00
	1886	—	15.00	22.50	35.00	65.00
	1889	—	15.00	25.00	40.00	65.00
	1891	—	—	—	Rare	—

UN (1) CENTAVO

BRONZE

Y#	Date	Mintage	VG	Fine	VF	XF
9	1878	.346	11.00	20.00	40.00	75.00
	1879	Inc. Ab.	9.00	15.00	30.00	65.00
	1880	Inc. Ab.	8.00	12.50	22.50	50.00

Plain and reeded edges

Y#	Date	Mintage	VG	Fine	VF	XF
14	1881	—	5.00	10.00	17.50	27.50
	1884	—	2.50	5.00	12.50	20.00
	1885	—	2.00	4.00	7.50	12.50
	1886	—	3.00	6.00	12.50	20.00
	1889	—	3.00	6.00	12.50	20.00
	1890	—	2.50	5.00	11.50	17.50
	1896	—	2.50	5.50	11.50	20.00
	1898	.180	2.50	5.50	11.50	20.00
	1899	Inc. Ab.	3.00	6.00	12.50	20.00
	1900	.030	2.50	5.50	11.50	22.50
	1901	.100	2.50	5.00	11.50	18.50
	1902	—	2.50	5.00	11.50	18.50
	1903	—	5.00	10.00	17.50	30.00
	1904	—	2.50	5.00	11.50	20.00
	1907/4	—	4.00	7.50	15.00	30.00
	1907	.802	3.00	6.00	12.50	22.50

Y#	Date	Mintage	VG	Fine	VF	XF
15	1890	—	5.00	10.00	15.00	30.00
	1893	—	5.00	10.00	15.00	30.00
	1895	—	2.50	5.00	8.00	17.50
	1900	—	2.50	5.00	8.00	17.50
	1907	Inc. Y#14	1.50	3.00	5.00	10.00
	1908	Inc. Y#17	2.50	5.00	8.00	17.50

Mule: Obv. of Y#14. Rev. of Y#9.

Y#	Date	Mintage	VG	Fine	VF	XF
16	Undated	—	—	100.00	125.00	150.00

Obv. of Y#21. Rev: Altered Y#21.

Y#	Date	Mintage	VG	Fine	VF	XF
17	1890	—	4.50	9.00	15.00	27.50
	1891	—	4.25	8.50	12.50	27.50
	1892	—	4.50	9.00	15.00	27.50
	1893	—	3.25	6.50	12.50	16.50
	1895	—	4.00	8.00	10.00	27.50
	1908	.236	3.00	6.00	12.50	18.50

Mule: Obv. of Y#6. Rev. of Y#9.

Y#	Date	Mintage	VG	Fine	VF	XF
18	1895	—	—	100.00	150.00	250.00

Obv. of Y#13. Rev: Altered Y#13.

Y#	Date	Mintage	VG	Fine	VF	XF
32	1910	.340	10.00	20.00	30.00	50.00
	1911	.060	7.50	15.00	25.00	40.00

Mule: Obv. of Y#19. Rev: Altered Y#13.

Y#	Date	Mintage	VG	Fine	VF	XF
34	1910	Inc. Ab.	12.00	22.50	32.50	50.00
	1610 (error) inverted 9					
		Inc. Ab.	12.00	22.50	32.50	50.00

Obv. of Y#19. Rev: Altered Y#19.

Y#	Date	Mintage	VG	Fine	VF	XF
35	1910	Inc. Ab.	5.00	9.00	17.50	32.50
	1911	Inc. Ab.	12.00	20.00	32.50	45.00

Mule: Obv. of Y#13. Rev: Altered Y#19.

Y#	Date	Mintage	VG	Fine	VF	XF
36	1910	Inc. Ab.	14.00	25.00	35.00	50.00

Similar to Y#32, CENTAVO omitted.

Y#	Date	Mintage	VG	Fine	VF	XF
37	1919	.168	1.00	2.00	3.00	5.00
	1920	.030	1.00	2.00	3.00	5.00

2 CENTAVOS

BRONZE
Rev: Altered Y#21.

Y#	Date	Mintage	VG	Fine	VF	XF
31	1907	Inc. Bl.	—	—	Rare	—
	1908	Inc. Bl.	17.50	27.50	50.00	75.00

Obv. of Y#14. Rev: Altered Y#14.

Y#	Date	Mintage	VG	Fine	VF	XF
33	1910	.520	.75	1.50	2.50	5.00
	1911	.070	1.25	2.50	5.00	7.00
	1912	.070	1.00	2.00	4.00	6.00
	1913	.260	1.00	2.00	4.00	6.00

Rev: CENTAVOS omitted.

Y#	Date	Mintage	VG	Fine	VF	XF
38	1919	.120	.75	1.50	3.00	5.00
	1920	.283	.50	1.00	2.00	3.50

NOTE: Several varieties exist.

5 CENTAVOS

1.3000 gm., .900 SILVER, .0376 oz ASW
Obv: Arms. Rev: Tree.

Y#	Date	Mintage	VG	Fine	VF	XF
5	1871	.002	425.00	800.00	1200.	1750.

Obv: Eagle. Rev: Standing Liberty.

Y#	Date	Mintage	VG	Fine	VF	XF
10	1879	—	300.00	500.00	800.00	1200.

Y#	Date	Mintage	VG	Fine	VF	XF
19	1883	—	—	—	Rare	—
	1884	—	9.50	17.50	27.50	45.00
	1885	—	10.00	17.50	27.50	45.00
	1886	—	8.00	15.00	25.00	42.50
	1890	—	—	—	Rare	—
	1902	—	22.00	30.00	45.00	75.00

Y#	Date	Mintage	VG	Fine	VF	XF
20	1886	—	4.25	8.50	15.00	27.50
	6188 Error	—	—	—	—	—
	1895	—	10.00	20.00	32.50	45.00
	1895/6	—	5.00	10.00	18.50	35.00
	1896	—	4.25	8.50	15.00	27.50

10 CENTAVOS

2.5000 gm., .900 SILVER, .0723 oz ASW
Obv: Arms. Rev: Tree.

Y#	Date	Mintage	VG	Fine	VF	XF
6	1871	.017	17.50	30.00	50.00	75.00

Obv: Eagle. Rev: Standing Liberty.

Y#	Date	Mintage	VG	Fine	VF	XF
11	1878	—	—	300.00	600.00	1000.

Y#	Date	Mintage	VG	Fine	VF	XF
21	1883	—	—	—	Rare	—
	1884	—	8.00	15.00	22.50	32.50
	1885	—	8.00	15.00	20.00	27.50
	1886	—	12.50	20.00	25.00	35.00
	1889	—	12.50	20.00	25.00	35.00
	1891	—	—	—	Rare	—
	1893	—	8.00	16.50	22.50	32.50
	1895	—	8.00	16.50	22.50	32.50
	1900	5,300	14.00	22.50	30.00	45.00

Mule: Obv. of Y#6. Rev. of Y#21.

Y#	Date	Mintage	VG	Fine	VF	XF
22.1	1886 w/P on rev.					
		—	15.00	25.00	40.00	65.00
	1895 w/P on rev.					
		—	15.00	25.00	45.00	75.00
22.2	Undated with P in place of date					
		—	20.00	32.50	50.00	80.00

25 CENTAVOS

6.3000 gm., .900 SILVER, .1823 oz ASW

Y#	Date	Mintage	VG	Fine	VF	XF
7	1871	.180	6.00	8.50	12.50	25.00

Y#	Date	Mintage	VG	Fine	VF	XF
23	1883	—	BV	6.00	7.50	10.00
	1884	—	BV	6.00	7.50	12.00
	1885	—	BV	6.00	7.50	10.00
	1886	—	BV	6.00	7.50	10.00
	1887	—	—	—	Rare	—
	1888/3	—	BV	6.00	7.50	12.00
	1888	—	BV	6.00	7.50	10.00
	1890	—	BV	6.00	7.50	12.00
	1891	—	BV	6.00	7.50	10.00
	1892	—	BV	6.00	7.50	12.00
	1892/1	—	BV	6.00	7.50	15.00
	1893	—	BV	6.00	7.50	10.00
	1895	—	BV	6.00	7.50	12.00
	1896	—	BV	6.00	7.50	12.00
	1897	—	Reported, not confirmed			
	1898	.077	Reported, not confirmed			

6.3000 gm., .835 SILVER, .1691 oz ASW

Y#	Date	Mintage	VG	Fine	VF	XF
23a	1899 sm. 99	I.A.	BV	5.50	7.50	12.00
	1899 lg. 99	I.A.	BV	5.50	7.50	12.00
	1900	.040	BV	5.50	7.50	12.00
	1901	—	BV	5.50	7.50	10.00
	1902F	—	BV	5.50	7.50	10.00
	1904	—	6.00	8.50	18.00	25.00
	1907	.014	5.50	7.50	15.00	20.00
	1908	—	—	—	—	—
	1910	7,000	—	—	—	—
	1912	.007	8.50	12.00	20.00	30.00
	1913	.051	BV	6.00	12.00	20.00

50 CENTAVOS

12.5000 gm., .900 SILVER, .3617 oz ASW

Y#	Date	Mintage	VG	Fine	VF	XF
8	1871	.040	BV	12.00	20.00	45.00

Obv: Eagle. Rev: Standing Liberty.

Y#	Date	Mintage	VG	Fine	VF	XF
12	1879	—	300.00	425.00	650.00	950.00

Y#	Date	Mintage	VG	Fine	VF	XF
24	1883	—	BV	12.00	15.00	20.00
	1883P	—	—	—	—	—
	1884	—	BV	12.00	15.00	25.00
	1885	—	BV	12.00	15.00	25.00
	1886	—	BV	12.00	15.00	25.00
	1887/5	—	BV	13.50	17.50	30.00
	1887	—	BV	12.00	15.00	25.00
	1896	—	15.00	20.00	35.00	50.00
	1897	—	15.00	20.00	35.00	50.00
	1910	1,022?	—	—	Rare	—

.835 SILVER

Y#	Date	Mintage	VG	Fine	VF	XF
24a	1908	447 pcs.	45.00	80.00	140.00	200.00
	1911	90 pcs.	Reported, not confirmed			

PESO

25.0000 gm., .900 SILVER, .7234 oz ASW
Rev: W/small CENTRO-AMERICA

Y#	Date	Mintage	VG	Fine	VF	XF
25	1881	.026	25.00	50.00	85.00	125.00
	1882	.076	22.50	40.00	70.00	110.00
	1883	—	22.50	40.00	70.00	110.00

Rev: W/large CENTRO-AMERICA

Y#	Date	Mintage	VG	Fine	VF	XF
25a	1883/1	—	200.00	325.00	450.00	600.00
	1884	—	25.00	35.00	60.00	110.00
	1885 lg. 8	—	25.00	35.00	60.00	110.00
	1885 sm. 8	—	22.50	30.00	60.00	110.00
	1886	—	25.00	35.00	60.00	110.00
	1887	—	25.00	35.00	60.00	110.00
	1888	—	25.00	35.00	60.00	110.00
	1889/8	—	—	—	—	—
	1889	—	25.00	35.00	60.00	110.00
	1890	—	25.00	35.00	60.00	110.00
	1891/89	—	30.00	40.00	75.00	130.00
	1891	—	25.00	35.00	60.00	110.00
	1892/0	—	30.00	40.00	75.00	130.00
	1892	—	25.00	35.00	60.00	110.00
	1893/1	—	—	—	Rare	—
	1893	—	325.00	500.00	800.00	1100.
	1895/0	—	25.00	35.00	70.00	125.00
	1895	—	25.00	35.00	60.00	130.00
	1899/87	1 pc.	—	—	Rare	—
	1899	—	600.00	900.00	1400.	2000.
	1902/1	—	25.00	35.00	65.00	125.00
	1902	—	22.50	30.00	65.00	100.00
	1903 flat top 3	—	22.50	30.00	55.00	100.00
	1903 round top 3	—	22.50	30.00	60.00	110.00
	1904	—	22.50	30.00	60.00	110.00
	1912	—	Reported, not confirmed			
	1913	—	Reported, not confirmed			
	1914	—	325.00	500.00	900.00	1350.

Mule: Obv. of Y#25, w/o 25 GMOS above UN PESO.
Rev: Of Y#25a.

Y#	Date	Mintage	VG	Fine	VF	XF
25b	1894/2 closed 4		35.00	50.00	85.00	150.00
	1894/2 open 4	—	35.00	50.00	85.00	150.00
	1894	—	30.00	40.00	70.00	125.00
	1895/3	—	30.00	40.00	75.00	120.00
	1895/4	—	30.00	40.00	75.00	120.00
	1895	—	25.00	35.00	60.00	100.00
	1896	—	25.00	35.00	75.00	120.00

1.6120 gm., .900 GOLD, .0467 oz AGW
Similar to 10 Pesos, Y#B27.

Y#	Date	Mintage	VF	XF	Unc
26	1871	—	550.00	825.00	1375.

Y#	Date	Mintage	VF	XF	Unc
27	1887	—	Reported, not confirmed		
	1888	—	400.00	550.00	825.00
	1889	—	—	—	—
	1890	—	Reported, not confirmed		
	1895	—	400.00	550.00	825.00
	1896	—	400.00	550.00	825.00
	1899	—	Reported, not confirmed		
	1901	—	—	—	—
	1902	—	—	—	—
	1907	—	400.00	550.00	825.00
	1912	—	Reported, not confirmed		
	1913	—	Reported, not confirmed		
	1919	—	400.00	550.00	825.00
	1920	—	—	—	—
	1922	—	400.00	550.00	825.00

5 PESOS

8.0645 gm., .900 GOLD
Similar to 10 Pesos, Y#B27.

Y#	Date	Mintage	VF	XF	Unc
A27	1871	—	—	Rare	—

Y#	Date	Mintage	VF	XF	Unc
28	1883	—	650.00	825.00	1100.
	1888	—	650.00	825.00	1100.
	1889	—	Reported, not confirmed		
	1890	—	650.00	825.00	1100.
	1895	—	650.00	825.00	1100.
	1896	—	650.00	825.00	1100.
	1897	—	650.00	825.00	1100.
	1900	—	750.00	950.00	1300.
	1902	—	750.00	950.00	1300.
	1908	—	650.00	825.00	1100.
	1913	—	900.00	1100.	1500.

10 PESOS

16.1290 gm., .900 GOLD

Y#	Date	Mintage	VF	XF	Unc
B27	1871	—	—	Rare	—

Y#	Date	Mintage	VF	XF	Unc
29	1889	—	—	Rare	—

20 PESOS

32.2580 gm., .900 GOLD

Y#	Date	Mintage	VF	XF	Unc
30	1888	—	3500.	5000.	8000.
	1895	—	3500.	5000.	8000.
	1908	—	3500.	5000.	8000.

MONETARY REFORM

100 Centavos = 1 Lempira

CENTAVO

BRONZE

Y#	Date	Mintage	Fine	VF	XF	Unc
39	1935	2.000	.10	.15	.25	.75
	1939	2.000	.10	.15	.25	.75
	1949	4.000	.10	.15	.20	.35
	1954	3.500	.10	.15	.20	.35
	1956	2.000	.10	.15	.20	.35
	1957	28.000	.10	.15	.20	.30

BRONZE-CLAD STEEL

Y#	Date	Mintage	Fine	VF	XF	Unc
39a	1974	—	.10	.15	.20	.25

2 CENTAVOS

BRONZE

Y#	Date	Mintage	Fine	VF	XF	Unc
40	1939	2.000	.10	.15	.25	.50
	1949	3.000	.10	.15	.25	.50
	1954	2.000	.10	.15	.25	.50
	1956	20.000	.10	.15	.20	.25

BRONZE-CLAD STEEL

Y#	Date	Mintage	Fine	VF	XF	Unc
40a	1974	—	.10	.15	.20	.25

5 CENTAVOS

COPPER-NICKEL

Y#	Date	Mintage	Fine	VF	XF	Unc
41	1931	2.000	.15	.25	.50	2.50
	1932	1.000	.15	.25	.35	1.50
	1949	2.000	.10	.15	.25	.75
	1954	1.400	.10	.15	.25	.50
	1956	10.000	.10	.15	.20	.35

Different style lettering.

Y#	Date	Mintage	Fine	VF	XF	Unc
41.1	1972	—	.10	.15	.20	.30

BRASS

Y#	Date	Mintage	Fine	VF	XF	Unc
41a	1975	20.000	.10	.15	.20	.25

10 CENTAVOS

COPPER-NICKEL

Y#	Date	Mintage	Fine	VF	XF	Unc
42	1932	1.500	.25	.50	1.00	4.00
	1951	1.000	.10	.25	.75	1.25
	1954	1.200	.10	.20	.35	.75
	1956	7.559	.10	.15	.35	.75
	1967	—	.10	.15	.25	.50
			BRASS			
42a	1976	—	.10	.15	.20	.30

20 CENTAVOS

2.5000 gm., .900 SILVER, .0723 oz ASW

Y#	Date	Mintage	Fine	VF	XF	Unc
43	1931	1.000	BV	BV	2.50	4.00
	1932	.750	BV	BV	2.75	4.50
	1951	1.500	BV	BV	2.25	3.50
	1952	2.500	BV	BV	2.25	3.50
	1958	2.000	BV	BV	2.25	3.50

COPPER-NICKEL

Y#	Date	Mintage	Fine	VF	XF	Unc
46	1967	12.000	.15	.20	.25	.50
			Different style lettering.			
46.1	1973	15.000	.15	.20	.25	.50

50 CENTAVOS

6.2500 gm., .900 SILVER, .1808 oz ASW

Y#	Date	Mintage	Fine	VF	XF	Unc
44	1931	.500	BV	BV	6.50	8.50
	1932	1.100	BV	BV	6.00	7.50
	1937	1.000	BV	BV	6.00	7.50
	1951	.500	BV	BV	6.50	8.50

COPPER-NICKEL

Y#	Date	Mintage	Fine	VF	XF	Unc
47	1967	4.800	.35	.50	.75	1.00

F.A.O. Issue

Y#	Date	Mintage	Fine	VF	XF	Unc
48	1973	4.400	.35	.50	.75	1.00

LEMPIRA

12.5000 gm., .900 SILVER, .3617 oz ASW

Y#	Date	Mintage	Fine	VF	XF	Unc
45	1931	.550	BV	BV	15.00	17.50
	1932	1.000	BV	BV	12.00	15.00
	1933	.400	BV	BV	15.00	17.50
	1934	.600	BV	BV	15.00	17.50
	1935	1.000	BV	BV	12.00	15.00
	1937	4.000	BV	BV	12.00	15.00

NCLT ISSUES

PATTERNS

KM#	Date	Mintage	Identification	Mkt.Val.
PT5	1862T A	—	16 Pesos, Bronze	—
PT5a	1862T A	—	16 Pesos, Silver	—
B27A	1871	—	10 Pesos, Copper	175.00

HONG KONG

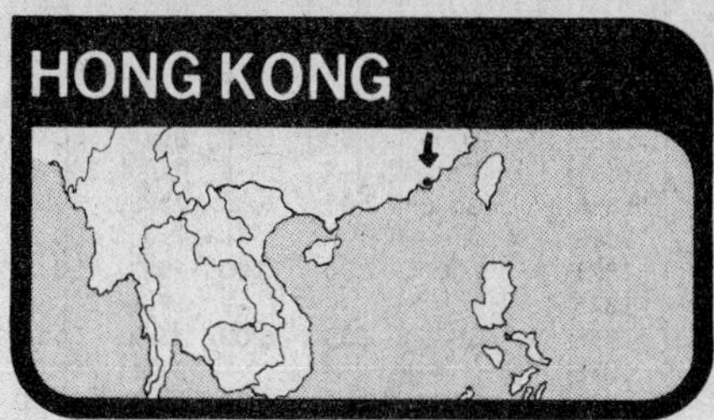

The colony of Hong Kong, a British colony situated at the mouth of the Canton or Pearl River 90 miles (145 km.) southeast of Canton, has an area of 404 sq. mi. (1,046 sq. km. and a population of 4.2 million. Capital: Victoria. The free port of Hong Kong, the commercial center of the Far East, is a trans-shipment point for goods destined for China and the countries of the Western Pacific. Light manufacturing and tourism are important components of the economy.

Long a haven for fishermen-pirates and opium smugglers, the island of Hong Kong was ceded to Britain at the conclusion of the first Opium War (1839-42). At the time, the acquisition of 'a barren rock' was ridiculed by both London and English merchants operating in the Far East. The so—called New Territories, comprising Kowloon Peninsula and Stonecutter's Island, were leased to Britain for 99 years in 1898.

The legends on Hong Kong coinage are bilingual: English and Chinese. The rare 1941 cent was dispatched to Hong Kong in several shipments. One fell into Japanese hands while another was melted down by the British.

RULERS

British

MINTMARKS

H - Heaton

KN - King's Norton

MONETARY SYSTEM

10 Mils = 1 Cent

100 Cents = 1 Dollar

MIL

文

BRONZE

Chinese value '1 WEN'

Y#	Date	Mintage	Fine	VF	XF	Unc
1	1863	20.000	1.00	4.00	8.00	12.00
	1863	—	—	—	Proof	70.00
	1864	—	800.00	1000.	1600.	3000.
	1865	40.000	1.00	4.00	6.00	10.00
			Rev: With hyphen between HONG KONG.			
1.1	1865	Inc. Ab.	—	—	350.00	500.00
			GILT BRONZE			
1.2	1863	—	—	—	Proof	110.00
			SILVER			
1.3	1863	—	—	—	Proof	150.00

千

BRONZE

Chinese value 'CH'IEN'

Y#	Date	Mintage	Fine	VF	XF	Unc
1a	1866	20.000	1.00	4.00	6.00	10.00

CENT

BRONZE

Obv: 14 pearls in left arch of crown.

Y#	Date	Mintage	Fine	VF	XF	Unc
2	1863	1.000	2.00	6.00	25.00	50.00

Y#	Date	Mintage	Fine	VF	XF	Unc
	1863	—	—	—	Proof	200.00
	1863 w/dot on reverse	—		—	Proof	250.00
	1865	2.000	2.00	6.00	25.00	50.00
	1865	—	—	—	Proof	200.00
	1866	1.000	2.00	6.00	25.00	50.00
	1866	—	—	—	Proof	200.00
	1875	1.000	2.00	6.00	25.00	50.00
	1875	—	—	—	Proof	200.00
	1876	1.000	2.00	6.00	25.00	50.00
	1876	—	—	—	Proof	200.00
	1877	2.000	2.00	6.00	25.00	50.00
	1877	—	—	—	Proof	200.00

Obv: 15 pearls in left arch of crown.

Y#	Date	Mintage	Fine	VF	XF	Unc
2.1	1877	2.000	2.00	6.00	25.00	50.00
	1877	—	—	—	Proof	200.00
	1879	Inc. Be.	2.00	6.00	25.00	50.00
	1879	—	—	—	Proof	200.00

Obv: 5 pearls in center of crown.

Y#	Date	Mintage	Fine	VF	XF	Unc
2.2	1879	1.000	2.00	8.00	30.00	60.00
	1879	—	—	—	Proof	200.00
	1880	1.000	2.00	8.00	30.00	60.00
	1880	—	—	—	Proof	200.00
	1881	1.000	2.00	8.00	30.00	60.00
	1881	—	—	—	Proof	200.00
	1899	1.000	2.00	8.00	30.00	60.00
	1899	—	—	—	Proof	150.00
	1900H	1.000	.75	2.00	10.00	25.00
	1901	5.000	.50	1.00	10.00	25.00
	1901H	10.000	.50	1.00	10.00	20.00

Y#	Date	Mintage	Fine	VF	XF	Unc
9	1902	5.000	.40	1.05	10.00	30.00
	1903	5.000	.40	1.00	10.00	30.00
	1904H	10.000	.40	1.00	5.00	25.00
	1905	2.500	.40	2.00	10.00	35.00
	1905H	12.500	.40	1.00	3.00	20.00

Y#	Date	Mintage	Fine	VF	XF	Unc
14	1919H	2.500	.40	1.00	3.00	10.00
	1923	2.500	.40	1.00	3.00	10.00
	1924	5.000	.40	1.00	3.00	8.00
	1925	2.500	.40	1.00	3.00	8.00
	1926	2.500	.40	1.00	3.00	8.00
	1926	—	—	—	Proof	150.00

Y#	Date	Mintage	Fine	VF	XF	Unc
15	1931	5.000	.20	.35	.75	2.25
	1933	6.500	.15	.30	.40	2.25
	1933	—	—	—	Proof	75.00
	1934	5.000	.20	.35	.75	2.25

Y#	Date	Mintage	Fine	VF	XF	Unc
19	1941	5.000	1000.	1600.	2000.	3000.
	1941	—	—	—	Proof	4500.

5 CENTS

1.3577 gm., .800 SILVER, .0349 oz ASW

Y#	Date	Mintage	Fine	VF	XF	Unc
3	1866	1.313	2.00	15.00	35.00	60.00
	1866	—	—	—	Proof	200.00
	1867	Inc. Ab.	2.00	15.00	35.00	60.00
	1867	—	—	—	Proof	200.00
	1868	Inc. Ab.	2.50	10.00	30.00	45.00
	1872H Arabic 1	.136	2.00	12.00	45.00	70.00
	1872H Roman I	Inc. Ab.	6.50	25.00	55.00	90.00
	1873/63	.387	2.50	20.00	45.00	80.00
	1873	Inc. Ab.	2.00	15.00	35.00	60.00
	1873	—	—	—	Proof	225.00
	1873/63H	—	1.50	3.50	9.00	35.00
	1873H	.256	2.00	15.00	35.00	60.00
	1874H	.280	2.00	15.00	35.00	60.00
	1875H	.280	2.00	15.00	35.00	60.00
	1875H	—	—	—	Proof	225.00
	1876H	.480	2.00	15.50	35.00	60.00
	1877H	.240	2.00	15.00	35.00	60.00
	1879	.288	2.00	15.00	35.00	60.00
	1880H	.300	2.00	10.00	25.00	40.00
	1881/71	.300	2.50	13.50	32.50	52.50
	1881	Inc. Ab.	2.00	10.00	25.00	40.00
	1881	—	—	—	Proof	200.00
	1882H	.600	2.00	8.00	20.00	35.00
	1883	.550	2.00	8.00	20.00	35.00
	1883	—	—	—	Proof	200.00
	1883H	.250	2.05	15.00	35.00	50.00
	1883-H	—	—	—	Proof	200.00
	1884	.960	2.00	6.00	15.00	25.00
	1884	—	—	—	Proof	200.00
	1885	3.120	1.00	2.00	10.00	17.50
	1886	2.100	1.00	2.00	10.00	17.50
	1887	2.448	1.00	2.00	10.00	17.50
	1888/78	5.952	1.50	2.50	8.00	20.00
	1888	Inc. Ab.	1.00	2.00	6.00	15.00
	1889	5.169	1.00	2.00	6.00	15.00
	1889H	2.100	1.00	2.00	6.00	15.00
	1890	1.500	1.00	2.00	6.00	15.00
	1890	—	—	—	Proof	200.00
	1890H	5.400	1.00	2.00	5.00	10.00
	1891	6.900	1.00	2.00	5.00	10.00
	1891H	2.100	1.00	2.00	5.00	10.00
	1892	4.200	1.00	2.00	5.00	10.00
	1892H	1.200	1.00	3.00	6.00	15.00
	1892H	—	—	—	Proof	100.00
	1893	3.000	1.00	2.00	5.00	10.00
	1894	4.600	1.00	2.00	5.00	10.00
	1894	—	—	—	Proof	200.00
	1895	4.000	1.00	2.00	5.00	10.00
	1897	4.000	1.00	2.00	5.00	10.00
	1898	3.500	1.00	2.00	5.00	10.00
	1899	9.377	1.00	2.00	3.00	5.00
	1900	1.623	1.00	2.00	5.00	10.00
	1900H	7.000	1.00	2.00	3.00	5.00
	1901	10.000	1.00	2.00	3.00	5.00

COPPER

Y#	Date	Mintage	Fine	VF	XF	Unc
3a	1866	—	—		Proof Only	300.00

1.3577 gm., .800 SILVER, .0349 oz ASW

Y#	Date	Mintage	Fine	VF	XF	Unc
10	1903	6.000	1.00	1.50	2.25	4.50
	1903	—	—	—	Proof	150.00
	1904	8.000	1.00	1.50	2.25	4.50
	1904	—	—	—	Proof	150.00
	1905	1.000	1.00	1.50	2.25	5.00
	1905H	7.000	1.00	1.50	2.25	4.50

Y#	Date	Mintage	Fine	VF	XF	Unc
18	1932	3.000	1.00	1.35	2.00	3.50
	1932	—	—	—	Proof	100.00
	1933	2.000	1.00	1.35	2.00	3.50

COPPER-NICKEL

Y#	Date	Mintage	Fine	VF	XF	Unc
16	1935	1.000	1.50	2.75	3.50	10.00
	1935	—	—	—	Proof	75.00

NICKEL

Y#	Date	Mintage	Fine	VF	XF	Unc
20	1937	3.000	.50	1.00	1.50	3.50
	1937	—	—	—	Proof	75.00

Y#	Date	Mintage	Fine	VF	XF	Unc
22	1938	3.000	.20	.35	.85	2.00
	1939H	7.800	.20	.35	.85	2.00
	1939KN	Inc. Ab.	.20	.35	.65	2.00
	1941H	.777	350.00	500.00	600.00	700.00
	1941KN	1.075	120.00	225.00	300.00	400.00

NICKEL-BRASS

Y#	Date	Mintage	Fine	VF	XF	Unc
24	1949	15.000	—	.15	.25	4.00
	1949	—	—	—	Proof	175.00
	1950	20.400	—	.15	.25	4.00

Reeded, security edges

Y#	Date	Mintage	Fine	VF	XF	Unc
27	1958H	5.000	—	.10	.15	.20
	1960	5.000	—	.10	.15	.20
	1963	7.000	—	.10	.15	.20
	1964H	—	6.00	8.00	15.00	75.00
	1965	18.000	—	—	.10	.20
	1967	10.000	—	—	.10	.20
	1968	15.000	—	—	.10	.20

Error: Reeded, without security edge.

Y#	Date	Mintage	Fine	VF	XF	Unc
27.1	1958	Inc. Ab.	1.75	3.50	6.50	12.50
	1960	Inc. Ab.	1.75	3.50	6.50	12.50

Reeded edges

Y#	Date	Mintage	Fine	VF	XF	Unc
27a	1971KN	20.000	—	—	—	.15
	1971H	Inc. Ab.	—	—	—	.15
	1972H	—	—	—	—	.15
	1977	—	—	—	—	.15
	1978	—	—	—	—	.15

10 CENTS

2.7154 gm., .800 SILVER, .0698 oz ASW

Y#	Date	Mintage	Fine	VF	XF	Unc
4	1863	.100	10.00	30.00	40.00	65.00
	1863	—	—	—	Proof	200.00
	1864	.200	150.00	300.00	475.00	675.00
	1864	—	—	—	Proof	825.00
	1865	.550	10.00	25.00	35.00	65.00
	1865	—	—	—	Proof	200.00

Obv: 10 pearls on right arch of crown.

Y#	Date	Mintage	Fine	VF	XF	Unc
4.1	1866	.300	10.00	15.00	25.00	55.00
	1866	—	—	—	Proof	200.00

Obv: 11 pearls on right arch of crown.

Y#	Date	Mintage	Fine	VF	XF	Unc
4.2	1866	2.479	8.00	15.00	25.00	60.00
	1867	Inc. Ab.	10.00	20.00	35.00	65.00
	1867	—	—	—	Proof	250.00
	1868	Inc. Ab.	8.00	12.00	18.00	40.00
	1869	—	8.00	12.00	17.50	40.00
	1869	—	—	—	Proof	400.00
	1872H	.088	25.00	40.00	60.00	100.00
	1872H	—	—	—	Proof	300.00

Y#	Date	Mintage	Fine	VF	XF	Unc
	1873	.197	10.00	15.00	25.00	60.00
	1873	—	—	—	Proof	250.00
	1873H	.128	12.50	18.00	30.00	65.00
	1874H	.200	12.50	18.00	30.00	65.00
	1875H	.200	10.00	15.00	25.00	60.00
	1875H	—	—	—	Proof	250.00
	1876H	.480	10.00	15.00	20.00	60.00
	1877H	.240	10.00	15.00	25.00	65.00
	1879	.288	10.00	15.00	25.00	70.00
	1879	—	—	—	Proof	250.00
	1880H	.300	10.00	15.00	25.00	60.00
	1880H	—	—	—	Proof	250.00
	1881	.300	10.00	15.00	25.00	60.00
	1881	—	—	—	Proof	250.00
	1882H	.500	8.50	15.00	20.00	60.00
	1883	.550	4.50	10.00	20.00	50.00
	1883	—	—	—	Proof	250.00
	1883H	.250	15.00	25.00	40.00	70.00
	1883H	—	—	—	Proof	300.00
	1884	.960	4.00	8.00	12.50	20.00
	1884	—	—	—	Proof	150.00
	1885	3.120	2.50	4.00	8.00	16.50
	1886	2.100	2.50	4.00	8.00	16.50
	1886	—	—	—	Proof	150.00
	1887	2.441	2.50	4.00	8.00	16.50
	1888	7.027	2.50	4.00	8.00	16.50
	1888	—	—	—	Proof	150.00
	1889	4.027	2.50	4.00	8.00	16.50
	1889	—	—	—	Proof	150.00
	1889H	2.100	2.50	4.00	8.00	16.50
	1890	1.500	2.50	4.00	8.00	16.50
	1890	—	—	—	Proof	150.00
	1890H	5.400	2.50	4.00	8.00	16.50
	1891	6.150	2.50	4.00	8.00	16.50
	1891H	1.750	2.50	4.00	8.50	37.50
	1892	5.500	2.50	4.00	8.00	16.50
	1892	—	—	—	Proof	150.00
	1892H	1.100	4.00	7.50	15.00	37.50
	1892H	—	—	—	Proof	150.00
	1893	11.250	2.50	4.00	6.00	14.00
	1894	16.750	2.50	4.00	6.00	14.00
	1894	—	—	—	Proof	150.00
	1895	19.000	2.50	4.00	6.00	14.00
	1896	16.500	2.50	4.00	6.00	14.00
	1897	23.500	2.50	3.50	6.00	14.00
	1897H	7.000	2.50	4.00	8.00	16.50
	1898	29.500	2.50	4.00	8.00	14.00
	1899	33.842	2.50	3.50	6.00	12.00
	1900	7.758	2.50	4.00	8.00	14.00
	1900H	41.500	2.50	3.50	6.00	12.00
	1901	25.000	2.50	3.50	6.00	12.00

COPPER

Y#	Date	Mintage	Fine	VF	XF	Unc
4a	1863	—	—		Proof Only	250.00
	1866	—	—		Proof Only	250.00
	1869	—	—		Proof Only	250.00
	1873	—	—		Proof Only	250.00

ALUMINUM
Obv: With SPECIMEN

Y#	Date	Mintage	Fine	VF	XF	Unc
4b	1894	—	—		Proof Only	350.00

2.7154 gm., .800 SILVER, .0698 oz ASW

Y#	Date	Mintage	Fine	VF	XF	Unc
11	1902	18.000	2.50	3.00	4.00	8.00
	1902	—	—	—	Proof	100.00
	1903	25.000	2.50	3.00	4.00	8.00
	1903	—	—	—	Proof	100.00
	1904	30.000	2.50	3.00	4.00	8.00
	1904	—	—	—	Proof	100.00
	1905	33.487	500.00	600.00	800.00	1200.
	1905	—	—	—	Proof	1500.

COPPER-NICKEL

Y#	Date	Mintage	Fine	VF	XF	Unc
17	1935	10.000	.25	.50	1.00	3.00
	1935	—	—	—	Proof	75.00
	1936	5.000	.25	.50	1.00	3.00

NICKEL

Y#	Date	Mintage	Fine	VF	XF	Unc
21	1937	17.500	.40	.70	1.00	3.00
	1937	—	—	—	Proof	75.00

Y#	Date	Mintage	Fine	VF	XF	Unc
23	1938	7.500	.25	.50	.75	2.00
	1939H	5.000	.25	.50	1.00	2.00
	1939KN	5.000	.15	.30	.50	2.00
	1939KN	—	—	—	Proof	50.00

NICKEL-BRASS
Reeded, security edge.

Y#	Date	Mintage	Fine	VF	XF	Unc
25	1948	30.000	.15	.25	.40	2.00
	1949	35.000	.15	.25	.40	2.00
	1949	—	—	—	Proof	50.00
	1950	20.000	.15	.25	.35	2.00
	1951	5.000	.15	.25	.40	4.00
	1951	—	.15	—	Proof	50.00

Error: Reeded, without security edge.

Y#	Date	Mintage	Fine	VF	XF	Unc
25a	1950	Inc. Ab.	2.00	3.75	7.50	15.00

Reeded, with security edges

Y#	Date	Mintage	Fine	VF	XF	Unc
28	1955	10.000	.10	.15	.35	.75
	1955	—	—	—	Proof	50.00
	1956	3.110	.10	.20	.50	15.00
	1956H	4.488	.10	.15	.35	1.00
	1956KN	2.500	.10	.15	.35	15.00
	1957H	5.250	.10	.15	.30	.90
	1957KN	2.800	.10	.15	.30	1.00
	1958KN	10.000	.10	.15	.25	.70
	1959H	20.000	.10	.15	.20	.25
	1960	12.500	.10	.15	.20	.50
	1960	—	—	—	Proof	50.00
	1960H	10.000	.10	.15	.20	.40
	1961	20.000	.10	.15	.20	.25
	1961H	5.000	.10	.15	.20	5.00
	1961KN	5.000	.10	.15	.20	.40
	1963	30.000	.10	.15	.20	5.00
	1963	—	—	—	Proof	50.00
	1963H	Inc. Ab.	.10	.15	.20	.30
	1963KN	Inc. Ab.	.10	.15	.20	.25
	1964	30.000	.10	.15	.20	.25
	1964H	Inc. Ab.	.10	.15	.20	.25
	1965	48.000	.10	.15	.20	.25
	1965H	Inc. Ab.	.10	.15	.20	.25
	1965KN	Inc. Ab.	.10	.15	.20	.25
	1967	10.000	.10	.15	.20	.25
	1968H	15.000	.10	.15	.20	.25

Error: Reeded, without security edge.

Y#	Date	Mintage	Fine	VF	XF	Unc
28.1	1956H	Inc. Ab.	2.25	4.50	8.50	17.50

Reeded edges

Y#	Date	Mintage	Fine	VF	XF	Unc
28a	1971KN	—	.10	.15	.20	.25
	1971H	Inc. Ab.	.10	.15	.20	.30
	1972KN	20.000	.10	.15	.20	.25
	1973	2.250	.10	.15	.20	.30
	1974	4.600	.10	.15	.20	.30
	1975	44.840	.10	.15	.20	.25
	1978	—	.10	.15	.20	.25
	1979	—	.10	.15	.20	.25

20 CENTS

5.4308 gm., .800 SILVER, .1397 oz ASW

Y#	Date	Mintage	Fine	VF	XF	Unc
5	1866	.445	15.00	30.00	80.00	140.00
	1866	—	—	—	Proof	325.00
5	1867	Inc. Ab.	15.00	30.00	80.00	140.00
	1867	—	—	—	Proof	325.00
	1868	Inc. Ab.	15.00	30.00	80.00	140.00
	1868	—	—	—	Proof	325.00
	1872H	.064	15.00	30.00	80.00	160.00
	1872H	—	—	—	Proof	350.00
	1873	.096	15.00	30.00	80.00	160.00
	1873H	.064	15.00	30.00	80.00	160.00
	1874H	.070	15.00	30.00	80.00	160.00
	1875H	.070	15.00	30.00	80.00	140.00
	1875H	—	—	—	Proof	325.00
	1876H	.120	15.00	30.00	80.00	140.00
	1877H	.060	15.00	35.00	80.00	160.00
	1879	.020	200.00	400.00	600.00	1000.
	1879	—	—	—	Proof	2000.
	1880H	.030	100.00	200.00	300.00	400.00
	1881	.030	200.00	400.00	500.00	800.00
	1881	—	—	—	Proof	975.00
	1882H	.100	15.00	30.00	80.00	140.00
	1883	.138	15.00	30.00	80.00	140.00
	1883	—	—	—	Proof	350.00
	1883H	.060	15.00	30.00	80.00	140.00
	1883H	—	—	—	Proof	350.00
	1884	.080	15.00	30.00	80.00	140.00
	1884	—	—	—	Proof	350.00
	1885	.260	15.00	25.00	60.00	100.00
	1886	.175	15.00	25.00	60.00	100.00
	1887	.200	12.00	20.00	60.00	100.00
	1888	.500	10.00	18.00	50.00	100.00
	1888	—	—	—	Proof	500.00
	1889	.440	10.00	18.00	50.00	100.00
	1889	—	—	—	Proof	500.00
	1889H	.175	10.00	18.00	50.00	125.00
	1890	.125	10.00	18.00	50.00	100.00
	1890H	.450	10.00	18.00	50.00	100.00
	1891	.575	10.00	18.00	50.00	100.00
	1891H	.175	10.00	18.00	50.00	125.00
	1892	.450	10.00	18.00	40.00	80.00
	1892H	.100	10.00	18.00	50.00	125.00
	1893	.750	10.00	18.00	40.00	80.00
	1894	.650	10.00	18.00	40.00	80.00
	1894	—	—	—	Proof	500.00
	1895	.500	10.00	18.00	40.00	80.00
	1896	.250	10.00	18.00	10.00	85.00
	1898	.125	10.00	18.00	60.00	100.00

Y#	Date	Mintage	Fine	VF	XF	Unc
12	1902	.250	30.00	50.00	70.00	200.00
	1902	—	—	—	Proof	425.00
	1904	.250	30.00	50.00	70.00	200.00
	1905	.750	500.00	800.00	1000.	1400.
	1905	—	—	—	Proof	1650.

NICKEL-BRASS

Y#	Date	Mintage	Fine	VF	XF	Unc
33	1975	71.000	.10	.15	.20	.25
	1976	42.000	.10	.15	.20	.25
	1977	Inc. Ab.	.10	.15	.20	.25
	1978	—	.10	.15	.20	.25
	1979	—	.10	.15	.20	.25

1/2 DOLLAR

13.478 gm., .900 SILVER, .3900 oz ASW

Y#	Date	Mintage	Fine	VF	XF	Unc
6	1866	.059	250.00	350.00	800.00	1200.
	1866	—	—	—	Proof	1000.
	1867	Inc. Ab.	700.00	900.00	1200.	2000.
	1867	—	—	—	Proof	1800.
	1868	—	—		Proof Only	2000.

50 CENTS

13.5769 gm., .800 SILVER, .3492 oz ASW

Y#	Date	Mintage	Fine	VF	XF	Unc
7	1890	.050	25.00	50.00	120.00	250.00
	1890	—	—	—	Proof	450.00
	1891	.150	20.00	35.00	85.00	200.00
	1891	—	—	—	Proof	450.00
	1891H	.070	20.00	40.00	85.00	200.00
	1892	.090	20.00	35.00	85.00	200.00
	1892	—	—	—	Proof	450.00
	1892H	.020	60.00	100.00	120.00	325.00
	1892H	—	—	—	Proof	800.00
	1893	.150	20.00	35.00	85.00	200.00
	1894	.130	25.00	35.00	85.00	200.00
	1894	—	—	—	Proof	450.00

Y#	Date	Mintage	Fine	VF	XF	Unc
13	1902	.100	15.00	25.00	40.00	75.00
	1902	—	—	—	Proof	225.00
	1904	.100	15.00	25.00	40.00	60.00
	1904	—	—	—	Proof	225.00
	1905	.300	15.00	20.00	35.00	60.00
	1905	—	—	—	Proof	175.00

COPPER-NICKEL
Reeded, security edge.

Y#	Date	Mintage	Fine	VF	XF	Unc
26	1951	15.000	1.00	2.00	4.00	6.00
	1951	—	—	—	Proof	125.00

Error: Reeded, without security edge.

Y#	Date	Mintage	Fine	VF	XF	Unc
26.1	1951	Inc. Ab.	2.50	5.00	10.00	20.00

Reeded, security edge

Y#	Date	Mintage	Fine	VF	XF	Unc
29	1958H	4.000	.15	.20	.50	1.00
	1960	4.000	.15	.20	.40	.50
	1961	6.000	.15	.20	.40	.80
	1963H	6.500	.15	.20	.40	.50
	1964	5.000	.15	.20	.30	.50
	1965KN	8.000	.15	.20	.25	.50
	1966	5.000	.15	.20	.25	.50
	1967	12.000	.15	.20	.25	.50
	1968H	12.000	.15	.20	.25	.50
	1970H	—	.15	.20	.25	.40

Error: Reeded, without security edge.

Y#	Date	Mintage	Fine	VF	XF	Unc
29.1	1958H	Inc. Ab.	2.50	5.00	10.00	20.00

Reeded edge

Y#	Date	Mintage	Fine	VF	XF	Unc
29a	1971KN	—	.15	.20	.25	.40
	1971H	Inc. Ab.	.15	.20	.25	.40
	1972	30.000	.15	.20	.25	.40
	1972KN	Inc. Ab.	.15	.20	.25	.40
	1973	36.800	.15	.20	.25	.40
	1974	6.000	.15	.20	.25	.40
	1975	8.000	.15	.20	.25	.40

NICKEL-BRASS

Y#	Date	Mintage	Fine	VF	XF	Unc
34	1977	—	.15	.20	.25	.40
	1978	—	.15	.20	.25	.40
	1979	—	—	—	—	—

DOLLAR

26.9568 gm., .900 SILVER, .7800 oz ASW

Y#	Date	Mintage	Fine	VF	XF	Unc
8	1866	2.109	60.00	80.00	160.00	300.00
	1866	—	—	—	Proof	800.00
	1867/6	Inc. Ab.	150.00	200.00	350.00	500.00
	1867	Inc. Ab.	60.00	80.00	160.00	300.00
	1868	Inc. Ab.	60.00	80.00	160.00	300.00

COPPER

Y#	Date	Mintage	Fine	VF	XF	Unc
8a	1866	—	—	Proof Only		500.00

COPPER-NICKEL
Reeded, security edge

Y#	Date	Mintage	Fine	VF	XF	Unc
30	1960H	68.225	.25	.30	.50	1.00
	1960KN	Inc. Ab.	.25	.30	.50	1.00
	1970H	20.000	.25	.35	.60	1.00

Error: Reeded, without security edge.

Y#	Date	Mintage	Fine	VF	XF	Unc
30.1	1960H	Inc. Ab.	3.00	6.00	11.50	22.50

Reeded edge

Y#	Date	Mintage	Fine	VF	XF	Unc
30a	1971H	—	.25	.30	.50	1.00
	1972	20.000	.25	.30	.40	.60
	1973	8.125	.25	.30	.45	.75
	1974	26.000	.25	.30	.40	.60
	1975	22.500	.25	.30	.40	.60

Y#	Date	Mintage	Fine	VF	XF	Unc
35	1978	—	.25	.30	.40	.75
	1979	—	—	—	—	—

2 DOLLARS

COPPER-NICKEL

Y#	Date	Mintage	Fine	VF	XF	Unc
36	1975	60.000	.50	.60	.75	1.00

5 DOLLARS

COPPER-NICKEL

Y#	Date	Mintage	Fine	VF	XF	Unc
37	1976	30.000	1.25	1.50	1.75	2.25
	1978	—	1.25	1.50	1.75	2.25

1000 DOLLARS

15.9700 gm., .917 GOLD, .4708 oz AGW
Visit Of Queen Elizabeth

Y#	Date	Mintage	Fine	VF	XF	Unc
31	1975	.015	—	—	—	600.00
	1975	5,005	—	—	Proof	1200.

Year of the Dragon

Y#	Date	Mintage	Fine	VF	XF	Unc
32	1976	.020	—	—	—	900.00
	1976	6,555	—	—	Proof	1400.

Year Of The Snake

Y#	Date	Mintage	Fine	VF	XF	Unc
38	1977	.027	—	—	—	550.00
	1977	.010	—		Proof	750.00

Year of the Horse

Y#	Date	Mintage	Fine	VF	XF	Unc
39	1978	.020	—	—	—	550.00
	1978	.010	—	—	Proof	750.00

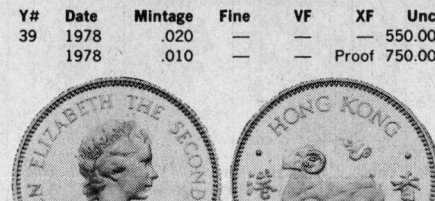

Year of the Goat

Y#	Date	Mintage	Fine	VF	XF	Unc
40	1979	.020	—	—	—	500.00
	1979	.010	—	—	Proof	750.00

Year of the Monkey

Y#	Date	Mintage	Fine	VF	XF	Unc
41	1980	.027	—	—	—	400.00
	1980	.013	—	—	Proof	800.00

NCLT ISSUES

PROOF SETS

STANDARD METALS

KM#	Date	Mintage	Identification	Issue Price	Mkt. Val.
101	1866(5)	—	Y3-6,8	—	1850.

HUNGARY

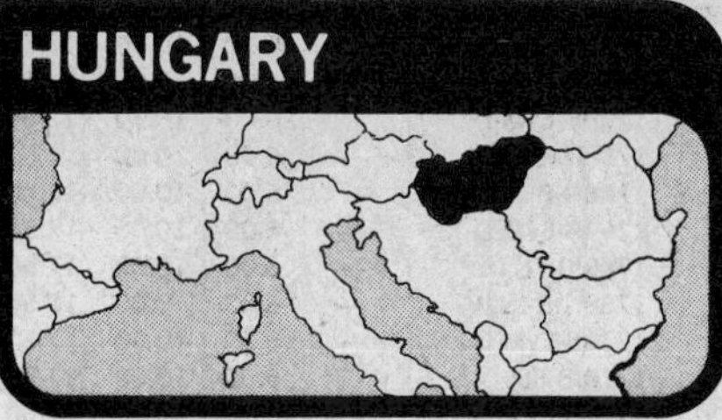

The Hungarian People's Republic, located in central Europe, has an area of 35,900 sq. mi. (92,980 sq. km.) and a population of 10.5 million. Capital: Budapest. The economy is based on agriculture, bauxite and a rapidly expanding industrial sector. Machinery, chemicals, iron and steel, and fruits and vegetables are exported.

The ancient kingdom of Hungary, founded by the Magyars in the 9th century, achieved its greatest extension in the mid-14th century when its dominions touched the Baltic, Black and Mediterranean seas. After suffering repeated Turkish invasions, Hungary accepted Hapsburg rule to escape Turkish occupation, regaining independence in 1867 with the Emperor of Austria as king of a dual Austro-Hungarian Empire. Sharing the defeat of the Central Powers in World War I, Hungary lost the greater part of its territory and population and underwent a period of drastic political revision. The short-lived republic of 1918 was followed by a chaotic interval of communist rule, 1919, and the restoration of the monarchy in 1920 with Admiral Horthy as regent of a kingdom without a king. Although a German ally in World War II, Hungary was occupied by German troops who imposed a pro-Nazi dictatorship, 1944. Soviet armies drove out the Germans in 1945 and assisted the communist minority in seizing power. A revised constitution published on Aug. 20, 1949, established Hungary as a 'people's republic' of the Soviet type.

NOTE: Many coins of Hungary through 1948, especially 1925-1945, have been restruck in recent times. These may be identified by a rosette in the vicinity of the mintmark. Restrike mintages for Y#1 to Y#30 are usually about 1000 pieces, later date mintages are not known.

RULERS

Austrian until 1916

MINTMARKS

A - Vienna
B,KB,K - Kremnitz (1792-1867)
BP - Budapest (since 1926)
KB - Kremnitz (1868-1915)
KB(r) - Kremnitz with rosette (restrikes)

GYF - Gyulafehervar (1868-1871)
G, NB - Nagyabanya (1849)
S - Schmollnitz
UP - Ungarische Praegung

KREMNITZ MINTMASTER'S INITIALS

D, PD - Paschal Josef V. Damiani
EvM - Edler V. Munzburg
K, SK - Sigmund Klemmer V. Klemmerberg

NAGYBANYA MINTMASTER'S INITIALS

B, IB - Josef Brunner
FL, L - Franz Anton Lochner
IV, V - Josef Vischer

MONETARY SYSTEM

(Until 1857)
2 Poltura = 3 Krajczar
60 Krajczar = 1 Forint (Gulden)
2 Forint = 1 Convention Thaler
1857-1891
100 Krajczar = 1 Forint
100 Filler = 1 Forint (since 1946)

POLTURA

COPPER
Obv: Veiled heads of Maria Theresa right.
Rev: Madonna and child over value

C#	Date	Mintage	VG	Fine	VF
4a	1775S	—	10.00	17.50	30.00

5/10 KRAJCZAR

COPPER

Y#	Date	Mintage	Fine	VF	XF	Unc
3	1882KB	2.400	2.50	4.00	5.50	7.50
	1882KB (restrike)		—	—	Proof	7.00

KRAJCZAR

COPPER

Y#	Date	Mintage	Fine	VF	XF	Unc
1	1868KB	12.530	.50	1.00	2.00	3.00
	1868KB (restrike)		—	—	Proof	7.50
	1868KB-GYF	—	—	—	Rare	—
	1869KB	5.070	.30	.75	2.00	3.00
	1872KB	—	.50	1.25	3.00	4.50
	1873KB	—	30.00	62.50	95.00	150.00

Y#	Date	Mintage	Fine	VF	XF	Unc
4	1878KB	4.480	10.00	16.50	27.50	40.00
	1879KB	10.101	3.00	6.50	10.00	15.00
	1881KB	12.233	3.00	6.50	10.00	15.00
	1882KB	19.800	4.00	9.00	15.00	22.50
	1883KB	8.535	7.50	12.50	22.50	30.00
	1885KB	26.606	1.25	3.00	6.00	10.00
	1886KB	17.671	2.00	5.00	7.50	12.50
	1887KB	11.989	2.00	5.00	10.00	15.00
	1888KB	10.334	3.00	6.50	10.00	15.00

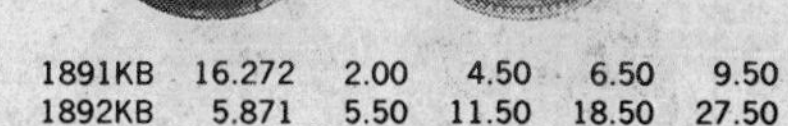

Y#	Date	Mintage	Fine	VF	XF	Unc
4a	1891KB	16.272	2.00	4.50	6.50	9.50
(5)	1892KB	5.871	5.50	11.50	18.50	27.50

3 KRAJCZAR

BILLON
Obv: Veiled head of Maria Theresa right
Rev: Madonna and child over value

C#	Date	Mintage	VG	Fine	VF
13a	1766B-EvM-D	—	5.00	10.00	15.00
	1767B-EvM-D	—	5.00	10.00	15.00
	1768B-EvM-D	—	5.00	10.00	15.00
	1769B-EvM-D	—	5.00	10.00	15.00
	1770B-EvM-D	—	5.00	10.00	15.00
	1771B-EvM-D	—	5.00	10.00	15.00
	1773B-EvM-D	—	5.00	10.00	15.00
	1778B-K-D	—	5.00	10.00	15.00
	1779B-K-D	—	5.00	10.00	15.00
	1779B-SK-PD	—	5.00	10.00	15.00
	1779B-V	—	5.00	10.00	15.00
	1779CM	—	5.00	10.00	15.00
	1779IB-IV	—	5.00	10.00	15.00
	1779K-B	—	5.00	10.00	15.00

4 KRAJCZAR

COPPER

Y#	Date	Mintage	Fine	VF	XF	Unc
2	1868KB	3.100	3.00	7.50	15.00	22.50
	1868KB (restrike)		—	—	Proof	20.00

10 KRAJCZAR

SILVER
Obv: Veiled head of Maria Theresa right.
Rev: Madonna and child over value

C#	Date	Mintage	Fine	VF	XF
19a	1769B EvM-D	—	7.50	12.50	20.00

.500 SILVER

C#	Date	Mintage	Fine	VF	XF	Unc
60	1837B	—	—	—	Rare	—
	1838B	—	11.50	22.50	45.00	85.00
	1839B	—	4.25	10.00	21.50	37.50
	1840B	—	5.00	12.50	25.00	45.00
	1841B	—	3.75	8.50	17.50	30.00
	1842B	—	3.75	8.50	17.50	30.00
	1843B	—	6.25	12.50	25.00	45.00
	1844B	—	3.75	7.50	15.00	27.50
	1845B	—	3.75	7.50	15.00	27.50
	1846B	—	3.25	6.50	12.50	22.50
	1847B	—	2.50	5.00	10.00	20.00
	1848B	—	2.00	4.00	10.00	20.00

.500 SILVER

Y#	Date	Mintage	Fine	VF	XF	Unc
6	1868KB	—	13.50	27.50	50.00	100.00
	1868KB (restrike)		—	—	Proof	60.00

.400 SILVER

Y#	Date	Mintage	Fine	VF	XF	Unc
7	1868GYF	1.010	17.50	35.00	70.00	135.00
	1868KB	3.250	10.00	20.00	32.50	55.00
	1868KB (restrike)		—	—	Proof	32.50
	1869GYF	2.750	10.00	21.50	35.00	60.00
	1869KB	12.750	5.00	17.50	30.00	50.00

Y#	Date	Mintage	Fine	VF	XF	Unc
10	1870GYF	3.030	5.00	10.00	20.00	35.00
	1870KB	21.930	3.00	5.00	10.00	20.00
	1870KB (restrike)		—	—	Proof	20.00
	1871GYF	3.380	5.00	10.00	20.00	35.00
	1872KB	1.150	6.50	13.50	27.50	45.00
	1873KB	1.070	6.50	13.50	27.50	45.00
	1874KB	1.320	6.50	13.50	27.50	45.00
	1875KB	.430	9.00	18.50	37.50	75.00
	1876KB	.520	10.00	30.00	55.00	85.00
	1877KB	.460	10.00	30.00	55.00	85.00
	1887KB	.025	60.00	90.00	140.00	200.00
	1888KB	.360	7.50	13.50	27.50	50.00

Mule, Obv: Y#10, Rev. Y#6

Y#	Date	Mintage	VF	XF	Unc
10a	1868 KB	(restrike)	—	Proof	60.00

20 KRAJCZAR

SILVER
Obv: Veiled head of Maria Theresa right.
Rev: Madonna and child over value

C#	Date	Mintage	Fine	VF	XF
22a	1766B-EvM-D	—	6.00	10.00	17.50
	1766IB-FL	—	6.00	10.00	17.50
	1767B-EvM-D	—	6.00	10.00	17.50
	1767IB-FL	—	6.00	10.00	17.50
	1768B-EvM-D	—	6.00	10.00	17.50
	1768IB-FL	—	6.00	10.00	17.50
	1768N-B	—	6.00	10.00	17.50
	1769B-EvM-D	—	6.00	10.00	17.50
	1769IB-FL	—	6.00	10.00	17.50
	1769N-B-IB-IV	—	6.00	10.00	17.50
	1770B-EvM-D	—	6.00	10.00	17.50
	1770IB-FL	—	6.00	10.00	17.50
	1771B-EvM-D	—	6.00	10.00	17.50
	1771IB-FL	—	6.00	10.00	17.50
	1771N-B-IB-FL	—	6.00	10.00	17.50
	1772B-EvM-D	—	6.00	10.00	17.50
	1773B-EvM-D	—	6.00	10.00	17.50
	1773IB-IV	—	6.00	10.00	17.50
	1773G-IB-IV	—	6.00	10.00	17.50
	1773G-IB-IV/N-B	—	6.00	10.00	17.50
	1774B-EvM-D	—	6.00	10.00	17.50
	1774B-SK-PD	—	6.00	10.00	17.50
	1774IB-IV	—	6.00	10.00	17.50
	1775B-SK-PD	—	6.00	10.00	17.50
	1775IB-IV	—	6.00	10.00	17.50
	1775N-B-IB-IV	—	6.00	10.00	17.50
	1776B-SK-PD	—	6.00	10.00	17.50
	1776IB-IV	—	6.00	10.00	17.50
	1776N-B-IB-IV	—	6.00	10.00	17.50
	1777B-SK-PD	—	6.00	10.00	17.50
	1777IB-IV	—	6.00	10.00	17.50
	1777N-B-IB-IV	—	6.00	10.00	17.50
	1778B-SK-PD	—	6.00	10.00	17.50
	1778IB-IV	—	6.00	10.00	17.50
	1779B-SK-PD	—	6.00	10.00	17.50
	1779IB-IV	—	6.00	10.00	17.50
	1779B-V	—	6.00	10.00	17.50
	1780B-SK-PD	—	6.00	10.00	17.50
	1780IB-IV	—	6.00	10.00	17.50

Obv: Ribbons on wreath forward across neck
Rev: Madonna With Child

C#	Date	Mintage	VF	XF	Unc
56	1830A	—	40.00	75.00	120.00

Obv: Left ribbon on wreath behind neck

C#	Date	Mintage	VF	XF	Unc
56b	1830A	—	180.00	325.00	550.00

Obv: Both ribbons on wreath behind neck

C#	Date	Mintage	VF	XF	Unc
56a	1832B	—	90.00	160.00	270.00
	1833B	—	40.00	75.00	120.00
	1834B	—	15.00	27.50	45.00
	1835B	—	25.00	45.00	75.00

Obv. leg: FERD. I. Rev. leg: S. MARIA...

C#	Date	Mintage	VF	XF	Unc
61	1837B	—	4.50	8.00	13.50
	1838B	—	4.25	7.50	12.50
	1839B	—	3.50	6.50	11.50
	1840B	—	2.50	4.50	7.50
	1841B	—	2.50	4.50	7.50
	1842B	—	3.00	6.00	9.50
	1843B	—	2.75	5.00	8.00
	1844B	—	2.75	5.00	8.00
	1845B	—	3.00	5.50	9.00
	1846B	—	2.50	4.50	7.50
	1847B	—	2.25	4.50	7.50
	1848B	—	3.00	5.00	7.00

.500 SILVER

Y#	Date	Mintage	Fine	VF	XF	Unc
8	1868GYF	—	30.00	65.00	95.00	140.00
	1868KB	—	15.00	30.00	42.50	60.00

Y#	Date	Mintage	Fine	VF	XF	Unc
9	1868GYF	1.040	9.00	20.00	38.50	75.00
	1868KB	3.220	6.25	13.50	27.50	50.00
	1868KB (restrike)		—	—	Proof	60.00
	1869GYF	2.300	7.50	15.00	30.00	55.00
	1869KB	9.490	5.00	13.50	27.50	50.00

Y#	Date	Mintage	Fine	VF	XF	Unc
11	1870GYF	7.210	21.50	45.00	75.00	110.00
	1870KB	4.430	21.50	45.00	75.00	110.00
	1870KB (restrike)		—	—	Proof	32.50
	1872KB	1.290	30.00	60.00	90.00	135.00

Mule, obv: Y#11. Rev: Y#8

Y#	Date	Mintage	VF	XF	Unc
11a	1868KB	(restrike)	—	Proof	60.00

30 KRAJCZAR

SILVER
Obv: Veiled head of Maria Theresa right
Rev: Crowned arms with angel supporters in rhombus

C#	Date	Mintage	Fine	VF	XF
24a	1767K-EvM-D		17.50	30.00	42.50
	1768K-EvM-D		17.50	30.00	42.50
	1768B-EvM-D		17.50	30.00	42.50
	1769K-EvM-D		17.50	30.00	42.50
	1770K-EvM-D		17.50	30.00	42.50
	1771K-EvM-D		17.50	30.00	42.50
	1772K-EvM-D		17.50	30.00	42.50
	1776K-SK-PD		17.50	30.00	42.50

1/2 THALER
(Convention)

SILVER

C#	Date	Mintage	Fine	VF	XF
27	1767K-EvM-D		30.00	45.00	65.00
	1768K-EvM-D		30.00	45.00	65.00
	1769K-EvM-D		30.00	45.00	65.00
	1770K-EvM-D		30.00	45.00	65.00
	1771K-EvM-D		30.00	45.00	65.00
	1772K-EvM-D		30.00	45.00	65.00
	1775K-SK-PD		30.00	45.00	65.00
	1776K-SK-PD		30.00	45.00	65.00
	1779B-SK-PD		30.00	45.00	65.00
	1780B-SK-PD		30.00	45.00	65.00

Obv. leg: IOS.II.D.G.R.IMP......
Rev: Madonna

C#	Date	Mintage	Fine	VF	XF
45.1	1782A	—	15.00	20.00	35.00
	1782B	—	15.00	20.00	35.00
	1783B	—	15.00	20.00	35.00
	1785B	—	15.00	20.00	35.00
	1786B	—	15.00	20.00	35.00
	1789B	—	15.00	20.00	35.00

C#	Date	Mintage	Fine	VF	XF
45.2	1785A	—	15.00	20.00	35.00
	1786A	—	15.00	20.00	35.00
	1787A	—	15.00	20.00	35.00
	1788A	—	15.00	20.00	35.00
	1789A	—	15.00	20.00	35.00
	1790A	—	15.00	20.00	35.00

.833 SILVER
Obv. leg: LEOP.II.D.-G.R.IMP.
Rev: Madonna

C#	Date	Mintage	Fine	VF	XF	Unc
50	1790A	—	200.00	500.00	750.00	1150.
	1791A	—	200.00	500.00	750.00	1150.
	1792A	—	225.00	550.00	825.00	1250.

Obv: Crowned arms with angels.
Rev: Madonna with child.

C#	Date	Mintage	VF	XF	Unc
53	1792A	—	120.00	180.00	300.00
	1793A	—	95.00	150.00	250.00
	1794A	—	110.00	165.00	275.00
	Obv: Ribbons on wreath forward across neck.				
	Rev: Madonna with child.				
57	1830A	—	85.00	125.00	200.00
	Obv: Both ribbons on wreath behind neck.				
57a	1831B	*	—	—	—
	1833B	*	60.00	90.00	150.00
	1834B	—	250.00	325.00	550.00
	1835B	—	—	—	—

*Restruck in 1841.

.833 SILVER
Obv: Head right, leg: FERD. I.D.G.....

C#	Date	Mintage	Fine	VF	XF	Unc
62	1837B	—	300.00	550.00	900.00	1250.
	1839B	—	—	—	Rare	—

FORINT

12.3457 gm., .900 SILVER, .3572 oz ASW

Y#	Date	Mintage	Fine	VF	XF	Unc
12	1868GYF	.270	12.00	17.50	25.00	45.00
	1868KB	.570	12.00	17.50	25.00	45.00
	1868KB (restrike)	—	—	—	—	30.00
	1869GYF	.360	11.50	15.00	20.00	30.00
	1869KB	.490	11.50	15.00	20.00	35.00

Y#	Date	Mintage	Fine	VF	XF	Unc
13	1870GYF	.570	35.00	60.00	90.00	130.00
	1870KB	1.250	15.00	25.00	40.00	60.00
	1871GYF	.240	35.00	60.00	90.00	125.00
	1871KB	2.440	15.00	25.00	40.00	60.00
	1872KB	3.456	12.00	17.50	30.00	50.00
	1873KB	2.338	15.00	30.00	45.00	75.00
	1874KB	2.082	15.00	25.00	35.00	50.00
	1875KB	2.074	BV	12.00	17.50	25.00
	1876KB	4.136	BV	12.00	15.00	20.00
	1877KB	2.241	BV	12.00	15.00	20.00
	1878KB	5.717	BV	12.00	15.00	20.00
	1879KB	25.756	BV	12.00	15.00	20.00
	Obv: Larger head and legends					
13a	1880KB	3.815	BV	12.00	17.50	22.50
	1881KB	15.495	BV	12.00	15.00	20.00

Y#	Date	Mintage	Fine	VF	XF	Unc
14	1882KB	1.897	BV	12.00	17.50	22.50
	1883KB	7.041	BV	12.00	15.00	20.00
	1884KB	1.722	BV	12.00	15.00	20.00
	1885KB	1.672	BV	12.00	15.00	20.00
	1886KB	1.566	BV	12.00	17.50	22.50
	1887KB	2.022	BV	12.00	15.00	20.00
	1888KB	1.841	BV	12.00	15.00	20.00
	1889KB	1.974	BV	12.00	15.00	20.00
	1890KB	2.022	12.00	15.00	20.00	30.00

Y#	Date	Mintage	Fine	VF	XF	Unc
15	1890KB	Inc. Ab.	BV	15.00	20.00	30.00
	1891KB	1.470	BV	15.00	20.00	30.00
	1892KB	1.607	BV	12.00	20.00	30.00
	1892KB (restrike)	—	—	Proof	25.00	

Reopening of the Joseph II Mine at Schemnitz

Y#	Date	Mintage	VF	XF	Unc
16	1878	4,000	1000.	1400.	2000.

THALER
(Convention)

SILVER
Obv: Crowned arms with angel supporters
Rev: Madonna and child

C#	Date	Mintage	Fine	VF	XF
30	1767K		50.00	65.00	100.00
	1767K EVM-D		50.00	65.00	100.00
	1768K EVM-D		50.00	65.00	100.00
	1769K EVM-D		50.00	65.00	100.00
	1770K EVM-D		50.00	65.00	100.00
	1771K EVM-D		50.00	65.00	100.00
	1772K EVM-D		50.00	65.00	100.00
	1773K EVM-D		50.00	65.00	100.00
	1775K SK-PD		50.00	65.00	100.00
	1776K SK-PD		50.00	65.00	100.00
	1777B SK-PD		50.00	65.00	100.00
	1778B SK-PD		50.00	65.00	100.00
	1779B SK-PD		50.00	65.00	100.00
	1780B SK-PD		50.00	65.00	100.00

Obv. leg: IOS.II.D.G.R.IMP.S.A....

C#	Date	Mintage	Fine	VF	XF
46.1	1781B	—	35.00	50.00	75.00
	1782B	—	35.00	50.00	75.00
	1783B	—	35.00	50.00	75.00
	Obv. leg: IOS.II.D.G.R.I.S.A.....				
46.2	1783A	—	35.00	50.00	75.00
	1785A	—	35.00	50.00	75.00
	Obv: Similar to C#46.2, but flying angels.				
46.3	1785A	—	35.00	50.00	75.00
	1786A	—	35.00	50.00	75.00
	1786B	—	35.00	50.00	75.00
	1789A	—	35.00	50.00	75.00

.833 SILVER
Obv. leg: LEOP.II.D.-G.HV.BO.GA.LOD....
Rev: Madonna.

C#	Date	Mintage	Fine	VF	XF	Unc
51	1790A	—	600.00	1200.	1750.	2250.
	Obv. leg: LEOP.II.D.G.R.IMP.....					
51a	1790A	—	450.00	900.00	1750.	2500.
	1791A	—	500.00	1000.	2000.	2750.

Obv: Crowned arms with angels, leg: FRANC D.G.
Rev: Madonna with child.

C#	Date	Mintage	VF	XF	Unc
54	1792A	—	300.00	450.00	750.00
	Obv. leg: FRANC II. D.G....				
54a	1792A	—	400.00	550.00	900.00
	Obv: Ribbons on wreath forward across neck.				
58	1830A	—	150.00	210.00	350.00
	1830B	—	—	—	—

Obv: Ribbons on wreath behind neck.

C#	Date	Mintage	VF	XF	Unc
58a	1831B	—	175.00	300.00	525.00
	1833B	—	100.00	275.00	450.00

Obv: Head right, leg: FERD I. D.G.....

C#	Date	Mintage	Fine	VF	XF	Unc
63	1837B	—	400.00	700.00	1000.	1400.
	1839B	—	—	—	Rare	—

REVOLUTIONARY ISSUES

1848-1849

EGY (1) KRAJCZAR

COPPER

C#	Date	Mintage	Fine	VF	XF	Unc
65	1848	—	1.75	3.50	7.00	13.50
	1849NB	—	1.00	2.00	3.25	4.50

HAROM (3) KRAJCZAR

COPPER

C#	Date	Mintage	Fine	VF	XF	Unc
66	1849NB	—	6.50	12.50	20.00	30.00

HAT (6) KRAJCZAR

.220 SILVER

C#	Date	Mintage	Fine	VF	XF	Unc
67	1849NB	—	3.25	6.50	12.50	16.50

10 KRAJCZAR

.500 SILVER
Similar to 20 Krajczar, C#69.

C#	Date	Mintage	Fine	VF	XF	Unc
68	1848KB	—	15.00	32.50	62.50	125.00

20 KRAJCZAR

.583 SILVER
Rev. leg: SZ. MARIA...

C#	Date	Mintage	Fine	VF	XF	Unc
69	1848KB	—	3.00	6.00	12.00	23.50

TRADE COINS

4 FORINT/10 FRANCS

3.2258 gm., .900 GOLD, .0934 oz AGW

Y#	Date	Mintage	Fine	VF	XF	Unc
17.1	1870KB	.081	BV	65.00	80.00	100.00
	1870KB-UP	(restrike)		—	Proof	75.00
	1870GYF	.049	BV	65.00	80.00	100.00
	1871KB	.111	BV	70.00	85.00	110.00
	1872KB	.053	BV	70.00	85.00	110.00
	1873KB	.013	75.00	100.00	130.00	160.00
	1874KB	8,229	100.00	125.00	150.00	175.00
	1875KB	.011	75.00	100.00	130.00	160.00
	1876KB	.024	BV	75.00	90.00	115.00
	1877KB	.024	BV	75.00	90.00	115.00
	1878KB	.015	BV	75.00	90.00	115.00
	1879KB	.012	BV	75.00	90.00	115.00

NOTE: Semi official restrikes have the letters UP below the bust.

Older head

Y#	Date	Mintage	Fine	VF	XF	Unc
17.2	1880KB	.013	65.00	75.00	85.00	100.00
	1881KB	.012	65.00	75.00	85.00	100.00
	1882KB	.013	65.00	75.00	85.00	100.00
	1883KB	.012	65.00	75.00	85.00	100.00
	1884KB	.054	BV	65.00	75.00	90.00
	1885KB	.064	BV	65.00	75.00	90.00
	1886KB	.039	BV	65.00	75.00	90.00
	1887KB	.039	BV	65.00	75.00	90.00
	1888KB	.049	BV	65.00	75.00	90.00
	1889KB	.019	100.00	150.00	225.00	300.00
	1890KB					
		Inc. Y#19	95.00	135.00	200.00	275.00

Rev: Fiume arms

Y#	Date	Mintage	Fine	VF	XF	Unc
19	1890KB	.029	200.00	275.00	350.00	425.00
	1891KB	.032	65.00	75.00	85.00	100.00
	1892	20 pcs.	800.00	1000.	1350.	1750.

DUCAT

3.4900 gm., .986 GOLD, .1106 oz AGW
Obv: Veiled head of Maria Theresa right
Rev: Madonna and child

C#	Date	Mintage	Fine	VF	XF
35a	1766B-L	—	250.00	350.00	500.00
	1767B-L	—	250.00	350.00	500.00
	1768B-L	—	250.00	350.00	500.00
	1769B-L	—	250.00	350.00	500.00
	1770B-L	—	250.00	350.00	500.00
	1771B-L	—	250.00	350.00	500.00
	1773	—	250.00	350.00	500.00
	1774B-V	—	250.00	350.00	500.00
	1775B-V	—	250.00	350.00	500.00
	1779IB-IV	—	250.00	350.00	500.00
	1779B-V	—	250.00	350.00	500.00
	1780IB-IV	—	250.00	350.00	500.00

Obv: Standing monarch, leg: IOS.II.D.G.R.I.S.A.— G.H.B.R.A.A.D.B.ET.L.
Rev: Madonna, leg: PATRONA REGNI HVNGARIAE.

C#	Date	Mintage	Fine	VF	XF
47	1781	—	150.00	225.00	275.00
	1782	—	150.00	225.00	275.00
	1783	—	150.00	225.00	275.00
	1784	—	150.00	225.00	275.00
	1785/4	—	150.00	225.00	275.00
	1785	—	150.00	225.00	275.00

Obv: Standing monarch, leg: LEOP.II.D.G.HV.BO.GA.- L.R.A.A.D.B.ET.L.M.D.H. Rev: Madonna, leg: S.MARIA MATER DEI-PATRONA HVNG.

C#	Date	Mintage	Fine	VF	XF	Unc
52	1790	—	225.00	275.00	425.00	600.00

C#	Date	Mintage	Fine	VF	XF	Unc
52a	1791	—	135.00	275.00	450.00	625.00
	1792	—	125.00	250.00	400.00	600.00

Obv: King standing, leg: FRAN II.D.G.
Rev: Madonna with child.

C#	Date	Mintage	VF	XF	Unc
55	1792	—	120.00	180.00	300.00
	1793	—	120.00	180.00	300.00
	1794	—	100.00	160.00	260.00
	1795	—	185.00	285.00	475.00
	1796	—	110.00	165.00	270.00
	1797	—	110.00	165.00	270.00
	1798	—	150.00	210.00	360.00
	1799	—	120.00	180.00	300.00

Obv. leg: FRANC I.D.G....

C#	Date	Mintage	VF	XF	Unc
59	1830	—	75.00	125.00	175.00
	1832	—	75.00	125.00	175.00
	1833	—	75.00	100.00	125.00
	1834	—	75.00	100.00	125.00
	1835	—	75.00	100.00	125.00

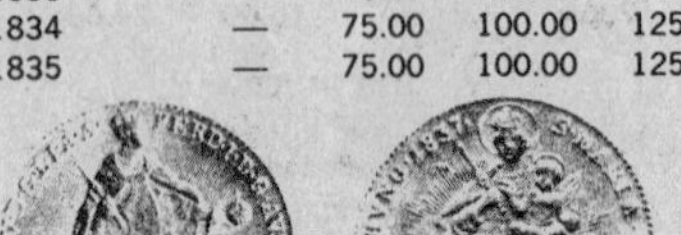

Obv. leg: FERDI. D.G....

C#	Date	Mintage	Fine	VF	XF	Unc
64	1837	—	150.00	250.00	400.00	600.00
	1838	—	150.00	250.00	400.00	600.00
	1839	—	90.00	125.00	200.00	350.00
	1840	—	75.00	100.00	160.00	275.00
	1841	—	90.00	125.00	200.00	350.00
	1842	—	90.00	125.00	160.00	275.00
	1843	—	100.00	150.00	250.00	450.00
	1844	—	90.00	125.00	200.00	350.00
	1845	—	100.00	150.00	250.00	450.00
	1846	—	90.00	125.00	200.00	350.00
	1847	—	75.00	100.00	160.00	275.00
	1848	—	75.00	100.00	150.00	250.00

.986 GOLD
Rev. leg: SZ. MARIA....

C#	Date	Mintage	Fine	VF	XF	Unc
70	1848	—	75.00	100.00	150.00	250.00

Y#	Date	Mintage	Fine	VF	XF	Unc
21	1868KB	.128	100.00	185.00	250.00	400.00
	1868GYF	.400	85.00	135.00	190.00	275.00
	1869KB	.107	100.00	185.00	250.00	400.00
	1869GYF	.270	85.00	135.00	190.00	275.00

Similar to 4 Forint, Y#17.

Y#	Date	Mintage	Fine	VF	XF	Unc
22a	1870KB	Restrike	—	—	Proof	75.00
	1877KB	452 pcs.	—	—	—	—
	1879KB	3,651	—	—	—	—
	1880KB	5,075	—	—	—	—

Y#	Date	Mintage	Fine	VF	XF	Unc
22a	1881KB	*43 pcs.	500.00	750.00	1250.	2750.

8 FORINT/20 FRANCS

6.4516 gm., .900 GOLD, .1867 oz AGW

Y#	Date	Mintage	Fine	VF	XF	Unc
18.1	1870KB	.046	BV	125.00	140.00	160.00
	1870GYF	.125	BV	120.00	135.00	150.00
	1871KB	.076	BV	120.00	135.00	150.00
	1871GYF	.177	BV	120.00	135.00	150.00
	1872KB	.273	BV	BV	125.00	135.00
	1873KB	.245	BV	BV	125.00	135.00
	1874KB	.240	BV	BV	125.00	135.00
	1875KB	.261	BV	BV	125.00	135.00
	1876KB	.304	BV	BV	125.00	135.00
	1877KB	.313	BV	BV	125.00	135.00
	1878KB	.308	BV	BV	125.00	135.00
	1879KB	.306	BV	BV	125.00	135.00
	1880KB	.301	BV	125.00	150.00	175.00

Obv: Larger head

Y#	Date	Mintage	Fine	VF	XF	Unc
18.2	1880KB	Inc. Ab.	BV	BV	120.00	125.00
	1881KB	.309	BV	BV	120.00	125.00
	1882KB	.304	BV	BV	120.00	125.00
	1883KB	.300	BV	BV	120.00	125.00
	1884KB	.284	BV	BV	120.00	125.00
	1885KB	.267	BV	BV	120.00	125.00
	1886KB	.313	BV	BV	120.00	125.00
	1887KB	.294	BV	BV	120.00	125.00
	1888KB	.296	BV	BV	120.00	125.00
	1889KB	.351	BV	BV	120.00	125.00
	1890KB	Inc. Be.	BV	BV	120.00	125.00

Rev: Fiume arms

Y#	Date	Mintage	Fine	VF	XF	Unc
20	1890KB	.329	BV	120.00	150.00	175.00
	1891KB	.378	BV	120.00	135.00	150.00
	1892KB	.232	BV	120.00	150.00	175.00

2 DUCATS

.986 GOLD

Y#	Date	Mintage	Fine	VF	XF
48	1781	—	600.00	750.00	900.00
	1782	—	600.00	750.00	900.00
	1783	—	—	Rare	—
	1784/3	—	600.00	750.00	900.00
	1784	—	—	Rare	—
	1785	—	600.00	750.00	900.00

MONETARY REFORM

(1892-1921)

100 Filler = 1 Korona

FILLER

BRONZE

Y#	Date	Mintage	Fine	VF	XF	Unc
23	1892KB	Inc. Be.	17.50	30.00	50.00	80.00
	1893KB	8.153	1.75	2.50	4.50	13.50
	1894KB	8.642	.50	1.00	1.75	5.00
	1895KB	9.121	.50	1.00	1.75	5.00
	1896KB	5.397	1.25	2.50	5.00	12.50
	1897KB	5.157	3.75	7.50	15.00	30.00
	1898KB	1.419	4.25	8.50	17.50	35.00
	1899KB	5.066	1.75	3.50	7.00	17.50
	1900KB	10.461	1.00	2.00	4.00	11.50
	1901KB	5.994	2.00	4.00	8.50	20.00
	1902KB	16.299	.20	.50	1.25	4.00
	1903KB	2.291	8.00	16.50	26.50	45.00
	1906KB	.061	100.00	150.00	200.00	300.00
	1914KB	—	65.00	90.00	135.00	200.00

2 FILLER

BRONZE

Y#	Date	Mintage	Fine	VF	XF	Unc
24	1892KB	Inc. Be.	27.50	40.00	65.00	100.00
	1893KB	17.176	1.75	3.50	5.00	7.50
	1894KB	39.150	.25	.50	1.00	1.50
	1895KB	65.017	.25	.50	1.00	1.50
	1896KB	53.716	.25	.50	1.00	1.50
	1897KB	37.297	.25	.50	1.00	1.50
	1898KB	14.073	2.25	4.50	8.50	12.50
	1899KB	21.570	2.25	4.50	8.50	12.50
	1900KB	.584	60.00	115.00	160.00	210.00
	1901KB	25.805	.25	.50	1.00	1.50
	1902KB	6.936	5.50	8.50	13.50	20.00
	1903KB	4.052	15.00	22.50	30.00	40.00
	1904KB	4.203	5.00	10.00	22.50	32.50
	1905KB	9.335	.50	1.00	1.75	2.50
	1906KB	3.140	1.75	2.50	3.50	5.00
	1907KB	9.443	4.50	7.00	10.00	15.00
	1908KB	16.486	.35	.50	.75	1.00
	1909KB	19.075	.35	.50	.75	1.00
	1910KB	6.025	3.75	6.25	8.50	12.50
	1914KB	—	.35	.50	.75	1.00
	1915KB	1.294	1.00	1.50	2.25	3.00

IRON
World War I Coinage

Y#	Date	Mintage	Fine	VF	XF	Unc
28	1916KB	—	3.75	7.00	11.00	15.00
	1917KB	—	1.00	2.00	4.00	7.50
	1918KB	—	1.75	3.50	6.50	10.25

10 FILLER

NICKEL

Y#	Date	Mintage	Fine	VF	XF	Unc
25	1892KB	Inc. Bel.	2.50	5.00	12.50	21.50
	1893KB	15.733	.25	.50	1.00	2.50
	1894KB	39.463	.25	.50	1.00	2.50
	1895KB	16.804	.25	.50	1.00	2.50
	1906KB	.056	75.00	175.00	250.00	325.00
	1908KB	6.819	.25	.50	.75	2.00
	1909KB	17.204	.30	.60	1.00	2.50
	1914KB	—	150.00	250.00	450.00	750.00

COPPER-NICKEL
World War I Coinage

Y#	Date	Mintage	Fine	VF	XF	Unc
26	1914KB	—	200.00	300.00	500.00	850.00
	1915KB	4.400	.25	.50	1.00	1.50
	1916KB	—	.50	1.25	2.50	5.00

IRON

Y#	Date	Mintage	Fine	VF	XF	Unc
29	1915KB	—	7.50	17.50	27.50	45.00
	1918KB	—	12.50	25.00	45.00	70.00
	1918KB	(restrike)		—	Proof	20.00
	1920KB	3.000	2.00	4.00	8.50	15.00

20 FILLER

NICKEL

Y#	Date	Mintage	Fine	VF	XF	Unc
27	1892KB	.696	2.00	4.00	8.00	12.00
	1893KB	27.187	.50	1.25	2.50	5.00
	1894KB	26.117	.50	1.25	2.50	5.00
	1906KB	.067	500.00	750.00	1100.	1650.
	1907KB	1.248	2.50	5.00	8.00	11.00
	1908KB	10.770	.75	1.75	3.75	7.50
	1914KB	—	3.75	6.50	9.00	13.50
	1914KB	(restrike)		—	Proof	15.00

IRON
World War I Coinage

Y#	Date	Mintage	Fine	VF	XF	Unc
30	1916KB	—	.50	1.25	2.50	4.50
	1917KB	—	.75	1.75	3.50	6.50
	1918KB	—	.75	1.75	3.50	6.50
	1918KB	(restrike)		—	Proof	8.50
	1920KB	—	2.25	4.50	8.00	12.50
	1921KB	—	18.50	37.50	55.00	80.00
	1921KB	(restrike)		—	Proof	20.00
	1922KB	—	—	—	Rare	—

BRASS

Y#	Date	Mintage	Fine	VF	XF	Unc
30a	1922KB	(restrike)		—	Proof	15.00

KORONA

5.0000 gm., .835 SILVER, .1342 oz ASW

Y#	Date	Mintage	Fine	VF	XF	Unc
32	1892KB	—	BV	BV	7.00	12.50
	1893KB	24.386	BV	BV	5.00	12.50
	1894KB	12.077	BV	BV	4.50	9.00
	1895KB	18.544	BV	BV	4.50	9.00
	1896KB	3.983	BV	4.25	7.00	12.50
	1906KB	.023	175.00	225.00	325.00	450.00

Millennium Commemorative

Y#	Date	Mintage	Fine	VF	XF	Unc
31	1896KB	1.000	BV	BV	4.50	9.00
	1896KB	(restrike)		—	Proof	35.00

NOTE: The above issue has been restruck in proof several times, both with and without edge inscriptions.

Y#	Date	Mintage	Fine	VF	XF	Unc
32a	1912KB	4.004	BV	5.00	10.00	15.00
	1913KB	5,214	35.00	60.00	100.00	150.00
	1914KB	—	BV	4.50	7.50	12.50
	1915KB	4.400	BV	4.25	5.00	7.50
	1916KB	—	BV	4.25	6.00	8.50

2 KORONA

10.0000 gm., .835 SILVER, .2685 oz ASW

Y#	Date	Mintage	Fine	VF	XF	Unc
33	1912KB	4.000	BV	BV	8.50	12.00
	1913KB	3.000	BV	BV	8.50	12.00
	1914KB	—	15.00	25.00	40.00	60.00

5 KORONA

24.0000 gm., .900 SILVER, .6944 oz ASW

Y#	Date	Mintage	Fine	VF	XF	Unc
34	1900KB	3.840	BV	22.00	35.00	90.00
	1900KB	(restrike)		—	Proof	75.00
	1906KB	1,263	1000.	1500.	2000.	2500.
	1907KB	.508	BV	22.00	40.00	100.00
	1908KB	1.742	BV	22.00	35.00	90.00
	1909KB	1.299	BV	22.00	35.00	90.00
	1909KB U.P.	(restrike)		—	Proof	75.00

40th Anniversary Coronation of Franz Josef

Y#	Date	Mintage	Fine	VF	XF	Unc
35	1907KB	.300	BV	22.00	32.50	60.00
	1907KB	(restrike)		—	Proof	50.00
	1907KB(U.P.)	(restrike)		—	Proof	75.00

10 KORONA

3.3875 gm., .900 GOLD, .0980 oz AGW

Y#	Date	Mintage	Fine	VF	XF	Unc
36	1892KB	1.087	BV	BV	65.00	70.00
	1893KB	Inc. Ab.	BV	BV	65.00	70.00
	1894KB	.099	BV	BV	65.00	70.00
	1895KB	—	900.00	1250.	1600.	2000.
	1896KB	.032	65.00	75.00	85.00	100.00
	1897KB	.259	BV	BV	65.00	70.00
	1898KB	.218	BV	BV	65.00	70.00
	1899KB	.231	BV	BV	65.00	70.00
	1900KB	.228	BV	BV	65.00	70.00
	1901KB	.230	BV	BV	65.00	70.00
	1902KB	.243	BV	BV	65.00	70.00
	1903KB	.228	BV	BV	65.00	70.00
	1904KB	1.531	BV	BV	65.00	70.00
	1905KB	.869	BV	BV	65.00	70.00
	1906KB	.748	BV	BV	65.00	70.00
	1907KB	.752	BV	BV	65.00	70.00
	1908KB	.509	BV	BV	65.00	70.00
	1909KB	.574	BV	BV	65.00	70.00
	1910KB	—	BV	BV	65.00	70.00
	1911KB	—	BV	BV	65.00	70.00
	1912KB	—	BV	65.00	75.00	90.00
	1913KB	—	70.00	85.00	125.00	170.00
	1914KB	—	70.00	85.00	125.00	170.00
	1915KB	—	1000.	2000.	3000.	4000.

20 KORONA

6.7750 gm., .900 GOLD, .1960 oz AGW

Y#	Date	Mintage	Fine	VF	XF	Unc
A36	1892KB	1.779	BV	BV	130.00	140.00
	1893KB	5.089	BV	BV	130.00	140.00
	1894KB	2.526	BV	BV	130.00	140.00
	1895KB	1.935	BV	BV	130.00	140.00
	1896KB	1.023	BV	BV	130.00	140.00
	1897KB	1.819	BV	BV	130.00	140.00
	1898KB	1.281	BV	BV	130.00	140.00
	1899KB	.712	BV	BV	130.00	140.00
	1900KB	.435	BV	BV	130.00	140.00
	1901KB	.510	BV	BV	130.00	140.00
	1902KB	.523	BV	BV	130.00	140.00
	1903KB	.505	BV	BV	130.00	140.00
	1904KB	.572	BV	BV	130.00	140.00
	1905KB	.526	BV	BV	130.00	140.00
	1906KB	.353	BV	BV	130.00	140.00
	1907KB	.194	130.00	150.00	175.00	200.00
	1908KB	.138	BV	BV	135.00	150.00
	1909KB	.459	BV	BV	135.00	150.00
	1910KB	—	150.00	200.00	250.00	300.00
	1911KB	—	BV	BV	135.00	165.00
	1912KB	—	BV	BV	135.00	165.00
	1913KB	—	135.00	150.00	175.00	200.00
	1914KB	—	BV	BV	135.00	150.00
	1915KB	—	135.00	150.00	175.00	200.00

Obv. of Y#A36. Rev. of Y#B36.

Y#	Date	Mintage	Fine	VF	XF	Unc
E36	1914KB	—	BV	BV	130.00	140.00

Y#	Date	Mintage	Fine	VF	XF	Unc
B36	1916KB	—	150.00	200.00	300.00	450.00

100 KORONA

33.8753 gm., .900 GOLD, .9802 oz AGW
40th Anniversary of Coronation

Y#	Date	Mintage	Fine	VF	XF	Unc
C36	1907KB	.011	650.00	750.00	850.00	1150.

Y#	Date	Mintage	Fine	VF	XF	Unc
D36	1907KB	1,088	700.00	1000.	1500.	2000.
	1908KB	4,038	650.00	750.00	1100.	1650.
	1908KB (restrike)		—	—	Proof	650.00

MONETARY REFORM

(1925-1945)

100 Filler = 1 Pengo

FILLER

BRONZE

Y#	Date	Mintage	VF	XF	Unc
37	1926BP	6.471	.30	1.00	2.25
	1927BP	16.529	.20	.50	1.25
	1928BP	7.000	.25	.60	1.50
	1929BP	.418	.90	2.00	4.75
	1930BP	3.734	.30	1.00	2.50
	1931BP	10.849	.20	.60	1.50
	1932BP	5.000	.25	.60	1.75
	1933BP	5.000	.25	.60	1.75
	1934BP	3.111	.30	1.00	2.50
	1935BP	6.889	.25	.60	1.50
	1936BP	10.000	.20	.60	1.25
	1938BP	10.575	.20	.60	1.25
	1939BP	10.425	.20	.60	1.25

2 FILLER

BRONZE

Y#	Date	Mintage	VF	XF	Unc
38	1926BP	17.777	.20	.40	1.00
	1927BP	44.836	.20	.40	1.00

Y#	Date	Mintage	VF	XF	Unc
38	1928BP	11.448	.20	.40	1.00
	1929BP	8.995	.25	.50	1.25
	1930BP	6.943	.25	.50	1.25
	1931BP	.826	.90	1.50	3.00
	1932BP	4.174	.25	.50	1.25
	1933BP	.501	1.00	2.00	3.25
	1934BP	9.499	.20	.40	1.00
	1935BP	10.000	.20	.40	1.00
	1936BP	2.049	.30	.60	1.25
	1937BP	7.951	.25	.50	1.00
	1938BP	14.125	.20	.40	.75
	1939BP	16.875	.20	.40	.75
	1940BP	7.000	.25	.50	1.00

STEEL
World War II Coinage

Y#	Date	Mintage	VF	XF	Unc
50	1940BP	1.500	1.25	2.50	4.00

Y#	Date	Mintage	VF	XF	Unc
50a	1940BP	141.000	.20	.50	1.25
	1941BP	22.000	.20	.50	1.25
	1942BP	20.000	.20	.50	1.25
	1942BP	— (restrike)		Proof	7.50

ZINC

Y#	Date	Mintage	VF	XF	Unc
51	1943BP	37.000	.20	.50	1.75
	1944BP	55.000	.20	.50	1.75

10 FILLER

COPPER-NICKEL
Regency Coinage

Y#	Date	Mintage	VF	XF	Unc
39	1926BP	20.000	.25	.40	1.00
	1927BP	12.255	.25	.40	1.10
	1935BP	4.740	.25	.50	1.25
	1936BP	3.005	.25	.50	1.25
	1938BP	6.700	.25	.50	1.25
	1939BP	4.460	.25	.50	1.25
	1940BP	.960	.25	1.00	2.50

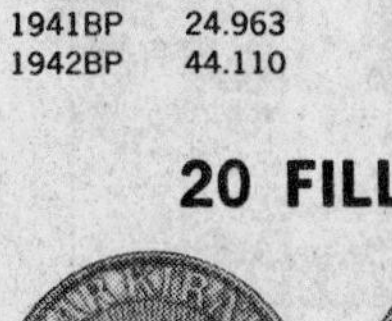

STEEL
World War II Coinage

Y#	Date	Mintage	VF	XF	Unc
52	1940BP	45.927	.15	.30	.90
	1941BP	24.963	.15	.30	.90
	1942BP	44.110	.15	.30	.90

20 FILLER

COPPER-NICKEL
Regency Coinage

Y#	Date	Mintage	VF	XF	Unc
40	1926BP	25.000	.25	.70	1.25
	1927BP	.830	1.00	2.00	4.00

Y#	Date	Mintage	VF	XF	Unc
40	1938BP	20.150	.25	.70	1.25
	1939BP	2.020	.50	1.00	2.50
	1940BP	2.470	.50	1.00	2.50

STEEL
World War II Coinage

Y#	Date	Mintage	VF	XF	Unc
53	1941BP	75.007	.20	.40	1.00
	1943BP	7.500	.20	.40	1.00
	1944BP	25.000	.20	.40	1.00
	1944BP	— (restrike)		Proof	10.00

50 FILLER

COPPER-NICKEL
Regency Coinage

Y#	Date	Mintage	VF	XF	Unc
41	1926BP	14.921	.40	1.00	2.00
	1938BP	20.079	.40	1.00	2.00
	1939BP	2.770	.65	1.25	3.00
	1939BP	— (restrike)		Proof	18.50
	1940BP	6.230	.45	1.00	2.25

PENGO

5.0000 gm., .640 SILVER, .1029 oz ASW
Regency Coinage

Y#	Date	Mintage	VF	XF	Unc
42	1926BP	17.770	BV	3.00	5.00
	1927BP	21.514	BV	3.00	5.00
	1937BP	4.000	BV	3.50	5.50
	1938BP	5.000	BV	3.50	5.50
	1939BP	13.000	BV	3.00	5.00

ALUMINUM
World War II Coinage

Y#	Date	Mintage	VF	XF	Unc
54	1941BP	80.000	.20	.60	.70
	1942BP	19.000	.20	.30	.70
	1943BP	2.000	20.00	—	—
	1944BP	20.650	.15	.50	.70

2 PENGO

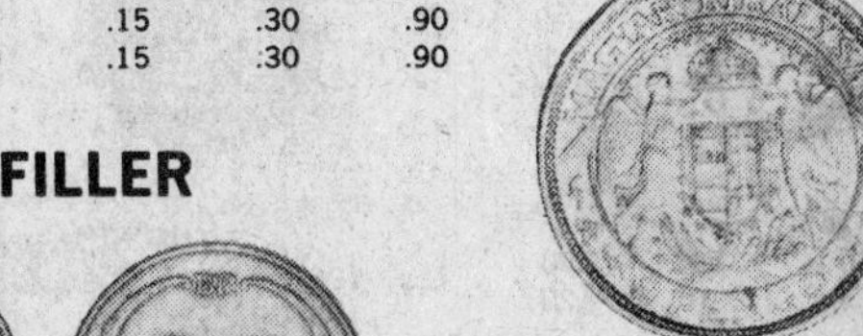

10.0000 gm., .640 SILVER, .2058 oz ASW
Regency Coinage

Y#	Date	Mintage	VF	XF	Unc
43	1929BP	.500	BV	6.50	8.50
	1931BP	.103	50.00	—	—
	1932BP	.610	BV	6.50	8.50
	1933BP	1.051	BV	6.50	8.50
	1935BP	.050	10.00	15.00	20.00
	1936BP	.711	BV	6.50	8.50
	1937BP	1.500	BV	6.50	8.50

Y#	Date	Mintage	VF	XF	Unc
43	1938BP	6.417	BV	6.50	8.50
	1939BP	2.103	BV	6.50	8.50

Pazmany University Tercentenary

Y#	Date	Mintage	VF	XF	Unc
45	1935BP	.050	6.50	8.50	11.00
	1935BP (restrike not marked)			Proof	35.00

Rakozi Bicentennial

Y#	Date	Mintage	VF	XF	Unc
46	1935BP	.100	6.50	8.50	12.00
	1935BP (restrike not marked)			Proof	45.00

50th Anniversary Death of Liszt

Y#	Date	Mintage	VF	XF	Unc
47	1936BP	.200	6.50	8.50	10.00
	1936BP (restrike not marked)			Proof	35.00

ALUMINUM
World War II Coinage

Y#	Date	Mintage	VF	XF	Unc
55.1	1941BP	24.000	.40	.60	1.00
	1942BP	8.000	.40	.60	1.00
	1943BP	10.000	.40	.60	1.00

Base of the number 2 is wavy

Y#	Date	Mintage	VF	XF	Unc
55.2	1941BP	—	—	—	—

5 PENGO

24.9300 gm., .640 SILVER, .5130 oz ASW
Admiral Horthy
Proof like with raised, sharp edge reeding.

Y#	Date	Mintage	VF	XF	Unc
44	1930BP	3.650	BV	16.00	17.50

25.33 gm., 36.1mm
Smooth edge with incuse reading

Y#	Date	Mintage	VF	XF	Unc
44a	1930BP	—	(restrike)	Proof	20.00

St. Stephan

Y#	Date	Mintage	VF	XF	Unc
48	1938BP	.300	BV	16.00	17.50
	1938BP	—	(restrike not identified)		
		—	—	Proof	25.00

Horthy Government

Y#	Date	Mintage	VF	XF	Unc
49	1939BP	.408	BV	16.00	17.50

ALUMINUM
75th Birthday of Admiral Horthy

Y#	Date	Mintage	VF	XF	Unc
57	1943BP	2.000	1.00	2.00	4.50
	1943BP	—	(restrike)	Proof	6.00

Provisional Government

Y#	Date	Mintage	VF	XF	Unc
56	1945BP	5.002	1.50	2.50	4.50
	1945BP	PROBAVERET	(restrike)	Proof	15.00

MONETARY REFORM

100 Filler = 1 Forint

2 FILLER

BRONZE
Republic Coinage

Y#	Date	Mintage	VF	XF	Unc
58	1946BP	13.660	.15	.30	.50
	1947BP	23.870	.15	.30	.50
	1947BP	—	(restrike)	Proof	3.00

ALUMINUM
People's Republic Coinage

Y#	Date	Mintage	VF	XF	Unc
70	1950BP	25.000	—	—	.10
	1952BP	5.600	—	—	.15
	1953BP	9.400	—	—	.10
	1954BP	10.000	—	—	.10
	1955BP	6.030	—	—	.15
	1956BP	4.000	—	—	.15
	1957BP	5.000	—	—	.10
	1960BP	3.000	—	—	.10
	1961BP	2.000	—	—	.10
	1962BP	3.000	—	—	.10
	1963BP	2.090	—	—	.10
	1965BP	.540	—	—	.10
	1966BP	—	—	—	.10
	1967BP	—	—	—	.10
	1971BP	—	—	—	.10
	1972BP	—	—	—	.10
	1973BP	—	—	—	.10
	1974BP	—	—	—	.10
	1975BP	.050	—	—	.10
	1976BP	.050	—	—	.10
	1977BP	—	—	—	.10

COPPER-NICKEL

Y#	Date	Mintage	VF	XF	Unc
70a	1966BP	5,000	(restrike)	Proof	1.25
	1967BP	5,000	(restrike)	Proof	1.25

5 FILLER

ALUMINUM
Republic Coinage

Y#	Date	Mintage	VF	XF	Unc
59	1948BP	24.000	.30	.50	1.00
	1951BP	15.000	.05	.10	.20

People's Republic Coinage

Y#	Date	Mintage	VF	XF	Unc
71	1953BP	10.000	.05	.10	.15
	1955BP	6.000	.05	.10	.20

Y#	Date	Mintage	VF	XF	Unc
71	1956BP	6.000	.05	.10	.15
	1957BP	5.000	.05	.10	.15
	1959BP	8.000	.05	.10	.15
	1960BP	7.000	.05	.10	.15
	1961BP	4.410	.05	.10	.15
	1962BP	5.590	.05	.10	.15
	1963BP	4.020	.05	.10	.15
	1964BP	3.600	—	—	.15
	1965BP	6.000	—	—	.15
	1966BP	—	—	—	.15
	1967BP	—	—	—	.15
	1970BP	—	—	—	.15
	1971BP	—	—	—	.15
	1972BP	—	—	—	.15
	1973BP	—	—	—	.15
	1974BP	—	—	—	.15
	1975BP	.060	—	—	.15
	1976BP	.050	—	—	.15
	1977BP	—	—	—	.15

COPPER-NICKEL

Y#	Date	Mintage	VF	XF	Unc
71a	1966BP	5,000	(restrike)	Proof	1.25
	1967BP	5,000	(restrike)	Proof	1.25

10 FILLER

ALUMINUM-BRONZE
Republic Coinage

Y#	Date	Mintage	VF	XF	Unc
60	1946BP	23.570	.10	.25	.60
	1947BP	29.580	.10	.25	.70
	1947BP	—	(restrike)	Proof	3.00
	1948BP	4.855	.20	.35	.75
	1950BP	1.000	.25	.50	1.00

ALUMINUM

Y#	Date	Mintage	VF	XF	Unc
60a	1950BP	—	.25	.50	1.00

People's Republic Coinage

Y#	Date	Mintage	VF	XF	Unc
72	1950BP	5.040	—	.10	.20
	1951BP	80.950	—	.10	.20
	1955BP	10.019	—	.10	.20
	1957BP	13.000	—	—	.20
	1958BP	12.015	—	.10	.20
	1959BP	15.000	—	—	.20
	1960BP	5.000	—	—	.20
	1961BP	13.000	—	—	.20
	1962BP	4.000	—	—	.20
	1963BP	8.000	—	—	.20
	1964BP	17.000	—	—	.20
	1965BP	21.880	—	.10	.20
	1966BP	8.120	—	—	.20

COPPER-NICKEL

Y#	Date	Mintage	VF	XF	Unc
72b	1966BP	5,000	(restrike)	Proof	1.25
	1967BP	5,000	(restrike)	Proof	1.25

ALUMINUM, reduced size

Y#	Date	Mintage	VF	XF	Unc
72a	1967BP	5,000	—	—	.15
	1968BP	—	—	—	.15
	1969BP	—	—	—	.15
	1970BP	—	—	—	.15
	1971BP	—	—	—	.15
	1972BP	—	—	—	.15
	1973BP	—	—	—	.15
	1974BP	—	—	—	.15
	1975BP	30.000	—	—	.15
	1976BP	20.025	—	—	.15
	1977BP	—	—	—	.15
	1978BP	—	—	—	.15

20 FILLER

ALUMINUM-BRONZE
Republic Coinage

Y#	Date	Mintage	VF	XF	Unc
61	1946BP	16.560	.30	.50	.75
	1946BP	—	(restrike)	Proof	5.00
	1947BP	18.260	.25	.50	.75
	1948BP	5.180	.30	.50	.85
	1950BP	5.000	—	—	.85

ALUMINUM
People's Republic

Y#	Date	Mintage	VF	XF	Unc
73	1953BP	45.000	—	.10	.25
	1955BP	10.020	—	.10	.25
	1957BP	5.000	—	.10	.25
	1958BP	10.000	—	.10	.25
	1959BP	13.000	—	.10	.25
	1961BP	9.000	—	.10	.25
	1963BP	7.000	—	.10	.25
	1964BP	10.400	—	.10	.20
	1965BP	15.000	—	.10	.25
	1966BP	5.000	—	.10	.25

COPPER-NICKEL

Y#	Date	Mintage	VF	XF	Unc
73b	1966BP	5,000	(restrike)	Proof	1.25
	1967BP	5,000	(restrike)	Proof	1.25

ALUMINUM
Reduced size

Y#	Date	Mintage	VF	XF	Unc
73a	1967BP	10.000	—	.10	.20
	1968BP	—	—	.10	.20
	1969BP	—	—	.10	.20
	1970BP	—	—	.10	.20
	1971BP	—	—	.10	.20
	1972BP	—	—	.10	.20
	1973BP	—	—	.10	.20
	1974BP	—	—	.10	.20
	1975BP	30.010	—	.10	.20
	1976BP	30.010	—	.10	.20
	1977BP	—	—	.10	.20

50 FILLER

ALUMINUM
Republic Coinage

Y#	Date	Mintage	VF	XF	Unc
62	1948BP	15.000	.80	1.50	2.25
	1948BP	—	(restrike)	Proof	6.50

People's Republic Coinage

Y#	Date	Mintage	VF	XF	Unc
74	1953BP	10.020	—	.15	.40
	1965BP	3.000	—	.15	.35
	1966BP	1.500	—	.15	.35
	1967BP	20.000	—	.15	.35

COPPER-NICKEL

Y#	Date	Mintage	VF	XF	Unc
74a	1966BP	5,000	(restrike)	Proof	1.25
	1967BP	5,000	(restrike)	Proof	1.25

ALUMINUM

Y#	Date	Mintage	VF	XF	Unc
97	1967BP	—	—	.10	.25
	1968BP	—	—	.10	.25
	1969BP	—	—	.10	.25
	1971BP	—	—	.10	.25
	1972BP	—	—	.10	.25
	1973BP	—	—	.10	.25
	1974BP	—	—	.10	.25
	1975BP	10.160	—	.10	.25
	1976BP	15.130	—	.10	.25
	1977BP	—	—	.10	.25

FORINT

ALUMINUM
Republic Coinage

Y#	Date	Mintage	VF	XF	Unc
63	1946BP	38.900	.60	1.00	2.00
	1947BP	2.600	.60	1.00	2.00
	1949BP	17.000	.60	1.00	2.00

People's Republic Coinage

Y#	Date	Mintage	VF	XF	Unc
75	1949BP	19.440	.10	.25	.65
	1950BP	39.060	.10	.25	.65
	1951BP	—	.10	.25	.65
	1952BP	63.018	.10	.25	.65

Y#	Date	Mintage	VF	XF	Unc
80	1957BP	7.500	.10	.25	.50
	1958BP	5.070	.10	.25	.50
	1960BP	5.000	.10	.25	.50
	1961BP	5,000	.10	.25	.50
	1962BP	3.000	.10	.25	.50
	1963BP	—	.10	.25	.50
	1964BP	6.080	.10	.25	.50
	1965BP	9.810	.10	.25	.50
	1966BP	5.680	.10	.25	.50

5.8500 gm., .835 SILVER, .1570 oz ASW

Y#	Date	Mintage	VF	XF	Unc
80b	1966BP	5,000	(restrike)	Proof	5.00
	1967BP	5,000	(restrike)	Proof	5.00

ALUMINUM
Reduced size, 22.8mm

Y#	Date	Mintage	VF	XF	Unc
80a	1967BP	60.000	.10	.40	.50
	1968BP	—	.10	.20	.50
	1969BP	—	.10	.20	.40
	1970BP	—	.10	.20	.50
	1971BP	—	.10	.20	.50
	1972BP	—	.10	.20	.50
80a	1973BP	—	.10	.20	.50
	1974BP	—	.10	.20	.50
	1975BP	10.000	.10	.20	.50
	1976BP	15.000	.10	.20	.50
	1977BP	—	.10	.20	.50

2 FORINT

ALUMINUM
Republic Coinage

Y#	Date	Mintage	VF	XF	Unc
64	1946BP	10.000	1.00	2.00	3.25
	1947BP	3.500	1.00	2.00	3.25

COPPER-NICKEL
People's Republic Coinage

Y#	Date	Mintage	VF	XF	Unc
76	1950BP	18.500	.15	.50	1.00
	1951BP	4.000	.20	.50	1.00
	1952BP	4.540	.20	.50	1.00
	1956BP	—	.20	.50	1.00

Y#	Date	Mintage	VF	XF	Unc
81	1957BP	5.000	.20	.50	.85
	1958BP	1.033	—	—	.85
	1960BP	4.000	.20	.50	.85
	1961BP	.690	—	—	.85

COPPER-NICKEL-ZINC

Y#	Date	Mintage	VF	XF	Unc
81a	1962BP	2.400	.20	.35	.75
	1963BP	3.100	.20	.35	.75
	1964BP	3.250	.20	.35	.75
	1965BP	4.395	.20	.35	.75
	1966BP	6.630	.20	.35	.75
	1967BP	—	.20	.35	.75

6.1200 gm., .835 SILVER, .1643 oz ASW

Y#	Date	Mintage	VF	XF	Unc
81b	1966BP	5,000	—	(restrike)	6.00
	1967BP	5,000	—	(restrike)	6.00

BRASS

Y#	Date	Mintage	VF	XF	Unc
115	1970BP	—	.15	.35	.75
	1971BP	—	.15	.35	.75
	1972BP	—	.15	.35	.75
	1973BP	—	.15	.35	.75
	1974BP	—	.15	.35	.75
	1975BP	20.030	.15	.35	.75
	1976BP	15.000	.15	.35	.75
	1977BP	—	.15	.35	.75

5 FORINT

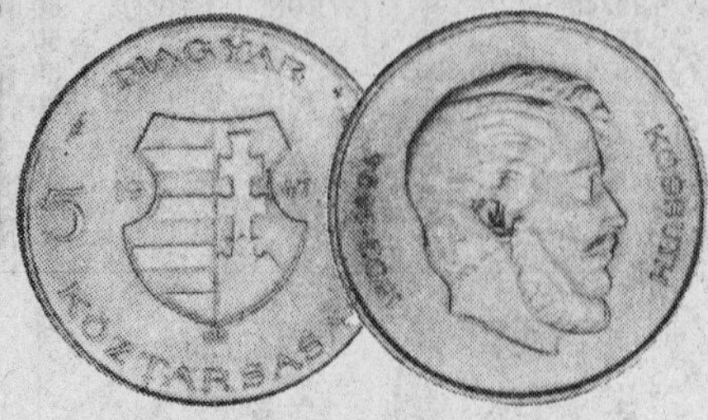

20.0000 gm., .835 SILVER, .5369 oz ASW
Thick planchet

Y#	Date	Mintage	VF	XF	Unc
65	1946BP	.040	BV	16.50	20.00

12.0000 gm., .500 SILVER, .1929 oz ASW
1.7mm thin planchet

66	1947BP	10.000	BU	6.00	7.50
	1947BP	— (restrike)		Proof	10.00

13.0000 gm., .835 SILVER, .3490 oz ASW

66a	1966BP	5,000 (restrike)		Proof	12.50
	1967BP	5,000 (restrike)		Proof	12.50

12.0000 gm., .500 SILVER, .1929 oz ASW
Petofi 1848 Revolution

67	1948BP	.106	BV	6.50	8.50
	1948BP	—	—	Proof	25.00

COPPER-NICKEL

98	1967BP	20.000	.50	.75	1.25
	1968BP	—	60.00	80.00	125.00

NICKEL

116	1971BP	—	.30	.60	1.00
	1972BP	—	.30	.60	1.50
	1973BP	—	.30	.60	1.00
	1974BP	—	.30	.60	1.00
	1975BP	.050	.30	.60	1.00
	1976BP	5.090	.30	.60	1.00

10 FORINT

20.0000 gm., .500 SILVER, .3215 oz ASW
Szechenyi 1848 Revolution

Y#	Date	Mintage	VF	XF	Unc
68	1948BP	.100	BV	10.00	12.00

12.0000 gm., .800 SILVER, .3086 oz ASW
10th Anniversary of Revision
of Monetary and Economic System

77	1956BP	.022	BV	10.00	12.50

NICKEL

117	1971BP	—	.75	1.25	2.00
	1972BP	—	.75	1.25	2.50
	1973BP	—	.65	1.00	1.75
	1974BP	—	.65	1.00	1.75
	1975BP	.050	.65	1.00	1.75
	1976BP	3.568	.65	1.00	1.75

20 FORINT

28.0000 gm., .500 SILVER, .4501 oz ASW
Tancsics 1848 Revolution

69	1948BP	.050	BV	15.00	17.50

20.0000 gm., .800 SILVER, .5144 oz ASW
10th Anniversary of Revision
of Monetary and Economic System

Y#	Date	Mintage	VF	XF	Unc
78	1956BP	.022	BV	16.00	20.00

HUSZONOT (25) FORINT

25.0000 gm., .800 SILVER, .6430 oz ASW
10th Anniversary of Revision
of Monetary and Economic System

79	1956BP	.022	BV	20.00	27.50

17.5000 gm., .750 SILVER, .4220 oz ASW
150th Anniversary of Birth of Liszt

82	1961BP	.015	— Proof only		20.00

80th Anniversary of Birth of Bartok

87	1961BP	.015	— Proof only		20.00

12.0000 gm., .640 SILVER, .2469 oz ASW
400th Anniversary of Death of Zrinyi

92	1966BP	.011	— Proof only		20.00

17.5000 gm., .750 SILVER, .4220 oz ASW
Kodaly 85th Birthday

Y#	Date	Mintage	VF	XF	Unc
99	1967BP	—	BV	BV	14.00
	1967BP	—	—	Proof	16.50

OTVEN (50) FORINT

20.0000 gm., .835 SILVER, .5369 oz ASW
150th Anniversary of Birth of Liszt

Y#	Date	Mintage	VF	XF	Unc
83	1961BP	.015	—	Proof only	27.50

3.8380 gm., .986 GOLD, .1217 oz AGW
150th Anniversary of Birth of Liszt

Y#	Date	Mintage	VF	XF	Unc
84	1961BP	2,500	—	Proof only	100.00

16.0000 gm., .750 SILVER, .3858 oz ASW
150th Anniversary of Birth of Liszt

Y#	Date	Mintage	VF	XF	Unc
88	1961BP	.015	—	Proof Only	27.50

3.8380 gm., .986 GOLD, .1217 oz AGW
80th Anniversary of Birth of Bartok

Y#	Date	Mintage	VF	XF	Unc
89	1961BP	2,500	—	Proof only	90.00

16.0000 gm., .640 SILVER, .3292 oz ASW
400th Anniversary of Death of Zrinyi

Y#	Date	Mintage	VF	XF	Unc
93	1966BP	—	—	Proof only	27.50

Kodaly 85th Birthday

Y#	Date	Mintage	VF	XF	Unc
100	1967BP	—	BV	BV	15.00
	1967BP	—	—	Proof	20.00

150th Anniversary of Birth of Semmelweis

Y#	Date	Mintage	VF	XF	Unc
104	1968BP	—	BV	BV	12.00
	1968BP	4,750	—	Proof	15.00

4.2050 gm., .900 GOLD, .1217 oz AGW
150th Anniversary of Birth of Semmelweis

Y#	Date	Mintage	VF	XF	Unc
106	1968BP	3,500	—	Proof only	100.00

16.0000 gm., .640 SILVER, .3292 oz ASW
50th Year of Republic

Y#	Date	Mintage	VF	XF	Unc
111	1969BP	.032	BV	BV	22.00
	1969BP	8,000	—	Proof	30.00

25th Anniversary of Liberation

Y#	Date	Mintage	VF	XF	Unc
113	1970BP	—	BV	BV	11.00
	1970BP	4,000	—	Proof	15.00

St. Stephen

Y#	Date	Mintage	VF	XF	Unc
118	1972BP	.024	BV	BV	12.50
	1972BP	6,000	—	Proof	15.00

Sandor Petofi

Y#	Date	Mintage	VF	XF	Unc
121	1973BP	.024	BV	BV	12.50
	1973BP	6,000	—	Proof	15.00

50th Anniversary National Bank

Y#	Date	Mintage	VF	XF	Unc
124	1974BP	.024	BV	BV	12.50
	1974BP	.006	—	Proof	30.00

SZAZ (100) FORINT

7.6760 gm., .986 GOLD, .2431 oz AGW
150th Anniversary of Birth of Liszt

Y#	Date	Mintage	VF	XF	Unc
85	1961BP	—	—	Proof	165.00

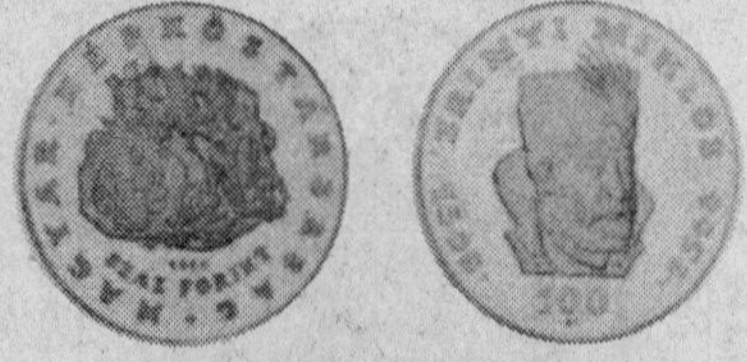

80th Anniversary of Birth of Bartok

Y#	Date	Mintage	VF	XF	Unc
90	1961	2,500	—	Proof	165.00

8.4100 gm., .900 GOLD, .2433 oz AGW
400th Anniversary of Death of Zrinyi

Y#	Date	Mintage	VF	XF	Unc
94	1966	330 pcs.	—	Proof	200.00

28.0000 gm., .750 SILVER, .6752 oz ASW
Kodaly 85th Birthday

Y#	Date	Mintage	VF	XF	Unc
101	1967BP	—	BV	22.50	30.00
	1967BP	—	—	Proof	40.00

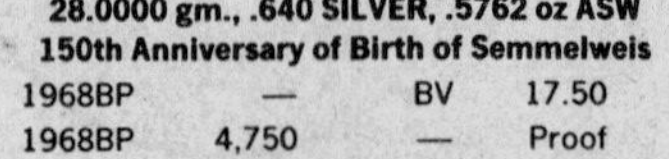

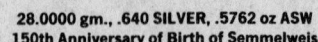

28.0000 gm., .640 SILVER, .5762 oz ASW
150th Anniversary of Birth of Semmelweis

Y#	Date	Mintage	VF	XF	Unc
105	1968BP	—	BV	17.50	20.00
	1968BP	4,750	—	Proof	40.00

8.4100 gm., .900 GOLD, .2433 oz AGW
150th Anniversary of Birth of Semmelweis

Y#	Date	Mintage	VF	XF	Unc
107	1968BP	—		Proof only	175.00

22.0000 gm., .640 SILVER, .4527 oz ASW
50th Year of Republic

Y#	Date	Mintage	VF	XF	Unc
112	1969BP	.032	BV	17.50	30.00
	1969BP	8,000	—	Proof	40.00

25th Anniversary of Liberation

Y#	Date	Mintage	VF	XF	Unc
114	1970BP	—	BV	BV	17.50
	1970BP	4,000	—	Proof	20.00

St. Stephen

Y#	Date	Mintage	VF	XF	Unc
119	1972BP	.024	BV	BV	17.50
	1972BP	6,000	—	Proof	20.00

Budapest Centennial

Y#	Date	Mintage	VF	XF	Unc
120	1972BP	.024	BV	BV	17.50
	1972BP	6,000	—	Proof	25.00

Sandor Petofi

Y#	Date	Mintage	VF	XF	Unc
122	1973BP	.024	BV	BV	17.50
	1973BP	6,000	—	Proof	20.00

CMEA Anniversary

Y#	Date	Mintage	VF	XF	Unc
123	1974BP	.020	BV	17.50	25.00
	1974BP	5,000	—	Proof	45.00

50th Anniversary National Bank

Y#	Date	Mintage	VF	XF	Unc
125	1974BP	.024	BV	BV	15.00
	1974BP	6,000	—	Proof	35.00

KETSZAS (200) FORINT

16.8210 gm., .900 GOLD, .4867 oz AGW
150th Anniversary of Birth of Semmelweis

Y#	Date	Mintage	VF	XF	Unc
108	1968BP	3,500	— Proof only		325.00

28.0000 gm., .640 SILVER, .5762 oz ASW
30th Anniversary of Liberation

Y#	Date	Mintage	VF	XF	Unc
126	1975BP	.020	—	—	25.00
	1975BP	.010	—	Proof	32.50

150th Anniversary Academy of Science

Y#	Date	Mintage	VF	XF	Unc
127	1975BP	.020	—	—	25.00
	1975BP	.010	—	Proof	32.50

Rakoczi

Y#	Date	Mintage	VF	XF	Unc
128	1976BP	.025	—	—	25.00
	1976BP	5,000	—	Proof	35.00

Mikaly Munkacsy

Y#	Date	Mintage	VF	XF	Unc
129	1976BP	.025	—	—	25.00
	1976BP	5,000	—	Proof	35.00

Pal Szinyei Merse
Obv: Similar to Y#129

Y#	Date	Mintage	VF	XF	Unc
130	1976BP	.025	—	—	25.00

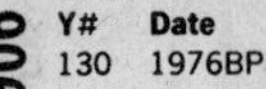
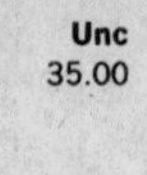

Y#	Date	Mintage	VF	XF	Unc
130	1976BP	5,000	—	Proof	35.00

Gyula Derkovits
Obv: Similar to Y#129

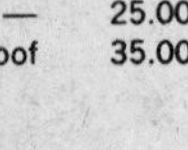

Y#	Date	Mintage	VF	XF	Unc
131	1976BP	.025	—	—	25.00
	1976BP	5,000	—	Proof	35.00

Adam Manyoki
Obv: Similar to Y#129

Y#	Date	Mintage	VF	XF	Unc
132	1977BP	.025	—	—	25.00
	1977BP	5,000	—	Proof	35.00

Tivadar C. Kosztka
Obv: Similar to Y#129

Y#	Date	Mintage	VF	XF	Unc
133	1977BP	.025	—	—	25.00
	1977BP	5,000	—	Proof	35.00

Jozsef Rippl-Ronai
Obv: Similar to Y#129

Y#	Date	Mintage	VF	XF	Unc
134	1977BP	.025	—	—	25.00
	1977BP	5,000	—	Proof	35.00

175th Anniversary of National Museum

Y#	Date	Mintage	VF	XF	Unc
135	1977BP	.030	—	—	25.00
	1977BP	5,000	—	Proof	35.00

First Gold Forint

Y#	Date	Mintage	VF	XF	Unc
136	1978BP	.025	—	—	25.00
	1978BP	5,000	—	Proof	35.00

International Year of the Child

Y#	Date	Mintage	VF	XF	Unc
137	1979	—	—	—	—

350th Anniversary of Death of Gabor Bethlen

Y#	Date	Mintage	VF	XF	Unc
138	1979	.015	—	—	—
	1979	5,000	—	Proof	—

OTSZAZ (500) FORINT

38.3800 gm., .986 GOLD, 1.2168 oz AGW
150th Anniversary of Birth of Liszt

Y#	Date	Mintage	VF	XF	Unc
86	1961BP	2,500	—	Proof	800.00

80th Anniversary of Birth of Bartok

Y#	Date	Mintage	VF	XF	Unc
91	1961BP	2,500	—	Proof	800.00

42.0500 gm., .900 GOLD, 1.2168 oz AGW
400th Anniversary of Death of Zrinyi

Y#	Date	Mintage	VF	XF	Unc
95	1966BP	1,100	—	Proof	1250.

Kodaly 85th Birthday

Y#	Date	Mintage	VF	XF	Unc
102	1967BP	—	—	—	800.00
	1967BP	1,000	—	Proof	1250.

42.0000 gm., .900 GOLD, 1.2154 oz AGW
150th Anniversary of Birth of Semmelweis

Y#	Date	Mintage	VF	XF	Unc
109	1968BP	3,500	—	Proof	800.00

EZER (1000) FORINT

84.1000 gm., .900 GOLD, 2.4337 oz AGW
400th Anniversary of Death of Zrinyi

Y#	Date	Mintage	VF	XF	Unc
96	1966BP	330 pcs.	—	Proof	2500.

Kodaly 85th Birthday

Y#	Date	Mintage	VF	XF	Unc
103	1967BP	500 pcs.		Proof Only	2000.

84.0000 gm., .900 GOLD, 2.4308 oz AGW
150th Anniversary of Birth of Semmelweis

Y#	Date	Mintage	VF	XF	Unc
110	1968BP	3,500	—	Proof	1600.

NCLT ISSUES

PATTERNS

KM#	Date	Mintage	Identification	Mkt.Val.
1	1849KB	—	Krajczar, Copper, C#65	—
2	1849KB	—	3 Krajczar, Copper, C#66	—
3	1867B	*1,000	10 Krajczar, Silver, Y#6	—
4	1868GYF	—	10 Krajczar, Silver, Y#6	—
5	1916KB	—	10 Filler, Iron, Y#29	—

6	1928BP	—	10 Pengo, Gold, FR#100	1500.

7	1928BP	—	20 Pengo, Gold, FR#99	1200.

8	1929BP	—	20 Pengo, Gold, FR#99a	1200.

SPECIMEN SETS

KM#	Date	Mintage	Identification	Issue Price	Mkt. Val.
S1	1966(8)	5,000	Y70a,71a,72b,73b,74a,80b, 81b,66a	15.00	30.00
S2	1967(8)	5,000	Y70a,71a,72b,73b,74a,80b, 81b,66a	—	30.00
S3	1977(9)	—	Y70,71,72a,73a,97,80a,115-117	—	5.00
S4	1978(9)	—	Y70,71,72a,73a,97,80a,115-117	—	5.00
S5	1979(9)	—	Y70,71,72a,73a,97,80a,115-117	—	5.00

PROOF SETS
STANDARD METALS

KM#	Date	Mintage	Identification	Issue Price	Mkt. Val.
101	1961(6)	2,500	Y84-86,89-91	—	2000.
102	1961(4)	—	Y82,83,87,88	—	95.00
103	1966(8)	—	Y66a,70a,71a,72b,73b, 74a,80b,81b	—	27.50
104	1966(3)	330	Y94-96	430.00	3750.
105	1966(2)	11,000	Y92,93	7.50	45.00
106	1967(8)	—	Same As KM#103	—	27.50
107	1967(2)	500	Y102,103	—	3250.
108	1968(5)	7,000	Y106-110	—	3000.
109	1968(2)	4,750	Y104,105	35.00	50.00
110	1969(2)	3,000	Y111,112	35.00	65.00
111	1970(2)	4,000	Y113,114	25.00	35.00

KM#	Date	Mintage	Identification	Issue Price	Mkt. Val.
112	1972(2)	6,000	Y118,119	25.00	35.00
113	1973(2)	6,000	Y121,122	—	35.00
114	1974(2)	—	Y124,125	—	65.00
115	1976(3)	5,000	Y129-131	—	100.00

ICELAND

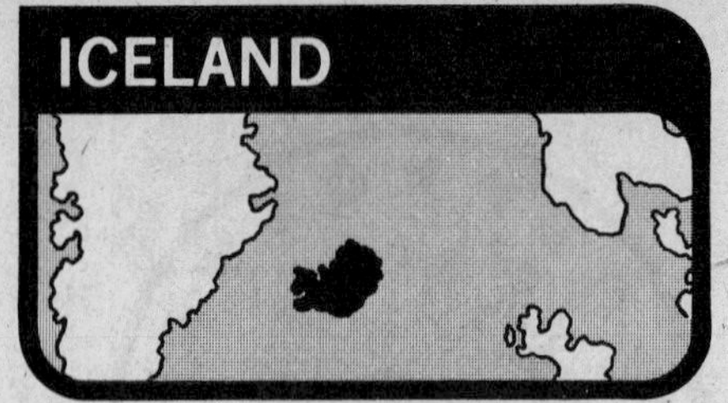

The Republic of Iceland, an island of recent volcanic origin in the North Atlantic east of Greenland and immediately south of the Arctic Circle, has an area of 39,709 sq. mi. (102,845 sq. km.) and a population of 224,472. Capital: Reykjavik. Fishing is the chief industry and accounts for more than 70 percent of the exports.

Iceland was settled by Norwegians in the 9th century and established as an independent republic in 930. The Icelandic assembly called the 'Althing', also established in 930, is the oldest parliament in the world. Iceland came under Norwegian sovereignty in 1262, and passed to Denmark when Norway and Denmark were united under the Danish crown in 1384. In 1918 it was established as a virtually independent kingdom in union with Denmark. On June 17, 1944, while Denmark was still under occupation by troops of the Third Reich, Iceland was established by plebiscite as an independent republic.

The 1930 10 kronur Althing commemorative is widely held to be one of the most attractive numismatic items of the modern period.

RULERS

Christian X, 1912-1944

MINTMARKS

L - London
Heart (h) - Copenhagen
No mintmark - London, Ottawa

MINTMASTERS INITIALS

HCN - Hans Christian Nielsen, 1919-1927
N - Niels Peter Nielsen, 1927-1955

MONEYERS INITIALS

GI, GJ - Knud Gunnar Jensen, 1901-1933

MONETARY SYSTEM

100 Aurar = 1 Krona

EYRIR

BRONZE

MINT: COPENHAGEN

Y#	Date	Mintage	Fine	VF	XF	Unc
1	1926(h)HCN-GJ	.405	1.25	2.25	4.00	10.00
	1931(h)N-GJ	.462	.75	1.75	3.00	7.00
	1937(h)N-GJ	.211	1.75	3.00	5.50	11.00
	1938(h)N-GJ	.279	.75	1.75	3.00	5.00
	1939(h)N-GJ large 3	.305	.75	1.75	3.00	5.00
	1939(h)N-GJ small 3	Inc. Ab.	.75	1.50	3.00	5.00

MINT: LONDON or Ottawa

Y#	Date	Mintage	Fine	VF	XF	Unc
1.1	1940	1.000	.25	.65	1.25	2.50
	1942	2.000	.25	.40	.75	1.50

Republic

Y#	Date	Mintage	Fine	VF	XF	Unc
11	1946	4.000	—	.15	.35	1.00
	1953	4.000	—	.15	.35	.75
	1956	2.000	—	.15	.35	.75
	1957	2.000	—	.15	.35	.75
	1958	2.000	—	.15	.35	.75
	1959	1.600	—	.15	.35	.75
	1966	1.000	—	.15	.35	.75
	1966	.015	—	—	Proof	5.00

2 AURAR

BRONZE

MINT: COPENHAGEN

Y#	Date	Mintage	Fine	VF	XF	Unc
2	1926(h)HCN-GJ	.498	.75	1.75	3.50	10.00
	1931(h)N-GJ	.446	.65	1.50	3.00	9.00
	1938(h)N-GJ	.206	3.00	6.00	12.00	25.00
	1940(h)N-GJ	.257	2.50	5.00	10.00	20.00

MINT: LONDON or OTTAWA

Y#	Date	Mintage	Fine	VF	XF	Unc
2.1	1940(London)	—				
		1.000	.40	.75	1.50	3.00
	1942	2.000	.25	.50	1.00	2.00

NOTE: Through 1939 all coins were struck at the Copenhagen Mint and bear a heart mintmark. Beginning in 1940 all issues have been struck at the London or Ottawa Mints and do not bear a mintmark. The 2-aurar and 1-krona issues of 1940 were struck at Copenhagen and London.

5 AURAR

BRONZE

MINT: COPENHAGEN

Y#	Date	Mintage	Fine	VF	XF	Unc
3	1926(h)HCN-GJ	.355	2.00	4.50	7.50	17.50
	1931(h)N-GJ	.311	2.00	4.50	7.50	17.50

MINT: LONDON or OTTAWA

Y#	Date	Mintage	Fine	VF	XF	Unc
3.1	1940	1.000	.40	.85	1.75	3.50
	1942	2.000	.20	.40	1.00	2.00

Republic

Y#	Date	Mintage	Fine	VF	XF	Unc
12	1946	4.000	—	.25	.50	1.25
	1958	.400	.40	1.00	2.00	4.00
	1959	.600	.30	.75	1.50	3.00
	1960	1.200	—	.25	.65	1.25
	1961	1.200	—	.25	.65	1.25
	1963	1.200	—	.20	.50	1.00
	1965	.800	—	.20	.50	1.00
	1966	1.000	—	.20	.35	.75
	1966	.015	—	—	Proof	5.00

10 AURAR

COPPER-NICKEL

MINT: COPENHAGEN

Y#	Date	Mintage	Fine	VF	XF	Unc
4	1922HCN(h)GJ	.300	1.25	2.50	5.00	20.00
	1923HCN(h)GJ	.302	1.50	3.00	6.00	20.00
	1925HCN(h)GJ	.321	6.50	12.50	25.00	75.00
	1929(h)N-GJ	.176	6.50	12.50	25.00	75.00
	1933(h)N-GJ	.157	5.00	10.00	20.00	50.00
	1936(h)N-GJ	.213	1.50	3.00	6.00	20.00
	1939/6(h)N-GJ	.208	4.00	7.50	15.00	30.00
	1939(h)N-GJ	I.A.	1.50	3.00	6.00	15.00

MINT: LONDON or OTTAWA

Y#	Date	Mintage	Fine	VF	XF	Unc
4.1	1940	1.500	.35	.65	1.25	3.50

ZINC

Y#	Date	Mintage	Fine	VF	XF	Unc
4a	1942	2.000	1.00	2.00	5.00	15.00

COPPER-NICKEL
Republic

Y#	Date	Mintage	Fine	VF	XF	Unc
13	1946	4.000	—	—	.30	.60
	1953	4.000	—	—	.25	.50
	1957	1.200	—	—	1.00	2.00
	1958	.500	—	—	.50	1.25
	1959	3.000	—	—	.75	1.50
	1960	1.000	—	—	.50	1.00
	1961	2.000	—	—	.10	.30
	1962	3.000	—	—	—	.20
	1963	4.000	—	—	—	.20
	1965	2.000	—	—	—	.20
	1966 plain edge		—			
		4.000	—	—	—	.20
	1966 coarse edge reeding					
		Inc. Ab.	—	—	—	—
	1967	2.000	—	—	—	.20
	1969 coarse edge reeding					
		3.200	—	—	—	.20
	1969 fine edge reeding	—				
		3.200	—	—	—	.20
	1969 smooth edge					
		Inc. Ab.	—	—	—	—

ALUMINUM

Y#	Date	Mintage	Fine	VF	XF	Unc
13a	1970	4.800	—	—	—	.10
	1971	11.200	—	—	—	.10
	1973	4.800	—	—	—	.10
	1974	4.800	—	—	—	.10
	1974	.015	—	—	Proof	5.00
	1976	—	—	—	—	.10

25 AURAR

COPPER-NICKEL

MINT: COPENHAGEN

Y#	Date	Mintage	Fine	VF	XF	Unc
5	1922HCN(h)GJ					
		.300	.90	1.75	5.00	25.00
	1923HCN(h)GJ					
		.304	.90	1.75	5.00	25.00
	1925HCN(h)GJ					
		.207	1.25	2.50	8.50	25.00
	1933(h)N-GJ	.104	3.50	6.50	13.50	35.00
	1937(h)N-GJ near 7					
		.201	1.25	2.50	5.00	12.50
	1937(h)N-GJ far 7					
		I.A.	1.25	2.50	5.00	12.50

MINT: LONDON or OTTAWA

Y#	Date	Mintage	Fine	VF	XF	Unc
5.1	1940	1.500	.25	.60	1.25	2.50

ZINC

Y#	Date	Mintage	Fine	VF	XF	Unc
5a	1942	2.000	.75	1.50	3.00	10.00

COPPER-NICKEL
Republic

Y#	Date	Mintage	Fine	VF	XF	Unc
14	1946	2.000	—	.15	.35	1.00
	1951	2.000	—	.15	.35	.75
	1954	2.000	—	.15	.35	.75
	1957	1.000	.15	.35	.75	1.50
	1958	.500	—	.10	.30	.75
	1959	2.000	—	.10	.50	1.00
	1960	1.000	—	.05	.10	.25
	1961	1.200	—	.05	.10	.25
	1962	2.000	—	—	—	.20
	1963	3.000	—	—	—	.20
	1965	4.000	—	—	—	.20
	1966	2.000	—	—	—	.20
	1967	3.000	—	—	—	.20
	1967	.015	—	—	Proof	5.00

50 AURAR

NICKEL-BRASS

Y#	Date	Mintage	Fine	VF	XF	Unc
A15	1969	1.000	—	—	.10	.15
	1970	2.000	—	—	.10	.15
	1971	2.000	—	—	.10	.15
	1973	1.000	—	—	.10	.15
	1974	2.000	—	—	.10	.15
	1974	.015	—	—	Proof	5.00
	1976	—	—	—	.10	.15

KRONA

ALUMINUM-BRONZE

MINT: COPENHAGEN

Y#	Date	Mintage	Fine	VF	XF	Unc
6	1925HCN(h)GJ					
		.252	1.75	4.50	15.00	40.00
	1929(h)N-GJ	.154	2.00	6.00	20.00	55.00
	1940(h)N-GJ	.209	.50	1.50	4.00	7.50

MINT: LONDON or OTTAWA

Y#	Date	Mintage	Fine	VF	XF	Unc
6.1	1940	.715	.75	1.50	3.00	6.00

Republic

Y#	Date	Mintage	Fine	VF	XF	Unc
15	1946	2.175	—	.10	.40	1.25

NICKEL-BRASS

Y#	Date	Mintage	Fine	VF	XF	Unc
15a	1957	1.000	—	.10	.40	1.25
	1959	.500	—	.20	.75	1.75
	1961	.500	—	.20	.75	1.75
	1962	1.000	—	—	.20	.50
	1963	1.500	—	—	—	.25
	1965	2.000	—	—	—	.25
	1966	2.000	—	—	—	.25
	1969	2.000	—	—	—	.25
	1970	3.000	—	—	—	.25
	1971	2.500	—	—	—	.10

Large Date, Royal Mint **Thin Date, Ottawa Mint**

Y#	Date	Mintage	Fine	VF	XF	Unc
	1973 large round knob 3					
		2.500	—	—	—	.25
	1973 thin, sharp end 3	—				
		3.500	—	—	—	.25
	1974	5.000	—	—	—	.25
	1975	10.500	—	—	—	.25
	1975	.015	—	—	Proof	5.00

ALUMINUM

Y#	Date	Mintage	Fine	VF	XF	Unc
15b	1976	10.000	—	—	—	.10
	1977	10,000	—	—	—	.10
	1978	—	—	—	—	.10
	1980	—	—	—	—	.10
	1980	.015	—	—	Proof	5.00

2 KRONUR

ALUMINUM-BRONZE

MINT: COPENHAGEN

Y#	Date	Mintage	Fine	VF	XF	Unc
7	1925HCN(h)GJ					
		.126	3.00	5.50	15.00	50.00
	1929(h)N-GJ	.077	5.00	10.00	25.00	100.00

MINT: LONDON or OTTAWA

Y#	Date	Mintage	Fine	VF	XF	Unc
7.1	1940	.546	.75	1.50	3.00	6.00

Republic

Y#	Date	Mintage	Fine	VF	XF	Unc
16	1946	1.086	.15	.35	.75	1.50

NICKEL-BRASS

Y#	Date	Mintage	Fine	VF	XF	Unc
16a	1958	.500	.10	.50	1.00	2.00
	1962	.500	.10	.50	1.00	2.00
	1963	.750	—	.30	.60	1.25
	1966	1.000	—	.20	.40	1.00
	1966	.015	—	—	Proof	5.00

Thick planchet, 11.5 gm.

Y#	Date	Mintage	Fine	VF	XF	Unc
16a.1	1966	300 pcs.	25.00	50.00	65.00	75.00

5 KRONUR

COPPER-NICKEL

Y#	Date	Mintage	Fine	VF	XF	Unc
18	1969	1.000	—	—	.10	.25
	1970	1.000	—	—	.10	.25
	1971	.500	—	—	.10	.20
	1973	1.100	—	—	—	.15
	1974	1.200	—	—	—	.10
	1975	1.500	—	—	—	.25
	1976	.500	—	—	—	.10
	1977	1.000	—	—	—	.10
	1978	—	—	—	—	—
	1980	—	—	—	—	.10
	1980	.015	—	—	Proof	5.00

10 KRONUR

COPPER-NICKEL

Y#	Date	Mintage	Fine	VF	XF	Unc
19	1967	1.000	—	—	.30	.50
	1969	.500	—	—	.40	1.00
	1970	1.000	—	—	—	.50
	1971	1.500	—	—	—	.20
	1973	1.500	—	—	—	.20
	1974	2.000	—	—	—	.20
	1975	2.500	—	—	—	.20
	1976	2.500	—	—	—	.20
	1977	2.000	—	—	—	.20
	1978	—	—	—	—	—
	1980	—	—	—	—	.20
	1980	.015	—	—	Proof	5.00

50 KRONUR

NICKEL
50th Anniversary of Sovereignty

Y#	Date	Mintage	Fine	VF	XF	Unc
20	1968	.100	1.00	2.00	3.00	4.00

COPPER-NICKEL

Y#	Date	Mintage	Fine	VF	XF	Unc
21	1970	.800	—	—	.50	1.50
	1971	.500	—	—	.50	.90
	1973	.050	—	—	1.25	1.75
	1974	.200	—	—	.50	.75
	1975	.700	—	—	—	.50
	1976	.500	—	—	—	.50
	1977	.200	—	—	—	.50
	1978	—	—	—	—	.50
	1980	—	—	—	—	.50
	1980	.015	—	—	Proof	5.00

500 KRONUR

8.9604 gm., .900 GOLD, .2593 oz AGW
Jon Sigurdsson Sesquicentennial

Y#	Date	Mintage	Fine	VF	XF	Unc
17	1961	.010	—	—	250.00	300.00
	1961	—	—	—	Proof	500.00

20.0000 gm., .925 SILVER, .5968 oz ASW
1100th Anniversary 1st Settlement

Y#	Date	Mintage	Fine	VF	XF	Unc
22	1974	.070	—	—	18.00	20.00
	1974	*.058	—	—	Proof	25.00

NOTE: A considerable amount of proof coins were remelted.

1000 KRONUR

30.0000 gm., .925 SILVER, .8923 oz ASW
1100th Anniversary 1st Settlement

Y#	Date	Mintage	Fine	VF	XF	Unc
23	1974	.070	—	—	27.50	30.00
	1974	*.058	—	—	Proof	35.00

NOTE: A considerable amount of proof coins were remelted.

10,000 KRONUR

15.5000 gm., .900 GOLD, .4485 oz AGW
1100th Anniversary 1st Settlement

Y#	Date	Mintage	Fine	VF	XF	Unc
24	1974	.012	—	—	—	275.00
	1974	8,000	—	—	Proof	350.00

NCLT ISSUES

MEDALLIC ISSUES

2 KRONUR

BRONZE

1000 Years Althing

Y#	Date	Mintage	Fine	VF	XF	Unc
8	1930	.020	—	—	30.00	50.00

5 KRONUR

SILVER
1000 Years Althing

Y#	Date	Mintage	Fine	VF	XF	Unc
9	1930	.010	—	—	100.00	150.00

10 KRONUR

SILVER
1000 Years Althing

Y#	Date	Mintage	Fine	VF	XF	Unc
10	1930	.010	—	—	150.00	250.00

MINT: Saxon State Mint, Dresden. Denominations on edges.

MINT SETS

KM#	Date	Mintage	Identification	Issue Price	Mkt. Val.
S1	1973(6)	—	Y13a,15A,18,19,21	3.25	5.00
S2	1974(6)	—	Y13a,15A,18,19,21	3.25	4.50
S3	1974(2)	70,000	Y22,23	30.00	50.00
S4	1975(4)	—	Y15a,18,19,21	—	—
S5	1976(4)	—	Y15b,18,19,21	—	4.00
S6	1977(4)	—	Y15b,18,19,21	—	4.00
S7	1978(4)	—	Y15b,18,19,21	—	—

PROOF SETS

STANDARD METALS

KM#	Date	Mintage	Identification	Issue Price	Mkt. Val.
101	1930(3)	10,000	Y8-10	—	400.00
102	1974(3)	8,000	Y22-24	272.00	400.00
103	1974(2)	58,000	Y22,23	38.00	60.00
104	1980(11)	15,000	(Mixed dates) 1966: Y-11,12,16a; 1967: y-14; 1974: Y-13a,A15; 1975: Y-15a; 1980: Y-15b,18,19,21	40.00	55.00

INDIA/Mughal Empire

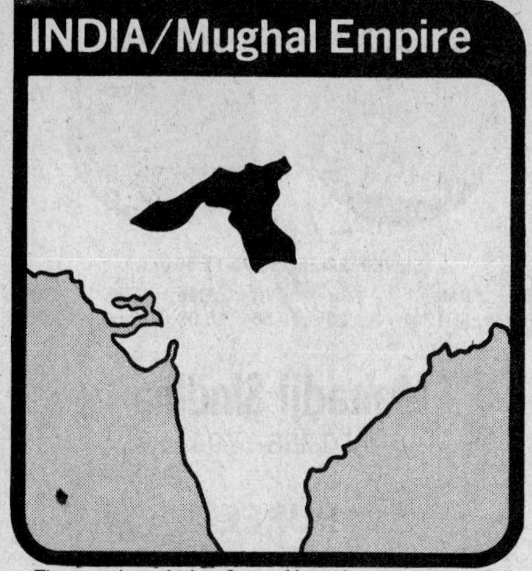

The empire of the Great Mughals encompassed its maximum territorial area during the reign of the emperor Aurangzeb Alamgir (AD1658-1707). At that time it included the greater part of the modern states of Afghanistan, Bangladesh, India and Pakistan. On Aurangzab's death the empire was in a condition of military exhaustion and financial impoverishment, unable to contain internal dissension or meet external challenge. By the mid-eighteenth century, large sections of the Mughal empire had attained independence.

Shah Alam II was the last Emperor who exercised any real control, but successive defeats at the hands of the British reduced him to little more than an East India Company pensioner by the end of his reign in 1806. The later Emperors were mere figureheads, allowed to 'rule' the city of Delhi and little else by favor of the Company. They were also permitted to strike coins at Delhi, and limited numbers were produced in all three metals by Muhammad Akbar II, and in silver by Bahadur II.

The importance of the later Emperors is that they remained the formal source of legitimacy for most of the rulers of the Native States, who, rather than strike coins in their own names, added their symbols to the official types of the later Mughal Emperors, which were often the same symbols earlier used by the Mughals themselves in conjunction with the mint name in the Persian script. These symbols are listed in all the major references on Mughal coinage, though no single book has a complete list.

INDEX

Emperors

Because it is often important to distinguish the legends of Shah Alam II, Muhammad Akbar II, and Bahadur Shah, the following drawings show the portions of the legend that are distinctive to the primary type of each ruler. However, there were other types used, and the key features are often off the flan, and in many cases it is therefore necessary to read the Persian legends:

Shah Alam II شاه عالم
حامی دین

(The first drawing is of his name, the second of the expression 'Hami-yi Din', Protector of the Faith)

Bedar Bakht محمد بیدار بخت

(Only his name is shown)

Muhammad Akbar II محمد اکبر شاه
صاحب قران

(The first drawing is of this name, the second of the expression 'Sahibqiran', a title he was granted)

Bahadur II بهادر

(Only his name is shown)

Dating

The Mughal coins were dated both in the Hejira era and in the regnal era of each emperor. The four-digit Hejira year usually was shown on the obverse, with the one or two-digit regnal (jalus) year on the reverse. Since the regnal and calendar years did not necessarily coincide, it was common for two different regnal years to appear on the coins produced during any calendar year. The first jalus year of each reign was usually written as a word, 'ahd', rather than as a numeral.

Legends

The Mughals had the unfortunate habit of striking many of their silver and gold coins from larger dies with the result that often much of the legend is off the coin.

Standard Coin Pattern

The Mughal Rupees and Mohurs from the time of Aurangzeb (d.1707AD), generally followed a standard pattern of layout.

Obverse:

Date (1174) Emperor's name (Shah Alam)

Legend, (read right to left, bottom to top) 'Auspicious coin of the fighter of infidels, the emperor Shah Alam'.

Reverse:

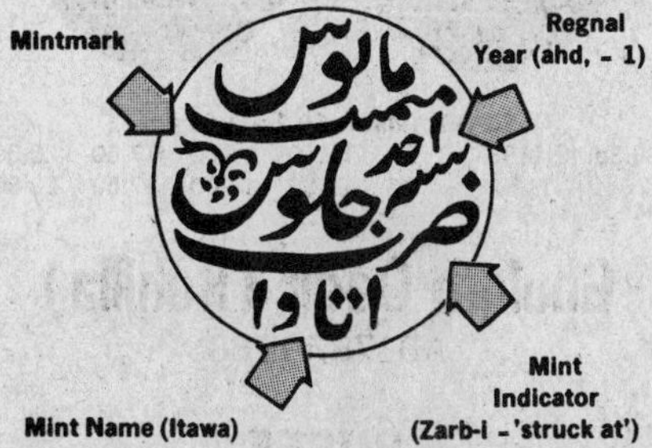

Legend, (read right to left, bottom to top) 'Struck in Itawa in the Year One of the accession associated with prosperity'.

There are many variations of this layout, especially as to the poetic couplet containing the king's name on the obverse. In general however the provincial mints and independent state mints used the simple standard pattern.

Shah Alam II

AH1173-1221/AD1759-1806

Except for the Delhi Mint, most of the later coins struck in the name of this Emperor were Native State issues, and can be found in their appropriate place under the States. earlier issues come from nearly 100 mints, and it is always a problem to determine in what year coins of a particular mint cease to be Mughal and become State issues.

The following mints, for the most part in the Delhi (Shahjahanabad) area, may be considered the nucleus of Mughal mints during Shah Alam's reign. They were located in provinces governed by Mughal functionaries, whose increasing independence is reflected in the growing eccentricity of coin design.

In some cases the distinctive geometric designs and floral devices found on the coins were true mintmarks, representative of a single mint. In other instances the 'mintmarks' listed below were temporary privy marks or simply decoration.

Shah Alam II legends were used in some states long after his death, until AH1314/1879AD at Ujjain, for example. This is not the case with true Mughal issues.

MINT NAMES

Ahmadabad احمداباد

Akbarabad (Mustagir-ul-khilafat) مستقر الخلافه اکبراباد

Allahabad الهاباد

Azimabad عظیم اباد

Chhachrauli چھچرولی

Gokulgarh گوکل گده

Hardwar (Tirath) تیرتھ هردوار

Hathras هاتهرس

Kora کورا

Murshidabad مرشداباد

Saharanpur (Dar-us-sarur) دارالسرور سهرنپور

Shahjahanabad (Dar-ul-khilafat) دارالخلافه شاهجهاناباد

Ahmadabad Mint

Mintmarks:

PAISA

COPPER, 21mm

C#	Date	Year	Good	VG	Fine	VF
71.1	AH1202	29	.85	1.50	2.50	4.00

RUPEE

SILVER, 21mm, 10.70-11.60 gm.

C#	Date	Year	VG	Fine	VF	XF
86.1	AH1201	28	12.50	15.00	17.50	23.50

MOHUR

GOLD, 19mm, 10.70-11.40 gm.

C#	Date	Year	VG	Fine	VF	XF
97.1	AH1202	29	220.00	240.00	265.00	300.00

Akbarabad Mint

The city and fort of Agra or Akbarabad fell to the Jats of Bharatpur after the battle of Panipat. For issues AH1175-1186 (AD1761-1773) see India Native States: Bharatpur. A succession of governors from 1770 controlled Agra nominally as officers of the Mughal emperor.

PRE-PANIPAT

RUPEE

SILVER, 25mm, 10.70-11.60 gm.
No mintmark.

C#	Date	Year	VG	Fine	VF	XF
86.3	AH1174	1	12.50	14.00	17.50	21.50

NAZARANA RUPEE

SILVER, 30mm

C#	Date	Year	VG	Fine	VF	XF
86.3a	AH1174	1	65.00	85.00	110.00	135.00

Najaf Khan (Rohilla)

AD1773-1779

RUPEE

Mintmark: 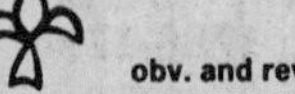 obv. and rev.

SILVER, 22mm, 10.70-11.60 gm.

C#	Date	Year	VG	Fine	VF	XF
86.3b	AH1185 (error)					
		14	12.50	15.00	18.50	25.00

Muhammad Beg Hamadani

AD1779-1784

1/4 RUPEE

SILVER, 16mm, 2.68-2.90 gm.

C#	Date	Year	VG	Fine	VF	XF
84.3c	—	22	7.00	9.00	12.00	16.00

RUPEE

Mintmark: 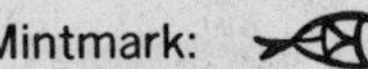 rev.

SILVER, 21mm, 10.70-11.60 gm.

C#	Date	Year	VG	Fine	VF	XF
86.3c	AH1193	20	11.50	14.00	17.50	23.50
	1196	24	11.50	14.00	17.50	23.50
	1197	25	11.50	14.00	17.50	23.50
	1198	25	11.50	14.00	17.50	23.50

Mahadji Sindhia

AD1784-1787

RUPEE

Mintmark:  obv.  rev.

SILVER, 23mm, 10.70-11.60 gm.

C#	Date	Year	VG	Fine	VF	XF
86.3d	AH1198	26	11.50	14.00	17.50	23.50
	1199	26	11.50	14.00	17.50	23.50

Ghulam Qadir (Rohilla)

AD1787-1788

RUPEE

Mintmark: rev.

SILVER, 22mm, 10.70-11.60 gm.

C#	Date	Year	VG	Fine	VF	XF
86.3e	AH1201	28	12.50	15.00	18.50	25.00

Mahadji Sindhia

AD1788-1794

RUPEE

Mintmark:  obv. 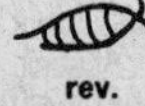 rev.

SILVER, 22mm, 10.70-11.60 gm.

C#	Date	Year	VG	Fine	VF	XF
86.3f	AH1203	30	12.50	15.00	18.50	25.00
	1207	34	12.50	15.00	18.50	25.00

Daulat Rao Sindhia

AD1794-1803

PAISA

COPPER, 15-18mm
Rev: Pistol

KM#	Date	Year	Good	VG	Fine	VF
71.3b	AH1217	44	5.00	7.00	10.00	15.00

1/2 RUPEE

SILVER, 20mm, 5.35-5.80 gm.
Rev: Fish mintmark.

C#	Date	Year	VG	Fine	VF	XF
85.3g	AH	40	8.00	10.00	12.50	16.50

RUPEE

SILVER, 21mm, 10.70-11.60 gm.
Rev: Fish mintmark.

C#	Date	Year	VG	Fine	VF	XF
86.3g	AH—	38	11.50	13.00	15.00	20.00
	—	42	11.50	13.00	15.00	20.00
	1215	43	11.50	13.00	15.00	20.00
	1217	44	11.50	13.00	15.00	20.00
	—	45	11.50	13.00	15.00	20.00

East India Company

RUPEE

SILVER, 21mm, 10.70-11.60 gm.
Obv: Legend different.
Rev: Fish mintmark.

C#	Date	Year	VG	Fine	VF	XF
86.3h	AH1220	47	12.50	14.00	17.50	23.50

Allahabad Mint

At the accession of Shah Alam II the city and fortress of Allahabad were in the possession of the Nawab-Vizier of Awadh. From 1765 to 1771 the Mughal emperor was in residence in Allahabad; subsequently it was seized by the E.I.C. and sold to Awadh once more in 1773.

For issues AH1173-1178 (AD1759-1765) and AH1187-1195 (AD1773-1781) see India Native States: Awadh.

RUPEE

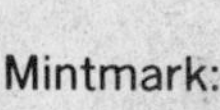

rev.

SILVER, 23mm, 10.70-11.60 gm.

C#	Date	Year	VG	Fine	VF	XF
86.4a	AH1185	13	12.50	14.00	17.50	23.50

East India Company

RUPEE

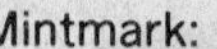

rev.

SILVER, 23mm, 10.70-11.60 gm.

C#	Date	Year	VG	Fine	VF	XF
86.4b	AH1198	23	11.50	13.00	15.00	20.00

Mintmark: rev.

Rev: Arabic numeral 2 in field.

C#	Date	Year	VG	Fine	VF	XF
86.4c	AH—	25	11.50	13.00	15.00	20.00
	1199	26	11.50	13.00	15.00	20.00
	1200	26	11.50	13.00	15.00	20.00

Obv: 9-pointed star.

C#	Date	Year	VG	Fine	VF	XF
86.4d	AH1207	26 (frozen)	11.50	13.00	15.00	20.00

21mm
Obv: Ball and sword.

C#	Date	Year	VG	Fine	VF	XF
86.4e	AH—	26 (frozen)	11.50	13.00	15.00	20.00

Azimabad Mint

Azimabad or Patna was lost by Shah Alam II to the East India Company in AD1765. For subsequent issues of the Patna mint in the mint-name Murshidabad, see India, British: Bengal Presidency.

RUPEE

Mintmark 

SILVER, 21mm, 10.70-11.60 gm.

C#	Date	Year	VG	Fine	VF	XF
86.5a	AH—	2	11.50	13.00	15.00	20.00
	—	3	11.50	13.00	15.00	20.00
	—	4	11.50	13.00	15.00	20.00
	—	5	11.50	13.00	15.00	20.00
	—	6	11.50	13.00	15.00	20.00

East India Company

RUPEE

SILVER, 10.70-11.60 gm.
Similar to C#86.5a.

C#	Date	Year	VG	Fine	VF	XF
86.5b	AH—	6	11.50	13.00	15.00	20.00
	—	7	11.50	13.00	15.00	20.00
	—	8	11.50	13.00	15.00	20.00
	—	9	11.50	13.00	15.00	20.00
	—	10	11.50	13.00	15.00	20.00

Chhachrauli Mint

A mint of the Mughal governor of Saharanpur.

PAISA

COPPER, 24mm

C#	Date	Year	Good	VG	Fine	VF
71.7	AH1214	41	1.50	2.50	4.00	6.00
	1215	42	1.50	2.50	4.00	6.00
	1216	41 (error)	1.50	2.50	4.00	6.00
	1218	44	1.50	2.50	4.00	6.00

GOKULGARH

Mintname: گوکل گڑہ

Mintmark: 

RUPEE

GOVERNOR: RAJA of REWARI

SILVER, 21-23mm., 10.70-11.60 gm.

KM#	Date	Year	VG	Fine	VF	XF
1	AH—	10	13.50	18.50	23.50	30.00
	1184	12	13.50	18.50	23.50	30.00
	1188	16	13.50	18.50	23.50	30.00
	1189	17	13.50	18.50	23.50	30.00
	1189	18	13.50	18.50	23.50	30.00
	1190	18	13.50	18.50	23.50	30.00
	1191	19	13.50	18.50	23.50	30.00
	1193	21	13.50	18.50	23.50	30.00
	—	24	13.50	18.50	23.50	30.00
	1196	24	13.50	18.50	23.50	30.00
	1197	25	13.50	18.50	23.50	30.00
	1197	26	13.50	18.50	23.50	30.00

ROHILLA GOVERNOR

KM#	Date	Year	VG	Fine	VF	XF
2	AH1202	29	13.50	18.50	23.50	30.00
	1202	30	13.50	18.50	23.50	30.00

SINDHIA GOVERNOR

KM#	Date	Year	VG	Fine	VF	XF
3	AH1202	31	13.50	18.50	23.50	30.00
	1203	31	13.50	18.50	23.50	30.00
	1204	31	13.50	18.50	23.50	30.00
	1204	32	13.50	18.50	23.50	30.00
	xx14	43	13.50	18.50	23.50	30.00
	1217	45	13.50	18.50	23.50	30.00
	1218	46	13.50	18.50	23.50	30.00

Hardwar Mint

A mint of the Mughal governor of Saharanpur.

RUPEE

SILVER, 23mm, 10.70-11.60 gm.

C#	Date	Year	VG	Fine	VF	XF
86.9	AH1205	31	22.50	26.00	30.00	40.00
	1212	39	22.50	26.00	30.00	40.00
	1214	41	22.50	26.00	30.00	40.00

Hathras Mint

Harthras, near Aligarh, was in the control of the Nawab-Vizier of Awadh until AD1782. For issues before AH1196-24, see India Native States: Awadh.

Madhoji Sindhia

as Amir-ul-Umara
AD1784-1788,
1788-1794

RUPEE

SILVER, 22.5mm, 10.70-11.60 gm.

C#	Date	Year	VG	Fine	VF	XF
86.10	AH—	26	22.50	26.00	30.00	40.00
	—	28	22.50	26.00	30.00	40.00
	—	29	22.50	26.00	30.00	40.00
	12xx	30	22.00	26.00	30.00	40.00

Coins of 1202-30 and 1203-30 may have been issued by Ghulam Qadir.

Kora Mint

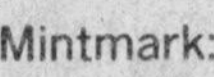

Mintmark: rev.

Shah Alam II received Kora from Awadh in AD1765/AH1178, and lost it to the E.I.C. in AD1771/AD1184 when he moved to Delhi.

Mirza Najaf Khan

Governor

RUPEE

SILVER, 19mm
Obv: No symbols.

C#	Date	Year	VG	Fine	VF	XF
86.12a	AH11xx	7	11.50	13.00	15.00	20.00
	11xx	8	11.50	13.00	15.00	20.00
	11xx	9	11.50	13.00	15.00	20.00
	11xx	10	11.50	13.00	15.00	20.00

Obv: Sword, 18mm.

C#	Date	Year	VG	Fine	VF	XF
86.12a	AH11xx	11	11.50	13.00	15.00	20.00
	11xx	12	11.50	13.00	15.00	20.00

For issues later than AH1187-R.Y. see India Native States: Awadh.

Murshidabad Mint

Bengal, including the mint-town of Murshidabad, was lost by Shah Alam II to the East India Company in AD1765. For coins later than AH1178-5, see India, British: Bengal Presidency.

RUPEE

Mintmark: 

SILVER, 22mm, 10.70-11.60 gm.

C#	Date	Year	VG	Fine	VF	XF
86.13	AH—	5	11.50	13.00	15.00	20.00

Saharanpur Mint

GOVERNORS:

Ghani Bahadur
AD1788-1791/AH1203-1205
Bhairon Pant Tantia
AD1791-1794/AH1206-1208
George Thomas and Bapù Sindhia
AD1796-1798/AH1211-1212
Imam Baksh
AD1799/AH1213-14
General Perron (for Sindhia)
AD1800-1803/AH1215-1218

OTHERS:

Sikhs AD1794-1796/AH1209-1210

1/2 PAISA

COPPER, 19mm
Mintname Seharanpur; dagger symbol.

C#	Date	Year	Good	VG	Fine	VF
70.18	AH12xx	44	7.00	9.00	11.00	15.00

PAISA

COPPER, 21mm
Mintname Dar-us-Sarur Saharanpur

C#	Date	Year	Good	VG	Fine	VF
71.18a	—	31	6.00	8.50	10.00	13.50

Mintmark:  stylized daggar

Mintname: Saharanpur

Annual variations in additional symbols.

24mm
Additional symbol three-pronged quadrafoil.

25mm
Additional symbol vertical and horizontal spray.

Additional symbols chakra and cingfoil.

C#	Date	Year	Good	VG	Fine	VF
71.18b	AH1206	33	4.00	6.00	9.00	12.00
	1207	33	4.00	6.00	9.00	12.00
	1212	39	4.00	6.00	9.00	12.00
	1212	40	4.00	6.00	9.00	12.00
	1214	41	4.00	6.00	9.00	12.00
	1215	42	4.00	6.00	9.00	12.00
	—	43	4.00	6.00	9.00	12.00
	1217	44	4.00	6.00	9.00	12.00
	1218	45	4.00	6.00	9.00	12.00

RUPEE

SILVER, 20.5mm, 10.70-11.60 gm.

C#	Date	Year	VG	Fine	VF	XF
86.18a	AH1204	31	20.00	25.00	30.00	40.00
	1205	33	20.00	25.00	30.00	40.00
	1207	34	20.00	25.00	30.00	40.00
	1211	38	20.00	25.00	30.00	40.00
	1212	40	20.00	25.00	30.00	40.00
	1214	41	20.00	25.00	30.00	40.00
	1216	43	20.00	25.00	30.00	40.00
	1218	45	20.00	25.00	30.00	40.00

23mm
Circled dot additional mark.

C#	Date	Year	VG	Fine	VF	XF
86.18b	AH1216	43	20.00	25.00	30.00	40.00
	1217	44	20.00	25.00	30.00	40.00

Sikh Occupation

RUPEE

SILVER, 19mm, 10.70-11.60 gm.
Rev: W/"Sri".

C#	Date	Year	VG	Fine	VF	XF
86.18c	AH1210	37	25.00	30.00	37.50	50.00

East India Company

PAISA

COPPER, 25mm.
Rev: St. Stephen's cross.

C#	Date	Year	Good	VG	Fine	VF
71.18d	AH1218	45	4.00	10.00	15.00	20.00

RUPEE

SILVER, 22mm, 10.70-11.60 gm.
Rev: St. Stephen's cross.

C#	Date	Year	VG	Fine	VF	XF
86.18d	AH1218	45	25.00	30.00	37.50	50.00

19mm
Symbols similar to C#86.18a.

C#	Date	Year	VG	Fine	VF	XF
86.18e	AH1219	46	20.00	25.00	30.00	40.00

20mm
Rev: Plain.

C#	Date	Year	VG	Fine	VF	XF
86.18f	AH1220	47	20.00	25.00	30.00	40.00
	1220	49	20.00	25.00	30.00	40.00

Shahjahanabad Mint

Mintmarks:

(Obverse of silver coins only)

PAISA

COPPER, 21mm

C#	Date	Year	Good	VG	Fine	VF
71.19	AH1185	12	1.00	1.75	2.50	4.00
	1186	13	1.00	1.75	2.50	4.00
	1187	15	1.00	1.75	2.50	4.00
	1190	18	1.00	1.75	2.50	4.00
	—	25	1.00	1.75	2.50	4.00
	—	28	1.00	1.75	2.50	4.00
	1205	32	1.00	1.75	2.50	4.00
	1206	33	1.00	1.75	2.50	4.00
	1206	34	1.00	1.75	2.50	4.00
	1207	35	1.00	1.75	2.50	4.00
	1207	36	1.00	1.75	2.50	4.00
	1208	35	1.00	1.75	2.50	4.00
	1208	36	1.00	1.75	2.50	4.00
	1209	36	1.00	1.75	2.50	4.00
	1210	38	1.00	1.75	2.50	4.00
	1211	39	1.00	1.75	2.50	4.00
	1214	41	1.00	1.75	2.50	4.00
	1219	46	1.00	1.75	2.50	4.00
	1219	47	1.00	1.75	2.50	4.00
	1220	48	1.00	1.75	2.50	4.00

1/4 RUPEE

SILVER, 14mm, 2.68-2.90 gm.
Obv. leg: "Hami Din"

C#	Date	Year	VG	Fine	VF	XF
84.19a	AH1197	25	8.00	11.00	15.00	20.00

11mm
Obv. leg: "Sahib Qiran"

C#	Date	Year	VG	Fine	VF	XF
84.19b	AH—	33	8.00	11.00	15.00	20.00

13mm
Obv: Cingfoil additional mark.

C#	Date	Year	VG	Fine	VF	XF
84.19e	AH1220	48	8.00	11.00	15.00	20.00

1/2 RUPEE

SILVER, 17mm, 5.35-5.80 gm.
Obv. leg: "Sahib Qiran"

C#	Date	Year	VG	Fine	VF	XF
85.19b	AH—	33	6.50	9.00	12.00	16.00
	1211	39	6.50	9.00	12.50	16.00
	1213	41	6.50	9.00	12.50	16.00

18mm
Obv: Cinqfoil additional mark.

C#	Date	Year	VG	Fine	VF	XF
85.19e	AH1220	47	6.50	9.00	12.50	16.00

RUPEE

NOTE: The size of the Shahjahanabad Rupees of Shah Alam II were subject to a wide variance. The early issues tended to be normal size for the hammered coinage (about 22mm). As the power of the emperor waned, the flan size of the Shahjahanabad Rupees waxed, reflecting the increasingly ceremonial role of the coinage. The later coins should not be confused with the Nazarana (presentation) coins, which always show a full border design around the legend.

SILVER, 22mm, 10.70-11.60 gm.
Obv. leg: "Hami Din"

C#	Date	Year	VG	Fine	VF	XF
86.19a	AH1174	2	11.50	13.00	15.00	20.00
	1175	2	11.50	13.00	15.00	20.00
	1175	3	11.50	13.00	15.00	20.00
	1176	4	11.50	13.00	15.00	20.00
	1177	5	11.50	13.00	15.00	20.00
	1178	5	11.50	13.00	15.00	20.00
	1178	6	11.50	13.00	15.00	20.00
	1179	6	11.50	13.00	15.00	20.00
	1179	7	11.50	13.00	15.00	20.00
	1180	8	11.50	13.00	15.00	20.00
	1181	9	11.50	13.00	15.00	20.00
	1183	11	11.50	13.00	15.00	20.00
	1184	12	11.50	13.00	15.00	20.00
	1185	13	11.50	13.00	15.00	20.00
	1186	13	11.50	13.00	15.00	20.00
	1186	14	11.50	13.00	15.00	20.00
	1187	14	11.50	13.00	15.00	20.00
	1188	16	11.50	13.00	15.00	20.00
	1189	17	11.50	13.00	15.00	20.00
	1190	18	11.50	13.00	15.00	20.00
	1191	18	11.50	13.00	15.00	20.00
	1191	19	11.50	13.00	15.00	20.00
	1192	19	11.50	13.00	15.00	20.00
	1192	20	11.50	13.00	15.00	20.00
	1193	21	11.50	13.00	15.00	20.00
	1194	21	11.50	13.00	15.00	20.00
	1194	22	11.50	13.00	15.00	20.00
	1195	22	11.50	13.00	15.00	20.00
	1195	23	11.50	13.00	15.00	20.00
	1196	23	11.50	13.00	15.00	20.00
	1196	24	11.50	13.00	15.00	20.00
	1197	25	11.50	13.00	15.00	20.00
	1198	25	11.50	13.00	15.00	20.00
	1198	26	11.50	13.00	15.00	20.00
	1199	26	11.50	13.00	15.00	20.00
	1199	27	11.50	13.00	15.00	20.00
	1200	27	11.50	13.00	15.00	20.00
	1200	28	11.50	13.00	15.00	20.00
	1201	29	11.50	13.00	15.00	20.00

21mm
Obv. leg: "Sahib Qiran"

C#	Date	Year	VG	Fine	VF	XF
86.19b	AH1202	30	11.50	13.00	15.00	20.00
	1203	31	11.50	13.00	15.00	20.00
	1204	31	11.50	13.00	15.00	20.00
	1205	32	11.50	13.00	15.00	20.00
	1205	33	11.50	13.00	15.00	20.00
86.19b	1206	34	11.50	13.00	15.00	20.00
	1207	34	11.50	13.00	15.00	20.00
	1207	35	11.50	13.00	15.00	20.00
	1208	36	11.50	13.00	15.00	20.00
	1209	36	11.50	13.00	15.00	20.00
	1209	37	11.50	13.00	15.00	20.00
	1210	38	11.50	13.00	15.00	20.00
	1211	39	11.50	13.00	15.00	20.00
	1212	39	11.50	13.00	15.00	20.00
	1213	41	11.50	13.00	15.00	20.00

Additional Mintmark:  obv.

29mm

C#	Date	Year	VG	Fine	VF	XF
86.19c	AH1216	44	13.50	17.50	21.50	28.50
	1217	44	13.50	17.50	21.50	28.50
	1218	45	13.50	17.50	21.50	28.50

Additional Mintmark:  obv.

27mm

C#	Date	Year	VG	Fine	VF	XF
86.19d	AH1218	46	25.00	30.00	35.00	47.50

Additional Mintmark:  obv.

C#	Date	Year	VG	Fine	VF	XF
86.19e	AH1218	46	15.00	18.50	22.50	30.00
	1221	49	15.00	18.50	22.50	30.00

Design surrounded by wreath of roses, thistles and shamrocks.

C#	Date	Year	VG	Fine	VF	XF
86.19f	AH1219	47	60.00	75.00	90.00	120.00
	1220	48	60.00	75.00	90.00	120.00
	1221	48	60.00	75.00	90.00	120.00

NAZARANA RUPEE

SILVER, 29-36mm, 10.70-11.60 gm.
From dies of 86.19a.

C#	Date	Year	VG	Fine	VF	XF
86.19g	AH1174	2	30.00	45.00	60.00	90.00

From dies of 86.19b.

C#	Date	Year	VG	Fine	VF	XF
86.19h	AH1202	30	30.00	45.00	60.00	90.00

C#	Date	Year	VG	Fine	VF	XF
86.19h	1209	37	30.00	45.00	60.00	90.00

MOHUR

GOLD, 21mm, 10.70-11.40 gm.

C#	Date	Year	VG	Fine	VF	XF
97.19	AH1174	2	220.00	240.00	265.00	300.00
	1175	2	220.00	240.00	265.00	300.00
	1176	3	220.00	240.00	265.00	300.00
	1197	24	220.00	240.00	265.00	300.00
	1197	25	220.00	240.00	265.00	300.00
	1204	31	220.00	240.00	265.00	300.00
	1205	32	220.00	240.00	265.00	300.00
	1206	34	220.00	240.00	265.00	300.00

NAZARANA MOHUR

GOLD, 35mm

C#	Date	Year	Fine	VF	XF	Unc
97.19a	AH1217	45	225.00	275.00	325.00	400.00
	1218	46	225.00	275.00	325.00	400.00

Wreath type, 26mm.

C#	Date	Year	Fine	VF	XF	Unc
97.19b	AH1219	47	250.00	300.00	375.00	450.00
	1221	48	250.00	300.00	375.00	450.00

Bedar Bakht

AH1202-1203/AD1788

Bedar Bakht was a pretender to the Mughal masnad who enjoyed a temporary power, only to be overthrown in favor of the incumbent Shah Alam II.

Ahmadabad Mint

PAISA

COPPER

C#	Date	Year	Good	VG	Fine	VF
100.1	AH1203	1	6.00	10.00	15.00	20.00

RUPEE

SILVER, 20mm, 10.70-11.60 gm.

C#	Date	Year	VG	Fine	VF	XF
106.1	AH1202	1	60.00	80.00	110.00	150.00
106.1	1203	1	60.00	80.00	110.00	150.00

MOHUR

GOLD, 18mm, 10.70-11.40 gm.

C#	Date	Year	VG	Fine	VF	XF
117.1	AH1203	1	400.00	550.00	675.00	800.00

Shahjahanabad Mint

RUPEE

SILVER, 10.70-11.60 gm.

C#	Date	Year	VG	Fine	VF	XF
106.2	AH1202	1	85.00	125.00	150.00	200.00

MOHUR

GOLD, 20mm

C#	Date	Year	VG	Fine	VF	XF
117.2	AH1202	1	400.00	550.00	675.00	800.00

Muhammad Akbar II

AH1221-1253/AD1806-1837

Saharanpur Mint

East India Company

RUPEE

SILVER, 21mm, 10.70-11.60 gm.

C#	Date	Year	VG	Fine	VF	XF
130	AH1203	1	—	—	Rare	—

Shahjahanabad Mint

PAISA

COPPER, 18mm

C#	Date	Year	Good	VG	Fine	VF
123.1	AH1222	1	1.25	2.00	3.00	4.00
	1222	2	1.25	2.00	3.00	4.00

Rev: With letter "S" by regnal year.

C#	Date	Year	Good	VG	Fine	VF
123.2	AH1225	4	1.25	2.00	3.00	4.00
123.2	1225	5	1.25	2.00	3.00	4.00
	1226	5	1.25	2.00	3.00	4.00
	1231	10	1.25	2.00	3.00	4.00
	1233	12	1.25	2.00	3.00	4.00

1/4 RUPEE

SILVER, 2.68-2.90 gm.

C#	Date	Year	VG	Fine	VF	XF
134	AH—	7	5.00	6.50	8.00	11.50

1/2 RUPEE

SILVER, 5.35-5.80 gm.

C#	Date	Year	VG	Fine	VF	XF
135	AH1221	1	6.00	7.00	8.50	11.50
	1225	4	6.00	7.00	8.50	11.50

RUPEE

SILVER, 22mm

C#	Date	Year	VG	Fine	VF	XF
136	AH1221	1	11.50	13.00	15.00	20.00
	1222	1	11.50	13.00	15.00	20.00
	1222	2	11.50	13.00	15.00	20.00
	1223	2	11.50	13.00	15.00	20.00
	1223	3	11.50	13.00	15.00	20.00
	1224	3	11.50	13.00	15.00	20.00
	1225	4	11.50	13.00	15.00	20.00
	1226	5	11.50	13.00	15.00	20.00
	1227	6	11.50	13.00	15.00	20.00
	1227	7	11.50	13.00	15.00	20.00
	1228	7	11.50	13.00	15.00	20.00
	1228	8	11.50	13.00	15.00	20.00
	1229	9	11.50	13.00	15.00	20.00
	12xx	11	11.50	13.00	15.00	20.00

NAZARANA RUPEE

SILVER, 29-31mm

C#	Date	Year	VG	Fine	VF	XF
136a	AH1223	3	22.50	35.00	50.00	65.00
	1224	3	22.50	35.00	50.00	65.00
	1225	4	22.50	35.00	50.00	65.00
	1227	7	22.50	35.00	50.00	65.00
	1235	15	22.50	35.00	50.00	65.00
	1237	17	22.50	35.00	50.00	65.00
	1239	19	22.50	35.00	50.00	65.00
	1240	20	22.50	35.00	50.00	65.00
	1241	21	22.50	35.00	50.00	65.00
	1242	22	22.50	35.00	50.00	65.00
	1248	28	22.50	35.00	50.00	65.00
	1249	29	22.50	35.00	50.00	65.00
	125x	30	22.50	35.00	50.00	65.00
	1251	31	22.50	35.00	50.00	65.00
	1252	32	22.50	35.00	50.00	65.00

MOHUR

GOLD, 19-24mm, 10.70-11.40 gm.

C#	Date	Year	VG	Fine	VF	XF
147	AH122x	2	220.00	240.00	265.00	300.00
	12xx	6	220.00	240.00	265.00	300.00

NAZARANA MOHUR

GOLD, 27mm, 10.70-11.40 gm.

C#	Date	Year	Fine	VF	XF	Unc
147a	AH1221	1	235.00	265.00	300.00	350.00
	1234	12	235.00	265.00	300.00	350.00

Bahadur II

AH1253-1273/AD1837-1857

NAZARANA RUPEE

SILVER, 28-30mm, 10.70-11.40 gm.

C#	Date	Year	VG	Fine	VF	XF
156	AH1255	3	100.00	150.00	200.00	275.00
	1257	5	100.00	150.00	200.00	275.00
	1258	6	100.00	150.00	200.00	275.00

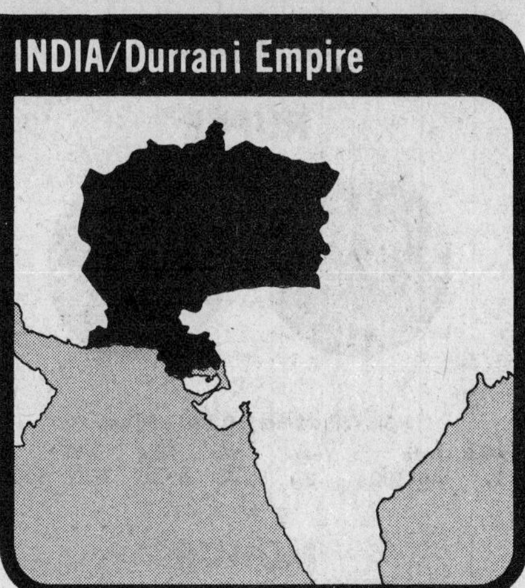

The Durrani kings of Afghanistan (q.v.), beginning with Ahmad Shah in AD1748, and continuing in succeeding decades, raided the Mughal empire in depth, capturing the capital Delhi and holding the emperor for ransom. Large sections of the north-west of India came under the direct rule of a Durrani viceroy, and the Mughal himself was made a vassal of the Afghan emperor. Ahmad Shah Durrani's Pyrrhic victory at Panipat (1761) was the last major armed incursion into Hindustan, although Durrani rule over the Punjab, Kashmir and Sindh continued some time after.

The Durranies had an unfortunate habit of striking many of their silver and gold coins from larger dies with the result that usually much of the legends are off the coin.

INDEX

Ahmad Shah

AH1160-1186/AD1747-1772

Ahmadnagar-Farrukhabad Mint

RUPEE

SILVER, 28mm, 10.70-11.60 gm.

KM#	Date	Year	VG	Fine	VF	XF
6	AH1174	14	12.50	14.00	17.50	23.50
	1176	15	12.50	14.00	17.50	23.50

MOHUR

GOLD, 27mm, 10.70-11.40 gm.

KM#	Date	Year	VG	Fine	VF	XF
9	AH1176	15	250.00	300.00	350.00	400.00

Anwala (Aonla) Mint

RUPEE

SILVER, 21mm, 10.70-11.60 gm.

KM#	Date	Year	VG	Fine	VF	XF
16	AH1173	14	20.00	25.00	32.50	45.00
	1174	14	20.00	25.00	32.50	45.00

Bareli Mint

RUPEE

SILVER, 21mm, 10.70-11.60 gm.

KM#	Date	Year	VG	Fine	VF	XF
26	AH1173	14	30.00	37.50	45.00	60.00
	1174	14	30.00	37.50	45.00	60.00

Kashmir Mint

DAM

COPPER

KM#	Date	Year	Good	VG	Fine	VF
32	—	23	5.00	6.50	7.50	10.00
	AH1187 (error)		5.00	6.50	7.50	10.00

RUPEE

SILVER, 24mm, 10.70-11.60 gm.

KM#	Date	Year	VG	Fine	VF	XF
36	AH1176	14	11.50	13.00	15.00	20.00
	1176	15	11.50	13.00	15.00	20.00
	1177	15	11.50	13.00	15.00	20.00
	1177	16	11.50	13.00	15.00	20.00
	1178	17	11.50	13.00	15.00	20.00
	—	18	11.50	13.00	15.00	20.00
	—	20	—	—	—	—
	—	21	11.50	13.00	15.00	20.00
	1182	22	11.50	13.00	15.00	20.00
	1184	23	11.50	13.00	15.00	20.00
	1184	24	11.50	13.00	15.00	20.00
	1185	24	11.50	13.00	15.00	20.00

MOHUR

GOLD, 21mm, 10.70-11.40 gm.

KM#	Date	Year	VG	Fine	VF	XF
39	AH1167	6	—	—	—	—

Lahore Mint

RUPEE

SILVER, 22mm, 10.70-11.60 gm.

KM#	Date	Year	VG	Fine	VF	XF
A46	AH1161	1	—	—	—	—

KM#	Date	Year	VG	Fine	VF	XF
B46	AH1165	5	12.50	14.00	17.50	23.50
	—	10	12.50	14.00	17.50	23.50
	1170	11	12.50	14.00	17.50	23.50
	1173	13	12.50	14.00	17.50	23.50
	1173	14	12.50	14.00	17.50	23.50
	1173	15	12.50	14.00	17.50	23.50
	1174	15	12.50	14.00	17.50	23.50
	1175	15	12.50	14.00	17.50	23.50
	1175	16	12.50	14.00	17.50	23.50
	1176	16	12.50	14.00	17.50	23.50
	1176	17	12.50	14.00	17.50	23.50
	1177	17	12.50	14.00	17.50	23.50
	1177	18	12.50	14.00	17.50	23.50
	1178	18	12.50	14.00	17.50	23.50
	1179	19	12.50	14.00	17.50	23.50
	1180	21	12.50	14.00	17.50	23.50

MOHUR

GOLD, 22mm, 10.70-11.40 gm.

KM#	Date	Year	VG	Fine	VF	XF
A39	AH1161	1	—	—	—	—

Similar to Rupee, KM#B46.

KM#	Date	Year	VG	Fine	VF	XF
B39	AH1175	15	—	—	—	—

Muradabad Mint

RUPEE

SILVER, 21mm, 10.70-11.60 gm.

KM#	Date	Year	VG	Fine	VF	XF
46	AH1173	14	25.00	30.00	37.50	50.00

Najibabad Mint

RUPEE

SILVER, 20mm, 10.70-11.60 gm.

KM#	Date	Year	VG	Fine	VF	XF
56	AH1180	21	50.00	62.50	75.00	100.00

MOHUR

GOLD, 10.70-11.40 gm.

KM#	Date	Year	VG	Fine	VF	XF
59	AH1180	21	—	—	—	—

Sarhind Mint

RUPEE

SILVER, 10.70-11.60 gm.

KM#	Date	Year	VG	Fine	VF	XF
66	—	1	17.50	25.00	32.50	45.00
	AH1164	4	17.50	25.00	32.50	45.00
	1174	14	17.50	25.00	32.50	45.00
	1174	15	17.50	25.00	32.50	45.00
	1175	16	17.50	25.00	32.50	45.00
	1176	—	17.50	25.00	32.50	45.00

MOHUR

GOLD, 21mm, 10.70-11.40 gm.

KM#	Date	Year	VG	Fine	VF	XF
69	—	1	—	—	—	—
	AH1172	—	—	—	—	—
	—	16	—	—	—	—

Shahjahanabad Mint

1/8 RUPEE

SILVER, 1.34-1.45 gm.

KM#	Date	Year	VG	Fine	VF	XF
73	AH1170	11	—	—	Rare	—

RUPEE

SILVER, 23mm, 10.70-11.60 gm.

KM#	Date	Year	VG	Fine	VF	XF
76	AH1170	11	50.00	62.50	75.00	100.00
	1173	14	50.00	62.50	75.00	100.00
	1174	15	50.00	62.50	75.00	100.00

NAZARANA RUPEE

SILVER, 37mm, 10.70-11.60 gm.
Similar to Rupee, KM#73.

KM#	Date	Year	VG	Fine	VF	XF
A76	AH1173	14	—	—	Rare	—

NISAR
(Presentation 1/3 Rupee)

SILVER, 28mm, 3.57-3.87 gm.

KM#	Date	Year	VG	Fine	VF	XF
B76	—	14	—	—	Rare	—

MOHUR

GOLD, 22mm, 10.70-11.40 gm.
Similar to Nazarana Mohur, KM#A79.

KM#	Date	Year	VG	Fine	VF	XF
79	AH1170	11	250.00	325.00	375.00	425.00
	1173	14	250.00	325.00	375.00	425.00
	1174	15	250.00	325.00	375.00	425.00

NAZARANA MOHUR

GOLD, 34mm, 10.70-11.40 gm.

KM#	Date	Year	VG	Fine	VF	XF
A79	AH1173	14	—	—	Rare	—

Tatta Mint

RUPEE

SILVER, 22mm, 10.70-11.60 gm.

KM#	Date	Year	VG	Fine	VF	XF
86	AH1171	—	11.50	13.00	15.00	20.00
	—	14	11.50	13.00	15.00	20.00
	1174	—	11.50	13.00	15.00	20.00

Taimur Shah

Governor, AH1170-1186/AD1757-72
King, AH1186-1207/AD1772-93

Kashmir Mint

DAM

COPPER, 22mm

KM#	Date	Year	Good	VG	Fine	VF
A91	AH119x	1	5.00	6.50	7.50	10.00

KM#	Date	Year	Good	VG	Fine	VF
A91	—	9	5.00	6.50	7.50	10.00
	1195	—	5.00	6.50	7.50	10.00
	1197	—	5.00	6.50	7.50	10.00

21mm

KM#	Date	Year	Good	VG	Fine	VF
B91	AH1199	—	5.50	7.50	9.00	12.50
	1200	13	5.00	6.50	7.50	10.00
	1201	13	5.00	6.50	7.50	10.00
	1201	14	5.00	6.50	7.50	10.00
	1201	15	5.00	6.50	7.50	10.00
	1202	15	5.00	6.50	7.50	10.00
	1204	17	5.00	6.50	7.50	10.00

RUPEE

SILVER, 24mm, 10.70-11.60 gm.

KM#	Date	Year	VG	Fine	VF	XF
A96	AH1187	1	11.50	13.00	15.00	20.00
	—	5	11.50	13.00	15.00	20.00
	1193	6	11.50	13.00	15.00	20.00
	1195	8	11.50	13.00	15.00	20.00
	1198	6	11.50	13.00	15.00	20.00
	1198	7	11.50	13.00	15.00	20.00
	1197	10	12.50	14.00	16.50	22.50

25mm

KM#	Date	Year	VG	Fine	VF	XF
B96	AH1199	12	11.50	13.00	15.00	20.00
	1200	12	11.50	13.00	15.00	20.00

22mm

KM#	Date	Year	VG	Fine	VF	XF
C96	AH1200	13	11.50	13.00	15.00	20.00
	1201	13	11.50	13.00	15.00	20.00
	1201	14	11.50	13.00	15.00	20.00
	1202	15	11.50	13.00	15.00	20.00
	1204	16	11.50	13.00	15.00	20.00
	1204	17	11.50	13.00	15.00	20.00
	1205	17	11.50	13.00	15.00	20.00
	1206	19	11.50	13.00	15.00	20.00
	1207	19	11.50	13.00	15.00	20.00
	1208	20	11.50	13.00	15.00	20.00

MOHUR

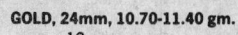

GOLD, 24mm, 10.70-11.40 gm.

KM#	Date	Year	VG	Fine	VF	XF
A99	—	12	—	—	—	—

26mm

KM#	Date	Year	VG	Fine	VF	XF
B99	AH1203	15	—	—	—	—

Lahore Mint

RUPEE

SILVER, 21mmm, 10.70-11.60 gm.

KM#	Date	Year	VG	Fine	VF	XF
106	AH1170	1	12.50	14.00	17.50	23.50
	1171	1	12.50	14.00	17.50	23.50
	1173	3	12.50	14.00	17.50	23.50

MOHUR

GOLD, 22mm, 10.70-11.40 gm.

KM#	Date	Year	VG	Fine	VF	XF
109	AH1170	1	—	—	—	—
	1171	1	—	—	—	—

Sind Mint

RUPEE

SILVER, 23mm, 10.70-11.60 gm.

KM#	Date	Year	VG	Fine	VF	XF
A116	AH1170	1	11.50	13.00	15.00	20.00

KM#	Date	Year	VG	Fine	VF	XF
B116	AH1198	—	11.50	13.00	15.00	20.00

Tatta Mint

RUPEE

SILVER, 10.70-11.60 gm.

KM#	Date	Year	VG	Fine	VF	XF
126	AH120x	—	11.50	13.00	15.00	20.00

Sulaiman

AH1186/AD1772

Kashmir Mint

RUPEE

SILVER, 24mm

KM#	Date	Year	VG	Fine	VF	XF
136	AH1186	1	30.00	45.00	60.00	80.00

Shah Zaman

AH1207-1216/AD1793-1801

Kashmir Mint

FALUS

COPPER, 20mm

KM#	Date	Year	Good	VG	Fine	VF
A141	AH1210	3	3.00	4.50	6.00	8.00
	1212	—	3.00	4.50	6.00	8.00

21mm

KM#	Date	Year	Good	VG	Fine	VF
B141	AH1212	5	3.00	4.50	6.00	8.00

22mm

KM#	Date	Year	Good	VG	Fine	VF
C141	AH1212	6	3.00	4.50	6.00	8.00
	1213	6	3.00	4.50	6.00	8.00

23mm

KM#	Date	Year	Good	VG	Fine	VF
D141	AH1214	7	3.00	4.50	6.00	8.00
	1214	8	3.00	4.50	6.00	8.00
	1215	8	3.00	4.50	6.00	8.00

RUPEE

SILVER, 24mm, 10.70-11.60 gm.

KM#	Date	Year	VG	Fine	VF	XF
A146	AH1208	2	12.50	15.00	17.50	23.50
	1209	2	12.50	15.00	17.50	23.50
	1209	3	12.50	15.00	17.50	23.50

KM#	Date	Year	VG	Fine	VF	XF
	1210	3	12.50	15.00	17.50	23.50
	1211	4	12.50	15.00	17.50	23.50
	1211	5	12.50	15.00	17.50	23.50
	1212	5	12.50	15.00	17.50	23.50

23mm

KM#	Date	Year	VG	Fine	VF	XF
B146	AH1211	5	12.50	15.00	17.50	23.50
	1212	5	12.50	15.00	17.50	23.50
	1213	6	12.50	15.00	17.50	23.50

Rev. legend in circle

KM#	Date	Year	VG	Fine	VF	XF
C146	AH1213	6	15.00	18.50	22.50	28.50
	1213	7	15.00	18.50	22.50	28.50
	1214	7	15.00	18.50	22.50	28.50

Rev. legend in lozenge

KM#	Date	Year	VG	Fine	VF	XF
D146	AH1214	7	15.00	18.50	22.50	28.50
	12xx	8	15.00	18.50	22.50	28.50

Lahore Mint

RUPEE

SILVER, 20mm, 10.70-11.60 gm.

KM#	Date	Year	VG	Fine	VF	XF
A156	AH1211	4	12.50	15.00	17.50	23.50

26mm

KM#	Date	Year	VG	Fine	VF	XF
B156	AH1213	6	12.50	15.00	17.50	23.50

MOHUR

GOLD, 19mm, 10.70-11.40 gm.

KM#	Date	Year	VG	Fine	VF	XF
159	AH1211	4	—	—	—	—

Mahmud Shah

AH1216-1218/AD1801-1803
AH1224-1233/AD1809-1818

Kashmir Mint

FRACTIONAL FALUS

COPPER
First Reign

KM#	Date	Year	Good	VG	Fine	VF
A171	AH1217	2	3.00	4.00	5.00	7.00

Second Reign

KM#	Date	Year	Good	VG	Fine	VF
B171	AH—	1	3.00	4.00	5.00	7.00

FALUS

COPPER
First Reign

KM#	Date	Year	Good	VG	Fine	VF
C171	AH1216	1	3.00	4.00	5.00	7.00

Second Reign
Rev: Legend

KM#	Date	Year	Good	VG	Fine	VF
D171	AH—	1	3.00	4.00	5.00	7.00
	1230	6	3.00	4.50	5.50	7.50
	1229	—	3.00	4.50	5.50	7.50

23mm
Rev: Swords and plume

KM#	Date	Year	Good	VG	Fine	VF
E171	AH12xx	—	3.00	4.00	5.00	7.00

1/4 RUPEE

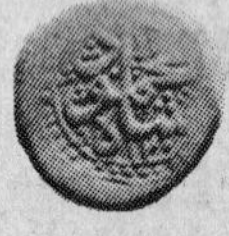
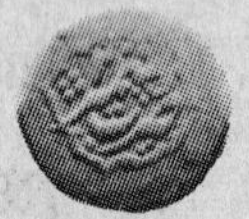

SILVER, 14mm, 2.68-2.90 gm.

KM#	Date	Year	VG	Fine	VF	XF
174	AH1217	2	8.00	14.00	20.00	26.50

RUPEE

SILVER, 22mm, 10.70-11.60 gm.

KM#	Date	Year	VG	Fine	VF	XF
A176	AH12xx	1	15.00	20.00	25.00	33.50
	1217	2	17.50	22.50	27.50	37.50
	1218	3	17.50	22.50	27.50	37.50

23mm
1st Reign

KM#	Date	Year	VG	Fine	VF	XF
B176	AH—	1	11.50	13.00	15.00	20.00
	1217	2	11.50	13.00	15.00	20.00
	1218	3	11.50	13.00	15.00	20.00

2nd Reign

KM#	Date	Year	VG	Fine	VF	XF
C176	AH1227	—	11.50	13.00	15.00	20.00
	1228	6	11.50	13.00	15.00	20.00
	1229	6	11.50	13.00	15.00	20.00
	1229	7	11.50	13.00	15.00	20.00
	1230	8	11.50	13.00	15.00	20.00
	1230	10	11.50	13.00	15.00	20.00
	1232	10	11.50	13.00	15.00	20.00
	1233	10	11.50	13.00	15.00	20.00
	1233	11	11.50	13.00	15.00	20.00

The sequence of regnal years at Kashmir is very confused.

Ladakh Mint

TIMASHA

In the name of Mahmud Khan

SILVER, 20mm

KM#	Date	Year	VG	Fine	VF	XF
183	ND	—	—	—	Rare	—

In the name of Mahmud Shah

21mm
Rev: Inscription

KM#	Date	Year	VG	Fine	VF	XF
184	ND	—	10.00	14.00	18.50	25.00

KM#	Date	Year	VG	Fine	VF	XF
185	ND	—	10.00	14.00	18.50	25.00

Shuja Al-Mulk

AH1218-1224/AD1803-1809

Kashmir Mint

FALUS

COPPER, 17mm

KM#	Date	Year	Good	VG	Fine	VF
200	AH1228	1	2.50	3.50	5.00	7.00
	—	2	3.00	4.50	6.50	9.00

KM#	Date	Year	Good	VG	Fine	VF
201	AH1219	—	3.00	4.00	6.00	8.50
	—	3	3.00	4.00	6.00	8.50
	1221	4	3.50	5.00	7.50	10.00

RUPEE

SILVER, 24mm, 10.70-11.60 gm.

KM#	Date	Year	Good	VG	Fine	VF
206	AH1218	1	11.50	13.00	15.00	20.00
	1219	2	11.50	13.00	15.00	20.00
	1220	3	11.50	13.00	15.00	20.00
	1221	4	11.50	13.00	15.00	20.00
	1222	5	11.50	13.00	15.00	20.00
	1223	6	11.50	13.00	15.00	20.00

Qaisar Shah

AH1222-1223/AD1807-1808

Kashmir Mint

RUPEE

SILVER, 23mm, 10.70-11.60 gm.

KM#	Date	Year	Good	VG	Fine	VF
216	AH1222	1	25.00	32.50	40.00	52.50
	1223	2	25.00	32.50	40.00	52.50

Ata Muhammad Bamizai Khan

(Rebel Governor of Kashmir)

AH1223-1228/AD1808-1813

In the name of Shah Nur-ud-din, the patron 'saint' of Kashmir.

FALUS

COPPER

KM#	Date	Year	Good	VG	Fine	VF
202	AH1225	—	3.50	5.00	8.00	12.50

RUPEE

SILVER, 22mm

KM#	Date	Year	VG	Fine	VF	XF
226	AH1223	1	11.50	13.00	15.00	20.00
	1224	1	11.50	13.00	15.00	20.00
	1224	2	11.50	13.00	15.00	20.00
	1225	2	11.50	13.00	15.00	20.00
	1225	3	11.50	13.00	15.00	20.00
	1226	4	11.50	13.00	15.00	20.00
	1227	4	11.50	13.00	15.00	20.00
	1227	5	11.50	13.00	15.00	20.00
	1228	5	11.50	13.00	15.00	20.00

1-1/4 RUPEES

SILVER, 26mm, 13.38-14.50 gm.

KM#	Date	Year	VG	Fine	VF	XF
227	AH1223	1	30.00	37.50	47.50	62.50

2 MOHURS

GOLD, 24mm, 21.40-22.80 gm.

KM#	Date	Year	VG	Fine	VF	XF
A230	AH1225	2	300.00	400.00	500.00	600.00

KM#	Date	Year	VG	Fine	VF	XF
B230	AH1225	3	300.00	400.00	500.00	600.00

Muhammad Azim Khan

Governor for Ayub Shah

AH1228-1234/AD1813-1819

FALUS

COPPER

KM#	Date	Year	Good	VG	Fine	VF
203	AH1228	1	4.00	6.00	8.50	12.00

Ayyub Shah

AH1233-1245/AD1818-1829

FALUS

COPPER

KM#	Date	Year	Good	VG	Fine	VF
204	AH1233	—	4.00	6.00	8.50	12.00

RUPEE

SILVER, 22mm

KM#	Date	Year	VG	Fine	VF	XF
236	AH1234	1	13.50	16.50	21.50	28.50
	1234	2	13.50	16.50	21.50	28.50

Kashmir fell to the Sikhs in 1234 (AD1819), ending the Durrani dominion in India. For later issues of the above mints see Indian Native and Independent States listings.

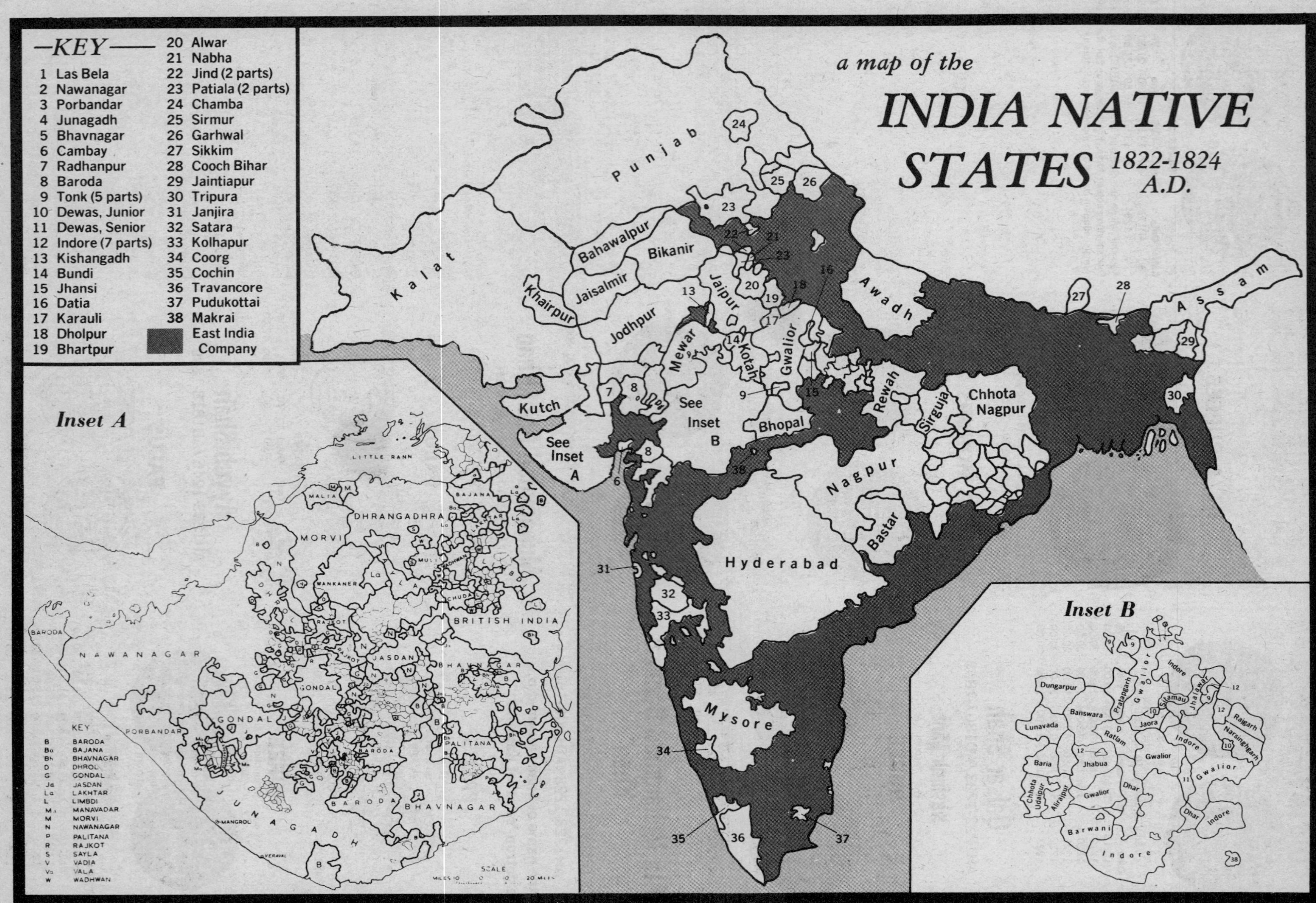
a map of the
INDIA NATIVE STATES 1822-1824 A.D.
—KEY—
1 Las Bela
2 Nawanagar
3 Porbandar
4 Junagadh
5 Bhavnagar
6 Cambay
7 Radhanpur
8 Baroda
9 Tonk (5 parts)
10 Dewas, Junior
11 Dewas, Senior
12 Indore (7 parts)
13 Kishangadh
14 Bundi
15 Jhansi
16 Datia
17 Karauli
18 Dholpur
19 Bhartpur
20 Alwar
21 Nabha
22 Jind (2 parts)
23 Patiala (2 parts)
24 Chamba
25 Sirmur
26 Garhwal
27 Sikkim
28 Cooch Bihar
29 Jaintiapur
30 Tripura
31 Janjira
32 Satara
33 Kolhapur
34 Coorg
35 Cochin
36 Travancore
37 Pudukottai
38 Makrai
East India Company
Kalat
Punjab
Bahawalpur
Bikanir
Jaisalmir
Khairpur
Jodhpur
Jaipur
Mewar
Kotah
Gwalior
Awadh
Assam
Kutch
See Inset A
See Inset B
Bhopal
Rewah
Sirguja
Chhota Nagpur
Nagpur
Bastar
Hyderabad
Mysore
Inset A
LITTLE RANN
MALIA
DHRANGADHRA
BAJANA
MORVI
WANKANER
CHUDA
BRITISH INDIA
BARODA
NAWANAGAR
JASDAN
GONDAL
BHAVNAGAR
PORBANDAR
PALITANA
JUNAGADH
MANGROL
VERAVAL
KEY
B BARODA
Ba BAJANA
Bh BHAVNAGAR
D DHROL
G GONDAL
Ja JASDAN
La LAKHTAR
L LIMBDI
Ma MANAVADAR
M MORVI
N NAWANAGAR
P PALITANA
R RAJKOT
S SAYLA
V VADIA
Va VALA
W WADHWAN
SCALE
Inset B
Dungarpur
Banswara
Pratapgarh
Gwalior
Indore
Jhalawar
Jaora
Rajgarh
Narsinghgarh
Lunavada
Ratlam
Baria
Jhabua
Chhota Udaipur
Alirajpur
Dhar
Barwani

INDIA INDEPENDENT AND NATIVE STATES

As the Mughal Empire began to disintegrate soon after 1700, dozens, and later, hundreds of districts and provinces slipped from Mughal control and became independent states. New political groupings arose, each seeking to establish its hegemony over its neighbors. One in particular, the Maratha Confederacy, came close to establishing a new imperium, only to be checked by the intrusions of the Durrani Afghans into North India. The resultant power vacuum permitted a devastating series of wars among contending secondary rulers. These latter sought protection from one of the European powers who were gradually gaining dominance over India. By the end of the Eighteenth Century, the Mughal Empire had disappeared in all but name, and the British East India Company had become the effective ruler of India, either directly or through the offices of local rulers of the states. The term 'Native States' came to be applied to those states which entered treaty relations with the British. Generally this involved the surrender of control of the state's foreign relations, and, in effect, its sovereign independence. The listings below include states both before and after their mediatization by the British; hence the classification rightfully is entitled Independent and Native States. By mid 19th century, after the suppression of the mutiny in 1857-58, all of India came under British rule, with the largest part directly administered, the remainder administered through more than 1,000 autonomous States, though that number was reduced to 675 by the time of Independence in 1947. After 1947, all the States were abolished, and their territories absorbed into the new dominions of India and Pakistan.

Many of the States preserved and exercised the right to mint coins, which had become the formal symbol of independence since the 14th century. The coinage is extremely varied, and with very few exceptions, imperfectly researched. For that reason, most of the listings below should be regarded not as definitive, but as preliminary. New types, denominations, and dates will be discovered that are not yet in the catalog.

Identification of the coins is difficult, and the large number of illustrations, and drawings of symbols and special legends, are intended to facilitate that task. Most of the legends are in the Persian or Nagari scripts, often quite barbarized. In many cases, it is not the legends, but special symbols that are the key to attribution, and wherever relevant, these symbols have been noted.

MONETARY SYSTEMS:

In each state, local rates of exchange prevailed. There was no fixed rate between copper, silver or gold coin but the rates varied in accordance with the values of the metal and by the edict of the local authority.

Within the subcontinent, different regions used distinctive coinage standards. In North India and the Deccan, the silver rupee (11.6 gm.) and gold mohur (11 gm.) predominated. In Gujarat, the silver kori (4.7 gm.) and gold kori (6.4 gm.) were the main currency. In South India the silver fanam (0.7-1 gm.) and gold hun or Pagoda (3.4 gm.) were current. Copper coins in all parts of India were produced to a myriad of local metrologies with seemingly endless varieties.

PRICING

As the market for Indian coins develops, and more dealers handle the material, sale records and price lists enable a firmer basis for pricing most series. For scarcer types in general no adequate sale record is presently available, and prices must be regarded as tentative. Inasmuch as date collectors of Native States series are few, dates known to be scarce are usually worth little more than common ones. Coins of a dated type which do not show the date on their flans should be evaluated at about 70 per cent of the prices indicated.

DATING

Coins are dated in several eras. Arabic and Devanagari numerals are used in conjunction with the Hijri era (AH), the Vikrama Samvat (VS), Saka Samvat (Saka), Falsi era (FE) Maulaudi era (AM), and Malabar era (ME).

GRADING

Copper coins are rarely found in better grade, as they were the workhorse of coinage circulation, and were everywhere used for day-to-day transactions. Moreover, they were carelessly struck and even when 'new', can often only be distinguished from VF coins with difficulty, if at all.

Silver coins were often hoarded, and not infrequently, turn up in nearly new condition. The silver coins of Hyderabad (dump coins) are common in high grades, and the rupees of some states are scarcer 'used' than 'new'. Great caution must be exercised in determining the value or scarcity of high grade dump coins.

Dump gold was rarely circulated, and usually occurs in high grades, or is found made into jewelry.

INDEX

ALMORA

Chand Rajas

(Until AD1790)

In The Name Of Shah Alam II

PAISA

COPPER, 18mm
Symbol like '41' above footprints.

C#	Date	Year	Good	VG	Fine	VF
5	—	14	4.50	8.50	13.50	20.00
	—	18	4.50	8.50	13.50	20.00

NOTE: For later issues, see Gurkhas: Kumaon.

ALWAR

RULERS

Pratap Singh, AD1772-1791
Bakhtawar Singh, AD1791-1815
Bani Singh, AD1815-1857

Rajgarh Mint

In the name of Shah Alam II,
(AD1759-1806)

PAISA

COPPER

C#	Date	Year	Good	VG	Fine	VF
5	—	28	3.00	4.00	6.00	8.00

RUPEE

SILVER, 22mm, 10.70-11.60 gm.

C#	Date	Year	VG	Fine	VF	XF
10	—	5	15.00	20.00	25.00	32.50
	—	19	15.00	20.00	25.00	32.50
	AH1195	24	15.00	20.00	25.00	32.50

In the name of Muhammad Akbar II
AD 1806-37

PAISA

Mintmark:  rev.

COPPER, 21mm

C#	Date	Year	Good	VG	Fine	VF
15	AH—	4	2.50	3.50	5.00	7.50
	-	11	2.50	3.50	5.00	7.50
	—	13	2.50	3.50	5.00	7.50
	—	14	2.50	3.50	5.00	7.50
	—	19	2.50	3.50	5.00	7.50
	—	20	2.50	3.50	5.00	7.50
	—	21	2.50	3.50	5.00	7.50
	—	22	2.50	3.50	5.00	7.50
	—	25	2.50	3.50	5.00	7.50
	—	27	2.50	3.50	5.00	7.50
	—	29	2.50	3.50	5.00	7.50
	—	30	2.50	3.50	5.00	7.50
	—	31	2.50	3.50	5.00	7.50
	—	33	2.50	3.50	5.00	7.50
	—	34	2.50	3.50	5.00	7.50
	—	37	2.50	3.50	5.00	7.50
	—	40	2.50	3.50	5.00	7.50

1/4 RUPEE

SILVER, 13mm, 2.68-2.90 gm.

C#	Date	Year	VG	Fine	VF	XF
18	ND	22	5.00	7.50	10.00	13.50

1/2 RUPEE

SILVER, 18mm, 5.35-5.80 gm.

C#	Date	Year	VG	Fine	VF	XF
19	ND	19-20	8.50	11.00	13.50	17.50

RUPEE

SILVER, 21-22mm, 10.70-11.40 gm.

C#	Date	Year	VG	Fine	VF	XF
20	—	6-28	12.50	16.50	21.50	26.50

In the name of Bahadur Shah II (AD 1837-57):

PAISA

COPPER, 20-21mm

C#	Date	Year	Good	VG	Fine	VF
25	—	2	1.50	2.50	3.00	4.00
	—	6	1.50	2.50	3.00	4.00
	—	12	1.50	2.50	3.00	4.00
	—	18	1.50	2.50	3.00	4.00
	—	20	1.50	2.50	3.00	4.00

1/4 RUPEE

SILVER, 16mm, 2.68-2.90 gm.

C#	Date	Year	VG	Fine	VF	XF
27	ND	20	6.50	8.50	11.00	15.00

1/2 RUPEE

SILVER, 18mm, 5.35-5.80 gm.

C#	Date	Year	VG	Fine	VF	XF
28	ND	17	6.50	10.00	12.00	16.00

RUPEE

SILVER, 20-22mm, 10.70-11.60 gm.

C#	Date	Year	VG	Fine	VF	XF
30	ND	1-20	15.00	20.00	25.00	32.50

NAZARANA RUPEE

SILVER, 29-30mm, 10.70-11.60 gm.

C#	Date	Year	VG	Fine	VF	XF
30a	AH1261	8	35.00	45.00	60.00	75.00
	126x	13	35.00	45.00	60.00	75.00

Sheodan Singh

AD 1857-74

In the names of Queen Victoria and Sheodan Singh.

PAISA

COPPER, 19-23mm

Y#	Date	Year	Good	VG	Fine	VF
1	(1865)	9	1.50	2.50	3.00	3.50

NAZARANA PAISA

COPPER

Y#	Date	Year	Good	VG	Fine	VF
1a	(1871)	15	12.50	20.00	27.50	35.00

RUPEE

SILVER, 20-24mm, 10.70-11.60 gm.

Y#	Date	Year	VG	Fine	VF	XF
2	(1860-65)	2-7	12.50	17.50	22.50	30.00

NAZARANA RUPEE

SILVER, 28-33mm, 10.70-11.60 gm.

Y#	Date	Year	VG	Fine	VF	XF
2a	(1859-74)	—	30.00	40.00	50.00	60.00

Mangal Singh

AD 1874-1892

NAZARANA PAISA

COPPER
Similar to Nazarana Rupee, Y#4.

Y#	Date	Year	VG	Fine	VF	XF
3	1874-91	—	7.50	15.00	22.50	30.00

NAZARANA RUPEE

SILVER, 25mm

Y#	Date	Year	VG	Fine	VF	XF
4	1894	—	25.00	40.00	50.00	65.00

NOTE: A few each of Y#3 and Y#4 were struck at the Rajgarh Mint each year for presentation purposes.

RUPEE

11.6600 gm., .917 SILVER, 3438 oz ASW

Y#	Date	Year	Fine	VF	XF	Unc
5	1788 (error)	—	15.00	18.50	25.00	50.00
	1877	—	12.50	15.00	20.00	40.00
	1878	—	13.50	16.50	22.50	45.00
	1880	—	12.50	15.00	20.00	40.00
	1881	—	15.00	18.50	25.00	50.00
	1882	—	12.50	15.00	20.00	40.00

Obv: Similar to Rupee, Y#1. Rev: Different legends.

Y#	Date	Year	Fine	VF	XF	Unc
5a	1891	—	12.50	15.00	20.00	40.00

ANDAMAN ISLANDS

The Andaman Islands are the northern group of 204 volcanic and coral isles in the east part of the Bay of Bengal about 400 miles directly west of the coast of lower Burma. They are united with the southern Nicobar group for administrative purposes.

RULERS
British

TOKEN ISSUES

RUPEE

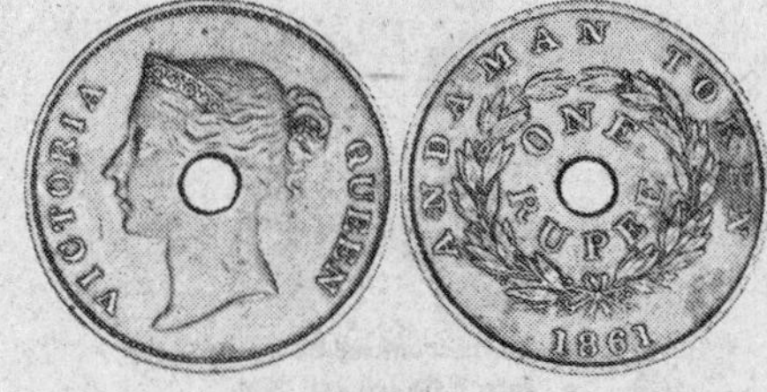

COPPER

KM#	Date	Mintage	Fine	VF	XF	Unc
1	1861	.020	225.00	300.00	375.00	500.00
	1861	—	—	—	Proof	650.00

KM#	Date	Mintage	Fine	VF	XF	Unc
2	1866	.021	275.00	350.00	425.00	550.00
	1866	—	—	—	Proof	700.00

NOTE: Proof issues are without center hole.

ARCOT

The Nawabs of Arcot used the title Wala-Jah which was often displayed prominently on the coins.

'Wala' والا

Muhammad Ali

AH1165-1209/AD1751-1795

Arkat Mint

In the name of Shah Alam II

PAISA

COPPER, 17mm

KM#	Date	Year	Good	VG	Fine	VF
3	AH1177	4	2.00	3.50	5.50	8.00
	1177	5	2.00	3.50	5.50	8.00

RUPEE

Rupees were coined by the Nawab of Arcot, his subsidiaries, and the English and French East India Companies, all in the mint name Arkat. The French issues were distinguishable by broad flan and dotted field, and the English by the lotus mintmark and anachronistic use of Alamgir II's legend (see respective sections). The actual issues of Arkat mint were differentiated from other mint products by the four-petal flower or star beside the regnal year on the reverse.

Other

SILVER, 19-22mm
Mintmark: Four petal flower

KM#	Date	Year	VG	Fine	VF	XF
5	AH1186	10	12.50	15.00	20.00	28.50
	119x	12	12.50	15.00	20.00	28.50
	1191	18	12.50	15.00	20.00	28.50
	1200	27	12.50	15.00	20.00	28.50
	1201	28	12.50	15.00	20.00	28.50
	1203	29	12.50	15.00	20.00	28.50
	1205	30	12.50	15.00	20.00	28.50

19-23mm
Mintmarks: Four petal flower and 'Wala'

KM#	Date	Year	VG	Fine	VF	XF
6	AH1206	31	15.00	17.50	22.50	30.00

With the title Wala or Wala Jah:

1/4 PAISA

COPPER, 12-15mm

KM#	Date	Year	Good	VG	Fine	VF
8	AH1183	—	.85	1.50	2.50	3.50
	1201	—	.85	1.50	2.50	3.50
	1202	—	.85	1.50	2.50	3.50

1/2 PAISA

COPPER, 13-20mm

KM#	Date	Year	Good	VG	Fine	VF
9	AH1200	27	.85	1.50	2.50	3.50
	1201	—	.85	1.50	2.50	3.50
	1203	—	.85	1.50	2.50	3.50
	1205	—	.85	1.50	2.50	3.50
	1206	34	.85	1.50	2.50	3.50
	1207	34	.85	1.50	2.50	3.50

PAISA

COPPER, 19-22mm

KM#	Date	Year	Good	VG	Fine	VF
10	AH1206	—	1.25	2.25	3.50	5.00
	1208	—	1.25	2.25	3.50	5.00

PAGODA

3.000 gm., .800 GOLD, 14mm, 0771 oz AGW
Obv: '3 Swamis'

KM#	Date	Year	VG	Fine	VF	XF
13	—	—	75.00	100.00	120.00	140.00

Obv: 3 Swamis. Rev: Arabic ain'.

KM#	Date	Year	VG	Fine	VF	XF
14	ND	—	80.00	110.00	130.00	150.00

15mm
Obv: Figure flanked by inscription Wa-La.

KM#	Date	Year	VG	Fine	VF	XF
15	—	—	75.00	100.00	120.00	140.00

Kadapa Mint
(Uncertain)

In the name of Shah Alam II:

1/2 PAISA

COPPER, 6-8mm

KM#	Date	Year	Good	VG	Fine	VF
18	AH1179	—	.60	1.00	1.50	2.00

PAISA

COPPER, 17-20mm
Rev: Without 'Wala'

KM#	Date	Year	Good	VG	Fine	VF
19	AH1175	7	.85	1.50	2.50	3.50
	1182	—	.85	1.50	2.50	3.50
	1198	—	.85	1.50	2.50	3.50

Madras/Tiruvallur Mint
With the title Wala: والا

1/4 PAISA

COPPER, 7-11mm

KM#	Date	Year	Good	VG	Fine	VF
21	AH1208	35	.85	1.50	2.50	3.50
	1209	36	.85	1.50	2.50	3.50

1/2 PAISA

COPPER, 17-20mm

KM#	Date	Year	Good	VG	Fine	VF
22	AH1207	34	2.50	4.00	5.50	7.00
	1208	35	2.50	4.00	5.50	7.00
	1209	36	2.50	4.00	5.50	7.00

PAISA

COPPER, 22-24mm

KM#	Date	Year	Good	VG	Fine	VF
23	AH1200	27	3.00	5.00	6.50	8.00
	1206	34	3.00	5.00	6.50	8.00
	1208	35	3.00	5.00	6.50	8.00

Madurai, Ramnad (Poliyagars) Mint

NAYAKA CASH

COPPER, 8-11mm
Obv: Wala Jah. Rev: Date.

KM#	Date	Year	Good	VG	Fine	VF
25	AH1196	—	.45	.75	1.25	2.00

Obv: Deities, animal figures, etc.
Rev: Wala Jah and date.

KM#	Date	Year	Good	VG	Fine	VF
27	AH1200	—	.60	1.00	2.00	3.00
	1201	—	.60	1.00	2.00	3.00
	1202	—	.60	1.00	2.00	3.00
	1204	—	.60	1.00	2.00	3.00
	1207	—	.60	1.00	2.00	3.00

Obv: Deities, geometric figures, etc.
Rev: Crude Wala Jah, no date.

KM#	Date	Year	Good	VG	Fine	VF
29	ND	—	.60	1.00	1.75	2.50

Tanjore Mint

CASH

COPPER, 13mm
Obv: Fish, bull, etc.
Rev: Tamil letter 'Na'.

KM#	Date	Year	Good	VG	Fine	VF
31	ND	—	1.75	3.00	4.50	6.00

8-11mm
Obv: Deities, bow and arrow, horse, etc.
Rev: Tamil legend 'Nawab'.

KM#	Date	Year	Good	VG	Fine	VF
32	ND	—	.60	1.00	1.75	2.50

Tinnevelly Mint

CASH

COPPER
Obv: Wala. Rev: Date.

KM#	Date	Year	Good	VG	Fine	VF
35	AH1207	—	.75	1.25	2.00	3.00

8-11mm
Obv: Deities, lingam, etc. Rev: Wala Jah.

KM#	Date	Year	Good	VG	Fine	VF
36	ND	—	.60	1.00	1.75	2.50

Obv: Sun, moon, bull, lingam, etc.
Rev: Tamil legend 'Kampani'.

KM#	Date	Year	Good	VG	Fine	VF
37	ND	—	1.25	2.00	3.50	5.00

Obv: Star within dots. Rev: Tamil legend 'Nawabu'.

KM#	Date	Year	Good	VG	Fine	VF
38	ND	—	.60	1.00	1.75	2.50

Trichinopoly (Nathanagar) Mint
With the title Wala Jah والاجاه

CASH

COPPER, 8-11mm
Obv: Wala Jah. Rev: Date.

KM#	Date	Year	Good	VG	Fine	VF
41	AH1181	—	1.25	2.00	3.00	4.00
	1186	—	1.25	2.00	3.00	4.00
	1189	—	1.25	2.00	3.00	4.00
	1195	—	1.25	2.00	3.00	4.00
	1197	—	1.25	2.00	3.00	4.00
	1203	—	1.25	2.00	3.00	4.00
	1206	—	1.25	2.00	3.00	4.00

Obv: Wala Jah. Rev: Ain

KM#	Date	Year	Good	VG	Fine	VF
42	ND	—	1.00	1.75	2.50	3.50

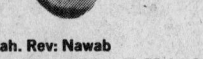

Obv: Wala Jah. Rev: Nawab

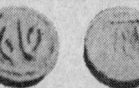

KM#	Date	Year	Good	VG	Fine	VF
43	ND	—	.60	1.00	1.75	2.50

Obv: Wala. Rev: Jah

KM#	Date	Year	Good	VG	Fine	VF
44	ND	—	.60	1.00	1.75	2.50

1/4 PAISA

COPPER, 10-13mm
Rev: NAHTARNAGAR

KM#	Date	Year	Good	VG	Fine	VF
47	AH—	—	.90	1.50	2.50	3.50

1/2 PAISA

COPPER, 14-17mm, octagonal

KM#	Date	Year	Good	VG	Fine	VF
48	AH1207	—	3.00	5.00	7.00	9.00

PAISA

COPPER, 18-22mm, octagonal

KM#	Date	Year	Good	VG	Fine	VF
49	AH1207	—	3.50	6.00	8.00	10.00

Uncertain Mints

RUPEE

SILVER, 21mm, 10.70-11.60 gm.
Mintmark: Bud or flower above J of Julus

KM#	Date	Year	VG	Fine	VF	XF
50	AH—	20	12.50	17.50	23.50	32.50

No mintmarks.

KM#	Date	Year	VG	Fine	VF	XF
51	AH—	23	12.50	17.50	23.50	32.50

18.5 mm
Mintmark: Trisul in S of JULUS.

KM#	Date	Year	VG	Fine	VF	XF
52	AH1183	11	12.50	17.50	23.50	32.50

NOTE: C#51 may be the issue of an European company.

Umdat-Ul-Umara

AH1209-1216/AD1795-1801

Arkat Mint

In the name of Shah Alam II:

Special Mark:  'Wa'

RUPEE

SILVER, 23mm, 10.70-11.60 gm.
Mintmarks: Four-petal flower and 'Wa'

KM#	Date	Year	VG	Fine	VF	XF
54	AH1212	—	12.50	17.50	23.50	32.50
	1213	—	12.50	17.50	23.50	32.50
	1214	—	12.50	17.50	23.50	32.50

Madras Mint

With the title Wala Jah: والاجاه

1/4 PAISA

COPPER, 13-14mm

KM#	Date	Year	Good	VG	Fine	VF
56	AH1213	—	1.50	2.50	3.50	5.00

1/2 PAISA

COPPER, 18-20mm

KM#	Date	Year	Good	VG	Fine	VF
57	AH1213	—	1.75	3.00	4.50	6.00

PAISA

COPPER, 21-23mm

KM#	Date	Year	Good	VG	Fine	VF
58	AH1213	—	2.00	3.50	5.00	7.00

Tinnevelly Mint

CASH

COPPER, 8-11mm
Obv: Lingam. Rev: Wala Jah and date.

KM#	Date	Year	Good	VG	Fine	VF
61	AH1210	—	.60	1.00	1.75	2.50

Trichinopoly Mint

CASH

COPPER, 8-11mm
Obv: Wala Jah. Rev: Date.

KM#	Date	Year	Good	VG	Fine	VF
63	AH1214	—	.60	1.00	1.75	2.50

ASSAM

AHOM KINGDOM

NOTE: All dated coins have Saka year (Saka year plus 78 ad year). Gold issues were struck from the same dies as silver coinage.

Surempha

(Rajesvara Simha)

I - Bengali Legends

1/16 RUPEE

SILVER, 10mm, octagonal, 0.67-0.72 gm

C#	Date	Year	VG	Fine	VF	XF
3	ND		3.00	4.00	6.00	9.00

1/8 RUPEE

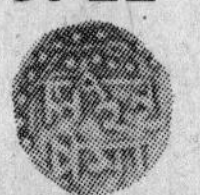

SILVER, 10mm, octagonal, 1.34-1.45 gm

C#	Date	Year	VG	Fine	VF	XF
4	ND		2.50	3.50	5.00	7.50

1/4 RUPEE

SILVER, 14mm, octagonal, 2.68-2.90 gm

C#	Date	Year	VG	Fine	VF	XF
5	SE1674	(1752)	3.50	4.50	6.50	10.00
	1676	(1754)	3.50	4.50	6.50	10.00
	1677	(1755)	3.50	4.50	6.50	10.00
	1678	(1756)	3.50	4.50	6.50	10.00
	1679	(1757)	3.50	4.50	6.50	10.00
	1680	(1758)	3.50	4.50	6.50	10.00
	1681	(1759)	3.50	4.50	6.50	10.00
	1682	(1760)	3.50	4.50	6.50	10.00
	1683	(1761)	3.50	4.50	6.50	10.00
	1684	(1762)	3.50	4.50	6.50	10.00
	1685	(1763)	3.50	4.50	6.50	10.00
	1686	(1764)	3.50	4.50	6.50	10.00
	1687	(1765)	3.50	4.50	6.50	10.00
	1687	(1766)	3.50	4.50	6.50	10.00
	1689	(1767)	3.50	4.50	6.50	10.00
	1690	(1768)	3.50	4.50	6.50	10.00

1/2 RUPEE

SILVER, 16mm, octagonal, 5.35-5.80 gm

C#	Date	Year	VG	Fine	VF	XF
6	ND	—	6.50	7.50	10.00	15.00

RUPEE

SILVER, 20-22mm, octagonal, 10.70-11.60 gm

C#	Date	Year	VG	Fine	VF	XF
7	SE1674	(1752)	12.50	15.00	18.50	23.50
	1675	(1753)	12.50	15.00	18.50	23.50
	1676	(1754)	12.50	15.00	18.50	23.50
	1677	(1755)	12.50	15.00	18.50	23.50
	1678	(1756)	12.50	15.00	18.50	23.50
	1679	(1757)	12.50	15.00	18.50	23.50
	1680	(1758)	12.50	15.00	18.50	23.50
	1681	(1759)	12.50	15.00	18.50	23.50
	1682	(1760)	12.50	15.00	18.50	23.50
	1683	(1761)	12.50	15.00	18.50	23.50
	1684	(1762)	12.50	15.00	18.50	23.50
	1685	(1763)	12.50	15.00	18.50	23.50
	1686	(1764)	12.50	15.00	18.50	23.50
	1687	(1765)	12.50	15.00	18.50	23.50
	1688	(1766)	12.50	15.00	18.50	23.50
	1689	(1767)	12.50	15.00	18.50	23.50
	1690	(1768)	12.50	15.00	18.50	23.50

1/16 MOHUR

GOLD, 10mm, octagonal, 0.67-0.71 gm

C#	Date	Year	VG	Fine	VF	XF
14	ND	—	20.00	30.00	50.00	70.00

1/8 MOHUR

GOLD, 12mm, octagonal, 1.34-1.42 gm

C#	Date	Year	VG	Fine	VF	XF
15	ND	—	35.00	45.00	55.00	70.00

Square

C#	Date	Year	VG	Fine	VF	XF
15a	ND	—	45.00	60.00	80.00	110.00

1/4 MOHUR

GOLD, 13mm, octagonal, 2.68-2.85 gm

C#	Date	Year	VG	Fine	VF	XF
16	SE1675	(1753)	60.00	75.00	90.00	125.00
	1676	(1754)	60.00	75.00	90.00	125.00
	1677	(1755)	60.00	75.00	90.00	125.00
	1678	(1756)	60.00	75.00	90.00	125.00
	1680	(1758)	60.00	75.00	90.00	125.00
	1681	(1759)	60.00	75.00	90.00	125.00
	1683	(1761)	60.00	75.00	90.00	125.00
	1688	(1766)	60.00	75.00	90.00	125.00

14mm, square

C#	Date	Year	VG	Fine	VF	XF
16a	SE1678	(1756)	65.00	90.00	120.00	160.00

1/2 MOHUR

GOLD, octagonal, 5.35-5.70 gm

C#	Date	Year	VG	Fine	VF	XF
17	ND	—	100.00	125.00	150.00	200.00

MOHUR

GOLD, 20mm, octagonal, 10.70-11.40 gm

C#	Date	Year	VG	Fine	VF	XF
18	SE1674	(1752)	220.00	240.00	265.00	300.00
	1678	(1756)	220.00	240.00	265.00	300.00
	1681	(1759)	220.00	240.00	265.00	300.00
	1684	(1762)	220.00	240.00	265.00	300.00
	1688	(1766)	220.00	240.00	265.00	300.00

C#	Date	Year	VG	Fine	VF	XF
18	1689	(1767)	220.00	240.00	265.00	300.00
	1690	(1768)	220.00	240.00	265.00	300.00

RUPEE

SILVER, 22mm, octagonal, 10.70-11.60 gm

C#	Date	Year	VG	Fine	VF	XF
9	SE1675	(1753)	15.00	22.50	35.00	50.00

MOHUR

GOLD, 10.70-11.40 gm

C#	Date	Year	VG	Fine	VF	XF
18.1	1675	(1753)	225.00	250.00	285.00	350.00

III - Persian Legends

1/4 RUPEE

SILVER, square, 2.68-2.90 gm

C#	Date	Year	VG	Fine	VF	XF
10	ND	—	40.00	55.00	75.00	110.00

RUPEE

SILVER, 19mm, square, 10.70-11.60 gm

C#	Date	Year	VG	Fine	VF	XF
12	SE1674	(1752)	40.00	55.00	75.00	110.00

23mm, octagonal

C#	Date	Year	VG	Fine	VF	XF
12a	SE1685	(1763)	27.50	35.00	45.00	60.00

1/4 MOHUR

GOLD, square, 2.68-2.85 gm

C#	Date	Year	VG	Fine	VF	XF
16b	ND	—	—	—	Rare	—

MOHUR

GOLD, square

C#	Date	Year	VG	Fine	VF	XF
A19	SE1674	(1652)	250.00	275.00	325.00	400.00

Octagonal

C#	Date	Year	VG	Fine	VF	XF
19	SE1685	(1763)	220.00	240.00	265.00	300.00

IV - Ahom Legends

RUPEE

SILVER, octagonal, 10.70-11.60 gm

C#	Date	Year	VG	Fine	VF	XF
8		(1751)	50.00	75.00	100.00	135.00

MOHUR

GOLD, 22mm, octagonal, 10.70-11.40 gm

C#	Date	Year	VG	Fine	VF	XF
20		(1751)	250.00	350.00	450.00	600.00

Sunyeopha

(Lakshmi Simha)

SAKA 1691-1702/AD 1769-1780

1/16 RUPEE

SILVER, 0.67-0.72 gm

C#	Date	Year	VG	Fine	VF	XF
21	ND	—	3.50	5.00	7.50	11.50

1/8 RUPEE

SILVER, 1.34-1.45 gm

C#	Date	Year	VG	Fine	VF	XF
22	ND	—	3.50	5.00	7.50	11.50

1/4 RUPEE

SILVER, 2.68-2.90 gm

C#	Date	Year	VG	Fine	VF	XF
23	SE1692	(1770)	3.50	4.50	6.50	10.00
	1693	(1771)	3.50	4.50	6.50	10.00
	1694	(1772)	3.50	4.50	6.50	10.00
	1695	(1773)	3.50	4.50	6.50	10.00
	1696	(1774)	3.50	4.50	6.50	10.00
	1697	(1775)	3.50	4.50	6.50	10.00
	1698	(1776)	3.50	4.50	6.50	10.00
	1699	(1777)	3.50	4.50	6.50	10.00
	1700	(1778)	3.50	4.50	6.50	10.00
	1701	(1779)	3.50	4.50	6.50	10.00
	1702	(1780)	3.50	4.50	6.50	10.00

1/2 RUPEE

SILVER, 5.35-5.80 gm
Rev. leg: HARA GAURI

C#	Date	Year	VG	Fine	VF	XF
24	ND	—	7.50	10.00	15.00	22.50

C#	Date	Year	VG	Fine	VF	XF
24.1	ND	—	6.50	7.50	10.00	15.00
24.2	—	1	6.50	8.50	11.50	16.50

RUPEE

SILVER, 10.70-11.60 gm
Rev. leg: HARI HARA....

C#	Date	Year	VG	Fine	VF	XF
25	SE1692	(1770)	12.50	14.50	17.50	23.50

Rev. leg: HARA GAURI....

C#	Date	Year	VG	Fine	VF	XF
25.1	SE1692	(1770)	11.50	13.50	16.50	21.50
	1693	(1771)	11.50	13.50	16.50	21.50
	1694	(1772)	11.50	13.50	16.50	21.50
	1695	(1773)	11.50	13.50	16.50	21.50
	1696	(1774)	11.50	13.50	16.50	21.50
	1697	(1775)	11.50	13.50	16.50	21.50
	1698	(1776)	11.50	13.50	16.50	21.50
	1699	(1777)	12.50	14.50	17.50	23.50
	1700	(1778)	12.50	14.50	17.50	23.50

1/16 MOHUR

GOLD, 0.67-0.71 gm

C#	Date	Year	VG	Fine	VF	XF
27	ND	—	17.50	22.50	32.50	50.00

1/8 MOHUR

GOLD, 1.34-1.42 gm

C#	Date	Year	VG	Fine	VF	XF
28	ND	—	27.50	35.00	45.00	60.00

1/4 MOHUR

GOLD, 2.68-2.85 gm

C#	Date	Year	VG	Fine	VF	XF
29	SE1692	(1770)	55.00	60.00	70.00	90.00
	1693	(1771)	55.00	60.00	70.00	90.00
	1694	(1772)	55.00	60.00	70.00	90.00
	1695	(1773)	55.00	60.00	70.00	90.00
	1696	(1774)	55.00	60.00	70.00	90.00
	1697	(1775)	55.00	60.00	70.00	90.00
	1702	(1780)	55.00	60.00	70.00	90.00

Square flan

C#	Date	Year	VG	Fine	VF	XF
29.1	SE1692	(1770)	70.00	90.00	125.00	175.00

1/2 MOHUR

GOLD, 5.35-5.70 gm

C#	Date	Year	VG	Fine	VF	XF
30	ND	—	90.00	110.00	135.00	185.00

MOHUR

GOLD, 10.70-11.40 gm

C#	Date	Year	VG	Fine	VF	XF
31	SE1692	(1770)	220.00	240.00	265.00	300.00
	1693	(1771)	220.00	240.00	265.00	300.00
	1694	(1772)	220.00	240.00	265.00	300.00
	1698	(1776)	220.00	240.00	265.00	300.00
	1701	(1779)	220.00	240.00	265.00	300.00

Suhitpanpha

(Guarinatha Simha)

SAKA 1702-1717/AD 1780-1795

1/32 RUPEE

SILVER, 0.34-0.36 gm

C#	Date	Year	VG	Fine	VF	XF
32	ND	—	4.00	5.00	7.00	10.00

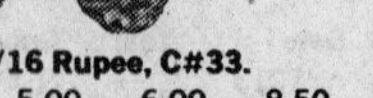

Similar to 1/16 Rupee, C#33.

C#	Date	Year	VG	Fine	VF	XF
32.1	ND	—	5.00	6.00	8.50	12.50

1/16 RUPEE

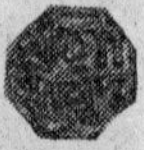

SILVER, 0.67-0.72 gm
Rev: Type 1

C#	Date	Year	VG	Fine	VF	XF
33	ND	—	4.00	5.50	7.50	11.50

Rev: Type 2

C#	Date	Year	VG	Fine	VF	XF
33.1	ND	—	4.00	5.50	7.50	11.50

Rev: Na below

C#	Date	Year	VG	Fine	VF	XF
33.2	ND	—	7.50	10.00	14.00	20.00

1/8 RUPEE

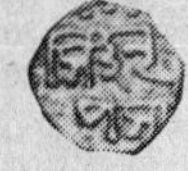

SILVER, 1.34-1.45 gm
Variety 1

C#	Date	Year	VG	Fine	VF	XF
34	ND	—	4.00	5.50	7.50	11.50

Variety 2

C#	Date	Year	VG	Fine	VF	XF
34.1	ND	—	4.00	5.50	7.50	11.50

Rev: Na below

C#	Date	Year	VG	Fine	VF	XF
34.2	ND	—	7.50	10.00	14.00	20.00

1/4 RUPEE

SILVER, 2.68-2.90 gm

C#	Date	Year	VG	Fine	VF	XF
35	SE1703	(1781)	5.00	7.00	10.00	15.00
	1704	(1782)	5.00	7.00	10.00	15.00
	1705	(1783)	5.00	7.00	10.00	15.00
	1706	Yr. 5	3.50	5.00	7.00	10.00
	1707	Yr. 6	3.50	5.00	7.00	10.00
	1708	Yr. 7	3.50	5.00	7.00	10.00
	1708	(1786)	5.00	7.00	10.00	15.00
	1709	Yr. 8	5.00	7.00	10.00	15.00
	1711	(1789)	10.00	12.50	17.50	25.00
	1712	Yr. 11	10.00	12.50	17.50	25.00
	1712	(1790)	10.00	12.50	17.50	25.00
	1713	(1791)	—	—	—	—
	1714	(1792)	10.00	12.50	17.50	25.00
	1715	Yr. 14	10.00	12.50	17.50	25.00
	1716	(1794)	3.50	5.00	7.00	10.00
	1717	(1795)	3.50	5.00	7.00	10.00

Rev: Regnal year 1

C#	Date	Year	VG	Fine	VF	XF
35.1	SE1716	Yr. 1	5.00	7.00	10.00	15.00

Obv: Regnal year 1

C#	Date	Year	VG	Fine	VF	XF
35.2	SE1716	Yr. 1	5.00	7.00	10.00	15.00

Obv: Regnal year 1 below

C#	Date	Year	VG	Fine	VF	XF
35.3	SE1717	Yr. 1	5.00	7.00	10.00	15.00

Rev: Regnal year 16 below

C#	Date	Year	VG	Fine	VF	XF
35.4	SE1717	Yr. 16	5.00	7.00	10.00	15.00

Obv: Regnal year 1 below
Rev: Regnal year 16 below

C#	Date	Year	VG	Fine	VF	XF
35.5	SE1717	Yr. 1/16	5.00	7.00	10.00	15.00

Rev: (Di) below

C#	Date	Year	VG	Fine	VF	XF
35.6	SE1717	(1795)	7.50	10.00	14.00	20.00

Square flan

C#	Date	Year	VG	Fine	VF	XF
35.7	SE1705	(1783)	22.50	30.00	37.50	50.00

1/2 RUPEE

SILVER, 5.35-5.80 gm
Without regnal year

C#	Date	Year	VG	Fine	VF	XF
36	ND	—	6.50	7.50	9.00	12.50

NOTE: 4 varieties are known.

With regnal year

C#	Date	Year	VG	Fine	VF	XF
36.1	ND	Yr. 5	7.00	8.50	11.00	15.00
	ND	Yr. 6	7.00	8.50	11.00	15.00
	ND	Yr. 7	7.00	8.50	11.00	15.00
	ND	Yr. 8	7.00	8.50	11.00	15.00
	ND	Yr. 12	12.50	15.00	21.50	30.00
	ND	Yr. 13	12.50	15.00	21.50	30.00
	ND	Yr. 14	12.50	15.00	21.50	30.00
	ND	Yr. 15	12.50	15.00	21.50	30.00
	ND	Yr. 16	7.00	9.00	11.50	15.00

NOTE: Two varieties of regnal year 5 are known.

Obv: Regnal year 1

C#	Date	Year	VG	Fine	VF	XF
36.2	ND	Yr. 1	7.50	10.00	14.00	20.00

Rev: Regnal year 1

C#	Date	Year	VG	Fine	VF	XF
36.3	ND	Yr. 1	7.00	9.00	12.00	17.50

Obv: With Di

C#	Date	Year	VG	Fine	VF	XF
36.4	ND	—	10.00	12.50	16.50	21.50

Rev: With Ha

C#	Date	Year	VG	Fine	VF	XF
36.5	ND	—	7.50	10.00	14.00	20.00

Obv: With Na

C#	Date	Year	VG	Fine	VF	XF
36.6	ND	—	7.50	10.00	14.00	20.00

Rev: With Na

C#	Date	Year	VG	Fine	VF	XF
36.7	ND	—	7.50	10.00	14.00	20.00

Obv. & Rev: With Na

C#	Date	Year	VG	Fine	VF	XF
36.8	ND	—	7.50	10.00	14.00	20.00

Obv: With Na. Rev: With Ha.

C#	Date	Year	VG	Fine	VF	XF
36.9	ND	—	7.50	10.00	14.00	20.00

RUPEE

SILVER, 10.70-11.60 gm
Obv: Lion faces right

C#	Date	Year	VG	Fine	VF	XF
37	SE1703	(1781)	12.50	14.50	17.50	22.50

Obv: Lion faces left

C#	Date	Year	VG	Fine	VF	XF
37.1	SE1703	(1781)	12.50	14.50	17.50	22.50
	1704	(1782)	12.50	14.50	17.50	22.50
	1705	(1783)	11.50	13.50	16.50	20.00
	1706	Yr. 5	11.50	13.50	16.50	20.00

C#	Date	Year	VG	Fine	VF	XF
37.2	SE1706	Yr. 5	11.50	13.50	16.50	20.00

C#	Date	Year	VG	Fine	VF	XF
37.3	SE1706	Yr. 5	12.50	14.50	17.50	22.50

C#	Date	Year	VG	Fine	VF	XF
37.4	SE1707	Yr. 6	11.50	13.50	16.50	20.00
	1708	Yr. 7	11.50	13.50	16.50	20.00
	1709	Yr. 8	11.50	13.50	16.50	20.00
	1711	(1789)	13.50	18.50	25.00	32.50
	1713	Yr. 12	13.50	18.50	25.00	32.50
	1715	Yr. 14	13.50	18.50	25.00	32.50
	1716	(1794)	—	5.00	6.00	7.50
	1716	Yr. 1	12.50	14.50	17.50	22.50
	1717	(1795)	12.50	14.50	17.50	22.50
	1718	Yr. 16	12.50	14.50	17.50	22.50

Rev: Regnal year 1

C#	Date	Year	VG	Fine	VF	XF
37.5	SE1716	Yr. 1	12.50	14.50	17.50	22.50

Obv: With Di

C#	Date	Year	VG	Fine	VF	XF
37.6	SE1716	(1794)	12.50	14.50	17.50	22.50
	1717	(1795)	12.50	14.50	17.50	22.50

Rev: With Ha

C#	Date	Year	VG	Fine	VF	XF
37.7	SE1716	(1794)	12.50	14.50	17.50	22.50

Rev: With Na

C#	Date	Year	VG	Fine	VF	XF
37.8	SE1716	(1794)	12.50	14.50	17.50	22.50

Rev: With 68

C#	Date	Year	VG	Fine	VF	XF
37.9	SE1716	(1794)	12.50	14.50	17.50	22.50

1/32 MOHUR

GOLD, 0.34-0.35 gm

C#	Date	Year	VG	Fine	VF	XF
38	ND	—	17.50	21.50	28.50	40.00

1/16 MOHUR

GOLD, 0.67-0.71 gm

C#	Date	Year	VG	Fine	VF	XF
39	ND	—	17.50	21.50	28.50	40.00

1/8 MOHUR

GOLD, 1.34-1.42 gm

C#	Date	Year	VG	Fine	VF	XF
40	ND	—	25.00	32.50	40.00	55.00

1/4 MOHUR

GOLD, 2.68-2.85 gm

C#	Date	Year	VG	Fine	VF	XF
41	SE1703	(1781)	55.00	65.00	80.00	110.00
	1706	Yr. 5	55.00	65.00	80.00	110.00
	1707	Yr. 6	55.00	65.00	80.00	110.00
	1711	(1789)	60.00	75.00	100.00	140.00
	1712	Yr. 11	55.00	65.00	80.00	110.00
	1716	(1794)	55.00	65.00	80.00	110.00

1/2 MOHUR

GOLD, 5.35-5.70 gm

C#	Date	Year	VG	Fine	VF	XF
42	ND	—	110.00	120.00	135.00	160.00
	ND	Yr. 13	120.00	135.00	150.00	200.00

MOHUR

GOLD, 10.70-11.40 gm

C#	Date	Year	VG	Fine	VF	XF
43	SE1703	(1781)	220.00	240.00	265.00	300.00
	1705	(1783)	220.00	240.00	265.00	300.00
43.1	SE1706	Yr. 5	220.00	240.00	265.00	300.00
43.2	SE1707	Yr. 6	220.00	240.00	265.00	300.00
	1709	Yr. 8	220.00	240.00	265.00	300.00
	1711	(1789)	225.00	250.00	285.00	325.00
	1712	Yr. 11	225.00	250.00	285.00	325.00
	1716	(1794)	220.00	240.00	265.00	300.00
	1716	Yr. 15	225.00	250.00	285.00	325.00

Rev: Regnal year 1

C#	Date	Year	VG	Fine	VF	XF
43.3	SE1716	(1794)	220.00	240.00	265.00	300.00

Ahom inscription

C#	Date	Year	VG	Fine	VF	XF
43.4	1781	Yr. 13	—	—	Rare	—

Kamalesvara Simha

SAKA 1717-1732/AD 1795-1810

1/8 RUPEE

SILVER, 10mm, round, 1.34-1.45 gm

C#	Date	Year	VG	Fine	VF	XF
46	ND	—	20.00	30.00	40.00	55.00

1/2 RUPEE

SILVER, 17mm, octagonal, 5.35-5.80 gm

C#	Date	Year	VG	Fine	VF	XF
48	ND	—	25.00	35.00	45.00	60.00

RUPEE

SILVER, 21mm, octagonal, 10.70-11.60 gm

C#	Date	Year	VG	Fine	VF	XF
49	SE1720	(1798)	35.00	45.00	60.00	80.00

1/8 MOHUR

GOLD, octagonal, 1.34-1.42 gm

C#	Date	Year	VG	Fine	VF	XF
52	ND	—	45.00	55.00	70.00	100.00

MOHUR

GOLD, octagonal, 10.70-11.40 gm

C#	Date	Year	VG	Fine	VF	XF
55	SE1720	(1798)	220.00	240.00	265.00	300.00

Chandrakanta Simha

SAKA 1732-39, 1741/
AD 1810-1818, 1819-1820

1/32 RUPEE

SILVER, oval, 0.34-0.36 gm

C#	Date	Year	VG	Fine	VF	XF
56	ND	—	15.00	20.00	26.50	35.00

1/16 RUPEE

SILVER, 7mm, octagonal, 0.67-0.72 gm

C#	Date	Year	VG	Fine	VF	XF
57	ND	—	15.00	20.00	26.50	35.00

1/8 RUPEE

SILVER, 10mm, round, 1.34-1.45 gm

C#	Date	Year	VG	Fine	VF	XF
58	ND	—	15.00	20.00	26.50	35.00

1/4 RUPEE

SILVER, octagonal, 2.68-2.90 gm

C#	Date	Year	VG	Fine	VF	XF
59	SE1741	(1819)	25.00	35.00	45.00	60.00
	1742	(1820)	25.00	35.00	45.00	60.00

1/2 RUPEE

SILVER, 16mm, 5.35-5.80 gm

C#	Date	Year	VG	Fine	VF	XF
60	ND	—	25.00	35.00	45.00	60.00

RUPEE

SILVER, 22mm, octagonal, 10.70-11.60 gm

C#	Date	Year	VG	Fine	VF	XF
61	SE1741	(1819)	30.00	40.00	50.00	70.00
61.1	SE1742	(1820)	30.00	40.00	50.00	70.00

MOHUR

GOLD, 10.70-11.40 gm

C#	Date	Year	VG	Fine	VF	XF
67	SE1741	(1819)	225.00	250.00	285.00	325.00

Brajnatha Simha

SAKA 1739-1740/AD 1818-1819

1/32 RUPEE

SILVER, 6mm, round, 0.34-0.36 gm

C#	Date	Year	VG	Fine	VF	XF
68	ND	—	15.00	20.00	26.50	35.00

1/16 RUPEE

SILVER, 8mm, round, 0.67-0.72 gm

C#	Date	Year	VG	Fine	VF	XF
69	ND	—	15.00	20.00	26.50	35.00

1/8 RUPEE

SILVER, 10mm, round, 1.34-1.45 gm

C#	Date	Year	VG	Fine	VF	XF
70	ND	—	15.00	20.00	26.50	35.00

1/4 RUPEE

SILVER, 13mm, octagonal, 2.68-2.90 gm

C#	Date	Year	VG	Fine	VF	XF
71	SE1739	(1817)	20.00	30.00	40.00	55.00
	1740	(1818)	20.00	30.00	40.00	55.00

1/2 RUPEE

SILVER, 16mm, octagonal, 5.35-5.80 gm

C#	Date	Year	VG	Fine	VF	XF
72	ND	—	20.00	30.00	40.00	55.00

RUPEE

SILVER, 22-23mm, octagonal, 10.70-11.60 gm

C#	Date	Year	VG	Fine	VF	XF
73	SE1739	(1817)	25.00	35.00	50.00	70.00
	1740	(1818)	25.00	35.00	50.00	70.00

1/8 MOHUR

GOLD, octagonal, 1.34-1.42 gm

C#	Date	Year	VG	Fine	VF	XF
76	ND	—	45.00	55.00	70.00	100.00

1/4 MOHUR

GOLD, 2.68-2.85 gm

C#	Date	Year	VG	Fine	VF	XF
77	SE1739	(1817)	55.00	65.00	75.00	100.00

MOHUR

GOLD, octagonal, 10.70-11.40 gm

C#	Date	Year	VG	Fine	VF	XF
79	SE1739	(1817)	225.00	250.00	285.00	325.00
	1740	(1818)	225.00	250.00	285.00	325.00

Jogesvara Simha

SAKA 1743/AD 1821

1/8 RUPEE

SILVER, octagonal, 1.34-1.45 gm

C#	Date	Year	VG	Fine	VF	XF
82	ND	—	17.50	25.00	32.50	45.00

1/4 RUPEE

SILVER, octagonal, 2.68-2.90 gm

C#	Date	Year	VG	Fine	VF	XF
83	SE1743	(1821)	20.00	27.50	37.50	50.00

1/2 RUPEE

SILVER, 16mm, octagonal, 5.35-5.80 gm

C#	Date	Year	VG	Fine	VF	XF
84	ND	—	30.00	40.00	50.00	70.00

RUPEE

SILVER, 23mm, octagonal, 10.70-11.60 gm

C#	Date	Year	VG	Fine	VF	XF
85	SE1743	(1821)	30.00	40.00	50.00	70.00

1/4 MOHUR

GOLD

C#	Date	Year	VG	Fine	VF	XF
89	1743	(1821)	—	—	—	—

MATAK

Sarvvananda Simha, Raja

SAKA 1715-1717/AD 1793-1795

1/16 RUPEE

SILVER, 0.67-0.72 gm

C#	Date	Year	VG	Fine	VF	XF
201	ND	—	10.00	13.50	18.50	27.50

1/8 RUPEE

SILVER, 0.34-0.36 gm

C#	Date	Year	VG	Fine	VF	XF
202	ND	—	12.50	16.50	21.50	30.00

1/4 RUPEE

SILVER, 2.68-2.90 gm

C#	Date	Year	VG	Fine	VF	XF
203	SE1715	(1793)	15.00	18.50	25.00	35.00
	1716	(1794)	15.00	18.50	25.00	35.00

1/2 RUPEE

SILVER, 5.35-5.80 gm
Obv. leg: Variety 1

C#	Date	Year	VG	Fine	VF	XF
204	ND	—	20.00	27.50	37.50	50.00

C#	Date	Year	VG	Fine	VF	XF
Obv. leg: variety 2. Rev: "KRISHNA PADA...."						
204.1	ND	—	20.00	27.50	37.50	50.00
Obv. leg: Variety 3. Rev: "Krishna Madhv...."						
204.2	ND	—	20.00	27.50	37.50	50.00
Obv. leg: variety 4. Rev: "KRISHNA CHARANA...."						
204.3	ND	—	20.00	27.50	37.50	50.00

RUPEE

SILVER, 10.70-11.60 gm
Obv. leg: Variety 1

C#	Date	Year	VG	Fine	VF	XF
205	SE1715	(1793)	20.50	27.50	37.50	50.00

C#	Date	Year	VG	Fine	VF	XF
Obv. leg: Variety 2						
205.1	SE1716	(1794)	20.50	27.50	35.00	50.00
Obv. leg: Variety 3						
205.2	SE1716	(1794)	20.50	27.50	35.00	50.00
	1717	(1795)	20.50	27.50	35.00	50.00

1/4 MOHUR

GOLD, 2.68-2.85 gm

C#	Date	Year	VG	Fine	VF	XF
208	SE1716	(1794)	60.00	75.00	100.00	140.00

1/2 MOHUR

GOLD, 5.35-5.70 gm

C#	Date	Year	VG	Fine	VF	XF
209	ND	—	100.00	125.00	150.00	185.00

MOHUR

GOLD, 10.70-11.40 gm

C#	Date	Year	VG	Fine	VF	XF
210	SE1715	(1793)	225.00	250.00	285.00	325.00

RANGPUR

Bharatha Simha, Raja

SAKA 1713-1715, 1718-1719/
AD 1791-1793, 1796-1797

1/16 RUPEE

SILVER, 0.67-0.72 gm

C#	Date	Year	VG	Fine	VF	XF
211	ND	—	10.00	13.50	18.50	26.50

1/8 RUPEE

SILVER, 1.34-1.45 gm

C#	Date	Year	VG	Fine	VF	XF
212	ND	—'	12.50	16.50	22.50	30.00

1/4 RUPEE

SILVER, 2.68-2.90 gm

C#	Date	Year	VG	Fine	VF	XF
213	SE1713	(1791)	15.00	20.00	28.50	40.00
	1714	(1792)	15.00	20.00	28.50	40.00
	1715	(1793)	15.00	20.00	28.50	40.00
	1718	(1796)	15.00	20.00	28.50	40.00
	1719	(1797)	15.00	20.00	28.50	40.00

1/2 RUPEE

SILVER, 5.35-5.80 gm

C#	Date	Year	VG	Fine	VF	XF
214	ND	—	12.50	17.50	23.50	32.50

RUPEE

SILVER, 10.70-11.60 gm

C#	Date	Year	VG	Fine	VF	XF
215	SE1713	(1791)	15.00	20.00	28.50	40.00
	1714	(1792)	15.00	20.00	28.50	40.00
	1715	(1793)	15.00	20.00	28.50	40.00
	1718	(1796)	12.50	20.00	28.50	40.00
	1719	(1797)	12.50	20.00	28.50	40.00

1/8 MOHUR

GOLD, 1.34-1.42 gm

C#	Date	Year	VG	Fine	VF	XF
217	ND	—	50.00	75.00	100.00	140.00

1/4 MOHUR

GOLD, 2.68-2.85 gm

C#	Date	Year	VG	Fine	VF	XF
218	SE1713	(1791)	60.00	85.00	120.00	165.00

1/2 MOHUR

GOLD, 5.35-5.70 gm

C#	Date	Year	VG	Fine	VF	XF
219	ND	—	100.00	125.00	150.00	185.00

AWADH (OUDH)

(OUDH)

RULERS

Shuja-ud-daula
AH1189/AD1756-1775
Asaf al-Dawla
AH1189-1212/1775-1797
Wazir Ali
AH 1212-1213/AD 1797-1798
Sa'adat Ali
AH 1213-1230/AD 1798-1814
Ghazi al-Din Haidar, as Nawab,
AH 1230-1234/AD 1814-1819

In the name of Shah Alam II:

Allahabad Mint

To Awadh AH1173-1178 and AH1187-1195. Administered by East India Company thereafter.

RUPEE

FIRST ISSUE

SILVER, 19mm, 10.70-11.60 gm

KM#	Date	Year	VG	Fine	VF	XF
6.1	AH1174	—	11.50	13.50	16.50	20.00

For issues AH1178-1187/AD1765-1773, see India, Mughal Empire: Allahabad.

SECOND ISSUE

23mm
Rev: Pataka (banner)

KM#	Date	Year	VG	Fine	VF	XF
6.2	AH1190	18	11.50	13.50	16.50	20.00
	1191	18	11.50	13.50	16.50	20.00
	1192	18	11.50	13.50	16.50	20.00
	1192	19	11.50	13.50	16.50	20.00
	1194	19	11.50	13.50	16.50	20.00

For issues after AH1195 - R.Y 22, see India, Mughal Empire: Allahabad.

Asafabad Mint

Mintname: 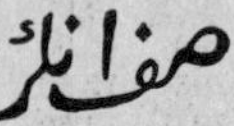

RUPEE

SILVER, 21mm, 10.70-11.60 gm
Rev: Cluster of four crosses, sword.

KM#	Date	Year	VG	Fine	VF	XF
16.1	AH	18	15.00	20.00	27.50	35.00

Rev: Cluster of four crosses, inverted Persian letter 'nun'

KM#	Date	Year	VG	Fine	VF	XF
16.2	AH1191	18	15.00	20.00	27.50	35.00

19mm
Rev: Danda (mace).

KM#	Date	Year	VG	Fine	VF	XF
16.3	AH	19	15.00	20.00	27.50	35.00
		21	15.00	20.00	27.50	35.00

Asafnagar Mint

Mintname: 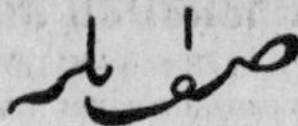

For issues prior to AD1774/AH1187 - R.Y. 15, see Rohilkhand.

RUPEE

SILVER, 21.5mm, 10.70-11.60 gm
Obv: Sword. Rev: Inverted Persian letter 'nun'.

KM#	Date	Year	VG	Fine	VF	XF
26.1		17	15.00	20.00	27.50	35.00

21mm
Rev: Fish and inverted Persian letter 'nun'.

KM#	Date	Year	VG	Fine	VF	XF
26.2	AH1189	17	15.00	20.00	27.50	35.00
	1190	18	15.00	20.00	27.50	35.00

Banares Mint

Under Awadh until AD1775/AH1189 - R.Y. 16

Mintname: Muhammadabad Banares

RUPEE

SILVER, 10.70-11.60 gm
Various symbols, generally including the pataka or banner
Similar to KM#37.

KM#	Date	Year	VG	Fine	VF	XF
36	AH1174	2	11.50	13.50	16.50	20.00
	1189	16	11.50	13.50	16.50	20.00

NAZARANA RUPEE

SILVER, 29.5mm, 10.70-11.60 gm

KM#	Date	Year	VG	Fine	VF	XF
37	AH1183	11	—	—	—	—

For later issues of Banares mint see India, British. Bengal Presidency, Banares. See also issues of Lucknow mint in mint-name "Muhammadabad Banares", below.

Bareli Mint

To Awadh in AH1188 - R.Y. 15. For issues prior to this see India Native States: Rohilkhand.

PAISA

COPPER, 22mm
Obv: Dagger. Rev: Fish.

KM#	Date	Year	Good	VG	Fine	VF
41	AH12xx	35	3.00	5.00	7.00	10.00
		37	3.00	5.00	7.00	10.00

1/2 RUPEE

SILVER, 5.35-5.80 gm

KM#	Date	Year	VG	Fine	VF	XF
45	AH1213	37	7.00	9.00	12.50	17.50

RUPEE

I- Obverse legend "Fazl-i-Hami Din"

SILVER, 22mm, 10-70-11.60 gm
Mintname: 'Bareli' lower left. No symbols.

KM#	Date	Year	VG	Fine	VF	XF
46.1	AH1189	17	11.50	13.50	16.50	20.00

21mm
Rev: Crescent.

KM#	Date	Year	VG	Fine	VF	XF
46.2	AH1190	17	11.50	13.50	16.50	20.00
	1191	18	11.50	13.50	16.50	20.00
	1191	19	11.50	13.50	16.50	20.00

20mm
Rev: Fish.

KM#	Date	Year	VG	Fine	VF	XF
46.3	AH1190	18	11.50	13.50	16.50	20.00

19mm
Rev: Danda (mace).

KM#	Date	Year	VG	Fine	VF	XF
46.4	AH1191	19	11.50	13.50	16.50	20.00
	1192	19	11.50	13.50	16.50	20.00
	1194	21	11.50	13.50	16.50	20.00

19.5mm
Rev: Sword.

KM#	Date	Year	VG	Fine	VF	XF
46.5	AH1193	20	11.50	13.50	16.50	20.00
	1193	21	11.50	13.50	16.50	20.00

24mm
Mintname: 'Bareli' upper rev.
Obv.: Pataka. Rev.: Fish.

KM#	Date	Year	VG	Fine	VF	XF
47.1	AH1199	26	11.50	13.50	16.50	20.00
	1199	27	11.50	13.50	16.50	20.00
	1200	27	11.50	13.50	16.50	20.00
	1201	27	11.50	13.50	16.50	20.00

24.5mm
Obv.: Cross. Rev.: Fish, Persian letter 'mim'.

KM#	Date	Year	VG	Fine	VF	XF
47.2	AH1202	28	11.50	13.50	16.50	20.00
	1202	29	11.50	13.50	16.50	20.00
	1203	29	11.50	13.50	16.50	20.00

22.5mm
Mintname: "Bareli Qita" upper rev.
Obv.: Cross. Rev.: Fish, Persian letters 'mim' and 'ain' trident.

KM#	Date	Year	VG	Fine	VF	XF
48.1	AH1205	29	11.50	13.50	16.50	20.00
	1206	29	11.50	13.50	16.50	20.00

23mm
Rev.: W/o trident.

KM#	Date	Year	VG	Fine	VF	XF
48.2	AH1207	29	11.50	13.50	16.50	20.00

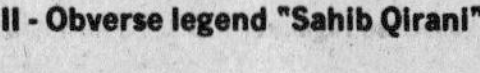

II - Obverse legend "Sahib Qirani"

25mm
Mintname "Bareli Qita" upper rev.
Obv: Cross. Rev: Fish, Persian letters 'mim'. and 'ain', trident with crescent.

KM#	Date	Year	VG	Fine	VF	XF
49.1	AH1209	31	11.50	13.50	16.50	20.00

22mm
Rev.: Fish, Persian letter. 're', star shaped flower.

KM#	Date	Year	VG	Fine	VF	XF
49.2	AH1209	31	11.50	13.50	16.50	20.00

22.5mm
Mintname 'Asafabad Bareli' center rev.
Obv.: Cross. Rev.: Persian letter 're', fish, crescent.

KM#	Date	Year	VG	Fine	VF	XF
50.1	AH1209	35	50.00	65.00	80.00	100.00
	1210	35	50.00	65.00	80.00	100.00

22mm
Rev: Persian letter 're', fish, swastika.

KM#	Date	Year	VG	Fine	VF	XF
50.2	AH1210	35	50.00	65.00	80.00	100.00

Rev: Fish. Persian letter 'alif'

KM#	Date	Year	VG	Fine	VF	XF
50.3	AH1210	35	50.00	65.00	80.00	100.00

Mintname 'Bareli Qita' upper rev.
Obv: Cross. Rev: Fish, Persian letter 'alif'

KM#	Date	Year	VG	Fine	VF	XF
51.1	AH1211	35	11.50	13.50	16.50	20.00
	1211	36	11.50	13.50	16.50	20.00

Rev: Fish, Persian letter 'mim', trident.

KM#	Date	Year	VG	Fine	VF	XF
51.2	AH1211	37	11.50	13.50	16.50	20.00
	1212	37	11.50	13.50	16.50	20.00

21mm
Rev: Fish, Persian letters 'mim' and 'nun', dagger

KM#	Date	Year	VG	Fine	VF	XF
51.3	AH1212	37	11.50	13.50	16.50	20.00
	1213	37	11.50	13.50	16.50	20.00

24mm
Rev: Fish, Persian letter 'mim', trident, dagger

KM#	Date	Year	VG	Fine	VF	XF
51.4	AH1213	37	11.50	13.50	16.50	20.00
	1214	37	11.50	13.50	16.50	20.00

Rev: Fish, Persian letter 'mim', star-shaped flower, dagger

KM#	Date	Year	VG	Fine	VF	XF
51.5	AH1215	37	11.50	13.50	16.50	20.00

21mm
Rev: Fish, Persian letter 'mim', star shaped flower, crescent

KM#	Date	Year	VG	Fine	VF	XF
51.6	AH1215	37	11.50	13.50	16.50	20.00

Rev: Fish, Persian letter 'mim', star-shaped flower, swastika

KM#	Date	Year	VG	Fine	VF	XF
51.7	AH1215	37	11.50	13.50	16.50	20.00

East India Company

RUPEE

SILVER, 21mm, 10.70-11.60 gm
Similar to KM#51.1 but Rev. fish, star-shaped flower, Persian letter 'alif'.

KM#	Date	Year	VG	Fine	VF	XF
52.1	AH1216	37	11.50	13.50	16.50	20.00

20mm
Rev: Fish, star-shaped flower, Persian letter 'he'.

KM#	Date	Year	VG	Fine	VF	XF
52.2	AH1216	37	11.50	13.50	16.50	20.00

21mm
Rev: Fish, star-shaped flower, Persian letter 'wa'.

KM#	Date	Year	VG	Fine	VF	XF
52.3	AH1216	37	11.50	13.50	16.50	20.00
	1217	37	11.50	13.50	16.50	20.00
	1218	37	11.50	13.50	16.50	20.00
	1219	37	11.50	13.50	16.50	20.00
	1220	37	11.50	13.50	16.50	20.00

The letter 'wa' on E.I.C. issues was reputedly the initial of the surname of the new settlement officer for Bareli, Henry Wellesley. The earlier issue, with letter 'he', may have been a less majestic initial of his personal name.

Hathras Mint

Under Awadh control until AD1782.

For later issues after AH1196 - R.Y. 24, see India-Mughal Empire: Hathras.

PAISA

COPPER, 16mm
Rev: Fish.

KM#	Date	Year	Good	VG	Fine	VF
61	ND	—	5.00	7.00	10.00	15.00

RUPEE

SILVER, 10.70-11.60 gm

KM#	Date	Year	VG	Fine	VF	XF
66	AH	22	20.00	25.00	30.00	40.00

Itawa Mint

To Awadh AD1774/AH1188

For issues before AH1188 - R.Y. 15, see India Native States, Maratha Confederacy, Peshwa, or India Native States, Rohilkhand. Ceded to the E.I.C. in AD1801.

RUPEE

SILVER, 27mm, 10.70-11.60 gm
Obv. mintmark: Umbrella.

KM#	Date	Year	VG	Fine	VF	XF
76.1	AH	15	11.50	13.50	16.50	20.00
	1189	17	11.50	13.50	16.50	20.00

26mm
Obv. mintmarks: Umbrella, pataka.

KM#	Date	Year	VG	Fine	VF	XF
76.2	AH1191	18	11.50	13.50	16.50	20.00

25mm
Obv. mintmarks: Umbrella, small fish.

KM#	Date	Year	VG	Fine	VF	XF
76.3	AH	19	11.50	13.50	16.50	20.00

24mm
Obv. mintmarks: Umbrella, stylized fish.

KM#	Date	Year	VG	Fine	VF	XF
76.4	AH	20	11.50	13.50	16.50	20.00
	—	21	11.50	13.50	16.50	20.00
	1194	22	11.50	13.50	16.50	20.00
	—	23	11.50	13.50	16.50	20.00
	1196	24	11.50	13.50	16.50	20.00
	1197	25	11.50	13.50	16.50	20.00
	1198	25	11.50	13.50	16.50	20.00

26mm
Obv. mintmarks: Umbrella, sword.

KM#	Date	Year	VG	Fine	VF	XF
76.5	AH	29	11.50	13.50	16.50	20.00

25mm
Obv. mintmarks: Umbrella, sword, shamrock.

KM#	Date	Year	VG	Fine	VF	XF
76.6	AH	30	11.50	13.50	16.50	20.00

26mm
Obv. mintmarks: Umbrella, stylized fish, shamrock.

KM#	Date	Year	VG	Fine	VF	XF
76.7	AH	31	11.50	13.50	16.50	20.00
	—	32	11.50	13.50	16.50	20.00
	—	33	11.50	13.50	16.50	20.00

24mm
Obv. mintmarks: Umbrella, stylized fish, star.

KM#	Date	Year	VG	Fine	VF	XF
76.8	AH	35	11.50	13.50	16.50	20.00

Kanauj Mint

Mintname: Shahabad Qanauj

1/2 RUPEE

SILVER, 20mm, 5.35-5.80 gm

KM#	Date	Year	VG	Fine	VF	XF
85	AH	26	20.00	25.00	32.50	45.00

RUPEE

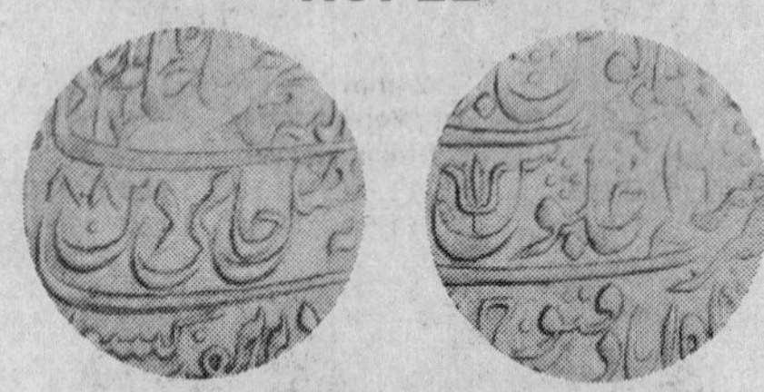

SILVER, 26.5mm, 10.70-11.60 gm
Rev. mintmark: Trisula.

KM#	Date	Year	VG	Fine	VF	XF
86.1	AH1188	16	15.00	20.00	27.50	35.00

29mm
Rev. mintmark: quadrafoil.

KM#	Date	Year	VG	Fine	VF	XF
86.2	AH1190	17	15.00	20.00	27.50	35.00

Kora Mint

To Awadh AD1773. For issues before AH1187 - R.Y. 14, see India Mughal Empire: Kora, or India Native States. Maratha Confederacy, Peshwa.

1/2 RUPEE

SILVER, 16mm, 5.35-5.80 gm

Obv. mintmark: Fish.

KM#	Date	Year	VG	Fine	VF	XF
95	AH119x	16	12.50	14.50	17.50	22.50

RUPEE

I - Obverse legend "SHAH ALAM BADSHAH"

SILVER, 18mm, 10.70-11.60 gm
Obv. mintmark: Vertical fish.

KM#	Date	Year	VG	Fine	VF	XF
96.1	AH1188	16	11.50	13.50	16.50	20.00
	1189	16	11.50	13.50	16.50	20.00
	1190	17	11.50	13.50	16.50	20.00

II - Obverse legend "FAZL-i-Shah Alam"

19mm
Obv. mintmark: Horizontal fish.

KM#	Date	Year	VG	Fine	VF	XF
96.2	AH	20	11.50	13.50	16.50	20.00

Lucknow Mint

Mintname: Muhammadabad Banaras

The issues of the Nawab-Vizier in this mintname are distinguished from E.I.C. issues on the basis of distinctive fabric and fixed regnal year: 26 for Awadh, 17 for E.I.C.

FALUS

COPPER, 16mm, irregular flan

C#	Date	Year	Good	VG	Fine	VF
1	AH1217	—	.75	1.50	2.25	3.50
	1218	—	.75	1.50	2.25	3.50
	1222	—	.75	1.50	2.25	3.50
	1224	—	.75	1.50	2.25	3.50
	1230	—	.75	1.50	2.25	3.50
	1231	—	.75	1.50	2.25	3.50
	1232	—	.75	1.50	2.25	3.50
	1233	—	.75	1.50	2.25	3.50

Round

C#	Date	Year	Good	VG	Fine	VF
2	AH—	24	1.75	3.00	4.50	7.00
	1208	26	1.75	3.00	4.50	7.00
	1229	29	1.75	3.00	4.50	7.00
	1233	—	1.75	3.00	4.50	7.00

1/8 RUPEE

SILVER, 12.5mm, 1.34-1.45 gm
Actual regnal year.

C#	Date	Year	VG	Fine	VF	XF
3.1	AH1 xx	23	8.00	10.00	13.50	18.50

14mm
Fixed regnal year.

C#	Date	Year	VG	Fine	VF	XF
3.2	AH1215	26	6.00	7.50	10.00	13.50
	1218	26	6.00	7.50	10.00	13.50
	1229	26	6.00	7.50	10.00	13.50

1/4 RUPEE

SILVER, 16.5mm, 2.68-2.90 gm
Actual regnal year.

KM#	Date	Year	VG	Fine	VF	XF
4.1	AH1196	23	8.00	10.00	13.50	18.50

Fixed regnal year.

C#	Date	Year	VG	Fine	VF	XF
4.2	AH1225	26	6.00	7.50	10.00	13.50

1/2 RUPEE

SILVER, 20mm, 5.35-5.80 gm
Actual regnal year

KM#	Date	Year	VG	Fine	VF	XF
5.1	AH1196	23	8.00	10.00	13.50	20.00

RUPEE

SILVER, 20-23mm, 10.70-11.60 gm

C#	Date	Year	VG	Fine	VF	XF
6	AH1201	26	12.50	14.50	17.50	22.50
	1202	26	12.50	14.50	17.50	22.50
	1203	26	12.50	14.50	17.50	22.50
	1204	26	12.50	14.50	17.50	22.50
	1205	26	12.50	14.50	17.50	22.50
	1206	26	12.50	14.50	17.50	22.50
	1207	26	12.50	14.50	17.50	22.50
	1208	26	12.50	14.50	17.50	22.50
	1209	26	12.50	14.50	17.50	22.50
	1210	26	12.50	14.50	17.50	22.50
	1211	26	12.50	14.50	17.50	22.50
	1212	26	12.50	14.50	17.50	22.50
	1213	26	12.50	14.50	17.50	22.50
	1214	26	12.50	14.50	17.50	22.50
	1215	26	12.50	14.50	17.50	22.50
	1216	26	12.50	14.50	17.50	22.50
	1217	26	12.50	14.50	17.50	22.50
	1218	26	12.50	14.50	17.50	22.50
	1219	26	12.50	14.50	17.50	22.50
	1220	26	12.50	14.50	17.50	22.50
	1221	26	11.50	13.50	16.50	20.00
	1222	26	11.50	13.50	16.50	20.00
	1223	26	11.50	13.50	16.50	20.00
	1224	26	11.50	13.50	16.50	20.00
	1225	26	11.50	13.50	16.50	20.00
	1226	26	11.50	13.50	16.50	20.00
	1227	26	11.50	13.50	16.50	20.00
	1228	26	11.50	13.50	16.50	20.00
	1229	26	11.50	13.50	16.50	20.00
	1230	26	11.50	13.50	16.50	20.00
	1231	26	11.50	13.50	16.50	20.00
	1232	26	11.50	13.50	16.50	20.00
	1233	26	11.50	13.50	16.50	20.00
	1234	26	11.50	13.50	16.50	20.00

NOTE: See C#130 for similar coins also dated AH1229/Yr. 26.

NAZARANA RUPEE

Similar to 1 Rupee, C#6, broad flan, 28mm.

6a	AH1216	26	35.00	45.00	60.00	85.00

MOHUR

GOLD, 10.70-11.40 gm

10	AH1230	26	220.00	240.00	265.00	300.00

Muradabad Mint

To Awadh AD1774. For issues before AH1188 - R.Y. 15, see India Native States: Rohikhand.

RUPEE

SILVER, 22.5mm, 10.70-11.60 gm
Rev: Star.

KM#	Date	Year	VG	Fine	VF	XF
106.1	AH1189	16	11.50	13.50	16.50	20.00
	1189	17	11.50	13.50	16.50	20.00
	1190	17	11.50	13.50	16.50	20.00
	1190	18	11.50	13.50	16.50	20.00
	1191	18	11.50	13.50	16.50	20.00

21mm
Rev: Shamrock.

106.2	AH1191	18	11.50	13.50	16.50	20.00

Rev: Danda (mace).

106.3	AH1193	21	11.50	13.50	16.50	20.00
	—	22	11.50	13.50	16.50	20.00

Najibabad Mint

To Awadh AD1774. For issues before AH1188 - R.Y. 15, see India Native States: Rohilkhand.

PAISA

Various weight standards

COPPER, 19mm
Obv: Crescent. Rev: Vertical fish.

KM#	Date	Year	Good	VG	Fine	VF
111	AH1198	23	1.50	2.50	3.50	5.00
	1199	26	1.50	2.50	3.50	5.00
	1207	33	1.50	2.50	3.50	5.00
	—	41	1.50	2.50	3.50	5.00
	1215	43	1.50	2.50	3.50	5.00

21mm
Rev: Stylized dagger.

112	AH1198	25	2.00	2.75	3.75	5.50
	—	27	2.00	2.75	3.75	5.50
	—	29	2.00	2.75	3.75	5.50
	1202	30	2.00	2.75	3.75	5.50
	—	31	2.00	2.75	3.75	5.50
	—	37	2.00	2.75	3.75	5.50
	1210	38	2.00	2.75	3.75	5.50
	1212	39	2.00	2.75	3.75	5.50

19.5mm
Rev: Horizontal fish.

KM#	Date	Year	Good	VG	Fine	VF
113	AH	38	5.00	7.00	10.00	15.00
	1216	43	5.00	7.00	10.00	15.00

22mm
Rev: Sword.

114	AH1214	41	5.00	7.00	10.00	15.00

RUPEE

SILVER, 10.70-11.60 gm
Obv: Horizontal fish. Rev: Crude dagger.

KM#	Date	Year	VG	Fine	VF	XF
116.1	AH1194	22	12.50	14.50	17.50	22.50
	1196	23	12.50	14.50	17.50	22.50
	1197	24	12.50	14.50	17.50	22.50
	1200	27	12.50	14.50	17.50	22.50

23mm
Mintname: 'Najibabad'
Obv: Crescent. Rev: Persian letter 'sad', fish.

116.2	AH1198	25	11.50	13.50	16.50	20.00
	1199	26	11.50	13.50	16.50	20.00
	1200	27	11.50	13.50	16.50	20.00

Rev: Persian letters 'mim' and 'ain', fish.

116.3	AH1204	30	11.50	13.50	16.50	20.00
	1205	31	11.50	13.50	16.50	20.00
	1208	34	11.50	13.50	16.50	20.00

22mm
Rev: Persian letter 'mim', bud or halberd, fish.

116.4	AH1206	32	11.50	13.50	16.50	20.00
	1207	33	11.50	13.50	16.50	20.00
	1213	40	11.50	13.50	16.50	20.00
	1214	41	11.50	13.50	16.50	20.00

21mm
Rev: Swastika, fish.

116.5	AH1210	36	11.50	13.50	16.50	20.00

22mm
Rev: Persian letter 'mim', bud, fish, dagger.

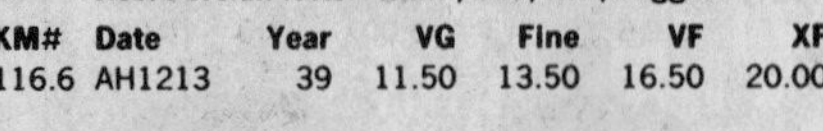

KM#	Date	Year	VG	Fine	VF	XF
116.6	AH1213	39	11.50	13.50	16.50	20.00

21mm
Rev: Persian letter 'mim' written as word; bud, fish.

KM#	Date	Year	VG	Fine	VF	XF
116.7	AH1215	42	11.50	13.50	16.50	20.00
	1216	42	11.50	13.50	16.50	20.00

20mm
Rev: Persian letter 'mim'.
Persian word 'ald', fish. Persian letter 'he'.

KM#	Date	Year	VG	Fine	VF	XF
116.8	AH1216	43	11.50	13.50	16.50	20.00

DOUBLE RUPEE

SILVER, 27mm, 21.40-23.20 gm

KM#	Date	Year	VG	Fine	VF	XF
118	AH1195	22	125.00	175.00	225.00	300.00

MOHUR

GOLD, 10.70-11.40 gm

KM#	Date	Year	VG	Fine	VF	XF
120	AH	24	220.00	240.00	265.00	300.00
	—	25	220.00	240.00	265.00	300.00
	—	26	220.00	240.00	265.00	300.00

Shahabad Mint

Mintname: Anupnagar Shahabad

RUPEE

SILVER, 26mm, 10.70-11.60 gm
Rev: Trident.

KM#	Date	Year	VG	Fine	VF	XF
126	AH1189	16	20.00	25.00	32.50	40.00

Tanda Mint

Mintname: Muhammadnagar Tanda

RUPEE

SILVER, 22mm, 10.70-11.60 gm
Obv: Crosses.

KM#	Date	Year	VG	Fine	VF	XF
136.1	AH1184	11	15.00	20.00	26.50	35.00

Obv: Pataka.

KM#	Date	Year	VG	Fine	VF	XF
136.2	AH1185	11	15.00	20.00	26.50	35.00
	1185	12	15.00	20.00	26.50	35.00
	1186	12	15.00	20.00	26.50	35.00

Ghaziu-D-Din Haidar

King, AH1234-1243/AD1819-1827

All coins from Lucknow Mint.

In the name of Shah Alam II:

FALUS

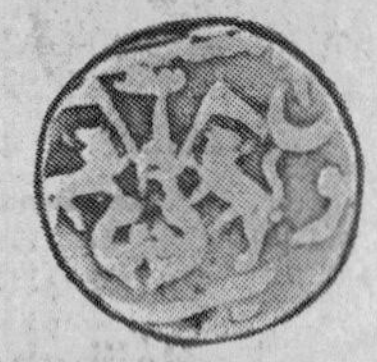

COPPER, 22mm

C#	Date	Year	Good	VG	Fine	VF
13	AH1234	26	1.50	2.25	2.75	3.75
	1235	26	1.50	2.25	2.75	3.75

1/4 RUPEE

SILVER, 2.68-2.90 gm

C#	Date	Year	VG	Fine	VF	XF
20	AH1234	26	10.00	13.50	18.50	25.00

RUPEE

SILVER, 26-27mm, 10.70-11.60 gm

C#	Date	Year	VG	Fine	VF	XF
22	AH1234	26	11.50	13.50	16.50	20.00

1/2 MOHUR

GOLD, 5.35-5.70 gm

C#	Date	Year	VG	Fine	VF	XF
25	AH1234	26	110.00	120.00	135.00	150.00

MOHUR

GOLD, 25-26mm, 10.70-11.40 gm

C#	Date	Year	VG	Fine	VF	XF
26	AH1234	26	225.00	250.00	285.00	325.00

In His Own Name

NOTE: Coins dated AH1234 have regnal year 5 for Haidar as Nawab; coins dated AH1235 and later have his regnal year as King AH1235 Yr. 1.

NOTE: The mint name comes with 2 different epithets:
AH1234-1235; Dar ul-Imaret Lakhnau Suba Awadh
AH1236-1243 Dar us-Saltanat Lakhnau Suba Awadh

FALUS

COPPER, 21-24mm

C#	Date	Year	Good	VG	Fine	VF
33	AH1234	5	1.50	2.50	3.50	5.00
	1235	1	1.25	2.00	2.50	3.50
	1236	2	.85	1.50	2.00	3.00
	1237	3	.85	1.50	2.00	3.00
	1238	4	1.25	2.00	2.50	3.50
	1239	5	.85	1.50	2.00	3.00
	1240	6	.85	1.50	2.00	3.00

1/16 RUPEE (ANNA)

SILVER, 10mm, 0.67-0.72 gm

C#	Date	Year	VG	Fine	VF	XF
35	AH1235	1	6.50	8.50	11.50	16.50

1/8 RUPEE (2 ANNAS)

SILVER, 12-14mm, 1.34-1.45 gm

C#	Date	Year	VG	Fine	VF	XF
36	AH1235	1	6.50	8.50	11.50	16.50

1/4 RUPEE

SILVER, 15-17mm, 2.68-2.90 gm

C#	Date	Year	VG	Fine	VF	XF
37	AH1236	2	6.50	8.50	11.50	16.50

1/2 RUPEE

SILVER, 20-21mm, 5.35-5.80 gm

C#	Date	Year	VG	Fine	VF	XF
38	AH1240	6	7.50	10.00	13.50	18.50
	1242	8	7.50	10.00	13.50	18.50

RUPEE

SILVER, 23-27mm, 10.70-11.60 gm
Mint name: Dar-ul-Amarat Lakhnau

C#	Date	Year	VG	Fine	VF	XF
39.1	AH1234	5	12.50	14.50	17.50	22.50
	1235	1	12.50	14.50	17.50	22.50

Mint name: Dar-us-Sultanat Lakhnau

C#	Date	Year	VG	Fine	VF	XF
39.2	AH1236	2	12.50	14.50	17.50	22.50
	1237	3	12.50	14.50	17.50	22.50
	1238	4	12.50	14.50	17.50	22.50
	1239	5	12.50	14.50	17.50	22.50
	1240	6	11.50	13.50	16.50	20.00
	1241	7	11.50	13.50	16.50	20.00
	1242	8	11.50	13.50	16.50	20.00
	1243	9	11.50	13.50	16.50	20.00

1/4 ASHRAFI

GOLD, 2.68-2.85 gm

C#	Date	Year	VG	Fine	VF	XF
43	AH1236-43	—	65.00	85.00	110.00	135.00

ASHRAFI

GOLD, 23-27mm, 10.70-11.40 gm

C#	Date	Year	VG	Fine	VF	XF
45	AH1235	1	250.00	285.00	325.00	400.00
	1236	1	250.00	285.00	325.00	400.00
	1241	7	250.00	285.00	325.00	400.00

Nasiru-D-Din Haidar

AH 1243-53/AD 1827-37

In the name of Sulayman Jah:

FALUS

COPPER, 21-23mm

C#	Date	Year	Good	VG	Fine	VF
47	AH1243	1	1.25	2.00	2.75	4.00
	1244	1	1.25	2.00	2.75	4.00
	1244	2	1.25	2.00	2.75	4.00

1/8 RUPEE

SILVER, 13mm, 1.34-1.45 gm

C#	Date	Year	VG	Fine	VF	XF
49	AH1244	2	5.00	7.00	10.00	14.00

1/4 RUPEE

SILVER, 14-15mm, 2.68-2.90 gm

C#	Date	Year	VG	Fine	VF	XF
50	AH1244	2	6.50	8.50	11.50	16.50

1/2 RUPEE

SILVER, 20mm, 5.35-5.80 gm

C#	Date	Year	VG	Fine	VF	XF
51	AH1244	2	7.00	9.00	12.50	17.50

RUPEE

SILVER, 22-26mm, 10.70-11.60 gm

C#	Date	Year	VG	Fine	VF	XF
52	AH1243	1	12.50	14.50	17.50	22.50
	1244	1	12.50	14.50	17.50	22.50
	1244	2	12.50	14.50	17.50	22.50
	1245	1	12.50	14.50	17.50	22.50

NOTE: This series comes in 2 major varieties, the difference being in the coat of arms and position of regnal year.

Variety I: Katar (knife) above fish, regnal year within fish.
Variety II: Katar within fish, regnal year in marginal inscription.

ASHRAFI

In the name of Nasir al-Din Haidar

GOLD, 10.70-11.40 gm

C#	Date	Year	VG	Fine	VF	XF
54	AH1243	1	250.00	285.00	325.00	400.00

FALUS

COPPER, 20-23MM
Variety I

C#	Date	Year	Good	VG	Fine	VF
56.1	AH1245	3	.85	1.50	2.00	2.75
	1246	3	.85	1.50	2.00	2.75
	1246	4	.85	1.50	2.00	2.75
	1247	4	.85	1.50	2.00	2.75
	1247	5	.85	1.50	2.00	2.75
	1248	5	.85	1.50	2.00	2.75
	1249	6	.85	1.50	2.00	2.75

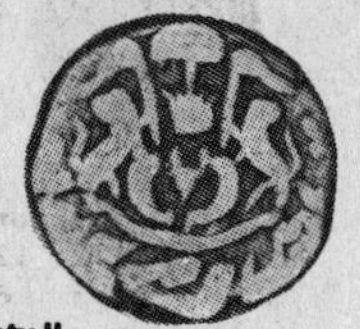

Variety II

C#	Date	Year	Good	VG	Fine	VF
56.2	AH1249	6	.85	1.50	2.00	2.75
	1250	—	1.50	2.50	3.00	5.00

1/16 RUPEE (ANNA)

SILVER, 9-13mm, 0.67-0.72 gm

Variety II

C#	Date	Year	VG	Fine	VF	XF
58a	AH1250	—	—	4.00	6.50	8.50
	1252	—	—	4.00	6.50	8.50

1/8 RUPEE

SILVER, 14mm, 1.34-1.45 gm
Variety I

C#	Date	Year	VG	Fine	VF	XF
59	AH125x	—	—	4.50	7.50	10.00

1/4 RUPEE

SILVER, 15-17mm, 2.68-2.90 gm
Variety I

C#	Date	Year	VG	Fine	VF	XF
60.1	AH1245	3	—	6.00	11.00	15.00
	124X	4	—	6.00	11.00	15.00
	1248	15	—	6.00	11.00	15.00

Variety II

C#	Date	Year	VG	Fine	VF	XF
60.2	AH1250	—	—	9.00	12.00	16.50

1/2 RUPEE

SILVER, 18-20mm, 5.35-5.80 gm
Variety 1

C#	Date	Year	VG	Fine	VF	XF
61	AH1248	5	7.00	9.00	12.00	16.50

RUPEE

SILVER, 22-28mm, 10.70-11.60 gm
Variety I

C#	Date	Year	VG	Fine	VF	XF
62.1	AH1246	3	11.50	13.50	16.50	20.00
	1246	4	11.50	13.50	16.50	20.00
	1247	4	11.50	13.50	16.50	20.00
	1247	5	11.50	13.50	16.50	20.00
	1248	5	11.50	13.50	16.50	20.00
	1248	6	11.50	13.50	16.50	20.00
	1249	6	11.50	13.50	16.50	20.00

Variety II

C#	Date	Year	VG	Fine	VF	XF
62.2	AH1249	7	11.50	13.50	16.50	20.00
	1250	7	11.50	13.50	16.50	20.00
	1250	8	11.50	13.50	16.50	20.00
	1251	7	11.50	13.50	16.50	20.00
	1251	8	11.50	13.50	16.50	20.00
	1252	7	12.50	14.50	17.50	21.50
	1252	8	12.50	14.50	17.50	21.50
	1252	9	11.50	13.50	16.50	20.00
	1253	9	13.50	16.50	20.00	26.50

ASHRAFI

GOLD, 25mm
Variety I

C#	Date	Year	VG	Fine	VF	XF
69	AH1246	3	250.00	285.00	325.00	400.00

Muhammad Ali Shah

AH 1253-58/AD 1837-42

NOTE: Mint name comes in 2 varieties.
Variety I. Suba Awadh Baitu-s-Saltanat Lakhnau, on all coins through 1256/Yr. 3.
Variety II. Mulk Awadh Baitu-s-Saltanat Lakhnau, on all coins beginning 1256/Yr. 4.

FALUS

COPPER, 20-22mm

C#	Date	Year	Good	VG	Fine	VF
72	AH1253	—	1.25	2.25	3.00	4.00
	1254	—	1.25	2.25	3.00	4.00
	1255	—	1.25	2.25	3.00	4.00

1/8 RUPEE

SILVER, 10mm, 1.34-1.45 gm

C#	Date	Year	VG	Fine	VF	XF
76	AH1253	1	4.50	6.50	9.00	13.50

1/4 RUPEE

SILVER, 13-16mm, 2.68-2.90 gm

C#	Date	Year	VG	Fine	VF	XF
77	AH1253	—	6.00	8.00	11.00	15.00

1/2 RUPEE

SILVER, 19mm, 5.35-5.80 gm

C#	Date	Year	VG	Fine	VF	XF
78	AH1254	—	7.00	9.00	12.00	16.50
	1258	—	7.00	9.00	12.00	16.50

RUPEE

SILVER, 23-26mm, 10.70-11.60 gm

C#	Date	Year	VG	Fine	VF	XF
79	AH1253	1	12.50	14.50	17.50	21.50
	1254	1	12.50	14.50	17.50	21.50
	1254	2	12.50	14.50	17.50	21.50
	1255	2	12.50	14.50	17.50	21.50
	1255	3	12.50	14.50	17.50	21.50
	1256	3	12.50	14.50	17.50	21.50
	1256	4	12.50	14.50	17.50	21.50
	1257	4	12.50	14.50	17.50	21.50
	1257	5	12.50	14.50	17.50	21.50
	1258	5	12.50	14.50	17.50	21.50

1/2 ASHRAFI

GOLD, 19mm, 5.35-5.70 gm

C#	Date	Year	VG	Fine	VF	XF
85	AH1253	1	125.00	150.00	185.00	225.00

ASHRAFI

GOLD, 24-26mm, 10.70-11.40 gm
Varieties

C#	Date	Year	VG	Fine	VF	XF
86	AH1253	—	225.00	250.00	285.00	325.00
	1255	3	225.00	250.00	285.00	325.00
	1258	—	225.00	250.00	285.00	325.00

Amjad Ali Shah

AH 1258-63/AD 1842-47

FALUS

COPPER, 20mm

C#	Date	Year	Good	VG	Fine	VF
95	AH1258	1	1.50	2.50	3.50	5.00
	1262	—	1.50	2.50	3.50	5.00
	Finer style, 27mm					
95a	AH1258	1	5.00	10.00	15.00	21.50

1/16 RUPEE

SILVER, 10-11mm, 0.67-0.72 gm

C#	Date	Year	VG	Fine	VF	XF
97	AH1262	—	5.00	6.50	8.50	11.50

1/8 RUPEE

SILVER, 13-14mm, 1.34-1.45 gm

C#	Date	Year	VG	Fine	VF	XF
98	AH1258	—	6.00	8.00	11.00	15.00
	1262	—	6.00	8.00	11.00	15.00

1/4 RUPEE

SILVER, 17mm, 2.68-2.90 gm

C#	Date	Year	VG	Fine	VF	XF
99	AH1259	2	12.50	16.50	21.50	27.50
	1260	3	6.00	7.50	9.00	12.50

1/2 RUPEE

SILVER, 18-20mm, 5.35-5.80 gm

C#	Date	Year	VG	Fine	VF	XF
100	AH1259	2	6.50	8.00	10.00	14.00
	1260	3	6.50	8.00	10.00	14.00
	1261	—	6.50	8.00	10.00	14.00

RUPEE

SILVER, 23-26mm, 10.70-11.60 gm

C#	Date	Year	VG	Fine	VF	XF
101	AH1258	1	12.50	14.50	17.50	22.50
	1259	1	12.50	14.50	17.50	22.50
	1259	2	12.50	14.50	17.50	22.50
	1260	2	12.50	14.50	17.50	22.50
	1260	3	12.50	14.50	17.50	22.50
	1261	3	12.50	14.50	17.50	22.50
	1261	4	12.50	14.50	17.50	22.50
	1262	4	12.50	14.50	17.50	22.50
	1262	5	12.50	14.50	17.50	22.50
	1263	5	12.50	14.50	17.50	22.50

1/2 ASHRAFI

GOLD, 18-19mm, 5.35-5.70 gm

C#	Date	Year	VG	Fine	VF	XF
107	AH1258	—	125.00	150.00	185.00	225.00

ASHRAFI

GOLD, 23mm, 10.70-11.40 gm

C#	Date	Year	VG	Fine	VF	XF
108	AH1258-63	—	225.00	250.00	285.00	325.00

Wajid Ali Shah

AH 1263-72/AD 1847-56

NOTE: Wajid Alis coins come in 3 varieties, depending on form of mint name:
Variety 1: Mulk Awadh Baitu-s-Saltanat Lakhnau, AH1263—1267/Yr. 4.
Variety 2: Mulk Awadh Akhtarnagar, AH1267/5 reported so far only for Rupees dated 1267/Yr. 5. The same date/year combination is also found in Var. 3.
Variety 3: Baitu-s-Saltanat Lakhnau Mulk Awadh Akhtar—nagar, 1267/Yr. 5-1272

1/8 FALUS

COPPER, 13mm

C#	Date	Year	Good	VG	Fine	VF
109	AH1270	8	3.50	6.00	8.00	11.50
	1271	—	3.00	5.00	7.00	10.00

1/4 FALUS

COPPER, 15mm

C#	Date	Year	Good	VG	Fine	VF
110	AH127X	7	3.00	5.00	7.00	10.00
	1270	8	3.50	6.00	8.50	12.00
	1272	9	3.00	5.00	7.00	10.00

1/2 FALUS

COPPER, 18mm

C#	Date	Year	Good	VG	Fine	VF
111	AH1269	—	2.75	4.50	6.00	8.50
	1270	—	2.75	4.50	6.00	8.50
	1270	8	2.75	4.50	6.00	8.50
	1271	—	2.75	4.50	6.00	8.50
	1272	—	2.75	4.50	6.00	8.50

FALUS

COPPER, 22-23mm

C#	Date	Year	Good	VG	Fine	VF
112	AH—	1	1.50	2.50	3.00	4.50
	1264	2	2.00	3.50	5.00	7.00
	1270	8	2.00	3.50	5.00	7.00
	1270	9	2.00	3.50	5.00	7.00
	1271?	—	2.00	3.50	5.00	7.00
	1272	—	2.00	3.50	5.00	7.00
	Rectangular, 14x18mm					
112.1	AH1271	—	2.00	3.50	5.00	7.00

NOTE: Barbarous versions of C#112, without legible date or year, are common and worth half of what a legible specimen commands.

1/16 RUPEE

SILVER, 9-10mm, 0.67-0.72 gm

C#	Date	Year	VG	Fine	VF	XF
114	AH126X	—	4.50	6.50	9.00	12.50
	1270	8	4.50	6.50	9.00	12.50
	1270	2(sic)	4.50	6.50	9.00	12.50
	1271	—	4.50	6.50	9.00	12.50
	1272	—	4.50	6.50	9.00	12.50

1/8 RUPEE

SILVER, 12-14mm, 1.34-1.45 gm

C#	Date	Year	VG	Fine	VF	XF
115	AH1265	—	5.00	6.50	8.50	11.50
	1266	—	5.00	6.50	8.50	11.50
	1269	—	5.00	6.50	8.50	11.50
	1270	8	5.00	6.50	8.50	11.50
	1271	9	5.00	6.50	8.50	11.50

1/4 RUPEE

SILVER, 15-16mm, 2.68-2.90 gm

C#	Date	Year	VG	Fine	VF	XF
116	AH1263	1	5.00	6.50	8.50	11.50
	1265	—	5.00	6.50	8.50	11.50
	1267	5	5.00	6.50	8.50	11.50
	1271	9	5.00	6.50	8.50	11.50

1/2 RUPEE

SILVER, 18-20mm, 5.35-5.80 gm

Variety I

C#	Date	Year	VG	Fine	VF	XF
117.1	AH1263	2	6.50	8.50	11.00	15.00
	1265	2	6.50	8.50	11.00	15.00
	1266	3	6.50	8.50	11.00	15.00

Variety III, 19mm

C#	Date	Year	VG	Fine	VF	XF
117.3	1268	5	6.50	8.50	11.00	15.00
	1271	8	6.50	8.50	11.00	15.00
	1271	9	6.50	8.50	11.00	15.00

RUPEE

SILVER, 22-26mm, 10.70-11.60 gm

C#	Date	Year	VG	Fine	VF	XF
	Variety I					
118.1	AH1263	1	11.50	13.50	16.50	20.00
	1264	1	11.50	13.50	16.50	20.00
	1264	2	11.50	13.50	16.50	20.00
	1265	1	11.50	13.50	16.50	20.00
	1265	2	11.50	13.50	16.50	20.00
	1265	3	11.50	13.50	16.50	20.00
	1266	3	11.50	13.50	16.50	20.00
	1266	4	11.50	13.50	16.50	20.00
	1267	3	11.50	13.50	16.50	20.00
	1267	4	11.50	13.50	16.50	20.00
	Variety II					
118.2	1267	5	17.50	25.00	35.00	50.00
	Variety III					
118.3	1267	5	11.50	13.50	16.50	20.00
	1268	5	11.50	13.50	16.50	20.00
	1268	6	11.50	13.50	16.50	20.00
	1269	6	11.50	13.50	16.50	20.00
	1269	2	(2- Backwards 6)			
			11.50	13.50	16.50	20.00
	1269	7	11.50	13.50	16.50	20.00
	1270	7	11.50	13.50	16.50	20.00
	1270	8	11.50	13.50	16.50	20.00
	1271	8	11.50	13.50	16.50	20.00
	1271	9	11.50	13.50	16.50	20.00
	1272	9	11.50	13.50	16.50	20.00
	1272	10	11.50	13.50	16.50	20.00

1/16 ASHRAFI

GOLD, 10mm, 0.67-0.71 gm

C#	Date	Year	VG	Fine	VF	XF
120	AH1270	—	35.00	45.00	55.00	70.00

1/8 ASHRAFI

GOLD, 1.34-1.42 gm

C#	Date	Year	VG	Fine	VF	XF
121	AH1263-72	—	40.00	50.00	60.00	80.00

1/4 ASHRAFI

GOLD, 2.68-2.85 gm

C#	Date	Year	VG	Fine	VF	XF
122	AH1263-72	—	60.00	75.00	90.00	120.00

1/2 ASHRAFI

GOLD, 18-19mm, 5.35-5.70 gm

C#	Date	Year	VG	Fine	VF	XF
123	AH1263-72	—	110.00	125.00	150.00	175.00

ASHRAFI

GOLD, 24mm, 10.70-11.40 gm

C#	Date	Year	VG	Fine	VF	XF
124	AH1263	—	220.00	240.00	265.00	300.00
	1265	2	220.00	240.00	265.00	300.00
	1266	3	220.00	240.00	265.00	300.00
	1267	4	220.00	240.00	265.00	300.00
	1272	—	220.00	240.00	265.00	300.00

Brijis Qadr

Nawab-Wazir during the Indian Mutiny

AD 1857-58

Subah Awadh Mint

FALUS

COPPER

C#	Date	Year	Good	VG	Fine	VF
125	AH1229	26	3.00	5.00	7.50	10.00

1/8 RUPEE

SILVER, 13-14mm, 1.34-1.45 gm

C#	Date	Year	VG	Fine	VF	XF
127	AH1229	26	7.00	10.00	14.00	20.00

Fictitious dating in imitation of coinage before AH1234/1819. Identifiable only by style and form of mint name, dated only AH1229/26.

1/2 RUPEE

SILVER, 2.68-2.90 gm

C#	Date	Year	VG	Fine	VF	XF
129	AH1229	26	9.00	13.50	18.50	26.50

RUPEE

SILVER, 22mm, 10.70-11.60 gm

C#	Date	Year	VG	Fine	VF	XF
130	AH1229	26	17.50	23.50	28.50	37.50

ASHRAFI

GOLD, 10.70-11.40 gm

C#	Date	Year	VG	Fine	VF	XF
135	AH1229	26	225.00	265.00	325.00	400.00

BAHAWALPUR

For earlier issues in the names of the Durrani rulers, see INDIA-DURRANI EMPIRE.

RULERS

Amirs of Bahawalpur:

Muhammad Bahawal Khan II,
AH1186-1224 (AD1772-1809)

Sadiq Muhammad Khan II,
AH1224-41 (AD1809-25)

Muhammad Bahawal Khan III,
AH1241-69 (AD1825-52)

Sadiq Muhammad Khan III,

AH1269-70 (AD1852-53)
Fateh Khan, AH1270-75 (AD1853-58)
Muhammad Bahawal Khan IV, AH1275-83 (AD1858-66)
Sir Sadiq Muhammad Khan IV, AH1283-1317 (AD1866-99)
Alhaj Muhammad Bahawal Khan V, AH1317-25 (AD1899-1907)
Sir Sadiq Muhammad Khan V, AH1325-1365 (AD1907-1947)

ANONYMOUS COINAGE

FALUS

COPPER

C#	Date	Year	Good	VG	Fine	VF
5	AH1194	—	3.50	6.50	10.00	15.00
	1195	—	3.50	6.50	10.00	15.00
	1196	—	3.50	6.50	10.00	15.00
	1197	—	3.50	6.50	10.00	15.00

Obv: Lion right.

C#	Date	Mintage	VG	Fine	VF
10	ND	—	—	—	—

Square or round, 14-16mm

Y#	Date	Year	Good	VG	Fine	VF
1	AH1225	—	4.00	7.50	10.00	15.00
	1248	—	3.00	5.00	7.00	10.00
	1254	—	3.00	5.00	7.00	10.00
	1259	—	3.00	5.00	7.00	10.00
	1261	—	3.00	5.00	7.00	10.00
	1269	—	3.00	5.00	7.00	10.00
	127x	—	2.50	4.00	6.00	8.50
	1276	—	3.00	5.00	7.00	10.00
	1277	—	2.00	3.50	5.00	7.50
	1281	—	3.50	6.00	8.00	11.00

PAISA

COPPER
Squarish, 15-16mm

Y#	Date	Year	Good	VG	Fine	VF
2	AH1301	—	Reported, not confirmed			
	1302	—	3.50	6.00	8.50	12.00
	1304	—	3.50	6.00	8.50	12.00
	1311	—	3.50	6.00	8.50	12.00
	1313	—	3.50	6.00	8.50	12.00
	1315	—	3.50	6.00	8.50	12.00
	1317	—	3.50	6.00	8.50	12.00
	1321	—	3.50	6.00	8.50	12.00

Ahmadpur Mint

Mintmark احمدپور

RUPEE

SILVER, 10.70-11.60 gm

In name of Mahmud Shah

C#	Date	Year	VG	Fine	VF	XF
18	AH1217	48	13.50	17.50	23.50	30.00
	—	49	13.50	17.50	23.50	30.00

Probably posthumous issue.

20-22mm, anonymous

Y#	Date	Year	VG	Fine	VF	XF
3	AH1275	—	14.00	18.50	25.00	32.50
	1276	—	14.00	18.50	25.00	32.50
	1277	—	14.00	18.50	25.00	32.50
	1278	—	14.00	18.50	25.00	32.50
	1280	—	14.00	18.50	25.00	32.50
	1281	—	14.00	18.50	25.00	32.50
	1282	—	14.00	18.50	25.00	32.50
	1284	—	14.00	18.50	25.00	32.50

Bahawalpur Mint

Mintmark بهاولپور

RUPEE

SILVER, 22mm, 11gm.

Y#	Date	Year	VG	Fine	VF	XF
4	AH1272	—	14.00	18.50	25.00	32.50
	1273	—	14.00	18.50	25.00	32.50

7 gm.

Y#	Date	Year	VG	Fine	VF	XF
4a	AH1280	—	14.00	18.50	25.00	32.50
	1281	—	14.00	18.50	25.00	32.50

Khanpur Mint

Mintmark خانپور

RUPEE

SILVER

Y#	Date	Year	VG	Fine	VF	XF
5	AH1280	—	15.00	20.00	27.50	35.00

Muhammad Bahawal Khan V

AD 1899-1907 (AH 1317-1325)

For anonymous paisas struck during the early years of his reign, see Y#2.

PAISA

COPPER, square, 15-16mm

Y#	Date	Year	Good	VG	Fine	VF
6	AH1324	—	3.50	6.00	9.00	12.50
	1325	—	3.50	6.00	9.00	12.50

Sadiq Muhammad Khan V

AD1907-1947 (AH1325-1365)

DUMP COINAGE

PAISA

COPPER, square, 15-19mm

Y#	Date	Year	Good	VG	Fine	VF
7	AH1326	—	3.50	6.00	9.00	12.50
	1327	—	3.50	6.00	9.00	12.50
	w/o date or star		5.50	9.00	13.50	20.00

14-16mm

Y#	Date	Year	Good	VG	Fine	VF
8	AH1342	—	7.50	11.00	15.00	20.00
	1343	—	7.50	11.00	15.00	20.00

MACHINE-STRUCK COINAGE

1/2 PICE

COPPER, 21mm

Y#	Date	Year	Fine	VF	XF	Unc
12	AH1359	—	.35	.75	1.25	2.00

PAISA (1/4 Anna)

COPPER, 24-25mm

Y#	Date	Year	Fine	VF	XF	Unc
9	AH1343	—	11.50	17.50	25.00	40.00

Y#	Date	Year	Fine	VF	XF	Unc
13	AH1359	—	.75	1.25	2.00	3.00

RUPEE

SILVER, 28mm, 10.70-11.40 gm

10	AH1343	—	175.00	250.00	325.00	400.00

Possibly a pattern issue.

MOHUR

GOLD, 22mm, 10.70-11.40 gm

11	AH1343	—	300.00	400.00	500.00	650.00

BAJRANGGARH

Jai Singh
AD 1797-1818

RUPEE

SILVER, 22-24mm, 10.70-11.60 gm
No symbols, thin flan.

C#	Date	Year	VG	Fine	VF	XF
6	—	13	11.50	13.50	16.50	20.00
	—	15	11.50	13.50	16.50	20.00
	—	16	11.50	13.50	16.50	20.00
	—	17	11.50	13.50	16.50	20.00
		Thick flan, 20mm				
6a	—	18	11.50	13.50	16.50	20.00
	—	20	11.50	13.50	16.50	20.00
	—	21	11.50	13.50	16.50	20.00

NAZARANA RUPEE

SILVER, 20mm
Octagonal

7	—	19	22.50	30.00	37.50	50.00

MOHUR

GOLD, 23.5mm, 10.70-11.40 gm.
Small lettering, no symbols.

C#	Date	Year	VG	Fine	VF	XF
12	—	16	225.00	250.00	285.00	325.00
		Octagonal				
13	ND	—	235.00	275.00	325.00	400.00

For later issues bearing lotus and bow and arrow symbols (issued by Sindhia) see Gwalior listings.

BANSWARA

RULERS
Lakshman Singh, AD 1862-1905
Shambu Singh AD 1905-1920's
NOTE: All coins are anonymous.

1/2 PAISA

COPPER, 18-19mm

Y#	Date	Year	Good	VG	Fine	VF
1	ND	—	2.50	3.75	5.00	7.00

3	ND	—	3.00	4.50	6.50	9.00

PAISA

COPPER

2	ND	—	1.50	3.00	4.50	6.50

Thick and thin flans.

		Tail of symbol turned right, obv. & rev.				
4	ND	—	1.50	3.00	4.00	5.50
		Tail of symbol turned left, obv. & rev.				
4.1	ND	—	1.50	3.00	4.00	5.50
		Tail left on obv., right on rev.				
4.2	ND	—	1.75	3.50	4.50	6.50
		Mule, obv. of Y#6, rev. of Y#7, tail left.				
4.3	ND	—	2.75	4.50	6.00	8.50

18-20mm, larger symbols

Y#	Date	Year	Good	VG	Fine	VF
6b	ND	—	3.00	4.50	6.50	9.00

1/8 RUPEE

SILVER, 10-11mm, 1.34-1.45 gm

Y#	Date	Year	VG	Fine	VF	XF
6	ND	—	11.50	15.00	18.50	25.00

1/4 RUPEE

SILVER, 13mm, 2.68-2.90 gm

7	ND	—	11.50	15.00	18.50	25.00

1/2 RUPEE

SILVER, 17mm, 5.35-5.80 gm

8	ND	—	12.50	16.50	20.00	26.50

RUPEE

SILVER, 18-23mm, 10.70-11.60 gm

9.1	ND (thick, dumpy, 18-20mm)		13.50	20.00	27.50	35.00
9.2	ND (thin, broad, 21-23mm)	—	15.00	18.50	25.00	

The authenticity of Y#6 and Y#9.2 has been questioned.

MOHUR

GOLD, 12 gm.
Similar to 1 Rupee, Y#9.1.

10	ND	—	225.00	250.00	285.00	325.00

BARODA

MINTMARKS

Ahmedabad Mint:

Ankus, Maratha mark.

Nagari letters denoting Baroda ruler:

गा 'Ga' - Anand Rao's Shah Alam II coins, Ahmedabad Mint (with two verticle stems).

'A' - Anand Rao's Shah Alam II coins, Petlad Mint.

मा 'Ma' - Anand Rao's Shah Alam II coins. Baroda Mint.

आा 'A' - Anand Rao's Muhammad Akbar II coins, Baroda Mint.

गा 'Ga' - Anand Rao's Muhammad Akbar II Coins, Ahmedabad Mint (with three verticle stems).

सा 'Sa' - Sayaji Rao II, Baroda Mint.

(श्री) ('Sri) S Ga' - Sayaji Rao II, Amreli Mint.

गा 'Ga' - Ganpat Rao, Baroda Mint.

श्री ग गा 'Sir G Ga' - Ganpat Rao, Amreli Mint.

खा 'Kha' - Khande Rao, Muhammad Akbar II coins, Baroda Mint.

ख· गा 'K HA GA' - Khande Rao, coins in own name, Baroda Mint.

श्री ख गा 'Sri Kh Ga' - Khande Rao, Amreli Mint.

मा गा 'MaGa' - Malhar Rao.

सा गा 'SaGa' - Sayaji Rao II, Baroda Mint.

सा गा 'SaGa' - Sayaji Rao II, Amreli Mint.

NOTE: The first two marks are found only on the coins of Ahmedabad Mint, and serve to identify it. The remaining 14 marks are used to indicate the ruler under whom the coin was struck; when no mint name is given after the ruler's name in the above list, that shows that the symbol was used at all his mints.

Note the variant forms of 'G' and 'Ga' used above.

RULERS

Govind Rao (first reign)
AH1182-85/AD1768-71
Sayaji Rao I
AH1185-92/AD1771-78
Fatah Singh
AH1192-1204/AD1778-89
Manaji Rao (regent)
AH1204-08/AD1789-93
Govind Rao (second reign)
AH1208-15/AD1793-1800

Anand Rao

AH 1215-35/AD 1800-19

In the name of Shah Alam II, AD 1800-1806

Years of Anand Rao

Petlad Mint

Nagari 'a'

PAISA

COPPER, 20mm

C#	Date	Year	Good	VG	Fine	VF
10	—	—	2.50	3.50	4.50	6.00

RUPEE

SILVER, 18mm, 10.70-11.60 gm

C#	Date	Year	VG	Fine	VF	XF
13	—	3	12.50	15.00	18.50	23.50
	—	4	12.50	15.00	18.50	23.50

Baroda Mint

Nagari 'Ma' and scimitar

1/2 RUPEE

SILVER, 15-16mm, 5.35-5.80 gm

C#	Date	Year	VG	Fine	VF	XF
14	—	4	7.00	9.00	11.50	15.00

RUPEE

SILVER, 19-20 mm, 10.70-11.60 gm

C#	Date	Year	VG	Fine	VF	XF
17	—	3	11.50	13.50	16.50	20.00
	—	4	11.50	13.50	16.50	20.00

Ahmedabad Mint

1/2 RUPEE

SILVER, 5.35-5.80 gm

C#	Date	Year	VG	Fine	VF	XF
18	—	—	8.00	10.00	13.50	16.50

Nagari 'GA' and ankus

RUPEE

SILVER, 23mm, 10.70-11.60 gm

C#	Date	Year	VG	Fine	VF	XF
19	—	4	11.50	13.50	16.50	20.00
	—	5	11.50	13.50	16.50	20.00

In the name of Muhammad Akbar II,

Years of Akbar (after 1221/1806)

Baroda Mint

Nagari 'A' and scimitar

1/2 PAISA

COPPER, 14mm

C#	Date	Year	Good	VG	Fine	VF
20	ND	14	2.00	3.00	4.00	5.00

PAISA

COPPER, 18-20mm

C#	Date	Year	Good	VG	Fine	VF
21	AH1226	6	1.25	2.50	3.50	5.00
	1227	7	1.25	2.50	3.50	5.00
	—	8	1.25	2.50	3.50	5.00
	1233	14	1.25	2.50	3.50	5.00
	1234	—	1.25	2.50	3.50	5.00

1/8 RUPEE

SILVER, 12mm, 1.34-1.45 gm

C#	Date	Year	VG	Fine	VF	XF
24	AH122x	—	3.50	4.50	6.00	8.00
	1234	—	4.00	6.00	8.00	11.00

1/4 RUPEE

SILVER, 2.68-2.90 gm

C#	Date	Year	VG	Fine	VF	XF
25	AH1228	—	4.00	6.00	8.50	12.00

1/2 RUPEE

SILVER, 17mm, 5.35-5.80 gm

C#	Date	Year	VG	Fine	VF	XF
26	AH1222	2	7.00	9.00	11.50	15.00
	1228	—	7.00	9.00	11.50	15.00
	1234	14	7.00	9.00	11.50	15.00

RUPEE

SILVER, 21-23mm, 10.70-11.60 gm

C#	Date	Year	VG	Fine	VF	XF
27	AH1222	2	11.50	13.50	16.50	20.00
	1224	4	11.50	13.50	16.50	20.00
	1225	5	11.50	13.50	16.50	20.00
	1226	6	11.50	13.50	16.50	20.00
	1227	7	11.50	13.50	16.50	20.00
	1228	8	11.50	13.50	16.50	20.00
	1229	9	11.50	13.50	16.50	20.00
	1232	12	11.50	13.50	16.50	20.00
	1233	13	11.50	13.50	16.50	20.00
	1234	14	11.50	13.50	16.50	20.00

Ahmedabad Mint

Nagari 'GA' and ankus

1/2 RUPEE

SILVER, 5.35-5.80 gm

C#	Date	Year	VG	Fine	VF	XF
A28	—	—	7.50	10.00	13.50	17.50

RUPEE

SILVER, 22-23mm

C#	Date	Year	VG	Fine	VF	XF
28	—	6	11.50	13.50	16.50	20.00
	AH1229	7	11.50	13.50	16.50	20.00
	1229	8	11.50	13.50	16.50	20.00
	1232	10	11.50	13.50	16.50	20.00
	1233	11	11.50	13.50	16.50	20.00

Sayaji Rao II

AH 1235-64/AD 1819-47

Baroda Mint

In the name of Muhammad Akbar II.

Years of Akbar II.

With Nagari 'SA' or 'SAGA' and other symbols as noted.

1/2 PAISA

COPPER, 14-15mm
Obv: Cross

C#	Date	Year	Good	VG	Fine	VF
31.2	ND	—	1.25	2.50	4.00	6.00
		Obv: Sun				
31.4	ND	—	1.25	2.50	4.00	6.00
		Obv: Shaded ball				
31.8	—	40	1.25	2.50	4.00	6.00

PAISA

All types have date on obverse, ruler's initial, symbol and regnal year on reverse.

COPPER, 18-24mm
Rev: No symbol

C#	Date	Year	Good	VG	Fine	VF
33.1	AH1236	16	1.25	2.00	3.00	4.50

Rev: Oblique cross

C#	Date	Year	Good	VG	Fine	VF
33.2	AH1240	20	1.25	2.25	3.50	5.00

Rev: Lotus

C#	Date	Year	Good	VG	Fine	VF
33.3	AH1243	23	1.25	2.25	3.50	5.00

Rev: Rayed sun

C#	Date	Year	Good	VG	Fine	VF
33.4	AH1247	27	1.25	2.25	3.50	5.00
		Rev: Flag				
33.5	AH12xx	28	1.25	2.25	3.50	5.00
	1249	29	1.25	2.25	3.50	5.00
	1250	—	1.25	2.25	3.50	5.00
	1253	—	1.25	2.25	3.50	5.00
		Rev: Upright cross				
33.6	AH1255	35	1.25	2.25	3.50	5.00

Rev: Five-petal flower

C#	Date	Year	Good	VG	Fine	VF
33.7	AH1255	—	1.25	2.25	3.50	5.00
	1256	36	1.25	2.25	3.50	5.00

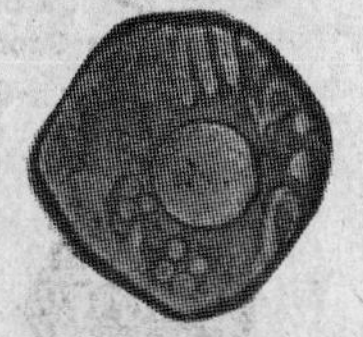

Rev: Shaded ball

C#	Date	Year	Good	VG	Fine	VF
33.8	AH1260	40	1.00	2.00	3.00	4.00
	—	41	1.00	2.00	3.00	4.00
	1263	43	1.00	2.00	3.00	4.00

1/8 RUPEE

SILVER, 11-14mm, 1.34-1.45 gm

C#	Date	Year	VG	Fine	VF	XF
35	—	26	3.00	4.50	6.00	7.50

1/4 RUPEE

SILVER, 14-15mm, 2.68-2.90 gm
Variety I

C#	Date	Year	VG	Fine	VF	XF
36.1	AH1238	18	5.00	7.00	10.00	13.50

Variety II

C#	Date	Year	VG	Fine	VF	XF
36.2	AH1249	29	5.00	7.00	10.00	13.00
	1250	29	5.00	7.00	10.00	13.00
	1257	37	5.00	7.00	10.00	13.00

1/2 RUPEE

SILVER, 16-17mm, 5.35-5.80 gm
Variety I

C#	Date	Year	VG	Fine	VF	XF
37.1	AH1239	19	7.00	8.50	10.00	13.00
	—	27	7.00	8.50	10.00	13.00

Variety II

C#	Date	Year	VG	Fine	VF	XF
37.2	AH125x	33	7.00	8.50	10.00	13.00
	—	35	7.00	8.50	10.00	13.00
	—	38	7.00	8.50	10.00	13.00
	1260	40	7.00	8.50	10.00	13.00

RUPEE

SILVER, 20-23mm, 10.70-11.60 gm
Variety I

C#	Date	Year	VG	Fine	VF	XF
38.1	AH1237	17	11.50	13.50	16.50	20.00
	1238	18	11.50	13.50	16.50	20.00
	1239	19	11.50	13.50	16.50	20.00
	1240	20	11.50	13.50	16.50	20.00
	1241	21	11.50	13.50	16.50	20.00
	1242	22	11.50	13.50	16.50	20.00

Variety II

C#	Date	Year	VG	Fine	VF	XF
38.2	AH1249	29	11.50	13.50	16.50	20.00
	1250	30	11.50	13.50	16.50	20.00
	1251	30	11.50	13.50	16.50	20.00
	1253	33	11.50	13.50	16.50	20.00
	1255	35	11.50	13.50	16.50	20.00
	1256	36	11.50	13.50	16.50	20.00
	1258	38	11.50	13.50	16.50	20.00
	1259	39	11.50	13.50	16.50	20.00
	1260	40	11.50	13.50	16.50	20.00

NOTE: The last 4 silver coins have two varieties each: (1) Sword in S of JULUS (to year 28) and (2) sword to right of JULUS (from year 29).

Ganpat Rao

AH 1264-73/AD 1847-56

Baroda Mint

In the name and with years of Muhammad Akbar II.

With Nagari 'GA' and scimitar.

1/2 PAISA

COPPER, 15mm
Shaded ball in center.

C#	Date	Year	Good	VG	Fine	VF
41	AH1264-1272	—	1.00	2.00	3.00	4.50

PAISA

COPPER, 18-21mm

C#	Date	Year	Good	VG	Fine	VF
42	AH1263	43	2.00	3.00	4.00	5.50
	1264	44	2.00	3.00	4.00	5.50
	1265	45	2.00	3.00	4.00	5.50
	1266	46	2.00	3.00	4.00	5.50
	1272	52	2.00	3.00	4.00	5.50

1/8 RUPEE

SILVER, 11mm, 1.34-1.45 gm

C#	Date	Year	VG	Fine	VF	XF
44	AH126x	—	2.50	3.50	4.50	6.00

1/4 RUPEE

SILVER, 13mm, 2.68-2.90 gm

C#	Date	Year	VG	Fine	VF	XF
45	AH126x	—	5.00	7.00	9.00	12.00

1/2 RUPEE

SILVER, 16-17mm, 5.35-5.80 gm

C#	Date	Year	VG	Fine	VF	XF
46	AH1267	—	6.00	8.00	10.00	12.50
	1271	—	6.00	8.00	10.00	12.50
	1272	—	6.00	8.00	10.00	12.50

RUPEE

SILVER, 19-20mm, 10.70-11.60 gm

C#	Date	Year	VG	Fine	VF	XF
47	AH1264	43	11.50	13.50	16.50	20.00
	1265	44	11.50	13.50	16.50	20.00
	—	45	11.50	13.50	16.50	20.00
	126x	46	11.50	13.50	16.50	20.00
	1268	47	11.50	13.50	16.50	20.00
	1271	50	11.50	13.50	16.50	20.00
	1272	51	11.50	13.50	16.50	20.00
	1272	52	11.50	13.50	16.50	20.00

Khande Rao

AH 1273-87/AD 1856-70

Baroda Mint

In the name of, and with years of Muhammad Akbar II.

With Nagari 'KHA' and scimitar.

1/2 PAISA

COPPER, 15mm
Rev: Pomegranate in center

Y#	Date	Year	Good	VG	Fine	VF
1	ND	—	1.25	2.00	3.00	4.00

PAISA

COPPER, 18-19mm
Rev: Pomegranate in center

Y#	Date	Year	Good	VG	Fine	VF
2	AH127x	52	1.50	2.50	3.50	5.00

1/4 RUPEE

SILVER, 13-14mm, 2.68-2.90 gm

Y#	Date	Year	VG	Fine	VF	XF
3	AH1273	—	5.00	7.00	9.00	12.00
	1278	—	5.00	7.00	9.00	12.00

1/2 RUPEE

SILVER, 16-17mm, 5.35-5.80 gm

Y#	Date	Year	VG	Fine	VF	XF
4	AH1267	—	6.50	8.00	10.00	13.50
	1275	—	6.50	8.00	10.00	13.50

RUPEE

SILVER, 21-22mm, 10.70-11.60 gm

Y#	Date	Year	VG	Fine	VF	XF
5	AH1274	53	11.50	13.50	16.50	20.00
	1275	—	11.50	13.50	16.50	20.00
	128x	—	11.50	13.50	16.50	20.00

In the name of the Commander of the Sovereign Band (a title of the Gaekwar, ruler of Baroda). No regnal year.

With Nagari 'KHA-GA' and scimitar.

1/2 PAISA

COPPER
Rev: Sword on center

Y#	Date	Year	Good	VG	Fine	VF
6	AH1275	—	2.00	3.00	4.00	5.50
	1276	—	2.00	3.00	4.00	5.50

Rev: Sword and hoof

Y#	Date	Year	Good	VG	Fine	VF
6a	AH128x	—	5.00	7.50	10.00	15.00

PAISA

COPPER, 16-18mm
Rev: Sword

Y#	Date	Year	Good	VG	Fine	VF
7	AH1274	—	2.00	3.00	4.00	5.50
	1275	—	1.25	2.25	3.25	4.00
	1276	—	1.25	2.25	3.25	4.00
	1277	—	2.00	3.00	4.00	5.50

Rev: Sword and hoof

Y#	Date	Year	Good	VG	Fine	VF
7a	AH1281	—	3.50	4.50	6.00	8.00
	1282	—	3.50	4.50	6.00	8.00
	1283	—	3.50	4.50	6.00	8.00
	1284	—	3.50	4.50	6.00	8.00
	1285	—	3.50	4.50	6.00	8.00

2 PAISA

COPPER, 21mm
Rev: Sword and hoof

Y#	Date	Year	Good	VG	Fine	VF
8	AH1281	—	2.50	4.00	5.50	7.50
	1285	—	2.50	4.00	5.50	7.50

1/8 RUPEE

SILVER, 10-12mm, 1.34-1.45 gm

Y#	Date	Year	VG	Fine	VF	XF
9	AH1282	—	3.50	5.50	7.50	10.00

1/4 RUPEE

SILVER, 13mm, 2.68-2.90 gm

Y#	Date	Year	VG	Fine	VF	XF
10	AH1274	—	4.50	6.50	9.00	12.00
	1286	—	4.50	6.50	9.00	12.00

1/2 RUPEE

SILVER, 15-17mm, 5.35-5.80 gm

Y#	Date	Year	VG	Fine	VF	XF
11	AH1276	—	6.50	8.00	10.00	12.50
	1278	—	6.50	8.00	10.00	12.50
	1280	—	6.50	8.00	10.00	12.50
	1282	—	6.50	8.00	10.00	12.50
	1285	—	6.50	8.00	10.00	12.50
	1286	—	6.50	8.00	10.00	12.50

Y#	Date	Year	VG	Fine	VF	XF
13	AH1287	—	60.00	90.00	120.00	160.00

RUPEE

SILVER, 20-21mm, 10.70-11.60 gm

Y#	Date	Year	VG	Fine	VF	XF
12	AH1274	—	11.50	13.50	16.50	20.00
	1275	—	11.50	13.50	16.50	20.00
	1276	—	11.50	13.50	16.50	20.00
	1278	—	11.50	13.50	16.50	20.00
	1280	—	11.50	13.50	16.50	20.00
	1281	—	11.50	13.50	16.50	20.00
	1282	—	11.50	13.50	16.50	20.00
	1283	—	11.50	13.50	16.50	20.00
	1284	—	11.50	13.50	16.50	20.00
	1286	—	11.50	13.50	16.50	20.00
	1287	—	11.50	13.50	16.50	20.00
	"87"	—	11.50	13.50	16.50	20.00

24mm

Y#	Date	Year	VG	Fine	VF	XF
14	AH1287	—	60.00	90.00	120.00	160.00

Malhar Rao

AH 1287-92/AD 1870-75

With Nagari 'MA GA' and scimitar.

1/2 PAISA

COPPER, 15mm

Y#	Date	Year	Good	VG	Fine	VF
15	AH1288	—	2.00	3.00	4.00	5.50
	1290	—	2.00	3.00	4.00	5.50

PAISA

COPPER, 17-18mm

Y#	Date	Year	Good	VG	Fine	VF
16	AH1288	—	1.25	2.50	3.50	5.00
	1289	—	1.25	2.50	3.50	5.00

Y#	Date	Year	Good	VG	Fine	VF
16	1290	—	1.25	2.50	3.50	5.00
	ND	—	1.25	2.50	3.50	5.00

2 PAISA

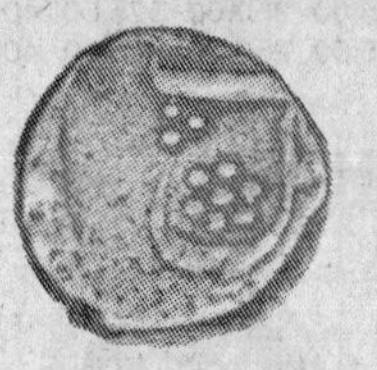

COPPER, 21-22mm

Y#	Date	Year	Good	VG	Fine	VF
17	AH1288	—	2.00	3.00	4.00	5.50
	1289	—	2.00	3.00	4.00	5.50

1/8 RUPEE

SILVER, 11mm, 1.34-1.45 gm

Y#	Date	Year	VG	Fine	VF	XF
18	AH129x	—	3.50	5.50	7.50	10.00

1/4 RUPEE

SILVER, 13mm, 2.68-2.90 gm

Y#	Date	Year	VG	Fine	VF	XF
19	AH1290	—	4.00	6.00	8.50	11.50

1/2 RUPEE

SILVER, 17mm, 5.35-5.80 gm

Y#	Date	Year	VG	Fine	VF	XF
20	AH1287	—	6.50	8.00	10.00	12.50
	1288	—	6.50	8.00	10.00	12.50
	1289	—	6.50	8.00	10.00	12.50
	1290	—	6.50	8.00	10.00	12.50

RUPEE

SILVER, 20-21mm, 10.70-11.60 gm

Y#	Date	Year	VG	Fine	VF	XF
21	AH1287	—	11.50	13.50	16.50	20.00
	1288	—	11.50	13.50	16.50	20.00
	1290	—	11.50	13.50	16.50	20.00
	—	122	12.50	15.00	18.50	22.50

2 RUPEES

SILVER, 32mm, 21.40-23.20 gm

Y#	Date	Year	VG	Fine	VF	XF
22	AH1288	—	—	—	Rare	—

Possibly unique. Recent counterfeits have been reported.

Sayaji Rao III

AH1292-1357/VS1932-1996/1875-1939AD

Baroda Mint

With Nagari 'SA GA' and scimitar.

1/2 PAISA

COPPER, about 15mm

Y#	Date	Year	Good	VG	Fine	VF
23	VS1937	(1880)	1.50	2.50	4.00	5.50
	1948	(1891)	1.50	2.50	4.00	5.50

PAISA

COPPER, 17-18mm, dump

Y#	Date	Year	Good	VG	Fine	VF
24	VS1937	(1880)	1.50	2.50	4.00	5.50
	1947	(1890)	1.50	2.50	4.00	5.50
	1948	(1891)	1.50	2.50	4.00	5.50

21mm, machine-punched planchets.

Y#	Date	Year	Good	VG	Fine	VF
24a	VS1949	(1892)	2.00	3.50	5.00	7.00

2 PAISA

COPPER, 22mm, dump

Y#	Date	Year	Good	VG	Fine	VF
25	VS1937	(1880)	3.50	5.00	6.50	8.50
	1947	(1890)	3.50	5.00	6.50	8.50
	1948	(1891)	3.50	5.00	6.50	8.50

24mm, machine-punched planchets.

Y#	Date	Year	Good	VG	Fine	VF
25a	VS1949	(1892)	3.75	5.50	7.50	10.00

1/8 RUPEE

SILVER, 10mm, 1.34-1.45 gm

Y#	Date	Year	VG	Fine	VF	XF
26	AH1294	—	3.50	5.00	6.50	8.00
	1295	—	3.50	5.00	6.50	8.00

1/4 RUPEE

SILVER, 13mm, 2.68-2.90 gm

Y#	Date	Year	VG	Fine	VF	XF
27	AH1299	—	4.00	6.00	8.00	11.00

1/2 RUPEE

SILVER, 15-16mm, 5.35-5.80 gm

Y#	Date	Year	VG	Fine	VF	XF
28	AH1293	—	6.50	8.00	10.00	13.00
	1294	—	6.50	8.00	10.00	13.00
	1297	—	6.50	8.00	10.00	13.00
	1298	—	6.50	8.00	10.00	13.00
	1299	—	6.50	8.00	10.00	13.00
	1300	—	6.50	8.00	10.00	13.00
	1301	—	6.50	8.00	10.00	13.00

RUPEE

SILVER, 20mm, 10.70-11.60 gm

Y#	Date	Year	VG	Fine	VF	XF
29	AH1292	—	11.50	13.50	16.50	20.00
	1293	—	11.50	13.50	16.50	20.00
	1294	—	11.50	13.50	16.50	20.00
	1298	—	11.50	13.50	16.50	20.00
	1299	—	11.50	13.50	16.50	20.00
	1300	—	11.50	13.50	16.50	20.00
	1301	—	11.50	13.50	16.50	20.00
	1302	—	11.50	13.50	16.50	20.00

MACHINE-STRUCK COINAGE

PIE

COPPER, 19mm

First obv: Annulets between letters

Y#	Date	Year	VG	Fine	VF	XF
30.1	VS1944	(1887)	.50	1.00	1.50	2.00

Second obv: No annulets

Thick planchet

Y#	Date	Year	VG	Fine	VF	XF
30.2	VS1944	(1887)	.75	1.50	2.00	2.50
	1945	(1888)	.35	.75	1.00	1.50
	1946	(1889)	.75	1.50	2.00	2.50
	1947	(1890)	.75	1.50	2.00	2.50

Thin planchet

Y#	Date	Year	VG	Fine	VF	XF
30.2a	VS1948	(1891)	.75	1.50	2.00	2.50
	1949	(1892)	.35	.75	1.00	1.50
	1950	(1893)	.35	.75	1.00	1.50

NOTE: Two varieties '5' in 1950 exist.

PAISA

COPPER, 24mm

First obv: Sarkar curved, long hoof.

Y#	Date	Year	VG	Fine	VF	XF
31.1	VS1940	(1883)	1.00	2.00	2.50	3.00
	1941	(1884)	1.00	2.00	2.50	3.00
	1942	(1885)	1.75	2.50	3.75	5.00

Second obv: Sarkar straight, short hoof.

Thick planchet

Y#	Date	Year	VG	Fine	VF	XF
31.2	VS1941	(1884)	.75	1.50	2.00	2.75
	1942	(1885)	.35	.75	1.25	1.75
	1943	(1886)	.35	.75	1.25	1.75
	1944	(1887)	.35	.75	1.25	1.75
	1945	(1888)	.50	1.00	1.50	2.00
	1946	(1889)	.50	1.00	1.50	2.00

Y#	Date	Year	VG	Fine	VF	XF
	1947	(1890)	.35	.75	1.25	1.75

Thin planchet, Obv: Smaller inner circle and scimitar.

Y#	Date	Year	VG	Fine	VF	XF
31.2a	VS1948	(1891)	.30	.60	1.00	1.50
	1949	(1892)	.30	.60	1.00	1.50
	1950	(1893)	.30	.60	1.00	1.50

2 PAISA

(= 1/2 Anna)

COPPER, 29.5mm

First obv: Sarkar curved, long hoof.

Y#	Date	Year	VG	Fine	VF	XF
32.1	VS1940	(1883)	2.00	3.50	5.00	6.50
	1941	(1884)	2.00	3.50	5.00	6.50

Second obv: Sarkar straight, short hoof.

Thick planchet

Y#	Date	Year	VG	Fine	VF	XF
32.2	VS1942	(1885)	1.00	2.00	3.00	4.50
	1943	(1886)	.75	1.50	2.25	3.00
	1944/3	(1887)	.75	1.50	2.25	3.00
	1944	(1887)	.75	1.50	2.25	3.00
	1945	(1888)	.75	1.50	2.25	3.00
	1946	(1889)	1.25	2.50	4.00	6.00
	1947	(1890)	.75	1.50	2.25	3.00

Thin planchet

Y#	Date	Year	VG	Fine	VF	XF
32.2a	VS1948	(1891)	.50	1.00	1.50	2.25
	1949/4	(1892)	.50	1.00	1.50	2.25
	1949/8	(1892)	.75	1.50	2.25	3.00
	1949	(1892)	.75	1.50	2.25	3.00
	1950	(1893)	.65	1.25	1.75	2.50

2 ANNAS

(= 1/8 Rupee)

SILVER, 16mm

Y#	Date	Year	Fine	VF	XF	Unc
33	VS1949	(1892)	5.50	8.50	13.50	20.00

14mm

Y#	Date	Year	Fine	VF	XF	Unc
33a	VS1951	(1894)	5.00	8.00	12.50	18.50
	1952	(1895)	5.00	8.00	12.50	18.50

4 ANNAS

(1/4 Rupee)

SILVER, 19mm

Y#	Date	Year	Fine	VF	XF	Unc
34	VS1949	(1892)	5.50	8.50	13.50	20.00

17-18mm

Y#	Date	Year	Fine	VF	XF	Unc
34a	VS1951	(1894)	5.00	7.50	11.50	17.50
	1952	(1895)	5.00	7.50	11.50	17.50

1/2 RUPEE

SILVER, 24mm

Y#	Date	Year	Fine	VF	XF	Unc
35	VS1948	(1891)	20.00	25.00	35.00	50.00
	1949	(1892)	20.00	25.00	35.00	50.00

22mm

Y#	Date	Year	Fine	VF	XF	Unc
35a	VS1951	(1894)	12.50	15.00	20.00	30.00
	1952	(1895)	12.50	15.00	20.00	30.00

RUPEE

SILVER, 30mm

Y#	Date	Year	Fine	VF	XF	Unc
36	VS1948	(1891)	12.50	15.00	18.50	27.50
	1949	(1892)	12.50	15.00	18.50	27.50

28mm

Y#	Date	Year	Fine	VF	XF	Unc
36a	VS1951	(1894)	11.50	13.50	16.50	23.50
	1952	(1895)	11.50	13.50	16.50	23.50
	1953	(1896)	11.50	13.50	16.50	23.50
	1954	(1897)	11.50	13.50	16.50	23.50
	1955	(1898)	11.50	13.50	16.50	23.50
	1956	(1899)	11.50	13.50	16.50	23.50

1/6 MOHUR

GOLD, 13mm

Y#	Date	Year	Fine	VF	XF	Unc
37	VS1943	(1886)	165.00	225.00	275.00	350.00
37	1959	(1902)	165.00	225.00	275.00	350.00

1/3 MOHUR

GOLD, 16mm

Y#	Date	Year	Fine	VF	XF	Unc
38	VS1942	(1886)	185.00	250.00	325.00	400.00
	1959	(1902)	185.00	250.00	325.00	400.00

MOHUR

GOLD, 20mm

Y#	Date	Year	Fine	VF	XF	Unc
39	VS1942	(1886)	250.00	325.00	425.00	500.00
	1959	(1902)	250.00	325.00	425.00	500.00

NOTE: Many varieties exist including muled obverses and reverses.

Pratap Singh

VS1995-2008/AD1939-1951

1/3 MOHUR

GOLD, 18mm

Y#	Date	Year	Fine	VF	XF	Unc
40	VS1995	(1939)	175.00	225.00	300.00	350.00

SILVER (OMS)

Y#	Date	Year			XF	Unc
40a	VS1995	(1939)	(Restrike)		13.50	20.00

MOHUR

GOLD, 21mm

Y#	Date	Year	Fine	VF	XF	Unc
41	VS1995	(1939)	220.00	250.00	300.00	350.00

SILVER (OMS)

Y#	Date	Year			XF	Unc
41a	VS1995	(1939)	(Restrike)		23.50	30.00

LOCAL ISSUES

Amreli Mint

Sayaji Rao II

AH1235-64/AD1819-47

PAISA

COPPER, 7-8 gm.

Obv: Scimitar (curved sword)

C#	Date	Year	Good	VG	Fine	VF
29.3	AH1253	—	2.50	4.50	7.00	10.00
	1257	—	2.50	4.50	7.00	10.00

Obv: Elephant, flag right.

C#	Date	Year	Good	VG	Fine	VF
29.1	AH1256	—	3.00	5.50	8.50	11.50

Obv: Elephant, flag left.

C#	Date	Year	Mintage	VG	Fine	VF
29.1a	AH1256	—	2.50	4.50	7.00	10.00

Obv: Kator (dagger)

C#	Date	Year	Good	VG	Fine	VF
29.2	AH1256	—	2.50	4.50	7.00	10.00
	Obv: Crescent					
29.4	AH1262	—	3.00	5.50	8.50	11.50

Obv: Legends only, large SA.

30	ND	—	1.50	2.50	4.00	5.50

Ganpat Rao

AH1264-73/AD1847-56

1/2 PAISA

COPPER, 14mm

A39	AH1266	—	2.50	4.50	6.00	8.50

PAISA

COPPER, 18-26mm

39	ND	—	3.00	5.50	7.00	9.00
	AH1266	—	3.00	5.50	7.00	9.00
	1272	—	3.00	5.50	7.00	9.00

Khande Rao

AH1273-87/AD1856-70

PAISA

COPPER, thin, 21-26mm, 7 gm.

Y#	Date	Year	Good	VG	Fine	VF
1	AH1277	—	2.00	3.50	5.50	8.00

Thick, 17-18mm, cruder types

Y#	Date	Year	Good	VG	Fine	VF
1a	ND	—	2.00	3.50	5.50	8.00

Sayaji Rao III

AH1292-1357/AD1875-1939

1/2 PAISA

COPPER, 16mm

2	AH1312	—	1.75	3.25	4.50	6.00

PAISA

COPPER, 19-25mm

3	AH1312(retrograde)	3.00	5.00	7.50	10.00
	1313(retrograde)	3.00	5.00	7.50	10.00

Rev: English S with serifs to left of SA GA and sword in S of JULUS.

3a	ND	—	6.00	10.00	14.00	18.50

These coins may have been issued by Sayaji Rao II with blundered dates.

BELA (BEYLAH)

(Beylah)

Mir Khan Jam

AD 1840-77

FALUS

COPPER, 17-20mm

C#	Date	Year	Good	VG	Fine	VF
5	AH1271	—	3.50	5.50	8.50	12.50
	1285	—	3.50	5.50	8.50	12.50

Mahmud Khan (of Kalat)

FALUS

COPPER, 20mm

10	AH1870	—	3.50	5.50	8.50	12.50
	1877	—	3.50	5.50	8.50	12.50

BHARATPUR

RULERS

Jawahir Singh, AD1763-1768
Ratan Singh, AD1768-1769
Kehri Singh, AD1769-1777
Ranjit Singh, AD1777-1805
Randhir Singh, AD1805-1823
Baldeo Singh, AD1823-1825
Balwant Singh, AD1826-1852
Jaswant Singh, AD1852-1893

In the name of Shah Alam II:

Akbarabad Mint

Agra or Akbarabad was controlled by the Bharatpur Jats from AH1175-1186/AD1761-1773. For earlier or later issues see India, Mughal Empire: Akbarabad Mint.

1/4 RUPEE

SILVER, 17mm, 2.68-2.90 gm.

KM#	Date	Year	VG	Fine	VF	XF
4	AH—	2	7.50	10.00	13.50	20.00

RUPEE

SILVER, 23mm, 10.70-11.60 gm.

6	AH1175	2	11.50	13.50	16.50	20.00
	1175	3	11.50	13.50	16.50	20.00
	1176	3	11.50	13.50	16.50	20.00
	1176	4	11.50	13.50	16.50	20.00
	1177	4	11.50	13.50	16.50	20.00
	1177	5	11.50	13.50	16.50	20.00
	1178	5	11.50	13.50	16.50	20.00
	1179	6	11.50	13.50	16.50	20.00
	1180	7	11.50	13.50	16.50	20.00
	1180	8	11.50	13.50	16.50	20.00
	1184	11	11.50	13.50	16.50	20.00

Bharatpur Mint

Mintname: Bharatpur or Braj Indrapur

Mintmarks  

PAISA

COPPER, 15-17mm

KM#	Date	Year	Good	VG	Fine	VF
11	AH—	4	1.25	2.50	4.00	5.50
	—	42	1.25	2.50	4.00	5.50
	—	45	1.25	2.50	4.00	5.50
	—	48	1.25	2.50	4.00	5.50
	1215	49	1.00	2.00	3.00	4.50
	—	50	1.25	2.50	4.00	5.50

RUPEE

SILVER, 22mm, 10.70-11.60 gm.

Mintname: Bharatpur

KM#	Date	Year	VG	Fine	VF	XF
16	AH1187	14	18.50	25.00	32.50	40.00

23.5mm
Mintname: Braj Indrapur

KM#	Date	Year	VG	Fine	VF	XF
26	AH12xx	29	11.50	13.50	16.50	20.00
	—	30	11.50	13.50	16.50	20.00
	12xx	31	11.50	13.50	16.50	20.00
	—	32	11.50	13.50	16.50	20.00
	1206	34	11.50	13.50	16.50	20.00
	1207	34	11.50	13.50	16.50	20.00
	12xx	35	11.50	13.50	16.50	20.00
	1209	37	11.50	13.50	16.50	20.00
	—	38	11.50	13.50	16.50	20.00
	—	39	11.50	13.50	16.50	20.00
	12xx	40	11.50	13.50	16.50	20.00
	1214	42	11.50	13.50	16.50	20.00
	1215	43	11.50	13.50	16.50	20.00
	1216	44	11.50	13.50	16.50	20.00
	1217	45	11.50	13.50	16.50	20.00
	1218	46	11.50	13.50	16.50	20.00
	1219	47	11.50	13.50	16.50	20.00

Dig Mint

Mintname: Maha Indrapur or (pseudo) Dar-ul-khilafat Shahjahanabad or (pseudo) Dar-ul-khilafat Najibabad

First Series: Type One, no mintmarks

PAISA

COPPER, 23mm
Mintname: Maha Indrapur

KM#	Date	Year	Good	VG	Fine	VF
31	AH12xx	35	7.00	10.00	13.50	18.50

RUPEE

SILVER, 22mm, 10.70-11.60 gm.
Mintname: Maha Indrapur

KM#	Date	Year	VG	Fine	VF	XF
36	AH117x	3	11.50	13.50	16.50	20.00
	1176	4	11.50	13.50	16.50	20.00
	1177	4	11.50	13.50	16.50	20.00
	—	5	11.50	13.50	16.50	20.00
	—	6	11.50	13.50	16.50	20.00
	1181	8	11.50	13.50	16.50	20.00

MOHUR

GOLD, 20mm, 10.70-11.40 gm.
Mintname: Maha Indrapur

KM#	Date	Year	VG	Fine	VF	XF
40	AH1175	2	220.00	240.00	265.00	300.00

First Series: Type Two

Mintmarks: III स
(Sa, - sanh, "year")

RUPEE

SILVER, 22.5mm, 10.70-11.60 gm.
Mintname: Maha Indrapur

KM#	Date	Year	VG	Fine	VF	XF
46	AH1182	9	12.50	14.50	18.50	23.50
	1183	10	12.50	14.50	18.50	23.50

MOHUR

GOLD, 22mm, 10.70-11.40 gm.
Mintname: Maha Indrapur

KM#	Date	Year	VG	Fine	VF	XF
50	AH118x	10	220.00	240.00	265.00	300.00

First Series: Type Three

Mintmark: 

RUPEE

SILVER, 22mm, 10.70-11.60 gm.
Mintname: Maha Indrapur

KM#	Date	Year	VG	Fine	VF	XF
56	AH1185	14	11.50	13.50	16.50	20.00
	1186	14	11.50	13.50	16.50	20.00
	1187	15	11.50	13.50	16.50	20.00
	118x	16	11.50	13.50	16.50	20.00

First Series: Type Four

Mintmarks: 

23mm
Mintname: Maha Indrapur

KM#	Date	Year	VG	Fine	VF	XF
66	AH1206	34	11.50	13.50	16.50	20.00
	12xx	40	11.50	13.50	16.50	20.00
	121x	41	11.50	13.50	16.50	20.00
	121x	42	11.50	13.50	16.50	20.00
	121x	46	11.50	13.50	16.50	20.00

Second Series:

Mintmarks * ·|·

21mm
Mintname: Dar-ul-khilafat Shahjahanabad
Obv: Umbrella mintmark.

KM#	Date	Year	VG	Fine	VF	XF
76.1	AH1200	29	20.00	25.00	32.50	40.00

20mm
Mintname: Dar-ul-khilafat Najibabad

KM#	Date	Year	VG	Fine	VF	XF
76.2	AH1210	38	20.00	25.00	32.50	40.00

21mm
Mintname: Maha Indrapur

KM#	Date	Year	VG	Fine	VF	XF
86	AH1206	34	13.50	17.50	23.50	30.00
	121x	46	13.50	17.50	23.50	30.00

Uncertain Mint

Possibly the fortress of Ver or Wair

Mintmarks: 
(Arabic 'wa' - ver?)

PAISA

COPPER, 20mm
Mintname unclear.

KM#	Date	Year	Good	VG	Fine	VF
91	AH—	27	4.00	6.50	10.00	15.00

RUPEE

SILVER, 20mm, 10.70-11.60 gm.
Possibly Maha Indrapur Mint

KM#	Date	Year	VG	Fine	VF	XF
96	AH12xx	46	13.50	17.50	22.50	30.00

In the name of Muhammad Akbar II (1806-37)

Bharatpur Mint

Mintname: Braj Indrapur

Mintmarks:  

PAISA

COPPER

KM#	Date	Year	Good	VG	Fine	VF
101	AH1279	49	2.50	4.00	6.50	10.00

NOTE: This date is posthumous.

1/4 RUPEE

SILVER, 15mm, 2.68-2.90 gm.

KM#	Date	Year	VG	Fine	VF	XF
104	AH—	—	6.00	8.00	11.00	15.00

1/2 RUPEE

SILVER, 16mm, 5.35-5.80 gm.

KM#	Date	Year	VG	Fine	VF	XF
105	AH—	22	6.50	8.50	11.50	16.50
	12xx	34	6.50	8.50	11.50	16.50

RUPEE

SILVER, 21mm, 10.70-11.60 gm.
Narrow flan. Rev: Tiger knife.

KM#	Date	Year	VG	Fine	VF	XF
106.1	AH1222	2	11.50	13.50	16.50	20.00
	1225	5	11.50	13.50	16.50	20.00
	1226	6	11.50	13.50	16.50	20.00
	1227	7	11.50	13.50	16.50	20.00
	1228	8	11.50	13.50	16.50	20.00
	122x	9	11.50	13.50	16.50	21.50
	1230	10	11.50	13.50	16.50	20.00
	1231	11	11.50	13.50	16.50	20.00
	1232	12	11.50	13.50	16.50	20.00
	12xx	13	11.50	13.50	16.50	21.50
	1234	14	11.50	13.50	16.50	20.00
	1238	18	11.50	13.50	16.50	20.00
	1239	19	11.50	13.50	16.50	21.50
	1243	22	11.50	13.50	16.50	21.50
	1244	23	11.50	13.50	16.50	21.50
	124x	24	11.50	13.50	16.50	21.50
	124x	25	11.50	13.50	16.50	21.50
	12xx	26	11.50	13.50	16.50	21.50
	1247	27	11.50	13.50	16.50	20.00
	1248	28	11.50	13.50	16.50	20.00
	1249	29	11.50	13.50	16.50	20.00
	12xx	30	11.50	13.50	16.50	21.50
	1251	31	11.50	13.50	16.50	20.00
	1252	32	11.50	13.50	16.50	20.00
	1253	34	11.50	13.50	16.50	21.50
	12xx	36	11.50	13.50	16.50	21.50
	125x	38	11.50	13.50	16.50	21.50
	1270	40	11.50	13.50	16.50	21.50
	—	46	11.50	13.50	16.50	21.50
	—	48	11.50	13.50	16.50	21.50

NOTE: Regnal years 34-48 (AH1253-1278) were posthumous, being struck during the reign of the Mughal emperor Bahadur Shah Zafar.

Wide flan

KM#	Date	Year	VG	Fine	VF	XF
106.2	AH1233	13	11.50	13.50	16.50	21.50
	1234	14	11.50	13.50	16.50	23.50
	1235	15	11.50	13.50	16.50	21.50
	1236	16	11.50	13.50	16.50	21.50
	1237	17	11.50	13.50	16.50	21.50
	1238	18	11.50	13.50	16.50	21.50

NAZARANA RUPEE

SILVER, 31mm

KM#	Date	Year	VG	Fine	VF	XF
107	AH1235	15	40.00	55.00	75.00	100.00

MOHUR

GOLD, 20mm, 10.70-11.40 gm.

KM#	Date	Year	VG	Fine	VF	XF
110	—	1	220.00	240.00	265.00	300.00

Dig Mint

Mintname: Maha Indrapur

First Series:

Mintmarks

RUPEE

SILVER, 21mm, 10.70-11.60 gm.
Narrow flan

KM#	Date	Year	VG	Fine	VF	XF
116.1	AH1222	3	11.50	13.50	16.50	21.50
	12xx	5	11.50	13.50	16.50	20.00
	12xx	6	11.50	13.50	16.50	21.50
	12xx	7	11.50	13.50	16.50	21.50
	122x	8	11.50	13.50	16.50	20.00
	1229	9	11.50	13.50	16.50	21.50
	122x	10	11.50	13.50	16.50	20.00
	—	11	11.50	13.50	16.50	20.00
	1233	13	11.50	13.50	16.50	20.00
	12xx	21	11.50	13.50	16.50	20.00
	1243	22	11.50	13.50	16.50	20.00
	12xx	23	11.50	13.50	16.50	20.00
	—	24	11.50	13.50	16.50	20.00
	124x	25	11.50	13.50	16.50	20.00
	124x	26	11.50	13.50	16.50	20.00
	12xx	27	11.50	13.50	16.50	21.50
	1248	28	11.50	13.50	16.50	21.50
	1249	29	11.50	13.50	16.50	20.00
	1262	48	11.50	13.50	16.50	21.50

NOTE: The issue of regnal year 48 is posthumous.

25.5mm, wide flan.

KM#	Date	Year	VG	Fine	VF	XF
116.2	AH1234	14	25.00	32.50	40.00	50.00
	1235	15	25.00	32.50	40.00	50.00
	1238	16	25.00	32.50	40.00	50.00

Second Series:

Mintmarks

21mm, narrow flan.

KM#	Date	Year	VG	Fine	VF	XF
126.1	AH12xx	7	11.50	13.50	16.50	23.50
	1229	9	11.50	13.50	16.50	21.50
	123x	11	11.50	13.50	16.50	21.50
	1232	12	11.50	13.50	16.50	20.00
	123x	13	11.50	13.50	16.50	21.50
	1237	18	11.50	13.50	16.50	21.50
	12xx	19	11.50	13.50	16.50	23.50
	12xx	24	11.50	13.50	16.50	21.50
	—	26	11.50	13.50	16.50	23.50
	12xx	27	11.50	13.50	16.50	21.50
	12xx	28	11.50	13.50	16.50	20.00
	12xx	29	11.50	13.50	16.50	21.50
	12xx	31	11.50	13.50	16.50	23.50
	—	32	11.50	13.50	16.50	23.50
	—	42	11.50	13.50	16.50	23.50

NOTE: The issue of regnal year 42 is posthumous.

25.5mm, wide flan.

KM#	Date	Year	VG	Fine	VF	XF
126.2	AH1234	14	20.00	26.50	33.50	42.50
	12xx	15	20.00	26.50	33.50	42.50
	123x	16	20.00	26.50	33.50	42.50
	—	17	18.50	25.00	31.50	40.00

Uncertain Mint

Possibly Ver (Wair)

Mintmarks: 

('wa')

RUPEE

SILVER, 21mm

KM#	Date	Year	VG	Fine	VF	XF
136	AH12xx	3	11.50	13.50	16.50	21.50
	12xx	5	11.50	13.50	16.50	23.50
	12xx	6	11.50	13.50	16.50	20.00
	122x	7	11.50	13.50	16.50	20.00
	12xx	8	11.50	13.50	16.50	20.00
	12xx	9	11.50	13.50	16.50	21.50
	123x	11	11.50	13.50	16.50	23.50
	123x	12	11.50	13.50	16.50	23.50
	—	19	11.50	13.50	16.50	23.50
	124x	21	11.50	13.50	16.50	21.50
	—	23	11.50	13.50	16.50	23.50
	124x	25	11.50	13.50	16.50	20.00
	12xx	26	11.50	13.50	16.50	21.50
	124x	28	11.50	13.50	16.50	20.00
	—	31	11.50	13.50	16.50	21.50
	1252	32	11.50	13.50	16.50	20.00

In the name of Bahadur Shah II
(1837-57)

Bharatpur Mint

Mintname: Braj Indrapur

Mintmarks:  

RUPEE

SILVER, 20mm, 10.70-11.60 gm.

KM#	Date	Year	VG	Fine	VF	XF
146	AH129x/vs1912					
		18	15.00	20.00	26.50	33.50
	AH1293/VS1913					
		19	15.00	20.00	26.50	33.50
	AH -/VS1914					
		20	15.00	20.00	26.50	33.50

In the names of Queen Victoria and Jaswant Singh:

Bharatpur Mint

Mintnames: Bharatpur and Braj Indrapur

Mintmarks:  

RUPEE

SILVER, 21-24mm, 10.70-11.60 gm.

KM#	Date	Year	VG	Fine	VF	XF
156	VS1910	AD1858	27.50	35.00	50.00	70.00

With titles of Queen Victoria only

25mm

KM#	Date	Year	VG	Fine	VF	XF
166	VS1914	(1858)	32.50	42.50	55.00	75.00
	1917	(1861)	32.50	42.50	55.00	75.00

Years after 1914/1858 on narrower flans.

MOHUR

GOLD, 21mm, 10.70-11.40 gm.

KM#	Date	Year	VG	Fine	VF	XF
170	VS1915	(1858)	250.00	300.00	350.00	425.00
	1919	(1862)	250.00	300.00	350.00	425.00

NOTE: For similar coins with dagger at left and sword at right of Queen's bust, see Bindraban State.

Dig Mint

Mintnames: Dig and Maha Indrapur

Mintmarks:

RUPEE

SILVER, 20mm, 10.70-11.60 gm.

KM#	Date	Year	VG	Fine	VF	XF
176	VS1910	(1858)	37.50	50.00	65.00	80.00

BHAUNAGAR

Anonymous types, bearing the distinguishing Nagari legend BAHADUR in addition to the Mughal legends. Monetary system as Kutch.

In the name of Shah Jahan III

1/4 TRAMBIYO

COPPER

C#	Date	Year	Good	VG	Fine	VF
13	ND	—	1.75	3.00	4.00	5.50

TRAMBIYO

COPPER, 13-16mm

C#	Date	Year	Good	VG	Fine	VF
14	ND	—	2.50	3.75	5.00	6.50

DOKDO

COPPER, 16-20mm
Rev: Without SRI

C#	Date	Year	Good	VG	Fine	VF
15	ND	—	2.50	3.75	5.00	6.50

NOTE: Varieties occur with sword curved up and down.

Rev: Nagari 'SRI' added

C#	Date	Year	Good	VG	Fine	VF
15a	ND	—	2.50	3.75	5.00	6.50

(Sri may be in relief or incuse, right-side-up or inverted)

Rev: 1825 incuse in panel

C#	Date	Year	Good	VG	Fine	VF
15b	1825	—	3.50	5.50	7.50	9.00

Actual date of striking unknown

DHINGLO

COPPER, 20-22mm

C#	Date	Year	Good	VG	Fine	VF
20	ND	—	2.50	4.00	5.50	7.50

In the name of Shah Alam II

DOKDO

COPPER

C#	Date	Year	Good	VG	Fine	VF
25	ND	—	2.50	4.00	5.50	7.50

In the name of Muhammad Akbar II

DHINGLO

COPPER, 22-23mm

C#	Date	Year	Good	VG	Fine	VF
30	ND	—	2.75	4.50	6.00	8.00

Anonymous coinage (modern):

DOKDA

COPPER, 18mm

KM#	Date	Year	Good	VG	Fine	VF
1	SE2004	(1926)	3.00	5.00	8.00	12.50

BHOPAL

RULERS

Kudsia Begam
AH 1235-53/AD 1819-1837
Jahangir Muhammad Khan
AH 1253-61/AD 1837-44
Sikandar Begam
AH 1261-1285/AD 1844-1868
Shah Jahan Begam
AH 1285-1319/AD 1868-1901

In the name of Shah Alam II:

RUPEE

SILVER, 18-22mm, 10.70-11.60 gm

C#	Date	Year	VG	Fine	VF	XF
12	AH—	1	11.50	13.50	16.50	20.00
	—	3	11.50	13.50	16.50	20.00
	1191	19	11.50	13.50	16.50	20.00
	1192	20	11.50	13.50	16.50	20.00
	—	21	11.50	13.50	16.50	20.00
	—	24	11.50	13.50	16.50	20.00
	1198	25	11.50	13.50	16.50	20.00
	1199	26	11.50	13.50	16.50	20.00
	1200	28	11.50	13.50	16.50	20.00
	1201	29	11.50	13.50	16.50	20.00
	1201	31	11.50	13.50	16.50	20.00
	1202	30	11.50	13.50	16.50	20.00
	1203	30	11.50	13.50	16.50	20.00
	1208	30	11.50	13.50	16.50	20.00
	120x	32	11.50	13.50	16.50	20.00
	—	33	11.50	13.50	16.50	20.00
	1206	34	11.50	13.50	16.50	20.00
	—	35	11.50	13.50	16.50	20.00
	1208	36	11.50	13.50	16.50	20.00
	1208	37	11.50	13.50	16.50	20.00
	1215	42	11.50	13.50	16.50	20.00

In the name of Muhammad Akbar II

1/8 RUPEE

SILVER, 12mm, 1.34-1.45 gm

C#	Date	Year	VG	Fine	VF	XF
24	—	16	3.50	4.50	6.00	8.00
	—	29	3.50	4.50	6.00	8.00

1/4 RUPEE

SILVER, 13mm, 2.68-2.90 gm

C#	Date	Year	VG	Fine	VF	XF
25	—	16	3.50	4.50	6.00	8.00
	—	29	3.50	4.50	6.00	8.00

1/2 RUPEE

SILVER, 15mm, 5.35-5.80 gm

C#	Date	Year	VG	Fine	VF	XF
26	—	16	6.50	8.50	11.00	14.00
	—	29	6.50	8.50	11.00	14.00

RUPEE

SILVER, 18-20mm, 10.70-11.60 gm

C#	Date	Year	VG	Fine	VF	XF
27	—	1	11.50	13.50	16.50	20.00
	—	4	11.50	13.50	16.50	20.00
	—	5	11.50	13.50	16.50	20.00
	—	7	11.50	13.50	16.50	20.00
	—	8	11.50	13.50	16.50	20.00
	—	11	11.50	13.50	16.50	20.00
	—	13	11.50	13.50	16.50	20.00
	—	14	11.50	13.50	16.50	20.00
	—	15	11.50	13.50	16.50	20.00
	—	16	11.50	13.50	16.50	20.00
	—	17	11.50	13.50	16.50	20.00
	—	18	11.50	13.50	16.50	20.00
	—	22	11.50	13.50	16.50	20.00
	—	25	11.50	13.50	16.50	20.00
	—	26	11.50	13.50	16.50	20.00
	—	30	11.50	13.50	16.50	20.00
	—	32	11.50	13.50	16.50	20.00
	—	33	11.50	13.50	16.50	20.00
	—	34	11.50	13.50	16.50	20.00

Anonymous issues:

PAISA

COPPER, 21-22mm
Obv: BHOPAL. Rev: Year in circle.

C#	Date	Year	Good	VG	Fine	VF
20	—	25	1.50	2.50	4.00	5.50
	—	29	1.50	2.50	4.00	5.50

Rev: Whisk

C#	Date	Year	Good	VG	Fine	VF
21	—	28	2.50	3.50	5.00	6.50

UNIFACE PAISAS

COPPER
Bhopal in circular depressed area.

C#	Date	Year	Good	VG	Fine	VF
20a	ND	—	1.75	2.75	4.00	6.00

SIKKA BHOPAL and date

C#	Date	Year	Good	VG	Fine	VF
21a	AH1255	—	2.50	3.50	5.00	7.00

Fly whisk and sword

C#	Date	Year	Good	VG	Fine	VF
21b	—	13	1.50	2.50	4.00	6.00
	ND	—	1.50	2.50	4.00	6.00

'Fateh' and sword

C#	Date	Year	Good	VG	Fine	VF
21c		8	1.50	2.50	4.00	6.00

Persian 'Jim' and year

C#	Date	Year	Good	VG	Fine	VF
21d		5	1.50	2.50	4.00	6.00
		10	1.50	2.50	4.00	6.00
		12	1.50	2.50	4.00	6.00
		47	1.75	2.75	4.50	6.50

First Series

Denomination on coin date on obverse and denomination alone on reverse.

1/4 ANNA (Paisa)

COPPER, 18-19mm

Y#	Date	Year	Good	VG	Fine	VF
1	AH1266	—	1.00	1.75	2.50	3.50
	1269	—	1.00	1.75	2.50	3.50
	1273	—	1.00	1.75	2.50	3.50
	1279	—	1.00	1.75	2.50	3.50

1/2 ANNA

COPPER, 20-21mm

Y#	Date	Year	Good	VG	Fine	VF
2	AH1276	—	1.50	2.50	3.50	5.00
	1278	—	1.50	2.50	3.50	5.00

ANNA

COPPER, 27mm

Y#	Date	Year	Good	VG	Fine	VF
3	AH1276	—	2.25	4.00	6.00	8.50

Second Series

Date and denomination on reverse.

1/4 ANNA

COPPER, 18-21mm

Y#	Date	Year	Good	VG	Fine	VF
4	AH1285	—	.75	1.25	2.00	3.00

Y#	Date	Year	Good	VG	Fine	VF
4.1	AH1286	—	.65	1.25	1.75	2.50
	1287	—	.65	1.25	1.75	2.50
	1288	—	.65	1.25	1.75	2.50
	1289	—	.65	1.25	1.75	2.50
	1292	—	.65	1.25	1.75	2.50
	1293	—	.65	1.25	1.75	2.50
	1299	—	.75	1.25	2.00	3.00

Two varieties of 1285 and differences in arrangement of most dates.

1/2 ANNA

COPPER, 21-26mm

Y#	Date	Year	Good	VG	Fine	VF
5	AH1286	—	1.00	1.75	2.50	3.50
	1289	—	1.25	2.00	3.00	4.50
	1300	—	1.00	1.75	2.50	3.50

ANNA

COPPER, 27-30mm

Y#	Date	Year	Good	VG	Fine	VF
6	AH1286	—	2.50	4.00	6.00	8.50
	1289	—	2.50	4.00	6.00	8.50
	1300	—	2.50	4.00	6.00	8.50

First Silver Series

ZARB above BHOPAL.

NOTE: AH dates and regnal years inconsistently paired.

1/8 RUPEE

SILVER, 11-13mm, 1.34-1.45 gm

Y#	Date	Year	VG	Fine	VF	XF
7	AH1275	—	2.00	3.00	4.50	6.50
	1288	7	2.00	3.00	4.50	6.50
	1291	8	2.00	3.00	4.50	6.50

1/4 RUPEE

SILVER, 13-16mm, 2.68-2.90 gm

Y#	Date	Year	VG	Fine	VF	XF
8	AH1275	—	3.50	4.50	6.00	8.00
	1282	—	3.50	4.50	6.00	8.00
	1288	8	3.50	4.50	6.00	8.00

1/2 RUPEE

SILVER, 16-18mm, 5.35-5.80 gm

Y#	Date	Year	VG	Fine	VF	XF
9	AH1275	—	6.50	8.00	10.00	13.00
	1278	—	6.50	8.00	10.00	13.00
	1280	—	6.50	8.00	10.00	13.00
	1281	—	6.50	8.00	10.00	13.00
	1282	2	6.50	8.00	10.00	13.00
	1283	8	6.50	8.00	10.00	13.00
	1288	7	6.50	8.00	10.00	13.00
	1288	8	6.50	8.00	10.00	13.00
	1291	8	6.50	8.00	10.00	13.00
	1292	—	6.50	8.00	10.00	13.00

RUPEE

SILVER, 18-20mm, 10.70-11.60 gm

Y#	Date	Year	VG	Fine	VF	XF
10	AH1271	—	11.50	13.50	16.50	20.00
	1271	5	11.50	13.50	16.50	20.00
	1272	—	11.50	13.50	16.50	20.00
	1275	—	11.50	13.50	16.50	20.00
	1277	—	11.50	13.50	16.50	20.00
	1278	2	11.50	13.50	16.50	20.00
	1279	3	11.50	13.50	16.50	20.00
	1279	4	11.50	13.50	16.50	20.00
	1279	5	11.50	13.50	16.50	20.00
	1280	5	11.50	13.50	16.50	20.00
	1281	8	11.50	13.50	16.50	20.00
	1282	2	11.50	13.50	16.50	20.00
	1282	6	11.50	13.50	16.50	20.00
	1283	7	11.50	13.50	16.50	20.00
	1283	8	11.50	13.50	16.50	20.00
	1285	5	11.50	13.50	16.50	20.00
	1285	8	11.50	13.50	16.50	20.00
	1288	7	11.50	13.50	16.50	20.00
	1292	—	11.50	13.50	16.50	20.00
	1293	—	11.50	13.50	16.50	20.00

Second Silver Series

ZARB below BHOPAL. Finer style.

NOTE: Regnal years and AH dates inconsistently paired.

1/8 RUPEE

SILVER, 11mm, 1.34-1.45 gm

Y#	Date	Year	VG	Fine	VF	XF
11	AH1294	9	3.00	4.50	6.00	8.00
	1303	15	3.00	4.50	6.00	8.00
	1306	17	3.00	4.50	6.00	8.00

1/4 RUPEE

SILVER, 13mm, 2.68-2.90 gm

Y#	Date	Year	VG	Fine	VF	XF
12	AH1293	8	4.00	5.50	7.50	10.00
	1294	9	4.00	5.50	7.50	10.00
	1297	12	4.00	5.50	7.50	10.00
	1303	15	4.00	5.50	7.50	10.00
	1305	16	4.00	5.50	7.50	10.00

1/2 RUPEE

SILVER, 16mm, 5.35-5.80 gm

Y#	Date	Year	VG	Fine	VF	XF
13	AH1294	9	6.50	7.50	9.00	12.00
	130(2)	14	6.50	7.50	9.00	12.00
	1306	17	6.50	7.50	9.00	12.00

RUPEE

SILVER, 19mm, 10.70-11.60 gm

Y#	Date	Year	VG	Fine	VF	XF
14	AH1293	8	11.50	13.50	16.50	20.00
	1294	9	11.50	13.50	16.50	20.00
	1295	10	11.50	13.50	16.50	20.00
	1295	11	11.50	13.50	16.50	20.00
	1296	—	11.50	13.50	16.50	20.00
	1297	12	11.50	13.50	16.50	20.00
	1298	9	11.50	13.50	16.50	20.00

Y#	Date	Year	VG	Fine	VF	XF
14	1298	10	11.50	13.50	16.50	20.00
	1302	14	11.50	13.50	16.50	20.00
	1304	15	11.50	13.50	16.50	20.00
	1305	16	11.50	13.50	16.50	20.00
	1306	17	11.50	13.50	16.50	20.00

In the name of Shah Jahan Begam:

PIE (or 1/2 Paisa)

COPPER, 16mm

Y#	Date	Year	Good	VG	Fine	VF
15	AH1305	—	1.50	2.25	3.25	4.50

1/4 ANNA

COPPER, 19-20mm

Y#	Date	Year	Good	VG	Fine	VF
16	AH1303	—	.50	1.00	1.50	2.25
	1305	—	.50	1.00	1.50	2.25
	1306	—	.50	1.00	1.50	2.25

1/2 ANNA

COPPER, 22-25mm

Y#	Date	Year	Good	VG	Fine	VF
17	AH1302	—	.75	1.50	2.50	4.00
	1303	—	.75	1.50	2.50	4.00
	1304	—	.75	1.50	2.50	4.00
	1306	—	.75	1.50	2.50	4.00
	1309	—	Reported, not confirmed			

ANNA

COPPER, 27-30mm

Y#	Date	Year	Good	VG	Fine	VF
18	AH1302	—	3.00	5.00	7.50	10.00
	1303	—	3.00	5.00	7.50	10.00
	1304	—	3.00	5.00	7.50	10.00
	1306	—	3.00	5.00	7.50	10.00

29mm
Struck from 1/2 Anna dies

Y#	Date	Year	Good	VG	Fine	VF
18a	—	—	3.00	5.00	7.00	10.00

FEUDATORY ISSUE

Narsinggarh

PAISA

COPPER, square, 14x14mm

Y#	Date	Year	Good	VG	Fine	VF
91	ND	—	3.00	5.00	7.00	10.00

BIJAWAR

RULERS

Lakshman Singh, AD 1833-1847
Bhau Pratap Singh, AD 1847-1900

In the Name of Shah Alam II

RUPEE

SILVER, 18mm, 10.70-11.60 gm.

KM#	Date	Year	VG	Fine	VF	XF
15	ND	—	11.50	13.50	16.50	20.00

BIKANIR

MINTMARKS:

1. Gaj Singh, AD 1746-1787 

2. (")

3. Surat Singh, 1787-1828 

4. (") 

5. (")

6. (2 vars.) Ratan Singh, 1828-1851 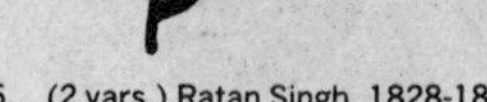 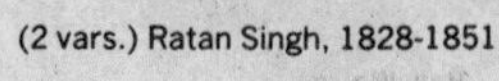 

7. Sardar Singh, 1851-1872 

8. Dungar Singh, 1872-1887 

9. Ganga Singh, 1887-1943 

NOTE: The above symbols normally occur in groups on the obverse or reverse of the coins; the various combinations are shown for each series.

Rupees and their fractions were probably struck in every year, but only a small representation of regnal years is listed; unlisted years are probably no rarer than the listed ones, and are worth no premium.

Gaj Singh

AD1746-1787

In the name of Alamgir II:

PAISA

COPPER

C#	Date	Year	Good	VG	Fine	VF
5	—	36	1.50	2.50	4.00	6.00

RUPEE

SILVER, 18-21mm, 10.70-11.60 gm

C#	Date	Year	VG	Fine	VF	XF
10	—	1	11.50	13.50	16.50	20.00
	—	37	11.50	13.50	16.50	20.00

NAZARANA RUPEE

SILVER, 26mm, 10.70-11.60 gm

C#	Date	Year	VG	Fine	VF	XF
10a	—	2	15.00	20.00	26.50	35.00
		6	15.00	20.00	26.50	35.00

In the name of Shah Alam II:

NAZARANA RUPEE

SILVER, 10.70-11.60 gm

C#	Date	VG	Fine	VF	XF
11	AH114(error)	20.00	30.00	40.00	55.00

Surat Singh

AD 1787-1828

In the name of Alamgir II:

1/2 PAISA

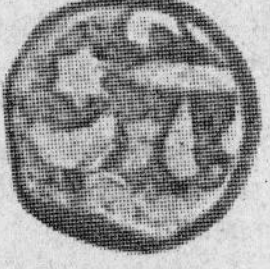

COPPER, 16-17mm
Years of Shah Alam II

C#	Date	Year	Good	VG	Fine	VF
12	—	47	.75	1.25	2.00	3.00

PAISA

COPPER, 19-21mm
Rev: Mark #3. Years of Shah Alam II.

C#	Date	Year	Good	VG	Fine	VF
13	—	42	1.50	2.25	3.00	4.00
	—	47	1.50	2.25	3.00	4.00

Year 47 is of much cruder fabric.

RUPEE

SILVER, 22-23mm, 10.70-11.60 gm
Obv: Mark #1. Rev: Mark #3. Years of Shah Alam II.

C#	Date	Year	VG	Fine	VF	XF
17	AH1204	28	11.50	13.50	16.50	20.00
	1229	42	11.50	13.50	16.50	20.00
	1229	43	11.50	13.50	16.50	20.00
	1229	47	11.50	13.50	16.50	20.00
	1229	51	11.50	13.50	16.50	20.00
	1229	52	11.50	13.50	16.50	20.00

In the name of Shah Alam II:

NAZARANA RUPEE

SILVER, 29mm, 10.70-11.60 gm

C#	Date	Year	VG	Fine	VF	XF
17a	AH1204	—	30.00	40.00	50.00	65.00

Ratan Singh

AD 1828-1851

Anonymous:

UNIFACE PAISA

COPPER, round or square, 12-18mm
Symbol of Ratan Singh only

C#	Date	Year	Good	VG	Fine	VF
20	ND	—	1.25	2.25	3.50	5.00

In the name of Alamgir II

1/2 PAISA

COPPER, 14mm
Rev: Mark #6.

C#	Date	Year	Good	VG	Fine	VF
22	ND	41	.75	1.25	2.00	3.00

PAISA

COPPER, 17-19mm
Rev: Mark #6.

C#	Date	Year	Good	VG	Fine	VF
23	ND	41	.75	1.25	2.00	3.00

NOTE: So called year 21 is debased copy of year 41.

RUPEE

SILVER, 22-23mm, 10.70-11.60 gm
Obv: Mark #1. Rev: Marks #3 and 6.
Years of Muhammad Akbar II

C#	Date	Year	VG	Fine	VF	XF
32	AH1229	21	11.50	13.50	16.50	20.00
	1229	25	11.50	13.50	16.50	20.00
	1229	31	11.50	13.50	16.50	20.00
	1229	32	11.50	13.50	16.50	20.00
	1229	41	11.50	13.50	16.50	20.00
	1229	47	11.50	13.50	16.50	20.00
	1229	52	11.50	13.50	16.50	20.00

In the name of Shah Alam II:

NAZARANA RUPEE

SILVER, 29mm, 10.70-11.60 gm

C#	Date	Year	VG	Fine	VF	XF
32a	AH1229	25	30.00	40.00	50.00	65.00

Sardar Singh

AD 1851-1872

In the Name of Alamgir II
Struck prior to AD 1859

1/2 PAISA

COPPER, 17mm

C#	Date	Year	Good	VG	Fine	VF
33	—	18	2.00	3.00	4.50	6.50

1/4 RUPEE

SILVER, 16mm, 2.68-2.90 gm

C#	Date	Year	VG	Fine	VF	XF
A34	—	—	5.50	7.50	10.00	13.50

1/2 RUPEE

SILVER, 18mm, 5.35-5.80 gm

C#	Date	Year	VG	Fine	VF	XF
B34	—	—	7.50	10.00	13.50	17.50

RUPEE

SILVER, 22-23mm, 10.70-11.60 gm
Rev: Marks #1, 4 (or 5), 6, and 7.
Years of Bahadur Shah II

C#	Date	Year	VG	Fine	VF	XF
34	AH1229	18	11.50	13.50	16.50	20.00
	1229	21	11.50	13.50	16.50	20.00

NAZARANA RUPEE

SILVER, 29mm, 10.70-11.60 gm

C#	Date	Year	VG	Fine	VF	XF
34a	AH1229	21	30.00	40.00	50.00	65.00

In the Name of Queen Victoria

Beginning AD 1859

Reverse marks from left to right: #6, 7, 2, 5.
Coined for many years without change of date.

PAISA

COPPER, 18-19mm

Y#	Date	Year	Good	VG	Fine	VF
1	VS1916	(1859)	.75	1.25	2.00	3.00

1/8 RUPEE

SILVER, 11-12mm, 1.34-1.45 gm

Y#	Date	Year	VG	Fine	VF	XF
2	VS1916	(1859)	5.50	7.50	10.00	13.50

1/4 RUPEE

SILVER, 15mm, 2.68-2.90 gm

Y#	Date	Year	VG	Fine	VF	XF
3	VS1916	(1859)	6.50	8.50	11.50	15.00

1/2 RUPEE

SILVER, 18mm, 5.35-5.80 gm

Y#	Date	Year	VG	Fine	VF	XF
4	VS1916	(1859)	7.50	9.00	12.50	16.50

RUPEE

SILVER, 22mm, 10.70-11.60 gm

Y#	Date	Year	VG	Fine	VF	XF
5	VS1916	(1859)	11.50	13.50	16.50	20.00

NAZARANA RUPEE

SILVER, 30mm, 10.70-11.60 gm

Y#	Date	Year	VG	Fine	VF	XF
5a	VS1916	(1859)	30.00	40.00	50.00	65.00

Dungar Singh

AD 1872-1887

Reverse marks, left to right: #6, 7, 8, 2, 5.
All coins spuriously dated AD 1859/SE 1916.

PAISA

COPPER

Y#	Date	Year	Good	VG	Fine	VF
6	VS1916	(1859)	.75	1.25	2.00	3.00

1/8 RUPEE

SILVER, 12mm, 1.34-1.45 gm

Y#	Date	Year	VG	Fine	VF	XF
7	VS1916	(1859)	6.00	8.00	10.00	13.50

1/4 RUPEE

SILVER, 14mm, 2.68-2.90 gm

Y#	Date	Year	VG	Fine	VF	XF
8	VS1916	(1859)	7.50	9.00	12.50	16.50

1/2 RUPEE

SILVER, 17mm, 5.35-5.80 gm

Y#	Date	Year	VG	Fine	VF	XF
9	VS1916	(1859)	7.50	9.00	12.50	16.50

RUPEE

SILVER, 22mm, 10.70-11.60 gm

Y#	Date	Year	VG	Fine	VF	XF
10	VS1916	(1859)	11.50	13.50	16.50	20.00

NAZARANA RUPEE

SILVER, 30mm, 10.70-11.60 gm

Y#	Date	Year	VG	Fine	VF	XF
10a	VS1916	(1859)	30.00	40.00	50.00	65.00

Ganga Singh

AD 1887-1943

Reverse marks, left to right: #6, 7, 9, 8, 2, 5.
All dump coins spuriously dated AD1859 VS1916.
Machine struck coins bear actual AD or VS dates.

PAISA

COPPER, 18mm

Y#	Date	Year	Good	VG	Fine	VF
11	VS1916	(1859)	1.75	2.50	3.50	5.00

1/8 RUPEE

SILVER, 12mm, 1.34-1.45 gm

Y#	Date	Year	VG	Fine	VF	XF
12	VS1916	(1859)	6.00	8.00	10.00	13.50

1/4 RUPEE

SILVER, 14mm, 2.68-2.90 gm

Y#	Date	Year	VG	Fine	VF	XF
13	VS1916	(1859)	6.00	8.00	10.00	13.50

NOTE: Counterfeits exist.

1/2 RUPEE

SILVER, 16-19 mm, 5.35-5.80 gm

Y#	Date	Year	VG	Fine	VF	XF
14	VS1916	(1859)	6.50	8.50	11.00	15.00

RUPEE

SILVER, 20-21mm, 10.70-11.60 gm

Y#	Date	Year	VG	Fine	VF	XF
15	VS1916	(1859)	11.50	13.50	16.50	20.00

NAZARANA RUPEE

SILVER, 30mm, 10.70-11.60 gm

Y#	Date	Year	VG	Fine	VF	XF
15a	VS1916	(1859)	30.00	40.00	50.00	65.00

MACHINE-STRUCK COINAGE

1/2 PICE

COPPER, 21mm

Y#	Date	Mintage	Fine	VF	XF	Unc
16	1894	—	5.00	7.50	11.50	16.50

1/4 ANNA

COPPER, 25mm

Y#	Date	Mintage	Fine	VF	XF	Unc
17	1895	—	4.00	6.50	10.00	15.00

RUPEE

SILVER, 31mm, 11.66 gm

Y#	Date	Mintage	Fine	VF	XF	Unc
18	1892	—	11.50	13.50	17.50	22.50
	1897	—	11.50	13.50	17.50	22.50

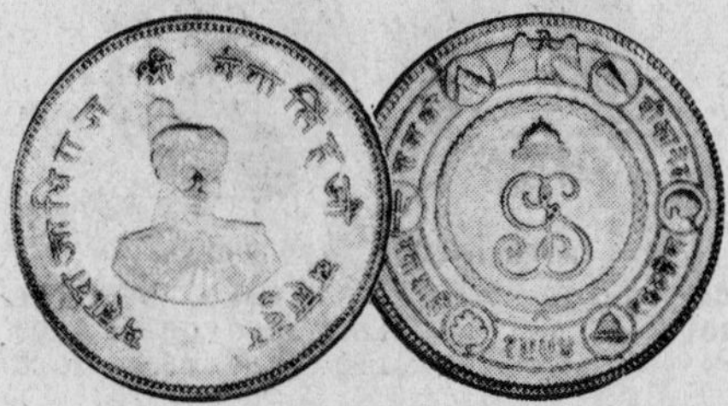

30mm

Y#	Date	Year	Fine	VF	XF	Unc
19	SE1994	(1916)	11.50	13.50	16.50	20.00
	1994	(1916)	—	—	Proof	50.00

1/2 MOHUR

GOLD, 17mm

Y#	Date	Year	Fine	VF	XF	Unc
20	SE1994	(1916)	110.00	130.00	160.00	200.00
	1994	(1916)			Proof Restrike	135.00

MOHUR

GOLD, 21mm

Y#	Date	Year	Fine	VF	XF	Unc
21	SE1994	(1916)	220.00	240.00	265.00	300.00
	1994	(1916)			Proof Restrike	235.00

Cast counterfeits reported to exist.

BINDRABAN

This city, the modern Vrindavan, was not a native state. The area surrounding the city, including the neighboring city of Mathura, was under Jat control in the mid-eighteenth century, although nominally subject to Awadh. After varying fortunes the area passed to the E.I.C. in 1803-05. The coins below display symbols of Awadh, Mughals, Delhi and Bhartpur, although it is clear that they were not mints of any of those authorities, especially in the British period.

Mominabad Bindraban Mint

In the name of Shah Alam II:

PAISA

COPPER, 20mm

Mintname: Ṣhahjahanabad

Fish left.

KM#	Date	Year	Good	VG	Fine	VF
2	—	32	3.00	5.00	7.50	10.00

21mm
Fish right.

KM#	Date	Year	Good	VG	Fine	VF
3	1206	33	2.50	3.50	5.00	7.00
	1208	35	2.50	3.50	5.00	7.00
	1209	36	2.50	3.50	5.00	7.00
	1210	38	2.50	3.50	5.00	7.00
	1212	39	2.50	3.50	5.00	7.00

Rev: Trident and Arabic 'N'.

Y#	Date	Year	Fine	VF	XF	Unc
4	—	27	2.50	3.50	5.00	7.00

KM#	Date	Year	Good	VG	Fine	VF
5	AH1211	40	1.75	2.50	4.00	6.00
	AH	36 (error)	—	2.50	4.00	6.00
	1212	40	1.75	2.50	4.00	6.00
	1212	41	1.75	2.50	4.00	6.00
	1212	36 (error)	1.75	2.50	4.00	6.00
	—	(4)3	1.75	2.50	4.00	6.00
	1216	44	1.75	2.50	4.00	6.00

1/4 RUPEE

SILVER, 14mm, 2.68-2.90 gm
Sword and dagger

KM#	Date	Year	VG	Fine	VF	XF
8a	—	4	3.50	5.50	8.00	11.50

1/2 RUPEE

SILVER, 16mm, 5.35-5.80 gm
Sword and dagger

KM#	Date	Year	VG	Fine	VF	XF
9a	—	4	7.50	10.00	13.50	16.50

RUPEE

SILVER, 21mm, 10.70-11.60 gm
Sword and trident.

KM#	Date	Year	VG	Fine	VF	XF
10.1	—	23	12.50	14.50	17.50	22.50

19mm
Sword, dagger and 'Sri'

KM#	Date	Year	VG	Fine	VF	XF
10.2	ND	23	11.50	13.50	16.50	20.00
	AH120x	37	11.50	13.50	16.50	20.00

20mm
Sword, 'Sri' and trident.

KM#	Date	Year	VG	Fine	VF	XF
10.3	AH120x	37	12.50	14.50	17.50	22.50

18mm
Sword, dagger and trident.

KM#	Date	Year	VG	Fine	VF	XF
10.4	AH12xx	44	11.50	13.50	16.50	20.00

Sword and dagger

KM#	Date	Year	VG	Fine	VF	XF
10.5	—	4	11.50	13.50	16.50	20.00

20mm
Trident and five-trident figure.

KM#	Date	Year	VG	Fine	VF	XF
10.6	AH1217	45	13.50	16.50	20.00	27.50

MOHUR

GOLD, 21mm, 10.70-11.40 gm

KM#	Date	Year	VG	Fine	VF	XF
15	AH1192	20	220.00	240.00	265.00	300.00

In the name of Queen Victoria:

1/4 RUPEE

SILVER, 15mm, 2.68-2.90 gm

Y#	Date	Year	VG	Fine	VF	XF
1	VS1915	(1858)	15.00	25.00	40.00	60.00
	1916	(1859)	15.00	25.00	40.00	60.00
	1924	(1867)	15.00	25.00	40.00	60.00

1/2 RUPEE

SILVER, 5.35-5.80 gm

Y#	Date	Year	VG	Fine	VF	XF
2	VS1915	(1858)	20.00	35.00	50.00	65.00
	1916	(1859)	20.00	35.00	50.00	65.00
	1924	(1867)	20.00	35.00	50.00	65.00

RUPEE

SILVER, 19mm, 10.70-11.60 gm

Y#	Date	Year	VG	Fine	VF	XF
3	VS1915	(1858)	25.00	35.00	50.00	70.00

Islamabad Mathura Mint

In the name of Shah Alam II:

Mintmark: 

PAISA

COPPER, 16-17mm, 6 gm.

KM#	Date	Year	Good	VG	Fine	VF
35	ND	—	2.50	3.50	5.00	7.00

20mm

KM#	Date	Year	Good	VG	Fine	VF
36	—	36	2.50	3.50	5.00	7.00

RUPEE

SILVER, 22mm, 10.70-11.60 gm
Rev: Sword.

KM#	Date	Year	VG	Fine	VF	XF
40	—	18	11.50	13.50	16.50	20.00
	AH119x	23	11.50	13.50	16.50	20.00
	—	30	11.50	13.50	16.50	20.00
	12xx	34	11.50	13.50	16.50	20.00

19mm
Rev: Cross, star and dagger.

KM#	Date	Year	VG	Fine	VF	XF
41	—	43	13.50	16.50	20.00	27.50

In the name of Muhammad Akbar II:

1/2 PAISA

COPPER, 3 gm.
Similar to 1 Paisa, KM#35, but for royal legends.

KM#	Date	Year	Good	VG	Fine	VF
51	ND	—	2.50	3.50	5.00	7.00

PAISA

COPPER, 6 gm.
Similar to 1/2 Paisa, KM#51.

KM#	Date	Year	Good	VG	Fine	VF
52	ND	—	2.25	3.25	4.50	6.00

BIRMAWAL

Raja Handa Singh

PAISA

COPPER, 17.5mm

KM#	Date	Year	Good	VG	Fine	VF
5	ND	—	3.00	5.00	7.50	10.00

BROACH

RULERS

Town ruled by Nawabs, 1736-1772
Nek Nam Khan, 1754-1768
Imtya-Ud-Daula, 1768-1772
To British 1772-1783 and 1803 on
To Gwalior 1783-1803

Mintmarks:

Flower (Nawabs)

Cross (Gwalior and E.I.C.)

Imtiy - ud - daula

AD 1768-1772

PAISA

COPPER, 18mm

C#	Date	Year	Good	VG	Fine	VF
20	AH1176	—	2.50	3.50	5.00	7.00

In the name of Shah Alam II:

PAISA

COPPER, 17mm
Similar to 1 Rupee, C#36.

C#	Date	Year	Good	VG	Fine	VF
25	ND	—	2.50	3.50	5.00	7.00

1/2 RUPEE

SILVER, 14mm, 5.35-5.80 gm

C#	Date	Year	VG	Fine	VF	XF
34	—	2x	6.50	7.50	9.00	11.50

RUPEE

SILVER, 20mm, 10.70-11.60 gm
Rev: Flower mark

C#	Date	Year	VG	Fine	VF	XF
35	AH11xx	4	11.50	13.50	16.50	20.00
	1172	5	11.50	13.50	16.50	20.00
	1181	9	11.50	13.50	16.50	20.00

East India Company

1/2 RUPEE

SILVER, 16mm, 5.35-5.80 gm
Rev: Cross mark

C#	Date	Year	VG	Fine	VF	XF
A36	ND	—	7.50	10.00	13.50	18.50

RUPEE

SILVER, 20mm, 10.70-11.60 gm

C#	Date	Year	VG	Fine	VF	XF
36	—	2x	12.50	15.00	18.50	25.00

These cross marked coins were probably also issued under the Sindhias. For other Broach issues see Gwalior.

BUNDI

RULERS

Bishen Singh, AD1804-21/SE1861-78
Ram Singh, AD1821-89/SE1878-1946
Raghubir Singh,
AD1889-1927/SE1946-84
Iswari Singh,
AD1927-47/SE1984-2004

NOTE: All of the coins of Bundi struck prior to the mutiny (1857) are in the name of the Mughal emperor and bear the following 2 marks on the reverse, to the left and right of the regnal year, respectively:

The same symbols appear on the coins of Kotah, but the difference is that the Kotah pieces have an additional cruci- form mark below the lotus, which NEVER appears on Bundi coinage.

In the name of Shah Alam II

1759-1806

PAISA

COPPER, 23mm

C#	Date	Year	Good	VG	Fine	VF
5	—	2	1.50	2.50	3.50	5.00
	—	20	1.50	2.50	3.50	5.00
	—	23	1.50	2.50	3.50	5.00
	—	25	1.50	2.50	3.50	5.00
	—	28	1.50	2.50	3.50	5.00
	—	32	1.50	2.50	3.50	5.00
	—	33	1.50	2.50	3.50	5.00
	—	35	1.50	2.50	3.50	5.00
	—	36	1.50	2.50	3.50	5.00
	—	39	1.50	2.50	3.50	5.00
	—	40	1.50	2.50	3.50	5.00
	—	41	1.50	2.50	3.50	5.00
	—	42	1.50	2.50	3.50	5.00
	—	43	1.50	2.50	3.50	5.00
	—	44	1.50	2.50	3.50	5.00
	—	46	1.50	2.50	3.50	5.00

RUPEE

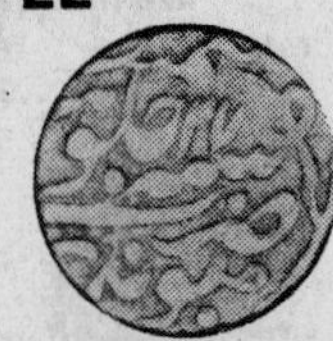

SILVER, round

C#	Date	Year	VG	Fine	VF	XF
10	—	2	11.50	13.50	16.50	20.00
	—	3	11.50	13.50	16.50	20.00
	—	7	11.50	13.50	16.50	20.00
	—	10	11.50	13.50	16.50	20.00
	—	12	11.50	13.50	16.50	20.00
	—	18	11.50	13.50	16.50	20.00
	—	21	11.50	13.50	16.50	20.00
	—	23	11.50	13.50	16.50	20.00
	—	25	11.50	13.50	16.50	20.00
	—	28	11.50	13.50	16.50	20.00
	—	29	11.50	13.50	16.50	20.00
	—	30	11.50	13.50	16.50	20.00
	—	32	11.50	13.50	16.50	20.00
	—	33	11.50	13.50	16.50	20.00
	—	34	11.50	13.50	16.50	20.00
	—	37	11.50	13.50	16.50	20.00
	—	40	11.50	13.50	16.50	20.00
	—	43	11.50	13.50	16.50	20.00
	—	44	11.50	13.50	16.50	20.00
	—	46	11.50	13.50	16.50	20.00
	—	47	11.50	13.50	16.50	20.00

NAZARANA RUPEE

SILVER, square

C#	Date	Year	VG	Fine	VF	XF
10a	—	28	27.50	32.50	40.00	50.00
	—	31	27.50	32.50	40.00	50.00

In the name of Muhammad Akbar II

1806-1837

1/2 PAISA

COPPER, 14-16mm, square

C#	Date	Year	Good	VG	Fine	VF
16	—	29	2.50	3.50	4.50	6.00

PAISA

COPPER, round

C#	Date	Year	Good	VG	Fine	VF
17	—	3	2.50	3.50	4.50	6.00
	—	13	2.50	3.50	4.50	6.00
	—	19	2.50	3.50	4.50	6.00

Square, 16-20mm

C#	Date	Year	Good	VG	Fine	VF
17a	—	4	1.50	2.50	3.50	5.00
	—	6	1.25	2.00	3.00	4.50
	—	8	1.50	2.50	3.50	5.00
	—	11	1.25	2.00	3.00	4.50
	—	12	1.25	2.00	3.00	4.50
	—	14	1.25	2.00	3.00	4.50
	—	15	1.50	2.50	3.50	5.00
	—	16	1.50	2.50	3.50	5.00

C#	Date	Year	Good	VG	Fine	VF
17a	—	24	1.50	2.50	3.50	5.00
	—	25	1.25	2.00	3.00	4.50
	—	26	1.25	2.00	3.00	4.50
	—	27	1.50	2.50	3.50	5.00
	—	28	1.50	2.50	3.50	5.00
	—	29	1.50	2.50	3.50	5.00
	—	30	1.50	2.50	3.50	5.00

1/4 RUPEE

SILVER, 12mm, 2.68-2.90 gm.

C#	Date	Year	VG	Fine	VF	XF
24	—	23	5.00	6.00	7.00	8.50
	—	25	5.00	6.00	7.00	8.50

1/2 RUPEE

SILVER, 15mm, 5.35-5.80 gm.

C#	Date	Year	VG	Fine	VF	XF
25	—	25	6.50	7.50	8.50	10.00

RUPEE

SILVER, 19mm, 10.7011.60 gm.

C#	Date	Year	VG	Fine	VF	XF
30	—	1	11.50	13.50	16.50	20.00
	—	2	11.50	13.50	16.50	20.00
	—	3	11.50	13.50	16.50	20.00
	—	5	11.50	13.50	16.50	20.00
	—	6	11.50	13.50	16.50	20.00
	—	9	11.50	13.50	16.50	20.00
	—	10	11.50	13.50	16.50	20.00
	—	11	11.50	13.50	16.50	20.00
	—	12	11.50	13.50	16.50	20.00
	—	13	11.50	13.50	16.50	20.00
	—	15	11.50	13.50	16.50	20.00
	—	16	11.50	13.50	16.50	20.00
	—	17	11.50	13.50	16.50	20.00
	—	18	11.50	13.50	16.50	20.00
	—	19	11.50	13.50	16.50	20.00
	—	20	11.50	13.50	16.50	20.00
	—	21	11.50	13.50	16.50	20.00
	—	22	11.50	13.50	16.50	20.00
	—	32	11.50	13.50	16.50	20.00

NAZARANA RUPEE

SILVER, square, 20mm, 10.70-11.60 gm.

C#	Date	Year	VG	Fine	VF	XF
30a	—	5	25.00	32.50	40.00	50.00
	—	11	25.00	32.50	40.00	50.00
	—	16	25.00	32.50	40.00	50.00
	—	19	25.00	32.50	40.00	50.00

Round, 27-31mm

C#	Date	Year	VG	Fine	VF	XF
30b	—	19	25.00	32.50	40.00	50.00
	—	24	25.00	32.50	40.00	50.00
	—	32	25.00	32.50	40.00	50.00

MOHUR

GOLD, 18mm, 10.70-11.40 gm.

C#	Date	Year	VG	Fine	VF	XF
33	—	17	220.00	240.00	265.00	300.00
	—	19	220.00	240.00	265.00	300.00
	—	32	220.00	240.00	265.00	300.00

In the name of Bahadur Shah II, AD 1837-1857

PAISA

COPPER, 20mm

C#	Date	Year	Good	VG	Fine	VF
35	—	15	4.50	6.50	8.50	12.50

RUPEE

SILVER, 19mm, 10.70-11.60 gm.

C#	Date	Year	VG	Fine	VF	XF
40	—	5	11.50	13.50	16.50	20.00
	—	6	11.50	13.50	16.50	20.00
	—	8	11.50	13.50	16.50	20.00
	—	18	11.50	13.50	16.50	20.00

NAZARANA RUPEE

SILVER, broad flan, 29mm, 10.70-11.60 gm.

C#	Date	Year	VG	Fine	VF	XF
40a	—	1	30.00	37.50	45.00	55.00
	—	3	30.00	37.50	45.00	55.00
	—	4	30.00	37.50	45.00	55.00
	—	9	30.00	37.50	45.00	55.00
	—	10	30.00	37.50	45.00	55.00

Square, 16 x 16mm

C#	Date	Year	VG	Fine	VF	XF
40b	—	11	20.00	30.00	40.00	50.00

In the name of Queen Victoria

AD date on obv., VS date on rev.

First Series

1/4 PAISA

COPPER, 9-11mm

Y#	Date	Year	Good	VG	Fine	VF
1	VS1924	(1867)	.75	1.25	2.25	3.50

1/2 PAISA

COPPER, 12-15mm square

Y#	Date	Year	Good	VG	Fine	VF
2	VS1915	(1858)	.35	.65	1.00	1.50
	1924	(1867)	.25	.50	.85	1.25

PAISA

COPPER, 18-21mm, usually squarish

Y#	Date	Year	Good	VG	Fine	VF
3	VS1919	(1862)	.35	.85	1.25	1.75
	1922	(1864)	.35	.85	1.25	1.75
	1922	(1865)	.35	.85	1.25	1.75
	1923	(1866)	.35	.85	1.25	1.75
	1924	(1867)	.35	.85	1.25	1.75
	1926	(1869)	.35	.85	1.25	1.75
	1928	(1871)	.35	.85	1.25	1.75
	1929	(1872)	.35	.85	1.25	1.75
	1934	(1877)	.25	.50	.85	1.25
	1935	(1878)	.25	.50	.85	1.25
	1936	(1879)	.25	.50	.85	1.25
	1940	(1883)	.25	.50	.85	1.25
	1942	(1885)	.25	.50	.85	1.25
	1943	(1886)	.25	.50	.85	1.25
	1944	(1887)	.25	.50	.85	1.25
	1945	(1888)	.25	.50	.85	1.25
	1946	(1889)	.25	.50	.85	1.25
	1955	(1898)	.85	1.25	2.00	3.00
	1956	(1899)	1.25	2.25	3.50	5.00

1/4 RUPEE

SILVER, 13mm, 2.68-2.90 gm.

Y#	Date	Year	VG	Fine	VF	XF
4	VS1915	(1858)	3.50	4.00	5.00	6.00
	1935	(1888)	3.50	4.00	5.00	6.00
	1936	(1879)	3.50	4.00	5.00	6.00

1/2 RUPEE

SILVER, 16-17mm, 5.35-5.80 gm.

Y#	Date	Year	VG	Fine	VF	XF
5	VS1915	(1858)	6.50	7.00	7.50	8.50
	1930	(1873)	6.50	7.00	7.50	8.50
	1937	(1880)	6.50	7.00	7.50	8.50
	1940	(1883)	6.50	7.00	7.50	8.50
	1941	(1884)	6.50	7.00	7.50	8.50
	1943	(1886)	6.50	7.00	7.50	8.50

RUPEE

SILVER, 21-24mm, 10.70-11.60 gm.

Y#	Date	Year	VG	Fine	VF	XF
6	VS1915	(1858)	11.50	12.50	14.00	16.50
	1916	(1860)	11.50	13.50	15.00	17.50
	1917	(1860)	11.50	12.50	14.00	16.50
	1918	(1861)	11.50	12.50	14.00	16.50
	1920	(1863)	11.50	12.50	14.00	16.50
	1921	(1864)	11.50	12.50	14.00	16.50
	1922	(1865)	11.50	12.50	14.00	16.50
	1923	(1866)	11.50	12.50	14.00	16.50
	1925	(1868)	11.50	12.50	14.00	16.50
	1926	(1869)	11.50	12.50	14.00	16.50
	1927	(1870)	11.50	12.50	14.00	16.50
	1928	(1871)	11.50	12.50	14.00	16.50
	1929	(1872)	11.50	12.50	14.00	16.50
	1930	(1873)	11.50	12.50	14.00	16.50
	1931	(1874)	11.50	12.50	14.00	16.50
	1932	(1875)	11.50	12.50	14.00	16.50
	1933	(1876)	11.50	12.50	14.00	16.50
	1934	(1877)	11.50	12.50	14.00	16.50
	1935	(1878)	11.50	12.50	14.00	16.50
	1936	(1879)	11.50	12.50	14.00	16.50
	1937	(1880)	11.50	12.50	14.00	16.50
	1938	(1881)	11.50	12.50	14.00	16.50
	1940	(1883)	11.50	12.50	14.00	16.50
	1941	(1884)	11.50	12.50	14.00	16.50
	1942	(1885)	11.50	12.50	14.00	16.50
	1943	(1886)	11.50	12.50	14.00	16.50

NAZARANA RUPEE

SILVER, Square, 17mm, 10.70-11.60 gm.

Y#	Date	Year	VG	Fine	VF	XF
6a	VS1915	(1858)	20.00	25.00	32.50	42.50
	1919	(1862)	20.00	25.00	32.50	42.50
	1925	(1868)	20.00	25.00	32.50	42.50
	1932	(1875)	20.00	25.00	32.50	42.50
	1934	(1877)	20.00	25.00	32.50	42.50

NOTE: On Y#1-6, both dates are not often visible, and specimens with both clearly distinguishable are worth about 50 percent more than given prices (except Nazarana coins, which are priced for specimens with both dates legible). Specimens with both dates off are of little value.

Second Series

Katar on obv., VS date on rev.

Specimens with date off worth considerably less, especially on smaller pieces.

1/4 RUPEE

SILVER, 12mm, 2.68-2.90 gm.

Y#	Date	Year	VG	Fine	VF	XF
7	VS1944	(1887)	5.00	6.00	7.00	8.50
	1947	(1890)	3.50	4.00	5.00	6.00
	1953	(1896)	3.50	4.00	5.00	6.00
	1955	(1898)	3.50	4.00	5.00	6.00

1/2 RUPEE

SILVER, 16-17mm

Y#	Date	Year	VG	Fine	VF	XF
8	VS1946	(1889)	6.50	7.50	8.50	10.00
	1948	(1891)	6.50	7.00	8.00	9.00
	1949	(1892)	6.50	7.00	8.00	9.00
	1953	(1896)	6.50	7.50	8.50	10.00
	1954	(1897)	6.50	7.00	8.00	9.00
	1955	(1898)	6.50	7.00	8.00	9.00

RUPEE

SILVER, 18-23mm, 10.70-11.60 gm.

Y#	Date	Year	VG	Fine	VF	XF
9	VS1943	(1886)	11.50	12.50	14.00	16.50
	1944	(1887)	11.50	12.50	14.00	16.50
	1945	(1888)	11.50	12.50	14.00	16.50
	1946	(1889)	11.50	12.50	14.00	16.50
	1947	(1890)	11.50	12.50	14.00	16.50
	1948	(1891)	11.50	12.50	14.00	16.50
	1949	(1892)	11.50	12.50	14.00	16.50
	1950	(1893)	11.50	12.50	14.00	16.50
	1953	(1896)	11.50	12.50	14.00	16.50
	1954	(1897)	11.50	12.50	14.00	16.50
	1955	(1898)	11.50	12.50	14.00	16.50
	1957	(1900)	11.50	12.50	14.00	16.50

NAZARANA RUPEE

SILVER, Square, 20mm, 10.70-11.60 gm.

Y#	Date	Year	VG	Fine	VF	XF
9a	VS1943	(1886)	15.00	20.00	25.00	32.50
	1945	(1888)	15.00	20.00	25.00	32.50
	1949	(1892)	15.00	20.00	25.00	32.50
	1951	(1894)	15.00	20.00	25.00	32.50
	1952	(1895)	15.00	20.00	25.00	32.50

RUPEE

SILVER, Round, 24mm, 10.70-11.60 gm.

Y#	Date	Year	VG	Fine	VF	XF
10	VS1958	(1901)	40.00	60.00	85.00	120.00

In the name of Edward VII:

First Coinage

Crude figure of king on obverse.

1/4 RUPEE

SILVER, 12-14mm, 2.68-2.90 gm.

Y#	Date	Year	VG	Fine	VF	XF
B11	VS1958	(1901)	20.00	25.00	30.00	37.50
	1961	(1904)	20.00	25.00	30.00	37.50

1/2 RUPEE

SILVER, 16-18mm, 5.35-5.80 gm.

Y#	Date	Year	VG	Fine	VF	XF
A11	VS1958	(1901)	20.00	25.00	30.00	37.50

RUPEE

SILVER, 23-25mm, 10.70-11.60 gm.

Y#	Date	Year	VG	Fine	VF	XF
11	VS1958	(1901)	11.50	12.50	14.00	16.50
	1959	(1902)	11.50	13.50	15.00	17.50
	1960	(1903)	11.50	13.50	15.00	17.50
	1961	(1904)	11.50	13.50	15.00	17.50
	1962	(1905)	11.50	13.50	15.00	17.50
	1963	(1906)	12.50	14.50	16.50	20.00

Second Coinage

Katar on obverse

PAISA

COPPER, 10-14mm

Y#	Date	Year	Good	VG	Fine	VF
A12	VS1963	(1906)	7.50	11.50	15.00	20.00
	1965	(1908)	6.00	9.00	12.50	16.50
	Date Off Flan		1.50	2.25	3.00	4.00

1/4 RUPEE

SILVER, 13-15mm, 2.68-2.90 gm.

Y#	Date	Year	VG	Fine	VF	XF
12	VS1963	(1906)	3.50	4.00	4.50	5.50
	1964	(1907)	3.50	4.00	4.50	5.50
	1965	(1908)	3.50	4.00	5.00	6.50
	1966	(1909)	3.50	4.00	4.50	5.50

1/2 RUPEE

SILVER, 16mm, 5.35-5.80 gm.

Y#	Date	Year	VG	Fine	VF	XF
13	VS1963	(1906)	6.50	7.50	8.50	10.00
	1964	(1907)	6.00	7.00	8.00	9.00
	1965	(1908)	6.00	7.00	8.00	9.00
	1966	(1909)	6.00	7.00	8.00	9.00

RUPEE

SILVER, 18-20mm, 10.70-11.60 gm.

Y#	Date	Year	VG	Fine	VF	XF
14	VS1963	(1906)	11.50	12.50	14.50	16.50
	1964	(1907)	11.50	12.50	14.50	16.50
	1965	(1908)	11.50	12.50	14.50	16.50
	1966	(1909)	11.50	12.50	14.50	16.50
	1967	(1910)	11.50	13.00	15.00	17.50
	1968	(1911)	11.50	13.00	15.00	17.50
	1969	(1912)	11.50	13.00	15.00	17.50

NAZARANA RUPEE

Silver, broad flan, 26mm, 10.70-11.60 gm.

Y#	Date	Year	VG	Fine	VF	XF
14b	VS1967	(1910)	17.50	22.50	30.00	40.00
	1968	(1911)	17.50	22.50	30.00	40.00

Squarish, 22mm

Y#	Date	Year	VG	Fine	VF	XF
14a	VS1966	(1909)	32.50	40.00	55.00	70.00
	1967	(1910)	32.50	40.00	55.00	70.00
	1968	(1911)	32.50	40.00	55.00	70.00
	1969	(1912)	32.50	40.00	55.00	70.00

In the name of George V:

PAISA

COPPER, 8-13mm, usually rectangular
Much variation in size and weight

Y#	Date	Year	Good	VG	Fine	VF
15	VS1973	(1916)	1.50	2.25	3.00	4.00
	1974	(1917)	1.50	2.25	3.00	4.00
	1981	(1924)	1.50	2.25	3.00	4.00
	1982	(1925)	1.50	2.25	3.00	4.00
	1984	(1927)	1.50	2.25	3.00	4.00
	1986	(1929)	2.00	3.00	4.00	5.00
	1987	(1930)	2.00	3.00	4.00	5.00
	199x	—	3.00	4.00	5.50	7.50
	Date Off Flan	—	.35	.65	1.00	1.50

1/4 RUPEE

SILVER, 13-15mm, 2.68-2.90 gm.

Y#	Date	Year	VG	Fine	VF	XF
16	VS1972	(1915)	3.50	4.00	4.50	6.00
	1973	(1916)	3.50	4.00	4.50	6.00
	1974	(1917)	3.50	4.00	4.50	6.00
	1980	(1923)	3.50	4.00	4.50	6.00
	1981	(1924)	3.50	4.00	4.50	6.00
	1982	(1925)	3.50	4.00	4.50	6.00

13mm, similar to 1/2 Rupee, Y#19 and 1 Rupee, Y#20.

Y#	Date	Year	VG	Fine	VF	XF
A19	1925	—	25.00	35.00	40.00	60.00

1/2 RUPEE

SILVER, 14-16mm, 5.35-5.80 gm.

Y#	Date	Year	VG	Fine	VF	XF
17	VS1972	(1915)	6.50	7.00	8.00	10.00
	1973	(1916)	6.50	7.00	8.00	10.00
	1974	(1917)	6.50	7.00	7.50	9.00
	1979	(1922)	6.50	7.00	7.50	9.00
	1980	(1923)	6.50	7.00	7.50	9.00
	1981	(1924)	6.50	7.00	7.50	9.00
	1982	(1925)	6.50	7.00	7.50	9.00
	1983	(1926)	6.50	7.00	7.50	9.00
	1984	(1927)	6.50	7.00	7.50	9.00

14-17mm

Y#	Date	Year	VG	Fine	VF	XF
19	1925	—	27.50	35.00	42.50	50.00

RUPEE

SILVER, 18-20mm, 10.70-11.60 gm.

Y#	Date	Year	VG	Fine	VF	XF
18	VS1972	(1915)	11.50	12.50	13.50	15.00
	1973	(1916)	11.50	12.50	13.50	15.00
	1974	(1917)	11.50	12.50	13.50	15.00
	1979	(1922)	11.50	12.50	13.50	15.00
	1980	(1923)	11.50	12.50	13.50	15.00
	1981	(1924)	11.50	12.50	13.50	15.00
	1982	(1925)	11.50	12.50	13.50	15.00
	1983	(1926)	11.50	12.50	13.50	15.00
	1984	(1927)	11.50	12.50	14.00	16.00
	1987	(1930)	11.50	12.50	14.00	16.00
	1989	(1932)	11.50	12.50	14.00	16.00

Y#	Date	Year	VG	Fine	VF	XF
20	1925	—	40.00	50.00	65.00	80.00

NAZARANA RUPEE

SILVER, square, 19-21mm

Y#	Date	Year	VG	Fine	VF	XF
18a	VS1975	(1918)	32.50	40.00	50.00	65.00
	1979	(1922)	32.50	40.00	50.00	65.00
	1980	(1923)	32.50	40.00	50.00	65.00
	1981	(1924)	32.50	40.00	50.00	65.00
	1983	(1926)	32.50	40.00	50.00	65.00
	1987	(1930)	32.50	40.00	50.00	65.00

Y#	Date	Mintage	VG	Fine	VF	XF
20a	1925	—	35.00	50.00	65.00	80.00

CAMBAY

Hussain Yafar Khanj

AH1257-1297/1841-1880AD

In the name of Shah Alam II

RUPEE

SILVER, 20mm, 10.70-11.60 gm

Y#	Date	Year	VG	Fine	VF	XF
1	AH1282	—	11.50	13.50	16.50	20.00
	1294	—	11.50	13.50	16.50	20.00

NOTE: Fractional denominations are reported to exist.

Ja'far Ali Khanji

AH1297-1333/VS1937-1972/1880-1915AD

ANONYMOUS COINS

1/4 PAISA

COPPER, 11mm
Obv: With 'SHAH'.

Y#	Date	Year	Good	VG	Fine	VF
2	ND	—	3.00	5.50	7.50	10.00

1/2 PAISA

COPPER, 13-15mm
Round or square. Obv: With 'SHAH'.

Y#	Date	Year	Good	VG	Fine	VF
3	VS194x	—	3.00	5.50	7.50	9.00
	(19)62	(1905)	3.00	5.50	7.50	9.00

14-15mm
Denomination in words

Y#	Date	Year	Good	VG	Fine	VF
5	VS1963	(1906)	3.50	6.50	9.00	12.50
	1964	(1907)	3.50	6.50	9.00	12.50

Denomination in numerals

Y#	Date	Year	Good	VG	Fine	VF
5a	VS1964	(1907)	3.00	5.00	7.50	10.00
	1965	(1908)	3.00	5.00	7.50	10.00
	1966	(1909)	3.00	5.00	7.50	10.00

PAISA

COPPER, Round, 18-19mm
Obv: With 'SHAH'.

Y#	Date	Year	Good	VG	Fine	VF
4	ND	—	1.25	2.00	3.00	4.25

Square

Y#	Date	Year	Good	VG	Fine	VF
4a	ND	—	1.50	2.25	3.25	4.50

16-20mm

Y#	Date	Year	Good	VG	Fine	VF
6	VS1963	(1906)	1.25	2.00	3.00	4.00
	1964	(1907)	1.50	2.50	3.50	4.50
	1965	(1908)	1.25	2.00	3.00	4.00
	1966	(1909)	1.25	2.00	3.00	4.00
	1968	(1911)	1.25	2.00	3.00	4.00
	1970	(1913)	2.00	3.00	4.00	5.00

NOTE: Several subvarieties of type.

In the name of Ja'far Ali Khan:

1/8 RUPEE

SILVER, 11mm, 1.34-1.45 gm

Y#	Date	Year	VG	Fine	VF	XF
7	AH1313	—	5.00	6.50	8.00	10.00

1/4 RUPEE

SILVER, 14mm, 2.68-2.90 gm

Y#	Date	Year	VG	Fine	VF	XF
8	AH1313	—	7.00	8.00	10.00	12.50

1/2 RUPEE

SILVER, 15mm, 5.35-5.80 gm

Y#	Date	Year	VG	Fine	VF	XF
9	AH1313	17	7.50	9.00	11.50	14.00

RUPEE

SILVER, 19mm, 10.70-11.60 gm

Y#	Date	Year	VG	Fine	VF	XF
10	AH1313	17	12.50	14.50	17.50	22.50
	1317	21	12.50	14.50	17.50	22.50
	1319	23	12.50	15.00	18.50	23.50

CANNANORE

Under The Ali Rajas, 'Lord's of the Deep'

1/5 RUPEE

SILVER, 14-15mm

C#	Date	Mintage	VG	Fine	VF	XF
10	AH1134	—	5.00	7.50	10.00	13.50
	1139	—	4.50	7.00	9.00	11.50
	1144	—	4.50	7.00	9.00	11.50
	1181	—	4.50	7.00	9.00	11.50
	1188	—	3.00	5.00	7.00	9.00
	1194	—	3.00	5.00	7.00	9.00
	1199	—	3.00	5.00	7.00	9.00
	1221	—	3.00	5.00	7.00	9.00
	1231	—	3.00	5.00	7.00	9.00
	1631 error for 1231					
		—	5.00	7.50	10.00	13.50
	8711 error for 1178					
		—	4.50	7.00	9.00	11.50

DOUBLE FANAM

GOLD, 16mm

KM#	Date	Year	VG	Fine	VF	XF
1	AH1194	—	85.00	125.00	150.00	175.00

CHAMBA

Charhat Singh

AD 1808-1844

PAISA

COPPER, 20-23mm

C#	Date	Year	Good	VG	Fine	VF
15	—	15	4.00	7.00	10.00	14.00
	—	16	4.00	7.00	10.00	14.00
	—	17	4.00	7.00	10.00	14.00
	ND	—	3.00	4.50	6.50	8.00

Lakar Shah of Basoli

Rebel, AD 1844

PAISA

COPPER, 18-22mm
No trident below legends

20	ND	—	5.00	8.00	11.00	15.00

Sri Singh

AD 1844-1870

PAISA

COPPER, 18-22mm
Trident countermarked on C#20

23	ND	—	7.50	12.50	18.50	25.00

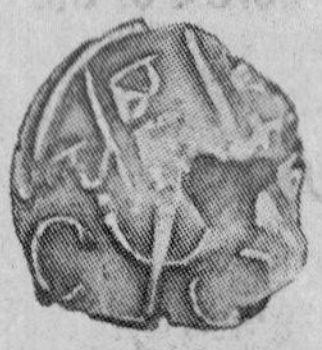

Crude copy of #15 over struck on C#20

24	ND	—	2.75	4.00	5.50	7.50

Crude, degenerate copy of C#15

25	ND	—	2.75	4.00	5.50	7.50

NOTE: Above coin also struck during reign of Sham Singh, AD1870-1904.

CHHATARPUR

Struck circa 1816 until 1882, with unchanging AH date 1192, sometimes blundered. Mark: Helianthus flower on obverse.

In the name of Shah Alam II:

1/4 RUPEE

SILVER, 14mm, 2.68-2.90 gm.

C#	Date	Year	VG	Fine	VF	XF
5	—	25	10.00	13.50	16.50	21.50

RUPEE

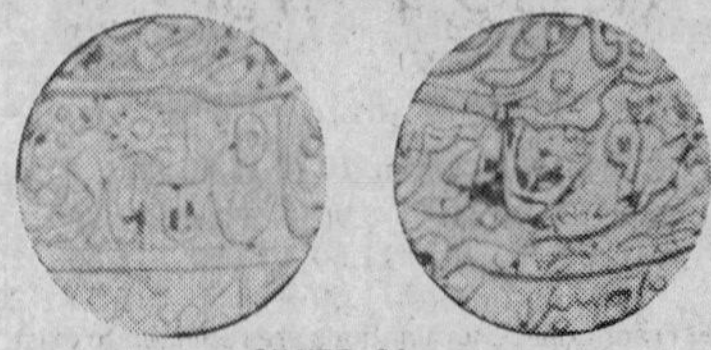

SILVER, 21mm
Obv: Trisul

15.1	—	9	11.50	13.50	16.50	20.00

18mm
Obv: Chakra

15.2	—	15	11.50	13.50	16.50	20.00

17mm
Obv: Pataka

15.3	—	24	11.50	13.50	16.50	20.00
	—	25	11.50	13.50	16.50	20.00

Uncertain types

15	—	11	11.50	13.50	16.50	20.00
	—	12	11.50	13.50	16.50	20.00
	—	16	11.50	13.50	16.50	20.00
	—	17	11.50	13.50	16.50	20.00
	—	20	11.50	13.50	16.50	20.00
	—	21	11.50	13.50	16.50	20.00
	—	22	11.50	13.50	16.50	20.00
	—	25	11.50	13.50	16.50	20.00

CHHOTA UDAIPUR

Guman Singhji

SE1744-1773/1822-1851AD

PAISA

COPPER, 7.4 gm

KM#	Date	Year	Good	VG	Fine	VF
10	—	—	4.00	6.00	8.50	11.50

2 PAISA

COPPER, 27mm, 13.4-14.0 gm

15	SE(1)765(1843)	3.50	5.50	7.50	10.00
	1767(1845)	3.50	5.50	7.50	10.00

Jitsinghji

SE1773-1803/VS1908-1938/1851-81AD

PAISA

COPPER, 22mm, 7.4 gm

Y#	Date	Year	Good	VG	Fine	VF
1	SE1787	(1865)	2.50	4.50	6.50	8.50

2 PAISA

COPPER, 27mm, 13.4-14.0 gm

Y#	Date	Year	Good	VG	Fine	VF
2	—	—	5.50	7.00	9.00	12.00

3	VS1919	(1862)	7.00	9.00	12.00	16.50
	1924	(1867)	7.00	9.00	12.00	16.50

Motisinghji

VS1938-52/AD1881-1905

PAISA

COPPER, 15mm, 7.4 gm

4	VS1948	(1891)	6.00	7.50	10.00	13.50

2 PAISA

COPPER, 20mm, 13.4-14.0 gm

5	VS1948	(1891)	5.00	6.50	8.50	11.50

CIS-SUTLEJ STATES

These States, originally under the Durranis of Afghanistan, were officially recognized by the E.I.C. over a period from 1803 to 1846; but independent coinages (nominally in the name of Ahmad Shah Durrani, mostly with the frozen regnal year 4) were issued with differentiating marks as noted under each state heading.

FARIDKOT

Harindar Singh

AD1918-1949

NAZARANA RUPEE

SILVER, 23mm

Y#	Date	Mintage	Fine	VF	XF	Unc
A1	1941	—	100.00	135.00	185.00	250.00

NAZARANA 1/3 MOHUR

GOLD, 20mm, 3.57-3.80 gm

Y#	Date	Mintage	Fine	VF	XF	Unc
1	1941	—	235.00	275.00	350.00	425.00

HANSI

Raja George Thomas

Hansi Sahibabad Mint

RUPEE

SILVER, 22mm
Obv: Umbrella. Rev: Sunface.

KM#	Date	Year	VG	Fine	VF	XF
1	AH1214	42	—	—	Rare	—

JIND

Identifying Marks:

On reverse of all hammered coinage

RULERS
Gajpat Singh, AD1764-1786
Sangat Singh, AD1822-1834
Sarup Singh, AD1834-1864

RUPEE

SILVER, 16-18mm, 10.70-11.60 gm
Reverse markings as above.
Same type for the three rulers.

#	Date	Year	VG	Fine	VF	XF
1	—	4 (frozen)	12.50	15.00	20.00	26.50

MOHUR

GOLD, 16-18mm, 10.70-11.40 gm
Reverse markings as above.
Same type for the three rulers.

#	Date	Year	VG	Fine	VF	XF
2	—	(4) (frozen)	225.00	240.00	265.00	300.00

Bhag Singh

AD1786-1819

RUPEE

SILVER, uniface, 16-18mm, 10.70-11.60 gm

#	Date	Year	VG	Fine	VF	XF
3	—	ND	13.50	17.50	24.50	33.50

Raghbir Singh

AD1864-1887

RUPEE

SILVER, 18mm, 10.70-11.60 gm
Reverse markings as above

but fine calligraphy.

Y#	Date	Year	VG	Fine	VF	XF
1	—	4 (frozen)	12.50	14.50	17.50	22.50

Ranbir Singh

VS1943-/1887-AD

NAZARANA RUPEE

SILVER, 30.5mm, 10.70-11.60 gm

#	Date	Year	VG	Fine	VF	XF
2	VS1993	(1937)	45.00	60.00	80.00	100.00

KAITHAL

Identifying Marks:

On reverse of all hammered coinage

RULERS
Desu Singh, AD1767-1781
Lal Singh, AD1781-1819
Pratap Singh, AD1819-1824
Udai Singh, AD1824-1843

RUPEE

SILVER, 15-16mm, 10.70-11.60 gm

KM#	Date	Year	VG	Fine	VF	XF
10	—	—	11.50	13.50	16.50	20.00

MALER KOTLA

Umar Khan

AD1768-1778

Identifying Marks:

On reverse

RUPEE

SILVER, 17mm, 10.70-11.60 gm

C#	Date	Year	VG	Fine	VF	XF
5	—	4 (frozen)	15.00	20.00	26.50	33.50

Asadullah Khan

AD1778-1782

Identifying Marks:

On reverse

RUPEE

SILVER, 17mm, 10.70-11.60 gm

C#	Date	Year	VG	Fine	VF	XF
10	—	4 (frozen)	11.50	13.50	16.50	20.00

Amir Khan

AD1821-1845

Identifying Marks:

On reverse

1/4 RUPEE

SILVER, 14mm, 2.68-2.90 gm

#	Date	Year	VG	Fine	VF	XF
13	—	4 (frozen)	6.50	8.50	11.00	15.00

1/2 RUPEE

SILVER, 16mm, 5.35-5.80 gm

#	Date	Year	VG	Fine	VF	XF
14	—	4 (frozen)	6.50	8.50	11.00	15.00

RUPEE

SILVER, 17mm, 10.70-11.60 gm

#	Date	Year	VG	Fine	VF	XF
15	—	4 (frozen)	11.50	13.50	16.50	20.00

NOTE: Counterfeit copies exist.

Sube Khan

Mahbub Ali Khan

AD1845-1859

Identifying Marks:

On reverse

1/2 RUPEE

SILVER, 15mm, 5.35-5.80 gm

#	Date	Year	VG	Fine	VF	XF
19	—	4 (frozen)	10.00	12.50	16.00	21.50

RUPEE

SILVER, 17mm, 10.70-11.60 gm

#	Date	Year	VG	Fine	VF	XF
20	ND	—	11.50	13.50	16.50	20.00

Sikandar Ali Khan

AD1859-1871

Identifying Marks:

On reverse

1/4 RUPEE

SILVER, 14mm, 2.68-2.90 gm

Y#	Date	Year	VG	Fine	VF	XF
1	ND	—	6.00	8.00	11.00	15.00

1/2 RUPEE

SILVER, 16mm, 5.35-5.80 gm
Marks as above

Y#	Date	Year	VG	Fine	VF	XF
2	ND	—	6.00	8.00	11.00	15.00

RUPEE

SILVER, 17mm, 10.70-11.60 gm
Fine style

Y#	Date	Year	VG	Fine	VF	XF
3	ND	—	11.50	13.50	16.50	20.00

Ibrahim Ali Khan

AD1871-1908

Identifying Marks:

On reverse

1/4 RUPEE

SILVER, 11-14mm, 2.68-2.90 gm

Y#	Date	Year	VG	Fine	VF	XF
4	ND	—	6.50	8.50	11.50	16.00

1/2 RUPEE

SILVER, 16mm, 5.35-5.80 gm

Y#	Date	Year	VG	Fine	VF	XF
5	ND	—	6.50	8.50	11.50	16.00

RUPEE

SILVER, 15-17mm, 10.70-11.60 gm

Y#	Date	Year	VG	Fine	VF	XF
6	ND	—	11.50	13.50	16.50	20.00
	AH1292	—	12.50	14.50	17.50	22.50

Ahmad Ali Khan

1908-After 1923

Identifying Marks:

On reverse

1/2 PAISA

COPPER

Y#	Date	Year	Good	VG	Fine	VF
7	ND	—	2.50	3.50	5.00	7.00

PAISA

COPPER

Y#	Date	Year	Good	VG	Fine	VF
8	AH3126 (error for 1326)		3.00	4.50	6.50	10.00

RUPEE

SILVER, 15-19mm, 10.70-11.60 gm

Y#	Date	Year	VG	Fine	VF	XF
9	ND	—	11.50	13.50	16.50	20.00
	AH1311	—	12.50	14.50	17.50	22.50

NAZARANA RUPEE

SILVER, 33mm, 10.70-11.60 gm

Y#	Date	Year	VG	Fine	VF	XF
10	AH1326	—	—	—	Rare	—

NABHA

Jaswant Singh

VS1840-1897/1783-1840AD

Identifying Marks:

On reverse. Various Arabic numerals are known.

RUPEE

SILVER, 15mm, 10.70-11.60 gm

C#	Date	Year	VG	Fine	VF	XF
20	ND	—	11.50	13.50	16.50	20.00

16mm

C#	Date	Year	VG	Fine	VF	XF
20.1	VS(18)77	(1820)	11.50	13.50	16.50	20.00

C#	Date	Year	VG	Fine	VF	XF
20.2	VS(18)82	(1825)	11.50	13.50	16.50	20.00
	83	(1826)	11.50	13.50	16.50	20.00
	93	(1836)	11.50	13.50	16.50	20.00

NAZARANA RUPEE

SILVER, 32mm

C#	Date	Year	VG	Fine	VF	XF
25	VS1893	(1836)	—	—	Rare	—

Bharpur Singh

VS1903-1920/1846-1863AD

Identifying Marks:

On reverse

In the name of Govind Singh, Sikh Saint:

RUPEE

SILVER, 18-21mm, 10.70-11.60 gm
Leaf to left of stylized '4'

Y#	Date	Year	VG	Fine	VF	XF
1	VS1907	(1850)	13.50	18.50	24.50	33.50
	1917	(1860)	13.50	18.50	24.50	33.50
	1920	(1863)	13.50	18.50	24.50	33.50

Hira Singh

VS1927-1968/1870-1911AD

Identifying Marks:

On reverse

RUPEE

SILVER, 18-21mm, 10.70-11.60 gm
Dagger to left of stylized '4'

Y#	Date	Year	VG	Fine	VF	XF
2	VS1927	(1870)	13.50	18.50	24.50	33.50
	1928	(1871)	13.50	18.50	24.50	33.50
	1929	(1872)	13.50	18.50	24.50	33.50

PATIALA

Amar Singh

AD1765-1781

Identifying Marks:

 **On reverse**

RUPEE

SILVER, 16-18mm, 10.70-11.60 gm

C#	Date	Year	VG	Fine	VF	XF
10	—	4 (frozen)				
			12.50	14.50	17.50	22.50

Sahib Singh

AD1781-1813

Identifying Marks:

 **On reverse (tentative)**

RUPEE

SILVER, 16-18mm, 10.70-11.60 gm

#	Date	Year	VG	Fine	VF	XF
20	—	—	12.50	14.50	17.50	22.50

Karm Singh

AD1813-1845

Identifying Marks:

 **On reverse**

1/4 RUPEE

SILVER, 2.68-2.90 gm

#	Date	Year	VG	Fine	VF	XF
28	—	—	10.00	13.50	16.50	21.50

RUPEE

SILVER, 16mm, 10.70-11.60 gm
No symbols around

C#	Date	Year	VG	Fine	VF	XF
30.1	—	—	12.50	14.50	17.50	23.50

'Alif' to left of

C#	Date	Year	VG	Fine	VF	XF
30.2	—	—	12.50	14.50	17.50	23.50

18mm
Crescent to right of

C#	Date	Year	VG	Fine	VF	XF
30.3	—	—	12.50	14.50	17.50	23.50

17mm
Three-pointed leaf to right of

C#	Date	Year	VG	Fine	VF	XF
30.4	—	—	12.50	14.50	17.50	23.50

18mm
Crescent to right, branch to left of

C#	Date	Year	VG	Fine	VF	XF
30.5	—	—	12.50	14.50	17.50	23.50

17mm
Branch to right of

C#	Date	Year	VG	Fine	VF	XF
30.6	—	—	12.50	14.50	17.50	23.50

Branches both sides of

C#	Date	Year	VG	Fine	VF	XF
30.7	—	—	12.50	14.50	17.50	23.50

 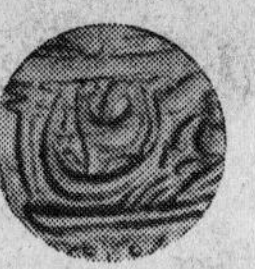

16mm
Double hilted sword.

C#	Date	Year	VG	Fine	VF	XF
31	—	—	13.50	17.50	23.50	30.00

NAZARANA RUPEE

SILVER, 24mm, 10.70-11.60 gm

C#	Date	Year	VG	Fine	VF	XF
30a	AH(18)98	—	—	—	Rare	—

MOHUR

GOLD, 16mm, 10.70-11.60 gm

C#	Date	Year	VG	Fine	VF	XF
35	—	—	220.00	240.00	265.00	300.00

Narindar Singh

VS1902-1919/1845-1862AD

Identifying Marks:

 **On reverse**

RUPEE

SILVER, 16-17mm, 10.70-11.60 gm

Y#	Date	Year	VG	Fine	VF	XF
1	VS1902	1845	13.50	16.50	20.00	28.50

MOHUR

GOLD, 17-18mm, 10.70-11.40 gm
Similar to 1 Rupee, Y#1.

Y#	Date	Year	VG	Fine	VF	XF
2	—	—	220.00	240.00	265.00	300.00

Mahindar Singh

VS1919-1933/1862-1876AD

Identifying Marks:

 **On reverse**

RUPEE

SILVER, 16-17mm, 10.70-11.60 gm

Y#	Date	Year	VG	Fine	VF	XF
3	—	—	12.50	14.50	17.50	22.50

Rajindar Singh

VS1933-1957/1876-1900AD

Identifying Marks:

 **On reverse**

1/4 RUPEE

SILVER, 13mm, 2.68-2.90 gm

Y#	Date	Year	VG	Fine	VF	XF
4	—	—	10.00	13.00	16.50	20.00

1/2 RUPEE

SILVER, 16mm, 5.35-5.80 gm
Marks as above

Y#	Date	Year	VG	Fine	VF	XF
5	—	—	10.00	13.00	16.50	20.00

RUPEE

SILVER, 16-18mm, 10.70-11.60 gm

Y#	Date	Year	VG	Fine	VF	XF
6	VS(19)45	4 (frozen)				
			11.50	13.50	16.50	20.00
	(19)46	(1889)	11.50	13.50	16.50	20.00
	(19)47	(1890)	11.50	13.50	16.50	20.00

NAZARANA RUPEE

SILVER, 32mm, 10.70-11.60 gm

Y#	Date	Year	VG	Fine	VF	XF
6a	—	4 (frozen)				
			—	—	Rare	—

Mint name, Sahrind, clearly legible on reverse.

1/3 MOHUR

GOLD, 15mm, 3.57-3.80 gm
Bayoneted rifle to left of stylized '4'.

7	(xx)94	—	75.00	100.00	125.00	165.00

2/3 MOHUR

GOLD, 18mm, 7.14-7.60 gm
Bayoneted rifle to left of stylized '4'

8	(xx)94	—	150.00	185.00	210.00	250.00

MOHUR

GOLD, 18mm, 10.70-11.40 gm
Similar to 1 Rupee, Y#6.

9	ND	—	—	—	—	—

Uncertain

Unknown, possibly early twentieth Century.

Identifying Marks:

On reverse

RUPEE

SILVER, 17mm, 10.70-11.60 gm

KM#	Date	Year	VG	Fine	VF	XF
1	—	4 (frozen)				
			—	—	—	—

1/3 MOHUR

GOLD, 15mm, 3.57-3.80 gm
Rev: Dagger to left.

15	(xx)58	—

COCHIN

Late 18th - early 19th century

PUTTUN

SILVER, 6-7mm, 0.324 gm.

C#	Date	VG	Fine	VF	XF
1	ND	2.00	3.00	5.00	8.00

.52 gm.
Similar to 2 Puttuns, C#6.

5	ND	3.00	4.00	6.00	9.00

2 PUTTUNS

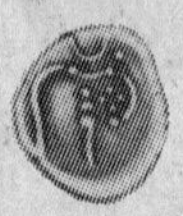

SILVER, 11mm, 1.0 gm.

2	ND	4.00	5.50	8.00	11.50

6	ND	4.00	5.50	8.00	11.50

FANAM

GOLD, 7-9mm

KM#	Date	VG	Fine	VF	XF
10	ND	7.00	9.00	11.50	15.00

COOCH BEHAR

Devendra Narayana

1764-1766

NOTE: Minimum portion of name necessary for identification. Refer to Bhutan listings for later copies in silver, brass, copper.

'Vendra' center left on obverse

1/2 RUPEE

SILVER, 20mm, 5.35-5.80 gm.

C#	Date	VG	Fine	VF	XF
111	ND	7.50	9.00	11.00	15.00

Dhairyendra Narayana

1766-1771, 1780-1783

Minimum portion of name necessary for identification:

'Y E NDRA' center left on obverse

1/2 RUPEE

SILVER, 19mm, 5.35-5.80 gm.

C#	Date	VG	Fine	VF	XF
121	ND	7.50	9.00	11.00	15.00

Rajendra Narayana

1771-1773

Minimum portion of name necessary for identification.

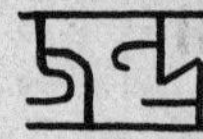

'J E NDRA' center left on obverse

1/2 RUPEE

SILVER, 20mm, 5.35-5.80 gm.

131	ND	7.50	9.00	11.00	15.00

Darendra Narayana

1773-1780

Harendra Narayana

1783-1839

These names usually cannot be differentiated. Minimum portion of name necessary for identification:

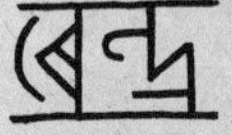

Rendra' center left on obverse

1/2 RUPEE

SILVER, 19mm, 5.35-5.80 gm.

151	ND	7.50	9.00	11.00	15.00

PRESENTATION ISSUES

The following half Rupees and Mohurs are all presentation (nazarana) issues. Silver and gold were struck from same dies. They are dated in a local era beginning with the founding of the Koch Kingdom in AD1510 (RE dates).

Sivendra Narayana

1839-1847

1/2 RUPEE

SILVER, 21mm, 5.35-5.80 gm.

C#	Date	Year	VG	Fine	VF	XF
161	ND	—	20.00	27.50	36.50	45.00

MOHUR

GOLD, 21mm, 10.70-11.40 gm.

165	ND	—	220.00	240.00	265.00	300.00

Narendra Narayana

1847-1863

1/2 RUPEE

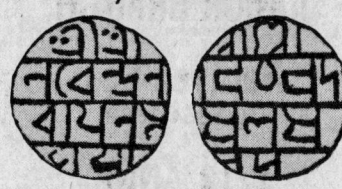

SILVER, 21mm, 5.35-5.80 gm.

Y#	Date	Mintage	VG	Fine	VF	XF
1	ND	1,000	18.50	25.00	33.50	42.50

MOHUR

GOLD, 21mm, 10.70-11.60 gm.

2	ND	—	225.00	250.00	300.00	350.00

Nrpendra Narayana

1863-1911

1/2 RUPEE

SILVER, 21mm

Y#	Date	Year	Fine	VF	XF	Unc
3	RE354	(1864)	20.00	25.00	31.50	40.00

MOHUR

GOLD, 21mm

4	RE354	(1864)	225.00	275.00	325.00	375.00

Raja Rajendra

1911-1913

1/2 RUPEE

SILVER, 21mm

Y#	Date	Year	Mintage	VF	XF	Unc
5	RE402	(1912)	1,001	22.50	30.00	37.50

MOHUR

GOLD, 21mm

6	RE402	(1912)	100 pcs.	265.00	300.00	350.00

Jitendra Narayana

AD1913-1922

1/2 RUPEE

SILVER, 21mm

Y#	Date	Year	Mintage	VF	XF	Unc
7	RE404	(1914)	1,002	20.00	27.50	36.50

MOHUR

GOLD, 21mm

8	RE404	(1914)	100 pcs.	265.00	300.00	350.00

Jagaddipendra Narayana

AD1922-1949

1/2 RUPEE

SILVER, 21mm

9	RE413	(1923)	—	32.50	40.00	50.00

COORG

Formerly listed under 'Malabar Coast'

FANAM

SILVER, 7-8mm, 0.39 gm.

C#	Date	Year	VG	Fine	VF	XF
10	ND	—	3.50	4.00	5.50	8.00

NOTE: Struck 18th-19th centuries.

GOLD, 7-8mm, 0.38 gm.
'Vira Raya'
Many minor variations

20	ND	—	7.00	9.00	11.50	15.00

NOTE: Struck Ca. 1770-1900AD.

DATIA

RULERS

Parachat, AD 1802-1839
Vijaya Bahadur, AD 1839-1857
Bhawahni Singh, AD 1857-1907
Govino Singh, AD 1907-1948

In the name of Shah Alam II:

Early issues:

Mintname: Dalipnagar

RUPEE

SILVER, 21mm, 10.70-11.60 gm
Prototype for 1 Rupee, C#27.

KM#	Date	Year	VG	Fine	VF	XF
6	1178	6	20.00	25.00	31.50	40.00

TEGH SHAHI PAISA

COPPER, 20mm

C#	Date	Year	Good	VG	Fine	VF
21	—	1	1.50	2.25	3.25	4.50

Raja Shahi Series

Spuriously dated AH1178 and yr. 6 (of Shah Alam II); identified by the following marks:

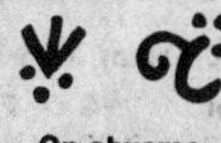

On obverse

On reverse

1/4 RUPEE

SILVER, 12-13mm, 2.68-2.90 gm

C#	Date	Year	VG	Fine	VF	XF
25	AH1178	6	4.00	5.50	7.00	10.00

1/2 RUPEE

SILVER, 14-15mm, 5.35-5.80 gm

26	AH1178	6	6.50	7.50	9.00	13.50

RUPEE

SILVER, 17-19mm, 10.70-11.60 gm

27	AH1178	6	11.50	13.50	16.50	20.00

NOTE: Known error dates include 1171, 1177, 1181, 1182, 8811, 11782 and 117112. No premiums.

Gaja Shahi Series

Struck for more than 100 years, with AH date on obverse and spurious regnal year on reverse. These are close copies of Orchha C#24-32 and can only be distinguished by the symbols, which are always different from those of Orchha, except for the 'Gaja' (mace):

'Gaja' always on reverse

On obverse (Datia Mint Symbol)

On reverse

1/2 PAISA

COPPER, 14mm, 6 gm.

C#	Date	Year	Good	VG	Fine	VF
22	—	4x	2.25	3.00	3.75	5.00

PAISA

COPPER, 16-20mm, round or squarish, 12-13 gm.

C#	Date	Year	Good	VG	Fine	VF
23	AH1246	3x	2.50	3.25	4.00	5.50
	—	39	2.50	3.25	4.00	5.50
	—	4x	2.50	3.25	4.00	5.50
	Date Off Flan		1.25	2.25	3.25	4.50

1/8 RUPEE

SILVER, 10-11mm, 1.34-1.45 gm

C#	Date	Year	VG	Fine	VF	XF
35	—	22	3.00	4.00	5.50	7.50
	—	4x	3.00	4.00	5.50	7.50

1/4 RUPEE

SILVER, 12-15mm, 2.68-2.90 gm

C#	Date	Year	VG	Fine	VF	XF
36	AH1317	23	4.50	5.50	7.00	10.00

1/2 RUPEE

SILVER, 15-17mm, 5.35-5.80 gm

C#	Date	Year	VG	Fine	VF	XF
37	AH1311	19	6.50	7.50	9.00	14.00
	—	23	6.50	7.50	9.00	14.00
	—	29	6.50	7.50	9.00	14.00

RUPEE

SILVER, 18-20mm, 10.70-11.60 gm

C#	Date	Year	VG	Fine	VF	XF
38	AH1215	23	11.50	13.50	16.50	20.00
	1233	24	11.50	13.50	16.50	20.00
	1233	28	11.50	13.50	16.50	20.00
	1249	28	11.50	13.50	16.50	20.00
	1262	29	11.50	13.50	16.50	20.00
	1270	36	11.50	13.50	16.50	20.00
	1272	38	11.50	13.50	16.50	20.00
	1273	39	11.50	13.50	16.50	20.00
	1277	44	11.50	13.50	16.50	20.00
	1278	45	11.50	13.50	16.50	20.00
	1282	46	11.50	13.50	16.50	20.00
	1311	19	11.50	13.50	16.50	20.00
	1312	25	11.50	13.50	16.50	20.00
	1313	24	11.50	13.50	16.50	20.00
	1315	23	11.50	13.50	16.50	20.00
	—	35	11.50	13.50	16.50	20.00

In the name of Muhammad Akbar II:

RUPEE

SILVER, 10.70-11.60 gm

C#	Date	Year	VG	Fine	VF	XF
45	AH1270	33	12.50	15.00	18.50	23.50

Govind Singh

AD 1907-1948

1/2 MOHUR

GOLD, 20mm, 5.35-5.70 gm

Y#	Date	Year	VG	Fine	VF	XF
1	ND		235.00	265.00	300.00	350.00

DEWAS

SENIOR BRANCH

Krishnaji Rao

AD 1860-1899

PAISA

COPPER, 20mm

C#	Date	Good	VG	Fine	VF
10	—	2.50	3.50	5.00	7.00

NOTE: This coin was struck in Allote from ca. 1750 until the beginning of this century. Several design and weight varieties exist.

MACHINE STRUCK COINAGE

1/12 ANNA

COPPER

Y#	Date	Mintage	Fine	VF	XF	Unc
1	1888	—	8.00	12.50	18.50	28.50
	1888	—	—	—	Proof	70.00

1/4 ANNA

COPPER

Y#	Date	Mintage	Fine	VF	XF	Unc
2	1888	—	8.00	12.50	20.00	30.00
	1888	—	—	—	Proof	70.00

Vikrama Simha Rao

AD 1937-1948

PAISA

COPPER

Y#	Date	Mintage	Fine	VF	XF	Unc
3	1944	—	45.00	60.00	80.00	100.00

JUNIOR BRANCH

Narayan Rao

AD 1864-1892

1/12 ANNA

COPPER

Y#	Date	Mintage	Fine	VF	XF	Unc
1	1888	—	15.00	25.00	35.00	45.00

1/4 ANNA

COPPER

Y#	Date	Mintage	Fine	VF	XF	Unc
3	1888	—	13.50	22.50	32.50	42.50

DHAR

Jaswant Rao

AH1250-1274/1834-1857AD

PAISA

COPPER, 17mm

C#	Date	Year	Good	VG	Fine	VF
1	AH1266	—	2.50	4.00	5.50	7.50

Anand Rao III

AH1276-1316/1860-1898AD

1/2 PAISA

COPPER, 16mm

Y#	Date	Year	Good	VG	Fine	VF
A1	AH1289	—	3.00	5.00	6.00	8.50

PAISA

COPPER, 17-20mm

Y#	Date	Year	Good	VG	Fine	VF
B1	AH1289	—	1.75	3.00	4.50	6.50

17mm

Y#	Date	Year	Good	VG	Fine	VF
C1	AH1266	—	1.75	3.00	4.50	6.00

MACHINE STRUCK COINAGE

1/12 ANNA

COPPER

Y#	Date	Mintage	Fine	VF	XF	Unc
1	1887	—	6.00	7.50	9.50	13.50
	1887	—	—	—	Proof	70.00

1/2 PICE

COPPER

Y#	Date	Mintage	Fine	VF	XF	Unc
2	1887	—	6.50	7.50	9.50	13.50
	1887	—	—	—	Proof	70.00

1/4 ANNA

COPPER

Y#	Date	Mintage	Fine	VF	XF	Unc
3	1887	—	7.50	10.00	15.00	22.50
	1887	—	—	—	Proof	80.00

Anand Rao IV

1943-1948

NAZARANA MOHUR

GOLD

KM#	Date	Year	Fine	VF	XF	Unc
1	1943	—	220.00	240.00	265.00	300.00

DHOLPUR

Kirat Singh

AD1788-1806 (In Gohad)

AD1806-1835 (In Dholpur)

In the name of Shah Alam II:

Struck at Gohad before Kirat Singh exchanged it forDholpur in AD1806/AH1221.

RUPEE

SILVER, 21-25mm, 10.70-11.60 gm.

C#	Date	Year	VG	Fine	VF	XF
5	AH1208	36	20.00	22.50	25.00	32.50
	1218	46	20.00	22.50	25.00	32.50

In the name of Muhammad Akbar II:

Mintmarks

On obverse

On reverse

1/2 RUPEE

SILVER, 17mm, 5.35-5.80 gm.

MINT: GOHAD

C#	Date	Year	VG	Fine	VF	XF
11g	—	—	14.00	18.00	22.50	28.50

RUPEE

SILVER, 20-25mm

MINT: DHOLPUR

C#	Date	Year	VG	Fine	VF	XF
12d	AH1221	—	15.00	20.00	25.00	31.50
	1225	4	20.00	25.00	30.00	37.50

The two dates differ in form of the mint name.

MINT: GOHAD

20-25mm

C#	Date	Year	VG	Fine	VF	XF
12g	AH—	21	15.00	20.00	25.00	31.50
	1245	24	15.00	20.00	25.00	31.50
	1251	30	15.00	20.00	25.00	31.50
	1252	31	17.50	22.50	27.50	35.00

NOTE: Coins dated AH1252/31 actually struck in 1857 (AH1274).

NAZARANA RUPEE

SILVER, 31mm, 10.70-11.60 gm.

C#	Date	Year	VG	Fine	VF	XF
13	AH1252	31	50.00	65.00	80.00	100.00

DUNGARPUR

BIJEY SINGH

VS1955-1975/1898-1918AD

1/2 PAISA

COPPER, 13mm

KM#	Date	Year	Good	VG	Fine	VF
1	VS1917	(1860)	3.50	5.50	8.00	11.50

PAISA

COPPER, 18mm

Y#	Date	Year	Good	VG	Fine	VF
A1	VS1916	(1859)	3.00	5.00	7.50	10.00
	1917	(1860)	3.00	5.00	7.50	10.00

Lakshman Singh

VS1975-2005/1918-1948AD

PAISA

COPPER, 17-19mm

Rev: Var. I, 2 bars above P of Paisa and dot to lower right of SA.

Y#	Date	Year	VG	Fine	VF	XF
1.1	VS2001	(1944)	25.00	30.00	37.50	45.00

Rev: Var. II, one bar above P of Paisa, no dot.

Y#	Date	Year	VG	Fine	VF	XF
1.2	VS2001	—	6.50	9.00	12.50	16.50

NOTE: Var. II is believed to be a restrike or fake.

NAZARANA MOHUR

GOLD

KM#	Date	Year	VG	Fine	VF	XF
2	VS1996	(1939)	225.00	250.00	285.00	325.00

FARRUKHABAD

Formerly listed as Mughal Empire: Ahmadnagar-Farrukhabad Mint.

BANGASH NAWABS

Ahmad Khan
AH1174-1185/AD1761-1771
Muzaffar Jang
AH1185-1210/AD1771-1796
Amin-ud-Daula
AH1210-1217/AD1796-1802

Ahmadnagar - Farrukhabad Mint

1/4 RUPEE

SILVER, 2.68-2.90 gm.

C#	Date	Year	VG	Fine	VF	XF
84.2	AH—	39	6.00	8.00	10.00	13.50

RUPEE

SILVER, 24-28mm, 10.70-11.60 gm.

C#	Date	Year	VG	Fine	VF	XF
86.2	AH1175	2	12.50	14.00	17.50	23.50
	1175	3	12.50	14.00	17.50	23.50
	1177	4	12.50	14.00	17.50	23.50
	1177	5	11.50	13.00	15.00	20.00
	1179	6	11.50	13.00	15.00	20.00
	1180	7	11.50	13.00	15.00	20.00
	1186	13	11.50	13.00	15.00	20.00
	1187	15	11.50	13.00	15.00	20.00
	1189	17	11.50	13.00	15.00	20.00
	1190	18	11.50	13.00	15.00	20.00
	1192	19	11.50	13.00	15.00	20.00
	1193	20	11.50	13.00	15.00	20.00
	1194	21	11.50	13.00	15.00	20.00
	1195	21	11.50	13.00	15.00	20.00
	1196	21	11.50	13.00	15.00	20.00
	1196	22	11.50	13.00	15.00	20.00
	1196	23	11.50	13.00	15.00	20.00
	1197	23	11.50	13.00	15.00	20.00
	1197	24	11.50	13.00	15.00	20.00
	1198	24	11.50	13.00	15.00	20.00
	1198	25	11.50	13.00	15.00	20.00
	1199	27	11.50	13.00	15.00	20.00
	1200	27	11.50	13.00	15.00	20.00
	1203	29	11.50	13.00	15.00	20.00
	1205	31	11.50	13.00	15.00	20.00
	1206	31	11.50	13.00	15.00	20.00
	1207	31	11.50	13.00	15.00	20.00
	1208	31	11.50	13.00	15.00	20.00
	1209	31	11.50	13.00	15.00	20.00
	1211	31	11.50	13.00	15.00	20.00
	1212	31	11.50	13.00	15.00	20.00
	1212	39	11.50	13.00	15.00	20.00
	1213	39	11.50	13.00	15.00	20.00
	1214	39	11.50	13.00	15.00	20.00
	1215	39	11.50	13.00	15.00	20.00
	1216	39	11.50	13.00	15.00	20.00
	1217	39	11.50	13.00	15.00	20.00
	1218	39	11.50	13.00	15.00	20.00
	1219	39	11.50	13.00	15.00	20.00
	1220	39	11.50	13.00	15.00	20.00
	1224	31	12.50	14.00	17.50	27.50
	1225	31	12.50	14.00	17.50	27.50
	1227	31	12.50	14.00	17.50	27.50
	1228	31	12.50	14.00	17.50	27.50

NAZARANA RUPEE

SILVER, 36mm, 10.70-11.60 gm.

C#	Date	Year	VG	Fine	VF	XF
86.2a	AH1218	39	65.00	85.00	110.00	135.00

MOHUR

GOLD, 24mm, 10.70-11.40 gm.

C#	Date	Year	VG	Fine	VF	XF
97.2	AH1194	21	220.00	240.00	265.00	300.00
	1196	23	220.00	240.00	265.00	300.00
	1211	31	220.00	240.00	265.00	300.00

GARHWAL

Srinagar Mint

Pradip Shah

VS1774-1829/1717-1772AD

In the name of Pradip Shah

TACA

COPPER, 20mm

C#	Date	Year	Good	VG	Fine	VF
5	VS1827	(1770)	3.00	4.50	6.50	9.00

In the name of Shah Alam II:

Dar-ul-Khilafat Shahjahanabad Mint

TIMASHA
TYPE I

SILVER, 17mm
Prototype of C#10.

C#	Date	Year	VG	Fine	VF	XF
3	ND	—	—	—	Rare	—

Srinagar Mint

TIMASHA
TYPE II, Jalus dates

SILVER, 18mm

C#	Date	Year	VG	Fine	VF	XF
10	—	1	7.50	9.00	11.00	15.00
		2	7.50	9.00	11.00	15.00
		3	7.50	9.00	11.00	15.00
		4	7.50	9.00	11.00	15.00
		5	7.50	9.00	11.00	15.00
		8	7.50	9.00	11.00	15.00
		11	7.50	9.00	11.00	15.00
		12	7.50	9.00	11.00	15.00
		15	7.50	9.00	11.00	15.00

TYPE III, Hijri dates

17mm

C#	Date	Year	VG	Fine	VF	XF
10a	AH1181	—	9.00	12.00	15.00	20.00
	1182	—	9.00	12.00	15.00	20.00

Lallat Shah

VS1829-1838/1772-1781AD

In the name of Lallat Shah

TACA

COPPER, 18mm

C#	Date	Year	Good	VG	Fine	VF
15	VS1830	(1773)	3.00	4.50	6.00	8.50
	1831	(1774)	3.00	4.50	6.00	8.50
	1835	(1778)	3.00	4.50	6.00	8.50
	1838	(1781)	4.00	6.00	7.50	10.00

In the name of Shah Alam II:

TIMASHA

SILVER, 17mm

C#	Date	Year	VG	Fine	VF	XF
20	AH1188	VS1831	10.00	15.00	20.00	27.50
	1189	1832	10.00	15.00	20.00	27.50
	1190	1833	10.00	15.00	20.00	27.50
	1191	1834	10.00	15.00	20.00	27.50
	1192	1835	10.00	15.00	20.00	27.50

18mm, trident instead of AH date.

C#	Date	Year	VG	Fine	VF	XF
20a	VS1837	(1780)	6.00	9.00	12.50	17.00

Parduman Shah

VS1842-1860/1785-1803AD

In the name of Parduman Shah

TACA

COPPER, 16-17mm

C#	Date	Year	Good	VG	Fine	VF
25	VS1845	(1788)	4.00	6.00	7.50	10.00
	1853	(1796)	3.00	4.50	6.00	8.50

Girvan Yuddha

(of Nepal)

VS1860-1872/1803-1815AD

In the names of Shah Alam II & Girvan Yuddha (1803-06):

TIMASHA

SILVER, 15-17mm

C#	Date	Year	VG	Fine	VF	XF
35	VS(18)66	(1809)	8.00	11.00	15.00	20.00
	ND	—	5.00	8.00	11.00	14.00

In the name of Muhammad Akbar II & Girvan Yuddha (1806-13):

TIMASHA

SILVER, 15-17mm

C#	Date	VG	Fine	VF	XF
36	(18)66 (1809)	8.00	11.00	15.00	20.00
	(18)67 (1810)	8.00	11.00	15.00	20.00
	(18)68 (1811)	8.00	11.00	15.00	20.00
	(18)69 (1812)	8.00	11.00	15.00	20.00
	(18)70 (1813)	8.00	11.00	15.00	20.00

In the name of Girvan Yuddha (1813-15)

PAISA

COPPER, 19mm

C#	Date	Year	Good	VG	Fine	VF
30	VS1859	(1802)	4.00	6.00	7.50	10.00
	1872	(1815)	3.00	4.50	6.00	8.00
	1873	(1816)	4.00	6.00	7.50	10.00

TIMASHA

SILVER, 16-17mm

C#	Date	Year	VG	Fine	VF	XF
37	ND	—	8.00	11.00	15.00	20.00

KUMAON

Almora Mint

For earlier issues, see Almora

Girvan Yuddha

(of Nepal)

VS1847-1872/1790-1815AD

PAISA

COPPER, 18-19mm

C#	Date	Year	Good	VG	Fine	VF
10	VS(18)66	(1809)	3.50	5.00	7.00	10.00

SIRMUR

Nahan Mint

Girvan Yuddha

(of Nepal)

AD1803-1815

1/2 PAISA

COPPER, 20mm

C#	Date	Year	Good	VG	Fine	VF
20	AH1227	—	3.00	4.50	6.00	8.00

PAISA

COPPER, 25mm

C#	Date	Year	Good	VG	Fine	VF
21	AH1227	—	4.00	5.50	7.50	10.00

GWALIOR

RULERS

Jankoji Rao
AH1173-1175/AD1759-1761
Mahadji Rao
AH 1175-1209/AD 1761-1794
Daulat Rao
AH 1209-1243/AD 1794-1827
Baija Bao, Regent,
(Widow of Daulat Rao)
AH 1243-1249/AD 1827-1833
Jankoji Rao
AH 1243-1259/AD 1827-1843
Jayaji Rao
AH 1259-1304/AD 1843-1886
Madho Rao
AH 1304-13/AD 1886-1925

NOTE: None of the coins of Gwalior prior to the beginning of machine-struck coinage in 1889 bears the name of the Sindhia (ruler of Gwalior), but beginning with the reign of Baija Bao, a Nagari letter is used to indicate the ruler under whom it was struck, as follows:

श्री	Sri	Baija Bao
ज	Ja	Jankoji Rao
जी	Ji	Jayaji Rao
मा	M	Madho Rao

However, not all the coins bear the initial of the ruler, especially the copper.

The coinage of Gwalior is extremely complicated and not fully understood. Each mint, and there were probably more than twenty in all, maintained its own styles and types, and operated fully independently of every other mint. Hence it is most logical to list the issues of each mint together, rather than attempt to list the coins by reign or denomination. The mints are best identified by the presence of special symbols on the obverse or reverse of the coins, and those symbols are noted whenever possible. Types are listed with designation of reign only when the initial of the ruler appears on the coin; others are assigned a single number for the full duration of their issuance.

Most of the coins of Gwalior are undated, or issued over long periods of time with frozen dates, in order to discourage the nefarious practice of devaluing coins of older dates (for example, one-year old coins might be devalued 1", two-year olds 2", and so forth). Many of the types were struck with frozen dates for several decades, and in many other cases, the dates remained frozen while the ruler's initial changed. The frozen dates may be either AH dates or regnal years, or both.

Regularly dated series often continued over long durations, such as the Ujjain rupees (C#259); the lists of such coins are probably very fragmentary, and many unlisted dates will be discovered. In general, unlisted dates are worth no more than listed dates of the same type.

Ajmir Mint

In the name of Shah Alam II

Mintmark 

NOTE: The Rupees (C#17) of Kuchawan are copied from Ajmir prototypes, but add a small sword to the obverse, by which they are distinguished from true Ajmir issues. See also Ajmir State (Maratha).

RUPEE

SILVER, 22mm, 10.70-11.60 gm
No mintmark.

C#	Date	Year	VG	Fine	VF	XF
1	AH1178	6	3.50	4.50	6.00	8.50
	—	10	11.50	13.50	16.50	20.00

Mintmark: 3 knots.

C#	Date	Year	VG	Fine	VF	XF
2	AH1188	14	11.50	13.50	16.50	20.00
	1189	14	11.50	13.50	16.50	20.00
	1190	14	11.50	13.50	16.50	20.00

20mm
Mintmark: 2 knots.

C#	Date	Year	VG	Fine	VF	XF
5	AH1196	24	11.50	13.50	16.50	20.00
	1197	24	11.50	13.50	16.50	20.00
	1198	24	11.50	13.50	16.50	20.00
	1203	31	11.50	13.50	16.50	20.00

23mm
With symbol 'SIR' of Baija Bao added, to left of regnal year.

C#	Date	Year	VG	Fine	VF	XF
7	AH1203	31	30.00	35.00	42.50	50.00

Bajranggarh Mint

Types of Jai Singh with added mintmarks.

1/8 RUPEE

SILVER, 16mm, 1.34-1.45 gm
Similar to 1 Rupee, C#12a.

C#	Date	Year	VG	Fine	VF	XF
9	ND	—	3.00	3.75	4.50	6.00

1/4 RUPEE

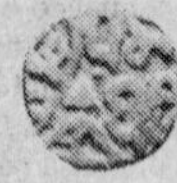

SILVER, 18mm, 2.68-2.90 gm

C#	Date	Year	VG	Fine	VF	XF
10	ND	—	5.00	6.00	7.50	10.00

1/2 RUPEE

SILVER, 5.35-5.80 gm.

C#	Date	Year	VG	Fine	VF	XF
11	ND	—	6.50	7.50	9.00	11.50

RUPEE

SILVER, 10.70-11.60 gm
Rev: Lotus, small flan.

C#	Date	Year	VG	Fine	VF	XF
12	—	21	11.50	13.50	16.50	20.00
	—	22	11.50	13.50	16.50	20.00

18-21mm
Obv: Bow and arrow. Rev: Lotus.

C#	Date	Year	VG	Fine	VF	XF
12a	—	23	11.50	13.50	16.50	20.00
	—	24	11.50	13.50	16.50	20.00
	—	25	11.50	13.50	16.50	20.00
	—	26	11.50	13.50	16.50	20.00
	—	27	11.50	13.50	16.50	20.00
	—	28	11.50	13.50	16.50	20.00
	—	29	11.50	13.50	16.50	20.00

MOHUR

GOLD, octagonal, 10.70-11.40 gm

C#	Date	Year	VG	Fine	VF	XF
13	ND	—	225.00	250.00	300.00	375.00

Broach Mint

PAISA

COPPER, 18mm

C#	Date	Year	Good	VG	Fine	VF
15	—	3	3.00	4.50	6.00	8.00

NAZARANA RUPEE

SILVER, 10.70-11.60 gm

C#	Date	Year	VG	Fine	VF	XF
18	AH1212	3	30.00	40.00	50.00	65.00

Basoda Mint

In the joint names of Muhammad Akbar II and Jankoji Rao

MINTMARKS

RUPEE

SILVER, 18mm, 10.70-11.60 gm

C#	Date	Year	VG	Fine	VF	XF
20	AH124x	18	11.50	13.50	16.50	20.00
	1252	32	11.50	13.50	16.50	20.00
	1254	32	11.50	13.50	16.50	20.00
	1274	3x	11.50	13.50	16.50	20.00
	1274	46	11.50	13.50	16.50	20.00

Bhilsa Mint

Mintmark

Frozen date AH(12)25

NOTE: The bow & arrow and trident appear on nearly all coins of Bhilsa, Gwalior Fort, and Lashkar Mints, and cannot be used to identify any one of them.

In the name of Shah Alam II, with initial of Jayaji Rao

Two varieties of C#30-32, with and without sword on obverse (no difference in value)

1/8 RUPEE

SILVER, 10-11mm, 1.34-1.45 gm

Y#	Date	Year	VG	Fine	VF	XF
1	AH(12)25	—	3.00	3.50	4.50	6.00

1/4 RUPEE

SILVER, 12-14mm, 2.68-2.90 gm

Y#	Date	Year	VG	Fine	VF	XF
2	AH(12)25	—	3.50	4.50	5.50	7.00

1/2 RUPEE

SILVER, 13-16mm, 5.35-5.80 gm
Variety I: No sword

Y#	Date	Year	VG	Fine	VF	XF
3.1	AH(12)25	—	6.50	7.50	8.50	10.00

Var. II: Sword on obv.

Y#	Date	Year	VG	Fine	VF	XF
3.2	AH(12)25	—	6.50	7.50	8.50	10.00

RUPEE

SILVER, 15mm, 10.70-11.60 gm

C#	Date	Year	VG	Fine	VF	XF
4	—	7	11.50	13.50	16.50	20.00
		11	11.50	13.50	16.50	20.00
		13	11.50	13.50	16.50	20.00
		14	11.50	13.50	16.50	20.00
		15	11.50	13.50	16.50	20.00
		16	11.50	13.50	16.50	20.00
		17	11.50	13.50	16.50	20.00
		26	11.50	13.50	16.50	20.00
		51	11.50	13.50	16.50	20.00

17-18mm
Var. I: No sword

Y#	Date	Year	VG	Fine	VF	XF
4.1	AH(12)25	—	11.50	13.50	16.50	20.00

Var. II: Sword on obv.

Y#	Date	Year	VG	Fine	VF	XF
4.2	AH(12)25	—	11.50	13.50	16.50	20.00

In the name of Shah Alam II, with initial of Madho Rao II

1/8 RUPEE

SILVER, 9-10mm, 1.34-1.45 gm

Y#	Date	Year	VG	Fine	VF	XF
5	AH(12)25	—	2.00	2.50	3.00	4.00

1/4 RUPEE

SILVER, 12mm, 2.68-2.90 gm

Y#	Date	Year	VG	Fine	VF	XF
6	AH(12)25	—	3.50	4.50	5.50	7.00

1/2 RUPEE

SILVER, 14mm, 5.35-5.80 gm

Y#	Date	Year	VG	Fine	VF	XF
7	AH(12)25	—	6.50	7.50	8.50	10.00

RUPEE

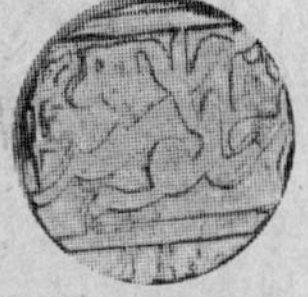

SILVER, 17-18mm, 10.70-11.60 gm

Y#	Date	Year	VG	Fine	VF	XF
8	AH(12)25	—	11.50	13.50	16.50	20.00

Burhanpur Mint

In the name of Shah Alam II:

Identifying mark:

on reverse

PAISA

COPPER, square, 16-18mm

C#	Date	Year	Good	VG	Fine	VF
40	—	—	2.50	3.50	4.50	6.00

NOTE: Struck 1795AD.

Round, 22mm

C#	Date	Year	Good	VG	Fine	VF
41	(Struck AD1805)		2.00	2.50	3.50	5.00

NOTE: The following silver coins bear the mintmark on reverse:

1/4 RUPEE

SILVER, 15mm, 2.68-2.90 gm

C#	Date	Year	VG	Fine	VF	XF
45	AH1214	—	8.00	10.00	12.50	16.50

1/2 RUPEE

SILVER, 17mm, 5.35-5.70 gm

C#	Date	Year	VG	Fine	VF	XF
46	AH1214	—	10.00	12.50	15.00	20.00

RUPEE

SILVER, 21-22mm, 10.70-11.60 gm

C#	Date	Year	VG	Fine	VF	XF
47	AH1195	—	11.50	13.50	16.50	20.00
	1196	23	11.50	13.50	16.50	20.00
	1197	21	11.50	13.50	16.50	20.00
	1198	24	11.50	13.50	16.50	20.00
	1200	26	11.50	13.50	16.50	20.00
	1201	2x	11.50	13.50	16.50	20.00
	1203	30	11.50	13.50	16.50	20.00
	1205	3x	11.50	13.50	16.50	20.00
	1209	—	11.50	13.50	16.50	20.00
	1210	84	11.50	13.50	16.50	20.00
	1211	3x	11.50	13.50	16.50	20.00
	1213	3x	11.50	13.50	16.50	20.00
	1214	—	11.50	13.50	16.50	20.00
	1215	4x	11.50	13.50	16.50	20.00
	1216	4x	11.50	13.50	16.50	20.00
	1217	4x	11.50	13.50	16.50	20.00
	1218	—	11.50	13.50	16.50	20.00
	1219	4x	11.50	13.50	16.50	20.00
	1221	4x	11.50	13.50	16.50	20.00
	1222	—	11.50	13.50	16.50	20.00
	1223	4x	11.50	13.50	16.50	20.00
	1224	4x	11.50	13.50	16.50	20.00
	1225	—	11.50	13.50	16.50	20.00
	1229	—	11.50	13.50	16.50	20.00
	1230	—	11.50	13.50	16.50	20.00
	1232	—	11.50	13.50	16.50	20.00
	1233	—	11.50	13.50	16.50	20.00
	1234	3x	11.50	13.50	16.50	20.00
	1235	39	11.50	13.50	16.50	20.00
	1237	—	11.50	13.50	16.50	20.00
	1238	—	11.50	13.50	16.50	20.00
	1239	—	11.50	13.50	16.50	20.00
	1242	—	11.50	13.50	16.50	20.00
	1243	—	11.50	13.50	16.50	20.00
	1247	—	11.50	13.50	16.50	20.00
	1255	—	11.50	13.50	16.50	20.00
	1259	—	11.50	13.50	16.50	20.00
	1260	—	11.50	13.50	16.50	20.00
	1261	—	11.50	13.50	16.50	20.00
	1262	—	11.50	13.50	16.50	20.00
	1266	—	11.50	13.50	16.50	20.00
	1271	—	11.50	13.50	16.50	20.00
	1273	—	11.50	13.50	16.50	20.00
	1274	—	11.50	13.50	16.50	20.00
47	1275	—	11.50	13.50	16.50	20.00
	1276	—	11.50	13.50	16.50	20.00
	1277	—	11.50	13.50	16.50	20.00

In the name of Alyjah Bahadur

Symbols:

to right of date

PAISA

COPPER, 24-26mm

C#	Date	Year	Good	VG	Fine	VF
50	AH1260	—	2.00	3.00	4.00	5.50
	1273	—	2.00	3.00	4.00	5.50
	1274	—	2.00	3.00	4.00	5.50
	1275	—	2.00	3.00	4.00	5.50

NOTE: Alyjah Bahadur was the hereditary title of the Sindhia rulers of Gwalior, and was used by all rulers of the dynasty.

Chanderi Mint

Mintmark

None, identified by style and mint name Kankurti, but struck at Chanderi.

In the name of Shah Alam II

RUPEE

SILVER, 18-19mm, 10.70-11.60 gm

C#	Date	Year	VG	Fine	VF	XF
58	ND	—	11.50	13.50	16.50	20.00

NOTE: This Rupee is identified by Arabic AL preceding MANUS on reverse.

Dohad Mint

Mintmark

PAISA

COPPER

Y#	Date	Year	Good	VG	Fine	VF
1	VS1912	—	3.00	4.50	6.50	9.00

Gwalior Fort Mint

In the name of Muhammad Shah

1/3 MOHUR

GOLD, 18mm, 3.57-3.80 gm

C#	Date	Year	VG	Fine	VF	XF
75	AH1130	2 (Frozen, struck AD1795)	125.00	165.00	200.00	235.00

Nagari SRI for Baija Bao

C#	Date	Year	VG	Fine	VF	XF
75a	AH1130	2 (Frozen, struck AD1827)	125.00	165.00	200.00	235.00
		Nagari JA for Jankoji				
75b	AH1130	2 (Frozen, struck AD1834)	125.00	165.00	200.00	235.00
		Nagari JI for Jayaji				
14	AH1130	2 (Frozen, struck AD1843)	125.00	165.00	200.00	235.00

In the Name of Shah Alam II

Mintmarks

copper coins (on obv.)

silver coins (on rev.)

PAISA

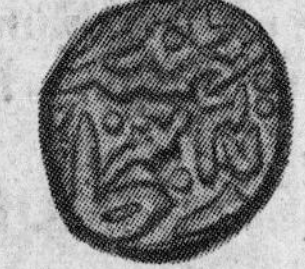

COPPER, 17-18mm

C#	Date	Year	Good	VG	Fine	VF
80	—	39	1.50	2.25	3.00	4.00

RUPEE

SILVER, 20-22mm, 10.70-11.60 gm

C#	Date	Year	VG	Fine	VF	XF
85	AH1174	1	12.50	14.50	17.50	21.50
	1191	19	11.50	13.50	16.50	20.00
	1197	25	11.50	13.50	16.50	20.00
	1210	—	11.50	13.50	16.50	20.00
	121x	40	11.50	13.50	16.50	20.00
	1213	41	11.50	13.50	16.50	20.00
	1216	—	11.50	13.50	16.50	20.00
	1221	48	11.50	13.50	16.50	20.00

In the name of Muhammad Akbar II:

PAISA

COPPER, 16-19mm

C#	Date	Year	Good	VG	Fine	VF
87	AH1256	—	.75	1.25	2.00	3.00
	1269	—	.75	1.25	2.00	3.00
	1277	48	.75	1.25	2.00	3.00
	—	49	.75	1.25	2.00	3.00
	1279	—	.75	1.25	2.00	3.00
	—	54	.75	1.25	2.00	3.00

RUPEE

Mintmarks

on obverse

on reverse

SILVER, 19-22mm

C#	Date	Year	VG	Fine	VF	XF
92	AH1222	—	11.50	13.50	16.50	20.00
	1227	6	11.50	13.50	16.50	20.00
	1228	7	11.50	13.50	16.50	20.00
	1229	8	11.50	13.50	16.50	20.00
	1230	9	11.50	13.50	16.50	20.00
	1231	10	11.50	13.50	16.50	20.00
	1231	11	11.50	13.50	16.50	20.00
	1232	11	11.50	13.50	16.50	20.00
	1234	13	11.50	13.50	16.50	20.00
	1235	14	11.50	13.50	16.50	20.00
	1236	15	11.50	13.50	16.50	20.00
	1239	19	11.50	13.50	16.50	20.00
	1240	19	11.50	13.50	16.50	20.00
	1241	19	11.50	13.50	16.50	20.00

In the name of Muhammad Akbar II, with 'Sri' for Baija Bao:

RUPEE

SILVER, 21mm, 10.70-11.60 gm
Obv. & Rev: Five-flowered symbol.

C#	Date	Year	VG	Fine	VF	XF
95	—	23(Frozen)	11.50	13.50	16.50	20.00

NOTE: The regnal year 23 becomes frozen with this issue on all silver coins of this mint (identified by five-flowered symbol) and of Lashkar Mint.

In the name of Muhammad Akbar II, with initial of Jankoji Rao:

Symbols

 on obverse

 on reverse (points up or down)

RUPEE

SILVER, 20mm, 10.70-11.60 gm

C#	Date	Year	VG	Fine	VF	XF
100	AH1244	23	11.50	13.50	16.50	20.00

In the name of Muhammad Akbar, with initial of Jayaji Rao

Symbols as on C#100, but more stylized.

1/16 RUPEE

SILVER, 9mm, 0.67-0.72 gm

Y#	Date	Year	VG	Fine	VF	XF
9	—	23	3.00	3.50	4.50	6.00

1/8 RUPEE

SILVER, 11mm, 1.34-1.45 gm

Y#	Date	Year	VG	Fine	VF	XF
10	—	23	3.00	3.50	4.50	6.00

1/4 RUPEE

SILVER, 13mm, 2.68-2.90 gm

Y#	Date	Year	VG	Fine	VF	XF
11	—	23	3.50	4.00	5.00	7.00

1/2 RUPEE

SILVER, 15mm, 5.35-5.70 gm

Y#	Date	Year	VG	Fine	VF	XF
12	—	23	6.50	7.50	9.00	13.00

RUPEE

SILVER, 17-19mm, 10.70-11.60 gm

Y#	Date	Year	VG	Fine	VF	XF
13	—	23	11.50	13.50	16.50	20.00

NAZARANA RUPEE

SILVER, 27mm

Y#	Date	Year	VG	Fine	VF	XF
13a	AH125x	23	20.00	30.00	42.50	60.00

In the name of Muhammad Shah with initial of Madho Rao II:

1/3 MOHUR

GOLD, 21mm, 3.57-3.80 gm

Y#	Date	Year	VG	Fine	VF	XF
15	AH1130	2 (struck AD1886)	125.00	165.00	200.00	235.00

Isagarh Mint

All issues in the name of Muhammad Akbar II with symbol of Jankoji Rao

First Series

Identifying mark:

on obverse

RUPEE

SILVER, 20mm, 10.70-11.60 gm

KM#	Date	Year	VG	Fine	VF	XF
121	ND	—	11.50	13.50	16.50	20.00

Second Series

Identifying marks:

 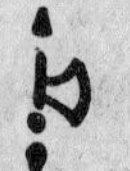 on reverse

RUPEE

SILVER, 18-19mm, 10.70-11.60 gm

KM#	Date	Year	VG	Fine	VF	XF
123	AH1248	28	11.50	13.50	16.50	20.00

Third Series

Identifying marks:

 on obverse

(no bow & battle-axe on reverse)

1/4 RUPEE

SILVER, 12mm, 2.68-2.90 gm

KM#	Date	Year	VG	Fine	VF	XF
125	ND	—	5.00	7.00	9.00	12.00

1/2 RUPEE

SILVER, 15-16mm, 5.35-5.80 gm

KM#	Date	Year	VG	Fine	VF	XF
126	ND	—	6.50	7.50	9.00	12.50

RUPEE

SILVER, 10.70-11.60 gm

KM#	Date	Year	VG	Fine	VF	XF
127	ND	—	11.50	13.50	16.50	20.00
	AH1252	—	11.50	13.50	16.50	20.00

Jawad Mint

PAISA

Without initial of Sindhia:

COPPER, 18-19mm

KM#	Date	Year	Good	VG	Fine	VF
129	VS1840	(1793)	3.00	5.00	7.00	10.00

With initial of Jankoji Rao

KM#	Date	Year	Good	VG	Fine	VF
130	ND	—	2.50	4.00	5.50	8.00

NOTE: For similar issues without the initial of the Sindhia, see Mewar, Jawad.

With initial of Jayaji Rao:

Y#	Date	Year	Good	VG	Fine	VF
1	ND	—	2.50	4.00	5.50	7.50

With initial of Madho Rao II:

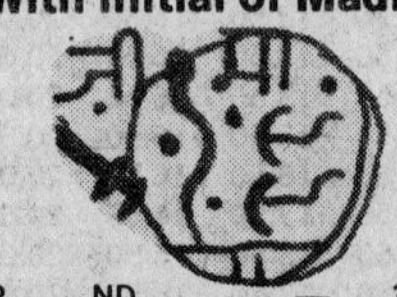 

Y#	Date	Year	Good	VG	Fine	VF
2	ND	—	3.00	5.00	6.50	8.50

Jhansi Mint

To Gwalior AD1865-86

Regular Jhansi types (q.v.), identifiable as Sindhia issues only by date, and by Persian Ji for Jayaji:

1/8 RUPEE

SILVER, 11mm, 1.34-1.45 gm

Y#	Date	Year	VG	Fine	VF	XF
16	ND	—	4.00	5.00	6.50	8.50

RUPEE

SILVER, 17mm, 10.70-11.60 gm

Y#	Date	Year	VG	Fine	VF	XF
19	AH—	48	11.50	13.50	16.50	20.00
	1282	5x	11.50	13.50	16.50	20.00
	1284	5x	11.50	13.50	16.50	20.00

Lashkar Mint

In the name of Shah Alam II:

NOTE: All dump coins of this mint are in name of Shah Alam II, with initials and mintmarks as shown, except C#173-174.

With regnal years of Shah Alam II:

RUPEE

SILVER, 20mm, 10.70-11.60 gm

C#	Date	Year	VG	Fine	VF	XF
143	AH1196	—	11.50	13.50	16.50	20.00
	—	13	11.50	13.50	16.50	20.00
	—	25	11.50	13.50	16.50	20.00
	—	66	11.50	13.50	16.50	20.00

With regnal years of Muhammad Akbar II

(Struck AD1821-27)

Symbol above regnal year:

1/8 RUPEE

SILVER, 12mm, 1.34-1.45 gm

C#	Date	Year	VG	Fine	VF	XF
145	—	17	2.00	2.50	3.50	5.00

1/4 RUPEE

SILVER, 14mm, 2.68-2.90 gm

C#	Date	Year	VG	Fine	VF	XF
146	—	17	3.50	4.50	6.00	8.00

1/2 RUPEE

SILVER, 16mm, 5.35-5.80 gm

C#	Date	Year	VG	Fine	VF	XF
147	—	17	6.50	7.50	9.00	12.00

RUPEE

SILVER, 20mm, 10.70-11.60 gm

C#	Date	Year	VG	Fine	VF	XF
148	—	16	11.50	13.50	16.50	20.00
	—	17	11.50	13.50	16.50	20.00
	—	21	11.50	13.50	16.50	20.00
	—	22	11.50	13.50	16.50	20.00

With initial 'SRI' for Baija Bao:

1/4 RUPEE

SILVER, 15mm, 2.68-2.90 gm

C#	Date	Year	VG	Fine	VF	XF
155	—	23	3.50	4.50	6.00	8.00

1/2 RUPEE

SILVER, 17mm, 5.35-5.80 gm

C#	Date	Year	VG	Fine	VF	XF
156	—	23	6.50	7.50	9.00	12.00

RUPEE

SILVER, 19mm, 10.70-11.60 gm

C#	Date	Year	VG	Fine	VF	XF
157	—	23	11.50	13.50	16.50	20.00

Without initial, but struck by Jankoji Rao:

Symbols:

1/2 PAISA

COPPER, 15-17mm

C#	Date	Year	Good	VG	Fine	VF
160	—	23	1.25	2.25	3.50	5.00

PAISA

COPPER, 18-21mm

C#	Date	Year	Good	VG	Fine	VF
161	—	12	1.00	2.00	3.00	4.50
		22	1.00	2.00	3.00	4.50
		23	1.00	2.00	3.00	4.50
		31	1.00	2.00	3.00	4.50

With initial of Jankoji Rao:

Bow & arrow, and trident, now appear on the silver coinage.

1/8 RUPEE

SILVER, 10mm, 1.34-1.45 gm

C#	Date	Year	VG	Fine	VF	XF
165	—	23	3.00	3.50	4.50	6.00

1/4 RUPEE

SILVER, 12mm, 2.68-2.90 gm

C#	Date	Year	VG	Fine	VF	XF
166	—	23	3.50	4.00	5.00	7.00

1/2 RUPEE

SILVER, 16mm, 5.35-5.80 gm

C#	Date	Year	VG	Fine	VF	XF
167	—	23	6.50	7.50	9.00	13.00

RUPEE

SILVER, 20mm, 10.70-11.60 gm

C#	Date	Year	VG	Fine	VF	XF
168	—	23	11.50	13.50	16.50	20.00

Anonymous coins struck by Jayaji Rao:

1/2 PAISA

COPPER, 12mm

Y#	Date	Year	Good	VG	Fine	VF
28	VS1926	(1869)	5.00	7.00	10.00	13.50

PAISA

COPPER

Y#	Date	Year	Good	VG	Fine	VF
29	VS1926	(1869)	.35	.75	1.25	2.25

NOTE: Struck for 30 years. 1869-99AD.

In name of Shah Alam II, with initials of Jayaji Rao:

Copper coins have symbols:

 or 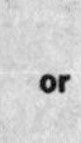 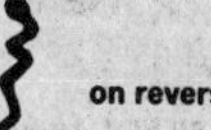

1/2 PAISA

COPPER, 13-17mm

C#	Date	Year	Good	VG	Fine	VF
20	—	23	.75	1.25	2.00	3.00

PAISA

COPPER, 19-22mm

C#	Date	Year	Good	VG	Fine	VF
21	—	23	.75	1.25	2.00	3.00

2 PAISA

COPPER, 22-24mm

Y#	Date	Year	Good	VG	Fine	VF
22	—	23	1.25	2.25	3.00	4.00

1/16 RUPEE

SILVER, 9mm, 0.67-0.72 gm

Y#	Date	Year	VG	Fine	VF	XF
23	—	23-25	2.50	3.00	4.00	6.00

1/8 RUPEE

SILVER, 10mm, 1.34-1.45 gm

Y#	Date	Year	VG	Fine	VF	XF
24	—	23	1.75	2.50	3.50	5.00
		25	1.75	2.50	3.50	5.00

1/4 RUPEE

SILVER, 12mm, 2.68-2.90 gm

Y#	Date	Year	VG	Fine	VF	XF
25	—	23	3.50	4.50	6.00	8.00
	—	25	3.50	4.50	6.00	8.00

1/2 RUPEE

SILVER, 15mm, 5.35-5.80 gm

Y#	Date	Year	VG	Fine	VF	XF
26	—	23	6.50	7.50	9.00	12.00
	—	25	6.50	7.50	9.00	12.00

RUPEE

SILVER, 18mm, 10.70-11.60 gm

Y#	Date	Year	VG	Fine	VF	XF
27	—	23	11.50	13.50	16.50	20.00
	—	27	11.50	13.50	16.50	20.00

With initial of Madho Rao II.

Symbols as on previous series.

1/8 RUPEE

SILVER, 9-11mm, 1.34-1.45 gm

Y#	Date	Year	VG	Fine	VF	XF
30	—	23	1.75	2.25	3.00	4.00

1/4 RUPEE

SILVER, 13mm, 2.68-2.90 gm

Y#	Date	Year	VG	Fine	VF	XF
31	—	23	3.50	4.50	6.00	8.00

1/2 RUPEE

SILVER, 15mm, 5.35-5.80 gm

Y#	Date	Year	VG	Fine	VF	XF
32	—	23	6.50	7.50	9.00	12.00

RUPEE

SILVER, 19mm, 10.70-11.60 gm

Y#	Date	Year	VG	Fine	VF	XF
33	—	23	11.50	13.50	16.50	20.00

MACHINE-STRUCK COINS

PIE

COPPER, 14mm

Y#	Date	Year	VG	Fine	VF	XF
41	VS1946	(1889)	20.00	30.00	40.00	47.50

1/2 PICE

COPPER, 20mm
Struck from 1/2 Anna dies.

Y#	Date	Year	VG	Fine	VF	XF
42	VS1946	(1889)	20.00	30.00	40.00	47.50

Y#	Date	Year	VG	Fine	VF	XF
45	VS1956	(1899)	.75	1.25	1.75	2.25
	1957	(1900)	.75	1.25	1.75	2.25
	1958	(1901)	.75	1.25	1.75	2.25

1/4 ANNA

18 point star, wide nose on sun.

Y#	Date	Year	VG	Fine	VF	XF
43.1	VS1944	(1887)	20.00	30.00	38.50	50.00

17 point star, wide nose on sun.

Y#	Date	Year	VG	Fine	VF	XF
43.2	VS1945	(1888)	20.00	30.00	38.50	50.00

16 point star, narrow nose on sun.

Y#	Date	Year	VG	Fine	VF	XF
43.3	VS1946	(1889)	20.00	30.00	38.50	50.00

22mm

Y#	Date	Year	VG	Fine	VF	XF
46	VS1953	(1896)	.50	.75	1.25	1.75
	1954	(1897)	.50	.75	1.25	1.75
	1956	(1899)	.50	.75	1.25	1.75
	1957	(1900)	.50	.75	1.25	1.75
	1958	(1901)	.50	.75	1.25	1.75

2.2mm thick planchet, 6.6gm.

Y#	Date	Year	VG	Fine	VF	XF
48	VS1970	(1913)	.50	1.00	1.50	2.00

1.6mm thin planchet, 5.1gm.

Y#	Date	Year	VG	Fine	VF	XF
48a	VS1970	(1913)	2.50	3.50	5.00	7.00
	1974	(1917)	.35	.75	1.25	1.75

1/2 ANNA

COPPER, 32mm

Y#	Date	Year	VG	Fine	VF	XF
44	VS1946	(1889)	35.00	50.00	65.00	90.00

RUPEE

SILVER, 32mm

Y#	Date	Year	VG	Fine	VF	XF
—	VS1954	(1897)	60.00	80.00	100.00	125.00

Perhaps a pattern.

1/3 MOHUR

GOLD, 19.4mm, 3.442 gm.

Y#	Date	Year	VG	Fine	VF	XF
47	VS1959	(1902)	165.00	225.00	275.00	325.00

Mandisor Mint

With initial of Jayaji Rao

PAISA

COPPER, 16-18mm

Y#	Date	Year	Good	VG	Fine	VF
1	VS1921	(1864)	1.75	2.75	4.00	6.00
	1927	(1870)	1.75	2.75	4.00	6.00

18-19mm

Y#	Date	Year	Good	VG	Fine	VF
2	VS1937	(1880)	1.75	2.75	4.00	6.00

Narwar Mint

To Gwalior From AD1805

Coins continued to be struck in the types of Narwar state, with dates after AH1221 (AD1806). The year 1230 was retained for several years.

In the name of Shah Alam II:

Symbol

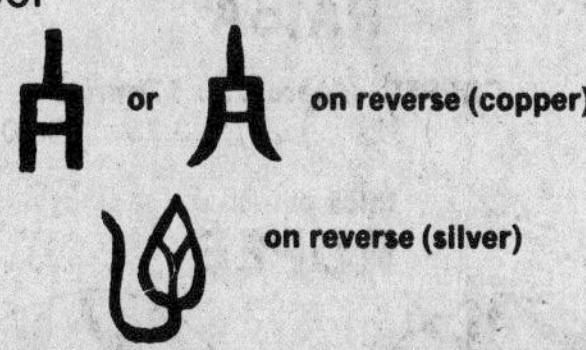

PAISA

COPPER, 20-22mm

C#	Date	Year	Good	VG	Fine	VF
198	AH1230	7	2.00	3.50	4.50	6.00
	1230	24	2.00	3.50	4.50	6.00

1/4 RUPEE

SILVER, 11-12mm, 2.68-2.90 gm

C#	Date	Year	VG	Fine	VF	XF
199	AH—	15	7.00	9.00	11.50	15.00

1/2 RUPEE

SILVER, 12-14mm, 5.35-5.80 gm

C#	Date	Year	VG	Fine	VF	XF
200	AH1230	21	7.00	9.00	11.50	15.00

RUPEE

SILVER, 18-20mm, 10.70-11.60 gm

C#	Date	Year	VG	Fine	VF	XF
201	AH1228	7	11.50	13.50	16.50	20.00
	1230	9	11.50	13.50	16.50	20.00
	1230	15	11.50	13.50	16.50	20.00
	1230	21	11.50	13.50	16.50	20.00

Rajod Mint

Symbol: Figure of Hanuman.

1/2 PAISA

COPPER, 17mm

Y#	Date	Year	Good	VG	Fine	VF
A2	VS19xx	—	4.00	6.00	9.00	12.50

PAISA

COPPER, 20-27mm

C#	Date	Year	VG	Fine	VF	XF
1	VS1930	(1873)	4.50	7.50	11.00	15.00

22mm

C#	Date	Year	VG	Fine	VF	XF
2	VS1936	(1879)	4.50	7.50	11.00	15.00

22-30mm

C#	Date	Year	VG	Fine	VF	XF
3	VS1940	(1883)	4.50	7.50	11.00	15.00

Shadorah Mint

Formerly listed as Seondha

In the name of Muhammad Akbar II

Symbols

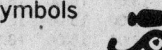

on C#222 and C#226 obverse

latter has  on reverse 

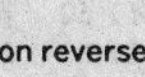

on C#225 and C#227 on reverse

C#225 also has  on reverse

PAISA

COPPER, 18mm

C#	Date	Year	Good	VG	Fine	VF
222	ND	—	1.75	2.75	4.00	5.50

RUPEE

SILVER, 21-23mm, 10.70-11.60 gm

C#	Date	Year	VG	Fine	VF	XF
225	AH1228	—	11.50	13.50	16.50	20.00

C#	Date	Year	VG	Fine	VF	XF
226	Date off flan	—	11.50	13.50	16.50	20.00

C#	Date	Year	VG	Fine	VF	XF
227	AH1229	8	11.50	13.50	16.50	20.00
	1230	10	11.50	13.50	16.50	20.00
	1231	11	11.50	13.50	16.50	20.00

Sheopur Mint

In the name of Muhammad Akbar II

Symbol

on reverse

RUPEE

SILVER, 20-23mm, 10.70-11.60 gm

C#	Date	Year	VG	Fine	VF	XF
235	AH1228	7	11.50	13.50	16.50	20.00
	1228	8	11.50	13.50	16.50	20.00
	1228	9	11.50	13.50	16.50	20.00
	1228	10	11.50	13.50	16.50	20.00
	1228	11	11.50	13.50	16.50	20.00
	1228	13	11.50	13.50	16.50	20.00
	1228	15	11.50	13.50	16.50	20.00
	1228	16	11.50	13.50	16.50	20.00
	1228	17	11.50	13.50	16.50	20.00
	1228	18	11.50	13.50	16.50	20.00
	1228	20	11.50	13.50	16.50	20.00
	1228	22	11.50	13.50	16.50	20.00
	1228	27	11.50	13.50	16.50	20.00
	1228	28	11.50	13.50	16.50	20.00

With initial of Jayaji Rao

20-22mm

Y#	Date	Year	VG	Fine	VF	XF
34.1	AH1270	1	11.50	13.50	16.50	20.00
	1271	1	11.50	13.50	16.50	20.00
	1274	1	11.50	13.50	16.50	20.00
	1276	1	11.50	13.50	16.50	20.00

Y#	Date	Year	VG	Fine	VF	XF
34.2	—	15	11.50	13.50	16.50	20.00

Sipri Mint

Mintname: Narwar

RUPEE

SILVER, 19mm, 10.70-11.60 gm
Flower in outline.

C#	Date	Year	VG	Fine	VF	XF
238	AH1106	47	11.50	13.50	16.50	20.00

Solid flower.

C#	Date	Year	VG	Fine	VF	XF
239	AH1106	47	11.50	13.50	16.50	20.00

Sri for Bija Bai

C#	Date	Year	VG	Fine	VF	XF
240	AH1106	17	11.50	13.50	16.50	20.00

17mm
Je for Jankoji

C#	Date	Year	VG	Fine	VF	XF
241	—	9	11.50	13.50	16.50	20.00

Ujjain Mint

Symbols

on most issues

on many copper issues

In the name of Shah Alam II

Without Sindhia's Initial

PAISA

COPPER, 15-21mm

C#	Date	Year	Good	VG	Fine	VF
250	AH1205	33	1.25	1.75	2.50	3.50

1/8 RUPEE

SILVER, 11mm, 1.34-1.45 gm

C#	Date	Year	VG	Fine	VF	XF
256	—	5x	3.00	3.75	4.50	6.00

1/4 RUPEE

SILVER, 13mm, 2.68-2.90 gm

C#	Date	Year	VG	Fine	VF	XF
257	—	15	3.50	4.50	6.00	9.00
		28	3.50	4.50	6.00	9.00
	—	36	3.50	4.50	6.00	9.00
		86	3.50	4.50	6.00	9.00

1/2 RUPEE

SILVER, 15mm, 5.35-5.80 gm

C#	Date	Year	VG	Fine	VF	XF
258	—	20	6.50	7.50	9.00	13.00
		86	6.50	7.50	9.00	13.00

RUPEE

SILVER, 18-21mm

C#	Date	Year	VG	Fine	VF	XF
259	AH1176	3	11.50	13.00	15.00	18.50
	1187	15	11.50	13.00	15.00	18.50
	1193	19	11.50	13.00	15.00	18.50
	1193	20	11.50	13.00	15.00	18.50
	1194	21	11.50	13.00	15.00	18.50
	1197	23	11.50	13.00	15.00	18.50
	1198	24	11.50	13.00	15.00	18.50
	1199	25	11.50	13.00	15.00	18.50
	1199	26	11.50	13.00	15.00	18.50
	1200	26	11.50	13.00	15.00	18.50
	1200	27	11.50	13.00	15.00	18.50
	1201	27	11.50	13.00	15.00	18.50
	1201	28	11.50	13.00	15.00	18.50
	1201	29	11.50	13.00	15.00	18.50
	1201	30	11.50	13.00	15.00	18.50
	1202	31	11.50	13.00	15.00	18.50
	1203	32	11.50	13.00	15.00	18.50
	1204	33	11.50	13.00	15.00	18.50
	1205	33	11.50	13.00	15.00	18.50
	1205	34	11.50	13.00	15.00	18.50
	1206	35	11.50	13.00	15.00	18.50
	1207	35	11.50	13.00	15.00	18.50
	1208	36	11.50	13.00	15.00	18.50
	1209	38	11.50	13.00	15.00	18.50
	1210	39	11.50	13.00	15.00	18.50
	1211	38	11.50	13.00	15.00	18.50
	1211	40	11.50	13.00	15.00	18.50
	1212	35	11.50	13.00	15.00	18.50
	1212	39	11.50	13.00	15.00	18.50
	1212	40	11.50	13.00	15.00	18.50
	1213	40	11.50	13.00	15.00	18.50
	1214	41	11.50	13.00	15.00	18.50
	1215	41	11.50	13.00	15.00	18.50
	1215	42	11.50	13.00	15.00	18.50
	1216	44	11.50	13.00	15.00	18.50
	—	45	11.50	13.00	15.00	18.50
	—	50	11.50	13.00	15.00	18.50
	—	52	11.50	13.00	15.00	18.50

C#	Date	Year	VG	Fine	VF	XF
259	—	53	11.50	13.00	15.00	18.50
	—	55	11.50	13.00	15.00	18.50
	—	58	11.50	13.00	15.00	18.50
	—	64	11.50	13.00	15.00	18.50
	—	68	11.50	13.00	15.00	18.50
	—	69	11.50	13.00	15.00	18.50
	—	70	11.50	13.00	15.00	18.50
	—	73	11.50	13.00	15.00	18.50
	—	23 (of Muhammad Akbar II)				
			11.50	13.00	15.00	18.50
	—	77	11.50	13.00	15.00	18.50
	—	78	11.50	13.00	15.00	18.50
	—	79	11.50	13.00	15.00	18.50
	—	84	11.50	13.00	15.00	18.50
	—	86	11.50	13.00	15.00	18.50
	—	89	11.50	13.00	15.00	18.50
	—	94	11.50	13.00	15.00	18.50
	—	95	11.50	13.00	15.00	18.50
	—	98	11.50	13.00	15.00	18.50
	—	99	11.50	13.00	15.00	18.50

With 'Sri' for Baija Bao:

PAISA

COPPER, 16 x 17mm, (square)
Similar to Y#35, except for initial.

C#	Date	Year	Good	VG	Fine	VF
265	—	23	1.25	2.25	3.00	4.00

With initial of Jankoji Rao:

PAISA

COPPER, square, 15 x 17mm

C#	Date	Year	Good	VG	Fine	VF
270	—	31	1.25	2.25	3.00	4.00

RUPEE

SILVER, 22mm, 10.70-11.60 gm

C#	Date	Year	VG	Fine	VF	XF
267	—	23	12.50	14.50	17.50	21.50

With initial of Jayoji Roa

PAISA

COPPER, round or square, 16-20mm

Y#	Date	Year	Good	VG	Fine	VF
35	AH1262	—	1.00	1.75	2.50	3.50
	1263	—	1.00	1.75	2.50	3.50
	1281	—	1.00	1.75	2.50	3.50
	1292	—	1.00	1.75	2.50	3.50
	1295	—	1.00	1.75	2.50	3.50

With initial of Madho Rao II:

Regnal years of the British Raj (Yr. 1 = AD1857)

1/16 RUPEE

SILVER, 8-9mm, 0.67-0.72 gm

Y#	Date	Year	VG	Fine	VF	XF
36	AH1313	37	3.50	5.00	6.50	8.00

1/8 RUPEE

SILVER, 9mm, 1.34-1.45 gm

Y#	Date	Year	VG	Fine	VF	XF
37	AH1310	34	2.50	3.50	4.50	6.00
	1312	36	2.50	3.50	4.50	6.00

1/4 RUPEE

SILVER, 12mm, 2.68-2.90 gm

Y#	Date	Year	VG	Fine	VF	XF
38	AH1310	34	3.50	4.50	6.00	8.00
	1312	36	3.50	4.50	6.00	8.00
	1313	37	3.50	4.50	6.00	8.00
	1314	38	3.50	4.50	6.00	8.00

1/2 RUPEE

SILVER, 14-15mm, 5.35-5.80 gm

Y#	Date	Year	VG	Fine	VF	XF
39	AH1310	34	6.50	7.50	9.00	12.00
	1311	35	6.50	7.50	9.00	12.00
	1312	36	6.50	7.50	9.00	12.00
	1313	37	6.50	7.50	9.00	12.00
	1314	38	6.50	7.50	9.00	12.00

RUPEE

SILVER, 19mm

Y#	Date	Year	VG	Fine	VF	XF
40	AH1310	34	11.50	13.50	16.50	20.00
	1311	35	11.50	13.50	16.50	20.00
	1312	34	Error			
			11.50	13.50	16.50	20.00
	1312	36	11.50	13.50	16.50	20.00
	1313	37	11.50	13.50	16.50	20.00
	1314	38	11.50	13.50	16.50	20.00

Uncertain Mint

PAISA

COPPER, 18mm

Y#	Date	Year	Good	VG	Fine	VF
2	—	23	5.00	8.50	12.50	18.50

21mm

Y#	Date	Year	Good	VG	Fine	VF
4	—	ND	5.00	8.00	12.00	16.50

MACHINE STRUCK COINS

Jivaji Rao

AD 1925-1948

1/4 ANNA

COPPER, 23mm

Thick planchet, 6.6gm.

Y#	Date	Year	Fine	VF	XF	Unc
49	VS1986	(1929)	.50	.60	1.00	2.00

NOTE: Two varieties of portrait.

Thin planchet

Y#	Date	Year	Fine	VF	XF	Unc
49a	VS1986	(1929)	1.50	2.50	3.50	6.00
	1999	(1942)	1.50	2.50	3.50	6.00

22mm
Rev: No inscriptions on side.

Y#	Date	Year	Fine	VF	XF	Unc
50	VS1999	(1942)	.35	.75	1.25	2.25

1/2 ANNA

BRASS

Y#	Date	Year	Fine	VF	XF	Unc
51	VS1999	(1942)	.35	.50	.85	1.50
	1999	(1942)	—	—	Proof	50.00

HASANABAD

Uncertain mint. Possibly a mint of Awadh or Rohilkhand.

RUPEE

In name of Shah Alam II:

I - Obverse "Badshah Ghazi"

SILVER, 21mm

KM#	Date	Year	VG	Fine	VF	XF
6.1	AH1174	1	—	—	Rare	—

II - Obverse "Fazl-i-Hami Din"

KM#	Date	Year	VG	Fine	VF	XF
6.2	AH1196	25	—	—	Rare	—

HUSENGARH

Uncertain mint. Possibly a mint of the Doab or eastern Rajasthan.

In name of Shah Alam II:

1/2 PAISA

COPPER, 18mm

KM#	Date	Year	Good	VG	Fine	VF
1	AH119x	23	7.00	10.00	14.50	20.00

PAISA

COPPER, 21mm

KM#	Date	Year	Good	VG	Fine	VF
2	AH119x	23	7.00	10.00	14.50	20.00

HYDERABAD

Nizam Ali Khan

AH1175-1218/AD1761-1803

In the name of Shah Alam II:

Distinguishing mark:

Arabic letter 'nun' for Nizam on the reverse

PAISA

COPPER, 19mm

C#	Date	Year	Good	VG	Fine	VF
20	—	—	2.00	2.50	3.50	5.00

DOUBLE PAISA

COPPER, 25mm

MINT: DAULATABAD

C#	Date	Year	Good	VG	Fine	VF
22	AH1213	40	6.00	9.00	14.50	20.00

RUPEE

SILVER, 21mm, 10.70-11.60 gm

MINT: KHUJISTA BUNYAD

C#	Date	Year	VG	Fine	VF	XF
28	AH1176	3	—	—	—	—
	1193	19	11.50	13.50	16.50	20.00

MINT: DAULATABAD

C#	Date	Year	VG	Fine	VF	XF
30	AH1187	14	15.00	20.00	26.50	35.00

Sikandar Jah

AH 1218-44/AD 1803-29

In the name of Shah Alam II:

PAISA

COPPER, 17-20mm

C#	Date	Year	Good	VG	Fine	VF
40	AH1217	—	1.25	2.00	3.00	4.50
	1218	—	1.25	2.00	3.00	4.50

RUPEE

SILVER, 20-21mm, 10.70-11.60 gm

C#	Date	Year	VG	Fine	VF	XF
41	AH1218	—	12.50	14.50	17.50	21.50
	1220	—	12.50	14.50	17.50	21.50

In the name of Muhammad Akbar II

PAISA

COPPER, 17-20mm

C#	Date	Year	Good	VG	Fine	VF
42	AH1229	—	1.25	2.00	2.75	3.50

NOTE: The following silver and gold coins all bear the mark of the ruler (Nizam) of Hyderabad on the reverse:

Each of the silver and gold types comprises two subtypes, the second differing from the first by the addition of the Persian letter 'S' (for Sikandar) on the obverse:

The 'S' is often off the flan on the fractional denomination.

1/4 RUPEE

SILVER, 14-15mm, 2.68-2.90 gm

C#	Date	Year	VG	Fine	VF	XF
46	AH1222-44		3.50	4.50	6.00	8.00

1/2 RUPEE

SILVER, 18mm, 5.35-5.80 gm

C#	Date	Year	VG	Fine	VF	XF
47	AH1235/14		6.50	7.50	9.00	12.00
	1238/—		6.50	7.50	9.00	12.00
	1242/23		6.50	7.50	9.00	12.00

RUPEE

SILVER, 20-23mm, 10.70-11.60 gm

MINT: HYDERABAD

Obv: Persian S

C#	Date	Year	VG	Fine	VF	XF
48	AH1225	4	11.50	13.50	16.50	20.00
	1226	—	11.50	13.50	16.50	20.00
	1228	7	11.50	13.50	16.50	20.00
	1229	—	11.50	13.50	16.50	20.00
	1230	9	11.50	13.50	16.50	20.00
	1231	10	11.50	13.50	16.50	20.00
	1232	11	11.50	13.50	16.50	20.00
	1234	13	11.50	13.50	16.50	20.00
	1235	15	11.50	13.50	16.50	20.00
	1236	15	11.50	13.50	16.50	20.00
	1237	16	11.50	13.50	16.50	20.00
	1238	—	11.50	13.50	16.50	20.00
	1239	21	11.50	13.50	16.50	20.00
	1240	21	11.50	13.50	16.50	20.00
	1240	22	11.50	13.50	16.50	20.00
	1241	22	11.50	13.50	16.50	20.00
	1242	23	11.50	13.50	16.50	20.00
	1243	24	11.50	13.50	16.50	20.00
	1244	25	11.50	13.50	16.50	20.00

MINT: AURANGABAD

Obv: No S

C#	Date	Year	VG	Fine	VF	XF
48a	AH1240	20	12.50	14.50	17.50	21.50
	1241	—	12.50	14.50	17.50	21.50

1/16 MOHUR

GOLD, 0.67-0.71 gm

C#	Date	Year	VG	Fine	VF	XF
56	—	—	35.00	50.00	70.00	100.00

1/8 MOHUR

GOLD, 1.34-1.42 gm

C#	Date	Year	VG	Fine	VF	XF
57	—	—	50.00	65.00	90.00	125.00

1/4 MOHUR

GOLD, 2.68-2.85 gm

C#	Date	Year	VG	Fine	VF	XF
58	—	—	75.00	90.00	120.00	160.00

1/2 MOHUR

GOLD, 5.35-5.70 gm

C#	Date	Year	VG	Fine	VF	XF
59	—	—	125.00	150.00	185.00	225.00

MOHUR

GOLD, 25mm, 10.70-11.40 gm

C#	Date	Year	VG	Fine	VF	XF
60	AH1226	—	225.00	250.00	285.00	325.00
	1231	—	225.00	250.00	285.00	325.00
	1234	—	225.00	250.00	285.00	325.00
	1237	16	225.00	250.00	285.00	325.00
	1244	—	225.00	250.00	285.00	325.00

Nasir Ad-Daula

AH 1244-1273/AD 1829-1857

The coins of Nasir ad-Daula bear the mark of the Nizam and the Persian letter 'N' for Nasir:

First Series

In the name of Muhammad Akbar II to AH1252; with his regnal years.

PAISA

COPPER, 17-18mm

C#	Date	Year	Good	VG	Fine	VF
61	AH1247	—	1.25	2.00	3.00	4.00
	1250	—	1.25	2.00	3.00	4.00

1/4 RUPEE

SILVER, 15mm, 2.68-2.90 gm

C#	Date	Year	VG	Fine	VF	XF
64	AH1246	—	3.50	4.50	6.00	8.00
	1247	—	3.50	4.50	6.00	8.00

1/2 RUPEE

SILVER, 18mm, 5.35-5.80 gm

C#	Date	Year	VG	Fine	VF	XF
65	AH1249-51		6.50	7.50	9.00	12.00

RUPEE

SILVER, 21-23 mm, 0.70-11.60 gm

MINT: HYDERABAD

C#	Date	Year	VG	Fine	VF	XF
66	AH1245	26	11.50	13.50	16.50	20.00
	1246	—	11.50	13.50	16.50	20.00
	1248	29	11.50	13.50	16.50	20.00
	1249	—	11.50	13.50	16.50	20.00
	1250	31	11.50	13.50	16.50	20.00
	1251	33	11.50	13.50	16.50	20.00
	1252	34	11.50	13.50	16.50	20.00
	1253	35	11.50	13.50	16.50	20.00

21mm

MINT: AURANGABAD

C#	Date	Year	VG	Fine	VF	XF
66a	AH1251	—	12.50	14.50	17.50	21.50

1/16 MOHUR

GOLD, 0.67-0.71 gm

C#	Date	Year	VG	Fine	VF	XF
68	—	—	25.00	35.00	45.00	60.00

1/8 MOHUR

GOLD, 1.34-1.42 gm

C#	Date	Year	VG	Fine	VF	XF
69	—	—	35.00	50.00	70.00	100.00

1/4 MOHUR

GOLD, 2.68-2.85 gm

C#	Date	Year	VG	Fine	VF	XF
70	—	—	65.00	85.00	120.00	150.00

1/2 MOHUR

GOLD, 5.35-5.70 gm

C#	Date	Year	VG	Fine	VF	XF
71	—	—	100.00	125.00	165.00	200.00

MOHUR

GOLD, 22-23mm

C#	Date	Year	VG	Fine	VF	XF
72	AH1244	—	225.00	250.00	285.00	325.00
	1251	—	225.00	250.00	285.00	325.00

Second Series

In the name of Bahadur Shah
Dates AH1253-1274; with his regnal years.

PAISA

COPPER, round or square, 16-21mm
Often irregular shape

C#	Date	Year	Good	VG	Fine	VF
73	AH1257	4	1.25	2.00	2.75	4.00
	1258	—	1.25	2.00	2.75	4.00
	1262	—	1.25	2.00	2.75	4.00
	1272	—	1.25	2.00	2.75	4.00
	1273	—	1.25	2.00	2.75	4.00

1/16 RUPEE

SILVER, 9-11mm, 0.67-0.72 gm

C#	Date	Year	VG	Fine	VF	XF
75	AH1272	—	4.00	5.50	7.50	10.00

1/8 RUPEE

SILVER, 11-13 mm, 1.34-1.45 gm

C#	Date	Year	VG	Fine	VF	XF
76	AH1272	—	4.00	5.50	7.50	10.00

1/4 RUPEE

SILVER, 14-15mm, 2.68-2.90 gm

C#	Date	Year	VG	Fine	VF	XF
77	AH1273	18	4.00	5.50	7.50	10.00

1/2 RUPEE

SILVER, 16-19mm, 5.35-5.80 gm

C#	Date	Year	VG	Fine	VF	XF
78	AH1257-73		6.50	7.50	9.00	12.00

RUPEE

SILVER, 20-25mm, 10.70-11.60 gm

MINT: HYDERABAD

C#	Date	Year	VG	Fine	VF	XF
79	AH1253	1	11.50	13.50	16.50	20.00
	1261	8	11.50	13.50	16.50	20.00
	1262	9	11.50	13.50	16.50	20.00
	1267	12	11.50	13.50	16.50	20.00
	1268	12	11.50	13.50	16.50	20.00
	1268	13	11.50	13.50	16.50	20.00
	1270	15	11.50	13.50	16.50	20.00
	1270	16	11.50	13.50	16.50	20.00
	1271	16	11.50	13.50	16.50	20.00
	1271	17	11.50	13.50	16.50	20.00
	1272	17	11.50	13.50	16.50	20.00
	1273	18	11.50	13.50	16.50	20.00

MINT: AURANGABAD

C#	Date	Year	VG	Fine	VF	XF
79a	AH1256	4	12.50	14.50	17.50	21.50

1/16 MOHUR

GOLD, 0.67-0.71 gm

C#	Date	Year	VG	Fine	VF	XF
80	—	—	35.00	50.00	70.00	100.00

1/8 MOHUR

GOLD, 1.34-1.42 gm

C#	Date	Year	VG	Fine	VF	XF
81	—	—	50.00	65.00	90.00	125.00

1/4 MOHUR

GOLD, 2.68-2.85 gm

C#	Date	Year	VG	Fine	VF	XF
82	—	—	75.00	90.00	120.00	160.00

1/2 MOHUR

GOLD, 5.35-5.70 gm

C#	Date	Year	VG	Fine	VF	XF
83	—	—	125.00	150.00	185.00	225.00

MOHUR

GOLD, 22mm, 10.70-11.40 gm

C#	Date	Year	VG	Fine	VF	XF
84	AH1258	—	220.00	240.00	265.00	300.00
	1260	—	220.00	240.00	265.00	300.00
	1261	—	220.00	240.00	265.00	300.00
	1263	—	220.00	240.00	265.00	300.00
	1264	—	220.00	240.00	265.00	300.00
	1265	—	220.00	240.00	265.00	300.00
	1266	—	220.00	240.00	265.00	300.00
	1267	—	220.00	240.00	265.00	300.00
	1268	—	220.00	240.00	265.00	300.00
	1269	—	220.00	240.00	265.00	300.00
	1270	—	220.00	240.00	265.00	300.00
	1271	—	220.00	240.00	265.00	300.00
	1273	—	220.00	240.00	265.00	300.00
	1276	—	220.00	240.00	265.00	300.00

Afzal Ad-Daula

AH 1273-1285/AD 1857-1869

First Series

In the name of Bahadur Shah II,

(For his last two years, 1274-75AH, regnal year 18) with Persian letter 'A' (symbol 3) above 'Padishah' on obverse.

Coppers have symbol #1, silver and gold have #2.

#1 

#2 

#3 ا

1/2 PAISA

COPPER, 16-17mm

MINT: AURANGABAD

C#	Date	Year	Good	VG	Fine	VF
85	AH1275	—	.85	1.50	2.50	3.50
	—	19	.85	1.50	2.50	3.50

PAISA

COPPER, 20-21mm

C#	Date	Year	Good	VG	Fine	VF
86	AH1275	18	1.00	1.50	2.25	3.25
	1276	19	1.00	1.50	2.25	3.25
	1277	19	1.00	1.50	2.25	3.25

1/8 RUPEE

SILVER, 13mm, 1.34-1.45 gm

MINT: HYDERABAD

C#	Date	Year	VG	Fine	VF	XF
88	AH1275	—	4.00	5.00	6.50	8.00

1/4 RUPEE

SILVER, 14mm, 2.68-2.90 gm

C#	Date	Year	VG	Fine	VF	XF
89	AH1274	—	5.50	6.50	8.00	10.00

1/2 RUPEE

SILVER, 17mm, 5.35-5.80 gm

C#	Date	Year	VG	Fine	VF	XF
90	AH1274	—	6.50	7.50	9.00	12.00

RUPEE

SILVER, 21-24mm, 10.70-11.60 gm

C#	Date	Year	VG	Fine	VF	XF
91	AH1273	18	11.50	13.50	16.50	20.00
	1274	18	11.50	13.50	16.50	20.00
	1275	18	11.50	13.50	16.50	20.00

MOHUR

GOLD, 23mm

C#	Date	Year	VG	Fine	VF	XF
96	AH1274	—	220.00	240.00	265.00	300.00
	1275	—	220.00	240.00	265.00	300.00

Second Series

In the name of Asaf Jah, Nizam al-Mulk, Founder of the Nizami line (AD1713-48).

Persian letter 'A' (for Afzal) above 'K' of Mulk on obverse.

All coins bear the numeral '92' on upper obverse.

PAISA (DUB)

COPPER
Irregular and regular shapes, 16-30mm

Y#	Date	Year	Good	VG	Fine	VF
1	AH1282	—	1.75	2.50	3.50	5.00
	1283	—	1.75	2.50	3.50	5.00
	Date off flan		.65	1.00	1.25	2.00

1/16 RUPEE (ANNA)

SILVER, 9mm, 0.67-0.72 gm

Y#	Date	Year	VG	Fine	VF	XF
2	AH1275	—	3.00	4.00	5.50	7.50

1/8 RUPEE

SILVER, 11-13mm, 1.34-1.45 gm

Y#	Date	Year	VG	Fine	VF	XF
3	AH1278	—	3.50	4.50	6.00	8.00
	1279	—	3.50	4.50	6.00	8.00

1/4 RUPEE

SILVER, 15-16mm, 2.68-2.90 gm

Y#	Date	Year	VG	Fine	VF	XF
4	AH1276	—	3.50	4.50	6.00	8.50
	1278	—	3.50	4.50	6.00	8.50
	1283	10	3.50	4.50	6.00	8.50

1/2 RUPEE

SILVER, 19-20mm, 5.35-5.80 gm

Y#	Date	Year	VG	Fine	VF	XF
5	AH1277	—	6.50	7.50	9.00	12.00

RUPEE

SILVER, 22-25mm, 10.70-11.60

Y#	Date	Year	VG	Fine	VF	XF
6	AH1275	2	11.50	13.50	16.50	20.00
	1276	3	11.50	13.50	16.50	20.00
	1276	4	11.50	13.50	16.50	20.00
	1277	4	11.50	13.50	16.50	20.00
	1278	5	11.50	13.50	16.50	20.00
	1279	6	11.50	13.50	16.50	20.00
	1280	7	11.50	13.50	16.50	20.00
	1281	7	11.50	13.50	16.50	20.00
	1281	8	11.50	13.50	16.50	20.00
	1282	9	11.50	13.50	16.50	20.00
	1283	10	11.50	13.50	16.50	20.00
	1284	11	11.50	13.50	16.50	20.00
	1285	12	11.50	13.50	16.50	20.00

1/16 MOHUR

GOLD, 8-9mm, 0.67-0.71 gm

Y#	Date	Year	VG	Fine	VF	XF
7	—		Reported, not confirmed			

1/8 MOHUR

GOLD, 11mm, 1.34-1.42 gm

Y#	Date	Year	VG	Fine	VF	XF
8	AH1279-81		45.00	55.00	70.00	90.00

1/4 MOHUR

GOLD, 14mm, 2.68-2.85 gm

Y#	Date	Year	VG	Fine	VF	XF
9	AH1281	—	70.00	85.00	110.00	140.00

1/2 MOHUR

GOLD, 16mm, 5.35-5.70 gm

Y#	Date	Year	VG	Fine	VF	XF
10	AH1281	—	110.00	135.00	165.00	200.00

MOHUR

GOLD, 22mm, 10.70-11.40 gm

Y#	Date	Year	VG	Fine	VF	XF
11	AH1275	—	220.00	240.00	265.00	300.00
	1276	—	220.00	240.00	265.00	300.00
	1277	—	220.00	240.00	265.00	300.00
	1278	—	220.00	240.00	265.00	300.00
	1279	—	220.00	240.00	265.00	300.00
	1280	—	220.00	240.00	265.00	300.00
	1281	—	220.00	240.00	265.00	300.00
	1282	—	220.00	240.00	265.00	300.00
	1283	—	220.00	240.00	265.00	300.00
	1284	—	220.00	240.00	265.00	300.00
	1285	—	220.00	240.00	265.00	300.00

Mir Mahbub Ali Khan II

AH 1285-1329/AD 1868-1911

First Series

In the name of Asaf Jah, Nizam al-Mulk, Founder of the Nizami line (AD1713-48).

Persian letter 'M' for Mahbub above 'K' of Mulk on obv.

PAISA (DUB)

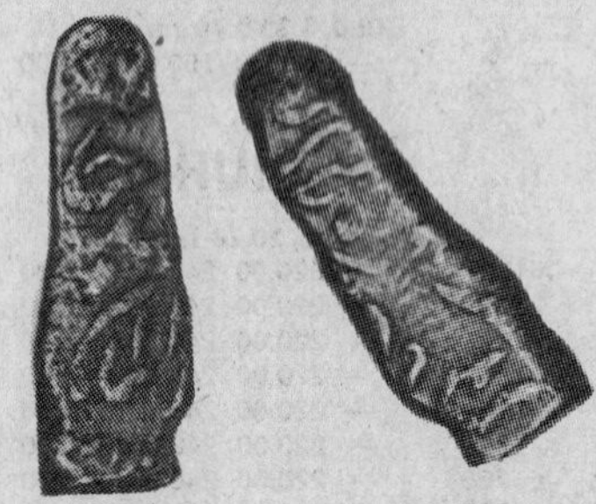

COPPER
Round, rectangular, irregular shape
Many sizes and weights

Y#	Date	Year	Good	VG	Fine	VF
12	AH1292	—	1.25	1.75	2.50	3.50
	1297	—	1.25	1.75	2.50	3.50
	1300	—	1.25	1.75	2.50	3.50
	1301	—	1.25	1.75	2.50	3.50
	1303	—	1.25	1.75	2.50	3.50
	Date off flan		.15	.35	.65	1.00

1/16 RUPEE

SILVER, 7-9mm, 0.67-0.72 gm

Y#	Date	Year	VG	Fine	VF	XF
13	AH1299	15	1.25	1.75	2.50	3.50
	1300	—	1.25	1.75	2.50	3.50
	1304	—	1.25	1.75	2.50	3.50
	1307	—	1.25	1.75	2.50	3.50
	1313	—	1.25	1.75	2.50	3.50

Y#	Date	Year	VG	Fine	VF	XF
	1314	—	1.25	1.75	2.50	3.50
	1321	37	1.25	1.75	2.50	3.50
	Date off flan		.75	1.00	1.35	2.00

1/8 RUPEE

SILVER, 10-13mm, 1.34-1.45 gm

Y#	Date	Year	VG	Fine	VF	XF
14	AH1286	—	1.75	2.25	3.00	3.75
	1290	—	1.75	2.25	3.00	3.75
	1297	—	1.75	2.25	3.00	3.75
	1298	—	1.75	2.25	3.00	3.75
	1299	—	1.75	2.25	3.00	3.75
	1300	—	1.75	2.25	3.00	3.75
	1301	—	1.75	2.25	3.00	3.75
	1302	18	1.75	2.25	3.00	3.75
	1304	20	1.75	2.25	3.00	3.75
	1305	—	1.75	2.25	3.00	3.75
	1306	—	1.75	2.25	3.00	3.75
	1307	—	1.75	2.25	3.00	3.75
	1308	24	1.75	2.25	3.00	3.75
	1316	—	1.75	2.25	3.00	3.75
	1317	33	1.75	2.25	3.00	3.75
	1321	37	1.75	2.25	3.00	3.75
	Date off flan		1.50	1.75	2.25	3.00

1/4 RUPEE

SILVER, 13-16mm, 2.68-2.90 gm

Y#	Date	Year	VG	Fine	VF	XF
15	AH1286	—	3.50	4.00	4.50	5.50
	1287	—	3.50	4.00	4.50	5.50
	1291	7	3.50	4.00	4.50	5.50
	1295	—	3.50	4.00	4.50	5.50
	1298	14	3.50	4.00	4.50	5.50
	1299	15	3.50	4.00	4.50	5.50
	1300	—	3.50	4.00	4.50	5.50
	1301	17	3.50	4.00	4.50	5.50
	1304	—	3.50	4.00	4.50	5.50
	1305	22	3.50	4.00	4.50	5.50
	1306	—	3.50	4.00	4.50	5.50
	1307	24	3.50	4.00	4.50	5.50
	1308	—	3.50	4.00	4.50	5.50
	1313	29	3.50	4.00	4.50	5.50
	1314	—	3.50	4.00	4.50	5.50
	1316	33	3.50	4.00	4.50	5.50
	1317	33	3.50	4.00	4.50	5.50
	Date off flan		2.50	3.00	3.50	4.00

1/2 RUPEE

SILVER, 17-19mm, 5.35-5.80 gm

Y#	Date	Year	VG	Fine	VF	XF
16	AH1286	—	6.50	7.00	8.00	10.00
	1294	10	6.50	7.00	8.00	10.00
	1299	—	6.50	7.00	8.00	10.00
	1301	17	6.50	7.00	8.00	10.00
	1304	—	6.50	7.00	8.00	10.00
	1305	22	6.50	7.00	8.00	10.00
	1306	22	6.50	7.00	8.00	10.00
	1307	—	6.50	7.00	8.00	10.00
	1308	—	6.50	7.00	8.00	10.00
	1310	—	6.50	7.00	8.00	10.00
	1316	32	6.50	7.00	8.00	10.00
	1317	—	6.50	7.00	8.00	10.00

RUPEE

SILVER, 22-24mm, 10.70-11.60 gm

Y#	Date	Year	VG	Fine	VF	XF
17	AH1286	1	11.50	13.00	15.00	18.50
	1287	—	11.50	13.00	15.00	18.50
	1288	—	11.50	13.00	15.00	18.50
	1289	—	11.50	13.00	15.00	18.50
	1293	—	11.50	13.00	15.00	18.50
	1294	10	11.50	13.00	15.00	18.50
	1295	11	11.50	13.00	15.00	18.50
	1299	15	11.50	13.00	15.00	18.50
	1299	16	11.50	13.00	15.00	18.50
	1300	16	11.50	13.00	15.00	18.50
	1301	—	11.50	13.00	15.00	18.50
	1302	18	11.50	13.00	15.00	18.50
	1306	22	11.50	13.00	15.00	18.50
	1307	23	11.50	13.00	15.00	18.50
	1308	24	11.50	13.00	15.00	18.50
	1308	25	11.50	13.00	15.00	18.50
	1309	25	11.50	13.00	15.00	18.50
	1310	26	11.50	13.00	15.00	18.50
	1315	32	11.50	13.00	15.00	18.50
	1316	32	11.50	13.00	15.00	18.50
	1317	33	11.50	13.00	15.00	18.50
	1317	34	11.50	13.00	15.00	18.50
	1318	34	11.50	13.00	15.00	18.50
	Date off flan		11.50	13.00	15.00	18.50

1/16 MOHUR

GOLD, 7mm, 0.67-0.71 gm

Y#	Date	Year	VG	Fine	VF	XF
18	AH1305	—	25.00	35.00	40.00	60.00
	1314	—	25.00	35.00	40.00	60.00
	1315	—	25.00	35.00	40.00	60.00
	1321	—	25.00	35.00	40.00	60.00

1/8 MOHUR

GOLD, 10mm, 1.34-1.42 gm

Y#	Date	Year	VG	Fine	VF	XF
19	AH1313	—	40.00	50.00	65.00	85.00
	1318	—	40.00	50.00	65.00	85.00
	1320	—	40.00	50.00	65.00	85.00
	1321	—	35.00	45.00	60.00	80.00

1/4 MOHUR

GOLD, 14mm, 2.68-2.85 gm

Y#	Date	Year	VG	Fine	VF	XF
20	AH1304	—	60.00	75.00	90.00	120.00
	1306	—	60.00	75.00	90.00	120.00
	1314	30	60.00	75.00	90.00	120.00
	1318	—	60.00	75.00	90.00	120.00

1/2 MOHUR

GOLD, 17mm, 5.35-5.70 gm

Y#	Date	Year	VG	Fine	VF	XF
21	AH1317	—	110.00	125.00	140.00	165.00

MOHUR

GOLD, 22mm, 10.70-11.40 gm

Y#	Date	Year	VG	Fine	VF	XF
22	AH1294	—	220.00	240.00	265.00	300.00
	1314	—	220.00	240.00	265.00	300.00

MACHINE-STRUCK COINS

First Provisional Issue:

AH1305-1307

RUPEE

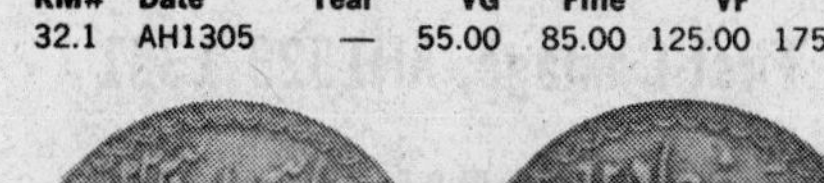

SILVER, 30mm, 11.66 gm.

KM#	Date	Year	VG	Fine	VF	XF
32.1	AH1305	—	55.00	85.00	125.00	175.00

32mm, modified design

KM#	Date	Year	VG	Fine	VF	XF
32.2	AH1307	—	55.00	85.00	125.00	175.00

Second Provisional Issue:

2 ANNAS

SILVER, 15mm, 1.46 gm

Y#	Date	Year	VG	Fine	VF	XF
29	AH1318	35	27.50	37.50	50.00	65.00

4 ANNAS

SILVER, 19mm, 2.92 gm

Y#	Date	Year	VG	Fine	VF	XF
30	AH1318	34	25.00	35.00	45.00	60.00
	1318	35	25.00	35.00	45.00	60.00

8 ANNAS

SILVER, 24mm, 5.83 gm

Y#	Date	Year	VG	Fine	VF	XF
31	AH1312	28	25.00	35.00	45.00	60.00
	1318	34	25.00	35.00	45.00	60.00
	1318	35	25.00	35.00	45.00	60.00

RUPEE

SILVER, 30mm, 11.66 gm

Y#	Date	Year	VG	Fine	VF	XF
32	AH1312	28	20.00	25.00	30.00	40.00
	1313	29	20.00	25.00	30.00	40.00
	1314	30	20.00	25.00	30.00	40.00
	1318	34	20.00	25.00	30.00	40.00

ASHRAFI

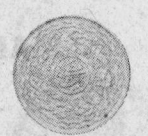

GOLD, 24mm

Y#	Date	Year	VG	Fine	VF	XF
33	AH1311	27	225.00	250.00	285.00	325.00

30mm

Y#	Date	Year	VG	Fine	VF	XF
33a	AH1311	—	225.00	250.00	285.00	325.00

REGULAR COINAGE

PAI

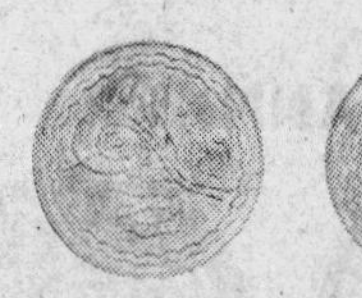

COPPER, 16mm

Y#	Date	Year	Fine	VF	XF	Unc
34	AH1326	42	1.75	2.50	3.50	5.50
	1327	42	1.75	2.50	3.50	5.50
	1329	—	—	Reported, not confirmed		

2 PAI

COPPER, 20mm

Y#	Date	Year	Fine	VF	XF	Unc
35	AH1322	37	1.00	1.25	1.75	2.75
	1322	38	.75	1.00	1.50	2.50
	1322	39	1.00	1.25	1.75	2.75
	1323	38	1.00	1.25	1.75	2.75
	1323	39	.60	.75	1.00	1.50
	1323	40	.75	1.00	1.50	2.50
	1323	41	.75	1.00	1.50	2.50
	1324	39	1.00	1.25	1.75	2.75
	1324	40	.60	.85	1.25	1.75
	1324	41	.75	1.00	1.50	2.50
	1325	40	1.00	1.25	1.75	2.75
	1325	41	.75	1.00	1.50	2.50
	1329	44	.50	.65	1.00	1.75

1/2 ANNA

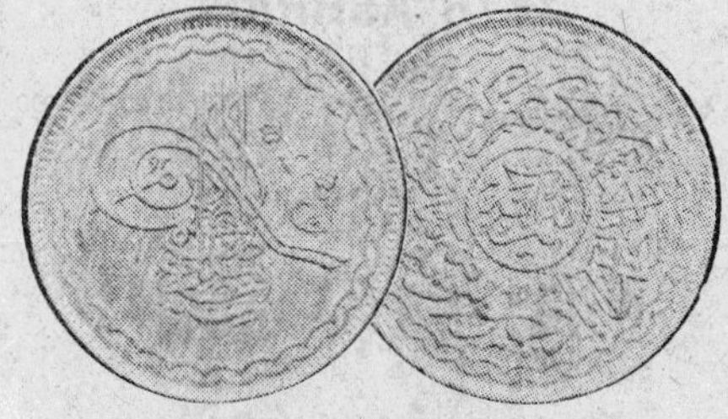

COPPER, 31mm

Y#	Date	Year	Fine	VF	XF	Unc
36	AH1324	40	1.00	1.50	2.00	3.25
	1324	41	1.75	2.25	2.75	4.50
	1325	40	1.50	2.50	3.00	5.00
	1325	41	1.50	2.50	3.00	5.00
	1326	41	2.00	3.00	4.00	6.50
	1329	44	1.00	1.75	2.25	3.50

2 ANNAS

SILVER, 15mm, 1.46 gm

Y#	Date	Year	Fine	VF	XF	Unc
37	AH1323	34(Sic)	1.50	2.50	5.00	8.00
	1323	39	.75	1.25	3.00	5.00

4 ANNAS

SILVER, 20mm, 2.92 gm

Y#	Date	Year	Fine	VF	XF	Unc
38	AH1323	39	4.00	4.75	5.50	9.00
	1328	43	4.00	4.75	6.00	10.00
	1329	44	4.00	4.75	5.50	9.00

8 ANNAS

SILVER, 24mm, 5.83 gm

Y#	Date	Year	Fine	VF	XF	Unc
39	AH1322	38	7.00	8.00	10.00	16.00
	1328	43	6.50	7.50	9.00	14.50
	1329	44	6.50	7.50	9.00	14.50

RUPEE

SILVER, 30mm, 11.66 gm

Y#	Date	Year	Fine	VF	XF	Unc
40	AH1321	37	11.50	13.50	16.50	26.50
	1321	38	11.50	13.50	15.00	24.00
	1322	38	11.50	13.50	15.00	24.00
	1322	39	11.50	13.50	15.00	24.00
	1323	39	11.50	13.50	15.00	24.00
	1324	40	11.50	13.50	15.00	24.00
	1325	41	11.50	13.50	15.00	24.00
	1326	41	11.50	13.50	15.00	24.00
	1328	43	11.50	13.50	15.00	24.00
	1329	44	11.50	13.50	15.00	24.00

1/8 ASHRAFI

GOLD, 1.46 gm

Y#	Date	Year	Fine	VF	XF	Unc
41	AH1325	41	35.00	50.00	60.00	75.00

1/4 ASHRAFI

GOLD, 2.91 gm

Y#	Date	Year	Fine	VF	XF	Unc
42	AH1325	41	55.00	65.00	85.00	100.00
	1329	44	55.00	65.00	85.00	100.00

1/2 ASHRAFI

GOLD, 5.83 gm

Y#	Date	Year	Fine	VF	XF	Unc
43	AH1325	41	110.00	125.00	145.00	165.00
	1326	41	110.00	125.00	145.00	165.00
	1329	44	110.00	125.00	145.00	165.00

NOTE: Y#24 has been observed struck in silver, AH 1324/40, probably a restrike or pattern.

ASHRAFI

GOLD, 24mm, 11.66 gm

Y#	Date	Year	Fine	VF	XF	Unc
44	AH1325	41	225.00	250.00	285.00	325.00
	1329	—	225.00	250.00	285.00	325.00

Mir Usman Ali Khan

AH1329-1368/1911-1948AD

First Coinage, AH1329-1361

PAI

BRONZE

Y#	Date	Year	Fine	VF	XF	Unc
45	AH1338	—	1.50	2.00	2.50	4.00
	1344	15	.60	.75	1.00	1.50
	1349	20	.60	.75	1.00	1.50
	1352	23	1.00	1.25	1.50	2.50
	1352	24	1.00	1.25	1.50	2.50
	1353	24	.70	.85	1.10	1.75

2 PAI

BRONZE
Obv: Short 'Ain' in toughra-not illustrated: see note for Y#A30.

Y#	Date	Year	Fine	VF	XF	Unc
46	AH1329	1	10.00	15.00	22.50	35.00
	1330	1	8.00	12.50	20.00	32.50

Obv: Full 'Ain' in toughra

Y#	Date	Year	Fine	VF	XF	Unc
46a	AH1330	1	1.50	2.00	2.50	3.50
	1330	2	.35	.50	.65	1.00
	1331	2	.35	.50	.65	1.00
	1331	3	.50	.65	.75	1.00
	1332	3	.35	.50	.65	1.00
	1332	4	.60	.75	1.00	1.50
	1333	4	.35	.50	.65	1.00
	1333	5	.75	1.00	1.25	2.00
	1335	6	.35	.50	.65	1.00
	1335	7	.35	.50	.65	1.00
	1336	7	.35	.50	.65	1.00
	1336	8	.50	.65	.80	1.25
	1337	7	.75	1.00	1.25	2.00
	1337	8	.60	.75	1.00	1.50
	1338	8	.75	1.00	1.25	2.00
	1338	9	.35	.50	.65	1.00
	1339	10	.75	1.00	1.25	2.00
	1339	11	.75	1.00	1.25	2.00
	1342	13	.60	.75	1.00	1.50
	1342	14	.35	.50	.65	1.00
	1343	14	.35	.50	.65	1.00
	1344	15	.50	.65	.80	1.25
	1345	16	.35	.50	.65	1.00
	1347	18	.75	1.00	1.25	2.00
	1347	19	.75	1.00	1.25	2.00
	1348	19	.35	.50	.65	1.00
	1349	20	.35	.50	.65	1.00

1/2 ANNA

BRONZE

Y#	Date	Year	Fine	VF	XF	Unc
47	AH1332	3	.75	1.00	1.25	2.00
	1334	4	1.25	1.50	2.00	3.25
	1344	15	1.25	1.50	2.00	3.25
	1347	—	—	Reported, not confirmed		

Y#	Date	Year	Fine	VF	XF	Unc
47	1348	20	1.00	1.35	1.75	2.75

ANNA

COPPER-NICKEL

Y#	Date	Year	Fine	VF	XF	Unc
48	AH1338	—	.50	.75	1.00	1.50
	1339	—	1.00	1.35	1.75	2.75
	1340	—	.60	.85	1.25	2.00
	1341	—	.75	1.00	1.25	2.00
	1344	—	.50	.75	1.00	1.50
	1347	—	.50	.75	1.00	1.50
	1349	—	.50	.75	1.00	1.50
	1351	—	.50	.75	1.00	1.50
	1352	—	1.00	1.35	1.75	2.75
	1353	—	.50	.75	1.00	1.50
	1354	—	.50	.75	1.00	1.50

Y#	Date	Year	Fine	VF	XF	Unc
49	AH1356	—	.35	.50	.65	1.00
	1357	—	.50	.65	.85	1.35
	1358	—	.35	.50	.65	1.00
	1359	—	.75	1.00	1.25	2.00
	1360	—	.75	1.00	1.25	2.00
	1361	—	.75	1.00	1.25	2.00

2 ANNAS

SILVER, 15mm, 1.46 gm

Y#	Date	Year	Fine	VF	XF	Unc
50	AH1335	6	2.00	2.25	2.50	4.00
	1338	10	1.75	2.00	2.50	4.00
	1340	11	1.75	2.00	2.50	4.00
	1341	13	1.75	2.00	2.50	4.00
	1341	14	2.00	2.50	3.00	5.00
	1342	13	1.75	2.00	2.50	4.00
	1343	14	1.75	2.00	2.25	3.50
	1347	—	2.00	2.50	3.00	5.00
	1348	19	1.75	2.00	2.25	3.50
	1351	22	1.75	2.00	2.50	4.00
	1355	26	1.75	2.00	2.50	4.00

4 ANNAS

SILVER, 20mm, 2.92 gm

Y#	Date	Year	Fine	VF	XF	Unc
51	AH1337	9	3.50	4.00	4.50	7.00
	1340	11	3.50	4.00	4.50	7.00
	1342	13	3.50	4.00	4.50	7.00
	1342	14	3.50	4.00	4.50	7.00
	1348	19	3.50	4.00	4.50	7.00
	1351	22	3.50	4.00	4.50	7.00
	1354	25	3.50	4.00	4.50	7.00
	1358	30	3.50	4.00	4.50	7.00

8 ANNAS

SILVER, 24mm, 5.83 gm

Y#	Date	Year	Fine	VF	XF	Unc
52	AH1337	9	6.50	7.00	8.00	12.00
	1342	13	6.50	7.00	8.00	12.00
	1343	13	6.50	7.00	8.00	12.00
	1354	25	6.50	7.00	8.00	12.00

RUPEE

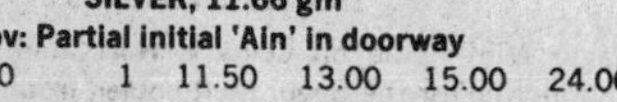

SILVER, 11.66 gm
Obv: Partial initial 'Ain' in doorway

Y#	Date	Year	Fine	VF	XF	Unc
53	AH1330	1	11.50	13.00	15.00	24.00

Obv: Full 'Ain' in doorway

Y#	Date	Year	Fine	VF	XF	Unc
53a	AH1330	1	12.50	14.50	17.50	28.50
	1330	2	12.50	14.50	16.50	27.50
	1331	2	11.50	13.00	15.00	24.00
	1331	3	11.50	13.00	15.00	24.00
	1332	3	11.50	13.00	15.00	24.00
	1334	6	11.50	13.00	15.00	24.00
	1335	6	11.50	13.00	15.00	24.00
	1335	7	11.50	13.00	15.00	24.00
	1336	7	11.50	13.00	15.00	24.00
	1337	8	11.50	13.00	15.00	24.00
	1337	9	12.50	14.50	16.50	27.50
	1338	9	11.50	13.00	15.00	24.00
	1339	9	11.50	13.00	15.00	24.00
	1340	11	11.50	13.00	15.00	24.00
	1341	12	11.50	13.00	15.00	24.00
	1342	13	11.50	13.00	15.00	24.00
	1343	14	11.50	13.00	15.00	24.00

1/8 ASHRAFI

GOLD, 1.46 gm

Y#	Date	Year	Fine	VF	XF	Unc
54	AH1337	8	35.00	50.00	60.00	75.00
	1344	15	35.00	50.00	60.00	75.00
	1354	—	35.00	50.00	60.00	75.00
	1368	39	35.00	50.00	60.00	75.00

1/4 ASHRAFI

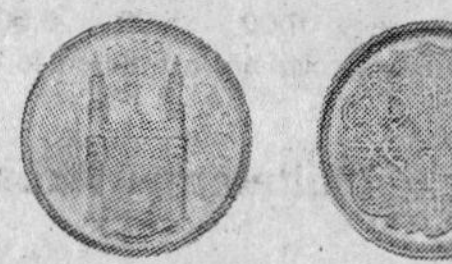

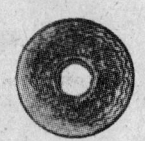

GOLD, 2.91 gm

Y#	Date	Year	Fine	VF	XF	Unc
55	AH1337	8	55.00	65.00	85.00	100.00
	1349	20	55.00	65.00	85.00	100.00
	1357	—	55.00	65.00	85.00	100.00

1/2 ASHRAFI

GOLD, 21mm, 5.83 gm

Y#	Date	Year	Fine	VF	XF	Unc
56	AH1337	8	110.00	125.00	145.00	165.00
	1345	16	110.00	125.00	145.00	165.00
	1349	20	110.00	125.00	145.00	165.00
	1354	25	110.00	125.00	145.00	165.00
	1357	—	110.00	125.00	145.00	165.00

ASHRAFI

GOLD, 24mm, 11.66 gm
Obv: Partial initial 'Ain' in doorway.

Y#	Date	Year	Fine	VF	XF	Unc
57	AH1330	1	250.00	300.00	375.00	450.00

Obv: Full 'Ain' in doorway.

Y#	Date	Year	Fine	VF	XF	Unc
57a	AH1331	3	225.00	250.00	285.00	325.00
	1333	4	225.00	250.00	285.00	325.00
	1337	8	225.00	250.00	285.00	325.00
	1337	9	225.00	250.00	285.00	325.00
	1338	9	225.00	250.00	285.00	325.00
	1340	11	225.00	250.00	285.00	325.00
	1343	14	225.00	250.00	285.00	325.00
	1344	15	225.00	250.00	285.00	325.00
	1348	19	225.00	250.00	285.00	325.00
	1349	20	225.00	250.00	285.00	325.00
	1354	25	225.00	250.00	285.00	325.00

Second Coinage: AH1361-1368

2 PAI

BRONZE

Y#	Date	Year	Fine	VF	XF	Unc
58	AH1362	33	.25	.35	.50	.75
	1363	34	.25	.35	.50	.75
	1363	35	.20	.25	.50	.75
	1364	35	.20	.25	.50	.75
	1365	36	.20	.25	.50	.75
	1366	37	.20	.25	.50	.75
	1368	39	.20	.25	.50	.75

ANNA

BRONZE

Y#	Date	Year	Fine	VF	XF	Unc
59	AH1361	—	.40	.50	.60	1.00
	1362	—	.40	.50	.60	1.00
	1364	—	.40	.50	.60	1.00
	1365	—	.40	.50	.60	1.00
	1366	—	.40	.50	.60	1.00
	1368	—	.40	.50	.60	1.00

2 ANNAS

SILVER

Y#	Date	Year	Fine	VF	XF	Unc
60	AH1362	33	.40	.50	.60	1.00

NICKEL

Y#	Date	Year	Fine	VF	XF	Unc
64	AH1366	37	.15	.25	.35	.60
	1368	39	.25	.35	.45	.90

4 ANNAS

SILVER

Y#	Date	Year	Fine	VF	XF	Unc
61	AH1362	33	.70	.80	1.00	1.65
	1362	34	.75	.90	1.10	1.75
	1364	35	.80	1.00	1.25	2.00
	1364	36	.80	1.00	1.25	2.00
	1365	36	.80	1.00	1.25	2.00

NICKEL

Y#	Date	Year	Fine	VF	XF	Unc
65	AH1366	37	.40	.50	.60	1.00
	1368	39	.40	.50	.60	1.00

8 ANNAS

SILVER, 5.83 gm

Y#	Date	Year	Fine	VF	XF	Unc
62	AH1363	34	6.50	7.00	8.50	12.00

NICKEL

Y#	Date	Year	Fine	VF	XF	Unc
66	AH1366	37	.70	.85	1.00	1.65

RUPEE

SILVER, 11.66 gm

Y#	Date	Year	Fine	VF	XF	Unc
63	AH1361	31	11.50	13.00	15.00	20.00
	1361	32	11.50	13.00	15.00	20.00
	1362	34	11.50	13.00	15.00	20.00
	1364	35	11.50	13.00	15.00	20.00
	1364	36	11.50	13.00	15.00	20.00
	1365	36	11.50	13.00	15.00	20.00

NCLT ISSUES

PATTERNS

KM#	Date	Mintage	Identification	Mkt.Val.
1	AH1312	—	Pai, Copper	—
2	AH1312	—	2 Pai, Copper	—
3	AH1312	—	1/4 Anna, Copper	—
4	AH1312	—	1/2 Anna, Copper	—

FEUDATORY STATES

Under Hyderabad

ELICHPUR

Anonymous Coinage:

PAISA

COPPER, 18-20mm
Obv: Tiger right

C#	Date	Year	Good	VG	Fine	VF
10	AH1250	—	3.50	4.00	6.00	10.00

Obv: Tiger left

C#	Date	Year	Good	VG	Fine	VF
10a	AH1250	—	5.00	6.00	8.00	11.50
	1285	—	5.00	6.00	8.00	11.50

2 PAISA

COPPER, 20-22mm

C#	Date	Year	Good	VG	Fine	VF
15	AH1250	—	5.00	6.00	8.00	11.50

GADWAL

LOCAL RAJAS

RUPEE

SILVER, 17-18mm, 10.70-11.60 gm

C#	Date	Year	VG	Fine	VF	XF
20	AH1186	11	12.50	14.50	17.50	21.50

TOKA

PAISA

COPPER
Rev: Battle-axe in canopy, date below.

C#	Date	Year	Good	VG	Fine	VF
28	FE1241	—	4.00	6.00	8.00	11.50

Date in Nagari numerals.

COPPER, 16mm

C#	Date	Year	Good	VG	Fine	VF
30	AH1273	—	3.50	5.00	7.00	10.00

NARAYANPETT

LOCAL RAJAS

Dilshadabad on coins.

MINTMARKS

ती 'Ti' obv. dated AH1186/1186, C#40

क 'K' rev. dated AH1186/1186, C#40

गो 'Go' obv. dated AH1186/1252, C#37-40

ल 'L' rev. dated AH1186/1252, C#37-40

In the name of Shah Alam II:

1/8 RUPEE

SILVER, 1.34-1.45 gm

C#	Date	Year	VG	Fine	VF	XF
37	AH1186		5.00	6.00	8.00	11.50

1/4 RUPEE

SILVER, 13mm, 2.68-2.90 gm

C#	Date	Year	VG	Fine	VF	XF
38	AH1186	1252	6.00	7.00	9.00	12.50

1/2 RUPEE

SILVER, 16mm, 5.35-5.80 gm

C#	Date	Year	VG	Fine	VF	XF
39	AH1186	1252	7.00	8.50	10.00	14.00

RUPEE

SILVER, 17-19mm, 10.70-11.60 gm

C#	Date	Year	VG	Fine	VF	XF
40	AH1186	1186	12.50	14.50	17.50	21.50
	1186	1239	12.50	14.50	17.50	21.50
	1186	1245	12.50	14.50	17.50	21.50
	1186	1252	12.50	14.50	17.50	21.50

PAISA

COPPER, 18mm
Reverse legend both sides

C#	Date	Year	Good	VG	Fine	VF
34	AH1202	—	4.00	5.50	7.00	10.00

Aurangabad Mint

Struck by Pestonji Meherji, a Bombay banker in the time of Nasir al-Daula, AD1829-57.

In the name of Bahadur Shah II:

1/8 RUPEE

SILVER, 11-13mm, 1.34-1.45 gm

C#	Date	Year	VG	Fine	VF	XF
57	AH1256	4	4.00	5.00	6.50	9.00

1/4 RUPEE

SILVER, 14mm, 2.68-2.90 gm

C#	Date	Year	VG	Fine	VF	XF
58	AH1256	4	4.50	5.50	7.00	10.00

1/2 RUPEE

SILVER, 17mm, 5.35-5.80 gm

C#	Date	Year	VG	Fine	VF	XF
59	AH1256	4	6.50	7.50	9.00	12.00

RUPEE

SILVER, 10.70-11.60 gm

C#	Date	Year	VG	Fine	VF	XF
60	AH1256	4	11.50	13.50	16.50	20.00
	1264	—	11.50	13.50	16.50	20.00

WANPARTI

BAHIRI RAJAS

Sagur Mint name on coins is Nasirabad. The latter is anhonorific for the Sagur Mint copied from the Rupees of Dharwar.

1/2 PAISA

COPPER, 13mm
Similar to 1 Paisa, C#66.

C#	Date	Year	Good	VG	Fine	VF
65	AH1262	—	4.00	5.00	6.50	9.00

PAISA

COPPER, 18mm

C#	Date	Year	Good	VG	Fine	VF
63	ND	—	3.00	4.00	5.00	7.00

Rev: Inscribed BAHIRI, 18mm.

C#	Date	Year	Good	VG	Fine	VF
64	ND	—	4.00	5.00	6.50	9.00

Rev: BAHIRI and date, 17-19mm.

C#	Date	Year	Good	VG	Fine	VF
66	AH1261	—	4.00	5.00	6.50	9.00
	1262	—	4.00	5.00	6.50	9.00

NOTE: The above Paisa coins are attributed to Shorapur by some authorities.

In the name of Muhammad Akbar II

RUPEE

SILVER, 17-18mm, 10.70-11.60 gm
Obv: 'J', Rev: 'RA' in Nagari

C#	Date	Year	VG	Fine	VF	XF
80	AH1235	14	11.50	13.50	16.50	20.00

INDORE

The Holkars were one of the three dominant Maratha powers (with the Peshwas and Sindhias), with major land holdings in Central India. The Holkar rulers survived major wars with the East India Company to become a Princely State generally called after its capital, Indore. The following section is based on S.K. Bhatt, R. Holkar and P.K. Sethi, A STUDY OF HOLKAR STATE COINAGE, and numbering (BHS nos.) follows that catalogue.

Anonymous issues in the name of Shah Alam II:

Until AD1880 (AH1296), all coinage of Indore was struck in the name of Shah Alam II, with the exception of a few rare special or nazarana issues. The coinage of the individual rulers (until AD1880) cannot be told apart except by the date, as no change of type was made for more than a century.

Regnal years refer to:

Alamgir II (AH1168-9 = Yr.1)
Shah Alam II (AH1173-4 = Yr. 1)
Muhammad Akbar II (AH1222-3 = Yr. 1)
Malhar Rao I as Subehdar (AH1170-71 = Yr. 1)

HOLKAR RULERS

Malhar Rao I
AH1141-79/AD1728-66
Ahalya Bai
AH1179-1210/AD1765-95
Tukoji Rao I, AH 1210-12/AD 1795-97
Kashi Rao, AH1212-13/AD1797-98
Jaswant Rao
AH1213-26/AD1798-1811
Mulhar Rao II
AH1226-48/AD1811-33
Martand Rao, AH1249/AD1834
Hari Rao, AH 1250-60/AD 1834-43
Khande Rao
AH1260-61/AD1843-44
Tukoji Rao II
AH1261-1304/AD1844-86

Chandor Mint

Mintname: J'afarabad 'urf Chandor

Mintmark

1/4 RUPEE

SILVER, 2.68-2.90 gm.

KM#	Date	Year	VG	Fine	VF	XF
1	ND	—	6.00	7.50	9.00	12.00

1/2 RUPEE

SILVER, 17mm, 5.35-5.80 gm.

KM#	Date	Year	VG	Fine	VF	XF
2	ND	—	6.50	7.50	9.00	12.00

RUPEE

SILVER, 20mm, 10.70-11.60 gm.

KM#	Date	Year	VG	Fine	VF	XF
3	ND	—	11.50	13.50	15.00	20.00

Chandwad Mint

RUPEE

SILVER, 20mm, 10.70-11.60 gm.

KM#	Date	Year	VG	Fine	VF	XF
4	ND	—	11.50	13.50	16.50	20.00

East India Company

Administrator of Kunch for Holkar from AD1805/AH1220-RY47.

RUPEE

SILVER, 10.70-11.60 gm.
Obv: Symbols #1, #2, #3.
Rev: Symbol #4.

KM#	Date	Year	VG	Fine	VF	XF
7	AH1220	47	12.50	14.50	16.50	21.50
	1221	47	12.50	14.50	16.50	21.50

Maheshwar Mint

Mintname: Malharnagar

Distinctive Marks:

Bilva Leaf.
Silver

Linga - yoni.
Copper and Silver.

1/4 ANNA

COPPER, 8.7 gm
Linga and flywhisk

BHS#	Date	Year	Good	VG	Fine	VF
130	AH1207	—	2.00	2.75	3.50	5.00

7.3 gm.
Linga

BHS#	Date	Year	Good	VG	Fine	VF
139	AH1207	—	2.00	2.75	3.50	5.00

1/2 ANNA

COPPER, 13.5-16.5 gm
Leaves and linga

BHS#	Date	Year	Good	VG	Fine	VF
39	AH1202	—	2.50	3.25	4.00	6.00

15.8-16.3 gm.
Linga and fly whisk

BHS#	Date	Year	Good	VG	Fine	VF
115	AH1203	—	2.50	3.25	4.00	6.00

1/8 RUPEE

SILVER, 1.34-1.45 gm
Linga only

BHS#	Date	Year	VG	Fine	VF	XF
84	1205	—	10.00	14.00	18.50	23.50

1/4 RUPEE

SILVER, 2.68-2.90 gm.
Linga only

BHS#	Date	Year	VG	Fine	VF	XF
79	AH1185	15	10.00	15.00	21.50	28.50

Bilva leaf and linga.

BHS#	Date	Year	VG	Fine	VF	XF
80	AH1202	—	8.50	12.50	16.50	21.50
	1203	—	8.50	12.50	16.50	21.50
	1205	—	8.50	12.50	16.50	21.50
	1211	38	8.50	12.50	16.50	21.50
	1215	—	8.50	12.50	16.50	21.50
	1217	—	8.50	12.50	16.50	21.50

1/2 RUPEE

SILVER, 5.35-5.80 gm.
Linga only

BHS#	Date	Year	VG	Fine	VF	XF
68	AH1192	2x	15.00	20.00	26.50	33.50
	1197	2x	15.00	20.00	26.50	33.50

Bilva leaf and linga

BHS#	Date	Year	VG	Fine	VF	XF
70	AH1202	—	11.00	15.00	20.00	27.50
	1203	3x	11.00	15.00	20.00	27.50
	1205	—	11.00	15.00	20.00	27.50
	1207	—	11.00	15.00	20.00	27.50
	1211	—	11.00	15.00	20.00	27.50

BHS#	Date	Year	VG	Fine	VF	XF
70	1216	44	11.00	15.00	20.00	27.50
	1217	—	11.00	15.00	20.00	27.50

RUPEE

SILVER, 10.70-11.60 gm.
Linga only

BHS#	Date	Year	VG	Fine	VF	XF
2	AH1179	25	11.50	15.00	20.00	27.50
	1180	11	11.50	15.00	20.00	27.50
	1181	11	11.50	15.00	20.00	27.50
	1185	15	11.50	15.00	20.00	27.50
	1186	15	11.50	15.00	20.00	27.50
	1186	16	11.50	15.00	20.00	27.50
	1186	17	11.50	15.00	20.00	27.50
	1190	18	11.50	15.00	20.00	27.50
	1190	19	11.50	15.00	20.00	27.50
	1190	20	11.50	15.00	20.00	27.50
	1191	19	11.50	15.00	20.00	27.50
	1191	20	11.50	15.00	20.00	27.50
	1191	21	10.00	15.00	20.00	27.50
	1192	22	10.00	15.00	20.00	27.50
	1193	23	10.00	15.00	20.00	27.50
	1194	24	10.00	15.00	20.00	27.50
	1197	24	10.00	15.00	20.00	27.50
	1197	25	10.00	15.00	20.00	27.50
	1198	2x	10.00	15.00	20.00	27.50
	1198	25	10.00	15.00	20.00	27.50

Bilva leaf and linga.

BHS#	Date	Year	VG	Fine	VF	XF
24	AH1201	28	11.50	13.50	16.50	20.00
	1202	29	11.50	13.50	16.50	20.00
	1203	31	11.50	13.50	16.50	20.00
	1203	38	11.50	13.50	16.50	20.00
	1205	33	11.50	13.50	16.50	20.00
	1207	35	11.50	13.50	16.50	20.00
	1208	35	11.50	13.50	16.50	20.00
	1209	3x	11.50	13.50	16.50	20.00
	1211	38	11.50	13.50	16.50	20.00
	1215	42	11.50	13.50	16.50	20.00
	1216	44	11.50	13.50	16.50	20.00
	1217	46	11.50	13.50	16.50	20.00

Malharnagar Mint

Mintname: Malharnagar

Distinctive Symbols:

Bilva Leaf
Copper

Sunface
Copper and Silver

1/2 PAISA

COPPER, 3.8 gm.

BHS#	Date	Year	Good	VG	Fine	VF
142	ND	—	5.00	7.50	10.00	13.50

1/4 ANNA

COPPER, 9.6-9.7 gm.

BHS#	Date	Year	Good	VG	Fine	VF
290	AH1244	—	3.00	4.00	5.50	7.50
	xx88	—	3.00	4.00	5.50	7.50

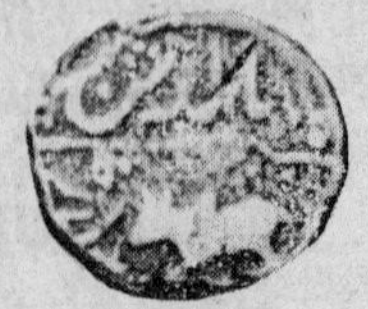

12.2-12.4 gm.
Hindi legend "Pau Anna"

BHS#	Date	Year	Good	VG	Fine	VF
518	AH1296	97	5.00	6.50	8.50	11.50

1/2 ANNA

COPPER, 18.7 - 20 gm.

BHS#	Date	Year	Good	VG	Fine	VF
287	AH1243	1251	3.00	4.00	5.50	7.50
	1244	—	3.00	4.00	5.50	7.50
	—	88	3.00	4.00	5.50	7.50

17.-17.3 gm.
Hindi leg: „Adha Anna"

BHS#	Date	Year	Good	VG	Fine	VF
484	AH1261	—	2.50	3.25	4.00	6.00
	1266	—	2.50	3.25	4.00	6.00
	1267	97	2.75	3.50	4.50	6.50
	1268	—	2.50	3.25	4.00	6.00
	1269	99	3.00	3.50	4.50	6.50
	1271	—	2.50	3.25	4.00	6.00
	1285	—	1.75	2.50	3.50	5.50
	1286	113	2.25	3.00	4.00	6.00
	1286	1286	3.00	3.50	4.00	6.00

1/8 RUPEE

SILVER, 9-10mm, 1.34-1.45 gm.

BHS#	Date	Year	VG	Fine	VF	XF
251	AH1236	—	3.50	4.00	5.00	7.50
	1268	—	2.50	3.25	4.00	6.00
	1279	—	2.50	3.25	4.00	6.00
	1282	—	2.00	3.25	4.00	6.00
	1289	—	2.50	3.25	4.00	6.00
	1291	—	2.50	3.25	4.00	6.00
	1294	—	2.50	3.25	4.00	6.00

1/4 RUPEE

SILVER, 11-13mm, 2.68-2.90 gm.

BHS#	Date	Year	VG	Fine	VF	XF
83	AH1232	—	3.50	4.00	4.50	6.00
	1233	—	3.50	4.00	4.50	6.00
	1234	—	3.50	4.00	4.50	6.00
	1235	—	3.50	4.00	4.50	6.00
	1237	—	3.50	4.00	4.50	6.00
	1240	—	3.50	4.00	4.50	6.00
	1241	—	3.50	4.00	4.50	6.00

BHS#	Date	Year	VG	Fine	VF	XF
	1244	—	3.50	4.00	4.50	6.00
	1249	—	3.50	4.00	4.50	6.00
	1250	—	3.50	4.00	4.50	6.00
	1251	—	3.50	4.00	4.50	6.00
	1252	—	3.50	4.00	4.50	6.00
	1253	—	3.50	4.00	4.50	6.00
	1256	—	3.50	4.00	4.50	6.00
	1261	—	3.50	4.00	4.50	6.00
	1263	—	3.50	4.00	4.50	6.00
	1265	—	3.50	4.00	4.50	6.00
	1266	—	3.50	4.00	4.50	6.00
	1268	—	3.50	4.00	4.50	6.00
	1269	—	3.50	4.00	4.50	6.00
	1272	—	3.50	4.00	4.50	6.00
	1275	—	3.50	4.00	4.50	6.00
	1278	—	3.50	4.00	4.50	6.00
	1285	—	3.50	4.00	4.50	6.00
	1286	—	3.50	4.00	4.50	6.00
	1288	—	3.50	4.00	4.50	6.00
	1291	—	3.50	4.00	4.50	6.00
	1292	—	3.50	4.00	4.50	6.00
	1293	—	3.50	4.00	4.50	6.00
	1294	—	3.50	4.00	4.50	6.00
	1295	—	3.50	4.00	4.50	6.00

25mm
Broad, thin planchet

BHS#	Date	Year	VG	Fine	VF	XF
451	AH1280	110	20.00	25.00	30.00	40.00

1/2 RUPEE

SILVER, 14-15mm, 5.35-5.80 gm.

BHS#	Date	Year	VG	Fine	VF	XF
74	AH1228	—	6.50	7.50	9.00	12.00
	1230	—	6.50	7.50	9.00	12.00
	1233	—	6.50	7.50	9.00	12.00
	1238	—	6.50	7.50	9.00	12.00
	1242	—	6.50	7.50	9.00	12.00
	1250	—	6.50	7.50	9.00	12.00
	1266	—	6.50	7.50	9.00	12.00
	1267	—	6.50	7.50	9.00	12.00
	1268	—	6.50	7.50	9.00	12.00
	1272	—	6.50	7.50	9.00	12.00
	1275	—	6.50	7.50	9.00	12.00
	1276	—	6.50	7.50	9.00	12.00
	1281	—	6.50	7.50	9.00	12.00
	1283	—	6.50	7.50	9.00	12.00
	1285	—	6.50	7.50	9.00	12.00
	1286	—	6.50	7.50	9.00	12.00
	1289	—	6.50	7.50	9.00	12.00
	1291	—	6.50	7.50	9.00	12.00
	1292	—	6.50	7.50	9.00	12.00
	1294	—	6.50	7.50	9.00	12.00
	1295	—	6.50	7.50	9.00	12.00
	—	121	6.50	7.50	9.00	12.00

Broad, thin planchet, 27mm

BHS#	Date	Year	VG	Fine	VF	XF
418	AH1236	69	25.00	32.50	40.00	50.00
	1280	110	35.00	45.00	55.00	67.50

RUPEE

SILVER, 17-21mm, 10.70-11.60 gm.

BHS#	Date	Year	VG	Fine	VF	XF
33	AH1185	15	11.50	13.50	16.50	20.00
	1187	17	11.50	13.50	16.50	20.00
	1191	2x	11.50	13.50	16.50	20.00
	1195	—	11.50	13.50	16.50	20.00
	1199	26	11.50	13.50	16.50	20.00
	1200	27	11.50	13.50	16.50	20.00
	1201	29	11.50	13.50	16.50	20.00
	1202	29	11.50	13.50	16.50	20.00
	1203	30	11.50	13.50	16.50	20.00

BHS#	Date	Year	VG	Fine	VF	XF
	1204	—	11.50	13.50	16.50	20.00
	1205	32	11.50	13.50	16.50	20.00
	1206	33	11.50	13.50	16.50	20.00
	1210	—	11.50	13.50	16.50	20.00
	1211	—	11.50	13.50	16.50	20.00
	1212	—	11.50	13.50	16.50	20.00
	1213	—	11.50	13.50	16.50	20.00
	1216	—	11.50	13.50	16.50	20.00
	1224	—	11.50	13.50	16.50	20.00
	1225	—	11.50	13.50	16.50	20.00
	1228	62	11.50	13.50	16.50	20.00
	1230	62	11.50	13.50	16.50	20.00
	1231	63	11.50	13.50	16.50	20.00
	1232	65	11.50	13.50	16.50	20.00
	1233	66	11.50	13.50	16.50	20.00
	1234	67	11.50	13.50	16.50	20.00
	1235	68	11.50	13.50	16.50	20.00
	1237	—	11.50	13.50	16.50	20.00
	1238	70	11.50	13.50	16.50	20.00
	1242	75	11.50	13.50	16.50	20.00
	1243	76	11.50	13.50	16.50	20.00
	1246	76	11.50	13.50	16.50	20.00
	1248	77	11.50	13.50	16.50	20.00
	1249	—	11.50	13.50	16.50	20.00
	1257	87	11.50	13.50	16.50	20.00
	1258	88	11.50	13.50	16.50	20.00
	1260	9x	11.50	13.50	16.50	20.00
	1262	—	11.50	13.50	16.50	20.00
	1263	—	11.50	13.50	16.50	20.00
	1264	—	11.50	13.50	16.50	20.00
	1265	—	11.50	13.50	16.50	20.00
	1266	9x	11.50	13.50	16.50	20.00
	1266	16	11.50	13.50	16.50	20.00
	1267	—	11.50	13.50	16.50	20.00
	1270	—	11.50	13.50	16.50	20.00
	1272	1xx	11.50	13.50	16.50	20.00
	1273	—	11.50	13.50	16.50	20.00
	1275	—	11.50	13.50	16.50	20.00
	1276	—	11.50	13.50	16.50	20.00
	1277	—	11.50	13.50	16.50	20.00
	1278	—	11.50	13.50	16.50	20.00
	1279	—	11.50	13.50	16.50	20.00
	1280	—	11.50	13.50	16.50	20.00
	1285	—	11.50	13.50	16.50	20.00
	1286	—	11.50	13.50	16.50	20.00
	1289	—	11.50	13.50	16.50	20.00
	1292	118	11.50	13.50	16.50	20.00
	1293	111	11.50	13.50	16.50	20.00
	1293	119	11.50	13.50	16.50	20.00
	1294	—	11.50	13.50	16.50	20.00
	1295	122	11.50	13.50	16.50	20.00
	1296	122	11.50	13.50	16.50	20.00

Broad, thinner planchet, 28mm

10a	AH1280	110	35.00	45.00	55.00	70.00

NAZARANA RUPEE

SILVER, 29mm, 10.70-11.60 gm.

164	AH1225	59	—	—	—	—

Sironj Mint

RUPEE

SILVER, 20mm, 10.70-11.60 gm.

KM#	Date	Year	VG	Fine	VF	XF
9	AH1188	16	10.00	13.50	18.50	25.00

Uncertain Mints

PAISA

I - "Raij" type

Obv: Sword

KM#	Date	Year	Good	VG	Fine	VF
11	AH	30	5.00	5.50	6.00	8.00

Obv: Branch

12	AH	30	4.00	4.50	5.00	7.00

13	AH	59	3.00	4.00	4.50	6.00

14	AH	59	4.00	4.50	5.00	7.00

15	AH	5x	4.00	4.50	5.50	7.50

1/2 ANNA

II - Symbols Type.

COPPER, 21mm

21	AH1203	—	4.00	4.50	5.50	7.50

22	AH1207	—	4.00	4.50	5.50	7.50

23	AH1228	—	4.00	4.50	5.50	7.50

23mm

KM#	Date	Year	Good	VG	Fine	VF
24	AH1230	—	4.00	4.50	5.50	7.50

22mm

25	AH1230	—	4.00	4.50	5.50	7.50

25mm

26	AH1230	—	4.00	4.50	5.50	7.50

21mm

27	AH1241	—	4.00	4.50	5.50	7.50

NOTE: These coins were issued from AH1202 to 1244 with many varieties of symbols of which the above are only a sample.

Coins struck in the names of the Holkars of Indore:

Jaswant Rao

SE1719-1734/AH1212-1226/
1797-1811AD

NAZARANA RUPEE

SILVER, 25mm, 10.70-11.60 gm.
In his own name, alone; Nagari legends.

C#	Date	Year	VG	Fine	VF	XF
52	SE1728	(1806)	65.00	80.00	100.00	135.00

28mm
In name of Md.Akbar II and Jaswant Rao;
Nagari legends.

53	SE1728	(1806)	—	—	Rare	—

30mm
Together with Muhammad Akbar II; Persian legends

C#	Date	Year	VG	Fine	VF	XF
58	AH1222	2	50.00	60.00	75.00	100.00

Tukoji Rao II

VS1891-1943/SE1766-1808/
AH1260-1304/1844-1886AD

The following issues are all of special or presentation nature, probably not intended primarily for circulation purposes.

COPPER 1/2 MUDRA

COPPER, 17mm, 4.3-5.1 gm.

BHS#	Date	Year	Good	VG	Fine	VF
520	SE1780	(1858)	20.00	30.00	40.00	55.00
	1788	VS1923	20.00	30.00	40.00	55.00

COPPER MUDRA

COPPER, 22mm, 7.8-11. gm.

515	SE1780	(1858)	15.00	25.00	35.00	50.00
	1788	VS1923	15.00	25.00	35.00	50.00

1/2 ANNA

COPPER, 16.6 gm.

513	VS1942	(1885)	30.00	40.00	50.00	65.00

13.4 gm.

514	VS1942/SE1807/1885	40.00	50.00	65.00	80.00

MUDRA

SILVER, 25mm, 11.2 gm.

BHS#	Date	Year	VG	Fine	VF	XF
388	SE1780	(1858)	20.00	30.00	40.00	55.00

Obv: Blank within wreath.

389	SE1780	(1858)	20.00	30.00	40.00	55.00

21mm
Obv: Two varieties of swirls.

391	SE1780	(1858)	40.00	50.00	60.00	75.00

24mm

392	SE1788	VS1923	25.00	35.00	45.00	60.00

20mm

393	VS1934	FE1287	60.00	75.00	90.00	110.00

18mm

393.1	VS1934	FE1287	—	—	Rare	—

1/2 RUPEE

SILVER, 14mm, 5.5 gm.

433	AH1289	—	55.00	70.00	85.00	110.00

RUPEE

SILVER, 18mm, 11.2 gm.

395	AH1289	—	25.00	35.00	45.00	60.00

19mm

BHS#	Date	Year	VG	Fine	VF	XF
399	AH1295	—	35.00	50.00	65.00	80.00

MACHINE-STRUCK COINAGE

Shivaji Rao

AD 1886-1903

No ruler's name

1/2 PAISA

COPPER
Var. 1: Denomination in 2 lines: 1/2 ADELA

Y#	Date	Year	Good	VG	Fine	VF
9.1	VS1944	(1887)	10.00	15.00	21.50	30.00

Var. II: Denomination in 3 lines 1/2 DHALEKA PAISA

9.2	VS1944	(1887)	10.00	15.00	21.50	30.00

In the name of Shivaji Rao

Var. III: Denomination in 2 lines: ADHA PESA

9a	VS1946	(1889)	11.50	16.50	23.50	32.50

No ruler's name

1/4 ANNA

COPPER
Obv: Date under bull.

10.1	VS1943	(1886)	1.50	3.00	5.00	7.50

Obv: Indore upside-down below bull.

Y#	Date	Year	Good	VG	Fine	VF
10.2	VS1943	(1886)	.35	.75	1.25	1.75
	1944	(1887)	.50	1.00	1.50	2.00
	1945	(1888)	.75	1.25	2.00	3.00

Obv: Indore upright below bull.

Y#	Date	Year	Good	VG	Fine	VF
10.3	VS1943	(1886)	.50	1.00	1.50	2.00

Obv: Cross with dot in each quadrant flanking INDORE.

Y#	Date	Year	Good	VG	Fine	VF
10.4	VS1943	(1886)	1.00	2.00	3.00	5.00

In the Name of Sivaji Rao

Obv: Name of ruler & state. Rev: Date.

Y#	Date	Year	Good	VG	Fine	VF
10a.1	VS1944	(1887)	.85	1.75	2.50	3.50
	1945	(1888)	.75	1.50	2.00	3.00
	1946	(1889)	.85	1.75	2.50	3.50
	1947	(1890)	.75	1.50	2.00	3.00

Obv: Name of ruler and "BAHADUR".
Rev: Date and state name.

Y#	Date	Year	Good	VG	Fine	VF
10a.2	VS1947	(1890)	.75	1.50	2.25	3.00
	1948	(1891)	.50	1.00	1.50	2.00
	1956	(1899)	.35	.75	1.25	1.75
	1958	(1901)	.65	1.25	1.75	2.50
	1959	(1902)	.65	1.25	1.75	2.50

No ruler's name

1/2 ANNA

COPPER
Obv: Date under bull. Rev: State name.

Y#	Date	Year	Good	VG	Fine	VF
11.1	VS1943	(1886)	3.00	5.00	8.00	12.50

Obv: Indore upside-down below bull.

Y#	Date	Year	Good	VG	Fine	VF
11.2	VS1943	1886	.50	1.00	1.50	2.75
	1944	(1887)	.50	1.00	1.50	2.75

State name on both sides.

Y#	Date	Year	Good	VG	Fine	VF
11.3	VS1943	(1886)	1.00	2.00	3.00	4.50

Obv: Indore upright below bull.

Y#	Date	Year	Good	VG	Fine	VF
11.4	VS1943	(1886)	.50	1.00	1.50	2.75

In the Name of Sivaji Rao

Obv: Name of ruler & state. Rev: Date.

Y#	Date	Year	Good	VG	Fine	VF
11a.1	1944	(1887)	.50	1.00	1.50	2.75
	1945	(1888)	.50	1.00	1.50	2.75

Obv: Bahadur upright below bull. Rev: State.

Y#	Date	Year	Good	VG	Fine	VF
11a.2	VS1943	—	—	2.00	3.00	4.00

Obv: Bahadur upside-down below bull. Rev: Date & state.

Y#	Date	Year	Good	VG	Fine	VF
11a.3	VS1945	(1888)	.75	1.50	2.25	4.00
	1947	(1890)	.65	1.25	2.00	3.25
	1948	(1891)	.50	1.00	1.50	2.75
	1956	(1899)	.50	1.00	1.50	2.50
	1957	(1900)	.50	1.00	1.50	2.50
	1958	(1901)	.65	1.25	2.00	3.25
	1959	(1902)	.65	1.25	2.00	3.25

'DUMP' SILVER COINAGE

First Series

1/4 RUPEE

SILVER, 2.68-2.90 gm.

Y#	Date	Year	VG	Fine	VF	XF
12	FE1895	VS1945	15.00	20.00	25.00	32.50

1/2 RUPEE

SILVER, 5.35-5.80 gm.

Y#	Date	Year	VG	Fine	VF	XF
13	FE1296	VS1947	15.00	20.00	25.00	32.50

RUPEE

SILVER, 21mm, 10.70-11.60 gm.
Obv: Large flames.

Y#	Date	Year	VG	Fine	VF	XF
14.1	FE1294	VS1945	25.00	30.00	37.50	47.50
	1295	1945	25.00	30.00	37.50	47.50
	1296	1945	25.00	30.00	37.50	47.50

Obv: Small flames, 20mm.

Y#	Date	Year	VG	Fine	VF	XF
14.2	FE1296	—	20.00	25.00	30.00	38.50

Obv: No flames

Y#	Date	Year	VG	Fine	VF	XF
14.3	FE1295	VS1947	20.00	30.00	40.00	55.00
	1296	1947	20.00	30.00	40.00	55.00
	1297	1947	20.00	30.00	40.00	55.00

Second Series

NOTE: There are 2 varieties, one with U-shaped mark on forehead of sunface, the other with solid forehead.

1/8 RUPEE

SILVER, 10mm, 1.34-1.45 gm.

Y#	Date	Year	VG	Fine	VF	XF
15	VS1947	(1890)	2.00	2.50	3.25	4.50
	1950	(1893)	2.00	2.50	3.25	4.50
	1951	(1894)	2.00	2.50	3.25	4.50

1/4 RUPEE

SILVER, 12mm, 2.68-2.90 gm.

Y#	Date	Year	VG	Fine	VF	XF
16	VS1947	(1890)	3.50	4.00	4.50	5.50
	1951	(1893)	3.50	4.00	4.50	5.50
	1954	(1897)	3.50	4.00	4.50	5.50

1/2 RUPEE

SILVER, 16mm, 5.35-5.80 gm.

Y#	Date	Year	VG	Fine	VF	XF
17	VS1947	(1890)	6.50	7.50	9.00	12.00
	1948	(1891)	6.50	7.50	9.00	12.00
	1949	(1892)	6.50	7.50	9.00	12.00
	1950	(1893)	6.50	7.50	9.00	12.00
	1951	(1894)	6.50	7.50	9.00	12.00
	1952	(1895)	6.50	7.50	9.00	12.00
	1953	(1896)	6.50	7.50	9.00	12.00
	1954	(1897)	6.50	7.50	9.00	12.00

RUPEE

SILVER, 22mm, 10.70-11.60 gm.

Y#	Date	Year	VG	Fine	VF	XF
18	VS1947	(1890)	11.50	13.50	16.50	20.00
	1948	(1891)	11.50	13.50	16.50	20.00
	1949	(1892)	11.50	13.50	16.50	20.00
	1950	(1893)	11.50	13.50	16.50	20.00
	1951	(1894)	11.50	13.50	16.50	20.00
	1952	(1895)	11.50	13.50	16.50	20.00
	1953	(1896)	11.50	13.50	16.50	20.00
	1954	(1897)	11.50	13.50	16.50	20.00
	1955	(1898)	11.50	13.50	16.50	20.00
	Date off flan		11.50	13.50	16.50	20.00

25mm
Full flan.

Y#	Date	Year	VG	Fine	VF	XF
18.1	VS1947	(1890)	30.00	35.00	40.00	50.00

MACHINE-STRUCK COINS

RUPEE

SILVER

Y#	Date	Year	Fine	VF	XF	Unc
19	VS1956	(1899)	125.00	175.00	250.00	325.00
	1958	(1901)	175.00	225.00	275.00	350.00

Yeshwant Rao

VS1983-2005/1926-1948AD

1/4 ANNA

COPPER

Y#	Date	Year	Fine	VF	XF	Unc
20	VS1992	(1935)	1.00	2.00	3.50	6.00

1/2 ANNA

COPPER

Y#	Date	Year	Fine	VF	XF	Unc
21	VS1992	(1935)	1.25	2.50	4.00	7.00

JAFARABAD

Anonymous coinage

3/4 KORI

BASE SILVER, 12mm, 3.4 gm.

KM#	Date	Year	Good	VG	Fine	VF
1	ND	—	5.00	6.00	7.00	10.00

KORI

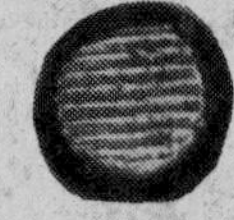

BASE SILVER, 13mm, 4.7 gm.

KM#	Date	Year	Good	VG	Fine	VF
2	ND	—	5.00	6.00	7.00	10.00

1-1/2 KORI

BASE SILVER, 14mm, 7.0 gm.

KM#	Date	Year	Good	VG	Fine	VF
3	ND	—	5.00	6.00	7.00	10.00

The attribution of these coins is very tentative. The denominations are suggested by the average weights.

JAINTIAPUR

All coins are dated to year of ruler's accession

Bar Gossain II

SE1653-1692/1731-1770AD

1/4 RUPEE

SILVER, 2.68-2.90 gm.

C#	Date	Year	VG	Fine	VF	XF
175	SE1653	(1731)	—	—	—	—

RUPEE

SILVER, 30mm, 10.70-11.60 gm.

C#	Date	Year	VG	Fine	VF	XF
177	SE1653	(1731)	15.00	20.00	25.00	35.00

Chattra Simha

SE1692-1704/1770-1782AD

RUPEE

SILVER, 10.70-11.60 gm.

C#	Date	Year	VG	Fine	VF	XF
180	SE1696	(1774)	25.00	30.00	37.50	50.00

Jatra Narayana

SE1704-1707/1782-1785AD

RUPEE

SILVER, 10.70-11.60 gm.

C#	Date	Year	VG	Fine	VF	XF
183	SE1704	(1782)	25.00	30.00	37.50	50.00

Vijaya Narayan

SE1707-1712/1785-1790AD

RUPEE

SILVER

C#	Date	Year	VG	Fine	VF	XF
186	SE1707	(1785)	25.00	30.00	37.50	50.00

Ram Simha II

SE1712-1754/1790-1832AD

1/4 RUPEE

SILVER, 2.68-2.90 gm.

C#	Date	Year	VG	Fine	VF	XF
189	SE1712	(1790)	—	—	Rare	—

RUPEE

SILVER, 10.70-11.60 gm.

C#	Date	Year	VG	Fine	VF	XF
191	SE1712	(1790)	20.00	25.00	30.00	42.50

JAIPUR

RULERS

Madho Singh, AD 1760-1778
Pratap Singh, AD 1778-1803
Jagat Singh II, AD 1803-1818
Mohan Singh, AD 1818-1819
Jai Singh III, AD 1819-1835
Ram Singh, AD 1835-1880
Madho Singh II, AD 1880-1922
Man Singh II, AD 1922-1949

All coins struck prior to 1857 are in the name of the Mughal emperor. They were struck at two mints, which bear the following characteristic marks on the reverse:

(Sawai) Jaipur Mint

(Sawai) Madhopur Mint

('Sawai' is merely an honorific title accorded each of the two cities.)

The name of the Maharaja of Jaipur does not appear on the pre-1857 coins. Beginning in 1857, coins were struck jointly in the names of the British sovereign and the Maharaja of Jaipur, with regnal years always referring to the Maharaja.

The broad, well-struck silver and copper Nazarana pieces have recently become available in large numbers, particularly Y#A1, A#5a, and 9. It is believed they are from old hoards, though some persons allege they are 'restrikes.'

The coins ordinarily bear both AH date (before 1857) or the AD date (after 1857) as well as the regnal year, but as it is found only at the extreme right of the obverse die, it almost never is visible on the regular coinage (but generally legible on the presentation pieces, which were struck from the entire die). Consequently, the regular coins are listed only by regnal year.

The listing of regnal years is very incomplete and many more years will turn up. In general, unlisted years are worth no more than listed years.

Jaipur Mint

In the name of Shah Alam II

AD1759-1806

PAISA

COPPER, 26mm
Type I: Jhar on reverse

C#	Date	Year	Good	VG	Fine	VF
29	—	12	1.25	2.00	4.00	6.00
29	—	13	1.25	2.00	4.00	6.00
	—	14	1.25	2.00	4.00	6.00
	—	15	1.25	2.00	4.00	6.00
	—	16	1.25	2.00	4.00	6.00
	—	17	1.25	2.00	4.00	6.00
	—	18	1.25	2.00	4.00	6.00
	—	19	1.25	2.00	4.00	6.00
			21mm			
			Type II: Cross on reverse.			
30	—	20	1.50	2.50	4.00	6.00
	—	21	1.50	2.50	4.00	6.00
	—	22	1.50	2.50	4.00	6.00
	—	23	1.50	2.50	4.00	6.00
	—	24	1.50	2.50	4.00	6.00
	—	25	1.50	2.50	4.00	6.00
			20mm			
			Type III: Three-lobed flower on reverse.			
31	—	25	2.00	3.00	5.00	7.50
			21mm			
			Type IV: Three-lobed leaf reverse.			
32	—	26	2.00	3.00	5.00	7.50
			23mm			
			Type V: Fish on reverse.			
33	—	26	1.50	2.50	4.00	6.00
	—	27	1.50	2.50	4.00	6.00
	—	28	1.50	2.50	4.00	6.00
	—	29	1.50	2.50	4.00	6.00
	—	30	1.50	2.50	4.00	6.00
	—	31	1.50	2.50	4.00	6.00
			24mm			
			Type VI: Leaf and fish on reverse.			
34	—	31	1.50	2.50	4.00	6.00
	—	32	1.50	2.50	4.00	6.00
	—	33	1.50	2.50	4.00	6.00
	—	34	1.50	2.50	4.00	6.00
	—	35	1.50	2.50	4.00	6.00
			19.5mm			
			Type VII: Large spray on reverse.			
35	—	35	1.00	2.00	3.00	4.50
	—	36	1.00	2.00	3.00	4.50
	—	37	1.00	2.00	3.00	4.50
	—	38	1.00	2.00	3.00	4.50
	—	39	1.00	2.00	3.00	4.50
	—	40	1.00	2.00	3.00	4.50
	—	41	1.00	2.00	3.00	4.50

NAZARANA PAISA

COPPER, 33mm

C#	Date	Year	Good	VG	Fine	VF
29a	—	23	6.00	9.00	12.50	15.00
	—	33	6.00	9.00	12.50	15.00
	—	37	6.00	9.00	12.50	15.00
	—	38	6.00	9.00	12.50	15.00
	—	39	6.00	9.00	12.50	15.00
	—	45	6.00	9.00	12.50	15.00

RUPEE

SILVER, 20-22mm, 10.70-11.60 gm.

C#	Date	Year	VG	Fine	VF	XF
36	AH1208	34	11.50	13.50	16.50	20.00
	—	38	11.50	13.50	16.50	20.00
	—	39	11.50	13.50	16.50	20.00
	1214	40	11.50	13.50	16.50	20.00
	—	46	11.50	13.50	16.50	20.00
	—	47	11.50	13.50	16.50	20.00

NAZARANA RUPEE

SILVER, 10.70-11.60 gm.

C#	Date	Year	VG	Fine	VF	XF
36a	AH1186	10	45.00	60.00	80.00	100.00
	1208	34	45.00	60.00	80.00	100.00

MOHUR

GOLD, 10.70-11.40 gm.

C#	Date	Year	VG	Fine	VF	XF
40	—	15	225.00	250.00	285.00	325.00

Madhopur Mint

RUPEE

SILVER, 20-22mm, 10.70-11.60 gm.

C#	Date	Year	VG	Fine	VF	XF
43	—	7	11.50	13.50	16.50	20.00
	—	14	11.50	13.50	16.50	20.00
	—	33	11.50	13.50	16.50	20.00
	—	38	11.50	13.50	16.50	20.00
	—	41	11.50	13.50	16.50	20.00
	—	43	11.50	13.50	16.50	20.00

For similar coins, see Bundi C#10.

In the name of Muhammad Akbar II,

AD1806-37

NAZARANA PAISA

COPPER, 32mm
Type I: Whisk on reverse

C#	Date	Year	Good	VG	Fine	VF
46	—	3	6.00	9.00	12.50	16.00
	—	8	6.00	9.00	12.50	16.00
	—	11	6.00	9.00	12.50	16.00

Type II: Jhar on reverse

C#	Date	Year	Good	VG	Fine	VF
47a	—	9	6.00	9.00	12.50	16.00
	—	22	6.00	9.00	12.50	16.00

PAISA

COPPER, 18-20mm
Similar to Nazarana Paisa, C#47a.

C#	Date	Year	Good	VG	Fine	VF
47	—	22	1.75	2.50	3.50	4.50
	—	26	1.75	2.50	3.50	4.50
	—	27	1.75	2.50	3.50	4.50
	—	29	1.75	2.50	3.50	4.50
	—	35	1.75	2.50	3.50	4.50

1/8 RUPEE

(2 Annas)

SILVER, 17-18mm, 1.34-1.45 gm.

C#	Date	Year	VG	Fine	VF	XF
52	—	22	2.00	2.75	4.00	5.50

1/4 RUPEE

SILVER, 18-19mm, 2.68-2.90 gm.

C#	Date	Year	VG	Fine	VF	XF
53	—	17	3.50	5.00	6.50	8.50
	—	28	3.50	5.00	6.50	8.50

1/2 RUPEE

SILVER, 18-20mm, 5.35-5.80 gm.

C#	Date	Year	VG	Fine	VF	XF
54	—	16	6.50	7.50	9.00	11.50
	—	31	6.50	7.50	9.00	11.50

RUPEE

SILVER, 20-24mm, 10.70-11.60 gm.

C#	Date	Year	VG	Fine	VF	XF
55	—	2	11.50	13.50	16.50	20.00
	AH122x	3	11.50	13.50	16.50	20.00
	—	9	11.50	13.50	16.50	20.00
	—	10	11.50	13.50	16.50	20.00
	—	13	11.50	13.50	16.50	20.00
	—	14	11.50	13.50	16.50	20.00
	—	15	11.50	13.50	16.50	20.00
	—	18	11.50	13.50	16.50	20.00
	—	27	11.50	13.50	16.50	20.00
	—	30	11.50	13.50	16.50	20.00

NAZARANA RUPEE

SILVER, 33mm, 10.70-11.60 gm.

C#	Date	Year	VG	Fine	VF	XF
55a	—	1	22.50	30.00	38.50	50.00
	—	9	22.50	30.00	38.50	50.00
	AH1232	11	22.50	30.00	38.50	50.00
	—	16	22.50	30.00	38.50	50.00
	1242	22	22.50	30.00	38.50	50.00
	1245	23	22.50	30.00	38.50	50.00
	1249	27	22.50	30.00	38.50	50.00
	1251	29	22.50	30.00	38.50	50.00
	—	30	22.50	30.00	38.50	50.00

MOHUR

GOLD, 20-22mm, 10.70-11.60 gm.

C#	Date	Year	VG	Fine	VF	XF
62	—	1	220.00	240.00	265.00	300.00
	—	7	220.00	240.00	265.00	300.00
	—	8	220.00	240.00	265.00	300.00
	—	9	220.00	240.00	265.00	300.00
	—	11	220.00	240.00	265.00	300.00
	—	12	220.00	240.00	265.00	300.00
	—	16	220.00	240.00	265.00	300.00
	—	19	220.00	240.00	265.00	300.00
	—	29	220.00	240.00	265.00	300.00
	—	30	220.00	240.00	265.00	300.00

Madhopur Mint

In the name of Bahadur Shah II,

AD1837-1857

PAISA

COPPER

C#	Date	Year	Good	VG	Fine	VF
71	—	13	1.75	2.75	4.00	5.50
	—	14	1.75	2.75	4.00	5.50

RUPEE

SILVER, 19-22mm, 10.70-11.60 gm.

C#	Date	Year	VG	Fine	VF	XF
75	—	2	11.50	13.50	16.50	20.00
	(AH1232)	4	11.50	13.50	16.50	20.00
	—	5	11.50	13.50	16.50	20.00
	—	6	11.50	13.50	16.50	20.00
	1238	7	11.50	13.50	16.50	20.00
	—	10	11.50	13.50	16.50	20.00
	—	11	11.50	13.50	16.50	20.00
	—	12	11.50	13.50	16.50	20.00
	—	13	11.50	13.50	16.50	20.00
	—	14	11.50	13.50	16.50	20.00
	—	15	11.50	13.50	16.50	20.00
	—	18	11.50	13.50	16.50	20.00
	—	21	11.50	13.50	16.50	20.00
	—	22	11.50	13.50	16.50	20.00
	—	23	11.50	13.50	16.50	20.00
	—	26	11.50	13.50	16.50	20.00
	—	30	11.50	13.50	16.50	20.00

Jaipur Mint

PAISA

COPPER, 19-23mm

C#	Date	Year	Good	VG	Fine	VF
85	—	13	1.75	2.50	3.50	5.00

NAZARANA PAISA

COPPER, 32mm

C#	Date	Year	Good	VG	Fine	VF
85a	—	2	6.00	9.00	12.50	16.00
	—	6	6.00	9.00	12.50	16.00
	—	11	6.00	9.00	12.50	16.00
	—	12	6.00	9.00	12.50	16.00
	—	13	6.00	9.00	12.50	16.00
	—	17	6.00	9.00	12.50	16.00

1/16 RUPEE

SILVER, 11mm, 0.67-0.72 gm.

C#	Date	Year	VG	Fine	VF	XF
89	—	7	4.00	6.00	8.00	11.00
	—	18	4.00	6.00	8.00	11.00

1/8 RUPEE

SILVER, 15mm, 1.34-1.45 gm.

C#	Date	Year	VG	Fine	VF	XF
90	—	18	4.00	6.00	8.00	11.00

1/4 RUPEE

SILVER, 16-18mm, 2.68-2.90 gm.

C#	Date	Year	VG	Fine	VF	XF
91	—	7	4.00	6.00	8.00	11.00
	—	20	4.00	6.00	8.00	11.00

1/2 RUPEE

SILVER, 18-19mm, 5.35-5.80 gm.

C#	Date	Year	VG	Fine	VF	XF
92	—	5	6.50	7.50	9.00	12.50
	—	18	6.50	7.50	9.00	12.50

RUPEE

SILVER, 22-25mm, 10.70-11.60 gm.

C#	Date	Year	VG	Fine	VF	XF
93	—	1	11.50	13.00	15.00	18.50
	(AH1256)	3	11.50	13.00	15.00	18.50
	—	4	11.50	13.00	15.00	18.50
	—	5	11.50	13.00	15.00	18.50
	—	8	11.50	13.00	15.00	18.50
	—	10	11.50	13.00	15.00	18.50
	—	12	11.50	13.00	15.00	18.50
	—	17	11.50	13.00	15.00	18.50
	—	20	11.50	13.00	15.00	18.50

NAZARANA RUPEE

SILVER, 32-35mm, 10.70-11.60 gm.

C#	Date	Year	VG	Fine	VF	XF
93a	—	3	22.50	30.00	38.50	50.00
	AH1268	8	22.50	30.00	38.50	50.00
	1266	13	22.50	30.00	38.50	50.00
	—	19	22.50	30.00	38.50	50.00

1/4 MOHUR

GOLD, 17mm, 2.68-2.85 gm.

C#	Date	Year	VG	Fine	VF	XF
98	—	12	60.00	80.00	100.00	125.00

1/2 MOHUR

GOLD, 18mm, 5.35-5.70 gm.

C#	Date	Year	VG	Fine	VF	XF
99	—	12	110.00	120.00	135.00	150.00

MOHUR

GOLD, 19-20mm

C#	Date	Year	VG	Fine	VF	XF
100	—	1	220.00	240.00	265.00	300.00
	—	7	220.00	240.00	265.00	300.00

C#	Date	Year	VG	Fine	VF	XF
100	—	9	220.00	240.00	265.00	300.00
	AH1264	10	220.00	240.00	265.00	300.00
	—	12	220.00	240.00	265.00	300.00
	—	13	220.00	240.00	265.00	300.00
	—	19	220.00	240.00	265.00	300.00

Madhopur Mint

RUPEE

SILVER, 20-22mm, 10.70-11.60 gm.

	Date	Year	VG	Fine	VF	XF
96	AH125x	3	11.50	13.00	15.00	18.50
	—	4	11.50	13.00	15.00	18.50
	1258	6	11.50	13.00	15.00	18.50
	—	8	11.50	13.00	15.00	18.50
	1263	10	11.50	13.00	15.00	18.50
	—	12	11.50	13.00	15.00	18.50
	—	17	11.50	13.00	15.00	18.50
	—	18	11.50	13.00	15.00	18.50

Ram Singh

AD 1835-1880

In the names of Queen Victoria & Ram Singh (AD 1857-80):

NEW PAISA

COPPER, 18-20mm

Y#	Date	Year	Good	VG	Fine	VF
1	—	36	.50	1.00	1.50	1.75
	—	37	.50	1.00	1.50	1.75
	—	38	.50	1.00	1.50	1.75
	—	39	.50	1.00	1.50	1.75
	—	40	.50	1.00	1.50	1.75
	—	41	.50	1.00	1.50	1.75
	—	42	.50	1.00	1.50	1.75
	—	45	.65	1.25	2.00	2.50

NAZARANA 'NEW' PAISA

COPPER, 28mm

	Date	Year	Good	VG	Fine	VF
1a	1858	23	5.00	7.50	10.00	12.50
	1864	29	5.00	7.50	10.00	12.50
	1865	30	5.00	7.50	10.00	12.50
	1872	37	5.00	7.50	10.00	12.50
	1876	41	5.00	7.50	10.00	12.50
	1880	45	5.00	7.50	10.00	12.50

1/8 RUPEE

(2 Annas)

SILVER, 14mm, 1.34-1.45 gm.

Y#	Date	Year	VG	Fine	VF	XF
3	—	22	2.25	2.75	3.50	4.50
	—	42	2.25	2.75	3.50	4.50

1/4 RUPEE

SILVER, 15-17mm, 2.68-2.90 gm.

Y#	Date	Year	VG	Fine	VF	XF
4	—	21	3.50	4.00	5.00	6.50
	—	26	3.50	4.00	5.00	6.50
	—	27	3.50	4.00	5.00	6.50
	—	32	3.50	4.00	5.00	6.50
	—	33	3.50	4.00	5.00	6.50
	—	41	3.50	4.00	5.00	6.50
	—	44	3.50	4.00	5.00	6.50

1/2 RUPEE

SILVER, 18-21mm, 5.35-5.80 gm.

Y#	Date	Year	VG	Fine	VF	XF
5	—	21-45	6.50	7.50	8.50	10.00

RUPEE

SILVER, 22mm, 10.70-11.60 gm.

Y#	Date	Year	VG	Fine	VF	XF
6	—	20	11.50	13.00	15.00	17.50
	—	21	11.50	13.00	15.00	17.50
	—	23	11.50	13.00	15.00	17.50
	—	25	11.50	13.00	15.00	17.50
	—	31	11.50	13.00	15.00	17.50
	—	32	11.50	13.00	15.00	17.50
	—	33	11.50	13.00	15.00	17.50
	1869	34	11.50	13.00	15.00	17.50
	—	35	11.50	13.00	15.00	17.50
	—	36	11.50	13.00	15.00	17.50
	—	38	11.50	13.00	15.00	17.50
	—	42	11.50	13.00	15.00	17.50
	—	43	11.50	13.00	15.00	17.50
	—	44	11.50	13.00	15.00	17.50
	1880	45	11.50	13.00	15.00	17.50

NAZARANA RUPEE

SILVER, 29mm, 10.70-11.60 gm.

Y#	Date	Year	VG	Fine	VF	XF
6a	—	24	10.00	15.00	20.00	30.00
	—	26	10.00	15.00	20.00	30.00
	—	29	10.00	15.00	20.00	30.00
	1865	30	15.00	20.00	28.50	40.00
	1866	31	10.00	15.00	20.00	30.00
	1867	32	10.00	15.00	20.00	30.00
	1870	35	10.00	15.00	20.00	30.00

MOHUR

GOLD, 18mm, 10.70-11.40 gm.

Y#	Date	Year	VG	Fine	VF	XF
7	—	23	200.00	240.00	265.00	300.00

Madho Singh

AD 1880-1922

In the names of Queen Victoria and Madho Singh II:

NOTE: Queen Victoria's name was retained on Madho Singh's coinage until 1922, no coins were struck with Edward VIII's or George V's name by Madho Singh II.

PAISA

COPPER, 15-20mm

Y#	Date	Year	Good	VG	Fine	VF
8	—	4	.30	.60	.75	1.00
	—	5	.30	.60	.75	1.00
	—	8	.30	.60	.75	1.00
	—	19	.20	.40	.50	.75
	—	20	.20	.40	.50	.75
	—	21	.20	.40	.50	.75
	—	22	.20	.40	.50	.75
	—	23	.20	.40	.50	.75
	—	24	.20	.40	.50	.75
	—	25	.20	.40	.50	.75
	—	27	.20	.40	.50	.75
	—	28	.20	.40	.50	.75
	—	29	.20	.40	.50	.75
	—	38	.20	.40	.50	.75
	—	39	.20	.40	.50	.75

NAZARANA PAISA

COPPER, 32-36mm

Y#	Date	Year	Good	VG	Fine	VF
8a	—	1	2.50	3.50	4.00	5.00
	1897	18	2.50	3.50	4.00	5.00
	1899	20	2.50	3.50	4.00	5.00
	1900	21	2.50	3.50	4.00	5.00
	1901	22	2.50	3.50	4.00	5.00
	1902	23	2.50	3.50	4.00	5.00
	1903	24	2.50	3.50	4.00	5.00
	1904	25	2.50	3.50	4.00	5.00
	1905	26	2.50	3.50	4.00	5.00
	1906	27	2.50	3.50	4.00	5.00
	1908	29	2.50	3.50	4.00	5.00
	1909	30	2.50	3.50	4.00	5.00
	1910	31	2.50	3.50	4.00	5.00
	1911	32	2.50	3.50	4.00	5.00
	1912	33	2.50	3.50	4.00	5.00
	1913	34	2.50	3.50	4.00	5.00
	1914	35	2.50	3.50	4.00	5.00
	1916	37	2.50	3.50	4.00	5.00

1/16 RUPEE

SILVER, 10mm, 0.67-0.72 gm.

Y#	Date	Year	VG	Fine	VF	XF
9	—	2	2.00	2.50	3.50	5.00
	—	10	2.00	2.50	3.50	5.00

1/8 RUPEE

SILVER, 13mm, 1.34-1.45 gm.

Y#	Date	Year	VG	Fine	VF	XF
10	—	4	1.75	2.25	3.00	4.00
	—	6	1.75	2.25	3.00	4.00
	—	12	1.75	2.25	3.00	4.00
	—	18	1.75	2.25	3.00	4.00
	—	19	1.75	2.25	3.00	4.00
	—	21	1.75	2.25	3.00	4.00

Y#	Date	Year	VG	Fine	VF	XF
10	—	22	1.75	2.25	3.00	4.00
	—	23	1.75	2.25	3.00	4.00
	—	26	1.75	2.25	3.00	4.00
	—	27	1.75	2.25	3.00	4.00
	—	28	1.75	2.25	3.00	4.00
	—	29	1.75	2.25	3.00	4.00
	—	41	1.75	2.25	3.00	4.00
	—	42	1.75	2.25	3.00	4.00

1/4 RUPEE

SILVER, 16mm, 2.68-2.90 gm.

Y#	Date	Year	VG	Fine	VF	XF
11	—	1	3.50	4.00	5.00	6.50
	—	8	3.50	4.00	5.00	6.50
	—	10	3.50	4.00	5.00	6.50
	—	11	3.50	4.00	5.00	6.50
	—	12	3.50	4.00	5.00	6.50
	—	14	3.50	4.00	5.00	6.50
	—	15	3.50	4.00	5.00	6.50
	—	15	3.50	4.00	5.00	6.50
	—	17	3.50	4.00	5.00	6.50
	—	20	3.50	4.00	5.00	6.50
	1900	21	3.50	4.00	5.00	6.50
	—	22	3.50	4.00	5.00	6.50
	—	23	3.50	4.00	5.00	6.50
	—	26	3.50	4.00	5.00	6.50
	—	27	3.50	4.00	5.00	6.50
	—	28	3.50	4.00	5.00	6.50
	—	29	3.50	4.00	5.00	6.50
	—	42	3.50	4.00	5.00	6.50
	—	44	3.50	4.00	5.00	6.50

1/2 RUPEE

SILVER, 18mm, 5.35-5.80 gm.

Y#	Date	Year	VG	Fine	VF	XF
12	—	1	6.50	7.50	8.50	10.00
	—	4	6.50	7.50	8.50	10.00
	—	5	6.50	7.50	8.50	10.00
	—	8	6.50	7.50	8.50	10.00
	—	9	6.50	7.50	8.50	10.00
	—	10	6.50	7.50	8.50	10.00
	—	14	6.50	7.50	8.50	10.00
	—	15	6.50	7.50	8.50	10.00
	1900	18	6.50	7.50	8.50	10.00
	1900	21	6.50	7.50	8.50	10.00
	—	22	6.50	7.50	8.50	10.00
	—	23	6.50	7.50	8.50	10.00
	—	30	6.50	7.50	8.50	10.00
	—	37	6.50	7.50	8.50	10.00

RUPEE

SILVER, 21mm, 10.70-11.60 gm.

Y#	Date	Year	VG	Fine	VF	XF
13	—	1	11.50	13.00	15.00	17.50
	1881	2	11.50	13.00	15.00	17.50
	—	4	11.50	13.00	15.00	17.50
	—	5	11.50	13.00	15.00	17.50
	—	6	11.50	13.00	15.00	17.50
	1886	7	11.50	13.00	15.00	17.50
	—	8	11.50	13.00	15.00	17.50
	1888	9	11.50	13.00	15.00	17.50
	—	10	11.50	13.00	15.00	17.50
	—	11	11.50	13.00	15.00	17.50
	—	12	11.50	13.00	15.00	17.50
	—	13	11.50	13.00	15.00	17.50
	—	14	11.50	13.00	15.00	17.50
	—	15	11.50	13.00	15.00	17.50
	—	16	11.50	13.00	15.00	17.50
	—	17	11.50	13.00	15.00	17.50
	—	18	11.50	13.00	15.00	17.50
	—	20	11.50	13.00	15.00	17.50
	—	23	11.50	13.00	15.00	17.50
	—	25	11.50	13.00	15.00	17.50

Y#	Date	Year	VG	Fine	VF	XF
13	—	26	11.50	13.00	15.00	17.50
	—	29	11.50	13.00	15.00	17.50
	—	30	11.50	13.00	15.00	17.50
	—	31	11.50	13.00	15.00	17.50
	—	33	11.50	13.00	15.00	17.50
	—	39	11.50	13.00	15.00	17.50
	—	42	11.50	13.00	15.00	17.50

NAZARANA RUPEE

SILVER, 30-31mm, 10.70-11.60 gm.

Y#	Date	Year	VG	Fine	VF	XF
13a	1880	1	11.50	13.50	16.50	20.00
	1883	4	11.50	13.50	16.50	20.00
	1884	5	11.50	13.50	16.50	20.00

36-37mm

Y#	Date	Year	VG	Fine	VF	XF
13b	1884	5	11.50	13.00	15.00	17.50
	1886	7	11.50	13.00	15.00	17.50
	1897	18	11.50	13.00	15.00	17.50
	1899	20	11.50	13.00	15.00	17.50
	1901	22	11.50	13.00	15.00	17.50
	1903	24	11.50	13.00	15.00	17.50
	1911	32	11.50	13.00	15.00	17.50
	1913	34	11.50	13.00	15.00	17.50
	—	37	11.50	13.00	15.00	17.50

MOHUR

GOLD, 18mm, 10.70-11.40 gm.

Y#	Date	Year	VG	Fine	VF	XF
14	1895	16	220.00	240.00	265.00	300.00
	—	40	220.00	240.00	265.00	300.00

NAZARANA MOHUR

GOLD, 29-36mm, 10.70-11.40 gm.

Y#	Date	Year	VG	Fine	VF	XF
14a	1880	1	225.00	250.00	300.00	350.00

Man Singh II

AD 1922-1949

In the name of George V and Man Singh II

AD 1922-36

RUPEE

SILVER, 22mm, 10.70 gm.

Y#	Date	Year	VG	Fine	VF	XF
15	1922	1	15.00	18.50	22.50	28.50

In the names of George VI and Man Singh II

AD 1936-49

1/2 PAISA

COPPER, 16-17mm

Y#	Date	Year	Good	VG	Fine	VF
16	—	21	.25	.50	.65	.85
	—	22	.25	.50	.65	.85
	—	23	.25	.50	.65	.85

NAZARANA PAISA

COPPER, 32mm

Y#	Date	Year	Good	VG	Fine	VF
17	1949	28	4.00	6.00	8.00	10.00

ANNA

BRASS

Y#	Date	Year	VG	Fine	VF	XF
18	1943	—	.15	.25	.50	.75
	1944	—	.15	.25	.50	.75

Y#	Date	Year	VG	Fine	VF	XF
19	1944	—	.10	.20	.40	.65

2 ANNA

BRASS

Y#	Date	Year	Good	VG	Fine	VF
20	1942	21	1.00	2.00	3.00	4.50

NAZARANA RUPEE

SILVER, 27-30mm, 10.70-11.60 gm.

Y#	Date	Year	VG	Fine	VF	XF
21	1938	17	11.50	13.50	16.00	18.50
	193(8)	20	11.50	13.50	16.00	18.50

Larger size, 37-38mm

Y#	Date	Year	VG	Fine	VF	XF
21a	1939	18	11.50	13.00	15.00	17.50

MOHUR

GOLD, 19-21mm, 10.70-11.40 gm.

Y#	Date	Year	VG	Fine	VF	XF
22	—	20	220.00	240.00	265.00	300.00

JAISALMIR

Anonymous:

DODIA PAISA

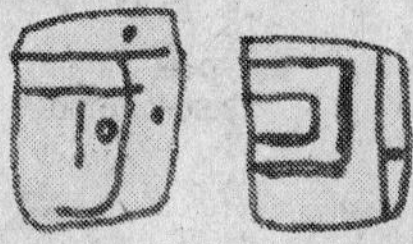

COPPER, 15-18mm, thick

C#	Date	Year	Good	VG	Fine	VF
4	ND		.75	1.50	2.00	2.75

NOTE: Struck 1660-1863.

In the name of Muhammad Shah
(AD 1719-48, struck 1756-1860):

1/8 RUPEE

SILVER, 11-12mm, 1.34-1.45 gm

C#	Date	Year	VG	Fine	VF	XF
7	AH1152	22	2.50	3.50	4.50	6.00

1/4 RUPEE

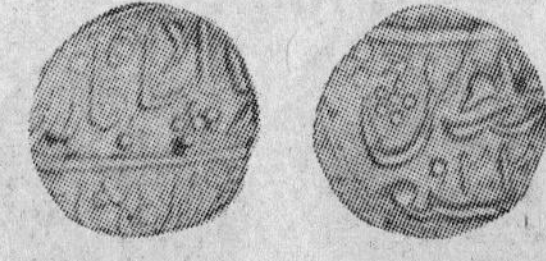

SILVER, 13-16mm, 2.68-2.90 gm

C#	Date	Year	VG	Fine	VF	XF
8	AH1152	22	4.00	5.00	6.50	8.50

1/2 RUPEE

SILVER, 18mm, 5.35-5.80 gm

C#	Date	Year	VG	Fine	VF	XF
9	AH1153	22	6.50	7.50	9.00	12.00

RUPEE

SILVER, 22mm, 10.70-11.60 gm

C#	Date	Year	VG	Fine	VF	XF
10	AH1153	22	11.50	13.50	16.50	20.00

MOHUR

GOLD, 22mm, 10.70-11.40 gm

C#	Date	Year	VG	Fine	VF	XF
—	AH1153	22	220.00	240.00	265.00	300.00

In the Name of Queen Victoria

No mintmarks on reverse.

1/8 RUPEE

SILVER, 12mm, 1.34-1.45 gm

Y#	Date	Year	VG	Fine	VF	XF
1		22	2.00	2.50	4.00	6.00

1/4 RUPEE

SILVER, 13-16mm, 2.68-2.90 gm

Y#	Date	Year	VG	Fine	VF	XF
2	—	22	3.50	4.50	6.00	8.00

1/2 RUPEE

SILVER, 17-18mm, 5.35-5.80 gm

Y#	Date	Year	VG	Fine	VF	XF
3	—	22	6.50	7.50	9.00	12.00

RUPEE

SILVER, 20-22mm, 10.70-11.60 gm

Y#	Date	Year	VG	Fine	VF	XF
4	—	22	11.50	13.50	16.50	20.00

NAZARANA RUPEE

SILVER, Square, 21X21mm, 10.70-11.60 gm

Y#	Date	Year	VG	Fine	VF	XF
4a	—	22	50.00	65.00	80.00	100.00

39mm

Y#	Date	Year	VG	Fine	VF	XF
4b	—	22	125.00	150.00	175.00	225.00

Reverse Mintmarks

Bird

Umbrella

1/8 RUPEE

SILVER, 10mm, 1.34-1.45 gm

Y#	Date	Year	VG	Fine	VF	XF
5	—	22	2.00	2.50	4.00	6.00

1/4 RUPEE

SILVER, 14mm, 2.68-2.90 gm

Y#	Date	Year	VG	Fine	VF	XF
6	—	22	3.50	4.50	6.00	8.00

1/2 RUPEE

SILVER, 17-18mm, 5.35-5.80 gm

Y#	Date	Year	VG	Fine	VF	XF
7	—	22	6.50	7.50	9.00	12.00

RUPEE

SILVER, 20-22mm, 10.70-11.60 gm

Y#	Date	Year	VG	Fine	VF	XF
8	—	22	11.50	13.50	16.50	20.00

NAZARANA RUPEE

SILVER, Square, 21mm, 10.70-11.60 gm

Y#	Date	Year	VG	Fine	VF	XF
8a	—	22	50.00	65.00	80.00	100.00

37mm

Y#	Date	Year	VG	Fine	VF	XF
8b	—	22	125.00	150.00	185.00	225.00

1/8 MOHUR

GOLD, 12mm, 1.34-1.42 gm

Y#	Date	Year	VG	Fine	VF	XF
9	—	22	45.00	60.00	80.00	100.00

1/4 MOHUR

GOLD, 15mm, 2.68-2.85 gm

Y#	Date	Year	VG	Fine	VF	XF
10	—	22	60.00	80.00	100.00	125.00

1/2 MOHUR

GOLD, 18mm, 5.35-5.70 gm

Y#	Date	Year	VG	Fine	VF	XF
11	—	22	110.00	130.00	150.00	175.00

MOHUR

GOLD, 21-23mm, 10.70-11.40 gm

Y#	Date	Year	VG	Fine	VF	XF
12	—	22	220.00	240.00	265.00	300.00

JAMMU

A hill state which maintained a precarious independence until conquered by the Sikh leader Ranjit Singh in AD1812. For later issues see India Native States : Kashmir.

DOGRA RAJAS

Ranjit Dev
AH1155-94/VS1799-1837/AD1742-80
Brij Raj Dev
AH1195- /VS1838- /AD1781

Mintname:

Jamun (Dar-ul-Aman) 

RUPEE

In the name of Shah Alam II:

SILVER, 20mm, 10.70-11.60 gm
No mintmarks.

KM#	Date	Year	VG	Fine	VF	XF
5.1	AH1195	23	15.00	20.00	26.50	35.00
	1196	24	15.00	20.00	26.50	35.00

Rev: Sword mintmark.

KM#	Date	Year	VG	Fine	VF	XF
5.2	AH1196	24	18.50	25.00	32.50	40.00

19mm
Obv: Fish mintmark.

KM#	Date	Year	VG	Fine	VF	XF
5.3	AH1197	25	18.50	25.00	32.50	40.00

In the name of Ranjit Dev:

23mm
Fine fabric

KM#	Date	Year	VG	Fine	VF	XF
10.1	VS1841	27	—	—	Rare	—
	1841	28	100.00	125.00	160.00	200.00

 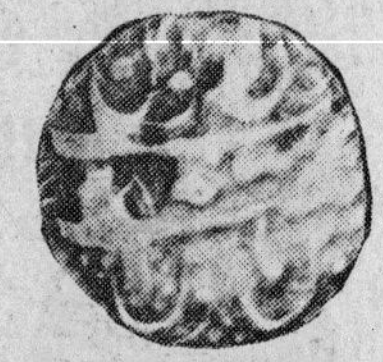

Crude, barbarous fabric

KM#	Date	Year	VG	Fine	VF	XF
10.2	VS1841	28	100.00	125.00	160.00	200.00

JANJIRA

Sidi Ibrahim Khan II

AD 1789-1792, 1804-1826

PAISA

COPPER, 17-18mm

C#	Date	Year	Good	VG	Fine	VF
5	ND	—	3.00	5.00	7.50	10.00

Sidi Muhammad Khan

AD 1826-1848

PAISA

COPPER, 17-18mm

C#	Date	Year	Good	VG	Fine	VF
15	ND	—	4.00	6.00	8.00	11.00

Sidi Ibrahim Khan III

AD 1848-1879

PAISA

COPPER, 23mm
Obv: Date

C#	Date	Year	Good	VG	Fine	VF
20.1	AH1284	—	3.50	5.50	7.50	10.00

Rev: Date

C#	Date	Year	Good	VG	Fine	VF
20.2	AH1284	—	3.00	5.00	7.00	9.00

Rev: Date

C#	Date	Year	Good	VG	Fine	VF
20.3	AH1288	—	4.00	6.00	8.50	12.00

JAORA

Muhammad Ismail

AD 1865-1895/AH 1282-1313

PAISA

COPPER, 19mm
Wheel left of flag

Y#	Date	Year	Good	VG	Fine	VF
A1	AH1282	—	7.50	10.00	13.00	18.50
	1284	—	7.50	10.00	13.00	18.50
	1285	—	7.50	10.00	13.00	18.50

Flag only

Y#	Date	Year	Good	VG	Fine	VF
B1	AH1295	—	2.75	4.50	6.00	8.50

MACHINE-STRUCK COINAGE

PAISA

COPPER, 26mm

Y#	Date	VG	Fine	VF	XF
1	1893/VS1950/AH1310	2.00	3.00	4.50	7.00
	1893/VS1950/AH1311	3.00	4.00	5.50	8.00
	1894/VS1950/AH1310	2.00	3.00	4.00	6.50
	1894/VS1950/AH1311	2.00	3.00	4.00	6.50
	1894/VS1951/AH1311	2.00	3.00	4.00	6.50
	1895/VS1951/AH1311	2.50	3.50	4.50	7.00
	1895/VS1952/AH1311	2.00	3.00	4.00	6.50
	1895/VS1952/AH1312	3.00	4.25	5.50	8.00
	1895/VS1952/AH1313	2.00	3.00	4.00	6.50
	1895/VS1953/AH1313	3.00	4.00	5.50	8.00
	1896/VS1953/AH1313	2.00	3.00	4.00	6.50
	1896/VS1953/AH1331 (error for 1313)	3.00	4.00	5.00	7.50
	1896/VS1953/AH1331 (error for 1313)	3.50	4.50	5.50	8.00

2 PAISA

COPPER, 31mm

Y#	Date	VG	Fine	VF	XF
2	1893/VS1950/AH1310	3.00	4.00	6.50	9.00
	1894/VS1950/AH1310	4.00	5.00	7.50	10.00

JHABUA

Gopal Singh

VS1897-1952/1840-1895AD

PAISA

COPPER, 18-19mm
Obv: JABUVA in Devanagari
Rev: JABUA in Arabic

KM#	Date	Year	Good	VG	Fine	VF
1	VS(19)29(1872)		8.50	11.50	15.00	21.50
	(19)35 (1878)		8.50	11.50	15.00	21.50

Obv: JHABUA in Devanagari. Rev: Date.

KM#	Date	Year	Good	VG	Fine	VF
2	VS(19)36(1879)		8.50	11.50	15.00	21.50

Obv: SA(mvat) 21 in Devanagari

KM#	Date	Year	Good	VG	Fine	VF
3	VS(19)21(1864)		8.50	11.50	15.00	21.50

Obv: Trident. Rev: Date.

KM#	Date	Year	Good	VG	Fine	VF
4	VS(19)31(1874)		3.50	5.00	6.50	8.50
	ND	—	3.50	5.00	6.50	8.50

Obv: Four-lobed flower. Rev: Date.

KM#	Date	Year	Good	VG	Fine	VF
5	VS(19)34(1877)		3.50	5.00	6.50	8.50

Obv: Stylized leaf

KM#	Date	Year	Good	VG	Fine	VF
6	VS(19)22(1865)		7.50	10.00	12.50	16.50
	23 (1866)		5.00	7.00	10.00	14.00
	24 (1867)		5.00	7.00	10.00	14.00
	28 (1871)		5.00	7.00	10.00	14.00
	32 (1875)		3.00	5.00	7.00	10.00
	33 (1876)		3.00	5.00	7.00	10.00
	35 (1878)		5.00	7.00	10.00	14.00

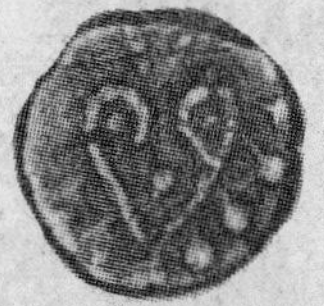

Rev: Curled branch with berry

KM#	Date	Year	Good	VG	Fine	VF
7	ND		5.00	7.00	10.00	14.00

Rev: Spear point

KM#	Date	Year	Good	VG	Fine	VF
8	ND		3.00	5.00	7.00	10.00

Rev: Curved dagger

KM#	Date	Year	Good	VG	Fine	VF
9	ND		5.00	7.00	10.00	14.00

Rev: Jhar and blossom

KM#	Date	Year	Good	VG	Fine	VF
10	ND		4.50	6.50	9.00	13.00

Rev: Six lobed flower

KM#	Date	Year	Good	VG	Fine	VF
11	ND		5.00	7.00	10.00	14.00

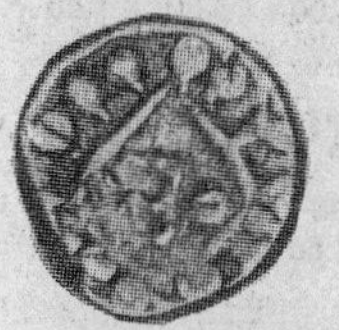
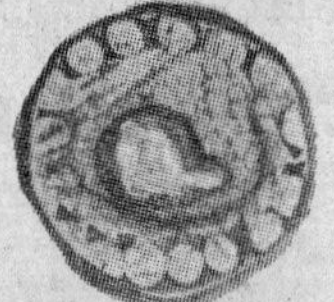

Rev: Tailed ball

KM#	Date	Year	Good	VG	Fine	VF
12	Yr. 30		4.00	6.00	8.00	12.00

Obv: Cross. Rev: Tailed ball.

KM#	Date	Year	Good	VG	Fine	VF
13	ND		3.00	5.00	7.00	11.00

Obv: Square. Rev: Indistinct.

KM#	Date	Year	Good	VG	Fine	VF
14	ND		4.00	6.00	8.00	12.00

Obv: Arabic 'Wa'. Rev: Groups of dots.

KM#	Date	Year	Good	VG	Fine	VF
15	ND		7.00	9.00	12.00	16.00

In addition to the above there are other symbols, and all these occur in different combinations. The crude fabric of these coins and uncommon variety of dies indicate that they were struck by bankers, with or without official sanction. They are commonly found overstruck on earlier types or on coins of other states.

JHALAWAR

RULERS

Madan Singh, AD1837-47/AH1253-64
Prithri Singh, AD1847-75/AH1264-92
Zalim Singh
AD1877-96/AH1294-1314

Mintmarks

Both marks on reverse

In the name of Bahadur Shah II:
REGNAL years of Bahadur Shah II.

PAISA

COPPER, (rectangular), 21mm

C#	Date	Year	Good	VG	Fine	VF
21	—	21	1.25	2.00	3.00	4.50

1/8 RUPEE

SILVER, 1.34-1.45 gm.

C#	Date	Year	VG	Fine	VF	XF
25	—	—	4.00	5.50	7.00	9.00

1/4 RUPEE

SILVER, 2.68-2.90 gm.

C#	Date	Year	VG	Fine	VF	XF
26	—	—	4.50	6.00	7.50	10.00

1/2 RUPEE

SILVER, 5.35-5.80 gm.

C#	Date	Year	VG	Fine	VF	XF
27	—	—	6.50	7.50	8.50	11.50

RUPEE

SILVER, 21mm, 10.70-11.60 gm.

C#	Date	Year	VG	Fine	VF	XF
28	—	19	11.50	13.50	16.50	20.00

NAZARANA RUPEE

SILVER, 30mm, 10.70-11.60 gm.

C#	Date	Year	VG	Fine	VF	XF
29	—	8	35.00	45.00	55.00	70.00
	—	21	35.00	45.00	55.00	70.00

In the name of Queen Victoria
Regnal years (Yr. 1 = 1857-58)

1/2 PAISA

COPPER, Rectangular, 14-20mm, 9.0 gm.

Y#	Date	Year	Good	VG	Fine	VF
1	—	5	1.50	2.50	3.50	5.00

PAISA

COPPER, Squarish, 19-21mm, 18.0 gm.

Y#	Date	Year	Good	VG	Fine	VF
2	—	5	1.25	2.25	3.25	4.50
	—	7	1.25	2.25	3.25	4.50
	—	8	1.25	2.25	3.25	4.50
	—	9	1.25	2.25	3.25	4.50
	—	10	1.25	2.25	3.25	4.50
	—	11	1.25	2.25	3.25	4.50
	—	12	1.25	2.25	3.25	4.50
2	—	18	1.25	2.25	3.25	4.50
	—	21	1.25	2.25	3.25	4.50
	—	28	1.25	2.25	3.25	4.50

1/8 RUPEE

SILVER, 13mm, 1.34-1.45 gm.

Y#	Date	Year	VG	Fine	VF	XF
3	—	5	4.00	5.50	7.00	9.00
	—	37	4.00	5.50	7.00	9.00

1/4 RUPEE

SILVER, 14mm, 2.68-2.90 gm.

Y#	Date	Year	VG	Fine	VF	XF
4	—	7	4.50	6.00	8.00	10.00
	—	37	4.50	6.00	8.00	10.00

1/2 RUPEE

SILVER, 17mm, 5.35-5.80 gm.

Y#	Date	Year	VG	Fine	VF	XF
5	—	1-35	6.50	7.50	9.00	13.50

RUPEE

SILVER, 18-20mm, 10.70-11.60 gm.

Y#	Date	Year	VG	Fine	VF	XF
6	—	(1-41)	11.50	13.50	16.50	20.00

NAZARANA 1/2 RUPEE

SILVER, 21mm

Y#	Date	Year	VG	Fine	VF	XF
5a	—	38	16.50	22.50	30.00	40.00

NAZARANA RUPEE

SILVER, 27mm

Y#	Date	Year	VG	Fine	VF	XF
6a	VS1915	2	30.00	40.00	55.00	70.00
	1915	5	30.00	40.00	55.00	70.00
	1915	15	30.00	40.00	55.00	70.00
	1915	21	30.00	40.00	55.00	70.00
	1915	22	30.00	40.00	55.00	70.00
	1915	39	30.00	40.00	55.00	70.00

37-38mm

Y#	Date	Year	VG	Fine	VF	XF
6b	VS1915	3	55.00	65.00	80.00	100.00
	1915	15	55.00	65.00	80.00	100.00

JODHPUR

RULERS:

Bijy Singh, AD 1752-1792
Bhim Singh, AD 1792-1803
Man Singh, AD 1803-1843
Takhat Singh, AD 1843-1873
Jaswant Singh, AD 1873-1895
Sardar Singh, AD 1895-1911
Sumar Singh, AD 1911-1918
Umaid Singh, AD 1918-1947
Hanwant Singh, AD 1947
As titular ruler until 1952

MINTS:

Mintmarks on the coinage struck before 1858:

Sujat Mint, always on reverse. (C#30 & C#34) 

Sujat, sometimes on obverse. (C#30 & C#34) 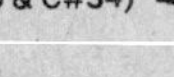

(*), (C#34)

Pali, sometimes on obverse. (On C#30) 

Pali, usually on obverse. (C#30 & C#55) 

Pali, sometimes on obverse of C#30. 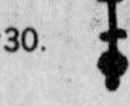

Jodhpur, on obverse of C#559

After 1858, the mintmarks vary, and are given for each listing, wherever there is a difference.

NOTE: All gold coins struck at Jodhpur Mint. All mints except Jodhpur closed by or before 1893 AD. All copper coins probably minted at Jodhpur, but if struck elsewhere, they bear no distinguishing marks.

In addition to the mintmarks indicating the mint cities, there are also the marks of the Darogas (mint overseers), which are very useful in identifying the mints, especially when the city marks are missing or off the flan. These are given by C# and mint: (Only one of the marks appears on any one coin, always on the obverse.)

Issues Of 1858-1873:

Jodhpur Y#1.1 रा

Sujat Y#1.2 ला

Jodhpur Y#3 गं न श्री

Jodhpur Y#19.1 ग रा 卐

Sujat Y#1a.2 मा

Pali Y#4.3 स ग कि

Sujat Y#4.3 के

Issues of Jaswant Singh:

Jodhpur Y#9.1 & 12 علی

Jodhpur Y#9.1 ३ ३ रु

Pali Y#9.2 卐 卐 मा

३ ३ँ बा ब्रा ग

Sujat Y#9.3 2 ट कि म

Victoria & Sardar Singh:

Jodhpur all

Edward VII & George V & Sardar Singh & Sumar Singh

Jodhpur Y#1,2,A2-C2,E2-G2,J2,K2 म

George V & Sumar Singh:

Jodhpur Y#D2,L2,M2 द

George V & Umaid Singh:

Jodhpur Y#37 & 38 अँ

Jodhpur Y#38 श्री

Edward VIII & Umaid Singh:

Jodhpur all रं

George VI & Umaid Singh;

Jodhpur Y#40 रं

Jodhpur Y#41 & 42 गो

George VI & Hanwant Singh:

Jodhpur all गो

NOTE: The Darogas' marks generally consist of a symbol or a single Nagari letter, sometimes inverted, and even lying on its side. Some letters are found on more than one series, so that the mark is not a positive identification, but taken together with the city mark and the style of the coin, will provide a correct attribution.

Coinage Of The First Four Rulers

Before AD 1858

NOTE: The AH and SE dates, as well as the regnal years, are rarely actual dates and years, but were used for many years without change, and were often quite indiscriminately applied. Mismatched regnal years and dates are frequently encountered, as well as blundered dates of all sorts. Dates lying outside the reign of the rulers named on the coin (after 1858) were often used. The date or year does not provide an actual dating of the coin.

Coinage of the first four rulers (until 1858) is not distinguished by reign, but by type of inscription, mint, and (pseudo-) date.

Anonymous copper with regnal years of Shah Alam II

(Struck AD1792-1858)

PAISA

COPPER, 20-27mm

C#	Date	Year	Good	VG	Fine	VF
21	AH1192	—	1.50	2.50	3.50	5.00
	1203	45	1.50	2.50	3.50	5.00
	1205	34	1.50	2.50	3.50	5.00
	1205	35	1.50	2.50	3.50	5.00
	1205	39	1.50	2.50	3.50	5.00
	1215	45	1.50	2.50	3.50	5.00
	1227	—	1.50	2.50	3.50	5.00

NOTE: Some specimens show a wide, floral border.

In the name of Shah Alam II

Jodhpur Mint, AD 1778-1826; Pali Mint, before AD 1803 to AD1860 or later; Sujat Mint, AD1807-48. Date range is tentative, most coins inscribed 'Jodhpur' regardless of where struck.

1/2 RUPEE

SILVER, 5.35-5.80 gm

C#	Date	Year	VG	Fine	VF	XF
29	AH1203	31	6.50	7.50	9.00	13.50

RUPEE

SILVER, 21mm, 10.70-11.60 gm

AJMIR MINT

C#	Date	Year	VG	Fine	VF	XF
A30	AH1203	31	11.50	13.50	16.50	20.00

20-23mm

JODHPUR MINT

C#	Date	Year	VG	Fine	VF	XF
30	AH1192	20	12.50	14.50	17.50	21.50
	1205	33	11.50	13.50	16.50	20.00
	1212	42	11.50	13.50	16.50	20.00
	1215	42	11.50	13.50	16.50	20.00
	1218	45	11.50	12.50	15.00	18.50

NOTE: Also mis-cut error dates of AH1128, 1228 and 128.

NAZARANA RUPEE

SILVER, 20x20mm
Similar to 1 Rupee, C#30, but square.

C#	Date	Year	VG	Fine	VF	XF
30a	AH1218	45	22.50	28.50	36.50	45.00

34.5mm

C#	Date	Year	VG	Fine	VF	XF
30b	AH1206	36	70.00	90.00	120.00	160.00

NAGORE MINT: Written on upper rev.

C#	Date	Year	VG	Fine	VF	XF
33	AH1194	—	12.50	14.50	17.50	21.50
	1197	—	12.50	14.50	17.50	21.50
	1218	—	12.50	14.50	17.50	21.50

Sujat Mint

C#	Date	Year	VG	Fine	VF	XF
34	AH1204	23	11.50	13.50	16.50	20.00
	1264	43	11.50	13.50	16.50	20.00

NOTE: Struck circa 1848-59AD.

MERTA MINT: Symbols not known

C#	Date	Year	VG	Fine	VF	XF
35	AH1188	—	12.50	14.50	17.50	23.50

MOHUR

GOLD, 19mm, 10.70-11.40 gm

JODHPUR MINT

C#	Date	Year	VG	Fine	VF	XF
40	AH1218	45	220.00	240.00	265.00	300.00

(Struck circa AD1803-58.)

In the name of Muhammad Akbar II:

PAISA

COPPER, 23-26mm

C#	Date	Year	Good	VG	Fine	VF
50	31 on obv., 22 on rev.	—	2.50	3.50	4.50	6.00

RUPEE

SILVER, 20-22mm, 10.70-11.60 gm

JODHPUR MINT

C#	Date	Year	VG	Fine	VF	XF
55	—	22	—	7.50	9.00	11.00
	—	23	—	8.00	10.00	12.00

NOTE: Struck circa 1816-1859AD.

NAGORE MINT

56	AH1222	—	12.50	15.00	18.50	23.50

MOHUR

GOLD, 20mm, 10.70-11.40 gm

JODHPUR MINT

59	—	22	220.00	240.00	265.00	300.00

Anonymous Copper:

PAISA

COPPER, 20mm

C#	Date	Year	Good	VG	Fine	VF
22	AH1267	—	1.75	2.50	3.50	5.00

Takhat Singh

AD 1843-1873

In the names of Queen Victoria and Takhat Singh (1858-1873):

First Issue

AD1858-1859

Jodhpur in Persian on obverse

RUPEE

SILVER, 20-22mm, 10.70-11.60 gm

JODHPUR MINT

Obv: Jhar. Rev: Sword.

Y#	Date	Year	VG	Fine	VF	XF
1.1	—	22	11.50	13.50	16.50	20.00
	—	52	11.50	13.50	16.50	20.00

SUJAT MINT

Rev: Mintmaster's mark, katar.

1.2	—	16	12.50	14.50	17.50	21.50
	—	22	12.50	14.50	17.50	21.50

MOHUR

GOLD, 20mm, 10.70-11.40 gm

JODHPUR MINT

2	—	22	220.00	240.00	265.00	300.00

Second Issue

Jodhpur in Persian on reverse.

RUPEE

SILVER, 21mm, 10.70-11.60 gm

JODHPUR MINT: (jhar & sword)

1.3	—	22 & 21	11.50	13.50	16.50	20.00
	—	22 only	11.50	13.50	16.50	20.00
	—	52 & 16	11.50	13.50	16.50	20.00
	—	52 only	11.50	13.50	16.50	20.00

NOTE: Struck circa 1860-69AD.

SUJAT MINT: Katar

1.4	—	13 & 16	12.50	14.50	17.50	21.50

NOTE: Struck 1869AD.

UNCERTAIN MINT: Swastika

1.5	—	—	12.50	14.50	17.50	21.50

In the name of Takhat Singh

AD1869-73

Queen Victoria mentioned without name, but with title 'Queen, Ruler of India and Europe'. Actual mint names used on this and all subsequent issues.

Third Issue

Nagari legend SRI MATAJI added on reverse.

RUPEE

SILVER, 21mm, 10.70-11.60 gm

JODHPUR MINT

3	—	22 & 61	11.50	13.50	16.50	20.00
	—	22 Only	11.50	13.50	16.50	20.00

NOTE: Struck 1859-60AD.

4.1	VS1926	(1869)	11.50	13.50	16.50	20.00
	1928	(1871)	11.50	13.50	16.50	20.00

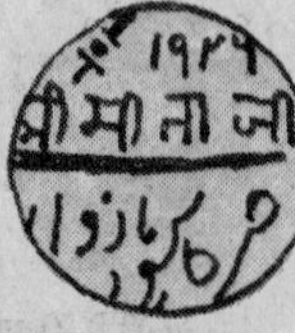

NAGORE MINT

Y#	Date	Year	VG	Fine	VF	XF
4.2	VS1926	(1869)	12.50	14.50	17.50	21.50

PALI MINT

Rev: Jhar & sword

4.3	VS1926	45	11.50	13.50	16.50	20.00

SUJAT MINT

4.4	VS1926	(1869)	12.50	14.50	17.50	21.50
	1928	(1871)	12.50	14.50	17.50	21.50

Jaswant Singh

AD 1873-1895

In the name of Queen Victoria:

PAISA

COPPER, 20-25mm

Y#	Date	Year	Good	VG	Fine	VF
5	VS1940	(1883)	1.25	2.25	3.00	4.00
	1941	(1884)	1.00	2.00	2.75	3.75
	1942	(1885)	1.25	2.25	3.00	4.00
	1945	(1888)	1.25	2.25	3.00	4.00
	1947	(1890)	1.25	2.25	3.00	4.00
	AH1293	61	1.00	2.00	2.75	3.75
	1305	65	1.25	2.25	3.00	4.00
	Date off flan		.50	1.00	1.50	2.25

In the names of Queen Victoria & Jaswant Singh:

Jodhpur Mint

Mintmaster's mark to right of jhar (leafy branch) on obverse; sword on reverse (to left of Jaswant's name).

1/8 RUPEE

SILVER, 11mm, 1.34-1.45 gm

Y#	Date	Year	VG	Fine	VF	XF
6	—	—	7.50	10.00	13.50	18.50

1/4 RUPEE

SILVER, 12-16mm, 2.68-2.90 gm

7	—	22	7.50	10.00	13.50	18.50

1/2 RUPEE

SILVER, 17mm, 5.35-5.80 gm

8	VS1945	(1888)	7.50	10.00	13.50	18.50

RUPEE

SILVER, 19-22mm, 10.70-11.60 gm

Y#	Date	Year	VG	Fine	VF	XF
9.1	AH1293	—	11.50	13.50	16.50	20.00
	VS1941	(1884)	11.50	13.50	16.50	20.00
	1942	(1885)	11.50	13.50	16.50	20.00
	2491 error for 1942					
			11.50	13.50	16.50	20.00
	1943	(1886)	11.50	13.50	16.50	20.00
	8941 error for 1948					
			11.50	13.50	16.50	20.00
	1950	—	11.50	13.50	16.50	20.00
	Date off flan		11.50	13.50	16.50	20.00

1/4 MOHUR

GOLD, 13mm, 2.68-2.85 gm

Y#	Date	Year	VG	Fine	VF	XF
10	AH1293	—	60.00	75.00	90.00	120.00

1/2 MOHUR

GOLD, 18mm, 5.35-5.70 gm

Y#	Date	Year	VG	Fine	VF	XF
11	AH1293	—	110.00	120.00	135.00	160.00

MOHUR

GOLD, 20mm, 10.70-11.40 gm

Y#	Date	Year	VG	Fine	VF	XF
12	AH1293	—	220.00	240.00	265.00	300.00

Pali Mint

Mintmaster's mark on obverse; jhar and sword both on reverse.

RUPEE

SILVER, 19-21mm, 10.70-11.60 gm

Y#	Date	Year	VG	Fine	VF	XF
9.2	VS1930	(1883)	11.50	13.50	16.50	20.00
	1931	(1884)	11.50	13.50	16.50	20.00
	1931	40	11.50	13.50	16.50	20.00
	1932	40	11.50	13.50	16.50	20.00
	1934	40	11.50	13.50	16.50	20.00
	1934	(1887)	11.50	13.50	16.50	20.00
	1935	(1888)	11.50	13.50	16.50	20.00
	1939	(1892)	11.50	13.50	16.50	20.00
	1941	(1894)	11.50	13.50	16.50	20.00
	1943	(1896)	11.50	13.50	16.50	20.00
	1944	(1897)	11.50	13.50	16.50	20.00
	1950	(1893)	11.50	13.50	16.50	20.00
	Date off flan		11.50	13.50	16.50	20.00

Sujat Mint

Mintmaster's mark to right of jhar on obverse; sword on reverse, far to right (right of name 'Jaswant')

RUPEE

SILVER, 20-21mm, 10.70-11.60 gm

Y#	Date	Year	VG	Fine	VF	XF
9.3	VS1929	(1882)	11.50	13.50	16.50	20.00
	AH1291	22	11.50	13.50	16.50	20.00
	VS1933	(1886)	11.50	13.50	16.50	20.00
	1936	(1889)	11.50	13.50	16.50	20.00
	1938	(1891)	11.50	13.50	16.50	20.00
	Date off flan		11.50	13.50	16.50	20.00

20mm
Obv: Devanagari "Sri Maheshji".

Y#	Date	Year	VG	Fine	VF	XF
9.4	ND	—	11.50	13.50	16.50	20.00

Obv: Devanagari "Sri Ragunathji".

Y#	Date	Year	VG	Fine	VF	XF
9.5	ND	—	11.50	13.50	16.50	20.00

Sardar Singh

AD 1895-1911

In the name of Queen Victoria & Sardar Singh:

Jodhpur Mint

Mintmaster's mark to right of jhar on obverse. Sword on reverse (to left of name).

RUPEE

SILVER, 10.70-11.60 gm

Y#	Date	Year	VG	Fine	VF	XF
16.1	VS1955	(1898)	12.50	14.50	17.50	21.50

Pali Mint

Mintmaster's mark on obverse. Jhar and sword both on reverse.

RUPEE

SILVER, 10.70-11.60 gm

Y#	Date	Year	VG	Fine	VF	XF
16.2	—	—	12.50	14.50	17.50	21.50

Uncertain Mint

All the following silver and gold coins, as well as those of the following reigns were not struck for circulation and are seldom seen below XF grade. They may be presentation pieces or jeweler's issues.

1/8 RUPEE

SILVER, 11-14mm, 1.34-1.45 gm

Y#	Date	Year	VG	Fine	VF	XF
13	—	—	8.50	11.50	15.00	20.00

1/4 RUPEE

SILVER, 13-17mm, 2.68-2.90 gm

Y#	Date	Year	VG	Fine	VF	XF
14	—	—	8.50	11.50	15.00	20.00

1/2 RUPEE

SILVER, 19mm, 5.35-5.80 gm

Y#	Date	Year	VG	Fine	VF	XF
15	—	—	8.50	11.50	15.00	20.00

RUPEE

SILVER, 22mm

Y#	Date	Year	VG	Fine	VF	XF
16.3	VS1955	(1898)	13.50	17.50	25.00	33.50
	1956	(1899)	13.50	17.50	25.00	33.50

1/4 MOHUR

GOLD, 15mm, 2.68-2.85 gm

Y#	Date	Year	VG	Fine	VF	XF
17	VS1952	(1895)	57.50	70.00	80.00	100.00

1/2 MOHUR

GOLD, 18mm, 5.35-5.70 gm

Y#	Date	Year	VG	Fine	VF	XF
18	VS1952	(1895)	110.00	120.00	135.00	150.00

MOHUR

GOLD, 21mm, 10.70-11.40 gm

Y#	Date	Year	VG	Fine	VF	XF
19	VS1952	(1845)	220.00	240.00	265.00	300.00

In the name of Edward VII and Sardar Singh:

1/4 ANNA

COPPER, 16mm

Y#	Date	Year	Good	VG	Fine	VF
20	1901	—	1.50	2.50	3.75	5.50
	1902	—	1.50	2.50	3.75	5.50
	1903	—	1.50	2.50	3.75	5.50
	1904	—	1.50	2.50	3.75	5.50
	1905	—	1.50	2.50	3.75	5.50
	1906	—	.50	1.00	1.75	2.50
	1609 (error)	—	1.50	2.50	3.75	5.50
	1907	—	.50	1.00	1.75	2.75
	1908	—	.50	1.00	1.75	2.75
	1909	—	.50	1.00	1.75	2.75
	1910	—	.50	1.00	1.75	2.75
	AH1290 (error)		1.25	2.25	3.00	4.00
	1291 (error)		1.00	2.00	2.75	3.75
	1291 (error)		1.25	2.25	3.00	4.00
	2091 (error)		1.25	2.25	3.00	4.00
	5201 (error)		1.25	2.25	3.00	4.00
	Date off flan		.35	.75	1.75	2.00

NOTE: Other blundered dates' exist.

1/2 ANNA

COPPER, 24mm

Y#	Date	Year	Good	VG	Fine	VF
21	1906	—	3.50	5.00	7.00	9.00
	1908	—	3.50	5.00	7.00	9.00

1/4 RUPEE

SILVER, 19mm, 2.68-2.90 gm

Y#	Date	Year	VG	Fine	VF	XF
22	VS1965	(1908)	5.00	8.50	12.50	17.50

1/4 MOHUR

GOLD, 13mm, 2.68-2.85 gm

Y#	Date	Year	VG	Fine	VF	XF
23	1906	—	60.00	70.00	85.00	110.00

1/2 MOHUR

GOLD, 18mm, 5.35-5.70 gm

Y#	Date	Year	VG	Fine	VF	XF
24	1906	—	110.00	120.00	135.00	150.00

MOHUR

GOLD, 20mm, 10.70-11.40 gm

Y#	Date	Year	VG	Fine	VF	XF
25	1906	—	220.00	240.00	265.00	300.00

Sumar Singh

AD 1911-1918

In the names of Edward VII and Sumar Singh:

1/2 MOHUR

GOLD, 19mm, 5.35-5.70 gm

Y#	Date	Year	VG	Fine	VF	XF
26	(1910)	—	120.00	140.00	165.00	200.00

In the names of George V and Sumar Singh:

1/4 ANNA

COPPER, 18mm

Y#	Date	Year	Good	VG	Fine	VF
27	1911	—	6.50	9.00	12.50	17.50
	1914	—	6.50	9.00	12.50	17.50
	Date off flan		2.00	3.50	4.50	6.00

1/2 ANNA

COPPER, 25mm

Y#	Date	Year	Good	VG	Fine	VF
28	1914	—	5.00	7.50	11.00	15.00
	1918	—	5.00	7.50	11.00	15.00

1/8 RUPEE

SILVER, 13mm, 1.34-1.45 gm

Y#	Date	Year	VG	Fine	VF	XF
29	Date off flan		4.00	7.00	10.00	15.00

1/4 RUPEE

SILVER, 14mm, 2.68-2.90 gm

Y#	Date	Year	VG	Fine	VF	XF
30	Date off flan		4.00	7.00	10.00	15.00

1/2 RUPEE

SILVER, 18mm, 5.35-5.80 gm

Y#	Date	Year	VG	Fine	VF	XF
31	Date off flan		7.50	11.00	15.00	20.00

RUPEE

SILVER, 21mm

Y#	Date	Year	VG	Fine	VF	XF
32	Date off flan		13.50	16.50	21.50	27.50

MOHUR

GOLD, 18mm, 10.70-11.40 gm

Y#	Date	Year	VG	Fine	VF	XF
33	ND	—	220.00	240.00	265.00	300.00

Umaid Singh

AD 1918-1947

In the names of George V and Umaid Singh:

1/4 ANNA

COPPER, 19mm
Obv: Sword, GEORGE, date.
Rev: Illegible crude legend.

Y#	Date	Year	Good	VG	Fine	VF
34	1910	—	3.50	5.50	7.50	10.00

Uncertain mint.

1/4 RUPEE

SILVER, 18mm, 2.68-2.90 gm

Y#	Date	Year	VG	Fine	VF	XF
35	Date off flan		7.50	11.50	15.00	20.00

1/4 MOHUR

GOLD, 16mm, 2.68-2.85 gm

Y#	Date	Year	VG	Fine	VF	XF
36	Date off flan		60.00	70.00	85.00	110.00

1/2 MOHUR

GOLD, 16-20mm, 5.35-5.70 gm

Y#	Date	Year	VG	Fine	VF	XF
37	Date off flan		110.00	120.00	135.00	150.00

MOHUR

GOLD, 19-20mm, 10.70-11.60 gm

Y#	Date	Year	VG	Fine	VF	XF
38	Date off flan		220.00	240.00	265.00	300.00

In the name of Edward VIII and Umaid Singh:

1/4 ANNA

COPPER, 18mm
Comes with and without Persian '8' to left of Edward on obv.

Y#	Date	Year	Good	VG	Fine	VF
39	1936	—	1.75	2.75	4.00	5.50

NOTE: Blundered legends occur.

In the name of George VI and Umaid Singh:

1/4 ANNA

COPPER, 19mm

Y#	Date	Year	Good	VG	Fine	VF
40	1937	—	1.25	1.75	2.50	3.50
	1938	—	1.25	1.75	2.50	3.50
	1939	—	1.25	1.75	2.50	3.50
	VS1996	(1939)	2.00	3.00	4.00	5.50
	Date off flan		.50	1.00	1.50	2.25

BRASS

Y#	Date	Year	Good	VG	Fine	VF
40a	Date off flan		1.75	2.75	4.00	5.50

18mm, thin flan

Y#	Date	Year	Good	VG	Fine	VF
41	VS2000	(1943)	1.75	2.75	4.00	5.50
	2001	(1944)	1.75	2.75	4.00	5.50
	2002	(1945)	1.75	2.75	4.00	5.50
	Date off flan		.35	.75	1.75	2.50

NOTE: VS2000 comes with and without Persian '6' below Daroga's mark.

MOHUR

GOLD, 18mm, 10.70-11.40 gm

Y#	Date	Year	VG	Fine	VF	XF
42	Date off flan		220.00	240.00	265.00	300.00

Hanwant Singh

AD 1947-1952/SE2004-2009

In the names of George VI and Hanwant Singh:

1/4 ANNA

COPPER, 15-16mm

Y#	Date	Year	Good	VG	Fine	VF
43	Date off		7.50	11.50	15.00	21.50

MOHUR

GOLD, 18mm, 10.70-11.40 gm

Y#	Date	Year	VG	Fine	VF	XF
44	Date off	—	220.00	240.00	265.00	300.00

FEUDATORY STATES

(Under Jodhpur)

Kuchawan

In the name of Shah Alam II:

Small sword added above 'H' of 'Padishah' on obverse.

1/4 RUPEE

SILVER, 13mm, 2.68-2.90 gm

C#	Date	Year	VG	Fine	VF	XF
15	AH1203	31	4.00	5.50	7.50	10.00

1/2 RUPEE

SILVER, 16-17mm, 5.35-5.80 gm

C#	Date	Year	VG	Fine	VF	XF
16	AH1203	31	6.50	7.50	9.00	12.50

RUPEE

SILVER, 19mm, 10.70-11.60 gm

C#	Date	Year	VG	Fine	VF	XF
17	AH1203	31	11.50	13.50	16.50	20.00

In the name of Queen Victoria

1/4 RUPEE

SILVER, 13mm, 2.68-2.90 gm

Y#	Date	Year	VG	Fine	VF	XF
1	1863	—	4.50	6.50	8.50	11.50

1/2 RUPEE

SILVER, 15-16mm, 5.35-5.80 gm

Y#	Date	Year	VG	Fine	VF	XF
2	1863	—	6.50	7.50	9.00	12.50

RUPEE

SILVER, 19-20mm, 10.70-11.60 gm

Y#	Date	Year	VG	Fine	VF	XF
3	1863	—	11.50	13.50	16.50	20.00

JUNAGADH

RULERS

Bahadur Khan,
VS1868-1897/1811-1840AD
Hamid Khan II,
VS1897-1908/1840-1851AD
Mahabat Khan II,
VS1908-1939/1851-1882AD

In the name of Muhammad Akbar II:

With title SRI DIWANA on obverse, AH and SE dates on reverse.

DOKDO

COPPER, 16-20mm

C#	Date	Year	Good	VG	Fine	VF
20	AH1239-48					
		VS1880-89	2.50	4.50	6.00	8.50

1/2 KORI

SILVER, 11-13mm, 2.3 gm.

C#	Date	Year	VG	Fine	VF	XF
27	AH1236	VS1877	2.75	3.50	5.00	7.50
	1251	1892	2.75	3.50	5.00	7.50
	1267	19xx	2.75	3.50	5.00	7.50
	1270	1910	2.75	3.50	5.00	7.50
	1271	1911	2.75	3.50	5.00	7.50
	1272	1912	2.75	3.50	5.00	7.50
	1273	1913	2.75	3.50	5.00	7.50
	1274	1914	2.75	3.50	5.00	7.50
	1275	1915	2.75	3.50	5.00	7.50
	1276	1916	2.75	3.50	5.00	7.50
	1278	1918	2.75	3.50	5.00	7.50
	1279	1919	2.75	3.50	5.00	7.50
	1280	1920	2.75	3.50	5.00	7.50

KORI

SILVER, 14-16mm, 4.6 gm.

C#	Date	Year	VG	Fine	VF	XF
28	AH1235	VS1875	5.00	6.50	8.50	11.50
	1235	1876	5.00	6.50	8.50	11.50
	1236	1877	4.50	6.00	8.00	11.00
	1245	1886	4.50	6.00	8.00	11.00
	1246	1886	4.50	6.00	8.00	11.00
	1247	1887	4.50	6.00	8.00	11.00
	1247	1888	4.50	6.00	8.00	11.00
	1249	1889	4.50	6.00	8.00	11.00
	1249	1890	5.00	6.50	8.00	11.00
	1251	1892	5.00	6.50	8.00	11.00
	1521	1892 (error)				
			5.00	6.50	8.50	11.50
	1252	1892	5.00	6.50	8.00	11.00
	1263	190x	5.00	6.50	8.00	11.00
	1267	1907	5.00	6.50	8.00	11.00
	1268	1908	5.00	6.50	8.00	11.00
	1270	1910	5.00	6.50	8.00	11.00
	1272	1912	5.00	6.50	8.00	11.00
	1273	1913	5.00	6.50	8.00	11.00
	1274	1914	5.00	6.50	8.00	11.00
	1275	1915	5.00	6.50	8.00	11.00
	1276	1915	5.00	6.50	8.00	11.00
	1277	1917	5.00	6.50	8.00	11.00
	1278	1918	5.00	6.50	8.00	11.00
	1279	1919	5.00	6.50	8.00	11.00
	1280	1920	5.00	6.50	8.00	11.00

In the name of Mahabat Khan II

DOKDO

COPPER, 20-21mm

Y#	Date	Year	Good	VG	Fine	VF
1	VS1931	(1874)	12.50	22.50	30.00	37.50
	1935	(1878)	10.00	20.00	27.50	35.00

1/2 KORI

SILVER, 12-14mm, 2.3 gm.

Y#	Date	Year	VG	Fine	VF	XF
E1	AH1293	VS1934	4.00	6.50	10.00	15.00

KORI

SILVER, 14-15mm, 4.6 gm.

Y#	Date	Year	VG	Fine	VF	XF
2	AH1292	VS1932	5.00	6.50	8.00	11.00
	1293	1933	5.00	6.50	8.00	11.00
	1293	1934	5.00	6.50	8.00	11.00
	1297	1935	5.00	6.50	8.00	11.00
	1297	1936	5.00	6.50	8.00	11.00
	1298	1937	5.00	6.50	8.00	11.00
	1299	1938	5.00	6.50	8.00	11.00

GOLD KORI.

GOLD, 15-16mm

Y#	Date	Year	VG	Fine	VF	XF
3	AH1292	VS1932	100.00	125.00	150.00	185.00

Bahadur Khan III

AD 1882-1892

1/2 KORI

GOLD, 15mm

Y#	Date	Year	VG	Fine	VF	XF
4	AH1309	VS1947	100.00	150.00	175.00	225.00

KORI

GOLD, 18mm

Y#	Date	Year	VG	Fine	VF	XF
5	AH1309	VS1947	175.00	250.00	300.00	375.00

Muhammad Khan

AD 1892-1911

DOKDO

COPPER, 19-20mm

Y#	Date	Year	Good	VG	Fine	VF
6.1	AH1325	VS1963	4.50	7.00	10.00	13.50

No stops flanking date

Y#	Date	Year	Good	VG	Fine	VF
6.2	VS1963	(1906)	1.25	2.00	3.00	4.50
	1964	(1907)	1.25	2.00	3.00	4.50

With stops flanking date

Y#	Date	Year	Good	VG	Fine	VF
6.3	VS1964	(1907)	.50	.85	1.25	1.75
	1965	(1908)	.50	.85	1.25	1.75
	1966	(1909)	.50	.85	1.25	1.75
	1967	(1910)	1.00	1.75	2.50	3.50

Y#	Date	Year	Good	VG	Fine	VF
6.4	ND	—	1.75	2.75	4.00	5.50

2 DOKDA

COPPER, 20mm
Thicker than Y#2

Y#	Date	Year	Good	VG	Fine	VF
7	VS1964	(1907)	7.50	11.50	16.50	23.50

KORI

SILVER, 15mm, 4.6 gm.

Y#	Date	Year	VG	Fine	VF	XF
8	VS1966	(1909)	12.50	20.00	26.50	35.00

Mahabat Khan III

AD 1911-1948

DOKDO

COPPER, 19mm

Y#	Date	Year	Good	VG	Fine	VF
9	VS1985	(1928)	7.50	13.50	18.50	25.00
	1990	(1933)	7.50	13.50	18.50	25.00

KACHAR

Laksmi Chandra Narayan

AD 1772-1780

RUPEE

SILVER, 10.70-11.60 gm.

KM#	Date	Year	VG	Fine	VF	XF
1	SE1694	(1772)	—	—	Rare	—

MOHUR

GOLD, 10.70-11.40 gm.

KM#	Date	Year	VG	Fine	VF	XF
2	SE1694	(1772)	—	—	Rare	—

Govinda Chandra

AD 1813-1830

RUPEE

SILVER, 25mm

KM#	Date	Year	VG	Fine	VF	XF
10	SE1736	(1814)	—	—	Rare	—

KALAT

Kasir Khan

AD1840-57

FALUS

COPPER, 20mm

C#	Date	Year	VG	Fine	VF	XF
5	AH1237	—	3.50	6.00	8.50	11.50
	1240	—	3.50	6.00	8.50	11.50

Khudadad

AD1857-1893/AH1274-1311

In the name of Mahmud Khan Durrani

FALUS

COPPER, 21-30mm
Round, irregular, or rough-cut octagonal

C#	Date	Year	VG	Fine	VF	XF
10	AH1186(error for 1286?)	—	2.50	4.00	6.00	8.50
	1293	—	2.50	4.00	6.00	8.50
	1294	—	2.50	4.00	6.00	8.50
	1295	—	2.00	3.50	5.00	7.50
	ND	—	1.50	2.50	4.00	6.00

KALAYANI (Kallian)

1/8 RUPEE

SILVER, 12mm, 1.34-1.45 gm.

KM#	Date	Year	VG	Fine	VF	XF
2	AH1226	—	12.00	15.00	18.50	25.00

RUPEE

SILVER, 19mm, 10.70-11.60 gm.

KM#	Date	Year	VG	Fine	VF	XF
5	AH1212	—	17.50	22.50	30.00	42.50
	1226	—	20.00	25.00	32.50	45.00
	ND	—	17.50	22.50	30.00	42.50

KARAULI

RULERS

Manak Pal, AD 1772-1804
Harbaksh Pal, AD 1804-1838
Pratap Pal, AD 1838-1848
Nar Singh Pal, AD 1848-1853
Madan Pal, AD 1853-1869

MINTMARK

(Jhar) on reverse

In the name of Shah Alam II:

PAISA

COPPER
Similar to Rupee, C#10.

C#	Date	Year	Good	VG	Fine	VF
5	—	44	3.00	4.50	6.00	8.50

RUPEE

SILVER, 20-21mm, 10.70-11.60 gm.

C#	Date	Year	VG	Fine	VF	XF
10	—	24	11.50	13.00	15.00	20.00
	—	29	11.50	13.00	15.00	20.00
	—	30	11.50	13.00	15.00	20.00
	—	41	11.50	13.00	15.00	20.00
	—	43	11.50	13.00	15.00	20.00

In the name of Muhammad Akbar II:

RUPEE

SILVER, 22mm, 10.70-11.60 gm.

C#	Date	Year	VG	Fine	VF	XF
20	AH1228	7	11.50	13.00	15.00	20.00
	1231	10	11.50	13.00	15.00	20.00
	1244	—	11.50	13.00	15.00	20.00

In the name of Bahadur Shah II:

RUPEE

SILVER, 20-23mm, 10.70-11.60 gm.

C#	Date	Year	VG	Fine	VF	XF
40	—	9	12.50	14.50	17.50	23.50
	AH1265	13	12.50	14.50	17.50	23.50
	1268	15	12.50	14.50	17.50	23.50

In the name of Queen Victoria, Years of Madan Pal:

PAISA

COPPER, 20mm

Y#	Date	Year	Good	VG	Fine	VF
1	1852 (error for 1859)					
		13	2.50	4.00	5.50	8.00

1/4 RUPEE

SILVER, 13mm, 2.68-2.90 gm.

Y#	Date	Year	VG	Fine	VF	XF
2	1852	7-14	4.00	6.00	8.00	11.00

1/2 RUPEE

SILVER, 18mm, 5.35-5.80 gm.

Y#	Date	Year	VG	Fine	VF	XF
3	1852	—	7.00	8.50	10.00	13.50
	1859	—	7.50	9.00	11.00	14.50

RUPEE

SILVER, 21-22mm, 10.70-11.60 gm.

Y#	Date	Year	VG	Fine	VF	XF
4	1859	7	11.50	13.00	15.00	20.00
	1859	9	11.50	13.00	15.00	20.00
	1852	10	11.50	13.00	15.00	20.00
	1852	11	11.50	13.00	15.00	20.00
	1852	12	11.50	13.00	15.00	20.00
	1852	13	11.50	13.00	15.00	20.00
	1852	14	11.50	13.00	15.00	20.00

Arjun Pal

AD 1875-1886

In the name of Empress Victoria, Years of Arjun Pal:

1/4 PAISA

COPPER, 13mm, 4.5 gm.

Y#	Date	Year	Good	VG	Fine	VF
5	—	11	3.00	4.50	6.00	8.50

1/2 PAISA

COPPER, 16mm, 9 gm.

Y#	Date	Year	Good	VG	Fine	VF
6	1886	11	1.75	2.75	4.00	6.00

PAISA

COPPER, 20-26mm, 18 gm.

Y#	Date	Year	Good	VG	Fine	VF
7	1881	—	1.75	2.75	4.00	6.00
	1882	11	error for 1886			
			1.75	2.75	4.00	6.00
	188-	9	1.75	2.75	4.00	6.00
	1885	10	1.75	2.75	4.00	6.00
	1886	11	1.75	2.75	4.00	6.00

RUPEE

SILVER, 20-22mm, 10.70-11.60 gm.

Y#	Date	Year	VG	Fine	VF	XF
8	1882	—	11.50	13.00	15.00	20.00
	1884	—	11.50	13.00	15.00	20.00
	1885	10	11.50	13.00	15.00	20.00
	1886	11	11.50	13.00	15.00	20.00

Bhanwar Pal

AD 1886-1927

In the name of Empress Victoria, Years of Bhanwal Pal:

1/2 PAISA

COPPER, 14-17mm

Y#	Date	Year	Good	VG	Fine	VF
9	1886	1	1.75	3.00	4.50	6.00
	1887	2	1.75	3.00	4.50	6.00

PAISA

COPPER, 18-21mm

Y#	Date	Year	Good	VG	Fine	VF
10	1886	1	1.75	2.75	3.75	5.00
	1887	2	1.75	2.75	3.75	5.00
	1891	6	1.75	2.75	3.75	5.00
	1893	8	1.75	2.75	3.75	5.00

1/4 RUPEE

SILVER, 12mm, 2.68-2.90 gm.

Y#	Date	Year	VG	Fine	VF	XF
11	1893	8	5.50	7.50	10.00	13.50
	1896	11	5.50	7.50	10.00	13.50

1/2 RUPEE

SILVER, 18mm, 5.35-5.80 gm.

Y#	Date	Year	VG	Fine	VF	XF
12	1893	8	6.50	8.50	11.50	15.00
	1896	10	6.50	8.50	11.50	15.00

RUPEE

SILVER, 22mm

Y#	Date	Year	VG	Fine	VF	XF
13	1882	2	11.50	13.00	15.00	20.00
	1885	1	11.50	13.00	15.00	20.00
	1886	2	11.50	13.00	15.00	20.00
	1888	2	11.50	13.00	15.00	20.00
	1888	3	11.50	13.00	15.00	20.00
	1889	4	11.50	13.00	15.00	20.00
	1890	4	11.50	13.00	15.00	20.00
	1890	—	11.50	13.00	15.00	20.00
	1891	6	11.50	13.00	15.00	20.00
	1892	8	11.50	13.00	15.00	20.00
	1893	8	11.50	13.00	15.00	20.00
	1896	11	11.50	13.00	15.00	20.00
	1897	11	11.50	13.00	15.00	20.00

KASHMIR

For earlier issues, see Durrani Empire and Sikhs.

UNDER DOGRA RULE

RULERS

Gulab Singh,
VS1903-1913/1846-1856AD
Ranbir Singh,
VS1914-1942/1857-1885AD
Pertab Singh,
VS1942-1979/1885-1925AD

First Copper Series

Many variations

PAISA

COPPER, 18-22mm

Y#	Date	Year	Good	VG	Fine	VF
1	VS1904	(1847)	2.00	3.50	5.00	6.50
	1908	(1851)	2.00	3.50	5.00	6.50

Second Copper Series

Sword on obv., fancy leaf on rev., denomination in Persian.

1/2 ANNA

COPPER, 19-20mm

Y#	Date	Year	Good	VG	Fine	VF
8	VS1920	(1863)	4.00	6.50	8.50	12.50

ANNA

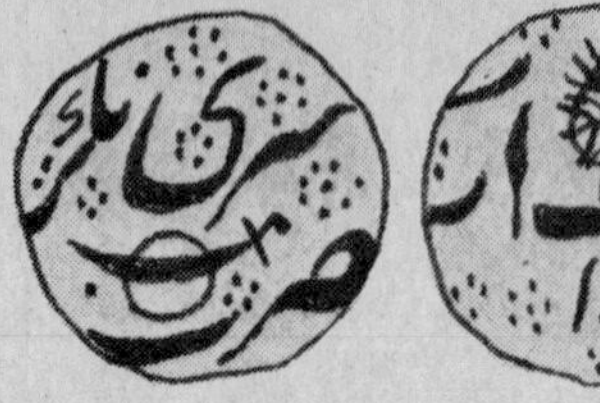

COPPER, 24mm

Y#	Date	Year	Good	VG	Fine	VF
9	VS1920	(1863)	6.00	9.00	12.50	17.50
	1924	(1867)	6.00	9.00	12.50	17.50

Third Copper Series

Date in cartouche on obverse.

1/2 PAISA

COPPER, 15-18mm, 2.5-3.0 gm.

Y#	Date	Year	Good	VG	Fine	VF
6	VS1922	(1865)	1.25	2.00	2.75	4.00

PAISA

COPPER, 18-20mm, 5.5-6.0 gm.

Y#	Date	Year	Good	VG	Fine	VF
7	VS1920	(1863)	.75	1.25	1.75	2.50
	1921	(1864)	.75	1.25	1.75	2.50
	1922	(1865)	1.00	1.50	2.00	2.75
	1923	(1866)	1.25	1.75	2.25	3.00
	1926	(1869)	1.25	1.75	2.25	3.00
	1927	(1870)	1.00	1.50	2.00	2.75
	1928	(1871)	1.00	1.50	2.00	2.75
	1931	(1874)	1.25	1.75	2.25	3.00

Fourth Copper Series

JHS on obverse, Takari legend on reverse.

1/4 PAISA

COPPER, 10mm, 1.5 gm.

Y#	Date	Year	Good	VG	Fine	VF
17	VS1935	(1878)	1.75	3.00	4.00	6.00
	1941	(1884)	1.75	3.00	4.00	6.00

1/2 PAISA

COPPER, 14-16mm, 3 gm.

Y#	Date	Year	Good	VG	Fine	VF
18	VS1932	(1875)		1.00	1.50	3.00
	1933	(1876)		1.00	1.50	3.00
	1933 on obv/1934 on rev. (1875/76)		1.75	2.50	3.50	5.00
	1934	(1877)	1.00	1.50	2.00	3.00
	1936	(1879)	1.00	1.50	2.00	3.00
	1937	(1880)	1.00	1.50	2.00	3.00
	1938	(1881)	1.00	1.50	2.00	3.00
	1939	(1882)	1.00	1.50	2.00	3.00
	1940	(1883)	1.00	1.50	2.00	3.00
	1941	(1884)	1.00	1.50	2.00	3.00

PAISA

COPPER, 19mm, 6 gm.

Y#	Date	Year	Good	VG	Fine	VF
19	VS1938	(1881)	1.75	2.75	4.00	6.00
	1939	(1882)	1.75	2.75	4.00	6.00
	1940	(1883)	1.75	2.75	4.00	6.00

First Silver Type

Leaf and date on obv. No JHS.

NOTE: The dot for 'O' in 1903, 1904, 1905 is sometimes omitted. The half and full Rupees of 1905-06 are of a slightly variant type.

1/8 RUPEE

SILVER, 10-12mm, 1.34-1.45 gm.

Y#	Date	Year	VG	Fine	VF	XF
2	VS1903	(1846)	7.00	10.00	13.50	20.00
	1904	(1847)	7.00	10.00	13.50	20.00
	1905	(1848)	7.00	10.00	13.50	20.00

1/4 RUPEE

SILVER, 13-15mm, 2.68-2.90 gm.

Y#	Date	Year	VG	Fine	VF	XF
3	VS1903	(1846)	5.50	8.00	11.00	15.00
	1904	(1847)	5.50	8.00	11.00	15.00

1/2 RUPEE

SILVER, 17-19mm, 5.35-5.80 gm.

Y#	Date	Year	VG	Fine	VF	XF
4	VS1903	(1846)	7.00	9.00	12.50	17.50
	1904	(1847)	7.00	9.00	12.50	17.50
	1905	(1848)	7.00	9.00	12.50	17.50

RUPEE

SILVER, 20-23mm

Y#	Date	Year	VG	Fine	VF	XF
5	VS1903	(1846)	11.50	13.00	15.00	20.00
	1904	(1847)	11.50	13.00	15.00	20.00
	1905	(1848)	12.50	14.50	17.50	23.50
	1906	(1849)	12.50	14.50	17.50	23.50

Second Silver Type

Persian legends, JHS added to reverse.

1/8 RUPEE

SILVER, 13mm, 1.34-1.45 gm.

Y#	Date	Year	VG	Fine	VF	XF
10	VS1914	(1857)	6.50	8.50	11.50	16.50
	1925	(1868)	6.50	8.50	11.50	16.50

1/4 RUPEE

SILVER, 14mm, 2.68-2.90 gm.

Y#	Date	Year	VG	Fine	VF	XF
11	VS1914	(1857)	7.00	9.00	12.50	17.50
	1922	(1865)	7.00	9.00	12.50	17.50
	1925	(1868)	7.00	9.00	12.50	17.50

1/2 RUPEE

SILVER, 16-17mm, 5.35-5.80 gm.

Y#	Date	Year	VG	Fine	VF	XF
12	VS1914	(1857)	6.50	8.50	11.50	16.50
	1922	(1865)	6.50	8.50	11.50	16.50

RUPEE

SILVER, 20-22mm, 10.70-11.60 gm.

Y#	Date	Year	VG	Fine	VF	XF
13	VS1907	(1850)	11.50	13.00	15.00	20.00
	1908	(1851)	11.50	13.00	15.00	20.00
	1909	(1852)	11.50	13.00	15.00	20.00
	1910	(1853)	11.50	13.00	15.00	20.00
	1911	(1854)	11.50	13.00	15.00	20.00
	1912	(1855)	11.50	13.00	15.00	20.00
	1913	(1856)	11.50	13.00	15.00	20.00
	1914	(1857)	11.50	13.00	15.00	20.00
	1915	(1858)	11.50	13.00	15.00	20.00
	1916	(1859)	11.50	13.00	15.00	20.00
	1917	(1860)	11.50	13.00	15.00	20.00
	1918	(1861)	11.50	13.00	15.00	20.00
	1919	(1862)	11.50	13.00	15.00	20.00
	1920	(1863)	11.50	13.00	15.00	20.00
	1921	(1864)	11.50	13.00	15.00	20.00
	1922	(1865)	11.50	13.00	15.00	20.00
	1923	(1866)	11.50	13.00	15.00	20.00
	1924	(1867)	11.50	13.00	15.00	20.00
	1925	(1868)	11.50	13.00	15.00	20.00
	1926	(1869)	11.50	13.00	15.00	20.00
	1927	(1870)	11.50	13.00	15.00	20.00

Third Silver Type

Persian legends and IHS obverse, Takari legends reverse. Weight reduced to 6.8 gr. (from ca. 10.3-10.8 gr.) Date in top line of obverse.

NOTE: VS1927-1929 struck in collar, 1929-1932 struck without collar.

1/4 RUPEE

SILVER, 15mm, 2.68-2.90 gm.

Y#	Date	Year	VG	Fine	VF	XF
14	VS1928	(1871)	4.50	6.50	9.00	13.50

1/2 RUPEE

SILVER, 17mm, 5.35-5.80 gm.

Y#	Date	Year	VG	Fine	VF	XF
15	VS1928	(1871)	4.50	6.50	9.00	13.50

RUPEE

SILVER, 23mm, 10.70-11.60 gm.
Machine-struck

Y#	Date	Year	VG	Fine	VF	XF
16	VS1927	(1870)	15.00	20.00	27.50	40.00

22mm
Struck on machine - cut planchets.

Y#	Date	Year	VG	Fine	VF	XF
16a	VS1927	(1870)	11.50	13.00	15.00	20.00
	1928	(1871)	11.50	13.00	15.00	20.00

Y#	Date	Year	VG	Fine	VF	XF
16a	1929	(1872)	12.50	14.50	17.50	23.50

Struck on dump planchets.

Y#	Date	Year	VG	Fine	VF	XF
16b	1929	(1872)	12.50	14.50	17.50	23.50
	1930	(1873)	12.50	14.50	17.50	23.50
	1931	(1874)	12.50	14.50	17.50	23.50
	1932	(1875)	12.50	14.50	17.50	23.50

Fourth Silver Type

Similar to above, but JHS.
Date in second line of obv. in Arabic, in second line of rev. in Davanajari.
Weight of Rupee reduced to 6.6 gm.

1/2 RUPEE

SILVER, 16mm, 5.35-5.80 gm.

Y#	Date	Year	VG	Fine	VF	XF
20	VS1946	(1889)	11.50	13.00	15.00	20.00
	1950	(1893)	11.50	13.00	15.00	20.00
	1951	(1894)	11.50	13.00	15.00	20.00

RUPEE

SILVER, 18-21mm, 10.70-11.60 gm.

Y#	Date	Year	VG	Fine	VF	XF
21	VS1932	(1875)	11.50	13.00	15.00	20.00
	1933	(1876)	11.50	13.00	15.00	20.00
	1934	(1877)	11.50	13.00	15.00	20.00
	1935	(1878)	11.50	13.00	15.00	20.00
	1936	(1879)	11.50	13.00	15.00	20.00
	1937	(1880)	11.50	13.00	15.00	20.00
	1939	(1882)	11.50	13.00	15.00	20.00
	1940	(1883)	11.50	13.00	15.00	20.00
	1941	(1884)	11.50	13.00	15.00	20.00
	1942	(1885)	11.50	13.00	15.00	20.00
	1943	(1886)	11.50	13.00	15.00	20.00
	1944	(1887)	11.50	13.00	15.00	20.00
	1945	(1888)	11.50	13.00	15.00	20.00
	1946	(1889)	11.50	13.00	15.00	20.00
	1947	(1890)	11.50	13.00	15.00	20.00
	1948	(1891)	11.50	13.00	15.00	20.00
	1949	(1892)	11.50	13.00	15.00	20.00
	1950	(1893)	11.50	13.00	15.00	20.00
	1951	(1894)	11.50	13.00	15.00	20.00
	1952	(1895)	11.50	13.00	15.00	20.00

NOTE: 1933 weighs 6.8gm., 1934 and after weigh 6.6gm.

Jammu Mint

UNDER DOGRA RULE

Anonymous Coins

RULERS

Gulab Singh,
VS1903-1913/1846-1856AD
Ranbir Singh,
VS1914-1942/1857-1885AD
Pertab Singh,
VS1942-1979/1885-1925AD

PAISA

COPPER, 18-20mm
Obv: Persian. Rev: Gurmukhi.

Y#	Date	Year	Good	VG	Fine	VF
1	VS1914	(1857)	.50	1.00	1.75	2.50
	1915	(1858)	.50	1.00	1.75	2.50
	1917	(1860)	.50	1.00	1.75	2.50
	1919	(1861)	.50	1.00	1.75	2.50
	1921	(1864)	.50	1.00	1.75	2.50
	1922	(1865)	.50	1.00	1.75	2.50

Obv: Persian. Rev: Takari.
15mm

Y#	Date	Year	Good	VG	Fine	VF
2	VS1935	(1876)	3.50	6.00	8.50	12.50

 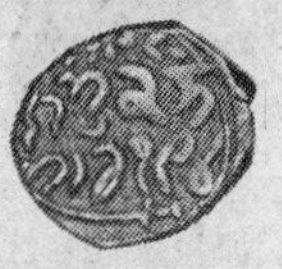

Dump style, uneven planchets, 14-16mm

Y#	Date	Year	Good	VG	Fine	VF
2a	VS1935	(1876)	.50	1.00	1.75	2.50
	1937	(1878)	.50	1.00	1.75	2.50
	1938	(1879)	.50	1.00	1.75	2.50
	1939	(1880)	.50	1.00	1.75	2.50
	1940	(1881)	.50	1.00	1.75	2.50
	1942	(1883)	.50	1.00	1.75	2.50
	1946	(1887)	.50	1.00	1.75	2.50
	1947	(1888)	.50	1.00	1.75	2.50
	1949	(1890)	.50	1.00	1.75	2.50

1/3 MOHUR

GOLD, 19mm, 3.57-3.80 gm.

Y#	Date	Year	VG	Fine	VF	XF
3	VS1921	(1864)	225.00	300.00	375.00	500.00

Ladakh Mint

Coins for Ladakh were struck at both Srinagar and Jammu

UNDER DOGRA RULE

AFTER AD 1834:

PAISA

COPPER, 19mm

Y#	Date	Year	Good	VG	Fine	VF
2	VS1924	(1867)	2.50	4.00	5.50	7.50
	1926	(1869)	2.50	4.00	5.50	7.50
	1927	(1870)	2.50	4.00	5.50	7.50

In the name of Gulab Singh:

TIMASHA

SILVER, 20-22mm
Rev: Large dagger.

Y#	Date	Mintage	VG	Fine	VF
1	ND	—	10.00	12.50	15.00

Anonymous Issue

Obv: Persian inscription. Rev: No dagger.

Y#	Date	Mintage	VG	Fine	VF
3	VS1928	—	25.00	32.50	40.00

For issues struck in the name of Mahmud Shah see Durrani Empire.

KISHANGARH

RULERS

Kalyan Singh, AD1797-1832
Mokham Singh, AD1832-1840
Prithui Singh, AD1840-1879

In the name of Shah Alam II (struck until 1857):

PAISA

COPPER, 18-19mm

C#	Date	Year	Good	VG	Fine	VF
4	AH119x	25	3.00	4.50	6.50	10.00

Degenerate copy of Jaipur, C#29

C#	Date	Year	Good	VG	Fine	VF
5	—	45	1.25	1.75	2.50	3.50

1/4 RUPEE

SILVER, 15mm, 2.68-2.90 gm.

C#	Date	Year	VG	Fine	VF	XF
8	AH1197	24	7.00	10.00	13.50	18.50
	1198	24	7.00	10.00	13.50	18.50

RUPEE

SILVER, 16mm, 10.70-11.60 gm.

C#	Date	Year	VG	Fine	VF	XF
10	AH1197	24	11.50	13.00	15.00	20.00
	1198	24	11.50	13.00	15.00	20.00
	1198	25	12.50	14.50	17.50	23.50

21mm

Rev: Flower instead of jhar.

Y#	Date	Year	VG	Fine	VF	XF
10.1	AH—	24	12.50	14.50	17.50	23.50

MOHUR

GOLD, 10.70-11.40 gm.

C#	Date	Year	VG	Fine	VF	XF
17	—	24	225.00	250.00	275.00	325.00

In the name of Muhammad Akbar II:

PAISA

COPPER, 18-19mm
Crude copy of Jaipur C#47

C#	Date	Year	Good	VG	Fine	VF
25	ND	—	1.00	1.50	2.25	3.50

In the names of Queen Victoria & Prithvi Singh
AD1858-1879

NOTE: Coins, starting in AD1857, and all subsequent coins bear the frozen regnal year 24 (of Shah Alam II!)

RUPEE

SILVER, 20-23mm, 10.70-11.60 gm.

Y#	Date	Year	VG	Fine	VF	XF
	Variety 1					
1.1	1858	24	11.50	13.00	15.00	20.00
	Variety 2					
1.2	1859	24	12.50	14.00	17.50	23.50

2 RUPEES

SILVER, 34mm, 21.40-23.20 gm.

KM#	Date	Year	VG	Fine	VF	XF
1	1858	24	—	—	Rare	—

In the names of Queen Victoria Unread Chief (probably Sardul Singh)
AD1879-1900

1/2 RUPEE

SILVER, 18mm, 5.35-5.80 gm.

Y#	Date	Year	VG	Fine	VF	XF
A2	ND	—	9.00	11.50	15.00	20.00

RUPEE

SILVER, 20-23mm, 10.70-11.60 gm.
Barbarous Persian legends

KM#	Date	Year	VG	Fine	VF	XF
2	1880	24	14.00	17.50	21.50	30.00

In the names of Edward VII and unread chief (probably Madan Singh):
AD1900-1926

1/2 RUPEE

SILVER, 20mm, 5.35-5.80 gm.

KM#	Date	Year	VG	Fine	VF	XF
3	1904	24	15.00	20.00	25.00	33.50

In the names of George V or VI and Yagyanarain
AD 1926-38

1/4 RUPEE

SILVER, 15mm, 2.68-2.90 gm.

KM#	Date	Year	VG	Fine	VF	XF
4	—	24	15.00	18.50	23.50	30.00

1/2 RUPEE

SILVER, 20mm, 5.35-5.80 gm.

KM#	Date	Year	VG	Fine	VF	XF
5	—	24	15.00	18.50	23.50	30.00

RUPEE

SILVER, 10.70-11.60 gm.

KM#	Date	Year	VG	Fine	VF	XF
6	—	24	20.00	30.00	40.00	55.00

NAZARANA RUPEE

SILVER, 26.5mm, 10.70-11.60 gm.

Y#	Date	Year	VG	Fine	VF	XF
6a	—	—	50.00	75.00	100.00	135.00

1/2 MOHUR

GOLD, 18mm, 5.35-5.70 gm.

KM#	Date	Year	VG	Fine	VF	XF
7	—	24	175.00	225.00	275.00	325.00

MOHUR

GOLD, 19mm, 10.70-11.40 gm.

KM#	Date	Year	VG	Fine	VF	XF
8	—	24	225.00	275.00	325.00	400.00

Anonymous 20th Century Issues

First Series

1/8 RUPEE

SILVER, 12mm, 1.34-1.45 gm.
Similar to 1 Mohur, KM#8.

Y#	Date	Year	VG	Fine	VF	XF
9	—	24	7.50	10.00	13.50	18.50

1/4 RUPEE

SILVER, 15mm, 2.68-2.90 gm.
Similar to 1 Mohur, KM#8.

Y#	Date	Year	VG	Fine	VF	XF
10	—	24	7.50	10.00	13.50	18.50

1/2 RUPEE

SILVER, 17-18mm, 5.35-5.70 gm.
Similar to 1 Mohur, KM#8.

Y#	Date	Year	VG	Fine	VF	XF
11	—	24	9.00	12.50	16.50	22.50

RUPEE

SILVER, 20-24mm, 10.70-11.60 gm.

Y#	Date	Year	VG	Fine	VF	XF
12	—	24	11.50	16.50	22.50	30.00

Second Series

Denomination in Nagari in Annas on reverse.

2 ANNAS

SILVER, 11mm, 1.34-1.45 gm.

Y#	Date	Year	VG	Fine	VF	XF
13	—	24	9.00	12.50	16.50	22.50

4 ANNAS

SILVER, 12-13mm, 2.68-2.90 gm.

Y#	Date	Year	VG	Fine	VF	XF
14	—	24	7.50	10.00	13.50	18.50

8 ANNAS

SILVER, 16mm, 5.35-5.70 gm.

Y#	Date	Year	VG	Fine	VF	XF
15	—	24	7.50	10.00	13.50	18.50

KOLHAPUR

In the name of Muhammad Shah with false mint name 'Azamnagar Gokak':
(struck until circa 1850 AD)

1/4 RUPEE

SILVER, 12mm, 2.68-2.90 gm.

C#	Date	Year	VG	Fine	VF	XF
14	ND	—	7.50	10.00	13.50	20.00

1/2 RUPEE

SILVER, 15mm, 5.35-5.80 gm.

C#	Date	Year	VG	Fine	VF	XF
15	ND	—	7.50	10.00	13.50	20.00

RUPEE

SILVER, 17-21mm, 10.70-11.60 gm.

C#	Date	Year	VG	Fine	VF	XF
16	ND	—	11.50	13.00	15.00	20.00
	Fine calligraphy					
25	1821	—	12.50	14.50	17.50	23.50

East India Company

Local issue from Shahupur in mintname Azamnagar Gokak.

RUPEE

SILVER, 20mm, 10.70-11.60 gm.

C#	Date	Year	VG	Fine	VF	XF
30	1821	—	12.50	14.50	17.50	23.50

KOTAH

RULERS

Ram Singh, AD 1828-1866
Chattar Sal, AD 1866-1889
Umed Singh, AD 1889-1945

MINTMARKS

1. 
4. 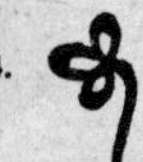
2.
3. 
5. 

Mintmark #1 appears beneath #4 on all Kotah coins, and serves to distinguish coins of Kotah from similar issues of Bundi in the pre-Victoria period.

C#28 has mm#2 on obverse, #1, 3 and 4 on reverse. All later issues have #1 on obverse, #1, 5 and 4 on reverse.

In the name of Shah Alam II:

RUPEE

SILVER, 19mm, 10.70-11.60 gm.

C#	Date	Year	VG	Fine	VF	XF
28	—	44	11.50	13.00	15.00	20.00
	—	45	11.50	13.00	15.00	20.00
	—	46	11.50	13.00	15.00	20.00
	—	47	11.50	13.00	15.00	20.00

In the name of Muhammad Akbar II
AD1806-1837

PAISA

COPPER, 25mm, square

C#	Date	Year	Good	VG	Fine	VF
29	—	25	2.50	3.50	5.00	7.00

RUPEE

SILVER, 20mm, 10.70-11.60 gm.

C#	Date	Year	VG	Fine	VF	XF
30	—	1	11.50	13.00	15.00	20.00
	—	12	11.50	13.00	15.00	20.00
	—	16	11.50	13.00	15.00	20.00
	—	20	11.50	13.00	15.00	20.00
	—	23	11.50	13.00	15.00	20.00
	—	28	11.50	13.00	15.00	20.00

In the name of Bahadur II
AD1837-1857

1/8 RUPEE

SILVER, 10mm, 1.34-1.45 gm.

C#	Date	Year	VG	Fine	VF	XF
31	—	—	3.50	5.00	7.00	10.00

1/4 RUPEE

SILVER, 12mm, 2.68-2.90 gm.

C#	Date	Year	VG	Fine	VF	XF
A31	—	—	4.50	6.50	8.50	12.50

1/2 RUPEE

SILVER, 5.35-5.80 gm.

C#	Date	Year	VG	Fine	VF	XF
B31	—	—	6.50	8.00	10.00	14.50

RUPEE

SILVER, 20-21mm, 10.70-11.60 gm.

C#	Date	Year	VG	Fine	VF	XF
32	—	9	11.50	13.00	15.00	20.00
	—	16	11.50	13.00	15.00	20.00
	—	18	11.50	13.00	15.00	20.00
	—	19	11.50	13.00	15.00	20.00
	—	21	11.50	13.00	15.00	20.00

NAZARANA RUPEE

SILVER, 32mm, 10.70-11.60 gm.

C#	Date	Year	VG	Fine	VF	XF
32a	—	4	25.00	35.00	45.00	60.00
	—	5	25.00	35.00	45.00	60.00
	—	6	25.00	35.00	45.00	60.00
	—	7	25.00	35.00	45.00	60.00
	—	8	25.00	35.00	45.00	60.00
	—	9	25.00	35.00	45.00	60.00
	—	12	25.00	35.00	45.00	60.00
	—	13	25.00	35.00	45.00	60.00
	—	14	25.00	35.00	45.00	60.00
	—	15	25.00	35.00	45.00	60.00
	—	17	25.00	35.00	45.00	60.00
	—	19	25.00	35.00	45.00	60.00
	—	20	25.00	35.00	45.00	60.00

NOTE: Most specimens show rudimentary traces of AH date on obverse.

MOHUR

GOLD, 19mm, 10.70-11.40 gm.

C#	Date	Year	VG	Fine	VF	XF
	—	1-21	225.00	250.00	285.00	325.00

In the name of Queen Victoria
From AD1857

1/2 PAISA

COPPER, 12-16mm, 9 gm.

Y#	Date	Year	Good	VG	Fine	VF
1	—	37	1.50	2.25	3.00	4.00
	—	39	1.50	2.25	3.00	4.00
	—	40	1.50	2.25	3.00	4.00

PAISA

COPPER, square, 15-20mm

Y#	Date	Year	Good	VG	Fine	VF
2	—	28	1.50	2.25	3.00	3.75
	—	31	1.50	2.25	3.00	3.75
	—	32	1.50	2.25	3.00	3.75
	—	37	1.50	2.25	3.00	3.75
	—	38	1.50	2.25	3.00	3.75
	—	39	1.50	2.25	3.00	3.75
	—	40	1.50	2.25	3.00	3.75
	—	41	1.50	2.25	3.00	3.75
	—	51	1.50	2.25	3.00	3.75

1/8 RUPEE

SILVER, 9mm, 1.34-1.45 gm.

Y#	Date	Year	VG	Fine	VF	XF
3	—	27	2.25	3.00	4.00	6.00
	—	29	2.25	3.00	4.00	6.00
	—	30	2.25	3.00	4.00	6.00
	—	31	2.25	3.00	4.00	6.00
	—	32	2.25	3.00	4.00	6.00
	—	33	2.25	3.00	4.00	6.00
	—	34	2.25	3.00	4.00	6.00
	—	36	2.25	3.00	4.00	6.00
	—	37	2.25	3.00	4.00	6.00
	—	38	2.25	3.00	4.00	6.00

1/4 RUPEE

SILVER, 12mm, 2.68-2.90 gm.

Y#	Date	Year	VG	Fine	VF	XF
4	—	1	3.50	4.50	5.50	7.50
	—	2	3.50	4.50	5.50	7.50
	—	8	3.50	4.50	5.50	7.50
	—	22	3.50	4.50	5.50	7.50

Y#	Date	Year	VG	Fine	VF	XF
	—	29	3.50	4.50	5.50	7.50
	—	30	3.50	4.50	5.50	7.50
	—	31	3.50	4.50	5.50	7.50
	—	32	3.50	4.50	5.50	7.50
	—	33	3.50	4.50	5.50	7.50
	—	35	3.50	4.50	5.50	7.50
	—	37	3.50	4.50	5.50	7.50
	—	38	3.50	4.50	5.50	7.50

1/2 RUPEE

SILVER, 13-15mm, 5.35-5.80 gm.

Y#	Date	Year	VG	Fine	VF	XF
5	—	1	6.50	8.00	10.00	15.00
	—	8	6.50	8.00	10.00	15.00
	—	18	6.50	8.00	10.00	15.00
	—	22	6.50	8.00	10.00	15.00
	—	24	6.50	8.00	10.00	15.00
	—	25	6.50	8.00	10.00	15.00
	—	28	6.50	8.00	10.00	15.00
	—	29	6.50	8.00	10.00	15.00
	—	30	6.50	8.00	10.00	15.00
	—	31	6.50	8.00	10.00	15.00
	—	32	6.50	8.00	10.00	15.00
	—	33	6.50	8.00	10.00	15.00
	—	35	6.50	8.00	10.00	15.00
	—	36	6.50	8.00	10.00	15.00
	—	38	6.50	8.00	10.00	15.00

RUPEE

SILVER, 18-20mm, 10.70-11.60 gm.

Y#	Date	Year	VG	Fine	VF	XF
6	—	1	11.50	13.00	15.00	20.00
	—	2	11.50	13.00	15.00	20.00
	—	4	11.50	13.00	15.00	20.00
	—	6	11.50	13.00	15.00	20.00
	—	8	11.50	13.00	15.00	20.00
	—	9	11.50	13.00	15.00	20.00
	—	15	11.50	13.00	15.00	20.00
	—	16	11.50	13.00	15.00	20.00
	—	18	11.50	13.00	15.00	20.00
	—	19	11.50	13.00	15.00	20.00
	—	20	11.50	13.00	15.00	20.00
	—	21	11.50	13.00	15.00	20.00
	—	22	11.50	13.00	15.00	20.00
	—	26	11.50	13.00	15.00	20.00
	—	28	11.50	13.00	15.00	20.00
	—	31	11.50	13.00	15.00	20.00
	—	32	11.50	13.00	15.00	20.00
	—	34	11.50	13.00	15.00	20.00
	—	38	11.50	13.00	15.00	20.00
	—	40	11.50	13.00	15.00	20.00
	—	41	11.50	13.00	15.00	20.00
	—	44	11.50	13.00	15.00	20.00

Rev: Full year, 20mm.

Y#	Date	Year	VG	Fine	VF	XF
7	VS1956	(1899)	15.00	18.00	21.50	28.50

NAZARANA RUPEE

SILVER, 27-30mm

Y#	Date	Year	VG	Fine	VF	XF
6a	—	1	27.50	37.50	47.50	60.00
	—	2	27.50	37.50	47.50	60.00
	—	3	27.50	37.50	47.50	60.00
	—	4	27.50	37.50	47.50	60.00
	—	6	27.50	37.50	47.50	60.00
	—	7	27.50	37.50	47.50	60.00
	—	8	27.50	37.50	47.50	60.00
	—	9	27.50	37.50	47.50	60.00
	—	14	27.50	37.50	47.50	60.00
	—	15	27.50	37.50	47.50	60.00
	—	16	27.50	37.50	47.50	60.00
	—	17	27.50	37.50	47.50	60.00
	—	18	27.50	37.50	47.50	60.00
	—	21	27.50	37.50	47.50	60.00
	—	22	27.50	37.50	47.50	60.00
	—	23	27.50	37.50	47.50	60.00
	—	25	27.50	37.50	47.50	60.00
	—	26	27.50	37.50	47.50	60.00
	—	27	27.50	37.50	47.50	60.00
	—	28	27.50	37.50	47.50	60.00
	—	29	27.50	37.50	47.50	60.00
	—	30	27.50	37.50	47.50	60.00
	—	31	27.50	37.50	47.50	60.00
	—	32	27.50	37.50	47.50	60.00
	—	44	27.50	37.50	47.50	60.00

Y#	Date	Year	VG	Fine	VF	XF
7a	VS1956	(1899)	30.00	40.00	50.00	65.00

MOHUR

GOLD, 18mm

Y#	Date	Year	VG	Fine	VF	XF
8	—	1	220.00	240.00	265.00	300.00
	—	6	220.00	240.00	265.00	300.00
	—	8	220.00	240.00	265.00	300.00
	—	9	220.00	240.00	265.00	300.00
	—	15	220.00	240.00	265.00	300.00
	—	31	220.00	240.00	265.00	300.00
	—	32	220.00	240.00	265.00	300.00
	—	44	220.00	240.00	265.00	300.00

KUTCH

MONETARY SYSTEM

2 Trambiyo = 1 Dokda
1-1/2 Dokda = 1 Dhingla
16 Dhinghla = 1 Kori (silver)
25 Kori (silver) = 1 Kori (gold)

NOTE: All coins of Lakhpatji through Bharmalji II bear a common type, derived from the Gujarati coinage of Muzaffar III (late 16th Century AD), and bear a stylized form of the date AH 978 (AD 1570) (the silver of Bharmalji also has the fictitious date AH 1165). The rulers name appears in the Nagari script on the obverse.

Lakhpatji

AD 1752-1761

DHINGLO

COPPER, 12 gm.

C#	Date	Good	VG	Fine	VF
8	ND	3.00	5.00	7.50	10.00

1/2 KORI

SILVER, 13mm, 2.35 gm.

C#	Date	VG	Fine	VF	XF
10	AH1165	7.50	10.00	13.50	17.50

17mm
Obv: Ahmad Shah inscriptions

C#	Date	VG	Fine	VF	XF
11	AH1165	7.50	10.00	13.50	17.50

16-18mm
Obv: Muzaffar Shah inscriptions

C#	Date	VG	Fine	VF	XF
12	ND	12.50	17.50	23.50	30.00

Gohodaji II

AD 1761-1778

1/2 TRAMBIYO

COPPER, 9mm, 2 gm.

C#	Date	Good	VG	Fine	VF
15	ND	—	—	Rare	—

TRAMBIYO

COPPER, 13mm, 4 gm.

C#	Date	Good	VG	Fine	VF
16	ND	1.75	2.50	3.50	5.00

DOKDO

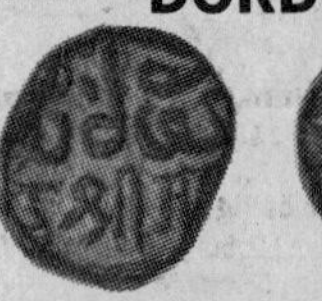

COPPER, 17mm, 8 gm.

C#	Date	Good	VG	Fine	VF
17	ND	1.75	2.50	3.50	5.00

DHINGLO

COPPER, 18mm, 12 gm.

C#	Date	Good	VG	Fine	VF
18	ND	1.75	2.50	3.50	5.00

1/4 KORI

SILVER, 9-11mm, 1.17 gm.

C#	Date	VG	Fine	VF	XF
20	ND	—	—	—	—

1/2 KORI

SILVER, 12mm, 2.35 gm.

C#	Date	VG	Fine	VF	XF
21	ND	6.00	8.50	11.50	15.00

KORI

SILVER, 15mm, 4.70 gm.

C#	Date	VG	Fine	VF	XF
22	ND	5.00	7.00	10.00	12.50

Rayadhanji II

AD 1778-1814

TRAMBIYO

COPPER, 12mm, 4 gm.

C#	Date	Good	VG	Fine	VF
25	ND	1.50	2.50	3.50	5.00

DOKDO

COPPER, 16mm, 8 gm.

C#	Date	Good	VG	Fine	VF
26	ND	1.50	2.50	3.50	5.00

DHINGLO

COPPER, 17mm, 12 gm.

C#	Date	Good	VG	Fine	VF
27	ND	1.75	2.75	4.00	5.50

1/4 KORI

SILVER, 7-8mm, 1.17 gm.

C#	Date	VG	Fine	VF	XF
28	ND	7.50	10.00	13.50	18.50

1/2 KORI

SILVER, 10-12mm, 2.35 gm.

C#	Date	VG	Fine	VF	XF
29	ND	6.00	8.00	11.00	16.00

KORI

SILVER, 14-15mm, 4.70 gm.

C#	Date	VG	Fine	VF	XF
30	ND	5.00	7.50	10.00	14.00

Bharmalji II

AD 1814-1819

TRAMBIYO

COPPER, 12mm, 4 gm.

C#	Date	Good	VG	Fine	VF
31	ND	2.50	4.00	5.50	7.50

DOKDO

COPPER, 16mm, 8 gm.

C#	Date	Good	VG	Fine	VF
32	ND	2.50	4.00	5.50	7.50

DHINGLO

COPPER, 17mm, 12 gm.

C#	Date	Good	VG	Fine	VF
33	ND	3.00	4.50	6.00	8.50

1/2 KORI

SILVER, 9-10mm, 1.17 gm.

C#	Date	VG	Fine	VF	XF
35	AH1165 (fictitious)				
35		3.00	4.50	6.00	8.50

KORI

SILVER, 14-16mm, 2.35 gm.

C#	Date	VG	Fine	VF	XF
36	SH1165 (fictitious)				
		2.75	3.50	4.50	6.50

Desalji II

AD 1819-1860

The coins of Desalji II may be divided into four basic series, which may be differentiated as follows:

FIRST SERIES: In the name of Muzaffar Shah of Gujarot, types similar to those of Bharmalji, but with Desalji's name instead.

SECOND SERIES: In the name of Muhammad Akbar II, Desalji's name in Nagari on obverse, mint and both dates in Persian inscription on reverse but actual SE date in Nagari numerals. AH date is unvarying (12)34, SE dates 1875-1887.

THIRD SERIES: Obverse in Persian, reverse in Nagari script. AH dates 1250-1266, VS dates 1892-1904. Many subvarieties of type, some with only AH dates, some only SE dates, some both. In the name of Muhammad Akbar II.

FOURTH SERIES: As above, but in the name of Bahadur II. VS dates only 1909-1916 on silver and gold, AH dates only on copper 1267-1274.

NOTE: Although Muhammad Akbar II was succeeded by Bahadur II on the Mughal throne in AH 1253, the change is not acknowledged on Kutch coinage until AH 1263!

First Series

Types of Bharmalji II continued, but with Desalji II's name in Nagari on obverse.

TRAMBIYO

COPPER, 13-14mm, 4 gm.

C#	Date	Good	VG	Fine	VF
38	ND	1.00	1.50	2.50	4.00

DOKDO

COPPER, 16mm, 8 gm.

C#	Date	Good	VG	Fine	VF
39	ND	1.00	1.50	2.50	4.00

DHINGLO

COPPER, 18mm, 12 gm.

C#	Date	Good	VG	Fine	VF
40	ND	1.25	2.00	3.00	4.50

Second Series

Obverse and reverse legends in Persian, Nagari name below obverse.

In the name of Muhammad Akbar II:

NOTE: The fixed date AH1234 on this series is the accession date of Desalji II.

TRAMBIYO

COPPER, 13-14mm, 4 gm.

C#	Date	Year	Good	VG	Fine	VF
41	AH1234	VS1880	2.50	3.50	5.00	7.50

DOKDO

COPPER, 16mm, 8 gm.

C#	Date	Year	Good	VG	Fine	VF
42	AH1234	VS1880	2.50	3.50	5.00	7.00

NOTE: Samvat date on reverse usually off the flan.

DHINGLO (1-1/2 DOKDA)

COPPER, 18mm, 12 gm.

C#	Date	Year	Good	VG	Fine	VF
43	AH1234	VS1880	2.75	4.00	5.50	7.50

1/2 KORI

SILVER, 11-13mm, 2.35 gm.

C#	Date	Year	VG	Fine	VF	XF
52	AH1234	—	3.50	5.50	8.50	12.50

KORI

SILVER, 13-15mm, 4.70 gm.

C#	Date	Year	VG	Fine	VF	XF
53	AH1234	VS1875	3.50	4.00	5.00	7.00
	1234	1876	4.00	4.75	6.00	8.00
	1234	1877	3.50	4.00	5.00	7.00
	1234	1879	4.00	4.75	6.00	8.00
	1234	1880	4.00	4.75	6.00	8.00
	1234	1881	4.00	4.75	6.00	8.00
	1234	1882	3.50	4.00	5.00	7.00
	1234	1884	4.00	4.75	6.00	8.00
	1234	1885	4.00	4.50	5.50	7.50
	1234	1887	4.00	4.50	5.50	7.50

Third Series

Obverse legends in Persian, reverse in Nagari.

In the name of Muhammad Akbar II:

TRAMBIYO

COPPER, 13-15mm, 4 gm.

C#	Date	Good	VG	Fine	VF
45	AH1255-1262	1.00	1.50	2.50	4.00

DOKDO

COPPER, 17-19mm, 8 gm.

C#	Date	Good	VG	Fine	VF
46	AH1259	1.00	1.50	2.50	4.00
	1261	1.00	1.50	2.50	4.00
	1262	1.00	1.50	2.50	4.00

DHINGLO

COPPER, 18-21mm, 12 gm.

C#	Date	Good	VG	Fine	VF
47	AH1255	1.75	3.00	4.00	5.50
	1257	1.25	2.00	3.00	4.50
	1258	1.25	2.00	3.00	4.50
	1259	1.25	2.00	3.00	4.50
	1261	1.25	2.00	3.00	4.50
	1262	1.25	2.00	3.00	4.50
	1266	1.50	2.50	3.50	5.00

1/2 KORI

SILVER, 2.35 gm.
11-13mm. Numerous varieties.

C#	Date	Year	VG	Fine	VF	XF
55	VS1892	(1835)	3.00	5.25	6.50	8.50
55a	AH1252	VS1894	3.25	5.50	7.00	9.00
58	VS1895	(1838)	2.50	4.00	5.00	7.00
58a	AH1262	VS1903	3.00	5.00	6.00	8.00
	1263	1904	3.00	5.00	6.00	8.00

KORI

SILVER, 4.70 gm.
14-16mm. Numerous varieties and subtypes.

C#	Date	Year	VG	Fine	VF	XF
56	AH1250	VS1892	4.50	6.00	8.00	11.50
	1251	1892	4.00	5.00	6.50	8.50
	1252	1893	4.00	5.00	6.50	8.50
56a	1252	1894	4.00	5.00	6.50	8.50
59	—	1895	3.50	4.00	5.00	7.00
	1899	—	4.00	5.00	6.00	7.50
	1901	—	4.00	5.00	6.00	7.50
	1902	—	4.00	5.00	6.00	7.50
59a	AH1262	VS1903	4.00	5.00	6.00	7.50
	1263	1904	Reported, not confirmed			

Fourth Series

In name of Bahadur II.

TRAMBIYO

COPPER, 14mm, 4 gm.

C#	Date	Good	VG	Fine	VF
61	AH1263	1.75	2.75	4.00	5.50
	1266	1.75	2.75	4.00	5.50

C#	Date	Good	VG	Fine	VF
61a	1267	1.00	1.50	2.00	3.50
	1269	1.00	1.50	2.00	3.50
	1274	1.00	1.50	2.00	3.50

NOTE: On this and the next two denominations (C#61-63) dated AH1263 and 1266 are of a somewhat different type.

DOKDO

COPPER, 17-19mm, 8 gm.

C#	Date	Good	VG	Fine	VF
62	AH1263	1.50	2.50	4.00	5.00
	1266	1.50	2.50	4.00	5.00

C#	Date	Good	VG	Fine	VF
62a	1267	1.50	2.50	4.00	5.00
	1269	1.00	1.50	2.00	2.50
	1274	—	Reported, not confirmed		

DHINGLO

COPPER, 18-21mm, 12 gm.

C#	Date	Good	VG	Fine	VF
63	AH1263	2.50	4.00	5.25	6.50
	1266	2.00	3.50	4.50	5.50

C#	Date	Good	VG	Fine	VF
63a	1267	1.25	2.00	2.50	3.00
	1268	1.25	2.00	2.50	3.00
	1269	1.25	2.00	2.50	3.00
	1271	1.75	3.00	3.50	4.00
	1272	1.25	2.00	2.50	3.00
	1274	1.75	3.00	3.50	4.00

1/2 KORI

SILVER, 11mm, 2.35 gm.

C#	Date	Year	VG	Fine	VF	XF
65	VS1909	(1852)	2.00	3.50	4.00	6.00
	1910	(1853)	2.00	3.50	4.00	6.00
	1911	(1854)	3.00	5.00	6.00	8.50
	1912	(1855)	2.00	3.50	4.00	6.00
	1913	(1856)	2.00	3.50	4.00	6.00
	1914	(1857)	2.00	3.50	4.00	6.00

KORI

SILVER, 15mm, 4.70 gm.

C#	Date	Year	VG	Fine	VF	XF
66	VS1909	(1852)	3.50	4.00	5.50	7.50
	1910	(1853)	3.50	4.00	5.50	7.00
	1911	(1854)	4.00	5.00	6.00	8.50
	1912	(1855)	3.50	4.00	5.50	7.00
	1913	(1856)	3.50	4.00	5.50	7.00
	1914	(1857)	3.50	4.00	5.50	7.00
	1915	(1858)	6.50	8.00	11.00	15.00
	1916	(1859)	8.00	10.00	13.50	17.50

25 KORI

.999 GOLD, 16mm, 4.67 gm.

C#	Date	Year	Fine	VF	XF	Unc
67	VS1912	(1855)	110.00	120.00	130.00	150.00
	1913	(1856)	110.00	120.00	130.00	150.00
	1914	(1857)	110.00	120.00	130.00	150.00
	1915	(1858)	110.00	120.00	130.00	150.00

Pragmalji II

AD 1860-1875

MACHINE-STRUCK COINAGE

TRAMBIYO

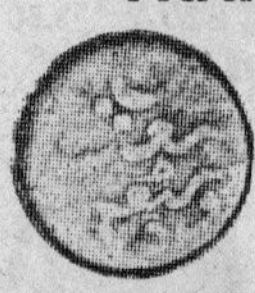

COPPER, 4 gm.

Y#	Date	Good	VG	Fine	VF
1	1865	1.25	2.00	3.00	4.50

2 letters right of trident

Y#	Date	Good	VG	Fine	VF
5	1865	.50	.85	1.50	2.50
	1866	1.50	2.50	3.50	5.00

No letters right of trident

Y#	Date	Good	VG	Fine	VF
5.1	1865	.75	1.25	1.75	2.50
	1866	.50	.85	1.50	2.50
	1867	1.25	2.00	3.00	4.50
	1767 (error)	.50	.85	1.50	2.50
	1868	.50	.85	1.50	2.50

Obv: 'Victoria' at bottom of legend.

Y#	Date	Year	Good	VG	Fine	VF
9	1869	VS1925	1.00	1.50	2.50	3.75
	1869	1926	1.50	2.50	3.50	4.50

Obv: 'Victoria' at top of legend.

Y#	Date	Year	Good	VG	Fine	VF
9.1	1869	VS1926	.50	1.00	2.00	3.00
	1873	1930	Reported, not confirmed			

DOKDO

COPPER, 8 gm.

Y#	Date	Good	VG	Fine	VF
6	1865	1.25	2.00	2.50	3.50
	1866	1.00	1.75	2.25	3.00
	1867	.90	1.50	1.75	2.50
	1868	.60	1.00	1.50	2.75
	1869 (retrograde 9)	1.50	2.50	3.75	5.00

Obv: 'Victoria' at top.

Y#	Date	Year	Good	VG	Fine	VF
10	1869	VS1925	1.25	2.00	3.00	4.50

Obv: 'Victoria' at bottom.

Y#	Date	Year	Good	VG	Fine	VF
10.1	1869	VS1925	.60	1.00	1.50	2.50
	1869	1926	1.00	1.50	2.00	3.00
	1869	1927	1.50	2.50	3.50	5.00

Obv: 'Victoria' right.

Y#	Date	Year	Good	VG	Fine	VF
10.2	1873	VS1930	1.00	1.50	2.00	3.00
	1874	1930	.60	1.00	1.50	2.50

1-1/2 DOKDA

COPPER, 12 gm.
Obv: 'Victoria' at top.

Y#	Date	Year	Good	VG	Fine	VF
11	1869	VS1925	— Reported, not confirmed			
	1869	1926	.75	1.25	1.75	2.25
	1780	1925 (error)				
			1.75	3.00	3.50	4.25
			.90	1.50	2.00	2.50
	1780	1926 (error)				
	1870	1927	.60	1.00	1.50	2.00
	1870	1928	.60	1.00	1.50	2.00
	1780	1928 (error)				
			.75	1.25	1.75	2.25
	1871	1928	.60	1.00	1.50	2.00
	1872	1928	.75	1.25	1.75	2.25

Obv: 'Victoria' to right.

Y#	Date	Year	Good	VG	Fine	VF
11.1	1871	VS1928	.90	1.50	2.00	2.50
	1872	1928	.90	1.50	2.00	2.50
	1872	1929	.75	1.25	1.75	2.25
	1873	1929	.60	1.00	1.50	2.25
	1879	1929 (error)				
			.75	1.25	1.75	2.25
	1873	1930	.60	1.00	1.50	2.25
	1783	1930 (error)				
			.75	1.25	1.75	2.50
	1874	1930	.60	1.00	1.50	2.00
	1874	1931	.60	1.00	1.50	2.00
	1874	1932	1.25	2.00	2.75	3.50
	1875	1931	.75	1.25	1.75	2.25
	1875	1932	.75	1.25	1.75	2.25

Obv: 'Victoria' to left.

Y#	Date	Year	Good	VG	Fine	VF
11.2	1872	VS1928	1.50	2.50	3.75	5.00
	1872	1929	1.50	2.50	3.75	5.00

3 DOKDA

COPPER, 24 gm.

Y#	Date	Year	Good	VG	Fine	VF
8	1868	VS1925	1.50	2.50	3.00	4.00

NOTE: Two varieties, based on position of reverse marginal legend.

Y#	Date	Year	Good	VG	Fine	VF
12	1868	VS1925	2.50	4.00	5.50	6.50
	1869	1925	2.00	3.50	4.50	5.75
	1869	1926	2.00	3.50	4.50	5.75

1/2 KORI

.610 SILVER, 2.35 gm.

Y#	Date	Year	VG	Fine	VF	XF
13	1862	VS1919	1.50	2.50	3.50	5.00
	1862	1920	1.25	2.00	2.50	3.50
	1863	1920	1.50	2.50	3.00	5.00
	1763	1920 (error)				
			2.00	3.50	4.50	5.50
	1863	1921	1.25	2.00	2.50	3.50

KORI

.610 SILVER, 4.70 gm.

Y#	Date	Year	VG	Fine	VF	XF
14	1862	VS1918	2.75	3.50	4.00	5.50
	1862	1919	3.00	3.75	5.00	6.50
	1862	1920	2.50	3.00	3.50	5.00
	1863	1920	2.75	3.50	4.00	5.50
	1863	1921	2.50	3.00	3.50	5.00

2-1/2 KORI

.937 SILVER, 6.93 gm.

Y#	Date	Year	VG	Fine	VF	XF
15	1875	VS1931	6.50	7.50	8.50	11.50
	1785	1931	7.50	10.00	12.50	16.00
	1875	1932	6.50	7.50	8.50	11.50

5 KORI

.937 SILVER, 13.87 gm.

Y#	Date	Year	VG	Fine	VF	XF
16	1863	VS1921	20.00	35.00	40.00	55.00

Obv: Inscriptions rearranged.

Y#	Date	Year	VG	Fine	VF	XF
16.1	1865	VS1921	13.50	16.50	20.00	27.50
	1865	1922	12.50	15.00	18.50	25.00
	1866	1922	12.00	13.50	15.00	18.50
	1866	1923	12.00	13.50	15.00	18.50
	1870	1927	12.50	14.50	17.50	22.50
	1874	1931	12.00	13.00	14.50	17.50
	1875	1931	12.00	13.00	14.50	17.50
	1875	1932	12.00	13.00	14.50	17.50

25 KORI

.999 GOLD, 4.67 gm.

Y#	Date	Year	Fine	VF	XF	Unc
17	1862	VS1919	110.00	120.00	130.00	150.00
	1863	1920	110.00	120.00	130.00	150.00
	1863	1921	110.00	120.00	130.00	150.00

Y#	Date	Year	Fine	VF	XF	Unc
17a	1870	VS1926	110.00	120.00	130.00	150.00
	1870	1927	110.00	120.00	130.00	150.00

50 KORI

.906 GOLD, 9.35 gm.

Y#	Date	Year	Fine	VF	XF	Unc
18	1866	VS1923	165.00	185.00	210.00	250.00
	1873	1930	165.00	185.00	210.00	250.00
	1874	1930	165.00	185.00	210.00	250.00
	1874	1931	165.00	185.00	210.00	250.00

100 KORI

.937 GOLD, 18.70 gm.

Y#	Date	Year	Fine	VF	XF	Unc
19	1866	VS1922	375.00	400.00	435.00	500.00
	1866	1923	375.00	400.00	435.00	500.00

Khengarji III

AD 1875-1942

First Series

'QUEEN VICTORIA MIGHTY QUEEN'

DOKDO

COPPER, 20mm, 8 gm.

Y#	Date	Year	Good	VG	Fine	VF
22	1878	VS1934	10.00	17.50	20.00	25.00
	1878	1935	13.50	22.50	25.00	30.00
	(1)878	1935	15.00	25.00	27.50	32.50

1-1/2 DOKDA

COPPER, 23-24mm, 12 gm.

Y#	Date	Year	Good	VG	Fine	VF
23	1876	VS1933	.90	1.50	2.00	2.50
	1877	1933	.90	1.50	2.00	2.50
	1877	1934	.90	1.50	2.00	2.50
	1877	1922	(error)			
			.90	1.50	2.00	2.50
	1878	1934	.90	1.50	2.00	2.50
	1878	1935	1.25	2.00	2.50	3.00
	1879	—	Reported, not confirmed			

Obv: Similar to 1 1/2 Dokda, Y#11.

Y#	Date	Year	Good	VG	Fine	VF
23.1	1876	VS1933	1.25	2.00	2.50	3.50

KORI

.610 SILVER, 16mm, 4.70 gm.

Y#	Date	Year	VG	Fine	VF	XF
26	1876	VS1932	60.00	100.00	125.00	150.00
	1876	1933	60.00	100.00	125.00	150.00

5 KORI

.937 SILVER, 13.87 gm.

Y#	Date	Year	VG	Fine	VF	XF
28	1876	VS1933	20.00	30.00	40.00	50.00

Second Series

'VICTORIA EMPRESS OF INDIA'

TRAMBIYO

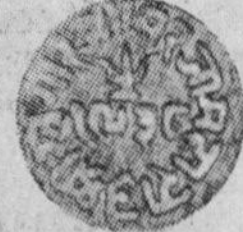

COPPER, 4 gm.

Y#	Date	Year	Good	VG	Fine	VF
30	1881	VS1938	.50	.75	1.00	1.50
	1882	1938	.30	.50	.75	1.25
	1883	1939	.30	.50	.75	1.25
	1883	1940	.50	.75	1.00	1.50

Rev: 'KUTCH' added below Vikrama date.

Y#	Date	Year	Good	VG	Fine	VF
30.1	1883	VS1940	.50	.75	1.00	1.50

DOKDO

COPPER, 8 gm.

Y#	Date	Year	Good	VG	Fine	VF
31	1882	VS1938	.50	.75	1.00	1.50
	1882	1939	.90	1.50	2.00	2.50
	1883	1939	.50	.75	1.00	1.50

Rev: 'KUTCH' added below Vikrama date.

Y#	Date	Year	Good	VG	Fine	VF
31.1	1883	VS1940	.50	.75	1.00	1.50
	1884	1940	.50	.75	1.00	1.50

Note spacing of obverse legend.

Y#	Date	Year	Good	VG	Fine	VF
31.2	1892	VS1948	2.50	4.00	6.00	8.50

Slight change in Urdu legend

Y#	Date	Year	Good	VG	Fine	VF
31.3	1899	VS1956	.90	1.50	2.00	3.00

1-1/2 DOKDA

COPPER, 12 gm.

Y#	Date	Year	Good	VG	Fine	VF
32	1882	VS1938	.60	1.00	1.25	1.75
	1882	1939	.60	1.00	1.25	1.75
	1883	1939	.60	1.00	1.25	1.75
	1883	1940	.60	1.00	1.25	1.75

Rev: 'KUTCH' added below Vikrama date.

Y#	Date	Year	Good	VG	Fine	VF
32.1	1883	VS1940	.60	1.00	1.25	1.75
	1884	1940	.60	1.00	1.25	1.75
	1884	1941	.60	1.00	1.25	1.75

Finer style

Y#	Date	Year	Good	VG	Fine	VF
32.2	1885	VS1942	.75	1.25	1.50	2.00
	1887	1944	.75	1.25	1.50	2.00
	1888	1944	.75	1.25	1.50	2.00

Y#	Date	Year	Good	VG	Fine	VF
32.3	1892	1948	.75	1.25	1.50	2.00
	1894	1950	.75	1.25	1.50	2.00

Y#	Date	Year	Good	VG	Fine	VF
32.4	1899	VS1955	1.25	2.00	2.50	3.00
	1899	1956	1.25	2.00	2.75	3.50

3 DOKDA

COPPER, 24 gm.

Y#	Date	Year	Good	VG	Fine	VF
33	1883	VS1940	1.25	2.00	2.50	3.00
	1885	1942	.90	1.50	2.00	2.50
	1886	1942	1.35	2.25	3.00	4.00
	1887	1944	.90	1.50	2.00	2.50
	1888	1944	1.25	2.00	2.50	3.00

Rev: Similar to 3 Dokda, Y#33.1.

Y#	Date	Year	Good	VG	Fine	VF
33.1	1894	VS1951	1.50	2.50	3.00	3.50
	1899	1955	1.50	2.50	3.00	3.50

1/2 KORI

.610 SILVER, 2.35 gm.

Y#	Date	Year	VG	Fine	VF	XF
34	1898	VS1954	1.75	3.00	4.00	5.50
	1899	1955	1.75	3.00	4.00	5.50
	1899	1956	1.75	3.00	4.00	5.50
	1900	1956	1.75	3.00	4.00	5.50
	1900	1957	2.50	4.00	5.00	6.50

KORI

.610 SILVER, 4.70 gm.
Rev: Closed crescent.

Y#	Date	Year	VG	Fine	VF	XF
35	1881	VS1938	3.00	3.50	4.25	5.50
	1882	1938	3.00	3.50	4.25	5.50
	1882	1939	2.75	3.25	4.00	5.00
	1883	1939	2.75	3.25	4.00	5.00
	1883	1940	2.75	3.25	4.00	5.00
	1884	1941	3.00	3.50	4.25	5.50
	1885	1941	2.75	3.00	3.50	5.00

Rev: Open crescent.

Y#	Date	Year	VG	Fine	VF	XF
35.1	1894	VS1950	2.75	3.00	3.50	5.00
	1896	1952	2.75	3.00	3.50	5.00
	1897	1953	2.75	3.00	3.50	4.50
	1897	1954	2.75	3.00	3.50	4.50
	1898	1954	2.75	3.00	3.50	4.50
	1898	1955	2.75	3.00	3.50	4.50
	1899	1955	2.75	3.00	3.50	4.50
	1899	1956	2.75	3.00	3.50	4.50
	1900	1956	2.75	3.00	3.50	4.50
	1900	1957	2.75	3.00	3.50	4.50
	1901	1957	2.75	4.00	5.50	7.00

2-1/2 KORI

.937 SILVER, 6.93 gm.
Rev: Closed crescent.

Y#	Date	Year	VG	Fine	VF	XF
36	1881	VS1938	6.50	7.50	9.00	12.50
	1882	1938	6.50	7.50	8.50	11.50

Rev: Open crescent.

Y#	Date	Year	VG	Fine	VF	XF
36.1	1894	VS1951	6.50	7.50	8.50	12.00
	1895	1951	6.50	7.50	8.50	11.50
	1897	1953	6.50	7.50	8.50	11.50
	1897	1954	6.50	7.50	8.50	11.50
	1898	1954	6.50	7.50	8.50	12.00
	1898	1955	6.50	7.50	8.50	12.00
	1899	1955	6.50	7.50	8.50	12.00

Y#	Date	Year	VG	Fine	VF	XF
36.2	1899	VS1955	6.50	7.50	8.50	12.00
	1899	1956	6.50	7.50	8.50	11.50

5 KORI

.937 SILVER, 13.87 gm.
Obv: Leaves of wreath point counter-clockwise

Y#	Date	Year	VG	Fine	VF	XF
37	1880	VS1937	12.00	13.00	16.00	20.00
	1881	1937	12.00	13.00	14.50	17.50
	1881	1938	12.00	13.00	14.50	17.50

Obv: Leaves of wreath point clockwise

Y#	Date	Year	VG	Fine	VF	XF
37.1	1881	VS1937	12.00	13.00	14.50	17.50
	1881	1938	12.00	13.00	14.50	17.50

Obv: Similar to Y#37.2.
Rev: Stops (bars) to left and right of center legend.

Y#	Date	Year	VG	Fine	VF	XF
37.2	1881	VS1937	12.00	13.00	14.50	17.50

Obv: Similar to Y#37.1. Rev: Similar to Y#37.3

Y#	Date	Year	VG	Fine	VF	XF
37.3	1880	VS1937	12.00	13.00	14.50	18.50

Obv: Changed wreath. Rev: Closed crescent.

Y#	Date	Year	VG	Fine	VF	XF
37.4	1881	VS1938	12.00	13.00	14.50	17.50
	1882	1938	12.00	13.00	14.50	17.50
	1882	1939	12.00	13.00	14.50	17.50
	1883	1939	12.00	13.00	14.50	17.50
	1883	1940	12.00	13.00	14.50	17.50
	1884	1940	12.00	13.00	14.50	17.50
	1884	1941	12.00	13.00	14.50	17.50
	1885	1941	12.00	13.00	14.50	17.50
	1885	1942	12.00	20.00	30.00	40.00
	1886	1943	12.00	20.00	30.00	40.00

Rev: Open Crescent

Y#	Date	Year	VG	Fine	VF	XF
37.5	1890	VS1947	12.00	17.50	25.00	37.50
	1893	1950	12.00	17.50	22.50	30.00
	1894	1950	12.00	13.00	14.50	17.50
	1894	1951	12.00	13.00	14.50	17.50
	1895	1951	12.00	13.00	14.50	17.50
	1895	1952	12.00	13.00	14.50	17.50
	1896	1952	12.00	13.00	14.50	18.50
	1896	1953	12.00	13.00	14.50	17.50
	1896	1954	(error)			
			12.50	20.00	27.50	35.00
	1897	1951	(error)			
			12.00	13.50	16.50	22.50
	1897	1953	12.00	13.00	14.50	17.50
	1897	1954	12.00	13.00	14.50	17.50
	1897	1957	(error)	Reported, not confirmed		
	1898	1954	12.00	13.00	14.50	17.50
	1898	1955	12.00	13.00	14.50	17.50
	1899	1955	12.00	13.50	15.00	20.00

Y#	Date	Year	VG	Fine	VF	XF
37.6	1899	VS1955	12.00	13.00	14.50	17.50
	1899	1956	12.00	13.00	14.50	17.50
	1901	1957	18.50	27.50	35.00	45.00

Third Series

In the name of Edward VII

TRAMBIYO

COPPER, 4 gm.

Y#	Date	Year	VG	Fine	VF	XF
38	1908	VS1965	1.50	2.50	3.50	4.50
	1909	1965	.60	1.00	1.50	2.50
	1909	1966	.60	1.00	1.50	2.00
	1910	1966	1.60	2.75	4.25	6.00

DOKDO

COPPER, 8 gm.

Y#	Date	Year	VG	Fine	VF	XF
39	1909	VS1965	.75	1.25	1.50	2.00
	1909	1966	.75	1.25	1.50	2.00

1-1/2 DOKDA

COPPER, 23mm, 12 gm.

Y#	Date	Year	VG	Fine	VF	XF
40	1909	VS1965	60.00	100.00	115.00	150.00

3 DOKDA

COPPER

Y#	Date	Year	VG	Fine	VF	XF
41	1909	VS1965	60.00	100.00	115.00	150.00

5 KORI

.937 SILVER, 13.87 gm.

Y#	Date	Year	VG	Fine	VF	XF
45	1902	VS1959	80.00	130.00	170.00	225.00
	1903	1960	80.00	130.00	170.00	225.00
	1904	1961	80.00	130.00	170.00	225.00
	1905	1962	80.00	130.00	170.00	225.00
	1906	1963	80.00	130.00	170.00	225.00
	1907	1964	80.00	130.00	170.00	225.00
	1908	1965	65.00	115.00	150.00	225.00
	1909	1966	65.00	115.00	150.00	225.00

Fourth Series

In the name of George V

TRAMBIYO

COPPER, 4 gm.

Y#	Date	Year	VG	Fine	VF	XF
46	1919	VS1976	.30	.50	.75	1.00
	1920	1976	.30	.50	.75	1.50
	1920	1977	.30	.50	.75	1.50

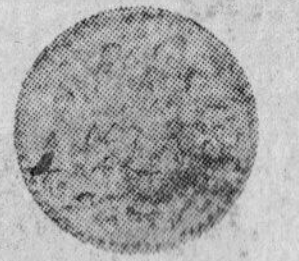

Y#	Date	Year	VG	Fine	VF	XF
54	1928	VS1984	.60	1.00	2.00	3.00
	1928	1985	.30	.50	.75	1.00

DOKDO

COPPER, 8 gm.

Y#	Date	Year	VG	Fine	VF	XF
47	1920	VS1976	.60	1.00	1.25	2.00
	1920	1977	.60	1.00	1.25	2.00

Y#	Date	Year	VG	Fine	VF	XF
55	1922	VS1982 (error)	1.25	1.75	2.50	3.50
	1928	1984	.60	1.00	1.25	1.50
	1929	1985	.60	1.00	1.25	1.50

1-1/2 DOKDA

COPPER, 12 gm.

Y#	Date	Year	VG	Fine	VF	XF
48	1926	VS1982	.90	1.50	2.50	3.00

Y#	Date	Year	VG	Fine	VF	XF
56	1928	VS1985	.50	.75	1.00	1.50
	1929	1985	.50	.75	1.00	1.50
	1929	1986	.50	.75	1.00	1.50
	1931	1987	.50	.75	1.00	1.50
	1931	1988	.50	.75	1.00	1.50
	1932	1988	1.00	1.50	2.50	4.00
	1932	1989	.50	.75	1.00	1.50

3 DOKDA

COPPER, 24 gm.

Y#	Date	Year	VG	Fine	VF	XF
49	1926	VS1982	1.50	2.50	3.50	4.50

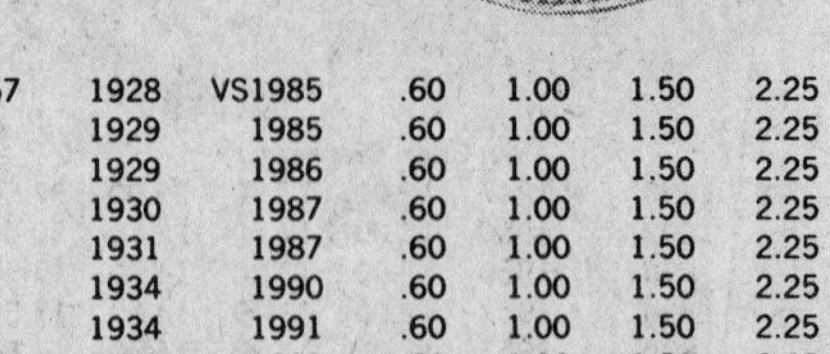

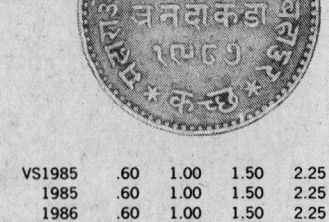

Y#	Date	Year	VG	Fine	VF	XF
57	1928	VS1985	.60	1.00	1.50	2.25
	1929	1985	.60	1.00	1.50	2.25
	1929	1986	.60	1.00	1.50	2.25
	1930	1987	.60	1.00	1.50	2.25
	1931	1987	.60	1.00	1.50	2.25
	1934	1990	.60	1.00	1.50	2.25
	1934	1991	.60	1.00	1.50	2.25
	1935	1992	.60	1.00	1.50	2.25

1/2 KORI

.601 SILVER, 2.35 gm.

Y#	Date	Year	VG	Fine	VF	XF
58	1928	VS1985	1.75	2.00	2.25	3.00

KORI

.601 SILVER, 4.70 gm.

Y#	Date	Year	Fine	VF	XF	Unc
51	1913	VS1970	2.25	2.00	2.50	3.50
	1923	1979	2.25	2.00	2.50	3.50
	1923	1980	2.25	2.00	2.50	3.50
	1927	1984	2.50	2.50	3.50	4.50
	1927	1985	Reported, not confirmed			

Y#	Date	Year	Fine	VF	XF	Unc
59	1928	VS1985	2.25	2.50	3.00	4.00
	1929	1985	2.25	2.50	3.00	4.00
	1931	1987	7.50	12.50	14.50	20.00
	1931	1988	2.25	2.50	3.00	4.00
	1932	1988	2.25	2.50	3.00	4.00
	1932	1989	2.25	2.50	3.00	4.00
	1933	1989	2.25	2.50	3.00	4.00
	1933	1990	2.25	2.50	3.00	4.00
	1934	1990	2.25	2.50	3.00	4.00
	1934	1991	2.25	2.50	3.00	4.00
	1935	1991	2.25	2.50	3.00	4.00
	1935	1992	2.25	2.50	3.00	4.00
	1936	1992	2.50	3.00	4.50	5.50

2-1/2 KORI

.937 SILVER, 6.93 gm.

Y#	Date	Year	Fine	VF	XF	Unc
52	1916	VS1973	6.50	7.00	8.00	10.00
	1917	1973	6.50	7.00	8.00	10.00
	1917	1974	6.50	7.00	8.00	10.00
	1918	1974	6.50	7.00	8.00	10.00
	1919	1975	6.50	7.00	8.00	10.00
	1922	1978	6.50	7.00	8.00	10.00
	1922	1979	6.50	7.00	8.00	10.00
	1924	1981	6.50	7.00	8.00	10.00
	1926	1983	6.50	7.00	8.00	10.00

Rev: Small lettering.

Y#	Date	Year	Fine	VF	XF	Unc
52a	1927	VS1984	6.50	7.50	9.00	12.50
	1928	1985	6.00	7.00	8.00	10.00
	1930	1986	6.00	7.00	8.00	10.00
	1930	1987	6.00	7.00	8.00	10.00
	1932	1988	6.00	7.00	8.00	10.00
	1932	1989	6.00	7.00	8.00	10.00
	1933	1989	6.00	7.00	8.00	10.00
	1933	1990	6.00	7.00	8.00	10.00
	1934	1990	6.00	7.00	8.00	10.00
	1934	1991	6.00	7.00	8.00	10.00
	1935	1991	6.00	7.00	8.00	10.00
	1935	1992	6.00	7.00	8.00	10.00

5 KORI

.937 SILVER, 13.87 gm.

Y#	Date	Year	Fine	VF	XF	Unc
53	1913	VS1970	12.00	13.50	15.00	18.50
	1915	1972	12.00	13.50	15.00	18.50
	1916	1973	12.00	13.00	14.50	17.50
	1917	1973	12.00	13.00	14.50	17.50
	1917	1974	12.00	13.00	14.50	17.50
	1918	1974	12.00	13.00	14.50	17.50
	1918	1975	12.00	13.00	14.50	17.50
	1919	1975	12.00	13.00	14.50	17.50
	1919	1976	25.00	40.00	50.00	60.00
	1920	1977	12.00	13.50	15.00	18.50
	1921	1977	12.00	13.00	14.50	17.50
	1921	1978	12.00	13.00	14.50	17.50
	1922	1978	12.00	13.00	14.50	17.50
	1922	1979	12.00	13.00	14.50	17.50
	1922	1982	(error)			
			10.00	13.50	16.50	20.00
	1923	1979	12.00	13.00	14.50	17.50
	1924	1978	(error)			
			17.50	30.00	40.00	50.00
	1924	1980	12.00	13.00	14.50	17.50
	1924	1981	12.00	13.00	14.50	17.50
	1925	1982	12.00	13.00	14.50	17.50
	1926	1982	12.00	13.00	14.50	17.50
	1926	1983	12.00	13.00	14.50	17.50
	1927	1984	15.00	27.50	35.00	45.00

Y#	Date	Year	Fine	VF	XF	Unc
53a	1928	VS1985	13.50	20.00	30.00	40.00
	1929	1986	12.00	13.00	14.50	18.50
	1930	1986	12.00	13.00	14.50	17.50
	1930	1987	12.00	13.00	14.50	17.50
	1931	1987	12.00	13.00	14.50	17.50
	1931	1988	12.00	13.00	14.50	17.50
	1932	1988	12.00	13.00	14.50	17.50
	1932	1989	12.00	13.00	14.50	17.50
	1933	1989	12.00	13.00	14.50	17.50
	1933	1990	12.00	13.00	14.50	17.50
	1934	1990	12.00	13.00	14.50	17.50
	1934	1991	12.00	13.00	14.50	17.50
	1935	1991	12.00	13.00	14.50	17.50
	1935	1992	12.00	13.00	14.50	17.50
	1936	1992	12.00	13.00	14.50	18.50

Fifth Series

In the name of Edward VIII

3 DOKDA

COPPER, 24 gm.

Y#	Date	Year	VG	Fine	VF	XF
63	1936	VS1993	3.00	5.00	7.50	10.00

KORI

.601 SILVER, 4.7 gm.

Y#	Date	Year	Fine	VF	XF	Unc
65	1936	VS1992	2.75	3.00	3.50	4.00
	1936	1993	2.75	3.00	3.25	4.50

2-1/2 KORI

.937 SILVER, 6.93 gm.

Y#	Date	Year	Fine	VF	XF	Unc
66	1936	VS1992	10.00	17.50	22.50	28.50
	1936	1993	10.00	17.50	22.50	28.50

5 KORI

.937 SILVER, 13.87 gm.

Y#	Date	Year	Fine	VF	XF	Unc
67	1936	VS1992	7.00	8.00	9.00	11.00
	1936	1993	7.00	8.00	9.00	11.00

Sixth Series

In the name of George VI

3 DOKDA

COPPER, 24 gm.

Y#	Date	Year	VG	Fine	VF	XF
71	1937	VS1993	.90	1.50	2.00	3.00

KORI

.601 SILVER, 4.70 gm.

Y#	Date	Year	Fine	VF	XF	Unc
73	1937	VS1993	2.75	3.00	3.50	4.00
	1937	1994	2.75	3.00	3.50	4.00
	1938	1995	2.75	3.00	3.50	4.00
	1939	1995	2.75	3.00	3.50	4.00
	1939	1996	2.75	3.00	3.50	4.00
	1940	1996	2.75	3.00	3.50	4.00

2-1/2 KORI

.937 SILVER, 6.93 gm.

Y#	Date	Year	Fine	VF	XF	Unc
74	1937	VS1993	6.50	7.00	8.00	10.00

5 KORI

.937 SILVER, 13.87 gm.

Y#	Date	Year	Fine	VF	XF	Unc
75	1936	VS1993	12.00	13.00	14.50	18.50
	1937	1993	12.00	13.00	14.50	17.50
	1937	1994	12.00	13.00	14.50	17.50
	1938	1994	12.00	13.00	14.50	17.50
	1938	1995	12.00	13.00	14.50	17.50
	1941	1998	12.00	13.00	14.50	17.50

Vijayarajji

AD 1942-1947

In the name of George VI:

TRAMBIYO

COPPER

Y#	Date	Year	VG	Fine	VF	XF
76	1943	VS2000	.25	.50	1.00	1.50
	1944	2000	.25	.50	1.00	1.50

DHINGLO

(1/16 Kori = 1-1/2 Dokda)

COPPER

Y#	Date	Year	VG	Fine	VF	XF
77	1943	VS2000	.20	.35	.60	1.00

Y#	Date	Year	Fine	VF	XF	Unc
77	1944	2000	.20	.35	.60	1.00
	1947	2004	.20	.35	.60	1.00

DHABU
(1/8 Kori = 3 Dokda)

COPPER

Y#	Date	Year	Fine	VF	XF	Unc
78	1943	VS1999	.25	.40	.60	1.00
	1943	2000	.25	.40	.60	1.00
	1944	2000	.25	.40	.60	1.00

PATHALO
(1/4 Kori)

COPPER

Y#	Date	Year	Fine	VF	XF	Unc
79	1943	VS1999	.75	1.00	1.50	2.50
	1943	2000	.75	1.00	1.50	2.50
	1944	2000	.75	1.00	1.50	2.50
	1944	2001	.75	1.00	1.50	2.50
	1945	2001	.35	.50	.75	1.25
	1945	2002	.35	.50	.75	1.25
	1946	2002	.35	.50	.75	1.25
	1946	2003	.35	.50	.75	1.25
	1947	2003	.75	1.00	1.50	2.50

ADHIO
(1/2 Kori)

COPPER

Y#	Date	Year	Fine	VF	XF	Unc
80	1943	VS1999	1.50	1.75	2.00	3.50
	1943	2000	1.50	1.75	2.00	3.50
	1944	2001	1.25	1.50	1.75	3.00
	1945	2001	1.50	1.75	2.00	3.50
	1945	2002	1.50	1.75	2.00	3.50
	1946	2002	1.50	1.75	2.00	3.50

KORI

.601 SILVER, 4.70 gm.

Y#	Date	Year	Fine	VF	XF	Unc
81	1942	VS1999	2.75	3.00	3.50	4.00
	1943	1999	2.75	3.00	3.50	4.00
	1943	2000	2.75	3.00	3.50	4.00
	1944	2000	2.75	3.00	3.50	4.00
	1944	2001	2.75	3.00	3.50	4.00

5 KORI

.937 SILVER, 13.87 gm.

Y#	Date	Year	Fine	VF	XF	Unc
82	1942	VS1998	12.00	13.00	14.50	17.50
	1942	1999	12.00	13.00	14.50	17.50
	1943	1998	Reported, not confirmed			

Madanasinghji
AD 1947-1948

DHABU
(1/8 Kori)

COPPER

Y#	Date	Year	Fine	VF	XF	Unc
83	VS2004	(1947)	.75	1.25	1.75	3.00

KORI

.601 SILVER, 4.70 gm.

Y#	Date	Year	Fine	VF	XF	Unc
84	VS2004	(1947)	4.00	6.50	8.50	11.50

5 KORI

.937 SILVER, 13.87 gm.

Y#	Date	Year	Fine	VF	XF	Unc
85	VS2004	(1947)	75.00	125.00	175.00	200.00

NCLT ISSUES

PRESENTATION ISSUES

In the last years of its coinage history, Kutch struck some non-circulating coins which stated denomination. At least one was a pattern which wasn't approved for circulation strikes and the others were probably presentation pieces.

Issues of Khengarji III
Vs1932-1999/1875-1942AD

5 KORI

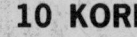

SILVER, 32mm
Obv: Small portrait.

KM#	Date	Year	Mintage	VF	XF	Unc
1	VS1985	1929	—	—	Rare	—

Obv: Large portrait.

KM#	Date	Year	Mintage	VF	XF	Unc
2	VS1985	1929	—	—	Rare	—

31mm
Similar to 10 Kori, KM#5.

KM#	Date	Year	Mintage	VF	XF	Unc
3	1942	VS1998	—	—	Rare	—

10 KORI

SILVER

KM#	Date	Year	Mintage	VF	XF	Unc
4	1941	VS1998	—	—	Rare	—

(Also struck in gold)

KM#	Date	Year	Mintage	VF	XF	Unc
5	1942	VS1998	—	—	Rare	—

GOLD (OMS)

KM#	Date	Year	Mintage	VF	XF	Unc
5a	1942	VS1998	—	—	Rare	—

Issues of Madanasinghji, 1947-1948

KORI

GOLD
Similar to Silver 1 Kori, Y#84.

KM#	Date	Year	Mintage	VF	XF	Unc
6	VS2004	(1947)	—	—	Rare	—

MOHUR

GOLD, 31mm

KM#	Date	Year	Mintage	VF	XF	Unc
7	VS2004	(1947)	—	—	—	—

LUNAVADA

Weight standard: 1 paisa = 7-8 gm.

Wakhat Singhji

VS1924-1986/1867-1929

1/2 PAISA

COPPER, rectangular or round
Obv: Open hand.
Rev: Mughal style Persian inscription.

Y#	Date	Year	Good	VG	Fine	VF
A4	ND	—	2.75	4.50	6.00	8.00

Obv: Open hand in square, "LUNAVADA" around clockwise. Rev: Date & inscription.

Y#	Date	Year	Good	VG	Fine	VF
7	VS1942	(1885)	3.00	5.00	7.50	10.00

Obv: Lion and "LUNAVADA" and date.
Rev: Inscriptions including ruler's name.

Y#	Date	Year	Good	VG	Fine	VF
5	VS1949	(1892)	2.75	4.50	6.00	8.50

PAISA

COPPER, round or rectangular
Obv: Two sabres

Y#	Date	Year	Good	VG	Fine	VF
1	ND	—	3.50	6.00	8.50	12.00

Obv: Cannon barrel

Y#	Date	Year	Good	VG	Fine	VF
2	ND	—	3.50	6.00	8.50	12.00

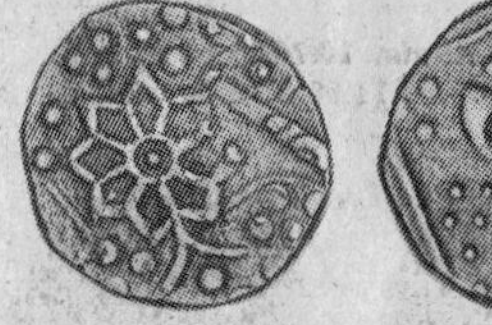

Obv: Lotus blossom. Rev: Persian inscription.

Y#	Date	Year	Good	VG	Fine	VF
3	ND	—	2.50	4.00	5.50	8.00

Open hand, similar to 1/2 Paisa, Y#A4.

Y#	Date	Year	Good	VG	Fine	VF
4	ND	—	2.50	4.00	5.50	8.00

Open hand in square, similar to 1/2 Paisa, Y#7.

Y#	Date	Year	Good	VG	Fine	VF
8	VS1942	(1885)	2.50	4.00	5.50	8.00
	1249 (error)		2.50	4.00	5.50	8.00

Lion, similar to 1/2 Paisa, Y#5.

Y#	Date	Year	Good	VG	Fine	VF
6	VS1949	(1892)	2.50	4.00	5.50	8.00

NOTE: Coins of Lunavada are frequently found counterstruck over earlier types, and over types of Rampur.

RAMPUR

The following pieces may be from Lunavada or from neighboring Rampur. They are often found c/s on coins of Lunavada, and other states, including Sailana.

PAISA

COPPER, 7-8 gm.
Obv: Spears. Rev: Spears.

KM#	Date	Year	Good	VG	Fine	VF
1	ND	—	2.50	4.00	5.50	8.00

Round or square.
Obv: Spears. Rev: 'Rampar'.

KM#	Date	Year	Good	VG	Fine	VF
2	ND	—	2.50	4.00	5.50	8.00

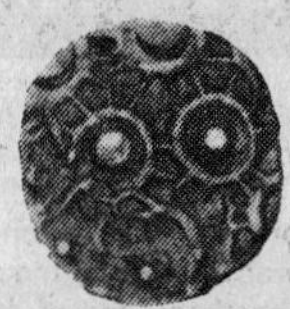

Round or square
Obv: Solar symbols. Rev: 'Rampar'.

KM#	Date	Year	Good	VG	Fine	VF
3	ND	—	2.50	4.00	5.50	8.00

MAKRAI

Raja Bharat Shah

AD 1866-1920

PAISA

COPPER, 18-23mm

KM#	Date	Year	Good	VG	Fine	VF
1	ND	—	2.50	4.00	5.50	7.00

MANIPUR

Gaura Singh

Saka 1678-1686/1756-1764

NAZARANA RUPEE

SILVER, 20x20mm, 10.70-11.60 gm.

C#	Date	Year	VG	Fine	VF	XF
23	SE1678	(1756)	50.00	75.00	100.00	—

1/4 MOHUR

GOLD, 13x13mm, 2.68-2.85 gm.

C#	Date	Year	VG	Fine	VF	XF
27	ND	—	135.00	165.00	200.00	250.00

1/2 MOHUR

GOLD, 17x17mm, 5.35-5.70 gm.

C#	Date	Year	VG	Fine	VF	XF
28	SE1684	(1762)	150.00	180.00	225.00	275.00

MOHUR

GOLD, 18mm, 10.70-11.40 gm.

C#	Date	Year	VG	Fine	VF	XF
29	SE1678	(1756)	235.00	265.00	300.00	350.00
	1684	(1762)	235.00	265.00	300.00	350.00

Jai Singh

Saka 1686-1720/1764-1798

1/2 RUPEE

SILVER, 18mm, 5.35-5.80 gm.

C#	Date	Year	VG	Fine	VF	XF
32	ND	—	45.00	60.00	90.00	125.00

MOHUR

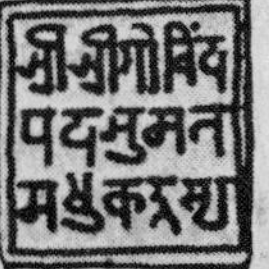

GOLD, 10.70-11.40 gm.

C#	Date	Year	VG	Fine	VF	XF
36	SE1694	(1772)	235.00	265.00	300.00	350.00

Chaurajit Singh

Saka 1725-1734/1803-1812

NAZARANA 1/4 RUPEE

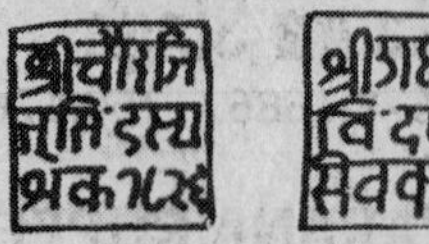

SILVER, square, 14mm

C#	Date	Year	VG	Fine	VF	XF
55	SE1726	(1804)	40.00	55.00	85.00	120.00
	1729	(1807)	40.00	55.00	85.00	120.00

NAZARANA 1/2 RUPEE

 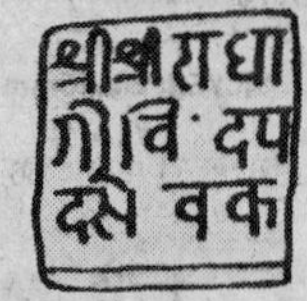

SILVER, square, 18mm, 5.35-5.80 gm.

C#	Date	Year	VG	Fine	VF	XF
56	SE1726	(1804)	45.00	60.00	90.00	125.00

NAZARANA RUPEE

SILVER, square, 22-24mm, 10.70-11.60 gm.

C#	Date	Year	VG	Fine	VF	XF
57	SE1728	(1806)	50.00	75.00	100.00	135.00
	1729	(1807)	50.00	75.00	100.00	135.00
	1732	(1810)	50.00	75.00	100.00	135.00
	1734	(1812)	50.00	75.00	100.00	135.00

Marjit Singh

Saka 1734-1741/1812-19

NAZARANA MOHUR

 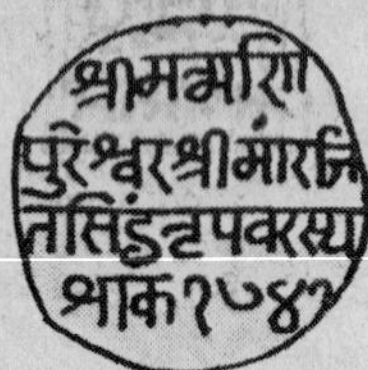

GOLD, 24mm, 10.70-11.40 gm.

C#	Date	Year	VG	Fine	VF	XF
75	SE1741	(1819)	225.00	250.00	275.00	325.00

Gambhir Singh

Saka 1748-1756/1826-1834

NAZARANA MOHUR

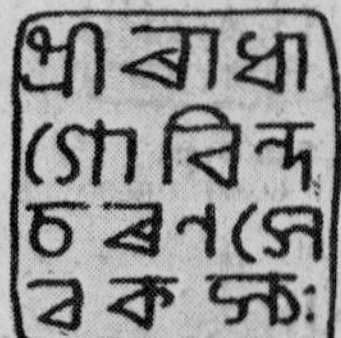 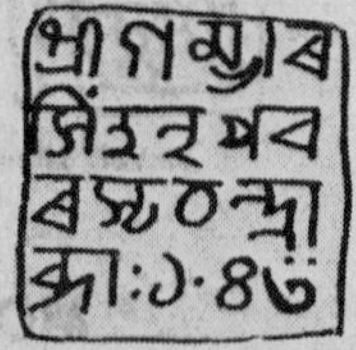

GOLD, square, 23mm, 10.70-11.40 gm.

85 Chandrabdah 1043 (a local date system)
235.00 265.00 300.00 350.00

ANONYMOUS BELL-METAL

These bear a single Bengali character, of uncertain significance, and cannot be assigned to particular rulers. The sel was valued at 900 to the rupee before 1838, and at between 420 and 480 to the rupee after 1838 until their demonetization by the British government in 1891. All are uniface.

SEL

BRONZE BELL-METAL, 10mm

SRI

C#	Date	Good	VG	Fine	VF
1	ND	3.50	6.00	8.00	10.00

(Many variations in style, 2 shown above)

MA

C#	Date	Good	VG	Fine	VF
2	ND	5.00	8.00	10.00	12.50

RA

C#	Date	Good	VG	Fine	VF
3	ND	6.00	10.00	12.50	15.00

(Said to be on issue of Nara Singh, 1843-50)

KA

C#	Date	Good	VG	Fine	VF
4	ND	6.00	10.00	12.50	15.00

(Struck before 1820)

LA

C#	Date	Good	VG	Fine	VF
5	ND	6.00	10.00	12.50	15.00

(Perhaps an issue of Sura Chandra, 1886-90)

KU

C#	Date	Good	VG	Fine	VF
6	ND	6.00	10.00	12.50	15.00

(Probably an issue of Kula Chandra Singh, 1890-91)

MARATHA CONFEDERACY

This powerful alliance of Marathi warriors owed nominal allegiance to the rajas of Satara (descendents of Shivaji) and drew their unity from the leadership of the Peshwa, the hereditary prime minister of the confederation. In the mid eighteenth century the Marathas were at the apogee of their influence, having hastened the end of effective Mughal power in the Deccan and western India. They successfully checked the intrusions of the Durranis into north India, although the experience left them so militarily exhausted that the dominance in Hindustan passed to other hands.

The great families of the lieutenants of the Peshwa gradually carved out regional power bases and became progressively less responsive to the authority of their formal superiors. The Maratha power as such was broken in a series of wars with the East India Company, bitterly fought and very close contests which settled the fate of large sections of India. Broadly speaking the Marathas may for convenience sake be listed in two categories, the lines which became extinct through British action and those which accomodated the English after defeat and survived to become Native States. These latter will be found elsewhere in the catalogue; the non-surviving political units are catalogued below.

BHONSLAS

RULERS

Januji, AD1753-1772
Raghoji II, AD1788-1816
Raghoji III, AD1816-1853

Most coins are imitations of Mughal coins of Ahmad Shah (1748-54), more or less barbarized.

Chanda Mint

RUPEE

SILVER, 20-22mm, 10.70-11.60 gm.
Mint name 'Surat' in barbarous form:

KM#	Date	Year	VG	Fine	VF	XF
3	—	27	11.50	13.00	15.00	20.00

Cuttack Mint

PAISA

COPPER, 17mm
Symbol: trident

KM#	Date	Year	Good	VG	Fine	VF
5	ND	—	1.50	2.50	3.50	4.50

(An issue of Raghoji II).

1/4 RUPEE

SILVER, 14mm, 2.68-2.90 gm.

Symbols  and 

KM#	Date	Year	VG	Fine	VF	XF
10	ND	—	4.50	5.50	7.00	9.00

RUPEE

SILVER, 19mm, 10.70-11.60 gm.

KM#	Date	Year	VG	Fine	VF	XF
12	ND	—	11.50	13.00	15.00	20.00

22mm
No mintmarks. Mintname: Katak.
Pseudo regnal years

KM#	Date	Year	VG	Fine	VF	XF
16	—	5	11.50	13.00	15.00	20.00
	—	51	11.50	13.00	15.00	20.00
	—	52	11.50	13.00	15.00	20.00
	—	512	11.50	13.00	15.00	20.00
	—	521	11.50	13.00	15.00	20.00

Hinganghat Mint

2 PAISA

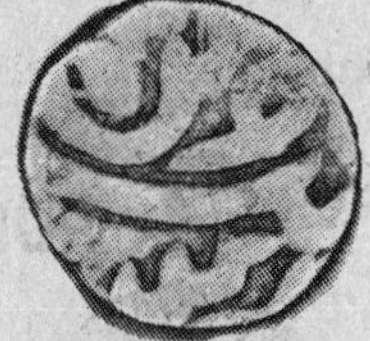

COPPER, 21-22mm

KM#	Date	Year	Good	VG	Fine	VF
22	ND	—	2.00	3.50	4.50	7.00

Nagpur Mint

Nagpur Mint probably produced varieties of KM#3 Rupee of Chanda Mint.

PAISA

COPPER, 24mm
Uniface, BARAKAT NAGPUR in recessed area.

26	ND	—	3.00	5.00	6.50	10.00

Uncertain Mint

PAISA

COPPER, 14mm
Barbarous designs

29	ND	2x	1.75	3.00	4.00	5.00

GAEKWARS

(See Baroda)

HOLKARS

(See Indore)

KOLHAPUR RAJAS

(See Kolhapur)

PESHWAS

RULERS

Madhoji Rao, AD1761-1771
Raghunath Rao, AD1772-1774
Madho Rao, AD1774-1795
Baji Rao, AD1796-1818

Ahmadabad Mint

One of Maratha Mints from 1757-1800A.D., it was leased to Baroda from 1800-1804, returned during 1804-1806, released to Baroda in 1806, and ceded to Baroda in 1817. Later, in 1818, it was annexed by the East India Company and finally closed in 1835.

MINTMARKS

Mint symbol, on all coins, reverse, lower left.

NOTE: Baroda coins of this mint have the Nagari initial of the ruler: British coins have the following mark on reverse:

In the name of Shah Alam II:

PAISA

COPPER

KM#	Date	Year	Good	VG	Fine	VF
35	—	—	2.50	3.50	5.00	7.50

1/2 RUPEE

SILVER, 18mm, 5.35-5.80 gm.
Mintmark: Ankus only

KM#	Date	Year	VG	Fine	VF	XF
39	—	27	6.00	7.50	9.00	13.50

RUPEE

SILVER, 24mm, 10.70-11.60 gm.
Mintmark: Ankus only

KM#	Date	Year	VG	Fine	VF	XF
40	AH1188	15	12.50	14.50	17.50	23.50
	118x	16	12.50	14.50	17.50	23.50
	—	17	12.50	14.50	17.50	23.50
	119x	21	12.50	14.50	17.50	23.50
	1197	24	12.50	14.50	17.50	23.50
	—	27	12.50	14.50	17.50	23.50

Mintmark: Ankus and Nagari 'RaM'

43	—	3x	12.50	14.50	17.50	23.50

In the name of Muhammad Akbar II:

1/2 RUPEE

SILVER, 18mm, 5.35-5.80 gm.
Mintmark: Ankus only

34	AH—	—	6.50	7.50	9.00	13.50

RUPEE

SILVER, 10.70-11.60 gm.
Mintmark: Ankus and scissors

36	AH1230	8	12.50	14.50	17.50	23.50

Mintmark: Ankus only

37	AH122x	8	11.50	13.00	15.00	20.00
		9	11.50	13.00	15.00	20.00

Mintmark: Ankus with pennant

38	AH1231	9	12.50	14.50	17.50	23.50

Ajmir Mint

A Maratha mint 1759-1787, taken by Jodhpur 1787-1792, and ruled by Gwalior 1792-1818. Ceded to the British 1818.

Mintmark: 

(For issues with only 2 dots, see Gwalior)

In the name of Shah Alam II:

PAISA

COPPER

KM#	Date	Year	Good	VG	Fine	VF
40	—	—	2.50	3.50	5.00	7.50

RUPEE

SILVER, 10.70-11.60 gm.
No mintmark

KM#	Date	Year	VG	Fine	VF	XF
45	AH1178	6	11.50	13.00	15.00	20.00
	—	10	11.50	13.00	15.00	20.00
	1197	24	11.50	13.00	15.00	20.00

Mintmark: 3 dots on vertical line.

50	AH1188	1	12.50	14.50	17.50	23.50
	1190	1	12.50	14.50	17.50	23.50

MOHUR

GOLD, 10.70-11.40 gm.
No mintmark

KM#	Date	Year	Mintage	VG	Fine	VF
55	—	—	—	—	—	—

Aurangnagar Mint

Possibly an issue of the Purandhare Sardars from Nasirabad in Khandesh, ca. AH1170-1205/AD1757-1790.

In the name of Shah Alam II:

RUPEE

SILVER, 21mm, 10.70-11.60 gm.
Rev: Nagari "Mu".

KM#	Date	Year	VG	Fine	VF	XF
56	AH—	—	17.50	25.00	32.50	45.00

Bagalkot Mint

A mint in the Bijapur region. The coins are attributed to the Rastias of Wai, ca. AH1170-1233/AD1757-1818, and are copies of the rupee of Dar-ul-khilafat Shahjahanabad.

Malhar Rao

AD1757-1778

RUPEE

In the name of "Aziz-ud-din" Shah Alam II:

SILVER, 22mm, 10.70-11.60 gm.
Mintname: Bagalkot
Fine fabric.

Crude fabric
Possibly an issue of Mudhol.

KM#	Date	Year	VG	Fine	VF	XF
57	AHxxx	9	(fixed)			
			15.00	20.00	27.50	40.00

In the name of Aziz-ud-din Alamgir II

Mintname: Bijapur

KM#	Date	VG	Fine	VF	XF
57.2	AH1121 (false)	17.50	25.00	32.50	45.00

24mm
Uncertain mintname (Iphani?).
Obv: Nagari "Ra".

KM#	Date	VG	Fine	VF	XF
57.3	AHxx81 (fixed)	15.00	20.00	27.50	40.00

Obv: Long-tailed Persian "Wa".

KM#	Date	VG	Fine	VF	XF
57.4	AHxx81 (fixed)	15.00	20.00	27.50	40.00

In the name of "Aziz-us-din" Shah Alam II:

KM#	Date	VG	Fine	VF	XF
57.5	AH1181 (fixed)	15.00	20.00	27.50	40.00

Burhanpur Mint

RUPEE

SILVER, 21mm

KM#	Date	Year	VG	Fine	VF	XF
58	AH1175	1	11.50	13.50	15.00	20.00
	1177	—	11.50	13.50	15.00	20.00
	1178	5	11.50	13.50	15.00	20.00
	1179	5	11.50	13.50	15.00	20.00
	1179	6	11.50	13.50	15.00	20.00
	1180	6	11.50	13.50	15.00	20.00
	1180	7	11.50	13.50	15.00	20.00
	1182	8	11.50	13.50	15.00	20.00
	1184	—	11.50	13.50	15.00	20.00
	1185	11	11.50	13.50	15.00	20.00
	1186	12	11.50	13.50	15.00	20.00
	1186	13	11.50	13.50	15.00	20.00
	1187	13	11.50	13.50	15.00	20.00
	1188	14	11.50	13.50	15.00	20.00
	1189	15	11.50	13.50	15.00	20.00
	1190	16	11.50	13.50	15.00	20.00
	1191	17	11.50	13.50	15.00	20.00
	1192	18	11.50	13.50	15.00	20.00

For coins struck after AH1192-R.Y.20 (AD1778), see India Native States: Gwalior.

Chinchwar Mint

Struck by the Patwardans of Miraj, possibly at Poona.

Puresham Bhau

AD1771?-1799

RUPEE

SILVER, 21mm, 10.70-11.60 gm.
Rev: Mintmark: Parasu (battleaxe).

KM#	Date	Year	VG	Fine	VF	XF
59	AH1189	—	—	12.00	14.00	19.00

Itawa Mint

Maratha to AD1762/AH1175-R.Y.3; Rohilla until reconquest by Marathas in AD1771/AH1184-R.Y.12. Ceded to Awadh AD1774/AH1188-R.Y.15. For early issues see also India Native States: Rohilkhand.

RUPEE

First Occupation

SILVER, 22mm, 10.70-11.60 gm.

KM#	Date	Year	VG	Fine	VF	XF
61.1	AH—	1	12.50	14.50	17.50	23.50

Second Occupation

27mm
Obv: Trident

KM#	Date	Year	VG	Fine	VF	XF
61.2	AH—	12	11.50	13.00	15.00	20.00
	—	13	11.50	13.00	15.00	20.00

Kunch Mint

Mintmarks: 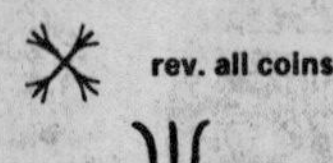 **rev. all coins**

 **#1 obv.** 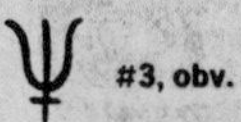 **#3, obv.**

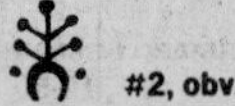 **#2, obv.**

 **#4, rev.** **#5, rev.**

Mintname: **"Kunch Hijri"**

RUPEE

SILVER, 21mm, 10.70-11.60 gm.
Obv: Symbols #1, #3.

KM#	Date	Year	VG	Fine	VF	XF
5	AH—	22	11.50	13.50	15.00	20.00
	—	25	11.50	13.50	15.00	20.00

Mintname: "Kuch Hijri"

Obv: Symbols #1, #2, #3.

KM#	Date	Year	VG	Fine	VF	XF
6.1	AH—	27	11.50	13.50	15.00	20.00
	—	28	11.50	13.50	15.00	20.00

19mm
Obv: Symbols #1, #2, #3.
Rev: Symbols #4, #5.

KM#	Date	Year	VG	Fine	VF	XF
6.2	AH1203	31	11.50	13.50	15.00	20.00
	1208(error)	31	11.50	13.50	15.00	20.00
	1203(error)	39	11.50	13.50	15.00	20.00
	1213	39	11.50	13.50	15.00	20.00
	3121(error)	39	11.50	13.50	15.00	20.00
	8121(error)	39	11.50	13.50	15.00	20.00

Jalaun Mint

Symbols **and**  **on obv**

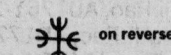

or **on reverse**

In the name of Shah Alam II
(CA. 1775-1818AD)

PAISA

COPPER, 19mm

KM#	Date	Year	Good	VG	Fine	VF
63	—	53	2.00	3.50	4.50	6.50

1/2 RUPEE

SILVER, 5.35-5.80 gm.

KM#	Date	Year	VG	Fine	VF	XF
64	—	17	8.00	10.00	12.50	16.50
	—	2x	8.00	10.00	12.50	16.50

RUPEE

Mintname: "Zarb ba Jalaun Hijri"

SILVER, 21mm, 10.70-11.60 gm.
Fine fabric, normal flan.

KM#	Date	Year	VG	Fine	VF	XF
65.1	AH—	46	11.50	13.00	15.00	20.00

17mm
Crude fabric, narrow flan.

KM#	Date	Year	VG	Fine	VF	XF
65.2	AH1224	49	11.50	13.00	15.00	20.00
	1222	55	11.50	13.00	15.00	20.00

Mintname: "Zarb Ku(nch), Kuna(r), Jalaun"

20mm
Fine fabric, normal flan.

KM#	Date	Year	VG	Fine	VF	XF
66.1	AH—	49	12.50	14.50	17.50	23.50

17mm
Crude fabric, narrow flan.

KM#	Date	Year	VG	Fine	VF	XF
66.2	AH1222	17 (error)	11.50	13.00	15.00	20.00
	1223	17 (error)	11.50	13.00	15.00	20.00
	1222	51	11.50	13.00	15.00	20.00
	1222	52	11.50	13.00	15.00	20.00
	1222	53	11.50	13.00	15.00	20.00
	1222	55	11.50	13.00	15.00	20.00
	1222	57	11.50	13.00	15.00	20.00

In joint names of Shah Alam II and Latif Khan:

20mm

KM#	Date	Year	VG	Fine	VF	XF
66.3	AH—	53	12.50	14.50	17.50	23.50

Jhansi Mint

Mintmark:

on reverse

In the name of Shah Alam II

Struck ca. 1766-1817AD

1/4 PAISA

COPPER
Similar to 1 Paisa, KM#73.

KM#	Date	Year	Good	VG	Fine	VF
71	ND	—	1.75	2.50	3.50	5.00

PAISA

COPPER, 17-19mm
With Nagari; Dhu right of Julus.

KM#	Date	Year	Good	VG	Fine	VF
73	AH1204	—	2.00	3.50	4.50	6.50

1/4 RUPEE

SILVER, 13mm, 2.68-2.90 gm.

KM#	Date	Year	VG	Fine	VF	XF
76	—	2x	4.00	6.00	8.50	12.50

RUPEE

SILVER, 22mm, 10.70-11.60 gm.
Fine fabric.

KM#	Date	Year	VG	Fine	VF	XF
78.1	AH1174	1	12.50	14.50	17.50	23.50
	1174	3	12.50	14.50	17.50	23.50
	1175	4	12.50	14.50	17.50	23.50
	1180	8	12.50	14.50	17.50	23.50
	1181	9	12.50	14.50	17.50	23.50
	1183	11	12.50	14.50	17.50	23.50
	1184	12	12.50	14.50	17.50	23.50
	1185	13	12.50	14.50	17.50	23.50

19mm
Crude fabric.

KM#	Date	Year	VG	Fine	VF	XF
78.2	AH1187	15	11.50	13.00	15.00	20.00
	1187	16	11.50	13.00	15.00	20.00
	1189	16	11.50	13.00	15.00	20.00
	1192	20	11.50	13.00	15.00	20.00
	1197	24	11.50	13.00	15.00	20.00
	1198	25	11.50	13.00	15.00	20.00

20mm
Rev: Symbol

KM#	Date	Year	VG	Fine	VF	XF
78.3	AH—	28	12.50	14.50	17.50	23.50
	1209	29	12.50	14.50	17.50	23.50

Obv: 2 added

KM#	Date	Year	VG	Fine	VF	XF
78.4	AH1204	3x	11.50	13.00	15.00	20.00
	—	33	11.50	13.00	15.00	20.00
	1206	34	11.50	13.00	15.00	20.00

Obv: 92 added.

KM#	Date	Year	VG	Fine	VF	XF
78.5	AH1206	34	11.50	13.00	15.00	20.00
	—	35	11.50	13.00	15.00	20.00
	1209	36	11.50	13.00	15.00	20.00
	1210	36	11.50	13.00	15.00	20.00

Obv: 99111 added.

KM#	Date	Year	VG	Fine	VF	XF
78.6	AH1220	47	11.50	13.00	15.00	20.00
	1221	48	11.50	13.00	15.00	20.00
	1224	52	11.50	13.00	15.00	20.00
	1234	—	11.50	13.00	15.00	20.00

Obv. and rev. leg: Different arrangement.

KM#	Date	Year	VG	Fine	VF	XF
79	AH—	3	12.50	14.50	17.50	23.50
	—	4	12.50	14.50	17.50	23.50

Kalpi Mint

Symbols: rev.

In the name of Shah Alam II

Mintname: "Kalpi Hijri"

RUPEE

SILVER, 21.5mm, 10.70-11.60 gm.

KM#	Date	Year	VG	Fine	VF	XF
82	AH—	22	12.50	14.50	17.50	23.50
	1198	25	12.50	14.50	17.50	23.50
	—	26	12.50	14.50	17.50	23.50
	—	27	12.50	14.50	17.50	23.50
	—	28	12.50	14.50	17.50	23.50
	—	29	12.50	14.50	17.50	23.50
	1201	30	12.50	14.50	17.50	23.50
	—	31	12.50	14.50	17.50	23.50
	—	33	12.50	14.50	17.50	23.50

Kora Mint

Mintmark:

Mintname: کورا "Kora"

RUPEE

SILVER, 19mm, 10.70-11.60 gm.
Obv: Trisula (trident)

KM#	Date	Year	VG	Fine	VF	XF
85.1	AH117x	1	11.50	13.00	15.00	20.00
	117x	2	11.50	13.00	15.00	20.00

22mm
Obv: Lotus and trisual.

KM#	Date	Year	VG	Fine	VF	XF
85.2	AH117x	1	12.50	14.50	17.50	23.50
	117x	2	12.50	14.50	17.50	23.50

20mm
Obv: Pataka (banner) and trisula.

KM#	Date	Year	VG	Fine	VF	XF
85.3	AH117x	2	12.50	14.50	17.50	23.50
	117x	3	12.50	14.50	17.50	23.50
	117x	4	12.50	14.50	17.50	23.50

19mm
Obv: Sword left and trisula.

KM#	Date	Year	VG	Fine	VF	XF
85.4	AH117x	2	12.50	14.50	17.50	23.50

20mm
Obv: Sword right and trisula.

KM#	Date	Year	VG	Fine	VF	XF
85.5	AH117x	2	12.50	14.50	17.50	23.50

For later issues of Kora mint from AD1765/AH1178/R.Y. 6, see India, Mughal Empire: Kora.

Kunar Mint

Symbols similar to Jalaun.

Mintname: 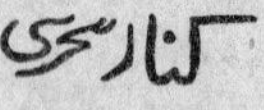
"Kunar Hijri"

In the name of Shah Alam II

RUPEE

SILVER, 22mm, 10.70-11.60 gm.
Obv: Axe head and trisula.

KM#	Date	Year	VG	Fine	VF	XF
86.1	AH—	22	12.50	14.50	17.50	23.50

Obv: Parasu (axe), axe head and trisula.

KM#	Date	Year	VG	Fine	VF	XF
86.2	AH—	25	12.50	14.50	17.50	23.50

For other issues in mintname Kunar see Jalaun rupee KM#66.1.

Mahoba Mint

Symbols: 
from left to right on middle line of obverse

In the name of Shah Alam II:

PAISA

COPPER, 22-24mm

KM#	Date	Year	Good	VG	Fine	VF
90	ND	—	3.00	4.50	6.00	8.50

Miraj Mint

Mintmarks: 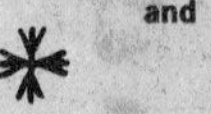 and 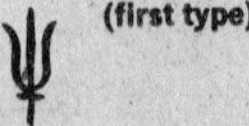 (first type)

or 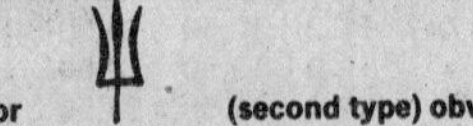 (second type) obv.

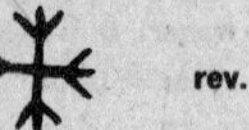 rev.

Mintname:
"Balanagar Gadha"

In the name of Shah Alam II

RUPEE

SILVER, 21mm, 10.70-11.60 gm.
Trisula first type.

KM#	Date	Year	VG	Fine	VF	XF
93.1	AH1198	25	12.50	14.50	17.50	23.50
	1199	26	12.50	14.50	17.50	23.50
	1200	27	12.50	14.50	17.50	23.50
	1201	28	12.50	14.50	17.50	23.50
	—	29	12.50	14.50	17.50	23.50

20mm
Trisula second type.

KM#	Date	Year	VG	Fine	VF	XF
93.2	AH—	30	12.50	14.50	17.50	23.50
	1202	31	12.50	14.50	17.50	23.50
	1205	32	12.50	14.50	17.50	23.50
	1207	33	12.50	14.50	17.50	23.50
	—	34	12.50	14.50	17.50	23.50
	—	35	12.50	14.50	17.50	23.50
	—	36	12.50	14.50	17.50	23.50
	—	38	12.50	14.50	17.50	23.50

Nasik Mint

In the name of Shah Alam II:

MINTMARKS

Symbols  on reverse

1/4 RUPEE

SILVER, 2.68-2.90 gm.

KM#	Date	Year	VG	Fine	VF	XF
98	ND	—	10.00	12.50	16.50	21.50

1/2 RUPEE

SILVER, 16mm, 5.35-5.80 gm.

KM#	Date	Year	VG	Fine	VF	XF
99	AH1235	—	10.00	12.50	16.50	21.50

RUPEE

SILVER, 20-21mm, 10.70-11.60 gm.

KM#	Date	Year	Mintage	VG	Fine	VF
100	AH1234	—	12.50	14.50	17.50	23.50
100	1251	—	12.50	14.50	17.50	23.50

Nipani Mint

Very degenerate legends. Identified by calligraphy and by large number of stars, especially 4-pointed ones, dispersed throughout legend.

Symbol: 

In the name of Shah Alam II:

1/4 RUPEE

SILVER, 2.68-2.90 gm.

KM#	Date	Year	VG	Fine	VF	XF
103	ND	—	10.00	14.00	17.50	23.50

RUPEE

SILVER, 23-24mm, 10.70-11.60 gm.

KM#	Date	Year	VG	Fine	VF	XF
105	ND	—	13.00	16.00	20.00	27.50

(Struck circa AD1759-1818)

Poona Mint

In the name of Ali Gauhar, the name of Shah Alam II before his accession.

NOTE: On Feb. 10, 1818 (AH1233, Fasli 1228) the British East India Co. took over Poona, so all coins of that date or later are British Colonial.

Mintmarks:

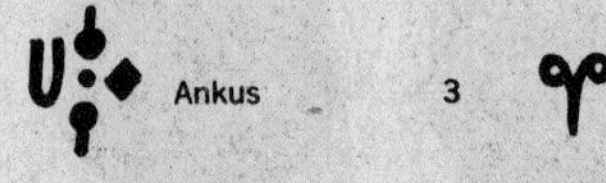

1 Ankus 3 (scissors)

2 Aze 4 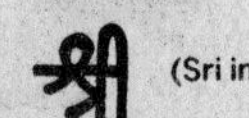 (Sri in Nagari)

PAISA

COPPER, square, 15mm
Mintmark #3

KM#	Date	Year	Good	VG	Fine	VF
110	—	—	1.50	2.50	3.00	3.50

1/4 RUPEE

SILVER, 2.68-2.90 gm.

KM#	Date	Year	VG	Fine	VF	XF
113	—	—	Reported, not confirmed			

14mm, with Fasli date

KM#	Date	Year	VG	Fine	VF	XF
114	FE1238	—	7.50	10.00	13.50	18.50

1/2 RUPEE

SILVER, 5.35-5.80 gm.

KM#	Date	Year	VG	Fine	VF	XF
116	—	—	Reported, not confirmed			

With Fasli date

KM#	Date	Year	VG	Fine	VF	XF
117	—	—	Reported, not confirmed			

RUPEE

SILVER, 19-20mm, 10.70-11.60 gm.
Mintmark #1

'Ankusi rupee', date in Arabic numerals.

KM#	Date	Year	VG	Fine	VF	XF
120	—	11	11.50	13.00	15.00	20.00
	—	12	11.50	13.00	15.00	20.00
	—	15	11.50	13.00	15.00	20.00
	AH1225	—	11.50	13.00	15.00	20.00
	1229	—	11.50	13.00	15.00	20.00

Mintmark #1

Fasli date in Nagari numerals

NOTE: Coins with Nagari dates are in the Fasli system, a solar calendar dating from the Conversion of Muhammnad, FE1 = AD591.

KM#	Date	Year	VG	Fine	VF	XF
122	FE1232	—	11.50	13.00	15.00	20.00
	1233	—	11.50	13.00	15.00	20.00
	1234	—	11.50	13.00	15.00	20.00
	1235	—	11.50	13.00	15.00	20.00
	1236	—	11.50	13.00	15.00	20.00
	1237	—	11.50	13.00	15.00	20.00
	1238	—	11.50	13.00	15.00	20.00
	1239	—	11.50	13.00	15.00	20.00
	1240	—	11.50	13.00	15.00	20.00
	1241	—	11.50	13.00	15.00	20.00
	1242	—	11.50	13.00	15.00	20.00
	1243	—	11.50	13.00	15.00	20.00
	1244	—	11.50	13.00	15.00	20.00

Mintmark #2

KM#	Date	Year	VG	Fine	VF	XF
124	ND	—	12.50	14.50	17.50	23.50

Mintmark #3, Nagari date.

KM#	Date	Year	VG	Fine	VF	XF
126	FE1230	—	11.50	13.00	15.00	20.00
	1231	—	11.50	13.00	15.00	20.00
	1234	—	11.50	13.00	15.00	20.00
	1240	—	11.50	13.00	15.00	20.00
	1241	—	11.50	13.00	15.00	20.00
	1243	—	11.50	13.00	15.00	20.00
	1244	—	11.50	13.00	15.00	20.00
	ND	30	12.50	14.50	17.50	23.50

Mintmark #4, AH dates.

KM#	Date	Year	VG	Fine	VF	XF
130	AH1206	—	12.50	14.50	17.50	23.50
	1211	—	12.50	14.50	17.50	23.50
	date off	—	11.50	13.00	15.00	20.00

Sangli Mint

Chintaman Rao

AD1799-1851

In the name of Muhammad Shah:

RUPEE

SILVER, 20-21mm, 10.70-11.60 gm.

KM#	Date	Year	VG	Fine	VF	XF
155	—	frozen	11.50	13.00	15.00	20.00

Sashti (Salsette) Mint

Under the Peshwa, 1739-1782

PAISA

COPPER, 16mm

KM#	Date	Year	Good	VG	Fine	VF
177	AH(11)96	—	2.50	3.50	5.00	7.00

Saugor Mint

In the name of Shah Alam II:

PAISA

COPPER, 22mm

KM#	Date	Year	Good	VG	Fine	VF
160	—	37	1.50	2.50	3.50	5.00

25mm

Symbol  on obverse

KM#	Date	Year	Good	VG	Fine	VF
162	ND	—	1.50	2.50	3.50	5.00

1/2 RUPEE

SILVER, 5.35-5.80 gm.

Type of KM#167.1.

KM#	Date	Year	VG	Fine	VF	XF
166.2	AH—	51	10.00	13.50	16.50	22.50

RUPEE

Mintmarks: obv.

Pataka First type — Trisul rev. First type

Second type — Second type

Mintname:

"Ravishnagar Sagar"

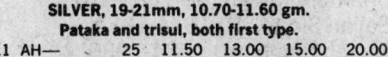

SILVER, 19-21mm, 10.70-11.60 gm.

Pataka and trisul, both first type.

KM#	Date	Year	VG	Fine	VF	XF
167.1	AH—	25	11.50	13.00	15.00	20.00

20mm

Pataka second type, trisul first type.

KM#	Date	Year	VG	Fine	VF	XF
167.2	AH1199	26	11.50	13.00	15.00	20.00
	—	27	11.50	13.00	15.00	20.00
167.2	—	28	11.50	13.00	15.00	20.00
	—	29	11.50	13.00	15.00	20.00
	—	30	11.50	13.00	15.00	20.00

19mm

Pataka and trisul, both second type.

KM#	Date	Year	VG	Fine	VF	XF
167.3	AH—	31	11.50	13.00	15.00	20.00
	—	32	11.50	13.00	15.00	20.00
	—	33	11.50	13.00	15.00	20.00
	1207	34	11.50	13.00	15.00	20.00
	—	35	11.50	13.00	15.00	20.00
	—	36	11.50	13.00	15.00	20.00
	—	37	11.50	13.00	15.00	20.00
	—	38	11.50	13.00	15.00	20.00
	—	39	11.50	13.00	15.00	20.00
	—	40	11.50	13.00	15.00	20.00
	—	41	11.50	13.00	15.00	20.00
	1216	42	11.50	13.00	15.00	20.00
	1218	43	11.50	13.00	15.00	20.00
	1218	44	11.50	13.00	15.00	20.00
	1219	44	11.50	13.00	15.00	20.00
	1220	45	11.50	13.00	15.00	20.00
	1222	47	11.50	13.00	15.00	20.00
	—	48	11.50	13.00	15.00	20.00
	—	49	11.50	13.00	15.00	20.00

18mm

Similar to 167.3 but very crude.

KM#	Date	Year	VG	Fine	VF	XF
167.4	AH—	52	11.50	13.00	15.00	20.00
	—	55	11.50	13.00	15.00	20.00

Srinagar Mint

(In Bundelkhand)

Symbols  on rev. (copper)

In the name of Shah Alam II

PAISA

COPPER, 18-20mm

KM#	Date	Year	Good	VG	Fine	VF
176	—	5	1.00	2.00	3.00	4.00

Squarish, 14-19mm

KM#	Date	Year	Good	VG	Fine	VF
176a	—	5	1.50	2.50	3.50	5.00

RUPEE

Mintmarks:  obv.

 rev.

Mintname:

"Nagar Ijhri (sic)"

SILVER, 20.5mm, 10.70-11.60 gm.

Rev: Asynchronous date in "Sin" of 'Jalus'.

KM#	Date	Year	VG	Fine	VF	XF
180	AH—	26	11.50	13.00	15.00	20.00
	—	27	11.50	13.00	15.00	20.00
	xxx2	28	11.50	13.00	15.00	20.00
	xx99	29	11.50	13.00	15.00	20.00

18mm
Obv: Hijri date.
Rev: Quadrafoil in "sin" of 'Jalus'.

KM#	Date	Year	VG	Fine	VF	XF
181	AH1206	32	11.50	13.00	15.00	20.00
	1206	33	11.50	13.00	15.00	20.00
	12012 (error)					
		35	11.50	13.00	15.00	20.00

17mm
Small flan, crude execution.

KM#	Date	Year	VG	Fine	VF	XF
182	AH—	39 (frozen)	11.50	13.00	15.00	20.00

Torgal Mint

PATWARDANS of Miraj

Pureshuram Bhau, AD1771?-1799

Mintmarks:

Nagari "Sa"

(Upside down on flan) Persian "Mim"

chhatra

trisula

Mintname: سرکارتور

"Sarkar Tor(gal)"

RUPEE

SILVER, 19mm, 10.70-11.60 gm.

KM#	Date	Year	VG	Fine	VF	XF
185	ND	—	—	—	Rare	—

SATARA RAJAS

In the name of Chhatrapati Sivaji:

Probably Satara Mint

1/2 PAISA

COPPER, 13-16mm

KM#	Date	Year	Good	VG	Fine	VF
180	ND	—	1.00	1.50	2.25	3.00

PAISA

COPPER, 18-22mm

KM#	Date	Year	Good	VG	Fine	VF
185	ND	—	1.50	2.00	2.75	3.50

18-20mm
Obv: Double lines.

KM#	Date	Year	Good	VG	Fine	VF
190	ND	—	.75	1.00	1.50	2.25

East India Company

Local issues post - AD1818/19

PAISA

With FE date.

KM#	Date	Year	Good	VG	Fine	VF
192	FE1230	—	1.50	2.00	2.75	3.50
	1231	—	1.50	2.00	2.75	3.50
	1232	—	1.50	2.00	2.75	3.50
	1233	—	1.50	2.00	2.75	3.50
	1234	—	1.50	2.00	2.75	3.50
	1235	—	1.50	2.00	2.75	3.50
	1237	—	1.50	2.00	2.75	3.50
	1238	—	1.50	2.00	2.75	3.50
	1240	—	1.50	2.00	2.75	3.50

RUPEE

SILVER, 20mm
Bagalkot Mint

KM#	Date	Year	VG	Fine	VF	XF
195	AD1819	—	15.00	20.00	27.50	40.00

TANJORE

FANAM

GOLD, 7mm, 0.4 gm.

KM#	Date	Year	VG	Fine	VF	XF
200	ND	—	7.00	9.00	11.00	13.50

MEWAR

RULERS

Raj Singh II, 1754-1761
Ari Singh II, 1761-1773
Hammir Singh II, 1773-1778
Bhim Singh, AD 1778-1828
Jawan Singh, AD 1828-1838
Sirdar Singh, AD 1838-1842
Swarup Singh, AD 1842-1861
Shambhu Singh, AD 1861-1874
Sajjan Singh, AD 1874-1884
Fatteh Singh, AD 1884-1930
Bhupal Singh, AD 1930-1948

NOTE: All Mewar coinage is struck without ruler's name, and is largely undated. Types were generally struck over several reigns.

Chitori Series:

Struck at Chitor Mint, before 1870, for at least 40 years.

MINTMARK

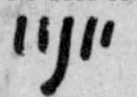

On obverse, without jhar.

1/16 RUPEE

SILVER, 0.67-0.72 gm

C#	Date	Year	VG	Fine	VF	XF
22	ND	—	2.00	3.00	4.00	6.00

1/8 RUPEE

SILVER, 1.34-1.45 gm

C#	Date	Year	VG	Fine	VF	XF
23	ND	—	2.00	2.50	3.50	5.00

1/4 RUPEE

SILVER, 2.68-2.90 gm

C#	Date	Year	VG	Fine	VF	XF
24	ND	—	3.50	4.00	5.00	7.50

1/2 RUPEE

SILVER, 14-15mm, 5.35-5.80 gm

C#	Date	Year	VG	Fine	VF	XF
25	ND	—	6.50	7.00	8.00	12.00

RUPEE

SILVER, 19mm, 10.70-11.60 gm

C#	Date	Year	VG	Fine	VF	XF
26	ND	—	12.50	13.50	15.00	22.50

Udaipuri Series:

Struck at Udaipur through middle of 19th century.

Mintmark:

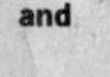 and   on obverse.

1/2 RUPEE

SILVER, 5.35-5.80 gm

C#	Date	Year	VG	Fine	VF	XF
31	ND	—	6.50	7.00	8.00	12.00

RUPEE

SILVER, 19-20mm, 10.70-11.60 gm

C#	Date	Year	VG	Fine	VF	XF
32	ND	—	12.50	13.50	15.00	22.50

note: 1/16, 1/8 and 1/4 rupees were reportedly also produced in this series.

Old Chandori Series:

Struck at Udaipur, ordered by Bhim Singh, and coined until 1842. Recalled by Swarup Shah.

Mintmark:

On obverse

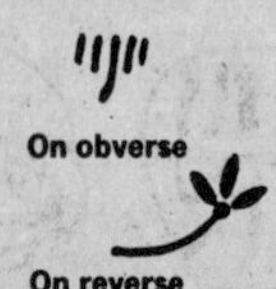

On reverse

RUPEE

SILVER, 19-21mm, 10.70-11.60 gm

C#	Date	Year	VG	Fine	VF	XF
44	ND	—	7.50	10.00	12.50	18.50

New Chandori Series:

Udaipur Mint. Struck circa 1842-1890. Many varieties.

Mintmark:

On obverse

1/16 RUPEE

SILVER, 9mm, 0.67-0.72 gm

Y#	Date	Year	VG	Fine	VF	XF
1	ND	—	1.50	2.00	3.00	4.50

1/8 RUPEE

SILVER, 10-11mm, 1.34-1.45 gm

Y#	Date	Year	VG	Fine	VF	XF
2	ND	—	1.75	2.25	2.75	4.25

1/4 RUPEE

SILVER, 12-14mm, 2.68-2.90 gm

Y#	Date	Year	VG	Fine	VF	XF
3	ND	—	3.50	4.00	4.75	7.00

1/2 RUPEE

SILVER, 14-16mm, 5.35-5.80 gm

Y#	Date	Year	VG	Fine	VF	XF
4	ND	—	6.50	7.00	8.00	12.00

RUPEE

SILVER, 20mm, 10.70-11.60 gm

Y#	Date	Year	VG	Fine	VF	XF
5	ND	—	12.50	13.50	15.00	22.50

MOHUR

GOLD, 22mm, 10.70-11.40 gm

Y#	Date	Year	VG	Fine	VF	XF
6	ND	—	220.00	240.00	265.00	300.00

Swarupshahi Series:

Udaipur Mint. Struck circa 1851-1930. Many minor varieties.

1/16 RUPEE

SILVER, 9mm, round, 0.67-0.72 gm

Y#	Date	Year	VG	Fine	VF	XF
7.1	ND	—	1.50	2.00	2.50	3.55

Irregular shape, 8-10mm.

Y#	Date	Year	VG	Fine	VF	XF
7.2	ND	—	2.00	2.75	3.50	4.50

1/8 RUPEE

SILVER, 11-12mm, 1.34-1.45 gm

Y#	Date	Year	VG	Fine	VF	XF
8	ND	—	1.75	2.25	2.75	3.75

1/4 RUPEE

SILVER, 15mm, 2.68-2.90 gm

Y#	Date	Year	VG	Fine	VF	XF
9	ND	—	3.50	4.00	4.75	6.50

1/2 RUPEE

SILVER, 18mm, 5.35-5.80 gm

Y#	Date	Year	VG	Fine	VF	XF
10	ND	—	6.50	7.00	8.00	11.00

RUPEE

SILVER, 22-25mm, 10.70-11.60 gm

Y#	Date	Year	VG	Fine	VF	XF
11	ND	—	12.50	13.50	15.00	20.00

MOHUR

GOLD, 22-24mm, 10.70-11.60 gm

Y#	Date	Year	VG	Fine	VF	XF
12	ND	—	220.00	240.00	265.00	300.00

Fatteh Singh

With names of Chitor and Udaipur.

PIE

COPPER, 16mm

Y#	Date	Year	Good	VG	Fine	VF
13	VS1975	(1918)	6.00	10.00	13.50	17.50

Y#	Date	Year	Good	VG	Fine	VF
14	VS1978	(1921)	5.00	8.00	10.00	14.00

MACHINE-STRUCK COINS

In the name of 'A Friend of London'.

(Dated VS1985 i.e. AD1928, but actually struck in AD1931 and 32.)

1/16 RUPEE

SILVER, 12mm, 0.67-0.72 gm

Y#	Date	Year	Mintage	Fine	VF	XF
18	VS1985	(1928)	3.262	1.00	1.50	2.50

1/8 RUPEE

SILVER, 15mm, 1.34-1.45 gm

Y#	Date	Year	Mintage	Fine	VF	XF
19	VS1985	(1928)	.800	1.75	2.25	3.50

1/4 RUPEE

SILVER, 19mm, 2.68-2.90 gm

Y#	Date	Year	Mintage	Fine	VF	XF
20	VS1985	(1928)	.839	3.50	4.50	6.00

GOLD, 2.68-2.85 gm

Y#	Date	Year	Mintage	Fine	VF	XF
20a	VS1985	(1928)	—	—	Proof	250.00

1/2 RUPEE

SILVER, 24.5mm, 5.35-5.80 gm

Y#	Date	Year	Mintage	Fine	VF	XF
21	VS1985	(1928)	.648	6.50	7.50	9.00

GOLD, 5.35-5.70 gm

Y#	Date	Year	Mintage	Fine	VF	XF
21a	VS1985	(1928)	—	—	Proof	350.00

RUPEE

SILVER, 30.5mm, 10.70-11.60 gm

Y#	Date	Year	Mintage	Fine	VF	XF
22	VS1985	(1928)	14.906	12.50	13.50	15.00

GOLD, 10.70-11.4 gm

Y#	Date	Year	Mintage	Fine	VF	XF
22a	VS1985	(1928)	—	—	Proof	450.00

Issues of Bhupal Singh:

1/4 ANNA

COPPER

Y#	Date	Year	Fine	VF	XF	Unc
15	VS1999	(1942)	.30	.45	.65	1.00

1/2 ANNA

COPPER

Y#	Date	Year	Fine	VF	XF	Unc
16	VS1999	(1942)	.25	.40	.60	.90

ANNA

COPPER

Y#	Date	Year	Fine	VF	XF	Unc
17	VS2000	(1943)	.30	.50	.75	1.10

NCLT ISSUES

PATTERNS

KM#	Date	Mintage	Identification	Mkt.Val.
1	VS1985	—	1/16 Rupee, Silver	—

KM#	Date	Mintage	Identification	Mkt.Val.
2	VS1985	—	1/8 Rupee, Silver	—

KM#	Date	Mintage	Identification	Mkt.Val.
3	VS1985	—	1/4 Rupee, Silver	—

KM#	Date	Mintage	Identification	Mkt.Val.
4	VS1985	—	1/2 Rupee, Silver	—

KM#	Date	Mintage	Identification	Mkt.Val.
5	VS1985	—	Rupee, Silver	—

LOCAL COINAGE

BHILWARA

In the name of Shah Alam II

Symbol:

On obverse

PAISA

COPPER
Obv: Symbol vertical

C#	Date	Year	Good	VG	Fine	VF
2.5	ND	—	3.00	5.00	7.00	9.00

note: Known as the old Bhilwari paisa.

Obv: Symbol oblique, 20-23mm

C#	Date	Year	Good	VG	Fine	VF
3	ND	—	1.50	2.50	3.50	5.00

note: Known as the new Bhilwari paisa.

CHITOR

Struck by local coppersmiths

2 PIES (?)

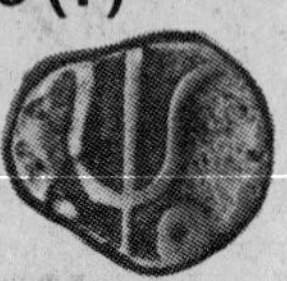

COPPER, 15-17mm

C#	Date	Year	Good	VG	Fine	VF
2	ND	—	.45	.75	1.00	1.50

C#	Date	Year	Good	VG	Fine	VF
2.1	ND	—	.60	1.00	1.25	1.50

JAWAD

Early 19th century.

PAISA

COPPER, 16-18mm

C#	Date	Year	Good	VG	Fine	VF
4	ND	—	3.50	6.00	7.50	10.00

NOTE: For later issues, see Gwalior.

UMARDA

PAISA

COPPER, 15mm
Many varieties

Y#	Date	Year	Good	VG	Fine	VF
23	ND	—	.45	.75	1.00	1.50

Square, 14mm
Innumerable varieties
Struck circa 1938-1941

Y#	Date	Year	Good	VG	Fine	VF
24	ND	—	.75	1.25	1.75	2.50

FEUDATORY STATES

BHINDA

Zurawar Singh

AD 1799-1827

PAISA

COPPER, 17mm

C#	Date	Year	Good	VG	Fine	VF
1	ND	—	3.00	5.00	6.00	7.50

SALUMBA

2 PIES

COPPER, 15mm

C#	Date	Year	Good	VG	Fine	VF
1	ND	—	1.75	3.00	5.00	6.50

Struck circa 1815-1870.

SHAHPUR

RULERS

Jagat Singh, AD 1845-1853
Lachman Singh, AD 1853-1870
Nahat Singh, AD 1870-1932

PAISA

COPPER, 22mm
Issued 1827-70

C#	Date	Year	Good	VG	Fine	VF
10	ND	—	.90	1.50	2.50	3.50

In the name of Alamgir II

Copy of his Dehli coin with Yr. 12 as a frozen fictitious year. Distinguished by the addition of a small trisul to lower obverse.

1/4 RUPEE

SILVER, 14mm, 2.68-2.90 gm

C#	Date	Year	VG	Fine	VF	XF
20	—	12	6.50	8.00	10.00	15.00

1/2 RUPEE

SILVER, 17mm, 5.35-5.80 gm

C#	Date	Year	VG	Fine	VF	XF
21	—	12	6.50	8.00	10.00	15.00

RUPEE

SILVER, 20mm, 10.70-11.60 gm

C#	Date	Year	VG	Fine	VF	XF
22	—	12	12.50	14.00	17.50	23.50

MOHUR

GOLD, 18mm, 10.70-11.40 gm

C#	Date	Year	VG	Fine	VF	XF
29	—	12	220.00	240.00	265.00	300.00

MUZAFFARGARH

Fortress and town founded in AD1794 by the Durrani governor of Multan, Nawab Muzaffar Khan. Why the coins were struck with the legends, symbols and style of Delhi issues of Shah Alam II remains unexplained. If earlier dates can be found, the mint may well be identified with the town of Muzaffarnagar, northeast of Delhi.

Mintmarks: 

RUPEE

SILVER, 21mm, 10.70-11.60 gm.

C#	Date	Year	VG	Fine	VF	XF
86.14	AH1208	35	12.50	14.00	17.50	23.50
	1209	36	12.50	14.00	17.50	23.50
	1209	37	12.50	14.00	17.50	23.50
	1211	39	12.50	14.00	17.50	23.50
	1212	40	12.50	14.00	17.50	23.50
	1213	41	12.50	14.00	17.50	23.50
	121x	42	12.50	14.00	17.50	23.50
	121x	43	12.50	14.00	17.50	23.50
	—	46	12.50	14.00	17.50	23.50
	12xx	47	12.50	14.00	17.50	23.50
	12xx	44	12.50	14.00	17.50	23.50

MYSORE

Haidar Ali

AD 1174-1197/AD 1761-1782

Balhari Mint

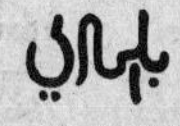 Balhari (Bellary)

PAISA

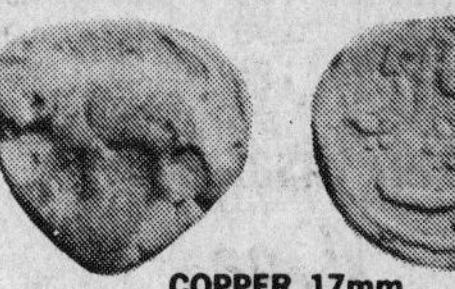

COPPER, 17mm

KM#	Date	Year	Good	VG	Fine	VF
1	ND	—	7.50	12.50	15.00	18.00

Gooty Mint

Gooty

In name of Muhammad Shah:

PAGODA

GOLD, 11mm, 3.4 gm.

KM#	Date	Year	VG	Fine	VF	XF
3	AH1194	—	55.00	67.50	80.00	100.00
	1198	—	55.00	67.50	80.00	100.00

Haidarnagar Mint

In the name of Shah Alam II:

RUPEE

SILVER, 10.70-11.60 gm.

KM#	Date	Year	VG	Fine	VF	XF
4	AH1191	14	45.00	60.00	75.00	100.00
	—	16	45.00	60.00	75.00	100.00

Patan Mint

Patan Seringapatan

PAISA

COPPER, 20mm

KM#	Date	Year	Good	VG	Fine	VF
5	AH1195	—	3.50	6.00	8.00	10.00
	1196	—	3.50	6.00	8.00	10.00

In the name of Shah Alam

MOHUR

GOLD, 22.5mm, 10.70-11.40 gm.

KM#	Date	Year	VG	Fine	VF	XF
6	AH1195	20	—	—	Rare	—

Uncertain Mint

FANAM

GOLD, 6mm, 0.4 gm.
Obv: God & Goddess
Rev: Letter HE (For Haidar)

Obv: Letter HE. Rev: Date.

KM#	Date	Year	VG	Fine	VF	XF
8	ND	—	5.00	7.00	9.00	12.00
9	AH1189	—	6.00	8.50	11.50	15.00
	1196	—	6.00	8.50	11.00	15.00

1/2 PAGODA

GOLD, 9mm, 1.7 gm.
Obv: God & Goddess
Rev: Letter HE

KM#	Date	Year	VG	Fine	VF	XF
11	ND	—	28.50	35.00	45.00	60.00

8mm
Obv: Seated God

KM#	Date	Year	VG	Fine	VF	XF
12	ND	—	28.50	35.00	45.00	60.00

PAGODA

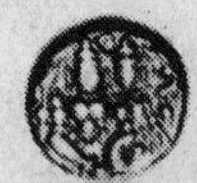

GOLD, 11mm, 3.4 gm.
Obv: God & Goddess
Rev: Letter HE

KM#	Date	Year	VG	Fine	VF	XF
15	ND	—	55.00	67.50	80.00	100.00

Uncertain Mint

CASH

COPPER, 10mm
Obv: Arabic 222, Kanarese 10
Rev: Crossed lines

KM#	Date	Year	Good	VG	Fine	VF
20	Kanarese	1-33	1.25	2.00	2.50	3.75

1/8 PAISA

COPPER, 8mm
Obv: Tiger. Rev: Battle axe.

KM#	Date	Year	Good	VG	Fine	VF
22	ND	—	2.75	4.50	6.00	9.00

1/4 PAISA

COPPER, 13mm

KM#	Date	Year	Good	VG	Fine	VF
23	ND	—	3.00	5.00	7.00	10.00

1/2 PAISA

COPPER, 16mm

KM#	Date	Year	Good	VG	Fine	VF
24	ND	—	3.00	5.00	7.00	10.00

Tipu Sultan

AH1197-1213/AM1211-1227/ 1782-1799AD

DATING: Tipu used Hijri years on his coins from AH1197 to AH1201. Thereafter he instituted the Mauludi era (AM), which used solar years, 14 years advanced from the Hijri year. They are indicated on the coins by being written in Arabic numerals from right to left, the opposite of normal usage. The Mauludi years were from 1215 to his death in 1227. The last four of these were often indicated by letters rather than numbers. Thus Arabic ALIF - Mauludi 1224, BE - 1225, TE - 1226, SE - 1227. Many blundered dates exist on the copper coins. Two digit regnal years were also written from right to left.

DENOMINATIONS: Tipu renamed his coins after the introduction of the Mauludi era. 1/8 Paisa - Qutb; 1/4 Paisa - Akhtar; 1/2 Paisa - Bahram; Paisa - Zohra; 2 Paisa - Osmani or Mushtari; 1/32 Rupee - Khizri; 1/16 Rupee - Kazimi; 1/8 Rupee - Jafari; 1/4 Rupee - Baqiri; 1/2 Rupee - Abidi; Rupee - Imami; 2 Rupees - Faruqi; Pagoda - Sadiqi; 4 Pagoda - Ahmadi. The system lapsed on his death. For simplicity sake the more familiar denominations will be used below.

NOTE: Significant varieties exist for many of the coins.

Bengalur Mint

Bengalur (Bangalore)

1/8 PAISA

COPPER, 10mm

KM#	Date	Year	Good	VG	Fine	VF
30	AM1216	(1787)	6.00	9.00	12.00	17.50
	1217	(1788)	6.00	9.00	12.00	17.50
	1218	(1789)	6.00	9.00	12.00	17.50
	1219	(1790)	6.00	9.00	12.00	17.50

1/4 PAISA

COPPER, 14mm

KM#	Date	Year	Good	VG	Fine	VF
31	AH1200	—	1.50	2.50	3.50	5.00
	AM1215	(1786)	1.25	2.00	3.00	4.50
	1216	(1787)	1.25	2.00	3.00	4.50
	1217	(1788)	1.25	2.00	3.00	4.50
	1218	(1789)	1.25	2.00	3.00	4.50
	1219	(1790)	1.25	2.00	3.00	4.50

1/2 PAISA

COPPER, 17mm

KM#	Date	Year	Good	VG	Fine	VF
32	AM1215	(1786)	1.50	2.50	3.50	5.00
	1216	(1787)	1.50	2.50	3.50	5.00
	1217	(1788)	1.50	2.50	3.50	5.00
	1218	(1789)	1.50	2.50	3.50	5.00
	1219	(1790)	1.50	2.50	3.50	5.00

PAISA

COPPER, 23mm

KM#	Date	Year	Good	VG	Fine	VF
33	AH1200	—	2.00	3.50	4.50	6.50
	AM1215	(1786)	1.75	3.00	4.00	6.00
	1216	(1787)	1.75	3.00	4.00	6.00
	1217	(1788)	1.75	3.00	4.00	6.00
	1218	(1789)	1.75	3.00	4.00	6.00
	1219	(1790)	1.75	3.00	4.00	6.00

Faiz Hisar Mint

Faiz Hisar (Gooty)

1/4 PAISA

COPPER, 12mm

KM#	Date	Year	Good	VG	Fine	VF
41	AM1215	(1786)	1.50	2.50	3.50	5.00
	1216	(1787)	1.50	2.50	3.50	5.00
	1217	(1788)	1.50	2.50	3.50	5.00
	1222	(1793)	1.50	2.50	3.50	5.00
	1223	(1794)	1.50	2.50	3.50	5.00
	1224(ALIF)	(1795)	1.50	2.50	3.50	5.00
	1225(BE)	(1796)	1.50	2.50	3.50	5.00
	1226(TE)	(1797)	1.50	2.50	3.50	5.00

1/2 PAISA

COPPER, 18mm

KM#	Date	Year	Good	VG	Fine	VF
42	AM1215	(1786)	1.75	3.00	4.00	6.00
	1216	(1787)	1.75	3.00	4.00	6.00
	1217	(1788)	1.75	3.00	4.00	6.00
	1218	(1789)	1.75	3.00	4.00	6.00
	1221	(1792)	1.75	3.00	4.00	6.00
	1222	(1793)	1.75	3.00	4.00	6.00
	1223	(1794)	1.75	3.00	4.00	6.00
	1224(ALIF)	(1795)	1.75	3.00	4.00	6.00
	1225(BE)	(1796)	1.75	3.00	4.00	6.00
	1226(TE)	(1797)	1.75	3.00	4.00	6.00

PAISA

COPPER, 21mm

KM#	Date	Year	Good	VG	Fine	VF
43	AM1215	(1786)	2.00	3.50	5.00	7.50
	1216	(1787)	2.00	3.50	5.00	7.50
	1217	(1788)	2.00	3.50	5.00	7.50
	1218	(1789)	2.00	3.50	5.00	7.50
	1220	(1791)	2.00	3.50	5.00	7.50
	1221	(1792)	2.00	3.50	5.00	7.50
	1222	(1793)	2.00	3.50	5.00	7.50
	1224(ALIF)	(1795)	2.00	3.50	5.00	7.50
	1225(BE)	(1796)	2.00	3.50	5.00	7.50

KM#	Date	Year	Good	VG	Fine	VF
43	1226(TE)	(1797)	2.00	3.50	5.00	7.50

Farrukhi Mint

Farrukhi (Feroke)

1/4 PAISA

COPPER, 15mm

KM#	Date	Year	Good	VG	Fine	VF
51	AM1216	(1787)	2.75	4.50	6.50	10.00
	1217	(1788)	2.75	4.50	6.50	10.00
	1218	(1789)	2.75	4.50	6.50	10.00

1/2 PAISA

COPPER, 18mm

KM#	Date	Year	Good	VG	Fine	VF
52	AM1217	(1788)	2.50	4.00	6.00	9.00
	1218	(1789)	2.50	4.00	6.00	9.00

PAISA

COPPER, 25mm

KM#	Date	Year	Good	VG	Fine	VF
53	AM1216	(1787)	2.00	3.50	5.50	8.00
	1217	(1788)	2.00	3.50	5.50	8.00
	1218	(1789)	2.00	3.50	5.50	8.00
	1219	(1790)	2.00	3.50	5.50	8.00

2 PAISA

COPPER, 32mm

KM#	Date	Year	Good	VG	Fine	VF
54	AM1218	(1789)	15.00	25.00	35.00	50.00

FANAM

GOLD, 7mm, 0.4 gm.

KM#	Date	Year	VG	Fine	VF	XF
58	AM1216	(1787)	6.00	9.00	12.00	15.00
	1217	(1788)	6.00	9.00	12.00	15.00
	1218	(1789)	6.00	9.00	12.00	15.00

Farrukhyab-Hisar Mint

Farrukhyab-Hisar Chitaldrug

1/8 PAISA

COPPER

KM#	Date	Year	Good	VG	Fine	VF
60	AM1217	(1788)	—	13.50	16.50	25.00

1/4 PAISA

COPPER, 15mm

KM#	Date	Year	Good	VG	Fine	VF
61	AM1216	(1787)	1.25	2.00	3.00	4.50
	1217	(1788)	1.25	2.00	3.00	4.50
	1218	(1789)	1.25	2.00	3.00	4.50
	1219	(1790)	1.25	2.00	3.00	4.50

1/2 PAISA

COPPER, 19mm

KM#	Date	Year	Good	VG	Fine	VF
62	AM1215	(1786)	1.50	2.50	3.50	5.00
	1216	(1787)	1.50	2.50	3.50	5.00
	1217	(1788)	1.50	2.50	3.50	5.00
	1218	(1789)	1.50	2.50	3.50	5.00
	1219	(1790)	1.50	2.50	3.50	5.00

PAISA

COPPER, 21mm

KM#	Date	Year	Good	VG	Fine	VF
63	AH1201	—	1.75	3.00	4.50	7.00
	AM1215	(1786)	1.75	3.00	4.50	7.00
	1216	(1787)	1.75	3.00	4.50	7.00
	1217	(1788)	1.75	3.00	4.50	7.00
	1218	(1789)	1.75	3.00	4.50	7.00
	1219	(1790)	1.75	3.00	4.50	7.00

2 PAISA

COPPER, 36mm

KM#	Date	Year	Good	VG	Fine	VF
64	AM1218	—	15.00	25.00	35.00	50.00
	1219	—	15.00	25.00	35.00	50.00

Kalikut Mint

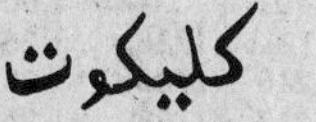

Kalikut (Calicut)

1/4 PAISA

COPPER, 11mm

KM#	Date	Year	Good	VG	Fine	VF
71	ND	—	3.50	6.00	9.00	13.50

PAISA

COPPER, 21mm

KM#	Date	Year	Good	VG	Fine	VF
73	AH1198	—	4.00	7.00	10.00	15.00
	1199	—	4.00	7.00	10.00	15.00
	1200	—	4.00	7.00	10.00	15.00
	AM1215	(1786)	4.00	7.00	10.00	15.00
	ND	—	6.00	10.00	15.00	22.50

RUPEE

SILVER, 10.70-11.60 gm.

KM#	Date	Year	VG	Fine	VF	XF
76	AM1215	5	35.00	45.00	60.00	90.00

2 RUPEES

SILVER, 21.40-23.20 gm.

KM#	Date	Year	VG	Fine	VF	XF
77	AM1215	(1786)	150.00	225.00	275.00	350.00

FANAM

GOLD, 7mm, 0.4 gm.

KM#	Date	Year	VG	Fine	VF	XF
78	AH1198	—	5.00	7.00	9.00	12.00
	1199	—	5.00	7.00	9.00	12.00
	1200	—	5.00	7.00	9.00	12.00
	AM1215	(1786)	5.00	7.00	9.00	12.00

Khaliqabad Mint

خالق اباد

Khaliqabad (Dindigul)

1/4 PAISA

COPPER, 12mm

KM#	Date	Year	Good	VG	Fine	VF
81	AM1215	(1786)	1.50	2.50	3.50	5.00
	1216	(1787)	1.50	2.50	3.50	5.00
	1217	(1788)	1.50	2.50	3.50	5.00
	1218	(1789)	1.50	2.50	3.50	5.00
	1225	(1796)	1.50	2.50	3.50	5.00

1/2 PAISA

COPPER, 17mm

KM#	Date	Year	Good	VG	Fine	VF
82	AM1215	(1786)	2.00	3.50	5.00	7.50
	1217	(1787)	2.00	3.50	5.00	7.50
	1218	(1788)	2.00	3.50	5.00	7.50

PAISA

COPPER, 22mm

KM#	Date	Year	Good	VG	Fine	VF
83	AM1215	(1786)	—	7.00	9.00	12.00
	1217	(1788)	—	7.00	9.00	12.00

FANAM

GOLD, 7mm, 0.4 gm.

KM#	Date	Year	VG	Fine	VF	XF
88	AM1215	(1786)	8.00	11.00	13.50	17.50
	1217	(1788)	8.00	11.00	13.50	17.50

Khurshed-Sawad Mint

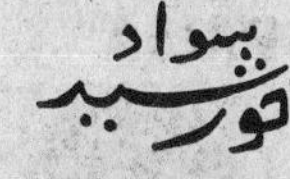

Khurshed-Sawad (Dharwar)

1/2 PAISA

COPPER, 19mm

KM#	Date	Year	Good	VG	Fine	VF
92	AM1217	(1788)	3.50	6.00	8.00	12.00

PAISA

COPPER, 23mm

KM#	Date	Year	Good	VG	Fine	VF
93	AM1217	(1788)	4.00	6.50	9.00	12.00
	1218	(1789)	4.00	6.50	9.00	12.00

RUPEE

SILVER, 10.70-11.60 gm.

KM#	Date	Year	VG	Fine	VF	XF
96	AM1216	(1787)	40.00	60.00	80.00	120.00
	1217	(1788)	40.00	60.00	80.00	120.00
	1218	(1789)	40.00	60.00	80.00	120.00

FANAM

GOLD, 7-8mm, 0.4 gm.

KM#	Date	Year	VG	Fine	VF	XF
98	AM1216	(1787)	11.50	15.00	18.00	22.50

PAGODA

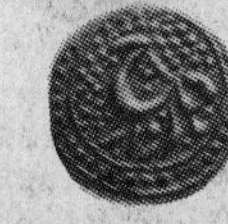

GOLD, 13mm

KM#	Date	Year	VG	Fine	VF	XF
99	AM1216	(1787)	55.00	67.50	80.00	100.00

KM#	Date	Year	VG	Fine	VF	XF
99a	AM1217	(1788)	55.00	67.50	80.00	100.00
	1218	(1789)	55.00	67.50	80.00	100.00

Nagar Mint

Nagar (Bednur)

1/8 PAISA

COPPER, 12mm

KM#	Date	Year	Good	VG	Fine	VF
100	AM1226(TE)	(1797)	6.00	10.00	15.00	22.50

1/4 PAISA

COPPER, 15mm

KM#	Date	Year	Good	VG	Fine	VF
101	AH1198	—	1.25	2.00	3.00	4.50
	1200	—	1.25	2.00	3.00	4.50
	AM1216	(1787)	1.25	2.00	3.00	4.50
	1217	(1788)	1.25	2.00	3.00	4.50
	1221	(1789)	1.25	2.00	3.00	4.50
	1224(ALIF)	(1792)	1.25	2.00	3.00	4.50
	1225(BE)	(1793)	1.25	2.00	3.00	4.50
	1226(TE)	(1794)	1.25	2.00	3.00	4.50

1/2 PAISA

COPPER, 18mm

KM#	Date	Year	Good	VG	Fine	VF
102	AH1200	—	1.50	2.50	3.50	5.00
	1201	—	1.75	3.00	5.00	7.50
	AM1215	(1786)	1.25	2.00	3.00	4.50
	1216	(1787)	1.25	2.00	3.00	4.50
	1217	(1788)	1.25	2.00	3.00	4.50
	1221	(1792)	1.25	2.00	3.00	4.50
	1222	(1793)	1.25	2.00	3.00	4.50
	1223	(1794)	1.25	2.00	3.00	4.50
	1224(ALIF)	(1795)	1.25	2.00	3.00	4.50
	1225(BE)	(1796)	1.25	2.00	3.00	4.50
	1226(TE)	(1797)	1.25	2.00	3.00	4.50
	1227(SE)	(1798)	1.75	3.00	4.50	6.50

PAISA

COPPER, 20mm

KM#	Date	Year	Good	VG	Fine	VF
103	AH1197	—	1.50	2.50	3.75	5.50
	1199	—	1.50	2.50	3.75	5.50
	1200	—	1.50	2.50	3.75	5.50
	1201	—	1.50	2.50	3.75	5.50
	AM1215	(1786)	1.50	2.50	3.75	5.50
	1216	(1787)	1.50	2.50	3.75	5.50
	1217	(1788)	1.50	2.50	3.75	5.50
	1218	(1789)	1.50	2.50	3.75	5.50
	1219	(1790)	1.50	2.50	3.75	5.50
	1220	(1791)	1.50	2.50	3.75	5.50
	1221	(1792)	1.50	2.50	3.75	5.50
	1222	(1793)	1.50	2.50	3.75	5.50
	1223	(1794)	1.50	2.50	3.75	5.50
	1224 (ALIF)	(1795)	1.50	2.50	3.75	5.50
	1225(BE)	(1796)	1.50	2.50	3.75	5.50
	1226(TE)	(1797)	1.50	2.50	3.75	5.50
	1227(SE)	(1798)	1.50	2.50	3.75	5.50

2 PAISA

COPPER, 29mm

KM#	Date	Year	Good	VG	Fine	VF
104	AM1218	(1789)	9.00	15.00	25.00	37.50
	1222	(1793)	9.00	15.00	25.00	37.50
	1223	(1794)	9.00	15.00	25.00	37.50
	1224(ALIF)	(1795)	9.00	15.00	25.00	37.50
	1225(BE)	(1796)	9.00	15.00	25.00	37.50
	1226(TE)	(1797)	9.00	15.00	25.00	37.50

1/2 RUPEE

SILVER, 5.35-5.80 gm.

KM#	Date	Year	VG	Fine	VF	XF
105	AM1215	(1786)	25.00	35.00	45.00	60.00

RUPEE

SILVER, 26mm, 10.70-11.60 gm.

KM#	Date	Year	VG	Fine	VF	XF
106	AH1200	—	50.00	60.00	75.00	110.00
	AM1216	(1787)	50.00	60.00	75.00	110.00

2 RUPEES

SILVER, 21.40-23.20 gm.

KM#	Date	Year	VG	Fine	VF	XF
107	AH1200	—	150.00	200.00	250.00	325.00
	AM1215	(1786)	150.00	200.00	250.00	325.00

FANAM

GOLD, 7mm

KM#	Date	Year	VG	Fine	VF	XF
108	AH1197	—	7.00	9.00	11.50	15.00
	1198	—	7.00	9.00	11.50	15.00
	1199	—	7.00	9.00	11.50	15.00
	1200	—	7.00	9.00	11.50	15.00
	AM1215	(1786)	7.00	9.00	11.50	15.00
	AM1216	(1787)	7.00	9.00	11.50	15.00
	AM1217	(1788)	7.00	9.00	11.50	15.00
	1220	(1791)	7.00	9.00	11.50	15.00
	1221	(1792)	7.00	9.00	11.50	15.00

PAGODA

GOLD, 12mm, 3.4 gm.

KM#	Date	Year	VG	Fine	VF	XF
109	AH1198	—	55.00	67.50	80.00	100.00
	1199	—	55.00	67.50	80.00	100.00
	1200	—	55.00	67.50	80.00	100.00
	AM1215	(1786)	55.00	67.50	80.00	100.00
	1216	(1787)	55.00	67.50	80.00	100.00
	1217	(1788)	55.00	67.50	80.00	100.00

4 PAGODAS

GOLD, 13.6 gm.

KM#	Date	Year	VG	Fine	VF	XF
109a	AM1216	(1787)	—	—	Rare	—

Nazarbar Mint

نظر بار

Nazarbar (City of Mysore)

1/4 PAISA

COPPER

KM#	Date	Year	Good	VG	Fine	VF
111	AM1216	(1787)	7.50	11.50	15.00	22.50

PAISA

COPPER

KM#	Date	Year	Good	VG	Fine	VF
112	AM1216	(1787)	7.50	11.50	15.00	22.50

25mm

KM#	Date	Year	Good	VG	Fine	VF
113	AM1216	(1787)	7.50	11.50	15.00	22.50

Patan Mint

(Seringapatan)

For drawing, see above KM#5.

1/8 PAISA

COPPER

KM#	Date	Year	Good	VG	Fine	VF
120	AM1216	(1787)	4.50	7.50	10.00	15.00
	1217	(1788)	4.50	7.50	10.00	15.00
	1218	(1789)	4.50	7.50	10.00	15.00
	1221	(1792)	4.50	7.50	10.00	15.00
	1222	(1793)	4.50	7.50	10.00	15.00
	1224(ALIF)	(1795)	4.50	7.50	10.00	15.00
	1225(BE)	(1796)	4.50	7.50	10.00	15.00
	1226(TE)	(1797)	4.50	7.50	10.00	15.00

1/4 PAISA

COPPER, 13mm

KM#	Date	Year	Good	VG	Fine	VF
121	AH1198	—	1.50	2.50	3.50	5.00
	1200	—	1.50	2.50	3.50	5.00
	1201	—	1.50	2.50	3.50	5.00
	AM1215	(1786)	1.25	2.00	3.00	4.50
	1216	(1787)	1.25	2.00	3.00	4.50
	1217	(1788)	1.25	2.00	3.00	4.50
	1218	(1789)	1.25	2.00	3.00	4.50

KM#	Date	Year	Good	VG	Fine	VF
121	1219	(1790)	1.25	2.00	3.00	4.50
	1220	(1791)	1.25	2.00	3.00	4.50
	1221	(1792)	1.25	2.00	3.00	4.50
	1222	(1793)	1.25	2.00	3.00	4.50
	1223	(1794)	1.25	2.00	3.00	4.50
	1224(ALIF)	(1795)	1.25	2.00	3.00	4.50
	1225(BE)	(1796)	1.25	2.00	3.00	4.50
	1226(TE)	(1797)	1.25	2.00	3.00	4.50

1/2 PAISA

COPPER, 17mm

KM#	Date	Year	Good	VG	Fine	VF
122	AH1200	—	1.50	2.50	3.50	5.00
	1201	—	1.50	2.50	3.50	5.00
	AM1215	(1786)	1.25	2.00	3.00	4.50
	1216	(1787)	1.25	2.00	3.00	4.50
	1217	(1788)	1.25	2.00	3.00	4.50
	1218	(1789)	1.25	2.00	3.00	4.50
	1219	(1790)	1.25	2.00	3.00	4.50
	1220	(1791)	1.25	2.00	3.00	4.50
	1221	(1792)	1.25	2.00	3.00	4.50
	1222	(1793)	1.25	2.00	3.00	4.50
	1223	(1794)	1.25	2.00	3.00	4.50
	1224(ALIF)	(1795)	1.25	2.00	3.00	4.50
	1225(BE)	(1796)	1.25	2.00	3.00	4.50
	1226(TE)	(1797)	1.25	2.00	3.00	4.50

PAISA

COPPER, 25mm

KM#	Date	Year	Good	VG	Fine	VF
123	AH1197	—	1.75	3.00	4.00	6.00
	1200	—	1.75	3.00	4.00	6.00
	1201	—	1.75	3.00	4.00	6.00
	AM1215	(1786)	1.50	2.50	3.50	5.00
	1216	(1787)	1.50	2.50	3.50	5.00
	1217	(1788)	1.50	2.50	3.50	5.00
	1218	(1789)	1.50	2.50	3.50	5.00
	1219	(1790)	1.50	2.50	3.50	5.00
	1220	(1791)	1.50	2.50	3.50	5.00
	1221	(1792)	1.50	2.50	3.50	5.00
	1222	(1793)	1.50	2.50	3.50	5.00
	1223	(1794)	1.50	2.50	3.50	5.00
	1224(ALIF)	(1795)	1.50	2.50	3.50	5.00
	1225(BE)	(1796)	1.50	2.50	3.50	5.00
	1226(TE)	(1797)	1.50	2.50	3.50	5.00

2 PAISA

COPPER, 32mm

KM#	Date	Year	Good	VG	Fine	VF
124	AM1218	(1789)	9.00	16.50	27.50	40.00
	1219	(1790)	9.00	16.50	27.50	40.00
	1220	(1791)	9.00	16.50	27.50	40.00
	1221	(1792)	9.00	16.50	27.50	40.00
	1222	(1793)	9.00	16.50	27.50	40.00
	1223	(1794)	9.00	16.50	27.50	40.00
	1224(ALIF)	(1795)	9.00	16.50	27.50	40.00
	1225(BE)	(1796)	9.00	16.50	27.50	40.00
	1226(TE)	(1797)	9.00	16.50	27.50	40.00

1/32 RUPEE

SILVER, 0.34-0.36 gm.

KM#	Date	Year	VG	Fine	VF	XF
A125	AM1222	(1793)	—	—	—	—

1/16 RUPEE

SILVER, 8mm, 0.68-0.72 gm.

KM#	Date	Year	VG	Fine	VF	XF
B125	AM1220	(1791)	10.00	15.00	20.00	30.00
	1221	(1792)	10.00	15.00	20.00	30.00
	1222	(1793)	10.00	15.00	20.00	30.00
	1223	(1794)	10.00	15.00	20.00	30.00
	1224	(1795)	10.00	15.00	20.00	30.00
	1225	(1796)	10.00	15.00	20.00	30.00
	1226	(1797)	10.00	15.00	20.00	30.00

1/8 RUPEE

SILVER, 11mm, 1.34-1.45 gm.

KM#	Date	Year	VG	Fine	VF	XF
C125	AM1218	(1789)	10.00	15.00	20.00	30.00
	1220	(1791)	10.00	15.00	20.00	30.00
	1221	(1792)	10.00	15.00	20.00	30.00
	1222	(1793)	10.00	15.00	20.00	30.00
	1223	(1794)	10.00	15.00	20.00	30.00
	1224	(1795)	10.00	15.00	20.00	30.00
	1225	(1796)	10.00	15.00	20.00	30.00
	1226	(1797)	10.00	15.00	20.00	30.00

1/4 RUPEE

SILVER, 16mm, 2.68-2.90 gm.

KM#	Date	Year	VG	Fine	VF	XF
D125	AM1216	(1787)	10.00	17.50	25.00	37.50
	1217	(1788)	10.00	17.50	25.00	37.50
	1218	(1789)	10.00	17.50	25.00	37.50
	1221	(1792)	10.00	17.50	25.00	37.50
	1222	(1793)	10.00	17.50	25.00	37.50
	1224	(1795)	10.00	17.50	25.00	37.50

1/2 RUPEE

SILVER, 21mm, 5.35-5.80 gm.

KM#	Date	Year	VG	Fine	VF	XF
125	AM1215	(1786)	20.00	30.00	40.00	60.00
	1216	(1787)	20.00	30.00	40.00	60.00
	1217	(1788)	20.00	30.00	40.00	60.00
	1218	(1789)	20.00	30.00	40.00	60.00
	1219	(1790)	20.00	30.00	40.00	60.00
	1220	(1791)	20.00	30.00	40.00	60.00
	1222	(1793)	20.00	30.00	40.00	60.00
	1224	(1795)	20.00	30.00	40.00	60.00

RUPEE

SILVER, 25mm, 10.70-11.60 gm.

KM#	Date	Year	VG	Fine	VF	XF
126	AH1200	—	25.00	37.50	47.50	70.00
	AM1216	(1787)	25.00	37.50	47.50	70.00
	1217	(1788)	25.00	37.50	47.50	70.00
	1218	(1789)	25.00	37.50	47.50	70.00
	1219	(1790)	25.00	37.50	47.50	70.00
	1220	(1791)	25.00	37.50	47.50	70.00
	1223	(1794)	25.00	37.50	47.50	70.00

2 RUPEES

SILVER, 36mm, 21.40-23.20 gm.

KM#	Date	Year	VG	Fine	VF	XF
127	AH1198	2	125.00	175.00	225.00	325.00
	1199	3	125.00	175.00	225.00	325.00
	1200	—	125.00	175.00	225.00	325.00
	AM1215	—	125.00	175.00	225.00	325.00
	1216	6	125.00	175.00	225.00	325.00
	1217	—	125.00	175.00	225.00	325.00
	1218	—	125.00	175.00	225.00	325.00
	1219	—	125.00	175.00	225.00	325.00
	1220	—	125.00	175.00	225.00	325.00

FANAM

GOLD, 7mm, 0.4 gm.

KM#	Date	Year	VG	Fine	VF	XF
128	AH1197	—	6.00	8.50	11.50	15.00
	1198	—	6.00	8.50	11.50	15.00
	1199	—	6.00	8.50	11.50	15.00
	1200	—	6.00	8.50	11.50	15.00
	1201	—	6.00	8.50	11.50	15.00
	AM1215	(1786)	6.00	8.50	11.50	15.00
	1216	(1787)	6.00	8.50	11.50	15.00
	1217	(1788)	6.00	8.50	11.50	15.00
	1218	(1789)	6.00	8.50	11.50	15.00
	1219	(1790)	6.00	8.50	11.50	15.00
	1220	(1791)	6.00	8.50	11.50	15.00
	1221	(1792)	6.00	8.50	11.50	15.00
	1222	(1793)	6.00	8.50	11.50	15.00
	1223	(1794)	6.00	8.50	11.50	15.00

PAGODA

GOLD, 12mm, 3.4 gm.

KM#	Date	Year	VG	Fine	VF	XF
129	AH1197	—	55.00	67.50	80.00	100.00
	1198	2	55.00	67.50	80.00	100.00
	1200	—	55.00	67.50	80.00	100.00
	AM1215	(1786)	55.00	67.50	80.00	100.00

KM#	Date	Year	VG	Fine	VF	XF
129a	AM1216	(1787)	55.00	67.50	80.00	100.00
	1217	(1788)	55.00	67.50	80.00	100.00
	1218	8	55.00	67.50	80.00	100.00
	1219	(1790)	55.00	67.50	80.00	100.00
	1220	(1791)	55.00	67.50	80.00	100.00
	1221	(1792)	55.00	67.50	80.00	100.00
	1223	(1794)	55.00	67.50	80.00	100.00

2 PAGODAS

GOLD, 19mm, 6.8 gm.

KM#	Date	Year	VG	Fine	VF	XF
A129	AM1216	(1787)		—	—	—
	1217	(1788)		—	—	—
	1218	8		—	—	—
	1219	(1790)		—	—	—

4 PAGODAS

GOLD, 24mm, 13.6 gm.

KM#	Date	Year	VG	Fine	VF	XF
B129	AH1198	2		—	—	—
	1199	—		—	—	—
	AM1215	(1786)		—	—	—
	1217	(1788)		—	—	—
	1218	8		—	—	—
	1219	(1790)		—	—	—

Salamabad Mint

Salamabad (Satyamangalam)

1/8 PAISA

COPPER, 12mm

KM#	Date	Year	Good	VG	Fine	VF
130	AM1218	(1789)	12.50	20.00	25.00	37.50

1/4 PAISA

COPPER, 16mm

KM#	Date	Year	Good	VG	Fine	VF
131	AM1216	(1787)	6.00	10.00	12.50	18.50

1/2 PAISA

COPPER, 19mm

KM#	Date	Year	Good	VG	Fine	VF
132	AM1216	(1787)	4.50	7.50	10.00	15.00
	1217	(1788)	4.50	7.50	10.00	15.00
	1218	(1789)	4.50	7.50	10.00	15.00

PAISA

COPPER, 24mm

Obv: Elephant

KM#	Date	Year	Good	VG	Fine	VF
133	AM1216	(1787)	6.00	10.00	12.50	18.50
	1217	(1788)	6.00	10.00	12.50	18.50
	1218	(1789)	6.00	10.00	12.50	18.50

Zafarabad Mint

ظفراباد

Zafarabad Gurramkonda

1/4 PAISA

COPPER, 16mm

KM#	Date	Year	Good	VG	Fine	VF
141	AM1218	(1789)	7.50	12.50	15.00	22.50

1/2 PAISA

COPPER, 19mm

KM#	Date	Year	Good	VG	Fine	VF
142	AM1215	(1786)	6.00	9.00	12.50	18.50
	1216	(1787)	6.00	9.00	12.50	18.50
	1217	(1788)	6.00	9.00	12.50	18.50
	1218	(1789)	6.00	9.00	12.50	18.50

PAISA

COPPER, 21mm

KM#	Date	Year	Good	VG	Fine	VF
143	AM1216	(1787)	9.00	13.50	18.50	28.50
	1218	(1788)	9.00	13.50	18.50	28.50

Dewan Purnaiya

Regent for Krishnaraja Wodeyar

AD 1799-1810

A Sardula (mythical tiger) is illustrated on all of Dewan Purnaiya's coins.

6-1/4 CASH

COPPER, 14mm
Without value, with Mysore.

C#	Date	Good	VG	Fine	VF
185	ND	1.75	3.00	4.00	6.00

Without value or Mysore.

C#	Date	Good	VG	Fine	VF
185a	ND	3.00	5.00	6.00	9.00

Value in English, with Mysore.

C#	Date	Good	VG	Fine	VF
185b	ND	3.00	5.00	6.00	9.00

12-1/2 CASH

COPPER, 17-18mm

C#	Date	Good	VG	Fine	VF
186	ND	2.75	4.50	6.00	9.00

25 CASH

COPPER, 24mm
English legends often blundered

C#	Date	Good	VG	Fine	VF
187	ND	2.50	4.00	6.00	9.00

NOTE: Silver coinage of Dewan Purnaiya is identical to that of Krishnaraja and they are all listed together following the copper issues.

Krishna Raja Wodeyar

AD 1810-1868

British control after 1831

Type I

Obv: Elephant. Rev: Three line Nagari legend.

All other elephant types have Kanarese on reverse.

6-1/4 CASH

COPPER, 14mm

C#	Date	Good	VG	Fine	VF
170	ND	6.00	10.00	13.50	20.00

Type II

Obv: Elephant. Rev: Two lines of Kanarese and one of English.

5 CASH

COPPER, 13mm

C#	Date	Good	VG	Fine	VF
171	ND (vars.)	1.75	3.00	4.50	6.50
	ND (X CASH in error)	3.00	5.00	7.50	11.00

20 CASH

COPPER, 19mm
English legends often blundered

C#	Date	Good	VG	Fine	VF
177	ND	1.25	2.00	3.00	4.50

40 CASH

COPPER, 23mm

C#	Date	Good	VG	Fine	VF
180	ND	4.50	7.50	10.00	15.00

Type III

Obv: Elephant. Rev: Three line Kanarese legend and value in English.

The 5 & 10 Cash have the English at bottom, whereas Type II has English at top on these two denominations.

10 CASH

COPPER, 16mm

C#	Date	Good	VG	Fine	VF
174a	ND	3.00	5.00	6.50	10.00
	With "2"	3.00	5.00	6.50	10.00

20 CASH

COPPER, 21mm

C#	Date	Good	VG	Fine	VF
177a	ND	1.00	1.75	2.50	3.50
	With "1"	1.00	1.75	2.50	3.50
	With "2"	1.00	1.75	2.50	3.50

Type IV

Obv: Elephant, Kanarese legend above.
Rev: Similar to Type III.

5 CASH

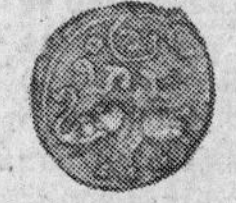 

COPPER, 13mm

C#	Date	Good	VG	Fine	VF
171b	ND	1.75	3.00	5.00	7.50

10 CASH

COPPER, 17mm

C#	Date	Good	VG	Fine	VF
174b	ND	2.75	4.50	6.00	9.00

20 CASH

COPPER, 21-22mm

C#	Date	Good	VG	Fine	VF
177b	ND	2.00	3.50	5.00	7.50

Type V

Obv: Sardula, date below.

2-1/2 CASH

COPPER, 10mm

C#	Date	Good	VG	Fine	VF
190.1	1833	4.50	7.50	9.00	13.50

5 CASH

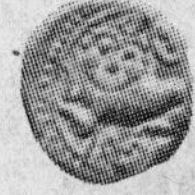 

COPPER, 13mm

C#	Date	Good	VG	Fine	VF
191.1	1833	2.50	4.00	5.50	8.00
	1834	2.50	4.00	5.50	8.00

10 CASH

COPPER, 18mm

C#	Date	Good	VG	Fine	VF
192.1	1833	3.00	5.00	6.00	9.00
	1834	3.00	5.00	6.00	9.00

22mm

C#	Date	Good	VG	Fine	VF
193.1	1833	2.00	3.50	5.00	7.50
	1834	2.00	3.50	5.00	7.50

Type VI

Obv: Lion, date below.

2-1/2 CASH

COPPER, 10-11mm

C#	Date	Good	VG	Fine	VF
190.2	1841	2.50	4.00	6.00	9.00
	1842	1.75	3.00	5.00	7.50
	1843	1.75	3.00	5.00	7.50

5 CASH

COPPER, 12-14mm

C#	Date	Good	VG	Fine	VF
191.2	1834	1.75	3.00	4.50	7.00
	1835	1.75	3.00	4.50	7.00
	1836	1.75	3.00	4.50	7.00
	1837	1.75	3.00	4.50	7.00
	1838	1.75	3.00	4.50	7.00
	1839	1.75	3.00	4.50	7.00
	1840	1.75	3.00	4.50	7.00
	1841	1.75	3.00	4.50	7.00
	1842	1.75	3.00	4.50	7.00
	1843	1.75	3.00	4.50	7.00

10 CASH

COPPER, 16-18mm

C#	Date	Good	VG	Fine	VF
192.2	1834	3.00	5.00	7.00	11.00
192.2	1835	2.00	3.50	5.00	7.50
	1836	2.00	3.50	5.00	7.50
	1837	2.00	3.50	5.00	7.50
	1838	2.00	3.50	5.00	7.50
	1839	2.00	3.50	5.00	7.50
	1840	2.00	3.50	5.00	7.50
	1841	2.00	3.50	5.00	7.50
	1842	2.00	3.50	5.00	7.50
	1843	2.00	3.50	5.00	7.50

20 CASH

COPPER, 20-26mm

C#	Date	Good	VG	Fine	VF
193.2	1833	1.75	3.00	4.50	7.00
	1834	1.75	3.00	4.50	7.00
	1835	1.50	2.50	4.00	6.00
	1836	1.50	2.50	4.00	6.00
	1837	1.50	2.50	4.00	6.00
	1838	1.50	2.50	4.00	6.00
	1839	1.50	2.50	4.00	6.00
	1840	1.50	2.50	4.00	6.00
	1841	1.50	2.50	4.00	6.00
	1843	1.50	2.50	4.00	6.00

NOTE: All dates have MEILEE on rev.; some 1834 have MILAY, and some 1837 have MILEE.

1/3 PAVALI

SILVER, 9mm, 0.89-0.96 gm.

C#	Date	Year	VG	Fine	VF	XF
200	ND	—	15.00	20.00	25.00	37.50

2/3 PAVALI

SILVER, 11mm, 1.78-1.92 gm.

C#	Date	Year	VG	Fine	VF	XF
201	ND	—	11.50	15.00	20.00	30.00

1/4 RUPEE (PAVALI)

SILVER, 14mm, 2.68-2.90 gm.
Dancing figure (Chamundi)

C#	Date	Year	VG	Fine	VF	XF
202	AH1214		5.00	7.50	11.50	17.50
	1226	—	5.00	7.50	11.50	17.50
	1229	—	5.00	7.50	11.50	17.50
	1243	—	5.00	7.50	11.50	17.50
	1244	—	5.00	7.50	11.50	17.50
	1245	—	5.00	7.50	11.50	17.50
	1246	—	5.00	7.50	11.50	17.50
	1247	—	5.00	7.50	11.50	17.50
	1248	—	5.00	7.50	11.50	17.50
	3421(Sic)	—	5.00	7.50	11.50	17.50
	4421(Sic)	—	5.00	7.50	11.50	17.50

Shah Alam II legends

C#	Date	Year	VG	Fine	VF	XF
205	AH1220	44	7.50	10.00	13.50	20.00
	1220	45	7.50	10.00	13.50	20.00
	—	76	7.50	10.00	13.50	20.00
	—	84	7.50	10.00	13.50	20.00

1/2 RUPEE

SILVER, 23mm, 5.35-5.80 gm.

MYSORE MINT

C#	Date	Year	VG	Fine	VF	XF
206	—	39	10.00	13.50	17.50	26.50
	—	76	10.00	13.50	17.50	26.50

NAGAR MINT

C#	Date	Year	VG	Fine	VF	XF
206a	—	74	12.50	15.00	20.00	30.00
	—	84	12.50	15.00	20.00	30.00

RUPEE

SILVER, 23mm

MYSORE MINT

C#	Date	Year	VG	Fine	VF	XF
207	AH1214	39	12.50	14.00	17.50	23.50
	1215	39	12.50	14.00	17.50	23.50
	1219	44	12.50	14.00	17.50	23.50
	1221	25(Sic)	12.50	14.00	17.50	23.50
	1221	45	12.50	14.00	17.50	23.50
	1222	46	12.50	14.00	17.50	23.50
	1222	64	12.50	14.00	17.50	23.50
	1223	64	12.50	14.00	17.50	23.50
	1224	64	12.50	14.00	17.50	23.50
	1224	74	12.50	14.00	17.50	23.50
	1225	74	12.50	14.00	17.50	23.50
	1225	94	12.50	14.00	17.50	23.50
	1226	94	12.50	14.00	17.50	23.50
	1227	95	12.50	14.00	17.50	23.50
	1228	95	12.50	14.00	17.50	23.50
	1229	96	12.50	14.00	17.50	23.50
	1230	97	12.50	14.00	17.50	23.50
	1231	98	12.50	14.00	17.50	23.50
	1232	99	12.50	14.00	17.50	23.50
	1234	98	12.50	14.00	17.50	23.50
	1235	98	12.50	14.00	17.50	23.50
	1236	98	12.50	14.00	17.50	23.50
	1237	37	12.50	14.00	17.50	23.50
	1238	37	12.50	14.00	17.50	23.50
	1239	3x	12.50	14.00	17.50	23.50
	1240	98	12.50	14.00	17.50	23.50
	1242	37	12.50	14.00	17.50	23.50
	1243	98	12.50	14.00	17.50	23.50
	1247	47	12.50	14.00	17.50	23.50
	1248	48	12.50	14.00	17.50	23.50
	x421	45	12.50	14.00	17.50	23.50
	x421	47	12.50	14.00	17.50	23.50

NAGAR MINT

21mm

C#	Date	Year	VG	Fine	VF	XF
207a	—	46	17.50	22.50	27.50	40.00
	AH1225	84	17.50	22.50	27.50	40.00

FANAM

GOLD, 7mm, 0.4 gm.
Narasimha

C#	Date	Year	VG	Fine	VF	XF
212	ND	—	7.50	10.00	13.50	20.00

PAGODA

GOLD, 12mm, 3.4 gm.
Shiva And Parvati

C#	Date	Year	VG	Fine	VF	XF
210	ND	—	55.00	67.50	80.00	100.00

NOTE: Fanams and 1/2 pagodas of this type are recent fabrications.

1/4 MOHUR

GOLD
Mughal type

C#	Date	Year	VG	Fine	VF	XF
215	—	45	—	—	Rare	—

NARWAR

Independent until AH1220/1805AD

In the name of Shah Alam II

PAISA

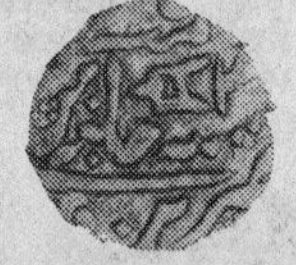

COPPER, 17mm
Horizontal Katar

C#	Date	Year	Good	VG	Fine	VF
10	AH1205	3x	—	—	—	—
	1207	35	1.75	3.00	4.00	5.00
	1207	46	1.75	3.00	4.00	5.00
	1208	4x	1.75	3.00	4.00	5.00

18mm
Vertical Katar

C#	Date	Year	Good	VG	Fine	VF
10.1	AH1215	43	1.75	3.00	4.00	5.00
	1216	44	1.75	3.00	4.00	5.00
	1217	4x	1.75	3.00	4.00	5.00

AH1215 dated coins are slightly different type.

1/4 RUPEE

SILVER, 2.68-2.90 gm

C#	Date	Year	VG	Fine	VF	XF
23	AH1207	3x	10.00	12.50	15.00	22.50

RUPEE

SILVER, 26mm, 10.70-11.60 gm
Rev: Plain.

C#	Date	Year	VG	Fine	VF	XF
25	AH	2	12.50	15.00	20.00	30.00
	1179	6	12.50	15.00	20.00	30.00

25mm

Rev: Katar

C#	Date	Year	VG	Fine	VF	XF
25.1	AH1179	6	12.00	15.00	20.00	30.00

24mm
Rev: Floral symbols.

C#	Date	Year	VG	Fine	VF	XF
25.2	AH1189	16	12.50	15.00	20.00	30.00
	1190	17	12.50	15.00	20.00	30.00
	1191	18	12.50	15.00	20.00	30.00

SILVER, 20-21mm
Pseudo - dated AH1106

C#	Date	Year	VG	Fine	VF	XF
25.3	AH1106	9	12.50	14.00	17.50	23.50
	1106	17	12.50	14.00	17.50	23.50
	1106	34	12.50	14.00	17.50	23.50
	1106	35	12.50	14.00	17.50	23.50
	1106	40	12.50	14.00	17.50	23.50
	1106	41	12.50	14.00	17.50	23.50
	1106	44	12.50	14.00	17.50	23.50
	1106	46	12.50	14.00	17.50	23.50
	1106	47	11.50	13.00	15.00	20.00

Actual date and regnal year

C#	Date	Year	VG	Fine	VF	XF
25.4	1201	29	11.50	13.00	15.00	20.00
	1202	30	11.50	13.00	15.00	20.00
	1202	31	11.50	13.00	15.00	20.00
	1203	31	11.50	13.00	15.00	20.00
	1205	33	11.50	13.00	15.00	20.00
	1206	34	11.50	13.00	15.00	20.00
	1207	35	11.50	13.00	15.00	20.00
	1208	35	11.50	13.00	15.00	20.00

For later dates, see Gwalior: Narwar.

NAWANAGER

Early Types: Stylized imitations of the coins of Muzaffar III of Gujarat (AD 1560-73), dated AH 978 (= AD 1570), were struck from the end of the 16th Century until the early part of the reign of Vibhaji. These show a steady degradation of style over the nearly 300 years of issue, but no types can be dated to specific rulers. The former attribution of these coins to Ranmalji II (AD 1820-52) is incorrect. All are inscribed 'SRI JAMJI', title of all rulers of Nawanager. varieties in this series are the rule, not the exception. These include legend style and small marks in the field such as a crescent, Katar (dagger), etc.

DUMP COINAGE

Crude style; ca. 1570's into the 19th Century AD

TRAMBIYO

COPPER, 11mm

C#	Date	Good	VG	Fine	VF
14	AH978 (frozen)	1.75	3.00	4.50	6.00

DOKDO

COPPER, 16-19mm

C#	Date	Good	VG	Fine	VF
15	AH978 (frozen)	.90	1.50	2.00	2.50

1-1/2 DOKDO

COPPER, 20mm

C#	Date	Good	VG	Fine	VF
16	AH978 (frozen)	1.75	3.00	4.00	5.00

1/2 KORI

SILVER, 12mm

C#	Date	Good	VG	Fine	VF
20	AH978 (frozen)	1.75	3.00	4.50	6.00

KORI

SILVER, 15mm

C#	Date	Good	VG	Fine	VF
21	AH978 (frozen)	1.50	2.50	3.25	4.00

LATER DUMP COINAGE

Finer style from ca. 1850AD.

1/2 DOKDO

COPPER, 14-16mm

Y#	Date	Good	VG	Fine	VF
2	AH978 (frozen)	.60	1.00	1.50	2.00

(Late style, perhaps of Vibhaji, illustrated)

DOKDO

COPPER, 17-19mm

Y#	Date	Good	VG	Fine	VF
3	AH978 (frozen)	.60	1.00	1.50	2.00

1-1/2 DOKDA

COPPER, 19-21mm

Y#	Date	Good	VG	Fine	VF
4	AH978 (frozen)	.90	1.50	2.00	2.50

1/2 KORI

SILVER, 12-13mm

Y#	Date	VG	Fine	VF	XF
5	AH978 (frozen)	2.50	3.50	4.50	6.00

KORI

SILVER, 14-16mm

Y#	Date	VG	Fine	VF	XF
6	AH978 (frozen)	3.00	4.00	5.00	6.50

Vibhaji

AD 1852-1895

1/2 DOKDO

COPPER, 15mm
Similar to 1/2 Dokdo, Y#2.

Y#	Date	Good	VG	Fine	VF
9	AH978 (frozen)	.75	1.25	2.00	2.75

DOKDO

COPPER, 18mm
Similar to 1 Dokdo, Y#3.

Y#	Date	Good	VG	Fine	VF
10	AH978 (frozen)	.90	1.50	2.50	3.50

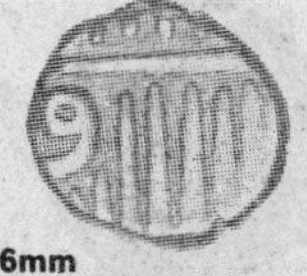

15-16mm

Y#	Date	Year	Good	VG	Fine	VF
1	VS1909	(1852)	3.50	6.00	7.50	9.00
	1917	(1860)	3.50	6.00	7.50	9.00

(Other dates probably exist)

2 DOKDA

COPPER, 22mm

Y#	Date	Year	Good	VG	Fine	VF
13	VS1943	(1886)	5.50	9.00	12.50	17.50

3 DOKDA

COPPER, 31mm

Y#	Date	Year	Good	VG	Fine	VF
11	VS1928	(1871)	4.50	7.50	12.50	15.00

27mm

Y#	Date	Year	Good	VG	Fine	VF
14	VS1942	(1885)	4.75	8.00	11.50	15.00

KORI

SILVER, (plain edge), 17mm
Crude striking

Y#	Date	Year	VG	Fine	VF	XF
12	VS1934	(1877)	5.00	7.00	10.00	15.00
	1935	(1878)	5.00	7.00	10.00	14.00
	1936	(1879)	4.50	6.50	9.50	13.50

2-1/2 KORI

SILVER, (milled edge), 17-19mm

Y#	Date	Year	VG	Fine	VF	XF
15	VS1949	(1892)	7.50	12.00	17.50	23.50
	1950	(1893)	7.50	12.00	17.50	23.50

5 KORI

SILVER, (milled edge), 22-26mm
Large inner circle

Y#	Date	Year	Fine	VF	XF	Unc
16	VS1945	(1888)	12.50	15.00	20.00	27.50
	1946	(1889)	12.50	16.00	20.00	27.50
	1947	(1890)	12.50	15.00	20.00	27.50

Redesigned

Y#	Date	Year	Fine	VF	XF	Unc
16.1	1948	(1891)	12.50	15.00	20.00	27.50
	1949	(1892)	12.50	15.00	20.00	27.50
	1950	(1893)	12.50	15.00	20.00	27.50

1/2 GOLD KORI

GOLD, 13mm

Y#	Date	VG	Fine	VF	XF
7	AH978 (frozen)	75.00	100.00	125.00	165.00

GOLD KORI

GOLD, 14-17mm

Y#	Date	VG	Fine	VF	XF
8	AH(9)78 (frozen)	125.00	150.00	185.00	250.00

Jaswant Singh

AD 1894-1907

1/2 DOKDO

COPPER, 19mm

Y#	Date	Year	Good	VG	Fine	VF
17	VS1956	(1899)	7.50	12.50	20.00	30.00

DOKDO

COPPER, 17mm

Y#	Date	Year	Good	VG	Fine	VF
18	VS1956	(1899)	7.50	12.50	20.00	30.00

1-1/2 DOKDA

COPPER, 20mm

Y#	Date	Year	Good	VG	Fine	VF
19	VS1956	(1899)	7.50	12.50	20.00	30.00

2 DOKDA

COPPER, 22mm

Y#	Date	Year	Good	VG	Fine	VF
20	VS1956	(1899)	7.50	12.50	20.00	30.00

3 DOKDA

COPPER, 26mm

Y#	Date	Year	Good	VG	Fine	VF
21	VS1956	(1899)	12.00	20.00	30.00	40.00

ORCHHA

RULERS

Vikramajit Mahendra, AD 1796-1817
Dharam Pal, AD 1817-1834
Taj Singh, AD 1834-1841
Surjain Singh, AD 1842-1848
Hamir Singh, AD 1848-1874
Pratap Singh, AD 1874-1930

MINTMARKS:

1 Reverse. (This is the symbol most characteristic of Orchha's coinage and is copied on the Datia imitations)

2 Obverse, most common.

3 Obverse, less common.

4 Reverse

5 Reverse

6 Reverse

7 Reverse

8 Reverse

9 Reverse

10 Reverse

NOTE: Marks #4 through #10 are found in addition to Mark #1.

NOTE: The Datia copies can only be distinguished by the mintmarks, other than #1, which is common to both series; for the list of Datia marks, see listings under that state.

NOTE: There seems to be no correspondence between AH dates on the obverse and regnal years on the reverse!

In the name of Shah Alam II:

1/2 PAISA

COPPER, 16mm

C#	Date	Year	Good	VG	Fine	VF
24	—	—	1.50	2.50	3.50	5.00

PAISA

COPPER, 20-24mm

C#	Date	Year	Good	VG	Fine	VF
25	AH1211	41	1.50	2.50	3.25	4.50
	1214	4x	1.50	2.50	3.25	4.50
	1278	45	1.50	2.50	3.25	4.50
	1282	42	1.50	2.50	3.25	4.50

1/8 RUPEE

SILVER, 10mm, 1.34-1.45 gm

C#	Date	Year	VG	Fine	VF	XF
29	AH—	4x	2.25	3.00	3.75	5.50

1/4 RUPEE

SILVER, 12mm, 2.68-2.90 gm

C#	Date	Year	VG	Fine	VF	XF
30	AH1233	45	3.50	4.25	5.00	6.50
	1233	5x	3.50	4.25	5.00	6.50
	1251	3x	3.50	4.25	5.00	6.50

1/2 RUPEE

SILVER, 14-15mm, 5.35-5.80 gm

C#	Date	Year	VG	Fine	VF	XF
31	AH1211	42	6.50	7.50	8.50	10.00
	1212	40	6.50	7.50	8.50	10.00
	1214	45	6.50	7.50	8.50	10.00
	1215	42	6.50	7.50	8.50	10.00

RUPEE

SILVER, 20mm

C#	Date	Year	VG	Fine	VF	XF
32	AH1211	39	11.50	13.00	15.00	20.00
	1211	41	11.50	13.00	15.00	20.00
	1212	45	11.50	13.00	15.00	20.00
	1214	40	11.50	13.00	15.00	20.00
	1214	43	11.50	13.00	15.00	20.00
	1214	44	11.50	13.00	15.00	20.00
	1214	45	11.50	13.00	15.00	20.00
	1214	46	11.50	13.00	15.00	20.00
	1216	46	11.50	13.00	15.00	20.00
	1218	47	11.50	13.00	15.00	20.00
	121x	47	11.50	13.00	15.00	20.00
	1233	40	11.50	13.00	15.00	20.00
	1245	43	11.50	13.00	15.00	20.00
	1252	32	11.50	13.00	15.00	20.00
	1257	39	11.50	13.00	15.00	20.00

NOTE: Varieties exist with different variations of obverse and reverse symbols.

In the name of Muhammad Akbar II:

PAISA

COPPER

C#	Date	Year	Good	VG	Fine	VF
38	AH—	3x	2.00	3.50	4.50	6.50

RUPEE

SILVER, 20mm

C#	Date	Year	VG	Fine	VF	XF
42	AH1257	48	12.50	14.00	17.50	23.50
	1258	3x	12.50	14.00	17.50	23.50
	1273	39	12.50	14.00	17.50	23.50
	1275	4X	12.50	14.00	17.50	23.50
	1321	9	13.50	15.00	18.50	25.00

PANNA

In the name of Shah Alam II:

MINTMARK
A running Hanuman (monkey god)

PAISA

COPPER, 25mm

C#	Date	Year	Good	VG	Fine	VF
10	ND	—	3.00	5.00	7.00	10.00

PARTABGARH

(PRATAPGARH)

Sawant Singh

AD1775-1825

In the name of Shah Alam II:

Deogarh Mint

First Type:

Actual dates

The series begins with coins of refined Mughal fabric which become cruder and more stylized with passing years.

1/4 RUPEE

SILVER, 2.68-2.90 gm

KM#	Date	Year	VG	Fine	VF	XF
3	AH1199	26	6.50	8.00	10.00	13.50

1/2 RUPEE

SILVER, 18mm, 5.35-5.80 gm

KM#	Date	Year	VG	Fine	VF	XF
4	AH1193	20	6.50	8.00	10.00	13.50
	1197	2x	6.50	8.00	10.00	13.50
	1199	26	6.50	8.00	10.00	13.50

RUPEE

SILVER, 21mm

KM#	Date	Year	VG	Fine	VF	XF
5	AH1184	11	12.50	14.50	17.50	23.50
	1189	16	12.50	14.50	17.50	23.50

KM#	Date	Year	VG	Fine	VF	XF
5	1190	17	12.50	14.50	17.50	23.50
	1192	19	12.50	14.50	17.50	23.50
	1193	20	12.50	14.50	17.50	23.50
	1195	22	12.50	14.50	17.50	23.50
	1196	24	12.50	14.50	17.50	23.50
	1197	24	12.50	14.50	17.50	23.50
	1198	25	12.50	14.50	17.50	23.50
	1199	26	11.50	13.00	15.00	20.00

Second Type:

Unchanging date 1199 & year 29

1/8 RUPEE

SILVER, 11mm, 1.34-1.45 gm

C#	Date	Year	VG	Fine	VF	XF
13	AH1199	29	3.75	5.00	6.50	8.50

1/4 RUPEE

SILVER, 11-14mm, 2.68-2.90 gm

C#	Date	Year	VG	Fine	VF	XF
14	AH1199	29	3.50	4.50	6.00	8.00

1/2 RUPEE

SILVER, 15-17mm, 5.35-5.80 gm

C#	Date	Year	VG	Fine	VF	XF
15	AH1199	29	6.50	7.50	9.00	12.00

RUPEE

SILVER, 19-20mm

C#	Date	Year	VG	Fine	VF	XF
16	AH1199	29	11.50	13.00	15.00	20.00

Dulep Singh

AD 1825-1864

In the name of Shah Alam II:

Fixed date AH 1236/Yr. 45. The meaning of Yr. 45 not known.

1/8 RUPEE

SILVER, 10mm, 1.34-1.45 gm

C#	Date	Year	VG	Fine	VF	XF
26	AH1236	45	3.75	5.00	6.50	8.50

1/4 RUPEE

SILVER, 11-12mm, 2.68-2.90 gm

C#	Date	Year	VG	Fine	VF	XF
27	AH1236	45	3.50	4.50	6.00	8.00

1/2 RUPEE

SILVER, 14-15mm, 5.35-5.80 gm

C#	Date	Year	VG	Fine	VF	XF
28	AH1236	45	6.50	7.50	9.00	12.00

RUPEE

SILVER, round 18-20mm

C#	Date	Year	VG	Fine	VF	XF
29	AH1236	45	11.50	13.00	15.00	20.00

Square, 18x18mm

C#	Date	Year	VG	Fine	VF	XF
29a	AH1236	45	30.00	40.00	50.00	70.00

Udaya Singh

VS1921-1947/1864-1890AD

PAISA

COPPER, 17mm

Y#	Date	Year	Good	VG	Fine	VF
1	VS1935	(1888)	1.25	2.25	3.00	4.50

Y#	Date	Year	Good	VG	Fine	VF
2	VS1942	(1895)	1.00	1.75	2.50	4.00
	1943	(1896)	1.00	1.75	2.50	4.00

In the name of the 'Shah of London'

(= Queen Victoria)

Fixed dated AH 1236/Yr. 45. To be distinguished from the C#27-29 series by the word 'London' directly below the date 1236:

لندن

1/8 RUPEE

SILVER, 10mm, 1.34-1.45 gm

Y#	Date	Year	VG	Fine	VF	XF
3	AH1236	45	3.50	4.50	5.50	7.50

1/4 RUPEE

SILVER, 13mm, 2.68-2.90 gm

Y#	Date	Year	VG	Fine	VF	XF
4	AH1236	45	3.50	4.50	5.50	7.50

1/2 RUPEE

SILVER, 15mm, 5.35-5.80 gm

Y#	Date	Year	VG	Fine	VF	XF
5	AH1236	45	6.50	7.50	8.50	11.50

RUPEE

SILVER, round, 17-19mm, 10.70-11.60 gm

Y#	Date	Year	VG	Fine	VF	XF
6	AH1236	45	11.50	13.00	15.00	20.00

Square

Y#	Date	Year	VG	Fine	VF	XF
6a	AH1236	45	30.00	40.00	50.00	70.00

Raganath Singh

VS1947-1986/1890-1929AD

PAISA

COPPER, 19-23mm

Y#	Date	Year	Good	VG	Fine	VF
7	VS1953	(1896)	1.50	2.50	3.50	5.00

PORBANDAR

Like the coins of Kutch & Navanager, the coins of Porbandar derive from a prototype struck in AH 978/AD 1570 by Muzaffar Shah III of Gujarat. They have, in Nagari, the additional inscription, 'SRI RANA':

All are dated AH 978. They were struck until about 1890, and cannot be assigned to a specific ruler.

1/2 TRAMBIYO (1/4 DOKDO)

COPPER, 10-11mm

C#	Date	Good	VG	Fine	VF
30	AH978 (fictitious)	1.50	2.50	3.50	5.00

TRAMBIYO (1/2 DOKDO)

COPPER, 9-13mm

C#	Date	Good	VG	Fine	VF
31	AH978 (fictitious)	1.50	2.50	3.50	5.00

DOKDO

COPPER, 13-17mm

C#	Date	Good	VG	Fine	VF
32	AH978 (fictitious)	1.25	2.00	2.75	4.00

DHINGLA

COPPER, 18-19mm

C#	Date	Year	Good	VG	Fine	VF
33	AH978 (fictitious)		1.75	3.00	4.00	6.00

Rectangular, 20x15mm
Cruder calligraphy

C#	Date	Year	Good	VG	Fine	VF
34	AH978 (fictitious)		3.50	5.50	7.00	10.00

NOTE: Said to have been struck by Khimji (1813-31).

1/4 KORI

SILVER, 8-9mm

C#	Date	Year	VG	Fine	VF	XF
36	AH978 (fictitious)		4.50	5.75	7.00	9.00

1/2 KORI

SILVER, 11-13mm

C#	Date	Year	VG	Fine	VF	XF
37	AH978 (fictitious)		4.00	5.00	6.50	8.50

KORI

SILVER, 13-15mm

C#	Date	Year	VG	Fine	VF	XF
38	AH978 (fictitious)		3.50	4.50	6.00	8.00

PUDUKKOTTAI

Martanda Bhairava

AD1886-1928

Rajagopala

AD1928-1947

1/20 ANNA

COPPER, hand struck, 10mm, 1.3 gm.

Y#	Date	VG	Fine	VF	XF
A1	ND	.90	1.50	2.00	3.00

Machine struck, 12mm, 1.25 gm.

Y#	Date	VG	Fine	VF	XF
1	ND	.25	.75	1.25	1.75

1/16 ANNA

COPPER, 1.65 gm.
Similar to 1/20 Anna, Y#A1 but broader flan, twisted cord border.

KM#	Date	Year	Good	VG	Fine	VF
1	ND	—	—	—	Rare	—

RADHANPUR

Zorawar Khan

AD 1825-1874

In the name of Queen Victoria and Zorawar Khan

2 ANNAS

SILVER, 15mm, 1.34-1.45 gm.

Y#	Date	Year	VG	Fine	VF	XF
5	AH1288	1871	20.00	27.50	35.00	50.00

4 ANNAS

SILVER, 18mm, 2.68-2.90 gm.

Y#	Date	Year	VG	Fine	VF	XF
6	AH1287	1869	18.50	25.00	32.50	45.00
	1287	1871	18.50	25.00	32.50	45.00
	1288	1872	18.50	25.00	32.50	45.00

8 ANNAS

SILVER, 23mm, 5.35-5.80 gm.

Y#	Date	Year	VG	Fine	VF	XF
7	AH1287	1869	20.00	27.50	35.00	50.00
	1288	1871	20.00	27.50	35.00	50.00
	1289	1871	20.00	27.50	35.00	50.00

50 FALUS

SILVER, 24mm

Y#	Date	Year	VG	Fine	VF	XF
3	AH1284	1867	30.00	37.50	45.00	60.00

RUPEE

SILVER, 28-29mm, 10.70-11.60 gm.

Y#	Date	Year	VG	Fine	VF	XF
8	AH1287	1870	18.50	25.00	32.50	45.00
	1287	1871	18.50	25.00	32.50	45.00
	1288	1871	18.50	25.00	32.50	45.00
	1289	1872	18.50	25.00	32.50	45.00

(Intermediate dates exist)

100 FALUS

SILVER, 28mm

Y#	Date	Year	VG	Fine	VF	XF
4	AH1284	1867	30.00	37.50	45.00	60.00
	1286	1868	30.00	37.50	45.00	60.00
	1286	1869	30.00	37.50	45.00	60.00

MOHUR

GOLD, 27mm, 10.70-11.40 gm.

Y#	Date	Year	VG	Fine	VF	XF
9	AH1277	1860	220.00	240.00	265.00	300.00

Bismilla Khan

AD 1874-1895

In the name of Queen Victoria and Bismillah Khan

2 ANNAS

SILVER, 15mm, 1.34-1.45 gm.

Y#	Date	Year	VG	Fine	VF	XF
10	AH—	1880	25.00	32.50	40.00	55.00

4 ANNAS

SILVER, 2.68-2.90 gm.
Obv: Type I legend; field divided twice, Nawab's name at top. Rev: Type A legend field divided once, Queen's name upper left.

Y#	Date	Year	VG	Fine	VF	XF
11	AH—	1880	20.00	27.50	35.00	50.00

8 ANNAS

SILVER, 24mm, 5.35-5.80 gm.
Obv: Type I legend: Rev: Type B legend: No field dividers, Queen's name lower left.

Y#	Date	Year	VG	Fine	VF	XF
12	AH1297	1881	18.50	25.00	32.50	45.00

23mm
Obv: Type I legend.
Rev: Type C legend; two field dividers, Queen's name center left, center line three words.

Y#	Date	Year	VG	Fine	VF	XF
12.1	AH1297	1880	18.50	25.00	32.50	45.00

24mm
Obv: Type I legend.
Rev: Type D legend; two field dividers,
Queen's name center left, center line three words.

Y#	Date	Year	VG	Fine	VF	XF
12.2	AH1299	1881	18.50	25.00	32.50	45.00

Obv: Type II legend; two field dividers,
Nawab's name center in one line.
Rev: Type B legend.

Y#	Date	Year	VG	Fine	VF	XF
12.3	AH129x	1881	18.50	25.00	32.50	45.00

23mm
Obv: Type III legend; two field dividers,
Nawab's name center in two lines.
No Muhammad.
Rev: Type E legend; as type A but title
Queen instead of Empress.

Y#	Date	Year	VG	Fine	VF	XF
12.4	AH1291	1875	18.50	25.00	32.50	45.00

RUPEE

SILVER, 28mm, 10.70-11.60 gm.
Obv: Type I legend.
Rev: Type D legend.

Y#	Date	Year	VG	Fine	VF	XF
13	AH1299	1881	25.00	32.50	40.00	55.00

Obv: Type II legend.
Rev: Type H legend, as Type E but field
divider over dak.

Y#	Date	Year	VG	Fine	VF	XF
13.1	AH1297	1880	25.00	32.50	40.00	55.00

Obv: Type II legend.
Rev: Type E legend: As Type A but
Queen's titles in different order.

Y#	Date	Year	VG	Fine	VF	XF
13.2	AH1298	1881	25.00	32.50	40.00	55.00

29mm
Obv: Type II legend.
Rev: Type F legend: One field divider,
no Queen's name, mint name above.

Y#	Date	Year	VG	Fine	VF	XF
13.3	AH1311	1894	25.00	32.50	40.00	55.00

Obv: Type IV legend: One field divider,
Nawab's name above.
Rev: Type G legend: As Type G
but mint name below.

Y#	Date	Year	VG	Fine	VF	XF
13.4	AH1311	1894	25.00	32.50	40.00	55.00

Anonymous Copper Coins

These uniface bronze or copper pieces bear a single Nagari letter, and were struck throughout the 19th Century and perhaps into the 20th. The significance of the letters is unknown, but it is certain they are not the initials of rulers.

PAISA

'JI' जी

COPPER or BRONZE

Y#	Date	Good	VG	Fine	VF
1	ND	1.75	2.25	3.00	4.50

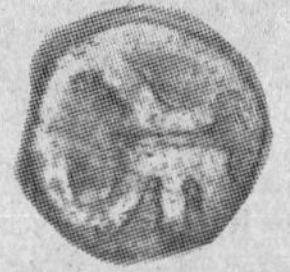

'GO' गो

Y#	Date	Good	VG	Fine	VF
2	ND	1.00	1.75	2.50	4.00

RAJKOT

Previously listed gold and silver restrike "Mohurs" of Rajkot have been determined to be medals.

RATLAM

Pardam Singh

AD 1773-1800

In the name of Shah Alam II

'RAYIJ' (current) in circle of dots.

PAISA

COPPER, 18-20mm

KM#	Date	Year	Good	VG	Fine	VF
1	—	20	2.00	3.00	4.00	6.00
	AH1197	24	2.50	3.50	4.50	6.50
	—	25	1.75	2.75	3.75	5.50
	1198	26	2.50	3.50	4.50	6.50
	—	27	1.75	2.75	3.75	5.50
	—	30	1.75	2.75	3.75	5.50
	—	31	1.75	2.75	3.75	5.50
	—	34	1.75	2.75	3.75	5.50

Ranjit Singh

VS1921-1950/1864-1893AD

PAISA

COPPER, 22mm

Y#	Date	Year	Good	VG	Fine	VF
1	VS1921	(1864)	6.00	9.00	12.50	18.50

17-20mm

Y#	Date	Year	Good	VG	Fine	VF
2	VS1927	(1870)	3.50	4.50	5.50	7.50
	1928	(1871)	1.50	2.25	3.00	4.50

20mm

Y#	Date	Year	Good	VG	Fine	VF
3	1885	—	2.50	4.00	6.00	9.00

MACHINE-STRUCK

COPPER, 24mm

Y#	Date	Year	VG	Fine	VF	XF
4	VS1945	(1888)	2.50	4.00	5.00	7.00
	1947	(1890)	.45	.75	1.25	2.00

Thin, crude restrike of Y#4.

Y#	Date	Year	VG	Fine	VF	XF
4a	VS1947	(1890)	.30	.50	.75	1.00

REWAH

Jai Singh Deo

AD 1809-1835

PAISA

COPPER, 16mm

C#	Date	Year	Good	VG	Fine	VF
20	VS1890		1.25	2.00	2.75	3.50

16-17mm

C#	Date	Year	Good	VG	Fine	VF
21	ND		1.75	2.75	4.00	6.00

2 PAISA

COPPER, 20-21mm

C#	Date	Year	Good	VG	Fine	VF
22	ND		2.50	4.00	6.00	9.00

Vishvanath Singh

AD 1835-1843

PAISA

COPPER, 17-19mm
Similar to 2 Paisa, C#34.

C#	Date	Year	Good	VG	Fine	VF
31	ND		2.50	3.50	5.00	7.50

2 PAISA

COPPER, 21-24mm

C#	Date	Year	Good	VG	Fine	VF
34	ND		2.50	3.50	5.00	7.00

Raghuraj Singh

AD 1843-1880

With name of "Agent Bushby Saheb"

PAISA

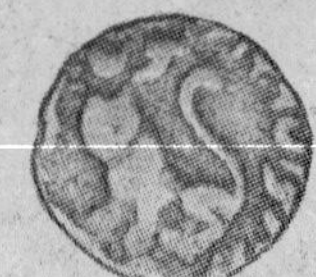

COPPER, 16-19mm

C#	Date	Year	Good	VG	Fine	VF
45	VS1906		2.75	4.50	6.50	9.00

2 PAISE

COPPER, 21-22mm
Obv: Lion left.

C#	Date	Year	Good	VG	Fine	VF
46	VS1906		2.75	4.50	6.50	9.00

21.5mm

Obv: Lion right.

C#	Date	Year	Good	VG	Fine	VF
46.1	VS1906		5.00	7.00	9.00	12.50

Gulab Singh

AD 1918-1946

MOHUR

GOLD, 25mm, 10.70-11.40gm
Accession Commemorative

Y#	Date	Year	VG	Fine	VF	XF
1	VS1975		235.00	265.00	300.00	375.00

NOTE: Copies exist in silver.

ROHILKHAND

During the early 18th century a Rohilla Afghan adventurer, Ali Muhammad, rose from bandit leader to control the country between Itawa and the Himalayas which subsequently came to bear the tribal name of his followers, Rohillakhant or (modern) Rohilkhand. In 1754 this territory was partitioned among his many sons, who thereafter formed a loose confederacy, alternately given to feuding internally and uniting to meet aggression by the Marathas, Awadh, and Imperial forces in turn. Eventually the Nawab-Vizier of Awadh succeeded in conquering most of the Rohilla possessions in A.D. 1774, with the exception of Saharanpur and Rampur. This latter survived as a remnant state until Indian Independence.

Anwala Mint

For issues in the name of Ahmad Shah Durrani, see India, Durrani Empire: Anwala. Anwala is the Persian rendition of the Hindi Aonla.

Mintname: Anwala انوله

In the name of Shah Alam II:

RUPEE

SILVER, 21mm, 10.70-11.60 gm
Obv: Four line legend.

KM#	Date	Year	VG	Fine	VF	XF
6	—	2	12.50	15.00	18.50	23.50

Mintmark:

Obv: Three line legend.
Additional mintmarks.

KM#	Date	Year	VG	Fine	VF	XF
16.1	AH1174	2	11.50	13.50	16.50	20.00
	1175	3	11.50	13.50	16.50	20.00
	1176	3	11.50	13.50	16.50	20.00
	1176	4	11.50	13.50	16.50	20.00

Additional mark cluster of crosses.

KM#	Date	Year	VG	Fine	VF	XF
16.2	AH1183	11	11.50	13.50	16.50	20.00
	1184	11	11.50	13.50	16.50	20.00

Additional mark fish.

KM#	Date	Year	VG	Fine	VF	XF
16.3	AH1184	12	12.50	16.50	22.50	30.00

20mm
Additional mark pretzel shape.

KM#	Date	Year	VG	Fine	VF	XF
16.4	AH	13	12.50	16.50	22.50	30.00

The Aonla mint became inactive after conquest by Awadh (AD1774-AH1188/R.V. 15).

Asafnagar Mint

Mintname: Asafnagar اصف نگر

In the name of Shah Alam II:

RUPEE

SILVER, 21mm, 10.70-11.60 gm

KM#	Date	Year	VG	Fine	VF	XF
26	—	14	12.50	17.50	25.00	32.50

For issues of Asafnagar later than AH1188/R.V. 15, see India Native States: Awadh.

Bareli Mint

For issues in the name of Ahmad Shah Durrani, see India, Durrani Empire: Bareli.

Mintname: Bareli 

RULERS

Hafiz Rahmat Khan
AD1754/1774/AH1167-1188

In the name of Shah Alam II:

RUPEE

SILVER, 19mm, 10.70-11.60 gm
Rev: Sword.

KM#	Date	Year	VG	Fine	VF	XF
36.1	AH1173	2	12.50	16.50	22.50	30.00

22mm
No mintmarks.

KM#	Date	Year	VG	Fine	VF	XF
36.2	AH1174	2	11.50	13.50	16.50	20.00
	1174	3	11.50	13.50	16.50	20.00
	1175	3	11.50	13.50	16.50	20.00
	1177	4	11.50	13.50	16.50	20.00
	1183	10	11.50	13.50	16.50	20.00
	1184	10	11.50	13.50	16.50	20.00
	1184	11	11.50	13.50	16.50	20.00
	1184	12	11.50	13.50	16.50	20.00
	1185	12	11.50	13.50	16.50	20.00

25mm
Rev: Crescent and stars.

KM#	Date	Year	VG	Fine	VF	XF
36.3	AH1177	4	12.50	14.50	17.50	22.50
	117	5	12.50	14.50	17.50	22.50

22mm
Rev: Lamp shape.

KM#	Date	Year	VG	Fine	VF	XF
36.4	AH1178	5	12.50	14.50	17.50	22.50

21mm
Rev: Danda (Mace).

KM#	Date	Year	VG	Fine	VF	XF
36.5	AH1181	9	—	9.00	12.00	15.00

For issues of Bareli mint later than AH1188/R.V. 15, see India Native States: Awadh.

INDIAN MUTINY
(GREAT REVOLT)

During the mutiny of AD1857-58, Khan Bahadur Khan, a descendent of Hafiz Rahmat Khan, declared himself subahdar of Rahilkhand under the Mughal Emperor Bahadur Shah Zafar. The independent government sat at Bareli, issuing rupees on the Mughal pattern of Shah Alam II, with current Hijri year and a regnal year dating from AH1202 (AD1788), the year Rohilla power ended with the death of Ghulam Qadir.

RUPEE

SILVER, 23mm

KM#	Date	Year	VG	Fine	VF	XF
46	AH1274	72	—	—	Rare	—

Bisauli Mint

Mintname: Bisauli

First Arrangement

Second Arrangement

RULERS

Abdullah Khan
AD1754-1761/AH1167-1174
Nasrulla Khan
AD1761-1770/AH1175-1183
Dunde Khan
AD1770/AH1184
Muhib-ud-daula
AD1770-1774/1184-1188

In the name of Shah Alam II:

RUPEE

SILVER, 22mm, 10.70-11.60 gm
Mintname first arrangement.

KM#	Date	Year	VG	Fine	VF	XF
56.1	AH1182	10	12.50	16.50	22.50	30.00
	1186	14	12.50	16.50	22.50	30.00

Mintname second arrangement.

KM#	Date	Year	VG	Fine	VF	XF
56.2	AH1182	10	12.50	16.50	22.50	30.00
	1183	11	12.50	16.50	22.50	30.00
	1184	11	12.50	16.50	22.50	30.00

The Bisauli mint became inactive after conquest by Awadh (AD1774-AH1888/R.Y. 15).

Itawa Mint

RULERS

Inayat Khan
AD1762-1771/AH1176-1184

Mintname: Itawa

In the name of Shah Alam II:

RUPEE

SILVER, 27mm, 10.70-11.60 gm
Obv: Sword.

KM#	Date	Year	VG	Fine	VF	XF
66	AH1176	3	11.50	13.50	16.50	20.00
	117X	4	11.50	13.50	16.50	20.00
	1179	5	11.50	13.50	16.50	20.00
	1180	6	11.50	13.50	16.50	20.00
	118X	7	11.50	13.50	16.50	20.00

For later issues from Itawa mint dated AH1185/R.Y.12 to AH1186/R.Y.13, see India Native States: Maratha Confederacy, Peshwa. For issues dated AH1187/R.Y. 14 and later, see India Native States: Awadh.

Muradabad Mint

For issues in the name of Ahmad Shah Durrani, see India, Durrani Empire: Muradabad.

Mintname: Muradabad

RULERS

Hafiz Rahmat Khan
AD1754-1774/AH1167-1188

In the name of Shah Alam II:

RUPEE

SILVER, 22mm, 10.70-11.60 gm
Obv: Trefoil.
Rev. leg: "JALUS SAUH".

KM#	Date	Year	VG	Fine	VF	XF
76.1	AH11XX	2	11.50	13.50	16.50	20.00

21mm
Rev. Quadrafoil, leg: "SAUH JALUS"

KM#	Date	Year	VG	Fine	VF	XF
76.2	AH1176	4	11.50	13.50	16.50	20.00

22mm
Rev: Quadrafoil (star like); leg: "MANUS SAUH"

KM#	Date	Year	VG	Fine	VF	XF
76.3	AH1176	4	11.50	13.50	16.50	20.00
	1178	8	11.50	13.50	16.50	20.00

23mm
Rev: Quadrafoil and Persian letter 'nun', leg: "JALUS SAUH".

KM#	Date	Year	VG	Fine	VF	XF
76.4	AH1178	5	11.50	13.50	16.50	20.00
	1179	7	11.50	13.50	16.50	20.00
	1180	7	11.50	13.50	16.50	20.00
	1180	8	11.50	13.50	16.50	20.00
	1182	10	11.50	13.50	16.50	20.00

For later issues of Muradabad mint dated after AH1188/R.Y. 15, see India Native States: Awadh.

Najafgarh Mint

RULERS

Nawab Najaf Khan
AD1766-1782/AH1180-1196
Afrasyab Khan
AD1782-1784/AH1196-1198

Mintname: Najafgarh 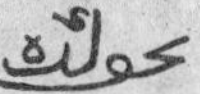

In the name of Shah Alam II:

RUPEE

SILVER, 20mm, 10.70-11.60 gm

KM#	Date	Year	VG	Fine	VF	XF
86	AH	21	13.50	18.50	25.00	32.50
	1198	26	13.50	18.50	25.00	32.50

Najibabad Mint

For issues in the name of Ahmad Shah Durrani, see India, Durrani Empire: Najibabad.

Mintname: Najibabad 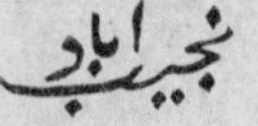

RULERS

Najib Khan alias Najib-ud-daula
AD1753-1770/AH1166-1183
Zabita Khan
AD1770-1774/AH1183-1188

In the name of Shah Alam II:

PAISA

COPPER, 22mm

KM#	Date	Year	Good	VG	Fine	VF
91	AH1176	3	2.00	3.50	5.00	7.50
	1177	4	2.00	3.50	5.00	7.50
	1178	5	2.00	3.50	5.00	7.50
	1179	6	2.00	3.50	5.00	7.50
	1179	7	2.00	3.50	5.00	7.50
	1180	8	2.00	3.50	5.00	7.50
	1182	9	2.00	3.50	5.00	7.50
	1182	10	2.00	3.50	5.00	7.50
	1185	12	2.00	3.50	5.00	7.50
	1185	13	2.00	3.50	5.00	7.50
	1186	13	2.00	3.50	5.00	7.50
	1187	15	2.00	3.50	5.00	7.50

RUPEE

SILVER, 20mm, 10.70-11.60 gm
No symbols.

KM#	Date	Year	VG	Fine	VF	XF
96.1	AH1174	2	11.50	13.50	16.50	20.00
	1175	3	11.50	13.50	16.50	20.00
	1176	3	11.50	13.50	16.50	20.00
	1176	4	11.50	13.50	16.50	20.00
	1177	4	11.50	13.50	16.50	20.00
	1177	5	11.50	13.50	16.50	20.00

21.5mm
Rev: Crude dagger.

KM#	Date	Year	VG	Fine	VF	XF
96.2	AH1177	5	11.50	13.50	16.50	20.00
	1178	6	11.50	13.50	16.50	20.00
	1179	6	11.50	13.50	16.50	20.00
	1179	7	11.50	13.50	16.50	20.00

KM#	Date	Year	VG	Fine	VF	XF
96.2	1180	7	11.50	13.50	16.50	20.00
	1180	8	11.50	13.50	16.50	20.00
	1181	8	11.50	13.50	16.50	20.00
	1181	9	11.50	13.50	16.50	20.00
	—	12	11.50	13.50	16.50	20.00
	—	14	11.50	13.50	16.50	20.00

MOHUR

GOLD, 10.70-11.40 gm

KM#	Date	Year	VG	Fine	VF	XF
100	AH	3	220.00	240.00	265.00	300.00
	1177	5	220.00	240.00	265.00	300.00
	1178	5	220.00	240.00	265.00	300.00

For issues of the Najibabad mint after AH1188/R.Y. 15, see India Native States: Awadh.

Nasrullanagar Mint

Mintname: Nasrullanagar

In the name of Shah Alam II:

RUPEE

SILVER, 22mm, 10.70-11.60 gm

KM#	Date	Year	VG	Fine	VF	XF
106	AH1181	9	20.00	27.50	37.50	50.00

Panipat Mint

A mint of Zabita Khan of Saharanpur.

Mintname: Qasbah Panipat

In the name of Shah Alam II:

RUPEE

SILVER, 23mm, 10.70-11.60 gm

KM#	Date	Year	VG	Fine	VF	XF
116	AH1198	25	12.50	17.50	22.50	30.00

Rampur Mint

Mintname: Mustafabad (Tentative)

RULERS

Faizullah Khan
AD1754-1794/AH1167-1208
Muhammad Ali Khan
AD1794- /AH1209

In the name of Shah Alam II:

RUPEE

SILVER, 22mm, 10.70-11.60 gm

Rev: Ten pointed star.

KM#	Date	Year	VG	Fine	VF	XF
126.1	AH1184	11	18.50	27.50	37.50	50.00
	1184	12	18.50	27.50	37.50	50.00
	1185	12	18.50	27.50	37.50	50.00

Rev: Floral symbol and trident quadrafoil.

KM#	Date	Year	VG	Fine	VF	XF
126.2	AH1185	13	18.50	27.50	37.50	50.00

SAILANA

General Issue, 19th Century

1/2 PAISA

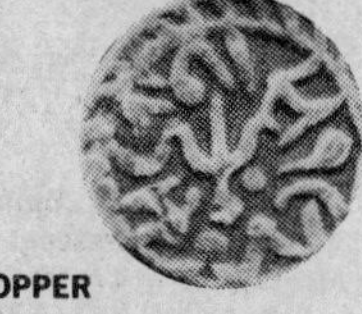

COPPER

C#	Date	Year	Good	VG	Fine	VF
4	ND	—	2.00	3.00	4.00	5.50

PAISA

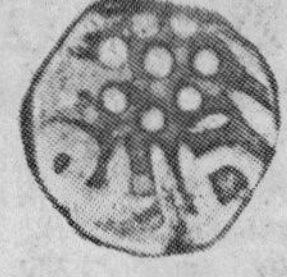

COPPER, 15-20mm
Pennant points either up or down.

C#	Date	Year	Good	VG	Fine	VF
5	ND	—	1.00	1.50	2.25	3.00

C#5 is known struck over an Egyptian 20 Para Y#3, cut down to an irregular shape. Other combinations could exist.

Dule Singh

VS1907-1947/1850-1890AD

1/2 PAISA

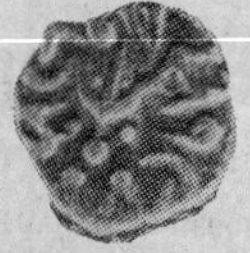

COPPER, 15mm

Y#	Date	Year	Good	VG	Fine	VF
A4	VS1944	(1887)	3.00	4.50	6.00	8.50

PAISA

COPPER, 17-20mm

Y#	Date	Year	Good	VG	Fine	VF
1	VS1937	(1880)	1.50	2.25	3.00	4.00

Obv: Sprig, Nagari date.

Y#	Date	Year	Good	VG	Fine	VF
2	VS1940	(1883)	2.25	3.50	4.50	6.00

Arabic numerals in Samvat date

Y#	Date	Year	Good	VG	Fine	VF
3	VS1941	(1884)	2.25	3.50	4.50	6.00

Trident

Y#	Date	Year	Good	VG	Fine	VF
4	VS1944	(1887)	2.25	3.50	4.50	6.00

Jaswant Singh

AD1890-1919

1/4 ANNA

COPPER

Y#	Date	Year	VG	Fine	VF	XF
5	1908	—	5.00	8.50	13.50	18.50

Y#	Date	Year	VG	Fine	VF	XF
6	1912	—	2.50	4.50	8.50	12.50

FEUDATORY STATE

BARMAWAL

PAISA

COPPER, 18-19mm

Y#	Date	Year	Good	VG	Fine	VF
1	ND	—	3.50	5.50	8.00	11.50

NOTE: Y#1 was struck prior to 1881.

SELAM

PAISA

COPPER, 20mm

C#	Date	Year	Good	VG	Fine	VF
5	AH1213	—	7.50	13.50	17.50	23.50

SIKHS

Khalsa (Military Government)

AD1765-1799

RULERS

Ranjit Singh, AD1799-1839
Kurruk Singh, AD1839-1840
Sher Singh, AD1840-1843
Dulip Singh, AD1843-1849

NOTE: Most coins struck after the accession of Ranjit Singh bear a large leaf on one side, and have Persian or Gurmukhi (Punjabi) legends in the name of Gobind Singh, the tenth and last guru of the Sikhs, AD1675-1708. Earlier pieces are similar, but lack the leaf. There is a great variety of coppers, and only representative types are catalogued here; many crude pieces were struck at the official and at unofficial mints, and bear illegible or semi-literate inscriptions. None of the coins bear the name of the Sikh ruler.

Ahluwalia Misl

RUPEE

SILVER, 22mm, 10.70-11.60 gm.
Obv: Trident. Rev: Lion.

KM#	Date	Year	VG	Fine	VF	XF
1	VS1862	(1805)	—	—	Rare	—

Amritsar Mint

First Copper Series

Persian legends. Various types.

1/2 PAISA

COPPER, 17mm

KM#	Date	Year	Good	VG	Fine	VF
3	VS1897	(1840)	2.75	4.00	5.50	8.00

PAISA

COPPER, 20mm

KM#	Date	Year	Good	VG	Fine	VF
4.1	VS1880	1823	1.50	2.75	4.00	5.50
	1881	(1824)	1.50	2.75	4.00	5.50
	1882	(1825)	1.50	2.75	4.00	5.50

21mm

KM#	Date	Year	Good	VG	Fine	VF
4.2	VS1896	(1839)	2.75	4.00	5.50	8.00
	1897	(1840)	2.75	4.00	5.50	8.00

2 PAISE

COPPER, 24mm

KM#	Date	Year	VG	Fine	VF	XF
6	VS1880	(1823)	3.00	5.50	8.50	12.50

Second Copper Series

Gurmukhi legends. Leaf in center obverse.

FALUS

COPPER, 20mm

KM#	Date	Year	Good	VG	Fine	VF
9	ND	—	2.00	3.50	4.50	6.50

PAISA

COPPER, 17-21mm
Date usually off flan

KM#	Date	Year	Good	VG	Fine	VF
7.1	VS1885	(1828)	.85	1.50	2.00	2.50
	1886	(1829)	.85	1.50	2.00	2.50

Rev: Banner

KM#	Date	Year	Good	VG	Fine	VF
7.2	ND	—	1.50	2.75	4.00	5.50

Rev: Flower

KM#	Date	Year	Good	VG	Fine	VF
7.3	ND	—	1.50	2.75	4.00	5.50

Rev: Cross

KM#	Date	Year	Good	VG	Fine	VF
7.4	VS188x	—	1.50	2.75	4.00	5.50

Rev: Trident

KM#	Date	Year	Good	VG	Fine	VF
7.5	ND	—	1.50	2.75	4.00	5.50

Rev: Katar

KM#	Date	Year	Good	VG	Fine	VF
7.6	ND	—	1.50	2.75	4.00	5.50

Rev: Lion

KM#	Date	Year	Good	VG	Fine	VF
7.7	ND	—	2.75	4.00	5.50	8.00

Rev: Pipal leaf spray.

KM#	Date	Year	Good	VG	Fine	VF
7.8	ND	—	2.75	4.00	5.50	8.00

2 PAISE

COPPER, 25mm

KM#	Date	Year	Good	VG	Fine	VF
8.1	VS1xxx	—	3.00	5.50	8.50	12.50

22x22x22mm

KM#	Date	Year	Good	VG	Fine	VF
8.2	VS—	—	5.00	7.50	11.00	15.00

24x22mm

KM#	Date	Year	Good	VG	Fine	VF
8.3	VS188x	—	3.50	6.00	9.00	13.50

MULTIPLE PAISAS

COPPER, 33mm

KM#	Date	Year	Good	VG	Fine	VF
9.1	VS1885	(1828)	—	—	—	—

31mm
Obv: Banner

KM#	Date	Year	Good	VG	Fine	VF
9.2	ND	—	—	—	—	—

Rev: Cross

KM#	Date	Year	Good	VG	Fine	VF
9.3	ND	—	—	—	—	—

Hexagonal, 30mm
Rev: Banner

KM#	Date	Year	Good	VG	Fine	VF
9.4	ND	—	—	—	—	—

Third Copper Series

Persian and Gurmukhi legends

FALUS

COPPER, 18mm

KM#	Date	Year	Good	VG	Fine	VF
10.1	ND	—	—	—	—	—

20mm

KM#	Date	Year	Good	VG	Fine	VF
10.2	VS1900	—	2.75	4.00	5.50	8.00
	1901	—	2.75	4.00	5.50	8.00
	ND	—	2.75	4.00	5.50	8.00

19mm

KM#	Date	Year	Good	VG	Fine	VF
10.3	ND	—	2.50	4.00	5.50	8.00

22mm

KM#	Date	Year	Good	VG	Fine	VF
10.4	ND	—	2.50	4.00	5.50	8.50

Silver Series

1/8 RUPEE

SILVER, 13mm, 1.34-1.45 gm.
Obv: Dated VS1884.

KM#	Date	Year	VG	Fine	VF	XF
17.1	VS(18)95	(1838)	9.00	15.00	22.50	30.00

Obv: Dated VS1885.

KM#	Date	Year	VG	Fine	VF	XF
17.2	VS(18)99	(1842)	9.00	15.00	22.50	30.00
	1900	(1843)	9.00	15.00	22.50	30.00

1/4 RUPEE

SILVER, 15mm, 2.68-2.90 gm.
Obv: Dated VS1884.

KM#	Date	Year	VG	Fine	VF	XF
18.1	VS(18)85	(1828)	8.50	14.00	20.00	27.50
	(18)89	(1832)	8.50	14.00	20.00	27.50
	(18)95	(1838)	8.50	14.00	20.00	27.50

Obv: Dated VS1885.

KM#	Date	Year	VG	Fine	VF	XF
18.2	VS(18)97	(1840)	8.50	14.00	20.00	27.50
	(18)98	(1841)	8.50	14.00	20.00	27.50
	1904	(1847)	8.50	14.00	20.00	27.50

KM#	Date	Year	VG	Fine	VF	XF
18.3	VS(18)99	—	8.50	14.00	20.00	27.50
	1900	—	8.50	14.00	20.00	27.50

1/2 RUPEE

SILVER, 18mm, 5.35-5.80 gm.
Obv: Actual date

KM#	Date	Year	VG	Fine	VF	XF
19.1	VS1880	(1823)	7.50	10.00	13.50	20.00

Obv: Dated VS1884

KM#	Date	Year	VG	Fine	VF	XF
19.2	VS(18)92	(1835)	8.50	11.50	15.00	22.50
	(18)95	(1838)	8.50	11.50	15.00	22.50
	(18)99	(1842)	8.50	11.50	15.00	22.50

Obv: Dated VS1885.

KM#	Date	Year	VG	Fine	VF	XF
19.3	VS(18)93	(1836)	8.50	11.50	15.00	22.50
	(18)97	(1840)	8.50	11.50	15.00	22.50
	(18)98	(1841)	8.50	11.50	15.00	22.50
	(18)99	(1842)	8.50	11.50	15.00	22.50
	1902	(1845)	8.50	11.50	15.00	22.50
	1904	(1847)	8.50	11.50	15.00	22.50
	1905	(1848)	8.50	11.50	15.00	22.50

19mm

KM#	Date	Year	VG	Fine	VF	XF
19.4	VS(18)98	—	8.50	14.00	20.00	27.50

17mm

KM#	Date	Year	VG	Fine	VF	XF
19.5	VS1902	—	9.00	15.00	22.50	30.00

RUPEE

SILVER, 21mm, 10.70-11.60 gm.
Obv: First legend arrangement.

KM#	Date	Year	VG	Fine	VF	XF
A20.1	VS1835	(1778)	13.50	17.50	22.50	30.00
	1836	(1779)	13.50	17.50	22.50	30.00
	1837	(1780)	13.50	17.50	22.50	30.00
	1838	(1781)	13.50	17.50	22.50	30.00

20mm
Obv: Second legend arrangement.
Rev: Dagger symbol.

KM#	Date	Year	VG	Fine	VF	XF
A20.2	VS1841	(1784)	11.50	13.00	15.00	20.00
	1842	(1785)	11.50	13.00	15.00	20.00
	1852	(1795)	11.50	13.00	15.00	20.00
	1854	(1797)	13.50	16.50	21.50	28.50
	1859	(1802)	13.50	16.50	21.50	28.50
	1864	(1807)	13.50	16.50	21.50	28.50
	1865	(1808)	13.50	16.50	21.50	28.50

21.5mm
Obv: Third legend arrangement.

KM#	Date	Year	VG	Fine	VF	XF
A20.3	VS1841	31	13.50	16.50	21.50	28.50
	1843	31	13.50	16.50	21.50	28.50

22mm
Rev: Branches

KM#	Date	Year	VG	Fine	VF	XF
B20.1	VS1862	(1805)	13.50	16.50	21.50	28.50

21mm
Rev: Leaves

KM#	Date	Year	VG	Fine	VF	XF
B20.2	VS1863	(1806)	13.50	16.50	21.50	28.50

22mm
Rev: Peacock tail.
(The 'Mora' Rupee)

KM#	Date	Year	VG	Fine	VF	XF
C20	VS1862	(1805)	13.50	20.00	27.50	37.50
	1863	(1806)	13.50	20.00	27.50	37.50

21.5mm
Obv: Hand. Rev: Dotted leaf.

KM#	Date	Year	VG	Fine	VF	XF
20.1	VS1859	(1802)	13.50	16.50	21.50	28.50

20.5mm
Obv: Double oval. Rev: Dotted leaf.

KM#	Date	Year	VG	Fine	VF	XF
20.2	VS1859	(1802)	13.50	16.50	21.50	28.50

21mm
Rev: Pipal leaf. Early fabric.

25mm
Late fabric.

KM#	Date	Year	VG	Fine	VF	XF
20.3	VS1851	(1794)	12.50	14.50	18.50	23.50
	1852	(1795)	12.50	14.50	18.50	23.50
	1853	(1796)	12.50	14.50	18.50	23.50
	1855	(1798)	12.50	14.50	18.50	23.50
	1856	(1799)	12.50	14.50	18.50	23.50
	1857	(1800)	12.50	14.50	18.50	23.50
	1859	(1802)	12.50	14.50	18.50	23.50
	1860	(1803)	11.50	13.00	15.00	20.00
	1861	(1804)	11.50	13.00	15.00	20.00
	1863	(1806)	11.50	13.00	15.00	20.00
	1864	(1807)	11.50	13.00	15.00	20.00
	1865	(1808)	11.50	13.00	15.00	20.00
	1866	(1809)	11.50	13.00	15.00	20.00
	1867	(1810)	11.50	13.00	15.00	20.00
	1868	(1811)	11.50	13.00	15.00	20.00
	1869	(1812)	11.50	13.00	15.00	20.00
	1871	(1814)	11.50	13.00	15.00	20.00
	1872	(1815)	11.50	13.00	15.00	20.00
	1873	(1816)	11.50	13.00	15.00	20.00
	1874	(1817)	11.50	13.00	15.00	20.00
	1875	(1818)	11.50	13.00	15.00	20.00
	1876	(1819)	11.50	13.00	15.00	20.00
	1877	(1820)	11.50	13.00	15.00	20.00

KM#	Date	Year	VG	Fine	VF	XF
20.3	1878	(1821)	11.50	13.00	15.00	20.00
	1879	(1822)	11.50	13.00	15.00	20.00
	1880	(1823)	11.50	13.00	15.00	20.00
	1881	(1824)	11.50	13.00	15.00	20.00
	1882	(1825)	11.50	13.00	15.00	20.00
	1883	(1826)	11.50	13.00	15.00	20.00
	1884	(1827)	11.50	13.00	15.00	20.00
	1888	(1831)	11.50	13.00	15.00	20.00
	1889	(1832)	11.50	13.00	15.00	20.00

23mm
Obv: Partial or full actual dates.
Rev: VS1884 fixed.

KM#	Date	Year	VG	Fine	VF	XF
21	VS(18)85	(1828)	11.50	13.00	15.00	20.00
	(18)86	(1829)	11.50	13.00	15.00	20.00
	(18)87	(1830)	11.50	13.00	15.00	20.00
	(18)89	(1832)	11.50	13.00	15.00	20.00
	(18)90	(1833)	11.50	13.00	15.00	20.00
	(18)91	(1834)	11.50	13.00	15.00	20.00
	(18)92	(1835)	11.50	13.00	15.00	20.00
	(18)93	(1836)	11.50	13.00	15.00	20.00
	(18)95	(1838)	11.50	13.00	15.00	20.00
	(18)96	(1839)	11.50	13.00	15.00	20.00
	(18)97	(1840)	11.50	13.00	15.00	20.00
	(18)98	(1841)	11.50	13.00	15.00	20.00
	(18)99	(1842)	11.50	13.00	15.00	20.00
	1901	(1844)	11.50	13.00	15.00	20.00
	1903	(1846)	11.50	13.00	15.00	20.00
	1904	(1847)	11.50	13.00	15.00	20.00

Obv: Partial actual dates.
Rev: VS1885 fixed.

KM#	Date	Year	VG	Fine	VF	XF
22.1	VS(18)93	(1836)	12.50	14.50	18.50	23.50
	(18)94	(1837)	12.50	14.50	18.50	23.50

24mm
Rev: Katar (dagger).

KM#	Date	Year	VG	Fine	VF	XF
22.2	VS(18)94	(1837)	11.50	13.00	15.00	20.00

22.5mm
Obv: Dot cluster.

KM#	Date	Year	VG	Fine	VF	XF
22.3	VS(18)94	(1837)	11.50	13.00	15.00	20.00
	(18)95	(1838)	11.50	13.00	15.00	20.00
	(18)96	(1839)	11.50	13.00	15.00	20.00
	(18)97	(1840)	11.50	13.00	15.00	20.00
	(18)98	(1841)	11.50	13.00	15.00	20.00

24mm
Obv: Nagari "Om"

KM#	Date	Year	VG	Fine	VF	XF
22.4	VS(18)97	(1840)	12.50	14.50	18.50	23.50

22.5mm

Obv: Trisul (trident)

KM#	Date	Year	VG	Fine	VF	XF
22.5	VS(18)98	(1841)	11.50	13.00	15.00	20.00
	(18)99	(1842)	11.50	13.00	15.00	20.00

23mm
Obv: Chhatra (umbrella).

KM#	Date	Year	VG	Fine	VF	XF
22.6	VS(18)99	(1842)	11.50	13.00	15.00	20.00
	1900	(1843)	11.50	13.00	15.00	20.00

Obv: Three-lobed leaf.
Similar to KM#19.5.

KM#	Date	Year	VG	Fine	VF	XF
22.7	VS1902	(1845)	11.50	13.00	15.00	20.00

22.5mm
Obv: Pataka (banner).

KM#	Date	Year	VG	Fine	VF	XF
22.8	VS1902	(1845)	11.50	13.00	15.00	20.00
	1903	(1846)	11.50	13.00	15.00	20.00

23mm
Obv: Gurmukhi "sate" beneath chhatra.

KM#	Date	Year	VG	Fine	VF	XF
22.9	VS1903	(1846)	11.50	13.00	15.00	20.00
	1904	(1847)	11.50	13.00	15.00	20.00

24mm
Obv: Lazy W beneath chhatra.

KM#	Date	Year	VG	Fine	VF	XF
22.10	VS1905	(1848)	11.50	13.00	15.00	20.00

23mm
Obv: Nagari "Shiva".

KM#	Date	Year	VG	Fine	VF	XF
22.11	VS1905	(1848)	12.50	14.50	18.50	23.50

MOHUR

GOLD, 10.70-11.40 gm.

KM#	Date	Year	VG	Fine	VF	XF
24	VS1861	(1804)	220.00	240.00	265.00	300.00
	1862	(1805)	220.00	240.00	265.00	300.00
	1863	(1806)	220.00	240.00	265.00	300.00
	1868	(1811)	220.00	240.00	265.00	300.00
	1901	(1844)	220.00	240.00	265.00	300.00

NCLT ISSUES

PATTERNS

KM#	Date	Mintage	Identification	Mkt.Val.
1	AD1830	—	1 Paisa, Copper, 27mm	75.00

Anandgarh Mint

RUPEE

SILVER, 22mm, 10.70-11.60 gm.

KM#	Date	Year	VG	Fine	VF	XF
30	VS1841	(1784)	27.50	35.00	45.00	60.00
	1842	(1785)	27.50	35.00	45.00	60.00
	1843	(1786)	27.50	35.00	45.00	60.00
	1844	(1787)	27.50	35.00	45.00	60.00
	1846	(1788)	27.50	35.00	45.00	60.00

Jammu Mint

PAISA

COPPER, 21mm

KM#	Date	Year	Good	VG	Fine	VF
35	ND	—	2.00	3.50	4.50	8.00

Jhang Mint

RUPEE

SILVER, 22mm

KM#	Date	Year	VG	Fine	VF	XF
105	VS1873	(1816)	25.00	35.00	45.00	60.00

Kashmir Mint

PAISA

COPPER, 20mm
Gurmukhi and Persian legends

KM#	Date	Year	Good	VG	Fine	VF
40.1	VS2078 (imaginary)					
		—	1.50	2.75	4.00	5.50

21.5mm
Persian and Gurmukhi legends.

KM#	Date	Year	Good	VG	Fine	VF
40.2	ND	—	1.50	2.75	4.00	5.50

Persian legends, sword.

KM#	Date	Year	Good	VG	Fine	VF
41.1	VS1894	(1837)	1.50	2.75	4.00	5.50

Persian legends, rosette.

KM#	Date	Year	Good	VG	Fine	VF
41.2	ND	—	1.50	2.75	4.00	5.50

RUPEE

SILVER, 23mm, 10.70-11.60 gm.
Gurmukhi legends

KM#	Date	Year	VG	Fine	VF	XF
45	VS189x	—	35.00	45.00	55.00	75.00

21mm
Obv: Flower spray. Rev: Date to right.

KM#	Date	Year	VG	Fine	VF	XF
46.1	VS1876	—	11.50	13.00	15.00	20.00

Obv: Flower spray. Rev: Legend divided horizonally.

KM#	Date	Year	VG	Fine	VF	XF
46.2	VS1876	(1819)	11.50	13.00	15.00	20.00

21mm
Obv: Flower spray. Rev: Legend divided vertically.

KM#	Date	Year	VG	Fine	VF	XF
46.3	VS1877	(1820)	11.50	13.00	15.00	20.00
	1878	(1821)	11.50	13.00	15.00	20.00

22mm
Obv: Gurmukhi "Hara".

KM#	Date	Year	VG	Fine	VF	XF
46.4	VS1878	(1821)	11.50	13.00	15.00	20.00
	1879	(1822)	11.50	13.00	15.00	20.00

Obv: Nagari "Om Sri".

KM#	Date	Year	VG	Fine	VF	XF
46.5	VS—	—	12.50	14.50	18.50	23.50

21mm
Obv: Nagari "Haraji".

KM#	Date	Year	VG	Fine	VF	XF
46.6	VS—	—	12.50	14.50	18.50	23.50

Obv: Floral symbol

KM#	Date	Year	VG	Fine	VF	XF
46.7	VS1881	(1824)	11.50	13.00	15.00	20.00

Obv: Banner, 23mm

KM#	Date	Year	VG	Fine	VF	XF
46.8	VS1882	(1825)	11.50	13.00	15.00	20.00

Obv: Dotted chakra, 22mm.

KM#	Date	Year	VG	Fine	VF	XF
46.9	VS1883	(1826)	11.50	13.00	15.00	20.00

21mm
Obv: Persian "Ram".

KM#	Date	Year	VG	Fine	VF	XF
46.10	VS—	—	11.50	13.00	15.00	20.00

22mm
Obv: Persian letter.

KM#	Date	Year	VG	Fine	VF	XF
46.11	VS1885	(1828)	11.50	13.00	15.00	20.00

Rev: Leaf splits legend.

KM#	Date	Year	VG	Fine	VF	XF
46.12	VS188x	—	11.50	13.00	15.00	20.00

22.5mm
Rev: Letter in field.

KM#	Date	Year	VG	Fine	VF	XF
46.13	VS1888	(1831)	11.50	13.00	15.00	20.00

Rev: Circled date

KM#	Date	Year	VG	Fine	VF	XF
48	VS1884	(1827)	11.50	13.00	15.00	20.00

20.5mm
Obv: Date

KM#	Date	Year	VG	Fine	VF	XF
49	VS1890	(1833)	11.50	13.00	15.00	20.00

Obv: Circled sword.

KM#	Date	Year	VG	Fine	VF	XF
50	VS1893	(1836)	12.50	14.50	18.50	23.50
	1894	(1837)	12.50	14.50	18.50	23.50
	1895	(1838)	12.50	14.50	18.50	23.50
	1896	(1839)	12.50	14.50	18.50	23.50
	1897	(1840)	12.50	14.50	18.50	23.50
	1898	(1841)	12.50	14.50	18.50	23.50
	1899	(1842)	12.50	14.50	18.50	23.50

19mm
Obv: Persian letter sin.

KM#	Date	Year	VG	Fine	VF	XF
51	VS1900	(1843)	11.50	13.00	15.00	20.00
	1901	(1844)	11.50	13.00	15.00	20.00
	1902	(1845)	11.50	13.00	15.00	20.00
	1903	(1846)	11.50	13.00	15.00	20.00

Lahore Mint
(Dar-us-Sultanat)

PAISA

COPPER, 20-22mm

KM#	Date	Year	Good	VG	Fine	VF
60	VS1881	(1824)	2.75	4.00	5.50	8.00

1/2 RUPEE

SILVER, 18mm, 5.35-5.80 gm.

KM#	Date	Year	VG	Fine	VF	XF
62	VS1889	(1832)	6.50	8.50	12.50	18.50

RUPEE

SILVER, 22mm, 10.70-11.60 gm.
No leaf symbol

KM#	Date	Year	VG	Fine	VF	XF
63	VS1822	(1765)	11.50	13.00	15.00	20.00
	1823	(1766)	11.50	13.00	15.00	20.00
	1824	(1767)	11.50	13.00	15.00	20.00
	1825	(1768)	11.50	13.00	15.00	20.00
	1826	(1769)	11.50	13.00	15.00	20.00
	1827	(1770)	11.50	13.00	15.00	20.00
	1828	(1771)	11.50	13.00	15.00	20.00
	1830	(1773)	11.50	13.00	15.00	20.00
	1832	(1775)	11.50	13.00	15.00	20.00
	1833	(1776)	11.50	13.00	15.00	20.00
	1834	(1777)	11.50	13.00	15.00	20.00
	1835	(1778)	11.50	13.00	15.00	20.00
	1836	(1779)	11.50	13.00	15.00	20.00
	1842	(1785)	11.50	13.00	15.00	20.00

Obv: Different legend.

KM#	Date	Year	VG	Fine	VF	XF
64	VS1853	(1796)	11.50	13.00	15.00	20.00

23-25mm, actual VS years.
Rev: Pipal leaf added.

KM#	Date	Year	VG	Fine	VF	XF
66.1	VS1843	(1786)	11.50	13.00	15.00	20.00
	1845	(1788)	11.50	13.00	15.00	20.00
	1855	(1798)	11.50	13.00	15.00	20.00
	1856	(1799)	11.50	13.00	15.00	20.00
	1857	(1800)	11.50	13.00	15.00	20.00
	1858	(1801)	11.50	13.00	15.00	20.00
	1859	(1802)	11.50	13.00	15.00	20.00
	1860	(1803)	11.50	13.00	15.00	20.00
	1861	(1804)	11.50	13.00	15.00	20.00
	1864	(1807)	11.50	13.00	15.00	20.00
	1869	(1812)	11.50	13.00	15.00	20.00
	1871	(1814)	11.50	13.00	15.00	20.00
	1872	(1815)	11.50	13.00	15.00	20.00
	1879	(1822)	11.50	13.00	15.00	20.00
	1882	(1825)	11.50	13.00	15.00	20.00
	1883	(1826)	11.50	13.00	15.00	20.00
	1887	(1830)	11.50	13.00	15.00	20.00

Obv: Actual date. Rev: VS1884.

KM#	Date	Year	VG	Fine	VF	XF
66.2	VS18(87)	(1831)	11.50	13.00	15.00	20.00
	18(88)	(1831)	11.50	13.00	15.00	20.00
	(18)90	(1833)	11.50	13.00	15.00	20.00
	(18)91	(1834)	11.50	13.00	15.00	20.00
	(18)92	(1835)	11.50	13.00	15.00	20.00

Rev: VS1885

KM#	Date	Year	VG	Fine	VF	XF
67	VS(18)95	(1838)	11.50	13.00	15.00	20.00
	1903	(1846)	11.50	13.00	15.00	20.00

23mm
Rev: Two seated figures and VS1885.

KM#	Date	Year	VG	Fine	VF	XF
68	VS(18)93	(1836)	—	—	Rare	—

Malkarian Mint

RUPEE

SILVER, 23mm, 10.70-11.60 gm.

KM#	Date	Year	VG	Fine	VF	XF
72	VS1880	(1823)	22.50	32.50	45.00	60.00

Multan Mint

PAISA

COPPER, 21mm
No leaf symbol.

KM#	Date	Year	Good	VG	Fine	VF
76	VS1834	(1777)	3.00	5.00	7.50	10.00

20-24mm

KM#	Date	Year	Good	VG	Fine	VF
77	VS1875	(1818)	1.50	2.75	4.00	5.50
	1878	(1821)	1.50	2.75	4.00	5.50

NOTE: Also found with botched or fictitious dates.

RUPEE

SILVER, 22-24mm
Rev: Without pipal leaf.

KM#	Date	Year	VG	Fine	VF	XF
83	VS1829	(1772)	13.50	20.00	27.50	40.00
	1830	(1773)	13.50	20.00	27.50	40.00
	1831	—	13.50	20.00	27.50	40.00

23mm
Obv: Plain.

KM#	Date	Year	VG	Fine	VF	XF
84	VS1875	(1818)	13.50	16.50	25.00	30.00
	1879	(1822)	13.50	16.50	25.00	30.00

24mm
Obv: Trident.

KM#	Date	Year	VG	Fine	VF	XF
85	VS1880	(1823)	13.50	16.50	22.50	30.00
	1881	(1824)	13.50	16.50	22.50	30.00
	1882	(1825)	13.50	16.50	22.50	30.00

23mm
Obv: Flower.

KM#	Date	Year	VG	Fine	VF	XF
86	VS1877	(1820)	12.50	16.50	22.50	30.00
	1879	(1822)	12.50	16.50	22.50	30.00
	1880	(1823)	12.50	16.50	22.50	30.00
	1881	(1824)	12.50	16.50	22.50	30.00
	1884	(1827)	12.50	16.50	22.50	30.00
	1887	(1830)	12.50	16.50	22.50	30.00
	1888	(1831)	12.50	16.50	22.50	30.00
	1891	(1834)	12.50	16.50	22.50	30.00
	1892	(1835)	12.50	16.50	22.50	30.00
	1894	(1837)	12.50	16.50	22.50	30.00
	1895	(1838)	12.50	16.50	22.50	30.00
	1896	(1839)	12.50	16.50	22.50	30.00
	1897	(1840)	12.50	16.50	22.50	30.00
	1899	(1842)	12.50	16.50	22.50	30.00
	1900	(1843)	12.50	16.50	22.50	30.00
	1901	(1844)	12.50	16.50	22.50	30.00
	1905	(1848)	12.50	16.50	22.50	30.00

Pathankot Mint

PAISA

COPPER

KM#	Date	Year	Good	VG	Fine	VF
90	VS1894	—	6.00	9.00	12.50	17.50

Peshawar Mint

FALUS

COPPER, 21-24mm
Rev: Persian legend.

KM#	Date	Year	Good	VG	Fine	VF
93	AH1248	—	1.25	2.50	3.50	5.00
	1249	—	1.25	2.50	3.50	5.00

Rev: Gurmukhi legend & Nagari date.

KM#	Date	Year	Good	VG	Fine	VF
94	VS1891	(1834)	3.50	5.50	8.50	12.50

KM#	Date	Year	Good	VG	Fine	VF
95	ND or date off flan	—	1.25	2.50	3.50	5.00

KM#	Date	Year	Good	VG	Fine	VF
96	AH126x	—	1.25	2.50	3.50	5.00

23mm

KM#	Date	Year	Good	VG	Fine	VF
97	VS1892	(1835)	6.00	9.00	12.50	17.50

RUPEE

SILVER, 21mm, 10.70-11.60 gm.
Rev: Plain pipal leaf.

KM#	Date	Year	VG	Fine	VF	XF
98.1	VS1891	(1834)	22.50	27.50	32.50	45.00

SILVER, 22-23mm
Rev: Dotted pipal leaf.

KM#	Date	Year	VG	Fine	VF	XF
98.2	VS1892	(1835)	15.00	22.50	30.00	42.50
	1893	(1836)	15.00	22.50	30.00	42.50
	1894	(1837)	15.00	22.50	30.00	42.50

Uncertain Mint

Attributed to the revolt of Diwan Mulraj (Apr. 1848-Jan. 1849/VS1905) at Multan:

1/20 MOHUR

GOLD, 0.57 gm.

KM#	Date	Year	VG	Fine	VF	XF
100	VS1905	—	17.50	25.00	32.50	42.50

SIKH FEUDATORIES

DERA

Sikh Protectorate

AD1819-1847

Dera is now known as Dera Ghazi Khan, to distinguish it from Dera Ismail Khan (Derajat).

PAISA

COPPER, 18-21mm

KM#	Date	Year	Good	VG	Fine	VF
101	VS1896	(1839)	3.00	5.00	7.50	11.50
	1898	(1841)	3.00	5.00	7.50	11.50
	ND	—	2.75	4.00	5.50	8.00

DERAJAT

Sikh Protectorate

AD1819-1847

Derajat was the region centered about Der Ismail Khan

where the mint was presumably located.

NOTE: There are many varieties of copper coins, only a sample of which are listed below.

PAISA

COPPER, 16-20mm
Obv: Rayij. Mint name: 'DERAJAT'

KM#	Date	Year	Good	VG	Fine	VF
105	AH1241	—	2.75	4.00	5.50	8.00
	1242	—	2.75	4.00	5.50	8.00
	Obv: Rayij. Rev: SAMADI monogram					
106	AH124x	—	3.00	5.00	7.50	11.50
	Obv: SAHIH. Rev: Mint name & date.					
108	AH1252	—	2.75	4.00	5.50	8.00

Obv: Lion left, AH date.

KM#	Date	Year	Good	VG	Fine	VF
111	AH1246	—	2.25	3.50	4.50	6.50
	1247	—	2.25	3.50	4.50	6.50
	1249	—	2.25	3.50	4.50	6.50
	1254	—	2.25	3.50	4.50	6.50
	1261	—	2.25	3.50	4.50	6.50
	1262	—	2.25	3.50	4.50	6.50
	1265	—	2.25	3.50	4.50	6.50
	1267	—	2.25	3.50	4.50	6.50
	1276	—	2.25	3.50	4.50	6.50

Obv: 'FATH'. Rev: Leaf.

KM#	Date	Year	Good	VG	Fine	VF
112	—	—	2.75	4.00	5.50	8.00

Obv: Lion right.

KM#	Date	Year	Good	VG	Fine	VF
113	VS1793 (error, for 1893)	(1836)	2.25	3.50	4.50	6.50

RUPEE

SILVER, 19mm, 10.70-11.60 gm.
Obv: Date below Gurmukhi letter.
Rev: Neat leaf.

KM#	Date	Year	VG	Fine	VF	XF
119	VS1892	(1835)	30.00	40.00	50.00	70.00
	1893	(1836)	30.00	40.00	50.00	70.00

19mm
Obv: Date above Gurmukhi letter.
Rev: Crude leaf.

KM#	Date	Year	VG	Fine	VF	XF
120	VS1894	(1837)	25.00	32.50	42.50	60.00
	1895	(1838)	25.00	32.50	42.50	60.00
	1896	(1839)	25.00	32.50	42.50	60.00
	1897	(1840)	25.00	32.50	42.50	60.00
	1898	(1841)	25.00	32.50	42.50	60.00
	1899	(1842)	25.00	32.50	42.50	60.00
	1900	(1843)	25.00	32.50	42.50	60.00
	1901	(1844)	25.00	32.50	42.50	60.00

NAJIBABAD

Symbols: 

on obv. and **on rev.**

PAISA

COPPER, 16-18mm
Obv: Date

KM#	Date	Year	Good	VG	Fine	VF
131	—	40	1.50	2.75	4.00	5.50

SIKKIM

Thutab Namgyel
VS1931-1968/1874-1911AD

PAISA

COPPER, 20-22mm

Y#	Date	Year	Good	VG	Fine	VF
1	VS1940	(1883)	3.00	5.00	7.50	11.50
	1942	(1885)	3.00	5.00	7.50	11.50

Usually found with date off flan. Many forgeries exist.

SIND

AMIRS OF HYDERABAD
In the name of Taimur Shah Durrani:

Hyderabad Sind Mint

RUPEE

SILVER, 10.70-11.60 gm.

KM#	Date	Year	VG	Fine	VF	XF
18	ND	—	13.50	18.50	25.00	35.00

Sind Mint

RUPEE

SILVER, 11.0-11.5 gm.

KM#	Date	Year	VG	Fine	VF	XF
19	AH1239	—	15.00	20.00	27.50	37.50
	1240	—	15.00	20.00	27.50	37.50
	1242	—	15.00	20.00	27.50	37.50

Rev: Mintmark star below SANA.

KM#	Date	Year	VG	Fine	VF	XF
19	ND	—	11.50	13.00	15.00	20.00
	Mintmark: Group of 6 dots.					
19.1	ND	—	11.50	13.00	15.00	20.00
	Reduced weight, 7.5-7.8 gm.					
20	AH1252	—	12.50	16.50	21.50	30.00
	1255	—	12.50	16.50	21.50	30.00
	1256	—	12.50	16.50	21.50	30.00
	1257	—	12.50	16.50	21.50	30.00
	Mintmark: 6-petal flower.					
20.1	ND	—	11.50	13.00	15.00	20.00
	Mintmark: Rosette of 6 dots.					
20.2	ND	—	11.50	13.00	15.00	20.00
	Mintmark: Cross.					
20.3	ND	—	11.50	13.00	15.00	20.00
	Mintmark: Sprig with 3 berries.					
20.3	ND	—	11.50	13.00	15.00	20.00
	Rev: No mark, with Fath ('Victory').					
21	ND	—	12.50	14.50	17.50	23.50

It is not known to which victory the reference is made.

AMIRS of KHAIRPUR
FORMALLY INDEPENDENT
AFTER 1832/1248

Bhakkar Mint

RUPEE

SILVER, 21mm

In the name of Mahmud Shah Durrani

NOTE: These Rupees bear 2 mintmarks, one on the obverse at the top of the central cartouche, one on the reverse, usually to the upper right of the J of Julus.

C#	Date	Year	VG	Fine	VF	XF
	Without mintmarks					
10	AH1245	—	12.50	14.50	17.50	23.50
	Mintmarks: Star/Star					
10.1	AH1252	—	12.50	14.50	17.50	23.50
	1254	—	12.50	14.50	17.50	23.50
	1255	—	12.50	14.50	17.50	23.50
	Mintmarks: Star/Branch					
10.2	AH1255	—	12.50	14.50	17.50	23.50
	Mintmarks: Branch/Branch					
10.3	AH1256	—	12.50	14.50	17.50	23.50
	Mintmarks: Pigeon/Plume					
10.4	AH1256	—	12.50	14.50	17.50	23.50
	Mintmarks: Pigeon/Peacock					
10.5	AH1258	—	12.50	14.50	17.50	23.50
	Mintmarks: Hare/Peacock					
10.6	AH1258	—	12.50	14.50	17.50	23.50

British Occupation
After 1843/1259

RUPEE

SILVER
Mintmarks: Hare/British lion

C#	Date	Year	VG	Fine	VF	XF
11	AH1259	—	13.50	20.00	27.50	40.00
	1261	—	13.50	20.00	27.50	40.00

Without British lion
With floral mintmarks of various kinds on obv. & rev.

C#	Date	Year	VG	Fine	VF	XF
12	AH1262	—	12.50	14.50	17.50	23.50
	1264	—	12.50	14.50	17.50	23.50
	1265	—	12.50	14.50	17.50	23.50
	1266	—	12.50	14.50	17.50	23.50
	1267	—	12.50	14.50	17.50	23.50
	1268	—	12.50	14.50	17.50	23.50
	1269	—	12.50	14.50	17.50	23.50

LOCAL ISSUES

SHIKARPUR

FALUS

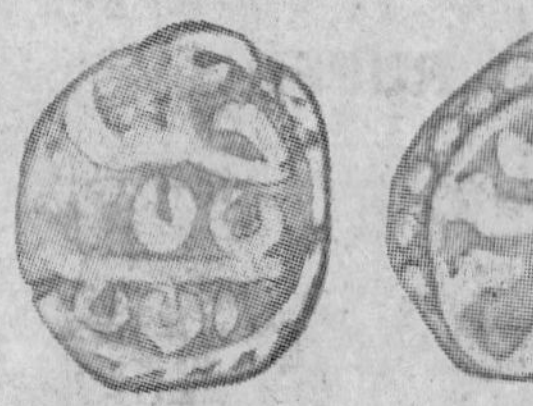

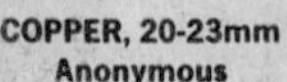

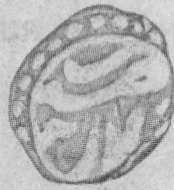

COPPER, 20-23mm
Anonymous

C#	Date	Year	Good	VG	Fine	VF
30	AH1255	—	1.75	2.75	4.00	6.00

TATTA

RUPEE

SILVER, 17-18mm, 10.70-11.60 gm.
In name of Taimur Shah Durrani

C#	Date	Year	VG	Fine	VF	XF
45	ND	—	12.50	14.50	17.50	23.50

SIRMUR

For earlier issues, see Gurkhas.

Fath Prakash

Restored,
VS1872-1890/1815-1833AD

PAISA

COPPER, 21mm

C#	Date	Year	Good	VG	Fine	VF
30	VS1877	(1820)	3.00	5.00	7.50	11.50

SITAMAU

Raja Ram Singh

VS1859-1924/1802-1867AD

PAISA

COPPER, 18-20mm

KM#	Date	Year	Good	VG	Fine	VF
1	1844	—	4.50	7.00	10.00	13.50

Bahadur Singh

VS1942-1956/1885-1899AD

PAISA

COPPER, 16-19mm

Y#	Date	Year	Good	VG	Fine	VF
1	VS1948	(1891)	3.00	5.00	7.50	11.50

Shardul Singh

VS1956-1957/1899-1900AD

1/2 PAISA

COPPER, 16-18mm

Y#	Date	Year	Good	VG	Fine	VF
2	VS1956	(1899)	4.50	7.00	10.00	13.50

NOTE: Varieties exist.

SURAT

RUPEE

SILVER, 10.70-11.60 gm.

C#	Date	Year	VG	Fine	VF	XF
25	—	2	11.50	13.50	15.00	20.00

TONK

MINTMARKS

Necklace (on C#50 only)

Flower (on all)

Leaf (several forms)

Leaf (on Sironj coins KM#3-6)

RULERS

Amir Khan,
AH1213-1250/AD1798-1834
Wazir Muhammad Khan,
AH1250-1281/AD1834-1864

In the name of Shah Alam II

RUPEE

SILVER, 21-24mm, 10.70-11.60 gm.

C#	Date	Year	VG	Fine	VF	XF
160	AH1172	10	12.50	14.50	17.50	23.50
	1184	12	12.50	14.50	17.50	23.50
	1189	16	12.50	14.50	17.50	23.50
	1200	—	12.50	14.50	17.50	23.50

In the name of Muhammad Akbar II

Sironj Mint

PAISA

COPPER, 23mm
Rev: Jhar.

C#	Date	Year	Good	VG	Fine	VF
45	AH1225	—	3.00	4.50	6.00	8.50

Rev: Horse.

C#	Date	Mintage	VG	Fine	VF
45a	AH1226	—	6.00	8.00	10.00

With uncertain symbols

C#	Date	Year	Good	VG	Fine	VF
45c	AH1247	—	2.50	3.50	5.00	7.00

With rosette & katar

C#	Date	Year	Good	VG	Fine	VF
45d	AH1250	—	3.00	4.50	6.00	8.50

20-21mm
With rosette & pearl loop

C#	Date	Year	Good	VG	Fine	VF
50	AH1252	—	2.50	3.50	5.00	7.00
	1253	—	2.50	3.50	5.00	7.00
	1269	—	2.50	3.50	5.00	7.00

1/4 RUPEE

SILVER, 13mm, 2.68-2.90 gm.

C#	Date	Year	VG	Fine	VF	XF
58	AH1253	—	3.50	4.50	6.00	8.50

1/2 RUPEE

SILVER, 15mm, 5.35-5.80 gm.

C#	Date	Year	VG	Fine	VF	XF
59	AH1253	—	6.50	7.50	9.00	13.50
	1267	—	6.50	7.50	9.00	13.50

RUPEE

SILVER, 20-21mm, 10.70-11.60 gm.

C#	Date	Year	VG	Fine	VF	XF
60	AH1233	—	11.50	13.00	16.00	20.00
	1235	—	11.50	13.00	16.00	20.00
	1245	—	11.50	13.00	16.00	20.00
	1252	—	11.50	13.00	16.00	20.00
	1253	—	11.50	13.00	16.00	20.00
	1264	—	11.50	13.00	16.00	20.00
	1269	—	11.50	13.00	16.00	20.00

In the names of Queen Victoria & Wazir Muhammad Khan

Sironj Mint

PAISA

COPPER, 18-20mm

Y#	Date	Year	Good	VG	Fine	VF
1	AH1278	—	1.75	3.00	4.00	6.00

RUPEE

SILVER, 20-21mm, 10.70-11.60 gm.

Y#	Date	Year	VG	Fine	VF	XF
2	AH1276	—	11.50	13.50	16.50	20.00
	1277	—	11.50	13.50	16.50	20.00
	1280	—	12.50	14.50	17.50	22.50

Muhammad Ali Khan

AH 1281-1285/AD 1864-1867

No coins can definitely be assigned to his reign, but coins continued to be struck in the names of Queen Victoria & Muhammad Ali Khan during the regency period of his successor, Muhammad Ibrahim Ali Khan (AD 1867-1872 - AH 1285-1290), as follows (Sironj Mint).

PAISA

COPPER, 23-24mm

Y#	Date	Year	Good	VG	Fine	VF
3	AH1283	—	1.75	2.50	3.50	5.00
	1285	—	1.75	2.50	3.50	5.00
	1286	—	1.75	2.50	3.50	5.00
	1288	—	1.75	2.50	3.50	5.00
	1289	—	1.75	2.50	3.50	5.00

1/8 RUPEE

SILVER, 12mm, 1.34-1.45 gm.

Y#	Date	Year	VG	Fine	VF	XF
4	ND (off flan)	—	2.00	3.50	5.00	7.50

1/4 RUPEE

SILVER, 15mm, 2.68-2.90 gm.

Y#	Date	Year	VG	Fine	VF	XF
5	AH1289	—	3.50	5.00	7.00	10.00

1/2 RUPEE

SILVER, 16-17mm, 5.35-5.80 gm.

Y#	Date	Year	VG	Fine	VF	XF
6	AH1289	—	6.50	8.00	10.00	14.00

RUPEE

SILVER, 20-24mm, 10.70-11.60 gm.

Y#	Date	Year	VG	Fine	VF	XF
7	AH1282	—	11.50	13.50	16.50	20.00
	1286	—	11.50	13.50	16.50	20.00
	1288	—	11.50	13.50	16.50	20.00
	1289	—	11.50	13.50	16.50	20.00

Muhammad Ibrahim Ali KHAN

AH1285-1348/AD1867-1930

Beginning with this reign, most coins have both AD and AH dates. Coins with both dates fully legible are worth about 20 per cent more than listed prices. Coins with one date fully legible are worth prices shown. Coins with both dates off are of little value.

There are many minor and major variations of type, varying with location of date, orientation of leaf, arrangement of legend. Although these fall into easily distinguished patterns, they are strictly for the specialist and are omitted here.

NOTE: It is anticipated that new Yeoman numbers will soon be assigned, the present numbers being cumbersome and incomplete. Temporary 'Krause' numbers are used.

NOTE: Coins of Sironj Mint (KM#3-6) are distinguished from coins of Tonk by the form of the leaf, the mint name (written in Persian), and the arrangement of the reverse legend (illustration of KM#6.)

In the names of Queen Victoria & Muhammad Ibrahim Ali Khan:

Tonk Mint

PAISA

COPPER, 20mm

Y#	Date	Year	Good	VG	Fine	VF
8	AH1290	—	1.25	1.75	2.50	3.50

1/8 RUPEE

SILVER, 1.34-1.45 gm.

Y#	Date	Year	VG	Fine	VF	XF
9	(Date off)	—	5.00	6.00	8.50	11.50

RUPEE

SILVER, 19-22mm, 6 vars., 10.70-11.60 gm.

NOTE: Var. 1, illustrated above, has no leaf, but a branch on obverse. All others have the leaf, as on the paisa (KM#1).

Y#	Date	Year	VG	Fine	VF	XF
10	—	1873	11.50	13.50	16.50	20.00
	AH1290	1873	12.50	14.50	17.50	22.50
	1290	—	11.50	13.50	16.50	20.00
	1292	—	11.50	13.50	16.50	20.00
	1293	—	11.50	13.50	16.50	20.00
	1294	—	11.50	13.50	16.50	20.00
10	1293	1876	12.50	14.50	17.50	21.50
	1294	1877	12.50	14.50	17.50	21.50

In the names of Empress Victoria and Muhammad Ibrahim Ali Khan:

Sironj Mint

PIE

COPPER, 16mm

Y#	Date	Year	Good	VG	Fine	VF
11	AH1314	—	—	—	—	—

PAISA

COPPER, 23mm

Y#	Date	Year	Good	VG	Fine	VF
12	AH1298	—	1.75	2.75	3.75	5.00
	1299	—	1.75	2.75	3.75	5.00
	1302	—	1.75	2.75	3.75	5.00

1/4 RUPEE

SILVER, about 12mm, 2.68-2.90 gm.

Y#	Date	Year	VG	Fine	VF	XF
13	AH1314	1896	5.00	7.00	9.00	13.00

1/2 RUPEE

SILVER, about 16mm, 5.35-5.80 gm.

Y#	Date	Year	VG	Fine	VF	XF
14	AH1310	1893	6.50	8.00	10.00	14.00
	1314	1896	6.50	8.00	10.00	14.00

RUPEE

SILVER, 19mm, 10.70-11.60 gm.

Y#	Date	Year	VG	Fine	VF	XF
15	AH1309	1892	12.50	14.50	17.50	21.50
	1310	1893	12.50	14.50	17.50	21.50

Tonk Mint

PAISA

COPPER, 17-18mm, 4 vars.

Y#	Date	Year	Good	VG	Fine	VF
16	AH1290	—	1.75	2.50	3.50	5.00
	1292	1876	1.75	2.50	3.50	5.00
	1294	1877	1.75	2.50	3.50	5.00
	1295	—	1.50	2.25	3.25	4.50
	1295	—	1.25	1.75	2.75	4.00
	1298	1881	1.50	2.25	3.25	4.50
	1302	1885	1.00	1.75	2.75	4.00
	1303	1885	1.00	1.75	2.75	4.00
	1303	1886	1.00	1.75	2.75	4.00
	—	1896	1.25	1.75	2.75	4.00

1/8 RUPEE

SILVER, 10mm, 1.34-1.45 gm.

Y#	Date	Year	VG	Fine	VF	XF
17	AH1309	1892	3.00	4.00	5.50	8.00
	1317	1899	3.00	4.00	5.50	8.00

1/4 RUPEE

SILVER, 14-15mm, 2.68-2.90 gm.

Y#	Date	Year	VG	Fine	VF	XF
18	AH1305	1888	3.50	4.50	6.00	8.50
	1309	1892	3.50	4.50	6.00	8.50

Y#	Date	Year	VG	Fine	VF	XF
18	1316	—	3.50	4.50	6.00	8.50
	1317	1899	3.50	4.50	6.00	8.50
	1318	—	3.50	4.50	6.00	8.50

1/2 RUPEE

SILVER, 16-17mm, 5.35-5.80 gm.

Y#	Date	Year	VG	Fine	VF	XF
19	AH129x	1882	—	—	—	—
	1305	1888	6.50	7.50	9.00	12.50
	1209	1892	6.50	7.50	9.00	12.50
	1309	1892	6.50	7.50	9.00	12.50
	1317	1899	6.50	7.50	9.00	12.50

RUPEE

SILVER, 19-21mm, 10.70-11.60 gm.

Y#	Date	Year	VG	Fine	VF	XF
20	AH1293	18xx	11.50	13.50	16.50	20.00
	1294	187x	11.50	13.50	16.50	20.00
	1295	—	11.50	13.50	16.50	20.00
	1296	18xx	11.50	13.50	16.50	20.00
	1295	1878	12.50	14.50	17.50	21.50
	1297	1879	11.50	13.50	16.50	20.00
	1297	1880	11.50	13.50	16.50	20.00
	1298	1881	11.50	13.50	16.50	20.00
	1299	1879	11.50	13.50	16.50	20.00
	1301	1884	11.50	13.50	16.50	20.00
	1302	—	—	Reported, not confirmed		
	1303	—	—	Reported, not confirmed		
	1304	1887	11.50	13.50	16.50	20.00
	1305	1888	11.50	13.50	16.50	20.00
	1306	—	—	Reported, not confirmed		
	1308	1891	11.50	13.50	16.50	20.00
	1309	1891	11.50	13.50	16.50	20.00
	1310	1xxx	11.50	13.50	16.50	20.00
	1312	xxxx	11.50	13.50	16.50	20.00
	1313	1895	11.50	13.50	16.50	20.00
	1315	1897	11.50	13.50	16.50	20.00

NAZARANA 2 RUPEES

SILVER, 32mm, 21.40-23.20 gm.

Y#	Date	Year	VG	Fine	VF	XF
21	AH1297	1880	125.00	150.00	225.00	300.00
	1298	1881	125.00	150.00	225.00	300.00

MOHUR

GOLD, 19mm, 10.70-11.40 gm.

Y#	Date	Year	VG	Fine	VF	XF
22	AH1297	1880	220.00	240.00	265.00	300.00
	1298	—	220.00	240.00	265.00	300.00

2 MOHURS

GOLD, 31mm, 21.40-22.80 gm.

Y#	Date	Year	VG	Fine	VF	XF
23	AH1297	1880	450.00	550.00	675.00	850.00

In the names of George V and Muhammad Ibrahim Ali Khan

PAISA

COPPER, 16-19mm

Y#	Date	Year	Good	VG	Fine	VF
24	AH1329	1911	1.25	1.75	2.50	3.50
	1329 (sic)					
		1329	1.25	1.75	2.50	3.50
	1335	1917	1.25	1.75	2.50	3.50
	1336	1917	1.25	1.75	2.50	3.50
	1342	1924	1.25	1.75	2.50	3.50
	1344	1925	1.25	1.75	2.50	3.50
	1344	1926	1.25	1.75	2.50	3.50
	1345	1927	1.25	1.75	2.50	3.50
	xxxx	1928	1.25	1.75	2.50	3.50

1/8 RUPEE

SILVER, 11mm, 1.34-1.45 gm.

Y#	Date	Year	Good	VG	Fine	VF
25	AH1346	1928	1.75	2.75	4.00	5.50

1/4 RUPEE

SILVER, 13mm, 2.68-2.90 gm.

Y#	Date	Year	VG	Fine	VF	XF
26	AH1346	1928	3.50	4.50	5.50	7.50

1/2 RUPEE

SILVER, 16mm, 5.35-5.80 gm.

Y#	Date	Year	VG	Fine	VF	XF
27	AH1346	1928	6.50	7.50	9.00	12.50

RUPEE

SILVER, 17-20mm

Y#	Date	Year	VG	Fine	VF	XF
28	AH1329	—	12.50	14.50	17.50	21.50
	1330	1912	12.50	14.50	17.50	21.50
	1341	1923	11.50	13.50	16.50	20.00
	1342	1924	11.50	13.50	16.50	20.00
	1344	1925	11.50	13.50	16.50	20.00
	1344	1926	11.50	13.50	16.50	20.00
	1345	1926	11.50	13.50	16.50	20.00
	1347	xxxx	11.50	13.50	16.50	20.00
	1348	1929	11.50	13.50	16.50	20.00
	—	1930	11.50	13.50	16.50	20.00

Muhammad Sa'adat Ali Khan

AH 1348-1368/AD 1930-1949

PICE (PAISA)

COPPER, 26mm

Y#	Date	Year	Mintage	Fine	VF	XF
29	AH1350	1932	.640	.75	1.25	2.00

1932 report.

21mm

Y#	Date	Year	Mintage	Fine	VF	XF
29a	AH1350	1932	.640	.25	.50	1.00

1934 report.

1/8 RUPEE

SILVER, 9mm, 1.34-1.45 gm

Y#	Date	Year	VG	Fine	VF	XF
30	AH1351	—	6.00	8.00	10.00	14.00
	1352	—	6.00	8.00	10.00	14.00
	1353	1934	6.00	8.00	10.00	14.00

TRAVANCORE

MONETARY SYSTEM

16 Cash = 1 Chuckram
4 Chuckram = 1 Fanam
2 Fanam = 1 Anantaraya
52-1/2 Fanam = 1 Pagoda

DATING

ME dates are in Malabar Era. Add 824 or 825 to the ME date for the AD date. e.g., ME1112 plus 824-825 = AD1936-1937.

Bala Rama Varma I

ME973-986 (1798-1810AD)

1/2 CHUCKRAM

COPPER, 14mm

KM#	Date	Year	Good	VG	Fine	VF
1	ND		1.75	2.75	4.00	6.00

SILVER, 5.5mm

C#	Date	Year	VG	Fine	VF	XF
10	ND	(1809-10)	2.50	4.00	5.50	8.00

CHUCKRAM

SILVER, 7mm

C#	Date	Year	VG	Fine	VF	XF
11	ND (1600-1860)		1.25	1.50	1.75	2.25

2 CHUCKRAMS

SILVER, 8mm

C#	Date	Year	VG	Fine	VF	XF
12	ND	(1809-10)	3.00	5.00	7.50	11.00

1/2 ANANTARAYA

(Fanam)

GOLD, 6mm

C#	Date	Year	VG	Fine	VF	XF
19	ND (1790-1830)		10.00	12.50	15.00	18.50

ANANTARAYA
(2 Fanam)

GOLD

C#	Date	Year	VG	Fine	VF	XF
22	ND	(1790-1860)	16.50	18.50	21.50	25.00

NOTE: For similar coins with leaf sprays on the obverse see Yeoman #11.

Rani Parvathi Bai
Regent, ME990-1004 (1815-29AD)

CASH
COPPER, 10mm
Similar to 4 Cash, C#27.

C#	Date	Year	Good	VG	Fine	VF
25	ME991-7	(1815-21)	1.00	1.75	2.50	5.00

2 CASH
COPPER, 12mm
Similar to 4 Cash, C#27.

C#	Date	Year	Good	VG	Fine	VF
26	ME991	(1815)	1.50	2.50	3.50	7.00
	ME997	(1821)	1.50	2.50	3.50	7.00

4 CASH

COPPER

C#	Date	Year	Good	VG	Fine	VF
27	ME991	(1815)	2.50	4.50	6.50	12.50

8 CASH
COPPER
Similar to 4 Cash, C#27.

C#	Date	Year	Good	VG	Fine	VF
28	ME991	(1814)	5.50	8.50	11.50	22.50

Rama Varma III
ME1004-22 (1829-47AD)

CASH

COPPER

C#	Date	Year	Good	VG	Fine	VF
36	ME1005	(1830)	1.00	1.75	2.50	5.00

C#	Date	Year	Good	VG	Fine	VF
38	ND	(1830-39)	1.00	1.75	2.50	5.50

Martanda Varma II
AD 1847-1860

CASH
COPPER, 8-10mm

Y#	Date	Year	Good	VG	Fine	VF
1	ND	(1848-60)	.50	1.00	1.50	2.25

2 CASH

COPPER, 10-11mm

Y#	Date	Year	Good	VG	Fine	VF
2	ND	(1848-49)	1.00	2.00	3.00	4.50

4 CASH

COPPER, 13-14mm

Y#	Date	Year	Good	VG	Fine	VF
3	ND		2.00	4.00	6.00	9.00

8 CASH

COPPER, 18mm

Y#	Date	Year	Good	VG	Fine	VF
A4	ND		4.00	8.00	12.00	18.00

Rama Varma IV
AD 1860-1880

CASH
COPPER, 8-10mm

Y#	Date	Year	Good	VG	Fine	VF
1a	ND	(1860-85)	.25	.50	.75	1.25

CHUCKRAM

SILVER, 6mm

Y#	Date	Year	Good	VG	Fine	VF
8	ND	(1860-1901)	1.25	1.50	1.75	2.25

VELLI FANAM

DUMP SILVER, 12mm

Y#	Date	Year	VG	Fine	VF	XF
9	ND	(1860-61)	2.50	3.25	4.00	7.00

Machine-struck, 15mm

Y#	Date	Year	VG	Fine	VF	XF
10	ND	(1864)	2.25	3.00	3.75	6.50

ANATARAYA (FANAM)

GOLD, 6mm

Y#	Date	Year	VG	Fine	VF	XF
11	ND	(1860-90)	9.00	11.50	14.00	17.50

1/2 PAGODA
GOLD

Y#	Date	Year	VG	Fine	VF	XF
15	1877		42.50	62.50	87.50	120.00

PAGODA

GOLD, 17mm

Y#	Date	Year	VG	Fine	VF	XF
16	1877		85.00	125.00	175.00	225.00

2 PAGODA

GOLD, 19mm

Y#	Date	Year	VG	Fine	VF	XF
17	1877		135.00	175.00	225.00	275.00

Rama Varma V
AD 1880-1885

ME dates are in Malabar Era. Add 824 or 825 to ME date for AD date. (E.g., ME 1112 and 824-825 - AD 1936-1937.

VIRARAYA FANAM

SILVER, 8mm

Y#	Date	Year	VG	Fine	VF	XF
18	ND	(1881)	1.75	2.50	3.50	5.00

VIRARAYA FANAM

GOLD, 8mm

Y#	Date	Year	VG	Fine	VF	XF
19	ND	(1881)	9.00	11.50	14.00	17.50

1/2 SOVEREIGN

GOLD, 20mm
Obv: Bust of Maharajah. Rev: Arms.

Y#	Date	Year	Mintage	VF	XF	Unc
20	ME1057	1881	2,000	300.00	400.00	500.00

SOVEREIGN
GOLD, 22mm
Obv: Bust of Maharajah. Rev: Arms.

Y#	Date	Year	Mintage	VF	XF	Unc
21	ME1057	1881	1,000	375.00	475.00	600.00

NOTE: Y#20 and Y#21 were presentation pieces struck to the British gold standard.

Rama Varma VI
AD 1885-1924

DUMP COINAGE

CASH

COPPER, 8-10mm

Y#	Date	Year	Good	VG	Fine	VF
1b	ND	(1885-95)	.25	.50	.75	1.25

No. 1b is a rather degenerated copy of Y#1.

1/4 CHUCKRAM

COPPER, 13mm

Y#	Date	Year	Good	VG	Fine	VF
22	ND	(1888-89)	1.25	2.00	2.75	5.50

1/2 CHUCKRAM

COPPER, 17-20mm

Y#	Date	Year	Good	VG	Fine	VF
23	ND		1.50	2.50	4.00	7.50

KALI FANAM

GOLD, 8mm

Y#	Date	Year	VG	Fine	VF	XF
24	ND	(1890-95)	9.00	11.50	14.00	17.50

MACHINE-STRUCK COINAGE

CASH

COPPER
Obv. leg: 'CASH 1'

Y#	Date	Year	VG	Fine	VF	XF
29	ND	(1901)	3.50	5.50	8.00	12.00

4 CASH

COPPER
Obv. leg: 'CASH FOUR'

Y#	Date	Year	VG	Fine	VF	XF
30	ND		1.50	2.25	3.00	5.00

Obv. leg: 'FOUR CASH'

Y#	Date	Year	VG	Fine	VF	XF
30a	ND	(1924-30)	.75	1.25	1.75	3.00

8 CASH

COPPER, 21mm
Obv. leg: 'CASH EIGHT'

Y#	Date	Year	VG	Fine	VF	XF
31	ND	(1901-03)	1.75	3.00	4.50	7.50

Obv. leg: 'EIGHT CASH'

Y#	Date	Year	VG	Fine	VF	XF
31a	ND	(1924-30)	.75	1.25	1.75	2.50

CHUCKRAM

COPPER, 27mm
Obv. leg: 'CHUCKRAM ONE'

Y#	Date	Year	VG	Fine	VF	XF
32	ND	(1901-03)	2.00	3.50	5.00	8.50

Obv. leg: 'ONE CHUCKRAM'

Y#	Date	Year	VG	Fine	VF	XF
32a	ND	(1927-28)	1.00	1.75	2.50	3.50

2 CHUCKRAMS

SILVER
Obv. leg: 'CHS. 2'

Y#	Date	Year	VG	Fine	VF	XF
33	ND	(1901)	1.50	2.50	3.50	5.50

Obv. leg: '2 CHS.'

Y#	Date	Year	VG	Fine	VF	XF
33a	ND	(1928)	1.25	2.25	3.25	5.00

FANAM

SILVER
Obv. leg: 'ONE FANAM'

Y#	Date	Year	VG	Fine	VF	XF
34	ND	(1889)	3.00	5.00	7.50	11.50

Obv. leg: 'FANAM ONE', undated.

Y#	Date	Year	VG	Fine	VF	XF
34a	ND	(1911)	2.00	2.75	3.50	5.50

With date

Y#	Date	Year	VG	Fine	VF	XF
34b	ME1087	—	2.25	3.00	4.00	6.00
	1100	—	2.25	3.00	4.00	6.00
	1106	—	2.25	3.00	4.00	6.00

NOTE: Undated Y#34a comes both with plain and reeded edge.

1/4 RUPEE

SILVER

Y#	Date	Year	VG	Fine	VF	XF
35.1	AD1889		4.00	6.00	9.00	13.50

Y#	Date	Year	VG	Fine	VF	XF
35.2	ME1083		7.00	10.00	13.50	20.00
	1085		7.00	10.00	13.50	20.00
	1087		3.50	5.50	8.50	13.00
	1096		3.50	4.50	6.00	8.00
	1099		3.50	4.50	6.00	8.00
	1100		3.50	4.50	6.00	8.00
	1103		3.50	4.50	6.00	8.00
	1106		3.50	4.50	6.00	8.00

1/2 RUPEE

SILVER

Y#	Date	Year	VG	Fine	VF	XF
36.1	1889		6.50	10.00	15.00	21.50

Rev: Shorter inscription on bottom.

Y#	Date	Year	VG	Fine	VF	XF
36.2	ME1086		8.50	13.50	18.50	25.00
	1087		7.50	10.00	15.00	21.50
	1106		6.50	8.50	11.50	15.00
	1107		6.75	9.00	13.50	18.50

Bala Rama Varma II

AD 1924-1949

CASH

COPPER, thick, 0.65gm

Y#	Date	Year	VG	Fine	VF	XF
41.1	ND		.25	.50	.75	1.25

Thin, 0.48gm

Y#	Date	Year	VG	Fine	VF	XF
41.2	ND		.10	.15	.25	.50

4 CASH

COPPER
Obv. monogram: BRV.

Y#	Date	Year	VG	Fine	VF	XF
42	ND		.25	.50	.75	1.00

8 CASH

COPPER
Obv. monogram: BRV

Y#	Date	Year	VG	Fine	VF	XF
43	ND		.25	.50	.75	1.00

CHUCKRAM

COPPER

Y#	Date	Year	VG	Fine	VF	XF
44	ME1114	(1938)	.50	1.00	2.00	3.50
	ND	(1931-45)	.25	.50	.75	1.25

FANAM

SILVER

Y#	Date	Year	VG	Fine	VF	XF
45	ME1112	(1936)	1.75	2.50	3.50	5.00

Y#	Date	Year	VG	Fine	VF	XF
45a	ME1116	(1940)	1.75	2.25	2.75	3.50
	1118	(1942)	1.75	2.25	2.75	3.50
	1121	(1945)	1.75	2.25	2.75	3.50

1/4 RUPEE

SILVER

Y#	Date	Year	VG	Fine	VF	XF
46	ME1112	(1936)	3.50	4.50	5.50	8.50

Y#	Date	Year	VG	Fine	VF	XF
46a	ME1116	(1940)	3.50	4.00	4.50	6.50
	ME1121	(1945)	3.50	4.00	4.50	6.50

1/2 RUPEE

SILVER

Y#	Date	Year	VG	Fine	VF	XF
47	ME1112	(1936)	6.50	8.00	10.00	14.50

1/2 'CHITRA' RUPEE

SILVER, reeded edge

Y#	Date	Year	VG	Fine	VF	XF
47a	ME1114	(1938)	6.50	8.00	10.00	13.50

Security edge

Y#	Date	Year	VG	Fine	VF	XF
47b	ME1116	(1940)	6.50	7.50	9.00	12.50
	ME1121	(1945)	6.50	7.50	9.00	12.50

NCLT ISSUES

TULABHARAM ISSUES

These presentation coins were struck prior to the weighing in ceremony of the Maharajah. The balance of his weight in these gold coins were distributed amongst the learned Brahmins and are referred to as 'Tulabhara Kasu'. The legend reads 'Sri Patmanabha', the national deity.

1/4 PAGODA

GOLD, uniface, 8.8mm, 0.63gm
Obv: 3 lines of Tamil legend

C#	Date	Year	Fine	VF	XF	Unc
42	ND	(1829,47)	50.00	70.00	100.00	150.00

Uniface, 12.7mm, 0.63gm
Obv: 3 lines of Tamil legend

Y#	Date	Year	Fine	VF	XF	Unc
4	ND	(1850,55)	50.00	70.00	100.00	150.00

10.9-12.7mm
Obv: Conch shell within wreath.
Rev: 3 lines of Tamil legend within wreath.

Fr#	Date	Mintage	Fine	VF	XF	Unc
338	ND(1870-1931)		45.00	65.00	90.00	135.00

1/2 PAGODA

GOLD, uniface, 10.9mm, 1.27gm
Obv: 3 lines of Tamil legend

C#	Date	Year	Fine	VF	XF	Unc
43	ND	(1829,47)	60.00	80.00	110.00	165.00

Uniface, 14.5mm, 1.27gm
Obv: 3 lines of Tamil legend

Y#	Date	Year	Fine	VF	XF	Unc
5	ND	(1850,55)	60.00	80.00	110.00	165.00

12.7-16mm, 1.28gm

Fr#	Date	Mintage	Fine	VF	XF	Unc
337	ND(1870-1931)		55.00	75.00	100.00	165.00

PAGODA

GOLD, uniface, 13mm, 2.54gm
Obv: 3 lines of Tamil legend

C#	Date	Year	Fine	VF	XF	Unc
44	ND	(1829,47)	100.00	135.00	175.00	235.00

Uniface, 17mm, 2.54gm
Obv: 3 lines of Tamil legend

Y#	Date	Year	Fine	VF	XF	Unc
6	ND	(1850,55)	100.00	135.00	175.00	235.00

17.0-20.3mm, 2.54gm

Fr#	Date	Mintage	Fine	VF	XF	Unc
336	ND(1870-1931)		90.00	125.00	150.00	200.00

2 PAGODAS

GOLD, uniface, 15.4mm, 5.06gm
Obv: 3 lines of Tamil legend

C#	Date	Year	Fine	VF	XF	Unc
45	ND	(1829,47)	150.00	185.00	225.00	300.00

Uniface, 20.3mm, 5.06gm
Obv: 3 lines of Tamil legend

Y#	Date	Year	Fine	VF	XF	Unc
7	ND	(1850,55)	150.00	185.00	225.00	300.00

20.0-23.9mm, 5.09gm
Obv: Conch shell within wreath
Rev: 3 lines of Tamil legend within wreath

Fr#	Date	Mintage	Fine	VF	XF	Unc
335	ND (1870-1931)		125.00	170.00	200.00	265.00

TRIPURA

NOTE: Until 1920 this state was named Hill Tippera. All modern Tripura coins were presentation pieces, more medallic than monetary in nature. They were struck in very limited numbers and although not intended for local circulation, they are often found in worn condition. They all bear the name of the ruler plus the name of his current wife. The late issues are dated in the Tripurabda era. To convert, TE Date plus 590 = AD Date. The dates appear to be accession years.

Krishna Manikya

SE1682-1705/1760-1783AD

1/4 RUPEE

SILVER, 15mm

KM#	Date	Year	VG	Fine	VF	XF
1	SE1682	(1760)	30.00	42.50	55.00	80.00

1/2 RUPEE

SILVER, 19mm

KM#	Date	Year	VG	Fine	VF	XF
2	SE1682	(1760)	50.00	60.00	75.00	100.00

RUPEE

SILVER, 25mm
Krishna Manikya alone

KM#	Date	Year	VG	Fine	VF	XF
3	SE1682	(1760)	35.00	47.50	60.00	85.00

23mm, with Queen Jahnavi

KM#	Date	Year	VG	Fine	VF	XF
4	SE1682	(1760)	35.00	47.50	60.00	85.00

1/4 MOHUR

GOLD

KM#	Date	Year	VG	Fine	VF	XF
5	SE1682	(1760)	175.00	200.00	250.00	300.00

MOHUR

GOLD
Krishna Manikya alone

KM#	Date	Year	VG	Fine	VF	XF
6	SE1682	(1760)	400.00	450.00	500.00	600.00

With Queen Jahnavi

KM#	Date	Year	VG	Fine	VF	XF
7	SE1682	(1760)	400.00	450.00	500.00	600.00

Rajadhara Manikya

SE1707-1726/1785-1804AD

RUPEE

SILVER, 25mm

KM#	Date	Year	VG	Fine	VF	XF
10	SE1707	(1785)	37.50	50.00	65.00	90.00

MOHUR

GOLD

KM#	Date	Year	VG	Fine	VF	XF
12	SE1707	(1785)	400.00	450.00	500.00	600.00

Rama Ganga Manikya

SE1728-1731/1806-1809AD

RUPEE

SILVER, plain edge
With Queen Tara

KM#	Date	Year	VG	Fine	VF	XF
15	SE1728	(1806)	40.00	60.00	85.00	110.00

Oblique edge milling

KM#	Date	Year	VG	Fine	VF	XF
16	SE1728	(1806)	80.00	100.00	125.00	150.00

MOHUR

GOLD

KM#	Date	Year	VG	Fine	VF	XF
18	SE1728	(1806)	400.00	450.00	500.00	600.00

Durga Manikya

1809-1813AD

RUPEE

SILVER
With Queen Sumitra

KM#	Date	Year	VG	Fine	VF	XF
21	SE1731	(1809)	40.00	60.00	85.00	110.00

MOHUR

GOLD

KM#	Date	Year	VG	Fine	VF	XF
23	SE1731	(1809)	400.00	450.00	500.00	600.00

Rama Ganga Manikya

SE1735-1748/1813-1826AD

RUPEE

SILVER
With Queen Chandratara

KM#	Date	Year	VG	Fine	VF	XF
26	SE1743	(1821)	40.00	60.00	85.00	110.00

MOHUR

GOLD

KM#	Date	Year	VG	Fine	VF	XF
28	SE1743	(1821)	400.00	450.00	500.00	600.00

Kasi Chandra Manikya

SE1748-1752/1826-1830AD

RUPEE

SILVER
With Queen Chandravethi

KM#	Date	Year	VG	Fine	VF	XF
31	SE1748	(1826)	80.00	100.00	125.00	150.00

With Queen Kirti Lakshmi

KM#	Date	Year	VG	Fine	VF	XF
32	SE1748	(1826)	80.00	100.00	125.00	150.00

Krishna Kishora Manikya

SE1752-1772/1830-1850AD

MOHUR

GOLD
With Queen Akhilesvari

KM#	Date	Year	VG	Fine	VF	XF
34	SE1752	(1830)	400.00	450.00	500.00	600.00

RUPEE

SILVER
With Queen Bidumukhi

KM#	Date	Year	VG	Fine	VF	XF
37	SE1752	(1830)	80.00	100.00	125.00	150.00

With Queen Purnakala

KM#	Date	Year	VG	Fine	VF	XF
38	SE1752	(1830)	80.00	100.00	125.00	150.00

With Queen Ratna Mala

KM#	Date	Year	VG	Fine	VF	XF
39	SE1752	(1830)	60.00	75.00	90.00	110.00

MOHUR

GOLD
With Queen Ratna Mala

KM#	Date	Year	VG	Fine	VF	XF
41	SE1752	(1830)	400.00	450.00	500.00	600.00

With Queen Sudakshina

KM#	Date	Year	VG	Fine	VF	XF
42	SE1752	—	400.00	450.00	500.00	600.00

Ishana Chandra Manikya

SE1772-1784/1850-1862AD

RUPEE

SILVER
With Queen Chandresvari

KM#	Date	Year	VG	Fine	VF	XF
45	SE1771	(1849)	60.00	75.00	90.00	110.00

MOHUR

GOLD
With Queen Chandresvari

KM#	Date	Year	VG	Fine	VF	XF
47	SE1771	—	400.00	450.00	500.00	600.00

RUPEE

With Queen Muktavali

KM#	Date	Year	VG	Fine	VF	XF
50	SE1771	(1849)	60.00	75.00	90.00	110.00

MOHUR

GOLD

KM#	Date	Year	VG	Fine	VF	XF
52	SE1771	(1849)	400.00	450.00	500.00	600.00

RUPEE

SILVER
With Queen Raja Lakshmi

KM#	Date	Year	VG	Fine	VF	XF
55	SE1771	(1849)	60.00	75.00	90.00	110.00

MOHUR

GOLD
With Queen Raja Lakshmi

KM#	Date	Year	VG	Fine	VF	XF
57	SE1771	(1849)	400.00	450.00	500.00	600.00

Vira Chandra Manikya

SE1784-1818/1862-1896AD

RUPEE

SILVER, hand struck, plain edge
With Queen Bhanumati Devi

KM#	Date	Year	VG	Fine	VF	XF
60	SE1791	(1869)	60.00	75.00	85.00	110.00

Machine struck, milled edge

KM#	Date	Year	VG	Fine	VF	XF
61	TE1279	(1869)	60.00	75.00	85.00	110.00

With Queen Manamohini

KM#	Date	Year	VG	Fine	VF	XF
62	TE1279	(1869)	50.00	65.00	80.00	100.00

MOHUR

GOLD

KM#	Date	Year	VG	Fine	VF	XF
64	TE1279	(1869)	250.00	300.00	400.00	500.00

RUPEE

SILVER, hand struck
With Queen Rajeswari Devi

KM#	Date	Year	VG	Fine	VF	XF
67	SE1791	(1869)	60.00	75.00	90.00	110.00

Machine struck

KM#	Date	Year	VG	Fine	VF	XF
68	TE1279	(1869)	50.00	65.00	80.00	100.00

MOHUR

GOLD
Similar to Rupee, KM#23.

KM#	Date	Year	VG	Fine	VF	XF
70	SE1791	(1869)	400.00	450.00	500.00	600.00

Radha Kishora Manikya

1897-1909AD

RUPEE

SILVER, 11.6 gm.
With Queen Ratna Manjari

KM#	Date	Year	VG	Fine	VF	XF
73	TE1306	(1896)	50.00	70.00	100.00	140.00

MOHUR

GOLD

KM#	Date	Year	VG	Fine	VF	XF
75	TE1306	(1896)	400.00	450.00	500.00	600.00

1/2 RUPEE

SILVER
With Queen Tulsiwati

KM#	Date	Year	VG	Fine	VF	XF
77	TE1306	(1896)	50.00	70.00	100.00	140.00

RUPEE

SILVER, 8.8 gm.

KM#	Date	Year	VG	Fine	VF	XF
78	TE1306	(1896)	40.00	60.00	85.00	110.00

Birendra Kishora MANIKYA

1909-1923AD

MOHUR

GOLD
With Queen Prabhavati

KM#	Date	Year	VG	Fine	VF	XF
80	TE1319	(1909)	400.00	450.00	500.00	600.00

Vira Vikrama Kishora MANIKYA

1923-1947AD

RUPEE

SILVER, milled edge
Without a queen

KM#	Date	Year	VG	Fine	VF	XF
83	TE1337	(1930)	25.00	35.00	50.00	70.00

Security edge

KM#	Date	Year	VG	Fine	VF	XF
84	TE1337	(1930)	40.00	60.00	90.00	110.00

With Queen Kirti Mani

KM#	Date	Year	VG	Fine	VF	XF
85	TE1341	(1934)	40.00	60.00	85.00	110.00

With Queen Kanchen Prabha

KM#	Date	Year	VG	Fine	VF	XF
86	TE1341	(1931)	20.00	30.00	40.00	52.50

Plains Tripura

The estates of lower or Plains Tripura were annexed by the East India Company, nominally under the authority of the Nawab of Murshidabad, in AD1760.

Roshnabad Tripura Mint

RUPEE

SILVER, 30mm

KM#	Date	Year	VG	Fine	VF	XF
111	AH1175	3	75.00	100.00	125.00	150.00

INDIAN ENCLAVES

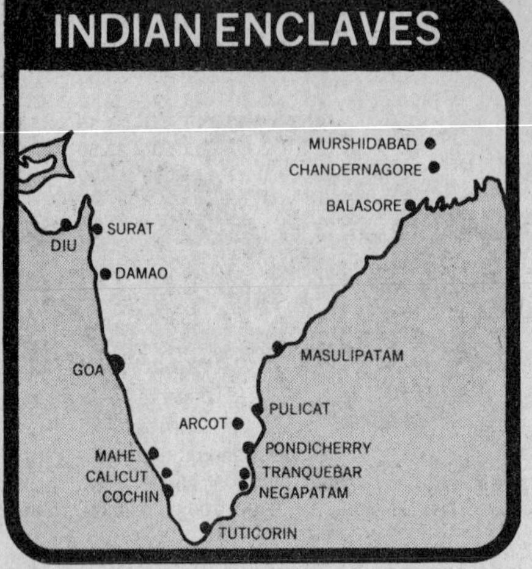

Danish India or Tranquebar is a town and former Danish colony on the southeast coast of India. In Danish times, 1620-1845, it was a factory site and seaport operated by the Danish Asiatic Company. Tranquebar and the other Danish settlements in India were sold to the British East India Company in 1845.

It was not until 1664, during the reign of Louis XIV, that the Compagnie des Indes Orientales was formed for the purpose of obtaining holdings on the subcontinent of India. Between 1666 and 1721, French settlements were established at Arcot, Mahe, Surat, Pondicherry, Masulipatam, Murshidabad, Chandernagore, Balasore and Calicut. War with Britain reduced the French holdings to a few unimportant coast settlements.

The Netherlands, operating as the United East India Company of the Netherlands, were the real successors to the Portuguese in India. They maintained a number of thriving establishments on the subcontinent until 1795, when Robert Clive, founder of the empire of British India, completed Britain's conquest of Bengal. Thereafter the Dutch holdings were gradually ceded to Britain, the most important to numismatics being Cochin, ceded in 1814; Negapatnam, ceded in 1784; Pulicat, ceded in 1824; and Tuticorin, ceded in 1795.

Vasco da Gama, the Portuguese explorer, first visited India in 1498. Portugal seized control of a number of islands and small enclaves on the west coast of India, and for the next hundred years enjoyed a monopoly on trade. With the arrival of powerful Dutch and English fleets in the first half of the 17th century, Portuguese power in the area declined until virtually all of India that remained under Portuguese control were the west coast enclaves of Goa, Damao and Diu. They were forcibly annexed by India in 1961.

INDIA-DANISH

Tranquebar

RULERS

Danish until 1845

MONETARY SYSTEM

80 Kas (Cash) = Royaliner (Fano or Fanam)
8 Royaliner = 1 Rupee
18 Royaliner = 1 Speciesdaler

KAS

COPPER, dump
Obv: Crowned C7 monogram.
Rev: Crowned DAC monogram between date, 1 below.

C#	Date	Mintage	Good	VG	Fine	VF
6	1767	—	40.00	65.00	100.00	140.00
	1768	—	20.00	35.00	55.00	85.00
	1770	—	20.00	35.00	55.00	85.00
	1777	—	20.00	35.00	55.00	85.00
	1780	—	20.00	35.00	55.00	85.00

Obv: Crowned FVIR monogram.
Rev: Value, date below.

C#	Date	Mintage	Good	VG	Fine	VF
16	1816	—	—	—	Rare	—
	1819	—	20.00	35.00	55.00	85.00

2 KAS

COPPER, dump
Obv: Crowned C7 monogram
Rev: Crowned DAC monogram between date, 2 below.

C#	Date	Mintage	Good	VG	Fine	VF
7	1767	—	—	—	—	—
	1768	—	20.00	35.00	55.00	85.00
	1770	—	20.00	35.00	55.00	85.00
	1777	—	20.00	35.00	55.00	85.00

Rev: W/o crown over DAC monogram.

C#	Date	Mintage	Good	VG	Fine	VF
7.1	1770	—	35.00	60.00	100.00	140.00

Rev: W/retrograde 2

C#	Date	Mintage	Good	VG	Fine	VF
7.2	1780	—	35.00	60.00	100.00	140.00

IV KAS

COPPER, dump
Obv: Crowned C7 monogram.
Rev: Crowned DAC monogram between date, 4 below.

C#	Date	Mintage	Good	VG	Fine	VF
8	1767	—	5.50	9.00	15.00	25.00
	1768	—	5.50	9.00	15.00	25.00
	1770	—	5.00	8.50	14.00	23.50
	1776	—	7.00	14.00	18.50	30.00
	1777	—	5.50	9.00	15.00	25.00

Rev: Second 7 in date retrograde.

C#	Date	Mintage	Good	VG	Fine	VF
8.1	1770	—	12.50	20.00	32.50	50.00

Obv: Crowned C7 monogram.

C#	Date	Mintage	Good	VG	Fine	VF
9	1782	—	5.00	8.50	15.00	25.00
	1786	—	5.00	8.50	15.00	25.00
	1787	—	5.00	8.50	15.00	25.00
	1788	—	5.00	8.50	15.00	25.00
	1790	—	4.00	7.50	13.50	22.50
	1797	—	5.00	8.50	15.00	25.00
	1807	—	6.50	11.50	21.50	33.50

R between date.

C#	Date	Mintage	Good	VG	Fine	VF
9.1	1786	—	12.50	20.00	32.50	50.00

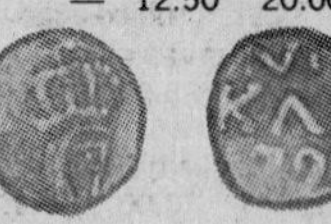

Rev: Error: Value retrograde .VI. for .IV.

C#	Date	Mintage	Good	VG	Fine	VF
9a	1797	—	8.00	13.50	23.50	35.00
	1799	—	9.00	15.00	25.00	37.50
	1800	—	8.00	13.50	23.50	35.00

C#	Date	Mintage	Good	VG	Fine	VF
17	1815	—	6.50	10.00	17.50	27.50
	1816	—	6.00	9.00	16.50	26.50
	1817	—	7.00	11.00	18.50	28.50
	1820	—	6.00	9.00	16.50	26.50
	1821	—	20.00	32.50	50.00	80.00
	1822	—	6.00	9.00	16.50	26.50
	1823	—	5.50	8.50	15.00	25.00
	1824	—	5.50	8.50	15.00	25.00

Crown design standardized.

C#	Date	Mintage	Good	VG	Fine	VF
17.1	1824	—	—	—	—	—
	1825	—	5.50	8.50	15.00	25.00
	1830	—	6.50	10.00	17.50	27.50
	1831	—	5.50	8.50	15.00	25.00
17.1	1832	—	5.50	8.50	15.00	25.00
	1833	—	5.50	8.50	15.00	25.00
	1834	—	5.50	8.50	15.00	25.00
	1837	—	5.50	8.50	15.00	25.00
	1838	—	5.50	8.50	15.00	25.00
	1839	—	5.00	8.00	13.50	22.50

Rev: S in KAS retrograde.

C#	Date	Mintage	Good	VG	Fine	VF
17.2	1817	—	5.00	8.50	13.50	22.50
	1831	—	12.50	20.00	32.50	50.00

Rev: Error-value retrograde .VI. for .IV.

C#	Date	Mintage	Good	VG	Fine	VF
17a	1824	—	20.00	32.50	50.00	80.00

Obv: Crowned C VIII R monogram.

C#	Date	Mintage	Good	VG	Fine	VF
21	1840	—	6.50	11.50	17.50	27.50
	1841	—	6.00	11.00	16.50	26.50
	1842	—	6.00	11.00	16.50	26.50
	1843	—	6.00	11.00	16.50	26.50
	1844	—	8.50	13.50	22.50	33.50

Obv: Crowned CR monogram.

C#	Date	Mintage	Good	VG	Fine	VF
21.1	1844	—	5.50	10.00	15.00	25.00
	1845	—	7.50	12.50	20.00	35.00

10 KAS

COPPER, dump
Obv: Crowned double C7 monogram.
Rev: Crowned DAC monogram, value 10, date below.

C#	Date	Mintage	Good	VG	Fine	VF
10	1768	—	50.00	75.00	125.00	200.00

Rev: Value appears as X KAS on one line.

C#	Date	Mintage	Good	VG	Fine	VF
11	1768	—	22.50	37.50	62.50	100.00
	1770	—	22.50	37.50	62.50	100.00
	1777	—	22.50	37.50	62.50	100.00

Rev: Value appears as X/KAS on two lines.

C#	Date	Mintage	Good	VG	Fine	VF
12	1782	—	17.50	30.00	50.00	80.00
	1786	—	17.50	30.00	50.00	80.00
	1788	—	17.50	30.00	50.00	80.00
	1790	—	16.50	26.50	45.00	75.00

C#	Date	Mintage	Good	VG	Fine	VF
18	1816	—	15.00	25.00	40.00	65.00
	1822	—	15.00	25.00	40.00	65.00
	1838	—	15.00	25.00	40.00	65.00
	1839	—	13.50	22.50	37.50	60.00

C#	Date	Mintage	Good	VG	Fine	VF
22	1842	—	25.00	40.00	65.00	100.00

ROYALIN

(Fano, Fanam)

SILVER, dump
Obv: Crowned C7 monogram.
Rev: Value, arms w/lion between date.

C#	Date	Mintage	Good	VG	Fine	VF
13	1767	—	20.00	32.50	55.00	85.00
	1768	—	20.00	32.50	55.00	85.00
	1769	—	20.00	32.50	55.00	85.00
	1770	—	20.00	32.50	55.00	85.00
	1771	—	20.00	32.50	55.00	85.00
	1772	—	20.00	32.50	55.00	85.00
	1773	—	20.00	32.50	55.00	85.00
	1774	—	20.00	32.50	55.00	85.00
	1775	—	20.00	32.50	55.00	85.00
	1776	—	20.00	32.50	55.00	85.00
	1779	—	20.00	32.50	55.00	85.00
	1780	—	20.00	32.50	55.00	85.00
	1781	—	20.00	32.50	55.00	85.00
	1783	—	20.00	32.50	55.00	85.00
	1784	—	20.00	32.50	55.00	85.00
	1786	—	20.00	32.50	55.00	85.00
	1787	—	20.00	32.50	55.00	85.00
	1788	—	20.00	32.50	55.00	85.00
	1789	—	20.00	32.50	55.00	85.00
	1791	—	20.00	32.50	55.00	85.00
	1792	—	20.00	32.50	55.00	85.00
	1793	—	20.00	32.50	55.00	85.00
	1794	—	20.00	32.50	55.00	85.00
	1795	—	20.00	32.50	55.00	85.00
	1796	—	20.00	32.50	55.00	85.00
	1797	—	20.00	32.50	55.00	85.00
	1799	—	20.00	32.50	55.00	85.00
	1807	—	20.00	32.50	55.00	85.00

C#	Date	Mintage	Good	VG	Fine	VF
13.1	1786R	—	57.50	90.00	165.00	250.00

C#	Date	Mintage	Good	VG	Fine	VF
19	1816	—	35.00	60.00	100.00	165.00
	1818	—	35.00	60.00	100.00	165.00

2 ROYALINER

(2 Fano, Fanams)

SILVER, dump
Obv: Crowned C7 monogram.

C#	Date	Mintage	Good	VG	Fine	VF
14	1767	—	20.00	32.50	55.00	85.00
	1768	—	20.00	32.50	55.00	85.00
	1769	—	20.00	32.50	55.00	85.00
	1770	—	20.00	32.50	55.00	85.00
	1771	—	20.00	32.50	55.00	85.00
	1772	—	20.00	32.50	55.00	85.00
	1773	—	20.00	32.50	55.00	85.00
	1774	—	20.00	32.50	55.00	85.00
	1775	—	20.00	32.50	55.00	85.00
	1776	—	20.00	32.50	55.00	85.00
	1779	—	20.00	32.50	55.00	85.00
	1780	—	20.00	32.50	55.00	85.00
	1781	—	20.00	32.50	55.00	85.00
	1783	—	20.00	32.50	55.00	85.00
	1784	—	20.00	32.50	55.00	85.00
	1786	—	20.00	32.50	55.00	85.00
	1787	—	20.00	32.50	55.00	85.00
	1788	—	20.00	32.50	55.00	85.00
	1789	—	20.00	32.50	55.00	85.00
	1792	—	20.00	32.50	55.00	85.00
	1793	—	20.00	32.50	55.00	85.00
	1794	—	20.00	32.50	55.00	85.00
	1795	—	20.00	32.50	55.00	85.00
	1796	—	20.00	32.50	55.00	85.00
	1797	—	20.00	32.50	55.00	85.00
	1799	—	—	—	—	—
	1807	—	20.00	32.50	55.00	85.00

C#	Date	Mintage	Good	VG	Fine	VF
14.1	1786R	—	57.50	90.00	165.00	250.00

C#	Date	Mintage	Good	VG	Fine	VF
20	1816	—	50.00	80.00	125.00	200.00
	1818	—	50.00	80.00	125.00	200.00

PAGODE, PAGODA

GOLD
Obv: Crowned C7 monogram in oval on granulated field.
Rev: Indian diety.

C#	Date	Mintage	VG	Fine	VF	XF
15	ND(1789)	—	1650.	2000.	2500.	3250.

NOTE: Modern counterfeits exist in both silver and gold.

INDIA-FRENCH

RULERS

French until 1848

MONETARY SYSTEM

Cache Kas or Cash
Doudou = 4 Caches
Biche = 1 Pice
2 Royalins = 1 Fanon Pondichery
5 Heavy Fanons = 1 Rupee Mahe
64 Biches = 1 Rupee

NOTE: Undated coinage struck 1720 - early 19th century.

ARCOT COINAGE

MINTMARKS

Although being copies of native issues bearing the name of the Arcot (Arkat) Mint, a crescent moon mintmark is found to left of the regnal year for those struck at Pondichery.

In the name of Shah Alam II

AH1173-1221 = AD1759-1806

1/2 RUPEE

SILVER, 5.7 gm.

C#	Date	Year	VG	Fine	VF	XF
45	AH1198	32 (sic)	15.00	25.00	35.00	50.00

RUPEE

SILVER, 11.4 gm.

C#	Date	Year	VG	Fine	VF	XF
46	AH117x	4	13.50	17.50	23.50	32.50
	1178	5	13.50	17.50	23.50	32.50
	1183	9	13.50	17.50	23.50	32.50
	1184	10	13.50	17.50	23.50	32.50
	1185	10	13.50	17.50	23.50	32.50
	1186	11	13.50	17.50	23.50	32.50
	1188	13	13.50	17.50	23.50	32.50
	1190	15	13.50	17.50	23.50	32.50
	1191	16	13.50	17.50	23.50	32.50
	1197	22	13.50	17.50	23.50	32.50
	1198	32(sic)	13.50	17.50	23.50	32.50
	1199	24	13.50	17.50	23.50	32.50
	1200	25	13.50	17.50	23.50	32.50
	1201	26	13.50	17.50	23.50	32.50
	1202	27	13.50	17.50	23.50	32.50
46	1203	28	13.50	17.50	23.50	32.50
	1204	29	13.50	17.50	23.50	32.50
	1205	30	13.50	17.50	23.50	32.50
	1206	31	13.50	17.50	23.50	32.50
	1207	32	13.50	17.50	23.50	32.50
	1208	34	13.50	17.50	23.50	32.50
	1218	43	12.50	16.50	21.50	27.50
	1218	44	12.50	16.50	21.50	27.50
	1219	44	12.50	16.50	21.50	27.50
	1219	45	12.50	16.50	21.50	27.50
	1220	43	12.50	16.50	21.50	27.50
	1220	45	12.50	16.50	21.50	27.50
	1221	43	12.50	16.50	21.50	27.50
	1221	49	12.50	16.50	21.50	27.50

NAZARANA RUPEE

SILVER, 32-33mm, 11.4 gm.

C#	Date	Year	Mintage	Fine	VF	XF
46a	AH1178	5	—	—	Rare	—
	1184	—	—	—	Rare	—
	1185	10	—	—	Rare	—
	1199	24	—	—	Rare	—

Karikal

CACHE

COPPER

C#	Date	Mintage	Good	VG	Fine	VF
47	ND	—	3.50	5.50	11.50	20.00

1/2 DOUDOU

COPPER

C#	Date	Mintage	Good	VG	Fine	VF
48	ND	—	6.00	10.00	17.50	25.00

DOUDOU

COPPER, 3.2 gm.

C#	Date	Mintage	Good	VG	Fine	VF
49	ND	—	6.00	10.00	17.50	25.00

Mahe

1/4 BICHE

COPPER, 1.1-1.4 gm.
Obv: 5 fleur de lis. Rev: Date.

C#	Date	Mintage	Good	VG	Fine	VF
51	1753-69	—	15.00	25.00	40.00	65.00

1/2 BICHE

COPPER, 2.2-3.6 gm.
Obv: 5 fleur de lis. Rev: Date.

C#	Date	Mintage	Good	VG	Fine	VF
52	1731-85	—	7.50	15.00	25.00	40.00

BICHE

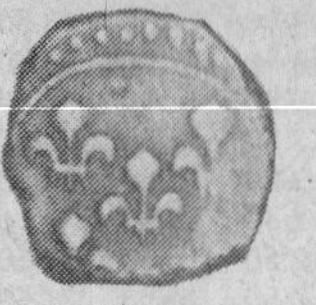

COPPER, 4.4-6.4 gm.

C#	Date	Mintage	Good	VG	Fine	VF
53	1730-90	—	6.50	13.50	20.00	35.00

FANAM (1/5 RUPEE)

SILVER

C#	Date	Mintage	VG	Fine	VF	XF
57a	1738-1820	—	6.00	10.00	16.50	25.00

Pondichery

CACHE

COPPER
LIS inscription 1.6 gm.

C#	Date	Mintage	Good	VG	Fine	VF
121	ND	—	6.00	10.00	16.50	25.00

1/2 DOUDOU

COPPER, 2.1 gm.

C#	Date	Mintage	Good	VG	Fine	VF
122	ND	—	3.50	6.00	10.00	20.00

DOUDOU

COPPER, 4.2 gm.

C#	Date	Mintage	Good	VG	Fine	VF
123	ND	—	1.25	2.50	5.00	9.00

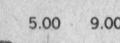

C#	Date	Mintage	Good	VG	Fine	VF
141	1836	—	1.75	3.50	6.50	13.50

ROYALIN(1/2 FANON)

SILVER, 0.7 gm.

C#	Date	Mintage	VG	Fine	VF	XF
131	ND	—	6.00	10.00	16.50	25.00

C#	Date	Mintage	VG	Fine	VF	XF
143	1837	—	12.50	23.50	35.00	50.00

2 ROYALINS(FANON)

SILVER
Obv: Royal crown, 1.500-1.593 gm.

C#	Date	Mintage	VG	Fine	VF	XF
132	ND	—	12.50	20.00	30.00	50.00

Obv: Hindu crown

C#	Date	Mintage	VG	Fine	VF	XF
132a	ND	—	12.50	20.00	30.00	50.00

C#	Date	Mintage	VG	Fine	VF	XF
144	1837	—	15.00	25.00	40.00	60.00

4 ROYALINS(2 FANON)

SILVER
Obv: Royal crown, 2.76 gm.

C#	Date	Mintage	VG	Fine	VF	XF
133	ND	—	7.50	15.00	25.00	35.00

Obv: Hindu crown

C#	Date	Mintage	VG	Fine	VF	XF
133a	ND	—	7.50	15.00	25.00	35.00

C#	Date	Mintage	VG	Fine	VF	XF
145	1837	—	15.00	27.50	42.50	65.00

INDIA DUTCH

MINTMARKS

NOTE: On native style coins the Dutch East India Company often used the mintmark: Lazy J.

MONETARY SYSTEM

(1724-1795)

8 Bazaruk = 1 Duit
4 Duiten = 1 Fanam
32 Fanam = 1 Stuiver

Cochin

BAZARUK

TIN
Obv: 8/VOC monogram.
Rev: Pear shaped shield.

Sch#	Date	Mintage	Good	VG	Fine	VF
1255	ND(1724-95)	—	—	—	—	—

1/2 RASI

COPPER, 5.42-5.89 gm.
Similar to 1 Rasi, Sch#1252.

Sch#	Date	Mintage	Good	VG	Fine	VF
1253	ND	—	20.00	35.00	60.00	100.00

RASI

COPPER, 10.84-11.79gm.

Sch#	Date	Mintage	Good	VG	Fine	VF
1252	ND	—	12.50	22.50	37.50	62.50

NOTE: Sch#1253 and 1252 were struck for trade with Muscat.

FANAM

GOLD

Sch#	Date	Mintage	VG	Fine	VF	XF
1249	ND(1740-80)	—	20.00	37.50	60.00	100.00

SILVER
Rev: Lazy 'J' over OC/ 3 rows of 4 dots each.

Sch#	Date	Mintage	VG	Fine	VF	XF
1250	ND(1782-91)	—	7.50	12.50	21.50	30.00

Negapatnam

MONETARY SYSTEM

80 Cash = 1 Fanam
24 Fanam = 1 Pagoda

CASH

LEAD
Obv: N/VOC monogram.
Rev: Tamil legend in 2 lines: NAKAPATTANAM.

Sch#	Date	Mintage	Good	VG	Fine	VF
1242	ND	—	20.00	32.50	50.00	90.00

COPPER

Sch#	Date	Mintage	Good	VG	Fine	VF
1241	ND	—	5.00	9.00	15.00	25.00

Obv: Retrograde 'N'/VOC monogram.

Sch#	Date	Mintage	Good	VG	Fine	VF
1241e	ND	—	—	—	—	—

2 CASH

COPPER
Obv: P/VOC monogram.
Rev: PA..../date in outer circle.

Sch#	Date	Mintage	Good	VG	Fine	VF
1224	1780	—	—	—	Rare	—

Rev: Tamil legend in 3 lines.

Sch#	Date	Mintage	Good	VG	Fine	VF
1240	ND	—	10.00	16.50	27.50	45.00

Obv: Retrograde N/VOC monogram.

Sch#	Date	Mintage	Good	VG	Fine	VF
1240b	ND	—	—	—	—	—

4 CASH

COPPER
Obv: N/VOC monogram/4.
Rev: Tamil legend in 2 lines.

Sch#	Date	Mintage	Good	VG	Fine	VF
1238	ND	—	20.00	32.50	55.00	90.00

Obv: N/VOC monogram/IV.

Sch#	Date	Mintage	Good	VG	Fine	VF
1239	ND	(1 Known)	—	—	—	—

10 CASH

COPPER
Obv: N/VOC monogram/10.

Sch#	Date	Mintage	Good	VG	Fine	VF
1237	ND	—	—	—	Rare	—

15 CASH

COPPER
Obv: N/VOC monogram/15.

Sch#	Date	Mintage	Good	VG	Fine	VF
1236	ND	—	—	Rare	—	—

FANAM

SILVER
Obv: Degenerated Kali.
Rev: Lazy 'J' over OC (without dots) /3 rows of 4 dots each.

Sch#	Date	Mintage	VG	Fine	VF	XF
1234	ND	—	17.50	28.50	45.00	75.00

GOLD
Obv: Degenerated Kali.
Rev: Degenerated Nagari legend: RAMA RAYA.

Sch#	Date	Mintage	VG	Fine	VF	XF
1232/1233	ND	—	7.50	11.50	17.50	27.50

PAGODA

GOLD
Obv: Degenerated Vishnu.
Rev: Granulated.

Sch#	Date	Mintage	VG	Fine	VF	XF
1229	ND(1747-84)	—	70.00	85.00	100.00	120.00

NOTE: Similar coins without Lazy 'J' at 3 o'clock on obverse were struck at Colombo, Ceylon (1783) and Tuticorin (1788). Coins with devices on reverse were struck in Tranquebar (C#15), Madras (C#421), Pondicherry (C#114) and possibly in Arcot with Arabic 'Ain' on reverse and Mysore with Arabic H on reverse. Three main varieties exist of the above coin: gold contents of .800 (1747-67), .769 (1767-1781) and .675 (1781-1784).

Pulicat

First Series

2 CASH

COPPER
Obv: II/VOC monogram.

Sch#	Date	Mintage	VG	Fine	VF	XF
1222	ND(1646-)	—	17.50	30.00	50.00	80.00

CASH

COPPER
Obv: P/VOC monogram.
Rev. Arabic legend in the name of Sultan Abd'Allah.

Sch#	Date	Mintage	VG	Fine	VF	XF
1223	ND(1646-)	—	17.50	30.00	50.00	80.00

4 CASH

COPPER
Obv: PAL/IIII/VOC monogram.
Rev: Similar to 1 Cash, Sch#1223.

Sch#	Date	Mintage	VG	Fine	VF	XF
1220	ND(1646-)	—	45.00	75.00	120.00	200.00

8 CASH

COPPER
Obv: PAL/VIII/VOC monogram.
Rev: Similar to 1 Cash, Sch#1223.

Sch#	Date	Mintage	VG	Fine	VF	XF
1218	ND(1646-)	—	27.50	45.00	75.00	125.00

Second Series

(Struck for circulation in Ceylon)

5 CASH

COPPER
Obv: V/VOC monogram.

Sch#	Date	Mintage	VG	Fine	VF	XF
1219	ND(1646-)	—	45.00	72.50	120.00	200.00

10 CASH

COPPER
Obv: X/VOC monogram.

Sch#	Date	Mintage	VG	Fine	VF	XF
1217	ND(1646-)	—	17.50	30.00	50.00	85.00

Third Series

CASH

COPPER
Obv: P/VOC monogram.
Rev: PALCATE, date around G (elria).

Sch#	Date	Mintage	VG	Fine	VF	XF
1226	1743	—	20.00	35.00	65.00	80.00

NOTE: Struck between 1740-1790, although 1743 is the only confirmed date. Many varieties in spelling.

2 CASH

COPPER

Sch#	Date	Mintage	VG	Fine	VF	XF
1224	178x	—	20.00	35.00	60.00	80.00

Tuticorin

FANAM

GOLD
Obv: Degenerated Kali.
Rev: Degenerated Nagari legend: RAMA RAYA

Sch#	Date	Mintage	VG	Fine	VF	XF
1257	ND(1738)	—	25.00	40.00	65.00	110.00

NOTE: Similar coins were struck for Negapatnam, Sch#1232-3. The difference is in the shape of the letter RA.

PAGODA

GOLD
Obv: Degenerated Vishnu, no lazy 'J' at 3 o'clock.
Rev: Granulated.

Sch#	Date	Mintage	VG	Fine	VF	XF
—	ND(1786)	7,100	70.00	100.00	150.00	200.00

INDIA - PORTUGUESE

RULERS

Portuguese until 1961

NOTE: The undated coppers are best identified by the shape of the coat of arms.

Maria I-Somewhat triangular shield (baroque style)
Joao VI, as Regent: oval shield
Joao VI, as King: square shield superimposed on globe
Maria II: square shield on plain background

The denomination of most copper coins appears in numerals on the reverse, though 30 Keri is often given as "1/2 T", and 60 Reis as "T" (T=tanga). The silver coins have the denomination in words, usually on the obverse until 1850, then on the reverse.

Damao

MONETARY SYSTEM

60 Reis = 1 Tanga

15 REIS

COPPER

C#	Date	Mintage	Good	VG	Fine	VF
21	1843	—	3.50	7.00	12.50	21.50

C#	Date	Mintage	Good	VG	Fine	VF
31	1854	—	3.00	6.50	11.50	20.00

30 REIS

COPPER

C#	Date	Mintage	Good	VG	Fine	VF
22	1840	—	2.25	4.50	7.50	12.50
32	1854	—	3.00	6.00	10.00	17.00

60 REIS

COPPER

C#	Date	Mintage	Good	VG	Fine	VF
23	1840	—	4.00	8.00	13.50	22.50

Diu

MONETARY SYSTEM

750 Bazarucos = 600 Reis
40 Atia = 10 Tanga = 1 Rupia

3 BAZARUCOS

LEAD or TIN, 15-18mm, 2.4 gm.

C#	Date	Mintage	Good	VG	Fine	VF
90	1800	—	10.00	17.50	27.50	40.00

1/4 ATTIA

COPPER

C#	Date	Mintage	Good	VG	Fine	VF
71	1778	—	6.50	12.50	17.50	30.00

5 BAZARUCOS

LEAD or TIN, 20-23mm
Obv: Crude crowned arms.
Rev: Date in angles of cross.

C#	Date	Mintage	Good	VG	Fine	VF
91	1800	—	6.50	12.50	17.50	25.00

21mm
Similar to 20 Bazarucos, C#93.

C#	Date	Mintage	Good	VG	Fine	VF
111	1807	—	12.50	25.00	35.00	50.00

20-22 mm

C#	Date	Mintage	Good	VG	Fine	VF
131	1827	—	5.00	10.00	15.00	22.50
	1828	—	5.00	10.00	15.00	22.50

1/2 ATIA

COPPER

C#	Date	Mintage	Good	VG	Fine	VF
95	1787	—	1.50	3.00	5.00	8.50
	1799	—	3.00	6.00	9.00	15.00

10 BAZARUCOS

LEAD or TIN

C#	Date	Mintage	Good	VG	Fine	VF
92	1799	—	5.00	10.00	15.00	22.50
	1800	—	5.00	10.00	15.00	22.50

27mm

C#	Date	Mintage	Good	VG	Fine	VF
132	1827	—	—	—	—	—

ATIA

COPPER

C#	Date	Mintage	Good	VG	Fine	VF
73	1778	—	1.50	3.00	5.00	8.50

C#	Date	Mintage	Good	VG	Fine	VF
96	1799	—	1.50	3.00	6.00	10.00

20 BAZARUCOS

LEAD or TIN

C#	Date	Mintage	Good	VG	Fine	VF
93	1799	—	5.00	10.00	15.00	22.50
	1800	—	6.50	12.50	20.00	30.00
	1801	—	6.50	12.50	20.00	30.00

33-36mm
Similar to C#93.

C#	Date	Mintage	Good	VG	Fine	VF
113	1807	—	15.00	27.50	40.00	60.00

C#	Date	Mintage	Good	VG	Fine	VF
133	1827	—	5.00	10.00	17.50	26.50
	1828	—	5.00	10.00	17.50	26.50

30 REIS

COPPER

C#	Date	Mintage	Good	VG	Fine	VF
116	1818	—	6.00	11.00	18.00	40.00

60 REIS

COPPER
Similar to 30 Reis, C#116.

C#	Date	Mintage	Good	VG	Fine	VF
117	1818	—	7.50	15.00	23.50	50.00

150 REIS

SILVER
Obv: Crowned arms. Rev: Date in angles of cross.

C#	Date	Mintage	Good	VG	Fine	VF
98	1806	—	30.00	50.00	110.00	225.00

C#	Date	Mintage	Good	VG	Fine	VF
155	1859	—	20.00	35.00	70.00	150.00

300 REIS

SILVER

C#	Date	Mintage	Good	VG	Fine	VF
99	1806	—	25.00	40.00	100.00	200.00

C#	Date	Mintage	Good	VG	Fine	VF
156	1859	—	25.00	40.00	100.00	200.00

600 REIS
(= 1 Rupia)

SILVER
Obv: Accolated bust of Maria and Pedro.
Rev: Crowned arms.

C#	Date	Mintage	Good	VG	Fine	VF
77	1781	—	95.00	150.00	300.00	600.00

Obv: Crowned arms.
Rev: Date in angles of cross.

C#	Date	Mintage	Good	VG	Fine	VF
100	1806	—	75.00	125.00	250.00	500.00

C#	Date	Mintage	Good	VG	Fine	VF
148	1841	—	100.00	150.00	300.00	600.00

NCLT ISSUES

PATTERNS

KM#	Date	Mintage	Identification	Mkt.Val.
1	1851	—	1/2 Attia, Copper, C141	—
2	1851	—	Attia, Copper, C142	—

Goa

MONETARY SYSTEM

480 Reis = 2 Pardao =
2 Xerafim = 1 Rupia

NOTE: The silver Xerafim was equal to the silver Pardao, but the gold Xerafim varied according to fluctuations in the gold/silver ratio.

3 REIS

COPPER

3 REIS

COPPER
Obv: Ornate arms. Rev: Value.

C#	Date	Mintage	Good	VG	Fine	VF
211	ND	—	8.50	15.00	40.00	80.00

Obv: Crowned oval arms of Joao VI as Prince Regent.

C#	Date	Mintage	Good	VG	Fine	VF
251	ND	—	5.00	7.50	12.50	25.00

Obv: Crowned arms on globe of Joao VI as King.

C#	Date	Mintage	Good	VG	Fine	VF
271	ND	—	5.00	7.50	12.50	25.00

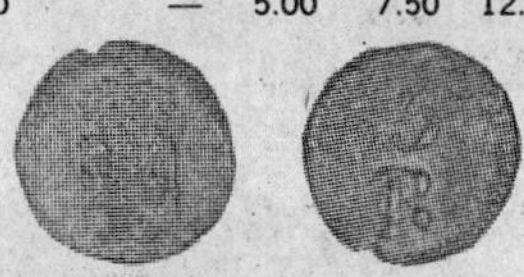

Obv: Crowned arms of Maria II.

C#	Date	Mintage	Good	VG	Fine	VF
333	ND	—	5.00	10.00	17.50	35.00
	1845	—	5.00	10.00	17.50	35.00
	1846	—	5.00	10.00	17.50	35.00
	1848	—	5.00	10.00	17.50	35.00

4-1/2 REIS

COPPER
Obv: Ornate arms. Rev: Value.

C#	Date	Mintage	Good	VG	Fine	VF
212	ND	—	8.50	15.00	40.00	80.00

Crowned oval arms of Joao VI as Prince Regent

C#	Date	Mintage	Good	VG	Fine	VF
252	ND	—	5.00	7.50	12.50	25.00

Crowned arms on globe of Joao VI as king

C#	Date	Mintage	Good	VG	Fine	VF
272	ND	—	5.00	7.50	12.50	25.00

Arms of Maria II

C#	Date	Mintage	Good	VG	Fine	VF
334	ND	—	4.00	6.50	11.50	22.50
	1845	—	4.00	7.00	12.50	25.00
	1846	—	4.00	7.00	12.50	25.00

6 REIS

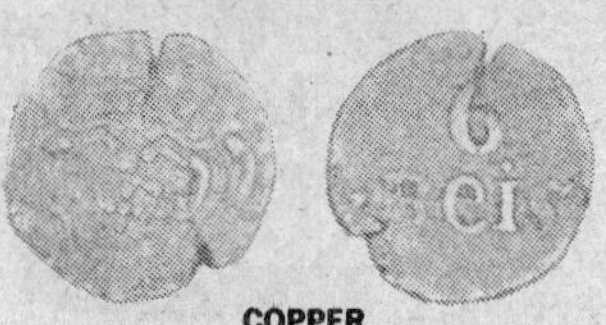

COPPER
Obv: Ornate arms.

C#	Date	Mintage	Good	VG	Fine	VF
213	ND	—	6.00	10.00	25.00	50.00

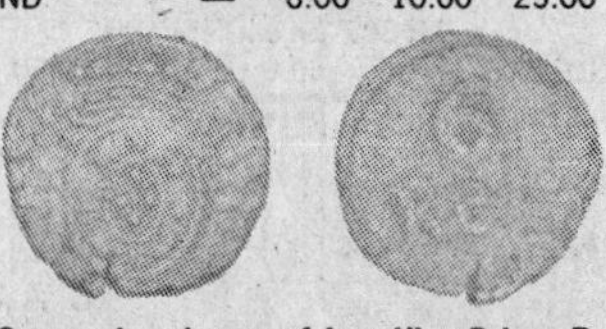

Obv: Crowned oval arms of Joao VI as Prince Regent.

C#	Date	Mintage	Good	VG	Fine	VF
253	ND	—	6.00	10.00	15.00	30.00

Obv: Crowned arms on globe of Joao VI as King.

C#	Date	Mintage	Good	VG	Fine	VF
273	ND	—	5.00	8.00	13.50	27.50

C#	Date	Mintage	Good	VG	Fine	VF
335	ND	—	4.00	7.00	12.50	25.00
	1845	—	4.00	7.00	12.50	25.00
	1846	—	4.00	7.00	12.50	25.00
	1848	—	4.00	7.00	12.50	25.00

7-1/2 REIS

COPPER
Obv: Crowned oval arms of Joao VI as Prince Regent.
Rev. denomination: 7-1/2 REIS

C#	Date	Mintage	Good	VG	Fine	VF
254	ND	—	6.50	12.50	17.50	35.00

Rev. denomination: 7-2/4 REIS

C#	Date	Mintage	Good	VG	Fine	VF
254a	ND	—	12.50	25.00	35.00	70.00

Obv: Crowned arms on globe of Joao VI as King.
Rev. denomination: 7-1/2 REIS

C#	Date	Mintage	Good	VG	Fine	VF
274	ND	—	6.00	11.50	17.50	35.00

Obv: Arms of Maria II.

C#	Date	Mintage	Good	VG	Fine	VF
336	ND	—	4.00	7.00	12.50	25.00
	1845	—	4.00	7.00	12.50	25.00
	1846	—	4.00	7.00	12.50	25.00
	1848	—	4.50	8.00	13.50	30.00

9 REIS

COPPER
Obv: Crowned arms on globe of Joao VI as King.
Rev. denomination: 9 REIS

C#	Date	Mintage	Good	VG	Fine	VF
275	ND	—	10.00	15.00	20.00	40.00

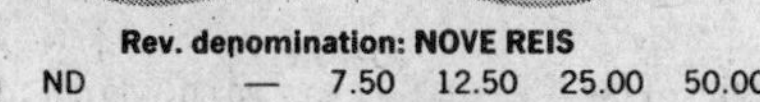

Rev. denomination: NOVE REIS

C#	Date	Mintage	Good	VG	Fine	VF
275a	ND	—	7.50	12.50	25.00	50.00

10 REIS

COPPER
Obv: Crowned oval arms of Joao VI as Prince Regent.

C#	Date	Mintage	Good	VG	Fine	VF
255	ND	—	6.00	11.00	17.50	35.00

Obv: Crowned arms on globe of Joao VI as King.

C#	Date	Mintage	Good	VG	Fine	VF
276	ND	—	5.00	10.00	15.00	30.00

Obv: Arms of Maria II.

C#	Date	Mintage	Good	VG	Fine	VF
337	ND	—	2.00	4.00	8.50	15.00
	1845	—	1.75	3.50	7.50	12.50

12 REIS

COPPER
Obv: Ornate arms. Rev: Value.

C#	Date	Mintage	Good	VG	Fine	VF
215	ND	—	6.00	10.00	25.00	50.00

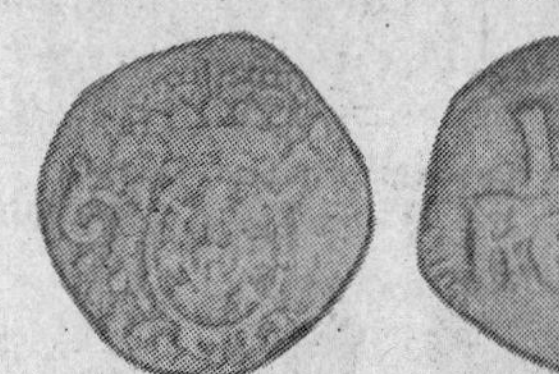

Obv: Crowned oval arms of Joao VI as Prince Regent.

C#	Date	Mintage	Good	VG	Fine	VF
256	ND	—	7.00	12.50	20.00	40.00

Obv: Crowned arms on globe of Joao VI as King.

C#	Date	Mintage	Good	VG	Fine	VF
277	ND	—	6.00	11.50	17.50	35.00

Obv: Arms of Maria II.

C#	Date	Mintage	Good	VG	Fine	VF
338	ND	—	7.00	12.50	20.00	40.00

15 REIS

COPPER
Obv: Crowned oval arms of Joao VI as Prince Regent.

C#	Date	Mintage	Good	VG	Fine	VF
257	ND	—	6.00	11.50	17.50	35.00

Obv: Crowned arms on globe of Joao VI as King.

C#	Date	Mintage	Good	VG	Fine	VF
278	ND	—	4.00	7.50	12.50	25.00

Obv: Arms of Maria II.

C#	Date	Mintage	Good	VG	Fine	VF
338.2	ND	—	2.00	4.00	8.50	16.50

Struck in 1846 over earlier coins

C#	Date	Mintage	Good	VG	Fine	VF
339	ND	—	1.75	3.50	7.50	15.00

20 REIS

COPPER
Obv: Ornate arms. Rev: Value.

C#	Date	Mintage	Good	VG	Fine	VF
216	ND	—	6.00	10.00	25.00	50.00

C#	Date	Mintage	Good	VG	Fine	VF
217	1787	—	13.50	22.50	37.50	75.00

30 REIS
(= 1/2 Tanga)

COPPER
Obv: Ornate arms. Rev: Value.

C#	Date	Mintage	Good	VG	Fine	VF
218	ND	—	6.00	10.00	25.00	50.00

Rev: Date below value in wreath.

C#	Date	Mintage	Good	VG	Fine	VF
219	1787	—	12.50	20.00	50.00	100.00

Obv: Crowned oval arms of Joao VI as Prince Regent.

C#	Date	Mintage	Good	VG	Fine	VF
258	ND	—	7.50	12.50	17.50	35.00

Obv: Crowned arms on globe of Joao VI as King.

C#	Date	Mintage	Good	VG	Fine	VF
279	ND	—	7.50	12.50	17.50	35.00

Obv: Arms of Miguel.

C#	Date	Mintage	Good	VG	Fine	VF
310	ND	—	5.00	8.00	12.50	25.00

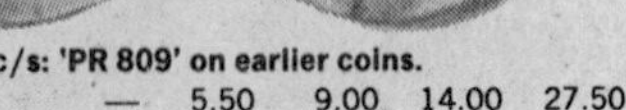

c/s: 'PR 809' on earlier coins.

C#	Date	Mintage	Good	VG	Fine	VF
315	ND	—	5.50	9.00	14.00	27.50

Obv: Arms of Maria II.

C#	Date	Mintage	Good	VG	Fine	VF
338.5	ND	—	5.00	9.00	14.00	27.50

c/s: '30' in circle over earlier coins.

C#	Date	Mintage	Good	VG	Fine	VF
340	ND(1846)	—	10.00	15.00	25.00	50.00

60 REIS

(= 1 Tanga)

COPPER

Obv: Ornate arms. Rev: Value.

C#	Date	Mintage	Good	VG	Fine	VF
220	ND	—	35.00	60.00	100.00	200.00

SILVER

C#	Date	Mintage	Good	VG	Fine	VF
231	1785	—	11.50	22.50	50.00	100.00

COPPER

C#	Date	Mintage	Good	VG	Fine	VF
221	1787	—	12.50	20.00	50.00	100.00

SILVER

Obv: Bust wtih widow's veil.

C#	Date	Mintage	Good	VG	Fine	VF
235	ND	—	11.50	22.50	50.00	100.00

Old head with bonnet.

C#	Date	Mintage	Good	VG	Fine	VF
239	1802	—	17.50	35.00	60.00	120.00
	1803	—	17.50	35.00	60.00	120.00

COPPER

Obv: Crowned oval arms of Joao VI as Prince Regent.

C#	Date	Mintage	Good	VG	Fine	VF
259	ND	—	5.50	10.00	16.50	28.50

Obv: Crowned arms on globe of Joao VI as King.

C#	Date	Mintage	Good	VG	Fine	VF
280	ND	—	12.50	20.00	30.00	60.00

SILVER

Obv: Crowned arms on globe of Joao VI as King.

C#	Date	Mintage	Good	VG	Fine	VF
285	1819	—	—	—	—	—
	1823	—	—	—	—	—

COPPER

Obv: Arms of Miguel.

C#	Date	Mintage	Good	VG	Fine	VF
311	ND	—	6.00	10.00	15.00	30.00

c/s: '60 REI' on C#311.

C#	Date	Mintage	Good	VG	Fine	VF
311a	ND	—	12.50	20.00	30.00	60.00

c/s: 'PR 809' on earlier coins.

C#	Date	Mintage	Good	VG	Fine	VF
316	ND	—	5.00	7.50	12.50	25.00

Obv: Arms of Maria II.

C#	Date	Mintage	Good	VG	Fine	VF
338.7	ND	—	8.00	15.00	25.00	50.00

c/s: '60' in circle over earlier coins.

C#	Date	Mintage	Good	VG	Fine	VF
341	(1846)	—	7.50	15.00	25.00	50.00

SILVER

Pedro V

C#	Date	Mintage	Good	VG	Fine	VF
361	1858	—	—	—	—	—

1/2 XERAFIM

(= 150 Reis)

SILVER

Rev: Crowned oval arms of Joao VI as Prince Regent.

C#	Date	Mintage	Good	VG	Fine	VF
261	1818	—	—	—	—	—

Rev: Crowned arms on globe of Joao VI as King.

C#	Date	Mintage	Good	VG	Fine	VF
286	1818	—	25.00	35.00	45.00	75.00
	1819/8	—	35.00	45.00	55.00	85.00
	1819	—	25.00	35.00	45.00	75.00
	1820	—	25.00	35.00	45.00	75.00
	1823	—	25.00	35.00	45.00	75.00

C#	Date	Mintage	Good	VG	Fine	VF
318	1831	—	40.00	65.00	100.00	200.00

1/2 PARDAO

(= 150 Reis)

SILVER

Value: MEIO PARDAO

C#	Date	Mintage	Good	VG	Fine	VF
223	1780	—	20.00	40.00	75.00	125.00
226	1781	—	18.50	37.50	65.00	110.00

Value: 150 R.

C#	Date	Mintage	Good	VG	Fine	VF
227	1782	—	18.50	37.50	65.00	110.00

C#	Date	Mintage	Good	VG	Fine	VF
232	1782	—	7.50	15.00	35.00	65.00
	1784	—	7.50	15.00	35.00	65.00
	1785	—	7.50	15.00	35.00	65.00
	1786	—	7.50	15.00	35.00	65.00

Obv: Bust with widow's veil.

C#	Date	Mintage	Good	VG	Fine	VF
236	1787	—	7.50	15.00	35.00	65.00
	1790	—	7.50	15.00	35.00	65.00
	1793	—	7.50	15.00	35.00	65.00
	1794	—	7.50	15.00	35.00	65.00

Obv. value: 150 R.

C#	Date	Mintage	Good	VG	Fine	VF
240	1796	—	17.50	35.00	60.00	100.00
	1797	—	17.50	35.00	60.00	100.00

Obv. value: 150 RES.

C#	Date	Mintage	Good	VG	Fine	VF
240a	1798	—	10.00	20.00	45.00	85.00
	1799	—	10.00	20.00	45.00	85.00
	1802	—	10.00	20.00	45.00	85.00
	1803	—	10.00	20.00	45.00	85.00
	1804	—	10.00	20.00	45.00	85.00

C#	Date	Mintage	Good	VG	Fine	VF
240a	1806	—	10.00	20.00	45.00	85.00

Maria II

C#	Date	Mintage	Good	VG	Fine	VF
348	1846	—	20.00	30.00	40.00	80.00
	1846/5	—	25.00	35.00	50.00	100.00
	1849	—	20.00	30.00	40.00	80.00

Pedro V

C#	Date	Mintage	Good	VG	Fine	VF
362	1857	—	25.00	35.00	45.00	90.00
	1860	—	25.00	35.00	45.00	90.00

PARDAO

(= 300 Reis)

SILVER

C#	Date	Mintage	Good	VG	Fine	VF
224	1779	—	20.00	40.00	75.00	125.00
	1780	—	20.00	40.00	75.00	125.00
228	1781	—	18.50	37.50	65.00	110.00

Obv: Similar to C#233a. Rev: Arms.

C#	Date	Mintage	Good	VG	Fine	VF
233	1782	—	11.50	22.50	50.00	100.00
	1783	—	11.50	22.50	50.00	100.00

Rev: More elaborate arms.

C#	Date	Mintage	Good	VG	Fine	VF
233a	1784	—	7.50	15.00	25.00	55.00
	1785	—	7.50	15.00	25.00	55.00
	1786	—	7.50	15.00	25.00	55.00
	1787	—	7.50	15.00	25.00	55.00

Obv: Bust with widow's veil.

C#	Date	Mintage	Good	VG	Fine	VF
237	1787	—	11.50	22.50	50.00	100.00
	1791	—	11.50	22.50	50.00	100.00
	1792	—	11.50	22.50	50.00	100.00
	1793	—	11.50	22.50	50.00	100.00

Obv: Older bust with bonnet.

C#	Date	Mintage	Good	VG	Fine	VF
241	1796	—	10.00	20.00	40.00	80.00
	1797	—	10.00	20.00	40.00	80.00
	1798	—	10.00	20.00	40.00	80.00
	1799	—	10.00	20.00	40.00	80.00
	1800	—	10.00	20.00	40.00	80.00
	1801	—	10.00	20.00	40.00	80.00
	1802	—	10.00	20.00	40.00	80.00
	1803	—	10.00	20.00	40.00	80.00
	1804	—	10.00	20.00	40.00	80.00
	1805	—	10.00	20.00	40.00	80.00
	1806	—	10.00	20.00	40.00	80.00

Rev: Crowned oval arms of Joao VI as Prince Regent.

C#	Date	Mintage	Good	VG	Fine	VF
262	1808	—	17.50	27.50	37.50	75.00
	1809	—	17.50	27.50	37.50	75.00
	1811	—	17.50	27.50	37.50	75.00
	1812/09	—	17.50	35.00	70.00	140.00
	1815/09	—	15.00	30.00	60.00	120.00
	1815	—	17.50	27.50	37.50	75.00
	1817	—	17.50	27.50	37.50	75.00
	1818	—	17.50	27.50	37.50	75.00

Rev: Crowned arms on globe of Joao VI as King.

C#	Date	Mintage	Good	VG	Fine	VF
287	1818	—	20.00	30.00	40.00	80.00
	1819	—	20.00	30.00	40.00	80.00
	1820	—	20.00	30.00	40.00	80.00
	1823	—	20.00	30.00	40.00	80.00

Pedro IV

C#	Date	Mintage	Good	VG	Fine	VF
300	ND	—	40.00	55.00	70.00	140.00

Miguel

C#	Date	Mintage	Good	VG	Fine	VF
319	1831	—	35.00	50.00	65.00	130.00

Maria II

C#	Date	Mintage	Good	VG	Fine	VF
345	1839	—	32.50	45.00	60.00	120.00
	1840	—	32.50	45.00	60.00	120.00
	1841	—	32.50	45.00	60.00	120.00

C#	Date	Mintage	Good	VG	Fine	VF
349	1845	—	20.00	30.00	40.00	80.00
	1846	—	20.00	30.00	40.00	80.00
	1847	—	20.00	30.00	40.00	80.00
	1848	—	20.00	30.00	40.00	80.00

Rev: Value and arms.

C#	Date	Mintage	Good	VG	Fine	VF
352	1851	—	30.00	37.50	50.00	100.00

Pedro V

C#	Date	Mintage	Good	VG	Fine	VF
363	1857	—	30.00	40.00	55.00	110.00
	1860	—	30.00	40.00	55.00	110.00
	1861	—	30.00	40.00	55.00	110.00

Luis I

C#	Date	Mintage	Good	VG	Fine	VF
371	1868	—	30.00	40.00	55.00	110.00

RUPIA

SILVER

Posthumous Issue of Joseph I

C#	Date	Mintage	Good	VG	Fine	VF
195a	1781	—	25.00	50.00	110.00	165.00
225	1778	—	20.00	40.00	75.00	125.00
	1779	—	20.00	40.00	75.00	125.00
	1780	—	20.00	40.00	75.00	125.00
	1781	—	20.00	40.00	75.00	125.00
229	1781	—	20.00	40.00	75.00	125.00

C#	Date	Mintage	Good	VG	Fine	VF
234	1782	—	6.50	13.50	30.00	55.00
	1783	—	6.50	13.50	30.00	55.00
	1784	—	6.50	13.50	30.00	55.00
	1785	—	6.50	13.50	30.00	55.00
	1786	—	6.50	13.50	30.00	55.00
	1786 inverted A for V in RVPIA	—	10.00	20.00	40.00	75.00
	1787	—	6.50	13.50	30.00	55.00
	1787 inverted A for V in RVPIA	—	10.00	20.00	40.00	75.00

Obv: Bust with widow's veil.

C#	Date	Mintage	Good	VG	Fine	VF
238	1787	—	10.00	20.00	40.00	75.00
	1788	—	10.00	20.00	40.00	75.00
	1790	—	10.00	20.00	40.00	75.00
	1791	—	10.00	20.00	40.00	75.00
	1792	—	10.00	20.00	40.00	75.00
	1793	—	10.00	20.00	40.00	75.00
	1794	—	10.00	20.00	40.00	75.00
	1795	—	10.00	20.00	40.00	75.00

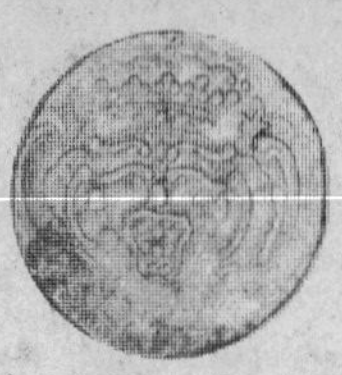

C#	Date	Mintage	Good	VG	Fine	VF
242	1796	—	7.50	15.00	25.00	45.00
	1797	—	7.50	15.00	25.00	45.00
	1798	—	7.50	15.00	25.00	45.00
	1799	—	7.50	15.00	25.00	45.00
	1800	—	7.50	15.00	25.00	45.00
	1801	—	7.50	15.00	25.00	45.00
	1802	—	7.50	15.00	25.00	45.00
	1803	—	7.50	15.00	25.00	45.00
	1804	—	7.50	15.00	25.00	45.00
	1805	—	7.50	15.00	25.00	45.00
	1806	—	7.50	15.00	25.00	45.00
	1807	—	7.50	15.00	25.00	45.00

Rev: Oval arms of Joao VI as Prince Regent.

C#	Date	Mintage	Good	VG	Fine	VF
263	1807	—	40.00	55.00	70.00	140.00
	1808	—	40.00	55.00	70.00	140.00
	1809	—	40.00	55.00	70.00	140.00
	1811	—	40.00	55.00	70.00	140.00
	1812	—	40.00	55.00	70.00	140.00
	1813	—	45.00	60.00	80.00	160.00
	1814	—	45.00	60.00	80.00	160.00
	1815	—	45.00	60.00	80.00	160.00
	1816	—	40.00	55.00	70.00	140.00
	1817	—	40.00	55.00	70.00	140.00

Rev: Arms on globe of Joao VI as King.

C#	Date	Mintage	Good	VG	Fine	VF
288	1818	—	40.00	55.00	70.00	140.00
	1819	—	40.00	55.00	70.00	140.00
	1820	—	40.00	55.00	70.00	140.00
	1822	—	40.00	55.00	70.00	140.00
	1823	—	40.00	55.00	70.00	140.00
	1824	—	40.00	55.00	70.00	140.00
	1825	—	40.00	55.00	70.00	140.00
	1826	—	40.00	55.00	70.00	140.00

Pedro IV

C#	Date	Mintage	Good	VG	Fine	VF
301	1827	—	80.00	100.00	125.00	250.00
	1828	—	80.00	100.00	125.00	250.00

Miguel

C#	Date	Mintage	Good	VG	Fine	VF
320	1829	—	70.00	85.00	110.00	225.00
	1830	—	60.00	75.00	90.00	180.00
	1831	—	55.00	65.00	80.00	160.00
	1832	—	55.00	65.00	80.00	160.00

Maria II.

C#	Date	Mintage	Good	VG	Fine	VF
346	1839	—	22.50	45.00	60.00	75.00
346	1840	—	22.50	45.00	60.00	75.00
	1841	—	22.50	45.00	60.00	75.00

Rev: Value

C#	Date	Mintage	Good	VG	Fine	VF
350	1845	—	20.00	40.00	55.00	70.00
	1846	—	20.00	40.00	55.00	70.00
	1847	—	20.00	40.00	55.00	70.00
	1848	—	20.00	40.00	55.00	70.00
	1849	—	20.00	40.00	55.00	70.00

Rev: Value and arms.

C#	Date	Mintage	Good	VG	Fine	VF
353	1850	—	25.00	50.00	70.00	90.00
	1851	—	25.00	50.00	70.00	90.00

Pedro V

C#	Date	Mintage	Good	VG	Fine	VF
364	1856	—	20.00	40.00	55.00	65.00
	1857	—	20.00	40.00	55.00	65.00
	1858	—	20.00	40.00	55.00	65.00
	1859	—	20.00	40.00	55.00	65.00
	1860	—	20.00	40.00	55.00	65.00
	1861	—	20.00	40.00	55.00	65.00

Luiz I

C#	Date	Mintage	Good	VG	Fine	VF
372	1866	—	25.00	50.00	65.00	80.00
	1868	—	25.00	50.00	65.00	80.00
	1869	—	25.00	50.00	65.00	80.00

XERAFIN

GOLD
Obv: Arms on crowned globe.
Rev: Value and date in angles of cross.

C#	Date	Mintage	VG	Fine	VF	XF
289	1819	—	75.00	125.00	200.00	300.00

2 XERAFINS

GOLD
Obv: Crowned arms.
Rev: Value and date in angles of cross.

C#	Date	Mintage	VG	Fine	VF	XF
244.5	1778	—	200.00	350.00	550.00	800.00
	1786	—	200.00	350.00	550.00	800.00
244.6	1799	—	150.00	250.00	350.00	400.00
244.7	1815	—	175.00	300.00	450.00	650.00
244.8	1819	—	125.00	200.00	300.00	450.00

4 XERAFINS

GOLD
Obv: Crowned arms.
Rev: Value and date in angles of cross.

C#	Date	Mintage	VG	Fine	VF	XF
A245	1778	—	325.00	500.00	750.00	1150.

C#	Date	Mintage	VG	Fine	VF	XF
245	1795	—	325.00	500.00	725.00	1100.
	1803	—	325.00	500.00	725.00	1100.
264	1819	—	275.00	400.00	600.00	900.00

8 XERAFINS

GOLD
Obv: Crowned arms.
Rev: Value and date in angles of cross.

C#	Date	Mintage	VG	Fine	VF	XF
A246	1778	—	175.00	275.00	425.00	600.00
246	1782	—	600.00	850.00	1250.	1850.
	1787	—	600.00	850.00	1250.	1850.
	1795	—	600.00	850.00	1250.	1850.

Obv: Oval arms of Joao VI as Prince Regent.

C#	Date	Mintage	VG	Fine	VF	XF
265	1819	—	300.00	550.00	750.00	1150.

Obv: Arms on globe of Joao VI as King.

C#	Date	Mintage	VG	Fine	VF	XF
A291	1819	—	500.00	750.00	1100.	1650.

12 XERAFINS

GOLD

C#	Date	Mintage	VG	Fine	VF	XF
A247	1779	—	600.00	850.00	1250.	1850.
247a	1781 mule	—	500.00	750.00	1100.	1650.

C#	Date	Mintage	VG	Fine	VF	XF
247	1781	—	500.00	750.00	1100.	1500.
	1782	—	500.00	750.00	1100.	1500.
	1791	—	500.00	750.00	1100.	1500.
	1792	—	500.00	750.00	1150.	1650.
	1793	—	450.00	650.00	1100.	1500.
	1795	—	450.00	650.00	1100.	1500.
	1796	—	450.00	650.00	1100.	1500.
	1802	—	450.00	650.00	1100.	1500.
	1803	—	250.00	450.00	600.00	900.00
	1804	—	325.00	450.00	600.00	900.00
	1806	—	325.00	600.00	800.00	1200.

Obv: Oval arms of Joao VI as Prince Regent.

C#	Date	Mintage	VG	Fine	VF	XF
266	1814	—	450.00	650.00	1100.	1500.
	1815	—	450.00	650.00	1100.	1500.

Obv: Arms on globe of Joao VI as King.

C#	Date	Mintage	VG	Fine	VF	XF
291	1819	—	550.00	800.00	1250.	1700.
	1824	—	550.00	800.00	1250.	1700.
	1825	—	550.00	800.00	1250.	1700.

MONETARY REFORM

960 Reis = 16 Tanga = 1 Rupia

3 REIS

COPPER

Y#	Date	Mintage	Fine	VF	XF	Unc
1	1871	—	3.75	7.50	12.50	25.00

5 REIS

COPPER

Y#	Date	Mintage	Fine	VF	XF	Unc
2	1871	—	2.50	5.00	10.00	20.00

1/12 TANGA

BRONZE
Roman numeral dating

Y#	Date	Mintage	Fine	VF	XF	Unc
15	1901	.960	1.00	2.00	5.00	10.00
	1903	.960	1.00	2.00	5.00	10.00

OITAVO DE (1/8) TANGA

COPPER

Y#	Date	Mintage	Fine	VF	XF	Unc
7	1881	—	1.25	2.25	5.00	10.00
	1884	—	1.25	2.25	5.00	10.00
	1886	—	1.25	2.25	5.00	10.00

BRONZE
Roman numeral dating

Y#	Date	Mintage	Fine	VF	XF	Unc
16	1901	.960	1.00	2.00	4.00	8.00
	1903	.960	1.00	2.00	4.00	8.00

10 REIS

COPPER

Y#	Date	Mintage	Fine	VF	XF	Unc
3	1871	—	2.50	5.00	10.00	20.00

1/4 TANGA
(= 15 Reis)

COPPER

Y#	Date	Mintage	Fine	VF	XF	Unc
4	1871	—	6.50	12.50	25.00	50.00

QUARTO DE (1/4) TANGA

COPPER

Y#	Date	Mintage	Fine	VF	XF	Unc
8	1881	—	1.50	3.00	6.00	12.00
	1884	—	1.50	3.00	6.00	12.00
	1886	—	1.50	3.00	6.00	12.00
	1888	—	12.50	25.00	50.00	100.00

BRONZE
Roman numeral dating

Y#	Date	Mintage	Fine	VF	XF	Unc
17	1901	.800	.85	1.75	3.50	7.00
	1903	.800	.85	1.75	3.50	7.00

1/2 TANGA
(= 30 Reis)

COPPER

Y#	Date	Mintage	Fine	VF	XF	Unc
5	1871	—	6.50	12.50	25.00	50.00

BRONZE
Roman numeral dating

Y#	Date	Mintage	Fine	VF	XF	Unc
18	1901	.800	1.25	2.50	5.00	10.00
	1903	.800	1.25	2.50	5.00	10.00

TANGA
(= 60 Reis)

COPPER

Y#	Date	Mintage	Fine	VF	XF	Unc
6	1871	—	11.50	22.50	45.00	90.00

BRONZE

Y#	Date	Mintage	Fine	VF	XF	Unc
21	1934	.100	1.25	2.50	5.00	10.00

Y#	Date	Mintage	Fine	VF	XF	Unc
26	1947	1.000	.15	.35	.75	1.50
26a	1952	9.600	.25	.50	1.00	2.00

OITAVO DE (1/8) RUPIA

1.4600 gm., .917 SILVER, .0430 oz ASW

Y#	Date	Mintage	Fine	VF	XF	Unc
11	1881	—	3.75	7.50	12.50	20.00

2 TANGAS

COPPER-NICKEL

Y#	Date	Mintage	Fine	VF	XF	Unc
22	1934	.150	2.00	4.00	6.00	10.00

QUARTO DE (1/4) RUPIA

2.9200 gm., .917 SILVER, .0860 oz ASW

Y#	Date	Mintage	Fine	VF	XF	Unc
12	1881	—	3.50	7.00	12.50	20.00

COPPER-NICKEL

Y#	Date	Mintage	Fine	VF	XF	Unc
27	1947	.800	.50	1.00	2.00	4.00
	1952	4.000	.35	.75	1.00	2.00

4 TANGAS

COPPER-NICKEL

Y#	Date	Mintage	Fine	VF	XF	Unc
23	1934	.100	2.25	4.50	9.00	15.00

MEIA (1/2) RUPIA

5.8300 gm., .917 SILVER, .1719 oz ASW

Y#	Date	Mintage	Fine	VF	XF	Unc
13	1881	—	BV	5.00	10.00	16.00
	1882	—	BV	5.00	10.00	16.00
24	1936	.100	BV	6.50	12.50	20.00

COPPER-NICKEL

Y#	Date	Mintage	Fine	VF	XF	Unc
28	1947	.600	.50	1.00	2.00	4.00
	1952	2.000	.35	.75	1.50	3.00

UMA (1) RUPIA

11.6600 gm., .917 SILVER, .3438 oz ASW

Y#	Date	Mintage	Fine	VF	XF	Unc
14	1881	—	BV	BV	12.50	20.00
	1882	—	BV	BV	12.50	20.00

Y#	Date	Mintage	Fine	VF	XF	Unc
19	1903	.050	BV	BV	20.00	35.00
	1904	.270	BV	BV	17.50	30.00

Y#	Date	Mintage	Fine	VF	XF	Unc
20	1912	.100	BV	BV	20.00	32.50

Y#	Date	Mintage	Fine	VF	XF	Unc
25	1935	.300	BV	BV	12.50	17.50

Y#	Date	Mintage	Fine	VF	XF	Unc
29	1947	.900	BV	BV	11.50	15.00

COPPER-NICKEL

Y#	Date	Mintage	Fine	VF	XF	Unc
29a	1952	1.132	.85	1.75	3.75	7.50

DECIMAL COINAGE

100 Centavos = 1 Escudo

10 CENTAVOS

BRONZE

Y#	Date	Mintage	Fine	VF	XF	Unc
34	1958	5.000	.20	.35	.60	1.00
	1959	—	.15	.25	.45	.75
	1961	—	.10	.20	.30	.50

30 CENTAVOS

BRONZE

Y#	Date	Mintage	Fine	VF	XF	Unc
35	1958	5.000	.20	.35	.60	1.00
	1959	Inc. Ab.	.20	.35	.60	1.00

60 CENTAVOS

COPPER-NICKEL

Y#	Date	Mintage	Fine	VF	XF	Unc
36	1958	5.000	.25	.45	.75	1.25
	1959	—	.35	.60	1.00	1.75

ESCUDO

COPPER-NICKEL

Y#	Date	Mintage	Fine	VF	XF	Unc
37	1958	6.000	.25	.45	.75	1.25
	1959	—	.30	.50	.90	1.50

3 ESCUDOS

COPPER-NICKEL

Y#	Date	Mintage	Fine	VF	XF	Unc
38	1958	5.000	.35	.60	1.00	1.75
	1959	—	.45	.75	1.25	2.00

6 ESCUDOS

COPPER-NICKEL

Y#	Date	Mintage	Fine	VF	XF	Unc
39	1959	4.000	1.00	1.50	2.50	4.00

NCLT ISSUES

PROVAS (Pr)

Standard metals unless otherwise noted
Stamped "PROVA" in field.

Y#	Date	Mintage	Identification	Issue Price	Mkt Val.
Pr28	1947	—	1/2 Rupia	—	30.00
Pr29	1947	—	1 Rupia	—	—
Pr27	1952	—	1/4 Rupia	—	20.00
Pr28	1952	—	1/2 Rupia	—	27.50
Pr30	1952	—	1 Tanga	—	17.50
Pr33	1952	—	1 Rupia	—	35.00
Pr33	1954	—	1 Rupia	—	150.00
Pr34	1958	—	10 Centavos	—	15.00
Pr35	1958	—	30 Centavos	—	16.50
Pr36	1958	—	60 Centavos	—	17.50
Pr37	1958	—	1 Escudo	—	20.00
Pr38	1958	—	3 Escudos	—	25.00
Pr34	1959	—	10 Centavos	—	15.00
Pr35	1959	—	30 Centavos	—	16.50
Pr36	1959	—	60 Centavos	—	17.50
Pr37	1959	—	1 Escudo	—	20.00
Pr38	1959	—	3 Escudos	—	25.00
Pr39	1959	—	6 Escudos	—	30.00
Pr34	1961	—	10 Centavos	—	15.00

INDIA-BRITISH

The civilization of India, which began about 2500 B.C., flourished under a succession of empires - notably those of Chandragupta, Asoka and the Mughals - until undermined in the 18th and 19th centuries by European Colonial powers.

The Portuguese were the first to arrive, off Calicut in May 1498. It wasn't until 1612, after the Portuguese and Spanish power had begun to wane, that the British East India Company established its initial settlement at Surat. Britain could not have chosen a more propitious time. The northern Mogul Empire, the central girdle of petty states, and the southern Vijayanagar Empire were crumbling and ripe for foreign exploitation. By the end of the century, English traders were firmly established in Bombay, Madras, Calcutta and lesser places elsewhere, and Britain was implementing its announced policy to create such civil and military institutions 'as may be the foundation of secure English domination for all time.' By 1757, following the successful conclusion of a war of colonial rivalry with France during which the military victories of Robert Clive, a young officer with the British East India Company, making him the most powerful man in India, the British were firmly settled in India as not only traders but as conquerors. During the next 60 years, the British East India Company acquired dominion over most of India by bribery and force, and governed it directly or through puppet princelings.

Because of the Sepoy Mutiny of 1857-58, a large scale mutiny among Indian soldiers of the Bengal army, control of the government of India was transferred from the East India Company to the British Crown, 1858. At this point in world history, India was the brightest jewel in the imperial diadem of the British lords of the earth, but even then a movement for greater Indian representation in government presaged the Indian Empire's twilight hour less than a century hence - it would pass into history on Aug. 15, 1947.

HINDU MONETARY SYSTEM

20 Cash = 1 Fulus
4 Faluce = 1 Fanam
42 Fanams = 1 Pagoda

MOSLEM MONETARY SYSTEM

12 Pie = 4 Pysa (Pice, Paisa) = 1 Anna
16 Annas = 1 Rupee
14 To 16 Rupees = 1 Mohur (Mohar)

WEIGHTS

Rupee = 10.7 to 11.6 grams (gm)
Mohur = 10.7 to 11.4 grams (gm)

NOTE: Fraction and multiples Mohurs and Rupees were struck in proportion.

BENGAL PRESIDENCY

East India Company

(UNTIL 1835 AD)

NOTE: Due to extensive revisions and new information the following section in part is listed by PRIDMORE (P#) numbers. These are in reference to the newly published "The Coins of the Commonwealth of Nations" Part 4, INDIA by F. Pridmore (Spink & Son Ltd.).

BENARES

(Banaras, Varanasi)

NOTE: Coins of similar dates with different legends are listed under Awadh.

1/2 PICE

COPPER, 3.1 gm.

MINT: CALCUTTA

C#	Date	Year	VG	Fine	VF	XF
710	(1795)	37	2.50	5.00	10.00	15.00
	(1795)	37	—	—	Proof	65.00

NOTE: Struck between 1808 and 1809.

PICE

COPPER, dump

C#	Date	Year	Good	VG	Fine	VF
825	(1775-6)	17	2.00	4.00	6.00	9.00
	(1777-8)	19	2.00	4.00	6.00	9.00

Trisul symbol added

C#	Date	Year	Good	VG	Fine	VF
826	(1786-7)	28	1.50	3.00	5.00	7.50
	(1792-3)	35	1.50	3.00	5.00	7.50
	(1806-7)	49	1.50	3.00	5.00	7.50

TRISUL PICE

COPPER, dump, 6.4 gm.

MINT: BENARES

C#	Date	Year	VG	Fine	VF	XF
714	(1815-21)	37	2.50	4.00	6.00	10.00

Reduced weight, 6.15 gm.

C#	Date	Year	VG	Fine	VF	XF
714a	(1821-7)	37	3.00	5.00	7.50	12.50

Large flan, 24.5-26.5mm.

C#	Date	Year	VG	Fine	VF	XF
714a.1	(1827-9)	37	4.00	6.00	8.50	13.50

With crossbar on trisul (trident), 21-24.5mm.

C#	Date	Year	VG	Fine	VF	XF
714b	(1827-9)	37	4.00	6.00	8.50	13.50
	(1827-9)	37	—	—	Proof	75.00

PICE

COPPER, 6.2 gm.

MINT: CALCUTTA

C#	Date	Year	VG	Fine	VF	XF
711	(1795)	37	10.00	15.00	20.00	27.50
	(1795)	37	—	—	Proof	85.00

NOTE: Struck between 1808 and 1809.

2 PICE

COPPER, 12.3 gm.

MINT: CALCUTTA

C#	Date	Year	VG	Fine	VF	XF
712	(1795)	37	11.50	16.50	22.50	30.00
	(1795)	37	—	—	Proof	100.00

NOTE: Struck between 1808 and 1809.

1/16 RUPEE

SILVER, dump, 0.67-0.72 gm.

C#	Date	Year	VG	Fine	VF	XF
830	AH1190-92 1193	17	5.00	10.00	15.00	21.50
		17/20-49	5.00	10.00	15.00	21.50

1/8 RUPEE

SILVER, dump, 1.34-1.45 gm.

C#	Date	Year	VG	Fine	VF	XF
831	AH1190-92 1193	17	3.75	7.50	10.00	15.00
		17/20-49	3.75	7.50	10.00	15.00

1/4 RUPEE

SILVER, dump, 2.68-2.90 gm.

C#	Date	Year	VG	Fine	VF	XF
832	AH1190-92 1193	17	4.00	8.00	11.50	17.50
		17/20-49	4.00	8.00	11.50	17.50

Struck w/o Darogah's marks

C#	Date	Year	VG	Fine	VF	XF
832.1	AH1229	17/49	3.75	7.50	10.00	15.00

Machine struck, broad flan, with oblique milling.

C#	Date	Year	
842	AH1229	17/49	Reported, not confirmed

1/2 RUPEE

SILVER, dump, 5.35-5.80 gm.

C#	Date	Year	VG	Fine	VF	XF
833	AH1190-92 1193	17	6.50	10.00	15.00	20.00
		17/20-49	6.50	10.00	15.00	20.00

Struck without Darogah's marks

C#	Date	Year	VG	Fine	VF	XF
833.1	AH1229	17/49	6.50	8.50	13.50	17.50

Machine struck, broad flan with oblique milling.

C#	Date	Year	VG	Fine	VF	XF
843	AH1229	17/49	—	—	Rare	—

RUPEE

SILVER, dump, 10.70-11.60 gm.

C#	Date	Year	VG	Fine	VF	XF
834	AH1190	17	11.50	13.50	16.50	20.00
	1191	17	11.50	13.50	16.50	20.00
	1192	17	11.50	13.50	16.50	20.00
	1193	17/20	11.50	13.50	16.50	20.00
	1193	17/21	11.50	13.50	16.50	20.00
	1194	17/22	11.50	13.50	16.50	20.00
	1195	17/23	11.50	13.50	16.50	20.00
	1196	17/24	11.50	13.50	16.50	20.00
	1197	17/25	11.50	13.50	16.50	20.00
	1198	17/26	11.50	13.50	16.50	20.00
	1199	17/26	11.50	13.50	16.50	20.00
	1199	17/27	11.50	13.50	16.50	20.00
	1200	17/27	11.50	13.50	16.50	20.00
	1201	17/29	11.50	13.50	16.50	20.00
	1202 (error)					
		17/28	12.50	15.00	18.50	23.50
	1202	17/29	11.50	13.50	16.50	20.00
	1202	17/30	11.50	13.50	16.50	20.00
	1203	17/30	11.50	13.50	16.50	20.00
	1203	17/31	11.50	13.50	16.50	20.00
	1204	17/32	11.50	13.50	16.50	20.00
	1205	17/33	11.50	13.50	16.50	20.00
	1206	17/33	11.50	13.50	16.50	20.00
	1206	17/34	11.50	13.50	16.50	20.00
	1207	17/34	11.50	13.50	16.50	20.00
	1207	17/35	11.50	13.50	16.50	20.00
	1208	17/35	11.50	13.50	16.50	20.00
	1208	17/36	11.50	13.50	16.50	20.00
	1209	17/36	11.50	13.50	16.50	20.00
	1209	17/37	11.50	13.50	16.50	20.00
	1210	17/37	11.50	13.50	16.50	20.00
	1210	17/38	11.50	13.50	16.50	20.00
	1211	17/38	11.50	13.50	16.50	20.00
	1211	17/39	11.50	13.50	16.50	20.00
	1212	17/39	11.50	13.50	16.50	20.00
	1212	17/40	11.50	13.50	16.50	20.00

C#	Date	Year	VG	Fine	VF	XF
	AH1213 (error)					
		17/33	12.50	15.00	18.50	23.50
	1213	17/40	11.50	13.50	16.50	20.00
	1213	17/41	11.50	13.50	16.50	20.00
	1214	17/41	11.50	13.50	16.50	20.00
	1214	17/42	11.50	13.50	16.50	20.00
	1215	17/42	11.50	13.50	16.50	20.00
	1215	17/43	11.50	13.50	16.50	20.00
	1216	17/43	11.50	13.50	16.50	20.00
	1216	17/44	11.50	13.50	16.50	20.00
	1217	17/44	11.50	13.50	16.50	20.00
	1217	17/45	11.50	13.50	16.50	20.00
	1218	17/45	11.50	13.50	16.50	20.00
	1218	17/46	11.50	13.50	16.50	20.00
	1219	17/46	11.50	13.50	16.50	20.00
	1219	17/47	11.50	13.50	16.50	20.00

C#	Date	Year	VG	Fine	VF	XF
	AH1219	17/47	15.00	20.00	27.50	37.50
	1220	17/47	11.50	13.50	16.50	20.00
	1220	17/48	11.50	13.50	16.50	20.00
	1221	17/48	11.50	13.50	16.50	20.00
	1221	17/49	11.50	13.50	16.50	20.00
	1222	17/49	11.50	13.50	16.50	20.00
	1223	17/49	11.50	13.50	16.50	20.00
	1224	17/49	11.50	13.50	16.50	20.00
	1225	17/49	11.50	13.50	16.50	20.00
	1226	17/49	11.50	13.50	16.50	20.00

Large full flan

C#	Date	Year	VG	Fine	VF	XF
834a	AH1217	17/45	13.50	17.50	23.50	30.00

Without Darogah's marks

C#	Date	Year	VG	Fine	VF	XF
834b	AH1228	17/49	11.50	13.00	15.00	20.00
	1229	17/49	11.50	13.00	15.00	20.00

Machine struck, broad flan with oblique milling

C#	Date	Year	VG	Fine	VF	XF
844	AH1229	17/49	13.50	17.50	22.50	30.00

MOHUR

GOLD, dump, 10.70-11.40 gm.

C#	Date	Year	VG	Fine	VF	XF
839	AH1209	37	225.00	250.00	285.00	325.00
	1213	41	225.00	250.00	285.00	325.00

BENGAL

Prinsep Issues

1780-1784 AD

1/16 ANNA

COPPER 15.8mm, 1.8 gm.
Large, thin flan

C#	Date	Year	VG	Fine	VF	XF
701	AH1195	22	2.50	3.50	7.00	10.00
	1195	22	—	—	Proof	65.00

14.5mm, 1.8 gm.
Small, thick flan

C#	Date	Year	VG	Fine	VF	XF
701a	AH1195	22	2.50	3.50	7.00	10.00

1/8 ANNA

COPPER, 19.6mm, 3.6 gm.
Large, thin flan

C#	Date	Year	VG	Fine	VF	XF
702	AH1195	22	2.00	3.00	6.00	9.00
	1195	22	—	—	Proof	70.00

18.3mm, 3.6 gm.
Small, thick flan

C#	Date	Year	VG	Fine	VF	XF
702a	AH1195	22	2.00	3.00	5.00	7.50

1/4 ANNA

COPPER, 23.7mm, 7.3 gm.
Large, thin flan

C#	Date	Year	VG	Fine	VF	XF
703	AH1195	22	2.00	3.00	6.00	9.00
	1195	22	—	—	Proof	75.00

22.8mm, 7.3 gm.
Small, thick flan

C#	Date	Year	VG	Fine	VF	XF
703a	AH1195	22	2.00	3.00	6.00	9.00

1/2 ANNA

COPPER, 29mm, 14.5 gm.
Large, thin flan

C#	Date	Year	VG	Fine	VF	XF
704	AH1195	22	3.00	4.50	9.00	13.00
	1195	22	—	—	Proof	85.00

26mm, 14.5 gm.
Small, thick flan

C#	Date	Year	VG	Fine	VF	XF
704a	AH1195	22	3.00	4.50	9.00	13.00

Calcutta Issues

PIE

COPPER

C#	Date	Year	VG	Fine	VF	XF
718	(1831)	—	.50	1.00	1.50	3.00

1/2 PICE

COPPER, 5.8 gm.

C#	Date	Year	VG	Fine	VF	XF
705	(1795)	37	7.50	10.00	13.50	20.00
	Reduced weight, 4.30 gm.					
705a	(1796)	37	4.00	6.00	10.00	15.00

PICE

COPPER, 11.6 gm.

C#	Date	Year	VG	Fine	VF	XF
706	(1795)	37	5.00	8.50	12.50	18.50
	Reduced weight, 8.7 gm., large and small flans.					
706a	(1796)	37	1.00	2.00	3.00	5.00
	Reduced weight, 6.54 gm.					
706b	(1809)	37	.75	1.75	2.50	4.50
	Reduced weight, 6.46 gm.					
706c	(1817)	37	.75	1.75	2.50	4.50

C#	Date	Year	VG	Fine	VF	XF
706d	(1829)	37	.75	1.75	2.50	4.50
	(1829)	37	—	—	Proof	65.00

C#	Date	Year	VG	Fine	VF	XF
706e	(1831)	37	.50	1.00	2.00	3.50
	(1831)	37	—	—	Proof	60.00

1/2 ANNA

COPPER

C#	Date	Year	VG	Fine	VF	XF
720	(1831-35)	—	2.00	3.50	6.00	9.00

FARRUKHABAD

TRISUL PICE

COPPER, 6.2 gm.

MINT: FARRUKHABAD

C#	Date	Year	VG	Fine	VF	XF
716	(1820)	45	2.50	4.00	6.00	9.00

MINT: SAGAR

Obv. & Rev. trident

C#	Date	Year	VG	Fine	VF	XF
716b	(1826)	45	3.00	4.00	5.50	7.50

MINT: SAGAR

Obv: 6-petalled rosette replaces trident

C#	Date	Year	VG	Fine	VF	XF
716a	(1833)	45	3.00	4.00	5.50	7.50

1/4 RUPEE

.955 SILVER, 2.80 gm.

MINT: FARRUKHABAD

Oblique milling (1806-1819)

C#	Date	Year	Fine	VF	XF	Unc
852	AH—	45	3.50	4.00	5.00	8.00
	.909 SILVER, 2.92 gm. MINT: FARRUKHABAD Vertical milling (1820-1831)					
852a	AH—	45	3.50	4.00	5.00	8.00
	MINT : CALCUTTA AND BENARES					
852b	AH1204	45	3.50	4.00	5.00	8.00

MINT: CALCUTTA

Plain edge (1831-1833)

C#	Date	Year	Fine	VF	XF	Unc
852c	AH1204	45	3.50	4.00	5.00	8.00
	AH1204	45	—	—	Proof	110.00

1/2 RUPEE

.955 SILVER, 5.60 gm.

MINT: FARRUKHABAD

Oblique milling (1806-1819)

C#	Date	Year	Fine	VF	XF	Unc
853	—	45	6.50	7.50	9.00	14.00
	.909 SILVER, 5.80 gm. MINTS: CALCUTTA AND BENARES Vertical milling (1820-1831) 5.8 gm.					
853a	—	45	6.50	7.50	9.00	14.00

MINT: CALCUTTA

Plain edge (1831-1833)

C#	Date	Year	Fine	VF	XF	Unc
853b	—	45	6.50	7.50	9.00	14.00
	—	45	—	—	Proof	120.00

RUPEE

.955 SILVER, 11.21 gm.

MINTS: FARRUKHABAD AND CALCUTTA

With oblique milling (1806-1819)

C#	Date	Year	Fine	VF	XF	Unc
854	—	45	11.50	13.00	15.00	20.00

.909 SILVER, 11.68 gm.

MINTS: FARRUKHABAD, CALCUTTA, BENARES, SAGAR

Vertical milling (1820-1831) 11.6 gm.

C#	Date	Year	Fine	VF	XF	Unc
854a	—	45	11.50	13.00	15.00	20.00

MINT: CALCUTTA

Obv. and rev: Large dots; plain edge (1831-1833)

C#	Date	Year	Fine	VF	XF	Unc
854b	—	45	11.50	13.00	15.00	20.00
	—	45	—	—	Proof	135.00

MINT: CALCUTTA

Obv. and rev: Small dots; plain edge (1833-1835)

C#	Date	Year	Fine	VF	XF	Unc
854c	—	45	11.50	13.00	15.00	20.00
	—	45	—	—	Proof	135.00

MURSHIDABAD

1/16 RUPEE

SILVER, dump, 0.73 gm.

MINT: MURSHIDABAD (1777-1793)

C#	Date	Year	VG	Fine	VF	XF
750	—	19	5.00	7.50	10.00	15.00

1/8 RUPEE

SILVER, dump, 1.45 gm.

MINT: MURSHIDABAD (1777-1793)

C#	Date	Year	VG	Fine	VF	XF
751	—	19	5.00	7.50	10.00	15.00

1/4 RUPEE

SILVER, dump, 2.90 gm.

MINT: MURSHIDABAD (1777-1793)

C#	Date	Year	VG	Fine	VF	XF
752	—	19	5.00	7.50	10.00	15.00

MINTS: CALCUTTA, DACCA, MURSHIDABAD, PATNA

Oblique milling (1793-1818).

C#	Date	Year	Fine	VF	XF	Unc
772	AH1204	19	3.50	4.50	5.50	7.50

MINT: CALCUTTA

Vertical milling (1819-1829)

C#	Date	Year	Fine	VF	XF	Unc
772a	AH1204	19	3.50	4.50	5.50	7.50

MINT: NEW CALCUTTA

Plain edge (1830-1833)

C#	Date	Year	Fine	VF	XF	Unc
772b	AH1204	19	3.50	4.50	5.50	7.50

1/2 RUPEE

SILVER, dump, 5.80 gm.

MINT: MURSHIDABAD (1777-1793)

C#	Date	Year	VG	Fine	VF	XF
753	—	19	6.50	7.50	8.50	12.50

MINTS: CALCUTTA, DACCA, MURSHIDABAD, PATNA

Oblique milling (1793-1818)

C#	Date	Year	Fine	VF	XF	Unc
773	—	19	6.50	7.50	8.50	12.50
	—	19	—	—	Proof	85.00

MINT: CALCUTTA

Vertical milling (1819-1829) 6.2 gm.

C#	Date	Year	Fine	VF	XF	Unc
773a	—	19	6.50	7.50	9.00	14.00
	—	19	—	—	Proof	110.00

MINT: NEW CALCUTTA

Plain edge, crescent added (1830-1833)

C#	Date	Year	Fine	VF	XF	Unc
773b	—	19	6.50	7.00	8.00	12.00
	—	19	—	—	Proof	110.00

RUPEE

SILVER, dump, 11.60 gm.

MINT: MURSHIDABAD

C#	Date	Year	VG	Fine	VF	XF
754	AH1179	5	12.50	15.00	17.50	23.50
	1179	7	12.50	15.00	17.50	23.50
	1185	12	12.50	15.00	17.50	23.50
	1191	19	11.50	13.50	16.50	20.00
	1192	19	11.50	13.50	16.50	20.00
	1193	19	11.50	13.50	16.50	20.00
	1194	19	11.50	13.50	16.50	20.00
	1195	19	11.50	13.50	16.50	20.00
	1196	19	11.50	13.50	16.50	20.00
	1197	19	11.50	13.50	16.50	20.00
	1198	19	11.50	13.50	16.50	20.00
	1199	19	11.50	13.50	16.50	20.00
	1201	19	11.50	13.50	16.50	20.00
	1202	19	11.50	13.50	16.50	20.00
	1203	19	11.50	13.50	16.50	20.00

C#	Date	Year	VG	Fine	VF	XF
754.1	AH1190 error, muled with obverse of 1770 series.	19	—	—	—	—

MINT: MURSHIDABAD

Partially machine struck, 11.6 gm.

C#	Date	Year	Fine	VF	XF	Unc
754.2	AH1205	19	11.50	13.50	16.50	20.00

MINT: CALCUTTA

Oblique milling, struck - type of Mohur, (1790)

C#	Date	Year	Fine	VF	XF	Unc
774	AH1202	19	12.50	15.00	18.50	23.50

NOTE: Dump Rupees and fractions of Murshidabad Mint, in the name of Shah Alam II, with regnal years 10-12, were struck by the French at Chandernagor, AD1769-71, and fall outside the scope of this catalog.

MINTS: CALCUTTA, DACCA, MURSHIDABAD

Oblique milling.

C#	Date	Year	Fine	VF	XF	Unc
774.1	AH1202	19	11.50	13.50	17.50	22.50

MINTS: CALCUTTA, DACCA, MURSHIDABAD, PATNA

Machine struck, oblique milling (1792-1818)

C#	Date	Year	Fine	VF	XF	Unc
774.2	—	19	11.50	13.50	16.50	20.00

MINT: CALCUTTA

Vertical milling

C#	Date	Year	Fine	VF	XF	Unc
774a	—	19	12.50	15.00	18.50	25.00

Obv: Star added.
Vertical milling (1819-1832)

C#	Date	Year	Fine	VF	XF	Unc
774a.1	—	19	11.50	13.00	15.00	18.50

MINT: CALCUTTA

Privy mark 'S' added.

C#	Date	Year	Fine	VF	XF	Unc
774a.2	—	19	11.50	13.50	16.50	20.00

MINT: NEW CALCUTTA

Plain edge (1830-1833)

C#	Date	Year	Fine	VF	XF	Unc
774b	—	19	11.50	13.00	15.00	18.50

1/16 MOHUR

GOLD, dump, 11mm, 0.77 gm.

MINT: MURSHIDABAD

C#	Date	Year	VG	Fine	VF	XF
760	AH1182	10	25.00	35.00	45.00	60.00
	1183	10	25.00	35.00	45.00	60.00
	1202	19	25.00	35.00	45.00	60.00
	1203	19	25.00	35.00	45.00	60.00

9mm

C#	Date	Year	VG	Fine	VF	XF
760.1	—	15	25.00	35.00	45.00	60.00

1/8 MOHUR

GOLD, dump, 14mm, 1.50 gm.

MINT: MURSHIDABAD

C#	Date	Year	Fine	VF	XF	Unc
761	AH1182	10	45.00	55.00	65.00	80.00
	1183	10	45.00	55.00	65.00	80.00
	1200	19	45.00	55.00	65.00	80.00
	1202	19	45.00	55.00	65.00	80.00
	1203	19	45.00	55.00	65.00	80.00

11mm

C#	Date	Year	Fine	VF	XF	Unc
761.1	—	15	35.00	45.00	55.00	70.00

1/4 MOHUR

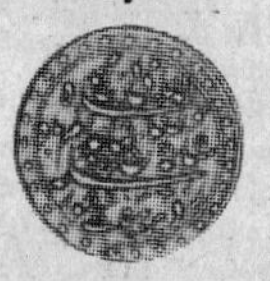

GOLD, dump, 16.5mm, 3.09 gm.

MINT: MURSHIDABAD

C#	Date	Year	Fine	VF	XF	Unc
762	AH1182	10	60.00	70.00	82.50	100.00
	1202	19	60.00	70.00	82.50	100.00
	1203	19	60.00	70.00	82.50	100.00

.996 GOLD, 3.09 gm.

MINTS: CALCUTTA, DACCA, MURSHIDABAD, PATNA

Oblique milling (1793-1818)

C#	Date	Year	Fine	VF	XF	Unc
777	AH1204	19	60.00	70.00	80.00	95.00

.917 GOLD, 3.31 gm.

MINT: CALCUTTA

Vertical milling (1819-1832)

C#	Date	Year	Fine	VF	XF	Unc
777a	AH1204	19	60.00	70.00	80.00	95.00

1/2 MOHUR

GOLD, dump, 19.5mm, 6.18 gm.

MINT: MURSHIDABAD

C#	Date	Year	Fine	VF	XF	Unc
763	AH1182	10	120.00	135.00	150.00	175.00
	1183	11	120.00	135.00	150.00	175.00

.996 GOLD, 6.18 gm.

MINTS: CALCUTTA, DACCA, MURSHIDABAD, PATNA

Machine struck, oblique milling (1793-1818)

C#	Date	Year	Fine	VF	XF	Unc
778	AH1202	19	120.00	130.00	145.00	165.00

.917 GOLD, 6.63 gm.

MINT: CALCUTTA

Vertical milling (1819-1832)

C#	Date	Year	Fine	VF	XF	Unc
778a	AH1202	19	120.00	130.00	140.00	160.00

MOHUR

GOLD, dump, 12.36 gm.

MINT: MURSHIDABAD

C#	Date	Year	Fine	VF	XF	Unc
764	AH1182	10	225.00	250.00	285.00	325.00
	1183	10	225.00	250.00	285.00	325.00
	1183	11	225.00	250.00	285.00	325.00
	1184	11	225.00	250.00	285.00	325.00
	1185	12	225.00	250.00	285.00	325.00
	1186	12	225.00	250.00	285.00	325.00
	1187	15	225.00	250.00	285.00	325.00
	1188	12	(error) old reverse die			
			—	—	—	—
	1188	15	225.00	250.00	285.00	325.00
	1189	12	(error) old reverse die			

MINT: MURSHIDABAD

Machine struck, oblique milling (1790-1792)

C#	Date	Year	Fine	VF	XF	Unc
779	AH1202	19	225.00	250.00	285.00	325.00

.996 GOLD, 12.36 gm.

MINTS: CALCUTTA, DACCA, MURSHIDABAD, PATNA (1793-1818)

C#	Date	Year	Fine	VF	XF	Unc
779.1	AH1202	19	225.00	250.00	285.00	325.00

.917 GOLD, 13.26 gm.

MINT: CALCUTTA

Vertical milling (1819-1825)

C#	Date	Year	Fine	VF	XF	Unc
779a	AH1202	19	225.00	250.00	285.00	325.00

.996 GOLD, 12.36 gm.

MINT: CALCUTTA

Low relief, oblique left milling (1825)

C#	Date	Year	Fine	VF	XF	Unc
779.2	AH1202	19	225.00	250.00	285.00	325.00

Low relief, oblique left milling, crescent added (1830)

C#	Date	Year	Fine	VF	XF	Unc
779.3	AH1202	19	225.00	250.00	285.00	325.00

BOMBAY PRESIDENCY

1/4 PICE

COPPER, dump, 2.65 gm.

C#	Date	Year	Good	VG	Fine	VF
575	1816	—	2.00	4.00	8.00	12.00
	1821	—	2.00	4.00	8.00	12.00
	1825	—	2.00	4.00	8.00	12.00

PIE

COPPER

MINT: BOMBAY

Obv: Center lion on helmet above shield.

C#	Date	Year	VG	Fine	VF	XF
591	AH1246	1830		Proof Only		—
	1246	1831	1.00	2.00	4.00	6.00
	1246	1831	—	—	Proof	75.00

MINT: CALCUTTA

Obv: Center lion on shield, value in letters 1.2mm high.

C#	Date	Year	VG	Fine	VF	XF
591a	AH1248	1833	.50	1.00	2.00	4.00
	1248	1833	—	—	Proof	65.00

Obv: Value in letters 0.8mm high.

C#	Date	Year	VG	Fine	VF	XF
591b	AH1248	1833	.50	1.00	2.00	4.00

Mule: Obv: Calcutta. Rev: Bombay.

C#	Date	Year	VG	Fine	VF	XF
591c	AH1246	1833	—	—	—	—

Mule: Obv: Bombay. Rev: Calcutta.

C#	Date	Year	VG	Fine	VF	XF
591d	AH1248	1831	—	—	—	—

1/2 PICE (2 REAS)

COPPER, 20mm, 3.23 gm.

C#	Date	Year	Good	VG	Fine	VF
581	1791	—	1.25	2.50	5.00	7.50
	1791	—	—	—	Proof	70.00
	1794	—	1.25	2.50	5.00	7.50
	1794	—	—	—	Proof	70.00

COPPER, dump, 5.31 gm.

C#	Date	Year	Good	VG	Fine	VF
576	1802	—	1.00	2.00	3.00	6.00
	1803	—	Reported, not confirmed			
	1808	—	1.00	2.00	3.00	6.00
	1810	—	1.00	2.00	3.00	6.00
	1813	—	1.00	2.00	3.00	6.00
	1815	—	1.00	2.00	3.00	6.00
	1816	—	1.00	2.00	3.00	6.00
	1818	—	1.00	2.00	3.00	6.00
	1819	—	1.00	2.00	3.00	6.00
	1825	—	1.00	2.00	3.00	6.00
	1826	—	1.00	2.00	3.00	6.00
	1827	—	1.00	2.00	3.00	6.00
	1829	—	Reported, not confirmed			

COPPER
Obv: Center lion on helmet above shield.

C#	Date	Year	VG	Fine	VF	XF
586	AH1219	1804	1.25	2.50	5.00	8.50
	1219	1804	—	—	Proof	70.00

COPPER, dump, 17-18mm, 3.76 gm.

MINT: LOCAL SOUTHERN CONCAN

C#	Date	Year	Good	VG	Fine	VF
687	1820	—	—	—	Rare	—
	1821	—	4.00	6.00	9.00	13.50

PICE (4 REAS)

(= 1/4 Anna)

COPPER, 25.4mm, 6.47 gm.

C#	Date	Year	VG	Fine	VF	XF
582	1791	—	2.00	4.00	6.00	8.00
	1791	—	—	—	Proof	80.00
	1794	—	2.00	4.00	6.00	8.00
	1794	—	—	—	Proof	80.00

COPPER, dump, 10.62 gm.

C#	Date	Year	Good	VG	Fine	VF
577	1802	—	1.25	2.50	3.50	6.00
	1803	—	1.25	2.50	3.50	6.00
	1804	—	1.25	2.50	3.50	6.00
	1808	—	1.25	4.50	7.00	10.00
	1809	—	1.25	2.50	3.50	6.00
	1810	—	1.25	2.50	3.50	6.00
	1813	—	1.25	2.50	3.50	6.00
	1815	—	1.25	2.50	3.50	6.00
	1816	—	1.25	2.50	3.50	6.00
	1818	—	1.25	2.50	3.50	6.00
	1819	—	1.25	2.50	3.50	6.00
	1825	—	1.25	2.50	3.50	6.00
	1826	—	1.25	2.50	3.50	6.00
	1827	—	1.25	2.50	3.50	6.00
	1828	—	1.25	2.50	3.50	6.00
	1829	—	1.25	2.50	3.50	6.00

C#	Date	Year	VG	Fine	VF	XF
587	AH1219	1804	2.00	4.00	6.50	10.00
	1219	1804	—	—	Proof	75.00

MINT: LOCAL SOUTHERN CONCAN

19-20mm, 7.53 gm.

C#	Date	Year	Good	VG	Fine	VF
688	1820	—	—	—	Rare	—
	1821	—	3.50	6.00	10.00	15.00

20mm, 6.7 gm.

C#	Date	Year	Good	VG	Fine	VF
688a	1829	—	—	—	—	—

1/4 ANNA

COPPER

MINT: BOMBAY

Obv: EAST INDIA COMPANY legend

C#	Date	Year	Fine	VF	XF	Unc
592	AH1246	1830	2.50	4.00	6.00	10.00
	1246	1830	—	—	Proof	60.00
	1246	1832	2.50	4.00	6.00	10.00
	1247	1832	2.50	4.00	6.00	10.00

Obv. Without E.I.C. legend, Rev. large letters

C#	Date	Year	Fine	VF	XF	Unc
592a	AH1247	1833	Mule, With Reverse Of C#592			
			—	—	—	—
	1249	1833	1.50	3.00	5.00	7.50
	1249	1833	—	—	Proof	70.00

Rev: Small English letters

C#	Date	Year	Fine	VF	XF	Unc
592a.1	AH1249	1833	2.50	4.00	6.00	10.00
	1249	1832	Mule, with obverse of C#592			
			5.00	8.50	17.50	27.50

1-1/2 PICE (6 REAS)

COPPER, 29mm, 9.71 gm.
Rev: Small scales, vertical milling

C#	Date	Year	VG	Fine	VF	XF
583	1791	—	—	—	Proof	90.00

Rev: Large scales, oblique milling.

C#	Date	Year	VG	Fine	VF	XF
583.1	1791	—	3.50	6.00	10.00	15.00
	1791	—	—	—	Proof	90.00
	1794	—	—	—	Proof	90.00

2 PICE (8 REAS)

COPPER, 30.5mm, 12.95 gm.

C#	Date	Year	VG	Fine	VF	XF
584	1791	—	2.50	3.50	6.00	10.00
	1791	—	—	—	Proof	100.00
	1794	—	2.50	3.50	6.00	10.00
	1794	—	—	—	Proof	100.00

COPPER, dump, 21.25 gm., without value '2'

C#	Date	Year	Good	VG	Fine	VF
578	1802	—	2.00	4.00	7.50	12.50
	1803	—	2.00	4.00	7.50	12.50
	1804	—	2.00	4.00	7.50	12.50

Without value "2"

C#	Date	Year	Good	VG	Fine	VF
578a	1808	—	1.75	3.50	6.00	9.00
	1809	—	1.75	3.50	6.00	9.00
	1810	—	1.75	3.50	6.00	9.00
	1812	—	Reported, not confirmed			
	1813	—	1.75	3.50	6.00	9.00
	1816	—	1.75	3.50	6.00	9.00
	1818	—	1.75	3.50	6.00	9.00
	1819	—	1.75	3.50	6.00	9.00
	1825	—	1.75	3.50	6.00	9.00
	1826	—	1.75	3.50	6.00	9.00
	1827	—	Reported, not confirmed			
	1828	—	1.75	3.50	6.00	9.00
	1829	—	1.75	3.50	6.00	9.00

C#	Date	Year	VG	Fine	VF	XF
588	AH1219	1804	1.75	3.50	6.50	10.00
	1219	1804	—	—	Proof	100.00

1/2 ANNA

COPPER, 30.5mm, 12.95 gm.

P#	Date	Mintage	Fine	VF	XF	Unc
204	AH1246	1832	—	—	Proof	100.00

Rev: English letters, 2mm.

C#	Date	Year	Fine	VF	XF	Unc
593	AH1249	1834	3.50	5.50	9.00	15.00
	1249	1834	—	—	Proof	90.00

Rev: English letters, 2.5mm.

C#	Date	Year	Fine	VF	XF	Unc
593.1	AH1249	1834	1.50	3.00	5.00	8.00

Rev: English letters, 1mm.

C#	Date	Year	Fine	VF	XF	Unc
593.2	AH1249	1834	3.50	5.50	8.50	13.50

SILVER
Rev: English letters, 1mm.

C#	Date	Year	Fine	VF	XF	Unc
593.3	AH1249	1834	—	—	Proof	125.00

COPPER, dump, 23-24mm, 15.6 gm.
Rev: W/Nagari value and date.

MINT: LOCAL SOUTHERN CONCAN

C#	Date	Year	Good	VG	Fine	VF
689	1820	—	—	—	Rare	—
	1821	—	5.00	8.50	12.50	18.50

22.5mm, 13.6 gm.
Rev: W/western date.

C#	Date	Year	Good	VG	Fine	VF
689a	1828	—	6.50	12.50	20.00	30.00
	1829	—	6.50	12.50	20.00	30.00

4 PICE

COPPER, 42.51 GM.

C#	Date	Year	Good	VG	Fine	VF
579	1802	—	6.50	12.50	20.00	30.00
	1803	—	6.50	12.50	20.00	30.00
	1804	—	6.50	12.50	20.00	30.00

SURAT

PAISA

COPPER

C#	Date	Year	VG	Fine	VF	XF
40	AH1234	12	3.00	5.50	8.50	13.50

1/8 RUPEE

SILVER, dump, 10-11mm, 1.44 gm.

MINT: SURAT (1800-1824)

C#	Date	Year	VG	Fine	VF	XF
661	—	46	3.00	6.00	10.00	15.00

1.46 gm.

C#	Date	Year	VG	Fine	VF	XF
661.1	1825	46	3.50	6.50	13.50	20.00

NOTE: Struck in the period of 1825-1831; the above issue exists with three varieties of privy marks.

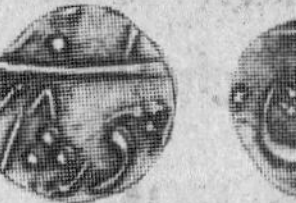

11-14mm

MINT: AHMADABAD

C#	Date	Year	VG	Fine	VF	XF
42	AH1234	12	3.00	4.00	5.50	7.50
	1248	—	3.00	4.00	5.50	7.50

See note after Rupee, C#45.

1/4 RUPEE

SILVER, dump, 13-14mm, 2.88 gm.

MINT: SURAT (1800-1824)

C#	Date	Year	VG	Fine	VF	XF
662	—	46	5.00	8.50	12.50	18.50

2.91 gm.

C#	Date	Year	VG	Fine	VF	XF
662.1	1825	46	6.00	9.00	13.50	20.00

NOTE: Struck in the period of 1825-1831; the above issue exists with four varieties of privy marks.

Machine struck, plain edge.

C#	Date	Year	Fine	VF	XF	Unc
676	AH1215	46	3.50	4.50	6.50	10.00
	1215	46	—	—	Proof	75.00

MINT: AHMADABAD

C#	Date	Year	VG	Fine	VF	XF
43	AH1234	12	3.50	4.50	6.00	9.00

See note after Rupee, C#45.

1/2 RUPEE

SILVER, dump, 15.5-16mm, 5.76 gm.

MINT: SURAT (1800-1824)

C#	Date	Year	VG	Fine	VF	XF
663	—	46	6.50	7.50	8.50	10.00

5.83 gm.

C#	Date	Year	VG	Fine	VF	XF
663.1	1825	46	6.50	8.50	11.50	15.00

NOTE: Struck in the period of 1825-1831; the above issue exists with five varieties of privy marks.

Machine struck, plain edge.

C#	Date	Year	Fine	VF	XF	Unc
677	AH1215	46	3.00	4.00	7.50	11.50
	1215	46	—	—	Proof	80.00

MINT: AHMADABAD

C#	Date	Year	VG	Fine	VF	XF
44	AH1248	—	6.50	8.00	10.00	13.50

See note after Rupee, C#45.

RUPEE

SILVER, dump, 20-21mm, 11.59 gm.

MINT: SURAT (1800-1824)

C#	Date	Year	VG	Fine	VF	XF
664	—	46	11.50	13.00	15.00	18.50

11.66 gm.

C#	Date	Year	VG	Fine	VF	XF
664.1	1825	46	11.50	13.50	16.50	20.00

NOTE: Struck in the period of 1825-1831; the above issue exists with five varieties of privy marks.

Machine struck, vertical milling.

C#	Date	Year	Fine	VF	XF	Unc
678	AH1215	46	12.50	13.50	16.50	23.50
	1215	46	—	—	Proof	85.00

Plain edge

C#	Date	Year	Fine	VF	XF	Unc
678a	AH1215	46	11.50	13.00	15.00	20.00
	1215	46	—	—	Proof	85.00

SILVER, dump, 22.23mm

MINT: AHMADABAD

C#	Date	Year	VG	Fine	VF	XF
45	AH1234	12	11.50	13.00	15.00	20.00
	1243	—	11.50	13.00	15.00	20.00
	1248	—	11.50	13.00	15.00	20.00

NOTE: Ahmadabad Mint was acquired by the British in 1817. for earlier issues, see Mughals, Baroda, and Ahmadabad. Symbols as an Ahmadabad State Issues Q.V.. in the name of Mahammad Akbar II.

1/15 MOHUR

(= Gold Rupee)

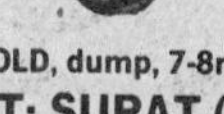

GOLD, dump, 7-8mm, 0.77 gm.

MINT: SURAT (1800-1815)

C#	Date	Year	VG	Fine	VF	XF
665	—	46	25.00	31.50	37.50	50.00

MINT: BOMBAY

Privy Mark: Crescent

C#	Date	Year	VG	Fine	VF	XF
665.1	ND(1801-2)	46	35.00	45.00	55.00	70.00

Privy Mark: Star

C#	Date	Year	VG	Fine	VF	XF
665.2	ND(1803-24)	46	35.00	45.00	55.00	70.00

Without Privy Mark

C#	Date	Year	VG	Fine	VF	XF
665.3	ND(1825-31)	46	35.00	45.00	55.00	70.00

PANCHIA (1/3 MOHUR)

GOLD, dump, 14-15mm, 3.86 gm.

C#	Date	Year	VG	Fine	VF	XF
667	—	46	75.00	85.00	100.00	120.00

Privy Mark: Crescent

C#	Date	Year	VG	Fine	VF	XF
667.1	ND(1801-2)	46	75.00	85.00	100.00	120.00

C#	Date	Year	VG	Fine	VF	XF
667.2	1802	46	75.00	85.00	100.00	120.00

Privy Mark: Crown normal

C#	Date	Year	VG	Fine	VF	XF
667.3	ND(1803-24)	46	75.00	85.00	100.00	120.00

Privy Mark: Crown inverted

C#	Date	Year	VG	Fine	VF	XF
667.4	—	46	75.00	85.00	100.00	120.00

Privy Marks: Crown normal and 6 petal rosette.

C#	Date	Year	VG	Fine	VF	XF
667.5	ND(1825-31)	46	75.00	85.00	100.00	120.00

Privy Marks: Crown inverted and 6 petal rosette.

C#	Date	Year	VG	Fine	VF	XF
667.6	—	46	75.00	35.00	100.00	120.00

MOHUR

GOLD, dump, 16-19mm, 11.59 gm.

MINT: SURAT (1800-1832)

C#	Date	Year	VG	Fine	VF	XF
669	—	46	225.00	250.00	285.00	325.00

MINT: BOMBAY

Privy Mark: Crescent

C#	Date	Year	VG	Fine	VF	XF
669.1	ND(1801-2)	46	225.00	250.00	285.00	325.00

Privy Mark: Crown normal.

C#	Date	Year	VG	Fine	VF	XF
669.2	ND(1803-24)	46	225.00	250.00	285.00	325.00

Privy Mark: Crown inverted

C#	Date	Year	VG	Fine	VF	XF
669.3	—	46	225.00	250.00	285.00	325.00

Privy Marks: Crown normal and 6 petal rosette

C#	Date	Year	VG	Fine	VF	XF
669.4	ND(1825-31)	46	225.00	250.00	285.00	325.00

MALABAR COAST

Tellicherry

1/5 RUPEE

SILVER, dump, 2.32 gm.

C#	Date	Year	VG	Fine	VF	XF
694	AH1214	—	3.50	6.50	9.00	13.50

C#	Date	Year	VG	Fine	VF	XF
695	1805	—	4.00	7.00	10.00	15.00

RUPEE

SILVER, dump, 11.59 gm.

MINT: OLD MUMBAI (BOMBAY) (1810-1813)

Machine struck, plain edge.

C#	Date	Mintage	VG	Fine	VF	XF
640	—	2.037	20.00	30.00	40.00	55.00

PAGODA

GOLD, dump, 3.0 gm.

C#	Date	Year	VG	Fine	VF	XF
699	1809	—	70.00	85.00	100.00	120.00

MADRAS PRESIDENCY

Pagoda System

CASH

COPPER, dump, 10mm, 0.97-1.23 gm.

C#	Date	Year	Good	VG	Fine	VF
407.1	VII(AH1211) (1796-7?)		3.00	6.00	9.00	13.50
407	AH1212	(1797)	3.00	6.00	9.00	13.50
407.2	ND	—	3.00	6.00	9.00	13.50

NOTE: Many varieties exist.

1.1 gm.

Obv: Balemark. Rev: Date.

C#	Date	Mintage	Good	VG	Fine	VF
408	1803	—	1.75	3.75	7.50	11.50

Machine struck, 11.5mm, 0.64 gm.

C#	Date	Mintage	Fine	VF	XF	Unc
431	1803	—	1.00	1.50	3.00	6.00
	1803	—	—	—	Proof	60.00

SILVER (OMS)

C#	Date	Mintage	Fine	VF	XF	Unc
431a	1803	—	—	—	Proof	60.00

2-1/2 CASH

COPPER, 16mm, 1.21 gm.

C#	Date	Year	Good	VG	Fine	VF
435	ND (1790-1800)		2.00	4.00	6.50	10.00

NOTE: The above exists struck on a V Cash planchet.

1/2 DUDU (5 CASH)

 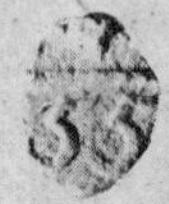

COPPER, 11-14mm, 3.15 gm.

C#	Date	Mintage	Good	VG	Fine	VF
410	1755	—	3.00	5.00	7.50	11.50
	1758	—	—	Reported, not confirmed		
	1761	—	—	Reported, not confirmed		
	1768	—	—	Reported, not confirmed		
	1777	—	3.00	5.00	7.50	11.50
	1784	—	3.00	5.00	7.50	11.50
	1785	—	—	Reported, not confirmed		
	1786	—	3.00	5.00	7.50	11.50
	1790	—	—	Reported, not confirmed		
	1791	—	—	Reported, not confirmed		
	1802	—	—	Reported, not confirmed		
	1804	—	—	Reported, not confirmed		

V (5) CASH

COPPER, 16mm, 1.21 gm.

Obv: Line of dots above denomination.

C#	Date	Year	Good	VG	Fine	VF
436	ND	(1807)	2.00	4.00	6.50	10.00

Obv: Solid line above denomination.

C#	Date	Year	Good	VG	Fine	VF
436.1	ND (1790-1800)		2.00	4.00	6.50	10.00

21mm, 3.23 gm.

Obv: Large lettering

C#	Date	Mintage	Fine	VF	XF	Unc
432	1803	—	1.50	2.00	3.75	7.50

Obv: Small lettering

C#	Date	Mintage	Fine	VF	XF	Unc
432.1	1803	—	1.50	2.00	3.50	7.00

Modified design

C#	Date	Mintage	Fine	VF	XF	Unc
432.2	1803	—	—	—	Proof	70.00

SILVER (OMS)

C#	Date	Mintage	Fine	VF	XF	Unc
432a	1803	—	—	—	Proof	100.00

1/4 DUB (5 CASH)

COPPER, 16.5mm, 2.57 gm.

C#	Date	Mintage	Good	VG	Fine	VF
530	(1807)	—	6.50	13.50	21.50	40.00

DUDU (10 CASH)

COPPER, 6.3 gm.

411	1755	—	2.00	3.00	5.00	8.50
	1756	—	2.00	3.00	5.00	8.50
	1761	—	2.00	3.00	5.00	8.50
	1765	—	—	Reported, not confirmed		
	1768	—	2.00	3.00	5.00	8.50
	1769	—	2.00	3.00	5.00	8.50
	1774	—	2.00	3.00	5.00	8.50
	1777	—	—	Reported, not confirmed		
	1780	—	—	Reported, not confirmed		
	1784	—	2.00	3.00	5.00	8.50
	1786	—	2.00	3.00	5.00	8.50
	1787	—	—	Reported, not confirmed		
	1788	—	—	Reported, not confirmed		
	1789	—	—	Reported, not confirmed		
	1790	—	—	Reported, not confirmed		
	1795	—	2.00	3.00	5.00	8.50
	1796	—	2.00	3.00	5.00	8.50
	1798	—	—	Reported, not confirmed		
	1800	—	2.00	3.00	5.00	8.50
	1801	—	2.00	3.00	5.00	8.50
	1805	—	2.00	3.00	5.00	8.50
	1806	—	—	Reported, not confirmed		

X (10) CASH

COPPER, 23.5mm, 4.83 gm.

437	(1807)	—	1.50	3.00	6.00	10.00

NOTE: Seven varieties exist; i.e. dividing lines, dots and star, etc. Also exists struck on a XX Cash planchet.

Heavy issue, 25.8mm, 6.47 gm.

C#	Date	Mintage	Fine	VF	XF	Unc
433	1803	—	1.50	2.00	4.00	7.00
	1803	—	—	—	Proof	80.00
	1808	—	1.50	2.00	4.00	7.50
	1808	—	—	—	Proof	80.00

SILVER (OMS)

433b	1808	—	—	—	Proof	120.00

COPPER, 25.8mm, 4.66 gm.

433a	1808	—	1.50	2.00	3.50	6.50
	1808	—	—	—	Proof	80.00

1/2 DUB (10 CASH)

COPPER, 22.7mm, 5.15 gm.

C#	Date	Mintage	Good	VG	Fine	VF
531	1807	—	4.00	7.50	15.00	25.00

26mm, 4.75 gm.

531a	1808	—	6.00	9.00	18.00	30.00

XX (20 CASH)

COPPER, 26.5mm, 9.65 gm.

438	(1807)	—	2.25	4.50	8.50	15.00

NOTE: Five varieties exist; i.e. dividing lines, dots and star.

Heavy issue, 30.7mm, 12.95 gm.

C#	Date	Mintage	Fine	VF	XF	Unc
434	1803	—	2.00	3.00	5.50	10.00
	1803	—	—	—	Proof	100.00
	1808	—	2.00	3.00	5.50	10.00
	1808	—	—	—	Proof	100.00

SILVER (OMS)

434b	1808	—	—	—	Proof	150.00

COPPER, 30.7mm, 9.33 gm.

434a	1808	—	1.50	2.00	3.50	6.50
	1808	—	—	—	Proof	100.00

DUB (20 CASH)

COPPER, 27.2mm, 7.56 gm.

C#	Date	Mintage	Good	VG	Fine	VF
535	1807	—	6.50	10.00	16.50	30.00
	1808	—	6.50	10.00	16.50	30.00

NOTE: An unusual issue refered to as a 'Regulating Dub'. The translation is 'This and three new Dubs are one small Fanam'.

26.5mm, 10.31 gm.

532	(1807)	—	5.00	8.50	15.00	25.00

26.8mm, 10 gm.

C#	Date	Mintage	Good	VG	Fine	VF
532a	1808	—	5.00	8.50	15.00	25.00

24.3mm, 9.9 gm.

532b	1808	—	5.00	8.50	15.00	25.00

XL (40) CASH

COPPER, 36mm, 19.31 gm.

439	(1807)	—	10.00	20.00	32.50	50.00

NOTE: Five varieties exist; i.e. dividing lines, dots and stars.

2 DUBS (40 CASH)

COPPER, 39.2mm, 20.61 gm.

533	1807	—	20.00	35.00	65.00	100.00

36mm, 19.69 gm.

C#	Date	Mintage	Good	VG	Fine	VF
533a	1808	—	10.00	20.00	32.50	50.00

FANAM

SILVER, 7-8mm, 0.91 gm.

C#	Date	Mintage	VG	Fine	VF	XF
416	(1764-1807)	—	2.75	4.00	7.50	12.50

10mm, 0.92 gm.
Obv. and rev: Center circle

C#	Date	Mintage	VG	Fine	VF	XF
445c	(1807)	.386	6.00	10.00	15.00	22.50

Obv: Without center circle.

C#	Date	Mintage	VG	Fine	VF	XF
445	(1807)	Inc. Ab.	5.00	8.00	12.00	20.00

Obv: Without branches below star.

C#	Date	Mintage	VG	Fine	VF	XF
445b	(1807)	Inc. Ab.	5.00	10.00	15.00	22.50

11-11.5mm

C#	Date	Mintage	VG	Fine	VF	XF
445a	(1808)	1.545	3.00	4.00	6.50	10.00

NOTE: Two varieties exist of the buckle at the bottom of the obverse.

DOUBLE (2) FANAM

SILVER, 10-11mm, 1.83 gm.

C#	Date	Mintage	VG	Fine	VF	XF
417	(1764-1807)	—	5.00	10.00	15.00	22.50

12.5mm, 1.85 gm.
Obv: With center circle. Rev: No center circle.

C#	Date	Mintage	VG	Fine	VF	XF
446	(1807)	1.511	6.00	8.00	10.00	16.50

Obv. and Rev: No center circle.

C#	Date	Mintage	VG	Fine	VF	XF
446b	(1807)	Inc. Ab.	2.75	4.50	7.50	12.50

Obv. and Rev: With center circles.

C#	Date	Mintage	VG	Fine	VF	XF
446c	(1807)	Inc. Ab.	2.75	4.50	7.50	12.50

Obv: No center circle. Rev: With center circle.

C#	Date	Mintage	VG	Fine	VF	XF
446d	(1807)	Inc. Ab.	2.75	4.50	7.50	12.50

C#	Date	Mintage	VG	Fine	VF	XF
446a	(1808)	6.044	2.75	4.50	7.50	12.50

NOTE: Four varieties exist of the buckle at the bottom of the obverse.

5 FANAMS

SILVER, 17.3mm, 4.65 gm.

C#	Date	Mintage	VG	Fine	VF	XF
447	(1807)	.988	10.00	17.50	27.50	40.00

21-22mm

C#	Date	Mintage	VG	Fine	VF	XF
447a	(1808)	3.954	6.50	11.50	16.50	25.00

NOTE: Eight varieties exist of the buckle at the bottom of the obverse.

1/4 PAGODA

SILVER, 27.2mm, 10.58 gm.

C#	Date	Mintage	VG	Fine	VF	XF
448	(1807)	1.773	22.50	30.00	45.00	65.00

NOTE: Two varieties exist, one with 9 stars to each side of the Gopuram, the other having 13 stars.

25.5mm

C#	Date	Mintage	VG	Fine	VF	XF
448a	(1808)	7.092	17.50	22.50	40.00	60.00

NOTE: Five varieties exist of the buckle at the bottom of the obverse.

1/2 PAGODA

SILVER, 36.5mm, 21.17 gm.

C#	Date	Mintage	VG	Fine	VF	XF
449	(1807)	.501	65.00	100.00	135.00	175.00

NOTE: Four varieties exist; 12, 14, 15 or 18 stars in the field to each side of the Gopuram.

35.5mm
Large English lettering

C#	Date	Mintage	VG	Fine	VF	XF
449a	(1808)	2.000	65.00	100.00	135.00	175.00

Small English lettering

C#	Date	Mintage	VG	Fine	VF	XF
449b	(1808)	Inc. Ab.	65.00	100.00	135.00	175.00

Error: "HALF PGODA"

C#	Date	Mintage	VG	Fine	VF	XF
449c	(1808)	Inc. Ab.	65.00	100.00	135.00	175.00

PAGODA

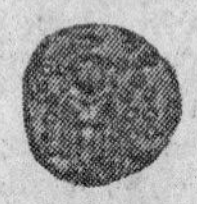

GOLD, 10-11mm, 3.40 gm.
Star Pagoda

C#	Date	Mintage	VG	Fine	VF	XF
426	(1740-1807)	—	65.00	80.00	100.00	150.00

12-14mm, 3.43 gm.
Three Swami Pagoda

C#	Date	Mintage	VG	Fine	VF	XF
421	(1740-1807)	—	65.00	75.00	90.00	125.00

17.4mm, 2.97 gm.

C#	Date	Mintage	VG	Fine	VF	XF
452	(1808-1815)	1.382	65.00	100.00	135.00	175.00

2 PAGODAS

GOLD, 20.5mm, 5.94 gm.

C#	Date	Mintage	VG	Fine	VF	XF
453	(1808-1815)	1.064	120.00	150.00	185.00	225.00

NOTE: Two varieties exist, one with 7 stars to each side of the Gopuram, the other having 9 stars.

Rupee System

1/2 DUB

COPPER, dump, 16mm, 6.6-6.9 gm.
Obv: Persian STRUCK AT MACHHLIPATANBANDAR.
Rev: Date legend.

C#	Date	Mintage	Good	VG	Fine	VF
504	AH1175-1222	—	5.00	9.00	13.50	20.00

1/96th RUPEE (1/2 DUB)

COPPER

Lettered edge

C#	Date	Mintage	Fine	VF	XF	Unc
521	1794	—	2.50	3.50	8.50	15.00
	1794	—	—	—	Proof	75.00

Mule: Obv. C#521a. Rev: C#521.

C#	Date	Mintage	Fine	VF	XF	Unc
521.1	1794	—	—	—	Proof	70.00

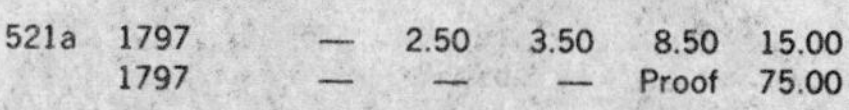

C#	Date	Mintage	Fine	VF	XF	Unc
521a	1797	—	2.50	3.50	8.50	15.00
	1797	—	—	—	Proof	75.00

PIE

COPPER

C#	Date	Year	Mintage	VF	XF	Unc
440	AH1240	1825	4.741	2.00	3.50	6.50
	1240	1825	Inc. Ab.	—	Proof	70.00
	1248	1833	—	2.00	3.50	6.50

DUB

COPPER, dump, 20mm, 13-14 gm.
Obv: Persian STRUCK AT MACHHLIPATANBANDAR.
Rev: Date legend.

C#	Date	Mintage	Good	VG	Fine	VF
506	AH1175-1222	—	5.00	10.00	16.50	25.00

Similar, English M on reverse.

C#	Date	Mintage	Good	VG	Fine	VF
507	AH1218	—	7.50	13.50	20.00	30.00

1/48th RUPEE (DUB)

COPPER
Lettered edge

C#	Date	Mintage	Fine	VF	XF	Unc
522	1794	—	3.50	6.50	11.50	20.00
	1794	—	—	—	Proof	85.00

Mule obv. C#522. Rev: C#522a.

C#	Date	Mintage	Fine	VF	XF	Unc
522b	1794	—	—	—	Proof	100.00

Plain edge

C#	Date	Mintage	Fine	VF	XF	Unc
522c	1794	—	—	—	—	—

C#	Date	Mintage	Fine	VF	XF	Unc
522a	1797	—	3.50	6.50	11.50	20.00
	1797	—	—	—	Proof	85.00

2 PIES

COPPER

C#	Date	Year	Mintage	VF	XF	Unc
441	AH1240	1825	7.126	4.00	7.50	13.50
	1240	1825	Inc. Ab.	—	Proof	90.00

4 PIES

COPPER
Rev: Right wreath tip points up.

C#	Date	Year	Mintage	VF	XF	Unc
442	AH1240	1824	7.136	4.50	8.00	15.00
	1240	1824	Inc. Ab.	—	Proof	100.00

Rev: Right wreath tip points down.

C#	Date	Year	Mintage	VF	XF	Unc
442a	1240	1825	Inc. Ab.	4.50	8.00	15.00
	1240	1825	Inc. Ab.	—	Proof	100.00

Rev: Right wreath tip points up.

C#	Date	Year	Mintage	VF	XF	Unc
442b	1240	1825	Inc. Ab.	4.50	8.00	15.00

Rev: Right wreath tip in straight line.

C#	Date	Year	Mintage	VF	XF	Unc
442c	1240	1825	Inc. Ab.	4.50	8.00	15.00

1/16 RUPEE

SILVER, 8.8mm, 0.11 gm.

MINT: ARCOT

Similar to 1 Rupee, C#514.

C#	Date	Year	VG	Fine	VF	XF
465	ND	6 (Frozen)	6.00	10.00	15.00	20.00

MINT: MADRAS

(mm: Lotus, 1817-1835)
Oblique milling, 10.5mm, 0.73 gm.

C#	Date	Year	VG	Fine	VF	XF
480	AH1172	6	2.50	3.50	5.00	8.50

MINT: CALCUTTA

(mm: Rose 1823-1825)
Oblique milling

C#	Date	Year	VG	Fine	VF	XF
480c	AH1172	6	2.00	3.00	4.50	8.00

2 ANNAS

SILVER, 16.4mm, 1.48 gm.

C#	Date	Mintage	VG	Fine	VF	XF
541	(1808)	.065	15.00	25.00	35.00	50.00

Rev: Without star

C#	Date	Mintage	VG	Fine	VF	XF
541a	(1808)	Inc. Ab.	25.00	40.00	50.00	65.00

1/8 RUPEE

SILVER, 11mm, 1.42 gm.

MINT: ARCOT

C#	Date	Year	VG	Fine	VF	XF
466	ND	6 (Frozen)	3.50	6.00	10.00	15.00

MINT: MADRAS

(mm: Lotus 1807)
Oblique milling, 16.5mm, 1.51 gm.

C#	Date	Year	Mintage	VF	XF	Unc
481	AH1172	6	.020	—	Rare	—

13.5mm, 1.46 gm.
Oblique milling
(mm: Lotus 1812-1817)

C#	Date	Year	Mintage	VF	XF	Unc
481a	AH1172	6	.104	3.75	5.50	8.50

Oblique milling
(mm: Closed form lotus 1817-1835)

C#	Date	Year	Mintage	VF	XF	Unc
481b	AH1172	6	10.790	3.00	4.50	6.50

MINT: CALCUTTA

(mm: Rose 1823-1825)
Oblique milling

C#	Date	Year	Mintage	VF	XF	Unc
481c	AH1172	6	—	3.50	5.00	7.50

4 ANNAS

SILVER, 17mm, 2.97 gm.

C#	Date	Mintage	VG	Fine	VF	XF
542	(1808)	.044	25.00	40.00	55.00	75.00

1/4 RUPEE

SILVER, 15.5mm, 2.86 gm.

MINT: ARCOT

C#	Date	Year	VG	Fine	VF	XF
467	ND	6 (frozen)	4.00	7.00	10.00	15.00

MINT: MASULIPATAM

(mm: Lotus)
13.2mm, 2.81gm.
Similar to 1/4 Rupee, C#467, but with AH date.

C#	Date					
512	AH1200	—	—	—	—	—
	1210	—	—	—	—	—

MINT: MADRAS
(mm: Lotus 1807)
16.5mm, 3.02 gm.
Oblique milling

C#	Date	Year	Mintage	VF	XF	Unc
482	AH1172	6	.018	—	Rare	—

17.4mm, 2.91 gm.
Indented cord milling
(mm: Lotus 1812-1817)

C#	Date	Year	Mintage	VF	XF	Unc
482a	AH1172	6	.784	5.00	7.50	12.50
	1176	6	Inc. Ab.	12.50	18.50	27.50

Indented cord milling
(mm: Closed form lotus 1817-1835)

C#	Date	Year	Mintage	VF	XF	Unc
482b	AH1172	6	5.227	4.50	6.00	9.00

MINT: CALCUTTA
(mm: Rose 1823-1825)
Vertical milling

C#	Date	Year	Mintage	VF	XF	Unc
482c	AH1172	6	—	5.00	6.50	10.00

Plain Edge
(mm: Rose, crescent added 1830-1835)

C#	Date	Year	Mintage	VF	XF	Unc
482d	AH1172	6	—	4.50	6.00	10.00
	1172	6	—	—	Proof	75.00

1/2 RUPEE

SILVER, 17mm, 5.72 gm.
MINT: ARCOT
(mm: Lotus)
Similar to 1/2 Rupee, C#513, but w/o date.

C#	Date	Year	VG	Fine	VF	XF
468	ND	6 (Frozen)	6.50	8.50	11.50	16.50

MINT: MASULIPATAM
16.4mm, 5.64 gm.

C#	Date	Year	VG	Fine	VF	XF
513	AH1198	—	—	—	—	—
	1199	2	—	—	—	—
	1204	—	—	—	—	—

MINT: MADRAS
(mm: Lotus 1807)
22mm, 6.05 gm.
Oblique milling

C#	Date	Year	Mintage	VF	XF	Unc
483	AH1172	6	.108	10.00	15.00	22.50

21.7mm, 5.83 gm.
Indented cord milling

C#	Date	Year	Mintage	VF	XF	Unc
483a	AH1172	6	3.392	6.50	8.50	12.50
	1176	6	Inc. Ab.	12.50	20.00	30.00

(mm: Closed formed lotus 1817-1835)

C#	Date	Year	Mintage	VF	XF	Unc
483b	AH1172	6	10.674	6.50	8.50	12.50

MINT: CALCUTTA
(mm: Rose 1823-1825)
Vertical milling

C#	Date	Year	Mintage	VF	XF	Unc
483c	AH1172	6	—	6.50	8.50	12.50

(mm: Rose, crescent added 1830-1835)
Plain edge

C#	Date	Year	Mintage	VF	XF	Unc
483d	AH1172	6	—	6.50	8.50	13.50
	1172	6	—	—	Proof	85.00

RUPEE

SILVER, 20-25mm, 11.43 gm.
MINT: ARCOT
(mm: Lotus)
Similar to C#514, but w/o date.

C#	Date	Year	VG	Fine	VF	XF
469	ND(1755)	2	12.50	14.50	17.50	22.50
	ND(1756)	3	12.50	14.50	17.50	22.50
	ND(1757)	4	12.50	14.50	17.50	22.50
	ND(1758)	5	12.50	14.50	17.50	22.50
	ND(1759)	6	11.50	14.00	16.50	20.00

NOTE: The year 6 was a frozen date struck until 1809.

MINT: MASULIPATAM
21.2mm, 11.26 gm.

C#	Date	Year	VG	Fine	VF	XF
514	AH1197	2	—	—	—	—
	1205	—	—	—	—	—
	1211	—	—	—	—	—
	1212	—	—	—	—	—
	1213	—	—	—	—	—

MINT: MADRAS
(mm: Lotus 1807)
28mm, 12.1 gm.
Oblique milling

C#	Date	Year	Mintage	VF	XF	Unc
484	AH1172	6	2.145	12.50	14.50	18.50

27.8mm, 11.66 gm.
Indented cord milling
(mm: Lotus 1812-1817)

C#	Date	Year	Mintage	VF	XF	Unc
484a	AH1172	6	10.939	12.00	14.00	17.50
	1176	6	Inc. Ab.	14.50	21.50	30.00

(mm: Closed form lotus 1817-1835)

C#	Date	Year	Mintage	VF	XF	Unc
484b	AH1172	6	63.116	4.50	6.50	11.50

MINT: CALCUTTA
(mm: Rose 1823-1825)
Vertical milling

C#	Date	Year	Mintage	VF	XF	Unc
484c	AH1172	6	—	5.50	7.50	12.50

(mm: Rose, crescent added 1830-1835)
Plain edge

C#	Date	Year	Mintage	VF	XF	Unc
484d	AH1172	6	—	5.50	7.50	12.50
	1172	6	—	—	Proof	150.00

NOTE: Dump rupees in the name of Alamgir, with a small crescent to left of regnal year and mint name "Arcot", were struck by the French (see INDIA-FRENCH) as were Arcot rupees in the names of other Mughal emperors.

2 RUPEES

SILVER, 32.4mm, 22.55 gm.

MINT: MASULIPATAM

P#	Date	Year	Mintage	Fine	VF	XF
291	AH1194	2	—	—	Rare	—

NOTE: Previously catalogued in BMC (#145) as a double rupee it is believed the above is a specimen strike.

MINT: MADRAS

(mm: Lotus 1807)

39.5mm, 24.19 gm.

C#	Date	Year	Mintage	VG	Fine	VF
485	AH1172	2	.165	100.00	160.00	225.00
	1172	6	Inc. Ab.	100.00	160.00	225.00

NOTE: Struck over Spanish or Spanish Colonial 8 Reales.

1/4 MOHUR

GOLD, 17.4mm, 2.91 gm.

(mm: Lotus 1817)

MINT: MADRAS

C#	Date	Year	Mintage	VF	XF	Unc
492	AH1172	6	2,000	200.00	275.00	375.00

17mm

C#	Date	Mintage	Fine	VF	XF	Unc
456	(1819)	.092	75.00	100.00	125.00	165.00

1/3 MOHUR

GOLD, 19.5mm, 3.88 gm.

C#	Date	Mintage	Fine	VF	XF	Unc
457	(1820)	2.180	100.00	135.00	165.00	225.00

1/2 MOHUR

GOLD, 21.7mm, 5.83 gm.

MINT: MADRAS

(mm: Lotus 1817)

C#	Date	Year	Mintage	VF	XF	Unc
493	AH1172	6	7,500	225.00	265.00	325.00

21.2mm

C#	Date	Mintage	Fine	VF	XF	Unc
458	(1819)	.213	175.00	200.00	250.00	300.00

MOHUR

GOLD, 27.8mm, 11.66 gm.

MINT: MADRAS

(mm: Lotus 1817)

C#	Date	Year	Mintage	VF	XF	Unc
494	AH1172	6	.059	225.00	275.00	335.00

28mm

C#	Date	Mintage	Fine	VF	XF	Unc
459	(1819)	1.118	165.00	200.00	250.00	300.00

COLONIAL ISSUES

This section lists the coins of British India from reign of William IV (1835) to the reign of George VI (1947). The issues are divided into two main parts:

Coins struck under the authority of the East India Company (E.I.C.) from 1835 to 1858 (1862).

Coins struck under the authority of the Crown (Regal issues) from 1862 until 1947.

The first regal issues bear the date 1862 and were struck with the date 1862 unchanged until 1874. From then onward all coins bear the year date. The copper coins dated 1862 have not yet been fully attributed and therefore are not listed by the mint of issue.

In 1877 Queen Victoria was proclaimed Empress of India and the title of the obverse legend was changed accordingly.

RULERS

British until 1947

MINT MARKS

The coins of British India were struck at the following mints, indicated in the catalogue by capital letters after the date.

B-Bombay, 1835-1947
C-Calcutta, 1835-1947
I-Bombay, 1918
L-Lahore, 1943-1945
M-Madras, 1869 (closed Sept. 1869)
P-Pretoria, South Africa, 1943-1944

In 1947 British rule came to an end and India was divided into two self-governing countries, India and Pakistan. In 1971 Bangladash seceded from Pakistan. All are now independent republics and although they are still members of the British Commonwealth of Nations, their coinages do not belong to the British India series.

MONETARY SYSTEM

3 Pies = 1 Pice
4 Pice = 1 Anna
16 Annas = 1 Rupee
15 Rupees = 1 Mohur

The transition from the coins of the Moslem monetary system began with the silver pattern Rupees of William IV, 1834, issued by the East India Company, with the value on the reverse, given in English, Bengali, Persian and Nagari characters. This coinage was struck for several years, as dated, except for the currency Rupee which was struck from 1835 to 1840, all dated 1835.

The portrait coins issued by the East India Company for Victoria show two different head designs on the obverse, which are called Type I and Type II. The coins with Type I head have a continuous obverse legend and were struck from 1840 to 1851. The coins with the Type II head have a divided obverse legend and were struck from 1850 (Calcutta) until 1862. The date on the coins remained unchanged, Rupee, 1/2 Rupee and 1/4 Rupee are dated 1840, the 2 Annas and the Mohur are dated 1841. Both issues were struck at the Calcutta, Bombay and Madras Mints.

Type I coins have on the reverse a dot after the date, those of Type II have no dot, except for some rare 1/4 Rupees and 2 Annas. The latter are mules, struck from reverse dies of the preceding issue.

The following initials appear on the obverse on the truncation of the head:

S Incuse (Type I)
WW raised or incuse (Type II)
WWS or SWW (Type II)
WWB raised (Type II)

On both issues, the "S" is the initial of Major, later Lt. Col., J. T. Smith, mintmaster at Madras from 1840-1855. The 'B' which occurs only on Rupees of Type II, is the initial of Major, later Lt. Col. J.H. Bell (mintmaster at Madras, 1855-1859). The initials WW which appear on all coins of Type II, are those of William Wyon, Chief Engraver of the Royal Mint, London, who prepared this obverse design in 1849.

East India Company

(Coinage for all India)

1/12 ANNA

(1 Pie)

COPPER

Bombay, 18.0mm; Madras, 17.8mm.

C#	Date	Mintage	Fine	VF	XF	Unc
865	1835B	72.313	1.00	2.50	4.00	6.00
	1835M	133.788	.75	2.00	3.00	4.50
	1848C	14.380	1.25	3.00	5.00	7.50

1/2 PICE

COPPER

C#	Date	Mintage	Fine	VF	XF	Unc
866	1853C	62.408	1.75	3.75	4.50	9.00

1/4 ANNA

COPPER

Obv: Large lions

Calcutta, 26.2mm; Bombay, 25.2mm; Madras, 25.5mm.

C#	Date	Mintage	Fine	VF	XF	Unc
867	1835C	755.059	1.00	2.00	3.75	7.50
	1835B	126.131	1.00	2.00	3.75	7.50
	1835M	186.529	1.00	2.00	3.75	7.50

Obv: Small lions

C#	Date	Mintage	Fine	VF	XF	Unc
867.1	1849	—	—	—	Proof	75.00
	1857H	47.040	1.00	2.00	3.00	6.00
	1858	Inc. Ab.	.75	1.50	2.25	4.50

1/2 ANNA

COPPER
Bombay, 29.7mm; Madras, 30.8mm.

C#	Date	Mintage	Fine	VF	XF	Unc
868	1835B	17.270	2.00	4.00	7.50	15.00
	1835M	95.202	2.00	4.00	7.50	15.00
	1845C	17.160	2.00	4.00	7.50	15.00

2 ANNAS

1.4600 gm., .917 SILVER, .0430 oz ASW
Obv: Legend continuous (Type I)
Calcutta, 15.4-15.5 mm. Rev: Type I, mintmark "crescent" on left ribbon bow; Bombay, 15.8mm; Madras, 'S' incuse.

Y#	Date	Mintage	Fine	VF	XF	Unc
1.1	1841C	—	2.00	3.75	6.00	11.50
	1841B	—	2.00	3.75	6.00	11.50

Obv: With S incuse on truncation.

Y#	Date	Mintage	Fine	VF	XF	Unc
1.2	1841M	11.880	3.50	6.00	9.00	18.00

Obv: Legend divided (Type II).
Rev: Type I, dot after date.

Y#	Date	Mintage	Fine	VF	XF	Unc
1a.1	1841	—	7.50	12.50	18.50	37.50

Obv: W.W. raised on truncation

Y#	Date	Mintage	Fine	VF	XF	Unc
1a.2	1841C	—	1.50	3.00	4.50	9.00

S incuse, W.W. raised.

Y#	Date	Mintage	Fine	VF	XF	Unc
1a.3	1841B	—	1.50	3.00	4.50	9.00

S incuse, W.W. raised.

Y#	Date	Mintage	Fine	VF	XF	Unc
1a.4	1841M	—	1.75	3.50	6.00	11.50

WW raised.

Y#	Date	Mintage	Fine	VF	XF	Unc
1a.5	1849	—	—		Proof Only	80.00

1/4 RUPEE

2.9200 gm., .917 SILVER, .0860 oz ASW
Obv: No initial on truncation.

Rev: Dot after date.

C#	Date	Mintage	Fine	VF	XF	Unc
872.1	1835.B	—	3.50	6.00	9.00	18.00

Obv: F raised on truncation (for mintmaster Forbes).

C#	Date	Mintage	Fine	VF	XF	Unc
872.2	1835.C	—	4.50	7.50	11.50	22.50

Obv: F incuse.

C#	Date	Mintage	Fine	VF	XF	Unc
872.3	1835.C	—	3.50	6.00	9.00	18.00

Obv: No initial on truncation.
Rev: No dot after date.

C#	Date	Mintage	Fine	VF	XF	Unc
872.4	1835B	—	5.00	10.00	15.00	30.00

Obv: F incuse on truncation.

C#	Date	Mintage	Fine	VF	XF	Unc
872.5	1835C	—	5.00	10.00	15.00	30.00

Obv: RS incuse on truncation.

C#	Date	Mintage	Fine	VF	XF	Unc
872.6	1835C	—	5.00	10.00	15.00	30.00

Obv: RS incuse. Rev: Urdu denomination variety.

C#	Date	Mintage	Fine	VF	XF	Unc
872.7	1835C	—	15.00	27.50	37.50	75.00

Obverse legend continuous (Type I)
Calcutta, 19.5mm, type I, mintmark "crescent" on left ribbon bow on Reverse Bombay, 19.7mm; Madras, "S" inc. or raised. Madras coins of type I have also a small, raised "V" on the lower part of the right ribbon bow.

First reverse: 20 berries

Y#	Date	Mintage	Fine	VF	XF	Unc
2.1	1840C	—	3.50	4.50	6.00	12.00
	1840B	—	3.50	4.50	6.00	12.00

First rev: S incuse on truncation.

Y#	Date	Mintage	Fine	VF	XF	Unc
2.2	1840M	7.320	4.50	7.50	11.50	22.50

Second reverse: 34 berries

Y#	Date	Mintage	Fine	VF	XF	Unc
2.3	1840C	—	3.50	4.50	7.50	13.50

Obv: Legend divided (Type II).
Dot after date, second reverse of Type I.

Y#	Date	Mintage	Fine	VF	XF	Unc
2a.1	1840.	—	15.00	20.00	30.00	60.00

Obv: W.W. raised on truncation.

Y#	Date	Mintage	Fine	VF	XF	Unc
2a.2	1840C	—	3.50	4.50	6.00	12.00

Obv: W.W. raised.

Y#	Date	Mintage	Fine	VF	XF	Unc
2a.3	1840B	—	3.50	4.50	6.50	13.50

Obv: W.W. and S raised.

Y#	Date	Mintage	Fine	VF	XF	Unc
2a.4	1840M	—	4.00	7.50	11.50	22.50

Obv: W.W. incuse.

Y#	Date	Mintage	Fine	VF	XF	Unc
2a.5	1846B	—	5.00	10.00	15.00	30.00
	1849	—	—		Proof only	80.00

Obv: W.W. raised

Y#	Date	Mintage	Fine	VF	XF	Unc
2a.6	1849	—	—		Proof only	80.00

1/2 RUPEE

5.8300 gm., .917 SILVER, .1719 oz ASW
Obv: Without initial on truncation.

C#	Date	Mintage	Fine	VF	XF	Unc
873.1	1835.B	—	8.00	15.00	22.50	45.00

Obv: F raised on truncation.

C#	Date	Mintage	Fine	VF	XF	Unc
873.2	1835.C	—	8.00	15.00	22.50	45.00

With F incuse

C#	Date	Mintage	Fine	VF	XF	Unc
873.3	1835.C	—	8.00	15.00	22.50	45.00

Obv: RS incuse.

C#	Date	Mintage	Fine	VF	XF	Unc
873.4	1835.C	—	10.00	20.00	30.00	60.00

Obv: Legend continuous (Type I)
Calcutta, 24.2-24.4mm, Type I, mintmark 'crescent' on left ribbon bow on reverse (Bombay, 24.5—24.6mm) Madras, 'S' incuse on truncation.

Obv: Without initial on truncation.

Y#	Date	Mintage	Fine	VF	XF	Unc
3.1	1840C	—	6.50	10.00	15.00	30.00
	1840B	—	6.50	9.00	12.50	25.00

Obv: S incuse on truncation.

Y#	Date	Mintage	Fine	VF	XF	Unc
3.2	1840M	1.870	12.00	20.00	30.00	60.00

Obv: Legend divided (Type II),
'W.W.' incuse on truncation.

Y#	Date	Mintage	Fine	VF	XF	Unc
3a.1	1840C	—	6.50	8.50	12.50	25.00

Obv: W.W. raised.

Y#	Date	Mintage	Fine	VF	XF	Unc
3a.2	1840C	—	6.50	7.50	9.00	18.00
	1840B	—	7.50	12.50	16.50	33.50

Obv: W.W. incuse and S raised.

Y#	Date	Mintage	Fine	VF	XF	Unc
3a.3	1840M	—	7.00	11.00	15.00	30.00

Obv: W.W. and S incuse.

Y#	Date	Mintage	Fine	VF	XF	Unc
3a.4	1840M	—	7.00	11.00	15.00	30.00

Obv: W.W. incuse.

Y#	Date	Mintage	Fine	VF	XF	Unc
3a.5	1849	—	—		Proof Only	90.00

RUPEE

11.6600 gm., .917 SILVER, .3438 oz ASW
Obv: No initial on truncation.

C#	Date	Mintage	Fine	VF	XF	Unc
874.1	1835.B	—	11.50	13.50	17.50	25.00

Obv: F raised on truncation.

C#	Date	Mintage	Fine	VF	XF	Unc
874.2	1835.C	—	11.50	13.50	17.50	25.00

Obv: F incuse.

C#	Date	Mintage	Fine	VF	XF	Unc
874.3	1835.C	—	11.50	13.50	18.50	27.50

Obv: RS incuse.

C#	Date	Mintage	Fine	VF	XF	Unc
874.4	1835.C	—	12.50	15.00	20.00	30.00

Obv: No initial.

C#	Date	Mintage	Fine	VF	XF	Unc
874.5	1840/35.	—	75.00	125.00	175.00	250.00

Obv: F raised on truncation.

C#	Date	Mintage	Fine	VF	XF	Unc
874.6	1840	—	50.00	70.00	100.00	150.00

Obverse legend continuous (Type I)

The major reverse varieties occur on the Type I Rupees of all three mints. The first reverse has 19 berries in the wreath, the second reverse has 34 and 35 berries (Calcutta) and 35 berries (Bombay and Madras). There are several minor varieties of the first reverse, but these are not listed. Type I Rupees are attributed to the mint of issue as follows: Calcutta, mintmark "crescent" on left ribbon bow on reverse, 1st reverse 31.5mm, 2nd reverse 31.1-31.3mm; Bombay, 31.6-31.8mm; Madras, 31.9-32.2mm. Madras specimens of Type I with the 1st reverse also have a small, raised "V" on the lower part of the right ribbon bow, 31.9-32mm.

Y#	Date	Mintage	Fine	VF	XF	Unc
	19 berries, large date, mm: U					
4.1	1840.C	—	11.50	13.50	15.00	22.50
	35 berries, no initial					
4.2	1840.B	—	11.50	13.50	15.00	22.50
	19 berries, small diamonds					
4.3	1840.B	—	11.50	13.50	15.00	22.50
	19 berries, large diamonds					
4.4	1840.B	—	11.50	13.50	15.00	22.50
	19 berries, small diamonds					
4.5	1840.M	23.300	12.50	15.00	18.50	27.50
	19 berries, large diamonds					
4.6	1840.M	Inc. Ab.	12.50	15.00	18.50	27.50
	19 berries, S incuse					
4.7	1840.M	Inc. Ab.	12.50	15.00	18.50	27.50
	35 berries, S incuse					
4.8	1840.M	Inc. Ab.	13.50	17.50	25.00	37.50

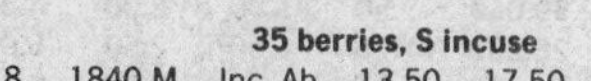

Obverse legend divided (Type II)
Calcutta, 30.5mm; Bombay, 30.8mm; Madras, W.W.S raised and W.W.B raised

Y#	Date	Mintage	Fine	VF	XF	Unc
	28 berries, W.W. raised, small diamonds					
4a.1	1840C	—	11.50	13.00	15.00	22.50
	28 berries, W.W. raised, large diamonds					
4a.2	1840C	—	11.50	13.00	15.00	22.50
	27 berries, W.W. raised					
4a.3	1840B	—	11.50	13.00	15.00	22.50
	28 berries, W.W.B raised, small B					
4a.4	1840M	—	12.50	15.00	18.50	27.50
	28 berries, W.W.B raised, large B					
4a.5	1840M	—	12.50	15.00	18.50	27.50
	28 berries, W.W.B raised, small letters					
4a.6	1840M	—	12.50	15.00	18.50	27.50
	28 berries, W.W.S raised					
4a.7	1840M	—	12.50	16.50	21.50	30.00
	Variety not specified					
4a.8	1849	—	—		Proof only	150.00

MOHUR

11.6600 gm., .917 GOLD, .3437 oz AGW
Obv: No initial

C#	Date	Mintage	Fine	VF	XF	Unc
878.1	1835	—	275.00	375.00	500.00	700.00
878a.1	1835	—	—		Proof Restrike	400.00
	Obv: RS incuse on truncation.					
878.2	1835	—	275.00	375.00	500.00	700.00
878a.2	1835	—	—		Proof Restrike	400.00

Obv: F incuse on truncation.

Y#	Date	Mintage	Fine	VF	XF	Unc
878.3	1835	—	275.00	375.00	500.00	700.00
878a.3	1835	—	—		Proof Restrike	400.00

Obverse legend continuous (Type I)

The Type I Mohur was struck at all three East India Company Mints, (b)-Bombay, (c)-Calcutta, and (m)-Madras. The Type II Mohur was struck only at Calcutta and Bombay. So far, it has not been possible to distinguish between the issues of the Calcutta and Bombay Mint but the coins are listed separately below as the Bombay issue eventually will be identified. Only a very small number of pieces were struck at the Bombay Mint of Type II.

Y#	Date	Mintage	Fine	VF	XF	Unc
A4	1841	4,736	—	—	Rare	—
	1841.C	.330	275.00	350.00	400.00	500.00
	Obv: S incuse on truncation.					
A4.1	1841.M	.030	300.00	375.00	450.00	600.00

Obverse legend divided (Type II)

Y#	Date	Mintage	Fine	VF	XF	Unc
A4a	1841.C with W.W. incuse, regular 4	—	275.00	325.00	375.00	450.00
	1841.C with W.W. incuse, crosslet 4	—	275.00	350.00	400.00	500.00
	1841B	—	—	—	Rare	—

2 MOHURS

23.3200 gm., .917 GOLD, .6873 oz AGW
With RS incuse on truncation

C#	Date	Mintage	Fine	VF	XF	Unc
879	1835.	1,000	850.00	1250.	1750.	2750.
	1835.	—	—	—	Proof	3000.
879a	1835. (restrike)		—	—	Proof	1250.

REGAL ISSUES

1/12 ANNA

NOTE: The coins dated 1862 were struck at Calcutta, Bombay and Madras but have not yet been attributed to the mint of issue. Calcutta Mint issues 1874-76 are 17.3mm in diameter. From 1877 the coins have a diameter of 17.5mm and the obverse legend at the lower right is distant from the bust. The issues dated 1882 and 1886 have a small incuse "C" on a bead of the circle below the date. Bombay issues 1874-76 have a diameter of 17.9mm, From 1877 the obverse legend at the lower right is close to the bust.

COPPER

Y#	Date	Mintage	Fine	VF	XF	Unc
5	1862C,B,M	—	1.00	1.50	2.50	5.00
	1874C	7.780	1.00	1.50	2.50	5.00
	1874B	Inc. Ab.	1.00	1.50	2.50	5.00
	1875C	7.714	1.00	1.50	2.50	5.00
	1875B	Inc. Ab.	1.00	1.50	2.50	5.00
	1876C	20.318	1.00	1.50	2.50	5.00
	1876B	Inc. Ab.	1.00	1.50	2.50	5.00

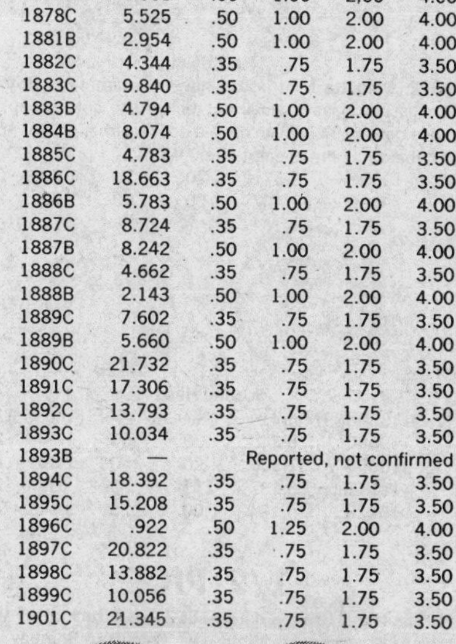

Y#	Date	Mintage	Fine	VF	XF	Unc
16	1877C	5.880	.50	1.00	2.00	4.00
	1877B	1.551	.50	1.00	2.00	4.00
	1878C	5.525	.50	1.00	2.00	4.00
	1881B	2.954	.50	1.00	2.00	4.00
	1882C	4.344	.35	.75	1.75	3.50
	1883C	9.840	.35	.75	1.75	3.50
	1883B	4.794	.50	1.00	2.00	4.00
	1884B	8.074	.50	1.00	2.00	4.00
	1885C	4.783	.35	.75	1.75	3.50
	1886C	18.663	.35	.75	1.75	3.50
	1886B	5.783	.50	1.00	2.00	4.00
	1887C	8.724	.35	.75	1.75	3.50
	1887B	8.242	.50	1.00	2.00	4.00
	1888C	4.662	.35	.75	1.75	3.50
	1888B	2.143	.50	1.00	2.00	4.00
	1889C	7.602	.35	.75	1.75	3.50
	1889B	5.660	.50	1.00	2.00	4.00
	1890C	21.732	.35	.75	1.75	3.50
	1891C	17.306	.35	.75	1.75	3.50
	1892C	13.793	.35	.75	1.75	3.50
	1893C	10.034	.35	.75	1.75	3.50
	1893B	—		Reported, not confirmed		
	1894C	18.392	.35	.75	1.75	3.50
	1895C	15.208	.35	.75	1.75	3.50
	1896C	.922	.50	1.25	2.00	4.00
	1897C	20.822	.35	.75	1.75	3.50
	1898C	13.882	.35	.75	1.75	3.50
	1899C	10.056	.35	.75	1.75	3.50
	1901C	21.345	.35	.75	1.75	3.50

Thick planchets

NOTE: All were struck at the Calcutta Mint. Until 1906 the pieces were struck in copper. Later issues are in bronze on thinner planchets. Both types occur dated 1906.

Y#	Date	Mintage	Fine	VF	XF	Unc
27	1903C	7.883	.25	.50	.85	1.75
	1904C	16.506	.25	.50	.85	1.75
	1905C	—	.25	.50	.85	1.75
	1906C	—	.25	.50	.85	1.75
	BRONZE, thinner planchets					
27a	1906C	—	.30	.75	1.75	3.50
	1907C	—	.25	.50	.85	1.75
	1908C	—	.25	.50	.85	1.75
	1909C	—	.25	.50	.85	1.75
	1910C	—	.25	.50	.85	1.75

NOTE: Calcutta Mint issues have no mintmark. Bombay Mint issues have a small raised bead or dot below the center of the date.

Y#	Date	Mintage	Fine	VF	XF	Unc
35	1912C	—	.25	.50	.75	1.50
	1913C	25.937	.15	.30	.45	.90
	1914C	29.184	.10	.25	.35	.65
	1915C	20.563	.10	.25	.35	.65
	1916C	12.230	.10	.25	.35	.65
	1917C	26.880	.10	.25	.35	.65
	1918C	29.088	.10	.25	.35	.65
	1919C	20.686	.10	.25	.35	.65
	1920C	42.201	.10	.25	.35	.65
	1921C	19.334	.10	.25	.35	.65
	1923C	6.662	.10	.25	.35	.65
	1923B	4.877	.10	.25	.35	.65
	1924C	2.515	.10	.30	.45	.90
	1924B	11.711	.10	.25	.35	.65
	1925C	6.106	.10	.25	.35	.65
	1925B	5.871	.10	.25	.35	.65
	1926C	4.147	.10	.25	.35	.65
	1926B	18.406	.10	.25	.35	.65
	1927C	2.880	.10	.30	.40	.80
	1927B	4.846	.10	.25	.35	.65
	1928C	11.846	.10	.15	.25	.50
	1928B	8.077	.10	.15	.25	.50
	1929C	15.130	.10	.15	.25	.50
	1930C	13.498	.10	.15	.25	.50

Y#	Date	Mintage	Fine	VF	XF	Unc
35	1931C	18.278	.10	.15	.25	.50
	1932C	23.213	.10	.15	.25	.50
	1933C	16.896	.10	.15	.25	.50
	1934C	17.146	.10	.15	.25	.50
	1935C	19.142	.10	.15	.25	.50
	1936C	23.213	.10	.15	.25	.50
	1936B	12.887	.10	.15	.25	.50

First Head

NOTE: Calcutta Mint issues have no mintmark. Bombay Mint issues have a small dot below the date except for those dated 1942 which have a dot on either side of ANNA and the date, and one dot after "INDIA".

Y#	Date	Mintage	Fine	VF	XF	Unc
47	1939C	3.571	.20	.50	1.00	2.00
	1939B	17.407	.20	.50	1.00	2.00

Second Head

Y#	Date	Mintage	Fine	VF	XF	Unc
47a	1938	(restrike)	—	—	Proof	12.50
	1939C	5.245	.20	.50	1.00	2.00
	1939B	31.306	.20	.50	1.00	2.00
	1941B	6.137	.15	.25	.50	1.00
	1942B	6.124	1.00	2.25	3.50	7.00

1/2 PICE

NOTE: The 1/2 Pice dated 1862 was struck at all three Indian Government Mints i.e. Calcutta, Bombay and Madras but a correct attribution to the mint of issue has not yet been possible. Two different busts and two reverses have been noted so far. It is hoped that these pieces can be listed correctly by mint of issue in future editions of this catalogue. All later issues were struck at the Calcutta Mint.

COPPER

Y#	Date	Mintage	Fine	VF	XF	Unc
6	1862C,B,M	—	1.25	2.25	4.50	9.00
	1875	—	—		Proof only	60.00
	1877	(restrike)	—	—	Proof	15.00

Y#	Date	Mintage	Fine	VF	XF	Unc
17	1885	6.206	1.25	2.50	3.75	7.50
	1886	7.733	1.25	2.50	3.75	7.50
	1887	6.464	1.25	2.50	3.75	7.50
	1888	3.190	1.25	2.50	3.75	7.50
	1889	7.587	1.25	2.50	3.75	7.50
	1890	3.504	1.25	2.50	3.75	7.50
	1891	5.139	1.25	2.50	3.75	7.50
	1892	4.774	1.25	2.50	3.75	7.50
	1893	7.005	1.00	1.75	3.50	7.00
	1894	7.777	1.25	2.50	3.75	7.50
	1895	9.874	1.00	1.75	3.50	7.00
	1896	6.113	1.25	2.50	3.75	7.50
	1897	8.484	1.25	2.50	3.75	7.50
	1898	12.940	1.00	1.75	3.50	7.00
	1899	7.936	1.25	2.50	3.75	7.50
	1900	5.219	1.25	2.50	3.75	7.50
	1901	16.057	1.25	2.50	3.75	7.50

NOTE: All were struck at the Calcutta Mint.

Y#	Date	Mintage	Fine	VF	XF	Unc
28	1903	5.376	.75	1.50	3.00	6.00
	1904	8.464	.75	1.50	3.00	6.00
	1905	—	.75	1.50	3.00	6.00
	1906	—	.75	1.50	3.00	6.00

BRONZE, thinner planchets

Y#	Date	Mintage	Fine	VF	XF	Unc
28a	1906	—	.75	1.50	3.00	6.00
	1907	—	.75	1.50	3.00	6.00
	1908	—	.75	1.50	3.00	6.00
	1909	—	.50	1.00	2.75	5.50
	1910	—	.75	1.50	3.00	6.00

NOTE: All were struck at the Calcutta Mint.

Y#	Date	Mintage	Fine	VF	XF	Unc
36	1912	—	.25	.50	.75	1.50
	1913	12.912	.25	.50	.75	1.50
	1914	10.022	.15	.30	.50	1.00
	1915	8.653	.15	.30	.50	1.00
	1916	5.875	.15	.30	.50	1.00
	1917	13.094	.15	.30	.50	1.00
	1918	4.608	.15	.30	.50	1.00
	1919	13.516	.15	.30	.50	1.00
	1920	7.436	.15	.30	.50	1.00
	1921	6.131	.15	.30	.50	1.00
	1922	4.941	.15	.30	.50	1.00
	1923	6.272	.15	.30	.50	1.00
	1924	10.624	.15	.30	.50	1.00
	1925	3.622	.15	.30	.50	1.00
	1926	6.528	.15	.30	.50	1.00
	1927	6.528	.15	.30	.50	1.00
	1928	7.332	.15	.30	.50	1.00
	1929	7.654	.15	.30	.50	1.00
	1930	7.181	.15	.30	.50	1.00
	1931	8.794	.15	.30	.50	1.00
	1932	5.440	.15	.30	.50	1.00
	1933	9.242	.15	.30	.50	1.00
	1934	8.947	.15	.30	.50	1.00
	1935	15.501	.10	.20	.35	.75
	1936	26.726	.10	.15	.30	.60

Obv: First head, high relief.

NOTE: Calcutta Mint issues have no mintmark. Bombay Mint issues have a small dot below the date.

Y#	Date	Mintage	Fine	VF	XF	Unc
49	1938C	11.162	.25	.50	.75	1.50
	1939C	8.834	.15	.40	.65	1.25
	1939B	2.456	.15	.40	.65	1.25
	1940C	30.668	.15	.40	.65	1.25

Obv: Second head, low relief.

Y#	Date	Mintage	Fine	VF	XF	Unc
49a	1939B	6.890	.35	.75	1.50	3.00

NOTE: 1942 proof restrikes exist in quantity, $8.00.

1/4 ANNA

COPPER

NOTE: The one quarter Anna dated 1862 was struck at Calcutta, Bombay and Madras but the coins have not yet been correctly attributed to the mint of issue. From 1874 onward the issues from the Calcutta and Bombay have a distinctive type of reverse and the coins are identified as follows:

On Calcutta Mint issues the floral design has a leaf below the center of the date. Some specimens dated 1879-1887 have also as a mintmark, a tiny incuse "C" on a bead of the beaded circle, below the center of the date.

On Bombay Mint issues the floral design has a leaf below the first and the last numeral of the date.

Y#	Date	Mintage	Fine	VF	XF	Unc
7	1862C,B,M	—	.75	1.50	2.25	4.50
	1874C	44.678	.75	1.50	2.50	5.00
	1875C	36.237	.75	1.50	2.50	5.00
	1875B	14.494	.75	1.50	2.50	5.00
	1876C	43.581	.75	1.50	2.50	5.00

Y#	Date	Mintage	Fine	VF	XF	Unc
18	1877C	65.210	.75	1.50	2.50	5.00
	1877B	9.320	.75	1.50	2.50	5.00
	1878C	40.813	.75	1.50	2.50	5.00
	1879C	43.072	.50	1.00	2.00	4.00
	1880C	10.278	.35	.75	1.50	3.00
	1882C	52.291	.40	1.00	2.00	4.00
	1882B	12.409	.75	1.50	2.50	5.00
	1883C	57.571	.75	1.50	2.50	5.00
	1883B	12.443	.75	1.50	2.50	5.00
	1884C	43.196	.50	1.00	2.00	4.00
	1884B	16.845	.75	1.50	2.50	5.00
	1885C	36.699	.50	1.00	2.00	4.00
	1886C	36.121	.50	1.00	2.00	4.00
	1886B	14.390	.75	1.50	2.50	5.00
	1887C	59.060	.50	1.00	2.00	4.00
	1887B	26.205	.75	1.50	2.50	5.00
	1888C	34.531	.75	1.50	2.50	5.00
	1888B	8.293	.75	1.50	2.50	5.00
	1889C	88.559	.35	.75	1.50	3.00
	1889B	19.110	.50	1.00	2.00	4.00
	1890C	82.909	.35	.75	1.50	3.00
	1891C	86.076	.35	.75	1.50	3.00
	1892C	68.131	.35	.75	1.50	3.00
	1893C	76.039	.35	.75	1.50	3.00
	1894C	45.744	.35	.75	1.50	3.00
	1895C	35.744	.35	.75	1.50	3.00
	1896C	109.853	.35	.75	1.50	3.00
	1897C	82.288	.35	.75	1.50	3.00
	1898C	12.118	.35	.75	1.50	3.00
	1899C	36.896	.35	.75	1.50	3.00
	1900C	30.534	.35	.75	1.50	3.00
	1901C	136.691	.35	.75	1.50	3.00

NOTE: All were struck at the Calcutta Mint.

Y#	Date	Mintage	Fine	VF	XF	Unc
29	1903C	105.974	.35	.75	1.50	3.00
	1904C	104.595	.35	.75	1.50	3.00
	1905C	—	.35	.75	1.50	3.00
	1906C	—	.35	.75	1.50	3.00

BRONZE, thinner planchets

Y#	Date	Mintage	Fine	VF	XF	Unc
29a	1906C	—	.35	.75	1.50	3.00
	1907C	—	.35	.75	1.50	3.00
	1908C	—	.35	.75	1.50	3.00
	1909C	—	.35	.75	1.50	3.00
	1910C	—	.35	.75	1.50	3.00

NOTE: Calcutta Mint issues have no mintmark. Bombay Mint issues have a small dot below the date. The pieces dated 1911, like the other coins with that date, show the "Pig" elephant.

Y#	Date	Mintage	Fine	VF	XF	Unc
37	1911C	—	.35	.75	1.50	3.00
	1912C	—	.20	.40	.75	1.50
	1913C	107.456	.20	.40	.75	1.50
	1914C	40.576	.15	.30	.50	1.00
	1916C	1.632	.15	.30	.50	1.00
	1917C	69.370	.15	.30	.50	1.00
	1918C	84.045	.15	.30	.50	1.00
	1919C	212.467	.15	.30	.50	1.00
	1920C	96.019	.15	.30	.50	1.00

Y#	Date	Mintage	Fine	VF	XF	Unc
37	1924B	16.322	.15	.30	.50	1.00
	1925C	14.253	.15	.30	.50	1.00
	1925B	14.588	.15	.30	.50	1.00
	1926C	17.389	.15	.30	.50	1.00
	1926B	16.073	.15	.30	.50	1.00
	1927C	—	.15	.30	.50	1.00
	1927B	12.440	.15	.30	.50	1.00
	1928C	25.779	.15	.30	.50	1.00
	1928B	10.057	.15	.30	.50	1.00
	1929C	64.000	.10	.20	.50	.75
	1930C	33.485	.15	.30	.50	1.00
	1930B	9.646	.15	.30	.50	1.00
	1931C	6.560	.15	.30	.50	1.00
	1933C	58.800	.10	.20	.35	.75
	1934C	85.862	.10	.35	.50	.75
	1935C	92.768	.10	.20	.35	.75
	1936C	225.344	.15	.30	.50	1.00
	1936B	81.812	.10	.20	.35	.75

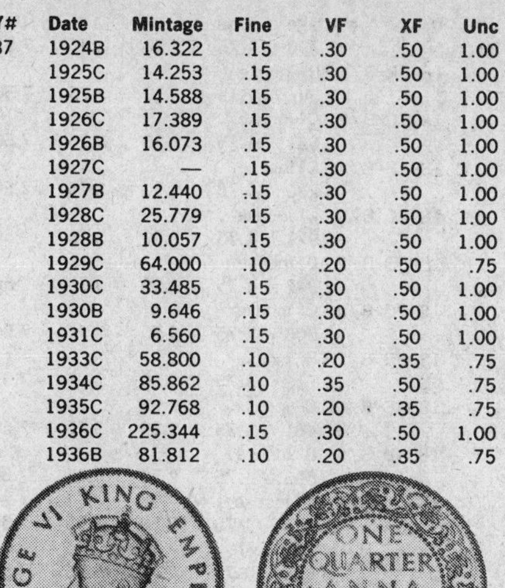

Obv: First head, high relief.

NOTE: Calcutta Mint issues have no mintmark. Bombay Mint issues have a small dot above N of "ONE."

Y#	Date	Mintage	Fine	VF	XF	Unc
50	1938C	33.465	.15	.25	.50	1.00
	1938B	63.000	.15	.25	.50	1.00
	1939C	28.843	.25	.50	1.00	2.00
	1939B	115.905	.25	.50	1.00	2.00
	1940B	164.241	.30	.75	1.50	3.00

Obv: Second head, low relief.

Y#	Date	Mintage	Fine	VF	XF	Unc
50a	1939C	Inc. Ab.	1.00	1.75	3.75	7.50
	1940C	93.510	.10	.20	.30	.60
	1940B	Inc. Ab.	.10	.20	.30	.60
	1941C	123.369	.15	.20	.35	.75
	1942C	34.298	.10	.20	.30	.60
	1942B	8.768	.10	.20	.30	.60

PICE

NOTE: There are three types of the crown, which is on the obverse at the top. These are shown below and are designated as (RC) Round Crown, (HC) High Crown, and (FC) Flat Crown. Calcutta Mint issues have no mintmark. The issues from the other mints have the mintmark below the date as following: Lahore, raised "L"; Pretoria, small round dot; Bombay, diamond dot or "large" round dot. On the Bombay issues dated 1944 the mintmark appears to be a large dot over a diamond.

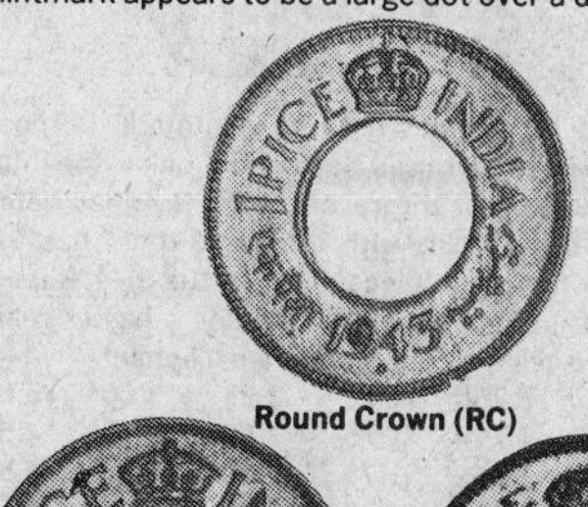

Round Crown (RC)

High Crown (HC) Flat Crown (FC)

BRONZE

Small date, small legend.

Y#	Date	Mintage	Fine	VF	XF	Unc
51	1943B (RC) diamond	164.659	.20	.40	.75	1.50

Large date, large legend.

Y#	Date	Mintage	Fine	VF	XF	Unc
51a	1943B (HC) large dot	—	.10	.20	.35	.75
	1943P (HC) small dot	—	.10	.20	.35	.75
	1944(C)HC	—	.10	.20	.35	.75
	1944B (HC) large dot	195.354	.10	.20	.35	.75
	1944B (HC) diamond	—	.10	.40	.65	1.35
	1944B FC large dot	—	—	.40	.65	1.35
	1944P (HC) small dot	—	.10	.40	.65	1.35
	1944L (HC)	—	.10	.20	.35	.75
	1945(C)FC	—	.10	.20	.35	.75
	1945B (FC) diamond	237.197	.10	.20	.35	.75
	1945B (FC) large dot	Inc. Ab.	.10	.20	.35	.75
	1945L (FC)	—	.10	.20	.35	.75
	1947(C)HC	97.092	.10	.30	.35	.75
	1947B (HC) diamond	43.654	.10	.20	.30	.60

1/2 ANNA

NOTE: The half Anna dated 1862 was struck at all three Indian Government Mints, i.e. Calcutta, Bombay and Madras but a correct attribution to the mint of issue has not yet been possible. The coins dated 1875-76 were struck at the Calcutta Mint, those dated 1877 were struck at Calcutta and Bombay. Two different busts occur on the 1877 issue.

BUST A-The bottom section of the front dress panel has a small flower in the upper left corner and a large flower at right of center.

BUST C-The bottom section of the front dress panel has a five-dotted flower at right of center.

NOTE: Bust B is the common obverse on 1862 issues and is not described here.

The Bombay issue dated 1877 was identified by the type of the date figure "7" which has a short horizontal stroke and a long downstroke. This type of "7" appears on most Bombay issues but not on any denomination of the Calcutta Mint.

COPPER

Y#	Date	Mintage	Fine	VF	XF	Unc
8	1862(C,B,M,)		5.00	10.00	18.50	37.50
	1875C, bust A	—	10.00	20.00	30.00	60.00
	1875	—	—	—	Proof	75.00
	1876C, bust A	3.437	8.50	15.00	25.00	50.00
19	1877C, bust C, wide short 7's in date	3.584	10.00	18.50	30.00	60.00
	1877B, bust A, narrow tall 7's in date	3.454	10.00	18.50	30.00	60.00
	1879B	—	—		Proof only	75.00
	1884C	—	—		Proof only	75.00
	1890B	—	—		Proof only	75.00
	1891B	—	—		Proof only	75.00
	1892B	—	—		Proof only	75.00
19	1893B	—	—		Proof only	75.00

NICKEL-BRASS

Obv: Second head

NOTE: Bombay Mint issues dated 1942-1945 have a dot before and after India and on each side of the date. Calcutta Mint issues dated 1942 have no dots. The Bombay Mint issues dated 1946 have "dash-dot-dash" before and after the date. Calcutta Mint issues dated 1946-47 have only a "dash" on both sides of the date.

Y#	Date	Mintage	Fine	VF	XF	Unc
52	1942C	159.000	.10	.15	.20	.30
	1942B	7.945	.15	.25	.35	.75
	1943B	437.760	.10	.15	.20	.30
	1944B	514.800	.10	.15	.20	.30
	1945B	222.996	.10	.15	.20	.30

COPPER-NICKEL

Obv: Second head

Y#	Date	Mintage	Fine	VF	XF	Unc
52a	1940B	(restrike)	—	—	Proof	10.00
	1946C	127.918	.10	.15	.25	.35
	1946B	38.214	.10	.15	.25	.35
	1947C	145.426	.10	.15	.25	.35

ANNA

NOTE: Struck only at the Bombay Mint, the pieces have as mintmark a small incuse "B" in the space below the cross pattee of the crown on the obverse.

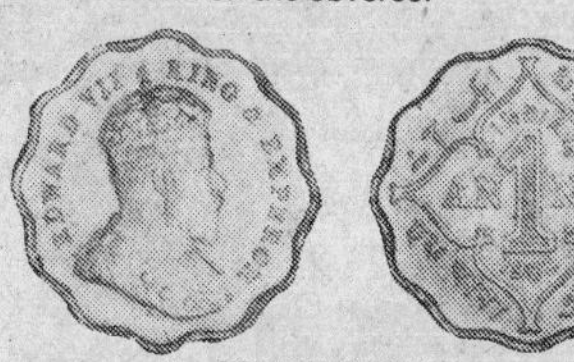

COPPER-NICKEL

Y#	Date	Mintage	Fine	VF	XF	Unc
30	1907B	37.256	.50	1.25	2.00	4.00
	1908B	22.536	.50	1.25	2.00	4.00
	1909B	24.800	.50	1.25	2.00	4.00
	1910B	40.200	.50	1.25	2.00	4.00

NOTE: Until 1920 all were struck at the Bombay Mint without mintmark. From 1923 on the Bombay Mint issues have a small raised bead or dot below the date. Calcutta Mint issues have no mintmark.

Y#	Date	Mintage	Fine	VF	XF	Unc
38	1912B	39.400	.40	1.00	1.50	3.00
	1913B	39.776	.40	1.00	1.50	3.00
	1914B	48.000	.25	.50	.85	1.75
	1915B	12.470	.25	.50	.85	1.75
	1916B	26.738	.25	.50	.85	1.75
	1917B	50.136	.25	.50	.85	1.75
	1918B	80.360	.25	.50	.85	1.75
	1919B	141.000	.25	.35	.75	1.50
	1920B	11.671	.25	.50	.85	1.75
	1923B	6.438	.25	.50	.85	1.75
	1924C	13.536	.25	.50	.85	1.75
	1924B	—	.25	.50	.85	1.75
	1925C	19.832	.25	.50	.85	1.75
	1925B	—	.25	.50	.85	1.75
	1926C	14.216	.25	.50	.85	1.75
	1926B	8.988	.25	.50	.85	1.75
	1927C	11.080	.25	.50	.85	1.75
	1927B	6.444	.25	.50	.85	1.75
	1928C	23.432	.25	.50	.85	1.75
	1928B	11.340	.25	.50	.85	1.75
	1929C	43.184	.25	.50	.85	1.75
	1930C	27.978	.25	.50	.85	1.75
	1933C	8.968	.25	.50	.85	1.75
	1934C	37.248	.25	.40	.75	1.50
	1935C	18.384	.25	.40	.75	1.50
	1935B	29.221	.25	.40	.75	1.50

Y#	Date	Mintage	Fine	VF	XF	Unc
38	1936C	4.008	.25	.40	.75	1.50
	1936B	91.689	.20	.35	.75	1.50

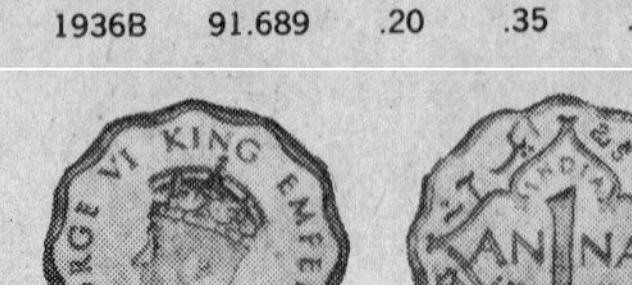

Obv: First head, high relief.

NOTE: Calcutta Mint issues have no mintmark. Bombay Mint issues have a small dot below the date.

Y#	Date	Mintage	Fine	VF	XF	Unc
53	1938C	—	.30	.75	1.50	3.00
	1938B	42.712	.30	.75	1.50	3.00
	1939C	47.192	.15	.40	.75	1.50
	1939B	10.057	.15	.40	.75	1.50
	1940B	—	.30	.75	1.50	3.00
	1940C	60.945	.30	.75	1.50	3.00

Obv: Second head, low relief.

Y#	Date	Mintage	Fine	VF	XF	Unc
53b	1940C	Inc. Ab.	.10	.25	.50	1.00
	1940B	144.712	.10	.25	.50	1.00
	1941C	98.967	.10	.15	.25	.50
	1941B	40.170	.10	.15	.25	.50
	1946C	130.872	.10	.15	.25	.50
	1946B	68.452	.10	.15	.25	.50
	1947C	126.093	.10	.25	.50	1.00
	1947B	50.096	.10	.15	.25	.50

NICKEL-BRASS
Obv: Second head.

Y#	Date	Mintage	Fine	VF	XF	Unc
53a	1942C	143.016	.10	.25	.50	1.00
	1942B	103.240	.10	.25	.50	1.00
	1943C	197.236	.10	.25	.50	1.00
	1943B	292.000	.10	.25	.50	1.00
	1944C	632.608	.10	.25	.50	1.00
	1944B	17.708	.10	.25	.50	1.00
	1945C	264.760	.10	.25	.50	1.00
	1945B	74.828	.10	.25	.50	1.00

2 ANNAS

NOTE: The distinguishing features of the two busts and two reverses are:

BUST A-The front dress panel has four sections. The last section has at left, three leaves, and a small indistinct flower in the upper right corner.

BUST B-The front dress panel has 3 1/2 sections. The last, incomplete section shows only three small leaf tops.

REVERSE I-Large top flower; the two large petals above the whorl are long and curved downward.

REVERSE II-Small top flower; the two large petals above the whorl are short and horizontal.

The 2 Annas dated 1862-76 have been re-attributed as a result of latest studies. The 2 Annas, dated 1877 having a bead in the tip of the top flower is now attributed to Calcutta. Calcutta issues dated 1862-78 have no mintmark. The diameter of the coins is 15.25mm, except for the 1877 issue with the bead in the top flower which is 15.4mm. From 1879 the mintmark is a small incuse "C" in the whorl below the center of the bottom flower. Calcutta coins dated 1874 have not yet been verified.

Bombay issues until 1877 are without mintmark and have a diameter of 15.8mm. From 1877-1883 the mintmark is a small raised bead directly above the bottom flower. From 1884 the coins have a small B raised or incuse, above the whorl of the top flower. Madras issues (1862 only) are 16mm in diameter.

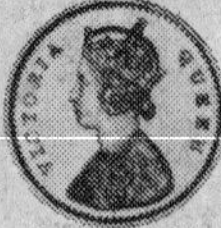

1.4600 gm., .917 SILVER, .0430 oz ASW
Obv: Bust "A"

Y#	Date	Mintage	Fine	VF	XF	Unc
9	1862C	—	1.75	3.50	5.00	10.00
	1862B	—	2.00	4.00	6.00	12.00
	1862M	—	2.75	5.00	7.50	15.00
	1874C	5.690	1.75	3.50	5.00	10.00
	1874B	9.510	1.75	2.50	3.75	7.50
	1874B dot	I.A.	1.75	4.00	6.00	12.00
	1875C	6.510	1.75	2.25	3.00	6.00
	1875B	1.710	1.75	2.25	3.00	6.00
	1876C	10.500	1.75	2.00	3.00	6.00
	1876B	3.910	1.75	4.00	6.00	12.00

Y#	Date	Mintage	Fine	VF	XF	Unc
20	1877C A/I, no mm.	3.575	1.75	2.50	3.75	7.50
	1877C A/I, dot below	Inc. Ab.	1.75	3.50	5.50	11.50
	1877C B/II, no mm.	Inc. Ab	1.75	3.50	5.50	11.50
	1877C B/II, dot in top flower	Inc. Ab.	1.75	2.50	3.75	7.50
	1878B A.I, dot	2.215	1.75	2.50	3.75	7.50
	1878C B/II, no mm.	3.994	1.75	2.50	3.75	7.50
	1879C B/II, "C" incuse	3.541	1.75	2.50	3.75	7.50
	1880C B/II, "C" incuse	2.539	1.75	2.50	3.75	7.50
	1881C B/II, "C" incuse	4.400	1.75	2.50	3.75	7.50
	1881B A/I, dot	2.449	1.75	2.50	3.75	7.50
	1881B B/II, dot	Inc. Ab.	1.75	2.50	3.75	7.50
	1882C B/II, "C" incuse	14.360	1.75	2.50	3.75	7.50
	1882B A/I, dot	2.629	1.75	2.50	3.75	7.50
	1882B B/II, dot	Inc. Ab.	1.75	2.50	3.75	7.50
	1883C B/II, "C" incuse	2.736	1.75	2.50	3.75	7.50
	1883B A/I, no mm.	Inc. Ab.	1.75	2.50	3.75	7.50
	1883B A/I, dot	4.417	1.75	2.50	3.75	7.50
	1883B B/II, dot	Inc. Ab.	1.75	2.50	3.75	7.50
	1884C B/II, "C" incuse	7.200	1.75	2.50	3.75	7.50
	1884B A/I, no mm.	1.638	1.75	2.50	3.75	7.50
	1884B A/I, dot	Inc. Ab.	1.75	2.50	3.75	7.50
	1884B A/I, "B" raised	Inc. Ab.	1.75	2.50	3.75	7.50
	1884B A/I, dot, "B" raised	Inc. Ab.	1.75	2.50	3.75	7.50
	1884B B/II, "B" incuse	Inc. Ab.	1.75	2.50	3.75	7.50
	1885C B/II, "C" incuse	1.335	1.75	2.50	3.75	7.50
	1885B B/II, "B" raised	2.262	1.75	2.50	3.75	7.50
	1886C B/II, "C" incuse	10.346	1.75	2.50	3.75	7.50
	1886B B/II, "B" incuse	3.155	1.75	2.50	3.75	7.50
	1887C B/II, "C" incuse	13.927	1.75	2.50	3.75	7.50
	1887B B/II, "B" incuse	3.283	1.75	2.50	3.75	7.50
	1888C B/II, no mm.	9.307	1.75	2.50	3.75	7.50
	1888B B/II, "B" incuse	8.039	1.75	2.50	3.75	7.50
	1889C B/II, "C" incuse	.135	1.50	3.50	5.50	11.00
	1889B B/II, "B" incuse	5.895	1.75	2.50	3.75	7.50
	1890C B/II, "C" incuse	9.836	1.75	2.50	3.75	7.50
	1890B B/II, "B" raised	7.790	1.75	2.50	3.75	7.50
	1890B B/II, "B" incuse	Inc. Ab.	1.75	2.50	3.75	7.50
	1891C B/II, "C" incuse	8.621	1.75	2.50	3.75	7.50
	1891B B/II, "B" incuse	4.230	1.75	2.50	3.75	7.50
	1892C B/II, "C" incuse	6.971	1.75	2.50	3.75	7.50
	1892B B/II, "B" incuse	9.347	1.75	2.50	3.75	7.50
	1893C B/II, "C" incuse	8.003	1.75	2.50	3.75	7.50
	1893B B/II, "B" incuse	10.716	1.75	2.50	3.75	7.50
	1894C B/II, "C" incuse	2.461	1.75	2.50	3.75	7.50
	1894B B/II, "B" incuse	Inc. 1893	1.75	2.50	3.75	7.50
	1895C B/II, "C" incuse	9.668	1.75	2.50	3.75	7.50
	1896C B/II, "C" incuse	6.616	1.75	2.50	3.75	7.50
	1896B B/II, "B" incuse	8.235	1.75	2.50	3.75	7.50
	1897C B/II, "C" incuse	12.103	1.75	2.50	3.75	7.50
	1897B B/II, "B" incuse	8.041	1.75	2.50	3.75	7.50
	1898C B/II, "C" incuse	4.011	1.75	2.50	3.75	7.50
	1898B B/II, "B" incuse	3.250	1.75	2.50	3.75	7.50
	1900C B/II, "C" incuse	1.705	1.75	2.50	3.75	7.50
	1900B B/II, "B" raised	4.439	1.75	2.50	3.75	7.50
	1901C B/II, "C" incuse	8.944	1.75	2.50	3.75	7.50
	1901B B/II, "B" incuse	1.706	1.75	2.50	3.75	7.50
	1901B B/II, "B" raised	Inc. Ab.	1.75	2.50	3.75	7.50

NOTE: All were struck at the Calcutta Mint without mintmark.

Y#	Date	Mintage	Fine	VF	XF	Unc
31	1903C	4.434	1.75	2.25	3.00	6.00
	1904C	14.632	1.75	2.25	3.00	6.00
	1905C	19.303	1.75	2.25	3.00	6.00
	1906C	1.629	1.75	2.25	3.75	7.50
	1907C	22.145	1.75	2.25	3.00	6.00
	1908C	21.600	1.75	2.25	3.00	6.00
	1909C	6.769	1.75	3.00	6.00	12.00
	1910C	Inc. Ab.	1.75	2.25	3.00	6.00

NOTE: Calcutta Mint issues have no mintmark. Bombay Mint issues have a small raised bead or dot below the lotus flower at the bottom of the reverse. The 2 Annas dated 1911, like the other coins with the same date, has the "Pig" elephant. On these pieces like on the 1/4 Rupee, the King's bust is slightly smaller and has a higher relief than the later issues with the redesigned elephant.

Y#	Date	Mintage	Fine	VF	XF	Unc
42	1911C	16.760	1.75	2.25	3.00	6.00
	1912C	7.724	1.75	2.25	2.75	4.50
	1912B	2.462	1.75	2.25	2.75	4.50
	1913C	13.959	1.75	2.25	2.75	4.50
	1913B	5.461	1.75	2.25	2.75	4.50
	1914C	8.861	1.75	2.25	2.75	4.50
	1914B	3.231	1.75	2.25	2.75	4.50
	1915C	1.620	1.75	2.25	2.75	4.50
	1915B	2.711	1.75	2.25	2.75	4.50
	1916C	9.849	1.75	2.25	2.75	3.75
	1917C	35.491	1.75	2.25	2.75	3.75

COPPER-NICKEL

NOTE: Calcutta Mint issues have no mintmark. Bombay Mint issues have a small raised dot on the reverse at the bottom near the rim.

Y#	Date	Mintage	Fine	VF	XF	Unc
39	1918C	53.412	1.75	2.25	2.75	4.50
	1918B	9.191	1.75	2.25	2.75	4.50
	1919C	8.904	1.75	2.25	2.75	4.50
	1920B	(restrike)	—	—	Proof	15.00
	1920C	13.520	1.75	2.25	2.75	4.50
	1923C	7.656	1.75	2.25	2.75	4.50
	1923B	6.431	1.75	2.25	2.75	4.50
	1924C	8.384	1.75	2.25	2.75	4.50
	1924B	4.818	1.75	2.25	2.75	4.50
	1925C	10.848	1.75	2.25	2.75	4.50
	1925B	8.348	1.75	2.25	2.75	4.50
	1926C	8.352	1.75	2.25	2.75	4.50
	1926B	2.927	1.75	2.25	2.75	4.50
	1927C	6.424	1.75	2.25	2.75	4.50
	1927B	4.835	1.75	2.25	2.75	4.50
	1928C	7.352	1.75	2.25	2.75	4.50
	1928B	4.876	1.75	2.25	2.75	4.50
	1929C	13.408	1.75	2.25	2.75	4.50
	1930C	8.888	1.75	2.25	2.75	4.50
	1933C	4.300	1.75	2.25	2.75	4.50
	1934C	7.016	1.75	2.25	2.75	4.50
	1935C	12.354	1.75	2.25	2.75	4.50
	1935B	21.017	1.75	2.25	2.75	3.50
	1936B	36.295	1.75	2.25	2.75	3.50

Obv: First head, high relief.

NOTE: Calcutta Mint issues have no mintmark. Bombay Mint issues have a small dot before and after the date.

Y#	Date	Mintage	Fine	VF	XF	Unc
54	1939C	2.916	1.75	2.00	2.50	3.00
	1939B	3.392	1.75	2.00	2.50	3.00
	1940B	5.898	1.75	2.00	2.50	4.00

Obv: Second head, low relief.

Y#	Date	Mintage	Fine	VF	XF	Unc
54b	1939C	12.528	1.75	2.00	2.50	3.00
	1939B	44.701	.20	.30	.50	1.00
	1940C	31.738	.20	.30	.50	1.00
	1940B	5.898	.20	.30	.50	1.00
	1941C	69.354	.20	.30	.50	1.00
	1941B	10.760	.20	.30	.50	1.00
	1946C	84.068	.20	.30	.50	1.00
	1946B	41.600	.20	.30	.50	1.00
	1947C	60.230	.20	.30	.50	1.00
	1947B	38.908	.20	.30	.50	1.00

NICKEL-BRASS
Obv: Second head.

Y#	Date	Mintage	Fine	VF	XF	Unc
54a	1942B	133.000	.25	.35	.50	1.00
	1943B	343.680	.25	.35	.50	1.00
	1944C	6.352	.50	1.25	2.00	3.50
	1944B	219.700	.25	.35	.50	1.00
	1945C	13.360	.25	.75	1.25	2.25
	1945B	147.588	.25	.35	.50	1.00

1/4 RUPEE

NOTE: The distinguishing features of the three busts and two reverses are as following:

BUST A-The front dress panel is divided into four sections. The last section has a five-dotted flower at right.

BUST B-The front dress panel is divided into four sections. The last section, which is incomplete has a five-petalled flower in the center.

BUST C-The front dress panel is divided into three sections. The last section has a five-dotted flower at left.

REVERSE I-The two large petals above the base of the top flower are long and curved downward; long stroke between "1/4".

REVERSE II-The two large petals above the base of the top flower are short and horizontal; short stroke between "1/4".

As a result of recent studies, the 1/4 Rupees dated 1862-1876 have been re-attributed.

CALCUTTA issues dated 1862-1878 have no mintmark. The diameter of the coins is 19-19.2mm and the milling is coarse. From 1879 the mintmark is a small incuse "C" which is in the whorl below the center of the bottom flower.

BOMBAY issues dated 1862, 1875 and 1876 have no mintmark. These have a diameter of 19.7-8mm and the milling is narrow. The coins dated 1874, 1877-1883 have as mintmark a small bead directly above the bottom flower. From 1884 the mintmark is a small "B" raised or incuse, which is above the whorl, in the top flower.

MADRAS issues (1862 only) have a diameter of 20mm.

2.9200 gm., .917 SILVER, .0860 oz ASW
Obv: Bust A. Rev: I.

Y#	Date	Mintage	Fine	VF	XF	Unc
10	1862C	—	3.50	4.50	6.00	12.00
	1862B	—	3.50	5.00	7.50	15.00
	1862M	—	3.50	6.00	10.00	20.00
	1874C	5.445	3.50	4.50	5.50	11.00
	1874B	1.612	3.50	4.50	5.50	11.00
	1875C	2.797	3.50	4.50	5.50	11.00
	1875B	5.240	3.50	4.50	5.50	11.00
	1876C	6.457	3.50	4.50	5.50	11.00
	1876B	1.430	3.50	4.50	5.50	11.00

Y#	Date	Mintage	Fine	VF	XF	Unc
21	1877C B/I, no mm.	3.440	3.50	4.00	5.00	10.00
	1877B A/I, dot	.884	3.50	4.50	6.00	12.00
	1877B B/I, dot	Inc. Ab.	3.50	4.00	4.50	9.00
	1878C C/II, no mm.	3.332	3.50	4.00	4.50	9.00
	1879C C/II, "C" incuse	Inc. Ab.	3.50	4.00	4.50	9.00
	1880C C/II, "C" incuse	Inc. In 1881	3.50	4.00	4.50	9.00
	1881C C/II, "C" incuse	3.244	3.50	5.00	7.50	15.00
	1881B A/II, dot	1.444	3.50	4.00	6.00	12.00
	1881B B/I, dot	Inc. Ab.	4.00	7.00	11.50	22.50
	1882C C/II, "C" incuse	.612	3.50	4.00	4.50	7.50
	1882B A/II, dot	2.775	3.50	4.00	5.50	11.00
	1882B B/I, dot	Inc. Ab.	4.00	7.00	10.00	18.50
	1882B C/II, dot	Inc. Ab.	3.50	5.00	7.50	15.00
	1883C C/II, "C" incuse	2.871	5.00	8.00	11.50	22.50
	1883B B/I, dot	.184	3.50	5.00	7.50	15.00
	1884C C/II "C" incuse	3.596	4.50	7.50	11.50	21.50
	1884B B/I, "B" raised	1.709	4.50	7.50	11.50	21.50
	1884B C/II, "B" raised	Inc. Ab.	4.50	7.50	11.50	21.50
	1885C C/II, "C" incuse	1.024	4.50	7.50	11.50	21.50
	1885B B/I, "B" raised	1.117	4.50	7.50	11.50	21.50
	1886C C/II, "C" incuse	7.087	3.50	4.50	6.50	13.50
	1886B C/II, "B" raised	1.684	4.00	7.50	11.50	21.50
	1887C C/II, "C" incuse	6.494	3.50	4.50	6.50	13.50
	1887B C/II, "B" raised	4.422	3.50	5.00	7.50	15.00
	1888C C/II, no mm.	4.945	3.50	5.00	7.50	15.00
	1888B C/II, "B" raised	2.228	4.00	6.50	9.00	18.50
	1888B C/II, "B" incuse	Inc. Ab.	4.00	7.50	11.50	21.50
	1889C C/II, "C" incuse	8.075	3.75	4.50	6.50	13.50
	1889B C/II, "B" incuse	4.298	3.50	5.00	7.50	15.00
	1890C C/II, "C" incuse	Inc. 1891	3.50	5.00	7.50	15.00
	1890B C/II, "B" incuse	.459	5.00	9.00	12.50	22.50
	1891C C/II, "C" incuse	13.770	3.50	4.50	6.50	13.50
	1891B C/I, "B" incuse	.883	4.00	7.50	11.50	21.50
	1892B C/I, "B" incuse	4.059	3.50	4.00	5.00	7.50
	1893C C/II, "C" incuse	6.435	3.50	4.00	5.00	7.50
	1893B C/I, "B" incuse	6.137	3.50	4.00	5.00	7.50
	1894C C/II, "C" incuse	2.653	3.50	4.00	5.00	7.50
	1894B C/I, "B" incuse	2.385	3.50	4.00	5.00	7.50
	1896C C/II, "C" incuse	6.811	3.50	4.00	5.00	7.50
	1897C C/II, "C" incuse	5.884	3.50	4.00	5.00	7.50
	1897B C/I, "B" incuse	2.893	3.50	4.00	5.00	7.50
	1898C C/II, "C" incuse	1.330	3.50	4.00	5.00	7.50
	1898B C/I, "B" incuse	2.056	3.50	4.00	5.00	7.50
	1900C C/II, "C" incuse	1.606	3.50	4.00	5.00	7.50
	1901C C/II, "C" incuse	4.476	3.50	4.00	5.00	7.50

NOTE: All were struck at the Calcutta Mint without mintmark.

Y#	Date	Mintage	Fine	VF	XF	Unc
32	1903C	2.472	3.50	4.00	5.00	7.50
	1904C	28.241	3.50	4.00	5.00	7.50
	1905C	10.026	3.50	4.00	5.00	7.50
	1906C	16.300	3.50	4.00	5.00	7.50
	1907C	10.672	3.50	4.00	5.00	7.50
	1908C	11.464	3.50	4.00	5.00	7.50
	1909C	—	—	Proof Only		100.00
	1910C	.801	3.50	4.00	5.00	9.00

NOTE: Calcutta Mint issues have no mintmark. Bombay Mint issues have a small raised bead or dot in the space below the lotus flower at the bottom of the reverse. The 1/4 Rupee dated 1911, like the other coins with the same date, has the "Pig" elephant. On these pieces the King's bust is slightly smaller and has a higher relief than later issues with the re-designed elephant.

Y#	Date	Mintage	Fine	VF	XF	Unc
43	1911C	8.024	3.50	4.00	5.00	9.00
	1912C	2.245	3.50	4.00	4.50	6.00
	1912B	1.168	3.50	4.00	4.50	6.00
	1913C	9.587	3.50	4.00	4.50	6.00
	1913B	2.276	3.50	4.00	4.50	6.00
	1914C	6.014	3.50	4.00	4.50	6.00
	1914B	3.967	3.50	4.00	4.50	6.00
	1915C	.851	3.50	4.00	5.00	9.00
	1915B	2.096	3.50	4.00	4.50	6.00
	1916C	10.716	3.50	4.00	4.50	6.00
	1917C	21.380	3.50	4.00	4.50	6.00
	1918C	43.306	3.50	4.00	4.50	6.00
	1919C	35.557	3.50	4.00	4.50	6.00
	1925B	2.003	3.50	4.00	4.50	6.00
	1926C	6.117	3.50	4.00	4.50	6.00
	1928B	4.023	3.50	4.00	4.50	6.00
	1929C	4.013	3.50	4.00	4.50	6.00
	1930C	3.942	3.50	4.00	4.50	6.00

Y#	Date	Mintage	Fine	VF	XF	Unc
43	1934C	3.947	3.50	4.00	4.50	6.00
	1936C	21.771	3.50	4.00	4.50	5.50
	1936B	7.142	3.50	4.00	4.50	5.50

NOTE: The silver coinage of George VI is a very complex series with numerous obverse and reverse die varieties. Two different designs of the head appear on the obverse of most denominations struck for George VI. The "First Head" shows the Kings effigy in high relief the "Second Head" in low relief. In 1941-42 the "Second Head" was slightly reduced in size and this type continued to be used on the silver coins and on some of the smaller denominations.

First Head

Second Head (small) **Second Head (large)**

From 1942 to 1945 the reverse designs of the silver coins change slightly every year. However, a distinct reverse variety occurs on Rupees and 1/4 Rupees dated 1943-44 and on the half Rupee dated 1944, all struck at Bombay. This variety may be distinguished from the other coins by the design of the center bottom flower as illustrated, and is designated as Reverse B.

On the normal common varieties dated 1943-44 the three "scalloped circles" are not connected to each other and the bead in the center is not attached to the nearest circle.

Obv: First head, reeded edge.

NOTE: Calcutta Mint issues have no mintmark. Bombay coins have a small bead below the lotus flower at the bottom on the reverse, except those dated 1943-1944 with reverse B which have a diamond. Lahore Mint issues have a small "L" in the same position. The nickel coins have a diamond below the date on the reverse.

Y#	Date	Mintage	Fine	VF	XF	Unc
55	1938	(restrike)	—	—	Proof	15.00
	1939C	14.807	3.50	4.00	4.50	6.00
	1939B	6.770	3.50	4.00	4.50	6.00
	1940B	24.635	3.50	4.00	4.50	6.00

2.9200 gm., .500 SILVER, .0469 oz ASW

Obv: Small second head, reeded edge.

Y#	Date	Mintage	Fine	VF	XF	Unc
55a	1940C	59.848	1.50	1.75	2.25	3.00
	1940B	28.947	1.50	1.75	2.25	3.00
	1942C	103.693	1.50	1.75	2.00	2.50
	1943C	33.844	1.50	1.75	2.00	2.50

Obv: Small second head, security edge.

Y#	Date	Mintage	Fine	VF	XF	Unc
55b	1943B	95.200	1.50	1.75	2.00	2.50
	1943B reverse B					
55b		Inc. Ab.	1.50	1.75	2.00	2.50
	1943L	62.294	1.50	1.75	2.00	2.50
	1944B	170.504	1.50	1.75	2.00	2.50
	1944B reverse B					
		Inc. Ab.	1.50	1.75	2.00	2.50
	1944L	86.400	1.50	1.75	2.00	2.50
	1945B	181.648	1.50	1.75	2.00	2.50
	1945L	29.751	1.50	1.75	2.00	2.50

NICKEL

Y#	Date	Mintage	Fine	VF	XF	Unc
58	1946B	57.200	.30	.60	.75	1.50
	1947B	*128.370	.40	.50	.75	1.50

***NOTE:** 3 varieties are known.

4 ANNAS

NOTE: Calcutta Mint issues have no mintmark. Bombay Mint issues have a small raised dot on the reverse at the bottom near the rim.

COPPER-NICKEL

Y#	Date	Mintage	Fine	VF	XF	Unc
40	1919C	9.168	2.00	3.50	7.50	15.00
	1919B	1.100	3.00	5.00	10.00	20.00
	1920C	22.258	2.00	3.50	7.50	15.00
	1920B	8.238	2.00	3.50	7.50	15.00
	1921B	1.200	3.00	5.00	10.00	20.00
	1921C	(restrike)	—	—	Proof	15.00

8 ANNAS

NOTE: Calcutta Mint issues have no mintmark. Bombay Mint issues have a small raised dot on the reverse at the bottom near the rim.

COPPER-NICKEL

Y#	Date	Mintage	Fine	VF	XF	Unc
41	1919C	2.980	3.25	6.00	9.00	13.50
	1919B	1.100	4.00	7.50	12.50	25.00
	1919B	(restrike)	—	—	Proof	17.50
	1920B	1.300	12.50	20.00	30.00	50.00

1/2 RUPEE

Distinguishing Features

BUST A-The front dress panel has four sections. The last section has a round flower at left and right.

BUST B-The dress panel has 4-1/2 or 4-2/3 sections. The last, incomplete section has a five- petalled flower at left of center.

BUST C-The dress panel is the same as on Bust B but the floral design of the dress differs.

Bust B **Bust C**

REVERSE I-The top flower is open and the two large petals above the whorl are short and horizontal.

REVERSE II-The top flower is closed and the two petals above the whorl are long and curved downward.

CALCUTTA issues have Bust A and Reverse I coins dated 1862-1878 have no mintmark. From 1879 the mintmark is a small incuse "C" located in the whorl, below the center of the bottom flower.

BOMBAY issues dated 1862 have no mintmark. From 1874-1884 the mintmark is a small bead directly above the center of the bottom flower. From 1885 the mintmark is a "B" raised or incuse, in the top flower.

MADRAS issues (1862 only) have Bust "C" and Reverse II.

.917 SILVER

Y#	Date	Mintage	Fine	VF	XF	Unc
11	1862C A/I	—	6.50	8.50	13.50	20.00
	1862B B/II	—	6.50	8.50	13.50	20.00
	1862M C/II	—	6.50	8.50	13.50	20.00
	1874B B/II, dot	1.654	6.50	10.00	17.50	26.50
	1875C A/I	2.257	6.50	8.50	14.00	21.50
	1875B B/II, dot	1.023	6.50	10.00	17.50	26.50
	1876B B/II, dot	.966	6.50	10.00	17.50	26.50

Y#	Date	Mintage	Fine	VF	XF	Unc
22	1877C A/I	.858	6.50	8.50	14.00	21.50
	1877B B/II, dot	.214	6.50	10.00	17.50	26.50
	1878C A/I	1.390	6.50	8.50	14.00	21.50
	1879C A/I, "C" incuse	1.008	6.50	8.50	14.00	21.50
	1880C A/I, " incuse	.180	6.50	10.00	20.00	30.00
	1881C A/I, "C" incuse	.921	6.50	8.50	14.00	21.50
	1881B B/II, dot	1.591	6.50	8.50	14.00	21.50
	1882C A/II, "C" incuse	1.161	6.50	8.50	14.00	21.50
	1882B B/II, dot	.308	6.50	10.00	17.50	26.50
	1882B A/II, dot	Inc. Ab.	7.50	16.50	22.50	33.50
	1883C A/I, "C" incuse	1.036	6.50	8.50	14.00	21.50
	1884C A/I, "C" incuse	—	6.50	8.50	14.00	21.50
	1884B A/II, dot	1.110	6.50	8.50	14.00	21.50
	1884B A/II, no mm.	Inc. Ab.	6.50	8.50	14.00	21.50
	1885C A/I, "C" incuse	1.408	6.50	8.00	11.00	16.50
	1885B A/II, "B" raised	.390	6.50	8.50	14.00	21.00
	1886C A/I, "C" incuse	2.645	6.50	8.00	11.00	16.50
	1886B A/II, "B" raised	1.116	6.50	8.00	11.00	16.50
	1887C A/I, "C" incuse	2.275	6.50	8.00	11.00	16.50
	1887B A/II, "B" raised	.407	6.50	8.50	14.00	21.00
	1888C A/I, "C" incuse	1.100	6.50	8.00	11.00	16.50
	1888B A/II, "B" raised	1.748	6.50	8.00	11.00	16.50
	1888B A/II, no mm.	Inc. Ab.	6.50	8.50	14.00	21.00
	1889C A/I, "C" incuse	2.331	6.50	8.00	11.00	16.50
	1889B A/II, "B" raised	1.083	6.50	8.00	11.00	16.50
	1889B A/I, "B" incuse	Inc. Ab.	6.50	8.00	11.00	16.50
	1891B A/I, "B" Incuse	—	—	Proof Only		100.00
	1892C A/I, "C" incuse	1.761	6.50	8.00	11.00	16.50
	18?2B A/I, "B" incuse	1.104	6.50	8.00	11.00	16.50
	1893C A/I, "C" incuse	—	6.50	8.00	11.00	16.50
	1893B A/I, "B" incuse	2.462	6.50	8.00	11.00	16.50

Y#	Date	Mintage	Fine	VF	XF	Unc
22	1894C A/I, "C" incuse	1.277	6.50	8.00	11.00	16.50
	1894B A/I, "B" incuse	—	6.50	8.00	11.00	16.50
	1896C A/I, "C" incuse	2.114	6.50	8.00	11.00	16.50
	1897C A/I, "C" incuse	—	6.50	8.00	11.00	16.50
	1897B A/I, "B" incuse	.560	6.50	8.00	11.00	16.50
	1898C A/I, "C" incuse	2.057	6.50	8.00	11.00	16.50
	1898B A/I, "B" incuse	.458	6.50	8.50	14.00	21.00
	1899C A/I, "C" incuse	6.893	6.50	8.00	11.00	16.50
	1899B A/I, "B" incuse	11.174	6.50	7.50	9.00	13.50
	1900C A/I	(restrike)		—	Proof	15.00

NOTE: Calcutta Mint issues have no mintmark. Bombay Mint issues have a small incuse "B" in the space below the cross pattee of the crown on the reverse.

Y#	Date	Mintage	Fine	VF	XF	Unc
33	1904	—	—		Proof only	100.00
	1905C	.823	6.50	8.50	12.50	18.50
	1906C	3.036	6.50	8.50	12.50	18.50
	1906B	.400	6.50	9.00	12.50	22.50
	1907C	2.786	6.50	8.50	12.50	18.50
	1907B	1.856	6.50	8.50	12.50	18.50
	1908C	1.577	6.50	8.50	12.50	18.50
	1909C	1.569	6.50	8.50	12.50	18.50
	1910C	3.413	6.50	8.50	12.50	18.50
	1910B	.809	6.50	8.50	12.50	18.50

NOTE: Calcutta Mint issues have no mintmarks. Bombay Mint issues have a small raised bead or dot in the space below the lotus flower at the bottom of the reverse. The half Rupee dated 1911 like the Rupee and all other issues of that year has the "Pig" elephant. It was struck only at the Calcutta Mint.

Y#	Date	Mintage	Fine	VF	XF	Unc
44	1911C	2.293	6.50	7.50	9.00	15.00
	1912C	3.390	6.50	7.50	8.50	11.50
	1912B	1.505	6.50	7.50	8.50	10.00
	1913C	Inc. Ab.	6.50	7.50	8.50	10.00
	1913B	Inc. Ab.	6.50	7.50	8.50	10.00
	1914C	1.639	6.50	7.50	8.50	10.00
	1914B	1.919	6.50	7.50	8.50	10.00
	1915C	1.600	6.50	7.50	8.50	10.00
	1915B	(restrike)	—	—	Proof	15.00
	1916C	1.402	6.50	7.50	8.50	10.00
	1916B	4.615	6.50	7.50	8.50	10.00
	1917B	8.422	6.50	7.50	8.50	10.00
	1918B	8.768	6.50	7.50	8.50	10.00
	1919B	12.180	6.50	7.50	8.50	10.00
	1921C	5.804	6.50	7.50	8.50	10.00
	1922C	4.405	6.50	7.50	8.50	10.00
	1922B	1.037	6.50	7.50	8.50	10.00
	1923C	3.464	6.50	7.50	8.50	10.00
	1923B	1.005	6.50	7.50	8.50	10.00
	1924C	3.646	6.50	7.00	8.00	10.00
	1924B	2.089	6.50	7.00	8.00	10.00
	1925C	3.975	6.50	7.00	8.00	10.00
	1925B	1.627	6.50	7.00	8.00	10.00
	1926C	6.139	6.50	7.00	8.00	10.00
	1926B	2.011	6.50	7.00	8.00	10.00
	1927C	2.032	6.50	7.00	8.00	10.00
	1928B	2.466	6.50	7.00	8.00	10.00
	1929C	4.050	6.50	7.00	8.00	10.00
	1930C	2.036	6.50	7.00	8.00	10.00
	1933/2C	—	6.50	7.00	8.50	11.50
	1933C	4.056	6.50	7.00	8.00	10.00
	1934C	1.971	6.50	7.00	8.00	10.00
	1936C	13.020	6.50	7.00	8.00	10.00
	1936B	1.700	6.50	7.00	8.00	10.00

NOTE: Some 1933C are overdated 1933/32, but no coins dated 1932 were struck, and none are known.

SILVER
Obv: First head, reeded edge.

NOTE: Calcutta Mint issues have no mintmark. Bombay coins dated 1938-43 and 1945 have a bead below the lotus flower at the bottom of the reverse. Specimens dated 1944 with Reverse B have a diamond in the same position. Those dated 1944 with the normal common reverse have either a bead or a diamond. Lahore Mint issues have a small raised "L" in the same position as the Bombay coins. Bombay Mint 1943 coins have either large or small denticles on obverse. The nickel pieces of the last issue have a diamond below the date on the reverse.

Y#	Date	Mintage	Fine	VF	XF	Unc
56	1938C	(restrike)	—	—	Proof	15.00
	1938B	2.200	6.50	7.00	9.00	12.00
	1939C	10.096	6.50	7.00	8.00	10.00
	1939B	10.180	6.50	7.00	8.00	10.00

Obv: Large second head, reeded edge.

Y#	Date	Mintage	Fine	VF	XF	Unc
56a	1939C	Inc. Ab.	6.50	7.00	8.00	10.00
	1939B	Inc. Ab.	6.50	7.00	8.00	10.00
	1940C	42.994	BV	6.50	7.50	9.00
	1940B	17.811	6.50	7.00	8.00	10.00

5.8300 gm., .500 SILVER, .0937 oz ASW
Obv: Large second head, security edge.

Y#	Date	Mintage	Fine	VF	XF	Unc
56b	1941B	24.100	BV	3.00	4.00	5.50

Obv: Small second head, security edge.

Y#	Date	Mintage	Fine	VF	XF	Unc
	1942B	61.600	BV	3.00	4.00	5.50
	1943B	90.400	BV	3.00	4.00	5.50
	1943L	9.000	BV	3.00	4.00	5.50
	1944B	51.200	BV	3.00	4.00	5.50
	1944B reverse B	Inc. Ab.	BV	3.00	4.00	5.50
	1944L	79.100	BV	3.00	4.00	5.50
	1945B	32.722	BV	3.00	4.00	5.50
	1945L small date	79.192	BV	3.00	4.00	5.50
	1945L large date	Inc. Ab.	3.00	4.50	7.50	15.00

NICKEL
Rev: New design, reeded edge.

Y#	Date	Mintage	Fine	VF	XF	Unc
59	1946B	34.300	.50	1.00	2.25	3.75
	1947B	81.850	.50	1.00	2.25	3.75

RUPEE

NOTE: The Rupees dated 1862 were struck with the date unchanged until 1874. However, in 1863 Bombay Mint adopted a method of adding dots or beads to its dies to indicate the exact year of minting.

The beads occur in the following positions:

1. Below the base or whorl of the top flower.
2. Above or around the top of the bottom flower.
3. In both positions together.

The different busts are identified as follows:

BUST A-The front dress panel has 3-3/4 sections with two dividing lines below the lowest string of pearls.

BUST B-The front dress panel has 4-1/4 sections with three dividing lines below the lowest string of pearls.

BUST C-Like bust A, but shorter at the bottom. The front panel has only 3-1/3 sections.

The reverses are identified by the design of the top center flower as illustrated.

I II III

A variety of Reverse II, designated as IIa, shows the flower buds with a pineapple like pattern above "ONE" and above right of the second "E" of "RUPEE". In the listing of 1862 Rupees, the date column indicates the year in which the coins are believed to have been struck. The variety column lists the Obverse/Reverse combination and the bead position. For example, A/1 0/0 means Bust A, Reverse 1 and no beads. A11 1/2 means Bust A, Reverse II, and one bead at the top and two beads at the bottom.

Mintage for 1862 Rupees

Calcutta	**269,427,222**
Bombay	**408,003,034**
Madras	**29,481,923**

NOTE: The B/II 0/0 coins are attributed to the mint of issue as follows:

CALCUTTA, 30.3mm, round pearls in crown arch.

BOMBAY, 30.5mm, elongated pearls in crown arch. The scroll like floral design of the dress is in flat relief and has a depression around it.

MADRAS, 30.55mm elongated pearls in crown arch. The floral design is in high relief and shows no depression.

11.6600 gm., .917 SILVER, .3438 oz ASW
Common date: 1862

Y#	Date	Year	Fine	VF	XF	Unc
12	B/II, 0/0	1862-63C	BV	11.50	15.00	22.50
	B/II, 0/0	1862-63B	BV	11.50	12.50	15.00
	B/II, 0/0	1862-69M?	BV	11.50	12.50	15.00
	A/III, 0/0	1863C	12.50	20.00	30.00	50.00
	B/III, 0/0	1863C	12.50	20.00	30.00	50.00
	A/I, 0/0	1863-74C	BV	11.50	12.50	15.00
	B/II, 1/0	1863B	11.50	12.50	16.50	25.00
	A/II, 0/2	1864B	13.50	25.00	40.00	60.00
	B/II, 2/0	1864B	13.50	25.00	40.00	60.00
	A/II, 2/0	1864B	12.00	20.00	30.00	45.00
	B/II, 0/3	1865B	BV	11.50	12.50	15.00
	B/II, 2/3	1865B	13.50	25.00	40.00	60.00
	A/I, 0/4	1866B	13.50	25.00	40.00	60.00
	B/I, 0/4	1866B	13.50	25.00	40.00	60.00
	A/II, 0/4	1866B	BV	11.50	12.50	15.00
	B/II, 0/4	1866B	BV	11.50	15.00	22.50
	A/IIa, 0/0	1866-69C	11.50	12.50	16.50	25.00
	B/IIa, 0/0	1866-69B or M	12.00	20.00	30.00	45.00
	A/II, 0/5	1867B	BV	11.50	13.50	18.50
	A/II, 0/0 (30.7mm)	1867-68B	12.00	20.00	30.00	45.00
	A/II, 0/6	1868B	BV	11.50	13.50	18.50
	A/II, 0/7	1869B	BV	11.50	13.50	18.50
	B/II, 0/7	1869B	12.50	22.50	35.00	50.00
	A/II, 1/7 (top dot in top flower)	1869-70B	—	—	Rare	—
	A/II, 1/7 (top dot in normal position)	1872B	13.50	25.00	40.00	60.00
	A/II, 0/8	1870B	13.50	25.00	40.00	60.00
	A/II, 0/9	1871B	13.50	25.00	40.00	60.00

Y#	Date	Year	Fine	VF	XF	Unc
12	A/II, 0/10	1872B	11.50	12.50	16.50	25.00
	A/II, 1/10 (top dot in top flower)	1872-73B	13.50	25.00	40.00	60.00
	A/II, 1/10 (top dot in normal position)	1873B	13.50	25.00	40.00	60.00
	A/II, 1/1	1873B	12.50	17.50	25.00	37.50
	A/II, 0/1	1873B	13.50	25.00	40.00	60.00
	A/II, 0/12	1874B	13.50	25.00	40.00	60.00
	A/II, 1/2	1874B	12.50	17.50	25.00	37.50
	A/I, 1/2	1874B	13.50	25.00	40.00	60.00
	C/I, 1/2	1874B	13.50	25.00	40.00	60.00
	C/II, 1/2	1874B	12.50	17.50	25.00	37.50

From 1874 onward the coins show the year date. The designs are similar to those on the 1862 Rupees but only Bust "A" and the Reverse I and II were used.

CALCUTTA Mint issues dated 1874-78 have no mintmark. From 1879 the mintmark is a small incuse "C" on the whorl below the center of the bottom lotus flower on the reverse. All Calcutta issues have Reverse I.

BOMBAY Mint issues dated 1875-83 have as mintmark a small bead directly above the center of the bottom lotus flower. From 1883 the mintmark is a small "B" raised or incuse above the whorl or base of the top flower. Both mintmarks occur on the coins dated 1883. The issues dated 1874—76 have Reverse II only, those dated 1877-85 have both Reverses I and II. Reverse II distinguishes the 1874 coins which have no mintmark from those of Calcutta.

NOTE: There are reverse varieties in most of the following Rupees. Reverse II flowers are found in various sizes. Two bottom rosettes are found rotated, i.e., one petal up or down.

Y#	Date	Mintage	Fine	VF	XF	Unc
12	1874C Rev.I	15.014	BV	11.50	14.50	18.50
	1874B Rev.II	25.509	BV	11.50	13.50	16.50
	1875C Rev.I	11.632	BV	11.50	13.00	15.00
	1875C Rev.II	—	BV	11.50	13.00	15.00
	1875B Rev.II, dot	19.360	BV	11.50	14.50	18.50
	1876C Rev.I	12.001	BV	11.50	13.00	15.00
	1876B Rev.II, dot	28.950	BV	11.50	13.00	15.00

Y#	Date	Mintage	Fine	VF	XF	Unc
23	1877C Rev.I	39.252	BV	11.50	13.00	15.00
	1877B Rev.I, dot	95.554	BV	11.50	13.00	15.00
	1877B Rev.II, dot	Inc. Ab.	BV	11.50	13.00	15.00
	1878C Rev.I	32.658	BV	11.50	13.00	15.00
	1878B Rev.I, dot	63.927	BV	11.50	13.00	15.00
	1878B Rev.II, dot	Inc. Ab.	BV	11.50	13.00	15.00
	1879C Rev.I, "C" incuse	15.928	BV	11.50	13.00	15.00
	1879B Rev.I, dot	72.800	12.50	17.50	25.00	37.50
	1879B Rev.II, dot	Inc. Ab.	BV	11.50	14.50	18.50
	1879B Rev.II, dot (rosette var.)	Inc. Ab.	BV	11.50	13.00	15.00
	1880C Rev.I, "C" incuse	18.400	BV	11.50	15.00	22.50
	1880B Rev.I, dot	53.786	BV	11.50	14.50	18.50
	1880B Rev.II, dot	Inc. Ab.	BV	11.50	13.00	15.00
	1881C Rev.I, "C" incuse	2.436	BV	12.50	16.50	25.00
	1881B Rev.I, dot	3.162	12.50	17.50	25.00	37.50
	1881B Rev.II, dot	Inc. Ab.	12.50	17.50	25.00	37.50
	1882C Rev.I, "C" incuse	15.090	BV	11.50	13.00	15.00
	1882B Rev.I, dot	56.397	BV	11.50	13.00	15.00
	1883C Rev.I, "C" incuse	5.123	BV	11.50	15.00	22.50
	1883C Rev.I, mo mm.	Inc. Ab.	Reported, not confirmed			
	1883B Rev.I, dot	18.023	12.50	17.50	25.00	37.50
	1883B Rev.I, "B" raised	Inc. Ab.	12.50	17.50	25.00	37.50
	1883B Rev.I, dot, "B" raised	Inc. Ab.	Reported, not confirmed			
	1884C Rev.I, "C" incuse	11.642	BV	11.50	14.50	18.50
	1884B Rev.I, "B" raised	35.847	BV	11.50	16.50	25.00
	1884B Rev. II, "B" raised on whorl be. ctr. of flower	I.A.	12.50	17.50	25.00	37.50
	1885C Rev.I, "C" incuse	34.152	BV	11.50	13.00	15.00
	1885B Rev.I, "B" raised	64.878	BV	11.50	13.00	15.00
	1885B Rev.II, "B" raised	Inc. Ab.	BV	11.50	13.00	15.00
	1885B Rev.I, "B" incuse	Inc. Ab	BV	11.50	13.00	15.00
	1886C Rev.I, "C" incuse	10.878	BV	11.50	13.00	15.00
	1886B Rev.I, "B" incuse	41.146	BV	11.50	13.00	15.00
	1887C Rev.I, "C" incuse	40.200	BV	11.50	13.00	15.00
	1887B Rev.I, "B" raised	48.400	BV	11.50	13.00	15.00
	1887B Rev.I, "B" incuse	Inc. Ab.	BV	11.50	13.00	15.00
	1887B Rev.I, "B" incuse, inverted B	Inc. Ab.	Rarity Not Determined			
	1888C Rev.I, "C" incuse	7.568	BV	11.50	13.00	15.00
	1888B Rev.I, "B" raised	63.200	BV	11.50	13.00	15.00
	1888B Rev.I, "B" incuse	Inc. Ab.	BV	11.50	13.00	15.00
	1889C Rev.I, "C" incuse	9.368	BV	11.50	13.00	15.00
	1889B Rev.I, "B" raised	65.300	BV	11.50	15.00	22.50
	1889B Rev.I, "B" incuse	Inc. Ab.	BV	11.50	13.00	15.00
	1890C Rev.I, "C" incuse	24.742	BV	11.50	13.00	15.00
	1890B Rev.I, "B" incuse	92.900	BV	11.50	13.00	15.00
	1891C Rev.I, "C" incuse	14.670	BV	11.50	13.00	15.00
	1891B Rev.I, "B" incuse	49.500	BV	11.50	13.00	15.00
	1892C Rev.I, "C" incuse	32.455	BV	11.50	13.00	15.00
	1892B Rev.I, "B" raised	72.200	BV	11.50	14.50	18.50
	1892B Rev.I, "B" incuse	Inc. Ab.	BV	11.50	13.00	15.00
	1893C Rev.I, "C" incuse	9.140	BV	11.50	13.00	15.00
	1893B Rev.I, "B" incuse	69.590	BV	11.50	13.00	15.00
	1897C Rev.I, "C" incuse	.470	13.50	18.50	30.00	45.00
	1897B Rev.I, "B" incuse	1.055	12.50	17.50	25.00	37.50
	1898C Rev.I, "C" incuse	1.251	BV	12.50	20.00	30.00
	1898B Rev.I, "B" incuse	6.268	BV	11.50	13.00	15.00
	1900C Rev.I, "C" incuse	5.291	BV	11.50	13.00	15.00
	1900B Rev.I, "B" incuse	65.237	BV	11.50	13.00	15.00
	1901C Rev.I, "C" incuse	72.017	BV	11.50	13.00	15.00
	1901B Rev.I, "B" incuse	103.258	BV	11.50	13.00	15.00

NOTE: Calcutta Mint issues have no mintmark. Bombay Mint issues have a small incuse "B" in the space below the cross pattee of the crown on the reverse.

Y#	Date	Mintage	Fine	VF	XF	Unc
34	1903C	49.403	BV	BV	11.50	15.00
	1903B	52.969	BV	BV	11.50	15.00
	1904C	58.339	BV	BV	11.50	15.00
	1904B	101.949	BV	BV	11.50	15.00
	1905C	51.258	BV	BV	11.50	15.00
	1905B	76.202	BV	BV	11.50	15.00
	1906C	104.797	BV	BV	11.50	15.00
	1906B	158.953	BV	BV	11.50	15.00
	1907C	81.338	BV	BV	11.50	15.00
	1907B	170.912	BV	BV	11.50	15.00
	1908C	20.218	BV	BV	12.50	16.50
	1908B	10.715	BV	BV	12.50	16.50
	1909C	12.759	BV	BV	12.50	16.50
	1909B	9.539	BV	BV	12.50	16.50
	1910C	12.627	BV	BV	12.50	16.50
	1910B	10.885	BV	BV	12.50	16.50

NOTE: Calcutta Mint issues have no mintmark. Bombay Mint issues have a small raised bead or dot in the space below the lotus flower at the bottom of the reverse.

The Rupees dated 1911 were rejected by the public as the elephant of the Order of the Indian Empire shown on the King's robe supposedly resembled a pig, an animal considered to be unclean by Indians. These coins were withdrawn from circulation. Out of a total of 9.4 million pieces struck at both mints, only 700,000 were issued. The remainder and the withdrawn pieces were melted down. The issues dated 1912 and later have a re-designed elephant.

Y#	Date	Mintage	Fine	VF	XF	Unc
45	1911C	4.300	BV	11.50	14.50	18.50
	1911B	5.143	BV	11.50	14.50	18.50
	1912C	45.122	BV	11.50	14.50	18.50
	1912B	79.067	BV	11.50	13.00	15.00
	1913C	75.800	BV	11.50	13.00	15.00
	1913B	87.466	BV	11.50	13.00	15.00
	1914C	33.100	BV	11.50	13.00	15.00
	1914B	15.270	BV	11.50	13.00	15.00
	1915C	9.900	BV	11.50	13.00	15.00
	1915B	5.372	BV	11.50	13.00	15.00
	1916C	115.000	BV	11.50	13.00	15.00
	1916B	97.900	BV	11.50	13.00	15.00
	1917C	114.974	BV	11.50	13.00	15.00
	1917B	151.583	BV	11.50	13.00	15.00
	1918C	205.420	BV	11.50	13.00	15.00
	1918B	210.550	BV	11.50	13.00	15.00
	1919C	211.206	BV	11.50	13.00	15.00
	1919B	226.706	BV	11.50	13.00	15.00
	1920C	50.500	BV	11.50	13.00	15.00
	1920B	55.940(?)	BV	11.50	13.00	15.00
	1921B	5.115	BV	11.50	13.00	15.00
	1922B	2.051	BV	11.50	12.50	16.50
	1935C	(restrike)	—	—	Proof	22.50
	1936C	—		Proof only		150.00

NOTE: No rupees with the "First Head" were struck for circulation. Those dated 1938-39 were struck in 1940 before the fineness of the silver coins was reduced to .500.

The pieces struck at Calcutta have no mintmark. Bombay issues dated 1938-41 and 1944-45 have a bead below the lotus flower at the bottom of the reverse while those dated 1942-44 have a small diamond mark in the same position. On the specimens dated 1944 with Reverse B the mintmark appears to be a "bead over a diamond." Lahore Mint issues have a small raised "L" in the same position as the Bombay coins. The last issue nickel rupees struck at Bombay have a small diamond below the date on the reverse. The rupees dated 1943 occur with large and small "Second Head" and with large and small date figure "3".

Obv: Large "Second Head", reeded edge.

Y#	Date	Mintage	Fine	VF	XF	Unc
57	1938C	—	BV	12.50	15.00	22.50
	1938B	9.802	BV	12.50	15.00	22.50
	1939B	—	100.00	175.00	250.00	350.00
	1939C	(restrike)	—	—	Proof	22.50

11.6600 gm., .500 SILVER, .1874 oz ASW
Security edge

Y#	Date	Mintage	Fine	VF	XF	Unc
57a	1939B	—	200.00	350.00	650.00	1000.
	1940B	153.120	BV	6.00	7.50	10.00
	1941B	111.480	BV	6.00	7.50	10.00
	1943B	Inc. Be.	BV	6.50	8.50	12.50

Obv: Small "Second Head", security edge.

Y#	Date	Mintage	Fine	VF	XF	Unc
57a	1942B	244.500	BV	6.00	7.50	10.00
	1943B	65.995	BV	6.00	7.50	10.00
	1943B Rev. B	Inc. Ab.	BV	6.00	7.50	10.00
	1944B Rev. B	146.206	BV	6.00	7.50	10.00
	1944B	Inc. Ab.	BV	6.00	7.50	10.00
	1944L	91.400	BV	6.00	7.50	10.00
	1945B small date	142.666	BV	6.00	7.50	10.00
	1945B large date	Inc. Ab.	BV	6.00	7.50	15.00
	1945L	118.126	BV	6.00	7.50	10.00

NICKEL
Rev: New design, security edge.

Y#	Date	Mintage	Fine	VF	XF	Unc
60	1947C	118.130	1.50	2.50	4.00	6.00
	1947B	Inc. Ab.	1.50	2.50	4.00	6.00

5 RUPEES

3.8870 gm., .917 GOLD, .1146 oz AGW
Obv: Young bust

Y#	Date	Year	Fine	VF	XF	Unc
13	1862	—	—	Proof Only		500.00
	1870	—	—	—	Rare	—
	1870	—	—	—	Proof	375.00
	1870	(restrike)	—	—	Proof	275.00
	1872	—	—	Proof Only		650.00
	1873	—	—	Proof Only		650.00

Obv: Mature bust

Y#	Date	Year	Fine	VF	XF	Unc
13a	1870	—	—	—	Rare	—
	1870	—	—	—	Proof	375.00
	1870	(restrike)	—	—	Proof	275.00
24	1879	—	—	—	Proof	375.00
24	1879	(restrike)	—	—	Proof	275.00

10 RUPEES

7.7740 gm., .917 GOLD, .2292 oz AGW
Obv: Young bust

Y#	Date	Mintage	Fine	VF	XF	Unc
14	1862	—	—	—	Proof	650.00
	1870	—	—	—	Rare	—
	1870	—	—	—	Proof	450.00
	1870	(restrike)	—	—	Proof	275.00
	1872	—	—	—	Proof	650.00
	1875	—	—	—	Proof	650.00

Obv: Mature bust

Y#	Date	Mintage	Fine	VF	XF	Unc
14a	1870	—	—	—	Rare	—
	1870	—	—	—	Proof	350.00
	1870	(restrike)	—	—	Proof	275.00
25	1879 Bom.	—	—	—	Rare	—
	1879 Bom.	(restrike)	—	—	Proof	275.00

15 RUPEES

7.9881 gm., .917 GOLD, .2354 oz AGW

Y#	Date	Mintage	Fine	VF	XF	Unc
46	1918B	—	225.00	275.00	325.00	400.00
	1918B	(restrike)	—	—	Proof	275.00

NOTE: The above issue was equal in weight and fineness to the British sovereign.

MOHUR

11.6600 gm., .917 GOLD, .3437 oz AGW
Obv: Young bust

Y#	Date	Mintage	Fine	VF	XF	Unc
15	1862	—	250.00	300.00	350.00	450.00
	1862	—	—	—	Proof	600.00
	1862	(restrike)	—	—	Proof	300.00
	1862V	—	250.00	325.00	400.00	500.00
	1870	—	—	—	Rare	—
	1870	—	—	—	Proof	600.00
	1870	(restrike)	—	—	Proof	300.00
	1875	—	250.00	300.00	350.00	450.00
	1875	—	—	—	Proof	600.00
	1875	(restrike)	—	—	Proof	300.00

Obv: Mature bust

Y#	Date	Mintage	Fine	VF	XF	Unc
15a	1870	—	—	—	Rare	—
	1870	—	—	—	Proof	650.00
	1870	(restrike)	—	—	Proof	300.00

Mule, obv. Y#26 and rev. Y#15a.

Y#	Date	Mintage	Fine	VF	XF	Unc
15b	1870	—	—	—	Proof	650.00

Obv: Young bust

Y#	Date	Mintage	Fine	VF	XF	Unc
26	1877	—	225.00	275.00	350.00	450.00
	1879	—	225.00	275.00	350.00	450.00
	1879	—	—	—	Proof	650.00
	1879	(restrike)	—	—	Proof	300.00
	1881	—	225.00	275.00	350.00	450.00
	1882C	—	225.00	275.00	350.00	450.00
	1884	—	235.00	300.00	375.00	500.00
	1885	—	225.00	275.00	350.00	450.00
	1888	—	235.00	300.00	375.00	500.00
	1889	—	225.00	275.00	350.00	450.00
	1889	(restrike)	—	—	Proof	300.00
	1891	—	225.00	275.00	350.00	450.00

TRADE COINS

SOVEREIGN

7.9881 gm., .917 GOLD, .2354 oz AGW

Y#	Date	Mintage	Fine	VF	XF	Unc
A46	1918I	1.295	165.00	180.00	200.00	250.00
	1918I	(restrike)	—	—	Proof	185.00

BULLION ISSUES

TOLA

.996 GOLD
Obv: King's royal crown

Fr#	Date	Mintage	VF	XF	Unc
18	ND	—	150.00	175.00	225.00

TOKEN ISSUES

1/2 RUPEE

COPPER
Famine Relief

KM#	Date	Mintage	Fine	VF	XF	Unc
2	1874	—	—	—	—	—

RUPEE

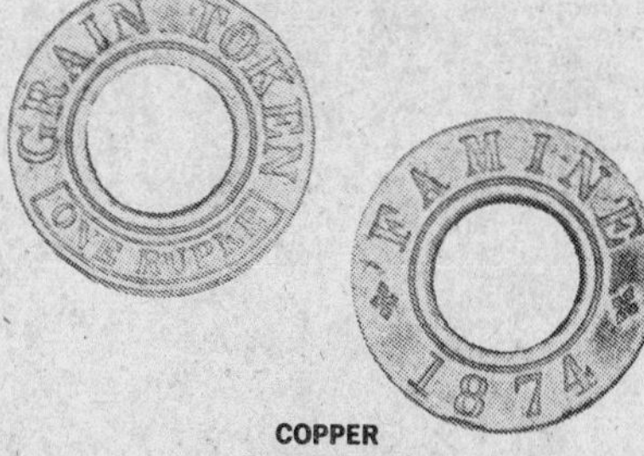

COPPER
Famine Relief

KM#	Date	Mintage	Fine	VF	XF	Unc
1	1874	—	50.00	75.00	100.00	135.00

NCLT ISSUES

PATTERNS

KM#	Date	Mintage	Identification	Mkt.Val.
1	1804	—	20 Cash, Copper, error, mule: Bombay/Madras	—

KM#	Date	Mintage	Identification	Mkt.Val.
2	1834	—	1 Rupee, .917 Silver	—

INDIA REPUBLIC

The Republic of India, a subcontinent jutting southward from the mainland of Asia, has an area of 1,211,000 sq. mi. (3,136,475 sq. km.) and a population of 629 million, second only to that of the People's Republic of China. Capital: New Delhi. India's economy is based on agriculture and industrial activity. Engineering goods, cotton apparel and fabrics, handicrafts, tea, iron and steel are exported.

The people of India have had a continuous civilization since about 2,500 B.C., when an urban culture based on commerce and trade, and to a lesser extent, agriculture, was developed by the inhabitants of the Indus River Valley. The origins of this civilization are uncertain, but it declined about 1,500 B.C., when the region was conquered by the Aryans. Over the following 2,000 years, the Aryans developed a Brahmanic civilization and introduced the caste system. Several successive empires flourished in India over the following centuries, notably those of the Mauryans, Guptas, and Mughals. In the 7th and 8th centuries A.D., the Arabs expanded into western India, bringing with them the Islamic faith. A Muslim dynasty (the Mughal Empire) controlled virtually the entire subcontinent during the period preceding the arrival of the Europeans; an Indo-Islamic style of art and architecture evolved, of which the Taj Mahal is a splendid example.

The Portuguese were the first to arrive, off Calicut in May 1498. It wasn't until 1612, after Portuguese and Spanish power began to wane, that the British East India Company established its initial settlement at Surat. By the end of the century, English traders were firmly established in Bombay, Madras, and Calcutta, as well as in some parts of the interior, and Britain was implementing a policy to create the civil and military institutions that would insure British dominion over the country. By 1757, following the successful conclusion of a war of colonial rivalry with France, the British were firmly established in India as not only traders, but as conquerors. During the next 60 years, the British East India Company acquired dominion over most of India by bribery and force, and ruled directly, or through puppet princelings.

The Indian Mutiny (also called Sepoy Mutiny) of 1857-59, begun by Indian troops in the service of the British East India Company, revealed the intensity of the growing resentment against British domination. The widespread rebellion against British rule was unsuccessful, but resulted in the transfer of government from the company to the British crown, and was a source of inspiration to later Indian nationalists. Agitation for representation in the government continued.

Following World War I, in which India sent six million troops to fight at the side of the Allies, Indian nationalism intensified under the banner of the Indian National Congress and the leadership of Mohandas Karamchand Gandhi, who called for non-violent revolt against British authority. The Government of India Act of 1935 proposed a federal status linking the British India provinces with the many princely states; in addition, provincial legislatures were to be created. The federal status was never implemented, but the legislatures were created after the election of 1937, with the National Congress winning majorities in most of the provinces.

When Britain declared war on Germany in Sept. 1939, the viceroy delcared India also to be at war with a common enemy. The Congress, however, demanded independence as a condition for cooperation,. Britain refused. But as the Japanese advanced into Asia, Britain offered to transfer to Indians power over all but military affairs during the war, and set forth a plan for postwar independence. Congress was willing to accept the wartime transfer of power, but both Congress and the Muslim League rejected Britain's plan for independence; Congress because it did not sufficiently safeguard Indian unity, the Muslims (who wanted a separate Muslim state) because of fears of what would happen to Muslims within a united India.

Early in 1947, Prime Minister Clement Attlee announced that Britain would leave India "by a date not later than June 1948," even though the Hindus and Muslims could not agree among themselves on a plan for self-government. The National Congress, aware that the Muslim League would revolt rather than accept an all-India government, reluctantly agreed to the formation of separate Muslim state. The Muslim-populated provinces of the northwest frontier, Sindh and West Punjab in the west, and East Bengal in the east were separated from India to form the Muslim state of Pakistan, which became independent on Aug. 14, 1947. India became independent on the following day. Initially, Pakistan consisted of East and West Pakistan, two areas separated by 1,000 miles of Indian territory. East Pakistan seceded from Pakistan on March 26, 1971, and with the support of India established itself as the independent People's Republic of Bangladesh.

The Republic of India is a member of the Commonwealth of Nations. The president is the Chief of State. The prime minister is the Head of Government.

MINTMARKS

(Most mintmarks appear directly below the date.)

B - Bombay, proof issues only
(B) - Bombay, diamond
(C) - Calcutta, no mintmark
(H) - Hyderabad, star
(Hd) - Hyderabad, split diamond
(Hy) - Hyderabad, dot in diamond

NOTE: The attribution of the split diamond (Hd) to Hyderabad remains tentative.

MONETARY SYSTEM

(Until 1957)

4 Pice = 1 Anna
16 Annas = 1 Rupee

PICE

BRONZE

Var. 1: 1.6mm thick, 0.3mm edge rim

Y#	Date	Mintage	VF	XF	Unc
61	1950(B)	32.080	.25	.40	.90

Var. 2: 1.6mm thick, 1.0mm edge rim

Y#	Date	Mintage	VF	XF	Unc
61	1950(B)	Inc. Ab.	.15	.25	.40
	1950(b)	—	—	Proof	.75
	1950(C)	14.000	.20	.35	.60

Var. 3: 1.2mm thick, 0.8mm edge rim

Y#	Date	Mintage	VF	XF	Unc
61a	1951(B)	104.626	—	.10	.20
	1951(C)	127.300	—	.10	.20
	1952(B)	213.830	—	.10	.20
	1953(B)	242.358	—	.10	.20
	1953(C)	111.000	—	.10	.20
	1953(Hd)	Inc. Ab.	2.00	3.50	5.00
	1954(B)	136.758	—	.10	.20
	1954(b)	—	—	Proof	2.50
	1954(C)	52.600	—	.10	.20
	1954(Hd)	Inc. Ab.	1.00	2.00	4.00
	1955(B)	24.423	—	.20	.35
	1955(Hd)	Inc. Ab.	—	2.75	4.50

NOTE: A variety of 1954HD exists with mintmark split horizontally, instead of vertically.

1/2 ANNA

COPPER-NICKEL

Y#	Date	Mintage	VF	XF	Unc
62	1950(B)	26.076	.10	.25	.35
	1950(b)	—	—	Proof	2.50
	1950(C)	3.100	.50	.75	1.50
	1954(B)	14.000	.10	.25	.40
	1954(b)	—	—	Proof	2.50
	1954(C)	20.800	.10	.25	.40
	1955(B)	22.488	.10	.25	.40

ANNA

COPPER-NICKEL

Y#	Date	Mintage	VF	XF	Unc
63	1950(B)	9.944	.20	.30	.50
	1950(b)	—	—	Proof	2.50
	1954(B)	20.388	.10	.25	.40
	1954(b)	—	—	Proof	1.00
	1955(B)	—	2.00	3.50	5.00

2 ANNAS

COPPER-NICKEL

Y#	Date	Mintage	VF	XF	Unc
64	1950(B)	7.536	—	.25	.65
	1950(b)	—	—	Proof	1.50
	1954(B)	10.548	.25	.35	.50
	1954(b)	—	—	Proof	1.25
	1955(B)	—	2.00	3.50	5.00

1/4 RUPEE

NICKEL

Var. 1: Large lion

Y#	Date	Mintage	VF	XF	Unc
65	1950(B)	7.650	.15	.30	.75
	1950(b)	—	—	Proof	2.00
	1950(C)	7.800	.15	.30	.75
	1951(B)	41.439	.15	.30	.75
	1951(C)	13.500	.15	.30	.75
	1954(b)	—	—	Proof	1.75
	1954(C)	58.300	.15	.30	.75
	1955(B)	57.936	.20	.40	1.00
	Var. 2: Small lion				
65a	1954(C)	Inc. Ab.	—	.30	.75
	1955(C)	28.900	—	.30	.75
	1956(C)	22.000	—	.30	.75
	1957(C)	7,324	Reported, not confirmed		

1/2 RUPEE

NICKEL

Var. 1: Large lion

Y#	Date	Mintage	VF	XF	Unc
66	1950(B)	12.352	.30	.50	.85
	1950(b)	—	—	Proof	2.50
	1950(C)	1.100	.50	1.00	1.50
	1951(B)	9.239	.50	1.00	1.50
	1954B	—	—	Proof	2.00
	1954(C)	36.300	.25	.50	1.00
	1955(B)	18.977	.50	1.00	1.50
	Var. 2: Small lion **Obv: Dots missing between words.**				
66a	1956(C)	24.900	.25	.40	.75
	1957(C)	1,551	Reported, not confirmed		

RUPEE

NICKEL

Y#	Date	Mintage	VF	XF	Unc
67	1950(B)	19.412	.50	1.00	2.25
	1950(b)	—	—	Proof	6.00
	1954(B)	Inc. Ab.	1.00	1.75	3.00
	1954(b)	—	—	Proof	6.00

DECIMAL COINAGE

100 Naye Paise = 1 Rupee (1957-63)

100 Paise = 1 Rupee (1964-)

NOTE: The Paisa was at first called "Naya Paisa" (= New Paisa), so that people would distinguish from the old non-decimal Paisa (or Pice, equal to 1/64 Rupee). After 7 years, the word 'new' was dropped, and the coin was simply called a "Paisa."

NOTE: Many of the Paisa standard types come with two obverse varieties: (three varieties for 25 Paise).

OBV. I: Asoka lion pedestal small. Short, squat 'D' in 'INDIA'.

OBV. II: Asoka lion pedestal larger. Lettering closer to rim. Tall, more elegant "D" in "INDIA"The shape of the "D" in INDIA is the easiest way to distinguish the 2 obverses.

Obv I

Obv II

NOTE: Paisa standard pieces with mintmark B, 1969 to date, were struck only in proof.

NOTE: Indian mintage figures are not divided by mint, and often include dates other than the year in which struck. They should be regarded with reserve.

NAYA PAISA

BRONZE

Y#	Date	Mintage	VF	XF	Unc
68	1957(B)	618.630	—	.10	.20
	1957(C)	Inc. Ab.	—	.10	.20
	1957(Hd)	Inc. Ab.	.10	.20	.35
	1958(B)	468.630	.20	.30	.50
	1958(Hd)	Inc. Ab.	.10	.20	.35
	1959(B)	351.120	.10	.20	.35
	1959(C)	Inc. Ab.	—	.15	.25
	1959(Hd)	Inc. Ab.	.10	.20	.35
	1960(B)	357.940	—	.10	.20
	1960B	—	—	Proof	—
	1960(C)	Inc. Ab.	.70	1.00	1.50
	1960(Hd)	Inc. Ab.	2.00	3.00	5.00
	1961(B)	573.170	—	.10	.20
	1961B	—	—	Proof	—
	1961(C)	Inc. Ab.	—	.15	.25
	1961(Hy)	Inc. Ab.	.25	.40	.70
	1962(B)	—	—	4.00	5.00

NOTE: 1962(B) has only been found in some of the 1962 uncirculated mint sets.

NICKEL-BRASS

Y#	Date	Mintage	VF	XF	Unc
68a	1962(B)	235.103	—	.15	.25
	1962B	—	—	Proof	—
	1962(C)	Inc. Ab.	—	.15	.30
	1962(Hy)	Inc. Ab.	.25	.40	.70
	1963(B)	343.313	—	.15	.25
	1963B	—	—	Proof	—
	1963(C)	Inc. Ab.	.25	.40	.70
68a	1963(H)	Inc. Ab.	—	.15	.25

PAISA

NICKEL-BRASS

Obverse 1

Y#	Date	Mintage	VF	XF	Unc
75	1964(B)	539.068	—	.10	.25
	1964(C)	Inc. Ab.	—	.10	.20
	1964(H)	Inc. Ab.	—	.10	.25
	BRONZE				
75a	1964(H)	Inc. Ab.	.35	.50	.80

ALUMINUM

Obverse 1

Y#	Date	Mintage	VF	XF	Unc
84	1965(B)	223.480	.20	.35	.60
	1965(Hy)	Inc. Ab.	.15	.25	.40
	1966(B)	404.200	.10	.20	.30
	1966(C)	Inc. Ab.	.15	.30	.50
	1966(Hy)	Inc. Ab.	—	—	.15
	1967(B)	450.433	—	—	.10
	1967(C)	Inc. Ab.	—	.10	.20
	1967(Hy)	Inc. Ab.	—	—	.15
	1968(B)	302.720	—	—	.10
	1968(C)	Inc. Ab.	—	.10	.20
	1968(Hy)	Inc. Ab.	—	—	.10
	1969(B)	125.930	.30	.50	.80
	1969B	9,147	—	Proof	2.00
	1969(H)	Inc. Ab.	.30	.50	.80
	1970(B)	15.800	1.75	2.00	2.25
	1970B	3,046	—	Proof	2.00
	1970(C)	—	—	—	—
	1971(H)	112.100	—	—	.10
	1971B	4,375	—	Proof	1.50
	1972(B)	62.090	—	—	.10
	1972B	7,895	—	Proof	1.25
	1972(H)	Inc. Ab.	—	—	.10
	1973B	7,562	—	Proof	1.25
	1974B	—	—	Proof	1.25
	1975B	—	—	Proof	1.25
	1976B	—	—	Proof	—
	1977B	—	—	Proof	1.25
	Obverse 2				
84.1	1969(C)	Inc. Ab.	.20	.25	.40
	1970(C)	Inc. Ab.	—	—	.10

2 NAYE PAISE

COPPER-NICKEL

Y#	Date	Mintage	VF	XF	Unc
69	1957(B)	406.230	—	.10	.25
	1957(C)	Inc. Ab.	—	.10	.25
	1958(B)	245.660	—	.10	.25
	1958(C)	Inc. Ab.	—	.15	.30
	1959(B)	171.445	.10	.20	.35
	1959(C)	Inc. Ab.	.25	.40	.80
	1960(B)	121.820	—	.10	.25
	1960B	—	—	Proof	—
	1960(C)	Inc. Ab.	.10	.20	.25
	1961(B)	190.610	—	.15	.15
	1961B	—	—	Proof	—
	1961(C)	Inc. Ab.	—	.15	.20
	1962(B)	318.181	—	.10	.25
	1962B	—	—	Proof	—
	1962(C)	Inc. Ab.	—	.10	.25
	1963(B)	372.380	—	.10	.15
	1963B	—	—	Proof	—
	1963(C)	Inc. Ab.	—	.15	.25

2 PAISE

COPPER-NICKEL
Obverse 1

Y#	Date	Mintage	VF	XF	Unc
76	1964(B)	323.504	—	—	.15
	1964(C)	Inc. Ab.	—	—	.15

ALUMINUM
Obverse 1, Rev: 10mm '2'

Y#	Date	Mintage	VF	XF	Unc
85	1965(B)	175.770	—	—	.20
	1965(C)	Inc. Ab.	.10	.20	.35
	1966(B)	386.795	—	—	.15
	1966(C)	Inc. Ab.	—	—	.15
	1967(B)	454.593	—	—	.15

Obverse 1, Rev: 10-1/2mm "2".

Y#	Date	Mintage	VF	XF	Unc
85.1	1967(C)	Inc. Ab.	—	—	.15

Obverse 1, Rev: 11mm "2".

Y#	Date	Mintage	VF	XF	Unc
85.2	1968(C)	—	—	—	—
	1977(B)	—	—	—	—
	1977(B)	—	—	Proof	—
	1978(B)	—	—	Proof	—

Obverse 2, Rev: 10mm "2".

Y#	Date	Mintage	VF	XF	Unc
85.3	1967(B)	—	—	—	—

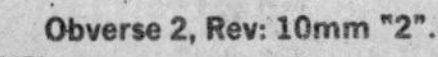

Obverse 2, Rev: 11mm '2'

Y#	Date	Mintage	VF	XF	Unc
85.4	1968(B)	305.205	—	—	.10
	1968(C)	Inc. Ab.	—	.15	.25
	1969(B)	5.335	1.00	1.25	1.75
	1969B	9,147	—	Proof	2.00
	1970(B)	—	1.00	1.50	2.00
	1970B	3,046	—	Proof	2.00
	1970(C)	79.100	—	—	.10
	1971B	4,375	—	Proof	1.25
	1971(C)	207.900	—	—	.10
	1972B	7,895	—	Proof	1.25
	1972(C)	261.270	—	—	.15
	1972(H)	Inc. Ab.	—	—	.10
	1973B	7,562	—	Proof	1.25
	1973(C)	—	—	—	.20
	1973(H)	—	—	—	.10
	1974B	—	—	Proof	1.25
	1974(C)	—	—	—	.10
	1974(H)	—	—	—	.10
	1975B	—	—	Proof	1.25
	1975(C)	184.500	—	—	.10
	1975(H)	Inc. Ab.	—	—	.10
	1976B	68.140	—	—	.10
	1976B	—	—	Proof	—
	1976(H)	—	—	—	—
	1977B	—	—	—	1.25
	1977(H)	—	—	—	—

3 PAISE

ALUMINUM
Obverse 1

Y#	Date	Mintage	VF	XF	Unc
77	1964(B)	138.890	—	—	.10
	1964(C)	Inc. Ab.	—	.10	.20
	1965(B)	459.825	—	—	.15
	1965(C)	Inc. Ab.	.10	.20	.35
	1966(B)	390.440	—	—	.10
	1966(C)	Inc. Ab.	—	—	.15
77	1966(Hy)	Inc. Ab.	.20	.35	.50
	1967(B)	167.018	—	—	.10
	1967(C)	Inc. Ab.	—	—	.10
	1967(H)	Inc. Ab.	.60	.90	1.35
	1968(B)	—	.60	.90	1.35
	1968(H)	—	2.00	2.50	3.00

Obverse 2

Y#	Date	Mintage	VF	XF	Unc
77	1967(C)	—	.65	.90	1.35
	1967(H)	Inc. Ab.	.65	.90	1.35
	1968(B)	246.390	—	—	.10
	1968(C)	Inc. Ab.	.30	.45	.70
	1968(H)	Inc. Ab.	—	—	.20
	1969B	9,147	—	Proof	2.00
	1969(C)	7.025	—	—	.20
	1969(H)	Inc. Ab.	.40	.60	1.00
	1970(B)	—	1.00	1.25	1.50
	1970B	3,046	—	Proof	2.00
	1970(C)	15.300	—	—	.10
	1971B	4,375	—	Proof	1.50
	1971(C)	203.100	—	—	.10
	1971(H)	Inc. Ab.	—	—	.10

Obverse 2

Y#	Date	Mintage	VF	XF	Unc
A93	1972B	7,895	—	Proof	1.25
	1973B	7,562	—	Proof	1.25
	1974B	—	—	Proof	1.25
	1975B	—	—	Proof	1.25
	1976B	—	—	Proof	1.25
	1977B	—	—	Proof	1.25

NOTE: Reportedly, 9,740,000 pieces were produced, but it is not known at which mint. To date, only proof coins with B mintmark have been confirmed.

5 NAYE PAISE

COPPER-NICKEL

Y#	Date	Mintage	VF	XF	Unc
70	1957(B)	227.210	—	.15	.35
	1957(C)	Inc. Ab.	—	.15	.35
	1958(B)	214.320	—	.20	.35
	1958(C)	Inc. Ab.	—	.20	.35
	1959(B)	137.105	—	.15	.40
	1959(C)	Inc. Ab.	—	.25	.65
	1960(B)	93.345	—	.15	.40
	1960B	—	—	Proof	—
	1960(C)	Inc. Ab.	—	.20	.55
	1960(Hy)	Inc. Ab.	—	.25	.65
	1961(B)	197.620	—	.15	.30
	1961B	—	—	Proof	—
	1961(C)	Inc. Ab.	.25	.45	.70
	1961(Hy)	Inc. Ab.	.75	1.25	1.75
	1962(B)	224.277	—	.15	.30
	1962B	—	—	Proof	—
	1962(C)	Inc. Ab.	—	.15	.30
	1962(Hy)	Inc. Ab.	—	.45	.70
	1963(B)	332.600	—	.15	.30
	1963B	—	—	Proof	—
	1963(C)	Inc. Ab.	—	.45	.70
	1963(H)	Inc. Ab.	.40	.60	1.00

5 PAISE

COPPER-NICKEL
Obverse 1

Y#	Date	Mintage	VF	XF	Unc
78	1964(B)	156.000	.40	.60	1.00
	1964(C)	Inc. Ab.	.25	.45	.70
	1964(H)	Inc. Ab.	.40	.60	1.00
	1965(B)	203.855	—	.10	.20
	1965(C)	Inc. Ab.	.25	.45	.70
	1965(H)	Inc. Ab.	.75	1.25	1.75
	1966(B)	101.395	.40	.60	1.00
	1966(C)	Inc. Ab.	.25	.45	.70

ALUMINUM
6mm Short 5 **7mm Tall 5**
Obverse 1

Y#	Date	Mintage	VF	XF	Unc
78.1	1967(B)short 5	608.533	—	—	.15
	1967(B)tall 5	Inc. Ab.	.25	.45	.80
	1967(c)short	I.A.	—	—	.15
	1967(H)tall	Inc. Ab.	—	—	.15
	1968(B)	—	2.00	2.50	3.00
	1968(C)	—	—	.30	1.75
	1968(H)	666.750	—	—	1.00
	1971(H)	499.200	—	—	.15

Obverse 2

Y#	Date	Mintage	VF	XF	Unc
78.2	1967(H)	—	1.00	1.50	2.00
	1968(B)	Inc. Ab.	—	—	.15
	1968(C)	Inc. Ab.	—	—	.15
	1968(H)	Inc. Ab.	—	—	.30
	1969(B)	3.740	.75	1.25	1.75
	1969B	9,147	—	Proof	2.00
	1970(B)	39.900	.15	.25	.45
	1970B	3,046	—	Proof	2.00
	1970(C)	Inc. Ab.	.15	.25	.45
	1970(H)	Inc. Ab.	.40	.60	1.00
	1971(B) Inc. w/1971(H) of Obverse 1	—	—	—	.15
	1971B	4,375	—	Proof	1.25
	1971(C)	Inc. Ab.	—	—	.15
	1971(H)	—	—	—	.15

Obverse 1

Y#	Date	Mintage	VF	XF	Unc
B93	1972(H)	512.430	—	—	.15
	1973(H)	—	1.00	1.40	2.00
	1977(B)	—	—	—	.10
	1978(B)	—	—	—	.10

Obverse 2

Y#	Date	Mintage	VF	XF	Unc
B93.1	1972(B)	Inc. Ab.	—	—	.15
	1972B	7,895	—	Proof	1.25
	1972(C)	Inc. Ab.	—	—	.15
	1972(H)	—	—	.30	.50

Different style date and larger "5".

Y#	Date	Mintage	VF	XF	Unc
B93.2	1973(B)	—	—	—	.15
	1973B	7,562	—	Proof	1.25
	1973(C)	—	—	—	.15

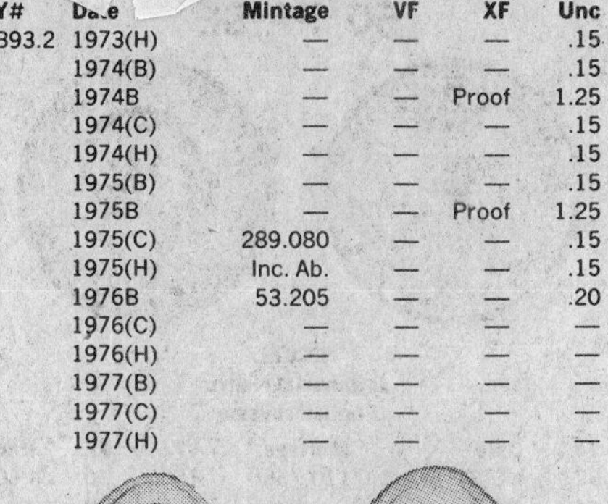

Y#	Date	Mintage	VF	XF	Unc
B93.2	1973(H)	—	—	—	.15
	1974(B)	—	—	—	.15
	1974B	—	—	Proof	1.25
	1974(C)	—	—	—	.15
	1974(H)	—	—	—	.15
	1975(B)	—	—	—	.15
	1975B	—	—	Proof	1.25
	1975(C)	289.080	—	—	.15
	1975(H)	Inc. Ab.	—	—	.15
	1976B	53.205	—	—	.20
	1976(C)	—	—	—	—
	1976(H)	—	—	—	—
	1977(B)	—	—	—	—
	1977(C)	—	—	—	—
	1977(H)	—	—	—	—

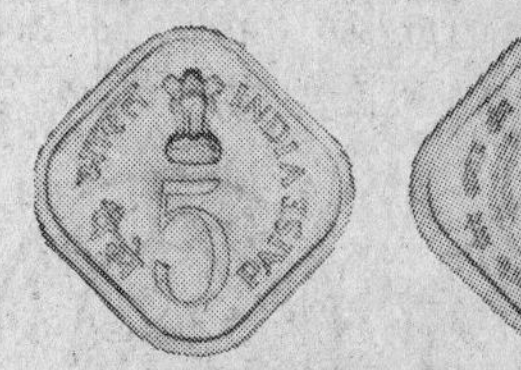

F.A.O. Issue, FOOD & WORK FOR ALL

Y#	Date	Mintage	VF	XF	Unc
107	1976(B)	160.000	—	—	.15
	1976B	—	—	Proof	1.25
	1976(C)	Inc. Ab.	—	—	.15
	1976H	—	—	—	—

F.A.O. Issue, SAVE FOR DEVELOPMENT

Y#	Date	Mintage	VF	XF	Unc
111	1977(B)	80.950	—	—	.15
	1977(B)	2,224	—	Proof	1.25
	1977(C)	Inc. Ab.	—	—	.15

F.A.O. Issue, FOOD & SHELTER FOR ALL

Y#	Date	Mintage	VF	XF	Unc
115	1978(B)	90.000	—	—	.15
	1978(B)	—	—	Proof	1.25
	1978(C)	Inc. Ab.	—	—	.15

International Year of the Child

Y#	Date	Mintage	VF	XF	Unc
119	1979(B)	—	—	—	.10
	1979(C)	—	—	—	—

10 NAYE PAISE

COPPER-NICKEL

Y#	Date	Mintage	VF	XF	Unc
71	1957(B)	139.655	.10	.20	.40
	1957(C)	Inc. Ab.	.10	.20	.40
	1958(B)	123.160	.10	.20	.40
	1958(C)	Inc. Ab.	.25	.40	.70
	1959(B)	148.570	.10	.20	.40
	1959(C)	Inc. Ab.	.10	.20	.40
	1960(B)	52.335	.10	.20	.40
	1960B	—	—	Proof	—
	1961(B)	172.545	.10	.20	.40
	1961B	—	—	Proof	—
	1961(C)	Inc. Ab.	.10	.20	.40
	1961(Hy)	Inc. Ab.	1.00	1.40	2.00
	1962(B)	172.777	.10	.20	.40
	1962B	—	—	Proof	—
	1962(C)	Inc. Ab.	.10	.20	.40
71	1962(Hy)	Inc. Ab.	.40	.60	1.00
	1963(B)	182.834	.10	.20	.40
	1963B	—	—	Proof	—
	1963(C)	Inc. Ab.	.10	.20	.40
	1963(H)	Inc. Ab.	.25	.40	.75

10 PAISE

COPPER-NICKEL
Obverse 1, Rev: 6.5mm '10'

Y#	Date	Mintage	VF	XF	Unc
79	1964(B) open 4	84.112	.10	.20	.35
	1964(B) closed 4	Inc. Ab.	1.00	1.40	2.00
	1964(C)	Inc. Ab.	.15	.25	.45
	1964(H)	Inc. Ab.	.40	.60	1.00
	1965(B)	253.430	—	.10	.30
	1965(C)	Inc. Ab.	—	.10	.30
	1965(Hy)	Inc. Ab.	.25	.40	.75
	1965(H)	Inc. Ab.	.25	.40	.75
	1966(B)	326.990	—	.10	.30
	1966(C)	Inc. Ab.	—	.10	.30
	1966(Hy)	Inc. Ab.	.15	.25	.45
	1967(B)	59.443	.40	.60	1.00
	1967(C)	Inc. Ab.	.40	.60	1.00
	1967(H)	Inc. Ab.	.40	.60	1.00

NICKEL-BRASS
Obverse 1

Y#	Date	Mintage	VF	XF	Unc
79a	1968(H)	55.940	1.00	1.40	2.00

Obverse 2, Rev: 6.5mm '10'

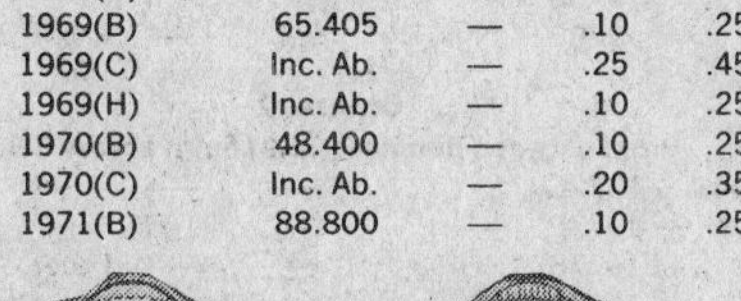

Y#	Date	Mintage	VF	XF	Unc
79a.1	1968(B)	Inc. Ab.	—	.20	.35
	1968(C)	Inc. Ab.	—	.10	.25
	1968(H)	Inc. Ab.	—	.20	.35
	1969(B)	65.405	—	.10	.25
	1969(C)	Inc. Ab.	—	.25	.45
	1969(H)	Inc. Ab.	—	.10	.25
	1970(B)	48.400	—	.10	.25
	1970(C)	Inc. Ab.	—	.20	.35
	1971(B)	88.800	—	.10	.25

Obverse 2, Rev: 7mm '10'

Y#	Date	Mintage	VF	XF	Unc
79a.2	1969B	9,147	—	Proof	2.50
	1970B	3,046	—	Proof	2.00
	1971B	4,375	—	Proof	2.00

ALUMINUM
Obverse 2

Y#	Date	Mintage	VF	XF	Unc
93	1971(B)	146.100	—	—	.15
	1971(C)	Inc. Ab.	—	—	.15
	1971(H)	Inc. Ab.	.10	.25	.45
	1972(B)	735.090	—	—	.15
	1972B	7,895	—	Proof	1.25
	1972(C)	Inc. Ab.	—	—	.15
	1973(B)	—	—	—	.15
	1973B	7,567	—	Proof	1.25
	1973(C)	—	—	—	.15
	1973(H)	—	—	.15	.30
	1974(B)	—	—	—	.20
93	1974(C)	—	—	—	.20
	1974(H)	—	—	—	.15
	1975B	—	—	—	.20
	1975(C)	298.830	—	—	.15
	1976B	1.115	—	—	.15
	1977B	—	—	—	.15
	1977C	—	—	—	.15
	1978B	—	—	—	.15
	1978C	—	—	—	.15

F. A. O. Issue

Y#	Date	Mintage	VF	XF	Unc
101	1974(B)	369.168	—	—	.15
	1974B	—	—	Proof	2.00
	1974(C)	Inc. Ab.	—	—	.20
	1974(H)	Inc. Ab.	.15	.25	.45

F.A.O. Issues, EQUALITY, DEVELOPMENT, PEACE

Y#	Date	Mintage	VF	XF	Unc
104	1975(B)	142.500	—	—	.15
	1975B	—	—	Proof	2.00
	1975(C)	Inc. Ab.	—	—	.15

NOTE: Mintmark is below wheat stalk.

F.A.O. Issue, FOOD & WORK FOR ALL

Y#	Date	Mintage	VF	XF	Unc
108	1976(B)	50.000	—	—	.25
	1976B	—	—	Proof	1.75
	1976(C)	Inc. Ab.	—	—	.25

F.A.O. Issue, SAVE FOR DEVELOPMENT

Y#	Date	Mintage	VF	XF	Unc
112	1977(B)	25.060	—	—	.25
	1977(B)	2,224	—	Proof	1.75
	1977(C)	Inc. Ab.	—	Proof	—

F.A.O. Issue, FOOD & SHELTER FOR ALL

Y#	Date	Mintage	VF	XF	Unc
116	1978(B)	112.500	—	—	.25
	1978(C)	Inc. Ab.	—	—	1.75
	1978(H)	Inc. Ab.	—	—	.25

International Year of the Child

Y#	Date	Mintage	VF	XF	Unc
120	1979(b)	—	—	—	.25

Y#	Date	Mintage	VF	XF	Unc
120	1979(C)	—	—	—	.25

20 PAISE

NICKEL-BRASS

Y#	Date	Mintage	VF	XF	Unc
86	1968(B)	10.585	.15	.25	.45
	1968(C)	Inc. Ab.	.20	.35	.60
	1969(B)	197.940	—	.15	.30
	1969C	—	—	.15	.30
	1970(B)	Inc. Ab.	—	.15	.30
	1970(C)	Inc. Ab.	—	.15	.30
	1970(H)	Inc. Ab.	—	.15	.30
	1971(B)	124.200	—	.15	.30

ALUMINUM-BRONZE
Mahatma Gandhi Centennial

Y#	Date	Mintage	VF	XF	Unc
87	ND (B)	100.000	—	.15	.30
	ND B	9,147	—	Proof	2.50
	ND (C)	Inc. Ab.	—	.15	.30
	ND (H)	Inc. Ab.	—	.20	.40

Struck in 1969 & 1970.

F.A.O. Issue, FOOD FOR ALL

Y#	Date	Mintage	VF	XF	Unc
91	1970(B)	10.173	—	.20	.30
	1970B	3,046	—	Proof	3.00
	1970(C)	—	.20	.30	.50
	1971(B)	.060	.15	.25	.40
	1971B	4,375	—	Proof	2.50

25 NAYE PAISE

NICKEL

Y#	Date	Mintage	VF	XF	Unc
72	1957(B)	5.640	.25	.50	1.00
	1957(C)	Inc. Ab.	.25	.50	1.00
	1959(B)	43.080	.15	.30	.70
	1959(C)	Inc. Ab.	.10	.30	.50
	1960(B)	115.320	—	.25	.50
	1960B	—	—	Proof	—
	1960(C)	Inc. Ab.	—	.25	.50
	1961(B)	109.008	—	.25	.50
	1961B	—	—	Proof	—
	1961(C)	Inc. Ab.	—	.25	.50
	1962(B)	79.242	—	.25	.50
	1962B	—	—	Proof	—
	1962(C)	Inc. Ab.	—	.25	.50
	1963(B)	101.565	—	.25	.50
	1963B	—	—	Proof	—
	1963(C)	Inc. Ab.	—	.25	.50

25 PAISE

NICKEL

Obverse 1, Reverse 1

Y#	Date	Mintage	VF	XF	Unc
80	1964(B)	85.321	—	.20	.40
	1964(C)	Inc. Ab.	—	.20	.40

Obverse 1, Reverse 2

Y#	Date	Mintage	VF	XF	Unc
80.1	1965(B)	143.662	—	.20	.40
	1965(C)	Inc. Ab.	—	.20	.40
	1966(B)	59.040	—	.20	.40
	1966(C)	Inc. Ab.	.15	.30	.60
	1967(B)	30.027	2.00	2.50	3.00

Obverse 2, Reverse 2

Y#	Date	Mintage	VF	XF	Unc
80.2	1967(C)	Inc. Ab.	—	.20	.50
	1968(B)	Inc. Ab.	—	.25	.60

COPPER-NICKEL
Obverse 1

Y#	Date	Mintage	VF	XF	Unc
94	1972(B)	367.640	—	—	.30
	1972B	7,895	—	Proof	2.00
	1972(H)	Inc. Ab.	—	.20	.40
	1973(B)	—	—	—	.30
	1973B	7,567	—	Proof	2.00
	1973(H)	—	—	—	.30
	1974(B)	—	—	—	.25
	1974B	—	—	Proof	2.00
	1974(H)	—	—	—	.35
	1975(B)	559.980	—	—	.25
	1975B	—	—	Proof	2.00
	1975(H)	Inc. Ab.	—	—	.25
	1976B	30.016	—	—	.25
	1976B	—	—	Proof	2.00
	1976H	—	—	—	.25
	1977B	—	—	Proof	—
	1977H	—	—	—	.25
	1978B	—	—	—	.25
	1978B	—	—	Proof	—

Obverse 2
9mm between lion nosetips, 15mm across field.

Y#	Date	Mintage	VF	XF	Unc
94.1	1972C	—	—	—	.25
	1977B	—	—	—	.25
	1977B	—	—	Proof	—
	1978B	—	—	—	.25

Obverse 2
10mm between lion nosetips, 16-16.3mm across field.

Y#	Date	Mintage	VF	XF	Unc
94.2	1972(C)	Inc. Ab.	1.00	1.40	2.00
	1973(C)	—	—	.15	.30
	1974(C)	—	—	.15	.30
	1975(C)	Inc. Ab.	—	.15	.30

50 NAYE PAISE

NICKEL

Y#	Date	Mintage	VF	XF	Unc
73	1960(B)	11.224	.40	.60	1.00
	1960B	—	—	Proof	—
	1960(C)	Inc. Ab.	.20	.40	.85
	1961(B)	45.992	.15	.30	.70
	1961B	—	—	Proof	—
	1961(C)	Inc. Ab.	.15	.30	.70
	1962(B)	64.228	.15	.30	.70
	1962B	—	—	Proof	—
	1962(C)	Inc. Ab.	.15	.30	.70
	1963(B)	58.168	.15	.30	.70
	1963B	—	—	Proof	—
	1963(C)	Inc. Ab.	.20	.40	.85

50 PAISE

NICKEL
Jawaharlal Nehru
English reverse

Y#	Date	Mintage	VF	XF	Unc
82	ND(B)	110.766	.15	.30	.60
	ND B	—	—	Proof	—
	ND (C)	—	.30	.45	.90

Hindi reverse

Y#	Date	Mintage	VF	XF	Unc
82.1	ND (B)	Inc. Ab.	.15	.30	.60
	ND (C)	Inc. Ab.	.15	.35	.70

NOTE: Nehru Commemorative issues were struck until 1967.

Obverse 1, Reverse 1

Y#	Date	Mintage	VF	XF	Unc
81	1964(C)	23.361	.15	.40	.80
	1967(B)	19.267	.15	.30	.65

Obverse 1, Reverse 2

Y#	Date	Mintage	VF	XF	Unc
81.1	1970(B)	Inc. w/1969 below			
		—	.15	.25	.60
	1970B	3,046	—	Proof	3.00
	1971B	4,375	—	Proof	2.50

Obverse 2, Reverse 2

Y#	Date	Mintage	VF	XF	Unc
81.2	1967(C)	—	.35	.60	1.00
	1968(B)	28.076	.15	.25	.50
	1968(C)	Inc. Ab.	.15	.25	.50
	1969(B)	59.388	.15	.25	.50
	1969(C)	Inc. Ab.	.35	.60	1.00
	1970(B)	Inc. Ab.	.15	.25	.50
	1970(C)	Inc. Ab.	.15	.25	.50
	1971(C)	57.900	.10	.20	.45

Mahatma Gandhi Centennial

Y#	Date	Mintage	VF	XF	Unc
88	ND (B)	20.000	.15	.25	.50
	ND B	9,147	—	Proof	3.00
	ND (C)	Inc. Ab.	.15	.25	.50

Struck during 1969 and 1970.

COPPER-NICKEL
25th Anniversary of Independence

Y#	Date	Mintage	VF	XF	Unc
96	ND(B)	55.960	.10	.20	.40
	ND(B)	7,895	—	Proof	2.50
	ND(C)	Inc. Ab.	.10	.20	.40

Obverse 2, Rev. Lettering spaced out.

Y#	Date	Mintage	VF	XF	Unc
95	1972(B)	Inc. Ab.	.10	.20	.35
	1972(C)	Inc. Ab.	.10	.20	.35
	1973(B)	—	.10	.20	.35
	1973(C)	—	.40	.60	1.00

Obverse 2, Rev. Lettering close.

Y#	Date	Mintage	VF	XF	Unc
95.1	1974(B)	—	.10	.20	.35
	1974B	—	—	Proof	2.00
	1974(C)	—	.10	.20	.35
	1975(B)	225.880	.10	.20	.35
	1975B	—	—	Proof	2.00
	1975(C)	Inc. Ab.	.10	.20	.35
	1975H	—	—	—	—
	1976B	99.564	.10	.15	.40
	1976B	—	—	Proof	—
	1976C	—	—	—	—
	1976H	—	—	—	—
	1977B	—	—	Proof	—
	1977B	—	—	—	—
	1977H	—	—	—	—
	1978B	—	—	Proof	—

F. A. O. Issue

Y#	Date	Mintage	VF	XF	Unc
98	1973(B)	47.086	.15	.20	.50
	1973B	.011	—	Proof	2.50
	1973(C)	—	.15	.25	.50

RUPEE

NICKEL, 10 gm.
Obverse 1

Y#	Date	Mintage	VF	XF	Unc
74	1962B	—	—	Proof	—
	1962(C)	3.689	.60	1.25	2.50
	1970(B)	Inc. Ab.	1.50	2.50	4.00
	1970B	3,046	—	Proof	4.00
	1971B	4,375	—	Proof	4.00
	1972B	7.895	—	Proof	3.00
	1973B	7,567	—	Proof	3.00
	1974B	—	—	Proof	3.00

COPPER-NICKEL, 8 gm.

Y#	Date	Mintage	VF	XF	Unc
74a	1975(B)	98.850	.15	.25	.50
	1975B	—	—	Proof	3.00
	1976B	161.895	.15	.25	.50
	1976B	—	—	Proof	—
	1977B	—	.15	.25	.50
	1977B	—	—	Proof	3.00
	1978(B)	—	—	—	—
	1978B	—	—	Proof	—
	1978C	—	—	—	—

Obverse 2

Y#	Date	Mintage	VF	XF	Unc
	1975(C)	Inc. Ab.	.20	.35	.75
	1976C	—	.20	.35	.75

NICKEL
Jawaharlal Nehru

Y#	Date	Mintage	VF	XF	Unc
83	ND (B)	20.036	.25	.50	1.00
	ND B	—	—	Proof	—
	ND (C)	Inc. Ab.	.25	.50	1.00

NOTE: Nehru commemorative issues were struck until 1967.

Mahatma Gandhi Centennial

Y#	Date	Mintage	VF	XF	Unc
89	ND (B)	11.851	.25	.40	.75
	ND B	9,147	—	Proof	5.00
	ND (C)	Inc. Ab.	.30	.60	1.25

Struck during 1969 and 1970.

10 RUPEES

15.0000 gm., .800 SILVER, .3858 oz ASW
Mahatma Gandhi Centennial

Y#	Date	Mintage	VF	XF	Unc
90	ND(B)	3.247	BV	BV	12.00
	ND B	9,147	—	Proof	15.00
	ND(C)	Inc. Ab.	BV	BV	12.00

Struck during 1969 and 1970.

F. A. O. Issue
Obv: Similar to Y#90.

Y#	Date	Mintage	VF	XF	Unc
92	1970(B)	.406	BV	12.00	15.00
	1970B	3,046	—	Proof	17.50
	1970(C)	Inc. Ab.	BV	12.00	15.00
	1971(B)	.020	BV	12.00	17.50
	1971B	1,594	—	Proof	25.00

22.3000 gm., .500 SILVER, .3585 oz ASW
25th Anniversary of Independence

Y#	Date	Mintage	VF	XF	Unc
97	1972(B)	.012	BV	BV	12.00
	1972B	—	—	Proof	15.00
	1972(C)	Inc. Ab.	BV	BV	12.00

F. A. O. Issue
Obv: Similar to Y#97.

Y#	Date	Mintage	VF	XF	Unc
99	1973(B)	.064	BV	BV	12.00
	1973B	.015	—	Proof	15.00

COPPER-NICKEL
F.A.O. Issue
Obv: Similar to Y#97.

Y#	Date	Mintage	VF	XF	Unc
102	1974(B)	.065	1.50	3.00	4.00
	1974B	.012	—	Proof	17.50

F.A.O. Issue, EQUALITY, DEVELOPMENT, PEACE
Obv: Similar to Y#97.

Y#	Date	Mintage	VF	XF	Unc
105	1975(B)	.049	1.50	2.75	4.00
	1975B	2,531	—	Proof	6.00

F.A.O. Issue
Obv: Similar to Y#97.

Y#	Date	Mintage	VF	XF	Unc
109	1976(B)	.042	1.50	2.50	3.75
	1976B	—	—	Proof	6.50

F.A.O. Issue
Obv: Similar to Y#97.

Y#	Date	Mintage	VF	XF	Unc
113	1977(B)	.026	1.75	3.00	4.50
	1977B	2,384	—	Proof	7.00

F.A.O. Issue

Obv: Similar to Y#97.

Y#	Date	Mintage	VF	XF	Unc
117	1978(B)	.025	—	3.00	4.00
	1978B	—	—	Proof	7.00

International Year of the Child
24.7000 gms.

Y#	Date	Mintage	VF	XF	Unc
121	1979(b)	—	—	3.00	4.00
	1979B	—	—	Proof	7.00

20 RUPEES

30.0000 gm., .500 SILVER, .4823 oz ASW
F. A. O. Issue

Y#	Date	Mintage	VF	XF	Unc
100	1973(B)	.064	BV	BV	15.00
	1973B	.012	—	Proof	20.00

50 RUPEES

34.9500 gm., .500 SILVER, .5618 oz ASW
F. A. O. Issue

Y#	Date	Mintage	VF	XF	Unc
103	1974(B)	.082	BV	17.50	20.00
	1974B	.013	—	Proof	25.00

F.A.O. Issue
Obv: Similar to Y#103.

Y#	Date	Mintage	VF	XF	Unc
106	1975(B)	.065	BV	17.50	20.00
	1975B	2,691	—	Proof	25.00

F.A.O Issue
Obv: Similar to Y#103.

Y#	Date	Mintage	VF	XF	Unc
110	1976(B)	.042	BV	17.50	20.00
	1976B	—	—	Proof	25.00

F.A.O. Issue
Obv: Similar to Y#103.

Y#	Date	Mintage	VF	XF	Unc
114	1977(B)	.026	BV	17.50	20.00
	1977B	2,544	—	Proof	25.00

F.A.O. Issue
Obv: Similar to Y#103.

Y#	Date	Mintage	VF	XF	Unc
118	1978(B)	.025	BV	17.50	20.00
	1978B	—	—	Proof	25.00

International Year of the Child

Y#	Date	Mintage	VF	XF	Unc
122	1979(b)	—	—	—	—

NCLT ISSUES

MINT SETS

KM#	Date	Mintage	Identification	Issue Price	Mkt. Val.
S1	1950(7)	—	—	—	—
S2	1954(7)	—	—	—	—
S3	1962(B)(6)	—	—	—	—
S4	1964(2)	—	—	—	—
S5	1967(8)	—	—	—	—
S6	ND(1969)B (4)	—	Y87-90, green plastic case	2.50	—
S7	1970(B)(8)	—	Y74,77,78a,79a,81.3,84-86, brown vinyl case, diamond below date	1.00	—
S8	1970B(2)	—	Y91,92, clear plastic case	2.00	—

PROOF SETS

NOTE: Beginning in 1969, all proof coins have B beneath date, for Bombay Mint. Normal Bombay coins have diamond mintmark.

Standard metals unless otherwise noted

KM#	Date	Mintage	Identification	Issue Price	Mkt. Val.
101	1950(7)	-*	Y61-67	8.40	15.00
102	1954(7)	-*	Y61a,62-67	8.40	12.00
103	1960(6)	-*	Y68-73	7.00	15.00
104	1961(6)	-*	Y68-73	7.00	15.00
105	1962(7)	-*	Y68a,69-74	8.40	12.00
106	1963(6)	-*	Y68a,69-73	7.00	15.00
107	1964(2)	-*	Y82,83	5.00	12.00

***NOTE:** Restrikes exist for KM#101-107.

KM#	Date	Mintage	Identification	Issue Price	Mkt. Val.
108	1969B(9)	9,147	Y77,78a,79a, 84,85,87-90	15.25	40.00
109	1970B(9)	3,046	Y74,77,78a,79a, 81.2,84,85,91,92	15.25	45.00
110	1971B(9)	4,375	As Above	15.25	35.00
111	1972B(9)	7,895	Y74,84,85,93, A93,B93,94.1,96,97a	15.25	25.00
112	1973B(10)	7,562	Y74,84,85,93,A93 B93,94.1,98-100	26.00	35.00
113	1973B(9)	3,326	As Above Less Y100	15.25	25.00
114	1973B(2)	2,408	Y99,100	17.50	35.00
115	1974B(10)	9,138	Y74,84,85,A93,B93, 94.1,95.2,101-103	29.00	45.00
116	1974B(2)	1,712	Y102,103	7.50	42.50
117	1975B(10)	—	Y74a,84,85,A93,B93, 94.1,95.2,104-106	35.00	35.00
118	1975B(2)	—	Y105,106	22.00	30.00
119	1976B(10)	—	Y74,84,85,A93,94.1,95.2,107-110	35.00	27.50
120	1976B(2)	—	Y109,110	22.00	30.00
121	1977B(6)	—	Y84,85,A93,94.1,95.2,74a	35.00	—

Listings For

INDO-CHINA: refer to French Indo-China

INDONESIA

The Republic of Indonesia, the world's largest archipelago, extends for more than 3,000 miles (4,827 km.) along the equator from the mainland of southeast Asia to Australia. The more than 13,500 islands comprising the archipelago have a combined area of 736,000 sq. mi. (1,906,230 sq. km.) and a population of 135 million, including East Timor. Capital: Jakarta. Petroleum, timber, rubber, and coffee are exported.

Had Columbus succeeded in reaching the fabled Spice Islands, he would have found advanced civilizations a millennium old, and temples still ranked among the finest examples of ancient art. During the opening centuries of the Christian era, the islands were influenced by Hindu priests and traders who spread their culture and religion. Moslem invasions began in the 13th century, fragmenting the island kingdoms into small states which were unable to resist Western colonial infiltration. Portuguese traders established posts in the 16th century, but they were soon outnumbered by the Dutch who arrived in 1602 and gradually asserted control over the islands comprising present-day Indonesia. Dutch dominance, interrupted by British incursions during the Napoleonic Wars, established the Netherlands East Indies as one of the richest colonial possessions in the world.

The Indonesian independence movement, which began between the two world wars, was encouraged by the Japanese during their 3-year occupation during World War II. Indonesia proclaimed its independence on Aug. 17, 1945, three days after the surrender of Japan, and established it on Dec. 28, 1949, after four years of Dutch effort to reassert control. Irian Jaya, formerly Netherlands New Guinea, came under the administration of Indonesia on May 1, 1963.

At the end of Nov. 1975 the Portuguese Province of Timor, an overseas province occupying the eastern half of the East Indian island of Timur, attained independence as the People's Democratic Republic of East Timur. In Dec., 1975 or early in 1976 the government of the People's Democratic Republic was seized by a guerrilla faction sympathetic to the Indonesian territorial claim to East Timur which ousted the constitutional government and replaced it with the Provisional Government of East Timur. On July 17, 1976, the Provisional Government enacted a law which dissolved the free republic and made East Timur the 24th province of Indonesia.

Coinage for the Indonesian Archipelago is varied and extensive. The Dutch struck coins for the islands at various mints in Holland and the islands under the auspices of the United East India Company and the Batavian Republic. The British issued a coinage during the various occupations by the British East Indian Company, 1811-24. Modern coinage issued by the Republic of Indonesia includes a separate coinage for West Irian and for the Riau Archipelago, an area of small islands between Singapore and Sumatra.

EAST INDIES - BRITISH

JAVA

A mountainous island, 661 miles long by 124 miles at widest part, in greater Sunda Island group. Early cultural influence from India. Islam introduced in late 1400's. Java was mainly a Dutch possession from 1619 to 1947 with the exception of a few periods of British occupation, principally 1811-1816.

BRITISH EAST INDIA COMPANY

Occupation 1811-1816

MONETARY SYSTEM:

4 Doit = 1 Stiver;
30 Stivers = 1 Rupee (Silver)
66 Stivers = 1 Dollar

DATING SYSTEM

The coins listed are found with AD (Christian) dates, AD and AH (Hejira) dates, and with AD, AH and AS (Aki Saki = Javanese) dates which are explained after the introduction in this catalog.

DOIT

COPPER

C#	Date	Mintage	VG	Fine	VF	XF
54	1811	—	5.00	10.00	15.00	25.00
	1812	—	4.00	7.50	12.50	20.00

NOTE: At least 5 varieties exist of each date.

BRASS

C#	Date	Mintage	VG	Fine	VF	XF
54a	1812	—	10.00	18.50	25.00	35.00

TIN

C#	Date	Mintage	VG	Fine	VF	XF
57	1813	16.747	17.50	35.00	70.00	140.00
	1814	33.656	15.00	30.00	60.00	120.00

1/2 STIVER

COPPER

C#	Date	Mintage	VG	Fine	VF	XF
55	1811	—	10.00	18.50	25.00	40.00
	1812	—	4.00	8.00	12.50	20.00
	1813	—	4.00	8.00	12.50	20.00
	1814	—	10.00	18.50	25.00	40.00
	1815	—	10.00	18.50	25.00	40.00

NOTE: At least 3 varieties exist of each date.

STIVER

COPPER

C#	Date	Mintage	VG	Fine	VF	XF
56	1812	—	—	—	Rare	—
	1813	—	10.00	20.00	30.00	50.00
	1814	—	13.50	27.50	40.00	70.00
	1815	—	40.00	80.00	120.00	200.00

NOTE: 3 varieties exist of 1814.

1/2 RUPEE

SILVER

C#	Date	Year	VG	Fine	VF	XF
58	AH1668	AS1740	(error - AH1228)			
			100.00	200.00	300.00	450.00
	1229	1741	100.00	200.00	300.00	450.00

NOTE: The 1/2 Rupee struck in silver is similar to the 1/2 Mohur struck in gold except a five- petaled flower replaces the Christian date on the silver coins.

RUPEE

.792 SILVER
Error date AH1668

C#	Date	Year	VG	Fine	VF	XF
59	AH1668	AS1740	(error - AH1228) 3 varieties			
			30.00	60.00	100.00	150.00
	1228	1740	(error with Y's for Arabic 2's)			
			30.00	60.00	100.00	150.00
	1229	1741	100.00	200.00	300.00	450.00
	1230	1743	w/OZ			
			40.00	80.00	140.00	200.00
	1230	1743	w/.Z			
			50.00	100.00	175.00	275.00
	1231	1743	—	—	Unique	—
	1232	1743	60.00	120.00	200.00	300.00
	1232	1744/3	60.00	120.00	200.00	300.00
	1232	1744	50.00	100.00	160.00	250.00

NOTE: Many varieties exist of the above.

1/2 MOHUR

.750 GOLD

C#	Date	Year	AD	VG	Fine	VF	XF
60	AH1668	AS1740	1813				
				—	—	Rare	—
	1229	1743	1814				
				650.00	1250.	1850.	2500.
	1230	1743	1815	w/OZ			
				650.00	1250.	1850.	2500.
	1230	1743	1815	w/Z			
				650.00	1250.	1850.	2500.
	1230	1743	1816AD (error - AH1231)				
				650.00	1250.	1850.	2500.
	1231/0	1743	—	—	—	—	—
	1231	1743	1816				
				650.00	1250.	1850.	2500.
	1231	1743	1816	.w/M Arabic legends			
				—	—	Rare	—
	1231	1743	1816				
				650.00	1250.	1850.	2500.

NOTE: Many die varieties exist of the above.

MALUKA

A private state in southern Borneo founded by the Englishman, Alexander Hare in 1812 acquired through a grant from the local sultan. The state existed from 1812 to 1818. The coins were made at a mint in the state in 1812 and 1813. The state ceased to exist when the area was repossessed by the Dutch in 1818.

DUIT

COPPER

C#	Date	Mintage	VG	Fine	VF	XF
11	—	—	—	—	Rare	—
12	AH1227	—	2.50	4.50	7.50	15.00

NOTE: 8 varieties exist.

C#	Date	Mintage	VG	Fine	VF	XF
13	AH1228	—	2.00	3.50	6.50	12.50

Rev. floral design

C#	Date	Mintage	VG	Fine	VF	XF
14	AH1228	—	—	—	Rare	—

Rev: Date within wreath.

C#	Date	Mintage	VG	Fine	VF	XF
15	AH1228	—	—	—	Rare	—

SUMATRA

An island, south of the Malay peninsula, was first reached by Europeans for trade in 1599. Competition between European powers for trading rights continued until 1824 at which time it became a Dutch possession. British coins for the island were struck at the Birmingham Mint by Matthew Boulton in 1786 and other issues were struck at Indian mints.

BRITISH EAST INDIA COMPANY

1685 - 1824

MONETARY SYSTEM

100 Kepings = 1 Suku
4 Suku = 1 Dollar (Spanish)

DENOMINATIONS

The following Arabic legends appear for the denomination with an Arabic number above.

كفڠ	سكفڠ	سات كڤڠ
(1) Keping	Sakeping	Satkeping
دوكڤڠ	تيك كفڠ	امڤت كڤڠ
(2) Dua Keping	(3) Tiga Keping	(4) Ampat Keping

KEPING

COPPER
Milled edge (oblique or vertical)

C#	Date	Year	VG	Fine	VF	XF
21	AH1200	1786	2.50	5.00	10.00	20.00
	1200	1786	—	—	Proof	75.00
	1200	1786	—		Gilt Proof	70.00
	1202	1786	Error AH1200			

C#	Date	Year	VG	Fine	VF	XF
			2.50	5.00	10.00	20.00
	1202	1787	—	—	Proof	75.00
	1202	1787	—		Gilt Proof	70.00

Plain edge

C#	Date	Year	VG	Fine	VF	XF
	1200	1786	1.75	3.50	7.50	15.00
	1202	1787	Error AH1200			
	1202	1787	—	—	Proof	75.00

Error: With Arabic denomination and '3' (for 1.)

C#	Date	Year	VG	Fine	VF	XF
21a	AH1213	1798	1.75	3.50	7.50	15.00
	1213	1798	—	—	Proof	75.00
	1213	1798	—		Gilt Proof	75.00

Thin planchet, 2.05 gm.

C#	Date	Year	VG	Fine	VF	XF
25a	AH1219	1804	1.25	2.50	5.00	10.00

Thick planchet, 3.476 gm.

C#	Date	Year	VG	Fine	VF	XF
25	AH1219	1804	1.25	2.50	5.00	10.00
	1219	1804	—	—	Proof	75.00
	1219	1804	—		Gilt Proof	70.00

2 KEPINGS

COPPER, 19-22mm
Milled edge (oblique or vertical)

C#	Date	Year	VG	Fine	VF	XF
20	AH1197	1783	3.50	6.50	12.50	25.00
	1197	1783	—	—	Proof	75.00

SILVER (OMS)

C#	Date	Year	VG	Fine	VF	XF
20a	AH1197	1783	—		Proof Only	Rare

GOLD (OMS)

C#	Date	Year	VG	Fine	VF	XF
20b	AH1197	1783	—		Proof Only	Rare

BRONZE (OMS)

C#	Date	Year	VG	Fine	VF	XF
20c	AH1197	1783	—		Proof Only	Rare

COPPER

C#	Date	Year	VG	Fine	VF	XF
22	1200	1786	2.50	5.00	10.00	20.00
	1200	1786	—	—	Proof	85.00
	1200	1786	—		Gilt Proof	80.00
	1200	1787	Error AH1202			
			5.00	10.00	20.00	40.00
	1202	1787	2.50	5.00	10.00	20.00
	1202	1787	—	—	Proof	85.00
	1202	1787	—		Gilt Proof	80.00

Error: With Arabic denomination and '3' (for 2).

C#	Date	Year	VG	Fine	VF	XF
22a	AH1213	1798	3.50	6.50	12.50	25.00
	1213	1798	—	—	Proof	85.00
	1213	1798	—		Gilt Proof	80.00

Thin planchet, 4.40 gm.

C#	Date	Year	VG	Fine	VF	XF
26a	AH1219	1804	1.50	3.00	6.00	12.00

Thick planchet, 6.47 gm.

C#	Date	Year	VG	Fine	VF	XF
26	AH1219	1804	1.25	2.50	5.00	10.00
		1804	—	—	Proof	85.00
		1804	—		Gilt Proof	80.00

3 KEPINGS

COPPER
Milled edge (oblique or vertical)

C#	Date	Year	VG	Fine	VF	XF
23	AH1200	1786	5.00	10.00	20.00	40.00
	1200	1786	—	—	Proof	100.00
	1200	1786	—		Gilt Proof	90.00
	1202	1787	3.75	7.50	15.00	30.00
	1202	1787	—	—	Proof	100.00
	1202	1787	—		Gilt Proof	90.00
	1213	1798	3.75	7.50	15.00	30.00
	1213	1798	—	—	Proof	100.00
	1213	1798	—		Gilt Proof	90.00

4 KEPINGS

COPPER
Thin planchet, 8.5 gm.

C#	Date	Year	VG	Fine	VF	XF
27a	AH1219	1804	2.50	5.00	10.00	20.00

Thick planchet, 12.8 gm.

C#	Date	Year	VG	Fine	VF	XF
27	AH1219	1804	1.75	3.75	7.50	15.00
	1219	1804	—	—	Proof	125.00
	1219	1804	—		Gilt Proof	110.00

FORT MARLBRO

This fort was the principal British settlement in the East Indies from its construction in 1714 until 1786. The name is a corrupted version of Marlborough, a popular British hero in 1714. The silver coins were made in Calcutta.

1/2 DOLLAR

COPPER

C#	Date	Year	VG	Fine	VF	XF
30		1797	—	—	Rare	—

2 SUKUS

SILVER

C#	Date	Year	Good	VG	Fine	VF
35	AH1197	1783	85.00	135.00	175.00	250.00
	1198	1784	125.00	175.00	225.00	300.00

NETHERLANDS EAST INDIES

RULERS:

United East India Company, 1602-1799
Batavian Republic 1799-1806
Louis Napoleon, King of Holland, 1806-1811
Kingdom Of The Netherlands
Willem I, 1815-1840
Willem II, 1840-1849
Willem III, 1849-1890
Wilhelmina, 1890-1945

MINT MARKS:

H = Amsterdam (H)
Hk - Harderwijk (various)
Hn - Hoorn (star)
E = Einkhuizen (Star)
Dt = Dordrecht (Rosette)
K - Kampen (eagle)
S = Utrecht (S)
Sa = Surabaya (Sa)

MONETARY SYSTEM:

120 Duits = 120 Cents
1 Gulden = 1 Java Rupee
16 Silver Rupees = 1 Gold Mohur

BONKS: Because of the slow delivery of coins from the Netherlands, the government in the East Indies often resorted to the manufacture of "Bonks". These were simply lumps cut from the copper (or tin) rods used for coining. This eliminated the problems inherent in casting round coins and allowed the production of large quantities of legal tender very quickly. The thicker rods were used for the 2 and 8 Stiver Bonks and the thinner rod for the smaller denominations.

DUITS: On many of the Duit and 1/2 Duit coins of the East Indies dated 1802-1826, the value appears as 5-1/32-G (1/2 Duit) and 5-1/16-G (Duit). This is interpreted as: 5 of the pieces equal 1/16 Guilder or 5 equal 1/32 Guilder. However, in 1802 the rate of exchange was set so that 6 Duits should equal 1/16 Guilder which would mean the Duit actually equaled 1/96 Guilder and the 1/2 Duit equaled 1/192 Guilder, but because of the perennial shortage of small coins, the error was ignored and the coins released to circulation.

CENTS: Although some coins in 1833-1841 appear with value as 1 CT (1 Cent) and 2 CT (2 Cent) they are considered Duits and Double Duits and were exchanged at the rate of 1 Duit - 1/96 Guilder, not on a decimal system.

GELDERLAND

MINTMASTER PRIVY MARKS

Date	Privy Mark
1758-76	Tree trunk

Date	Privy Mark
1782-1806	Ear of corn

1/2 DUIT

COPPER
Obv: Crowned arms of Gelderland
Rev: VOC monogram above date.

C#	Date	Mintage	VG	Fine	VF	XF
A1	1788	—	4.00	8.50	12.50	20.00
	1789	—	4.00	8.50	12.50	20.00
	1790	—	4.00	8.50	12.50	20.00
	SILVER (OMS)					
A1a	1789 plain edge		75.00	125.00	200.00	300.00

DUIT

COPPER
Obv: Crowned arms of Gelderland

C#	Date	Mintage	VG	Fine	VF	XF
A2	1771	—	2.00	4.00	7.50	12.50
	1772	—	2.00	4.00	7.50	12.50
	1776	—	2.00	4.00	7.50	12.50
	1785	—	2.00	4.00	7.50	12.50
	1786	—	2.00	4.00	7.50	12.50
	1787	—	2.00	4.00	7.50	12.50
	1788	—	2.00	4.00	7.50	12.50
	1789	—	2.00	4.00	7.50	12.50
	1790	—	2.00	4.00	7.50	12.50
	1791	—	2.00	4.00	7.50	12.50
	1792	—	2.00	4.00	7.50	12.50
	1793	—	2.00	4.00	7.50	12.50
	1794	—	2.00	4.00	7.50	12.50

SILVER
Obv: Crowned arms of Gelderland.
Rev: VOC monogram over date.

C#	Date	Mintage	VG	Fine	VF	XF
A2b	1789	—	30.00	50.00	85.00	150.00
	1791	—	30.00	50.00	85.00	150.00

10 STUIVER

(1/2 Gulden)

.920 SILVER

C#	Date	Mintage	VG	Fine	VF	XF
A4	1786	—	40.00	100.00	175.00	275.00

GULDEN

.920 SILVER

C#	Date	Mintage	VG	Fine	VF	XF
A5	1786	—	40.00	80.00	135.00	200.00
	1790	—	40.00	80.00	135.00	200.00

3 GULDEN

.920 SILVER
Similar to Westfriesland C#G6.

C#	Date	Mintage	VG	Fine	VF	XF
A6	1786	—	250.00	500.00	750.00	1150.

HOLLAND

MINTMASTER PRIVY MARKS

Date	Privy Mark
1771-93	Rosette

1/2 DOIT

COPPER
Obv: Crowned arms of Holland.
Rev: VOC monogram over date.

C#	Date	Mintage	VG	Fine	VF	XF
C1	1769	—	4.00	8.00	13.50	25.00
	1770	—	4.00	8.00	13.50	25.00
	SILVER (OMS)					
C1a	1760	—	17.50	30.00	60.00	100.00
	1761	—	17.50	30.00	60.00	100.00
	1762	—	17.50	30.00	60.00	100.00
	1763	—	17.50	30.00	60.00	100.00
	GOLD (OMS)					
C1b	1760	—	—	—	—	—
	1761	—	—	—	—	—
	1763	—	—	—	—	—

DOIT

COPPER
Obv: Crowned arms of Holland
Rev: VOC monogram over date.

C#	Date	Mintage	VG	Fine	VF	XF
C2	1764	—	1.50	3.50	6.50	11.50
	1765/64	—	4.00	8.00	13.50	25.00
	1765	—	1.50	3.50	6.50	11.50
	1766	—	1.50	3.50	6.50	11.50
	1767	—	1.50	3.50	6.50	11.50
	1768	—	4.00	8.00	13.50	25.00
	1770	—	1.50	3.50	6.50	11.50
	1771	—	1.50	3.50	6.50	11.50
	1772	—	3.00	7.50	12.50	22.50
	1776	—	3.00	7.50	12.50	22.50
	1777	—	3.00	7.50	12.50	22.50
	1778	—	1.50	3.50	6.50	11.50
	1779	—	1.50	3.50	6.50	11.50
	1780	—	1.50	3.50	6.50	11.50
	1781	—	1.50	3.50	6.50	11.50
	1784	—	4.00	8.50	13.50	22.50
	1788	—	1.50	3.50	6.50	11.50
	1789	—	1.50	3.50	6.50	11.50
	1790/89	—	4.00	8.00	13.50	22.50
	1790	—	1.50	3.50	6.50	11.50
	1791	—	1.50	3.50	6.50	11.50
	1792	—	1.50	3.50	6.50	11.50
	1793	—	1.50	3.50	6.50	11.50
	SILVER (OMS)					
C2a	1760	—	12.50	22.50	40.00	75.00
	1761	—	12.50	22.50	40.00	75.00
	1762	—	12.50	22.50	40.00	75.00
	1763	—	12.50	22.50	40.00	75.00
	GOLD (OMS)					
C2b	1763	—	—	—	—	—

UTRECHT

MINTMARKS

Date	Privy Mark
1771-94	City shield

MINTMASTER PRIVY MARKS

Date	Privy Mark
1827	Star between dots
1815-38	Child in swaddling clothes
1840-43	Star

1/2 DUIT

COPPER
Obv: Crowned arms of Utrecht.
Rev: VOC monogram over date.

C#	Date	Mintage	VG	Fine	VF	XF
F1	1769	—	4.00	8.50	12.50	21.50
	1770	—	4.00	8.50	12.50	21.50
	Rev: With star mm.					
F1a	1790 struck C.1842	—	—	—	Rare	—

SILVER (OMS)

C#	Date	Mintage	VG	Fine	VF	XF
F1b	1760	—	17.50	30.00	60.00	100.00
	1761	—	17.50	30.00	60.00	100.00
	1762	—	17.50	30.00	60.00	100.00
	1763	—	17.50	30.00	60.00	100.00
	1764	—	17.50	30.00	60.00	100.00
	1765	—	17.50	30.00	60.00	100.00
	1766	—	17.50	30.00	60.00	100.00
	1767	—	17.50	30.00	60.00	100.00
	1768	—	17.50	30.00	60.00	100.00
	1769	—	17.50	30.00	60.00	100.00
	1770	—	17.50	30.00	60.00	100.00
	1771	—	40.00	75.00	125.00	200.00
	1773	—	—	—	Rare	—
	1792	—	—	—	Rare	—
	1793	—	22.50	40.00	75.00	125.00
	1794	—	22.50	40.00	75.00	125.00
	GOLD (OMS)					
F1c	1761	—	Unique	—	—	—
	1762	—	—	—	—	—
	1764	—	—	—	—	—
	1767	—	—	—	—	—
	1793	—	—	—	Rare	—

DUIT

COPPER
Obv: Crowned arms of Utrecht supported by lions.
Rev: VOC monogram over date.

C#	Date	Mintage	VG	Fine	VF	XF
F2	1764	—	1.50	3.50	6.50	11.50
	1765	—	1.50	3.50	6.50	11.50
	1766	—	1.50	3.50	6.50	11.50
	1767	—	1.50	3.50	6.50	11.50
	1769	—	—	—	—	—
	1770	—	1.50	3.50	6.50	11.50
	1771	—	8.50	17.50	27.50	40.00
	1776	—	1.50	3.50	6.50	11.50
	1777	—	1.50	3.50	6.50	11.50
	1778	—	1.50	3.50	6.50	11.50
	1779	—	1.50	3.50	6.50	11.50
	1780	—	1.50	3.50	6.50	11.50
	1781	—	2.00	4.00	8.50	15.00
	1784	—	2.00	4.00	8.50	15.00
	1785	—	1.50	3.50	6.50	11.50
	1786	—	1.50	3.00	5.50	10.00
	1787	—	1.50	3.00	5.50	10.00
	1788	—	1.50	3.00	5.50	10.00
	1789	—	1.50	3.00	5.50	10.00
	1790	—	1.50	3.50	6.50	11.50
	1791	—	1.50	3.00	5.50	10.00
	1792	—	1.50	3.00	5.50	10.00
	1793	—	4.00	8.00	13.50	22.50
	1794	—	1.50	3.00	5.50	10.00
	SILVER					
F2b	1760	—	17.50	30.00	60.00	100.00
	1761	—	—	—	Rare	—
	1762	—	30.00	50.00	85.00	150.00
	1763	—	10.00	20.00	40.00	75.00
	1764	—	10.00	20.00	40.00	75.00
	1765	—	30.00	50.00	85.00	150.00
	1766	—	10.00	20.00	40.00	75.00
	1767	—	30.00	50.00	85.00	150.00
	1768	—	10.00	20.00	40.00	75.00
	1769	—	—	—	Rare	—
	1770	—	—	—	Rare	—
	1771	—	10.00	20.00	40.00	75.00
	1772	—	10.00	20.00	40.00	75.00
	1773	—	10.00	20.00	40.00	75.00
	1784	—	—	—	Rare	—
	1790	—	10.00	20.00	40.00	75.00
	1794	—	10.00	20.00	40.00	75.00
	GOLD (OMS)					
F2c	1760	—	—	—	—	—
	1762	—	—	—	—	—
	1766	—	—	—	—	—
	1792	—	—	—	Rare	—

COPPER
MM: Babe in swaddling clothes.

C#	Date	Mintage	VG	Fine	VF	XF
F2a	1790	—	4.00	8.50	13.50	22.50

NOTE: Struck in 1827.

MM: Star between dots.

C#	Date	Mintage	VG	Fine	VF	XF
F2.1	1790	—	2.00	4.00	8.50	15.00

NOTE: Struck in 1827.

SILVER

C#	Date	Mintage	VG	Fine	VF	XF
F2.1a	1790	—	—	—	Rare	—

NOTE: Struck in 1827.

COPPER
MM: Star

C#	Date	Mintage	VG	Fine	VF	XF
F2.2	1790	—	2.00	4.00	6.00	10.00

NOTE: Struck in 1840-43.

MM - Star over child

C#	Date	Mintage	VG	Fine	VF	XF
F2.3	1790	—	6.00	12.50	18.50	25.00

NOTE: Struck in 1840-43.

SILVER (OMS)

C#	Date	Mintage	VG	Fine	VF	XF
F2.2a	1790	—	20.00	40.00	75.00	110.00

NOTE: Struck in 1840-43.

Piefort (double thick flan).

C#	Date	Mintage	VG	Fine	VF	XF
F2.2b	1790	—	—	—	Rare	—

NOTE: Struck 1840-43 Piefort.

2 DUITS

COPPER
Obv: Crowned arms supported by lions; MM: Star.
Rev: VOC monogram over date.

C#	Date	Mintage	VG	Fine	VF	XF
F3	1790	—	3.00	6.50	10.00	18.50

NOTE: Struck in 1840-43.

SILVER

C#	Date	Mintage	VG	Fine	VF	XF
F3a	1790	—	75.00	125.00	200.00	300.00

NOTE: Struck in 1840-43.

10 STUIVER

(1/2 Gulden)

.920 SILVER
Similar to Gelderland C#A4.
Rev. leg. ends: TRAI

C#	Date	Mintage	VG	Fine	VF	XF
F4	1786	—	25.00	60.00	100.00	165.00

GULDEN

.920 SILVER
Rev. leg. ends: TRAI

C#	Date	Mintage	VG	Fine	VF	XF
F4	1786	—	60.00	100.00	150.00	225.00
	1790	—	70.00	120.00	175.00	275.00

3 GULDEN

.920 SILVER
Similar to Westfriesland C#G6.
Rev. leg. ends: TRAI

C#	Date	Mintage	VG	Fine	VF	XF
F6	1786	—	175.00	350.00	600.00	900.00

WESTFRIESLAND

MINTMASTER PRIVY MARKS

Date	Privy Mark
1771-81	Boat
1781-96	Rosette

1/2 DOIT

COPPER
Obv: Crowned arms of Westfriesland.
Rev: VOC monogram over date.

C#	Date	Mintage	VG	Fine	VF	XF
G1	1769	—	6.50	12.50	16.50	27.50
	1770	—	6.50	12.50	16.50	27.50

DUIT

COPPER
Obv: Crowned arms of Westfriesland.
Rev: VOC monogram over date.

C#	Date	Mintage	VG	Fine	VF	XF
G2	1764	—	10.00	16.50	25.00	37.50
	1765	—	3.00	6.50	10.00	16.50
	1766	—	3.00	6.50	10.00	16.50
	1767	—	3.00	6.50	10.00	16.50
	1768	—	3.00	7.50	10.00	15.00
	1770	—	6.50	10.00	12.50	20.00
	1771	—	2.00	4.00	8.50	15.00
	1772	—	2.00	4.00	8.50	15.00
	1773	—	4.00	8.50	13.50	21.50
	1776/3	—	4.00	8.50	15.00	23.50
	1776	—	1.50	3.50	6.50	11.50
	1777/6	—	3.00	7.50	12.50	20.00
	1777	—	1.50	3.50	6.50	11.50
	1778/7	—	3.00	7.50	12.50	20.00
	1778	—	1.50	3.50	6.50	11.50
	1779	—	1.50	3.50	6.50	11.50
	1780	—	3.00	7.00	12.50	20.00
	1781	—	3.00	7.00	12.50	20.00
	1784/1	—	3.00	7.50	12.50	20.00
	1784	—	1.50	3.50	6.50	11.50
	1785/4	—	3.00	7.50	12.50	20.00
	1785	—	1.50	3.50	6.50	11.50
	1786	—	1.50	3.50	6.50	11.50
	1787	—	2.00	4.00	8.50	15.00
	1788	—	1.50	3.50	6.50	11.50
	1789/8	—	3.00	7.50	12.50	20.00
	1789/9871	—	8.50	20.00	35.00	55.00
	1789	—	1.50	3.50	6.50	11.50
	1790	—	1.50	3.50	6.50	11.50
	1791/0	—	2.00	4.00	8.50	15.00
	1791	—	1.50	3.50	6.50	11.50
	1792	—	1.50	3.50	6.50	11.50
	1794	—	8.00	20.00	35.00	55.00

10 STUIVER

(1/2 Gulden)

.920 SILVER
Similar to Gelderland C#A4
Rev. leg. ends: WESTF.

C#	Date	Mintage	VG	Fine	VF	XF
G4	1786	—	25.00	50.00	100.00	160.00
	1787/6	—	50.00	90.00	140.00	200.00
	1787	—	25.00	50.00	100.00	160.00

GULDEN

.920 SILVER
Similar to Gelderland C#A5.
Rev. leg. ends: WESTF.

C#	Date	Mintage	VG	Fine	VF	XF
G5	1786	—	50.00	90.00	140.00	200.00
	1786/64	—	50.00	90.00	140.00	200.00
	1787	—	50.00	100.00	160.00	235.00
	1790/87	—	60.00	100.00	180.00	265.00
	1790	—	50.00	100.00	160.00	235.00

3 GULDEN

.920 SILVER
Rev. leg. ends: WESTF.

C#	Date	Mintage	VG	Fine	VF	XF
G6	1786	—	175.00	350.00	600.00	900.00

ZEELAND

MINTMARKS

Date	Privy Mark
1714-94	Tower

1/2 DUIT

COPPER
Obv: Crowned arms of Zeeland.
Rev: VOC monogram divides date.

C#	Date	Mintage	VG	Fine	VF	XF
H1	1770	—	12.50	25.00	35.00	50.00
	1771	—	12.50	25.00	35.00	50.00
	1772	—	12.50	25.00	35.00	50.00
	1789 milled edge	—	16.50	30.00	50.00	80.00

DUIT

COPPER
Obv: Crowned arms of Zeeland.

C#	Date	Mintage	VG	Fine	VF	XF
H2a	1764	—	3.50	5.50	8.50	15.00
	1765	—	1.50	3.50	6.50	11.50
	1766	—	1.50	3.50	6.50	11.50
	1767	—	2.00	4.00	10.00	16.50
	1768 sm.8	—	4.00	7.50	12.50	17.50
	1768 lg.8	—	1.50	3.50	6.50	16.50
	1770	—	1.50	3.50	6.50	16.50
	1771	—	1.50	3.50	6.50	16.50
	1772	—	1.50	3.50	6.50	11.50
	1773	—	6.50	12.50	20.00	35.00
	1777	—	1.50	3.50	6.50	11.50
	1778	—	2.00	4.00	8.50	15.00
	1779	—	2.00	4.00	8.50	15.00
	1780	—	1.50	3.00	5.00	8.50
	1784	—	1.50	3.00	5.00	8.50
	1785	—	1.50	3.00	5.00	8.50
	1786	—	1.50	3.00	5.00	8.50
	1787	—	1.50	3.00	5.00	8.50
	1788	—	1.50	3.00	5.00	8.50
	1789	—	1.50	3.50	6.50	11.50
	1790	—	1.50	3.50	6.50	11.50
	1791	—	1.50	3.50	6.50	11.50
	1792	—	2.00	4.00	8.50	15.00

Rev: Garland around top border.

C#	Date	Mintage	VG	Fine	VF	XF
—	1792	—	8.50	16.50	30.00	50.00
	1793	—	2.00	4.00	8.50	15.00
	1794/3	—	4.00	8.50	15.00	25.00
	1794	—	2.00	4.00	8.50	15.00

SILVER (OMS)

C#	Date	Mintage	VG	Fine	VF	XF
H2b	1788	—	40.00	75.00	110.00	150.00

10 STUIVER

(1/2 Gulden)

SILVER
Similar to Gelderland C#a4, date above crown.
Rev. leg. ends: ZEL

C#	Date	Mintage	VG	Fine	VF	XF
H4	1791	—	30.00	60.00	100.00	165.00

Similar to Gelderland C#A5, date below Liberty.

C#	Date	Mintage	VG	Fine	VF	XF
H4.1	1791	—	—	—	—	—

GULDEN

.920 SILVER
Similar to Gelderland C#A5.
Rev. leg. ends: ZEL.

C#	Date	Mintage	VG	Fine	VF	XF
H5	1791	—	50.00	100.00	135.00	185.00
	1791/86	—	60.00	110.00	150.00	200.00

3 GULDEN

.920 SILVER
Similar to Westfriesland C#G6.
Rev. leg. ends: ZEL.

C#	Date	Mintage	VG	Fine	VF	XF
H6	1789	—	175.00	350.00	600.00	900.00

UNITED EAST INDIA CO.

DUIT

COPPER
Obv: Wreath

C#	Date	Mintage	VG	Fine	VF	XF
10A	1783	—	20.00	60.00	110.00	160.00

TIN
With center hole.
Obv: VOC monogram with B above.
Rev: Value.

C#	Date	Mintage	Good	VG	Fine
11	ND (1796)	No surviving specimens			

Obv: VOC monogram with N above.
Rev: Value over date.

C#	Date	Mintage	VG	Fine	VF	XF
12	1796	—	—	—	Rare	—
	1797	—	—	—	Rare	—

STUIVER

COPPER BONK

C#	Date	Mintage	VG	Fine	VF	XF
13	1796	—	27.50	55.00	80.00	110.00
	1797	—	25.00	50.00	70.00	100.00
	1798	—	27.50	55.00	80.00	110.00
	1799	—	50.00	100.00	140.00	180.00

2 STUIVERS

COPPER BONK
Obv: 2 S in rectangle.
Rev: Date in rectangle.

C#	Date	Mintage	VG	Fine	VF	XF
14	1796	—	40.00	80.00	120.00	160.00
	1797	—	35.00	70.00	100.00	140.00
	1798	—	35.00	70.00	100.00	140.00
	1799	—	—	—	Rare	—

1/2 RUPEE

.792 GOLD
Obv. and Rev: Crude Arabic legend.

C#	Date	Mintage	VG	Fine	VF	XF
22	1783	1,610	—	—	Rare	—
	1784	Inc. Ab.	—	—	Rare	—
	1785	5,147	—	—	Rare	—
	1798	—	400.00	800.00	1250.	1750.
	1799	3,321	400.00	800.00	1250.	1750.

RUPEE

.833 SILVER
Obv. and Rev: Crude Arabic legend.

C#	Date	Mintage	VG	Fine	VF	XF
17	1764	—	—	—	Rare	—
	1765	—	22.50	45.00	70.00	100.00
	1766	—	22.50	45.00	70.00	100.00
	1767	—	40.00	80.00	125.00	175.00
	1782	—	—	—	Rare	—
	1783	—	30.00	60.00	90.00	135.00
	1784	—	50.00	100.00	140.00	200.00
	1785	—	50.00	100.00	140.00	200.00
	1786	—	50.00	100.00	140.00	200.00
	1787	—	—	—	Rare	—
	1788	—	50.00	100.00	140.00	200.00
	1789	—	—	—	—	—
	1795	—	50.00	100.00	140.00	200.00
	1796	—	30.00	60.00	90.00	135.00
	1798	—	50.00	100.00	140.00	200.00
	1799	.018	50.00	100.00	140.00	200.00

NOTE: No known specimens exist of coins dated 1782, 1787 and 1789.

.792 GOLD

C#	Date	Mintage	VG	Fine	VF	XF
23	1783	3,822	—	—	Rare	—
	1784	.010	—	—	Rare	—
	1796	1,435	1200.	2400.	3250.	4250.
	1797	.013	600.00	1200.	2000.	2850.

BATAVIAN REPUBLIC

1/2 DUIT

COPPER

C#	Date	Mintage	VG	Fine	VF	XF
26	1802	.157	2.00	4.00	6.50	11.50
	1803	—	3.00	7.50	12.50	20.00
	1804	—	3.00	7.50	12.50	20.00
	1805	—	2.00	4.00	6.50	11.50
	1806	—	2.00	4.00	6.50	11.50

C#	Date	Mintage	VG	Fine	VF	XF
49	1807	—	2.00	4.00	6.50	11.50
	1808	—	2.00	4.00	6.50	11.50
	1809	—	3.00	5.00	7.50	13.50

NOTE: Many varieties of above 3 coins exist.

Obv. Crowned shield with lion and value as 5 1/32 G
Rev. INDIAE BATAV

C#	Date	Mintage	VG	Fine	VF	XF
61	1814	—	—	—	Rare	—

NOTE:2 varieties exist.

C#	Date	Mintage	VG	Fine	VF	XF
	1815	—	.75	2.00	4.00	7.50
	1816	—	.60	1.50	3.50	6.00

NOTE: Several varieties exist.

C#	Date	Mintage	VG	Fine	VF	XF
61a	1816	23.818	.80	2.00	4.00	7.50
61b	1816	—	2.00	5.00	10.00	18.50

NOTE: 3 varieties exist.

C#	Date	Mintage	VG	Fine	VF	XF
	1818	—	.80	2.00	4.00	7.50
	1821	—	.80	2.00	4.00	7.50
	1822	—	2.00	5.00	10.00	17.50

NOTE: Many varieties of the above 3 coins exist.

1/8 STUIVER (1/2 DUIT)

COPPER
Lion redesigned

C#	Date	Mintage	VG	Fine	VF	XF
64	1822S	1.300	1.50	4.00	8.50	15.00
	1823S	33.000	.75	2.00	4.00	7.50

NOTE: 2 varieties exist.

C#	Date	Mintage	VG	Fine	VF	XF
	1824S	21.000	.75	2.00	4.00	7.50
	1825S	44.000	.75	2.00	4.00	7.50
	1826S	69.000	.60	1.50	3.50	6.00

NOTE: Several varieties exist. Type with lion of 1825 very rare.

DUIT

COPPER
Arms of Gelderland

C#	Date	Mintage	VG	Fine	VF	XF
24	1802	—	4.00	6.00	8.00	15.00
	1803	—	4.00	6.00	8.00	15.00

NOTE: 2 varieties exist.

C#	Date	Mintage	VG	Fine	VF	XF
	1804	—	5.00	8.00	12.50	20.00

NOTE: 2 varieties exist.

C#	Date	Mintage	VG	Fine	VF	XF
	1805	—	4.00	6.00	10.00	17.50

NOTE: 5 varieties exist, including date as: 1085.

C#	Date	Mintage	VG	Fine	VF	XF
	1806	—	4.00	6.00	10.00	17.50

NOTE: 2 varieties exist.

Obv. Arms of Holland. Rev. as C#24.

C#	Date	Mintage	VG	Fine	VF	XF
25	1802	—	4.00	8.00	12.50	20.00
	1802	—	6.00	10.00	15.00	25.00
	1803	—	4.00	8.00	12.50	20.00

NOTE: 3 varieties exist.

C#	Date	Mintage	VG	Fine	VF	XF
	1804	—	6.00	12.50	20.00	35.00

Value: 1/80 Gulden 'Holland Arms'

C#	Date	Mintage	VG	Fine	VF	XF
27	1802	.358	3.00	5.00	8.50	15.00

NOTE: 3 varieties exist.

C#	Date	Mintage	VG	Fine	VF	XF
	1803	—	2.00	4.00	6.50	10.00

NOTE: Many varieties exist.

C#	Date	Mintage	VG	Fine	VF	XF
	1804	—	2.00	4.00	6.50	10.00
	1805	—	2.00	4.00	6.50	10.00

NOTE: 2 varieties exist.

C#	Date	Mintage	VG	Fine	VF	XF
	1806	—	2.00	4.00	6.50	10.00

SILVER (OMS)

C#	Date	Mintage	VG	Fine	VF	XF
27a	1802	—	—	—	—	—

COPPER
Value: 1/80 Gulden 'Overyssel Arms'

C#	Date	Mintage	VG	Fine	VF	XF
28	1803	—	2.00	4.00	6.50	10.00

NOTE: 5 varieties exist.

C#	Date	Mintage	VG	Fine	VF	XF
	1804	—	2.00	4.00	6.50	10.00
	1805	—	2.00	4.00	6.50	10.00

NOTE: Many varieties of 1804 and 1805 exist.

C#	Date	Mintage	VG	Fine	VF	XF
	1806K	—	4.00	6.00	10.00	17.50

NOTE: 2 varieties exist.

SILVER (OMS)

C#	Date	Mintage	VG	Fine	VF	XF
28a	1804	— Unique	—	—	—	—
	1807 plain edge	—	—	—	—	—
	1807 milled edge	—	—	—	—	—

COPPER
Obv: VOC and star above. Rev: JAVA/1806.

C#	Date	Mintage	VG	Fine	VF	XF
29	1806	—	10.00	20.00	32.50	50.00

Rev: JAVA/date

C#	Date	Mintage	VG	Fine	VF	XF
42	1807	—	3.00	7.50	12.50	20.00

NOTE: 4 varieties exist.

C#	Date	Mintage	VG	Fine	VF	XF
	1808	—	3.00	7.50	12.50	20.00

NOTE: 3 varieties exist.

C#	Date	Mintage	VG	Fine	VF	XF
	1809	—	4.00	8.50	15.00	25.00

NOTE: 3 varieties exist.

C#	Date	Mintage	VG	Fine	VF	XF
	1810	—	—	—	Rare	—

Obv. Block LN. Rev. JAVA/date.

C#	Date	Mintage	VG	Fine	VF	XF
43	1808	—	3.00	5.00	7.50	13.50

NOTE: 2 varieties exist.

C#	Date	Mintage	VG	Fine	VF	XF
	1809	—	2.00	4.00	6.50	10.00
	1810	—	2.00	4.00	6.50	10.00

NOTE: Several varieties of above 2 coins exist.

C#	Date	Mintage	VG	Fine	VF	XF
44	1810	—	2.00	4.00	6.50	10.00
	1811	—	2.00	4.00	6.50	10.00

NOTE: Several varieties of above 2 coins exist.

With circles of arrowheads around border on both sides.

C#	Date	Mintage	VG	Fine	VF	XF
44a	1810	—	8.00	16.50	25.00	40.00

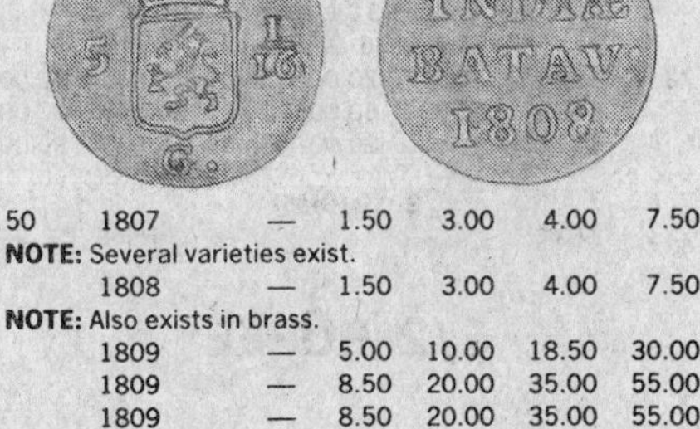

C#	Date	Mintage	VG	Fine	VF	XF
50	1807	—	1.50	3.00	4.00	7.50

NOTE: Several varieties exist.

C#	Date	Mintage	VG	Fine	VF	XF
	1808	—	1.50	3.00	4.00	7.50

NOTE: Also exists in brass.

C#	Date	Mintage	VG	Fine	VF	XF
	1809	—	5.00	10.00	18.50	30.00
	1809	—	8.50	20.00	35.00	55.00
	1809	—	8.50	20.00	35.00	55.00

Obv: Overyssel arms. Rev: INDI AE/BATAV and date

C#	Date	Mintage	VG	Fine	VF	XF
51	1807	—	3.00	7.50	12.50	20.00

Obv: Crowned shield. Rev: INDIAE/BATAV/date.

C#	Date	Mintage	VG	Fine	VF	XF
62	1814H	—	—	—	Rare	—

NOTE: This coin has a larger planchet than following dates.

C#	Date	Mintage	VG	Fine	VF	XF
	1815H	—	1.25	3.00	6.50	10.00
	1816H	—	1.25	3.00	6.50	10.00

NOTE: Several varieties of the above two coins exist.

C#	Date	Mintage	VG	Fine	VF	XF
62a	1816S	64.562	.50	1.25	3.00	5.00

NOTE: Actually minted 1820-22.

C#	Date	Mintage	VG	Fine	VF	XF
62b	1816	—	4.00	10.00	16.50	28.50

NOTE: 2 varieties exist. Actually minted in 1820.

C#	Date	Mintage	VG	Fine	VF	XF
	1818	—	.50	1.25	2.50	4.00
	1819	—	2.00	5.00	10.00	18.50
	1820	—	.50	1.25	2.50	4.00
	1821	—	.50	1.25	2.50	4.00
	1822	—	.75	2.00	4.00	7.50
	1823	—	1.25	3.00	6.50	11.50

NOTE: Many varieties of the above 6 coins exist.

C#	Date	Mintage	VG	Fine	VF	XF
	1824	—	2.00	4.00	8.50	15.00

NOTE: 2 varieties exist.

C#	Date	Mintage	VG	Fine	VF	XF
	1825	—	.75	2.00	4.00	7.50

NOTE: Many varieties exist.

C#	Date	Mintage	VG	Fine	VF	XF
	1826	—	4.00	10.00	20.00	32.50

1/4 STUIVER (DUIT)

COPPER

C#	Date	Mintage	VG	Fine	VF	XF
65	1822S	30.000	.75	2.00	4.00	7.50
65	1823S	29.000	.75	2.00	4.00	7.50
	1824S	26.000	.75	2.00	4.00	7.50
	1825S	125.000	.40	1.00	2.00	3.50
	1826S	208.000	.40	1.00	2.00	3.50

NOTE: 2 varieties exist and counterfeits with border of dots.

C#	Date	Mintage	VG	Fine	VF	XF
	1836S	33.453	.75	2.00	4.00	7.50

NOTE: Several varieties exist.

CENT (DUIT)

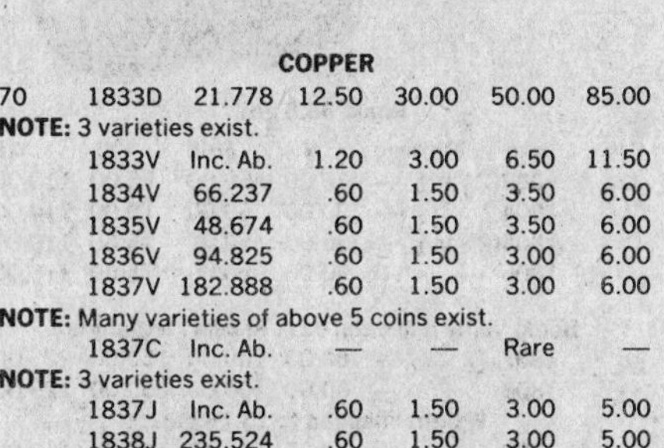

COPPER

C#	Date	Mintage	VG	Fine	VF	XF
70	1833D	21.778	12.50	30.00	50.00	85.00

NOTE: 3 varieties exist.

C#	Date	Mintage	VG	Fine	VF	XF
	1833V	Inc. Ab.	1.20	3.00	6.50	11.50
	1834V	66.237	.60	1.50	3.50	6.00
	1835V	48.674	.60	1.50	3.50	6.00
	1836V	94.825	.60	1.50	3.00	6.00
	1837V	182.888	.60	1.50	3.00	6.00

NOTE: Many varieties of above 5 coins exist.

C#	Date	Mintage	VG	Fine	VF	XF
	1837C	Inc. Ab.	—	—	Rare	—

NOTE: 3 varieties exist.

C#	Date	Mintage	VG	Fine	VF	XF
	1837J	Inc. Ab.	.60	1.50	3.00	5.00
	1838J	235.524	.60	1.50	3.00	5.00
	1839J	314.953	.60	1.50	3.00	5.00
	1839W	Inc. Ab.	.60	1.50	3.00	5.00
	1840W	461.726	.60	1.50	3.00	5.00

NOTE: Many varieties of above 5 coins exist.

SILVER

C#	Date	Mintage	VG	Fine	VF	XF
70a	1833	—	—	—	Rare	—
	1834	—	—	—	Rare	—
	1835	—	—	—	Rare	—
	1836	—	—	—	Rare	—
	1837	—	—	—	Rare	—
	1838	—	—	—	Rare	—

1/2 STUIVER

COPPER

Bonk, 7.72 gm. Value and date each in pearled rectangle.

C#	Date	Mintage	VG	Fine	VF	XF
30	1804	—	60.00	100.00	140.00	200.00
	1805	—	—	—	Rare	—

Obv: Ornate LN below value. Rev: JAVA/date.

C#	Date	Mintage	VG	Fine	VF	XF
45	1810	—	80.00	200.00	300.00	450.00

NOTE: 3 varieties exist.

C#	Date	Mintage	VG	Fine	VF	XF
45a	1810	—	3.00	6.00	12.50	20.00

NOTE: Many varieties exist.

C#	Date	Mintage	VG	Fine	VF	XF
	1811Z	—	3.00	6.00	12.50	20.00

NOTE: Several varieties exist.

Obv: G below shield.

C#	Date	Mintage	VG	Fine	VF	XF
63	1818	—	2.00	4.00	8.50	15.00
	1819	—	2.00	4.00	8.50	15.00
	1820	—	2.50	5.00	10.00	17.50

NOTE: Several varieties of above 3 coins exist.

Obv: G removed.

C#	Date	Mintage	VG	Fine	VF	XF
63a	1820	—	2.00	4.00	8.50	15.00
	1821	—	2.00	4.00	8.50	15.00
	1822	—	2.50	5.00	10.00	17.50
	1823	—	2.00	4.00	8.50	15.00
	1824	—	2.00	4.00	8.50	15.00
	1825	—	2.00	4.00	8.50	15.00
	1826	—	4.00	10.00	12.50	22.50

NOTE: Many varieties of above 7 coins exist.

C#	Date	Mintage	VG	Fine	VF	XF
66	1821S	10.000	.50	2.00	4.00	7.00
	1822S	7.000	.50	2.00	4.00	7.00
	1823S	19.000	.50	2.00	4.00	7.00
	1824S	5.500	1.00	3.00	6.00	11.50
	1825S	42.000	.50	2.00	4.00	7.00
	1826S	66.000	.50	2.00	4.00	7.00

Bonk, value/date in rectangle, 7.72 gm.

C#	Date	Mintage	VG	Fine	VF	XF
67	1818	—	30.00	70.00	120.00	185.00

NOTE: 3 varieties exist.

2 CENTS (DOUBLE DUIT)

COPPER

C#	Date	Mintage	VG	Fine	VF	XF
71	1833D	11.305*	20.00	40.00	80.00	135.00

***NOTE:** 3 varieties exist.

C#	Date	Mintage	VG	Fine	VF	XF
	1833V	Inc. Ab.	1.25	3.00	6.00	10.00
	1834V	32.997	.75	2.00	4.00	7.00
	1835V	24.627	.75	2.00	4.00	7.00
	1836V	48.612	.75	2.00	4.00	7.00
	1837J	54.812	1.50	3.00	5.00	9.00
	1837V	Inc. Ab.	.75	2.00	4.00	7.00
	1838J	93.809	.75	2.00	4.00	7.00
	1839J	90.964	.75	2.00	4.00	7.00
	1839W	Inc. Ab.	1.00	3.00	6.00	10.00
	1840W	98.086	2.00	5.00	10.00	17.50

NOTE: Many varieties of the above 10 coins exist.

SILVER (OMS)

C#	Date	Mintage	VG	Fine	VF	XF
71a	1836	— Unique	—	—	—	
	1837	— Unique	—	—	—	
	1838	— Unique	—	—	—	

COPPER

Obv: Crowned shield. Rev: NEDERL/INDIE/date.

C#	Date	Mintage	VG	Fine	VF	XF
75	1841W	115.321	2.00	5.00	10.00	17.50

NOTE: Many varieties exist.

STUIVER

COPPER BONK, 23.16 gm.

C#	Date	Mintage	VG	Fine	VF	XF
31	1800	—	35.00	70.00	100.00	150.00
	1801	—	35.00	70.00	100.00	150.00
	1802	—	25.00	45.00	60.00	90.00

Bonk, 19.3 gm. Value and date each in pearl rectangle.

C#	Date	Mintage	VG	Fine	VF	XF
31a	1803	—	25.00	45.00	60.00	90.00
	1804	—	25.00	45.00	60.00	90.00

NOTE: 2 varieties exist.

C#	Date	Mintage	VG	Fine	VF	XF
	1805	—	25.00	45.00	60.00	90.00
	1806	—	30.00	60.00	90.00	135.00

LEAD-BRONZE

C#	Date	Mintage	VG	Fine	VF	XF
34	1799	—	25.00	40.00	55.00	75.00
	1800	—	25.00	40.00	55.00	75.00

NOTE: Many varieties exist.

COPPER

Obv: Ornate LN, value. Rev: JAVA/date.

C#	Date	Mintage	VG	Fine	VF	XF
46	1810	—	80.00	200.00	300.00	450.00

NOTE: 2 varieties exist.

19.30 gm:

C#	Date	Mintage	VG	Fine	VF	XF
47	1807	—	60.00	100.00	150.00	225.00
	1808	—	—	—	Rare	—
	1809	—	25.00	45.00	60.00	90.00

NOTE: 2 varieties exist.

11.58 gm.

C#	Date	Mintage	VG	Fine	VF	XF
47a	1810	—	25.00	45.00	60.00	90.00

NOTE: 2 varieties exist.

Bonk. Value and date each in rectangle, 15.44 gm.

C#	Date	Mintage	VG	Fine	VF	XF
68	1818	—	16.50	40.00	70.00	110.00

NOTE: Several varieties exist.

1/16 GULDEN

.916 SILVER, 18mm

C#	Date	Mintage	VG	Fine	VF	XF
38	1802	—	20.00	35.00	65.00	100.00

NOTE: 4 varieties exist.

16mm

C#	Date	Mintage	VG	Fine	VF	XF
38a	1802	—	20.00	35.00	65.00	100.00

NOTE: 3 varieties exist.

2 STUIVER

COPPER

Bonk 46.32 gm. Value and date each in pearl rectangle.

C#	Date	Mintage	VG	Fine	VF	XF
32	1800	—	60.00	100.00	150.00	200.00
	1801	—	60.00	100.00	150.00	200.00
	1802	—	40.00	80.00	125.00	175.00

Bonk, 38.6 gm.

C#	Date	Mintage	VG	Fine	VF	XF
32a	1803(2 var.)	—	30.00	50.00	75.00	110.00
	1804	—	30.00	50.00	75.00	110.00
	1805(2 var.)	—	30.00	50.00	75.00	110.00
	1806	—	30.00	50.00	75.00	110.00

Bonk. Value and date, each in pearl rectangle.

C#	Date	Mintage	VG	Fine	VF	XF
48	1807	—	60.00	100.00	150.00	225.00
	1808	—	60.00	100.00	150.00	225.00

Weight changed to 23.16 gm.

C#	Date	Mintage	VG	Fine	VF	XF
	1809	—	35.00	70.00	100.00	150.00
	1810	—	30.00	60.00	90.00	125.00

NOTE: Many counterfeits exist.

Bonk. Value and date each in rectangle. 30.88 gm.

C#	Date	Mintage	VG	Fine	VF	XF
69	1818	—	16.50	40.00	75.00	110.00

NOTE: Many varieties exist.

C#	Date	Mintage	VG	Fine	VF	XF
	1819	—	37.50	75.00	125.00	185.00

NOTE: 4 varieties exist.

1/8 GULDEN

.916 SILVER, 20mm

C#	Date	Mintage	VG	Fine	VF	XF
39	1802	—	16.50	30.00	50.00	80.00

NOTE: 4 varieties exist.

18mm

C#	Date	Mintage	VG	Fine	VF	XF
39a	1802	—	16.50	30.00	50.00	80.00

NOTE: 3 varieties exist.

1/4 GULDEN

.916 SILVER

C#	Date	Mintage	VG	Fine	VF	XF
40	1802	—	20.00	35.00	65.00	100.00

NOTE: 6 varieties exist.

GOLD (OMS)

C#	Date	Mintage	VG	Fine	VF	XF
40a	1802	—	—	—	Rare	—

.568 SILVER

C#	Date	Mintage	VG	Fine	VF	XF
72.1	1826	1.238	17.50	30.00	45.00	65.00
	1827	1.003	17.50	30.00	45.00	65.00
	1834	1.002	17.50	30.00	45.00	65.00
	1840	.973	17.50	30.00	45.00	65.00

Coarse milling

C#	Date	Mintage	VG	Fine	VF	XF
72.2	1826	Inc. Ab.	18.50	32.50	50.00	70.00

GOLD (OMS)

C#	Date	Mintage	VG	Fine	VF	XF
72a	1834	—	—	—	Rare	—

8 STUIVERS

COPPER

Bonk. Value and date in pearl circles.

C#	Date	Mintage	VG	Fine	VF	XF
33	1803	.395	225.00	325.00	450.00	600.00

1/2 GULDEN

.916 SILVER

Obv: Crowned shield and value.

Rev: Ship with INDIAE BATAV, date around.

C#	Date	Mintage	VG	Fine	VF	XF
40.1	1802	—	25.00	50.00	85.00	135.00

NOTE: 2 varieties exist.

GOLD (OMS)

C#	Date	Mintage	VG	Fine	VF	XF
40.1a	1802	—	—	—	Rare	—

.893 SILVER

Obv. Head. Rev. Value.

C#	Date	Mintage	VG	Fine	VF	XF
73	1826	.517	20.00	35.00	60.00	90.00
	1827	.037	60.00	125.00	200.00	325.00
	1834	.501	20.00	35.00	60.00	90.00

GOLD (OMS)

C#	Date	Mintage	VG	Fine	VF	XF
73a	1834	—	—	—	Rare	—

1/2 RUPEE

.750 GOLD

Obv. Arabic legend, AD date.

C#	Date	Mintage	VG	Fine	VF	XF
41	1800	—	—	—	Rare	—
	1801	—	400.00	800.00	1250.	1750.
	1802	—	400.00	800.00	1250.	1750.
	1803	—	—	Unique	—	—

.792 SILVER

C#	Date	Mintage	VG	Fine	VF	XF
35	1805	—	40.00	80.00	135.00	200.00

NOTE: 12 varieties exist.

C#	Date	Mintage	VG	Fine	VF	XF
	1806	—	32.50	70.00	125.00	185.00

NOTE: 12 varieties exist.

GOLD

C#	Date	Mintage	VG	Fine	VF	XF
53	1807	—	750.00	1250.	1850.	2500.

GULDEN

.916 SILVER

C#	Date	Mintage	VG	Fine	VF	XF
40.2	1802	—	35.00	70.00	110.00	185.00

NOTE: 5 varieties exist.

GOLD (OMS)

C#	Date	Mintage	VG	Fine	VF	XF
40.2a	1802	—	—	—	Rare	—

.893 SILVER, 10.77gm

C#	Date	Mintage	VG	Fine	VF	XF
74	1821	.099	100.00	200.00	350.00	500.00

.945 SILVER, 10.0gm

C#	Date	Mintage	VG	Fine	VF	XF
74a	1839	2.217	20.00	40.00	65.00	100.00
	1840	1.981	30.00	60.00	85.00	135.00

RUPEE

.792 SILVER

C#	Date	Mintage	VG	Fine	VF	XF
36	1800	—	200.00	400.00	600.00	850.00
	1801	—	40.00	65.00	100.00	135.00

NOTE: 4 varieties exist.

C#	Date	Mintage	VG	Fine	VF	XF
	1802	—	60.00	100.00	150.00	200.00
	1803	—	35.00	55.00	90.00	125.00

NOTE: 2 varieties exist.

C#	Date	Mintage	VG	Fine	VF	XF
37	1804	—	40.00	65.00	100.00	135.00

NOTE: 3 varieties exist.

C#	Date	Mintage	VG	Fine	VF	XF
	1805Z	—	40.00	65.00	100.00	135.00
	1806Z	—	30.00	50.00	75.00	110.00

NOTE: 2 varieties exist.

C#	Date	Mintage	VG	Fine	VF	XF
52z	1808	—	45.00	80.00	125.00	165.00

DECIMAL COINAGE

MINTMASTER PRIVY MARKS

Date	Privy Mark
1854-74	Caduceus - Sword
1875-87	Caduceus - Axe
1888-1909	Caduceus - Halberd
1909-33	Caduceus - Sea Horse
1933-42	Caduceus - Grapes

MONETARY SYSTEM

100 Cents = 1 Gulden

1/2 CENT

COPPER

Y#	Date	Mintage	Fine	VF	XF	Unc
1	1855	—	—	—	Rare	—
	1856	10.800	1.50	3.00	5.00	8.50
	1857	36.800	1.25	2.50	4.00	6.00
	1858	53.588	1.25	2.50	4.00	6.00
	1859	219.600	1.25	2.50	4.00	6.00
	1860	107.124	1.25	2.50	4.00	6.00
	1902	20.000	.60	1.25	2.50	4.00
	1908	10.600	.75	1.50	3.00	5.00
	1909	4.400	1.25	2.50	4.00	6.00

SILVER (OMS)

Y#	Date	Mintage	Fine	VF	XF	Unc
1a	1902	—	—	—	Rare	—

GOLD (OMS)

Y#	Date	Mintage	Fine	VF	XF	Unc
1b	1860	—	—	—	Unique	—
	1902	—	—	—	Rare	—

BRONZE

Mintmaster's mark: Sea horse

Y#	Date	Mintage	Fine	VF	XF	Unc
18.1	1914	50.000	.50	1.00	2.00	3.00
	1916	10.000	.60	1.25	2.50	4.00
	1921	4.000	.80	1.50	3.00	5.00
	1932	10.000	.60	1.25	2.50	4.00
	1933	15.000	.60	1.25	2.50	4.00

Mintmaster's mark: Grapes

Y#	Date	Mintage	Fine	VF	XF	Unc
18.2	1933	5.000	.80	1.50	3.00	5.00
	1934	30.000	.50	1.00	2.00	3.00
	1935	14.000	.60	1.25	2.50	4.00
	1936	12.000	.60	1.25	2.50	4.00
	1937	8.400	.60	1.25	2.50	4.00
	1938	3.600	.80	1.50	3.00	5.00
	1939	2.000	.80	1.50	3.00	5.00
	1945P	400.000	.25	.40	.75	1.25

CENT

COPPER

Y#	Date	Mintage	Fine	VF	XF	Unc
2	1855	.100	27.50	45.00	60.00	80.00
	1856	67.900	1.50	3.00	5.00	8.00
	1857	162.000	1.25	2.50	4.00	6.00
	1858	119.431	1.25	2.50	4.00	6.00
	1859	40.800	1.50	3.00	5.00	8.00
	1860	14.455	1.50	3.00	5.00	8.00
	1896	60.400	1.50	3.00	5.00	8.00
	1897	69.600	1.50	3.00	5.00	8.00
	1898	36.600	1.50	3.00	5.00	8.00
	1899	18.400	1.50	3.00	5.00	8.00
	1901	15.000	1.50	3.00	5.00	8.00
	1902	10.000	1.50	3.00	5.00	8.00
	1907	7.500	1.50	3.00	5.00	8.00
	1908	12.500	1.50	3.00	5.00	8.00
	1909	7.500	1.25	2.50	4.00	6.00
	1912	25.000	.75	1.50	3.00	5.00

YELLOW BRONZE (OMS)

Y#	Date	Mintage	Fine	VF	XF	Unc
2a	1898	—	—	—	Rare	—

SILVER (OMS)

Y#	Date	Mintage	Fine	VF	XF	Unc
2b	1902	—	—	—	Rare	—

GOLD (OMS)

Y#	Date	Mintage	Fine	VF	XF	Unc
2c	1860	—	—	—	Unique	—
	1902	—	—	—	Rare	—

BRONZE

Y#	Date	Mintage	Fine	VF	XF	Unc
19	1914	85.000	.75	1.50	3.00	5.00
	1916	16.440	1.25	2.50	4.00	6.00
	1919	20.000	1.25	2.50	4.00	6.00
	1920	120.000	.60	1.25	2.50	4.00
	1926	10.000	1.25	2.50	4.00	6.00
	1929	50.000	.60	1.25	2.50	4.00

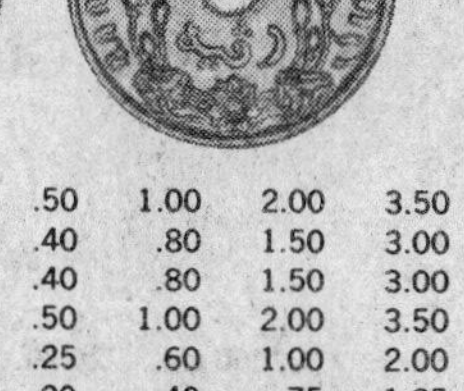

Y#	Date	Mintage	Fine	VF	XF	Unc
21	1936	52.000	.50	1.00	2.00	3.50
	1937	120.400	.40	.80	1.50	3.00
	1938	150.000	.40	.80	1.50	3.00
	1939	81.400	.50	1.00	2.00	3.50
	1942P	100.000	.25	.60	1.00	2.00
	1945P	335.000	.20	.40	.75	1.25
	1945D	133.800	.25	.60	1.00	2.00
	1945S	102.568	.20	.40	.75	1.50

2-1/2 CENTS

COPPER

Y#	Date	Mintage	Fine	VF	XF	Unc
3	1856	2.480	5.00	10.00	16.50	20.00
	1857	36.560	3.00	6.00	10.00	15.00
	1858	40.990	3.00	6.00	10.00	15.00
	1896	1.120	3.00	6.00	10.00	15.00
	1897	18.105	1.00	1.50	3.00	5.00
	1898	7.600	2.50	5.00	10.00	15.00
	1899	10.400	2.00	4.00	8.00	12.50
	1902	6.000	2.50	5.00	10.00	15.00
	1907	3.000	3.00	6.00	12.50	16.50
	1908	5.940	2.50	5.00	10.00	15.00
	1909	3.060	2.50	5.00	10.00	15.00
	1913	4.000	2.50	5.00	10.00	15.00

SILVER (OMS)

Y#	Date	Mintage	Fine	VF	XF	Unc
3a	1902	—	—	—	Rare	—

GOLD (OMS)

Y#	Date	Mintage	Fine	VF	XF	Unc
3b	1858	—	—	—	Unique	—
	1902	—	—	—	Rare	—

BRONZE

Y#	Date	Mintage	Fine	VF	XF	Unc
20	1914	22.000	.75	3.00	5.00	8.00
	1915	6.000	1.50	4.00	6.00	10.00
	1920	48.000	.75	1.50	3.00	5.00
	1945P	200.000	.50	1.00	2.00	3.00

1/20 GULDEN

.6100 gm., .720 SILVER, .0141 oz ASW

Y#	Date	Mintage	Fine	VF	XF	Unc
4	1854	—	150.00	225.00	350.00	450.00
	1855	.492	6.00	12.50	18.50	27.50

GOLD (OMS)

Y#	Date	Mintage	Fine	VF	XF	Unc
4a	1855	—	—	—	Unique	—

5 CENTS

COPPER-NICKEL

Y#	Date	Mintage	Fine	VF	XF	Unc
17	1913	60.000	.75	1.50	3.00	5.00
	1921	40.000	1.25	2.50	4.00	6.00
	1922	20.000	2.00	4.00	6.00	10.00

1/10 GULDEN

1.2500 gm., .720 SILVER, .0289 oz ASW

Y#	Date	Mintage	Fine	VF	XF	Unc
5	1854	3.550	3.00	6.00	10.00	15.00
	1855	6.452	3.00	6.00	8.00	12.50
	1856	3.000	4.00	8.00	12.50	16.50
	1857	11.000	3.00	6.00	8.00	12.50
	1858	14.000	2.00	4.00	6.00	10.00
	1882	7.500	3.00	6.00	10.00	15.00
	1884	3.550	4.00	8.00	12.50	16.50
	1885	.825	7.50	16.50	25.00	35.00
	1891	5.000	2.00	4.00	6.00	10.00
	1893	5.000	2.00	4.00	6.00	10.00
	1896	3.075	2.00	4.00	6.00	10.00
	1898	2.500	3.00	6.00	10.00	15.00
	1900	6.850	2.00	4.00	6.00	10.00
	1901	5.000	2.00	4.00	6.00	10.00

GOLD (OMS)

Y#	Date	Mintage	Fine	VF	XF	Unc
5a	1854	—	—	—	Unique	—

1.2500 gm., .720 SILVER, .0289 oz ASW

Y#	Date	Mintage	Fine	VF	XF	Unc
7	1903	5.000	2.00	4.00	6.00	10.00
(12)	1904	5.000	2.00	4.00	6.00	10.00
	1905	5.000	2.00	4.00	6.00	10.00
	1506	7.500	2.00	4.00	6.00	10.00
	1907	14.000	1.50	3.50	5.00	8.00
	1908	3.000	3.00	6.00	8.00	12.50
	1909	10.000	1.50	3.50	5.00	8.00

GOLD (OMS)

Y#	Date	Mintage	Fine	VF	XF	Unc
7a (12a)	1903	—	—	—	Rare	—

1.2500 gm., .720 SILVER, .0289 oz ASW
Obv. & rev: Wide rims and small legends.

Y#	Date	Mintage	Fine	VF	XF	Unc
14	1910	15.000	1.25	2.50	4.00	6.00
	1911	10.000	1.25	2.50	4.00	6.00
	1912	25.000	1.00	1.50	3.00	5.00
	1913	15.000	1.25	2.50	4.00	6.00
	1914	25.000	1.00	1.50	3.00	5.00
	1915	15.000	1.25	2.50	4.00	6.00
	1918	30.000	1.00	1.50	3.00	5.00
	1919	20.000	1.00	1.50	3.00	5.00
	1920	85.000	1.25	2.50	4.00	6.00
	1928	30.000	1.00	1.50	3.00	5.00
	1930	15.000	1.25	2.50	4.00	6.00

Obv. & rev: Narrow rims and large legends.

Y#	Date	Mintage	Fine	VF	XF	Unc
14a	1937	20.000	BV	1.25	2.50	4.00
	1938	30.000	BV	1.25	2.50	4.00
14a	1939	5.400	1.50	3.00	5.00	8.00
	1940	10.000	1.25	2.50	4.00	6.00
	1941P	41.850	BV	1.00	1.25	2.50
	1941S	58.150	BV	1.00	1.50	3.00
	1942S	75.000	BV	1.00	1.25	2.50
	1945P	100.720	BV	1.00	1.25	2.50
	1945S	19.280	BV	1.25	2.00	3.50

1/4 GULDEN

3.1800 gm., .720 SILVER, .0736 oz ASW

Y#	Date	Mintage	Fine	VF	XF	Unc
6	1854	11.460	4.00	8.00	12.50	16.50
	1855	4.541	4.00	8.00	12.50	16.50
	1857	2.400	8.00	15.00	22.50	30.00
	1858	4.800	4.00	8.00	12.50	16.50
	1882	2.200	10.00	20.00	30.00	40.00
	1883	.800	16.50	27.50	40.00	60.00
	1885	1.750	12.50	25.00	35.00	50.00
	1890	1.140	7.50	15.00	17.50	22.50
	1891	.860	8.50	16.50	22.50	30.00
	1893	2.000	4.00	8.50	12.50	16.50
	1896	1.230	7.50	15.00	18.50	22.50
	1898	3.000	3.50	7.50	10.00	15.00
	1900	2.800	3.50	7.50	10.00	15.00
	1901	2.000	4.00	8.50	12.50	16.50

GOLD (OMS)

Y#	Date	Mintage	Fine	VF	XF	Unc
6a	1885	—	—	—	Unique	—

3.1800 gm., .720 SILVER, .0736 oz ASW

Y#	Date	Mintage	Fine	VF	XF	Unc
8	1903	2.000	4.00	8.00	12.50	16.50
(13)	1904	2.000	4.00	8.00	12.50	16.50
	1905	2.000	4.00	8.00	12.50	16.50
	1906	4.000	3.50	6.00	10.00	15.00
	1907	4.400	3.00	6.00	10.00	15.00
	1908	2.000	4.00	8.00	12.50	16.50
	1909	4.000	3.50	6.00	10.00	15.00

GOLD (OMS)

Y#	Date	Mintage	Fine	VF	XF	Unc
8a (13a)	1903	—	—	—	Rare	—

3.1800 gm., .720 SILVER, .0736 oz ASW
Obv. & rev: Wide rims and small legends.

Y#	Date	Mintage	Fine	VF	XF	Unc
15	1910	6.000	3.00	6.00	10.00	15.00
	1911	4.000	3.00	6.00	10.00	15.00
	1912	10.000	3.00	6.00	8.50	12.50
	1913	6.000	3.00	6.00	10.00	15.00
	1914	10.000	3.00	6.00	8.50	12.50
	1915	6.000	3.00	6.00	10.00	15.00
	1917	12.000	3.00	6.00	8.50	12.50
	1919	6.000	3.00	6.00	10.00	15.00
	1920	20.000	BV	2.75	4.00	6.00
	1921	24.000	BV	2.75	4.00	6.00
	1929	5.000	2.50	4.00	6.00	10.00
	1930	7.000	BV	3.00	5.00	8.50

Obv. & rev: Narrow rims and large legends.

Y#	Date	Mintage	Fine	VF	XF	Unc
15a	1937	8.000	BV	3.00	5.00	8.50
	1938	12.000	BV	3.00	5.00	8.50
	1939	10.400	BV	3.00	5.00	8.50
	1941P	34.947	BV	2.25	3.00	5.00
	1941S	5.053	2.25	4.00	6.00	8.50
	1942S	32.000	BV	2.25	3.00	5.00
	1945S	56.000	BV	2.25	2.75	4.00

WORLD WAR II ISSUES

Netherlands and Netherlands East Indies coins of the 1941-45 period were struck at U.S. Mints (P-Philadelphia, D-Denver, S-San Francisco) and bear the mint mark and a palm tree (Acorn on Homeland Issues) flanking the date. The following issues-Y46a and Y47a-are of the usual Netherlands types, being distinguished from similar 1944-45 issues produced in the name of the Homeland by the presence of the palm tree, but were produced for release in the colony. See other related issues under Curacao and Surinam.

Homeland Types

GULDEN

10.0000 gm., .720 SILVER, .2315 oz ASW

Y#	Date	Mintage	Fine	VF	XF	Unc
46a	1943D	20.000	BV	7.50	10.00	15.00

2 1/2 GULDEN

25.0000 gm., .720 SILVER, .5787 oz ASW

Y#	Date	Mintage	Fine	VF	XF	Unc
47a	1943D	2.000	BV	BV	17.50	22.50

TRADE COINS

DUCAT

.986 GOLD

These gold coins, intended primarily for circulation in the Netherlands East Indies will be found listed as Y#15 in the Netherlands section.

NOTE: For later coinage see Indonesia.

Japanese Occupation

10 SEN

TIN ALLOY

Three coins were struck primarily for circulation in the East Indies. The Sen, 5 Sen and 10 Sen are inscribed DAI NIHON (Great Japan) and are found listed under Japan - Occupation Issues.

LOCAL ISSUES

KEPING

COPPER
Obv: Arabic leg: PULU PERCHA (Island of Sumatra).

P#	Date	Year	VG	Fine	VF	XF
—	AH1247	—	Reported, not confirmed			
39	1251	—	5.00	10.00	16.50	25.00
39A	1251	—	—	—	Proof	100.00

Obv: Arabic leg: TANAH MALAYU (Land of the Malays).

P#	Date	Year	VG	Fine	VF	XF
49	AH1251	—	5.00	10.00	16.50	25.00
49A	1251	—	—	—	Proof	125.00

Obv: .date misformed, Arabic legend above rooster, TATAH MALAYU SATU KEPING (Land of the Malays - One Keping). C.R.READ under rooster. Rev. leg: IN BUGI, WANOEWA TANA OEGI SEDI KEPING (Land of the Oegi - One Keping) around 16-petal rosette.

P#	Date	Year	VG	Fine	VF	XF
33	AH1250	—	2.00	4.00	8.00	15.00
33A	1250	—	—	—	Proof	125.00

Obv: Arabic leg: PULU MALAYU (Island of the Malays).

P#	Date	Year	VG	Fine	VF	XF
28	AH1411	—	3.00	6.00	12.50	20.00

Obv: Arabic leg: TANAH MALAYU (Land of the Malays).

P#	Date	Year	VG	Fine	VF	XF
31	AH1250	—	2.50	5.00	10.00	16.50

Obv: Arabic leg: TANAH UGI (Land of the Bugis—Celebes). Rev. leg: SEUWA DUWI (One Doit).

P#	Date	Year	VG	Fine	VF	XF
53	AH1250	—	5.00	10.00	16.50	25.00
53A	1250	—	—	—	Proof	125.00

Obv: Two lions supporting shield below island of Sumatra. Rev. value: P for Arabic 1, date.

P#	Date	Year	VG	Fine	VF	XF
1	AH1219	1804	2.00	4.00	8.00	15.00

Rev: Q for Arabic 1

P#	Date	Year	VG	Fine	VF	XF
2	AH1219	1804	7.50	15.00	22.50	35.00

Rev: 1 for Arabic 1

P#	Date	Year	VG	Fine	VF	XF
3	AH1247	1804	1.25	2.50	5.00	10.00

Obv: leg: ISLAND OF SULTANA. Rev. leg: Meaningless.

P#	Date	Year	VG	Fine	VF	XF
4	AH1411	1804	.75	1.50	3.00	6.00

Obv. leg: ISLAND OF SULTANA above arms.

P#	Date	Year	VG	Fine	VF	XF
5	AH1219	1804	.65	1.25	2.50	5.00

Obv: Similar to P#4. Rev: Similar to P#3.

P#	Date	Year	VG	Fine	VF	XF
6	AH1247	1804	.65	1.25	2.50	5.00

P#	Date	Year	VG	Fine	VF	XF
7	AH1250	1804	2.00	4.00	8.00	15.00

Obv. leg: ISLAND OF SULTANA, horses supporting shield with two flags. Rev: Meaningless legends.

P#	Date	Year	VG	Fine	VF	XF
8	AH1411	1835	3.00	6.00	12.00	20.00

Similar to P#8 with one flag above arms, flying right.

P#	Date	Year	VG	Fine	VF	XF
9a	AH1411	1835	4.00	8.00	15.00	25.00

Obv: One flag above arms, flying left.

P#	Date	Year	VG	Fine	VF	XF
9b	AH1411	1835	4.00	8.00	15.00	25.00

Obv: W/o leg. Rev: Similar to P#8.

P#	Date	Year	VG	Fine	VF	XF
10	AH1411	1835	4.00	8.00	15.00	20.00

NOTE: Although it was once thought that Island of Sultana referred to the Island of Labuan, it now appears to be a name given to the Island of Sumatra.

2 KEPINGS

COPPER
Obv: Arabic leg: PULAU PERCHA (Island of Sumatra).

P#	Date	Year	VG	Fine	VF	XF
36	AH1247	—	4.00	8.00	15.00	25.00
36A	1247	—	—	—	Proof	125.00
38	1251	—	4.00	8.00	15.00	25.00
38A	1251	—	—	—	Proof	125.00

ATCHEH

KEPING

TIN
Arabic legends.

C#	Date	Mintage	Good	VG	Fine	VF
10	AH1220	—	12.50	20.00	32.50	50.00

2 KEPINGS

COPPER
Obv. Arabic leg: NEGRI ACHEH (State of Acheh).

P#	Date	Year	VG	Fine	VF	XF
40	AH1247	—	2.00	4.00	8.00	15.00
40A	1247	—	—	—	Proof	125.00
41	1251	—	—	—	Proof	125.00

BANDARMASSIN

KEPING

COPPER
Obv: Arabic legend BANJARMASIN.
Rev: Date and value.

C#	Date	Mintage	VG	Fine	VF	XF
23a	AH1221	—	12.50	20.00	32.50	50.00

DELI

KEPING

COPPER
Obv: Arabic legend: NEGRI DILLI (State of Deli).

P#	Date	Year	VG	Fine	VF	XF
—	AH1247	—	Reported, not confirmed			
47	1251	—	2.00	4.00	8.00	15.00
47A	1251	—	—	—	Proof	100.00

MENANGKABAU

KEPING

COPPER
Obv: Arabic leg: MENANGKABAU.

P#	Date	Year	VG	Fine	VF	XF
—	AH1247	—	Reported, not confirmed			
46	1251	—	2.00	4.00	8.00	15.00
46A	1251	—	—	—	Proof	100.00

2 KEPING

COPPER

P#	Date	Year	VG	Fine	VF	XF
44	AH1247	—	—	—	Proof	125.00
45	1251	—	2.00	4.00	8.00	15.00
45A	1251	—	—	—	Proof	125.00

PALEMBANG

PITIS

TIN
Octagonal shape, 14mm. Obv: Arabic legends.
Rev: Blank.

C#	Date	Mintage	Good	VG	Fine	VF
120	AH1219	—	6.00	10.00	16.50	25.00
	Hole in center					
123	AH1219	—	7.00	12.00	18.50	28.50

PONTIANAQ

KEPING

COPPER
Obv: Two lions supporting arms. Rev: Scales.

C#	Date	Mintage	VG	Fine	VF	XF
135	1810	—	5.00	10.00	17.50	27.50
	Obv: Arabic legend. 22mm					
138	AH1226	—	5.00	10.00	17.50	27.50

2 KEPINGS

COPPER, 26mm

C#	Date	Mintage	VG	Fine	VF	XF
139	AH1226	—	6.00	12.00	20.00	32.50

SIAK

KEPING

COPPER
Obv. Arabic legend: NEGRI SIAK (State of Siak).

P#	Date	Year	VG	Fine	VF	XF
48	AH1251	—	2.00	4.00	8.00	15.00
48A	1251	—	—	—	Proof	100.00

SUMENEP

COUNTERSTAMP ISSUES

RUPEE

SILVER
c/s: Five-petaled flower on various Rupees.

C#	Date	Mintage	Good	VG	Fine	VF
170	ND	—	25.00	35.00	45.00	60.00

1/2 REAL BATU

SILVER
c/s: SUMENEP and 5 petaled flowers on
Spanish or Spanish Colonial 'cob' 4 Reales.

C#	Date	Mintage	Good	VG	Fine	VF
172	ND	—	150.00	200.00	265.00	350.00

REAL BATU

SILVER
c/s: SUMENEP and (1)230 in Arabic on
Spanish or Spanish Colonial 'cob' 8 Reales.

C#	Date	Mintage	Good	VG	Fine	VF
173	AH(1)230	—	120.00	165.00	225.00	300.00

DOLLAR

SILVER
c/s: Five petaled flower on various crown size coins.

C#	Date	Mintage	Good	VG	Fine	VF
174	ND	—	75.00	90.00	135.00	200.00

RUPEE

GOLD
c/s: SUMENEP and (1)230 in Arabic on
Spanish or Spanish Colonial 2 Escudos.

C#	Date	Mintage	Good	VG	Fine	VF
178	AH1230	—	—	—	Rare	—

TARUMON

2 KEPINGS

COPPER
Obv: Arabic legend NEGRI TARUMON (State of Tarumon).

P#	Date	Year	VG	Fine	VF	XF
42	AH1247	—	2.00	4.00	8.00	12.00
43	1251	—	2.00	4.00	8.00	12.00
43A	1251	—	—	—	Proof	100.00

INDONESIA

MONETARY SYSTEM

100 Sen = 1 Rupiah

SEN

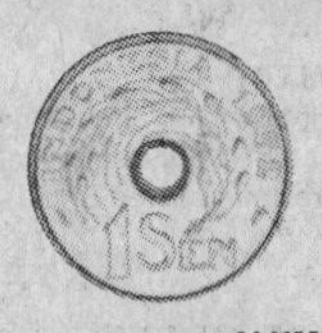

ALUMINUM

Y#	Date	Mintage	VF	XF	Unc
1	1952	100.000	.30	.50	1.00

5 SEN

ALUMINUM

Y#	Date	Mintage	VF	XF	Unc
2	1951	—	.25	.40	.60
	1954	—	.25	.40	.50

10 SEN

ALUMINUM

Y#	Date	Mintage	VF	XF	Unc
3	1951	—	.25	.40	.75
	1954	50.000	.20	.30	.50

Y#	Date	Mintage	VF	XF	Unc
3a	1957	50.224	.75	1.10	1.25

25 SEN

ALUMINUM

Y#	Date	Mintage	VF	XF	Unc
4	1952	200.00	.30	.40	.60

Y#	Date	Mintage	VF	XF	Unc
6	1955	25.767	.20	.30	.40
	1957	100.000	.25	.30	.40

50 SEN

COPPER-NICKEL

Y#	Date	Mintage	VF	XF	Unc
5	1952	100.000	.20	.30	.40

Y#	Date	Mintage	VF	XF	Unc
5a	1954	—	2.00	2.50	4.00
	1955	15.000	.25	.30	.40
	1957	24.977	.25	.30	.40

Head size is significantly different with larger lettering on the 1957 issue.

ALUMINUM

Y#	Date	Mintage	VF	XF	Unc
7	1958	100.000	.25	.35	.60

Modified eagle

Y#	Date	Mintage	VF	XF	Unc
	1959	100.000	.20	.25	.50
	1961	128.528	.25	.35	.50

RUPIAH

ALUMINUM

Y#	Date	Mintage	VF	XF	Unc
13	1970	136.010	.10	.15	.25

2 RUPIAH

ALUMINUM

Y#	Date	Mintage	VF	XF	Unc
14	1970	139.230	.10	.15	.30

5 RUPIAH

ALUMINUM

Y#	Date	Mintage	VF	XF	Unc
15	1970	448.000	.25	.35	.50

F.A.O. Issue

Y#	Date	Mintage	VF	XF	Unc
20	1974	283.600	.10	.20	.30

F.A.O. Issue
1.3800gm.

Y#	Date	Mintage	VF	XF	Unc
26	1979	—	—	.25	.50

10 RUPIAH

COPPER-NICKEL
F.A.O. Issue

Y#	Date	Mintage	VF	XF	Unc
18	1971	286.360	.10	.20	.25
	1973	80.000	.15	.25	.40

BRASS-CLAD STEEL
F.A.O. Issue

Y#	Date	Mintage	VF	XF	Unc
21	1974	204.753	.10	.20	.40

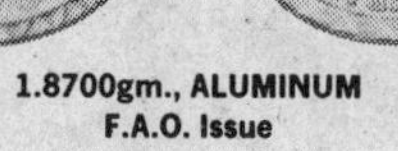

1.8700gm., ALUMINUM
F.A.O. Issue

Y#	Date	Mintage	VF	XF	Unc
27	1979	—	—	.25	.50

25 RUPIAH

COPPER-NICKEL

Y#	Date	Mintage	VF	XF	Unc
16	1971	390.000	.15	.35	.60

50 RUPIAH

COPPER-NICKEL

Y#	Date	Mintage	VF	XF	Unc
17	1971	336.900	.25	.50	1.00

100 RUPIAH

COPPER-NICKEL

Y#	Date	Mintage	VF	XF	Unc
19	1973	270.000	.30	.60	1.25

F.A.O. Issue

Y#	Date	Mintage	VF	XF	Unc
25	1978	68.820	—	—	2.00

200 RUPIAH

8.0000 gm., .999 SILVER, .2569oz ASW

H#	Date	Mintage	XF	Unc	Proof
1	1970	—	—	—	12.50

250 RUPIAH

10.0000 gm., .999 SILVER, .3212oz ASW

H#	Date	Mintage	XF	Unc	Proof
2	1970	—	—	—	15.00

500 RUPIAH

20.0000 gm., .999 SILVER, .6424oz ASW
Obv: Similar to 10,000 Rupiah, H#9.

H#	Date	Mintage	XF	Unc	Proof
3	1970	—	—	—	22.50

750 RUPIAH

30.0000 gm., .999 SILVER, .9636oz ASW
Obv: Similar to 20,000 Rupiah, H#10.

H#	Date	Mintage	XF	Unc	Proof
4	1970	4,650	—	—	35.00

1000 RUPIAH

40.0000 gm., .999 SILVER, 1.2848oz ASW
Obv: Similar to 25,000 Rupiah, H#11.

H#	Date	Mintage	XF	Unc	Proof
5	1970	1,200	—	—	40.00

2000 RUPIAH

4.9300 gm., .900 GOLD, .1426oz AGW

H#	Date	Mintage	XF	Unc	Proof
7	1970	4,150	—	—	100.00

25.3100 gm., .500 SILVER, .4069oz ASW
Conservation Commemorative
Obv: Similar to 100,000 Rupiah, Y#24.

Y#	Date	Mintage	VF	XF	Unc
22	1974	.106	—	—	25.00

28.2800 gm., .925 SILVER, .8411oz ASW

Y#	Date	Mintage	VF	XF	Unc
22a	1974	.030	—	Proof	30.00

5000 RUPIAH

12.3400 gm., .900 GOLD, .3571oz AGW
Rev: Similar to 2000 Rupiah, H#7.

H#	Date	Mintage	XF	Unc	Proof
8	1970	4,200	—	—	250.00

31.6500 gm., .500 SILVER, .5007oz ASW
Conservation Commemorative
Obv: Similar to 100,000 Rupiah, Y#24.

Y#	Date	Mintage	VF	XF	Unc
23	1974	.118	—	—	40.00

35.0000 gm., .925 SILVER, 1.0410oz ASW

Y#	Date	Mintage	VF	XF	Unc
	1974	.031	—	Proof	50.00

10,000 RUPIAH

24.6800 gm., .900 GOLD, .7142oz AGW
Obv: Similar to 500 Rupiah, H#3.

H#	Date	Mintage	XF	Unc	Proof
9	1970	4,100	—	—	500.00

20,000 RUPIAH

49.3700 gm., .900 GOLD, 1.4391oz AGW
Obv: Similar to 750 Rupiah, H#4.

H#	Date	Mintage	XF	Unc	Proof
10	1970	4,180	—	—	1000.

25,000 RUPIAH

61.7100 gm., .900 GOLD, 1.7858oz AGW
Obv: Similar to 1000 Rupiah, H#5.

H#	Date	Mintage	XF	Unc	Proof
11	1970	4,070	—	—	1250.

100,000 RUPIAH

33.4370 gm., .900 GOLD, .9676oz AGW
Conservation Commemorative

Y#	Date	Mintage	VF	XF	Unc
24	1974	.010	—	BV	650.00
	1974	3,459	—	Proof	750.00

NCLT ISSUES

PROOF SETS
STANDARD METALS

KM#	Date	Mintage	Identification	Issue Price	Mkt. Val.
101	1970(10)	—	H1-5,7-11	488.00	3000.
102	1970(5)	—	H1-5	45.00	125.00
103	1974(2)	30,000	Y22,23	50.00	75.00

RIAU ARCHIPELAGO

A group of islands off the tip of the Malay Peninsula. Coins were issued near the end of 1963 (although dated 1962) and recalled as worthless on Sept. 30, 1964. They were legal tender from Oct. 15, 1963 to July 1, 1964.

INSCRIPTION ON EDGE
KEPULAUAN RIAU

SEN

ALUMINUM

Y#	Date	Mintage	VF	XF	Unc
8	1962	—	.35	.80	1.25

5 SEN

ALUMINUM

Y#	Date	Mintage	VF	XF	Unc
9	1962	—	.30	.75	1.00

10 SEN

ALUMINUM

Y#	Date	Mintage	VF	XF	Unc
10	1962	—	.35	.85	1.25

25 SEN

ALUMINUM

Y#	Date	Mintage	VF	XF	Unc
11	1962	—	.50	.95	1.50

Rev: Different style "5".

Y#	Date	Mintage	VF	XF	Unc
11.1	1962	—	4.00	8.00	12.00

50 SEN

ALUMINUM

Y#	Date	Mintage	VF	XF	Unc
12	1962	—	.70	1.00	2.25

12 Var. 1962 - Struck on different obverse and reverse dies, different style edge lettering, 16 leaves on right branch unique.

IRIAN JAYA

WEST IRIAN, WEST NEW GUINEA, IRIAN BARAT, NETHERLANDS NEW GUINEA

A province of Indonesia comprising the western half of the island of New Guinea. A special set of coins dated 1962 were issued in 1964 and were no longer legal tender after June 1, 1971.

Coins of West Irian were recalled December 31, 1971 and are no longer legal tender.

NO INSCRIPTION ON EDGE

SEN

ALUMINUM
Plain edge

Y#	Date	Mintage	Fine	VF	XF	Unc
8a	1962	—	.25	.60	.85	1.50

5 SEN

ALUMINUM
Plain edge

Y#	Date	Mintage	Fine	VF	XF	Unc
9a	1962	—	.25	.60	.85	1.50

10 SEN

ALUMINUM
Plain edge

Y#	Date	Mintage	Fine	VF	XF	Unc
10a	1962	—	.30	.65	1.00	2.00

25 SEN

ALUMINUM
Reeded edge

Y#	Date	Mintage	Fine	VF	XF	Unc
11a	1962	—	.35	.80	1.25	2.50

Rev: Different style "5".

Y#	Date	Mintage	Fine	VF	XF	Unc
11a.1	1962	—	1.50	3.00	6.00	10.00

50 SEN

ALUMINUM
Reeded edge

Y#	Date	Mintage	Fine	VF	XF	Unc
12a	1962	—	.55	.90	1.50	3.00

TIMOR

An island in the Lesser Sunda group, presently part of Indonesia but formerly divided between Portugal and the Netherlands. Portugal owned the eastern half of the island and made coins for this colony. Made part of Indonesia in 1975.

MONETARY SYSTEM
100 Avos = 1 Pataca

COLONIAL ISSUES

10 AVOS

BRONZE

Y#	Date	Mintage	Fine	VF	XF	Unc
1	1945	.050	12.00	20.00	30.00	50.00
	1948	.500	.60	1.50	2.25	4.00
	1951	6.250	.50	1.25	1.75	3.00

20 AVOS

NICKEL-BRONZE

Y#	Date	Mintage	Fine	VF	XF	Unc
2	1945	.050	5.00	7.50	15.00	30.00

50 AVOS

.650 SILVER

Y#	Date	Mintage	Fine	VF	XF	Unc
3	1945	.100	20.00	30.00	40.00	60.00
	1948	.500	4.50	7.50	12.50	20.00
	1951	6.250	4.50	6.50	8.50	15.00

MONETARY REFORM

100 Centavos = 1 Escudo

10 CENTAVOS

BRONZE

Y#	Date	Mintage	Fine	VF	XF	Unc
4	1958	1.000	.50	1.00	2.00	5.00

20 CENTAVOS

BRONZE

Y#	Date	Mintage	Fine	VF	XF	Unc
12	1970	1.000	—	.10	.20	.40

30 CENTAVOS

BRONZE

Y#	Date	Mintage	Fine	VF	XF	Unc
5	1958	2.000	.15	.35	.65	1.00

50 CENTAVOS

BRONZE

Y#	Date	Mintage	Fine	VF	XF	Unc
13	1970	1.000	—	.10	.25	.65

60 CENTAVOS

COPPER-NICKEL

Y#	Date	Mintage	Fine	VF	XF	Unc
6	1958	1.000	.25	.50	1.00	2.00

ESCUDO

COPPER-NICKEL

Y#	Date	Mintage	Fine	VF	XF	Unc
7	1958	1.200	.50	.75	1.25	3.00

BRONZE

Y#	Date	Mintage	Fine	VF	XF	Unc
14	1970	1.200	.15	.35	.65	1.00

2-1/2 ESCUDOS

COPPER-NICKEL

Y#	Date	Mintage	Fine	VF	XF	Unc
15	1970	1.000	—	.25	.50	1.50

3 ESCUDOS

3.5000 gm., .650 SILVER, .0731 oz ASW

Y#	Date	Mintage	Fine	VF	XF	Unc
8	1958	1.000	2.25	2.75	3.50	5.00

5 ESCUDOS

COPPER-NICKEL

Y#	Date	Mintage	Fine	VF	XF	Unc
16	1970	1.200	.40	.65	1.00	2.00

6 ESCUDOS

7.0000 gm., .650 SILVER, .1463 oz ASW

Y#	Date	Mintage	Fine	VF	XF	Unc
9	1958	1.000	4.50	5.50	7.00	10.00

10 ESCUDOS

7.0000 gm., .650 SILVER, .1463 oz ASW

Y#	Date	Mintage	Fine	VF	XF	Unc
10	1964	.600	4.50	5.50	7.00	10.00

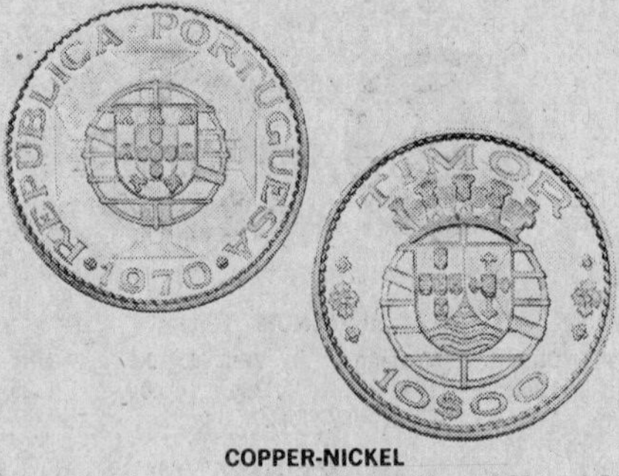

COPPER-NICKEL

Y#	Date	Mintage	Fine	VF	XF	Unc
17	1970	.700	.60	1.00	1.75	3.50

Listings For

IONIAN ISLANDS: refer to Greece

IRAN

The Islamic Republic of Iran, located between the Caspian Sea and the Persian Gulf in southwestern Asia, has an area of 636,000 sq. mi. (1,647,240 km.) and a population of 34.4 million. Capital: Tehran. Although predominantly an agricultural state, Iran depends heavily on oil for foreign exchange. Crude oil, carpets and agricultural products are exported.

Iran (historically known as Persia) is one of the world's most ancient and resilient nations. Strategically astride the lower land gate to Asia, it has been conqueror and conquered, sovereign nation and vassal state, ever emerging from its periods of glory or travail with its culture and political individuality intact. Iran (Persia) was a powerful empire under Cyrus the Great (600-529 B.C.), its borders extending from the Indus to the Nile. It has also been conquered by the predatory empires of antique and recent times - Assyrian, Medean, Macedonian, Seljuq, Turk, Mongol - and more recently been coveted by Russia, the Third Reich and Great Britain. Revolts against the absolute power of the Persian shahs resulted in the establishment of a constitutional monarchy in 1906. In 1979, the monarchy was toppled and an Islamic republic proclaimed.

RULERS

Qajar Dynasty

Agha Muhammad Khan
AH1193-1211/AD1779-97
Crowned, AH1210/AD1796
Baba Khan (Fath'ali before coronation) AH1211-12/AD1797-98
Fath'ali Shah,
AH1212-50/AD1797-1834
Sultan Ali Shah,
AH1250/AD1834 (30 days)
Husayn Ali Shah,
AH1250/AD1834 (6 months)
(in Southern Iran only)
Muhammad Shah,
AH1250-64/AD1834-48
Nasir al-Din Shah,
AH1264-1313/AD1848-96
Muzaffar al-Din Shah,
AH1313-24/AD1896-1907
Muhammad Ali Shah,
AH1324-27/AD1907-09
Sultan Ahmad Shah,
AH1327-44/AD1909-25

PAHLAVI DYNASTY

Reza Shah,
SH1304-20/AD1925-41
Muhammad Reza Shah,
SH1320-1358/AD1941-1979

COIN DATING

Iranian coins were dated according to the Moslem lunar calendar until March 21, 1925 (AD), when dating was switched to a new calendar based on the solar year, indicated by the notation SH. The monarchial calender system was adopted in 1976 - MS2535 and was abandoned in 1978 - MS2537. The previously used solar year calendar was restored at that time.

MONETARY SYSTEM

1797-98 (AH 1211-12)

50 Dinars = 1 Shahi
15 Shahis = 1 Rupee (?)
12 Rupees and 2 Shahis = 1 Toman
300 Dinars = 1 Abbasi

NOTE: The Shahi was a fixed unit, first coined in AD1501, equal to 50 Dinars. The Toman, introduced as a unit of account about AD1240, was always fixed at 10,000 Dinars. The value of the Rupee for this period is not known with certainty.

1798-1825 (AH 1212-1241)

1250 Dinars = 1 Riyal
8 Riyals = 1 Toman

1825-1931 (AH1241-1344, SH1304-09)

50 Dinars = 1 Shahi
20 Shahis = 1 Kran (Qiran)
10 Krans = 1 Toman

NOTE: From AD1830-34 (AH1245-50) the gold Toman was known as a 'Keshwarsetan.'

1932-Date (SH1310-Date)

5 Dinars = 1 Shahi
20 Shahis = 1 Rial (100 Dinars)
10 Rials = 1 Toman

NOTE: The Toman ceased to be an official unit in 1932, but continues to be applied in popular usage. Thus, '135 Rials' is always expressed as '13 Toman, 5 Rials.' The term 'Rial' is often used in conversation, as well as either 'Kran' or 'Ezar' (short for Hazar - 1000) is used.

NOTE: The Law of 18 March 1930 fixed the gold Pahlavi at 20 Rials. No gold coins were struck. The Law of 13 March 1932 divided the Pahlavi into 100 Rials, instead of 20. The Rial's weight was reduced from 0.3661 grams of pure gold to 0.0732. Since 1937 it has been allowed to float and is quoted daily in Rials in the marketplaces.

HAMMERED COINAGE

Copper Coin System

During the nineteenth century, copper coins (falus) were issued at some 40 or more local mints, each of which coined Falus for local use only. Copper coins did not circulate generally, but were restricted to the city of their origin and its immediate environs. The local mintmaster, often in collaboration with the local governor, determined the type, design, and weight of the coinage, and regulated its circulation.

In theory, copper coins were recalled and changed every year, with a substantial fee payable to the mintmaster for the exchange of old coin for new. To discourage further use the old coin was either demonetized or tariffed at a lower value, usually about half its original.

In order to facilitate the recognition of new and old coin, the type was changed annually, the type being the obverse pictorial design, so that illiterate shopkeepers could tell the difference and not be deceived by obsolete coins. However, after a number of years, the same types would be reinstated for another year. In practice, the system worked more informally, and surviving coins show that at some mints, identical types were struck for several years running and were not recalled annually.

The metrology of the copper Falus is uncertain. While it seems that Falus were intended to follow an assigned weight standard, great tolerance was permitted. The weight standard was frequently changed (or the mintmaster issued lighter coins and pocketed the difference), and each mint city maintained its own standard and copper currency policies.

As a result of the frequent recoinage of copper and its frequent demonetization, copper coins were not hoarded or saved, and are consequently quite scarce today. Annual change meant that each mint had a multiplicity of types and varieties, most of which are uncommon today. The following listings are not an attempt at completeness, but give a representative selection of the products of each mint.

IMPORTANT: Most types were used at many different mints. The type can therefore not be used to attribute a coin to the mint of its issue. The ONLY certain way of attributing the coin is to read the mint name on the reverse.

LP# - Lane-Poole reference 'Coins of the Shahs of Persia.'

LOCAL COPPER FALUS

ABUSHAHR (BUSHIRE)

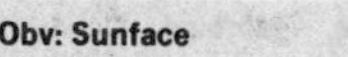

Obv: Sunface

KM#	Date	Mintage	Good	VG	Fine	VF
1	ND	—	3.50	7.50	12.50	20.00

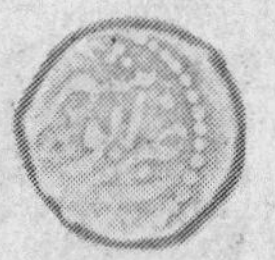

Rev: Lion

KM#	Date	Mintage	Good	VG	Fine	VF
2	ND	—	2.00	3.50	7.00	11.00

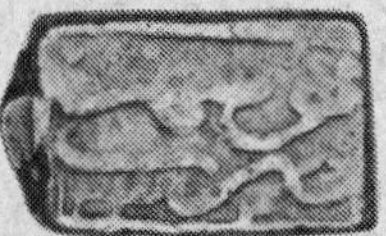

Bale Mark

KM#	Date	Mintage	Good	VG	Fine	VF
3	AH1234	—	5.00	10.00	16.50	26.50

Obv: Peacock

KM#	Date	Mintage	Good	VG	Fine	VF
4	AH1239	—	3.50	7.50	12.50	20.00

Fish

KM#	Date	Mintage	Good	VG	Fine	VF
5	AH1231	—	3.50	7.50	12.50	20.00

ARDABIL

Obv: Peacock holding worm in beak.

KM#	Date	Mintage	Good	VG	Fine	VF
6	AH1232	—	4.00	8.50	15.00	23.50

ASTARABAD

Obv: 2 Ibexes

KM#	Date	Mintage	Good	VG	Fine	VF
7	ND	—	5.00	10.00	16.50	26.50

BANDAR (ABBAS)

Obv: Lion

KM#	Date	Mintage	Good	VG	Fine	VF
8	ND	—	5.50	11.00	17.50	28.50

BEHBEHAN

Obv: Lion attacking stag

KM#	Date	Mintage	Good	VG	Fine	VF
9	ND	—	5.00	10.00	16.50	26.50

BORUJERD

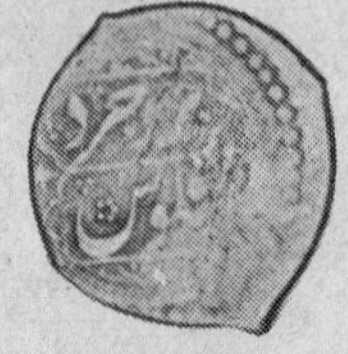

Obv: Soldier leaning on his rifle

KM#	Date	Mintage	Good	VG	Fine	VF
10	AH124x	—	5.00	10.00	16.50	26.50

Obv: Small bird

KM#	Date	Mintage	Good	VG	Fine	VF
11	ND	—	3.50	7.50	12.50	20.00

DEZFUL

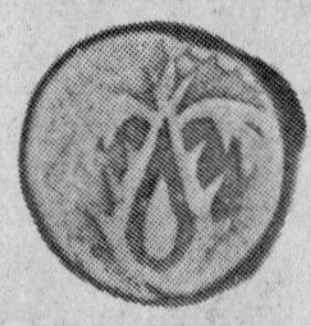

Obv: Lyre-bird

KM#	Date	Mintage	Good	VG	Fine	VF
12	ND	—	3.00	6.00	10.00	16.50

Obv: Fish

KM#	Date	Mintage	Good	VG	Fine	VF
13	ND	—	3.50	7.50	12.50	20.00

FARAHABAD

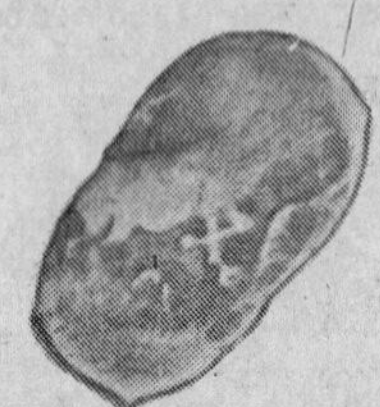

Obv: Bull

KM#	Date	Mintage	Good	VG	Fine	VF
14	ND	—	6.00	12.50	20.00	32.50

GANJEH (GANJA) (ELIZABETPOL)

Obv: Goose

KM#	Date	Mintage	Good	VG	Fine	VF
15	ND	—	6.00	12.50	20.00	32.50

GILAN

Obv: Camel & rider

KM#	Date	Mintage	Good	VG	Fine	VF
16	ND	—	3.50	7.50	12.50	20.00

HAMADAN

Obv: Lion attacking wolf

KM#	Date	Mintage	Good	VG	Fine	VF
17	ND	—	3.50	7.50	12.50	20.00

Obv: Eagle carrying off chicken

KM#	Date	Mintage	Good	VG	Fine	VF
18	AH1204	—	4.00	8.50	15.00	23.50

IRAVAN
(Yerivan in Armenia)

Obv: Camel

KM#	Date	Mintage	Good	VG	Fine	VF
19	AH1223	—	8.50	15.00	23.50	35.00

Obv: Lion & Sun

KM#	Date	Mintage	Good	VG	Fine	VF
20	ND	—	7.50	12.50	20.00	32.50

ISFAHAN

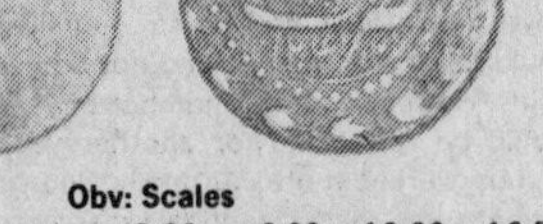

Obv: Scales

KM#	Date	Mintage	Good	VG	Fine	VF
21	AH1242	—	3.00	6.00	10.00	16.50

KASHAN

Obv: Boar

KM#	Date	Mintage	Good	VG	Fine	VF
22	AH1206	—	3.50	7.50	12.50	20.00

Obv: Sunface

KM#	Date	Mintage	Good	VG	Fine	VF
23	ND	—	3.50	7.50	12.50	20.00

Obv: Lion & sun within wreath.

Denomination: 50 Dinars

KM#	Date	Mintage	Good	VG	Fine	VF
24	AH1293	—	3.50	7.50	12.50	20.00

NOTE: This type was an attempt to reform the copper coinage by Nasir Al-Din Shah, and was also struck at Isfahan, Tehran, Tabriz and Shiraz in 1293 and 1294. Kashan is the rarest mint, Tehran and Isfahan the most plentiful.

KHUY

Obv: Lion & sun

KM#	Date	Mintage	Good	VG	Fine	VF
25	AH1189	—	3.50	7.50	12.50	20.00

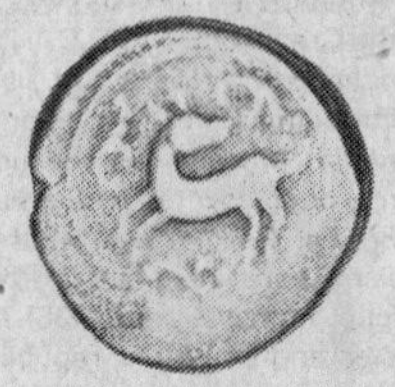
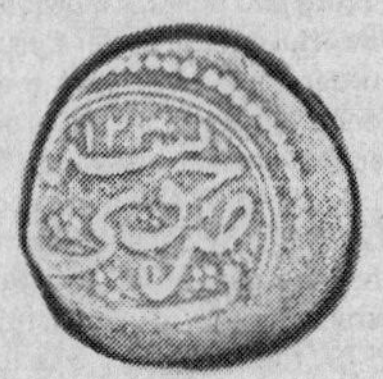

Obv: Gazelle

KM#	Date	Mintage	Good	VG	Fine	VF
26	AH1230	—	3.50	7.50	12.50	20.00

KIRMAN

Obv: Lion in wreath

KM#	Date	Mintage	Good	VG	Fine	VF
27	AH1287	—	3.50	7.50	12.50	20.00

KIRMANSHAHAN

Obv: Sunface

KM#	Date	Mintage	Good	VG	Fine	VF
28	AH1245	—	3.50	7.00	11.50	18.50

Obv: Lion

KM#	Date	Mintage	Good	VG	Fine	VF
29	ND	—	3.50	7.00	11.50	18.50

LAHIJAN

Obv: Peacock

KM#	Date	Mintage	Good	VG	Fine	VF
30	ND	—	5.00	10.00	16.50	26.50

MARAGHEH

Obv: Peacock

KM#	Date	Mintage	Good	VG	Fine	VF
31	AH1270	—	5.00	10.00	16.50	26.50

MASHHAD

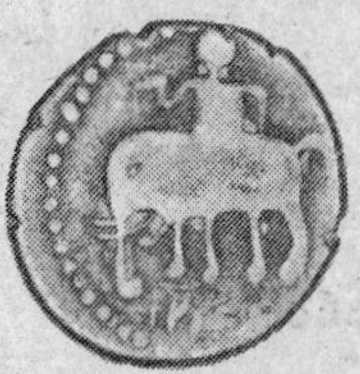

Obv: Elephant & rider

KM#	Date	Mintage	Good	VG	Fine	VF
32	AH1246	—	2.50	4.50	9.00	14.50

MAZANDARAN

Obv: Peacock

KM#	Date	Mintage	Good	VG	Fine	VF
33	AH1167	—	3.50	7.50	12.50	20.00

NIHAVAND

Obv: Lion sitting

KM#	Date	Mintage	Good	VG	Fine	VF
34	AH1240	—	5.50	11.50	18.50	30.00

QAZVIN

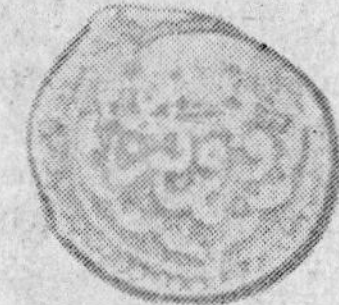

Obv: Lion and sun

KM#	Date	Mintage	Good	VG	Fine	VF
35	ND	—	3.00	6.00	10.00	16.50

RASHT

Obv: Lion & sun

KM#	Date	Mintage	Good	VG	Fine	VF
36	AH1246	—	3.50	7.00	11.50	18.50

Obv: Lion

KM#	Date	Mintage	Good	VG	Fine	VF
37	AH1233	—	3.50	7.50	12.50	20.00

SARI

Obv: Sunface

KM#	Date	Mintage	Good	VG	Fine	VF
38	ND	—	3.50	7.50	12.50	20.00

SA'UJBULAGH (MAHABAD)

Obv: 2 guinea hens

KM#	Date	Mintage	Good	VG	Fine	VF
39	ND	—	3.50	7.50	12.50	20.00

Obv: Lion & sun, stylized

KM#	Date	Mintage	Good	VG	Fine	VF
40	AH1230	—	3.50	7.50	12.50	20.00

SHIRAZ

Obv: Scales

KM#	Date	Mintage	Good	VG	Fine	VF
41	AH126x	—	3.00	6.00	10.00	16.50

SHUSHTAR

Inscriptions only

KM#	Date	Mintage	Good	VG	Fine	VF
42	ND	—	3.00	6.00	10.00	16.50

SULTANABAD

Obv: Lion & sun

KM#	Date	Mintage	Good	VG	Fine	VF
43	ND	—	5.50	11.50	18.50	30.00

TABARISTAN

Obv: Lion & sun

KM#	Date	Mintage	Good	VG	Fine	VF
44	ND	—	3.50	7.50	12.50	20.00

TABRIZ

Obv: Lion & sun

KM#	Date	Mintage	Good	VG	Fine	VF
45	AH1236	—	3.00	6.00	10.00	16.50

Obv: Bullock & fish

KM#	Date	Mintage	Good	VG	Fine	VF
46	AH1202	—	3.50	7.50	12.50	20.00

(Coin originally round, but shaped for ornamental purposes)

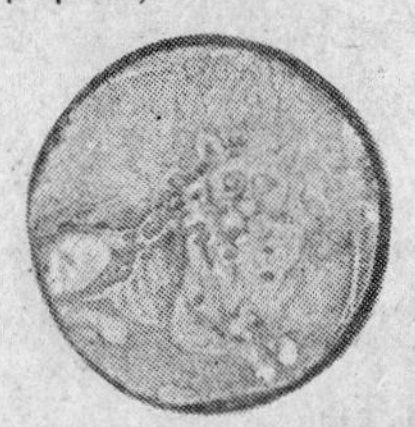

Obv: Lion passant

KM#	Date	Mintage	Good	VG	Fine	VF
47	AH125x	—	3.00	6.00	10.00	16.50

TEHRAN

Obv: Peacock

KM#	Date	Mintage	Good	VG	Fine	VF
48	AH1222	—	3.00	6.00	10.00	16.50

Obv: Russian eagle

KM#	Date	Mintage	Good	VG	Fine	VF
49	ND	—	5.50	11.50	18.50	30.00

URUMI (REZA'IYEH)

Obv: Lion with fancy tail

KM#	Date	Mintage	Good	VG	Fine	VF
50	AH1210	—	3.50	7.50	12.50	20.00

Obv: Scorpion

KM#	Date	Mintage	Good	VG	Fine	VF
51	Uncertain	—	7.50	12.50	20.00	32.50

Obv: Small bird

KM#	Date	Mintage	Good	VG	Fine	VF
52	AH120x	—	3.50	7.50	12.50	20.00

YAZD

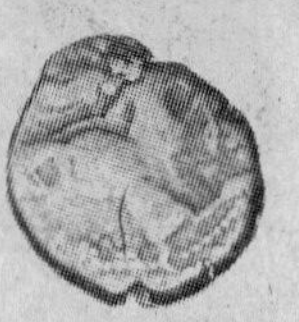

Obv: Man riding uncertain beast

KM#	Date	Mintage	Good	VG	Fine	VF
53	AH1188	—	3.00	6.00	10.00	16.50

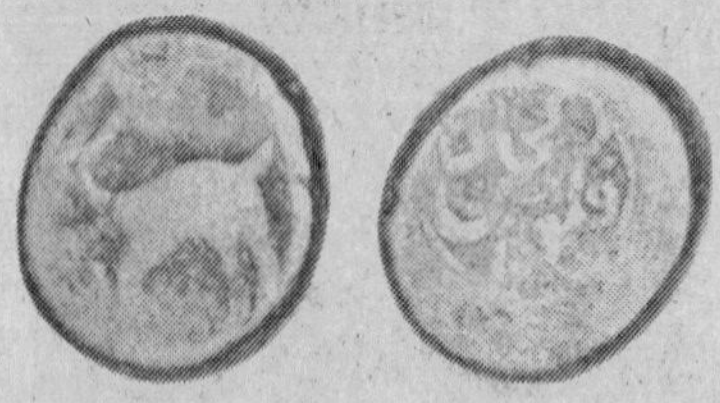

Obv: Lion & sun

KM#	Date	Mintage	Good	VG	Fine	VF
54	ND	—	3.50	7.50	12.50	20.00

ZANJAN

Obv: Deer

KM#	Date	Mintage	Good	VG	Fine	VF
55	ND	—	5.00	10.00	16.50	26.50

NOTE: Other mints also produced local Falus, for which examples were not available to illustrate. Still other mints operated only or largely at earlier dates. These include Damavand, Damghan, Darabjird, Ja'farafad, Kangan, Ra'nash, Semnan, Tuy, Tus and more.

SILVER AND GOLD COINAGE

The precious metal monetary system of Qajar Persia prior to the reforms of 1878 was the direct descendant of the Mongol system introduced by Ghazan Mahmud in AD 1297, and was the last example of a medieval Islamic coinage. It is not a modern system, and cannot be understood as such. It is not possible to list types, dates, and mints as for other countries, both because of the nature of the coinage, and because very little research has been done on the series. The following comments should help elucidate its nature.

STANDARDS: The weight of the primary silver and gold coins was set by law and was expressed in terms of the Mesqal (about 4.61 gm.) and the Nokhod (24 Nokhod = 1 Mesqal). The primary silver coin was the Rupee from AH1211- 1212, the Riyal from 1212-1241, and the Qeran from 1241-1344. The standard gold coin was the Toman. Currently the price of gold is quoted in Mesqals.

DENOMINATIONS: In addition to the primary denominations, noted in the last paragraph, fractional pieces were coined, valued at one-eighth, one-fourth, and one-half the primary denomination, usually in much smaller quantities. These were ordinarily struck from the same dies as the larger pieces, sometimes on broad, thin flans, sometimes on thick, dumpy flans. On the smaller coins, the denomination can best be determined only by weighing the coin. The denomination is almost never expressed on the coin!

DEVALUATIONS: From time to time, the standard for silver and gold was reduced, and the old coin recalled and replaced with lighter coin, the difference going to the government coffers. The effect was that of a devaluation of the primary silver and gold coins, or inversely regarded, an increase in the price of silver and gold. The durations of each standard varied from about 2 to 20 years. The standards are given for each ruler, as the denomination can only be determined when the standard is known.

LIGHTWEIGHT AND ALLOYED PIECES: Most of the smaller denomination coins were issued at lighter weights than those prescribed by law, with the difference going to the pockets of the mintmasters. Other mints, notably Hamadan, added excessive amounts of alloy to the coins, and some mintmasters lost their heads as a result. Discrepancies in weight of as much as 15 per cent and more are observed, with the result that it is often quite impossible to determine the denomination of a coin!

OVERSIZE COINS: Occasionally, multiples of the primary denominations were produced, usually on special occasions for presentation by the Shah to his favorites. These 'coins' did not circulate (except as bullion), and were usually worn as ornaments. They were the 'NCLT's' of the day.

MINTS & EPITHETS: Qajar coinage was struck at 34 mints (plus at least a dozen others striking only copper Falus), which are listed below, with drawings of the mint names in Persian, as they appear on the coins. However, the Persian script admits of infinite variation and stylistic whimsy, so the forms given are only guides, and not absolute. Only a knowledge of the script will assure correct reading. In addition to the city name, most mint names were given identifying epithets, which occasionally appear in lieu of the mint name, particularly at Iravan and Mashhad.

TYPES: There were no types in the modern sense, but the arrangement of the legends and the ornamental borders were frequently changed. These changes do not coincide with changes in standards, and cannot be used to determine the mint, which must be found by actually reading the reverse inscriptions.

MINTS FOR SILVER AND GOLD

The following mints struck silver and/or gold coins during the period AD1796-1878 (AH1211-1296). All except the Central Mint at Tehran were suppressed by order of Nasir Al-Din Shah in 1295/1878.

The first column lists the mint name, the second a symbol used for cataloging purposes. The third column shows the normal written form of the mint name in Persian script. The following three columns provide valuation adjustments for silver coins of each mint for each reign. Special premiums are not applicable to gold coins from the rarer mints. A dash (-) means that no coins are known from the mint for the respective reign.

Mint Identification

Mint	Symbol	Form
Ardabil	Ar	اردبیل
Astarabad	As	استراباد
Burujerd	Br	بروجرد
Ganja	Ga	گنجه
Hamadan	Hm	همدان
Herat	Hr	هرات
Iravan	Ir	ایروان
Isfahan	Is	اصفهان
Kashan	Ka	کاشان
Khuy	Kh	خوی
Kirman	Kr	کرمان
Kirmanshahan	Ks	کرمانشاهان
Lahijan	La	لاهیجان
Maragheh	Mr	مراغه
Mashhad	Ms	مشهد
Mazandaran	Mz	مازندران
Nihavand	Nh	نهاوند
Nukhwi	Nw	نخوی
Qazvin	Qz	قزوین
Qumm	Qm	قم
Rasht	Rs	رشت
Rikab	Rk	رکاب
Sarakhs	Ss	سرخس
Shiraz	Sh	شیراز
Shushtar	Su	شوشتر
Simnan	Sm	سمنان
Tabaristan	Tb	طبرستان
Tabriz	Tz	تبریز
Tehran	Th	طهران
Tuyserkan	Tu	توی سرکان
Urumi	Ur	ارومی
Yazd	Yz	یزد
Zanjan	Zn	زنجان

Relative Scarcity

(For silver coins only)
(plus percent premium)

Mint	Fath'Ali	Muhammad	Nasir Al-din
Ardabil	100	—	—
Astarabad	25	25	None
Burujerd	50	—	—
Ganja	150	—	—
Hamadan	50	None	None
Herat	—	—	100
Iravan	50	—	—
Isfahan	None	None	None
Kashan	None	—	25
Khuy	50	—	50
Kirman	25	50	50
Kirmanshahan	None	None	25
Lahijan	50	—	—
Maragheh	150	—	—
Mashhad	None	None	None
Mazandaran	25	—	—
Nihavand	150	—	—
Nukhwi	200	—	—
Qazvin	None	—	25
Qumm	75	—	—
Rasht	None	25	25
Rikab	75	—	—
Sarakhs	—	—	200
Shiraz	None	25	25
Shushtar	150	—	See Note
Simnan	100	—	—
Tabaristan	50	25	None
Tabriz	None	None	None
Tehran	None	None	None
Tuyserkan	100	—	—
Urumi	25	—	—
Yazd	None	25	25
Zanjan	75	—	—

NOTE: A coin of Shushtar is reported for Nasir Al-Din Shah, but not confirmed.

None = No premium. A dash means coins of that mint for that ruler are unknown.

The following listings are arranged by ruler, first, the various standards are explained. Then, the coins are listed by denomination within each reign. For each denomination, one or more pieces, when available, are illustrated, with the mint and date noted beneath each photo. For each type, a date range is given, but this range indicates the years during which the particular type was current, and does not imply that every year of the interval is known on actual coins. Because dates were carelessly engraved, and old dies were used until they wore out or broke, we occasionally find coins of a particular type dated before or after the indicated interval. Such coins command no premium. No attempt has been made to determine which mints actually exist for which types.

Baba Khan

(AH1211-1212/AD1797)

NOTE: Baba Khan was the name used by Fath'ali Shah prior to his official julus, or coronation. Mint premiums as for Fath'ali Shah. All known coins of Baba Khan are dated 1212. They fall into two standards, the first based on a Rupee of 60 Nokhod (= 11.5 gm.), the second on a Riyal of 54 Nokhod (= 10.4 gm.).

ABBASI (300 DINARS)

SILVER, 4.6 gm. (- 1 Mesqal)
Shiraz, AH1212

C#	Date	Mintage	Good	VG	Fine	VF
180	AH1212	—	20.00	30.00	40.00	55.00

RUPEE (750 DINARS)

SILVER, 11.5 gm.
Shiraz, AH1212

C#	Date	Mintage	Good	VG	Fine	VF
181	AH1212	—	22.50	35.00	55.00	80.00

RIYAL (1250 DINARS)

SILVER, 10.4 gm.
Maragheh, AH1212

C#	Date	Mintage	Good	VG	Fine	VF
185	AH1212	—	25.00	40.00	60.00	85.00

No gold coins are known in the name of Baba Khan. Known mints that struck silver coinage include Kashan, Maragheh, Tehran, Shiraz, Astarabad, Isfahan and Tabriz.

Fath'Ali Shah

(AH1212-1250/AD1797-1834)

STANDARDS EMPLOYED BY FATH'ALI SHAH

SILVER COINAGE

I. Rupee Standard, used only for coronation piece (C#188) AH1212. 1 Rupee - 60 Nokhod.

1 Rupee	**11.5 gm.**

II. First Riyal Standard, AH1212-1232, 1 Riyal - 54 Nokhod

1/8 Riyal	**1.3 gm.**
1/4 Riyal	**2.6 gm.**
1/2 Riyal	**5.2 gm.**
1 Riyal	**10.4 gm.**

III. Second Riyal Standard, AH1232-1241, 1 Riyal - 2 Mesqal - 48 Nokhod

1/8 Riyal	**1.15 gm.**
1/4 Riyal	**2.3 gm.**
1/2 Riyal	**4.6 gm.**
1 Riyal	**9.2 gm.**

IV. Kran Standard, AH1241-1250, 1 Kran - 1-1/2 Mesqal Nokhod

1/8 Kran	**0.9 gm.**
1/4 Kran	**1.7 gm.**
1/2 Kran	**3.5 gm.**
1 Kran	**6.9 gm.**

GOLD COINAGE

I. First Standard, AH1213-?? (after 1214), 1 Toman - 32 Nokhod

1/2 Toman	**3.1 gm.**
1 Toman	**6.1 gm.**

II. Second Standard, AH1220-1224, 1 Toman - 30 Nokhod

1/4 Toman	**1.5 gm.**
1/2 Toman	**2.9 gm.**
1 Toman	**5.8 gm.**

III. Third Standard, AH1224-1227, 1 Toman - 28 Nokhod

1/2 Toman	**2.7 gm.**
1 Toman	**5.4 gm.**

IV. Fourth Standard, AH1227-1229, 1 Toman - 25 Nokhod

1/2 Toman	**2.4 gm.**
1 Toman	**4.8 gm.**

V. Fifth Standard, AH1230-1244, 1 Toman - 24 Nokhod - 1 Mesqal

1/4 Toman	**1.15 gm.**
1/2 Toman	**2.3 gm.**
1 Toman	**4.6 gm.**

NOTE: Some mints were using this standard as early as AH1228 if the dates on the coins are correct. However, the similarity of the '2' and '3' in Persian may have led to 1232 being read as 1222, etc.

VI. Sixth Standard, AH1246-1250, 1 Toman - 18 Nokhod

1/2 Toman	**1.7 gm.**
1 Toman (Keshvarsetan)	**3.5 gm.**

NOTE: It is probable that all fractions exist for each standard.

TYPES

Although there are no clearly distinguishable 'types' in the European sense, changes in the obverse legend and calligraphic style enable us to divide the coinage into a sequence of five basic 'types'. Since the same dies, or similar dies, were used for all denominations, gold and silver, the following division applies to all.

TYPE I: With title 'Sultan' and thick, interlaced, coarse calligraphy. Used AH1213-1217.

TYPE II: With title 'Sultan, Son of the Sultan' and thick, coarse calligraphy, but letters separate and flowing (script known as Nasta'liq). Plain background. Used AH1217-22.

TYPE III: As last, but background filled with dots, vines, and tendrils. Used AH1222-1241.

TYPE IV: Style as Type III, but with title 'Sahibqiran' (literally, a title for a person born under an auspicious conjunction of the planets. After the title was assumed by Tamerlane in the 14th century, it lost its astrological meaning and came to denote 'Conqueror'). The coins of this type were named 'Sahibqiran' on account of this title, which was shortened in the popular idiom to 'Qiran' (Kran). Used AH1241-1245 (but the fifth type never caught on, and most coins dated AH1246-1250 are of the fourth type).

TYPE V: As the third, but with title 'Keshvarsetan' (Conqueror of Nations). Used AH1245-1250.

NOTE: Due to mint carelessness, the use of old dies, and the whims of mintmasters, the above types are found dated before and after their 'official' spans of existence.

NOTE: Type I normally bears dates on obverse and reverse, quite frequently mismatched (no premium for such coins: they are almost as common as those with matched dates!). All other types are normally dated only on the reverse.

NOTE: The obverse is the side bearing the king's name and titles. The reverse is the side with the mint.

All silver coins of the first and second types are on the first Riyal Standard. The third type is divided into two subtypes: III A on the first Riyal Standard (AH1222-1232), III B on the reduced second Riyal Standard (AH1232-41). Types IV and V are on the Kran Standard.

RUPEE STANDARD

SILVER, 11.5 gm.
Tehran, AH1212
Coronation Commemorative

C#	Date	Mintage	Good	VG	Fine	VF
188	AH1212	—	25.00	37.50	60.00	100.00

RIYAL STANDARDS

1/8 RIYAL

SILVER, 1.3 gm.

Iravan, AH1227

TYPE III A.

C#	Date	Mintage	Good	VG	Fine	VF
191b	AH1222-32	—	3.50	6.50	10.00	16.00

1.15 gm.

TYPE III B.

C#	Date	Mintage	Good	VG	Fine	VF
191c	AH1232-41	—	3.50	6.50	10.00	16.00

1/4 RIYAL

SILVER, 2.6 gm.
Tabriz, AH1228

TYPE III A.

C#	Date	Mintage	Good	VG	Fine	VF
192b	AH1222-32	—	3.00	5.50	9.00	15.00

Tabriz, AH1237

Borujerd, AH1236
2.3 gm.

TYPE III B.

C#	Date	Mintage	Good	VG	Fine	VF
192c	AH1232-41	—	3.00	5.50	9.00	15.00

1/2 RIYAL

SILVER, 5.2 gm.
Isfahan, AH1217

TYPE I

C#	Date	Mintage	Good	VG	Fine	VF
193	AH1213-17	—	7.50	12.50	20.00	30.00

Isfahan, date missing, 5.2 gm.

TYPE II

C#	Date	Mintage	Good	VG	Fine	VF
193a	AH1217-22	—	5.50	9.00	12.50	18.50

Yazd, AH1229

TYPE III.A

C#	Date	Mintage	Good	VG	Fine	VF
193b	AH1222-32	—	5.00	8.00	11.50	17.50

Kashan, AH123x, 4.5 gm.

C#	Date	Mintage	Good	VG	Fine	VF
193c.3	AH123x	—	5.00	8.00	11.50	17.50

Tehran, AH1237, 4.6 gm.

TYPE III.B

C#	Date	Mintage	Good	VG	Fine	VF
193c.2	AH1232-41	—	5.00	8.00	11.00	16.50

RIYAL

SILVER, 10.4 gm.
Tehran, AH1215

TYPE I

C#	Date	Mintage	Good	VG	Fine	VF
194	AH1212-17	—	10.00	12.50	15.00	20.00

Khuy, AH1220

TYPE II

C#	Date	Mintage	Good	VG	Fine	VF
194a	AH1217-22	—	10.00	11.50	13.50	17.50

Isfahan, AH1227

TYPE III.A

C#	Date	Mintage	Good	VG	Fine	VF
194b	AH1222-32	—	10.00	11.50	13.50	17.50

9.2 gm.

TYPE III.B

C#	Date	Mintage	Good	VG	Fine	VF
194c	AH1232-41	—	10.00	11.50	13.50	17.50

KRAN STANDARD

1/8 KRAN

SILVER, 0.9 gm.
Khuy, AH1243

TYPE IV

C#	Date	Mintage	Good	VG	Fine	VF
200	AH1241-45	—	3.00	6.00	10.00	16.50

Found both uniface and with two faces.

Isfahan, AH1230

TYPE V

C#	Date	Mintage	Good	VG	Fine	VF
200a	AH1246-50	—	7.50	15.00	25.00	40.00

NOTE: Use of obsolete dated reverse die.

1/4 KRAN

SILVER, 1.7 gm.

TYPE IV

C#	Date	Mintage	Good	VG	Fine	VF
201	AH1241-45	—	5.00	10.00	16.50	26.50

1/2 KRAN

SILVER, 3.5 gm.
Kashan, AH1241

TYPE IV

C#	Date	Mintage	Good	VG	Fine	VF
202	AH1241-45	—	3.50	6.00	10.00	16.50

KRAN

SILVER
Hamadan, AH1241

Mashhad, AH1244, 6.9 gm.

TYPE IV

C#	Date	Mintage	Good	VG	Fine	VF
203	AH1241-45	—	7.00	9.00	11.50	15.00

Tabaristan, AH1246, 6.9 gm.

TYPE V

C#	Date	Mintage	Good	VG	Fine	VF
203a	AH1246-50	—	8.50	15.00	25.00	45.00

MISCELLANEOUS ISSUE

SILVER
Ganjeh, AH1215

C#	Date	Mintage	Good	VG	Fine	VF
189	AH1212—	—	40.00	70.00	100.00	150.00

Name of Denomination unknown. Struck at Ganjeh only and priced for that mint.

GOLD COINAGE

At present, it is not yet possible to determine which types were used with which standard. Until more research is done, and more coins are brought to light, we shall list the gold by standard. The fifth standard comes in two varieties, without 'Sahibaqiran' AH1230-1241 and with 'Sahibqiran' (AH1241-1245), referred to as standards 5A and 5B, respectively.

1/4 TOMAN

GOLD, 1.5 gm.

C#	Date	Mintage	VG	Fine	VF	XF
SECOND STANDARD						
204a	AH1220-24	—	35.00	55.00	85.00	125.00
Fourth Standard, Isfahan						
204c	AH1228	—	35.00	55.00	85.00	125.00
1.15 gm. FIFTH STANDARD (5A)						
204d.1	AH1230-41	—	35.00	55.00	85.00	125.00
1.15 gm. FIFTH STANDARD, SAHIBQERAN (5B)						
204d.2	AH1241-45	—	32.50	50.00	70.00	100.00

1/2 TOMAN

GOLD, 3.1 gm.

C#	Date	Mintage	VG	Fine	VF	XF
FIRST STANDARD						
205	AH1213-17	—	65.00	80.00	100.00	125.00
2.9 gm. SECOND STANDARD						
205a	AH1220-24	—	65.00	80.00	100.00	125.00
2.7 gm. THIRD STANDARD						
205b	AH1224-27	—	67.50	85.00	110.00	140.00

Tabriz, AH1231

C#	Date	Mintage	VG	Fine	VF	XF
2.3 gm. FIFTH STANDARD, WITHOUT 'SAHIBQIRAN' (5A)						
205d.1	AH1230-41	—	65.00	80.00	100.00	125.00
2.3 gm. FIFTH STANDARD, WITH 'SAHIBQIRAN' (5B)						
205d.2	AH1241-45	—	67.50	85.00	110.00	140.00
1.75 gm. SIXTH STANDARD, (KESHVARESTAN)						
205e	AH1246-50	—	75.00	100.00	135.00	175.00

TOMAN

GOLD, 6.1 gm.
Isfahan, AH1213

FIRST STANDARD

C#	Date	Mintage	VG	Fine	VF	XF
206.1	AH1213-17	—	125.00	145.00	175.00	200.00

Tehran, AH1216

C#	Date	Mintage	VG	Fine	VF	XF
206.2	AH1216	—	125.00	145.00	175.00	200.00
Mazandaran, AH1213						
206.3	AH1213	—	—	—	—	—
Qazvin, AH12x4						
206.4	AH12x4	—	—	—	—	—

Isfahan, AH1221, 5.8 gm.

C#	Date	Mintage	VG	Fine	VF	XF
SECOND STANDARD						
206a	AH1220-24	—	125.00	140.00	160.00	185.00
5.4 gm. THIRD STANDARD						
206b	AH1224-27	—	115.00	130.00	150.00	175.00

Isfahan, AH1228, 4.8 gm.

FOURTH STANDARD

C#	Date	Mintage	VG	Fine	VF	XF
206c	AH1227-29	—	125.00	140.00	160.00	185.00

Iravan, AH1230

Borujerd, AH1236, 4.6 gm.

FIFTH STANDARD, WITHOUT 'SAHIBQIRAN' (5A)

C#	Date	Mintage	VG	Fine	VF	XF
206d.1	AH1230-41	—	100.00	115.00	135.00	160.00

Rasht, AH1232

C#	Date	Mintage	VG	Fine	VF	XF
206d.2	AH1232	—	100.00	115.00	135.00	160.00

Tabriz, AH1244, 4.6 gm.

FIFTH STANDARD, WITH 'SAHIBQIRAN' (5B)

C#	Date	Mintage	VG	Fine	VF	XF
206d.3	AH1241-45	—	100.00	115.00	135.00	160.00

Tehran, AH1248, 3.5 gm.

SIXTH STANDARD (KESHVARSETAN)

C#	Date	Mintage	VG	Fine	VF	XF
206e	AH1246-50	—	130.00	150.00	170.00	200.00

Zanjan, AH1236, 4.5 gm.

SPECIAL ISSUE: King on horseback

C#	Date	Mintage	VG	Fine	VF	XF
207	AH1236	—	250.00	400.00	600.00	800.00

Isfahan, AH1249

Isfahan, AH1245, 3.5 gm.

SPECIAL ISSUE: King on throne. Several varieties.

C#	Date	Mintage	VG	Fine	VF	XF
208.1	AH1245-49	—	250.00	400.00	600.00	800.00

C#	Date	Mintage	VG	Fine	VF	XF
208.2	AH1245	—	250.00	400.00	600.00	800.00

3 TOMANS

NOTE: (Coins of this denomination were probably intended more for presentation purposes than as a circulating medium)

GOLD, 18.4 gm.
Yazd, AH1221

SECOND STANDARD

C#	Date	Mintage	VG	Fine	VF	XF
209	AH1221	—	400.00	600.00	850.00	1150.

Zanjan, AH1236, 13.9 gm.

SPECIAL ISSUE (FIFTH STANDARD)

C#	Date	Mintage	VG	Fine	VF	XF
210	AH1236	—	650.00	1000.	1500.	2000.

5 TOMANS

GOLD
Tehran, AH1227

C#	Date	Mintage	VG	Fine	VF	XF
212	AH1227	—	—	—	Rare	—

MEDALLIC ISSUES

10 TOMANS

GOLD
Tabriz, Rev: w/date divided 122/0.

KM#	Date	Year	Mintage	Fine	VF	XF
1	AH1220	—	—	—	Rare	—

Obv: Similar to KM#1.
Rev: Different border design; date divided 12/20.

KM#	Date	Year	Mintage	Fine	VF	XF
2	AH1220	—	—	—	Rare	—

Mints of Fath'Ali Shah

The following illustrations are of coins, mostly Riyals and Krans, for each of Fath Ali's mints. Usually only one example is shown but considerable variation exists, as die cutters emphasized artistic stylization of legends rather than standardization. In each case, the mint name, date and C# are indicated below the illustration.

Ardabil, AH1245, C#203

Astarabad, AH1215, C#194

NOTE: Dated AH1213 on obverse, AH1215 on reverse.

Borujerd, AH1244, C#203

Hamadan, AH1250, C#203

NOTE: This AH1250 date is an example of C#203 struck five years after the introduction of C#203a!

Iravan, AH1216, C#194

Isfahan, AH1225, C#194b

Kashan, AH1233, C#194c

Khuy, AH1214, C#194
NOTE: Dated AH1215 on obverse, AH1214 on reverse.

Kirman, AH1238, C#193c

 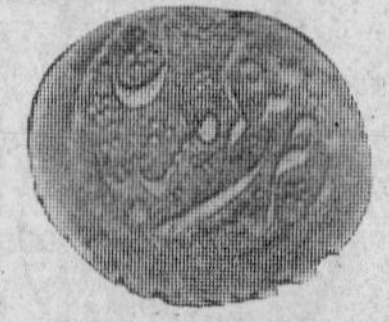

Kirmanshahan, AH1233, C#194c

Lahijan, AH1219, C#194a

Mashhad, AH1222, C#194a
Dated both obverse and reverse

Mazandaran, AH1218, C#194a

Nihavand, AH1242, C#203

Qazvin, AH1227, C#194b

Qumm, AH1246, C#203

Rasht, AH1222, C#194a

Rikab, AH1213, C#194

Shiraz, AH1214, C#194
Dated on reverse only

Shushtar, AH1243, C#203

Simnan, AH12xx, C#194

Tabaristan, AH1246, C#203a

Tabriz, AH1221, C#193a

Tehran, AH1217, C#194a

Tuyserkan, AH1241, C#203

Urumi, AH1233, C#194c

Yazd, AH1222, C#194b

Zanjan, AH1244, C#203

For coins of Panahabad struck in the name of Fath'ali Shah, see listings under Russian Caucasia, Khanate of Karabagh.

Sultan Ali Shah

(AH1250/AD1834)

(Ruled only 30 days)

Silver and gold struck to Fath'ali Shah's Kran and Sixth Gold Standard, respectively. Known only from Mint of Tehran.

KRAN

SILVER, 6.9 gm.
Tehran, AH1250

C#	Date	Mintage	VG	Fine	VF	XF
215	AH1250	—	35.00	50.00	75.00	110.00

TOMAN

GOLD, 3.5 gm.
Tehran, AH1250

C#	Date	Mintage	VG	Fine	VF	XF
216	AH1250	—	150.00	250.00	400.00	550.00

Husain Ali Shah

AH1250/AD1834

For six months in southern Iran

Standards as for Sultan Ali mints of Kirman, Shiraz and Yazd struck silver coins. The mint at Shiraz also struck gold coins.

KRAN

SILVER, 6.9 gm.

C#	Date	Mintage	VG	Fine	VF	XF
219	AH1250	—	35.00	50.00	75.00	110.00

Muhammad Shah

(AH1250-1264/AD1834-1848)

SILVER COINAGE

I. FIRST STANDARD AH1250-1251:

1 Kran - 1-1/2 Mesqal - 36 Nokhod

1/4 Kran	**1.7 gm.**
1/2 Kran	**3.5 gm.**
1 Kran	**6.9 gm.**

II. SECOND STANDARD, AH1252-1255:

1 Kran - 30 Nokhod

1/8 Kran	**0.72 gm.**
1/4 Kran	**1.5 gm.**
1/2 Kran	**2.9 gm.**
1 Kran	**5.8 gm.**

III. THIRD STANDARD, AH1254-1264:

1 Kran - 28 Nokhod

1/8 Kran	**0.68 gm.**
1/4 Kran	**1.35 gm.**
1/2 Kran	**2.7 gm.**
1 Kran	**5.4 gm.**
Krans	**10.8 gm.**

GOLD COINAGE

Only one Standard: 1 Toman - 18 Nokhod

1/4 Toman	**0.9 gm.**
1/2 Toman	**1.7 gm.**
1 Toman	**3.5 gm.**

NOTE: All coins of Muhammad Shah are essentially of a single type, with the ruler's name on the obverse, the mint & date on the reverse. The exception is the lion & sun type (C# 228 below).

1/8 KRAN

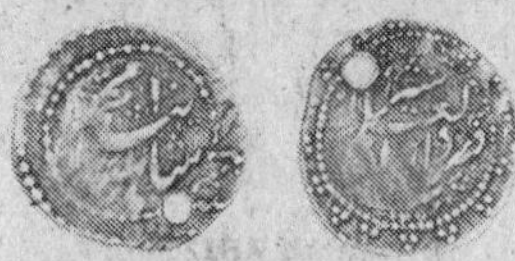

SILVER, 0.72 gm.
Shiraz, AH1252

SECOND STANDARD

C#	Date	Mintage	Good	VG	Fine	VF
224a	AH1252-55	—	4.50	8.50	15.00	25.00

0.68 gm.

THIRD STANDARD

C#	Date	Mintage	Good	VG	Fine	VF
224b	AH1255-64	—	4.00	8.00	13.50	22.50

1/4 KRAN

SILVER, 1.7 gm.

FIRST STANDARD

C#	Date	Mintage	Good	VG	Fine	VF
225	AH1250-51	—	5.00	10.00	17.50	27.50

1.5 gm.

SECOND STANDARD

C#	Date	Mintage	Good	VG	Fine	VF
225a	AH1252-55	—	4.00	8.00	13.50	22.50

Kirman, AH1255, 1.35 gm.

THIRD STANDARD

C#	Date	Mintage	Good	VG	Fine	VF
225b	AH1255-64	—	3.00	6.00	12.00	17.50

1/2 KRAN

SILVER, 3.5 gm.
Tehran, AH1251

FIRST STANDARD

C#	Date	Mintage	Good	VG	Fine	VF
226	AH1250-51	—	5.00	10.00	17.50	27.50

Tabriz, AH1252, 2.9 gm.

SECOND STANDARD

C#	Date	Mintage	Good	VG	Fine	VF
226a	AH1252-54	—	4.00	8.00	13.50	22.50

Tabaristan, AH1255, 2.7 gm.

THIRD STANDARD

C#	Date	Mintage	Good	VG	Fine	VF
226b	AH1254-64	—	3.00	6.00	11.00	16.50

KRAN

SILVER, 6.9 gm.
Tabriz, AH1251

FIRST STANDARD

C#	Date	Mintage	Good	VG	Fine	VF
227	AH1250-51	—	7.50	10.00	15.00	20.00

Mashhad, AH1252, 5.8 gm.

SECOND STANDARD

C#	Date	Mintage	Good	VG	Fine	VF
227a	AH1252-55	—	7.00	8.00	9.00	11.00

Isfahan, AH1261, 5.4 gm.

THIRD STANDARD

C#	Date	Mintage	Good	VG	Fine	VF
227b	AH1254-64	—	7.00	8.00	9.00	11.00

Tehran, AH1255, 5.4 gm.
Machine-milled with obliquely reeded edge. Possibly a pattern, but found circulated. Tehran Mint only.

C#	Date	Mintage	Good	VG	Fine	VF
227r	AH1255	—	8.50	13.50	25.00	40.00

Tehran, AH1261
Lion & sun type, 5.4 gm.

C#	Date	Mintage	Good	VG	Fine	VF
228	AH1258-63	—	7.50	10.00	16.50	25.00

2 KRANS

SILVER, 10.8 gm.
Tehran, AH1263
Lion & sun type

C#	Date	Mintage	Good	VG	Fine	VF
229	AH1263	—	17.50	30.00	50.00	85.00

1/4 TOMAN

GOLD, 0.9 gm.

C#	Date	Mintage	VG	Fine	VF	XF
231	AH1250-64	—	45.00	70.00	100.00	135.00

1/2 TOMAN

GOLD, 1.7 gm.

C#	Date	Mintage	VG	Fine	VF	XF
232	AH1250-64	—	80.00	110.00	140.00	185.00

TOMAN

GOLD, 3.5 gm.
Mashhad, AH1263

C#	Date	Mintage	VG	Fine	VF	XF
233	AH1250-64	—	80.00	100.00	120.00	155.00

Tehran, AH1261
Lion & sun type, 3.5 gm.

C#	Date	Mintage	VG	Fine	VF	XF
234	AH1262-64	—	85.00	110.00	130.00	165.00

Hasan Khan Salar

(Rebel, AH1264-66)

No coins known. Former C#241 is a coin of Muhammad Shah, dated AH1265 postumously (or error for AH1260).

Nasir Al-Din Shah

(AH1264-1313/AD1848-1896)

HAMMERED COINAGE

(AH1264-1296)

STANDARDS: SILVER COINAGE

FIRST STANDARD, AH1264-1273: 1 Kran - 28 Nokhod

1/8 Kran	**0.68 gm.**
1/4 Kran	**1.35 gm.**
1/2 Kran	**2.7 gm.**
1 Kran	**5.4 gm.**

SECOND STANDARD, AH1273-1296: 1 Kran - 26 Nokhod

1/8 Kran	**0.63 gm.**
1/4 Kran	**1.3 gm.**
1/2 Kran	**2.5 gm.**
1 Kran	**5.0 gm.**

With the introduction of machine-made coinage in AH1296/AD1879, the Kran was reduced to 24 Nokhod (4.6 gm.).

GOLD COINAGE

ONLY ONE STANDARD, based on a Toman of 18 Nokhod

1/4 Toman	**0.9 gm.**
1/2 Toman	**1.7 gm.**
1 Toman	**3.5 gm.**
2 Tomans	**6.0 gm.**

25 DINARS

COPPER

C#	Date	Mintage	Good	VG	Fine	VF
249	AH1271-73	—	1.25	2.50	4.50	7.00

This and C#250 bear no mint name. Several variations of type.

50 DINARS (1 SHAHI)

COPPER

250	AH1270-86	—	1.25	2.00	4.00	6.50

1/8 KRAN

SILVER, uniface, 0.68 gm.
Rasht, AH1272

FIRST STANDARD

C#	Date	Mintage	VG	Fine	VF	XF
260	AH1264-73	—	3.00	6.00	8.50	12.50

Uniface, 0.68 gm.
Tehran, AH1293

SECOND STANDARD

260a	AH1273-94	—	3.00	6.00	8.50	12.50

1/4 KRAN

SILVER, 1.35 gm.
Tabriz, AH1265

FIRST STANDARD

261	AH1264-73	—	3.00	6.00	8.50	12.50

Tehran, AH1288

Tehran, AH1294, 1.3 gm.

SECOND STANDARD

261a	AH1273-94	—	2.50	5.00	7.50	11.50

1/2 KRAN

SILVER
Isfahan, AH1265

Khuy, AH1271

Tabaristan, AH1272, 2.7 gm.

FIRST STANDARD

C#	Date	Mintage	VG	Fine	VF	XF
262	AH1264-73	—	2.75	4.50	7.50	12.50

Astarabad, AH1275

Hamadan, AH1274, 2.5 gm.

SECOND STANDARD

262a	AH1273-95	—	2.50	3.50	5.00	7.00

Tehran, AH1273
Portrait type, 2.5 gm.

265	AH1273-75	—	3.00	6.00	10.00	15.00

KRAN

SILVER
Astarabad, AH1267

Kirman, AH1269

Astarabad, AH1272

Herat, AH1273, 5.4 gm.

FIRST STANDARD

263	AH1264-73	—	5.50	6.50	8.00	10.00

Herat, AH1273

Astarabad, AH1279

Hamadan, AH1279

Tabriz, AH1279

Tabriz, AH1293, 5.0 gm.

SECOND STANDARD

C#	Date	Mintage	VG	Fine	VF	XF
263a	AH1273-96	—	5.50	6.50	8.00	10.00

Mashad, AH1286
Toughra in wreath, 5.0 gm.

264.1	AH1286	—	7.00	10.00	15.00	22.50

Mashad Mint only

Mashad, AH1287
Plain toughra, 5.0 gm.

264.2	AH1287	—	7.00	10.00	15.00	22.50

Mashad Mint only

TRANSITIONAL TYPES

Tehran, AH1272
Obv: Shah's portrait facing left above wreath between Arabic legends. Rev: Arabic legends within wreath.

266.1	AH1272	—	—	—	Rare	—

Kirman, AH1282
Machine-made planchet, reeded edge, 5.0 gm.

266.2	AH1282	—	9.00	15.00	22.50	30.00

Kirmanshahan, AH1294, 4.6 gm.

Broad flan, machine-made planchet, plain edge.

C#	Date	Mintage	VG	Fine	VF	XF
266.3	AH1294	—	12.50	20.00	30.00	45.00

Yazd, AH1294
With title Sahibqiran, 5.0 gm.

C#	Date	Mintage	VG	Fine	VF	XF
267	AH1294	—	12.50	20.00	32.50	50.00

Known only from Yazd, muled with AH1289-dated reverse.

Tehran, AH1295
Machine-struck (?), but crude, 5.0 gm.

C#	Date	Mintage	VG	Fine	VF	XF
268.1	AH1295	—	7.50	12.50	20.00	30.00

Tehran, AH1295, 5.0 gm.
Rev: Crowned lion & sun, date beneath lion.

C#	Date	Mintage	VG	Fine	VF	XF
268.2	AH1295	—	7.50	12.50	20.00	30.00

Tehran, AH1296, 5.0 gm.
Obv: Date beneath wreath.

C#	Date	Mintage	VG	Fine	VF	XF
268.3	AH1296	—	7.50	12.50	20.00	30.00

Tehran, AH1296
Rev: Crowned mint name, 5.0 gm.

C#	Date	Mintage	VG	Fine	VF	XF
268.4	AH1296	—	12.50	20.00	25.00	37.50

All varieties 268.1-4 from Tehran only.

1/4 TOMAN

.900 GOLD, 0.9 gm.

C#	Date	Mintage	VG	Fine	VF	XF
270	AH1264-93	—	50.00	80.00	110.00	140.00

1/2 TOMAN

.900 GOLD, 1.7 gm.
Tehran, AH1280

C#	Date	Mintage	VG	Fine	VF	XF
271	AH1264-93	—	42.50	65.00	90.00	110.00

TOMAN

.900 GOLD, 3.5 gm.
Mashad, AH1266

C#	Date	Mintage	VG	Fine	VF	XF
272.1	AH1266	—	75.00	85.00	100.00	120.00

Qazvin, AH1267

C#	Date	Mintage	VG	Fine	VF	XF
272.2	AH1267	—	75.00	85.00	100.00	120.00

Rasht, AH1277

C#	Date	Mintage	VG	Fine	VF	XF
272.3	AH1277	—	75.00	80.00	90.00	110.00

Sarakhs, AH1276

C#	Date	Mintage	VG	Fine	VF	XF
272.4	AH1264-94	—	75.00	80.00	90.00	110.00

Shiraz

C#	Date	Mintage	VG	Fine	VF	XF
272.5	AH1269	—	75.00	80.00	90.00	110.00

Tabriz, AH1272

C#	Date	Mintage	VG	Fine	VF	XF
272.6	AH1272	—	75.00	80.00	90.00	110.00

Tehran, Facing portrait.

C#	Date	Mintage	VG	Fine	VF	XF
275.1	AH1271	—	125.00	175.00	250.00	350.00

Tehran, AH1272
Obv: Portrait left, 3.5 gm.

C#	Date	Mintage	VG	Fine	VF	XF
275.2	AH1272-75	—	100.00	140.00	200.00	275.00

2 TOMANS

.900 GOLD, 6.9 gm.
Kirmanshahan, AH1271
Obv: Portrait facing

C#	Date	Mintage	VG	Fine	VF	XF
276	AH1271	—	175.00	300.00	500.00	700.00

Mashad, AH1281
Obv: Toughra, 6.9 gm.

C#	Date	Mintage	VG	Fine	VF	XF
273	AH1281	—	135.00	250.00	375.00	550.00

NOTE: Struck at Mashad mint only.

MACHINE-STRUCK COINAGE

KRAN STANDARD

(AH1293-1344, SH1304-09)
(AD1876-1931)

12 DINARS (1/4 SHAHI)

COPPER, 15mm

Y#	Date	Mintage	Good	VG	Fine	VF
1	AH1301	—	4.00	10.00	18.00	30.00
	1303	—	4.00	10.00	18.00	30.00
	ND	—	3.00	8.00	10.00	20.00

25 DINARS (1/2 SHAHI)

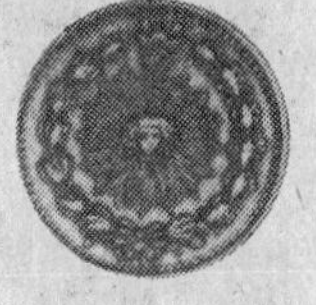

COPPER, 20mm
NOTE: On AH1294 & 1295 coins, initials FP appear on rev.

Y#	Date	Mintage	VG	Fine	VF	XF
2	AH1294	—	.60	1.75	3.50	6.00
	1295	—	.60	1.75	3.50	6.00
	1296	—	.60	1.75	3.50	6.00
	1297	—	1.00	2.50	4.00	8.00
	1298	—	1.00	2.50	4.00	8.00
	1299	—	.60	1.75	3.50	6.00
	1300	—	.60	1.75	3.50	6.00
	1303	—	1.00	2.50	4.00	5.00
	ND	—	1.00	2.50	4.00	5.00

50 DINARS (1 SHAHI)

۵۰ دینار

COPPER, 25mm
NOTE: On AH1294 & 1295, initials FP appear on rev.

Y#	Date	Mintage	VG	Fine	VF	XF
4	AH1293	—	4.00	6.00	12.50	20.00
	1294	—	.75	1.50	4.00	8.00
	1295	—	.50	1.00	3.00	6.00
	1296	—	.50	1.00	3.00	6.00
	1297	—	.60	1.25	3.50	7.00
	1298	—	.60	1.25	3.50	7.00
	1299	—	.60	1.25	3.50	7.00
	1300	—	1.00	2.00	5.00	10.00
	1301	—	.75	1.50	3.50	7.00
	1302	—	4.00	8.00	15.00	25.00
	1303	—	.75	1.50	4.00	8.00
	1304	—	4.00	8.00	15.00	25.00
	1305	—	.85	1.75	4.00	8.00
	1330 (error) for 1303					
		—	Reported, not confirmed			
	ND	—	1.50	3.00	5.00	10.00

SHAHI

یکشاهی

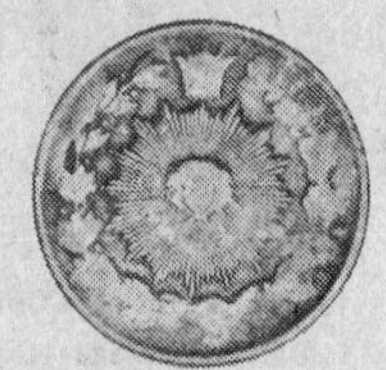

COPPER

Y#	Date	Mintage	Good	VG	Fine	VF
4a	AH1305	—	18.50	30.00	50.00	75.00
	ND	—	12.50	20.00	30.00	40.00

50 DINARS

COPPER-NICKEL, 19mm

Y#	Date	Mintage	VG	Fine	VF	XF
23	AH1318	10.000	.40	.75	1.50	4.00
	1319	12.000	.40	.75	1.50	4.00
	1321	10.000	.40	.75	1.50	4.00
	1326	8.000	.50	1.00	2.50	8.00
	1332	6.000	.35	.75	1.50	4.00
	1337	7.000	.35	.75	1.50	4.00

Y#	Date	Mintage	VG	Fine	VF	XF
95	SH1305	11.000	.30	.60	1.00	2.50
	1307	2.500	.40	.80	1.25	3.00

100 DINARS (2 SHAHIS)

COPPER, 29mm

Y#	Date	Mintage	VG	Fine	VF	XF
5	AH1297	—	1.00	3.00	6.00	10.00
	1298	—	1.00	3.00	6.00	10.00
	1299	—	1.00	3.00	6.00	10.00
	1300	—	1.00	3.00	6.00	10.00
	1301	—	1.00	3.00	6.00	10.00
	1302	—	6.00	15.00	30.00	50.00
	1303	—	2.50	3.50	10.00	20.00
	1304	—	6.00	15.00	30.00	50.00
	1305	—	3.00	5.00	12.50	25.00
	1307	—	Reported, not confirmed			
	1308	—	6.00	15.00	30.00	50.00
	1313 (error) for 1303	—	6.00	15.00	30.00	50.00
	1330 (error) for 1303	—	2.00	4.00	10.00	20.00
	ND	—	1.00	3.00	6.00	10.00

2 SHAHIS

COPPER

Y#	Date	Mintage	Good	VG	Fine	VF
5a	AH1305	—	30.00	50.00	85.00	125.00
	ND	—	20.00	37.50	60.00	100.00

100 DINARS

COPPER-NICKEL, 21mm

Y#	Date	Mintage	VG	Fine	VF	XF
24	AH1318	10.000	.40	1.00	2.00	5.00
	1319	9.000	.40	1.00	2.00	5.00
	1321/19	5.000	1.25	2.50	6.00	10.00
	1321	Inc. Ab.	.50	1.00	3.00	6.00
	1326	6.000	.60	1.25	3.00	6.00
	1332	5.000	.50	1.00	3.00	6.00
	1337	6.500	.40	1.00	2.00	5.00

Y#	Date	Mintage	VG	Fine	VF	XF
96	SH1305	4.500	.35	1.00	2.00	5.00
	1307	3.750	.35	1.00	2.00	5.00

200 DINARS

COPPER, 34mm

Y#	Date	Mintage	VG	Fine	VF	XF
6	AH1300	—	15.00	30.00	60.00	100.00
	1301	—	12.50	20.00	40.00	70.00

SHAHI SEFID

(WHITE SHAHI)

Called the white (i.e., silver) Shahi to distinguish it from the black or copper Shahi, the Shahi Sefid was actually worth 3 Shahis. It was used primarily for distribution on New Year's day (Now-Ruz) as good-luck gifts. Since 1926 special privately struck tokens, having no monetary value, have been used instead of coins.

The Shahi Sefid, worth 150 Dinars, was broader, but much thinner, than the 1/4 Kran (Rob'i), worth 250 Dinars.

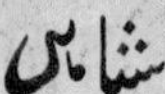

0.6908 gm., .900 SILVER, 17mm, .0200 oz ASW

Y#	Date	Mintage	VG	Fine	VF	XF
7	AH1296	—	4.00	8.00	15.00	27.50

Date below lion instead of denomination, which is omitted.

Date below wreath

Y#	Date	Mintage	VG	Fine	VF	XF
7a	AH1297	—	1.50	3.00	5.00	10.00
	1298	—	1.50	3.00	5.00	10.00
	1299	—	1.50	3.00	5.00	10.00
	1300	—	1.50	3.00	5.00	10.00
	1301	—	1.00	2.00	3.50	6.00
	1302	—	2.00	4.00	8.00	12.50
	1303	—	2.00	4.00	8.00	12.50
	1304	—	2.50	5.00	10.00	15.00
	1305	—	2.50	5.00	10.00	15.00
	1307/1	—	3.00	6.00	12.50	18.50
	1307	—	3.00	6.00	12.50	18.50
	1309/01 (error) 13019	—	3.50	7.50	15.00	30.00
	1309	—	3.00	6.00	12.50	18.50
	'13' only	—	3.00	6.00	12.50	18.50
	ND	—	1.50	3.00	5.00	10.00

Rev: Date amidst lion's legs.
(Variations exist)

Y#	Date	Mintage	VG	Fine	VF	XF
7b	AH1313	—	1.50	3.00	5.00	10.00
	1--3	—	1.50	3.00	5.00	10.00

Obv. of Nasir al-din (Y#7a)
Rev. of 'Sahib al-zaman' (-obv. of Y#B44)

Y#	Date	Mintage	VG	Fine	VF	XF
8	ND	—	2.50	5.00	10.00	20.00

Obv. of Muzaffar al-din Shah

Y#	Date	Mintage	VG	Fine	VF	XF
25	AH1314	—	5.00	7.50	15.00	25.00
	1315	—	5.00	7.50	15.00	25.00
	1316	—	5.00	7.50	15.00	25.00
	1317	—	4.00	6.50	10.00	20.00
	1318	—	4.00	6.50	10.00	20.00
	1319	—	3.00	5.00	7.50	15.00
	1320	.150	4.00	6.00	10.00	20.00
	8310 (error)	—	—	—	—	—
	1039 (error)	—	—	—	—	—
	ND	—	3.00	5.00	7.50	15.00

Mule, obv. of Y#25 and rev. of Y#7b.

Y#	Date	Mintage	VG	Fine	VF	XF
25.1	AH1313	—	4.00	6.00	10.00	20.00

With denomination omitted

Y#	Date	Mintage	VG	Fine	VF	XF
25a	ND	—	3.00	5.00	7.50	15.00

NOTE: A number of varieties and mulings of Y#25 and Y#25a with other denominations, esp. 1/4 Krans & 500 Dinar pieces, are reported. These command a premium over others of the same types.)

NOTE: Many Shahis of Muzaffar al-Din are muled with reverses of Nasir al-Din, especially with date 1301 and 1303. Worth $5 in Fine, $7.50 in VF. Many also have the Mouzaffer date of issue engraved amid the legs of old Nasir dies from which the date beneath the wreath wasn't removed. No premium for those showing old Nasir dates.

NOTE: A total of 58,000 pieces were reported struck in AH1322, 1323 & 1324, but none are known with those dates. The specimens were either struck from old dies or were undated types.

Obv. of Muzaftar al-din Shah
Rev. of Sahib al-Zaman

Y#	Date	Mintage	VG	Fine	VF	XF
A25	ND	—	5.00	7.50	15.00	25.00

NOTE: Two varieties are known with thick and thin script lettering.

Obv. of Muhammad Ali Shah

Y#	Date	Mintage	VG	Fine	VF	XF
44	AH1325	—	5.00	7.50	15.00	25.00
	1326	—	5.00	7.50	15.00	25.00
	1327	—	5.00	7.50	15.00	25.00

Obv. of Sahib al-Zaman

Y#	Date	Mintage	VG	Fine	VF	XF
B44	AH1326	—	5.00	7.50	15.00	25.00

Obv. of Y#44, rev. is obv. of Y#B44

Y#	Date	Mintage	VG	Fine	VF	XF
A44	ND	—	5.00	10.00	25.00	50.00

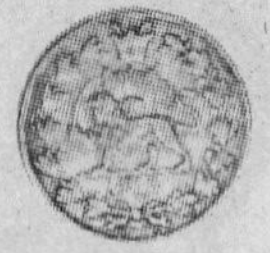

Obv. of Ahmad Shah
Dated below wreath

Y#	Date	Mintage	VG	Fine	VF	XF
64	AH1328	—	1.50	2.50	4.00	6.00
	1329	—	1.50	2.50	4.00	6.00
	1330	.189	1.50	2.50	4.00	6.00

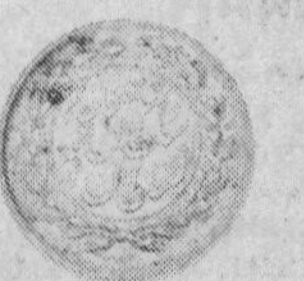

Rev: Date amidst lion's legs.

Y#	Date	Mintage	VG	Fine	VF	XF
A64	AH1332	.010	2.50	5.00	8.50	12.50

Obv: Ahmad Shah. Rev: Sahib-Al-Zaman.

Y#	Date	Mintage	VG	Fine	VF	XF
B64	ND	—	2.50	5.00	12.50	20.00

Y#	Date	Mintage	VG	Fine	VF	XF
A70	AH1333	.078	1.50	2.00	3.00	5.00
	1334	.006	2.00	4.00	6.50	10.00
	1335	.073	1.50	2.00	3.00	5.00
	1335 dated 1337 on rev. amid legs					
		Inc. Ab.	2.50	5.00	10.00	20.00
	1337	.076	1.50	2.00	3.00	5.00
	1337 also dated on rev.					
		—	2.50	5.00	10.00	17.50
	1339	.010	1.50	2.50	4.00	7.50
	1342	.020	1.50	2.50	4.00	7.50

Obv. of Y#A70. Rev: Sahib-Al-Zaman.

Y#	Date	Mintage	VG	Fine	VF	XF
A70a	AH1335	—	5.00	10.00	17.50	30.00

(Mintage included in Y#A70 of AH1335)

Obv. of Sahib al-Zaman

Y#	Date	Mintage	VG	Fine	VF	XF
B70	AH1332	(Inc. with Y#64a)				
			1.50	3.00	5.00	9.00
	1333	(Inc. with Y#A70)				
			1.50	3.00	5.00	9.00
	1337	(Inc. with Y#A70)				
			1.50	3.00	5.00	9.00
	1341	.003	2.00	4.00	7.50	15.00
	1342	(Inc. with Y#A70)				
			2.00	4.00	7.50	15.00
	ND	—	1.50	3.00	5.00	9.00

NOTE: Numerous silver Now Ruz tokens, some with dates 1329-1331, are available in Tehran for a fraction of the price of true Shahis.

1/4 KRAN

(Rob'i = 5 Shahis)

ربعی

1.1513 gm., .900 SILVER, 15mm, .0333 oz ASW
Date below wreath

Y#	Date	Mintage	VG	Fine	VF	XF
9	AH1296	—	2.00	4.00	6.00	10.00
	1297	—	2.00	4.00	6.00	10.00
	1298	—	2.00	4.00	6.00	10.00
	1299	—	2.00	4.00	6.00	10.00
	1300	—	2.00	4.00	6.00	10.00
	1301	—	2.00	4.00	6.00	10.00
	1303	—	2.00	4.00	6.00	10.00
	1305	—	3.00	5.00	8.00	12.50
	1306	—	2.00	4.00	6.00	10.00
	1307	—	2.00	4.00	6.00	10.00
	1308	—	3.00	5.00	8.00	12.50
	1309	—	3.00	5.00	8.00	12.50
	1311	—	5.00	10.00	15.00	25.00
	ND	—	3.00	5.00	8.00	12.50

NOTE: Many examples of Y#9 bear broken or partial dates. These command no premium.

Rev: Date amidst legs

Y#	Date	Mintage	VG	Fine	VF	XF
9d	AH1311	—	5.00	10.00	20.00	35.00
	1312	—	5.00	10.00	20.00	35.00

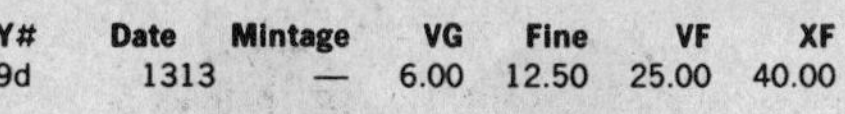

Y#	Date	Mintage	VG	Fine	VF	XF
9d	1313	—	6.00	12.50	25.00	40.00

Obv. of Muzaffar al-din Shah

Y#	Date	Mintage	VG	Fine	VF	XF
26	AH1316	—	5.00	10.00	20.00	35.00
	1318	—	6.00	12.50	22.50	40.50
	1319	—	5.00	10.00	20.00	35.00
	ND	—	3.00	6.00	11.50	17.50

NOTE: 300 specimens reportedly struck in AH1322, but none known to exist.

Obv. of Muhammad Ali Shah

Y#	Date	Mintage	VG	Fine	VF	XF
45	AH1325	—	6.00	12.50	18.50	25.00
	1326	—	4.00	8.00	12.50	20.00
	1327	—	4.00	8.00	12.50	20.00

Obv. of Ahmad Shah

Y#	Date	Mintage	VG	Fine	VF	XF
65	AH1327	—	2.00	4.00	8.50	12.50
	1328	—	2.00	4.00	8.50	12.50
	1329	.130	2.00	4.00	8.50	12.50
	1330	.156	2.00	4.00	8.50	12.50
	1331	.030	5.00	10.00	20.00	30.00

Obv: Changed. Rev: Date amidst legs.

Y#	Date	Mintage	VG	Fine	VF	XF
C70	AH1327 (error), probably due to use of old rev. die of Y#45		2.00	4.00	8.00	12.50
	1332	.252	2.00	4.00	8.00	12.50
	1333	Inc. Ab.	2.00	4.00	8.00	12.50
	1334	.070	3.00	6.00	10.00	17.50
	1335	.260	2.00	4.00	8.00	12.50
	1336	.160	2.00	4.00	8.00	12.50
	1337	.080	3.00	6.00	10.00	17.50
	1339	.028	4.00	8.00	12.50	20.00
	1341	.022	4.00	8.00	12.50	20.00
	1342	.110	3.00	6.00	10.00	17.50
	1343	.186	2.00	4.00	8.00	12.50
	ND	—	2.00	4.00	8.00	12.50

Obv. as Y#C70, date below wreath

Y#	Date	Mintage	VG	Fine	VF	XF
C70a	AH1334 (Inc. with Y#C70)		5.00	10.00	17.50	30.00

Y#	Date	Mintage	VG	Fine	VF	XF
100	SH1304	.024	5.00	10.00	20.00	35.00

NOTE: 8,000 reported struck in 1305, but that year not yet found.

500 DINARS

(10 Shahis = 1/2 Kran)

First Nasir al-din legend

Second Nasir al-din legend with 'Sahibqiran' added

Forms of the denomination:

500 DINARS: ۵۰۰ دینار

پانصد دینار

10 SHAHIS: ده شاهی

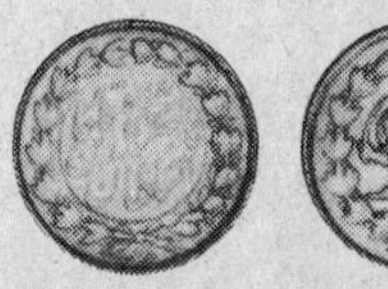

2.3025 gm., .900 SILVER, 18mm, .0666 oz ASW
First legend, '500 DINARS'

Y#	Date	Mintage	VG	Fine	VF	XF
10	AH1296	—	5.00	8.00	12.50	18.50
	1297	—	5.00	8.00	12.50	18.50
	1298	—	5.00	8.00	12.50	18.50
	1299	—	6.00	10.00	15.00	25.00
	1301	—	5.00	8.00	12.50	18.50
	1306	—	10.00	20.00	35.00	60.00
	1311	—	7.50	15.00	20.00	40.00
	ND	—	5.00	8.00	12.50	18.50

NOTE: The undated issue is often found in higher grades than dated coins.

First legend, '10 SHAHIS'
Rev: Date amid legs.

Y#	Date	Mintage	VG	Fine	VF	XF
10b	AH1310	—	10.00	25.00	50.00	80.00

Second legend, '10 SHAHIS'
Obv: Crown added above legend.
Rev: Date amid legs.

Y#	Date	Mintage	VG	Fine	VF	XF
10c	AH1310	—	10.00	25.00	50.00	80.00
	1311	—	10.00	25.00	50.00	80.00

First legend, '500 DINARS'
Rev: Date amidst legs.

Y#	Date	Mintage	VG	Fine	VF	XF
10d	AH1311	—	10.00	25.00	40.00	60.00
	1312	—	10.00	20.00	30.00	50.00
	1313	—	Reported, Not Confirmed			

'500 DINARS'
Nasir al-Din's Return From Europe
Rev: w/1306 date.

Y#	Date	Mintage	VG	Fine	VF	XF
A15	AH1307	—	30.00	85.00	150.00	225.00

Obv. of Muzaffar al-Din, '500 DINARS'
Rev: Date amid legs, arranged variously

Y#	Date	Mintage	VG	Fine	VF	XF
27	AH1298 error, or muling with old rev. die					
		—	5.00	10.00	18.50	30.00
	1313	—	5.00	10.00	18.50	30.00
	1314	—	4.00	8.50	15.00	25.00
	1315	—	6.00	12.50	20.00	40.00
	1316	—	6.00	12.50	20.00	40.00
	1317	—	6.00	12.50	20.00	40.00
	1318	—	6.00	12.50	20.00	40.00
	1319	—	4.00	8.50	15.00	25.00
	1322	—	4.00	8.50	15.00	25.00
	ND	—	3.00	6.50	10.00	20.00

Y#	Date	Mintage	VG	Fine	VF	XF
30	AH1323	.130	5.00	10.00	20.00	35.00

Obv. of Muhammad Ali Shah

Y#	Date	Mintage	VG	Fine	VF	XF
46	AH1325	.218	7.50	20.00	40.00	80.00
	1326	.218	5.00	15.00	35.00	60.00
	1336(Error for 1326)	Inc. Ab.	5.00	17.50	30.00	50.00

Obv: Date

Y#	Date	Mintage	VG	Fine	VF	XF
48	AH1326	(Inc. with Y#46)	8.00	20.00	35.00	60.00
	1327	—	8.00	20.00	35.00	60.00

Obv. of Y#48, Rev. of Y#46
(Date both sides)

Y#	Date	Mintage	VG	Fine	VF	XF
48a	AH1325	—	10.00	25.00	45.00	75.00
	1326	—	8.00	20.00	35.00	60.00

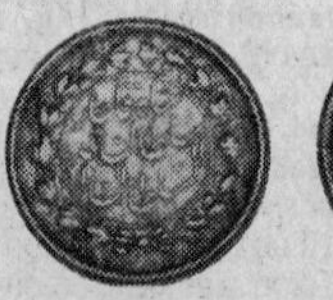

Obv. of Ahmad Shah

Y#	Date	Mintage	VG	Fine	VF	XF
66	AH1327	—	3.50	5.00	8.50	15.00
	1328	—	3.50	5.00	8.50	15.00
	1329	.044	5.00	7.50	12.50	20.00
	1330	.627	3.00	4.00	6.50	12.50

Obv: Date

Y#	Date	Mintage	VG	Fine	VF	XF
70	AH1331	(Inc. with 1330)	3.00	5.00	8.50	12.50
	1332	.560	3.00	4.00	6.00	8.50
	1333	.292	3.00	4.00	8.50	12.50
	1334	.065	3.00	4.00	8.50	12.50
	1335	.150	3.00	4.00	8.00	12.50
	1336	.240	3.00	4.00	8.00	12.50
	1339	—	3.50	6.00	10.00	15.00
	1343	.160	3.50	6.00	10.00	15.00

NOTE: 10,000 reported struck in AH1337 probably dated AH1336.

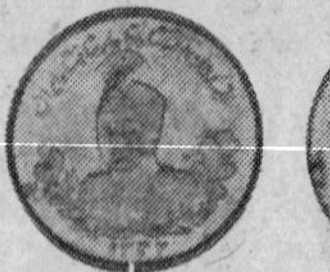

Dated obv. and rev.

Y#	Date	Mintage	VG	Fine	VF	XF
70a	AH1332	(Inc. with Y#70)	7.50	15.00	30.00	50.00

Y#	Date	Mintage	VG	Fine	VF	XF
A101	SH1304	—	50.00	100.00	200.00	300.00

Obv. of Reza Shah

Y#	Date	Mintage	VG	Fine	VF	XF
105	SH1305	.010	30.00	60.00	90.00	150.00

Y#	Date	Mintage	VG	Fine	VF	XF
A109	SH1306	.005	15.00	25.00	50.00	100.00
	1307	.046	5.00	7.50	12.50	18.50
	1308	.464	5.00	7.50	12.50	18.50

NOTE: Some of the coins reported in AH1308 were dated 1307.

1000 DINARS

(KRAN)

Forms of the denomination:

1000 DINARS: یکهزار دینار

1 KRAN: یکقران

4.6050 gm., .900 SILVER, 23mm, .1332 oz ASW
Obv. of Nasir al-din Shah, first legend
'1000 DINARS'

Y#	Date	Mintage	VG	Fine	VF	XF
11	AH1296	—	4.00	4.50	5.50	8.00
	1297	—	4.00	4.50	5.50	8.00
	1298/7	—	5.00	7.50	12.50	22.50
	1298	—	4.50	6.00	10.00	18.50
	12-—	—	4.00	4.50	5.50	8.50
	ND	—	4.00	4.50	6.00	10.00

Obv: Second legend, '1000 DINARS'

Y#	Date	Mintage	VG	Fine	VF	XF
11a	AH1298	—	4.00	5.00	6.50	10.00
	1299	—	4.00	5.00	6.50	10.00
	1303	—	25.00	50.00	100.00	200.00
	ND	—	4.00	5.00	6.50	10.00

Obv: Second legend, crown above legend.
'1 KRAN'

Y#	Date	Mintage	VG	Fine	VF	XF
11c	AH1310	—	10.00	15.00	25.00	40.00
	1311	—	12.50	20.00	35.00	60.00

Obv: Second legend, no crown.
'1 KRAN'

Y#	Date	Mintage	VG	Fine	VF	XF
11b	AH1311	—	13.50	25.00	50.00	85.00

Obv: Second legend, no crown.
'1000 DINARS'

Y#	Date	Mintage	VG	Fine	VF	XF
11d	AH1311	—	10.00	15.00	25.00	40.00
	1312	—	12.50	20.00	40.00	60.00

Obv. of Muzaffar al-Din Shah,
no crown.

Y#	Date	Mintage	VG	Fine	VF	XF
A27	AH1314	—	15.00	50.00	80.00	150.00

Obv: Crown added above legend.

Y#	Date	Mintage	VG	Fine	VF	XF
A27a	AH1317	—	10.00	20.00	40.00	75.00
	1318	—	10.00	20.00	40.00	75.00
	1319	—	12.50	20.00	40.00	75.00
	1322	—	10.00	15.00	30.00	60.00

Y#	Date	Mintage	VG	Fine	VF	XF
31	AH1323	.125	12.50	20.00	30.00	50.00

Obv. legend of Muhammad Ali Shah

Y#	Date	Mintage	VG	Fine	VF	XF
A47	AH1325	.289	40.00	85.00	135.00	250.00
	1326	.289	40.00	85.00	135.00	250.00

Obv: Date

Y#	Date	Mintage	VG	Fine	VF	XF
49	AH1326	(Inc. with A47)	20.00	30.00	50.00	85.00
	1327	—	20.00	30.00	50.00	100.00

Dated on obv. & rev.
(Obv. of Y#49, Rev. of Y#47)

Y#	Date	Mintage	VG	Fine	VF	XF
49a	AH1326	(Inc. with A#47)	25.00	50.00	100.00	150.00

Obv. of Ahmad Shah

Y#	Date	Mintage	VG	Fine	VF	XF
67	AH1327	—	4.00	5.00	6.00	9.00
	1328	—	4.00	5.00	6.50	10.00
	1329	3.000	4.00	5.00	6.50	10.00
	1330	—	4.00	5.00	6.00	9.00

24mm

Y#	Date	Mintage	VG	Fine	VF	XF
67a	AH1330	—	4.00	4.50	6.00	8.00
	1330	—	—	—	Proof	—

NOTE: Y#67a differs from Y#67 in that it is about 1mm broader and has a much thicker rim and more clearly defined dentices. Struck in Germany, without Iranian authorization, for circulation in western Iran during World War I.) Also, the lion lacks the triangular face & fierce expression of Y#67 and the point of the Talwar (scimitar) does not touch the sunburst as it does on Tehran issues.

23mm

Y#	Date	Mintage	VG	Fine	VF	XF
71	AH1330	—	10.00	20.00	40.00	80.00
	1331	1.310	4.00	4.50	5.50	7.00
	1332	1.891	4.00	4.50	5.50	7.00
	1333	2.179	4.00	4.50	5.50	7.00
	1334	1.273	4.00	4.50	5.50	7.50
	1335	2.162	4.00	4.50	5.50	7.50
	1336	1.412	4.00	4.50	5.50	7.50
	1337	3.330	4.00	4.50	5.50	7.50
	1339	.035	4.50	6.00	9.00	13.50
	1340	.028	4.50	5.50	8.50	13.50
	1341	.170	4.50	5.50	8.50	13.50
	1342	.255	4.50	5.50	8.50	13.50
	1343	1.345	4.00	5.00	6.00	8.00
	1344	2.978	4.00	5.00	6.00	8.00

Transitional Issue
Obv. of Y#67. Rev. of Y#49a.

Y#	Date	Mintage	VG	Fine	VF	XF
A71	AH1336	—	—	—	—	—

10th Year of Reign

Y#	Date	Mintage	VG	Fine	VF	XF
73	AH1337	.975	12.50	25.00	50.00	80.00

Y#	Date	Mintage	VG	Fine	VF	XF
101	SH1304	2.573	4.50	5.50	7.50	12.50
	1305	2.265	4.50	5.50	7.00	10.00

Obv. of REZA SHAH

Y#	Date	Mintage	VG	Fine	VF	XF
106	SH1305	Inc. Ab.	4.00	5.00	6.00	8.00
	1306/5	3.130	4.00	5.00	6.50	9.00
	1306	Inc. Ab.	4.00	5.00	6.00	8.00

Y#	Date	Mintage	VG	Fine	VF	XF
109	SH1306	Inc. Ab.	4.00	4.50	5.50	7.00
	1307	4.300	4.00	4.50	5.50	7.00
	1308	.603	4.00	4.50	5.50	7.50

2000 DINARS

(2 KRANS)

Forms of the denomination

2 KRANS: دو قران

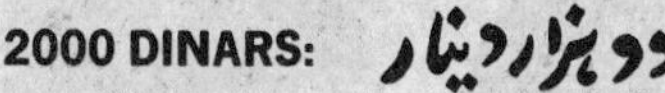

2000 DINARS: دو هزار دینار

9.2100 gm., .900 SILVER, 27mm, .2665 oz ASW
Obv. of Nasir al-din Shah, first legend
'2000 DINARS'

Y#	Date	Mintage	VG	Fine	VF	XF
12	AH1296	—	8.00	9.00	11.00	14.00
	1297	—	8.00	9.00	11.00	14.00
	1298	—	8.00	9.00	11.50	17.50
	ND	—	8.00	9.00	11.00	14.00

Obv: Second legend, '2000 DINARS'

Y#	Date	Mintage	VG	Fine	VF	XF
12a	AH1298	—	8.00	9.00	11.00	14.00
	1299	—	8.00	9.00	11.00	14.00
	1300	—	8.00	9.00	11.00	14.00
	1301	—	8.00	9.00	11.00	14.00
	1303	—	8.00	9.00	12.50	18.50
	1304	—	10.00	12.50	17.50	30.00
	1305	—	8.00	9.00	13.50	20.00
	1306	—	10.00	12.50	15.00	25.00
	1307	—	8.50	11.50	14.00	22.50
	1308	—	8.50	10.00	12.50	18.50
	ND	—	8.00	9.00	11.50	15.00

(All dates after 1301 struck from worn dies & hence incomplete even in high grades.

(Coins dated AH1300-1305 show a 'B' to the lower left obv., often missing on poorly struck specimens or specimens from filled dies.)

Obv: Second legend, date below wreath.
Crown above legend, '2 KRANS'

Y#	Date	Mintage	VG	Fine	VF	XF
12b.1	AH1310 (in blundered form as 13010)					
		—	12.50	17.50	30.00	45.00

Obv: No crown, '2 KRANS'

Y#	Date	Mintage	VG	Fine	VF	XF
12b.2	AH1310 (in blundered form as 13010)					
		—	16.50	25.00	40.00	60.00

Obv: Second legend, no crown, '2 KRANS'
Rev: Date amid legs.

Y#	Date	Mintage	VG	Fine	VF	XF
12c.1	AH1311	—	16.50	25.00	40.00	60.00

Obv: Crown

Y#	Date	Mintage	VG	Fine	VF	XF
12c.2	AH1310	—	8.00	11.00	15.00	25.00
	1311	—	8.00	11.00	15.00	25.00

Obv: No crown, '2000 DINARS'

Y#	Date	Mintage	VG	Fine	VF	XF
12d	AH1311	—	8.00	11.00	15.00	25.00
	1312	—	8.00	11.00	15.00	25.00

50th Year of Reign
Special legend: 'Dhu'l-qarneyn'

Y#	Date	Mintage	VG	Fine	VF	XF
C15	AH1313	—	—	275.00	450.00	600.00

NOTE: This coin was struck in quantity and was due to be released at Nasir's 50th Anniversary as a largesse piece. A number of specimens were passed out to persons close to the royal court before the celebration which accounts for the few known today. Nasir Al-Din was assassinated just before the fiftieth year of his reign began and the balance of the issue was melted.

Obv. of Muzaffar al-Din Shah,
no crown, '2000 DINARS'.

Y#	Date	Mintage	VG	Fine	VF	XF
28	AH1313	—	12.50	20.00	30.00	55.00
	1314	—	10.00	13.50	22.50	40.00

Obv: Crown added, '2000 DINARS'
Rev: Position of date amid legs varies
Blundered dates exist

Y#	Date	Mintage	VG	Fine	VF	XF
28a	AH1314	—	10.00	13.50	22.50	40.00
	1315	—	10.00	13.50	20.00	35.00
	1316	—	10.00	13.50	20.00	35.00
	1317	—	10.00	13.50	18.50	25.00
	1318	—	10.00	13.50	18.50	25.00
	1319	—	8.00	10.00	12.50	15.00
	1320	13.959	8.00	10.00	12.50	15.00

'2 KRANS'

Y#	Date	Mintage	VG	Fine	VF	XF
28b	AH1320	Inc. Ab.	8.00	9.00	11.00	13.50
	1321 (always '13201')					
		18.108	8.00	9.00	11.00	13.50
	1322	8.640	8.00	9.00	11.00	13.50

Y#	Date	Mintage	VG	Fine	VF	XF
32	AH1323					
		Inc. w/1322	12.50	17.50	25.00	35.00
	'13'*	—	16.50	28.50	42.50	75.00

*(23 of 1323 filled in or never punched)
(AH1319 is a pattern)

Obv. of Muhammad Ali Shah
'2 KRANS'

Y#	Date	Mintage	VG	Fine	VF	XF
47	AH1325	3.076	8.00	10.00	13.50	25.00
	1326	3.069	8.00	10.00	13.50	25.00
	1327	—	8.00	10.00	13.50	25.00
	1328	—	40.00	55.00	75.00	150.00

Portrait of Shan

Y#	Date	Mintage	VG	Fine	VF	XF
50	AH1326					
		Inc. w/Y#47	200.00	325.00	550.00	800.00

BEWARE: Counterfeits exist.

Obv. of Ahmad Shah
date below wreath, '2 KRANS'

Y#	Date	Mintage	VG	Fine	VF	XF
68	AH1327w/1328		8.00	9.00	11.00	14.00
	1328	30.000	8.00	9.00	11.00	14.00
	1329	29.250	8.00	9.00	11.00	14.00

Obv: Date below wreath, '2000 DINARS'
Tehran strike. Rev: Fierce, triangular face on lion.

Y#	Date	Mintage	VG	Fine	VF	XF
68a.1	AH1330	2.901	8.00	9.00	11.00	14.00

Berlin strike. Rev: Lion's face has friendly expression.

Y#	Date	Mintage	VG	Fine	VF	XF
68a.2	AH1330	—	8.50	10.00	12.50	16.50

Rev: Date amid legs, '2000 DINARS'

Y#	Date	Mintage	VG	Fine	VF	XF
68b	AH1330	Inc. Ab.	8.00	9.00	10.00	12.50
	1331	13.412	8.00	9.00	10.00	12.50

Y#	Date	Mintage	VG	Fine	VF	XF
72	AH1330					
		Inc. w/Y#68a	25.00	40.00	65.00	100.00
	1331					
		Inc. w/Y#68b	8.50	12.50	20.00	30.00
	1332	12.926	8.00	9.00	10.00	12.50
	1333					
		Inc. w/1332	8.00	9.00	10.00	12.50
	1334	4.299	8.00	9.00	10.00	12.50
	1335	9.777	8.00	9.00	10.00	12.50
	1336	5.401	8.00	9.00	10.00	12.50
	1337	2.951	8.00	9.00	11.50	16.50
	1339	1.085	8.00	9.00	11.50	16.50
	1340	.254	8.50	11.50	15.00	25.00
	1341	4.460	8.00	9.00	10.00	12.50
	1342	2.245	8.00	9.00	10.00	12.50
	1343	5.205	8.00	9.00	10.00	12.50

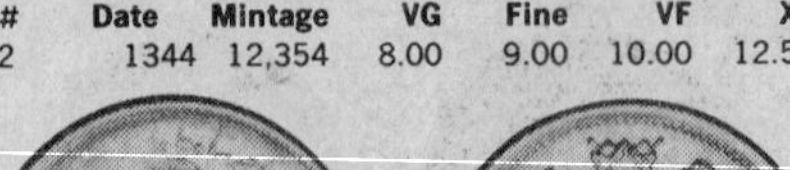

Y#	Date	Mintage	VG	Fine	VF	XF
72	1344	12.354	8.00	9.00	10.00	12.50

10th Anniversary of Reign

Y#	Date	Mintage	VG	Fine	VF	XF
74	AH1337	3.503	20.00	35.00	65.00	100.00

Y#	Date	Mintage	VG	Fine	VF	XF
102	SH1304	11.920	8.00	9.00	11.00	15.00
	1305	9.785	8.00	9.00	11.00	15.00

Y#	Date	Mintage	VG	Fine	VF	XF
107	SH1305	Inc. Ab.	8.00	9.00	10.00	12.50
	1306	9.380	8.00	9.00	10.00	12.50

Y#	Date	Mintage	VG	Fine	VF	XF
110	SH1306 no mintmark (Tehran)					
		Inc. Ab.	8.00	8.50	9.00	11.00
	1306 muled with reverse of Y#72					
		—	—	—	Rare	—
	1306H	11.714	BV	8.00	9.00	11.00
	1306L	7.500	BV	8.00	9.00	11.00
	1307	11.146	BV	8.00	9.00	11.00
	1308	1.611	BV	8.00	9.00	12.50

H - Heaton Mint
L - Leningrad Mint

5000 DINARS

(5 KRANS)

23.0251 gm., .900 SILVER, 36mm, .6662 oz ASW

Y#	Date	Mintage	Good	VG	Fine	VF
13	AH1296	—	65.00	110.00	175.00	250.00
	1297	—	85.00	135.00	200.00	275.00

Obv: Crown above legend, value is '5 KRANS'.

Y#	Date	Mintage	VG	Fine	VF	XF
13c	AH1311	—	—	—	Rare	—

Muzaffar al-din Shah

Y#	Date	Mintage	VG	Fine	VF	XF
29	AH1320	.250	13.50	17.50	20.00	25.00

(Actual mintage must be considerably greater; struck in Leningrad)

Royal Birthday

Y#	Date	Mintage	VG	Fine	VF	XF
A40	AH1322	—	225.00	450.00	700.00	1000.

Obv: Without additional inscriptions flanking head.

Y#	Date	Mintage	VG	Fine	VF	XF
33	AH1324	3,000	225.00	450.00	700.00	1000.

(AH1319 is a pattern)

Y#	Date	Mintage	Good	VG	Fine	VF
A50	AH1327	—	225.00	450.00	700.00	1000.

Y#	Date	Mintage	VG	Fine	VF	XF
69	AH1331	—	35.00	50.00	70.00	100.00
	1332	3.000	BV	21.50	23.50	28.50
	1333	.667	BV	21.50	23.50	28.50
	1334	.443	BV	21.50	23.50	28.50
	1335	1.884	BV	21.50	23.50	28.50
	1337	.165	22.50	25.00	35.00	50.00
	1339	.090	22.50	25.00	35.00	50.00
	1340	.303	BV	21.50	23.50	28.50
	1341	.757	BV	21.50	23.50	28.50
	1342	.546	BV	21.50	23.50	28.50
	1343	.935	BV	21.50	23.50	28.50
	1344	2.284	BV	21.50	23.50	28.50

NOTE: Specimens are known dated AH1338 but are believed to be 1337 dated with the 7 inverted. (9000 reported minted in AH1336, but probably dated earlier)

Beware of altered date 1331 specimens.

Y#	Date	Mintage	VG	Fine	VF	XF
103	SH1304	.500	BV	21.50	25.00	35.00
	1305	1.363	21.50	25.00	35.00	55.00

Y#	Date	Mintage	VG	Fine	VF	XF
108	SH1305	Inc. Ab.	BV	21.50	23.50	26.50
	1306	3.186	BV	21.50	23.50	26.50

Y#	Date	Mintage	VG	Fine	VF	XF
111	SH1306	Inc. Ab.	BV	21.50	22.50	25.00
	1306 muled with reverse of Y#69					
		—	—	—	Rare	—
	1306H	4.710	BV	21.50	23.50	26.50
	1306L	3.000	BV	21.50	23.50	26.50
	1307	3.928	BV	21.50	23.50	26.50
	1308	.584	BV	21.50	23.50	28.50

(Mintmarks located as on 2000 Dinars Y#110)

MEDALLIC ISSUES

(5 KRANS)

23.0251 gm., .900 SILVER, .6662 oz ASW
50th Year of Reign Commemorative

KM#	Date	Fine	VF	XF	Unc
M3	AH1313	35.00	50.00	70.00	100.00

The above piece is a medal, not a coin, though equal in weight to the 5 Kran piece. It is dated AH1313 and was formerly listed as Y#14 in error. Restrikes are known.

(10 KRANS)

46.0501 gm., .900 SILVER, 1.3325 oz ASW

Y#	Date	Mintage	Fine	VF	XF	Unc
15	AH1301	—	250.00	375.00	450.00	650.00

50th Anniversary of Reign

KM#	Date	Fine	VF	XF	Unc
M4	AH1313	200.00	325.00	400.00	550.00

GOLD COINAGE

Counterfeits exist of many pieces, particularly the small 1/5, 1/2 and 1 Toman coins. These are often underweight (or overweight), and are sold in the bazars by weight for use as jewelry. They are usually crude and not intended to deceive collectors, but as a convenient form of bullion. Some are dated outside the reign of the ruler whose name or portrait they bear.

A few deceptive counterfeits are known of the large 10 Toman pieces. Many of the larger pieces are medals, which have been mistaken for coins.

NOTE: Dates in parenthesis are reported, not confirmed.

1/5 TOMAN

0.5749 gm., .900 GOLD, .0166 oz AGW
Obv. leg: First Nasir type.

Y#	Date	Mintage	Fine	VF	XF	Unc
A16	AH1295	—	—	—	Rare	—

Obv: Bust of Nasir al-Din Shah, AH1292-1305.

Y#	Date	Mintage	Fine	VF	XF	Unc
16	AH1297	—	20.00	30.00	50.00	75.00
	1298	—	20.00	30.00	50.00	75.00
	1299	—	20.00	30.00	50.00	75.00
	1300	—	20.00	30.00	50.00	75.00
	1301	—	20.00	30.00	50.00	75.00
A38	AH1309 (error)	—	—	—	—	

Obv: Bust of Muhammad Ali-Shah, AH1326 turned half-left, divided date.

Y#	Date	Mintage	Fine	VF	XF	Unc
52	AH1326	—	75.00	110.00	150.00	200.00

Obv. leg: AHMAD SHAH, AH1328-1332.
Rev: Lion & sun

Y#	Date	Mintage	Fine	VF	XF	Unc
75	AH1329	—	40.00	65.00	100.00	140.00

Obv: Portrait type of Ahmad Shah, Ah1332-1343.
Rev: Legend.

Y#	Date	Mintage	Fine	VF	XF	Unc
79	AH1332	—	30.00	40.00	50.00	70.00
	1335	—	30.00	40.00	50.00	70.00
	1337	—	30.00	40.00	50.00	70.00
	1339	—	30.00	40.00	50.00	70.00
	1341	—	30.00	40.00	50.00	70.00

1/4 TOMAN

Obv. leg: First Nasir type. Rev: Lion and sun.

Y#	Date	Mintage	Fine	VF	XF	Unc
B16	AH1295	—	75.00	125.00	175.00	250.00
	1297	—	75.00	125.00	175.00	250.00

Obv: First bust of Nasir.

Y#	Date	Mintage	Fine	VF	XF	Unc
—	AH1297	—	75.00	125.00	175.00	250.00

Obv: Bust of Muzaffar Al-Din Shah, AH1319-1324, 3/4 left.

Rev: Legend in wreath.

Y#	Date	Mintage	Fine	VF	XF	Unc
A34a	AH1319	—	40.00	50.00	65.00	85.00
A34	ND	—	60.00	80.00	100.00	135.00

Obv: Bust 1/2 right.

Y#	Date	Mintage	Fine	VF	XF	Unc
34	AH1319	—	40.00	50.00	65.00	85.00
	1323	—	40.00	50.00	65.00	85.00
	1324	—	40.00	50.00	65.00	85.00

1/2 TOMAN

1.4372 gm., .900 GOLD, .0416 oz AGW
Nasir al-din Shah, AH1292-1298
Rev: Lion & sun type

Y#	Date	Mintage	Fine	VF	XF	Unc
C16	AH1296	—	75.00	90.00	125.00	165.00
	1298	—	75.00	90.00	125.00	165.00

Obv: First Nasir portrait type, AH1303-1307.

Y#	Date	Mintage	Fine	VF	XF	Unc
17	AH1297	—	60.00	80.00	100.00	135.00
	1303	—	60.00	80.00	100.00	135.00
	1305	—	60.00	80.00	100.00	135.00
	(1)3(0)5	—	60.00	80.00	100.00	135.00
	1307	—	60.00	80.00	100.00	135.00

Obv. leg: NASIR DHU'L GARNEYN.

Y#	Date	Mintage	Fine	VF	XF	Unc
—	AH1313	—	—	—	Rare	—

Obv. leg: MUZAFFAR AL-DIN SHAH, AH1313-1314.
Rev: Lion & sun type.

Y#	Date	Mintage	Fine	VF	XF	Unc
38	AH1314	—	90.00	140.00	200.00	275.00
	1315	—	90.00	140.00	200.00	275.00

Obv: Mouzaffer bust, 3/4 left. Rev: Divided date.

Y#	Date	Mintage	Fine	VF	XF	Unc
—	AH1317	—	60.00	80.00	100.00	135.00

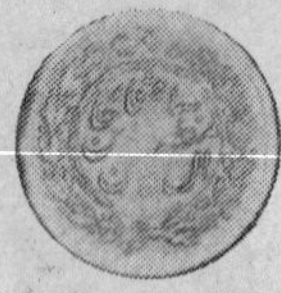

AH1316-1324

Y#	Date	Mintage	Fine	VF	XF	Unc
35	AH1316	—	45.00	60.00	75.00	100.00
	1318	—	45.00	60.00	75.00	100.00
	1319	—	45.00	60.00	75.00	100.00
	1321	—	45.00	60.00	75.00	100.00
	1322	—	45.00	60.00	75.00	100.00
	1323	—	45.00	60.00	75.00	100.00
	1324	—	45.00	60.00	75.00	100.00

Mule. Rev. of 3 Shahi, Y#A25.

Y#	Date	Mintage	Fine	VF	XF	Unc
35a	AH1323	—	—	—	—	—

Obv. leg: MUHAMMAD ALI SHAH.
Rev: Lion & sun.

Y#	Date	Mintage	Fine	VF	XF	Unc
56	AH1324	—	100.00	140.00	200.00	275.00
	1325	—	100.00	140.00	200.00	275.00

Obv: Mohammad Ali bust half-left, AH1326 divided date.

Y#	Date	Mintage	Fine	VF	XF	Unc
53	AH1326	—	100.00	140.00	200.00	275.00
	1362 (error)		100.00	140.00	200.00	275.00
	1327	—	100.00	140.00	200.00	275.00

Obv. leg: AHMAD SHAH, AH1328-1832.
Rev: Lion & sun.

Y#	Date	Mintage	Fine	VF	XF	Unc
76	AH1328	—	60.00	80.00	100.00	135.00
	1329	—	60.00	80.00	100.00	135.00

Obv: Portrait type, AH1332-1343. Rev. leg: Ahmad type.

Y#	Date	Mintage	Fine	VF	XF	Unc
80	AH1332	—	45.00	55.00	65.00	80.00
	1333	—	45.00	55.00	65.00	80.00
	1334	—	45.00	55.00	65.00	80.00
	1335	—	45.00	55.00	65.00	80.00
	1336	—	45.00	55.00	65.00	80.00
	1337	—	45.00	55.00	65.00	80.00
	1339	—	45.00	55.00	65.00	80.00
	1342	—	45.00	55.00	65.00	80.00
	1343	—	45.00	55.00	65.00	80.00

Mule. Obv: Ahmed portrait. Rev. leg: SAHIB AL-ZAMAN.

Y#	Date	Mintage	Fine	VF	XF	Unc
80a	AH1340	—	75.00	90.00	140.00	200.00

TOMAN

2.8744 gm., .900 GOLD, .0832 oz AGW
30th Year of Reign
Obv: Legend. Rev: Lion and sun.

Y#	Date	Mintage	Fine	VF	XF	Unc
—	AH1293	—	150.00	200.00	260.00	325.00

Obv. leg: First Nasir type.
Rev: Lion and sun.

Y#	Date	Mintage	Fine	VF	XF	Unc
D16	AH1296	—	125.00	150.00	190.00	240.00

Obv: First portrait, w/o legend.
Rev: First Nasir legend.

Y#	Date	Mintage	Fine	VF	XF	Unc
A18	ND	—	125.00	150.00	190.00	240.00

Obv: Portrait.
Rev. legend: First Nasir type.

Y#	Date	Mintage	Fine	VF	XF	Unc
18	AH1294	—	75.00	90.00	110.00	135.00
	1297	—	75.00	90.00	110.00	135.00
	1299	—	75.00	90.00	110.00	135.00
	13xx	—	75.00	90.00	110.00	135.00
	1301	—	75.00	90.00	110.00	135.00
	1305	—	75.00	90.00	110.00	135.00
	1306	—	75.00	90.00	110.00	135.00
	1309	—	75.00	90.00	110.00	135.00

Shah's return from Europe, AH1307.

Y#	Date	Mintage	Fine	VF	XF	Unc
D15	AH1307	—	150.00	250.00	350.00	500.00

Obv: Second portrait. Rev: First Nasir legend.

Y#	Date	Mintage	Fine	VF	XF	Unc
22	AH1310	—	100.00	135.00	175.00	225.00

Rev: Second Nasir legend.

Y#	Date	Mintage	Fine	VF	XF	Unc
22a	AH1311	—	100.00	135.00	175.00	225.00

Obv. leg: MUZAFFAR AL-DIN SHAH, AH1313-1314.
Rev: Lion & sun.

Y#	Date	Mintage	Fine	VF	XF	Unc
39	AH1314	—	125.00	165.00	225.00	300.00

Obv: Mouzaffer bust 1/2 right, AH1316-1322.

Y#	Date	Mintage	Fine	VF	XF	Unc
36	AH1316	—	75.00	90.00	115.00	150.00
	1318	—	75.00	90.00	115.00	150.00
	1321	—	75.00	90.00	115.00	150.00
	1322	—	75.00	90.00	115.00	150.00
	1323	—	75.00	90.00	115.00	150.00
	1324	—	75.00	90.00	115.00	150.00

Royal Birthday AH1322
Obv: Mouzaffer bust 3/4 left.

Y#	Date	Mintage	Fine	VF	XF	Unc
40	AH1322	—	125.00	200.00	300.00	450.00

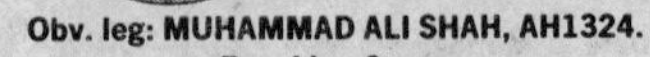

Obv. leg: MUHAMMAD ALI SHAH, AH1324.
Rev: Lion & sun.

Y#	Date	Mintage	Fine	VF	XF	Unc
A56	AH1324	—	130.00	175.00	250.00	350.00

Obv: Mohammad Ali portrait half-left, AH1326.

Y#	Date	Mintage	Fine	VF	XF	Unc
54	AH1326	—	130.00	175.00	250.00	350.00
	1327	—	130.00	175.00	250.00	350.00

Obv. leg: AHMAD SHAH AH1328-1332.
Rev: Lion & sun.

Y#	Date	Mintage	Fine	VF	XF	Unc
77	AH1329	—	—	—	Rare	—

Obv: Portrait, AH1332-1344
Rev. leg: Ahmad Shah type.

Y#	Date	Mintage	Fine	VF	XF	Unc
81	AH1332	—	75.00	85.00	100.00	125.00
	1334	—	75.00	85.00	100.00	125.00
	1335	—	75.00	85.00	100.00	125.00
	1337	—	75.00	85.00	100.00	125.00
	1339	—	75.00	85.00	100.00	125.00
	1340	—	75.00	85.00	100.00	125.00
	1343	—	75.00	85.00	100.00	125.00

Reza's First New Year Celebration
Obv. leg: Reza type. Rev: Lion and sun.

Y#	Date	Mintage	Fine	VF	XF	Unc
119	AH1305	—	200.00	275.00	350.00	450.00

2 TOMANS

5.7488 gm., .900 GOLD, .1663 oz AGW
Discovery of Gold in Kurdistan
Obv: Legend within wreath, crown above.
Rev: Legend within wreath.

Y#	Date	Mintage	Fine	VF	XF	Unc
—	AH1295	—	—	—	Rare	—

Obv: First Nasir portrait. Rev. leg: First Nasir type.

Y#	Date	Mintage	Fine	VF	XF	Unc
20	AH1294	—	150.00	200.00	275.00	375.00
	1297	—	150.00	200.00	275.00	375.00
	1299	—	150.00	200.00	275.00	375.00
	1309	—	150.00	200.00	275.00	375.00

7th Iman Commemorative
Obv: First Nasir portrait. Rev: Legend and crown.

Y#	Date	Mintage	Fine	VF	XF	Unc
—	AH1295	—	—	—	Rare	—

Shah's return from Europe, AH1307

Y#	Date	Mintage	Fine	VF	XF	Unc
B15	AH1307	—	—	—	Rare	—

Shah's visit to Tehran Mint, AH1308

Y#	Date	Mintage	Fine	VF	XF	Unc
E15	AH1308	—	—	—	Rare	—

Y#	Date	Mintage	Fine	VF	XF	Unc
37	AH1316	—	165.00	225.00	300.00	400.00
	1321	—	165.00	225.00	300.00	400.00
	1322	—	165.00	225.00	300.00	400.00
	1323	—	165.00	225.00	300.00	400.00

Similar to 1 Toman, Y#39.

Y#	Date	Mintage	Fine	VF	XF	Unc
A39	AH1311 (error)		Reported, not confirmed			

Obv: Bust 3/4 left.

Y#	Date	Mintage	Fine	VF	XF	Unc
40	AH1322	—	200.00	300.00	400.00	550.00

Royal Birthday
Obv: Bust 3/4 left.

Y#	Date	Mintage	Fine	VF	XF	Unc
41	AH1322	—	200.00	300.00	400.00	550.00

Obv: Mohammad Ali bust, 1/2 left.

Y#	Date	Mintage	Fine	VF	XF	Unc
55	AH1326	—	—	—	Rare	—

NOTE: 2 Toman pieces of Ahmad Shah are reported dated AH1333 (Y#84) and AH1337 (Y#85); but it cannot at this time be verified if these are indeed coins, or if they are medals.

5 TOMANS

14.3720 gm., .900 GOLD, .4159 oz AGW
The following pieces are noted, but all are believed to be medals:

Y#39 Muzaffar al-din Shah, AH1317 - this is a medal of valor.
Y#51 Muhammad Ali Shah, AH1324 - not seen.
Y#78 Ahmad Shah, AH1332 - not seen.
Y#82 Ahmad Shah, AH1333 - not seen.
Y#86 Ahmad Shah, AH1332 - not seen (probably same as Y#78).
Y#87 Ahmad Shah, AH1334 - This is a medal & bears no denomination.
Y#88 Ahmad Shah, AH1337 - This is a medal & bears no denomination.
Y#89 Ahmad Shah, AH1337 - This is an off-metal strike of the 2000 Dinar coin of Y#72 or 74.

10 TOMANS

28.7440 gm., .900 GOLD, .8317 oz AGW
Obv. leg: First Nasir type. Rev: Lion and sun.

Y#	Date	Mintage	Fine	VF	XF	Unc
—	AH1293	—	—	—	Rare	—

Obv: First portrait of Nasir al-din Shah, AH1296-1297.

Y#	Date	Mintage	Fine	VF	XF	Unc
21	AH1296	—	1500.	2000.	2500.	3350.
	1297	—	1500.	2000.	2500.	3350.
	1301	—	1500.	2000.	2500.	3350.
	1311	—	1500.	2000.	2500.	3350.

Obv: Second portrait of Nasir Al-Din Shah, AH1311.

Y#	Date	Mintage	Fine	VF	XF	Unc
A23	AH1311	—	450.00	500.00	600.00	750.00

NOTE: Restrikes may exist.

Obv: Bust of Muzaffar al-Din, 3/4 left.
Rev: Mouzaffer legend.

Y#	Date	Mintage	Fine	VF	XF	Unc
B34	AH1314	—	1500.	2000.	2500.	3350.

Restrikes may exist.

Obv: Ahmed portrait. Rev: Legend in wreath.

Y#	Date	Mintage	Fine	VF	XF
83	AH1331	—	—	—	—

Rev: Lion and sun.

Y#	Date	Mintage	Fine	VF	XF
91	AH1337	—	—	—	—

NOTE: Gold coins similar to Y#70-72 with values of 2, 58 and 15 Ashrafi are believed to be patterns.

MEDALLIC ISSUES

25 TOMANS

.900 GOLD, 50mm.
Obv. and rev. similar to 10 Krans KM#M4.

KM#	Date	Fine	VF	XF	Unc
M5	AH1301	—	—	—	—

Shah's Return From Europe Commemorative
Obv: First Nasir portrait circled with laurel leaves.

Rev: Legend with crown above and date below.

Y#	Date	Mintage	Fine	VF	XF	Unc
M6	AH1307	—	—	—	Rare	—

NEW COINAGE

5 Dinars = 1 Shahi
100 Dinars = 1 Rial
10 Rials = 1 Toman (unofficial)

DINAR

BRONZE

Y#	Date	Mintage	Fine	VF	XF	Unc
93	SH1310	10.000	1.00	2.50	5.00	8.50

2 DINARS

BRONZE

Y#	Date	Mintage	Fine	VF	XF	Unc
94	SH1310	5.000	1.00	2.50	5.00	8.50

5 DINARS

COPPER-NICKEL

Y#	Date	Mintage	Fine	VF	XF	Unc
97	SH1310	3.750	2.00	4.00	6.00	10.00

COPPER

Y#	Date	Mintage	Fine	VF	XF	Unc
97a	SH1314	.480	12.50	17.50	25.00	50.00

ALUMINUM-BRONZE

Y#	Date	Mintage	Fine	VF	XF	Unc
125	SH1315	5.665	1.00	2.00	4.00	8.50
	1316	Inc. Ab.	.20	.50	1.00	2.00
	1317	13.025	.20	.50	1.00	2.00
	1318	—	.20	.50	1.00	2.00
	1319	—	.20	.50	1.00	2.00
	1320	—	.20	.50	1.00	2.00
	1321	—	.25	.60	1.00	2.00

10 DINARS

COPPER-NICKEL

Y#	Date	Mintage	Fine	VF	XF	Unc
98	SH1310	3.750	2.50	4.00	6.00	10.00

COPPER

Y#	Date	Mintage	Fine	VF	XF	Unc
98a	SH1314	11.350	3.00	6.00	12.50	20.00

ALUMINUM-BRONZE

Y#	Date	Mintage	Fine	VF	XF	Unc
126	SH1315	6.195	1.00	2.00	4.00	8.50
	1316	Inc. Ab.	.20	.75	1.50	3.00
	1317	17.120	.20	.50	1.00	2.00
	1318	—	.20	.50	1.00	2.00
	1319	—	.20	.50	1.00	2.00

Y#	Date	Mintage	Fine	VF	XF	Unc
126	1320	—	.20	.50	1.00	2.00
	1321	—	.20	.75	1.00	2.00

25 DINARS

COPPER-NICKEL

Y#	Date	Mintage	Fine	VF	XF	Unc
99	SH1310	.750	10.00	15.00	25.00	40.00

COPPER

Y#	Date	Mintage	Fine	VF	XF	Unc
99a	SH1314	1.152	15.00	25.00	40.00	60.00

ALUMINUM-BRONZE

Y#	Date	Mintage	Fine	VF	XF	Unc
127	SH1326	—	.75	1.50	3.00	5.00
	1327	—	1.00	2.00	4.00	7.50
	1329	—	.75	1.50	3.00	5.00

Mule: Obv. of 25 Dinars, Y#127 with rev. of Rial, Y#129.

Y#	Date	Mintage	Fine	VF	XF	Unc
127a	1329	—	7.50	12.50	20.00	35.00

1/4 RIAL

SILVER

Y#	Date	Mintage	Fine	VF	XF	Unc
104	SH1315	.600	.50	.75	1.25	1.50

(The second '1' is often short, so that the date looks like 1305).

1/2 RIAL

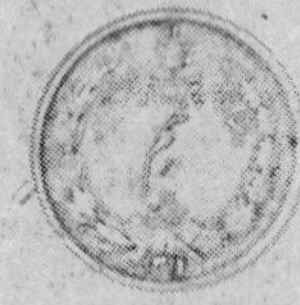

2.5000 gm., .828 SILVER, .0665 oz ASW

Y#	Date	Mintage	Fine	VF	XF	Unc
112	SH1310	2.000	BV	2.00	3.00	4.00
	1311	Reported, Not Confirmed				
	1312	—	BV	2.00	3.00	4.00
	1313	1.945	BV	2.00	3.00	4.00
	1314	.100	2.50	7.50	12.50	18.50
	1315	.800	BV	2.00	3.00	4.00

All 1/2 Rials dated AH1311-1315 are recut dies, usually from AH1310.

10 SHAHIS

COPPER

Y#	Date	Mintage	Fine	VF	XF	Unc
92	SH1314	15.714	3.00	6.00	10.00	18.50

50 DINARS

ALUMINUM-BRONZE

Y#	Date	Mintage	Fine	VF	XF	Unc
128	SH1315	15.968	1.00	2.00	4.00	8.00
	1316	34.200	.25	.75	1.50	3.00
	1317	17.314	.25	.75	1.50	3.00
	1318	—	.25	.75	1.50	3.00
	1319	—	.25	.75	1.50	3.00
	1320	—	.25	.75	1.50	3.00
	1321/0	—	.25	.75	1.50	3.00
	1322/12	—	.50	1.00	2.00	4.00
	1322/0	—	.50	1.00	2.00	4.00
	1322/1	—	.50	1.00	2.00	4.00

COPPER

Y#	Date	Mintage	Fine	VF	XF	Unc
128a	SH1322	—	1.00	3.00	5.00	10.00

ALUMINUM-BRONZE

Y#	Date	Mintage	Fine	VF	XF	Unc
128	SH1331	8.162	.50	1.00	2.00	4.00
	1332	22.892	.50	1.00	2.00	4.00

Reduced thickness

Y#	Date	Mintage	Fine	VF	XF	Unc
137	SH1333	4.036	.25	.50	1.00	2.00
	1334	1.370	.30	.60	1.25	2.50
	1335	.926	.30	.60	1.25	2.50
	1336	-*	.30	.60	1.25	2.50
	1342	.800	.30	.60	1.25	2.50
	1343	1.400	.10	.20	.75	1.50
	1344	1.600	.10	.15	.50	1.00
	1345	1.690	.10	.15	.50	1.00
	1346 153.648**		—	.10	.25	.40
	1347	2.000	—	.10	.15	.20
	1348	1.500	—	.10	.20	.30
	1349	.360	1.00	2.00	3.00	4.00
	1351	—	—	.10	.20	.30
	1353	.060	—	.10	.20	.30
	1354	.016	.20	.30	.40	.60

*Mint reports record 126,500 in SH1337 & 20,000 in SH1338; these were probably dated SH1336.

**Mintage report seems excessive for this and all SH1346 coinage.

BRASS-COATED STEEL

Y#	Date	Mintage	Fine	VF	XF	Unc
137a	MS2535	.027	—	.20	.30	1.00
	2536	—	—	—	.10	.30
	2537	—	—	—	—	—
	SH1357	—	—	—	—	—

NOTE: Sold only in mint sets.

RIAL

5.0000 gm., .828 SILVER, .1331 oz ASW

Y#	Date	Mintage	Fine	VF	XF	Unc
113	SH1310	2.190	BV	BV	4.00	6.00
	1311	10.256	BV	BV	4.00	6.00
	1312	25.768	BV	BV	4.00	6.00
	1313	6.670	BV	BV	4.50	8.00

All coins dated SH1311-13 recut from SH1310.

1.6000 gm., .600 SILVER, .0308 oz ASW

Y#	Date	Mintage	Fine	VF	XF	Unc
129	SH1322	—	BV	1.00	1.50	2.50
	1323	—	BV	1.00	1.50	2.50
	1324	—	BV	1.00	1.50	2.50
	1325	—	BV	1.50	2.00	4.00
	1326	.567	5.00	10.00	15.00	25.00
	1327	5.795	1.00	2.00	3.00	4.00
	1328	1.565	1.00	2.50	4.00	6.00
	1329	.144	4.00	6.00	8.00	11.50
	1330	—	1.50	2.50	4.00	6.00

COPPER-NICKEL

Y#	Date	Mintage	Fine	VF	XF	Unc
138	SH1331	4.735	.10	.50	1.00	1.50
	1332	3.320*	1.00	1.75	3.50	5.00
	1333	16.405	.10	.50	1.00	1.50
	1334	8.980	.10	.50	1.00	1.50
	1335	8.910	.10	.50	1.00	1.50
	1336	4.450	.10	.50	1.00	1.50

*Much rarer than mintage would indicate.

Only the last 2 digits of the date appear on Y#138.

2 gm.

Y#	Date	Mintage	Fine	VF	XF	Unc
A140	SH1337	8.005	.15	.30	.50	1.50

1.75 gm.

Y#	Date	Mintage	Fine	VF	XF	Unc
A140a	SH1338	14.940	.10	.20	.40	.60
	1339	8.400	.10	.20	.40	.60
	1340	8.490	.10	.20	.40	.60
	1341	8.680	.10	.20	.40	.60
	1342	13.332	.10	.15	.25	.40
	1343	14.746	.10	.15	.25	.40
	1344	12.050	.10	.15	.20	.40
	1345	13.786	.10	.15	.20	.40
	1346	155.321	.10	.15	.20	.40
	1347	20.664	.10	.15	.20	.40
	1348	22.960	.10	.15	.20	.30
	1349	19.918	.10	.15	.20	.30
	1350	24.248	.10	.15	.20	.30
	1351/0	21.825	.10	.25	.40	.75
	1351	Inc. Ab.	.10	.15	.20	.30
	1352	31.449	.10	.15	.20	.30
	1353 large date	33.700	.10	.20	.25	.35
	1353 sm.dt.	I.A.	.10	.15	.20	.30
	1354	—	.10	.15	.20	.30
	MS2536	—	.10	.15	.20	.30

COPPER-NICKEL
F.A.O. Coinage

Y#	Date	Mintage	Fine	VF	XF	Unc
152	SH1350	2.770	.10	.15	.25	.40
	1351	8.605	.10	.15	.25	.40
	1353	2.000	.10	.15	.25	.40
	1354	1.000	.10	.15	.25	.40

50th Anniversary of Pahlavi Rule

Y#	Date	Mintage	Fine	VF	XF	Unc
154	MS2535	61.945	—	.10	.20	.30

Obv: ARY AMEHR added to legend.

Y#	Date	Mintage	Fine	VF	XF	Unc
154a	MS2536	—	.10	.15	.25	.50
	2537	—	.10	.15	.25	.50
	SH1357	—	.10	.15	.25	.50

Y#	Date	Mintage	Fine	VF	XF	Unc
162	SH1358	—	.15	.35	.75	1.50

2 RIALS

10.0000 gm., .828 SILVER, .2662 oz ASW

Y#	Date	Mintage	Fine	VF	XF	Unc
114	SH1310	6.145	BV	BV	8.00	10.00
	1311	8.838	BV	BV	8.00	10.00
	1312	19.175	BV	BV	8.00	10.00
	1313	4.015	BV	BV	8.50	11.50

NOTE: All coins dated SH1311-13 recut over SH1310.

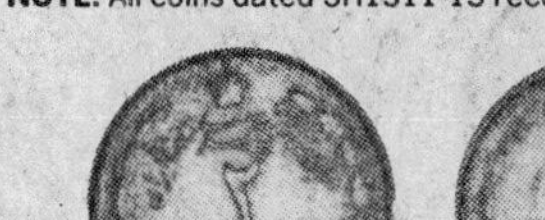

3.2000 gm., .600 SILVER, .0617 oz ASW

Y#	Date	Mintage	Fine	VF	XF	Unc
130	SH1322	—	BV	2.00	3.50	6.00
	1323	—	BV	2.00	2.50	5.00
	1324	—	BV	2.00	2.50	5.00
	1325	—	BV	2.00	2.75	5.50
	1326	.187	10.00	20.00	30.00	50.00
	1327	3.140	BV	2.00	3.00	5.00
	1328	1.198	2.50	5.00	7.50	12.00
	1329	—	2.50	5.00	7.50	12.00
	1330	—	2.50	5.00	7.50	12.00

COPPER-NICKEL

Y#	Date	Mintage	Fine	VF	XF	Unc
139	SH1331	5.335	.40	.75	2.00	4.00
	1332	6.870	.40	.75	2.00	4.00
	1333	13.668	.40	.75	2.00	4.00
	1334	7.185	.40	.75	2.00	4.00
	1335	2.400	.40	.75	2.00	4.00
	1336	.325	1.00	2.00	4.00	8.00

Y#	Date	Mintage	Fine	VF	XF	Unc
B140	SH1338	17.610	.10	.25	.50	1.00
	1339	8.575	.10	.25	.50	.80
	1340	5.668	.10	.25	.50	.80
	1341	5.820	.10	.25	.50	.80
	1342	8.570	.10	.25	.50	.80
	1343	11.250	.10	.25	.50	.80
	1344	5.155	.10	.25	.50	.80
	1345	2.267	.15	.30	.60	1.00
	1346	92.792	—	.15	.20	.25
	1347	10.300	—	.15	.30	.50
	1348	9.319	—	.15	.30	.50
	1349	9.895	—	.15	.20	.30
	1350	9.545	—	.15	.20	.30
	1351	13.305	—	.15	.20	.30
	1352	15.910	—	—	.10	.30
	1353	28.477	—	—	.10	.30
	1354	41.700	—	—	.10	.30
	MS2536	—	—	—	.10	.30

Obv: ARY AMEHR added to legend.

Y#	Date	Mintage	Fine	VF	XF	Unc
B140a	MS2536	—	—	—	.25	.50
	2537	—	—	—	.25	.50
	SH1357	—	—	—	.25	.50

50th Anniversary of Pahlavi Rule

Y#	Date	Mintage	Fine	VF	XF	Unc
155	MS2535	59.568	—	.10	.30	.50

1.7600 gm.

Y#	Date	Mintage	Fine	VF	XF	Unc
163	SH1358	—	—	—	1.00	1.75

5 RIALS

25.0000 gm., .828 SILVER, .6655 oz ASW

Y#	Date	Mintage	Fine	VF	XF	Unc
115	SH1310	5.471	BV	BV	20.00	25.00
	1311	4.527	BV	BV	20.00	25.00
	1312	5.502	BV	BV	20.00	25.00
	1313	1.208	20.00	22.50	27.50	40.00

NOTE: All coins dated SH1311-13 are recut from SH1310.

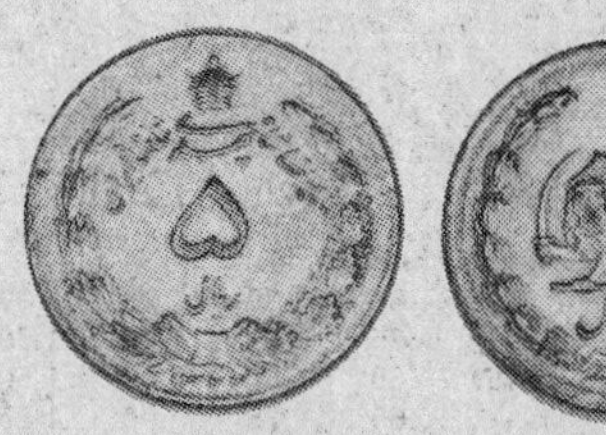

8.0000 gm., .600 SILVER, .1543 oz ASW

Y#	Date	Mintage	Fine	VF	XF	Unc
131	SH1322	—	BV	BV	4.75	6.50
	1323	—	BV	BV	4.75	6.50
	1324	—	BV	BV	4.75	6.50
	1325	—	BV	BV	5.00	7.50
	1326	.061	15.00	25.00	40.00	75.00
	1327	.836	BV	BV	5.50	10.00
	1328	.282	BV	5.00	6.50	12.50
	1329	—	25.00	45.00	75.00	125.00

COPPER-NICKEL

Y#	Date	Mintage	Fine	VF	XF	Unc
140	SH1331	3.660	.50	1.50	3.00	5.00
	1332	16.350	.50	1.00	2.50	3.50
	1333	6.582	.50	1.00	2.50	3.50
	1334	.300	1.00	2.50	5.00	7.50
	1336	1.410	.50	1.50	3.00	5.00

7 gm., 26mm

Y#	Date	Mintage	Fine	VF	XF	Unc
C140	SH1337	3.660	.25	.50	1.00	2.50
	1338	10.467	.25	.60	1.00	2.50

5 gm.

Y#	Date	Mintage	Fine	VF	XF	Unc
C140a	SH1338	Inc. Ab.	.25	.40	.60	1.00
	1339	3.980	.25	.40	.60	1.00
	1340	3.814	.25	.40	.60	1.00
	1341	2.332	.25	.40	.60	1.00
	1342	7.838	.25	.40	.60	1.00
	1343	9.484	.25	.40	.60	1.00
	1344	3.468	.25	.40	.60	1.00
	1345	6.092	.20	.30	.50	.80
	1346	74.781	.20	.30	.50	.80

4.6 gm., 24.5mm
Obv. legend changed, ARYA MEHR added.

Y#	Date	Mintage	Fine	VF	XF	Unc
C140b	SH1347	7.745	.20	.25	.40	.60
	1348	9.193	.20	.25	.40	.60
	1349	7.300	.20	.25	.40	.60
	1350	10.160	.20	.25	.35	.50
	1351	20.582	.20	.25	.30	.40
	1352	23.590	.20	.25	.30	.40
	1353	28.367	.20	.25	.30	.40
	1353 lg. date					
		Inc. Ab.	.20	.25	.30	.40
	1354	27.294	.20	.25	.30	.40
	MS2536	—	.20	.25	.30	.40
	2537	—	.20	.25	.35	.50
	SH1357	—	.20	.25	.35	.50

50th Anniversary of Pahlavi Rule

Y#	Date	Mintage	Fine	VF	XF	Unc
156	MS2535	37.144	.25	.50	.75	1.00

4.5500 gm.

Y#	Date	Mintage	Fine	VF	XF	Unc
164	SH1358	—	.25	.50	1.00	2.00

10 RIALS

16.0000 gm., .600 SILVER, .3086 oz ASW

Y#	Date	Mintage	Fine	VF	XF	Unc
132	SH1323	—	BV	10.00	12.50	15.00
	1324	—	BV	10.00	12.50	15.00
	1325	—	10.00	12.50	14.50	17.50
	1326	—	40.00	75.00	100.00	140.00

Counterfeits are known dated SH1322.

COPPER-NICKEL, 12 gm.

Y#	Date	Mintage	Fine	VF	XF	Unc
D140	SH1334	—	Reported, not confirmed			
	1335	6.225	.50	1.00	2.50	5.00
	1336	4.415	.50	1.00	2.50	5.00
	1337	.715	1.50	3.00	6.00	10.00
	1338	1.210	.50	1.00	2.50	5.00
	1339	2.775	.50	1.00	2.50	5.00
	1340	3.660	.50	1.00	2.50	5.00
	1341	.744	2.50	5.00	10.00	20.00
	1343	6.874	1.50	3.00	6.00	10.00

Thin flan, 9 gm.

Y#	Date	Mintage	Fine	VF	XF	Unc
D140a	SH1341	Inc. D140	1.00	2.50	4.00	8.00
	1342	3.763	.50	1.00	2.50	4.00
	1343	Inc. D140	.50	1.00	1.50	2.50
	1344	1.627	.50	1.00	1.50	2.50

Rev: Value in words.

Y#	Date	Mintage	Fine	VF	XF	Unc
149	SH1345	1.699	.35	.60	1.00	2.50
	1346	38.897	.35	.50	.70	1.00
	1347	8.220	.35	.50	.70	1.00
	1348	7.156	.35	.50	.70	1.00
	1349	7.397	.35	.50	.70	1.00
	1350	8.972	.35	.50	.70	1.00
	1351	9.912	.35	.50	.70	1.00
	1352	28.776	.35	.60	1.00	3.50

Rev: Value in numerals.

Y#	Date	Mintage	Fine	VF	XF	Unc
149a	SH1352	Inc. Ab.	.30	.50	.70	1.00
	1353	22.234	.30	.50	.70	1.00
	1354	23.482	.30	.50	.60	.75
	MS2536	—	.30	.50	.60	.75
	2537	—	.30	.50	.60	.75
	SH1357	—	.30	.50	.60	.75

F.A.O. Coinage

Y#	Date	Mintage	Fine	VF	XF	Unc
150	SH1348	.150	.35	.60	1.00	2.00

50th Anniversary of Pahlavi Rule

Y#	Date	Mintage	Fine	VF	XF	Unc
157	MS2535	29.859	.30	.50	.70	1.00

Y#	Date	Mintage	Fine	VF	XF	Unc
165	SH1358	—	.35	.75	1.25	2.25

1st Anniversary of Revolution

Y#	Date	Mintage	Fine	VF	XF	Unc
167	SH1358	—	.35	.75	1.25	2.25

20 RIALS

COPPER-NICKEL
Rev: Value in words.

Y#	Date	Mintage	Fine	VF	XF	Unc
151	SH1350	2.349	.75	1.00	1.50	2.50
	1351	11.416	.65	.85	1.25	2.00
	1352	7.172	.75	1.00	1.50	2.50

Rev: Value in numerals.

Y#	Date	Mintage	Fine	VF	XF	Unc
151a	SH1352	Inc. Ab.	.65	.85	1.25	2.00
	1353	12.601	.65	.80	1.00	1.50
	1354	16.246	.65	.80	1.00	1.50
	MS2536	—	.65	.75	.90	1.25
	2537	—	.65	.75	.90	1.25
	SH1357	—	.65	.75	.90	1.25

7th Asian Games

Y#	Date	Mintage	Fine	VF	XF	Unc
153	SH1353	Inc. Ab.	.65	.80	1.00	2.50

50th Anniversary of Pahlavi Rule

Y#	Date	Mintage	Fine	VF	XF	Unc
158	MS2535	—	.75	1.25	1.75	2.50

F.A.O. Issue

Y#	Date	Mintage	Fine	VF	XF	Unc
159	MS2535	10.000	.75	1.25	1.75	2.25
	2536	—	1.00	1.50	2.00	3.00

50th Anniversary of Bank Melli

Y#	Date	Mintage	Fine	VF	XF	Unc
160	SH1357	—	.65	.80	1.00	1.50

F.A.O. Issue

Y#	Date	Mintage	Fine	VF	XF	Unc
161	SH1357	5.000	.65	.80	1.00	2.50

8.9600 gm.

Y#	Date	Mintage	Fine	VF	XF	Unc
166	SH1358	—	.65	.85	1.25	2.50

1400th Anniversary of Mohammed's Flight

Y#	Date	Mintage	Fine	VF	XF	Unc
168	SH1358	—	.65	.85	1.25	2.75

25 RIALS

7.5000 gm., .999 SILVER, .2409 oz ASW

KM#	Date	Year	Mintage	XF	Unc	Proof
2	AH1350	1971	6,010	—	—	20.00

50 RIALS

15.0000 gm., .999 SILVER, .4818 oz ASW

KM#	Date	Year	Mintage	XF	Unc	Proof
3	AH1350	1971	5,796	—	—	25.00

75 RIALS

22.5000 gm., .999 SILVER, .7227 oz ASW
Obv: Similar to H#3, 50 Rials.

KM#	Date	Year	Mintage	XF	Unc	Proof
4	AH1350	1971	5,744	—	—	35.00

100 RIALS

30.0000 gm., .999 SILVER, .9636 oz ASW
Obv: Similar to H#3, 50 Rials.

KM#	Date	Year	Mintage	XF	Unc	Proof
5	AH1350	1971	5,755	—	—	40.00

200 RIALS

60.0000 gm., .999 SILVER, 1.9273 oz ASW
Rev: Similar to H#3, 50 Rials.

KM#	Date	Year	Mintage	XF	Unc	Proof
6	AH1350	1971	5,765	—	—	65.00

500 RIALS

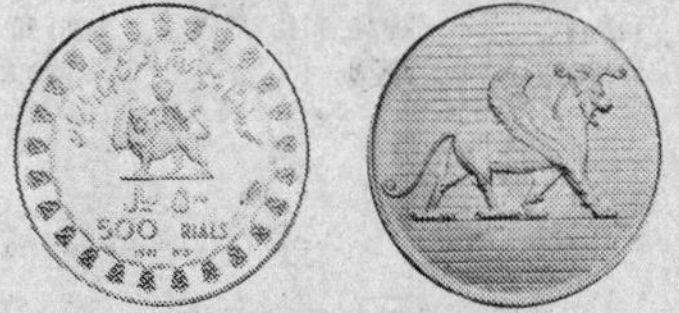

6.5100 gm., .900 GOLD, .1883 oz AGW

KM#	Date	Year	Mintage	XF	Unc	Proof
8	AH1350	1971	4,950	—	—	200.00

750 RIALS

9.7700 gm., .900 GOLD, .2827 oz AGW

KM#	Date	Year	Mintage	XF	Unc	Proof
9	AH1350	1971	4,796	—	—	300.00

1000 RIALS

13.0300 gm., .900 GOLD, .3770 oz AGW

KM#	Date	Year	Mintage	XF	Unc	Proof
10	AH1350	1971	4,759	—	—	400.00

2000 RIALS

26.0600 gm., .900 GOLD, .7541 oz AGW

KM#	Date	Year	Mintage	XF	Unc	Proof
11	AH1350	1971	4,711	—	—	750.00

1/4 PAHLAVI

2.0340 gm., .900 GOLD, 14mm, .0589 oz AGW

Y#	Date	Mintage	Fine	VF	XF	Unc
141	SH1332	.041	BV	BV	40.00	50.00
	1333	.007	BV	40.00	75.00	125.00
	1334	—	BV	BV	40.00	50.00
	1335	.041	BV	BV	40.00	50.00
	Thinner & broader, 16mm					
141a	SH1336	.007	BV	40.00	50.00	60.00
	1337	.033	BV	BV	40.00	45.00
	1338	.136	BV	BV	40.00	45.00
	1339	.156	BV	BV	40.00	45.00
	1340	.060	BV	BV	40.00	45.00
	1342	.080	BV	BV	40.00	50.00
	1343	.040	BV	BV	40.00	50.00
	1344	.030	BV	BV	40.00	50.00
	1345	.040	BV	BV	40.00	50.00
	1346	.030	BV	BV	40.00	45.00
	1347	.060	BV	BV	40.00	45.00
	1348	.060	BV	BV	40.00	45.00
	1349	.080	BV	BV	40.00	45.00
	1350	.080	BV	BV	40.00	45.00
	1351	.103	BV	BV	40.00	45.00
	1352	.050	BV	BV	40.00	45.00
141a	1353	—	BV	BV	40.00	45.00
	Obv. leg: ARYAMEHR added.					
141b	1354	.106	BV	BV	40.00	45.00
	1355	.186	BV	BV	40.00	45.00
	MS2536	—	BV	BV	40.00	45.00
	2537	—	BV	BV	40.00	45.00

1/2 PAHLAVI

4.0680 gm., .900 GOLD, .1177 oz AGW

Y#	Date	Mintage	Fine	VF	XF	Unc
123	SH1310	696 pcs.	BV	BV	90.00	125.00
	1311	286 pcs.	BV	BV	90.00	125.00
	1312	892 pcs.	BV	BV	90.00	125.00
	1313	531 pcs.	BV	BV	90.00	125.00
	1315	1,042	BV	BV	90.00	125.00

Y#	Date	Mintage	Fine	VF	XF	Unc
133	SH1322	—	BV	BV	80.00	90.00
	1323	.076	BV	BV	80.00	90.00
	1324	—	BV	BV	80.00	90.00
	Obv: High relief head.					
135	SH1324	—	BV	BV	80.00	90.00
	1325	—	BV	BV	80.00	90.00
	1326	.036	BV	BV	80.00	90.00
	1327	.036	BV	BV	80.00	90.00
	1328	—	BV	BV	80.00	90.00
	1329	75 pcs.	90.00	120.00	150.00	175.00
	1330	.098	BV	BV	80.00	90.00

Obv: Low relief head.

Y#	Date	Mintage	Fine	VF	XF	Unc
142	SH1330	Inc. Ab.	BV	BV	80.00	90.00
	1334	—	BV	85.00	100.00	125.00
	1335	—	BV	85.00	100.00	125.00
	1336	.132	BV	BV	80.00	90.00
	1337	.102	BV	BV	80.00	90.00
	1338	.140	BV	BV	80.00	90.00
	1339	.142	BV	BV	80.00	90.00
	1340	.439	BV	BV	80.00	90.00
	1342	.040	BV	BV	80.00	90.00
	1343	.040	BV	BV	80.00	90.00
	1344	.030	BV	BV	80.00	90.00
	1345	.040	BV	BV	80.00	90.00
	1346	.040	BV	BV	80.00	90.00
	1347	.050	BV	BV	80.00	90.00
	1348	.040	BV	BV	80.00	90.00
	1349	.080	BV	BV	80.00	90.00
	1350	.080	BV	BV	80.00	90.00
	1351	.103	BV	BV	80.00	90.00
	1352	.067	BV	BV	80.00	90.00
	1353	—	BV	BV	80.00	90.00
	Obv. leg: ARYAMEHR added.					
142a	1354	.037	BV	BV	80.00	90.00
	1355	.153	BV	BV	80.00	90.00
	MS2536	—	BV	BV	80.00	90.00
	2537	—	BV	BV	80.00	90.00

PAHLAVI

1.9180 gm., .900 GOLD, .0555 oz AGW

Y#	Date	Mintage	Fine	VF	XF	Unc
116	SH1305	5,000	100.00	150.00	225.00	325.00

Y#	Date	Mintage	Fine	VF	XF	Unc
120	SH1306	.021	80.00	90.00	120.00	150.00
	1307	5,000	85.00	100.00	140.00	200.00
	1308	989 pcs.	100.00	135.00	185.00	250.00

8.1360 gm., .900 GOLD, .2354 oz AGW

Y#	Date	Mintage	Fine	VF	XF	Unc
124	SH1310	304 pcs.	165.00	250.00	375.00	550.00

Y#	Date	Mintage	Fine	VF	XF	Unc
134	SH1322	—	BV	BV	160.00	175.00
	1323	.311	BV	BV	160.00	175.00
	1324	—	BV	BV	160.00	175.00

Obv: High relief head.

Y#	Date	Mintage	Fine	VF	XF	Unc
136	SH1324	—	BV	BV	160.00	175.00
	1325	—	BV	BV	160.00	175.00
	1326	.151	BV	BV	160.00	175.00
	1327	.020	BV	BV	160.00	175.00
	1328	4,000	BV	BV	185.00	200.00
	1329	4,000	BV	BV	185.00	200.00
	1330	.048	BV	BV	160.00	175.00

Obv: Low relief head.

Y#	Date	Mintage	Fine	VF	XF	Unc
143	SH1330	—	BV	BV	160.00	175.00
	1333	—	Reported, not confirmed			
	1334	—	BV	BV	160.00	175.00
	1335	—	BV	BV	160.00	175.00
	1336	.453	BV	BV	160.00	175.00
	1337	.665	BV	BV	160.00	175.00
	1338	.776	BV	BV	160.00	175.00
	1339	.847	BV	BV	160.00	175.00
	1340	.528	BV	BV	160.00	175.00
	1342	.020	BV	BV	175.00	225.00
	1343	.010	BV	BV	175.00	225.00
	1344	—	BV	BV	160.00	175.00
	1345	.020	BV	BV	175.00	225.00
	1346	.030	BV	BV	160.00	175.00
	1347	.040	BV	BV	160.00	175.00
	1348	.070	BV	BV	160.00	175.00
	1349	.070	BV	BV	160.00	175.00
	1350	.060	BV	BV	160.00	175.00
	1351	.100	BV	BV	160.00	175.00
	1352	.320	BV	BV	160.00	175.00
	1353	—	BV	BV	160.00	175.00

Obv. leg: ARYAMEHR added.

Y#	Date	Mintage	Fine	VF	XF	Unc
143a	SH1354	.021	BV	BV	160.00	175.00
	1355	.203	BV	BV	160.00	175.00
	MS2536	—	BV	BV	160.00	175.00
	2537	—	BV	BV	160.00	175.00

2 PAHLAVI

3.8360 gm., .900 GOLD, .1110 oz AGW

Y#	Date	Mintage	Fine	VF	XF	Unc
117	SH1305	1,134	175.00	250.00	350.00	500.00

Y#	Date	Mintage	Fine	VF	XF	Unc
121	SH1306	2,494	75.00	90.00	125.00	225.00
	1307	7,000	75.00	90.00	125.00	225.00
	1308	749 pcs.	150.00	225.00	325.00	450.00

2-1/2 PAHLAVI

20.3400 gm., .900 GOLD, .5885 oz AGW

Y#	Date	Mintage	Fine	VF	XF	Unc
144	SH1339	.002	BV	BV	425.00	450.00
	1340	.003	BV	BV	425.00	450.00
	1342	30 pcs.	—	—	Rare	—
	1347	.002	BV	BV	425.00	450.00
	1348	—	BV	BV	425.00	450.00
	1349	3,000	BV	BV	425.00	450.00
	1350	—	BV	BV	400.00	425.00
	1351	.003	BV	BV	400.00	425.00
	1352	.003	BV	BV	400.00	425.00
	1353	—	BV	BV	400.00	425.00

Obv. leg: ARYAMEHR added.

Y#	Date	Mintage	Fine	VF	XF	Unc
144a	SH1354	.018	BV	BV	400.00	425.00
	1355	.016	BV	BV	400.00	425.00
	MS2536	—	BV	BV	400.00	425.00
	2537	—	BV	BV	400.00	425.00

5 PAHLAVI

9.5900 gm., .900 GOLD, .2775 oz AGW

Y#	Date	Mintage	Fine	VF	XF	Unc
118	SH1305	271 pcs.	500.00	650.00	850.00	1100.

Y#	Date	Mintage	Fine	VF	XF	Unc
122	SH1306	909 pcs.	400.00	500.00	650.00	850.00
	1307	785 pcs.	400.00	500.00	650.00	850.00
	1308	121 pcs.	500.00	600.00	750.00	1000.

40.6799 gm., .900 GOLD, 1.1772 oz AGW

Y#	Date	Mintage	Fine	VF	XF	Unc
145	SH1339	.002	BV	BV	775.00	800.00
	1340	.002	BV	BV	775.00	800.00
	1342	20 pcs.	—	—	Rare	—
	1347	500 pcs.	BV	BV	775.00	1000.
	1348	.002	BV	BV	775.00	800.00
	1349	700 pcs.	BV	BV	775.00	1000.
	1350	.002	BV	BV	775.00	800.00
	1351	.003	BV	BV	775.00	800.00
	1352	.002	BV	BV	775.00	800.00
	1353	—	BV	BV	775.00	800.00

Obv. leg: ARYAMEHR added

Y#	Date	Mintage	Fine	VF	XF	Unc
145a	SH1354	.010	BV	BV	775.00	800.00
	1355	.017	BV	BV	775.00	800.00
	MS2536	—	BV	BV	775.00	800.00
	2537	—	BV	BV	775.00	800.00

NOTE: Beware of 1339 and 1340 counterfeits which have portrait in very flat relief.

10 PAHLAVI

81.3598 gm., .900 GOLD, 2.3544 oz AGW
50th Anniversary of Pahlavi Rule

Y#	Date	Mintage	Fine	VF	XF	Unc
—	MS2535	—	—	1550.	1650.	1800.
	2536	—	—	1550.	1650.	1800.

Similar to 5 Pahlavi, Y#145a.

Y#	Date	Mintage	Fine	VF	XF	Unc
—	MS2537	—	—	1550.	1650.	1800.
	SH1358	—	—	1550.	1650.	1800.

NCLT ISSUES

PATTERNS

KM#	Date	Mintage	Identification	Mkt.Val.
1	AH1293	—	500 Dinars, Silver	—
2	AH1319	—	500 Dinars, Silver, Y30	—
3	AH1319	—	1000 Dinars, Silver, Y31	—
4	AH1381	—	25 Dinars, Bronze	—
5	AH1381	—	50 Dinars, Bronze	—
6	AH1381	—	1/4 Kran, Silver	—
7	AH1381	—	500 Dinars, Silver	—
8	AH1381	—	1000 Dinars, Silver	—
9	AH1381	—	2000 Dinars, Silver	—

MINT SETS

KM#	Date	Mintage	Identification	Issue Price	Mkt. Val.
S1	SH1342(4)	—	YA140a,B140,C140a,D14a	—	—
S2	SH1343(4)	—	YA140a,B140,C140a,d140a	—	—
S3	SH1348(5)	—	Y137,140a,B140,C140b,149	2.00	—
S4	SH1350(5)	—	Y137,140a,B140,C140b,149	2.00	—
S5	SH1353(6)	—	Y137, 140a, B140, C140b, 149a, 151a	2.00	—
S6	SH1354(6)	—	Y137,140a,B140,C140b,149a,151a	2.00	—
S7	MS2535(6)	—	Y137a,154-158	2.50	—
S8	MS2536	—	—	2.50	—

PROOF SETS

STANDARD METALS

KM#	Date	Mintage	Identification	Issue Price	Mkt. Val.
101	1928(4)	20	Y10, 11*	—	—
102	1971(9)	—	KM2-6, 8-11	261.50	1500.
103	1971(5)	—	KM2-6	59.50	185.00

*Two each type.

IRAQ

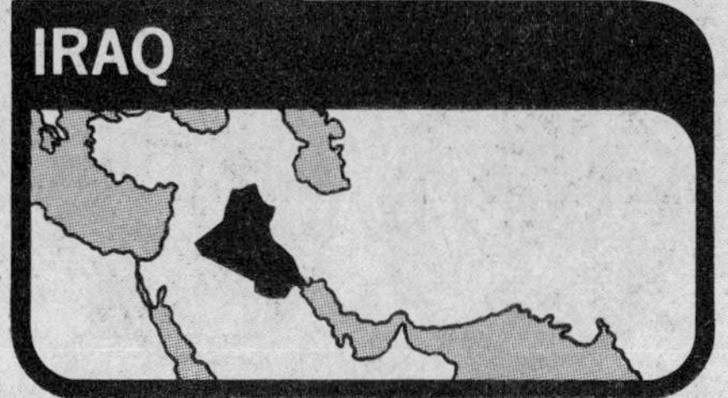

The Republic of Iraq, historically known as Mesopotamia, is located in the Near East and is bordered by Kuwait, Iran, Turkey, Syria, Jordan and Saudi Arabia. It has an area of 172,000 sq. mi. (445,000 sq. km.) and a population of 12.2 million. Capital: Baghdad. The economy of Iraq is based on agriculture and petroleum. Crude oil accounts for 94 percent of the exports.

Iraq was the site of a number of flourishing civilizations of antiquity - Sumerian, Assyrian, Babylonian, Parthian, Persian - and of the Biblical cities of Ur, Nineveh and Babylon. Desired because of its favored location which embraced the fertile alluvial plains of the Tigris and Euphrates Rivers, Mesopotamia - 'land between the rivers' - was conquered by Cyrus the Great of Persia, Alexander of Macedonia and by Arabs who made the legendary city of Baghdad the capital of the ruling caliphate. Great Britain, given a League of Nations mandate over the territory in 1920, recognized Iraq as a kingdom in 1922. Iraq became an independent constitutional monarchy presided over by the Hashemite family, direct descendants of the prophet Mohammed, in 1932. In 1958, the army-led revolution of July 14 overthrew the monarchy and proclaimed a republic.

NOTE: The 'I' mintmark on 1938 and 1943 issues appears on the obverse near the point of the bust. Some of the issues of 1938 have a dot to denote a composition change from nickel to copper-nickel.

RULERS

Abdul Hamid I,
AH1187-1203/AD1773-1789
Faisal I, 1921-1933
Ghazi I, 1933-1939
Faisal II, 1939-1958

MINTMARKS

I - Bombay

MONETARY SYSTEM

50 Fils = 1 Dirham
200 Fils = 1 Riyal
1000 Fils = 1 Dinar (Pound)

PROVINCIAL COINAGE

OTTOMAN EMPIRE

MONETARY SYSTEM

40 Para = 1 Piastre (Kurus)

MAHMUD II

AH1223-55/AD1808-39

NOTE: The denominations of the following coins are tentative, and all authorities are not in agreement of the classification. Until a better system is available, that of C.Olcer will be followed. Most types are similar to Turkish coins, but with mint name Baghdad.

*Coins omitted by Craig are given numbers to Olcer (O#'s).

FALS

The copper coins (Fals) of Mahmud II were probably valued at 5 Para (1/8 Piastre), but no definite information is available. Some bear AH dates, others have AH1223 (accessional) and regnal year.

COPPER, 16-23mm
Obv: Toughra. Rev: Mint and date.

C#	Date	Year	Good	VG	Fine	VF
118	AH1238	—	5.00	10.00	18.50	27.50
	1240	—	5.00	10.00	18.50	27.50
	1241	—	5.00	10.00	18.50	27.50
	1244	—	5.00	10.00	18.50	27.50

17-25mm
Rev: Star and crescent within hexagram

C#	Date	Year	Good	VG	Fine	VF
125	AH1223	22	5.00	10.00	18.50	27.50
	1223	25	5.00	10.00	20.00	30.00

Rev: Star and crescent only, 21-25mm.

C#	Date	Year	Good	VG	Fine	VF
127	AH1223	25	6.00	12.00	20.00	30.00
139	AH1223	26	5.00	10.00	17.50	26.50

Rev: Hexagram only, 29mm.

C#	Date	Year	Good	VG	Fine	VF
141	AH1248	—	6.00	12.50	20.00	30.00

20-22mm Obv: Toughra within wavy border
Rev: Mint and date within wavy border

C#	Date	Year	Good	VG	Fine	VF
*485a	AH1223	28	2.50	5.00	10.00	16.50

5 PARA

BILLON, 0.80gm., 18mm

C#	Date	Year	Good	VG	Fine	VF
150	AH1223	17	6.00	12.50	22.50	32.50

10 PARA

BILLON, 24mm, 2.1 gm.
Obv: Toughra. Rev: Mint and date within beaded borders.

C#	Date	Year	Good	VG	Fine	VF
152	AH1223	13	4.50	9.00	16.50	26.50

26mm, 1.6-1.8 gm.
Obv: Toughra, mint and date. Rev: 4-line legend.

C#	Date	Year	Good	VG	Fine	VF
*413	AH1223	15	5.00	10.00	17.50	27.50
*420b	AH1223	17	6.00	12.50	20.00	28.50

(Ornamental border added on #420b)

22mm, 1.4 gm.
Similar to C#152, but floral borders.

C#	Date	Year	Good	VG	Fine	VF
*420	AH1223	17	6.00	12.50	20.00	28.50

20 PARA

BILLON, 28mm, 3.5-4.2 gm.
Obv: Toughra. Rev: Mint and date within beaded borders.

C#	Date	Year	Good	VG	Fine	VF
159	AH1223	13	5.00	10.00	20.00	30.00

27mm, 3.2 gm.
Obv: Toughra, mint and date. Rev: 4-line legend.

C#	Date	Year	Good	VG	Fine	VF
165	AH1223	15	5.00	10.00	20.00	30.00

28mm, 3.0 gm.
Similar to C#159, but floral borders.

C#	Date	Year	Good	VG	Fine	VF
166	AH1223	17	5.00	10.00	20.00	30.00

Reduced weight; 22mm, 1.2-1.6 gm.

C#	Date	Year	Good	VG	Fine	VF
*435	AH1223	21	5.00	10.00	20.00	30.00

22mm, 1.8-2.0 gm.
Similar to C#159, but extra legends around central design.

C#	Date	Year	Good	VG	Fine	VF
*437	AH1223	22	5.00	10.00	20.00	30.00

Similar to C#165, 26mm, 2.0 gm.

C#	Date	Year	Good	VG	Fine	VF
*438	AH1223	22	5.00	10.00	20.00	30.00

30 PARA(ZOLTA)

BILLON, 31mm, 4.5 gm.
Obv. and rev.: 4-line legend.

C#	Date	Year	Good	VG	Fine	VF
170	AH1223	15	7.50	15.00	30.00	45.00

PIASTRE (40 PARA)

BILLON, 31mm, 8.0-9.5 gm.
Obv: Toughra. Rev: Mint and date with beaded borders.

C#	Date	Year	Good	VG	Fine	VF
*402	AH1223	13	6.00	12.50	25.00	40.00

Reduced weight; 29mm, 3.2-4.0 gm.

C#	Date	Year	Good	VG	Fine	VF
168	AH1223	21	6.00	12.50	25.00	40.00

Extra legends added around central device.

C#	Date	Year	Good	VG	Fine	VF
*436	AH1223	21	6.00	12.50	25.00	40.00

100 PARA

BILLON, 31mm, 3.0-3.2 gm.

C#	Date	Year	Good	VG	Fine	VF
*455	AH1223	26	10.00	20.00	35.00	50.00

5 PIASTRES

BILLON, 36mm, 5.5-6.9 gm.

C#	Date	Year	Good	VG	Fine	VF
175	AH1223	26	7.50	15.00	25.00	40.00
	—	27	7.50	15.00	25.00	40.00

HAYRIYE ALTIN

GOLD, 21mm, 1.4 gm.

C#	Date	Year	Good	VG	Fine	VF
185	AH1223	25	50.00	100.00	185.00	275.00

Governor Sait Pasa

Coins Without Name Or Toughra Of Mahmud II

2 PARA

COPPER, 15-18mm
Lion, mint and date

C#	Date	Year	Good	VG	Fine	VF
101	AH1230	—	8.50	16.50	30.00	50.00

5 PARA

COPPER, 27mm
Obv: Name of Sait Pasa within octagram.

C#	Date	Year	Good	VG	Fine	VF
111	AH1231	—	8.50	16.50	30.00	50.00

NOTE: This is the only Ottoman coin ever struck with a governor's name. Sait Pasa was beheaded for this infringement of tradition.

Obv: Tamgha within octogram.

C#	Date	Year	Good	VG	Fine	VF
111a	AH1231	—	6.00	12.50	22.50	37.50

NOTE: The Tamgha was originally a sheep and cattle brand, later seal or brand. Each Turkish clan formerly kept its own Tamgha, to use both as a brand and as a seal on documents.

Abdul Mejid

AH1255-1277/AD1839-1861

5 PARA (?)

BILLON, 19-21mm

C#	Date	Year	Good	VG	Fine	VF
201	AH1255	1	20.00	40.00	65.00	100.00

IRAQ

FILS

BRONZE

Y#	Date	Mintage	Fine	VF	XF	Unc
1	1931	4.000	.75	1.50	2.50	10.00
	1933	6.000	.50	1.00	2.00	8.00

Y#	Date	Mintage	Fine	VF	XF	Unc
8	1936	3.000	1.00	2.00	4.00	10.00
	1938	36.000	.25	.35	.60	1.50
	1938-I	3.000	.50	1.00	3.00	5.00

Y#	Date	Mintage	Fine	VF	XF	Unc
15	1953	41.000	.25	.40	.60	1.00
	1953	200 pcs.	—	—	Proof	25.00

Y#	Date	Mintage	Fine	VF	XF	Unc
24	1959	72.000	.15	.25	.40	.75
	1959	400 pcs.	—	—	Proof	20.00

2 FILS

BRONZE

Y#	Date	Mintage	Fine	VF	XF	Unc
2	1931	2.500	1.25	2.50	5.00	12.50
	1933	1.000	1.50	3.00	7.50	17.50

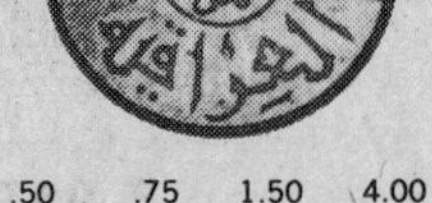

Y#	Date	Mintage	Fine	VF	XF	Unc
16	1953	.500	.50	.75	1.50	4.00
	1953	200 pcs.	—	—	Proof	30.00

4 FILS

NICKEL

Y#	Date	Mintage	Fine	VF	XF	Unc
3	1931	4.500	1.00	2.00	4.50	17.50
	1933	6.500	1.00	2.00	4.50	17.50

Y#	Date	Mintage	Fine	VF	XF	Unc
9	1938	1.000	1.50	2.50	5.00	12.50
	1939	1.000	2.50	4.00	8.00	15.00

COPPER-NICKEL

Y#	Date	Mintage	Fine	VF	XF	Unc
9a	1938	2.750	.75	1.00	1.50	5.50
	1938-I	2.500	1.00	2.00	4.50	12.50

BRONZE

Y#	Date	Mintage	Fine	VF	XF	Unc
9b	1938	8.000	.50	.75	1.50	2.50

Y#	Date	Mintage	Fine	VF	XF	Unc
13	1943-I	1.500	2.00	3.00	5.00	12.50

COPPER-NICKEL

Y#	Date	Mintage	Fine	VF	XF	Unc
17	1953	20.750	.60	.75	.90	1.50
	1953	200 pcs.	—	—	Proof	35.00

5 FILS

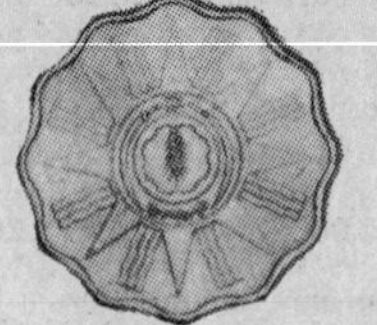

COPPER-NICKEL

Y#	Date	Mintage	Fine	VF	XF	Unc
25	1959	30.000	.15	.25	.50	1.00
	1959	400 pcs.	—	—	Proof	25.00

Y#	Date	Mintage	Fine	VF	XF	Unc
31	1967	17.000	.15	.25	.35	.50
	1971	15.000	.15	.25	.35	.50

STAINLESS STEEL

Y#	Date	Mintage	Fine	VF	XF	Unc
31a	1971	2.000	.20	.30	.50	.75
	1974	15.000	—	.15	.25	.35
	1975	75.600	—	.15	.25	.35

F.A.O. Issue

Y#	Date	Mintage	Fine	VF	XF	Unc
47	1975	2.000	—	.15	.25	.35

10 FILS

NICKEL

Y#	Date	Mintage	Fine	VF	XF	Unc
4	1931	2.400	2.00	5.00	7.50	20.00
	1933	2.200	2.00	5.00	7.50	20.00

Y#	Date	Mintage	Fine	VF	XF	Unc
10	1937	.400	4.00	6.00	12.50	25.00
	1938	.600	3.00	5.00	10.00	20.00

COPPER-NICKEL

Y#	Date	Mintage	Fine	VF	XF	Unc
10a	1938 dot	1.100	1.00	2.00	4.00	10.00
	1938-I	1.500	1.50	2.50	6.00	15.00

BRONZE

Y#	Date	Mintage	Fine	VF	XF	Unc
10b	1938 dot	8.250	.75	1.00	2.00	5.00

Y#	Date	Mintage	Fine	VF	XF	Unc
14	1943-I	1.500	3.00	5.00	8.00	16.50

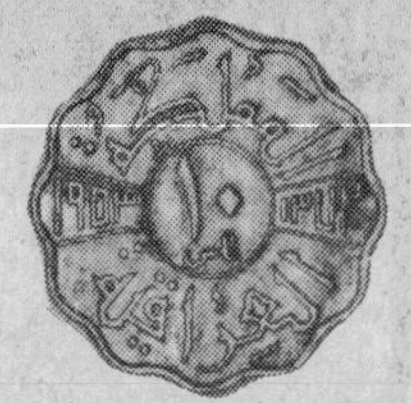

COPPER-NICKEL

Y#	Date	Mintage	Fine	VF	XF	Unc
18	1953	11.400	.50	.75	1.00	2.50
	1953	200 pcs.	—	—	Proof	40.00

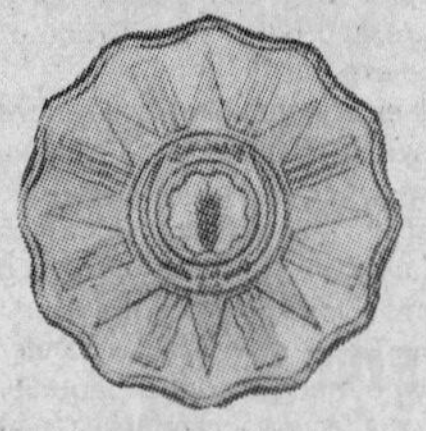

Y#	Date	Mintage	Fine	VF	XF	Unc
26	1959	24.000	.20	.30	.50	1.00
	1959	400 pcs.	—	—	Proof	30.00

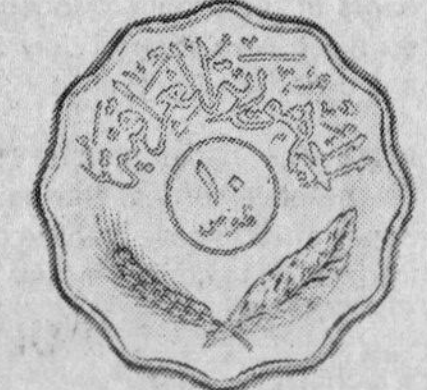

Y#	Date	Mintage	Fine	VF	XF	Unc
32	1967	13.400	.15	.25	.35	.60
	1971	12.000	.15	.25	.35	.60

STAINLESS STEEL

Y#	Date	Mintage	Fine	VF	XF	Unc
32a	1971	1.550	.15	.25	.35	.60
	1974	12.000	.15	.25	.35	.50
	1975	49.800	.15	.25	.35	.50

F.A.O. Issue

Y#	Date	Mintage	Fine	VF	XF	Unc
48	1975	1.000	.15	.25	.35	.50

20 FILS

3.6000 gm., .500 SILVER, .0579 oz ASW

Y#	Date	Mintage	Fine	VF	XF	Unc
5	1931	1.500	2.00	4.00	12.50	20.00
	1931	—	—		Specimen	—
	1933	1.100	2.00	4.00	12.50	25.00
	1933 (error) 1252	Inc. Ab.	10.00	20.00	40.00	85.00

Y#	Date	Mintage	Fine	VF	XF	Unc
11	1938	1.200	1.75	2.50	5.00	12.50
	1938-I	1.350	1.75	2.50	5.00	12.50

Y#	Date	Mintage	Fine	VF	XF	Unc
19	1953	.250	25.00	35.00	65.00	100.00
	1953	200 pcs.	—	—	Proof	45.00

Y#	Date	Mintage	Fine	VF	XF	Unc
22	1955	4.000	2.00	4.00	6.00	10.00
	1955	—	—	—	Proof	—

25 FILS

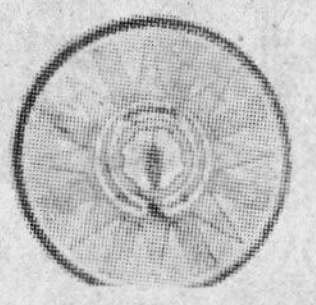

2.5000 gm., .500 SILVER, .0401 oz ASW

Y#	Date	Mintage	Fine	VF	XF	Unc
27	1959	12.000	BV	BV	1.50	3.00
	1959	400 pcs.	—	—	Proof	35.00

COPPER-NICKEL

Y#	Date	Mintage	Fine	VF	XF	Unc
33	1969	6.000	.15	.25	.35	.50
	1970	6.000	.15	.25	.35	.50
	1972	12.000	.15	.25	.35	.50
	1975	48.000	.15	.25	.35	.50

50 FILS

9.0000 gm., .500 SILVER, .1447 oz ASW

Y#	Date	Mintage	Fine	VF	XF	Unc
6	1931	8.800	4.50	6.50	10.00	20.00
	1933	.800	6.00	10.00	15.00	30.00

Y#	Date	Mintage	Fine	VF	XF	Unc
12	1937	1.200	4.50	6.50	10.00	20.00
	1938	5.300	BV	4.50	6.50	10.00
	1938-I	7.500	BV	4.50	6.50	10.00

Y#	Date	Mintage	Fine	VF	XF	Unc
20	1953	.560	15.00	25.00	50.00	75.00
	1953	200 pcs.	—	—	Proof	50.00

Y#	Date	Mintage	Fine	VF	XF	Unc
23	1955	12.000	BV	5.00	7.50	10.00
	1955	—	—	—	Proof	—

5.0000 gm., .500 SILVER, .0803 oz ASW

Y#	Date	Mintage	Fine	VF	XF	Unc
28	1959	24.000	BV	BV	2.50	5.00
	1959	400 pcs.	—	—	Proof	75.00

COPPER-NICKEL

Y#	Date	Mintage	Fine	VF	XF	Unc
34	1969	12.000	.20	.30	.50	.75
	1970	12.000	.20	.30	.50	.75
	1972	12.000	.20	.30	.50	.75
	1975	36.000	.20	.30	.50	.75

100 FILS

10.0000gm., .500 SILVER, .1607 oz ASW

Y#	Date	Mintage	Fine	VF	XF	Unc
21	1953	1.200	BV	5.00	10.00	20.00
	1953	200 pcs.	—	—	Proof	85.00

Y#	Date	Mintage	Fine	VF	XF	Unc
A24	1955	1.000	—	—	Rare	—
	1955	—	—	—	Proof	—

Y#	Date	Mintage	Fine	VF	XF	Unc
29	1959	6.000	2.25	2.75	3.50	5.00
	1959	400 pcs.	—	—	Proof	125.00

COPPER-NICKEL

Y#	Date	Mintage	Fine	VF	XF	Unc
35	1970	6.000	.35	.50	.75	1.00
	1972	6.000	.35	.50	.75	1.00
	1975	12.000	.35	.50	.75	1.00

RIYAL(200 FILS)

20.0000 gm., .500 SILVER, .3215 oz ASW

Y#	Date	Mintage	Fine	VF	XF	Unc
7	1932	.500	BV	12.50	25.00	60.00
	1932	—	—	—	Proof	Rare

250 FILS

NICKEL

F.A.O.Issue

Y#	Date	Mintage	Fine	VF	XF	Unc
36	1970	.500	1.50	2.50	4.00	6.00
	1970	1,000	—	—	Proof	15.00

Edge inscription-FAO-250-repeated three times.

1st Anniversary Peace With Kurds

Y#	Date	Mintage	Fine	VF	XF	Unc
40	1971	.500	1.50	2.50	4.00	6.00
	1971	1,000	—	—	Proof	15.00

Al Baath Party

Y#	Date	Mintage	Fine	VF	XF	Unc
41	1972	.250	2.00	4.00	6.00	10.00

25th Anniversary of Central Bank

Y#	Date	Mintage	Fine	VF	XF	Unc
42	1972	.250	2.00	4.00	6.00	10.00

Oil Nationalization

Y#	Date	Mintage	Fine	VF	XF	Unc
44	1973	.260	2.00	4.00	6.00	10.00
	1973	5,000	—	—	Proof	9.00

International Year of the Child

Y#	Date	Mintage	Fine	VF	XF	Unc
50	1979	.010	—	—	Proof	7.50

500 FILS

NICKEL
50th Anniversary of Iraqi Army

Y#	Date	Mintage	Fine	VF	XF	Unc
37	1971	.100	3.00	6.00	9.00	12.50
	1971	5,000	—	—	Proof	15.00

20.0000gm., .500 SILVER, .3215oz ASW
Oil Nationalization

Y#	Date	Mintage	Fine	VF	XF	Unc
45	1973	.260	BV	BV	10.00	12.50
	1973	5,000	—		Proof	15.00

DINAR

31.0000 gm., .900 SILVER, .8971 oz ASW
50th Anniversary of Iraqi Army

Y#	Date	Mintage	Fine	VF	XF	Unc
38	1971	.020	BV	BV	27.50	30.00

25th Anniversary of Central Bank

Y#	Date	Mintage	Fine	VF	XF	Unc
43	1972	.050	BV	BV	27.50	30.00
	1972	—	—	—	Proof	40.00

Oil Nationalization

Y#	Date	Mintage	Fine	VF	XF	Unc
46	1973	.060	BV	BV	27.50	30.00
	1973	5,000	—	—	Proof	40.00

1st Anniversary of Tharthat-Euphrates Canal

Y#	Date	Mintage	Fine	VF	XF	Unc
49	1977	7,000	—	—	Proof	35.00

International Year of the Child

Y#	Date	Mintage	Fine	VF	XF	Unc
51	1979	5,000	—	—	—	35.00

5 DINARS

13.5700gm., .917 GOLD, .4001oz AGW
50th Anniversary of Iraqi Army

Y#	Date	Mintage	Fine	VF	XF	Unc
39	1971	.020	BV	BV	265.00	275.00

NCLT ISSUES

MEDALLIC ISSUES

37.50000gm., .500 SILVER, .6028oz ASW

Y#	Date	Mintage	Fine	VF	XF	Unc
(30)	1959	.500	BV	BV	20.00	25.00
	1959	—	—	—	Proof	30.00

NOTE: This piece does not carry a designation of value and is considered a medal by most athorities.

PATTERNS

KM#	Date	Mintage	Identification	Mkt.Val.
1	1935	—	20 Fils,Y11	—
2	1935	—	50 Fils, Y12	—
3	1936	—	2 Fils, Y2	—
4	1936	—	4 Fils, Y9	—
5	1936	—	10 Fils, Y10	—
6	1936	—	20 Fils, Y11	—
7	1936	—	50 Fils, Y12	—

PROOF SETS
STANDARD METALS

KM#	Date	Mintage	Identification	Issue Price	Mkt. Val.
101	1953(7)	200	Y15-21	—	225.00
102	1955(3)	—	Y22,23,A24	—	—
103	1959(6)	400	Y24-29	—	375.00
104	1959(7)	—	Y24-30	—	—
106	1973(3)	5,000	Y44-46	—	62.50

IRELAND

Ireland, which occupies five-sixths of the island of Ireland located in the Atlantic Ocean west of Great Britain, has an area of 27,136 sq. mi. (70,282 sq. km.) and a population of 3 million. Capital: Dublin. Agriculture and dairy farming are the principal industries. Meat, livestock, dairy products and textiles are exported.

A race of tall, red-haired Celts from Gaul arrived in Ireland about 400 B.C., assimilated the native Erainn and Picts, and established a Gaelic civilization. After the arrival of St. Patrick in A.D. 432, Ireland evolved into a center of Latin learning which sent missionaries to Europe and possibly North America. In 1154, Pope Adrian IV gave all of Ireland to English King Henry II to administer as a Papal fief. Because of the enactment of anti-Catholic laws and the awarding of vast tracts of Irish land to Protestant absentee landowners, English control did not become reasonably absolute until 1800 when England and Ireland became the 'United Kingdom of Great Britain and Ireland'. Religious freedom was restored to the Irish in 1829, but agitation for political autonomy continued until the Irish Free State was established as a dominion on Dec. 6, 1921. Ireland withdrew from the Commonwealth and proclaimed itself a republic on April 18, 1949. The government, however, does not use the term "Republic of Ireland," which tacitly acknowledges the partitioning of the island into Ireland and Northern Ireland, but refers to the country simply as "Ireland."

RULERS

British, until 1949

MONETARY SYSTEM

4 Farthings = 1 Penny
12 Pence = 1 Shilling
2 Shillings = 1 Florin
5 Shillings = 1 Crown
20 Shillings = 1 Pound

TRADESMENS' TOKENS

Various token issues exist which include the following: "VOCE POPULI" with HIBERNIA reverse of the 1760's, many varieties of imitation regal harp Halfpennies of the 18th century, genuine trade tokens issued by various merchants between 1789-1804, lead tokens ca 1780-1820, silver issues including countermarked foreign coins ca 1804, copper tokens ca 1805-1830 followed by the Farthing tokens of 1830-1856. These are found listed in Seaby's COINS AND TOKENS OF IRELAND.

1/2 PENNY

1760-61

COPPER
'VOCE POPULI' 1/2 Penny token of 1760

1789-1804

Dublin 1/2 Penny token of 1795

PENNY
1805-1830

COPPER
Stephen's Dublin Penny token of 1816

REGULAR COINAGE

FARTHING

COPPER

C#	Date	Mintage	Fine	VF	XF	Unc
3	1805	—	—	—	Proof	75.00
	1806	—	2.50	4.00	15.00	45.00
	1806	—	—	—	Proof	135.00
			COPPER GILT			
	1805	—	—	Proof Only		75.00
			BRONZE			
3a	1805	—	—	Proof Only		55.00
			SILVER			
3b	1805	—	—	Proof Only		Rare
			GOLD			
3c	1805	—	—	Proof Only		Rare

COPPER

Fr#	Date	Mintage	Fine	VF	XF	Unc
209	1822	—	—	Proof Only		1000.

1/2 PENNY

COPPER

Obv: Type I, short bust.

C#	Date	Mintage	Fine	VF	XF	Unc
4	1766	—	4.00	10.00	30.00	50.00
	1769	—	4.50	12.50	30.00	55.00

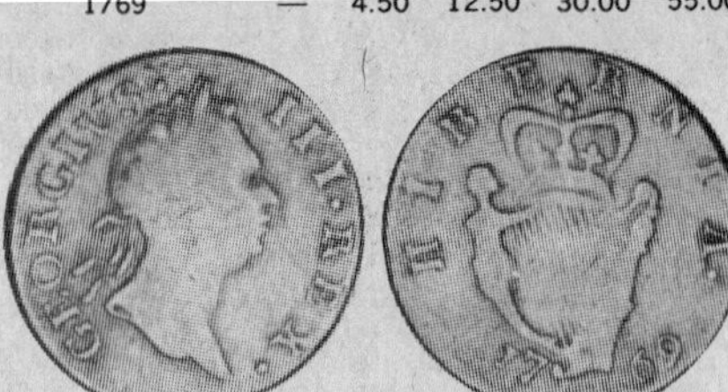

Obv: Type 2, long bust.

C#	Date	Mintage	Fine	VF	XF	Unc
4	1769	—	4.50	12.50	32.50	60.00

Obv: Type 3, long hair.

C#	Date	Mintage	Fine	VF	XF	Unc
4a	1774	—	—	Proof Only		250.00
	1775	—	7.50	30.00	75.00	125.00
	1775	—	—	—	Proof	200.00
	1776	—	6.00	12.50	30.00	90.00
	1781	—	6.00	10.00	27.50	60.00
	1782	—	5.00	10.00	27.50	55.00
	1782	—	—	—	Proof	250.00

C#	Date	Mintage	Fine	VF	XF	Unc
5	1805	—	4.00	4.50	17.50	37.50
	1805	—	—	—	Proof	100.00
			COPPER, Gilt			
	1805	—	Proof Only		—	200.00
			BRONZE			
5a	1805	—	Proof Only		—	200.00
			SILVER			
5b	1805	—	Proof Only		—	Rare
			GOLD			
5c	1805	—	Proof Only		—	Rare

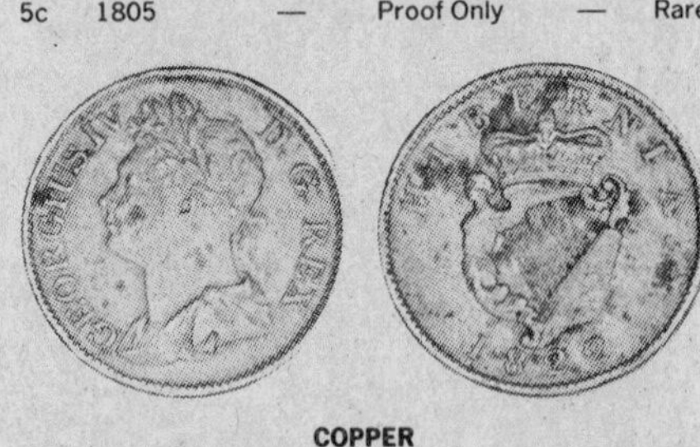

COPPER

C#	Date	Mintage	Fine	VF	XF	Unc
12	1822	—	5.00	15.00	35.00	100.00
	1822	—	—	—	Proof	300.00
	1823	—	5.00	12.00	32.50	90.00
	1823	—	—	—	Proof	300.00

PENNY

COPPER

C#	Date	Mintage	Fine	VF	XF	Unc
6	1805	—	5.00	17.50	45.00	100.00
	1805	—	—	—	Proof	250.00
			COPPER, Gilt			
	1805	—	Proof Only		—	300.00
			BRONZE			
6a	1805	—	Proof Only		—	250.00
			SILVER			
6b	1805	—	Proof Only		—	750.00
			GOLD			
6c	1805	—	Proof Only		—	3500.

COPPER

C#	Date	Mintage	Fine	VF	XF	Unc
13	1822	—	6.00	15.00	50.00	100.00
	1822	—	—	—	Proof	375.00
	1823	—	6.50	15.00	50.00	100.00
	1823	—	—	—	Proof	375.00

BANK TOKENS

BANK OF IRELAND

5 PENCE

SILVER

C#	Date	Mintage	Fine	VF	XF	Unc
7	1805	—	5.00	15.00	40.00	90.00
	1806	—	5.00	17.50	45.00	100.00

10 PENCE

SILVER

C#	Date	Mintage	Fine	VF	XF	Unc
8	1805	—	6.00	20.00	35.00	90.00
	1806	—	6.50	22.50	37.50	100.00

C#	Date	Mintage	Fine	VF	XF	Unc
9	1813	—	7.50	25.50	50.00	100.00
	1813	—	—	—	Proof	250.00

30 PENCE
BANK OF IRELAND

SILVER

C#	Date	Mintage	Fine	VF	XF	Unc
10	1808	—	15.00	35.00	125.00	250.00

6 SHILLINGS

SILVER

C#	Date	Mintage	Fine	VF	XF	Unc
11	1804	—	50.00	95.00	200.00	450.00
	1804	—	—	—	Proof	450.00

NOTE: The silver proofs were struck on specially prepared flans while circulation strikes were struck over Spanish and Spanish Colonial 8 Reales.

COPPER

C#	Date	Mintage	Fine	VF	XF	Unc
11a	1804	—	—	Proof	—	Rare

COPPER GILT

C#	Date	Mintage	Fine	VF	XF	Unc
11b	1804	—	—	Proof	—	Rare

COUNTERSTAMP ISSUES

Merchant

5 SHILLINGS 5 PENCE

.903 SILVER
c/s: PAYABLE AT CASTLE COMER COLLIERY, 5s. 5d. on Spanish or Spanish Colonial 8 Reales.

KM#	Date	Mintage	VG	Fine	VF
1	ND(1804)	—	500.00	900.00	1400.

MODERN COINAGE

FARTHING

BRONZE

Y#	Date	Mintage	Fine	VF	XF	Unc
1	1928	.300	2.00	4.00	6.00	12.00
	1928	6,001	—	—	Proof	20.00
	1930	.288	1.50	3.00	7.50	15.00
	1931	.192	4.00	7.50	12.00	20.00
	1932	.192	5.00	9.00	15.00	25.00
	1933	.480	1.00	3.00	5.00	10.00
	1935	.192	7.00	12.00	25.00	45.00
	1936	.192	6.00	10.00	27.50	60.00
	1937	.480	1.00	1.50	4.00	12.00

Y#	Date	Mintage	Fine	VF	XF	Unc
9	1939	.768	1.00	1.50	3.50	10.00
	1939	—	—	—	Proof	Rare
	1940	.192	4.00	7.50	12.00	24.00
	1941	.480	1.00	1.50	3.00	6.50
	1943	.480	1.00	1.00	2.00	4.00
	1944	.480	1.00	1.50	3.50	7.50
	1946	.480	.60	1.00	2.00	4.00
	1949	.192	1.00	2.25	5.00	10.00
	1949	—	—	—	Proof	425.00
	1953	.192	.20	.60	1.00	1.75
	1953	—	—	—	Proof	350.00
	1959	.192	.10	.60	1.00	1.50
	1959				Proof	250.00
	1966	.096	.20	1.00	1.50	3.50

1/2 PENNY

BRONZE

Y#	Date	Mintage	Fine	VF	XF	Unc
2	1928	2.880	1.00	3.00	7.50	20.00
	1928	6,001	—	—	Proof	50.00
	1933	.720	3.50	15.00	100.00	600.00
	1935	.960	2.00	10.00	50.00	250.00
	1937	.960	1.00	3.50	12.50	35.00

Y#	Date	Mintage	Fine	VF	XF	Unc
10	1939	.240	7.50	16.00	60.00	150.00
	1939	—	—	—	Proof	400.00
	1940	1.680	.50	3.00	45.00	250.00
	1941	2.400	.40	1.50	5.00	20.00
	1942	6.931	.20	1.00	3.00	10.00
	1943	2.669	.40	1.50	5.50	25.00
	1946	.720	1.00	3.50	17.50	65.00
	1949	1.344	.20	1.00	4.50	20.00
	1953	2.400	.20	.40	1.00	2.00
	1953				Proof	200.00
	1964	2.160	.10	.20	.40	.75
	1965	1.440	.15	.35	.75	2.50
	1966	1.680	—	.10	.25	.60
	1967	1.200	—	.10	.25	.75

PENNY

BRONZE

Y#	Date	Mintage	Fine	VF	XF	Unc
3	1928	9.000	.40	1.00	5.00	20.00
3	1928	6,001	—	—	Proof	25.00
	1931	2.400	.60	2.00	20.00	70.00
	1931				Proof	500.00
	1933	1.680	1.00	3.00	27.50	125.00
	1935	5.472	.40	1.00	7.50	27.50
	1937	5.400	.40	1.50	17.5	70.00
	1937				Proof	500.00

Y#	Date	Mintage	Fine	VF	XF	Unc
	1938				Unique	15,000.
11	1940	.312	4.00	10.00	100.00	1750.
	1941	4.680	.40	.75	7.50	50.00
	1942	17.520	.20	.50	1.75	12.50
	1943	3.360	.60	1.50	8.00	30.00
	1946	4.800	.20	.75	7.50	25.00
	1948	4.800	.40	.75	5.00	12.50
	1949	4.080	.40	.75	3.50	18.50
	1949	—	—	—	Proof	350.00
	1950	2.400	.40	.85	4.00	22.50
	1952	2.400	.20	.50	1.50	3.50
	1952	—	—	—	Proof	200.00
	1962	1.200	.50	.75	3.00	9.00
	1962	—	—	—	Proof	100.00
	1963	9.600	.15	.35	.75	1.75
	1963	—	—	—	Proof	200.00
	1964	6.000	.20	.30	.50	1.00
	1965	11.160	.10	.15	.35	.75
	1966	6.000	—	.10	.15	.40
	1967	2.400	—	.10	.25	.50
	1968	42.000	—	.10	.15	.25

3 PENCE

NICKEL

Y#	Date	Mintage	Fine	VF	XF	Unc
4	1928	1.500	.60	2.00	4.50	20.00
	1928	6,001	—	—	Proof	22.50
	1933	.320	2.00	5.50	65.00	450.00
	1934	.800	1.00	2.50	6.50	50.00
	1935	.240	2.00	5.00	30.00	275.00

Y#	Date	Mintage	Fine	VF	XF	Unc
12	1939	.064	7.50	12.50	65.00	300.00
	1939	—	—	—	Proof	350.00
	1940	.720	1.00	2.50	5.00	40.00

COPPER-NICKEL

Y#	Date	Mintage	Fine	VF	XF	Unc
12a	1942	4.000	.50	1.00	6.00	32.50
	1942				Proof	300.00
	1943	1.360	.50	2.00	15.00	100.00
	1946	.800	.75	2.00	9.00	42.50
	1948	1.600	.25	2.50	27.50	150.00
	1949	1.200	.25	1.00	5.00	20.00
	1949	—	—	—	Proof	150.00
	1950	1.600	.25	1.00	3.00	20.00
	1950				Proof	325.00
	1953	1.600	.25	.75	2.50	10.00
	1956	1.200	.25	.50	2.00	8.00
	1961	2.400	.25	.50	1.00	4.25
	1962	3.200	.25	.50	1.00	4.00
	1963	4.000	.25	.50	.75	3.00
	1964	4.000	.25	.40	.50	1.50
	1965	3.600	—	.25	.40	1.00
	1966	4.000	—	.25	.40	.75
	1967	2.400	—	.25	.40	.75
	1968	12.000	—	.10	.25	.50

6 PENCE

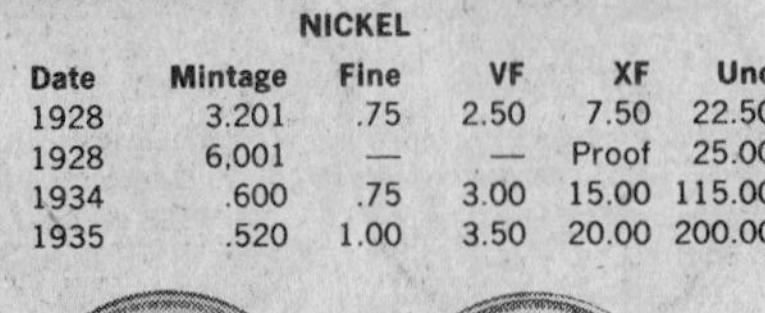

NICKEL

Y#	Date	Mintage	Fine	VF	XF	Unc
5	1928	3.201	.75	2.50	7.50	22.50
	1928	6,001	—	—	Proof	25.00
	1934	.600	.75	3.00	15.00	115.00
	1935	.520	1.00	3.50	20.00	200.00

Y#	Date	Mintage	Fine	VF	XF	Unc
13	1939	.876	.75	2.00	10.00	90.00
	1939	—	—	—	Proof	450.00
	1940	1.120	.60	1.50	8.00	40.00
		COPPER-NICKEL				
13a	1942	1.320	.75	1.75	7.50	50.00
	1945	.400	1.50	7.50	60.00	175.00
	1946	.720	1.00	4.50	65.00	500.00
	1947	.800	.75	4.50	20.00	160.00
	1948	.800	.75	2.50	10.00	50.00
	1949	.600	1.00	2.00	10.00	35.00
	1950	.800	.75	2.50	18.50	200.00
	1952	.800	.50	1.50	5.00	30.00
	1952	—	—	—	Proof	175.00
	1953	.800	.50	1.50	5.00	30.00
	1953	—	—	—	Proof	150.00
	1955	.600	.75	2.00	6.00	20.00
	1955	—	—	—	Proof	150.00
	1956	.600	.50	1.50	3.50	13.50
	1956	—	—	—	Proof	150.00
	1958	.600	.50	2.00	9.00	70.00
	1958				Proof	300.00
	1959	2.000	.25	1.00	4.00	27.50
	1960	2.020	.25	.75	3.00	15.00
	1961	3.000	.25	.50	2.50	7.50
	1962	4.000	.25	1.00	5.50	60.00
	1963	4.000	.10	.50	1.00	1.75
	1964	6.000	.10	.50	.75	1.50
	1966	2.000	.10	.50	.75	1.00
	1967	4.000	.10	.25	.40	.75
	1968	8.000	—	.25	.40	.75
	1969	2.000	—	.25	.40	.75

SHILLING

5.6552gm., SILVER, .1364oz ASW

Y#	Date	Mintage	Fine	VF	XF	Unc
6	1928	2.700	BV	5.00	15.00	35.00
	1928	6,001	—	—	Proof	30.00
	1930	.460	4.50	20.00	150.00	500.00
	1930				Proof	650.00
	1931	.400	4.50	15.00	75.00	200.00
	1933	.300	4.50	20.00	125.00	400.00
	1935	.400	4.50	10.00	35.00	135.00
	1937	.100	10.00	32.50	400.00	1250.

Y#	Date	Mintage	Fine	VF	XF	Unc
14	1939	1.140	BV	5.00	15.00	40.00
	1939	—	—	—	Proof	400.00
	1940	.580	BV	5.00	12.00	27.50
	1941	.300	4.25	6.00	20.00	45.00
	1942	.286	4.50	7.00	17.50	27.50

COPPER-NICKEL

Y#	Date	Mintage	Fine	VF	XF	Unc
14a	1951	2.000	.50	2.25	4.00	15.00
	1951	—	—	—	Proof	275.00
	1954	3.000	.25	1.50	3.00	6.50
	1955	1.000	.50	2.00	4.50	16.50
	1959	2.000	.25	1.25	5.50	40.00
	1960	—	—	—	—	—
	1962	4.000	.25	1.00	1.50	6.00
	1963	4.000	.25	.50	1.25	2.50
	1964	4.000	.25	.50	.75	2.00
	1966	3.000	—	.25	.50	1.50
	1968	4.000	—	.25	.50	1.50

FLORIN

11.3104 gm., .750 SILVER, .2727 oz ASW

Y#	Date	Mintage	Fine	VF	XF	Unc
7	1928	2.025	BV	10.00	25.00	45.00
	1928	6,001	—	—	Proof	45.00
	1930	.330	10.00	27.50	200.00	500.00
	1930				Proof	1000.
	1931	.200	10.00	30.00	150.00	450.00
	1933	.300	10.00	30.00	200.00	650.00
	1934	.150	12.50	40.00	300.00	800.00
	1934				Proof	2000.
	1935	.390	8.50	15.00	100.00	300.00
	1937	.150	10.00	25.00	200.00	500.00

Y#	Date	Mintage	Fine	VF	XF	Unc
15	1939	1.080	BV	10.00	20.00	40.00
	1939	—	—	—	Proof	450.00
	1940	.670	BV	10.00	20.00	50.00
	1941	.400	BV	10.00	20.00	45.00
	1942	.109	10.00	12.50	25.00	45.00
	1943	*	2750.	5000.	7500.	—

*Approximately 40 known.

COPPER-NICKEL

Y#	Date	Mintage	Fine	VF	XF	Unc
15a	1951	1.000	.60	2.00	7.50	30.00
	1951	—	—	—	Proof	300.00
	1954	1.000	.60	1.75	7.50	27.50
	1955	1.000	.60	1.75	7.50	25.00
	1955	—	—	—	Proof	200.00
	1959	2.000	.40	1.50	5.00	17.50
	1961	2.000	.40	1.25	6.00	65.00
	1962	2.400	.40	1.00	3.50	15.00
	1963	3.000	.40	.75	1.75	7.00
	1964	4.000	.40	.50	1.25	3.50
	1965	2.000	.25	.50	1.00	3.00
	1966	3.625	—	.35	.75	1.50
	1968	1.000	—	.40	.75	2.25

1/2 CROWN

14.1380gm., .750 SILVER, .3409oz ASW
Rev: Close O and I in COROIN, 8 tufts in horse's tail, with 156 beads in border.

Y#	Date	Mintage	Fine	VF	XF	Unc
8	1928	2.160	BV	12.00	27.50	50.00
	1928	6,001	—	—	Proof	50.00
	1930	.352	12.00	20.00	175.00	450.00
	1931	.160	15.00	30.00	200.00	450.00
	1931	—	—	—	Proof	450.00
	1933	.336	12.00	22.50	240.00	550.00
	1934	.480	11.00	15.00	50.00	200.00
	1937	.040	50.00	175.00	550.00	1750.

Rev: Normal spacing between O and I in COROIN, 7 tufts in horse's tail, with 151 beads in border.

Y#	Date	Mintage	Fine	VF	XF	Unc
16	1939	.888	BV	10.00	20.00	50.00
	1939	—	—	—	Proof	450.00
	1940	.752	BV	12.00	22.50	50.00
	1941	.320	11.00	12.50	27.50	90.00
	1941				Proof	500.00
	1942	.286	11.00	12.50	25.00	50.00
	1943	*	150.00	300.00	1000.	2400.

*Approximately 5000-6000 known.

COPPER-NICKEL

Y#	Date	Mintage	Fine	VF	XF	Unc
16a	1951	.800	1.00	2.00	7.50	40.00
	1951	—	—	—	Proof	350.00
	1954	.400	1.50	2.50	7.50	35.00
	1954	—	—	—	Proof	350.00
	1955	1.080	1.00	2.00	6.00	30.00
	1955	—	—	—	Proof	200.00
	1959	1.600	.75	1.50	5.00	15.00
	1961	1.600	.75	1.50	5.00	18.50
	1962	3.200	.50	1.50	3.00	10.00
	1963	2.400	.50	1.00	2.00	8.50
	1964	3.200	.50	1.00	2.00	4.00
	1966	.700	.50	.75	1.50	3.00
	1967	2.000	.50	.50	1.00	3.00

NOTE: 1967 exists struck with a polished reverse die. Estimated value is $10.00 in uncirculated.

Y#8 long base 2 Y#16-16a short base 2

Y#	Date	Mintage	VG	Fine	VF	XF
16b	1961 obverse muled with Y#8 reverse					
		Inc. Ab.	—	5.00	15.00	300.00

10 SHILLINGS

18.1400gm., .833 SILVER, .4858oz ASW

Y#	Date	Mintage	Fine	VF	XF	Unc
17	1966	*2.000	BV	BV	15.00	17.50
	1966	.020	—	—	Proof	30.00

NOTE: *Approximately 1.270 melted down.

DECIMAL COINAGE

5 New Pence = 1 Shilling
25 New Pence = 1 Crown
100 Pence = 1 Pound

1/2 PENNY

BRONZE

Y#	Date	Mintage	Fine	VF	XF	Unc
18	1971	100.500	—	—	—	.15
	1971	.050	—	—	Proof	1.00
	1975	11.000	—	—	—	.10
	1976	—	—	—	—	.10
	1978	—	—	—	—	.10

PENNY

BRONZE

Y#	Date	Mintage	Fine	VF	XF	Unc
19	1971	100.500	—	—	.10	.15
	1971	.050	—	—	Proof	1.25
	1974	10.000	—	—	—	.10
	1975	10.000	—	—	—	.10
	1976	—	—	—	—	.15
	1978	—	—	—	—	.15
	1979	—	—	—	—	.15

2 PENCE

BRONZE

Y#	Date	Mintage	Fine	VF	XF	Unc
20	1971	75.500	—	—	.15	.25
	1971	.050	—	—	Proof	1.50
	1975	35.010	—	—	—	.15
	1976	—	—	—	—	.25
	1978	—	—	—	—	.25
	1979	—	—	—	—	.25

5 PENCE

COPPER-NICKEL

Y#	Date	Mintage	Fine	VF	XF	Unc
21	1969	5.000	—	.15	.35	1.00
	1970	10.000	—	—	.20	.40
	1971	8.000	—	—	.15	.35
	1971	.050	—	—	Proof	2.00
	1974	—	—	—	.15	.25
	1975	10.000	—	—	.15	.25
	1976	—	—	—	.15	.25
	1978	—	—	—	—	.25

10 PENCE

COPPER-NICKEL

Y#	Date	Mintage	Fine	VF	XF	Unc
22	1969	27.000	.25	.30	.40	.75
	1971	3.160	.25	.30	.35	.65
	1971	.050	—	—	Proof	2.50
	1973	2.500	.25	.30	.35	.65
	1974	7.500	.25	.30	.35	.50
	1975	30.000	.25	.30	.35	.50
	1976	—	.25	.30	.35	.50
	1978	—	—	—	—	.50

50 PENCE

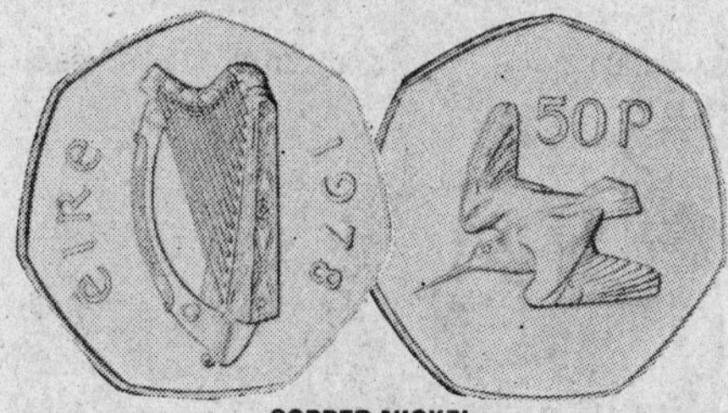

COPPER-NICKEL

Y#	Date	Mintage	Fine	VF	XF	Unc
23	1970	9.000	1.20	1.35	1.50	3.00
	1971	.600	1.20	1.35	1.50	2.50
	1971	.050	—	—	Proof	3.50
	1974	5.000	1.20	1.35	1.50	2.50
	1975	3.000	1.20	1.35	1.50	2.25
	1976	1.500	1.20	1.35	1.50	2.00
	1977	—	1.20	1.35	1.50	2.00
	1978	—	1.20	1.35	1.50	2.00

NCLT ISSUES

PROOF SETS

STANDARD METALS

KM#	Date	Mintage	Identification	Issue Price	Mkt. Val.
101	1928(8)	6,001	Y1-8	—	175.00
102	1971(6)	50,000	Y18-23	8.40	11.50

Listings For

IRIAN BARAT: refer to Indonesia

ISLE DE BOURBON: refer to Reunion

ISLE OF MAN

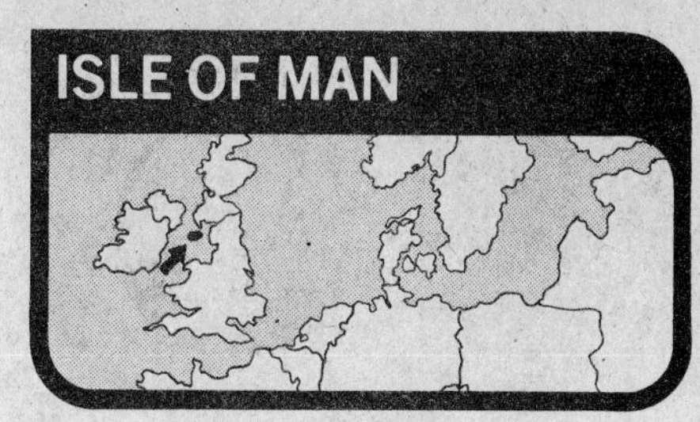

The Isle of Man, a dependency of the British Crown located in the Irish Sea equidistant from Ireland, Scotland and England, has an area of 227 sq. mi. (588 sq. km.) and a population of 62,000. Capital: Douglas. Agriculture, dairy farming, fishing and tourism are the chief industries.

The prevalence of prehistoric artifacts and monuments on the island give evidence that its mild, almost sub—tropical climate was enjoyed by mankind before the dawn of history. Vikings came to the Isle of Man during the 9th century and remained until ejected by Scotland in 1266. The island came under the protection of the British Crown in 1288, and in 1406 was granted, in perpetuity, to the earls of Derby, from whom it was inherited, 1736, by the Duke of Atholl. Rights and title were purchased from the Duke of Atholl in 1765 by the British Crown; the remaining privileges of the Atholl family were transferred to the crown in 1829. The Isle of Man is ruled by its own legislative council and the House of Keys, one of the oldest legislative assemblies in the world. Acts of Parliament passed in London do not affect the island unless it is specifically mentioned.

RULERS

British

MINTMARKS

PM - Pobjoy Mint

MONETARY SYSTEM

14 Pence (Manx) = 1 Shilling (Br.)
5 Shillings = 1 Crown
20 Shillings = 1 Pound

TRADESMEN'S TOKENS

1/2 PENNY

COPPER

Obv: Peel Castle. Rev. leg: DOUGLAS BANK TOKEN.....

P#	Date	Mintage	VG	Fine	VF	XF
57	1811	—	25.00	50.00	110.00	165.00
	1811	—	—	—	Proof	250.00

P#	Date	Mintage	VG	Fine	VF	XF
58	1811	—	3.50	7.50	12.50	25.00

Obv: Similar to P#60 with OFFICE DOUGLAS below Atlas

P#	Date	Mintage	VG	Fine	VF	XF
59	1811	—	3.50	7.50	12.50	25.00

P#	Date	Mintage	VG	Fine	VF	XF
60	1811	—	7.50	15.00	25.00	50.00

Obv: Roman numeral I in date

P#	Date	Mintage	VG	Fine	VF	XF
61	1830	—	3.50	7.50	12.50	25.00

NOTE: P#61 was issued by John Caine, a miller and baker of Castletown.

Obv: Arabic numeral 1 in date

62	1830	—	20.00	40.00	75.00	150.00

63	1815	—	3.50	7.50	12.50	25.00

64	1831	—	1.75	3.50	7.50	15.00

PENNY

COPPER

Rev. leg: DOUGLAS BANK TOKEN.....

51	1811	—	10.00	20.00	40.00	80.00
	1811 thin flan	—				
		—	—	—	Proof	125.00
	1811 thick flan	—				
		—	—	—	Proof	125.00

Obv: Similar to P#51

Rev. leg: DOUGLAS TOKEN.....

52	1811	—	10.00	20.00	40.00	80.00
	1811	—	—	—	Proof	125.00

P#	Date	Mintage	VG	Fine	VF	XF
53	1811	—	5.00	10.00	17.50	35.00

54	1811	—	5.00	10.00	17.50	35.00

Obv: Arabic 1 and round top 3 in date

55	1830	—	5.00	10.00	22.50	45.00

Similar to P#55 with I and flat top 3 in date.

56	1830	—	7.50	15.00	35.00	70.00

NOTE: P#55 and 56 were issued by John Caine, a miller and baker of Castletown.

SHILLING

SILVER

Similar to 5 Shillings, P#46.

48	1811	—	37.50	75.00	125.00	225.00
	1811	—	—	—	Proof	500.00

2 SHILLINGS 6 PENCE

SILVER

Similar to 5 Shillings, P#46.

47	1811	—	150.00	250.00	350.00	600.00

COPPER

P#	Date	Mintage	VG	Fine	VF	XF
47a	1811	—	—	—	Proof	1000.

5 SHILLINGS

SILVER

46	1811	—	150.00	250.00	450.00	800.00
	1811	—	—	—	Proof	1250.

REGULAR COINAGE

FARTHING

COPPER

C#	Date	Mintage	Fine	VF	XF	Unc
7	1839	.213	5.00	15.00	30.00	70.00
	1839	—	—	—	Proof	400.00
	1841	—	—	—	Proof	550.00
	1860	—	—	—	Proof	650.00

1/2 PENNY

COPPER

3	1786 engrailed edge	7.50	25.00	120.00	200.00	
	1786 engrailed edge	—	—	Proof	275.00	
	1786 plain edge	—	—	Proof	1000.	

4	1798	—	8.00	40.00	130.00	200.00
	1798	—	—	—	Proof	275.00
	1813	—	7.00	20.00	90.00	200.00
	1813	—	—	—	Proof	275.00

GILT COPPER

4a	1798	—	—	—	Proof	Rare

COPPER

C#	Date	Mintage	Fine	VF	XF	Unc
8	1839	.214	6.00	12.00	35.00	70.00
	1839	—	—	—	Proof	400.00
	1841	—	—	—	Proof	—
	1860	—	—	—	Proof	—

PENNY

COPPER

C#	Date	Mintage	Fine	VF	XF	Unc
5	1786 engrailed edge	—	12.50	40.00	125.00	200.00
	1786 engrailed edge			—	Proof	300.00
	1786 plain edge			—	Proof	1000.

C#	Date	Mintage	Fine	VF	XF	Unc
6	1798	—	20.00	40.00	150.00	225.00
	1798	—	—	—	Proof	350.00
	1813	—	10.00	25.00	125.00	200.00
	1813	—	—	—	Proof	300.00
	GILT COPPER					
6a	1798	—	—	Proof only		Rare
	1813	—	—	Proof only		Rare
	SILVER					
6b	1798	—	—	Proof only		Rare

COPPER

C#	Date	Mintage	Fine	VF	XF	Unc
9	1839	.080	10.00	17.50	60.00	100.00
	1839	—	—	—	Proof	350.00
	1841	—	—	—	Proof	—
	1859	—	—	—	Proof	—

DECIMAL COINAGE

5 New Pence = 1 Shilling
25 New Pence = 1 Crown
100 New Pence = 1 Pound

1/2 NEW PENNY

BRONZE

Y#	Date	Mintage	VF	XF	Unc
2	1971	.495	—	.50	1.00
	1971	.010	—	Proof	3.00
	1972PM	1,000	25.00	40.00	60.00
	1973PM	1,000	25.00	40.00	60.00
	1974PM	1,000	25.00	40.00	60.00
	1975PM	.825	—	—	.50
	2.1000 gm., .925 SILVER, .0624 oz ASW				
2a	1975PM	.020	—	—	7.50
	PLATINUM				
2b	1975PM	600 pcs.	—	Proof	175.00

1/2 PENNY

BRONZE

Y#	Date	Mintage	VF	XF	Unc
15	1976PM	.600	—	—	.15
	2.1000 gm., .925 SILVER, .0624 oz ASW				
15a	1976PM	.020	—	—	6.00
	1978PM	.010	—	—	—
	PLATINUM				
15b	1976PM	600 pcs.	—	Proof	175.00
	1978PM	600 pcs.	—	Proof	225.00

BRONZE
Rev: Without mintmark

Y#	Date	Mintage	VF	XF	Unc
15.1	1977	—	—	—	—

Rev: MM: Small circle with stylized triskelion.

Y#	Date	Mintage	VF	XF	Unc
15.2	1979(PM)	—	—	—	—

F.A.O. Issue

Y#	Date	Mintage	VF	XF	Unc
24	1977PM	.700	—	—	.15
	2.1000 gm., .925 SILVER, .0624 oz ASW				
24a	1977PM	.010	—	Proof	5.00

1.7800 gm., BRONZE

Y#	Date	Mintage	VF	XF	Unc
40	1980PM	—	—	—	—
	SILVER				
40a	1980PM	—	—	—	—
	.917 GOLD				
40b	1980PM	—	—	—	—
	.950 PLATINUM				
40c	1980PM	—	—	—	—

NEW PENNY

BRONZE

Y#	Date	Mintage	VF	XF	Unc
3	1971	.100	.15	.35	.85
	1971	.010	—	Proof	2.00
	1972PM	1,000	25.00	40.00	60.00
	1973PM	1,000	25.00	40.00	60.00
	1974PM	1,000	25.00	40.00	60.00
	1975PM	.855	—	.10	.15
	4.2000 gm., .925 SILVER, .1249 oz ASW				
3a	1975PM	.020	—	—	8.50
	8.0000 gm., .950 PLATINUM, .2443 oz APW				
3b	1975PM	600 pcs.	—	Proof	200.00

PENNY

BRONZE

Y#	Date	Mintage	VF	XF	Unc
16	1976PM	.900	—	—	.10
	1977PM	1.000	—	—	.10
	1978PM	—	—	—	.10
	4.2000 gm., .925 SILVER, .1249 oz ASW				
16a	1976PM	.020	—	Proof	6.50
	1977PM	.010	—	Proof	6.50
	1978PM	.010	—	Proof	—
	PLATINUM				
16b	1976PM	600 pcs.	—	Proof	200.00
	1978	600 pcs.	—	Proof	250.00

BRONZE

Rev: MM: Small circle containing stylized triskelion.

Y#	Date	Mintage	VF	XF	Unc
16.1	1979PM	—	—	—	—

3.5600 gm.

Y#	Date	Mintage	VF	XF	Unc
41	1980PM	—	—	—	—
	SILVER				
41a	1980PM	—	—	—	—
	.917 GOLD				
41b	1980PM	—	—	—	—
	.950 PLATINUM				
41c	1980PM	—	—	—	—

2 NEW PENCE

BRONZE

Y#	Date	Mintage	VF	XF	Unc
4	1971	.100	.35	.75	1.25
	1971	.010	—	Proof	2.50
	1972PM	1,000	25.00	40.00	60.00
	1973PM	1,000	25.00	40.00	60.00
	1974PM	1,000	25.00	40.00	60.00
	1975PM	.725	.10	.20	.35
	8.4000 gm., .925 SILVER, .2498 oz ASW				
4a	1975PM	.020	—	—	12.00
	PLATINUM				
4b	1975PM	600 pcs.	—	Proof	225.00

2 PENCE

BRONZE

Y#	Date	Mintage	VF	XF	Unc
17	1976PM	.800	—	.10	.15
	1977PM	1.000	—	.10	.15
	1978PM	—	—	—	.10
	8.4000 gm., .925 SILVER, .2498 oz ASW				
17a	1976PM	.020	—	Proof	10.00
	1977PM	.010	—	Proof	10.00
	1978PM	.010	—	—	—
	PLATINUM				
17b	1976PM	600 pcs.	—	Proof	250.00
	1977PM	600 pcs.	—	Proof	275.00

BRONZE

Rev: MM: Small circle containing stylized triskelion.

Y#	Date	Mintage	VF	XF	Unc
17.1	1979PM	—	—	—	—

7.0000 gm.

Y#	Date	Mintage	VF	XF	Unc
42	1980PM	—	—	—	—
	SILVER				
42a	1980PM	—	—	—	—
	.917 GOLD				
42b	1980PM	—	—	—	—
	.950 PLATINUM				
42c	1980PM	—	—	—	—

5 NEW PENCE

COPPER-NICKEL

Y#	Date	Mintage	VF	XF	Unc
5	1971	.100	.35	.75	1.35
	1971	.010	—	Proof	3.00
	1972PM	1,000	25.00	40.00	60.00
	1973PM	1,000	25.00	40.00	60.00
	1974PM	1,000	25.00	40.00	60.00
	1975PM	1.400	.15	.20	.35
	6.5000 gm., .925 SILVER, .1933 oz ASW				
5a	1975PM	.020	—	—	12.00
	PLATINUM				
5b	1975PM	600 pcs.	—	Proof	250.00

5 PENCE

COPPER-NICKEL

PM mintmark on obverse and reverse

Y#	Date	Mintage	VF	XF	Unc
18	1976PM	.800	.15	.20	.35
	1977PM	—	.15	.20	.25
	1978PM	—	—	—	—
	6.5000 gm., .925 SILVER, .1933 oz ASW				
18a	1976PM	.020	—	Proof	10.00
	1977PM	.010	—	Proof	10.00
	1978PM	.010	—	—	—
	PLATINUM				
18b	1976PM	600 pcs.	—	Proof	250.00
	1978PM	600 pcs.	—	Proof	275.00
	COPPER-NICKEL PM mintmark on obverse only.				
18.1	1976PM	Inc. Ab.	.25	.35	.75

Rev: MM: Small circle containing stylized triskelion.

Y#	Date	Mintage	VF	XF	Unc
18.2	1979PM	—	—	—	—

5.6500 gm.

Y#	Date	Mintage	VF	XF	Unc
43	1980PM	—	—	—	—
	SILVER				
43a	1980PM	—	—	—	—
	.917 GOLD				
43b	1980PM	—	—	—	—
	.950 PLATINUM				
43c	1980PM	—	—	—	—

10 NEW PENCE

COPPER-NICKEL

Y#	Date	Mintage	VF	XF	Unc
6	1971	.100	.35	.75	1.35
	1971	.010	—	Proof	3.50
	1972PM	1,000	25.00	40.00	60.00
	1973PM	1,000	25.00	40.00	60.00
	1974PM	1,000	25.00	40.00	60.00
	1975PM	1.500	.25	.35	.50
	13.0000 gm., .925 SILVER, .3866 oz ASW				
6a	1975PM	.020	—	—	17.50
	25.0000 gm., .950 PLATINUM, .7636 oz APW				
6b	1975PM	600 pcs.	—	Proof	400.00

10 PENCE

COPPER-NICKEL

PM mintmark on obverse and reverse

Y#	Date	Mintage	VF	XF	Unc
19.1	1976PM	2.800	.25	.35	.50
	1977PM	—	.25	.35	.75
	1978PM	—	—	—	.40
	PM mintmark on obverse only				
19.2	1976PM	Inc. Ab.	.25	.35	.75
	13.0000 gm., .925 SILVER, .3866 oz ASW				
19.1a	1976PM	.020	—	Proof	12.50
	1977PM	.010	—	Proof	12.50
	1978PM	.010	—	Proof	12.50
	PLATINUM				
19.1b	1976PM	600 pcs.	—	Proof	350.00
	1978PM	600 pcs.	—	Proof	350.00

COPPER-NICKEL

Rev: MM: Small circle containing stylized triskelion.

Y#	Date	Mintage	VF	XF	Unc
19.3	1979PM	—	—	—	—

11.5000 gm.

Y#	Date	Mintage	VF	XF	Unc
44	1980PM	—	—	—	.75
		SILVER			
44a	1980PM	—	—	—	—
		.917 GOLD			
44b	1980PM	—	—	—	—
		.950 PLATINUM			
44c	1980PM	—	—	—	—

CROWN (25 NEW PENCE)

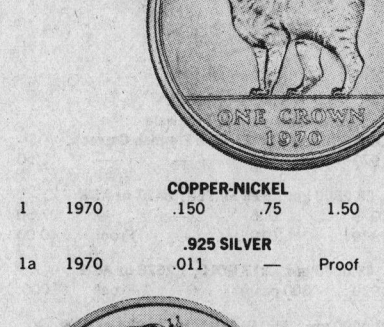

COPPER-NICKEL

Y#	Date	Mintage	VF	XF	Unc
1	1970	.150	.75	1.50	5.00
		.925 SILVER			
1a	1970	.011	—	Proof	50.00

COPPER-NICKEL
25th Wedding Anniversary

Y#	Date	Mintage	VF	XF	Unc
8	1972	.070	1.00	2.00	8.00
		28.2800 gm., .925 SILVER, .8411 oz ASW			
8a	1972	.015	—	Proof	30.00

COPPER-NICKEL
Winston Churchill Centenary

Y#	Date	Mintage	VF	XF	Unc
13	1974	.045	.75	1.50	3.00
		28.2800 gm., .925 SILVER, .8411 oz ASW			
13a	1974	—	—	—	27.50
	1974	.030	—	Proof	30.00

COPPER-NICKEL

Y#	Date	Mintage	VF	XF	Unc
14	1975PM	.035	.75	1.25	2.00
		28.2800 gm., .925 SILVER, .8411 oz ASW			
14a	1975PM	—	—	—	27.50
	1975PM	.030	—	Proof	30.00

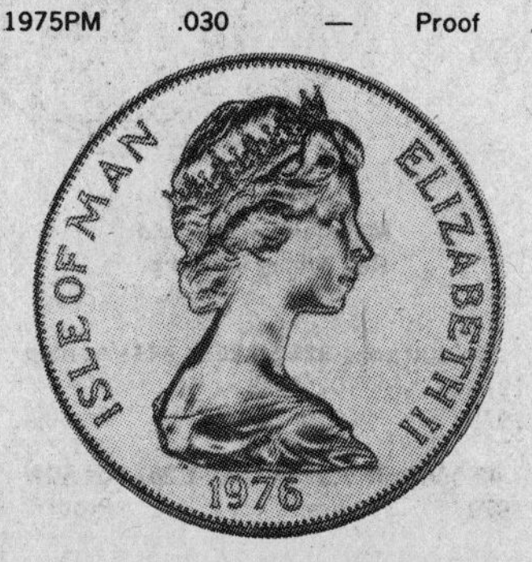

COPPER-NICKEL
Bicentenary Of American Independence

Y#	Date	Mintage	VF	XF	Unc
21	1976PM	.050	.75	1.25	2.50
		28.2800 gm., .925 SILVER, .8411 oz ASW			
21a	1976PM	—	—	—	27.50
	1976PM	.030	—	Proof	35.00

COPPER-NICKEL
Centenary of Horse Drawn Tram

Y#	Date	Mintage	VF	XF	Unc
22	1976PM	.050	.75	1.00	2.50
		28.2800 gm., .925 SILVER, .8411 oz ASW			
22a	1976PM	—	—	—	27.50
	1976PM	.030	—	Proof	35.00

COPPER-NICKEL
Silver Jubilee

Y#	Date	Mintage	VF	XF	Unc
23	1977PM	—	.75	1.00	6.00
		28.2800 gm., .925 SILVER, .8411 oz ASW			
23a	1977PM	—	—	—	27.50

Y#	Date	Mintage	VF	XF	Unc
23a	1977PM	.030	—	Proof	45.00

COPPER-NICKEL
Queen's Jubilee Appeal

Y#	Date	Mintage	VF	XF	Unc
25	1977PM	—	.75	1.00	2.50
	28.2800 gm., .925 SILVER, .8411 oz ASW				
25a	1977PM	.070	—	—	27.50
	1977PM	.030	—	Proof	30.00

COPPER-NICKEL
25th Anniversary of Coronation

Y#	Date	Mintage	VF	XF	Unc
26	1978	—	—	—	2.50
	28.2800 gm., .925 SILVER, .8411 oz ASW				
26a	1978	.070	—	—	27.50
	1978	.030	—	Proof	35.00

Mule, obv. of Isle of Man. Rev., Ascension Island, Y#1.

Y#	Date	Mintage	VF	XF	Unc
—	1978	—	—	—	250.00

COPPER-NICKEL
300th Anniversary of Manx Coinage

Y#	Date	Mintage	VF	XF	Unc
28	1979PM	—	—	—	2.50
	1979PM	—	—	Proof	—
	28.2800 gm., .925 SILVER, .8411 oz ASW				
28a	1979PM	.070	—	—	27.50
	1979PM	.030	—	Proof	40.00

COPPER-NICKEL
Millenium of Tynwald
Rev: Viking longship.

Y#	Date	Mintage	VF	XF	Unc
29	1979	.100	—	—	2.50
	28.2800 gm., .925 SILVER, .8411 oz ASW				
29a	1979	.025	—	—	27.50
	1979	.010	—	Proof	40.00
	43.0000 gm., .917 GOLD, 1.2678 oz AGW				
29b	1979	300 pcs.	—	Proof	1000.

52.0000 gm., .950 PLATINUM, 1.5884 oz APW

Y#	Date	Mintage	VF	XF	Unc
29c	1979	100 pcs.	—	Proof	1750.

COPPER-NICKEL
Millenium of Tynewald
Obv: Similar to Y#29. Rev: English Cog.

Y#	Date	Mintage	VF	XF	Unc
30	1979	.100	—	—	2.50
	28.2800 gm., .925 SILVER, .8411 oz ASW				
30a	1979	.025	—	—	27.50
	1979	.010	—	Proof	40.00
	43.0000 gm., .917 GOLD, 1.2678 oz AGW				
30b	1979	300 pcs.	—	Proof	1000.
	52.0000 gm., .950 PLATINUM, 1.5884 oz APW				
30c	1979	100 pcs.	—	Proof	1750.

COPPER-NICKEL
Millenium of Tynewald
Obv: Similar to Y#29. Rev: Flemish Carrack.

Y#	Date	Mintage	VF	XF	Unc
31	1979	.100	—	—	2.50
	28.2800 gm., .925 SILVER, .8411 oz ASW				
31a	1979	.025	—	—	27.50
	1979	.010	—	Proof	40.00
	43.0000 gm., .917 GOLD, 1.2678 oz AGW				
31b	1979	300 pcs.	—	Proof	1000.
	52.0000 gm., .950 PLATINUM, 1.5884 oz APW				
31c	1979	100 pcs.	—	Proof	1750.

COPPER-NICKEL
Millenium of Tynewald
Obv: Similar to Y#29.
Rev: Royalist Soldier and English Man-of-War.

Y#	Date	Mintage	VF	XF	Unc
32	1979	.100	—	—	2.50
	28.2800 gm., .925 SILVER, .8411 oz ASW				
32a	1979	.025	—	—	27.50
	1979	.010	—	Proof	40.00
	43.0000 gm., .917 GOLD, 1.2678 oz AGW				
32b	1979	300 pcs.	—	Proof	1000.
	52.0000 gm., .950 PLATINUM, 1.5884 oz APW				
32c	1979	100 pcs.	—	Proof	1750.

COPPER-NICKEL
Millenium of Tynewald
Obv: Similar to Y#29.
Rev: Lifeboat and Sir Hillary portrait.

Y#	Date	Mintage	VF	XF	Unc
33	1979	.100	—	—	2.50
	28.2800 gm., .925 SILVER, .8411 oz ASW				
33a	1979	.025	—	—	27.50
	1979	.010	—	Proof	40.00
	43.0000 gm., .917 GOLD, 1.2678 oz AGW				
33b	1979	300 pcs.	—	Proof	1000.
	52.0000 gm., .950 PLATINUM, 1.5884 oz APW				
33c	1979	100 pcs.	—	Proof	1750.

28.2800 gm., COPPER-NICKEL
Derby Bicentennial
Obv: Similar to Y#29.

Y#	Date	Mintage	VF	XF	Unc
35	1980PM	.100	—	—	2.50
	28.2800 gm., .925 SILVER, .8411 oz ASW				
35a	1980PM	.035	—	—	—
	1980PM	.020	—	Proof	—
	52.0000 gm., .950 PLATINUM, 1.5884 oz APW				
35b	1980PM	500 pcs.		Proof only	—

28.2800 gm., COPPER-NICKEL
1980 Winter Olympics - Lake Placid
Obv: Similar to Y#29.

Y#	Date	Mintage	VF	XF	Unc
36	1980PM	.100	—	—	—
	28.2800 gm., .925 SILVER, .8411 oz ASW				
36a	1980PM	.050	—	—	—
	1980PM	.030	—	Proof	—
	39.8000 gm., .917 GOLD, 1.1735 oz AGW				
36b	1980PM	1,500	—	—	—
	1980PM	500 pcs.	—	Proof	—
	52.0000 gm., .950 PLATINUM, 1.5884 oz APW				
36c	1980PM	100 pcs.	—	Proof	—

28.2800 gm., COPPER-NICKEL
22nd Olympiad Moscow
Obv: Similar to Y#29. Rev: Runner at top.

Y#	Date	Mintage	VF	XF	Unc
37	1980PM	.030	—	—	—
	28.2800 gm., .925 SILVER, .8411 oz ASW				
37a	1980PM	.010	—	Proof	—
	39.8000 gm., .917 GOLD, 1.1735 oz AGW				
37b	1980PM	1,500	—	—	—
	52.0000 gm., .950 PLATINUM, 1.5884 oz APW				
37c	1980PM	100 pcs.	—	Proof	—

28.2800 gm., COPPER-NICKEL
22nd Olympiad Moscow
Obv: Similar to Y#29. Rev: Javelin thrower at top.

Y#	Date	Mintage	VF	XF	Unc
38	1980PM	.030	—	—	—
	28.2800 gm., .925 SILVER, .8411 oz ASW				
38a	1980PM	.010	—	Proof	—
	39.8000 gm., .917 GOLD, 1.1735 oz AGW				
38b	1980PM	1,500	—	—	—
	52.0000 gm., .950 PLATINUM, 1.5884 oz APW				
38c	1980PM	100 pcs.	—	Proof	—

28.2800 gm., COPPER-NICKEL
22nd Olympiad Moscow
Obv: Similar to Y#29. Rev: Judo match at top.

Y#	Date	Mintage	VF	XF	Unc
39	1980PM	.030	—	—	—
	28.2800 gm., .925 SILVER, .8411 oz ASW				
39a	1980PM	.010	—	Proof	—
	39.8000 gm., .917 GOLD, 1.1735 oz AGW				
39b	1980PM	1,500	—	—	—
	52.0000 gm., .950 PLATINUM, 1.5884 oz APW				
39c	1980PM	100 pcs.	—	Proof	—

28.2800 gm., COPPER-NICKEL
80th Birthday of Queen Mother
Obv: Similar to Y#29.

Y#	Date	Mintage	VF	XF	Unc
46	1980PM	.100	—	—	—
	28.2800 gm., .500 SILVER, .4546 oz ASW				
46a	1980PM	.050	—	—	—
	28.2800 gm., .925 SILVER, .8411 oz ASW				
46a.1	1980PM	.030	—	Proof	—
	5.0000 gm., .3744 GOLD, .0601 oz AGW				
46b	1980PM	.050	—	—	—
	7.9600 gm., .917 GOLD, .2347 oz AGW				
46c	1980PM	1,000	—	—	—

50 NEW PENCE

COPPER-NICKEL

Y#	Date	Mintage	VF	XF	Unc
7	1971	.100	1.00	1.25	3.25
	1971	.010	—	Proof	8.50
	1972PM	1,000	25.00	40.00	60.00
	1973PM	1,000	25.00	40.00	60.00
	1974PM	1,000	25.00	40.00	60.00
	1975PM	.227	1.00	1.25	2.00
	15.5000 gm., .925 SILVER, .4610 oz ASW				
7a	1975PM	.020	—	—	17.50
	30.4000 gm., .950 PLATINUM, .9286 oz APW				
7b	1975PM	600 pcs.	—	Proof	500.00

50 PENCE

COPPER-NICKEL

Y#	Date	Mintage	VF	XF	Unc
20	1976PM	.250	1.00	1.25	3.00
	1977PM	—	—	—	2.50
	1978PM	—	—	—	2.50
	15.5000 gm., .925 SILVER, .4610 oz ASW				
20a	1976PM	.020	—	Proof	17.50
	1977PM	.010	—	Proof	17.50
	1978PM	.010	—	Proof	—
	30.4000 gm., .950 PLATINUM, .9286 oz APW				
20b	1976PM	600 pcs.	—	Proof	500.00
	1978PM	600 pcs.	—	Proof	500.00

COPPER-NICKEL
Rev: MM: Small circle containing stylized triskelion.

Y#	Date	Mintage	VF	XF	Unc
20.1	1979PM	—	—	—	—

Manx Millenium Viking Voyage
Edge inscription: H.M.Q.E.II ROYAL VISIT I.O.M. JULY 1979

Y#	Date	Mintage	VF	XF	Unc
34	1979PM	.050	—	—	4.00
	SILVER				
34a	1979PM	.010	—	—	—
	1979PM	5,000	—	Proof	—
	30.4000 gm., .950 PLATINUM, .9286 oz APW				
34b	1979PM	500 pcs.		Proof	—
	COPPER-NICKEL Edge inscription upside down.				
34.1	1979PM	—	—	—	4.00
	Plain edge				
34.2	1979PM	—	—	—	2.50

Y#	Date	Mintage	VF	XF	Unc
45	1980PM	—	—	—	—
	SILVER				
45a	1980PM	—	—	—	—
	.917 GOLD				
45b	1980PM	—	—	—	—
	.950 PLATINUM				
45c	1980PM	—	—	—	—

1/2 SOVEREIGN (POUND)

3.9940 gm., .917 GOLD, .1177 oz AGW
200th Anniversary of Acquisition

Fr#	Date	Mintage	VF	XF	Unc
3	1965	1,500	BV	BV	80.00
	.980 GOLD				
3a	1965	1,000	—	Proof	125.00

3.9813 gm., .917 GOLD, .1173 oz AGW

Y#	Date	Mintage	VF	XF	Unc
9	1973	.014	BV	BV	85.00
	1973	1,250	—	Proof	90.00
	1974	6,566	BV	BV	85.00
	1974	2,500	—	Proof	90.00
	1975	1,956	BV	BV	85.00
	1975	—	—	Proof	90.00
	1976	2,558	BV	BV	85.00
	1976	—	—	Proof	90.00
	1977	—	BV	BV	85.00
	1977	1,250	—	Proof	90.00
	Millenium of Tynewald				
35	1979PM	—	BV	BV	85.00
	1979PM	1,000	—	Proof	90.00

SOVEREIGN (POUND)

7.9881 gm., .917 GOLD, .2355 oz AGW
200th Anniversary of Acquisition

Fr#	Date	Mintage	VF	XF	Unc
2	1965	2,000	BV	BV	165.00
	.980 GOLD				
2a	1965	1,000	—	Proof	225.00

7.9627gm., .917 GOLD, .2347 oz AGW

Y#	Date	Mintage	VF	XF	Unc
10	1973	.040	BV	BV	155.00
	1973	1,250	—	Proof	165.00
	1974	8,604	BV	BV	160.00
	1974	2,500	—	Proof	160.00
	1975	956 pcs.	BV	175.00	200.00
	1975	—	—	Proof	160.00
	1976	1,238	BV	165.00	175.00
	1976	—	—	Proof	160.00
	1977	—	BV	165.00	175.00
	1977	1,250	—	Proof	160.00
	1978	Reported, not confirmed			

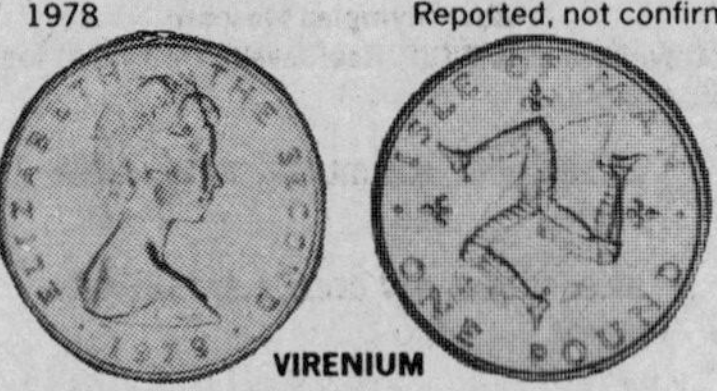

VIRENIUM

Y#	Date	Mintage	VF	XF	Unc
27	1978 w/'A.A' die mark	—	—	—	5.00
	1978 w/'A.B' die mark	—	—	—	4.00
	1978 w/'A.C' die mark	—	—	—	3.25
	1978 w/'A.D' die mark	3,780	—	—	12.00
	1978	.150	—	Proof	12.00
	1979 w/'A.A' die mark	—	—	—	3.50
	1979 w/'A.B' die mark	—	—	—	3.25
	1979 w/'A.C' die mark	—	—	—	3.25
	1979 w/crossed oars die mark	—	—	—	3.50
	.925 SILVER				
27a	1978PM	.100	—	Proof	21.00
	1979PM	.075	—	Proof	21.00
	PLATINUM				
27b	1978PM	1,000	—	Proof	300.00

VIRENIUM
Rev: MM: Circle containing stylized triskelion.

Y#	Date	Mintage	VF	XF	Unc
27.1	1979PM	—	—	—	—
	.917 GOLD Millenium of Tynewald				
36	1979PM	—	—	—	160.00
	1979PM	1,000	—	Proof	200.00

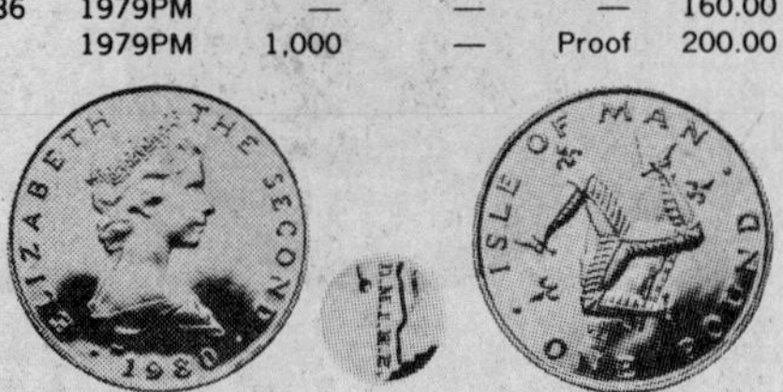

Rev: Privy mark "D.M.I.H.E." between legs.

Y#	Date	Mintage	VF	XF	Unc
27.2	1980PM	—	—	—	—

2 POUNDS

15.9253 gm., .917 GOLD, .4695 oz AGW

Y#	Date	Mintage	VF	XF	Unc
11	1973	3,612	BV	BV	310.00
	1973	1,250	—	Proof	350.00
	1974	1,257	BV	325.00	350.00
	1974	2,500	—	Proof	325.00
	1975	456 pcs.	350.00	375.00	400.00
	1975	—	—	Proof	325.00
	1976	578 pcs.	325.00	350.00	375.00
	1976	—	—	*Proof	325.00
	1977	—	BV	325.00	350.00
	1977	1,250	—	Proof	350.00
	Millenium of Tynewald				
37	1979	—	BV	325.00	350.00
	1979PM	1,000	—	Proof	375.00

5 POUNDS

39.9403 gm., .917 GOLD, 1.1776 oz AGW
200th Anniversary of Acquisition

Fr#	Date	Mintage	VF	XF	Unc
1	1965	500 pcs.	775.00	800.00	850.00
	.980 GOLD				
1a	1965	1,000	—	Proof	850.00

39.8134 gm., .917 GOLD, 1.1739 oz AGW

Y#	Date	Mintage	VF	XF	Unc
12	1973	3,035	BV	BV	775.00
	1973	1,250	—	Proof	800.00
	1974	481 pcs.	—	800.00	850.00
	1974	2,500	—	Proof	775.00
	1975	306 pcs.	—	800.00	850.00
	1975	—	—	Proof	775.00
	1976	370 pcs.	—	800.00	850.00
	1976	—	—	Proof	775.00
	1977	—	—	800.00	850.00
	1977	1,250	—	Proof	775.00
	1978		Reported, not confirmed		
	Millenium of Tynewald				
38	1979PM	—	—	—	800.00
	1979PM	1,000	—	Proof	—

WWII P.O.W. TOKENS

Issued in 1941 at Onchan internment camp for German prisoners of war.

1/2 PENNY

BRASS

P#	Date	Mintage	VF	XF	Unc
67	ND(1941)	—	35.00	45.00	65.00

PENNY

BRASS

P#	Date	Mintage	VF	XF	Unc
66	ND(1941)	—	7.50	12.50	20.00

6 PENCE

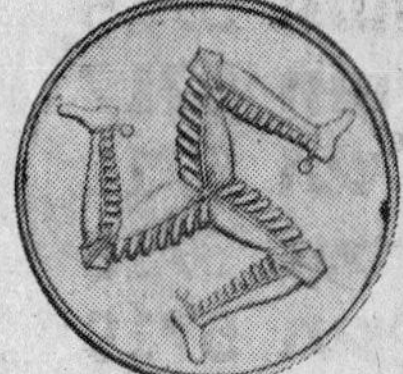

BRASS

P#	Date	Mintage	VF	XF	Unc
65	ND(1941)	—	17.50	25.00	35.00

NCLT ISSUES

MINT SETS

KM#	Date	Mintage	Identification	Issue Price	Mkt. Val.
S1	1965(3)	1,500	FR1-3	—	1100.
S2	1971(6)	50,000	Y2-7	3.00	5.00
S3	1973(4)	2,500	Y9-12	760.00	1300.
S4	1974(4)	250	Y9-12	—	1400.
S5	1975(6)	20,000	Y2-7	—	5.00
S6	1975(6)	20,000	Y2a-7a	56.50	75.00
S7	1975(4)	200	Y9-12	—	1500.
S8	1976(6)	20,000	Y17-22 wallet	—	3.50
S9	1976(6)	—	Y17-22 cased	—	8.00
S10	1976(6)	20,000	Y15a-20a	—	80.00
S11	1976(4)	—	Y9-12	—	1400.
S12	1977(6)	50,000	Y16-20,24	—	2.75
S13	1977(4)	180	Y9-12	—	1400.
S14	1978(7)	10,000	Y15a-20a, 27a	—	80.00
S15	1978(6)	—	—	—	4.00
S16	1979(4)	—	Y35-38	—	1350.

PROOF SETS

KM#	Date	Mintage	Identification	Issue Price	Mkt. Val.
101	1965(3)	1,000	Fr1a-3a	—	1200.
102	1971(6)	10,000	Y2-7	20.00	25.00
103	1973(4)	1,250	Y9-12	950.00	1400.
104	1974(4)	2,500	Y9-12	900.00	1350.
105	1975(6)	600	Y2b-7b	1175.	1600.
106	1975(4)	—	Y9-12	—	1350.
107	1976(6)	600	Y2b-7b	—	1600.
108	1976(4)	—	Y9-12	—	1350.
109	1977(6)	10,000	Y24a,16a-20a	—	75.00
110	1977(4)	1,250	Y9-12	—	1375.
111	1978(7)	600	Y15b-20b,27b	—	1750.
112	1978(6)	—	Y15-20	—	—
113	1979(7)	10,000	Y15a-20a,27a	110.00	—
114	1979(7)	500	Y15b-20b,27b	2765.	—
115	1979(4)	1,000	Y35-38	—	—
116	1980(6)	—	Y40a-45a	—	—
117	1980(6)	—	Y40b-45b	—	—
118	1980(6)	—	Y40c-45c	—	—

ISRAEL

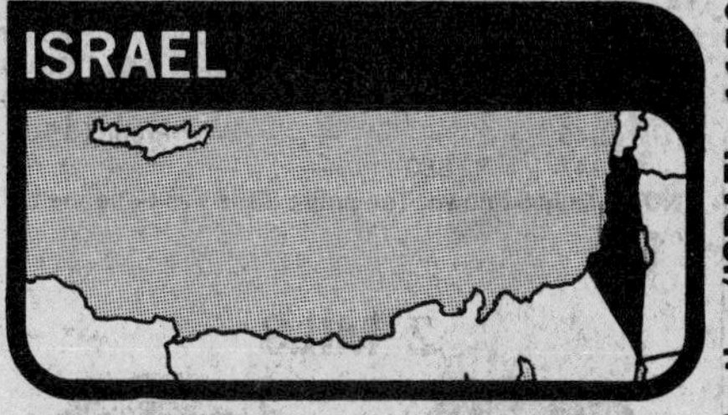

Israel, a Middle Eastern republic at the eastern end of the Mediterranean Sea, bounded by Lebanon on the north, Syria on the northeast, Jordan on the east, and Egypt on the southwest, has an area of 7,993 sq. mi. (20,701 sq. km.) and a population of 3.7 million. Capital: Jerusalem. Diamonds, chemicals, citrus, textiles, and minerals are exported.

Palestine, which corresponds to Canaan of the Bible, was settled by the Philistines about the 12th century B.C. and shortly thereafter was invaded by the Jews who established the kingdoms of Israel and Judah. Because of its position as part of the land bridge connecting Asia and Africa, Palestine was invaded and conquered by nearly all of the historic empires of ancient Europe and Asia. In the 16th century it became a Turkish satrap. After falling to the British in World War I, it, together with Transjordan, was mandated to Great Britain by the League of Nations, 1922.

For more than half a century prior to the termination of the British mandate over Palestine, 1948, Zionist leaders had sought to create a Jewish homeland for Jews dispersed throughout the world. For almost as long, Jews fleeing persecution had immigrated to Palestine. The Nazi persecutions of the 1930s and 1940s increased the Jewish movement to Palestine and generated international support for the creation of a Jewish state, first promulgated by the Balfour Declaration of 1917 which asserted British support for the endeavor. The dream of a Jewish homeland was realized on May 14, 1948 when Palestine was proclaimed the State of Israel.

MONETARY SYSTEM

1000 Mils = 1 Pound

PALESTINE

SOUVENIR MIL

(Holy Land)

BRONZE

KM#	Date	Mintage	VF	XF	Unc
1	1927	—	150.00	200.00	500.00

NOTE: This token which incorporates a reproduction of a 1927 1 Mil coin of Palestine is thought to have been created for sale to pilgrims as a souvenir of their visit to the Holyland. It is not known who produced them, nor how many were produced.

MIL

BRONZE

Y#	Date	Mintage	Fine	VF	XF	Unc
1	1927	10.000	.50	1.00	2.75	35.00
	1927	66 pcs.	—	—	Proof	750.00
	1935	.704	1.75	3.50	7.50	45.00
	1937	1.200	2.50	5.00	10.00	50.00
	1939	3.700	.50	1.00	4.00	35.00
	1939	—	—	—	Proof	150.00

Y#	Date	Mintage	Fine	VF	XF	Unc
1	1943	2.800	.75	1.50	2.50	25.00
	1944	1.400	.50	1.00	3.00	35.00
	1946	1.632	2.00	3.00	5.00	50.00
	1946	—	—	—	Proof	10,500.
	1947	*2.880	—	—	—	—

***NOTE:** Only 5 known. The entire issue was to be melted down.

2 MILS

BRONZE

Y#	Date	Mintage	Fine	VF	XF	Unc
2	1927	5.000	.50	1.00	4.00	35.00
	1927	66 pcs.	—	—	Proof	500.00
	1941	1.600	.65	1.25	7.00	45.00
	1941	—	—	—	Proof	85.00
	1942	2.400	.65	1.25	6.00	35.00
	1945	.960	3.00	6.00	10.00	65.00
	1946	.960	3.00	7.00	15.00	75.00
	1947	*.480	—	—	—	—

***NOTE:** The entire issue was melted down.

5 MILS

COPPER-NICKEL

Y#	Date	Mintage	Fine	VF	XF	Unc
3	1927	10.000	1.00	2.00	5.00	50.00
	1927	66 pcs.	—	—	Proof	500.00
	1934	.500	7.00	10.00	15.00	95.00
	1935	2.700	.50	1.00	4.00	45.00
	1939	2.000	.50	1.00	4.50	40.00
	1939	—	—	—	Proof	250.00
	1941	.400	5.50	11.00	16.00	75.00
	1941	—	—	—	Proof	100.00
	1946	1.000	.50	1.00	5.00	35.00
	1946	—	—	—	Proof	100.00
	1947	*1.000	—	—	—	—

***NOTE:** The entire issue was melted down.

BRONZE

Y#	Date	Mintage	Fine	VF	XF	Unc
3a	1942	2.700	.75	1.50	6.00	35.00
	1944	1.000	.75	1.50	4.50	45.00

10 MILS

COPPER-NICKEL

Y#	Date	Mintage	Fine	VF	XF	Unc
4	1927	5.000	1.00	2.00	10.00	75.00
	1927	66 pcs.	—	—	Proof	675.00
	1933	.500	3.50	7.00	20.00	90.00
	1933	—	—	—	Proof	100.00
	1934	.500	5.00	8.50	22.50	95.00
	1934	—	—	—	Proof	100.00
	1935	1.150	.75	1.50	11.00	50.00
	1935	—	—	—	Proof	100.00
	1937	.750	3.00	5.00	15.00	70.00
	1937	—	—	—	Proof	100.00
	1939	1.000	1.00	2.00	7.50	45.00
	1939	—	—	—	Proof	100.00
	1940	1.500	1.00	2.00	6.50	45.00
	1940	—	—	—	Proof	100.00
	1941	.400	10.00	20.00	50.00	90.00
	1941	—	—	—	Proof	200.00
	1942	.600	2.00	4.00	10.00	75.00
	1942	—	—	—	Proof	100.00
	1946	1.000	3.50	7.00	10.00	70.00
	1946	—	—	—	Proof	100.00
	1947	*1.000	—	—	—	—

***NOTE:** The entire issue was melted down.

BRONZE

Y#	Date	Mintage	Fine	VF	XF	Unc
4a	1942	1.000	2.00	4.00	15.00	70.00
	1943	1.000	6.00	10.00	20.00	75.00

20 MILS

COPPER-NICKEL

Y#	Date	Mintage	Fine	VF	XF	Unc
5	1927	1.500	4.00	10.00	20.00	90.00
	1927	66 pcs.	—	—	Proof	575.00
	1933	.250	17.50	35.00	75.00	125.00
	1934	.125	40.00	75.00	125.00	300.00
	1935	.575	5.00	10.00	20.00	90.00
	1940	.200	25.00	40.00	75.00	150.00
	1940	—	—	—	Proof	150.00
	1941	.100	50.00	75.00	100.00	200.00
	1941	—	—	—	Proof	250.00

BRONZE

Y#	Date	Mintage	Fine	VF	XF	Unc
5a	1942	1.100	5.00	7.00	25.00	90.00
	1944	1.000	20.00	50.00	100.00	500.00

50 MILS

5.8319 gm., .720 SILVER, .1350 oz ASW

Y#	Date	Mintage	Fine	VF	XF	Unc
6	1927	8.000	4.50	10.00	20.00	50.00
	1927	66 pcs.	—	—	Proof	750.00
	1931	.500	12.00	20.00	35.00	125.00
	1933	1.000	5.00	10.00	20.00	75.00
	1934	.399	10.00	20.00	50.00	125.00
	1935	5.600	4.50	7.50	10.00	40.00
	1939	3.000	4.50	7.50	10.00	40.00
	1939	—	—	—	Proof	140.00
	1940	2.000	5.00	10.00	20.00	50.00
	1940	—	—	—	Proof	140.00
	1942	5.000	4.75	7.00	15.00	40.00

100 MILS

11.6638 gm., .720 SILVER, .2700 oz ASW

Y#	Date	Mintage	Fine	VF	XF	Unc
7	1927	2.000	9.00	15.00	25.00	85.00
	1927	66 pcs.	—	—	Proof	1250.
	1931	.250	50.00	100.00	200.00	350.00
	1931	—	—	—	Proof	350.00
	1933	.500	20.00	40.00	65.00	150.00
	1934	.200	75.00	150.00	250.00	750.00
	1935	2.850	9.00	15.00	25.00	45.00
	1939	1.500	9.00	15.00	25.00	50.00
	1939	—	—	—	Proof	250.00
	1940	1.000	9.00	15.00	25.00	65.00
	1942	2.500	9.00	15.00	25.00	75.00

NCLT ISSUES

PROOF SETS

STANDARD METALS

KM#	Date	Mintage	Identification	Issue Price	Mkt. Val.
1	1927(14)	34	Y1-7, two each	—	13,500.
2	1927(7)	4	Y1-7	—	6750.

ISRAEL

HEBREW COIN DATING

Modern Israel's coins carry Hebrew dating formed from a combination of the 22 consonant letters of the Hebrew alphabet and read from right to left. The Jewish calendar dates back more than 5700 years, but only five milleniums are assumed in the dating of coins. Thus, the year 5735 (1975 AD) appears as 735, with the first two characters from the right indicating the number of years in hundreds; tav (400), plus shin (300). The next is Lamedh (30), followed by a separation mark which has the appearance of double quotation marks, then heh (5).

The separation mark - generally similar to a single quotation mark through 5718 (1958 AD), and like a double quotation mark thereafter - serves the purpose of indicating that the letters form a number, not a word, and on some issues can be confused with the character yodh (10), which in a stylized rendering can appear quite similar, although slightly larger and thicker. The separation mark does not appear in either form on a few commemorative issues.

The Jewish New Year falls in September or October by Christian calendar reckoning. Where dual dating is encountered, with but a few exceptions the Hebrew dating on the coins of modern Israel is 3760 years greater than the Christian dating; 5735 is equivalent to 1975 AD, with the 5000 assumed. These exceptions include the Chanuka (Feast of Lights) Pound 5719-24 (1958-63AD) and five Pound 5733-36 (1972-75AD) issues, along with the Bank of Israel gold 50 Pound commemorative of 5725 (1964AD). In such special instances the differential from Christian dating is 3761 years, except in the instance of the 5720 Chanuka Pound, which is dated 1960AD, as is the issue of 5721, an arrangement which reflects the fact that the events fall early in the Jewish year and late in the Christian.

The Star of David is not a mintmark. It appears only on some coins sold by the government Coin and Medal Co. for collectors.

1948	תש'ח	5708
1949	תש'ט	5709
1952	תשי'ב	5712
1954	תשי'ד	5714
1955	תשט'ו	5715
1957	תשי'ז	5717
1958	תשי"ח	5718
1958	תשי"ח	5718
1959	תשיט	5719
1959	תשי"ט	5719
1960	תש"ך	5720
1960	תשך	5720
1961	תשכ"א	5721
1962	תשכ"ב	5722
1963	תשכ"ג	5723
1964	תשכ"ד	5724
1965	תשכ"ה	5725
1966	תשכ"ו	5726
1967	תשכ"ז	5727

1968	תשכ"ח	5728
1969	תשכ"ט	5729
1970	תש"ל	5730
1971	תשל"א	5731
1972	תשל"ב	5732
1973	תשל"א	5733
1974	תשל"ד	5734
1975	תשל"ה	5735
1976	תשל"ו	5736
1977	תשל"ז	5737
1978	תשל"ח	5738
1979	תשל"ט	5739
1980	תש"ד	5740

MONETARY SYSTEM

1000 Mils = 1 Pound

25 MILS

ALUMINUM

Y#	Date	Year	Mintage	VF	XF	Unc
1	5708	(1948)	.043	100.00	350.00	1000.
	5709	(1949) open link	.650	20.00	35.00	150.00
	5709	(1949) closed link	—	15.00	25.00	40.00

NOTE: Above 3 coins were issued April 6, 1949.

NEW COINAGE SYSTEM

1000 Prutot = 1 Lira

NOTE: The 1949 Prutot coins, except for the 100 and 500 Prutot values, occur with (w/p) and without (wo/p) a small pearl under the bar connecting the wreath on the reverse.

PRUTA

ALUMINUM

Y#	Date	Year	Mintage	VF	XF	Unc
2	5709	(1949) w/pearl	5.185	.50	1.00	2.50
	5709	(1949)w/o pearl	Inc. Ab.	2.00	5.00	10.00

5 PRUTOT

BRONZE

Y#	Date	Year	Mintage	VF	XF	Unc
3	5709	(1949) w/pearl	10.045	.50	2.00	8.00
	5709	(1949)w/o pearl	Inc. Ab.	1.50	5.00	15.00

10 PRUTOT

BRONZE

Y#	Date	Year	Mintage	VF	XF	Unc
4	5709	(1949) w/pearl	14.948	2.00	10.00	35.00
	5709	(1949)w/o pearl	Inc. Ab.	.75	1.50	5.00

ALUMINUM

Y#	Date	Year	Mintage	VF	XF	Unc
5	5712	(1952)	26.042	.25	.75	5.00

Y#	Date	Year	Mintage	VF	XF	Unc
5a	5717	(1957)	1.000	.25	1.00	5.00
	COPPER ELECTROPLATED ALUMINUM					
5b	5717	(1957)	1.088	.25	1.00	5.00

25 PRUTOT

COPPER-NICKEL

Y#	Date	Year	Mintage	VF	XF	Unc
6	5709	(1949) w/pearl	13.020	.50	1.25	3.50
	5709	(1949)w/o pearl	Inc. Ab.	10.00	20.00	50.00

NICKEL-CLAD STEEL

Y#	Date	Year	Mintage	VF	XF	Unc
6a (7)	5714	(1954)	3.697	.75	1.00	4.00

50 PRUTOT

COPPER-NICKEL

Reeded Edge

Y#	Date	Year	Mintage	VF	XF	Unc
8	5709	(1949) w/pearl	12.040	5.00	12.50	30.00
	5709	(1949)w/o pearl	Inc. Ab.	1.00	2.00	5.00
	5714	(1954)	.250	12.50	30.00	80.00
	Plain Edge					
8a	5714	(1954)	4.500	.50	1.50	5.00
	NICKEL-CLAD STEEL **Plain Edge**					
8b (9)	5714	(1954)	17.774	.50	1.00	4.00

100 PRUTOT

COPPER-NICKEL

Y#	Date	Year	Mintage	VF	XF	Unc
10	5709	(1949)	6.062	1.00	2.00	4.00
	5715	(1955)	5.868	1.00	2.00	4.00

NICKEL-CLAD STEEL

Reduced size, 25.6mm -Bern die — Rev: Wreath large, close to edge.

Y#	Date	Year	Mintage	VF	XF	Unc
10a (11.1)	5714	(1954)	.700	1.50	2.25	3.50

UTRECHTdie.Rev:Small Wreath, Away From Edge.

Y#	Date	Year	Mintage	VF	XF	Unc
10a.2 (11.2)	5714	(1954)	.020	500.00	750.00	1200.

250 PRUTOT

COPPER-NICKEL

Y#	Date	Year	Mintage	VF	XF	Unc
12	5709	(1949)	w/pearl			
			2.020	1.50	10.00	25.00
	5709	(1949)	w/o pearl			
			Inc. Ab.	1.00	2.50	6.00

14.4000gm., .500 SILVER, .2315oz ASW

Y#	Date	Year	Mintage	VF	XF	Unc
12a (13)	5709H	(1949)	.044	7.50	10.00	15.00

500 PRUTOT

25.5000 gm., .500 SILVER, .4099 oz ASW

Y#	Date	Year	Mintage	VF	XF	Unc
14	5709	(1949)	.034	15.00	25.00	40.00

NEW MONETARY SYSTEM

100 Agorot = 1 Lira

AGORA

1960 normal date

1960 large date

1961 thick date

1961 wide date

1962 large date

1962 small date

ALUMINUM

Y#	Date	Year	Mintage	VF	XF	Unc
22	5720	(1960)	"Lamed" with serif			
			12.768	.50	1.00	12.50
	5720	(1960)	"Lamed" w/o lower serif			
			Inc. Ab.	5.00	25.00	200.00
	5720	(1960)	large date			
			300 pcs.	250.00	550.00	1500.
	5721	(1961)	19.262	.50	5.00	10.00
	5721	(1961)	thick date			
			Inc. Ab.	5.00	20.00	200.00
	5721	(1961)	wide date			
			Inc. Ab.	5.00	22.50	200.00
	5722	(1962)	large date			
			14.500	.25	.40	.50
	5722	(1962)	small date, small serifs			
			Inc. Ab.	5.00	8.00	20.00
	5723	(1963)	14.804	.25	.50	1.00
	5723	(1963)	inverted reverse			
			.010	4.00	7.00	25.00
	5724	(1964)	27.552	.25	.50	.85
	5725	(1965)	20.708	—	.15	.30
	5726	(1966)	10.165	—	.15	.30
	5727	(1967)	6.781	—	.15	.25
	5728	(1968)	20.899	—	.15	.30
	5729	(1969)	22.120	—	.15	.30
	5730	(1970)	18.205	—	.15	.25
	5731	(1971)	7.488	—	.10	.30
	5732	(1972)	24.912	—	.10	.20
	5733	(1973)	20.548	—	.10	.20
	5734	(1974)	42.080	—	.10	.20
	5735	(1975)	1.574	—	.10	.20
	5736	(1976)	6.496	—	—	.15

With star of David in field

Y#	Date	Year	Mintage	VF	XF	Unc
22a	5731	(1971)	.126	.10	.20	.35
	5732	(1972)	.068	.10	.20	.45
	5734	(1974)	.093	—	.15	.35
	5735	(1975)	.062	.10	.20	.40
	5736	(1976)	—	—	.10	.25
	5737	(1977)	—	—	.10	.20
	5738	(1978)	—	—	—	—
	5739	(1979)	—	—	—	—

25th Anniversary of Independence

Y#	Date	Year	Mintage	VF	XF	Unc
59	5733	(1973)	.100			
			In sets only	.50	1.25	2.50

NICKEL
25th Anniversary of Bank of Israel

Y#	Date	Year	Mintage	VF	XF	Unc
92	5740	1980	—	—	—	1.50

5 AGOROT

1961 normal 1961 I.C.I.

ALUMINUM-BRONZE

Y#	Date	Year	Mintage	VF	XF	Unc
24	5720	(1960)	8.019	.35	1.00	12.50
	5721	(1961)	sharp, flat date			
			15.090	.30	.75	2.00
	5721	(1961)	I.C.I. issue w/ high date w/ serifs			
			5.000	15.00	75.00	375.00
	5722	(1962)	large date			
			11.198	.25	.40	1.00
	5722	(1962)	small date			
			Inc. Ab.	3.50	6.50	13.50
	5723	(1963)	1.429	.35	.60	1.50
	5724	(1964)	.021	20.00	50.00	500.00
	5725	(1965)	.201	.15	.35	.90
	5726	(1966)	.291	.15	.30	.80
	5727	(1967)	2.195	—	.15	.40
	5728	(1968)	4.020	—	.15	.40
	5729	(1969)	2.200	—	.10	.20
	5730	(1970)	6.071	—	.15	.35
	5731	(1971)	11.090	—	.15	.35
	5732	(1972)	8.305	—	.10	.30
	5733	(1973)	17.330	—	—	.35
	5734	(1974)	10.470	—	.10	.30
	5735	(1975)	—	—	.10	.30

COPPER-NICKEL
With star of David in field

Y#	Date	Year	Mintage	VF	XF	Unc
24a	5731	(1971)	.126	.10	.20	.50
	5732	(1972)	.069	—	.15	.45
	5733	(1973)	.098	—	—	—
	5734	(1974)	.093	—	.15	.35
	5735	(1975)	.062	—	.15	.35
	5736	(1976)	—	—	.10	.25
	5737	(1977)	—	—	.10	.25

ALUMINUM

Y#	Date	Year	Mintage	VF	XF	Unc
24b	5736	(1976)	13.896	—	.10	.20
	5737	(1977)	—	—	—	.10
	5738	(1978)	—	—	—	—
	5739	(1979)	—	—	—	—

COPPER-NICKEL
25th Anniversary of Independence

Y#	Date	Year	Mintage	VF	XF	Unc
60	5733	(1973)	.100			
			In sets only	.35	.75	1.50

NICKEL
25th Anniversary of Bank of Israel

Y#	Date	Year	Mintage	VF	XF	Unc
93	5740	1980	—	—	—	2.00

10 AGOROT

ALUMINUM-BRONZE

Y#	Date	Year	Mintage	VF	XF	Unc
25	5720	(1960)	14.397	.50	1.25	11.50
	5721	(1961)	12.821	.50	1.00	10.00
	5721	(1961)	"PATCHA" in Arabic, leg: "ISRAEL"			
			Inc. Ab.	50.00	100.00	350.00

Large date-thick letters Small date-thin letters

Y#	Date	Year	Mintage	VF	XF	Unc
25	5722	(1962)	large date, thick letters 8.845	.25	.50	1.00
	5722	(1962)	small date, thin letters Inc. Ab.	.50	4.50	15.00
	5723	(1963)	3.931	.25	.50	1.00
	5724	(1964)	lg. date 3.612	.25	.50	1.50
	5724	(1964)	sm. date Inc. Ab.	5.00	15.00	55.00
	5725	(1965)	.201	.25	.50	1.50
	5726	(1966)	7.276	.15	.30	.75
	5727	(1967)	6.426	.10	.20	.50
	5728	(1968)	4.825	.10	.20	.50
	5729	(1969)	6.810	.10	.20	.40
	5730	(1970)	5.191	—	.15	.40
	5731	(1971)	7.700	—	.15	.40
	5732	(1972)	9.663	—	.15	.40
	5733	(1973)	14.480	—	.15	.40
	5734	(1974)	22.040	—	.10	.35
	5735	(1975)	25.135	—	.10	.35
	5736	(1976)	48.716	—	.10	.25
	5737	(1977)	—	—	—	—

COPPER-NICKEL
With star of David in field

Y#	Date	Year	Mintage	VF	XF	Unc
25a	5731	(1971)	.126	.10	.20	.50
	5732	(1972)	.069	.10	20	.50
	5734	(1974)	.093	—	.15	.40
	5735	(1975)	.062	—	.10	.35
	5736	(1976)	3.901	—	—	.20
	5737	(1977)	—	—	—	.20

ALUMINUM

Y#	Date	Year	Mintage	VF	XF	Unc
25b	5737	(1977)	—	—	—	.15
	5738	(1978)	—	—	—	.15
	5739	(1979)	—	—	—	—

COPPER-NICKEL
25th Anniversary of Independence

Y#	Date	Year	Mintage	VF	XF	Unc
61	5733	(1973)	.100 In sets only	.65	1.25	2.50

NICKEL
25th Anniversary of Bank of Israel

Y#	Date	Year	Mintage	VF	XF	Unc
94	5740	1980	—	—	—	2.50

25 AGOROT

ALUMINUM-BRONZE

Y#	Date	Year	Mintage	VF	XF	Unc
26	5720	(1960)	4.391	.50	1.50	2.00
	5721	(1961)	5.009	.35	1.00	1.50
	5722	(1962)	.882	.50	.80	2.00
	5723	(1963)	.194	.50	2.00	5.00
	5724	(1964)	Five trial pieces only			
	5725	(1965)	.187	.25	.50	2.00
	5726	(1966)	.320	.15	.30	.50
	5727	(1967)	.325	.10	.20	.50
	5728	(1968)	.445	.10	.25	.60
	5729	(1969)	.432	.10	.20	.50
	5730	(1970)	.677	.10	.20	.50
	5731	(1971)	.308	.10	.20	.50
	5732	(1972)	1.633	—	.15	.30
	5733	(1973)	2.916	—	.15	.30
	5734	(1974)	2.320	—	.15	.30
	5735	(1975)	—	—	.10	.40
	5736	(1976)	1.215	—	.10	.25
		(1978)	—	—	—	—

COPPER-NICKEL
With star of David in field

Y#	Date	Year	Mintage	VF	XF	Unc
26a	5731	(1971)	.126	.10	.20	.50
	5732	(1972)	.069	.10	.25	.65
	5734	(1974)	.093	.10	.20	.50
	5735	(1975)	.062	.10	.20	.60
	5736	(1976)	3.901	—	.10	.35
	5737	(1977)	—	—	.10	.30
	5739	(1979)	—	—	—	—

25th Anniversary of Independence

Y#	Date	Year	Mintage	VF	XF	Unc
62	5733	(1973)	.100 In sets only	.50	1.00	2.00

NICKEL
25th Anniversary of Bank of Israel

Y#	Date	Year	Mintage	VF	XF	Unc
95	5740	1980	—	—	—	3.00

1/2 LIRA (POUND)

COPPER-NICKEL

Y#	Date	Year	Mintage	VF	XF	Unc
36	5723	(1963)	5.607	1.50	3.50	7.50
	5724	(1964)	3.762	.35	.85	2.00
	5725	(1965)	1.551	.30	.75	1.75
	5726	(1966)	2.139	.15	.40	1.00
	5727	(1967)	1.942	.15	.35	.90
	5728	(1968)	1.183	.20	.40	1.00
	5729	(1969)	.450	.20	.40	1.00
	5730	(1970)	.972	.15	.35	.90
	5731	(1971)	.398	.20	.40	1.00
	5732	(1972)	.211	.20	.40	1.00
	5733	(1973)	3.425	.10	.20	.50
	5734	(1974)	4.275	.10	.20	.50
	5735	(1975)	11.066	—	.15	.35
	5736	(1976)	1.833	—	.10	.25
	5737	(1977)	—	—	.10	.25

With star of David in field.

Y#	Date	Year	Mintage	VF	XF	Unc
36a	5731	(1971)	.126	.15	.40	1.00
	5732	(1972)	.069	.15	.40	1.00
	5734	(1974)	.093	.15	.35	.75
	5735	(1975)	.062	.15	.35	.75
	5736	(1976)	—	.10	.20	.50
	5737	(1977)	—	.10	.20	.50
	5738	(1978)	—	—	—	—
	5739	(1979)	—	—	—	—

25th Anniversary of Independence

Y#	Date	Year	Mintage	VF	XF	Unc
63	5733	(1973)	.100 In sets only	.50	1.00	2.00

NICKEL
25th Anniversary of Bank of Israel

Y#	Date	Year	Mintage	VF	XF	Unc
96	5740	1980	—	—	—	3.50

LIRA (POUND)

COPPER-NICKEL

Y#	Date	Year	Mintage	VF	XF	Unc
37	5723	(1963)	4.212	.75	2.00	5.00
	5724	(1964)	Only ten trial pieces struck			
	5725	(1965)	.166	.75	1.00	2.25
	5726	(1966)	.290	.60	1.00	1.75
	5727	(1967)	.180	.75	1.00	2.00

Y#	Date	Year	Mintage	VF	XF	Unc
46	5727	(1967)	3.830	.50	1.00	1.50
	5728	(1968)	3.932	.50	1.00	1.50
	5729	(1969)	12.484	.35	.75	1.50
	5730	(1970)	4.805	.50	1.00	1.50
	5731	(1971)	3.058	.50	1.00	1.50
	5732	(1972)	2.489	.15	.35	.75
	5733	(1973)	10.365	.10	.25	.50
	5734	(1974)	6.287	.25	.50	1.50
	5735	(1975)	.225	.15	.35	.75
	5736	(1976)	10.364	.10	.25	.50
	5737	(1977)	—	.15	.35	.75
	5738	(1978)	—	—	—	—

With star of David in field.

Y#	Date	Year	Mintage	VF	XF	Unc
46a	5731	(1971)	.126	.25	.50	1.00
	5732	(1972)	.069	.25	.50	1.00
	5734	(1974)	.093	.20	.40	.85
	5735	(1975)	.062	.20	.40	.85
	5736	(1976)	—	.15	.35	.75
	5737	(1977)	—	.15	.35	.75
	5738	(1978)	—	—	—	—
	5739	(1979)	—	—	—	—

25th Anniversary of Independence

Y#	Date	Year	Mintage	VF	XF	Unc
64	5733	(1973)	.100 In sets only	.50	1.00	2.00

COMMEMORATIVE COINS

NOTE: All proof commemoratives with the exception of the 1 and 5 Lirot issues of 1958 are distinguished from the uncirculated editions by the presence of the Hebrew letter "mem".

1/2 SHEKELS

COPPER-NICKEL
Feast Of Purim

Y#	Date	Year	Mintage	XF	Unc	Proof
29	5721	(1961)	.020	20.00	35.00	—
	5721	(1961)	5,000	—	—	85.00
	5722	(1962)	.020	13.50	22.50	—
	5722	(1962)	.010	—	—	35.00

LIRA(POUND)

COPPER-NICKEL
Chanuka-Law Is Light

Y#	Date	Year	Mintage	XF	Unc	Proof
17	5718	1958	.150	3.00	6.00	—
	5718	1958	5,000	—	—	65.00

Deganya

Y#	Date	Year	Mintage	XF	Unc	Proof
19	5719	1960	.050	4.00	10.00	—
	5719	1960	5,000	—	—	100.00

Henrietta Szold

Y#	Date	Year	Mintage	XF	Unc	Proof
27	5720	1960	.017	60.00	150.00	—
	5720	1960	3,000	—	—	500.00

Heroism And Sacrifice

Y#	Date	Year	Mintage	XF	Unc	Proof
30	5721	1961	.019	20.00	30.00	—
	5721	1961	9,428	—	—	45.00

Chanuka - Italian Lamp

Y#	Date	Year	Mintage	XF	Unc	Proof
34	5722	1962	9,657	75.00	125.00	—
	5722	1962	6,040	—	—	175.00

18th Century

Chanuka-North Africa Lamp

Y#	Date	Year	Mintage	XF	Unc	Proof
38	5723	1963	.010	75.00	120.00	—
	5723	1963	5,500	—	—	165.00

NICKEL
25th Anniversary ofBank of Israel

Y#	Date	Year	Mintage	XF	Unc	Proof
97	5740	1980	—	—	—	4.00

5 LIROT (POUNDS)

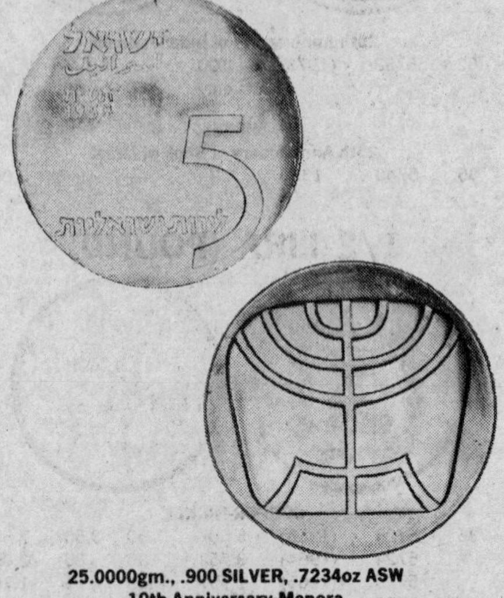

25.0000gm., .900 SILVER, .7234oz ASW
10th Anniversary-Menora

Y#	Date	Year	Mintage	XF	Unc	Proof
16	5718	1958	.098	22.50	35.00	—
	5718	1958	2,000	—	—	950.00

11th Anniversary
Ingathering Of The Exiles

Y#	Date	Year	Mintage	XF	Unc	Proof
18	5719	1959	.027	35.00	55.00	—
	5719	1959	4,792	—	—	175.00

12th Anniversary-Dr. Theodor Herzl

Y#	Date	Year	Mintage	XF	Unc	Proof
20	5720	1960	.034	35.00	50.00	—
	5720	1960	4,923	—	—	175.00

13th Anniversary-Bar Mitzvah

Y#	Date	Year	Mintage	XF	Unc	Proof
28	5721	1961	.020	65.00	125.00	—
	5721	1961	4,561	—	—	165.00

14th Anniversary
Negev Industrialization

Y#	Date	Year	Mintage	XF	Unc	Proof
31	5722	1962	.010	100.00	'75.00	—
	5722	1962	5,050	—	—	200.00

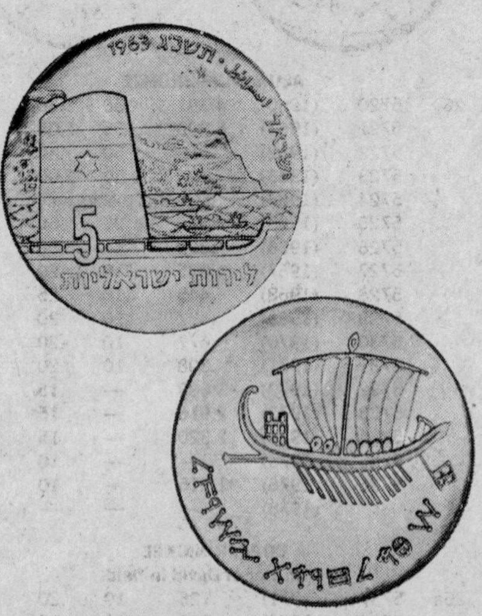

15th Anniversary-Seafaring

Y#	Date	Year	Mintage	XF	Unc	Proof
35	5723	1963	5,990	525.00	700.00	—
	5723	1963	4,500	—	—	800.00

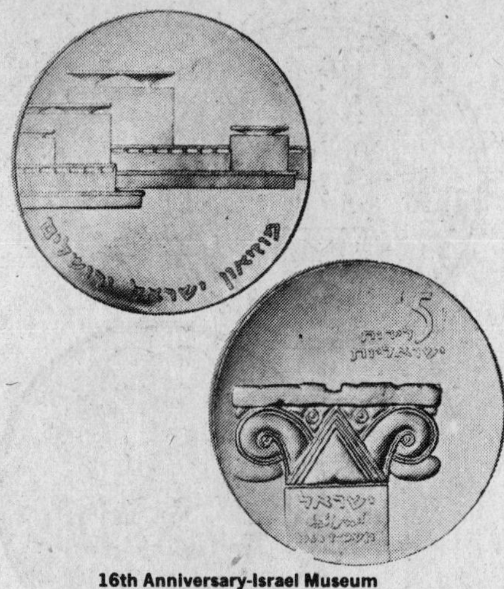

16th Anniversary-Israel Museum

Y#	Date	Year	Mintage	XF	Unc	Proof
39	5724	1964	.011	100.00	175.00	—
	5724	1964	4,500	—	—	200.00

17th Anniversary-Knesset Building

Y#	Date	Year	Mintage	XF	Unc	Proof
41	5725	1965	.025	35.00	55.00	—
	5725	1965	7,660	—	—	75.00

18th Anniversary-Crown of Life

Y#	Date	Year	Mintage	XF	Unc	Proof
42	5726	1966	.033	25.00	35.00	—
	5726	1966	.011	—	—	50.00

19th Anniversary-Port of Eilat

Y#	Date	Year	Mintage	XF	Unc	Proof
43	5727	1967	.030	40.00	50.00	—
	5727	1967	7,755	—	—	75.00

20.0000gm., .750 SILVER, .4823oz ASW
Chanuka-Russian Lamp

Y#	Date	Year	Mintage	XF	Unc	Proof
57	5732	1972	0.75	BV	15.00	—
	5732	1972	.022	—	—	17.50

20.0000gm., .500 SILVER, .3215oz ASW
Chanuka-Babylonian Lamp

Y#	Date	Year	Mintage	XF	Unc	Proof
69	5733	1973	.095	BV	10.00	—
	5733	1973	.045	—	—	12.50

COPPER-NICKEL

Y#	Date	Year	Mintage	XF	Unc	Proof
86	5738	1978	—	—	—	—

20.0000gm., .500 SILVER

Y#	Date	Year	Mintage	XF	Unc	Proof
	5739	1979	—	—	—	1.25

NICKEL
25th Anniversary ofBank of Israel

Y#	Date	Year	Mintage	XF	Unc	Proof
98	5740	1980	—	—	—	5.00

26.0000gm., .900 SILVER, .7524oz ASW
Victory Commemorative

Y#	Date	Year	Mintage	XF	Unc	Proof
44	5727	1967	.235	BV	25.00	—
44a	5727	1967	.050	—	—	25.00

20th Anniversary-Jerusalem

Y#	Date	Year	Mintage	XF	Unc	Proof
47	5728	1968	.050	BV	30.00	—
	5728	1968	.021	—	—	25.00

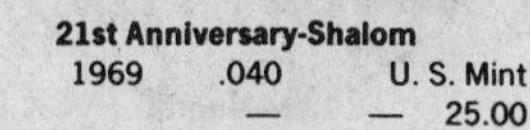

21st Anniversary-Shalom

Y#	Date	Year	Mintage	XF	Unc	Proof
49	5729	1969	.040	U. S. Mint		
				—	— 25.00	—

Rev: K A F under helmet.

Y#	Date	Year	Mintage	XF	Unc	Proof
49a	5729	1969	.020	Jerusalem Mint		
			—	25.00	32.50	—
	5729	1969	.020	U. S. Mint		
			—	—	—	50.00

Y#	Date	Year	Mintage	XF	Unc	Proof
51a	5731	1971	.030	—	27.50	—
	5731	1971	.014	—	—	32.50

Star of David
Jerusalem Mint

22nd Anniversary Mikveh Israel School

Y#	Date	Year	Mintage	XF	Unc	Proof
52	5730	1970	.048	BV	25.00	—
	5730	1970	.023	—	—	27.50

Pidyon Haben

Y#	Date	Year	Mintage	XF	Unc	Proof
51b	5732	1972	star			
			.030	BV	25.00	—
	5732	1972	no star			
			.015	22.50	35.00	—
51e	5732	1972	.013	—	—	30.00

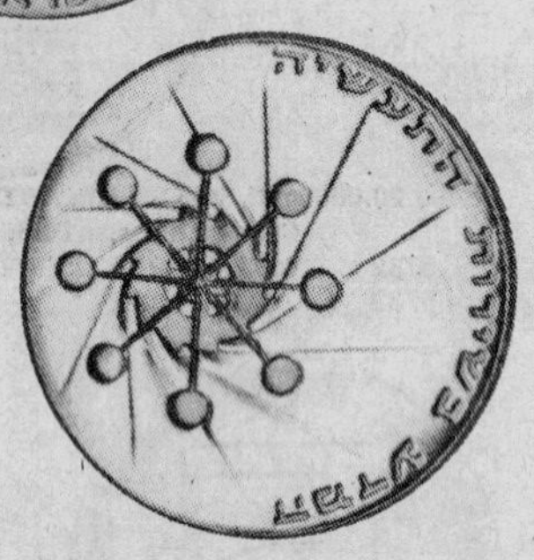

23rd Anniversary-Science and Industry

Y#	Date	Year	Mintage	XF	Unc	Proof
53.1	5731	1971	.030	Utrecht Mint		
				22.50	32.50	—
53.2	5731	1971	.023	Jerusalem Mint		
				27.50	40.00	—
53a	5731	1971	.018	—	—	40.00

24th Anniversary-Aviation

Y#	Date	Year	Mintage	XF	Unc	Proof
56	5732	1972	.050	BV	25.00	—
	5732	1972	.015	—	—	40.00

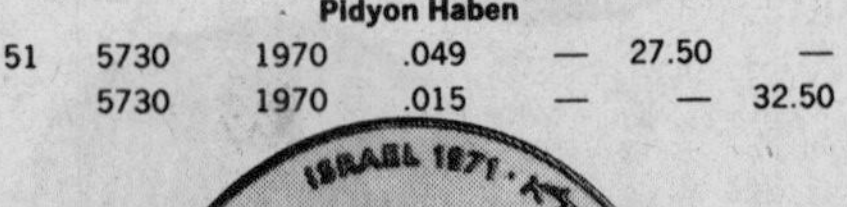

Pidyon Haben

Y#	Date	Year	Mintage	XF	Unc	Proof
51	5730	1970	.049	—	27.50	—
	5730	1970	.015	—	—	32.50

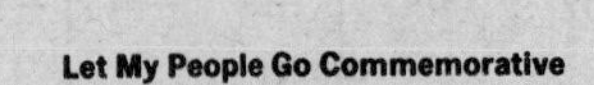

Let My People Go Commemorative

Y#	Date	Year	Mintage	XF	Unc	Proof
54	5731	1971	.074	BV	25.00	—
	5731	1971	.020	—	—	30.00

Pidyon Haben

Y#	Date	Year	Mintage	XF	Unc	Proof
58	5733	1973	.105	BV	22.50	—
	5733	1973	.015	—	—	25.00

25th Anniversary of Independence

Y#	Date	Year	Mintage	XF	Unc	Proof
65	5733	1973	.124	BV	22.50	—
	5733	1973	.042	—	—	22.50

Pidyon Haben

Y#	Date	Year	Mintage	XF	Unc	Proof
58a	5734	1974	.109	BV	25.00	—
	5734	1974	.044	—	—	25.00

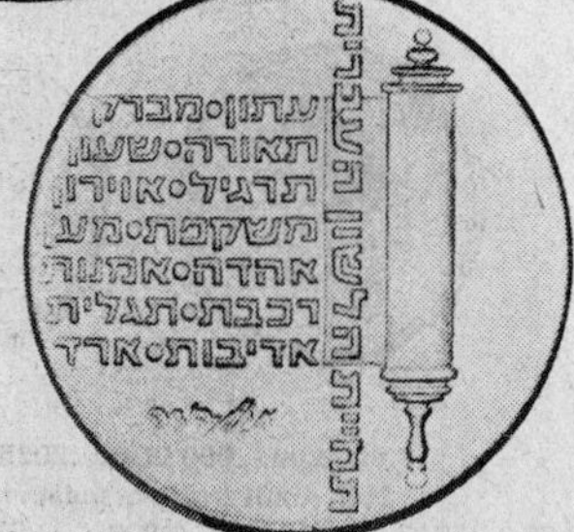

Hebrew Language Revival

Y#	Date	Year	Mintage	XF	Unc	Proof
70	5734	1974	.127	BV	22.50	—
	5734	1974	.050	—	—	22.50

20.0000gm., .500 SILVER, .3215oz ASW
Damascus Hannuka Lamp

Y#	Date	Year	Mintage	XF	Unc	Proof
73	5734	1974	.074	BV	12.50	—
	5734	1974	.059	—	—	20.00

Holland Hannuka Lamp

Y#	Date	Year	Mintage	XF	Unc	Proof
77	5735	1975	.068	12.50	25.00	—
	5735	1975	.050	—	—	32.50

26.0000gm., .900 SILVER, .7524oz ASW
U.S. Hannuka Lamp

Y#	Date	Year	Mintage	XF	Unc	Proof
80	5736	1976	.044	45.00	60.00	—
	5736	1976	.034	—	—	70.00

COPPER-NICKEL
Hanukka
Open style "mem"

Y#	Date	Year	Mintage	XF	Unc	Proof
83	5738	1977	.046	5.00	10.00	—
	5738	1977	.012	—	—	30.00

Closed style "mem"

Y#	Date	Year	Mintage	XF	Unc	Proof
—	5738	1977	.017	—	—	25.00

20 LIROT

7.9880gm., .917 GOLD, .2355oz AGW
Dr. Theodor Herzl

Y#	Date	Year	Mintage	XF	Unc	Proof
21	5720	1960	.010	450.00	650.00	—

25 LIROT

26.0000gm., .935 SILVER, .7816oz ASW
David Ben Gurion

Y#	Date	Year	Mintage	XF	Unc	Proof
71	5734	1974	.100	BV	25.00	—
	5734	1974	.065	—	—	30.00

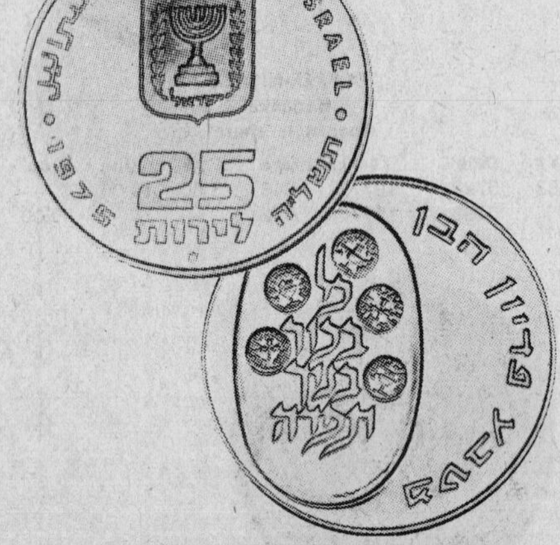

26.0000gm., .900 SILVER, .7524oz ASW
Pidyon Haben

Y#	Date	Year	Mintage	XF	Unc	Proof
74	5735	1975	.063	BV	22.50	—
	5735	1975	.049	—	—	25.00
	5736	1976	.050	BV	22.50	—
	5736	1976	.030	—	—	25.00

30.0000gm., .800 SILVER, .7717oz ASW
25th Anniversary of Israel Bond Program

Y#	Date	Year	Mintage	XF	Unc	Proof
75	5735	1975	.053	BV	25.00	—
	5735	1975	.041	—	—	30.00

26.0000gm., .900 SILVER, .7524oz ASW
28th Anniversary of Independence

Y#	Date	Year	Mintage	XF	Unc	Proof
78	5736	1976	.045	BV	22.50	
	5736	1976	.035	—	—	45.00

30.0000gm., .800 SILVER, .7717oz ASW
Pidyon Haben

Y#	Date	Year	Mintage	XF	Unc	Proof
79	5736	1976	.050	BV	25.00	—
	5736	1976	.030	—	—	45.00

20.0000gm., .500 SILVER, .3215oz ASW
29th Anniversary of Independence

Y#	Date	Year	Mintage	XF	Unc	Proof
81	5737	1977	.037	15.00	25.00	—
	5737	1977	.027	—	—	40.00

20.0000gm., .900 SILVER, .5787oz ASW
Pidyon Haben

Y#	Date	Year	Mintage	XF	Unc	Proof
82	5737	1977	.032	20.00	25.00	—
	5737	1977	.019	—	—	40.00

COPPER-NICKEL
Hannuka 1978

Y#	Date	Year	Mintage	XF	Unc	Proof
87	5738	1978	.036	7.00	10.00	—
	5738	1978	.022	—	—	15.00

50 LIROT

13.3400gm., .917 GOLD, .3933oz AGW
10th Anniversary ofDeath of Weizmann

Y#	Date	Year	Mintage	XF	Unc	Proof
32	5722	1962	5,941	275.00	350.00	600.00

10th Anniversary of Bank of Israel

Y#	Date	Year	Mintage	XF	Unc	Proof
40	5724	1964	5,201	500.00	700.00	—
	5724	1964	*1,502	—	—	4500.

*The Bank of Israel presented 702 pieces.

7.0000gm., .900 GOLD, .2025oz AGW
25th Anniversary of Independence

Y#	Date	Year	Mintage	XF	Unc	Proof
66	5733	1973	9,800	BV	BV	150.00

20.0000gm., .500 SILVER, .3215oz ASW
30th Anniversary

Y#	Date	Year	Mintage	XF	Unc	Proof
84	—	1978	.041	20.00	25.00	—
	—	1978	.022	—	—	50.00

31st Anniversary

88	—	1979	—	—	22.00	—
	—	1979	—	—	—	35.00

100 LIROT

26.6800gm., .917 GOLD, .7866oz AGW
10th Anniversary of Death of Weizmann

33	5723	1962	5,940	—	—	700.00

Victory Commemorative

Y#	Date	Year	Mintage	XF	Unc	Proof
45	5727	1967	8,202	—	—	850.00

25.0000gm., .800 GOLD, .6430oz AGW
20th Anniversary - Jerusalem

48	5728	1968	.012	—	—	500.00

21st Anniversary - Shalom

50	5729	1969	.012	—	—	450.00

22.0000gm., .900 GOLD, .6366oz AGW
Let My People Go

Y#	Date	Year	Mintage	XF	Unc	Proof
55	5731	1971	9,502	—	—	550.00

13.5000gm., .900 GOLD, .3906oz AGW
25th Anniversary of Independence

67	5733	1973	9,550	—	—	275.00

.900 GOLD
30th Anniversary

85	—	1978	.012		Proof only	400.00

20.0000gm., .500 SILVER, .3215oz ASW
Hanukka - Egyptian Lamp

89	—	1979	—	—	25.00	—
	—	1979	—	—	—	40.00

200 LIROT

27.0000gm., .900 GOLD, .7813oz AGW
25th Anniversary ofIndependence

68	5733	1973	.018	BV	525.00	650.00

26.0000gm., .900 SILVER, .7524oz ASW
Egyptian - Israeli Peace Treaty

Y#	Date	Year	Mintage	XF	Unc	Proof
90	—	1980	—	—	45.00	—
	—	1980	—	—	—	60.00

500 LIROT

28.0000gm., .900 GOLD, .8102oz AGW
David Ben Gurion

Y#	Date	Year	Mintage	XF	Unc	Proof
72	5734	1974	.048	—	—	550.00

20.0000gm., .900 GOLD, .5787oz AGW
27th Anniversary of Israel Bond Program

Y#	Date	Year	Mintage	XF	Unc	Proof
76	5735	1975	32,275	—	—	400.00

5000 LIROT

17.2800 gm., .900 GOLD, .5000 oz AGW

Y#	Date	Year	Mintage	XF	Unc	Proof
91	5740	1980	—		Proof only	410.00

MONETARY REFORM

MONETARY SYSTEM

10 Agorot = 1 New Agora
1 Lira = 10 New Agorot
1 Lira = 1/2 Shekel

NEW AGORA

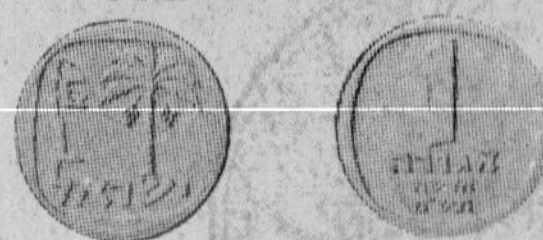

0.6000 gm., ALUMINUM

Y#	Date	Year	Mintage	XF	Unc	Proof
99	5740	1980	—	—	.10	.25

5 NEW AGOROT

0.9000 gm., ALUMINUM

Y#	Date	Year	Mintage	XF	Unc	Proof
100	5740	1980	—	—	.10	.25

10 NEW AGOROT

2.1000 gm., BRONZE

Y#	Date	Year	Mintage	XF	Unc	Proof
101	5740	1980	—	—	.10	.25

1/2 SHEKEL

3.0000 gm., COPPER-NICKEL

Y#	Date	Year	Mintage	XF	Unc	Proof
102	5740	1980	—	—	.25	.35

NCLT ISSUES

MINT SETS

KM#	Date	Mintage	Identification	Issue Price	Mkt. Val.
SA1	1927(14)	—	Palestine Mandate	—	13,000.
SB1	1927(7)	—	Palestine Mandate	—	7000.
SC1	1949(10)	—	Y1-4,6,8w/p,10,12w/p,13,14	—	250.00
S1	1962(16)	4,000	Y2-5,5a,5b,7,9,11, 12,14,22,24,25,26.	18.50	85.00
S2	1963(18)	7,000	As H-S1 plus Y36,37, in presentation holder	22.50	75.00

Trade coin sets as above, and six coin sets of 1964 and 1965 often contained circulated and cleaned coins, thus do not qualify as Mint Sets as usually defined.

KM#	Date	Mintage	Identification	Issue Price	Mkt. Val.
S4	1963(6)	*200	Y22,24,25(1962),Y26,36, 37 (white folder)	—	—

1963 ISRAEL COIN ISSUES
ISSUED BY THE BANK OF ISRAEL
UNCIRCULATED
25 AGOROT 10 AGOROT 5 AGOROT
1 AGORA ONE HALF-POUND ONE POUND

KM#	Date	Mintage	Identification	Issue Price	Mkt. Val.
S5	1963(6)	2,000	Y22,24-26,36,37 (plain white card)	2.50	125.00

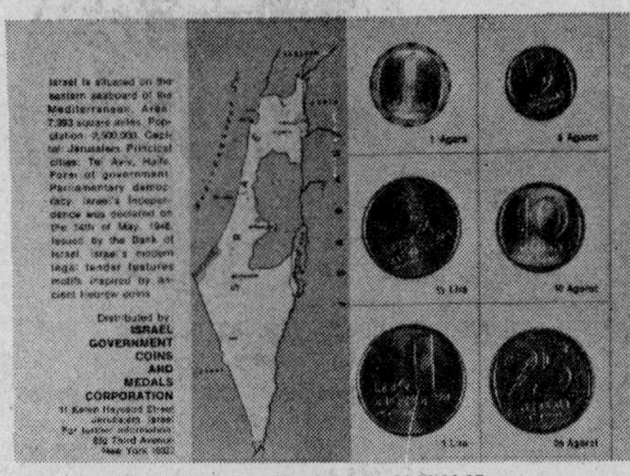

KM#	Date	Mintage	Identification	Issue Price	Mkt. Val.
S6	1963(6)	10,000	Y22 w/inv. rev., 24-26,36,37 (card w/map)	2.60	50.00
S7	1963(6)*	10,544	Y22,24-26,36,37 (card w/map)	2.60	20.00

NOTE: #S7 was issued in 1964.

KM#	Date	Mintage	Identification	Issue Price	Mkt. Val.
S8	1965(6)	153,500	Y22,24-26,36,37	3.50	3.75
S9	1966(6)	114,800	Y22,24-26,36,37	3.50	3.75
S10	1967(6)	128,600	Y22,24-26,36,37	3.50	3.75
S11	1968(6)	184,600	Y22,24-26,36,46	3.50	3.75
S12	1969(6)	158,000	Y22,24-26,36,46	3.50	3.75
S13	1970(6)	64,800	As above, in red wallet	3.75	3.85
S13	1970(6)	64,100	As above, in plastic case	3.75	4.75
S14	1971(6)	32,600	As above, in blue wallet	3.50	3.85
S14a	1971(6)**	126,100	As above, in pink plastic case	3.00	4.25
S15	1972(6)	21,500	As above, in violet wallet	3.00	6.00
S15a	1972(6)**	68,700	As above, in violet plastic case	3.50	5.75
S16	1973(6)	98,700	Y59-64, in blue plastic case	3.50	7.00
S17	1974(3)	—	Y71,72(Proof),71(Unc)	—	—

NON STANDARD METALS

KM#	Date	Mintage	Identification	Issue Price	Mkt. Val.
S18	1974(6)	93,050	Y22,24a,25a,26a,36,46, in brown plastic case	3.50	6.00
S19	1975(6)	61,885	Y22,24a-26a,36a,46a, in brown plastic case	3.50	7.00
S20	1976(6)	65,000	Y77-82, in green plastic case	3.50	25.00
S21	1977(6)	37,376	Y22a,24A-26A,36A,46A	3.50	5.00
S22	1978(6)	12,100	Y22a,24a-26a,36a,46a	—	—
S23	1979(7)	—	Y22a,24b,25b,26a,36a,46a,86	1.80	—

**Star of David mintmark on reverse.

SPECIMEN SETS

STANDARD METALS

KM#	Date	Mintage	Identification	Issue Price	Mkt. Val.
SB1	1949(6)	20,000	Y2,3,4,6,8,10	—	—

Listings For

Italian Somaliland: refer to Somalia

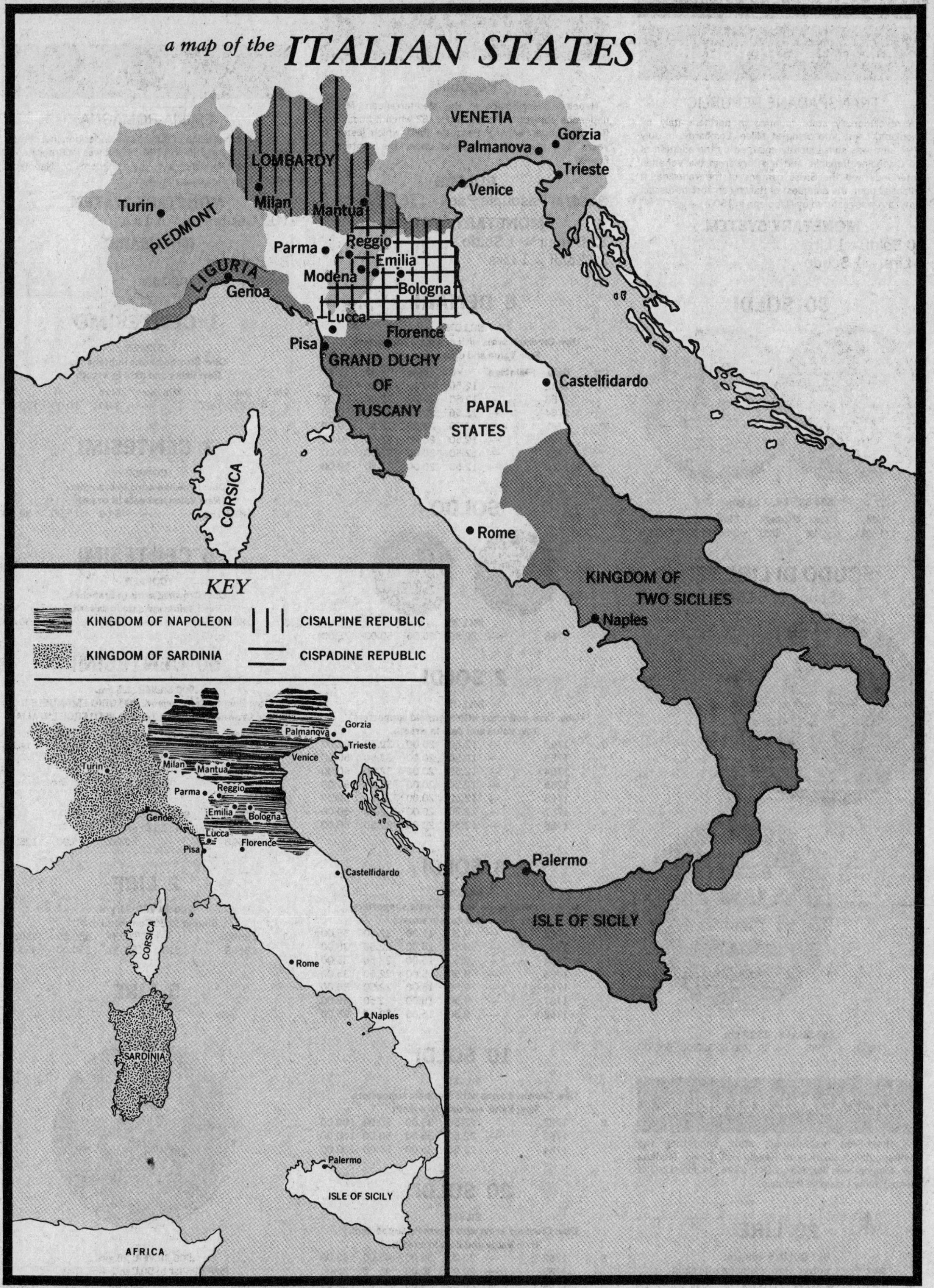
a map of the ITALIAN STATES
VENETIA
Gorzia
Palmanova
Trieste
Venice
LOMBARDY
Milan
Mantua
Turin
PIEDMONT
Parma
Reggio
Emilia
Modena
Bologna
LIGURIA
Genoa
Lucca
Florence
Pisa
GRAND DUCHY OF TUSCANY
PAPAL STATES
Castelfidardo
CORSICA
Rome
KINGDOM OF TWO SICILIES
Naples
Palermo
ISLE OF SICILY
KEY
KINGDOM OF NAPOLEON
CISALPINE REPUBLIC
KINGDOM OF SARDINIA
CISPADINE REPUBLIC
SARDINIA
AFRICA

ITALIAN STATES

CISALPINE REPUBLIC

TRANSPADANE REPUBLIC

A revolutionary state founded in northern Italy by Napoleon, came into being at Milan, Lombardy, in July 1797, and was subsequently enlarged by the addition of the Cispadine Republic and territory from the Venetian hinterlands and the Swiss cantons of the Valtellina. It collapsed upon the conquest of Italy by an Austro-Russian army, but was restored by Napoleon in 1800.

MONETARY SYSTEM

20 Soldi = 1 Lira
6 Lire = 1 Scudo

30 SOLDI

.684 SILVER, 7.33 gm.

C#	Date	Year	Mintage	Fine	VF	XF
1	(1801)	IX	.300	50.00	75.00	150.00

SCUDO DI LIRE SEI

(Scudo of 6 Lire)

.896 SILVER, 23.13 gm.

C#	Date	Year	Mintage	Fine	VF	XF
2	(1800)	VIII	.150	200.00	300.00	500.00

CISPADANE REPUBLIC

A short-lived revolutionary state comprising the northern Italian districts of Reggio nell' Emilia, Modena and Bologna, was formed in Oct. 1796. In July 1797 it merged in the Cisalpine Republic.

20 LIRE

.917 GOLD, 5.469 gm.
Obv: Flags, quiver, Rev: Madonna with child

C#	Date	Mintage	Fine	VF	XF
1	1797	—	1000.	1750.	2500.

CORSICA

Republic

Napoleon's birthplace in the Mediterranean. Mostly under the control of Genoa until 1762 when it became a Republic under General Pasquale Paoli which lasted 6 years. The island then became under the control of France.

RULERS

General Pasquale Paoli - 1762-1768

MONETARY SYSTEM

12 Denair = 1 Soldo
20 Soldi = 1 Lira

8 DENARI

BILLON
Obv: Crowned arms with mermaid supporters.
Rev: Value and date in wreath.

C#	Date	Mintage	VG	Fine	VF	XF
4	1762	—	12.50	20.00	32.50	50.00
	1763	—	12.50	20.00	32.50	50.00
	1764	—	12.50	20.00	32.50	50.00
	1765	—	12.50	20.00	32.50	50.00
	1766	—	12.50	20.00	32.50	50.00
	1767	—	12.50	20.00	32.50	50.00
	1768	—	12.50	20.00	32.50	50.00

SOLDO

BILLON

C#	Date	Mintage	VG	Fine	VF	XF
5	1768	—	22.50	35.00	50.00	75.00

2 SOLDI

BILLON
Obv: Crowned arms with mermaid supporters.
Rev: Value and date in wreath.

C#	Date	Mintage	VG	Fine	VF	XF
6	1762	—	12.50	20.00	32.50	50.00
	1763	—	12.50	20.00	32.50	50.00
	1764	—	12.50	20.00	32.50	50.00
	1765	—	12.50	20.00	32.50	50.00
	1766	—	12.50	20.00	32.50	50.00
	1767	—	12.50	20.00	32.50	50.00
	1768	—	12.50	20.00	32.50	50.00

4 SOLDI

BILLON
Obv: Crowned arms with mermaid supporters.
Rev: Value and date in wreath.

C#	Date	Mintage	VG	Fine	VF	XF
7	1762	—	9.50	15.00	22.50	35.00
	1763	—	9.50	15.00	22.50	35.00
	1764	—	9.50	15.00	22.50	35.00
	1765	—	9.50	15.00	22.50	35.00
	1766	—	9.50	15.00	22.50	35.00
	1767	—	9.50	15.00	22.50	35.00
	1768	—	9.50	15.00	22.50	35.00

10 SOLDI

SILVER
Obv: Crowned arms with mermaid supporters.
Rev: Value and date in wreath.

C#	Date	Mintage	VG	Fine	VF	XF
8	1762	—	22.50	35.00	50.00	100.00
	1763	—	22.50	35.00	50.00	100.00
	1764	—	22.50	35.00	50.00	100.00

20 SOLDI

SILVER
Obv: Crowned arms with mermaid supporters.
Rev: Value and date in wreath.

C#	Date	Mintage	VG	Fine	VF	XF
9	1762	—	20.00	30.00	45.00	85.00
	1763	—	20.00	30.00	45.00	85.00
	1764	—	20.00	30.00	45.00	85.00
	1765	—	20.00	30.00	45.00	85.00
	1766	—	20.00	30.00	45.00	85.00

C#	Date	Mintage	VG	Fine	VF	XF
9	1767	—	20.00	30.00	45.00	85.00
	1768	—	20.00	30.00	45.00	85.00

EMILIA

EMILIA-ROMAGNA

A northern division of Italy, came under nominal control of the papacy in 755. In 1796-1814 it was incorporated in the Italian Republic and the Kingdom of Napoleon, returning to the papacy in 1815.

MONETARY SYSTEM

100 Centesimi = 1 Lira

MINTMARKS

B - Bologna
(none) - Birmingham

1 CENTESIMO

COPPER
Obv: Crowned arms in branches.
Rev: Value and date in wreath.

KM#	Date	Mintage	Fine	VF	XF
1	1826(1860)	—	3.00	10.00	30.00

3 CENTESIMI

COPPER
Obv: Crowned arms in branches.
Rev: Value and date in wreath.

KM#	Date	Mintage	Fine	VF	XF
2	1826(1860)	—	5.00	15.00	32.50

5 CENTESIMI

COPPER
Obv: Crowned arms in branches.
Rev.: Value and date in wreath.

KM#	Date	Mintage	Fine	VF	XF
3	1826(1860)	—	10.00	25.00	50.00

50 CENTESIMI

.900 SILVER, 2.5 gm.
Obv: Bust to right, legend: VITTORIO EMANUELE II
Rev: Crowned arms, legend: DIO PROTEGGE L'ITALIA

C#	Date	Mintage	Fine	VF	XF
1	1859B	—	30.00	50.00	75.00

LIRA

.900 SILVER, 5 gm.
Similar to 50 Centesimi, C#1

C#	Date	Mintage	Fine	VF	XF
2	1859B	—	50.00	75.00	125.00

2 LIRE

.900 SILVER, 10 gm.
Similar to 50 Centesimi, C#1

C#	Date	Mintage	Fine	VF	XF
3	1859B	—	200.00	350.00	450.00
	1860B	.013	150.00	250.00	350.00

5 LIRE

.900 SILVER, 25 gm.
Rev: Similar to 50 Centesimi, C#1

C#	Date	Mintage	Fine	VF	XF
4	1859	—	200.00	400.00	800.00
	1860	—	200.00	350.00	650.00

10 LIRE

.900 GOLD, 3.22 gm.
Obv: Similar to 50 Centesimi, C#1
Rev: Value within wreath, legend:
REGIE PROVINCIE DELL EMILIA

C#	Date	Mintage	Fine	VF	XF
5	1860B	1,145	400.00	750.00	1250.

20 LIRE

.900 GOLD, 6.45 gm.
Similar to 10 Lire, C#5

C#	Date	Mintage	Fine	VF	XF
6	1860B	150 pcs.	3000.	4000.	5000.

NOTE: For similar coins of Vittorio Emanuele II, see Sardinia and Tuscany.

GENOA

Repubblica Ligure
1798-1805
Repubblica Genuensis
1814

A seaport in Liguria, was a dominant republic and colonial power in the Middle Ages. In 1798 Napoleon remodeled it into the Ligurian Republic, and in 1805 it was incorporated in the Kingdom of Napoleon. Following a brief restoration of the republic, it was absorbed by the Kingdom of Sardinia, 1815.

MINTMARKS

NOTE: During the occupation by the French forces regular French coins, 1/2, 1, 2, 5, 20 and 40 Francs were struck between 1813 and 1814 with the mintmark C.L.

After Sardinia absorbed Genoa in 1815, regular Sardinian coins were struck until 1860 with a fouled anchor mintmark.

MONETARY SYSTEM

12 Denari = 1 Soldo
20 Soldi = 1 Lira

3 DENARI

COPPER
Obv: R.L.A.V. 1802 around D. 3, Rev: Cross

C#	Date	Year	Mintage	Fine	VF	XF
25	(1802)	V	—	5.00	7.50	10.00

QUATRO (4) DENARI

BILLON
Obv: Arms. Rev: Value.

C#	Date	Mintage	Good	VG	Fine
5	1767	—	1.50	2.25	3.50
	1772	—	1.50	2.25	3.50
	1773	—	1.50	2.25	3.50
	1777	—	1.50	2.25	3.50
	1780	—	1.50	2.25	3.50
	1781	—	1.50	2.25	3.50
	1783	—	1.50	2.25	3.50
	1793	—	1.50	2.25	3.50

Value as QUATTRO.

C#	Date	Mintage	Good	VG	Fine
5a	1794	—	1.25	1.75	2.75
	1795	—	1.25	1.75	2.75
	1796	—	1.25	1.75	2.75
	1797	—	1.25	1.75	2.75

COPPER

C#	Date	Mintage	Fine	VF	XF
35	1814	—	3.00	5.00	10.00

8 DENARI

BILLON
Obv: Arms, DUX.ET GUB REIP GENU around.
Rev: Madonna, ET REGE EOS around.

C#	Date	Mintage	Good	VG	Fine
6a	1767	—	1.50	2.25	3.50
	1772	—	1.50	2.25	3.50
	1773	—	1.50	2.25	3.50
	1774	—	1.50	2.25	3.50
	1780	—	1.50	2.25	3.50
	1782	—	1.50	2.25	3.50
	1793	—	1.50	2.25	3.50
	1794	—	1.50	2.25	3.50
	1795	—	1.50	2.25	3.50
	1796	—	1.50	2.25	3.50

2 SOLDI

BILLON

C#	Date	Mintage	Fine	VF	XF
36	1814	—	5.00	8.00	12.00

NOTE: Exists with PRAESIDIUM and PRESIDIUM.

4 SOLDI

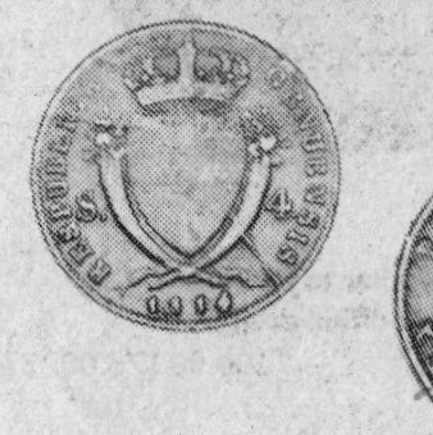

BILLON

C#	Date	Mintage	Fine	VF	XF
37	1814	—	8.00	10.00	15.00

CINQE (5) SOLDI

BILLON
Obv: Figure, DUX ET G.R.GEN around. Rev: Value, date.

C#	Date	Mintage	Good	VG	Fine
9a	1793	—	1.75	3.00	4.50
	1794	—	1.75	3.00	4.50

10 SOLDI

BILLON
Obv: Arms, DUX ET GUB REIP GENU around.
Rev: Value, date in wreath.

C#	Date	Mintage	Good	VG	Fine
10	1792	—	3.00	5.00	10.00

Value as DIECI (-10) SOLDI.

C#	Date	Mintage	Good	VG	Fine
10a	1792	—	2.50	4.50	9.00
	1793	—	2.50	4.50	9.00
	1794	—	2.50	4.50	9.00
	1796	—	2.50	4.50	9.00
	1797	—	2.50	4.50	9.00

C#	Date	Year	Mintage	Fine	VF	XF
26	1798	I	—	4.00	10.00	20.00
	1799	II	—	4.00	10.00	20.00

.889 SILVER, 2.1 gm.
Obv: Crowned shield, GENUENSIS
Rev: John The Baptist standing

C#	Date	Mintage	Fine	VF	XF
38	1814	—	8.00	10.00	15.00

Obv: JANUENSIS

C#	Date	Mintage	Fine	VF	XF
38a	1814	—	8.00	10.00	15.00

LIRA

.889 SILVER, 4.16 gm.

C#	Date	Mintage	Fine	VF	XF
12	1793	—	12.00	25.00	50.00
	1794	—	12.00	25.00	50.00
	1795	—	12.00	25.00	50.00

C#	Date	Mintage	Fine	VF	XF
27	1798	—	40.00	60.00	125.00

2 LIRE

.889 SILVER, 8.32 gm.

C#	Date	Mintage	Fine	VF	XF
14	1792	—	35.00	60.00	100.00
	1793	—	35.00	60.00	100.00
	1794	—	35.00	60.00	100.00
	1795	—	35.00	60.00	100.00
	1796	—	35.00	60.00	100.00

C#	Date	Mintage	Fine	VF	XF
28	1798	—	200.00	300.00	600.00

4 LIRE

.889 SILVER, 16.64 gm.

C#	Date	Mintage	Fine	VF	XF
15	1792	—	75.00	125.00	200.00
	1793	—	75.00	125.00	200.00
	1794	—	75.00	125.00	200.00
	1795	—	75.00	125.00	200.00
	1796	—	75.00	125.00	200.00
	1797	—	75.00	125.00	200.00

C#	Date	Year	Mintage	Fine	VF	XF
29	1798	I	—	50.00	100.00	250.00
	1799	II	—	50.00	100.00	250.00
	1804	VII	—	50.00	100.00	250.00

8 LIRE

.889 SILVER, 33.27 gm.

C#	Date	Mintage	Fine	VF	XF
16a	1792	—	80.00	150.00	300.00
	1793	—	80.00	150.00	300.00
	1794	—	80.00	150.00	300.00
	1795	—	80.00	150.00	300.00
	1796	—	80.00	150.00	300.00
	1797	—	80.00	150.00	300.00

.889 SILVER, 33.27 gm.

C#	Date	Year	Mintage	Fine	VF	XF
30.1	1798	I	—	100.00	175.00	375.00
	1799	II	—	100.00	175.00	375.00

Obv: Similar to C#30.1
Rev: Modified design

C#	Date	Year	Mintage	Fine	VF	XF
30.2	1804	VII	—	100.00	175.00	375.00

12 LIRE

.909 GOLD, 3.151 gm.
Similar to 24 Lire, C#22.

C#	Date	Mintage	Fine	VF	XF
21	1793	—	600.00	1500.	3000.
	1794	—	600.00	1500.	3000.
	1795	—	600.00	1500.	3000.

Obv: Liguria seated. Rev: Fasces within wreath.

C#	Date	Year	Mintage	VF	XF	Unc
31	1798	I	—	900.00	2000.	3500.

24 LIRE

.909 GOLD, 6.28-6.31 gm.

C#	Date	Mintage	Fine	VF	XF
22	1793	—	600.00	1500.	3000.
	1795	—	700.00	1500.	3000.

.909 GOLD, 6.303 gm.
Obv: Liguria seated. Rev: Fasces within wreath.

C#	Date	Year	Mintage	VF	XF	Unc
32	1798	I	—	500.00	650.00	1200.

48 LIRE

GOLD, 12.54-12.63 gm.
Obv: Arms, leg: DUX ET GUB REIP GENU.
Rev: Madonna, leg: ET REGE EOS.

C#	Date	Mintage	Fine	VF	XF
23	1793	—	700.00	1000.	2200.
	1794	—	700.00	1000.	2200.
	1796	—	700.00	1000.	2200.
	1797	—	700.00	1000.	2200.

.909 GOLD, 12.607 gm.

C#	Date	Year	Mintage	VF	XF	Unc
33	1798	I	—	450.00	600.00	1000.
	1801	IV	—	450.00	600.00	1000.
	1804	VII	—	450.00	600.00	1000.

96 LIRE

.909 GOLD, 24.96-25.47 gm.

C#	Date	Mintage	Fine	VF	XF
24	1793	—	1000.	1500.	2500.
	1795	—	1000.	1500.	2500.
	1796	—	1000.	1500.	2500.
	1797	—	1000.	1500.	2500.

.909 GOLD, 25.214 gm.

C#	Date	Year	Mintage	VF	XF	Unc
34	1798	I	—	1000.	1500.	2500.
	1801	IV	—	1000.	1500.	2500.
	1803	VI	—	1000.	1500.	2500.
	1804	VII	—	1000.	1500.	2500.
	1805	VIII	—	1000.	1500.	2500.

GORIZIA

GORIZIA, GORZ

A city in Venetia, passed to Maximilian I of Austria in 1500, and became the holding of Charles, son of Austrian emperor Ferdinand I in 1564.

RULERS

Joseph II, 1780-1790
Leopold II, 1790-1792
Franz II (Austria) 1792-1835

MINTMARKS

A - Wien - Vienna
F - Hall
G - Nagybanya
H - Gunzburg
K - Kremnitz
S - Schmollnitz
A - Wien - Vienna

MONETARY SYSTEM

20 Soldi = 1 Lira

1/2 SOLDO

COPPER
Obv: Crowned arms.

Rev: Value and date in cartouche.

C#	Date	Mintage	VG	Fine	VF
3	1783F	—	3.00	5.00	10.00
	1785F	—	3.00	5.00	10.00
	1788F	—	3.00	5.00	10.00
	1788K	—	3.00	5.00	10.00
	1789F	—	3.00	5.00	10.00
	1789K	—	3.00	5.00	10.00
	1790F	—	3.00	5.00	10.00

C#	Date	Mintage	Fine	VF	XF	Unc
5	1791A	—	8.50	17.50	35.00	65.00
	1791F	—	11.50	22.50	45.00	75.00

C#	Date	Mintage	Fine	VF	XF
7	1792F	—	4.00	12.00	30.00
	1793F	—	4.00	12.00	30.00
	1794F	—	4.00	12.00	30.00
	1799F	—	—	Rare	—
	1800H	—	Reported, not confirmed		
	1801H	—	Reported, not confirmed		

SOLDO

COPPER
Obv: Crowned arms.
Rev: Value and date in cartouche.

C#	Date	Mintage	VG	Fine	VF
4	1783F	—	3.00	5.00	10.00
	1785F	—	3.00	5.00	10.00
	1786F	—	3.00	5.00	10.00
	1787F	—	6.50	10.00	15.00
	1788F	—	3.00	5.00	10.00
	1788K	—	3.00	5.00	10.00
	1789F	—	3.00	5.00	10.00
	1790F	—	3.00	5.00	10.00
	1790H	—	5.00	8.50	12.50

C#	Date	Mintage	Fine	VF	XF	Unc
6	1791A	—	—	—	Rare	—
	1791F	—	12.50	25.00	50.00	90.00

C#	Date	Mintage	Fine	VF	XF
8	1792F	—	10.00	20.00	40.00
	1793F	—	4.00	8.00	15.00
	1794F	—	4.00	8.00	15.00
	1794K	—	—	Rare	—
	1795F	—	4.00	8.00	15.00
	1796F	—	4.00	8.00	15.00
	1796G	—	—	Rare	—
	1797F	—	2.50	5.00	9.00
	1798F	—	3.00	5.50	10.00
	1798H	—	3.50	6.00	10.00
	1799F	—	3.00	5.50	9.00
	1799H	—	3.00	5.00	9.00
	1800F	—	4.50	8.00	17.00
	1800H	—	3.50	6.50	13.50
	1801F	—	—	Rare	—
	1801H	—	6.00	12.50	25.00
	1802H	—	—	Rare	—

2 SOLDI

COPPER

C#	Date	Mintage	Fine	VF	XF
9	1799	—	—	Rare	—
	1799F	—	3.00	6.00	12.00
	1799H	—	16.50	30.00	50.00
	1799K	—	4.00	9.50	20.00
	1799S	—	2.50	4.00	9.00
	1799W	—	Reported, not confirmed		
	1801F	—	—	Rare	—
	1801H	—	4.00	7.00	17.00
	1802H	—	4.00	7.00	17.00

15 SOLDI

(= 8-1/2 Kreuzer)

BILLON

Obv: Crowned double headed eagle
Rev: Value in shield

C#	Date	Mintage	Fine	VF	XF
10	1802A	—	10.00	20.00	50.00
	1802F	—	10.00	20.00	40.00
	1802H	—	15.00	35.00	75.00

ITALIAN REPUBLIC

REPUBBLICA ITALIANA

Created in 1802 out of the Cisalpine Republic (q.v.) with some additions. Converted into the Kingdom of Italy in 1805. Capital: Milan. Years 1-4 of the republic = 1802-05.

RULERS

Napoleon, 1802-1805

MONETARY SYSTEM

(1803)

10 Denari = 1 Soldo
20 Soldi = 1 Lira

NCLT ISSUES

PATTERNS

KM#	Date	Mintage	Identification	Mkt.Val.
1	A.II(1803)M	—	Denaro, Copper	300.00

KM#	Date	Mintage	Identification	Mkt.Val.
2	A.II(1803)M	—	2 Denari, Copper	400.00

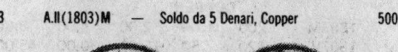

KM#	Date	Mintage	Identification	Mkt.Val.
3	A.II(1803)M	—	Soldo da 5 Denari, Copper	500.00

KM#	Date	Mintage	Identification	Mkt.Val.
4	A.II(1803)M	—	5 Soldi, .900 Silver	1700.

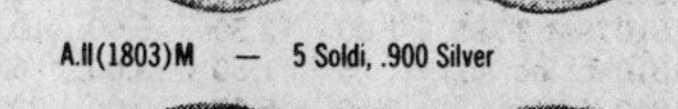

KM#	Date	Mintage	Identification	Mkt.Val.
5	A.II(1803)M	—	10 Soldi, .900 Silver	2250.

KM#	Date	Mintage	Identification	Mkt.Val.
6	A.II(1803)M	—	Lira da 20 Soldi, .900 Silver	3250.

KM#	Date	Mintage	Identification	Mkt.Val.
7	A.II(1803)M	—	30 Soldi, .900 Silver	4000.

KM#	Date	Mintage	Identification	Mkt.Val.
8	A.II(1803)M	—	Scudo da 5 Lire, .900 Silver	12,500.
9	A.II(1803)M	—	Mezzo (1/2) Doppia, .900 Gold	Rare
10	A.II(1803)M	—	Mezzo (1/2) Doppia (in wreath) .900 Gold	Rare
11	A.II(1803)M	—	Doppia, .900 Gold	Rare
12	A.II(1803)M	—	Doppia (in wreath), .900 Gold	Rare

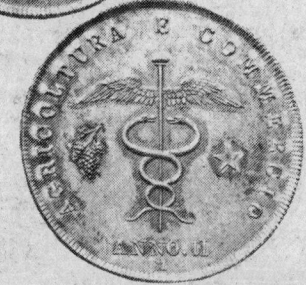

KM#	Date	Mintage	Identification	Mkt.Val.
13	1804M	—	1/100 (Centesimo), Copper	250.00

KM#	Date	Mintage	Identification	Mkt.Val.
14	1804M	—	Centesimo, Copper	300.00

KM#	Date	Mintage	Identification	Mkt.Val.
15	1804M	—	1/2 Soldo, Copper	350.00
16	1804M	—	Mezzo (1/2) Soldo, Copper	450.00

KM#	Date	Mintage	Identification	Mkt.Val.
17	1804M	—	Soldo, Copper	500.00

KM#	Date	Mintage	Identification	Mkt.Val.
18	1804M	—	5 Soldi, .900 Silver	1100.

KM#	Date	Mintage	Identification	Mkt.Val.
19	1804M	—	10 Soldi, .900 Silver	1700.

KM#	Date	Mintage	Identification	Mkt.Val.
20	1804M	—	1 Lira, .900 Silver	3200.

KM#	Date	Mintage	Identification	Mkt.Val.
21	1804M	—	2 Lire, .900 Silver, 8 gm.	4500.
21a	1804M	—	2 Lire, .900 Silver, 8.21 gm.	4500.

KM#	Date	Mintage	Identification	Mkt.Val.
22	1804M	—	5 Lire, .900 Silver	16,000.

KM#	Date	Mintage	Identification	Mkt.Val.
23	1804M	—	(Venti-20 Lire) Denari 8, .900 Gold	42,500.
23a	1804M	—	(Venti-20 Lire) Denari 8, Copper	1450.
24	1804M	—	(Venti-20 Lire) Denari 8, .900 Gold	42,500.
24a	1804M	—	(Venti-20 Lire) Denari 8, Copper	1600.

KINGDOM OF NAPOLEON

Came into being shortly after the first French empire was proclaimed on May 18, 1804; Napoleon's Italian coronation took place at Naples on May 26, 1805.

(FRENCH RULE)

RULERS

Napoleon I,1804-1814

MINT MARKS

M - Milan
B - Bologna
V - Venice

MONETARY SYSTEMS

100 Centesimi = 20 Soldi
20 Soldi = 1 Lira

CENTESIMO

COPPER

C#	Date	Mintage	VG	Fine	VF	XF
1	1807M	.100	2.50	5.00	10.00	20.00
	1807V	.130	2.50	5.00	10.00	20.00
	1807B	.085	.75	1.50	5.00	10.00
	1808M	3.390	.75	1.50	4.50	9.00
	1808M (error) IMPERAPORE					
		.020	5.00	10.00	20.00	35.00
	1808V	.375	2.50	5.00	10.00	20.00
	1808V/M	Inc Ab	2.50	5.00	10.00	20.00
	1808B	2.420	.75	1.50	4.50	9.00
	1809M	2.313	.75	1.50	4.50	9.00
	1809V	3.079	1.00	2.00	4.50	9.00
	1809B	4.321	.75	1.50	4.50	9.00
	1810M	2.375	.75	1.50	4.50	9.00
	1810V	.267	2.50	5.00	10.00	20.00
	1810/9B	3.811	5.00	10.00	15.00	20.00
	1810B	Inc. Ab.	.75	1.50	4.50	9.00
	1811M	1.190	.75	1.50	4.50	9.00
	1811V	7.836	1.00	2.00	4.50	9.00
	1811B	1.350	.75	1.50	4.50	9.00
	1812M	2.780	.75	1.50	4.50	9.00
	1812V	1.421	1.00	2.00	4.50	9.00
	1812B	4.814	.75	1.50	4.50	9.00
	1813M	3.719	.75	1.50	4.50	9.00
	1813V	4.433	1.00	2.00	4.50	9.00

3 CENTESIMI

COPPER

C#	Date	Mintage	VG	Fine	VF	XF
2	1807M	.200	1.00	2.00	4.00	8.00
	1807V	.120	7.50	15.00	30.00	45.00
	1807B	.053	.75	1.50	4.00	8.00
	1808M	1.980	.75	1.50	3.00	6.00
	1808V	.570	2.00	4.00	8.00	17.50
	1808B	.205	.75	1.50	3.00	6.00
	1809M	2.020	.75	1.50	3.00	6.00
	1809V	.123	2.00	4.00	8.00	16.00
	1810/9M	2.795	1.00	2.50	5.00	10.00
	1810M	Inc. Ab.	.75	1.50	3.00	6.00
	1810/00V	—	2.50	5.00	10.00	20.00
	1810V	—	2.00	4.00	8.00	16.00
	1810B	1.863	.75	1.50	3.00	6.00
	1811M	2.788	.75	1.50	3.00	6.00
	1812M	3.005	.75	1.50	3.00	6.00
	1813M	2.567	.75	1.50	3.00	6.00
	1813B	.884	.75	1.50	3.00	6.00

SOLDO

COPPER

C#	Date	Mintage	VG	Fine	VF	XF
3	1807M	.100	1.00	2.00	6.00	15.00
	1807V	.300	1.25	2.50	5.00	10.00
	1807B	.325	.75	1.50	5.00	10.00
	1808M	1.341	.75	1.50	5.00	10.00
	1808V	.311	1.25	2.50	5.00	10.00
	1808B	.303	.75	1.50	3.50	7.50
	1809M	1.356	.75	1.50	5.00	13.50
	1809B	1.346	.75	1.50	3.50	7.50
	1810M	1.387	.75	1.50	5.00	12.50
	1811M	—	.75	1.50	5.00	12.50
	1812M	2.234	.75	1.50	5.00	12.50
	1812V	1.096	1.25	2.50	5.00	10.00
	1813M	2.948	.75	1.50	5.00	12.50

10 CENTESIMI

BILLON

C#	Date	Mintage	VG	Fine	VF	XF
4	1808M	.012	6.50	12.50	22.50	45.00
	1809M	.875	1.25	2.50	5.00	10.00
	1810M	.721	1.25	2.50	5.00	10.00
	1811M	1.592	1.25	2.50	5.00	10.00
	1812M	.797	1.25	2.50	5.00	10.00
	1813M	2.677	1.25	2.50	5.00	10.00

5 SOLDI

.900 SILVER, 1.25 gm.

C#	Date	Mintage	VG	Fine	VF	XF
5	1808M with stars in relief on edge					
		.134	12.50	25.00	50.00	100.00
	1808M with stars incused on edge					
		Inc. Ab.	2.00	4.00	5.00	10.00
	1809M	.602	2.00	4.00	5.00	10.00
	1810M	1.047	2.00	4.00	5.00	10.00
	1811/0M	2.984	3.00	5.00	7.50	15.00
	1811M	Inc. Ab.	2.00	4.00	5.00	10.00
	1812M	1.719	2.00	4.00	5.00	10.00
	1812V	.120	3.75	7.50	15.00	30.00
	1812B	.730	2.50	5.00	7.50	15.00
	1812B/M	.279	2.50	5.00	7.50	15.00
	1813M	2.842	2.00	4.00	5.00	10.00
	1813B	2.911	2.00	4.00	7.00	14.00
	1813B/M	.032	2.50	5.00	7.00	14.00
	1814M	.740	2.00	4.00	5.00	10.00
	1814M (error: IMPERARORE)					
		Inc. Ab.	—	—	—	—

10 SOLDI

.900 SILVER, 2.5 gm.

C#	Date	Mintage	VG	Fine	VF	XF
6	1808M with stars in relief on edge					
		.174	7.50	15.00	25.00	50.00
	1808M with stars incused on edge					
		Inc. Ab.	2.50	4.00	5.00	15.00
	1809M	.426	2.50	4.00	5.00	15.00
	1810M	.529	2.50	4.00	5.00	15.00
	1811M	2.044	2.50	4.00	5.00	15.00
	1811V	.300	2.25	3.50	5.00	15.00
	1812M	.608	2.50	4.00	5.00	15.00
	1812V	.166	3.00	5.00	10.00	17.50
	1812B	.038	2.50	4.00	6.00	17.50
	1812B/M	—	4.00	8.00	12.50	17.50
	1813M	.490	2.50	4.00	5.00	15.00
	1813V	.320	2.25	3.50	5.00	15.00
	1813B	.351	2.50	4.00	6.00	15.00
	1814M	.458	2.50	4.00	5.00	15.00

15 SOLDI

.900 SILVER, 3.75 gm.

C#	Date	Mintage	VG	Fine	VF	XF
7	1808M	.037	15.00	30.00	50.00	100.00
	1809M	.014	15.00	30.00	50.00	100.00
	1810M	—	40.00	80.00	150.00	300.00
	1814M	—	40.00	80.00	150.00	300.00

LIRA

.900 SILVER, 5.00 gm.

C#	Date	Mintage	VG	Fine	VF	XF
8	1808M with stars in relief on edge					
		.492	10.00	20.00	25.00	50.00
	1808M with stars incused on edge					
		Inc. Ab.	10.00	20.00	25.00	50.00
	1808B	.102	5.00	10.00	20.00	40.00
	1809M	.339	4.50	7.50	10.00	20.00
	1810M	.495	4.50	7.50	10.00	20.00
	1810M (error) NATOLEON					
		Inc. Ab.	20.00	40.00	65.00	100.00
	1810B with stars in relief on edge					
		.336	5.00	10.00	20.00	40.00
	1810B with stars incused on edge					
		.308	5.00	10.00	20.00	40.00
	1811M	1.184	4.50	7.50	10.00	20.00
	1811V	.045	10.00	20.00	30.00	60.00
	1811B with stars in relief on edge					
		.306	5.00	10.00	20.00	40.00
	1811B with stars incused on edge					
		.310	5.00	10.00	20.00	40.00
	1812M	.332	4.50	7.50	10.00	20.00
	1812V	.089	10.00	20.00	30.00	60.00
	1813M	.227	4.50	7.50	10.00	20.00
	1813V	.341	7.50	15.00	25.00	50.00
	1813B	.218	5.00	10.00	20.00	40.00
	1814M	.276	4.50	7.50	10.00	20.00
	1814M/V	I.A.	27.50	55.00	110.00	225.00

2 LIRE

.900 SILVER, 10.00 gm.

C#	Date	Mintage	VG	Fine	VF	XF
9	1807M	.010	20.00	40.00	75.00	150.00
	1808M with edge inscription in relief					
		—	125.00	250.00	300.00	400.00
	1808B	2,207	25.00	50.00	100.00	200.00
	1808M with edge inscription incuse					
		.311	17.50	35.00	70.00	100.00
	1809M	.326	15.00	30.00	50.00	70.00
	1810M	.364	15.00	30.00	50.00	70.00
	1811M	.520	15.00	30.00	50.00	70.00
	1811V	.010	25.00	50.00	100.00	150.00
	1812M	.343	15.00	30.00	50.00	70.00
	1812V	.241	10.00	20.00	50.00	100.00
	1812B	.047	10.00	15.00	35.00	50.00
	1813M	.215	15.00	30.00	50.00	70.00
	1813V	.213	10.00	12.50	20.00	30.00
	1813B	.347	10.00	15.00	30.00	50.00
	1814M	3,130	35.00	60.00	75.00	110.00

5 LIRE

.900 SILVER, 25.00 gm.
DIO PROTEGGE L'ITALIA on edge in relief

C#	Date	Mintage	VG	Fine	VF	XF
10.1	1807M	.039	30.00	50.00	80.00	165.00
	1807V	—	—	—	Rare	—
	1808M	3.287	30.00	50.00	80.00	165.00
	1808V	—	—	—	Rare	—
	1808B	.023	30.00	50.00	80.00	165.00
	1809M	2.483	30.00	50.00	80.00	165.00
	1809B	.219	25.00	40.00	65.00	100.00
	1810M	.263	35.00	60.00	100.00	200.00
	1810B	.314	25.00	40.00	65.00	100.00
	1811B	—	22.50	35.00	60.00	100.00

Edge inscription incuse.

C#	Date	Mintage	VG	Fine	VF	XF
10.2	1809M	—	27.50	40.00	80.00	165.00
	1810M	—	27.50	40.00	80.00	165.00
	1810B	—	22.50	35.00	50.00	100.00
	1811M	—	27.50	40.00	80.00	165.00
	1811V	.368	27.50	40.00	80.00	165.00
	1812M	1.849	27.50	40.00	80.00	165.00
	1812V	.207	27.50	40.00	80.00	165.00
	1813M	.772	27.50	40.00	80.00	165.00
	1813V	.071	27.50	40.00	80.00	165.00
	1814M	.102	27.50	40.00	80.00	165.00

Letters in legend smaller, edge inscription incuse.

C#	Date	Mintage	VG	Fine	VF	XF
10.3	1808M	—	27.50	40.00	80.00	165.00
	1810V	.014	27.50	40.00	80.00	165.00
	1811M	2.827	27.50	40.00	80.00	165.00
	1811B	.450	22.50	35.00	50.00	125.00
	1812B	—	22.50	35.00	50.00	100.00
	1813B	—	22.50	35.00	50.00	100.00

20 LIRE

.900 GOLD, 6.451 gm.

C#	Date	Mintage	VG	Fine	VF	XF
11	1808M	.087	BV	125.00	150.00	225.00
	1809M	.052	BV	125.00	150.00	225.00
	1810M	.117	BV	125.00	150.00	200.00
	1811M	.055	BV	125.00	150.00	200.00
	1812M	.045	BV	125.00	150.00	200.00
	1813M	.039	BV	125.00	150.00	175.00
	1814M	.057	BV	125.00	150.00	175.00

40 LIRE

.900 GOLD, 12.903 gm.

C#	Date	Mintage	VG	Fine	VF	XF
12	1807M	3,418	300.00	400.00	500.00	600.00
	1808 no mintmark					
		.352	BV	250.00	275.00	300.00
	1808M with edge inscription in relief					
		Inc. Ab.	BV	265.00	300.00	325.00
	1808M with edge inscription incuse					
		.212	BV	265.00	300.00	325.00
	1809M	.038	BV	265.00	325.00	375.00
	1810M	.157	BV	250.00	275.00	300.00
	1811M	.105	BV	250.00	275.00	300.00
	1812M	.055	BV	265.00	325.00	375.00
	1813M	.040	BV	265.00	325.00	375.00
	1814M	.264	BV	250.00	275.00	300.00

NCLT ISSUES

PATTERNS

KM#	Date	Mintage	Identification	Mkt.Val.
1	1806M	—	Centesimo, Copper	100.00
2	1806M	—	2 Centesimi, Copper	200.00
3	1806M	—	3 Centesimi, Copper	200.00

KM#	Date	Mintage	Identification	Mkt.Val.
4	1806M	—	Soldo, Copper	100.00
5	1806M	—	5 Soldi, Silver	150.00
6	1806M	—	10 Soldi, Silver	150.00
7	1806M	—	15 Soldi, Silver	150.00
8	1806M	—	1 Lira, Silver	200.00
9	1806M	—	2 Lire, Silver	200.00
10	1806M	—	5 Lire, Silver	500.00
11	1806M	—	20 Lire, Gold	Rare
11		—	40 Lire, Gold	Rare

LOMBARDY - VENETIA

Comprised the northern Italian duchies of Milan and Mantua and the Venetian republic which were absorbed by the Kingdom of Napoleon in 1805. After Napoleon's fall they were awarded to Austria and incorporated in the Habsburg monarchy as the kingdom of Lombardy-Venetia.

RULERS

Franz I (Austria), 1814-1835
Ferdinand, 1835-1848

Franz Joseph, 1848-1866

MINTMARKS

A - Vienna
B - Kremnitz
M - Milan
V - Venice

MONETARY SYSTEM

(Until 1857)
100 Centesimi = 20 Soldi = 1 Lira
6 Lire = 1 Scudo
40 Lire = 1 Sovrano

CENTESIMO

COPPER

C#	Date	Mintage	VF	XF	Unc
1	1822A	—	Reported, not confirmed		
	1822M	—	5.00	12.00	30.00
	1822V	—	5.00	12.00	30.00
	1834M	—	5.00	12.50	30.00
	1834V	—	5.00	12.50	30.00

C#	Date	Mintage	Fine	VF	XF	Unc
12	1839M	—	3.75	7.50	15.00	30.00
	1839V	—	3.00	6.00	30.00	22.50
	1843M	—	3.75	7.50	30.00	27.50
	1843V	—	3.00	6.00	12.50	30.00
	1846M	—	3.25	6.50	13.50	30.00
	1846V	—	3.25	6.50	13.50	30.00

C#	Date	Mintage	Fine	VF	XF	Unc
25	1849M	—	6.25	12.50	17.50	30.00
	1850M	—	5.00	10.00	20.00	30.00
	1852M	—	7.50	10.00	20.00	40.00

C#	Date	Mintage	Fine	VF	XF	Unc
29	1852M	—	6.25	12.50	17.50	30.00
	1852V	—	2.50	5.00	8.50	20.00

5/10 SOLDO

COPPER

C#	Date	Mintage	VF	XF	Unc
34	1862A	—	3.50	7.00	15.00
	1862B	—	7.00	13.00	20.00
	1862V	—	7.50	14.00	25.00

3 CENTESIMI

COPPER

C#	Date	Mintage	VF	XF	Unc
2	1822A	—	Reported, not confirmed		
	1822M	—	7.50	12.00	20.00
	1822V	—	7.50	12.00	20.00
	1834M	—	12.00	22.00	35.00
	1834V	—	8.00	15.00	25.00

C#	Date	Mintage	Fine	VF	XF	Unc
13	1839M	—	4.25	8.50	17.50	32.50
	1839V	—	4.00	8.00	16.00	30.00
	1843M	—	4.25	8.50	17.50	32.50
	1843V	—	3.25	6.50	13.50	26.50
	1846M	—	3.00	6.50	12.50	23.50
	1846V	—	3.00	6.50	12.50	23.50

C#	Date	Mintage	Fine	VF	XF	Unc
26	1849M	—	10.00	20.00	40.00	70.00
	1850M	—	10.00	20.00	40.00	70.00
	1852M	—	10.00	20.00	40.00	70.00

C#	Date	Mintage	Fine	VF	XF	Unc
30	1852M	—	3.00	7.50	15.00	30.00
	1852V	—	3.00	7.50	15.00	30.00

5 CENTESIMI

COPPER

C#	Date	Mintage	VF	XF	Unc
3	1822A	—	—	Rare	—
	1822M	—	5.00	12.50	25.00
	1822V	—	5.00	12.50	25.00
	1823M	—	Reported, not confirmed		
	1834M	—	10.00	20.00	32.50
	1834V	—	8.00	14.00	25.00

C#	Date	Mintage	Fine	VF	XF	Unc
14	1839M	—	7.50	15.00	30.00	55.00
	1839V	—	7.50	15.00	30.00	55.00
	1843M	—	6.25	12.50	25.00	45.00
	1843V	—	6.25	12.50	25.00	45.00
	1846M	—	6.25	12.50	25.00	45.00
	1846V	—	5.50	11.50	22.50	40.00

C#	Date	Mintage	Fine	VF	XF	Unc
27	1849M	—	7.50	15.00	30.00	50.00
	1850M	—	10.00	17.50	35.00	62.50

C#	Date	Mintage	Fine	VF	XF	Unc
31	1852M	—	10.00	17.50	35.00	60.00
	1852V	—	3.75	7.50	15.00	25.00

SOLDO

COPPER

C#	Date	Mintage	VF	XF	Unc
35	1862A	22.000	3.00	7.00	10.00
	1862B	9.000	5.00	12.00	18.00
	1862V	9.000	5.00	13.00	20.00

10 CENTESIMI

COPPER
Similar to 5 Centesimi, C#3.

C#	Date	Mintage	Fine	VF	XF	Unc
28	1849M	—	30.00	50.00	70.00	100.00
32	1852M	—	—	—	Rare	—
	1852V	—	5.50	8.50	17.50	35.00

15 CENTESIMI

COPPER

C#	Date	Mintage	Fine	VF	XF	Unc
33	1852V	—	170.00	240.00	350.00	500.00

1/4 LIRA

.600 SILVER, 1.62 gm.

C#	Date	Mintage	VF	XF	Unc
4	1822A	—	45.00	80.00	160.00
	1822M	—	15.00	30.00	50.00
	1822V	—	15.00	30.00	50.00
	1823A	—	165.00	320.00	600.00
	1823/2M	—	25.00	40.00	60.00
	1823M	—	20.00	35.00	55.00
	1823V	—	100.00	300.00	500.00
	1824M	—	100.00	300.00	500.00
	1824V	—	20.00	40.00	60.00
	1835A	—	Reported, not confirmed		

C#	Date	Mintage	Fine	VF	XF	Unc
15	1835A	—	Reported, not confirmed			
	1837A	—	Reported, not confirmed			
	1837V	—	75.00	150.00	300.00	450.00
	1838V	—	75.00	150.00	300.00	450.00
	1839V	—	100.00	200.00	375.00	550.00
	1840V	—	100.00	200.00	375.00	550.00
	1841V	—	100.00	200.00	375.00	550.00
	1842V	—	75.00	150.00	275.00	425.00
	1843V	—	100.00	200.00	275.00	550.00
	1844V	—	100.00	200.00	375.00	550.00

Obv: FRANZ I, Rev: Arms

C#	Date	Mintage	VF	XF	Unc
4a	1843V	—	15.00	20.00	40.00

Obv: FERDINAND, Rev: Arms

C#	Date	Mintage	VF	XF	Unc
—	1837V	—	15.00	20.00	40.00
	1841V	—	15.00	20.00	40.00
	1842V	—	15.00	20.00	40.00

1/2 LIRA

.900 SILVER, 2.165 gm.

C#	Date	Mintage	VF	XF	Unc
5	1822A	—	75.00	175.00	300.00
	1822M	—	10.00	20.00	50.00
	1822V	—	20.00	40.00	70.00
	1823A	—	80.00	170.00	260.00
	1823M	—	16.00	22.00	50.00
	1823/2V	—	25.00	50.00	75.00
	1823V	—	125.00	300.00	475.00
	1824M	—	17.00	25.00	75.00
	1824V	—	Reported, not confirmed		
	1835A	—	Reported, not confirmed		

C#	Date	Mintage	Fine	VF	XF	Unc
16	1835A	—	Reported, not confirmed			
	1837A	—	Reported, not confirmed			
	1837V	—	100.00	200.00	400.00	600.00
	1838V	—	125.00	250.00	500.00	725.00
	1840V	—	125.00	250.00	500.00	725.00
	1841V	—	150.00	300.00	600.00	850.00
	1842V	—	125.00	250.00	500.00	725.00
	1843V	—	125.00	250.00	500.00	725.00
	1844V	—	100.00	325.00	650.00	900.00
36	1854V	—	90.00	150.00	225.00	325.00
	1855V	—	170.00	240.00	350.00	500.00

LIRA

.900 SILVER, 4.33 gm.

C#	Date	Mintage	VF	XF	Unc
6	1822A	—	150.00	475.00	650.00
	1822M	—	30.00	55.00	125.00
	1822V	—	25.00	50.00	100.00
	1823A	—	25.00	50.00	100.00
	1823M	—	25.00	50.00	100.00
	1823V	—	115.00	275.00	450.00
	1824M	—	25.00	50.00	100.00
	1825M	—	45.00	80.00	140.00
	1835A	—	Reported, not confirmed		

C#	Date	Mintage	Fine	VF	XF	Unc
17	1835A	—	Reported, not confirmed			
	1837A	—	Reported, not confirmed			
	1837V	—	135.00	275.00	550.00	750.00
	1838V	—	150.00	300.00	600.00	800.00
	1839V	—	175.00	350.00	700.00	900.00
	1840V	—	135.00	275.00	550.00	750.00
	1841V	—	150.00	300.00	600.00	800.00
	1842V	—	—	—	Rare	—
	1843V	—	135.00	275.00	550.00	750.00
	1844V	—	125.00	250.00	500.00	725.00
37	1852V	—	75.00	125.00	175.00	250.00
	1853M	—	75.00	125.00	175.00	250.00
	1854M	—	200.00	350.00	500.00	750.00
	1855M	—	200.00	350.00	500.00	750.00
	1856M	—	150.00	250.00	350.00	500.00
	1858M	—	200.00	350.00	500.00	750.00

1/2 SCUDO

.900 SILVER, 12.345 gm.

C#	Date	Mintage	VF	XF	Unc
7	1822A	—	75.00	150.00	250.00
	1822M	—	70.00	130.00	200.00
	1822V	—	40.00	70.00	150.00
	1823A	—	75.00	150.00	200.00
	1823M	—	35.00	60.00	150.00
	1823V	—	125.00	325.00	525.00
	1824M	—	30.00	55.00	150.00
	1824V	—	45.00	75.00	175.00
	1825A	—	Reported, not confirmed		
	1825M	—	—	Rare	—
	1825V	—	40.00	75.00	175.00

C#	Date	Mintage	VF	XF	Unc
7	1826M	—	—	Rare	—
	1826V	—	45.00	90.00	175.00
	1827M	—	—	Rare	—
	1827V	—	75.00	150.00	250.00
	1835A	—	Reported, not confirmed		

C#	Date	Mintage	Fine	VF	XF	Unc
18	1835A	—	Reported, not confirmed			
	1837A	—	Reported, not confirmed			
	1837V	—	125.00	250.00	500.00	725.00
	1838V	—	150.00	300.00	600.00	800.00
	1839V	—	125.00	250.00	500.00	725.00
	1840V	—	125.00	250.00	500.00	725.00
	1841V	—	125.00	250.00	500.00	725.00
	1842V	—	125.00	250.00	500.00	725.00
	1843V	—	125.00	250.00	500.00	725.00
	1844V	—	150.00	300.00	600.00	800.00
	1845V	—	175.00	350.00	700.00	900.00
	1846V	—	150.00	300.00	600.00	800.00

Without value

C#	Date	Mintage	Fine	VF	XF	Unc
38	1853V	—	165.00	275.00	425.00	625.00

SCUDO

.900 SILVER, 26.00 gm.

C#	Date	Mintage	VF	XF	Unc
8	1816M	—	—	Proof	1800.
	1821A	—	—	Proof	—
	1822A	—	100.00	250.00	400.00
	1822M	—	55.00	125.00	200.00
	1822V	—	85.00	175.00	275.00
	1823A	—	100.00	250.00	400.00
	1823M	—	75.00	150.00	225.00
	1823V	—	250.00	600.00	950.00
	1824A	—	125.00	325.00	525.00
	1824M	—	75.00	175.00	275.00
	1824V	—	75.00	175.00	275.00
	1825A	—	Reported, not confirmed		
	1825M	—	60.00	140.00	275.00
	1825V	—	—	Rare	—
	1826M	—	100.00	250.00	500.00
	1826V	—	60.00	150.00	225.00
	1827M	—	75.00	160.00	335.00
	1827V	—	100.00	200.00	400.00
	1828M	—	275.00	475.00	800.00
	1828V	—	200.00	475.00	675.00
	1829M	—	90.00	200.00	400.00
	1829V	—	200.00	450.00	700.00
	1830M	—	80.00	175.00	350.00
	1830V	—	90.00	200.00	400.00
	1831M	—	65.00	150.00	225.00
	1831V	—	80.00	175.00	350.00
	1832V	—	90.00	200.00	400.00
	1835A	—	Reported, not confirmed		

C#	Date	Mintage	Fine	VF	XF	Unc
19	1835A	—	Reported, not confirmed			
	1837A	—	Reported, not confirmed			
	1837M	—	200.00	400.00	800.00	1000.
	1837V	—	125.00	250.00	500.00	700.00
	1838V	—	125.00	250.00	500.00	700.00
	1839V	—	125.00	250.00	500.00	700.00
	1840V	—	100.00	200.00	400.00	600.00
	1841V	—	150.00	300.00	600.00	800.00
	1842V	—	125.00	250.00	500.00	700.00
	1843V	—	150.00	300.00	600.00	800.00
	1844V	—	150.00	300.00	600.00	800.00
	1845V	—	125.00	250.00	500.00	700.00
	1846V	—	125.00	250.00	500.00	700.00

Without value

C#	Date	Mintage	Fine	VF	XF	Unc
39	1853V	—	150.00	250.00	400.00	600.00

TRADE COINS

ZECCHINO

.900 GOLD
Obv: Doge kneeling before St. Mark, FRANC. I., etc.
Rev: Christ standing

C#	Date	Mintage	VF	XF	Unc
9	ND(1815)	—	400.00	700.00	1000.

1/2 SOVRANO

.900 GOLD, 5.67 gm.

C#	Date	Mintage	VF	XF	Unc
10	1820M	—	600.00	1000.	1350.
	1823A		200.00	400.00	600.00
	1822A	—	250.00	400.00	550.00
	1822M	—	225.00	400.00	550.00
	1822V	—	400.00	700.00	1000.
	1823A	—	200.00	400.00	600.00
	1823V	—	200.00	400.00	600.00
	1831A	—	200.00	400.00	600.00
	1831M	—	150.00	300.00	500.00

C#	Date	Mintage	VF	XF	Unc
10a	1835A	—	Reported, not confirmed		
	1835M	—	250.00	400.00	550.00

C#	Date	Mintage	Fine	VF	XF
20	1837A	—	Reported, not confirmed		
	1837M	—	1750.	2250.	2850.
	1837V	—	1000.	1500.	2100.
	1838M	—	500.00	850.00	1350.
	1838V	—	1250.	1750.	2350.
	1839A	—	900.00	1350.	1850.
	1839M	—	500.00	850.00	1350.
	1839V	—	800.00	1250.	1750.
	1840V	—	800.00	1250.	1750.
	1841M	—	500.00	850.00	1350.
	1841V	—	900.00	1350.	1850.
	1842M	—	700.00	1100.	1600.
	1842V	—	1000.	1500.	2000.
	1843M	—	1350.	1850.	2450.
	1843V	—	1000.	1500.	2000.
	1844M	—	800.00	1250.	1750.
	1844V	—	800.00	1250.	1750.
	1845M	—	600.00	1000.	1500.
	1845V	—	1000.	1500.	2000.
	1846M	—	600.00	1000.	1500.
	1846V	—	700.00	1100.	1600.
	1847M	—	600.00	1000.	1500.
	1847V	—	1500.	2000.	2600.
	1848M	—	500.00	850.00	1350.
20a	1849M	—	550.00	900.00	1400.

C#	Date	Mintage	Fine	VF	XF	Unc
40	1854M	—	600.00	900.00	1600.	2500.
	1854V	—	750.00	1150.	2000.	3000.
	1855M	—	600.00	900.00	1600.	2500.
	1855V	—	750.00	1150.	2000.	3000.
	1856M	—	600.00	900.00	1600.	2500.
	1856V	—	675.00	1000.	1650.	2500.

SOVRANO

.900 GOLD, 11.33 gm.

C#	Date	Mintage	VF	XF	Unc
11	1820M	—	1000.	1500.	1800.
	1822A	—	350.00	500.00	750.00
	1822M	—	350.00	500.00	1000.
	1822V	—	500.00	900.00	1200.
	1823A	—	350.00	500.00	850.00
	1823M	—	400.00	600.00	900.00
	1824M	—	600.00	900.00	1200.
	1826M	—	—	Rare	—
	1827M	—	700.00	1200.	1600.
	1828M	—	700.00	1200.	1600.
	1829M	—	375.00	550.00	1000.
	1830M	—	325.00	500.00	900.00
	1831A	—	325.00	500.00	625.00
	1831/21M	—	850.00	1000.	1250.
	1831M	—	275.00	400.00	800.00
11a	1835A	—	Reported, not confirmed		
	1835M	—	700.00	1000.	1500.

C#	Date	Mintage	Fine	VF	XF
21	1837A	—	700.00	1100.	1600.
	1837M	—	1750.	2250.	2850.
	1837V	—	700.00	1100.	1600.
	1838A	—	—	Rare	—
	1838M	—	1500.	2000.	2600.
	1838V	—	1000.	1500.	2000.
	1839A	—	700.00	1100.	1600.
	1839V	—	1250.	1750.	2350.
	1840A	—	—	Rare	—
	1840M	—	1500.	2000.	2600.
	1840V	—	1250.	1750.	2350.
	1841A	—	900.00	1350.	1850.
	1841M	—	1800.	2300.	3000.
	1841V	—	900.00	1350.	1850.
	1842A	—	Reported, not confirmed		
	1842V	—	1200.	1750.	2350.
	1843A	—	—	Rare	—
	1843V	—	1350.	1850.	2450.
	1844V	—	1000.	1500.	2000.
	1845A	—	—	Rare	—
	1845V	—	1350.	1850.	2450.
	1846V	—	1250.	1750.	2350.
	1847A	—	1750.	2250.	2850.
	1847V	—	1250.	1750.	2350.
	1848M	—	1750.	2250.	2850.

C#	Date	Mintage	Fine	VF	XF	Unc
41	1853M	—	850.00	1250.	2000.	3000.
	1854V	—	1150.	1650.	2500.	3500.
	1855M	—	850.00	1250.	2000.	3000.
	1855V	—	1150.	1650.	2500.	3500.
	1856M	—	850.00	1250.	2000.	3000.
	1856V	—	1000.	1500.	2500.	3500.

REVOLUTIONARY PROVISIONAL GOV'T

5 LIRE

.900 SILVER, 25.00 gm.

Obv: Short stems on branches.

C#	Date	Mintage	Fine	VF	XF	Unc
22.1	1848M	—	35.00	65.00	125.00	250.00
	Obv: Long stems on branches.					
22.2	1848M	—	75.00	150.00	275.00	400.00
	Obv: Short stems on branches. Rev: Star near crown.					
22.3	1848M	—	50.00	100.00	175.00	300.00

20 LIRE

.900 GOLD, 6.45 gm.

C#	Date	Mintage	Fine	VF	XF	Unc
23	1848M	—	300.00	450.00	600.00	1200.

40 LIRE

.900 GOLD, 12.9 gm.

C#	Date	Mintage	Fine	VF	XF	Unc
24	1848M	—	500.00	750.00	1100.	1650.

NCLT ISSUES

PATTERNS

KM#	Date	Mintage	Identification	Mkt.Val.
1	1821V	—	1/2 Lira, C#5, Silver	—
2	1848M	—	1 Lira, Silver	—
2a	1848M	—	1 Lira, Copper	—
2b	1848M	—	1 Lira, Zinc	—
3	1848M	—	2 Lira, Silver	—
3a	1848M	—	2 Lira, Copper	—
3b	1848M	—	2 Lira, Zinc	—
5	1852M	—	15 Centesimi, C#33, Copper	—

LUCCA

Luca, Lucensis
Lucca and Piombino
Principality, 1805-1814
Lucca, Duchy, 1817-1847

A town in Tuscany and the residence of a marquis, was nominally a fief but managed to maintain a de facto independence until awarded by Napoleon to his sister Elisa in 1805. In 1814 it was occupied by the Neapolitans, and from 1817 to 1847 was a duchy of the queen of Etruria, after which it became a division of Tuscany.

RULERS

Felix and Elisa (Bonaparte), 1805-1810
Maria Luisa di Borbone
Duchess, 1817-1824
Carlo Lodovico di Borbone
Duke, 1824-1847

MONETARY SYSTEM

100 Centesimi = 1 Franco

3 CENTESIMI

COPPER

Similar to 5 Franchi, C#24, with jugate busts left.

C#	Date	Mintage	Fine	VF	XF
21	1806	—	10.00	20.00	40.00

5 CENTESIMI

COPPER

C#	Date	Mintage	Fine	VF	XF
22	1806	—	10.00	20.00	40.00

FRANCO

.900 SILVER, 5.00 gm.

C#	Date	Mintage	Fine	VF	XF
23	1805	—	—	Rare	—
	1806	—	15.00	25.00	75.00
	1807	—	15.00	25.00	80.00
	1808	—	15.00	25.00	75.00

5 FRANCHI

.900 SILVER, 24.84 gm.

C#	Date	Mintage	Fine	VF	XF
24	1805	—	60.00	125.00	250.00
	1806	—	75.00	150.00	300.00
	1807	—	75.00	150.00	300.00
	1808/7	—	75.00	85.00	125.00
	1808	—	75.00	150.00	300.00

MONETARY REFORM

4 Denari - 1 Quattrino
3 Quattrini - 1 Soldo
20 Soldi - 1 Lira

QUATTRINO

COPPER
Obv: DUCATO DI LUCCA, Rev: Value, date

C#	Date	Mintage	Fine	VF	XF
31	1826	—	6.00	10.00	15.00

MEZZO (1/2) SOLDO

COPPER
Obv: DUCATO DI LUCCA, crown, Rev: Value, date

C#	Date	Mintage	Fine	VF	XF
32	1826	—	6.00	10.00	15.00
	1835	—	6.00	10.00	15.00

2 QUATTRINI

COPPER

C#	Date	Mintage	Fine	VF	XF
33	1826	—	6.00	10.00	17.50

SOLDO

COPPER
Obv: CARLO L. D. B. I. D. S. DUCA DI LUCCA

C#	Date	Mintage	Fine	VF	XF
34	1826	—	6.00	10.00	17.50

C#	Date	Mintage	Fine	VF	XF
34a	1841	—	6.00	10.00	17.50

5 QUATTRINI

COPPER
Obv: Crowned arms, Rev: Value, date

C#	Date	Mintage	Fine	VF	XF
35	1826	—	6.00	10.00	17.50

2 SOLDI

.200 SILVER, 1.4 gm.
Obv: Crowned arms, Rev: Value, date

C#	Date	Mintage	Fine	VF	XF
36	1835	—	15.00	17.00	25.00

BOLOGNINO (2 Soldi)

.200 SILVER, 3.07 gm.
Obv: Branch with 6 leaves

C#	Date	Year	Mintage	Fine	VF	XF
4a	1790	(1835) (restrike)				
			—	20.00	25.00	30.00

3 SOLDI

.200 SILVER, 1.6 gm.
Obv: Crowned CL monogram, Rev: Value, date

C#	Date	Mintage	Fine	VF	XF
37	1835	—	25.00	45.00	65.00

5 SOLDI

.200 SILVER, 3.00 gm.
Obv: Crowned shield, Rev: Value, date

C#	Date	Mintage	Fine	VF	XF
38	1833 flat top 3's				
		—	6.00	10.00	20.00
	1833 round top 3's				
		—	6.00	10.00	20.00
	1838	—	6.00	10.00	20.00

10 SOLDI

.666 SILVER, 2.36 gm.
Obv: Head right, Rev: Value, date within wreath.

C#	Date	Mintage	VF	XF	Unc
39	1833	—	15.00	25.00	75.00
	1838	—	15.00	25.00	75.00

LIRA

.666 SILVER, 4.72 gm.
Obv: Head right, Rev: Value within wreath

C#	Date	Mintage	VF	XF	Unc
40	1834	—	20.00	35.00	100.00
	1837	—	20.00	35.00	100.00
	1838	—	20.00	35.00	100.00

2 LIRE

.666 SILVER, 9.43 gm.

C#	Date	Mintage	VF	XF	Unc
41	1837	—	60.00	150.00	300.00

MANTUA

MANTOVA

A city of Lombardy, was taken by the Lombards in 568, became a fief of the princely Italian Gonzaga family in 1328, formed part of the Cisalpine and Italian republics, and fell to Austria in 1799. It was restored to the French in 1801, but reverted to Austria as part of the kingdom of Lombardy-Venetia, 1814-1866.

RULERS

Austrian until 1797, 1814-35

MONETARY SYSTEM

6 Denari - 1 Sesino
2 Sesini - 1 Soldo
20 Soldi - 1 Lira

1/2 SOLDO

COPPER
Obv: Crowned arms. Rev: Value, DI MANTOVA

C#	Date	Mintage	VG	Fine	VF
19	1793	—	5.50	9.00	16.50

MEZZA (1/2) LIRA

.552 SILVER, 3.1 gm.
Obv: Crowned arms within legend.
Rev: Value within wreath.

C#	Date	Mintage	Fine	VF	XF	Unc
16	1791	—	50.00	100.00	200.00	375.00

UNA (1) LIRA

.552 SILVER, 6.25 gm.
Obv. leg. ends: MANT. Rev: Similar to Mezza Lira C#16.

C#	Date	Mintage	Fine	VF	XF	Unc
17	1791	—	50.00	100.00	200.00	350.00
	Obv. leg. ends: ...MAN.					
17a	1791	—	—	—	—	—

20 SOLDI

SILVER

C#	Date	Mintage	VG	Fine	VF
20	1796	84,776	120.00	225.00	375.00
	1796 (error) retrograde S in SOLDI				
		Inc. Ab.	180.00	300.00	525.00

NOTE: The above issue was struck by the Austrian defenders during the siege by the French.

SIEGE OF 1799

(Issued by the French Defenders)

UN (1) SOLDO

CAST BELL METAL

C#	Date	Year	Mintage	VG	Fine	VF
31	(1799)	7	—	16.50	25.00	40.00

V (5) SOLDI

SILVER
Obv: Fasces with cap, leg: ASSEDIO.DI.MANT.AN. VII.R Rev: Value, DI MILANO within wreath.

C#	Date	Year	Mintage	VG	Fine	VF
32	(1799)	VII	—	35.00	65.00	120.00

X (10) SOLDI

SILVER
Obv. and rev: Similar to 5 Soldi, C#32.

C#	Date	Year	Mintage	VG	Fine	VF
33	(1799)	VII	—	42.50	70.00	150.00

SIEGE OF 1848

NOTE: For 3 Kreutzer, 20 Kreutzer and 1/2 Thaler Austrian coins dated 1848 with GM mintmark see Austria Craig #188a, 191a, and 192a.

MASSA — CARRARA

A small state in Tuscany, a territorial division consisting of the western part of the center of the Italian peninsula, attained the ranking of a principality in 1568 and of a duchy in 1663. The minting privilege was granted to the Marquis of Massa in 1559.

RULERS

Austrian until 1796, 1814-29

MONETARY SYSTEM

3 Quattrini = 1 Soldo
20 Soldi = 1 Lira

UN (1) QUATRINO

COPPER
Obv: Crowned arms within legends.
Rev: Value within wreath.

C#	Date	Mintage	VG	Fine	VF
1	1792	—	7.50	12.50	20.00

DUE (2) SOLDI

COPPER
Obv. & rev: Similar to Un Quattrino, C#1.

C#	Date	Mintage	VG	Fine	VF
2	1792	—	8.50	13.50	25.00

4 SOLDI

BILLON
Obv. & rev: Similar to Un Quattrino, C#1.

C#	Date	Mintage	VG	Fine	VF
3	1792	—	7.50	12.50	20.00

X (10) SOLDI

BILLON
Obv. & rev: Similar to Un Quattrino, C#1.

C#	Date	Mintage	VG	Fine	VF
4	1792	—	8.50	13.50	25.00

MILAN

A city in Lombardy, was ruled by the Lombards before falling to the Franks in 774. It was a dependency of the Spanish Crown from 1535 to 1714, became part of the Cisalpine Republic in 1797, became part of the Italian Republic in 1802, and was part of the Kingdom of Napoleon from 1805 to 1814. From 1814 to 1859 it was incorporated in Lombardy-Venetia.

5 SOLDI

.552 SILVER, 1.55 gm.
Obv: Biscia in shield. Rev: Value.

C#	Date	Mintage	Fine	VF	XF
31	1778	—	8.50	12.50	20.00
	1779	—	8.50	12.50	20.00
	1780	—	8.50	12.50	20.00

Obv: Biscia shield. Rev: Value.

C#	Date	Mintage	Fine	VF	XF
41	1780	—	5.00	8.50	15.00
	1781	—	5.00	8.50	15.00
	1782	—	5.00	8.50	15.00
	1783	—	5.00	8.50	15.00
	1784	—	5.00	8.50	15.00
	1785	—	5.00	8.50	15.00
	1786	—	5.00	8.50	15.00
	1787	—	5.00	8.50	15.00

MEZZA (1/2) LIRA

.552 SILVER, 3.1 gm.
Similar to 6 Lire, C#36.

C#	Date	Mintage	Fine	VF	XF
33	1778	—	22.50	40.00	65.00
	1779	—	22.50	40.00	65.00
	1780	—	22.50	40.00	65.00

Similar to 6 Lire, C#45

C#	Date	Mintage	Fine	VF	XF
42	1781	—	10.00	16.50	30.00
	1782	—	10.00	16.50	30.00
	1783	—	10.00	16.50	30.00
	1784	—	10.00	16.50	30.00
	1785	—	10.00	16.50	30.00
	1786	—	10.00	16.50	30.00
	1787	—	10.00	16.50	30.00

UNA (1) LIRA

.552 SILVER, 6.25 gm.
Similar to 6 Lire, C#36.

C#	Date	Mintage	Fine	VF	XF
34	1778	—	30.00	55.00	85.00
	1779	—	30.00	55.00	85.00
	1780	—	30.00	55.00	85.00

Similar to 6 Lire, C#45

C#	Date	Mintage	Fine	VF	XF
43	1781	—	11.50	20.00	35.00
	1782	—	11.50	20.00	35.00
	1783	—	11.50	20.00	35.00
	1784	—	11.50	20.00	35.00
	1785	—	11.50	20.00	35.00
	1786	—	11.50	20.00	35.00
	1787	—	11.50	20.00	40.00
	1788	—	11.50	20.00	40.00
	1789	—	11.50	20.00	40.00
	1790	—	11.50	20.00	40.00

.552 SILVER, 6.25 gm.
Obv: Bust of Leopold II within legend.
Rev. leg: MEDIOLANI ET MANT. DUX ...

C#	Date	Mintage	Fine	VF	XF	Unc
52	1790M	—	100.00	200.00	325.00	600.00
	1791M	—	125.00	250.00	400.00	750.00

30 SOLDI

.689 SILVER, 7.36 gm.
Obv: Bust to right within legend.
Rev: Crowned arms, legend.

C#	Date	Mintage	Fine	VF	XF
58	1792	—	Reported, not confirmed		
	1793	—	Reported, not confirmed		
	1794	—	50.00	90.00	150.00
	1795	—	75.00	125.00	200.00
	1796	—	50.00	90.00	150.00
	1797	—	Reported, not confirmed		
	1798	—	Reported, not confirmed		
	1799	—	75.00	125.00	200.00
	1800	—	50.00	90.00	150.00
58a	1794 (error) MEDILANI				
		—	100.00	175.00	300.00

3 LIRE

.896 SILVER, 11.55 gm.
Similar to 6 Lire, C#36.

C#	Date	Mintage	Fine	VF	XF
35	1777	—	65.00	100.00	150.00
	1778	—	65.00	100.00	150.00
	1779	—	65.00	100.00	150.00
	1780	—	65.00	100.00	150.00

Similar to 6 Lire, C#45.

C#	Date	Mintage	Fine	VF	XF
44	1781	—	40.00	60.00	90.00
	1782	—	40.00	60.00	100.00
	1783	—	40.00	60.00	100.00
	1784	—	40.00	60.00	100.00
	1785	—	40.00	60.00	100.00
	1786	—	40.00	60.00	100.00

1/2 CROCIONE

(1/2 Kronenthaler)

.873 SILVER, 14.72 gm.

C#	Date	Mintage	Fine	VF	XF
48	1786M	—	15.00	25.00	50.00
	1787M	—	15.00	25.00	50.00
	1788M	—	15.00	25.00	50.00
	1789M	—	15.00	25.00	50.00
	1790M	—	15.00	25.00	50.00

Rev: Similar to Crocione, C#54.

C#	Date	Mintage	Fine	VF	XF
53	1791M	—	20.00	30.00	50.00

6 LIRE

.896 SILVER, 23.1 gm.

C#	Date	Mintage	Fine	VF	XF
36	1778	—	110.00	150.00	225.00
	1779	—	110.00	150.00	225.00
	1780	—	110.00	150.00	225.00

C#	Date	Mintage	Fine	VF	XF
45	1781	—	100.00	140.00	200.00
	1782	—	100.00	140.00	200.00
	1783	—	100.00	140.00	200.00
	1784	—	100.00	140.00	200.00
	1785	—	100.00	140.00	200.00
	1786	—	100.00	140.00	200.00

CROCIONE

(Kronenthaler)

.873 SILVER, 29.44 gm.
Similar to 1/2 Crocione, C#48.

C#	Date	Mintage	Fine	VF	XF
49	1786M	—	30.00	45.00	60.00
	1787M	—	30.00	45.00	60.00
	1788M	—	30.00	45.00	60.00
	1789M	—	30.00	45.00	60.00
	1790M	—	30.00	45.00	60.00

Rev: Similar to Crocione, C#59.1.

C#	Date	Mintage	Fine	VF	XF
54	1791M	—	50.00	75.00	120.00
	1792M	—	50.00	75.00	120.00

C#	Date	Mintage	Fine	VF	XF
59.1	1792M	—	30.00	55.00	110.00
	1793M	—	20.00	35.00	70.00
	1794M	—	20.00	35.00	70.00
	1795M	—	22.50	37.50	70.00
	1796M	—	17.50	32.50	60.00
	1799M	—	30.00	55.00	110.00
	1800M	—	21.50	40.00	70.00

Edge inscription: IVSTITIA ET FIDE

C#	Date	Mintage	Fine	VF	XF
59.2	1799M	—	50.00	90.00	150.00
	1800M	—	40.00	75.00	120.00

1/4 SOVRANO

GOLD, 2.77 gm.
Similar to Crocione, C#54.

C#	Date	Mintage	Fine	VF	XF
55	1791M	—	Reported, not confirmed		

ZECCHINO

.986 GOLD, 3.49 gm.
Obv: Veiled bust of Maria Theresa.
Rev: Standing figure of St. Ambrose.

C#	Date	Mintage	Fine	VF	XF
37	ND	—	—	Rare	—

Rev: Biscia in shield.

C#	Date	Mintage	Fine	VF	XF
38	1778	—	450.00	650.00	1000.
	1779	—	450.00	650.00	1000.
	1780	—	450.00	650.00	1000.

.998 GOLD, 3.49 gm.

Similar to Mezza Lira, C#42.

C#	Date	Mintage	Fine	VF	XF
46	1781	—	300.00	375.00	500.00
	1782	—	300.00	375.00	500.00
	1783	—	300.00	375.00	500.00
	1784	—	300.00	375.00	500.00
	1785	—	300.00	375.00	500.00
	1786	—	300.00	375.00	500.00
	1787	—	300.00	375.00	500.00
	1788	—	300.00	375.00	500.00

1/2 SOVRANO

.900 GOLD, 5.67 gm.

C#	Date	Mintage	Fine	VF	XF	Unc
50	1787M	—	250.00	500.00	750.00	1100.
	1788M	—	300.00	600.00	900.00	1350.
	1789M	—	350.00	700.00	1000.	1500.
	1790M	—	350.00	700.00	1000.	1500.

Similar to Crocione, C#54.

C#	Date	Mintage	Fine	VF	XF	Unc
56	1790M	—	350.00	700.00	1000.	1500.
	1791M	—	300.00	600.00	900.00	1350.
	1792M	—	350.00	700.00	1000.	1500.

Rev: Larger crowned arms.

C#	Date	Mintage	Fine	VF	XF	Unc
56a	1791M	—	—	—	—	—

Similar to Sovrano, C#61.

C#	Date	Mintage	Fine	VF	XF
60	1800M	—	—	Rare	—

NOTE: For similar coins with other mintmarks refer to Austrian Netherlands.

DOPPIA

.910 GOLD, 6.3 gm.

C#	Date	Mintage	Fine	VF	XF
39	1778	—	950.00	1750.	3000.
	1779	—	950.00	1750.	3000.
	1780	—	950.00	1750.	3000.

Similar to Mezza Lira, C#42.

C#	Date	Mintage	Fine	VF	XF
47	1781	—	725.00	850.00	1000.
	1782	—	725.00	850.00	1000.
	1783	—	725.00	850.00	1000.
	1784	—	725.00	850.00	1000.

SOVRANO

.900 GOLD, 11.33 gm.

C#	Date	Mintage	Fine	VF	XF
51	1786M	—	225.00	275.00	400.00
	1787M	—	225.00	275.00	400.00
	1788M	—	225.00	275.00	400.00
	1789M	—	225.00	275.00	400.00
	1790M	—	225.00	275.00	400.00

Similar to Crocione, C#54.

C#	Date	Mintage	Fine	VF	XF	Unc
57	1790M	—	600.00	1500.	2000.	2500.
	1791M	—	750.00	1750.	2500.	3000.
	1792M	—	750.00	1750.	2500.	3000.

C#	Date	Mintage	Fine	VF	XF
61	1793M	—	350.00	550.00	900.00
	1794M	—	325.00	500.00	800.00
	1795M	—	275.00	450.00	650.00
61	1796M	—	250.00	425.00	625.00
	1799M	—	475.00	750.00	1200.
	1800M	—	350.00	550.00	900.00

NOTE: For similar coins with other mintmarks refer to Austrian Netherlands.

2 DOPPIE

.910 GOLD, 12.6 gm.
Obv: Veiled bust of Maria Theresa.
Rev: Biscia in shield.

C#	Date	Mintage	Fine	VF	XF
40	1778	—	1500.	3500.	6000.
	1779	—	1500.	3500.	6000.

MODENA

MUTINA

A territorial division of Italy fronting on the Adriatic Sea between Venetia and Marches, is the ancient Mutina which became Roman in 215-212 B.C. Ravaged by Attila and Lombard attacks, it was rebuilt in the 9th century. Obizzo d'Este became its lord in 1288 and it was constituted a duchy in favor of Borso d'Este in 1452. Modena was included in the Napoleonic complex from 1796 to 1813, after which it was governed by the House of Austria-Este. In 1859 it became a part of the new kingdom of Italy. Modena began coining in the 13th century and ceased in 1796.

RULERS

Ercole (Hercules) III d'Este
1780-1796

QVATTRO (4) DENARI

COPPER
Obv: Crowned lily. Rev: Value.

C#	Date	Mintage	VG	Fine	VF
13	ND	—	4.25	7.00	15.00

UN (VN = 1) SOLDO

COPPER
Obv: Date within wreath.
Rev: Value within wreath.

C#	Date	Mintage	VG	Fine	VF
14	1783	—	4.25	7.00	15.00
	1784	—	4.25	7.00	15.00

NOTE: Varieties exist.

UN (VN = 1) BOLOGNINO

COPPER
Obv: d' Este eagle. Rev: Value.

C#	Date	Mintage	VG	Fine	VF
15	1783	—	4.25	7.00	15.00
	1784	—	4.25	7.00	15.00

DUE (2) BOLOGNINI

BILLON
Obv: Eagle. Rev: Value.

C#	Date	Mintage	VG	Fine	VF
16	1783	—	7.00	15.00	30.00
	1784	—	7.00	15.00	30.00

SCUDO

.910 SILVER, 9.231 gm.

C#	Date	Mintage	Fine	VF	XF
17	1782	—	70.00	110.00	180.00
	1783	—	70.00	110.00	180.00

2 SCUDI

.910 SILVER, 18.462 gm.
Similar to Tallero, C#20

C#	Date	Mintage	Fine	VF	XF
18	1782	—	90.00	150.00	200.00
	1783	—	90.00	150.00	200.00

3 SCUDI

.910 SILVER, 27.6930 gm.
Similar to Tallero, C#20

C#	Date	Mintage	Fine	VF	XF
19	1782	—	150.00	225.00	375.00
	1783	—	150.00	225.00	375.00

TALLERO

.910 SILVER, 25.81 gm.

C#	Date	Mintage	Fine	VF	XF
20	1795	—	160.00	200.00	300.00
	1796	—	160.00	200.00	300.00

NAPLES & SICILY

TWO SICILIES

Consists of Sicily and the south of Italy which came into being in 1130. It passed under Spanish control in 1502; Naples was conquered by Austria in 1707. In 1733 Don Carlos of Spain was recognized as king. From then until becoming part of the united Kingdom of Italy, Naples and Sicily, together and separately, were contested for by Spain, Austria, France, and the republican and monarchial factions of Italy.

RULERS

Ferdinando IV, 1759-1799 (1st reign)
1799-1805 (2nd reign)
1815-1816 (restored in Naples)
1816-1825 (as King of the Two Sicilies)
Neapolitan Republic, 1799
Joseph Napoleon, 1806-1808
Joachim Murat, 1808-1815
(Gioacchino Napoleone)

Two Sicilies

Francesco I, 1825-1830
Ferdinand II, 1830-1859
Francesco II, 1859-1869

MONETARY SYSTEMS

(Until 1813)

6 Cavalli = 1 Tornese
240 Tornese = 120 Grana = 12 Carlini = 6 Tari = 1 Piastra
5 Grana = 1 Cinquina
100 Grana = 1 Ducato (Tallero)

3 CAVALLI

COPPER

C#	Date	Mintage	VG	Fine	VF
29	1788	—	1.50	2.75	5.00
	1789	—	1.50	2.75	5.00
	1790	—	1.50	2.75	5.00
	1791	—	1.50	2.75	5.00
	1792	—	1.50	2.75	5.00

4 CAVALLI

COPPER

C#	Date	Mintage	VG	Fine	VF
31	1788	—	3.50	6.00	9.50
	1789	—	3.50	6.00	9.50
	1790	—	3.50	6.00	9.50
	1791	—	3.50	6.00	9.50
	1792	—	3.50	6.00	9.50

TORNESE
(6 Cavalli)

COPPER

C#	Date	Mintage	VG	Fine	VF
33	1788	—	2.50	4.50	7.50
	1789	—	2.50	4.50	7.50
	1790	—	2.50	4.50	7.50
	1791	—	2.50	4.50	7.50
	1792	—	2.50	4.50	7.50

9 CAVALLI

COPPER

C#	Date	Mintage	VG	Fine	VF
37	1788	—	4.50	7.50	11.50
	1789	—	4.50	7.50	11.50
	1790	—	4.50	7.50	11.50
	1791	—	4.50	7.50	11.50
	1792	—	4.50	7.50	11.50

GRANO
(12 Cavalli)

COPPER

C#	Date	Mintage	VG	Fine	VF
39	1788	—	5.00	8.50	12.50
	1789	—	5.00	8.50	12.50
	1790	—	5.00	8.50	12.50
	1791	—	5.00	8.50	12.50
	1792	—	5.00	8.50	12.50
	1793	—	5.00	8.50	12.50
	1797	—	8.50	12.50	20.00

C#	Date	Mintage	VG	Fine	VF
39	1798	—	15.00	25.00	40.00

3 TORNESI

COPPER
Obv: Head of Ferdinand right.
Rev: PUBLI/CA/LETI/TIA in wreath.

C#	Date	Mintage	VG	Fine	VF
—	1778	—	—	Rare	—
	1779	—	—	Rare	—

C#	Date	Mintage	VG	Fine	VF
43	1788	—	8.50	12.50	20.00
	1789	—	8.50	12.50	20.00
	1790	—	8.50	12.50	20.00
	1791	—	8.50	12.50	20.00
	1792	—	8.50	12.50	20.00
	1793	—	8.50	12.50	20.00

5 TORNESI

COPPER, 26-27mm

C#	Date	Mintage	VG	Fine	VF
45	1797	—	5.00	8.50	12.50
	1798	—	8.50	12.50	20.00

30mm.

C#	Date	Mintage	VG	Fine	VF
45a	1798	—	5.00	8.50	12.50

8 TORNESI

COPPER

C#	Date	Mintage	VG	Fine	VF
49	1796	—	15.00	25.00	40.00
	1797	—	15.00	25.00	40.00

10 TORNESI

COPPER

C#	Date	Mintage	VG	Fine	VF
51	1798	—	15.00	25.00	40.00

CARLINO

.833 SILVER, 2.294 gm.
Obv: Head of Ferdinand right.
Rev: Radiant cross; date below.

C#	Date	Mintage	Fine	VF	XF
53	1788	—	6.00	10.00	25.00
	1791	—	6.00	10.00	25.00
	1792	—	6.00	10.00	25.00
	1794	—	6.00	10.00	25.00
	1795	—	6.00	10.00	25.00
	1798	—	6.00	10.00	25.00

20 GRANA

.833 SILVER, 5.544 gm.
Obv: Head of Ferdinand right.
Rev: Crowned arms; value below.

C#	Date	Mintage	Fine	VF	XF
55	1788	—	7.00	12.50	30.00
	1789	—	7.00	12.50	30.00
	1790	—	7.00	12.50	30.00

Rev: Crown in wreath, value below.

C#	Date	Mintage	Fine	VF	XF
57	1790	—	7.00	12.50	30.00
	1792	—	7.00	12.50	30.00
	1793	—	7.00	12.50	30.00
	1794	—	7.00	12.50	30.00
	1795	—	7.00	12.50	30.00
	1796	—	7.00	12.50	30.00
	1798	—	7.00	12.50	30.00

50 GRANA

.833 SILVER, 11.35 gm.
Obv: Head of Ferdinand right.
Rev: Crowned arms; value in exergue.

C#	Date	Mintage	Fine	VF	XF
59	1784	—	35.00	60.00	100.00
	1785	—	30.00	50.00	75.00

60 GRANA

.917 SILVER, 12.741 gm.
Obv: Young, small bust of Ferdinand right.
Rev: Crowned arms over value.

C#	Date	Mintage	Fine	VF	XF
60	1760	—	35.00	60.00	100.00

.833 SILVER, 13.766 gm.
Obv: Older bust of Ferdinand right.

C#	Date	Mintage	Fine	VF	XF
61	1785	—	35.00	60.00	100.00
	1786	—	35.00	60.00	100.00
	1788	—	35.00	60.00	100.00
	1791	—	—	Rare	—
	1792	—	30.00	50.00	75.00
	1793	—	50.00	75.00	125.00
	1794	—	—	—	—

Obv: Head of Ferdinand right.

C#	Date	Mintage	Fine	VF	XF
61a	1796	—	30.00	50.00	75.00
	1798	—	30.00	50.00	75.00

DUCATO

.833 SILVER, 22.5 gm.
Obv: Head of Ferdinand right.
Rev: Crowned arms in sprays; value below.

C#	Date	Mintage	Fine	VF	XF
63	1784	—	50.00	75.00	125.00
	1785	—	50.00	75.00	125.00

PAISTRA OF 120 GRANA

.917 SILVER, 25.483 gm.
Obv: Large youthful bust of Ferdinand right.
Rev: Crowned arms over value.

C#	Date	Mintage	Fine	VF	XF
64	1766	—	65.00	100.00	200.00

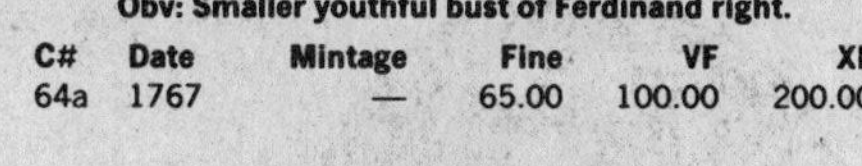

Obv: Smaller youthful bust of Ferdinand right.

C#	Date	Mintage	Fine	VF	XF
64a	1767	—	65.00	100.00	200.00

Birth of Princess Maria Theresa

C#	Date	Mintage	Fine	VF	XF
65	1772	—	60.00	95.00	175.00

.833 SILVER, 27.265 gm.
Obv: Head of Ferdinand right.
Rev: Crowned plain arms over value.

C#	Date	Mintage	Fine	VF	XF
66	1784	—	50.00	75.00	150.00
	1785	—	50.00	75.00	150.00

C#	Date	Mintage	Fine	VF	XF
66a	1786	—	50.00	75.00	150.00
	1787	—	50.00	75.00	150.00
	1788	—	50.00	75.00	150.00
	1789	—	60.00	95.00	175.00
	1790	—	50.00	75.00	150.00
	1791	—	50.00	75.00	150.00
	1792	—	50.00	75.00	150.00
	1793	—	50.00	75.00	150.00
	1794	—	50.00	75.00	150.00

Obv: Older head of Ferdinand right.

C#	Date	Mintage	Fine	VF	XF
66b	1795	—	50.00	75.00	150.00
	1796	—	50.00	75.00	150.00
	1798	—	50.00	75.00	150.00

.833 SILVER, 27.532 gm.
Obv: Accolated busts of Ferdinand and Maria Carolina.
Rev: Seated god at left, standing goddess at right; volcano between.

C#	Date	Mintage	Fine	VF	XF
67	1791	—	75.00	110.00	200.00

C#	Date	Mintage	Fine	VF	XF
68	1791	—	75.00	110.00	200.00

2 DUCATI

.906 GOLD, 2.932 gm.
Obv: Young bust of Ferdinand right.
Rev: Crowned arms over value.

C#	Date	Mintage	Fine	VF	XF
69	1762	—	600.00	900.00	1500.

Obv: Older bust of Ferdinand right.
Rev: Crowned arms in sprays over value.

C#	Date	Mintage	Fine	VF	XF
71	1771	—	500.00	750.00	1250.

4 DUCATI

.906 GOLD, 5.865 gm.
Obv: Young bust of Ferdinand right.
Rev: Crowned arms over value.

C#	Date	Mintage	Fine	VF	XF
73	1760	—	500.00	750.00	1500.
	1761	—	500.00	750.00	1500.
	1762	—	500.00	750.00	1500.
	1763	—	500.00	750.00	1500.
	1764	—	500.00	750.00	1500.
	1765	—	500.00	750.00	1500.
	1767	—	500.00	750.00	1500.
	1768	—	500.00	750.00	1500.

Obv: Older bust of Ferdinand right.

C#	Date	Mintage	Fine	VF	XF
74	1769	—	650.00	1000.	2000.
	1770	—	650.00	1000.	2000.
	1772	—	650.00	1000.	2000.
	1774	—	650.00	1000.	2000.
	1776	—	650.00	1000.	2000.

6 DUCATI

.906 GOLD, 8.798 gm.

C#	Date	Mintage	Fine	VF	XF
75	1759	—	450.00	750.00	1500.
	1760	—	450.00	750.00	1500.
	1761	—	450.00	750.00	1500.
	1762	—	375.00	600.00	1250.
	1763	—	375.00	600.00	1250.
	1764	—	375.00	600.00	1250.
	1765	—	375.00	600.00	1250.
	1766	—	375.00	600.00	1250.
	1767	—	375.00	600.00	1250.
	1768	—	375.00	600.00	1250.

C#	Date	Mintage	Fine	VF	XF
76	1768	—	375.00	600.00	1250.
	1769	—	375.00	600.00	1250.
	1770	—	375.00	600.00	1250.
	1771	—	375.00	600.00	1250.
	1772	—	375.00	600.00	1250.
	1773	—	375.00	600.00	1250.
	1774	—	375.00	600.00	1250.
	1775	—	375.00	600.00	1250.
	1776	—	375.00	600.00	1250.
	1777	—	375.00	600.00	1250.
	1778	—	375.00	600.00	1250.
	1780	—	—	Rare	—
	1781	—	—	Rare	—

Obv: Old bust of Ferdinand right.

C#	Date	Mintage	Fine	VF	XF
76a	1783	—	1500.	2250.	3500.
	1784	—	1500.	2250.	3500.
	1785	—	1500.	2250.	3500.

Neapolitan Republic

A revoultionary government in Naples 23 January - 13 June 1799. (Year 7 - Anno Settimo - 1799)

QVATTRO (4) TORNESI

COPPER
Obv: Fasces. Rev: Value.

C#	Date	Year	Mintage	Fine	VF	XF
81	(1799)	7	—	5.00	10.00	25.00

NOTE: Two varieties exist.

SEI (6) TORNESI

COPPER
Obv: Fasces. Rev: TORNESI.

C#	Date	Year	Mintage	Fine	VF	XF
82	(1799)	7	—	10.00	35.00	75.00

Obv: Fasces. Rev: TORNESI Z. N.

C#	Date	Year	Mintage	Fine	VF	XF
	(1799)	7	—	10.00	35.00	75.00

SEI (6) CARLINI

.833 SILVER, 13.95 gm.
Obv: Liberty standing. Rev: Value.

C#	Date	Year	Mintage	Fine	VF	XF
83	(1799)	7	—	50.00	100.00	150.00

DODI CI (12) CARLINI

.833 SILVER, 27.53 gm.
Obv: NAPOLITAN, Liberty standing. Rev: Value.

C#	Date	Year	Mintage	Fine	VF	XF
84	(1799)	7	—	50.00	125.00	250.00

Obv: NAPOLITANA

C#	Date	Year	Mintage	Fine	VF	XF
84	(1799)	7	—	40.00	75.00	150.00

Kingdom Of Naples

3 CAVALLI

COPPER

C#	Date	Mintage	Fine	VF	XF
91	1804	—	2.50	4.00	8.50

4 CAVALLI

COPPER
Obv: Head right. Rev: Grapes.

C#	Date	Mintage	Fine	VF	XF
92	1804LD	—	4.00	6.00	9.00

TORNESE (= 6 CAVALLI)

COPPER
Obv: Head right, Rev: Value within wreath

C#	Date	Mintage	Fine	VF	XF
93	1804LD	—	6.00	10.00	17.50

9 CAVALLI

COPPER
Obv: Head right, Rev: Castle

C#	Date	Mintage	Fine	VF	XF
94	1801	—	27.50	40.00	59.50
	1804	—	6.00	10.00	17.00
	1804LD	—	6.00	10.00	17.00

VN (1) GRANO

COPPER
Obv: Head right, Rev: Value within wreath

C#	Date	Mintage	Fine	VF	XF
94.5	1800	—	—	Rare	—

4 TORNESI

COPPER
Obv: Head right, Rev: Value

C#	Date	Mintage	Fine	VF	XF
95	1799RC	—	5.00	10.00	15.00
	1800AP	—	5.00	10.00	15.00

2 GRANA

COPPER

C#	Date	Mintage	Fine	VF	XF
101	1810	—	40.00	110.00	300.00

6 TORNESI

COPPER

C#	Date	Mintage	Fine	VF	XF
96	1799RC	—	5.00	10.00	18.00
	1799AP	—	5.00	10.00	18.00
	1800RC	—	5.00	10.00	18.00
	1800AP	—	5.00	10.00	18.00
	1801AP	—	5.00	10.00	18.00
	1802AP	—	5.00	10.00	18.00
	1803AP	—	5.00	10.00	18.00
	1803RC	—	12.50	25.00	45.00

3 GRANA

COPPER
Rev: Date within wreath

C#	Date	Mintage	Fine	VF	XF
102	1810	—	45.00	80.00	135.00

Rev: Date below wreath

C#	Date	Mintage	Fine	VF	XF
102a	1810	—	45.00	80.00	135.00

60 GRANA

.833 SILVER, 13.76 gm.
Obv: Head right, Rev: Crown above shield

C#	Date	Mintage	Fine	VF	XF
97	1805LD	—	15.00	25.00	50.00

120 GRANA

.833 SILVER, 27.53 gm.

C#	Date	Mintage	Fine	VF	XF
98	1799RP	—	30.00	50.00	100.00
	1800AP	—	30.00	50.00	100.00
	1802AP	—	35.00	60.00	100.00

Obv: Head right with smooth hair
Rev: Crown above small shield

C#	Date	Mintage	VG	Fine	VF
99.1	1805LD	—	25.00	40.00	60.00

Plain edge

C#	Date	Mintage	VG	Fine	VF
99.2	1805LD	—	22.50	30.00	50.00

Obv: Head right with curly hair

C#	Date	Mintage	VG	Fine	VF
99.3	1805LD	—	25.00	40.00	60.00

NOTE: Varieties exist.

C#	Date	Mintage	Fine	VF	XF
100	1806	—	175.00	275.00	400.00
	1807/6	—	175.00	250.00	350.00
	1807	—	150.00	225.00	300.00
	1808	—	150.00	225.00	300.00

DODICI (12) CARLINI

.833 SILVER, 27.53 gm.

C#	Date	Mintage	Fine	VF	XF
103	1809	—	100.00	300.00	400.00
	1810	—	100.00	275.00	350.00

NOTE: Many varieties including mules exist.

MONETARY REFORM

100 Centesimi = 1 Franco = 1 Lira

3 CENTESIMI

BRONZE
Obv: Head left, Rev: Value

C#	Date	Mintage	VF	XF	Unc
105	1813	1.350	1100.	1500.	2000.

5 CENTESIMI

BRONZE

C#	Date	Mintage	VF	XF	Unc
106	1813	1.280	1100.	1500.	2000.

10 CENTESIMI

BRONZE
Obv: Head left, Rev: Value

C#	Date	Mintage	VF	XF	Unc
107	1813	.450	1100.	1500.	2000.

MEZZA (1/2) LIRA

.900 SILVER, 2.5 gm.

C#	Date	Mintage	VF	XF	Unc
108	1813	.166	20.00	30.00	100.00

LIRA

.900 SILVER, 5.00 gm.

C#	Date	Mintage	VF	XF	Unc
109	1812	.027	40.00	70.00	150.00
	1813	.199	20.00	35.00	125.00

2 LIRE

.900 SILVER, 10.00 gm.

C#	Date	Mintage	VF	XF	Unc
110	1812	.028	125.00	175.00	250.00
	1813	.220	40.00	70.00	150.00

5 LIRE

.900 SILVER, 25.00 gm.

C#	Date	Mintage	VF	XF	Unc
111	1812	2,921	1000.	2000.	3000.
	1813	.037	250.00	400.00	1000.

20 LIRE

.900 GOLD, 6.45 gm.

C#	Date	Mintage	VF	XF	Unc
112	1813	.042	400.00	600.00	1000.

40 FRANCHI

.900 GOLD, 12.9 gm.

C#	Date	Mintage	VF	XF	Unc
104	1810	18 pcs.	10,000.	15,000.	20,000.

40 LIRE

.900 GOLD, 12.9 gm.

C#	Date	Mintage	VF	XF	Unc
113	1813	.024	400.00	500.00	1500.

TWO SICILIES

NOTE: Coins bearing legends FERDINANDO IV were for Naples and those with FERDINANDO I were for Two Sicilies.

MONETARY REFORM

6 Cavalli = 1 Tornese
240 Tornese = 120 Grana = 12 Carlini
= 6 Tari (Naples) = 1 Piastra
5 Grana = 1 Cinquina
100 Grana = 1 Ducato (Tallero)

MEZZO (1/2) TORNESE

COPPER

Obv: Young head without beard

C#	Date	Mintage	VF	XF	Unc
142	1832	—	3.50	7.50	16.50
	1833	—	3.50	7.50	16.50
	1835	—	3.50	7.50	16.50
	1836	—	3.50	7.50	16.50
	1838	—	5.00	8.50	16.50
	1839	—	3.50	7.50	16.50
	1840	—	10.00	18.00	25.00
	1844	—	3.50	7.50	16.50
	1845	—	8.00	10.00	16.50
	1846	—	3.50	7.50	16.50
	1847	—	3.50	7.50	16.50

Obv: Older head with beard

C#	Date	Mintage	VF	XF	Unc
142a	1848	—	6.50	10.00	20.00
	1849	—	6.50	10.00	20.00
	1851	—	6.50	10.00	20.00
	1852	—	6.50	10.00	20.00
	1853	—	6.50	10.00	20.00
	1854	—	6.50	10.00	20.00

UNO (1) TORNESE

COPPER

C#	Date	Mintage	Fine	VF	XF
119	1817	—	2.50	5.00	10.00

C#	Date	Mintage	Fine	VF	XF
130	1827	—	2.00	4.00	8.50

Obv: Young head without beard, large letters.

C#	Date	Mintage	VF	XF	Unc
143	1832	—	4.00	7.00	18.00
	1833	—	4.00	7.00	18.00
	1835	—	6.00	9.00	18.00
	1836	—	15.00	20.00	30.00

Obv: Legend with small letters

C#	Date	Mintage	VF	XF	Unc
143a	1838	—	4.00	7.00	18.00
	1839	—	4.00	7.00	18.00
	1840	—	4.00	7.00	18.00
	1843	—	15.00	20.00	30.00
	1844	—	4.00	7.00	18.00
	1845	—	4.00	7.00	18.00
	1846	—	4.00	7.00	18.00
	1847	—	4.00	7.00	18.00
	1848	—	15.00	20.00	30.00

Obv: Older head with beard

C#	Date	Mintage	VF	XF	Unc
143b	1845	—	3.00	6.00	15.00
	1849	—	3.00	6.00	15.00
	1851	—	3.00	6.00	15.00
	1852	—	3.00	6.00	15.00
	1853	—	3.00	6.00	15.00
	1854	—	3.00	6.00	15.00
	1855	—	15.00	20.00	30.00
	1857	—	3.00	6.00	15.00
	1858	—	3.00	6.00	15.00
	1859	—	3.00	6.00	15.00

UNO E MEZZO (1-1/2) TORNESE

COPPER

Obv: Young head without beard

C#	Date	Mintage	VF	XF	Unc
144	1832	—	10.00	15.00	25.00
	1835	—	5.00	8.00	20.00
	1836	—	5.00	8.00	20.00
	1839	—	15.00	20.00	30.00
	1840	—	6.00	9.00	20.00

Obv: Young head with beard

C#	Date	Mintage	VF	XF	Unc
144a	1844	—	5.00	8.00	20.00
	1847	—	8.00	11.00	20.00
	1848	—	8.00	11.00	20.00

Obv: Older head with beard

C#	Date	Mintage	VF	XF	Unc
144b	1849	—	4.00	7.00	18.00
	1850	—	4.00	7.00	18.00
	1851	—	15.00	20.00	30.00
	1853	—	4.00	7.00	18.00
	1854	—	4.00	7.00	18.00

DUE (2) TORNESI

COPPER

C#	Date	Mintage	Fine	VF	XF
131	1825	—	3.00	5.00	10.00
	1826	—	2.50	5.00	8.00

Obv: Young head without beard

C#	Date	Mintage	VF	XF	Unc
145	1832	—	15.00	22.00	30.00
	1835	—	15.00	22.00	30.00

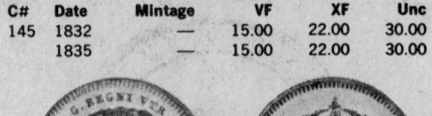

Obv: Young head with beard

C#	Date	Mintage	VF	XF	Unc
145a	1838	—	7.00	10.00	20.00

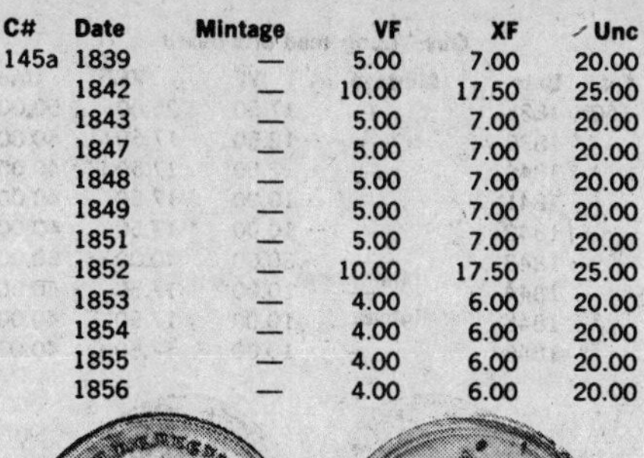

C#	Date	Mintage	VF	XF	Unc
145a	1839	—	5.00	7.00	20.00
	1842	—	10.00	17.50	25.00
	1843	—	5.00	7.00	20.00
	1847	—	5.00	7.00	20.00
	1848	—	5.00	7.00	20.00
	1849	—	5.00	7.00	20.00
	1851	—	5.00	7.00	20.00
	1852	—	10.00	17.50	25.00
	1853	—	4.00	6.00	20.00
	1854	—	4.00	6.00	20.00
	1855	—	4.00	6.00	20.00
	1856	—	4.00	6.00	20.00

C#	Date	Mintage	VF	XF	Unc
	1857	—	4.00	6.00	20.00
	1858	—	4.00	6.00	20.00
	1859	—	4.00	6.00	20.00

NOTE: Many minor varieties exist such as position of the obverse legend, placement of dots in the legend, large and small dates, etc.

C#	Date	Mintage	VF	XF	Unc
158	1859	—	4.00	7.50	22.50

TRE (3) TORNESI

COPPER
Obv: Young head without beard

C#	Date	Mintage	VF	XF	Unc
146	1833	—	5.00	9.00	25.00
	1835	—	5.00	9.00	25.00
	1837	—	5.00	9.00	25.00
	1838	—	20.00	25.00	30.00

Obv: Young head with beard

C#	Date	Mintage	VF	XF	Unc
146a	1839	—	5.00	9.00	25.00
	1842	—	5.00	9.00	25.00
	1847	—	5.00	9.00	25.00
	1848	—	5.00	9.00	25.00
	1849	—	5.00	9.00	25.00
	1851	—	5.00	9.00	25.00
	1852	—	15.00	23.00	32.50
	1854	—	5.00	9.00	25.00
	1858	—	15.00	23.00	32.50

QUATTRO (4) TORNESI

COPPER

C#	Date	Mintage	Fine	VF	XF
120	1817	—	15.00	30.00	50.00

CINQUE (5) TORNESI

COPPER
Obv: FERDINANDVS IV. D. G., etc.

C#	Date	Mintage	Fine	VF	XF
114	1816	—	5.00	8.00	12.00

Obv: FERD. I.D.G., etc.

C#	Date	Mintage	Fine	VF	XF
121	1816	—	18.00	40.00	55.00
	1817	—	6.75	12.00	18.00
	1818	—	6.75	12.00	18.00

C#	Date	Mintage	Fine	VF	XF
121a	1819	—	9.00	15.00	21.00

C#	Date	Mintage	Fine	VF	XF
132	1826	—	—	Rare	—
	1827	—	5.00	7.00	10.00

NOTE: Many varieties exist of 1827.

Obv: Young head without beard

C#	Date	Mintage	VF	XF	Unc
147	1831	—	6.00	9.00	25.00
	1832	—	6.00	9.00	25.00
	1833	—	6.00	9.00	25.00
	1838	—	6.00	9.00	25.00
	1839	—	12.50	17.50	35.00
	1840	—	6.00	9.00	25.00
	1841	—	10.00	15.00	32.50

Obv: Young head with beard

C#	Date	Mintage	VF	XF	Unc
147a	1841	—	6.00	9.00	22.50
	1842	—	6.00	9.00	22.50
	1843	—	6.00	9.00	22.50
	1845	—	6.00	9.00	22.50

Obv: Older head with beard

C#	Date	Mintage	VF	XF	Unc
147b	1846	—	6.00	8.50	22.50
	1847	—	6.00	8.50	22.50
	1848	—	6.00	8.50	22.50
	1849	—	6.00	8.50	22.50
	1851	—	6.00	8.50	22.50
	1853	—	6.00	8.50	22.50
	1854	—	6.00	8.50	22.50
	1857	—	6.00	8.50	22.50
	1858	—	11.50	17.50	25.00
	1859	—	6.00	8.50	22.50

6 TORNESI

BRONZE
Overstruck on 10 Centesimi, 1813, C#107

C#	Date	Mintage	Fine	VF	XF
107a	ND	—	900.00	1500.	3000.

OTTO (8) TORNESI

COPPER
Obv: FERDINANDUS IV D. G., etc.
Rev: Similar to C#122

C#	Date	Mintage	Fine	VF	XF
115	1816	—	5.00	8.00	12.00

Obv: FERD. I. D. G., etc.

C#	Date	Mintage	Fine	VF	XF
122	1816	—	9.00	15.00	21.00
	1817	—	9.00	15.00	21.00
	1818	—	9.00	15.00	21.00

DIECI (10) TORNESI

COPPER
Rev: Similar to C#148

C#	Date	Mintage	Fine	VF	XF
123	1819	—	3.00	7.00	15.00

Rev: Similar to C#148

C#	Date	Mintage	Fine	VF	XF
133	1825	—	4.00	8.00	20.00

Obv: Young head without beard.

C#	Date	Mintage	VF	XF	Unc
148	1831	—	6.00	10.00	30.00
	1832	—	6.00	10.00	30.00
	1833	—	6.00	10.00	30.00
	1834	—	—	Rare	—
	1835	—	7.00	10.00	30.00
	1836	—	20.00	30.00	40.00
	1837	—	7.00	11.00	30.00
	1838	—	7.00	11.00	30.00
	1839	—	7.00	11.00	30.00

Obv: Young head with beard.

C#	Date	Mintage	VF	XF	Unc
148a	1839	—	6.00	10.00	30.00
	1840	—	25.00	32.50	45.00
	1841	—	6.00	10.00	30.00
	1844	—	6.00	10.00	30.00
	1846	—	6.00	10.00	30.00
	1847	—	6.00	10.00	30.00
	1848	—	6.00	10.00	30.00
	1849	—	6.00	10.00	30.00
	1851	—	20.00	30.00	40.00

Obv: Older head with beard.

C#	Date	Mintage	VF	XF	Unc
148b	1851	—	6.00	10.00	27.50
	1852	—	6.00	10.00	27.50
	1853	—	6.00	10.00	27.50
	1854	—	6.00	10.00	27.50
	1855	—	6.00	10.00	27.50
	1856	—	6.00	10.00	27.50
	1857	—	6.00	10.00	27.50

C#	Date	Mintage	VF	XF	Unc
148b	1858	—	9.00	14.00	30.00
	1859	—	6.00	10.00	27.50

NOTE: Minor varieties exist, i.e., legend size, location.

C#	Date	Mintage	VF	XF	Unc
159	1859	—	9.00	20.00	40.00

CINQUE (5) GRANA

.833 SILVER, 1.15 gm.

Obv: Young head right without beard, Rev: Arms

C#	Date	Mintage	VF	XF	Unc
149	1836	—	6.00	15.00	50.00
	1838	—	6.00	15.00	50.00
	1844	—	6.00	15.00	50.00
	1845	—	6.00	15.00	50.00
	1846	—	6.00	15.00	50.00
	1847	—	6.00	15.00	50.00

Obv: Young head with beard.

C#	Date	Mintage	VF	XF	Unc
149a	1848	—	12.50	20.00	50.00
	1851	—	6.00	15.00	50.00
	1853	—	6.00	15.00	50.00

10 GRANA

.833 SILVER, 2.29 gm.

Obv: Head right, Rev: Arms

C#	Date	Mintage	Fine	VF	XF
116	1815	—	6.00	10.00	20.00
	1816	—	6.00	10.00	20.00

Obv: Crowned head right.

C#	Date	Mintage	Fine	VF	XF
124	1818	—	6.00	10.00	20.00

Obv: Head right.

C#	Date	Mintage	Fine	VF	XF
134	1826	—	7.00	12.00	20.00

Obv: Young head without beard, continuous legend.

C#	Date	Mintage	VF	XF	Unc
150	1832	—	12.50	17.50	40.00
	1833	—	12.50	17.50	40.00
	1834	—	12.50	17.50	40.00
	1835	—	12.50	17.50	40.00

Obv: Legend divided over young head without beard

C#	Date	Mintage	VF	XF	Unc
150a	1835	—	12.50	17.50	40.00
	1836	—	12.50	17.50	40.00
	1837	—	12.50	17.50	40.00
	1838	—	12.50	17.50	40.00
	1839	—	12.50	17.50	40.00

Obv: Young head with beard

C#	Date	Mintage	VF	XF	Unc
150b	1838	—	17.50	25.00	50.00
	1839	—	12.50	17.50	40.00
	1840	—	12.50	17.50	40.00
	1841	—	10.00	17.50	40.00
	1842	—	10.00	17.50	40.00
	1843	—	30.00	40.00	60.00
	1844	—	10.00	17.50	40.00
	1845	—	10.00	17.50	40.00
	1846	—	10.00	17.50	40.00

Obv: Older head with beard

C#	Date	Mintage	VF	XF	Unc
150c	1847	—	7.50	12.00	35.00
	1848	—	7.50	12.00	35.00
	1849	—	15.00	20.00	35.00
	1850	—	12.50	17.50	35.00
	1851	—	12.50	17.50	35.00
	1853	—	7.50	12.00	35.00
	1854	—	7.50	12.00	35.00
	1855	—	7.50	12.00	35.00
	1856	—	7.50	12.00	35.00
	1859	—	7.50	12.00	35.00

20 GRANA

.833 SILVER, 4.59 gm.

C#	Date	Mintage	Fine	VF	XF
135	1826	—	25.00	40.00	75.00

Obv: Young head without beard

C#	Date	Mintage	VF	XF	Unc
151	1831	—	15.00	20.00	50.00
	1832	—	12.00	20.00	50.00
	1833	—	12.00	20.00	50.00
	1834	—	12.00	20.00	50.00
	1835	—	12.00	20.00	50.00
	1836	—	12.00	20.00	50.00
	1837	—	15.00	25.00	50.00
	1838	—	12.00	20.00	50.00
	1839	—	12.00	20.00	50.00

Obv: Young head with beard

C#	Date	Mintage	VF	XF	Unc
151a	1839	—	22.50	30.00	50.00
	1840	—	12.00	20.00	50.00
	1841	—	12.00	20.00	50.00
	1842	—	10.00	15.00	50.00
	1843	—	10.00	15.00	50.00
	1844	—	10.00	15.00	50.00
	1845	—	10.00	15.00	50.00
	1846	—	10.00	15.00	50.00
	1847	—	10.00	15.00	50.00
	1848	—	10.00	15.00	50.00
	1850	—	10.00	15.00	50.00
	1851	—	10.00	15.00	50.00
	1852	—	10.00	15.00	50.00
	1853	—	10.00	15.00	50.00
	1854	—	10.00	15.00	50.00
	1855	—	10.00	15.00	50.00
	1856	—	10.00	15.00	50.00
	1857	—	10.00	15.00	50.00
	1858	—	10.00	15.00	50.00
	1859	—	10.00	15.00	50.00

Obv: Head left, Rev: Arms

C#	Date	Mintage	VF	XF	Unc
160	1859	—	10.00	20.00	50.00

60 GRANA

.833 SILVER, 13.77 gm.

Obv: Head right, FERD IV. D. G., etc.

C#	Date	Mintage	Fine	VF	XF
117	1816	—	25.00	40.00	75.00

Obv: Crowned head right, FERD I D. G., etc.

C#	Date	Mintage	Fine	VF	XF
125	1818	—	35.00	50.00	75.00

Obv: Head right. Rev: Arms within wreath.

C#	Date	Mintage	Fine	VF	XF
136	1826	—	45.00	75.00	100.00

Obv: Young head without beard, legend continuous.

C#	Date	Mintage	VF	XF	Unc
152	1831	—	25.00	50.00	85.00
	1832	—	25.00	50.00	85.00
	1833	—	25.00	50.00	85.00
	1834	—	25.00	50.00	85.00

Obv: Legend divided

C#	Date	Mintage	VF	XF	Unc
152a	1835	—	25.00	50.00	85.00
	1836	—	25.00	50.00	85.00
	1837	—	75.00	110.00	160.00
	1838	—	25.00	50.00	85.00
	1839	—	50.00	75.00	100.00

Obv: Young head with beard

C#	Date	Mintage	VF	XF	Unc
152b	1841	—	50.00	75.00	100.00
	1842	—	50.00	75.00	100.00
	1845	—	50.00	75.00	100.00

Obv: Older head with beard

C#	Date	Mintage	VF	XF	Unc
152c	1846	—	50.00	85.00	100.00
	1847	—	50.00	85.00	100.00
	1848	—	50.00	85.00	100.00
	1850	—	50.00	85.00	100.00
	1851	—	50.00	85.00	100.00
	1852	—	50.00	85.00	100.00
	1854	—	50.00	85.00	100.00
	1855	—	50.00	85.00	100.00
	1856	—	50.00	85.00	100.00
	1857	—	50.00	85.00	100.00
	1858	—	50.00	85.00	100.00
	1859	—	50.00	85.00	100.00

120 GRANA

.833 SILVER, 27.53 gm.

C#	Date	Mintage	Fine	VF	XF
118	1815	—	60.00	100.00	140.00
	1816R	*	75.00	125.00	175.00

***NOTE:** The R(istampato) issues were struck over the coins of Joseph Napoleon and Joachim Murat.

Obv: Large crowned head.

C#	Date	Mintage	Fine	VF	XF
126	1817	—	50.00	75.00	100.00
	1818	—	40.00	65.00	90.00

Obv: Small crowned head.

C#	Date	Mintage	Fine	VF	XF
126	1818	—	35.00	55.00	80.00

C#	Date	Mintage	VF	XF	Unc
137	1825	—	50.00	75.00	100.00

Obv: Young head without beard, legend continuous.
Rev: Similar to C#153b

C#	Date	Mintage	VF	XF	Unc
153	1831	—	30.00	40.00	80.00
	1832	—	30.00	40.00	80.00
	1833	—	50.00	75.00	100.00
	1834	—	50.00	75.00	100.00
	1835	—	30.00	40.00	80.00

Obv: Legend divided

C#	Date	Mintage	VF	XF	Unc
153a	1835	—	40.00	75.00	100.00
	1836	—	30.00	45.00	90.00
	1837	—	30.00	45.00	90.00
	1838	—	30.00	45.00	90.00
	1839	—	40.00	75.00	100.00

Obv: Young head with beard

C#	Date	Mintage	VF	XF	Unc
153b	1840	—	30.00	40.00	75.00
	1841	—	30.00	40.00	75.00
	1842	—	30.00	40.00	75.00
	1843	—	30.00	40.00	75.00
	1844	—	30.00	40.00	75.00
	1845	—	30.00	40.00	75.00
	1846	—	30.00	40.00	75.00
	1847	—	30.00	40.00	75.00
	1848	—	30.00	40.00	75.00
	1850	—	30.00	40.00	75.00
	1851	—	30.00	40.00	75.00

NOTE: Many varieties exist.

Obv: Older head with beard

C#	Date	Mintage	VF	XF	Unc
153c	1851	—	27.50	40.00	75.00
	1852	—	27.50	40.00	75.00
	1853	—	27.50	40.00	75.00
	1854	—	27.50	40.00	75.00
	1855	—	27.50	40.00	75.00
	1856	—	27.50	40.00	75.00
	1857	—	27.50	40.00	75.00
	1858	—	27.50	40.00	75.00
	1859	—	27.50	40.00	75.00

C#	Date	Mintage	VF	XF	Unc
161	1859	—	50.00	80.00	110.00

3 DUCATI

.996 GOLD, 3.79 gm.

C#	Date	Mintage	Fine	VF	XF
127	1818	—	375.00	500.00	1250.

Obv: Head right. Rev: Winged Genius.

C#	Date	Mintage	Fine	VF	XF
138	1826	—	475.00	650.00	1400.

Obv: Young head without beard

C#	Date	Mintage	VF	XF	Unc
154	1831	—	—	Rare	—
	1832	—	450.00	600.00	1250.
	1835	—	450.00	600.00	1250.
154a	1837	—	450.00	600.00	2000.

Obv: Young head with beard

C#	Date	Mintage	VF	XF	Unc
154b	1839	—	450.00	600.00	2000.
	1840	—	450.00	600.00	2000.

C#	Date	Mintage	VF	XF	Unc
154c	1842	—	450.00	600.00	2000.
	1845	—	450.00	600.00	2000.
	1846	—	450.00	600.00	2000.
	1848	—	450.00	600.00	2000.

Obv: Older head with beard

C#	Date	Mintage	VF	XF	Unc
154d	1850	—	400.00	650.00	2000.
	1851	—	400.00	650.00	2000.
	1852	—	400.00	650.00	2000.
	1854	—	400.00	650.00	2000.
	1856	—	400.00	650.00	2000.

6 DUCATI

.996 GOLD, 7.57 gm.

C#	Date	Mintage	Fine	VF	XF
139	1826	—	475.00	750.00	1750.

Obv: Young head without beard. Rev: Winged Genius.

C#	Date	Mintage	VF	XF	Unc
155	1831	—	450.00	600.00	1750.
	1833	—	450.00	600.00	1750.
	1835	—	550.00	750.00	1750.

Obv: Young head with beard

C#	Date	Mintage	VF	XF	Unc
155b	1840	—	450.00	600.00	1750.

Obv: Older head with beard

C#	Date	Mintage	VF	XF	Unc
155c	1842	—	500.00	650.00	1750.
	1845	—	500.00	650.00	1750.
	1847	—	500.00	650.00	1750.
	1848	—	500.00	650.00	1750.
	1850	—	500.00	650.00	1750.
	1851	—	500.00	650.00	1750.
	1852	—	500.00	650.00	1750.
	1854	—	500.00	650.00	1750.
	1856	—	500.00	650.00	1750.

15 DUCATI

.996 GOLD, 18.93 gm.

C#	Date	Mintage	Fine	VF	XF
128	1818	—	700.00	1500.	3000.

Obv: Head left. Rev: Genius.

C#	Date	Mintage	VF	XF	Unc
140	1825	—	—	Rare	—

Obv: Young head without beard

C#	Date	Mintage	VF	XF	Unc
156	1831	—	1000.	1750.	3000.

Obv: Young head with beard. Rev: Winged Genius.

C#	Date	Mintage	VF	XF	Unc
156c	1842	—	1000.	1900.	3250.
	1844	—	850.00	1600.	3000.
	1845	—	850.00	1600.	3000.
	1847	—	850.00	1600.	3000.

Obv: Older head with beard

C#	Date	Mintage	VF	XF	Unc
156d	1848	—	850.00	1600.	3000.
	1850	—	850.00	1400.	3000.
	1851	—	850.00	1400.	3000.
	1852	—	850.00	1400.	3000.
	1854	—	850.00	1400.	3000.
	1856	—	850.00	1400.	3000.

30 DUCATI

.996 GOLD, 37.87 gm.

C#	Date	Mintage	Fine	VF	XF
129	1818	—	800.00	1400.	3000.

Obv: Head right. Rev: Genius.

C#	Date	Mintage	Fine	VF	XF
141	1825	—	800.00	1500.	3100.
	1826	—	800.00	1400.	3000.

Obv: Large young head without beard
Rev: Similar to C#141.

C#	Date	Mintage	VF	XF	Unc
157	1831	—	800.00	1500.	2650.
	1833	—	800.00	1500.	2650.
	1835	—	800.00	1650.	2900.

Obv: Young medium head with beard
Rev: Similar to C#141.

C#	Date	Mintage	VF	XF	Unc
157b	1839	—	800.00	1550.	2800.
	1840	—	800.00	1650.	2900.
157c	1842	—	—	Rare	—
	1844	—	800.00	1400.	2650.
	1845	—	800.00	1600.	2900.
	1847	—	800.00	1500.	2600.
	1848	—	800.00	1600.	2900.
	1851	—	800.00	1000.	3200.
	1854	—	900.00	1800.	3000.

Obv: Large older head with beard

C#	Date	Mintage	VF	XF	Unc
157e	1850	—	800.00	1650.	2900.
	1851	—	800.00	1675.	2900.
	1852	—	800.00	1450.	2600.

Obv: Small older head with beard

C#	Date	Mintage	VF	XF	Unc
157d	1854	—	800.00	1650.	2900.

C#	Date	Mintage	VF	XF	Unc
157d	1856	—	800.00	1650.	2900.

ORBETELLO

REALI PRESIDII

A small province in southwestern Tuscany, was a possession of the kingdom of Naples and Sicily until 1808.

RULERS

Ferdinand IV, 1759-1808

MONETARY SYSTEM

60 Quattrini = 1 Lira

QUATTRINO

BILLON

C#	Date	Mintage	Fine	VF	XF
1	1782	—	10.00	15.00	25.00
	1791	—	10.00	15.00	25.00
	1798	—	10.00	15.00	25.00

2 QUATTRINI

BILLON
Obv: Head right. Rev: Value.

C#	Date	Mintage	Fine	VF	XF
2	1782	—	12.50	17.50	30.00
	1791	—	12.50	17.50	30.00
	1798	—	12.50	17.50	30.00

4 QUATTRINI

BILLON

C#	Date	Mintage	Fine	VF	XF
3	1782	—	15.00	25.00	40.00
	1791	—	15.00	25.00	40.00
	1798	—	15.00	25.00	40.00

PARMA

A town in Emilia which was a papal possession from 1512 to 1545, was seized by France in 1796, and was attached to the Napoleonic empire in 1808. In 1814 Parma was assigned to Marie Louise, empress of Napoleon I. It was annexed to Sardinia in 1860.

RULERS

Filippo di Borbone, 1737-1765
Ferdinando di Borbone, 1765-1802
Maria Luigia, Duchess, 1815-1847
Carlo II di Borbone, 1848-1854
Roberto di Borbone, 1854-1859

MONETARY SYSTEM

UNTIL 1802

12 Denair = 2 Sesini = 1 Soldo
20 = Soldi = 1 Lira
7 Lire = 1 Ducato

SESINO

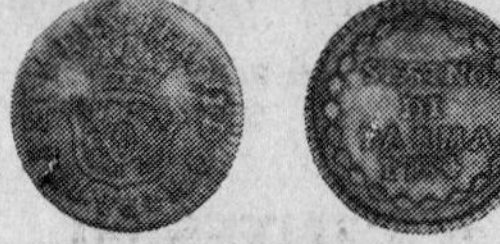

COPPER

C#	Date	Mintage	Fine	VF	XF
3	1784	—	5.00	8.50	12.50
	1785	—	5.00	8.50	12.50
	1787	—	5.00	8.50	12.50
	1788	—	5.00	8.50	12.50
	1790	—	5.00	8.50	12.50
	1792	—	5.00	8.50	12.50
	1795	—	5.00	8.50	12.50
	1796	—	5.00	8.50	12.50
	1797	—	5.00	8.50	12.50
	1798	—	5.00	8.50	12.50

5 SOLDI

BILLON
Obv: Arms. Rev: Madonna.

C#	Date	Mintage	Fine	VF	XF
4	1784	—	5.00	9.50	16.50
	1785	—	5.00	9.50	16.50
			Obv: Madonna. Rev: Value.		
5	1792	—	4.00	8.50	15.00
	1793	—	4.00	8.50	15.00
	1795	—	4.00	8.50	15.00
	1796	—	4.00	8.50	15.00
	1797	—	4.00	8.50	15.00
	1798	—	4.00	8.50	15.00
	1799	—	4.00	8.50	15.00

10 SOLDI

BILLON
Obv: Arms. Rev: St. Hilary.

C#	Date	Mintage	Fine	VF	XF
6	1784	—	5.00	9.50	16.50
	1786	—	5.00	9.50	16.50
	1789	—	5.00	9.50	16.50
	1790	—	5.00	9.50	16.50
	1792	—	5.00	9.50	16.50
	1793	—	5.00	9.50	16.50
	1795	—	5.00	9.50	16.50

20 SOLDI

BILLON
Obv: Arms. Rev: St. Thomas.

C#	Date	Mintage	Fine	VF	XF
7	1783	—	6.50	10.00	17.50
	1784	—	6.50	10.00	17.50
	1785	—	6.50	10.00	17.50
	1786	—	6.50	10.00	17.50
	1787	—	6.50	10.00	17.50
	1789	—	6.50	10.00	17.50
	1790	—	6.50	10.00	17.50
	1792	—	6.50	10.00	17.50
	1793	—	6.50	10.00	17.50
	1795	—	6.50	10.00	17.50
	1796	—	6.50	10.00	17.50
	1797	—	6.50	10.00	17.50

3 LIRE

.833 SILVER, 3.672 gm.
Obv: Head right. Rev: Value.

C#	Date	Mintage	Fine	VF	XF
8	1790	—	65.00	100.00	150.00
	1791	—	65.00	100.00	150.00
	1792	—	65.00	100.00	150.00
	1793	—	65.00	100.00	150.00
	1795	—	65.00	100.00	150.00

SEI (6) LIRE

.833 SILVER, 7.344 gm.

C#	Date	Mintage	Fine	VF	XF
9	1795	—	225.00	275.00	375.00
	1796	—	225.00	275.00	375.00

1/14 DUCATO

.902 SILVER, 1.83 gm.
Obv: Head right. Rev: Oval arms.

C#	Date	Mintage	Fine	VF	XF
10	1784	—	35.00	55.00	100.00
	1786	—	35.00	55.00	100.00

1/7 DUCATO

.902 SILVER, 3.672 gm.

C#	Date	Mintage	Fine	VF	XF
11	1784	—	40.00	65.00	100.00
	1785	—	40.00	65.00	100.00
	1787	—	40.00	65.00	100.00

1/2 DUCATO

.902 SILVER, 12.852 gm.
Obv: Head right. Rev: Arms in order chain.

C#	Date	Mintage	Fine	VF	XF
12	1784	—	85.00	125.00	200.00
			Rev: Oval arms.		
13	1786	—	55.00	85.00	125.00
	1787	—	55.00	85.00	125.00
	1790	—	55.00	85.00	125.00

DUCATO

.902 SILVER, 25.704 gm.
Obv: Head right.
Rev: Arms in order chain.

C#	Date	Mintage	Fine	VF	XF
14	1784	—	300.00	450.00	650.00
			Rev: Oval arms.		
15	1786	—	200.00	300.00	500.00
	1789	—	200.00	300.00	500.00
	1790	—	200.00	300.00	500.00
	1796	—	200.00	300.00	500.00
	1797	—	200.00	300.00	500.00
	1799	—	200.00	300.00	500.00

ZECCHINO

.900 GOLD, 3.5 gm.
Obv: Head right.
Rev: Arms in order chain.

C#	Date	Mintage	Fine	VF	XF
16	1784	—	1000.	1500.	2000.

1/2 DOPPIA

.891 GOLD, 3.57 gm.
Obv: Head right. Rev: Arms.

C#	Date	Mintage	Fine	VF	XF
17	1785	—	200.00	300.00	500.00
	1786	—	200.00	300.00	500.00
	1787	—	200.00	300.00	500.00
	1788	—	200.00	300.00	500.00
	1789	—	200.00	300.00	500.00
	1790	—	200.00	300.00	500.00
	1791	—	200.00	300.00	500.00
	1792	—	200.00	300.00	500.00
	1793	—	200.00	300.00	500.00
	1797	—	200.00	300.00	500.00

DOPPIA

.891 GOLD, 7.141 gm.
Obv: Head right.
Rev: Arms in order chain.

C#	Date	Mintage	Fine	VF	XF
18	1784	—	300.00	450.00	650.00

C#	Date	Mintage	Fine	VF	XF
18a	1786	—	225.00	350.00	550.00
	1787	—	225.00	350.00	550.00
	1788	—	225.00	350.00	550.00

C#	Date	Mintage	Fine	VF	XF
	1789	—	225.00	350.00	550.00
	1790	—	225.00	350.00	550.00
	1791	—	225.00	350.00	550.00
	1792	—	225.00	350.00	550.00
	1793	—	225.00	350.00	550.00
	1796	—	225.00	350.00	550.00

3 DOPPIE

.891 GOLD, 21.423 gm.
Obv: Head right. Rev: Oval arms.

C#	Date	Mintage	Fine	VF	XF
19	1786	—	5000.	8000.	12,500.

4 DOPPIE

.891 GOLD, 22.48 gm.
Obv: Head right. Rev: Arms in order chain.

C#	Date	Mintage	Fine	VF	XF
20	1784	—	2000.	3000.	4500.

.891 GOLD, 28.564 gm.
Rev: Arms.

C#	Date	Mintage	Fine	VF	XF
20a	1787	—	1500.	2500.	3750.
	1790	—	1500.	2500.	3750.
	1792	—	1500.	2500.	3750.
	1796	—	1500.	2500.	3750.

6 DOPPIE

.891 GOLD, 42.846 gm.
Obv: Head right. Rev: Arms.

C#	Date	Mintage	Fine	VF	XF
21	1786	—	4000.	7500.	12,000.

8 DOPPIE

.891 GOLD, 57.128 gm.

C#	Date	Mintage	Fine	VF	XF
22a	1786 S	—	3500.	4000.	7000.
	1789	—	3500.	4000.	7000.
	1791	—	3500.	4000.	7000.
	1792	—	3500.	4000.	7000.
	1796	—	3500.	4000.	7000.

MONETARY REFORM

100 Centesimi = 20 Soldi = 1 Lira

CENTESIMO

COPPER
Similar to 5 Centesimi, C#25.

C#	Date	Mintage	VF	XF	Unc
23	1830	2.029	7.50	12.50	25.00

Obv: Head left. Rev: Oval arms.

C#	Date	Mintage	VF	XF	Unc
33	1854	—	300.00	375.00	500.00

3 CENTESIMI

COPPER
Similar to 5 Centesimi, C#25.

C#	Date	Mintage	VF	XF	Unc
24	1830	.511	30.00	45.00	80.00

Obv: Head left, Rev: Oval arms

C#	Date	Mintage	VF	XF	Unc
34	1854	—	500.00	600.00	1000.

5 CENTESIMI

COPPER

C#	Date	Mintage	VF	XF	Unc
25	1830	1.506	5.00	10.00	50.00

Obv: Head left, Rev: Oval arms

C#	Date	Mintage	VF	XF	Unc
35	1854	—	1000.	1400.	2000.

5 SOLDI

.900 SILVER, 1.25 gm.

C#	Date	Mintage	VF	XF	Unc
26	1815/3	—	15.00	25.00	75.00
	1815	.682	12.50	20.00	50.00
	1830	Scarce	20.00	35.00	100.00

10 SOLDI

.900 SILVER, 2.5 gm.
Obv: Maria bust left, Rev: ML monogram

C#	Date	Mintage	VF	XF	Unc
27	1815	.530	20.00	30.00	85.00
	1830	Scarce	500.00	600.00	1000.

LIRA

.900 SILVER, 5.00 gm.
Similar to 5 Lire, C#30.

C#	Date	Mintage	VF	XF	Unc
28	1815	.066	35.00	50.00	125.00

2 LIRE

.900 SILVER, 10.00 gm.

C#	Date	Mintage	VF	XF	Unc
29	1815	.022	80.00	150.00	350.00

5 LIRE

.900 SILVER, 25.00 gm.

C#	Date	Mintage	VF	XF	Unc
30	1815	.093	500.00	600.00	800.00
	1821	—	—	Rare	—
	1832	.044	800.00	500.00	1000.

C#	Date	Mintage	VF	XF	Unc
36	1858	—	500.00	600.00	1000.

20 LIRE

.900 GOLD, 6.45 gm.

C#	Date	Mintage	VF	XF	Unc
31	1815	.012	500.00	600.00	1000.
	1832	1,550	2000.	2500.	3000.

40 LIRE

.900 GOLD, 12.9 gm.

C#	Date	Mintage	VF	XF	Unc
32	1815	.220	500.00	600.00	1000.
	1821	.037	700.00	1000.	2000.

PIACENZA

PLACENTIA

A town and episcopal see that is located in the northwestern corner of the Italian territorial division of Emilia. It was made a Roman colony in 218 B.C., later becoming an important road center of the Roman Empire. Once a leading member of the Lombard League, it was united with Parma in 1545 to form a hereditary duchy in favor of the son of Pope Paul III. In 1731 it passed again to Parma, then to the house of Hapsburg, and again to

Parma in 1748.

RULERS

Ferdinando di Borbone, 1765-1802

MONETARY SYSTEM

12 Denari = 2 Sesini = 1 Soldo
20 Soldi = 1 Lira

SESINO

COPPER
Obv: Arms. Rev: Cross.

C#	Date	Mintage	Fine	VF	XF
5	1784	—	3.50	6.50	10.00
	ND	—	3.50	6.50	10.00

5 SOLDI

BILLON
Obv: Arms. Rev: St. Justina.

C#	Date	Mintage	Fine	VF	XF
6	1785	—	5.00	8.50	15.00
	1786	—	5.00	8.50	15.00
	1788	—	5.00	8.50	15.00
	1792	—	5.00	8.50	15.00
	1793	—	5.00	8.50	15.00
	1794	—	5.00	8.50	15.00
	1795	—	5.00	8.50	15.00

10 SOLDI

BILLON
Obv: Arms. Rev: St. Anthony on horseback.

C#	Date	Mintage	Fine	VF	XF
7	1785	—	12.50	17.50	30.00
	1786	—	12.50	17.50	30.00
	1787	—	12.50	17.50	30.00
	1788	—	12.50	17.50	30.00
	1789	—	12.50	17.50	30.00
	1790	—	12.50	17.50	30.00
	1791	—	12.50	17.50	30.00
	1792	—	12.50	17.50	30.00
	1793	—	12.50	17.50	30.00
	1794	—	12.50	17.50	30.00
	1795	—	12.50	17.50	30.00

PIEDMONT REPUBLIC

Was established by Napoleon in 1798 in the Piedmont area of northwest Italy which was the mainland possession of the kingdom of Sardinia. The republic was overthrown by Austro-Russian forces in 1799.

REPUBBLICA PIEMONTESE

1798-1799

QUARTO (1/4) / DI SCUDO

.906 SILVER, 8.79 gm.

C#	Date	Year	Mintage	Fine	VF	XF
1	ANNO VII	(1799)	.140	125.00	175.00	250.00

MEZZO (1/2) SCUDO

.906 SILVER, 17.58 gm.

C#	Date	Year	Mintage	Fine	VF	XF
2	ANNO VII	(1799)	.300	150.00	300.00	400.00
	Obv: With designers name "LAVY".					
2a	ANNO VII	(1799)	.150	150.00	300.00	500.00

NAZIONE PIEMONTESE

1800

DUE (2) SOLDI

BRONZE

C#	Date	Year	Mintage	Fine	VF	XF
3	A(nno)9	(1800)	—	10.00	25.00	40.00

SUBALPINE REPUBLIC

1800-1801

5 FRANCS

.900 SILVER, 25.00 gm.

C#	Date	Year	Mintage	Fine	VF	XF
4	L'AN 9	(1800)	—	50.00	100.00	150.00
	L'AN 10	(1801)	—	50.00	100.00	150.00

20 FRANCS

.900 GOLD, 6.45 gm.

C#	Date	Year	Mintage	Fine	VF	XF
5	L'AN 9	(1800)	—	450.00	600.00	800.00
	L'AN 10	(1801)	—	500.00	750.00	900.00

SARDINIA

A Roman see in the 11th century occupied by the competitive cities of Pisa and Genoa. In 1297 it was granted to James II of Aragon, and remained under Spanish control until passing to the house of Savoy in 1720. In 1861 it became the nucleus about which the United Kingdom of Italy was formed.

RULERS

Vittorio Amedeo III 1773-1796
Carlo Emanuele IV 1796-1802
Vittorio Emanuele I 1802-1821
Carlo Felice 1821-1831
Carlo Alberto 1831-1849
Vittorio Emanuele II 1849-1878

MONETARY SYSTEMS

Mainland until 1816

12 Denari = 1 Soldo
20 Soldi = 1 Lira
6 Lire = 1 Scudo
2 Scudi = 1 Doppia

Island of Sardinia until 1816

12 Denari = 6 Cagliarese = 1 Soldo
50 Soldi = 10 Reales =
2- 1/2 Lire = 1 Scudo Sardo
2 Scudi Sardo = 1 Doppietta

Entire kingdom after 1816

100 Centesimi = 1 Lira

MINTMARKS

None Before 1802 = Turin (Torino)
After 1802 - Eagles Head = Turin (Torino)
Anchor = Genoa
Firenze = Florence
B = Bologna
M = Milan

MAINLAND COINAGE

2 DENARI

COPPER
Obv: Cross, VIC.AM.D.G.R.SAR. around.
Rev: Crowned knot, date.

C#	Date	Mintage	Fine	VF	XF
50	1773	—	5.00	10.00	20.00
	1774	—	5.00	10.00	20.00
	1775	—	25.00	50.00	100.00
	1776	—	50.00	100.00	300.00
	1777	—	5.00	10.00	20.00
	1778	—	5.00	10.00	20.00
	1779	—	5.00	10.00	20.00
	1780	—	5.00	10.00	20.00
	1781	—	5.00	10.00	20.00
	1782	—	50.00	100.00	300.00
	1783	—	5.00	10.00	20.00
	1784	—	5.00	10.00	20.00
	1785	—	50.00	100.00	300.00
	1786	—	100.00	200.00	500.00
	1787	—	5.00	10.00	20.00
	1789	—	25.00	50.00	100.00
	1790	—	5.00	10.00	20.00
	1791	—	5.00	10.00	20.00
	1792	—	5.00	10.00	20.00
	1796	—	5.00	10.00	20.00

Obv: Cross, CAROLUS.EM.IV.D.G.REX.CYP.ET.IER. around. Rev: Crowned knot, date.

C#	Date	Mintage	Fine	VF	XF
79	1798	—	—	Rare	—
	1799	—	5.00	7.50	15.00
	1800	—	5.00	7.50	15.00

1/2 SOLDO

BILLON

Obv: Cross, date, VIC. AM. D.G.R.SA.CY.ET.IE around. Rev: Crown over VA monogram.

C#	Date	Mintage	Fine	VF	XF
52	1780	—	75.00	150.00	400.00
	1781	—	25.00	50.00	100.00
	1782	—	25.00	50.00	100.00
	1783	—	25.00	50.00	100.00
	1784	—	25.00	50.00	100.00
	1785	—	25.00	50.00	100.00
	1787	—	100.00	200.00	500.00
	1789	—	50.00	100.00	300.00

SOLDO

BILLON

Obv: Cross, VIC.AM.D.G.REX.SAR.CVP.ET.IER. around date. Rev: Crowned ornate monogram.

C#	Date	Mintage	Fine	VF	XF
53	1773	—	100.00	200.00	500.00
	1774	—	50.00	100.00	300.00
	1775	—	50.00	100.00	300.00
	1780	—	25.00	50.00	100.00
	1781	—	25.00	50.00	100.00
	1782	—	25.00	50.00	100.00
	1783	—	25.00	50.00	100.00
	1785	—	25.00	50.00	100.00
	1789	—	100.00	200.00	600.00

COPPER

Obv: Cross, CAROLUS EMANUEL IV around, date. Rev: Ornate monogram, crown above.

C#	Date	Mintage	Fine	VF	XF
80	1797	—	5.00	10.00	20.00
	1798	—	5.00	10.00	20.00

2.6 SOLDI

BILLON

Obv: Head right, VIC.AM.D.G.REX.SAR.CYP.ET.IER. around date. Rev: Eagle, Savoy cross on breast.

C#	Date	Mintage	Fine	VF	XF
54	1781	—	25.00	50.00	100.00
	1782	—	25.00	50.00	100.00
	1783	—	25.00	50.00	100.00
	1784	—	25.00	50.00	100.00
	1785	—	25.00	50.00	100.00

C#	Date	Mintage	VF	XF	Unc
81	1798	—	6.50	16.00	35.00
	1799	—	6.50	16.00	35.00

Obv: Head right, VICTORIVS EMANVEL around, date. Rev: Similar to C#81.

C#	Date	Mintage	VF	XF	Unc
90	1814	—	6.00	15.00	35.00
	1815	—	6.00	15.00	35.00

5 SOLDI

COPPER

Obv: Bust right, VIC. AMED. D.G.REX.SARD. around, date. Rev: St. Maurice standing.

C#	Date	Mintage	Fine	VF	XF
51	1794	—	25.00	50.00	100.00
	1795	—	25.00	50.00	100.00
	1796	—	25.00	50.00	100.00

7.6 SOLDI

BILLON

Obv: Bust right, VIC.AM.D.G.REX.SAR.CYP.ET.TER. around, date. Rev: Eagle on shield, crown above.

C#	Date	Mintage	Fine	VF	XF
55	1781	—	50.00	100.00	200.00
	1782	—	150.00	300.00	1000.
	1783	—	50.00	100.00	200.00
	1784	—	100.00	200.00	500.00
	1785	—	100.00	200.00	500.00
	1789	—	500.00	1000.	2000.
	1793	—	100.00	200.00	500.00
55	1794	—	100.00	200.00	500.00
	1795	—	650.00	1500.	3000.

Obv: Head right, CAROLUS EMANUEL IV around, date. Rev: Eagle on shield, crown above.

C#	Date	Mintage	VF	XF	Unc
82	1798	—	—	Rare	—
	1799	—	15.00	25.00	50.00
	1800	—	10.00	15.00	35.00

10 SOLDI

BILLON

Obv: Bust right, VIC.AMED.D.G.REX.SARD. around, date. Rev: Arms.

C#	Date	Mintage	Fine	VF	XF
56	1794	—	50.00	100.00	200.00
	1795	—	50.00	100.00	200.00
	1796	—	50.00	100.00	200.00

15 SOLDI

BILLON

Obv: Bust right, VIC.AM.D.G.REX.SAR.CYP.ET.IER. around, date. Rev: Value in wreath.

C#	Date	Mintage	Fine	VF	XF
57	1794	—	50.00	100.00	200.00
	1798	—	500.00	1000.	2000.

20 SOLDI

BILLON

Obv: Bust right, VICT.AMED.D.G.REX. around, date. Rev: Arms.

C#	Date	Mintage	Fine	VF	XF
58	1794	—	50.00	100.00	200.00
	1795	—	50.00	100.00	200.00
	1796	—	50.00	100.00	200.00

1/4 SCUDO

.904 SILVER, 8.791 gm.

Obv: Bust left, VIC.AM.D.G.REX.SAR.CYP.ET.IER. around, date. Rev: Arms.

C#	Date	Mintage	Fine	VF	XF
59	1773	—	—	1500.	2500.
	1774	—	—	1500.	2500.
	1775	—	—	250.00	800.00
	1776	—	—	250.00	800.00
	1777	—	—	2000.	3000.
	1778	—	—	250.00	800.00
	1779	—	150.00	200.00	800.00
	1780	—	800.00	1000.	2000.
	1781	—	1500.	1800.	3000.
	1786	—	1500.	1800.	3000.
	1787	—	800.00	1000.	3000.
	1788	—	1500.	2200.	3000.
	1789	—	800.00	1000.	2000.
	1790	—	800.00	1000.	2000.
	1791	—	800.00	1000.	2000.
	1792	—	800.00	1000.	2000.
	1793	—	800.00	1000.	2000.

.905 SILVER, 8.79 gm.

C#	Date	Mintage	VF	XF	Unc
83	1797	—	—	Rare	—
	1798	—	300.00	500.00	1000.
	1799	—	300.00	500.00	1000.

1/2 SCUDO

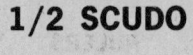

.904 SILVER, 17.582 gm.

Obv. leg: VIC.AM.D.G.REX.CYP.ET.IER.

C#	Date	Mintage	Fine	VF	XF
60	1773	—	300.00	500.00	2000.
	1774	—	300.00	500.00	2000.
	1775	—	300.00	500.00	2000.
	1776	—	300.00	500.00	2000.
	1777	—	300.00	500.00	2000.
	1778	—	300.00	500.00	2000.
	1779	—	300.00	500.00	2000.
	1780	—	300.00	500.00	2000.
	1781	—	4000.	8000.	10,000.
	1782	—	3000.	5000.	8000.
	1784	—	3000.	5000.	8000.
	1785	—	4000.	8000.	10,000.
	1786	—	300.00	500.00	2000.
	1787	—	300.00	500.00	2000.
	1788	—	1500.	3000.	5000.
	1789	—	1500.	3000.	5000.
	1790	—	1500.	3000.	5000.
	1791	—	3000.	5000.	8000.
	1792	—	300.00	500.00	2000.
	1793	—	300.00	500.00	2000.

.905 SILVER, 17.582 gm.

C#	Date	Mintage	VF	XF	Unc
84	1797	—	600.00	800.00	1500.
	1798	—	600.00	800.00	1500.
	1799	—	600.00	800.00	1500.
	1800	—	600.00	800.00	1500.

C#	Date	Mintage	VF	XF	Unc
91	1814	—	600.00	700.00	1000.
	1815	—	900.00	1250.	2000.

1/4 DOPPIA

.905 GOLD
Obv: Head left, VIC.AM.D.G.REX.SAR.CYP.ET.IER. around, date. Rev: Arms.

C#	Date	Mintage	Fine	VF	XF
62	1773	—	1000.	2000.	3000.
	1777	—	—	Rare	—
	1782	—	1000.	1500.	2000.

2.279 gm.
Obv: Head left, VIC.AM.D.G.REX.SARDINIAE. around, date. Rev: Eagle on crossed baton and scepter.

C#	Date	Mintage	Fine	VF	XF
63	1786	—	1500.	2000.	2500.

1/2 DOPPIA

.905 GOLD, 4.75 gm.
Obv: Head left, VIC.AM.D.G.REX.SAR.CYP.ET.IER. around, date. Rev: Arms.

C#	Date	Mintage	Fine	VF	XF
64	1773	—	1000.	2000.	3000.
	1774	—	1000.	2000.	4000.
	1775	—	1000.	2000.	4000.
	1776	—	1000.	2000.	4000.
	1777	—	1000.	2000.	4000.
	1778	—	1000.	2000.	4000.
	1781	—	—	Rare	—

4.558 gm.
Obv: Head left, VIC.AM.D.G.SARDINIAE. around, date. Rev: Crowned eagle on crossed baton and scepter.

C#	Date	Mintage	Fine	VF	XF
65	1786	—	1500.	3000.	4000.
	1787	—	1500.	3000.	4000.
	1788	—	1500.	3000.	4000.
	1789	—	1500.	3000.	4000.
	1790	—	2000.	3000.	6000.
	1791	—	1500.	3000.	4000.
	1792	—	1500.	3000.	4000.
	1793	—	2000.	4000.	6000.
	1794	—	3000.	5000.	10,000.
	1795	—	—	Rare	—
	1796	—	—	Rare	—

Obv: Head left, CAROLUS EMANUEL IV around, date.

C#	Date	Mintage	VF	XF	Unc
85	1797	—	1000.	1500.	3500.
	1798	—	1000.	1500.	3500.

SCUDO

.904 SILVER, 35.164 gm.

C#	Date	Mintage	Fine	VF	XF
61	1773	—	1000.	2000.	3000.
	1776	—	—	Rare	—

DOPPIA

.905 GOLD, 9.6 gm.
Obv: Head left, VIC.AM.D.G.REX.SAR.CYP.ET.IER. around, date. Rev: Arms.

C#	Date	Mintage	Fine	VF	XF
66	1773	—	1500.	2500.	3500.
	1776	—	1500.	2500.	3500.
	1777	—	1500.	2500.	3000.
	1778	—	1500.	2500.	3500.
	1779	—	1500.	2500.	3500.
	1780	—	1500.	2500.	3500.
	1782	—	1500.	2500.	3500.

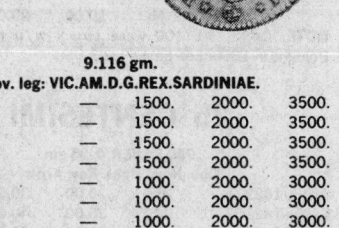

9.116 gm.
Obv. leg: VIC.AM.D.G.REX.SARDINIAE.

C#	Date	Mintage	Fine	VF	XF
67	1786	—	1500.	2000.	3500.
	1787	—	1500.	2000.	3500.
	1788	—	1500.	2000.	3500.
	1789	—	1500.	2000.	3500.
	1790	—	1000.	2000.	3000.
	1791	—	1000.	2000.	3000.
	1792	—	1000.	2000.	3000.
	1793	—	1000.	2000.	3000.
	1794	—	1500.	2500.	3500.
	1796	—	1500.	2500.	3500.

C#	Date	Mintage	VF	XF	Unc
86	1797	—	1000.	1500.	3000.
	1798	—	1000.	1500.	3000.
	1799	—	1000.	1500.	3000.
	1800	—	1000.	1500.	3000.

C#	Date	Mintage	VF	XF	Unc
94	1814	—	750.00	1000.	1500.
	1815	—	1200.	1500.	2000.

2-1/2 DOPPIA

.905 GOLD, 22.78 gm.

C#	Date	Mintage	Fine	VF	XF
68	1786	—	3000.	5000.	6000.

5 DOPPIA

.905 GOLD, 45.56 gm.
Head left, VIC.AM.D.G.REX.SARDINIAE. around, date. Rev: Eagle on crossed baton and scepter.

C#	Date	Mintage	Fine	VF	XF
69	1786	—	—	Rare	—

ISLAND COINAGE

CAGLIARESE

COPPER, 17mm.
Obv: Cross, VIC.AM.D.G.REX.SAR around. Rev: Knot inside wreath.

C#	Date	Mintage	Fine	VF	XF
70	1788	—	25.00	100.00	150.00
	1792	—	25.00	100.00	150.00

TRE (3) CAGLIARESE

COPPER
Obv: Cross on arms. Rev: Value.

C#	Date	Mintage	VF	XF	Unc
88	(1813)	—	90.00	125.00	250.00

SOLDO

BILLON
Obv: Cross in wreath, VIC.AM.D.G.REX.CYP.ET.IER. around, date. Rev: Crown above crossed scepter and baton, value below.

C#	Date	Mintage	Fine	VF	XF
71	1773	—	500.00	1000.	2000.
	1774	—	250.00	500.00	800.00
	1786	—	25.00	50.00	200.00
	1788	—	50.00	100.00	300.00
	1792	—	50.00	100.00	300.00

1/2 REALE

BILLON, 21mm.
Obv: Head right, VIĆ.AM.D.G.REX.SAR.CYP.ET.IER. around, date. Rev: Crown above cross, value.

C#	Date	Mintage	Fine	VF	XF
72	1773	—	—	Rare	—
	1774	—	25.00	50.00	300.00
	1786	—	25.00	50.00	300.00
	1788	—	25.00	50.00	300.00
	1790	—	25.00	50.00	300.00
	1793	—	25.00	50.00	300.00
	1795	—	25.00	50.00	300.00
	1796	—	150.00	300.00	500.00

REALE

BILLON, 22mm.
Obv: Head right, VIC.AM.D.G.REX.SAR.CYP.ET.IER

around, date. Rev: Arms.

C#	Date	Mintage	Fine	VF	XF
73	1773	—	500.00	1000.	2000.
	1774	—	50.00	100.00	300.00
	1785	—	50.00	100.00	300.00
	1786	—	50.00	100.00	300.00
	1788	—	50.00	100.00	300.00
	1790	—	50.00	100.00	300.00
	1792	—	25.00	50.00	100.00
	1793	—	25.00	50.00	100.00
	1795	—	25.00	50.00	100.00
	1796	—	25.00	50.00	100.00

Obv: Head, CAROLUS EMANUEL IV around.
Rev: Legend, date.

C#	Date	Mintage	VF	XF	Unc
87	1797	—	35.00	50.00	150.00
	1798	—	35.00	50.00	150.00
	1799	—	35.00	50.00	150.00

.500 SILVER, 3.18 gm.
Obv: Head right, VIC.EM.D.G.REX.SAR.CYP.ET.IER. around, date.
Rev: Eagle on shield with head to right, crown above.

89.1	1812	—	90.00	125.00	250.00

Rev: Eagle's head to left.

89.2	1812	—	90.00	125.00	250.00

1/4 SCUDO

.895 SILVER, 5.896 gm., 28mm
Obv: Head left, VIC.AM.D.G.REX.SAR.CYP.ET.IER. around, date. Rev: Arms, legend.

C#	Date	Mintage	Fine	VF	XF
75	1773	—	300.00	500.00	1500.
	1774	—	1000.	1500.	3000.
	1792	—	300.00	500.00	1500.

1/2 SCUDO

.895 SILVER, 11.793 gm., 33mm
Obv: Head left, VIC.AM.D.G.REX.SAR.CYP.ET.IER. around, date. Rev: Arms, legend.

76	1773	—	3000.	5000.	10,000.
	1774	—	3000.	5000.	10,000.
	1792	—	3000.	5000.	10,000.
	1793	—	3000.	5000.	10,000.

SCUDO

.895 SILVER, 23.586 gm., 38mm
Obv: Head left, VIC.AM.D.G.REX.SAR.CYP.ET.IER. around, date. Rev: Arms, legend.

77	1773	—	10,000.	15,000.	20,000.

DOPPIETTA

.891 GOLD, 3.2 gm., 22mm
Obv: Bust left, VIC.AM.D.G.REX.SAR.CYP.ET. IER. around, date. Rev: Arms, legend.

77.5	1773	—	3000.	5000.	8000.
	1786	—	3000.	5000.	8000.

2-1/2 DOPPIETTA

.891 GOLD, 8.026 gm., 27mm
Obv: Bust left, VIC.AM.D.G.REX.SAR.CYP.ET.IER. around, date. Rev: Arms, legend.

77.7	1773	—	—	Rare	—
	1786	—	—	Rare	—

5 DOPPIETTA

.891 GOLD, 16.053 gm., 31mm
Obv: Bust left, VIC.AM.D.G.REX.SAR.CYP.ET.IER. around, date. Rev: Arms, legend.

78	1773	—	—	Rare	—
	1774	—	—	Rare	—

MAINLAND COINAGE

CENTESIMO

COPPER

C#	Date	Mintage	VF	XF	Unc
98	1826-G-P	11.485	4.00	6.00	15.00
	1826-T with L	—	4.00	6.00	15.00
	1826-T with P	4.812	4.00	6.00	15.00

3 CENTESIMI

COPPER

99	1826	—	7.50	15.00	25.00
	1826-G	.844	5.00	10.00	20.00
	1826-T	5.778	5.00	10.00	20.00

5 CENTESIMI

COPPER

100	1826-G	10.514	10.00	20.00	40.00
	1826-T with L	32.177	10.00	20.00	40.00
	1826-T with P	Inc. Ab.	10.00	20.00	40.00

NOTE: C#98, 99, 100 were struck w/o mintmark at Bologna in 1860. See Emilia 1,2,3.

25 CENTESIMI

.900 SILVER, 1.25 gm.
Obv: Head right. Rev: Arms.

101	1829-G	.450	20.00	30.00	60.00
	1829-T	.110	30.00	40.00	70.00
	1830-G	.143	20.00	25.00	60.00
	1830-T with L	.234	20.00	25.00	60.00
	1830-T with P	Inc. Ab.	20.00	25.00	60.00

109	1832-T	.120	—	Rare	—
	1833-G	7,921	40.00	60.00	120.00
	1833-T	—	20.00	30.00	75.00
	1837-T	.230	—	Rare	—

50 CENTESIMI

.900 SILVER, 2.5 gm.

C#	Date	Mintage	VF	XF	Unc
102	1823-T	—	—	Rare	—
	1824-T	—	—	Rare	—
102	1825-T	.492	20.00	30.00	75.00
	1826-G	.079	20.00	30.00	75.00
	1826-T	.640	20.00	30.00	75.00
	1827-G	.143	30.00	60.00	120.00
	1827-T	.401	20.00	30.00	75.00
	1828-G	.194	80.00	90.00	120.00
	1828-T with L	.611	30.00	40.00	75.00
	1828-T with P	Inc. Ab.	30.00	40.00	75.00
	1829-G	.107	30.00	40.00	75.00
	1829-T	.255	80.00	90.00	120.00
	1830-T with L	.456	30.00	40.00	75.00
	1830-T with P	Inc. Ab.	150.00	200.00	300.00
	1831-T with L	.143	30.00	40.00	75.00
	1831-T with P	Inc. Ab.	80.00	90.00	120.00

Obv: Head right. Rev: Arms.

110	1832-T	—	—	Rare	—
	1833-G	136 pcs.	—	Rare	—
	1833-T	.062	35.00	100.00	150.00
	1834-T	.061	—	Rare	—
	1835-T	—	—	Rare	—
	1836-T	.022	—	Rare	—
	1837-T	.012	—	Rare	—
	1841-T	6,600	—	Rare	—
	1842-T	.010	30.00	40.00	50.00
	1843-T	.014	30.00	40.00	50.00
	1844-G	.023	—	Rare	—
	1844-T	9,100	—	Rare	—
	1845-T	.016	—	Rare	—
	1846-T	.023	—	Rare	—
	1847-T	.011	—	Rare	—

Obv: Head with beard.

121	1850-G	9,268	50.00	100.00	200.00
	1850-T	—	20.00	30.00	75.00
	1852-T	.055	10.00	15.00	60.00
	1853-T	.021	20.00	30.00	75.00
	1855-T	—	50.00	100.00	200.00
	1856-T	9,754	15.00	25.00	75.00
	1857-T	.015	10.00	20.00	60.00
	1858-T	8,114	10.00	20.00	60.00
	1860-G	15 pcs.	—	Rare	—
	1860-M	.982	10.00	15.00	60.00
	1860-T	6,484	10.00	20.00	60.00
	1861-M	—	50.00	100.00	200.00

LIRA

.900 SILVER, 5.00 gm.

103	1823-T	—	—	Rare	—
	1824-G	5,670	25.00	75.00	200.00
	1824-T	.092	35.00	55.00	100.00
	1825-G	—	35.00	55.00	100.00
	1825-T	.131	35.00	55.00	100.00
	1826-G	.154	35.00	55.00	100.00
	1826-T	.547	35.00	55.00	100.00
	1827-G	.251	35.00	55.00	100.00
	1827-T	.836	35.00	55.00	100.00
	1828-G	.388	35.00	55.00	100.00
	1828-T with L	.345	35.00	55.00	100.00
	1828-T with P	Inc. Ab.	35.00	55.00	100.00
	1829-G	.159	35.00	55.00	100.00
	1829-T	.111	25.00	75.00	200.00
	1830-G	.060	25.00	75.00	200.00
	1830-T	.313	35.00	55.00	100.00

Obv: Head right. Rev: Arms.

111	1831-G	.019	50.00	100.00	200.00
	1831-T	5,000	100.00	150.00	300.00
	1832-G	.035	30.00	50.00	100.00
	1832-T	.030	30.00	50.00	100.00
	1833-G	7,620	30.00	50.00	100.00
	1833-T	85 pcs.	—	Rare	—
	1834-G	.040	—	Rare	—
	1835-G	.023	30.00	40.00	100.00
	1835-T	—	—	Rare	—
	1837-G	.018	—	Rare	—
	1837-T	.028	30.00	40.00	100.00
	1838-G	—	30.00	40.00	80.00

C#	Date	Mintage	VF	XF	Unc
111	1838-T	.011	30.00	40.00	80.00
	1839-T	8,558	—	Rare	—
	1841-G	.011	—	Rare	—
	1841-T	.020	—	Rare	—
	1842-T	5,184	—	Rare	—
	1843-T	.015	30.00	40.00	100.00
	1844-G	.033	—	Rare	—
	1844-T	.015	—	Rare	—
	1845-T	.010	30.00	40.00	100.00
	1846-T	.019	—	Rare	—
	1847-T	.011	30.00	40.00	100.00
	1848-T	8,110	300.00	500.00	1000.
	1849-T	3,037	—	Rare	—

C#	Date	Mintage	VF	XF	Unc
122	1850-G	—	70.00	110.00	200.00
	1850-T	.092	25.00	35.00	75.00
	1851-T	—	Possibly Unique		—
	1852-T	—	Possibly Unique		—
	1853-G	7,051	—	Rare	—
	1853-T	.022	25.00	35.00	75.00
	1854-T	—	Possibly Unique		—
	1855-T	.016	30.00	60.00	120.00
	1856-T	.058	30.00	60.00	120.00
	1857-T	.031	25.00	35.00	75.00
	1858-T	—	Possibly Unique		—
	1859-G	.012	70.00	110.00	200.00
	1859-M	—	25.00	35.00	75.00
	1859-T	5,150	30.00	60.00	120.00
	1860-G	—	—	Rare	—
	1860-M	.603	25.00	35.00	75.00
	1860-T	4,752	80.00	100.00	150.00

2 LIRE

.900 SILVER, 10.00 gm.

C#	Date	Mintage	VF	XF	Unc
104	1823-T	—	—	Rare	—
	1825-G	—	30.00	100.00	300.00
	1825-T	.261	30.00	100.00	200.00
	1826-G	.157	30.00	100.00	250.00
	1826-T	.235	30.00	100.00	250.00
	1827-G	.366	30.00	100.00	250.00
	1827-T	.170	30.00	100.00	250.00
	1828-T	.102	30.00	200.00	300.00
	1829-T	—	Possibly Unique		—
	1830-G	.115	30.00	100.00	250.00
	1830-T with L				
		.049	30.00	100.00	250.00
	1830-T with P				
		Inc. Ab.	50.00	150.00	300.00
	1831-G	.072	30.00	100.00	250.00

Obv: Younger head right.

C#	Date	Mintage	VF	XF	Unc
112	1832-G	.035	50.00	150.00	300.00
	1832-T	Pattern?	—	Rare	—
	1833-G	187 pcs.	50.00	100.00	250.00
	1833-T	287 pcs.	50.00	100.00	250.00
	1834-T	—	Possibly Unique		—
	1835-G	5,142	—	Rare	—
	1835-T	.024	50.00	100.00	250.00
	1836-G	.030	—	Rare	—
	1836-T	—	50.00	100.00	250.00
	1838-T	.020	—	Rare	—
	1839-T	.014	—	Rare	—
	1841-T	4,259	250.00	350.00	550.00
	1842-T	.010	50.00	100.00	250.00
	1843-T	.012	50.00	100.00	250.00
	1844-G	.030	50.00	100.00	250.00
	1844-T	.012	50.00	100.00	250.00
	1845-G	.052	—	Rare	—
	1845-T	.015	50.00	100.00	250.00
	1846-T	.015	50.00	100.00	250.00
	1847-G	—	—	Rare	—
	1847-T	.015	—	Rare	—
	1848-T	.013	—	Rare	—
	1849-T	3,159	—	Rare	—

Obv: Head with beard right.

C#	Date	Mintage	VF	XF	Unc
123	1850-G	—	200.00	500.00	1000.
	1850-T	.018	200.00	500.00	1000.
	1852-T	.023	200.00	500.00	1000.
	1853-G	5,401	—	Rare	—
	1853-T	4,859	200.00	500.00	1000.
	1854-G	2,748	200.00	500.00	1000.
	1854-T	.018	200.00	500.00	1000.
	1855-T	9,414	200.00	500.00	1000.
	1856-T	.011	200.00	500.00	1000.
	1860-T	8,963	200.00	500.00	1000.

5 LIRE

.900 SILVER, 25.00 gm.
Obv: Similar to C#93.

C#	Date	Mintage	VF	XF	Unc
92	1816-T	.023	500.00	750.00	1500.
	1817-T	.044	300.00	400.00	800.00
	1818-T	.055	300.00	500.00	1000.
	1819-T	.035	300.00	500.00	1000.
	1820-T	.101	300.00	500.00	1000.

C#	Date	Mintage	VF	XF	Unc
93	1821-T	—	800.00	1000.	2000.

C#	Date	Mintage	VF	XF	Unc
105	1821-T	.035	500.00	600.00	800.00
	1822-T	.037	150.00	200.00	300.00
105	1823-T	.035	150.00	200.00	300.00
	1824-G	.016	150.00	200.00	300.00
	1824-T	.162	150.00	200.00	300.00
	1825-G	.017	500.00	600.00	800.00
	1825-T	.395	50.00	100.00	200.00
	1826-G	.489	50.00	100.00	250.00
	1826-T	.907	50.00	100.00	250.00
	1827-G	2.137	50.00	100.00	250.00
	1827-T	.724	50.00	100.00	250.00
	1828-G	1.149	50.00	100.00	250.00
	1828-T	.253	50.00	100.00	250.00
	1829-G	.597	50.00	100.00	250.00
	1829-T	.312	50.00	100.00	250.00
	1830-G	1.122	50.00	100.00	250.00
	1830-T with L				
		.913	50.00	100.00	250.00
	1830-T with P				
		Inc. Ab.	50.00	150.00	250.00
	1831-G	.451	500.00	600.00	800.00
	1831-T	.049	150.00	200.00	300.00

Obv: F on truncation. Rev: Arms.

C#	Date	Mintage	VF	XF	Unc
113.1	1831-G	.451	60.00	250.00	500.00
	1831-T	.049	60.00	250.00	500.00

Obv: FERRARIS on truncation

C#	Date	Mintage	VF	XF	Unc
113.2	1831-G	—	60.00	250.00	500.00
	1831-T	—	60.00	250.00	500.00
	1832-G	.317	40.00	100.00	250.00
	1832-T	.095	30.00	100.00	200.00
	1833-G	.275	40.00	100.00	250.00
	1833-T	.060	40.00	100.00	250.00
	1834-G	.154	60.00	250.00	500.00
	1834-T	.037	60.00	150.00	300.00
	1835-G	.336	40.00	100.00	250.00
	1835-T	.069	40.00	100.00	250.00
	1836-G	.595	60.00	120.00	300.00
	1836-T	.051	60.00	120.00	300.00
	1837-G	.359	60.00	100.00	250.00
	1837-T	.036	60.00	200.00	500.00
	1838-G	.307	60.00	100.00	250.00
	1838-T	.042	60.00	250.00	600.00
	1839-G	.141	60.00	100.00	250.00
	1839-T	.205	60.00	100.00	250.00
	1840-G	.193	60.00	100.00	250.00
	1840-T	.050	60.00	250.00	500.00
	1841-G	.313	60.00	250.00	500.00
	1841-T	.015	60.00	300.00	600.00
	1842-G*	.396	60.00	100.00	250.00
	1842-T	.042	60.00	120.00	300.00
	1843-G	.787	60.00	100.00	250.00
	1843-T	.037	60.00	200.00	500.00
	1844-G	1.043	60.00	100.00	250.00
	1844-T	.171	60.00	100.00	250.00
	1845-G	.302	40.00	90.00	250.00
	1845-T	.042	60.00	125.00	300.00
	1846-G	.264	60.00	200.00	500.00
	1846-T	.046	60.00	200.00	500.00
	1847-G	.142	40.00	100.00	250.00
	1847-T	.037	60.00	200.00	500.00
	1848-G	.778	40.00	100.00	250.00
	1848-T	.079	40.00	100.00	250.00
	1849-G	.739	40.00	100.00	250.00
	1849-T	.104	750.00	1400.	2200.

***NOTE:** Beware of forgeries.

C#	Date	Mintage	VF	XF	Unc
124	1850-G	.721	100.00	500.00	1000.
	1850-T	.058	100.00	500.00	1000.
	1851-G	.316	100.00	500.00	1000.
	1851-T	.049	100.00	500.00	1000.
	1852-G	.391	100.00	500.00	1000.
	1852-T	.097	100.00	500.00	1000.
	1853-G	.167	100.00	500.00	1000.
	1854-G	.284	100.00	500.00	1000.
	1854-T	.074	100.00	500.00	1000.
	1855-G	.084	100.00	500.00	1000.
	1855-T	.052	100.00	500.00	1000.
	1856-G	.058	100.00	500.00	1000.
	1856-T	.037	100.00	500.00	1000.
	1857-G	.035	100.00	500.00	1000.
	1857-T	.019	100.00	500.00	1000.
	1858-G	.030	100.00	500.00	1000.
	1858-T	.011	100.00	500.00	1000.
	1859-G	.049	100.00	500.00	1000.
	1859-T	.012	100.00	500.00	1000.
	1860-T	5,044	100.00	500.00	1000.
	1861-T	.012	100.00	500.00	1000.

10 LIRE

.900 GOLD, 3.22 gm.

C#	Date	Mintage	VF	XF	Unc
114	1832-T	—	—	Rare	—
	1833-G	1,550	150.00	200.00	300.00
	1833-T	5,004	150.00	200.00	300.00
	1835-G	—	—	Rare	—
	1835-T	5,118	—	Rare	—
	1838-T	2,826	—	Rare	—
	1839-T	2,237	150.00	200.00	300.00
	1841-G	2,809	—	Rare	—
	1841-T	1,583	—	Rare	—
	1842-T	759 pcs.	—	Rare	—
	1843-G	4,566	—	Rare	—
	1843-T	950 pcs.	—	Rare	—
	1844-G	.011	150.00	200.00	300.00
	1845-G	1,535	—	Rare	—
	1845-T	3,009	—	Rare	—
	1846-G	3,373	—	Rare	—
	1846-T	970 pcs.	—	Rare	—
	1847-G	—	—	Rare	—
	1847-T	405 pcs.	500.00	1000.	2000.
125	1850-G	4,141	200.00	250.00	350.00
	1850-T	2,326	200.00	250.00	350.00
	1852-T	—	—	Rare	—
	1853-T	—	200.00	250.00	350.00
	1854-T	1,833	—	Rare	—
	1855-T	2,566	200.00	250.00	350.00
	1856-T	2,526	—	Rare	—
	1857-T	7,193	200.00	250.00	350.00
125	1858-T	2,931	—	Rare	—
	1860-T	6,036	200.00	250.00	350.00

20 LIRE

.900 GOLD, 6.45 gm.

C#	Date	Mintage	VF	XF	Unc
95	1816-T	.019	300.00	400.00	600.00
	1817-T	.040	200.00	300.00	400.00
	1818-T	.035	200.00	300.00	400.00
	1819-T	.022	200.00	300.00	400.00
	1820-T	.033	200.00	300.00	400.00
96	1821-T	—	2000.	2500.	3000.

C#	Date	Mintage	VF	XF	Unc
106	1821-T	.018	150.00	175.00	225.00
	1822-T	7,460	125.00	150.00	175.00
	1823-T	.022	125.00	150.00	175.00
	1824-G	2,394	125.00	175.00	225.00
	1824-T	2,381	125.00	175.00	225.00
	1825-G	313 pcs.	500.00	600.00	800.00
	1825-T	.028	125.00	150.00	175.00
	1826-T	.144	125.00	150.00	175.00
	1827-G	1,766	300.00	400.00	500.00
	1827-T	.150	125.00	150.00	175.00
	1828-G	—	—	Rare	—
	1828-T with L				
		.095	125.00	150.00	175.00
	1828-T with P	—	150.00	200.00	250.00
	1829-G	—	300.00	400.00	500.00
	1829-T with L				
		.061	300.00	400.00	500.00
	1829-T with P	—	300.00	400.00	500.00
	1830-G	3,270	500.00	600.00	800.00
	1830-T with L	—	200.00	250.00	300.00
	1830-T with P				
		.035	150.00	175.00	200.00
	1831-G	—	—	Rare	—
	1831-T	.042	125.00	150.00	200.00

C#	Date	Mintage	VF	XF	Unc
115	1831-G	—	125.00	150.00	200.00
	1831-T	—	125.00	150.00	200.00
	1832-G	.074	125.00	150.00	200.00
	1832-T	.053	125.00	150.00	200.00
	1833-G	.080	—	Rare	—
	1833-T	.016	125.00	150.00	200.00
	1834-G	.133	125.00	150.00	200.00
	1834-T	.261	125.00	150.00	200.00
	1834	—	150.00	200.00	300.00
	1835-G	.052	125.00	150.00	250.00
	1836-G	.090	125.00	150.00	250.00
	1836-T	.014	—	Rare	—
	1837-G	.056	—	Rare	—
	1837-T	.015	—	Rare	—
	1838-G	.120	125.00	150.00	250.00
	1838-T	.031	125.00	150.00	250.00
	1839-G	.074	—	Rare	—
	1839-T	.070	125.00	150.00	250.00
	1840-G	.176	125.00	150.00	250.00
	1840-T	.028	125.00	150.00	250.00
	1841-G	.206	175.00	250.00	400.00
	1841-T	.031	—	Rare	—
	1842-G	.066	125.00	150.00	250.00
	1842-T	.026	125.00	150.00	250.00
	1843-G	.045	—	Rare	—
115	1843-T	.024	—	Rare	—
	1844-G	.034	—	Rare	—
	1844-T	.030	125.00	150.00	250.00
	1845-G	.043	125.00	150.00	250.00
	1845-T	.035	125.00	150.00	250.00
	1846-G	.043	—	Rare	—
	1846-T	.030	125.00	150.00	250.00
	1847-G	.052	125.00	150.00	250.00
	1847-T	.033	125.00	150.00	250.00
	1847	—	150.00	175.00	300.00
	1848-G	.059	150.00	175.00	300.00
	1848-T	.059	—	Rare	—
	1849-G	.111	125.00	150.00	175.00
	1849-T	.058	125.00	150.00	175.00

C#	Date	Mintage	VF	XF	Unc
126	1850-G	.139	125.00	135.00	150.00
	1850-T	.066	125.00	135.00	150.00
	1851-G	.296	125.00	135.00	150.00
	1851-T	.163	125.00	135.00	150.00
	1852-G	.103	125.00	135.00	150.00
	1852-T	.046	125.00	135.00	150.00
	1853-G	.137	125.00	135.00	150.00
	1853-T	.041	None Exist Or Possibly Unique		
	1854-G	.142	125.00	135.00	150.00
	1855-G	.148	125.00	135.00	150.00
	1855-T	.041	125.00	135.00	150.00
	1855-T (error) EMMANVEL H for II				
		—	125.00	135.00	150.00
	1856-G	.113	125.00	150.00	200.00
	1856-T	.061	500.00	750.00	1000.
	1857-G	.059	125.00	150.00	200.00
	1857-T	.067	125.00	150.00	200.00
	1858-G	.176	125.00	150.00	200.00
	1858-T	.103	200.00	250.00	300.00
	1859-G	.436	125.00	150.00	200.00
	1859-T	.187	125.00	150.00	200.00
	1860-G	.163	125.00	150.00	200.00
	1860-M	.023	150.00	175.00	200.00
	1860-T	.111	125.00	150.00	200.00
	1861-T	.156	125.00	150.00	200.00

40 LIRE

.900 GOLD, 12.9 gm.

C#	Date	Mintage	VF	XF	Unc
107	1822-T	5,011	350.00	450.00	750.00
	1823-T	—	—	Rare	—
	1825-G	3,994	350.00	450.00	750.00
	1825-T	.039	350.00	450.00	750.00
	1826-G	2,844	—	Rare	—
	1831-T with L	—	—	Rare	—
	1831-T with P				
		7,711	350.00	450.00	750.00

50 LIRE

.900 GOLD, 16.12 gm.

C#	Date	Mintage	VF	XF	Unc
116	1832-T	93 pcs.	800.00	1200.	2000.
	1833-G	92 pcs.	800.00	1200.	2000.
	1833-T	1,773	1000.	1500.	2500.
	1834-T	657 pcs.	1000.	1500.	2000.
	1835-G	—	1000.	1500.	2000.
	1835-T	1,296	1000.	1500.	2000.
	1836-T	385 pcs.	750.00	1000.	2000.
	1838-T	992 pcs.	1000.	1500.	2000.
	1839-T	553 pcs.	1000.	1500.	2000.
	1840-T	1,402	1000.	1500.	2000.

C#	Date	Mintage	VF	XF	Unc
116	1841-G	562 pcs.	1000.	1500.	2000.
	1841-T	2,753	1000.	1500.	2000.
	1843-T	586 pcs.	1000.	1500.	2000.

80 LIRE

.900 GOLD, 25.8 gm.

C#	Date	Mintage	VF	XF	Unc
97	1821-T	965 pcs.	5000.	6000.	8000.

C#	Date	Mintage	VF	XF	Unc
108	1823-T	—	—	Rare	—
	1824-G	3,904	800.00	1000.	1500.
	1824-T	5,919	800.00	1000.	1500.
	1825-G	8,465	600.00	1000.	1500.
	1825-T	.014	600.00	1000.	1500.
	1826-G	2,305	—	Rare	—
	1826-T	.076	600.00	1000.	1500.
	1827-G	.015	600.00	1000.	1500.
	1827-T	.038	600.00	1000.	1500.
	1828-G	8,961	800.00	1000.	1500.
	1828-T with L	.023	600.00	1000.	1500.
	1828-T with P	Inc. Ab.	3000.	3500.	4000.
	1829-G	7,436	600.00	1000.	1500.
	1829-T	8,181	—	Rare	—
	1830-G	.026	600.00	1000.	1500.
	1830-T	5,972	600.00	1000.	1500.
	1831-G	.021	—	Rare	—
	1831-T	740 pcs.	—	Rare	—

100 LIRE

.900 GOLD, 32.25 gm.

C#	Date	Mintage	VF	XF	Unc
117	1832-G	—	650.00	750.00	1250.
	1832-T	—	700.00	850.00	1400.
	1833-G	2,587	—	Rare	—
	1833-T	6,769	700.00	850.00	1400.
	1834-G	.012	650.00	750.00	1000.
	1834-T	.037	650.00	750.00	1000.
	1835-G	8,513	650.00	750.00	1000.
	1835-T	.026	650.00	750.00	1000.
	1836-G	703 pcs.	1000.	1200.	1500.
	1836-T	6,236	650.00	750.00	1000.
	1837-G	250 pcs.	—	Rare	—
	1837-T	3,885	700.00	800.00	1200.
	1838-G	4,774	—	Rare	—
	1838-T	3,616	—	Rare	—
	1839-G	2,922	—	Rare	—
	1840-G	1,003	700.00	800.00	1000.
	1840-T	2,898	700.00	800.00	1000.
	1841-G	8,889	—	Rare	—
	1841-T	1,207	—	Rare	—
	1842-G	3,606	—	Rare	—
	1842-T	864 pcs.	1000.	1500.	3000.
	1843-G	424 pcs.	—	Rare	—
	1843-T	827 pcs.	—	Rare	—
	1844-G	2,213	—	Rare	—
	1844-T	91 pcs.	—	Rare	—
	1845-G	646 pcs.	—	Rare	—

ISLAND COINAGE

CENTESIMO

COPPER
Obv: Arms. Rev: Value and date.

C#	Date	Mintage	VF	XF	Unc
118	1842-T	1.933	80.00	100.00	160.00

3 CENTESIME

COPPER
Obv: Arms. Rev: Value and date.

C#	Date	Mintage	VF	XF	Unc
119	1842-T	2.169	8.00	12.00	25.00

5 CENTESIMI

COPPER
Obv: Arms. Rev: Value and date.

C#	Date	Mintage	VF	XF	Unc
120	1842-T	1.845	8.00	14.00	30.00

SICILY

Has a history of occupation extending back to the ancient Phoenicians. In more recent times it was part of the Kingdom of Naples and Sicily.

RULERS

Ferdinando III, 1759-1825
(became Ferdinando I in 1816 as King of Two Sicilies)
Ferdinando II, 1830-1859

MONETARY SYSTEM

6 Cavalli = 1 Grano
20 Grani = 2 Carlini = 1 Taro
12 Tari = 1 Piastra
15 Tari = 1 Scudo
2 Scudi = 1 Oncia

3 PICCOLI

COPPER
Obv: Crowned eagle.
Rev: Value and date in ornamental cartouche.

C#	Date	Mintage	VG	Fine	VF
16	1775	—	3.50	5.00	7.50
	1776	—	3.50	5.00	7.50
	1779	—	3.50	5.00	7.50
	1782	—	3.50	5.00	7.50
	1783	—	3.50	5.00	7.50
	1791	—	3.50	5.00	7.50
	1793	—	3.50	5.00	7.50
	1794	—	3.50	5.00	7.50
	1795	—	3.50	5.00	7.50

MEZZO (1/2) GRANO

COPPER
Obv: Head right. Rev: Value, SICILIANO, date.

C#	Date	Mintage	Fine	VF	XF
52	1836	—	15.00	25.00	50.00

UN (1) GRANO

COPPER
Obv: Crowned eagle.
Rev: VT COMMODIUS and date in ornamental cartouche.

C#	Date	Mintage	Fine	VF	VF
18	1775 lg.eagle	—	6.00	8.50	12.50
	1775 sm.eagle	—	6.00	8.50	12.50
	1776	—	6.00	8.50	12.50
	1777	—	6.00	8.50	12.50
	1778	—	6.00	8.50	12.50
	1779	—	6.00	8.50	12.50
	1780	—	6.00	8.50	12.50
	1782	—	6.00	8.50	12.50
	1783	—	6.00	8.50	12.50
	1784	—	6.00	8.50	12.50
	1785	—	6.00	8.50	12.50
	1791	—	6.00	8.50	12.50
	1793	—	6.00	8.50	12.50
	1794	—	6.00	8.50	12.50

Obv: Larger crowned eagle.

C#	Date	Mintage	Fine	VF	VF
18a	1795	—	6.00	8.50	12.50

Obv: Eagle, legend. Rev: Value, date within wreath.

C#	Date	Mintage	Fine	VF	XF
41	1801	—	8.50	15.00	30.00
	1802	—	15.00	25.00	50.00
	1803	—	30.00	50.00	100.00

C#	Date	Mintage	Fine	VF	XF
42	ND(1814)	—	15.00	25.00	50.00
	1814	—	4.50	7.50	15.00
	1815	—	4.50	7.50	15.00

NOTE: Varieties exist.

Obv: Head right. Rev: SICILIANO, value, date.

C#	Date	Mintage	Fine	VF	XF
53	1836	—	30.00	50.00	100.00

DUE (2) GRANI

COPPER
Obv: Crowned eagle, head left.
Rev: VT COMMODIUS and date in ornamental cartouche.

C#	Date	Mintage	VG	Fine	VF
20	1775 lg.eagle	—	6.50	10.00	15.00
	1775 sm.eagle	—	6.50	10.00	15.00
	1776	—	5.00	7.00	10.00
	1777	—	5.00	7.00	10.00
	1778	—	5.00	7.00	10.00
	1779	—	5.00	7.00	10.00
	1780	—	5.00	7.00	10.00
	1782	—	5.00	7.00	10.00
	1783	—	5.00	7.00	10.00
	1784	—	5.00	7.00	10.00
	1785	—	5.00	7.00	10.00
	1791	—	6.50	10.00	15.00
	1793	—	6.50	10.00	15.00
	1794	—	5.00	7.00	10.00

Obv: Crowned eagle, head right.
Rev: UT COMMODIUS and date in different ornamental cartouche.

C#	Date	Mintage	VG	Fine	VF
20.1	1795	—	5.00	7.00	10.00

Obv: Eagle, legend. Rev: Value, date within wreath.

C#	Date	Mintage	Fine	VF	XF
43	1801	—	30.00	50.00	100.00
	1802	—	8.50	15.00	30.00
	1803	—	8.50	15.00	30.00
	1804	—	8.50	15.00	30.00

C#	Date	Mintage	Fine	VF	XF
44	1814	—	15.00	25.00	50.00
	1815	—	7.50	12.50	25.00

NOTE: 1814 exists with large and small G.2.

Obv: Head right. Rev: SICILIANI, value, date.

C#	Date	Mintage	Fine	VF	XF
54	1836	—	30.00	50.00	100.00

CINQUE (5) GRANI

COPPER
Obv: Eagle, legend. Rev: Value, date within wreath.

C#	Date	Mintage	Fine	VF	XF
45	1801	—	45.00	75.00	150.00
	1802	—	22.50	37.50	75.00
	1803	—	22.50	37.50	75.00
	1804	—	22.50	37.50	75.00

Large head

C#	Date	Mintage	Fine	VF	XF
46	ND(1814)	—	45.00	75.00	150.00
	1814	—	15.00	25.00	50.00
	1815	—	15.00	25.00	50.00

NOTE: Varieties exist of 1815.

Small head

C#	Date	Mintage	Fine	VF	XF
46a	1815	—	15.00	25.00	50.00
	1816	—	30.00	50.00	100.00

Obv: Head right. Rev: SICILIANI, crown, value, date.

C#	Date	Mintage	Fine	VF	XF
55	1836	—	75.00	125.00	250.00

DIECI (10) GRANI

.833 SILVER, 1.15 gm.
Obv: Head of Ferdinand right; value below.
Rev: Crowned eagle, date above.

C#	Date	Mintage	VG	Fine	VF
23	1796	—	7.50	12.50	20.00

COPPER
Obv: Eagle, legend. Rev: Value, date within wreath.

C#	Date	Mintage	Fine	VF	XF
47	1801	—	8.50	15.00	30.00
	1802	—	8.50	15.00	30.00
	1803	—	8.50	15.00	30.00
	1804	—	30.00	50.00	100.00

C#	Date	Mintage	Fine	VF	XF
48	ND(1814)	—	45.00	75.00	150.00
	1814	—	15.00	25.00	50.00
	1815	—	15.00	25.00	50.00

NOTE: 1815 exists with G.10. and G.10, and with lower right tip of bust pointing to E in REX; also tip of bust pointing to X in REX.

Obv: Head right. Rev: SICILIANI, crown, value, date.

C#	Date	Mintage	Fine	VF	XF
56	1835	—	—	Rare	—
	1836	—	8.50	15.00	25.00

20 GRANI

.833 SILVER, 2.2 gm.
Obv: Head of Ferdinand right.
Rev: Small crowned eagle, leg: HISP. INF.

C#	Date	Mintage	VG	Fine	VF
—	1785	—	8.50	15.00	25.00
	1786	—	8.50	15.00	25.00

Obv: Larger head of Ferdinand right.
Rev: Larger crowned eagle. Rev. leg: HISPAN. INFANS.

C#	Date	Mintage	VG	Fine	VF
—	1787	—	8.50	15.00	25.00
	1788	—	8.50	15.00	25.00
	1789	—	8.50	15.00	25.00
	1796	—	8.50	15.00	25.00

2 TARI

.833 SILVER, 4.5 gm.
Obv: Head of Ferdinand right.
Rev: Crowned eagle.

C#	Date	Mintage	Fine	VF	XF
27	1785	—	12.50	20.00	35.00
	1786	—	12.50	20.00	35.00
	1787	—	12.50	20.00	35.00
	1788	—	12.50	20.00	35.00
	1789	—	12.50	20.00	35.00

Rev: Crowned eagle, date below.

C#	Date	Mintage	Fine	VF	XF
27.1	1789	—	12.50	20.00	35.00
	1793	—	12.50	20.00	35.00

Obv: Value below head.

C#	Date	Mintage	Fine	VF	XF
27.2	1796	—	8.50	15.00	25.00

3 TARI

.833 SILVER, 6.4 gm.
Obv: Head of Ferdinand right, value below.
Rev: Crowned cross, date below, leg: HI SPAN. INFANS.

C#	Date	Mintage	Fine	VF	XF
29	1785 HISP.INF.	—	20.00	35.00	60.00
	1786	—	20.00	35.00	60.00
	1787	—	20.00	35.00	60.00
	1788	—	20.00	35.00	60.00
	1793	—	20.00	35.00	60.00
	1796	—	12.50	20.00	35.00
	1798	—	20.00	35.00	60.00

4 TARI

.833 SILVER, 8.7 gm.
Obv: Crude portrait of Ferdinand right.
Rev: Crowned eagle.

C#	Date	Mintage	Fine	VF	XF
—	1785	—	40.00	65.00	95.00

Obv: Head of Ferdinand right, date below.
Rev: Crowned eagle, leg: HISPAN INFANS.

C#	Date	Mintage	Fine	VF	XF
—	1785	—	35.00	55.00	85.00
	1786	—	35.00	55.00	85.00
	1787	—	35.00	55.00	85.00
	1793 HISPANIARVM INFANS	—	35.00	55.00	85.00
	1796 HISPANIARVM INFANS	—	35.00	55.00	85.00

6 TARI

.833 SILVER, 13.632 gm.

C#	Date	Mintage	Fine	VF	XF
31	1785	—	55.00	85.00	125.00
	1786	—	55.00	85.00	125.00
	1787	—	55.00	85.00	125.00
	1788	—	55.00	85.00	125.00
	1789	—	55.00	85.00	125.00
	1793	—	55.00	85.00	125.00
	1794	—	55.00	85.00	125.00
	1795	—	55.00	85.00	125.00

13.766 gm.
O Bv: Head FerdinandRIGHT, VALUE BELOW.
Rev: Crowned eagle,date below

C#	Date	Mintage	Fine	VF	XF
33	1796		65.00	100.00	135.00
	1797		65.00	100.00	135.00
	1798		65.00	100.00	135.00
	1799		65.00	100.00	135.00

.854 SILVER, 13.66 gm.
Obv: Head right, Rev: Eagle

C#	Date	Mintage	Fine	VF	XF
48.5	1799	—	15.00	25.00	50.00
	1799 (error) T.12 for T.6	—	30.00	50.00	100.00
	1800	—	15.00	25.00	50.00
	1801	—	20.00	35.00	70.00

PIASTRA OF 12 TARI

.833 SILVER, 27.265 gm.
Obv: Head of Ferdinand right, date below.
Rev: Large crowned eagle.

C#	Date	Mintage	Fine	VF	XF
35	1785	—	55.00	85.00	125.00

Obv: Date in legend. Rev: Small crowned eagle.

C#	Date	Mintage	Fine	VF	XF
	1786	—	55.00	85.00	125.00

Obv: Head of Ferdinand right, value below.
Rev: Large crowned eagle, wings to border, date below.

C#	Date	Mintage	Fine	VF	XF
35a	1787	—	75.00	110.00	150.00
	1788	—	75.00	110.00	150.00
	1789	—	65.00	95.00	135.00
	1790	—	65.00	95.00	135.00
	1793	—	55.00	85.00	125.00

27.533 gm.
Obv: T. 12 below head. Rev: Continuous legend.

C#	Date	Mintage	Fine	VF	XF
	1794	—	55.00	85.00	125.00
	1795	—	55.00	85.00	125.00

C#	Date	Mintage	Fine	VF	XF
36	1796	—	50.00	75.00	110.00
	1797	—	50.00	75.00	110.00
	1798	—	50.00	75.00	110.00
	1799	—	50.00	75.00	110.00

12 TARI

.883 SILVER, 27.533 gm.
Obv: Bust right, FERDINAN.D.G.SICIL....
Rev: Eagle, date

C#	Date	Mintage	Fine	VF	XF
49	1799	—	25.00	40.00	80.00
	1800	—	25.00	40.00	80.00
	1801	—	30.00	50.00	100.00
	1803	—	30.00	50.00	100.00

NOTE: 1799 and 1801 exist with REX. and REX

Obv. leg: FERDINAN. III. D.G.SICIL....

C#	Date	Mintage	Fine	VF	XF
49a	1799	—	25.00	40.00	80.00
	1800	—	25.00	40.00	80.00
	1801	—	30.00	50.00	100.00
	1802	—	25.00	40.00	80.00
	1803	—	30.00	50.00	100.00
	1804	—	40.00	65.00	130.00

NOTE: 1799 exists with REX. and REX

Rev: J.U.I. above eagle within wreath

C#	Date	Mintage	Fine	VF	XF
50	1805	—	45.00	75.00	150.00
	1806	—	45.00	75.00	150.00
	1807	—	45.00	75.00	150.00

Rev: V. eagle B. within wreath

C#	Date	Mintage	Fine	VF	XF
50a	1810	—	45.00	75.00	150.00

NOTE: Seven varieties exist.

ONCIA OF 30 TARI

.833 SILVER, 69.00 gm.
Obv: Head of Ferdinand right, date below.
Rev: Large phoenix arising from flames, sun above.

C#	Date	Mintage	Fine	VF	XF
37	1785	—	500.00	750.00	1400.

Obv: Bust of Ferdinand right, 55mm.
Rev: Date below Phoenix.

C#	Date	Mintage	Fine	VF	XF
37a	1791	—	600.00	850.00	1500.

C#	Date	Mintage	Fine	VF	XF
38	1793	—	450.00	650.00	1250.

2 ONCIA

.906 GOLD, 8.815 gm.

C#	Date	Mintage	VF	XF	Unc
51	1814	—	1000.	1350.	2500.

TUSCANY

ETRURIA

An Italian territorial division on the west-central peninsula, belonged to the Medici from 1530 to 1737, when it was given to Francis, duke of Lorraine. In 1800 the French established it as part of the Spanish dominions; from 1807 to 1809 it was a French department. After the fall of Napoleon it reverted to its pre-Napoleonic owner, Ferdinand III.

RULERS

Pietro Leopoldo, 1765-1790
As Emperor Leopold II, 1790-1792
Ferdinando III, 1791-1801
Louis I, 1801-1803
Charles Louis, under regency of his mother Maria Louisa, 1803-1807
Annexed To France 1807-1814
Ferdinando III Restored 1814-1824
Leopold II 1824-1848, 1849-1859
Provisional Government 1859
United to Italian Provisional Government 1859-1861

MINTMARKS

Firenze = Florence

MONETARY SYSTEM

Until 1826

12 Denari = 3 Quattrini = 1 Soldo
20 Soldi = 1 Lira
10 Lire = 1 Dena
40 Quattrini = 1 Paolo
1-1/2 Paoli = 1 Lira
10 Paoli = 1 Francescone, Scudo, Tallero
3 Zecchini = 1 Ruspone = 40 Lire

1826-1859

100 Quattrini = 1 Fiorino
4 Fiorini = 10 Paoli

1859

100 Centesimi = 1 Lira

QUATTRINO

COPPER
Obv: Crowned arms. Rev: Value and date.

C#	Date	Mintage	VG	Fine	VF
12	1771	—	4.50	6.50	9.50
	1778	—	4.50	6.50	9.50
	1779	—	4.50	6.50	9.50
	1780	—	4.50	6.50	9.50
	1781	—	4.50	6.50	9.50
	1782	—	4.50	6.50	9.50
	1783	—	4.50	6.50	9.50
	1784	—	4.50	6.50	9.50
	1787	—	4.50	6.50	9.50
	1788	—	4.50	6.50	9.50
	1789	—	4.50	6.50	9.50
	1790	—	4.50	6.50	9.50

C#	Date	Mintage	VG	Fine	VF
29	1791	—	2.75	4.00	6.00
	1792	—	2.75	4.00	6.00
	1795	—	2.75	4.00	6.00
	1796	—	2.75	4.00	6.00
	1798	—	2.75	4.00	6.00
	1799	—	2.75	4.00	6.00
	1800	—	2.75	4.00	6.00

Obv: Square arms.

C#	Date	Mintage	VG	Fine	VF
30	1801	—	2.75	4.00	6.00

Obv: Crowned arms. Rev: Value.

C#	Date	Mintage	Fine	VF	XF
40	1802	—	20.00	80.00	125.00
	1803	—	8.00	35.00	60.00
	1805 (error date)		8.00	35.00	60.00
44	1803	—	8.00	40.00	80.00
	1804	—	8.00	40.00	80.00
	1805	—	8.00	40.00	80.00
	1806	—	8.00	40.00	80.00
	1807	—	8.00	40.00	80.00
53	1819	—	4.00	15.00	30.00
	1820	—	4.00	15.00	30.00
	1821	—	4.00	15.00	30.00
	1822	—	4.00	15.00	30.00
	1824	—	4.00	15.00	30.00

Obv. leg: LEOP. II A.D.'A. GRAND. DI TOSC.

C#	Date	Mintage	Fine	VF	XF
62	1827	—	4.00	12.00	25.00
	1828	—	4.00	12.00	25.00
	1829	—	4.00	12.00	25.00
	1830	—	4.00	12.00	25.00
	1831	—	4.00	12.00	25.00
	1832	—	4.00	12.00	25.00
	1833	—	4.00	12.00	25.00
	1834	—	4.00	12.00	25.00
	1835	—	4.00	12.00	25.00
	1836	—	4.00	12.00	25.00
	1837	—	4.00	12.00	25.00
	1838	—	4.00	12.00	25.00
	1840	—	4.00	12.00	25.00
	1841	—	7.50	35.00	60.00
	1843	—	7.50	35.00	60.00

Obv. leg: LEOP. II A.D.'A. G-D. DI TOSC.

C#	Date	Mintage	Fine	VF	XF
62a	1842	—	7.50	35.00	60.00
	1843	—	4.00	12.00	25.00
	1844	—	4.00	12.00	25.00
	1845	—	4.00	12.00	25.00
	1846	—	4.00	12.00	25.00
	1847	—	4.00	12.00	25.00
	1848	—	4.00	12.00	25.00
	1849	—	4.00	12.00	25.00
	1850	—	4.00	12.00	25.00
	1851	—	4.00	12.00	25.00
	1852	—	4.00	12.00	25.00
	1853	—	4.00	12.00	25.00
	1854	—	4.00	12.00	25.00
	1856	—	4.00	12.00	25.00
	1857	—	4.00	12.00	25.00

MEZZO (1/2) SOLDO

COPPER

C#	Date	Mintage	Fine	VF	XF
45	ND(1804)	—	5.00	40.00	65.00

2 QUATTRINI

COPPER

Obv: Crowned arms. Rev: Value and date.

C#	Date	Mintage	VG	Fine	VF
13	1778	—	4.50	6.50	9.50
	1783	—	4.50	6.50	9.50
	1785	—	4.50	6.50	9.50

3 QUATTRINI

COPPER

C#	Date	Mintage	Fine	VF	XF
64	1826	—	4.00	10.00	30.00
	1827	—	4.00	10.00	30.00
	1828	—	4.00	10.00	30.00
	1829	—	9.00	35.00	60.00
	1830	—	4.00	10.00	30.00
	1832	—	4.00	10.00	30.00
	1833	—	4.00	10.00	30.00
	1834	—	4.00	10.00	30.00
	1835	—	4.00	10.00	30.00
	1836	—	4.00	10.00	30.00
	1838	—	4.00	10.00	30.00
	1839	—	4.00	10.00	30.00
	1840	—	4.00	10.00	30.00
	1843	—	4.00	10.00	30.00
	1845	—	4.00	10.00	30.00
	1846	—	4.00	10.00	30.00
	1851	—	4.00	10.00	30.00
	1853	—	4.00	10.00	30.00
	1854	—	9.00	35.00	60.00

SOLDO

COPPER

Obv: Crowned arms. Rev: Value and date.

C#	Date	Mintage	VG	Fine	VF
14	1778	—	5.00	7.50	12.50
	1780	—	5.00	7.50	12.50
	1782	—	5.00	7.50	12.50
	1785	—	5.00	7.50	12.50
	1790	—	5.00	7.50	12.50

Obv: Crowned arms in sprays.
Rev: Value in cartouche.

C#	Date	Mintage	VG	Fine	VF
31	1791	—	4.50	6.50	9.50

Obv: Legend, arms. Rev: Value.

C#	Date	Mintage	Fine	VF	XF
54	1822	—	4.00	10.00	30.00
	1823	—	4.00	10.00	30.00

Obv: Arms. Rev: Value.

C#	Date	Mintage	Fine	VF	XF
63	1824	—	30.00	50.00	100.00

5 QUATTRINI

BILLON

C#	Date	Mintage	Fine	VF	XF
65	1826	—	7.00	28.00	40.00
	1828	—	9.00	31.00	44.00
	1829	—	7.00	28.00	40.00
	1830	—	7.00	28.00	40.00

2 SOLDI

COPPER

Obv: Legend, arms. Rev: Value.

C#	Date	Mintage	Fine	VF	XF
46	1804	—	12.00	50.00	75.00
	1805	—	12.00	50.00	75.00
55	1818	—	4.00	10.00	30.00
	1822	—	4.00	10.00	30.00

DIECI (10) QUATTRINI

BILLON

C#	Date	Mintage	VG	Fine	VF
15	1778	—	3.75	5.00	7.50
	1780	—	3.75	5.00	7.50
	1781	—	3.75	5.00	7.50
	1782	—	3.75	5.00	7.50
	1785	—	3.75	5.00	7.50
	1786	—	3.75	5.00	7.50
	1787	—	3.75	5.00	7.50
	1788	—	3.75	5.00	7.50

Obv: Cross. Rev: Value.

C#	Date	Mintage	VG	Fine	VF
32	1800	—	4.50	6.50	9.50
	1801	—	4.50	6.50	9.50

Obv: Arms. Rev: Value on Sarcophagus.

C#	Date	Mintage	Fine	VF	XF
41	1801	—	10.00	35.00	75.00

Obv: Arms and date. Rev: Value in field.

C#	Date	Mintage	Fine	VF	XF
41a	1802	—	20.00	50.00	100.00

Obv: Arms. Rev: Value and date.

C#	Date	Mintage	Fine	VF	XF
41b	1802	—	10.00	20.00	50.00

Rev: "10 QUATTRINI"

C#	Date	Mintage	Fine	VF	XF
66	1826	—	10.00	15.00	25.00
	1827	—	10.00	15.00	25.00
	1853	—	10.00	15.00	25.00
	1854	—	10.00	15.00	25.00

Obv: Head right. Rev: Arms.

C#	Date	Mintage	Fine	VF	XF
67	1858	—	18.00	30.00	50.00

1/2 PAOLO

.920 SILVER, 1.37 gm.

Obv: Bust right. Rev: Arms.

C#	Date	Mintage	Fine	VF	XF
16	1783	—	15.00	25.00	40.00
	1784	—	15.00	25.00	40.00

1.375 gm.
Rev: Crowned arms.

C#	Date	Mintage	Fine	VF	XF
33	1792		17.50	30.00	50.00

1.37 gm.

C#	Date	Mintage	Fine	VF	XF
68	1832	—	10.00	35.00	65.00
	1839	—	10.00	15.00	25.00

Obv: Older bearded head.

C#	Date	Mintage	Fine	VF	XF
68a	1853	—	10.00	35.00	65.00
	1856	—	10.00	35.00	65.00
	1857	—	10.00	35.00	65.00
	1859	—	10.00	35.00	65.00

1/4 DI FIORINO

.916 SILVER, 1.719 gm.
Obv: Arms. Rev: Value.

C#	Date	Mintage	Fine	VF	XF
69	1827	—	20.00	50.00	100.00

10 SOLDI

.913 SILVER, 2.51 gm.
Obv: Arms. Rev: Value.

C#	Date	Mintage	Fine	VF	XF
56	1821	—	10.00	15.00	25.00
	1823	—	10.00	15.00	25.00

PAOLO

.920 SILVER, 2.74 gm.
Obv: Bust right. Rev: Arms.

C#	Date	Mintage	Fine	VF	XF
17	1783	—	15.00	25.00	50.00
17a	1788	—	15.00	25.00	50.00
	1789	—	15.00	25.00	50.00
	1790	—	15.00	25.00	50.00

2.751 gm.
Rev: Crowned arms.

C#	Date	Mintage	Fine	VF	XF
34	1791		45.00	75.00	110.00

2.74 gm.

C#	Date	Mintage	Fine	VF	XF
70	1831	—	10.00	30.00	75.00
	1832	—	10.00	30.00	75.00
	1838	—	10.00	30.00	75.00

Obv: Older bearded head.

C#	Date	Mintage	Fine	VF	XF
70a	1842	—	10.00	30.00	75.00
	1843	—	10.00	30.00	75.00
	1845	—	10.00	30.00	75.00
	1846	—	10.00	30.00	75.00
	1856	—	10.00	30.00	75.00
	1857	—	10.00	30.00	75.00
	1858	—	10.00	30.00	75.00

LIRA

.920 SILVER, 3.9 gm.

C#	Date	Mintage	Fine	VF	XF
47	1803	—	15.00	30.00	75.00
	1806	—	15.00	30.00	75.00

.913 SILVER, 4.103 gm.
Obv: Head right.

C#	Date	Mintage	Fine	VF	XF
57	1821	—	20.00	50.00	100.00
	1823	—	20.00	50.00	100.00

2 PAOLI

.920 SILVER, 5.48 gm.
Obv: Bust right. Rev: Crowned oval arms.

C#	Date	Mintage	Fine	VF	XF
18	1770	—	25.00	40.00	75.00
	1780	—	25.00	40.00	75.00
	1782	—	25.00	40.00	75.00
	1787	—	25.00	40.00	75.00

.917 SILVER, 5.502 gm.

C#	Date	Mintage	Fine	VF	XF
35	1791	—	65.00	100.00	150.00

1/2 FIORINO

.916 SILVER, 3.438 gm.
Obv: Arms. Rev: Value.

C#	Date	Mintage	Fine	VF	XF
71	1827	—	15.00	30.00	75.00

FIORINO

.916 SILVER, 6.876 gm.

C#	Date	Mintage	Fine	VF	XF
72	1826	—	10.00	25.00	75.00
	1828	—	10.00	25.00	75.00
	1830	—	10.00	25.00	75.00
	1840	—	10.00	25.00	75.00
	1842	—	10.00	25.00	75.00

Obv: Older head.

C#	Date	Mintage	Fine	VF	XF
72a	1843	—	10.00	25.00	75.00
	1844	—	10.00	25.00	75.00
	1847	—	10.00	25.00	75.00
	1848	—	10.00	25.00	75.00
	1856	—	10.00	25.00	75.00
	1857	—	10.00	25.00	75.00
	1858	—	10.00	25.00	75.00

5 PAOLI

.917 SILVER, 13.75 gm.
Obv: Bust right with loose hair.
Rev: Crowned arms.

C#	Date	Mintage	Fine	VF	XF
19	1777	—	135.00	175.00	225.00
	1778	—	135.00	175.00	225.00
	1779	—	135.00	175.00	225.00

Obv: Bust right with bound hair.

C#	Date	Mintage	Fine	VF	XF
19a	1778	—	65.00	100.00	150.00
	1779	—	65.00	100.00	150.00
	1787	—	65.00	100.00	150.00

Obv: Bust right. Rev: Square arms.

C#	Date	Mintage	Fine	VF	XF
20	1790	—	65.00	100.00	150.00

Obv: Head right. Rev: Oval arms.

C#	Date	Mintage	Fine	VF	XF
36	1791	—	65.00	100.00	150.00

.913 SILVER, 13.75 gm.

C#	Date	Mintage	Fine	VF	XF
58	1819	—	50.00	200.00	350.00
	1820	—	50.00	200.00	350.00

Obv: Longer hair.

C#	Date	Mintage	Fine	VF	XF
58a	1823	—	100.00	250.00	500.00

.916 SILVER

C#	Date	Mintage	Fine	VF	XF
73	1827	—	40.00	100.00	250.00
	1828	—	40.00	100.00	250.00
	1829 PC	—	40.00	100.00	250.00

C#	Date	Mintage	Fine	VF	XF
73a	1834	—	500.00	1400.	2000.

5 LIRE

.958 SILVER, 19.723 gm.

C#	Date	Mintage	Fine	VF	XF
48	1803	—	40.00	125.00	250.00
	1804	—	40.00	100.00	200.00

10 PAOLI

.917 SILVER, 27.5 gm.
Obv: Bust right. Rev: Crowned thin oval arms.

C#	Date	Mintage	Fine	VF	XF
21	1765	—	150.00	200.00	300.00
	1766	—	200.00	250.00	325.00

Obv: Bust right with bound hair.

C#	Date	Mintage	Fine	VF	XF
21a	1766	—	200.00	250.00	325.00

Obv: Bust right with loose hair.

C#	Date	Mintage	Fine	VF	XF
21b	1766	—	150.00	200.00	300.00
	1767	—	150.00	200.00	300.00
	1768	—	150.00	200.00	300.00
	1769	—	150.00	200.00	300.00
	1770	—	150.00	200.00	300.00
	1771	—	150.00	200.00	300.00

Rev: Similar to C#21a.

C#	Date	Mintage	Fine	VF	XF
22	1767	—	100.00	135.00	250.00
	1768	—	100.00	135.00	250.00

.917 SILVER, 28.25 gm.

Tallero For Use In The Levant States
Obv: Armored bust right.
Rev: Crowned and supported arms.

C#	Date	Mintage	Fine	VF	XF
23	1769 LSF	—	200.00	300.00	500.00
	1773 LSF	—	200.00	300.00	500.00
	1774 LSF	—	200.00	300.00	500.00

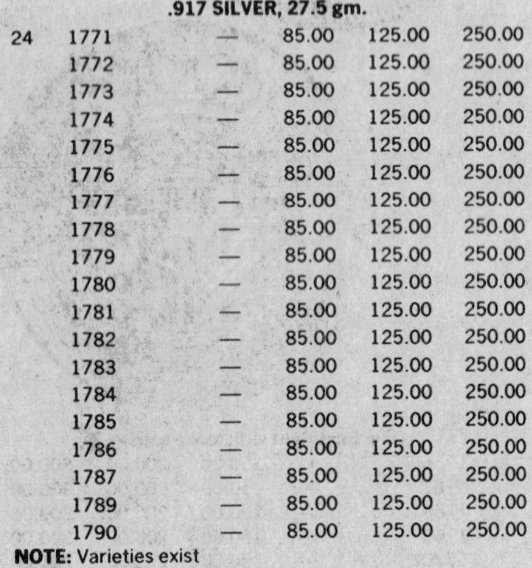

.917 SILVER, 27.5 gm.

C#	Date	Mintage	Fine	VF	XF
24	1771	—	85.00	125.00	250.00
	1772	—	85.00	125.00	250.00
	1773	—	85.00	125.00	250.00
	1774	—	85.00	125.00	250.00
	1775	—	85.00	125.00	250.00
	1776	—	85.00	125.00	250.00
	1777	—	85.00	125.00	250.00
	1778	—	85.00	125.00	250.00
	1779	—	85.00	125.00	250.00
	1780	—	85.00	125.00	250.00
	1781	—	85.00	125.00	250.00
	1782	—	85.00	125.00	250.00
	1783	—	85.00	125.00	250.00
	1784	—	85.00	125.00	250.00
	1785	—	85.00	125.00	250.00
	1786	—	85.00	125.00	250.00
	1787	—	85.00	125.00	250.00
	1789	—	85.00	125.00	250.00
	1790	—	85.00	125.00	250.00

NOTE: Varieties exist

Obv: Bust right.
Rev: Crowned and supported arms.

C#	Date	Mintage	Fine	VF	XF
25	1790	—	300.00	400.00	600.00

Rev: Crowned double eagle.

C#	Date	Mintage	Fine	VF	XF
26	1790	—	200.00	300.00	500.00

C#	Date	Mintage	Fine	VF	XF
37	1791	—	50.00	90.00	150.00
	1792	—	50.00	90.00	150.00
	1793	—	50.00	90.00	150.00
	1794	—	50.00	90.00	150.00
	1795	—	50.00	90.00	150.00
	1796	—	50.00	90.00	150.00
	1797	—	50.00	90.00	150.00
	1798	—	50.00	90.00	150.00
	1799	—	50.00	90.00	150.00
	1800	—	50.00	90.00	150.00
	1801	—	50.00	90.00	150.00

FRANCESCONE

.934 SILVER, 27.5 gm.

C#	Date	Mintage	Fine	VF	XF
42	1801	—	50.00	80.00	175.00
	1802	—	50.00	100.00	200.00
	1803	—	40.00	75.00	165.00

.913 SILVER

C#	Date	Mintage	Fine	VF	XF
50	1803	—	50.00	75.00	125.00
	1806	—	50.00	75.00	125.00
	1807	—	50.00	75.00	125.00

Obv: Head right. Rev: Arms.

C#	Date	Mintage	Fine	VF	XF
59	1814	—	45.00	65.00	100.00
	1815	—	45.00	65.00	100.00
	1819	—	45.00	65.00	100.00
	1820	—	45.00	65.00	100.00
	1824	—	45.00	65.00	100.00

QUATTRO (4) FIORINI

.916 SILVER, 27.5 gm.

C#	Date	Mintage	Fine	VF	XF
74	1826	—	200.00	400.00	700.00

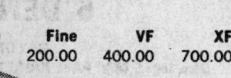

C#	Date	Mintage	Fine	VF	XF
75	1830	—	200.00	400.00	700.00

C#	Date	Mintage	Fine	VF	XF
75a	1833	—	200.00	400.00	700.00
	1834	—	200.00	400.00	700.00
	1836	—	200.00	400.00	700.00
	1839	—	200.00	400.00	700.00
	1840	—	200.00	400.00	700.00
	1841	—	200.00	400.00	700.00
	1845	—	200.00	400.00	700.00
	1846	—	200.00	400.00	700.00

C#	Date	Mintage	Fine	VF	XF
75b	1856	—	50.00	100.00	200.00
	1858	—	50.00	100.00	200.00
	1859	—	50.00	100.00	200.00

10 LIRE

.958 SILVER, 39.447 gm.

C#	Date	Mintage	Fine	VF	XF
49	1803	—	45.00	65.00	150.00
	1804	—	45.00	65.00	150.00
	1805	—	40.00	60.00	140.00
	1806	—	60.00	100.00	200.00
	1807	—	45.00	70.00	150.00

ZECCHINO

1.000 GOLD, 3.488 gm.

C#	Date	Mintage	Fine	VF	XF
27	1779	—	250.00	400.00	600.00
	1780	—	250.00	400.00	600.00
	1787	—	250.00	400.00	600.00
	1788	—	250.00	400.00	600.00
	1789	—	250.00	400.00	600.00
38	1791	—	375.00	500.00	650.00
	1792	—	375.00	500.00	650.00

For Levant Trade

.998 GOLD, 3.49 gm.
Obv: St. Zenobio kneeling before Christ. Rev: St. John.

C#	Date	Mintage	Fine	VF	XF
51	ND(1805)	—	—	Rare	—

C#	Date	Mintage	Fine	VF	XF
60	1816	—	250.00	400.00	1000.
	1821	—	250.00	400.00	1000.

3.452 gm.

C#	Date	Mintage	Fine	VF	XF
76	1824	—	200.00	250.00	650.00
	1826	—	200.00	250.00	650.00
	1829	—	200.00	250.00	650.00
	1832	—	200.00	250.00	650.00
	1853	—	200.00	250.00	650.00

RUSPONE (= 3 ZECCHINI)

1.000 GOLD, 10.464 gm.

C#	Date	Mintage	Fine	VF	XF
28	1765	—	450.00	650.00	1250.
	1766	—	450.00	650.00	1250.
	1768	—	450.00	650.00	1250.
	1769	—	450.00	650.00	1250.
	1770	—	450.00	650.00	1250.
	1771	—	450.00	650.00	1250.
	1772	—	450.00	650.00	1250.
	1773	—	450.00	650.00	1250.
	1774	—	450.00	650.00	1250.
	1775	—	450.00	650.00	1250.
	1776	—	450.00	650.00	1250.
	1777	—	450.00	650.00	1250.
	1778	—	450.00	650.00	1250.
	1779	—	450.00	650.00	1250.
	1780	—	450.00	650.00	1250.
	1781	—	450.00	650.00	1250.
	1783	—	450.00	650.00	1250.
	1784	—	450.00	650.00	1250.
	1786	—	450.00	650.00	1250.
	1789	—	450.00	650.00	1250.
	1790	—	450.00	650.00	1250.

Obv. leg: LEOPOLDUS II D.G.H.

C#	Date	Mintage	Fine	VF	XF
28a	1790	—	600.00	800.00	1500.

Obv. leg: LEOPOLDUS II D.G.R.I.

C#	Date	Mintage	Fine	VF	XF
28b	1790	—	500.00	750.00	1400.

10.461 gm.
Obv: Lily. Rev: St. John.

C#	Date	Mintage	Fine	VF	XF
39	1791		600.00	800.00	1500.
	1793		600.00	800.00	1500.
	1794		600.00	800.00	1500.
	1796		600.00	800.00	1500.
	1797		600.00	800.00	1500.
	1798		600.00	800.00	1500.
	1799		600.00	800.00	1500.
	1800		600.00	800.00	1500.
	1801		600.00	800.00	1500.

.998 GOLD, 10.411 gm.
Obv: Lily. Rev: St. John.

C#	Date	Mintage	Fine	VF	XF
43	1801	—	1000.	2000.	2800.
	1803	—	800.00	1500.	2400.

C#	Date	Mintage	Fine	VF	XF
52	1803	—	750.00	1000.	2000.
	1804	—	750.00	1000.	2000.
	1805	—	600.00	900.00	1750.
	1806	—	600.00	900.00	1750.
	1807	—	600.00	900.00	1750.

C#	Date	Mintage	Fine	VF	XF
61	1815	—	750.00	1000.	2000.
	1816	—	750.00	1000.	2000.
	1818	—	750.00	1000.	2000.
	1820	—	750.00	1000.	2000.
	1823	—	750.00	1000.	2000.

C#	Date	Mintage	Fine	VF	XF
77	1824	—	500.00	800.00	1500.
	1825	—	500.00	800.00	1500.
	1829	—	500.00	800.00	1500.
	1834	—	500.00	800.00	1500.
	1836	—	500.00	800.00	1500.

OTTANTA (80) FIORINI

1.000 GOLD, 32.65gm.

C#	Date	Mintage	Fine	VF	XF
78	1827	—	1200.	2200.	4000.
	1828	—	1200.	2200.	4000.

1ST PROVISIONAL GOV'T.

(1859)

FIORINO

.917 SILVER, 6.88 gm.

C#	Date	Mintage	Fine	VF	XF
79	1859	—	20.00	40.00	75.00

RUSPONE

.998 GOLD 10.47 gm
Obv: Lily. Rev: St. John.

C#	Date	Mintage	Fine	VF	XF
80	1859	—	1000.	2200.	3400.

2ND PROVISIONAL GOV'T.

(Italian 1859-1861)

CENTESIMO

COPPER

C#	Date	Mintage	VF	XF	Unc
81	1859	13.163	10.00	25.00	50.00

2 CENTESIMI

COPPER

C#	Date	Mintage	VF	XF	Unc
82	1859	11.012	5.00	15.00	30.00

5 CENTESIMI

COPPER

C#	Date	Mintage	VF	XF	Unc
83	1859	13.705	5.00	20.00	50.00

CINQUANTA (50) CENTESIMI

.900 SILVER, 2.5 gm.

C#	Date	Mintage	VF	XF	Unc
84	1860	2.430	60.00	75.00	100.00
	1861	1.222	500.00	700.00	1000.

LIRA

.900 SILVER, 5.00 gm.

Rev: No dash between FIRENZE and date.

C#	Date	Mintage	VF	XF	Unc
85.1	1859	.061	20.00	50.00	150.00
	1860	1.655	20.00	50.00	100.00

Rev: With dash between FIRENZE and date.

C#	Date	Mintage	VF	XF	Unc
85.2	1860	Inc. Ab.	10.00	30.00	80.00

2 LIRE

.900 SILVER, 10.00 gm.

C#	Date	Mintage	VF	XF	Unc
86	1860	.559	50.00	150.00	300.00
	1861	.164	300.00	700.00	1500.

VENICE

VENEZIA

A seaport of Venetia was founded by refugees from the Hun invasions. From that time until the arrival of Napoleon in 1797, it maintained a state of quasi-independence despite the antagonism of jealous Italian states and the Ottoman Turks. Napoleon handed it to Austria. Upon defeat of the Austrians by Prussia in 1860, Venice became a part of the united Kingdom of Italy.

RULERS

Alvise Mocenigo IV (Doge) 1763-1778
Paulo Renier (Doge) 1779-1789
Lodovico Manin (Doge) 1789-1797
Franz II (of Austria) 1798-1806

MINTMARKS

A - Vienna
F - Hall
V - Venice
ZV - Zecca Venezia - Venice

MONETARY SYSTEM

12 Denari = 1 Soldo
20 Soldi = 1 Lira
124 Soldi = 1 Ducatone
140 Soldi = 1 Scudo = 1 Tallero
= 1 Zecchino
2 Scudi = 1 Doppia

WEIGHTS

Zechhino = 3.4 gm.
Doppia = 6.8 gm.

NOTE: Venice struck many types of gold coins using billon or silver coinage dies. They also struck many denominations from the same dies, so it is most important to check the weight to determine the proper denomination.

DOGES OF VENICE

6 DENARI

BILLON
Obv. leg: S.M.V. PAVL RAINER around figures, value.
Rev. leg: DEFENS NOSTER, standing figure.

C#	Date	Mintage	Fine	VF	XF
84	ND	—	3.50	10.00	25.00

12 DENARI

BILLON
Obv. leg: S.M.V. ALOY....

C#	Date	Mintage	Fine	VF	XF
49	ND	—	5.00	8.50	20.00

Obv. leg: S M V PAVL RAINER around figures, value.
Rev. leg: DEFENS NOSTER around standing figure.

C#	Date	Mintage	Fine	VF	XF
85	ND	—	4.00	7.00	20.00

Obv. leg: SMV LVDO MANIN around figures, value.
Rev. leg: DEFENS NOSTER around standing figure.

C#	Date	Mintage	Fine	VF	XF
118	ND	—	50.00	100.00	200.00

5 SOLDI

.900 SILVER
Obv. leg: S.M.V. ALOY MOCENI around lion, date.
Rev. leg: IVDICIVM RECTVM around Justice.

C#	Date	Mintage	Fine	VF	XF
50	1763	—	6.50	10.00	20.00
	1777	—	6.50	10.00	20.00
	1778	—	6.50	10.00	20.00

Obv. leg: SMV LVDOV MANIN around lion, date.
Rev: Similar to C#50.

C#	Date	Mintage	Fine	VF	XF
119	1789	—	15.00	30.00	100.00
	1797	—	15.00	30.00	100.00

10 SOLDI

.900 SILVER, 21mm.
Obv. leg: ALOY MOCENI D., standing figure, date.
Rev. leg: SANCT MARCVS around lion.

C#	Date	Mintage	Fine	VF	XF
51	1763	—	6.50	10.00	20.00
	1777	—	6.50	10.00	20.00
	1778	—	6.50	10.00	20.00

Obv. leg: PAVL RAINER D., standing figure, date.
Rev: Similar to C#51.

C#	Date	Mintage	Fine	VF	XF
87	1781	—	7.50	12.00	25.00

Obv. leg: LVDO MANIN D. around standing figure, date.
Rev: Similar to C#51.

C#	Date	Mintage	Fine	VF	XF
120	1789	—	30.00	60.00	150.00
	1791	—	30.00	60.00	150.00
	1797	—	30.00	60.00	150.00

15 SOLDI

SILVER, 24mm.
Similar to 10 Soldi, C#51.

C#	Date	Mintage	Fine	VF	XF
52	1763	—	7.50	15.00	35.00
	1777	—	7.50	15.00	35.00
	1778	—	7.50	15.00	35.00

Similar to 10 Soldi, C#87.

C#	Date	Mintage	Fine	VF	XF
88	1781	—	8.50	20.00	50.00

Similar to 10 Soldi, C#120.

C#	Date	Mintage	Fine	VF	XF
121	1789*	—	150.00	300.00	500.00
	1791	—	150.00	300.00	500.00
	1797	—	150.00	300.00	500.00

***NOTE:** A variety exists in which 8 appears as 3.

1/8 DUCATO

SILVER, 26mm.
Obv. leg: SMV ALOY MOCENI around lion.
Rev: Figure, legend.

C#	Date	Mintage	Fine	VF	XF
58	ND	—	12.50	20.00	50.00

25mm.
Obv. leg: SMV PAVL RAINER around lion.

C#	Date	Mintage	Fine	VF	XF
94	ND	—	15.00	25.00	60.00

Obv. leg: SMV LUDOVICO MANIN DUCE, lion.

C#	Date	Mintage	Fine	VF	XF
127	ND	—	17.50	30.00	75.00

1/8 TALLERO
(= 17-1/2 Soldi)

SILVER
Obv. leg: ALOY MOCENI around lion.
Rev. leg: REPVBLICA VENETA around bust.

C#	Date	Mintage	Fine	VF	XF
54	ND	—	15.00	25.00	50.00

Obv. leg: PAVL RAINER DUCE, around lion.

C#	Date	Mintage	Fine	VF	XF
90	ND	—	10.00	20.00	40.00

Obv. leg: PAULO RAINERIO DUCE around lion, date.
Rev. leg: RESPUBLICA VENETA around bust.

C#	Date	Mintage	Fine	VF	XF
101	1780	—	12.50	20.00	50.00
	1781	—	12.50	20.00	50.00
	1786	—	12.50	20.00	50.00

Obv. leg: LUDIVICO MANIN DUCE around cross.
Rev. leg: SANCTVS MARCVS, lion.

C#	Date	Mintage	Fine	VF	XF
123	ND	—	9.00	15.00	40.00

Obv. leg: LUDIVICO MANIN DUCE around lion, date.
Rev. leg: RESPUBLICA VENETA, bust.

C#	Date	Mintage	Fine	VF	XF
134	1790	—	50.00	100.00	150.00
	1794	—	50.00	100.00	150.00
	1796	—	50.00	100.00	150.00

30 SOLDI

SILVER
Obv. leg: SANCTVS MARCVS VENETA around winged lion.
Rev: Seated ruler, legend around, date.

C#	Date	Mintage	Fine	VF	XF
53	1767	—	10.00	20.00	40.00
	1768	—	10.00	20.00	40.00
	1769	—	10.00	20.00	40.00
	1770	—	10.00	20.00	40.00
	1771	—	10.00	20.00	40.00
	1772	—	10.00	20.00	40.00
	1773	—	10.00	20.00	40.00
	1774	—	10.00	20.00	40.00
	1775	—	10.00	20.00	40.00
	1776	—	10.00	20.00	40.00
	1777	—	10.00	20.00	40.00
	1778	—	10.00	20.00	40.00

Similar to C#53.

C#	Date	Mintage	Fine	VF	XF
89	1781	—	12.50	25.00	50.00
	1782	—	12.50	25.00	50.00
	1783	—	12.50	25.00	50.00
	1784	—	12.50	25.00	50.00

Similar to C#53.

C#	Date	Mintage	Fine	VF	XF
122	1789	—	10.00	20.00	40.00

31 SOLDI = 1/4 DUCATO

SILVER, 29mm.
Obv. leg: S.M.V. ALOY MOCENI around lion.
Rev: Figure, legend.

C#	Date	Mintage	Fine	VF	XF
59	ND	—	20.00	35.00	75.00

Obv. leg: S.M.V. PAVL RAINER around lion.

C#	Date	Mintage	Fine	VF	XF
95	ND	—	20.00	40.00	75.00

Obv. leg: S.M.V. LUDIVICO MANIN around lion.

C#	Date	Mintage	Fine	VF	XF
128	ND	—	40.00	65.00	110.00

QVAR (1/4) DUCATO

SILVER, 27-30mm.
Obv. leg: SMV ALOY MOCENI around St. Mark.
DG mintmark. Rev: Winged lion, legend.

C#	Date	Mintage	Fine	VF	XF
62	ND	—	15.00	25.00	50.00

28 or 30 mm.
Obv. leg: SMV PAVL RAINER around St. Mark.
Rev: Similar to C#62.

C#	Date	Mintage	Fine	VF	XF
98	ND	—	15.00	25.00	50.00

Obv. leg: SMV LUDIVICO MANIN around St. Mark.
Rev: Similar to C#62.

C#	Date	Mintage	Fine	VF	XF
131	ND	—	15.00	25.00	50.00

35 SOLDI

SILVER, 29mm.
Obv. leg: ALOY MOCENI DUCE around winged lion, date.
Rev: Similar to C#102.

C#	Date	Mintage	Fine	VF	XF
65	1766	—	45.00	75.00	125.00

33mm
Obv. leg: SMV ALOY MOCENI around cross. Mint master's initials D.G. Rev. leg: SANCTVS MARCVS around lion.

C#	Date	Mintage	Fine	VF	XF
55	ND	—	20.00	40.00	75.00

GOLD, 15-16mm.
Obv. leg: S.M. VEN. MOCEN around St. Mark and kneeling doge. Rev. leg: EGO SVM LVX MVN around Christ.

C#	Date	Mintage	Fine	VF	XF
69	ND	—	250.00	400.00	675.00

SILVER

C#	Date	Mintage	Fine	VF	XF
102	1780	—	25.00	40.00	75.00

Obv. leg: SMV PAVL RAINER around cross.
Rev. leg: SANCTVS MARCVS around lion.

C#	Date	Mintage	Fine	VF	XF
91	ND	—	15.00	25.00	50.00

GOLD, 15-16mm.
Obv. leg: S.M.VEN. PAVL RAINE around St. Mark and kneeling Doge.
Rev. leg: EGO SVM LVX MVN around Christ.

C#	Date	Mintage	Fine	VF	XF
105	ND	—	150.00	250.00	500.00

SILVER, 28mm.
Obv. leg: LUDIVICO MANIN DUCE, winged lion, date.
Rev: Similar to C#102.

C#	Date	Mintage	Fine	VF	XF
135	1790	—	75.00	150.00	300.00
	1794	—	75.00	150.00	300.00
	1796	—	75.00	150.00	300.00

GOLD, 14-16mm.
Obv. leg: LVDO MANIN....

C#	Date	Mintage	Fine	VF	XF
138	ND	—	400.00	800.00	1500.

62 SOLDI

SILVER, 32mm.
Obv. leg: ALOY MOCENI around lion.
Mint master's initials D.G.

C#	Date	Mintage	Fine	VF	XF
60	ND	—	35.00	60.00	100.00

33mm.
Obv. leg: PAVL RAINER....

C#	Date	Mintage	Fine	VF	XF
96	ND	—	45.00	75.00	125.00

34mm.
Obv. leg: LUDIVICO MANIN around lion.

C#	Date	Mintage	Fine	VF	XF
129	ND	—	55.00	90.00	150.00

MEDI (1/2) DUCATONE

SILVER, 32-34mm.
Obv. leg: ALOY MOCENI around St. Mark.
Rev: Winged lion, legend.

C#	Date	Mintage	Fine	VF	XF
63	ND	—	17.50	30.00	50.00

Obv. leg: PAVL RAINER around St. Mark.
Rev: Similar to C#63.

C#	Date	Mintage	Fine	VF	XF
99	ND	—	15.00	25.00	45.00

Obv. leg: LUDIVICO MANIN around St. Mark.
Rev: Similar to C#63.

C#	Date	Mintage	Fine	VF	XF
132	ND	—	15.00	25.00	45.00

70 SOLDI

SILVER, 33mm.
Obv. leg: S.M.V. ALOY MOCENI around winged lion, date.
Rev: Similar to 1/2 Tallero, C#136.

C#	Date	Mintage	Fine	VF	XF
66	1764	—	60.00	100.00	175.00
	1766	—	60.00	100.00	175.00

Obv. leg: S.M.V. ALOY MOCENI around cross.
mint master's initials D.G.
Rev. leg: SANCTVS MARCVS around lion.

C#	Date	Mintage	Fine	VF	XF
56	ND	—	30.00	50.00	85.00

GOLD, 18-19mm.
Obv. leg: S.M. VEN ALOY MOCEN around St. Mark and kneeling Doge.
Rev. leg: EGO SVM LVX MVN around Christ.

C#	Date	Mintage	Fine	VF	XF
70	ND	—	275.00	600.00	1000.

Obv. leg: ALOY MOCENI around cross.
Rev. leg: SANCTVS MARCVS, lion.
Mintmaster's initials: G.P.

C#	Date	Mintage	Fine	VF	XF
81	ND	—	—	—	—

SILVER, 33mm.
Obv. leg: PAVL RAINER DUCE around winged lion, date.
Rev: Similar to 140 Soldi, C#104.

C#	Date	Mintage	Fine	VF	XF
103	1780	—	30.00	50.00	85.00
	1781	—	30.00	50.00	85.00
	1786	—	30.00	50.00	85.00

Obv. leg: SMV PAVL RAINER DUCE around cross, date.
Rev. leg: SANCTVS MARCVS around lion.

C#	Date	Mintage	Fine	VF	XF
92	ND	—	20.00	35.00	60.00

GOLD, 18mm.
Obv. leg: S.M. VENET PAVL RAINE around St. Mark and kneeling Doge.
Rev. leg: EGO SVM LVX MVN around Christ.

C#	Date	Mintage	Fine	VF	XF
106	ND	—	150.00	250.00	600.00

Obv. leg: PAVL RAINER around cross.
Rev. leg: SANCTVS MARCVS around lion.

C#	Date	Mintage	Fine	VF	XF
115	ND	—	—	—	—

C#	Date	Mintage	Fine	VF	XF
136	1789	—	200.00	400.00	750.00
	1790	—	200.00	400.00	750.00
	1791	—	200.00	400.00	750.00
	1792	—	200.00	400.00	750.00
	1796	—	200.00	400.00	750.00
	1797	—	200.00	400.00	750.00

Obv. leg: SMV LUDIVICO MANIN DUCE around cross.
Rev. leg: SANCTVS MARCVS around lion.

C#	Date	Mintage	Fine	VF	XF
125	ND	—	20.00	35.00	60.00

.997 GOLD, 20mm.
Obv. leg: LVDOV MANIN SM VENET around St. Mark and kneeling Doge.
Rev. leg: EGO SVM LVX MVN around Christ.

C#	Date	Mintage	Fine	VF	XF
139	ND	—	400.00	800.00	1500.

Obv. leg: LVD. MANIN around cross.
Rev. leg: SANCTVS MARCVS around lion.

C#	Date	Mintage	Fine	VF	XF
149	ND	—	750.00	1250.	2000.

124 SOLDI

SILVER, 41mm.
Obv. leg: S.M.V. ALOY MOCENI D. around winged lion.
Rev: Standing figure, legend, value.

C#	Date	Mintage	Fine	VF	XF
61	ND	—	90.00	150.00	250.00

Obv. leg: S.M.V. PAVL RAINER D. around winged lion,

Doge. Rev: Similar to C#61.

C#	Date	Mintage	Fine	VF	XF
97	ND	—	90.00	150.00	250.00

Obv. leg: S.M.V. LVDOVI MANIN DUX around winged lion, Dodge. Rev: Similar to C#61.

C#	Date	Mintage	Fine	VF	XF
130	ND	—	90.00	150.00	250.00

DUCATO

SILVER

C#	Date	Mintage	Fine	VF	XF
64	ND*	—	40.00	65.00	100.00

Rev: Similar to C#64.

C#	Date	Mintage	Fine	VF	XF
100	ND *BC	—	35.00	50.00	75.00
	*FD	—	35.00	50.00	75.00

NOTE: Many different mint masters' initials appear on the obverse of these coins.

Obv. leg: S.M.V. LVDOV MANIN around St. Mark and kneeling Doge. Rev: Similar to C#64.

C#	Date	Mintage	Fine	VF	XF
133	ND	—	35.00	50.00	75.00

140 SOLDI

SILVER

Obv. leg: S.M.V. ALOY MOCENI around cross. Rev. leg: SANCTVS MARCVS around winged lion.

C#	Date	Mintage	Fine	VF	XF
57	ND	—	45.00	75.00	125.00

Obv. leg: ALOY MOCENI DUCE around winged lion, date. Rev. leg: RESPUBLICA VENETA around bust.

C#	Date	Mintage	Fine	VF	XF
67	1764	—	100.00	175.00	300.00
	1766	—	100.00	175.00	300.00

Similar to C#67, modified design.

C#	Date	Mintage	Fine	VF	XF
68	1768	—	75.00	125.00	200.00
	1769	—	75.00	125.00	200.00

GOLD

C#	Date	Mintage	Fine	VF	XF
71	ND	—	150.00	200.00	350.00

Similar to C#57.

C#	Date	Mintage	Fine	VF	XF
82	ND	—	—	—	—

SILVER

Obv. leg: S.M.V. PAVL RAINER around cross. Rev. leg: SANCTVS MARCVS around winged lion.

C#	Date	Mintage	Fine	VF	XF
93	ND	—	45.00	75.00	100.00

C#	Date	Mintage	Fine	VF	XF
104	1781	—	50.00	80.00	125.00
	1782	—	50.00	80.00	125.00
	1783	—	50.00	80.00	125.00
	1784	—	50.00	80.00	125.00
	1785	—	50.00	80.00	125.00
	1786	—	50.00	80.00	125.00
	1787	—	50.00	80.00	125.00
	1788	—	50.00	80.00	125.00

GOLD

Obv. leg: PAVL RAINE....

C#	Date	Mintage	Fine	VF	XF
107	ND	—	150.00	200.00	350.00

Similar to C#93.

C#	Date	Mintage	Fine	VF	XF
116	ND	—	—	—	—

SILVER

Obv. leg: S.M.V. LVDOV MANIN around cross. Rev. leg: SANCTVS MARCVS around winged lion.

C#	Date	Mintage	Fine	VF	XF
126	ND	—	40.00	65.00	100.00

C#	Date	Mintage	Fine	VF	XF
137	1789	—	75.00	150.00	500.00
	1790	—	75.00	150.00	500.00
	1791	—	75.00	150.00	500.00
	1792	—	75.00	150.00	500.00
	1794	—	75.00	150.00	500.00
	1795	—	75.00	150.00	500.00
	1796	—	75.00	150.00	500.00
	1797	—	75.00	150.00	500.00

Obv. leg: LVDOV MANIN....

C#	Date	Mintage	Fine	VF	XF
140	ND	—	400.00	800.00	1000.

Similar to C#126.

C#	Date	Mintage	Fine	VF	XF
150	ND	—	850.00	1400.	2400.

DOPPIA

SILVER

Similar to Ducato, C#64, but twice as thick.

C#	Date	Mintage	Fine	VF	XF
64a	ND	—	275.00	450.00	750.00

GOLD

Obv. leg: ALOY MOCENI around cross. Rev. leg: SANCTVS MARCVS around winged lion.

C#	Date	Mintage	Fine	VF	XF
83	ND	—	—	—	—

SILVER

Similar to Ducato, C#100, but twice as thick.

C#	Date	Mintage	Fine	VF	XF
100a	ND	—	200.00	350.00	575.00

GOLD

Obv. leg: PAVL RAINE around cross. Rev. leg: SANCTVS MARCVS around winged lion.

C#	Date	Mintage	Fine	VF	XF
117	ND	—	—	—	—

SILVER

Similar to Ducato, C#133, but twice as thick.

C#	Date	Mintage	Fine	VF	XF
133a	ND	—	250.00	425.00	700.00

GOLD

Obv. leg: LVD. MANIN around cross. Rev. leg: SANCTVS MARCVS around winged lion.

C#	Date	Mintage	Fine	VF	XF
151	ND	—	500.00	1000.	2000.

Obv. leg: LVDO MANIN SM VENET around St. Mark and kneeling Doge. Rev. leg: SIT. T. XPE. DAT. Q. TV. REGIS. ISTE. DVCA around Christ.

C#	Date	Mintage	Fine	VF	XF
141	ND	—	1800.	3000.	5000.

4 ZECCHINI

GOLD, 21-22mm., 3.20-3.45 gm.
Similar to 10 Zecchini, C#110, leg: PAVL RAINE....

C#	Date	Mintage	Fine	VF	XF
108	ND	—	—	—	—

5 ZECCHINI

.997 GOLD, 24.5mm., 18.75 gm.
Similar to 10 Zecchini, C#146, leg: LVD.MANIN....

C#	Date	Mintage	Fine	VF	XF
142	ND	—	—	Rare	—

6 ZECCHINI

.997 GOLD, 18mm., 20.17 gm.
Similar to 10 Zecchini, C#146, leg: LVD.MANIN....

C#	Date	Mintage	Fine	VF	XF
143	ND	—	—	—	—

8 ZECCHINI

.986 GOLD, 50mm., 27.60 gm.
Similar to 50 Zecchini, C#79, leg: ALOY MOCENICO.

C#	Date	Mintage	Fine	VF	XF
72	ND	—	—	—	—

Similar to 10 Zecchini, C#110.

C#	Date	Mintage	Fine	VF	XF
109	ND	—	—	—	—

50mm., 27.87-28.04 gm.
Similar to 10 Zecchini, C#146, leg: LVD.MANIN....

C#	Date	Mintage	Fine	VF	XF
144	ND	—	—	—	—

9 ZECCHINI

.986 GOLD, 50mm., 34.83-44.77 gm.
Similar to 10 Zecchini, C#146, leg: LVD.MANIN....

C#	Date	Mintage	Fine	VF	XF
145	ND	—	—	—	—

10 ZECCHINI

.986 GOLD, 50mm., 34.82-35.2 gm.
Similar to 50 Zecchini, C#79, leg: ALOY MOCENICO....

C#	Date	Mintage	Fine	VF	XF
73	ND	—	—	—	—

34.65 gm.
Obv. leg: PAVL RAINER....
Rev: Similar to 50 Zecchini, C#79.

C#	Date	Mintage	Fine	VF	XF
110	ND	—	—	—	—

.997 GOLD, 34.50 gm.
Obv. leg: LUDOV.MANIN.
Rev: Similar to 50 Zecchini, C#79.

C#	Date	Mintage	Fine	VF	XF
146	ND	—	—	Rare	—

12 ZECCHINI

.986 GOLD, 50mm., 39.6-41.8 gm.
Similar to 50 Zecchini, C#79, leg: ALOY MOCENICO....

C#	Date	Mintage	Fine	VF	XF
74	ND	—	—	—	—

18 ZECCHINI

.986 GOLD, 62.67 gm.
Similar to 50 Zecchini, C#79, leg: ALOY MOCENICO....

C#	Date	Mintage	Fine	VF	XF
75	ND	—	—	—	—

65.59 gm.
Similar to 10 Zecchini, C#110, leg: PAVL RAINE....

C#	Date	Mintage	Fine	VF	XF
111	ND	—	—	—	—

20 ZECCHINI

.986 GOLD, 20mm., 69.7 gm.
Similar to 50 Zecchini, C#79, leg: ALOY MOCENI....

C#	Date	Mintage	Fine	VF	XF
76	ND	—	—	—	—

24 ZECCHINI

.986 GOLD, 83.63 gm.
Similar to 10 Zecchini, C#110, leg: PAVL RAINE....

C#	Date	Mintage	Fine	VF	XF
112	ND	—	—	—	—

25 ZECCHINI

.986 GOLD, 51mm., 86.65 gm.
Similar to 50 Zecchini, C#79, leg: ALOY MOCENI....

C#	Date	Mintage	Fine	VF	XF
77	ND	—	—	—	—

30 ZECCHINI

.986 GOLD, 51mm., 104.7 gm.
Similar to 50 Zecchini, C#79, leg: ALOY MOCENI....

C#	Date	Mintage	Fine	VF	XF
78	ND	—	—	—	—

Similar to 10 Zecchini, C#110, leg: PAVL RAINE....

C#	Date	Mintage	Fine	VF	XF
112.5	ND	—	—	—	—

40 ZECCHINI

.986 GOLD
Similar to 10 Zecchini, C#110, leg: PAVL RAINE....

C#	Date	Mintage	Fine	VF	XF
113	ND	—	—	—	—

50 ZECCHINI

.986 GOLD, 50mm., 174.77 gm.
Obv. leg: ALOY MOCENI....

C#	Date	Mintage	Fine	VF	XF
79	ND	—	—	—	—

76mm., 192.50 gm.
Similar to 10 Zecchini, C#110, leg: PAVL RAINE....

C#	Date	Mintage	Fine	VF	XF
114	ND	—	—	—	—

174.25 gm.
Similar to 10 Zecchini, C#146, leg: LVD.MANIN....

C#	Date	Mintage	Fine	VF	XF
147	ND	—	—	—	—

55 ZECCHINI

.986 GOLD
Similar to 10 Zecchini, C#110, leg: PAVL RAINE....

C#	Date	Mintage	Fine	VF	XF
114.5	ND	—	—	—	—

60 ZECCHINI

.986 GOLD
Similar to 50 Zecchini, C#79, leg: ALOY MOCENI....

C#	Date	Mintage	Fine	VF	XF
79.5	ND	—	—	—	—

100 ZECCHINI

.986 GOLD, 76mm., 349.5 gm.
Similar to 50 Zecchini, C#79, leg: ALOY MOCENI....

C#	Date	Mintage	Fine	VF	XF
80	ND	—	—	—	—

105 ZECCHINI

.986 GOLD, 79mm., 367.41 gm.
Similar to 10 Zecchini, C#146, leg: LVD.MANIN....

C#	Date	Mintage	Fine	VF	XF
148	ND	—	—	—	—

PROVISIONAL GOV'T

(1797-1798)

DIECE (10) LIRE

.826 SILVER, 28.47 gm.
Obv: ZECCA. V: below Liberty.

C#	Date	Mintage	Fine	VF	XF
155	1797	—	150.00	250.00	500.00
	1.797	—	150.00	250.00	500.00

Obv: Z V below Liberty.

C#	Date	Mintage	Fine	VF	XF
155a	1797	—	150.00	250.00	500.00

AUSTRIAN OCCUPATION

MEZZA (1/2) LIRA

.250 SILVER, 2.2 gm.
Obv: Imperial eagle. Rev: Value, date within wreath.

C#	Date	Mintage	Fine	VF	XF
160	1800	—	30.00	60.00	125.00

NOTE: Two varieties exist.

4.5 gm.
Rev: Value, date within ornate border.

C#	Date	Mintage	Fine	VF	XF
163	1802	—	40.00	80.00	125.00
	1802A		Reported, not confirmed.		
	1802F		Reported, not confirmed.		

UNA (1) LIRE

.250 SILVER, 5.3 gm.

C#	Date	Mintage	Fine	VF	XF
161	1800	—	30.00	50.00	100.00

11.36 gm.
Rev: Value, date within ornate border.

C#	Date	Mintage	Fine	VF	XF
164	1802	—	50.00	100.00	200.00
	1802A	—	Reported, not confirmed		
	1802F	—	Reported, not confirmed		

1-1/2 LIRE

.250 SILVER, 8.49 gm.
Obv: Imperial eagle. Rev: Value, date within wreath.

C#	Date	Mintage	Fine	VF	XF
165	1802	—	Reported, not confirmed		
	1802A	—	30.00	50.00	100.00
	1802F	—	45.00	70.00	140.00

DUE (2) LIRE

.250 SILVER, 7.95-9.46 gm.
Obv: Large imperial eagle.
Rev: Value, date within wreath.

C#	Date	Mintage	Fine	VF	XF
162	1801	—	40.00	70.00	175.00

NOTE: Three varieties exist.

Obv: Smaller imperial eagle, uncollared strike.

C#	Date	Mintage	Fine	VF	XF
162a	1801	—	60.00	100.00	225.00

ZECCHINO

.987 GOLD, 3.49 gm.
Obv: St. Mark, Doge FRANC. II. S.M. VENET.
Rev: Imperial eagle SIT.T.XPE.DAT.Q.TV-REGIS.
ISTE.DVCA

C#	Date	Mintage	Fine	VF	XF
166	ND	—	500.00	750.00	1500.

Rev: Christ holding orb.

C#	Date	Mintage	Fine	VF	XF
166a	ND	—	500.00	750.00	1500.

REVOLUTIONARY ISSUES

(1848-1849)

MONETARY SYSTEM

100 Centesimi = 1 Lire

CENTESIMO

COPPER

C#	Date	Mintage	Fine	VF	XF	Unc
181	1849ZV	—	5.50	11.50	22.50	40.00

3 CENTESIMI

COPPER

C#	Date	Mintage	Fine	VF	XF	Unc
182	1849ZV	—	3.00	6.00	12.00	22.50

5 CENTESIMI

COPPER

C#	Date	Mintage	Fine	VF	XF	Unc
183	1849ZV	—	3.00	6.00	12.00	22.50

15 CENTESIMI

.229 SILVER, 1.26 gm.

C#	Date	Mintage	Fine	VF	XF	Unc
184	1848	—	3.25	6.50	13.50	25.00

25 CENTESIMI

.900 SILVER, 1.25 gm.

C#	Date	Mintage	Fine	VF	XF	Unc
A184	1848ZV	—	75.00	150.00	300.00	500.00

5 LIRE

.900 SILVER, 25 gm.

C#	Date	Mintage	Fine	VF	XF	Unc
185	1848	—	75.00	125.00	250.00	375.00

Edge inscription: DIO BENEDITE L'ITALIA.

C#	Date	Mintage	Fine	VF	XF	Unc
186	1848V	—	70.00	110.00	225.00	375.00

Edge inscription: DIO BENEDETE L'ITALIA.

C#	Date	Mintage	Fine	VF	XF	Unc
186a	1848V	—	125.00	250.00	350.00	500.00

20 LIRE

.900 GOLD, 6.45 gm.
Similar to 5 Lire, C#185.

C#	Date	Mintage	Fine	VF	XF	Unc
187	1848	—	400.00	650.00	900.00	1250.

PALMA NOVA

Was ceded to France by Austria in 1806 and was returned to Austria in 1814. In 1860 it was incorporated in the united Kingdom of Italy.

(In Venetia)

EMERGENCY ISSUES

(French Defenders 1814)

25 CENTESIMI

BILLON

C#	Date	Mintage	Fine	VF	XF
1	1814	(Pattern?)	—	Rare	—

50 CENTESIMI

BILLON

C#	Date	Mintage	Fine	VF	XF
2	1814	—	115.00	175.00	250.00

ITALY

The Italian Republic, a 700-mile-long peninsula extending into the heart of the Mediterranean Sea, has an area of 116,303 sq. mi. (301,223 sq. km.) and a population of 56.2 million. Capital: Rome. The economy centers about agriculture, manufacturing, forestry and fishing. Machinery, textiles, clothing and motor vehicles are exported.

From the fall of Rome until modern times, 'Italy' was little more than a geographical expression. Although nominally included in the Empire of Charlemagne and the Holy Roman Empire, it was in reality divided into a number of independent states and kingdoms presided over by wealthy families, soldiers of fortune or hereditary rulers. The 19th century unification movement fostered by Mazzini, Garibaldi and Cavour attained fruition in 1860-70 with the creation of the Kingdom of Italy and the installation of Victor Emmanuel, king of Sardinia, as king of Italy. Benito Mussolini came to power during the post-World War I period of economic and political unrest, installed a Fascist dictatorship with a figurehead king as titular Head of State, and allied with Germany for the pursuit of World War II. Following the defeat of the Axis powers, the Italian monarchy was dissolved by plebiscite, and the Italian Republic proclaimed.

RULERS

Vittorio Emanuele II, 1861-1878
Umberto I, 1878-1900
Vittorio Emanuele III, 1900-1946

MINTMARKS

B - Bologna (1861)
BI - Birmingham (1893-1894)
FIRENZE - Florence (1861)
H - Birmingham (1866-1867)
KB - Berlin (1894)
M - Milan (1861-1875)
N - Naples (1861-1867)
OM - Strasbourg (1866-1867)
R - Rome (All coins from 1878 have R except where noted).
T - Turin (1861-1867)
No MM - Paris (1862-1866)

MONETARY SYSTEM

100 Centesimi = 1 Lira

CENTESIMO

COPPER

Y#	Date	Mintage	Fine	VF	XF	Unc
6	1861M	26.720	.60	1.50	3.00	6.00
	1861N	48.280	3.75	9.00	20.00	30.00
	1862/1N	37.500	25.00	40.00	55.00	75.00
	1862N	Inc. Ab.	1.25	2.00	3.25	7.00
	1867M	72.759	.80	1.25	2.75	5.00
	1867T	5.000	10.00	20.00	35.00	60.00

Y#	Date	Mintage	Fine	VF	XF	Unc
22	1895R	13.860	.80	1.30	2.25	4.50
	1896R	3.730	.80	1.30	2.25	4.50
	1897R	1.845	10.00	17.50	35.00	75.00
	1899R	1.287	1.25	1.50	2.75	5.00
	1900R	10.000	.85	1.30	2.25	5.00

BRONZE

Y#	Date	Mintage	Fine	VF	XF	Unc
35	1902R	.026	125.00	200.00	350.00	500.00
	1903R	5.655	.85	1.30	2.00	4.00
	1904/0R	14.626	5.00	10.00	20.00	40.00
	1904R	Inc. Ab.	.85	1.30	2.25	4.00
	1905/0R	8.531	5.00	10.00	20.00	40.00
	1905R	Inc. Ab.	1.00	1.50	2.25	4.00
	1908R	3.859	.65	2.00	2.25	4.00

Y#	Date	Mintage	Fine	VF	XF	Unc
43	1908R	.057	90.00	150.00	225.00	375.00
	1909R	3.539	.50	1.25	2.00	4.00
	1910R	3.599	.50	1.25	2.00	4.00
	1911R	.700	5.00	10.00	15.00	30.00
	1912R	3.995	.50	1.25	2.00	4.00
	1913R	3.200	.50	1.25	2.00	4.00
	1914R	11.585	.50	1.25	2.00	4.00
	1915R	9.757	.50	1.25	2.00	4.00
	1916R	9.845	.50	1.25	2.00	4.00
	1917R	2.400	.50	1.25	2.50	4.00
	1918R	2.710	4.00	7.50	15.00	30.00

2 CENTESIMI

COPPER

Y#	Date	Mintage	Fine	VF	XF	Unc
7	1861M	37.500	.60	1.50	3.50	10.00
	1861N	23.055	.60	1.50	3.50	10.00
	1862N	33.195	.60	1.50	3.50	10.00
	1867M	54.212	.60	1.50	3.50	10.00
	1867T	5.000	2.00	4.25	8.50	17.50

Y#	Date	Mintage	Fine	VF	XF	Unc
23	1895R	.305	8.00	13.50	37.50	70.00
	1896R	.282	25.00	50.00	100.00	175.00
	1897R	4.415	.60	1.50	4.50	10.00
	1898R	4.161	.60	1.50	4.00	10.00
	1900R	2.735	.60	1.50	4.00	10.00

BRONZE

Y#	Date	Mintage	Fine	VF	XF	Unc
36	1903R	5.000	.60	1.50	3.00	10.00
	1905R	1.260	2.25	5.00	10.00	25.00
	1906R	3.145	.60	1.50	3.00	10.00
	1907R	.230	20.00	40.00	60.00	100.00
	1908R	1.518	.60	1.50	3.00	10.00

Y#	Date	Mintage	Fine	VF	XF	Unc
44	1908R	.298	9.00	15.00	25.00	100.00

Y#	Date	Mintage	Fine	VF	XF	Unc
44	1909R	2.419	.60	1.50	3.00	10.00
	1910R	.590	2.00	4.00	9.00	30.00
	1911R	2.777	.60	1.50	3.00	8.00
	1912R	.840	.60	1.50	3.00	10.00
	1914R	1.648	.50	1.30	2.00	7.00
	1915R	4.860	.50	1.30	2.50	7.00
	1916R	1.540	.50	1.30	2.00	7.00
	1917R	3.638	.50	1.30	2.00	7.00

5 CENTESIMI

COPPER

Y#	Date	Mintage	Fine	VF	XF	Unc
8	1861B	3.809	20.00	40.00	80.00	175.00
	1861M	210.000	.60	1.50	5.00	15.00
	1861N	103.707	.60	1.50	5.00	15.00
	1862N	106.293	.60	1.50	5.00	15.00
	1867M	24.000	.60	1.50	5.00	20.00
	1867N	46.000	.60	1.50	5.00	17.50
24	1895R	.508	7.50	12.50	25.00	75.00
	1896R	.380	7.50	12.50	25.00	75.00
	1900R	2,000	—	—	Rare	—

BRONZE

Y#	Date	Mintage	Fine	VF	XF	Unc
45	1908R	.824	12.00	25.00	50.00	75.00
	1909R	1.734	.80	1.75	3.50	20.00
	1912R	.743	1.75	3.00	6.00	30.00
	1913R	1.964	4.50	11.50	22.50	50.00
	1915R	1.038	3.50	7.50	12.50	30.00
	1918R	4.242	.80	1.75	4.00	10.00

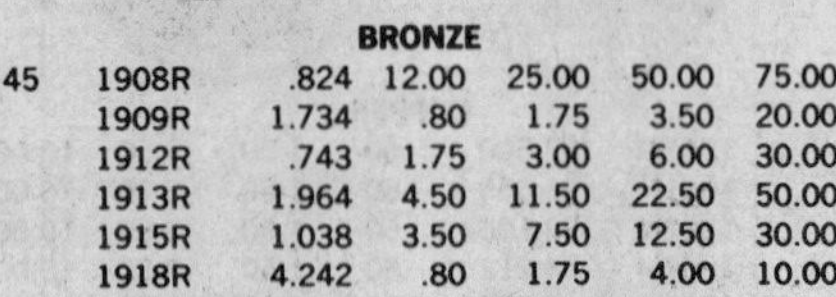

Y#	Date	Mintage	Fine	VF	XF	Unc
61	1919R	13.208	.75	2.00	2.75	10.00
	1920R	33.372	.50	1.25	2.00	5.50
	1921R	80.111	.50	1.25	2.00	5.50
	1922R	42.914	.50	1.25	2.00	5.50
	1923R	29.614	.30	.75	1.50	5.00
	1924R	20.352	.30	.75	1.50	5.00
	1925R	40.460	.30	.75	1.50	5.00
	1926R	21.158	.30	.75	1.50	5.00
	1927R	15.800	.30	.75	1.50	5.00
	1928R	16.090	.30	.75	1.50	5.00
	1929R	29.000	.30	.75	1.50	5.00
	1930R	22.694	.30	.75	1.50	5.00
	1931R	20.000	.30	.75	1.50	5.00
	1932R	11.456	.30	.75	1.50	5.00
	1933R	20.720	.30	.75	1.50	5.00
	1934R	16.000	.30	.75	1.50	5.00
	1935R	11.000	.30	.75	1.50	5.00
	1936R	9.462	.30	.75	1.50	5.00
	1937R	.972	4.50	7.00	11.50	22.50

Y#	Date	Mintage	Fine	VF	XF	Unc
77	1936R, yr. XIV	Inc. Ab.	1.75	4.00	9.00	17.50
	1937R, yr. XV	7.207	.30	.75	1.00	2.00
	1938R, yr. XVI	24.000	.20	.65	1.00	1.50
	1939R, yr. XVII	22.000	.20	.65	1.00	1.75

ALUMINUM-BRONZE

Y#	Date	Mintage	Fine	VF	XF	Unc
77a	1939R, yr. XVII	1.000	.30	.75	1.25	2.00
	1940R, yr. XVIII	9.630	.30	.75	1.00	1.75
	1941R, yr. XIX	16.340	.30	.75	.90	1.75
	1942R, yr. XX	25.200	.30	.75	1.25	2.25
	1943R, yr. XXI	13.922	.75	1.50	3.00	9.00

10 CENTESIMI

COPPER

Y#	Date	Mintage	Fine	VF	XF	Unc
9	1862M	40.000	1.00	2.50	5.50	50.00
	1862	—	1.00	2.50	5.50	25.00
	1863	80.000	1.00	2.50	5.50	25.00
	1866H	40.000	1.00	2.50	5.50	25.00
	1866M	36.000	1.00	2.50	5.50	25.00
	1866N	67.650	1.00	2.50	5.50	30.00
	1866OM	20.000	1.00	2.50	6.00	35.00
	1866.OM	Inc. Ab.	1.50	2.75	7.00	37.50
	1866T	16.350	1.00	2.50	5.50	30.00
	1866	—	15.00	25.00	50.00	150.00
	1867H	50.000	1.25	3.00	5.50	20.00
	1867M	—	3.00	3.75	6.00	25.00
	1867N	31.360	1.00	2.50	5.50	25.00
	1867OM	—	1.00	2.50	6.00	25.00
	1867.OM.	—	4.00	5.50	12.50	35.00
	1867T	18.640	1.00	2.50	5.50	25.00

Y#	Date	Mintage	Fine	VF	XF	Unc
25	1893BI	8.547	1.50	3.50	10.00	50.00
	1893R	28.000	1.50	3.50	10.00	50.00
	1894BI	32.000	1.50	3.00	10.00	50.00
	1894R	5.910	6.50	15.00	37.50	150.00

BRONZE

Y#	Date	Mintage	Fine	VF	XF	Unc
46	1908R	—	1250.	2500.	3500.	5000.

50th Anniversary of Kingdom

Y#	Date	Mintage	Fine	VF	XF	Unc
57	1911R	2.000	4.00	7.50	10.00	27.50

Y#	Date	Mintage	Fine	VF	XF	Unc
62	1919R	.986	35.00	60.00	90.00	250.00
	1920R	37.995	.30	.70	1.75	5.50
	1921R	66.510	.30	.70	1.75	5.50
	1922R	45.217	.30	.70	1.75	5.50
	1923R	31.529	.30	.70	1.75	5.50
	1924R	35.312	.30	.70	1.75	5.50
	1925R	22.370	.30	.70	1.75	5.50
	1926R	25.190	.30	.70	1.75	5.50
	1927R	22.673	.30	.70	1.75	5.50
	1928R	15.680	1.50	3.00	5.00	30.00
	1929R	15.593	.30	.70	1.75	5.50
	1930R	17.115	.60	.85	1.75	5.50
	1931R	10.750	.60	.85	1.75	5.50
	1932R	5.678	2.00	3.50	8.00	35.00
	1933R	10.250	.60	.85	1.75	5.50
	1934R	18.300	.60	.85	1.75	5.50
	1935R	10.500	.60	.85	1.75	5.50
	1936R	8.770	.90	1.50	3.75	10.00
	1937R	5.500	.50	1.00	2.75	7.50

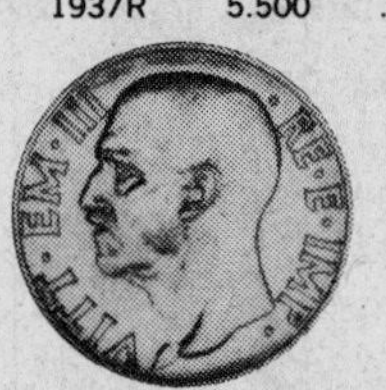

Y#	Date	Mintage	Fine	VF	XF	Unc
78	1936R, yr. XIV	Inc. Ab.	.90	1.50	2.50	8.50
	1937R, yr. XV	7.212	.50	1.00	2.50	4.00
	1938R, yr. XVI	18.750	.50	1.00	2.50	4.00
	1939R, yr. XVII	24.750	.50	1.00	2.50	4.00

ALUMINUM-BRONZE

Y#	Date	Mintage	Fine	VF	XF	Unc
78a	1939R, yr. XVII	.750	.70	1.75	2.75	5.00
	1940R, yr. XVIII	23.355	.25	.60	1.50	3.25
	1941R, yr. XIX	27.050	.25	.60	1.50	3.25
	1942R, yr. XX	18.100	.25	.60	1.50	3.25
	1943R, yr. XXI	25.400	.25	.60	1.50	2.75

20 CENTESIMI

1.0000 gm., .835 SILVER, .0268 oz ASW

Y#	Date	Mintage	Fine	VF	XF	Unc
10	1863T	461 pcs.	—	—	Rare	—

Y#	Date	Mintage	Fine	VF	XF	Unc
15	1863M	28.845	1.75	4.00	7.50	15.00
	1863T	6.289	4.00	5.50	10.00	20.00
	1867T	.866	20.00	35.00	60.00	100.00

COPPER-NICKEL

Y#	Date	Mintage	Fine	VF	XF	Unc
26	1894KB	75.000	.40	1.00	3.25	15.00
	1894R	13.901	.60	1.50	5.50	30.00
	1895R	11.099	.60	1.50	5.50	30.00

NICKEL

Y#	Date	Mintage	Fine	VF	XF	Unc
47	1908R	14.315	1.00	2.00	4.00	13.00
	1909R	19.280	1.00	2.00	4.00	15.00
	1910R	21.887	.75	1.50	2.75	10.00
	1911R	13.671	.75	1.75	2.75	13.00
	1912R	21.040	.60	1.50	2.75	10.00
	1913R	20.729	.60	1.50	2.75	10.00
	1914R	14.308	.60	1.50	2.75	10.00
	1919R	3.475	4.00	9.00	16.00	35.00
	1920R	27,284	.60	1.50	2.50	10.00
	1921R	50.372	.55	1.50	2.00	9.00
	1922R	17.134	.60	1.50	2.50	11.50
	1926R	500 pcs.	—	—	Rare	—
	1927R	100 pcs.	—	—	Rare	—

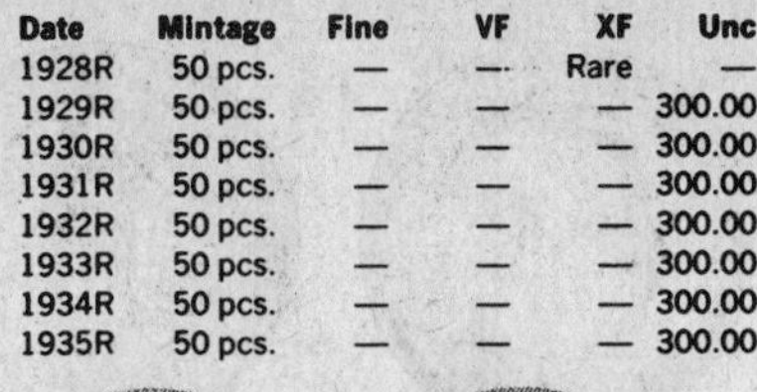

Y#	Date	Mintage	Fine	VF	XF	Unc
47	1928R	50 pcs.	—	—	Rare	—
	1929R	50 pcs.	—	—	—	300.00
	1930R	50 pcs.	—	—	—	300.00
	1931R	50 pcs.	—	—	—	300.00
	1932R	50 pcs.	—	—	—	300.00
	1933R	50 pcs.	—	—	—	300.00
	1934R	50 pcs.	—	—	—	300.00
	1935R	50 pcs.	—	—	—	300.00

COPPER-NICKEL
Plain and reeded edges, overstruck on Y#26.

Y#	Date	Mintage	Fine	VF	XF	Unc
63	1918R	43.097	.60	1.50	3.00	10.00
	1919R	33.432	.60	1.50	3.00	10.00
	1920R	.923	3.00	5.00	10.00	30.00

NICKEL

Y#	Date	Mintage	Fine	VF	XF	Unc
79	1936R, yr. XIV	.117	10.00	17.50	25.00	60.00
	1937R, yr. XV	50 pcs.	—	—	—	300.00
	1938R, yr. XVII	20 pcs.	—	—	—	300.00

STAINLESS STEEL (non-magnetic)

Y#	Date	Mintage	Fine	VF	XF	Unc
79a	1939R, yr. XVII	.460	.35	.75	1.50	4.00
	1939R, yr. XVIII	Inc. Ab.	.35	.75	1.50	4.00
	1940R, yr. XVIII	35.350	.25	.70	1.25	2.25

STAINLESS STEEL (magnetic)

Y#	Date	Mintage	Fine	VF	XF	Unc
79b	1939R, yr. XVII	Inc. Ab.	.30	.70	1.00	2.25
	1940R, yr. XVIII	Inc. Ab.	.30	.70	1.00	2.25
	1941R, yr. XIX	107.300	.30	.70	1.00	2.25
	1942R, yr. XX	99.900	.30	.70	1.00	2.25
	1943R, yr. XXI	57.003	.30	.75	.90	2.50

25 CENTESIMI

NICKEL

Y#	Date	Mintage	Fine	VF	XF	Unc
37	1902R	7.773	10.00	20.00	30.00	60.00
	1903R	5.895	10.00	20.00	30.00	60.00

50 CENTESIMI

.900 SILVER

Y#	Date	Mintage	Fine	VF	XF	Unc
11	1861FIRENZE	1.222	50.00	100.00	150.00	300.00
	1861M	—	250.00	500.00	750.00	1000.
	1861T	.045	250.00	500.00	750.00	1000.
	1862N	.630	25.00	50.00	100.00	200.00
	1862T	.185	25.00	50.00	75.00	150.00

2.5000 gm., .835 SILVER, .0671 oz ASW

Y#	Date	Mintage	Fine	VF	XF	Unc
11a	1863M	38.366	3.50	7.50	15.00	30.00
	1863T	9.054	7.50	15.00	30.00	75.00

Y#	Date	Mintage	Fine	VF	XF	Unc
16	1863M	—	2.75	5.00	12.50	32.50
	1863N	16.062	3.25	7.00	15.00	50.00
	1863T	—	3.00	6.00	20.00	50.00
	1866M	19.199	17.50	40.00	70.00	100.00
	1867M	10.984	3.00	6.50	12.00	32.50
	1867N	7.838	3.25	6.00	13.00	32.50
	1867T	.396	50.00	115.00	275.00	500.00

Y#	Date	Mintage	Fine	VF	XF	Unc
27	1889R	.635	20.00	35.00	75.00	150.00
	1892R	.148	30.00	50.00	100.00	200.00

NICKEL
Plain Edge

Y#	Date	Mintage	Fine	VF	XF	Unc
64	1919R	Inc. Bl.	2.50	5.00	20.00	50.00
	1920R	Inc. Bl.	.75	2.00	4.00	15.00
	1921R	Inc. Bl.	.75	2.00	4.00	15.00
	1924R	Inc. Bl.	125.00	250.00	350.00	500.00
	1925R	Inc. Bl.	2.50	5.00	10.00	35.00
	1926R	500 pcs.	—	—	—	300.00
	1927R	100 pcs.	—	—	—	300.00
	1928R	50 pcs.	—	—	—	500.00

Reeded Edge

Y#	Date	Mintage	Fine	VF	XF	Unc
64a	1919R	3.700	2.50	5.00	10.00	60.00
	1920R	29.450	1.50	3.00	5.00	12.50
	1921R	16.849	1.50	3.00	5.00	12.50
	1924R	.599	25.00	50.00	75.00	200.00
	1925R	24.884	5.00	10.00	20.00	50.00
	1929R	50 pcs.	—	—	—	300.00
	1930R	50 pcs.	—	—	—	300.00
	1931R	50 pcs.	—	—	—	300.00
	1832R	50 pcs.	—	—	—	300.00
	1933R	50 pcs.	—	—	—	300.00
	1934R	50 pcs.	—	—	—	300.00
	1935R	50 pcs.	—	—	—	300.00

Y#	Date	Mintage	Fine	VF	XF	Unc
80	1936R, yr. XIV	.118	6.50	12.50	20.00	32.50
	1937R, yr. XV	50 pcs.	—	—	—	300.00
	1938R, yr. XVII	20 pcs.	—	—	—	300.00

STAINLESS STEEL (non-magnetic)

Y#	Date	Mintage	Fine	VF	XF	Unc
80a	1939R, yr. XVII	.370	.25	.75	1.50	3.50
	1939R, yr. XVIII	Inc. Ab.	.25	.75	1.50	3.50
	1940R, yr. XVIII	19.005	.20	.35	.60	2.25

STAINLESS STEEL (magnetic)

Y#	Date	Mintage	Fine	VF	XF	Unc
80b	1939R, yr. XVII	Inc. Ab.	.25	.75	1.50	3.50
	1940R, yr. XVIII	Inc. Ab.	.25	.65	1.30	2.25
	1941R, yr. XIX	58.100	.25	.55	1.30	2.25
	1942R, yr. XX	26.450	.25	.60	1.40	2.50
	1943R, yr. XXI	3.681	4.50	7.00	12.50	20.00

LIRA

.900 SILVER

Y#	Date	Mintage	Fine	VF	XF	Unc
12	1861FIRENZE	.432	65.00	125.00	200.00	300.00
	1861T	.019	500.00	1000.	1500.	2000.
	1862N	.497	30.00	60.00	100.00	150.00
	1862T	.105	50.00	100.00	200.00	300.00

5.0000 gm., .835 SILVER, .1342 oz ASW

Y#	Date	Mintage	Fine	VF	XF	Unc
12a	1863M	53.891	BV	5.00	10.00	40.00
	1863T	6.109	5.00	10.00	20.00	50.00
	1867/3M	—	6.00	12.50	22.50	60.00
	1867M	7.665	4.50	9.00	17.50	50.00
	1867T	.033	25.00	40.00	80.00	200.00

Y#	Date	Mintage	Fine	VF	XF	Unc
17	1863M	—	BV	5.50	17.50	50.00
	1863T	—	75.00	150.00	200.00	400.00

Y#	Date	Mintage	Fine	VF	XF	Unc
28	1883R	5,420	500.00	800.00	1500.	3000.
	1884R	1.995	5.00	10.00	12.50	50.00
	1886R	6.095	5.00	10.00	16.50	40.00
	1887M	16.305	5.00	10.00	16.50	35.00
	1892R	.032	300.00	600.00	800.00	1000.
	1899R	1.798	6.50	12.50	17.50	45.00
	1900R	.318	6.50	13.50	18.50	50.00

Y#	Date	Mintage	Fine	VF	XF	Unc
38	1901R	2.590	5.00	9.00	16.50	45.00
	1902R	4.084	BV	6.00	12.50	30.00
	1905R	.700	30.00	60.00	100.00	300.00
	1906R	4.665	BV	6.00	10.00	30.00
	1907R	8.472	BV	6.00	10.00	30.00

Y#	Date	Mintage	Fine	VF	XF	Unc
48	1908R	2.212	20.00	35.00	50.00	100.00
	1909R	3.475	BV	6.50	15.00	30.00
	1910R	5.525	BV	5.50	12.50	25.00
	1912R	5.865	BV	5.50	12.50	25.00
	1913R	16.177	BV	3.50	6.00	17.50

Y#	Date	Mintage	Fine	VF	XF	Unc
50	1915R	5.229	BV	4.00	9.00	20.00
	1916R	1.835	4.50	8.50	17.50	30.00
	1917R	9.744	BV	3.00	5.00	12.50

NICKEL

Y#	Date	Mintage	Fine	VF	XF	Unc
65	1922R	82.267	.60	1.50	3.50	12.50
	1923R	20.175	.60	1.50	3.50	13.50
	1924R	29.288	.60	1.50	3.50	13.50
	1926R	500 pcs.	—	—	—	—
	1927R	100 pcs.	—	—	—	—
	1928R	19.996	.60	1.50	4.00	13.50
	1929R	50 pcs.	—	—	—	300.00
	1930R	50 pcs.	—	—	—	300.00
	1931R	50 pcs.	—	—	—	300.00
	1932R	50 pcs.	—	—	—	300.00
	1933R	50 pcs.	—	—	—	300.00
	1934R	50 pcs.	—	—	—	300.00
	1935R	50 pcs.	—	—	—	300.00

Y#	Date	Mintage	Fine	VF	XF	Unc
81	1936R, yr. XIV	.119	6.00	9.00	15.00	32.50
	1937R, yr. XV	50 pcs.	—	—	—	500.00
	1938R, yr. XVII	20 pcs.	—	—	—	500.00

STAINLESS STEEL (non-magnetic)

Y#	Date	Mintage	Fine	VF	XF	Unc
81a	1939R, yr. XVII	—	.65	1.75	3.50	9.00
	1939R, yr. XVIII	—	.40	.90	1.75	4.50
	1940R, yr. XVIII	25.997	.30	.80	1.50	2.50

STAINLESS STEEL (magnetic)

Y#	Date	Mintage	Fine	VF	XF	Unc
81b	1940R, yr. XVIII	Inc. Ab.	.30	.80	1.50	2.75
	1941R, yr. XIX	8.550	.30	.80	1.50	2.75
	1942R, yr. XX	5.700	.30	.80	1.50	2.75
	1943R, yr. XXI	11.500	1.75	3.50	7.50	15.00

ALUMINUM

Y#	Date	Mintage	Fine	VF	XF	Unc
95	1946R	.104	20.00	25.00	35.00	65.00
	1947R	.012	25.00	50.00	75.00	125.00
	1948R	9.000	.40	1.00	2.00	4.00
	1949R	13.200	.40	1.00	2.00	3.00
	1950R	1.942	1.50	3.50	5.00	9.00

Y#	Date	Mintage	Fine	VF	XF	Unc
99	1951R	3.680	.15	.40	.75	2.50
	1952R	2.720	.15	.40	.75	2.50
	1953R	2.800	.15	.40	.75	2.50
	1954R	41.040	.10	.30	.60	1.00
	1955R	32.640	.10	.30	.60	1.00
	1956R	1.840	.20	.40	.75	4.00
	1957R	7.440	.15	.35	.70	1.50
	1958R	5.280	.15	.35	.70	1.50
	1959R	1.680	.15	.35	.70	1.50
	1968R	.100	In mint sets only			10.00
	1969R	.310	In mint sets only			3.50
	1970R	1.011	In mint sets only			1.75

2 LIRE

.900 SILVER

Y#	Date	Mintage	Fine	VF	XF	Unc
13	1861T	9,871	250.00	500.00	1000.	2000.
	1862N	.062	125.00	250.00	500.00	800.00

10.0000 gm., .835 SILVER, .2684 oz ASW

Y#	Date	Mintage	Fine	VF	XF	Unc
13a	1863N	10.090	10.00	20.00	40.00	100.00
	1863T	4.910	12.50	25.00	50.00	100.00

Y#	Date	Mintage	Fine	VF	XF	Unc
18	1863N	—	8.50	25.00	90.00	200.00
	1863T	—	8.50	25.00	90.00	200.00

Y#	Date	Mintage	Fine	VF	XF	Unc
29	1881R	4.141	BV	8.50	15.00	50.00
	1882R	2.859	BV	8.50	15.00	50.00
	1883R	3.500	BV	8.50	15.00	50.00
	1884R	4.500	BV	8.50	15.00	50.00
	1885R	.598	25.00	40.00	80.00	150.00
	1886R	1.902	BV	8.50	15.00	50.00
	1887R	7.500	BV	8.50	14.00	50.00
	1897R	.848	8.50	10.00	17.50	60.00
	1898R	1.320	22.50	45.00	90.00	200.00
	1899R	.610	8.50	15.00	22.50	50.00

Y#	Date	Mintage	Fine	VF	XF	Unc
39	1901R	.072	150.00	300.00	600.00	1000.
	1902R	.549	35.00	75.00	125.00	200.00
	1903R	.054	250.00	500.00	1000.	2000.
	1904R	.157	100.00	200.00	275.00	400.00
	1905R	1.643	13.50	22.50	40.00	125.00
	1906R	.970	20.00	30.00	50.00	100.00
	1907R	1.245	13.50	22.50	45.00	100.00

Y#	Date	Mintage	Fine	VF	XF	Unc
49	1908R	2.283	8.50	15.00	35.00	80.00
	1910R	.719	25.00	45.00	60.00	150.00
	1911R	.535	65.00	100.00	150.00	350.00
	1912R	2.166	BV	8.50	13.50	35.00

50th Anniversary of Kingdom

Y#	Date	Mintage	Fine	VF	XF	Unc
58	1911R	1.000	10.00	15.00	25.00	45.00

Y#	Date	Mintage	Fine	VF	XF	Unc
51	1914R	10.390	BV	8.50	12.00	20.00
	1915R	7.948	BV	9.00	12.50	22.50
	1916R	10.923	BV	8.50	12.00	20.00
	1917R	6.123	BV	12.50	20.00	35.00

NICKEL

Y#	Date	Mintage	Fine	VF	XF	Unc
66	1923R	32.260	1.00	2.50	6.00	20.00
	1924R	45.051	1.00	2.50	6.00	20.00
	1925R	14.628	1.00	2.50	6.00	25.00
	1926R	5.101	5.00	10.00	32.50	100.00
	1927R	1.632	15.00	27.50	45.00	160.00
	1928R	50 pcs.	—	—	—	300.00
	1929R	50 pcs.	—	—	—	300.00
	1930R	50 pcs.	—	—	—	300.00
	1931R	50 pcs.	—	—	—	300.00
	1932R	50 pcs.	—	—	—	300.00
	1933R	50 pcs.	—	—	—	300.00
	1934R	50 pcs.	—	—	—	300.00
	1935R	50 pcs.	—	—	—	300.00

Y#	Date	Mintage	Fine	VF	XF	Unc
82	1936R, yr. XIV	.120	7.50	10.00	15.00	32.50
	1937R, yr. XV	50 pcs.	—	—	Rare	—
	1938R, yr. XVII	20 pcs.	—	—	Rare	—

STAINLESS STEEL (non-magnetic)

Y#	Date	Mintage	Fine	VF	XF	Unc
82a	1939R, yr. XVII	—	.50	1.00	2.50	4.00
	1939R, yr. XVIII	—	.50	1.00	2.75	4.50
	1940R, yr. XVIII	13.483	.35	.75	1.50	2.25

STAINLESS STEEL (magnetic)

Y#	Date	Mintage	Fine	VF	XF	Unc
82b	1940R, yr. XVIII	—	.40	.90	1.50	2.50
	1941R, yr. XIX	1.865	.40	.90	1.50	2.50
	1942R, yr. XX	2.450	6.50	12.50	30.00	50.00
	1943R, yr. XXI	.600	3.50	7.50	15.00	35.00

ALUMINUM

Y#	Date	Mintage	Fine	VF	XF	Unc
96	1946R	.123	15.00	25.00	40.00	80.00
	1947R	.012	25.00	40.00	55.00	150.00
	1948R	7.200	.50	1.25	2.50	4.50
	1949R	1.350	1.00	2.50	4.50	17.50
	1950R	2.640	.60	1.50	2.75	5.50

Y#	Date	Mintage	Fine	VF	XF	Unc
100	1953R	4.125	—	.50	1.00	2.00
	1954R	22.500	—	.50	1.00	1.25
	1955R	2.750	—	.50	1.00	1.50
	1956R	1.500	—	.50	1.00	2.50
	1957R	6.313	—	.50	1.00	1.00
	1958R	.125	—	20.00	40.00	80.00
	1959R	2.000	—	.50	1.00	1.50
	1968R	.100	In mint sets only			10.00
	1969R	.310	In mint sets only			4.00
	1970R	1.011	In mint sets only			1.75

5 LIRE

25.0000 gm., .900 SILVER, .7234 oz ASW
Accession To Throne Of Unified Italy

Y#	Date	Mintage	Fine	VF	XF	Unc
5	1861FIRENZE	.021	200.00	400.00	650.00	1000.

Y#	Date	Mintage	Fine	VF	XF	Unc
14	1861T	.160	125.00	250.00	400.00	600.00
14	1862N	.142	35.00	75.00	125.00	275.00
	1862T	.051	50.00	100.00	200.00	300.00
	1864N	.120	25.00	50.00	100.00	200.00
	1865N	.312	22.50	37.50	75.00	150.00
	1865T	.491	25.00	37.50	75.00	150.00
	1866N	.460	1500.	3000.	4000.	6000.
	1869M	3.995	BV	22.50	30.00	50.00
	1870M	5.969	BV	22.50	30.00	50.00
	1870R	—	22.50	27.50	50.00	100.00
	1871M	6.697	BV	22.50	30.00	50.00
	1871R	.404	25.00	50.00	100.00	200.00
	1872M	7.093	BV	22.50	30.00	45.00
	1872R	.029	500.00	1000.	1850.	3000.
	1873M	8.438	BV	22.50	30.00	50.00
	1873R	.017	1000.	2000.	3250.	5000.
	1874M	12.000	BV	22.50	30.00	50.00
	1875M	8.982	BV	22.50	30.00	50.00
	1875R	1.018	BV	25.00	35.00	60.00
	1876R	6.390	BV	22.50	30.00	50.00
	1877R	4.410	BV	22.50	30.00	50.00
	1878R	1.700	BV	25.00	35.00	60.00

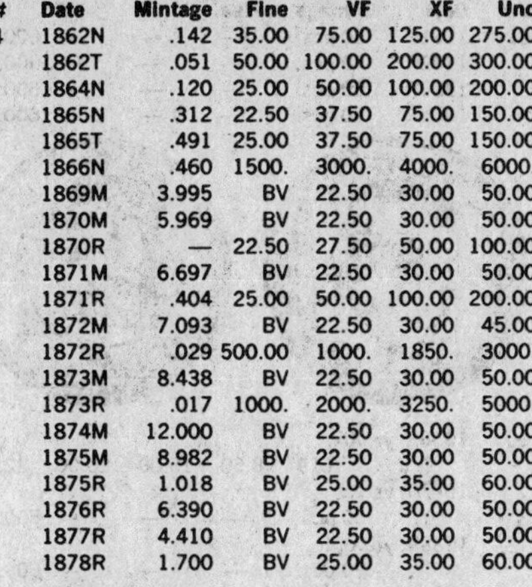

1.6129 gm., .900 GOLD, .0466 oz AGW

Y#	Date	Mintage	Fine	VF	XF	Unc
A18	1863T	.197	50.00	100.00	125.00	200.00
	1865T	.408	75.00	150.00	200.00	250.00

25.0000 gm., .900 SILVER, .7234 oz ASW

Y#	Date	Mintage	Fine	VF	XF	Unc
30	1878R	.100	250.00	500.00	700.00	1000.
	1879R	4.000	25.00	50.00	100.00	250.00

Y#	Date	Mintage	Fine	VF	XF	Unc
40	1901R	114 pcs.	2500.	5000.	6500.	10,000.

50th Anniversary of Kingdom

Y#	Date	Mintage	Fine	VF	XF	Unc
59	1911R	.060	150.00	300.00	400.00	1000.

Y#	Date	Mintage	Fine	VF	XF	Unc
52	1914R	.273	750.00	1500.	2000.	4000.

5.0000 gm., .835 SILVER, .1342 oz ASW

Y#	Date	Mintage	Fine	VF	XF	Unc
67	1926R	5.405	4.50	6.50	12.50	30.00
	1927R	92.887	BV	4.50	6.50	12.00
	1928R	9.908	BV	5.00	10.00	25.00
	1929R	33.803	BV	4.50	6.50	12.00
	1930R	19.525	BV	4.50	6.50	12.00
	1931R	50 pcs.	—	—	—	400.00
	1932R	50 pcs.	—	—	—	400.00
	1933R	50 pcs.	—	—	—	400.00
	1934R	50 pcs.	—	—	—	400.00
	1935R	50 pcs.	—	—	—	400.00

Y#	Date	Mintage	Fine	VF	XF	Unc
89	1936R, yr. XIV	1.016	5.00	9.00	13.50	27.50
	1937R, yr. XV	.100	10.00	22.50	27.50	45.00
	1938R, yr. XVIII	20 pcs.	—	—	—	500.00

Y#	Date	Mintage	Fine	VF	XF	Unc
89	1939R, yr. XVIII					
		20 pcs.	—	—	—	500.00
	1940R, yr. XIX					
		20 pcs.	—	—	—	500.00
	1941R, yr. XX					
		20 pcs.	—	—	—	500.00

ALUMINUM

Y#	Date	Mintage	Fine	VF	XF	Unc
97	1946R	.081	50.00	75.00	100.00	225.00
	1947R	.017	35.00	50.00	80.00	150.00
	1948R	25.125	.50	1.00	3.00	7.50
	1949R	71.100	.30	.75	2.00	6.00
	1950R	114.790	.30	.75	1.50	5.50

Y#	Date	Mintage	Fine	VF	XF	Unc
101	1951R	40.260	.15	.40	.75	2.00
	1952R	57.400	.15	.40	.75	2.00
	1953R	196.200	.15	.40	.75	2.00
	1954R	436.400	.15	.40	.75	2.00
	1955R	159.000	.15	.40	.75	1.50
	1956R	.400	10.00	20.00	40.00	125.00
	1966R	.120	1.00	2.50	3.50	6.00
	1967R	10.600	.20	.25	.50	1.00
	1968R	7.500	.20	.25	.50	1.00
	1969R	7.910	.20	.25	.50	1.00
	1970R	4.211	.20	.25	.50	1.00
	1971R	9.610	.20	.25	.50	1.00
	1972R	28.800	.20	.25	.50	1.00
	1973R	—	.15	.20	.40	.75
	1974R	6.600	.15	.20	.40	.75
	1975R	7.000	—	—	—	.75
	1976R	9.000	—	—	.20	.75
	1977R	—	—	—	.10	.25
	1978R	—	—	—	.10	.75
	1979R	—	—	—	.10	.25

10 LIRE

3.2258 gm., .900 GOLD, 18mm, .0933 oz AGW

Y#	Date	Mintage	Fine	VF	XF	Unc
B18.1	1861T	1,916	500.00	1000.	2000.	3000.
	18.5mm					
B18.2	1863T	.543	65.00	85.00	120.00	200.00
	1865T	.444	85.00	100.00	150.00	300.00
	19mm					
B18.3	1863T	Inc. Ab.	65.00	85.00	120.00	200.00
	19.5mm					
B18.4	1863T	Inc. Ab.	65.00	85.00	120.00	200.00

Y#	Date	Mintage	Fine	VF	XF	Unc
53	1910R	5,202	—	—	—	—
	1912R	5,796	500.00	1000.	1500.	2500.
	1926R	40 pcs.	1000.	2000.	4000.	6000.
	1927R	30 pcs.	1150.	2250.	4500.	7000.

10.0000 gm., .835 SILVER, .2684 oz ASW

Y#	Date	Mintage	Fine	VF	XF	Unc
68	1926R	1.748	45.00	80.00	150.00	275.00
	1927R	44.801	8.50	12.00	17.50	35.00
	1928R	6.652	10.00	17.50	40.00	80.00
	1929R	6.800	10.00	17.50	40.00	80.00
	1930R	3.668	30.00	65.00	125.00	200.00
68	1931R	50 pcs.	—	—	—	600.00
	1932R	50 pcs.	—	—	—	600.00
	1933R	50 pcs.	—	—	—	600.00
	1934R	50 pcs.	—	—	—	600.00

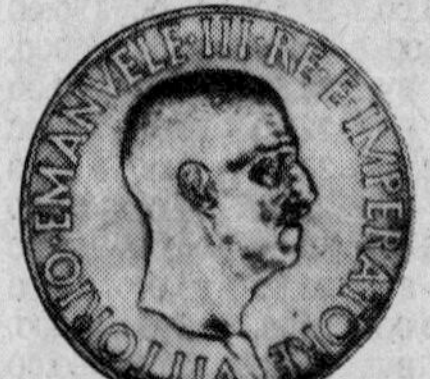

Y#	Date	Mintage	Fine	VF	XF	Unc
90	1936R, yr. XIV					
		.619	8.50	15.00	20.00	32.50
	1937R, yr. XV					
		50 pcs.	—	—	—	600.00
	1938R, yr. XVII					
		20 pcs.	—	—	—	600.00
	1939R, yr. XVIII					
		20 pcs.	—	—	—	600.00
	1940R, yr. XIX					
		20 pcs.	—	—	—	600.00
	1941R, yr. XX					
		20 pcs.	—	—	—	600.00

ALUMINUM

Y#	Date	Mintage	Fine	VF	XF	Unc
98	1946R	.101	15.00	30.00	50.00	100.00
	1947R	.012	150.00	250.00	325.00	700.00
	1948R	14.400	.40	1.00	2.00	8.50
	1949R	49.500	.50	1.25	2.50	8.00
	1950R	53.311	.40	1.00	2.00	9.00

Y#	Date	Mintage	Fine	VF	XF	Unc
102	1951R	96.600	.10	.25	.75	4.00
	1952R	105.150	.10	.25	.75	4.00
	1953R	151.500	.10	.25	.75	2.50
	1954R	95.250	.20	.30	1.25	6.50
	1955R	274.950	.10	.15	.65	3.00
	1956R	76.650	.10	.15	.65	3.00
	1965R	1.050	.25	.50	1.25	2.50
	1966R	16.500	.10	.25	.60	1.50
	1967R	30.450	.10	.25	.50	1.00
	1968R	32.200	—	.15	.50	.75
	1969R	23.710	—	.15	.50	.75
	1970R	15.111	.10	.25	.60	1.00
	1971R	24.560	—	.15	.50	.75
	1972R	61.200	—	.15	.25	.50
	1973R	140.100	—	.15	.25	.50
	1974R	90.000	—	.15	.25	.50
	1975R	85.800	—	—	.15	.40
	1976R	83.550	—	.10	.15	.25
	1977R	—	—	.10	.15	.25
	1978R	—	—	—	.10	.25
	1979R	—	—	—	.10	.30

20 LIRE

6.4516 gm., .900 GOLD, .1867 oz AGW

Y#	Date	Mintage	Fine	VF	XF	Unc
19	1861T	3,267	150.00	300.00	450.00	700.00
	1862T	1.955	BV	125.00	135.00	150.00
	1863T	2.981	BV	125.00	135.00	150.00
	1864T	.609	BV	130.00	140.00	165.00
	1865T	3.109	BV	125.00	135.00	150.00
	1866T	.196	BV	130.00	140.00	165.00
	1867T	.276	BV	125.00	135.00	150.00
	1868T	.340	BV	125.00	135.00	150.00
19	1869T	.185	BV	125.00	135.00	150.00
	1870T	.055	125.00	200.00	250.00	300.00
	1870R	—	150.00	300.00	400.00	500.00
	1871R	—	BV	150.00	175.00	200.00
	1872M	—	BV	150.00	175.00	200.00
	1873M	1.018	BV	125.00	135.00	150.00
	1873R	2,174	300.00	600.00	800.00	1000.
	1874M	.255	BV	130.00	140.00	165.00
	1874R	.041	BV	140.00	160.00	185.00
	1875R	.051	BV	140.00	160.00	185.00
	1876R	.108	BV	125.00	135.00	150.00
	1877R	.247	BV	125.00	135.00	150.00
	1878R	.316	BV	125.00	135.00	150.00

Y#	Date	Mintage	Fine	VF	XF	Unc
32	1879R	.146	BV	125.00	135.00	150.00
	1880R	.129	BV	125.00	135.00	150.00
	1881R	.843	BV	125.00	135.00	150.00
	1882R	6.970	BV	125.00	135.00	150.00
	1883R	.182	BV	130.00	140.00	165.00
	1884R	9,775	175.00	350.00	450.00	500.00
	1885R	.165	BV	125.00	135.00	150.00
	1886R	.059	BV	125.00	135.00	150.00
	1888R	.111	BV	125.00	135.00	150.00
	1889R	—	125.00	175.00	200.00	250.00
	1890R	.068	BV	130.00	140.00	165.00
	1891R	.032	BV	140.00	160.00	185.00
	1893R	.041	BV	140.00	160.00	185.00
	1897R	.038	BV	140.00	160.00	185.00

Y#	Date	Mintage	Fine	VF	XF	Unc
41	1902R	181 pcs.	3000.	5000.	6250.	8000.
	1903R	1,800	250.00	400.00	500.00	650.00
	1905R	8,715	175.00	300.00	400.00	500.00
	1908R	—	—	—	Rare	—

Obv: Small anchor bottom indicates gold in coin is from Eritrea.

Y#	Date	Mintage	Fine	VF	XF	Unc
41a	1902R	115 pcs.	3000.	5000.	6250.	8000.

Uniformed bust

Y#	Date	Mintage	Fine	VF	XF	Unc
54	1910R	.033	—	—	Rare	—
	1912R	.060	150.00	200.00	325.00	500.00
	1926R	40 pcs.	—	—	Rare	—
	1927R	30 pcs.	—	—	Rare	—

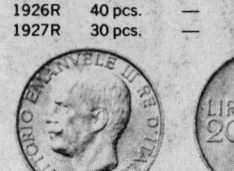

1st Anniversary of Fascist Government

Y#	Date	Mintage	Fine	VF	XF	Unc
72	1923R	.020	200.00	350.00	400.00	500.00

15.0000 gm., .800 SILVER, .3858 oz ASW

Y#	Date	Mintage	Fine	VF	XF	Unc
69	1927R, yr. V					

Y#	Date	Mintage	Fine	VF	XF	Unc
69		100 pcs.	500.00	1000.	1850.	3000.
	1927R, yr. VI	3.518	30.00	60.00	100.00	175.00
	1928R, yr. VI	2.487	40.00	80.00	125.00	225.00
	1929R, yr. VII	50 pcs.	—	—	—	3000.
	1930R, yr. VIII	50 pcs.	—	—	—	3000.
	1931R, yr. IX	50 pcs.	—	—	—	3000.
	1932R, yr. X	50 pcs.	—	—	—	3000.
	1933R, yr. XI	50 pcs.	—	—	—	3000.
	1934R, yr. XII	50 pcs.	—	—	—	3000.

.600 SILVER
10th Anniversary End of World War I

Y#	Date	Mintage	Fine	VF	XF	Unc
75	1928R, yr. VI	—	50.00	90.00	175.00	350.00

15.0000 gm., .800 SILVER, .3858 oz ASW

Y#	Date	Mintage	Fine	VF	XF	Unc
91	1936R, yr. XIV	.010	200.00	400.00	650.00	1000.
	1937R, yr. XV	50 pcs.	—	—	—	1500.
	1938R, yr. XVII	20 pcs.	—	—	—	1500.
	1939R, yr. XVIII	20 pcs.	—	—	—	1500.
	1940R, yr. XIX	20 pcs.	—	—	—	1500.
	1941R, yr. XX	20 pcs.	—	—	—	1500.

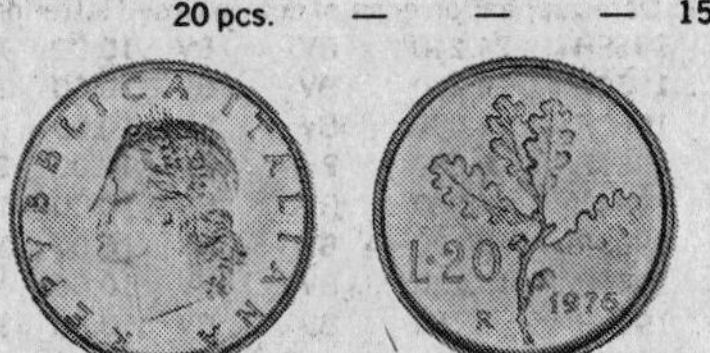

ALUMINUM-BRONZE

Y#	Date	Mintage	Fine	VF	XF	Unc
A102	1957R	*60.075	.25	1.00	2.25	5.00
	1958R	80.550	.20	.50	2.00	5.00
A102	1959R	4.005	.75	2.00	4.00	20.00

***NOTE:** Two different types of sevens.

Plain edge

Y#	Date	Mintage	Fine	VF	XF	Unc
A102a	1968R	—	—	—	—	—
	1969R	16.740	.10	.25	.50	.75
	1970R	32.511	.10	.25	.50	.75
	1971R	13.390	.10	.25	.50	.75
	1972R	33.980	.10	.25	.50	.75
	1973R	19.575	.10	.25	.50	.75
	1974R	16.875	.10	.25	.50	.75
	1975R	24.750	.10	.25	.50	.70
	1976R	17.325	.10	.25	.50	.70
	1977R	—	—	—	.25	.50
	1978R	—	—	—	.25	.50
	1979R	—	—	—	.15	.35

50 LIRE

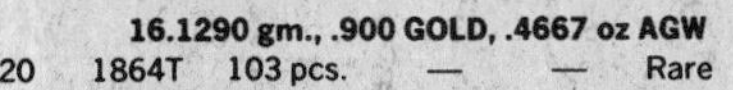

16.1290 gm., .900 GOLD, .4667 oz AGW

Y#	Date	Mintage	Fine	VF	XF	Unc
20	1864T	103 pcs.	—	—	Rare	—

Y#	Date	Mintage	Fine	VF	XF	Unc
33	1884R	2,532	400.00	650.00	850.00	1200.
	1888R	2,125	600.00	1000.	1200.	1750.
	1891R	414 pcs.	800.00	1350.	1650.	3000.

50th Anniversary of Kingdom

Y#	Date	Mintage	Fine	VF	XF	Unc
60	1911R	.020	350.00	500.00	700.00	1000.

Y#	Date	Mintage	Fine	VF	XF	Unc
55	1910R	2,096	—	—	Rare	—
	1912R	.011	350.00	500.00	700.00	1000.
	1926R	40 pcs.	—	—	Rare	—
	1927R	30 pcs.	—	—	Rare	—

4.3995 gm., .900 GOLD, .1273 oz AGW

Y#	Date	Mintage	Fine	VF	XF	Unc
70	1931R, yr. IX	.032	135.00	150.00	175.00	225.00
	1931R, yr. X	Inc. Ab.	150.00	225.00	325.00	500.00
	1932R, yr. X	.012	150.00	200.00	250.00	325.00
	1933R, yr. XI	6,463	250.00	350.00	450.00	600.00
92	1936R, yr. XIV	790 pcs.	500.00	1000.	1500.	2500.

STAINLESS STEEL

Y#	Date	Mintage	Fine	VF	XF	Unc
103	1954R	17.600	.25	.50	.75	3.00
	1955R	70.500	.25	.50	.75	3.00
	1956R	69.400	.25	.50	.75	3.00
	1957R	8.925	.25	.50	.75	4.00
	1958R	.825	.25	.50	1.50	6.00
	1959R	8.800	.25	.50	.75	3.00
	1960R	2.025	.25	.50	.75	3.00
	1961R	11.100	.25	.50	.75	2.00
	1962R	17.700	.25	.50	.75	2.00
	1963R	31.600	.20	.35	.60	2.00
	1964R	37.900	.20	.35	.60	2.00
	1965R	25.300	.20	.35	.60	2.00
	1966R	27.400	.20	.35	.60	2.00
	1967R	28.000	.20	.35	.50	1.75
	1968R	17.800	.20	.35	.50	1.75
	1969R	23.010	.20	.35	.50	1.25
	1970R	21.411	.20	.35	.50	1.00
	1971R	33.410	.20	.35	.50	1.00
	1972R	39.000	.20	.35	.50	1.00
	1973R	48.700	.20	.35	.50	1.00
	1974R	64.100	.20	.35	.50	1.00
	1975R	87.000	.20	.35	.50	1.00
	1976R	180.600	.20	.35	.50	1.00
	1977R	—	.20	.35	.50	1.00
	1978R	—	.20	.35	.50	1.00
	1979R	—	.20	.35	.50	1.00

100 LIRE

32.2580 gm., .900 GOLD, .9334 oz AGW

Y#	Date	Mintage	Fine	VF	XF	Unc
21	1864T	579 pcs.	1500.	2500.	3500.	5000.
	1872R	661 pcs.	1500.	2500.	3500.	5000.
	1878R	294 pcs.	2000.	3500.	4500.	6000.

Y#	Date	Mintage	Fine	VF	XF	Unc
34	1880R	145 pcs.	—	—	Rare	—
	1882R	1,229	625.00	1000.	1750.	3500.

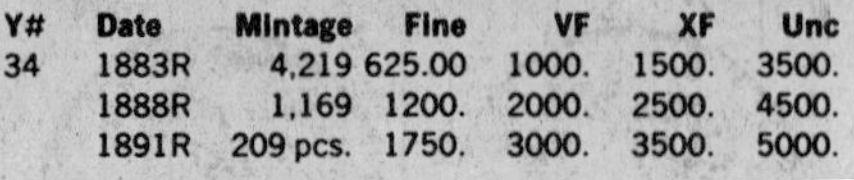

Y#	Date	Mintage	Fine	VF	XF	Unc
34	1883R	4,219	625.00	1000.	1500.	3500.
	1888R	1,169	1200.	2000.	2500.	4500.
	1891R	209 pcs.	1750.	3000.	3500.	5000.

Y#	Date	Mintage	Fine	VF	XF	Unc
42	1903R	916 pcs.	1500.	2500.	3500.	6000.
	1905R	1,012	1000.	1750.	2500.	4000.

Y#	Date	Mintage	Fine	VF	XF	Unc
56	1910R	2,013	—	—	Rare	—
	1912R	4,946	625.00	1000.	1850.	3000.
	1926R	40 pcs.	—	—	Rare	—
	1927R	30 pcs.	—	—	Rare	—

8.7990 gm., .900 GOLD, .2546 oz AGW
1st Anniversary of Fascist Government

Y#	Date	Mintage	Fine	VF	XF	Unc
73	1923R (frosted finish)	.020	350.00	600.00	1250.	2000.
	1923R (bright finish)			—	Rare	—

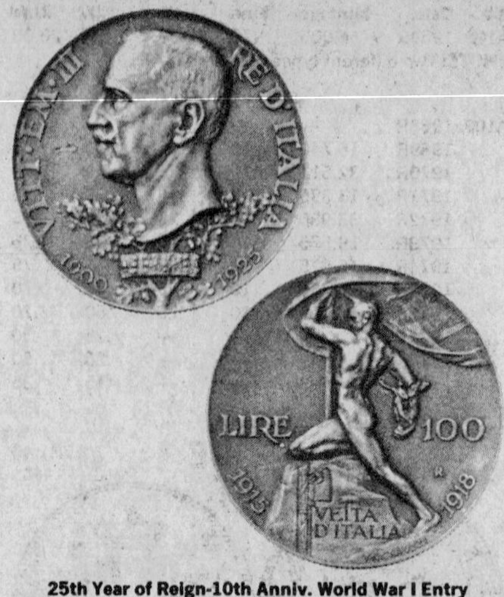

25th Year of Reign-10th Anniv. World War I Entry

Y#	Date	Mintage	Fine	VF	XF	Unc
74	1925R	5,000	800.00	1350.	2200.	3500.

Y#	Date	Mintage	Fine	VF	XF	Unc
71	1931R, yr. IX	.034	175.00	200.00	250.00	300.00
	1931R, yr. X	Inc. Ab.	200.00	275.00	375.00	500.00
	1932R, yr. X	9,081	200.00	275.00	325.00	375.00
	1933R, yr. XI	6,464	250.00	400.00	550.00	750.00

23mm

Y#	Date	Mintage	Fine	VF	XF	Unc
93	1936R, yr. XIV	812 pcs.	1000.	1850.	2350.	3000.

5.1900 gm., .900 GOLD, .1502 oz AGW
20mm

Y#	Date	Mintage	Fine	VF	XF	Unc
93a (94)	1937R, yr. XVI	249 pcs.	3000.	5000.	7000.	10,000.
	1940R, yr. XVIII	2 pcs.	—	—	Rare	—

STAINLESS STEEL

Y#	Date	Mintage	Fine	VF	XF	Unc
104	1955R	8.600	.25	.60	1.00	15.00
	1956R	99.800	.25	.50	.75	8.00
	1957R	90.600	.25	.50	.75	8.00
	1958R	25.640	.25	.50	.90	8.00
	1959R	19.500	.25	.50	.90	8.00
	1960R	20.700	.25	.50	.75	8.00
	1961R	11.860	.25	.50	.75	8.00
	1962R	21.700	.25	.50	.75	4.00
	1963R	33.100	.25	.50	.75	2.50
	1964R	31.300	.25	.50	.75	2.50
	1965R	37.000	.25	.50	.75	1.25
	1966R	52.500	.25	.50	.75	1.25
	1967R	23.700	.25	.50	.75	1.00
	1968R	34.200	.25	.50	.75	1.00
	1969R	27.710	.25	.50	.75	1.00
	1970R	25.011	.25	.50	.75	1.00
	1971R	25.910	.25	.50	.75	1.00
	1972R	31.170	.25	.50	.75	1.00
	1973R	30.780	.25	.50	.75	1.00
	1974R	83.880	.25	.50	.75	1.00
	1975R	106.650	.25	.50	.75	1.00
	1976R	160.020	.25	.50	.75	1.00
	1977R	—	.25	.50	.75	1.00
	1978R	—	.25	.50	.75	1.00
	1979R	—	.25	.50	.75	1.00

Guglielmo Marconi

Y#	Date	Mintage	Fine	VF	XF	Unc
109	1974R	50.000	.20	.40	.75	1.75

F.A.O. Issue

Y#	Date	Mintage	Fine	VF	XF	Unc
113	1979R	100.000	.20	.40	.75	1.00

200 LIRE

BRONZE

Y#	Date	Mintage	Fine	VF	XF	Unc
112	1977	16.000	.20	.40	.75	1.75
	1978	400.000	.20	.40	.75	1.75

5.0000 gm., ALUMINUM-BRONZE
F.A.O. and International Women's Year

Y#	Date	Mintage	Fine	VF	XF	Unc
116	1980	—	—	—	.50	1.00

500 LIRE

11.0000 gm., .835 SILVER, .2953 oz ASW

NOTE: Dates appear on edge of coin in raised lettering.

Y#	Date	Mintage	Fine	VF	XF	Unc
105	1958R	24.240	BV	BV	10.00	12.00
	1959R	19.360	BV	BV	10.00	12.00
	1960R	24.080	BV	BV	10.00	12.00
	1961R	6.560	BV	BV	12.00	25.00
	1964R	4.880	BV	BV	10.00	12.00
	1965R	3.120	BV	BV	10.00	12.00
	1966R	13.120	BV	BV	10.00	12.00
	1967R	1.760	BV	BV	10.00	12.00
	1968R		(In mint sets only)			50.00
	1969R	.310	In mint sets only			15.00
	1970R	1.011	In mint sets only			12.00

***NOTE:** Varieties exist in the 1966 issue.

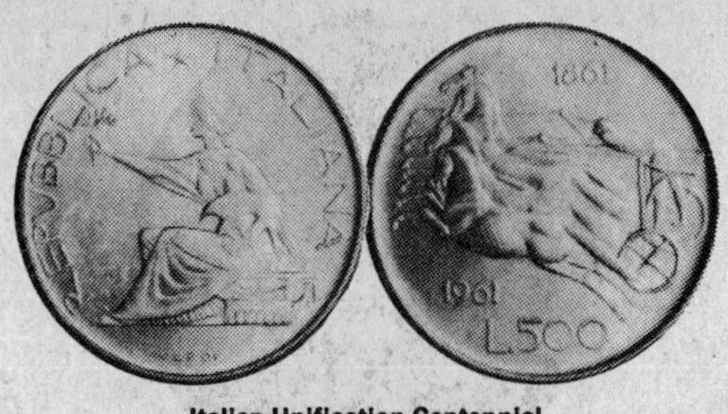

Italian Unification Centennial

Y#	Date	Mintage	Fine	VF	XF	Unc
106	1961R	27.120	BV	BV	10.00	12.00

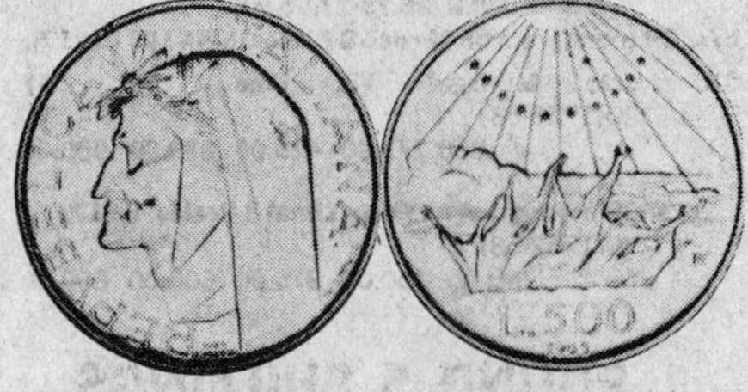

Dante Commemorative

Y#	Date	Mintage	Fine	VF	XF	Unc
107	1965R	5.000	BV	BV	10.00	12.00

Guglielmo Marconi

Y#	Date	Mintage	Fine	VF	XF	Unc
110	1974R	—	BV	BV	12.00	17.50

300th Anniversary Death of Carlo Maderno

Y#	Date	Mintage	Fine	VF	XF	Unc
114	1979	—	—	—	—	—

1000 LIRE

14.0000 gm., .835 SILVER, .3758 oz ASW
Centennial Of Rome As Capital

Y#	Date	Mintage	Fine	VF	XF	Unc
108	1970R	3.011	BV	BV	12.50	15.00

1900th Anniversary of Destruction of Pompeii

Y#	Date	Mintage	Fine	VF	XF	Unc
115	1979	—	—	—	—	—

NCLT ISSUES

PATTERNS

KM#	Date	Mintage	Identification	Mkt.Val.
XA102	1956R	1,200	20 Lire, Aluminum-Bronze	—

PROVAS (Pr)

(PROVA in field)
Standard metals unless otherwise noted

Y#	Date	Mintage	Identification	Issue Price	Mkt Val.
Pr54	1907R	—	20 Lire	—	—
Pr56	1907R	—	100 Lire	—	—
Pr52.1	1914R	—	5 Lire	—	2500.
Pr52.2	1914R	—	5 Lire, "PROVA DI STAMPA"	—	2000.
Pr52.2a	1914R	—	5 Lire, Copper	—	—
Pr52.2b	1914R	—	5 Lire, White metal	—	—
Pr66.1	1923R	—	2 Lire	—	—
Pr66.2	1923R	—	2 Lire, "PROVA DI STAMPA"	—	—
Pr72	1923R	—	20 Lire	—	—
Pr73.1	1923R	—	100 Lire	—	—
Pr73.2	1923R	—	100 Lire, 'P' (for PROVA)	—	—
Pr74	1925R	—	100 Lire	—	—
Pr69.1	1927R	—	20 Lire	—	—
Pr69.2	1927R	—	20 Lire, "PROVA DI STAMPA"	—	—
Pr69.3	1927R	—	20 Lire, "PROVA SEUZA RATOCCO"	—	—
Pr75.1	ND(1928)R	—	20 Lire, "PRIMA PROVA"	—	—
Pr75.2	1928R	—	20 Lire, "PROVA DI STAMPA"	—	—
Pr75a	1928R	—	20 Lire, Gold	—	—
Pr70	1931R	—	50 Lire	—	—
Pr71	1931R	—	100 Lire	—	—
Pr93	1936R	—	100 Lire	—	—
Pr77a	1939R	—	5 Centesimi	—	—
Pr78a	1939R	—	10 Centesimi	—	—
Pr79a	1939R	—	20 Centesimi	—	—
Pr80a	1939R	—	50 Centesimi	—	—
Pr81a	1939R	—	1 Lira	—	—
Pr82a	1939R	—	2 Lire	—	—
Pr95	1946R	—	1 Lire	—	75.00
Pr96	1946R	—	2 Lire	—	100.00
Pr97	1946R	—	5 Lire	—	125.00
Pr98	1946R	—	10 Lire	—	125.00
Pr99	1951R	—	1 Lire	—	65.00
Pr101	1951R	—	5 Lire	—	75.00
Pr102	1951R	—	10 Lire	—	80.00
Pr100	1953R	—	2 Lire	—	70.00
PrA102	1956R	—	20 Lire, 'P' (for PROVA)	—	200.00
Pr105	1957R	—	500 Lire	—	750.00
Pr107	1965R	570	500 Lire	—	350.00
Pr102a	1968R	—	20 Lire	—	75.00
Pr108	1970R	—	1000 Lire	—	275.00
Pr104	1974R	—	100 Lire	—	150.00
Pr109	1974R	—	100 Lire	—	75.00
Pr110	1974R	—	500 Lire	—	200.00

MINT SETS

KM#	Date	Mintage	Identification	Issue Price	Mkt. Val.
S1	1968(8)	100,000	Y99-102,A102,103-105	6.50	90.00
S2	1969(8)	310,000	As above	6.50	20.00
S3	1970(9)	1,011,000	As above plus 108	—	20.00
	1971(5)	—	Y101,102,A102a,103,104	—	5.00
	1972(5)	—	Y101,102,A102a,103,104	—	5.00
	1973(5)	—	Y101,102,A102a,103,104	—	7.00
	1974(6)	—	Y101,102,A102a,103,104,109	—	4.00
	1974(7)	—	Y101,102,A102a,103,104,109,111	—	20.00
	1975(5)	—	Y101,102,A102a,103,104	—	3.50
	1976(5)	—	Y101,102,A102a,103,104	—	3.50
	1977(6)	—	Y101,102,A102a,103,104,112	—	3.50
	1978(6)	—	Y101,102,A102a,103,104,112	—	4.50
	1979(7)	—	Y101,102,A102a,103,104,112,113	—	3.75

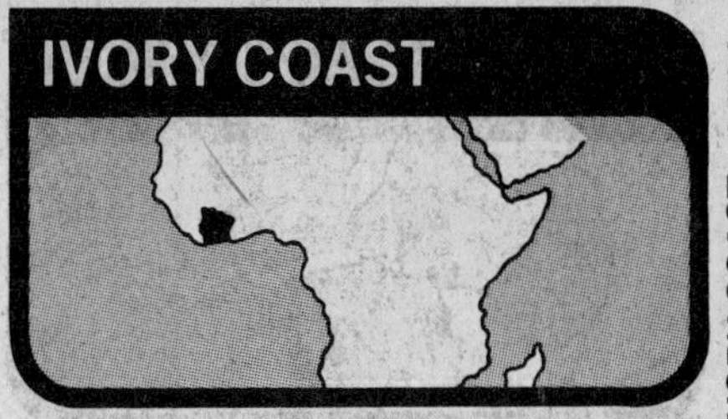

IVORY COAST

The Republic of Ivory Coast, a former French Overseas territory located on the south side of the African bulge between Nigeria and Ghana, has an area of 124,500 sq. mi. (322,500 sq. km.) and a population of 7.3 million. Capital: Abidjan. The predominantly agricultural economy is one of Africa's most prosperous. Coffee, tropical woods, cocoa, and bananas are exported.

The Ivory Coast was first visited by French and Portuguese navigators in the 15th century. French traders set up establishments in the 19th century, and gradually extended their influence along the coast and inland. The area was organized as a territory in 1893, and from 1904 to 1958 was a constituent unit of the Federation of French West Africa - as a Colony under the Third Republic and an Overseas Territory under the Fourth. In 1958 Ivory Coast became an autonomous republic within the French Community. Independence was attained on Aug. 7, 1960.

10 FRANCS

SILVER

H#	Date	Mintage	XF	Unc	Proof
1	1966	—	—	—	17.50

3.2000gm., .900 GOLD, .0926oz AGW

H#	Date	Mintage	XF	Unc	Proof
2	1966	2,000	—	—	75.00

25 FRANCS

8.0000gm., .900 GOLD, .2315oz AGW

H#	Date	Mintage	XF	Unc	Proof
3	1966	2,000	—	—	150.00

50 FRANCS

16.0000gm., .900 GOLD, .4630oz AGW
Similar to 25 Francs, H#3.

H#	Date	Mintage	XF	Unc	Proof
4	1966	2,000	—	—	300.00

100 FRANCS

32.0000gm., .900 GOLD, .9260oz AGW
Similar to 25 Francs, H#3.

H#	Date	Mintage	XF	Unc	Proof
5	1966	2,000	—	—	600.00

NCLT ISSUES

PROOF SETS

STANDARD METALS

KM#	Date	Mintage	Identification	Issue Price	Mkt. Val.
101	1966	2,000	H2-5	—	1125.

JAMAICA

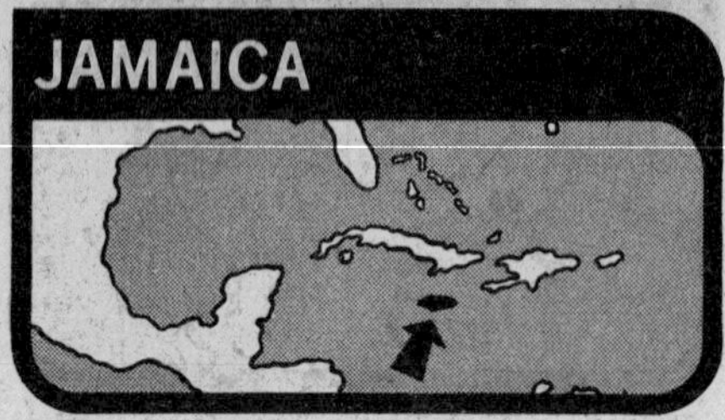

Jamaica, a member of the British Commonwealth situated in the Caribbean Sea 90 miles south of Cuba, has an area of 4,411 sq. mi. (11,424 sq. km.) and a population of 2.1 million. Capital: Kingston. The economy is founded chiefly on mining, tourism and agriculture. Alumina, bauxite, sugar, rum and molasses are exported.

Jamaica was discovered by Columbus on May 3, 1494, and settled by Spain in 1509. The island was captured in 1655 by a British naval force under the command of Admiral William Penn, and ceded to Britain by the Treaty of Madrid, 1670. For more than 150 years, the Jamaican economy of sugar, slaves and piracy was one of the most prosperous in the new world. Dissension between the property-oriented island legislature and the home government prompted parliament to establish a crown colony government for Jamaica in 1866. From 1958 to 1961 Jamaica was a member of the West Indies Federation, withdrawing when Jamaican voters rejected the association. The colony attained independence on Aug. 6, 1962. Jamaica is a member of the Commonwealth of Nations. The Queen of England is Chief of State.

A decimal standard currency system was adopted on Sept. 8, 1969.

RULERS

British, until 1962

MINTMARKS

H - Heaton
C - Ottawa
FM - Franklin Mint, U.S.A.**
(fm) - Franklin Mint, U.S.A.*
(RM) - Royal Mint

***NOTE:** During 1970 the Franklin Mint produced matte and proof coins (1 cent-1 dollar) using dies similar to/or Royal Mint without the FM mintmark.

****NOTE:** During 1975-77 the Franklin Mint produced coinage in up to 3 different qualities. Qualities of issue are designated in ( ) after each date and are defined as follows:

(M) MATTE - Normal circulation strike or a dull finish produced by sandblasting special uncirculated (polish finish) or proof quality dies.

(U) SPECIAL UNCIRCULATED - Polished or proof-like in appearance without any frosted features.

(P) PROOF - The highest qualitty obtainable having mirror-like fields and frosted features.

MONETARY SYSTEM

4 Farthings = 1 Penny
12 Pence = 1 Shilling
8 Reales = 6 Shillings, 8 Pence
(Commencing 1969)
100 Cents = 1 Dollar

COUNTERSTAMP ISSUES

1758

A flowery 'GR' monogram in a circular indentation is the only official Jamaican c/s and is always found on silver Spanish Colonial coins of the 'Pillar' type and on gold Spanish coins of the portrait type. Each coin was counterstamped on obverse and reverse.

5 PENCE

.903 SILVER, 1.65 gm.
c/s: GR monogram on Mexico 1/2 Real, KM#66 (C#2).

C#	Date	Mintage	VG	Fine	VF	XF
1	ND(1755-58)	.320	100.00	160.00	275.00	425.00

c/s: GR monogram on Peru (Lima) 1/2 Real, C#8.

C#	Date	Mintage	VG	Fine	VF	XF
1.1	ND(1755-58)	Inc. Ab.	80.00	130.00	225.00	350.00

10 PENCE

.903 SILVER, 3.4 gm.
c/s: GR monogram on Peru (Lima) 1 Real, C#9.

C#	Date	Mintage	VG	Fine	VF	XF
2	ND(1755-58)	.320	250.00	375.00	525.00	750.00

1 SHILLING 8 PENCE

.903 SILVER, 6.8 gm.
c/s: GR monogram on Mexico 2 Reales, KM#86 (C#15).

C#	Date	Mintage	VG	Fine	VF	XF
3	ND(1755-58)	.127	475.00	800.00	950.00	1300.

c/s: GR monogram on Peru (Lima) 2 Reales, C#10.

C#	Date	Mintage	VG	Fine	VF	XF
3.1	ND(1755-58)	Inc. Ab.	350.00	600.00	775.00	1100.

3 SHILLINGS 4 PENCE

SILVER, 13 gm.
c/s: GR monogram on Mexico 4 Reales, KM#95 (C#16).

C#	Date	Mintage	VG	Fine	VF	XF
4	ND(1755-58)	.060	775.00	1350.	2100.	3100.

6 SHILLINGS 8 PENCE

SILVER, 26.75-27.05 gm.
c/s: GR monogram on Mexico 8 Reales, KM#104 (C#17).

C#	Date	Mintage	VG	Fine	VF	XF
5	ND(1755-58)	.060	275.00	425.00	650.00	950.00

c/s: GR monogram on Peru (Lima) 8 Reales, C#12.

C#	Date	Mintage	VG	Fine	VF	XF
5.1	ND(1752-58)	Inc. Ab.	250.00	375.00	600.00	800.00

1 POUND 5 SHILLINGS

GOLD, 6.7 gm.
c/s: GR monogram on Colombia (Popayan) 2 Escudos, C#8a.

C#	Date	Mintage	VG	Fine	VF	XF
10	ND(1758)	1 known	—	—	Rare	—

5 POUNDS

GOLD, 27 gm.
c/s: GR monogram on Peru (Lima) 8 Escudos, C#22.

C#	Date	Mintage	VG	Fine	VF	XF
12	ND(1751-58)	*2,000	—	—	Rare	—

***NOTE:** Authorized mintage.

REGULAR COINAGE

FARTHING

COPPER-NICKEL

Y#	Date	Mintage	Fine	VF	XF	Unc
1	1880	.192	1.75	3.25	8.00	30.00

Y#	Date	Mintage	Fine	VF	XF	Unc
1	1880	—	—	—	Proof	100.00
	1882H	.384	1.50	3.00	7.00	25.00
	1882H	—	—	—	Proof	100.00
	1884	.096	1.75	3.25	8.00	30.00
	1884	—	—	—	Proof	100.00
	1885	.096	1.75	3.25	8.00	30.00
	1885	—	—	—	Proof	100.00
	1887	.192	1.50	3.00	8.00	25.00
	1887	—	—	—	Proof	100.00
	1888	.192	1.50	3.00	8.00	25.00
	1888	—	—	—	Proof	100.00
	1889	.192	1.50	3.00	8.00	25.00
	1890H	.096	1.85	3.75	8.00	25.00
	1891	.096	2.25	4.50	12.00	60.00
	1893	.096	1.75	4.00	10.00	37.50
	1894	.144	1.50	3.00	7.00	25.00
	1894	—	—	—	Proof	125.00
	1895	.144	1.50	3.00	7.00	25.00
	1897	.144	1.50	3.00	7.00	25.00
	1899	.144	1.75	3.25	10.00	35.00
	1900	.144	1.50	3.00	7.00	25.00

Rev: Horizontal shading in arms.

Y#	Date	Mintage	Fine	VF	XF	Unc
4	1902	.144	1.85	3.75	7.00	25.00
	1903	.144	1.85	3.75	9.00	30.00

Rev: Vertical shading in arms.

Y#	Date	Mintage	Fine	VF	XF	Unc
7	1904	.192	1.00	2.00	6.00	20.00
	1904	—	—	—	Proof	300.00
	1905	.192	1.00	2.00	5.00	20.00
	1906	.528	1.35	2.75	6.00	20.00
	1907	.192	1.00	2.00	4.00	20.00
	1909	.144	1.00	2.00	4.00	20.00
	1910	.048	1.35	2.75	6.00	22.00

Y#	Date	Mintage	Fine	VF	XF	Unc
10	1914	.192	3.00	8.00	22.50	55.00
	1916H	.480	.75	1.50	7.00	30.00
	1918C	.208	.75	2.00	6.00	22.00
	1919C	.401	.75	1.50	4.00	17.00
	1926	.240	.75	2.00	6.00	26.00
	1928	.480	.75	1.50	3.00	12.00
	1928	—	—	—	Proof	85.00
	1932	.480	.75	1.50	3.00	10.00
	1934	.480	.65	1.25	3.00	10.00

NICKEL-BRASS

Y#	Date	Mintage	Fine	VF	XF	Unc
13	1937	.480	.85	1.75	3.50	6.00
	1937	—	—	—	Proof	80.00

Obv: Larger head

Y#	Date	Mintage	Fine	VF	XF	Unc
16	1938	.480	.20	.40	2.00	4.00
	1942	.480	.20	.40	2.00	6.00
	1945	.480	.20	.40	.75	1.25
	1945	—	—	—	Proof	80.00
	1947	.192	.40	.75	2.25	7.00
	1947	—	—	—	Proof	80.00

Obv: EMPEROR OF INDIA dropped.

Y#	Date	Mintage	Fine	VF	XF	Unc
19	1950	.288	.10	.15	.25	1.00
	1950	—	—	—	Proof	80.00
	1952	.288	.10	.15	.25	1.00
	1952	—	—	—	Proof	80.00

1/2 PENNY

COPPER-NICKEL

Y#	Date	Mintage	Fine	VF	XF	Unc
2	1869	.192	1.75	3.50	8.00	35.00
	1869	—	—	—	Proof	100.00
	1870	.240	1.75	3.50	10.00	40.00
	1870	—	—	—	Proof	100.00
	1871	.240	1.75	3.50	10.00	40.00
	1871	—	—	—	Proof	100.00
	1880	.192	2.00	4.00	12.00	45.00
	1880	—	—	—	Proof	100.00
	1882H	.096	4.00	8.00	18.00	60.00
	1882H	—	—	—	Proof	125.00
	1884	.096	2.00	4.00	12.00	45.00
	1884	—	—	—	Proof	100.00
	1885	.096	2.00	4.00	12.00	45.00
	1885	—	—	—	Proof	100.00
	1887	.072	1.75	3.50	10.00	40.00
	1888	.096	1.75	3.50	12.00	45.00
	1888	—	—	—	Proof	100.00
	1889	.096	2.00	4.00	12.00	50.00
	1890H	.120	1.75	3.50	10.00	40.00
	1891	.120	2.25	5.00	14.00	55.00
	1893	.144	2.25	5.00	14.00	55.00
	1894	.096	2.50	5.00	14.00	55.00
	1895	.096	2.50	5.00	15.00	55.00
	1897	.120	1.75	3.50	9.00	35.00
	1899	.120	1.75	3.50	9.00	35.00
	1900	.120	1.75	3.50	9.00	35.00

BRASS

Y#	Date	Mintage	Fine	VF	XF	Unc
2a	1869	—	—	—	Proof	250.00

COPPER-NICKEL

Rev: Horizontal shading in arms.

Y#	Date	Mintage	Fine	VF	XF	Unc
5	1902	.048	2.50	5.00	12.00	30.00
	1903	.048	3.00	6.00	14.00	35.00

Rev: Vertical shading in arms.

Y#	Date	Mintage	Fine	VF	XF	Unc
8	1904	.048	5.00	10.00	20.00	65.00
	1905	.048	1.50	3.00	6.50	20.00
	1906	.432	1.75	3.50	8.50	25.00
	1907	.504	1.75	3.50	8.50	25.00
	1909	.144	1.75	3.50	7.50	20.00
	1910	.144	1.75	3.50	7.50	20.00

Y#	Date	Mintage	Fine	VF	XF	Unc
11	1914	.096	4.50	9.00	24.00	65.00
	1916H	.192	1.25	2.50	8.00	30.00
	1918C	.251	.75	1.50	5.00	17.50
	1919C	.312	.75	1.50	5.00	17.50
	1920	.480	.75	1.50	5.00	17.50
	1926	.240	.75	1.50	6.00	25.00
	1928	.120	.75	1.50	4.00	12.50
	1928	—	—	—	Proof	80.00

NICKEL-BRASS

Y#	Date	Mintage	Fine	VF	XF	Unc
14	1937	.960	1.00	2.00	4.00	7.00
	1937	—	—	—	Proof	75.00

Obv: Larger head

Y#	Date	Mintage	Fine	VF	XF	Unc
17	1938	.960	.30	.60	2.00	6.00
	1938	—	—	—	Proof	75.00
	1940	.960	.30	.60	2.00	6.00
	1940	—	—	—	Proof	75.00
	1942	.960	.30	.60	3.00	8.00
	1945	.960	.30	.60	2.00	8.00
	1945	—	—	—	Proof	75.00
	1947	.960	.30	.60	3.00	8.00
	1947	—	—	—	Proof	75.00

Obv: EMPEROR OF INDIA dropped.

Y#	Date	Mintage	Fine	VF	XF	Unc
20	1950	1.440	.10	.20	.30	1.25
	1950	—	—	—	Proof	75.00
	1952	1.200	.10	.20	.30	1.25
	1952	—	—	—	Proof	75.00

Y#	Date	Mintage	Fine	VF	XF	Unc
22	1955	1.440	.10	.15	.40	.75
	1955	—	—	—	Proof	70.00
	1957	.600	.10	.20	.75	1.50
	1958	.960	.10	.20	.75	2.25
	1958	—	—	—	Proof	70.00
	1959	.960	.10	.20	.75	3.25
	1961	.480	.10	.15	.30	.50
	1962	.960	.10	.15	.30	.50
	1962	—	—	—	Proof	70.00
	1963	.960	.10	.15	.30	.50
	1963	—	—	—	Proof	70.00

Rev: New arms.

Y#	Date	Mintage	Fine	VF	XF	Unc
24	1964	1.440	.10	.15	.20	.30
	1965	1.200	.10	.15	.20	.30
	1966	1.680	.10	.15	.20	.30

COPPER-NICKEL-ZINC
Jamaican Coinage Centennial

Y#	Date	Mintage	Fine	VF	XF	Unc
27	1969	.030	.10	.20	.35	.75
	1969	5,000	—	—	Proof	5.00

PENNY

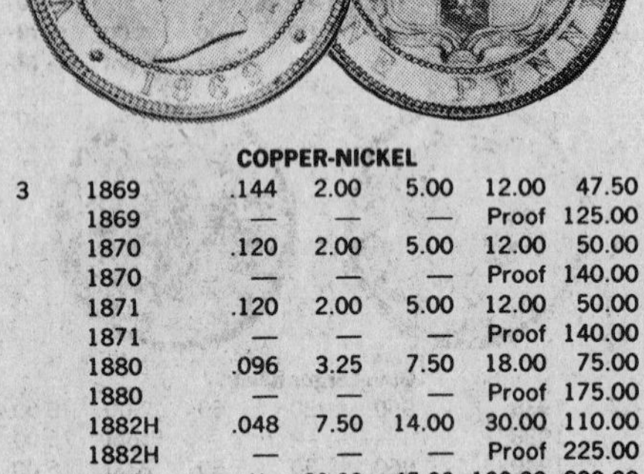

COPPER-NICKEL

Y#	Date	Mintage	Fine	VF	XF	Unc
3	1869	.144	2.00	5.00	12.00	47.50
	1869	—	—	—	Proof	125.00
	1870	.120	2.00	5.00	12.00	50.00
	1870	—	—	—	Proof	140.00
	1871	.120	2.00	5.00	12.00	50.00
	1871	—	—	—	Proof	140.00
	1880	.096	3.25	7.50	18.00	75.00
	1880	—	—	—	Proof	175.00
	1882H	.048	7.50	14.00	30.00	110.00
	1882H	—	—	—	Proof	225.00
	1882	Inc. Ab.	20.00	45.00	100.00	200.00
	1882	—	—	—	Proof	250.00
	1884	.048	3.00	7.50	18.00	75.00
	1884	—	—	—	Proof	150.00
	1885	.048	3.50	7.50	22.00	75.00
	1885	—	—	—	Proof	150.00
	1887	.024	3.00	7.50	18.00	70.00
	1888	.024	3.00	7.50	22.00	85.00
	1888	—	—	—	Proof	150.00
	1889	.024	4.00	8.00	24.00	85.00
	1890	.036	3.00	7.00	18.00	75.00
	1891	.036	6.00	14.00	34.00	100.00
	1893	.024	6.00	14.00	34.00	100.00
	1894	.036	3.50	9.00	22.00	80.00
	1895	.036	3.50	9.00	22.00	80.00
	1897	.024	4.50	10.00	24.00	100.00
	1899	.024	4.50	10.00	24.00	100.00
	1900	.024	3.50	9.00	22.00	90.00

BRASS

Y#	Date	Mintage	Fine	VF	XF	Unc
3a	1869	—	—	—	Proof	250.00
	1870	—	—	—	Proof	350.00

COPPER-NICKEL
Rev: Horizontal shading in arms.

Y#	Date	Mintage	Fine	VF	XF	Unc
6	1902	.060	2.50	5.00	12.50	30.00
	1903	.060	2.50	5.00	15.00	40.00

Rev: Vertical shading in arms.

Y#	Date	Mintage	Fine	VF	XF	Unc
9	1904	.024	5.00	12.00	27.50	80.00
	1904	—	—	—	Proof	300.00
	1905	.048	1.50	3.00	8.00	25.00
	1906	.156	1.75	3.50	8.00	30.00
	1907	.108	1.75	3.50	8.00	27.50
	1909	.144	1.75	3.50	8.00	25.00
	1910	.144	1.75	3.50	8.00	25.00

Y#	Date	Mintage	Fine	VF	XF	Unc
12	1914	.024	18.50	37.50	65.00	140.00
	1916H	.024	17.50	35.00	60.00	140.00
	1918C	.187	.75	1.50	6.00	20.00
	1919C	.251	.75	1.50	6.00	20.00
	1920	.360	.75	1.50	5.00	17.50
	1926	.240	.75	1.50	7.00	25.00
	1928	.360	.75	1.50	4.50	15.00
	1928	—	—	—	Proof	80.00

NICKEL-BRASS

Y#	Date	Mintage	Fine	VF	XF	Unc
15	1937	1.200	1.25	2.50	5.00	8.00
	1937	—	—	—	Proof	75.00

Obv: Larger head

Y#	Date	Mintage	Fine	VF	XF	Unc
18	1938	1.200	.35	.75	3.00	8.00
	1938	—	—	—	Proof	80.00
	1940	1.200	.35	.75	3.00	8.00
	1940	—	—	—	Proof	80.00
	1942	1.200	.35	.75	3.00	8.00
	1942	—	—	—	Proof	80.00
	1945	1.200	.35	.75	1.75	4.00
	1945	—	—	—	Proof	80.00
	1947	.480	.35	.75	2.00	6.00
	1947	—	—	—	Proof	80.00

Obv: EMPEROR OF INDIA dropped.

Y#	Date	Mintage	Fine	VF	XF	Unc
21	1950	.600	.20	.35	1.50	3.00
	1950	—	—	—	Proof	75.00
	1952	.725	.20	.35	1.50	3.00
	1952	—	—	—	Proof	75.00

Y#	Date	Mintage	Fine	VF	XF	Unc
23	1953	1.200	.10	.20	.75	1.50
	1953	—	—	—	Proof	70.00
	1955	.960	.10	.25	1.00	1.50
	1955	—	—	—	Proof	70.00

Y#	Date	Mintage	Fine	VF	XF	Unc
23	1957	.600	.10	.25	1.00	3.00
	1958	1.080	.10	.20	.35	.75
	1958	—	—	—	Proof	75.00
	1959	1.368	.10	.20	.35	.75
	1960	1.368	.10	.20	.30	.60
	1961	1.368	.10	.20	.30	.50
	1962	1.920	.10	.20	.30	.50
	1962	—	—	—	Proof	75.00
	1963	.720	5.00	10.00	20.00	40.00
	1963	—	—	—	Proof	60.00

Rev: New arms.

Y#	Date	Mintage	Fine	VF	XF	Unc
25	1964	.480	.10	.15	.25	.35
	1965	1.200	.10	.15	.20	.30
	1966	1.200	.10	.15	.20	.30
	1967	2.760	.10	.15	.20	.30

COPPER-NICKEL-ZINC
Jamaican Coinage Centennial

Y#	Date	Mintage	Fine	VF	XF	Unc
28	1969	.030	.10	.15	.35	.75
	1969	5,000	—	—	Proof	5.00

1-1/2 PENCE

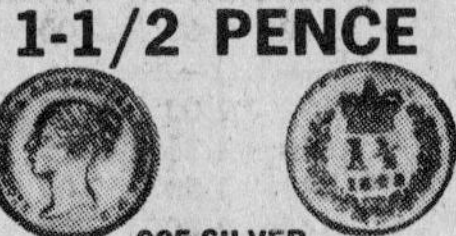

.925 SILVER

From 1834 through 1870 colonial issue 1 1/2 Pence or Three-half pence were circulated in Ceylon and Jamaica. These are listed under Great Britain.

5 SHILLINGS

COPPER-NICKEL
VIII Commonwealth Games

Y#	Date	Mintage	Fine	VF	XF	Unc
26	1966	.190	.75	1.00	1.50	3.00
	1966	.020	—	—	Proof	12.50

DECIMAL COINAGE

NOTE: The Franklin Mint and Royal Mint have both been striking the 1 cent through 1 dollar coinage. The 1970 issues were all struck with dies similar to/or Royal Mint without the FM mintmark. The Royal Mint issues have the name JAMAICA extending beyond the native head dress feathers. Those struck after 1970 by the Franklin Mint have the name JAMAICA within the head dress feathers.

CENT

BRONZE

Y#	Date	Mintage	VF	XF	Unc
29	1969	30.200	—	.10	.25
	1969	.019	—	Proof	1.50
	1970(RM) small date	10.000	—	.10	.25
	1970FM(M) large date	5,000	.50	.75	1.25
	1970FM(P)	.012	—	Proof	2.00
	1971RM	—	—	.10	.25

Y#	Date	Mintage	VF	XF	Unc
29.1	1971FM(M)	4,834	.50	.75	1.25
	1971FM(P)	.014	—	Proof	1.00
	1972FM(M)	7,982	.35	.60	1.00
	1972FM(P)	.017	—	Proof	1.00
	1973FM(M)	.029	.15	.25	.35
	1973FM(P)	.028	—	Proof	1.00
	1974FM(M)	.028	.15	.25	.35
	1974FM(P)	.022	—	Proof	1.00
	1975FM(M)	.036	—	.15	.25
	1975FM(U)	4,683	—	.60	1.00
	1975FM(P)	.016	—	Proof	1.00

F.A.O. Issue

Y#	Date	Mintage	VF	XF	Unc
36	1971	.645	—	.10	.25
	1972	5.000	—	.10	.25
	1973	5.500	—	.10	.25
	1974	3.000	—	.10	.25

ALUMINUM
F.A.O. Issue

Y#	Date	Mintage	VF	XF	Unc
36a	1975	15.000	—	.10	.20
	1976	16.000	—	.10	.20

Y#	Date	Mintage	VF	XF	Unc
36a.1	1976FM(M)	.028	—	.10	.15
	1976FM(U)	1,802	—	1.25	2.00
	1976FM(P)	.024	—	Proof	1.00
	1977FM(M)	.028	—	.10	.15
	1977FM(U)	597pcs.	—	2.00	3.00
	1977FM(P)	.010	—	Proof	1.00
	1978FM(M)	.028	—	—	—
	1978FM(u)	1,282	—	.10	.15
	1978FM(P)	6,058	—	Proof	1.00
	1979FM(M)	.028	—	—	—
36a.1	1979FM(U)	2,608	—	—	—
	1979FM(P)	4,049	—	Proof	—
	1980FM	—	—	—	—
	1980FM(P)	—	—	Proof	—

5 CENTS

COPPER-NICKEL

Y#	Date	Mintage	VF	XF	Unc
30	1969	12.008	—	.10	.20
	1969	.030	—	Proof	2.00
	1970FM(M)	5,000	.60	.90	1.50
	1970FM(P)	.012	—	Proof	2.50
	1972	6.000	—	.10	.20
	1975	6.010	—	.10	.15
	1977	1.600	—	.10	.15

Y#	Date	Mintage	VF	XF	Unc
30.1	1971FM(M)	4,834	.60	.90	1.50
	1971FM(P)	.014	—	Proof	1.25
	1972FM(M)	7,982	.50	.75	1.25
	1972FM(P)	.017	—	Proof	1.25
	1973FM(M)	.017	.35	.60	1.00
	1973FM(P)	.028	—	Proof	1.00
	1974FM(M)	.016	.30	.50	.75
	1974FM(P)	.022	—	Proof	1.00
	1975FM(M)	6,240	.35	.60	1.00
	1975FM(U)	4,683	—	.75	1.25
	1975FM(P)	.016	—	Proof	1.00
	1976FM(M)	5,560	.35	.60	1.00
	1976FM(U)	1,802	—	1.35	2.25
	1976FM(P)	.024	—	Proof	1.25
	1977FM(M)	5,560	.50	.75	1.25
	1977FM(U)	597pcs.	—	2.50	4.00
	1977FM(P)	.010	—	Proof	1.00
	1978FM(M)	5,560	—	—	—
	1978FM(U)	1,282	.35	.60	1.00
	1978FM(P)	6,058	—	Proof	1.00
	1979FM(M)	5,560	—	—	—
	1979FM(U)	2,608	—	—	—
	1979FM(P)	4,049	—	Proof	—
	1980FM	—	—	—	—
	1980FM(P)	—	—	Proof	—

10 CENTS

COPPER-NICKEL

Y#	Date	Mintage	VF	XF	Unc
31	1969	19.508	.10	.20	.35
	1969	.030	—	Proof	2.50
	1970FM(M)	5,000	.65	1.00	1.75
	1970FM(P)	.012	—	Proof	2.50
	1972	6.000	.10	.20	.35
	1975	10.010	.10	.15	.25
	1977	8.000	.10	.15	.25

Y#	Date	Mintage	VF	XF	Unc
31.1	1971FM(M)	4,834	.65	1.00	1.75
	1971FM(P)	.014	—	Proof	1.50
	1972FM(M)	7,982	.60	.90	1.50
	1972FM(P)	.017	—	Proof	1.50
	1973FM(M)	.015	.50	.75	1.25
	1973FM(P)	.028	—	Proof	1.25
	1974FM(M)	.014	.50	.75	1.25
	1974FM(P)	.022	—	Proof	1.25
	1975FM(M)	3,120	.60	.90	1.50
	1975FM(U)	4,683	—	1.00	1.75
31.1	1975FM(P)	.016	—	Proof	1.25
	1976FM(M)	2,780	.75	1.25	2.00
	1976FM(U)	1,802	—	1.75	3.00
	1976FM(P)	.024	—	Proof	1.50
	1977FM(M)	2,780	.75	1.25	2.00
	1977FM(U)	597pcs.	—	2.75	4.50
	1977FM(P)	.010	—	Proof	1.25
	1978FM(M)	2,780	—	—	—
	1978FM(u)	4,062	.60	1.00	1.75
	1978FM(P)	6,058	—	Proof	1.25
	1979FM(M)	2,780	—	—	—
	1979FM(U)	2,608	—	—	—
	1979FM(P)	4,049	—	Proof	—

20 CENTS

COPPER-NICKEL

Y#	Date	Mintage	VF	XF	Unc
32	1969	3.758	.30	.50	1.00
	1969	.030	—	Proof	3.00
	1970FM(M)	5,000	.75	1.25	2.00
	1970FM(P)	.012	—	Proof	3.50
	1975	.010	—	—	1.50

Y#	Date	Mintage	VF	XF	Unc
32.1	1971FM(M)	4,834	.75	1.25	2.00
	1971FM(P)	.014	—	Proof	1.75
	1972FM(M)	7,982	.60	1.00	1.75
	1972FM(P)	.017	—	Proof	2.50
	1973FM(M)	.013	.50	.90	1.50
	1973FM(P)	.028	—	Proof	2.50
	1974FM(M)	.012	.50	.90	1.50
	1974FM(P)	.022	—	Proof	1.50
	1975FM(M)	1,560	1.00	1.75	3.00
	1975FM(U)	4,683	—	1.25	2.25
	1975FM(P)	.016	—	Proof	1.50
	1976FM(M)	1,390	1.00	1.75	3.00
	1976FM(U)	1,802	—	1.75	3.00
	1976FM(P)	.024	—	Proof	2.50

F.A.O. Issue

Y#	Date	Mintage	VF	XF	Unc
42	1976	3.000	.30	.65	1.25

Y#	Date	Mintage	VF	XF	Unc
42.1	1977FM(M)	1,390	1.00	1.75	3.00
	1977FM(U)	597pcs.	2.00	3.50	5.50
	1977FM(P)	.010	—	Proof	1.75
	1978FM(M)	1,390	—	—	—
	1978FM(U)	1,282	.75	1.25	2.00
	1978FM(P)	6,058	—	Proof	1.75
	1979FM(M)	1,390	—	—	—
	1979FM(U)	2,608	—	—	—
	1979FM(P)	4,049	—	Proof	—
	1980FM	—	—	—	—
	1980FM(P)	—	—	Proof	—

25 CENTS

COPPER-NICKEL

Y#	Date	Mintage	VF	XF	Unc
33	1969	.758	.30	.65	1.00
	1969	.030	—	Proof	3.50
	1970FM(M)	5,000	.90	1.50	2.50
	1970FM(P)	.012	—	Proof	4.00
	1973	.160	.35	.75	1.25
	1975	3.110	.35	.75	1.25

Y#	Date	Mintage	VF	XF	Unc
33.1	1971FM(M)	4,834	.90	1.50	2.50
	1971FM(P)	.014	—	Proof	2.25
	1972FM(M)	8,382	.85	1.35	2.25
	1972FM(P)	.017	—	Proof	3.50
	1973FM(M)	.013	.75	1.25	2.00
	1973FM(P)	.028	—	Proof	3.50
	1974FM(M)	.012	.75	1.25	2.00
	1974FM(P)	.022	—	Proof	2.00
	1975FM(M)	1,503	1.75	2.75	4.50
	1975FM(U)	4,683	—	1.75	2.75
	1975FM(P)	.016	—	Proof	2.00
	1976FM(M)	1,112	1.75	2.75	4.50
	1976FM(U)	1,802	—	2.00	3.50
	1976FM(P)	.024	—	Proof	3.50
	1977FM(M)	1,112	1.75	2.75	4.50
	1977FM(U)	597pcs.	—	4.50	7.00
	1977FM(P)	.010	—	Proof	2.00
	1978FM(M)	1,112	—	—	—
	1978FM(U)	1,282	1.00	1.75	3.00
	1978FM(P)	6,058	—	Proof	2.00
	1979FM(M)	1,112	—	—	—
	1979FM(U)	2,608	—	—	—
	1979FM(P)	4,049	—	Proof	—
	1980FM	—	—	—	—
	1980FM(P)	—	—	Proof	—

50 CENTS

COPPER-NICKEL
Marcus Garvey

Y#	Date	Mintage	VF	XF	Unc
43	1975	12.010	.75	1.00	1.50

Y#	Date	Mintage	VF	XF	Unc
43.1	1976FM(M)	1,112	3.50	6.00	10.00
	1976FM(U)	1,802	—	4.00	6.50
	1976FM(P)	.024	—	Proof	4.00
	1977FM(M)	556pcs.	3.50	6.00	10.00
	1977FM(U)	597pcs.	—	6.00	10.00
	1977FM(P)	.010	—	Proof	2.00
43.1	1978FM(M)	556pcs.	—	—	—
	1978FM(U)	1,838	1.75	3.00	5.00
	1978FM(P)	6,058	—	Proof	2.00
	1979FM(M)	556pcs.	—	—	—
	1979FM(U)	1,282	—	—	—
	1979FM(P)	4,049	—	Proof	—
	1980FM	—	—	—	—
	1980FM(P)	—	—	Proof	—

DOLLAR

COPPER-NICKEL
Rev: Similar to Y#34.2.

Y#	Date	Mintage	VF	XF	Unc
34	1969	.047	2.50	4.00	6.50
	1969	.030	—	Proof	30.00
	1970FM(M)	5,000	3.50	5.50	8.50
	1970FM(P)	.014	—	Proof	23.50

Y#	Date	Mintage	VF	XF	Unc
34.1	1971FM	5,024	3.50	5.50	8.50
	1971FM(P)	.015	—	Proof	12.50
	1972FM	7,982	2.75	4.50	7.50
	1972FM(P)	.017	—	Proof	12.50
	1973FM	.010	2.75	4.50	7.50
	1973FM(P)	.028	—	Proof	12.50
	1974FM(M)	8,961	2.75	4.50	7.50
	1974FM(P)	.022	—	Proof	7.00
	1975FM(M)	5,312	2.75	4.50	7.50
	1975FM(U)	4,683	—	5.50	8.50
	1975FM(P)	.016	—	Proof	7.00
	1976FM(M)	284 pcs.	15.00	25.00	40.00
	1976FM(U)	1,802	—	7.50	12.50
	1976FM(P)	.024	—	Proof	12.50
	1977FM(M)	284pcs.	—	—	—
	1977FM(U)	597.Pcs.	—	6.00	10.00
	1977FM(P)	.010	—	Proof	7.00
	1978FM(U)	1,566	3.50	6.00	10.00
	1978FM(P)	6,058	—	Proof	12.50
	1979FM(M)	284pcs.	—	—	—
	1979FM(U)	2,608	—	—	—
	1979FM(P)	4,049	—	Proof	—

Reduced size, 34mm

Y#	Date	Mintage	VF	XF	Unc
34.2	1980FM	—	—	—	—
	1980FM(P)	—	—	Proof	—

5 DOLLARS

42.1500 gm., .925 SILVER, 1.2536 oz ASW
Norman W.Manley

Y#	Date	Mintage	VF	XF	Unc
35	1971FM	4,072	BV	45.00	50.00
	1971FM(P)	.013	—	Proof	45.00

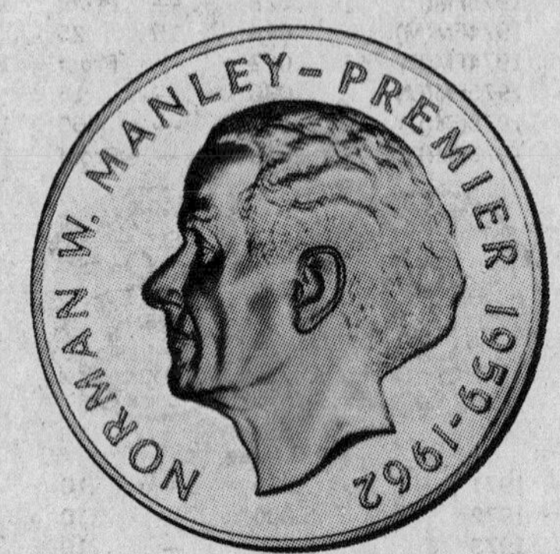

Obv: Similar to 5 Dollars, Y#35.

Y#	Date	Mintage	VF	XF	Unc
A36	1972FM	3,232	BV	40.00	50.00
	1972FM(P)	.021	—	Proof	45.00
	1973FM	6,484	BV	40.00	50.00
	1973FM(P)	.036	—	Proof	45.00

COPPER-NICKEL
Similar to Y#A36, reduced size, 42mm.

Y#	Date	Mintage	VF	XF	Unc
A36a	1974FM(M)	8,661	5.00	6.50	8.50
	1975FM(M)	65 pcs.	—	—	—
	1975FM(U)	4,683	6.00	8.00	10.00
	.1976FM(M)	56 pcs.	—	—	—
	1976FM(U)	1,802	—	10.00	12.50
	1977FM(M)	56pcs.	—	—	—
	1977FM(U)	597pcs.	—	12.50	15.00
	1978FM(U)	1,338	6.50	11.00	13.50
	1979FM(M)	56pcs.	—	—	—
	1979FM(U)	2,608	—	—	—

Reduced size, 36mm

Y#	Date	Mintage	VF	XF	Unc
A36a.1	1980FM	—	—	—	—

42.15000 gm., .500 SILVER, .6776 oz ASW

Y#	Date	Mintage	VF	XF	Unc
A36b	1974FM(P)	.022	—	Proof	20.00
	1975FM(P)	.016	—	Proof	22.50
	1976FM(P)	.023	—	Proof	22.50
	1977FM(P)	.010	—	Proof	22.50
	1978FM(P)	6,058	—	Proof	25.00
	1979FM(P)	4,049	—	Proof	—

Reduced size, 36mm

Y#	Date	Mintage	VF	XF	Unc
A36b.1	1980FM(P)	—	—	Proof	—

10 DOLLARS

48.6000 gm., .925 SILVER, 1.4454 oz ASW
10th Anniversary of Independence

Y#	Date	Mintage	VF	XF	Unc
37	1972	.042	BV	BV	45.00
	1972	.033	—	Proof	50.00

COPPER-NICKEL
Sir Henry Morgan

Y#	Date	Mintage	VF	XF	Unc
39	1974FM(M)	.015	—	9.00	15.00

48.6000 gm., .925 SILVER, 1.4454 oz ASW

Y#	Date	Mintage	VF	XF	Unc
39a	1974FM(P)	.042	—	Proof	50.00

COPPER-NICKEL
Christopher Columbus
Obv: Similar to Y#39.

Y#	Date	Mintage	VF	XF	Unc
40	1975FM(M)	30 pcs.	—	—	—
	1975FM(U)	5,758	—	13.50	20.00

48.6000 gm., .925 SILVER, 1.4454 oz ASW

Y#	Date	Mintage	VF	XF	Unc
40a	1975FM(P)	.029	—	Proof	50.00

COPPER-NICKEL
Admiral Horatio Nelson
Obv: Similar to Y#39.

Y#	Date	Mintage	VF	XF	Unc
44	1976FM(M)	27 pcs.	—	—	—
	1976FM(U)	2,302	—	15.00	22.50

48.6000 gm., .925 SILVER, 1.4454 oz ASW

Y#	Date	Mintage	VF	XF	Unc
44a	1976FM(P)	.031	—	Proof	50.00

COPPER-NICKEL
Admiral George Rodney
Obv: Similar to Y#39.

Y#	Date	Mintage	VF	XF	Unc
46	1977FM(M)	27 pcs.	—	—	—
	1977FM(U)	847pcs.	—	17.50	25.00

48.6000 gm., .925 SILVER, 1.4454 oz ASW

Y#	Date	Mintage	VF	XF	Unc
46a	1977FM(P)	.014	—	Proof	50.00

COPPER-NICKEL
Jamaican Unity
Obv: Similar to Y#39.

Y#	Date	Mintage	VF	XF	Unc
47	1978FM(U)	1,559	15.00	25.00	40.00

48.6000 gm., .925 SILVER, 1.4454 oz ASW

Y#	Date	Mintage	VF	XF	Unc
47a	1978FM(P)	.012	—	Proof	50.00

COPPER-NICKEL
Homerus Swallowtails

Y#	Date	Mintage	VF	XF	Unc
51	1979FM(M)	27 pcs.	—	—	—
	1979FM(U)	2,608	—	—	—

48.6000 gm., .925 SILVER, 1.4454 oz ASW

Y#	Date	Mintage	VF	XF	Unc
51a	1979FM(P)	8,308	—	Proof	50.00

International Year of the Child

Y#	Date	Mintage	VF	XF	Unc
55	1979	—	—	—	—

COPPER-NICKEL
Trochilus Polytmas Hummingbirds

Y#	Date	Mintage	VF	XF	Unc
56	1980FM	—	—	—	—

.925 SILVER

Y#	Date	Mintage	VF	XF	Unc
56a	1980FM(P)	—	—	—	—

20 DOLLARS

15.7484 gm., .500 GOLD, .2531 oz AGW
10th Anniversary of Independence

Y#	Date	Mintage	VF	XF	Unc
38	1972	.030	BV	BV	175.00
	1972	.020	—	Proof	200.00

25 DOLLARS

136.0800 gm., .925 SILVER, 4.0473 oz ASW
25th Anniversary of Coronation

Y#	Date	Mintage	VF	XF	Unc
48	1978	.011	—	—	—
	1978	.022	—	Proof	125.00

10th Anniversary of Investiture of Prince Charles

Y#	Date	Mintage	VF	XF	Unc
52	1979	—	—	—	125.00
	1979	.025	—	Proof	135.00

100 DOLLARS

7.8300 gm., .900 GOLD, .2265 oz AGW
Christopher Columbus

Y#	Date	Mintage	VF	XF	Unc
41	1975FM(M)	100 pcs.	—	—	—
	1975FM(U)	.010	BV	150.00	165.00
	1975FM(P)	1975FM(P)	—	Proof	175.00

Admiral Horatio Nelson

Y#	Date	Mintage	VF	XF	Unc
45	1976FM(M)	100 pcs.	—	350.00	450.00
	1976FM(P)	8,952	—	Proof	200.00

11.3400 gm., .900 GOLD, .3281 oz AGW
25th Anniversary of Coronation

Y#	Date	Mintage	VF	XF	Unc
49	1978	—	—	—	—
	1978	5,835	—	Proof	225.00

10th Anniversary of Investiture of Prince Charles

Y#	Date	Mintage	VF	XF	Unc
53	1979	.025		Proof only	235.00

250 DOLLARS

43.2200 gm., .900 GOLD, 1.2507 oz AGW
25th Anniversary of Coronation

Y#	Date	Mintage	VF	XF	Unc
50	1978	3,005	—	Proof	850.00

10th Anniversary of Investiture of Prince Charles

Y#	Date	Mintage	VF	XF	Unc
54	1979	.025		Proof only	825.00

NCLT ISSUES

MINT SETS
STANDARD METALS

KM#	Date	Mintage	Identification	Issue Price	Mkt. Val.
S1	1969(2)	30,000	Y27,28	.90	2.00
S2	1969(6)	30,000	Y29-34	—	8.00
S3	1970(6)	5,000	Y29-34	16.00	17.50
S4	1971(7)	4,072	Y29.1-34.1,35	19.50	65.00
S5	1971(6)	4,834	Y29.1-34.1	—	17.50
S6	1972(7)	2,982	Y29.1-34.1,A36	19.75	65.00
S7	1972(6)	4,000	Y29.1-34.1	10.00	15.00
S8	1973(7)	6,404	Y29.1-34.1,A36	19.75	60.00
S9	1973(6)	3,000	Y29.1-34.1	9.95	12.50
S10	1974(8)	8,361	Y29.1-34.1,A36,A39	25.00	35.00
S11	1975(8)	4,683	Y29.1-34.1,A36a,40,43	27.50	45.00
S12	1976(9)	1,802	Y30.1-34.1,A36a,36a.1,43.1,44	27.50	65.00
S13	1977(9)	600	36a.1,42.1,43.1,46 Y30.1,31.1,33.1,34.1,A36a	27.50	85.00
S14	1978(9)	1,282	Y30.1,31.1,34.1,A36a,36a.1, 42.1,43.1,47	27.50	75.00
S15	1979(9)	2,608	Y30.1,31.1,33.1,A36a,36a.1,42.1 43.1,50	27.50	—
S16	1980(9)	—	Y30.1,31.1,33.1,34.1,A36a,36a.2,42.1 43.1,56	30.00	—

PROOF SETS
STANDARD METALS

KM#	Date	Mintage	Identification	Issue Price	Mkt. Val.
101	1928(3)	20	Y10-12	—	225.00
102	1937(3)	—	Y13-15	—	200.00
103	1969(6)	8,530	Y29-34	15.00	40.00
104	1969(2)	5,000	Y27,28	2.70	10.00
105	1970(6)	11,540	Y29-34	15.00	35.00
106	1971(7)	12,739	Y29.1-34.1,35	26.50	65.00
107	1971(6)	1,048	Y29.1-34.1	15.00	20.00
108	1972(7)	16,967	Y29.1-34.1,A36	27.50	65.00
109	1973(7)	28,405	Y29.1-34.1,A36	27.50	65.00
110	1974(8)	22,026	Y29.1-34.1,A36b,39a	50.00	80.00
111	1975(8)	15,638	Y29.1-34.1,A36b,40a	55.00	85.00
112	1976(9)	22,900	Y30.1-34.1,A36b,36a.1,40a,43.1	55.00	95.00
113	1976(7)	1,503	Y30.1-34.1,A36b,36a.1	22.50	40.00
114	1977(9)	10,054	Y30.1,31.1,33.1,34.1,A36b,36a.1,42.1 43.1,46a	55.00	85.00
115	1978(9)	6,058	Y30.1,31.1,33.1,34.1,A36b,36a.1,42.1 43.1,47a	59.00	95.00
116	1979(9)	4,049	Y30.1,31.1,33.1,34.1,A36b,36a.1,42.1 43.1,51a	59.00	—
117	1980(9)	—	Y30.1,31.1,33.1,34.2,A36b,36a.1, 43.1,56a	90.00	—

JAPAN

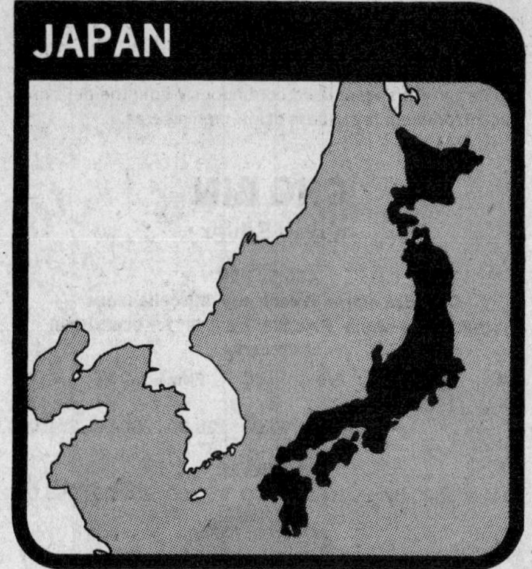

Japan, a constitutional monarchy situated off the east coast of Asia, has an area of 147,470 sq. mi. (381,945 sq. km.) and a population of 113 million. Capital: Tokyo. Japan, one of the three major industrial nations of the free world, exports machinery, motor vehicles, textiles and chemicals.

Japan, founded (so legend holds) in 660 B.C. by a direct descendant of the Sun Goddess, was first brought into contact with the west by a storm-blown Portuguese ship in 1542. European traders and missionaries proceeded to enlarge the contact until the Shogunate, sensing a military threat in the foreign presence, expelled all foreigners and severed relations with the outside world in the 17th century. After contact was reestablished by Commodore Perry of the U. S. Navy in 1854, Japan rapidly industrialized, abolished the Shogunate and established a parliamentary form of government, and by the end of the 19th century achieved the status of a modern economic and military power. A series of wars with China and Russia, and participation with the Allies in World War I, enlarged Japan territorially but brought its interests into contact with the Far Eastern interests of the United States and Britain, causing it to align with the Axis Powers for the pursuit of World War II. After its defeat in World War II, Japan renounced military aggression as a political instrument, established democratic self-government, and quickly reasserted its position as an economic world power.

Japanese coinage of concern to this catalog includes those issued for the Ryukyu Islands (also called Lauchu), a chain of islands extending southwest from Japan toward Taiwan (Formosa), before the Japanese government converted the islands into a prefecture under the name Okinawa. Many of the provinces of Japan issued their own definitive coinage under the Shogunate.

RULERS

(Shoguns)

Iyenari, 1787-1837
Iyeoshi, 1837-1853
Iyesada, 1853-1858
Iyemochi, 1858-1866
Yoshinobu, 1866-1867

(Emperors)

Komei, 1847-1866
Mutsuhito (Meiji), 1867-1912
Yoshihito (Taisho), 1912-1926
Hirohito (Showa), 1926-

NOTE: The personal name of the emperor is followed by the name that he chose for his regnal era.

MONETARY SYSTEM

(Until 1870)

Prior to the Meiji currency reform, there was no fixed exchange rate between the various silver, gold and copper coins in circulation. Each coin exchanged on the basis of its own merits and the prevailing market conditions. The size and weight of the copper coins and the weight and fineness of the silver and gold coins varied widely. From time to time the government would declare an official exchange rate, but this was usually ignored. For gold and silver, nominal equivalents were: 16 Shu = 4 Bu = 1 Ryo.

(Commencing 1870)

10 Rin = 1 Sen
100 Sen = 1 Yen

MINTMARKS ON MON

A - 文 - Tokyo
B - 佐佐佐 - Sado
C - 十 - Fukagawa
D - 小 - Honjo-kamme
E - 一 - Ichi-no-se
F - 川 - Onagi-gawa
G - 元 - Osaka
H - 長 - Nagasaki
I - 足 - Ashio
J - 仙 - Sendai
K - 千 - Sendai
L - 久 - Kuji (Kizaki)
M - ト,ト - Mito
N - ノ - Aizu
O - イ - Ise
P - 盛 - Morioka
Q - 了 - Hiroshima
R - 山 - Yamanouchi

NOTE: Dates shown in parentheses are the first year of minting. Most pieces were minted for several years afterwards, but the exact years minting took place are not known.

LEGENDS

Reading top-bottom, right-left.

Kanei Tsuho

Bunkyu-Eiho

EARLY COINAGE

MON

COPPER or BRASS
Rev: Plain

C#	Date	Mint	VG	Fine	VF	XF
1.1	(1626-1769)	—	.15	.30	.50	.75

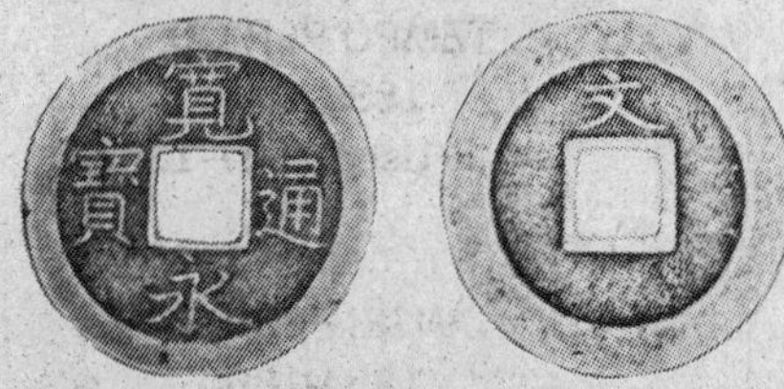

Rev: Character bun.

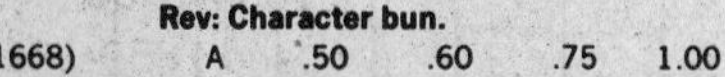

C#	Date	Mint	VG	Fine	VF	XF
1.2	(1668)	A	.50	.60	.75	1.00

Rev: Various mintmarks (Osaka illustrated).

C#	Date	Mint	VG	Fine	VF	XF
1.3	(1714;1717)	B	1.00	2.00	3.00	4.00
1.5	(1736)	C	20.00	30.00	40.00	60.00
1.6	(1737)	D	1.00	2.00	3.00	4.00
1.10	(1740)	E	3.00	5.00	10.00	15.00
1.7	(1740)	F	—	—	Rare	—
1.8	(1741)	G	.35	.75	1.25	2.00
1.11	(1767)	H	.50	1.00	2.00	4.00
1.9	(1741)	I	.50	1.00	2.00	4.00
1.4	(1728)	J	7.50	10.00	15.00	25.00

Obv: Mintmark on outer rim. Rev: Plain.

C#	Date	Mint	VG	Fine	VF	XF
1.5a	(1736)	C	3.00	5.00	7.00	10.00
1.7a	(1740)	F	3.00	5.00	7.00	10.00

IRON
Rev: Plain.

C#	Date	Mint	VG	Fine	VF	XF
1.1a	(1739-1867)	—	2.50	5.00	8.50	15.00

Rev: Various mintmarks.

C#	Date	Mint	VG	Fine	VF	XF
1.3a	(1740;1862)	B	3.00	5.00	10.00	15.00
1.6a	(1739)	D	2.00	4.00	8.00	15.00
1.10a	(1741)	E	3.00	5.00	10.00	15.00
1.12	1739;1838	K	2.50	4.00	8.00	15.00
—	(1769;1774)	L	2.50	4.00	8.00	15.00
—	1844	M	75.00	100.00	150.00	200.00

Obv: Mintmark on outer rim. Rev: Plain.

C#	Date	Mint	VG	Fine	VF	XF
1.5b	(1739)	C	3.00	5.00	10.00	15.00
1.10b	1740	E	3.00	5.00	10.00	15.00
1.7b	(1740)	F	7.50	10.00	15.00	20.00

NOTE: Copper 1 Mon pieces similar to those listed only under iron issues are "Tane Sen" - seed or mother coins.

4 MON

COPPER
Rev: 21 waves.

C#	Date	Mint	VG	Fine	VF	XF
4.1	(1768)	—	1.00	1.50	2.00	4.00

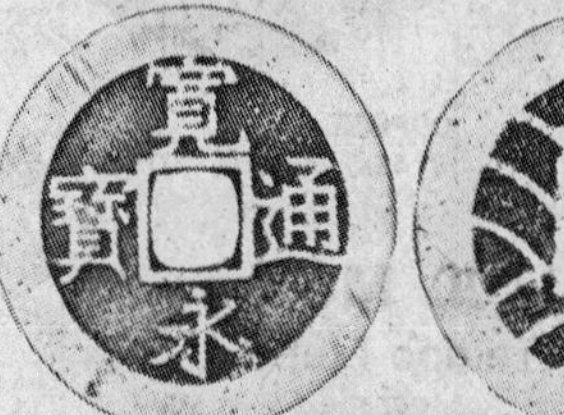

COPPER and BRASS
Rev: 11 waves.

C#	Date	Mint	VG	Fine	VF	XF
4.2	(1769-1860)	—	.30	.50	.75	1.00
6	(1863-67)	—	.50	1.00	1.50	2.00

Obv: Different legend. Rev: 11 waves.

C#	Date	Mint	VG	Fine	VF	XF
6.a	(1863-67)	—	.50	1.00	1.50	2.00

Obv: As above but character at left abbreviated. Rev: 11 waves.

C#	Date	Mint	VG	Fine	VF	XF
6.b	(1863-67)	—	1.00	1.50	2.00	4.00

IRON
Rev: 11 waves; no mintmark.

C#	Date	Mint	VG	Fine	VF	XF
4.2a	1866	—	2.50	5.00	8.00	15.00

Rev: 11 waves and various mintmarks.

C#	Date	Mint	VG	Fine	VF	XF
4.12	(1866)	K	2.50	5.00	8.00	15.00
4.14	1866	M	5.00	10.00	15.00	25.00
4.15	(1866)	N	4.00	8.00	12.50	20.00
4.16	(1866)	O	5.00	10.00	15.00	25.00
4.17	(1866)	P	2.50	5.00	8.00	15.00
4.18	(1866)	Q	100.00	150.00	200.00	300.00
4.19	(1866)	R	—	—	Rare	—

NOTE: Copper 4 Mon pieces similar to those listed only under iron issues are "Tane Sen" - seed or mother coins.

10 MON

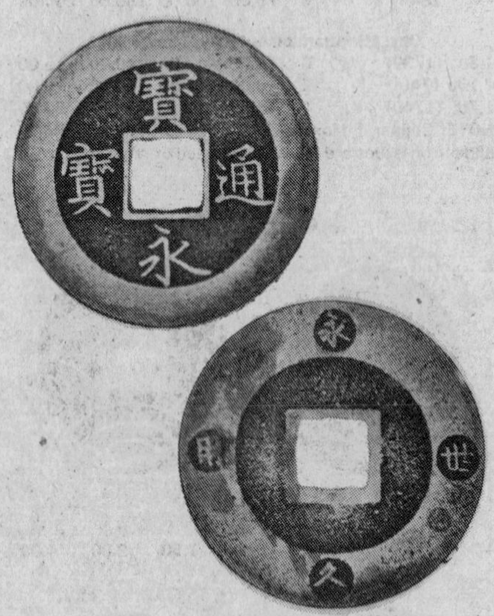

COPPER

C#	Date	Mint	VG	Fine	VF	XF
—	1707-09	—	4.00	6.50	10.00	15.00

100 MON
(Tempo Tsuho)

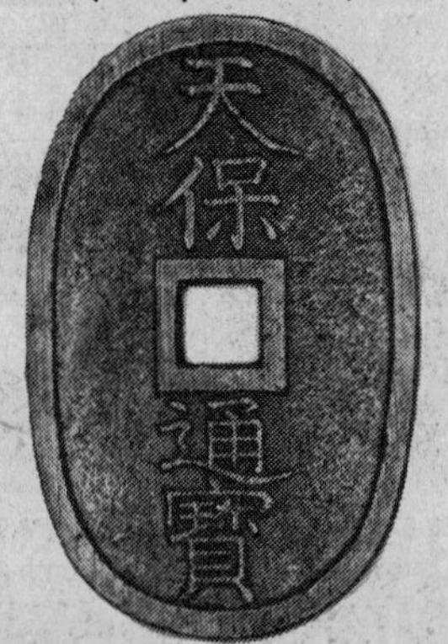

COPPER

C#	Date	Mint	VG	Fine	VF	XF
7	(1835-70)	—	1.50	2.00	3.00	4.50

MAMEITA 'BEAN' GIN

NOTE: Values are for pieces weighing 5-8 grams. Pieces over 10 grams may command up to twice the values shown; pieces under 5 grams somewhat less.

.460 SILVER
Obv: One or more characters, with or without 'God of Plenty'. Rev: Blank.

C#	Date	Era	VG	Fine	VF	XF
8.1	(1736)	Genbun	5.00	10.00	15.00	20.00
		.360 SILVER				
8.2	(1820)	Bunsei	6.00	12.50	17.50	25.00

.261 SILVER

C#	Date	Era	VG	Fine	VF	XF
8.3	(1837)	Tempo	3.50	7.50	10.00	17.50

.135 SILVER

C#	Date	Era	VG	Fine	VF	XF
8.4	(1859)	Ansei	3.00	6.00	9.00	15.00

.450 SILVER
'God of Plenty' design both sides, era designator on belly.

C#	Date	Era	VG	Fine	VF	XF
8a.1	(1736)	Genbun	60.00	90.00	120.00	100.00
		.360 SILVER				
8a.2	(1820)	Bunsei	60.00	90.00	120.00	150.00

.261 SILVER

C#	Date	Era	VG	Fine	VF	XF
8a.3	(1837)	Tempo	50.00	75.00	100.00	125.00

.135 SILVER

C#	Date	Era	VG	Fine	VF	XF
8a.4	(1859)	Ansei	40.00	55.00	75.00	100.00

KEY TO DATING MAMEITA GIN

文 'BUN'
GENBUN PERIOD
1736-1741
(Used 1736-1818)

'BUN'
BUNSEI PERIOD
1818-1830
(Used 1820-1837)

保 'HO'
TEMPO PERIOD
1830-1844
(Used 1837-1858)

政 'SEI'
ANSEI PERIOD
1854-1860
(Used 1859-1865)

One of the above characters is usually found on the obverse of C#8 or both sides of C#8a. The same characters are found at both ends of chogin pieces C#9. Era designators were used continuously until the next one was introduced, regardless of intervening eras.

CHO GIN
Long Silver

.460 SILVER
Obv: Era marks at each end. Miscellaneous marks elsewhere. Rev: Blank except for occasional chopmarks.

C#	Date	Era	VG	Fine	VF	XF
9	1736-1818	Genbun	100.00	150.00	200.00	250.00
		.360 SILVER				
9a	1820-37	Bunsei	100.00	150.00	200.00	265.00

.261 SILVER

C#	Date	Era	VG	Fine	VF	XF
9b	1837-58	Tempo	90.00	120.00	150.00	200.00
		.135 SILVER				
9c	1859-65	Ansei	80.00	110.00	140.00	175.00

KEY TO DATING CHO GIN

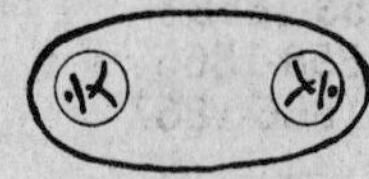

GENBUN

BUNSEI

TEMPO

ANSEI

ISSHU GIN
(One Shu silver)

.989 SILVER, 2.63gm.

C#	Date	Mintage	VG	Fine	VF	XF
11	(1829-37)					
		139.915	25.00	30.00	35.00	45.00

KEY TO DATING LATER ISSHU GIN

常 KAEI PERIOD
1848-1854
(Used 1853-1865)

常 MEIJI PERIOD
1868-1912
(Used 1868-1869)

.968 SILVER, 1.89 gm.

C#	Date	Mintage	VG	Fine	VF	XF
12	(1853-65)					
		159.245	3.00	3.50	4.00	5.00

.880 SILVER, 1.88 gm.

C#	Date	Mintage	VG	Fine	VF	XF
12a	(1868-69)					
		18.742	5.00	7.00	10.00	12.50

NOTE: C#12 TYPE ISSHU GIN are dated according to how the character illustrated is written on the reverse. Meiji Isshu Gin are also known as Kaheishi Isshu Gin.

NISSHU GIN
(Two Shu silver)

.978 SILVER, 10.19 gm.

C#	Date	Mintage	VG	Fine	VF	XF
13	(1772-1824)					
		47.464	35.00	45.00	60.00	90.00

.978 SILVER, 7.53 gm., 13X22mm

C#	Date	Mintage	VG	Fine	VF	XF
13a	(1824-30)					
		60.624	15.00	20.00	30.00	40.00

.845 SILVER, 13.62 gm.

C#	Date	Mintage	VG	Fine	VF	XF
15	(1859)	.706	250.00	400.00	550.00	700.00

KEY TO DATING ICHIBU GIN

常是 TEMPO PERIOD
1830-1844
(Used 1837-1854)

常是 ANSEI PERIOD
1854-1860
Used 1859-1868

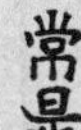

MEIJI PERIOD
1868-1912
(Used 1868-1869)

NOTE: Ichibu gin are dated according to how the two characters above are written on the reverse of the piece. There are other variations as well. Meiji Bu Gin also are known as Kaheishi Bu Gin.

ICHIBU GIN
(One Bu Silver)

是

.991 SILVER, 8.66 gm.
Varieties of countermark

C#	Date	Mintage	VG	Fine	VF	XF
16	(1837-54)					
		78.917	8.50	10.00	12.50	15.00

是

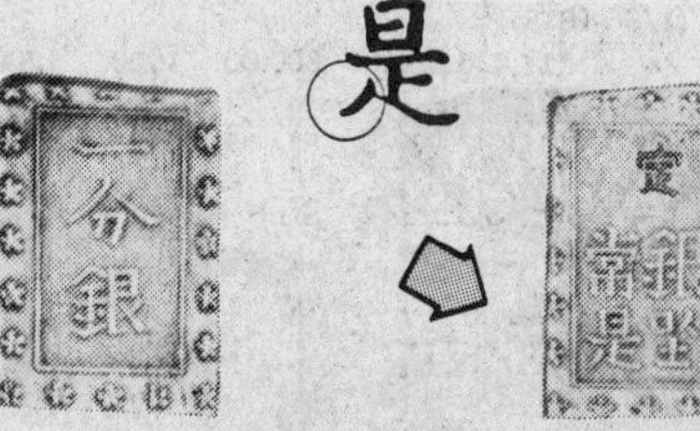

.873 SILVER, 8.63 gm.

C#	Date	Mintage	VG	Fine	VF	XF
16a	(1859-68)					
		11.399	8.00	9.00	11.00	13.50

.807 SILVER, 8.66 gm.

C#	Date	Mintage	VG	Fine	VF	XF
16b	(1868-69)	4.267	100.00	125.00	150.00	200.00

GO (5) - MOMME

.460 SILVER, 18.75 gm.

C#	Date	Era	VG	Fine	VF	XF
10	(1765-72)	Meiwa	350.00	450.00	600.00	800.00

SANBU GIN
(Three Bu Silver)

.903 SILVER

"Ansei Trade Dollar"
c/s: 4 characters on Mexico 8 Reales, KM#377. (Y#19).

C#	Date	Mintage	VG	Fine	VF	XF
—	ND(1859)	—	1500.	1750.	2000.	2400.

ISSHU KIN
(One Shu Gold)

.123 GOLD/.877 SILVER, 1.39 gm.

C#	Date	Mintage	VG	Fine	VF	XF
17	(1824-32)					
		46.723	70.00	90.00	120.00	175.00

NISSHU KIN
(Two Shu Gold)

.298 GOLD/.702 SILVER, 1.62 gm.

C#	Date	Mintage	VG	Fine	VF	XF
18	(1832-58)					
		103.070	10.00	12.00	15.00	20.00

.229 GOLD/.771 SILVER, 0.75 gm.

C#	Date	Mintage	VG	Fine	VF	XF
18a	(1860-69)					
		25.120	8.50	13.50	17.50	22.50

KEY TO DATING ICHIBU AND NIBU KIN

文 GENBUN PERIOD
1736-1741
(Used 1737-1818)

文 BUNSEI PERIOD
1818-1830
TYPE A DATE MARK
(Used 1818-1828)

文 BUNSEI PERIOD
1818-1830
TYPE B DATE MARK
(Used 1819-1832)

保 TEMPO PERIOD
1830-1844
(Used 1837-1858)

正 ANSEI PERIOD
1854-1860
(Used 1859)

One of these dating marks will be found in the upper right corner of C#20 and C#21. C#21b is dated according to its weight. C#21c and C#21d can be distinguished by the character to the left on the obverse. These are the most common types but others do exist.

KEY TO DATING C#21c and C#21d

分 MANEN PERIOD
1860-1861
(Used 1860)

分 MEIJI PERIOD
1868-1912
(Used 1868-1869)

ICHIBU KIN
(One Bu Gold)

.653 GOLD/.347 SILVER, 3.25 gm.
Obv: Written as flourish. Dating mark in upper right corner.

C#	Date	Era	VG	Fine	VF	XF
19	(1736-1818)	Genbun	45.00	50.00	65.00	80.00

.560 GOLD/.440 SILVER, 3.27 gm

C#	Date	Era	VG	Fine	VF	XF
20	(1819-29)	Bunsei	75.00	100.00	125.00	175.00

.568 GOLD/.432 SILVER, 2.80 gm.

C#	Date	Era	VG	Fine	VF	XF
20a	(1837-58)	Tempo	100.00	125.00	175.00	225.00

.570 GOLD/.430 SILVER, 2.24 gm.

C#	Date	Era	VG	Fine	VF	XF
20b	(1859)	Ansei	800.00	1000.	1250.	1750.

.574 GOLD/.426 SILVER, 0.82 gm.
Rev: No dating mark.

C#	Date	Era	VG	Fine	VF	XF
20c	(1860-67)	Manen	200.00	300.00	400.00	500.00

NOTE: Pieces without dating mark but weighing about 4 grams were made during the 17th and 18th centuries.

NIBU KIN
(Two Bu Gold)

.563 GOLD/.437 SILVER, 6.52 gm.
Obv: Type A date mark in upper right corner.

C#	Date	Mintage	VG	Fine	VF	XF
21	(1818-28)	5.972	200.00	250.00	300.00	350.00

.490 GOLD/.510 SILVER, 6.56 gm.
Obv: Type B date mark.

C#	Date	Mintage	VG	Fine	VF	XF
21a	(1828-32)	4.066	200.00	225.00	250.00	300.00

.209 GOLD/.791 SILVER, 5.62 gm.
Obv: w/o date mark.

C#	Date	Mintage	VG	Fine	VF	XF
21b	(1856-60)	7.103	60.00	80.00	100.00	120.00

.229 GOLD/.771 SILVER, 3 gm.
Obv: w/o date mark.

C#	Date	Mintage	VG	Fine	VF	XF
21c	(1860-68)	100.201	75.00	100.00	130.00	175.00

.223 GOLD/.777 SILVER, 3 gm.

C#	Date	Mintage	VG	Fine	VF	XF
21d	(1868-69)	—	12.50	15.00	20.00	27.50

KOBAN
(1 Ryo)

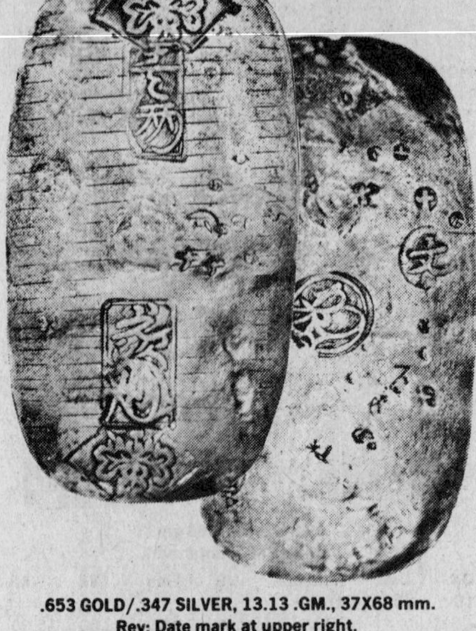

.653 GOLD/.347 SILVER, 13.13 .GM., 37X68 mm.
Rev: Date mark at upper right.

C#	Date	Mintage	VG	Fine	VF	XF
22	(1736-1818)	*17.436	600.00	800.00	1000.	1200.

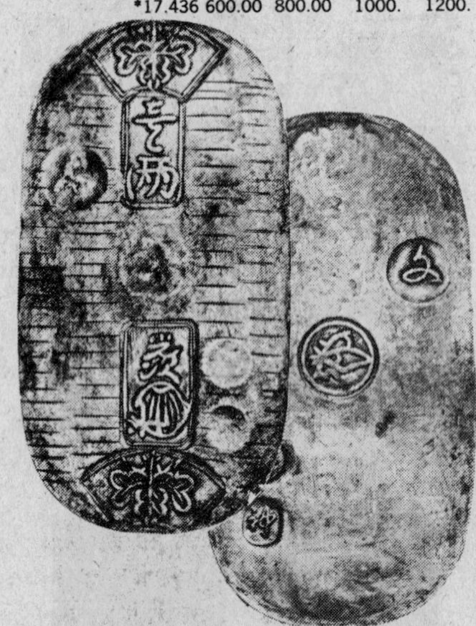

.559 GOLD/.441 SILVER, 13.13 gm. 33X62 mm.
Rev: Date mark at upper right.

C#	Date	Mintage	VG	Fine	VF	XF
22a	(1819-28)	*11.043	550.00	750.00	950.00	1150.

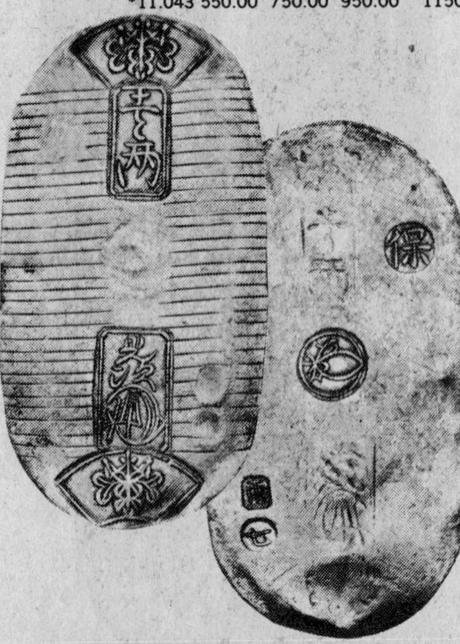

.568 GOLD/.432 SILVER, 11.25 gm., 32X61 mm.

C#	Date	Mintage	VG	Fine	VF	XF
22b	(1837-1858)	*8.120	500.00	700.00	900.00	1100.

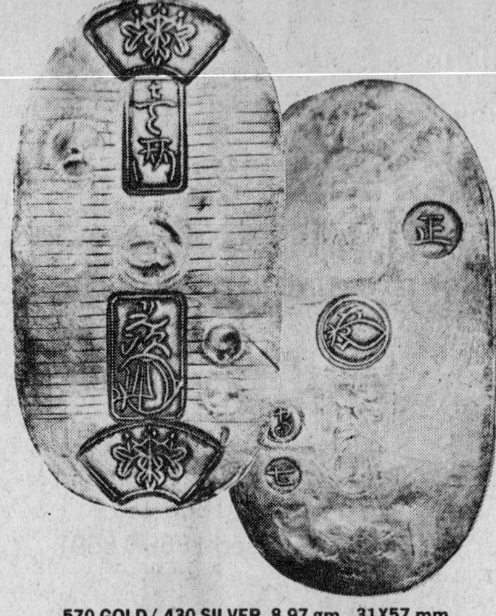

.570 GOLD/.430 SILVER, 8.97 gm., 31X57 mm.

C#	Date	Mintage	VG	Fine	VF	XF
22c	(1859)	.351	2500.	3000.	3500.	4250.

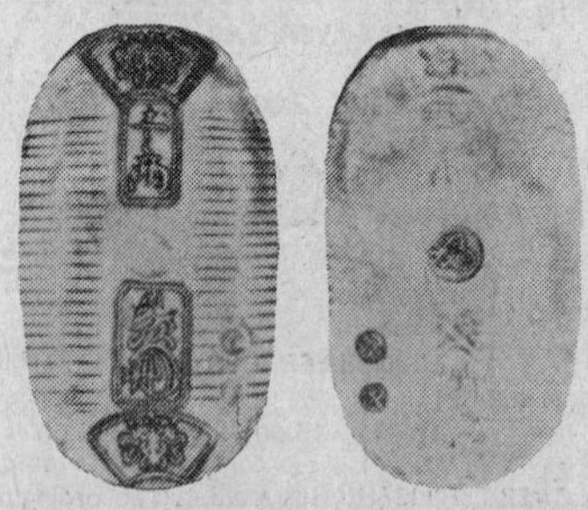

.574 GOLD/.426 SILVER, 3.3 gm., 21X36 mm.

C#	Date	Mintage	VG	Fine	VF	XF
22d	(1860-67)	.625	275.00	375.00	500.00	650.00

***NOTE:** Koban mintage figures include Ichibu Kin.

GORYOBAN (5 RYO)

.842 GOLD/.158 SILVER, 33.75 gm., 51X89 mm.
Rev: Date mark to upper right.

C#	Date	Mintage	VG	Fine	VF	XF
23	(1837-43)	.034	3000.	3750.	4750.	6000.

OBAN
(**NOTE:** Oban illustrations are reduced by 50 per cent.)

.676 GOLD/.324 SILVER, 165.38 gm., 94X153 mm.

C#	Date	Mintage	VG	Fine	VF	XF
24	(1725-1837)	8.515	—	—	Rare	—

Obv: Larger brush markings.

C#	Date	Mintage	VG	Fine	VF	XF
24.1	(1725-1837)	Inc. Ab.	—	—	Rare	—

.674 GOLD/.326 SILVER, 165.38 gm., 95X157 mm.

Rev: Various marks.

C#	Date	Mintage	VG	Fine	VF	XF
24.2	(1838-60)	1,887	—	—	Rare	—

.344 GOLD/.639 SILVER, 112.4 gm., 81X137 mm.
Hand made horizontal crenulations.

C#	Date	Mintage	VG	Fine	VF	XF
24a	(1860-62)	.017	—	5000.	7000.	9500.

Machine made horizontal crenulations.

C#	Date	Mintage	VG	Fine	VF	XF
24a.1	(1860-62)	I.A.	—	4000.	6000.	8500.

DECIMAL COINAGE

10 Rin = 1 Sen
100 Sen = 1 Yen

RIN

COPPER

Y#	Date	Year Meiji	Mintage	VF	XF	Unc
15	(1873)	6	6.979	3.00	5.00	27.50
	(1874)	7	Inc. Ab.	2.00	3.25	15.00
	(1875)	8	3.718	3.00	6.00	30.00
	(1876)	9	.023	400.00	800.00	1250.
	(1877)	10	Inc. Ab.	100.00	250.00	750.00
	(1880)	13	810 pcs.	500.00	1000.	1750.
	(1882)	15	3.632	2.00	3.00	6.50
	(1883)	16	14.128	2.00	3.00	6.50
	(1884)	17	16.009	2.00	3.00	6.50

NOTE: Two varieties of 17 exist.

5 RIN

BRONZE

Y#	Date	Year Taisho	Mintage	VF	XF	Unc
41	1916	5	8.000	.25	.75	6.00
	1917	6	5.287	.25	.75	8.50
	1918	7	11.661	.25	.75	3.00
	1919	8	17.130	.25	1.00	3.00

1/2 SEN

COPPER

Obv: Square scales on dragon's body.

Y#	Date	Year Meiji	Mintage	VF	XF	Unc
16	(1873)	6	16.804	1.00	3.00	275.00
	(1874)	7	Inc. Ab.	1.00	2.50	275.00
	(1875)	8	17.037	.50	2.00	200.00
	(1876)	9	24.292	.50	2.00	200.00
	(1877)	10	29.278	45.00	75.00	800.00

Obv: V scales on dragon's body.

Y#	Date	Year Meiji	Mintage	VF	XF	Unc
16.1	(1877)	10	Inc. Ab.	.75	1.50	20.00
	(1879)	12	29.963	10.00	20.00	350.00
	(1880)	13	14.090	.75	1.50	20.00
	(1881)	14	17.929	.75	1.50	20.00
	(1882)	15	26.458	.75	1.50	20.00
	(1883)	16	38.202	.75	1.50	20.00
	(1884)	17	38.480	.75	1.50	20.00
	(1885)	18	31.166	.25	1.00	15.00
	(1886)	19	31.831	.25	1.00	20.00
	(1887)	20	35.651	.25	1.00	20.00
	(1888)	21	25.744	1.00	2.00	40.00
	(1892)	25	(none struck for circulation)			

SEN

COPPER

Square scales on dragon's body

Y#	Date	Year Meiji	Mintage	VF	XF	Unc
17	(1873)	6	1.301	1.50	7.50	250.00
	(1874)	7	25.564	1.00	3.25	125.00
	(1875)	8	32.832	.90	3.00	65.00
	(1876)	9	38.048	.90	3.00	65.00
	(1877)	10	98.041	.90	3.00	65.00

V scales on dragon's body

Y#	Date	Year Meiji	Mintage	VF	XF	Unc
17.1	(1880)	13	33.947	.90	2.50	60.00
	(1881)	14	16.123	1.20	4.00	100.00
	(1882)	15	19.150	.90	2.25	60.00
	(1883)	16	47.613	.90	2.25	60.00
	(1884)	17	53.702	.90	2.25	60.00
	(1885)	18	46.846	.90	2.25	60.00
	(1886)	19	26.886	.90	2.25	60.00
	(1887)	20	22.249	.90	2.25	60.00
	(1888)	21	25.864	.90	4.00	65.00
	(1892)	25	(none struck for circulation)			

BRONZE

Y#	Date	Year Meiji	Mintage	VF	XF	Unc
20	(1898)	31	3.649	.90	2.75	100.00
	(1899)	32	9.764	.90	2.25	75.00
	(1900)	33	3.086	1.00	3.50	125.00
	(1901)	34	5.555	.90	2.25	75.00
	(1902)	35	4.444	1.10	2.75	120.00
	(1906)	39	(none struck for circulation)			
	(1909)	42	(none struck for circulation)			

Y#	Date	Year	Mintage	VF	XF	Unc
		Taisho				
35	(1913)	2	15.000	.70	1.25	22.50
	(1914)	3	10.000	.70	1.25	22.50
	(1915)	4	13.000	.70	1.25	22.50

Y#	Date	Year	Mintage	VF	XF	Unc
		Taisho				
42	(1916)	5	19.193	—	.50	60.00
	(1917)	6	27.183	—	.50	22.50
	(1918)	7	121.794	—	.50	7.50
	(1919)	8	209.959	—	.50	2.75
	(1920)	9	118.829	—	.50	2.75
	(1921)	10	252.440	—	.50	2.75
	(1922)	11	253.210	—	.50	2.75
	(1923)	12	155.500	—	.50	2.75
	(1924)	13	106.250	—	.50	2.75

Y#	Date	Year	Mintage	VF	XF	Unc
		Showa				
47	(1927)	2	26.500	.40	.60	7.50
	(1929)	4	3.000	3.50	10.00	80.00
	(1930)	5	5.000	2.25	4.50	125.00
	(1931)	6	25.001	—	.50	10.00
	(1932)	7	35.066	—	.50	2.50
	(1933)	8	38.936	—	.50	2.50
	(1934)	9	100.004	—	.50	2.25
	(1935)	10	200.009	—	.50	2.25
	(1936)	11	109.170	—	.50	2.25
	(1937)	12	133.196	—	.50	2.25
	(1938)	13	87.649	—	.50	2.25

Y#	Date	Year	Mintage	VF	XF	Unc
55	(1938)	13	113.605	—	.50	1.50

四 四

TYPE A ALUMINUM TYPE B

Y#	Date	Year	Mintage	VF	XF	Unc
56	(1938)	13	45.502	—	.40	.90
	(1939)	14	Type A 444.602	1.00	1.75	4.50
	(1939)	14	Type B Inc. Ab.	—	.30	.70
	(1940)	15	602.110	—	.30	.70

0.6500 gm.

Y#	Date	Year	Mintage	VF	XF	Unc
59	(1941)	16	1016.620	.10	.20	.40
	(1942)	17	119.709	.10	.20	.40
	(1943)	18	1,163.949	.10	.20	.60

Thinner, 0.5500 gm.

Y#	Date	Year	Mintage	VF	XF	Unc
59a	(1943)	18	627.191	.15	.25	.60

TIN-ZINC

Y#	Date	Year	Mintage	VF	XF	Unc
62	(1944)	19	1,641.661	.10	.20	.70
	(1945)	20	Inc. Ab.	.10	.25	.75

REDDISH BROWN BAKED CLAY

Y#	Date	Year	Mintage	VF	XF	Unc
—	ND(1945)	—	—	7.00	14.00	20.00

2 SEN

BRONZE

Obv: Square scales on dragon's body.

Y#	Date	Year	Mintage	VF	XF	Unc
		Meiji				
18	(1873)	6	3.949	16.50	25.00	800.00
	(1874)	7	Inc. Ab.	3.25	7.00	325.00
	(1875)	8	22.835	2.50	3.75	200.00
	(1876)	9	25.817	1.75	3.25	200.00
	(1877)	10	33.897	1.75	3.50	200.00

Obv: V scales on dragon's body.

Y#	Date	Year	Mintage	VF	XF	Unc
18.1	(1877)	10	43.290	1.50	2.50	85.00
	(1880)	13	33.142	1.50	2.50	85.00
	(1881)	14	38.475	1.50	2.50	85.00
	(1882)	15	43.527	1.50	2.50	85.00
	(1883)	16	19.476	1.50	2.50	85.00
	(1884)	17	12.090	2.00	3.75	250.00
	(1892)	25	None struck for circulation			

5 SEN

1.3400gm., .800 SILVER, .0344oz ASW

Y#	Date	Year	Mintage	VF	XF	Unc
		Meiji				
1	(1870)w/shallow scales	3	1.501	80.00	115.00	190.00
	(1870)w/deep scales	3	Inc. Ab.	80.00	115.00	190.00
—	(1871)	4	Inc. Ab.	125.00	170.00	300.00

Y#	Date	Year	Mintage	VF	XF	Unc
6	(1871)	4	1.665	25.00	37.50	110.00

Y#	Date	Year	Mintage	VF	XF	Unc
22	(1873)	6	5.593	6.00	10.00	25.00
	(1874)	7	7.806	55.00	90.00	180.00
	(1875)	8	6.396	6.00	10.00	25.00
	(1876)	9	5.546	7.00	11.50	30.00
	(1877)	10	22.024	6.00	10.00	25.00
	(1880)	13	79 pcs.	—	7500.	—

COPPER-NICKEL

Y#	Date	Year	Mintage	VF	XF	Unc
19	(1889)	22	28.841	1.25	2.50	50.00
	(1890)	23	39.258	1.25	2.50	50.00
	(1891)	24	15.924	1.25	2.50	60.00
	(1892)	25	9.510	1.35	2.75	60.00
	(1893)	26	8.531	1.35	2.75	60.00
	(1894)	27	14.680	1.25	2.50	60.00
	(1895)	28	1.030	50.00	65.00	700.00
	(1896)	29	5.119	2.25	10.00	130.00
	(1897)	30	7.857	1.40	2.75	60.00

Y#	Date	Year	Mintage	VF	XF	Unc
21	(1897)	30	4.167	5.00	15.00	150.00
	(1898)	31	18.197	2.25	4.00	50.00
	(1899)	32	10.658	2.25	4.00	50.00
	(1900)	33	2.426	4.00	10.00	130.00
	(1901)	34	7.124	2.25	4.00	70.00
	(1902)	35	2.448	8.50	16.50	175.00
	(1903)	36	.372	110.00	150.00	750.00
	(1904)	37	1.628	10.00	20.00	225.00
	(1905)	38	6.000	2.50	4.00	70.00
	(1909)	42	None struck for circulation			

20.6mm

Y#	Date	Year	Mintage	VF	XF	Unc
		Taisho				
43	(1917)	6	6.781	8.50	13.50	27.50
	(1918)	7	9.131	7.00	10.00	17.50
	(1919)	8	44.980	4.00	6.00	10.00
	(1920)	9	21.906	4.00	6.00	10.00

19.1mm

Y#	Date	Year	Mintage	VF	XF	Unc
44	(1920)	9	100.455	.20	.75	2.50
	(1921)	10	133.020	.20	.50	1.75
	(1922)	11	163.908	.20	.50	1.75
	(1923)	12	80.000	.20	.50	1.75

Y#	Date	Year	Mintage	VF	XF	Unc
		Showa				
48	(1932)	7	8.000	.60	1.25	2.75

NICKEL

Y#	Date	Year	Mintage	VF	XF	Unc
53	(1933)	8	16.150	.50	1.20	4.00
	(1934)	9	33.851	.50	.80	2.00
	(1935)	10	13.680	.50	.80	2.00
	(1936)	11	36.321	.50	.80	2.00
	(1937)	12	44.402	.50	.80	2.00
	(1938)	13	10.000			

4 known, balance remelted

ALUMINUM-BRONZE

Y#	Date	Year	Mintage	VF	XF	Unc
57	(1938)	13	40.001	.25	.55	2.00
	(1939)	14	97.903	.25	.55	2.00

Y#	Date	Year	Mintage	VF	XF	Unc
57	(1940)	15	34.501	.25	.55	3.00

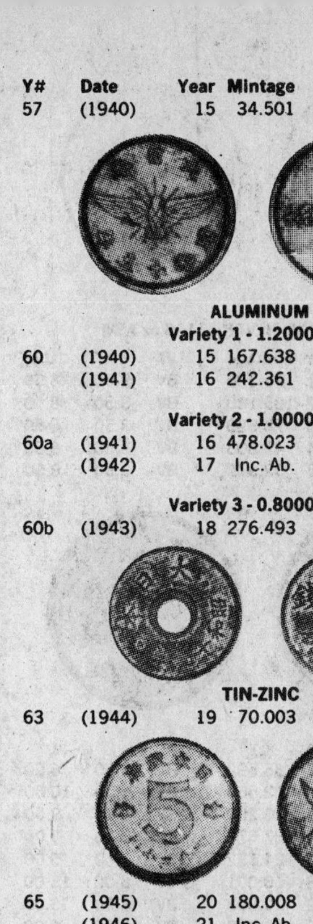

ALUMINUM

Variety 1 - 1.2000 gm.

Y#	Date	Year	Mintage	VF	XF	Unc
60	(1940)	15	167.638	—	.40	1.50
	(1941)	16	242.361	—	.40	1.00

Variety 2 - 1.0000 gm.

Y#	Date	Year	Mintage	VF	XF	Unc
60a	(1941)	16	478.023	2.00	3.50	7.50
	(1942)	17	Inc. Ab.	—	.35	.90

Variety 3 - 0.8000 gm.

Y#	Date	Year	Mintage	VF	XF	Unc
60b	(1943)	18	276.493	—	.35	.90

TIN-ZINC

Y#	Date	Year	Mintage	VF	XF	Unc
63	(1944)	19	70.003	—	.50	1.40
65	(1945)	20	180.008	—	.55	1.15
	(1946)	21	Inc. Ab.	—	.55	1.15

REDDISH BROWN BAKED CLAY

Y#	Date	Year	Mintage	VF	XF	Unc
—	(1945)	20	—	35.00	50.00	70.00

10 SEN

2.6957 gm. .800 SILVER, .0693oz ASW

Meiji

Y#	Date	Year	Mintage	VF	XF	Unc
2	(1870)w/shallow scales	3	6.102	10.00	16.50	45.00
	(1870)w/deep scales	3	Inc. Ab.	10.00	16.50	45.00

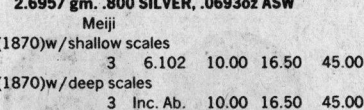

Y#	Date	Year	Mintage	VF	XF	Unc
23	1873 Type 1	6	5.109	—	—	—
	1873 Type 2 —	—	—	—	—	—
		6	Inc. Ab.	4.50	6.50	20.00
	(1874)	7	10.221	100.00	175.00	350.00

明 明

Type I Character Connected — **Type II Character not connected**

Y#	Date	Year	Mintage	VF	XF	Unc
	(1875) Type I	8	8.977	8.00	15.00	50.00
	(1875) Type II	8	Inc. Ab.	4.50	6.00	20.00
	(1876)	9	11.890	4.50	6.00	20.00
	(1877)	10	20.352	8.00	15.00	50.00
	(1880)	13	77 pcs.	—	7250.	—
	(1885)	18	9.763	2.50	4.50	12.50
	(1887)	20	10.421	2.50	4.50	12.50
	(1888)	21	8.177	3.00	6.50	15.00
	(1891)	24	5.000	6.00	10.00	30.00
	(1892)	25	5.000	6.00	10.00	30.00
	(1893)	26	12.000	3.50	5.00	15.00
	(1894)	27	11.000	2.00	3.50	10.00

Y#	Date	Year	Mintage	VF	XF	Unc
23	(1895)	28	13.719	2.00	3.00	8.50
	(1896)	29	15.080	2.00	3.00	8.50
	(1897)	30	20.357	2.00	3.00	7.50
	(1898)	31	13.643	2.00	3.50	10.00
	(1899)	32	26.216	2.00	3.50	10.00
	(1900)	33	8.183	5.00	8.50	30.00
	(1901)	34	.797	70.00	120.00	250.00
	(1902)	35	1.204	50.00	90.00	250.00
	(1904)	37	11.106	2.00	3.00	6.50
	(1905)	38	34.182	2.00	3.00	6.50
	(1906)	39	4.710	2.00	3.00	6.50

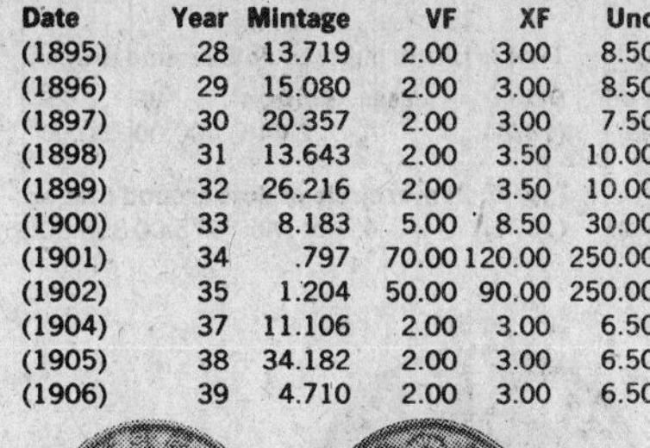

2.2500gm., .720 SILVER, .0521oz ASW

Y#	Date	Year	Mintage	VF	XF	Unc
29	(1907)	40	12.000	1.75	2.50	10.00
	(1908)	41	12.273	2.00	3.50	17.50
	(1909)	42	20.279	BV	1.75	4.00
	(1910)	43	20.339	BV	1.75	4.00
	(1911)	44	38.729	BV	1.75	4.00
	(1912)	45	10.755	1.75	2.50	10.00

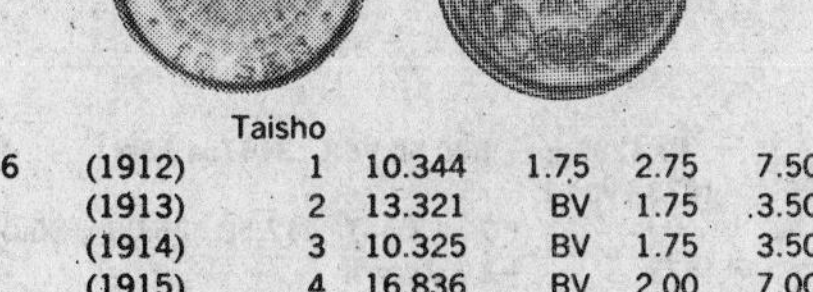

Taisho

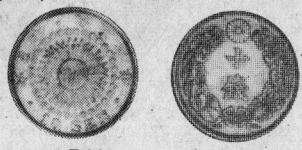

Y#	Date	Year	Mintage	VF	XF	Unc
36	(1912)	1	10.344	1.75	2.75	7.50
	(1913)	2	13.321	BV	1.75	3.50
	(1914)	3	10.325	BV	1.75	3.50
	(1915)	4	16.836	BV	2.00	7.00
	(1916)	5	10.324	BV	1.75	5.00
	(1917)	6	35.170	BV	1.75	3.00

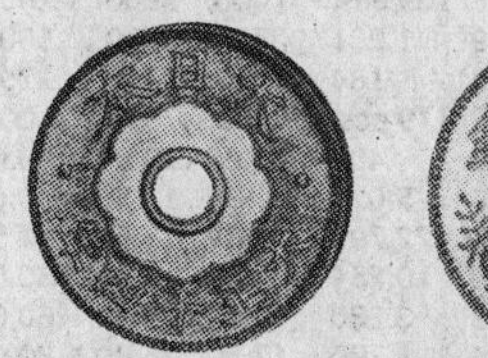

COPPER-NICKEL

Y#	Date	Year	Mintage	VF	XF	Unc
45	(1920)	9	4.894	.50	.90	3.50
	(1921)	10	61.870	.20	.25	1.00
	(1922)	11	159.770	.20	.25	1.00
	(1923)	12	190.010	.20	.25	1.00
	(1925)	14	54.475	.20	.25	1.00
	(1926)	15	58.675	.20	.25	1.00

Showa

Y#	Date	Year	Mintage	VF	XF	Unc
49	(1927)	2	36.050	.30	.50	1.00
	(1928)	3	41.450	.30	.50	1.00
	(1929)	4	10.000	.30	.50	2.00
	(1931)	6	1.850	.60	.90	2.50
	(1932)	7	23.151	.40	.60	1.75

NICKEL

Y#	Date	Year	Mintage	VF	XF	Unc
54	(1933)	8	14.570	—	.60	3.50
	(1934)	9	37.351	—	.60	1.75
	(1935)	10	35.586	—	.60	2.50
	(1936)	11	77.948	—	.60	1.75
	(1937)	12	40.001	—	.60	1.75

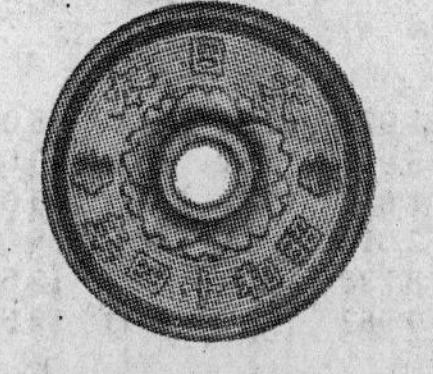 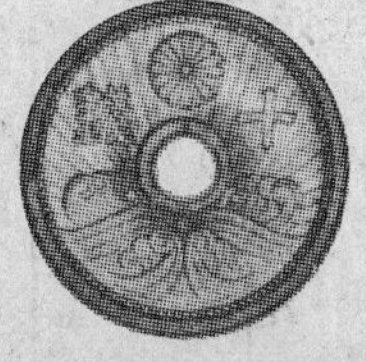

ALUMINUM-BRONZE

Y#	Date	Year	Mintage	VF	XF	Unc
58	(1938)	13	47.077	.30	.60	1.25
	(1939)	14	121.796	.30	.60	1.25
	(1940)	15	16.135	.30	.75	2.75

ALUMINUM, 1.5000 gm.

Y#	Date	Year	Mintage	VF	XF	Unc
61	(1940)	15	575.628	—	.30	.60
	(1941)	16	Inc. Ab.	—	.30	.60

1.2000 gm.

Y#	Date	Year	Mintage	VF	XF	Unc
61a	(1941)	16	944.947	—	.55	1.25
	(1942)	17	Inc. Ab.	—	.25	.50

1.0000 gm.

Y#	Date	Year	Mintage	VF	XF	Unc
61b	(1943)	18	756.037	—	.25	.50

TIN-ZINC

Y#	Date	Year	Mintage	VF	XF	Unc
64	(1944)	19	450.022	—	.30	1.50

REDDISH BROWN BAKED CLAY

Y#	Date	Year	Mintage	VF	XF	Unc
—	(1945)	20	—	25.00	35.00	50.00

ALUMINUM

Y#	Date	Year	Mintage	VF	XF	Unc
68	(1945)	20	237.590	—	.30	.60
	(1946)	21	Inc. Ab.	—	.25	.50

20 SEN

5.0000 gm., .800 SILVER, .1286 oz ASW

Meiji

Y#	Date	Year	Mintage	VF	XF	Unc
3	(1870)w/shallow scales	3	4.313	10.00	15.00	50.00
	(1870)w/deep scales	3	Inc. Ab.	10.00	15.00	50.00
	(1871)	4	Inc. Ab.	8.50	11.50	40.00

Y#	Date	Year	Mintage	VF	XF	Unc
24	(1873)	6	6.214	5.00	6.50	25.00
	(1874)	7	3.024	15.00	25.00	90.00
	(1875)	8 Type I w/sm. chrysanthemum rev.	.612	75.00	125.00	300.00
	(1875)	8 Type II w/lg.chrysanthemum rev.	Inc. Ab.	60.00	90.00	225.00

明 明

Type I — **Type II**

Y#	Date	Year	Mintage	VF	XF	Unc
24	(1876)	9	Type I w/char. MEI connected			
			9.200	16.50	22.50	70.00
	(1876)	9	Type II w/char. MEI not connected			
			Inc. Ab.	4.50	7.50	22.50
	(1877)	10	5.199	15.00	25.00	85.00
	(1880)	13	96 pcs.	—	Rare	—
	(1885)	18	4.205	4.25	5.00	14.00
	(1887)	20	4.794	4.25	5.00	14.00
	(1888)	21	.703	27.50	60.00	300.00
	(1891)	24	2.500	6.50	11.50	35.00
	(1892)	25	3.054	5.00	7.50	25.00
	(1893)	26	3.445	5.00	7.50	25.00
	(1894)	27	4.500	BV	4.50	12.00
	(1895)	28	7.000	BV	4.50	12.00
	(1896)	29	2.599	5.00	8.00	25.00
	(1897)	30	7.516	BV	4.50	10.00
	(1898)	31	17.984	BV	4.50	11.50
	(1899)	32	15.000	BV	4.50	11.50
	(1900)	33	.800	12.50	20.00	70.00
	(1901)	34	.500	85.00	125.00	400.00
	(1904)	37	5.250	BV	4.50	10.00
	(1905)	38	8.444	BV	4.50	10.00

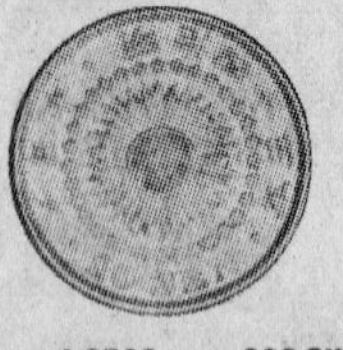

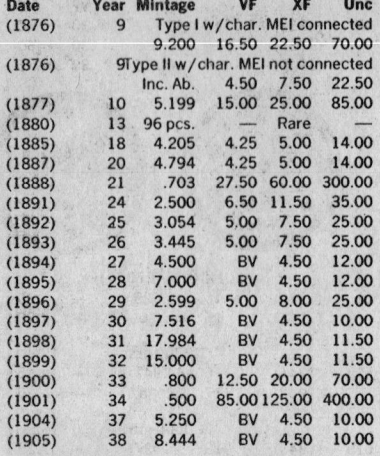

4.0500gm., .800 SILVER, .1042oz ASW

Y#	Date	Year	Mintage	VF	XF	Unc
30	(1906)	39	6.555	3.25	4.50	75.00
	(1907)	40	20.000	BV	3.25	22.50
	(1908)	41	15.000	BV	3.25	22.50
	(1909)	42	8.824	BV	3.25	22.50
	(1910)	43	21.175	BV	3.25	22.50
	(1911)	44	.500	45.00	60.00	200.00

50 SEN

12.5000 gm., .800 SILVER, 32mm, .3215 oz ASW

Meiji

Y#	Date	Year	Mintage	VF	XF	Unc
4	(1870)	3	1.806	20.00	30.00	100.00
	(1871)	4	Inc. Ab.	20.00	30.00	90.00

Type II, large dragon

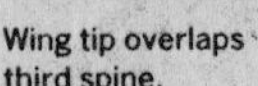

Wing tip overlaps third spine.

Type I, small dragon

Wing tip extends between third & fourth spine.

30.5mm

Type I: 19mm circle of dots around dragon.

Y#	Date	Year	Mintage	VF	XF	Unc
4a	(1871)	4	2.648	30.00	50.00	110.00

Type II: 21mm circle of dots around dragon.

Y#	Date	Year	Mintage	VF	XF	Unc
4a.1	(1871)	4	Inc. Ab.	275.00	350.00	675.00

13.4785gm., .800 SILVER, .3467oz ASW

Y#	Date	Year	Mintage	VF	XF	Unc
25	1873 Type 1					
		*6	3.447	17.50	25.00	90.00
	1873	—	Type II			
		*6	Inc.Ab.	20.00	30.00	120.00
	(1874)	7	.095	4000.	7000.	8500.
	(1875)	8	109 pcs.	7000.	8500.	11,000.
	(1876)	9	1,251	2500.	3500.	5000.
	(1877)	10	.184	1250.	1750.	2750.
	(1880)	13	179 pcs.	5500.	7500.	10,000.
	(1885)	18	.409	75.00	110.00	350.00
	(1897)	30	5.078	BV	12.50	40.00
	(1898)	31	22.797	BV	12.50	32.50
	(1899)	32	10.254	BV	12.50	30.00
	(1900)	33	3.280	12.50	15.00	60.00
	(1901)	34	1.790	17.50	25.00	80.00
	(1902)	35	1.023	37.50	65.00	175.00
	(1903)	36	1.503	22.50	30.00	100.00
	(1904)	37	5.373	BV	12.50	30.00
	(1905)	38	9.566	BV	12.50	30.00

NOTE: Two varieties exist in the character Nien (-year). The type 2 has a very long lower horizontal stroke.

10.1250gm., .800 SILVER, .2604oz ASW

Y#	Date	Year	Mintage	VF	XF	Unc
31	(1906)	39	12.478	BV	8.50	100.00
	(1907)	40	24.062	BV	8.00	25.00
	(1908)	41	25.470	BV	8.00	25.00
	(1909)	42	21.998	BV	8.00	25.00
	(1910)	43	15.323	BV	8.00	25.00
	(1911)	44	9.900	BV	8.00	25.00
	(1912)	45	3.677	8.50	10.00	45.00

Taisho

Y#	Date	Year	Mintage	VF	XF	Unc
37	(1912)	1	1.928	8.50	12.00	45.00
	(1913)	2	5.910	BV	8.00	20.00
	(1914)	3	1.872	15.00	25.00	65.00
	(1915)	4	2.011	15.00	25.00	65.00
	(1916)	5	8.736	BV	8.00	12.50
	(1917)	6	9.963	BV	8.00	12.50

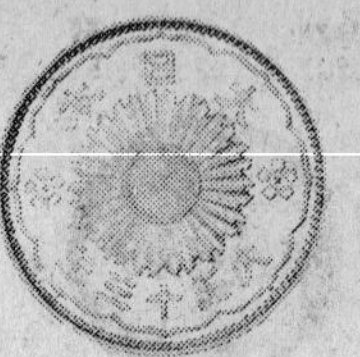

4.9500 gm. .720 SILVER, .1146 oz ASW

Y#	Date	Year	Mintage	VF	XF	Unc
46	(1922)	11	76.320	BV	3.50	8.50
	(1923)	12	185.180	BV	3.50	8.50
	(1924)	13	78.520	BV	3.50	8.50
	(1925)	14	47.808	BV	3.50	8.50
	(1926)	15	32.572	BV	3.50	8.50

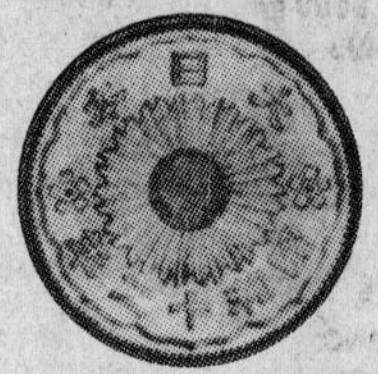

Showa

Y#	Date	Year	Mintage	VF	XF	Unc
50	(1928)	3	38.592	BV	3.50	6.00
	(1929)	4	12.568	BV	4.00	10.00
	(1930)	5	10.200	BV	3.75	8.50
	(1931)	6	27.677	BV	3.50	5.00
	(1932)	7	24.132	BV	3.50	5.00
	(1933)	8	10.001	3.50	6.00	15.00
	(1934)	9	20.003	BV	3.50	5.00
	(1935)	10	11.738	BV	3.50	6.00
	(1936)	11	44.272	BV	3.50	5.00
	(1937)	12	48.000	BV	3.50	5.00
	(1938)	13	3.600	55.00	80.00	110.00

BRASS

Y#	Date	Year	Mintage	VF	XF	Unc
67	(1946)	*21	268.187	.40	.55	1.50
	(1947)	22	Inc. Ab.	200.00	350.00	600.00

NOTE: Coins dated Showa 22 (1947) were not released to circulation.

***NOTE:** Varieties exist.

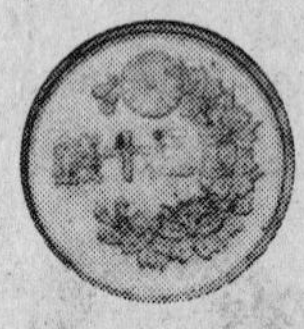

Y#	Date	Year	Mintage	VF	XF	Unc
69	(1947)	22	849.234	.15	.30	.90
	(1948)	23	Inc. Ab.	.15	.30	.40

YEN

.900 GOLD

13.5 mm, 1.67 gm.

Meiji

Y#	Date	Year	Mintage	VF	XF	Unc
9	(1871)	4	1.913	200.00	275.00	375.00

Reduced size, 12.1mm, 1.67 gm.

Y#	Date	Year	Mintage	VF	XF	Unc
9a	(1874)	7	.116	1200.	1500.	2000.
	(1876)	9	138 pcs.	—	Rare	—
	(1877)	10	7,246	—	Rare	—
	(1880)	13	112 pcs.	—	Rare	—
	(1892)	25	None struck for circulation			

圓	圓	圓
普通	正貝円	欠貝円
Type I	**Type II**	**Type III**

26.9568 gm., .900 SILVER, .7800 oz ASW

Y#	Date	Year	Mintage	VF	XF	Unc
	Meiji					
5	(1870)	3	Type 1 3.685	135.00	200.00	275.00
5.1	1870	3	Type 2 Inc.Ab.	175.00	225.00	350.00
5.2	1870	3	Type 3 Inc. Ab.	275.00	375.00	650.00

Type I: 38.6mm
Spiral on pearl held by dragon curls in counter clock wise direction from center.

Y#	Date	Year	Mintage	VF	XF	Unc
A25	(1874)	*7	.942	550.00	800.00	1600.

Spiral on pearl curls clockwise from center.

Y#	Date	Year	Mintage	VF	XF	Unc
A25.1	(1874)	*7	Inc. Ab.	425.00	650.00	1250.
	(1875)	8	.139	2000.	3250.	6000.
	(1878)	11	.856	225.00	325.00	625.00
	(1879)	12	1.913	700.00	1000.	2000.
	(1880)	13	5.427	75.00	100.00	200.00
	(1881)	14	2.927	85.00	120.00	275.00
	(1882)	15	5.089	45.00	70.00	165.00
	(1883)	16	3.636	50.00	75.00	175.00
	(1884)	17	3.599	75.00	115.00	250.00
	(1885)	18	4.296	55.00	75.00	200.00
	(1886)	19	9.084	65.00	85.00	215.00
	(1887)	20	8.275	130.00	175.00	350.00

***NOTE:** Two other varieties exist.

Type II: Reduced size, 38.1mm.

Y#	Date	Year	Mintage	VF	XF	Unc
A25.2	(1886)	19	Inc. Ab.	700.00	1000.	1800.
	(1887)	20	Inc. Ab.	70.00	90.00	200.00
	(1888)	21	9.477	30.00	45.00	85.00
	(1889)	22	9.295	30.00	45.00	70.00
	(1890)	23	7.292	30.00	45.00	70.00
A25.2	(1891)	24	7.518	30.00	40.00	60.00
	(1892) Flame overlaps third spine of dragon					
		*25	11.187	30.00	40.00	60.00
	(1892) Flame extends between fourth and fifth spine	*25	Inc. Ab.	—	—	—
	(1893)	26	10.403	30.00	40.00	60.00
	(1894)	27	22.118	25.00	35.00	50.00
	(1895)	28	21.098	25.00	35.00	50.00
	(1896)	29	11.363	25.00	35.00	50.00
	(1897)	30	2.448	30.00	40.00	55.00
	(1901)	34	1.256	35.00	45.00	65.00
	(1902)	35	.668	50.00	65.00	90.00
	(1903)	36	5.131	25.00	35.00	50.00
	(1904)	37	6.970	25.00	35.00	50.00
	(1905)	38	5.031	25.00	35.00	50.00
	(1906)	39	3.471	50.00	70.00	115.00
	(1908)	41	.334	150.00	225.00	350.00
	(1912)	45	5.000	25.00	35.00	50.00

Y#	Date	Year	Mintage	VF	XF	Unc
		Taisho				
38	(1914)	3	11.500	25.00	35.00	55.00

'GIN' COUNTERSTAMPS

c/s: 'Gin' right on 1 Yen Meiji Year 3, (1870), Y#5.

c/s: 'Gin' left on 1 Yen, Meiji Years 7-30, (1874-1897), Y#A25.

In 1897 Japan demonetized the silver one Yen and Trade Dollar coins, and many were melted to provide bullion from which to produce subsidiary coins. However, some 20 million Trade Dollars and one Yen coins were counterstamped with the character "gin" (meaning silver) and shipped to Taiwan, Korea and Southern Manchuria for use in circulation there. The counterstamp was applied to indicate that the coin was to be treated simply as bullion and to prevent the coins from returning to Japan where they could be sold to the government for gold.

The actual counterstamping was done by the Tokyo and Osaka Mints; the Osaka Mint putting its "gin" on the left side, the Tokyo Mint putting its "gin" on the right side. Only 2,100,000 coins were counterstamped at the Tokyo Mint as opposed to 18,350,000 counterstamped at Osaka, making the Tokyo pieces scarcer than the Osaka pieces.

Formerly "gin" stamped coins were regarded as damaged and sold for about 80 per cent of the price of the same coin without counterstamp. Now, however, the 'gin' coins are being collected by date and placement of the stamp, and some sell for more than a non-counterstamped piece.

MINT: OSAKA

c/s: 'Gin' left on 1 Yen, Y#5.

Y#	Date	Year	Mintage	Fine	VF	XF
		Meiji				
28	1870	3	—	75.00	125.00	175.00

Type I, 38.6mm
c/s: 'Gin' left on 1 Yen, Y#A25.
Counterclockwise spiral on pearl.

Y#	Date	Year	Mintage	Fine	VF	XF
28a	1874	7	—	300.00	500.00	750.00

Clockwise spiral on pearl.

Y#	Date	Year	Mintage	Fine	VF	XF
28a.1	1874	7	—	200.00	350.00	550.00
	1875	8	—	—	5000.	—
	1878	11	—	150.00	250.00	350.00
	1879	12	—	300.00	500.00	750.00
	1880	13	—	50.00	75.00	100.00
	1881	14	—	60.00	85.00	125.00
	1882	15	—	30.00	50.00	75.00
	1883	16	—	30.00	50.00	75.00
	1884	17	—	40.00	75.00	125.00
	1885	18	—	40.00	65.00	85.00
	1886	19	—	50.00	75.00	100.00
	1887	20	—	75.00	125.00	175.00

Type II, 38.1mm

Y#	Date	Year	Mintage	Fine	VF	XF
28a.2	1886	19	—	50.00	75.00	100.00
	1887	20	—	50.00	75.00	100.00
	1888	21	—	27.50	32.50	45.00
	1889	22	—	23.50	30.00	35.00
	1890	23	—	23.50	30.00	35.00
	1891	24	—	23.50	30.00	35.00
	1892	25	—	23.50	30.00	35.00
	1893	26	—	23.50	30.00	35.00
	1894	27	—	23.50	27.50	32.50
	1895	28	—	23.50	27.50	32.50
	1896	29	—	23.50	27.50	32.50
	1897	30	—	23.50	30.00	35.00

MINT: TOKYO

c/s: 'Gin' right on 1 Yen, Y#5.

Y#	Date	Year	Mintage	Fine	VF	XF
28.1	1870	3	—	60.00	125.00	200.00

Type I, 38.6mm
c/s: 'Gin' right on 1 Yen, Y#A25.
Counterclockwise spiral on pearl.

Y#	Date	Year	Mintage	Fine	VF	XF
28a.3	1874	7	—	325.00	525.00	775.00

Clockwise spiral on pearl.

Y#	Date	Year	Mintage	Fine	VF	XF
28a.4	1874	7	—	225.00	375.00	600.00
	1875	8	—	1100.	2250.	3500.
	1878	11	—	150.00	275.00	375.00
	1879	12	—	325.00	525.00	800.00
	1880	13	—	60.00	85.00	120.00
	1881	14	—	70.00	100.00	150.00
	1882	15	—	40.00	60.00	90.00
	1883	16	—	40.00	60.00	90.00
	1884	17	—	50.00	85.00	150.00
	1885	18	—	50.00	75.00	100.00
	1886	19	—	60.00	85.00	125.00
	1887	20	—	85.00	140.00	200.00

Type II, 38.1mm

Y#	Date	Year	Mintage	Fine	VF	XF
28a.5	1886	19	—	300.00	600.00	900.00
	1887	20	—	60.00	85.00	125.00
	1888	21	—	30.00	40.00	60.00
	1889	22	—	25.00	35.00	45.00
	1890	23	—	25.00	35.00	45.00
	1891	24	—	25.00	35.00	45.00
	1892	25	—	25.00	35.00	45.00
	1893	26	—	25.00	35.00	45.00
	1894	27	—	23.50	27.50	35.00

YEN

BRASS

Y#	Date	Year	Mintage	VF	XF	Unc
		Showa				
70	(1948)	23	451.209	.15	.40	1.00
	(1949)	24	Inc. Ab.	.15	.40	.75
	(1950)	25	Inc. Ab.	.15	.40	.75

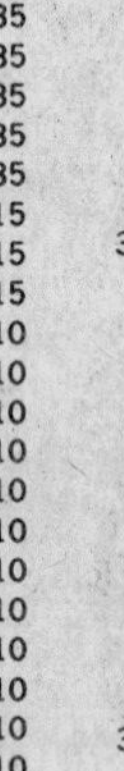

ALUMINUM

Y#	Date	Year	Mintage	VF	XF	Unc
74	(1955)	30	381.700	—	—	.35
	(1956)	31	500.900	—	—	.35
	(1957)	32	492.000	—	—	.35
	(1958)	33	374.900	—	—	.35
	(1959)	34	208.600	—	—	.35
	(1960)	35	300.000	—	—	.35
	(1961)	36	432.400	—	—	.15
	(1962)	37	572.000	—	—	.15
	(1963)	38	788.700	—	—	.15
	(1964)	39	1665.100	—	—	.10
	(1965)	40	1743.256	—	—	.10
	(1966)	41	807.344	—	—	.10
	(1967)	42	220.600	—	—	.10
	(1969)	44	184.700	—	—	.10
	(1970)	45	556.400	—	—	.10
	(1971)	46	904.950	—	—	.10
	(1972)	47	1274.950	—	—	.10
	(1973)	48	1470.000	—	—	.10
	(1974)	49	1750.000	—	—	.10
	(1975)	50	1656.150	—	—	.10
	(1976)	51	928.850	—	—	.10
	(1977)	52	895.000	—	—	.10
	(1978)	53	864.000	—	—	—
	(1979)	54	1.015	—	—	—
	(1980)	55	—	—	—	—

2 YEN

3.3333 gm., .900 GOLD, 17.48 mm

Y#	Date	Year	Mintage	VF	XF	Unc
		Meiji				
10	(1870)	3	.883	325.00	525.00	800.00

Reduced size 16.96mm

Y#	Date	Year	Mintage	VF	XF	Unc
10a	(1874)	7	—Reported, not confirmed			
	(1876)	9	178 pcs.	—	Rare	—
	(1877)	10	39 pcs.	—	Rare	—
	(1880)	13	87 pcs.	—	Rare	—

5 YEN

8.3333 gm., .900 GOLD, 23.8mm, .2411 oz AGW

Y#	Date	Year	Mintage	VF	XF	Unc
11	(1870)	3	.273	700.00	1100.	1450.
	(1871)	4	Inc. Ab.	625.00	1000.	1350.

Reduced size, 21.8 mm.

Y#	Date	Year	Mintage	VF	XF	Unc
11a	(1872)	5	1.057	550.00	850.00	1000.
11a	(1873)	6	3.148	550.00	850.00	1000.
	(1874)	7	.728	600.00	950.00	1400.
	(1875)	8	.181	600.00	950.00	1400.
	(1876)	9	.146	700.00	1300.	1500.
	(1877)	10	.136	700.00	1300.	1700.
	(1878)	11	.101	700.00	1300.	1700.
	(1880)	13	.078	700.00	1300.	1700.
	(1881)	14	.149	700.00	1300.	1700.
	(1882)	15	.113	700.00	1300.	1700.
	(1883)	16	.108	700.00	1300.	1700.
	(1884)	17	.113	700.00	1300.	1700.
	(1885)	18	.200	700.00	1300.	1700.
	(1886)	19	.179	700.00	1300.	1700.
	(1887)	20	.179	700.00	1300.	1700.
	(1888)	21	.165	700.00	1300.	1700.
	(1889)	22	.353	700.00	1300.	1700.
	(1890)	23	.238	700.00	1300.	1700.
	(1891)	24	.216	700.00	1300.	1700.
	(1892)	25	.263	700.00	1300.	1700.
	(1893)	26	.260	1650.	1900.	2250.
	(1894)	27	.314	700.00	1300.	1700.
	(1895)	28	.320	700.00	1300.	1700.
	(1896)	29	.224	1500.	1650.	2000.
	(1897)	30	.107	800.00	1300.	1700.

4.1666 gm., .900 GOLD, .1205 oz AGW

Y#	Date	Year	Mintage	VF	XF	Unc
32	(1897)	30	.111	350.00	500.00	700.00
	(1898)	31	.055	350.00	500.00	700.00
	(1903)	36	.021	500.00	650.00	900.00
	(1911)	44	.059	500.00	650.00	900.00
	(1912)	45	.059	350.00	500.00	700.00

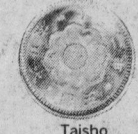

Y#	Date	Year	Mintage	VF	XF	Unc
		Taisho				
39	(1913)	2	.089	500.00	700.00	1000.
	(1924)	13	.076	350.00	550.00	900.00
		Showa				
51	(1930)	5	.852	4000.	8000.	12,000.

BRASS

Y#	Date	Year	Mintage	VF	XF	Unc
71	(1948)	23	74.520	.25	.40	12.50
	(1949)	24	179.692	.25	.30	8.00

Old script

Y#	Date	Year	Mintage	VF	XF	Unc
72	(1949)	24	111.896	.15	.30	7.00
	(1950)	25	181.824	.15	.30	4.50
	(1951)	26	197.980	.15	.30	4.50
	(1952)	27	55.000	.20	.30	4.50
	(1953)	28	45.000	.20	.30	5.00
	(1957)	32	10.000	1.75	2.25	11.00
	(1958)	33	50.000	.15	.30	4.00

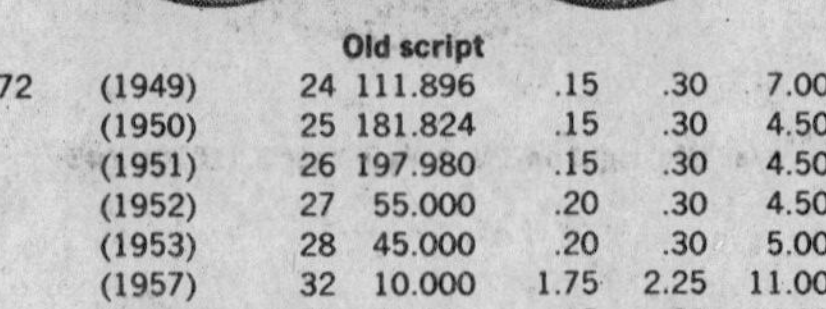

New script

Y#	Date	Year	Mintage	VF	XF	Unc
72a	(1959)	34	33.000	—	.10	2.50
	(1960)	35	34.800	—	.10	3.00
	(1961)	36	61.000	—	.10	3.00
	(1962)	37	126.700	—	.10	2.50
	(1963)	38	171.800	—	.10	2.00
	(1964)	39	379.700	—	—	.20
	(1965)	40	384.200	—	—	.20
72a	(1966)	41	163.100	—	—	.30
	(1967)	42	26.000	.15	.20	1.00
	(1968)	43	114.000	—	—	.20
	(1969)	44	240.000	—	—	.20
	(1970)	45	340.000	—	—	.20
	(1971)	46	362.050	—	—	.20
	(1972)	47	562.950	—	—	.20
	(1973)	48	745.000	—	—	.15
	(1974)	49	950.000	—	—	.20
	(1975)	50	970.000	—	—	.20
	(1976)	51	200.000	—	—	.15
	(1977)	52	340.000	—	—	.15
	(1978)	53	318.000	—	—	—
	(1979)	54	317.000	—	—	—
	(1980)	55	—	—	—	—

10 YEN

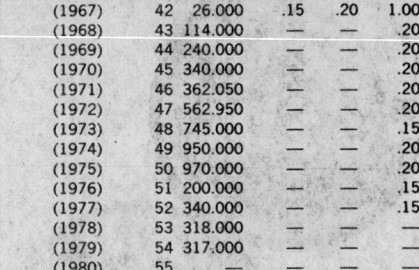

16.6666 gm. .900 GOLD, 29.4 mm. 4823 oz AGW

Y#	Date	Year	Mintage	VF	XF	Unc
		Meiji				
12	(1871)	4	1.867	1750.	2150.	3100.

Modified design

Y#	Date	Year	Mintage	VF	XF	Unc
12a	(1876)	9	1,925	—	Rare	—
	(1877)	10	36 pcs.	—	Rare	—
	(1880)	13	136 pcs.	—	Rare	—
	(1892)	25	None struck for circulation			

8.3333 gm., .900 GOLD, .2411 oz AGW

Y#	Date	Year	Mintage	VF	XF	Unc
33	(1897)	30	2.422	300.00	400.00	600.00
	(1898)	31	3.176	300.00	400.00	600.00
	(1899)	32	1.743	300.00	400.00	600.00
	(1900)	33	1.114	350.00	450.00	700.00
	(1901)	34	1.654	300.00	400.00	600.00
	(1902)	35	3.023	350.00	450.00	650.00
	(1903)	36	2.902	350.00	450.00	650.00
	(1904)	37	.724	350.00	450.00	650.00
	(1907)	40	.157	350.00	450.00	650.00
	(1908)	41	1.160	300.00	400.00	600.00
	(1909)	42	2.165	300.00	375.00	600.00
	(1910)	43	8,982	2500.	3000.	3500.

BRONZE
Reeded edge

Y#	Date	Year	Mintage	VF	XF	Unc
		Showa				
73	(1951)	26	101.068	.15	.25	45.00
	(1952)	27	486.632	.15	.25	5.00
	(1953)	28	466.300	.15	.25	5.00
	(1954)	29	520.900	.15	.25	5.00
	(1955)	30	123.100	.15	.25	8.00
	(1957)	32	50.000	.15	.25	5.50
	(1958)	33	25.000	.15	.40	17.50

Plain edge

Y#	Date	Year	Mintage	VF	XF	Unc
73a	(1959)	34	62.400	—	.15	4.00
	(1960)	35	225.900	—	.15	3.00
	(1961)	36	229.900	—	.15	3.00
	(1962)	37	284.200	—	.15	2.50
	(1963)	38	411.300	—	.15	1.00
	(1964)	39	479.200	—	.15	1.00

Y#	Date	Year	Mintage	VF	XF	Unc
73a	(1965)	40	387.600	—	.15	1.00
	(1966)	41	395.900	—	.15	.35
	(1967)	42	158.900	—	.15	.35
	(1968)	43	363.600	—	.15	.25
	(1969)	44	414.800	—	.15	.25
	(1970)	45	382.700	—	—	.25
	(1971)	46	610.050	—	—	.25
	(1972)	47	634.950	—	—	.25
	(1973)	48	1345.000	—	—	.25
	(1974)	49	1780.000	—	—	.15
	(1975)	50	1280.260	—	—	.25
	(1976)	51	1369.740	—	—	.15
	(1977)	52	1467.000	—	—	.15
	(1978)	53	1436.000	—	—	—
	(1979)	54	1207.000	—	—	—
	(1980)	55	—	—	—	—

20 YEN

33.3332 gm., .900 GOLD, .9646 oz AGW

Meiji

Y#	Date	Year	Mintage	VF	XF	Unc
13	(1870)	3	.046	7500.	8500.	13,500.
13a	(1876)	9	954 pcs.	—	Rare	—
	(1877)	10	29 pcs.	—	Rare	—
	(1880)	13	103 pcs.	—	Rare	—
	(1892)	25	None struck for circulation			

16.6666 gm., .900 GOLD, .4823 oz AGW

Y#	Date	Year	Mintage	VF	XF	Unc
34	(1897)	30	1.861	700.00	900.00	1200.
	(1903)	36	—	—	Rare	—
	(1904)	37	2.759	700.00	900.00	1200.
	(1905)	38	1.045	750.00	1000.	1250.
	(1906)	39	1.331	950.00	1150.	1350.
	(1907)	40	.817	1000.	1250.	1500.
	(1908)	41	.458	1100.	1300.	1600.
	(1909)	42	.557	1100.	1300.	1600.
	(1910)	43	2.163	750.00	1000.	1250.
	(1911)	44	1.470	750.00	950.00	1250.
	(1912)	45	1.272	1000.	1150.	1400.

Taisho

Y#	Date	Year	Mintage	VF	XF	Unc
40	(1912)	1	.177	1100.	1350.	1600.
	(1913)	2	.869	750.00	950.00	1200.
	(1914)	3	1.042	750.00	950.00	1200.
	(1915)	4	1.509	750.00	950.00	1200.
	(1916)	5	2.376	700.00	900.00	1200.
	(1917)	6	6.208	725.00	900.00	1150.
	(1918)	7	3.118	725.00	900.00	1200.
	(1919)	8	1.531	750.00	1000.	1250.
40	(1920)	9	.370	1000.	1150.	1400.

Showa

Y#	Date	Year	Mintage	VF	XF	Unc
52	(1930)	5	11.055	—	Rare	—
	(1931)	6	7.526	—	Rare	—
	(1932)	7	—	—	Rare	—

50 YEN

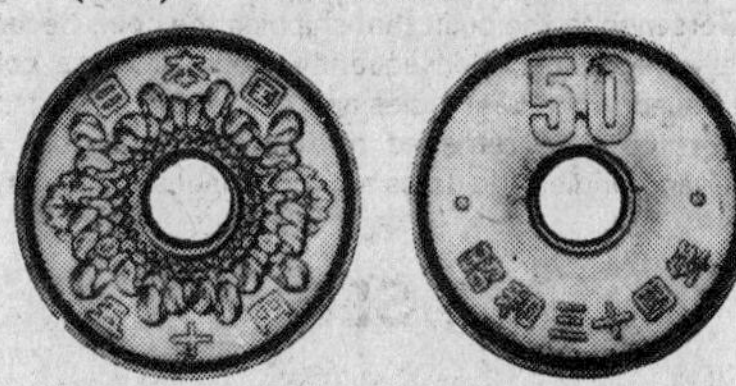

NICKEL

Showa

Y#	Date	Year	Mintage	VF	XF	Unc
75	(1955)	30	63.700	.25	.50	3.00
	(1956)	31	91.300	.75	1.00	3.00
	(1957)	32	39.000	.25	.60	3.75
	(1958)	33	18.000	1.00	1.75	6.00

Y#	Date	Year	Mintage	VF	XF	Unc
76	(1959)	34	23.900	1.25	1.80	3.75
	(1960)	35	6.000	6.50	8.50	15.00
	(1961)	36	16.000	1.50	2.00	4.50
	(1962)	37	50.300	1.25	1.75	3.00
	(1963)	38	55.000	1.25	1.75	2.50
	(1964)	39	69.200	1.25	1.75	2.50
	(1965)	40	189.300	1.25	1.75	2.50
	(1966)	41	171.500	1.25	1.75	2.50

COPPER-NICKEL

Y#	Date	Year	Mintage	VF	XF	Unc
81	(1967)	42	238.400	.20	.35	.50
	(1968)	43	200.000	.20	.25	.40
	(1969)	44	210.900	.20	.25	.40
	(1970)	45	269.800	.20	.25	.40
	(1971)	46	80.950	.20	.25	.40
	(1972)	47	138.980	.20	.25	.35
	(1973)	48	200.970	.20	.25	.35
	(1974)	49	470.000	.20	.25	.35
	(1975)	50	238.120	.20	.25	.35
	(1976)	51	241.880	.20	.25	.35
	(1977)	52	—	.20	.25	.35
	(1978)	53	234.000	—	—	—
	(1979)	54	110.000	—	—	—
	(1980)	55	—	—	—	—

100 YEN

4.8000 gm., .600 SILVER .0926 oz ASW

Showa

Y#	Date	Year	Mintage	VF	XF	Unc
77	(1957)	32	30.000	BV	3.00	5.00
	(1958)	33	70.000	BV	3.00	5.00

Y#	Date	Year	Mintage	VF	XF	Unc
78	(1959)	34	110.000	BV	3.00	4.00
	(1960)	35	50.000	BV	3.00	4.00
	(1961)	36	15.000	BV	3.00	5.00
	(1963)	38	45.000	BV	3.00	4.00
	(1964)	39	10.000	3.00	3.50	4.50
	(1965)	40	62.500	BV	3.00	4.00
	(1966)	41	97.500	BV	3.00	4.00

COPPER-NICKEL

Y#	Date	Year	Mintage	VF	XF	Unc
82	(1967)	42	432.200	.40	.50	.75
	(1968)	43	471.000	.40	.50	.75
	(1969)	44	323.700	.40	.50	.75
	(1970)	45	237.100	.40	.50	.75
	(1971)	46	481.050	.40	.50	.65
	(1972)	47	468.950	.40	.50	.65
	(1973)	48	680.000	.40	.50	.65
	(1974)	49	660.000	.40	.50	.65
	(1975)	50	437.160	.40	.50	.65
	(1976)	51	322.840	.40	.50	1.00
	(1977)	52	440.000	.40	.50	.65
	(1978)	53	292.000	—	—	—
	(1979)	54	382.000	—	—	—
	(1980)	55	—	—	—	—

4.8000 gm., .600 SILVER, .0926 oz ASW

1964 Olympic Games

Y#	Date	Year	Mintage	VF	XF	Unc
79	(1964)	39	80.000	BV	3.00	3.75

COPPER-NICKEL

Expo 70

Y#	Date	Year	Mintage	VF	XF	Unc
83	(1970)	45	40.000	1.00	1.50	3.50

Winter Olympic Games

Y#	Date	Year	Mintage	VF	XF	Unc
84	(1972)	47	30.000	2.00	3.00	5.00

Okinawa Expo 75

Y#	Date	Year	Mintage	VF	XF	Unc
85	(1975)	50	120.000	.50	.75	2.00

50th Anniversary of Reign

Y#	Date	Year	Mintage	VF	XF	Unc
86	(1976)	51	70.000	1.00	2.25	3.00

1000 YEN

20.0000 gm., .925 SILVER, .5948 oz ASW
1964 Olympic Games

Y#	Date	Year	Mintage	VF	XF	Unc
		Showa				
80	(1964)	39	15.000	20.00	30.00	45.00

NOTE: Counterfeits exist.

TRADE COINS

TRADE DOLLAR

.900 SILVER

Y#	Date	Year	Mintage	VF	XF	Unc
		Meiji				
14	(1875)	8	.097	400.00	525.00	1000.
	(1876)	9	1.514	400.00	525.00	1000.
	(1877)	10	1.444	425.00	625.00	1250.

'GIN' COUNTERSTAMPS

MINT: OSAKA

c/s: 'GIN' left on Trade Dollar, Y#14.

Y#	Date	Year	Mintage	Fine	VF	XF
28b.1	1875	8	—	100.00	250.00	400.00
	1876	9	—	100.00	250.00	400.00
	1877	10	—	100.00	250.00	400.00

MINT: TOKYO

c/s: 'GIN' right on Trade Dollar, Y#14.

Y#	Date	Year	Mintage	Fine	VF	XF
28b.2	1875	8	—	110.00	225.00	450.00
	1876	9	—	110.00	225.00	450.00
	1877	10	—	110.00	225.00	450.00

OCCUPATION ISSUES

The following issues were struck at the Osaka Mint for use in the Netherlands East Indies. The only inscription found on them is DAI NIPPON: Great Japan. The war situation had worsened to the point that shipping the coins became virtually impossible. Consequently, none of these coins were issued in the East Indies and almost the entire issue was lost or were remelted at the mint. Y#'s are for Netherlands Indies and dates are for Japanese calendar.

1 SEN

ALUMINUM

Y#	Date	Year	Mintage	VF	XF	Unc
22	2603	1943	233.190	55.00	75.00	135.00
	2604	1944	66.810	45.00	60.00	125.00

10 SEN

TIN ALLOY

Y#	Date	Year	Mintage	VF	XF	Unc
24	2603	1943	69.490	35.00	50.00	75.00
	2604	1944	110.510	30.00	40.00	50.00

NCLT ISSUES

PATTERNS

KM#	Date	Mintage	Identification	Mkt.Val.
1	(1869)	—	1 Rin, Yr.2, Copper, holed	—

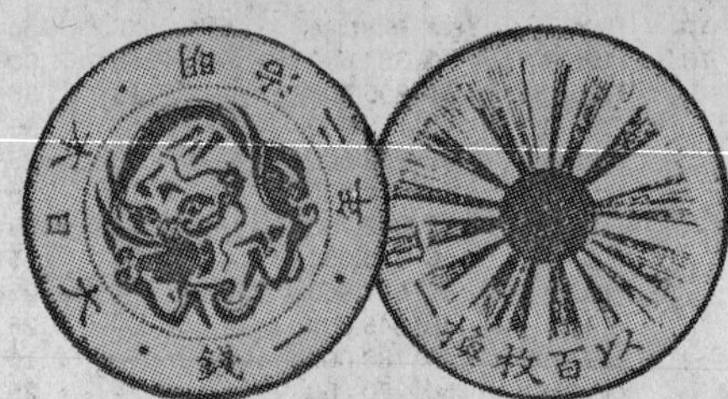

KM#	Date	Mintage	Identification	Mkt.Val.
2	(1869)	—	1 Sen, Yr.2, Copper	3500.

KM#	Date	Mintage	Identification	Mkt.Val.
3	(1870)	—	1 Rin, Yr.3, Copper	9000.

KM#	Date	Mintage	Identification	Mkt.Val.
4	(1870)	—	1/2 Sen, Yr.3, Copper	Rare

KM#	Date	Mintage	Identification	Mkt.Val.
5	(1870)	—	1 Sen, Yr.3, Copper	2000.

KM#	Date	Mintage	Identification	Mkt.Val.
6	(1870)	—	1 Yen, Yr.3, Silver	—

KM#	Date	Mintage	Identification	Mkt.Val.
7	(1870)	—	10 Yen, Yr.3, Gold, 32mm	Rare

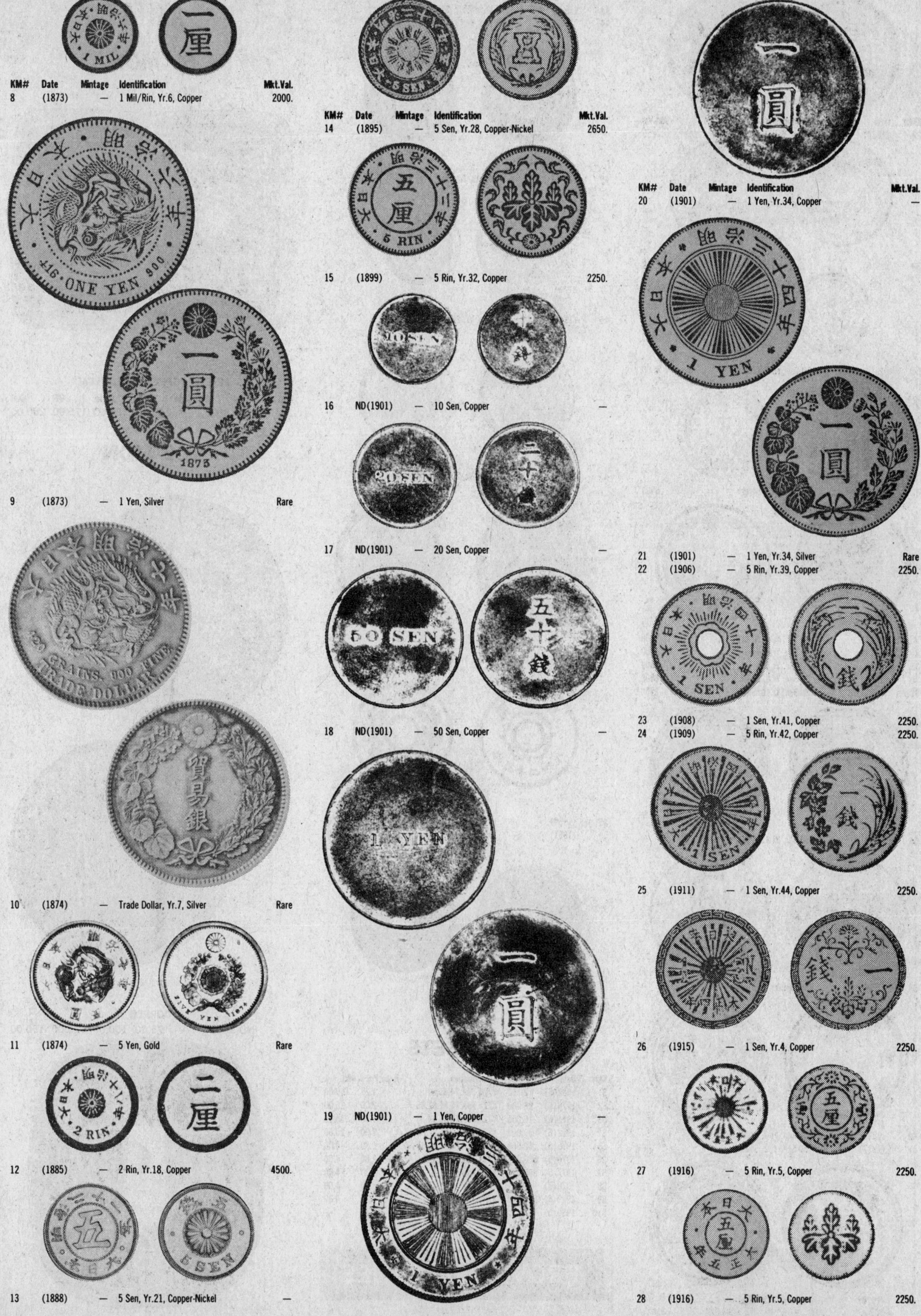

KM#	Date	Mintage	Identification	Mkt.Val.
8	(1873)	—	1 Mil/Rin, Yr.6, Copper	2000.
9	(1873)	—	1 Yen, Silver	Rare
10	(1874)	—	Trade Dollar, Yr.7, Silver	Rare
11	(1874)	—	5 Yen, Gold	Rare
12	(1885)	—	2 Rin, Yr.18, Copper	4500.
13	(1888)	—	5 Sen, Yr.21, Copper-Nickel	—

KM#	Date	Mintage	Identification	Mkt.Val.
14	(1895)	—	5 Sen, Yr.28, Copper-Nickel	2650.
15	(1899)	—	5 Rin, Yr.32, Copper	2250.
16	ND(1901)	—	10 Sen, Copper	—
17	ND(1901)	—	20 Sen, Copper	—
18	ND(1901)	—	50 Sen, Copper	—
19	ND(1901)	—	1 Yen, Copper	—

KM#	Date	Mintage	Identification	Mkt.Val.
20	(1901)	—	1 Yen, Yr.34, Copper	—
21	(1901)	—	1 Yen, Yr.34, Silver	Rare
22	(1906)	—	5 Rin, Yr.39, Copper	2250.
23	(1908)	—	1 Sen, Yr.41, Copper	2250.
24	(1909)	—	5 Rin, Yr.42, Copper	2250.
25	(1911)	—	1 Sen, Yr.44, Copper	2250.
26	(1915)	—	1 Sen, Yr.4, Copper	2250.
27	(1916)	—	5 Rin, Yr.5, Copper	2250.
28	(1916)	—	5 Rin, Yr.5, Copper	2250.

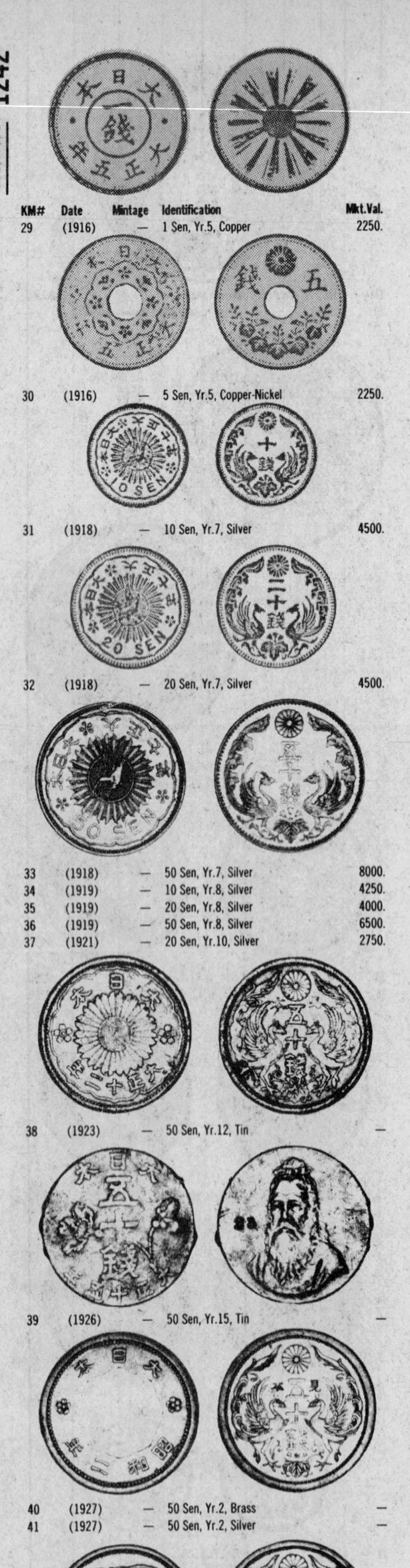

KM#	Date	Mintage	Identification	Mkt.Val.
29	(1916)	—	1 Sen, Yr.5, Copper	2250.
30	(1916)	—	5 Sen, Yr.5, Copper-Nickel	2250.
31	(1918)	—	10 Sen, Yr.7, Silver	4500.
32	(1918)	—	20 Sen, Yr.7, Silver	4500.
33	(1918)	—	50 Sen, Yr.7, Silver	8000.
34	(1919)	—	10 Sen, Yr.8, Silver	4250.
35	(1919)	—	20 Sen, Yr.8, Silver	4000.
36	(1919)	—	50 Sen, Yr.8, Silver	6500.
37	(1921)	—	20 Sen, Yr.10, Silver	2750.
38	(1923)	—	50 Sen, Yr.12, Tin	—
39	(1926)	—	50 Sen, Yr.15, Tin	—
40	(1927)	—	50 Sen, Yr.2, Brass	—
41	(1927)	—	50 Sen, Yr.2, Silver	—
42	(1927)	—	50 Sen, Yr.2, Brass	—

KM#	Date	Mintage	Identification	Mkt.Val.
43	(1927)	—	50 Sen, Yr.2, Silver	—
44	(1938)	—	1 Sen, Yr.13, Aluminum, 23mm	—

KM#	Date	Mintage	Identification	Mkt.Val.
45	(1943)	—	5 Cents, Tin alloy, Y#23	—

KM#	Date	Mintage	Identification	Mkt.Val.
46	(1945)	—	1 Sen, Yr. 20, white baked clay	—

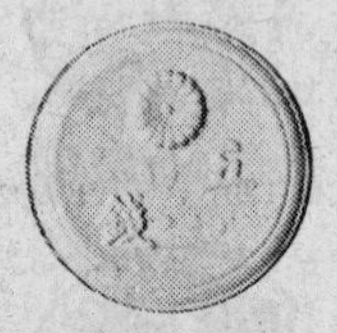

KM#	Date	Mintage	Identification	Mkt.Val.
47	(1945)	—	5 Sen, Yr. 20, white baked clay	—

KM#	Date	Mintage	Identification	Mkt.Val.
48	(1945)	—	10 Sen, Yr. 20, white baked clay	—

KM#	Date	Mintage	Identification	Mkt.Val.
49	(1950)	—	10 Yen, Yr.25, Copper-Nickel	1000.
50	(1951)	—	10 Yen, Yr.26, Copper-Nickel	1100.

KM#	Date	Mintage	Identification	Mkt.Val.
51	(1958)	—	5 Yen, Yr.33, Brass	—

MINT SETS

KM#	Date	Mintage	Identification	Issue Price	Mkt. Val.
S1	1969(5)	2,162	Y72A,73A,74,81,82	1.25	150.00
S2	1970(6)	26,000	Y72a,73A,74,81,82,83	2.00	25.00
S3	1971(5)	16,000	Y72a,73a,74,81,82	1.60	35.00
S4	1972(6)	30,000	Y72a,73a,74,81,82,84	2.90	20.00
S5	1975(6)	60,000	Y72a,73a,74,81,82,84	2.30	4.00
S6	1976(5)	580,000	Y72a,73a,74,81,82	2.80	4.00
S7	1977(5)	800,000	Y74,72a,73a,81,82	3.00	4.00
S8	1978(5)	—	Y72a,73a,74,81,82	3.50	4.00
S9	1979(5)	700,000	Y72a,73a,74,81,82	3.80	4.00
S10	1980(5)		Y72a,73a,74,81,82	3.20	—

PROVINCIAL ISSUES

AKITA

50 MON

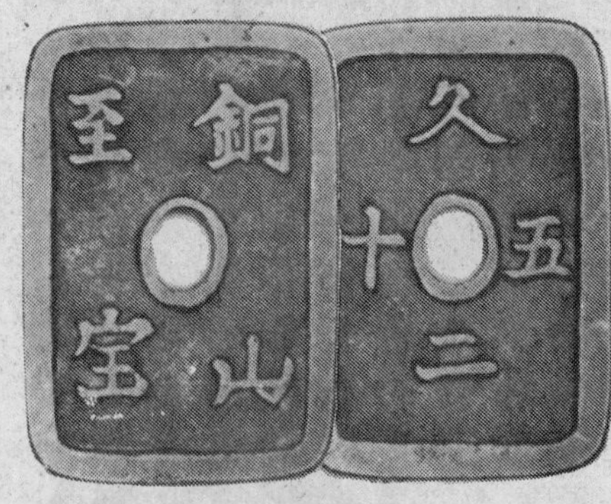

LEAD or COPPER-PLATED LEAD

KM#	Date	Mintage	VG	Fine	VF	XF
2	ND(1862)	—	100.00	125.00	175.00	250.00

100 MON

COPPER

KM#	Date	Mintage	VG	Fine	VF	XF
4	ND(1862)	—	75.00	100.00	125.00	150.00

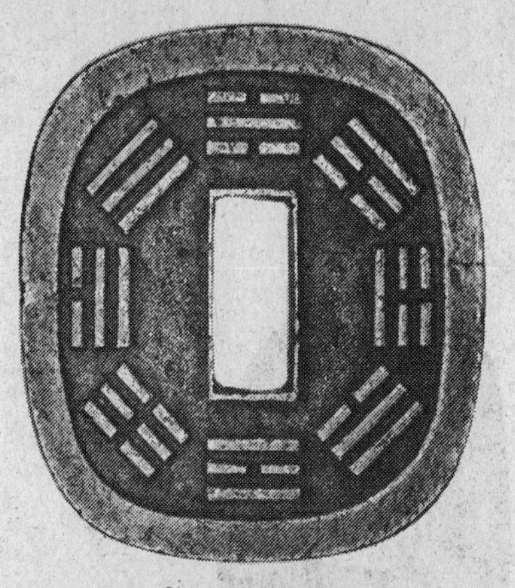

Short tail phoenix

KM#	Date	Mintage	VG	Fine	VF	XF
6	ND(1862)	—	25.00	30.00	40.00	60.00

Medium tail phoenix

KM#	Date	Mintage	VG	Fine	VF	XF
6.1	ND(1862)	—	35.00	50.00	70.00	90.00

Long tail phoenix

KM#	Date	Mintage	VG	Fine	VF	XF
6.2	ND(1862)	—	30.00	35.00	45.00	65.00

LEAD or COPPER-PLATED LEAD

KM#	Date	Mintage	VG	Fine	VF	XF
8	ND(1862)	—	40.00	55.00	80.00	125.00

BU

SILVER

KM#	Date	Mintage	VG	Fine	VF	XF
9	ND	—	250.00	275.00	325.00	400.00

4 MOMME 6 BU

SILVER

KM#	Date	Mintage	VG	Fine	VF	XF
10	ND(1863)	—	100.00	125.00	175.00	225.00

9 MOMME 2 BU

SILVER

KM#	Date	Mintage	VG	Fine	VF	XF
12	ND(1863)	—	225.00	275.00	325.00	400.00

HAKODATE

MON

IRON
Obv: 4 characters around round hole.
Rev: 1 character above hole.

KM#	Date	Mintage	VG	Fine	VF	XF
20	ND(1856)	—	3.00	6.00	10.00	15.00

HOSOKURA

100 MON

LEAD

KM#	Date	Mintage	VG	Fine	VF	XF
30	ND(1863)	—	75.00	125.00	175.00	225.00

KAGA

NAN RYO

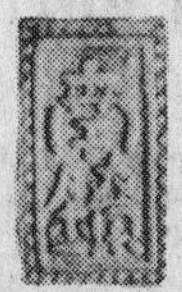

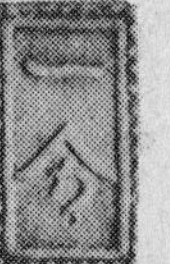

SILVER

KM#	Date	Mintage	VG	Fine	VF	XF
35	ND	—	300.00	500.00	800.00	1250.

KANRAGORI

16 MON

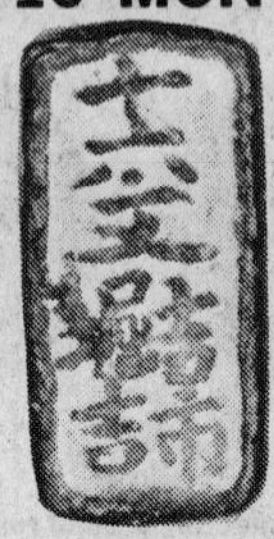

LEAD
Rev: Blank

KM#	Date	Mintage	VG	Fine	VF	XF
40	ND	—	25.00	40.00	60.00	80.00

24 MON

Rev: Blank

KM#	Date	Mintage	VG	Fine	VF	XF
42	ND	—	25.00	40.00	60.00	80.00

KM#	Date	Mintage	VG	Fine	VF	XF
44	ND	—	30.00	50.00	70.00	90.00

KOSHU

The following listings are representative of a very complex series of gold coinage. Other obscure or odd denominations may exist. This series contains many varieties. The characters usually found stamped on the reverse are hallmarks.

KAKU SHU-NAKA KIN
(Rectangular Half Shu Gold)

GOLD, .4 gm., 6x8mm

KM#	Date	Mintage	VG	Fine	VF	XF
90	ND	—	300.00	500.00	800.00	1200.

SHU-NAKA KIN
(Half Shu Gold)

GOLD, .4-.5 gm., 8.5-9.5mm
Similar to Ichi-Bu, KM#94.

KM#	Date	Mintage	VG	Fine	VF	XF
91	ND	—	700.00	1000.	1400.	1800.

ISSHU KIN
(One Shu Gold)

GOLD, .93-1.0 gm., 11-12mm
Similar to Ichi-Bu, KM#94.

KM#	Date	Mintage	VG	Fine	VF	XF
92	ND	—	175.00	225.00	275.00	325.00

NISSHU KIN
(Two Shu Gold)

GOLD, 1.87 gm., 12-13mm
Similar to Ichi-Bu, KM#94.

KM#	Date	Mintage	VG	Fine	VF	XF
93	ND	—	200.00	250.00	300.00	350.00

ICHI-BU KIN
(One Bu Gold)

GOLD, 3.75-4.00 gm., 14-17mm

KM#	Date	Mintage	VG	Fine	VF	XF
94	ND	—	150.00	200.00	250.00	300.00

ICHI-BU ISSHU KIN
(One Bu One Shu Gold)

GOLD, 4.8 gm., 18mm
Similar to Ichi-bu, KM#94.

KM#	Date	Mintage	VG	Fine	VF	XF
95	ND	—	—	—	Rare	—

ICHI-BU NISSHU KIN
(One Bu Two Shu Gold)

GOLD, 5.00 gm., 16mm
Similar to Ichi-bu, KM#94.

KM#	Date	Mintage	VG	Fine	VF	XF
96	ND	—	—	—	Rare	—

NI-BU KIN
(Two Bu Gold)

GOLD, 7.00-7.50 gm., 18-19mm
Similar to Ichi-Bu, KM#94.

KM#	Date	Mintage	VG	Fine	VF	XF
97	ND	—	—	—	Rare	—

NI-BU ISSHU KIN
(Two Bu One Shu Gold)

GOLD, 8.8 gm., 24mm
Similar to Ichi-Bu, KM#94.

KM#	Date	Mintage	VG	Fine	VF	XF
98	ND	—	—	—	Rare	—

RYO KIN
(One Ryo Gold)

GOLD, 14.7-15.3 gm., 16-19mm
Similar to Ichi-Bu, KM#94.

KM#	Date	Mintage	VG	Fine	VF	XF
99	ND	—	—	3000.	4000.	5500.

MINASAKA

BU

SILVER

KM#	Date	Mintage	VG	Fine	VF	XF
46	ND	—	250.00	450.00	700.00	1000.

MORIOKA

100 MON

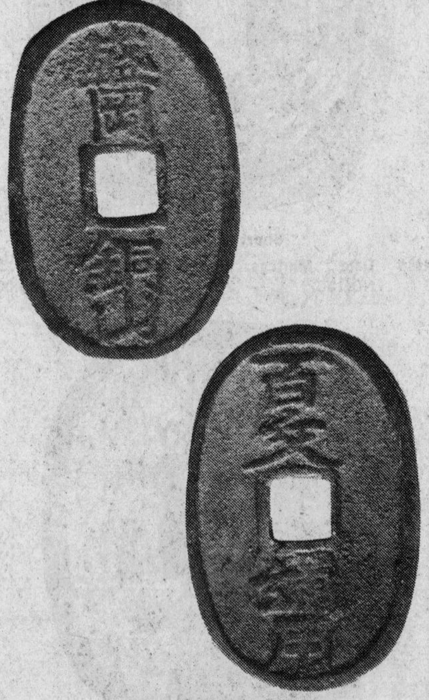

COPPER

KM#	Date	Mintage	VG	Fine	VF	XF
50	ND	—	300.00	400.00	500.00	600.00

8 MOMME

SILVER

KM#	Date	Mintage	VG	Fine	VF	XF
52	1868	—	300.00	500.00	700.00	900.00

SENDAI

MON

IRON
Rev: Blank.

KM#	Date	Mintage	VG	Fine	VF	XF
60	ND(1784)	—	3.00	6.00	10.00	15.00
	COPPER					
60a	ND(1784)	—	50.00	75.00	100.00	125.00

NOTE: KM#60a is the 'tane' or mother coin used in making the sand molds for casting KM#60.

TAJIMA

NAN RYO

SILVER

KM#	Date	Mintage	VG	Fine	VF	XF
65	ND	—	150.00	250.00	500.00	850.00

TOSA

100 MON

COPPER
Similar to 200 Mon, KM#72 but smaller.

KM#	Date	Mintage	VG	Fine	VF	XF
70	(1865)	—	—	—	Rare	—

200 MON

COPPER

KM#	Date	Mintage	VG	Fine	VF	XF
72	(1865)	—	—	—	Rare	—

NOTE: A total of 8 types are reported for Tosa Province.

YONEZAWA

200 MON

LEAD

KM#	Date	Mintage	VG	Fine	VF	XF
80	ND(1866)	—	80.00	110.00	140.00	175.00

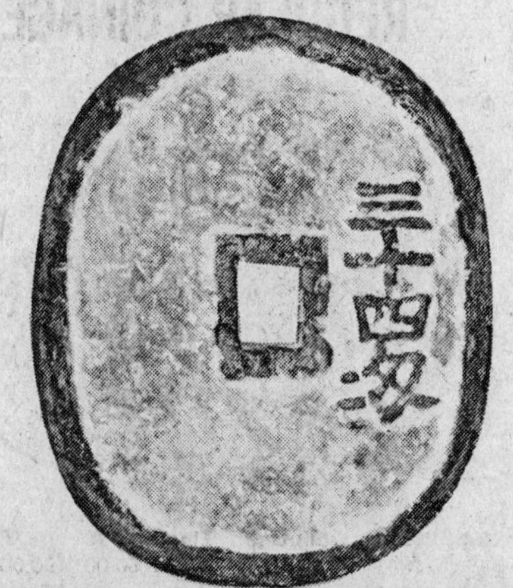

KM#	Date	Mintage	VG	Fine	VF	XF
82	ND(1866)	—	50.00	75.00	100.00	150.00

RYUKYU ISLANDS

(Also called Liu-kiu and Loo-choo)

100 MON

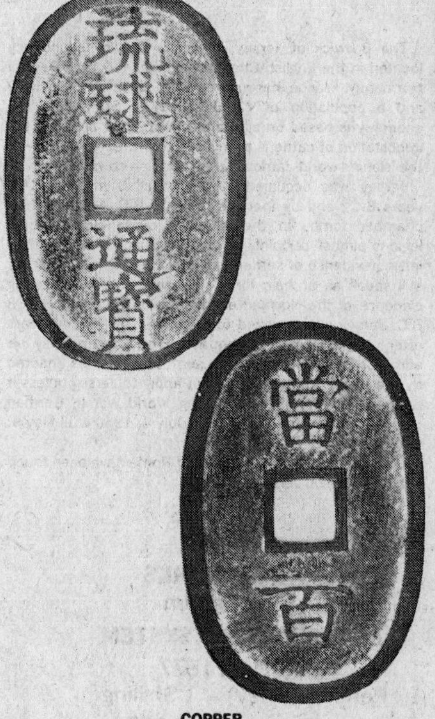

COPPER

C#	Date	Mintage	VG	Fine	VF	XF
100	(1862)	—	15.00	20.00	25.00	40.00

1/2 SHU

COPPER

C#	Date	Mintage	VG	Fine	VF	XF
115	(1862)	—	15.00	20.00	30.00	50.00

JERSEY

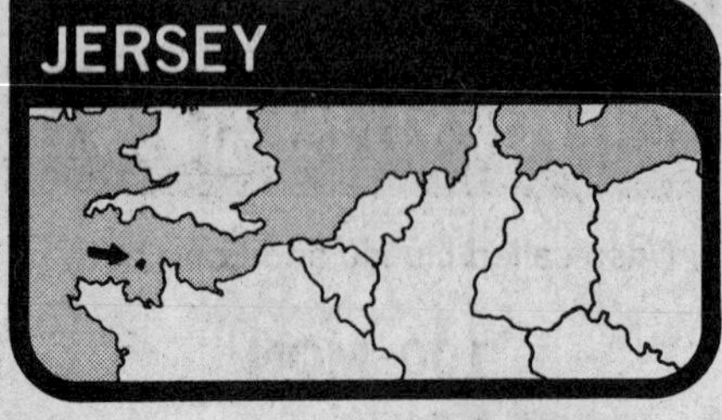

The Bailwick of Jersey, a British Crown dependency located in the English Channel 12 miles (19 km.) west of Normandy, France, has an area of 45 sq. mi. (117 sq. km.) and a population of 72,691. Capital: St. Helier. The economy is based on agriculture and cattle breeding-the importation of cattle is prohibited to protect the purity of the island's world- famous strain of milch cows.

Jersey was occupied by Neanderthal man 100,000 years B.C., and by Iberians of 2000 B.C. who left their chamber tombs in the island's granite cliffs. Roman legions almost certainly visited the island although they left no evidence of settlement. The country folk of Jersey still speak an archaic form of Norman-French, lingering evidence of the Norman annexation of the island in 933 B.C. Jersey was annexed to England in 1206, 140 years after the Norman Conquest. The dependency is administered by its own laws and customs; laws enacted by the British Parliament do not apply to Jersey unless it is specifically mentioned. During World War II, German troops occupied the island from July 1, 1940 until May 9, 1945.

Coins of pre-Roman Gaul and of Rome have been found in abundance on Jersey.

RULERS

British

MINTMARKS

H - Heaton, Birmingham

MONETARY SYSTEM

Until 1877

13 Pence (Jersey) = 1 Shilling

Commencing 1877

12 Pence = 1 Shilling

5 Shillings = 1 Crown

20 Shillings = 1 Pound

BANK TOKENS

1/2 PENNY

COPPER

Obv: JERSEY, GUERNSEY & ALDERNEY, value
Rev: TO FACILITATE TRADE, date, 3 plumes

P#	Date	Mintage	VG	Fine	VF
63	1813	—	—	Rare	—

PENNY

COPPER

Obv: JERSEY BANK TOKEN, bust of George III
Rev: ELIAS NEEL JERSEY, A BANK OF ENGLAND....

P#	Date	Mintage	VG	Fine	VF
60	1812	—	75.00	125.00	200.00

Obv: JERSEY BANK, bust of George III
Rev: Seated female, value.

P#	Date	Mintage	VG	Fine	VF
61	1813	—	35.00	65.00	100.00

P#	Date	Mintage	Fine	VF	XF
62	1813	—	17.50	25.50	40.00

18 PENCE

.891 SILVER

C#	Date	Mintage	VG	Fine	VF	XF
1	1813	*.091	20.00	35.00	60.00	90.00
	1813	—	—	—	Proof	275.00

3 SHILLINGS

.891 SILVER

Obv: Arms, Rev: Value within wreath

C#	Date	Mintage	VG	Fine	VF	XF
2	1813	*.045	35.00	50.00	70.00	125.00
	1813	—	—	—	Proof	300.00
		COPPER				
2a	1813	—	—	—	Proof	—

REGULAR COINAGE

1/52 SHILLING

COPPER

Y#	Date	Mintage	Fine	VF	XF	Unc
1	1841	.116	30.00	60.00	90.00	150.00
	1841	—	—	—	Proof	200.00
	1861	—	—	Proof only		275.00

1/48 SHILLING

BRONZE

Y#	Date	Mintage	Fine	VF	XF	Unc
6	1877H	*.288	15.00	32.50	60.00	90.00
	1877H	—	—	—	Proof	125.00
	1877	—	—	Proof only		225.00

NOTE: Issue withdrawn except for 38,400 pieces.

1/26 SHILLING

COPPER

Y#	Date	Mintage	Fine	VF	XF	Unc
2	1841	.233	4.00	10.00	25.00	50.00
	1841	—	—	—	Proof	150.00
	1844	.233	4.00	10.00	30.00	50.00
	1851	.160	3.50	8.50	22.50	40.00
	1858	.173	3.00	7.00	20.00	35.00
	1858	—	—	—	Proof	150.00
	1861	.173	2.50	5.00	17.50	30.00
	1861	—	—	—	Proof	135.00

BRONZE

Y#	Date	Mintage	Fine	VF	XF	Unc
4	1866	.173	1.50	5.00	12.00	25.00
	1866	—	—	—	Proof	120.00
	1870	.160	1.50	6.00	12.00	27.50
	1870	—	—	—	Proof	120.00
	1871	.160	1.50	6.00	12.00	27.50
	1871	—	—	—	Proof	120.00

1/24 SHILLING

BRONZE

Y#	Date	Mintage	Fine	VF	XF	Unc
7	1877H	.336	1.00	2.00	6.00	15.00
	1877H	—	—	—	Proof	90.00
	1877	—	—	Proof only		200.00
	1888	.120	1.50	3.00	8.00	20.00
	1894	.120	1.00	2.50	7.00	15.00
	1894	—	—	—	Proof	90.00

Y#	Date	Mintage	Fine	VF	XF	Unc
9	1909	.120	3.00	5.00	12.00	25.00

Y#	Date	Mintage	Fine	VF	XF	Unc
11	1911	.072	2.00	5.00	10.00	20.00
	1913	.072	2.00	5.00	10.00	20.00
	1923	.072	3.00	7.00	15.00	27.50

Y#	Date	Mintage	Fine	VF	XF	Unc
13	1923	.072	1.50	4.00	10.00	17.50
	1923	—	—	—	Proof	80.00
	1926	.120	1.00	2.25	6.00	9.00
	1926	—	—	—	Proof	80.00

Y#	Date	Mintage	Fine	VF	XF	Unc
15	1931	.072	1.00	2.25	5.00	10.00
	1931	—	—	—	Proof	90.00
	1933	.072	1.00	2.25	5.00	10.00
	1933	—	—	—	Proof	90.00
	1935	.072	1.00	2.25	5.00	10.00
	1935	—	—	—	Proof	90.00

Y#	Date	Mintage	Fine	VF	XF	Unc
17	1937	.072	1.00	2.25	5.00	10.00
	1937	—	—	—	Proof	90.00
	1946	.072	.75	2.00	5.00	8.00
	1946	—	—	—	Proof	80.00
	1947	.072	.75	2.00	5.00	8.00
	1947	—	—	—	Proof	80.00

1/13 SHILLING

COPPER

Y#	Date	Mintage	Fine	VF	XF	Unc
3	1841	.116	10.00	20.00	60.00	100.00
	1841	—	—	—	Proof	225.00
	1844	.027	15.00	30.00	90.00	175.00
	1844	—	—	—	Proof	275.00
	1851	.160	7.00	12.00	35.00	70.00
	1851	—	—	—	Proof	175.00

Y#	Date	Mintage	Fine	VF	XF	Unc
3	1858	.173	7.00	12.00	35.00	70.00
	1858	—	—	—	Proof	175.00
	1861	.173	6.00	10.00	30.00	70.00
	1861	—	—	—	Proof	175.00
	1865	—	—		Proof only	350.00

BRONZE

Y#	Date	Mintage	Fine	VF	XF	Unc
5	1866	.173	2.00	4.00	12.00	30.00
	1866	—	—	—	Proof	150.00
	1866 without LCW on bust					
		—	—		Proof only	275.00
	1870	.160	3.00	6.00	14.00	27.50
	1870	—	—	—	Proof	120.00
	1871	.160	3.00	6.00	14.00	27.50
	1871	—	—	—	Proof	120.00

1/12 SHILLING

BRONZE

Y#	Date	Mintage	Fine	VF	XF	Unc
8	1877H	.240	1.00	2.00	8.00	20.00
	1877H	—	—	—	Proof	100.00
	1877	—	—		Proof only	125.00
	1881	.075	3.00	7.00	15.00	35.00
	1888	.180	1.50	2.50	10.00	20.00
	1894	.180	1.00	2.00	6.00	15.00
	1894	—	—	—	Proof	100.00

NICKEL

Y#	Date	Mintage	Fine	VF	XF	Unc
8a	1877-H	—	—		Proof only	275.00
	1877	—	—		Proof only	275.00

ALUMINUM

Y#	Date	Mintage	Fine	VF	XF	Unc
8b	1877	—	—		Proof only	350.00

BRONZE

Y#	Date	Mintage	Fine	VF	XF	Unc
10	1909	.180	1.50	2.50	9.00	25.00

Y#	Date	Mintage	Fine	VF	XF	Unc
12	1911	.204	1.00	2.00	6.00	15.00
	1913	.204	1.00	2.00	6.00	15.00
	1923	.204	.75	1.50	5.00	14.00

Y#	Date	Mintage	Fine	VF	XF	Unc
14	1923	.301	.50	1.25	4.00	10.00
	1926	.083	2.00	4.00	8.00	17.50

Y#	Date	Mintage	Fine	VF	XF	Unc
16	1931	.204	.40	1.00	2.50	7.50
	1933	.204	.40	.80	2.50	7.50
	1933	—	—	—	Proof	90.00
	1935	.204	.40	.80	2.50	7.50
	1935	—	—	—	Proof	90.00

Y#	Date	Mintage	Fine	VF	XF	Unc
18	1937	.204	.40	.80	2.50	6.50
	1937	—	—	—	Proof	90.00
	1946	.204	.20	.40	2.00	5.50
	1946	—	—	—	Proof	90.00
	1947	.444	.30	.60	1.50	4.50
	1947	—	—	—	Proof	90.00

Liberation Commemorative

Y#	Date	Mintage	Fine	VF	XF	Unc
19	1945	1.000	.20	.40	.75	2.00
	1945	—	—	—	Proof	80.00

NOTE: Struck between 1949-52.

Y#	Date	Mintage	Fine	VF	XF	Unc
20	1945	.720	.20	.40	.75	2.00
	1945	—	—	—	Proof	70.00

NOTE: Struck 1954.

Y#	Date	Mintage	Fine	VF	XF	Unc
21	1957	.720	.10	.20	.40	.75

Y#	Date	Mintage	Fine	VF	XF	Unc
21	1957	2,100	—	—	Proof	12.50
	1964	1.200	.10	.15	.20	.40
	1964	.020	—	—	Proof	3.00

King Charles II Commemorative

Y#	Date	Mintage	Fine	VF	XF	Unc
23	1960	1.200	.10	.15	.20	.60
	1960	4,200	—	—	Proof	6.00

Mule 1/12 Shilling
Obverse of Y#20. Reverse of Y#23.

Y#	Date	Mintage	Fine	VF	XF	Unc
20/23	1960	—	—	Proof only		125.00

Norman Conquest

Y#	Date	Mintage	Fine	VF	XF	Unc
25	1966	1.200	.10	.15	.20	.40
	1966	.030	—	—	Proof	1.50

1/4 SHILLING (3 PENCE)

NICKEL-BRASS

Y#	Date	Mintage	Fine	VF	XF	Unc
22	1957	2.000	.10	.15	.20	.75
	1957	6,300	—	—	Proof	12.50
	1960	4,200	—	Proof only		15.00

Y#	Date	Mintage	Fine	VF	XF	Unc
24	1964	1.200	.10	.15	.20	1.00
	1964	.020	—	—	Proof	2.50

Norman Conquest

Y#	Date	Mintage	Fine	VF	XF	Unc
26	1966	1.200	.10	.15	.20	.50
	1966	.030	—	—	Proof	1.50

5 SHILLINGS

COPPER-NICKEL
Norman Conquest

Y#	Date	Mintage	Fine	VF	XF	Unc
27	1966	.300	.75	1.00	1.50	2.50
	1966	.030	—	—	Proof	8.50

DECIMAL COINAGE

100 New Pence = 1 Pound

1/2 NEW PENNY

BRONZE

Y#	Date	Mintage	VF	XF	Unc
28	1971	3.000	—	.10	.15

NEW PENNY

BRONZE

Y#	Date	Mintage	VF	XF	Unc
29	1971	4.000	—	.10	.20

2 NEW PENCE

BRONZE

Y#	Date	Mintage	VF	XF	Unc
30	1971	2.250	—	.10	.30
	1975	.750	—	.10	.30

5 NEW PENCE

COPPER-NICKEL

Y#	Date	Mintage	VF	XF	Unc
31	1968	3.000	.10	.15	.50

10 NEW PENCE

COPPER-NICKEL

Y#	Date	Mintage	VF	XF	Unc
32	1968	.400	.20	.25	.35
	1975	.300	.20	.30	.75

25 PENCE

COPPER-NICKEL
Queen's Silver Jubilee

Y#	Date	Mintage	VF	XF	Unc
43	1977	—	.60	1.00	1.50

.925 SILVER

Y#	Date	Mintage	VF	XF	Unc
43a	1977	.035	—	Proof	30.00

50 NEW PENCE

COPPER-NICKEL

Y#	Date	Mintage	VF	XF	Unc
33	1969	.400	1.00	1.25	2.50

50 PENCE

5.4200 gm., .925 SILVER, .1612 oz ASW
25th Wedding Anniversary

Y#	Date	Mintage	VF	XF	Unc
34	1972	.024	BV	5.00	6.00
	1972	1,500	—	Proof	12.00

POUND

10.8400 gm., .925 SILVER, .3224 oz ASW
25th Wedding Anniversary

Y#	Date	Mintage	VF	XF	Unc
35	1972	.024	BV	10.00	12.00
	1972	1,500	—	Proof	20.00

2 POUNDS

21.6400 gm., .925 SILVER, .6436 oz ASW
25th Wedding Anniversary
Obv: Similar to 1 Pound, Y#35.

Y#	Date	Mintage	VF	XF	Unc
36	1972	.024	BV	20.00	22.50
	1972	1,500	—	—	40.00

2 POUNDS 50 PENCE

27.1000 gm., .925 SILVER, .8060 oz ASW
25th Wedding Anniversary
Obv: Similar to 1 Pound, Y#35.

Y#	Date	Mintage	VF	XF	Unc
37	1972	.024	BV	25.00	27.50
	1972	1,500	—	Proof	40.00

5 POUNDS

2.6200 gm., .917 GOLD, .0772 oz AGW
25th Wedding Anniversary
Obv: Similar to 50 pounds, Y#42.

Y#	Date	Mintage	VF	XF	Unc
38	1972	8,500	BV	BV	60.00
	1972	1,500	—	Proof	100.00

10 POUNDS

4.6400 gm., .917 GOLD, .1368 oz AGW
25th Wedding Anniversary
Obv: Similar to 50 Pounds, Y#42.

Y#	Date	Mintage	VF	XF	Unc
39	1972	8,500	BV	BV	90.00
	1972	1,500	—	Proof	125.00

20 POUNDS

9.2600 gm., .917 GOLD, .2729 oz AGW
25th Wedding Anniversary
Obv: Similar to 50 Pounds, Y#42.

Y#	Date	Mintage	VF	XF	Unc
40	1972	8,500	BV	BV	180.00
	1972	1,500	—	Proof	200.00

25 POUNDS

11.9000 gm., .917 GOLD, .3507 oz AGW
25th Wedding Anniversary

Y#	Date	Mintage	VF	XF	Unc
41	1972	8,500	BV	BV	235.00
	1972	1,500	—	Proof	275.00

50 POUNDS

22.6300 gm., .917 GOLD, .6670 oz AGW
25th Wedding Anniversary

Y#	Date	Mintage	VF	XF	Unc
42	1972	8,500	BV	BV	450.00
	1972	1,500	—	Proof	500.00

NCLT ISSUES

MINT SETS

KM#	Date	Mintage	Identification	Issue Price	Mkt. Val.
S1	1972(4)	23,500	Y34-37	24.00	45.00
S2	1972(9)	—	Y34-42	348.00	1000.

PROOF SETS
STANDARD METALS

KM#	Date	Mintage	Identification	Issue Price	Mkt. Val.
101	1957(4)	1,050	Y21,22 two each	—	50.00
102	1960(4)	2,100	Y22,23 two each	—	40.00
103	1964(4)	10,000	Y21,24 two each	—	10.00
104	1966(4)	15,000	Y25,26 two each	—	6.00
105	1966(2)	15,000	Y27 two pcs.	—	15.00
106	1972(9)	1,500	Y34-42	648.00	1300.

JORDAN

The Hashemite Kingdom of Jordan, a constitutional monarchy in southwest Asia, has an area of 37,100 sq. mi. (96,088 sq. km.) and a population of 2.7 million. Capital: Amman. Agriculture and tourism comprise Jordan's economic base. Chief exports are phosphates, tomatoes and oranges.

Jordan is the Edom and Moab of the time of Moses. It became part of the Roman province of Arabia in 106 A.D., was conquered by the Arabs in 633-36, and was part of the Ottoman Empire from the 16th century until World War I. At that time, the regions presently known as Jordan and Israel were mandated to Great Britain by the League of Nations as Transjordan and Palestine. In 1922 Transjordan was established as the semi-autonomous Emirate of Trans- jordan, ruled by the Hashemite Prince Abdullah but still nominally a part of the British mandate. The mandate over Transjordan was terminated in 1946, the country becoming the independent Hashemite Kingdom of Transjordan. The kingdom was renamed the Hashemite Kingdom of Jordan in 1950.

NOTE: Several 1964 and 1965 issues were limited to respective quantities of 3,000 and 5,000 examples struck to make up sets for sale to collectors.

RULERS

Abdullah Ibn Al Hussein, 1946-1951
Hussein I, 1952—

MONETARY SYSTEM

100 Fils = 1 Dirham
1000 Fils = 10 Dirhams = 1 Dinar

FIL

BRONZE

Y#	Date	Year	Mintage	VF	XF	Unc
1	AH1368	1949	.350	1.25	1.75	3.00

NOTE: FIL is an error for FILS, the correct Arabic singular.

FILS

BRONZE

Y#	Date	Year	Mintage	VF	XF	Unc
2	AH1368	1949	Inc. Ab.	.65	1.00	2.00
	1368	1949	25 pcs.	—	Proof	65.00

Y#	Date	Year	Mintage	VF	XF	Unc
8	AH1374	1955	.200	.35	.50	1.00
	1379	1960	.150	.40	.60	1.25
	1382	1963	.200	.25	.50	1.00
	1383	1964	3,000	1.50	3.00	5.00
	1385	1965	5,000	1.00	2.00	4.00
	1385	1965	.010	—	Proof	3.00

Y#	Date	Year	Mintage	VF	XF	Unc
13	AH1387	1968	.060	—	—	.50
	1398	1978	.020	—	Proof	—

GOLD

Y#	Date	Year	Mintage	VF	XF	Unc
13a	AH1387	1968	2 pcs.	—	Rare	—

5 FILS

BRONZE

Y#	Date	Year	Mintage	VF	XF	Unc
3	AH1368	1949	3.300	.40	.75	1.50
	1368	1949	25 pcs.	—	Proof	80.00

Y#	Date	Year	Mintage	VF	XF	Unc
9	AH1374	1955	3.500	.35	.50	.75
	1380	1960	.540	.50	.70	1.25
	1382	1962	.250	.45	.70	1.25
	1383	1964	3,000	—	4.50	7.50
	1384	1964	2.500	.30	.50	1.00
	1385	1965	5,000	1.25	2.50	4.00
	1385	1965	.010	—	Proof	5.00
	1387	1967	2.000	.10	.20	.40

5 FILS (1/2 QIRSH)

BRONZE

Y#	Date	Year	Mintage	VF	XF	Unc
14	AH1387	1968	.800	.10	.25	.50
	1390	1970	1.400	—	.20	.40
	1392	1972	.400	.10	.25	.50
	1394	1974	2.000	—	.15	.40
	1395	1975	9.000	—	.10	.30
	1398	1978	.020	—	Proof	—

GOLD

Y#	Date	Year	Mintage	VF	XF	Unc
14a	AH1387	1968	2 pcs.	—	Rare	—

10 FILS

BRONZE

Y#	Date	Year	Mintage	VF	XF	Unc
4	AH1368	1949	2.700	.75	1.25	2.00
	1368	1949	25 pcs.	—	Proof	100.00

Y#	Date	Year	Mintage	VF	XF	Unc
10	AH1374	1955	1.500	.60	1.00	2.00
	1380	1960	.060	1.25	2.00	3.50
	1382	1962	2.300	.30	.50	1.00
	1383	1964	1.253	.30	.50	1.00
	1385	1965	1.003	.20	.40	.85
	1385	1965	.010	—	Proof	2.00
	1386	1967	1.000	.20	.35	.65

10 FILS (QIRSH, PIASTRE)

BRONZE

Y#	Date	Year	Mintage	VF	XF	Unc
15	AH1387	1968	.500	.20	.40	.75
	1390	1970	1.000	.20	.35	.60
	1392	1972	.600	.20	.40	.75
	1394	1974	1.000	.20	.40	.65
	1395	1975	5.000	.20	.35	.50
	1398	1978	.020	—	Proof	—

GOLD

Y#	Date	Year	Mintage	VF	XF	Unc
15a	AH1387	1968	2 pcs.	—	Rare	—

20 FILS

COPPER-NICKEL

Y#	Date	Year	Mintage	VF	XF	Unc
5	AH1368	1949	1.570	.75	1.25	2.00
	1368	1949	25 pcs.	—	Proof	110.00

Y#	Date	Year	Mintage	VF	XF	Unc
A10	AH1383	1964	3,000	1.50	3.00	5.00
	1385	1965	5,000	1.50	3.00	5.00
	1385	1965	.010	—	Proof	5.00

25 FILS (1/4 DIRHAM)

COPPER-NICKEL

Y#	Date	Year	Mintage	VF	XF	Unc
16	AH1387	1968	.200	—	.35	.75
	1390	1970	.240	—	.35	.75
	1394	1974	.800	—	.35	.75
	1395	1975	2.000	—	.35	.75
	1398	1978	.020	—	Proof	—

GOLD

Y#	Date	Year	Mintage	VF	XF	Unc
16a	AH1387	1968	2 pcs.	—	Rare	—

50 FILS

COPPER-NICKEL

Y#	Date	Year	Mintage	VF	XF	Unc
6	AH1368	1949	2.500	.75	2.00	3.50
	1368	1949	25 Pcs.	—	Proof	125.00

Y#	Date	Year	Mintage	VF	XF	Unc
11	AH1374	1955	2.500	.75	1.50	3.50
	1382	1962	.750	.85	1.00	1.50
	1383	1964	1.003	.50	.75	1.25
	1385	1965	1.505	.75	1.00	1.50
	1385	1965	.010	—	Proof	3.50

50 FILS (1/2 DIRHAM)

COPPER-NICKEL

Y#	Date	Year	Mintage	VF	XF	Unc
17	AH1387	1968	.400	.40	.75	1.25
	1390	1970	1.000	.40	.60	1.00
		1973	—	.40	.60	1.00
	1394	1974	1.000	.40	.60	1.00
	1395	1975	2.000	.40	.60	1.00
	1397	1977	—	.40	.60	1.00
	1398	1978	.020	—	Proof	—

GOLD

Y#	Date	Year	Mintage	VF	XF	Unc
17a	AH1387	1968	2 pcs.	—	Rare	—

100 FILS

COPPER-NICKEL

Y#	Date	Year	Mintage	VF	XF	Unc
7	AH1368	1949	2.000	2.00	3.00	5.00
	1368	1949	25 pcs.	—	Proof	150.00

Y#	Date	Year	Mintage	VF	XF	Unc
12	AH1374	1955	.500	2.00	2.50	4.00
	1382	1962	.600	1.00	1.50	2.50
	1383	1964	3,000	1.50	3.00	5.00
	1385	1965	.405	1.00	1.25	2.00
	1385	1965	.010	—	Proof	4.00

DIRHAM (100 FILS)

COPPER-NICKEL

Y#	Date	Year	Mintage	VF	XF	Unc
18	AH1387	1968	.175	—	1.25	2.00
	1395	1975	2.500	—	—	—
	1398	1978	.020	—	Proof	—

Y#	Date	Year	Mintage	VF	XF	Unc
			GOLD			
18a	AH1387	1968	2 pcs.	—	Rare	—

1/4 DINAR

COPPER-NICKEL
F.A.O.Issue

19	AH1389	1969	.060	2.25	3.00	4.00

Obv: Similar to Y#19.

20	AH1390	1970	.500	1.25	2.00	3.50
	1394	1974	—	1.25	2.00	3.50
	1398	1978	.020	—	Proof	—

25th Anniversary of Reign

21	AH1397	1977	—	2.75	3.75	5.50

250 FILS

COPPER-NICKEL

—	—	1974	.400 Reported, not confirmed
	—	1975	.100 Reported, not confirmed

1/2 DINAR

20.0000 gm., 1.000 SILVER, .6430 oz ASW

H#	Date	Year	Mintage	XF	Unc	Proof
4	AH1389	1969	.012	—	—	25.00

3/4 DINAR

30.0000 gm., 1.0000 SILVER, .9646 oz ASW
Obv: Similar to 1/2 Dinar, H#4.

5	AH1389	1969	.012	—	—	45.00

DINAR

40.0000 gm., 1.0000 SILVER, 1.2861 oz ASW
Obv: Similar to 1/2 Dinar, H#4.

6	AH1389	1969	.012	—	—	60.00

2 DINARS

5.5200 gm., .900 GOLD, .1597 oz ASW

Obv: Similar to 1/2 Dinar, H#4.

H#	Date	Year	Mintage	XF	Unc	Proof
8	AH1389	1969	6,000	—	—	125.00

2-1/2 DINARS

28.3000 gm., .925 SILVER, .8417 oz ASW
Conservation Series

Y#	Date	Year	Mintage	XF	Unc	Proof
23	AH1397	1977	—	—	25.00	—
	1397	1977	.010	—	—	30.00

3 DINARS

35.0000 gm., .925 SILVER, 1.0409 oz ASW
Conservation Series
Obv: Similar to 2- 1/2 Dinars, Y#23.

24	AH1397	1977	—	—	40.00	—
	1397	1977	.010	—	—	50.00

5 DINARS

13.8200 gm., .900 GOLD, .3999 oz AGW
Obv: Similar to 1/2 Dinar, H#4.

H#	Date	Year	Mintage	XF	Unc	Proof
9	AH1389	1969	6,000	—	—	265.00

10 DINARS

27.6400 gm., .900 GOLD, .7998 oz AGW
Obv: Similar to 1/2 Dinar, H#4.

H#	Date	Year	Mintage	XF	Unc	Proof
10	AH1389	1969	6,000	—	—	525.00

25 DINARS

69.1100 gm., .900 GOLD, 1.9999 oz AGW
Obv: Similar to 1/2 Dinar, H#4.

H#	Date	Year	Mintage	XF	Unc	Proof
11	AH1389	1969	6,000	—	—	1300.

15.0000 gm., .917 GOLD, .4422 oz AGW
25th Anniversary of Reign

Y#	Date	Year	Mintage	XF	Unc	Proof
22	AH1397	1977FM	4,724	—	—	300.00

50 DINARS

33.4400 gm., .900 GOLD, .9677 oz AGW
Conservation Series
Obv: Similar to 2-1/2 Dinars, Y#23.

Y#	Date	Year	Mintage	XF	Unc	Proof
25	AH1397	1977	—	—	650.00	—
	1397	1977	1,000	—	—	800.00

NCLT ISSUES

SPECIMEN SETS

KM#	Date	Mintage	Identification	Issue Price	Mkt. Val.
SS1	1964(6)	3,000	Y8-12	—	20.00
SS2	1965(6)	5,000	Y8-12	—	13.50
SS3	1968(6)	50	Y13-18	—	500.00
SS4	1968(6)	2	Y13a-18a	—	—

PROOF SETS
STANDARD METALS

KM#	Date	Mintage	Identification	Issue Price	Mkt. Val.
101	1949(6)	25	Y2-7	—	500.00
102	1965(6)	10,000	Y8-12	14.40	18.00
103	1969(7)	6,000	H4-6,8-11	396.00	2300.
104	1969(3)	5,800	H4-6	36.00	125.00
105	1977(3)	1,000	Y23-25	780.00	875.00
106	1977(2)	9,000	Y23,24	60.00	75.00
107	1978(7)	20,000	Y13-18,20	27.00	—

Listings For

KATANGA: refer to Zaire

KAMPUCHEA

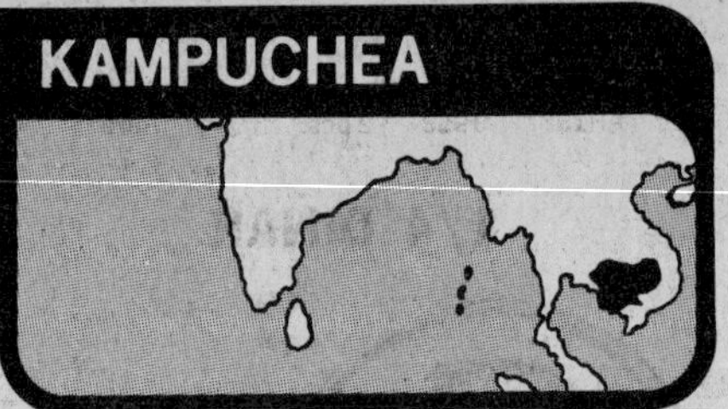

People's Democratic Republic of Kampuchea formerly the Republic of Cambodia, the Khmer Republic, and Democratic Kampuchea, a land of paddy fields and forest-clad hills located on the Southeast Asian peninsula, fronting on the Gulf of Thailand, has an area of 69,900 sq. mi. (181,040 sq. km.) and a population of 5 million. Capital: Phnom Penh. Agriculture is the basis of the economy, with rice the chief crop. Native industries include cattle breeding, weaving and rice milling. Rubber, cattle, corn, and timber are exported.

The region was the nucleus of the Khmer empire which flourished from the 5th to the 12th century and attained an excellence in art and architecture still evident in the magnificent ruins at Angkor. The Khmer empire once ruled over most of Southeast Asia, but began to decline in the 13th century as the Siamese, Thai and Vietnamese invaded the region and attached its territories. At the request of the Cambodian king, a French protectorate was established over the country in 1863, saving it from dissolution, and in 1877 Cambodia was included in the French Union of Indo-China. France granted Cambodia a constitution in 1947 and independence within the Union in 1949. The 1954 Geneva Convention resulted in full independence for the Kingdom of Cambodia. King Sihanouk abdicated to his father and won the office of Prime Minister.

Prince Sihanouk was toppled by a bloodless coup led by Lon Nol in March of 1970. Sihanouk moved to Peking to head a government-in-exile. On Oct. 9, 1970, Cambodia became the Khmer Republic, and Lon Nol its President. The Government of Lon Nol was in turn toppled, April 17, 1975, by the Khmer Rouge insurgents who took control of the government and renamed the country Democratic Cambodia.

In accordance with the constitution of Jan. 5, 1976, the name of the country was changed from Democratic Cambodia to Democratic Kampuchea.

Kampuchea has become a land of mystery; there is scant information concerning the present political and social situation. It would appear that an attempt is underway to attain agricultural self-sufficiency by relocating entire city populations in the countryside. Refugees tell of a barter system replacing the use of money.

RULERS

Ang Dong (Pra Ong Harizak) 1841-1859
Norodom I, 1859-1904
Norodom Sihanouk 1941-1955
Norodom Suramarit 1955-1960
Norodom Sihanouk (As Chief of State) 1960-1970

MINTMARKS

(a) - Paris, privy marks only

MONETARY SYSTEM

(Until 1860)
2 Att = 1 Pei (Pey)
4 Pei = 1 Fuang (Fuong)
8 Fuang = 1 Tical
4 Salong = 1 Tical
(Commencing 1860)
100 Centimes = 1 Franc
100 Sen = 1 Riel

CAMBODIA

Kingdom

AH

COPPER, 1.4-2.5 gm., uniface
Obv: Similar to 1 Pe, KM#2.

KM#	Date	Year	VG	Fine	VF	XF
1	1208	(1847)	4.00	6.50	9.00	20.00

PE

COPPER, 4.0-4.6 gm., uniface
With or without silver wash

KM#	Date	Year	VG	Fine	VF	XF
2	1208	(1847)	9.00	15.00	27.50	55.00

COPPER or BILLON 0.2-0.9 gm., uniface

KM#	Date	Year	VG	Fine	VF	XF
3	ND		6.00	8.50	12.50	27.50

Uniface
Obv: Cocoa bean.

KM#	Date	Year	VG	Fine	VF	XF
4	ND		6.00	9.00	15.00	30.00

Uniface

KM#	Date	Year	VG	Fine	VF	XF
5	ND		9.00	15.00	27.50	50.00

2 PE

(1/2 Fuang)

COPPER or BILLON 1.0-2.0 gm., uniface

KM#	Date	Year	VG	Fine	VF	XF
7	ND		3.00	4.50	7.00	12.00

Uniface

KM#	Date	Year	VG	Fine	VF	XF
9	ND		5.50	8.00	12.50	27.50

Uniface

KM#	Date	Year	VG	Fine	VF	XF
11	ND		3.00	4.50	7.00	12.50

Uniface

KM#	Date	Year	VG	Fine	VF	XF
13	ND		4.00	7.00	12.00	20.00

Uniface

KM#	Date	Year	VG	Fine	VF	XF
14	ND		4.00	7.00	12.00	20.00

Uniface

KM#	Date	Year	VG	Fine	VF	XF
15	ND		5.50	8.00	12.50	27.50

Uniface

KM#	Date	Year	VG	Fine	VF	XF
17	ND		5.50	8.00	12.50	27.50

Uniface
Obv: Similar to KM#5.

KM#	Date	Year	VG	Fine	VF	XF
19	ND		10.00	15.00	27.50	55.00

Uniface

KM#	Date	Year	VG	Fine	VF	XF
21	ND		10.00	15.00	27.50	55.00

Uniface

KM#	Date	Year	VG	Fine	VF	XF
23	ND		10.00	15.00	27.50	55.00

Rev: Legend in Cambodian script. Hand struck.

KM#	Date	Year	VG	Fine	VF	XF
25	ND		5.00	8.00	15.00	25.00

Obv: Similar to KM#25 but w/o border around Garuda bird. Machine struck.

KM#	Date	Year	VG	Fine	VF	XF
26	ND		2.50	4.00	6.50	12.00

FUANG

COPPER or BILLON, 2.7-3.0 gm., uniface

KM#	Date	Year	VG	Fine	VF	XF
27	ND		3.00	4.50	7.50	15.00

Uniface
Obv: A hippogriff walking to right. Similar to KM#21.

KM#	Date	Year	VG	Fine	VF	XF
29	ND		10.00	15.00	27.50	55.00

NOTE: KM#'s 1 through 29 above were struck between 1650 and 1850. All are believed to have been struck at Battambang except KM#25 which is thought to have been made at Siem Reap.

1/8 TICAL

(1 Fuang)

BILLON, 1.5-1.75 gm., 11-16mm, uniface

KM#	Date	Year	VG	Fine	VF	XF
32	1208	(1847)	3.50	5.00	8.00	15.00

SILVER, 14mm
Machine struck

KM#	Date	Year	VG	Fine	VF	XF
33	ND	(1847)	—	—	Rare	—

NOTE: Counterfeits exist in brass and silver.

1/4 TICAL

(1 Salong)

SILVER, 3.2 gm., 20mm

KM#	Date	Year	VG	Fine	VF	XF
34	1208	(1847)	—	—	Rare	—

3.6 gm. 22mm

KM#	Date	Year	VG	Fine	VF	XF
35	1208	(1847)	—	—	Rare	—

TICAL

SILVER, 15 gm., 30mm, thick flan

KM#	Date	Year	VG	Fine	VF	XF
36	1208	(1847)	35.00	55.00	110.00	250.00

35mm, thin flan

KM#	Date	Year	VG	Fine	VF	XF
37	1208	(1847)	55.00	90.00	200.00	325.00

3 TICALS

SILVER

KM#	Date	Year	VG	Fine	VF	XF
39	1208	(1847)	—	—	Rare	—

French Protectorate

MONETARY SYSTEM

100 Centimes = 1 Franc

TOKEN ISSUES

CENTIME

BRASS
With center hole

Y#	Date	Year	Fine	VF	XF	Unc
1	ND	1897	25.00	40.00	75.00	—
		Without center hole				
1.1	ND	1897	25.00	40.00	75.00	—
		With square center hole.				
1.2	ND	1897	60.00	100.00	250.00	—

REGULAR COINAGE

NOTE: The following issues were first struck in France in 1864 as souvenirs engraved by FACONNET. Another set was produced in Belgium in 1875 by WURDEN.

RESTRIKES: In 1899 after the death of the Queen Mother of Cambodia, many of the 1860 series coins were restruck with the original dies. These dies were rusty and dirty from long storage and these restrike coins have a grainy appearance to them.

CINQ (5) CENTIMES

BRONZE

Y#	Date	Mintage	VG	Fine	VF	XF
2	1860	11.467	4.00	8.00	15.00	35.00

GOLD (OMS)

2a	1860	(restrike)	—	—	—	—

DIX (10) CENTIMES

BRONZE

3	1860	10.267	3.50	7.00	12.00	27.50

Rev: Local manufacture, with error: CENTINES

3.1	1860	—	10.00	25.00	45.00	70.00

GOLD (OMS)

3a	1860	—	—	—	—	—

NOTE: Y#2 and Y#3 were restruck in 1879, 1882 and 1889 from original dies.

25 CENTIMES

SILVER

4	1860	—	6.00	17.50	45.00	80.00
	1860	(restrike)	4.00	12.00	25.00	45.00

GOLD (OMS)

4a	1860	—	—	—	—	—

50 CENTIMES

SILVER

5	1860	—	7.00	30.00	55.00	150.00
	1860	(restrike)	4.00	15.00	25.00	65.00

GOLD (OMS)

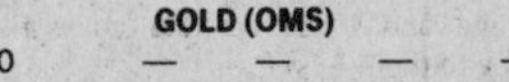

5a	1860	—	—	—	—	—

UN (1) FRANC

SILVER

Y#	Date	Mintage	VG	Fine	VF	XF
6	1860	—	7.00	45.00	75.00	175.00
	1860	(restrike)	5.00	25.00	50.00	75.00

GOLD (OMS)

6a	1860	—	—	—	—	—

DEUX (2) FRANCS

SILVER

7	1860	—	15.00	65.00	110.00	200.00
	1860	(restrike)	8.00	25.00	45.00	125.00

GOLD (OMS)

7a	1860	—	—	—	—	—

QUATRE (4) FRANCS

SILVER

8	1860	—	45.00	85.00	200.00	300.00
	1860	(restrike)	30.00	50.00	75.00	125.00

GOLD (OMS)

8a	1860	—	—	—	—	—

PIASTRE/PESO

SILVER

Y#	Date	Mintage	Fine	VF	XF	Unc
9	1860	—	350.00	700.00	1250.	4000.
	1860	(restrike)	150.00	300.00	700.00	1800.

GOLD (OMS)

Y#	Date	Mintage	VG	Fine	VF	XF
9a	1860	—	—	—	—	—

GOLD FRANC

(= 25 Silver Francs)

GOLD

10	—	—	—	Rare	—	

NOTE: Although dated 1860, Y#2-9 were actually minted about 1895.

Independent Kingdom

10 CENTIMES

ALUMINUM

Y#	Date	Mintage	Fine	VF	XF	Unc
11	1953(a)	4.000	.35	.75	1.50	3.00

20 CENTIMES

ALUMINUM

12	1953(a)	3.000	.35	.75	2.25	4.50

50 CENTIMES

ALUMINUM

13	1953(a)	3.170	.65	1.25	3.50	6.50

MONETARY REFORM

100 Sen = 1 Riel

10 SEN

ALUMINUM

Y#	Date	Mintage	Fine	VF	XF	Unc
11a	1959(a)	1.000	.15	.35	1.00	2.00

20 SEN

ALUMINUM

Y#	Date	Mintage	Fine	VF	XF	Unc
12a	1959(a)	1.004	.20	.40	1.25	2.50

50 SEN

ALUMINUM

Y#	Date	Mintage	Fine	VF	XF	Unc
13a	1959(a)	3.399	.30	.60	1.75	3.50

NCLT ISSUES

ESSAIS (E)

Standard metals unless otherwise noted

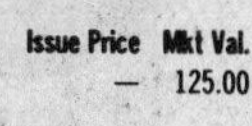

Y#	Date	Mintage	Identification	Issue Price	Mkt Val.
E1	1860	—	5 Centimes	—	125.00

Obv: Small bust with ESSAI below truncation.

Y#	Date	Mintage	Identification	Issue Price	Mkt Val.
E2	1860	—	10 Centimes	—	200.00
E2a	1860	—	10 Centimes, Silver	—	250.00

Obv: Large bust with E left of truncation.

Y#	Date	Mintage	Identification	Issue Price	Mkt Val.
E2b	1860	—	10 Centimes	—	100.00
E3	1860	—	25 Centimes	—	175.00

Y#	Date	Mintage	Identification	Issue Price	Mkt Val.
E4	1860	—	50 Centimes	—	250.00

Y#	Date	Mintage	Identification	Issue Price	Mkt Val.
E5	1860	—	1 Franc	—	300.00

Y#	Date	Mintage	Identification	Issue Price	Mkt Val.
E6	1860	—	2 Francs	—	400.00

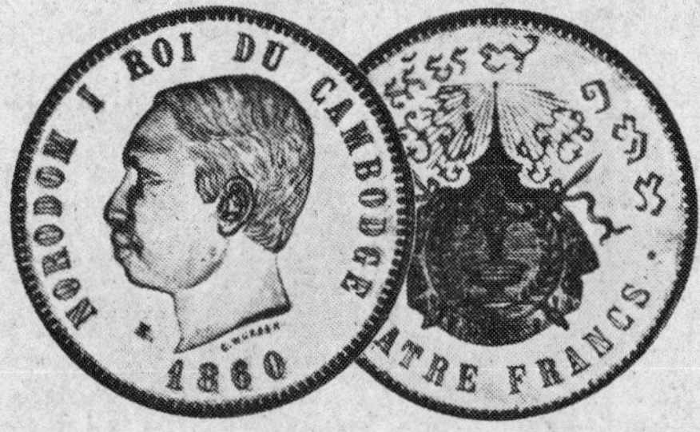

Y#	Date	Mintage	Identification	Issue Price	Mkt Val.
E7	1860	—	4 Francs	—	600.00
E8	1860	—	1 Piastre	—	Rare
E9	1953	1,200	10 Centimes	—	12.00
E10	1953	1,200	20 Centimes	—	13.00
E11	1953	1,200	50 Centimes	—	14.00

PIEFORTS (P)

PIEFORTS with ESSAI (PE)

(Double thickness)

Standard metals unless otherwise noted

Y#	Date	Mintage	Identification	Issue Price	Mkt Val.
P1	1860	—	5 Centimes	—	125.00
P2	1860	—	10 Centimes	—	150.00
P3	1860	—	20 Centimes	—	200.00
P4	1860	—	50 Centimes	—	300.00
P5	1860	—	1 Franc	—	400.00
P6	1860	—	2 Francs	—	500.00
P7	1860	—	4 Francs	—	700.00
P8	1860	—	1 Piastre	—	1750.
PE9	1953	104	10 Centimes	—	75.00
PE10	1953	104	20 Centimes	—	80.00
PE11	1953	104	50 Centimes	—	85.00

KHMER REPUBLIC

RIEL

COPPER-NICKEL
F.A.O. Coinage

Y#	Date	Mintage	Fine	VF	XF	Unc
14	1970	5.000	—	—	Not Released	

NOTE: According to the Royal Mint of Great Britain, this coin was minted at the Llantrissant Branch Mint in 1972 but dated 1969. According to the FAO, the coin was to have been dated 1971, but was not minted due to the fall of the Cambodian government in 1970. The photograph of the coin, supplied by the FAO, is dated 1970.

5000 RIELS

23.7600 gm., .925 SILVER, .7066 oz ASW

KM#	Date	Mintage	VF	XF	Unc
2	1974	.070	BV	BV	22.50
	1974	Inc. Ab.	—	Proof	30.00

Rev: Similar to KM#2.

KM#	Date	Mintage	VF	XF	Unc
6	1974	Inc. Ab.	BV	BV	22.50
	1974	Inc. Ab.	—	Proof	30.00

10,000 RIELS

47.5300 gm., .925 SILVER, 1.4136 oz ASW
President Lon Nol
Rev: Similar to 5,000 Riels, KM#2.

KM#	Date	Mintage	VF	XF	Unc
3	1974	.050	BV	BV	45.00
	1974	Inc. Ab.	—	Proof	60.00

Ancient sculpture
Rev: Similar to 5,000 Riels, KM#2.

KM#	Date	Mintage	VF	XF	Unc
7	1974	Inc. Ab.	BV	BV	45.00
	1974	Inc. Ab.	—	Proof	60.00

50,000 RIELS

6.7100 gm., .900 GOLD, .1941 oz AGW

KM#	Date	Mintage	VF	XF	Unc
4	1974	.011	BV	BV	150.00
	1974	Inc. Ab.	—	Proof	200.00

Obv: Ancient sculpture

KM#	Date	Mintage	VF	XF	Unc
8	1974	Inc. Ab.	BV	BV	150.00
	1974	Inc. Ab.	—	Proof	200.00

100,000 RIELS

19.1700 gm., .900 GOLD, .5547 oz AGW
President Lon Nol
Rev: Similar to 50,000 Riels, KM#8.

KM#	Date	Mintage	VF	XF	Unc
5	1974	7,000	BV	BV	375.00
	1974	Inc. Ab.	—	Proof	450.00

NOTE: The above coins were authorized by the Cambodian government shortly before its fall in 1975. The new Communist regime laid claim to the coins and for a time, their fate was uncertain. it was not until May, 1975, that the set was offered for sale.

NCLT ISSUES

PROOF SETS
STANDARD METALS

KM#	Date	Mintage	Identification	Issue Price	Mkt. Val.
101	1974(7)	—	KM2-8	—	1000.

Listings For

KANTANGA: refer to Zaire

KEELING-COCOS ISLANDS: refer to

KIAO CHAU: refer to China

KENYA

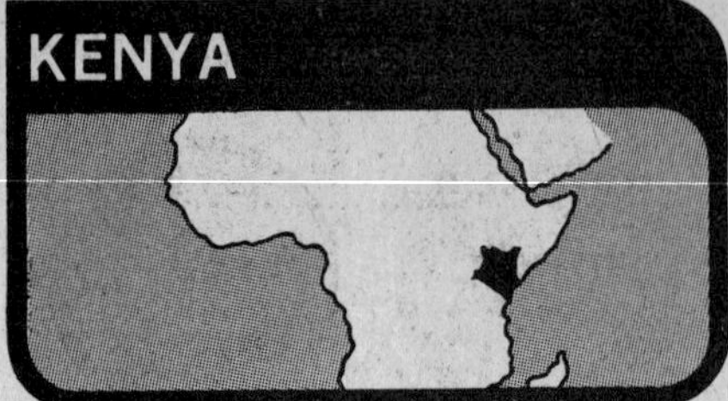

The Republic of Kenya, located on the east coast of Central Africa, has an area of 224,900 sq. mi. (582,488 sq. km.) and a population of 14.2 million. Capital: Nairobi. The predominantly agricultural country exports coffee, tea and petroleum products.

The Arabs came to the coast of Kenya in the 8th century and established posts to conduct an ivory and slave trade. The Portuguese, the inveterate wanderers of the Age of Exploration, followed in the 16th century. After a lengthy and bitter struggle with the sultans of Zanzibar who controlled much of the southeastern coast of Africa, the Portuguese were driven away (late 17th century) and for many years Kenya was simply a port of call on the route to India. German and British interests in the 19th century produced agreements defining their respective spheres of influence. The British sphere was administrated by the Imperial East Africa Co. until 1895, when the British government purchased the company's rights in the East Africa Protectorate which, in 1920, was designated as Kenya Colony and protectorate - the latter being a 10-mile wide coastal strip together with Mombasa, Lamu and other small islands nominally retained by the Sultan of Zanzibar. Kenya achieved self-government in June of 1963 as a consequence of the 1952-60 Mau Mau terrorist campaign to secure land reforms and political rights for Africans. Independence was attained on Dec. 12, 1963. Kenya became a republic in 1964. It is a member of the Commonwealth of Nations. The president is Chief of State and Head of Government.

Mombasa was a thriving Arabic commercial center when first visited by Portuguese navigator Vasco da Gama in 1498. During the following two centuries Portugal made repeated efforts to capture the island stronghold but was unable to hold it against the assaults of the Muscat Arabs. In 1823 the ruling Mazuri family placed the city under British protection. Britain repudiated the protectorate and it was then seized by Seyyid Said of Oman, 1837, and annexed to Zanzibar. In 1887 the sultan of Zanzibar relinquished the port of British administration. It was occupied by the Imperial British East Africa Company and for the following two decades was the capital of British East Africa.

MOMBASA

MINT MARKS

H - Birmingham
CM - Calcutta

MONETARY SYSTEM

4 Pice = 1 Anna
16 Anna = 1 Rupee

PICE

BRONZE
Small letters

Y#	Date	Year	Mintage	VF	XF	Unc
1	AH1306					
		1888CM	.630	4.50	7.00	10.00

Medium letters

Y#	Date	Year	Mintage	VF	XF	Unc
1.1	AH1306					
		1888CM	Inc. Ab.	3.00	5.00	8.00

Medium letters

Y#	Date	Year	Mintage	VF	XF	Unc
1.2	AH1306	1888H	—	5.00	8.00	12.50

Modified design, medium letters without serifs.

1.3	AH1306	1888H	—	—	Proof	65.00

SILVER

1a	AH13061888CM	—	—	—	300.00

2 ANNAS

.917 SILVER

Y#	Date	Mintage	VF	XF	Unc
2	1890H	—	10.00	15.00	35.00
	1890H	—	—	Proof	75.00

1/4 RUPEE

.917 SILVER

3	1890H	—	17.50	25.00	50.00
	1890H	—	—	Proof	100.00

1/2 RUPEE

.917 SILVER

4	1890H	—	22.50	35.00	80.00
	1890H	—	—	Proof	125.00

RUPEE

.917 SILVER

5	1888H	.050	22.50	35.00	80.00
	1888H	—	—	Proof	150.00

NCLT ISSUES

PROOF SETS
STANDARD METALS

KM#	Date	Mintage	Identification	Issue Price	Mkt. Val.
101	1888H(2)	—	Y1.3,5	—	150.00
102	1890H(3)	—	Y2-4	—	300.00

KENYA

MONETARY SYSTEM
100 Cents = 1 Shilling

5 CENTS

NICKEL-BRASS

Y#	Date	Mintage	VF	XF	Unc
1	1966	28.000	—	.10	.20
	1966	27 pcs.	—	Proof	—
	1967	9.600	—	.10	.20
	1968	12.000	—	.10	.20

7	1969	.800	—	.10	.20
	1969	15 pcs.	—	Proof	—
	1970	8.320	—	.10	.20
	1971	29.680	—	.10	.20
	1973	500 pcs.	—	Proof	—
	1974	5.599	—	.10	.20
	1975	6.000	—	.10	.20

10 CENTS

NICKEL-BRASS

2	1966	26.000	—	.10	.25
	1966	27 pcs.	—	Proof	—
	1967	7.300	—	.10	.25
	1968	12.000	—	.10	.25

8	1969	3.900	—	.10	.25
	1969	15 pcs.	—	Proof	—
	1970	7.200	—	.10	.25

Y#	Date	Mintage	VF	XF	Unc
8	1971	32.400	—	.10	.30
	1973	3.000	—	.10	.25
	1973	500 pcs.	—	Proof	—
	1974	3.000	—	.10	.25
	1975	3.000	—	.10	.25
	1977	—	—	—	—

25 CENTS

COPPER-NICKEL

3	1966	8.000	.20	.25	.40
	1966	27 pcs.	—	Proof	—
	1967	4.000	.20	.25	.40

9	1969	.200	.20	.25	.50
	1969	15 pcs.	—	Proof	—
	1973	500 pcs.	—	Proof	—

50 CENTS

COPPER-NICKEL

4	1966	14.000	.25	.35	.50
	1966	27 pcs.	—	Proof	—
	1967	5.120	.25	.35	.50
	1968	6.000	.25	.35	.50

10	1969	.400	.20	.25	.50
	1969	15 pcs.	—	Proof	—
	1971	9.600	.20	.30	.40
	1973	3.360	.15	.25	.40
	1973	500 pcs.	—	Proof	—
	1974	12.640	.15	.35	.50
	1975	8.000	.15	.25	.40

SHILLING

COPPER-NICKEL

5	1966	20.000	.30	.40	.70
	1966	27 pcs.	—	Proof	—
	1967	4.000	.35	.45	.70
	1968	8.000	.30	.40	.70

11	1969	4.000	.30	.40	.75
	1969	15 pcs.	—	Proof	—

Y#	Date	Mintage	VF	XF	Unc
11	1971	24.000	.20	.30	.60
	1973	2.480	.20	.35	.60
	1973	500 pcs.	—	Proof	—
	1974	13.520	.20	.30	.60
	1975	8.000	.20	.30	.60

2 SHILLINGS

COPPER-NICKEL

Y#	Date	Mintage	VF	XF	Unc
6	1966	3.000	.50	.85	1.25
	1966	27 pcs.	—	Proof	—
	1968	1.100	.40	.85	1.25

Y#	Date	Mintage	VF	XF	Unc
12	1969	.100	.75	1.00	1.75
	1969	15 pcs.	—	Proof	—
	1971	1.920	.40	.85	1.25
	1973	500 pcs.	—	Proof	—

5 SHILLINGS

BRASS
10th Anniversary

Y#	Date	Mintage	VF	XF	Unc
13	1973	.100	5.00	7.50	10.00
	1973	1,500	—	Proof	—

100 SHILLINGS

7.6000 gm., .917 GOLD, .2240 oz AGW

Fr#	Date	Mintage	VF	XF	Unc
3	1966	—	—	—	150.00
	1966	7,500	—	Proof	175.00

250 SHILLINGS

19.0000 gm., .917 GOLD, .5602 oz AGW

Fr#	Date	Mintage	VF	XF	Unc
2	1966	—	—	—	375.00
2	1966	1,000	—	Proof	450.00

500 SHILLINGS

38.0000 gm., .917 GOLD, 1.1204 oz AGW

Fr#	Date	Mintage	VF	XF	Unc
1	1966	—	—	—	750.00
		500 pcs.	—	Proof	1000.

NCLT ISSUES

MINT SETS

KM#	Date	Mintage	Identification	Issue Price	Mkt. Val.
S1	1966(3)	—	Fr 1-3	—	1275.

MINT SETS

PROOF SETS
STANDARD METALS

KM#	Date	Mintage	Identification	Issue Price	Mkt. Val.
101	1966(6)	27	Y1-6	—	—
102	1966(3)	500	Fr 1-3	152.60	1625.
103	1969(6)	15	Y7-12	—	—
104	1973(7)	500	Y7-13	—	150.00

KIRIBATI

Kiribati (formerly the Gilbert Islands), 30 coral stolls and islands spread over more than 1,000,000 sq. mi. (2,590,000 sq. km.) of the southwest Pacific Ocean, has an area of 264 sq. mi. (684 sq. km.) and a population of 53,000. Capital: Bairiki, on Tarawa. In addition to the Gilbert Islands proper, Kiribati includes Ocean Island, the Central and Southern Line Islands, and the Phoenix Islands, though possession of Canton and Enderbury of the Phoenix Islands is disputed with the United States. Most families engage in subsistence fishing. Copra and phosphates are exported, mostly to Australia and New Zealand.

The Gilbert Islands and the group formerly called the Ellice Islands (now Tuvalu) comprised a single British crown colony, the Gilbert and Ellice Islands.

The Islands were first sighted by Spanish mutineers in 1537. Succeeding visits were made by the English navigators John Byron (1764), James Cook (1777), and Thomas Golbert and John Marshall (1788). An American, Edward Fanning, arrived in 1798. Britain declared a protectorate over the Gilbert and Ellice Islands, and in 1915 began the formation of a colony which was completed with the addition of the Phoenix Islands in 1937. The Central and Southern Line Islands were administratively attached to the Gilbert and Ellice Islands colony in 1972, and remained attached to the Gilberts when Tuvalu was created in 1975. The colony became self-governing in 1971. Kiribati attained independence on July 12, 1979.

RULERS

British until 1979

MONETARY SYSTEM

100 Cents = 1 Dollar

CENT

BRONZE

Y#	Date	Mintage	VF	XF	Unc
1	1979	—	—	—	.15
	1979	—	—	Proof	—

2 CENTS

BRONZE

Y#	Date	Mintage	VF	XF	Unc
2	1979	—	—	—	.20
	1979	—	—	Proof	—

5 CENTS

COPPER-NICKEL

Y#	Date	Mintage	VF	XF	Unc
3	1979	—	—	—	.50
	1979	—	—	Proof	—

10 CENTS

COPEPR-NICKEL

Y#	Date	Mintage	VF	XF	Unc
4	1979	—	—	—	1.00
	1979	—	—	Proof	—

20 CENTS

COPPER-NICKEL

Y#	Date	Mintage	VF	XF	Unc
5	1979	—	—	—	1.50
	1979	—	—	Proof	—

50 CENTS

COPPER-NICKEL

Y#	Date	Mintage	VF	XF	Unc
6	1979	—	—	—	2.00
	1979	—	—	Proof	—

DOLLAR

COPPER-NICKEL
Obv: Arms. Rev: Sailing canoe.

Y#	Date	Mintage	VF	XF	Unc
7	1979	—	—	—	4.00
	1979	—	—	Proof	—

5 DOLLARS

28.1600 gm., .925 SILVER, .8375 oz ASW

Y#	Date	Mintage	VF	XF	Unc
8	1979				30.00
—		5,000		Proof	40.00

150 DOLLARS

15.9800 gm., .917 GOLD, .4711 oz AGW

Y#	Date	Mintage	VF	XF	Unc
9	1979	1,000	—	—	325.00
	1979	1,000		Proof	400.00

NCLT ISSUES

PROOF SETS

KM#	Date	Mintage	Identification	Issue Price	Mkt. Val.
101	1979(7)	10,000	Y1-7	34.00	50.00

KOREA

Korea, 'Land of the Morning Calm', occupies a mountainous peninsula in northeast Asia bounded by Manchuria, the Yellow Sea and the Sea of Japan.

According to legend, the first Korean dynasty, that of the House of Tangun, ruled from 2333 B.C. to 1122 B.C. It was followed by the dynasty of Kija, a Chinese scholar, which continued until 193 B.C. and brought a high civilization to Korea. The first recorded period in the history of Korea, the Period of the Three Kingdoms, lasted from 57 B.C. to 935 A.D. and achieved the first political unification of the peninsula. The Kingdom of Koryo, from which Korea derived its name, was founded in 935 and continued until 1392, when it was superseded by the Y I Dynasty of King Yi, Sung Kyewas to last until the Japanese annexation in 1910.

At the end of the 16th century Korea was invaded and occupied for 7 years by Japan, and from 1627 until the late 19th century it was a semi-independent tributary of China. Japan replaced China as the predominant foreign influence at the end of the Sino-Japanese War (1894-95), only to find its position threatened by Russian influence from 1896 to 1904. The Russian threat was eliminated by the Russo-Japanese War (1904-05) and in 1905 Japan established a direct protectorate over Korea. On Aug. 22, 1910, the last Korean ruler signed the treaty that annexed Korea to Japan as a government general in the Japanese Empire. Japanese suzerainty was maintained until the end of World War II.

From 1633 to 1891 the monetary system of Korea employed cast coins with a square center hole. Fifty-two mints were authorized to produce these coins, which exist in thousands of varieties. Seed, or mother coins, were used to make the impressions in the molds in which the regular cash coins were cast. Seed coins are readily recognized as they have a larger diameter than regular coinage, the characters are in high relief, and the rims are rounded, polished, or beveled to facilitate their removal from the mold. Seed coins have a value five to ten times greater than that of regular coinage. Czarist-Russian Korea experimented with Korean coins when Aliexiev of Russia, Korea's Financial Advisor, founded the First Asian Branch of the Russo-Korean Bank on March 1, 1898, and authorized the issuing of a set of new Korean coins with a crowned Russian-style quasi-eagle. British-Japanese opposition and the Russo-Japanese War operated to end the Russian coinage experiment in 1904.

RULERS

Sunjo, 1800-1834
Honjong, 1834-1849
Ch'olchong, 1850-1863
Kojong, 1863-1897
Kuang Mu, 1897-1907
Yung Hi, 1907-1910

MONETARY UNITS

文 Mun　兩 Yang, Niang

分 Fun　圜 Hwan

錢 Chon　圓 Won

CHARACTERS USED AS NUMERALS

The following characters are taken from a Chinese literary work known as the THOUSAND CHARACTER CLASSIC. This work consists of exactly 1000 characters, none of which is used twice, and for this reason the characters are often used as 'FURNACE NUMBERS' on the cash coins of Korea.

天	1	張	16	調	31
地	2	寒	17	陽	32
玄	3	來	18	雲	33
黃	4	暑	19	騰	34
宇	5	往	20	致	35
宙	6	秋	21	雨	36
洪	7	收	22	露	37
荒	8	冬	23	結	38
日	9	藏	24	為	39
月	10	閏	25	霜	40
盈	11	餘	26	金	41
昃	12	成	27	生	42
辰	13	歲	28	麗	43
宿	14	律	29	水	44
列	15	呂	30	玉	45

IDENTIFICATION CHART

Obverse:

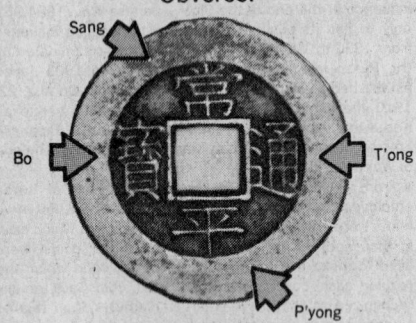

Sang

Bo

T'ong

P'yong

Sang P'yong T'ong Bo

Reverse:

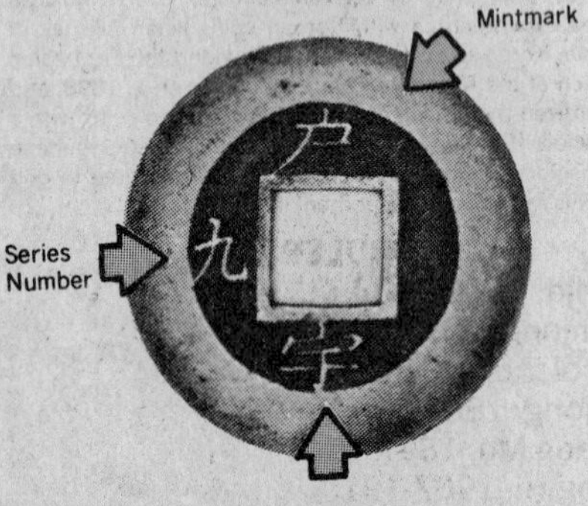

Furnace Number

NOTE: The series number may be to the left or right of the center hole. The furnace number may be either a numeral or a character from the THOUSAND CHARACTER CLASSIC.

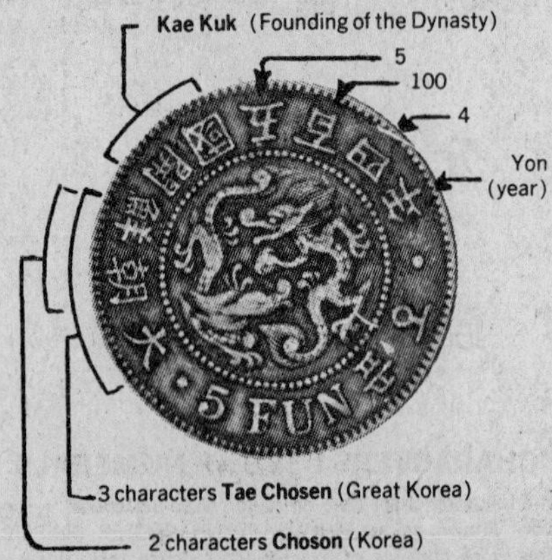

MINTMARKS

A 戸 or 户 or 戶 HO
Treasury Department

B 工 KONG
Ministry of Industry

C 均 KYUN
Government Tithe Office

D 冏 KYONG
Bureau of Royal Transportation

E 賑 CHIN
Charity Office in Seoul

F 向 HYANG
Food Supply Office

G 宣 SON
Rice & Cloth Department

H 惠 HYE
Rice & Cloth Department

I 典 CHON
Central Government Mint

J 兵 PYONG
Ministry of Defense

K 備 or 俻 PI
National Defense Bureau

L 摠 CH'ONG
General Military Office

M 營 or 营 YONG
Special Army Unit

N 武 MU
Armaments Bureau
Guard Office at the Palace

O 禁 KUM
Court Guard Military Unit

P 訓 or 訓 HUN
Military Training Command

Q 抄 CH'O
Commando Military Unit

R 統 or 統 T'ONG
T'ongyong Naval Office
Military Office in Seoul

S 经 KYONG
Government Office of
Pukhan Mountain Fortress

T 守 SU
Seoul Defense Fort

U 沁 SIM
Kanghwa Township Military Office

V 開 KAE
Kaesong Township Military Office

W 松 SONG
Kaesong Township Military Office

X 利 I
Iwon Township Military Office

Y 水 SU
Suwon Township Military Office

Z 原 WON
Wonju Township Military Office

AA 海 HAE
Haeju Township Military Office

BB 春 or 春 CH'UN
Ch'unch'on Township Military Office

CC 川 CH'ON
Tanch'on Township Military Office

DD 昌 CH'ANG
Ch'angdok Palace Mint
Ch'angwon Township Military Office

EE 圻 KI
Kwangju Township Military Office
in Kyonggi Province

FF 京 KYONG
Kyonggi Provincial Office

GG 京水 KYONG SU
Kyonggi Naval Station

HH 黃 HWANG
Hwanghae Provincial Office

II 平 P'YONG
P'yongan Provincial Office

JJ 平兵 P'YONG PYONG
P'yongan Military Fort

KK 咸 HAM
Hamgyong Provincial Office

LL 咸北 HAM PUK
North Hamgyong Provincial Office

MM 咸南 HAM NAM
South Hamgyong Provincial Office

NN 江 KANG
Kangwon Provincial Office

OO 尙 SANG
Kyongsang Provincial Office

PP 尙水 SANG SU
Kyongsang Naval Station

QQ 尙右 SANG U
Kyongsang Right Naval Base

RR 尙左 SANG CHWA
Kyongsang Left Naval Base

SS 全 CHON
Cholla Provincial Office

TT 全兵 CHON PYONG
Cholla Military Fort

UU 全右 CHON U
Cholla Right Naval Base

VV 全左 CHON CHWA
Cholla Left Naval Base

WW 忠 CH'UNG
Ch'ungch'ong Provincial Office

MUN

Minted: 1633

CAST COPPER or BRASS
Rev: Plain

KM#	Mint	Good	VG	Fine	VF
1	—	225.00	300.00	450.00	600.00

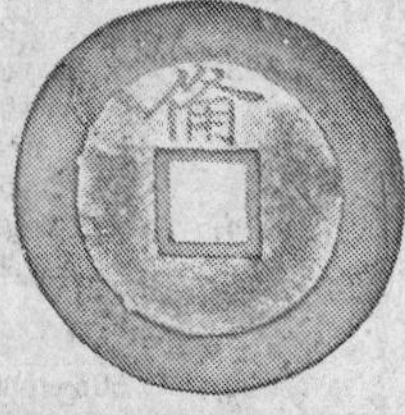

Rev: Mintmark only (one or two characters)

Minted: 1678 - 1742

KM#	Mint	Good	VG	Fine	VF
3	A	35.00	65.00	100.00	150.00
	B	75.00	150.00	225.00	300.00
	D	50.00	85.00	125.00	175.00
	F	50.00	100.00	150.00	225.00
	G	50.00	100.00	150.00	225.00
	J	25.00	50.00	75.00	100.00
	K	20.00	30.00	45.00	60.00
	L	175.00	275.00	400.00	550.00
	M	50.00	75.00	110.00	150.00
	N	50.00	100.00	150.00	225.00
	P	50.00	75.00	110.00	150.00
	Q	60.00	125.00	175.00	250.00
	R	75.00	150.00	225.00	325.00
	T	60.00	125.00	175.00	250.00
	V	50.00	75.00	110.00	150.00
	Y	75.00	150.00	250.00	350.00
	Z	60.00	125.00	200.00	275.00
	AA	60.00	125.00	175.00	250.00
	DD	60.00	125.00	175.00	250.00
	EE	75.00	150.00	225.00	325.00
	FF	60.00	125.00	175.00	250.00
	GG	100.00	175.00	225.00	300.00
	HH	75.00	150.00	225.00	325.00
	II	50.00	100.00	150.00	200.00
	JJ	75.00	150.00	225.00	325.00
	KK	75.00	150.00	250.00	350.00
	LL	100.00	175.00	275.00	375.00
	MM	125.00	200.00	300.00	400.00
	NN	75.00	150.00	225.00	300.00
	OO	40.00	75.00	110.00	150.00
	PP	60.00	110.00	175.00	250.00
	QQ	50.00	100.00	150.00	225.00
	RR	50.00	100.00	175.00	250.00
	SS	40.00	75.00	110.00	150.00
	TT	75.00	150.00	225.00	300.00
	UU	75.00	150.00	250.00	350.00
	VV	75.00	150.00	250.00	350.00
	WW	75.00	150.00	225.00	325.00

Rev: With mintmark, furnace and series number and sometimes various dots, circles or crescents.

Minted: 1742-1891

KM#	Mint	Good	VG	Fine	VF
5	A	.20	.40	.60	.75
	C	.25	.50	.75	1.00
	E	.40	.75	1.00	1.50
	G	.50	1.00	1.50	2.00
	H	.40	.75	1.00	1.50
	L	.15	.30	.45	.60
	M	.30	.60	.90	1.25
	N	.30	.60	.90	1.25
	O	.30	.60	.90	1.25
	P	.20	.40	.60	.75
	S	.45	.90	1.35	1.75
	U	6.00	12.00	17.50	25.00
	V	.40	.75	1.00	1.50
	W	.40	.75	1.00	1.50
	X	2.00	3.50	5.00	7.00

KM#	Mint	Good	VG	Fine	VF
5	DD	5.00	10.00	15.00	20.00
	EE	.75	1.50	2.00	2.75
	II	.15	.25	.35	.50
	KK	.75	1.50	2.25	3.00

2 MUN

CAST COPPER or BRASS
Rev: Mintmark at top, numeral two below indicating denomination. Dots, circles or crescents may also be present.

Minted: 1679-1752

KM#	Mint	Good	VG	Fine	VF
7	A	.15	.25	.50	.75
	B	.25	.50	.75	1.00
	D	4.00	7.50	11.00	15.00
	E	.15	.25	.50	.75
	F	3.00	6.00	9.00	12.00
	G	.60	1.25	1.75	2.50
	J	3.00	6.00	9.00	12.00
	K	2.00	4.00	6.00	8.00
	L	1.25	2.50	3.75	5.00
	M	.20	.35	.60	1.00
	N	.60	1.25	1.75	2.50
	O	.25	.50	.75	1.00
	P	3.00	6.00	9.00	12.00
	Q	1.50	3.00	5.00	7.50
	R	7.00	14.00	20.00	27.50
	T	1.00	2.00	3.00	4.00
	V	.25	.50	1.00	1.50
	Y	7.50	15.00	22.50	30.00
	Z	40.00	80.00	120.00	160.00
	AA	.25	.50	1.00	1.50
	EE	.60	1.25	1.75	2.50
	GG	.75	1.25	2.25	3.00
	HH	4.00	8.00	12.00	16.00
	II	.25	.50	.75	1.00
	JJ	40.00	80.00	120.00	160.00
	KK	3.00	6.00	9.00	12.00
	NN	.75	1.50	2.25	3.00
	OO	4.50	9.00	13.00	18.00
	PP	5.50	11.00	16.00	22.00
	QQ	5.50	11.00	16.00	22.00
	RR	5.00	10.00	15.00	20.00
	SS	.50	1.00	1.50	2.00
	TT	45.00	90.00	135.00	180.00
	WW	40.00	85.00	130.00	175.00

NOTE: Where the mintmark is given with two characters, one appears above and the other below the hole. The numeral two appears to the left or right of the hole.

Rev: Mintmark and furnace number. Series numbers, dots, circles or crescents may also be present.

Minted: 1742 - 1753

KM#	Mint	Good	VG	Fine	VF
9	A	.30	.60	.90	1.25
	G	1.00	1.75	2.50	3.50
	L	.75	1.25	1.75	2.50
	M	.50	1.00	1.50	2.00
	O	1.00	1.75	2.50	3.50
	P	.50	1.00	1.50	2.00
	R	.75	1.50	2.25	3.00
	V	1.00	2.25	3.50	4.50
	II	3.00	6.00	9.00	12.00
	KK	1.50	3.00	4.50	6.00
	OO	1.50	3.25	4.75	6.50
	SS	.75	1.25	1.75	2.50

5 MUN

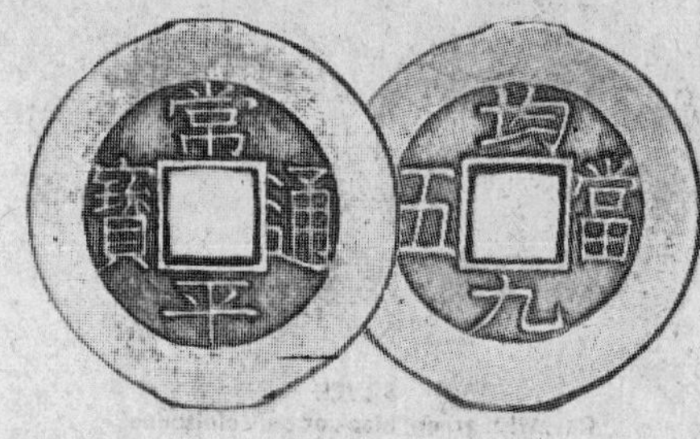

CAST COPPER or BRASS
Rev: Mintmark above hole, furnace number below. "Tang O" meaning "worth five (mun)" to left and right of hole.

Minted: 1883

KM#	Mint	Good	VG	Fine	VF
11	A	.75	1.50	2.25	3.00
	C	.50	1.00	1.50	2.00
	I	.50	1.00	1.50	2.00
	R	1.00	2.00	3.00	4.00
	U	1.00	2.00	3.00	4.00
	BB	.60	1.25	1.75	2.50
	CC	2.00	4.00	6.00	8.00
	DD	2.00	3.50	5.00	7.00
	FF	.30	.60	.90	1.25
	II	1.25	2.50	3.25	5.00

100 MUN

COPPER or BRASS

Minted: 1866

KM#	Mint	VG	Fine	VF	XF
15	A	2.00	3.00	4.00	6.00

CHON

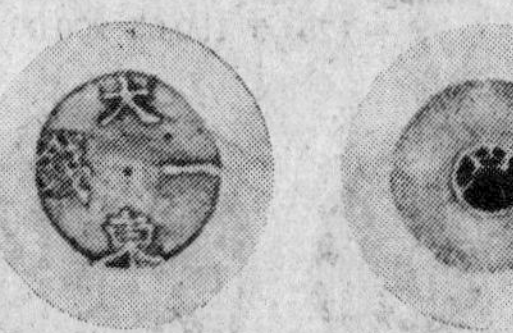

SILVER
Rev: With green, black or blue cloisonne' enamel in center circle.

C#	Date	Mintage	VG	Fine	VF	XF
5	(1882-83)	*—	60.00	85.00	125.00	175.00

2 CHON

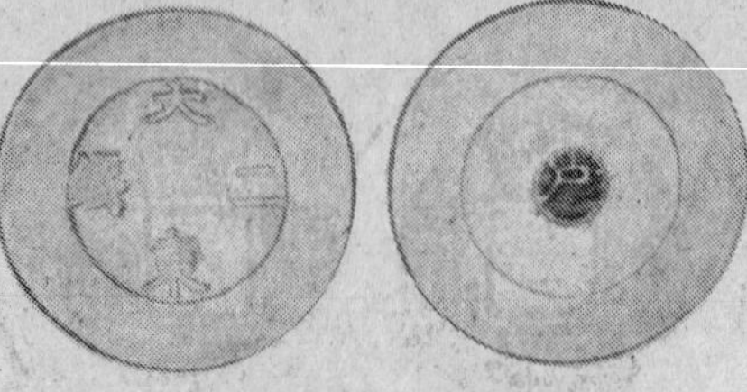

SILVER
Rev: With green, black or blue cloisonne' enamel in center circle.

C#	Date	Mintage	VG	Fine	VF	XF
6	(1882-83)	*—	90.00	125.00	175.00	250.00

3 CHON

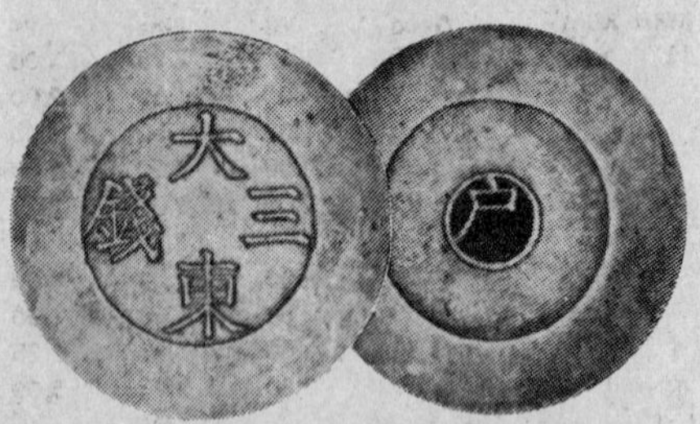

SILVER
Rev: With green, black or blue cloisonne' enamel in center circle.

C#	Date	Mintage	VG	Fine	VF	XF
7	(1882-83)	*—	175.00	250.00	350.00	500.00

***NOTE:** Due to the added expense of adding the cloisonne' enamel during production the silver one, two & three chon C#5-7 were discontinued in June, 1883. Examples with cloisonne missing are valued at one half normal valuations. There are many types of trial sets of 1, 2 & 3 Chon in existance. Counterfeits are reported.

MODERN COINAGE

During the 1880's and 1890's, Korea experimented with several different types of machine-struck coins including a struck "Cash" coin with round center hole, (Y#A1). A number of pattern coins of this period exist, some of which may have actually entered circulation.

FIRST MONETARY SYSTEM

1888-1891AD
1000 Mun = 1 Warn

5 MUN

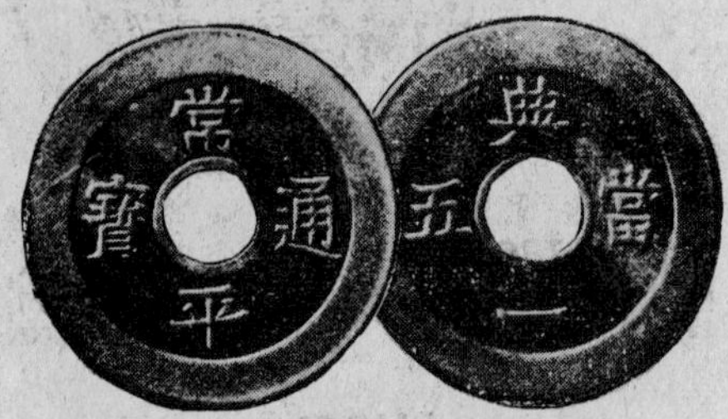

BRASS

Y#	Date	Mintage	Fine	VF	XF	Unc
A1	(1890)	—	125.00	150.00	200.00	300.00

COPPER, 3.25gm.

Y#	Date	Mintage	Fine	VF	XF	Unc
1	(1888)yr.497	—	30.00	60.00	100.00	200.00

10 MUN

COPPER, 6.5gm.

Y#	Date	Mintage	Fine	VF	XF	Unc
2	(1888)yr.497	—	50.00	100.00	175.00	325.00

WARN

.900 SILVER, 26.96gm.

Y#	Date	Mintage	Fine	VF	XF	Unc
3	(1888)yr.491	1,300	2250.	2750.	3750.	5500.

NOTE: Estimated mintage figure. Beware of counterfeits.

MONETARY REFORM

1892 - 1902 AD
100 Fun = 1 Yang
5 Yang = 1 Whan

FUN

BRASS, 3.5gm.
Obv: 3 characters, TAE CHO-SON (Great Korea), to left of denomination.

Y#	Date	Year	Fine	VF	XF	Unc
4	(1892)	501	6.00	13.50	20.00	50.00
	(1895)	504	8.50	17.50	45.00	65.00
	(1896)	505	10.00	20.00	50.00	75.00

Obv: 2 characters, CHO-SON (Korea), to left of denomination.

Y#	Date	Year	Fine	VF	XF	Unc
4.1	(1893)	502	6.00	12.00	40.00	55.00
	(1894)	503	Reported, not confirmed			
	(1895)	504	3.00	11.00	20.00	45.00
	(1896)	505	Reported, not confirmed			

5 FUN

COPPER, 17.2gm.
Obv: 2 characters, CHO-SON (Korea), to left of denomination.

Y#	Date	Year	Fine	VF	XF	Unc
5	(1893)	502 small characters obverse	2.00	5.00	10.00	30.00
	(1893)	502 large characters obverse	10.00	20.00	50.00	125.00
	(1894)	503 small character obverse	5.00	15.00	55.00	120.00
	(1894)	503 large characters obverse	2.50	6.00	12.50	35.00
	(1895)	504	2.00	5.00	10.00	30.00
	(1896)	505 small characters obverse	1.50	3.00	7.50	25.00

Obv: Three large characters, TAE CHO-SON (Great Korea) to left of denomination, no dot in legend above dragon.

Y#	Date	Year	Fine	VF	XF	Unc
5.1	(1895)	504	1.00	2.50	7.00	20.00
	(1896)	505	2.00	5.00	10.00	30.00

Obv: Three small characters, TAE CHO-SON legend above dragon divided into two parts by a dot.

Y#	Date	Year	Fine	VF	XF	Unc
5.2	(1892)	501	1.50	3.00	6.00	20.00
	(1896)	505	2.00	4.00	8.00	22.50

Obv: Date given as year of Kuang Mu reign.

Y#	Date	Year	Fine	VF	XF	Unc
A10	(1898)	2 small characters obverse	1.00	2.50	7.00	15.00
	(1898)	2 medium characters obverse	5.00	10.00	20.00	60.00
	(1898)	2 large characters obverse	15.00	25.00	50.00	125.00
	(1899)	3	60.00	125.00	325.00	575.00
	(1902)	6	2.50	5.00	10.00	25.00

1/4 YANG

COPPER-NICKEL
Obv: 2 characters, CHO-SON (Korea), to left of denomination.

Y#	Date	Year	Fine	VF	XF	Unc
6	(1893)	502	2.00	4.00	12.50	35.00
	(1894)	503	7.50	15.00	40.00	60.00

Y#	Date	Year	Fine	VF	XF	Unc
6	(1895)	504	50.00	100.00	155.00	250.00
	(1896)	505	2.00	4.00	12.50	35.00

Obv: 3 characters, TAE CHO-SON (Great Korea), to left of denomination.

Y#	Date	Year	Fine	VF	XF	Unc
6.1	(1892)	501	5.00	12.50	35.00	85.00
	(1895)	504	4.00	7.50	30.00	65.00
	(1896)	505	80.00	120.00	200.00	350.00

Obv: Dragon crowded by small tight circle, 11.25mm, date given as year of Kuang Mu reign.

Y#	Date	Year	Fine	VF	XF	Unc
B10	(1897)	1	30.00	60.00	150.00	250.00
	(1898)	2	1.50	3.00	7.50	17.50
	(1899)	3 large characters obverse	25.00	50.00	125.00	250.00
	(1899)	3 small characters obverse	27.50	55.00	130.00	250.00
	(1900)	4	27.50	55.00	130.00	250.00
	(1901)	5	27.50	55.00	130.00	250.00

Obv: Larger circle around dragon, making it less crowded.

Y#	Date	Year	Fine	VF	XF	Unc
B10.1	(1898)	2	.50	1.00	2.00	6.50
			.50	1.50	2.00	6.50

NOTE: Many varieties of character size and style exist.

NOTE: Counterfeits were made on machinery supplied by the Japanese. These counterfeits were authorized for circulation by the Koreans. Many other crudely struck and cast counterfeits, in various metals, exist.

YANG

.800 SILVER, 5.2gm.
Obv: 3 characters, TAE CHO-SON.

Y#	Date	Year	Fine	VF	XF	Unc
7	(1892)	501	15.00	30.00	90.00	175.00

Obv: 2 characters, CHO-SON.

Y#	Date	Year	Fine	VF	XF	Unc
7.1	(1893)	502	15.00	30.00	90.00	175.00

Obv: Date given as year of Kuang Mu reign.
Rev: Wide spaced 'Yang'

Y#	Date	Year	Fine	VF	XF	Unc
C10	(1898)	2	20.00	35.00	100.00	200.00

Rev: Closely spaced 'Yang'

Y#	Year	Mintage	Fine	VF	XF	Unc
C10.1	2	—	20.00	35.00	100.00	200.00

COPPER-NICKEL

Y#	Year	Mintage	Fine	VF	XF	Unc
C10A	2	—	40.00	80.00	—	—

5 YANG

.900 SILVER, 26.6gm.

Y#	Year	Mintage	Fine	VF	XF	Unc
8	501	.020	500.00	700.00	1000.	1750.

WHAN

SILVER, 27gm.

Y#	Year	Mintage	Fine	VF	XF	Unc
9	502	Inc. Ab.	1500.	2200.	4000.	6000.

MONETARY REFORM

1902 - 1910AD

100 Chon = 1 Won

1/2 CHON

BRONZE, 3.56gm.
Obv: Date given as year of Kuang Mu reign.

Y#	Year	Mintage	Fine	VF	XF	Unc
13	10	24.000	1.00	2.25	5.00	20.00

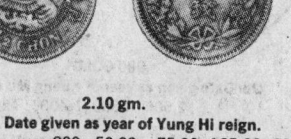

2.10 gm.
Obv: Date given as year of Yung Hi reign.

Y#	Year	Mintage	Fine	VF	XF	Unc
22	1	.800	50.00	75.00	125.00	200.00
	2	21.000	1.50	4.00	10.00	30.00
	3	8.200	2.00	5.00	12.00	35.00
	4	5.070	30.00	60.00	100.00	150.00

CHON

BRONZE, 6.8gm.
Obv: Date given as year of Kuang Mu reign.

Y#	Year	Mintage	Fine	VF	XF	Unc
10	6	3.001	400.00	850.00	1500.	2200.

NOTE: Most of the above coins were melted.

Obv: Date given as year of Kuang Mu reign, 7.13 gm.

Y#	Year	Mintage	Fine	VF	XF	Unc
14	9	Inc. Be.	3.00	7.50	17.50	50.00
	10	11.800	2.50	6.50	15.00	45.00

Obv: Date given as year of Kuang Mu reign, 4.25 gm.

Y#	Year	Mintage	Fine	VF	XF	Unc
B22	11	11.200	1.50	4.00	10.00	25.00

Obv: Date given as year of Yung Hi reign, 4.2 gm.

Y#	Year	Mintage	Fine	VF	XF	Unc
23	1	Inc. Ab.	2.00	5.00	12.50	40.00
	2	6.800	1.50	3.50	8.50	35.00
	3	9.200	1.25	3.25	8.50	35.00
	4	3.500	2.00	4.50	11.50	37.50

5 CHON

COPPER-NICKEL, 4.3gm.
Obv: Date given as year of Kuang Mu reign.

Y#	Year	Mintage	Fine	VF	XF	Unc
11	6	2.800	750.00	950.00	1500.	3000.

NOTE: Most of these coins were melted.

Obv: Date given as year of Kuang Mu reign, 4.5gm.

Y#	Year	Mintage	Fine	VF	XF	Unc
15	9	20.000	2.00	5.50	12.50	45.00
	11	160.000	4.00	8.50	20.00	60.00

Obv: Date given as year of Yung Hu reign.

Y#	Year	Mintage	Fine	VF	XF	Unc
—	3	4.001	350.00	650.00	1250.	2500.

10 CHON

.800 SILVER, 17.5mm, 2.7 gm.

Obv: Date given as year of Kuang Mu reign, 1.5mm thick.

Y#	Year	Mintage	Fine	VF	XF	Unc
16	10	2.000	4.00	10.00	25.00	55.00

Obv: Date given as year of Kuang Mu reign, 1.0mm thick.

Y#	Year	Mintage	Fine	VF	XF	Unc
C22	11	2.400	3.50	8.00	22.50	50.00

Obv: Date given as year of Yung Hi reign, 17mm, 2.25 gm.

Y#	Year	Mintage	Fine	VF	XF	Unc
25	2	6.300	2.50	6.00	12.50	35.00
	3	—	—	—	Rare	—
	4	9.500	2.50	5.00	11.50	30.00

20 CHON

.800 SILVER, 22.4mm, 5.39 gm.

Obv: Date given as year of Kuang Mu reign.

Y#	Year	Mintage	Fine	VF	XF	Unc
17	9	1.000	15.00	22.50	60.00	135.00
	10	2.500	12.50	17.50	40.00	100.00

Obv: Date given as year of Kuang Mu reign, 4.05 gm.

Y#	Year	Mintage	Fine	VF	XF	Unc
D22	11	1.500	8.00	12.00	30.00	65.00

Obv: Date given as year of Yung Hi reign.

Y#	Year	Mintage	Fine	VF	XF	Unc
26	2	3.000	6.00	10.00	25.00	55.00
	3	2.000	6.00	10.00	22.50	55.00
	4	2.000	8.00	12.00	25.00	60.00

1/2 WON

.800 SILVER, 13.50gm.

Obv: Date given as year of Kuang Mu reign.

Y#	Year	Mintage	Fine	VF	XF	Unc
12	5	1.831	900.00	1200.	1750.	4000.

NOTE: Most of these coins were melted.

Obv: Date given as year of Kuang Mu reign, 13.48gm.

Y#	Year	Mintage	Fine	VF	XF	Unc
18	9	.600	25.00	32.50	85.00	180.00
	10	1.200	25.00	35.00	85.00	200.00

Obv: Date given as year of Kuang Mu reign, 10.13gm.

Y#	Year	Mintage	Fine	VF	XF	Unc
E22	11	1.000	35.00	55.00	100.00	225.00

Obv: Date given as year of Yung Hi reign.

Y#	Year	Mintage	Fine	VF	XF	Unc
27	2	1.400	35.00	55.00	100.00	225.00
	3	—	—	—	Rare	—

5 WON

.900 GOLD

Obv: Date given as year of Yung Hi reign.

Y#	Year	Mintage	Fine	VF	XF	Unc
19	2	.010	1500.	3000.	9000.	17,500.
	3	—	—	—	Rare	—

10 WON

.900 GOLD

Obv: Date given as year of Kuang Mu reign.

Y#	Year	Mintage	Fine	VF	XF	Unc
20	10	5,012	1000.	2000.	7000.	9500.

Obv: Date given as year of Yung Hi reign.

Y#	Year	Mintage	Fine	VF	XF	Unc
—	3	—	—	—	Rare	—

20 WON

.900 GOLD

Ob: Date given as year of Kuang Mu reign.

Y#	Year	Mintage	Fine	VF	XF	Unc
21	10	2,506	2500.	4000.	12,000.	26,000.

Obv: Date given as year of Yung Hi reign.

Y#	Year	Mintage	Fine	VF	XF	Unc
—	2	.040	2600.	4000.	10,000.	26,000.
	3	.025	3000.	4000.	10,000.	26,000.
	4	.040	—	—	Rare	—

NCLT ISSUES

PATTERNS

KM#	Date	Mintage	Identification	Mkt.Val.
1	(1884)	—	5 Fun, Silver	—
2	(1884)	—	5 Chon, Silver	—
3	(1884)	—	2 Chon, Silver	—
4	(1884)	—	5 Chon, Silver	—
5	(1884)	—	1 Yang, Silver	—

KM#	Date	Mintage	Identification	Mkt.Val.
6	1885	—	5 Mun, White Metal (Tin alloy)	—

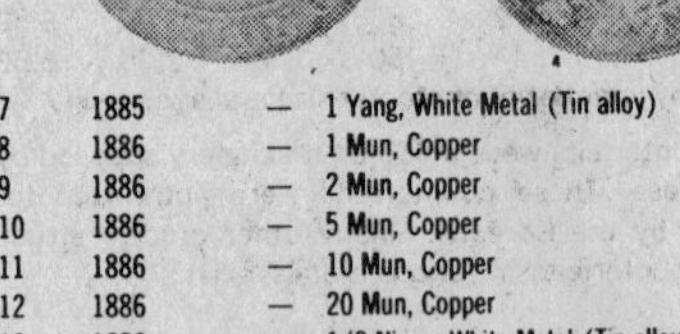

KM#	Date	Mintage	Identification	Mkt.Val.
7	1885	—	1 Yang, White Metal (Tin alloy)	—
8	1886	—	1 Mun, Copper	—
9	1886	—	2 Mun, Copper	—
10	1886	—	5 Mun, Copper	—
11	1886	—	10 Mun, Copper	—
12	1886	—	20 Mun, Copper	—
13	1886	—	1/2 Niang, White Metal (Tin alloy)	—

KM#	Date	Mintage	Identification	Mkt.Val.
14	1886	—	1 Niang, White Metal (Tin alloy)	—
15	1886	—	2 Niang, White Metal (Tin alloy)	—

KM#	Date	Mintage	Identification	Mkt.Val.
16	1886	—	5 Niang, White Metal (Tin alloy)	—
17	1886	—	1 Warn, White Metal (Tin alloy)	—
18	1886	—	1 Warn, gilt Copper	—
19	1886	—	2 Warn, gilt Copper	—
20	1886	—	5 Warn, gilt Copper	—
21	1886	—	10 Warn, gilt Copper	—
22	1886	—	20 Warn, gilt Copper	—
23	1891	—	5 Mun, Brass	—
24	1891	—	5 Mun, Copper	—
25	1891	—	10 Mun, Copper	—
26	1891	—	1 Warn, Silver	—
27	1896	—	5 Fun, Bronze, cast	—
28	1896	—	1 Chon, Copper, cast	—
29	1896	—	5 Chon, Pewter, cast, value not circled	—
30	1896	—	5 Chon, Bronze, cast, value circled	—
31	1899	—	Half Dollar, Yr.3, Silver	—
32	1900	—	20 Won, Yr.4, Copper	—
33	1901	—	5 Won, Yr.5, Copper	—
34	1901	—	10 Won, Yr.5, Copper	—
35	1902	—	20 Chon, Yr.6, Copper	—
36	1902	—	20 Won, Yr.6, Copper	—
37	1903	—	10 Won, Yr.7, Copper	—

KOREA-NORTH

The Democratic People's Republic of Korea, situated in northeastern Asia on the northern half of the Korean peninsula between the People's Republic of China and the Republic of Korea, has an area of 46,800 sq. mi. (121,200 sq. km.) and a population of 15.4 million. Capital: Pyongyang. The economy is based on heavy industry and agriculture. Metals, minerals and farm produce are exported.

Japan replaced China as the predominant foreign influence in Korea in 1895 and annexed the peninsular country in 1910. Defeat in World War II brought an end to Japanese rule. U.S. troops entered Korea from the south and Soviet forces entered from the north. The Cairo conference (1943) had established that Korea should be 'free and independent'. The Potsdam conference (1945) set the 38th parallel as the line dividing the occupation forces of the United States and Russia. When Russia refused to permit a U.N. commission designated to supervise reunification elections to enter North Korea, an election was held in South Korea which established the Republic of Korea on Aug. 15, 1948. North Korea held an unsupervised election on Aug. 25, 1948, and on the following day proclaimed the establishment of the Democratic People's Republic of Korea.

NOTE: For earlier coinage see Korea.

MONETARY SYSTEM

100 Chon = 1 Won

CHON

ALUMINUM

Y#	Date	Mintage	Fine	VF	XF	Unc
1	1959	—	1.50	2.00	3.00	4.00
	1970	—	2.00	3.00	4.00	5.00

5 CHON

ALUMINUM

Y#	Date	Mintage	Fine	VF	XF	Unc
2	1959	—	2.00	2.50	4.00	5.00
	1974	—	1.00	1.50	2.50	3.50

10 CHON

ALUMINUM

Y#	Date	Mintage	Fine	VF	XF	Unc
3	1959	—	2.00	3.00	4.50	6.00

SOUTH KOREA

The Republic of Korea, situated in northeastern Asia on the southern half of the Korean peninsula between North Korea and the Korean Strait, has an area of 38,022 sq. mi. (98,477 sq. km.) and a population of 33.5 million. Capital: Seoul. The economy is based on agriculture and textiles. Clothing, plywood and textile products are exported.

Japan replaced China as the predominant foreign influence in Korea in 1895 and annexed the peninsular country in 1910. Defeat in World War II brought an end to Japanese rule. U.S. troops entered Korea from the south and Soviet forces entered from the north. The Cairo conference (1943) had established that Korea should be 'free and independent'. The Potsdam conference (1945) set the 38th parallel as the line dividing the occupation forces of the United States and Russia. When Russia refused to permit a U.N. commission designated to supervise reunification elections to enter North Korea, an election was held in South Korea on May 10, 1948. By its determination, the Republic of Korea was inaugurated on Aug. 15, 1948.

NOTE: For earlier coinage see Korea.

MONETARY SYSTEM

100 Chon = 1 Hwan

10 HWAN

BRONZE

Y#	Date	Mintage	Fine	VF	XF	Unc
1	4292, (Yr.1959)	100.000	.15	.30	.50	3.00
	4294, (Yr.1961)	100.000	.10	.15	.30	.60

50 HWAN

NICKEL-BRASS

Y#	Date	Mintage	Fine	VF	XF	Unc
2	4292, (Yr.1959)	24.640	.15	.30	.40	1.10
	4294, (Yr.1961)	20.000	.10	.20	.30	.70

100 HWAN

COPPER-NICKEL

Y#	Date	Mintage	Fine	VF	XF	Unc
3	4292, (Yr.1959)	49.640	.30	.50	.75	2.00

NOTE: Quantities of Y#1-3 dated 4292 in uncirculated condition were counterstamped 'SAMPLE' in Korean for distribution to government and banking agencies. Y#3 did not circulate and Y#1 and Y#2 were withdrawn from circulation June 10, 1962 and melted.

MONETARY REFORM

10 Hwan = 1 Won

WON

BRASS

Y#	Date	Mintage	VF	XF	Unc
4	1966	7.000	—	.10	.30
	1967	48.500	—	.10	.15

ALUMINUM

Y#	Date	Mintage	VF	XF	Unc
4a	1968	66.500	—	—	.15
	1969	85.000	—	—	.15
	1970	45.000	—	—	.15
	1974	12.000	—	—	.15
	1975	10.000	—	—	.10
	1976	20.000	—	—	.10
	1977	30.000	—	—	.10
	1978	30.000	—	—	.10
	1979	—	—	—	.10

5 WON

BRONZE

Y#	Date	Mintage	VF	XF	Unc
5	1966	4.500	.15	.50	1.00
	1967	18.000	—	.10	.25
	1968	20.000	—	.10	.25
	1969	25.000	—	.10	.20
	1970	50.000	—	.10	.20

BRASS

Y#	Date	Mintage	VF	XF	Unc
5a	1970	Inc. Ab.	—	—	—
	1971	64.038	—	.10	.15
	1972	60.084	—	.10	.15
	1977	1.000	—	.10	.15
	1978	1.000	—	.10	.15
	1979	—	—	.10	.15

10 WON

BRONZE

Y#	Date	Mintage	VF	XF	Unc
6	1966	10.600	.15	.20	.50
	1967	22.500	.10	.15	.40
	1968	35.000	—	.10	.25
	1969	46.500	—	.10	.25
	1970	157.000	—	.10	.15

BRASS

Y#	Date	Mintage	VF	XF	Unc
6a	1970	Inc. Ab.	—	.10	.20
	1971	220.132	—	.10	.20
	1972	270.162	—	.10	.20
	1973	30.000	—	.10	.20
	1974	15.000	—	.10	.20
	1975	20.000	—	.10	.20
	1977	1.000	—	.10	.20
	1978	60.000	—	.10	.20
	1979	—	—	.10	.20

50 WON

2.8000 gm., 1.0000 SILVER, .0900 oz ASW

H#	Date	Mintage	XF	Unc	Proof
1	1970	—	—	—	30.00

COPPER-NICKEL
F.A.O. Issue

Y#	Date	Mintage	VF	XF	Unc
A7	1972	6.000	.20	.50	.75
	1973	40.000	.15	.20	.75
	1974	25.000	.15	.20	.75
	1977	1.000	.15	.20	.60
	1978	1.000	.15	.20	.55
	1979	—	.15	.20	.55

100 WON

5.6000 gm., 1.000 SILVER, .1800 oz ASW

H#	Date	Mintage	XF	Unc	Proof
2	1970	—	—	—	45.00

COPPER-NICKEL

Y#	Date	Mintage	VF	XF	Unc
7	1970	1.500	.75	1.00	1.50
	1971	13.037	.20	.75	1.25
	1972	20.012	.20	.30	.50
	1973*	80.000	.20	.30	1.25
	1974*	50.000	.20	.30	.50
	1975	70.000	.20	.30	1.00
	1977	3.000	.20	.30	.50
	1978	40.000	.20	.30	.50
	1979	—	—	.30	.50

***NOTE:** Die varieties exist.

30th Anniversary of Liberation

Y#	Date	Mintage	VF	XF	Unc
8	1975	4.998	.35	.75	2.50
	1975	2,000	—	Proof	90.00

200 WON

11.2000 gm., 1.000 SILVER, .3601 oz ASW

H#	Date	Mintage	XF	Unc	Proof
3	1970	—	—	—	60.00

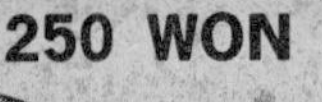

250 WON

14.0000 gm., 1.000 SILVER, .4501 oz ASW

H#	Date	Mintage	XF	Unc	Proof
4	1970	—	—	—	75.00

500 WON

28.0000 gm., 1.000 SILVER, .9003 oz ASW
Rev: Similar to 200 Won, H#3.

H#	Date	Mintage	XF	Unc	Proof
5	1970	—	—	—	100.00

COPPER-NICKEL
42nd World Shooting Championships

Y#	Date	Mintage	XF	Unc	Proof
9	1978	.980	—	6.50	—
	1978	.020	—	—	—

1000 WON

56.0000 gm., 1.000 SILVER, 1.8006 oz ASW
Rev: Similar to 200 Won, H#3.

H#	Date	Mintage	XF	Unc	Proof
6	1970	—	—	—	200.00

3.8700 gm., .900 GOLD, .1119 oz AGW

H#	Date	Mintage	XF	Unc	Proof
8	1970	900 pcs.	—	—	250.00

2500 WON

9.6800 gm., .900 GOLD, .2801 oz AGW

H#	Date	Mintage	XF	Unc	Proof
9	1970	1,200	—	—	400.00

5000 WON

19.3600 gm., .900 GOLD, .5602 oz AGW

H#	Date	Mintage	XF	Unc	Proof
10	1970	670 pcs.	—	—	800.00

23.0000 gm., .900 SILVER, .6655 oz ASW
42nd World Shooting Championships

Y#	Date	Mintage	XF	Unc	Proof
10	1978	.080	40.00	65.00	—
	1978	.020	—	—	—

10,000 WON

38.7200 gm., .900 GOLD, 1.1205 oz AGW

H#	Date	Mintage	XF	Unc	Proof
11	1970	430 pcs.	—	—	1200.

20,000 WON

77.4000 gm., .900 GOLD, 2.2398 oz AGW

H#	Date	Mintage	XF	Unc	Proof
12	1970	310 pcs.	—	—	2000.

25,000 WON

96.8000 gm., .900 GOLD, 2.8012 oz AGW
Actual diameter - 60 mm

H#	Date	Mintage	XF	Unc	Proof
13	1970	225 pcs.	—	—	3000.

NCLT ISSUES

PROOF SETS

STANDARD METALS

KM#	Date	Mintage	Identification	Issue Price	Mkt. Val.
101	1970(12)	—	H1-6,8-13	752.00	10,000.
102	1970(6)	—	H1-6	53.50	750.00
103	1970(6)	225	H8-13	698.00	8000.

KUWAIT

The State of Kuwait, a constitutional monarchy located on the Arabian Peninsula at the northwestern corner of the Persian Gulf, has an area of 7,780 sq. mi. (20,150 sq. km.) and a population of 1.1 million. Capital: Kuwait. Petroleum, the basis of the economy, provides 95 per cent of the exports.

The modern history of Kuwait began with the founding of the city of Kuwait, 1740, by tribesmen who wandered northward from the region of the Qatar Peninsula of eastern Arabia. Fearing that the Turks would take over the sheikhdom, Sheikh Mubarak entered into an agreement with Great Britain, 1899, placing Kuwait under the protection of Britain and empowering Britain to conduct its foreign affairs. Britain terminated the protectorate on June 19, 1961, giving Kuwait its independence (by a simple exchange of notes) but agreeing to furnish military aid on request.

The Kuwait dinar, one of the world's strongest currencies, is backed 100 percent by gold and foreign exchange holdings.

MONETARY SYSTEM

1000 Fils = 1 Dinar

FILS

NICKEL-BRASS

Y#	Date	Year	Mintage	VF	XF	Unc
1	1961	AH1380	2.000	.35	.50	1.00
	1961	1380	60 pcs.	—	Proof	30.00

Y#	Date	Year	Mintage	VF	XF	Unc
8	1962	AH1382	.500	.35	.50	1.00
	1962	1382	60 pcs.	—	Proof	30.00
	1964	1384	.600	.35	.50	1.00
	1966	1385	.500	.35	.50	1.00
	1967	1386	1.875	.35	.50	1.00
	1970	1389	.375	.60	1.00	1.50
	1971	1390	.500	.35	.50	1.00
	1971	1391	.500	.35	.50	1.00
	1972	1392	.500	.25	.30	.50
	1973	1393	.375	.25	.30	.50
	1975	1395	.500	.25	.30	.50
	1976	1396	2.500	.25	.30	.50

5 FILS

NICKEL-BRASS

Y#	Date	Year	Mintage	VF	XF	Unc
2	1961	AH1380	2.400	.20	.30	.50
	1961	1380	60 pcs.	—	Proof	35.00

Y#	Date	Year	Mintage	VF	XF	Unc
9	1962	AH1382	1.800	.20	.30	.50
	1962	1382	60 pcs.	—	Proof	35.00
	1964	1384	.600	.20	.30	.50
	1967	1386	1.600	.20	.30	.50
	1968	1388	.800	.20	.30	.50
	1970	1389	.600	.20	.30	.50
	1971	1390	.600	.20	.30	.50
9	1971	1391	.600	.20	.30	.50
	1972	1392	.800	.20	.30	.50
	1973	1393	.800	.20	.30	.50
	1974	1394	1.200	.20	.10	.25
	1975	1395	5.020	—	.10	.25
	1976	1396	.180	—	—	—

10 FILS

NICKEL-BRASS

Y#	Date	Year	Mintage	VF	XF	Unc
3	1961	AH1380	2.600	.20	.30	.50
	1961	1380	60 pcs.	—	Proof	40.00

Y#	Date	Year	Mintage	VF	XF	Unc
10	1962	AH1382	1.360	.20	.30	.50
	1962	1382	60 pcs.	—	Proof	40.00
	1964	1384	.800	.20	.30	.50
	1967	1386	1.360	.20	.30	.50
	1968	1388	.672	.20	.30	.50
	1969	1389	.480	.40	.60	1.20
	1970	1389	.640	.20	.30	.50
	1971	1390	.480	.40	.60	1.20
	1971	1391	.800	.20	.30	.50
	1972	1392	1.120	.20	.30	.50
	1973	1393	1.440	.20	.30	.50
	1974	1394	1.280	.20	.30	.50
	1975	1395	5.280	—	.15	.35
	1977	1397	—	—	.15	.35

20 FILS

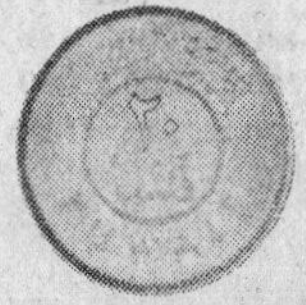

COPPER-NICKEL

Y#	Date	Year	Mintage	VF	XF	Unc
4	1961	AH1380	2.000	.30	.50	1.00
	1961	1380	60 pcs.	—	Proof	45.00

Y#	Date	Year	Mintage	VF	XF	Unc
11	1962	AH1382	1.200	.25	.35	.75
	1962	1382	60 Pcs.	—	Proof	45.00
	1964	1384	.480	.25	.35	.70
	1967	1386	1.280	.25	.35	.70
	1968	1388	.672	.25	.35	.70
	1969	1389	.800	.25	.35	.70
	1970	1389	.480	.25	.35	.70
	1971	1390	.480	.25	.35	.70
	1971	1391	.960	.25	.35	.70
	1972	1392	1.440	.25	.35	.70
	1973	1393	1.280	.25	.35	.70
	1974	1394	1.600	.25	.35	.70
	1975	1395	2.400	.20	.30	.50
	1976	1396	3.200	.20	.30	.50

50 FILS

COPPER-NICKEL

Y#	Date	Year	Mintage	VF	XF	Unc
5	1961	AH1380	1.720	.65	.80	1.00

Y#	Date	Year	Mintage	VF	XF	Unc
5	1961	1380	60 pcs.	—	Proof	50.00

Y#	Date	Year	Mintage	VF	XF	Unc
12	1962	AH1382	.900	.60	.80	1.00
	1962	1382	60 pcs.		Proof	50.00
	1964	1384	.300	.75	1.00	2.00
	1967	1386	.800	.60	.80	1.00
	1968	1388	.200	1.00	1.50	2.50
	1969	1389	.400	.60	.80	1.00
	1970	1389	.500	.60	.80	1.00
	1971	1390	.300	.75	1.00	2.00
	1971	1391	.500	.60	.80	1.00
	1972	1392	.900	.60	.80	1.00
	1973	1393	.800	.60	.80	1.00
	1974	1394	1.000	.60	.80	1.00
	1975	1395	1.950	.60	.80	1.00
	1976	1396	2.250	.60	.80	1.00
	1977	1397	—	—	.60	.80

100 FILS

COPPER-NICKEL

Y#	Date	Year	Mintage	VF	XF	Unc
6	1961	AH1380	1.260	1.00	1.50	2.00
	1961	1380	60 pcs.	—	Proof	70.00

Y#	Date	Year	Mintage	VF	XF	Unc
13	1962	AH1382	.640	1.00	1.50	2.00
	1962	1382	60 pcs.	—	Proof	70.00
	1964	1384	.160	1.60	2.75	4.00
	1967	1386	.640	1.00	1.50	2.00
	1968	1388	.160	1.60	2.75	4.00
	1969	1389	.320	1.00	1.50	2.00
	1971	1391	.240	1.00	1.50	2.00
	1972	1392	.400	1.00	1.50	2.00
	1973	1393	.480	1.00	1.50	2.00
	1974	1394	.480	1.00	1.50	2.00
	1975	1395	3.040	1.00	1.50	2.00
	1977	1397	—	1.00	1.25	1.50

2 DINARS

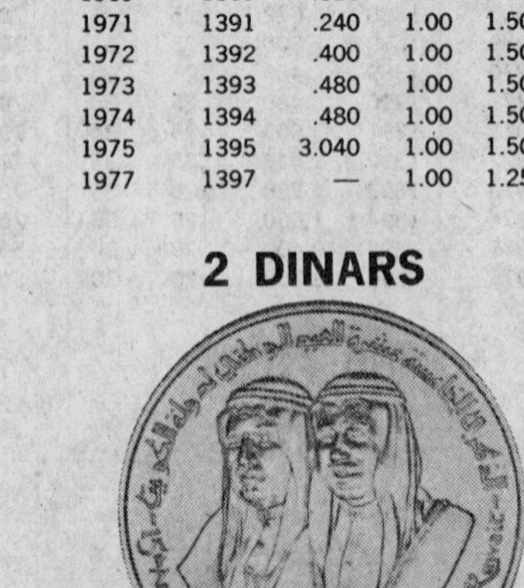

28.2700 gm., .500 SILVER, .4545 oz ASW
15th Anniversary of Independence

Y#	Date	Year	Mintage	VF	XF	Unc
14	1976	—	.035	BV	15.00	20.00
			.925 SILVER			
14a	1976	—	.072	—	Proof	50.00

5 DINARS

GOLD

Y#	Date	Year	Mintage	VF	XF	Unc
7	—	AH1380	1,000	275.00	375.00	500.00

NCLT ISSUES

MINT SETS

KM#	Date	Mintage	Identification	Issue Price	Mkt. Val.
S1	1393-1394(6)	74	Y8-13	1.75	—
S2	1396-1397(6)	—	Y8-13	3.50	—

PROOF SETS

STANDARD METALS

KM#	Date	Mintage	Identification	Issue Price	Mkt. Val.
101	1961(6)	60	Y1-6	—	250.00
102	1962(6)	60	Y8-13	—	250.00

LAOS

The Lao People's Democratic Republic, located on the Southeast Asian Peninsula between the Socialist Republic of Vietnam and the Kingdom of Thailand, has an area of 91,428 sq. mi. (236,802 km.) and a population of 3.3 million. Capital: Vientiane. Agriculture employs 95 per cent of the people. Tin, lumber and coffee are exported.

The first united kingdom of Laos was established in the mid-14th century by King Fa Ngum who ruled an area including present Laos, northeastern Thailand, and the southern part of China's Yunnan province from his capital at Luang Prabang. Siam (now Thailand) and Vietnam obtained control over much of the present Laotian territory in the 18th century and remained dominant until France established a protectorate over the area in 1893 and incorporated it into the Union of Indo-China. The Kingdom of Laos was proclaimed in March of 1945, during the last days of the Japanese occupation of World War II. France reoccupied Laos in 1946, and established it as a constitutional monarchy within the French Union in 1949. In 1953 war erupted between the government and the Pathet Lao, a Communist motivated movement supported by the Viet Minh (Vietnamese) Communist forces. Peace was declared in 1954 with Laos becoming fully independent and the Pathet Lao being permitted to occupy the country's two northern provinces. Civil war broke out again in 1960 with the United States supporting the government of the Kingdom of Laos and the North Vietnamese helping the pro-Communist Pathet Lao, and continued, with intervals of truce and political compromise, until the formation of the Lao People's Democratic Republic on Dec. 2, 1975.

NOTE: For earlier coinage see French Indo-China.

RULERS

Sisavang Vong, 1949-1959
Savang Vatthana, 1959-1975

MONETARY SYSTEM

100 Centimes = 1 Piastre
100 Att 1 Kip 1955—

MINTMARKS

(a) - Paris, privy marks only

10 CENTIMES

ALUMINUM

Y#	Date	Mintage	VF	XF	Unc
1	1952(a)	2.000	.25	.50	1.00

20 CENTIMES

ALUMINUM

Y#	Date	Mintage	VF	XF	Unc
2	1952(a)	3.000	.25	.50	1.00

50 CENTIMES

ALUMINUM

Y#	Date	Mintage	VF	XF	Unc
3	1952(a)	1.400	.50	1.00	2.00

1000 KIP

2.4000 gm., .925 SILVER, .0713 oz ASW
King Savang Vatthana Coronation

H#	Date	Mintage	XF	Unc	Proof
7	1971	—	—	—	20.00

2500 KIP

5.9000 gm., .925 SILVER, .1745 oz ASW
King Savang Vatthana Coronation

8	1971	—	—	—	35.00

4000 KIP

4.0000 gm., .900 GOLD, .1157 oz AGW
King Savang Vatthana Coronation

Fr#	Date	Mintage	XF	Unc	Proof
5	1971	—	—	—	75.00

5000 KIP

11.8000 gm., .925 SILVER, .3509 oz ASW
King Savang Vatthana Coronation

H#	Date	Mintage	XF	Unc	Proof
9	1971	—	—	—	65.00
12	1975	.150	—	13.50	—
	1975	Inc. Ab.	—	—	17.50

13	1975	Inc. Ab.	—	13.50	—
	1975	Inc. Ab.	—	—	17.50

8000 KIP

8.0000 gm., .900 GOLD, .2315 oz AGW
King Savang Vatthana Coronation

Fr#	Date	Mintage	XF	Unc	Proof
4	1971	—	—	—	150.00

10,000 KIP

23.6000 gm., .925 SILVER, .7019 oz ASW
King Savang Vatthana Coronation

H#	Date	Mintage	XF	Unc	Proof
10	1971	—	—	—	100.00

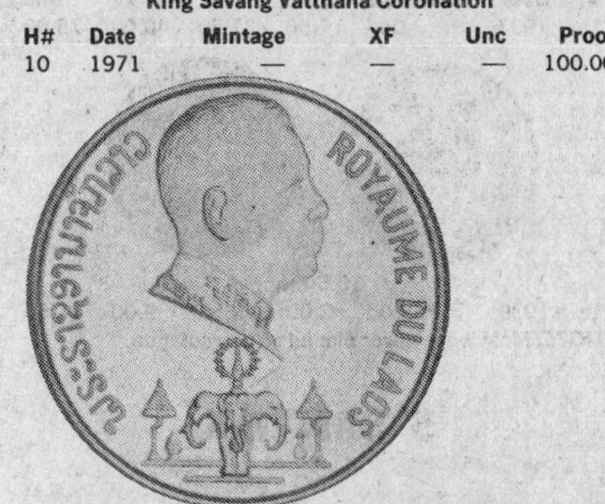

14	1975	.120	—	25.00	—
	1975	Inc. Ab.	—	—	35.00

20,000 KIP

20.0000 gm., .900 GOLD, .5787 oz AGW
King Savang Vatthana Coronation

Fr#	Date	Mintage	XF	Unc	Proof
3	1971	—	—	—	375.00

40,000 KIP

40.0000 gm., .900 GOLD, 1.1575 oz AGW
King Savang Vatthana Coronation

2	1971	—	—	—	775.00

50,000 KIP

3.6000 gm., .900 GOLD, .1041 oz AGW
Obv: Bust of King Savang Vatthana
Rev. That Luang Temple

7	1975	.022	—	—	70.00

Obv: Similar to 5,000 Kip, H#12.

8	1975	Inc. Ab.	—	—	70.00

80,000 KIP

80.0000 gm., .900 GOLD, 2.3151 oz AGW
King Savang Vatthana Coronation
Obv: Similar to 20,000 Kip, Fr#3.

Fr#	Date	Mintage	XF	Unc	Proof
1	1971	—	—	—	1500.

100,000 KIP

7.3200 gm., .900 GOLD, .2118 oz AGW
Obv: Bust of King Savang Vatthana.
Rev: Statue of Buddha.

6	1975	.012	—	—	150.00

NCLT ISSUES

ESSAIS (E)

Standard metals unless otherwise noted

Y#	Date	Mintage	Identification	Issue Price	Mkt Val.
E1	1952(a)	1,200	10 Centimes	—	16.00
E2	1952(a)	1,200	20 Centimes	—	18.00
E3	1952(a)	1,200	50 Centimes	—	20.00

PIEFORTS (P)

PIEFORTS with ESSAI (PE)

Double Thickness
Standard metals unless otherwise noted

PE1	1952(a)	104	10 Centimes	—	75.00
PE2	1952(a)	104	20 Centimes	—	80.00
PE3	1952(a)	104	50 Centimes	—	85.00

PROOF SETS

STANDARD METALS

KM#	Date	Mintage	Identification	Issue Price	Mkt. Val.
101	1971(5)	10,000	F1-5	467.00	2875.
102	1971(4)	—	H7-10	163.00	200.00
103	1975(3)	—	H12-14	256.00	70.00
104	1975(3)	—	F6-8	349.00	300.00

Listings For

LAHEJ: refer to Yemen Democratic Republic

LATVIA

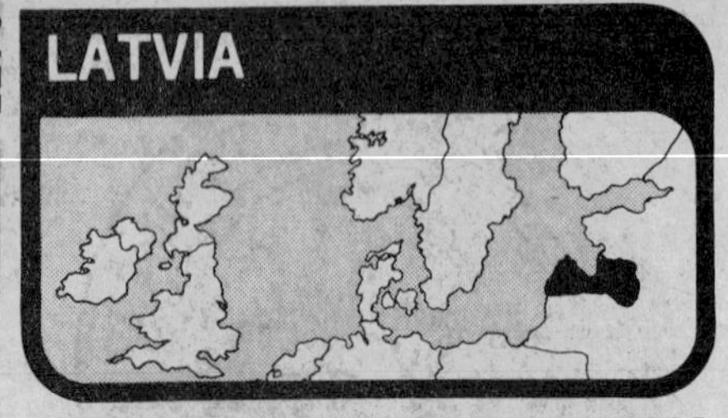

The Latvian Soviet Socialist Republic of the U.S.S.R., the central Baltic state in east Europe, has an area of 24,595 sq. mi. (43,601 sq. km.) and a population of 2.4 million. Capital: Riga. Livestock raising and manufacturing are the chief industries. Butter, bacon, fertilizers and telephone equipment are exported.

The Latvians, of Aryan descent, were nomadic tribesmen who settled along the Baltic prior to the 13th century. Lacking a central government, they were easily conquered by the German Teutonic knights, Russia, Sweden and Poland. Following the third partition of Poland by Austria, Prussia and Russia in 1795, Latvia came under Russian domination and did not experience autonomy until the Russian Revolution of 1917 provided an opportunity for freedom. The Latvian republic was established on Nov. 18, 1918. The republic was occupied by Soviet troops in 1939 and annexed to the Soviet Union in 1940. Following the German occupation of 1941-44, it was retaken by Russia and reestablished as a member republic of the Soviet Union. Western countries, including the United States, did not recognize Latvia's incorporation into the Soviet Union until the Treaty of Helsinki, 1975.

The coinage, issued during Latvia's short tenure as a republic, is obsolete.

MONETARY SYSTEM

100 Santimu = 1 Lats

SANTIMS

BRONZE

Y#	Date	Mintage	Fine	VF	XF	Unc
1	1922	5.000	.90	1.75	3.00	7.00
	1924	4.990	.90	1.75	3.00	7.00
	1926	5.000	.90	1.75	4.50	9.50
	1928 with designer's name below ribbon	5.000	.90	1.75	4.50	9.50
	1928 without designer's name below ribbon	Inc. Ab.	3.50	8.00	13.50	30.00
	1932	5.000	.90	1.75	4.50	9.50
	1935	5.000	.90	1.75	3.00	7.00

Y#	Date	Mintage	Fine	VF	XF	Unc
10	1937	2.700	2.00	3.25	5.00	9.00
	1938	1.900		3.25	6.50	11.00
	1939	*	3.00	5.00	9.00	12.50

***NOTE:** Reports show 3,400,000 minted, but most were never placed into circulation.

2 SANTIMI

BRONZE

Y#	Date	Mintage	Fine	VF	XF	Unc
2	1922 with designer's name below wreath	10.000	.90	2.00	2.75	6.50
	1922 without designer's name below wreath	Inc. Ab.	5.00	10.00	17.50	35.00
	1926	5.000	.90	2.00	3.00	7.00
	1928	5.000	.90	2.00	4.50	9.50
	1932	5.000	.90	2.00	3.00	7.00

19mm

Y#	Date	Mintage	Fine	VF	XF	Unc
11	1937	.044	17.50	27.50	40.00	75.00

19.5mm

Y#	Date	Mintage	Fine	VF	XF	Unc
11a	1939	*5.000	2.00	3.50	9.00	21.50

***NOTE:** Most were never placed into circulation.

5 SANTIMI

BRONZE

Y#	Date	Mintage	Fine	VF	XF	Unc
3	1922 with designer's name on reverse	15.000	.90	2.25	3.25	8.50
	1922 without designer's name	Inc. Ab.	6.00	12.00	20.00	37.50

10 SANTIMU

NICKEL

Y#	Date	Mintage	Fine	VF	XF	Unc
4	1922	15.000	1.25	3.00	5.00	9.50

20 SANTIMU

NICKEL

Y#	Date	Mintage	Fine	VF	XF	Unc
5	1922	15.000	1.25	3.25	5.00	10.00

50 SANTIMU

NICKEL

Y#	Date	Mintage	Fine	VF	XF	Unc
6	1922	9.000	2.00	4.50	7.00	14.50

LATS

5.0000 gm., .835 SILVER, .1342 oz ASW

Y#	Date	Mintage	Fine	VF	XF	Unc
7	1924	10.000	BV	BV	5.00	10.00

2 LATI

10.0000 gm., .835 SILVER, .2684 oz ASW

Y#	Date	Mintage	Fine	VF	XF	Unc
8	1925	6.386	BV	BV	10.00	12.50
	1926	1.114	BV	10.00	15.00	17.50

5 LATI

25.0000 gm., .835 SILVER, .6712 oz ASW

Y#	Date	Mintage	Fine	VF	XF	Unc
9	1929	1.000	BV	BV	22.50	30.00
	1931	2.000	BV	BV	22.50	30.00
	1932	.600	BV	22.50	27.50	35.00

NCLT ISSUES

PATTERNS

KM#	Date	Mintage	Identification	Mkt.Val.
1	1922	—	10 Santimu, Silver, Y#4	150.00
2	1922	—	10 Santimu, Aluminum-Bronze, Y#4	250.00
3	1938	—	2 Santimi, Bronze, Y#11a	500.00

LEBANON

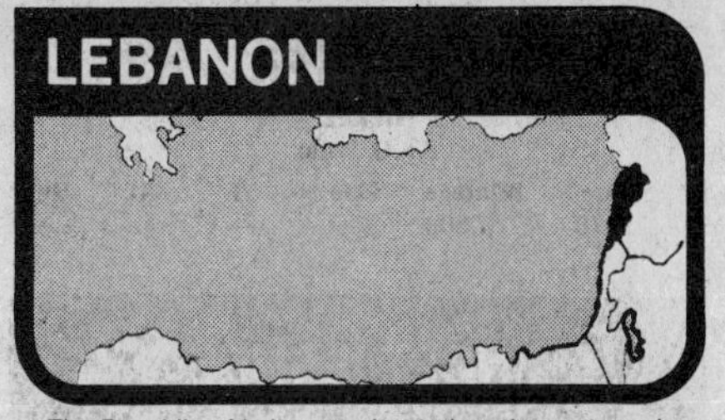

The Republic of Lebanon, situated on the eastern shore of the Mediterranean Sea between Syria and Israel, has an area of 4,000 sq. mi. (10,350 sq. km.) and a population of 3.5 million. Capital: Beirut. The economy is based on agriculture, trade and tourism. Fruit, other foodstuffs and textile's are exported.

Almost at the beginning of recorded history, Lebanon appeared as the well-wooded hinterland of the Phoenicians who exploited its famous forests of cedar. The mountains were a Christian refuge and a Crusader stronghold. Lebanon, the history of which is essentially the same as that of Syria, came under control of the Ottoman Turks early in the 16th century. Following the collapse of the Ottoman Empire after World War I, Lebanon, along with Syria, became a French mandate. The French drew a border around the predominantly Christian Lebanon sanjak or administrative subdivision in 1926, and proclaimed the area a republic under French control. France announced the independence of Lebanon on Nov. 26, 1941, but factual freedom wasn't attained until Nov. 22, 1943.

MINTMARKS

(a) - Paris, privy marks only
(u) - Utrecht, privy marks only

MONETARY SYSTEM

100 Piastres = 1 Livre (Pound)

1/2 PIASTRE

COPPER-NICKEL

Y#	Date	Mintage	Fine	VF	XF	Unc
5	1934(a)	.200	1.25	2.50	6.00	17.50
	1936(a)	1.200	1.25	2.50	5.00	15.00

ZINC

Y#	Date	Mintage	Fine	VF	XF	Unc
5a	1941(a)	1.000	.50	1.00	2.50	3.50

BRASS
World War II Provisional Issue

Y#	Date	Mintage	Fine	VF	XF	Unc
11	ND	—	1.00	1.25	1.50	4.00

NOTE: Three varieties known. Usually crudely struck, off center, etc. Perfectly struck, centered unc. specimens command a considerable premium.

PIASTRE

COPPER-NICKEL

Y#	Date	Mintage	Fine	VF	XF	Unc
6	1925(a)	1.500	.50	1.00	2.50	10.00
	1931(a)	.300	.60	1.50	4.00	17.50
	1933(a)	.500	.60	1.25	3.50	12.50
	1936(a)	2.200	.50	.75	2.00	9.00

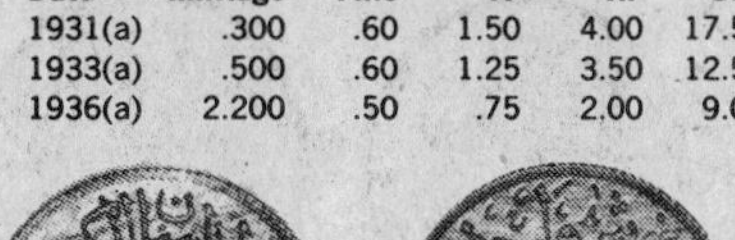

ZINC

Y#	Date	Mintage	Fine	VF	XF	Unc
6a	1940(a)	2.000	.50	.75	1.50	6.00

BRASS
World War II Provisional Issue

Y#	Date	Mintage	Fine	VF	XF	Unc
12	ND	—	1.00	1.50	2.50	7.50

NOTE: Two varieties known. Usually crudely struck, off center, etc. Perfectly struck, centered unc. specimens command a considerable premium.

ALUMINUM-BRONZE

Y#	Date	Mintage	Fine	VF	XF	Unc
18	1955(a)	4.000	—	.10	.15	.20

2 PIASTRES

ALUMINUM-BRONZE

Y#	Date	Mintage	Fine	VF	XF	Unc
1	1924(a)	1.800	1.25	2.50	8.50	35.00

Y#	Date	Mintage	Fine	VF	XF	Unc
3	1925(a)	1.000	2.25	5.00	13.50	45.00

2-1/2 PIASTRES

ALUMINUM-BRONZE

Y#	Date	Mintage	Fine	VF	XF	Unc
7	1940(a)	1.000	.50	1.00	1.50	6.00

ALUMINUM
World War II Provisional Issue

Y#	Date	Mintage	Fine	VF	XF	Unc
13	ND	—	1.00	1.75	2.50	4.50

NOTE: Seven varieties known. Usually crudely struck, off center, etc. Perfectly struck, centered unc. specimens command a considerable premium.

ALUMINUM-BRONZE

Y#	Date	Mintage	Fine	VF	XF	Unc
19	1955(a)	5.000	.10	.15	.20	.25

5 PIASTRES

ALUMINUM-BRONZE

Y#	Date	Mintage	Fine	VF	XF	Unc
2	1924(a)	1.000	1.00	2.00	6.50	25.00

Both privy marks to left of '5'

Y#	Date	Mintage	Fine	VF	XF	Unc
4	1925(a)	1.500	1.00	2.00	6.00	13.50

Privy marks to left and right of 5 Piastres

Y#	Date	Mintage	Fine	VF	XF	Unc
4.1	1925(a)	Inc. Ab.	1.25	2.25	6.00	17.50
	1931(a)	.400	1.25	2.25	6.00	17.50
	1933(a)	.500	1.25	2.25	6.00	14.00
	1936(a)	.900	1.25	2.25	5.00	12.50
	1940(a)	1.000	.50	1.25	2.50	6.50

ALUMINUM

Y#	Date	Mintage	Fine	VF	XF	Unc
14	1952(a)	3.600	.50	1.00	1.50	5.00

Y#	Date	Mintage	Fine	VF	XF	Unc
20	1954	4.440	.10	.30	.50	1.00

ALUMINUM-BRONZE

Y#	Date	Mintage	Fine	VF	XF	Unc
22	1955(a)	3.000	.10	.20	.30	.50
	1961(a)	—	.10	.15	.20	.30

NICKEL-BRASS

Y#	Date	Mintage	Fine	VF	XF	Unc
25	1968	2.000	—	.10	.15	.20
	1969	4.000	—	.10	.15	.20
	1970	—	—	—	.10	.15
	1972(a)	12.000	—	—	.10	.15

10 PIASTRES

2.0000 gm., .680 SILVER, .0437 oz ASW

Y#	Date	Mintage	Fine	VF	XF	Unc
8	1929	.880	4.00	10.00	22.50	50.00

ALUMINUM

Y#	Date	Mintage	Fine	VF	XF	Unc
15	1952(a)	3.600	.50	1.00	5.00	15.00

ALUMINUM-BRONZE

Y#	Date	Mintage	Fine	VF	XF	Unc
21	1955	2.175	.25	.60	.70	1.00

Y#	Date	Mintage	Fine	VF	XF	Unc
23	1955(a)	6.000	.10	.25	.50	.75

COPPER-NICKEL

Y#	Date	Mintage	Fine	VF	XF	Unc
24	1961	7.000	—	.10	.20	.40

NICKEL-BRASS

Y#	Date	Mintage	Fine	VF	XF	Unc
26	1968(a)	2.000	—	.10	.15	.25
	1969(a)	5.000	—	—	.10	.20
	1970(a)	8.000	—	—	.10	.20
	1972(a)	12.000	—	—	.10	.20

25 PIASTRES

5.0000 gm., .680 SILVER, .1093 oz ASW

Y#	Date	Mintage	Fine	VF	XF	Unc
9	1929	.600	3.50	6.00	17.50	40.00
	1933(a)	.200	3.50	6.50	16.50	50.00
	1936(a)	.400	3.50	6.50	16.00	42.50

ALUMINUM-BRONZE

Y#	Date	Mintage	Fine	VF	XF	Unc
16	1952(u)	7.200	.10	.50	.75	1.00
	1961(u)	5.000	.10	.40	.50	.75

NOTE: The 1961 issue was actually struck by the Berne Mint.

NICKEL-BRASS

Y#	Date	Mintage	Fine	VF	XF	Unc
27	1968	1.500	.10	.15	.25	.50
	1969	2.500	.10	.15	.20	.40
	1970	—	.10	.15	.20	.40
	1972	8.000	.10	.15	.20	.30

50 PIASTRES

10.0000 gm., .680 SILVER, .2186 oz ASW

Y#	Date	Mintage	Fine	VF	XF	Unc
10	1929	.500	6.50	7.00	22.50	75.00
	1933(a)	.100	7.00	10.00	27.50	95.00
	1936(a)	.100	7.00	10.00	27.50	85.00

.600 SILVER

Y#	Date	Mintage	Fine	VF	XF	Unc
17	1952(u)	7.200	1.00	1.50	1.75	3.00

NICKEL

Y#	Date	Mintage	Fine	VF	XF	Unc
28	1968	2.000	.25	.50	.70	1.00
	1969	3.488	.10	.30	.50	.75
	1970	2.000	.10	.30	.40	.50
	1971	2.000	.10	.30	.40	.50
	1975	—	.10	.30	.40	.50

LIVRE

NICKEL
F.A.O.Issue

Y#	Date	Mintage	Fine	VF	XF	Unc
29	1968	.300	—	.60	1.00	1.75

Y#	Date	Mintage	Fine	VF	XF	Unc
30	1975	—	—	.60	.75	1.00
	1975	—	—	—	Proof	—

5 LIVRES

NICKEL
F.A.O. Issue

Y#	Date	Mintage	Fine	VF	XF	Unc
31	1978	.500	—	—	—	—

NCLT ISSUES

ESSAIS

Standard metals unless otherwise noted

Y#	Date	Mintage	Identification	Issue Price	Mkt Val.
E2	1924(a)	—	5 Piastres	—	60.00
E5	1934A	—	1/2 Piastre	—	50.00
E6	1925(a)	—	1 Piastre	—	50.00
E1	1925(a)	—	2 Piastres	—	55.00
E4.1	1925(a)	—	5 Piastres	—	60.00
E6	1929(a)	—	1 Piastre	—	65.00
E8	1929	—	10 Piastres	—	75.00
E9	1929	—	25 Piastres	—	80.00
E10	1929	—	50 Piastres	—	90.00
E7	1940(a)	—	2-1/2 Piastres	—	45.00
E25	1972	—	5 Piastres	—	16.00
E26	1972(a)	—	10 Piastres	—	17.50

LESOTHO

The Kingdom of Lesotho, a constitutional monarchy located within the east-central part of the Republic of South Africa, has an area of 11,716 sq. mi. (30,344 sq. km.) and a population of 1.2 million. Capital: Maseru. The economy is based on subsistence agriculture and livestock raising. Wool, mohair, and cattle are exported. Lesotho is the only country in the world completely surrounded by another, and is without white settlers or landowners.

Lesotho (formerly Basutoland) was sparsely populated until the end of the 16th century. Between the 16th and 19th centuries an influx of refugees from tribal wars led to the development of a distinct Basotho group. During the reign of tribal chief Moshesh I (1823-70), a series of wars with the Orange Free State resulted in the loss of large areas of territory to South Africa. Moshesh appealed to the British for help, and Basutoland was constituted a native state under British protection. In 1871 it was annexed to Cape Colony, but was restored to direct control by the Crown in 1884. From 1884 to 1959 legislative and executive authority was vested in a British High Commissioner. The constitution of 1959 recognized the expressed wish of the people for independence, which was attained on Oct. 4, 1966.

Lesotho is a member of the Commonwealth of Nations. The King of Lesotho is Chief of State.

MONETARY SYSTEM

100 Licente/Lisente = 1 Loti

SENTE

NICKEL-BRASS

Y#	Date	Mintage	VF	XF	Unc
1	1979	—	—	—	—

2 LISENTE

NICKEL-BRASS

Y#	Date	Mintage	VF	XF	Unc
2	1979	—	—	—	—

5 LICENTE/LISENTE

2.8300 gm., .900 SILVER, .0818 oz ASW

H#	Date	Mintage	XF	Unc	Proof
1	1966	5,000	—	—	7.50

NICKEL-BRASS

Y#	Date	Mintage	VF	XF	Unc
3	1979	—	—	—	—

10 LICENTE/LISENTE

5.6600 gm., .900 SILVER, .1637 oz ASW

H#	Date	Mintage	XF	Unc	Proof
2	1966	5,000	—	—	10.00

COPPER-NICKEL

Y#	Date	Mintage	VF	XF	Unc
4	1979	—	—	—	—

20 LICENTE

11.3200 gm., .900 SILVER, .3275 oz ASW

H#	Date	Mintage	XF	Unc	Proof
3	1966	5,000	—	—	16.50

25 LISENTE

COPPER-NICKEL

Y#	Date	Mintage	VF	XF	Unc
5	1979	—	—	—	—

50 LICENTE/LISENTE

28.2800 gm., .900 SILVER, .8183 oz ASW
Small 900/1000 at right of date.

H#	Date	Mintage	XF	Unc	Proof
4.1	1966	—	—	25.00	—
		5,000	—	—	30.00

Large 900/1000 at right of date.

H#	Date	Mintage	XF	Unc	Proof
4.2	1966	Inc. Ab.	—	—	30.00

Mintmark and fineness below date

H#	Date	Mintage	XF	Unc	Proof
4a	1966	—	—	—	30.00

COPPER-NICKEL

Y#	Date	Mintage	VF	XF	Unc
6	1979	—	—	—	—

1 MALOTI

3.9940 gm., .917 GOLD, .1177 oz AGW

Fr#	Date	Mintage	XF	Unc	Proof
3	1966	3,500	—	—	75.00

F.A.O. Issue

Fr#	Date	Mintage	XF	Unc	Proof
12	1969	3,000	—	—	75.00

COPPER-NICKEL

Y#	Date	Mintage	VF	XF	Unc
7	1979	—	—	—	—

2 MALOTI

7.9880 gm., .917 GOLD, .2355 oz. AGW

Fr#	Date	Mintage	XF	Unc	Proof
2	1966	3,500	—	—	175.00

F.A.O. Issue

Fr#	Date	Mintage	XF	Unc	Proof
11	1966	3,000	—	—	150.00

4 MALOTI

15.9760 gm., .917 GOLD, .4710 oz AGW

Fr#	Date	Mintage	XF	Unc	Proof
1	1966	3,500	—	—	350.00

F.A.O. Issue

Fr#	Date	Mintage	XF	Unc	Proof
10	1969	3,000	—	—	325.00

10 MALOTI

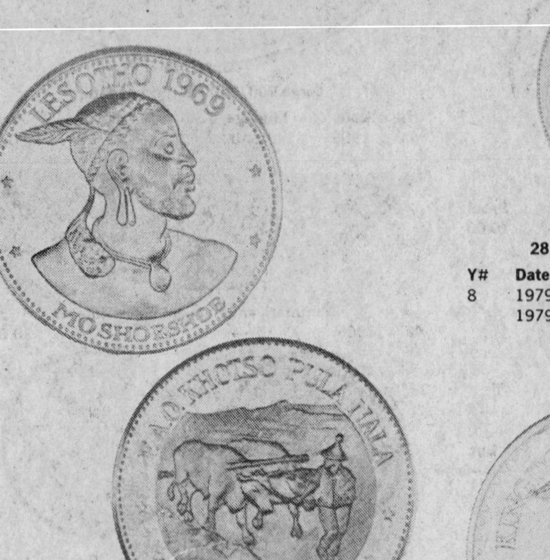

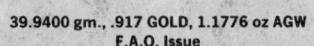

39.9400 gm., .917 GOLD, 1.1776 oz AGW
F.A.O. Issue

Fr#	Date	Mintage	XF	Unc	Proof
9	1969	3,000	—	—	800.00

25.0800 gm., .925 SILVER, .7459 oz ASW
10th Anniversary of Independence

17	1976	—	—	25.00	—
	1976	—	—	—	30.00

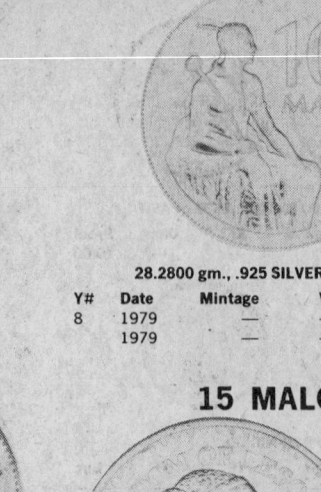

28.2800 gm., .925 SILVER, .8411 oz ASW

Y#	Date	Mintage	VF	XF	Unc
8	1979	—	—	25.00	—
	1979	—	—	Proof	30.00

15 MALOTI

33.6250 gm., .925 SILVER, 1.0000 oz ASW
International Year of the Child

9	1979	.018	—	30.00	—
	1979	7,500	—	Proof	35.00

20 MALOTI

79.8810 gm., .917 GOLD, 2.3553 oz AGW
F.A.O. Issue

Fr#	Date	Mintage	XF	Unc	Proof
8	1969	3,000	—	—	1600.

50 MALOTI

4.5000 gm., .900 GOLD, .1302 oz AGW
10th Anniversary of Independence

14	1976	—	—	85.00	—
	1976	—	—	—	125.00

100 MALOTI

9.0000 gm., .900 GOLD, .2604 oz AGW
10th Anniversary of Independence

13	1976	—	—	175.00	—

Fr#	Date	Mintage	XF	Unc	Proof
13	1976	—	—	—	250.00

250 MALOTI

33.9300 gm., .917 GOLD, 1.0000 oz AGW
International Year of the Child
Similar to 15 Maloti, Y#9.

Y#	Date	Mintage	XF	Unc	Proof
10	1979	2,500	—	650.00	—
	1979	2,000	—	—	675.00

NCLT ISSUES

PATTERNS

Obv: Moshoeshoe bareheaded.

KM#	Date	Mintage	Identification	Mkt.Val.
1	1966	2 pcs.	5 Licente, .900 Silver	—
2	1966	2 pcs.	10 Licente, .900 Silver	—
3	1966	2 pcs.	20 Licente, .900 Silver	—
4	1966	2 pcs.	50 Licente, .900 Silver	—
5	1966	7 pcs.	1 Maloti, .916 Gold	—
6	1966	7 pcs.	2 Maloti, .916 Gold	—
7	1966	7 pcs.	4 Maloti, .916 Gold	—
8	1966	7 pcs.	10 Maloti, .916 Gold	—
9	1966	7 pcs.	20 Maloti, .916 Gold	—

PROOF SETS

STANDARD METALS

KM#	Date	Mintage	Identification	Issue Price	Mkt. Val.
101	1966(7)	1,500	H1-4,Fr 1-3	301.00	650.00
102	1966(5)	7	KM X5-9 (patterns)	—	—
103	1966(4)	2	KM X1-4 (patterns)	—	—
104	1966(4)	3,500	H1-4	28.00	60.00
105	1966(3)	2,000	Fr 1-3	301.00	600.00
106	1969(5)	3,000	Fr 8-12	450.00	3000.
107	1976(3)	—	Fr 13,14,17	285.00	400.00
108	1976(2)	—	Fr 13-14	—	375.00
109	1976(2)	—	—	270.00	—

LIBERIA

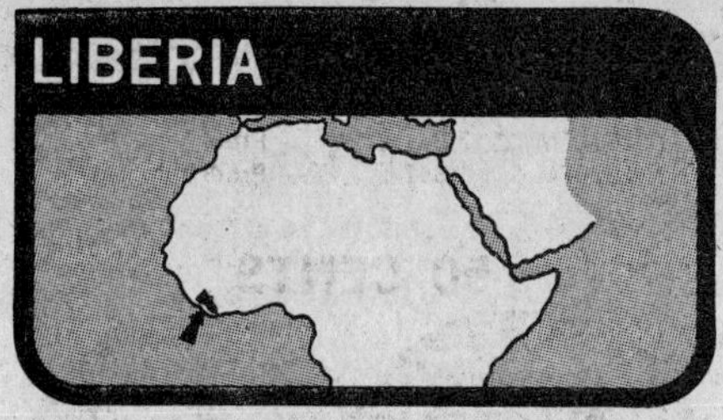

The Republic of Liberia, located on the southern side of the west African bulge between Sierra Leone and Ivory Coast, has an area of 43,000 sq. mi. (111,370 sq. km.) and a population of 1.7 million. Capital: Monrovia. The major industries are agriculture, mining and lumbering. Iron ore, diamonds, rubber, coffee and coca are exported.

The Liberian coast was explored and charted by Portuguese navigator Pedro de Cintra in 1461. For the following three centuries Portuguese traders visited the area regularly to trade for gold, slaves and pepper. The modern country of Liberia, Africa's first republic, was settled in 1822 by the American Colonization Society as a homeland for American freed slaves, with the U.S. government furnishing funds and assisting in negotiations for procurement of land from the native chiefs. The various settlements united in 1839 to form the Commonwealth of Liberia, and in 1847 established the country as a republic with a constitution modeled after that of the United States.

U.S. money was declared legal tender in Liberia in 1943, replacing British West African currency.

Most of the Liberian pattern series, particularly of the 1888-90 period are acknowledged to have been 'unofficial' privately sponsored issues, but they are without exception avidly collected by most collectors of Liberian coins. The 'K' number designations on these pieces refer to a listing of Liberian patterns compiled and published by Ernst Kraus.

MINTMARKS

B - Bern, Switzerland
H - Heaton, Birmingham
(d) - Denver, U.S.
(l) - London
(s) - San Francisco, U.S.
FM - Franklin Mint, U.S.A.*

***NOTE:** During 1975-77 the Franklin Mint produced coinage in up to 3 different qualities. Qualities of issue are designated in ( ) after each date and are defined as follows:

(M) MATTE - Normal circulation strike or a dull finish produced by sandblasting special uncirculated (polish finish) or proof quality dies.

(U) SPECIAL UNCIRCULATED - Polished or prooflike in appearance without any frosted features.

(P) PROOF - The highest quality obtainable having mirror-like fields and frosted features.

MONETARY SYSTEM

100 Cents = 1 Dollar

1/2 CENT

BRASS

Y#	Date	Mintage	VF	XF	Unc
9	1937	1.000	.25	.35	.50

COPPER-NICKEL

Y#	Date	Mintage	VF	XF	Unc
9a	1941	0.25	.35	.50	.75

CENT TOKEN

COPPER

Obv: Large ship (Ch-2,3,4,6)

Y#	Date	Mintage	VF	XF	Unc
1	1833	—	12.50	22.50	50.00

Obv: Small ship (Ch-1,5)

Y#	Date	Mintage	VF	XF	Unc
	1833	—	10.00	20.00	40.00

This piece has been attributed in six distinctive varieties by Charles G. Colver and Dan Harley, who have designated them in their order of incidence in a large hoard examined.

CH-1-Obverse; 1 in date left of tree trunk, small ship, 15 rays, 13 palm tree leaves, bush top at water line. Reverse; wide-spaced AD, single period between.

CH-2-Obverse; 1 in date under tree trunk, large ship, 14 rays, 12 palm tree leaves, bush top above water. Reverse; narrow-spaced AD, double periods between.

CH-3-Obverse; 1 in date under tree trunk, large ship, 14 rays with second touching ship, 10 palm tree leaves with leaf between LI, bush top at water line. Reverse; narrow-spaced AD, double periods between.

CH-4-Obverse; 1 in date left of tree trunk, large ship, 11 rays, 12 palm tree leaves with leaf between BE, bush top above water. Reverse; wide spaced AD, single period between, and first "N" in "COLONIZATION" tilted upward.

CH-5 Obverse; as CH-1. Reverse; very narrow AD.

CH-6 Obverse; as CH-2. Reverse; as CH-4.

CENT

COPPER

Y#	Date	Mintage	VF	XF	Unc
2	1847 2 star rev	—	15.00	22.50	50.00
	1847 2 star rev	—	—	Proof	75.00

Y#	Date	Mintage	VF	XF	Unc
2.1	1862 4 star rev	—	15.00	30.00	60.00
	1862 4 star rev	—	—	Proof	100.00

BRONZE

Y#	Date	Mintage	VF	XF	Unc
4	1896H	.358	6.00	15.00	25.00
	1896H	—	—	Proof	150.00
	1906H	.179	12.00	30.00	50.00
	1906H	—	—	Proof	150.00

BRASS

Y#	Date	Mintage	VF	XF	Unc
10	1937	1.000	.50	1.50	6.00

COPPER-NICKEL

Y#	Date	Mintage	VF	XF	Unc
10a	1941	.250	2.50	5.00	20.00

BRONZE

Y#	Date	Mintage	VF	XF	Unc
12	1960	.500	—	.10	.25
	1961	7.000	—	.10	.30
	1968(L)	3.000	—	.10	.15
	1968(S)	.014	—	Proof only	1.00
	1969	5,056	—	Proof only	1.25
	1970	3,466	—	Proof only	1.75
	1971	3,012	—	Proof only	1.75
	1972(D)	10.000	—	.15	—
	1972(S)	4,866	—	Proof only	1.50
	1973	.011	—	Proof only	1.00
	1974	4,050	—	Proof only	1.00
	1975	5.000	—	.10	.15
	1975	5,056	—	Proof	1.50
	1976	.010	—	Proof only	2.00
	1977	—	—	Proof only	2.00
	1978FM	7,311	—	Proof only	2.00
	1979FM	1,857	—	Proof only	—

2 CENTS

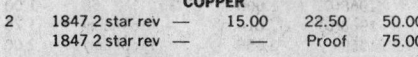

COPPER

Y#	Date	Mintage	VF	XF	Unc
3	1847 2 star rev.		12.50	22.50	50.00
	1847 2 star rev.	—	—	Proof	75.00
3.1	1862 4 star rev.		12.00	30.00	75.00
	1862 4 star rev.	—	—	Proof	250.00

Y#	Date	Mintage	VF	XF	Unc
5	1896H	.323	4.00	10.50	25.00
	1896H	—	—	Proof	200.00
	1906H	.108	10.00	25.00	65.00
	1906H	—	—	Proof	200.00

BRASS

Y#	Date	Mintage	VF	XF	Unc
11	1937	1.000	.35	1.00	5.00

COPPER-NICKEL

Y#	Date	Mintage	VF	XF	Unc
11a	1941	.810	.25	.75	2.25
	1977	—	—	—	—
	1978FM	7,311	—	Proof only	—
	1979FM	1,857	—	Proof only	—

5 CENTS

COPPER-NICKEL

Y#	Date	Mintage	VF	XF	Unc
13	1960	1.000	.15	.25	.50
	1961	3.200	.15	.25	.40
	1968	.015	—	Proof only	1.25
	1969	5,056	—	Proof only	1.50
	1970	3,466	—	Proof only	2.00
	1971	3,012	—	Proof only	2.00
	1972(D)	3.000	.10	.15	.25
	1972(S)	4,866	—	Proof only	1.75
	1973	.011	—	Proof only	1.25
	1974	4,050	—	Proof only	1.25
	1975	2.000	.10	.15	.25
	1975	5,055	—	Proof	1.75
	1976	.010	—	Proof only	2.25
	1977	—	—	Proof only	2.25
	1978FM	7,311	—	Proof only	2.25
	1979FM	1,857	—	Proof only	—

10 CENTS

2.0700 gm., .900 SILVER, .0599 oz ASW

Y#	Date	Mintage	VF	XF	Unc
6	1896H	.020	10.00	20.00	80.00
	1896H	—	—	Proof	250.00
	1906H	3,500	12.00	20.00	80.00
	1906H	—	—	Proof	250.00

Y#	Date	Mintage	VF	XF	Unc
14	1960	1.000	BV	BV	2.50
	1961	1.200	BV	BV	2.50

COPPER-NICKEL

Y#	Date	Mintage	VF	XF	Unc
14a	1966	2.000	.20	.30	.50
	1968	.014	—	Proof only	1.50
	1969	5,056	—	Proof only	1.75
	1970(D)	2.500	—	.40	.50
	1970(S)	3,466	—	Proof only	2.25
	1971	3,012	—	Proof only	2.25
	1972	4,866	—	Proof only	2.00
	1973	.011	—	Proof only	1.50
	1974	4,050	—	Proof only	1.50
	1975	4.000	.15	.20	.30
	1975	5,056	—	Proof	2.00
	1976	.010	—	Proof only	2.50
	1977	—	—	Proof only	2.50
	1978FM	7,311	—	Proof only	2.50
	1979FM	1,857	—	Proof only	—

25 CENTS

5.1800 gm., .900 SILVER, .1499 oz ASW

Y#	Date	Mintage	VF	XF	Unc
7	1896H	.015	12.00	35.00	90.00
	1896H	—	—	Proof	325.00
	1906H	4,000	15.00	40.00	100.00
	1906H	—	—	Proof	325.00

Y#	Date	Mintage	VF	XF	Unc
15	1960	.900	BV	BV	5.00
	1961	1.200	BV	BV	5.00

COPPER-NICKEL

Y#	Date	Mintage	VF	XF	Unc
15a	1966	.800	.40	.75	1.25
	1968(D)	1.600	.35	.50	1.00
	1968(S)	.014	—	Proof only	1.75
	1969	5,056	—	Proof only	2.00
	1970	3,466	—	Proof only	2.50
	1971	3,012	—	Proof only	2.50
	1972	4,866	—	Proof only	2.25
	1973	2.000	.35	.50	.75
	1973	.011	—	Proof	1.75
	1974	4,050	—	Proof only	1.75
	1975	1.600	.35	.50	.75
	1975	5,056	—	Proof	2.25
	1976	.800	—	—	—
	1976	100 pcs.	—	Proof	—

F.A.O. Issue

Y#	Date	Mintage	VF	XF	Unc
38	1976	.800	—	—	.75

Y#	Date	Mintage	VF	XF	Unc
	1976	.010	—	Proof	3.50
	1977	—	—	Proof only	3.50
	1978FM	7,311	—	Proof only	2.25
	1979FM	1,857	—	Proof only	—

50 CENTS

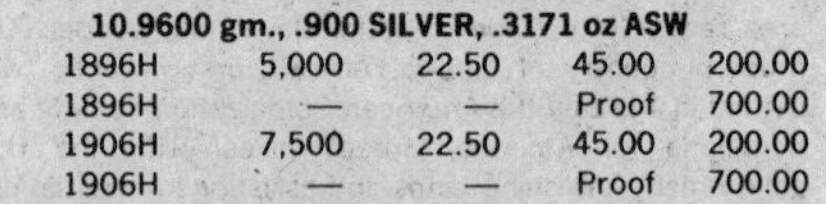

10.9600 gm., .900 SILVER, .3171 oz ASW

Y#	Date	Mintage	VF	XF	Unc
8	1896H	5,000	22.50	45.00	200.00
	1896H	—	—	Proof	700.00
	1906H	7,500	22.50	45.00	200.00
	1906H	—	—	Proof	700.00

Y#	Date	Mintage	VF	XF	Unc
16	1960	1.100	BV	BV	10.00
	1961	.800	BV	BV	11.00

COPPER-NICKEL

Y#	Date	Mintage	VF	XF	Unc
16a	1966	.200	1.00	1.25	1.50
	1968(L)	1.000	.75	1.00	1.50
	1968(S)	.014	—	Proof Only	2.00
	1969	5,056	—	Proof Only	2.50
	1970	3,446	—	Proof Only	3.50
	1971	3,012	—	Proof Only	3.50
	1972	4,866	—	Proof Only	3.00
	1973	1.000	.60	.75	1.00
	1973	.011	—	Proof	2.00
	1974	—	—	Proof Only	2.00
	1975	.800	.60	.75	1.00
	1975	5,056	—	Proof	3.00
	1976	1.000	—	—	—
	1976	100 pcs.	—	Proof	—
	1978FM	7,311	—	Proof only	3.50
	1979FM	1,857	—	Proof only	—

DOLLAR

20.7400 gm., .900 SILVER, .6001 oz ASW

Y#	Date	Mintage	VF	XF	Unc
17	1961	.200	BV	18.00	20.00
	1962	1.000	BV	BV	18.00

COPPER-NICKEL

Y#	Date	Mintage	VF	XF	Unc
17a	1966	1.000	1.25	2.00	3.50
	1968(L)	1.000	1.25	2.00	3.50
	1968(S)	.014	—	Proof Only	3.50
	1969	5,056	—	Proof Only	4.00
	1970(D)	2.000	1.25	1.50	3.00
	1970(S)	3,466	—	Proof Only	10.00

Y#	Date	Mintage	VF	XF	Unc
17a	1971	3,012	—	Proof Only	10.00
	1972	4,866	—	Proof Only	6.50
	1973	.011	—	Proof Only	3.50
	1974	—	—	Proof Only	3.50
	1975	.400	1.50	2.00	3.00
	1975	5,056	—	Proof Only	6.50
	1976	2,000	—	—	—
	1976	100 pcs.	—	Proof	—

Y#	Date	Mintage	VF	XF	Unc
40	1976	.010	—	Proof	11.50
	1977	—	—	Proof only	11.50
	1978FM	7,311	—	Proof only	12.50
	1979FM	1,857	—	Proof only	—

2-1/2 DOLLARS

4.1796 gm., .900 GOLD, .1209 oz AGW
Obv: The capitol; Rev: Arms.

Fr#	Date	Mintage	VF	XF	Unc
9	1972	—	BV	80.00	90.00

5 DOLLARS

8.3592 gm., .900 GOLD, .2419 oz AGW
Obv: Ship; Rev: Arms.

Fr#	Date	Mintage	VF	XF	Unc
8	1972	—	BV	160.00	175.00

34.1000 gm., .900 SILVER, .9868 oz ASW

Y#	Date	Mintage	VF	XF	Unc
18	1973	500 pcs.	BV	BV	30.00
	1973	.028	—	Proof	30.00
	1974	.020	—	Proof	30.00
	1975	9,112	—	Proof only	30.00
	1976	3,833	—	Proof only	35.00
	1977	1,635	—	Proof only	35.00
	1978FM	7,311	—	Proof only	35.00
	1979FM	1,857	—	Proof only	—

10 DOLLARS

16.7185 gm., .900 GOLD, .4838 oz AGW
Obv: Liberty; Rev: Arms.

Fr#	Date	Mintage	VF	XF	Unc
7	1972	—	BV	325.00	350.00

12 DOLLARS

6.0000 gm., .900 GOLD, .1736 oz AGW

Fr#	Date	Mintage	VF	XF	Unc
5	1965	400 pcs.	—	Proof	200.00

20 DOLLARS

18.6500 gm., .900 GOLD, .5397 oz AGW

Y#	Date	Mintage	VF	XF	Unc
27	1964B	.010	BV	BV	350.00

18.6500 gm., .999 GOLD, .5990 oz AGW

Y#	Date	Mintage	VF	XF	Unc
27a	1964B-L	100 pcs.	—	Proof	450.00

Of the total issue, 10,200 were struck of fine gold and bear the "B" mintmark of the Bern Mint below the date, while 100 were struck (restrikes suspected) as proofs and are designated by the presence of a small "l" above the date.

33.4370 gm., .900 GOLD, .9675 oz AGW
President Tolbert Inauguration

Fr#	Date	Mintage	VF	XF	Unc
6	1972	—	BV	650.00	700.00

25 DOLLARS

23.3120 gm., .900 GOLD, .6746 oz AGW
President Tubman 70th Birthday

Y#	Date	Mintage	VF	XF	Unc
28	1965B	3,000	BV	450.00	500.00
	1965B	—	—	Proof	500.00

.999 GOLD

Y#	Date	Mintage	VF	XF	Unc
28a	1965B-L	100 pcs.	—	—	500.00

President Tubman 75th Birthday

Fr#	Date	Mintage	VF	XF	Unc
A5	1970	—	—	Proof	600.00

23.3700 gm., .910 GOLD, .6838 oz AGW
Sesquicentennial of Founding of Liberia

Y#	Date	Mintage	VF	XF	Unc
A38	1972	3,000	—	Proof	—

30 DOLLARS

15.0000 gm., .900 GOLD, .4340 oz AGW
President Tubman 70th Birthday

Fr#	Date	Mintage	VF	XF	Unc
4	1965	400 pcs.	—	Proof	450.00

100 DOLLARS

6.0000 gm., .900 GOLD, .1736 oz AGW
Obv: President Tolbert. Rev: People stretching upward.

Y#	Date	Mintage	VF	XF	Unc
35	1976	175 pcs.	—	Proof	250.00

10.9300 gm., .900 GOLD, .3163 oz AGW
130th Anniversary

Y#	Date	Mintage	VF	XF	Unc
41	1977FM(U)	787 pcs.	—	225.00	250.00
	1977FM(P)	4,250	—	Proof	225.00

Organization of African Unity Summit Conference

Y#	Date	Mintage	VF	XF	Unc
42	1979FM(P)	1,656	—	Proof	225.00

.900 GOLD, .3241 oz AGW
Organization of African Unity
11.2000 gm.

Y#	Date	Mintage	VF	XF	Unc
—	1979FM(P)	—		Proof only	—

200 DOLLARS

12.0000 gm., .900 GOLD, .3472 oz AGW
Obv: President Tolbert. Rev: President Tolbert blowing a horn.

Y#	Date	Mintage	VF	XF	Unc
36	1976	100 pcs.	—	Proof	400.00

400 DOLLARS

24.0000 gm., .900 GOLD, .6945 oz AGW
Obv: President Tolbert. Rev: Map of Liberia.

Y#	Date	Mintage	VF	XF	Unc
37	1976	25 pcs.	—	Proof	700.00

NCLT ISSUES

PATTERNS

KM#	Date	Mintage	Identification	Mkt.Val.
1	1847	—	1 Cent, Copper	60.00

KM#	Date	Mintage	Identification	Mkt.Val.
2	1847	—	2 Cents, Copper, K1	50.00

KM#	Date	Mintage	Identification	Mkt.Val.
3	1847	—	10 Cents, Silver, K3	—
4	1847	—	10 Cents, Bronze, K3	—

KM#	Date	Mintage	Identification	Mkt.Val.
5	1862	—	1 Cent, Copper, thick planchet, KA8	50.00
6	1862	—	2 Cents, Copper, 2-1/2mm thick planchet, K8	50.00

KM#	Date	Mintage	Identification	Mkt.Val.
7	1864	—	10 Cents, Silver, K9	—
8	1864	—	10 Cents, Bronze, K9	—

KM#	Date	Mintage	Identification	Mkt.Val.
9	1865	—	25 Cents, Silver, K11	410.00
10	1865	—	25 Cents, Bronze, K11	125.00

KM#	Date	Mintage	Identification	Mkt.Val.
11	1866	—	1 Cent, Copper, w/star on cap, K13	50.00

KM#	Date	Mintage	Identification	Mkt.Val.
12	1866	—	1 Cent, Copper, w/o star on cap, K15	50.00

KM#	Date	Mintage	Identification	Mkt.Val.
13	1866	—	2 Cents, Copper, K14	50.00

KM#	Date	Mintage	Identification	Mkt.Val.
14	1866	—	2 Cents, Copper, K14a	50.00

KM#	Date	Mintage	Identification	Mkt.Val.
15	1868	—	1 Cent, Copper, K16	145.00
16	1868	—	2 Cents, Copper, K17	100.00

KM#	Date	Mintage	Identification	Mkt.Val.
17	1888	—	1 Cent, Copper, large shield, K18	35.00
18	1889	—	1 Cent, Copper, small shield, K19	30.00

KM#	Date	Mintage	Identification	Mkt.Val.
19	1889	—	25 Cents, Silver, K20	100.00
20	1889	—	25 Cents, Bronze, K20	50.00
21	1889	—	25 Cents, Aluminum, K20	50.00
22	1889	—	25 Cents, Copper-Nickel, K20	50.00

KM#	Date	Mintage	Identification	Mkt.Val.
23	1889	—	25 Cents, Silver, K22	100.00
24	1889	—	25 Cents, Bronze, K22	50.00
25	1889	—	25 Cents, Aluminum, K22	50.00
26	1889	—	25 Cents, Copper-Nickel, K22	50.00

KM#	Date	Mintage	Identification	Mkt.Val.
27	1889	—	25 Cents, Silver, K24	—
28	1889	—	25 Cents, Bronze, K24	50.00
29	1889	—	25 Cents, Aluminum, K24	50.00
30	1889	—	25 Cents, Copper-Nickel, K24	50.00

KM#	Date	Mintage	Identification	Mkt.Val.
31	1889	—	50 Cents, Silver, 1-3/4mm thick, K21	—
32	1889	—	50 Cents, Silver, 2-1/2mm thick, K21	—
33	1889	—	50 Cents, Silver Plated Copper, K21	—
34	1889	—	50 Cents, Bronze, K21	100.00
35	1889	—	50 Cents, Aluminum, K21	100.00
36	1889	—	50 Cents, Copper-Nickel, K21	100.00

KM#	Date	Mintage	Identification	Mkt.Val.
37	1889	—	50 Cents, Silver, 1-3/4mm thick, K23	—
38	1889	—	50 Cents, Silver, 2-1/2mm thick, K23	—
39	1889	—	50 Cents, Bronze, K23	100.00
40	1889	—	50 Cents, Aluminum, K23	100.00
41	1889	—	50 Cents, Copper-Nickel, K23	140.00

KM#	Date	Mintage	Identification	Mkt.Val.
42	1889	—	50 Cents, Silver, 1-3/4mm thick, K25	—
43	1889	—	50 Cents, Silver, 2-1/2mm thick, K25	—
44	1889	—	50 Cents, Bronze, K25	100.00
45	1889	—	50 Cents, Aluminum, K25	100.00
46	1889	—	50 Cents, Copper-Nickel, K25	100.00

KM#	Date	Mintage	Identification	Mkt.Val.
47	1890	—	1 Cent, Copper, K30	40.00

KM#	Date	Mintage	Identification	Mkt.Val.
48	1890	—	1 Cent, Copper, K32	30.00
49	1890	—	1 Cent, Copper, K34	30.00

KM#	Date	Mintage	Identification	Mkt.Val.
50	1890	—	1 Cent, Copper, K36	45.00

KM#	Date	Mintage	Identification	Mkt.Val.
51	1890	—	2 Cents, Copper, K31	60.00
52	1890	—	2 Cents, Copper, K33	50.00
53	1890	—	2 Cents, Copper, K35	30.00
54	1890	—	2 Cents, Copper, K37	45.00

PROOF SETS
STANDARD METALS

KM#	Date	Mintage	Identification	Issue Price	Mkt. Val.
101	1896H(5)	—	Y4-8	—	1500.
102	1906H(5)	—	Y4-8	—	1500.
103	1968(6)	14,396	Y12,13,14a-17a	15.25	10.00
104	1969(6)	5,158	Y12,13,14a-17a	15.25	11.50
105	1970(6)	3,464	Y12,13,14a-17a	15.25	20.00
106	1971(6)	3,032	Y12,13,14a-17a	15.25	20.00
107	1972(6)	4,866	Y12,13,14a-17a	15.50	15.00
108	1972(4)	—	F6-9	—	1300.
109	1973(7)	10,542	Y12,13,14a-17a,18	27.00	40.00
110	1974(7)	9,362	Y12,13,14a-17a,18	27.00	40.00
111	1975(7)	5,056	Y12,13,14a-17a,18	31.50	45.00
112	1976(7)	2,281	Y12,13,14a,18,38-40	45.00	50.00
113	1977(7)	920	Y12,13,14a,18,38-40	45.00	50.00
114	1978(8)	7,311	Y11a,12,13,14a,16a,18,38,40	47.00	—
115	1979(8)	1,857	Y11a,12,13,14a,16a,18,38,40 marked O.A.U. JULY,1979	45.00	—

LIBYA

The Socialist People's Libyan Arab Jamahiriya, located on the north-central coast of Africa between Tunisia and Egypt, has an area of 679,536 sq. mi. (1,759,998 sq. km.) and a population of 2.5 million. Capital: Tripoli. Crude oil, which accounts for 90 per cent of the export earnings, is the mainstay of the economy.

Libya has been subjected to foreign rule throughout most of its history, various parts of it having been ruled by the Phoenicians, Carthaginians, Vandals, Byzantines, Greeks, Romans, Egyptians, and in the following centuries the Arabs' language, culture and religion were adopted by the indigenous population. Libya was conquered by the Ottoman Turks in 1553, and remained under Turkish domination, becoming a Turkish vilayet in 1835, until it was conquered by Italy and made into a colony in 1911. The name 'Libya', the ancient Greek name for North Africa exclusive of Egypt, was given to the colony by Italy in 1934. Libya came under Allied administration after the fall of Tripoli on Jan. 23, 1943, divided into zones of British and French control. On Dec. 24, 1951, in accordance with a United Nations resolution, Libya proclaimed its independence as a constitutional monarchy, thereby becoming the first country to achieve independence through the United Nations. The monarchy was overthrown by a coup d'etat on Sept. 1, 1969, and Libya was established as a republic.

TRIPOLI

Tripoli (formerly Oea of antique Tripolitania, 700-146 B.C.), the capital city and chief port of the Libyan Arab Jamahiriya, is situated on the North African coast on a promontory stretching out into the Mediterranean Sea. It was probably founded by Phoenicians from Sicily, but was under Roman control from 146 B.C. until 450 A.D. Invasion by the Vandals and conquest by the Byzantines preceded the Arab invasions of the 11th century which, by destroying the commercial centers of Sabratha and Leptis, greatly enhanced the importance of Tripoli, an importance maintained through periods of Norman and Spanish control. Tripoli fell to the Turks, who made it the capital of the vilayet of Tripoli, in 1551 and remained in their hands until 1911, when it was occupied by the Italians who made it the capital of the Italian province of Tripolitania. British forces entered the city on Jan. 23, 1943, and administered it until establishment of the independent Kingdom of Libya on Dec. 24, 1951.

RULERS

(of Turkey)

Sultan Abdul Hamid I,
AH1187-1203/AD1774-1789

Sultan Selim III,
AH1203-1222/AD1789-1807

Mustafa IV
AH1222/AD1807

Mahmud II
AH1223-55/AD1808-39

LOCAL PASHAS:

Yusuf Qaramanli until
AH1248/AD1832

Ali Qaramanli and Muhammad Qaramanli, rivals for power
Until AH1251/AD1835

Najib Pasha (from Istanbul Gov't)
AH1251/AD1835

MINT

طرابلس غرب

Trablus Gharb – Tripoli West

The appellation 'West' serving to distinguish it from Tripoli in Lebanon, which had been an Ottoman Mint in the 16th century. On some of the copper coins, 'Gharb' is omitted; several types come both with and without 'Garb'. The mint closed between the 28th and 29th year of the reign of Mahmud II.

MONETARY SYSTEM

The monetary system of Tripoli was confused and is poorly understood. Theoretically, 40 Para were equal to one Piastre, but due to the debasement of the silver coinage, later issues are virtually pure copper, though the percentage of alloy varies radically even within a given year. The 10 Para and 20 Para pieces were little heavier than the copper Paras, with which they could easily be confounded, except that the copper Paras are generally thicker, and bear simpler inscriptions. It is not known how many of the coppers were tariffed to the debased Piastre and its fractions. Some authorities consider the copper pieces to be Beshliks (5 Para coins).

The gold coinage came in two denominations, the Zeri Mahbub (2.4-2.5 gr.), and the Sultani Altin (3.3-3.4 gr.). The ratio of the billon Piastres to the gold coins fluctuated from day to day.

COPPER COINAGE

Under this rubric are included all pieces intended as Paras. Many of the billon coins are so debased as to be nearly pure copper, but they can be distinguished from those coins intended as Paras as they are much thinner, and bear different devices and inscriptions. Some pieces are also struck in brass.

In addition to pieces bearing no regnal year, the issuance of coppers seems to be restricted to two series, one bearing year 12-13, the other years 20-27. The first group is related to an anomalous billon issue in the same years (Type D below), the second issue seems to be connected to the reduced weight series of yrs. 21-25. The undated pieces were most probably struck during one of these two periods.

All of the following pieces appear to be of one denomination, probably a Para, but vary in size from about 17-23mm.

PARA

COPPER

C#	Date	Year	Good	VG	Fine	VF
92	AH1223	w/o year	2.50	5.00	10.00	15.00
		13	3.75	7.50	15.00	22.50
		20	3.00	6.00	12.00	18.00

Obv. changed: SULTAN/MAHMUD KHAN/AZZA NASRUHU

C#	Date	Year	Good	VG	Fine	VF
92.1	AH1223	w/o year	3.75	7.50	15.00	22.50
		20	4.00	8.00	16.00	24.00

Obv: Sultan/1223. Rev: Mahmud/24.

C#	Date	Year	Good	VG	Fine	VF
93	AH1223	24	4.00	8.00	16.00	24.00

Obv: Tughra. Rev: as C#92, w/Gharb.

C#	Date	Year	Good	VG	Fine	VF
94	AH1223	w/o year	2.50	5.00	10.00	15.00

w/o Gharb

C#	Date	Year	Good	VG	Fine	VF
94.1	AH1223	w/o year	3.00	6.00	12.00	18.00

Obv. and rev. enclosed in lozenge.

C#	Date	Year	Good	VG	Fine	VF
94a	AH1223	2	3.75	7.50	15.00	22.50

COPPER or BRASS

C#	Date	Year	Good	VG	Fine	VF
94b	AH1223	2	5.00	10.00	20.00	30.00

COPPER

Obv: Arabesque; SULTAN MAHMUD KHAN 1223.

C#	Date	Year	Good	VG	Fine	VF
96	AH1223	25	3.00	6.00	12.00	18.00
		26	3.00	6.00	12.00	18.00
		62	(error) for year 26			
			3.75	7.50	15.00	22.50

Several variations are found in the arrangement of the obverse legend. Year 29 is reported, but is likely a misreading of year 26. Center ornament on obverse small.

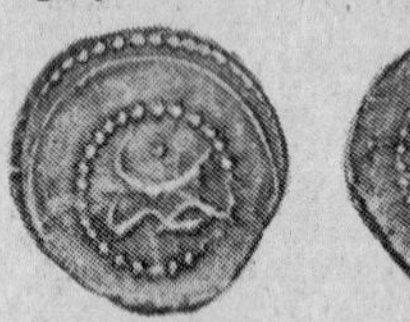

Obv: DURIBA. Rev: FI TRABLUS.

C#	Date	Year	Good	VG	Fine	VF
101	ND	no year	2.75	5.50	11.00	16.50

Inscriptions in lozenge.

C#	Date	Year	Good	VG	Fine	VF
101.1	AH1223	no year	2.75	5.50	11.00	16.50

COPPER or BRASS

Different arrangement of legends.

C#	Date	Year	Good	VG	Fine	VF
101.2	AH1223	23	3.00	6.00	12.00	18.00

COPPER

Legends within a 10-pointed star.

C#	Date	Year	Good	VG	Fine	VF
101.3	AH1223	23	3.00	6.00	12.00	18.00

Obv: DURIBA/FI/1223. Rev: TRABLUS.

C#	Date	Year	Good	VG	Fine	VF
101.4	AH1223	12	4.00	8.00	16.00	24.00
		13	4.00	8.00	16.00	24.00
		20	4.00	8.00	16.00	24.00

Obv: DURIBA/FI/1223. Rev: TRABLUS 21

C#	Date	Year	Good	VG	Fine	VF
101.5	AH1223	21	4.00	8.00	16.00	24.00

Obv: Similar to rev. of C#92
Rev: 5 dots within wreath

C#	Date	Year	Good	VG	Fine	VF
103	AH1223	20	3.75	7.50	15.00	22.50

Rev: With arabesque.

C#	Date	Year	Good	VG	Fine	VF
103.1	AH1223	21	4.00	8.00	16.00	24.00

Obv: Without GHARB.
Rev: Rosette within knotted border.

C#	Date	Year	Good	VG	Fine	VF
103.2	AH1223	22	3.75	7.50	15.00	22.50

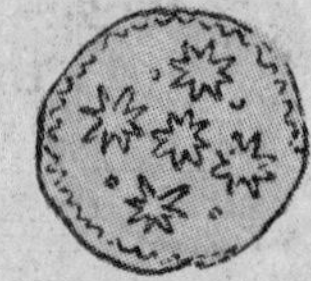

Rev: 5 stars.

C#	Date	Year	Good	VG	Fine	VF
103.3	AH1223	25	4.00	8.00	16.00	24.00

Obv: DURIBA/FI/TRABLUS/1223. Rev: GHARB.

C#	Date	Year	Good	VG	Fine	VF
105	AH1223	21	3.00	6.00	12.00	18.00

Similar to C#105, with obv. and rev. legends enclosed in wavy hexagrams.

C#	Date	Year	Good	VG	Fine	VF
105a	AH1223	22	4.00	8.00	16.00	24.00

Obv: Similar to C#105. Rev: Hexagram.

C#	Date	Year	Good	VG	Fine	VF
106	AH1223	25	3.00	6.00	12.00	18.00
		27	3.75	7.50	15.00	22.50

Rev: Hexagram with dots.

C#	Date	Year	Good	VG	Fine	VF
106.1	AH1223	—	3.00	6.00	12.00	18.00

Obv: Similar to C#105. Rev: Hexagram with '23'.

C#	Date	Year	Good	VG	Fine	VF
106.2	AH1223	23	4.50	9.00	18.00	24.00

Obv: Tughra with word 'NUHAS' to right.
Rev: DURIBA/FI/TRABLUS GHARB/1223.

C#	Date	Year	Good	VG	Fine	VF
106.3	AH1223	28	7.50	15.00	30.00	45.00

BILLON COINAGE

The billon coinage of Mahmud II is extremely varied, with a plethora of types deriving largely from contemporary Turkish, Egyptian, and Tunisian prototypes. There is considerable controversy over the denominations of these coins, although they seem to be based on a Piastre (40 Paras, Kurus) of about 16 grams from Yrs. 1-13, of about 12 grams from Yrs. 13-21, and of 10 grams from Yrs. 21-25. A new style coinage was introduced in Yr. 28, but it was apparently never issued in sizable quantities and confined to the one year.

There is considerable variation in the weight of the various denominations, up to 20 per cent above or below the theoretical norm. There does not appear to be any significant correlation between type, denomination, and standard; not uncommonly do 2 or 3 distinct types exist for the same denomination and regnal year. It is possible that there is a correlation between type and actual silver content, but no specimens have been analyzed to test such a hypothesis. Furthermore, it is possible that several distinct series were issued simultaneously over a stretch of years, but due to the extreme paucity of surviving specimens, such cannot be determined.

Except for a few isolated miscellaneous types, all of the billon coinage can be classed into five basic types:

TYPE A: Obv: Toughra, sometimes with adjacent symbol.
Rev: Year/mint/1223.

TYPE B: Obv: Toughra/mint/1223.
Rev: 4-line legend giving sultan's titles: SULTAN AL-BAHRAYN WA KHAQAN AL-BAHRAYN AL-SULTAN IBN AL-SULTAN.

TYPE C: Obv: Sultan's name/benediction/mint/1223 (4-line legend).
Rev: Same as reverse of Type B.

TYPE D: Obv: Sultan's name (sometimes with 1223).
Rev: Year/mint/1223 (1223 omitted when on obv.)

TYPE E: Obv: 4-line legend: SULTAN AL-BARRAYN WA KHAQAN AL-BAHRAYN AL-SULTAN MAHMUD KHAN AZZA NASRUHU & (year).
Rev: Mint/1223 (this type copied from Tunis piastre & fractions).

In addition to the variations in type, there is considerable variation in the borders. No attempt has been made in these listings to distinguish the various types of borders, though it is quite possible that such distinctions may have been monetarily important.

STANDARD COINAGE

The following listings are arranged by standard, and then by denomination within each standard. The sizes of the coins can vary considerably within each issue. The weight can vary by up to 20 per cent higher or lower than the amounts shown.

All of the coins were struck in low-grade billon, tending toward pure copper on some of the later issues. Most of the coins originally were lightly silver-washed, and specimens with the silver wash intact are now quite scarce.

First Standard

Based on a Piastre (40 Para) of about 16 grams.

5 PARA

BILLON, 22-23mm, Type B

C#	Date	Year	Good	VG	Fine	VF
162	AH1223	7	9.00	18.50	36.50	55.00
		9	9.00	18.50	36.50	55.00
		10	9.00	18.50	36.50	55.00
		11	9.00	18.50	36.50	55.00

10 PARA

BILLON, 22-24mm. Type A

C#	Date	Year	Good	VG	Fine	VF
129	AH1223	no year	12.50	25.00	50.00	75.00
		7	12.50	25.00	50.00	75.00
		10	12.50	25.00	50.00	75.00

Yrs. 7 and 10 are of slightly different type from the piece without regnal year. Yr. 7 is about 28.mm in diameter; Yr. 10 is about 31mm.

29-31mm

C#	Date	Year	Good	VG	Fine	VF
131a	AH1223	no year	7.50	15.00	30.00	45.00

20 PARA

BILLON, 31mm, Type A

C#	Date	Year	Good	VG	Fine	VF
131	AH1223	7	12.50	25.00	50.00	75.00

40 PARA

BILLON, 37mm, 15.68 gm., Type A

C#	Date	Year	Good	VG	Fine	VF
—	AH1223	ND	17.50	35.00	70.00	100.00

(Olcer #833)

Second Standard

YEARS 12-13

Based on a Piastre of about 14 grams.

100 PARA

BILLON, 25 gm., 44mm
Ornament with dot on either side.

C#	Date	Year	Good	VG	Fine	VF
—	AH1223	ND	100.00	175.00	275.00	400.00

10 PARA

BILLON, 19mm. Type D

C#	Date	Year	Good	VG	Fine	VF
191	AH1223	12	11.50	23.50	45.00	60.00

15 PARA

BILLON, 23mm. Type D

C#	Date	Year	Good	VG	Fine	VF
192	AH1223	12	11.50	23.50	45.00	60.00
		13	11.50	23.50	45.00	60.00

20 PARA

BILLON, 28mm. Type B

C#	Date	Year	Good	VG	Fine	VF
164	AH1223	13	7.50	15.00	30.00	60.00

Third Standard

YEARS 14-21

Based on a Piastre of about 12 grams.

10 PARA

C#	Date	Year	Good	VG	Fine	VF
BILLON, 26mm. Type A						
112	AH1223	19	11.50	22.50	45.00	60.00
Type B, 26-27mm.						
163	AH1223	16	7.50	15.00	30.00	45.00
	1223	17	7.50	15.00	30.00	45.00
Type C, 25mm.						
172	AH1223	14	12.50	25.00	50.00	75.00

The authenticity of C#172 is questionable, but if counterfeit, it is contemporary.

Unusual type: Both sides have devices in center and marginal legends around. 22mm.

C#	Date	Year	Good	VG	Fine	VF
198	AH1223	20	20.00	40.00	80.00	120.00

15 PARA

BILLON, 29mm. Type E.

C#	Date	Year	Good	VG	Fine	VF
183	AH1223	17	12.50	25.00	50.00	75.00

20 PARA

C#	Date	Year	Good	VG	Fine	VF
BILLON, 23mm. Type A						
125	AH1223	20	10.00	20.00	40.00	60.00
Type A, larger flan, 31mm.						
125a	AH1223	21	12.50	25.00	50.00	75.00
Type B, 29mm.						
164	AH1223	15	7.50	15.00	30.00	45.00
Type C, 29mm.						
174	AH1222	—	20.00	40.00	80.00	120.00
	AH1223	20	10.00	20.00	40.00	60.00
Type D, 28mm.						
174.1	AH1223	20	10.00	20.00	40.00	60.00

30 PARA

C#	Date	Year	Good	VG	Fine	VF
BILLON, 29mm, Type A						
126	AH1223	20	8.50	17.50	35.00	52.50
Type E, 33-34mm.						
185	AH1223	17	12.50	25.00	50.00	75.00
		18	12.50	25.00	50.00	75.00

40 PARA

C#	Date	Year	Good	VG	Fine	VF
BILLON, Type A, 35mm. Lozenge borders.						
127	AH1223	21	15.00	30.00	60.00	90.00
Type A, 32mm, plain borders						
117	AH1223	20	12.50	25.00	50.00	75.00
Type A, 36-39mm. Circular ornate borders.						
132	AH1223	19	15.00	30.00	60.00	90.00
		21	15.00	30.00	60.00	90.00
Type B, 35-37mm.						
166	AH1223	14	15.00	30.00	60.00	90.00
		18	12.50	25.00	50.00	75.00
		20	12.50	25.00	50.00	75.00
Type C, 36mm.						
176	AH1223	19	17.50	35.00	70.00	100.00
Type D, 34mm.						
194	AH1223	20	12.50	25.00	50.00	75.00
Type E, 33mm.						
187	AH1243	—	15.00	30.00	60.00	90.00

Dated to the actual year, as on similar coins of Tunis.

50 PARA

BILLON, 37mm, Type A.

C#	Date	Year	Good	VG	Fine	VF
117a	AH1243	—	17.50	35.00	70.00	100.00

See note to C#117. The denomination of the above coin is very uncertain.

60 PARA

BILLON, 37-40mm. Type A.

C#	Date	Year	Good	VG	Fine	VF
140	AH1223	20	12.50	25.00	50.00	75.00
	AH1243	—	—	—	Rare	—

Fourth Standard

YEARS 21-25

Based on a Piastre of approximately 10 grams.

10 PARA

BILLON, 24mm, Type B.

C#	Date	Year	Good	VG	Fine	VF
163	AH1223	22	7.50	15.00	30.00	45.00
		24	7.50	15.00	30.00	45.00
		25	7.50	15.00	30.00	45.00

20 PARA

BILLON, 29-30mm, Type A.

C#	Date	Year	Good	VG	Fine	VF
—	AH1223	23	10.00	20.00	40.00	60.00

Type B.

C#	Date	Year	Good	VG	Fine	VF
164	AH1223	22	8.50	17.50	35.00	52.50
		24	8.50	17.50	35.00	52.50

30 PARA

BILLON, Type D, 32mm.

C#	Date	Year	Good	VG	Fine	VF
193	AH1223	22	10.00	20.00	40.00	60.00

34mm
Obv. and rev: Circular Legends Around Central Devices.

C#	Date	Year	Good	VG	Fine	VF
199	AH1223	23	20.00	40.00	80.00	120.00

35mm
Similar to Type A, but with large crescents at both sides similar to Turkey C#197, but no wreaths.

C#	Date	Year	Good	VG	Fine	VF
141	AH1223	24	20.00	40.00	80.00	120.00

40 PARA

BILLON, 35mm, Type A.

C#	Date	Year	Good	VG	Fine	VF
—	AH1223	21	15.00	30.00	60.00	90.00

Type B, 35-37mm.

C#	Date	Year	Good	VG	Fine	VF
166	AH1223	13	12.50	25.00	50.00	75.00
		21	12.50	25.00	50.00	75.00
		22	12.50	25.00	50.00	75.00
		24	12.50	25.00	50.00	75.00
		25	12.50	25.00	50.00	75.00

Fifth Standard

Year 28 Only
Uncertain metrology

5 (?) PIASTRES (200 PARA)

BILLON, 14.5 gm., 38mm.
As Type A, but legends enclosed within wreaths, both sides. Word FIDDA (= SILVER) to right of toughra, regnal year at left.

C#	Date	Year	Good	VG	Fine	VF
148	AH1223	28	25.00	50.00	100.00	150.00

NOTE: Possibly a pattern.

ZERI MAHBUB

GOLD, 21-24mm, 2.3-2.5 gm.
Type B

C#	Date	Year	VG	Fine	VF	XF
210	AH1223	12	65.00	80.00	100.00	150.00
		13	65.00	80.00	100.00	150.00

Type E

C#	Date	Year	VG	Fine	VF	XF
212	AH1223	18	65.00	80.00	100.00	150.00

C#	Date	Year	VG	Fine	VF	XF
214	AH1223	20	75.00	90.00	110.00	165.00

SULTANI

GOLD, 24-26mm, 3.2-3.4 gm.
Type C (variant)

C#	Date	Year	VG	Fine	VF	XF
218	AH1223	6	100.00	125.00	150.00	200.00

Similar, but broader and thinner.

C#	Date	Year	VG	Fine	VF	XF
218a	AH1223	19	110.00	135.00	165.00	225.00

LIBYA

RULERS

Idris I, 1951-1969

MONETARY SYSTEM

10 Milliemes = 1 Piastre
100 Piastres = 1 Pound

MILLIEME

BRONZE

Y#	Date	Year	Mintage	VF	XF	Unc
1	—	1952	7.750	.10	.15	.25
	—	1952	32 pcs.	—	Proof	125.00

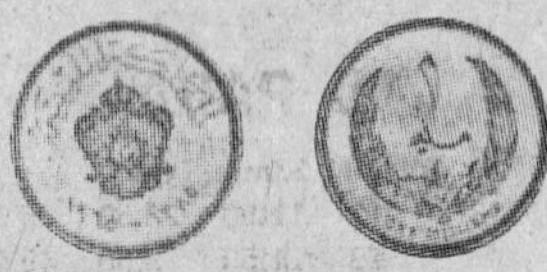

NICKEL-BRASS

Y#	Date	Year	Mintage	VF	XF	Unc
6	AH1385	1965	11.000	—	.10	.15

2 MILLIEMES

BRONZE

Y#	Date	Year	Mintage	VF	XF	Unc
2	—	1952	6.650	.10	.15	.35
	—	1952	32 pcs.	—	Proof	130.00

5 MILLIEMES

BRONZE

Y#	Date	Year	Mintage	VF	XF	Unc
3	—	1952	7.680	.10	.20	.60
	—	1952	32 pcs.	—	Proof	150.00

NICKEL-BRASS

Y#	Date	Year	Mintage	VF	XF	Unc
7	AH1385	1965	8.500	.10	.15	.20

PIASTRE

COPPER-NICKEL

Y#	Date	Year	Mintage	VF	XF	Unc
4	—	1952	10.200	.35	.55	.85
	—	1952	32 pcs.	—	Proof	175.00

10 MILLIEMES

COPPER-NICKEL

Y#	Date	Year	Mintage	VF	XF	Unc
8	AH1385	1965	17.000	.10	.20	.35

2 PIASTRES

COPPER-NICKEL

Y#	Date	Year	Mintage	VF	XF	Unc
5	—	1952	6.075	.25	.65	1.35
	—	1952	32 pcs.	—	Proof	200.00

20 MILLIEMES

COPPER-NICKEL

Y#	Date	Year	Mintage	VF	XF	Unc
9	AH1385	1965	8.750	.10	.20	.35

50 MILLIEMES

COPPER-NICKEL

Y#	Date	Year	Mintage	VF	XF	Unc
10	AH1385	1965	8.000	.25	.40	.75

100 MILLIEMES

COPPER-NICKEL

Y#	Date	Year	Mintage	VF	XF	Unc
11	AH1385	1965	8.000	.50	.80	1.50

MONETARY REFORM

1000 Dirhams = 1 Dinar

DIRHAM

BRASS-CLAD STEEL

Y#	Date	Year	Mintage	VF	XF	Unc
12	AH1395	1975	20.000	—	—	.10

5 DIRHAMS

BRASS-CLAD STEEL

Y#	Date	Year	Mintage	VF	XF	Unc
13	AH1395	1975	23.000	—	.10	.15

10 DIRHAMS

COPPER-NICKEL-CLAD STEEL

Y#	Date	Year	Mintage	VF	XF	Unc
14	AH1395	1975	44.000	—	.10	.25

20 DIRHAMS

COPPER-NICKEL-CLAD STEEL

Y#	Date	Year	Mintage	VF	XF	Unc
15	AH1395	1975	18.000	.10	.15	.35

50 DIRHAMS

COPPER-NICKEL

Y#	Date	Year	Mintage	VF	XF	Unc
16	AH1395	1975	13.000	.25	.40	.65

100 DIRHAMS

COPPER-NICKEL

Y#	Date	Year	Mintage	VF	XF	Unc
17	AH1395	1975	9.000	.50	.75	1.25

NCLT ISSUES

PROOF SETS

STANDARD METALS

KM#	Date	Mintage	Identification	Issue Price	Mkt. Val.
101	1952(5)	32	Y1-5	—	700.00

LIECHTENSTEIN

The Principality of Liechtenstein, located in central Europe on the east bank of the Rhine between Austria and Switzerland, has an area of 61 sq. mi. (160 sq. km.) and a population of 24,750. Capital: Vaduz. The economy is based on agriculture and light manufacturing. Canned goods, textiles, ceramics and precision instruments are exported.

Liechtenstein assumed its present form in 1719 when the lordships of Schellenburg and Vaduz were merged into a principality. It was a member of the Rhine Confederation from 1806 to 1815, and of the German Confederation from 1815 to 1866 when it became independent. Liechtenstein's long and close association with Austria was terminated by World War I. In 1921 it adopted the coinage of Switzerland, and two years later entered into a customs union with the Swiss, who also operate its postal and telegraph systems and represent it in international affairs. The tiny principality abolished its army in 1868 and has avoided involvement in all European wars since that time.

RULERS

Franz Joseph I, 1772-1781
Prince John II, 1858-1929
Prince Franz I, 1929-1938
Prince Franz Josef II, 1938-

MINTMARKS

A - Vienna
B - Bern
M - Munich (restrikes)

MONETARY SYSTEM

(1857-1868)

1-1/2 Florins = 1 Vereinsthaler

20 KREUZER

SILVER

C#	Date	Mintage	Fine	VF	XF
4	1778	—	40.00	60.00	80.00

1/2 THALER

(Convention)

SILVER

C#	Date	Mintage	Fine	VF	XF
5	1778	—	75.00	110.00	140.00

THALER

(Convention)

SILVER

C#	Date	Mintage	Fine	VF	XF
6	1778	—	250.00	350.00	450.00

EIN (1) VEREINSTHALER

.900 SILVER

Y#	Date	Mintage	VF	XF	Unc
1	1862A	1,920	1250.	1900.	2600.
	1862A-M	(restrike)		—	25.00

29.5000 gm., .900 GOLD, .8536 oz AGW

Y#	Date	Mintage	XF	Unc	Proof
1a	1862A-M	.050	(restrike)	—	575.00

TRADE COINS

DUCAT

3.4900 gm., .986 GOLD, .1106 oz AGW

C#	Date	Mintage	VF	XF	Unc
7	1778	—	1000.	1500.	2000.
7a	1778	Restrike	BV	75.00	100.00

MONETARY REFORM

100 Heller = 1 Krone to 1923
100 Rappen = 1 Frank from 1924

1/2 FRANK

.835 SILVER

Y#	Date	Mintage	Fine	VF	XF	Unc
7	1924B	*.030	35.00	70.00	120.00	175.00

***NOTE:** 15,745 pieces were remelted.

KRONE

5.0000 gm., .835 SILVER, .1342 oz ASW

Y#	Date	Mintage	Fine	VF	XF	Unc
2	1900A	.050	10.00	15.00	22.50	30.00
	1904A	.075	10.00	12.50	17.50	27.50
	1910A	.045	10.00	12.50	17.50	27.50
	1915A	.075	8.00	12.50	17.50	27.50

FRANK

.835 SILVER

Y#	Date	Mintage	Fine	VF	XF	Unc
8	1924B	*.060	40.00	60.00	100.00	125.00

***NOTE:** 45,355 pieces were remelted.

2 KRONEN

10.0000 gm., .835 SILVER, .2684 oz ASW

Y#	Date	Mintage	Fine	VF	XF	Unc
3	1912A	.050	9.00	12.50	20.00	30.00
	1915A	.038	10.00	15.00	25.00	35.00

2 FRANKEN

.835 SILVER

Y#	Date	Mintage	Fine	VF	XF	Unc
9	1924B	*.050	35.00	75.00	100.00	150.00

***NOTE:** 41,707 pieces were remelted.

5 KRONEN

24.0000 gm., .900 SILVER, .6945 oz ASW

Y#	Date	Mintage	Fine	VF	XF	Unc
4	1900A	5,000	325.00	450.00	700.00	900.00
	1904A	.015	90.00	120.00	180.00	225.00
	1910A	.010	100.00	125.00	200.00	275.00
	1915A	.010	75.00	115.00	190.00	275.00

5 FRANKEN

.900 SILVER

Y#	Date	Mintage	Fine	VF	XF	Unc
10	1924B	*.015	350.00	500.00	850.00	1000.

***NOTE:** 11,260 pieces were remelted.

10 KRONEN

3.3875 gm., .900 GOLD, .0980 oz AGW
Obv: Head left. Rev: Crowned shield with arms.

Y#	Date	Mintage	Fine	VF	XF	Unc
5	1900A	1,500	—	2250.	3500.	4500.

10 FRANKEN

3.2258 gm., .900 GOLD, .0933 oz AGW

Y#	Date	Mintage	Fine	VF	XF	Unc
11	1930B	2,500	—	650.00	900.00	1250.

Y#	Date	Mintage	Fine	VF	XF	Unc
13	1946B	.010	—	110.00	175.00	250.00

20 KRONEN

6.7750 gm., .900 GOLD, .1960 oz AGW

Y#	Date	Mintage	Fine	VF	XF	Unc
6	1898A	1,500	—	2150.	3000.	4000.

20 FRANKEN

6.4516 gm., .900 GOLD, .1867 oz AGW

Y#	Date	Mintage	Fine	VF	XF	Unc
12	1930B	2,500	—	650.00	800.00	1250.

Y#	Date	Mintage	Fine	VF	XF	Unc
14	1946B	.010	BV	125.00	180.00	225.00

25 FRANKEN

5.6450 gm., .900 GOLD, .1633 oz AGW
Franz Josef II and Princess Gina

Y#	Date	Mintage	Fine	VF	XF	Unc
15	1956B	.015	BV	125.00	180.00	225.00

100th Anniversary of National Bank

Y#	Date	Mintage	Fine	VF	XF	Unc
18	1961	.020	—	—	—	—

NOTE: Not released.

50 FRANKEN

11.2900 gm., .900 GOLD, .3267 oz AGW
Franz Josef II and Princess Gina

Y#	Date	Mintage	Fine	VF	XF	Unc
16	1956	.015	BV	BV	225.00	275.00

100th Anniversary of National Bank

Y#	Date	Mintage	Fine	VF	XF	Unc
19	1961	.020	—	—	—	—

NOTE: Not released.

100 FRANKEN

32.2580 gm., .900 GOLD, .9335 oz AGW
Franz Josef II and Princess Gina

Y#	Date	Mintage	VF	XF	Unc
17	1952	4,000	1500.	2500.	3500.

NCLT ISSUES

ESSAIS (E)

Standard metals unless otherwise noted

Y#	Date	Mintage	Identification	Issue Price	Mkt Val.
E2	1898	125	1 Krone	—	—
E4	1898	100	5 Kronen	—	—
E5	1898	35	10 Kronen	—	—
E6	1898	35	20 Kronen	—	—

LITHUANIA

The Lithuanian Soviet Federated Socialist Republic, southernmost of the Baltic states in east Europe, has an area of 25,174 sq. mi. (65,201 sq. km.) and a population of 3.1 million. Capital: Vilnius. The economy is based on livestock raising and manufacturing. Hogs, cattle, hides and electric motors are exported.

Lithuania emerged as a grand duchy joined to Poland through royal marriage in the 14th century. In the 15th century it was a major power of central Europe, stretching from the Baltic to the Black Sea. Following the third partition of Poland by Austria, Prussia and Russia, 1795, Lithuania came under Russian domination and did not regain its independence until shortly before the end of World War I when it declared itself a sovereign republic. The republic was occupied by Soviet troops in 1939 and annexed to the U.S.S.R. in 1940. Following the German occupation of 1940-44, it was retaken by Russia and reestablished as a member republic of the Soviet Union. Western countries, including the United States, have not recognized Lithuania's incorporation into the Soviet Union.

The coinage issued during Lithuania's short tenure as a republic, is obsolete.

MONETARY SYSTEM

100 Centu = 1 Litas

CENTAS

ALUMINUM-BRONZE

Y#	Date	Mintage	Fine	VF	XF	Unc
1	1925	5.000	1.00	2.00	4.00	10.00

BRONZE

Y#	Date	Mintage	Fine	VF	XF	Unc
9	1936	9.995	1.50	2.50	4.00	8.50

2 CENTAI

BRONZE

Y#	Date	Mintage	Fine	VF	XF	Unc
10	1936	4.951	2.00	3.50	4.50	8.50

5 CENTAI

ALUMINUM-BRONZE

Y#	Date	Mintage	Fine	VF	XF	Unc
2	1925	12.000	1.00	2.50	3.50	8.00

BRONZE

Y#	Date	Mintage	Fine	VF	XF	Unc
11	1936	4.800	1.50	3.00	6.00	12.00

10 CENTU

ALUMINUM-BRONZE

Y#	Date	Mintage	Fine	VF	XF	Unc
3	1925	12.000	1.00	2.50	3.75	10.00

20 CENTU

ALUMINUM-BRONZE

Y#	Date	Mintage	Fine	VF	XF	Unc
4	1925	8.000	1.25	3.50	6.00	12.00

50 CENTU

ALUMINUM-BRONZE

Y#	Date	Mintage	Fine	VF	XF	Unc
5	1925	5.000	2.50	5.00	7.50	15.00

LITAS

2.7000 gm., .500 SILVER, .0434 oz ASW

Y#	Date	Mintage	Fine	VF	XF	Unc
6	1925	5.985	2.00	4.00	7.00	12.00

2 LITU

5.4000 gm., .500 SILVER, .0868 oz ASW

Y#	Date	Mintage	Fine	VF	XF	Unc
7	1925	3.000	3.00	6.00	12.00	17.50

5 LITAI

13.5000 gm., .500 SILVER, .2170 oz ASW

Y#	Date	Mintage	Fine	VF	XF	Unc
8	1925	1.000	8.00	12.50	17.50	27.50

9.0000 gm., .750 SILVER, .2170 oz ASW
Obv: Designer's initials below bust, lettered edge

Y#	Date	Mintage	Fine	VF	XF	Unc
12	1936	2.612	7.00	10.00	12.50	20.00

10 LITU

18.0000 gm., .750 SILVER, .4340 oz ASW
Lettered edge

Y#	Date	Mintage	Fine	VF	XF	Unc
13	1936	.720	13.50	17.50	25.00	37.50

20th Anniversary of Founding

Y#	Date	Mintage	Fine	VF	XF	Unc
14	1938	.180	17.50	25.00	30.00	60.00

NCLT ISSUES

PATTERNS

KM#	Date	Mintage	Identification	Mkt.Val.
1	1936	—	5 Litai, Silver, plain edge, Y12	550.00
2	1936	—	5 Litai, Silver, plain edge, designer's name below bust, Y12	550.00
3	1936	—	10 Litu, Silver, plain edge, y13	600.00

KM#	Date	Mintage	Identification	Mkt.Val.
4	1938	—	2 Litai, Brass, lettered edge	350.00
5	1938	—	2 Litai, Silver, reeded edge, 5.56 gm.	375.00
6	1938	—	2 Litai, Silver, reeded edge, 4.9 gm.	450.00
7	1938	—	2 Litai, Silver, lettered edge	375.00
8	1938	—	2 Litai, Silver, plain edge	375.00

KM#	Date	Mintage	Identification	Mkt.Val.
9	1938	—	2 Litai, Silver, plain edge	1000.
10	1938	—	10 Litai, Silver, lettered edge	1250.

LUNDY

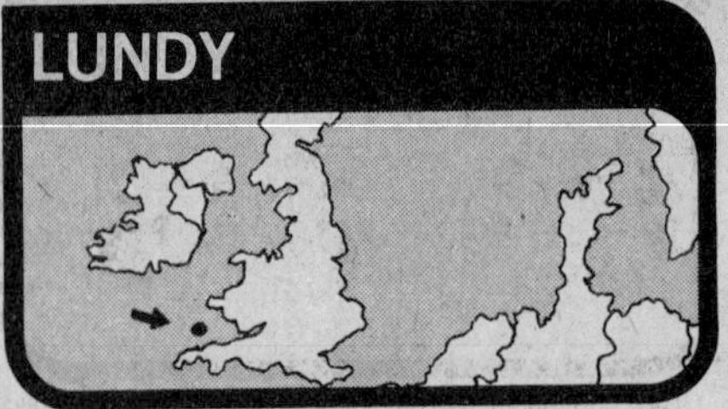

The island of Lundy, located at the entrance to the Bristol Channel 12 miles (19 km.) northwest of Hartford Point, Devonshire, has an area of 1.6 sq. mi. (4.22 sq. km.) and a population of about 32. The island, cliffbound and beautiful, maintains two lighthouses and is a bird sanctuary and popular tourist attraction. In former times, the chief industry was granite quarrying. The economy today is based on tourism and the breeding of ponies for sale on the mainland.

For seven centuries prior to 1969, Lundy was privately owned but under the British Crown. Pre-historic remains hint of an earlier and obscure habitation. Surrounded by unpredictable seas and walled with granite cliffs, Lundy was for several centuries the lair and refuge of pirates and smugglers. Martin Coles Harman purchased the island in 1925 for 16,000 pounds, and four years later issued the controversial puffin (sea parrot) token coinage which, by virtue of being ruled illegal by a British court, acquired a sentimental value greatly in excess of its dubious numismatic one. Jack Haywood, a British millionaire, purchased Lundy in 1969 for 150,000 pounds and gave it to the British people.

RULERS

British

TOKEN ISSUES

1/2 PUFFIN

BRONZE

Y#	Date	Mintage	Fine	VF	XF	Unc
1	1929	.050	1.75	2.75	4.50	7.50

H#	Date	Mintage	Fine	VF	XF	Unc
3	1965	3,000	—	—	Proof	6.50
		NICKEL-BRASS				
3a	1965	3,000	—	—	Proof	6.50
		GOLD				
3b	1965	50 pcs.	—	—	Proof	—

PUFFIN

BRONZE

Y#	Date	Mintage	Fine	VF	XF	Unc
2	1929	.050	3.00	4.00	7.50	12.50

H#	Date	Mintage	Fine	VF	XF	Unc
4	1965	3,000	—	—	Proof	6.50
		NICKEL-BRASS				
4a	1965	3,000	—	—	Proof	6.50
		GOLD				
4b	1965	50 pcs.	—	—	Proof	—

NCLT ISSUES

PROOF SETS

STANDARD METALS

KM#	Date	Mintage	Identification	Issue Price	Mkt. Val.
101	1965(4)	3,000	H3,3a,4,4a	—	22.50
102	1965(4)	25	3b, 4b (Two each)	—	—

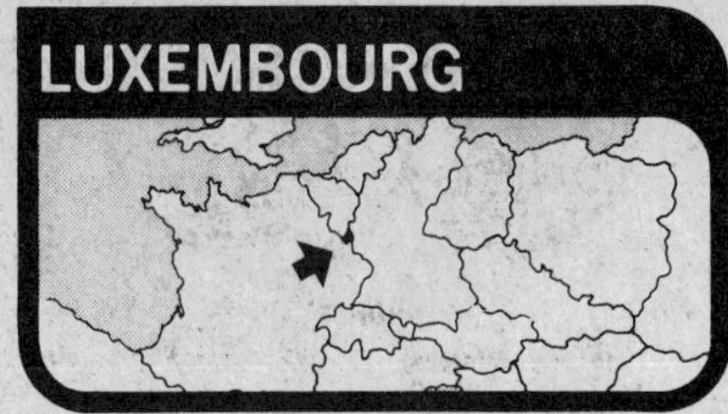

The Grand Duchy of Luxembourg, a sovereign constitutional monarchy located in western Europe between Belgium, Germany and France, has an area of 999 sq. mi. (2,587 sq. km.) and a population of 358,000. Capital: Luxembourg. The economy is based on steel - Luxembourg's per capita production of 16 tons is the highest in the world.

Founded about 963, Luxembourg was a prominent country of the Holy Roman Empire; one of its sovereigns became Holy Roman Emperor as Henry VII, 1308. After being made a duchy by Emperor Charles IV, 1534, Luxembourg passed under the domination of Burgundy, Spain, Austria and France, 1443-1815, regaining autonomy under the Treaty of Vienna, 1815, as a grand duchy in union with the Netherlands, though ostensibly a member of the German Confederation. When Belgium seceded from the Kingdom of the Netherlands, 1830, Luxembourg was forced to cede its greater western section to Belgium. The tiny duchy left the German Confederation in 1867 when the Treaty of London recognized it as an independent state and guaranteed its perpetual neutrality. Luxembourg was occupied by Germany and liberated by American troops in both World Wars, and is the resting place of 5,000 American soldiers, including Gen. George S. Patton.

RULERS

Austrian 1780-1795
William III (Netherlands), 1849-1890
Adolphe, 1890-1905
William IV, 1905-1912
Marie Adelaide, 1912-1919
Charlotte, 1919-1964
Jean, 1964—

MINT MARKS

A - Paris
(b) - Brussels, privy marks only
H - Gunzburg
(u) - Utrecht, privy marks only

PRIVY MARKS

Brussels - angels head, two headed eagle
Paris - anchor, hand, (1846-60)
Paris - anchor, bee, (1860-79)
Utrecht - sword, Mercury's staff

MONETARY SYSTEM

(Until 1795)
4 Liards = 1 Sol

DEMI (1/2) LIARD

COPPER
Obv: Rampant lion on crowned shield. Rev: Value, date.

C#	Date	Mintage	VG	Fine	VF
11	1783	1.362	3.75	7.50	12.50
	1784	1.466	3.75	7.50	12.50
	1789	1.566	3.75	7.50	12.50

2 LIARDS

COPPER

12	1789	.459	22.50	47.50	75.00

SOL

COPPER
Obv: Arms, IOS.D.G.R.I.H.B.R.DUX. LUXEMB. around. Rev: Value, date.

C#	Date	Mintage	VG	Fine	VF
13	1786	.400	15.00	30.00	50.00

Obv: Arms, IOS. II. D.G.R.IMP.S.A.H.B.R.DUX. LUXEMB. around.

13.1	1789	.071	15.00	30.00	50.00

16	1790H	.648	11.50	22.50	35.00

COPPER, cast

C#	Date	Mintage	Good	VG	Fine
19	1795	—	17.50	35.00	60.00

COPPER, struck

C#	Date	Mintage	VG	Fine	VF
19a	1795	—	Reported, not confirmed		

3 SOLS

BILLON
Obv: Arms, LEOP.II.D.G.HV.BO.REX.DVX.LVXEMB. around. Rev: Value, date.

C#	Date	Mintage	Fine	VF	XF
17	1790H	1.164	22.50	45.00	75.00

6 SOLS

BILLON
Obv: Arms, IOS.II.D.G.R.IMP.S.A.H.B.R.DUX. LUXEMB. around. Rev: Value, date.

14	1786	.071	17.50	35.00	60.00

Obv: Legend rotated 180 degrees.

14a	1789	.053	35.00	70.00	125.00

Obv: Arms, LEOP.II.D.G.HV.BO.REX.DVX.LVXEMB. around.

18	1790H	.728	35.00	70.00	125.00

12 SOLS

BILLON

15	1786	.037	45.00	90.00	150.00
	1789	.054	45.00	90.00	150.00

72 ASSES (SOLS)

SILVER

C#	Date	Mintage	VF	XF	Unc
20	1795	—	750.00	1650.	2850.

MONETARY REFORM

100 Centimes = 1 Franc

2-1/2 CENTIMES

BRONZE

Y#	Date	Mintage	VF	XF	Unc
1	1854A	.640	3.00	7.00	20.00
	1870(u)	.210	5.00	10.00	25.00
	1901(u)	.800	2.00	3.50	11.50
	1908(u)	.400	2.50	4.00	12.50

5 CENTIMES

BRONZE

2	1854(u)	.680	4.00	10.00	20.00
	1855A	.600	4.00	10.00	20.00
	1860A	.200	30.00	45.00	85.00
	1870(u)	.300	4.50	11.50	23.50

COPPER-NICKEL

10 (5)	1901	2.000	.75	1.50	3.00

12	1908	1.500	1.00	1.75	4.50

Y#	Date	Mintage	VF	XF	Unc
(8)					

ZINC

Y#	Date	Mintage	VF	XF	Unc
4 (9)	1915	1.200	2.50	5.50	12.50

IRON

Y#	Date	Mintage	VF	XF	Unc
7 (12)	1918	1.200	2.50	5.00	10.00
	1921	.600	3.50	7.50	15.00
	1922	.400	15.00	30.00	50.00

COPPER-NICKEL

Y#	Date	Mintage	VF	XF	Unc
13 (18)	1924	3.000	.35	.75	2.50

BRONZE

Y#	Date	Mintage	VF	XF	Unc
21 (25)	1930	5.000	.25	.60	2.00

10 CENTIMES

BRONZE

Y#	Date	Mintage	VF	XF	Unc
3	1854(u)	.500	30.00	50.00	100.00
	1855A	1.200	3.00	7.50	20.00
	1860A	.900	3.50	8.50	23.50
	1865A	1.000	3.00	7.50	20.00
	1870(u) dot above engravers name on reverse	1.300	3.00	6.50	17.50
	1870(u) w/o dot above engravers name on reverse	Inc. Ab.	3.00	6.50	17.50

COPPER-NICKEL

Y#	Date	Mintage	VF	XF	Unc
11 (6)	1901	4.000	.75	1.50	4.50

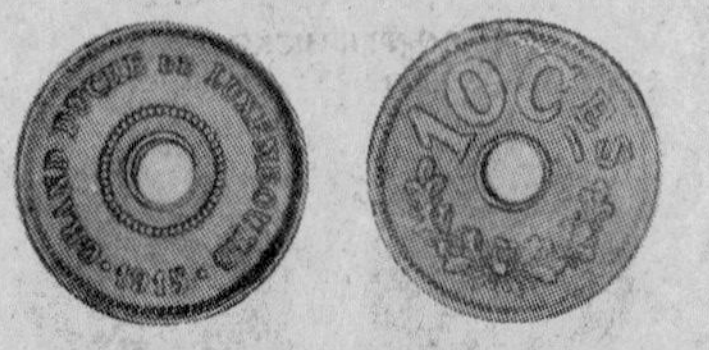

ZINC

Y#	Date	Mintage	VF	XF	Unc
5 (10)	1915	1.400	3.00	5.00	15.00

IRON

Y#	Date	Mintage	VF	XF	Unc
8 (13)	1918	1.603	3.50	7.50	17.50
	1921	.626	4.50	9.00	20.00
	1923	.350	15.00	30.00	50.00

COPPER-NICKEL

Y#	Date	Mintage	VF	XF	Unc
14 (19)	1924	3.500	.40	.85	2.50

BRONZE

Y#	Date	Mintage	VF	XF	Unc
22 (26)	1930	5.000	.25	.60	2.00

25 CENTIMES

ZINC

Y#	Date	Mintage	VF	XF	Unc
6 (11)	1916	.800	3.50	7.50	15.00

IRON

Y#	Date	Mintage	VF	XF	Unc
9 (14)	1919	.804	6.50	12.50	25.00
	1920	.800	5.00	10.00	21.50
	1922	.600	5.00	10.00	21.50

COPPER-NICKEL

Y#	Date	Mintage	VF	XF	Unc
15 (22)	1927	2.500	.75	1.25	3.00

BRONZE

Y#	Date	Mintage	VF	XF	Unc
15b (27)	1930	1.000	.75	1.50	4.00

COPPER-NICKEL

Y#	Date	Mintage	VF	XF	Unc
15a (27a)	1938	2.000	.75	1.50	4.00

BRONZE

Y#	Date	Mintage	VF	XF	Unc
25 (30)	1946	4.000	.15	.25	.75
	1947	4.000	.15	.25	.75

ALUMINUM

Y#	Date	Mintage	VF	XF	Unc
25a (30a)	1954	7.000	—	—	.10
	1957	3.020	—	—	.10
	1960	3.020	—	—	.10
	1963	4.000	—	—	.10
	1965	2.000	—	—	.10
	1967	3.000	—	—	.10
	1968	.600	—	.10	.25
	1970	4.000	—	—	.10
	1972	4.000	—	—	.10

50 CENTIMES

NICKEL

Y#	Date	Mintage	VF	XF	Unc
16 (28)	1930	2.000	.40	.75	2.25

FRANC

NICKEL

Y#	Date	Mintage	VF	XF	Unc
17 (20)	1924	1.000	.75	1.25	2.25
	1928	2.000	.50	1.00	2.00
	1935	1.000	.75	1.25	2.25

COPPER-NICKEL

Y#	Date	Mintage	VF	XF	Unc
24 (29)	1939	5.000	.75	1.75	4.00

Y#	Date	Mintage	VF	XF	Unc
26 (31)	1946	4.000	.35	.50	1.00
	1947	2.000	.40	.75	1.00

Y#	Date	Mintage	VF	XF	Unc
26a (32)	1952	5.000	.25	.50	1.00

Y#	Date	Mintage	VF	XF	Unc
26b	1953	2.000	.10	.15	.35
(32a)	1955	1.000	.10	.15	.35
	1957	2.000	.10	.15	.35
	1960	2.000	.10	.15	.35
	1962	2.000	.10	.15	.35
	1964	2.000	.10	.15	.30

Y#	Date	Mintage	VF	XF	Unc
34	1965	3.000	—	.10	.15
(41)	1966	1.000	—	.10	.15
	1968	3.000	—	.10	.15
	1970	3.000	—	.10	.15
	1972	3.000	—	.10	.15
	1973	3.000	—	.10	.15
	1976	3.000	—	.10	.15
	1977	1.000	—	.10	.15
	1978	1.000	—	.10	.15
	1980	—	—	—	—

2 FRANCS

NICKEL

Y#	Date	Mintage	VF	XF	Unc
18	1924	1.000	2.25	4.00	7.50
(21)					

5 FRANCS

8.0000 gm., .750 SILVER, .1607 oz ASW

Y#	Date	Mintage	VF	XF	Unc
19	1929	2.000	BV	5.00	15.00
(23)					

COPPER-NICKEL

Y#	Date	Mintage	VF	XF	Unc
27	1949	2.000	.75	1.25	2.50
(36)					

Y#	Date	Mintage	VF	XF	Unc
31	1962	2.000	.25	.40	.75
(37)					

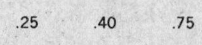

Y#	Date	Mintage	VF	XF	Unc
35	1971	1.000	.20	.30	.50
(42)	1976	1.000	.20	.30	.50
	1979	1.000	.20	.30	.50

10 FRANCS

13.3000 gm., .750 SILVER, .3207 oz ASW

Y#	Date	Mintage	VF	XF	Unc
20	1929	1.000	BV	12.00	30.00
(24)					

NICKEL

Y#	Date	Mintage	VF	XF	Unc
36	1971	3.000	.40	.50	.75
(43)	1972	3.000	.40	.50	.75
	1974	3.000	.40	.50	.75
	1976	3.000	.40	.50	.75
	1977	3.000	.40	.50	.75
	1978	3.000	.40	.50	.75

20 FRANCS

8.5000 gm., .835 SILVER .2282 oz ASW
600th Anniversary John the Blind

Y#	Date	Mintage	VF	XF	Unc
28	1946	.100	7.00	8.50	10.00
(33)					

6.4516 gm., .900 GOLD .1867 oz AGW
Marriage Commemorative
Prince Jean and Princess Josephine Charlotte

Fr#	Date	Mintage	VF	XF	Unc
12	1953	—	BV	125.00	150.00

BRONZE

Y#	Date	Mintage	VF	XF	Unc
37	1980	—	—	—	—

50 FRANCS

12.5000 gm., .835 SILVER .3356 oz ASW
600th Anniversary John the Blind

Y#	Date	Mintage	VF	XF	Unc
29	1946	.100	10.00	12.00	15.00
(34)					

100 FRANCS

25.0000 gm., .835 SILVER .6711 oz ASW
600th Anniversary John the Blind

Y#	Date	Mintage	VF	XF	Unc
30	1946	.100	20.00	27.50	35.00
(35)	1946 without designer's name (restrike)		—	—	125.00

18.0000 gm., .835 SILVER .4832 oz ASW

Y#	Date	Mintage	VF	XF	Unc
32	1963	.050	BV	17.50	22.50
(38)					

Y#	Date	Mintage	VF	XF	Unc
38 (40)	1964	.054	BV	15.00	20.00

250 FRANCS

25.0000 gm., .900 SILVER, .7234 oz ASW
Millennium Commemorative

Y#	Date	Mintage	VF	XF	Unc
33 (39)	1963	.020	50.00	100.00	150.00

8500 of the above pieces were 'dark toned' at the Mint, and as such command a premium.

NCLT ISSUES

PATTERNS

KM#	Date	Mintage	Identification	Mkt.Val.
1	1889	100	5 Centimes, w/ESSAI, Copper	85.00
2	1889	—	5 Centimes, w/ESSAI, Silver	200.00
3	1889	100	10 Centimes, w/ESSAI, Copper, large arms	90.00
4	1889	—	10 Centimes, w/ESSAI, Silver	200.00
5	1889	50	10 Centimes, w/ESSAI, Copper, small arms	—

KM#	Date	Mintage	Identification	Mkt.Val.
6	1889	—	5 Francs, w/ESSAI, Copper	100.00
7	1889	50	5 Francs, w/ESSAI, Tin	—
8	1889	—	5 Francs, w/ESSAI,Piefort, Tin	—
9	1889	50	5 Francs, w/ESSAI, Silver	400.00
10	1901	—	2-1/2 Centimes, Copper	—
11	1901	100	2-1/2 Centimes, Silver	—
12	1901	100	5 Centimes, Copper, w/o denomination	—
13	1901	100	5 Centimes, Nickel, w/o denomination	—
14	1901	100	5 Centimes, Nickel, w/o denomination	—
15	1901	50	5 Centimes, Silver, w/o denomination	—
16	1901	20	5 Centimes, Gold, w/o denomination	—
17	1901	100	10 Centimes, Copper, w/o denomination	—
18	1901	100	10 Centimes, Nickel, w/o denomination	—
19	1901	100	10 Centimes, Nickel, large letters, plain edge	—
20	1901	100	10 Centimes, Nickel, large letters, milled edge	—
21	1901	50	10 Centimes, Silver, large letters	—
22	1901	20	10 Centimes, Gold, w/o denomination	—
23	ND	50	1 Franc, Nickel, head of William	—
24	1914	100	50 Centimes, w/ESSAI, Copper	—
25	1914	3,000	50 Centimes, w/ESSAI, Silver	40.00

KM#	Date	Mintage	Identification	Mkt.Val.
26	1914	100	1 Franc, w/ESSAI, Copper	—
27	1914	3,000	1 Franc, w/ESSAI, Silver	50.00
28	1914	100	2 Francs, w/ESSAI, Copper	—
29	1914	3,000	2 Francs, w/ESSAI, Silver	60.00

NOTE: Restruck after WW I.

KM#	Date	Mintage	Identification	Mkt.Val.
30	1917	—	5 Centimes, Copper, crossed L's on rev.	—
31	1917	—	10 Centimes, Copper, crossed L's on rev.	—
32	1923	100	1 Franc, Aluminum	—
33	1923	100	1 Franc, Bronze	—
34	1923	100	1 Franc, Nickel	—
35	1923	100	1 Franc, Silver	—
36	1923	100	2 Francs, Pewter	—
37	1923	100	2 Francs, Aluminum	—
38	1923	100	2 Francs, Bronze	—
39	1923	100	2 Francs, Nickel	—
40	1923	100	2 Francs, Silver	—
41	1924	100	1 Franc, Copper	—
42	1924	100	1 Franc, Bronze	—
43	1924	100	1 Franc, Silver	—
44	1924	100	2 Francs, Copper	—
45	1924	100	2 Francs, Bronze	—
46	1927	100	25 Centimes, Bronze, Piefort	—
47	1929	50	5 Francs, w/ESSAI, Copper	30.00
48	1929	50	5 Francs, w/ESSAI, Bronze	30.00
49	1929	50	10 Francs, w/ESSAI, Copper	40.00
50	1929	50	10 Francs, w/ESSAI, Bronze	40.00
51	1938	100	25 Centimes, Copper-Nickel, Piefort	—
52	1939	50	1 Franc, Silver	—
53	1939	—	1 Franc, Gold	—
54	1942	—	5 Francs, Zinc	—
55	1942	—	5 Francs, Nickel	—
56	1945	100	25 Centimes, w/ESSAI, Copper, 25 at top	20.00
57	1945	100	25 Centimes, w/ESSAI, Copper, 25 at upper right	—
58	1946	100	25 Centimes, w/ESSAI, Copper	15.00
59	1946	500	25 Centimes, w/ESSAI, Copper	—
60	1946	500	25 Centimes, w/ESSAI, Silver	35.00
61	1946	500	1 Franc, w/ESSAI, Copper, plain edge	25.00
62	1946	100	1 Franc, w/ESSAI, Copper, milled edge	20.00
63	1946	500	1 Franc, w/ESSAI, Silver, plain edge	—
64	1946	100	1 Franc, w/ESSAI, Silver, milled edge	45.00
65	1946	100	1 Franc, w/ESSAI, Silver, small letters	—
66	1946	100	20 Francs, w/ESSAI, Copper	—
67	1946	50	20 Francs, w/ESSAI, Silver	50.00
68	1946	—	20 Francs, w/ESSAI, Gold	—
69	1946	100	50 Francs, w/ESSAI, Copper	—
70	1946	50	50 Francs, w/ESSAI, Silver	75.00
71	1946	—	50 Francs, w/ESSAI, Gold	—
72	1946	100	100 Francs, w/ESSAI, Copper	—
73	1946	50	100 Francs, w/ESSAI, Silver	125.00
74	1946	—	100 Francs, w/ESSAI, Gold	—
75	1947	100	2 Francs, Copper-Nickel	—

KM#	Date	Mintage	Identification	Mkt.Val.
76	1947	100	5 Francs, Copper-Nickel	—
77	1949	50	5 Francs, w/ESSAI, Copper	15.00
78	1949	50	5 Francs, w/ESSAI, Bronze	—
79	1962	50	5 Francs, w/ESSAI, Copper-Nickel	15.00
80	1962	50	5 Francs, w/ESSAI, Silver	45.00
81	1962	50	5 Francs, w/ESSAI, Gold	150.00
82	1963	50	100 Francs, w/ESSAI, Bronze	—
83	1963	50	100 Francs, w/ESSAI, Silver	150.00
84	1963	50	100 Francs, w/ESSAI, Gold	300.00
85	1963	200	250 Francs, w/ESSAI, Bronze	40.00
86	1963	200	250 Francs, w/ESSAI, Silver	250.00
87	1963	200	250 Francs, w/ESSAI, Gold	600.00
88	1964	200	100 Francs, w/ESSAI, Bronze	40.00
89	1964	200	100 Francs, w/ESSAI, Silver	110.00
90	1964	200	100 Francs, w/ESSAI, Gold	300.00

MACAO

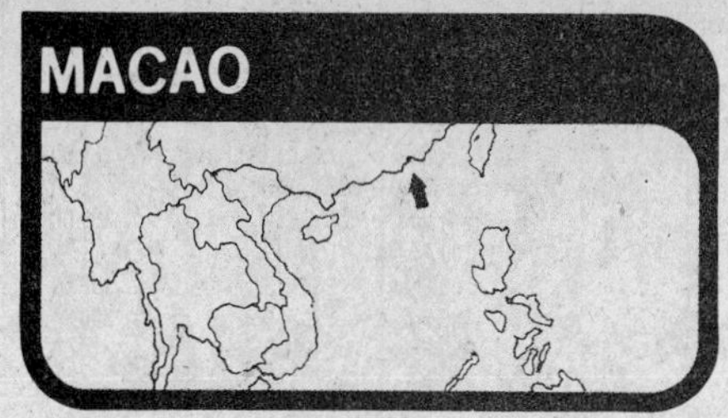

The Province of Macao, a Portuguese overseas province located in the South China Sea 35 miles southwest of Hong Kong, consists of the peninsula of Macao and the islands of Taipa and Coloane. It has an area of 6 sq. mi. (15.5 sq. km.) and a population of 266,000. Capital: Macao. Macao's economy is based on light industry, commerce, tourism, fishing, and gold trading -- Macao is one of the few entirely free markets for gold in the world. Cement, textiles, firecrackers, vegetable oils, and metal products are exported.

Established by the Portuguese in 1557, Macao is the oldest European settlement in the Far East. The Chinese, while agreeing to Portuguese settlement, did not recognize Portuguese sovereign rights and the Portuguese remained largely under control of the Chinese until 1849, when the Portuguese abolished the Chinese custom house and declared the independence of the port. The Manchu government formally recognized the Portuguese right to 'perpetual occupation' of Macao in 1887, but its boundaries are still not delimited.

RULERS

Portuguese

MONETARY SYSTEM

100 Avos = 1 Pataca

5 AVOS

BRONZE

Y#	Date	Mintage	VF	XF	Unc
1	1952	.500	.50	1.25	3.50

NICKEL-BRASS

Y#	Date	Mintage	VF	XF	Unc
1a	1967	5.000	—	.10	.25

10 AVOS

BRONZE

Y#	Date	Mintage	VF	XF	Unc
2	1952	12.500	.25	.50	1.25

NICKEL-BRASS

Y#	Date	Mintage	VF	XF	Unc
2a	1967	6.625	.15	.20	.30
	1968	5.675	.15	.20	.30
	1969	2.380	—	.10	.30
	1975	20.000	—	.10	.25
	1976	Inc. Ab.	—	.10	.25

50 AVOS

COPPER-NICKEL

Y#	Date	Mintage	VF	XF	Unc
3	1952	2.560	.30	.60	1.50

Y#	Date	Mintage	VF	XF	Unc
3a	1972	6.440	.15	.35	.75
	1973	2.295	.25	.35	.75

Y#	Date	Mintage	VF	XF	Unc
A3	1978	—	—	.30	.65

PATACA

2.5000 gm., .720 SILVER, .0578 oz ASW

Y#	Date	Mintage	VF	XF	Unc
4	1952	4.500	2.00	2.50	4.00

NICKEL

Y#	Date	Mintage	VF	XF	Unc
6	1968	5.000	.35	.50	1.25
	1972	.130	—	—	—
	1975	6.000	.20	.30	1.00

5 PATACAS

15.0000 gm., .720 SILVER, .3472 oz ASW

Y#	Date	Mintage	VF	XF	Unc
5	1952	.900	11.00	12.00	13.50

9.8700 gm., .650 SILVER, .2062 oz ASW

Y#	Date	Mintage	VF	XF	Unc
5a	1971	.500	6.50	7.50	9.00

20 PATACAS

18.0000 gm., .650 SILVER, .3762 oz ASW
Opening Of Macao-Taipa Bridge

Y#	Date	Mintage	VF	XF	Unc
7	1974	1.000	11.50	12.50	15.00
	1974	.010	—	Proof	25.00

100 PATACAS

28.2800 gm., .925 SILVER, .8411 oz ASW
25th Anniversary of Grand Prix
Obv: Similar to Y#8a.

Y#	Date	Mintage	VF	XF	Unc
8	1978	5,500		— Proof only	—

NOTE: Very few coins were released because of sponsors appearing on race car.

Y#	Date	Mintage	VF	XF	Unc
8a	1978	5,500		— Proof only	—

Year of the Goat
Obv: Similar to 500 Patacas, Y#11.

Y#	Date	Mintage	VF	XF	Unc
10	1979	5,500	— Proof only		50.00
		Year Of The Monkey			
12	1980		Proof only		—

500 PATACAS

7.9600 gm., .917 GOLD, .2347 oz AGW
25th Anniversary of Grand Prix
Similar to 100 Patacas, Y#8.

Y#	Date	Mintage	VF	XF	Unc
9	1978	5,500	— Proof only		—
		Similar to 100 Patacas, Y#8a.			
9a	1978	5,500	— Proof only		—

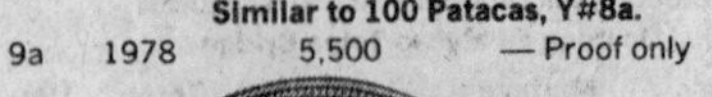

Year of the Goat

Y#	Date	Mintage	VF	XF	Unc
11	1979	5,500	— Proof only		200.00

1000 PATACAS

15.9800 gm., .917 GOLD, .4711 oz AGW
Year Of The Monkey

Y#	Date	Mintage	VF	XF	Unc
13	1980	5,500	Proof only		750.00

NCLT ISSUES

PROVAS (Pr)

STANDARD METALS
Stamped 'PROVA' in field

Y#	Date	Mintage	Identification	Issue Price	Mkt Val.
Pr1	1952	—	5 Avos	—	20.00
Pr1a	1967	—	5 Avos	—	20.00
Pr2	1952	—	10 Avos	—	20.00
Pr2a	1967	—	10 Avos	—	20.00
Pr2a	1968	—	10 Avos	—	20.00
Pr2a	1969	—	10 Avos	—	20.00
Pr3	1952	—	50 Avos	—	30.00
Pr3a	1972	—	50 Avos	—	30.00
Pr3a	1973	—	50 Avos	—	30.00
Pr4	1952	—	Pataca	—	45.00
Pr6	1968	—	Pataca	—	30.00
Pr6	1975	—	Pataca	—	30.00
Pr5	1952	—	5 Patacas	—	45.00
Pr5a	1971	—	5 Patacas	—	45.00
Pr7	1971	—	20 Patacas	—	50.00

MADAGASCAR

The Democratic Republic of Madagascar, an independent member of the French Community located in the Indian Ocean 250 miles (402 km.) off the southeast coast of Africa, has an area of 228,000 sq. mi. (590,517 sq. km.) and a population of 8.1 million. Capital: Antananarivo. The economy is primarily agricultural; large bauxite deposits are presently being developed. Coffee, vanilla, graphite, and rice are exported.

Diago Diaz, a Portuguese navigator, sighted the island of Madagascar on Aug. 10, 1500, when his ship became separated from an India-bound fleet. Attempts at settlement by the British during the reign of Charles I and by the French during the 17th and 18th centuries were of no avail, and the island became a refuge and supply base for Indian Ocean pirates. Despite considerable influence on the island, the British accepted the imposition of a French protectorate in 1886 in return for French recognition of Britain's sphere of influence in Zanzibar. Madagascar was made a French colony in 1896 after absolute control had been established by military force. Britain occupied the island after the fall of France, 1942, to prevent its seizure by the Japanese, returning it to the Free French in 1943. On Oct. 14, 1958, following a decade of intermittent but bitter warfare, Madagascar, as the Malagasy Republic, became an autonomous state within the French Community. On June 27, 1960, it became a sovereign, independent nation, though remaining nominally within the French Community. The Malagasy Republic was renamed the Democratic Republic of Madagascar in 1976.

MONETARY SYSTEM

100 Centimes = 1 Franc

MINTMARKS

(a) - Paris, privy marks only

50 CENTIMES

BRONZE

Y#	Date	Mintage	VF	XF	Unc
1	1943(a)	4.000	2.50	5.00	10.00

FRANC

BRONZE

Y#	Date	Mintage	VF	XF	Unc
2	1943(a)	5.000	5.00	9.00	35.00

ALUMINUM

Y#	Date	Mintage	VF	XF	Unc
3	1948(a)	7.400	.20	.30	1.00
	1958(a)	2.600	.10	.20	1.00

2 FRANCS

ALUMINUM

Y#	Date	Mintage	VF	XF	Unc
4	1948(a)	10.000	.25	.40	1.25

5 FRANCS

ALUMINUM

Y#	Date	Mintage	VF	XF	Unc
5	1953(a)	30.012	.40	.50	1.00

10 FRANCS

ALUMINUM-BRONZE

Y#	Date	Mintage	VF	XF	Unc
6	1953(a)	25.000	.15	.50	1.50

20 FRANCS

ALUMINUM-BRONZE

Y#	Date	Mintage	VF	XF	Unc
7	1953(a)	15.000	.20	.60	2.00

NCLT ISSUES

ESSAIS (E)

Standard metals unless otherwise noted

Y#	Date	Mintage	Identification	Issue Price	Mkt Val.
E3a	1948(a)	2,000	1 Franc, Copper-Nickel	—	15.00
E4a	1948(a)	2,000	2 Francs, Copper-Nickel	—	16.00
E5	1953(a)	1,200	5 Francs	—	20.00
E6	1953(a)	1,200	10 Francs	—	23.00
E7	1953(a)	1,200	20 Francs	—	25.00

PIEFORTS WITH ESSAI (PE)

Double Thickness
Standard metals unless otherwise noted

Y#	Date	Mintage	Identification	Issue Price	Mkt Val.
PE3	1948(a)	104	1 Franc	—	100.00
PE4	1948(a)	104	2 Francs	—	110.00
PE5	1953(a)	104	5 Francs	—	120.00
PE6	1953(a)	104	10 Francs	—	130.00
PE7	1953(a)	104	20 Francs	—	140.00

MALAGASY REPUBLIC

MINTMARKS

(a) - Paris, privy marks only

MONETARY SYSTEM

100 Centimes = 1 Franc

FRANC

STAINLESS STEEL

Y#	Date	Mintage	VF	XF	Unc
8	1965(a)	1.170	.10	.15	.30
(1)	1966(a)	—	.10	.15	.35
	1970(a)	—	.10	.15	.30
	1974(a)	1.250	.10	.15	.30

2 FRANCS

STAINLESS STEEL

Y#	Date	Mintage	VF	XF	Unc
9	1965(a)	.760	.15	.25	.75
(2)	1970(a)	—	.10	.15	.40
	1974(a)	1.250	.10	.15	.40

5 FRANCS

STAINLESS STEEL

Y#	Date	Mintage	VF	XF	Unc
10	1966(a)	—	.10	.20	.50
(3)	1967(a)	—	.10	.20	.50
	1968(a)	7.500	.10	.20	.50
	1970(a)	—	.10	.20	.50
	1972(a)	12.400	.10	.20	.50

10 FRANCS

ALUMINUM-BRONZE
F.A.O. Issue

Y#	Date	Mintage	VF	XF	Unc
11	1970(a)	25.000	.15	.25	.75
(4)	1971(a)	Inc. Ab.	.15	.25	.60
	1972(a)	Inc. Ab.	.15	.25	.60
	1973(a)	Inc. Ab.	.15	.25	.60
	1974(a)	—	—	—	—
	1975(a)	—	—	—	—
	1976(a)	—	—	—	—

20 FRANCS

ALUMINUM-BRONZE
F.A.O. Issue

Y#	Date	Mintage	VF	XF	Unc
12	1970(a)	15.000	.20	.40	1.00
(5)	1971(a)	Inc. Ab.	.20	.50	1.35
	1972(a)	Inc. Ab.	.20	.40	1.00
	1973(a)	Inc. Ab.	.20	.40	1.00
	1974(a)	—	—	—	—
	1975(a)	—	—	—	—
	1976(a)	—	—	—	—

NCLT ISSUES

ESSAIS (E)

Standard metals unless otherwise noted

Y#	Date	Mintage	Identification	Issue Price	Mkt Val.
E1	1965(a)	—	1 Franc	—	25.00
E2	1965(a)	—	2 Francs	—	25.00
E3	1966(a)	—	5 Francs	—	25.00
E4	1970(a)	—	10 Francs	—	27.00
E5	1970(a)	—	20 Francs	—	30.00

FLEUR DE COIN SETS

KM#	Date	Mintage	Identification	Issue Price	Mkt. Val.
S1	1970(5)	1,500	Y1-5	2.75	20.00

DEMOCRATIC REPUBLIC

FRANC

STAINLESS STEEL

Y#	Date	Mintage	VF	XF	Unc
1	1975	2.355	.15	.25	.40

2 FRANCS

STAINLESS STEEL

Y#	Date	Mintage	VF	XF	Unc
2	1975	3.250	.25	.50	.75

MONETARY REFORM

MONETARY SYSTEM

5 Frances = 1 Ariary

10 ARIARY

9.0000 gm., .925 SILVER

Y#	Date	Mintage			
13 (6)	1978	5,000	— Proof only		15.00

NICKEL
F.A.O. Issue

Y#	Date	Mintage			
13a (6a)	1978	8.000	—	—	—

20 ARIARY

12.0000 gm., .925 SILVER

Y#	Date	Mintage			
14 (7)	1978	5,000	— Proof only		20.00

NICKEL
F.A.O. Issue

Y#	Date	Mintage			
14a (7a)	1978	8.000	—	—	—

NCLT ISSUES

PROOF SETS

KM#	Date	Mintage	Identification	Issue Price	Mkt. Val.
101	1978	5,000	Y6,7	38.00	

MADEIRA

The Madeira Islands, which belong to Portugal, are located 360 miles (492 km.) off the northwest coast of Africa. They have an area of 308 sq. mi. (797 sq. km.) and a population of 253,000. The group consists of two inhabited islands named Madeira and Porto Santo and two groups of uninhabited rocks named Desertas and Selvagens. Capital: Funchal. The two staple products are wine and sugar. Bananas and pineapples are also produced for export.

Although the evidence is insufficient, it is thought that the Phoenicians visited Madeira at an early period. It is also probable that the entire archipelago was explored in early times by Genoese adventurers; an Italian map dated 1351 shows the Madeira Islands quite clearly. The Portuguese navigator Goncalvez Zarco first sighted Porto Santo in 1418, having been driven there by a storm while he was exploring the coast of West Africa. Madeira itself was discovered in 1420. The islands were uninhabited when visited by Zarco, but their colonization was immediately begun by Prince Henry the Navigator, aided by the knights of the Order of Christ. British troops occupied the islands in 1801, and again in 1807-14.

RULERS

Portuguese

V (5) REIS

COPPER

Similar to 10 Reis, C#2.

C#	Date	Mintage	VG	Fine	VF	XF
1	1850	—	15.00	30.00	45.00	70.00

X (10) REIS

COPPER

C#	Date	Mintage	VG	Fine	VF	XF
2	1842	—	3.50	8.00	15.00	30.00
	1850	—	15.00	30.00	45.00	70.00
	1852	—	3.00	7.50	13.50	27.50

XX (20) REIS

COPPER

Similar to 10 Reis, C#2.

C#	Date	Mintage	VG	Fine	VF	XF
3	1842	—	6.00	15.00	25.00	50.00
	1852	—	8.00	20.00	30.00	55.00

MALAWI

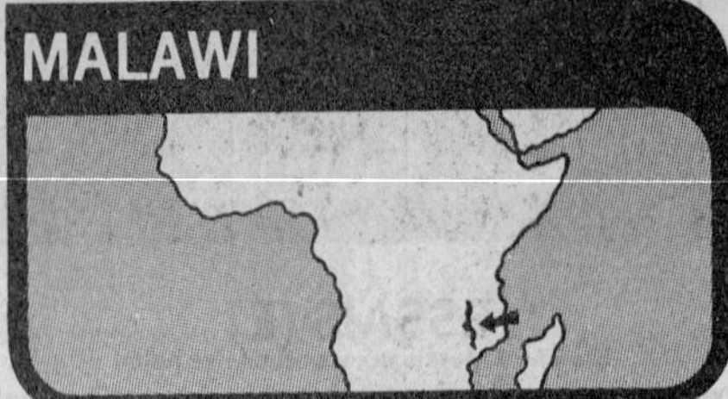

The Republic of Malawi (formerly Nyasaland), located in southeastern Africa to the west of Lake Malawi (Nyasa), has an area of 45,747 sq. mi. (118,484 sq. km.) and a population of 5.6 million. Capital: Lilongwe. The economy is predominantly agricultural. Tobacco, tea, peanuts and cotton are exported.

Although the Portuguese, heirs to the restless spirit of Prince Henry, were the first Europeans to reach the Malawi area, the first meaningful contact was made by missionary—explorer Dr. David Livingstone who arrived at Lake Malawi on Sept. 16, 1859, and remained to make extensive explorations in the 1860's. Subsequent clashes between settlements of Scottish missionaries and Arab slave traders, and the procurement of development rights by Cecil Rhodes, 1884, stimulated British interest and brought about the establishment of the Nyasaland protectorate in 1891. In 1953 Nyasaland reluctantly joined the Federation of Rhodesia and Nyasaland and, after prolonged protest, was granted self-government within the federation. Nyasaland became the independent nation of Malawi on July 6, 1964, and became a republic two years later. Malawi is a member of the Commonwealth of Nations. The president is the Chief of State and Head of Government.

NOTE: For earlier coinage see Rhodesia and Nyasaland.

RULERS

British, until 1964

MONETARY SYSTEM

12 Pence = 1 Shilling
2 Shillings = 1 Florin
5 Shillings = 1 Crown
20 Shillings = 1 Pound

PENNY

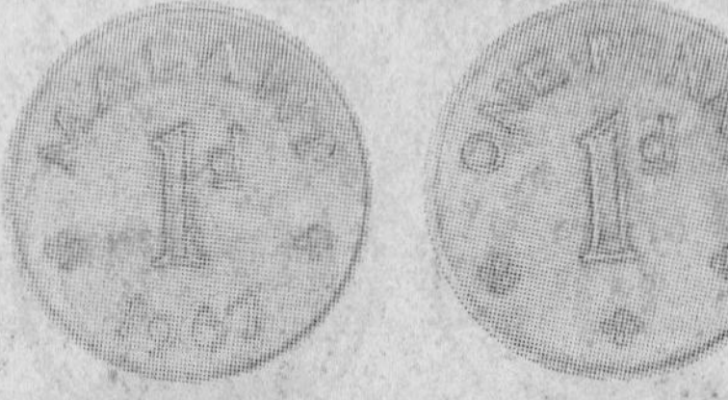

BRONZE

Y#	Date	Mintage	VF	XF	Unc
6	1967	6.000	.40	.50	1.00
	1968	3.600	1.00	1.50	3.50

6 PENCE

COPPER-NICKEL-ZINC

Y#	Date	Mintage	VF	XF	Unc
1	1964	14.800	.25	.40	.75
	1964	.010	—	Proof	2.50
	1967	6.000	1.00	2.50	5.00

SHILLING

COPPER-NICKEL-ZINC

Y#	Date	Mintage	VF	XF	Unc
2	1964	11.900	.50	.75	1.25
	1964	.010	—	Proof	3.00
	1968	3.000	2.50	4.00	6.00

FLORIN

COPPER-NICKEL-ZINC

Y#	Date	Mintage	VF	XF	Unc
3	1964	6.500	.75	1.25	2.00
	1964	.010	—	Proof	3.50

1/2 CROWN

COPPER-NICKEL-ZINC

Y#	Date	Mintage	VF	XF	Unc
4	1964	6.400	1.00	1.75	2.75
	1964	.010	—	Proof	4.50

CROWN

NICKEL-BRASS

Republic Day

Y#	Date	Mintage	VF	XF	Unc
5	1966	.020	—	Proof	8.50

DECIMAL COINAGE

100 Tambala = 1 Kwacha

TAMBALA

BRONZE

Y#	Date	Mintage	VF	XF	Unc
7	1971	15.000	—	.10	.15
	1971	4,000	—	Proof	1.00
	1973	5.000	—	.10	.15
	1974	12.500	—	.10	.15
	1975	—	—	.10	.15
	1976	10.000	—	—	.15

2 TAMBALA

BRONZE

Y#	Date	Mintage	VF	XF	Unc
8	1971	10.000	—	.10	.25
	1971	4,000	—	Proof	1.50
	1973	5.000	—	.10	.25
	1974	5.000	—	.10	.25
	1975	—	—	.10	.25
	1976	5.000	—	—	.25

5 TAMBALA

COPPER-NICKEL

Y#	Date	Mintage	VF	XF	Unc
9	1971	7.000	.10	.15	.35
	1971	4,000	—	Proof	2.00

10 TAMBALA

COPPER-NICKEL

Y#	Date	Mintage	VF	XF	Unc
10	1971	4.000	.15	.25	.50
	1971	4,000	—	Proof	2.50

20 TAMBALA

COPPER-NICKEL

Y#	Date	Mintage	VF	XF	Unc
11	1971	3.000	.30	.50	1.00
	1971	4,000	—	Proof	3.00

KWACHA

COPPER-NICKEL
Obv: Similar to 20 Tambala, Y#11.

Y#	Date	Mintage	VF	XF	Unc
12	1971	.020	1.50	2.25	4.00
	1971	4,000	—	Proof	4.50

5 KWACHA

28.2800 gm., .925 SILVER, .8411 oz ASW
Conservation Series

Y#	Date	Mintage	VF	XF	Unc
15	1978	—	—	27.50	30.00
	1978	—	—	Proof	40.00

35.0000 gm., .925 SILVER, 1.0409 oz ASW
Conservation Series

Y#	Date	Mintage	VF	XF	Unc
16	1978	—	—	32.50	40.00
	1978	—	—	Proof	50.00

10 KWACHA

35.0000 gm., .925 SILVER, 1.0409 oz ASW
10th Anniversary of Independence

Y#	Date	Mintage	VF	XF	Unc
13	1974	7,556	—	32.50	35.00
	1974	4,937	—	Proof	40.00

10th Anniversary of the Reserve Bank
Obv: Similar to Y#13.

Y#	Date	Mintage	VF	XF	Unc
14	1975	.020	—	32.50	35.00
	1975	.020	—	Proof	40.00

.900 GOLD

Y#	Date	Mintage	VF	XF	Unc
14a	1975	6,870	—	—	—

250 KWACHA

33.4300 gm., .900 GOLD, .9674 oz AGW
Conservation Series

Y#	Date	Mintage	VF	XF	Unc
17	1978	—	BV	BV	650.00
	1978	1,000	—	Proof	800.00

NCLT ISSUES

MINT SETS

KM#	Date	Mintage	Identification	Issue Price	Mkt. Val.
S1	1971(6)	10,000	Y7-12	3.30	5.00
S2	1978(2)	—	Y15,16	—	70.00

PROOF SETS

STANDARD METALS

KM#	Date	Mintage	Identification	Issue Price	Mkt. Val.
101	1964(4)	10,000	Y1-4	10.00	10.00
102	1971(6)	4,000	Y7-12	8.70	14.00
103	1978(2)	—	Y15,16	—	90.00

Listings For

MALAYA: refer to Malaysia

MALAYA & BRITISH BORNEO: refer to Malaysia

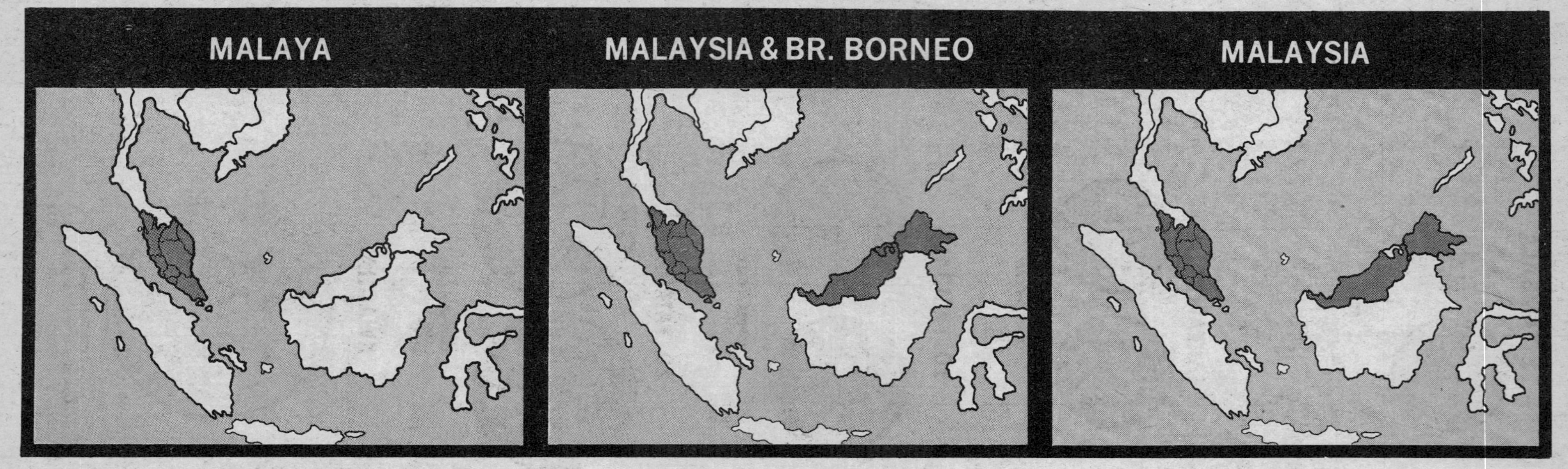
MALAYSIA
STRAITS SETTLEMENTS 1826-1939
PERLIS
KEDAH
PENANG
PERAK
SELANGOR
MALACCA
KELANTAN
TRENGGANU
PAHANG
NEGRI SEMBILAN
JOHORE
SINGAPORE
SUMATRA
BRUNEI
SABAH (NORTH BORNEO)
SARAWAK
BORNEO
CELEBES
MALAYA
MALAYSIA & BR. BORNEO
MALAYSIA
1939-1952
1952-1963
1963–

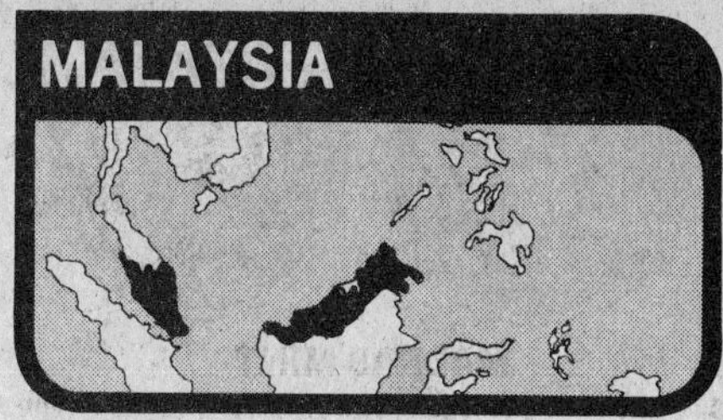

Malaysia, an independent federation of southeast Asia consisting of 11 states of West Malaysia on the Malay Peninsula and two states of East Malaysia on the island of Borneo, has an area of 127,316 sq. mi. (329,747 sq. km.) and a population of 12.1 million. Capital: Kuala Lumpur. The federation came into being on Sept. 16, 1963. Rubber, timber, tin, iron ore and bauxite are exported.

The constituent states of Malaysia are Johore, Kedah, Kelantan, Malacca, Negri Sembilan, Pahang, Penang, Perak, Perlis, Selangor and Trengganu of West Malaysia; and Sabah and Sarawak of East Malaysia. Singapore joined the federation in 1963, but broke away on Aug. 9, 1965, to become an independent republic. Malaysia is a member of the Commonwealth of Nations. The "Paramount Ruler" is Chief of State. The prime minister is Head of Government.

LOCAL ISSUES

MONETARY SYSTEM

10 Pitis = 1 Keping
900-4,000 Pitis = 1 Ringgit (Dollar)
1280 Trah = 1 Ringgit
100 Pice(Cents) = 1 Ringgit

NOTE: Many local merchant tokens, inscribed mainly in Chinese, exist for most of the Malay states. These have not been listed.

KEDAH

A state in northwestern Malaysia. Islam introduced in 15th century. Subject to Thailand from 1821-1909. Coins issued under governor TENGKU ANUM.

SULTANS

Ahmad Tajud-Din Halim, 1798-1843
Zainal Rashid al-Muazzam, 1843-1854
Ahmad Tajud-Din Mukarram, 1854-1879
Abdul-Hamim, 1882-1909

From 1821-1843, Kedah was actually under the control of the Siamese, and was ruled by Governor Tengku Anum.

TRAH

TIN, 23mm
Obv: Arabic leg: TAHUN ALIF 1224. Rev: Arabic leg: BALAD KEDAH DARU'L aman. Irregular center hole.

C#	Date	Mintage	Good	VG	Fine	VF
120	AH1224	—	10.00	20.00	30.00	40.00

24mm
Obv: Five-petaled lotus blossom. Rev: Arabic leg: BELANJA BALAD AL-PERLIS KEDAH-SANAT 1262. Irregular center hole.

C#	Date	Mintage	Good	VG	Fine	VF
140	AH1262	—	10.00	20.00	30.00	40.00

18mm
Obv: Crude 12-pointed star. Rev: Arabic leg: BELANJA BALAD KEDAH DARU'L-AMAN. Irregular center hole.

C#	Date	Mintage	Good	VG	Fine	VF
130	ND	—	12.50	17.50	25.00	35.00

KELANTAN

A state in northern Malaysia. Colonized by Javanese in 1300's. Subject to Thailand from 1780 to 1909.

SULTANS

Muhammed I 1800-1835
Muhammed II 1835-1886
Ahmad 1886-1889
Muhammed III 1889-1891
Mansur 1891-1899
Interregnum 1899-1902
Muhammed IV 1902-1919

PITIS

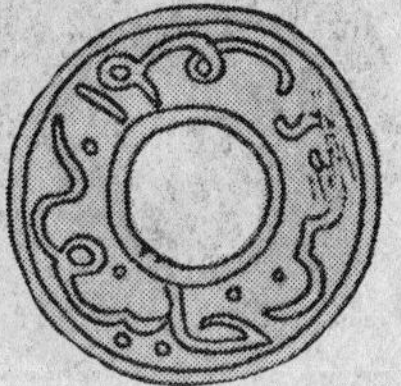

TIN, 24-29mm
Obv. Arabic leg: KHALIFAT AL-MU'MININ
Rev: Same. Many minor variations.

KM#	Date	Mintage	VG	Fine	VF	XF
1	ND	—	7.00	10.00	20.00	25.00

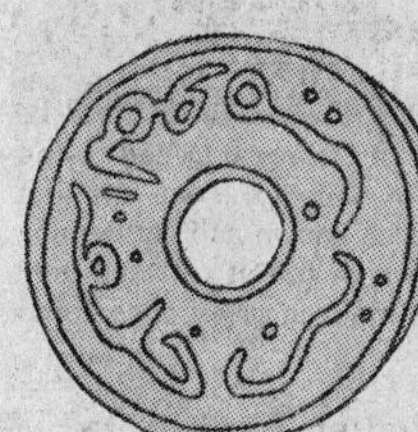

Obv: Similar to KM#1. Rev. Arabic leg: AL-JULUS KELANTAN

KM#	Date	Mintage	VG	Fine	VF	XF
2	ND	—	12.00	15.00	30.00	45.00

28mm
Obv. Arabic leg: Similar to KM#1. Rev: SANAT 1256.

KM#	Date	Mintage	VG	Fine	VF	XF
4	AH1256	—	15.00	20.00	25.00	35.00

NOTE: This type has also been attributed to Legeh.

Obv. Arabic leg: DURIBA FI JAMADAL AKHIR 1300. Rev. Arabic leg: DAMA SAMA MULKA DAULAT KELANTAN.

KM#	Date	Mintage	VG	Fine	VF	XF
5	AH1300	—	12.00	20.00	25.00	30.00

Obv. Arabic leg: ADIM MULKAHU BELANJAAN KERA JAAN KELANTAN. Rev. Arabic leg: SUNIA FI JUMADAL ULA SANAT 1314.

KM#	Date	Mintage	VG	Fine	VF	XF
10	AH1314	—	7.50	15.00	20.00	25.00

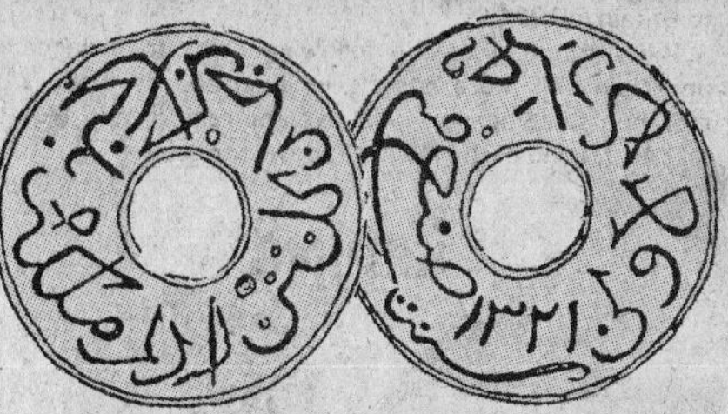

Obv. Arabic leg: BELANJAAN NEGRI KELANTAN ADAMA MULKAHU. Rev. Arabic leg: SUNIA FI JUMADAL ULA SANAT 1321.

KM#	Date	Mintage	VG	Fine	VF	XF
12	AH1321	—	7.50	15.00	20.00	25.00

Obv. Arabic leg: BELANJAAN KERAJAAN KELAN TAN. Rev. Arabic leg: DURIBA FI DHUL HIJJA SANAT 1321.

KM#	Date	Mintage	VG	Fine	VF	XF
15	AH1321	—	1.50	3.00	5.00	10.00

LEAD

KM#	Date	Mintage	VG	Fine	VF	XF
15a	AH1321	—	—	—	—	—

KEPING

TIN
Obv. Arabic leg: NEGRI KELANTAN SATU KEPING SANAT 1323. Rev: Uninscribed but obverse legend shows through in negative form.

KM#	Date	Mintage	VG	Fine	VF	XF
18	AH1323	—	10.00	15.00	20.00	30.00

10 KEPING

TIN
Obv. Arabic leg: BELANJAAN KERAJAAN KELANTIN SEPULOH KEPING. Rev. Arabic leg: SUNIA FI DHUL HIJJA SANAT 1321. Border of diamonds around legends.

KM#	Date	Mintage	VG	Fine	VF	XF
20	AH1321	—	10.00	16.00	25.00	35.00

LOCAL ISSUES

Kemasin

Town in Kelantan State

JOKOH

TIN, 29-30mm
Obv. Jawi leg: INI PAKAI DI KEMASIN SANAT 1300. Rev: Chinese inscription & 5 c/s. Two vars.

KM#	Date	Mintage	VG	Fine	VF	XF
30	AH1300	—	15.00	20.00	30.00	45.00

PATANI, PATTANI

Refer to Thailand Local Issues.

MALACCA

A state of Malaysia on the west coast. It was settled from Sumatra in the 1300's. Occupied by the Portuguese in 1511. Captured by the Dutch in 1641. Held by the British from 1795 to 1802 and 1811 to 1818. Ceded to Britain in 1824.

The attribution of the following coins to Malacca is uncertain. All were struck in England, on behalf of merchants in Singapore. All have an Arabic legend TANAH MELAYU (Land of the Malays) above a rooster.

KEPING

COPPER

Rev: Denomination at top written like a fraction.

KM#	Date	Mintage	Fine	VF	XF	Unc
8.1	AH1247	—	1.50	3.00	5.00	10.00
	Rev: Denomination written simply 1.					
8.2	AH1247	—	1.50	2.50	5.00	10.00
	AH1251	—	Reported, not confirmed			
	AH1147(error)		15.00	25.00	35.00	50.00
	AH1219(error)		2.25	5.00	8.00	15.00
	AH1241(error)		15.00	25.00	35.00	50.00
	AH1411(error)		3.50	7.50	12.50	18.00

NOTE: Some of these tokens may have been restruck at a later time. Some also exist in proof.

2 KEPING

COPPER

KM#	Date	Mintage	Fine	VF	XF	Unc
14	AH1247	—	8.50	12.50	20.00	32.50

PAHANG

A state on the east coast of Malaysia. Subject to the Suvyaya kingdom in Sumatra in the 1200's. Shuttled from native kingdom to native kingdom after 1450. Became one of the Federated Malay States in 1895.

The following coins were minted by prominent Chinese in Pahang by permission of Sultan Ahmed. They were intended for general circulation within Pahang. Many other pieces issued by merchants and gambling houses exist, but will not be listed here.

GOVERNORS

Bendahara Sewa Raja Tun Ali
1806-1857
Bendahara Sewa Raja Tun Mutahir
1857-1863

SULTANS

Ahmed Al Muazzam 1884-1914
Ruled As Governor Bendahara
Sewa Raja Ahmad From 1863 To 1884

1/2 CENT

TIN

Obv: Four Chinese characters CH'IEN SHENG T'UNG PAO. Rev. Arabic leg: PAHANG COMPANY and 1/2C.

KM#	Date	Mintage	Good	VG	Fine	VF
6	ND	—	10.00	15.00	18.00	22.00

Minted between 1884 and 1896.

CENT

TIN

Rev: 1 C

KM#	Date	Mintage	Good	VG	Fine	VF
9	ND	—	10.00	14.00	18.00	22.00

Minted between 1884 and 1896.

Obv: Value and four Chinese characters.
Rev: Date and Arabic legend.

KM#	Date	Mintage	Good	VG	Fine	VF
11	AH1301	—	14.00	20.00	30.00	42.50

PENANG (Pulu Penang-Prince of Wales Island)

An island off the west coast of Malaysia. Ceded to the British in 1791 by the sultan of Kedah and was the first British settlement in Malaya. Also known as Pulu Penang and Prince of Wales Island - which title it retained until 1867. Coins for the island were made in silver, copper and tin.

Acquired by the British East India Company in 1786.

MONETARY SYSTEM

100 Cents (Pice) = 1 Dollar

1/10 CENT (PICE)

COPPER, dump, 12-14mm
Similar to 1/2 Cent, C#273.

C#	Date	Mintage	VG	Fine	VF	XF
272	1787 with star		10.00	20.00	30.00	50.00
	1787 no star		12.50	25.00	35.00	60.00

NOTE: Varieties exist of 'with star' type.

1/2 CENT (PICE)

COPPER, dump, 18-20mm

C#	Date	Mintage	VG	Fine	VF	XF
273	1787	—	10.00	20.00	30.00	50.00

NOTE: Varieties exist.

COPPER

ROYAL MINT

C#	Date	Mintage	Fine	VF	XF	Unc
291.1	1810	1.720	10.00	15.00	20.00	40.00
	1810	—	—	—	Proof	120.00

MADRAS MINT

C#	Date	Mintage	Fine	VF	XF	Unc
291.2	1825	.145	12.00	20.00	30.00	60.00
	1828	.414	10.00	16.00	24.00	50.00

NOTE: Wreath varies from 21 to 26 lily cups.

CENT (PICE)

COPPER, dump, uniface

C#	Date	Mintage	VG	Fine	VF	XF
271	(1786)	—	10.00	25.00	35.00	60.00
	25-27mm **Similar to 1/2 Cent, C#273.**					
274	(1787)	—	10.00	25.00	35.00	60.00
	1787 last '7' inverted	—	16.50	30.00	55.00	75.00

TIN, uniface, 30.5 gm.
Obv: Initials GF (Governor Farguhar) in ring, counterstamped with Chinese character Ch'i.

C#	Date	Mintage	VG	Fine	VF	XF
281	(c.1805)	—	—	—	Rare	—

TIN, uniface, 30-32 gm.
Obv: Initials A & C (Anderson & Clubley) counterstamped with Chinese character Mei.

C#	Date	Mintage	VG	Fine	VF	XF
282	1809	—	—	—	Rare	—

COPPER

ROYAL MINT

Leaves on wreath go clockwise.

C#	Date	Mintage	Fine	VF	XF	Unc
292	1810 small date, small shield					
		1.827	6.00	15.00	25.00	40.00
	1810	—	—	—	Proof	120.00

MADRAS MINT

292.3	1825	.136	10.00	20.00	35.00	60.00
	1828	.235	5.00	17.50	30.00	50.00

NOTE: Wreath varies from 21 to 27 lily cups.

2 CENT (2 PICE)

COPPER

MADRAS MINT

293	1825	.130	10.00	20.00	40.00	75.00
	1828	.721	8.00	15.00	30.00	60.00

NOTE: Wreath varies from 24 to 28 lily cups.

1/10 DOLLAR

.903 SILVER, dump, 16-17mm
Similar to 1/4 Dollar, C#276.

C#	Date	Mintage	VG	Fine	VF	XF
275	1788	—	150.00	250.00	400.00	600.00

NOTE: Two varieties exist.

1/4 DOLLAR

.903 SILVER, dump

276	1788	—	450.00	700.00	1200.	1800.

1/2 DOLLAR

.903 SILVER, dump

277	1788	—	400.00	600.00	1000.	1500.

NOTE: Two varieties exist.

NCLT ISSUES

PATTERNS

KM#	Date	Mintage	Identification	Mkt.Val.
1	1810	—	Cent (Pice), Copper, leaves on wreath go counterclockwise	Rare
2	1810	—	Cent (Pice), Copper, leaves on wreath go clockwise	Rare

PERAK

A state on the west coast of Malaysia. Important tin deposits are in this state. Part of Malay kingdoms from early times. Perak was an independent state from 1824-1874. The only coin is one made in Birmingham, England and distributed by a Singapore importer.

SULTANS

Ahmadin ?-1806
Abdul-Malik Mansur 1806-1825
Abdullah Muazzam 1825-1830
Shahabud-Din Riayat 1831-1851
Abdullah Muhammad 1851-1857
Jafar Muazzam 1857-1865
Ali Al-Mukammal Inayat 1865-1871
Ismail Muabidin 1871-1874
Abdullah Muhammad 1874-1877
Yusuf Sharifud-Din Mufzal 1877-1887
Sir Idris Murshid Al-Azzam 1887-1916
Abdul-Jalil 1916-1918
Iskander 1918-?

KEPING

COPPER
Obv. Arabic leg: NEGRI PERAK (State of Perak).
Rev. Arabic leg: SATU KEPANG 1251 (one Keping AH 1251).

KM#	Date	Mintage	Fine	VF	XF	Unc
4	AH1251	—	8.00	12.00	18.00	25.00
	1251	—	—	—	Proof	80.00

This coin also exists in tin and in silvered bronze.

PERLIS

See State of Kedah

SELANGOR

A state on the west coast of Malaysia. Played a part in the trading programs of both the Dutch and the British. Signed a treaty with Britain in 1818 and Britain took control of the state in 1874. The only coin is one made in Birmingham, England and distributed by a Singapore importer.

SULTANS

Ibrahim ?-1826
Muhammad 1826-1857
Abdul-Samad 1857-1898
Sulaiman 1898-?

KEPING

COPPER
Obv. Arabic leg: NEGRI SELANGOR.
Rev. Arabic leg: SATU KEPING 1251.

3	AH1251	—	8.00	12.50	18.00	25.00

TRENGGANU

A state in eastern Malaysia on the shore of the South China Sea. Area of dispute between Malacca and Thailand with the latter emerging with possession. Trengganu became a British dependency in 1909.

SULTANS

Zainal Abidin II 1793-1808
Ahmad I 1808-1827
Abdul Rahman 1827-1831
Daud 1831
Mansur II 1831-1836
Muhammed 1836-1839
Baginda Omar 1839-1876
Ahmad II 1876-1881
Zainal Abidin III 1881-1918
Muhammed 1918-1920
Sulaiman 1920-1942

PITIS

TIN, 16-17mm
Obv: MALIK AL-ADIL. Rev: KHALIFAT AL-MU'MININ.

KM#	Date	Mintage	VG	Fine	VF	XF
4	ND	—	15.00	20.00	30.00	40.00

Believed struck during reign of Zainal Abidin II or shortly afterwards.

20-21mm. Blank reverse.
Arabic inscription: KALI MALIK AL-ADIL

6	ND	—	15.00	25.00	35.00	50.00

18mm. Uniface
Arabic inscription MALIK AL-ADIL

8	ND	—	15.00	20.00	30.00	40.00

24-28mm. Arabic legends on obv. MALIK AL-ADIL. Uniface.

10	ND(Vars)	—	10.00	15.00	20.00	30.00

Probably issued throughout first half of 19th century.

Similar to KM#10.

11	ND	—	15.00	25.00	35.00	50.00

Reverse blank.

KM#	Date	Mintage	VG	Fine	VF	XF
13	AH1213	—	15.00	25.00	35.00	50.00

16	AH1222	—	15.00	25.00	35.00	50.00

Legend points outward instead of inward.

17	AH1222	—	15.00	25.00	35.00	50.00

19	AH1251	—	17.50	30.00	45.00	60.00

21	AH1265	—	15.00	25.00	35.00	50.00

23	AH1299	—	15.00	25.00	35.00	50.00

KEPING

COPPER
Obv. Arabic leg: NEGRI TRENGGANU (State of Trengganu). Rev. Arabic leg: SATU KEPING 1251.

KM#	Date	Mintage	VG	Fine	VF	XF
25	AH1251	—	10.00	15.00	20.00	32.50
	AH1251	—	—	—	Proof	100.00

10 KEPING

TIN

27	AH1310	—	16.50	25.00	35.00	50.00

1/4 CENT

TIN

KM#	Date	Mintage	VG	Fine	VF	XF
29	AH1325	—	Reported, not confirmed			

Similar to following types.

1/2 CENT

TIN

31	AH1322	—	10.00	15.00	20.00	30.00

32	AH1325	—	10.00	15.00	20.00	30.00

CENT

TIN

35	AH1325	—	6.50	10.00	15.00	25.00

39	AH1325	—	6.00	10.00	15.00	25.00

Although dated AH 1325(1907) this coin was actually struck in 1920 under Sultan Sulaiman. Authorized mintage was one million pieces. Beware of thin lead counterfeits.

KUPANG

GOLD, 0.6 gm.
Issues of Zaynal Abidin II
Obv. Arabic: SULTAN ZAYN AL-ABIDIN SHAH
Rev. Arabic: KHALIFAT AL-MU'MININ

KM#	Date	Mintage	Fine	VF	XF	Unc
45	ND	—	40.00	60.00	80.00	120.00

A similar piece of finer style is attributed to Zaynal Abidin I (1708-33) (Pridmore 85).

MAS

GOLD
Legends & attribution as on KM#45.

KM#	Date	Mintage	Fine	VF	XF	Unc
48	ND	—	60.00	80.00	120.00	200.00

MALAYSIA/Straits Settlements

The independent limited constitutional monarchy of Malaysia, which occupies the southern part of the Malay Peninsula in southeast Asia and the northern part of the island of Borneo, has an area of 127,316 sq. mi. (329,747 sq. km.) and a population of 12.1 million. Capital: Kuala Lumpur. The economy is based on agriculture, mining and forestry. Rubber, tin, timber and palm oil are exported.

Malaysia came into being on Sept. 16, 1963, as a federation of Malaya (Johore, Kelantan, Kedah, Perlis, Trengganu, Negri-Sembilian, Pahang, Perak, Selangor, Penang, and Malacca), Singapore, Sabah (British North Borneo) and Sarawak. Following two serious racial riots involving Malayans and Chinese, Singapore withdrew from the federation on Aug. 9, 1965, to become an independent republic within the British Commonwealth.

STRAITS SETTLEMENTS

Straits Settlements, a former British crown colony situated on the Malay Peninsula of Asia, was formed in 1826 by combining the territories of Singapore, Penang and Malacca.

RULERS

Victoria, 1837-1901
Edward VII, 1901-1910
George V, 1910-1936
Edward VIII, 1936
George VI, 1936-1952

MINT MARKS

H- Heaton, Birmingham
W- Soho Mint
B-Bombay

MONETARY SYSTEM

100 Cents = 1 Dollar

1/4 CENT

COPPER
Rev. leg: EAST INDIA COMPANY

Y#	Date	Mintage	Fine	VF	XF	Unc
1	1845	34.327	3.50	7.50	12.50	40.00
	1845 WW on base of bust				Proof only	175.00

Rev. leg: INDIA STRAITS

Y#	Date	Mintage	Fine	VF	XF	Unc
4	1862	3.367	40.00	75.00	100.00	375.00
	1862	—	—	—	Proof	400.00

Rev. leg: STRAITS SETTLEMENTS, plain edge.

Y#	Date	Mintage	Fine	VF	XF	Unc
7	1872	—	—		Proof only	250.00
	1872H	9.240	6.50	12.50	30.00	80.00
	1872H	—	—		Proof	225.00
	1873	—	35.00	75.00	125.00	350.00
	1873	—	—	—	Proof	425.00
	1875	—	—		Proof only	225.00
	1875W	—	—		Proof only	450.00

Y#	Date	Mintage	Fine	VF	XF	Unc
7	1883	.200	150.00	300.00	350.00	400.00
	1884	8.000	2.00	4.00	11.50	50.00
	1884	—	—	—	Proof	150.00

Reeded edge

Y#	Date	Mintage	Fine	VF	XF	Unc
7a	1889	2.000	3.50	7.50	15.00	35.00
	1889	—	—	—	Proof	125.00
	1890	—	—		Proof only	140.00
	1891	—	—		Proof only	190.00
	1898	1.600	1.50	3.00	10.00	25.00
	1898	—	—	—	Proof	125.00
	1899	2.400	1.50	3.00	10.00	25.00
	1901	2.000	1.50	3.00	10.00	25.00

SILVER (OMS)

Y#	Date	Mintage	Fine	VF	XF	Unc
7b	1891	—	—		Proof only	250.00
	1898	—	—		Proof only	250.00

GOLD (OMS)

Y#	Date	Mintage	Fine	VF	XF	Unc
7c	1891	—	—		Proof only	3150.

COPPER

Y#	Date	Mintage	Fine	VF	XF	Unc
17	1904 plain edge		—		Proof only	300.00
	1904 milled edge		—		Proof only	300.00
	1905	2.008	1.75	3.50	5.50	16.50
	1908	1.200	2.00	3.75	6.50	13.50

Y#	Date	Mintage	Fine	VF	XF	Unc
27	1916	4.000	.90	1.75	2.50	8.00
	1916	—	—	—	Proof	125.00

1/2 CENT

COPPER

Y#	Date	Mintage	Fine	VF	XF	Unc
2	1845	18.737	4.50	10.00	15.00	40.00
	1845	—	—	—	Proof	125.00
	1845 WW on truncation	—	5.00	10.00	18.50	37.50
	1845 WW on truncation				Proof	150.00

Y#	Date	Mintage	Fine	VF	XF	Unc
5	1862	4.590	22.50	32.50	60.00	150.00
	1862	—	—	—	Proof	300.00

Plain edge

Y#	Date	Mintage	Fine	VF	XF	Unc
8	1872	—	—		Proof only	250.00
	1872H	5.610	8.50	17.50	40.00	80.00
	1872H	—	—	—	Proof	275.00
	1873	—	17.50	35.00	55.00	90.00
	1874	—	—		Proof only	275.00
	1875	—	—		Proof only	250.00
	1875W	—	—		Proof only	275.00
	1883	2.740	15.00	30.00	60.00	120.00
	1884	4.000	7.50	15.00	27.50	45.00

Reeded edge

Y#	Date	Mintage	Fine	VF	XF	Unc
8a	1889	2.000	11.50	22.50	35.00	50.00
	1890	—	—		Proof only	300.00
	1891	—	—		Proof	300.00

SILVER (OMS)

Y#	Date	Mintage	Fine	VF	XF	Unc
8b	1891	—	—		Proof only	300.00

GOLD (OMS)

Y#	Date	Mintage	Fine	VF	XF	Unc
8c	1891	—	—		Proof only	3150.

COPPER

Y#	Date	Mintage	Fine	VF	XF	Unc
18	1904	—	—		Proof only	250.00
	1908	2.000	4.50	9.00	15.00	25.00

Y#	Date	Mintage	Fine	VF	XF	Unc
28	1916	3.000	3.00	6.00	10.00	18.50
	1916	—	—	—	Proof	250.00

BRONZE

Y#	Date	Mintage	Fine	VF	XF	Unc
29	1932	5.000	.50	1.00	3.00	4.00
	1932	—	—	—	Proof	250.00

CENT

COPPER

Y#	Date	Mintage	Fine	VF	XF	Unc
3	1845	18.525	2.50	5.00	10.00	20.00
	1845 WW on truncation				Proof only	125.00

Y#	Date	Mintage	Fine	VF	XF	Unc
6	1862	9.321	5.00	10.00	30.00	170.00
	1862	—	—	—	Proof	250.00

Plain edge

Y#	Date	Mintage	Fine	VF	XF	Unc
9	1872	—	—		Proof only	200.00
	1872H	5.770	12.50	25.00	40.00	70.00
	1873	—	4.00	10.00	25.00	55.00
	1874	—	2.25	5.00	15.00	40.00
	1874H	10.000	2.25	5.00	15.00	40.00
	1874H	—	—	—	Proof	175.00
	1875	—	4.00	10.00	20.00	45.00
	1875	—	—	—	Proof	175.00
	1875W	6.000	4.00	10.00	20.00	45.00
	1875 W on truncation			—	Proof	225.00
	1876	—	5.00	10.00	20.00	45.00

Y#	Date	Mintage	Fine	VF	XF	Unc
9	1877	—	4.50	10.00	20.00	50.00
	1878	—	45.00	90.00	150.00	250.00
	1883	8.640	6.50	13.50	40.00	70.00
	1884	6.000	2.50	6.00	15.00	35.00
	1884	—	—	—	Proof	150.00
	1885	7.412	5.00	15.00	25.00	50.00
	1886	1.512	10.00	20.00	30.00	65.00

Reeded edge

Y#	Date	Mintage	Fine	VF	XF	Unc
9a	1887	8.988	2.00	4.00	10.00	30.00
	1888	10.000	2.00	4.00	10.00	30.00
	1889	6.010	2.00	4.00	10.00	30.00
	1890	11.006	2.00	4.00	10.00	30.00
	1890	—	—	—	Proof	150.00
	1891	6.004	2.00	4.00	10.00	30.00
	1894	9.034	2.00	4.00	10.00	30.00
	1895	4.446	2.00	4.00	10.00	30.00
	1897	18.040	3.50	7.50	15.00	40.00
	1898	2.086	4.00	10.00	20.00	40.00
	1900	2.914	2.00	4.00	10.00	30.00
	1901	15.229	2.00	4.00	15.00	30.00

SILVER (OMS)

Y#	Date	Mintage	Fine	VF	XF	Unc
9b	1890	—	—		Proof only	525.00
	1891	—	—		Proof only	450.00
	1898	—	—		Proof only	400.00

GOLD (OMS)

Y#	Date	Mintage	Fine	VF	XF	Unc
9c	1891	—	—		Proof only	3150.

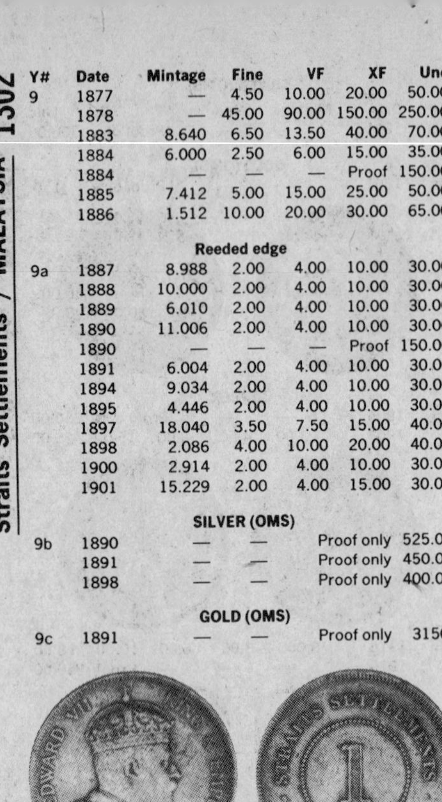

COPPER

Y#	Date	Mintage	Fine	VF	XF	Unc
19	1903	7.052	2.00	6.00	15.00	30.00
	1903	—	—	—	Proof	200.00
	1904	6.467	1.50	4.00	10.00	20.00
	1904	—	—	—	Proof	200.00
	1906	7.504	1.50	4.00	10.00	20.00
	1907	5.015	1.50	3.00	8.00	18.50
	1908	Inc. Ab.	1.00	2.00	5.00	16.50
	1908	—	—	—	Proof	200.00

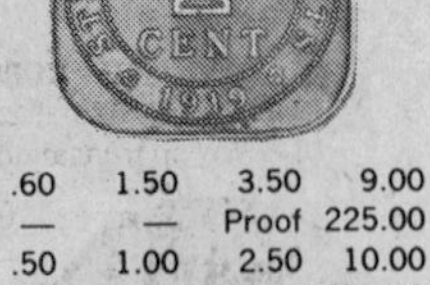

Y#	Date	Mintage	Fine	VF	XF	Unc
30	1919	20.165	.60	1.50	3.50	9.00
	1919	—	—	—	Proof	225.00
	1920	55.000	.50	1.00	2.50	10.00
	1920	—	—	—	Proof	150.00
	1926	5.000	.60	1.50	4.00	12.50
	1926/0	Inc. Ab.	3.50	7.50	20.00	50.00

5 CENTS

1.3600 gm., .800 SILVER, .0349 oz ASW

Y#	Date	Mintage	Fine	VF	XF	Unc
13	1871	.062	80.00	120.00	180.00	300.00
	1871	—	—	—	Proof	525.00
	1873	.060	150.00	200.00	300.00	500.00
	1874H	.060	55.00	75.00	100.00	180.00
	1876H	.040	150.00	200.00	300.00	400.00
	1877	.060	120.00	160.00	225.00	350.00
	1878	.260	15.00	25.00	50.00	120.00
	1878	—	—	—	Proof	200.00
	1879H	.100	50.00	80.00	120.00	200.00
	1880H	.090	60.00	100.00	150.00	200.00
	1881	.180	10.00	18.50	30.00	60.00
	1881	—	—	—	Proof	250.00
	1882H	.380	10.00	18.00	30.00	60.00
	1882H	—	—	—	Proof	250.00
	1883	.080	40.00	75.00	200.00	300.00
	1884	.440	3.00	6.50	12.00	30.00
	1884	—	—	—	Proof	250.00
	1885	.200	15.00	25.00	35.00	70.00
	1885	—	—	—	Proof	250.00
	1886	.340	2.50	5.00	10.00	25.00
	1887	.440	2.50	5.00	10.00	25.00
13	1887	—	—	—	Proof	250.00
	1888	.590	2.50	5.00	7.50	20.00
	1889	1.000	2.25	4.50	6.50	20.00
	1889	—	—	—	Proof	250.00
	1890H	.440	3.00	6.50	15.00	35.00
	1891	.800	1.25	2.50	6.50	25.00
	1893	.440	1.25	2.50	5.00	16.50
	1894	.340	2.00	4.00	5.00	16.50
	1895	1.480	1.75	3.50	10.00	20.00
	1896	.960	1.25	3.00	5.00	10.00
	1897	.320	1.50	3.00	5.50	18.50
	1897H	.440	7.50	15.00	25.00	45.00
	1898	1.200	1.25	3.00	5.00	10.00
	1899	.078	3.00	6.50	9.00	35.00
	1900	2.720	1.25	2.50	5.00	16.50
	1900H	.400	2.00	4.00	6.50	20.00
	1901	3.000	1.25	2.50	5.00	16.50

Y#	Date	Mintage	Fine	VF	XF	Unc
20	1902	1.920	3.00	6.00	12.00	20.00
	1902	—	—	—	Proof	225.00
	1903	2.270	3.00	6.00	12.00	20.00
	1903	—	—	—	Proof	225.00

1.3600 gm., .600 SILVER, .0262 oz ASW

Y#	Date	Mintage	Fine	VF	XF	Unc
20a	1910B	13.012	1.50	3.00	7.50	12.50
	1910B	—	—	—	Proof	175.00

1.3600 gm., .400 SILVER, .0174 oz ASW

Y#	Date	Mintage	Fine	VF	XF	Unc
32	1918	3.100	.75	1.50	2.50	7.50
	1919	6.900	.75	1.50	2.50	7.50
	1920	4.000	60.00	120.00	180.00	250.00

COPPER-NICKEL

Y#	Date	Mintage	Fine	VF	XF	Unc
31	1920	20.000	2.00	5.00	15.00	45.00
	1920	—	—	—	Proof	175.00

1.3600 gm., .600 SILVER, .0262 oz ASW
Similar to Y#32, smaller bust, broader rim.

Y#	Date	Mintage	Fine	VF	XF	Unc
32a	1926	10.000	.80	1.60	3.50	7.00
(33)	1935	3.000	.80	1.50	2.50	8.00
	1935	—	—	—	Proof	175.00

10 CENTS

2.7100 gm., .800 SILVER, .0697 oz ASW

Y#	Date	Mintage	Fine	VF	XF	Unc
14	1871	.248	6.50	12.50	25.00	60.00
	1871	—	—	—	Proof	300.00
	1872H	.230	10.00	20.00	35.00	55.00
	1872H	—	—	—	Proof	300.00
	1873	.210	10.00	20.00	35.00	60.00
	1873	—	—	—	Proof	300.00
	1874H	.180	5.00	10.00	20.00	40.00
	1876H	.120	12.50	25.00	50.00	80.00
	1877	.160	10.00	20.00	40.00	60.00
	1878	.470	3.50	7.50	15.00	40.00
	1879H	.250	5.00	10.00	15.00	32.50
	1879H	—	—	—	Proof	250.00
	1880H	.235	5.00	10.00	20.00	45.00
	1881	.460	2.50	5.00	13.50	37.50
	1881	—	—	—	Proof	250.00
	1882H	.430	2.50	5.00	17.50	45.00
	1882H	—	—	—	Proof	250.00
	1883	.160	10.00	30.00	40.00	60.00
	1883H	.610	40.00	60.00	80.00	175.00
14	1884	1.240	4.50	9.00	15.00	40.00
	1884	—	—	—	Proof	300.00
	1885	.400	3.50	7.00	10.00	18.50
	1885	—	—	—	Proof	300.00
	1886	.790	2.25	3.00	5.00	12.50
	1886	—	—	—	Proof	300.00
	1887	.640	BV	2.25	5.00	12.50
	1888	1.075	BV	2.25	5.00	10.00
	1888	—	—	—	Proof	250.00
	1889	1.500	BV	2.25	5.00	10.00
	1889	—	—	—	Proof	250.00
	1890H	.730	2.50	5.00	10.50	20.00
	1891	1.380	BV	2.25	5.00	12.50
	1891	—	—	—	Proof	200.00
	1893	.980	BV	2.25	7.00	25.00
	1893	—	—	—	Proof	250.00
	1894	1.640	BV	2.25	5.00	12.50
	1895	2.324	BV	3.50	8.00	22.50
	1896	2.255	BV	2.50	6.00	12.50
	1897	.700	3.00	6.50	15.00	25.00
	1897H	.390	3.00	6.00	10.00	25.00
	1898	1.960	BV	3.00	6.00	12.50
	1899	.286	BV	3.00	10.00	22.50
	1900	2.960	2.25	4.00	9.00	15.00
	1900H	1.000	2.25	6.00	10.00	18.00
	1901	2.700	BV	3.75	8.00	15.00

COPPER (OMS)

Y#	Date	Mintage	Fine	VF	XF	Unc
14a	1872H	—	—		Proof only	200.00

2.7100 gm., .800 SILVER, .0697 oz ASW

Y#	Date	Mintage	Fine	VF	XF	Unc
21	1902	6.118	BV	3.00	6.00	12.50
	1902	—	—	—	Proof	150.00
	1903	1.401	2.50	6.00	10.00	20.00
	1903	—	—	—	Proof	150.00

2.7100 gm., .600 SILVER, .0522 oz ASW

Y#	Date	Mintage	Fine	VF	XF	Unc
21a	1909B	11.088	3.00	6.00	12.00	20.00
	1910B	1.657	1.50	2.50	5.00	12.50
	1910B	—	—	—	Proof	190.00

Y#	Date	Mintage	Fine	VF	XF	Unc
34	1916	.600	1.50	2.50	5.00	11.50
	1917	5.600	BV	1.75	4.00	11.50

2.7100 gm., .400 SILVER, .0348 oz ASW

Y#	Date	Mintage	Fine	VF	XF	Unc
34a	1918	7.500	BV	1.25	3.25	9.00
	1919	11.500	BV	1.25	3.25	6.50
	1920	4.000	2.00	6.00	12.50	20.00

2.7100 gm., .600 SILVER, .0522 oz ASW

Y#	Date	Mintage	Fine	VF	XF	Unc
34b	1926	20.000	BV	BV	2.50	8.00
	1926	—	—	—	Proof	150.00
	1927	23.000	BV	BV	2.00	4.00
	1927	—	—	—	Proof	175.00

20 CENTS

5.4300 gm., .800 SILVER, .1396 oz ASW

Y#	Date	Mintage	Fine	VF	XF	Unc
15	1871	.015	200.00	300.00	400.00	600.00
	1871	—	—	—	Proof	800.00
	1872H	.040	50.00	100.00	150.00	200.00
	1873	.030	60.00	120.00	180.00	250.00
	1874H	.045	20.00	40.00	60.00	150.00
	1876H	.030	60.00	125.00	180.00	250.00
	1877	.055	40.00	80.00	175.00	275.00
	1878	.150	10.00	25.00	40.00	90.00
	1878	—	—	—	Proof	300.00
	1879H	.050	20.00	40.00	90.00	140.00
	1880H	.085	10.00	20.00	45.00	80.00
	1881	.100	8.00	14.00	27.50	50.00
	1882H	.245	10.00	15.50	30.00	50.00
	1882H	—	—	—	Proof	325.00
	1883	.200	10.00	15.00	30.00	55.00
	1884	.220	7.50	15.00	35.00	90.00
	1884	—	—	—	Proof	350.00

Y#	Date	Mintage	Fine	VF	XF	Unc
15	1885	.100	10.00	15.00	30.00	50.00
	1886	.245	4.25	6.50	12.50	35.00
	1886	—	—	—	Proof	350.00
	1887	.220	4.25	6.50	12.50	35.00
	1888	.295	5.00	10.00	25.00	60.00
	1889	.420	4.25	6.50	15.00	35.00
	1890H	.270	4.50	7.50	20.00	40.00
	1891	.510	4.25	5.50	12.50	30.00
	1893	.310	4.25	5.50	10.00	25.00
	1894	.495	5.00	10.00	25.00	70.00
	1895	.580	4.25	6.00	12.50	30.00
	1896	.600	5.00	8.50	20.00	60.00
	1897	.150	5.00	10.00	22.50	60.00
	1897H	.185	4.50	7.50	17.50	40.00
	1898	.580	5.00	8.50	22.50	60.00
	1899	.204	4.25	5.50	8.00	20.00
	1900	.620	4.50	7.50	20.00	50.00
	1900H	.300	4.25	6.00	15.00	30.00
	1901	.600	4.50	7.50	20.00	50.00

Y#	Date	Mintage	Fine	VF	XF	Unc
22	1902	1.105	5.00	8.00	20.00	40.00
	1902	—	—	—	Proof	300.00
	1903	1.150	5.00	8.00	20.00	50.00
	1903	—	—	—	Proof	300.00

5.4300 gm., .600 SILVER, .1047 oz ASW

Y#	Date	Mintage	Fine	VF	XF	Unc
22a	1910B	3.276	BV	4.00	9.00	20.00
	1910B	—	—	—	Proof	250.00

Y#	Date	Mintage	Fine	VF	XF	Unc
35	1916B	.545	4.00	6.00	15.00	30.00
	1917B	.652	3.25	5.00	12.00	25.00

5.4300 gm., .400 SILVER, .0698 oz ASW

Y#	Date	Mintage	Fine	VF	XF	Unc
35a	1919B	2.500	2.25	4.00	10.00	20.00
	1919B	—	—	—	Proof	200.00

5.4300 gm., .600 SILVER, .1047 oz ASW

Y#	Date	Mintage	Fine	VF	XF	Unc
35b	1926	2.500	3.50	5.00	12.50	25.00
	1926	—	—	—	Proof	200.00
	1927	3.000	3.25	4.00	10.00	20.00
	1935 round top 3	1.000	3.25	4.00	7.00	15.00
	1935 flat top 3	Inc. Ab.	3.25	3.75	6.00	16.50

50 CENTS

10.1100 gm., .800 SILVER, .2600 oz ASW

Y#	Date	Mintage	Fine	VF	XF	Unc
16	1886	.060	40.00	60.00	90.00	160.00
	1886	—	—	—	Proof	450.00
	1887	.094	25.00	40.00	60.00	125.00
	1888	.096	25.00	40.00	60.00	125.00
	1889	.032	400.00	500.00	600.00	800.00
	1890H	.042	40.00	60.00	90.00	160.00
	1891	.112	25.00	40.00	60.00	100.00
	1891	—	—	—	Proof	450.00
	1893	.024	150.00	300.00	600.00	1000.
	1894	.052	30.00	50.00	70.00	140.00
	1895	.056	30.00	50.00	70.00	140.00
	1896	.120	20.00	30.00	55.00	125.00
	1897	.036	40.00	60.00	90.00	175.00
	1897H	.044	40.00	65.00	90.00	150.00
	1898	.160	20.00	30.00	50.00	100.00
	1899	.136	20.00	30.00	50.00	100.00
	1900	.088	25.00	40.00	90.00	150.00
	1900H	.040	40.00	60.00	90.00	175.00
	1901	.120	25.00	30.00	50.00	100.00

Rev: Similar to Y#16.

Y#	Date	Mintage	Fine	VF	XF	Unc
23	1902	.148	30.00	50.00	70.00	150.00
	1902	—	—	—	Proof	350.00
	1903	.193	30.00	50.00	70.00	150.00
	1903	—	—	—	Proof	350.00
	1904	—	—		Proof only	950.00
	1905B raised	.497	30.00	50.00	80.00	100.00
	1905B raised	—	—	—	Proof	300.00
	1905B incuse	—	—		Proof only	525.00

10.1100 gm., .900 SILVER, .2925 oz ASW

Y#	Date	Mintage	Fine	VF	XF	Unc
24	1907	.464	BV	BV	10.00	15.00
	1907H	2.667	BV	BV	10.00	15.00
	1907H	—	—	—	Proof	100.00
	1908	2.869	BV	BV	10.00	15.00
	1908H	Inc. 1907H	BV	10.00	12.00	20.00

8.4200 gm., .500 SILVER, .1353 oz ASW

Y#	Date	Mintage	Fine	VF	XF	Unc
36	1920 cross under bust	3.900	BV	BV	4.25	6.00
	1920 cross under bust	—	—	—	Proof	80.00
	1920 dot under bust	Inc. Ab.	40.00	65.00	90.00	200.00
	1921	2.579	BV	BV	4.25	6.50
	1921	—	—	—	Proof	80.00

DOLLAR

26.9500 gm., .900 SILVER, .7799 oz ASW

Y#	Date	Mintage	Fine	VF	XF	Unc
25	1903	—	—		Proof only	1000.
	1903B incuse	15.010	BV	27.50	35.00	50.00
	1903B raised	Inc. Ab.	35.00	75.00	125.00	250.00
	1903B raised	—	—	—	Proof	450.00
	1904B	20.365	BV	25.00	35.00	45.00
	1904B	—	—	—	Proof	425.00

20.2100 gm., .900 SILVER, .5848 oz ASW
Reduced size, 34.5mm.

Y#	Date	Mintage	Fine	VF	XF	Unc
25a	1907	6.841	BV	BV	18.00	25.00
(26)	1907H	4.000	BV	BV	18.00	25.00
	1907H	—	—	—	Proof	350.00
	1908	4.152	BV	BV	18.00	25.00
	1908	—	—	—	Proof	350.00
	1909	1.014	BV	BV	20.00	30.00
	1909	—	—	—	Proof	350.00

16.8500 gm., .500 SILVER, .2709 oz ASW
Rev: Similar to Y#25.

Y#	Date	Mintage	Fine	VF	XF	Unc
37	1919	6.000	10.00	12.50	20.00	40.00
	1920	8.164	8.50	11.00	17.50	35.00
	1925	—	—		Proof only	700.00
	1926	—	—		Proof only	700.00

Restrikes

Y#	Date	Mintage	XF	Unc	Proof
37	1919	—	—	—	45.00
	1920	—	—	—	45.00
	1925	—	—	—	125.00
	1926	—	—	—	125.00

NOTE: For later coinage see Brunei and Singapore.

SARAWAK

Sarawak is a former British colony located on the northwest coast of Borneo. Japanese occupation during World War II so thoroughly devastated the country that rajah Sir Charles Vyner Brooke ceded it to Great Britain on July 1, 1946.

RULERS

James Brooke, Rajah, 1841-1868
Charles J. Brooke, Rajah, 1868-1917
Charles V. Brooke, Rajah, 1917-1946

MINT MARKS

H- Heaton, Birmingham

DOIT

COPPER
Obv: Animal to left above J.B., date.
Rev: Arabic legends

Y#	Date	Mintage	Fine	VF	XF	Unc
1	AH1247	—	350.00	500.00	700.00	800.00

BRASS

Y#	Date	Mintage	Fine	VF	XF	Unc
1a	AH1247	—	400.00	550.00	750.00	900.00

DECIMAL COINAGE

100 Cents = 1 Dollar

1/4 CENT

COPPER

Y#	Date	Mintage	Fine	VF	XF	Unc
2	1863	—	17.50	30.00	60.00	130.00
	1863	—	—	—	Proof	175.00

Y#	Date	Mintage	Fine	VF	XF	Unc
5	1870	—	6.50	12.50	25.00	40.00
	1870	—	—	—	Proof	155.00
	1896H	.283	5.50	10.00	20.00	40.00
	1896H	—	—	—	Proof	175.00

1/2 CENT

COPPER

Y#	Date	Mintage	Fine	VF	XF	Unc
3	1863	—	10.00	22.50	50.00	100.00
	1863	—	—	—	Proof	200.00

Y#	Date	Mintage	Fine	VF	XF	Unc
6	1870	—	5.00	14.00	25.00	50.00
	1879	—	6.50	15.00	22.50	35.00
	1879	—	—	—	Proof	175.00
	1896H	.326	5.00	12.00	17.50	30.00

Y#	Date	Mintage	Fine	VF	XF	Unc
13	1933H	2.000	1.00	1.50	2.00	3.00

CENT

COPPER

Y#	Date	Mintage	Fine	VF	XF	Unc
4	1863	—	4.00	8.50	15.00	50.00
	1863	—	—	—	Proof	150.00

Y#	Date	Mintage	Fine	VF	XF	Unc
7	1870	—	2.00	5.00	8.00	20.00
	1870	—	—	—	Proof	120.00
	1879	—	3.50	7.00	15.00	30.00
	1879	—	—	—	Proof	120.00
	1880	—	2.00	5.00	10.00	20.00
	1882	—	2.00	5.00	10.00	17.50
	1882	—	—	—	Proof	120.00
	1884	1.070	2.00	5.00	10.00	17.50
	1885	2.140	2.00	5.00	10.00	17.50
	1885	—	—	—	Proof	120.00
	1886	2.014	2.00	5.00	10.00	17.50
	1887	1.605	2.00	5.00	10.00	17.50
	1887	—	—	—	Proof	120.00
	1888	2.133	2.00	5.00	10.00	17.50
	1889	3.200	2.00	5.00	10.00	17.50
	1889H	Inc. Ab.	2.00	5.00	10.00	17.50
	1890H	3.210	2.00	5.00	10.00	17.50

Y#	Date	Mintage	Fine	VF	XF	Unc
7	1891	1.624	3.50	8.00	17.50	35.00
	1891H	Inc. Ab.	2.00	5.00	10.00	17.50

Y#	Date	Mintage	Fine	VF	XF	Unc
8	1892H	1.089	1.50	2.50	5.00	15.00
	1892H	—	—	—	Proof	125.00
	1893H	1.634	1.50	2.50	5.00	15.00
	1894H	1.633	1.50	2.50	5.00	15.00
	1896H	1.089	1.50	2.50	5.00	15.00
	1897H	1.089	1.50	2.50	5.00	15.00

COPPER-NICKEL

Y#	Date	Mintage	Fine	VF	XF	Unc
15	1920H	5.000	2.50	5.00	10.00	15.00

BRONZE

Y#	Date	Mintage	Fine	VF	XF	Unc
14	1927H	5.000	.75	1.50	3.50	7.00
	1929H	2.000	.75	1.50	3.50	7.00
	1930H	3.000	.75	1.50	3.00	6.00
	1937H	3.000	.75	1.25	2.00	3.50
	1941H	2.016	110.00	180.00	300.00	400.00

5 CENTS

.800 SILVER

Y#	Date	Mintage	Fine	VF	XF	Unc
9	1900H	.200	7.50	11.50	17.50	30.00
	1908H	.040	10.00	17.50	25.00	40.00
	1908H	—	—	—	Proof	175.00
	1911H	.040	10.00	15.00	22.50	35.00
	1913H	.100	6.50	12.50	22.50	35.00
	1913H	—	—	—	Proof	175.00
	1915H	.100	7.50	13.50	22.50	35.00
	1915H	—	—	—	Proof	175.00

Y#	Date	Mintage	Fine	VF	XF	Unc
18	1920H	.100	11.50	20.00	32.50	60.00

COPPER-NICKEL

Y#	Date	Mintage	Fine	VF	XF	Unc
16	1920H	.400	1.00	2.50	4.00	10.00
	1927H	.600	.75	2.00	3.50	9.00

10 CENTS

.800 SILVER

Y#	Date	Mintage	Fine	VF	XF	Unc
10	1900H	.150	4.50	8.50	15.00	25.00
	1906H	.050	7.00	13.50	20.00	30.00
	1906H	—	—	—	Proof	175.00
	1910H	.050	7.00	13.50	20.00	30.00
	1911H	.100	5.50	10.00	17.50	35.00
	1913H	.100	5.50	10.00	17.50	27.50
	1915H	.100	7.00	13.50	22.50	37.50

Y#	Date	Mintage	Fine	VF	XF	Unc
19	1920H	.150	7.00	15.00	20.00	35.00

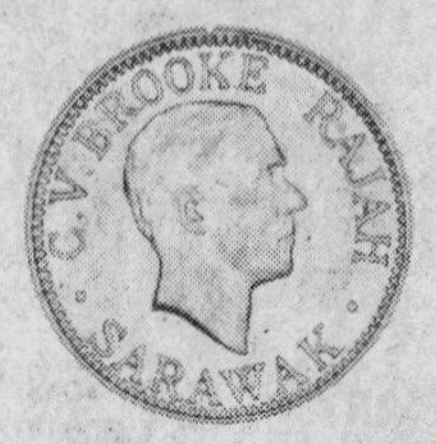

COPPER-NICKEL

Y#	Date	Mintage	Fine	VF	XF	Unc
17	1920H	.800	1.25	2.00	4.00	10.00
	1927H	1.000	.90	1.75	3.00	10.00
	1934H	2.000	.75	1.25	2.00	8.50

20 CENTS

.800 SILVER

Y#	Date	Mintage	Fine	VF	XF	Unc
11	1900H	.075	10.00	15.00	25.00	70.00
	1906H	.025	11.50	16.50	27.50	45.00
	1906H	—	—	—	Proof	175.00
	1910H	.025	11.50	16.50	27.50	40.00
	1911H	.025	11.50	16.50	27.50	40.00
	1913H	.025	11.50	16.50	27.50	40.00
	1913H	—	—	—	Proof	175.00
	1915H	.025	25.00	45.00	85.00	140.00

Y#	Date	Mintage	Fine	VF	XF	Unc
20	1920H	.025	25.00	50.00	75.00	100.00
	1927H	.250	4.00	6.50	10.00	20.00

50 CENTS

.800 SILVER

Y#	Date	Mintage	Fine	VF	XF	Unc
12	1900H	.040	20.00	30.00	50.00	150.00
	1906H	.010	30.00	45.00	65.00	110.00
	1906H	—	—	—	Proof	750.00

Y#	Date	Mintage	Fine	VF	XF	Unc
21	1927H	.200	8.00	12.50	25.00	30.00

BRITISH NORTH BORNEO

British North Borneo (now known as Sabah), a former British protectorate and crown colony, occupies the northern tip of the island of Borneo. The island of Labuan, which lies 6 miles off the northwest coast of the island of Borneo, was incorporated with British North Borneo in 1946.

MINT MARKS

H- Heaton, Birmingham

MONETARY SYSTEM

100 Cents = 1 Straits Dollar

1/2 CENT

BRONZE

Y#	Date	Mintage	Fine	VF	XF	Unc
1	1885H	1.000	4.00	7.50	15.00	20.00
	1885H	—	—	—	Proof	40.00
	1886H	1.000	3.50	7.00	12.50	16.50
	1886H	—	—	—	Proof	40.00
	1887H	5.000	3.00	6.00	10.00	15.00
	1891H	2.000	2.00	3.50	8.00	12.50
	1891H	—	—	—	Proof	35.00
	1907H	1.000	8.00	12.50	20.00	40.00

CENT

BRONZE

Y#	Date	Mintage	Fine	VF	XF	Unc
2	1882H	2.000	1.00	4.00	10.00	15.00
	1882H	—	—	—	Proof	40.00
	1884H	2.000	1.00	4.00	10.00	15.00
	1884H	—	—	—	Proof	40.00
	1885H	1.000	1.50	5.00	12.50	18.50
	1886H	5.000	.80	3.00	8.50	12.50
	1886H	—	—	—	Proof	30.00
	1887H	6.000	.80	3.00	8.50	12.50
	1887H	—	—	—	Proof	30.00
	1888H	6.000	.80	3.00	8.50	12.50
	1888H	—	—	—	Proof	30.00
	1889H	9.000	.50	2.00	6.00	10.00
	1890H	8.000	.50	2.00	6.00	10.00
	1890H	—	—	—	Proof	30.00
	1891H	3.000	.50	2.00	5.00	8.00
	1891H	—	—	—	Proof	25.00
	1894H	1.000	4.00	10.00	20.00	40.00
	1896H	1.000	4.00	10.00	20.00	40.00
	1907H	1.000	8.00	15.00	30.00	50.00

COPPER-NICKEL

Y#	Date	Mintage	Fine	VF	XF	Unc
3	1904H	4.000	.50	2.00	3.00	8.50
	1921H	1.000	.80	3.00	5.00	12.50
	1935H	1.000	.80	1.50	2.50	6.00
	1938H	1.000	.40	1.25	2.00	5.00
	1941H	1.000	.40	1.25	2.00	5.00

2-1/2 CENTS

COPPER-NICKEL

Y#	Date	Mintage	Fine	VF	XF	Unc
4	1903H	2.000	.80	3.00	8.00	15.00
	1920H	.280	1.00	4.00	10.00	20.00

5 CENTS

COPPER-NICKEL

Y#	Date	Mintage	Fine	VF	XF	Unc
5	1903H	1.000	.50	2.00	5.00	10.00
	1920H	.100	.80	3.00	8.00	20.00
	1921H	.500	.50	2.00	5.00	10.00
	1927H	.150	.80	3.00	8.00	18.50
	1928H	.151	.80	3.00	6.00	15.00
	1938H	.500	.40	1.50	3.00	4.00
	1940H	.500	.40	1.50	3.00	3.50
	1941H	1.000	.30	1.00	1.50	2.50

25 CENTS

.500 SILVER

Y#	Date	Mintage	Fine	VF	XF	Unc
6	1929H	.400	5.00	10.00	15.00	22.50

MALAYA

Malaya, a former member of the British Commonwealth located in the southern part of the Malay peninsula, consisted of 11 states: the unfederated Malay states of Johore, Kelantan, Kedah, Perlis and Trengganu; the federated Malay states of Negri-Sembilan, Pahang, Perak and Selangor; former members of the Straits Settlements Penang and Malacca. Malaya was granted full independence on Aug. 31, 1957.

RULERS

George VI, 1936-1952

MINT MARKS

I = Calcutta Mint(1941)

I = Bombay Mint(1945)

No Mintmark = Royal Mint

MONETARY SYSTEM

100 Cents = 1 Dollar

1/2 CENT

BRONZE

Y#	Date	Mintage	Fine	VF	XF	Unc
1	1940	6.000	.40	.80	1.50	2.00

CENT

BRONZE

Y#	Date	Mintage	Fine	VF	XF	Unc
2	1939	20.000	.25	.40	.60	1.50
	1939	—	—	—	Proof	125.00
	1940	23.600	.25	.40	.60	1.50
	1941-I	33.620	.15	.35	.50	1.00

Y#	Date	Mintage	Fine	VF	XF	Unc
2a	1943	50.000	.10	.20	.40	.80
	1945	40.033	.10	.20	.40	.60

5 CENTS

1.3600 gm., .750 SILVER, .0327 oz ASW

Y#	Date	Mintage	Fine	VF	XF	Unc
3	1939	2.000	BV	BV	1.50	3.00
	1939	—	—	—	Proof	100.00
	1941	4.000	BV	BV	1.00	2.00
	1941	—	—	—	Proof	100.00
	1941-I	Inc. Ab.	BV	BV	1.00	2.00

1.3600 gm., .500 SILVER, .0218 oz ASW

Y#	Date	Mintage	Fine	VF	XF	Unc
3a	1943	10.000	BV	BV	.65	1.25
	1943	—	—	—	Proof	100.00
	1945	8.800	BV	BV	.65	1.25
	1945-I	4.600	BV	BV	.80	1.50

COPPER-NICKEL

Y#	Date	Mintage	Fine	VF	XF	Unc
7	1948	30.000	.10	.20	.40	.80
	1948	—	—	—	Proof	90.00
	1950	40.000	.10	.20	.40	.80

10 CENTS

2.7100 gm., .750 SILVER, .0653 oz ASW

Y#	Date	Mintage	Fine	VF	XF	Unc
4	1939	10.000	BV	BV	2.00	2.50
	1939	—	—	—	Proof	100.00
	1941	17.000	BV	BV	2.00	2.50
	1941	—	—	—	Proof	100.00

2.7100 gm., .500 SILVER, .0435 oz ASW

Y#	Date	Mintage	Fine	VF	XF	Unc
4a	1943	5.000	BV	BV	1.35	2.00
	1943	—	—	—	Proof	100.00
	1945	3.152	BV	BV	1.35	2.00
	1945-I	Unique	—	—	—	—

COPPER-NICKEL

Y#	Date	Mintage	Fine	VF	XF	Unc
8	1948	23.885	—	.20	.40	.80
	1948	—	—	—	Proof	85.00
	1949	26.115	.25	.40	.80	1.50
	1950	65.000	—	.20	.40	.80

20 CENTS

5.4300 gm., .750 SILVER, .1309 oz ASW

Y#	Date	Mintage	Fine	VF	XF	Unc
5	1939	8.000	BV	BV	4.00	5.00
	1939	—	—	—	Proof	120.00

5.4300 gm., .500 SILVER, .0872 oz ASW

Y#	Date	Mintage	Fine	VF	XF	Unc
5a	1943	5.000	BV	BV	2.75	4.50
	1943	—	—	—	Proof	120.00
	1945	10.000	BV	BV	3.50	5.00

COPPER-NICKEL

Y#	Date	Mintage	Fine	VF	XF	Unc
9	1948	40.000	.30	.60	1.00	2.00
	1948	—	—	—	Proof	100.00
	1950	20.000	.30	.60	1.00	2.00

MALAYA & BRITISH BORNEO

Malaya & British Borneo, a Currency Commission named the Board of Commissioners of Currency, Malaya and British Borneo, was initiated on Jan. 1, 1952, for the purpose of providing a common currency for use in Johore, Kelantan, Kedah, Perlis, Trengganu, Negri Sembilan, Pahang, Perak, Selangor, Penang, Malacca, Singapore, North Borneo, Sarawak and Brunei.

RULERS

Elizabeth II, 1952-1963

MINTMARKS

KN - King's Norton, Birmingham
H - Heaton, Birmingham
No Mintmark - Royal Mint

MONETARY SYSTEM

100 Cents = 1 Dollar

CENT

BRONZE

Y#	Date	Mintage	VF	XF	Unc
A1	1956	6.250	.10	.25	.50
	1956	—	—	Proof	120.00
	1957	12.500	.10	.25	.50
	1958	5.000	.10	.25	.50
	1958	—	—	Proof	120.00
	1961	10.000	.10	.20	.50
	1961	—	—	Proof	120.00

Y#	Date	Mintage	VF	XF	Unc
5	1962	45.000	—	.15	.40
	1962	*25 pcs.	—	Proof	125.00

5 CENTS

COPPER-NICKEL

Y#	Date	Mintage	VF	XF	Unc
1	1953	20.000	.20	.40	1.50
	1953	—	—	Proof	120.00
	1957	20.000	.20	.40	1.50
	1957H	Inc. Ab.	.20	.40	1.50
	1957KN	Inc. Ab.	.40	.80	3.00
	1958	20.000	.20	.40	1.50
	1958H	Inc. Ab.	.30	.60	2.50
	1961	95.000	.15	.30	1.00
	1961H	Inc. Ab.	.80	1.50	6.00
	1961KN	Inc. Ab.	.30	.50	2.00

10 CENTS

COPPER-NICKEL

Y#	Date	Mintage	VF	XF	Unc
2	1953	20.000	.30	.60	2.50
	1953	—	—	Proof	120.00
	1956	10.000	.25	.50	2.00
	1957H	20.000	.30	.60	2.50
	1957KN	Inc. Ab.	.30	.60	2.50
	1958	10.000	.25	.50	2.00
	1960	10.000	.25	.50	2.00
	1961	130.004	.20	.40	1.50
	1961H	Inc. Ab.	.20	.40	1.50
	1961KN	Inc. Ab.	.20	.40	1.50

20 CENTS

COPPER-NICKEL

Y#	Date	Mintage	VF	XF	Unc
3	1954	10.000	.40	.80	3.00
	1954	—	—	Proof	120.00
	1956	5.000	.40	.80	3.00
	1957H	5.000	.40	.80	3.00
	1957KN	Inc. Ab.	.60	1.20	4.00
	1961	55.500	.40	.70	2.50
	1961H	Inc. Ab.	.40	.70	2.50

50 CENTS

COPPER-NICKEL, security edge

Y#	Date	Mintage	VF	XF	Unc
4	1954	8.000	.60	1.20	4.00
	1954	—	—	Proof	150.00
	1955H	2.560	.80	1.50	6.00
	1956	3.440	.80	1.50	6.00
	1956	—	—	Proof	300.00
	1957H	4.000	.80	1.50	6.00

Y#	Date	Mintage	VF	XF	Unc
4	1957KN	Inc. Ab.	1.00	2.00	7.00
	1958H	4.000	.80	1.50	6.00
	1961	21.000	.60	1.00	3.00
	1961H	Inc. Ab.	.60	1.00	3.00

Error, without security edge

Y#	Date	Mintage	VF	XF	Unc
	1954	Inc. Ab.	8.50	12.50	15.00
	1958	Inc. Ab.	8.50	12.50	15.00
	1961	Inc. Ab.	7.50	10.00	14.00

MALAYSIA

MINT MARKS

FM - Franklin Mint, U.S.A.*

***NOTE:** During 1976-77 the Franklin Mint produced coinage in up to 3 different qualities. Qualities of issue are designated in ( ) after each date and are defined as follows:

(M) MATTE - Normal circulation strike or a dull finish produced by sandblasting special uncirculated (polish finish) or proof quality dies.

(U) SPECIAL UNCIRCULATED - Polished or proof-like in appearance without any frosted features.

(P) PROOF - The highest quality obtainable having mirror-like fields and frosted features.

MONETARY SYSTEM

100 Sen = 1 Ringgit Dollar

SEN

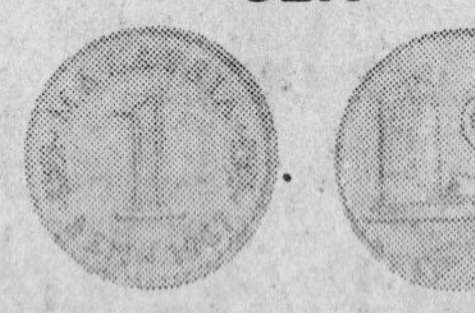

BRONZE

Y#	Date	Mintage	Fine	VF	XF	Unc
1	1967	45.000	—	.10	.15	
	1967	500 pcs.	—	Proof	7.50	
	1968	10.500	.10	.30	.40	
	1970	2.535	.15	.35	.50	
	1971	30.012	—	.10	.15	
	1973	57.675	—	.10	.15	

COPPER-CLAD STEEL

Y#	Date	Mintage	VF	XF	Unc
1a	1973	Inc. Ab.	—	.10	.15
	1976	24.694	—	.10	.15
	1977	24.437	—	—	.15

5 SEN

COPPER-NICKEL

Y#	Date	Mintage	VF	XF	Unc
2	1967	75.464	—	.15	.20
	1967	500 pcs.	—	Proof	10.00
	1968	74.536	—	.15	.20
	1971	16.668	—	.10	.15
	1973	172.148	—	.10	.15
	1976	66.659	—	.10	.15
	1977	10.609	—	.10	.15

10 SEN

COPPER-NICKEL

Y#	Date	Mintage	VF	XF	Unc
3	1967	106.708	.10	.15	.25
	1967	500 pcs.	—	Proof	12.50
	1968	128.292	.10	.15	.25
	1971	.042	10.00	15.00	20.00
	1973	353.372	.10	.15	.25
	1975	1.792	—	—	—
	1976	148.809	.10	.15	.25
	1977	52.724	.10	.15	.25

20 SEN

COPPER-NICKEL

Y#	Date	Mintage	VF	XF	Unc
4	1967	49.560	.15	.30	.40
	1967	500 pcs.	—	Proof	15.00
	1968	40.440	.15	.30	.40
	1969	15.000	.20	.35	.50
	1970	1.054	.50	.75	1.00
	1971	9.968	.15	.25	.35
	1973	172.546	.15	.20	.30
	1975	7.409	—	—	—
	1976	61.534	.15	.20	.30
	1977	52.002	.15	.20	.30

50 SEN

COPPER-NICKEL

Y#	Date	Mintage	VF	XF	Unc
5	1967	15.000	.40	.60	1.00
	1967	500 pcs.	—	Proof	20.00
	1968	12.000	.40	.60	.85
	1969	2.000	.50	.75	1.00

Error, without security edge

Y#	Date	Mintage	VF	XF	Unc
5c	1967	Inc. Ab.	5.00	6.50	9.50
	1968	Inc. Ab.	5.00	6.50	9.50
	1969	Inc. Ab.	5.00	6.50	9.50

Lettered edge

Y#	Date	Mintage	VF	XF	Unc
5a	1971	8.414	.45	.65	1.00
	1973	67.543	.25	.40	1.00
	1975	15.268	—	—	—
	1977	17.721	—	—	—

RINGGIT

COPPER-NICKEL
10th Anniversary Bank Negara

Y#	Date	Mintage	VF	XF	Unc
6	1969	1.000	.50	.75	2.00

.925 SILVER

Y#	Date	Mintage	VF	XF	Unc
6a	1969	1,000	—	Proof	75.00

COPPER-NICKEL

Y#	Date	Mintage	VF	XF	Unc
7	1971	7.389	.50	.65	2.00
	1971	500 pcs.	—	Proof	120.00

Kuala Lumpur Anniversary

Y#	Date	Mintage	VF	XF	Unc
10	1972	.500	.50	1.00	2.00
	1972	500 pcs.	—	Proof	100.00

25th Anniversary Employee Provident Fund

Y#	Date	Mintage	VF	XF	Unc
17	1976	.500	.60	.85	1.75
	1976FM(P)	8,003	—	Proof	4.50

Malaysian 3rd Five Year Plan

Y#	Date	Mintage	VF	XF	Unc
14	1976	.585	—	—	—
	1976FM(P)	.018	—	Proof Only	5.00

9th South-East Asian Games

Y#	Date	Mintage	VF	XF	Unc
20	1977	—	.60	.85	1.75
	1977FM(P)	.011	—	Proof	—

20th Anniversary of Independence

Y#	Date	Mintage	VF	XF	Unc
23	1977	—	.60	.75	1.75
	1977FM(P)	3,102	—	Proof	4.50

100th Anniversary of Natural Rubber Production

Y#	Date	Mintage	VF	XF	Unc
24	1977	—	—	—	1.75
	1977	—	—	Proof	—

20th Anniversary of Bank Negara

Y#	Date	Mintage	VF	XF	Unc
25	1979	—	—	—	1.75
	.925 SILVER				
25a	1979	—	—	Proof	—

5 RINGGIT

COPPER-NICKEL

Y#	Date	Mintage	VF	XF	Unc
8	1971	2.000	2.25	2.50	3.25
	1971	500 pcs.	—	Proof	125.00

10 RINGGIT

10.9000 gm., .917 SILVER, .3213 oz ASW
Malaysian 3rd Five Year Plan

Y#	Date	Mintage	VF	XF	Unc
15	1976FM(U)	.200	BV	BV	10.00
	1976FM(P)	.011	—	Proof	12.50

15 RINGGIT

28.2800 gm., .925 SILVER, .8411 oz ASW
Conservation Series

Y#	Date	Mintage	VF	XF	Unc
11	1976	.044	BV	BV	25.00
	1976	8,000	—	Proof	30.00

25 RINGGIT

35.0000 gm., .925 SILVER, 1.0409 oz ASW
Conservation Series
Obv: Similar to 15 Ringgit, Y#11.

Y#	Date	Mintage	VF	XF	Unc
12	1976	.045	BV	35.00	40.00
	1976	8,000	—	Proof	50.00

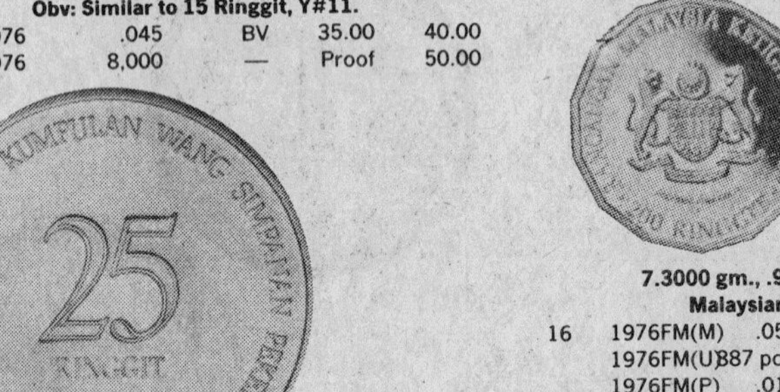

25th Anniversary Employee Provident Fund

Y#	Date	Mintage	VF	XF	Unc
18	1976FM(U)	.100	BV	BV	32.00
	1976FM(P)	8,094	—	Proof	22.50

9th South-East Asian Games

Y#	Date	Mintage	VF	XF	Unc
21	1977FM(U)	.100	BV	BV	32.00
	1977FM(P)	6,077	—	Proof	22.50

100 RINGGIT

.917 GOLD
Prime Minister Abdul Rahman Putra Al-haj

Y#	Date	Mintage	VF	XF	Unc
9	1971	.100	75.00	100.00	140.00
	1971	500 pcs.	—	Proof	600.00

200 RINGGIT

7.3000 gm., .900 GOLD, .2112 oz AGW
Malaysian 3rd Five Year Plan

Y#	Date	Mintage	VF	XF	Unc
16	1976FM(M)	.050	BV	140.00	150.00
	1976FM(U)387 pcs.		140.00	175.00	200.00
	1976FM(P)	.012	—	Proof	175.00

7.2200 gm., .900 GOLD, .2089 oz AGW
9th South-East Asian Games

Y#	Date	Mintage	VF	XF	Unc
22	1977FM(M)	.012	BV	135.00	150.00
	1977FM(U)357 pcs.		—	—	—
	1977FM(P),578 pcs.		—	Proof	175.00

250 RINGGIT

10.1100 gm., .900 GOLD, .2925 oz AGW
25th Anniversary Employee Provident Fund

Y#	Date	Mintage	VF	XF	Unc
19	1976FM(U)	.030	BV	185.00	200.00
	1976FM(P)	8,000	—	Proof	225.00

500 RINGGIT

33.4300 gm., .900 GOLD, .9674 oz AGW
Conservation Series

Y#	Date	Mintage	VF	XF	Unc
13	1976	2,000	BV	BV	650.00
	1976	100 pcs.	—	Proof	750.00

NCLT ISSUES

MINT SETS

KM#	Date	Mintage	Identification	Issue Price	Mkt. Val.
S1	1967(5)	10,000	Y1-5	—	2.50
S2	1976(2)	—	Y11,12	35.00	35.00

PROOF SETS

STANDARD METALS

KM#	Date	Mintage	Identification	Issue Price	Mkt. Val.
101	1967(5)	500	Y1-5	—	60.00
102	1976(3)	100	Y11-13	808.00	830.00
103	1976(2)	400	Y11,12	—	80.00
104	1976(3)	.011	Y14-16	—	190.00
105	1977(3)	975	Y17-19	164.00	265.00

MALDIVE ISLANDS

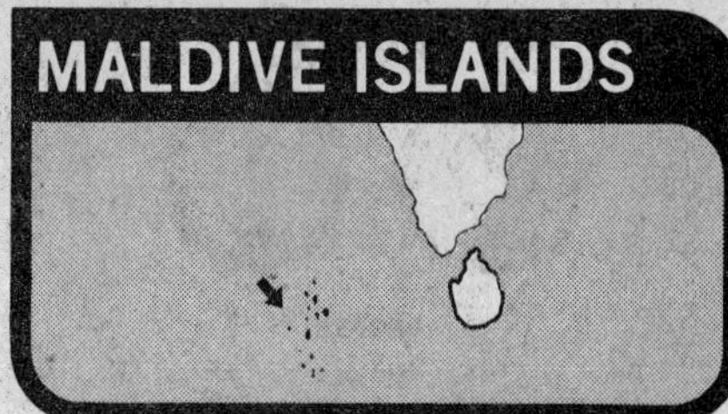

The Republic of Maldives, an archipelago of 2,000 coral islets in the northern Indian Ocean 417 miles (671 km.) southwest of Ceylon, has an area of 115 sq. mi. (298 sq. km.) and a population of 136,000. Capital: Male. Fishing employs 95 percent of the male work force. Dried fish, copra and coir yarn are exported.

The Maldive Islands were visited by Arab traders and converted to Islam in 1153. After being harassed in the 16th and 17th centuries by Mopla pirates of the Malabar coast and Portuguese raiders, the Maldivians voluntarily placed themselves under the suzerainty of Ceylon. In 1887 the islands became an internally self-governing British protectorate and a nominal dependency of Ceylon. Traditionally a sultanate, the Maldives became a republic in 1953 but restored the sultanate in 1954. The Sultanate of the Maldive Islands attained complete internal and external autonomy on July 26, 1965, and on Nov. 11, 1968, became again a republic.

The coins of the Maldives, issued by request of the Sultan and without direct British sponsorship, are not definitively coins of the British Commonwealth.

RULERS

Hasan Izz al-Din, AH1173-1180/AD1759-1767
Muhammad Ghiyas al-Din, AH1180-1187/AD1767-1773
Muhammad Shams al-Din II AH1187-1188/AD1773-1774 (no coinage known)
Muhammad Muiz al-Din, AH1188-1192/AD1774-1778
Hasan Nur al-Din I, AH1192-1213/AD1778-1798
Muhammad Mu'in al-Din, AH1213-1250/AD1798-1835
Muhammad Imad al-Din IV, AH1250-1300/AD1835-1882
Ibrahim Nur al-Din, AH1300-1318/AD1882-1900
Muhammad Imad al-Din V, AH1318-1322/AD1900-1904
Muhammad Shams al-Din III, AH1322-1353/AD1904-1935
Hasan Nur al-Din II, AH1353-1364/AD1935-1945
Abdul-Majid Didi, AH1364-1371 AD1945-1953
First Republic, AH1371-1372 AD1953-1954
Muhammad Farid Didi, AH1372-1388/AD1954-1968
Second Republic, AH1388 to date/AD1968 to date

NOTE: The metrology of the early coinage is problematical. There seem to be two denominations, a double Larin of 8-10 gm., and a half Larin that varies from 1.1 to 2.3 gm., known as the Bodu Larin and Kuda Larin, respectively. In some years, probably when copper was cheap (AH1276 & 1294), the Kuda (1/2) Larin is found with weights as high as 3.7 gm.

MONETARY SYSTEM

100 Lari = 1 Rupee

KUDA (1/2) LARIN

BRONZE, 9-13mm, 1.1-3.7 gm.
Muhammad Ghiyas al-Din.

C#	Date	Mintage	VG	Fine	VF	XF
16	AH1184	—	4.00	6.00	8.00	12.00
	1186	—	4.00	6.00	8.00	12.00

C#	Date	Mintage	VG	Fine	VF	XF
	Muhammad Muiz al-Din.					
21	AH1188	—	4.00	6.00	8.50	13.50
	Hasan Nur al-Din I					
26	AH1194	—	3.00	6.00	8.00	12.00
	1197	—	3.00	5.00	7.50	10.00
	1200	—	3.00	5.00	7.50	10.00
	1202	—	3.00	5.00	7.50	10.00
	Muhammad Mu'in al-Din					
41	AH1216	—	3.00	5.00	7.50	10.00
	1219	—	3.00	5.00	7.50	10.00
	1221	—	3.00	5.00	7.50	10.00
	1230	—	Reported, not confirmed			
	1238	—	3.50	6.00	9.00	12.00
	1248	—	3.00	5.00	7.00	9.00

C#	Date	Mintage	VG	Fine	VF	XF
	Muhammad Imad Al-Din IV					
46	AH1255	—	Reported, not confirmed			
	1257	—	2.50	3.00	6.00	8.00
	1276	—	2.50	3.00	6.00	8.00
	1286	—	2.00	2.50	4.50	6.00
	1287	—	Reported, not confirmed			
	1292	—	2.50	3.50	6.00	8.00
	1294	—	3.00	5.00	7.50	10.00
	1298	—	2.00	3.00	4.50	6.00

NOTE: The previously listed AH1251 is a misreading of 1257.

Rectangular flan

C#	Date	Mintage	VG	Fine	VF	XF
46	AH1257	—	3.00	4.50	6.50	9.00

BRONZE, 10-11mm
Ibrahim Nur Al-Din

Y#	Date	Mintage	Fine	VF	XF	Unc
A1	AH1300	—	2.00	3.50	5.00	8.50

Some authorities consider Y-A1 a 1/4 Larin, while others call it a full Larin!

LARIN

BILLON or BRONZE, 14-16mm, 4.8-4.9gm.

C#	Date	Mintage	VG	Fine	VF	XF
12	AH1173	—	4.50	7.00	10.00	14.00
	Muhammad Ghiyas al-Din					
17	AH1180	—	4.00	6.00	8.00	10.00
	1184	—	4.50	7.00	10.00	14.00

NOTE: No Larins are known after this until the machine-made coinage of AH1318/1900AD, Y#1 below. Later coins formerly listed in this denomination are now considered to be heavy examples of the 1/2 Larin, or Kuda Larin.

BODU (2) LARI

BILLON or BRONZE, 18-20mm, 7-10 gm.

C#	Date	Mintage	VG	Fine	VF	XF
	Hasan Izz al-Din.					
14	AH1173	—	6.00	8.00	11.00	14.00
	1177	—	6.00	8.00	11.00	14.00
	Muhammad Ghiyas al-Din.					
18	AH1182	—	6.00	8.00	11.00	14.00
	Muhammad Muiz al-Din.					
24	AH1189	—	5.00	8.00	12.50	16.50
	Hasan Nur al-Din I.					
28	AH1197	—	5.00	8.00	11.00	14.00
	1200	—	5.00	8.00	11.00	14.00
	1201	—	6.00	9.00	12.50	16.00
	*1207	—	5.00	8.00	11.00	14.00

***NOTE:** Many varieties exist.

C#	Date	Mintage	VG	Fine	VF	XF
	Muhammad Mu'in al-Din					
43	AH1214	—	5.00	8.00	11.00	14.00
	Muhammad Imad al-Din IV					
48	AH1294	—	6.00	9.00	12.50	17.50
	1298	—	7.50	13.50	20.00	30.00

MOHUR

GOLD, 12.4 gm.
Hasan Nur al-Din I

C#	Date	Mintage	VG	Fine	VF	XF
35	AH1207	—	—	—	Rare	—

MONETARY REFORM

NOTE: Y#1-3 were struck with little care to adhere to the theoretical weight standards. The three denominations can only be distinguished by date, 1318 for the one, 1319 for the 2, and 1320 for the 4 Lari. Coins formerly listed in brass are actually gold-plated examples made privately for jewelry purposes. Similar platings in silver are also encountered.

LARIN

13mm, 1.2-2.7 gm.

Y#	Date	Mintage	Fine	VF	XF	Unc
1	AH1311 (error for 1319					
(2)		—	3.00	4.50	8.50	18.50
	1319	—	1.25	2.00	4.50	8.50

COPPER, 10mm, 0.8-1.4 gm.

Y#	Date	Mintage	Fine	VF	XF	Unc
1.1	AH1318	—	1.50	2.00	3.00	6.00
	1319	—	2.50	4.00	6.00	8.50

Y#	Date	Mintage	Fine	VF	XF	Unc
5	AH1331	—	1.00	1.25	1.75	2.50

Struck at Birmingham, England.

4 LARI

COPPER, 16mm, 2.6-5.2 gm.

Y#	Date	Mintage	Fine	VF	XF	Unc
3	AH1320	—	2.00	3.50	5.00	10.00

Rev: Arabic for 'SANAT' below date.

Y#	Date	Mintage	Fine	VF	XF	Unc
3.1	AH1320	—	3.50	7.00	10.00	16.00

NOTE: Y#3 and 3.1 are found with silver plating which apparently was done for jewelry purposes.

Y#	Date	Mintage	Fine	VF	XF	Unc
6	AH1331	—	1.50	2.50	3.50	5.00

Struck at Birmingham, England.

DECIMAL CURRENCY

100 LARI = 1 RUPEE

LARIN

BRONZE

Y#	Date	Year	Mintage	VF	XF	Unc
10	AH1379	1960	.300	.20	.30	.50
(7)	1379	1960	1,270	—	Proof	3.50
	ALUMINUM					
10a (7a)	AH1389	1970	.500	.10	.15	.30
	F.A.O. Issue					
—	AH1395	1975	*1.000	Reported, not confirmed		

*Projected mintage.

2 LARI

BRONZE

Y#	Date	Year	Mintage	VF	XF	Unc
11	AH1379	1960	.600	.20	.35	.60
(8)	1379	1960	1,270	—	Proof	4.00
	ALUMINUM					
11a (8a)	AH1389	1970	.500	.15	.25	.40
	F.A.O. Issue					
—	AH1395	1975	*1.000	Reported, not confirmed		

*Projected mintage.

5 LARI

NICKEL-BRASS

Y#	Date	Year	Mintage	VF	XF	Unc
12	AH1379	1960	.300	.25	.40	.75
(9)	1379	1960	1,270	—	Proof	5.00
	1389	1970	.300	.20	.30	.40
	ALUMINUM F.A.O. Issue					
—	AH1395	1975	*.500	Reported, not confirmed		

*Projected mintage.

10 LARI

NICKEL-BRASS

Y#	Date	Year	Mintage	VF	XF	Unc
13	AH1379	1960	.600	.50	.75	1.50
(10)	1379	1960	1,270	—	Proof	6.50

25 LARI

NICKEL-BRASS

Y#	Date	Year	Mintage	VF	XF	Unc
14	AH1379	1960	.300	.60	1.00	1.50
(11)	1379	1960	1,270	—	Proof	7.50

50 LARI

NICKEL-BRASS

Y#	Date	Year	Mintage	VF	XF	Unc
15	AH1379	1960	.300	1.00	1.75	2.50
(12)	1379	1960	1,270	—	Proof	10.00

5 RUFIYAA

COPPER-NICKEL
F.A.O. Issue

Y#	Date	Year	Mintage	VF	XF	Unc
16	AH1397	1977	.015	—	4.00	5.00

F.A.O. Issue

Y#	Date	Year	Mintage	VF	XF	Unc
18	AH1398	1978	7,000	—	5.00	6.50
	SILVER					
18a	AH1398	1978	—	—	Proof	45.00
	COPPER-NICKEL F.A.O. Issue					
20	—	1979	—	—	—	—

20 RUFIYAA

.500 SILVER
F.A.O. Issue
Obv: Similar to 5 Rufiyaa, Y#13.

Y#	Date	Year	Mintage	VF	XF	Unc
17	AH1397	1977	.015	—	12.00	15.00

25 RUFIYAA

28.1600 gm., .500 SILVER
F.A.O. Issue
Obv: Similar to 5 Rufiyaa, Y#15.

Y#	Date	Year	Mintage	VF	XF	Unc
19	AH1398	1978	7,000	—	16.50	22.50
	1398	1978	—	—	Proof	50.00
	F.A.O. Issue					
21	—	1979	—	—	—	—

NCLT ISSUES

PROOF SETS

STANDARD METALS

KM#	Date	Mintage	Identification	Issue Price	Mkt. Val.
101	1960(6)	1,270	Y7-12	—	35.00

MALI

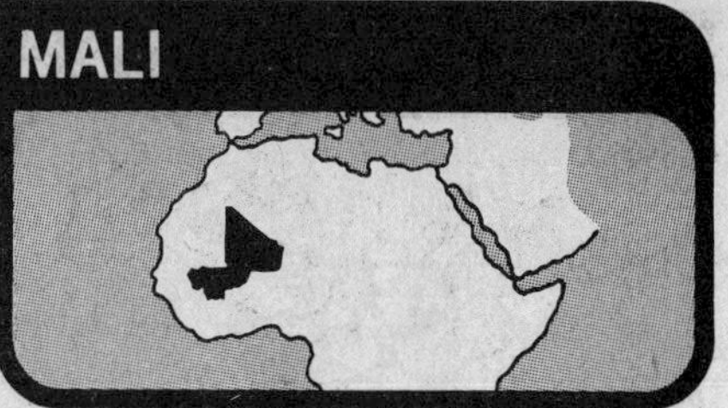

The Republic of Mali, a landlocked country in the interior of West Africa southwest of Algeria, has an area of 464,873 sq. mi. (1,204,015 sq. km.) and a population of 6.3 million. Capital: Bamako. Livestock, fish, cotton and peanuts are exported.

Malians are descendants of the ancient Malinke Kingdom of Mali that controlled the middle Niger from the 11th to the 17th centuries. The French penetrated the Sudan (now Mali) about 1880, and established their rule in 1898 after subduing fierce native resistance. In 1904 the area became the colony of Upper Senegal-Niger (changed to French Sudan in 1920), and became part of the French Union in 1946. In 1958 French Sudan became the Sudanese Republic with complete internal autonomy. Senegal joined with the Sudanese Republic in 1959 to form the Mali Federation which, in 1960, became a fully independent member of the French Community. Upon Senegal's subsequent withdrawal from the Federation, the Sudanese, on Sept. 22, 1960, proclaimed their nation the fully independent Republic of Mali and severed all ties with France.

MINT MARKS

(a) - Paris, privy marks only

5 FRANCS

ALUMINUM

Y#	Date	Mintage	VF	XF	Unc
1	1961	—	.50	.75	1.25

10 FRANCS

25.0000 gm., .900 SILVER, .7234 oz ASW
Independence Day

H#	Date	Mintage	XF	Unc	Proof
1	1960	.010	—	—	22.50

ALUMINUM

Y#	Date	Mintage	VF	XF	Unc
2	1961	—	.25	.50	1.00

3.2000 gm., .900 GOLD, .0926 oz AGW
Obv: Bust of President Keita. Rev: Coat of arms.

Fr#	Date	Mintage	XF	Unc	Proof
4	1967	—	—	—	75.00

ALUMINUM

Y#	Date	Mintage	VF	XF	Unc
6	1976	5.000	—	—	—

25 FRANCS

ALUMINUM

Y#	Date	Mintage	VF	XF	Unc
3	1961	—	.50	1.50	2.25

8.0000 gm., .900 GOLD, .2315 oz AGW
Similar to 10 Francs, Fr#4

Fr#	Date	Mintage	XF	Unc	Proof
3	1967	—	—	—	150.00

ALUMINUM

Y#	Date	Mintage	VF	XF	Unc
7	1976(a)	5.000	.35	.75	1.25

50 FRANCS

16.0000 gm., .900 GOLD, .4630 oz AGW
Similar to 10 Francs, Fr#4

Fr#	Date	Mintage	XF	Unc	Proof
2	1967	—	—	—	300.00

NICKEL-BRASS
F.A.O. Issue

Y#	Date	Mintage	VF	XF	Unc
4	1975(a)	10.000	.50	.75	1.50
	1977	—	—	—	—

100 FRANCS

32.0000 gm., .900 GOLD, .9260 oz AGW
Similar to 10 Francs, Fr#4

Fr#	Date	Mintage	XF	Unc	Proof
1	1967	—	—	—	625.00

NICKEL-BRASS
F.A.O. Issue

Y#	Date	Mintage	VF	XF	Unc
5	1975(a)	23.000	1.00	1.75	2.50

NCLT ISSUES

ESSAIS

Standard metals unless otherwise noted.

Y#	Date	Mintage	Identification	Issue Price	Mkt Val.
E4	1975	—	50 Francs	—	20.00
E5	1975	—	100 Francs	—	20.00
E2	1976	—	10 Francs	—	22.00
E6	1976	—	25 Francs	—	22.00

PROOF SETS

Standard metals unless otherwise noted.

KM#	Date	Mintage	Identification	Issue Price	Mkt. Val.
101	1967(4)	—	Fr#1-4	—	1150.

MALTA

The Republic of Malta, an independent parliamentary democracy within the British Commonwealth, is situated in the Mediterranean Sea between Sicily and North Africa. With the islands of Gozo and Comino, Malta has an area of 121 sq. mi. (313 sq. km.) and a population of 320,000. Capital: Valletta. Malta has no proven mineral resources, an agriculture insufficient to its needs, and a small, but expanding, manufacturing facility. Clothing, textile yarns and fabrics, and knitted wear are exported.

For more than 3,500 years Malta was ruled, in succession, by Phoenicians, Carthaginians, Romans, Arabs, Normans, the Knights of Malta, France and Britain. Napoleon seized Malta by treachery in 1798. The French were ousted by a Maltese insurrection assisted by Britain, and in 1814 Malta, of its own free will, became a part of the British Empire. Malta obtained full independence in Sept., 1964; electing to remain within the Commonwealth with the British monarch as the nominal head of state.

Malta became a republic on Dec. 13, 1974, but remained a member of the Commonwealth of Nations. The president is Chief of State. The prime minister is the Head of Government.

RULERS

British, until 1964

BRITISH COINAGE

MONETARY SYSTEM

4 Farthings = 1 Penny

1/3 FARTHINGS

COPPER

NOTE: From 1827 through 1913 homeland type 1/3 Farthings along with other coinage of Great Britain circulated in Malta. The 1/3 Farthings corresponded to the copper Grano or 1/12 penny. These are found listed under Great Britain.

DECIMAL COINAGE

MINTMARKS

FM - Franklin Mint, U.S.A.*

***NOTE:** During 1975-78 the Franklin Mint produced coinage in up to 3 different qualities. Qualities of issue are designated in ( ) after each date and are defined as follows:

(M) MATTE - Normal circulation strike or a dull finish produced by sandblasting special uncirculated (polish finish) or proof quality dies.

(U) SPECIAL UNCIRCULATED - Polished or prooflike in appearance without any frosted features.

(P) PROOF - The highest quality obtainable having mirror-like fields and frosted features.

MONETARY SYSTEM

10 Mils = 1 Cent
100 Cents = 1 Pound

2 MILS

ALUMINUM

Y#	Date	Mintage	VF	XF	Unc
5	1972	.030	—	.10	.25
5	1972	.013	—	Proof	1.00
	1976FM(M)	5,000	—	—	—
	1976FM(P)	.026	—	Proof	3.00
	1977FM(M)	5,000	—	—	—
	1977FM(U)	252 pcs.	—	—	—
	1977FM(P)	6,884	—	Proof	3.00
	1978FM(M)	5,000	—	—	—
	1978FM(U)	252 pcs.	—	—	—
	1978FM(P)	3,244	—	Proof	3.00
	1979FM(U)	537 pcs.	—	—	—
	1979FM(P)	6,577	—	Proof	1.50

3 MILS

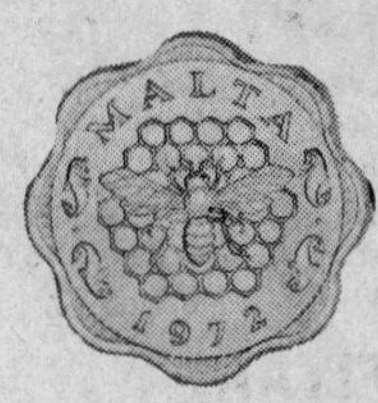

ALUMINUM

Y#	Date	Mintage	VF	XF	Unc
6	1972	—	—	—	.30
	1972	8,000	—	Proof	1.50
	1976FM(M)	5,000	—	—	—
	1976FM(P)	.026	—	Proof	6.00
	1977FM(M)	5,000	—	—	—
	1977FM(U)	252 pcs.	—	—	—
	1977FM(P)	6,884	—	Proof	6.00
	1978FM(M)	5,000	—	—	—
	1978FM(U)	252 pcs.	—	—	—
	1978FM(P)	3,244	—	Proof	6.00
	1979FM(U)	537 pcs.	—	—	—
	1979FM(P)	6,577	—	Proof	2.00

5 MILS

ALUMINUM

Y#	Date	Mintage	VF	XF	Unc
7	1972	4.320	.10	.15	.40
	1972	.013	—	Proof	2.50
	1976FM(M)	5,000	—	—	—
	1976FM(P)	.026	—	Proof	6.00
	1977FM(M)	5,000	—	—	—
	1977FM(U)	252 pcs.	—	—	—
	1977FM(P)	6,884	—	Proof	6.00
	1978FM(M)	5,000	—	—	—
	1978FM(U)	252 pcs.	—	—	—
	1978FM(P)	3,244	—	Proof	6.00
	1979FM(U)	537 pcs.	—	—	—
	1979FM(P)	6,577	—	Proof	2.50

CENT

BRONZE

Y#	Date	Mintage	VF	XF	Unc
8	1972	5.650	.10	.20	.40
	1972	.013	—	Proof	2.50
	1975	1.500	.10	.20	.30
	1976FM(M)	5,000	—	—	—
	1976FM(P)	.026	—	Proof	9.00
	1977	—	—	.10	.20
	1977FM(M)	5,000	—	—	—
	1977FM(U)	252 pcs.	—	—	—
	1977FM(P)	6,884	—	Proof	9.00
	1978FM(M)	5,000	—	—	—
	1978FM(U)	252 pcs.	—	—	—
	1978FM(P)	3,244	—	Proof	9.00
	1979FM(U)	537 pcs.	—	—	—
	1979FM(P)	6,527	—	Proof	3.00

2 CENTS

COPPER-NICKEL

Y#	Date	Mintage	VF	XF	Unc
9	1972	5.640	.15	.25	.50
	1972	.013	—	Proof	3.00
	1976	1.000	.15	.25	.60
	1976FM(M)	2,500	—	—	.50
	1976FM(P)	.026	—	Proof	10.00
	1977	—	.15	.25	.50
	1977FM(M)	2,500	—	—	—
	1977FM(U)	252 pcs.	—	—	—
	1977FM(P)	6,884	—	Proof	9.00
	1978(M)	2,500	—	—	—
	1978FM(U)	252 pcs.	—	—	—
	1978FM(P)	3,244	—	Proof	9.00
	1979FM(U)	537 pcs.	—	—	—
	1979FM(P)	6,577	—	Proof	4.00

5 CENTS

COPPER-NICKEL

Y#	Date	Mintage	VF	XF	Unc
10	1972	4.180	.20	.30	.50
	1972	.013	—	Proof	3.50
	1976	—	.20	.30	.75
	1976FM(M)	2,500	—	—	—
	1976FM(P)	.026	—	Proof	12.00
	1977FM(M)	2,500	—	—	—
	1977FM(U)	252 pcs.	—	—	—
	1977FM(P)	6,884	—	Proof	10.00
	1978FM(M)	252 pcs.	—	—	—
	1978FM(U)	252 pcs.	—	—	—
	1978FM(P)	3,244	—	Proof	10.00
	1979FM(U)	537 pcs.	—	—	—
	1979FM(P)	6,577	—	Proof	6.00

10 CENTS

COPPER-NICKEL

Y#	Date	Mintage	VF	XF	Unc
11	1972	7.180	.30	.75	1.50
	1972	.013	—	Proof	4.00
	1976FM(M)	1,000	—	—	—
	1976FM(P)	.026	—	Proof	18.00
	1977FM(M)	1,000	—	—	—
	1977FM(U)	252 pcs.	—	—	—
	1977FM(P)	6,884	—	Proof	18.00
	1978FM(M)	1,000	—	—	—
	1978FM(U)	252 pcs.	—	—	—
	1978FM(P)	3,244	—	Proof	18.00
	1979FM(U)	537 pcs.	—	—	—
	1979FM(P)	6,577	—	Proof	8.00

25 CENTS

BRASS

1st Anniversary of Republic of Malta

Y#	Date	Mintage	VF	XF	Unc
39	1975	.500	.75	1.00	2.00

BRONZE

Y#	Date	Mintage	VF	XF	Unc
39a	1975	6,000	—	Proof	14.00

COPPER-NICKEL

Y#	Date	Mintage	VF	XF	Unc
39b	1976FM(M)	300 pcs.	—	—	—
	1976FM(P)	.026	—	Proof	20.00
	1977FM(M)	300 pcs.	—	—	—
	1977FM(U)	252 pcs.	—	—	—
	1977FM(P)	6,884	—	Proof	20.00
	1977FM(M)	300 pcs.	—	—	—
	1978FM(U)	252 pcs.	—	—	—
	1978FM(P)	3,244	—	Proof	20.00
	1979FM(U)	537 pcs.	—	—	—
	1979FM(P)	6,577	—	Proof	9.00

50 CENTS

COPPER-NICKEL

Y#	Date	Mintage	VF	XF	Unc
12	1972	2.680	.75	1.50	2.75
	1972	.013	—	Proof	5.00
	1976FM(M)	150 pcs.	—	—	—
	1976FM(P)	.026	—	Proof	25.00
	1977FM(M)	150 pcs.	—	—	—
	1977FM(U)	252 pcs.	—	—	—
	1977FM(P)	6,884	—	Proof	25.00
	1978FM(M)	150 pcs.	—	—	—
	1978FM(U)	150 pcs.	—	—	—
	1978FM(P)	3,244	—	Proof	25.00
	1979FM(U)	537 pcs.	—	—	—
	1979FM(P)	6,577	—	Proof	10.00

POUND

10.0000 gm., .987 SILVER, .3173 oz ASW

Y#	Date	Mintage	VF	XF	Unc
13	1972	.055	BV	10.00	15.00

Y#	Date	Mintage	VF	XF	Unc
19	1973	.030	BV	10.00	15.00

5.6600 gm., .925 SILVER, .1683 oz ASW

Y#	Date	Mintage	VF	XF	Unc
45	1977	.015	BV	5.00	10.00
	1977	2,500	BV	Proof	25.00

Departure of Foreign Forces

Y#	Date	Mintage	VF	XF	Unc
51	1979	—	BV	5.00	7.00
	1979	1,294	—	Proof	15.00

2 POUNDS

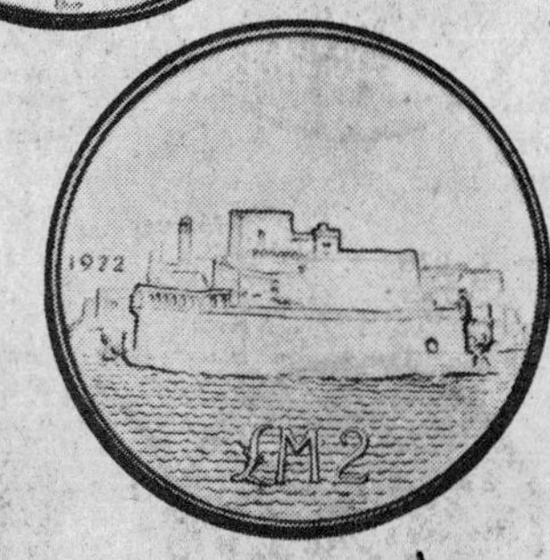

20.0000 gm., .987 SILVER, .6347 oz ASW

Y#	Date	Mintage	VF	XF	Unc
14	1972	.053	BV	20.00	30.00

Y#	Date	Mintage	VF	XF	Unc
20	1973	.030	BV	20.00	30.00

10.0000 gm., .987 SILVER, .3173 oz ASW

Y#	Date	Mintage	VF	XF	Unc
24	1974	.025	BV	10.00	15.00

Galea

Obv: Similar to Y#24. Rev: Similar to Y#34.

Y#	Date	Mintage	VF	XF	Unc
29	1975	2,000	BV	10.00	30.00

Galea

Y#	Date	Mintage	VF	XF	Unc
34	1975	.018	BV	10.00	15.00

Mercer

Y#	Date	Mintage	VF	XF	Unc
40	1976	.011	BV	10.00	15.00

11.3100 gm., .925 SILVER, .3363 oz ASW

Y#	Date	Mintage	VF	XF	Unc
46	1977	.015	BV	10.00	15.00
	1977	2,500	—	Proof	45.00

4 POUNDS

20.0000 gm., .987 SILVER, .6347 oz ASW

Y#	Date	Mintage	VF	XF	Unc
25	1974	.024	BV	20.00	25.00

Obv: Same as Y#25. Rev: Similar to Y#35.

Y#	Date	Mintage	VF	XF	Unc
30	1975	2,000	—	20.00	40.00

Y#	Date	Mintage	VF	XF	Unc
35	1975	.018	BV	20.00	25.00

Obv: Similar to Y#35.

Y#	Date	Mintage	VF	XF	Unc
41	1976	.010	BV	20.00	25.00

5 POUNDS

3.0000 gm., .917 GOLD, .0884 oz AGW

Y#	Date	Mintage	VF	XF	Unc
15	1972	.018	BV	60.00	65.00

28.2800 gm., .925 SILVER, .8411 oz ASW
Obv: Similar to 2 Pounds, Y#34.

Y#	Date	Mintage	VF	XF	Unc
47	1977	.015	—	25.00	30.00
	1977	2,500	—	Proof	75.00

10 POUNDS

6.0000 gm., .917 GOLD, .1769 oz AGW

Y#	Date	Mintage	VF	XF	Unc
16	1972	.016	BV	115.00	130.00

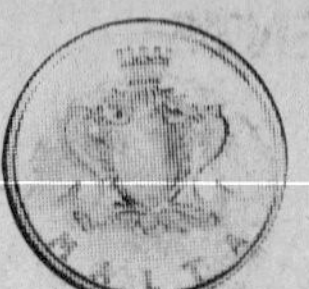

3.0000 gm., .917 GOLD, .0884 oz AGW

Y#	Date	Mintage	VF	XF	Unc
21	1973	9,078	BV	60.00	65.00

Y#	Date	Mintage	VF	XF	Unc
26	1974	9,124	BV	60.00	65.00

Obv: Similar to Y#26. Rev: Similar to Y#36.

Y#	Date	Mintage	VF	XF	Unc
31	1975	2,000	BV	60.00	120.00

Y#	Date	Mintage	VF	XF	Unc
36	1975	6,448	BV	60.00	70.00

Y#	Date	Mintage	VF	XF	Unc
42	1976	4,448	BV	60.00	70.00

20 POUNDS

12.0000 gm., .917 GOLD, .3538 oz AGW

Y#	Date	Mintage	VF	XF	Unc
17	1972	.016	BV	230.00	260.00

6.0000 gm., .917 GOLD, .1769 oz AGW

Y#	Date	Mintage	VF	XF	Unc
22	1973	9,075	BV	115.00	130.00

Y#	Date	Mintage	VF	XF	Unc
27	1974	8,700	BV	115.00	130.00

Obv: Similar to Y#27. Rev: Similar to Y#37.

Y#	Date	Mintage	VF	XF	Unc
32	1975	2,000	BV	115.00	230.00

Y#	Date	Mintage	VF	XF	Unc
37	1975	5,698	BV	115.00	125.00

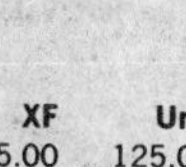

Obv: Similar to Y#27.

Y#	Date	Mintage	VF	XF	Unc
43	1976	4,098	BV	115.00	125.00

25 POUNDS

8.0000 gm., .917 GOLD, .2358 oz AGW

Y#	Date	Mintage	VF	XF	Unc
48	1977	4,000	BV	150.00	175.00
	1977	750 pcs.	—	Proof	300.00

50 POUNDS

30.0000 gm., .917 GOLD, .8845 oz AGW

Y#	Date	Mintage	VF	XF	Unc
18	1972	.016	BV	575.00	600.00

15.0000 gm., .917 GOLD, .4422 oz AGW

Y#	Date	Mintage	VF	XF	Unc
23	1973	9,075	BV	290.00	300.00

Y#	Date	Mintage	VF	XF	Unc
28	1974	8,667	BV	290.00	300.00

Obv: Similar to Y#28. Rev: Similar to Y#38.

Y#	Date	Mintage	VF	XF	Unc
33	1975	2,000	BV	290.00	480.00

Y#	Date	Mintage	VF	XF	Unc
38	1975	5,500	BV	290.00	300.00

Obv: Similar to Y#33.

Y#	Date	Mintage	VF	XF	Unc
44	1976	3,748	BV	290.00	300.00

16.0000 gm., .917 GOLD, .4717 oz AGW

Y#	Date	Mintage	VF	XF	Unc
49	1977	4,000	BV	300.00	350.00
	1977	750 pcs.	—	Proof	600.00

100 POUNDS

32.0000 gm., .917 GOLD, .9435 oz AGW

Y#	Date	Mintage	VF	XF	Unc
50	1977	4,000	BV	610.00	650.00
	1977	750 pcs.	—	Proof	1200.

NCLT ISSUES

MINT SETS

KM#	Date	Mintage	Identification	Issue Price	Mkt. Val.
S1	1972(8)	8,000	Y5-12	—	7.00
S2	1972(4)	8,000	Y15-18	210.00	1100.
S3	1972(2)	—	Y13,14	8.50	50.00
S4	1973(3)	9,075	Y21-23	—	525.00
S5	1973(2)	—	Y19,20	—	50.00
S6	1974(3)	—	Y26-28	256.00	515.00
S7	1974(2)	—	Y24,25	19.60	28.00
S8	1975(5)	2,000	Y29-33	—	900.00
S9	1975(3)	—	Y31-33	256.00	510.00
S10	1975(2)	—	Y29-30	20.00	29.00
S11	1975(3)	—	Y36-38	—	825.00
S12	1976(2)	—	Y34-35	—	29.00
S13	1976(3)	—	Y42-44	—	510.00
S14	1977(9)	252	Y5-12,39b	—	110.00
S15	1977(3)	4,000	Y48-50	610.00	1100.
S16	1977(3)	15,000	Y45-47	34.50	55.00
S17	1978(9)	252	Y5-12,39b	—	110.00
S18	1978(3)	—	Y54-56	—	—
S19	1978(3)	—	Y51-53	—	—
S20	1979(9)	537	Y15-12,39b	—	23.50

PROOF SETS

STANDARD METALS

KM#	Date	Mintage	Identification	Issue Price	Mkt. Val.
101	1972(8)	8,000	Y5-12 (plastic case)	—	24.00
102	1976(9)	26,117	Y5-12,39b	27.50	95.00
103	1977(9)	6,884	Y5-12,39b	31.50	110.00
104	1977(3)	750	Y48-50	909.00	1450.
105	1977(3)	2,500	Y45-47	72.00	140.00
106	1978(9)	3,244	Y5-12,39b	—	110.00
109	1979(10)	6,577	Y5-11,39b,12,51	41.50	58.00

ORDER OF MALTA

The Order of Malta, modern successor to the Sovereign Military Hospitaller Order of St. John of Jerusalem (the crusading Knights Hospitallers), derives its sovereignty from grants of extraterritoriality by Italy (1928) and the Vatican City (1953), and from its supranational character as a religious military Order owing suzerainty to the Holy See. Its territory is confined to Palazzo Malta on Via Condotti, Villa Malta and the crest of the Aventine Hill, all in the city of Rome. The Order maintains diplomatic relations with about 35 governments, including Italy, Spain, Austria, State of Malta, Portugal, Brazil, Guatemala, Panama, Peru, Iran, Lebanon, Philippines, Liberia, Ethiopia, etc.

The Knights Hospitallers were founded in 1099 just before the crusaders' capture of Jerusalem. Father Gerard (died 1120) was the founder and first rector of the Jerusalem hospital. The headquarters of the Order was successively at Jerusalem 1099-1187; Acre 1187-1291; Cyprus 1291-1310; Rhodes 1310-1522; Malta 1530-1798; Trieste 1798-1799; St. Petersburg 1799-1803; Catania 1803-1825; Ferrara 1826-1834; Rome 1834-Present.

The symbolic coins issued by the Order since 1961 are intended to continue the last independent coinage of the Order on Malta in 1798. In traditional tari and scudi denominations, they are issued only in proof condition. They have a theoretical fixed exchange value with the Italian lira, but are not used in commerce.

The coinage fits in neither the NCLT category, since it is not legal tender; the fantasy category, since a sovereign state issues it; nor medal category, since they carry denominations. They are perhaps the world's last symbolic coinage, just as their issuer is the world's last sovereign order of knighthood. Proceeds from the sale of Order coinage maintain the Order's hospitals, clinics and leprosaria around the world.

RULERS

Knights of St. John of Jerusalem until 1798, 1800-1802
Emmanuel de Rohan, Grand Master, 1775-1797
Ferdinand Hompesch, Grand Master, 1797-1798
French, 1798-1800
Ernesto Paterno-Castello di Carcaci, lieutenant grand master, 1955-1962
Angelo de Mojana di Cologna, grand master, 1962-

MINTMARKS

Rome (no mark) 1961
Paris (no mark) 1962
Arezzo (no mark) 1963
Order of Malta Mint in Rome - SMOM in angles of a cross - 1964-

MONETARY SYSTEM

(Until ca. 1800)

6 Piccioli = 1 Grano
20 Grani = 2 Carlini = 1 Taro (= 40 Lire, Italy)
12 Tari = 1 Scudo (= 480 Lire, Italy)
30 Tari = 1 Pezza or Oncia

NOTE: The exchange value of symbolic Order coinage was established in 1968 in connection with its F.A.O. commemorative coins. According to the United Nations agency:

GRANO

COPPER

Obv. leg: F. EMMANVEL DE ROHAN M, arms. Rev: Maltese cross with date in angles.

C#	Date	Mintage	VG	Fine	VF
36.1	1776	—	2.50	4.00	6.00

Obv. leg: F. EMMANYEL DE ROHAN M M.

C#	Date	Mintage	VG	Fine	VF
36.2	1776	—	2.50	4.00	6.00

Obv. leg: F. EMMANVEL DE ROHAN M. Rev: G-I in circle; date in legend.

C#	Date	Mintage	VG	Fine	VF
37.1	1776	—	2.00	3.00	4.50

Obv. leg: F EMMANUEL DE ROHAN M. M.

C#	Date	Mintage	VG	Fine	VF
37.2	1777	—	2.00	3.00	4.50
	1778	—	2.00	3.00	4.50

Obv. leg: F. EMMANUEL DE ROHAN M. Rev: G. I in circle; date in legend.

C#	Date	Mintage	VG	Fine	VF
37.3	1777	—	2.00	3.00	4.50
	1780	—	2.00	3.00	4.50

Obv. leg: F. EMMANVEL DE ROHAN M.

C#	Date	Mintage	VG	Fine	VF
37a.1	1785	—	2.00	3.00	4.50

Obv. leg: F. EMMANUEL DE ROHAN M.

C#	Date	Mintage	VG	Fine	VF
37a.2	1785	—	2.00	3.00	4.50

XV (15) PICCIOLI

COPPER

C#	Date	Mintage	VG	Fine	VF
38	1776	—	5.00	7.50	11.50
	1777	—	5.00	7.50	11.50

NOTE: Two varieties of 1776 exist.

V (5) GRANI

COPPER

Obv. leg: F EMMANUEL DE ROHAN M, crowned arms over eagle. Rev: Clasped hands, date above, value below.

C#	Date	Mintage	VG	Fine	VF
39.1	1776	—	3.00	4.50	7.00
	1780	—	3.00	4.50	7.00
	1790	—	3.00	4.50	7.00

Obv. leg: F. EMMANVEL ....

C#	Date	Mintage	VG	Fine	VF
39.2	1780	—	3.00	4.50	7.00

X (10) GRANI

COPPER

Obv. leg: F. EMMANUEL DE ROHAN M M H, crowned arms over eagle. Rev: Clasped hands, date above, value below.

C#	Date	Mintage	VG	Fine	VF
40.1	1776	—	5.00	7.50	11.50

Obv. leg: F. EMMANUEL DE ROHAN M.

C#	Date	Mintage	VG	Fine	VF
40.2	1776	—	5.00	7.50	11.50

Obv. leg: F. EMMANVEL DE ROHAN M.M.H.

C#	Date	Mintage	VG	Fine	VF
40.3	1776	—	5.00	7.50	11.50

Obv. leg: F. EMMANUEL DE ROHAN M.M.

C#	Date	Mintage	VG	Fine	VF
40.4	1786	—	5.00	7.50	11.50

Obv. leg: F. EMMANVEL DE ROHAN M.M.

C#	Date	Mintage	VG	Fine	VF
40.5	1786	—	5.00	7.50	11.50

BRONZE

KM#	Date	Mintage	XF	Unc	Proof
1	1967	.010	—	—	4.00
	1969	.010	—	—	4.00
	1970	3,000	—	—	4.00

Battle of Lepanto

Obv: Similar to 9 Tari, KM#9. Rev: Similar to KM#1.

KM#	Date	Mintage	XF	Unc	Proof
2	1971	6,000	—	—	4.00

Obv: Military bust of del Monte facing right, date at left, value at right. Rev: Scene of naval battle.

KM#	Date	Mintage	XF	Unc	Proof
3	1971	2,500	—	—	4.00

KM#	Date	Mintage	XF	Unc	Proof
4	1972	5,000	—	—	4.00
	1973	5,000	—	—	4.00
5	1974	5,000	—	—	4.00
	1975	5,000	—	—	4.00
	1976	5,000	—	—	4.00
	1977	5,000	—	—	4.00

KM#	Date	Mintage	XF	Unc	Proof
55	1978	5,000	—	—	4.00
	1979	5,000	—	—	3.00

TARO

COPPER

Obv. leg: F. EMMANUEL DE ROHAN M.M, crowned arms over eagle. Rev: Head of John the Baptist on platter.

C#	Date	Mintage	VG	Fine	VF
41.1	1786	—	10.00	15.00	22.50

Obv. leg: F. EMMANUEL DE ROHAN M.

C#	Date	Mintage	VG	Fine	VF
41.2	1786	—	10.00	15.00	22.50

Obv. leg: F. EMMANUEL DE ROHAN M.M.H. Rev. leg: CONCUTIATIS NEMINEM.

C#	Date	Mintage	VG	Fine	VF
41a.1	ND	—	11.50	17.50	26.50

Obv. leg: F. EMMANUEL DE ROHAN M., no value.

C#	Date	Mintage	VG	Fine	VF
41b	ND	—	11.50	17.50	26.50

SILVER

Obv: Crowned oval arms in sprays. Rev: Value in wreath; date in legend.

C#	Date	Mintage	VG	Fine	VF
42.1	1777	—	4.50	6.50	10.00

Obv: Crowned oval arms in sprays; retrograde N in ROHAN.

C#	Date	Mintage	VG	Fine	VF
42.2	1777	—	6.50	9.50	15.00

2 TARI

SILVER, 21mm

Obv: Crowned arms over eagle. Rev: Maltese cross in circle, date in angles; SPUL in legend.

C#	Date	Mintage	Fine	VF	XF
43.1	1776	—	4.50	6.50	10.00

Rev. leg: SPU for SEPUL.

C#	Date	Mintage	Fine	VF	XF
43.2	1779	—	6.50	9.50	15.00

BRONZE
F.A.O. Issue

KM#	Date	Mintage	XF	Unc	Proof
6	1968	.027	—	—	1.50

4 TARI

SILVER
Obv: Crowned arms over eagle.
Rev: Date, value in wreath.

C#	Date	Mintage	Fine	VF	XF
44	1776	—	6.00	9.00	13.50
	1779	—	6.00	9.00	13.50

VI (6) TARI

SILVER
Obv: Crowned arms over eagle.
Rev: Value, date in wreath.

C#	Date	Mintage	Fine	VF	XF
46	1776	—	8.00	12.00	20.00
	1780	—	8.00	12.00	20.00

NOTE: Varieties exist.

9 TARI

9.0000 gm., .900 SILVER, .2604 oz ASW
Obv: Similar to KM#9. Rev: Similar to 2 Scudi, KM#30.

KM#	Date	Mintage	XF	Unc	Proof
7	1967	.010	—	—	8.00

Obv: Similar to KM#9. Rev: Similar to 1 Scudo, KM#16.

KM#	Date	Mintage	XF	Unc	Proof
8	1969	.010	—	—	8.00
9	1970	3,000	—	—	8.00
	1971	6,000	—	—	8.00

Battle of Lepanto
Obv: Military bust of del Monte facing right, date at left, value at right. Rev: Scene of naval battle.

KM#	Date	Mintage	XF	Unc	Proof
10	1971	2,500	—	—	8.00

Obv: Similar to 1 Scudo, KM#16. Rev: Similar to KM#9.

KM#	Date	Mintage	XF	Unc	Proof
11	1972	2,500	—	—	8.00
12	1973	—	—	—	8.00
13	1974	—	—	—	8.00
	1975	—	—	—	8.00
13	1976	—	—	—	8.00
	1977	—	—	—	8.00
56	1978	—	—	—	8.00
	1979	5,000	—	—	8.00

SCUDO

SILVER

C#	Date	Mintage	Fine	VF	XF
47.1	1776	—	40.00	60.00	90.00

Obv: Large bust. Rev: Crown divides date.

C#	Date	Mintage	Fine	VF	XF
47.2	1776	—	40.00	60.00	90.00
48	1796	—	20.00	30.00	45.00

12.0000 gm., .986 SILVER, .3804 oz ASW
Obv: Similar to KM#16 reverse. Rev: Similar to KM#22.

KM#	Date	Mintage	XF	Unc	Proof
14	1961	1,200	—	—	15.00
15	1962	200 pcs.	—	—	125.00
	1963	600 pcs.	—	—	20.00
A15	1964	4,000	—	—	20.00
16	1965	4,000	—	—	20.00
	1966	3,600	—	—	20.00

Obv: Similar to 10 Grani, KM#3. Rev: Crowned Maltese Cross bearing collar of Santo Rosario, lower part of cross dividing date, value below.

KM#	Date	Mintage	XF	Unc	Proof
17	1967	4,000	—	—	15.00
18	1968	4,000	—	—	15.00
19	1969	5,000	—	—	15.00
20	1970	4,000	—	—	15.00
21	1971	4,000	—	—	15.00

KM#	Date	Mintage	XF	Unc	Proof
22	1972	4,000	—	—	15.00

Obv: Similar to C#49.

C#	Date	Mintage	Fine	VF	XF
50	1779	—	35.00	50.00	75.00

Obv: Similar to KM#27.

KM#	Date	Mintage	XF	Unc	Proof
28	1965	5,000	—	—	35.00
	1966	4,500	—	—	35.00

Obv: Same as KM#28. Rev: Two scrolled oval shields of arms, surmounted by a crowned Maltese cross.

29	1967	4,000	—	—	25.00

50a	1781	—	25.00	37.50	55.00

Obv: Bust left. Rev: Crowned imperial eagle with arms on breast, date and value above.

57	1798	—	20.00	30.00	45.00

23	1973	4,000	—	—	15.00

Obv: Similar to KM#23. Rev: Similar to KM#16.

24	1974	4,000	—	—	15.00
	1975	4,000	—	—	15.00
	1976	4,000	—	—	15.00
	1977	4,000	—	—	15.00

Obv: Left facing portrait, date.
Rev: Sailing ship with oars, value.

57	1978	4,000	—	—	15.00

16 TARI

SILVER

Obv: Bust right. Rev: Crowned arms over eagle, date in legend, crown divides value.

50b	1781	—	35.00	50.00	75.00

2 SCUDI

SILVER

Obv: Bust right.
Rev: Crowned oval, arms in wreath, date above, value below.

53	1796	—	25.00	37.50	55.00

24.0000 gm., .986 SILVER, .7608 oz ASW
Obv: Similar to 1 Scudo, KM#14.
Rev: Similar to 1 Scudo, KM#22.

KM#	Date	Mintage	XF	Unc	Proof
25	1961	1,200	—	—	30.00

30	1968	4,000	—	—	25.00

12.0000 gm.
Castle in Magione, Italy

60	1979	4,000	—	—	15.00

XV (15) TARI

SILVER

C#	Date	Mintage	Fine	VF	XF
49	1776	—	35.00	50.00	75.00
	1777	—	35.00	50.00	75.00

Obv: Similar to 5 Scudi, KM#40.

26	1962	200 pcs.	—	—	200.00
	1963	1,600	—	—	35.00

Obv: Similar to 1 Scudo, KM#16.

27	1964	6,000	—	—	35.00

31	1969	5,000	—	—	25.00

Obv: Similar to KM#31, date below bust: MCMLXX

KM#	Date	Mintage	XF	Unc	Proof
32	1970	4,000	—	—	25.00

Obv: Similar to KM#31.

KM#	Date	Mintage	XF	Unc	Proof
33	1971	4,000	—	—	25.00
	1973	—	—	—	25.00

Obv: Similar to KM#31.

KM#	Date	Mintage	XF	Unc	Proof
34	1972	4,000	—	—	25.00

Obv: Similar to KM#31. Rev: Crowned quartered arms on Maltese Cross separating 2-S.

KM#	Date	Mintage	XF	Unc	Proof
36	1974	3,000	—	—	25.00

Obv: Similar to KM#31.

KM#	Date	Mintage	XF	Unc	Proof
37	1975	4,000	—	—	25.00

Obv: Similar to KM#31. Rev: View of baptism of Jesus.

KM#	Date	Mintage	XF	Unc	Proof
53	1976	4,000	—	—	25.00
	1977	4,000	—	—	25.00

Obv: Left facing portrait, date.
Rev: Sailing ship with oars, value.

KM#	Date	Mintage	XF	Unc	Proof
58	1978	—	—	—	25.00

Castle in Ipplis Premariacco, Italy

KM#	Date	Mintage	XF	Unc	Proof
61	1979	4,000	—	—	25.00

XXX (30) TARI

SILVER

C#	Date	Mintage	Fine	VF	XF
51	1777	—	60.00	85.00	125.00

Obv: Bust. Rev: Crowned arms on imperial eagle.

C#	Date	Mintage	Fine	VF	XF
52	1779	—	40.00	60.00	90.00

Similar to C#52. Rev. leg: HOSPITA.

C#	Date	Mintage	Fine	VF	XF
52a	1779	—	40.00	60.00	90.00
	1781	—	40.00	60.00	90.00
	1785	—	40.00	60.00	90.00
	1789	—	40.00	60.00	90.00
	1790	—	40.00	60.00	90.00
	1796	—	40.00	60.00	90.00

C#	Date	Mintage	Fine	VF	XF
58.1	1798	—	75.00	125.00	175.00

Obv: Eight pointed cross below shoulder.

C#	Date	Mintage	Fine	VF	XF
58.2	1798	—	75.00	125.00	175.00

Obv: Dot below bust.

C#	Date	Mintage	Fine	VF	XF
58.3	1798	—	80.00	135.00	200.00

Obv: Dot in front of Grand Masters' nose.

C#	Date	Mintage	Fine	VF	XF
58.4	1798	—	80.00	135.00	200.00

NOTE: It is believed that C#58.3 and 58.4 were struck during the French occupation of Malta.

3 SCUDI

.800 SILVER
F.A.O. Issue
Rev: Similar to 5 Scudi, KM#40.

KM#	Date	Mintage	XF	Unc	Proof
38	1968	.027	—	—	4.50

5 SCUDI

.840 GOLD

C#	Date	Mintage	VF	XF	Unc
54	1779	—	300.00	400.00	600.00

4.0000 gm., .920 GOLD, .1183 oz AGW
Obv: Same as KM#40. Rev: Similar to 1 Scudo, KM#22, but date below cross.

KM#	Date	Mintage	XF	Unc	Proof
39	1961	1,200	—	—	100.00
40	1962	200 pcs.	—	—	500.00
	1963	600 pcs.	—	—	120.00
41	1964	1,000	—	—	120.00
	1965	1,000	—	—	120.00
	1966	600 pcs.	—	—	120.00

Obv: Similar to 2 Scudi, KM#35.

Rev: Similar to 2 Scudi, KM#27.

KM#	Date	Mintage	XF	Unc	Proof
42	1967	1,000	—	—	80.00
	1968	1,000	—	—	80.00
	1969	1,000	—	—	80.00

Obv: Similar to 2 Scudi, KM#35.
Rev: Similar to 10 Grani, KM#1 obverse.

KM#	Date	Mintage	XF	Unc	Proof
43	1970	1,000	—	—	80.00
	1971	1,000	—	—	80.00
44	1972	1,000	—	—	80.00
	1973	1,000	—	—	80.00
	1974	1,000	—	—	80.00
	1975	1,000	—	—	80.00

Similar to KM#44.

KM#	Date	Mintage	XF	Unc	Proof
54	1976	1,000	—	—	80.00
	1977	1,000	—	—	80.00
	1978	1,000	—	—	80.00
62	1979	1,000	—	—	80.00

10 SCUDI

.840 GOLD

C#	Date	Mintage	VF	XF	Unc
55.1	1778	—	500.00	650.00	850.00

Rev. leg: HOSPITAL ET S. SEPUL ...

C#	Date	Mintage	VF	XF	Unc
55.2	1778	—	500.00	650.00	850.00
	1782	—	500.00	650.00	850.00

Rev. legend ends: ... HIERUSA.

C#	Date	Mintage	VF	XF	Unc
55.3	1782	—	500.00	650.00	850.00

8.0000 gm., .900 GOLD, .2315 oz AGW
Obv: Same as 5 Scudi, KM#40. Rev: Similar to 1 Scudo, KM#22, but date below cross.

KM#	Date	Mintage	XF	Unc	Proof
45	1961	1,200	—	—	220.00
46	1962	200 pcs.	—	—	1000.
	1963	600 pcs.	—	—	260.00
47	1964	1,000	—	—	260.00
	1965	1,000	—	—	260.00
	1966	500 pcs.	—	—	260.00

Obv: Similar to 2 Scudi, KM#31.
Rev: Similar to KM#46.

KM#	Date	Mintage	XF	Unc	Proof
48	1967	1,000	—	—	175.00
	1968	1,000	—	—	175.00
	1969	1,000	—	—	175.00

Obv: Similar to 2 Scudi, KM#31.
Rev: Similar to 5 Scudi, KM#40.

KM#	Date	Mintage	XF	Unc	Proof
49	1970	1,000	—	—	175.00

Obv: Similar to 2 Scudi, KM#31.
Rev: Similar to 2 Scudi, KM#34.

KM#	Date	Mintage	XF	Unc	Proof
50	1971	1,000	—	—	175.00
51	1972	1,000	—	—	175.00
	1973	1,000	—	—	175.00
	1974	1,000	—	—	175.00

Obv: Same as KM#51. Rev: Coat of arms superimposed on center of Maltese Cross.

KM#	Date	Mintage	XF	Unc	Proof
52	1975	1,000	—	—	175.00
	1976	1,000	—	—	175.00
	1977	1,000	—	—	175.00

Obv: Portrait left, date. Rev: John baptizing Jesus, value.

KM#	Date	Mintage	XF	Unc	Proof
59	1978	1,000	—	—	175.00

8.0000 gm.
Castle in Chignolo, Italy

KM#	Date	Mintage	XF	Unc	Proof
63	1979	1,000	—	—	175.00

20 SCUDI

.840 GOLD

C#	Date	Mintage	VF	XF	Unc
56.1	1778	—	750.00	1000.	1350.

Similar to C#56.1, date on obverse.

C#	Date	Mintage	VF	XF	Unc
56.2	1778	—	750.00	1000.	1350.

Rev: Stars divide legends, date.

C#	Date	Mintage	VF	XF	Unc
56.3	1781	—	750.00	1000.	1350.

Rev: Dots divide legend.

C#	Date	Mintage	VF	XF	Unc
56.4	1782	—	750.00	1000.	1350.

Obv: Crowned arms on imperial eagle.
Rev: John the Baptist stands holding banner.

KM#	Date	Mintage	VF	XF	Unc
59	1778(error)	—	—	Rare	—

SIEGE COINAGE

Emergency issue struck by the French defenders between 1798-1800. They consist of cut silver and gold of various weights c/s in three lines: (issue number)/(value)/(assayer's mark). All are rare.

NCLT ISSUES

PATTERNS

KM#	Date	Mintage	Identification	Mkt.Val.
1	1776	—	1 Scudo, Copper, C47a	—
2	1778	—	5 Scudi, Copper, C54a	—
3	1778	—	10 Scudi, Copper, C55.1a	—
4	1778	—	20 Scudi, Copper, C56.2a	—
5	1779	—	5 Scudi, Copper, C54a	—
6	1782	—	10 Scudi, Copper, C55.2a	—
7	1790	—	30 Tari, Copper, C52b	—

PROOF SETS

Standard metals unless otherwise noted.

KM#	Date	Mintage	Identification	Issue Price	Mkt. Val.
101	1961(4)	1,200	KM14,25,39,45	—	275.00
102	1962(4)	200	KM15,26,40,46	—	1850.
103	1963(4)	600	KM15,26,40,46	—	325.00
104	1963(2)	1,000	KM15,26	—	60.00
105	1964(4)	1,000	KMA15,27,41,47	—	325.00
107	1964(2)	4,000	KMA15,27	—	25.00
108	1965(4)	1,000	KM16,27,41,47	—	325.00
109	1965(2)	4,000	KM16,27	—	25.00
110	1966(4)	500	KM16,28,41,47	—	325.00
111	1966(2)	4,000	KM16,28	—	25.00
112	1967(4)	1,000	KM17,29,42,48	62.50	225.00
113	1967(2)	3,000	KM17,29	14.00	25.00
114	1967(2)	10,000	KM1,7	3.50	8.50
115	1968(4)	1,000	KM18,30,42,48	62.50	225.00
116	1968(2)	3,000	KM18,30	14.00	25.00
117	1968(2)	20,000	KM6,38	3.00	8.50
118	1969(4)	1,000	KM19,31,42,48	75.00	225.00
119	1969(2)	4,000	KM19,31	17.00	25.00
120	1969(2)	10,000	KM1,8	3.00	8.50
121	1970(4)	1,000	KM20,32,43,49	75.00	225.00
122	1970(2)	3,000	KM20,32	17.00	25.00
123	1970(2)	3,000	KM1,9	3.00	8.50
124	1971(6)	1,000	KM2,9,21,33,43,50	78.00	235.00
125	1971(2)	3,000	KM21,33	17.00	25.00
126	1971(2)	5,000	KM2,9	3.00	8.50
127	1971(2)	2,500	KM3,10	5.00	8.50
128	1972(4)	1,000	KM22,34,44,51	82.00	225.00
129	1972(2)	3,000	KM22,34	18.00	25.00
130	1972(2)	5,000	KM4,11	5.00	8.50
131	1973(6)	1,000	KM4,12,23,33,44,51	110.00	235.00
132	1973(2)	3,000	KM23,33	12.00	25.00
133	1973(2)	5,000	KM4,12	6.00	8.50
134	1974(6)	1,000	KM5,13,24,36,44,51	170.00	235.00
135	1974(2)	3,000	KM24,36	33.00	35.00
136	1974(2)	5,000	KM5,13	8.00	8.50
137	1975(6)	1,000	KM24,37,44,52	170.00	225.00
138	1975(2)	3,000	KM24,37	30.00	35.00
139	1975(2)	5,000	KM5,13	8.00	8.50
140	1976(4)	1,000	KM24,44,51,53	180.00	225.00
141	1976(2)	3,000	KM24,53	35.00	35.00
142	1976(2)	5,000	KM5,13	10.00	8.50
143	1977(4)	1,000	—	—	225.00
144	1977(2)	3,000	—	—	35.00
145	1977(2)	5,000	—	—	8.50
146	1978(4)	1,000	—	—	225.00
147	1978(2)	3,000	—	—	35.00
148	1978(2)	5,000	—	—	8.50
149	1979(4)	1,000	—	—	250.00
150	1979(2)	3,000	—	—	50.00
151	1979(2)	5,000	—	—	11.00

Listings For

MANCHUKUO: refer to China

MARTINIQUE

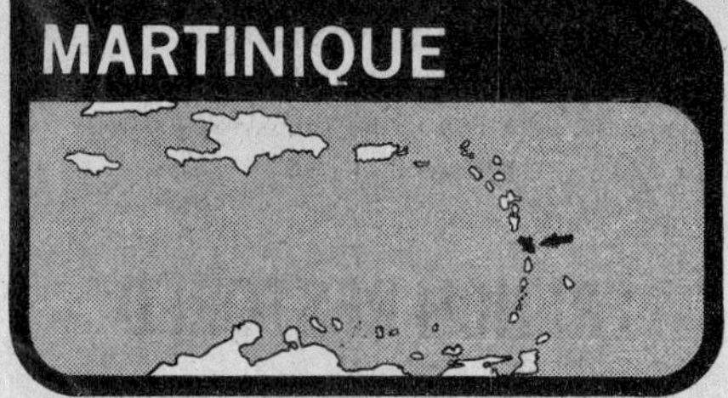

The French Overseas Department of Martinique, located in the Lesser Antilles of the West Indies between Dominica and Saint Lucia, has an area of 425 sq. mi. (1,101 sq. km.) and a population of 346,300. Capital: Fort-de-France. Agriculture and tourism are the major sources of income. Bananas, sugar, and rum are exported.

Christopher Columbus discovered Martinique, probably on June 15, 1502. France took possession on June 25, 1635, and has maintained possession since that time except for three short periods of British occupation during the Napoleonic Wars. A French department since 1946, Martinique voted a reaffirmation of that status in 1958, remaining within the new French Community. Martinique was the birthplace of Napoleon's Empress Josephine, and the site of the eruption of Mt. Pelee in 1902 that claimed 40,000 lives.

The official currency of Martinique is the French franc. The 1897-1922 coinage of the Colony of Martinique is now obsolete.

RULERS

British, 1793-1801
French, 1802-1809

MONETARY SYSTEM

15 Sols = 1 Escalin
20 Sols = 1 Livre
66 Livres = 4 Escudos = 6400 Reis

COUNTERSTAMP ISSUES

It is believed that circulating coins were holed in order to lower their intrinsic value below their face value thus keeping the coins from leaving the island.

Type I

(1761-64)

1/2 BIT

SILVER
Spanish or Colonial 1/2 Real with crude heart-shaped hole.

C#	Date	Mintage	Fine	VF	XF
1	ND	—	—	Rare	—

BIT

SILVER
Spanish or Colonial 1/2 Real with crude heart-shaped hole.

C#	Date	Mintage	Fine	VF	XF
2	ND	—	—	Rare	—

2 BITS

SILVER
Spanish or Colonial 1 Real with crude heart-shaped hole.

C#	Date	Mintage	Fine	VF	XF
3	ND	—	75.00	120.00	200.00

5 BITS

SILVER
Spanish or Colonial 4 Reales with crude heart-shaped hole.

C#	Date	Mintage	Fine	VF	XF
4	ND	—	—	Rare	—

10 BITS

SILVER
Spanish or Colonial 8 Reales with crude heart-shaped hole.

C#	Date	Mintage	Fine	VF	XF
5	ND	—	700.00	1000.	2000.

Type II

(1764)

1/2 BIT

SILVER
Spanish or Colonial 1/2 Real with heart-shaped hole.

C#	Date	Mintage	Fine	VF	XF
6	ND	—	—	Rare	—

BIT

SILVER
Spanish or Colonial 1 Real with heart-shaped hole.

C#	Date	Mintage	Fine	VF	XF
7	ND	—	—	Rare	—

2 BITS

SILVER
Spanish or Colonial 2 Reales with heart-shaped hole.

C#	Date	Mintage	Fine	VF	XF
8	ND	—	35.00	50.00	100.00

5 BITS

SILVER
Spanish or Colonial 4 Reales with heart-shaped hole.

C#	Date	Mintage	Fine	VF	XF
9	ND	—	—	Rare	—

10 BITS

SILVER
Spanish or Colonial 8 Reales with heart-shaped hole.

C#	Date	Mintage	Fine	VF	XF
10	ND	—	1100.	1500.	2000.

Type III

(1765)

1/2 BIT

 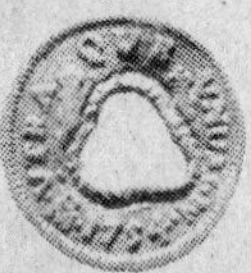

SILVER
Spanish or Colonial 1/2 Real with heart-shaped hole.

C#	Date	Mintage	Fine	VF	XF
11	ND	—	100.00	150.00	200.00

BIT

SILVER
Spanish or Colonial 1 Real with heart-shaped hole.

C#	Date	Mintage	Fine	VF	XF
12	ND	—	100.00	130.00	175.00

2 BITS

SILVER
Spanish or Colonial 2 Reales with heart-shaped hole.

C#	Date	Mintage	Fine	VF	XF
13	ND	—	150.00	300.00	500.00

5 BITS

SILVER
Spanish or Colonial 4 Reales with heart-shaped hole.

C#	Date	Mintage	Fine	VF	XF
14	ND	—	900.00	1200.	1500.

10 BITS

SILVER

Spanish or Colonial 8 Reales with heart-shaped hole.

C#	Date	Mintage	Fine	VF	XF
15	ND	—	1000.	1300.	1500.

Type IV

(1770-72)

1/2 BIT

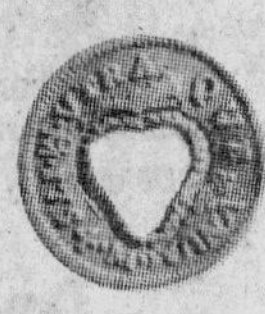

SILVER
Spanish or Colonial 1/2 Real with blunt heart-shaped hole with ornamented edges.

C#	Date	Mintage	Fine	VF	XF
16	ND	—	25.00	35.00	50.00

BIT

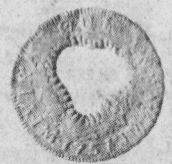

SILVER
Spanish or Colonial 1 Real with blunt heart-shaped hole with ornamented edges.

C#	Date	Mintage	Fine	VF	XF
17	ND	—	55.00	85.00	150.00

2 BITS

SILVER
Spanish or Colonial 2 Reales with blunt heart-shaped hole with ornamented edges.

C#	Date	Mintage	Fine	VF	XF
18	ND	—	150.00	175.00	250.00

5 BITS

SILVER
Spanish or Colonial 4 Reales with blunt heart-shaped hole with ornamented edges.

C#	Date	Mintage	Fine	VF	XF
19	ND	—	—	Rare	—

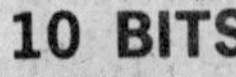

10 BITS

SILVER
Spanish or Colonial 8 Reales with blunt heart-shaped hole with ornamented edges.

C#	Date	Mintage	Fine	VF	XF
20	ND	—	375.00	475.00	600.00

The heart shaped center punches were never circulated and did not have any legal tender status. Most were melted at the time of minting.

BRITISH OCCUPATION

COUNTERMARKS

(1793-1801)

AR = Mr. Ruffy, Goldsmith at St. Pierre
FA = Francois Arnaud, Goldsmith at Fort Royal
22 or 20 = Fineness of gold
Eagle = Mr. Costet, Goldsmith at St. Pierre

ESCALIN

SILVER
Unmarked 1/3 cut of 2 Reales with crenated edges

C#	Date	Mintage	VG	Fine	VF
11	ND(1798)	—	20.00	35.00	60.00

3 ESCALINS

SILVER
Unmarked 1/4 cut of 8 Reales with crenated edges

C#	Date	Mintage	VG	Fine	VF
13	ND(1798)	—	40.00	60.00	90.00

66 LIVRES

GOLD
c/s: 'AR or FA' on plug in Portuguese 6400 Reis.

C#	Date	Mintage	VG	Fine	VF
21	ND(1798)	—	—	Rare	—

FRENCH RESTORED

(1802-1809)

MONETARY SYSTEM

6400 Reis = 22 Livres

20 LIVRES

GOLD
c/s: '20 over eagle' on lightweight Brazil 6400 Reis.

C#	Date	Mintage	VG	Fine	VF
31	ND(1805)	—	1000.	1200.	1500.

22 LIVRES

GOLD
c/s: '22/eagle' on Brazil 6400 Reis, C#53.

C#	Date	Mintage	VG	Fine	VF
32	(1777-86)	—	700.00	1000.	1200.

c/s: '22/eagle' on Brazil 6400 Reis, C#74.

C#	Date	Mintage	VG	Fine	VF
32.1	(1786-90)	—	700.00	1000.	1200.

c/s: '22/eagle on Brazil 6400 Reis, C#75.

C#	Date	Mintage	VG	Fine	VF
32.2	(1789-1805)	—	700.00	1000.	1200.

NOTE: There are many merchant c/s from Martinique during this period, but the above are probably the only official issues. There are also many counterfeits or fantasies attributed to the West Indies.

MODERN COINAGE

MONETARY SYSTEM

100 Centimes = 1 Franc

50 CENTIMES

COPPER-NICKEL

Y#	Date	Mintage	Fine	VF	XF
1	1897	.600	8.00	15.00	40.00
	1922	.500	7.00	14.00	30.00

FRANC

COPPER-NICKEL

Y#	Date	Mintage	Fine	VF	XF
2	1897	.300	12.00	27.50	60.00
	1922	.350	11.00	25.00	40.00

NCLT ISSUES

PIEFORTS with ESSAI (PE)

(DOUBLE THICKNESS)

Standard metals unless otherwise noted

Y#	Date	Mintage	Identification	Issue Price	Mkt Val.
PE1	1897	—	50 Centimes	—	130.00
PE2	1897	—	1 Franc	—	200.00
PE1	1922	—	50 Centimes	—	100.00
PE2	1922	—	1 Franc	—	140.00

STANDARD THICKNESS

Y#	Date	Mintage	Identification	Issue Price	Mkt Val.
PE1a	1897	—	50 Centimes, .900 Silver	—	200.00
PE2a	1897	—	1 Franc, .900 Silver	—	300.00
PE1a	1922	—	50 Centimes, .900 Silver	—	175.00
PE2a	1922	—	1 Franc, .900 Silver	—	225.00

MAURITANIA

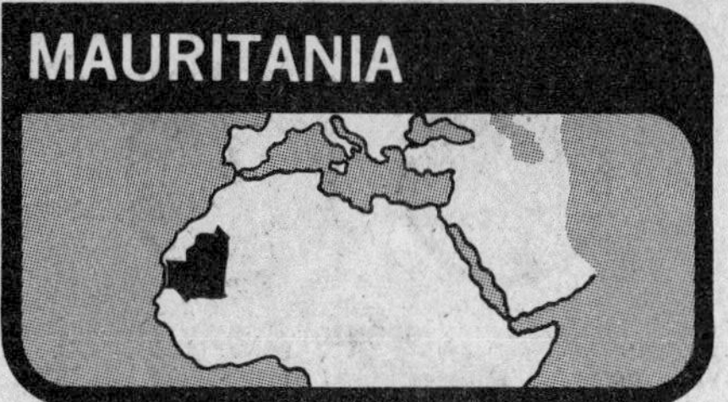

The Islamic Republic of Mauritania, located in northwest Africa bounded by Spanish Sahara, Mali, Algeria, Senegal and the Atlantic Ocean, has an area of 419,229 sq. mi. (1,085,760 sq. km.) and a population of 1.4 million. Capital: Nouakchott. The economy centers about herding, agriculture, fishing and mining. Iron ore, copper concentrates and fish products are exported.

The indigenous Negroid inhabitants were driven out of Mauritania by Berber invaders of the Islamic faith in the 11th century. The Berbers in turn were conquered by Arab invaders, the Beni Hassan, in the 16th century. Arab traders carried on a gainful trade in gum arabic, gold and slaves with Portuguese, Dutch, English and French traders until late in the 19th century when France took control of the area and made it a part of French West Africa, in 1920. Mauritania became a part of the French Union in 1946 and was made an autonomous republic within the new French Community in 1958, when the Islamic Republic of Mauritania was proclaimed. The republic became independent on November 28, 1960, and withdrew from the French Community in 1966.

On June 28, 1973, in a move designed to emphasize its non-alignment with France, Mauritania converted its currency from the old French-supported C.F.A. franc unit to a new unit called the ouguiya.

MONETARY SYSTEM

5 Khoum = 1 Ouguiya

100 Ouguiya = 500 CFA Francs

1/5 OUGUIYA (KHOUM)

ALUMINUM

Y#	Date	Year	Mintage	VF	XF	Unc
1	AH1393	1973	1,000	20.00	30.00	50.00

OUGUIYA

COPPER-NICKEL-ALUMINUM

Y#	Date	Year	Mintage	VF	XF	Unc
2	AH1393	1973	—	6.50	11.50	25.00
	1394	1974	—	6.50	11.50	30.00

5 OUGUIYA

COPPER-NICKEL-ALUMINUM

Y#	Date	Year	Mintage	VF	XF	Unc
3	AH1393	1973	—	7.50	11.50	25.00
	1394	1974	—	7.50	11.50	35.00

10 OUGUIYA

COPPER-NICKEL

Y#	Date	Year	Mintage	VF	XF	Unc
4	AH1393	1973	—	7.50	11.50	25.00
	1394	1974	—	7.50	11.50	35.00

20 OUGUIYA

COPPER-NICKEL

Y#	Date	Year	Mintage	VF	XF	Unc
5	AH1393	1973	—	7.50	11.50	25.00
	1394	1974	—	7.50	11.50	35.00

500 OUGUIYA

26.0800 gm., .920 GOLD, .7714 oz AGW
15th Anniversary of Independence

Y#	Date	Year	Mintage	VF	XF	Unc
6	—	1975(a)	1,800	BV 500.00	525.00	

NCLT ISSUES

MINT SETS

KM#	Date	Mintage	Identification	Issue Price	Mkt. Val.
S1	1973(10)	—	Y1-5, Two Each	20.00	350.00

MAURITIUS

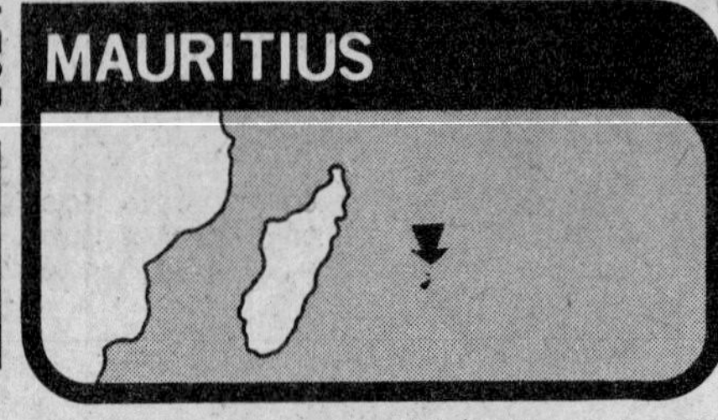

The island of Mauritius, a member nation of the British Commonwealth located in the Indian Ocean 500 miles (805 km.) east of Madagascar, has an area of 720 sq. mi. (1,865 sq. km.) and a population of 900,000. Capital: Port Louis. Sugar provides 90 percent of the export revenue.

Cartographic evidence indicates that Arabs and Malays arrived at Mauritius during the Middle Ages. Domingo Fernandez, a Portuguese navigator, visited the island in the early 16th century, but Portugal made no attempt at settlement. The Dutch took possession, and named the island, in 1598. Their colony failed to prosper and was abandoned in 1710. France claimed Mauritius in 1715 and developed a strong and prosperous colony that endured until the island was captured by the British, 1810, during the Napoleonic Wars. British possession was confirmed by the Treaty of Paris, 1814. Mauritius became independent on March 12, 1968. It is a member of the Commonwealth of Nations. The Queen of England if Chief of State.

The first coins struck under British auspices for Mauritius were undated (1822) and bore French legends.

RULERS

BRITISH

MINTMARKS

H - Heaton, Birmingham
SA - Pretoria Mint

MONETARY SYSTEM

20 Sols (Sous) = 1 Livre

25 SOUS

.500 SILVER

C#	Date	Mintage	Fine	VF	XF
31	Nd(1822)	—	30.00	60.00	100.00

50 SOUS

.500 SILVER

C#	Date	Mintage	Fine	VF	XF
32	Nd(1822)	—	35.00	70.00	135.00

ANCHOR COINAGE

(1/16, 1/8, 1/4 & 1/2 Dollar)

NOTE: Coins dated 1820 were struck for Mauritius and colonies of the British West Indies. These circulated in Mauritius until 1826 when they were shipped to the British West Indies where they will be found listed.

REGULAR COINAGE

100 Cents = 1 Rupee

CENT

BRONZE

Y#	Date	Mintage	VF	XF	Unc
1	1877	—	5.00	12.00	40.00
	1877	—	—	Proof	100.00
	1877H	.700	5.00	12.00	40.00
	1877H	—	—	Proof	100.00
	1878	.250	7.00	16.00	70.00
	1878	—	—	Proof	150.00
	1882H	.300	7.00	16.00	40.00
	1883	.500	5.00	12.00	30.00
	1883	—	—	Proof	100.00
	1884	.500	6.00	16.00	35.00
	1884	—	—	Proof	100.00
	1888	.500	4.00	10.00	25.00
	1890H	.500	4.00	10.00	25.00
	1896	.500	4.00	10.00	25.00
	1897	1.000	4.00	10.00	25.00
	1897	—	—	Proof	100.00

Y#	Date	Mintage	VF	XF	Unc
6	1911	1.000	2.00	4.00	8.50
	1912	.500	4.00	10.00	25.00
	1917	.500	3.50	9.00	20.00
	1920	.500	3.50	10.00	25.00
	1921	.500	5.00	14.00	35.00
	1922	1.800	2.00	4.00	8.50
	1923	.200	4.50	12.00	30.00
	1924	.200	4.50	12.50	35.00

Y#	Date	Mintage	VF	XF	Unc
12	1943SA	.520	1.25	2.75	7.50
	1944SA	.500	1.25	2.75	8.50
	1945SA	.500	1.25	2.75	8.50
	1946SA	.500	1.25	2.75	8.50
	1947SA	.500	1.25	2.75	7.50

Y#	Date	Mintage	VF	XF	Unc
23	1949	.500	.50	1.50	2.50
	1949	—	—	Proof	85.00
	1952	.500	.50	1.50	2.50

Y#	Date	Mintage	VF	XF	Unc
25	1953	.500	.25	.50	1.00
	1955	.501	.25	.50	1.50
	1956	.500	.20	.50	1.50
	1957	.501	.20	.50	2.00
	1959	.501	.20	.50	2.00
	1960	.500	.20	.50	2.00
	1961	.500	.20	.50	2.00
	1962	.500	.10	.25	.75
	1962	—	—	Proof	30.00
	1963	.500	.10	.25	.75
	1964	1.500	—	.20	.50
	1965	1.500	—	.15	.40
	1968	—	—	.15	.40
	1969	.500	—	.10	.20
	1970	1.500	—	.10	.20
	1971	1.000	—	.10	.20
	1971	750 pcs.	—	Proof	25.00
	1978	.020	—	Proof	—

F.A.O. Issue

Y#	Date	Mintage	VF	XF	Unc
—	1975	10.400	—	.10	.20

2 CENTS

BRONZE

Y#	Date	Mintage	VF	XF	Unc
2	1877	—	7.00	14.00	45.00
	1877	—	—	Proof	120.00
	1877H	.350	7.00	14.00	45.00
	1877H	—	—	Proof	120.00
	1878	.130	10.00	20.00	70.00
	1878	—	—	Proof	140.00
	1882H	.150	10.00	25.00	85.00
	1883	.250	9.00	18.00	50.00
	1884	.250	9.00	18.00	50.00
	1884	—	—	Proof	120.00
	1888	.250	5.00	11.00	35.00
	1888	—	—	Proof	—
	1890H	.250	7.00	15.00	35.00
	1896	.188	7.00	9.00	25.00
	1897	1.000	5.00	7.00	15.00
	1897	—	—	Proof	75.00

Y#	Date	Mintage	VF	XF	Unc
7	1911	.500	3.00	6.00	12.50
	1912	.250	8.00	15.00	30.00
	1917	.250	5.50	6.50	18.00
	1920	.250	5.50	6.50	18.00
	1921	.250	5.50	6.50	18.00
	1922	.900	3.50	4.00	12.50
	1923	.400	3.00	6.00	16.00
	1924	.400	3.00	6.00	22.00

Y#	Date	Mintage	VF	XF	Unc
13	1943SA	.290	2.00	3.00	11.00
	1944SA	.500	2.00	3.00	11.00
	1945SA	.250	2.25	3.00	11.00
	1946SA	.400	2.00	8.00	15.00
	1947SA	.250	1.25	2.00	5.00

Y#	Date	Mintage	VF	XF	Unc
24	1949	.250	1.00	2.00	3.00
	1949	—	—	Proof	100.00
	1952	.250	1.00	2.00	3.00

Y#	Date	Mintage	VF	XF	Unc
26	1953	.250	.25	.50	1.50
	1953	—	—	Proof	75.00
	1955	.501	.25	.50	1.50
	1956	.250	.25	.50	2.00
	1957	.501	.25	.50	2.00
	1959	.503	.25	.50	2.00
	1960	.250	.25	.50	2.00
	1961	.500	.25	.50	2.00
	1962	.500	.25	.50	2.00
	1962	—	—	Proof	—
	1963	.500	.25	.50	2.00
	1964	1.00	.10	.25	.50
	1964	—	—	Proof	45.00
	1965	.750	.10	.20	.45

Y#	Date	Mintage	VF	XF	Unc
26	1966	.500	.10	.20	.35
	1967	.250	.10	.20	.35
	1968	—	.10	.20	.35
	1969	.500	.10	.20	.35
	1970	—	.10	.20	.35
	1971	1.000	.10	.20	.30
	1971	750 pcs.	—	Proof	25.00
	1978	.020	—	Proof	—

F.A.O. Issue

Y#	Date	Mintage	VF	XF	Unc
—	1975	1.200	.10	.20	.35

5 CENTS

BRONZE

Y#	Date	Mintage	VF	XF	Unc
3	1877	—	—	Proof only	300.00
	1877H	.140	10.00	20.00	60.00
	1877H	—	—	Proof	140.00
	1878	.050	15.00	30.00	80.00
	1878	—	—	Proof	175.00
	1882H	.050	20.00	50.00	130.00
	1883	.100	12.00	24.00	65.00
	1884	.100	14.00	30.00	75.00
	1884	—	—	Proof	150.00
	1888	.100	7.00	14.00	40.00
	1890H	.100	10.00	20.00	60.00
	1897	.600	7.00	14.00	30.00
	1897	—	—	Proof	125.00

Y#	Date	Mintage	VF	XF	Unc
8	1917	.600	6.00	11.00	28.00
	1920	.200	7.00	12.00	35.00
	1921	.100	8.00	14.50	40.00
	1922	.360	7.00	12.00	35.00
	1923	.400	8.00	14.00	40.00
	1924	.400	7.00	12.00	35.00

Y#	Date	Mintage	VF	XF	Unc
14	1942SA	.940	2.50	6.00	18.00
	1944SA	1.000	2.50	6.00	18.00
	1945SA	.500	1.50	3.00	7.50

Y#	Date	Mintage	VF	XF	Unc
27	1956	.201	.30	.75	2.50
	1957	.203	.30	.75	4.00
	1959	.801	.25	.50	2.00
	1959	—	—	Proof	50.00
	1960	.400	.25	.50	2.00
	1960	—	—	Proof	50.00
	1963	.200	.25	.50	2.00
	1964	.600	.25	.50	2.00
	1965	.200	.20	.35	1.50
	1966	.200	.50	.75	1.00
	1967	.200	.20	.35	1.50
	1968	—	.15	.25	.50
	1969	.500	.15	.25	.50

Y#	Date	Mintage	VF	XF	Unc
27	1970	.800	.15	.25	.50
	1971	.500	.15	.25	.50
	1971	750 pcs.	—	Proof	25.00
	1978	.020	—	Proof	—

F.A.O. Issue

Y#	Date	Mintage	VF	XF	Unc
—	1975	2.800	.15	.25	.50

10 CENTS

1.4100 gm., .800 SILVER, .0362 oz ASW

Y#	Date	Mintage	VF	XF	Unc
4	1877	—	—	Proof only	300.00
	1877H	—	8.00	18.00	55.00
	1877H	—	—	Proof	125.00
	1878	.050	14.00	30.00	100.00
	1878	—	—	Proof	200.00
	1882H	.030	50.00	95.00	225.00
	1883	.100	17.50	35.00	95.00
	1883	—	—	Proof	175.00
	1886	.750	5.00	10.00	45.00
	1886	—	—	Proof	125.00
	1889H	.500	5.00	10.00	40.00
	1889	—	—	Proof	110.00
	1897	.500	5.00	10.00	37.50
	1897	—	—	Proof	110.00

COPPER-NICKEL

Y#	Date	Mintage	VF	XF	Unc
15	1947	.500	2.50	4.00	7.50

Y#	Date	Mintage	VF	XF	Unc
19	1952	.250	1.50	2.50	4.00
	1952	—	—	Proof	135.00

Y#	Date	Mintage	VF	XF	Unc
28	1954	.252	.35	.75	1.50
	1954	—	—	Proof	135.00
	1957	.250	.35	.75	1.50
	1959	.253	.35	.75	1.50
	1960	.501	.35	.75	1.25
	1963	.200	.30	.60	1.00
	1964	.200	.30	.60	1.00
	1965	.200	.30	.60	1.00
	1966	.200	.25	.50	.75
	1968	—	.25	.50	.75
	1969	.200	.25	.50	.75
	1970	.500	.25	.50	.75
	1971	.300	.25	.50	.75
	1971	750 pcs.	—	Proof	25.00
	1975	2.650	.25	.50	.75
	1978	.020	—	Proof	—

20 CENTS

2.8300 gm., .800 SILVER, .0727 oz ASW

Y#	Date	Mintage	VF	XF	Unc
5	1877		—	Proof	300.00
	1877H	—	8.00	18.00	55.00
	1877H	—	—	Proof	125.00
	1878	.050	20.00	40.00	110.00
	1878	—	—	Proof	150.00

Y#	Date	Mintage	VF	XF	Unc
5	1882H	.030	60.00	120.00	275.00
	1883	.100	20.00	35.00	90.00
	1883	—	—	Proof	150.00
	1886	.750	6.00	14.00	50.00
	1886	—	—	Proof	100.00
	1889H	.500	6.00	14.00	50.00
	1899	.500	7.00	16.00	60.00
	1899	—	—	Proof	125.00

1/4 RUPEE

2.8300 gm., .916 SILVER, .0833 oz ASW

Y#	Date	Mintage	VF	XF	Unc
9	1934	.400	4.00	7.00	15.00
	1935	.400	4.00	7.50	18.00
	1936	.400	4.00	7.50	18.00

Y#	Date	Mintage	VF	XF	Unc
16	1938	.2000	4.00	7.00	15.00
	1938	—	—	Proof	125.00

2.8300 gm., .500 SILVER .0454 oz ASW

Y#	Date	Mintage	VF	XF	Unc
	1946	2.000	2.25	6.00	15.00

COPPER-NICKEL

Y#	Date	Mintage	VF	XF	Unc
20	1950	2.000	1.00	2.25	3.50
	1951	1.000	1.00	3.00	4.50
	1951	—	—	Proof	125.00

Y#	Date	Mintage	VF	XF	Unc
30	1960	1.000	.75	1.00	1.50
	1964	.400	.50	.75	1.25
	1964	—	—	Proof	100.00
	1965	.400	.50	.75	1.25
	1968	—	.35	.60	1.00
	1969	—	.35	.60	1.00
	1970	.400	.35	.60	1.00
	1971	.540	.50	.75	1.50
	1971	750 pcs.	—	Proof	25.00
	1975	2.040	—	—	—
	1978	.020	—	Proof	—

1/2 RUPEE

5.6600 gm., .916 SILVER, .1667 oz ASW

Y#	Date	Mintage	VF	XF	Unc
10	1934	1.000	5.50	8.00	15.00
	1934	—	—	Proof	100.00

5.6600 gm., .500 SILVER, 0909 oz ASW

Y#	Date	Mintage	VF	XF	Unc
17	1946	1.000	12.00	30.00	150.00

COPPER-NICKEL

Y#	Date	Mintage	VF	XF	Unc
21	1950	1.000	1.00	1.75	3.00
	1951	.570	1.25	2.00	3.50

Y#	Date	Mintage	VF	XF	Unc
31	1965	.200	.75	1.50	2.50
	1968	—	.50	.75	1.00
	1969	—	.50	.75	1.00
	1970	—	.50	.75	1.00
	1971 w/reeded edge	—	—	—	—
	1971 w/security edge	.400	.50	.75	1.00
	1971	750 pcs.	—	Proof	35.00
	1975	.480	.50	.75	1.00
	1978	.020	—	Proof	—

RUPEE

11.3100 gm., .916 SILVER, .3331 oz ASW

Y#	Date	Mintage	VF	XF	Unc
11	1934	1.500	10.00	12.50	20.00

Y#	Date	Mintage	VF	XF	Unc
18	1938	.200	12.00	20.00	35.00
	1938	—	—	Proof	250.00

COPPER-NICKEL

Y#	Date	Mintage	VF	XF	Unc
22	1950	1.500	1.75	3.25	5.00
	1950	—	—	Proof	125.00
	1951 w/reeded edge	—	—	—	—
	1951 w/security edge	1.000	1.25	2.00	4.00
	1951	—	—	Proof	125.00

Y#	Date	Mintage	VF	XF	Unc
29	1956	1.001	.75	1.00	1.50
	1956	—	—	Proof	100.00
	1964	.200	.75	1.50	2.00
	1968	—	.60	1.00	1.50
	1969	—	.60	1.00	1.50
	1970	—	.60	1.00	1.50
	1971 with security edge	.600	.60	1.00	1.50
	1971 with reeded edge	Inc. Ab.	—	—	—
	1971	750 Pcs.	—	Proof	35.00
	1975	1.650	.60	1.00	1.50
	1978	.020	—	Proof	—

10 RUPEES

COPPER-NICKEL
Independence Commemorative

Y#	Date	Mintage	VF	XF	Unc
32	1971	.050	—	—	4.00

SILVER

Y#	Date	Mintage	VF	XF	Unc
32a	1971	750 pcs.	—	Proof	375.00

25 RUPEES

25.3100 gm., .500 SILVER, .4069 oz ASW
Conservation Series

Y#	Date	Mintage	VF	XF	Unc
34	1975	.104	BV	17.50	25.00

28.2800 gm., .925 SILVER, .8411 oz ASW

Y#	Date	Mintage	VF	XF	Unc
34a	1975	.036	—	Proof	30.00

25.3100 gm., .500 SILVER, .4069 oz ASW
Queen's Silver Jubilee

Y#	Date	Mintage	VF	XF	Unc
37	1977	—	BV	12.50	15.00

28.2800 gm., .925 SILVER, .8411 oz ASW

Y#	Date	Mintage	VF	XF	Unc
37a	1977	.025	—	Proof	30.00

10th Anniversary of Independence
Obv: Similar to 1000 Rupees, Y#39.

Y#	Date	Mintage	VF	XF	Unc
38	1978	.010	—	—	—
	1978	5,000	—	Proof	35.00

50 RUPEES

31.6500 gm., .500 SILVER, .5088 oz ASW
Conservation Series
Obv: Similar to 25 Rupees, Y#34.

Y#	Date	Mintage	VF	XF	Unc
35	1975	3,880	17.50	22.50	30.00

35.0000 gm., .925 SILVER, 1.0409 oz ASW

Y#	Date	Mintage	VF	XF	Unc
35a	1975	.036	—	Proof	50.00

200 RUPEES

15.5600 gm., .917 GOLD, .4587 oz AGW
Independence Commemorative

Y#	Date	Mintage	VF	XF	Unc
33	1971	2,500	—	—	350.00
	1971	750 pcs.	—	Proof	1000.

1000 RUPEES

33.4000 gm., .900 GOLD, .9665 oz AGW
Conservation Series

Y#	Date	Mintage	VF	XF	Unc
36	1975	.012	BV	BV	650.00
	1975	3,000	—	Proof	750.00

15.9800 gm., .917 GOLD, .4711 oz AGW
10th Anniversary of Independence

Y#	Date	Mintage	VF	XF	Unc
39	1978	1,000	BV	BV	325.00
	1978	1,000	—	Proof	400.00

NCLT ISSUES

PROOF SETS
STANDARD METALS

KM#	Date	Mintage	Identification	Issue Price	Mkt. Val.
101	1971(9)	750	Y25-31,32a,33	220.00	1500.
102	1972(2)	30,000	Y34a,35a	50.00	7500.
103	1978(7)	20,000	Y25-31	22.00	25.00

MAURITIUS & REUNION

Mauritius and Reunion (Isles de France et de Bourbon), located in the Indian Ocean about 500 miles east of Madagascar, were at one time administered by France as a single colony. Ownership of Mauritius passed to Great Britain in 1810-14. Isle de Bourbon, renamed Reunion in 1793, remained a French possession and is now an overseas department.

RULERS

French until 1810

MONETARY SYSTEM

20 Sols (Sous) = 1 Livre

ISLE DE FRANCE ET DE BOURBON

Isles de France et de Bourbon (now the separate entities of Mauritius and Reunion, located in the Indian Ocean about 500 miles east of Madagascar), were at one time administered by France as a single colony, at which time they utilized a common currency issue. Ownership of Mauritius passed to Great Britain in 1810-14. Isle de Bourbon, renamed Reunion in 1793, remained a French possession and is now an overseas department.

3 SOLS

BILLON

C#	Date	Mintage	Good	VG	Fine	VF
2	1779A	—	8.50	16.00	35.00	60.00
	1780A	—	10.00	22.00	50.00	70.00

3 SOUS

BILLON
Similar to 3 Sols, C#2.

C#	Date	Mintage	Good	VG	Fine	VF
2a	1781A	—	17.50	30.00	50.00	100.00

NCLT ISSUES

PATTERNS

KM#	Date	Mintage	Identification	Mkt.Val.
1	1780A	—	2 Sols, billon, C#1.	950.00

ISLES DE FRANCE ET BONAPARTE

Reunion became the official name in 1792 but after the French Revolution and the beginning of the Napoleonic era the name was changed to Isle de Bonaparte (1801-1814).

DIX (10) LIVRES

SILVER

C#	Date	Mintage	VG	Fine	VF	XF
11	1810	—	250.00	400.00	600.00	800.00

MINTS OF MEXICO

Locations of the various mints where coins were produced in Mexico.

MILLED COLONIAL

The United Mexican States, located immediately south of the United States has an area of 764,000 sq. mi. (1,978,750 sq. km.) and a population of 66.9 million. Capital: Mexico City. The economy is based on agriculture, manufacturing and mining. Cotton, sugar, coffee, and shrimp are exported.

Mexico was the site of highly advanced Indian civilizations. 1,500 years before conquistador Hernando Cortes conquered the wealthy Aztec empire of Montenzuma. 1519- 21, and founded a Spanish colony which lasted for nearly 300 years. During the Spanish period, Mexico, then called New Spain, stretched from Guatemala to the present states of Wyoming and California, its present northern boundary having been established by the secession of Texas (1836) and the 1846-48 war with the United States.

Independence from Spain was declared by Father Miguel Hidalgo on Sept. 16, 1810, (Mexican Independence Day) and was achieved by General Agustin de Iturbide in 1821. Iturbide became emperor in 1822 but was deposed when a republic was established a year later. For more than half a century following the birth of the republic, the political scene of Mexico was characterized by turmoil which saw two emperors (including the unfortunate Maximilian), several dictators and an average of one new government every nine months passing swiftly from obscurity to oblivion. The land, social, economic and labor reforms promulgated by the Reform Constitution of 1917 established the basis for a sustained economic development and participative democracy that have made Mexico one of the most politically stable countries of modern Latin America.

RULERS

Philip V, 1700-1746
Ferdinand VI, 1746-1759
Charles III, 1760-1788
Charles IV, 1788-1808
Ferdinand VII, 1808-1821

ASSAYER'S INITIALS

Letter	Date	Name
F	1733-1784	Francisco de la Pena
M	1733-1763	Manuel de la Pena
M	1754-1770	Manuel Assorin
F	1762-1770	Francisco de Rivera
M	1770-1777	Manuel de Rivera
F	1777-1803	Francisco Arance Cobos
M	1784-1801	Mariano Rodriguez
T	1801-1810	Tomas Butron Miranda
H	1803-1814	Henrique Buenaventura Azorin
J	1809-1833	Joaquin Davila Madrid
J	1812-1833	Jose Garcia Ansaldo

MONETARY SYSTEM

16 Reales = 1 Escudo

1/8 REAL

COPPER

MEXICO CITY MINT

Obv: Crowned F VII monogram.
Rev: Castles and lions in wreath.

KM#	Date	Mintage	VG	Fine	VF	XF
59	1814	—	15.00	25.00	50.00	85.00
	1815	—	15.00	25.00	50.00	85.00

1/4 REAL

.8450 gm., .903 SILVER, .0245 oz ASW

MEXICO CITY MINT

Obv: Castle. Rev: Lion.

KM#	Date	Mintage	VG	Fine	VF	XF
62	1796	—	15.00	25.00	35.00	60.00
	1797	—	10.00	15.00	20.00	37.50
	1798	—	12.50	6.00	27.50	45.00
	1799/8	—	15.00	25.00	35.00	60.00
	1799	—	10.00	15.00	27.50	45.00
	1800	—	10.00	15.00	27.50	45.00
	1801	—	10.00	15.00	27.50	45.00
	1802	—	12.50	20.00	27.50	45.00
	1803	—	12.50	20.00	12.50	45.00
	1804	—	10.00	15.00	20.00	37.50
	1805/4	—	10.00	15.00	20.00	37.50
	1805	—	10.00	15.00	20.00	37.50
	1806	—	10.00	15.00	20.00	37.50
	1807	—	12.50	13.50	27.50	45.00
	1807/1797	—	12.50	20.00	27.50	45.00
	1808	—	12.50	20.00	27.50	45.00
	1809	—	15.00	22.50	35.00	60.00
	1810	—	27.50	20.00	27.50	45.00
	1811	—	12.50	20.00	27.50	45.00
	1812	—	12.50	20.00	27.50	45.00
	1813	—	12.50	20.00	27.50	45.00
	1815	—	3.00	15.00	20.00	37.50
	1816	—	3.00	15.00	20.00	37.50

COPPER
Obv. leg: FERDIN. VII... around crowned F.VII.
Rev: Castles and lions in wreath.

KM#	Date	Mintage	VG	Fine	VF	XF
63	1814	—	8.50	17.50	35.00	80.00
	1815	—	2.50	20.00	8.50	90.00
	1816	—	3.00	12.50	30.00	60.00

2/4 REAL

COPPER
Obv. leg: FERDIN. VII... around crowned F.VII.
Rev: Castles.

KM#	Date	Mintage	VG	Fine	VF	XF
64	1814	—	12.00	20.00	50.00	80.00
	1815	—	12.00	20.00	50.00	80.00
	1816	—	12.00	20.00	50.00	80.00
	1821	—	20.00	40.00	75.00	110.00

1/2 REAL

1.6900 gm., .916 SILVER, .0497 oz ASW

MEXICO CITY MINT

Philip V
Obv. leg: PHILIP.V.D.G. HISPAN.ET IND. REX.

KM#	Date	Mintage	VG	Fine	VF	XF
65	1732 F	—	500.00	800.00	1200.	2000.
	1732 MF	—	400.00	650.00	1100.	1600.
	1733 F(MX)	—	375.00	600.00	1000.	1500.
	1733 MF(MX)	—	400.00	600.00	1000.	1500.
	1733 F	—	200.00	325.00	550.00	800.00
	1733 MF	—	300.00	400.00	600.00	800.00
	1734 MF	—	10.00	25.00	30.00	60.00
	1735 MF	—	5.00	10.00	20.00	40.00
	1736 MF	—	5.00	10.00	20.00	40.00
	1737 MF	—	5.00	10.00	20.00	40.00
	1738 MF	—	5.00	10.00	20.00	40.00
	1739 MF	—	4.00	7.50	15.00	30.00
	1740 MF	—	4.00	7.50	15.00	30.00
	1741 MF	—	4.00	7.50	15.00	30.00

Obv. leg:.PHS.V.D.G. HISP.ET IND.R.

KM#	Date	Mintage	VG	Fine	VF	XF
66	1742 M	—	4.00	7.50	15.00	30.00
	1743 M	—	4.00	7.50	15.00	30.00
	1744/3 M	—	4.00	7.50	15.00	30.00
	1744 M	—	4.00	7.50	15.00	30.00
	1745 M	—	4.00	7.50	15.00	30.00
	1746 M	—	4.00	7.50	15.00	30.00
	1747 M	—	5.00	10.00	20.00	40.00

Ferdinand VI
Obv. leg: FRD.VI.D.G.HISP.ET IND.R.

KM#	Date	Mintage	VG	Fine	VF	XF
67	1747 M	—	6.00	12.00	25.00	50.00
	1748/7 M	—	6.00	12.00	25.00	50.00
	1748 M	—	6.00	12.00	25.00	50.00
	1749 M	—	6.00	12.00	25.00	50.00
	1750 M	—	6.00	12.00	25.00	50.00
	1751 M	—	6.00	12.00	25.00	50.00
	1752 M	—	6.00	12.00	25.00	50.00
	1753 M	—	6.00	12.00	25.00	50.00
	1754 M	—	6.00	12.00	25.00	50.00
	1755 M	—	6.00	12.00	25.00	50.00
	1756/5 M	—	7.50	15.00	27.50	50.00
	1756 M	—	6.00	12.00	25.00	50.00
	1757 M	—	6.00	12.00	25.00	50.00
	1758 M	—	6.00	12.00	25.00	50.00
	1759 M	—	6.00	12.00	25.00	50.00
	1760 M	—	7.50	15.00	30.00	60.00

1.6900 gm., .903 SILVER, .0490 oz ASW
Charles III
Obv. leg: CAR.III.D.G.HISP.ET IND.R.

KM#	Date	Mintage	VG	Fine	VF	XF
68	1760 M	—	5.00	7.50	12.50	25.00
	1761 M	—	5.00	7.50	12.50	25.00
	1762 M	—	4.00	6.00	10.00	20.00
	1763/2 M	—	4.00	6.00	10.00	20.00
	1763 M	—	4.00	6.00	10.00	20.00
	1764 M	—	5.00	7.50	13.50	27.50
	1765 M	—	5.00	7.50	13.50	27.50
	1766 M	—	5.00	7.50	13.50	27.50
	1767 M	—	5.00	7.50	13.50	27.50
	1768 M	—	4.00	6.00	12.50	25.00
	1768/6 M	—	6.00	10.00	18.00	37.50
	1769 M	—	6.00	10.00	20.00	40.00
	1770 M	—	6.00	10.00	20.00	40.00
	1770 F	—	7.50	13.50	27.50	55.00
	1771 F	—	5.00	7.50	13.50	27.50

Obv. leg: CAROLUS.III.DEI.GRATIA.

KM#	Date	Mintage	VG	Fine	VF	XF
69	1772 FF	—	27.50	45.00	70.00	120.00
	1772 FM with inverted FM	—	3.00	6.50	12.50	25.00
	1773 FM	—	2.00	5.00	10.00	20.00
	1773 FM with inverted FM	—	5.00	8.00	15.00	30.00
	1774 FM	—	3.00	5.00	10.00	20.00
	1775 FM	—	3.00	5.00	10.00	20.00
	1776 FM	—	3.00	5.00	10.00	20.00
	1777 FM	—	6.00	10.00	20.00	40.00
	1778 FF	—	4.50	9.00	18.50	37.50
	1779 FF	—	3.00	5.00	10.00	20.00
	1780 FF	—	3.00	5.00	10.00	20.00
	1781 FF	—	2.50	4.00	8.50	17.50
	1782 FF	—	3.00	5.00	10.00	20.00
	1783 FF	—	3.00	5.00	10.00	20.00
	1784 FF	—	3.00	5.00	10.00	20.00
	1784 FM	—	6.00	10.00	20.00	40.00
	1785 FM	—	3.50	6.00	13.50	27.50
	1786 FM	—	3.00	5.00	10.00	20.00
	1787 FM	—	3.00	5.00	10.00	20.00
	1788 FM	—	3.00	5.00	10.00	20.00
	1789 FM	—	6.00	10.00	30.00	60.00

Charles IV
Obv: Armored bust of Charles III; leg: .CAROLUS.IV....

KM#	Date	Mintage	VG	Fine	VF	XF
70	1789 FM	—	6.00	10.00	20.00	40.00
	1790 FM	—	6.00	10.00	20.00	40.00

Obv: Armored bust of Charles III; leg: .CAROLUS.IIII....

KM#	Date	Mintage	VG	Fine	VF	XF
71	1790 FM	—	6.00	10.00	20.00	40.00

Obv: Armored bust of Charles IIII.

KM#	Date	Mintage	VG	Fine	VF	XF
72	1792 FM	—	6.00	10.00	20.00	40.00
	1793 FM	—	6.00	10.00	20.00	40.00
	1794/3 FM	—	7.50	12.50	25.00	50.00
	1794 FM	—	5.00	6.00	10.00	20.00
	1795 FM	—	4.00	6.00	10.00	22.50
	1796 FM	—	4.00	6.00	10.00	22.50
	1797 FM	—	4.00	6.00	10.00	20.00
	1798 FM	—	4.00	6.00	10.00	20.00
	1799 FM	—	4.00	6.00	10.00	20.00
	1800/799 FM	—	4.00	6.50	10.00	20.00
	1800 FM	—	4.00	6.50	7.50	15.00
	1801 FM	—	6.50	10.00	20.00	40.00
	1801 FT	—	4.00	6.00	10.00	20.00
	1802 FT	—	4.00	6.00	10.00	20.00
	1803 FT	—	5.00	9.00	15.00	30.00
	1804 TH	—	4.00	6.00	10.00	20.00
	1805 TH	—	4.00	6.00	10.00	20.00
	1806 TH	—	4.00	6.00	10.00	20.00
	1807/6 TH	—	4.00	6.00	10.00	20.00
	1807 TH	—	4.00	6.00	10.00	20.00
	1808/7 TH	—	4.00	6.00	10.00	20.00
	1808 TH	—	4.00	6.00	10.00	20.00

Obv: Armored bust of Ferdinand VII.

KM#	Date	Mintage	VG	Fine	VF	XF
73	1808 TH	—	3.00	5.00	8.50	17.50
	1809 TH	—	3.00	5.00	8.50	17.50
	1810 TH	—	5.00	8.00	12.00	20.00
	1810 HJ	—	3.00	5.00	8.50	17.50
	1811 HJ	—	3.00	5.00	8.50	17.50
	1812 HJ	—	3.00	5.00	8.50	17.50
	1813 TH	—	3.50	6.00	10.00	20.00
	1813 JJ	—	10.00	20.00	40.00	75.00
	1813 HJ	—	7.50	15.00	30.00	60.00
	1814 JJ	—	3.00	5.50	10.00	20.00

Obv: Draped bust of Ferdinand VII.

KM#	Date	Mintage	VG	Fine	VF	XF
74	1814 JJ	—	3.00	5.00	10.00	20.00
	1815 JJ	—	3.00	5.00	10.00	17.50
	1816 JJ	—	3.00	5.00	10.00	17.50
	1817 JJ	—	3.00	5.00	10.00	17.50
	1818/7 JJ	—	3.00	5.00	10.00	17.50
	1818 JJ	—	3.00	5.00	10.00	17.50
	1819 JJ	—	3.00	5.00	10.00	17.50
	1820 JJ	—	3.00	5.00	10.00	17.50
	1821 JJ	—	3.00	5.00	10.00	17.50

REAL

3.3800 gm., .916 SILVER, .0995 oz ASW

MEXICO CITY MINT

Philip V

Obv. leg: PHILIP.V.D.G.HISPAN.ET IND.REX.

KM#	Date	Mintage	VG	Fine	VF	XF
75	1732 F	—	125.00	225.00	350.00	500.00
	1733 F(MX)	—	150.00	300.00	425.00	600.00
	1733 MF(MX)	—	150.00	350.00	425.00	600.00
	1733 F	—	250.00	500.00	700.00	1000.
	1733 MF	—	85.00	150.00	225.00	325.00
	1734/3 MF	—	15.00	35.00	65.00	125.00
	1734 MF	—	12.00	25.00	40.00	75.00
	1735 MF	—	6.00	15.00	27.50	50.00
	1736 MF	—	12.00	20.00	30.00	60.00
	1737 MF	—	8.00	15.00	27.50	50.00
	1738 MF	—	8.00	15.00	27.50	50.00
	1739 MF	—	8.00	15.00	27.50	50.00
	1740 MF	—	8.00	15.00	27.50	50.00
	1741 MF	—	8.00	15.00	27.50	50.00
	1742 M	—	8.00	15.00	27.50	50.00
75	1743 M	—	8.00	15.00	27.50	50.00
	1744/3 M	—	8.00	15.00	27.50	50.00
	1744 M	—	8.00	15.00	27.50	50.00
	1745 M	—	8.00	10.00	15.00	27.50
	1746/5 M	—	8.00	10.00	17.50	32.50
	1746 M	—	8.00	10.00	17.50	32.50
	1747 M	—	8.00	15.00	27.50	50.00

Ferdinand VI

Obv. leg: .FRD.VI.D.G.HISP.ET IND.R.

KM#	Date	Mintage	VG	Fine	VF	XF
76	1747 M	—	10.00	20.00	30.00	60.00
	1748/7 M	—	10.00	20.00	30.00	60.00
	1748 M	—	8.00	15.00	27.50	50.00
	1749 M	—	8.00	15.00	27.50	50.00
	1750/49 M	—	8.00	15.00	27.50	50.00
	1750 M	—	8.00	15.00	27.50	50.00
	1751 M	—	8.00	15.00	27.50	50.00
	1752 M	—	8.00	15.00	27.50	50.00
	1753 M	—	8.00	15.00	27.50	50.00
	1754 M	—	8.00	15.00	27.50	50.00
	1755/4 M	—	8.00	15.00	27.50	50.00
	1755 M	—	8.00	15.00	27.50	50.00
	1756 M	—	8.00	15.00	27.50	50.00
	1757 M	—	8.00	15.00	27.50	50.00
	1758/5 M	—	10.00	20.00	30.00	60.00
	1758 M	—	8.00	15.00	27.50	50.00
	1759 M	—	8.00	15.00	27.50	50.00
	1760 M	—	10.00	20.00	30.00	60.00

3.3800 gm., .903 SILVER, .0981 oz ASW

Charles III

Obv. leg: CAR.III.D.G.HISP.ET IND.R.

KM#	Date	Mintage	VG	Fine	VF	XF
77	1760 M	—	6.50	12.50	20.00	40.00
	1761 M	—	6.00	9.00	15.00	27.50
	1762 M	—	6.00	9.00	15.00	27.50
	1763/2 M	—	6.00	10.00	20.00	40.00
	1763 M	—	6.00	9.00	17.50	37.50
	1764 M	—	6.00	9.00	17.50	37.50
	1765 M	—	6.00	9.00	17.50	37.50
	1766 M	—	6.00	9.00	17.50	37.50
	1767 M	—	6.00	9.00	17.50	37.50
	1768 M	—	6.00	9.00	17.50	37.50
	1769 M	—	6.00	9.00	17.50	37.50
	1770 M	—	10.00	20.00	40.00	70.00
	1770 F	—	10.00	22.00	35.00	60.00
	1771 F	—	18.50	35.00	50.00	90.00

Obv. leg: CAROLUS.III.DEI.GRATIA.

KM#	Date	Mintage	VG	Fine	VF	XF
78	1772 FM with inverted FM					
		—	6.00	10.00	18.50	37.50
	1773 FM with inverted FM					
		—	6.00	10.00	18.50	37.50
	1773 FM	—	6.50	12.50	20.00	40.00
	1774 FM	—	4.00	7.50	12.50	25.00
	1775 FM	—	4.00	7.50	12.50	25.00
	1776 FM	—	4.00	7.50	12.50	25.00
	1777 FM	—	4.00	7.50	12.50	25.00
	1778 FF	—	4.00	7.50	12.50	25.00
	1779 FF	—	5.00	8.50	15.50	30.00
	1780 FF	—	4.00	7.50	12.50	25.00
	1781 FF	—	4.00	7.50	15.00	22.50
	1782 FF	—	4.00	7.50	12.50	25.00
	1783 FF	—	5.00	8.50	15.00	30.00
	1784 FF	—	5.00	8.50	15.00	30.00
	1785 FM	—	4.00	7.50	12.50	25.00
	1785 FF	—	5.00	8.50	13.50	30.00
	1786 FM	—	4.00	7.50	12.50	25.00
	1787 FM	—	4.00	7.50	12.50	25.00
	1787 FF	—	4.00	7.50	12.50	25.00
	1788 FM	—	6.00	9.00	15.00	37.50
	1788 FF	—	4.00	7.50	12.50	25.00
	1789 FM	—	4.00	7.50	12.50	25.00

Charles IV

Obv: Armored bust of Charles III; leg: CAROLUS.IV....

KM#	Date	Mintage	VG	Fine	VF	XF
79	1789 FM	—	8.50	18.50	37.50	75.00
	1790 FM	—	5.00	10.00	20.00	40.00

Obv: Armored bust of Charles III; leg: CAROLUS.IIII.

KM#	Date	Mintage	VG	Fine	VF	XF
80	1790 FM	—	8.50	16.50	32.50	65.00

Obv: Armored bust of Charles IIII.

KM#	Date	Mintage	VG	Fine	VF	XF
81	1792 FM	—	4.00	6.00	15.00	30.00
	1793 FM	—	4.00	6.00	13.50	27.50
	1794 FM	—	8.00	15.00	22.00	37.50
	1795 FM	—	4.00	7.50	12.50	25.00
	1796 FM	—	4.00	7.50	12.50	25.00
	1797 FM	—	4.00	7.50	12.50	25.00
	1798/7 FM	—	4.00	7.50	12.50	25.00
	1798 FM	—	4.00	7.50	12.50	25.00
	1799 FM	—	4.00	7.50	13.50	27.50
	1800 FM	—	4.00	7.50	13.50	27.50
	1801 FM	—	6.00	10.00	20.00	40.00
	1801 FT	—	5.50	8.50	16.50	32.50
	1802 FM	—	5.50	8.50	16.50	32.50
	1802 FT	—	4.00	7.50	12.50	25.00
	1803 FT	—	5.00	8.50	16.50	32.50
	1804 TH	—	4.00	7.50	12.50	25.00
	1805 TH	—	5.00	8.50	16.50	32.50
	1806 TH	—	4.00	7.50	12.50	25.00
	1807/6 TH	—	4.00	7.50	12.50	25.00
	1807 TH	—	4.00	7.50	12.50	20.00
	1808/7 TH	—	4.00	7.50	12.50	27.50
	1808 TH	—	4.00	7.50	12.50	27.50

Obv: Imaginary bust of Ferdinand VII.

KM#	Date	Mintage	VG	Fine	VF	XF
82	1809 TH	—	6.00	10.00	20.00	40.00
	1810 TH	—	4.00	7.50	12.50	27.50
	1810 HJ	—	6.00	10.00	20.00	40.00
	1811 HJ	—	5.50	8.50	16.50	32.50
	1811 TH	—	6.50	11.50	22.50	45.00
	1812 HJ	—	5.50	8.50	17.50	35.00
	1812 JJ	—	6.00	10.00	20.00	40.00
	1813 HJ	—	5.50	8.50	17.50	35.00
	1813 JJ	—	4.00	7.50	12.50	27.50
	1814 HJ	—	15.00	32.50	65.00	110.00

Obv: Draped bust of Ferdinand VII.

KM#	Date	Mintage	VG	Fine	VF	XF
83	1814 JJ	—	5.50	8.50	17.50	35.00
	1815 JJ	—	5.50	8.50	16.50	32.50
	1815 HJ	—	5.50	8.50	17.50	35.00
	1816 JJ	—	4.00	7.50	12.50	25.00
	1817 JJ	—	4.00	7.50	12.50	25.00
	1818 JJ	—	5.50	8.50	17.50	35.00
	1819 JJ	—	5.50	8.50	17.50	35.00
	1820 JJ	—	5.00	8.50	17.50	35.00
	1821/0 JJ	—	5.00	8.50	17.50	35.00
	1821 JJ	—	27.50	70.00	100.00	150.00

2 REALES

6.7700 gm., .916 SILVER, .1993 oz ASW

MEXICO CITY MINT

Philip V

Obv. leg: PHILIP.V.D.G.HISPAN.ET IND. REX.

KM#	Date	Mintage	VG	Fine	VF	XF
84	1732 F	—	800.00	1200.	1600.	2500.
	1733 F(MX)	—	500.00	750.00	1200.	2000.
	1733 F	—	500.00	675.00	1000.	1750.
	1733 MF(MX)	—	350.00	600.00	1000.	1500.
	1733 MF	—	500.00	750.00	1200.	2000.
	1734/3 MF	—	15.00	30.00	45.00	75.00
	1734 MF	—	17.50	35.00	50.00	85.00
	1735/4 MF	—	20.00	40.00	75.00	100.00
	1735 MF	—	10.00	20.00	30.00	60.00
	1736/33 MF	—	15.00	30.00	45.00	75.00
	1736/34 Mf	—	15.00	30.00	45.00	75.00
	1736/35 MF	—	15.00	30.00	45.00	75.00
	1736 MF	—	10.00	15.00	25.00	50.00
	1737 MF	—	10.00	20.00	30.00	60.00
	1738 MF	—	10.00	15.00	25.00	50.00
	1739 MF	—	10.00	15.00	25.00	50.00
	1740/30 MF	—	15.00	30.00	45.00	75.00
	1740 MF	—	10.00	20.00	30.00	60.00
	1741 MF	—	10.00	15.00	25.00	50.00

Obv. leg: PHS.V.D.G.HISP.ET IND.R.

KM#	Date	Mintage	VG	Fine	VF	XF
85	1742 M	—	7.50	15.00	25.00	50.00
	1743 M	—	7.50	15.00	25.00	50.00
	1744/43 M	—	15.00	30.00	45.00	75.00
	1744 M	—	7.50	15.00	25.00	50.00
	1745 M	—	7.50	15.00	25.00	50.00
	1746 M	—	7.50	15.00	25.00	50.00
	1747 M	—	7.50	15.00	25.00	50.00
	1749 M	—	150.00	225.00	300.00	600.00
	1750 M	—	150.00	225.00	300.00	600.00

Ferdinand VI

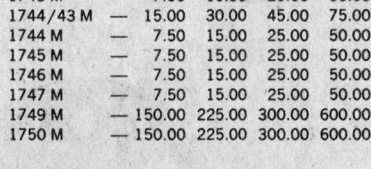

Obv. leg: FED.VI.D.G.HISP.ET IND.R.

KM#	Date	Mintage	VG	Fine	VF	XF
86	1747 M	—	12.00	24.00	42.00	65.00
	1748/7 M	—	12.00	25.00	45.00	65.00
	1748 M	—	10.00	20.00	30.00	60.00
	1749 M	—	10.00	20.00	30.00	60.00
	1750 M	—	10.00	20.00	30.00	60.00
	1751/41 M	—	15.00	30.00	45.00	75.00
	1751 M	—	10.00	20.00	30.00	60.00
	1752 M	—	10.00	20.00	30.00	60.00
	1753/2 M	—	10.00	20.00	30.00	60.00
	1753 M	—	10.00	20.00	30.00	60.00
	1754 M	—	10.00	20.00	30.00	60.00
	1755 M	—	10.00	20.00	30.00	60.00
	1756 M	—	10.00	20.00	30.00	60.00
	1757 M	—	10.00	20.00	30.00	60.00
	1758 M	—	10.00	20.00	30.00	60.00
	1759/8 M	—	10.00	20.00	30.00	60.00
	1759 M	—	10.00	20.00	30.00	60.00
	1760 M	—	15.00	30.00	42.50	85.00

6.7700 gm., .903 SILVER, .1965 oz ASW

Charles III

Obv. leg: CAR.III.D.G.HISP.ET IND.R.

KM#	Date	Mintage	VG	Fine	VF	XF
87	1760 M	—	8.00	11.50	20.00	40.00
	1761 M	—	8.00	12.50	25.00	50.00
	1762 M	—	8.00	12.50	25.00	50.00
	1763/2 M	—	8.00	12.50	25.00	50.00
	1763 M	—	8.00	13.50	27.50	55.00
	1764 M	—	8.00	12.50	25.00	50.00
	1765 M	—	8.00	12.50	25.00	50.00
	1766 M	—	8.00	12.50	25.00	50.00
	1767 M	—	9.00	15.00	30.00	60.00
	1768/6 M	—	9.00	15.00	30.00	60.00
	1768 M	—	9.00	15.00	30.00	60.00
	1769 M	—	10.00	16.50	32.50	65.00
	1770 M	—	—	—	Rare	—
	1770 F	—	—	—	Rare	—
	1771 F	—	8.00	12.50	25.00	50.00

Obv. leg: CAROLUS.III.DEI.GRATIA.

KM#	Date	Mintage	VG	Fine	VF	XF
88	1772FM with inverted FM					
		—	7.50	10.00	18.50	30.00
	1773 FM	—	7.50	10.00	17.50	27.50
	1773 FM with inverted FM					
		—	7.50	10.00	18.50	32.50
	1774 FM	—	7.50	10.00	18.50	32.50
	1775 FM	—	7.50	10.00	18.50	32.50
	1776 FM	—	7.50	10.00	17.50	27.50
	1777 FM	—	7.50	10.00	17.50	27.50
	1778 FF	—	7.50	10.00	17.50	27.50
	1779 FF	—	7.50	10.00	17.50	27.50
	1780 FF	—	7.50	10.00	17.50	27.50
	1781 FF	—	7.50	10.00	17.50	27.50
	1782 FF	—	7.50	10.00	17.50	27.50
	1783 FF	—	7.50	10.00	17.50	27.50
	1784 FF	—	7.50	10.00	17.50	27.50
	1784 FF (error) DEI GRTIA					
		—	—	—	Rare	—
	1784 FM	—	13.50	30.00	45.00	75.00
	1785 FM	—	7.50	10.00	17.50	27.50
	1786 FM	—	7.50	10.00	17.50	27.50
	1786 FF	—	60.00	85.00	135.00	200.00
	1787 FM	—	7.50	10.00	17.50	27.50
	1788 FM	—	7.50	10.00	17.50	27.50
	1789 FM	—	11.50	25.00	40.00	60.00

Charles IV

Obv: Armored bust of Charles III; leg: CAROLUS.IV....

KM#	Date	Mintage	VG	Fine	VF	XF
89	1789 FM	—	11.50	25.00	40.00	60.00
	1790 FM	—	11.50	25.00	40.00	60.00

Obv: Armored bust of Charles III; leg: CAROLUS.IIII....

KM#	Date	Mintage	VG	Fine	VF	XF
90	1790 FM	—	12.50	27.50	45.00	75.00

Obv: Armored bust of Carolus IIII.

KM#	Date	Mintage	VG	Fine	VF	XF
91	1792 FM	—	6.50	10.00	17.50	35.00
	1793 FM	—	6.50	10.00	15.00	25.00
	1794/3 FM	—	50.00	100.00	200.00	375.00
	1794 FM	—	6.50	10.00	17.50	27.50
	1795 FM	—	6.50	10.00	17.50	27.50
	1796 FM	—	6.50	10.00	17.50	27.50
	1797 FM	—	6.50	10.00	17.50	27.50
	1798 FM	—	6.50	10.00	17.50	27.50
	1799/8 FM	—	6.50	10.00	20.00	37.50
	1799 FM	—	6.50	10.00	17.50	27.50
	1800 FM	—	6.50	10.00	17.50	27.50
	1801 FT	—	6.50	10.00	17.50	27.50
	1801 FH	—	6.50	11.50	20.00	40.00
	1802 FT	—	6.50	10.00	17.50	27.50
	1803 FT	—	6.50	10.00	17.50	27.50
	1804 TH	—	6.50	10.00	17.50	27.50
	1805 TH	—	6.50	10.00	17.50	27.50
	1806 TH	—	6.50	10.00	17.50	27.50
	1807 TH	—	6.50	10.00	17.50	27.50
	1807/5 TH	—	6.50	10.00	17.50	27.50
	1808/7 Th	—	6.50	10.00	17.50	27.50
	1808 TH	—	6.50	10.00	17.50	27.50

Obv: Imaginary bust of Ferdinand VII.

KM#	Date	Mintage	VG	Fine	VF	XF
92	1809 TH	—	6.50	10.00	17.50	27.50
	1810 TH	—	6.50	10.00	17.50	27.50
	1810 HJ	—	6.50	10.00	17.50	27.50
	1811 HJ	—	6.50	10.00	18.50	32.50
	1811 TH	—	10.00	25.00	40.00	75.00
	1812 HJ	—	7.50	16.50	37.70	60.00
	1812 TH	—	6.50	12.50	27.50	50.00

Obv: Draped bust of Ferdinand VII.

KM#	Date	Mintage	VG	Fine	VF	XF
93	1812 HJ	—	6.50	11.50	20.00	40.00
	1812 TH	—	8.50	16.50	37.50	60.00
	1812 JJ	—	6.50	12.50	27.50	50.00
	1813 HJ	—	8.50	16.50	37.50	60.00
	1813 JJ	—	6.50	10.00	17.50	27.50
	1813 TH	—	6.50	10.00	18.50	32.50
	1814 JJ	—	6.50	10.00	17.50	27.50
	1815 JJ	—	6.50	10.00	17.50	27.50
	1816JJ	—	6.50	10.00	17.50	27.50
	1817 JJ	—	6.50	10.00	18.50	32.50
	1818 JJ	—	6.50	10.00	18.50	32.50
	1819 JJ	—	6.50	10.00	17.50	27.50
	1820 JJ	—	6.50	10.00	17.50	27.50
	1821/0 JJ	—	6.50	10.00	17.50	27.50
	1821 JJ	—	6.50	10.00	17.50	27.50

4 REALES

13.5400 gm., .916 SILVER, .3987 oz ASW

MEXICO CITY MINT

Philip V

Obv. leg: PHILLIP.V.D.G.HISPAN.ET IND.REX

KM#	Date	Mintage	VG	Fine	VF	XF
94	1732 F	—	2000.	3000.	5000.	10,000.
	1733 F	—	1500.	2000.	4000.	6000.
	1733 MF	—	1000.	1500.	2500.	4000.
	1733 MF(MX)	—	1500.	2200.	3000.	5000.
	1733 F(MX)	—	1500.	2500.	3500.	6000.
	1734/3 MF	—	125.00	200.00	350.00	500.00
	1734 MF	—	125.00	200.00	350.00	500.00
	1735 MF	—	125.00	200.00	350.00	500.00
	1736 MF	—	125.00	200.00	350.00	500.00
	1737 MF	—	125.00	200.00	350.00	500.00
	1738/7 MF	—	125.00	200.00	350.00	500.00
	1738 MF	—	125.00	200.00	350.00	500.00
	1739 MF	—	125.00	200.00	350.00	500.00
	1740 MF	—	125.00	200.00	350.00	500.00
	1741 MF	—	125.00	200.00	350.00	500.00
	1742 MF	—	125.00	200.00	350.00	500.00
	1743 MF	—	125.00	200.00	350.00	500.00
	1744/3 MF	—	150.00	225.00	350.00	600.00
	1744 MF	—	125.00	200.00	350.00	500.00
	1745 MF	—	125.00	200.00	350.00	500.00
	1746 MP	—	125.00	200.00	350.00	500.00
	1747 MF	—	125.00	200.00	350.00	500.00

Ferdinand VI

Obv. leg: FERDND.VI.D.G.HISPAN.ET IND.REX

KM#	Date	Mintage	VG	Fine	VF	XF
95	1747 MF	—	100.00	150.00	300.00	500.00
	1748/7 MF	—	100.00	150.00	300.00	500.00
	1748 MF	—	100.00	120.00	225.00	400.00
	1749 MF	—	100.00	120.00	225.00	400.00
	1750 MF	—	100.00	120.00	225.00	400.00
	1751 MF	—	100.00	120.00	225.00	400.00
	1752 MF	—	100.00	120.00	225.00	400.00
	1753 MF	—	100.00	120.00	225.00	400.00
	1754 MM	—	300.00	400.00	500.00	600.00
	1754 MF	—	200.00	300.00	500.00	800.00
	1755 MM	—	100.00	120.00	225.00	400.00
	1756 MM	—	100.00	150.00	300.00	400.00
	1757 MM	—	100.00	150.00	300.00	400.00
	1758 MM	—	100.00	120.00	225.00	400.00
	1759 MM	—	100.00	150.00	300.00	400.00
	1760/59 MM	—	100.00	150.00	300.00	400.00
	1760 MM	—	100.00	150.00	300.00	400.00

13.5400 gm., .903 SILVER, .3931 oz ASW

Charles III

Obv. leg: CAROLUS.III.D.G.HISPAN.ET IND.REX

KM#	Date	Mintage	VG	Fine	VF	XF
96	1760 MM	—	100.00	120.00	150.00	350.00
	1761 MM	—	100.00	120.00	150.00	275.00
	1762 MM	—	100.00	120.00	150.00	350.00
	1763/1 MM	—	100.00	135.00	200.00	350.00
	1763 MM	—	200.00	250.00	400.00	600.00
	1764 MM	—	400.00	600.00	800.00	1200.
	1765 MF	—	300.00	400.00	600.00	1000.
	1766 MF	—	250.00	350.00	500.00	800.00
	1767 MF	—	200.00	250.00	300.00	400.00
	1768 MF	—	100.00	120.00	150.00	350.00
	1769 MF	—	100.00	120.00	150.00	350.00
	1770 MF	—	100.00	120.00	150.00	275.00
	1771 MF	—	100.00	120.00	165.00	400.00
	1771 FM	—	120.00	200.00	300.00	500.00

Obv. leg: CAROLUS.III.DEI.GRATIA.

KM#	Date	Mintage	VG	Fine	VF	XF
97	1772 FM with inverted FM					
		—	100.00	150.00	200.00	300.00
	1773 FM with inverted FM					
		—	100.00	150.00	200.00	300.00
	1774 FM	—	40.00	60.00	90.00	150.00
	1775 FM	—	40.00	60.00	90.00	150.00
	1776 FM	—	40.00	60.00	90.00	150.00
	1777 FM	—	40.00	60.00	90.00	150.00
	1778 FF	—	40.00	60.00	90.00	150.00
	1779 FF	—	40.00	60.00	90.00	150.00
	1780 FF	—	40.00	60.00	90.00	150.00
	1781 FF	—	40.00	60.00	90.00	150.00
	1782 FF	—	40.00	60.00	90.00	150.00
	1783 FF	—	40.00	60.00	90.00	150.00
	1784 FF	—	60.00	100.00	150.00	200.00
	1784 FM	—	80.00	100.00	235.00	300.00
	1785 FM	—	40.00	60.00	100.00	150.00
	1786 FM	—	40.00	90.00	150.00	200.00
	1787 FM	—	40.00	90.00	150.00	200.00
	1788 FM	—	40.00	60.00	85.00	135.00
	1789 FM	—	100.00	120.00	150.00	300.00

Charles IV

Obv: Armored bust of Charles III; leg: CAROLUS.IV....

KM#	Date	Mintage	VG	Fine	VF	XF
98	1789 FM	—	60.00	100.00	120.00	200.00
	1790 FM	—	40.00	65.00	100.00	150.00

Obv: Armored bust of Charles III; leg: CAROLUS.IIII....

KM#	Date	Mintage	VG	Fine	VF	XF
99	1790 FM	—	50.00	100.00	200.00	300.00

Obv: Armored bust of Charles IIII.

KM#	Date	Mintage	VG	Fine	VF	XF
100	1792 FM	—	30.00	45.00	85.00	135.00
	1793 FM	—	30.00	45.00	85.00	135.00
	1794/3 FM	—	30.00	45.00	85.00	135.00
	1794 FM	—	30.00	45.00	85.00	135.00
	1795 FM	—	30.00	45.00	85.00	135.00
	1796 FM	—	30.00	45.00	85.00	135.00
	1797 FM	—	65.00	100.00	150.00	225.00
	1798/7 FM	—	30.00	45.00	85.00	135.00
	1798 FM	—	30.00	45.00	85.00	135.00
	1799 FM	—	30.00	45.00	85.00	135.00
	1800 FM	—	30.00	45.00	85.00	135.00
	1801 FM	—	30.00	45.00	85.00	135.00
	1801 FT	—	80.00	100.00	150.00	200.00
	1802 FT	—	30.00	45.00	85.00	135.00
	1803 FT	—	50.00	60.00	100.00	200.00
	1803 FM	—	60.00	80.00	105.00	250.00
	1804 TH	—	30.00	45.00	85.00	135.00
	1805 TH	—	50.00	60.00	100.00	200.00
	1806 TH	—	50.00	60.00	100.00	200.00
	1807 TH	—	50.00	60.00	100.00	200.00
	1808/7 TH	—	50.00	60.00	100.00	200.00
	1808 TH	—	50.00	60.00	100.00	200.00

Obv: Imaginary bust Ferdinand VII.

KM#	Date	Mintage	VG	Fine	VF	XF
101	1809 HJ	—	125.00	165.00	250.00	400.00
	1810 TH	—	125.00	165.00	250.00	400.00
	1810 HJ	—	125.00	165.00	250.00	400.00
	1811 HJ	—	125.00	165.00	250.00	400.00
	1812 HJ	—	125.00	165.00	250.00	400.00

Obv: Draped bust of Ferdinand VII.

KM#	Date	Mintage	VG	Fine	VF	XF
102	1816 JJ	—	200.00	300.00	400.00	500.00
	1817 JJ	—	200.00	300.00	400.00	500.00
	1818 JJ	—	200.00	300.00	400.00	500.00
	1819 JJ	—	200.00	300.00	400.00	500.00
	1820 JJ	—	200.00	300.00	400.00	500.00
	1821 JJ	—	100.00	160.00	250.00	400.00

8 REALES

27.0700 gm., .916 SILVER, .7973 oz ASW

MEXICO CITY MINT

Philip V

Obv. leg: PHILIP.V.D.G.HISPAN.ET IND.REX

KM#	Date	Mintage	VG	Fine	VF	XF
103	1732 F	—	3000.	6000.	8000.	10,000.
	1733/2 F	—	2000.	4000.	5000.	6500.
	1733 F	—	1600.	3250.	3000.	5000.
	1733 F(MX)	—	2250.	3250.	4000.	6000.
	1733 MF(MX)	—	1600.	2250.	3000.	4000.
	1733 MF	—	1200.	1500.	2000.	3000.
	1734/3 MF	—	300.00	450.00	600.00	1000.
	1734 MF	—	100.00	150.00	250.00	400.00
	1735 MF	—	100.00	150.00	250.00	400.00
	1736 MF	—	100.00	150.00	250.00	400.00
	1737 MF	—	80.00	120.00	200.00	350.00
	1738/6 MF	—	50.00	100.00	150.00	250.00
	1738/7 MF	—	40.00	100.00	150.00	250.00
	1738 MF	—	50.00	100.00	150.00	250.00
	1739/6 MF	—	50.00	100.00	150.00	250.00
	1739 MF	—	50.00	100.00	150.00	250.00
	1740/30 MF	—	50.00	100.00	150.00	250.00
	1740/39 MF	—	50.00	100.00	150.00	250.00
	1740 MF	—	50.00	100.00	150.00	250.00
	1741/31 MF	—	50.00	100.00	150.00	250.00
	1741 MF	—	50.00	100.00	150.00	250.00
	1742/32 MF	—	50.00	100.00	150.00	250.00
	1742/1 MF	—	50.00	100.00	150.00	250.00
	1742 MF	—	50.00	100.00	150.00	250.00
	1743/2 MF	—	40.00	100.00	150.00	250.00
	1743 MF	—	50.00	100.00	150.00	250.00
	1744/34 MF	—	40.00	100.00	150.00	250.00
	1744/3 MF	—	40.00	100.00	150.00	250.00
	1744 MF	—	50.00	100.00	150.00	250.00
	1745 MF	—	50.00	100.00	150.00	250.00
	1746 MF	—	50.00	100.00	150.00	250.00
	1747 MF	—	50.00	100.00	150.00	250.00

Ferdinand VI

Obv. leg: FERDND.VI.D.G.HISPAN.ET IND.REX

KM#	Date	Mintage	VG	Fine	VF	XF
104	1747 MF	—	40.00	100.00	150.00	250.00
	1748/7 MF	—	75.00	150.00	250.00	400.00
	1748 MF	—	50.00	100.00	150.00	250.00
	1749 MF	—	50.00	100.00	150.00	250.00
	1750 MF	—	50.00	100.00	150.00	250.00
	1751/0 MF	—	50.00	100.00	150.00	250.00
	1751 MF	—	50.00	100.00	150.00	250.00
	1752/1 MF	—	50.00	100.00	150.00	250.00
	1752 MF	—	50.00	100.00	150.00	250.00
	1753/2 MF	—	50.00	100.00	150.00	250.00
	1753 MF	—	50.00	100.00	150.00	250.00
	1754/3 MF	—	50.00	100.00	150.00	250.00
	1754/3 MM/MF		50.00	100.00	150.00	250.00

KM#	Date	Mintage	VG	Fine	VF	XF
104	1754 MF	—	100.00	150.00	200.00	300.00
	1754 MM	—	400.00	600.00	1000.	2000.
	1754 MF Rev. with imperial crown on left pillar	—	250.00	300.00	400.00	600.00
	1754 MM Rev. with imperial crown on left pillar	—	100.00	120.00	200.00	300.00
	1755 MM	—	50.00	100.00	150.00	250.00
	1756/5 MM	—	80.00	120.00	200.00	350.00
	1756 MM	—	50.00	100.00	150.00	250.00
	1757/6 MM	—	50.00	100.00	150.00	250.00
	1757 MM	—	50.00	100.00	150.00	250.00
	1758 MM	—	50.00	100.00	150.00	250.00
	1759 MM	—	50.00	100.00	150.00	250.00
	1760 MM	—	80.00	120.00	200.00	350.00

27.0700 gm., .903 SILVER, .7859 oz ASW

Charles III

Obv. leg: CAROLUS.III.D.G.HISPAN.ET IND.REX

KM#	Date	Mintage	VG	Fine	VF	XF
105	1760 MM with CAROLUS.III/FERDIN. VI. recut die	—	60.00	100.00	175.00	300.00
	1760 MM	—	50.00	100.00	150.00	250.00
	1761 MM tip of cross between H and I in legend	—	50.00	100.00	150.00	250.00
	1761 MM tip of cross between I and S in legend	—	18.00	100.00	150.00	250.00
	1762/1 MM	—	30.00	100.00	150.00	250.00
	1762 MM	—	14.00	100.00	150.00	250.00
	1762 MF	—	325.00	460.00	600.00	900.00
	1763/2 MM	—	30.00	100.00	150.00	250.00
	1763/53 MF	—	30.00	100.00	150.00	250.00
	1763/1 MF	—	30.00	100.00	150.00	250.00
	1763/2 MF	—	30.00	100.00	150.00	250.00
	1763/1772 MF	—	30.00	100.00	150.00	250.00
	1763 MM	—	450.00	625.00	800.00	1250.
	1763 MF	—	50.00	100.00	150.00	250.00
	1764/54 MF	—	50.00	100.00	150.00	250.00
	1764/1 MF	—	50.00	100.00	150.00	250.00
	1764/3 MF	—	50.00	100.00	150.00	250.00
	1764 MF	—	50.00	100.00	150.00	250.00
	1765 MF	—	50.00	100.00	150.00	250.00
	1766/5 MF	—	50.00	100.00	150.00	250.00
	1766 MF	—	50.00	100.00	150.00	250.00
	1767/17 MF	—	50.00	100.00	150.00	250.00
	1767/6 MF	—	50.00	100.00	150.00	250.00
	1767 MF	—	50.00	100.00	150.00	250.00
	1768/6 MF	—	50.00	100.00	150.00	250.00
	1768/7 MF	—	50.00	100.00	150.00	250.00
	1768 MF	—	50.00	100.00	150.00	200.00
	1769 MF	—	50.00	100.00	150.00	200.00
	1770/60 MF	—	50.00	100.00	150.00	250.00
	1770 MF	—	50.00	100.00	150.00	250.00
	1770/60 FM	—	50.00	100.00	150.00	250.00
	1770/69 FM	—	50.00	100.00	150.00	250.00
	1770 FM	—	50.00	100.00	150.00	250.00
	1771/0 FM	—	50.00	100.00	150.00	250.00
	1771 FM	—	50.00	100.00	150.00	250.00

MF (error)

FM (normal)
Obv. leg: CAROLUS.III.DEI.GRATIA.

KM#	Date	Mintage	VG	Fine	VF	XF
106	1772 FM with inverted FM					
		—	40.00	60.00	100.00	200.00
	1772 MF with inverted MF					
		—	200.00	300.00	400.00	650.00
	1773 FM	—	40.00	60.00	85.00	135.00
	1773 FM with inverted FM					
		—	30.00	60.00	85.00	135.00
	1774 FM	—	30.00	40.00	60.00	80.00
	1775 FM	—	30.00	40.00	60.00	80.00
	1776 FM	—	30.00	40.00	60.00	85.00
	1777 FM	—	30.00	40.00	60.00	85.00
	1777 FF	—	30.00	40.00	60.00	90.00
	1778 FF	—	30.00	40.00	60.00	85.00
	1779 FF	—	30.00	40.00	60.00	85.00
	1780 FF	—	30.00	40.00	60.00	85.00
	1781 FF	—	30.00	40.00	60.00	85.00
	1782 FF	—	30.00	40.00	60.00	85.00
	1783 FF	—	30.00	40.00	60.00	90.00
	1783 FM	—	200.00	400.00	600.00	900.00
	1784 FF	—	75.00	125.00	200.00	350.00
	1784 FM	—	30.00	40.00	60.00	85.00
	1785 FM	—	30.00	40.00	60.00	85.00
	1786/5 FM	—	30.00	40.00	60.00	85.00
	1786 FM	—	30.00	40.00	60.00	85.00
	1787 FM	—	30.00	40.00	60.00	85.00
	1788 FM	—	30.00	40.00	60.00	85.00
	1789 FM	—	100.00	150.00	200.00	350.00

Charles IV
Obv: Armored bust of Charles III; leg: CAROLUS.IV....

KM#	Date	Mintage	VG	Fine	VF	XF
107	1789 FM	—	60.00	80.00	100.00	150.00
	1790 FM	—	50.00	60.00	80.00	100.00

Obv: Armored bust of Charles III; leg: CAROLUS.IIII....

KM#	Date	Mintage	VG	Fine	VF	XF
108	1790 FM	—	50.00	60.00	80.00	150.00

Obv: Armored bust of Charles IIII.

KM#	Date	Mintage	VG	Fine	VF	XF
109	1791 FM	—	25.00	32.50	45.00	75.00
	1792 FM	—	25.00	30.00	40.00	70.00
	1793 FM	—	25.00	30.00	40.00	65.00
	1794 FM	—	25.00	30.00	40.00	65.00
	1795 FM	—	25.00	30.00	40.00	65.00
	1796 FM	—	25.00	30.00	40.00	65.00
	1797 FM	—	25.00	30.00	40.00	65.00
	1798 FM	—	25.00	30.00	40.00	65.00
	1799 FM	—	25.00	30.00	40.00	65.00
	1800 FM	—	25.00	30.00	40.00	65.00
	1801 FM	—	80.00	120.00	160.00	225.00
	1801/1791 FM		35.00	85.00	150.00	210.00
	1801 FT	—	25.00	30.00	40.00	65.00
	1802 FT	—	25.00	30.00	40.00	65.00

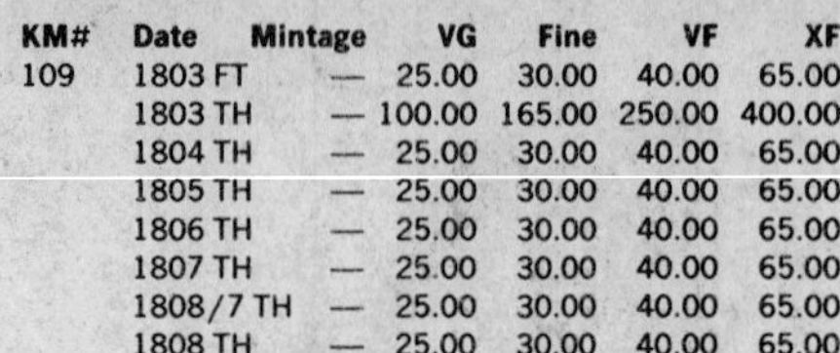

KM#	Date	Mintage	VG	Fine	VF	XF
109	1803 FT	—	25.00	30.00	40.00	65.00
	1803 TH	—	100.00	165.00	250.00	400.00
	1804 TH	—	25.00	30.00	40.00	65.00
	1805 TH	—	25.00	30.00	40.00	65.00
	1806 TH	—	25.00	30.00	40.00	65.00
	1807 TH	—	25.00	30.00	40.00	65.00
	1808/7 TH	—	25.00	30.00	40.00	65.00
	1808 TH	—	25.00	30.00	40.00	65.00

Ferdinand VII
Obv: Armored bust of Ferdinand VII.

KM#	Date	Mintage	VG	Fine	VF	XF
110	1808 TH	—	26.50	36.50	50.00	90.00
	1809 HJ	—	40.00	70.00	120.00	200.00
	1809 TH	—	26.50	36.50	50.00	90.00
	1810/09 HJ	—	27.50	40.00	60.00	110.00
	1810 HJ	—	25.00	60.00	80.00	135.00
	1810 TH	—	250.00	300.00	500.00	800.00
	1811/0 HJ	—	30.00	45.00	70.00	110.00
	1811 HJ	—	26.50	36.50	50.00	90.00

Obv: Draped bust of Ferdinand VII.

KM#	Date	Mintage	VG	Fine	VF	XF
111	1811 HJ	—	100.00	200.00	300.00	500.00
	1812 HJ	—	80.00	100.00	150.00	250.00
	1812 JJ	—	25.00	30.00	40.00	65.00
	1813 HJ	—	120.00	160.00	250.00	350.00
	1813 JJ	—	25.00	30.00	40.00	65.00
	1814/3 HJ	—	150.00	200.00	300.00	450.00
	1814/13 JJ	—	150.00	200.00	300.00	450.00
	1814 JJ	—	26.50	36.50	50.00	90.00
	1814 HJ	—	400.00	600.00	800.00	1100.
	1815 JJ	—	25.00	30.00	40.00	65.00
	1816/5 JJ	—	25.00	30.00	40.00	65.00
	1816 JJ	—	25.00	30.00	40.00	65.00
	1817 JJ	—	25.00	30.00	40.00	65.00
	1818 JJ	—	25.00	30.00	40.00	65.00
	1819 JJ	—	25.00	30.00	40.00	65.00

KM#	Date	Mintage	VG	Fine	VF	XF
111	1820 JJ	—	25.00	30.00	40.00	65.00
	1821 JJ	—	25.00	30.00	40.00	70.00

1/2 ESCUDO

1.6900 gm., .875 GOLD, .0475 oz AGW

MEXICO CITY MINT

Ferdinand VII

Obv. leg: FERD.VII.D.G.HISP.ET IND.

Rev: Oval arms in chain.

KM#	Date	Mintage	VG	Fine	VF	XF
112	1814 HJ	—	425.00	600.00	800.00	1000.
	1815/4 HJ	—	300.00	450.00	650.00	850.00
	1815 JJ	—	200.00	300.00	500.00	650.00
	1816 JJ	—	200.00	300.00	500.00	650.00
	1817 JJ	—	250.00	350.00	500.00	650.00
	1818 JJ	—	250.00	350.00	500.00	650.00
	1819 JJ	—	275.00	400.00	500.00	650.00
	1820 JJ	—	275.00	400.00	500.00	650.00

ESCUDO

3.3800 gm., .917 GOLD, .0996 oz AGW

MEXICO CITY MINT

Philip V

Obv. leg: PHILIP.V.D.G.HISPAN.ET IND.REX

KM#	Date	Mintage	VG	Fine	VF	XF
113	1732 F	—	800.00	1600.	2500.	4000.
	1733 F	—	800.00	1000.	1500.	2500.
	1734 MF	—	250.00	300.00	600.00	850.00
	1735 MF	—	250.00	300.00	600.00	850.00
	1736 MF	—	250.00	300.00	600.00	850.00
	1737 MF	—	250.00	300.00	600.00	850.00
	1738 MF	—	250.00	300.00	600.00	850.00
	1739 MF	—	250.00	300.00	600.00	850.00
	1740 MF	—	250.00	300.00	450.00	600.00
	1741 MF	—	250.00	300.00	450.00	600.00
	1742 MF	—	250.00	300.00	450.00	600.00
	1743 MF	—	250.00	300.00	450.00	600.00
	1744 MF	—	250.00	300.00	450.00	600.00
	1745 MF	—	250.00	300.00	450.00	600.00
	1746 MF	—	250.00	300.00	450.00	600.00

Ferdinand VI

Obv: Long bust; Leg: FERD.VI.D.G.HISPAN.ET IND.REX.

KM#	Date	Mintage	VG	Fine	VF	XF
114	1747 MF	—	600.00	850.00	1350.	2250.

Obv: Short bust

KM#	Date	Mintage	VG	Fine	VF	XF
115	1748 MF	—	250.00	300.00	450.00	800.00
	1749 MF	—	250.00	300.00	450.00	800.00
	1750 MF	—	250.00	300.00	400.00	600.00
	1751 MF	—	250.00	300.00	400.00	600.00
	1752 MF	—	250.00	300.00	400.00	600.00
	1753 MF	—	250.00	300.00	400.00	600.00
	1754 MF	—	250.00	300.00	400.00	600.00
	1755 MM	—	250.00	300.00	400.00	600.00
	1756 MF	—	250.00	300.00	400.00	600.00
	1756 MM	—	250.00	300.00	400.00	600.00
	1757 MM	—	250.00	300.00	400.00	600.00

Charles III

Obv. leg: CAROLVS.III.D.G.HISPAN.ET IND.REX

Rev. leg: NOMINA MAGNA SEQUOR

KM#	Date	Mintage	VG	Fine	VF	XF
116	1760 MM	—	300.00	600.00	800.00	1000.
	1761 MM	—	300.00	600.00	800.00	1000.

Obv: Large bust; leg: CAR.III.D.G.HISP.ET IND.R.

Rev. leg: IN.UTROQ. FELIX.

KM#	Date	Mintage	VG	Fine	VF	XF
117	1762 MF	—	300.00	400.00	600.00	800.00
	1762 MM	—	300.00	400.00	600.00	800.00
	1763 MF	—	300.00	400.00	600.00	800.00
	1763 MM	—	300.00	400.00	600.00	800.00
	1764 MM	—	300.00	400.00	600.00	800.00
	1765 MF	—	300.00	400.00	600.00	800.00
	1766 MF	—	300.00	400.00	600.00	800.00
	1767 MF	—	300.00	400.00	600.00	800.00
	1768 MF	—	300.00	400.00	600.00	800.00
	1769 MF	—	300.00	400.00	600.00	800.00
	1770 MF	—	300.00	400.00	600.00	800.00
	1771 MF	—	300.00	400.00	600.00	800.00

Obv. leg: CAROL.III.D.G. HISPAN.ET IND.R.

Rev: IN.UTROQ.FELIX.A.D.

KM#	Date	Mintage	VG	Fine	VF	XF
118	1772 FM	—	160.00	200.00	300.00	450.00
	1772 MF	—	160.00	200.00	300.00	450.00
	1773 MF	—	160.00	200.00	300.00	450.00
	1773 FM	—	160.00	200.00	300.00	450.00
	1774 FM	—	160.00	200.00	300.00	450.00
	1775 FM	—	160.00	200.00	300.00	450.00
	1776 FM	—	160.00	200.00	300.00	450.00
	1777 FM	—	160.00	200.00	300.00	450.00
	1778 FF	—	160.00	200.00	300.00	450.00
	1779 FF	—	160.00	200.00	300.00	450.00
	1780 FF	—	160.00	200.00	300.00	450.00
	1781 FF	—	160.00	200.00	300.00	450.00
	1782 FF	—	160.00	200.00	300.00	450.00
	1783 FF	—	160.00	200.00	300.00	450.00
	1784 FF	—	160.00	200.00	300.00	450.00
	1784 FM	—	160.00	200.00	300.00	450.00
	1785 FM	—	160.00	200.00	300.00	450.00

3.3800 gm., .875 GOLD, .0950 oz AGW

KM#	Date	Mintage	VG	Fine	VF	XF
118a	1786 FM	—	160.00	200.00	300.00	450.00
	1787 FM	—	160.00	200.00	300.00	450.00
	1788 FM	—	160.00	200.00	300.00	450.00

Charles IV

Obv: Bust of Charles III; leg: CAROLUS.IV.D.G....

KM#	Date	Mintage	VG	Fine	VF	XF
119	1789 FM	—	160.00	200.00	300.00	500.00
	1790 FM	—	160.00	200.00	300.00	500.00

Obv: Armored bust of Charles IV.

KM#	Date	Mintage	VG	Fine	VF	XF
120	1792 MF	—	150.00	200.00	250.00	350.00
	1793 FM	—	150.00	200.00	250.00	350.00
	1794 FM	—	150.00	200.00	250.00	350.00
	1795 FM	—	150.00	200.00	250.00	350.00
	1796 FM	—	150.00	200.00	250.00	350.00
	1797 FM	—	150.00	200.00	250.00	350.00
	1798 FM	—	150.00	200.00	250.00	350.00
	1799 FM	—	150.00	200.00	250.00	350.00
	1800 FM	—	150.00	200.00	250.00	350.00
	1801 FT	—	150.00	200.00	250.00	350.00
	1801 FM	—	150.00	200.00	250.00	350.00
	1802 FT	—	150.00	200.00	250.00	350.00
	1803 FT	—	150.00	200.00	250.00	350.00
	1804 TH	—	150.00	200.00	250.00	350.00
	1805 TH	—	150.00	200.00	250.00	350.00
	1806 TH	—	150.00	200.00	250.00	350.00
	1807 TH	—	150.00	200.00	250.00	350.00
	1808 TH	—	150.00	200.00	250.00	350.00

Ferdinand VII

Obv: Imaginary bust of Ferdinand VII.

KM#	Date	Mintage	VG	Fine	VF	XF
121	1809 HJ	—	120.00	200.00	250.00	400.00
	1810 HJ	—	120.00	200.00	250.00	400.00
	1811 HJ	—	120.00	200.00	250.00	400.00
	1812 HJ	—	120.00	200.00	250.00	400.00

Obv: Undraped bust Ferdinand VII.

KM#	Date	Mintage	VG	Fine	VF	XF
122	1814 HJ	—	120.00	200.00	250.00	400.00
	1815 JJ	—	120.00	200.00	250.00	400.00
	1815 HJ	—	120.00	200.00	250.00	400.00
	1816 JJ	—	120.00	200.00	250.00	400.00
	1817 JJ	—	120.00	200.00	250.00	400.00
	1818 JJ	—	120.00	200.00	250.00	400.00
	1819 JJ	—	120.00	200.00	250.00	400.00
	1820 JJ	—	120.00	200.00	250.00	400.00

2 ESCUDOS

6.7700 gm., .917 GOLD, .1996 oz AGW

MEXICO CITY MINT

Philip V

Obv. leg: PHILIP.V.D.G.HISPAN.ET IND.REX

Rev. leg: INITIUM SAPIENTIAE TIMOR DOMINI

KM#	Date	Mintage	VG	Fine	VF	XF
124	1732 F	—	1000.	1500.	2000.	3000.
	1733 F	—	600.00	800.00	1500.	2400.
	1734 MF	—	500.00	600.00	800.00	1000.
	1735 MF	—	500.00	600.00	800.00	1000.
	1736 MF	—	500.00	600.00	800.00	1000.
	1737 MF	—	500.00	600.00	800.00	1200.
	1738 MF	—	500.00	600.00	800.00	1200.
	1739 MF	—	500.00	600.00	800.00	1000.
	1740 MF	—	500.00	600.00	800.00	1200.
	1741 MF	—	500.00	600.00	800.00	1200.
	1742 MF	—	500.00	600.00	800.00	1200.
	1743 MF	—	500.00	600.00	800.00	1200.
	1744 MF	—	500.00	600.00	800.00	1200.
	1745 MF	—	500.00	600.00	800.00	1000.
	1746 MF	—	500.00	600.00	800.00	1000.
	1747 MF	—	500.00	600.00	800.00	1200.

Ferdinand VI

Obv: Large bust; Leg: FERD.VI.D.G..; Rev. leg: INITIUM....

KM#	Date	Mintage	VG	Fine	VF	XF
125	1747 MF	—	1000.	1200.	2000.	2500.

Obv: Small young bust; leg: FERD.VI.D.G...

Rev. leg: NOMINA MAGNA SEQUOR

KM#	Date	Mintage	VG	Fine	VF	XF
126	1748 MF	—	400.00	500.00	600.00	850.00
	1749 MF	—	400.00	500.00	600.00	800.00
	1750 MF	—	400.00	500.00	600.00	850.00
	1751 MF	—	400.00	500.00	600.00	850.00
	1752 MF	—	400.00	500.00	600.00	850.00
	1753 MF	—	400.00	500.00	600.00	850.00
	1754 MF	—	400.00	500.00	600.00	850.00
	1755 MM	—	400.00	500.00	600.00	850.00
	1756 MM	—	400.00	500.00	600.00	1000.
	1756 MF	—	400.00	500.00	600.00	1200.

Obv: Armored bust; leg: FERDND.VI.D.G....

KM#	Date	Mintage	VG	Fine	VF	XF
127	1757 MM	—	450.00	600.00	700.00	1000.
	1758 MM	—	450.00	600.00	750.00	1100.
	1759 MM	—	450.00	600.00	700.00	1000.

Charles III

Obv: Young bust; leg: CAROLVS.III.D.G....

KM#	Date	Mintage	VG	Fine	VF	XF
128	1760 MM	—	400.00	600.00	800.00	1500.
	1761 MM	—	400.00	600.00	800.00	1500.

Obv: Large young bust; leg: CAROLUS.III.D.G....

Rev. leg: IN.UTROQ.FELIX.AUSPICE.DEO

KM#	Date	Mintage	VG	Fine	VF	XF
129	1762 MF	—	500.00	600.00	800.00	1100.
	1763 MF	—	500.00	600.00	800.00	1100.
	1764 MF	—	500.00	600.00	800.00	1100.
	1764 MM	—	500.00	600.00	800.00	1100.
	1765 MF	—	500.00	600.00	800.00	1200.
	1766 MF	—	500.00	600.00	800.00	1200.
	1767 MF	—	500.00	600.00	800.00	1100.
	1768 MF	—	500.00	600.00	800.00	1100.

KM#	Date	Mintage	VG	Fine	VF	XF
129	1769 MF	—	500.00	600.00	800.00	1100.
	1770 MF	—	500.00	600.00	1000.	1500.
	1771 MF	—	500.00	600.00	800.00	1100.

Obv: Older bust; leg: CAROLUS.III.D.G....
Rev: Crowned arms in chain.

KM#	Date	Mintage	VG	Fine	VF	XF
130	1772 FM	—	300.00	400.00	500.00	650.00
	1773 FM	—	300.00	400.00	500.00	650.00
	1774 FM	—	300.00	400.00	500.00	650.00
	1775 FM	—	300.00	400.00	500.00	650.00
	1776 FM	—	300.00	400.00	500.00	650.00
	1777 FM	—	300.00	400.00	500.00	650.00
	1778 FF	—	300.00	400.00	500.00	650.00
	1779 FF	—	300.00	400.00	500.00	650.00
	1780 FF	—	300.00	400.00	500.00	650.00
	1781 FF	—	300.00	400.00	500.00	650.00
	1782 FF	—	300.00	400.00	500.00	650.00
	1783 FF	—	300.00	400.00	500.00	650.00
	1784 FF	—	300.00	400.00	500.00	650.00
	1784 FM	—	300.00	400.00	500.00	650.00
	1785 FM	—	300.00	400.00	500.00	650.00

6.7700 gm., .875 GOLD, .1904 oz AGW

KM#	Date	Mintage	VG	Fine	VF	XF
130a	1786 FM	—	300.00	400.00	500.00	600.00
	1787 FM	—	300.00	400.00	500.00	650.00
	1788 FM	—	300.00	400.00	500.00	650.00

Charles IV
Obv: Bust of Charles III; Leg: CAROL.IV.D.G....

KM#	Date	Mintage	VG	Fine	VF	XF
131	1789 FM	—	300.00	400.00	650.00	900.00
	1790 FM	—	300.00	400.00	650.00	900.00
	1791 FM	—	300.00	400.00	650.00	900.00

Obv: Armored bust of Charles IV.

KM#	Date	Mintage	VG	Fine	VF	XF
132	1792 FM	—	200.00	300.00	400.00	500.00
	1793 FM	—	200.00	300.00	400.00	500.00
	1794 FM	—	200.00	300.00	400.00	500.00
	1795 FM	—	200.00	300.00	400.00	500.00
	1796 FM	—	200.00	300.00	400.00	500.00
	1797 FM	—	200.00	350.00	500.00	700.00
	1798 FM	—	200.00	300.00	400.00	500.00
	1799 FM	—	200.00	300.00	400.00	500.00
	1800 FM	—	200.00	300.00	400.00	500.00
	1801 FM	—	200.00	300.00	400.00	550.00
	1802 FT	—	200.00	300.00	400.00	500.00
	1803 FT	—	200.00	300.00	400.00	500.00
	1804 TH	—	200.00	300.00	400.00	500.00
	1805 TH	—	200.00	300.00	400.00	500.00
	1806 TH	—	200.00	300.00	400.00	500.00
	1807 TH	—	200.00	300.00	400.00	500.00
	1808 TH	—	200.00	300.00	400.00	500.00

Ferdinand VII
Obv: Imaginary bust of Ferdinand VII.

KM#	Date	Mintage	VG	Fine	VF	XF
133	1808 TH	—	425.00	600.00	800.00	1200.
	1809 HJ	—	350.00	500.00	750.00	1150.
	1810 HJ	—	350.00	500.00	700.00	1100.
	1811 HJ	—	275.00	400.00	600.00	1000.

Obv: Undraped bust of Ferdinand VII.

KM#	Date	Mintage	VG	Fine	VF	XF
134	1814 HJ	—	200.00	250.00	400.00	550.00
	1814 JJ	—	200.00	250.00	400.00	550.00
	1815 JJ	—	200.00	250.00	400.00	550.00
	1816 JJ	—	200.00	250.00	400.00	550.00
	1817 JJ	—	200.00	250.00	400.00	550.00
	1818 JJ	—	200.00	250.00	400.00	550.00
	1819 JJ	—	200.00	250.00	400.00	550.00
	1820 JJ	—	200.00	250.00	400.00	550.00

4 ESCUDOS

13.5400 gm., .917 GOLD, .3992 oz AGW

MEXICO CITY MINT

Philip V
Obv. leg: PHILIP.V.D.G.HISPAN.ET IND.REX
Rev. leg: INITIUM SAPIENTIAE TIMOR DOMINI

KM#	Date	Mintage	VG	Fine	VF	XF
135	1732	—	2500.	5000.	8000.	12,500.
	1732 F	—	2000.	3000.	5000.	8000.
	1733 F	—	1000.	2000.	3000.	5000.
	1734/3 F	—	850.00	1500.	2000.	3500.
	1734 MF	—	600.00	1000.	1350.	1850.
	1735 MF	—	600.00	1000.	1350.	1850.
	1736 MF	—	600.00	1000.	1350.	1850.
	1737 MF	—	600.00	1000.	1350.	1850.
	1738 MF	—	600.00	1000.	1350.	1850.
	1739 MF	—	600.00	1000.	1350.	1850.
	1740 MF	—	600.00	1000.	1350.	1850.
	1741 MF	—	600.00	1000.	1350.	1850.
	1742 MF	—	600.00	1000.	1350.	1850.
	1743 MF	—	600.00	1000.	1350.	1850.
	1744 MD	—	600.00	1000.	1350.	1850.
	1745 MF	—	600.00	1000.	1350.	1850.
	1746 MF	—	600.00	1000.	1350.	1850.
	1747 MF	—	600.00	1000.	1500.	2000.

Ferdinand VI
Obv: Large bust; leg: FERDND.V.D.G....

KM#	Date	Mintage	VG	Fine	VF	XF
136	1747 MF	—	1500.	3000.	5000.	8500.

Obv: Small bust; leg: FERDND.VI.D.G.....
Rev. leg: NOMINA MAGNA SEQUOR, 4S by arms.

KM#	Date	Mintage	VG	Fine	VF	XF
137	1748 MF	—	800.00	1000.	1500.	2250.
	1749 MF	—	800.00	1000.	1500.	2250.
	1750MF	—	800.00	1000.	1500.	2250.
	1750 MF	—	800.00	1000.	1500.	2250.
	1751 MF	—	800.00	1000.	1500.	2250.

Rev: Without 4 S by arms.

KM#	Date	Mintage	VG	Fine	VF	XF
138	1752 MF	—	800.00	1000.	1500.	2250.
	1753 MF	—	800.00	1000.	1500.	2250.
	1754 MF	—	800.00	1000.	1500.	2250.
	1755 MM	—	800.00	1000.	1500.	2250.
	1756 MM	—	800.00	1000.	1500.	2250.

Obv: Large full bust; leg: FERDND.VI.D.G....

KM#	Date	Mintage	VG	Fine	VF	XF
139	1757 MM	—	800.00	1000.	1500.	2250.
	1758 MM	—	800.00	1000.	1500.	2250.
	1759 MM	—	800.00	1000.	1500.	2250.

Charles III
Obv: Young bust; leg: CAROLVS.III.D.G....
Rev. leg: NOMINA MAGNA SEQUOR

KM#	Date	Mintage	VG	Fine	VF	XF
140	1760 MM	—	800.00	1150.	1650.	2750.
	1761 MM	—	800.00	1150.	1650.	2750.

Obv: Large young bust; leg: CAROLUS.III.D.G....
Rev. leg: IN.UTROQ.FELIX.AUSPICE.DEO.

KM#	Date	Mintage	VG	Fine	VF	XF
141	1762 MF	—	800.00	1000.	1500.	2250.
	1763 MF	—	800.00	1000.	1500.	2250.
	1764 MF	—	800.00	1000.	1500.	2250.
	1765 MF	—	800.00	1000.	1500.	2250.
	1766 MF	—	800.00	1000.	1500.	2250.
	1767 MF	—	800.00	1000.	1500.	2250.
	1768 MF	—	800.00	1000.	1500.	2250.
	1769 MF	—	800.00	1000.	1500.	2250.
	1770 MF	—	800.00	1000.	1500.	2250.
	1771 MF	—	800.00	1000.	1500.	2250.

Obv. leg: CAROL.III.D.G....

KM#	Date	Mintage	VG	Fine	VF	XF
142	1772 FM	—	400.00	600.00	850.00	1350.
	1773 FM	—	400.00	600.00	850.00	1350.
	1774 FM	—	400.00	600.00	850.00	1350.
	1775 FM	—	400.00	600.00	850.00	1350.
	1776 FM	—	400.00	600.00	850.00	1350.
	1777 FM	—	400.00	600.00	850.00	1350.
	1778 FF	—	400.00	600.00	850.00	1350.
	1779 FF	—	400.00	600.00	850.00	1350.
	1780 FF	—	400.00	600.00	850.00	1350.
	1781 FF	—	400.00	600.00	850.00	1350.
	1782 FF	—	400.00	600.00	850.00	1350.
	1783 FF	—	400.00	600.00	850.00	1350.
	1784 FF	—	400.00	600.00	850.00	1350.
	1784 FM	—	400.00	600.00	850.00	1350.
	1785 FM	—	400.00	600.00	850.00	1350.

13.5400 gm., .875 GOLD, .3809 oz AGW

KM#	Date	Mintage	VG	Fine	VF	XF
142a	1786 FM	—	400.00	600.00	850.00	1350.
	1787 FM	—	400.00	600.00	850.00	1350.
	1788 FM	—	400.00	600.00	850.00	1350.
	1788 JM	—	400.00	600.00	850.00	1350.
	1789 FM	—	400.00	600.00	850.00	1350.

Charles IV
Obv: Bust of Charles III; leg: CAROL.IV.D.G....

KM#	Date	Mintage	VG	Fine	VF	XF
143	1789 FM	—	500.00	700.00	1000.	1600.
	1790 FM	—	500.00	700.00	1000.	1600.
	1791 FM	—	500.00	700.00	1000.	1600.

Obv: Armored bust of Charles IIII.

KM#	Date	Mintage	VG	Fine	VF	XF
144	1792 FM	—	300.00	500.00	850.00	1350.
	1793 FM	—	300.00	500.00	850.00	1350.
	1794 FM	—	300.00	500.00	850.00	1350.
	1795 FM	—	300.00	500.00	850.00	1350.
	1796 FM	—	300.00	500.00	850.00	1350.
	1797 FM	—	300.00	500.00	850.00	1350.
	1798/7 FM	—	350.00	500.00	650.00	900.00
	1798 FM	—	300.00	500.00	850.00	1350.
	1799 FM	—	300.00	500.00	850.00	1350.
	1800 FM	—	300.00	500.00	850.00	1350.
	1801 FM	—	300.00	500.00	850.00	1350.
	1801 FT	—	300.00	500.00	850.00	1350.
	1802 FT	—	300.00	500.00	850.00	1350.
	1803 FT	—	300.00	500.00	850.00	1350.
	1804 TH	—	300.00	500.00	850.00	1350.
	1805 TH	—	300.00	500.00	850.00	1350.
	1806 TH	—	300.00	500.00	850.00	1350.
	1807 TH	—	300.00	500.00	850.00	1350.
	1808 TH	—	300.00	500.00	850.00	1350.

Ferdinand VII
Obv: Imaginary bust of Ferdinand VII.

KM#	Date	Mintage	VG	Fine	VF	XF
145	1810 HJ	—	400.00	650.00	900.00	1500.
	1811 HJ	—	350.00	500.00	850.00	1350.
	1812 HJ	—	350.00	500.00	850.00	1350.

Obv: Undraped bust of Ferdin. VII.

KM#	Date	Mintage	VG	Fine	VF	XF
146	1814 HJ	—	400.00	650.00	900.00	1400.
	1815 HJ	—	400.00	650.00	900.00	1400.
	1815 JJ	—	400.00	650.00	900.00	1400.
	1816 JJ	—	400.00	650.00	900.00	1400.
	1817 JJ	—	400.00	650.00	900.00	1400.
	1818 JJ	—	400.00	650.00	900.00	1400.
	1819 JJ	—	400.00	650.00	900.00	1400.
	1820 JJ	—	400.00	650.00	900.00	1400.

8 ESCUDOS

27.0700 gm., .917 GOLD, .7981 oz AGW

MEXICO CITY MINT

Philip V

Obv. leg: PHILIP.V.D.G.HISPAN.ET IND.REX

Rev. leg: INITIUM SAPIENTIAE TIMOR DOMINI

KM#	Date	Mintage	VG	Fine	VF	XF
148	1732	—	3000.	6000.	10,000.	15,000.
	1732 F	—	2500.	3750.	6500.	12,000.
	1733 F	—	2500.	3750.	6500.	12,000.
	1734 MF	—	1200.	1600.	3000.	4000.
	1735 MF	—	1200.	1600.	3000.	4000.
	1736 MF	—	1200.	1600.	3000.	4000.
	1737 MF	—	1200.	1600.	3000.	4000.
	1738 MF	—	1200.	1600.	3000.	4000.
	1739 MF	—	1200.	1600.	3000.	4000.
	1740 MF	—	1200.	1600.	3000.	4000.
	1741 MF	—	1200.	1600.	3000.	4000.
	1742 MF	—	1200.	1600.	3000.	4000.
	1743 MF	—	1200.	1600.	3000.	4000.
	1744 MF	—	1200.	1600.	3000.	4000.
	1745 MF	—	1200.	1600.	3000.	4000.
	1746 MF	—	1200.	1600.	3000.	4000.
	1747 MF	—	1200.	1600.	3000.	4000.

Ferdinand VI

Obv: Large bust; leg: FERDND.VI.D.G....

KM#	Date	Mintage	VG	Fine	VF	XF
149	1747 MF	—	3500.	5000.	7500.	12,000.

Obv: Medium bust; leg: FERDND.VI.D.G....

Rev. leg: NOMINA MAGNA SEQUOR

KM#	Date	Mintage	VG	Fine	VF	XF
150	1748 MF	—	1000.	2000.	3000.	4000.
	1749 MF	—	1000.	2000.	3000.	4000.
	1750 MF	—	1000.	2000.	3000.	4000.
	1751 MF	—	1000.	2000.	3000.	4000.

Obv: Small bust; leg: FERDND.VI.D.G....

KM#	Date	Mintage	VG	Fine	VF	XF
151	1752 MF	—	1200.	2000.	3000.	4000.
	1753 MF	—	1200.	2000.	3000.	4000.
	1754 MF	—	1200.	2000.	3000.	4000.
	1755 MM	—	1200.	2000.	3000.	4000.
	1756 MM	—	1200.	2000.	3000.	4000.

Obv: Large, full bust; leg: FERDND.VI.D.G...

KM#	Date	Mintage	VG	Fine	VF	XF
152	1757 MM	—	1200.	2000.	3000.	4000.
	1758 MM	—	1200.	2000.	3000.	4000.
	1759 MM	—	1200.	2000.	3000.	4000.

Charles III

Obv: Young bust; leg: CAROLVS.III.D.G....

with order of the Golden Fleece at date.

KM#	Date	Mintage	VG	Fine	VF	XF
153	1760 MM	—	2000.	3000.	4000.	5000.
	1761 MM	—	2000.	3000.	4000.	5000.

Obv: Young bust; leg: CAROLVS.III.D.G....

with order of the Golden Fleece on chest.

KM#	Date	Mintage	VG	Fine	VF	XF
154	1761 MM	—	1500.	2000.	3000.	5000.

Obv: Large bust; leg: CAROLUS.III.D.G....

Rev. leg: IN.UTROQ.FELIX.AUSPICE

KM#	Date	Mintage	VG	Fine	VF	XF
155	1762 MF	—	1000.	1500.	2500.	4000.
	1762 MM	—	1000.	1500.	2500.	4000.
	1763 MF	—	1000.	1500.	2500.	4000.
	1763 MM	—	1000.	1500.	2500.	4000.
	1764 MF	—	1000.	1500.	2500.	4000.
	1764 MM	—	1000.	1500.	2500.	4000.
	1765 MF	—	1000.	1500.	2500.	4000.
	1765 MM	—	1000.	1500.	2500.	4000.
	1766 MF	—	1000.	1500.	2500.	4000.
	1767 MF	—	1000.	1500.	2500.	4000.
	1768 MF	—	1000.	1500.	2500.	4000.
	1769 MF	—	1000.	1500.	2500.	4000.
	1770 MF	—	1000.	1500.	2500.	4000.
	1771 MF	—	1000.	1500.	2500.	4000.

Obv: Mature bust; leg: CAROL.III.D.G....

Rev. leg: IN.UTROQ.FELIX.AUSPICE.DEO.

KM#	Date	Mintage	VG	Fine	VF	XF
156	1772 FM	—	550.00	700.00	1150.	1750.
	1772 FM with inverted FM	—	550.00	700.00	1150.	1750.

KM#	Date	Mintage	VG	Fine	VF	XF
	1773 FM	—	550.00	700.00	1150.	1850.
	1773 FM with inverted FM	—	550.00	700.00	1150.	1850.
	1774 FM	—	550.00	700.00	1150.	1750.
	1775 FM	—	550.00	700.00	1150.	1750.
	1776 FM	—	800.00	1200.	1500.	2500.
	1777 FM	—	550.00	700.00	1150.	1750.
	1778 FF	—	550.00	700.00	1150.	1750.
	1779 FF	—	550.00	700.00	1150.	1750.
	1780 FF	—	550.00	700.00	1150.	1750.
	1781 FF	—	550.00	700.00	1150.	1750.
	1782 FF	—	550.00	700.00	1150.	1750.
	1783 FF	—	550.00	700.00	1150.	1750.
	1784 FF	—	550.00	700.00	1150.	1750.
	1784 FM	—	550.00	700.00	1150.	1750.
	1785 FM	—	550.00	700.00	1150.	1750.

27.0700 gm., .875 GOLD, .7616 oz AGW

KM#	Date	Mintage	VG	Fine	VF	XF
156a	1786 FM	—	550.00	700.00	1150.	1750.
	1787 FM	—	550.00	700.00	1150.	1750.
	1787 FM with inverted FM	—	550.00	700.00	1150.	1750.
	1788 FM	—	550.00	700.00	1150.	1750.
	1788 FM with inverted FM	—	550.00	700.00	1150.	1750.

Charles IV
Obv: Bust of Charles III; leg: CAROL.IV.D.G....
Rev: IN UTROQ...A.D., arms, order chain.

KM#	Date	Mintage	VG	Fine	VF	XF
157	1789 FM	—	550.00	750.00	1250.	2000.
	1790 FM	—	550.00	750.00	1200.	2000.

Obv: Bust of Charles III; leg: CAROL.IIII.D.G....

KM#	Date	Mintage	VG	Fine	VF	XF
158	1790 FM	—	550.00	800.00	1200.	2000.

Obv: Armored bust of Charles IIII.
Rev: IN UTROQ. FELIX., arms, order chain.

KM#	Date	Mintage	VG	Fine	VF	XF
159	1791 FM	—	550.00	650.00	800.00	1000.
	1792 FM	—	550.00	650.00	800.00	1000.
	1793 FM	—	550.00	650.00	800.00	1000.
	1794 FM	—	550.00	650.00	800.00	1000.
	1795 FM	—	550.00	650.00	800.00	1000.
	1796 FM	—	550.00	650.00	800.00	1000.
	1797 FM	—	550.00	650.00	800.00	1000.
	1798 FM	—	550.00	650.00	800.00	1000.
	1799 FM	—	550.00	650.00	800.00	1000.

KM#	Date	Mintage	VG	Fine	VF	XF
159	1800 FM	—	550.00	650.00	800.00	1000.
	1801 FM	—	550.00	650.00	850.00	1250.
	1801 FT	—	550.00	650.00	850.00	1250.
	1802 FT	—	550.00	650.00	800.00	1000.
	1803 FT	—	550.00	650.00	800.00	1000.
	1804 TH	—	550.00	650.00	800.00	1000.
	1805 TH	—	550.00	650.00	800.00	1000.
	1806 TH	—	550.00	650.00	800.00	1000.
	1807 TH	—	550.00	650.00	800.00	1000.
	1808 TH	—	650.00	850.00	1250.	2000.

Ferdinand VII
Obv: Imaginary bust of Ferdinand VII.

KM#	Date	Mintage	VG	Fine	VF	XF
160	1808 TH	—	550.00	650.00	850.00	1200.
	1809 HJ	—	550.00	650.00	900.00	1500.
	1810 HJ	—	550.00	650.00	850.00	1200.
	1811 HJ	—	550.00	650.00	850.00	1200.
	1811 JJ	—	550.00	650.00	850.00	1200.
	1812 JJ	—	550.00	650.00	850.00	1250.

Obv: Undraped bust of Ferdinand VII.

KM#	Date	Mintage	VG	Fine	VF	XF
161	1814 JJ	—	550.00	650.00	850.00	1200.
	1815 JJ	—	550.00	650.00	850.00	1200.
	1815 HJ	—	550.00	650.00	850.00	1200.
	1816 JJ	—	550.00	650.00	850.00	1200.
	1817 JJ	—	550.00	650.00	850.00	1200.
	1818 JJ	—	550.00	650.00	850.00	1200.
	1819 JJ	—	550.00	650.00	850.00	1200.
	1820 JJ	—	550.00	650.00	850.00	1200.
	1821 JJ	—	550.00	650.00	850.00	1200.

WAR OF INDEPENDENCE

ROYALIST ISSUES

(1810-1821)

Provisional Mints

RULER

Ferdinand VII, 1808-1821

MINTMARKS

CA, Ca - Chihuahua
D,Do,DO - Durango
G,Ga,GA - Guadalajara
G,Go,GO - Guanajuato
Z,Zs,ZS - Zacatecas

MONETARY SYSTEM

16 Reales = 1 Escudo

CHIHUAHUA

The Chihuahua Mint was established by a decree of October 8, 1810 as a temporary mint. Their first coins were cast 8 reales using Mexico City coins as patterns and obleterating/changing the mintmark and moneyer initials. Two c/s were placed on the obverse—on the left, a T designating its having been received by the Royal Treasurer and on the right crowned pillars of Hercules with pomegranate beneath; the symbol of the comptroller.

In 1814 standard dies were available and from 1814 to 1822 standard 8 reales were struck. Only the one denomination was made at this mint.

MINTMARKS CA, Ca

8 REALES

CAST SILVER
Obv: Imaginary bust of Ferdinand VII; leg: FERDIN.VII. DEI.GRATIA. c/s: 'T' at left and head of Ferdinand in crowned arbor at right.

KM#	Date	Mintage	Good	VG	Fine	VF
123	1810 RP	—	—	—	Rare	—
	1811 RP	—	45.00	60.00	100.00	150.00
	1812 RP	—	30.00	40.00	65.00	100.00
	1813 RP	—	30.00	40.00	65.00	100.00

.903 SILVER, 27.07 gm.
Obv: Draped bust of Ferdinand VII.

KM#	Date	Mintage	VG	Fine	VF	XF
111.1	1813 RP	—	Reported, not confirmed			
	1814 RP	—	Reported, not confirmed			
	1815 RP	—	175.00	250.00	350.00	500.00
	1816 RP	—	100.00	150.00	185.00	250.00
	1817 RP	—	100.00	150.00	185.00	250.00
	1818 RP	—	100.00	150.00	185.00	250.00
	1819 RP	—	100.00	150.00	180.00	250.00
	1820 RP	—	100.00	150.00	200.00	300.00
	1821 RP	—	300.00	400.00	650.00	800.00
	1822 RP	—	400.00	600.00	800.00	1000.

NOTE: #111.1 is normally found struck over earlier cast 8 Reales.

DURANGO

The Durango mint was authorized as a temporary mint at the same time as the Chihuahua Mint, October 8, 1810. The mint opened sometime in 1811 and made coins of 6 denominations - 5 silver and 1 copper - during the period 1811 to 1822.

MINTMARKS D, DO, Do

1/8 REAL

COPPER
Obv: Crown over double F7 monogram.
Rev: EN DURANGO, value, date.

KM#	Date	Mintage	VG	Fine	VF	XF
60	1812	—	21.00	35.00	80.00	100.00
	1813	—	12.00	20.00	60.00	90.00

Rev: Spray added above date.

KM#	Date	Mintage	VG	Fine	VF	XF
61	1814	—	15.00	25.00	50.00	75.00
	1815	—	15.00	25.00	50.00	75.00
	1816	—	15.00	25.00	50.00	75.00
	1817	—	15.00	25.00	50.00	75.00
	1818	—	15.00	25.00	50.00	75.00

1/2 REAL

.903 SILVER, 1.69 gm.
Obv: Draped bust of Ferdinand VII.

KM#	Date	Mintage	VG	Fine	VF	XF
74.1	1814 MZ	—	75.00	100.00	125.00	200.00
	1816 MZ	—	75.00	100.00	125.00	200.00

REAL

.903 SILVER, 3.38 gm.
Obv: Draped bust of Ferdinand VII.

KM#	Date	Mintage	VG	Fine	VF	XF
83.1	1813 RM	—	180.00	300.00	450.00	750.00
	1814 MZ	—	180.00	350.00	450.00	750.00
	1815 MZ	—	150.00	300.00	375.00	600.00

2 REALES

.903 SILVER
Obv: Draped bust of Ferdinand VII.

KM#	Date	Mintage	VG	Fine	VF	XF
93.1	1811 MZ	—	200.00	300.00	400.00	800.00
	1812 MZ	—	100.00	200.00	300.00	400.00
	1812 RM	—	Reported, not confirmed			
	1813 MZ	—	60.00	100.00	150.00	250.00
	1813 RM	—	Reported, not confirmed			
	1814 MZ	—	60.00	100.00	150.00	250.00
	1815 MZ	—	60.00	100.00	150.00	250.00
	1816 MZ	—	60.00	100.00	150.00	250.00
	1817 MZ	—	60.00	100.00	150.00	250.00

4 REALES

.903 SILVER, 13.54 gm.
Obv: Draped bust of Ferdinand VII.

KM#	Date	Mintage	VG	Fine	VF	XF
102.1	1814 MZ	—	240.00	600.00	800.00	1500.
	1816 MZ	—	150.00	200.00	300.00	600.00
	1817 MZ	—	150.00	200.00	300.00	600.00

8 REALES

.903 SILVER, 27.07 gm.
Obv: Draped bust of Ferdinand VII.

KM#	Date	Mintage	VG	Fine	VF	XF
111.2	1812 MZ	—	300.00	400.00	600.00	1000.
	1812 RM	—	125.00	175.00	275.00	450.00
	1813 RM	—	125.00	175.00	275.00	450.00
	1813 MZ	—	100.00	150.00	250.00	400.00
	1814 MZ	—	90.00	225.00	275.00	400.00
	1815 MZ	—	50.00	120.00	175.00	300.00
	1816 MZ	—	50.00	120.00	175.00	300.00
	1817 MZ	—	50.00	120.00	175.00	300.00
	1818 MZ	—	50.00	120.00	200.00	350.00
	1818 RM	—	50.00	120.00	175.00	300.00
	1818 CG/RM	—	—	—	—	—
	1818 CG	—	50.00	120.00	175.00	300.00
	1819 CG	—	40.00	100.00	160.00	300.00
	1820 CG	—	50.00	120.00	160.00	300.00
	1821 CG	—	35.00	50.00	75.00	150.00
	1822 CG	—	40.00	90.00	150.00	200.00

NOTE: Occasionally these are found struck over Guadalajara 8 reales and are very rare in general, specimens dated prior to 1816 are rather weakly struck.

GUADALAJARA

The Guadalajara Mint made its first coins in 1812 and the mint operated until April 30, 1815. It was to reopen in 1818 and continue operations until 1823. It was the only Royalist mint to strike gold coins, both 4 and 8 escudos. In addition to these it struck the standard 5 denominations in silver.

MINTMARKS G, GA, Ga

1/2 REAL

.903 SILVER, 1.69 gm.
Obv: Draped bust of Ferdinand VII.

KM#	Date	Mintage	VG	Fine	VF	XF
74.2	1812 MR	—	—	—	—	—
	1814 MR	—	42.50	80.00	135.00	200.00
	1815 MR	—	80.00	175.00	300.00	450.00

REAL

.903 SILVER, 3.38 gm.
Obv: Draped bust of Ferdinand VII.

KM#	Date	Mintage	VG	Fine	VF	XF
83.2	1814 MR	—	100.00	125.00	150.00	250.00
	1815 MR	—	200.00	275.00	350.00	450.00

2 REALES

.903 SILVER, 6.77 gm.
Obv: Draped bust of Ferdinand VII.

KM#	Date	Mintage	VG	Fine	VF	XF
93.2	1812 MR	—	—	—	—	—
	1814 MR	—	20.00	35.00	50.00	80.00
	1815/4 MR	—	40.00	75.00	110.00	165.00
	1815 MR	—	30.00	50.00	85.00	125.00
	1821 FS	—	—	—	—	—

4 REALES

.903 SILVER, 13.54 gm.
Obv: Draped bust of Ferdinand VII.

KM#	Date	Mintage	VG	Fine	VF	XF
102.2	1814 MR	—	40.00	65.00	100.00	165.00
	1815 MR	—	100.00	200.00	300.00	500.00

8 REALES

.903 SILVER, 27.07 gm.
Obv: Draped bust of Ferdinand VII.

KM#	Date	Mintage	VG	Fine	VF	XF
111.3	1812 MR	—	1000.	1500.	3000.	4000.
	1813/2 MR	—	150.00	200.00	275.00	450.00
	1813 MR	—	120.00	180.00	250.00	400.00
	1814 MR	—	60.00	80.00	100.00	175.00
	1815 MR	—	100.00	175.00	225.00	300.00
	1818 FS	—	32.50	50.00	85.00	135.00
	1820 FS	—	40.00	60.00	100.00	150.00
	1821/0 FS	—	40.00	60.00	100.00	200.00
	1821 FS	—	30.00	50.00	75.00	125.00
	1822/1 FS	—	50.00	80.00	150.00	225.00
	1822 FS	—	40.00	60.00	100.00	200.00
	1823 FS	—	—	—	Rare	—

4 ESCUDOS

.875 GOLD, 13.54 gm.
Obv: Uniformed bust of Ferdinand VII.

KM#	Date	Mintage	VG	Fine	VF	XF
147	1812 MR	—	—	—	Rare	—

8 ESCUDOS

.875 GOLD, 27.07 gm.
Obv: Large uniformed bust of Ferdinand VII.

KM#	Date	Mintage	VG	Fine	VF	XF
162	1812 MR	—	3500.	5000.	8000.	Rare
	1813 MR	—	2800.	4000.	7000.	Rare

Obv: Small uniformed bust of Ferdinand VII.

KM#	Date	Mintage	VG	Fine	VF	XF
163	1813 MR	—	2800.	4000.	7000.	Rare

Obv: Undraped bust of Ferdinand VII.

KM#	Date	Mintage	VG	Fine	VF	XF
161.1	1821 FS	—	1200.	1500.	3000.	5000.

Obv: Draped bust of Ferdinand VII.

KM#	Date	Mintage	VG	Fine	VF	XF
164	1821 FS	—	1500.	2250.	3750.	6500.

GUANAJUATO

Guanajuato Mint was authorized December 24, 1812 and started production shortly thereafter. For unknown reasons it closed on May 15, 1813. The mint was reopened in April of 1821 by the insurgent forces. They continued to make coins of the Spanish design to pay their army. After independence coins were made into the year 1822. Only the 2 and 8 reales coins were made.

MINTMARKS G, GO, Go

2 REALES

.903 SILVER, 6.77 gm.
Obv: Draped bust of Ferdinand VII.

KM#	Date	Mintage	VG	Fine	VF	XF
93.3	1821 JM	—	18.50	30.00	50.00	85.00
	1822 JM	—	16.50	27.50	35.00	65.00
	1822 JJM	—	20.00	35.00	60.00	100.00

8 REALES

.903 SILVER, 27.07 gm.
Obv: Draped bust of Ferdinand VII.

KM#	Date	Mintage	VG	Fine	VF	XF
111.4	1812 JJ	—	750.00	1250.	1750.	2500.
	1813 JJ	—	200.00	300.00	400.00	550.00
	1821 JM	—	30.00	50.00	75.00	125.00
	1821 JM	—	300.00	500.00	800.00	1000.
	1822/0 JM	—	40.00	100.00	150.00	200.00
111.4	1822 JM	—	35.00	60.00	85.00	150.00

NUEVA VISCAYA

(Later became Durango State)

This 8 reales, intended for the province of Nueva Viscaya was minted in the newly opened Durango mint during the months of February and March of 1811 before the regular coinage of Durango was started.

8 REALES

0.903 SILVER
Obv. leg: MON.PROV. DE NUEV.VYZCA, arms of Durango. Rev: Royal arms.

C#	Date	Mintage	Good	VG	Fine	VF
181	1811 RM	—	1000.	3000.	5000.	8000.

NOTE: Several varieties exist.

OAXACA

The city of Oaxaca was in the midst of a coin shortage when it became apparent the the city would be taken by insurgent forces. The Royalist forces under Lt. Gen. Saravia had some coins made. They were cast in a blacksmith shop and were made in 3 denominations - 1/2, 1 and 8 reales. They were made only briefly in 1812 before the city fell to the opposing forces.

1/2 REAL

.903 SILVER
Obv: Cross separating castle, lion, F,7O.
Rev. leg: OAXACA around shield.

KM#	Date	Mintage	Good	VG	Fine	VF
166	1812	—	75.00	125.00	200.00	350.00

REAL

.903 SILVER

KM#	Date	Mintage	Good	VG	Fine	VF
167	1812	—	100.00	200.00	300.00	500.00

8 REALES

.903 SILVER

KM#	Date	Mintage	Good	VG	Fine	VF
168	1812 c/s A	—	800.00	1200.	2000.	3000.
	1812 c/s:B	—	800.00	1200.	2000.	3000.
	1812 c/s:C	—	800.00	1200.	2000.	3000.
	1812 c/s:D	—	800.00	1200.	2000.	3000.
	1812 c/s:K	—	800.00	1200.	2000.	3000.
	1812 c/s:Mo	—	800.00	1200.	2000.	3000.
	1812 c/s:N	—	800.00	1200.	2000.	3000.
	1812 c/s:O	—	800.00	1200.	2000.	3000.
	1812 c/s:R	—	800.00	1200.	2000.	3000.
	1812 c/s:V	—	800.00	1200.	2000.	3000.
	1812 c/s:Z	—	800.00	1200.	2000.	3000.

NOTE: The above issue usually has a second c/s: O between crowned pillars.

REAL DEL CATORCE

(City in San Luis Potosi)

Real de Catorce is an important mining center in the State of San Luis Potosi. In 1811 an 8 reales coin was issued under very tedious conditions while the city was still in Royalist hands. Few survive.

8 REALES

.903 SILVER
Obv. leg: EL R.D. CATORC. POR FERNA. VII.
Rev. leg: MONEDA. PROVISIONAL.VALE.8R.

C#	Date	Mintage	VG	Fine	VF	XF
169	1811	—	1200.	3000.	6000.	10,000.

SAN FERNANDO DE BEXAR

Struck by Jose Antonio de la Garza, the 'Jolas' are the only known coins issued under Spanish rule in the continental United States of America.

1/8 REAL

COPPER

KM#	Date	Mintage	Good	VG	Fine	VF
170	1818	8,000	500.00	750.00	1200.	1600.

171	1818	Inc. Ab.	500.00	750.00	1200.	1600.

SOMBRERETE

(Under Royalist General Vargas)

The Sombrerete Mint opened on October 8, 1810 in an area that boasted some of the richest mines in Mexico. The mint operated until July 16, 1811 when it closed only to reopen in 1812 and finally to close for good at the end of 1812. The man in charge of the mines, Fernando Vargas, was also in charge of the coinage. All of the coins bear his name.

1/2 REAL

.903 SILVER
Obv. leg: FERDIN.VII.SOMBRETE..., around crowned globes. Rev. leg: VARGAS over lys in oval, sprays.

172	1811	—	37.50	60.00	100.00	175.00
	1812	—	37.50	60.00	100.00	175.00

REAL

.903 SILVER
Obv. leg: FERDIN.VII.SOMBRETE.., around crowned globes. Rev. leg: VARGAS over lys in oval, sprays.

173	1811	—	42.50	55.00	100.00	160.00
	1812	—	40.00	50.00	90.00	150.00

2 REALES

.903 SILVER
Obv: R.CAXA.DE.SOMBRETE, royal arms.
Rev. c/s: VARGAS, 1811, S between crowned pillars.

174	1811 SE	—	65.00	200.00	400.00	650.00

4 REALES

.903 SILVER
Obv. leg: R.CAXA.SOMBRETE, royal arms.
Rev. leg: VARGAS/1812/3

KM#	Date	Mintage	Good	VG	Fine	VF
175	1812	—	65.00	175.00	350.00	550.00

8 REALES

.903 SILVER
Obv. leg: R.CAXA. DE SOMBRETE.
Rev. c/s: VARGAS, date, S between crowned pillars.

176	1810	—	1500.	2500.	4000.	5000.
	1811	—	200.00	300.00	400.00	500.00

Obv. leg: R.CAXA DE SOMBRETE, crowned arms.
Rev. leg: VARGAS/date/3

177	1811	—	150.00	200.00	250.00	400.00
	1812	—	100.00	150.00	225.00	300.00

VALLADOLID/DE MICHOACAN

MICHOACAN

(Now Morelia)

Valladolid, capitol of Michoacan province, was a strategually important center for military thrusts into the adjoining provinces. The Royalists made every effort to retain the position. In 1813, with the advance of the insurgent forces, it became apparent that to maintain the position would be very difficult. During 1813 it was necessary to make coins in the city due to lack of traffic with other areas. These were made only briefly before the city fell and were also used by the insurgents with appropriate counterstamps.

8 REALES

.903 SILVER
Obv: Royal arms in wreath, value at sides.
Rev: PROVISIONAL DE VALLADOLID, date.

KM#	Date	Mintage	Good	VG	Fine	VF
178	1813	—	1000.	2000.	3000.	5000.

Obv: Bust FERDIN. VII.
Rev: Arms, pillars.

179	1813	—	1500.	2500.	3500.	5500.

ZACATECAS

MINTMARKS: Z, ZS, Zs

The city of Zacatecas, in a rich mining area, has a long history of providing silver for the world. From the mid-1500's silver poured from its mines. On November 14, 1810 a mint began production for the Royalist cause. Zacatecas was the most prolific of the mints during the War of Independence. The 5 silver denominations were made here. The first type was a local type with the mountains of silver shown on the coins. These were made only in 1810 and 1811. Some of the 1811 were made by the insurgents after the town fell on April 15, 1811. The town was retaken by the Royalists on May 21, 1811. From then until 1822 the standard bust type of Ferdinand VII was made.

1/2 REAL

.903 SILVER
Similar to KM#181 but with local arms.
Flowers 1 and 4, castles 2 and 3.

180	1810	—	45.00	75.00	100.00	200.00
	1811	—	30.00	50.00	75.00	100.00

Obv: Royal arms.
Rev. leg: MONEDA PROVISIONAL DE ZACATECAS., mountain.

181	1811	—	30.00	50.00	75.00	100.00

Obv: Provincial bust FERDIN. VII.
Rev: 'MONEDA PROVISIONAL DE ZACATECAS'
Arms, pillars.

182	1811	—	30.00	40.00	60.00	80.00
	1812	—	30.00	40.00	60.00	80.00

.903 SILVER, 1.69 gm.
Obv: Imaginary bust Ferdinand VII.

73.1	1813 AZ	—	15.00	30.00	60.00	100.00
	1815 AG	—	12.50	25.00	40.00	60.00
	1816 AG	—	7.50	15.00	25.00	50.00
	1817 AG	—	7.50	15.00	25.00	50.00
	1818 AG	—	7.50	15.00	25.00	50.00
	1819 AG	—	7.50	15.00	25.00	50.00

Obv: Draped bust Ferdinand VII.

KM#	Date	Mintage	VG	Fine	VF	XF
74.3	1819 AG	—	9.00	12.00	25.00	50.00
	1820 AG	—	5.00	10.00	20.00	40.00
	1820 RG	—	5.00	10.00	20.00	40.00
	1821 AG	—	5.00	10.00	20.00	40.00
	1821 RG	—	5.00	10.00	20.00	40.00

REAL

.903 SILVER
Similar to KM#184 but with local arms.
Flowers 1 and 4, castles 2 and 3.

KM#	Date	Mintage	Good	VG	Fine	VF
183	1810	—	100.00	150.00	200.00	250.00
	1811	—	15.00	27.50	50.00	100.00

Obv: Royal arms.
Rev. leg: MONEDA PROVISIONAL DE ZACATECAS., mountain.

KM#	Date	Mintage	Good	VG	Fine	VF
184	1811	—	15.00	27.50	40.00	80.00

Obv: Provincial bust FERDIN. VII.
Rev. leg: MONEDA PRIVINSIONAL DE ZACATECAS, arms, pillars.

KM#	Date	Mintage	Good	VG	Fine	VF
185	1811	—	45.00	75.00	100.00	150.00
	1812	—	45.00	75.00	100.00	150.00

3.38 gm.
Obv: Imaginary bust of Ferdinand VII.

KM#	Date	Mintage	Good	VG	Fine	VF
82.1	1813 FP	—	50.00	100.00	150.00	250.00
	1814 FP	—	30.00	50.00	70.00	100.00
	1814 AG	—	20.00	35.00	50.00	70.00
	1815 AG	—	20.00	35.00	50.00	70.00
	1816 AG	—	10.00	17.50	25.00	50.00
	1817 AG	—	6.50	12.50	20.00	40.00
	1818 AG	—	12.50	22.50	30.00	42.50
	1819 AG	—	5.00	9.00	15.00	30.00
	1820 AG	—	3.75	7.50	12.50	25.00

Obv: Draped bust of Ferdinand VII.

KM#	Date	Mintage	VG	Fine	VF	XF
83.3	1820 RG	—	4.50	9.00	15.00	30.00
	1821 AG	—	15.00	25.00	37.50	75.00
	1821 AZ	—	4.50	9.00	15.00	30.00
	1821 RG	—	3.75	7.50	12.50	25.00
	1822 AZ	—	4.50	9.00	15.00	30.00
	1822 RG	—	4.50	9.00	15.00	30.00

2 REALES

.903 SILVER
Similar to KM#187 but with local arms.
Flowers 1 and 4, castles 2 and 3.

KM#	Date	Mintage	Good	VG	Fine	VF
186	1810	—	—	—	Rare	—
	1811	—	25.00	40.00	60.00	100.00

Obv: Royal arms.

Rev. leg: MONEDA PROVISIONAL DE ZACATECAS., mountain over L.V.O.

KM#	Date	Mintage	Good	VG	Fine	VF
187	1811	—	18.00	30.00	40.00	50.00

Obv: Provincial bust FERDIN. VII.
Rev. leg: MONEDA PROVISIONAL DE ZACATECAS, crowned arms, pillars.

KM#	Date	Mintage	Good	VG	Fine	VF
188	1811	—	40.00	75.00	150.00	225.00
	1812	—	40.00	75.00	150.00	225.00

6.77 gm.
Obv: Large imaginary bust of Ferdinand VII.

KM#	Date	Mintage	Good	VG	Fine	VF
92.1	1813	—	37.50	50.00	75.00	125.00
	1814 FP	—	37.50	50.00	75.00	125.00
	1814 AG	—	37.50	50.00	75.00	125.00

Obv: Large imaginary bust of Ferdinand VII.

KM#	Date	Mintage	Good	VG	Fine	VF
A92	1815 AG	—	7.50	15.00	25.00	50.00
	1816 AG	—	6.50	12.50	20.00	40.00
	1817 AG	—	6.50	12.50	20.00	40.00

Obv: Small imaginary bust of Ferdinand VII.

KM#	Date	Mintage	Good	VG	Fine	VF
B92	1819 AG	—	6.50	17.50	20.00	40.00

Obv: Draped bust of Ferdinand VII.

KM#	Date	Mintage	VG	Fine	VF	XF
93.4	1818 AG	—	6.50	12.50	20.00	40.00
	1819 AG	—	6.50	10.00	17.50	35.00
	1820 AG	—	6.50	12.50	20.00	40.00
	1820 RG	—	6.50	12.50	20.00	40.00
	1821 AG	—	6.50	10.00	17.50	35.00
	1821 AZ/RG	—	7.50	15.00	25.00	50.00
	1821 AZ	—	6.50	12.50	20.00	40.00
	1821 RG	—	6.50	10.00	17.50	35.00
	1822 AG	—	7.50	15.00	25.00	50.00
	1822 AZ	—	8.50	17.50	30.00	60.00
	1822 RG	—	8.50	17.50	30.00	60.00

8 REALES

.903 SILVER
Rev: Similar to KM#190.

KM#	Date	Mintage	Good	VG	Fine	VF
189	1810	—	300.00	500.00	800.00	1000.
	1811	—	100.00	150.00	225.00	350.00

Obv. leg: FERDIN.VII.DEI.., royal arms.
Rev. leg: MONEDA PROVISIONAL DE ZACATECAS, mountain over L.V.O.

KM#	Date	Mintage	Good	VG	Fine	VF
190	1811	—	75.00	125.00	160.00	250.00

Obv: Imaginary bust of Ferdinand VII.
Rev. leg: MONEDA PROVISIONAL DE ZACATECAS, crowned arms, pillars.

KM#	Date	Mintage	Good	VG	Fine	VF
191	1811	—	35.00	50.00	100.00	150.00
	1812	—	42.50	75.00	150.00	225.00

Obv: Draped bust of Ferdinand VII.
Rev. leg: MONEDA PROVISIONAL DE ZACATECAS

crowned arms, pillars.

KM#	Date	Mintage	Good	VG	Fine	VF
192	1812	—	50.00	85.00	175.00	250.00

.903 SILVER, 27.07 gm.
Obv: Draped bust of Ferdinand VII.

KM#	Date	Mintage	VG	Fine	VF	XF
111.5	1813 AG	—	—	—	—	—
	1813 FP	—	200.00	250.00	325.00	450.00
	1814 AG	—	150.00	200.00	250.00	350.00
	1814 FP	—	150.00	250.00	350.00	500.00
	1815 AG	—	100.00	150.00	200.00	275.00
	1816 AG	—	40.00	55.00	75.00	125.00
	1817 AG	—	40.00	55.00	75.00	125.00
	1818 AG	—	40.00	55.00	75.00	125.00
	1819 AG	—	40.00	55.00	75.00	125.00
	1820 AG	—	40.00	55.00	75.00	125.00
	1820 RG	—	50.00	65.00	100.00	150.00
	1821 RG	—	25.00	37.50	55.00	90.00
	1821/81 RG	—	60.00	150.00	200.00	300.00
	1821 AZ	—	100.00	150.00	200.00	250.00
	1822 RG	—	60.00	85.00	125.00	200.00

COUNTERSTAMP ISSUES

Crown and Flag

(Refer to Multiple Counterstamps)

LCM - La Comandancia Militar

NOTE: This counterstamp exists in 15 various sizes.

2 REALES

.903 SILVER
c/s: LCM on Mexico KM#92.

KM#	Date	Mintage	Good	VG	Fine	VF
193.1	1809 TH	—	100.00	135.00	185.00	250.00

c/s: LCM on Zacatecas KM#185.

KM#	Date	Mintage	Good	VG	Fine	VF
193.2	1811	—	100.00	135.00	185.00	250.00

8 REALES

CAST SILVER
c/s: LCM on Chihuahua KM#123.

KM#	Date	Mintage	Good	VG	Fine	VF
194.1	1811 RP	—	150.00	250.00	375.00	500.00

.903 SILVER
c/s: LCM on Chihuahua KM#111.1 struck over KM#123.

KM#	Date	Mintage	Good	VG	Fine	VF
194.2	1815 RP	—	200.00	275.00	400.00	550.00
	1817 RP	—	125.00	175.00	225.00	300.00
	1820 RG	—	125.00	175.00	225.00	300.00
	1821 RP	—	125.00	175.00	225.00	300.00

c/s: LCM on Durango KM#111.2.

KM#	Date	Mintage	Good	VG	Fine	VF
194.3	1812 RM	—	70.00	125.00	190.00	250.00
	1821 CG	—	70.00	125.00	190.00	250.00

c/s: LCM on Guadalajara KM#111.3.

KM#	Date	Mintage	Good	VG	Fine	VF
194.4	1813 MR	—	150.00	225.00	300.00	475.00
	1820 FS	—	60.00	100.00	150.00	200.00

c/s: LCM on Guanajuato KM#111.4.

KM#	Date	Mintage	Good	VG	Fine	VF
194.5	1813 JM	—	225.00	350.00	475.00	650.00

c/s: LCM on Nueva Vizcaya KM#165.

KM#	Date	Mintage	Good	VG	Fine	VF
194.6	1811 RM	—	—	—	Rare	—

c/s: LCM on Mexico KM#111.

KM#	Date	Mintage	Good	VG	Fine	VF
194.7	1811 HJ	—	125.00	225.00	350.00	600.00
	1812 JJ	—	110.00	135.00	190.00	325.00
	1817 JJ	—	50.00	65.00	85.00	125.00
	1818 JJ	—	50.00	65.00	85.00	125.00
	1820 JJ	—	—	—	—	—

c/s: LCM on Sombrerete KM#177.

KM#	Date	Mintage	Good	VG	Fine	VF
194.8	1811	—	—	—	Rare	—
	1812	—	—	—	Rare	—

c/s: LCM on Zacatecas KM#191.

KM#	Date	Mintage	Good	VG	Fine	VF
194.9	1811	—	225.00	350.00	450.00	—

c/s: LCM on Zacatecas KM#111.5.

KM#	Date	Mintage	Good	VG	Fine	VF
194.10	1813 FP	—	—	—	—	—
	1814 AG	—	—	—	—	—
	1822 RG	—	—	—	—	—

LCV - Las Cajas de Veracruz

(The Royal Treasury of the City of Veracruz)

7 REALES

SILVER
c/s: LCV and 7 on underweight 8 Reales.

KM#	Date	Mintage	Good	VG	Fine	VF
195	—	—	—	—	Rare	—

7-1/4 REALES

SILVER
c/s: LCV and 7.1/4 on underweight 8 Reales.

KM#	Date	Mintage	Good	VG	Fine	VF
196	—	—	—	—	Rare	—

7-1/2 REALES

SILVER
c/s: LCV and 7-1/2 on underweight 8 Reales.

KM#	Date	Mintage	Good	VG	Fine	VF
197	—	—	—	—	Rare	—

7-3/4 REALES

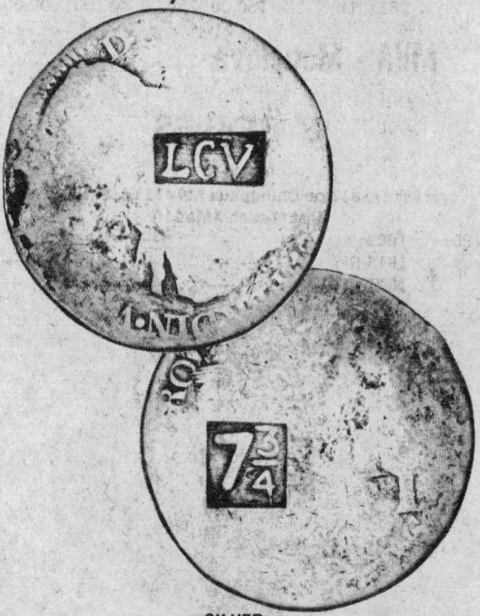

SILVER
c/s: LCV and 7-3/4 on underweight 8 Reales.

KM#	Date	Mintage	Good	VG	Fine	VF
198	—	—	300.00	375.00	450.00	600.00

8 REALES

CAST SILVER
c/s: LCV on Chihuahua KM#123.

KM#	Date	Mintage	Good	VG	Fine	VF
A198	1811 RP	—	150.00	250.00	400.00	500.00

SILVER
c/s: LCV on Zacatecas KM#191.

KM#	Date	Mintage	Good	VG	Fine	VF
199	1811	—	175.00	225.00	275.00	350.00
	1812	—	175.00	225.00	275.00	350.00

MS (Monogram) - Manuel Salcedo

8 REALES

SILVER
c/s: MS monogram on Mexico KM#110.

KM#	Date	Mintage	Good	VG	Fine	VF
200	1809 TH	—	150.00	250.00	400.00	500.00
	1810 HJ	—	150.00	250.00	400.00	500.00
	1811 HJ	—	150.00	250.00	400.00	500.00

MVA - Monclova

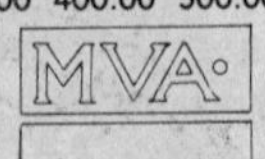

8 REALES

SILVER
c/s: MVA/1811 on Chihuahua KM#111.1; struck over cast Mexico KM#110.

KM#	Date	Mintage	Good	VG	Fine	VF
201	1809	—	—	—	Rare	—
	1816 RP	—	—	—	Rare	—
	1821 RP	—	—	—	Rare	—

c/s: MVA/1812 on Chihuahua KM#111.1; struck over cast Mexico KM#109.

KM#	Date	Mintage	Good	VG	Fine	VF
202.1	—	—	125.00	175.00	250.00	350.00

c/s: MVA/1812 on cast Mexico KM#109.

KM#	Date	Mintage	Good	VG	Fine	VF
202.2	1798 FM	—	100.00	150.00	250.00	350.00
	1802 FT	—	100.00	150.00	250.00	350.00

c/s: MVA/1812 on cast Mexico KM#110.

KM#	Date	Mintage	Good	VG	Fine	VF
202.3	1809 HJ	—	100.00	150.00	250.00	350.00
202.3	1809 TH	—	100.00	150.00	250.00	350.00
	1810 HJ	—	100.00	150.00	250.00	350.00

c/s: MVA/1812 on cast Mexico KM#111.

KM#	Date	Mintage	Good	VG	Fine	VF
202.4	1812 HJ	—	125.00	175.00	250.00	350.00

c/s: MVA/1812 on Zacatecas KM#189.

KM#	Date	Mintage	Good	VG	Fine	VF
202.4	1813	—	300.00	350.00	450.00	550.00

PDV - Provisional de Valladolid

VTIL - (util = useful)

(Refer to Multiple Countermarks)

INSURGENT ISSUES

Supreme National Congress Of America

1/2 REAL

COPPER
Obv: FERDIN. VII DEI GRATIA, eagle on bridge.
Rev: S.P.CONG.NAT.IND.
GUV.T., value, bow, quiver, etc.

KM#	Date	Mintage	Good	VG	Fine	VF
203	1811	—	30.00	45.00	60.00	100.00

REAL

SILVER
Similar to 1/2 Real, KM#203.

KM#	Date	Mintage	Good	VG	Fine	VF
204	1811	—	50.00	75.00	125.00	200.00

2 REALES

SILVER

KM#	Date	Mintage	Good	VG	Fine	VF
205	1812	—	250.00	350.00	500.00	700.00

8 REALES

CAST SILVER

KM#	Date	Mintage	Good	VG	Fine	VF
206	1811	—	150.00	250.00	350.00	500.00
	1812	—	150.00	250.00	350.00	500.00

STRUCK SILVER

KM#	Date	Mintage	Good	VG	Fine	VF
207	1811	—	—	Rare	—	—
	1812	—	—	Rare	—	—

COPPER
Obv. leg: FERDIN.VII...., eagle on bridge.
Rev: PROVICIONAL POR LA SUPREMA JUNTA DE AMERICA, bow, sword and quiver.

KM#	Date	Mintage	Good	VG	Fine	VF
208	1811	—	100.00	150.00	225.00	300.00
	1812	—	100.00	150.00	225.00	300.00

National Congress

1/2 REAL

COPPER
Obv: VICE FERD. VII DEI GRATIA ET.
Eagle on bridge.
Rev: S. P. CONG. NAT. IND.
GUV. T., value, bow, quiver, etc.

KM#	Date	Mintage	Good	VG	Fine	VF
209	1811	—	50.00	100.00	150.00	200.00
	1812	—	50.00	100.00	150.00	200.00
	1813	—	50.00	100.00	150.00	200.00
	1814	—	50.00	100.00	150.00	200.00

.903 SILVER

KM#	Date	Mintage	Good	VG	Fine	VF
210	1812	—	65.00	125.00	200.00	300.00
	1813	—	65.00	125.00	200.00	300.00

NOTE: 1812 exists with the date reading inwards and outwards.

REAL

.903 SILVER

KM#	Date	Mintage	Good	VG	Fine	VF
211	1812	—	50.00	75.00	125.00	200.00
	1813	—	50.00	75.00	125.00	200.00

NOTE: 1812 exists with the date reading inwards and outwards.

2 REALES

COPPER
Similar to 1 Real, KM#211.

KM#	Date	Mintage	Good	VG	Fine	VF
212	1812	—	35.00	75.00	110.00	150.00
	1813	—	25.00	50.00	75.00	100.00
	1814	—	35.00	75.00	110.00	150.00

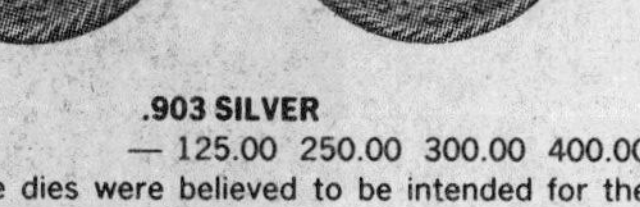

.903 SILVER

KM#	Date	Mintage	Good	VG	Fine	VF
213	1813	—	125.00	250.00	300.00	400.00

NOTE: These dies were believed to be intended for the striking of 2 Escudos.

4 REALES

.903 SILVER

KM#	Date	Mintage	Good	VG	Fine	VF
214	1813	—	500.00	1000.	2000.	3000.

8 REALES

.903 SILVER
Similar to 4 Reales, KM#214.

KM#	Date	Mintage	Good	VG	Fine	VF
215	1812	—	500.00	1000.	2000.	3500.
	1813	—	500.00	1000.	2000.	3500.

American Congress

REAL

.903 SILVER
Obv: Eagle on cactus, leg: AMERICANO CONGRESO.
Rev: F.7 on spread mantle, leg: DEPOSIT D.L.AUCTORI J.

KM#	Date	Mintage	Good	VG	Fine	VF
216	ND(1813)	—	35.00	65.00	100.00	150.00

Obv: Eagle on cactus, leg: CONGR.AMER.
Rev: F.7 on spread mantle, leg: DEPOS.D.L.AUT.D.

KM#	Date	Mintage	Good	VG	Fine	VF
217	ND(1813)	—	35.00	65.00	100.00	150.00

NUEVA GALICIA

(Later became Jalisco State)

Nueva Galicia was a province in early colonial times that was similar to modern Zacatecas, etc. The name was adopted again during the War of Independence. The only issue was an 1812 2 Reales of rather enigmatic origin.

2 REALES

.903 SILVER
Obv: PROVYCIONAL etc., N.G. in center, date.

KM#	Date	Mintage	Good	VG	Fine	VF
218	1813	—	1000.	3000.	6000.	10,000.

OAXACA

Oaxaca was the hub of insurgent activity in the south. The issues of Oaxaca represent various episodic strikings of coins, usually under dire circumstances, by various individuals. The copper coins were made because of urgency and were to be redeemed at its face value in gold or silver. The silver coins were made after the copper coins when silver was available to the insurgent forces. Coinage Started In July, 1811 and ran until October 1814.

SUD

(Under General Morelos)

1/2 REAL

COPPER
Obv: Bow, SUD.
Rev: Morelos monogram Mo, date.

KM#	Date	Mintage	Good	VG	Fine	VF
219	1811	—	7.50	15.00	30.00	60.00
	1812	—	7.50	15.00	30.00	60.00
	1813	—	7.50	15.00	30.00	60.00

NOTE: Uniface strikes exist of #219.

CAST SILVER

KM#	Date	Mintage	Good	VG	Fine	VF
220	1813	—	—	—	—	—
	1814	—	—	—	—	—

NOTE: Most specimens available on todays market are considered spurious.

SILVER
Obv. leg: PROVICIONAL DE OAXACA, bow, arrow.
Rev. leg: AMERICA MORELOS, lion.

KM#	Date	Mintage	Good	VG	Fine	VF
221	1813		100.00	200.00	350.00	500.00

REAL

COPPER

KM#	Date	Mintage	Good	VG	Fine	VF
222	1811	—	8.50	17.50	37.50	75.00
	1812	—	6.50	12.50	25.00	50.00
	1813	—	8.50	17.50	37.50	75.00

STRUCK SILVER

KM#	Date	Mintage	Good	VG	Fine	VF
222a	1812	—	—	—	—	—

CAST SILVER

KM#	Date	Mintage	Good	VG	Fine	VF
223	1813	—	—	—	—	—

NOTE: Most specimens available on todays market are considered spurious.

Obv: Bow, arrow/SUD.
Rev. leg: AMERICA MORELOS, lion.

KM#	Date	Mintage	Good	VG	Fine	VF
224	1813	—	—	—	Rare	—

SILVER

KM#	Date	Mintage	Good	VG	Fine	VF
225	1813	—	—	—	Rare	—

2 REALES

COPPER

KM#	Date	Mintage	Good	VG	Fine	VF
226	1811	—	12.50	25.00	50.00	100.00
	1812	—	3.75	7.50	15.00	30.00
	1813	—	3.75	7.50	15.00	30.00

Obv. leg: SUD-OXA, bow, arrow.
Rev: Morelos monogram, value, date.

KM#	Date	Mintage	Good	VG	Fine	VF
227	1813	—	60.00	100.00	200.00	300.00
	1814	—	60.00	100.00	200.00	300.00

Obv. leg: SUD. OAXACA

KM#	Date	Mintage	Good	VG	Fine	VF
228	1814	—	60.00	100.00	200.00	400.00

CAST SILVER

KM#	Date	Mintage	Good	VG	Fine	VF
229	1812	—	—	—	—	—

NOTE: Most specimens available on todays market are considered spurious.

4 REALES

CAST SILVER

KM#	Date	Mintage	Good	VG	Fine	VF
230	1811	—	—	—	—	—
	1812	—	—	—	—	—

NOTE: Most specimens available on todays market are considered spurious.

Obv. leg: SUD-OXA, bow, arrow.
Rev: Morelos monogram.

KM#	Date	Mintage	Good	VG	Fine	VF
231	1813	—	125.00	250.00	400.00	800.00

COPPER
Obv. leg: SUD-OXA, bow, arrow.
Rev: Morelos monogram.

KM#	Date	Mintage	Good	VG	Fine	VF
232	1814	—	100.00	150.00	200.00	400.00

8 REALES

COPPER
Plain fields

KM#	Date	Mintage	Good	VG	Fine	VF
233*	1811-14	—	—	—	—	—

***NOTE:** #233 are considered to be spurious.

Ornate flowery fields

KM#	Date	Mintage	Good	VG	Fine	VF
234	1811	—	75.00	125.00	150.00	250.00
	1812	—	4.00	5.00	7.50	15.00
	1813	—	4.00	5.00	7.50	15.00
	1814	—	8.00	10.00	15.00	25.00

CAST SILVER

KM#	Date	Mintage	Good	VG	Fine	VF
235	1811	—	—	—	—	—
	1812	—	—	—	—	—
	1813	—	—	—	—	—

NOTE: Most specimens available on todays market are considered spurious.

.903 SILVER, struck
Obv: PROV. D. OAXACA, M monogram.
Rev: Lion shield with or without bow above.

KM#	Date	Mintage	Good	VG	Fine	VF
236	1812	—	—	Rare	—	—

Without obverse legend

KM#	Date	Mintage	Good	VG	Fine	VF
237	1813	—	—	Rare	—	—

Obv: BOW/M/SUD..
Rev: PROV. DE, etc., arms.

KM#	Date	Mintage	Good	VG	Fine	VF
238	1813	—	—	Rare	—	—

CAST SILVER
Similar to 4 Reales, KM#231.

KM#	Date	Mintage	Good	VG	Fine	VF
239	1814	—	—	Rare	—	—

COPPER

KM#	Date	Mintage	Good	VG	Fine	VF
240	1814	—	75.00	100.00	150.00	225.00

OAXACA spelled out

KM#	Date	Mintage	Good	VG	Fine	VF
241	1814	—	—	—	Rare	—

Huautla

8 REALES

COPPER
Obv. leg: MONEDA PROVI.CIONAL PS.ES. around bow, arrow/SUD.
Rev. leg: FABRICADO EN HUAÚTLA

KM#	Date	Mintage	Good	VG	Fine	VF
242	1812	—	—	—	Rare	—

Tierra Caliente
(Hot Country)
Under General Morelos

1/2 REAL

COPPER
Obv: Bow, T.C., SUD.
Rev: Morelos monogram, value, date.

KM#	Date	Mintage	Good	VG	Fine	VF
243	1813	—	25.00	50.00	87.50	175.00

REAL

COPPER
Similar to 1/2 Real, KM#243.

KM#	Date	Mintage	Good	VG	Fine	VF
244	1813	—	22.50	45.00	75.00	150.00

2 REALES

COPPER
Similar to 1/2 Real, KM#243.

KM#	Date	Mintage	Good	VG	Fine	VF
245	1813	—	22.50	45.00	75.00	150.00

Rev: Lion divides value; AMERICA MORELOS above, date below.

KM#	Date	Mintage	Good	VG	Fine	VF
246	1814	—	26.50	52.50	87.50	175.00

CAST SILVER

KM#	Date	Mintage	Good	VG	Fine	VF
247	1814	—	—	—	Rare	—

8 REALES

COPPER

KM#	Date	Mintage	Good	VG	Fine	VF
248	1813	—	11.50	22.50	37.50	75.00

CAST SILVER

KM#	Date	Mintage	Good	VG	Fine	VF
249	1813	—	—	—	—	—

NOTE: Most specimens available on todays market are considered spurious.

PUEBLA

The coins of Puebla emanated from Zacatlan, the headquarters of the hit-and-run insurgent leader Osorno. The mint opened in April of 1812 and operated until the end of 1813. The coins were 2 reales in silver and 1 and 1/2 reales in copper.

Zacatlan
(Struck by General Osorno)

1/2 REAL

COPPER
Obv: Osorno monogram, Zacatlan, date.
Rev: Crossed arrows, wreath, value.

KM#	Date	Mintage	Good	VG	Fine	VF
250	1813	—	—	Rare	—	—

REAL

COPPER

KM#	Date	Mintage	Good	VG	Fine	VF
251	1813	—	100.00	150.00	250.00	450.00

2 REALES

COPPER

KM#	Date	Mintage	Good	VG	Fine	VF
252	1813	—	125.00	175.00	275.00	500.00

VERA CRUZ

Vera Cruz was the province that housed the town of Zongolica. In this town 2 priests and a lawyer decided to raise an army to fight for independence. Because of their isolation from other insurgent forces they decided to make coins for their area. Records show that they planned to or did mint coins of 1/2, 1, 2, 4, and 8 reales denominations. Extant specimens are known for only the three higher values.

Zongolica

2 REALES

.903 SILVER
Obv. leg: VIVA FERNANDO VII Y AMERICA, bow and arrow.
Rev. leg: SONGOLICA, value, crossed palm branch, sword, date.

KM#	Date	Mintage	Good	VG	Fine	VF
253	1812	—	45.00	80.00	125.00	250.00

4 REALES

.903 SILVER
Similar to 2 Reales, KM#253.

KM#	Date	Mintage	Good	VG	Fine	VF
254	1812	—	600.00	800.00	1200.	2000.

8 REALES

.903 SILVER

KM#	Date	Mintage	Good	VG	Fine	VF
255	1812	—	1200.	1600.	3000.	6000.

COUNTERSTAMP ISSUES

Congress Of Chilpanzingo

Type A: Hand holding bow and arrow between quiver with arrows, sword and bow.

Type B: Crowned eagle on bridge.

1/2 REAL

SILVER
c/s: Type A on cast Mexico City KM#72.

KM#	Date	Mintage	Good	VG	Fine	VF
256.1	1812	—	45.00	70.00	90.00	120.00

c/s: Type A on Zacatecas KM#181.

KM#	Date	Mintage	Good	VG	Fine	VF
256.2	1811	—	55.00	75.00	100.00	125.00

REAL

SILVER
c/s: Type A on cast Mexico City KM#81.

KM#	Date	Mintage	Good	VG	Fine	VF
A257	1803	—	20.00	35.00	65.00	100.00

2 REALES

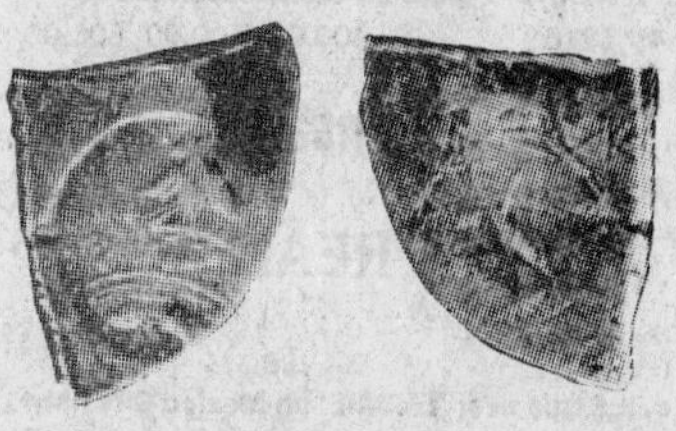

SILVER
c/s: Type B on 1/4 cut of 8 Reales.

KM#	Date	Mintage	Good	VG	Fine	VF
257.1	—	—	75.00	100.00	135.00	175.00

c/s: Type B on Zacatecas KM#186.

KM#	Date	Mintage	Good	VG	Fine	VF
257.2	1811	—	125.00	150.00	185.00	225.00

8 REALES

SILVER

KM#	Date	Mintage	Good	VG	Fine	VF
	c/s: Type A on cast Mexico City KM#109.					
258.1	1805 TH	—	50.00	75.00	100.00	150.00
	c/s: Type A on cast Mexico City KM#110.					
258.2	1810 HJ	—	50.00	75.00	100.00	150.00
	c/s: Type A on cast Mexico City KM#111.					
258.3	1811 HJ	—	45.00	65.00	85.00	125.00
	1812 HJ	—	105.00	125.00	175.00	275.00

SILVER

KM#	Date	Mintage	Good	VG	Fine	VF
	c/s: Type B on Chihuahua KM#111.1.					
259.1	1816 RP	—	200.00	250.00	300.00	350.00
	c/s: Type B on cast Mexico City KM#111.					
259.2	1811 HJ	—	130.00	140.00	150.00	175.00

c/s: Type B on Valladolid KM#178.

KM#	Date	Mintage	Good	VG	Fine	VF
259.3	1813	—	1000.	2000.	3000.	5000.

c/s: Type B on Zacatecas KM#190.

KM#	Date	Mintage	Good	VG	Fine	VF
259.4	1810	—	400.00	500.00	600.00	750.00

Ensaie

8 REALES

SILVER

c/s: Eagle over 'ENSAIE' on Mexico City KM#110.

KM#	Date	Mintage	Good	VG	Fine	VF
260.1	1811 HJ	—	150.00	200.00	275.00	350.00

c/s: Eagle over 'ENSAIE' crude sling below on Zacatecas KM#189.

KM#	Date	Mintage	Good	VG	Fine	VF
260.2	1811	—	—	—	—	—

c/s: Eagle over 'ENSAI', crude sling below on Zacatecas KM#190.

KM#	Date	Mintage	Good	VG	Fine	VF
260.3	1810	—	—	—	—	—
	1811	—	—	—	—	—

c/s: Eagle over 'ENSAIE', crude sling below on Zacatecas KM#191.

KM#	Date	Mintage	Good	VG	Fine	VF
260.4	1810	—	500.00	700.00	900.00	1200.
	1811	—	275.00	325.00	400.00	500.00
	1812	—	225.00	275.00	300.00	350.00

Jose Maria Liceaga

J.M.L. with banner on cross, crossed olive branches. (J.M.L./V., D.s, S.M.,S.Y.S.L., Ve, A.P., s.r.a., Sea, P.G.,S.,S.M.,E.)

1/2 REAL

SILVER

c/s: JML/SM on cast Mexico City 1/2 Real.

KM#	Date	Mintage	Good	VG	Fine	VF
A260	—	—	100.00	150.00	200.00	275.00

2 REALES

SILVER

c/s: J.M.L./Ve on 1/4 cut of 8 Reales.

KM#	Date	Mintage	Good	VG	Fine	VF
261.1	ND	—	185.00	225.00	300.00	—

c/s: J.M.L./V. on Zacatecas KM#186-187.

KM#	Date	Mintage	Good	VG	Fine	VF
261.2	1811	—	200.00	235.00	265.00	300.00

c/s: J.M.L./DS on Zacatecas KM#186-187.

KM#	Date	Mintage	Good	VG	Fine	VF
261.3	1811	—	200.00	235.00	275.00	325.00

c/s: J.M.L./S.M. on Zacatecas KM#186-187.

KM#	Date	Mintage	Good	VG	Fine	VF
261.4	1811	—	200.00	235.00	275.00	325.00

c/s: J.M.L./S.Y. on Zacatecas KM#186-187.

KM#	Date	Mintage	Good	VG	Fine	VF
261.5	1811	—	200.00	235.00	275.00	325.00

SILVER

c/s: J.M.L./D.S. on Zacatecas KM#189-190.

KM#	Date	Mintage	Good	VG	Fine	VF
262.1	1811	—	300.00	350.00	425.00	550.00

c/s: J.M.L./E on Zacatecas KM#189-190.

KM#	Date	Mintage	Good	VG	Fine	VF
262.2	1811	—	300.00	350.00	425.00	550.00

c/s: J.M.L./P.G. on Durango KM#111.2.

KM#	Date	Mintage	Good	VG	Fine	VF
262.3	1813 RM	—	275.00	350.00	450.00	600.00

c/s: J.M.L./S.M. on Zacatecas KM#189-190.

KM#	Date	Mintage	Good	VG	Fine	VF
262.4	1811	—	250.00	325.00	425.00	550.00

c/s: J.M.L./VE on Zacatecas KM#189-190.

KM#	Date	Mintage	Good	VG	Fine	VF
262.5	1811	—	250.00	325.00	425.00	550.00

Don Jose Maria De Linares

8 REALES

SILVER

c/s: LINA/RES* on Mexico City KM#110.

KM#	Date	Mintage	Good	VG	Fine	VF
263.1	1808 TH	—	300.00	350.00	425.00	500.00

c/s: LINA RES * on Zacatecas KM#189-190.

KM#	Date	Mintage	Good	VG	Fine	VF
263.2	1811	—	350.00	425.00	500.00	600.00
	1812	—	300.00	350.00	425.00	500.00

L.V.S. - Labor Vincit Semper

NOTE: Some authorities believe L.V.S. is for 'La Villa de Sombrerete'.

8 REALES

CAST SILVER

c/s: L.V.S. on Chihuahua KM#123.

KM#	Date	Mintage	Good	VG	Fine	VF
264.1	1811 RP	—	275.00	350.00	450.00	550.00
	1812 RP	—	200.00	250.00	300.00	350.00

c/s: L.V.S. on Chihuahua KM#111.1 overstruck on KM#123.

KM#	Date	Mintage	Good	VG	Fine	VF
264.2	1816 RP	—	250.00	300.00	325.00	350.00
	1817 RP	—	250.00	300.00	325.00	350.00
	1818 RP	—	250.00	300.00	325.00	350.00
	1820 RP	—	450.00	500.00	550.00	650.00

c/s: L.V.S. on Guadalajara KM#111.3.

KM#	Date	Mintage	Good	VG	Fine	VF
264.3	1817	—	185.00	220.00	250.00	300.00

c/s: L.V.S. on Nueva Vizcaya KM#165.

KM#	Date	Mintage	Good	VG	Fine	VF
264.4	1811 RM	—	1150.	3150.	5250.	8250.

c/s: L.V.S. on Sombrerete KM#177.

KM#	Date	Mintage	Good	VG	Fine	VF
264.5	1811	—	300.00	350.00	450.00	550.00
	1812	—	300.00	350.00	450.00	550.00

c/s: L.V.S. on Zacatecas KM#189-190.

KM#	Date	Mintage	Good	VG	Fine	VF
264.6	1811	—	350.00	400.00	450.00	550.00

c/s: L.V.S. on Zacatecas KM#192.

KM#	Date	Mintage	Good	VG	Fine	VF
264.7	1813	—	350.00	400.00	450.00	550.00

Morelos

Morelos monogram

Type A: Stars above and below monogram in circle.

Type B: Dots above and below monogram in oval.

Type C: Monogram in rectangle.

NOTE: Many specimens of Type C available on todays market are considered spurious.

8 REALES

SILVER

c/s: Type A on cast Mexico City KM#109.

KM#	Date	Mintage	Good	VG	Fine	VF
265.1	1797 FM	—	45.00	50.00	55.00	75.00
	1798 FM	—	45.00	50.00	55.00	75.00
	1800 FM	—	45.00	50.00	55.00	75.00
	1807 TH	—	45.00	50.00	55.00	75.00

c/s: Type A on Mexico City KM#110.

KM#	Date	Mintage	Good	VG	Fine	VF
265.2	1809 TH	—	55.00	65.00	75.00	100.00
	1811 HJ	—	55.00	65.00	75.00	100.00

c/s: Type A on Mexico City KM#111.

KM#	Date	Mintage	Good	VG	Fine	VF
265.3	1812 JJ	—	50.00	55.00	60.00	70.00

COPPER

c/s: Type A on Oaxaca Sud KM#233.

KM#	Date	Mintage	Good	VG	Fine	VF
265.4	1811	—	12.50	17.50	25.00	35.00
	1812	—	12.50	17.50	25.00	35.00
	1813	—	12.50	17.50	25.00	35.00
	1814	—	12.50	17.50	25.00	35.00

CAST SILVER

c/s: Type A on Supreme National Congress KM#206.

KM#	Date	Mintage	Good	VG	Fine	VF
265.5	1811	—	300.00	400.00	600.00	800.00

SILVER

c/s: Type A on Zacatecas KM#189-190.

KM#	Date	Mintage	Good	VG	Fine	VF
265.6	1811	—	200.00	275.00	375.00	500.00

c/s: Type A on Zacatecas KM#191.

KM#	Date	Mintage	Good	VG	Fine	VF
265.7	1811	—	200.00	275.00	375.00	500.00

c/s: Type B on Guatemala 8 Reales, C#67.

KM#	Date	Mintage	Good	VG	Fine	VF
266.1	1810 M	—	—	—	Rare	—

c/s: Type B on Mexico City KM#110.

KM#	Date	Mintage	Good	VG	Fine	VF
266.2	1809 TH	—	45.00	55.00	65.00	90.00

c/s: Type C on Zacatecas KM#189-190.

KM#	Date	Mintage	Good	VG	Fine	VF
267	1811	—	300.00	350.00	400.00	500.00

Norte

Issued by the Supreme National Congress and the Army of the North.

c/s: Eagle on cactus; star to left; 'NORTE' below.

1/2 REAL

SILVER

c/s: On Zacatecas KM#180.

KM#	Date	Mintage	Good	VG	Fine	VF
268	1811	—	250.00	300.00	375.00	450.00

2 REALES

SILVER

c/s: On Zacatecas KM#186.

KM#	Date	Mintage	Good	VG	Fine	VF
269	1811	—	225.00	275.00	325.00	400.00

4 REALES

SILVER

c/s: On Sombrerete KM#175.

KM#	Date	Mintage	Good	VG	Fine	VF
A269	1812	—	100.00	150.00	200.00	275.00

8 REALES

SILVER

c/s: On Chihuahua KM#111.1.

KM#	Date	Mintage	Good	VG	Fine	VF
270.1	1813 RP	—	250.00	350.00	450.00	500.00

c/s: On Guanajuato KM#111.4.

KM#	Date	Mintage	Good	VG	Fine	VF
270.2	1813 JM	—	400.00	550.00	700.00	800.00

c/s: On Zacatecas KM#188-189.

KM#	Date	Mintage	Good	VG	Fine	VF
270.3	1811	—	300.00	400.00	500.00	650.00

c/s: On Zacatecas KM#191.

KM#	Date	Mintage	Good	VG	Fine	VF
270.4	1811	—	200.00	300.00	400.00	550.00
	1812	—	200.00	300.00	400.00	550.00

Osorno

c/s: OSORNO monogram.
(Jose Francisco Osorno)

1/2 REAL

SILVER

c/s: On Mexico City KM#72.

KM#	Date	Mintage	Good	VG	Fine	VF
271.1	1798 FM	—	65.00	100.00	150.00	200.00
	1802 FT	—	65.00	100.00	150.00	200.00
	1806	—	65.00	100.00	150.00	200.00

c/s: On Mexico City KM#73.

KM#	Date	Mintage	Good	VG	Fine	VF
271.2	1809	—	65.00	100.00	150.00	200.00

REAL

SILVER

c/s: On Mexico City KM#81.

KM#	Date	Mintage	Good	VG	Fine	VF
272.1	1803 FT	—	65.00	100.00	150.00	200.00

c/s: On Potosi Real.

KM#	Date	Mintage	Good	VG	Fine	VF
272.2	ND	—	65.00	100.00	150.00	200.00

2 REALES

SILVER

c/s: On cast Mexico City KM#92.

KM#	Date	Mintage	Good	VG	Fine	VF
A272.1	1809 TH	—	75.00	125.00	175.00	250.00

c/s: On Zacatlan KM#252.

KM#	Date	Mintage	Good	VG	Fine	VF
A272.2	1813	—	150.00	200.00	300.00	400.00

4 REALES

SILVER

c/s: On Mexico City KM#97.

KM#	Date	Mintage	Good	VG	Fine	VF
273	1782 FF	—	—	—	—	—

8 REALES

SILVER

c/s: On Lima 8 Reales, C#101.

KM#	Date	Mintage	Good	VG	Fine	VF
274.1	1811 JP	—	200.00	225.00	250.00	300.00

c/s: On Mexico City KM#110.

KM#	Date	Mintage	Good	VG	Fine	VF
274.2	1809 TH	—	125.00	150.00	200.00	250.00
	1810 HJ	—	125.00	150.00	200.00	250.00
	1811 HJ	—	125.00	150.00	200.00	250.00

S.J.N.G. - Suprema Junta National Gubernativa

(Refer to Multiple Counterstamps)

VILLA/GRAN

(Julian Villagran)

2 REALES

SILVER

c/s: On cast Mexico City KM#91.

KM#	Date	Mintage	Good	VG	Fine	VF
298	1799 FM	—	150.00	200.00	250.00	350.00

8 REALES

SILVER

c/s: VILLA/GRAN on cast Mexico City KM#109.

KM#	Date	Mintage	Good	VG	Fine	VF
275	1796 FM	—	200.00	250.00	300.00	350.00
	1806 TH	—	200.00	250.00	300.00	350.00

UNCLASSIFIED COUNTERSTAMPS

General Vicente Guerrero

The counterstamp of an eagle facing left within a pearled oval has been attributed by some authors as that of General Vicente Guerrero, a leader of the insurgents in the south, 1816-1821.

1/2 REAL

SILVER
c/s: Eagle on Mexico City 1/2 Real.

KM#	Date	Mintage	Good	VG	Fine	VF
276	—	—	50.00	85.00	125.00	175.00

REAL

SILVER
c/s: Eagle on Mexico City KM#78.

KM#	Date	Mintage	Good	VG	Fine	VF
277	1772 FM	—	40.00	65.00	100.00	150.00

2 REALES

SILVER
c/s: Eagle on Mexico City KM#88.

KM#	Date	Mintage	Good	VG	Fine	VF
278.1	1784 FM	—	75.00	125.00	175.00	250.00

c/s: Eagle on Mexico City KM#91.

KM#	Date	Mintage	Good	VG	Fine	VF
278.2	1807 PJ	—	75.00	125.00	175.00	250.00

8 REALES

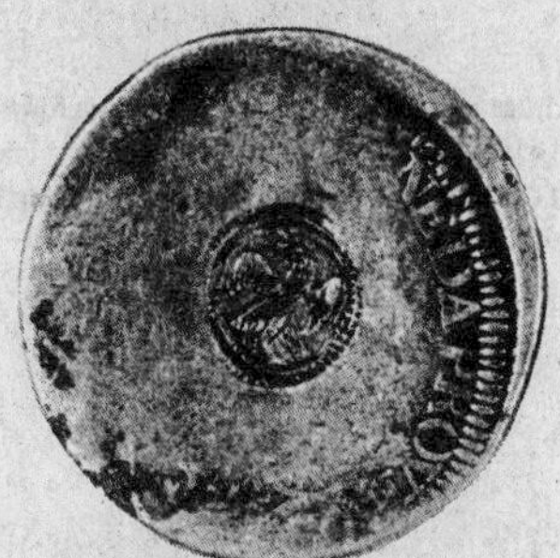

SILVER
c/s: Eagle on Zacatecas KM#191.

KM#	Date	Mintage	Good	VG	Fine	VF
279	1811	—	—	—	Rare	—

ZMY

8 REALES

SILVER
c/s: ZMY on Zacatecas KM#191.

KM#	Date	Mintage	Good	VG	Fine	VF
286	1812	—	100.00	150.00	210.00	275.00

MULTIPLE COUNTERSTAMPS

Many combinations of Royalist and Insurgent counterstamps are found usually on the cast copies produced by the Chihuahua and Mexico City Mints and also the crude provisional mint issues of this period. Struck Mexico mint coins were used for molds to cast necessity coinage and were counterstamped to show issuing authority. Some were stamped again by opposing forces or by friendly forces to allow circulation in their area of occupation. Some counterstamps are only obtainable with companion markings.

Chilpanzingo Crown and Flag

8 REALES

SILVER
c/s: Chilpanzingo Type B and crown and flag on Zacatecas KM#189-190.

KM#	Date	Mintage	Good	VG	Fine	VF
280	1811	—	—	—	—	—

Chilpanzingo/LVA

8 REALES

SILVER
c/s: Chilpanzingo Type A and LVA on Mexico City KM#109.

KM#	Date	Mintage	Good	VG	Fine	VF
297	1805 TH	—	—	—	—	—

Chilpanzingo/LVS

8 REALES

SILVER
c/s: Chilpanzingo Type A and script LVS on cast Mexico City KM#110.

KM#	Date	Mintage	Good	VG	Fine	VF
281	1809 HJ	—	—	—	—	—

Chilpanzingo/Morelos

8 REALES

SILVER
c/s: Chilpanzingo Type A and Morelos monogram Type A on cast Mexico City KM#109.

KM#	Date	Mintage	Good	VG	Fine	VF
284	1806 TH	—	—	—	—	—
	1807 TH	—	—	—	—	—

c/s: Chilpanzingo Type A and Morelos monogram type a on struck Mexico City KM#110.

KM#	Date	Mintage	Good	VG	Fine	VF
285.1	1809 TH	—	75.00	125.00	175.00	250.00

c/s: Chilpanzingo Type A and Morelos monogram Type A on cast Mexico City KM#110.

KM#	Date	Mintage	Good	VG	Fine	VF
285.2	1810 HJ	—	—	—	—	—
	1811 HJ	—	—	—	—	—

c/s: Chilpanzingo Type A and Morelos monogram Type A on cast Mexico City KM#111.

KM#	Date	Mintage	Good	VG	Fine	VF
285.3	1811 HJ	—	—	—	—	—

Chilpanzingo/P.D.V.

8 REALES

SILVER
c/s: Chilpanzingo Type B and P.D.V. (Provisional De Valladolid) on Valladolid KM#178.

KM#	Date	Mintage	Good	VG	Fine	VF
287	1813	—	—	—	—	—

Chilpanzingo/S.J.N.G.

8 REALES

SILVER
c/s: Chilpanzingo Type B and S.J.N.G. (Suprema Junta Nacional Gubernatine) on Zacatecas KM#189-190.

KM#	Date	Mintage	Good	VG	Fine	VF
288	1811	—	—	—	—	

C.M.S./S.C.M.

2 REALES

SILVER
c/s: C.M.S. (Comandancia Militar Suriana) and eagle with S.C.M. (Soberano Congreso Mexicano) on Mexico City 2 Reales.

KM#	Date	Mintage	Good	VG	Fine	VF
289	—	—	—	—	—	—

ENSAIE/VTIL

8 REALES

SILVER
c/s: ENSAIE and VTIL on Zacatecas KM#189-190.

KM#	Date	Mintage	Good	VG	Fine	VF
290	1811	—	—	—	—	

J.M.L./VTIL

2 REALES

SILVER
c/s: J.M.L./V E and VTIL on Zacatecas KM#186.

KM#	Date	Mintage	Good	VG	Fine	VF
286	1810	—	75.00	125.00	175.00	250.00
	1811	—	75.00	125.00	175.00	250.00

8 REALES

SILVER
c/s: J.M.L./D.S. and VTIL on Mexico City KM#110.

KM#	Date	Mintage	Good	VG	Fine	VF
291	1810 HJ	—	—	—	—	—

L.C.M./Morelos

8 REALES

SILVER
c/s: LCM and Morelos monogram Type A on cast Mexico City KM#109.

KM#	Date	Mintage	Good	VG	Fine	VF
282	1792 FM	—	—	—	—	—

Morelos/Morelos

8 REALES

SILVER
c/s: Morelos Type A and C on cast Mexico City KM#109.

KM#	Date	Mintage	Good	VG	Fine	VF
283	1806 TH	—	—	—	—	—

LCM/MVA-1812

8 REALES

SILVER
c/s: LCM and MVA/1812 on Chihuahua KM#123.

KM#	Date	Mintage	Good	VG	Fine	VF
292	1810 RP	—	—	—	—	—

c/s: LCM and MVA/1812 on Chihuahua KM#111.1.

KM#	Date	Mintage	Good	VG	Fine	VF
293	1818	—	—	—	—	—

L.V.A./Morelos

8 REALES

SILVER
c/s: Script LVA and Morelos monogram Type A on cast Mexico City KM#110.

KM#	Date	Mintage	Good	VG	Fine	VF
294	- HJ	—	—	—	—	—

M.d.S./S.C.M.

2 REALES

SILVER
c/s: M.d.S. (Militar del Sur) and eagle with S.C.M. (Soberno Congreso Mexicano) on Mexico City 2 Reales.

KM#	Date	Mintage	Good	VG	Fine	VF
295	—	—	—	—	—	—

Osorno/Villagram

8 REALES

SILVER
c/s: Osorno monogram and VILLA/GRAN on cast Mexico City KM#110.

KM#	Date	Mintage	Good	VG	Fine	VF
296	1809 TH	—	—	—	—	—

S.J.N.G./VTIL

8 REALES

c/s: S.J.N.G. and VTIL on Zacatecas KM#191.

KM#	Date	Mintage	Good	VG	Fine	VF
297	—	—	—	—	—	—

EMPIRE OF ITURBIDE

RULERS

Augustin I Iturbide, 1822-1823

MINTMARKS

Mo - Mexico City

ASSAYER'S INITIALS

JA - Jose Garcia Ansaldo, 1812-1833
JM - Joaquin Davila Madrid, 1809-1833

1/8 REAL

COPPER
NUEVA VISCAYA MINT

KM#	Date	Mintage	Fine	VF	XF	Unc
299	1821	—	10.00	17.50	25.00	40.00
	1822	—	7.50	12.50	17.50	30.00
	1823	—	8.50	13.50	20.00	35.00

1/4 REAL

COPPER
NUEVA VISCAYA MINT

KM#	Date	Mintage	Fine	VF	XF	Unc
300	1822	—	200.00	300.00	400.00	600.00

1/2 REAL

.903 SILVER
MEXICO MINT

KM#	Date	Mintage	Fine	VF	XF	Unc
301	1822 JM	—	16.50	25.00	45.00	175.00
	1823 JM	—	15.00	22.50	35.00	125.00

REAL

.903 SILVER
MEXICO MINT

KM#	Date	Mintage	Fine	VF	XF	Unc
302	1822 JM	—	100.00	165.00	250.00	450.00

2 REALES

.903 SILVER
MEXICO MINT

KM#	Date	Mintage	Fine	VF	XF	Unc
303	1822 JM	—	40.00	75.00	125.00	250.00
	1823 JM	—	35.00	65.00	100.00	200.00

8 REALES

.903 SILVER
MEXICO MINT

KM#	Date	Mintage	Fine	VF	XF	Unc
304	1822 JM	—	65.00	110.00	175.00	300.00

Obv: Bust similar to 8 Escudos, KM#313.

KM#	Date	Mintage	Fine	VF	XF	Unc
305	1822 JM	—	225.00	375.00	600.00	900.00

Type I. Obv Legend divided. Rev '8 R.J.M.' at upper left of eagle

KM#	Date	Mintage	Fine	VF	XF	Unc
306	1822 JM	—	160.00	250.00	400.00	650.00

Type II. Obv: Legend divided. Rev: '8 R.J.M.' below eagle.

KM#	Date	Mintage	Fine	VF	XF	Unc
307	1822 JM	—	160.00	250.00	375.00	600.00

Type III. Obv: Continuous legend with long smooth truncation. Rev: '8 R.J.M.' at upper left.

KM#	Date	Mintage	Fine	VF	XF	Unc
308	1822 JM	—	400.00	600.00	850.00	1100.

Type IV. Obv: Continuous legend with long smooth truncation. Rev: '8 R.J.M.' below eagle.

KM#	Date	Mintage	Fine	VF	XF	Unc
309	1822 JM	—	100.00	125.00	200.00	350.00

Type V. Obv. continuous legend with short irregular truncation. Rev: '8 R.J.M.' below eagle.

KM#	Date	Mintage	Fine	VF	XF	Unc
310	1822 JM	—	80.00	110.00	165.00	250.00
	1823 JM	—	80.00	110.00	165.00	250.00

Type VI. Obv: Bust with long truncation. Rev: '8 R.J.M. below eagle.

KM#	Date	Mintage	Fine	VF	XF	Unc
311	1823 JM	—	—	—	Rare	—

4 SCUDOS

.875 GOLD
MEXICO MINT

KM#	Date	Mintage	Fine	VF	XF	Unc
312	1823 JM	—	600.00	1000.	2000.	3000.

8 SCUDOS

.875 GOLD

MEXICO MINT

KM#	Date	Mintage	Fine	VF	XF	Unc
313	1822 JM	—	1000.	1500.	2250.	3500.

KM#	Date	Mintage	Fine	VF	XF	Unc
314	1823 JM	—	1000.	1650.	2500.	4250.

REPUBLIC OF MEXICO

MINTMARKS

A,As - Alamos
Ce - Real de Catorce
C,CH,Ch - Chihuahua
C,Cn,Gn(error)-Culiacan
D,Do - Durango
EoMo - Estado de Mexico
Ga - Guadalajara
GC - Guadalupe y Calvo
G,Go - Guanajuato
H,Ho - Hermosillo
M,Mo - Mexico City
O,Oa - Oaxaca
SLP, Pi - San Luis Potosi
Z,Zs - Zacatecas

ASSAYER'S INITIALS

ALAMOS MINT

PG - Pascual Gaxiola, 1862-1868
DL, L - Domingo Larraguibel, 1866-1879
AM - Antonio Moreno, 1872-1874
ML, L - Manuel Larraguibel, 1878-1895

REAL DE CATORCE MINT

ML - Mariano Leon, 1863

CHIHUAHUA MINT

MR - Mariano Cristobal Ramirez, 1831-1834
AM - Jose Antonio Mucharraz, 1833-1839
MJ - Jose Mariano Jimenez, 1832
RG - Rodrigo Garcia, 1839-1856
JC - Joaquin Campa, 1856-1865
BA - Bruno Arriada, 1858
FP - Francisco Potts, 1866
JG - Jose Maria Gomez del Campo, 1866-1868
MM, M - Manuel Merino, 1868-1895
AV - Antonio Valero, 1873-1880
EA - Eduardo Avila, 1877
JM - Jacobo Mucharraz, 1877
GR - Guadalupe Rocha, 1877
MG - Manuel Gameros, 1880-1882

CULIACAN MINT

CE - Clemente Espinosa de los Monteros, 1846-1870;
C - 1870
PV - Pablo Viruega, 1860-1861
MP, P - Manuel Onofre Parodi, 1871-1876
GP - Celso Gaxiola & Manuel Onofre Parodi, 1876
CG, G - Celso Gaxiola, 1876-1878
JD, D - Juan Dominguez, 1878-1882
AM, M - Antonio Moreno, 1882-1899
F - Fernando Ferrari, 1870
JQ, Q - Jesus S. Quiroz, 1899-1903
FV, V - Francisco Valdez, 1903
MH, H - Merced Hernandez, 1904
RP, P - Ramon Ponce de Leon, 1904-1905

DURANGO MINT

RL - ???, 1825-1832
RM - Ramon Mascarenas, 1830-1848
OMC - Octavio Martinez de Castro, 1840
CM - Clemente Moron, 1848-1876
JMR - Jose Maria Ramirez, 1849-1852
CP, P - Carlos Leon de la Pena, 1853-64, 1867-73
LT - ???, 1864-1865
JMP, P - Carlos Miguel de la Palma, 1877
PE, E - Pedro Espejo, 1878
TB, B - Trinidad Barrera, 1878-1880
JP - J. Miguel Palma, 1880-1894
MC, C - Manuel M. Canseco or Melchor Calderon, 1882-1890
JB - Jacobo Blanco, 1885
ND, D - Norberto Dominguez, 1892-1895

ESTADO DE MEXICO MINT

L - Luis Valazquez de la Cadena, 1828-1830
F - Francisco Parodi, 1828-1830

GUADALAJARA MINT

FS - Francisco Suarez, 1818-1835
JM - ???, 1830-1832
JG - Juan de Dios Guzman, 1836-39, 1842-67
MC - Manuel Cueras, 1839-1846
JM - Jesus P. Manzano, 1867-1869
IC, C - Ignacio Canizo y Soto, 1869-1877
MC - Manuel Contreras, 1874-1875
JA, A - Julio Arancivia, 1877-1881
FS, S -Fernando Sayago, 1880-1882
TB, B - Trinidad Barrera, 1883-1884
AH, H - Antonio Hernandez y Prado, 1884-1885
JS, S - Jose s. Schiafino, 1885-1895

GUADALUPE Y CALVO MINT

MP - Manuel Onofre Parodi, 1844-1852

GUANAJUATO MINT

JJ - Jose Mariano Jimenez, 1825-1826
MJ,MR,JM,PG,PJ,PF - ???
PM - Patrick Murphy, 1841-1848,1853-1861
YF - Yldefonso Flores, 1862-1868
YE - Ynocencio Espinoza, 1862-1863
FR - Faustino Ramirez, 1870-1878
SB, RR - ???
RS - Rosendo Sandoval, 1891-1900

HERMOSILLO MINT

PP - Pedro Peimbert, 1835-1836
FM - Florencio Monteverde, 1871-1876
MP - Manuel Onofre Parodi, 1866
PR - Pablo Rubio, 1866-1875; **R** - 1874-1875
GR - Guadalupe Rocha, 1877
AF, F - Alejandro Fourcade, 1876-1877
JA, A - Jesus Acosta, 1877-1883
FM, M - Fernando Mendez, 1883-1886
FG, G - Fausto Gaxiola, 1886-1895

MEXICO CITY MINT

Because of the great number of assayers for this mint (Mexico City is a much larger mint than any of the others) there is much confusion as to which initial stands for which assayer at any one time. Therefore we feel that it would be of no value to list the assayers.

OAXACA MINT

AE - Agustin Endner, 1859-1891; **E** - 1889-1890
FR - Francisco de la Rosa, 1861-1864
EN - Eduardo Navarro Luna, 1890; **N** - 1890

POTOSI MINT

JS - Juan Sanabria, 1827-1842
AM - Jose Antonio Mucharraz, 1838,1843-1849
PS - Pomposo Sanabria, 1842-1843,1848-1849, 1857-1861;1867-1870; **S** - 1869-1870
MC - Mariano Catano, 1849-1859
RO - Romualdo Obregon, 1859-1865
MH, H - Manuel Herrera Rozo, 1870-1885
O - Juan R. Ochoa, 1870-1873
CA, G - Carlos Aguirre Gomez, 1867-1870
BE, E - Blas Escontria, 1879-1881
LC, C - Uis Cuevas, 1885-1886
MR, R - Mariano Reyes, 1886-1893

ZACATECAS MINT

A - Adalco, 1825-1829
Z - Mariano Zaldivar, 1825-1826
V - Jose Mariano Vela, 1824-1831
O - Manuel Ochoa, 1829-1867
M - Manuel Miner, 1831-1867
VL - Vicente Larranaga, 1860-1866
JS - J.S. de Santa Ana, 1867-1868,1876-1886
YH - Ygnacio Hierro, 1868-1874
JA - Juan H. Acuna, 1874-1876
FZ - Francisco de P. Zarate, 1886-1905
FM - Francisco Mateos, 1904-1905

State and Federal Issues

1/16 REAL

(Medio Octavo)

COPPER

JALISCO MINT

Obv. leg: DEPARTAMENTO DE JALISCO

KM#	Date	Mintage	Good	VG	Fine	VF
316	1860	—	2.00	3.50	5.50	10.00
	Obv. leg: ESTADO LIBRE DE JALISCO					
317	1861	—	2.00	3.50	5.50	10.00

MEXICO CITY MINT

Obv. leg: REPUBLICA MEXICANA

KM#	Date	Mintage	VG	Fine	VF	XF
315	1831	—	6.50	9.00	14.50	20.00
	1832/1	—	7.50	10.00	15.00	22.50
	1832	—	6.50	9.00	14.50	20.00
	1833	—	6.50	9.00	14.50	20.00

BRASS

KM#	Date	Mintage	VG	Fine	VF	XF
315a	1833	—	7.00	10.00	15.00	22.50
	1836/3	—	—	—	Rare	—

1/8 REAL

(Octavo Real)

COPPER

CHIHUAHUA MINT

Obv. leg: ESTADO SOBERANO DE CHIHUAHUA

KM#	Date	Mintage	Good	VG	Fine	VF
318	1833	—	4.50	6.50	10.00	15.00
	1834	—	4.50	6.50	10.00	15.00

Obv. leg: ESTADO DE CHIHUAHUA

KM#	Date	Mintage	Good	VG	Fine	VF
319	1855	—	3.50	5.00	7.50	12.50

DURANGO MINT

Rev. leg: LIBERTAD

KM#	Date	Mintage	Good	VG	Fine	VF
320	1824	—	6.00	10.00	18.50	30.00
	1828	—	100.00	150.00	250.00	450.00

NOTE: These pieces were frequently struck over 1/8 Reals, dated 1821-23 of Nueva Vizcaya.

Rev. leg: OCTo.DE.R.DE DO., date.

KM#	Date	Mintage	Good	VG	Fine	VF
321	1828	—	7.50	10.00	16.50	25.00

Obv. leg: ESTADO DE DURANGO

KM#	Date	Mintage	Good	VG	Fine	VF
322	1833	—	150.00	200.00	300.00	450.00

Obv. leg: REPUBLICA MEXICANA

KM#	Date	Mintage	Good	VG	Fine	VF
323	1842/33	—	17.50	22.50	28.50	37.50
	1842	—	15.00	20.00	25.00	35.00

Obv. leg: REPUBLICA MEXICANA
Rev. leg: DEPARTAMENTO DE DURANGO

KM#	Date	Mintage	Good	VG	Fine	VF
324	1845	—	6.00	10.00	15.00	25.00
	1846	—	4.00	6.00	10.00	15.00
	1847	—	3.00	5.00	8.00	12.50

Obv. leg: REPUBLICA MEXICANA
Rev. leg: ESTADO DE DURANGO

KM#	Date	Mintage	Good	VG	Fine	VF
325	1851	—	2.50	3.50	5.50	10.00
	1852/1	—	3.50	4.50	6.00	9.00
	1852	—	2.00	3.00	4.50	7.50
	1854	—	4.50	6.50	10.00	15.00

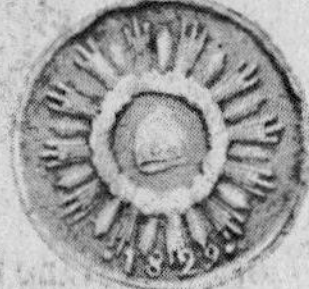

GUANAJUATO MINT

Obv. leg: ESTADO LIBRE DE GUANAJUATO

KM#	Date	Mintage	Good	VG	Fine	VF
326	1829	—	3.00	4.50	7.50	12.00
	1829 error with GUANJUATO					
		—	5.00	7.00	9.00	13.50
	1830	—	5.00	7.50	10.00	16.50

Obv. leg: EST. LIB. DE GUANAXUATO
Rev. leg: OMNIA VINCIT LABOR,

oval arms 29mm.

KM#	Date	Mintage	Good	VG	Fine	VF
327	1856	—	3.00	5.00	7.00	10.00

25mm

KM#	Date	Mintage	Good	VG	Fine	VF
328	1856	—	3.50	5.00	7.00	10.00
	1857	—	3.00	4.50	7.00	10.00

BRASS

KM#	Date	Mintage	Good	VG	Fine	VF
328a	1857	—	3.00	5.00	7.00	10.00

COPPER

JALISCO MINT

Obv. leg: ESTADO LIBRE DE JALISCO

KM#	Date	Mintage	Good	VG	Fine	VF
329	1828	—	2.50	3.50	6.00	9.00
	1831	—	75.00	100.00	150.00	200.00
	1832/28	—	2.50	3.50	6.00	9.00
	1832	—	2.50	3.50	6.00	9.00
	1833	—	2.50	3.50	6.00	9.00
	1834	—	3.00	4.50	6.50	10.00

KM#	Date	Mintage	Good	VG	Fine	VF
330	1856	—	1.75	2.50	4.00	7.00
	1857	—	1.75	2.50	4.00	7.00
	1858	—	2.00	3.00	5.00	10.00
	1861	—	2.00	3.00	4.50	7.00
	1862	—	2.00	3.00	4.50	7.00

Obv. leg: DEPARTAMENTO DE JALISCO

KM#	Date	Mintage	Good	VG	Fine	VF
331	1858	—	2.00	3.50	5.50	10.00
	1859	—	1.75	2.50	4.50	7.00
	1860/59	—	2.00	3.50	5.50	10.00
	1860	—	1.75	2.50	4.50	7.00
	1862	—	3.00	4.00	5.00	9.00

MEXICO CITY MINT

27mm
Obv. leg: REPUBLICA MEXICANA

KM#	Date	Mintage	Good	VG	Fine	VF
332	1829	—	50.00	75.00	100.00	150.00

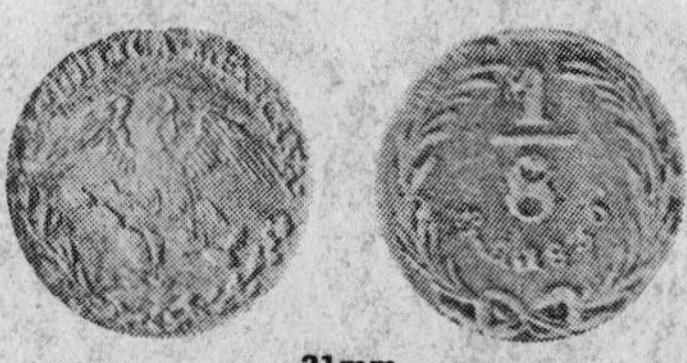

21mm
Obv. leg: REPUBLICA MEXICANA

KM#	Date	Mintage	Good	VG	Fine	VF
333	1829	—	4.00	5.00	12.00	25.00
	1830	—	2.50	4.00	5.50	10.00
	1831	—	2.50	4.00	5.50	10.00
	1832	—	2.50	4.00	5.50	10.00
	1833/2	—	3.25	6.00	10.00	16.50
	1833	—	2.50	4.00	5.50	10.00
	1834	—	2.50	4.00	5.50	10.00
	1835/4	—	3.25	6.00	10.00	16.50
	1835	—	2.50	4.00	5.50	10.00

Obv. leg: LIBERTAD

KM#	Date	Mintage	Good	VG	Fine	VF
334	1841	—	2.50	3.75	5.00	8.00
	1842	—	2.00	3.00	4.00	7.00
	1850	—	15.00	20.00	25.00	35.00
	1861	—	6.00	9.00	13.50	20.00

OCCIDENTE MINT

Obv. leg: ESTADO DE OCCIDENTE

KM#	Date	Mintage	Good	VG	Fine	VF
335	1828 reverse S	—	30.00	35.00	55.00	85.00
	1829	—	25.00	32.50	50.00	75.00

POTOSI MINT

Obv. leg: ESTADO LIBRE DE SAN LUIS POTOSI

KM#	Date	Mintage	Good	VG	Fine	VF
336	1829	—	4.50	7.00	10.00	15.00
	1830	—	6.00	9.00	12.50	20.00
	1831	—	3.50	6.00	8.00	12.00
	1859	—	3.00	4.50	7.00	10.00
	1865/1	—	—	—	—	—

SONORA MINT

Obv. leg: ETO LIBEY SOBO DE SONORA, 28mm.

KM#	Date	Mintage	Good	VG	Fine	VF
337	1859	—	—	Rare	—	—

ZACATECAS MINT

Obv. leg: ESTo LIBe FEDo DE ZACATECAS

KM#	Date	Mintage	Good	VG	Fine	VF
338	1825	—	2.25	3.00	4.50	8.00
	1827	—	2.25	3.00	4.50	8.00
	1827 with turned A for V in OCTAVO					
		—	3.00	4.00	6.00	12.00
	1829	—	2.25	3.00	4.50	8.00
	1830	—	2.00	3.00	4.00	8.00
	1831	—	2.50	4.50	6.50	10.00
	1832	—	2.00	2.50	4.00	8.00
	1833	—	2.00	2.50	4.00	8.00
	1835	—	2.25	3.00	4.50	9.00
	1846	—	2.00	4.00	6.00	10.00
	1851	—	2.50	5.50	7.00	12.00
	1852	—	2.00	4.50	6.00	10.00
	1858	—	1.75	3.25	4.00	8.00
	1859	—	1.75	3.25	4.00	8.00
	1862	—	1.75	3.25	4.00	8.00
	1863 with reversed 6 in date					
		—	2.00	4.00	6.00	10.00

Obv. leg: DEPARTAMENTO DE ZACATECAS

KM#	Date	Mintage	Good	VG	Fine	VF
339	1836	—	2.50	4.00	6.00	10.00
	1845	—	4.50	8.00	14.00	20.00
	1846	—	2.50	4.00	6.50	10.00

1/4 REAL

(Un Quarto/Una Quartilla)

(Copper/Brass Series)

COPPER

CHIHUAHUA MINT

Obv. leg: ESTADO SOBERANO DE CHIHUAHUA

KM#	Date	Mintage	Good	VG	Fine	VF
340	1833	—	2.25	4.50	7.50	14.00
	1834	—	2.25	4.50	7.50	14.00
	1835	—	2.25	4.50	7.50	14.00

Obv. leg: ESTADO LIBRE DE CHIHUAHUA

KM#	Date	Mintage	Good	VG	Fine	VF
341	1846	—	1.50	2.50	5.00	10.00

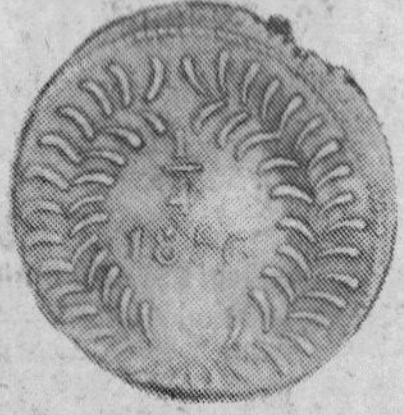

Obv. leg: ESTADO DE CHIHUAHUA

KM#	Date	Mintage	Good	VG	Fine	VF
342	1854	—	3.25	6.00	9.00	16.00
	1855	—	1.50	2.50	5.00	8.00
	1856	—	1.50	2.50	5.00	8.00

Obv. leg: DEPARTMENTO DE CHIHUAHUA

KM#	Date	Mintage	Good	VG	Fine	VF
343	1855	—	2.00	4.00	6.00	10.00
	1855 DE/OE	—	2.00	4.00	6.00	10.00

Obv. leg: E. CHIHA LIBERTAD

KM#	Date	Mintage	Good	VG	Fine	VF
344	1860	—	1.00	2.50	4.50	8.00
	1861	—	1.00	3.00	5.00	9.00
	1865/1	—	—	—	—	—
	1865	—	1.00	2.50	4.50	8.00
	1866	—	1.00	2.50	4.50	8.00

DURANGO MINT

Obv. leg: REPUBLICA MEXICANA

KM#	Date	Mintage	Good	VG	Fine	VF
345	1845	—	—	—	Rare	—

Obv. leg: REPUBLICA MEXICANA
Rev: DURANGO, date, value.

KM#	Date	Mintage	Good	VG	Fine	VF
346	1858	—	—	—	Rare	—

Obv. leg: ESTADO DE DURANGO
Rev. leg: CONSTITUCION

KM#	Date	Mintage	Good	VG	Fine	VF
347	1858	—	2.00	4.00	7.50	14.00

Obv. leg: DEPARTAMENTO DE DURANGO
Rev. leg: LIBERTAD EN EL ORDEN.

KM#	Date	Mintage	Good	VG	Fine	VF
348	1860	—	2.00	3.00	4.00	7.00
	1866	—	2.00	3.00	4.00	7.00

Obv. leg: ESTADO DE DURANGO
Rev. leg: INDEPENDENCIA Y LIBERTAD

KM#	Date	Mintage	Good	VG	Fine	VF
349	1866	—	3.00	4.50	7.00	12.50

Rev. leg: SUFRAGIO LIBRE

KM#	Date	Mintage	Good	VG	Fine	VF
350	1872	—	1.00	2.00	4.00	8.00

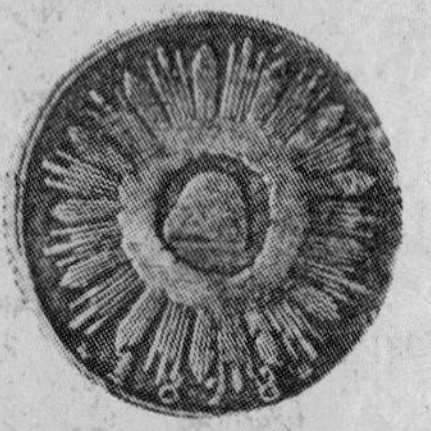

GUANAJUATO MINT

Obv. leg: ESTADO LIBRE DE GUANAJUATO

KM#	Date	Mintage	Good	VG	Fine	VF
351	1828	—	2.50	5.00	8.50	15.00
	1828 error with GUANJUATO	—	3.50	6.50	10.00	18.00
	1829	—	2.50	5.00	9.00	15.00

Obv. leg: EST. LIB. DE GUANAXUATO
Rev. leg: OMNIA VINCIT LABOR

KM#	Date	Mintage	Good	VG	Fine	VF
352	1856	—	4.00	6.00	9.00	14.00
	1857	—	3.00	5.50	10.00	15.00

BRASS

KM#	Date	Mintage	Good	VG	Fine	VF
352a	1856	—	3.50	6.00	9.00	12.00
	1857	—	3.50	6.00	9.00	12.00

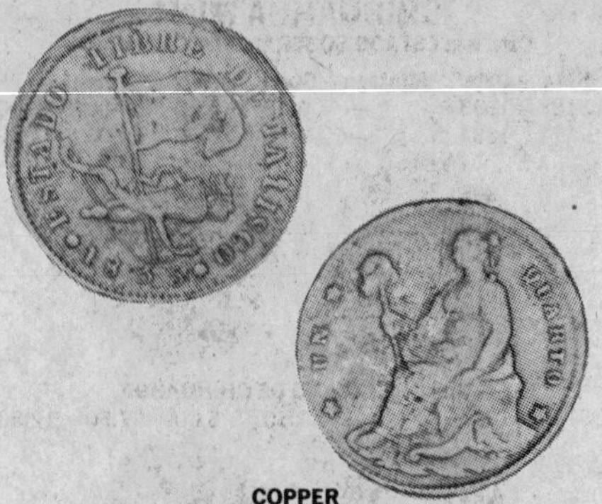

COPPER

JALISCO MINT

Obv. leg: ESTADO LIBRE DE JALISCO

KM#	Date	Mintage	Good	VG	Fine	VF
353	1828	—	2.50	4.50	7.00	11.50
	1829/8	—	3.50	5.00	8.00	12.50
	1829	—	2.00	4.00	6.00	11.00
	1830/20	—	2.00	3.00	5.00	8.00
	1830/29	—	2.00	3.00	5.00	8.00
	1830	—	2.00	3.00	5.00	8.00
	1832/20	—	3.00	5.00	8.00	12.50
	1832/28	—	2.00	3.00	7.00	11.00
	1832	—	2.00	3.00	7.00	11.50
	1833	—	2.00	3.00	7.00	11.00
	1834	—	2.00	3.00	5.50	8.50
	1835/3	—	—	—	—	—
	1835	—	2.00	3.00	5.50	8.50

Obv. leg: DEPARTAMENTO DE JALISCO

KM#	Date	Mintage	Good	VG	Fine	VF
354	1836	—	6.00	9.00	13.50	18.50

Obv. leg: ESTADO LIBRE DE JALISCO

KM#	Date	Mintage	Good	VG	Fine	VF
355	1858	—	2.00	4.00	6.50	10.00
	1861	—	2.50	4.00	7.00	12.00
	1862	—	2.00	4.50	7.50	12.50

Obv. leg: DEPARTAMENTO DE JALISCO

KM#	Date	Mintage	Good	VG	Fine	VF
356	1858	—	2.00	4.00	6.50	10.00
	1859/8	—	2.50	5.00	7.50	12.50
	1859	—	2.00	4.00	6.50	10.00
	1860	—	2.00	4.00	6.00	10.00

MEXICO CITY MINT

Obv. leg: REPUBLICA MEXICANA.

KM#	Date	Mintage	VG	Fine	VF	XF
357	1829	—	3.50	8.50	22.50	45.00

Reduced size.

KM#	Date	Mintage	VG	Fine	VF	XF
357a	1829	—	3.50	8.50	22.50	45.00
	1830	—	1.00	2.00	3.50	7.50
	1831	—	1.00	2.00	3.50	7.50
	1832	—	5.50	10.00	15.00	25.00
	1833	—	2.00	3.00	6.00	12.00
	1834	—	2.00	3.00	6.00	12.00
	1835	—	5.00	10.00	15.00	30.00
	1836	—	7.00	10.00	17.50	35.00
	1837	—	5.00	10.00	15.00	30.00

BRASS
c/s: JM

KM#	Date	Mintage	VG	Fine	VF	XF
358a	1831	—	5.50	10.00	15.00	25.00

Without counterstamp

KM#	Date	Mintage	VG	Fine	VF	XF
358b	1831	—	—	—	—	—

COPPER

POTOSI MINT

Obv. leg: MEXICO LIBRE
Rev. leg: ESTADO LIBRE DE SAN LUIS POTOSI

KM#	Date	Mintage	Good	VG	Fine	VF
359	1828	—	2.00	3.00	4.00	7.00
	1829	—	2.00	3.00	4.00	7.00
	1830	—	2.00	3.00	4.00	7.00
	1832	—	2.00	3.00	4.00	7.00
	1859 LIBRE-large	—	2.00	3.00	4.00	7.00
	1859 LIBRE-small	—	2.00	3.00	4.00	7.00
	1860	—	2.00	3.00	4.00	7.00

Obv. leg: REPUBLICA MEXICANA

KM#	Date	Mintage	Good	VG	Fine	VF
360	1862	1,367	1.50	2.50	4.00	7.00
	1862 LIBR	Inc. Ab.	2.00	3.50	6.00	11.00

Milled edge
Obv. leg: LIBERTAD Y REFORMA
Rev. leg: ESTADO LIBRE Y SOBERANO DE S.L. POTOSI

KM#	Date	Mintage	Good	VG	Fine	VF
361	1867	3,177	4.00	7.00	12.00	20.00
	1867 AFG	I.A.	2.00	4.00	6.50	12.00

Plain edge

KM#	Date	Mintage	Good	VG	Fine	VF
362	1867	Inc. Ab.	4.00	7.00	10.00	17.50
	1867 AFG	I.A.	2.00	4.00	6.50	12.00

SINALOA MINT

Obv. leg: ESTADO LIBRE Y SOBERANO DE SINALOA

KM#	Date	Mintage	Good	VG	Fine	VF
363	1847	—	2.00	4.00	6.50	12.50
	1848	—	2.00	4.50	5.50	8.50
	1859	—	2.00	3.00	5.00	8.00
	1861	—	2.00	3.00	5.00	8.00
	1862	—	2.00	3.00	5.00	8.00
	1863	—	2.00	3.50	5.50	8.50
	1864/3	—	2.50	3.50	6.00	10.00
	1864	—	2.00	3.00	5.00	8.00
	1865	—	2.00	3.00	6.00	10.00
	1866	7,401	2.00	3.00	6.00	10.00

BRASS

KM#	Date	Mintage	Good	VG	Fine	VF
363a	1847	—	2.00	4.00	6.50	12.50

COPPER

SONORA MINT

Obv. leg: EST.D.SONORA UNA CUART

KM#	Date	Mintage	Good	VG	Fine	VF
364	1832	—	2.50	4.00	7.50	12.00
	1833	—	2.50	4.00	6.00	10.00
	1834	—	2.50	4.00	6.00	10.00
	1835	—	2.50	4.00	6.00	10.00
	1836	—	2.50	4.00	6.00	10.00

Obv. leg: ESTO.LIBE.Y SOBO.DE SONORA

KM#	Date	Mintage	Good	VG	Fine	VF
365	1859	—	2.25	3.50	6.50	12.00
	1861/59	—	3.00	4.50	8.50	15.00
	1861	—	2.25	3.50	6.50	12.00
	1862	—	2.25	3.50	7.50	14.00
	1863/2	—	5.00	10.00	20.00	30.00

ZACATECAS MINT

Obv. leg: ESTO LIBE FEDO DE ZACATECAS

KM#	Date	Mintage	Good	VG	Fine	VF
366	1824	—	—	—	Rare	—
	1825	—	1.75	2.25	4.00	7.00
	1826	—	2.00	2.25	4.00	7.50
	1827/17	—	1.75	2.25	4.00	7.50
	1829	—	2.00	2.50	5.00	10.00
	1830	—	1.75	2.00	4.50	7.50
	1831	—	1.50	2.00	4.00	7.50
	1832	—	1.75	2.25	3.50	7.50
	1833	—	1.00	1.75	4.00	7.50
	1835	—	1.00	1.75	4.00	7.50
	1846	—	1.25	2.00	3.50	6.50
	1847	—	1.50	2.50	4.50	8.50
	1852	—	1.25	2.00	3.50	6.00
	1853	—	1.50	2.50	4.50	8.50
	1855	—	4.50	8.50	12.50	25.00
	1858	—	1.25	2.00	3.50	6.00
	1859	—	1.50	2.50	4.00	8.00
	1860	—	1.25	2.00	3.50	6.00
	1862/57	—	1.25	2.00	3.50	6.00
	1862/59	—	3.00	4.50	7.00	12.50
	1862	—	1.25	2.00	3.50	6.00
	1863/2	—	2.00	3.00	4.50	7.00
	1863	—	1.25	2.50	4.00	6.00
	1864/58	—	4.50	8.50	12.50	25.00

Obv. leg: DEPARTAMENTO DE ZACATECAS

KM#	Date	Mintage	Good	VG	Fine	VF
367	1836	—	3.00	5.00	10.00	15.00
	1846	—	2.00	4.00	8.00	12.00

SILVER SERIES

0.8450 gm., .903 SILVER, .0245 oz ASW

CHIHUAHUA MINT (Ca)

KM#	Date	Mintage	VG	Fine	VF	XF
368	1843 RG	—	20.00	27.50	37.50	60.00

CULIACAN MINT (C, Cn)

KM#	Date	Mintage	VG	Fine	VF	XF
368.1	1855 LR	—	20.00	27.50	37.50	60.00

DURANGO MINT (Do)

KM#	Date	Mintage	VG	Fine	VF	XF
368.2	1842 LR	—	6.00	10.00	15.00	25.00
	1843 LR	—	10.00	12.50	16.50	30.00

GUADALAJARA MINT (Ga)

KM#	Date	Mintage	VG	Fine	VF	XF
368.3	1842 JG	—	2.50	5.50	8.00	15.00
	1843 JG	—	6.00	9.00	12.50	22.50
	1843 MC	—	4.00	6.50	9.00	16.50
	1844 MC	—	4.00	6.50	9.00	16.50
	1844 LR	—	2.50	5.00	7.50	13.50
	1845 LR	—	2.50	4.50	7.50	13.50
	1846 LR	—	5.00	8.00	10.00	18.50
	1847 LR	—	4.00	6.50	9.00	16.50
	1851 LR	—	6.00	10.00	16.50	30.00
	1852 LR	—	6.00	10.00	15.00	27.50
	1854 LR	—	5.00	10.00	12.50	22.50
	1855 LR	—	5.00	8.00	10.00	18.50
	1857 LR	—	6.50	10.00	15.00	27.50
	1862 LR	—	5.50	10.00	15.00	27.50

GUADALUPE Y CALVO MINT (GC)

KM#	Date	Mintage	VG	Fine	VF	XF
368.4	1844 LR	—	45.00	60.00	85.00	125.00

GUANAJUATO MINT (Go)

KM#	Date	Mintage	VG	Fine	VF	XF
368.5	1842 PM	—	4.00	6.00	10.00	18.50
	1842 LR	—	2.00	4.00	8.00	15.00
	1843/2 LR	—	4.50	6.50	10.00	18.50
	1843 LR	—	2.50	5.00	8.00	15.00

KM#	Date	Mintage	VG	Fine	VF	XF
368.5	1844 LR	—	2.00	3.50	6.00	10.00
	1845 LR	—	4.00	6.50	9.00	16.50
	1846 LR	—	4.00	6.50	9.00	16.50
	1847 LR	—	1.50	3.00	5.00	8.00
	1848/7 LR	—	2.00	3.50	6.00	10.00
	1848 LR	—	2.00	3.50	6.00	10.00
	1849/7 LR	—	3.50	5.00	7.50	13.50
	1849 LR	—	1.50	3.00	5.50	9.00
	1850 LR	—	2.00	3.50	5.50	10.00
	1851 LR	—	2.00	3.50	5.50	10.00
	1852 LR	—	1.50	3.00	5.00	9.00
	1853 LR	—	2.00	3.50	6.00	10.00
	1855 LR	—	5.50	9.00	12.00	20.00
	1856 LR	—	6.00	9.00	12.50	22.50
	1862 LR	—	1.75	3.50	5.00	9.00
	1863 LR	—	1.50	4.00	7.00	13.50

MEXICO CITY MINT (Mo)

KM#	Date	Mintage	VG	Fine	VF	XF
368.6	1842 LR	—	2.00	4.00	5.00	9.00
	1843 LR	—	2.00	4.00	6.00	10.00
	1844 LR	—	5.00	8.00	10.00	18.50
	1845 LR	—	5.00	8.00	10.00	18.50
	1846 LR	—	4.00	5.00	8.00	15.00
	1850 LR	—	5.00	10.00	15.00	27.50
	1858 LR	—	6.00	10.00	12.50	22.50
	1859 LR	—	4.00	6.50	9.00	16.50
	1860 LR	—	4.00	6.50	9.00	16.50
	1861 LR	—	1.50	4.50	7.00	13.50
	1862 LR	—	4.00	6.50	9.00	16.50
	1863 LR	—	5.00	8.00	10.00	18.50

POTOSI MINT (S.L.Pi)

KM#	Date	Mintage	VG	Fine	VF	XF
368.7	1842	—	2.00	4.00	6.00	10.00
	1843/2	—	3.50	5.00	7.50	13.50
	1843	—	1.50	3.00	5.00	9.00
	1844	—	1.50	3.00	5.00	9.00
	1845/3	—	5.00	8.00	10.00	18.50
	1845	—	1.50	3.00	4.50	8.00
	1847/5	—	3.50	5.50	8.00	15.00
	1847	—	2.00	3.50	6.00	10.00
	1851	—	5.50	9.00	12.50	22.50
	1854	—	5.50	9.00	13.50	25.00
	1856	—	7.00	8.00	11.50	20.00
	1857	—	5.50	9.00	13.50	25.00

ZACATECAS MINT (Zs)

KM#	Date	Mintage	VG	Fine	VF	XF
368.8	1842/1 LR	—	3.50	6.50	10.00	18.50
	1842 LR	—	2.00	4.50	7.50	13.50

1/2 REAL

1.6900 gm., .903 SILVER, .0490 oz ASW

MEXICO CITY MINT (Mo)

Obv: Hooked neck eagle

KM#	Date	Mintage	Fine	VF	XF	Unc
369	1824 JM	—	25.00	50.00	100.00	175.00

ALAMOS MINT (A)

Obv: Facing eagle

KM#	Date	Mintage	Fine	VF	XF	Unc
370	1862 PG	—	—	—	Rare	—

CHIHUAHUA MINT (Ca)

KM#	Date	Mintage	Fine	VF	XF	Unc
370.1	1844 RG	—	75.00	100.00	150.00	250.00
	1845 RG	—	75.00	100.00	135.00	225.00

CULIACAN MINT (C)

KM#	Date	Mintage	Fine	VF	XF	Unc
370.2	1846 CE	—	25.00	42.50	65.00	125.00
	1848/7 CE	—	12.00	20.00	37.50	75.00
	1849/8 CE	—	10.00	15.00	20.00	50.00
	1852 CE	—	5.75	8.00	15.00	40.00
	1853/1 CE	—	8.00	12.50	25.00	50.00
	1854 CE	—	17.50	30.00	45.00	85.00
	1856 CE	—	9.00	15.00	22.50	55.00
	1857/6 CE	—	14.00	20.00	32.50	75.00
	1857 CE	—	14.00	20.00	32.50	75.00
	1858 CE	—	8.00	14.00	20.00	45.00
	1858 CE error 1 for 1/2					
		—	9.00	15.00	22.50	55.00
	1860 PV	—	3.00	4.50	17.50	35.00
	1861 PV	—	5.00	9.00	20.00	40.00
	1863 CE error 1 for 1/2					
		—	12.00	20.00	35.00	70.00
370.2	1867 CE	—	13.50	25.00	30.00	60.00
	1869 CE error 1 for 1/2					
		—	10.00	15.00	25.00	50.00

DURANGO MINT (Do)

KM#	Date	Mintage	Fine	VF	XF	Unc
370.3	1832 RM	—	17.00	30.00	40.00	80.00
	1833 RL	—	11.00	14.00	20.00	50.00
	1833/1 RM/L	—	12.50	15.00	22.50	65.00
	1833 RM	—	11.00	14.00	20.00	60.00
	1834 RM	—	11.00	14.00	20.00	40.00
	1837/6 RM	—	10.00	13.00	20.00	40.00
	1841/33 RM	—	14.50	20.00	30.00	55.00
	1842/32 RM	—	6.00	10.00	17.50	45.00
	1842 RM	—	6.00	10.00	17.50	45.00
	1843/33 RM	—	12.00	17.00	35.00	65.00
	1845/31 RM	—	8.00	15.00	20.00	50.00
	1845/34 RM	—	8.00	15.00	20.00	50.00
	1845/35 RM	—	8.00	15.00	20.00	50.00
	1846 RM	—	30.00	45.00	70.00	100.00
	1848/5 RM	—	13.50	35.00	37.50	75.00
	1848/6 RM	—	13.50	25.00	37.00	75.00
	1849 JMR	—	24.00	35.00	45.00	85.00
	1850 JMR	—	22.50	35.00	50.00	90.00
	1850 RM	—	—	—	—	—
	1851 JMR	—	20.00	30.00	50.00	80.00
	1852 JMR	—	30.00	45.00	75.00	125.00
	1853 CP	—	5.00	8.50	15.00	40.00
	1854 CP	—	20.00	30.00	40.00	75.00
	1855 CP	—	20.00	32.00	50.00	90.00
	1856/5 CP	—	12.00	15.00	20.00	50.00
	1857 CP	—	15.00	23.00	32.00	60.00
	1858/7 CP	—	12.00	14.00	25.00	50.00
	1859 CP	—	12.50	18.50	30.00	60.00
	1860/59 CP	—	15.00	22.00	32.50	55.00
	1861 CP	—	18.00	30.00	45.00	75.00
	1862 CP	—	18.50	30.00	45.00	75.00
	1864 LT	—	15.00	25.00	35.00	65.00
	1869 CP	—	15.00	25.00	35.00	65.00

ESTADO DE MEXICO MINT (Eo Mo)

KM#	Date	Mintage	Fine	VF	XF	Unc
370.4	1829 LF	—	140.00	225.00	325.00	500.00

GUADALAJARA MINT (Ga)

KM#	Date	Mintage	Fine	VF	XF	Unc
370.5	1825 FS	—	30.00	40.00	50.00	80.00
	1826 FS	—	11.00	14.50	20.00	45.00
	1828/7 FS	—	12.50	17.50	25.00	70.00
	1829 FS	—	4.50	7.00	17.50	50.00
	1830/29 FS	—	25.00	35.00	50.00	85.00
	1831 LP	—	20.00	30.00	42.50	90.00
	1832 FS	—	9.00	12.00	17.00	30.00
	1834 FS	—	9.00	12.00	18.50	50.00
	1835/4/3 FS/LP		10.00	17.50	22.50	40.00
	1837/6 JG	—	10.00	12.50	20.00	50.00
	1838/7 JG	—	12.00	15.00	20.00	45.00
	1839/8 JG/FS	—	8.50	12.00	17.50	40.00
	1839 MC	—	8.50	12.00	17.50	40.00
	1840 MC	—	12.00	15.00	20.00	45.00
	1841 MC	—	10.00	14.00	25.00	55.00
	1842 JG	—	4.00	7.00	15.00	35.00
	1843/2 JG	—	10.00	16.50	25.00	55.00
	1843 JG	—	8.50	15.00	27.50	60.00
	1843 MC/JG	—	8.00	14.00	25.00	55.00
	1843 MC	—	2.50	5.00	15.00	37.50
	1844 MC	—	2.00	5.00	15.00	37.50
	1845 MC	—	4.75	7.00	15.00	45.00
	1845 JG	—	4.75	7.00	15.00	45.00
	1846 MC	—	3.75	5.00	15.00	45.00
	1846 JG	—	3.75	5.00	15.00	40.00
	1847 JG	—	2.00	4.00	15.00	40.00
	1848/7 JG	—	5.75	8.00	15.00	45.00
	1849 JG	—	5.00	7.00	15.00	45.00
	1850 JG	—	3.75	5.00	15.00	45.00
	1851/0 JG	—	3.75	5.00	15.00	40.00
	1852 JG	—	4.00	8.00	15.00	50.00
	1853 JG	—	2.00	4.00	15.00	35.00
	1854 JG	—	6.00	10.00	15.00	45.00
	1855/4 JG	—	6.00	8.50	15.00	40.00
	1855 JG	—	6.00	10.00	15.00	45.00
	1856 JG	—	4.00	5.75	15.00	40.00
	1857 JG	—	5.00	7.75	15.00	45.00
	1858/7 JG	—	7.50	10.00	15.00	45.00
	1858 JG	—	6.50	9.00	15.00	45.00
	1859/7 JG	—	2.00	3.00	15.00	40.00
	1860/59 JG	—	3.00	5.00	15.00	35.00
	1861 JG	—	2.00	3.00	15.00	35.00
	1862/1 JG	—	8.50	12.00	16.00	55.00

GUADALUPE Y CALVO (GC)

KM#	Date	Mintage	Fine	VF	XF	Unc
370.6	1844 MP	—	25.00	42.50	60.00	100.00
	1845 MP	—	28.00	40.00	60.00	100.00
	1846 MP	—	25.00	37.50	55.00	125.00
	1847 MP	—	25.00	35.00	45.00	100.00
	1848 MP	—	22.50	35.00	45.00	90.00
	1849 MP	—	25.00	35.00	50.00	100.00
	1850 MP	—	30.00	37.50	55.00	115.00
	1851 MP	—	22.50	30.00	45.00	90.00

GUANAJUATO MINT (Go)

KM#	Date	Mintage	Fine	VF	XF	Unc
370.7	1826 MJ	—	4.00	8.00	17.00	40.00
	1827/6 MJ	—	2.50	3.50	15.00	25.00
	1828/7 MJ	—	3.00	4.50	15.00	60.00
	1828 MR	—	3.50	8.00	17.50	45.00
	1829 MJ	—	2.50	4.50	15.00	25.00
	1829 MJ with reversed N in MEXICANA					
		—	3.00	5.00	15.00	25.00
	1830 MJ	—	2.25	7.00	15.00	30.00
	1831/29 MJ	—	3.50	8.50	17.50	35.00
	1831 MJ	—	2.25	7.00	15.00	35.00
	1832/1 MJ	—	3.50	4.50	15.00	30.00
	1832 MJ	—	2.00	6.00	15.00	25.00
	1833 MJ with round top 3					
		—	2.00	5.00	15.00	30.00
	1833 MJ with flat top 3					
		—	2.00	5.00	15.00	30.00
	1834 PJ	—	2.00	5.00	15.00	25.00
	1835 PJ	—	2.00	5.00	15.00	25.00
	1836 PJ	—	2.00	5.00	15.00	30.00
	1837 PJ	—	2.00	5.00	15.00	30.00
	1838/7 PJ	—	4.50	5.75	15.00	25.00
	1839 PJ	—	2.00	5.00	15.00	30.00
	1839 PJ with error: REPUBLIGA					
		—	2.00	5.00	15.00	35.00
	1840 PJ straight J					
		—	2.00	5.00	15.00	25.00
	1840 PJ curved J					
		—	2.00	5.00	15.00	25.00
	1841/31 PJ	—	2.50	5.00	15.00	25.00
	1841 PJ	—	2.00	5.00	15.00	25.00
	1842/1 PJ	—	2.00	5.00	15.00	30.00
	1842 PJ	—	2.00	5.00	15.00	30.00
	1842/1 PM	—	2.00	5.00	15.00	30.00
	1842 PM/J	—	2.00	5.00	15.00	30.00
	1842 PM	—	2.00	5.00	15.00	30.00
	1843/33 PM with 1/2 over 8					
		—	3.50	4.50	15.00	25.00
	1843 PM with convex wings					
		—	2.50	5.00	15.00	25.00
	1843 PM with concave wings					
		—	2.50	5.00	15.00	25.00
	1844/3 PM	—	3.00	4.00	15.00	25.00
	1844 PM	—	2.00	4.00	15.00	25.00
	1845/4 PM	—	2.00	4.00	15.00	25.00
	1845 PM	—	2.00	4.00	15.00	25.00
	1846/4 PM	—	4.00	5.00	15.00	25.00
	1846/5 PM	—	4.00	5.00	15.00	25.00
	1846 PM	—	2.00	3.50	15.00	25.00
	1847/6 PM	—	3.00	4.00	15.00	25.00
	1847 PM	—	2.00	3.00	15.00	25.00
	1848 PM	—	2.00	4.00	15.00	25.00
	1848 PF/M	—	2.50	5.00	15.00	25.00
	1849/39 PF	—	4.00	6.50	15.00	35.00
	1849 PF	—	3.00	5.00	15.00	25.00
	1849 PF with error: MEXCANA					
		—	7.50	10.00	15.00	50.00
	1850 PF	—	2.00	4.00	15.00	25.00
	1851 PF	—	3.00	4.00	15.00	25.00
	1852/1 PF	—	2.00	3.00	15.00	25.00
	1852 PF	—	2.00	3.00	15.00	25.00
	1853 PF	—	2.00	3.00	15.00	25.00
	1854 PF	—	2.00	3.00	15.00	25.00
	1855 PF	—	2.00	3.00	15.00	25.00
	1856/4 PF	—	3.25	4.00	15.00	30.00
	1856/5 PF	—	3.25	4.00	15.00	30.00
	1856 PF	—	2.00	3.00	15.00	25.00
	1857/6 PF	—	3.00	4.00	15.00	30.00
	1857 PF	—	2.00	3.00	15.00	25.00
	1858/7 PF	—	4.50	7.00	15.00	30.00
	1858 PF	—	3.00	5.00	15.00	30.00
	1859 PF	—	2.00	3.00	15.00	25.00
	1860/59 PF small 1/2					
		—	2.00	3.00	15.00	30.00
	1860/59 PF large 1/2					
		—	2.00	3.00	15.00	30.00
	1861 PF sm.1/2		2.00	3.00	15.00	25.00
	1861 PF lg.1/2		2.00	3.00	15.00	25.00
	1862/1 YE	—	3.00	4.00	15.00	25.00
	1862 YE	—	2.00	3.00	15.00	25.00
	1862 YF	—	2.00	3.00	15.00	25.00
	1867 YF	—	2.00	3.00	15.00	20.00
	1868 YF	—	2.00	3.00	15.00	20.00
	1870 YF	—	—	—	—	—

HERMOSILLO MINT (Ho)

KM#	Date	Mintage	Fine	VF	XF	Unc
370.8	1839 PP	—	—	—	Unique	—
	1862 FM	—	50.00	75.00	125.00	200.00
	1867 PR/FM 6/inverted 6, & 7/1					
		—	32.50	50.00	85.00	125.00

MEXICO CITY MINT (Mo)

KM#	Date	Mintage	Fine	VF	XF	Unc
370.9	1825 JM	—	6.00	10.00	20.00	45.00
	1826 JM	—	2.50	6.50	15.00	30.00
	1827/6 JM	—	3.50	4.50	15.00	30.00

KM#	Date	Mintage	Fine	VF	XF	Unc
370.9	1827 JM		2.50	6.50	15.00	30.00
	1828/7 JM	—	11.00	15.00	20.00	50.00
	1828 JM	—	9.00	15.00	25.00	55.00
	1829 JM	—	4.25	7.00	15.00	35.00
	1830 JM	—	3.00	7.50	15.00	30.00
	1831 JM	—	2.25	7.00	15.00	35.00
	1832 JM	—	6.50	10.00	22.50	40.00
	1833 MJ	—	10.00	14.00	23.00	35.00
	1834 ML	—	2.00	6.00	15.00	28.00
	1835 ML	—	2.50	6.00	15.00	28.00
	1836/5 ML	—	5.50	7.00	15.00	35.00
	1836 ML	—	6.50	8.75	17.50	35.00
	1838 ML	—	2.00	6.00	15.00	30.00
	1839/8 ML	—	3.50	5.50	15.00	30.00
	1839 ML	—	2.00	5.00	15.00	30.00
	1840 ML	—	2.00	5.00	15.00	25.00
	1841 ML	—	2.00	5.00	15.00	25.00
	1842 ML	—	2.00	5.00	15.00	30.00
	1842 MM	—	2.00	5.00	15.00	30.00
	1844 MF	—	2.00	4.00	15.00	25.00
	1845/4 MF	—	2.00	4.00	15.00	25.00
	1845 MF	—	2.00	4.00	15.00	25.00
	1846 MF	—	2.00	4.00	15.00	25.00
	1847 RC	—	2.00	4.00	15.00	25.00
	1848/7 GC/~~RG~~		2.00	4.00	15.00	25.00
	1849 GC	—	2.00	3.00	15.00	25.00
	1850 GC	—	2.00	4.00	15.00	25.00
	1851 GC	—	2.00	3.00	15.00	25.00
	1852 GC	—	2.00	3.00	15.00	25.00
	1853 GC	—	2.00	3.00	10.00	25.00
	1854 GC	—	2.00	3.50	10.00	25.00
	1855 GC	—	2.00	3.00	10.00	25.00
	1855 GF/GC	—	2.00	3.00	10.00	25.00
	1856/5 GF	—	2.00	3.00	10.00	25.00
	1857 GF	—	2.00	3.00	10.00	25.00
	1858 FH	—	2.00	3.00	10.00	25.00
	1858/9 FH	—	3.25	4.00	10.00	30.00
	1859 FH	—	2.00	3.00	10.00	25.00
	1860/50 FH/GC		3.50	4.50	10.00	25.00
	1860 FH	—	2.00	3.00	10.00	25.00
	1860 TH	—	3.50	5.00	10.00	25.00
	1861 CH	—	2.00	3.00	10.00	20.00
	1862/52 CH	—	3.00	4.00	10.00	20.00
	1862 CH	—	2.00	3.00	10.00	20.00
	1863/55 TH/GC		3.50	5.00	10.00	20.00
	1863 CH	—	2.00	3.00	10.00	20.00

POTOSI MINT (Pi)

KM#	Date	Mintage	Fine	VF	XF	Unc
370.10	1831 JS	—	5.50	10.00	18.50	40.00
	1841/36 JS	—	25.00	35.00	45.00	75.00
	1842/1 PS/~~JS~~	—	25.00	35.00	50.00	90.00
	1842 JS	—	30.00	40.00	55.00	100.00
	1843/2 PS	—	13.50	17.50	25.00	55.00
	1843 PS	—	15.00	20.00	30.00	60.00
	1843 AM	—	11.00	15.00	20.00	50.00
	1844 AM	—	10.00	15.00	30.00	60.00
	1845 AM	—	27.50	40.00	60.00	90.00
	1846/5 AM	—	18.00	32.50	60.00	90.00
	1847/6 AM	—	10.00	15.00	20.00	45.00
	1848 AM	—	15.00	25.00	35.00	55.00
	1849 MC	—	12.50	21.50	35.00	55.00
	1850 MC	—	10.00	15.00	25.00	50.00
	1851 MC	—	8.50	14.00	23.00	45.00
	1852 MC	—	4.75	6.00	12.50	37.50
	1853 MC	—	7.00	11.50	17.00	45.00
	1854 MC	—	5.00	9.00	12.00	40.00
	1855 MC	—	15.00	20.00	30.00	50.00
	1856 MC	—	4.50	6.75	12.00	35.00
	1857 MC	—	8.50	12.00	20.00	45.00
	1857 PS	—	10.00	15.00	25.00	50.00
	1858 MC	—	11.00	20.00	30.00	60.00
	1859 MC	—	11.50	16.00	25.00	55.00
	1860/59 PS	—	12.00	15.00	22.00	45.00
	1861 RO	—	10.00	15.00	25.00	50.00
	1862 RO	—	8.00	11.00	15.00	40.00
	1863/2 RO	—	13.00	22.00	35.00	60.00

ZACATECAS MINT (Zs)

KM#	Date	Mintage	Fine	VF	XF	Unc
370.11	1826 AZ	—	2.50	6.50	15.00	30.00
	1826 AO	—	4.00	8.00	17.50	50.00
	1827 AO	—	2.50	6.50	15.00	40.00
	1828/7 AO	—	2.50	3.50	15.00	25.00
	1829 AO	—	4.00	8.00	15.00	30.00
	1830 OV	—	2.25	7.00	15.00	30.00
	1831 OV	—	2.25	6.00	15.00	25.00
	1831 OM	—	2.00	6.00	15.00	25.00
	1832 OM	—	2.00	6.00	15.00	25.00
	1833 OM	—	2.00	5.00	15.00	25.00
	1834 OM	—	2.00	6.00	15.00	30.00
	1835/4 OM	—	3.50	4.50	15.00	25.00
	1835 OM	—	2.00	5.00	15.00	25.00
	1836 OM	—	2.00	5.00	15.00	35.00
	1837 OM	—	2.00	5.00	15.00	30.00
	1838 OM	—	2.00	5.00	15.00	25.00
	1839 OM	—	2.00	5.00	15.00	30.00
	1840 OM	—	2.50	5.00	15.00	25.00
370.11	1841 OM	—	15.00	20.00	30.00	60.00
	1842/1 OM	—	2.00	5.00	15.00	30.00
	1843 OM	—	8.00	12.00	18.00	45.00
	1844 OM	—	4.00	6.00	15.00	30.00
	1845 OM	—	2.75	5.00	15.00	25.00
	1846 OM	—	2.00	4.00	15.00	30.00
	1847 OM	—	2.00	4.00	15.00	25.00
	1848 OM	—	2.00	4.00	15.00	25.00
	1849 OM	—	2.00	3.00	15.00	25.00
	1850 OM	—	3.75	5.00	15.00	30.00
	1851 OM	—	2.00	3.00	15.00	25.00
	1852 OM	—	2.00	3.00	15.00	25.00
	1853 OM	—	5.00	6.50	15.00	30.00
	1854/3 OM	—	5.00	6.50	15.00	30.00
	1854 OM	—	3.00	4.00	15.00	25.00
	1855 OM	—	3.00	5.00	15.00	30.00
	1856 OM	—	3.50	5.00	15.00	30.00
	1857 MO	—	2.00	3.00	15.00	25.00
	1858 MO	—	2.00	3.00	15.00	25.00
	1859 MO	—	5.00	6.50	15.00	30.00
	1859 VL	—	5.00	6.50	15.00	30.00
	1860 MO	—	2.00	3.00	15.00	25.00
	1860 VL	—	2.00	3.00	15.00	25.00
	1861 VL	—	2.00	3.00	15.00	25.00
	1862 VL	—	5.00	7.00	15.00	30.00
	1863 VL	—	5.00	8.00	15.00	25.00
	1869 YH	—	2.00	3.00	15.00	20.00

REAL

3.3800 gm., .903 SILVER, .0981 oz ASW

DURANGO MINT (Do)

Obv: Hooked-neck eagle

KM#	Date	Mintage	Fine	VF	XF	Unc
371	1824 RL	—	750.00	900.00	1500.	2250.

CHIHUAHUA MINT (Ca)

KM#	Date	Mintage	Fine	VF	XF	Unc
372	1844 RG	—	—	—	—	—
	1845 RG	—	90.00	110.00	135.00	175.00
	1855 RG	—	60.00	70.00	85.00	135.00

CULIACAN MINT (C)

KM#	Date	Mintage	Fine	VF	XF	Unc
372.1	1846 CE	—	12.50	15.00	30.00	75.00
	1848 CE	—	11.50	15.00	25.00	70.00
	1850 CE	—	7.00	9.00	20.00	65.00
	1851/0 CE	—	11.50	25.00	35.00	70.00
	1852/1 CE	—	4.50	5.75	15.00	45.00
	1853/2 CE	—	7.50	10.00	15.00	60.00
	1854 CE	—	7.50	10.00	18.00	65.00
	1856 CE	—	7.50	10.00	15.00	55.00
	1857/4 CE	—	7.00	9.00	15.00	60.00
	1857/6 CE	—	7.00	9.00	15.00	60.00
	1858 CE	—	4.00	5.50	12.00	50.00
	1859 CE	—	—	—	—	—
	1860 PV	—	5.00	7.00	15.00	60.00
	1861 PV	—	4.00	5.00	12.00	55.00
	1869 CE	—	3.50	4.50	10.00	50.00

DURANGO MINT (Do)

KM#	Date	Mintage	Fine	VF	XF	Unc
372.2	1832 RM	—	4.00	6.00	15.00	60.00
	1832/1 RM	—	5.00	6.50	15.00	60.00
	1832 RM/RL	—	5.00	6.00	15.00	55.00
	1834/2 RM/~~RL~~	—	10.00	12.50	25.00	65.00
	1834/3 RM/~~RL~~	—	10.00	12.50	25.00	65.00
	1834 RM	—	10.00	12.50	25.00	65.00
	1836/4 RM	—	4.50	6.00	12.00	50.00
	1836 RM	—	3.25	4.50	15.00	55.00
	1837 RM	—	12.50	15.00	30.00	60.00
	1841 RM	—	7.00	9.00	20.00	60.00
	1842/32 RM	—	8.50	11.00	18.00	60.00
	1842 RM	—	7.00	9.00	18.00	55.00
	1843 RM	—	4.50	5.75	15.00	55.00
	1844/34 RM	—	11.00	15.00	20.00	60.00
	1845 RM	—	3.25	5.50	15.00	60.00
	1846 RM	—	7.00	9.00	20.00	60.00
	1847 RM	—	10.00	15.00	20.00	50.00
	1848/31 RM	—	9.00	12.50	20.00	60.00
	1848/33 RM	—	9.00	12.00	20.00	60.00
	1848/5 RM	—	9.00	12.50	20.00	60.00
	1848 RM	—	7.50	10.00	18.00	55.00
	1849/8 CM	—	7.00	9.00	18.00	55.00
372.2	1850 JMR	—	15.00	24.00	35.00	70.00
	1851 JMR	—	15.00	20.00	30.00	65.00
	1852 JMR	—	15.00	25.00	35.00	70.00
	1853 CP	—	12.50	16.00	25.00	65.00
	1854/1 CP	—	9.00	12.00	20.00	60.00
	1854 CP	—	7.50	10.00	18.00	60.00
	1855 CP	—	9.00	12.00	20.00	65.00
	1856 CP	—	12.50	17.50	25.00	65.00
	1857 CP	—	11.50	15.00	20.00	65.00
	1858 CP	—	12.50	16.50	25.00	65.00
	1859 CP	—	7.50	10.00	15.00	60.00
	1860/59 CP	—	5.00	7.00	15.00	60.00
	1861 CP	—	14.00	20.00	35.00	65.00
	1862/1 CP	—	12.50	15.00	30.00	75.00
	1864 LT	—	15.00	20.00	30.00	75.00

ESTADO DE MEXICO MINT (EoMo)

KM#	Date	Mintage	Fine	VF	XF	Unc
372.3	1828 LF	—	175.00	275.00	450.00	600.00

GUADALAJARA MINT (Ga)

KM#	Date	Mintage	Fine	VF	XF	Unc
372.4	1826 FS	—	14.00	17.50	30.00	70.00
	1828/7 FS	—	18.00	25.00	40.00	75.00
	1829 FS	—	12.50	18.00	30.00	65.00
	1830 FS	—	12.00	18.00	30.00	65.00
	1831 LP	—	15.00	23.50	30.00	65.00
	1831 LP/FS	—	16.50	25.00	32.50	75.00
	1832 FS	—	15.00	26.00	35.00	70.00
	1833 FS	—	10.00	15.00	30.00	65.00
	1834/3 FS	—	10.00	15.00	30.00	65.00
	1835 FS	—	—	—	—	—
	1837/6 JG/~~FS~~		12.50	15.00	30.00	60.00
	1838/7 JG/~~FS~~		7.50	10.00	20.00	65.00
	1839 JG	—	12.50	15.00	30.00	65.00
	1840 JG	—	12.00	15.00	30.00	60.00
	1840 MC	—	7.50	10.00	18.00	50.00
	1841 MC	—	15.00	20.00	30.00	65.00
	1842/0 JG/~~MG~~		7.50	10.00	18.00	55.00
	1842 JG	—	6.00	8.00	15.00	55.00
	1843 JG	—	12.50	16.00	30.00	70.00
	1843 MC	—	4.00	5.00	15.00	50.00
	1844 MC	—	6.00	8.50	20.00	60.00
	1845 MC	—	10.00	12.50	20.00	60.00
	1845 JG	—	4.00	6.00	15.00	55.00
	1846 JG	—	12.50	15.00	30.00	65.00
	1847/6 JG	—	10.00	15.00	20.00	50.00
	1847 JG	—	10.00	15.00	20.00	50.00
	1848 JG	—	—	—	—	—
	1849 JG	—	7.00	9.00	18.00	55.00
	1850 JG	—	12.00	15.00	30.00	70.00
	1851 JG	—	10.00	12.50	18.00	55.00
	1852 JG	—	10.00	12.50	20.00	55.00
	1853/2 JG	—	10.00	12.50	18.00	55.00
	1854 JG	—	11.00	15.00	25.00	60.00
	1855 JG	—	18.00	22.50	30.00	70.00
	1856 JG	—	7.00	9.00	15.00	50.00
	1857/6 JG	—	12.50	17.50	25.00	65.00
	1858/7 JG	—	15.00	22.50	25.00	70.00
	1859/8 JG	—	12.50	16.50	25.00	65.00
	1860/59 JG	—	5.00	7.00	15.00	60.00
	1861/0 JG	—	16.00	22.50	35.00	70.00
	1861 JG	—	14.00	20.00	35.00	65.00
	1862 JG	—	7.00	9.00	15.00	65.00

GUADALUPE Y CALVO MINT (GC)

KM#	Date	Mintage	Fine	VF	XF	Unc
372.5	1844 MP	—	45.00	65.00	85.00	150.00
	1845 MP	—	40.00	50.00	75.00	135.00
	1846 MP	—	30.00	50.00	75.00	135.00
	1847 MP	—	40.00	55.00	75.00	135.00
	1848 MP	—	35.00	50.00	70.00	125.00
	1849/7 MP	—	32.50	50.00	80.00	140.00
	1849/8 MP	—	32.50	50.00	80.00	140.00
	1849 MP	—	30.00	45.00	75.00	135.00
	1850 MP	—	30.00	45.00	75.00	135.00
	1851 MP	—	30.00	50.00	75.00	135.00

GUANAJUATO MINT (Go)

KM#	Date	Mintage	Fine	VF	XF	Unc
372.6	1826/5 JJ	—	3.00	4.00	10.00	45.00
	1826 MJ	—	2.25	3.00	10.00	45.00
	1827 MJ	—	3.75	5.00	12.00	50.00
	1827 JM	—	7.75	10.00	18.50	55.00
	1828/7 MR	—	3.25	4.00	10.00	45.00
	1828 MJ, straight J, small 8	—	2.25	3.00	10.00	45.00
	1828Go MJ, full J, large 8	—	2.25	3.00	10.00	45.00
	1828G MJ, full J, large 8	—	2.25	3.00	10.00	45.00
	1828 MR	—	2.25	3.00	10.00	45.00
	1829/8 MG with small eagle	—	2.25	3.00	10.00	40.00
	1829 MJ with small eagle	—	2.25	3.00	10.00	40.00
	1829 MJ with large eagle	—	2.25	3.00	10.00	40.00
	1830 MJ with small initials	—	2.25	3.00	10.00	40.00

KM#	Date	Mintage	Fine	VF	XF	Unc
372.6	1830 MJ with medium initials	—	2.25	3.00	10.00	40.00
	1830 MJ with large initials	—	2.25	3.00	10.00	40.00
	1830 MJ with reversed N in MEXICANA	—	2.25	3.00	10.00	40.00
	1831/0 MJ with reversed N in MEXICANA	—	2.75	3.50	12.50	55.00
	1831 MJ	—	2.25	3.00	10.00	45.00
	1832 MJ	—	2.25	3.00	10.00	45.00
	1833 MJ top of 3 round	—	2.25	3.00	10.00	40.00
	1833 MJ top of 3 flat	—	2.25	3.00	10.00	40.00
	1834 PJ	—	2.25	3.00	10.00	40.00
	1835 PJ	—	5.50	6.50	10.00	40.00
	1836 PJ	—	2.00	4.00	10.00	40.00
	1837 PJ	—	2.25	3.00	10.00	40.00
	1838/7 PJ	—	2.00	3.00	10.00	40.00
	1839 PJ	—	2.25	3.00	10.00	45.00
	1840/39 PJ	—	3.50	4.50	10.00	45.00
	1840 PJ	—	2.25	3.00	10.00	45.00
	1841/31 PJ	—	3.00	4.50	12.00	50.00
	1841 PJ	—	2.00	3.00	10.00	40.00
	1842 PJ	—	4.00	5.00	10.00	45.00
	1842 PM	—	3.00	4.00	10.00	45.00
	1843 PM with convex wings	—	2.25	4.00	10.00	45.00
	1843 PM with concave wings	—	2.25	4.00	10.00	45.00
	1844 PM	—	2.00	4.00	10.00	40.00
	1845/4 PM	—	2.50	4.00	12.00	45.00
	1845 PM	—	1.50	3.00	10.00	40.00
	1846 PM	—	2.00	3.00	10.00	40.00
	1847/6 PM	—	2.00	3.00	10.00	40.00
	1847 PM	—	2.00	3.00	10.00	40.00
	1848 PM	—	3.25	4.50	10.00	40.00
	1849 PF	—	2.00	3.00	10.00	40.00
	1850 PF	—	3.25	4.50	10.00	40.00
	1851 PF	—	3.25	4.50	10.00	40.00
	1853 PF	—	2.00	3.00	10.00	40.00
	1854/3 PF	—	3.50	4.50	10.00	45.00
	1854 PF, large eagle	—	2.00	3.00	10.00	40.00
	1854 PF, small eagle	—	2.00	3.00	10.00	40.00
	1855/3 PF	—	3.50	4.50	12.00	45.00
	1855/4 PF	—	3.50	4.50	12.00	45.00
	1855 PF	—	2.00	3.00	10.00	40.00
	1856/5 PF	—	3.50	4.50	10.00	45.00
	1856 PF	—	2.00	3.00	10.00	40.00
	1857/6 PF	—	3.50	4.50	12.00	50.00
	1857 PF	—	2.00	3.00	10.00	45.00
	1858 PF	—	2.00	3.00	10.00	45.00
	1859 PF	—	2.00	3.00	10.00	50.00
	1860/50 PF	—	3.00	4.00	10.00	50.00
	1860 PF	—	2.00	3.00	10.00	50.00
	1861 PF	—	2.00	3.00	10.00	50.00
	1862 YE	—	2.00	3.00	10.00	50.00
	1862 YF	—	2.00	3.00	12.00	55.00
	1867 YF	—	2.00	3.00	12.00	50.00
	1868/7 YF	—	2.00	3.00	12.00	50.00

HERMOSILLO MINT (Ho)

KM#	Date	Mintage	Fine	VF	XF	Unc
372.7	1867/1 PR	—	38.50	55.00	75.00	125.00
	1867/7 PR	—	38.50	55.00	75.00	125.00
	1868 PR	—	55.00	65.00	90.00	150.00

MEXICO CITY MINT (Mo)

KM#	Date	Mintage	Fine	VF	XF	Unc
372.8	1825 JM	—	7.00	9.00	18.00	60.00
	1826 JM	—	2.25	3.00	10.00	45.00
	1827 JM	—	2.25	3.00	10.00	50.00
	1828 JM	—	4.00	6.00	15.00	65.00
	1830/29 JM	—	3.25	4.50	10.00	40.00
	1830 JM	—	2.25	3.00	10.00	45.00
	1831 JM	—	4.50	6.00	10.00	45.00
	1832 JM	—	3.25	4.50	10.00	40.00
	1833/2 MJ	—	3.25	4.50	9.00	40.00
	1850 GC	—	3.25	4.50	10.00	40.00
	1852 GC	—	3.25	4.50	10.00	40.00
	1854 GC	—	7.50	10.00	15.00	45.00
	1855 GF	—	2.00	3.00	10.00	40.00
	1856 GF	—	2.00	3.50	10.00	40.00
	1857 GF	—	3.00	4.00	10.00	45.00
	1858 FH	—	2.00	3.00	10.00	45.00
	1859 FH	—	2.00	3.00	10.00	50.00
	1861 CH	—	2.00	3.00	10.00	45.00
	1862 CH	—	2.00	3.00	12.00	55.00
	1863/2 CH	—	2.00	3.00	12.00	55.00

POTOSI MINT (Pi)

KM#	Date	Mintage	Fine	VF	XF	Unc
372.9	1831 JS	—	5.00	7.00	18.00	55.00
	1837 JS	—	7.50	10.00	18.00	55.00
	1838 JS	—	20.00	30.00	40.00	75.00
	1840/39 JS	—	7.50	10.00	20.00	50.00
	1840 JS	—	6.00	8.00	20.00	55.00
372.9	1841 JS	—	8.50	10.00	18.00	55.00
	1842 JS	—	10.00	15.00	30.00	60.00
	1842 PS	—	4.50	5.75	18.00	50.00
	1843 PS	—	11.00	15.00	20.00	65.00
	1843 AM	—	11.00	15.00	20.00	60.00
	1844 AM	—	10.00	12.50	20.00	65.00
	1845 AM	—	7.00	9.00	18.00	55.00
	1846/5 AM	—	3.25	4.50	12.00	55.00
	1847/6 AM	—	7.00	9.00	18.00	55.00
	1847 AM	—	7.00	9.00	18.00	55.00
	1848/7 AM	—	7.00	9.00	18.00	55.00
	1849 PS	—	7.00	9.00	18.00	60.00
	1849 SP	—	15.00	25.00	40.00	75.00
	1850 MC	—	4.00	5.00	10.00	40.00
	1851/0 MC	—	7.50	10.00	15.00	45.00
	1851 MC	—	6.00	8.00	12.00	55.00
	1852/1 MC	—	8.00	11.00	20.00	65.00
	1852 MC	—	7.00	9.00	15.00	60.00
	1853/1 MC	—	11.50	15.00	18.50	60.00
	1853 MC	—	9.50	12.50	16.00	55.00
	1854/3 MC	—	13.00	17.50	25.00	55.00
	1855/4 MC	—	14.00	20.00	27.50	55.00
	1855 MC	—	12.50	17.50	25.00	55.00
	1856 MC	—	14.00	20.00	30.00	65.00
	1857 PS	—	20.00	30.00	40.00	80.00
	1858 MC	—	12.50	16.50	25.00	65.00
	1859 PS	—	10.00	12.50	18.00	65.00
	1860/59 PS	—	10.00	12.50	18.00	55.00
	1861 PS	—	7.50	10.00	20.00	60.00
	1861 RO	—	12.50	15.00	30.00	70.00
	1862/1 RO	—	8.50	11.00	17.00	65.00
	1862 RO	—	7.00	9.00	15.00	60.00

ZACATECAS MINT (Zs)

KM#	Date	Mintage	Fine	VF	XF	Unc
372.10	1826 AZ	—	2.25	3.00	10.00	45.00
	1826 AO	—	3.25	5.00	15.00	50.00
	1827 AO	—	3.25	5.00	10.00	45.00
	1828 AO	—	2.25	4.00	10.00	45.00
	1828 VO	—	2.25	4.00	10.00	45.00
	1829 AO	—	2.25	3.00	10.00	40.00
	1830 ZsOV	—	3.00	4.50	10.00	40.00
	1830 ZOV	—	4.00	5.00	10.00	40.00
	1831 OV	—	2.25	3.00	10.00	45.00
	1831 OM	—	3.25	5.00	10.00	40.00
	1832 OM	—	2.25	3.00	10.00	40.00
	1833/2 OM	—	3.50	4.50	12.00	45.00
	1833 OM	—	2.25	3.00	10.00	40.00
	1834/3 OM	—	3.50	4.50	10.00	45.00
	1834 OM	—	2.25	3.00	10.00	40.00
	1835/4 OM	—	2.50	4.00	10.00	40.00
	1835 OM	—	2.25	3.00	10.00	40.00
	1836/5 OM	—	3.50	4.50	12.00	45.00
	1836 OM	—	2.25	3.00	10.00	40.00
	1837 OM	—	2.25	3.00	10.00	40.00
	1838 OM	—	2.25	3.00	10.00	45.00
	1839 OM	—	2.25	3.00	10.00	45.00
	1840 OM	—	2.25	3.00	10.00	40.00
	1841 OM	—	2.00	3.00	10.00	40.00
	1842/1 OM	—	3.50	4.50	10.00	45.00
	1842 OM	—	2.00	3.00	10.00	45.00
	1843 OM	—	2.00	3.00	10.00	45.00
	1844 OM	—	2.00	3.00	10.00	45.00
	1845 OM	—	2.00	3.00	10.00	40.00
	1846 OM using old font and obv.	—	2.00	3.00	10.00	40.00
	1846 OM using new font and obv.	—	2.00	3.00	10.00	40.00
	1847 OM	—	2.00	3.00	10.00	40.00
	1848 OM	—	2.00	3.00	10.00	40.00
	1849 OM	—	2.00	3.00	10.00	40.00
	1850 OM	—	3.25	4.50	10.00	40.00
	1851 OM	—	2.00	3.00	10.00	40.00
	1852 OM	—	2.00	3.00	10.00	40.00
	1853 OM	—	2.00	3.00	10.00	40.00
	1854/2 OM	—	3.50	4.50	12.00	45.00
	1854/3 OM	—	3.50	4.50	12.00	45.00
	1854 OM	—	2.00	3.00	10.00	40.00
	1855/4 OM	—	3.50	4.50	12.00	55.00
	1855 OM	—	2.00	3.00	10.00	40.00
	1855 MO	—	2.00	3.50	10.00	40.00
	1856 MO	—	2.00	3.00	10.00	40.00
	1857 MO	—	2.00	3.00	10.00	45.00
	1858 MO	—	2.25	3.00	10.00	45.00
	1859 MO	—	1.50	3.00	10.00	50.00
	1860 VL	—	2.00	3.00	10.00	50.00
	1861 VL	—	2.00	3.00	12.00	50.00
	1862 VL	—	2.00	3.00	12.00	55.00
	1868 JS	—	15.00	25.00	60.00	135.00
	1869 YH	—	2.00	3.00	12.00	50.00

2 REALES

6.7600 gm., .903 SILVER, .1962 oz ASW

DURANGO MINT (Do)

Obv: Hooked-neck eagle

KM#	Date	Mintage	Fine	VF	XF	Unc
373.1	1824 RL	—	60.00	125.00	300.00	550.00

DURANGO MINT (D)

KM#	Date	Mintage	Fine	VF	XF	Unc
373.2	1824 RL	—	100.00	200.00	500.00	1000.

MEXICO CITY MINT (Mo)

KM#	Date	Mintage	Fine	VF	XF	Unc
373.3	1824 JM	—	15.00	25.00	45.00	85.00

ALAMOS MINT (A)

Obv: Facing eagle with reeded edge

KM#	Date	Mintage	Fine	VF	XF	Unc
374	1872 AM	.015	42.50	55.00	85.00	150.00

REAL DE CATORCE MINT (Ce)

KM#	Date	Mintage	Fine	VF	XF	Unc
374.1	1863 ML	—	100.00	165.00	250.00	400.00

CHIHUAHUA MINT (Ca)

KM#	Date	Mintage	Fine	VF	XF	Unc
374.2	1832 MR	—	45.00	60.00	75.00	120.00
	1833 MR	—	25.00	50.00	75.00	115.00
	1834 MR	—	35.00	50.00	75.00	120.00
	1834 AM	—	40.00	60.00	80.00	125.00
	1835 AM	—	30.00	45.00	65.00	100.00
	1836 AM	—	20.00	28.50	37.50	80.00
	1845 RG	—	25.00	35.00	45.00	100.00
	1855 RG	—	30.00	37.50	50.00	80.00

CULIACAN MINT (C)

KM#	Date	Mintage	Fine	VF	XF	Unc
374.3	1846/1146 CE	—	15.00	22.50	30.00	75.00
	1847 CE	—	8.50	13.00	18.00	75.00
	1848 CE	—	12.50	20.00	25.00	70.00
	1850 CE	—	30.00	37.50	47.50	90.00
	1851 CE	—	11.50	15.00	25.00	75.00
	1852/1 CE	—	6.50	10.00	18.00	60.00
	1853/2 CE	—	10.00	15.00	22.50	65.00
	1854 CE	—	15.00	22.50	35.00	75.00
	1856 CE	—	17.50	25.00	35.00	65.00
	1857 CE	—	10.00	15.00	22.50	55.00
	1860 PV	—	10.00	15.00	22.50	60.00
	1861 PV	—	18.00	22.50	30.00	75.00
	1869 CE	—	10.00	16.00	30.00	75.00

DURANGO MINT (Do)

KM#	Date	Mintage	Fine	VF	XF	Unc
374.4	1826 RL	—	17.50	25.00	35.00	75.00
	1832 RM style of pre-1832	—	17.50	25.00	35.00	80.00
	1832 RM style of post-1832	—	17.50	25.00	35.00	80.00
	1834/2 RM	—	5.50	8.50	18.50	70.00
	1834/3 RM	—	5.50	8.50	18.00	70.00
	1835/4 RM/RL	—	10.00	16.00	25.00	65.00
	1841 RM	—	9.00	15.00	20.00	75.00
	1842/32 RM	—	11.50	15.00	25.00	75.00
	1843 RM/RL	—	6.50	10.00	15.00	70.00
	1844 RM	—	17.50	25.00	35.00	80.00
	1845/34 RM/RL	—	8.50	13.00	20.00	65.00
	1846/36 RM	—	8.50	13.00	25.00	75.00
	1848/36 RM	—	12.00	18.50	25.00	75.00
	1848/7 RM	—	11.50	17.50	25.00	75.00
	1848 RM	—	10.50	16.00	25.00	75.00
	1849 CM	—	6.00	9.00	18.00	65.00
	1851 JMR/RL	—	12.00	16.00	25.00	75.00
	1852 JMR	—	10.00	18.00	26.00	60.00
	1854 CP/CR	—	30.00	37.50	50.00	80.00
	1855 CP	—	50.00	60.00	75.00	100.00
	1856 CP	—	50.00	60.00	85.00	110.00
	1858 CP	—	12.50	20.00	26.00	55.00
	1859/8 CP	—	10.00	20.00	32.50	70.00
	1861 CP	—	12.50	20.00	30.00	75.00

ESTADO DE MEXICO MINT (Eo Mo)

KM#	Date	Mintage	Fine	VF	XF	Unc
374.5	1828 LF	—	250.00	400.00	600.00	850.00

GUADALAJARA MINT (Ga)

KM#	Date	Mintage	Fine	VF	XF	Unc
374.6	1825 FS	—	15.00	18.00	28.00	75.00
	1826 FS	—	7.00	9.00	18.00	70.00
	1828/7 FS	—	17.50	25.00	35.00	75.00
	1829 FS	—	10.00	15.00	25.00	75.00
	1832 FS	—	6.50	10.00	18.00	70.00
	1833/2 FS/LP	—	12.00	15.00	25.00	75.00
	1834 FS	—	10.00	15.00	25.00	75.00
	1837 JG	—	10.00	14.00	25.00	70.00
	1838 JG	—	10.00	15.00	22.00	75.00
	1840/30 MC	—	6.00	9.00	18.00	75.00
	1841 MC	—	11.50	15.00	20.00	75.00
	1842/32 JC	—	6.50	10.00	15.00	70.00
	1842 JG	—	6.50	10.00	15.00	70.00
	1842 JG/MC	—	6.00	9.00	12.50	70.00
	1843 JG	—	9.00	15.00	22.50	75.00
	1843 MC/JG	—	8.00	11.50	17.00	70.00
	1844 MC	—	6.50	11.50	18.00	70.00
	1845/3 MC/JG		6.50	10.00	15.00	65.00
	1845 JG	—	6.50	10.00	20.00	75.00
	1846 JG	—	6.50	10.00	18.00	70.00
	1847/6 JG	—	6.50	10.00	18.00	75.00
	1848/7 JG	—	10.00	13.00	20.00	70.00
	1849 JG	—	10.00	13.00	25.00	75.00
	1850/40 JG	—	7.50	11.50	16.00	60.00
	1851 JG	—	—	—	—	—
	1852 JG	—	10.00	15.00	22.00	55.00
	1853/1 JG	—	6.00	9.00	18.00	60.00
	1854 JG	—	42.50	50.00	65.00	85.00
	1855 JG	—	18.00	22.50	30.00	70.00
	1856 JG	—	10.00	15.00	20.00	60.00
	1857 JG	—	10.00	16.00	25.00	60.00
	1859/8 JG	—	12.00	18.00	25.00	60.00
	1859 JG	—	10.00	16.00	25.00	60.00
	1862/1 JG	—	7.50	11.50	20.00	65.00

GUADALUPE Y CALVO MINT (GC)

KM#	Date	Mintage	Fine	VF	XF	Unc
374.7	1844 MP	—	35.00	55.00	75.00	150.00
	1845 MP	—	35.00	45.00	65.00	135.00
	1846 MP	—	35.00	55.00	75.00	150.00
	1847 MP	—	35.00	47.50	65.00	150.00
	1848 MP	—	30.00	45.00	65.00	125.00
	1850 MP	—	42.50	60.00	80.00	160.00
	1851/0 MP	—	46.50	60.00	90.00	175.00
	1851 MP	—	42.50	55.00	80.00	160.00

GUANAJUATO MINT (Go)

KM#	Date	Mintage	Fine	VF	XF	Unc
374.8	1825 JJ	—	6.50	11.50	18.00	70.00
	1826/5 JJ	—	6.50	11.50	18.00	65.00
	1826 JJ	—	6.00	8.00	12.00	65.00
	1826 MJ	—	6.00	8.00	12.00	65.00
	1827/6 MJ	—	6.00	8.50	14.00	65.00
	1827 MJ	—	6.00	8.00	12.00	65.00
	1828/7 MR	—	7.50	11.50	20.00	70.00
	1828 MJ	—	6.00	8.00	12.00	65.00
	1828 JM	—	6.00	8.00	14.00	70.00
	1829 MJ	—	6.00	8.00	12.00	65.00
	1831 MJ	—	6.00	8.00	14.00	65.00
	1832 MJ	—	6.00	8.00	12.00	60.00
	1833 MJ	—	6.00	8.00	12.00	60.00
	1834 PJ	—	6.00	8.00	12.00	60.00
	1835 PJ	—	6.00	8.00	12.00	60.00
	1836 PJ	—	6.00	8.00	12.00	60.00
	1837/6 PJ	—	6.00	8.00	12.00	60.00
	1837 PJ	—	6.00	8.00	12.00	60.00
	1838/7 PJ	—	6.00	8.00	17.00	65.00
	1838 PJ	—	6.00	8.00	12.00	60.00
	1839 PJ	—	6.00	8.00	12.00	60.00
	1840 PJ	—	6.00	8.00	12.00	60.00
	1841 PJ	—	6.00	8.00	12.00	60.00
	1842 PJ	—	6.00	8.00	12.00	60.00
	1842 PM/PJ	—	6.00	8.00	12.00	60.00
	1842 PM	—	6.00	8.00	12.00	60.00
	1843/2 PM concave wings, thin rays, sm. letters	—	6.00	8.00	12.00	60.00
	1843 PM convex wings, thick rays & lg. letters	—	6.00	8.00	9.00	60.00
	1844 PM	—	6.00	8.00	12.00	60.00
	1845/4 PM	—	6.00	8.00	14.00	65.00
	1845 PM	—	6.00	8.00	12.00	60.00
	1846 PM	—	6.00	8.00	12.00	60.00
	1847 PM	—	6.00	8.00	12.00	60.00
	1848/7 PM	—	9.00	12.50	17.50	75.00
	1848 PM	—	7.50	11.00	15.00	60.00
	1848 PF	—	30.00	37.50	47.50	80.00
	1849/8 PF/PM		6.00	8.00	12.00	60.00
	1849 PF	—	6.00	8.00	12.00	60.00
	1850/40 PF	—	6.00	8.00	18.00	65.00
	1850 PF	—	6.00	8.00	12.00	60.00
	1851 PF	—	6.00	8.00	12.00	60.00
	1852/1 PF	—	6.00	8.00	12.00	45.00
	1852 PF	—	6.00	8.00	12.00	45.00
374.8	1853 PF	—	6.00	8.00	12.00	45.00
	1854 PF old font and obv.	—	6.00	8.00	12.00	40.00
	1854 PF new font and obv.	—	6.00	8.00	12.00	40.00
	1855 PF	—	6.00	8.00	12.00	45.00
	1855 PF with star in G of mintmark	—	6.00	8.50	14.00	55.00
	1856 PF	—	10.00	13.00	17.50	55.00
	1857/6 PF	—	6.00	8.50	16.00	45.00
	1857 PF	—	6.00	8.00	12.00	40.00
	1858/7 PF	—	6.00	8.00	17.00	45.00
	1858 PF	—	6.00	8.00	12.00	40.00
	1859/7 PF	—	6.00	8.00	15.00	45.00
	1859 PF	—	6.00	8.00	14.00	45.00
	1860/50 PF	—	6.00	8.00	16.00	50.00
	1860/59 PF	—	6.00	8.00	16.00	50.00
	1860 PF	—	6.00	8.00	14.00	45.00
	1861/51 PF	—	6.00	8.50	17.00	65.00
	1861/57 PF	—	6.00	8.50	17.00	65.00
	1861/0 PF	—	6.00	8.50	17.00	65.00
	1861 PF	—	6.00	8.00	12.00	45.00
	1862/1 YE	—	6.00	8.50	17.00	60.00
	1862 YE	—	6.00	8.00	14.00	55.00
	1862 YE/PF	—	6.00	8.50	17.00	60.00
	1862 YF	—	6.00	8.00	14.00	55.00
	1863/52 YF	—	6.00	8.00	15.00	65.00
	1863 YF	—	6.00	8.00	15.00	65.00
	1867/57 YF	—	6.00	8.00	14.00	55.00
	1868/57 YF	—	10.00	13.50	25.00	65.00

HERMOSILLO MINT (Ho)

KM#	Date	Mintage	Fine	VF	XF	Unc
374.9	1861 FM	—	120.00	165.00	250.00	375.00
	1862/52 FM/C CE	—	150.00	200.00	275.00	400.00
	1867/1 PR/FM		47.50	65.00	80.00	135.00

MEXICO CITY MINT (Mo)

KM#	Date	Mintage	Fine	VF	XF	Unc
374.10	1825 JM	—	6.00	8.00	13.00	80.00
	1826 JM	—	6.00	8.00	14.00	90.00
	1827 JM	—	6.00	8.00	12.00	85.00
	1828 JM	—	6.00	8.00	12.00	85.00
	1829/8 JM	—	6.00	8.00	14.00	85.00
	1829 JM	—	6.00	8.00	12.00	85.00
	1830 JM	—	6.00	8.00	12.00	85.00
	1831 JM	—	6.00	8.50	14.00	85.00
	1832 JM	—	6.00	8.50	14.00	80.00
	1833/2 MJ/JM		10.00	15.00	22.00	80.00
	1834 ML	—	6.00	8.00	12.00	75.00
	1836 ML	—	6.00	8.00	15.00	75.00
	1836 MF	—	6.00	8.00	12.00	70.00
	1837 ML	—	7.50	14.00	22.00	80.00
	1840 ML	—	6.00	8.00	16.00	70.00
	1841 ML	—	6.00	8.00	10.00	70.00
	1842 ML	—	6.00	8.00	12.00	70.00
	1847 RC	—	6.00	8.00	12.00	70.00
	1848 GC	—	6.00	8.00	12.00	70.00
	1849 GC	—	6.00	8.00	12.00	70.00
	1850 GC	—	6.00	8.00	12.00	70.00
	1851 GC	—	6.00	8.00	12.00	70.00
	1852 GC	—	6.00	8.00	12.00	70.00
	1853 GC	—	6.00	8.00	18.00	70.00
	1854/44 GC	—	6.00	8.00	12.00	70.00
	1855 GC	—	6.00	8.50	12.00	75.00
	1855 GF/GC	—	6.00	10.00	18.00	80.00
	1855 GF	—	6.00	8.00	12.00	75.00
	1856/5 GF/GC		6.00	8.00	12.00	70.00
	1857 GF	—	6.00	8.00	13.00	75.00
	1858 FH	—	6.00	8.00	12.00	70.00
	1858 FH/GH	—	6.00	8.00	17.00	75.00
	1859 FH	—	6.00	8.00	12.00	70.00
	1860 FH	—	6.00	8.00	15.00	75.00
	1860 TH	—	6.00	8.00	14.00	75.00
	1861 TH	—	6.00	8.00	15.00	85.00
	1861 CH	—	6.00	8.00	15.00	80.00
	1862 CH	—	6.00	8.00	14.00	75.00
	1863 CH	—	6.00	8.00	15.00	75.00
	1863 TH	—	6.00	8.00	15.00	75.00
	1867 CH	—	6.00	8.00	13.50	70.00
	1868 CH	—	9.00	12.00	18.00	75.00
	1868 PH	—	6.00	8.00	15.00	75.00

POTOSI MINT (Pi)

KM#	Date	Mintage	Fine	VF	XF	Unc
374.11	1829 JS	—	9.00	14.00	25.00	75.00
	1830/20 JS	—	10.00	15.00	25.00	75.00
	1837 JS	—	10.00	15.00	22.00	70.00
	1841 JS	—	6.00	9.00	14.00	70.00
	1842/1 JS	—	6.50	10.00	18.50	70.00
	1842 JS	—	6.00	8.00	14.00	65.00
	1842 PS	—	17.50	25.00	35.00	75.00
	1843 PS	—	10.00	16.00	22.00	65.00
	1843 AM	—	6.00	9.00	20.00	65.00
	1844 AM	—	6.00	8.00	14.00	65.00
	1845 AM	—	6.00	9.00	15.00	70.00
	1846 AM	—	6.50	10.00	18.00	70.00
	1849 MC	—	7.50	11.50	18.00	70.00
374.11	1850 MC	—	7.50	11.50	18.00	70.00
	1856 MC	—	40.00	50.00	65.00	90.00
	1858 MC	—	12.50	20.00	30.00	65.00
	1859 MC	—	50.00	70.00	100.00	110.00
	1861 PS	—	10.00	15.00	25.00	75.00
	1862 RO	—	10.00	16.00	30.00	75.00
	1863 RO	—	18.00	22.50	35.00	75.00
	1868 PS	—	6.00	9.00	16.00	60.00
	1869/8 PS	—	10.00	13.50	22.00	75.00
	1869 PS	—	8.50	13.00	20.00	65.00

ZACATECAS MINT (Zs)

KM#	Date	Mintage	Fine	VF	XF	Unc
374.12	1825 AZ	—	7.50	11.50	18.50	70.00
	1826 AV (A is inverted V)	—	6.00	9.00	18.00	70.00
	1826 AZ A is inverted V	—	6.00	8.00	12.00	60.00
	1826 AO	—	7.50	11.50	18.00	70.00
	1827 AO (A is inverted V)	—	6.00	8.00	12.00	65.00
	1828/7 AO	—	—	—	—	—
	1828 AO	—	6.00	8.00	12.00	65.00
	1828 AO (A is inverted V)	—	6.00	8.00	12.00	65.00
	1829 AO	—	6.00	8.00	12.00	65.00
	1829 OV	—	6.00	8.00	12.00	65.00
	1830 OV	—	6.00	8.00	12.50	60.00
	1831 OV	—	6.00	8.00	12.00	60.00
	1831 OM/OV	—	6.00	8.00	12.00	60.00
	1831 OM	—	6.00	8.00	12.00	60.00
	1832 OM	—	6.00	8.00	14.00	65.00
	1833/27 OM	—	6.00	8.00	14.00	65.00
	1833/2 OM	—	6.00	8.00	14.00	65.00
	1833 OM	—	6.00	8.00	12.00	60.00
	1834 OM	—	6.00	8.00	12.00	60.00
	1835 OM	—	6.00	8.00	12.00	60.00
	1836 OM	—	6.00	8.00	12.00	60.00
	1837 OM	—	6.00	8.00	12.00	60.00
	1838 OM	—	6.00	8.00	12.00	60.00
	1839 OM	—	6.00	8.00	12.00	60.00
	1840 OM	—	6.00	8.00	12.00	60.00
	1841/0 OM	—	6.00	8.00	12.00	65.00
	1841 OM	—	6.00	8.00	12.00	65.00
	1842 OM	—	6.00	8.00	12.00	60.00
	1843 OM	—	6.00	8.00	12.00	60.00
	1844 OM	—	6.00	8.00	12.00	60.00
	1845 OM small letters and small leaves	—	6.00	8.00	12.00	60.00
	1845 OM large letters and small leaves	—	6.00	8.00	12.00	60.00
	1846 OM	—	6.00	8.00	12.00	60.00
	1847 OM	—	6.00	8.00	12.00	60.00
	1848 OM	—	6.00	8.00	12.00	60.00
	1849 OM	—	6.00	8.00	12.00	60.00
	1850 OM	—	6.00	8.00	12.00	60.00
	1851 OM	—	6.00	8.00	12.00	60.00
	1852 OM	—	6.00	8.00	12.00	45.00
	1853 OM	—	6.00	8.00	10.00	40.00
	1854/3 OM	—	6.00	8.00	15.00	50.00
	1854 OM	—	6.00	8.00	12.00	40.00
	1855/4 OM	—	6.00	8.00	12.00	45.00
	1855 OM	—	6.00	8.00	12.00	45.00
	1855 MO	—	6.00	8.00	12.00	45.00
	1856/5 MO	—	6.00	8.00	12.00	40.00
	1856 MO	—	6.00	8.00	12.00	40.00
	1857 MO	—	6.00	8.00	12.00	40.00
	1858 MO	—	6.00	8.00	12.00	40.00
	1859 MO	—	6.00	8.00	12.00	45.00
	1860/50 MO	—	6.00	8.00	14.00	45.00
	1860 MO	—	6.00	8.00	14.00	45.00
	1860 VL	—	6.00	8.00	13.00	40.00
	1861 VL	—	6.00	8.00	15.00	45.00
	1862 VL	—	6.00	8.00	15.00	60.00
	1863 MO	—	6.00	8.00	15.00	65.00
	1863 VL	—	6.00	8.00	15.00	60.00
	1864 MO	—	6.00	8.00	15.00	60.00
	1864 VL	—	6.00	8.00	14.00	60.00
	1865 MO	—	6.00	8.00	16.00	60.00
	1867 JS	—	6.00	8.00	14.00	60.00
	1868 JS	—	6.00	8.00	15.00	60.00
	1868 YH	—	6.00	8.00	14.00	55.00
	1869 YH	—	6.00	8.00	14.50	60.00
	1870 YH	—	6.00	8.00	15.00	60.00

4 REALES

13.5400 gm., .903 SILVER, .3925 oz ASW

REAL DE CATORCE MINT (Ce)

Obv: Facing eagle

KM#	Date	Mintage	Fine	VF	XF	Unc
375	1863 ML	—	125.00	200.00	300.00	500.00

CULIACAN MINT (C)

KM#	Date	Mintage	Fine	VF	XF	Unc
375.1	1846 CE	—	60.00	75.00	100.00	200.00
	1850 CE	—	30.00	37.50	50.00	150.00
	1852 CE	—	30.00	40.00	75.00	175.00
	1857 CE	—	80.00	100.00	150.00	225.00
	1858 CE	—	42.50	55.00	80.00	165.00
	1860 PV	—	25.00	32.50	50.00	140.00

GUADALAJARA MINT (Ga)

KM#	Date	Mintage	Fine	VF	XF	Unc
375.2	1842/1 JG	—	36.50	50.00	75.00	175.00
	1842 JG	—	35.00	47.50	65.00	150.00
	1843 MC	—	13.50	20.00	30.00	130.00
	1844/3 MC	—	15.00	22.50	35.00	125.00
	1844 MC	—	12.50	17.50	25.00	120.00
	1845 MC	—	11.50	13.50	22.50	125.00
	1845 JG	—	12.00	22.50	24.00	125.00
	1846 JG	—	12.50	20.00	30.00	135.00
	1847 JG	—	11.50	16.00	35.00	135.00
	1848/7 JG	—	12.50	22.50	32.50	125.00
	1849 JG	—	25.00	35.00	45.00	135.00
	1850 JG	—	65.00	90.00	115.00	165.00
	1852 JG	—	23.50	35.00	45.00	130.00
	1854 JG	—	13.50	18.50	25.00	125.00
	1855 JG	—	13.50	18.50	28.00	125.00
	1856 JG	—	25.00	47.50	65.00	140.00
	1857/6 JG	—	11.50	17.50	23.50	115.00
	1858 JG	—	15.00	21.00	35.00	130.00
	1859/8 JG	—	17.50	23.50	31.50	125.00
	1860 JG	—	35.00	47.50	60.00	130.00
	1863/2 JG	—	10.00	15.00	35.00	125.00
	1863 JG	—	10.00	15.00	35.00	125.00

GUADALUPE Y CALVO MINT (GC)

KM#	Date	Mintage	Fine	VF	XF	Unc
375.3	1844 MP	—	400.00	500.00	650.00	900.00
	1845 MP	—	—	—	—	—
	1846 MP	—	400.00	500.00	650.00	900.00
	1847 MP	—	400.00	500.00	650.00	900.00
	1849 MP	—	400.00	500.00	650.00	900.00
	1850 MP	—	400.00	500.00	600.00	800.00

GUANAJUATO MINT (Go)

KM#	Date	Mintage	Fine	VF	XF	Unc
375.4	1835 PJ	—	12.50	20.00	30.00	125.00
	1836/5 PJ	—	11.50	15.00	25.00	125.00
	1836 PJ	—	11.50	16.50	28.50	140.00
	1837 PJ	—	11.50	17.50	30.00	125.00
	1838/7 PJ	—	11.50	18.50	35.00	140.00
	1838 PJ	—	11.50	17.50	35.00	140.00
	1839 PJ	—	11.50	13.50	20.00	125.00
	1840/30 PJ	—	13.50	18.50	27.50	150.00
	1840 PJ	—	16.50	22.50	30.00	140.00
	1841/31 PJ	—	18.00	25.00	32.50	140.00
	1842 PJ	—	20.00	27.50	60.00	250.00
	1842 PM	—	11.50	17.50	30.00	125.00
	1843/2 PM eagle with convex wings					
		—	11.50	15.00	25.00	140.00
	1843 PM eagle with concave wings					
		—	11.50	15.00	25.00	140.00
	1844/3 PM	—	11.50	15.00	25.00	125.00
	1844 PM	—	11.50	15.00	25.00	125.00
	1845/4 PM	—	11.50	15.00	25.00	125.00
	1845 PM	—	11.50	15.00	25.00	125.00
	1846/5 PM	—	11.50	15.00	25.00	125.00
	1846 PM	—	11.50	15.00	25.00	125.00
	1847/6 PM	—	11.50	15.00	25.00	125.00
	1847 PM	—	11.50	15.00	25.00	125.00

KM#	Date	Mintage	Fine	VF	XF	Unc
375.4	1848/7 PM	—	11.50	25.00	40.00	140.00
	1848 PM	—	11.50	17.50	27.50	130.00
	1849 PF	—	12.50	17.50	26.00	125.00
	1850 PF	—	11.50	15.00	22.50	125.00
	1851 PF	—	11.50	15.00	25.00	125.00
	1852 PF	—	11.50	15.00	25.00	125.00
	1853 PF	—	12.50	17.50	27.50	125.00
	1854 PF large eagle					
		—	12.50	17.00	28.50	140.00
	1854 PF small eagle					
		—	12.50	17.00	28.00	140.00
	1855/4 PF	—	11.50	15.00	25.00	125.00
	1855 PF	—	11.50	13.50	22.50	125.00
	1856 PF	—	11.50	15.00	25.00	125.00
	1857 PF	—	11.50	15.00	24.00	125.00
	1858 PF	—	11.50	15.00	25.00	125.00
	1859 PF	—	11.50	13.50	22.50	125.00
	1860/59 PF	—	11.50	15.00	25.00	125.00
	1860 PF	—	11.50	15.00	25.00	125.00
	1861/51 PF	—	11.50	13.50	22.50	125.00
	1862/1 YE	—	11.50	15.00	25.00	125.00
	1862/1 YF	—	11.50	12.50	20.00	125.00
	1862 YE/PF	—	11.50	15.00	25.00	125.00
	1862 YE	—	11.50	15.00	25.00	125.00
	1862 YF	—	11.50	16.50	28.50	125.00
	1863/53 YF	—	11950	16.50	28.50	125.00
	1863 YF/PF	—	11.50	16.50	28.50	125.00
	1863 YF	—	11.50	15.00	25.00	125.00
	1867/57 YF	—	11.50	15.00	25.00	125.00
	1867 YF/PF	—	11.50	15.00	25.00	125.00
	1868/58 YF	—	11.50	15.00	25.00	125.00
	1868 YF/PF	—	11.50	15.00	25.00	125.00
	1869 YF	—	12.50	17.50	28.50	125.00
	1870 FR	—	11.50	12.50	20.00	125.00

HERMOSILLO MINT (Ho)

KM#	Date	Mintage	Fine	VF	XF	Unc
375.5	1861 FM	—	200.00	250.00	325.00	450.00
	1867/1 PR/FM		75.00	100.00	165.00	275.00

MEXICO CITY MINT (Mo)

KM#	Date	Mintage	Fine	VF	XF	Unc
375.6	1827 JM	—	47.50	60.00	85.00	175.00
	1850 GC	—	12.50	17.50	25.00	125.00
	1852 GC	—	23.50	35.00	45.00	150.00
	1854 GC	—	12.50	17.50	22.50	140.00
	1855 GF/GC	—	35.00	47.50	60.00	165.00
	1856 GF/GC	—	13.50	18.50	25.00	140.00
	1859 FH	—	10.00	13.50	22.50	125.00
	1861 CH	—	11.50	12.50	22.00	125.00
	1862 CH	—	13.50	20.00	30.00	140.00
	1863/2 CH	—	15.00	22.50	35.00	150.00
	1863 CH	—	13.50	20.00	30.00	140.00
	1867 CH	—	13.50	20.00	30.00	140.00
	1868 CH/PH	—	11.50	15.00	25.00	140.00
	1868 PH	—	11.50	15.00	25.00	125.00

OAXACA MINT (Oa)

KM#	Date	Mintage	Fine	VF	XF	Unc
375.7	1861 FR with ornamented edge					
		—	180.00	225.00	300.00	450.00
	1861 FR with herringbone edge					
		—	180.00	225.00	300.00	450.00
	1861 FR with oblique reeding					
		—	180.00	225.00	300.00	450.00

POTOSI MINT (Pi)

KM#	Date	Mintage	Fine	VF	XF	Unc
375.8	1837 JS	—	18.50	25.00	35.00	150.00
	150.00	—	30.00	37.50	45.00	150.00
	150.00	—	12.50	20.00	35.00	150.00
	1843/2 PS	—	15.00	27.50	43.50	150.00
	1843/2 PS (3 cut from 8 punch)					
		—	15.00	27.50	43.50	150.00
	1843 PS	—	13.50	25.00	40.00	150.00
	1843 AM	—	12.50	18.50	35.00	140.00
	1843 PS	—	15.00	20.00	30.00	140.00
	1844 AM	—	11.50	16.50	28.50	140.00
	1845/4 AM	—	14.00	20.00	30.00	140.00
	1845 AM	—	12.00	18.50	25.00	140.00
	1846 AM	—	12.50	20.00	35.00	140.00
	1847 AM	—	15.00	20.00	25.00	140.00
	1848 AM	—	12.50	17.50	32.50	140.00
	1849 MC/AM	—	11.50	15.00	25.00	140.00
	1849 MC	—	11.50	15.00	25.00	140.00
	1849 PS	—	11.50	15.00	25.00	140.00
	1850 MC	—	17.50	23.50	28.50	140.00
	1851 MC	—	12.50	18.50	28.50	140.00
	1852 MC	—	12.00	20.00	27.50	140.00
	1853 MC	—	13.50	18.50	35.00	140.00
	1854 MC	—	17.50	30.00	37.50	150.00
	1855 MC	—	11.50	15.00	25.00	150.00
	1856 MC	—	16.50	22.50	30.00	150.00
	1857 MC	—	27.50	37.50	50.00	150.00
	1857 PS	—	27.50	37.50	50.00	150.00
	1858 MC	—	80.00	100.00	150.00	275.00
	1859 MC	—	16.50	22.50	30.00	150.00
	1860 PS	—	23.50	31.50	40.00	150.00
	1861 PS	—	12.50	17.50	32.50	150.00
	1861 PS/RO	—	13.50	20.00	35.00	150.00

KM#	Date	Mintage	Fine	VF	XF	Unc
375.8	1862 RO	—	11.50	16.50	28.50	150.00
	1863 RO	—	11.50	15.00	25.00	150.00
	1864 RO	—	13.50	20.00	30.00	150.00
	1868 PS	—	11.50	15.00	25.00	150.00
	1869/8 PS	—	11.50	16.50	28.50	150.00
	1869 PS	—	11.50	15.00	25.00	150.00

ZACATECAS MINT (Zs)

KM#	Date	Mintage	Fine	VF	XF	Unc
375.9	1830 OM	—	18.50	25.00	38.50	150.00
	1831 OM	—	10.00	15.00	35.00	150.00
	1832/1 OM	—	11.50	15.00	25.00	125.00
	1832 OM	—	11.50	15.00	25.00	125.00
	1833/27 OM	—	11.50	16.50	28.50	125.00
	1833/2 OM	—	11.50	16.50	28.50	125.00
	1833 OM	—	11.50	18.50	30.00	125.00
	1834 OM	—	11.50	18.50	30.00	125.00
	1835 OM	—	11.50	16.50	28.00	125.00
	1836 OM	—	11.50	15.00	28.00	125.00
	1837/5 OM	—	12.50	17.50	30.00	140.00
	1837/6 OM	—	12.50	17.50	30.00	140.00
	1837 OM	—	12.50	17.50	30.00	140.00
	1838/7 OM	—	12.50	17.50	30.00	140.00
	1839 OM	—	13.50	18.50	30.00	125.00
	1841 OM	—	11.50	13.50	20.00	125.00
	1842 OM large letters					
		—	11.50	14.50	28.00	125.00
	1842 OM small letters					
		—	11.50	16.50	28.00	125.00
	1843 OM	—	11.50	15.00	25.00	125.00
	1844 OM	—	11.50	15.00	25.00	125.00
	1845 OM	—	11.50	15.00	25.00	125.00
	1846 OM	—	11.50	15.00	25.00	125.00
	1847 OM	—	11.50	15.00	25.00	125.00
	1848 OM	—	11.50	16.50	27.50	125.00
	1849 OM	—	11.50	15.00	25.00	125.00
	1850 OM	—	11.50	13.50	22.50	125.00
	1851 OM	—	11.50	15.00	25.00	125.00
	1852 OM	—	11.50	13.50	22.00	125.00
	1853 OM	—	11.50	15.00	25.00	125.00
	1854/3 OM	—	13.50	22.50	35.00	140.00
	1854 OM	—	12.50	20.00	30.00	140.00
	1855/4 OM	—	11.50	15.00	25.00	125.00
	1855 OM	—	11.50	13.50	22.50	125.00
	1856 OM	—	11.50	15.00	25.00	125.00
	1856 MO	—	11.50	15.00	25.00	125.00
	1857/5 MO	—	11.50	15.00	25.00	125.00
	1857 MO	—	11.50	15.00	25.00	125.00
	1858 MO	—	11.50	15.00	25.00	125.00
	1859 MO	—	11.50	13.50	22.50	125.00
	1860/59 MO	—	11.50	15.00	25.00	150.00
	1860 MO	—	11.50	15.00	25.00	125.00
	1860 VL	—	11.50	13.50	22.50	125.00
	1861/0 VL	—	11.50	16.50	28.50	140.00
	1861 VL	—	11.50	16.50	28.50	125.00
	1862/1 VL	—	11.50	13.50	22.50	125.00
	1862 VL	—	11.50	16.50	28.50	125.00
	1863 VL	—	11.50	15.00	25.00	125.00
	1863 MO	—	11.50	15.00	25.00	125.00
	1864 VL	—	11.50	15.00	25.00	125.00
	1868 JS	—	11.50	13.50	20.00	125.00
	1868 YH	—	11.50	15.00	25.00	125.00
	1869 YH	—	11.50	15.00	25.00	125.00
	1870 YH	—	11.50	13.50	22.00	125.00

8 REALES

27.0700 gm., .903 SILVER, .7859 oz ASW

DURANGO MINT (Do)

Obv: Hooked neck eagle

KM#	Date	Mintage	Fine	VF	XF	Unc
376	1824 RL	—	150.00	250.00	500.00	1200.

GUANAJUATO MINT (Go)

KM#	Date	Mintage	Fine	VF	XF	Unc
376.1	1824 JM	—	125.00	275.00	450.00	1100.
	1825/4 JJ	—	350.00	500.00	750.00	1350.
	1825 JJ	—	450.00	600.00	850.00	1500.

MEXICO CITY MINT (Mo)

KM#	Date	Mintage	Fine	VF	XF	Unc
376.2	1823 JM	—	100.00	185.00	300.00	700.00
	1824 JM	—	100.00	175.00	275.00	600.00
	1824 JM with error REPULICA					
		—	—	—	—	—

NOTE: These are rarely found with detail on the eagles breast and bring a premium if even slight feather detail is present there.

ALAMOS MINT (A, As)

KM#	Date	Mintage	Fine	VF	XF	Unc
377	1864 PG	—	300.00	400.00	500.00	650.00
	1865 PG	—	300.00	400.00	500.00	700.00
	1866 PG	—	400.00	500.00	700.00	800.00
	1866 DL	—	400.00	500.00	700.00	800.00
	1867 DL	—	400.00	500.00	600.00	850.00
	1868 DL	—	60.00	80.00	100.00	135.00
	1869 DL	—	65.00	80.00	120.00	140.00
	1870 DL	—	77.50	90.00	125.00	150.00
	1871 DL	—	17.50	25.00	37.50	75.00
	1872 AM	—	37.50	50.00	75.00	100.00
	1873 AM	.509	BV	25.00	35.00	80.00
	1874 DL	—	BV	25.00	35.00	70.00
	1875A DL	—	BV	25.00	35.00	60.00
	1875AsDL	—	BV	25.00	35.00	60.00
	1876 DL	—	BV	25.00	35.00	60.00
	1877 DL	.515	BV	25.00	35.00	55.00
	1878 DL	.513	BV	25.00	35.00	55.00
	1879 DL	—	BV	25.00	38.50	85.00
	1879 ML	—	BV	25.00	35.00	75.00
	1880 ML	—	BV	25.00	35.00	55.00
	1881 ML	.966	BV	25.00	35.00	60.00
	1882 ML	.480	BV	25.00	35.00	55.00
	1883 ML	.464	BV	25.00	35.00	55.00
	1884 ML	—	BV	25.00	35.00	50.00
	1885 ML	.280	BV	25.00	35.00	55.00
	1886 ML	.857	BV	25.00	38.50	85.00
	1887 ML	.650	BV	25.00	35.00	60.00
	1888 ML	.508	BV	25.00	35.00	60.00
	1889 ML	.427	BV	25.00	35.00	60.00
	1890 ML	.450	BV	25.00	35.00	55.00
	1891 ML	.533	BV	25.00	35.00	55.00
	1892 ML	.465	BV	25.00	35.00	55.00
	1893 ML	.734	BV	25.00	35.00	55.00
	1894 ML	.725	BV	25.00	35.00	55.00
	1895 ML	.477	BV	25.00	35.00	60.00

REAL DE CATORCE MINT (Ce)

KM#	Date	Mintage	Fine	VF	XF	Unc
377.1	1863 ML	—	350.00	450.00	650.00	900.00
	1863 CeML/PiMC					
		—	325.00	550.00	750.00	1100.

CHIHUAHUA MINT (Ca)

KM#	Date	Mintage	Fine	VF	XF	Unc
377.2	1831 CM	—	300.00	400.00	500.00	800.00
	1831 MR	—	200.00	300.00	400.00	700.00
	1832 MR	—	65.00	85.00	110.00	160.00
	1833 MR	—	75.00	125.00	175.00	225.00
377.2	1834 MR	—	300.00	500.00	700.00	1000.
	1834 AM	—	300.00	500.00	700.00	1000.
	1835 AM	—	60.00	80.00	125.00	250.00
	1836 AM	—	45.00	60.00	80.00	225.00
	1837 AM	—	70.00	110.00	185.00	225.00
	1838 AM	—	60.00	80.00	125.00	250.00
	1839 RG	—	200.00	250.00	300.00	400.00
	1840 RG 1 dot after date					
		—	200.00	250.00	300.00	400.00
	1840 RG 3 dots after date					
		—	200.00	250.00	300.00	400.00
	1841 RG	—	60.00	80.00	100.00	140.00
	1842 RG	—	27.50	40.00	60.00	100.00
	1843 RG	—	22.50	32.50	60.00	100.00
	1844/1 RG	—	30.00	45.00	60.00	100.00
	1845 RG	—	25.00	60.00	90.00	150.00
	1846 RG	—	60.00	80.00	100.00	175.00
	1847 RG	—	50.00	70.00	90.00	150.00
	1848 RG	—	35.00	100.00	150.00	225.00
	1849 RG	—	27.50	40.00	60.00	100.00
	1850/40 RG	—	BV	28.50	42.50	65.00
	1850 RG	—	BV	25.00	37.50	60.00
	1851/41 RG	—	30.00	45.00	60.00	100.00
	1851 RG	—	30.00	45.00	60.00	100.00
	1852/42 RG	—	70.00	100.00	125.00	250.00
	1853/43 RG	—	100.00	150.00	200.00	350.00
	1854/44 RG	—	42.50	60.00	80.00	110.00
	1854 RG	—	40.00	55.00	75.00	100.00
	1855/45 RG	—	32.50	48.50	65.00	110.00
	1855 RG	—	30.00	45.00	60.00	100.00
	1856/45 RG	—	80.00	100.00	135.00	180.00
	1856/5 JC	—	200.00	250.00	325.00	450.00
	1857 JC/RG	—	BV	26.50	37.50	85.00
	1857 JC	—	BV	25.00	32.50	80.00
	1858 JC	—	25.00	30.00	45.00	75.00
	1858 BA	—	55.00	85.00	125.00	200.00
	1859 JC	—	BV	25.00	32.50	55.00
	1860 JC	—	BV	25.00	35.00	75.00
	1861 JC	—	BV	25.00	30.00	60.00
	1862 JC	—	BV	25.00	32.50	55.00
	1863 JC	—	25.00	35.00	60.00	100.00
	1864 JC	—	45.00	60.00	80.00	125.00
	1865 JC	—	45.00	60.00	80.00	125.00
	1865 FP	—	200.00	300.00	400.00	600.00
	1866 JG	—	150.00	200.00	250.00	350.00
	1866 FP	—	200.00	300.00	600.00	1000.
	1866 JG	—	150.00	200.00	275.00	400.00
	1867 JG	—	BV	25.00	47.50	75.00
	1868 JG	—	60.00	100.00	135.00	175.00
	1868 MM	—	65.00	110.00	150.00	200.00
	1869 MM	—	BV	25.00	30.00	60.00
	1869 CE	—	BV	25.00	37.50	85.00
	1870 MM	—	BV	21.00	32.50	55.00
	1871/0 MM	—	BV	27.50	38.50	65.00
	1871 Mm	—	BV	25.00	35.00	60.00
	1871 MM first M over inverted M					
		—	BV	25.00	35.00	65.00
	1873 MM	—	BV	25.00	30.00	50.00
	1873 MM over T					
		—	BV	25.00	30.00	50.00
	1874 MM	—	BV	25.00	30.00	50.00
	1875 MM	—	BV	25.00	30.00	50.00
	1876 MM	—	BV	25.00	30.00	50.00
	1877 EA	.472	BV	25.00	30.00	50.00
	1877 GR	Inc. Ab.	27.50	40.00	60.00	80.00
	1877 JM	Inc. Ab.	BV	25.00	30.00	40.00
	1877 AV	Inc. Ab.	30.00	50.00	75.00	100.00
	1878 AV	.439	BV	25.00	30.00	50.00
	1879 AV	—	BV	25.00	30.00	50.00
	1880 AV	—	BV	25.00	30.00	50.00
	1880 PM	—	—	—	Rare	—
	1880 MG with normal initials					
		—	BV	25.00	30.00	50.00
	1880 MG with tall initials					
		—	BV	25.00	30.00	50.00
	1880 MM	—	BV	25.00	30.00	50.00
	1881 MG	1.085	BV	25.00	30.00	50.00
	1882 MG	.779	BV	25.00	30.00	50.00
	1882 MM	I.A.	BV	25.00	30.00	55.00
	1882 MM M sideways					
		Inc. Ab.	BV	25.00	30.00	60.00
	1883 MM	.818	BV	25.00	30.00	50.00
	1884/3 MM	I.A.	BV	25.00	30.00	50.00
	1884 MM	—	BV	25.00	30.00	50.00
	1885/4 MM	—	BV	2K.00	30.00	50.00
	1885 MM	1.345	BV	25.00	30.00	50.00
	1886 MM	2.483	BV	25.00	30.00	50.00
	1887 MM	2.625	BV	25.00	30.00	50.00
	1888/7 MM	I.A.	BV	25.00	30.00	50.00
	1888 MM	2.434	BV	25.00	30.00	50.00
	1889 MM	2.681	BV	25.00	30.00	50.00
	1890 MM	2.137	BV	25.00	30.00	50.00
	1891/0 MM					
		2.268	BV	25.00	30.00	50.00
	1891 MM	I.A.	BV	25.00	30.00	50.00
	1892 MM	2.527	BV	25.00	30.00	50.00
	1893 MM	2.632	BV	25.00	30.00	50.00
377.2	1894 MM	2.642	BV	25.00	30.00	50.00
	1895 MM	1.112	BV	25.00	30.00	50.00

CULIACAN MINT (C, Cn)

KM#	Date	Mintage	Fine	VF	XF	Unc
377.3	1846 CE	—	50.00	65.00	90.00	125.00
	1847 CE	—	80.00	100.00	135.00	180.00
	1848 CE	—	65.00	85.00	125.00	225.00
	1849 CE	—	100.00	175.00	275.00	400.00
	1850 CE	—	75.00	150.00	235.00	350.00
	1851 CE	—	100.00	175.00	275.00	400.00
	1852/1 CE	—	45.00	60.00	80.00	115.00
	1853 CE thick rays					
		—	150.00	200.00	300.00	400.00
	1853 CE with error MEXIGANA					
		—	150.00	200.00	300.00	400.00
	1853/0 CE	—	150.00	200.00	300.00	400.00
	1854 CE	—	27.50	40.00	60.00	100.00
	1854 CE large eagle & hat					
		—	27.50	40.00	60.00	100.00
	1855 CE	—	30.00	45.00	60.00	100.00
	1855/6 CE	—	32.50	50.00	65.00	100.00
	1856 CE	—	25.00	30.00	40.00	85.00
	1857 CE	—	BV	25.00	30.00	55.00
	1858 CE	—	BV	25.00	37.50	65.00
	1859 CE	—	BV	25.00	30.00	55.00
	1860 CE	—	32.50	50.00	65.00	100.00
	1860/9 PV/CV		45.00	60.00	80.00	125.00
	1860 PV	—	45.00	60.00	80.00	125.00
	1861/0 CE	—	BV	25.00	32.50	65.00
	1861 PV/CE	—	90.00	150.00	225.00	325.00
	1861 CE	—	BV	26.50	35.00	70.00
	1862 CE	—	BV	25.00	30.00	55.00
	1863 CE	—	BV	25.00	32.50	65.00
	1864 CE	—	BV	25.00	32.50	60.00
	1865 CE	—	45.00	60.00	80.00	125.00
	1866 CE	—	90.00	115.00	150.00	300.00
	1867 CE	—	65.00	85.00	110.00	165.00
	1868/7 CE	—	BV	25.00	32.50	65.00
	1868 CE	—	BV	25.00	32.50	60.00
	1869 CE	—	25.00	32.50	45.00	85.00
	1870 CE	—	30.00	45.00	60.00	100.00
	1873 MP	—	25.00	35.00	55.00	90.00
	1874 MC	—	BV	25.00	30.00	55.00
	1874 MP	—	80.00	100.00	165.00	225.00
	1875 MP	—	BV	25.00	30.00	55.00
	1876 GP	—	BV	27.50	45.00	75.00
	1876 CG	—	BV	25.00	30.00	50.00
	1877 CG	.339	BV	25.00	40.00	85.00
	1877 GnCG (error)					
		—	BV	25.00	30.00	50.00
	1877 JA	Inc. Ab.	25.00	35.00	55.00	90.00
	1878 CG	.483	25.00	30.00	40.00	70.00
	1878 JD	Inc. Ab.	BV	25.00	30.00	50.00
	1878 JD D over retrograde D					
		—	BV	25.00	30.00	50.00
	1879 JD	—	BV	25.00	40.00	75.00
	1880/70 JD	—	BV	25.00	30.00	65.00
	1881 JC	1.032	BV	25.00	30.00	50.00
	1881C JD	I.A.	BV	25.00	30.00	50.00
	1881CnJD	I.A.	BV	25.00	30.00	50.00
	1882 JD	.397	BV	28.50	45.00	80.00
	1882 AM	I.A.	BV	25.00	32.50	60.00
	1883 AM	.333	BV	25.00	32.50	60.00
	1884 AM	—	BV	25.00	32.50	60.00
	1885C AM	.227	80.00	100.00	140.00	200.00
	1885CnAM	I.A.	BV	25.00	30.00	50.00
	1885/6 AM	I.A.	BV	25.00	30.00	50.00
	1885GnAM (error)					
		Inc. Ab.	45.00	60.00	80.00	120.00
	1886 AM	.571	BV	25.00	30.00	50.00
	1887 AM	.732	BV	25.00	30.00	50.00
	1888 AM	.768	BV	25.00	30.00	50.00
	1889 AM	1.075	BV	25.00	30.00	50.00
	1890 AM	.874	BV	25.00	30.00	50.00
	1891 AM	.777	BV	25.00	30.00	50.00
	1892 AM	.681	BV	25.00	30.00	50.00
	1893 AM	1.144	BV	25.00	30.00	50.00
	1894 AM	2.118	BV	25.00	30.00	50.00
	1895 AM	1.834	BV	25.00	30.00	50.00
	1896 AM	2.134	BV	25.00	30.00	50.00
	1897 AM	1.580	BV	25.00	30.00	50.00

DURANGO MINT (Do)

KM#	Date	Mintage	Fine	VF	XF	Unc
377.4	1825 RL	—	25.00	30.00	40.00	85.00
	1826 RL	—	26.50	32.50	47.50	90.00
	1827/6 RL	—	27.50	37.50	55.00	90.00
	1827 RL	—	25.00	35.00	50.00	85.00
	1828/7 RL	—	25.00	30.00	42.50	70.00
	1828 RL	—	25.00	28.50	37.50	65.00
	1829 RL	—	25.00	28.50	37.50	70.00
	1830 RM	—	25.00	35.00	55.00	90.00
	1831 RM	—	25.00	32.50	47.50	80.00
	1832 RM	—	BV	27.50	35.00	70.00
	1832 RM/RL (European dies)					
		—	BV	25.00	28.50	65.00
	1833/2 RM/RL		BV	26.50	38.50	75.00
	1833 RM	—	BV	25.00	35.00	70.00
	1834/3/2 RM/RL					
		—	BV	25.00	35.00	70.00
	1834 RM	—	BV	25.00	37.50	65.00
	1835/4 RM/RL		BV	26.50	38.50	70.00
	1835 RM	—	35.00	70.00	100.00	175.00
	1836/1 RM	—	BV	25.00	30.00	60.00
	1836/4 RM	—	BV	25.00	30.00	60.00
	1836 RM	—	BV	25.00	30.00	55.00
	1836 RM with M on snake					
		—	BV	25.00	30.00	65.00
	1837/1 RM	—	BV	27.50	40.00	85.00
	1837 RM	—	BV	27.50	40.00	85.00
	1838/1 RM	—	BV	25.00	32.50	65.00
	1838/7 RM	—	BV	25.00	32.50	65.00
	1838 RM	—	BV	25.00	30.00	60.00
	1839/1 RM/RL		BV	25.00	30.00	55.00
	1840/38/31 RM		BV	25.00	37.50	60.00
	1840/39 RM	—	BV	35.00	50.00	85.00
	1841/31 RM	—	35.00	50.00	75.00	125.00
	1842/31 RM B below cactus					
		—	25.00	30.00	45.00	75.00
	1842/31 RM	—	25.00	30.00	45.00	75.00
	1842/32 RM	—	25.00	30.00	45.00	75.00
	1842 RM eagle of 1832-41					
		—	25.00	30.00	35.00	75.00
	1842 RM pre 1832 eagle resumed					
		—	25.00	30.00	35.00	80.00
	1843/33 RM	—	40.00	100.00	150.00	225.00
	1844/34 RM	—	55.00	75.00	100.00	165.00
	1844/35 RM	—	55.00	75.00	100.00	165.00
	1844 RM	—	55.00	75.00	100.00	165.00
	1845/31 RM	—	25.00	35.00	55.00	85.00
	1845/34 RM	—	25.00	35.00	55.00	85.00
	1845/35 RM	—	25.00	35.00	55.00	85.00
	1845 RM	—	BV	25.00	32.50	70.00
	1846/31 RM	—	25.00	30.00	35.00	70.00
	1846/36 RM	—	25.00	30.00	37.50	65.00
	1846 RM	—	BV	25.00	32.50	70.00
	1847 RM	—	25.00	30.00	40.00	80.00
	1848/7 RM	—	47.50	65.00	85.00	150.00
	1848/7 CM/RM		25.00	30.00	40.00	70.00
	1848 CM/RM	—	25.00	30.00	40.00	65.00
	1848 RM	—	45.00	60.00	80.00	140.00
	1848 CM	—	25.00	30.00	37.50	60.00
	1849/39 RM	—	27.50	40.00	60.00	100.00
	1849 JMR/CM		100.00	150.00	200.00	300.00
	1849 DoJMR oval O					
		—	100.00	150.00	200.00	300.00
	1849 DoJMR round O					
		—	100.00	150.00	200.00	300.00
	1850 J.M.R.	—	155.00	175.00	200.00	300.00
	1851/0 JMR	—	75.00	125.00	180.00	275.00
	1851 JMR	—	75.00	125.00	175.00	275.00
	1852 CP/JMR		150.00	170.00	225.00	350.00
	1852 JMR	—	55.00	75.00	100.00	165.00
	1853 CP/JMR		45.00	60.00	80.00	140.00
	1854 CP	—	25.00	35.00	55.00	90.00
	1855 CP	—	27.50	40.00	55.00	90.00
	1856 CP	—	45.00	60.00	80.00	140.00
	1857 CP	—	36.00	50.00	75.00	135.00
	1858/7 CP	—	25.00	30.00	40.00	90.00
	1858 CP	—	25.00	30.00	35.00	85.00
	1859 CP	—	25.00	30.00	40.00	90.00
	1860/59 CP	—	25.00	30.00	40.00	90.00
	1860 CP	—	25.00	30.00	40.00	70.00
	1861 CP	—	25.00	30.00	35.00	50.00
	1862/1 CP	—	25.00	40.00	60.00	80.00
	1862 CP	—	25.00	30.00	40.00	85.00
	1863/2 CP	—	25.00	45.00	65.00	95.00
	1863 CP	—	25.00	50.00	75.00	125.00
	1864 CP	—	25.00	30.00	40.00	70.00
	1864 LT	—	25.00	30.00	40.00	70.00
	1865 LT	—	300.00	400.00	500.00	650.00
	1866 CM	—	500.00	600.00	750.00	1000.
	1867 CP	—	25.00	30.00	40.00	70.00
	1867 CP/CM	—	25.00	30.00	40.00	70.00
	1867 CP/LT	—	25.00	30.00	40.00	70.00
	1867 CM	—	25.00	30.00	37.50	65.00
	1868 CP	—	25.00	50.00	75.00	125.00
	1869 CP	—	25.00	30.00	35.00	60.00
	1870/69 CP	—	26.50	37.50	55.00	90.00
377.4	1870/9 CP	—	25.00	35.00	50.00	85.00
	1870 CP	—	25.00	35.00	50.00	85.00
	1873 CP	—	37.50	50.00	75.00	125.00
	1873 CM	—	35.00	50.00	75.00	125.00
	1874/3 CM	—	25.00	30.00	35.00	50.00
	1874 CM	—	25.00	30.00	35.00	50.00
	1874 JH	—	45.00	60.00	75.00	100.00
	1875 CM	—	25.00	30.00	35.00	50.00
	1875 JH	—	25.00	30.00	37.50	70.00
	1876 CM	—	25.00	30.00	35.00	50.00
	1877 CM	.431	25.00	30.00	37.50	65.00
	1877 CP	Inc. Ab.	25.00	30.00	37.50	60.00
	1877 JMP	I.A.	600.00	800.00	1200.	1750.
	1878 PE	.409	25.00	30.00	37.50	70.00
	1878 TB	Inc. Ab.	BV	25.00	30.00	50.00
	1879 TB	—	BV	25.00	30.00	50.00
	1880/70 TB	—	BV	25.00	30.00	50.00
	1880/70 TB/JP		BV	25.00	30.00	50.00
	1880/70 JP	—	BV	25.00	30.00	55.00
	1880 TB	—	BV	25.00	30.00	45.00
	1880 JP	—	BV	25.00	30.00	50.00
	1881 JP	.928	BV	25.00	30.00	45.00
	1882 JP	.414	BV	25.00	30.00	45.00
	1882 MC/JP	I.A.	28.50	42.50	65.00	100.00
	1882 MC	I.A.	27.50	40.00	60.00	90.00
	1883/73 MC					
		.452	BV	25.00	30.00	50.00
	1883 MC	I.A.	BV	25.00	30.00	50.00
	1884/3 MC	—	BV	25.00	30.00	50.00
	1884 MC	—	BV	25.00	30.00	50.00
	1885 MC	.547	BV	25.00	30.00	50.00
	1885 JB	Inc. Ab.	22.50	32.50	50.00	100.00
	1886/3 MC	.955	BV	25.00	30.00	50.00
	1886 MC	I.A.	BV	25.00	30.00	50.00
	1887 MC	1.004	BV	25.00	30.00	50.00
	1888 MC	.996	BV	25.00	30.00	50.00
	1889 MC	.874	BV	25.00	30.00	50.00
	1890 MC	1.119	BV	25.00	30.00	50.00
	1890 JP	Inc. Ab.	BV	25.00	30.00	50.00
	1891 JP	1.487	BV	25.00	30.00	50.00
	1892 JP	1.597	BV	25.00	30.00	50.00
	1892 ND	Inc. Ab.	40.00	60.00	100.00	165.00
	1893 ND	1.617	BV	25.00	30.00	50.00
	1894 ND	1.537	BV	25.00	30.00	50.00
	1895/3 ND	.761	BV	25.00	30.00	50.00
	1895 ND	I.A.	BV	25.00	30.00	50.00

ESTADO DE MEXICO MINT (Eo Mo)

KM#	Date	Mintage	Fine	VF	XF	Unc
377.5	1828 LF	—	350.00	500.00	750.00	1000.
	1829 LF	—	350.00	500.00	750.00	1000.
	1830/20 LF	—	1000.	1350.	1850.	2500.
	1830 LF	—	650.00	850.00	1100.	1500.

GUADALAJARA MINT (Ga)

KM#	Date	Mintage	Fine	VF	XF	Unc
377.6	1825 FS	—	90.00	150.00	225.00	275.00
	1826/5 FS	—	65.00	85.00	125.00	200.00
	1827 FS	—	65.00	85.00	125.00	200.00
	1827/87 FS	—	70.00	90.00	125.00	200.00
	1828 FS	—	55.00	75.00	125.00	200.00
	1829/8 FS	—	70.00	90.00	125.00	200.00
	1829 FS	—	65.00	85.00	125.00	200.00
	1830/29 FS	—	55.00	75.00	100.00	165.00
	1830 FS	—	55.00	75.00	100.00	165.00
	1830 LP/FS	—	600.00	700.00	850.00	1350.
	1831 LP	—	60.00	80.00	100.00	165.00
	1831 FS/LP	—	60.00	80.00	100.00	165.00
	1831 FS	—	250.00	300.00	400.00	650.00
	1832/1 FS	—	40.00	55.00	75.00	135.00
	1832/1 FS/LP		40.00	55.00	80.00	135.00
	1832 FS	—	45.00	100.00	150.00	250.00
	1833/2/1 FS/LP					
		—	50.00	70.00	90.00	150.00
	1833 FS	—	50.00	125.00	150.00	250.00
	1834/2 FS	—	32.50	50.00	65.00	110.00
	1834/3 FS	—	32.50	50.00	65.00	110.00
	1834 FS	—	30.00	45.00	60.00	100.00
	1835 FS	—	40.00	50.00	65.00	100.00
	1836/1 JG/FS		60.00	80.00	125.00	200.00
	1836 FS	—	75.00	100.00	165.00	250.00
	1836 JG/FS	—	50.00	70.00	100.00	165.00
	1836 JG	—	50.00	70.00	90.00	150.00
	1837/6 JG/FS		32.50	48.50	65.00	110.00
377.6	1837 JG	—	30.00	45.00	60.00	100.00
	1838/7 JG	—	55.00	75.00	100.00	165.00
	1838 JG	—	60.00	140.00	180.00	260.00
	1839 MC	—	47.50	65.00	85.00	150.00
	1839 MC/JG	—	50.00	70.00	90.00	150.00
	1839 JG	—	25.00	35.00	55.00	90.00
	1840/30 MC	—	50.00	70.00	90.00	150.00
	1840 MC	—	47.50	65.00	85.00	140.00
	1841 MC	—	50.00	70.00	90.00	150.00
	1842 JG	—	27.50	40.00	55.00	90.00
	1842 JG/MG	—	27.50	40.00	55.00	90.00
	1843/2 MC/JG		27.50	38.50	55.00	90.00
	1843 MC/JG	—	27.50	38.50	55.00	90.00
	1843 JG	—	37.50	65.00	85.00	140.00
	1843 MC	—	50.00	125.00	200.00	300.00
	1844 MC	—	27.50	40.00	70.00	125.00
	1845 MC	—	60.00	80.00	100.00	165.00
	1845 JG	—	60.00	80.00	100.00	165.00
	1846 JG	—	37.50	55.00	75.00	125.00
	1847 JG	—	100.00	150.00	200.00	300.00
	1848/7 JG	—	37.50	55.00	80.00	135.00
	1848 JG	—	35.00	60.00	85.00	140.00
	1849 JG	—	90.00	115.00	150.00	250.00
	1850 JG	—	40.00	100.00	150.00	250.00
	1851 JG	—	300.00	400.00	550.00	850.00
	1852 JG	—	60.00	80.00	100.00	165.00
	1853/2 JG	—	90.00	115.00	150.00	250.00
	1853 JG	—	90.00	115.00	150.00	250.00
	1854/3 JG	—	50.00	70.00	100.00	165.00
	1854 JG	—	50.00	70.00	90.00	150.00
	1855/4 JG	—	47.50	65.00	85.00	140.00
	1856/4 JG	—	60.00	80.00	100.00	160.00
	1856 JG	—	60.00	80.00	100.00	160.00
	1857 JG	—	25.00	32.50	45.00	75.00
	1858 JG	—	BV	25.00	32.50	70.00
	1859/7 JG	—	BV	25.00	30.00	60.00
	1859/8 JG	—	BV	25.00	30.00	60.00
	1859 JG	—	35.00	50.00	75.00	125.00
	1860 JG	—	60.00	80.00	100.00	165.00
	1860 JG with dot in loop of eagles tail					
	(base alloy)	—	60.00	80.00	100.00	165.00
	1862 JG	—	200.00	300.00	450.00	650.00
	1863/59 JG	—	25.00	32.50	55.00	80.00
	1863/2 JG	—	25.00	30.00	45.00	70.00
	1863/4 JG	—	25.00	32.50	55.00	80.00
	1863 JG	—	27.50	37.50	60.00	100.00
	1863 FV	—	300.00	400.00	550.00	750.00
	1867 JM	—	100.00	125.00	200.00	350.00
	1868/7 JM	—	40.00	60.00	75.00	135.00
	1868 JM	—	37.50	55.00	70.00	130.00
	1869 JM	—	50.00	70.00	90.00	150.00
	1869 IC	—	65.00	85.00	110.00	175.00
	1870/60 IC	—	50.00	70.00	90.00	150.00
	1873 IC	—	25.00	35.00	55.00	90.00
	1874 IC	—	25.00	30.00	35.00	50.00
	1874 MC	—	25.00	35.00	55.00	75.00
	1875 IC	—	BV	25.00	30.00	50.00
	1875 MC	—	BV	25.00	30.00	50.00
	1876 IC	.559	BV	25.00	30.00	50.00
	1876 MC	Inc. Ab.	100.00	175.00	275.00	400.00
	1877 IC	.928	BV	25.00	30.00	50.00
	1877 JA	Inc. Ab.	BV	25.00	35.00	60.00
	1878 JA	.764	BV	25.00	30.00	50.00
	1879 JA	—	BV	25.00	30.00	50.00
	1880/70 FS	—	BV	2K.00	30.00	50.00
	1880 JA	—	25.00	32.50	42.50	70.00
	1880 FS	—	BV	25.00	30.00	50.00
	1881 FS	1.300	BV	25.00	30.00	50.00
	1882/1 FS	.537	BV	25.00	30.00	50.00
	1882 FS	I.A.	BV	25.00	30.00	50.00
	1882 TB/FS	I.A.	BV	25.00	30.00	55.00
	1882 TB	I.A.	BV	25.00	30.00	55.00
	1883 TB	.561	BV	25.00	30.00	50.00
	1884 TB	—	BV	25.00	30.00	50.00
	1884 AH	—	BV	25.00	30.00	50.00
	1885 AH	.443	BV	25.00	30.00	50.00
	1885 JS	Inc. Ab.	BV	25.00	30.00	50.00
	1886 JS	1.039	BV	25.00	30.00	50.00
	1887 JS	.878	BV	25.00	30.00	50.00
	1888 JS	1.159	BV	25.00	30.00	50.00
	1889 JS	1.583	BV	25.00	30.00	50.00
	1890 JS	1.658	BV	25.00	30.00	50.00
	1891 JS	1.507	BV	25.00	30.00	50.00
	1892/1 JS	1.627	BV	25.00	30.00	50.00
	1892 JS	I.A.	BV	25.00	30.00	50.00
	1893 JS	1.952	BV	25.00	30.00	50.00
	1894 JS	2.046	BV	25.00	30.00	50.00
	1895 JS	1.146	BV	25.00	30.00	50.00

GUADALUPE Y CALVO MINT (GC)

KM#	Date	Mintage	Fine	VF	XF	Unc
377.7	1844 MP	—	300.00	400.00	650.00	1000.
	1844 MP (error) reversed S in Ds,Gs	—				Rare
	1845 MP	—	150.00	225.00	350.00	500.00
	1846 MP eagle's tail square					
		—	125.00	200.00	350.00	500.00
	1846 MP eagle's tail rounded					
		—	125.00	200.00	350.00	500.00
	1847 MP	—	125.00	200.00	350.00	500.00
	1848 MP	—	150.00	225.00	400.00	600.00
	1849 MP	—	150.00	225.00	400.00	600.00
	1850 MP	—	150.00	225.00	400.00	600.00
	1851 MP	—	300.00	400.00	550.00	750.00
	1852 MP	—	300.00	400.00	550.00	750.00

GUANAJUATO MINT (Go)

KM#	Date	Mintage	Fine	VF	XF	Unc
377.8	1825 JJ	—	45.00	60.00	80.00	150.00
	1826 JJ with straight J's					
		—	37.50	50.00	70.00	130.00
	1826 JJ with full J's					
		—	37.50	50.00	70.00	130.00
	1826 MJ	—	65.00	90.00	120.00	200.00
	1827 MJ	—	50.00	75.00	100.00	150.00
	1827 MJ/JJ	—	50.00	75.00	100.00	150.00
	1827 MR	—	55.00	75.00	100.00	150.00
	1828 MJ	—	25.00	30.00	35.00	60.00
	1828 MR	—	50.00	70.00	90.00	135.00
	1829 MJ	—	25.00	30.00	40.00	70.00
	1830 MJ with oblong beading and narrow J's					
		—	BV	25.00	30.00	55.00
	1830 MJ with regular beading and wide J's					
		—	BV	25.00	30.00	55.00
	1831 MJ with colon after date					
		—	BV	25.00	30.00	50.00
	1831 MJ with two stars after date					
		—	BV	25.00	30.00	50.00
	1832 MJ	—	BV	25.00	30.00	50.00
	1832 MJ inverted 1 above 1 in date					
		—	BV	25.00	30.00	50.00
	1833 MJ	—	BV	25.00	30.00	50.00
	1833 JM	—	BV	25.00	30.00	55.00
	1834 PJ	—	BV	25.00	30.00	50.00
	1835 PJ	—	BV	25.00	30.00	50.00
	1836 PJ	—	BV	25.00	30.00	50.00
	1837 PJ	—	BV	25.00	30.00	50.00
	1838 PJ	—	BV	25.00	30.00	50.00
	1839 PJ/JJ	—	27.50	38.50	55.00	85.00
	1840/30 PJ	—	BV	25.00	32.50	50.00
	1840 PJ	—	BV	25.00	32.50	50.00
	1841/31 PJ	—	BV	25.00	32.50	50.00
	1841 PJ	—	BV	25.00	32.50	50.00
	1842 PJ	—	BV	25.00	32.50	50.00
	1842 PM/PJ	—	BV	25.00	32.50	50.00
	1842 PM	—	BV	25.00	32.50	50.00
	1843 PM	—	BV	25.00	32.50	50.00
	1843 PM with traingle of dots after date					
		—	BV	25.00	32.50	50.00
	1844 PM	—	BV	25.00	32.50	50.00
	1845 PM	—	BV	25.00	32.50	50.00
	1846/5 PM	—	BV	25.00	32.50	50.00
	1846 PM	—	BV	25.00	32.50	50.00
	1847 PM	—	BV	25.00	40.00	70.00
	1848/7 PM	—	BV	25.00	32.50	50.00
	1848 PM	—	BV	25.00	32.50	50.00
	1848 PF	—	BV	25.00	32.50	50.00
	1849 PF	—	BV	25.00	32.50	50.00
	1850 MP (error)					
		—	—	—	—	—
	1850 PF	—	BV	25.00	32.50	50.00
	1851/0 PF	—	BV	25.00	32.50	50.00
	1851 PF	—	BV	25.00	32.50	50.00
	1852/1 PF	—	BV	25.00	32.50	50.00
	1852 PF	—	BV	25.00	32.50	50.00
	1853/2 PF	—	BV	25.00	32.50	50.00
	1853 PF	—	BV	25.00	32.50	50.00
	1854 PF	—	BV	25.00	32.50	50.00
	1855 PF large letters					
		—	BV	25.00	32.50	50.00
	1855 PF small letters					
		—	BV	25.00	32.50	50.00
377.8	1856/5 PF	—	BV	25.00	32.50	50.00
	1856 PF	—	BV	25.00	32.50	50.00
	1857/6 PF	—	BV	25.00	32.50	50.00
	1857 PF	—	BV	25.00	32.50	50.00
	1858 PF	—	BV	25.00	32.50	50.00
	1859/7 PF	—	BV	25.00	32.50	50.00
	1859/8 PF	—	BV	25.00	32.50	50.00
	1859 PF	—	BV	25.00	32.50	50.00
	1860/50 PF	—	BV	25.00	32.50	50.00
	1860/59 PF	—	BV	25.00	32.50	50.00
	1860 PF	—	BV	25.00	32.50	50.00
	1861/51 PF	—	BV	25.00	32.50	50.00
	1861/0 PF	—	BV	25.00	32.50	50.00
	1861 PF	—	BV	25.00	32.50	50.00
	1862 JG	—	BV	25.00	32.50	50.00
	1862 YE/PF	—	BV	25.00	32.50	50.00
	1862 YF	—	BV	25.00	32.50	50.00
	1862 YF/PF	—	25.00	30.00	40.00	70.00
	1863/53 YF	—	BV	25.00	32.50	50.00
	1863 YF	—	BV	25.00	32.50	50.00
	1867/57 YF	—	27.50	38.50	55.00	90.00
	1867 YF	—	25.00	30.00	42.50	65.00
	1868/58 YF	—	BV	25.00	32.50	50.00
	1868 YF	—	BV	25.00	32.50	50.00
	1870/60 FR	—	BV	25.00	35.00	60.00
	1870 YF	—	50.00	75.00	125.00	200.00
	1870 FR/YF	—	25.00	30.00	37.50	60.00
	1870 FR	—	BV	25.00	32.50	55.00
	1873 FR	—	BV	25.00	32.50	50.00
	1874/3 FR	—	BV	25.00	32.50	50.00
	1874 FR	—	BV	25.00	32.50	50.00
	1875/6 FR	—	BV	25.00	32.50	50.00
	1875 FR	—	BV	25.00	32.50	50.00
	1876 FR	—	BV	25.00	32.50	50.00
	1877 FR	2.477	BV	25.00	32.50	50.00
	1878/7 FR					
		2.273	BV	25.00	32.50	50.00
	1878 FR	I.A.	BV	25.00	32.50	50.00
	1878/7 SM	—	BV	25.00	32.50	50.00
	1878 SM	—	BV	25.00	32.50	50.00
	1879/7 SM	—	BV	25.00	32.50	50.00
	1879/8 SM	—	BV	25.00	32.50	50.00
	1879 SM	—	BV	25.00	32.50	50.00
	1880/70 SB	—	BV	25.00	32.50	50.00
	1880 SB/SM	—	BV	25.00	32.50	50.00
	1881/71 SB					
		3.974	BV	25.00	32.50	50.00
	1881/0 SB	I.A.	BV	25.00	32.50	50.00
	1881 SB	I.A.	BV	25.00	32.50	50.00
	1882 SB	2.015	BV	25.00	32.50	50.00
	1883 SB	2.100	BV	25.00	32.50	50.00
	1883 BR	Inc. Ab.	BV	25.00	32.50	50.00
	1883 BR/SR	—	BV	25.00	32.50	50.00
	1883 BR/SB	I.A.	BV	25.00	32.50	50.00
	1884/73 BR	—	BV	25.00	32.50	50.00
	1884/74 BR	—	25.00	30.00	40.00	70.00
	1884/3 BR	—	BV	25.00	32.50	50.00
	1884 BR	—	BV	25.00	32.50	50.00
	1884 RR	—	25.00	30.00	40.00	65.00
	1885/75 PR					
		2.363	BV	25.00	30.00	50.00
	1885 RR	I.A.	BV	25.00	30.00	50.00
	1886/75 RR					
		4.127	BV	25.00	30.00	50.00
	1886/76 RR	I.A.	BV	25.00	30.00	50.00
	1886 RR	I.A.	BV	25.00	30.00	50.00
	1887 RR	4.205	BV	25.00	30.00	50.00
	1888 RR	3.985	BV	25.00	30.00	50.00
	1889 RR	3.646	BV	25.00	30.00	50.00
	1890 RR	3.615	BV	25.00	30.00	50.00
	1891 RR	3.197	250.00	400.00	600.00	850.00
	1891 RS	Inc. Ab.	BV	25.00	32.50	50.00
	1892 RS	3.672	BV	25.00	32.50	50.00
	1893 RS	3.854	BV	25.00	32.50	50.00
	1894 RS	4.127	BV	25.00	32.50	50.00
	1895/1 RS					
		3.768	BV	25.00	32.50	55.00
	1895 RS	I.A.	BV	25.00	32.50	50.00
	1896 RS	5.229	BV	25.00	32.50	50.00
	1896 RS with Go 1896 RS over As 1891 ML					
		Inc. Ab.	BV	25.00	35.00	60.00
	1897 RS	4.344	BV	25.00	32.50	50.00

HERMOSILLO MINT (Ho)

KM#	Date	Mintage	Fine	VF	XF	Unc
377.9	1835 PP	—	Known in illustration only			
	1836 PP	—	—	Unique	—	—
	1839 PR	—	—	Unique	—	—
	1861 FM	—	600.00	850.00	1350.	2000.
	1862 FM	—	100.00	200.00	350.00	550.00
	1862 FM with reeded edge					
		—	100.00	200.00	300.00	500.00
	1863 FM	—	100.00	200.00	300.00	500.00
	1864 FM	—	150.00	250.00	350.00	550.00
	1864 PR	—	150.00	250.00	350.00	550.00
	1865 FM	—	100.00	135.00	175.00	325.00
	1866 FM	—	125.00	175.00	225.00	400.00
	1866 MP	—	400.00	500.00	600.00	900.00
377.9	1867 PR	—	65.00	85.00	125.00	200.00
	1868 PR	—	25.00	30.00	45.00	85.00
	1869 PR	—	55.00	75.00	100.00	165.00
	1870 PR	—	90.00	115.00	165.00	225.00
	1871/0 PR	—	60.00	75.00	100.00	165.00
	1871 PR	—	55.00	70.00	100.00	165.00
	1872/1 PR	—	55.00	70.00	85.00	150.00
	1872 PR	—	50.00	65.00	80.00	140.00
	1873 PR	.351	35.00	50.00	75.00	135.00
	1874 PR	—	25.00	32.50	45.00	85.00
	1875 PR	—	25.00	30.00	35.00	70.00
	1876 AF	—	25.00	35.00	50.00	90.00
	1877 AF	.410	25.00	30.00	40.00	80.00
	1877 GR	Inc. Ab.	55.00	70.00	100.00	165.00
	1877 JA	Inc. Ab.	25.00	30.00	40.00	65.00
	1878 JA	.451	BV	25.00	32.50	50.00
	1879 JA	—	BV	25.00	32.50	55.00
	1880 JA	—	BV	25.00	32.50	50.00
	1881 JA	.586	BV	25.00	32.50	55.00
	1882 HoJA with O above H					
		.240	25.00	40.00	70.00	125.00
	1882 HoJA with O after H					
		Inc. Ab.	25.00	40.00	70.00	125.00
	1883/2 JA	.204	50.00	70.00	90.00	150.00
	1883/2 FM/JA					
		Inc. Ab.	25.00	30.00	40.00	60.00
	1883 JA	Inc. Ab.	50.00	70.00	100.00	165.00
	1884/3 FM	—	BV	25.00	32.50	55.00
	1884 FM	—	BV	25.00	32.50	50.00
	1885 FM	.132	BV	25.00	32.50	55.00
	1886 FM	.225	25.00	30.00	40.00	70.00
	1886 FG	Inc. Ab.	BV	25.00	32.50	65.00
	1887 FG	.150	BV	25.00	32.50	70.00
	1888 FG	.364	BV	25.00	32.50	50.00
	1889 FG	.490	BV	25.00	32.50	50.00
	1890 FG	.565	BV	25.00	32.50	50.00
	1891 FG	.738	BV	25.00	32.50	50.00
	1892 FG	.643	BV	25.00	32.50	50.00
	1893 FG	.518	BV	25.00	32.50	50.00
	1894 FG	.504	BV	25.00	32.50	50.00
	1895 FG	.320	BV	25.00	32.50	50.00

MEXICO CITY MINT (Mo)

KM#	Date	Mintage	Fine	VF	XF	Unc
377.10	1824 JM	—	65.00	85.00	110.00	225.00
	1825 JM	—	25.00	30.00	40.00	75.00
	1826/5 JM	—	25.00	30.00	40.00	70.00
	1826 JM	—	25.00	30.00	40.00	65.00
	1827 JM	—	25.00	30.00	40.00	55.00
	1828 JM	—	25.00	30.00	40.00	85.00
	1829 JM	—	25.00	30.00	40.00	70.00
	1830/20 JM	—	25.00	32.50	50.00	85.00
	1830 JM	—	30.00	55.00	75.00	125.00
	1831 JM	—	25.00	30.00	47.50	65.00
	1832/1 JM	—	25.00	30.00	40.00	55.00
	1832 JM	—	25.00	30.00	40.00	55.00
	1833 MJ	—	27.50	40.00	55.00	85.00
	1833 ML	—	70.00	100.00	150.00	250.00
	1834/3 ML	—	25.00	30.00	40.00	55.00
	1834 ML	—	25.00	30.00	40.00	50.00
	1835 ML	—	25.00	30.00	40.00	50.00
	1836 ML	—	47.50	65.00	85.00	140.00
	1836 ML/MF	—	50.00	65.00	85.00	140.00
	1836 MF	—	25.00	30.00	45.00	70.00
	1836 MF/ML	—	25.00	30.00	45.00	70.00
	1837/6 ML	—	30.00	43.50	65.00	125.00
	1837/6 MM	—	25.00	30.00	40.00	70.00
	1837/6 MM/ML		25.00	30.00	40.00	70.00
	1837 ML	—	27.50	35.00	55.00	100.00
	1837 MM	—	25.00	30.00	36.50	65.00
	1838 MM	—	40.00	60.00	80.00	140.00
	1838 ML	—	25.00	35.00	55.00	85.00
	1838 ML/MM	—	25.00	30.00	40.00	60.00
	1839 ML	—	BV	25.00	32.50	50.00
	1840 ML	—	BV	25.00	32.50	50.00
	1841 ML	—	BV	25.00	32.50	50.00
	1842 ML	—	BV	25.00	32.50	50.00
	1842 MM	—	BV	25.00	32.50	50.00
	1843 MM	—	30.00	55.00	85.00	140.00
	1844 MF	—	BV	25.00	32.50	50.00
	1845/4 MF	—	BV	25.00	32.50	50.00
	1845 MF	—	BV	25.00	32.50	50.00
	1846/5 MF	—	BV	25.00	32.50	50.00

KM#	Date	Mintage	Fine	VF	XF	Unc
377.10	1849/8 GC	—	BV	25.00	32.50	50.00
	1849 GC	—	BV	25.00	32.50	50.00
	1850/40 GC	—	BV	25.00	32.50	50.00
	1850 GC	—	BV	25.00	32.50	50.00
	1851 GC	—	BV	25.00	32.50	50.00
	1852 GC	—	BV	25.00	32.50	65.00
	1853 GC	—	BV	25.00	32.50	60.00
	1854 GC	—	BV	25.00	32.50	60.00
	1855 GC	—	25.00	35.00	55.00	90.00
	1855 GF	—	BV	25.00	32.50	55.00
	1855 GF/GC	—	BV	25.00	32.50	60.00
	1856/4 GF	—	BV	25.00	32.50	60.00
	1856/5 GF	—	BV	25.00	32.50	60.00
	1856 GF	—	BV	25.00	32.50	55.00
	1857 FH	—	BV	25.00	32.50	60.00
	1858 FH	—	BV	25.00	32.50	55.00
	1859 FH	—	BV	25.00	32.50	55.00
	1860/59 FH	—	BV	25.00	32.50	55.00
	1860 FH	—	BV	25.00	32.50	50.00
	1861 TH	—	BV	25.00	32.50	55.00
	1861 CH	—	BV	25.00	32.50	50.00
	1862 CH	—	BV	25.00	32.50	50.00
	1863 CH	—	BV	25.00	32.50	55.00
	1863 CH/TH	—	BV	25.00	32.50	55.00
	1863 TH	—	BV	25.00	32.50	50.00
	1863 MM	—	100.00	200.00	350.00	500.00
	1863 MF	—	100.00	200.00	350.00	500.00
	1867 CH	—	25.00	30.00	40.00	65.00
	1868 CH	—	BV	25.00	32.50	50.00
	1868 PH	—	BV	25.00	32.50	50.00
	1869 CH	—	BV	25.00	32.50	50.00
	1873 MH	—	BV	25.00	32.50	50.00
	1873 MH/HH	—	BV	25.00	32.50	50.00
	1874/69 MH	—	BV	25.00	32.50	50.00
	1874 MH	—	BV	25.00	32.50	50.00
	1874 CP	—	400.00	500.00	700.00	1000.
	1874 BH/MH	—	BV	25.00	32.50	50.00
	1875 BH	—	BV	25.00	32.50	50.00
	1876/4 BH	—	BV	25.00	32.50	50.00
	1876/5 BH	—	BV	25.00	32.50	50.00
	1876 BH	—	BV	25.00	32.50	50.00
	1877 MH	.898	BV	25.00	32.50	50.00
	1877 MH/BH	—	BV	25.00	32.50	50.00
	1878 MH	2.154	BV	25.00	32.50	50.00
	1879/8 MH	—	BV	25.00	32.50	50.00
	1879 MH	—	BV	25.00	32.50	50.00
	1880/79 MH	—	BV	25.00	32.50	50.00
	1880 MH	—	BV	25.00	32.50	50.00
	1881 MH	5.712	BV	25.00	32.50	50.00
	1882/1 MH	2.746	BV	25.00	32.50	50.00
	1882 MH	I.A.	BV	25.00	32.50	50.00
	1883/2 MH	2.726	BV	25.00	32.50	50.00
	1883 MH	I.A.	BV	25.00	32.50	50.00
	1884/3 MH	—	BV	25.00	32.50	50.00
	1884 MH	—	BV	25.00	32.50	50.00
	1885 MH	3.649	BV	25.00	32.50	50.00
	1886 MH	7.559	BV	25.00	32.50	50.00
	1887 MH	7.681	BV	25.00	32.50	50.00
	1888 MH	7.179	BV	25.00	32.50	50.00
	1889 MH	7.332	BV	25.00	32.50	50.00
	1890 MH	7.412	BV	25.00	32.50	50.00
	1890 AM	Inc. Ab.	BV	25.00	32.50	50.00
	1891 AM	8.076	BV	25.00	32.50	50.00
	1892 AM	9.392	BV	25.00	32.50	50.00
	1893 AM	10.773	BV	25.00	32.50	50.00
	1894 AM	12.394	BV	25.00	32.50	50.00
	1895 AM	10.474	BV	25.00	32.50	50.00
	1895 AB	Inc. Ab.	BV	25.00	32.50	50.00
	1896 AB	9.327	BV	25.00	32.50	50.00
	1896 AM	Inc. Ab.	BV	25.00	32.50	50.00
	1897 AM	8.621	BV	25.00	32.50	50.00

OAXACA MINT (O, Oa)

KM#	Date	Mintage	Fine	VF	XF	Unc
377.11	1858O AE	—	200.00	300.00	450.00	700.00
	1858OaAE	—	200.00	300.00	450.00	700.00
	1859 AE	—	100.00	200.00	350.00	500.00
	1860 AE	—	55.00	75.00	100.00	165.00
	1861OaFR	—	80.00	100.00	150.00	225.00
	1861OaFR A in O	—	75.00	100.00	125.00	225.00
	1862O FR	—	45.00	75.00	125.00	225.00
	1862OaFR	—	60.00	80.00	100.00	175.00
	1863 FR	—	27.50	40.00	60.00	100.00
	1863 AE	—	27.50	40.00	60.00	100.00
	1863OaAE with A in O of mm	—	100.00	150.00	250.00	400.00
	1863OaAE with A above O in mm	—	300.00	400.00	550.00	850.00
	1864 FR	—	27.50	40.00	60.00	100.00
	1867 AE	—	40.00	55.00	75.00	125.00
	1868 AE	—	25.00	32.50	47.50	70.00
	1869 AE	—	40.00	75.00	100.00	150.00
	1870 AE	—	—	—	—	—
	1871/69 E	—	—	—	—	—
	1871 E	—	—	—	—	—
	1872 E	—	—	—	—	—
	1873 AE	—	42.50	60.00	80.00	115.00
	1873 E	—	—	—	—	—
	1874 AE	.142	25.00	30.00	40.00	60.00
	1875/4 AE	.131	25.00	30.00	40.00	60.00
	1875 AE	I.A.	25.00	30.00	40.00	60.00
	1876 AE	.140	BV	25.00	32.50	55.00
	1877 AE	.139	BV	25.00	32.50	55.00
	1878 AE	.125	BV	25.00	32.50	55.00
	1879 AE	.153	BV	25.00	32.50	55.00
	1880 AE	.143	BV	25.00	32.50	55.00
	1881 AE	.134	BV	25.00	32.50	60.00
	1882 AE	1.000	BV	25.00	32.50	55.00
	1883 AE	.122	BV	25.00	32.50	55.00
	1884 AE	.142	BV	25.00	32.50	55.00
	1885 AE	.158	BV	25.00	32.50	55.00
	1886 AE	.120	BV	25.00	32.50	55.00
	1887/6 AE	.115	25.00	32.50	40.00	70.00
	1887 AE	I.A.	25.00	32.50	40.00	65.00
	1888 AE	.145	25.00	32.50	40.00	65.00
	1889 AE	.150	BV	25.00	32.50	55.00
	1890 AE	.181	BV	25.00	32.50	55.00
	1891 EN	.160	BV	25.00	32.50	55.00
	1892 EN	.120	BV	25.00	32.50	60.00
	1893 EN	.066	32.50	45.00	60.00	100.00

POTOSI MINT (Pi)

KM#	Date	Mintage	Fine	VF	XF	Unc
377.12	1827 JS	—	400.00	550.00	750.00	1000.
	1828/7 JS	—	70.00	90.00	120.00	200.00
	1828 JS	—	65.00	85.00	110.00	175.00
	1829 JS	—	55.00	75.00	100.00	165.00
	1830 JS	—	35.00	50.00	75.00	125.00
	1831/0 JS	—	27.50	38.50	55.00	90.00
	1831 JS	—	25.00	35.00	55.00	90.00
	1832/22 JS	—	27.50	38.50	55.00	90.00
	1832 JS	—	25.00	35.00	55.00	90.00
	1833/2 JS	—	25.00	30.00	38.50	60.00
	1833 JS	—	25.00	30.00	35.00	55.00
	1834/3 JS	—	25.00	31.50	45.00	75.00
	1834 JS	—	25.00	30.00	40.00	65.00
	1835 JS w/8R		25.00	32.50	47.50	75.00
	1835 JS w/8Rs		25.00	32.50	47.50	70.00
	1836 JS	—	25.00	30.00	40.00	65.00
	1837 JS	—	27.50	40.00	60.00	100.00
	1838 JS	—	25.00	30.00	40.00	60.00
	1839 JS	—	25.00	35.00	52.50	85.00
	1840 JS	—	BV	25.00	32.50	50.00
	1841PiJS		25.00	30.00	40.00	60.00
	1841iPJS (error)	—	100.00	150.00	225.00	350.00
	1842/1 JS	—	25.00	37.50	55.00	90.00
	1842/1 PS/JS		25.00	30.00	40.00	70.00
	1842 JS	—	25.00	32.50	47.50	80.00
	1842 PS	—	25.00	30.00	40.00	70.00
	1842 PS/JS	—	25.00	30.00	40.00	65.00
	1843/2 PS 3 with round top	—	30.00	45.00	65.00	100.00
	1843 PS 3 with flat top	—	30.00	45.00	65.00	100.00
	1844 AM	—	25.00	30.00	40.00	70.00
	1845/4 AM	—	25.00	30.00	35.00	55.00
	1845 AM	—	27.50	40.00	50.00	85.00
	1846/5 AM	—	25.00	30.00	40.00	75.00
	1846 AM	—	25.00	30.00	40.00	70.00
	1847 AM	—	25.00	30.00	40.00	60.00
	1848/7 AM	—	25.00	30.00	40.00	70.00
	1848 AM	—	25.00	30.00	40.00	70.00
	1849/8 PS/AM		300.00	450.00	650.00	900.00
	1849 PS/AM	—	300.00	450.00	650.00	900.00
	1849 MC/PS	—	25.00	30.00	40.00	85.00
	1849 AM	—	100.00	135.00	185.00	265.00
	1849 MC	—	25.00	30.00	40.00	85.00
	1850 MC	—	25.00	30.00	40.00	85.00
	1851 MC	—	100.00	125.00	185.00	250.00
	1852 MC	—	30.00	45.00	65.00	100.00
	1853 MC	—	30.00	45.00	60.00	85.00
	1854 MC	—	25.00	35.00	55.00	85.00
	1855 MC	—	25.00	30.00	37.50	75.00
	1856 MC	—	25.00	32.50	45.00	85.00
	1857 MC	—	45.00	70.00	100.00	150.00
	1857 PS/MC	—	40.00	60.00	85.00	120.00
	1857 PS	—	32.50	45.00	70.00	110.00
	1858 MC/PS	—	150.00	275.00	400.00	700.00
	1858 PS	—	200.00	300.00	450.00	700.00
	1859/8 MC/PS		500.00	600.00	800.00	1000.
	1859 PS/PC	—	500.00	600.00	800.00	1000.
	1859 PS	—	500.00	600.00	800.00	1000.
	1860 PS	—	300.00	400.00	550.00	850.00
	1860 MC	—	100.00	200.00	350.00	550.00
	1861 RS	—	25.00	30.00	45.00	70.00
	1861 RO	—	25.00	30.00	40.00	65.00
	1862/1 RO	—	25.00	30.00	40.00	60.00
	1862 RO	—	BV	25.00	32.50	55.00
	1862 RO oval O in RO	—	25.00	30.00	37.50	55.00
	1862 RO round O in RO, 6 is inverted 9	—	25.00	30.00	40.00	65.00
	1863/2 RO	—	25.00	30.00	45.00	80.00
	1863 RO	—	25.00	30.00	40.00	75.00
	1863 6 over inverted 6	—	25.00	30.00	40.00	80.00
	1863 FC	—	45.00	60.00	85.00	140.00
	1864 RO	—	100.00	200.00	285.00	400.00
	1867 CA	—	400.00	500.00	650.00	1000.
	1867 LR	—	50.00	70.00	90.00	120.00
	1867 PS	—	25.00	32.50	47.50	70.00
	1868/7 PS	—	25.00	45.00	65.00	100.00
	1868 PS	—	30.00	40.00	55.00	85.00
	1869/8 PS	—	BV	25.00	32.50	55.00
	1869 PS	—	BV	25.00	32.50	55.00
	1870 PS	—	100.00	125.00	175.00	250.00
	1873 MH	—	BV	25.00	32.50	50.00
	1874/3 MH	—	BV	25.00	32.50	50.00
	1874 MH	—	BV	25.00	32.50	50.00
	1875 MH	—	BV	25.00	32.50	50.00
	1876/5 MH	—	BV	25.00	32.50	50.00
	1876 MH	—	BV	25.00	32.50	50.00
	1877 MH	1.018	BV	25.00	32.50	50.00
	1878 MH	1.046	BV	25.00	32.50	50.00
	1879/8 MH	—	BV	25.00	32.50	50.00
	1879 MH	—	BV	25.00	32.50	50.00
	1879 BE	—	25.00	37.50	55.00	85.00
	1879 MR	—	40.00	60.00	85.00	140.00
	1880 MR	—	25.00	35.00	55.00	75.00
	1880 MH	—	BV	25.00	32.50	50.00
	1881 MH	2.100	BV	25.00	35.00	60.00
	1882 MH	1.602	BV	25.00	32.50	50.00
	1882/1 MH	I.A.	BV	25.00	32.50	50.00
	1883 MH	1.545	BV	25.00	32.50	50.00
	1884/3 MH	—	BV	25.00	32.50	50.00
	1884 MH/MM	—	BV	25.00	32.50	50.00
	1884 MH	—	BV	25.00	32.50	50.00
	1885/4 MH	1.736	BV	25.00	32.50	50.00
	1885/8 MH	I.A.	BV	25.00	32.50	50.00
	1885 MH	I.A.	BV	25.00	32.50	50.00
	1885 LC	I.A.	BV	25.00	32.50	50.00
	1886 LC	3.347	BV	25.00	32.50	50.00
	1886 MR	I.A.	BV	25.00	32.50	50.00
	1887 MR	2.922	BV	25.00	32.50	50.00
	1888 MR	2.438	BV	25.00	32.50	50.00
	1889 MR	2.103	BV	25.00	32.50	50.00
	1890 MR	1.562	BV	25.00	32.50	50.00
	1891 MR	1.184	BV	25.00	32.50	50.00
	1892 MR	1.336	BV	25.00	32.50	50.00
	1893 MR	.530	BV	25.00	32.50	50.00

ZACATECAS MINT (Zs)

KM#	Date	Mintage	Fine	VF	XF	Unc
377.13	1825 AZ	—	25.00	30.00	40.00	80.00
	1826 AZ	—	25.00	30.00	37.50	55.00
	1826 AV	—	25.00	30.00	45.00	85.00
	1826 AO	—	150.00	250.00	375.00	500.00
	1827 AO/Z	—	25.00	30.00	37.50	60.00
	1827 AO/AZ	—	25.00	30.00	37.50	55.00
	1828 AO	—	25.00	30.00	37.50	55.00
	1829 AO	—	25.00	30.00	37.50	65.00
	1829 OV	—	37.50	55.00	85.00	150.00
	1830 OV	—	25.00	30.00	37.50	50.00
	1831 OV	—	20.00	40.00	60.00	100.00
	1831 OM	—	BV	25.00	32.50	55.00
	1832/1 OM	—	BV	25.00	32.50	55.00
	1832 OM	—	BV	25.00	32.50	50.00
	1833/2 OM	—	BV	25.00	32.50	55.00
	1833 OM/MM	—	BV	25.00	32.50	50.00
	1833 OM	—	BV	25.00	32.50	50.00
	1834 OM	—	BV	25.00	32.50	55.00
	1835 OM	—	BV	25.00	32.50	50.00

KM#	Date	Mintage	Fine	VF	XF	Unc
377.13	1836/5 OM	—	BV	25.00	32.50	55.00
	1836 OM	—	BV	25.00	32.50	50.00
	1837 OM	—	BV	25.00	32.50	50.00
	1838/7 OM	—	BV	25.00	32.50	50.00
	1838 OM	—	BV	25.00	32.50	50.00
	1839 OM	—	BV	25.00	32.50	50.00
	1840 OM	—	BV	25.00	32.50	50.00
	1841 OM	—	BV	25.00	32.50	50.00
	1842 OM	—	BV	25.00	32.50	50.00
	1843 OM	—	BV	25.00	32.50	50.00
	1844 OM	—	BV	25.00	32.50	50.00
	1845 OM	—	BV	25.00	32.50	50.00
	1846 OM	—	BV	25.00	32.50	50.00
	1847 OM	—	BV	25.00	32.50	50.00
	1848/7 OM	—	BV	25.00	32.50	50.00
	1848 OM	—	BV	25.00	32.50	50.00
	1849 OM	—	BV	25.00	32.50	50.00
	1850 OM	—	BV	25.00	32.50	50.00
	1851 OM	—	BV	25.00	32.50	50.00
	1852 OM	—	BV	25.00	32.50	50.00
	1853 OM	—	25.00	32.50	50.00	80.00
	1854 OM	—	BV	25.00	32.50	50.00
	1855 OM	—	25.00	30.00	37.50	70.00
	1855 MO	—	27.50	42.50	60.00	100.00
	1856/5 MO	—	BV	25.00	32.50	50.00
	1856 MO	—	BV	25.00	32.50	50.00
	1857/5 MO	—	BV	25.00	32.50	50.00
	1857 MO	—	BV	25.00	32.50	50.00
	1858/7 MO	—	BV	25.00	32.50	50.00
	1858 MO	—	BV	25.00	32.50	50.00
	1859/8 MO	—	BV	25.00	32.50	50.00
	1859 MO	—	BV	25.00	32.50	50.00
	1859 VL/MO	—	25.00	30.00	37.50	60.00
	1859 VL	—	BV	25.00	32.50	55.00
	1860/59 MO	—	BV	25.00	32.50	50.00
	1860 MO	—	BV	25.00	32.50	50.00
	1860 VL/MC	—	BV	25.00	32.50	50.00
	1860 VL	—	BV	25.00	32.50	50.00
	1861/0 VL/MO		27.50	40.00	60.00	100.00
	1861 VL	—	BV	25.00	32.50	50.00
	1862 VL	—	BV	25.00	32.50	50.00
	1863 VL	—	BV	25.00	32.50	50.00
	1863 MO	—	BV	25.00	32.50	50.00
	1864/3 VL	—	25.00	30.00	37.50	70.00
	1864 VL	—	25.00	30.00	37.50	65.00
	1864 MO	—	25.00	30.00	37.50	60.00
	1865/4 MO	—	135.00	185.00	250.00	350.00
	1865 MO	—	125.00	175.00	235.00	325.00
	1866 VL contemporary counterfeit					
	1867 JS	—	400.00	500.00	700.00	1000.
	1868 JS	—	BV	25.00	32.50	50.00
	1868 YH	—	BV	25.00	32.50	55.00
	1869 YH	—	BV	25.00	32.50	50.00
	1873 YH	—	BV	25.00	32.50	70.00
	1874 YH	—	BV	25.00	32.50	50.00
	1874 JA/YA	—	BV	25.00	32.50	50.00
	1874 JA	—	BV	25.00	32.50	50.00
	1875 JA	—	BV	25.00	32.50	50.00
	1876 JA	—	BV	25.00	32.50	50.00
	1876 JS	—	BV	25.00	32.50	50.00
	1877 JS	2.700	BV	25.00	32.50	50.00
	1878 JS	2.310	BV	25.00	32.50	50.00
	1879/8 JS	—	BV	25.00	32.50	50.00
	1879 JS	—	BV	25.00	32.50	50.00
	1880 JS	—	BV	25.00	32.50	50.00
	1881 JS	5.592	BV	25.00	32.50	50.00
	1882/1 JS	2.480	BV	25.00	32.50	50.00
	1882 JS	I.A.	BV	25.00	32.50	50.00
	1882 JS straight J	Inc. Ab.	BV	25.00	32.50	50.00
	1882 JS full J	Inc. Ab.	BV	25.00	32.50	50.00
	1883/2 JS	2.563	BV	25.00	32.50	50.00
	1883 JS	I.A.	BV	25.00	32.50	50.00
	1884 JS	—	BV	25.00	32.50	50.00
	1885 JS	2.252	BV	25.00	32.50	50.00
	1886/5 JS	5.303	BV	25.00	32.50	50.00
	1886/8 JS	I.A.	BV	25.00	32.50	50.00
	1886 JS	I.A.	BV	25.00	32.50	50.00
	1886 FZ	I.A.	BV	25.00	32.50	50.00
	1887ZsFZ	4.733	BV	25.00	32.50	50.00
	1887Z FZ	I.A.	25.00	30.00	45.00	80.00
	1888/7 FZ	5.132	BV	25.00	32.50	50.00
	1888 FZ	I.A.	BV	25.00	32.50	50.00
	1889 FZ	4.344	BV	25.00	32.50	50.00
	1890 FZ	3.887	BV	25.00	32.50	50.00
	1891 FZ	4.114	BV	25.00	32.50	50.00
	1892/1 FZ	4.238	BV	25.00	32.50	55.00
	1892 FZ	I.A.	BV	25.00	32.50	50.00
	1893 FZ	3.872	BV	25.00	32.50	50.00
	1894 FZ	3.081	BV	25.00	32.50	50.00
	1895 FZ	4.718	BV	25.00	32.50	50.00
	1896 FZ	4.226	BV	25.00	32.50	50.00
	1897 FZ	4.877	BV	25.00	32.50	50.00

1/2 ESCUDO

1.6900 gm., .875 GOLD, .0475 oz ASW

CULIACAN MINT (C, Cn)

Obv: Facing eagle

KM#	Date	Mintage	VG	Fine	VF	XF
378	1848 CE	—	40.00	50.00	65.00	100.00
	1853 CE	—	35.00	47.50	60.00	85.00
	1854 CE	—	40.00	50.00	65.00	100.00
	1857 CE	—	40.00	50.00	65.00	100.00
	1859 CE	—	40.00	50.00	65.00	100.00
	1860 CE	—	35.00	47.50	60.00	85.00
	1862 CE	—	30.00	42.50	50.00	70.00
	1863 CE	—	30.00	42.50	50.00	70.00
	1866 CE	—	45.00	65.00	80.00	110.00
	1867 CE	—	35.00	47.50	60.00	85.00
	1870 CE	—	—	—	—	—

DURANGO MINT (Do)

KM#	Date	Mintage	VG	Fine	VF	XF
378.1	1833 RM/RL	—	35.00	47.50	60.00	85.00
	1834/3 RM	—	35.00	47.50	60.00	85.00
	1835/3 RM	—	35.00	47.50	60.00	85.00
	1836/4 RM	—	35.00	47.50	60.00	85.00
	1837 RM	—	42.50	55.00	70.00	100.00
	1838 RM	—	50.00	70.00	90.00	120.00
	1843 RM	—	50.00	70.00	90.00	120.00
	1844/33 RM	—	55.00	75.00	90.00	120.00
	1846 RM	—	50.00	70.00	90.00	120.00
	1848 RM	—	42.50	55.00	70.00	100.00
	1850/33 JMR	—	50.00	70.00	90.00	120.00
	1851 JMR	—	55.00	80.00	100.00	135.00
	1852 JMR	—	55.00	80.00	100.00	135.00
	1853 CP	—	35.00	50.00	65.00	90.00
	1854 CP	—	42.50	55.00	70.00	100.00
	1855 CP	—	35.00	47.50	60.00	85.00
	1859 CP	—	42.50	55.00	70.00	100.00
	1861 CP	—	40.00	50.00	65.00	90.00
	1864 LT	—	55.00	75.00	100.00	135.00

GUADALAJARA MINT (Ga)

KM#	Date	Mintage	VG	Fine	VF	XF
378.2	1825 FS	—	50.00	70.00	90.00	120.00
	1829 FS	—	42.50	60.00	75.00	100.00
	1831 FS	—	55.00	75.00	90.00	120.00
	1834 FS	—	47.50	70.00	80.00	110.00
	1835 FS	—	42.50	60.00	75.00	100.00
	1837 JG	—	55.00	75.00	90.00	120.00
	1838 JG	—	55.00	75.00	90.00	120.00
	1839 JG	—	55.00	80.00	100.00	135.00
	1842 JG	—	55.00	80.00	100.00	135.00
	1847 JG	—	55.00	80.00	100.00	135.00
	1850 JG	—	40.00	50.00	65.00	90.00
	1852 JG	—	40.00	50.00	65.00	90.00
	1859 JG	—	50.00	70.00	90.00	120.00
	1861 JG	—	35.00	47.50	60.00	85.00

GUADALUPE Y CALVO MINT (GC)

KM#	Date	Mintage	VG	Fine	VF	XF
378.3	1843/2 MP	—	60.00	70.00	90.00	120.00
	1846 MP	—	45.00	65.00	80.00	110.00
	1847 MP	—	42.50	55.00	70.00	100.00
	1848/7 MP	—	42.50	55.00	70.00	100.00
	1851 MP	—	45.00	65.00	80.00	110.00

GUANAJUATO MINT (Go)

KM#	Date	Mintage	VG	Fine	VF	XF
378.4	1845 PM	—	32.50	42.50	50.00	75.00
	1849 PF	—	32.50	42.50	50.00	75.00
	1851 PF	—	27.50	37.50	47.50	65.00
	1852 PF	—	27.50	37.50	47.50	65.00
	1853 PF	—	32.50	42.50	50.00	75.00
	1855 PF	—	35.00	47.50	60.00	85.00
	1857 PF	—	27.50	37.50	47.50	65.00
	1858/7 PF	—	27.50	37.50	47.50	65.00
	1859 PF	—	27.50	37.50	47.50	65.00
	1860 PF	—	27.50	37.50	47.50	65.00
	1861 PF	—	27.50	37.50	47.50	65.00

KM#	Date	Mintage	VG	Fine	VF	XF
378.4	1862/1 YE	—	27.50	37.50	47.50	65.00
	1863 YF	—	27.50	37.50	47.50	65.00

MEXICO CITY MINT (Mo)

KM#	Date	Mintage	VG	Fine	VF	XF
378.5	1825/4 JM	—	35.00	47.50	57.50	80.00
	1825 JM	—	32.50	45.00	52.50	75.00
	1827/6 JM	—	35.00	47.50	57.50	80.00
	1827 JM	—	32.50	45.00	52.50	75.00
	1829 JM	—	40.00	52.50	67.50	90.00
	1831/0 JM	—	30.00	42.50	52.50	70.00
	1831 JM	—	27.50	37.50	47.50	65.00
	1832 JM	—	27.50	37.50	47.50	65.00
	1833 MF olive & oak branches reversed	—	32.50	42.50	52.50	75.00
	1834 ML	—	32.50	42.50	52.50	75.00
	1835 ML	—	40.00	52.50	67.50	90.00
	1838 ML	—	55.00	75.00	100.00	135.00
	1839 ML	—	55.00	75.00	100.00	135.00
	1840 ML	—	27.50	37.50	47.50	65.00
	1841 ML	—	27.50	37.50	47.50	65.00
	1842 ML	—	35.00	47.50	60.00	85.00
	1842 MM	—	35.00	47.50	60.00	85.00
	1843 MM	—	32.50	42.50	50.00	75.00
	1844 MF	—	27.50	37.50	47.50	65.00
	1845 MF	—	27.50	37.50	47.50	65.00
	1846/5 MF	—	30.00	40.00	50.00	75.00
	1846 MF	—	27.50	37.50	47.50	65.00
	1848 GC	—	32.50	42.50	50.00	75.00
	1850 GC	—	27.50	37.50	47.50	65.00
	1851 GC	—	27.50	37.50	47.50	65.00
	1852 GC	—	27.50	37.50	47.50	65.00
	1853 GC	—	27.50	37.50	47.50	65.00
	1854 GC	—	27.50	37.50	47.50	65.00
	1855 GF	—	32.50	42.50	50.00	75.00
	1856/4 GF	—	27.50	37.50	47.50	65.00
	1857 GF	—	27.50	37.50	47.50	65.00
	1858 FH	—	27.50	37.50	47.50	65.00
	1859 FH	—	32.50	42.50	50.00	75.00
	1860/59 FH	—	27.50	37.50	45.00	65.00
	1861 CH/FH	—	35.00	47.50	60.00	85.00
	1862 CH	—	32.50	42.50	50.00	75.00
	1863/57 CH/GF		27.50	37.50	47.50	65.00
	1868/58 PH	—	42.50	55.00	70.00	110.00
	1869/59 CH	—	42.50	55.00	70.00	110.00

ZACATECAS MINT (Zs)

KM#	Date	Mintage	VG	Fine	VF	XF
378.6	1860 VL	—	32.50	42.50	50.00	75.00
	1862/1 VL	—	32.50	42.50	50.00	70.00
	1862 VL	—	27.50	37.50	47.50	65.00

ESCUDO

3.3800 gm., .875 GOLD, .0950 oz ASW

CULIACAN MINT (C, Cn)

Obv: Facing eagle

KM#	Date	Mintage	VG	Fine	VF	XF
379	1846 CE	—	65.00	80.00	110.00	150.00
	1847 CE	—	65.00	80.00	110.00	150.00
	1848 CE	—	65.00	80.00	110.00	150.00
	1849/8 CE	—	65.00	80.00	110.00	150.00
	1850 CE	—	65.00	80.00	110.00	150.00
	1851/0 CE	—	65.00	80.00	110.00	150.00
	1853/1 CE	—	65.00	80.00	110.00	150.00
	1854 CE	—	75.00	90.00	125.00	170.00
	1856/5/4 CE	—	65.00	80.00	110.00	160.00
	1856 CE	—	65.00	80.00	110.00	150.00
	1857/1 CE	—	65.00	80.00	110.00	160.00
	1857 CE	—	65.00	80.00	110.00	160.00
	1861 PV	—	75.00	90.00	125.00	170.00
	1862 CE	—	75.00	90.00	125.00	170.00
	1863 CE	—	65.00	80.00	110.00	160.00
	1866 CE	—	75.00	90.00	125.00	170.00
	1870 CE	—	75.00	90.00	125.00	170.00

DURANGO MINT (Do)

KM#	Date	Mintage	VG	Fine	VF	XF
379.1	1832 RL	—	90.00	110.00	150.00	185.00
	1833/2 RM/RL		70.00	90.00	125.00	160.00
	1834 RM	—	80.00	110.00	135.00	170.00
	1836 RM/RL	—	70.00	90.00	125.00	160.00
	1838 RM	—	80.00	110.00	135.00	170.00
	1846/38 RM	—	80.00	110.00	135.00	170.00
	1850 JMR	—	100.00	120.00	160.00	200.00
	1851 JMR	—	100.00	120.00	160.00	200.00
	1853 CP	—	90.00	110.00	150.00	185.00

KM#	Date	Mintage	VG	Fine	VF	XF
379.1	1854/34 CP	—	90.00	120.00	160.00	200.00
	1854/44 CP/RP	—	90.00	110.00	150.00	185.00
	1855 CP	—	90.00	110.00	150.00	185.00
	1859 CP	—	90.00	110.00	150.00	185.00
	1861 CP	—	90.00	110.00	150.00	185.00
	1864 LT/CP	—	90.00	110.00	150.00	185.00

GUADALAJARA MINT (Ga)

KM#	Date	Mintage	VG	Fine	VF	XF
379.2	1825 FS	—	65.00	80.00	110.00	165.00
	1826 FS	—	75.00	90.00	135.00	175.00
	1831 FS	—	75.00	90.00	135.00	175.00
	1834 FS	—	65.00	80.00	110.00	165.00
	1842 JG/MC	—	75.00	90.00	125.00	175.00
	1843 MC	—	65.00	80.00	110.00	165.00
	1847 JG	—	75.00	90.00	125.00	175.00
	1848/7 JG	—	65.00	80.00	110.00	165.00
	1849 JG	—	75.00	90.00	125.00	175.00
	1850 JG	—	75.00	90.00	125.00	175.00
	1851/1 JG	—	65.00	80.00	110.00	165.00
	1856 JG	—	75.00	90.00	125.00	175.00
	1857 JG	—	65.00	80.00	110.00	165.00
	1859/7 JG	—	75.00	90.00	125.00	175.00
	1860/59 JG	—	67.50	85.00	110.00	165.00
	1860 JG	—	65.00	80.00	110.00	165.00

GUADALUPE Y CALVO MINT (GC)

KM#	Date	Mintage	VG	Fine	VF	XF
379.3	1844 MP	—	100.00	120.00	160.00	220.00
	1845 MP	—	90.00	110.00	150.00	200.00
	1846 MP	—	100.00	120.00	160.00	220.00
	1847 MP	—	90.00	110.00	150.00	200.00
	1848 MP	—	90.00	110.00	150.00	200.00
	1849 MP	—	100.00	120.00	160.00	220.00
	1850 MP	—	90.00	110.00	150.00	200.00
	1851 MP	—	100.00	120.00	160.00	200.00

GUANAJUATO MINT (Go)

KM#	Date	Mintage	VG	Fine	VF	XF
379.4	1845 PM	—	57.50	72.50	100.00	140.00
	1849 PF	—	57.50	72.50	100.00	140.00
	1851 PF	—	57.50	72.50	100.00	140.00
	1853 PF	—	57.50	72.50	100.00	140.00
	1860 PF	—	57.50	72.50	100.00	140.00
	1862 YE	—	57.50	72.50	100.00	140.00

MEXICO CITY MINT (Mo)

KM#	Date	Mintage	VG	Fine	VF	XF
379.5	1825 JM	—	50.00	65.00	90.00	140.00
	1827/6 JM	—	50.00	65.00	90.00	140.00
	1827 JM	—	50.00	65.00	90.00	140.00
	1830/29 JM	—	50.00	65.00	90.00	140.00
	1831 JM	—	50.00	65.00	90.00	140.00
	1832 JM	—	65.00	80.00	110.00	170.00
	1833 MJ	—	50.00	65.00	90.00	140.00
	1834 ML	—	65.00	80.00	110.00	170.00
	1841 ML	—	50.00	65.00	90.00	140.00
	1843 MM	—	50.00	65.00	90.00	140.00
	1845 MF	—	50.00	65.00	90.00	140.00
	1846/5 MF	—	50.00	65.00	90.00	140.00
	1848 GC	—	57.50	75.00	100.00	150.00
	1850 GC	—	65.00	80.00	110.00	170.00
	1856/4 GF	—	50.00	60.00	80.00	130.00
	1856/5 GF	—	50.00	60.00	80.00	130.00
	1856 GF	—	50.00	60.00	80.00	130.00
	1858 FH	—	57.50	75.00	100.00	150.00
	1859 FH	—	50.00	65.00	90.00	140.00
	1860 TH	—	57.50	75.00	100.00	150.00
	1861 CH	—	50.00	65.00	90.00	140.00
	1862 CH	—	57.50	75.00	100.00	150.00
	1863 TH	—	50.00	65.00	90.00	140.00
	1869 CH	—	50.00	65.00	90.00	140.00

ZACATECAS MINT (Zs)

KM#	Date	Mintage	VG	Fine	VF	XF
379.6	1853 OM	—	90.00	120.00	150.00	200.00
	1860/59 VL V is inverted A	—	75.00	90.00	125.00	175.00
	1860 VL	—	75.00	90.00	125.00	175.00
	1862 VL	—	75.00	90.00	125.00	175.00

2 ESCUDOS

6.7700 gm., .875 GOLD, .1904 oz ASW

CULIACAN MINT (C, Ca)

Obv: Facing eagle

KM#	Date	Mintage	VG	Fine	VF	XF
380	1846 CE	—	125.00	160.00	200.00	265.00
	1847 CE	—	125.00	160.00	200.00	265.00
	1848 CE	—	125.00	160.00	200.00	265.00
	1852 CE	—	125.00	160.00	200.00	265.00
	1854 CE	—	135.00	175.00	225.00	275.00
	1856/1 CE	—	135.00	175.00	225.00	275.00
	1857 CE	—	125.00	165.00	200.00	265.00

DURANGO MINT (Do)

KM#	Date	Mintage	VG	Fine	VF	XF
380.1	1833 RM	—	300.00	450.00	700.00	1000.
	1844 RM	—	275.00	400.00	600.00	850.00

ESTADO DE MEXICO MINT (Eo, Mo)

KM#	Date	Mintage	VG	Fine	VF	XF
380.2	1828 LF	—	700.00	900.00	1500.	2000.

GUADALAJARA MINT (Ga)

KM#	Date	Mintage	VG	Fine	VF	XF
380.3	1835 FS	—	125.00	160.00	200.00	265.00
	1836/5 JG	—	125.00	160.00	200.00	265.00
	1839 JG	—	125.00	160.00	200.00	265.00
	1840 MC	—	125.00	160.00	200.00	265.00
	1841 MC	—	125.00	160.00	200.00	265.00
	1847/6 JG	—	125.00	160.00	200.00	265.00
	1848/7 JG	—	125.00	160.00	200.00	265.00
	1850 JG	—	125.00	160.00	200.00	265.00
	1851 JG	—	125.00	160.00	200.00	265.00
	1853 JG	—	125.00	160.00	200.00	265.00
	1858 JG	—	125.00	160.00	200.00	265.00
	1859/8 JG	—	125.00	160.00	200.00	265.00
	1859 JG	—	125.00	160.00	200.00	265.00
	1860/50 JG	—	125.00	160.00	200.00	265.00
	1861/59 JG	—	125.00	160.00	200.00	265.00
	1861/0 JG	—	125.00	160.00	200.00	265.00
	1863/1 JG	—	125.00	160.00	200.00	265.00
	1870 IC	—	125.00	160.00	200.00	265.00

GUADALUPE Y CALVO MINT (GC)

KM#	Date	Mintage	VG	Fine	VF	XF
380.4	1844 MP	—	125.00	175.00	250.00	350.00
	1847 MP	—	125.00	175.00	350.00	500.00
	1848 MP	—	135.00	185.00	350.00	450.00
	1849 MP	—	150.00	200.00	300.00	400.00
	1850 MP	—	150.00	200.00	300.00	400.00

GUANAJUATO MINT (Go)

KM#	Date	Mintage	VG	Fine	VF	XF
380.5	1845 PM	—	125.00	160.00	200.00	265.00
	1849 PF	—	125.00	160.00	200.00	265.00
	1853 PF	—	125.00	160.00	200.00	265.00
	1856 PF	—	125.00	160.00	200.00	265.00
	1859 PF	—	125.00	160.00	200.00	265.00
	1860 PF	—	125.00	160.00	200.00	265.00
	1862 YE	—	125.00	160.00	200.00	265.00

HERMOSILLO MINT (Ho)

KM#	Date	Mintage	VG	Fine	VF	XF
380.6	1861 FM	—	500.00	900.00	1500.	2000.

MEXICO CITY MINT (Mo)

KM#	Date	Mintage	VG	Fine	VF	XF
380.7	1825 JM	—	125.00	160.00	200.00	250.00
	1827/6 JM	—	125.00	160.00	200.00	250.00
	1827 JM	—	125.00	160.00	200.00	250.00
	1830/29 JM	—	125.00	160.00	200.00	250.00
	1833 ML	—	125.00	160.00	200.00	250.00
	1841 ML	—	125.00	160.00	200.00	250.00
	1844 MF	—	125.00	160.00	200.00	250.00
	1845 MF	—	125.00	160.00	200.00	250.00
	1846 MF	—	125.00	160.00	200.00	250.00
	1848 GC	—	125.00	160.00	200.00	250.00
	1850 GC	—	125.00	160.00	200.00	250.00
	1856/5 GF	—	125.00	160.00	200.00	250.00
	1856 GF	—	125.00	160.00	200.00	250.00
	1858 FH	—	125.00	160.00	200.00	250.00
	1859 FH	—	125.00	160.00	200.00	250.00
	1861 TH	—	125.00	160.00	200.00	250.00
	1861 CH	—	125.00	160.00	200.00	250.00
	1862 CH	—	125.00	160.00	200.00	250.00
	1863 TH	—	125.00	160.00	200.00	250.00
	1868 PH	—	125.00	160.00	200.00	265.00
	1869 CH	—	125.00	160.00	200.00	250.00

ZACATECAS MINT (Zs)

KM#	Date	Mintage	VG	Fine	VF	XF
380.8	1860 VL	—	125.00	160.00	225.00	350.00
	1862 VL	—	125.00	160.00	225.00	350.00
	1864 MO	—	135.00	175.00	250.00	400.00

4 ESCUDOS

13.5400 gm., .875 GOLD, .3809 oz AGW

CULIACAN MINT (C, Cn)

Facing eagle

KM#	Date	Mintage	VG	Fine	VF	XF
381	1847 CE	—	300.00	500.00	700.00	1000.
	1848 CE	—	500.00	750.00	1000.	1350.

DURANGO MINT (Do)

KM#	Date	Mintage	VG	Fine	VF	XF
381.1	1832 RM	—	500.00	750.00	1000.	1650.
	1833 RM	—	250.00	500.00	750.00	1100.

GUADALAJARA MINT (Ga)

KM#	Date	Mintage	VG	Fine	VF	XF
381.2	1844 MC	—	500.00	750.00	1000.	1350.
	1844 JG	—	300.00	500.00	700.00	1000.

GUADALUPE Y CALVO MINT (GC)

KM#	Date	Mintage	VG	Fine	VF	XF
381.3	1844 MP	—	300.00	500.00	700.00	1100.
	1845 MP	—	250.00	300.00	400.00	700.00
	1846 MP	—	300.00	500.00	700.00	1000.
	1848 MP	—	425.00	475.00	575.00	900.00
	1850 MP	—	500.00	750.00	1000.	1350.

GUANAJUATO MINT (Go)

KM#	Date	Mintage	VG	Fine	VF	XF
381.4	1829/8 MJ	—	300.00	350.00	450.00	700.00
	1829 JM	—	300.00	350.00	450.00	700.00
	1832 MJ	—	300.00	350.00	450.00	700.00
	1833 MJ	—	300.00	350.00	450.00	700.00
	1834 PJ	—	350.00	450.00	550.00	850.00
	1835 PJ	—	350.00	450.00	550.00	850.00
	1836 PJ	—	300.00	350.00	450.00	700.00
	1837 PJ	—	300.00	350.00	450.00	700.00
	1838 PJ	—	300.00	350.00	450.00	700.00
	1839 PJ	—	350.00	450.00	550.00	850.00
	1840 PJ	—	300.00	350.00	450.00	700.00
	1841 PJ	—	350.00	450.00	550.00	850.00
	1845 PM	—	300.00	350.00	450.00	700.00
	1847 PM	—	350.00	450.00	550.00	850.00
	1849 PF	—	350.00	450.00	550.00	850.00
	1851 PF	—	350.00	450.00	550.00	850.00
	1852 PF	—	300.00	350.00	450.00	700.00
	1855 PF	—	300.00	350.00	450.00	700.00
	1857 PF	—	300.00	350.00	450.00	700.00
	1858 PF	—	300.00	350.00	450.00	700.00
	1859 PF	—	350.00	450.00	550.00	850.00
	1860 PF	—	300.00	350.00	450.00	700.00
	1862 YE	—	300.00	350.00	450.00	700.00
	1863 YF	—	300.00	350.00	450.00	700.00

HERMOSILLO MINT (Ho)

KM#	Date	Mintage	VG	Fine	VF	XF
381.5	1861 FM	—	750.00	1250.	2250.	3250.

MEXICO CITY MINT (Mo)

KM#	Date	Mintage	VG	Fine	VF	XF
381.6	1825 JM	—	350.00	450.00	550.00	850.00
	1827 JM	—	300.00	350.00	450.00	700.00
	1832 JM	—	350.00	450.00	550.00	850.00
	1844 MF	—	350.00	450.00	550.00	850.00
	1850 GC	—	350.00	450.00	550.00	850.00
	1856 GF	—	300.00	350.00	450.00	700.00
	1857 GF	—	300.00	350.00	450.00	700.00
	1858 FH	—	350.00	450.00	550.00	850.00
	1859/8 FH	—	300.00	350.00	450.00	700.00
	1861 CH	—	350.00	450.00	550.00	850.00
	1863 CH	—	300.00	350.00	450.00	700.00
	1868 PH	—	300.00	350.00	450.00	700.00
	1869 CH	—	300.00	350.00	450.00	700.00

OAXACA MINT (O, Oa)

KM#	Date	Mintage	VG	Fine	VF	XF
381.7	1861 FR	—	1500.	2500.	4000.	6500.

ZACATECAS MINT (Zs)

KM#	Date	Mintage	VG	Fine	VF	XF
381.8	1862 VL	—	300.00	400.00	500.00	800.00

8 ESCUDOS

27.0700 gm., .875 GOLD, .7616 oz ASW

MEXICO CITY MINT (Mo)

Obv: Hooked-neck eagle

KM#	Date	Mintage	Fine	VF	XF	Unc
382	1823 JM	—	1500.	3000.	5000.	8000.

ALAMOS MINT (A, As)

Obv: Facing eagle

KM#	Date	Mintage	Fine	VF	XF	Unc
383	1864 PG	—	600.00	800.00	1000.	1500.
	1868/7 DL	—	1350.	2000.	2650.	3500.
	1869 DL	—	575.00	700.00	900.00	1350.
	1870 DL	—	1350.	2000.	2650.	3500.
	1872 AM	—	1350.	2000.	2850.	3750.

CHIHUAHUA MINT (Ca)

KM#	Date	Mintage	Fine	VF	XF	Unc
383.1	1841 RG	—	500.00	600.00	750.00	1150.
	1842 RG	—	500.00	600.00	750.00	1150.
	1843 RG	—	525.00	650.00	800.00	1250.
	1844 RG	—	525.00	650.00	800.00	1250.
	1845 RG	—	525.00	650.00	800.00	1250.
	1846 RG	—	500.00	600.00	750.00	1150.
	1848 RG	—	500.00	600.00	750.00	1150.
	1849 RG	—	500.00	600.00	750.00	1150.
	1850/40 RG	—	500.00	600.00	750.00	1150.
	1851/41 RG	—	500.00	600.00	750.00	1150.
	1852/42 RG	—	500.00	600.00	750.00	1150.
	1853/43 RG	—	500.00	600.00	750.00	1150.
	1854/44 RG	—	500.00	600.00	750.00	1150.
	1855/43 RG	—	500.00	600.00	750.00	1150.
	1856 RG	—	500.00	600.00	750.00	1150.
	1857 JC/RG	—	500.00	600.00	750.00	1150.
	1858 JC	—	500.00	600.00	750.00	1150.
	1858 BA/RG	—	500.00	600.00	750.00	1150.
	1859 JC/RC	—	500.00	600.00	750.00	1150.
	1860 JC/RC	—	500.00	600.00	750.00	1150.
	1861 JC	—	500.00	600.00	750.00	1150.
	1862 JC	—	525.00	650.00	800.00	1250.
	1863 JC	—	500.00	600.00	750.00	1150.
	1864 JC	—	500.00	600.00	750.00	1150.
	1865 JC	—	500.00	600.00	750.00	1150.
	1866 JC	—	500.00	600.00	750.00	1150.
383.1	1866 FP	—	650.00	800.00	1000.	1400.
	1866 JG	—	650.00	800.00	1000.	1400.
	1867 JG	—	500.00	600.00	750.00	1150.
	1868 JG	—	500.00	600.00	750.00	1150.
	1869 MM	—	500.00	600.00	750.00	1150.
	1870 MM	—	500.00	600.00	750.00	1150.
	1871/61 MM	—	500.00	600.00	750.00	1150.

CULIACAN MINT (C, Ca)

KM#	Date	Mintage	Fine	VF	XF	Unc
383.2	1846 CE	—	500.00	600.00	750.00	1150.
	1847 CE	—	500.00	600.00	750.00	1150.
	1848 CE	—	500.00	600.00	750.00	1150.
	1849 CE	—	500.00	600.00	750.00	1150.
	1850 CE	—	500.00	600.00	750.00	1150.
	1851 CE	—	500.00	600.00	750.00	1150.
	1852 CE	—	500.00	600.00	750.00	1150.
	1853/1 CE	—	500.00	600.00	750.00	1150.
	1854 CE	—	500.00	600.00	750.00	1150.
	1855 CE	—	500.00	600.00	750.00	1150.
	1856 CE	—	500.00	600.00	750.00	1150.
	1857 CE	—	500.00	600.00	750.00	1150.
	1858 CE	—	500.00	600.00	750.00	1150.
	1859 CE	—	500.00	600.00	750.00	1150.
	1860 CE	—	500.00	600.00	750.00	1150.
	1860 PV	—	500.00	600.00	750.00	1150.
	1861 PV	—	500.00	600.00	750.00	1150.
	1861 CE	—	500.00	600.00	750.00	1150.
	1862 CE	—	500.00	600.00	750.00	1150.
	1863 CE	—	500.00	600.00	750.00	1150.
	1864 CE	—	500.00	600.00	750.00	1150.
	1865 CE	—	500.00	600.00	750.00	1150.
	1866/5 CE	—	500.00	600.00	750.00	1150.
	1866 CE	—	500.00	600.00	750.00	1150.
	1867 CE	—	500.00	600.00	750.00	1150.
	1868 CE	—	500.00	600.00	750.00	1150.
	1869 CE	—	500.00	600.00	750.00	1150.
	1870 CE	—	500.00	600.00	750.00	1150.

DURANGO MINT (Do)

KM#	Date	Mintage	Fine	VF	XF	Unc
383.3	1832 RM	—	800.00	1100.	1250.	1750.
	1833 RM/RL	—	500.00	600.00	750.00	1150.
	1834 RM	—	500.00	600.00	750.00	1150.
	1835 RM	—	500.00	600.00	750.00	1150.
	1836 RM/RL	—	500.00	600.00	750.00	1150.
	1837 RM	—	500.00	600.00	750.00	1150.
	1838 RM	—	500.00	600.00	750.00	1150.
	1839 RM	—	500.00	600.00	750.00	1150.
	1840/30 RM/RL		500.00	600.00	750.00	1150.
		—	500.00	600.00	750.00	1150.
	1841/31 RM	—	500.00	600.00	750.00	1150.
	1841/34 RM/RL					
		—	500.00	600.00	750.00	1150.
	1842/32 RM	—	500.00	600.00	750.00	1150.
	1843/1 RM	—	500.00	600.00	750.00	1150.
	1844/34 RM/RL		700.00	850.00	1000.	1400.
	1844 RM	—	700.00	850.00	1000.	1400.
	1845/36 RM	—	700.00	850.00	1000.	1400.
	1845 RM	—	700.00	850.00	1000.	1400.
	1846 RM	—	500.00	600.00	750.00	1150.
	1847 RM	—	500.00	600.00	750.00	1150.
	1848 CM	—	500.00	600.00	750.00	1150.
	1849/39 CM	—	500.00	600.00	750.00	1150.
	1849 JMR	—	550.00	700.00	900.00	1300.
	1850 JMR	—	550.00	700.00	900.00	1300.
	1851 JMR	—	550.00	700.00	900.00	1300.
	1852/1 JMR	—	550.00	700.00	950.00	1350.
	1852 CP	—	650.00	800.00	1000.	1400.
	1853 CP	—	500.00	600.00	750.00	1150.
	1854 CP	—	500.00	600.00	750.00	1150.
	1855/4 CP	—	500.00	600.00	750.00	1150.
	1856 CP	—	550.00	600.00	750.00	1150.
	1857 CP	—	550.00	600.00	750.00	1150.
	1858 CP	—	550.00	600.00	750.00	1150.
	1859 CP	—	550.00	600.00	750.00	1150.
	1861/0 CP	—	500.00	600.00	750.00	1150.
	1862 CP	—	500.00	600.00	750.00	1150.
	1863 CP	—	500.00	600.00	750.00	1150.
	1864 LT	—	700.00	850.00	1000.	1400.
	1866 CM	—	500.00	600.00	750.00	1150.
	1867/6 CP	—	500.00	600.00	750.00	1150.
	1869 CP	—	500.00	600.00	750.00	1150.
	1870 CP	—	500.00	600.00	750.00	1150.

ESTADO DE MEXICO MINT (Eo, Mo)

KM#	Date	Mintage	Fine	VF	XF	Unc
383.4	1828 LF	—	1350.	2500.	4000.	6000.
	1829 LF	—	1350.	2500.	4000.	6000.

GUADALAJARA MINT (Ga)

KM#	Date	Mintage	Fine	VF	XF	Unc
383.5	1825 FS	—	650.00	750.00	900.00	1300.
	1826 FS	—	650.00	800.00	1000.	1400.
	1830 FS	—	650.00	750.00	900.00	1300.
	1836 FS	—	900.00	1350.	1600.	2000.
	1837 JG	—	650.00	850.00	1200.	1650.
	1840 MC	—	900.00	1350.	1600.	2000.
	1843 MC	—	—	—	—	—
	1845 MC	—	550.00	650.00	800.00	1200.
	1849 JG	—	550.00	650.00	800.00	1200.
	1850 JG	—	550.00	650.00	800.00	1200.
	1851 JG	—	550.00	650.00	800.00	1200.
	1852/1 JG	—	550.00	650.00	800.00	1200.
	1855 JG	—	550.00	650.00	800.00	1200.
	1856 JG	—	550.00	650.00	800.00	1200.
	1857 JG	—	550.00	650.00	800.00	1200.
	1861/0 JG	—	550.00	650.00	800.00	1200.
	1863/1 JG	—	550.00	650.00	800.00	1200.
	1866 JG	—	550.00	650.00	800.00	1200.

GUADALUPE Y CALVO MINT (GC)

KM#	Date	Mintage	Fine	VF	XF	Unc
383.6	1844 MP	—	600.00	750.00	900.00	1350.
	1845 MP	—	600.00	750.00	900.00	1350.
	1846 MP	—	600.00	750.00	900.00	1350.
	1847 MP	—	600.00	750.00	900.00	1350.
	1848 MP	—	600.00	750.00	900.00	1350.
	1849 MP	—	600.00	750.00	900.00	1350.
	1850 MP	—	600.00	750.00	900.00	1350.
	1851 MP	—	600.00	750.00	900.00	1350.
	1852 MP	—	600.00	750.00	900.00	1350.

GUANAJUATO MINT (Go)

KM#	Date	Mintage	Fine	VF	XF	Unc
383.7	1828 MJ	—	500.00	600.00	750.00	1150.
	1829 MJ	—	500.00	600.00	750.00	1150.
	1830 MJ	—	500.00	600.00	750.00	1150.
	1831 MJ	—	500.00	600.00	750.00	1150.
	1832 MJ	—	500.00	600.00	750.00	1150.
	1833 MJ	—	500.00	600.00	750.00	1150.
	1834 PJ	—	500.00	600.00	750.00	1150.
	1835 PJ	—	500.00	600.00	750.00	1150.
	1836 PJ	—	500.00	600.00	750.00	1150.
	1837 PJ	—	500.00	600.00	750.00	1150.
	1838/7 PJ	—	500.00	600.00	750.00	1150.
	1839/8 PJ	—	500.00	600.00	750.00	1150.
	1840 PJ	—	500.00	600.00	750.00	1150.
	1841 PJ	—	500.00	600.00	750.00	1150.
	1842 PJ	—	500.00	600.00	750.00	1150.
	1842 RM	—	500.00	600.00	750.00	1150.
	1843 PM	—	500.00	600.00	750.00	1150.
	1844/3 PM	—	500.00	600.00	750.00	1150.
	1844 PM	—	500.00	600.00	750.00	1000.
	1845 PM	—	500.00	600.00	750.00	1000.
	1846 PM	—	500.00	600.00	750.00	1000.
	1847 PM	—	500.00	600.00	750.00	1000.
	1848/7 PM	—	500.00	600.00	750.00	1000.
	1848 PM	—	500.00	600.00	750.00	1000.
	1848 PF	—	500.00	600.00	750.00	1000.
	1849 PF	—	500.00	600.00	750.00	1000.
	1850 PF	—	500.00	600.00	750.00	1000.
	1851 PF	—	500.00	600.00	750.00	1000.
	1852 PF	—	500.00	600.00	750.00	1000.
	1853 PF	—	500.00	600.00	750.00	1000.
	1854 PF	—	500.00	600.00	750.00	1000.
	1855/4 PF	—	—	—	—	—
	1855 PF	—	500.00	600.00	750.00	1000.
	1856 PF	—	500.00	600.00	750.00	1000.
	1857 PF	—	500.00	600.00	750.00	1000.
	1858 PF	—	500.00	600.00	750.00	1000.
	1859 PF	—	500.00	600.00	750.00	1000.
	1860/59 PF	—	—	—	—	—
	1860 PF	—	500.00	600.00	750.00	1000.
	1861/0 PF	—	500.00	600.00	750.00	1000.
	1861 PF	—	500.00	600.00	750.00	1000.
	1862/1 YE	—	500.00	600.00	750.00	1000.
	1862 YE	—	500.00	600.00	750.00	1000.
	1863 YF	—	500.00	600.00	750.00	1000.
	1863 PF	—	500.00	600.00	750.00	1000.
	1867 YF	—	500.00	600.00	750.00	1000.

KM#	Date	Mintage	Fine	VF	XF	Unc
383.7	1868 YF	—	500.00	600.00	750.00	1000.
	1870 FR	—	500.00	600.00	750.00	1000.

HERMOSILLO MINT (Ho)

KM#	Date	Mintage	Fine	VF	XF	Unc
383.8	1863 FM	—	600.00	700.00	800.00	1200.
	1864 FM	—	700.00	850.00	1500.	2000.
	1864 PR/FM	—	700.00	850.00	1500.	2000.
	1865 FM/PR	—	600.00	750.00	900.00	1300.
	1867 PR	—	550.00	650.00	850.00	1250.
	1868 PR	—	550.00	650.00	850.00	1250.
	1869 PR	—	550.00	650.00	800.00	1200.
	1870 PR	—	550.00	650.00	800.00	1200.
	1871 PR	—	550.00	650.00	800.00	1200.
	1872/1 PR	—	600.00	700.00	850.00	1250.
	1873 PR	—	550.00	650.00	800.00	1200.

MEXICO CITY MINT (Mo)

KM#	Date	Mintage	Fine	VF	XF	Unc
383.9	1824 JM	—	400.00	600.00	700.00	1000.
	1825/3 JM	—	400.00	475.00	625.00	800.00
	1825 JM	—	500.00	600.00	750.00	1000.
	1826/5 JM	—	500.00	600.00	750.00	900.00
	1827 JM	—	500.00	600.00	750.00	900.00
	1828 JM	—	500.00	600.00	750.00	900.00
	1829 JM	—	500.00	600.00	750.00	900.00
	1830 JM	—	500.00	600.00	750.00	900.00
	1831 JM	—	500.00	600.00	750.00	900.00
	1832/1 JM	—	500.00	600.00	750.00	900.00
	1833 MJ	—	500.00	600.00	750.00	900.00
	1833 ML	—	500.00	600.00	750.00	900.00
	1834 ML	—	500.00	600.00	750.00	900.00
	1835/4 ML	—	500.00	600.00	750.00	900.00
	1836 ML	—	500.00	600.00	750.00	900.00
	1837/6 ML	—	500.00	600.00	750.00	900.00
	1838 ML	—	500.00	600.00	750.00	900.00
	1839 ML	—	500.00	600.00	750.00	900.00
	1840 ML	—	500.00	600.00	750.00	900.00
	1841 ML	—	500.00	600.00	750.00	900.00
	1842 ML	—	500.00	600.00	750.00	900.00
	1843 MM	—	500.00	600.00	750.00	900.00
	1844 MF	—	500.00	600.00	750.00	900.00
	1845 MF	—	500.00	600.00	750.00	900.00
	1846 MF	—	500.00	600.00	750.00	900.00
	1847 RC	—	500.00	600.00	750.00	900.00
	1848 GC	—	500.00	600.00	750.00	900.00
	1849 GC	—	500.00	600.00	750.00	900.00
	1850 GC	—	500.00	600.00	750.00	900.00
	1851 GC	—	500.00	600.00	750.00	900.00
	1852 GC	—	500.00	600.00	750.00	900.00
	1853 GC	—	500.00	600.00	750.00	900.00
	1854/44 GC	—	500.00	600.00	750.00	900.00
	1854/3 GC	—	500.00	600.00	750.00	900.00
	1855 GF	—	500.00	600.00	750.00	900.00
	1856/5 GF	—	500.00	600.00	750.00	900.00
	1857 GF	—	500.00	600.00	750.00	900.00
	1858 FH	—	500.00	600.00	750.00	900.00
	1859 FH	—	500.00	600.00	750.00	900.00
	1860 FH	—	500.00	600.00	750.00	900.00
	1860 TH	—	500.00	600.00	750.00	900.00
	1861/51 CH	—	500.00	600.00	750.00	900.00
	1862 CH	—	500.00	600.00	750.00	900.00
	1863/53 CH	—	500.00	600.00	750.00	900.00
	1863/53 TH	—	500.00	600.00	750.00	900.00
	1867 CH	—	500.00	600.00	750.00	900.00
	1868 CH	—	500.00	600.00	750.00	900.00
	1868 PH	—	500.00	600.00	750.00	900.00
	1869 CH	—	500.00	600.00	750.00	900.00

OAXACA MINT (O, Oa)

KM#	Date	Mintage	Fine	VF	XF	Unc
383.10	1858 AE	—	2000.	3000.	4000.	6000.
	1859 AE	—	700.00	1000.	1500.	2500.
	1860 AE	—	700.00	1000.	1500.	3000.
	1861 FR	—	550.00	650.00	800.00	1200.
	1862 FR	—	550.00	650.00	850.00	1300.
	1863 FR	—	550.00	650.00	850.00	1300.
	1864 FR	—	550.00	650.00	800.00	1200.
	1867 AE	—	550.00	650.00	750.00	1150.
	1868 AE	—	550.00	650.00	750.00	1150.
	1869 AE	—	550.00	650.00	750.00	1150.

ZACATECAS MINT (Z, Zs)

KM#	Date	Mintage	Fine	VF	XF	Unc
383.11	1858 MO	—	500.00	600.00	750.00	900.00
	1859 MO	—	500.00	600.00	750.00	900.00
	1860 MO	—	500.00	600.00	750.00	900.00
383.11	1861/0 VL	—	—	—	—	—
	1861 VL	—	500.00	600.00	750.00	900.00
	1862 VL	—	500.00	600.00	750.00	900.00
	1863 VL	—	500.00	600.00	750.00	900.00
	1863 MO	—	500.00	600.00	750.00	900.00
	1864 MO	—	500.00	600.00	750.00	900.00
	1865 MO	—	500.00	600.00	750.00	900.00
	1868 JS	—	500.00	600.00	750.00	900.00
	1868 YH	—	500.00	600.00	750.00	900.00
	1869 YH	—	500.00	600.00	750.00	900.00
	1870 YH	—	500.00	600.00	750.00	900.00
	1871 YH	—	500.00	600.00	750.00	900.00

EMPIRE OF MAXIMILIAN

RULER

Maximilian, Emperor, 1864-1867

MINTMARKS

Refer To Republic Coinage

ASSAYER'S INITIALS

Refer To Republic Coinage

MONETARY SYSTEM

100 Centavos = 1 Peso (8 Reales)

CENTAVO

COPPER

MEXICO CITY MINT (M)

KM#	Date	Mintage	Fine	VF	XF	Unc
384	1864	—	35.00	50.00	100.00	550.00

5 CENTAVOS

1.3537 gm., .903 SILVER, .0393 oz ASW

GUANAJUATO MINT (G)

KM#	Date	Mintage	Fine	VF	XF	Unc
385	1864	.090	35.00	50.00	100.00	225.00
	1865	—	35.00	45.00	85.00	175.00
	1866	—	125.00	180.00	300.00	500.00

MEXICO CITY MINT (M)

KM#	Date	Mintage	Fine	VF	XF	Unc
385.1	1864	—	25.00	45.00	85.00	175.00
	1866	—	50.00	90.00	175.00	350.00

POTOSI MINT (P)

KM#	Date	Mintage	Fine	VF	XF	Unc
385.2	1864	—	200.00	300.00	650.00	1150.

ZACATECAS MINT (Z)

KM#	Date	Mintage	Fine	VF	XF	Unc
385.3	1865	—	45.00	75.00	125.00	275.00

10 CENTAVOS

2.7073 gm., .903 SILVER, .0786 oz ASW

GUANAJUATO MINT (G)

KM#	Date	Mintage	Fine	VF	XF	Unc
386	1864	.045	25.00	40.00	80.00	170.00
	1865	—	27.50	50.00	100.00	225.00

MEXICO CITY MINT (M)

KM#	Date	Mintage	Fine	VF	XF	Unc
386.1	1864	—	20.00	35.00	75.00	175.00
	1866	—	20.00	30.00	75.00	175.00

POTOSI MINT (P)

KM#	Date	Mintage	Fine	VF	XF	Unc
386.2	1864	—	65.00	110.00	200.00	500.00

ZACATECAS MINT (Z)

KM#	Date	Mintage	Fine	VF	XF	Unc
386.3	1865	—	45.00	60.00	100.00	225.00

50 CENTAVOS

13.5365 gm., .903 SILVER, .3929 oz ASW

MEXICO CITY MINT (Mo)

KM#	Date	Mintage	Fine	VF	XF	Unc
387	1866	.031	30.00	45.00	100.00	450.00

PESO

27.0700 gm., .903 SILVER, .7857 oz ASW

GUANAJUATO MINT (Go)

KM#	Date	Mintage	Fine	VF	XF	Unc
388	1866	—	350.00	450.00	800.00	1250.

MEXICO CITY MINT (Mo)

KM#	Date	Mintage	Fine	VF	XF	Unc
388.1	1866	2.148	25.00	45.00	100.00	425.00
	1867	1.238	27.50	60.00	115.00	450.00

POTOSI MINT (Pi)

KM#	Date	Mintage	Fine	VF	XF	Unc
388.2	1866	—	35.00	60.00	150.00	550.00

20 PESOS

33.8400 gm., .875 GOLD, .9520 oz AGW

MEXICO CITY MINT (Mo)

KM#	Date	Mintage	Fine	VF	XF	Unc
389	1866	8.274	650.00	1000.	1750.	3000.

GOLD PESO FANTASIES

Modern gold 'Peso' fantasies of Maximilian exist. Five varieties exist, some dated 1865. One has an eagle in a plain field above a wreath on the reverse. On the second type a numeral '1' appears to either side of the eagle, and the metallic content is designated below: LEY-ORO-K22.

DECIMAL COINAGE

UN (1) CENTAVO

COPPER

MEXICO CITY MINT (Mo)

Obv: Seated Liberty

KM#	Date	Mintage	Fine	VF	XF	Unc
390	1863 round top 3	—	10.00	15.00	30.00	90.00
	1863 flat top 3	—	8.00	12.50	25.00	75.00

POTOSI MINT (S.L.P.)

KM#	Date	Mintage	Fine	VF	XF	Unc
390.1	1863	1.025	9.00	15.00	40.00	125.00

ALAMOS MINT (As)

Obv: Standing eagle

KM#	Date	Mintage	Fine	VF	XF	Unc
391	1876	.049	40.00	60.00	150.00	300.00
	1880	—	25.00	50.00	100.00	225.00
	1881	—	30.00	40.00	65.00	135.00

CULIACAN MINT (Cn)

KM#	Date	Mintage	Fine	VF	XF	Unc
391.1	1874	.266	6.00	9.00	20.00	50.00
	1875/4	.153	10.00	12.50	16.00	55.00
	1875	Inc. Ab.	8.00	11.00	14.00	50.00
	1876	.154	5.00	8.00	15.00	40.00
	1877	.993	6.00	9.00	13.50	40.00
	1880	.142	7.50	10.00	12.50	35.00
	1881	.167	7.50	10.00	21.50	65.00
	1897 w/large N in mm.	.300	2.50	5.00	10.00	30.00
	1897 w/small N in mm.	Inc. Ab.	2.50	5.00	10.00	30.00

DURANGO MINT (Do)

KM#	Date	Mintage	Fine	VF	XF	Unc
391.2	1879	.110	14.00	18.00	35.00	90.00
	1880	.069	11.50	17.50	35.00	90.00
	1891	—	8.00	11.00	30.00	60.00
391.2	1891 Do/Mo	—	8.00	11.00	30.00	60.00

GUADALAJARA MINT (Ga)

KM#	Date	Mintage	Fine	VF	XF	Unc
391.3	1872	.263	6.00	9.00	25.00	80.00
	1873	.333	7.00	10.00	25.00	80.00
	1874	.076	6.00	9.00	20.00	60.00
	1875	—	4.00	6.00	15.00	30.00
	1876	.303	4.00	6.00	17.50	40.00
	1877	.108	4.00	6.00	18.50	50.00
	1878	.543	4.00	6.00	15.00	40.00
	1881/71	.975	5.50	7.50	15.00	40.00
	1881	Inc. Ab.	4.25	6.00	13.50	35.00
	1889 Ga/Mo	—	3.50	5.00	15.00	40.00
	1890	—	4.00	5.75	18.50	50.00

GUANAJUATO MINT (Go)

KM#	Date	Mintage	Fine	VF	XF	Unc
391.4	1874	—	13.50	18.00	40.00	90.00
	1875	.190	11.50	14.50	35.00	70.00
	1876	—	100.00	150.00	275.00	400.00
	1877	—	—	—	Rare	—
	1878	.576	8.00	11.00	30.00	65.00
	1880	.890	6.00	10.00	25.00	50.00

HERMOSILLO MINT (Ho)

KM#	Date	Mintage	Fine	VF	XF	Unc
391.5	1875	3,500	—	—	Rare	—
	1876	8,508	35.00	60.00	125.00	250.00
	1880 short H, round O	.102	6.75	10.00	25.00	50.00
	1880 tall H, oval O	Inc. Ab.	6.75	10.00	25.00	50.00
	1881	.459	5.00	7.50	17.50	55.00

MEXICO CITY MINT (Mo)

KM#	Date	Mintage	Fine	VF	XF	Unc
391.6	1869	1.874	7.50	15.00	35.00	75.00
	1870	1.200	8.00	11.00	35.00	75.00
	1871	.918	8.00	11.00	30.00	70.00
	1872/1	1.625	6.50	10.00	27.50	85.00
	1872	Inc. Ab.	6.00	9.00	25.00	75.00
	1873	1.605	4.00	5.50	12.50	30.00
	1874/3	1.700	5.00	7.00	13.50	35.00
	1874	Inc. Ab.	3.00	5.50	12.50	30.00
	1874.	Inc. Ab.	5.00	7.00	13.50	35.00
	1875	1.495	6.00	8.00	20.00	45.00
	1876	1.600	3.00	5.50	12.50	30.00
	1877	1.270	3.00	5.50	13.50	40.00
	1878/5	1.900	7.50	11.00	22.50	50.00
	1878/6	Inc. Ab.	7.50	11.00	22.50	50.00
	1878/7	Inc. Ab.	7.50	11.00	20.00	45.00
	1878	Inc. Ab.	6.00	9.00	13.50	30.00
	1879/8	1.505	4.50	6.50	12.50	30.00
	1879	Inc. Ab.	3.00	5.50	11.50	27.50
	1880/70	1.130	5.50	7.50	15.00	40.00
	1880	Inc. Ab.	4.25	6.00	12.50	35.00
	1881	1.060	4.50	7.00	15.00	45.00
	1886	12.687	1.50	2.00	8.50	22.50
	1887	7.292	1.50	2.00	8.50	22.50
	1888/78	9.984	2.50	3.00	10.00	30.00
	1888/7	Inc. Ab.	2.50	3.00	10.00	30.00
	1888	Inc. Ab.	1.50	2.00	8.50	25.00
	1889	19.970	2.00	3.00	8.50	25.00
	1890/89	18.726	2.50	3.00	8.50	30.00
	1890/990	I.A.	2.75	3.25	8.50	30.00
	1890	Inc. Ab.	1.50	2.00	8.50	25.00
	1891	14.544	1.50	2.00	8.50	25.00
	1892	12.907	1.50	2.00	8.50	25.00
	1893/2	5.078	2.50	3.00	8.50	30.00
	1893	Inc. Ab.	1.50	2.00	8.50	25.00
	1894	1.896	2.00	3.00	10.00	27.50
	1895	3.453	2.00	3.00	8.50	25.00
	1896	3.075	2.00	3.00	8.50	25.00
	1897	4.150	1.50	2.00	8.50	25.00

OAXACA MINT (Oa)

KM#	Date	Mintage	Fine	VF	XF	Unc
391.7	1872	.015	—	—	Rare	—
	1873	.011	—	—	Rare	—
	1874	4,835	—	—	Rare	—
	1875	2,860	—	—	Rare	—

POTOSI MINT (Pi)

KM#	Date	Mintage	Fine	VF	XF	Unc
391.8	1871	—	—	—	Rare	—
	1877	.249	10.00	13.50	25.00	60.00
	1878	.751	8.00	10.00	20.00	50.00
	1891 Pi/Mo	—	10.00	15.00	30.00	70.00
	1891	—	8.00	11.00	25.00	60.00

ZACATECAS MINT (Zs)

KM#	Date	Mintage	Fine	VF	XF	Unc
391.9	1872	.055	22.50	30.00	75.00	200.00
	1873	1.460	4.00	6.00	15.00	45.00
	1874/3	.685	5.50	7.50	15.00	40.00
	1874	Inc. Ab.	4.00	6.00	15.00	35.00
	1875/4	.200	8.50	11.50	25.00	60.00
	1875	Inc. Ab.	7.00	10.00	23.50	55.00
	1876	—	5.00	8.00	20.00	40.00
	1877	—	50.00	125.00	275.00	500.00
	1878	—	4.50	7.00	15.00	35.00
	1880	.100	5.00	8.00	20.00	45.00
391.9	1881	1.200	4.25	6.00	15.00	40.00

COPPER-NICKEL

MEXICO CITY MINT (Mo)

KM#	Date	Mintage	Fine	VF	XF	Unc
392	1882	99.955	8.00	12.00	18.50	35.00
	1883	Inc. Ab.	.50	.75	1.00	2.75

MEXICO CITY MINT (Mo)

Obv: Restyled eagle

KM#	Date	Mintage	Fine	VF	XF	Unc
393	1898	1.529	4.00	6.00	15.00	50.00

CULIACAN MINT (C)

Reduced size

KM#	Date	Mintage	Fine	VF	XF	Unc
394	1901	.220	17.50	25.00	40.00	80.00
	1902	.320	15.00	22.50	45.00	85.00
	1903	.536	6.00	8.50	15.00	40.00
	1904/3	.148	32.50	40.00	65.00	100.00
	1904	Inc. Ab.	30.00	40.00	50.00	65.00
	1905	.110	35.00	70.00	125.00	300.00

MEXICO CITY MINT (Mo, M)

KM#	Date	Mintage	Fine	VF	XF	Unc
394.1	1899	.051	75.00	125.00	200.00	450.00
	1900	4.010	2.00	3.00	7.50	25.00
	1901	1.494	4.00	6.50	15.00	45.00
	1902/899	2.090	15.00	25.00	40.00	100.00
	1902	Inc. Ab.	2.00	3.00	8.50	26.50
	1903	8.400	1.50	2.00	5.00	12.50
	1904	10.250	1.50	2.00	5.00	15.00
	1905	3.643	2.00	3.00	10.00	37.50

2 CENTAVOS

COPPER-NICKEL

MEXICO CITY MINT (Mo)

KM#	Date	Mintage	Fine	VF	XF	Unc
395	1882	50.022	2.00	3.00	7.50	15.00
	1883	Inc. Ab.	.50	.75	1.50	3.00

5 CENTAVOS

1.3530 gm., .903 SILVER, .0392 oz ASW

CHIHUAHUA MINT (Ca)

Eagle/wreath

KM#	Date	Mintage	Fine	VF	XF	Unc
396	1868	—	23.50	40.00	90.00	160.00
	1869	*.030	21.50	35.00	70.00	140.00
	1870	.035	21.50	35.00	70.00	140.00

POTOSI MINT (S.L.P.)

KM#	Date	Mintage	Fine	VF	XF	Unc
396.1	1863	—	75.00	125.00	250.00	500.00

MEXICO CITY MINT (Mo)

Rev: Cap and rays

KM#	Date	Mintage	Fine	VF	XF	Unc
397	1867/3	—	20.00	40.00	80.00	160.00
	1867	—	18.50	37.50	75.00	150.00
	1868	—	18.50	37.50	75.00	150.00

POTOSI MINT (P)

KM#	Date	Mintage	Fine	VF	XF	Unc
397.1	1868	.034	18.50	37.50	75.00	150.00

KM#	Date	Mintage	Fine	VF	XF	Unc
397.1	1869	.014	25.00	50.00	100.00	200.00

ALAMOS MINT (As)

Obv: Standing eagle

KM#	Date	Mintage	Fine	VF	XF	Unc
398	1874 DL	—	11.00	15.00	25.00	60.00
	1875 DL	—	6.50	8.00	17.50	45.00
	1876 L	—	11.00	14.50	24.00	60.00
	1878 L mule, gold peso obverse					
		—	—	—	Rare	—
	1879 L mule, gold peso obverse					
		—	12.50	25.00	47.50	120.00
	1880 L mule, gold peso obverse					
		.012	22.50	37.50	65.00	125.00
	1886 L	.043	8.00	11.00	24.00	60.00
	1886 L mule, gold peso obverse					
		Inc. Ab.	21.50	30.00	60.00	100.00
	1887 L	.020	7.50	10.00	22.50	55.00
	1888 L	.032	5.75	7.50	12.50	30.00
	1889 L	.016	7.25	10.00	16.50	40.00
	1890 L	.030	11.50	17.50	30.00	75.00
	1891 L	8,000	25.00	32.50	50.00	125.00
	1892 L	.013	6.50	8.75	13.50	35.00
	1893 L	.024	5.75	7.50	13.50	35.00
	1895 L	.020	5.00	6.50	10.00	25.00

CHIHUAHUA MINT (CH, Ca)

KM#	Date	Mintage	Fine	VF	XF	Unc
398.1	1871 M	.014	15.00	18.00	27.50	65.00
	1873 M crude date					
		—	40.00	65.00	90.00	225.00
	1874 M crude date					
		—	6.50	12.50	24.00	60.00
	1886 M	.025	5.00	6.50	13.50	35.00
	1887 M	.037	5.00	7.50	12.50	30.00
	1887 Ca/MoM					
		Inc. Ab.	6.00	9.00	13.50	35.00
	1888 M	.145	1.25	1.75	3.50	8.00
	1889 M	.044	3.00	4.00	6.50	17.50
	1890 M	.102	1.25	1.75	3.00	7.50
	1891 M	.164	1.25	1.75	3.00	7.50
	1892 M	.085	1.50	2.00	3.00	7.50
	1892 M 9/inverted 9					
		Inc. Ab.	2.50	3.50	4.50	10.00
	1893 M	.133	1.25	1.75	3.00	7.50
	1894 M	.108	1.25	1.75	3.00	7.50
	1895 M	.074	1.75	2.50	4.00	10.00

CULIACAN MINT (Cn)

KM#	Date	Mintage	Fine	VF	XF	Unc
398.2	1871 P	—	14.00	18.50	32.50	80.00
	1873 P	4,992	12.50	16.50	27.50	65.00
	1874 P	—	11.00	15.00	25.00	60.00
	1875 P	—	—	—	Rare	—
	1876 P	—	10.00	12.50	22.50	55.00
	1886 M	.010	7.50	10.00	16.50	40.00
	1887 M	.010	9.00	13.50	25.00	60.00
	1888 M	.119	1.25	1.75	4.00	10.00
	1889 M	.066	3.50	4.50	8.50	22.50
	1890 M	.180	1.25	1.75	3.00	7.50
	1890 D (error)	—	—	—	Rare	—
	1891 M	.087	1.75	2.50	4.00	10.00
	1894 M	.024	3.50	5.00	10.00	25.00
	1896 M	.016	6.50	9.50	16.50	40.00
	1897 M	.223	1.25	1.75	3.00	7.50

DURANGO MINT (Do)

KM#	Date	Mintage	Fine	VF	XF	Unc
398.3	1874 M	—	50.00	85.00	150.00	300.00
	1877 P	4,795	10.00	12.50	22.50	55.00
	1878/7 E/P					
		4,300	11.50	15.00	27.50	65.00
	1879 B	—	10.00	12.50	45.00	110.00
	1880 B	—	—	—	Rare	—
	1881 P	3,020	50.00	75.00	140.00	350.00
	1887 C	.042	4.25	5.50	11.50	27.50
	1888 C	.091	3.50	4.50	10.00	25.00
	1889 C	.049	3.00	4.00	8.00	20.00
	1890 C	.136	3.50	4.50	10.00	25.00
	1890 P	Inc. Ab.	4.00	5.00	11.50	27.50
	1891/0 P	.047	4.00	5.50	8.50	21.50
	1891 P	Inc. Ab.	3.00	4.00	7.50	18.50
	1894D	.038	3.50	4.50	8.50	21.50

GUADALAJARA MINT (Ga)

KM#	Date	Mintage	Fine	VF	XF	Unc
398.4	1877 A	—	8.50	11.50	22.50	55.00
	1881 S	.156	3.00	4.00	8.00	20.00
	1886 S	.087	1.75	2.50	4.00	10.00
	1888 GaS	.262	1.75	2.25	5.00	12.50
	1888 gaS	I.A.	1.75	2.25	5.00	12.50
	1889 S	.178	1.10	1.50	4.00	10.00
	1890 S	.068	2.75	4.00	7.00	17.50
	1891 S	.050	2.50	3.50	6.00	15.00
	1892 S	.078	1.80	2.50	4.00	10.00
398.4	1893 S	.044	3.00	4.00	8.00	20.00

GUANAJUATO MINT (Go)

KM#	Date	Mintage	Fine	VF	XF	Unc
398.5	1869 S	.080	7.50	17.50	35.00	85.00
	1871 S	.100	4.00	7.50	17.50	45.00
	1872 S	.030	20.00	37.50	75.00	150.00
	1873 S	.040	11.00	14.00	24.00	60.00
	1874 S	—	6.50	8.00	16.50	40.00
	1875 S	—	8.00	10.00	17.50	45.00
	1876 S	—	8.00	10.00	17.50	45.00
	1877 S	—	6.50	8.00	13.50	35.00
	1878/7 S	.020	5.00	7.50	13.50	35.00
	1879 S	—	7.50	10.00	15.00	37.50
	1880 S	.055	12.50	25.00	50.00	125.00
	1881/0 S	.160	4.00	5.50	8.50	21.50
	1881 S	Inc. Ab.	3.00	4.00	8.00	20.00
	1886 R	.230	1.25	2.00	4.00	10.00
	1887 R	.230	1.25	1.75	3.50	9.00
	1888 R	.320	1.25	1.50	3.50	8.50
	1889 R	.060	3.50	4.50	8.50	22.50
	1890 R	.250	1.25	1.50	3.00	7.50
	1891/0 R	.168	1.00	1.75	3.50	8.50
	1891 R	Inc. Ab.	1.25	1.75	3.00	7.50
	1892 R	.138	1.25	2.25	4.00	10.00
	1893 R	.200	1.25	1.50	3.00	7.50
	1894 R	.200	1.25	1.50	3.00	7.50
	1896 R	.525	1.25	1.35	2.50	6.00
	1897 R	.596	1.25	1.35	2.50	6.00

HERMOSILLO MINT (Ho)

KM#	Date	Mintage	Fine	VF	XF	Unc
398.6	1874/69 R	—	7.50	15.00	30.00	75.00
	1874 R	—	6.50	12.50	25.00	65.00
	1878 A	.022	10.00	12.50	22.50	55.00
	1878 A mule, gold peso obverse					
		Inc. Ab.	12.50	20.00	50.00	100.00
	1880 A	.043	4.50	6.00	12.50	35.00
	1886 G	.044	4.50	5.50	8.50	25.00
	1887 G	.020	5.75	7.50	11.50	32.50
	1888 G	.012	7.25	10.00	13.50	40.00
	1889 G	.067	3.00	4.00	8.00	20.00
	1890 G	.050	3.00	4.00	8.00	20.00
	1891 G	.046	2.50	3.25	6.00	15.00
	1893 G	.084	2.00	2.75	6.00	15.00
	1894 G	.068	1.40	2.00	4.00	10.00

MEXICO CITY MINT (Mo)

KM#	Date	Mintage	Fine	VF	XF	Unc
398.7	1869/8 C	*.040	6.50	9.00	25.00	65.00
	1870 C	.140	3.50	4.50	4.00	35.00
	1871 C	.103	8.00	10.00	16.50	45.00
	1871 M	Inc. Ab.	6.50	8.00	16.50	40.00
	1872 M	.266	2.00	3.00	10.00	25.00
	1873 M	.020	5.00	7.50	16.50	40.00
	1874/69 M	—	4.50	7.00	16.50	40.00
	1874 M	—	3.50	4.50	12.00	30.00
	1874 B	—	3.50	4.50	14.00	35.00
	1875 B	—	4.00	5.50	10.00	25.00
	1875 B/M	—	5.50	7.00	12.50	30.00
	1876/5 B	—	4.50	6.00	10.00	25.00
	1876 B	—	3.50	4.50	8.50	20.00
	1877/6 M	.080	4.00	6.00	10.00	25.00
	1877 M	Inc. Ab.	3.50	4.50	8.50	21.50
	1878/7 M	*.100	4.00	6.00	10.00	25.00
	1878 M	Inc. Ab.	2.00	3.00	8.50	21.50
	1879/8 M	—	7.50	10.00	15.00	35.00
	1879 M	—	4.00	6.00	10.00	25.00
	1879 M 9/inverted 9					
		—	8.50	11.50	16.50	40.00
	1880/76 M/B	—	5.00	6.50	10.00	25.00
	1880/76 M	—	5.00	6.50	10.00	25.00
	1880 M	—	3.00	5.00	8.00	20.00
	1881/0 M	.180	3.50	5.00	7.50	18.50
	1881 M	Inc. Ab.	2.75	3.75	6.00	15.00
	1886/0 M	.398	1.25	2.00	5.00	12.50
	1886/1 M	I.A.	1.25	2.00	5.00	12.50
	1886 M	Inc. Ab.	1.25	1.75	4.00	10.00
	1887 M	.720	1.25	1.50	3.50	9.00
	1887 m	Inc. Ab.	1.25	1.75	4.00	10.00
	1887 M/m	I.A.	1.25	1.75	4.00	10.00
	1888/7 M	1.360	1.25	1.50	3.50	9.00
	1888 M	Inc. Ab.	1.25	1.50	3.00	7.50
	1889 M	1,242	1.25	1.50	3.00	7.50
	1890/00 M					
		1,064	1.25	1.75	4.00	10.00
	1890 M	Inc. Ab.	1.25	1.50	3.00	7.50
	1891 M	1,030	1.25	1.50	3.00	7.50
	1892 M	1,400	1.25	1.50	3.00	7.50
	1892 M 9/inverted 9					
		Inc. Ab.	1.50	2.00	5.00	12.50
	1893 M	.220	1.25	1.50	3.00	7.50
	1894 M	.320	1.25	1.50	3.00	7.50
	1895 M	.078	1.25	1.75	3.50	8.50
398.7	1896 B	.080	1.25	1.75	3.50	8.50
	1897 M	.160	1.25	1.50	3.00	7.50

OAXACA MINT (Oa)

KM#	Date	Mintage	Fine	VF	XF	Unc
398.8	1890 E	.048	—	—	Rare	—
	1890 N	Inc. Ab.	50.00	85.00	135.00	300.00

POTOSI MINT (Pi)

KM#	Date	Mintage	Fine	VF	XF	Unc
398.9	1869 S	—	20.00	30.00	60.00	150.00
	1870 PiG/MoC					
		.020	12.50	16.50	35.00	90.00
	1870 O	Inc. Ab.	12.50	16.50	30.00	75.00
	1871 O	5,400	—	—	Rare	—
	1872 O	—	60.00	85.00	150.00	250.00
	1873	5,000	—	—	Rare	—
	1874 H	—	11.00	14.50	26.50	65.00
	1875 H	—	6.50	8.00	24.00	60.00
	1876 H	—	18.50	25.00	60.00	150.00
	1877 H	—	8.00	10.00	16.50	40.00
	1878 H	—	50.00	75.00	100.00	250.00
	1880 H	6,200	9.50	12.50	22.50	55.00
	1881 H	4,500	—	—	Rare	—
	1886 R	.033	8.00	11.00	16.50	40.00
	1887/0 R	.169	2.50	3.50	8.00	20.00
	1887 R	Inc. Ab.	2.25	3.00	6.00	15.00
	1888 R	.210	1.25	1.75	5.00	12.50
	1889/7 R	.197	1.75	2.50	6.00	15.00
	1889 R	Inc. Ab.	1.25	1.75	5.00	12.50
	1890 R	.221	1.25	1.50	3.00	7.50
	1891/89 R/B					
		.176	1.50	2.50	4.00	10.00
	1891 R	Inc. Ab.	1.25	1.50	3.00	7.50
	1892/89 R	.182	1.50	2.50	4.00	10.00
	1892/0 R	I.A.	1.50	2.50	4.00	10.00
	1892 R	Inc. Ab.	1.25	1.50	3.00	7.50
	1893 R	.041	3.50	4.50	9.00	22.50

ZACATECAS MINT (Zs)

KM#	Date	Mintage	Fine	VF	XF	Unc
398.10	1870 H	.040	11.00	14.50	24.00	60.00
	1871 H	.040	5.00	7.50	14.00	35.00
	1872 H	.040	6.50	10.00	20.00	50.00
	1873/2 H	.020	7.50	12.50	27.50	70.00
	1873 H	Inc. Ab.	11.00	14.50	24.00	60.00
	1874 H	—	8.00	10.00	16.50	40.00
	1874 A	—	10.00	12.50	27.50	65.00
	1875 A	—	5.50	8.50	16.50	40.00
	1876 A	—	8.00	10.00	20.00	50.00
	1876 S	—	10.00	12.50	22.50	55.00
	1877 S	—	3.00	5.00	7.50	18.50
	1878 S	.060	3.00	5.00	8.00	20.00
	1879/8 S	—	2.75	4.00	9.00	22.50
	1879 S	—	2.00	3.00	8.00	20.00
	1880/79 S	.130	5.50	7.50	12.00	30.00
	1880 S	Inc. Ab.	4.50	6.00	10.00	25.00
	1881 S	.210	2.75	3.75	6.00	15.00
	1886 S	.360	1.25	1.50	3.00	7.50
	1886 Z	Inc. Ab.	4.50	7.50	15.00	36.50
	1887 Z	.400	1.25	1.50	3.00	7.50
	1888/7 Z	.500	1.25	1.50	3.50	8.50
	1888 Z	Inc. Ab.	1.25	1.50	3.00	7.50
	1889 Z	.520	1.25	1.50	3.00	7.50
	1889 Z 9/inverted 9					
		Inc. Ab.	1.50	2.50	4.00	10.00
	1889 ZsZ/MoM					
		Inc. Ab.	1.50	2.50	4.00	10.00
	1890 Z	.580	1.25	1.50	3.00	7.50
	1890 ZsZ/MoM					
		Inc. Ab.	1.50	2.50	4.00	10.00
	1891 Z	.420	1.25	1.50	3.00	7.50
	1892 Z	.346	1.25	1.50	3.00	7.50
	1893 Z	.258	1.25	1.50	3.00	7.50
	1894 Z	.228	1.25	1.50	3.50	8.50
	1894 ZoZ (error)					
		Inc. Ab.	1.50	2.50	4.00	10.00
	1895 Z	.260	1.25	1.50	3.00	7.50
	1896 Z	.200	1.25	1.50	3.00	7.50
	1896 6/inverted 6					
		Inc. Ab.	1.50	2.50	4.00	10.00
	1897/6 Z	.200	1.50	2.50	4.00	10.00
	1897 Z	Inc. Ab.	1.25	1.50	3.00	7.50

COPPER-NICKEL

MEXICO CITY MINT (Mo)

KM#	Date	Mintage	Fine	VF	XF	Unc
399	1882	40.000	.75	1.50	3.00	5.00
	1883	Inc. Ab.	75.00	125.00	175.00	350.00

.903 SILVER

CULIACAN MINT (Cn)

Obv: Restyled eagle

KM#	Date	Mintage	Fine	VF	XF	Unc
400	1898 M	.044	1.75	3.50	6.50	20.00
	1899 M	.111	5.50	8.50	20.00	50.00
	1899 Q	Inc. Ab.	1.25	1.50	3.00	7.50
	1900 Q round Q, single tail					
		.239	1.25	1.75	4.00	10.00
	1900 CnQ narrow C, oval Q					
		Inc. Ab.	1.25	1.75	4.00	10.00
	1900 CnQ wide C, oval Q					
		Inc. Ab.	1.25	1.75	4.00	10.00
	1901 Q	.148	1.25	1.50	3.00	7.50
	1902 CnQ narrow C, heavy serifs					
		.262	1.25	1.75	4.00	10.00
	1902 CnQ wide C, light serifs					
		Inc. Ab.	1.25	1.75	4.00	10.00
	1903/1 Q	.331	1.25	1.75	4.00	10.00
	1903 Q	Inc. Ab.	1.25	1.50	3.00	7.50
	1903 V	Inc. Ab.	1.25	1.50	3.00	7.50
	1904 H	.352	1.25	1.50	3.50	8.50

GUANAJUATO MINT (Go)

KM#	Date	Mintage	Fine	VF	XF	Unc
400.1	1898 R mule, gold peso obverse					
		.180	5.00	10.00	20.00	50.00
	1899 R	.260	1.25	1.50	3.00	7.50
	1900 R	.200	1.75	1.50	3.00	7.50

MEXICO CITY MINT (Mo)

KM#	Date	Mintage	Fine	VF	XF	Unc
400.2	1898 M	.080	1.25	1.50	3.00	7.50
	1899 M	.168	1.25	1.50	3.00	7.50
	1900 M	.300	1.25	1.50	3.00	7.50
	1901 M	.100	1.25	1.50	3.00	7.50
	1902 M	.144	BV	1.25	2.50	6.00
	1903 M	.500	BV	1.25	2.50	6.00
	1904/94 M					
		1.090	1.25	1.75	4.00	10.00
	1904 M	Inc. Ab.	BV	1.25	2.50	6.00
	1905 M	.344	1.35	2.00	5.00	12.00

ZACATECAS MINT (Zs)

KM#	Date	Mintage	Fine	VF	XF	Unc
400.3	1898 Z	.100	1.25	1.50	3.00	7.50
	1899 Z	.050	1.25	1.75	3.50	8.50
	1900 Z	.055	1.25	1.75	3.50	8.50
	1901 Z	.040	1.25	1.75	3.50	8.50
	1902/1 Z	—	1.50	3.00	6.00	15.00
	1902 Z	.034	1.35	2.50	4.50	12.00
	1903 Z	.217	BV	1.25	2.50	6.00
	1904 Z	.191	1.25	1.75	3.50	8.50
	1904 M	Inc. Ab.	1.25	1.75	4.00	10.00
	1905 M	.046	1.50	2.50	6.00	15.00

10 CENTAVOS

2.7070 gm., .903 SILVER, .0785 oz ASW

CHIHUAHUA MINT (Ca)

Obv: Eagle. Rev: Value within wreath.

KM#	Date	Mintage	Fine	VF	XF	Unc
401	1868/7	—	30.00	60.00	150.00	350.00
	1868	—	25.00	50.00	135.00	325.00
	1869	*.015	20.00	40.00	125.00	300.00
	1870	.017	17.50	35.00	100.00	275.00

POTOSI MINT (S.L.P.)

KM#	Date	Mintage	Fine	VF	XF	Unc
401.2	1863	—	120.00	175.00	300.00	550.00

MEXICO CITY MINT (M)

KM#	Date	Mintage	Fine	VF	XF	Unc
402	1867/3	—	20.00	40.00	80.00	240.00
	1867	—	18.50	37.50	75.00	225.00
	1868/7	—	20.00	40.00	80.00	240.00
	1868	—	18.50	37.50	75.00	225.00

POTOSI MINT (P)

KM#	Date	Mintage	Fine	VF	XF	Unc
402.1	1868/7	.038	22.50	45.00	90.00	270.00
	1868	Inc. Ab.	20.00	40.00	80.00	240.00
	1869/7	4,900	25.00	50.00	100.00	300.00

ALAMOS MINT (As)

Obv: Standing eagle. Rev: Value above branches.

KM#	Date	Mintage	Fine	VF	XF	Unc
403	1874 DL	—	13.50	18.00	40.00	100.00
	1875 L	—	4.00	5.50	10.00	25.00
	1876 L	—	8.00	11.00	16.50	42.50
	1878/5 L	—	5.00	7.50	16.00	40.00
	1878 L	—	5.00	7.50	14.00	35.00
	1879 L	—	7.50	10.00	18.00	45.00
	1880 L	.013	4.50	6.00	10.00	25.00
	1882 L	.022	4.00	5.50	12.00	30.00
	1883 L	8,520	9.00	12.50	22.50	55.00
	1884 L	—	4.00	5.50	12.00	30.00
	1885 L	.015	4.00	5.50	12.00	30.00
	1886 L	.045	4.50	6.00	12.00	30.00
	1887 L	.015	5.00	7.50	14.00	35.00
	1888 L	.038	3.50	5.00	10.00	25.00
	1889 L	.020	4.50	6.00	12.00	30.00
	1890 L	.040	3.00	4.00	6.00	15.00
	1891 L	.038	4.00	5.00	10.00	25.00
	1892 L	.057	2.75	3.75	7.50	18.50
	1893 L	.070	7.50	11.50	22.50	55.00

CHIHUAHUA MINT (Ca, CH)

KM#	Date	Mintage	Fine	VF	XF	Unc
403.1	1871 M	8,150	6.00	8.00	16.50	40.00
	1873 M crude date					
		—	7.50	11.50	20.00	50.00
	1874 M	—	7.50	11.50	20.00	50.00
	1880 G/g	7,620	11.00	14.00	26.50	65.00
	1881	340 pcs.	—	—	Rare	—
	1883 M	9,000	10.00	13.50	25.00	60.00
	1884 M	—	11.00	15.00	30.00	75.00
	1886 M	.045	4.50	6.00	12.00	30.00
	1887 M	.096	3.00	4.00	8.00	20.00
	1888 M	.299	BV	1.50	3.00	7.50
	1888 Ca/Mo	—	BV	3.00	6.00	15.00
	1889/8 M	.115	BV	BV	3.00	7.50
	1889 M small 89 (5 Centavo font)					
		Inc. Ab.	BV	3.00	6.00	15.00
	1890/80 M	.139	BV	2.50	4.00	10.00
	1890 M	Inc. Ab.	BV	BV	3.00	7.50
	1891 M	.163	BV	BV	3.00	7.50
	1892 M	.169	BV	BV	3.00	7.50
	1892 M 9/inverted 9					
		Inc. Ab.	BV	3.00	6.00	15.00
	1893 M	.246	BV	BV	3.00	7.50
	1894 M	.163	BV	BV	3.00	7.50
	1895 M	.127	BV	BV	3.00	7.50

CULIACAN MINT (Cn)

KM#	Date	Mintage	Fine	VF	XF	Unc
403.2	1871 P	—	—	—	Rare	—
	1873 P	8,732	12.50	15.00	28.50	70.00
	1881 D	9,440	40.00	65.00	100.00	175.00
	1882 D	.012	14.00	17.50	35.00	85.00
	1885 M mule gold 2-1/2 peso obverse					
		.018	17.50	25.00	50.00	125.00
	1886 M mule, gold 2-1/2 peso obverse					
		.013	20.00	30.00	60.00	150.00
	1887 M	.011	8.00	10.00	17.50	45.00
	1888 M	.056	4.00	5.50	10.00	25.00
	1889 M	.042	2.50	3.25	6.00	15.00
	1890 M	.132	BV	2.50	4.00	10.00
	1891 M	.084	BV	2.50	5.00	12.50
	1892/1 M	.037	3.00	4.50	7.00	17.50
	1892 M	Inc. Ab.	2.50	3.75	6.00	15.00
	1894 M	.043	BV	2.75	5.50	14.00
	1895 M	.023	2.50	4.00	7.00	17.50
	1896 M	.121	BV	BV	3.00	7.50

DURANGO MINT (Do)

KM#	Date	Mintage	Fine	VF	XF	Unc
403.3	1878 E	2,500	11.00	20.00	40.00	100.00
	1879 B	—	65.00	100.00	175.00	350.00
	1880/79 B	—	—	—	Rare	—
	1884 C	—	9.00	12.50	24.00	60.00
	1886 C	.013	14.00	18.00	35.00	90.00
	1887 C	.081	2.50	4.00	8.00	20.00
	1888 C	.031	3.00	4.50	8.50	21.50
	1889 C	.055	2.75	3.75	7.00	17.50
	1890 C	.050	2.75	3.75	7.00	17.50
	1891 P	.139	BV	2.50	5.00	12.50
	1892 P	.212	BV	2.50	5.00	12.50
	1892 D	Inc. Ab.	BV	2.50	5.00	12.50
	1893 D	.258	BV	BV	3.00	7.50
	1893 D/C	I.A.	2.50	3.00	6.00	15.00
	1894 D	.184	BV	BV	3.00	7.50
	1895 D	.142	BV	BV	3.00	7.50

GUADALAJARA MINT (Ga)

KM#	Date	Mintage	Fine	VF	XF	Unc
403.4	1871 C	4,734	17.50	25.00	50.00	125.00
	1873 C	.025	7.50	10.00	20.00	50.00
	1874 C	—	11.00	15.00	27.50	65.00
	1877 A	—	9.00	12.00	20.00	50.00
	1881 A	.115	40.00	60.00	100.00	250.00
	1881 S	Inc. Ab.	3.50	5.00	10.00	25.00
	1883 B	.090	3.50	5.00	10.00	25.00
	1884 B	—	5.00	8.00	16.00	40.00
	1884 B/S	—	6.00	10.00	18.00	45.00

KM#	Date	Mintage	Fine	VF	XF	Unc
403.4	1884 H	—	3.00	4.00	8.00	20.00
	1885 H	.093	BV	2.50	5.00	12.50
	1886 S	.151	2.50	4.00	8.00	20.00
	1887 S	.162	BV	BV	3.00	7.50
	1888 S	.225	BV	BV	3.00	7.50
	1888 GaS/HoG					
		Inc. Ab.	2.50	3.00	6.00	15.00
	1889 S	.310	BV	BV	3.00	7.50
	1890 S	.303	BV	BV	3.00	7.50
	1891 S	.199	BV	BV	3.00	7.50
	1892 S	.329	BV	BV	3.00	7.50
	1893 S	.225	BV	BV	3.00	7.50
	1894 S	.243	2.50	3.50	7.00	17.50
	1895 S	.080	BV	BV	3.00	7.50

GUANAJUATO MINT (Go)

KM#	Date	Mintage	Fine	VF	XF	Unc
403.5	1869 S	7,000	12.50	25.00	50.00	125.00
	1871/0 S	.060	3.50	7.00	14.00	35.00
	1872 S	.060	3.00	5.00	10.00	25.00
	1873 S	.050	2.75	5.50	11.50	27.50
	1874 S	—	5.00	6.50	12.50	30.00
	1875 S	—	5.00	6.50	12.50	30.00
	1876 S	—	5.25	6.00	12.00	30.00
	1877 S	—	13.50	18.00	36.00	90.00
	1878/7 S	.010	9.00	12.00	20.00	50.00
	1878 S	Inc. Ab.	7.50	10.00	18.00	45.00
	1879 S	—	3.00	4.00	8.00	20.00
	1880 S	—	—	—	Rare	—
	1881/71 S	.100	3.00	4.00	6.00	15.00
	1881/0 S	I.A.	3.50	4.00	6.00	15.00
	1881 S	Inc. Ab.	BV	2.50	5.00	12.50
	1882/1 S	.040	BV	2.50	5.00	12.50
	1883 B	—	2.50	4.00	8.00	20.00
	1884 B	—	BV	2.50	4.00	10.00
	1884 S	—	5.50	8.50	16.50	40.00
	1885 R	.100	BV	BV	3.00	7.50
	1886 R	.095	BV	BV	3.00	7.50
	1887 R	.330	2.50	4.00	8.00	20.00
	1888 R	.270	BV	BV	3.00	7.50
	1889 R	.205	BV	2.50	4.00	10.00
	1889 GoR/HoG					
		Inc. Ab.	2.50	3.50	6.00	15.00
	1890 R	.270	BV	BV	3.00	7.50
	1891 R	.523	BV	BV	3.00	7.50
	1892 R	.440	BV	BV	3.00	7.50
	1893/1 R	.389	2.50	3.50	6.00	15.00
	1893 R	Inc. Ab.	BV	BV	3.00	7.50
	1894 R	.400	BV	BV	3.00	7.50
	1895 R	.355	BV	BV	3.00	7.50
	1896 R	.190	BV	BV	3.00	7.50
	1897 R	.205	BV	BV	3.00	7.50

HERMOSILLO MINT (Ho)

KM#	Date	Mintage	Fine	VF	XF	Unc
403.6	1874 R	—	8.00	12.00	20.00	50.00
	1876 F	3,140	16.50	22.50	40.00	100.00
	1878 A	—	7.50	11.50	20.00	50.00
	1879 A	—	8.00	12.00	20.00	50.00
	1880 A	—	2.75	4.00	8.00	20.00
	1881 A	.028	6.00	9.00	18.00	45.00
	1882/1 A	.025	7.50	11.00	20.00	50.00
	1882/1 a	I.A.	7.50	11.00	20.00	50.00
	1882 A	Inc. Ab.	6.00	9.00	18.00	45.00
	1883	7,000	50.00	75.00	150.00	300.00
	1884 A	—	5.00	7.50	14.00	35.00
	1884 M	—	3.00	5.00	10.00	25.00
	1885 M	.021	10.00	15.00	25.00	60.00
	1886 M	.010	—	—	—	—
	1886 G	Inc. Ab.	6.50	8.50	16.00	40.00
	1887 G	—	12.50	16.50	30.00	75.00
	1888 G	.025	4.50	6.00	12.00	30.00
	1889 G	.042	2.50	4.00	8.00	20.00
	1890 G	.048	2.50	3.50	6.00	15.00
	1891/80 G	.136	3.50	4.50	8.00	20.00
	1891 G	Inc. Ab.	2.50	3.50	6.00	15.00
	1892 G	.067	2.50	3.50	7.00	17.50
	1893 G	.067	2.50	3.50	7.00	17.50

MEXICO CITY MINT (Mo)

KM#	Date	Mintage	Fine	VF	XF	Unc
403.7	1869/8 C	.030	10.00	15.00	30.00	75.00
	1869 C	Inc. Ab.	8.00	14.00	28.00	65.00
	1870 C	.110	3.00	6.00	12.00	30.00
	1871 C	.084	4.50	6.00	12.00	30.00
	1871 M	Inc. Ab.	6.00	8.00	16.00	40.00
	1872 M	.198	BV	2.50	5.00	12.50
	1873 M	.040	7.00	9.00	15.00	37.50
	1874 M	—	3.50	7.00	14.00	35.00
	1874/64 B	—	4.50	6.00	12.00	30.00
	1874 B/M	—	4.50	6.00	12.00	30.00
	1874 B	—	3.00	5.00	10.00	25.00
	1875 B	—	3.50	5.00	10.00	25.00
	1876/5 B	—	3.00	4.00	6.00	15.00
	1876/5 B/M	—	3.00	4.00	6.00	15.00
	1876 B	—	BV	3.00	5.50	13.50
	1877/6 M	—	3.00	4.50	7.00	17.50
	1877/6 M/B	—	3.00	4.50	7.00	17.50
	1877 M	—	BV	3.00	6.00	15.00

KM#	Date	Mintage	Fine	VF	XF	Unc
403.7	1878/7 M	.100	3.00	4.50	7.00	17.50
	1878 M	Inc. Ab.	BV	3.00	6.00	15.00
	1879/69 M	—	3.50	5.00	7.50	18.50
	1879 M/C	—	2.50	3.50	6.50	17.50
	1879 M	—	BV	3.00	6.00	15.00
	1880/79 M	—	2.50	3.50	6.50	17.50
	1881/0 M	.510	BV	2.50	4.00	10.00
	1881 M	Inc. Ab.	BV	BV	3.00	7.50
	1882/1 M	.550	BV	3.00	6.00	15.00
	1882 M	Inc. Ab.	BV	2.50	5.00	12.50
	1883/2 M	.250	BV	3.00	6.00	15.00
	1884 M	—	BV	BV	3.00	7.50
	1885 M	.470	BV	BV	3.00	7.50
	1886 M	.603	BV	BV	3.00	7.50
	1887 M	.580	BV	BV	3.00	7.50
	1888/7 M	.710	BV	2.50	4.00	10.00
	1888 MoM	I.A.	BV	2.50	4.00	10.00
	1888 MOM	I.A.	BV	2.50	4.00	10.00
	1889 M	.622	BV	BV	3.00	7.50
	1890/89 M	.815	BV	2.50	4.00	10.00
	1890 M	Inc. Ab.	BV	BV	3.00	7.50
	1891 M	.859	BV	BV	3.00	7.50
	1892 M	1.030	BV	BV	3.00	7.50
	1893 M	.310	BV	BV	3.00	7.50
	1893 M/C	I.A.	BV	2.50	4.00	10.00
	1894 M	.350	BV	BV	3.00	7.50
	1895 M	.320	BV	BV	3.00	7.50
	1896 B	.340	BV	BV	3.00	7.50
	1896 B/G	I.A.	BV	2.50	4.00	10.00
	1896 M	Inc. Ab.	10.00	16.50	32.50	80.00
	1897 M	.170	BV	BV	3.00	7.50

OAXACA MINT (Oa)

KM#	Date	Mintage	Fine	VF	XF	Unc
403.8	1889 E	.021	—	—	Rare	—
	1890 E	.031	75.00	125.00	200.00	400.00
	1890 N	Inc. Ab.	—	—	Rare	—

POTOSI MINT (Pi)

KM#	Date	Mintage	Fine	VF	XF	Unc
403.9	1869/8 S	4,000	15.00	25.00	50.00	125.00
	1870 G	Inc. Ab.	10.00	14.00	28.00	70.00
	1870/69 O	.018	—	—	Rare	—
	1871 O	.021	11.00	15.00	30.00	75.00
	1872 O	.016	10.00	14.00	28.00	70.00
	1873 O	4,750	16.50	25.00	50.00	125.00
	1874 H	—	5.75	7.50	14.00	35.00
	1875 H	—	11.00	15.00	30.00	75.00
	1876 H	—	5.00	7.50	14.00	35.00
	1877 H	—	11.00	15.00	30.00	75.00
	1878 H	—	17.50	24.00	48.00	120.00
	1879 H	—	15.00	20.00	40.00	100.00
	1880 H	—	15.00	20.00	40.00	100.00
	1881 H	7,600	11.00	15.00	30.00	75.00
	1882 H	4,000	11.00	15.00	30.00	75.00
	1883 H	—	11.00	15.00	30.00	75.00
	1884 H	—	5.00	7.50	14.00	35.00
	1885 H	.051	10.00	14.00	28.00	70.00
	1885 C	Inc. Ab.	7.50	12.50	25.00	50.00
	1886 C	.052	6.50	8.00	16.00	40.00
	1886 R	Inc. Ab.	2.50	4.00	8.00	20.00
	1887 R	.118	BV	BV	3.00	7.50
	1888 R	.136	BV	BV	3.00	7.50
	1889/7 R	.131	6.00	8.00	16.00	40.00
	1890 R	.204	BV	BV	3.00	7.50
	1891/89 R	.163	2.50	3.50	6.00	15.00
	1891 R	Inc. Ab.	BV	2.50	4.00	10.00
	1892/0 R	.200	BV	2.50	4.00	10.00
	1892 R	Inc. Ab.	BV	BV	3.00	7.50
	1893 R	.048	BV	BV	3.00	7.50

ZACATECAS MINT (Zs)

KM#	Date	Mintage	Fine	VF	XF	Unc
403.10	1870 H	.020	5.00	6.50	14.00	35.00
	1871/0 H	.010	7.00	10.00	16.00	40.00
	1871 H	Inc. Ab.	6.00	7.50	15.00	37.50
	1872 H	.010	—	—	Rare	—
	1873 H	.010	7.00	10.00	16.00	40.00
	1874 H	—	10.00	12.50	22.50	55.00
	1874 A	—	13.50	20.00	32.50	80.00
	1875 A	—	3.50	7.00	14.00	35.00
	1876 A	—	4.00	5.50	11.50	27.50
	1876 S	—	4.50	6.00	12.00	30.00
	1877 S small S	—	5.50	7.50	15.00	37.50
	1877 S large S	—	5.50	7.50	15.00	37.50
	1878/7 S	.030	4.00	5.50	11.50	27.50
	1878 S	Inc. Ab.	3.00	5.00	10.00	25.00
	1879 S	Inc. Ab.	2.50	4.50	9.00	22.50
	1880 S	—	3.00	5.00	10.00	17.50
	1881/0 S	.120	3.00	5.00	10.00	17.50
	1881 S	Inc. Ab.	BV	3.00	6.00	15.00
	1882/1 S	.064	4.50	6.00	8.00	20.00
	1882 S	Inc. Ab.	3.00	4.00	6.00	15.00
	1883/73 S	.102	BV	3.00	5.00	12.50
	1883 S	Inc. Ab.	BV	BV	3.00	7.50
	1884/3 S	—	BV	3.00	5.00	12.50
	1884 S	—	BV	BV	3.00	7.50
	1885 S	.297	BV	BV	3.00	7.50
	1885 S small S in mintmark					

KM#	Date	Mintage	Fine	VF	XF	Unc
		Inc. Ab.	BV	3.00	6.00	15.00
	1885 (error) I.A.		2.50	5.00	10.00	25.00
	1886 S	.274	—	—	3.00	7.50
	1886 Z	Inc. Ab.	2.50	4.00	8.00	20.00
	1887 ZsZ	.233	BV	BV	3.00	7.50
	1887 Z Z (error)					
		Inc. Ab.	2.50	5.00	10.00	25.00
	1888 ZsZ	.270	BV	BV	3.00	7.50
	1888 Z Z (error)					
		Inc. Ab.	2.50	5.00	10.00	25.00
	1889/7 Z/S	240	BV	3.00	6.00	15.00
	1889 Z/S	I.A.	BV	3.00	6.00	15.00
	1889 Z	Inc. Ab.	BV	BV	3.00	7.50
	1890 ZsZ	.410	BV	BV	3.00	7.50
	1890 Z Z (error)					
		Inc. Ab.	2.50	5.00	10.00	25.00
	1891 Z	1.105	BV	BV	3.00	7.50
	1891 ZsZ dbl. s					
		Inc. Ab.	BV	3.00	6.00	15.00
	1892 Z	1.102	BV	BV	3.00	7.50
	1893 Z	1.011	BV	BV	3.00	7.50
	1894 Z	.892	BV	BV	3.00	7.50
	1895 Z	.920	BV	BV	3.00	7.50
	1896 ZsZ	.700	BV	BV	3.00	7.50
	1896 Z Z (error)					
		Inc. Ab.	2.50	5.00	10.00	25.00
	1897/6 ZsZ	.900	BV	3.00	6.00	15.00
	1897/6 Z Z (error)					
		Inc. Ab.	2.50	5.00	10.00	25.00
	1897 Z	Inc. Ab.	BV	BV	3.00	7.50

CULIACAN MINT (Cn)

Obv: Restyled eagle

KM#	Date	Mintage	Fine	VF	XF	Unc
404	1898 M	9,870	20.00	30.00	60.00	150.00
	1899 Q round Q, single tail					
		.080	3.50	6.00	12.00	30.00
	1899 Q oval Q, double tail					
		Inc. Ab.	3.50	6.00	12.00	30.00
	1900 Q	.160	BV	BV	3.00	7.50
	1901 Q	.235	BV	BV	3.00	7.50
	1902 Q	.186	BV	BV	3.00	7.50
	1903 Q	.256	BV	BV	3.00	7.50
	1903 V	Inc. Ab.	BV	BV	3.00	7.50
	1904 H	.307	BV	BV	3.00	7.50

GUANAJUATO MINT (Go)

KM#	Date	Mintage	Fine	VF	XF	Unc
404.1	1898 R	.435	BV	BV	3.00	7.50
	1899 R	.270	BV	BV	3.00	7.50
	1900 R	.130	6.00	10.00	18.00	45.00

MEXICO CITY MINT (Mo)

KM#	Date	Mintage	Fine	VF	XF	Unc
404.2	1898 M	.130	BV	BV	3.00	7.50
	1899 M	.190	BV	BV	3.00	7.50
	1900 M	.311	BV	BV	3.00	7.50
	1901 M	.080	BV	BV	3.00	7.50
	1902 M	.181	BV	BV	3.00	7.50
	1903 M	.581	BV	BV	3.00	7.50
	1904 M	1.266	BV	BV	3.00	7.50
	1904 MM (error)					
		Inc. Ab.	2.00	3.00	6.00	15.00
	1905 M	.266	BV	2.50	4.00	10.00

ZACATECAS MINT (Zs)

KM#	Date	Mintage	Fine	VF	XF	Unc
404.3	1898 Z	.240	BV	BV	3.00	7.50
	1899 Z	.105	BV	BV	3.00	7.50
	1900 Z	.219	6.00	8.50	16.00	40.00
	1901 Z	.070	2.50	4.50	9.00	22.50
	1902 Z	.120	2.50	4.50	9.00	22.50
	1903 Z	.228	BV	BV	3.00	7.50
	1904 Z	.638	BV	BV	3.00	7.50
	1904 M	Inc. Ab.	BV	2.50	4.00	10.00
	1905 M	.066	6.00	10.00	20.00	50.00

20 CENTAVOS

5.4150 gm., .903 SILVER, .1572 oz ASW

CULIACAN MINT (Cn)

Obv: Restyled eagle

KM#	Date	Mintage	Fine	VF	XF	Unc
405	1898 M	.114	5.00	8.00	16.00	40.00
	1899 M	.044	11.50	17.50	27.50	65.00
405	1899 Q	Inc. Ab.	20.00	32.50	65.00	160.00
	1900 Q	.068	6.50	8.00	16.00	40.00
	1901 Q	.185	BV	5.00	9.00	22.50
	1902/802 Q	098	6.00	8.50	16.00	40.00
	1902 Q	Inc. Ab.	BV	6.00	12.00	30.00
	1903 Q	.093	BV	5.00	10.00	25.00
	1904 H	.258	BV	7.00	14.00	35.00

GUANAJUATO MINT (Go)

KM#	Date	Mintage	Fine	VF	XF	Unc
405.1	1898 R	.135	BV	6.00	12.00	30.00
	1899 R	.215	BV	5.00	10.00	25.00
	1900/800 R	038	8.50	13.50	27.50	65.00

MEXICO CITY MINT (Mo)

KM#	Date	Mintage	Fine	VF	XF	Unc
405.2	1898 M	.150	BV	5.00	10.00	25.00
	1899 M	.425	BV	5.00	8.00	20.00
	1900 M	.295	BV	5.00	8.00	20.00
	1901 M	.110	BV	5.00	10.00	25.00
	1902 M	.120	BV	5.00	8.00	20.00
	1903 M	.213	BV	7.00	14.00	35.00
	1904 M	.276	5.00	8.00	16.00	40.00
	1905 M	.117	6.50	13.00	26.00	65.00

ZACATECAS MINT (Zs)

KM#	Date	Mintage	Fine	VF	XF	Unc
405.3	1898 Z	.195	BV	5.00	10.00	25.00
	1899 Z	.210	BV	5.00	8.00	20.00
	1900/800 Z	097	BV	5.00	10.00	25.00
	1901 Z	.130	BV	5.00	10.00	25.00
	1902 Z	.105	BV	5.00	8.00	20.00
	1903 Z	.143	BV	5.00	10.00	25.00
	1904 Z	.246	5.00	8.00	16.00	40.00
	1904 M	Inc. Ab.	BV	7.00	14.00	35.00
	1905 M	.059	8.00	16.00	32.00	80.00

25 CENTAVOS

6.7680 gm., .9903 SILVER, .1965 oz ASW

ALAMOS MINT (A, As)

Rev: Balance scale

KM#	Date	Mintage	Fine	VF	XF	Unc
406	1874 L	—	8.50	16.50	33.50	82.50
	1875 L	—	8.50	16.50	33.50	82.50
	1876 L	—	10.00	20.00	40.00	100.00
	1877 L	.011	17.50	35.00	70.00	175.00
	1878 L	.025	7.00	14.00	28.00	70.00
	1879 L	—	9.00	18.00	36.00	90.00
	1880 L	—	7.00	14.00	28.00	70.00
	1881 L	8,800	—	—	Rare	—
	1882 L	7,777	8.00	16.00	32.00	80.00
	1883 L	.028	7.00	14.00	28.00	70.00
	1884 L	—	8.00	16.00	32.00	80.00
	1885 L	—	9.00	18.00	36.00	90.00
	1886 L	.046	7.50	15.00	30.00	75.00
	1887 L	.012	6.00	12.00	24.00	60.00
	1888 L	.020	7.00	14.00	28.00	70.00
	1889 L	.014	8.00	16.00	32.00	80.00
	1890 L	.023	7.00	14.00	28.00	70.00

CHIHUAHUA MINT Ca, CH, CA

KM#	Date	Mintage	Fine	VF	XF	Unc
406.1	1871 M	.018	12.50	25.00	50.00	125.00
	1872 M very crude date					
		.024	13.50	27.50	55.00	140.00
	1883 M	.012	7.50	15.00	30.00	75.00
	1885 M	.035	7.00	14.00	28.00	70.00
	1886 M	.022	7.50	15.00	30.00	75.00
	1887 M	.026	6.50	13.50	27.50	65.00
	1888 M	.014	7.50	15.00	30.00	75.00
	1889 M	.050	6.00	12.00	24.00	60.00

CULIACAN MINT (Cn)

KM#	Date	Mintage	Fine	VF	XF	Unc
406.2	1871 P	—	—	—	Rare	—
	1872 P	2,780	—	—	Rare	—
	1873 P	.020	7.50	15.00	30.00	75.00
	1874 P	—	6.00	12.00	24.00	60.00
	1875 P	—	—	—	Rare	—
	1876 P	—	—	—	Rare	—
	1878 D	—	6.00	10.00	20.00	50.00
	1879 D	—	6.50	13.50	27.50	65.00
	1880 D	—	—	—	Rare	—
	1881/0 D	.018	8.00	16.00	32.00	80.00
	1882 D	—	—	—	Rare	—
	1882 M	—	—	—	Rare	—
	1883 M	.015	9.00	18.00	36.00	90.00
	1884 M	—	10.00	20.00	40.00	100.00
	1885/4 M	.019	7.00	14.00	28.00	70.00
	1886 M	.022	6.00	12.00	24.00	60.00

KM#	Date	Mintage	Fine	VF	XF	Unc
	1887 M	.032	6.00	11.50	22.50	55.00
	1888 M	.086	7.00	14.00	28.00	70.00
	1889 M	.050	7.00	14.00	28.00	70.00
	1890 M	.091	6.00	12.00	24.00	60.00
	1892 M	.016	6.00	12.00	24.00	60.00

DURANGO MINT (Do)

KM#	Date	Mintage	Fine	VF	XF	Unc
406.3	1873	892 pcs.	—	—	Rare	—
	1877 P	—	12.50	25.00	50.00	125.00
	1878/7 E	—	—	—	Rare	—
	1878 B	—	—	—	Rare	—
	1879 B	—	12.50	25.00	50.00	125.00
	1880/70 B	—	—	—	Rare	—
	1880 B	—	—	—	Rare	—
	1882 C	.017	8.50	17.50	35.00	85.00
	1884/3 C	—	15.00	30.00	60.00	150.00
	1885 C	.015	7.50	15.00	30.00	75.00
	1886 C	.033	6.50	13.50	26.50	65.00
	1887 C	.027	7.00	14.00	28.00	70.00
	1888 C	.025	7.50	15.00	30.00	75.00
	1889 C	.029	7.00	14.00	28.00	70.00
	1890 C	.068	6.00	12.00	24.00	60.00

GUADALAJARA MINT (Ga)

KM#	Date	Mintage	Fine	VF	XF	Unc
406.4	1880 A	.038	7.00	14.00	28.00	70.00
	1881 S	.039	7.00	14.00	28.00	70.00
	1882 S	.018	7.00	14.00	28.00	70.00
	1883/2 B/S	—	6.00	12.00	24.00	60.00
	1884 B	—	7.50	15.00	30.00	75.00
	1889 S	.030	7.00	14.00	28.00	70.00

GUANAJUATO MINT (Go)

KM#	Date	Mintage	Fine	VF	XF	Unc
406.5	1870 S	.128	6.00	10.00	20.00	50.00
	1871 S	.172	6.00	10.00	20.00	50.00
	1872/1 S	.178	6.00	12.00	24.00	60.00
	1872 S	Inc. Ab.	6.00	10.00	20.00	50.00
	1873 S	.120	7.00	14.00	28.00	70.00
	1874 S	—	6.00	10.00	20.00	50.00
	1875/4 S	—	6.00	12.00	24.00	60.00
	1875 S	—	6.00	10.00	20.00	50.00
	1876 S	—	7.00	14.00	28.00	70.00
	1877 S	.124	6.00	10.00	20.00	50.00
	1878 S	.146	6.00	10.00	20.00	50.00
	1879 S	—	6.00	10.00	20.00	50.00
	1880 S	—	7.50	15.00	30.00	75.00
	1881 S	.408	6.00	10.00	20.00	50.00
	1882 S	.204	6.00	10.00	20.00	50.00
	1883 B	.168	6.00	10.00	20.00	50.00
	1884/69 B	—	6.00	12.00	24.00	60.00
	1884 B	—	6.00	10.00	20.00	50.00
	1885/65 R	.300	6.00	12.00	24.00	60.00
	1885/69 R	I.A.	6.00	12.00	24.00	60.00
	1885 R	Inc. Ab.	6.00	10.00	20.00	50.00
	1886/66 R	.322	6.00	12.00	24.00	60.00
	1886/69 R/S		6.00	12.00	24.00	60.00
	1886/5/69R		6.00	12.00	24.00	60.00
	1886 R	Inc. Ab.	6.00	10.00	20.00	50.00
	1887 R	.254	6.00	10.00	20.00	50.00
	1888 R	.312	6.00	10.00	20.00	50.00
	1889/8 R	.304	6.00	12.00	24.00	60.00
	1889 R	Inc. Ab.	6.00	10.00	20.00	50.00
	1890 R	.236	6.00	10.00	20.00	50.00

HERMOSILLO MINT (Ho)

KM#	Date	Mintage	Fine	VF	XF	Unc
406.6	1874 R	.023	7.50	15.00	30.00	75.00
	1875 R	—	—	—	Rare	—
	1876/4 F/R	.034	10.00	20.00	40.00	100.00
	1876 F/R	I.A.	9.00	18.00	36.00	90.00
	1877 F	—	8.00	16.00	32.00	80.00
	1878 A	.023	6.00	12.00	24.00	60.00
	1879 A	—	7.00	14.00	28.00	70.00
	1880 A	—	7.00	14.00	28.00	70.00
	1881 A	.019	7.00	14.00	28.00	70.00
	1882 A	8,120	7.00	14.00	28.00	70.00
	1883 M	2,000	15.00	30.00	60.00	150.00
	1884 M	—	10.00	20.00	40.00	100.00
	1885 M	—	6.00	12.00	24.00	60.00
	1886 G	6,400	10.00	20.00	40.00	100.00
	1887 G	.012	15.00	30.00	60.00	150.00
	1888 G	.020	7.00	14.00	28.00	70.00
	1889 G	.028	6.00	10.00	20.00	50.00
	1890 G	.018	12.50	25.00	50.00	125.00

MEXICO CITY MINT (Mo)

KM#	Date	Mintage	Fine	VF	XF	Unc
406.7	1869 C	.076	7.00	14.00	28.00	70.00
	1870 C	.136	6.00	10.00	20.00	50.00
	1871 M	.138	6.00	10.00	20.00	50.00
	1872 M	.220	6.00	10.00	20.00	50.00
	1873/1 M	.048	6.00	12.00	24.00	60.00
	1873 M	Inc. Ab.	6.00	10.00	20.00	50.00
	1874/69 B/M		6.00	10.00	20.00	50.00
	1874/3 M	—	8.00	16.00	32.00	80.00
	1874 M	—	7.00	14.00	28.00	70.00
	1875 B	—	6.00	10.00	20.00	50.00
	1876/5 B	—	6.00	12.00	24.00	60.00
	1876 B	—	6.00	10.00	20.00	50.00

KM#	Date	Mintage	Fine	VF	XF	Unc
406.7	1877 M	.056	6.00	10.00	20.00	50.00
	1878/1 M	.120	6.00	12.00	24.00	60.00
	1878/7 M	I.A.	6.00	12.00	24.00	60.00
	1878 M	Inc. Ab.	6.00	10.00	20.00	50.00
	1879 M	—	6.00	10.00	20.00	50.00
	1880 M	—	6.00	10.00	20.00	50.00
	1881/0 M	.300	6.00	12.00	24.00	60.00
	1881 M	Inc. Ab.	6.00	10.00	20.00	50.00
	1882 M	.212	6.00	10.00	20.00	50.00
	1883 M	.108	6.00	12.00	24.00	60.00
	1884 M	—	6.00	10.00	20.00	50.00
	1885 M	.216	6.00	10.00	20.00	50.00
	1886/5 M	.436	6.00	12.00	24.00	60.00
	1886 M	Inc. Ab.	6.00	10.00	20.00	50.00
	1887 M	.376	6.00	10.00	20.00	50.00
	1888 M	.192	6.00	12.00	24.00	60.00
	1889 M	.132	6.00	10.00	20.00	50.00
	1890 M	.060	6.00	12.00	24.00	60.00

POTOSI MINT (Pi)

KM#	Date	Mintage	Fine	VF	XF	Unc
406.8	1869 S	—	15.00	30.00	60.00	150.00
	1870 G	.050	7.00	14.00	28.00	70.00
	1870 O	Inc. Ab.	7.00	14.00	28.00	70.00
	1871 O	.030	7.00	14.00	28.00	70.00
	1872 O	.046	7.00	14.00	28.00	70.00
	1873 O	.013	6.00	12.00	24.00	60.00
	1874 H	—	9.00	18.00	36.00	90.00
	1875 H	—	6.00	12.00	24.00	60.00
	1876/5 H	—	8.50	17.00	34.00	85.00
	1876 H	—	7.50	15.00	30.00	75.00
	1877 H	.019	7.50	15.00	30.00	75.00
	1878 H	—	6.00	11.00	22.00	55.00
	1879 H	—	6.00	12.00	24.00	60.00
	1879 E	—	—	—	Rare	—
	1880 H	—	5.00	10.00	20.00	50.00
	1881 H	.050	7.00	14.00	28.00	70.00
	1881 E	Inc. Ab.	—	—	Rare	—
	1882 H	.020	6.00	12.00	24.00	60.00
	1883 H	.017	7.00	14.00	28.00	70.00
	1884 H	—	6.00	12.00	24.00	60.00
	1885 H	.043	6.00	10.00	20.00	50.00
	1886 C	.078	7.50	15.00	30.00	75.00
	1886 R	Inc. Ab.	6.00	10.00	20.00	50.00
	1886 R 6/inverted 6	Inc. Ab.	6.00	12.00	24.00	60.00
	1887 Pi/ZsR	.092	6.00	12.00	24.00	60.00
	1887 Pi/ZsB	I.A.	10.00	20.00	40.00	100.00
	1888 R	.106	6.00	12.00	24.00	60.00
	1888 Pi/ZsR	I.A.	7.00	14.00	28.00	70.00
	1888 R/B	I.A.	7.00	14.00	28.00	70.00
	1889 R	.115	6.00	12.00	24.00	60.00
	1889 Pi/ZsR	I.A.	7.00	14.00	28.00	70.00
	1889 R/B	I.A.	7.00	14.00	28.00	70.00
	1890 R	.064	6.00	10.00	20.00	50.00
	1890 Pi/ZsR/B	Inc. Ab.	6.00	12.00	24.00	60.00
	1890 R/B	I.A.	6.00	12.00	24.00	60.00

ZACATECAS MINT (Zs)

KM#	Date	Mintage	Fine	VF	XF	Unc
406.9	1870 H	.152	6.00	10.00	20.00	50.00
	1871 H	.250	6.00	10.00	20.00	50.00
	1872 H	.260	6.00	10.00	20.00	50.00
	1873 H	.132	6.00	10.00	20.00	50.00
	1874 H	—	6.00	10.00	20.00	50.00
	1874 A	—	6.00	12.00	24.00	60.00
	1875 A	—	6.00	12.00	24.00	60.00
	1876 A	—	6.00	10.00	20.00	50.00
	1876 S	—	6.00	10.00	20.00	50.00
	1877 S	.350	6.00	10.00	20.00	50.00
	1878 S	.252	6.00	10.00	20.00	50.00
	1879 S	—	6.00	10.00	20.00	50.00
	1880 S	—	6.00	10.00	20.00	50.00
	1881 S	.570	6.00	10.00	20.00	50.00
	1882/1 S	.300	6.00	12.00	24.00	60.00
	1882 S	Inc. Ab.	6.00	10.00	20.00	50.00
	1883/2 S	.193	6.00	12.00	24.00	60.00
	1883 S	Inc. Ab.	6.00	10.00	20.00	50.00
	1884/3 S	—	6.00	12.00	24.00	60.00
	1884 S	—	6.00	10.00	20.00	50.00
	1885 S	.309	6.00	10.00	20.00	50.00
	1886/5 S	.613	6.00	12.00	24.00	60.00
	1886 S	Inc. Ab.	6.00	10.00	20.00	50.00
	1886 Z	Inc. Ab.	6.00	10.00	20.00	50.00
	1887 Z	.389	6.00	10.00	20.00	50.00
	1888 Z	.408	6.00	10.00	20.00	50.00
	1889 Z	.400	6.00	10.00	20.00	50.00
	1890 Z	.269	6.00	10.00	20.00	50.00

50 CENTAVOS

13.5360 gm., .903 SILVER, .3930 oz ASW

ALAMOS MINT (A, As)

Rev: Balance scale

KM#	Date	Mintage	Fine	VF	XF	Unc
407	1875 L	—	15.00	30.00	60.00	150.00
	1876 L	—	15.00	30.00	60.00	150.00
	1877 L	.026	16.00	32.00	64.00	160.00
	1878 L	—	15.00	30.00	60.00	150.00
	1879 L	—	12.50	25.00	50.00	125.00
	1880 L	.057	12.50	25.00	50.00	125.00
	1881 L	.018	13.50	26.50	52.50	135.00
	1884 L	6,286	35.00	70.00	140.00	350.00
	1885 As/HoL	.021	15.00	30.00	60.00	150.00

CHICHUAHUA MINT Ca, CH, CA

KM#	Date	Mintage	Fine	VF	XF	Unc
407.1	1883 M	.012	16.00	32.00	64.00	160.00
	1884 M	—	17.50	35.00	70.00	175.00
	1885 M	.013	13.50	26.50	52.50	135.00
	1886 M	.018	13.00	26.00	52.00	130.00
	1887 M	.026	25.00	50.00	100.00	250.00

CULIACAN MINT (Cn)

KM#	Date	Mintage	Fine	VF	XF	Unc
407.2	1871 P	—	15.00	30.00	60.00	150.00
	1873 P	—	30.00	60.00	120.00	300.00
	1874 P	—	—	—	Rare	—
	1875 P	—	13.00	26.00	52.00	130.00
	1876 P	—	13.00	26.00	52.00	130.00
	1877/6 G	—	13.50	26.50	52.50	135.00
	1877 G	—	12.50	25.00	50.00	125.00
	1878 G	.018	13.50	26.50	52.50	135.00
	1878 D	Inc. Ab.	13.50	26.50	52.50	135.00
	1879 D	—	12.50	25.00	50.00	125.00
	1879 D/G	—	13.50	26.50	52.50	135.00
	1880 D	—	15.00	30.00	60.00	150.00
	1881/0 D	.188	14.00	28.00	56.00	140.00
	1881 D	Inc. Ab.	13.50	26.50	52.50	135.00
	1881 G	Inc. Ab.	30.00	60.00	120.00	300.00
	1882 D	—	—	—	Rare	—
	1882 G	—	—	—	Rare	—
	1883 D	.019	16.50	32.50	65.00	165.00
	1885/3 M/G	9,254	13.50	27.50	55.00	140.00
	1886 M	7,030	35.00	70.00	140.00	350.00
	1887 M	.076	13.50	27.50	55.00	140.00
	1888 M	—	—	—	Rare	—
	1892 M	8,200	35.00	70.00	140.00	350.00

DURANGO MINT (Do)

KM#	Date	Mintage	Fine	VF	XF	Unc
407.3	1871 P	591 pcs.	—	—	Rare	—
	1873 P	4,010	35.00	70.00	140.00	350.00
	1873 M/P	I.A.	13.50	27.50	55.00	140.00
	1874 M	—	25.00	50.00	100.00	250.00
	1875 M	—	13.50	27.50	55.00	140.00
	1875 H	—	35.00	70.00	140.00	350.00
	1876/5 M	—	15.00	30.00	60.00	150.00
	1876 M	—	13.50	27.50	55.00	140.00
	1877 P	2,000	15.00	30.00	60.00	150.00
	1878 B	—	—	—	Rare	—
	1879 B	—	—	—	Rare	—
	1880 P	—	17.50	35.00	70.00	175.00
	1881 P	.010	15.00	30.00	60.00	150.00
	1882 C	8,957	40.00	80.00	160.00	400.00
	1884/2 C	—	16.50	32.50	65.00	165.00
	1884 C	—	15.00	30.00	60.00	150.00
	1885 B	—	16.50	32.50	65.00	165.00
	1886 C	.016	16.50	32.50	65.00	165.00
	1887 Do/MoC	.028	35.00	70.00	140.00	350.00

GUANAJUATO MINT (Go)

KM#	Date	Mintage	Fine	VF	XF	Unc
407.4	1869 S	—	15.00	30.00	60.00	150.00
	1870 S	.166	12.50	25.00	50.00	125.00
	1871 S	.148	12.50	25.00	50.00	125.00
	1872/1 S	.144	15.00	30.00	60.00	150.00
	1872 S	Inc. Ab.	13.50	27.50	55.00	140.00
	1873 S	.050	12.50	25.00	50.00	125.00
	1874 S	—	12.50	25.00	50.00	125.00
	1875 S	—	12.50	25.00	50.00	125.00
	1876 S	—	12.50	25.00	50.00	125.00
	1877 S	.076	13.50	27.50	55.00	140.00
	1878 S	.037	12.50	25.00	50.00	125.00
	1879 S	—	12.50	25.00	50.00	125.00

KM#	Date	Mintage	Fine	VF	XF	Unc
407.4	1880 S	—	13.50	27.50	55.00	140.00
	1881/79 S	.032	13.50	27.50	55.00	140.00
	1881 S	Inc. Ab.	12.50	25.00	50.00	125.00
	1882 S	.018	12.50	25.00	50.00	125.00
	1883/2 B/S	—	13.50	27.50	55.00	140.00
	1883 B	—	12.50	25.00	50.00	125.00
	1884 B/S	—	12.50	25.00	50.00	125.00
	1885 R	.053	12.50	25.00	50.00	125.00
	1886/5 R/B	.059	13.50	27.50	55.00	140.00
	1886/5 R/S	I.A.	13.50	27.50	55.00	140.00
	1886 R	Inc. Ab.	12.50	25.00	50.00	125.00
	1887 R	.018	13.50	27.50	55.00	140.00

HERMOSILLO MINT (Ho)

KM#	Date	Mintage	Fine	VF	XF	Unc
407.5	1874 R	—	12.50	25.00	50.00	125.00
	1875/4 R	—	16.50	32.50	65.00	165.00
	1875 R	—	15.00	30.00	60.00	150.00
	1876/5 F/R	—	22.50	45.00	90.00	225.00
	1876 F	—	20.00	40.00	80.00	200.00
	1877 F	—	13.50	27.50	55.00	140.00
	1880/70 A	—	12.50	25.00	50.00	125.00
	1880 A	—	15.00	30.00	60.00	150.00
	1881 A	.013	13.50	27.50	55.00	140.00
	1882 A	—	12.50	25.00	50.00	125.00
	1894 G	.059	25.00	50.00	100.00	250.00
	1895 G	8,000	55.00	110.00	220.00	550.00

MEXICO CITY MINT (Mo)

KM#	Date	Mintage	Fine	VF	XF	Unc
407.6	1869 C	.046	20.00	40.00	80.00	200.00
	1870 C	.052	12.50	25.00	50.00	125.00
	1871 C	.014	17.50	35.00	70.00	175.00
	1871 M/C	I.A.	12.50	25.00	50.00	125.00
	1872/1 M	.060	13.50	27.50	55.00	140.00
	1872 M	Inc. Ab.	12.50	25.00	50.00	125.00
	1873 M	6,000	15.00	30.00	60.00	150.00
	1874/3 M	—	15.00	30.00	60.00	150.00
	1874/2 B	—	13.50	27.50	55.00	140.00
	1874/3 B/M	—	13.50	27.50	55.00	140.00
	1874 B	—	12.50	25.00	50.00	125.00
	1875 B	—	15.00	30.00	60.00	150.00
	1876/5 B	—	13.50	27.50	55.00	140.00
	1876 B	—	12.50	25.00	50.00	125.00
	1877/2 M	—	13.50	27.50	55.00	140.00
	1877 M	—	12.50	25.00	50.00	125.00
	1878/7 M	8,000	15.00	30.00	60.00	150.00
	1878 M	Inc. Ab.	12.50	25.00	50.00	125.00
	1879 M	—	12.50	25.00	50.00	125.00
	1880 M	—	25.00	50.00	100.00	250.00
	1881 M	.016	15.00	30.00	60.00	150.00
	1882/1 M	2,000	16.50	32.50	65.00	160.00
	1883 M	4,000	—	—	Rare	—
	1884 M	—	—	—	Rare	—
	1885 M	.012	17.50	35.00	70.00	175.00
	1886/5 M	.066	13.50	27.50	55.00	140.00
	1886 M	Inc. Ab.	12.50	25.00	50.00	125.00
	1887/6 M	.088	13.50	27.50	55.00	140.00
	1887 M	Inc. Ab.	12.50	25.00	50.00	125.00

POTOSI MINT (Pi)

KM#	Date	Mintage	Fine	VF	XF	Unc
407.7	1870/780 G	.050	15.00	30.00	60.00	150.00
	1870 G	Inc. Ab.	13.50	27.50	55.00	140.00
	1870 O	I.A.	15.00	30.00	60.00	150.00
	1871 O/G	.064	15.00	30.00	60.00	150.00
	1872 O	.052	12.50	25.00	50.00	125.00
	1872 O/G	I.A.	13.50	27.50	55.00	140.00
	1873 O	.032	18.50	37.50	75.00	150.00
	1873 H	Inc. Ab.	17.50	35.00	70.00	140.00
	1874 H/O	—	12.50	25.00	50.00	125.00
	1875 H	—	13.50	27.50	55.00	140.00
	1876 H	—	30.00	60.00	120.00	300.00
	1877 H	.034	12.50	25.00	50.00	125.00
	1878 H	9,700	12.50	25.00	50.00	125.00
	1879/7 H	—	13.50	27.50	55.00	140.00
	1879 H	—	12.50	25.00	50.00	125.00
	1880 H	—	12.50	25.00	50.00	125.00
	1881 H	.028	13.50	27.50	55.00	140.00
	1882 H	.022	12.50	25.00	50.00	125.00
	1883 H	.029	13.50	27.50	55.00	140.00
	1884 H	—	12.50	25.00	50.00	125.00
	1885/0 H	.045	13.50	27.50	55.00	140.00
	1885/4 H	I.A.	13.50	27.50	55.00	140.00
	1885 H	Inc. Ab.	12.50	25.00	50.00	125.00
	1885 C	Inc. Ab.	12.50	25.00	50.00	125.00
	1886/1 R	.092	15.00	30.00	60.00	150.00
	1886 C	Inc. Ab.	16.50	32.50	65.00	165.00
	1886 R	Inc. Ab.	15.00	30.00	60.00	150.00
	1887 R	.032	13.50	27.50	55.00	140.00

NOTE: Coins dated 1888 R are considered to be counterfeit.

ZACATECAS MINT (Zs)

KM#	Date	Mintage	Fine	VF	XF	Unc
407.8	1870 H	.086	13.50	27.50	55.00	140.00
	1871 H	.146	13.50	27.50	55.00	140.00
	1872 H	.132	12.50	25.00	50.00	125.00
	1873 H	.056	13.50	27.50	55.00	140.00
	1874 H	—	12.50	25.00	50.00	125.00
	1875 A	—	12.50	25.00	50.00	125.00
407.8	1876/5 A	—	13.50	27.50	55.00	140.00
	1876 A	—	12.50	25.00	50.00	125.00
	1876 S	—	12.50	25.00	50.00	125.00
	1877 S	.100	12.50	25.00	50.00	125.00
	1878/7 S	.254	13.50	27.50	55.00	140.00
	1878 S	Inc. Ab.	12.50	25.00	50.00	125.00
	1879 S	—	12.50	25.00	50.00	125.00
	1880 S	—	12.50	25.00	50.00	125.00
	1881 S	.201	12.50	25.00	50.00	125.00
	1882 S	*2,000	12.50	25.00	50.00	125.00
	1883 Zs/Za S	.031	12.50	25.00	50.00	125.00
	1884/3 S	—	13.50	27.50	55.00	140.00
	1884 S	—	12.50	25.00	50.00	125.00
	1885/4 S	2,000	15.00	30.00	60.00	150.00
	1885 S	Inc. Ab.	13.50	27.50	55.00	140.00
	1886 Z	2,000	—	—	Rare	—
	1887 Z	.063	16.50	32.50	65.00	165.00

PESO

27.0730 gm., .903 SILVER, .7860 oz ASW

CHIHUAHUA MINT (CH)

Rev: Balance scale

KM#	Date	Mintage	Fine	VF	XF	Unc
408	1872 P/M	.747	—	—	Rare	—
	1872 M	Inc. Ab.	BV	32.50	55.00	165.00
	1873 M	.320	BV	30.00	50.00	150.00
	1873 M/P	I.A.	BV	32.50	55.00	165.00

CULIACAN MINT (Cn)

KM#	Date	Mintage	Fine	VF	XF	Unc
408.1	1870 E	—	35.00	60.00	100.00	300.00
	1871/11 P	.478	25.00	42.50	70.00	210.00
	1871 P	Inc. Ab.	BV	32.50	55.00	165.00
	1872 P	.209	BV	30.00	50.00	150.00
	1873 P	.527	25.00	42.50	70.00	210.00

DURANGO MINT (Do)

KM#	Date	Mintage	Fine	VF	XF	Unc
408.2	1870 P	—	BV	32.50	55.00	165.00
	1871 P	.427	BV	27.50	45.00	135.00
	1872 P	.296	BV	30.00	50.00	150.00
	1872 Pt	Inc. Ab.	45.00	90.00	150.00	450.00
	1873 P	.203	BV	35.00	60.00	180.00

GUADALAJARA MINT (Ga)

KM#	Date	Mintage	Fine	VF	XF	Unc
408.3	1870 C	—	350.00	550.00	900.00	1500.
	1871 C	.829	BV	32.50	55.00	165.00
	1872 C	.485	BV	32.50	55.00	165.00
	1873/2 C	.277	BV	35.00	60.00	180.00
	1873 C	Inc. Ab.	BV	32.50	55.00	165.00

GUANAJUATO MINT (Go)

KM#	Date	Mintage	Fine	VF	XF	Unc
408.4	1871/3 S	3.946	BV	32.50	55.00	165.00
	1871 S	I.A.	BV	27.50	45.00	135.00
	1872 S	4.067	BV	25.00	40.00	120.00
	1873/2 S	1.560	BV	27.50	45.00	135.00
	1873 S	Inc. Ab.	BV	25.00	40.00	120.00
	1873/Go/Mo/S/M	—	BV	30.00	50.00	150.00

MEXICO CITY MINT (Mo)

KM#	Date	Mintage	Fine	VF	XF	Unc
408.5	1869 C	—	25.00	42.50	70.00	210.00
	1870/69 C	5.115	BV	27.50	45.00	135.00
	1870 C	Inc. Ab.	BV	25.00	40.00	120.00
	1870 M/C	I.A.	BV	27.50	45.00	135.00
	1870 M	Inc. Ab.	BV	25.00	40.00	120.00
	1871/0 M	6.974	BV	27.50	45.00	135.00
	1871 M	Inc. Ab.	BV	25.00	40.00	120.00
	1872/1 M	4.801	BV	27.50	45.00	135.00
	1872 M	Inc. Ab.	BV	25.00	40.00	120.00
	1873 M	1.765	BV	25.00	40.00	120.00

OAXACA MINT (Oa)

KM#	Date	Mintage	Fine	VF	XF	Unc
408.6	1869 E	—	225.00	350.00	650.00	1000.
	1870 OAE small A	.177	BV	30.00	50.00	150.00
	1870 OA E large A	Inc. Ab.	200.00	325.00	550.00	900.00
	1871/69 E	.140	BV	32.50	55.00	165.00
	1871 OaE small A	Inc. Ab.	BV	25.00	40.00	120.00
	1871 OA E large A	Inc. Ab.	BV	30.00	50.00	150.00
	1872 OaE small A	.180	BV	25.00	40.00	120.00
	1872 OA E large A	Inc. Ab.	165.00	275.00	450.00	750.00
	1873 E	.105	BV	30.00	50.00	150.00

POTOSI MINT (Pi)

KM#	Date	Mintage	Fine	VF	XF	Unc
408.7	1870 S	1.967	130.00	200.00	330.00	550.00
	1870 S/A	I.A.	120.00	200.00	330.00	550.00
	1870 G	Inc. Ab.	BV	27.50	45.00	135.00
	1870 H	Inc. Ab.	—	—	Rare	—
	1870 O/G	I.A.	25.00	42.50	70.00	210.00
	1870 O	Inc. Ab.	BV	35.00	60.00	180.00
	1871/69 O	2.103	BV	30.00	50.00	150.00
	1871 O/G	I.A.	BV	30.00	50.00	150.00
	1872 O	1.873	—	27.50	45.00	135.00
	1873 O	.893	—	27.50	45.00	135.00
	1873 H	Inc. Ab.	BV	25.00	50.00	150.00

ZACATECAS MINT (Zs)

KM#	Date	Mintage	Fine	VF	XF	Unc
408.8	1870 H	4.519	25.00	42.50	70.00	210.00
	1871 H	4.459	BV	27.50	45.00	135.00
	1872 H	4.039	BV	25.00	40.00	120.00
	1873 H	1.782	BV	BV	30.00	90.00

CULIACAN MINT (Cn)

Liberty cap

KM#	Date	Mintage	Fine	VF	XF	Unc
409	1898 AM	1.720	BV	25.00	40.00	65.00
	1898 Cn/MoAM	Inc. Ab.	BV	27.50	45.00	75.00
	1899 AM	1.722	35.00	60.00	100.00	175.00
	1899 JQ	Inc. Ab.	BV	25.00	42.50	70.00
	1900 JQ	1.804	BV	BV	30.00	50.00
	1901 JQ	1.473	BV	BV	35.00	60.00
	1902 JQ	1.194	BV	BV	30.00	50.00
	1903 JQ	1.514	BV	BV	35.00	60.00
	1903 FV	Inc. Ab.	BV	27.50	45.00	75.00
	1904 MH	1.554	BV	BV	35.00	60.00
	1904 RP	Inc. Ab.	32.50	55.00	90.00	150.00
	1905 RP	.598	29.00	47.50	80.00	135.00

GUANAJUATO MINT (Go)

KM#	Date	Mintage	Fine	VF	XF	Unc
409.1	1898 RS	4.256	BV	25.00	40.00	65.00
	1898 Go/MoRS					
		Inc. Ab.	BV	27.50	45.00	75.00
	1899 RS	3.207	BV	BV	25.00	40.00
	1900 RS	1.489	BV	BV	32.50	55.00

MEXICO CITY MINT (Mo)

KM#	Date	Mintage	Fine	VF	XF	Unc
409.2	1898 AM original strike - rev. w/139 beads					
		10.156	BV	BV	25.00	40.00
	1898 AM restrike (1949) - rev. w/134 beads					
		10.250	BV	BV	25.00	40.00
	1899 AM	7.930	BV	BV	25.00	40.00
	1900 AM	8.226	BV	BV	25.00	40.00
	1901 AM	14.505	BV	BV	25.00	40.00
	1902/1 AM					
		16.224	25.00	50.00	100.00	175.00
	1902 AM	Inc. Ab.	BV	BV	25.00	40.00
	1903 AM	22.396	BV	BV	25.00	40.00
	1903 MA (error)					
		Inc. Ab.	500.00	600.00	800.00	1200.
	1904 AM	14.935	BV	BV	25.00	40.00
	1905 AM	3.557	BV	32.50	55.00	90.00
	1908 AM	7.575	BV	BV	25.00	40.00
	1908 GV	Inc. Ab.	BV	BV	25.00	40.00
	1909 GV	2.924	BV	BV	25.00	40.00

ZACATECAS MINT (Zs)

KM#	Date	Mintage	Fine	VF	XF	Unc
409.3	1898 FZ	5.714	BV	BV	25.00	40.00
	1899 FZ	5.618	BV	BV	25.00	40.00
	1900 FZ	5.357	BV	BV	27.50	45.00
	1901 AZ	5.706	400.00	500.00	600.00	850.00
	1901 FZ	Inc. Ab.	BV	BV	25.00	40.00
	1902 FZ	7.134	BV	BV	27.50	45.00
	1903/2 FZ	3.080	BV	27.50	45.00	75.00
	1903 FZ	Inc. Ab.	BV	BV	27.50	45.00
	1904 FZ	2.423	BV	BV	27.50	45.00
	1904 FM	Inc. Ab.	BV	27.50	45.00	75.00
	1905 FM	.995	27.50	45.00	75.00	125.00

1.6920 gm., .875 GOLD, .0476 oz ASW

ALAMOS MINT (As)

Obv: Standing eagle

KM#	Date	Mintage	Fine	VF	XF	Unc
410	1888 L	—	—	—	Rare	—
	1888 AsL/MoM		—	—	Rare	—

CHIHUAHUA MINT (Ca)

KM#	Date	Mintage	Fine	VF	XF	Unc
410.1	1888 Ca/MoM					
		104 pcs.	—	—	Rare	—

CULIACAN MINT (Cn)

KM#	Date	Mintage	Fine	VF	XF	Unc
410.2	1873 P	1,221	85.00	125.00	175.00	300.00
	1875 P	—	100.00	150.00	225.00	375.00
	1878 G	248 pcs.	175.00	250.00	350.00	600.00
	1879 D	—	140.00	200.00	275.00	450.00
	1881/0 D					
		338 pcs.	140.00	200.00	275.00	450.00
410.2	1882 D	340 pcs.	140.00	200.00	275.00	450.00
	1883 D	—	140.00	200.00	275.00	450.00
	1884 M	—	140.00	200.00	275.00	450.00
	1886/4 M					
		277 pcs.	140.00	200.00	300.00	500.00
	1888 M	2,586	70.00	100.00	150.00	250.00
	1889 M	—	—	—	Rare	—
	1891/89 M					
		969 pcs.	85.00	125.00	175.00	300.00
	1892 M	780 pcs.	85.00	125.00	175.00	300.00
	1893 M	498 pcs.	100.00	150.00	225.00	375.00
	1894 M	493 pcs.	100.00	150.00	225.00	375.00
	1895 M	1,143	85.00	125.00	175.00	300.00
	1896/5 M	1,028	85.00	125.00	175.00	300.00
	1897 M	785 pcs.	100.00	150.00	225.00	375.00
	1898 M	3,521	70.00	100.00	150.00	250.00
	1898 Cn/MoM					
		Inc. Ab.	100.00	150.00	225.00	375.00
	1899 Q	2,000	70.00	100.00	150.00	250.00
	1901/0 Q	2,350	75.00	125.00	165.00	275.00
	1902 Q	2,480	70.00	100.00	150.00	250.00
	1902 Cn/MoQ/C					
		—	85.00	125.00	175.00	300.00
	1904 H	3,614	70.00	100.00	150.00	250.00
	1904 Cn/Mo/ H					
		Inc. Ab.	85.00	125.00	175.00	300.00
	1905 P	1,000	85.00	125.00	175.00	300.00

GUANAJUATO MINT (Go)

KM#	Date	Mintage	Fine	VF	XF	Unc
410.3	1870 S	—	100.00	150.00	225.00	375.00
	1871 S	500 pcs.	140.00	200.00	300.00	500.00
	1888 R	210 pcs.	175.00	250.00	350.00	600.00
	1890 R	1,916	85.00	125.00	175.00	300.00
	1892 R	533 pcs.	150.00	200.00	275.00	450.00
	1894 R	180 pcs.	200.00	300.00	425.00	700.00
	1895 R	676 pcs.	150.00	200.00	275.00	450.00
	1896/5 R	4,671	85.00	125.00	175.00	300.00
	1897/6 R	4,280	85.00	125.00	175.00	300.00
	1897 R	Inc. Ab.	70.00	100.00	150.00	250.00
	1898 R regular obverse					
		5,193	70.00	100.00	150.00	250.00
	1898 R mule, 5 Centavos obv., normal rev.					
		Inc. Ab.	85.00	125.00	175.00	300.00
	1899 R	2,748	70.00	100.00	150.00	250.00
	1900/800 R					
		864 pcs.	100.00	150.00	225.00	375.00

HERMOSILLO MINT (Ho)

KM#	Date	Mintage	Fine	VF	XF	Unc
410.4	1874 R	—	Reported, not confirmed			
	1875 R	310 pcs.	—	—	Rare	—
	1876 F	—	—	—	Rare	—
	1888 G	—	—	—	Rare	—

MEXICO CITY MINT (Mo)

KM#	Date	Mintage	Fine	VF	XF	Unc
410.5	1870 C	2,540	100.00	150.00	225.00	375.00
	1871 M/C	1,000	85.00	125.00	175.00	300.00
	1872 M/C	3,000	85.00	125.00	175.00	300.00
	1873/1 M	2,900	85.00	125.00	175.00	300.00
	1874 M	—	85.00	125.00	175.00	300.00
	1875 B/M	—	85.00	125.00	175.00	300.00
	1876/5 B/M	—	85.00	125.00	175.00	300.00
	1877 M	—	85.00	125.00	175.00	300.00
	1878 M	2,000	85.00	125.00	175.00	300.00
	1879 M	—	85.00	125.00	175.00	300.00
	1880/70 M	—	85.00	125.00	175.00	300.00
	1881/71 M	1,000	85.00	125.00	175.00	300.00
	1882/72 M	—	85.00	125.00	175.00	300.00
	1883/72 M	1,000	85.00	125.00	175.00	300.00
	1884 M	—	85.00	125.00	175.00	300.00
	1885/71 M	—	85.00	125.00	175.00	300.00
	1885 M	—	85.00	125.00	175.00	300.00
	1886 M	1.700	85.00	125.00	175.00	300.00
	1887 M	2,200	70.00	100.00	150.00	250.00
	1888 M	1,000	85.00	125.00	175.00	300.00
	1889 M	500 pcs.	130.00	185.00	275.00	450.00
	1890 M	570 pcs.	130.00	185.00	275.00	450.00
	1891 M	746 pcs.	130.00	185.00	275.00	450.00
	1892/0 M	2,895	85.00	125.00	175.00	300.00
	1893 M	5,917	70.00	100.00	150.00	250.00
	1894 M	6,244	70.00	100.00	150.00	250.00
	1895 M	8,994	70.00	100.00	150.00	250.00
	1895 B	Inc. Ab.	85.00	125.00	175.00	300.00
	1896 B	7,166	70.00	100.00	150.00	250.00
	1896 M	Inc. Ab.	70.00	100.00	150.00	250.00
	1897 M	5,131	85.00	125.00	175.00	300.00
410.5	1899 M	9,515	70.00	100.00	150.00	250.00
	1900/800 M					
		9,301	85.00	125.00	175.00	300.00
	1900/890 M	I.A.	85.00	125.00	175.00	300.00
	1900 M	Inc. Ab.	70.00	100.00	150.00	250.00
	1901 M	8,293	70.00	100.00	150.00	250.00
	1902 M large date					
		.011	70.00	100.00	150.00	250.00
	1902 M small date					
		Inc. Ab.	70.00	100.00	150.00	250.00
	1903 M	.010	70.00	100.00	150.00	250.00
	1904 M	9,845	70.00	100.00	150.00	250.00
	1905 M	3,429	70.00	100.00	150.00	250.00

ZACATECAS MINT (Zs)

KM#	Date	Mintage	Fine	VF	XF	Unc
410.6	1872 H	2,024	85.00	125.00	175.00	300.00
	1875/3 A	—	85.00	125.00	175.00	300.00
	1878 S	—	85.00	125.00	175.00	300.00
	1888 Z	280 pcs.	200.00	300.00	425.00	700.00
	1889 Z	492 pcs.	130.00	185.00	275.00	450.00
	1890 Z	738 pcs.	140.00	200.00	300.00	500.00

2-1/2 PESOS

4.2300 gm., .875 GOLD, .1190 oz ASW

ALAMOS MINT (As)

Obv: Standing eagle

KM#	Date	Mintage	Fine	VF	XF	Unc
411	1888 As/MoL	—	—	—	Rare	—

CULIACAN MINT (Cn)

KM#	Date	Mintage	Fine	VF	XF	Unc
411.1	1893 M	141 pcs.	700.00	1000.	1400.	2000.

DURANGO MINT (Do)

KM#	Date	Mintage	Fine	VF	XF	Unc
411.2	1888 C	—	—	—	Rare	—

GUANAJUATO MINT (Go)

KM#	Date	Mintage	Fine	VF	XF	Unc
411.3	1871 S	600 pcs.	250.00	350.00	500.00	700.00
	1888 Go/MoR					
		110 pcs.	350.00	500.00	750.00	1100.

HERMOSILLO MINT (Ho)

KM#	Date	Mintage	Fine	VF	XF	Unc
411.4	1874 R	—	—	—	Rare	—
	1888 G	—	—	—	Rare	—

MEXICO CITY MINT (Mo)

KM#	Date	Mintage	Fine	VF	XF	Unc
411.5	1870 C	820 pcs.	200.00	300.00	425.00	700.00
	1872 M/C					
		800 pcs.	200.00	300.00	425.00	700.00
	1873/2 M	—	175.00	250.00	350.00	600.00
	1874 M	—	200.00	300.00	425.00	700.00
	1874 B/M	—	175.00	250.00	350.00	600.00
	1875 B	—	175.00	250.00	350.00	600.00
	1876 B	—	175.00	250.00	350.00	600.00
	1877 M	—	175.00	250.00	350.00	600.00
	1878 M	400 pcs.	175.00	250.00	350.00	600.00
	1879 M	—	200.00	300.00	425.00	700.00
	1880/79 M	—	200.00	300.00	425.00	700.00
	1881 M	400 pcs.	200.00	300.00	425.00	700.00
	1882 M	—	200.00	300.00	425.00	700.00
	1883/73 M					
		400 pcs.	175.00	250.00	350.00	600.00
	1884 M	—	200.00	300.00	425.00	700.00
	1885 M	—	200.00	300.00	425.00	700.00
	1886 M	400 pcs.	200.00	300.00	425.00	700.00
	1887 M	400 pcs.	200.00	300.00	425.00	700.00
	1888 M	540 pcs.	200.00	300.00	425.00	700.00
	1889 M	240 pcs.	250.00	350.00	500.00	800.00
	1890 M	420 pcs.	200.00	300.00	425.00	700.00
	1891 M	188 pcs.	325.00	450.00	650.00	1100.
	1892 M	240 pcs.	325.00	450.00	650.00	1100.

ZACATECAS MINT (Zs)

KM#	Date	Mintage	Fine	VF	XF	Unc
411.6	1872 H	1,300	175.00	250.00	350.00	600.00
	1873 H	—	175.00	250.00	350.00	600.00
	1875/3 A	—	200.00	300.00	425.00	700.00
	1877 S	—	250.00	350.00	500.00	800.00
	1878 S	300 pcs.	200.00	300.00	425.00	700.00
	1888 Zs/MoS					
		80 pcs.	500.00	700.00	1000.	1500.
	1889 Zs/MoZ					
		184 pcs.	350.00	500.00	750.00	1100.
	1890 Z	326 pcs.	250.00	350.00	500.00	700.00

5 PESOS

8.4600 gm., .875 GOLD, .2380 oz ASW

ALAMOS MINT (As)

Rev: Balance scale

KM#	Date	Mintage	Fine	VF	XF	Unc
412	1878 L	383 pcs.	450.00	625.00	900.00	1500.

CHIHUAHUA MINT (Ca)

KM#	Date	Mintage	Fine	VF	XF	Unc
412.1	1888 M	120 pcs.	—	—	Rare	—

CULIACAN MINT (Cn)

KM#	Date	Mintage	Fine	VF	XF	Unc
412.2	1873 P	—	210.00	300.00	450.00	750.00
	1875 P	—	210.00	300.00	450.00	750.00
	1876 P	—	210.00	300.00	450.00	750.00
	1877 G	—	210.00	300.00	450.00	750.00
	1882	174 pcs.	—	—	Rare	—
	1890 M	435 pcs.	200.00	300.00	450.00	750.00
	1891 M	1,390	210.00	300.00	450.00	750.00
	1894 M	484 pcs.	210.00	300.00	450.00	750.00
	1895 M	142 pcs.	300.00	425.00	600.00	1000.
	1900 Q	1,536	210.00	300.00	450.00	750.00
	1903 Q	1,000	265.00	375.00	550.00	900.00

DURANGO MINT (Do)

KM#	Date	Mintage	Fine	VF	XF	Unc
412.3	1873/2 P	—	365.00	525.00	750.00	1250.
	1877 P	—	365.00	525.00	750.00	1250.
	1878 E	—	375.00	550.00	800.00	1350.
	1879/7 B	—	365.00	525.00	750.00	1250.
	1879 B	—	350.00	500.00	700.00	1150.

GUANAJUATO MINT (Go)

KM#	Date	Mintage	Fine	VF	XF	Unc
412.4	1871 S	1,600	200.00	275.00	450.00	750.00
	1887 R	140 pcs.	350.00	500.00	700.00	1150.
	1888 R	65 pcs.	—	—	Rare	—
	1893 R	16 pcs.	—	—	Rare	—

HERMOSILLO MINT (Ho)

KM#	Date	Mintage	Fine	VF	XF	Unc
412.5	1874 R	—	1000.	1400.	2000.	3500.
	1877 R	990 pcs.	425.00	625.00	900.00	1500.
	1877 A	Inc. Ab.	375.00	550.00	800.00	1350.
	1888G	—	—	—	Rare	—

MEXICO CITY MINT (Mo)

KM#	Date	Mintage	Fine	VF	XF	Unc
412.6	1870 C	550 pcs.	210.00	300.00	450.00	750.00
	1871/69 M	,600	210.00	300.00	450.00	750.00
	1871/9 M	I.A.	210.00	300.00	450.00	750.00
	1872 M	1,600	175.00	250.00	350.00	600.00
	1873/2 M	—	175.00	250.00	350.00	600.00
	1874 M	—	175.00	250.00	350.00	600.00
	1875 B	—	210.00	300.00	450.00	750.00
	1876/5 B/M	—	175.00	250.00	350.00	600.00
	1877 M	—	265.00	375.00	550.00	900.00
	1878/7 M	400 pcs.	210.00	300.00	450.00	750.00
	1878 M	Inc. Ab.	210.00	300.00	450.00	750.00
	1879/8 M	—	210.00	300.00	450.00	750.00
	1880 M	—	210.00	300.00	450.00	750.00
	1881 M	—	175.00	250.00	350.00	600.00
	1882 M	200 pcs.	265.00	375.00	550.00	900.00
	1883 M	200 pcs.	265.00	375.00	550.00	900.00
	1884 M	—	175.00	250.00	350.00	600.00
	1886 M	200 pcs.	265.00	375.00	550.00	900.00
	1887 M	200 pcs.	265.00	375.00	550.00	900.00
	1888 M	250 pcs.	225.00	325.00	475.00	800.00
	1889 M	190 pcs.	265.00	375.00	550.00	900.00
	1890 M	149 pcs.	300.00	425.00	600.00	1000.
	1891 M	156 pcs.	265.00	375.00	550.00	900.00
	1892 M	214 pcs.	265.00	375.00	550.00	900.00
	1893 M	1,058	175.00	275.00	400.00	650.00
	1897 M	370 pcs.	225.00	325.00	475.00	800.00
	1898 M	376 pcs.	225.00	325.00	475.00	800.00
	1900 M	1,014	175.00	275.00	400.00	650.00
	1901 M	1,071	175.00	275.00	400.00	650.00
	1902 M	1,478	175.00	275.00	400.00	650.00
	1903 M	1,162	175.00	275.00	400.00	650.00
	1904 M	1,415	175.00	275.00	400.00	650.00
	1905 M	563 pcs.	225.00	325.00	475.00	800.00

ZACATECAS MINT (Zs)

KM#	Date	Mintage	Fine	VF	XF	Unc
412.7	1874 A	—	210.00	300.00	450.00	750.00
	1875 A	—	225.00	325.00	475.00	800.00
	1877 S/A	—	210.00	300.00	450.00	750.00
	1878/7 S/A	—	210.00	300.00	450.00	750.00
	1883 S	—	225.00	325.00	475.00	800.00
	1888 Z	70 pcs.	425.00	625.00	900.00	1500.
	1889 Z	373 pcs.	225.00	325.00	475.00	800.00
	1892 Z	1,229	210.00	300.00	450.00	750.00

10 PESOS

16.9200 gm., .875 GOLD, .4760 oz ASW

ALAMOS MINT (As)

Rev: Balance scale

KM#	Date	Mintage	Fine	VF	XF	Unc
413	1874 DL	—	—	—	Rare	—
	1875 L	642 pcs.	435.00	625.00	900.00	1500.
	1878 L	977 pcs.	385.00	550.00	800.00	1350.
	1879 L	1,078	350.00	500.00	700.00	1150.
	1880 L	2,629	375.00	525.00	750.00	1250.
	1881 L	2,574	375.00	525.00	750.00	1250.
	1882 L	3,403	375.00	525.00	750.00	1250.
	1883 L	3,597	375.00	525.00	750.00	1250.
	1884 L	—	375.00	525.00	750.00	1250.
	1885 L	4,562	350.00	500.00	700.00	1150.
	1886 L	4,643	350.00	500.00	700.00	1150.
	1887 L	3,667	385.00	550.00	800.00	1350.
	1888 L	4,521	385.00	550.00	800.00	1350.
	1889 L	5,615	385.00	550.00	800.00	1350.
	1890 L	4,920	350.00	500.00	700.00	1150.
	1891 L	568 pcs.	385.00	550.00	800.00	1350.
	1893 L	817 pcs.	385.00	550.00	800.00	1350.
	1894 L	1,658	350.00	500.00	700.00	1150.
	1895 L	1,237	325.00	425.00	600.00	1000.

CHIHUAHUA MINT (Ca)

KM#	Date	Mintage	Fine	VF	XF	Unc
413.1	1888 M	175 pcs.	—	—	Rare	—

CULIACAN MINT (Cn)

KM#	Date	Mintage	Fine	VF	XF	Unc
413.2	1882 E	874 pcs.	385.00	550.00	800.00	1350.
	1883 M	221 pcs.	385.00	550.00	800.00	1350.
	1884 D	—	375.00	525.00	750.00	1250.
	1884 M	—	350.00	500.00	700.00	1150.
	1885 M	1,235	350.00	500.00	700.00	1150.
	1886 M	981 pcs.	375.00	525.00	750.00	1250.
	1887 M	2,289	385.00	550.00	800.00	1350.
	1888 M	767 pcs.	385.00	550.00	800.00	1350.
	1889 M	859 pcs.	385.00	550.00	800.00	1350.
	1890 M	1,427	375.00	525.00	750.00	1250.
	1891 M	670 pcs.	385.00	550.00	800.00	1350.
	1892 M	379 pcs.	375.00	525.00	750.00	1250.
	1893 M	1,806	325.00	425.00	600.00	1000.
	1895 M	179 pcs.	600.00	850.00	1200.	2000.
	1903 Q	774 pcs.	375.00	525.00	750.00	1250.

DURANGO MINT (Do)

KM#	Date	Mintage	Fine	VF	XF	Unc
413.3	1872 P	1,755	385.00	550.00	800.00	1350.
	1873/2 P	1,091	385.00	550.00	800.00	1350.
	1873/2 P/M	I.A.	435.00	625.00	900.00	1500.
	1874 M	—	385.00	550.00	800.00	1350.
	1875 M	—	385.00	550.00	800.00	1350.
	1876 M	—	600.00	850.00	1200.	2000.
	1877 P	—	385.00	550.00	800.00	1350.
	1878 E	582 pcs.	385.00	550.00	800.00	1350.
	1879 B	—	385.00	550.00	800.00	1350.
	1880 P	2,030	375.00	525.00	750.00	1250.
	1881/79 P	2,617	375.00	525.00	750.00	1250.
	1882 P	1,528	—	—	Rare	—
	1882 C	Inc. Ab.	375.00	525.00	750.00	1250.
	1883 C	793 pcs.	600.00	850.00	1200.	2000.
	1884 C	108 pcs.	600.00	850.00	1200.	2000.

GUADALAJARA MINT (Ga)

KM#	Date	Mintage	Fine	VF	XF	Unc
413.4	1870 C	490 pcs.	385.00	550.00	800.00	1350.
	1871 C	1,910	385.00	550.00	800.00	1350.
	1872 C	780 pcs.	385.00	550.00	800.00	1350.
	1873 C	422 pcs.	385.00	550.00	800.00	1350.
	1874/3 C	477 pcs.	500.00	700.00	1000.	1650.
	1875 C	710 pcs.	385.00	550.00	800.00	1350.
	1878 A	183 pcs.	600.00	850.00	1200.	2000.
	1879 A	200 pcs.	600.00	850.00	1200.	2000.
	1880 S	404 pcs.	500.00	700.00	1000.	1650.
	1881 S	239 pcs.	600.00	850.00	1200.	2000.
	1891 S	196 pcs.	600.00	850.00	1200.	2000.

GUANAJUATO MINT (Go)

KM#	Date	Mintage	Fine	VF	XF	Unc
413.5	1872 S	1,400	435.00	625.00	900.00	1500.
	1887 R	80 pcs.	700.00	1000.	1500.	2500.
	1888 R	68 pcs.	875.00	1250.00	1800.	3000.

HERMOSILLO MINT (Ho)

KM#	Date	Mintage	Fine	VF	XF	Unc
413.6	1874 R	—	—	—	Rare	—
	1876 F	357 pcs.	—	—	Rare	—
413.6	1878 A	814 pcs.	1000.	1400.	2000.	3500.
	1880 A	—	385.00	550.00	800.00	1350.
	1881 A	—	—	—	Rare	—

MEXICO CITY MINT (Mo)

KM#	Date	Mintage	Fine	VF	XF	Unc
413.7	1870 C	480 pcs.	435.00	625.00	900.00	1500.
	1872/1 M	2,100	385.00	550.00	800.00	1350.
	1873 M	—	385.00	550.00	800.00	1350.
	1874/3 M	—	385.00	550.00	800.00	1350.
	1875 B/M	—	385.00	550.00	800.00	1350.
	1878 M	300 pcs.	385.00	550.00	800.00	1350.
	1881 M	100 pcs.	600.00	850.00	1200.	2000.
	1882 M	—	385.00	550.00	800.00	1350.
	1883 M	100 pcs.	600.00	850.00	1200.	2000.
	1884 M	—	600.00	850.00	1200.	2000.
	1885 M	—	375.00	525.00	750.00	1250.
	1886 M	100 pcs.	600.00	850.00	1200.	2000.
	1887 M	100 pcs.	625.00	900.00	1300.	2200.
	1888 M	144 pcs.	435.00	625.00	900.00	1500.
	1889 M	88 pcs.	600.00	850.00	1200.	2000.
	1890 M	137 pcs.	600.00	850.00	1200.	2000.
	1891 M	133 pcs.	600.00	850.00	1200.	2000.
	1892 M	45 pcs.	—	—	Rare	—
	1893 M	1,361	300.00	425.00	600.00	1000.
	1897 M	239 pcs.	385.00	550.00	800.00	1350.
	1898/7 M	244 pcs.	385.00	550.00	800.00	1350.
	1900 M	733 pcs.	375.00	525.00	750.00	1250.
	1901 M	562 pcs.	375.00	525.00	750.00	1250.
	1902 M	719 pcs.	375.00	525.00	750.00	1250.
	1903 M	713 pcs.	375.00	525.00	750.00	1250.
	1904 M	694 pcs.	375.00	525.00	750.00	1250.
	1905 M	401 pcs.	385.00	550.00	800.00	1350.

OAXACA MINT (Oa)

KM#	Date	Mintage	Fine	VF	XF	Unc
413.8	1870 E	4,614	350.00	500.00	700.00	1150.
	1871 E	2,705	350.00	500.00	700.00	1150.
	1872 E	5,897	350.00	500.00	700.00	1150.
	1873 E	3,537	350.00	500.00	700.00	1150.
	1874 E	2,205	350.00	500.00	700.00	1150.
	1875 E	312 pcs.	385.00	550.00	800.00	1350.00
	1876 E	766 pcs.	385.00	550.00	800.00	1350.00
	1877 E	463 pcs.	385.00	550.00	800.00	1350.00
	1878 E	229 pcs.	385.00	550.00	800.00	1350.00
	1879 E	210 pcs.	385.00	550.00	800.00	1350.00
	1880 E	238 pcs.	385.00	550.00	800.00	1350.00
	1881 E	961 pcs.	385.00	550.00	800.00	1350.00
	1882 E	170 pcs.	600.00	850.00	1200.	2000.
	1883 E	111 pcs.	600.00	850.00	1200.	2000.
	1884 E	325 pcs.	385.00	550.00	800.00	1350.
	1885 E	370 pcs.	385.00	550.00	800.00	1350.
	1886 E	400 pcs.	385.00	550.00	800.00	1350.
	1887 E	—	700.00	1000.	1500.	2500.

ZACATECAS MINT (Zs)

KM#	Date	Mintage	Fine	VF	XF	Unc
413.9	1871 H	2,000	375.00	525.00	750.00	1250.
	1872 H	3,092	375.00	525.00	750.00	1250.
	1873 H	936 pcs.	385.00	550.00	800.00	1350.
	1874 H	—	385.00	550.00	800.00	1350.
	1875/3 A	—	385.00	550.00	800.00	1350.
	1876/5 S	—	385.00	550.00	800.00	1350.
	1877 S/H		385.00	550.00	800.00	1350.
		506 pcs.	385.00	550.00	800.00	1350.
	1878 S	711 pcs.	385.00	550.00	800.00	1350.
	1879 S	—	375.00	525.00	750.00	1250.
	1880 S	2,089	375.00	525.00	750.00	1250.
	1881 S	736 pcs.	385.00	550.00	800.00	1350.
	1882 S	1,599	375.00	525.00	750.00	1250.
	1883/2 S	256 pcs.	385.00	550.00	800.00	1350.
	1884/3 S	—	385.00	550.00	800.00	1350.
	1885 S	1,588	385.00	550.00	800.00	1350.
	1886 S	5,364	375.00	525.00	750.00	1250.
	1887 Z	2,330	385.00	550.00	800.00	1350.
	1888 Z	4,810	385.00	550.00	800.00	1350.
	1889 Z	6,154	385.00	550.00	800.00	1350.
	1890 Z	1,321	375.00	525.00	750.00	1250.
	1891 Z	1,930	350.00	500.00	700.00	1150.
	1892 Z	1,882	300.00	425.00	600.00	1000.
	1893 Z	2,899	300.00	425.00	600.00	1000.
	1894 Z	2,501	300.00	425.00	600.00	1000.
	1895 Z	1,217	300.00	425.00	600.00	1000.

20 PESOS

33.8400 gm., .875 GOLD, .9520 oz AGW

ALAMOS MINT (As)

Rev: Balance scale

KM#	Date	Mintage	Fine	VF	XF	Unc
414	1876 L	276 pcs.	—	—	Rare	—
	1877 L	166 pcs.	—	—	Rare	—
	1888 L	—	—	—	Rare	—

CHIHUAHUA MINT (Ca, CH)

KM#	Date	Mintage	Fine	VF	XF	Unc
414.1	1872 M	995 pcs.	700.00	875.00	1100.	1800.
	1873 M	950 pcs.	700.00	875.00	1100.	1800.
	1874 M	1,116	700.00	875.00	1100.	1800.
	1875 M	750 pcs.	700.00	875.00	1100.	1800.
	1876 M	600 pcs.	750.00	950.00	1200.	2000.
	1877	55 pcs.	—	—	Rare	—
	1882 M	1,758	650.00	800.00	1000.	1650.
	1883 M	161 pcs.	950.00	1200.	1500.	2500.
	1884 M	496 pcs.	650.00	800.00	1100.	1800.
	1885 M	122 pcs.	1000.	1300.	1600.	2800.
	1887 M	550 pcs.	650.00	800.00	1000.	1650.
	1888 M	351 pcs.	700.00	875.00	1100.	1800.
	1889 M	464 pcs.	650.00	800.00	1000.	1650.
	1890 M	1,209	650.00	800.00	1000.	1650.
	1891 M	2,004	650.00	800.00	1000.	1650.
	1893 M	418 pcs.	700.00	875.00	1100.	1800.
	1895 M	133 pcs.	950.00	1200.	1500.	2500.

CULIACAN MINT (Cn)

KM#	Date	Mintage	Fine	VF	XF	Unc
414.2	1870 E	3,749	700.00	875.00	1100.	1800.
	1871 P	3,046	750.00	950.00	1200.	2000.
	1872 P	972 pcs.	750.00	950.00	1200.	2000.
	1873 P	1,317	750.00	950.00	1200.	2000.
	1874 P	—	750.00	950.00	1200.	2000.
	1875 P	—	750.00	950.00	1200.	2000.
	1876 P	—	750.00	950.00	1200.	2000.
	1876 G	—	750.00	950.00	1200.	2000.
	1877 G	167 pcs.	950.00	1200.	1500.	2500.
	1878	842 pcs.	—	—	Rare	—
	1881 D	2,039	750.00	950.00	1200.	2000.
	1882/1 D	736 pcs.	750.00	950.00	1200.	2000.
	1883 M	1,836	650.00	800.00	1000.	1650.
	1884 M	—	750.00	950.00	1200.	2000.
	1885 M	544 pcs.	700.00	875.00	1100.	1800.
	1886 M	882 pcs.	700.00	875.00	1100.	1800.
	1887 M	837 pcs.	700.00	875.00	1100.	1800.
	1888 M	473 pcs.	750.00	950.00	1200.	2000.
	1889 M	1,376	700.00	875.00	1100.	1800.
	1890 M	—	750.00	950.00	1200.	2000.
	1891 M	237 pcs.	950.00	1200.	1500.	2500.
	1892 M	526 pcs.	750.00	950.00	1200.	2000.
	1893 M	2,062	700.00	875.00	1100.	1800.
	1894 M	4,516	650.00	800.00	1000.	1650.
	1895 M	3,193	650.00	800.00	1000.	1650.
	1896 M	4,072	650.00	800.00	1000.	1650.
	1897/6 M	959 pcs.	750.00	950.00	1200.	2000.
	1897 M	Inc. Ab.	700.00	875.00	1100.	1800.
	1898 M	1,660	700.00	875.00	1100.	1800.

KM#	Date	Mintage	Fine	VF	XF	Unc
414.2	1899 M	1,243	650.00	800.00	1000.	1650.
	1899 Q	Inc. Ab.	950.00	1200.	1500.	2500.
	1900 Q	1,558	650.00	800.00	1000.	1650.
	1901 Q	1,496	700.00	875.00	1100.	1800.
	1902 Q	1,059	700.00	875.00	1100.	1800.
	1903 Q	1,121	700.00	875.00	1100.	1800.
	1904 H	4,646	700.00	875.00	1100.	1800.
	1905 P	1,738	950.00	1200.	1500.	2500.

DURANGO MINT (Do)

KM#	Date	Mintage	Fine	VF	XF	Unc
414.3	1870 P	416 pcs.	950.00	1200.	1500.	2500.
	1871/0 P	1,073	950.00	1200.	1500.	2500.
	1871 P	Inc. Ab.	750.00	950.00	1200.	2000.
	1872 PT	—	—	—	Rare	—
	1876 M	—	875.00	1100.	1350.	2250.
	1877 P	94 pcs.	950.00	1200.	1500.	2500.
	1878	258 pcs.	—	—	Rare	—

GUANAJUATO MINT (Go)

KM#	Date	Mintage	Fine	VF	XF	Unc
414.4	1870 S	3,250	700.00	875.00	1100.	1800.
	1871 S	.020	650.00	800.00	1000.	1650.
	1872 S	.018	650.00	800.00	1000.	1650.
	1873 S	7,000	650.00	800.00	1000.	1650.
	1874 S	—	700.00	875.00	1100.	1800.
	1875 S	—	700.00	875.00	1100.	1800.
	1876 S	—	650.00	800.00	1000.	1650.
	1877 M/S	.015	—	—	Rare	—
	1877 R	Inc. Ab.	650.00	800.00	1000.	1650.
	1877 S	—	—	—	Rare	—
	1878 S	.013	700.00	875.00	1100.	1800.
	1879	8,202	950.00	1200.	1500.	2500.
	1880 S	7,375	700.00	875.00	1100.	1800.
	1881 S	4,909	650.00	800.00	1000.	1650.
	1882 S	4,020	750.00	875.00	1100.	1800.
	1883 B	3,705	750.00	875.00	1100.	1800.
	1884 B	1,798	750.00	875.00	1100.	1800.
	1885 R	2,660	650.00	800.00	1000.	1650.
	1886 R	1,090	700.00	875.00	1100.	1800.
	1887 R	1,009	700.00	875.00	1100.	1800.
	1888 R	1,011	700.00	875.00	1100.	1800.
	1889 R	956 pcs.	750.00	950.00	1200.	2000.
	1890 R	879 pcs.	875.00	1100.	1350.	2250.
	1891 R	818 pcs.	875.00	1100.	1350.	2250.
	1892 R	730 pcs.	875.00	1100.	1350.	2250.
	1893 R	3,343	700.00	875.00	1100.	1800.
	1894 R	6,734	650.00	800.00	1000.	1650.
	1895/3 R	7,118	700.00	875.00	1100.	1800.
	1895 R	Inc. Ab.	650.00	800.00	1000.	1650.
	1896 R	9,219	650.00	800.00	1000.	1650.
	1897 R	6,781	650.00	800.00	1000.	1650.
	1898 R	7,710	650.00	800.00	1000.	1650.
	1899 R	8,527	650.00	800.00	1000.	1650.
	1900 R	4,512	650.00	800.00	1000.	1650.

HERMOSILLO MINT (Ho)

KM#	Date	Mintage	Fine	VF	XF	Unc
414.5	1874 R	—	—	—	Rare	—
	1875 R	—	—	—	Rare	—
	1876 F	—	—	—	Rare	—
	1888 G	—	—	—	Rare	—

MEXICO CITY MINT (Mo)

KM#	Date	Mintage	Fine	VF	XF	Unc
414.6	1870 C	.014	650.00	800.00	1000.	1650.
	1871 M	.021	650.00	800.00	1000.	1650.
	1872/1 M	.011	700.00	875.00	1100.	1800.
	1872 M	Inc. Ab.	700.00	875.00	1100.	1800.
	1873 M	5,600	700.00	875.00	1100.	1800.
	1874/2 M	—	750.00	950.00	1200.	2000.
	1874/2 B	—	950.00	1200.	1500.	2500.
	1875 B	—	700.00	875.00	1100.	1800.
	1876 B	—	650.00	800.00	1000.	1650.
	1877 M	2,000	700.00	875.00	1100.	1800.
	1878 M	7,000	700.00	875.00	1100.	1800.
	1879 M	—	700.00	875.00	1100.	1800.
	1881/0 M	.011	700.00	875.00	1100.	1800.
	1881 M	Inc. Ab.	650.00	800.00	1000.	1650.
	1882/1 M	5,800	700.00	875.00	1100.	1800.
	1882 M	Inc. Ab.	650.00	800.00	1000.	1650.
	1883 M	4,000	650.00	800.00	1000.	1650.
	1884/3 M	—	750.00	950.00	1200.	2000.
	1884 M	—	700.00	875.00	1100.	1800.
	1885 M	6,000	650.00	800.00	1000.	1650.
	1886 M	.010	650.00	800.00	1000.	1650.
	1887 M	.012	650.00	800.00	1000.	1650.
	1888 M	7,300	650.00	800.00	1000.	1650.
	1889 M	6,477	650.00	800.00	1000.	1650.
	1890 M	7,852	650.00	800.00	1000.	1650.
	1891/0 M	8,725	700.00	875.00	1100.	1800.
	1891 M	Inc. Ab.	650.00	800.00	1000.	1650.
	1892 M	.011	650.00	800.00	1000.	1650.
	1893 M	.015	650.00	800.00	1000.	1650.
	1894 M	.014	650.00	800.00	1000.	1650.
	1895 M	.013	650.00	800.00	1000.	1650.
	1896 B	.014	650.00	800.00	1000.	1650.
	1897 M	.012	650.00	800.00	1000.	1650.
	1898 M	.020	650.00	800.00	1000.	1650.
	1899 M	.023	650.00	800.00	1000.	1650.
	1900 M	.021	650.00	800.00	1000.	1650.
	1901 M	.029	650.00	800.00	1000.	1650.
	1902 M	.038	650.00	800.00	1000.	1650.
	1903/2 M	.031	700.00	875.00	1100.	1800.
	1903 M	Inc. Ab.	650.00	800.00	1000.	1650.
	1904 M	.052	650.00	800.00	1000.	1650.
	1905 M	9,757	700.00	875.00	1100.	1800.

OAXACA MINT (Oa)

KM#	Date	Mintage	Fine	VF	XF	Unc
414.7	1870 E	1,131	750.00	950.00	1200.	2000.
	1871 E	1,591	750.00	950.00	1200.	2000.
	1872 E	255 pcs.	950.00	1200.	1500.	2500.
	1888 E	170 pcs.	950.00	1200.	1500.	2500.

ZACATECAS MINT (Zs)

KM#	Date	Mintage	Fine	VF	XF	Unc
414.8	1871 H	1,000	950.00	1200.	1500.	2500.
	1875 A	—	950.00	1200.	1500.	2500.
	1878 S	441 pcs.	950.00	1200.	1500.	2500.
	1888 Z	50 pcs.	—	—	Rare	—
	1889 Z	640 pcs.	950.00	1200.	1500.	2500.

CENTAVO

BRONZE, 20mm

KM#	Date	Mintage	Fine	VF	XF	Unc
415	1905	6.040	2.50	4.50	6.00	22.50
	1906	67.505	.50	.75	1.00	15.00
	1910	8.700	1.50	2.50	4.00	45.00
	1911	16.450	.75	1.00	1.50	15.00
	1912	12.650	.75	1.00	2.50	22.50
	1913	12.850	.75	1.00	2.50	22.50
	1914	17.350	.75	1.00	2.50	8.00
	1915	2.276	7.50	15.00	45.00	125.00
	1916	.500	20.00	35.00	60.00	200.00
	1920	1.433	5.00	12.00	20.00	65.00
	1921	3.470	3.00	7.50	15.00	100.00
	1922	1.880	4.00	6.00	18.50	150.00
	1923	4.800	.50	.75	1.50	12.00
	1924/3	2.000	15.00	30.00	60.00	—
	1924	Inc. Ab.	3.00	5.00	15.00	150.00
	1925	1.550	3.00	6.00	10.00	65.00
	1926	5.000	.50	1.00	3.00	15.00
	1927	6.000	.35	.75	1.50	12.00
	1928	5.000	.50	1.00	1.50	10.00
	1929	4.500	.50	1.00	1.50	12.00
	1930	7.000	.20	.50	1.00	12.00
	1933	10.000	.15	.20	.35	9.00
	1934	7.500	.15	.25	.50	15.00
	1935	12.400	.10	.15	.20	6.00
	1936	20.100	.10	.15	.20	6.00
	1937	20.000	.10	.15	.20	2.00
	1938	10.000	.10	.15	.50	1.50
	1939	30.000	.10	.15	.20	.50
	1940	10.000	.10	.20	.30	5.00
	1941	15.800	.10	.15	.20	2.00
	1942	30.400	.10	.15	.20	1.00
	1943	4.310	.15	.25	.50	5.00
	1944	5.645	.10	.15	.25	2.00
	1945	26.375	.10	.15	.20	.40
	1946	42.135	.10	.15	.20	.25
	1947	13.445	.10	.15	.20	.35
	1948	20.040	.10	.15	.20	.75
	1949	6.235	.10	.15	.20	.75

Reduced size, 16mm, Zapata Issue

KM#	Date	Mintage	Fine	VF	XF	Unc
416	1915	.179	15.00	18.50	22.50	32.50

BRASS, 16mm.

KM#	Date	Mintage	Fine	VF	XF	Unc
417	1950	12.815	—	.10	.25	1.00
	1951	25.740	—	—	.10	.40
	1952	24.610	—	—	.10	.25
	1953	21.160	—	—	.10	.25
	1954	25.675	—	—	.10	.25
	1955	9.820	—	—	.10	.65
	1956	11.285	—	—	.10	.35
	1957	9.805	—	—	.10	.50
	1958	12.155	—	—	.10	.25
	1959	11.875	—	—	.10	.35
	1960	10.360	—	—	.10	.15
	1961	6.385	—	—	.10	.25
	1962	4.850	—	—	.10	.25
	1963	7.775	—	—	—	.10
	1964	4.280	—	—	—	.10
	1965	2.255	—	—	—	.10
	1966	1.760	—	—	.10	.20
	1967	1.290	—	—	.10	.20
	1968	1.000	—	—	.10	.50
	1969	1.000	—	—	.10	.50

Reduced size, 13mm.

KM#	Date	Mintage	Fine	VF	XF	Unc
418	1970	1.000	—	—	.10	.60
	1971	—	—	—	.10	.75
418	1972	1.000	—	—	.10	2.00
	1973	1.000	—	—	.10	3.00

2 CENTAVOS

BRONZE, 25mm.

KM#	Date	Mintage	Fine	VF	XF	Unc
419	1905	.050	50.00	100.00	125.00	450.00
	1906	9.998	5.00	9.00	17.50	75.00
	1920	1.325	6.00	15.00	25.00	90.00
	1921	4.275	2.00	4.00	9.00	75.00
	1922	—	300.00	500.00	750.00	2500.
	1924	.750	6.00	18.50	35.00	150.00
	1925	3.650	1.00	2.00	5.00	25.00
	1926	4.750	1.00	2.00	5.00	25.00
	1927	7.250	.50	1.00	2.00	17.50
	1928	3.250	.50	1.00	4.00	20.00
	1929	.250	15.00	35.00	65.00	225.00
	1935	1.250	4.00	7.00	15.00	70.00
	1939	5.000	.30	.50	1.00	15.00
	1941	3.550	.30	.50	1.00	15.00

Reduced size, 20mm, Zapata Issue

KM#	Date	Mintage	Fine	VF	XF	Unc
420	1915	.487	4.00	5.00	7.50	25.00

5 CENTAVOS

NICKEL

KM#	Date	Mintage	Fine	VF	XF	Unc
421	1905	1.420	6.00	10.00	20.00	75.00
	1906	10.615	.50	.75	2.50	40.00
	1907	4.000	.75	1.50	10.00	50.00
	1909	2.052	3.00	6.00	15.00	70.00
	1910	6.181	.50	1.00	6.00	50.00
	1911	4.487	.50	1.00	4.00	45.00
	1912 w/small mintmark	.420	35.00	50.00	135.00	250.00
	1912 w/large mintmark	Inc. Ab.	35.00	50.00	135.00	250.00
	1913	2.035	1.25	2.50	6.00	40.00
	1914	2.000	.75	2.00	3.00	35.00

BRONZE

KM#	Date	Mintage	Fine	VF	XF	Unc
422	1914	2.500	7.50	15.00	25.00	65.00
	1915	11.424	1.00	4.00	8.00	35.00
	1916	2.860	10.00	25.00	65.00	250.00
	1917	.800	37.50	85.00	150.00	350.00
	1918	1.332	20.00	50.00	100.00	250.00
	1919	.400	40.00	100.00	200.00	450.00
	1920	5.920	3.50	7.50	15.00	50.00
	1921	2.080	8.00	20.00	50.00	100.00
	1924	.780	20.00	50.00	100.00	250.00
422	1925	4.040	2.00	5.00	12.00	60.00
	1926	3.160	2.00	6.00	18.00	80.00
	1927	3.600	2.00	5.00	12.00	60.00
	1928	1.740	8.00	12.00	35.00	100.00
	1928 small date	Inc. Ab.	10.00	15.00	30.00	70.00
	1929	2.400	3.00	7.00	20.00	50.00
	1930 w/large oval 0 in date	2.600	3.50	8.50	25.00	60.00
	1930 w/small square 0 in date	Inc. Ab.	25.00	60.00	125.00	300.00
	1931	—	375.00	550.00	800.00	2000.
422	1933	8.000	.75	1.00	2.00	25.00
	1934	10.000	.75	1.00	2.00	25.00
	1935	21.980	.50	1.00	1.50	20.00

COPPER-NICKEL

KM#	Date	Mintage	Fine	VF	XF	Unc
423	1936	46.700	.25	.40	.75	4.50
	1937	49.060	.20	.25	.75	4.00
	1938	3.340	3.00	4.00	5.00	40.00
	1940	22.800	.20	.25	.75	4.00
	1942	7.100	.75	1.00	2.00	16.50

BRONZE
'Josefa' Ortiz de Dominguez

KM#	Date	Mintage	Fine	VF	XF	Unc
424	1942	.900	5.00	15.00	35.00	175.00
	1943	54.660	.15	.25	.50	2.50
	1944	53.463	.10	.15	.25	.35
	1945	44.262	.10	.15	.25	.50
	1946	49.054	.10	.15	.25	1.50
	1951	50.758	.15	.25	.50	2.50
	1952	17.674	.25	.50	1.00	7.00
	1953	31.568	.15	.20	.75	2.00
	1954	58.680	.15	.25	.75	2.00
	1955	31.114	.20	.35	.75	8.00

COPPER-NICKEL
'White Josefa'

KM#	Date	Mintage	Fine	VF	XF	Unc
425	1950	5.700	.40	.50	.75	3.50

BRASS

KM#	Date	Mintage	Fine	VF	XF	Unc
426	1954 w/dot	—	3.00	6.00	10.00	80.00
	1954 w/o dot	—	3.00	6.00	10.00	80.00
	1955	12.136	.15	.25	.50	5.00
	1956	60.216	.10	.15	.20	.75
	1957	55.288	.10	.15	.20	.50
	1958	104.624	.10	.15	.20	.35
	1959	106.000	.10	.15	.20	.80
	1960	99.144	.10	.15	.20	.25
	1961	61.136	.10	.15	.20	.25
	1962	47.232	.10	.15	.20	.25
	1963	156.680	—	—	—	.10
	1964	71.168	—	—	—	.10
	1965	155.720	—	—	—	.10
	1966	124.944	—	.10	.15	.25
	1967	118.816	—	.10	.15	.20
	1968	189.588	—	—	.10	.15
	1969	210.492	—	—	.10	.15

Reduced size, 18mm.

KM#	Date	Mintage	Fine	VF	XF	Unc
427	1970	163.368	—	—	—	.10
	1971	198.844	—	—	—	.10
	1972	225.000	—	—	—	.10
	1973 flat top 3	595.070	—	—	—	.10
	1973 round top 3	Inc. Ab.	—	—	—	.10
	1974	401.584	—	—	—	.10
	1975	—	—	—	—	.10
	1976	—	—	—	—	.10

10 CENTAVOS

2.5000 gm., .800 SILVER, .0643 oz ASW

KM#	Date	Mintage	Fine	VF	XF	Unc
428	1905	3.920	2.00	2.50	4.00	15.00
	1906	8.410	BV	2.00	3.00	9.00
	1907/6	5.950	2.00	3.00	7.00	20.00
	1907	Inc. Ab.	2.00	2.50	4.00	13.50
	1909	2.620	3.00	4.50	12.00	35.00
	1910/00	3.450	5.00	7.50	12.50	40.00
	1910	Inc. Ab.	2.00	2.50	3.50	10.00
	1911	2.550	2.25	3.00	5.00	20.00
	1912	1.350	4.00	5.50	9.00	85.00
	1913	1.990	2.50	3.50	6.00	22.50
	1914	3.110	2.00	2.50	3.50	7.50

Reduced size, 15mm.

KM#	Date	Mintage	Fine	VF	XF	Unc
429	1919	8.360	3.00	5.00	10.00	25.00

BRONZE

KM#	Date	Mintage	Fine	VF	XF	Unc
430	1919	1.232	10.00	20.00	50.00	275.00
	1920	6.612	8.50	12.50	40.00	225.00
	1921	2.255	10.00	15.00	45.00	250.00
	1935	5.970	4.50	8.50	20.00	60.00

1.6600 gm., .720 SILVER, .0384 oz ASW

KM#	Date	Mintage	Fine	VF	XF	Unc
431	1925/3	5.350	6.00	8.50	12.50	25.00
	1925	Inc. Ab.	BV	1.25	2.00	12.00
	1926	2.650	1.25	2.00	4.00	16.50
	1927	2.810	BV	1.25	2.00	10.00
	1928	5.270	BV	BV	1.25	4.00
	1930	2.000	1.25	1.50	2.50	11.50
	1933	5.000	BV	BV	1.25	2.50
	1934	8.000	BV	BV	1.25	2.50
	1935	3.500	2.00	3.00	4.50	10.00

COPPER-NICKEL

KM#	Date	Mintage	Fine	VF	XF	Unc
432	1936	33.030	.20	.35	.50	7.00
	1937	3.000	1.00	2.00	7.50	25.00
	1938	3.650	.75	1.00	3.00	40.00
	1939	6.920	.50	1.00	2.00	18.50
	1940	12.300	.20	.35	.75	4.00
	1942	14.380	.25	.40	1.00	8.00
	1945	9.557	.25	.30	.50	2.50
	1946	46.230	.15	.20	.35	1.00

BRONZE
Benito Juarez

KM#	Date	Mintage	Fine	VF	XF	Unc
433	1955	1.817	.50	.75	2.00	20.00
	1956	5.255	.15	.25	1.00	15.00
	1957	11.925	.10	.15	.25	4.00
	1959	26.140	—	—	.10	.15
	1966	5.873	—	—	.10	.15
	1967	32.318	—	—	.10	.15

COPPER-NICKEL
Variety I
Rev: 5 full rows of kernels, sharp stem.

KM#	Date	Mintage	Fine	VF	XF	Unc
434.1	1974	6.000	—	—	.10	.20
	1975	—	—	—	.10	.20
	1976	—	—	—	—	.10
	1977	—	—	—	—	.10
	1978	271.870	—	—	—	—

Variety II
Rev: 5 full, plus 2 partial rows of kernels, blunt stem.

KM#	Date	Mintage	Fine	VF	XF	Unc
434.2	1977	—	—	—	.10	.20
	1978	Inc. Ab.	—	—	—	.10

20 CENTAVOS

5.0000 gm., .800 SILVER, .1286 oz ASW

KM#	Date	Mintage	Fine	VF	XF	Unc
435	1905	2.565	BV	5.00	12.00	50.00
	1906	6.860	BV	4.00	7.00	40.00
	1907 w/straight 7	9.435	BV	4.00	8.00	40.00
	1907 w/curved 7	Inc. Ab.	BV	4.00	8.00	40.00
	1908	.350	15.00	25.00	50.00	150.00
	1910	1.135	4.00	7.00	12.00	60.00
	1911	1.150	4.00	7.00	15.00	75.00
	1912	.625	12.00	20.00	50.00	135.00
	1913	1.000	BV	4.00	10.00	60.00
	1914	1.500	BV	4.00	9.00	35.00

Reduced size, 19mm.

KM#	Date	Mintage	Fine	VF	XF	Unc
436	1919	4.155	10.00	17.50	50.00	225.00

BRONZE

KM#	Date	Mintage	Fine	VF	XF	Unc
437	1920	4.835	11.50	20.00	40.00	250.00
	1935	20.000	2.00	4.00	6.50	35.00

3.3300 gm., .720 SILVER, .0770 oz ASW

KM#	Date	Mintage	Fine	VF	XF	Unc
438	1920	3.710	2.50	4.00	10.00	75.00
	1921	6.160	2.50	4.00	9.00	70.00
	1925	1.450	4.00	7.50	15.00	80.00
	1926	1.465	2.50	3.00	8.00	60.00
	1927	1.405	2.50	3.50	6.00	50.00
	1928	3.630	BV	BV	2.50	12.00
	1930	1.000	BV	2.50	5.00	20.00
	1933	2.500	BV	BV	2.50	7.00
	1934	2.500	BV	BV	2.50	9.00
	1935	2.460	BV	BV	2.50	6.00
	1937	10.000	BV	BV	2.50	3.00
	1939	8.800	BV	BV	2.50	3.00
	1940	3.000	BV	BV	2.50	3.00
	1941	5.740	BV	BV	2.50	3.00
	1942	12.460	BV	BV	2.50	3.00
	1943	3.955	BV	BV	2.50	3.00

BRONZE
Obv: Small eagle.
Rev: Pyramid of the Sun.

KM#	Date	Mintage	Fine	VF	XF	Unc
439	1943	46.350	.25	.50	1.00	15.00
	1944	83.650	.20	.30	.40	8.00
	1945	26.800	.20	.30	.40	5.00
	1946	25.695	.25	.35	.50	5.00
	1951	11.385	1.00	3.00	6.00	75.00
	1952	6.559	.75	1.50	4.00	20.00
	1953	26.948	.15	.25	.40	4.00
	1954	40.108	.15	.25	.40	9.00
	1955	16.950	.40	2.00	4.00	55.00

Obv: Large eagle

KM#	Date	Mintage	Fine	VF	XF	Unc
440	1955	Inc. Y#38	.35	.75	2.00	9.00
	1956	22.431	.15	.20	.25	2.00
	1957	13.455	.20	.35	.75	7.00
	1959	6.016	2.00	5.00	10.00	60.00
	1960	39.756	—	.10	.15	.25
	1963	14.869	—	.10	.15	.35
	1964	28.654	—	—	.10	.25
	1965	74.161	—	—	.10	.25
	1966	43.745	—	.10	.15	.25
	1967	46.486	—	.10	.15	.25
	1968	15.477	—	.10	.15	.25
	1969	63.647	—	.10	.15	.25

KM#	Date	Mintage	Fine	VF	XF	Unc
	1970	76.287	—	.10	.15	.25
	1971	29.894	—	.10	.15	.50

Obv: Stylized eagle

KM#	Date	Mintage	Fine	VF	XF	Unc
441	1971	Inc. Ab.	—	.10	.15	.50
	1973	78.398	—	—	.10	.25
	1974	34.200	—	.10	.15	.40

COPPER-NICKEL
Madero

KM#	Date	Mintage	Fine	VF	XF	Unc
442	1974	112.000	—	—	—	.10
	1975	—	—	—	—	.10
	1976	—	—	—	—	.10
	1977	—	—	—	—	.10
	1978	527.950	—	—	—	.10
	1979	—	—	—	—	.10

VEINTICINCO (25) CENTAVOS

3.3300 gm., .300 SILVER, .0321 oz ASW

KM#	Date	Mintage	Fine	VF	XF	Unc
443	1950	77.060	BV	BV	BV	1.00
	1951	41.172	BV	BV	BV	1.00
	1952	29.264	BV	BV	BV	1.00
	1953	38.144	BV	BV	BV	1.25

COPPER-NICKEL
Francisco Madero

KM#	Date	Mintage	Fine	VF	XF	Unc
444	1964	20.686	—	—	.10	.15
	1966	.180	.15	.35	.75	1.50

50 CENTAVOS

12.5000 gm., .800 SILVER, .3215 oz ASW

KM#	Date	Mintage	Fine	VF	XF	Unc
445	1905	2.446	BV	10.00	15.00	50.00
	1906	16.966	BV	BV	10.00	20.00
	1907 w/straight 7					
		33.761	BV	BV	10.00	15.00
	1907 w/curved 7					
		Inc. Ab.	BV	BV	10.00	15.00
	1908	.488	20.00	50.00	100.00	200.00
	1912	3.736	BV	BV	10.00	15.00
	1913/07	10.510	10.00	12.00	15.00	50.00
	1913/2	Inc. Ab.	BV	BV	10.00	30.00
	1913	Inc. Ab.	BV	BV	10.00	15.00
	1914	7.710	BV	BV	10.00	15.00
	1916	.480	12.50	20.00	30.00	125.00
	1917	37.112	BV	BV	10.00	12.50
	1918	1.320	13.50	22.50	35.00	150.00

Reduced size, 27mm.

KM#	Date	Mintage	Fine	VF	XF	Unc
446	1918	2.760	10.00	12.50	27.50	135.00
	1919	29.670	BV	BV	15.00	90.00

8.3300 gm., .720 SILVER, .1928 oz ASW

KM#	Date	Mintage	Fine	VF	XF	Unc
447	1919	10.200	BV	8.00	12.50	50.00
	1920	27.166	BV	BV	7.50	50.00
	1921	21.864	BV	BV	7.50	50.00
	1925	3.280	6.00	7.50	10.00	75.00
	1937	20.000	BV	BV	6.00	7.50
	1938	.100	15.00	20.00	35.00	150.00
	1939	10.440	BV	BV	6.00	7.50
	1942	.800	BV	BV	6.00	10.00
	1943	41.512	BV	BV	6.00	7.50
	1944	55.806	BV	BV	6.00	7.50
	1945	56.766	BV	BV	6.00	7.50

.420 SILVER

KM#	Date	Mintage	Fine	VF	XF	Unc
448	1935	70.800	BV	BV	5.00	6.00

6.6600 gm., .300 SILVER, .0642 oz ASW
Cuauhtemoc

KM#	Date	Mintage	Fine	VF	XF	Unc
449	1950	13.570	BV	BV	BV	2.00
	1951	3.650	BV	BV	BV	2.50

BRONZE

KM#	Date	Mintage	Fine	VF	XF	Unc
450	1955	3.502	.50	.75	1.50	20.00
	1956	34.643	.15	.25	.50	1.50
	1957	9.675	.15	.25	.35	3.00
	1959	4.540	—	.10	.15	.50

COPPER-NICKEL

KM#	Date	Mintage	Fine	VF	XF	Unc
451	1964	43.806	—	—	.10	.15
	1965	14.326	—	—	.10	.15
	1966	1.726	.10	.20	.40	.60
	1967	55.144	—	—	.10	.20
	1968	80.438	—	—	.10	.25
	1969	87.640	—	.10	.20	.50

Obv: Stylized eagle

KM#	Date	Mintage	Fine	VF	XF	Unc
452	1970	76.236	—	.10	.15	.25
	1971	125.288	—	—	.10	.20
	1972	16.000	—	.10	.15	.35
	1975	—	—	.10	.15	.50
	1976	—	—	—	.10	.30
	1978	85.400	—	—	.10	.30
	1979 round 2nd 9 in date					
		—	—	—	.10	.30
	1979 square 9's in date					
		—	—	—	.10	.30

PESO

27.0700 gm., .903 SILVER, .7859 oz ASW
'Caballito'

KM#	Date	Mintage	Fine	VF	XF	Unc
453	1910	3.814	25.00	30.00	37.50	110.00
	1911 w/long lower left ray on rev.					
		1.227	30.00	35.00	45.00	125.00
	1911 w/short lower left ray on rev.					
		Inc. Ab.	65.00	100.00	150.00	500.00
	1912	.322	35.00	60.00	100.00	160.00
	1913/2	2.880	30.00	35.00	50.00	150.00
	1913	Inc. Ab.	25.00	30.00	40.00	90.00
	1914	.120	300.00	400.00	550.00	1000.

18.1300 gm., .800 SILVER, .4663 oz ASW

KM#	Date	Mintage	Fine	VF	XF	Unc
454	1918	3.050	BV	20.00	50.00	300.00
	1919	6.151	BV	15.00	30.00	175.00

16.6600 gm., .720 SILVER, .3856 oz ASW
Rev: Similar to KM#454.

KM#	Date	Mintage	Fine	VF	XF	Unc
455	1920/10	8.830	12.50	17.50	25.00	100.00
	1920	Inc. Ab.	BV	BV	15.00	60.00
	1921	5.480	BV	BV	15.00	60.00
	1922	33.620	BV	BV	12.00	14.00
	1923	35.280	BV	BV	12.00	15.00
	1924	33.060	BV	BV	12.00	16.00
	1925	9.160	BV	BV	12.00	25.00
	1926	28.840	BV	BV	12.00	15.00
	1927	5.060	BV	BV	12.00	25.00
	1932	50.770	BV	BV	12.00	14.00
	1933	43.920	BV	BV	12.00	14.00
	1934	22.070	BV	BV	12.00	14.00
	1935	8.050	BV	BV	12.00	15.00
	1938	30.000	BV	BV	12.00	14.00
	1940	20.000	BV	BV	12.00	14.00
	1943	47.662	BV	BV	12.00	14.00
	1944	39.522	BV	BV	12.00	14.00
	1945	37.300	BV	BV	12.00	14.00

14.0000 gm., .500 SILVER, .2250 oz ASW
Morelos

KM#	Date	Mintage	Fine	VF	XF	Unc
456	1947	61.460	BV	BV	7.00	8.50
	1948	22.915	BV	BV	7.00	8.50
	1949	*4.000	500.00	650.00	850.00	1350.

***NOTE:** Not released for circulation.

13.3300 gm., .300 SILVER, .1285 oz ASW
Morelos

KM#	Date	Mintage	Fine	VF	XF	Unc
457	1950	3.287	BV	BV	4.00	5.00

16.0000 gm., .100 SILVER, .0514 oz ASW
Juarez-Constitution

KM#	Date	Mintage	Fine	VF	XF	Unc
458	1957	.500	BV	BV	2.00	10.00

16.0000 gm., .100 SILVER, .0514 oz ASW
Morelos
Obv: Similar to KM#458.

KM#	Date	Mintage	Fine	VF	XF	Unc
459	1957	28.273	BV	BV	BV	3.00
	1958	41.899	BV	BV	BV	3.00
	1959	27.369	BV	BV	BV	3.50
	1960	26.259	BV	BV	BV	3.50
	1961	52.601	BV	BV	BV	3.50
	1962	61.094	BV	BV	BV	1.75
	1963	26.394	BV	BV	BV	2.00
	1964	15.615	BV	BV	BV	1.75
	1965	5.004	BV	BV	BV	1.75
	1966	30.998	BV	BV	BV	1.75
	1967	9.308	BV	BV	BV	1.75

COPPER-NICKEL

KM#	Date	Mintage	Fine	VF	XF	Unc
460	1969	—	—	—	—	—
	1970	102.715	—	.10	.15	.35
	1971	426.222	—	.10	.15	.35
	1972	120.000	—	.10	.15	.35
	1974	63.700	—	.10	.15	.40
	1975 tall narrow date	—	—	.10	.15	.50
	1975 short wide date	—	—	.10	.15	.50
	1976	—	—	.10	.15	.35
	1977 thick date	—	—	.10	.15	.50
	1977 thin date	—	—	.10	.15	.50
	1978 closed 8 in date	263.440	—	.10	.15	.50
	1978 open 8 in date	Inc. Ab.	—	.10	.15	.30
	1979	—	—	.10	.15	.30

2 PESOS

1.6666 gm., .900 GOLD, .0482 oz AGW

KM#	Date	Mintage	Fine	VF	XF	Unc
461	1919	1.670	BV	BV	32.00	35.00
	1920	4.282	BV	BV	32.00	35.00
	1944	.010	BV	BV	35.00	65.00
	1945	*.140	BV	BV	32.00	35.00
	1946	.168	BV	BV	50.00	125.00
	1947	.025	BV	BV	40.00	70.00
	1948	.045	—	(No specimens known)		

***NOTE:** During 1951-1972 a total of 4,590,493 pieces were restruck, most likely dated 1945.

30.0000 gm., .900 SILVER, .8681 oz ASW
Independence Commemorative

KM#	Date	Mintage	Fine	VF	XF	Unc
462	1921	1.278	BV	32.00	45.00	250.00

DOS Y MEDIO (2-1/2) PESOS

2.0833 gm., .900 GOLD, .0602 oz AGW

KM#	Date	Mintage	Fine	VF	XF	Unc
463	1918	1.704	BV	BV	40.00	45.00
	1919	.984	BV	BV	40.00	45.00
	1920/10	.607	BV	BV	40.00	45.00
	1920	Inc. Ab.	BV	BV	40.00	45.00

KM#	Date	Mintage	Fine	VF	XF	Unc
463	1944	.020	BV	40.00	60.00	80.00
	1945	*.180	BV	BV	40.00	45.00
	1946	.163	BV	40.00	60.00	75.00
	1947	.024	200.00	325.00	450.00	600.00
	1948	.063	BV	BV	40.00	75.00

***NOTE:** During 1951-1972 a total of 5,025,087 pieces were restruck, most likely dated 1945.

CINCO (5) PESOS

4.1666 gm., .900 GOLD, .1205 oz AGW

KM#	Date	Mintage	Fine	VF	XF	Unc
464	1905	.018	150.00	275.00	400.00	600.00
	1906	4.638	BV	BV	BV	85.00
	1907	1.088	BV	BV	BV	85.00
	1910	.100	BV	BV	BV	90.00
	1918/7	.609	BV	BV	BV	100.00
	1918	Inc. Ab.	BV	BV	BV	90.00
	1919	.506	BV	BV	BV	90.00
	1920	2.385	BV	BV	BV	90.00
	1955	*.048	BV	BV	BV	90.00

***NOTE:** During 1955-1972 a total of 1,767,645 pieces were restruck, most likely dated 1955.

30.0000 gm., .900 SILVER, .8681 oz ASW
Cuauhtemoc

KM#	Date	Mintage	Fine	VF	XF	Unc
465	1947	5.110	BV	BV	BV	30.00
	1948	26.740	BV	BV	BV	27.50

27.7800 gm., .720 SILVER, .6431 oz ASW
Southeast Railroad

KM#	Date	Mintage	Fine	VF	XF	Unc
466	1950	.200	20.00	25.00	35.00	50.00

Miguel Hidalgo y Costilla
Obv: Similar to KM#466.

KM#	Date	Mintage	Fine	VF	XF	Unc
467	1951	4.958	BV	BV	BV	20.00
	1952	9.595	BV	BV	BV	20.00
	1953	20.376	BV	BV	BV	20.00
	1954	.030	40.00	60.00	75.00	125.00

Hidalgo
Obv: Similar to KM#466.

KM#	Date	Mintage	Fine	VF	XF	Unc
468	1953	1.000	BV	BV	BV	20.00

18.0500 gm., .720 SILVER, .4178 oz ASW
Reduced size, 36mm.

KM#	Date	Mintage	Fine	VF	XF	Unc
469	1955	4.271	BV	BV	BV	12.50
	1956	4.596	BV	BV	BV	12.50
	1957	3.464	BV	BV	BV	12.50

Juarez-Constitution

KM#	Date	Mintage	Fine	VF	XF	Unc
470	1957	.200	BV	BV	12.00	15.00

Carranza

KM#	Date	Mintage	Fine	VF	XF	Unc
471	1959	1.000	BV	BV	BV	12.50

Small date

Large date

COPPER-NICKEL
Guerrero

KM#	Date	Mintage	Fine	VF	XF	Unc
472	1971	28.457	.30	.40	.50	1.50
	1972	75.000	.30	.40	.50	1.00
	1973	19.405	.30	.50	.75	1.75
	1974	34.500	.30	.40	.50	1.00
	1976 small date	—	.35	.75	1.25	2.50
	1976 large date	—	.30	.40	.50	1.00
	1977	—	.30	.40	.75	1.25
	1978	25.700	.30	.40	.50	1.75

KM#	Date	Mintage	Fine	VF	XF	Unc
Y#107	1980	—	—	—	—	—

DIEZ (10) PESOS

8.3333 gm., .900 GOLD, .2411 oz AGW

KM#	Date	Mintage	Fine	VF	XF	Unc
473	1905	.039	BV	BV	BV	200.00
	1906	2.949	BV	BV	BV	175.00
	1907	1.589	BV	BV	BV	175.00
	1908	.890	BV	BV	BV	175.00
	1910	.451	BV	BV	BV	175.00
	1916	.026	BV	BV	BV	200.00
	1917	1.967	BV	BV	BV	175.00
	1919	.266	BV	BV	BV	175.00
	1920	.011	300.00	500.00	750.00	1000.
	1959	*.050	BV	BV	160.00	170.00

***NOTE:** During 1961-1972 a total of 954,983 pieces were restruck, most likely dated 1959.

28.8800 gm., .900 SILVER, .8357 oz ASW
Hidalgo

KM#	Date	Mintage	Fine	VF	XF	Unc
474	1955	.585	BV	BV	BV	27.50
	1956	3.535	BV	BV	BV	25.00

Juarez-Constitution

KM#	Date	Mintage	Fine	VF	XF	Unc
475	1957	.100	BV	25.00	27.50	35.00

Hidalgo-Madero

KM#	Date	Mintage	Fine	VF	XF	Unc
476	1960	1.000	BV	BV	BV	25.00

COPPER-NICKEL
Hidalgo

KM#	Date	Mintage	Fine	VF	XF	Unc
477	1974	3.900	.75	1.00	1.25	2.00
	1975	—	1.50	2.50	4.00	6.00
	1976	—	.50	.65	1.00	1.50
	1977	—	.50	.65	1.00	1.50
	1978	124.850	.50	.65	1.00	2.00
	1979	—	.50	.65	1.00	1.50

VEINTE (20) PESOS

16.6666 gm., .900 GOLD, .4823 oz AGW

KM#	Date	Mintage	Fine	VF	XF	Unc
478	1917	.852	BV	BV	BV	325.00
	1918	2.831	BV	BV	BV	325.00
	1919	1.094	BV	BV	BV	325.00
	1920/10	.462	BV	BV	BV	335.00
	1920	Inc. Ab.	BV	BV	BV	325.00
	1921/11	.922	BV	BV	BV	335.00
	1921	Inc. Ab.	BV	BV	BV	325.00
	1959	*.013	BV	BV	BV	325.00

***NOTE:** During 1960-1971 a total of 1,158,414 pieces were restruck, most likely dated 1959.

VEINTICINCO (25) PESOS

.720 SILVER
22.5000 gm., .720 SILVER, .5209 oz ASW
Type I, rings aligned.

KM#	Date	Mintage	Fine	VF	XF	Unc
479.1	1968	30.000	BV	BV	BV	16.00

Type II, center ring low.

KM#	Date	Mintage	Fine	VF	XF	Unc
479.2	1968	Inc. Ab.	BV	BV	BV	17.50

Normal tongue **Long curved tongue**
Type III, center rings low. Snake with long curved tongue.

KM#	Date	Mintage	Fine	VF	XF	Unc
479.3	1968	Inc. Ab.	BV	BV	BV	20.00

CIEN (100) PESOS

Benito Juarez

KM#	Date	Mintage	Fine	VF	XF	Unc
480	1972	2.000	BV	BV	BV	16.00

50 PESOS

41.6666 gm., .900 GOLD, 1.2057 oz AGW

KM#	Date	Mintage	Fine	VF	XF	Unc
481	1921	.180	BV	BV	BV	800.00
	1922	.463	BV	BV	BV	800.00
	1923	.432	BV	BV	BV	800.00
	1924	.439	BV	BV	BV	800.00
	1925	.716	BV	BV	BV	800.00
	1926	.600	BV	BV	BV	800.00
	1927	.606	BV	BV	BV	800.00
	1928	.538	BV	BV	BV	800.00
	1929	.458	BV	BV	BV	800.00
	1930	.372	BV	BV	BV	800.00
	1931	.137	BV	BV	BV	800.00
	1944	.593	BV	BV	BV	800.00
	1945	1.012	BV	BV	BV	800.00
	1946	1.588	BV	BV	BV	800.00
	1947	*.309	BV	BV	BV	800.00

***NOTE:** During 1949-1972 a total of 3,975,654 pieces were restruck, most likely dated 1947.

Rev: Denomination omitted

KM#	Date	Mintage	Fine	VF	XF	Unc
482	1943	.089	BV	BV	BV	800.00

Low 7's

High 7's

27.7700 gm., .720 SILVER, .6429 oz ASW

KM#	Date	Mintage	Fine	VF	XF	Unc
483	1976	Pattern	—	—	Rare	—
	1977 Low 7's, plain 'C' in CIEN					
		—	BV	BV	BV	20.00
	1977 High 7's, C serif in CIEN					
		—	BV	BV	BV	20.00

KM#	Date	Mintage	Fine	VF	XF	Unc
484	1977 Date in line, redesigned bust.					
		—	BV	BV	BV	20.00
	1978	9.879	BV	BV	BV	20.00
	1979	*—	—	—	20.00	25.00

***NOTE:** The 1979 dated 100 Pesos were not released for circulation and were only issued in mint sets.

BULLION ISSUES

'TROY ONZA'

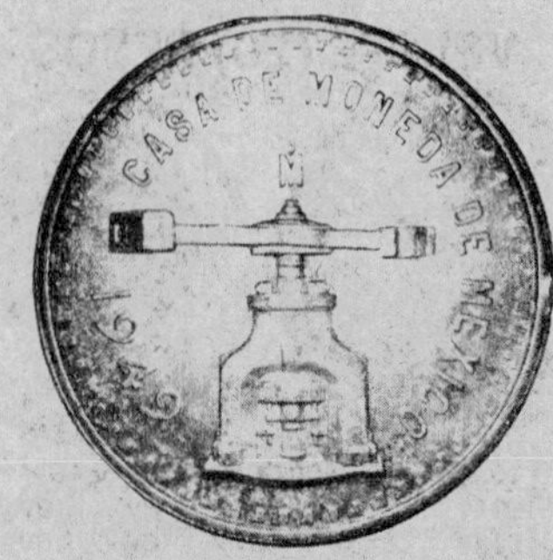

33.6250 gm., .925 SILVER, 1.0000 oz ASW
One Troy ounce of pure silver

KM#	Date	Mintage	Fine	VF	XF	Unc
M49a	1949	1.000	BV	BV	30.00	35.00

Type 1. Obv: Wide spacing between DE MONEDA

KM#	Date	Mintage	Fine	VF	XF	Unc
—	1978	—	—	—	30.00	35.00

Type 2. Obv: Close spacing between DE MONEDA

KM#	Date	Mintage	Fine	VF	XF	Unc
—	1978	—	—	—	BV	30.00
	1979	—	—	—	BV	30.00

NCLT ISSUES

MINT SETS

KM#	Date	Mintage	Identification	Issue Price	Mkt. Val.
S1	1977(16)	500	—	—	—
S2	1978(9)	500	—	—	—
S3	1979(8)	—	KM# , Type 1 (flat pack)	11.00	22.50
S4	1979(8)	—	KM# , Type 2 (for 3 ring binders)	11.00	22.50

NOTE: The 1978 and 1979 sets were issued in 2 varieties of plastic holders, one of which has holes for insertion in an official 3 ring binder which is sold for $3.30.

LOCAL ISSUES

Campeche

CENTAVO

BRASS

KM#	Date	Good	VG	Fine	VF
L1	1861	7.50	15.00	25.00	40.00

Catorce

1/4 REAL

COPPER
Obv: "FONDOS PUBLICO" around border. 1/4 below flower and raised rectangle. Rev: "DE CATORCE 1822" around border. Eagle on cactus.

KM#	Date	Good	VG	Fine	VF
L2	1822	8.50	17.50	30.00	50.00

Colima

OCTAVO - 1/8 REAL

COPPER, 24mm.
Obv: "VILLA DE COLIMA" around border as continuous legend. Rev: Blank.

KM#	Date	Good	VG	Fine	VF
L3	1813	10.00	20.00	35.00	60.00

15x16mm.
Obv: "VILLA DE COLIMA" and date in 3 lines. Rev: Blank.

KM#	Date	Good	VG	Fine	VF
L4	1814	8.50	17.50	30.00	50.00

26mm.
Obv: "QUART COLIMA 1816" in 3 lines in wreath. Rev: Colima monogram in wreath.

KM#	Date	Good	VG	Fine	VF
L5	1816	10.00	20.00	35.00	60.00

24mm.
Obv: "QUARTo DE COLIMA" around border; date in center circle. Rev: Colima monogram in wreath.

KM#	Date	Good	VG	Fine	VF
L6	1824	10.00	20.00	35.00	60.00

Obv: "OCTO DE COLIMA" around border; date in center circle. Rev: "OCTAVO" within wreath; pellet in center.

KM#	Date	Good	VG	Fine	VF
L7	1824	11.50	22.50	45.00	75.00

KM#	Date	Good	VG	Fine	VF
L8	1819	11.50	22.50	45.00	75.00

22mm.
Obv: "OCTO DE COLA" in 3 lines. Rev: "ANO DE 1824" in 3 lines.

KM#	Date	Good	VG	Fine	VF
L9	1824	11.50	22.50	45.00	75.00

23mm.
Obv: "OCTo DE COLIMA" in 3 lines. Rev: "ANO DE 1830" in 3 lines.

KM#	Date	Good	VG	Fine	VF
L10	1830	11.50	22.50	45.00	75.00

Merida

1/2 GRANO

LEAD
Obv: "PART/DE LA SO/CIED" in center. "MERIDADE YUCATAN" around border. 1859 below. Rev: 1/2/GRANO/DE PESO/FUERTE

KM#	Date	Good	VG	Fine	VF
L11	1859	7.50	15.00	30.00	50.00

Paztucaro

OCTAVO

COPPER
Obv: Town at base of mountains; lake in foreground; value "1/8" above. Rev: Woman walking right, carrying bag, fish net and fish.

KM#	Date	Good	VG	Fine	VF
L12	ND	6.50	12.50	25.00	40.00

NOTE: Also in brass and cast in bronze.

Progreso

OCTAVO

COPPER
Obv: Radiant star above open book. Rev: Value "1/8" in double wreath.

KM#	Date	Good	VG	Fine	VF
L13	1858	8.50	17.50	35.00	60.00

Tacambaro

OCTAVO

COPPER
Obv: Winged caduceus in sprays. Rev: Value "1/8" in sprays.

KM#	Date	Good	VG	Fine	VF
L14	ND	7.50	15.00	30.00	50.00

Taretan

OCTAVO

COPPER, 19mm.
Obv: Head of man right. Rev: Tree.

KM#	Date	Good	VG	Fine	VF
L15	1858	11.50	22.50	45.00	75.00

Tlazasalca

OCTAVO

COPPER
Obv: 2 mountains, date below. Rev: Value "1/8" in wreath.

KM#	Date	Good	VG	Fine	VF
L16	1853	8.50	17.50	35.00	60.00

Zamora

OCTAVO

COPPER
Obv: Eagle on cactus above sprays. Rev: Liberty, bow and arrows above sprays. W/or w/o various c/s.

KM#	Date	Good	VG	Fine	VF
L17	1852	6.50	12.50	25.00	40.00
	1853	6.50	12.50	25.00	40.00
	1856	6.50	12.50	25.00	40.00
	1857	6.50	12.50	25.00	40.00

NOTE: These pieces come with various counterstamps. Za in a dentilated circle is the most common. 1/8 in a circular c/s is also encountered.

PATTERNS

1/4 REAL

Culiacan

COPPER
Obv: Liberty head left. Rev: Value and date in branches.

Cat.#	Date	Mintage	VF	XF	Unc
P1	1861	—	75.00	100.00	175.00

Guanajuato

COPPER
Obv: Seated Liberty plain edge left. Rev: Rays surrounding wreath; Liberty cap within.

Cat.#	Date	Mintage	VF	XF	Unc
P2	1828	—	—	—	—

Thick Planchet
Obv: Eagle on cactus holding snake.

Cat.#	Date	Mintage	VF	XF	Unc
P3	1836	—	—	—	—

Thin Planchet

Cat.#	Date	Mintage	VF	XF	Unc
P3a	1836	—	—	—	—

1/2 REAL

SILVER PLATED BRONZE

DURANGO MINT

Obv: Eagle on cactus holding snake. Rev: Radiant Liberty cap.

Cat.#	Date	Mintage	VF	XF	Unc
P4	1833 RL	—	—	—	—

GILT BRONZE

Cat.#	Date	Mintage	VF	XF	Unc
P4a	1833 RL	—	100.00	135.00	225.00

SILVER

Cat.#	Date	Mintage	VF	XF	Unc
P4b	1833 RL	—	110.00	175.00	275.00

REAL

SILVER PLATED BRONZE

DURANGO MINT

Obv: Eagle on cactus holding snake. Rev: Radiant Liberty cap.

Cat.#	Date	Mintage	VF	XF	Unc
P5	1833 RL	—	—	—	—

GILT BRONZE

Cat.#	Date	Mintage	VF	XF	Unc
P5a	1833 RL	—	65.00	100.00	175.00

SILVER

ZACATECAS MINT

Obv: Eagle left holding snake w/wings arched.

Rev: Different radiant Liberty cap.

Cat.#	Date	Mintage	VF	XF	Unc
P6	1834 OM	—	—	—	—

2 REALES

SILVER PLATED BRONZE

DURANGO MINT

Obv: Eagle on cactus holding snake.
Rev: Radiant Liberty cap.

Cat.#	Date	Mintage	VF	XF	Unc
P7	1832 RL	—	100.00	200.00	325.00

8 REALES

SILVER PLATED BRONZE

DURANGO MINT

Obv: Eagle on cactus holding snake.
Rev: Radiant Liberty cap.

Cat.#	Date	Mintage	VF	XF	Unc
P8	1831 RL	—	175.00	300.00	500.00

SILVER

Cat.#	Date	Mintage	VF	XF	Unc
P9	1840 OMC	—	600.00	950.00	1500.

WHITE METAL

Cat.#	Date	Mintage	VF	XF	Unc
P9a	1840 OMC	—	600.00	950.00	1500.

STERLING SILVER

GUANAJUATO MINT

Designer: William Wyon

Cat.#	Date	Mintage	VF	XF	Unc
P10	1827 WW	—	750.00	1000.	1750.

SILVER

Cat.#	Date	Mintage	VF	XF	Unc
P11	1843 PM	—	500.00	850.00	1250.

HERMOSILLO MINT

Designer: William Wyon

Cat.#	Date	Mintage	VF	XF	Unc
P12	1882 JA	—	850.00	1350.	2250.

MEXICO CITY MINT

Rev: Different radiant Liberty cap.

Cat.#	Date	Mintage	VF	XF	Unc
P13	1823 JM	—	—	—	—

Obv: Hooked neck eagle on cactus holding snake.
Rev: Radiant Liberty cap.

Cat.#	Date	Mintage	VF	XF	Unc
P14	1823 JM	—	—	—	—

Obv: Eagle on cactus with wings spread holding snake.
Obverse of above.

Cat.#	Date	Mintage	VF	XF	Unc
P15	1824 JM	—	—	—	—

Reverse of above.

Cat.#	Date	Mintage	VF	XF	Unc
P15a	1824 JM	—	—	—	—

WHITE METAL

Obv: Hooked neck eagle on cactus holding snake.
Rev: Radiant Liberty cap.
Obverse of above.

Cat.#	Date	Mintage	VF	XF	Unc
P16	1825 JM	—	—	—	—

Reverse of above.

Cat.#	Date	Mintage	VF	XF	Unc
P16a	1825 JM	—	—	—	—

SILVER

Obv: Eagle on cactus holding snake.
Rev: Radiant Liberty cap.

Cat.#	Date	Mintage	VF	XF	Unc
P17	1843 MM	—	500.00	850.00	1250.

COPPER

Cat.#	Date	Mintage	VF	XF	Unc
P17a	1843 MM	—	350.00	450.00	600.00
	1844 MM	—	350.00	450.00	600.00

SILVER

POTOSI MINT

Obv: Eagle on cactus holding snake.
Rev: Radiant Liberty cap.

Cat.#	Date	Mintage	VF	XF	Unc
P18	1827 SA	—	850.00	1350.	1950.
P19	1829 JS	—	375.00	600.00	950.00

COPPER

Cat.#	Date	Mintage	VF	XF	Unc
P19a	1829 JS	—	250.00	375.00	500.00

ZACATECAS MINT

19mm.
Obv: Eagle holding snake, wings arched left.
Rev: Different radiant Liberty cap.

Cat.#	Date	Mintage	VF	XF	Unc
P20	1834 OM	—	—	—	—

SILVER, reeded edge
Rev: Radiant Liberty cap.

Cat.#	Date	Mintage	VF	XF	Unc
P20a	1834 OM	—	—	Rare	—

Obv: Eagle on cactus holding snake.

Cat.#	Date	Mintage	VF	XF	Unc
P21	1843 OM	—	500.00	850.00	1250.

COPPER

Cat.#	Date	Mintage	VF	XF	Unc
P21a	1843 OM	—	350.00	475.00	650.00
	1844 OM	—	350.00	475.00	650.00

1/2 ESCUDO

GILT BRONZE

DURANGO MINT

Obv: Eagle on cactus holding snake.
Rev: Hand holding Liberty cap on pole, above book.

Cat.#	Date	Mintage	VF	XF	Unc
P22	1833/2 RL	—	150.00	225.00	300.00

ESCUDO

GILT BRONZE

DURANGO MINT

Obv: Eagle on cactus holding snake.
Rev: Hand holding Liberty cap on pole, above book.

Cat.#	Date	Mintage	VF	XF	Unc
P23	1831 RL	—	125.00	200.00	250.00

2 ESCUDOS

GILT BRONZE

DURANGO MINT

Obv: Eagle on cactus holding snake.
Rev: Hand holding Liberty cap on pole, above book.

Cat.#	Date	Mintage	VF	XF	Unc
P24	1832 RL	—	125.00	200.00	300.00

4 ESCUDOS

GILT BRONZE

DURANGO MINT

Obv: Eagle on cactus holding snake.
Rev: Hand holding Liberty cap on pole, above book.

Cat.#	Date	Mintage	VF	XF	Unc
P25	1832 RL	—	150.00	275.00	400.00

8 ESCUDOS

GILT BRONZE

DURANGO MINT

Obv: Eagle on cactus holding snake.
Rev: Hand holding Liberty cap on pole, above book.

Cat.#	Date	Mintage	VF	XF	Unc
P26	1832 RL	—	375.00	500.00	750.00

GOLD
Designer: William Wyon
Obv: Ealge on cactus holding snake.
Rev: Radiant Liberty cap.

Cat.#	Date	Mintage	VF	XF	Unc
P27	1826 WW	—	—	Rare	—

CENTAVO

COPPER

MEXICO CITY MINT

Obv: Liberty seated right.
Rev: Value, date and mintmark in wreath.

Cat.#	Date	Mintage	VF	XF	Unc
P28	1841	—	125.00	225.00	300.00

Obv: Eagle on cactus holding snake.

Cat.#	Date	Mintage	VF	XF	Unc
P29	1862	—	—	—	—

SILVER

Cat.#	Date	Mintage	VF	XF	Unc
P29a	1862	—	—	—	—

SILVER PLATED COPPER

Cat.#	Date	Mintage	VF	XF	Unc
P29b	1862	—	—	—	—

COPPER
Obv: Eagle on cactus holding snake.
Rev: Value, date and mintmark in wreath.

Cat.#	Date	Mintage	VF	XF	Unc
P30	1868	—	—	—	—

WHITE METAL
Rev: Radiant Liberty cap.

Cat.#	Date	Mintage	VF	XF	Unc
P31	1889	—	—	—	—

5 CENTAVOS

SILVER

MEXICO CITY MINT

Obv: Eagle on cactus holding snake.
Rev: Radiant Liberty cap.

Cat.#	Date	Mintage	VF	XF	Unc
P32	1863	—	225.00	350.00	450.00

Rev: Value in branches.

Cat.#	Date	Mintage	VF	XF	Unc
P33	1868 C	—	125.00	200.00	275.00

WHITE METAL
Rev: Radiant Liberty cap.

Cat.#	Date	Mintage	VF	XF	Unc
P34	1889 AM	—	—	—	—

10 CENTAVOS

SILVER

MEXICO CITY MINT

Obv: Eagle on cactus holding snake.
Rev: Radiant Liberty cap.

Cat.#	Date	Mintage	VF	XF	Unc
P35	1863	—	325.00	450.00	600.00

Rev: Value in branches.

Cat.#	Date	Mintage	VF	XF	Unc
P36	1868 C	—	225.00	325.00	450.00

BRONZE
Rev: Bust of Allende right.

Cat.#	Date	Mintage	VF	XF	Unc
P37	1970	—	100.00	200.00	350.00

20 CENTAVOS

WHITE METAL

MEXICO CITY MINT

Obv: Eagle on cactus holding snake.
Rev: Radiant Liberty cap.

Cat.#	Date	Mintage	VF	XF	Unc
P38	1889 AM	—	—	Rare	—

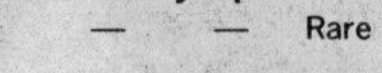

Cat.#	Date	Mintage	VF	XF	Unc
P39	1892 AM	—	—	Rare	—

50 CENTAVOS

WHITE METAL

MEXICO CITY MINT

Obv: Eagle on cactus holding snake.
Rev: Radiant Liberty cap.

Cat.#	Date	Mintage	VF	XF	Unc
P40	1889 AM	—	—	—	—

SILVER
Rev: Liberty on horseback left.
Plain edge

Cat.#	Date	Mintage	VF	XF	Unc
P41	1907	—	—	—	—

Lettered edge-incuse

Cat.#	Date	Mintage	VF	XF	Unc
P41a	1907	—	—	—	—

Lettered edge-raised

Cat.#	Date	Mintage	VF	XF	Unc
P41b	1907	—	—	—	—

BRONZE, 30.5mm, 11.65 gm.
Obv: Eagle left on cactus holding snake.
Rev: Head of Cuauhtemoc left.
Reeded edge.

Cat.#	Date	Mintage	VF	XF	Unc
P42	1955	—	150.00	300.00	500.00

PESO

SILVER

MEXICO CITY MINT

Obv: Head of Maximilian right, small letters in legend.
Rev: Crowned and supported arms, value and date below, minor differences in arms.

Cat.#	Date	Mintage	VF	XF	Unc
P43	1866	—	—	—	—

SILVER PLATED COPPER

Cat.#	Date	Mintage	VF	XF	Unc
P43a	1866	—	—	—	—

COPPER-NICKEL

Cat.#	Date	Mintage	VF	XF	Unc
P43b	1866	—	—	—	—

COPPER

Cat.#	Date	Mintage	VF	XF	Unc
P43c	1866	—	—	—	—

LEAD

Cat.#	Date	Mintage	VF	XF	Unc
P43d	1866	—	—	—	—

WHITE METAL
Obv: Eagle on cactus holding snake.
Rev: Radiant Liberty cap.

Cat.#	Date	Mintage	VF	XF	Unc
P44	1889AM	—	—	—	—

BRONZE, 39mm.
Rev: Liberty head left.

Cat.#	Date	Mintage	VF	XF	Unc
P45	1898	—	—	—	—

SILVER
Rev: Liberty on horseback left.
Plain edge.

Cat.#	Date	Mintage	VF	XF	Unc
P46	1908	—	—	—	—
	1909	—	—	—	—
	1911	—	—	—	—

Lettered edge-incuse.

Cat.#	Date	Mintage	VF	XF	Unc
P47	1908	—	—	—	—
	1909	—	—	—	—

Lettered edge-raised.

Cat.#	Date	Mintage	VF	XF	Unc
P48	1908	—	—	—	—
	1909	—	—	—	—

BRONZE PLATED LEAD
Reverse of above

Cat.#	Date	Mintage	VF	XF	Unc
P49	190-	—	—	—	—

SILVER
Obv: Eagle left on cactus holding snake.
Rev: Head of Morelos right, value behind head.

Cat.#	Date	Mintage	VF	XF	Unc
P50	1936	—	500.00	850.00	1250.

Rev: Head of Morelos right, value below.

Cat.#	Date	Mintage	VF	XF	Unc
P51	1947	—	350.00	500.00	750.00

Rev: Head of Juarez left, value below.

Cat.#	Date	Mintage	VF	XF	Unc
P52	1947	—	500.00	850.00	1250.

COPPER-NICKEL
Rev: Uniformed bust of Morelos, value behind head.

Cat.#	Date	Mintage	VF	XF	Unc
P53	1955	—	300.00	500.00	850.00

2-1/2 PESOS

WHITE METAL

MEXICO CITY MINT

Obv: Eagle on cactus holding snake.
Rev: Radiant Liberty cap.

Cat.#	Date	Mintage	VF	XF	Unc
P54	1889 AM	—	—	—	—

5 PESOS

SILVER

MEXICO CITY MINT

Obv: Eagle on cactus holding snake.
Rev: Balance scales, sword, scroll and radiant Liberty cap.

Cat.#	Date	Mintage	VF	XF	Unc
P55	1947	—	—	—	—

Cat.#	Date	Mintage	VF	XF	Unc
P56	1950	—	500.00	750.00	1000.

Rev: Head of Hidalgo left, name below; wreath does not join at top.

Cat.#	Date	Mintage	VF	XF	Unc
P57	1950	—	500.00	750.00	1000.

10 PESOS

COPPER

MEXICO CITY MINT

Obv: Eagle on cactus holding snake, date below.
Rev: Balance scales, sword, scroll and radiant Liberty cap, value below.

Cat.#	Date	Mintage	VF	XF	Unc
P58	1869 C	—	—	—	—

WHITE METAL
Obv: Eagle on cactus holding snake.
Rev: Radiant Liberty cap.

Cat.#	Date	Mintage	VF	XF	Unc
P59	1889 AM	—	—	—	—

GOLD
Rev: Head of Hidalgo right, date below.

Cat.#	Date	Mintage	VF	XF	Unc
P60	1892 AM	—	—	—	—

20 PESOS

GOLD

MEXICO CITY MINT

Obv: Eagle on cactus holding snake, in ornamental frame, date below.

Cat.#	Date	Mintage	VF	XF	Unc
P61	1868	—	—	Rare	—

COPPER

Cat.#	Date	Mintage	VF	XF	Unc
P62	1878	—	—	—	—

WHITE METAL
Obv: Eagle on cactus holding snake.
Rev: Radiant Liberty cap.

Cat.#	Date	Mintage	VF	XF	Unc
P63	1889 AM	—	—	—	—

GOLD
Rev: Head of Hidalgo right, date below.

Cat.#	Date	Mintage	VF	XF	Unc
P64	1892 AM	—	—	—	—

COPPER
Rev: Aztec calendar stone, date below.

Cat.#	Date	Mintage	VF	XF	Unc
P65	1916	—	—	—	—

ONZA BULLION PIECE

SILVER
Obv: Coining press.
Rev: Balance scales.

Cat.#	Date	Mintage	VF	XF	Unc
P66	1947	—	—	—	—

NON-CIRCULATING ISSUES

UNA(1)QUARTILLA

1/4 REAL

Chihuahua

BRASS
Obv: Liberty head right, date below.
Rev: Value and mintmark in inner circle, heavy wreath in outer circle.

Cat.#	Date	Mintage	VF	XF	Unc
NC1	1838	—	50.00	85.00	125.00

SILVER

Cat.#	Date	Mintage	VF	XF	Unc
NC1a	1838	—	95.00	125.00	175.00

COPPER
Rev: Standing Indian.

C#	Date	Mintage	Fine	VF	XF
NC2	1838	—	150.00	275.00	400.00

Durango

BRASS
Obv: Liberty head right, date below.
Rev: Value and mintmark over sprays.

Cat.#	Date	Mintage	VF	XF	Unc
NC3	1838	—	50.00	85.00	125.00

Guadalajara

BRASS
Obv: Liberty head right, date below.
Rev: Value and mintmark in quatrefoil.

Cat.#	Date	Mintage	VF	XF	Unc
NC4	1838	—	50.00	85.00	125.00

Guanajuato

BRASS
Obv: Liberty head right, date below.
Rev: Value and mintmark in branches.

Cat.#	Date	Mintage	VF	XF	Unc
NC5	1838	—	100.00	175.00	225.00

Mexico

BRASS
Obv: Liberty head right, date below.
Rev: Value and mintmark in branches.

Cat.#	Date	Mintage	VF	XF	Unc
NC6	1838	—	100.00	175.00	225.00

Rev: Value and mintmark in ornamental border.

Cat.#	Date	Mintage	VF	XF	Unc
NC7	1838	—	100.00	175.00	225.00

Rev: Column with flying eagle above in wreath.

Cat.#	Date	Mintage	VF	XF	Unc
NC8	1838	—	125.00	200.00	275.00

Potosi

BRASS
Obv: Liberty head right, date below.
Rev: Numeral "1" in shaded inner circle.

Cat.#	Date	Mintage	VF	XF	Unc
NC9	1838	—	125.00	200.00	275.00

Tuxtla

COPPER
Obv: Liberty head right, date below.
Rev: Eagle holding snake in beak.

Cat.#	Date	Mintage	VF	XF	Unc
NC10	1838	—	100.00	175.00	225.00

Zacatecas

BRASS
Obv: Liberty head right, date below.
Rev: Value and mintmark in branches.

Cat.#	Date	Mintage	VF	XF	Unc
NC11	1838	—	85.00	125.00	200.00

SILVER

Cat.#	Date	Mintage	VF	XF	Unc
NC11a	1838	—	135.00	175.00	250.00

CENTAVOS

Campeche

BRONZE

Cat.#	Date	Mintage	VF	XF	Unc
NC12	1890	—	45.00	65.00	85.00

Coahuila

BRONZE
Similar to NC12.

Cat.#	Date	Mintage	VF	XF	Unc
NC13	1890	—	45.00	65.00	85.00

Mexico

BRONZE
Similar to NC12.

Cat.#	Date	Mintage	VF	XF	Unc
NC14	1890	—	45.00	65.00	85.00

Nuevo Leon

BRONZE
Similar to NC12.

Cat.#	Date	Mintage	VF	XF	Unc
NC15	1890	—	45.00	65.00	85.00

Puebla

BRONZE
Similar to NC12.

Cat.#	Date	Mintage	VF	XF	Unc
NC16	1890	—	45.00	65.00	85.00

Queretaro

BRONZE
Similar to NC12.

Cat.#	Date	Mintage	VF	XF	Unc
NC17	1890	—	45.00	65.00	85.00

San Luis Potosi

BRONZE
Similar to NC12.

Cat.#	Date	Mintage	VF	XF	Unc
NC18	1890	—	45.00	65.00	85.00

Tlaxcala

BRONZE
Similar to NC12.

Cat.#	Date	Mintage	VF	XF	Unc
NC19	1890	—	45.00	65.00	85.00

Zacatecas

BRONZE
Similar to NC12.

Cat.#	Date	Mintage	VF	XF	Unc
NC20	1890	—	45.00	65.00	85.00

80th Anniversary of Independence
Obv: Liberty head left.
Rev: Inscription and dates.

Cat.#	Date	Mintage	VF	XF	Unc
NC21	1890	—	55.00	70.00	95.00

Republic Of North Mexico

BRONZE
Obv: Flag and inscription.
Rev: Value and date in branches.

Cat.#	Date	Mintage	VF	XF	Unc
NC22	1890	—	125.00	165.00	225.00

MEXICO/REVOLUTIONARY

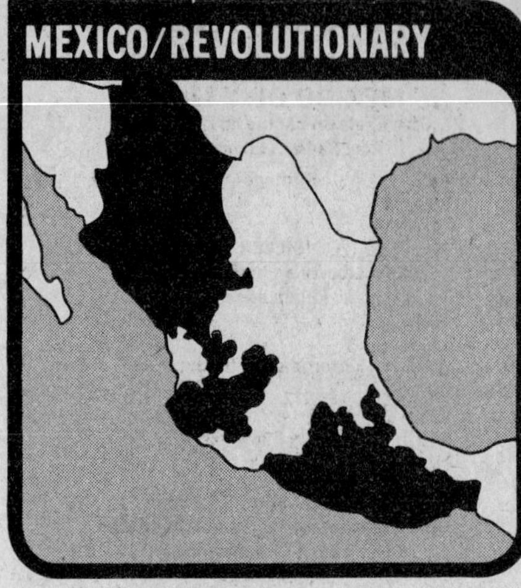

The Mexican independence movement, which is of interest and concern to collectors because of the warfare-induced activity of local and state mints, began with the Sept. 16, 1810 march on the capital led by Father Miguel Hidalgo, a well-intentioned man of imagination and courage who proved to be an inept organizer and leader. Hidalgo was captured and executed within 10 months. His revolution, led by such as Morelos, Guerrero and Iturbide, continued and culminated in Mexican independence in 1821. Turbulent years followed. From 1821 to 1877 there were two emperors, several dictators and enough presidents to provide a change of government on the average of once every nine months. Porfirio Diaz, who had the longest tenure of any dictator in Latin American history, seized power in 1877 and did not relinquish it until 1911.

The final phase of Mexico's lengthy revolutionary period began in 1910 and lasted through the adoption of a liberal constitution and the election of a new congress in 1917. The 1910-1917 revolution was agrarian in character and intended to destroy the regime of Diaz and to make Mexico economically and diplomatically independent. The republic experienced a state of upheaval that saw most of the leading figures of the revolution (Villa, Carranza, Obregon, Zapata, Calles) fighting each other at one time or another. Carranza eventually emerged as the most powerful figure of the early revolution. As de facto president in 1916, he convened a constitutional convention which produced a constitution in which the aims of the revolution were formulized. Obregon, perhaps the ablest general and wiliest politician of the lot, became Mexico's elected president in 1920, bringing the most disasterous but significant decade in Mexico's history to an end.

AGUASCALIENTES

Aguacalientes is a state in central Mexico. Its coin issues, struck by authority of Pancho Villa, represent his deepest penetration into the Mexican heartland. Lack of silver made it necessary to make all denominations in copper.

CENTAVO

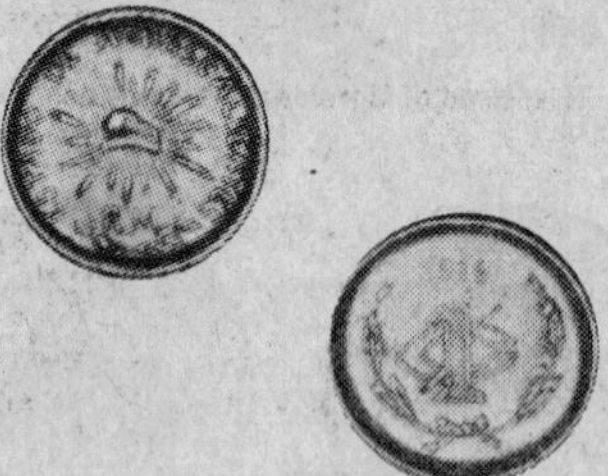

COPPER

KM#	Date	VG	Fine	VF	XF
601	1915 lg. date	15.00	30.00	50.00	70.00
	1915 sm. date	15.00	25.00	35.00	55.00

SILVER

KM#	Date	VG	Fine	VF	XF
601a	1915 lg. date	—	—	250.00	400.00
	1915 sm. date	—	—	250.00	400.00

2 CENTAVOS

COPPER

KM#	Date	VG	Fine	VF	XF
602	1915 round front	36.00	100.00	200.00	350.00
	1915 square front	36.00	60.00	85.00	200.00
	SILVER				
602a	1915	—	—	500.00	800.00

5 CENTAVOS

COPPER

KM#	Date	VG	Fine	VF	XF
603	1915	9.00	15.00	20.00	35.00

KM#	Date	VG	Fine	VF	XF
604	1915	6.00	10.00	17.00	25.00
	SILVER				
604a	1915	—	—	900.00	1200.

20 CENTAVOS

COPPER

Rev: With flat bottomed "2"

KM#	Date	VG	Fine	VF	XF
605	1915	4.50	6.00	8.50	15.00
	SILVER				
605a	1915	—	—	1200.	2000.

Rev: With wavy bottomed "2"

KM#	Date	VG	Fine	VF	XF
606	1915	4.50	6.00	8.50	15.00

NOTE: Varieties exist with both plain and milled edges and many variations in the shading of the numerals.

CHIHUAHUA

Chihuahua is a northern state of Mexico bordering the U.S. It was the arena that introduced Pancho Villa to the world. Villa, an outlaw, was given a title when asked by Madero to participate in maintaining order during Madero's presidency. After Madero's death in February 1913 Villa became a persuasive leader. Chihuahua was where he made his first coins - the Parral series. The "Army of the North" pesos also came from this state. This coin helped Villa recruit soldiers because of his ability to pay in silver while others were paying in worthless paper.

HIDALGO DEL PARRAL

"FUERZAS CONSTITUCIONALISTAS"

2 CENTAVOS

COPPER

KM#	Date	VG	Fine	VF	XF
607	1913	2.50	4.00	8.00	15.00

50 CENTAVOS

SILVER

Reeded edge

KM#	Date	VG	Fine	VF	XF
608	1913	9.00	15.00	20.00	32.50
	Plain edge				
609	1913	17.50	30.00	37.50	50.00

PESO

SILVER

Rev: "1" over ball "BOLITA"

KM#	Date	VG	Fine	VF	XF
610	1913	1200.	1500.	1850.	3500.

Rev: "1" above PESO

KM#	Date	VG	Fine	VF	XF
611	1913	50.00	100.00	150.00	200.00

CONSTITUTIONALIST ARMY

"EJERCITO CONSTITUCIONALISTA"

5 CENTAVOS

COPPER

Rev: Ornaments at each side of 1914

KM#	Date	VG	Fine	VF	XF
612	1914	20.00	30.00	50.00	75.00

KM#	Date	VG	Fine	VF	XF
613	1914	.75	1.25	1.75	2.50
	1915	.75	1.25	1.75	2.50

NOTE: Numerous varieties exist.

BRASS

KM#	Date	VG	Fine	VF	XF
613a	1914	2.50	4.00	6.50	9.00
	1915	2.50	4.00	6.50	9.00

NOTE: Numerous varieties exist.

COPPER

KM#	Date	VG	Fine	VF	XF
614	1915	150.00	250.00	325.00	415.00

10 CENTAVOS

KM#	Date	VG	Fine	VF	XF
		COPPER			
615	1915	1.25	2.00	2.50	4.00
		BRASS			
615a	1915	2.00	3.50	5.00	6.50

NOTE: Many varieties exist.

NCLT ISSUES

PATTERNS

KM#	Date	Mintage	Identification	Mkt.Val.
1	1913	—	Peso, Silver	—

KM#	Date	Mintage	Identification	Mkt.Val.
2	1914	—	Peso, Copper	1600.

NOTE: Silver or silver plated copper pieces are modern fantasies.

KM#	Date	Mintage	Identification	Mkt.Val.
3	1914	—	50 Centavos, Copper	500.00

NOTE: Specimens exist in copper & silver plated copper.

ARMY OF THE NORTH

"EJERCITO DEL NORTE"

KM#	Date	VG	Fine	VF	XF
		SILVER			
619	1915	20.00	30.00	40.00	50.00

DURANGO

A state in north central Mexico. Another area of operation for Pancho Villa. The "Muera Huerta" peso originates in this state. The coins were made in Cuencame under the orders of Generals Cemceros and Contreras.

CUENCAME

"MUERA HUERTA"

(Death to Huerta)

PESO

SILVER

1914 below UN PESO with 3 stars at each side

KM#	Date	VG	Fine	VF	XF
620	1914	1000.	1600.	2300.	3250.

Obverse and reverse continuous border

KM#	Date	VG	Fine	VF	XF
621	1914	100.00	150.00	200.00	300.00

Obverse with dot and dash border

KM#	Date	VG	Fine	VF	XF
622	1914	100.00	120.00	150.00	200.00

20 PESOS

NOTE: The so called 20 Pesos gold Muera Huerta pieces are modern fantasies. These pieces come in 22 and 14 K gold, also brass and copper.

ESTADO DE DURANGO

CENTAVO

COPPER

KM#	Date	VG	Fine	VF	XF
625	1914	2.00	3.00	5.00	7.50

BRASS

KM#	Date	VG	Fine	VF	XF
625a	1914	9.00	15.00	20.00	30.00

LEAD

KM#	Date	VG	Fine	VF	XF
625b	1914	12.50	22.50	45.00	60.00

COPPER

KM#	Date	VG	Fine	VF	XF
626	1914	12.00	20.00	40.00	60.00

BRASS

KM#	Date	VG	Fine	VF	XF
626a	1914	12.50	20.00	30.00	45.00

LEAD

KM#	Date	VG	Fine	VF	XF
626b	1914	20.00	35.00	50.00	75.00

COPPER

KM#	Date	VG	Fine	VF	XF
627	1914	6.00	10.00	13.50	17.50

LEAD

KM#	Date	VG	Fine	VF	XF
627a	1914	20.00	37.50	50.00	65.00

ALUMINUM

KM#	Date	VG	Fine	VF	XF
628	1914	.65	1.00	2.00	3.00

5 CENTAVOS

COPPER
Obv. leg: ESTADO DE DURANGO

KM#	Date	VG	Fine	VF	XF
629	1914	1.25	2.00	4.00	7.50

Obv. leg: E. DE DURANGO. Rev: Thin 5.

KM#	Date	VG	Fine	VF	XF
630	1914	20.00	30.00	40.00	60.00

Rev: Thick 5.

KM#	Date	VG	Fine	VF	XF
631	1914	1.25	2.00	4.00	7.50

BRASS

KM#	Date	VG	Fine	VF	XF
631a	1914	6.50	10.00	13.50	20.00

LEAD

KM#	Date	VG	Fine	VF	XF
631b	1914	29.50	40.00	55.00	75.00

COPPER

KM#	Date	VG	Fine	VF	XF
632	1914	3.00	5.00	9.00	15.00

LEAD

KM#	Date	VG	Fine	VF	XF
632a	1914	30.00	45.00	60.00	80.00

Obv: 3 stars below 1914. Rev: 5 CVS.

KM#	Date	VG	Fine	VF	XF
633	1914	—	400.00	800.00	—

BRASS

KM#	Date	VG	Fine	VF	XF
634	1914	.50	1.00	1.50	2.00

NOTE: There are numerous varieties of these general types of the Durango 1 and 5 Centavo pieces.

GUERRERO

Guerrero is a state on the southwestern coast of Mexico. It was one of the areas of operation of Zapata and his forces in the south of Mexico. Seven different mints were operated by the Zapata forces in this state. The date ranges were from 1914 to 1917 and denominations from 2 centavos to 2 pesos. Some were cast but most were struck and the rarest coin of the group is the Suriana 1915 2 pesos.

3 CENTAVOS

COPPER

KM#	Date	VG	Fine	VF	XF
635	1915	600.00	1000.	1600.	2000.

5 CENTAVOS

COPPER

KM#	Date	VG	Fine	VF	XF
636	1915GRO	600.00	1000.	1300.	1750.

10 CENTAVOS

COPPER

KM#	Date	VG	Fine	VF	XF
637	1915GRO	4.50	7.50	10.00	12.50

20 CENTAVOS

Previously listed #638 dated 1915GRO existing in copper and in silver has been determined to be spurious.

25 CENTAVOS

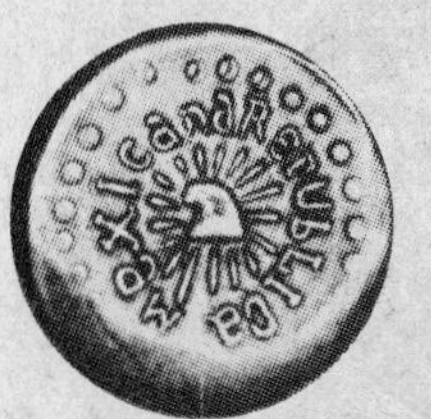

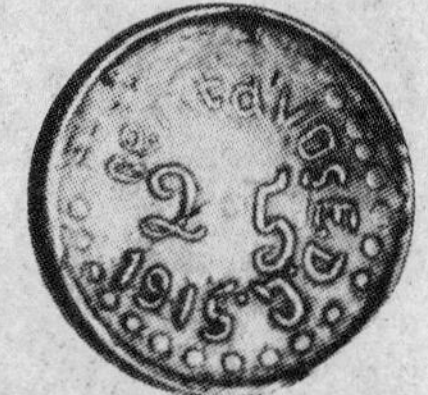

SILVER

KM#	Date	VG	Fine	VF	XF
639	1915	300.00	400.00	500.00	600.00

50 CENTAVOS

SILVER

KM#	Date	VG	Fine	VF	XF
640	1915	900.00	1500.	2100.	3000.

UN (1) PESO

.3 gm., 1.000 FINE GOLD/SILVER
Obv: Star before UN PESO

KM#	Date	VG	Fine	VF	XF
641	1914	20.00	30.00	50.00	75.00

NOTE: Many die varieties exist.

Obv: Star before and after UN PESO

KM#	Date	VG	Fine	VF	XF
642	1914	75.00	100.00	125.00	150.00
	1915	600.00	1000.	1500.	2000.

DOS (2) PESOS

.595 gm., 1.000 FINE GOLD/SILVER

KM#	Date	VG	Fine	VF	XF
643	1914	12.50	22.50	35.00	50.00

NOTE: Many varieties exist.

KM#	Date	VG	Fine	VF	XF
644	1915	100.00	125.00	160.00	200.00

COPPER

KM#	Date	VG	Fine	VF	XF
644a	1915	400.00	600.00	800.00	1000.

ATLIXTAC

10 CENTAVOS

COPPER

KM#	Date	VG	Fine	VF	XF
645	1915	3.00	4.00	6.50	9.00

Obv: Stars in legend

KM#	Date	VG	Fine	VF	XF
646	1915	3.00	4.00	6.50	9.00

CACAHUATEPEC

5 CENTAVOS

COPPER

KM#	Date	VG	Fine	VF	XF
648	1917	25.00	50.00	100.00	150.00

20 CENTAVOS

SILVER

KM#	Date	VG	Fine	VF	XF
649	1917	100.00	150.00	200.00	250.00

50 CENTAVOS

SILVER

KM#	Date	VG	Fine	VF	XF
650	1917	50.00	75.00	100.00	150.00

UN (1) PESO

SILVER

KM#	Date	VG	Fine	VF	XF
651	1917	1500.	2500.	3750.	4500.

CACALOTEPEC

20 CENTAVOS

SILVER

KM#	Date	VG	Fine	VF	XF
652	1917	1000.	1500.	2000.	2500.

CAMPO MORADO

C.M., C.M.GRO, CoMoGro, CAMPO Mo

5 CENTAVOS

COPPER

KM#	Date	VG	Fine	VF	XF
653	1915C.M.	9.00	15.00	22.50	35.00

10 CENTAVOS

COPPER

KM#	Date	VG	Fine	VF	XF
654	1915C.M.Gro	6.00	10.00	17.50	27.50

20 CENTAVOS

COPPER

KM#	Date	VG	Fine	VF	XF
655	1915C.M.Gro	15.00	25.00	35.00	50.00

50 CENTAVOS

COPPER
Obv: UN PESO effaced below eagle.

656	1915C.M.Gro	12.00	20.00	27.50	32.50

Regular obverse

657	1915C.M.Gro	6.00	10.00	13.50	20.00

BASE SILVER

657a	1915C.M. Gro	165.00	275.00	400.00	575.00

UN (1) PESO

.300 gm., 1.000 FINE GOLD/SILVER
Obv: Date below eagle.

658	1914Co Mo Gro	500.00	700.00	900.00	1100.

Rev: Date below Liberty cap.

659	1914 CAMPO Mo	15.00	20.00	35.00	50.00

DOS (2) PESOS

.595 gm., 1.000 FINE GOLD/SILVER

KM#	Date	VG	Fine	VF	XF
660	1915 Co. Mo.	20.00	35.00	50.00	65.00

Rev: Star before and after Co. Mo.

661	1915 Co.Mo.	1200.	2000.	3000.	4500.

662	1915 C.M.Gro	20.00	30.00	50.00	75.00

CHILPANCINGO

10 CENTAVOS

SILVER (cast)

KM#	Date	VG	Fine	VF	XF
663	1914	—	—	1500.	—

20 CENTAVOS

SILVER (cast)

664	1914	—	—	1500.	—

SURIANA

DOS (2) PESOS

.595 gm., 1.000 FINE GOLD/SILVER

665	1915	—	—23,000.*	—

*Munoz Part 1 Sale by Superior Galleries June, 1978 (The Bothamely Specimen).

TAXCO

2 CENTAVOS

COPPER

666	1915	90.00	150.00	200.00	450.00

Obv: EDO.DE.GRO above eagle.

KM#	Date	VG	Fine	VF	XF
667	1915 O/T	30.00	50.00	80.00	100.00

5 CENTAVOS

COPPER

KM#	Date	VG	Fine	VF	XF
668	1915	9.00	15.00	20.00	25.00

10 CENTAVOS

COPPER

KM#	Date	VG	Fine	VF	XF
669	1915	9.00	15.00	20.00	27.50

50 CENTAVOS

COPPER
Obv. leg: Large letters

KM#	Date	VG	Fine	VF	XF
670	1915	15.00	25.00	45.00	60.00

SILVER

KM#	Date	VG	Fine	VF	XF
671	1915	20.00	30.00	45.00	70.00

UN (1) PESO

.300 gm., 1.000 FINE GOLD/SILVER
Obv: Star before UN PESO and star before G.

KM#	Date	VG	Fine	VF	XF
672	1915	12.00	20.00	25.00	32.50

Obv: Star before UN PESO, no star before G.

KM#	Date	VG	Fine	VF	XF
673	1915	250.00	300.00	400.00	500.00

Obv: Without star before UN PESO.

KM#	Date	VG	Fine	VF	XF
674	1915	75.00	125.00	200.00	300.00

NCLT ISSUES

PATTERNS

KM#	Date	Mintage	Identification	Mkt.Val.
647	1914	—	2 Pesos, .300 gm., 1.000 Fine Gold/Silver, Atlixtac	—

JALISCO

Jalisco is a state on the west coast of Mexico. The few coins made for this state show that the "Army of the North" did not restrict their operations to the northern border states. The coins were made in Guadalajara under the watchful eye of General Dieguez, commander of this segment of Villa's forces.

GUADALAJARA

CENTAVO

COPPER

KM#	Date	VG	Fine	VF	XF
675	1915	9.50	15.00	20.00	25.00

2 CENTAVOS

COPPER

KM#	Date	VG	Fine	VF	XF
676	1915	9.50	15.00	17.50	22.50

5 CENTAVOS

COPPER

KM#	Date	VG	Fine	VF	XF
677	1915	6.50	12.00	15.00	20.00

10 CENTAVOS

COPPER

KM#	Date	VG	Fine	VF	XF
678	1915	—	—	2250.	—

PESO

COPPER

KM#	Date	VG	Fine	VF	XF
A678	1915	—	—	—	8000.

MEXICO

Estado de Mexico is a state of central Mexico that surrounds the Federal District on 3 sides. The issues by the Zapata forces in this state have two distinctions - the Amecameca pieces are the crudest and the Touluca cardboard piece is the most unusual. General Tenorio authorized the crude incuse Amecameca pieces.

AMECAMECA

5 CENTAVOS

BRASS, HAND STAMPED

KM#	Date	VG	Fine	VF	XF
679	ND	—	—	Unique	—

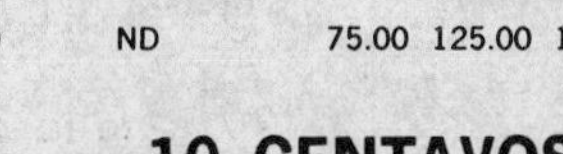

680	ND	75.00	125.00	170.00	200.00

10 CENTAVOS

BRASS, HAND STAMPED

681	ND	50.00	75.00	100.00	125.00

20 CENTAVOS

BRASS, HAND STAMPED

682	ND	22.50	37.50	50.00	75.00

COPPER, HAND STAMPED
Obv: Eagle over A.D.J.

683	ND	7.50	12.50	18.00	30.00

BRASS

683a	ND	—	—	125.00	175.00

25 CENTAVOS

BRASS, HAND STAMPED

684	ND	—	—	Unique	—

COPPER, HAND STAMPED
Obv: Eagle over sprays.

685	ND	25.00	40.00	55.00	90.00

BRASS, HAND STAMPED

685a	ND	—	—	50.00	100.00

50 CENTAVOS

COPPER, HAND STAMPED
Obverse: Eagle over sprays

KM#	Date	VG	Fine	VF	XF
686	ND	5.00	8.00	12.00	20.00

BRASS, HAND STAMPED

686a	ND	75.00	100.00	150.00	200.00

COPPER
Contemporary counterfeit, hand engraved.

687	ND	12.00	20.00	32.50	50.00

NOTE: Cat. #687 - ¢ clears top of 5 while Cat. #686a has the stem of ¢ above the 5.

TENANCINGO, TOWN

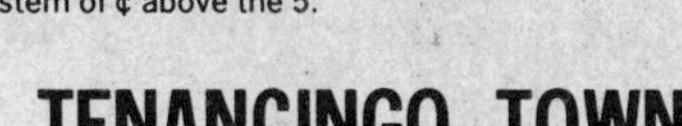

2 CENTAVOS

COPPER

688	1915	—	—	350.00	—

5 CENTAVOS

COPPER

689	1915	4.50	7.50	12.50	20.00

10 CENTAVOS

COPPER

690	1916	10.00	17.50	22.50	35.00

20 CENTAVOS

COPPER

KM#	Date	VG	Fine	VF	XF
691	1915	25.00	42.50	57.50	75.00

TOLUCA, CITY

5 CENTAVOS

GREY CARDBOARD

KM#	Date	VG	Fine	VF	XF
692	1915	15.00	25.00	35.00	50.00

20 CENTAVOS

COPPER
20 within C in circular counterstamp on regular 1 Centavo.

KM#	Date	VG	Fine	VF	XF
693	ND	20.00	30.00	40.00	50.00

40 CENTAVOS

COPPER
40 within C in circular counterstamp on regular 2 Centavos.

694	ND	25.00	42.50	55.00	70.00

MORELOS

Morelos is a state in south central Mexico, adjoining the federal district on the south. It was the headquarters of Emiliano Zapata. His personal quarters were at Tlaltezapan in Morelos. The Morelos coins from 2 centavos to 1 peso were all copper except one type of 1 peso in silver. The 2 operating Zapatista mints in Morelos Were Atlihuayan and Tlaltizapan.

2 CENTAVOS

COPPER
"E.L.DE MORELOS"

KM#	Date	VG	Fine	VF	XF
695	1915	1200.	1500.	2000.	2500.

5 CENTAVOS

COPPER
"E. DE MOR. 1915."

KM#	Date	VG	Fine	VF	XF
696	1915	200.00	350.00	500.00	700.00

10 CENTAVOS

COPPER

KM#	Date	VG	Fine	VF	XF
697	1915	12.00	20.00	27.50	35.00

Date effaced from die

KM#	Date	VG	Fine	VF	XF
698	—	12.00	20.00	32.50	50.00

KM#	Date	VG	Fine	VF	XF
699	1915	1000.	1500.	2000.	2500.

KM#	Date	VG	Fine	VF	XF
700	1916	5.00	10.00	15.00	20.00

20 CENTAVOS

COPPER

KM#	Date	VG	Fine	VF	XF
701	1915	9.00	15.00	21.50	30.00

50 CENTAVOS

COPPER

Obv: 'MOR' beneath eagle. Rev: 50C monogram.

KM#	Date	VG	Fine	VF	XF
702	1915	300.00	500.00	900.00	1300.

Obv: Sprays beneath eagle

KM#	Date	VG	Fine	VF	XF
703	1915	12.50	17.50	27.50	32.50

NOTE: The above exists with a silver and also a brass wash.

Obv: MORELOS below eagle.

KM#	Date	VG	Fine	VF	XF
704	1916	12.50	17.50	27.50	32.50

UN (1) PESO

SILVER

KM#	Date	VG	Fine	VF	XF
708	1916	450.00	750.00	1000.	1500.

COPPER

KM#	Date	VG	Fine	VF	XF
708a	1916	450.00	750.00	1000.	1500.

NCLT ISSUES

PATTERNS

KM#	Date	Mintage	Identification	Issue Price	Mkt. Val.
705	1915	—	50 Centavos, Silver	—	1500.

KM#	Date	Mintage	Identification	Issue Price	Mkt. Val.
706	1915	—	50 Centavos, Copper	—	1000.

KM#	Date	Mintage	Identification	Issue Price	Mkt. Val.
707	191-	—	1 Peso, Silver	—	4000.

KM#	Date	Mintage	Identification	Issue Price	Mkt. Val.
707a	191-	—	1 Peso, Copper	—	3000.
707b	1916	—	1 Peso, Copper	—	2750.

OAXACA

Oaxaca is one of the southern states in Mexico. The coins issued in this state represents the most prolific series of the Revolution. Most of the coins bear the portrait of Benito Juarez and were issued by a provisional government in the state. The exceptions are the rectangular 1 and 3 centavos pieces that begin the series.

UN (1) CENTAVO

COPPER

KM#	Date	VG	Fine	VF	XF
709	1915	65.00	110.00	140.00	160.00

KM#	Date	VG	Fine	VF	XF
710	1915	12.00	20.00	25.00	32.50

TRES (3) CENTAVOS

COPPER
Rev: PROVISIO on top line

KM#	Date	VG	Fine	VF	XF
711	1915	60.00	100.00	125.00	150.00

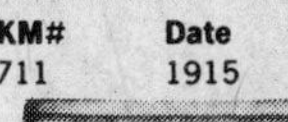

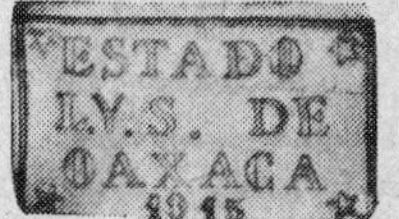

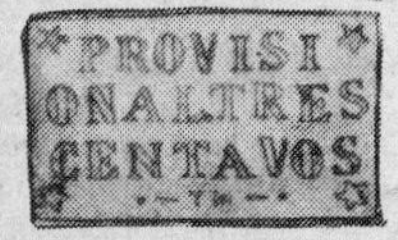

Rev: PROVISI on top line

KM#	Date	VG	Fine	VF	XF
712	1915	600.00	1000.	1500.	2000.

Rev: Large flat top 3

KM#	Date	VG	Fine	VF	XF
713	1915	3.00	5.00	10.00	12.00

Rev: Small round 3

KM#	Date	VG	Fine	VF	XF
714	1915	7.50	12.50	15.00	20.00

5 CENTAVOS

COPPER
JAN.15 1915, incuse lettering

KM#	Date	VG	Fine	VF	XF
715	1915	—	—	Rare	—

Obv: Facing bust of Juarez

KM#	Date	VG	Fine	VF	XF
716	1915	—	—	—	1800.

Obv: 2nd bust, low relief with long pointed truncation.

KM#	Date	VG	Fine	VF	XF
717	1915	2.75	4.00	6.00	8.00

Obv: 5th bust, heavy with short unfinished lapels centered high.

KM#	Date	VG	Fine	VF	XF
718	1915	3.00	5.00	7.00	9.00

Obv: 6th bust, curved bottom.

KM#	Date	VG	Fine	VF	XF
719	1915	3.00	5.00	7.00	9.00

Obv: 7th bust, short truncation with closed lapels.

KM#	Date	VG	Fine	VF	XF
720	1915	2.50	4.00	6.00	8.00

Obv: 8th bust, short curved truncation.

KM#	Date	VG	Fine	VF	XF
721	1915	3.00	5.00	7.00	9.00

10 CENTAVOS

COPPER
Obv: 2nd bust, low relief with long-pointed truncation.

KM#	Date	VG	Fine	VF	XF
722	1915	3.00	5.00	7.00	9.00

Legend retrograde

KM#	Date	VG	Fine	VF	XF
723	1915	—	—	450.00	—

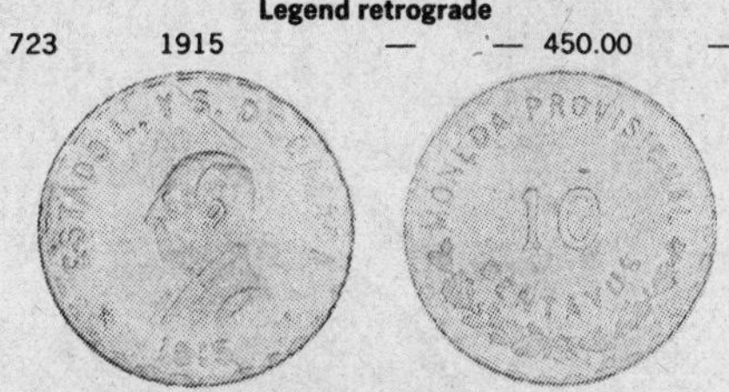

Obv: 4th bust, bold, unfinished truncation. using 1 Peso obverse die

KM#	Date	VG	Fine	VF	XF
724	1915	3.00	5.00	7.00	9.00

Obv: 5th bust, heavy with short unfinished lapels centered high.

KM#	Date	VG	Fine	VF	XF
725	1915	3.00	5.00	7.00	9.00

Obv: 6th bust, curved bottom.

KM#	Date	VG	Fine	VF	XF
726	1915	2.50	4.00	6.00	8.00

Obv: 7th bust, short truncation with closed lapels.

KM#	Date	VG	Fine	VF	XF
727	1915	2.50	4.00	6.00	8.00

20 CENTAVOS

SILVER
Obv: 2nd bust, low relief with long-pointed truncation.

KM#	Date	VG	Fine	VF	XF
728	1915	500.00	750.00	1200.	1500.

COPPER
Obv: 4th bust, bold unfinished truncation using 1 Peso obverse die

KM#	Date	VG	Fine	VF	XF
729	1915	9.00	15.00	22.50	30.00

Obv: 5th bust, heavy, with short unfinished lapels centered high.

KM#	Date	VG	Fine	VF	XF
730	1915	2.50	4.00	6.00	8.00

Obv: 6th bust, curved bottom, 31mm.

KM#	Date	VG	Fine	VF	XF
731	1915	4.50	6.00	8.00	10.00

Obv: 6th bust, 28mm.

KM#	Date	VG	Fine	VF	XF
732	1915	5.00	7.50	10.00	15.00

Obv: 7th bust, short truncation with closed lapels.

KM#	Date	VG	Fine	VF	XF
733	1915	3.00	5.00	7.00	9.00

50 CENTAVOS

SILVER, 22mm
Obv: 7th bust, heavy with short unfinished lapels, centered high.

KM#	Date	VG	Fine	VF	XF
734	1915	6.00	10.00	12.50	17.50

Obv: 6th bust, curved bottom.

KM#	Date	VG	Fine	VF	XF
735	1915	9.00	15.00	20.00	25.00

Obv: 7th bust, short truncation with closed lapels.

KM#	Date	VG	Fine	VF	XF
736	1915	7.50	12.50	17.50	22.50

Obv: 8th bust, short truncation with pronounced curve.

KM#	Date	VG	Fine	VF	XF
737	1915	12.50	17.50	25.00	32.50

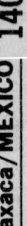

Obv: 5th bust, medium truncation with closed lapels.

KM#	Date	VG	Fine	VF	XF
738	1915	7.50	12.50	17.50	25.00

BILLON

KM#	Date	VG	Fine	VF	XF
739	1915	—	—	—	2000.

COPPER

KM#	Date	VG	Fine	VF	XF
739a	1915	—	—	—	—

UN (1) PESO

SILVER

Obv: 4th bust, with heavy unfinished truncation.

KM#	Date	VG	Fine	VF	XF
740	1915	4.75	8.00	12.00	17.50

Obv: 5th bust, heavy, with short unfinished lapels, centered high.

KM#	Date	VG	Fine	VF	XF
741	1915	4.75	8.00	12.00	17.50

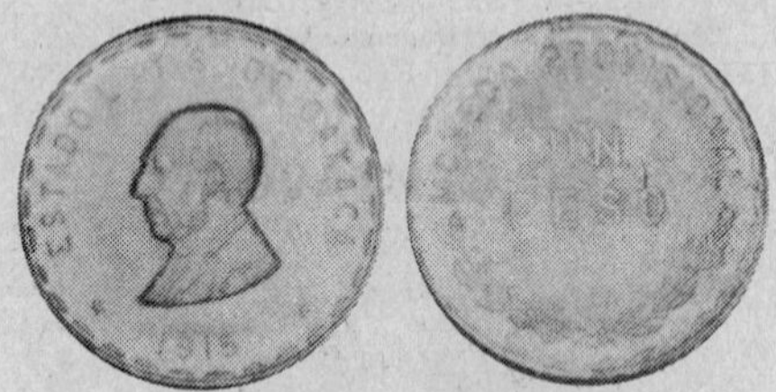

Obv: 6th bust, curved bottom line.

KM#	Date	VG	Fine	VF	XF
742	1915	4.75	8.00	12.00	17.50

Obv: 7th bust, short truncation with closed lapels.

KM#	Date	VG	Fine	VF	XF
743	1915	6.00	10.00	17.50	25.00

DOS (2) PESOS

SILVER

Obv: 4th bust, using 1 Peso obverse die.

KM#	Date	VG	Fine	VF	XF
744	1915	12.00	20.00	26.00	35.00

.902 SILVER/.010 GOLD, 22mm

Obv: 5th bust. Rev: Curved bottomed 2 over PESOS

KM#	Date	VG	Fine	VF	XF
745	1915	12.00	20.00	26.00	35.00

COPPER

KM#	Date	VG	Fine	VF	XF
745a	1915	15.00	25.00	45.00	75.00

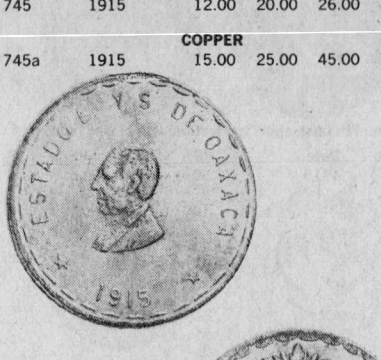

SILVER

Obv: 6th bust. Rev: 2 PESOS

KM#	Date	VG	Fine	VF	XF
746	1915	12.00	20.00	32.50	50.00

Obv: 6th bust. Rev: DOS PESOS

KM#	Date	VG	Fine	VF	XF
747	1915	13.50	22.50	40.00	70.00

.902 SILVER

Obv: 7th bust, short truncation with closed lapels, 22mm.

KM#	Date	VG	Fine	VF	XF
748	1915	12.00	20.00	30.00	40.00

SILVER

Obv: 10th, small nude bust.

KM#	Date	VG	Fine	VF	XF
749	1915	—	—	Unique	2300.

5 PESOS

GOLD

Obv: 3rd bust, heavy, with short unfinished lapels.

KM#	Date	VG	Fine	VF	XF
750	1915	100.00	150.00	250.00	350.00

.902 SILVER

Obv: 7th bust, short truncation with closed lapels.

KM#	Date	VG	Fine	VF	XF
751	1915	30.00	50.00	80.00	125.00

COPPER

KM#	Date	VG	Fine	VF	XF
751a	1915	25.00	45.00	65.00	100.00

10 PESOS

GOLD

Obv: 5th bust

KM#	Date	VG	Fine	VF	XF
752	1915	125.00	200.00	350.00	450.00

20 PESOS

GOLD

Obv: 5th bust, heavy, with short unfinished lapels, centered high.

KM#	Date	VG	Fine	VF	XF
753	1915	300.00	400.00	500.00	700.00

Obv: 7th bust, short truncation with closed lapels.

KM#	Date	VG	Fine	VF	XF
754	1915	—	400.00	500.00	700.00

60 PESOS

.903 GOLD

KM#	Date	VG	Fine	VF	XF
755	1916	—	6000.	8000.	10,000.

PUEBLA

A state of central Mexico. Puebla was a state that occassionally saw Zapata forces active within its boundaries. Also active, and an issuer of coins, was the Madero brigade who issued coins with their name 2 years after Madero's death. The state issue of 2, 5, 10 and 20 centavos saw limited circulation and recent hoards have been found of some values.

CHICONCUAUTLA

"MADERO BRIGADE"

10 CENTAVOS

COPPER

756	1915	9.00	15.00	18.50	25.00

20 CENTAVOS

COPPER
Rev: 'TRANSITORIO' between rosettes.

757	1915	5.00	7.50	10.00	12.50

Rev: 'TRANSITORIO' without rosettes.

758	1915	7.00	12.00	17.00	25.00

TETELA DEL ORO Y OCAMPO

2 CENTAVOS

COPPER, 17mm

KM#	Date	VG	Fine	VF	XF
759	1915	3.50	6.00	8.00	12.00

Rev. leg. ends: 'E.DE PU.,' 20mm

760	1915	15.00	25.00	32.50	47.50

Rev. leg. ends: 'E.DE PUE.,'

761	1915	9.00	15.00	20.00	30.00

5 CENTAVOS

COPPER

762	1915	175.00	300.00	450.00	600.00

20 CENTAVOS

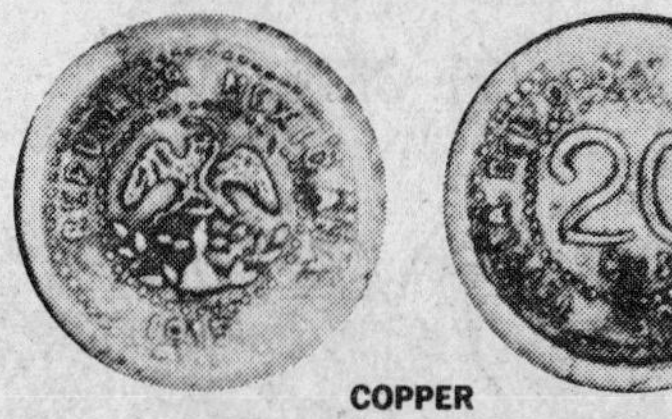

COPPER

764	1915	150.00	250.00	300.00	450.00

NCLT ISSUES

DIE TRIALS

KM#	Date	Mintage	Identification	Mkt.Val.
1	1915	—	10 Centavos, Copper, Uniface, KM#763	475.00

SINALOA

A state along the west coast of Mexico. The cast pieces of this state have been attributed to two people - Generals Rafael Buelna and Juan Carrasco. The cap and rays 8 reales is usually attributed to General Buelna and the rest of the series to Carrasco. Because of their crude nature it is questionable whether separate series or mints can be determined.

BUELNA/CARRASCO ISSUES

NOTE: These are all crude sand cast coins using regular coins to prepare the mold. Prices below give a range for how much of the original coin from which the mold was prepared is visible.

20 CENTAVOS

SILVER (cast)
Sand molded using regular 20 Centavos

KM#	Date	Good	VG	Fine	VF
765		100.00	175.00	300.00	350.00

50 CENTAVOS

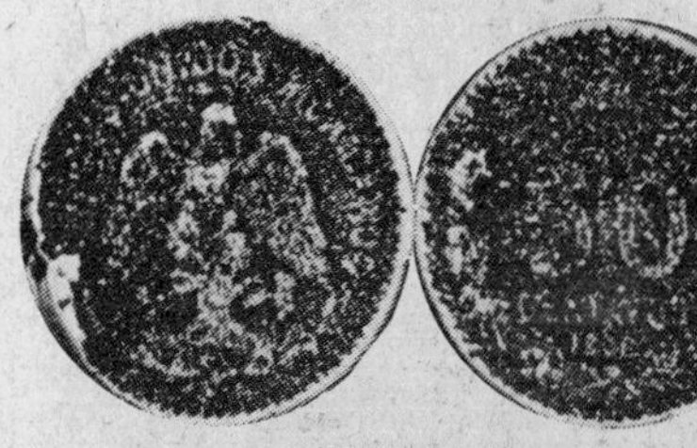

SILVER (cast)
Sand molded using regular 50 Centavos

766		75.00	125.00	200.00	250.00

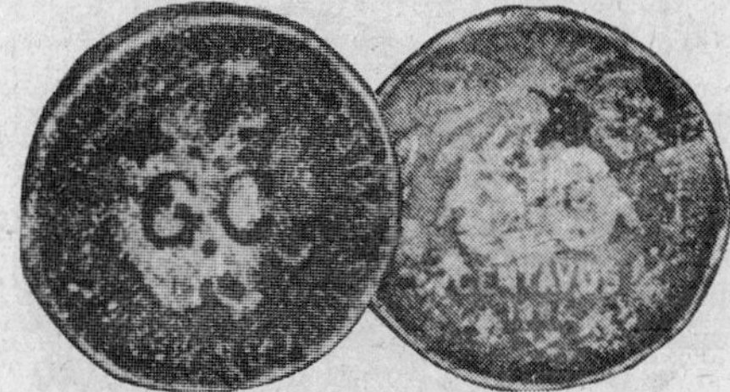

Obv: c/s G.C. on eagle

767		200.00	350.00	500.00	600.00

PESO

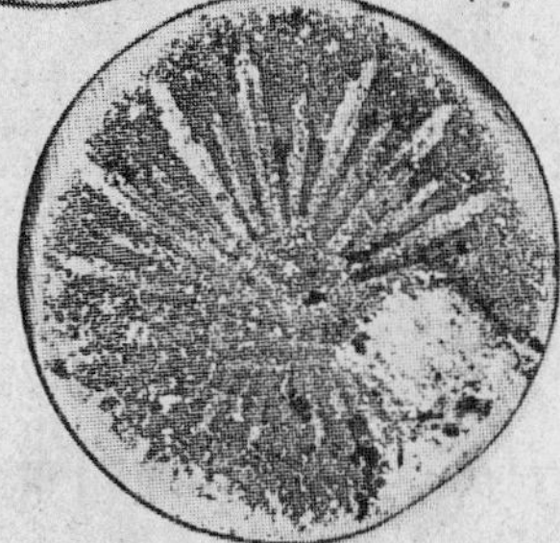

SILVER (cast)
Sand molded using regular Liberty cap 8 Reales

768		17.50	35.00	45.00	65.00

Sand molded using regular Liberty peso

KM#	Date	Good	VG	Fine	VF
769		17.50	35.00	45.00	65.00

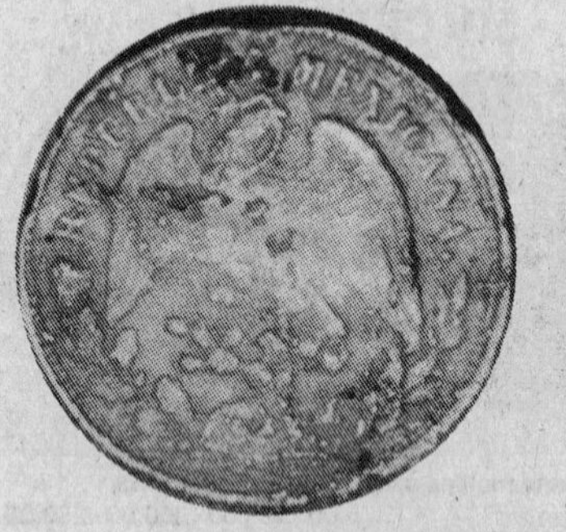

With additional counterstamp GC

KM#	Date	Good	VG	Fine	VF
770		60.00	90.00	150.00	200.00

Listings For

MOMBASA: refer to Kenya

MONACO

The Principality of Monaco, located on the Mediterranean coast nine miles off Nice, has an area of 0.8 sq. mi. (2.07 sq. km.) and a population of 25,000. Capital: Monaco-Ville. The economy is based on tourism and the manufacture of perfumes and liqueurs. Monaco derives most of its revenue from a tobacco monopoly, the sale of postage stamps for philatelic purpose, and the gambling tables of Monte Carlo Casino.

Monaco derived its name from 'Monoikos', the Greek surname for Hercules, the mythological strong man in whose honor the Greeks erected a temple on the Monacan headland. Probably founded by the Phoenicians, Monaco has been ruled by the Genoa Grimmaldi family since 1297 - Prince Rainier III, the present and 30th monarch of Monaco, is still of that line - except for a period during the French Revolution and the First Republic when it was annexed to France. Since 1865, Monaco has maintained a customs union with France which guarantees its privileged position as long as the royal male line remains intact. Under the new constitution proclaimed on December 17, 1962, the Prince shares his power with an 18-member unicameral National Council.

RULERS

Honore V, 1819-1841
Charles III, 1856-1889
Albert I, 1889-1922
Louis II, 1922-1949
Rainier III, 1949-

MINTMARKS

M - Monte Carlo
A - Paris

PRIVY MARKS

(a) - Paris (privy marks only)
C - Cabanis, 1837-1838
(P) - Thunderbolt - Poissy

MONETARY SYSTEM

10 Centimes = 1 Decime
10 Decimes = 1 Franc

Monetary Reform of 1960
100 Old Francs = 1 New Franc

CINQ (5) CENTIMES

CAST BRASS
Obv: Large head

C#	Date	Mintage	Fine	VF	XF
1	1837M C	—	7.50	14.00	27.50
	Obv: Small head				
	1837M C	—	6.00	12.00	17.50

COPPER, struck

C#	Date	Mintage	Fine	VF	XF
1a	1837M C	—	5.50	12.00	25.00
1a	1838M C	—	5.50	12.00	25.00
	1838M C	—	—	Proof	100.00

UN (1)DECIME

COPPER, struck

C#	Date	Mintage	Fine	VF	XF
2	1838M C	—	9.00	25.00	45.00
	1838M C	—	—	Proof	150.00
	BRASS, struck				
	1838M C	—	9.00	25.00	45.00

CENTIME

STAINLESS STEEL

Y#	Date	Mintage	VF	XF	Unc
34	1976(a)	.025	—	—	2.50
	1977(a)	.025	—	—	2.50
	1979	—	—	—	2.50

5 CENTIMES

COPPER-ALUMINUM-NICKEL

Y#	Date	Mintage	VF	XF	Unc
35	1976(a)	.025	—	—	3.00
	1977	.025	—	—	3.00
	1979	—	—	—	3.00

10 CENTIMES

ALUMINUM-BRONZE

Y#	Date	Mintage	VF	XF	Unc
20	1962(a)	.750	—	.15	.50
	1974(a)	.179	—	—	2.00
	1975(a)	.172	—	—	2.00
	1976(a)	.178	—	—	1.50
	1977(a)	.172	—	—	1.50
	1979	—	—	—	1.50

20 CENTIMES

ALUMINUM-BRONZE

Y#	Date	Mintage	VF	XF	Unc
21	1962(a)	.750	—	.20	1.00
	1974(a)	.104	—	—	2.50
	1975(a)	.097	—	—	2.50
	1976	.103	—	—	1.50
	1977	.097	—	—	1.50
	1979	—	—	—	1.50

50 CENTIMES

ALUMINUM-BRONZE

Y#	Date	Mintage	VF	XF	Unc
2	1924(p)	.150	15.00	25.00	40.00

Rev: No inscription in inner circle.

Y#	Date	Mintage	VF	XF	Unc
5	1926(p)	.100	17.00	25.00	45.00

Y#	Date	Mintage	VF	XF	Unc
22	1962(a)	.375	.75	1.25	3.00

1/2 FRANC

NICKEL

Y#	Date	Mintage	VF	XF	Unc
A18	1965(a)	.375	—	.60	1.25
	1968(a)	.250	—	.60	1.25
	1974(a)	.069	—	—	2.00
	1975(a)	.070	—	—	2.00
	1976(a)	.068	—	—	2.00
	1977(a)	.062	—	—	2.00
	1979	—	—	—	2.00

FRANC

ALUMINUM-BRONZE

Y#	Date	Mintage	VF	XF	Unc
3	1924(p)	.150	18.00	27.50	40.00

Rev: No inscription in inner circle.

Y#	Date	Mintage	VF	XF	Unc
6	1926(p)	.100	20.00	30.00	50.00

ALUMINUM

Y#	Date	Mintage	VF	XF	Unc
8a	ND(1943a)	2.500	.75	1.00	3.50

ALUMINUM-BRONZE

Y#	Date	Mintage	VF	XF	Unc
8	ND(1945a)	1.509	1.00	2.50	5.00

NICKEL

Y#	Date	Mintage	VF	XF	Unc
18	1960(a)	.500	.50	1.00	2.25
	1966(a)	.175	.50	1.00	2.25
	1968(a)	.250	.50	1.00	2.25
	1974(a)	.194	—	—	3.50
	1975(a)	.195	—	—	3.50
	1976(a)	.193	—	—	3.50
	1977(a)	.188	—	—	3.50
	1979	—	—	—	3.50

2 FRANCS

ALUMINUM-BRONZE

Y#	Date	Mintage	VF	XF	Unc
4	1924(p)	.075	20.00	30.00	55.00

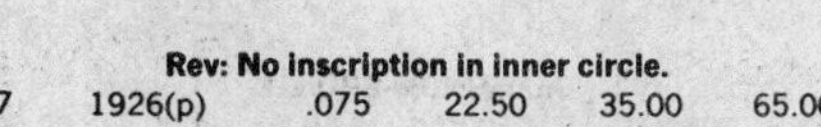

Rev: No inscription in inner circle.

Y#	Date	Mintage	VF	XF	Unc
7	1926(p)	.075	22.50	35.00	65.00

ALUMINUM

Y#	Date	Mintage	VF	XF	Unc
9a	ND(1943a)	1.250	1.00	3.00	5.00

ALUMINUM-BRONZE

Y#	Date	Mintage	VF	XF	Unc
9	ND(1945a)	1.080	1.25	4.00	7.00

7.4500 gm., nickel

Y#	Date	Mintage	VF	XF	Unc
36	1979(a)	.162			

5 FRANCS

.900 SILVER

Obv: Head right. Rev: Crowned, supported arms.

C#	Date	Mintage	VF	XF	Unc
3	1837M	—	300.00	500.00	800.00

C#	Date	Mintage	VF	XF	Unc
3a	1837M	—	1000.	2500.	Rare

NOTE: Restrikes exist.

ALUMINUM

Y#	Date	Mintage	VF	XF	Unc
10	1945(a)	1.000	1.50	3.00	7.00

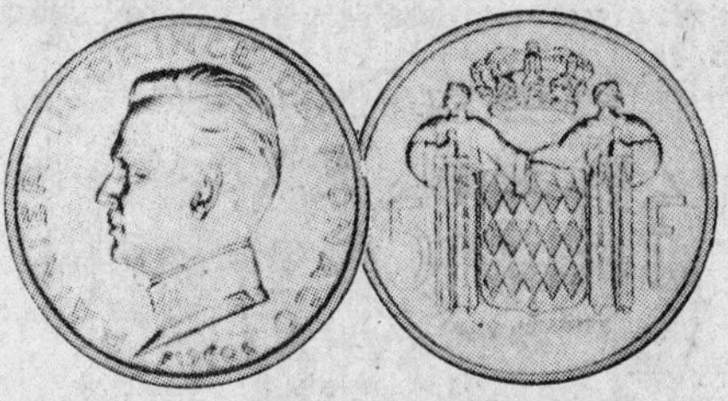

12.0000 gm., .835 SILVER, .3221 oz ASW

Y#	Date	Mintage	VF	XF	Unc
19	1960(a)	.125	10.00	11.00	12.50
	1966(a)	.125	10.00	11.00	12.50

NICKEL-CLAD COPPER-NICKEL

Y#	Date	Mintage	VF	XF	Unc
26	1971(a)	.250	1.50	2.00	3.75
	1974(a)	.152	1.25	1.75	3.75
	1975(a)	.008	—	—	15.00
	1976(a)	.008	—	—	8.00
	1977(a)	—	—	—	8.00
	1979	—	—	—	8.00

10 FRANCS

COPPER-NICKEL

Y#	Date	Mintage	VF	XF	Unc
11	1946(a)	1.000	1.25	2.00	6.50

ALUMINUM-BRONZE

Y#	Date	Mintage	VF	XF	Unc
13	1950(a)	.500	.50	1.00	2.50
	1951(a)	.500	.50	1.00	2.50

25.0000 gm., .900 SILVER, .7234 oz ASW
Charles III

Y#	Date	Mintage	VF	XF	Unc
25	1966(a)	.038	BV	30.00	40.00

10th Wedding Anniversary

Y#	Date	Mintage	VF	XF	Unc
23	1966(a)	.024	BV	25.00	40.00
	1966(a)	1,000	—	Proof	150.00

COPPER-NICKEL
25th Anniversary of Reign

Y#	Date	Mintage	VF	XF	Unc
27	1974(a)	.025	—	—	9.00

Y#	Date	Mintage	VF	XF	Unc
33	1975(a)	.025	—	—	6.00
	1976(a)	.016	—	—	8.00
	1977(a)	.050	—	—	4.00

VINGT (20)FRANCS

6.4516 gm., .900 GOLD, .1867 oz AGW

Y#	Date	Mintage	VF	XF	Unc
A1	1878A	.025	150.00	200.00	300.00
	1879A	.050	135.00	175.00	275.00

COPPER-NICKEL

Y#	Date	Mintage	VF	XF	Unc
12	1947(a)	1.000	2.50	3.50	7.50

ALUMINUM-BRONZE

Y#	Date	Mintage	VF	XF	Unc
14	1950(a)	.500	.50	1.00	2.50
	1951(a)	.500	.50	1.00	2.50

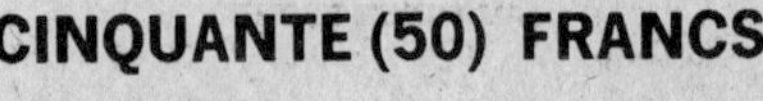

CINQUANTE (50) FRANCS

ALUMINUM-BRONZE

Y#	Date	Mintage	VF	XF	Unc
15	1950(a)	.500	2.50	4.00	9.00

30.0000 gm., .900 SILVER, .8681 oz ASW
25th Anniversary of Reign

Y#	Date	Mintage	VF	XF	Unc
28	1974(a)	.025	—	35.00	50.00

NOTE: The above has a commemorative edge inscription.

Plain edge

Y#	Date	Mintage	VF	XF	Unc
28a	1975(a)	7,500	—	35.00	45.00
	1976a	6,000		40.00	50.00

CENT (100)FRANCS

32.2580 gm., .900 GOLD, .9335 oz AGW

Y#	Date	Mintage	VF	XF	Unc
B1	1882A	5,000	—	—	2000.
	1884A	.015	BV	700.00	1000.
	1886A	.015	BV	700.00	1000.

Y#	Date	Mintage	VF	XF	Unc
1	1891A	.020	BV	625.00	800.00
	1892A	—	Proof Only		1250.
	1893A	.020	BV	625.00	—
	1895A	.020	BV	625.00	800.00
	1896A	.020	BV	625.00	800.00
	1901A	.015	BV	625.00	875.00
	1904A	.010	BV	625.00	1000.

COPPER-NICKEL

Y#	Date	Mintage	VF	XF	Unc
16	1950(a)	.500	6.00	10.00	20.00

Y#	Date	Mintage	VF	XF	Unc
17	1956(a)	.500	2.00	4.00	8.00

36.0000 gm., .999 SILVER, 1.1563 oz ASW
25th Anniversary of Reign

Y#	Date	Mintage	VF	XF	Unc
29	1974(a)	.025	—	Proof	50.00

200 FRANCS

32.0000 gm., .920 GOLD, .9466 oz AGW
10th Wedding Anniversary

Y#	Date	Mintage	VF	XF	Unc
24	1966(a)	5,000	BV	BV	625.00
	1966(a)	1,000	—	Proof	800.00

1000 FRANCS

.500 GOLD
Monte Carlo Casino Centennial

Y#	Date	Mintage	VF	XF	Unc
36	1979	—	—	—	—

MEDALLIC ISSUES

1000 FRANCS

.997 PLATINUM
25th Anniversary of Reign

Y#	Date	Mintage	VF	XF	Unc
30	1974(a)	.010	—	Proof	—

2000 FRANCS

.997 PLATINUM

25th Anniversary of Reign

Y#	Date	Mintage	VF	XF	Unc
31	1974(a)	.010	—	Proof	—

3000 FRANCS

.999 GOLD
25th Anniversary of Reign

Y#	Date	Mintage	VF	XF	Unc
32	1974(a)	5,000	—	Proof	—

NCLT ISSUES

ESSAIS (E)

Standard metals unless otherwise noted.

Y#	Date	Mintage	Identification	Issue Price	Mkt Val.
—	1934(a)	—	500 Francs, .900 Gold, Louis II		1750.
E8b	ND(1943a)	—	1 Franc, .900 Gold	—	400.00
E9b	ND(1943a)	—	2 Francs, .900 Gold	—	500.00
E10a	1945(a)	—	5 Francs, .900 Gold	—	750.00
E11	1945(a)	—	10 Francs	—	30.00

Y#	Date	Mintage	Identification	Issue Price	Mkt Val.
E12	1945(a)	—	20 Francs	—	35.00
E11a	1946(a)	—	10 Francs, .900 Gold	—	450.00
E12a	1947(a)	—	20 Francs, .900 Gold	—	500.00
E13	1950(a)	—	10 Francs	—	15.00
E13a	1950(a)	*450	10 Francs, Silver	—	30.00
E13b	1950(a)	500	10 Francs, .900 Gold	—	425.00
E14	1950(a)	—	20 Francs	—	20.00
E14a	1950(a)	*450	20 Francs, Silver	—	40.00
E14b	1950(a)	500	20 Francs, .900 Gold	—	450.00
E15	1950(a)	—	50 Francs	—	25.00
E15a	1950(a)	*450	50 Francs, Silver	—	50.00
E15b	1950(a)	500	50 Francs, .900 Gold	—	475.00
E16	1950(a)	—	100 Francs	—	40.00
E16a	1950(a)	*450	100 Francs, Silver	—	60.00
E16b	1950(a)	500	100 Francs, .900 Gold	—	650.00
E17a	1956(a)	500	100 Francs, .900 Gold	—	475.00
E18	1960(a)	—	Franc	—	25.00
E18a	1960(a)	500	Franc, .920 Gold	—	100.00
E19	1960(a)	*400	5 Francs	—	40.00
E19a	1960(a)	500	5 Francs, .920 Gold	—	175.00
E20	1962(a)	1,200	10 Centimes	—	13.50
E20a	1962(a)	502	10 Centimes, .950 Silver	—	60.00
E20b	1962(a)	502	10 Centimes, .920 Gold	—	175.00
E21	1962(a)	1,200	20 Centimes	—	16.50
E21a	1962(a)	502	20 Centimes, .950 Silver	—	75.00
E21b	1962(a)	502	20 Centimes, .920 Gold	—	200.00
E22	1962(a)	1,200	50 Centimes	—	20.00
E22a	1962(a)	502	50 Centimes, .950 Silver	—	150.00
E22b	1962(a)	502	50 Centimes, .920 Gold	—	250.00
EA18a	1965(a)	1,000	1/2 Franc, .920 Gold	—	100.00
E19a	1966(a)	500	5 Francs, .920 Gold	—	175.00
E25	1966(a)	100	10 Francs	—	100.00
E25a	1966(a)	1,000	10 Francs, .920 Gold	—	375.00
E26	1971(a)	—	5 Francs	—	60.00
E26a	1971(a)	—	5 Francs, Silver	—	100.00
E26b	1971(a)	—	5 Francs, .920 Gold	—	175.00
E26a	1974(a)	—	5 Francs, Silver	—	60.00
E26b	1974(a)	—	5 Francs, Gold	—	350.00
E27	1974(a)	—	10 Francs	—	40.00
E27a	1974(a)	—	10 Francs, Silver	—	—
E27b	1974(a)	—	10 Francs, Gold	—	500.00
E28	1974(a)	—	50 Francs	—	65.00
E28a	1974(a)	—	50 Francs, Gold	—	1000.

PIEFORTS - (P)

PIEFORTS WITH ESSAI (PE)

(DOUBLE THICKNESS)
Standard metals unless otherwise noted.

Y#	Date	Mintage	Identification	Issue Price	Mkt Val.
PE8b	ND(1943a)	—	1 Franc, .900 Gold	—	550.00
PE9b	ND(1943a)	—	2 Francs, .900 Gold	—	800.00
PE10a	1945(a)	—	5 Francs, .900 Gold	—	900.00
PE11a	1946(a)	—	10 Francs, .900 Gold	—	650.00
PE12a	1947(a)	—	20 Francs, .900 Gold	—	800.00
PE13	1950(a)	—	10 Francs	—	30.00
PE13a	1950(a)	*450	10 Francs, Silver	—	45.00
PE13b	1950(a)	350	10 Francs, .900 Gold	—	550.00
PE14	1950(a)	—	20 Francs	—	40.00
PE14a	1950(a)	*450	20 Francs, Silver	—	60.00
PE14b	1950(a)	350	20 Francs, .900 Gold	—	600.00
PE15	1950(a)	—	50 Francs	—	75.00
PE15a	1950(a)	*450	50 Francs, Silver	—	75.00
PE15b	1950(a)	350	50 Francs, .900 Gold	—	675.00
PE16	1950(a)	—	100 Francs	—	100.00
PE16a	1950(a)	*450	100 Francs, Silver	—	90.00
PE16b	1950(a)	350	100 Francs, .900 Gold	—	750.00
PE17a	1956(a)	20	100 Francs, .900 Gold	—	1000.
PE18a	1960(a)	25	1 Franc, .920 Gold	—	250.00
PE19a	1960(a)	25	5 Francs, .920 Gold	—	400.00
PE20a	1962(a)	100	10 Centimes, .950 Silver	—	125.00
PE20b	1962(a)	25	10 Centimes, .920 Gold	—	750.00
PE21a	1962(a)	100	20 Centimes, .950 Silver	—	150.00
PE21b	1962(a)	25	20 Centimes, .920 Gold	—	850.00
PE22a	1962(a)	100	50 Centimes, .950 Silver	—	200.00
PE22b	1962(a)	25	50 Centimes, .920 Gold	—	1000.
PE26	1966(a)	—	5 Francs	—	60.00
PE26b	1971(a)	—	5 Francs, .920 Gold	—	325.00
PE26a	1974(a)	—	5 Francs, Silver	—	—
PE26b	1974(a)	—	5 Francs, Gold	—	—
PE27a	1974(a)	—	10 Francs, Silver	—	—
PE27b	1974(a)	—	10 Francs, Gold	—	—
PE28	1974(a)	—	50 Francs	—	—
PE28(a)	1974(a)	—	50 Francs, Gold	—	—

SPECIMEN SETS

(Fleur de Coin)
STANDARD METALS

KM#	Date	Mintage	Identification	Issue Price	Mkt. Val.
SS1	1974(7)	*7,000	Y18,A18,20,21,26-28	45.00	110.00
*NOTE: 3,000 of the above sets were not released.					
SS2	1975(7)	7,500	Y18,A18,20,21,26,28a,33	—	100.00
SS3	1976(9)	7,000	Y34,35,20,21,A18,18,26,33,28a	—	85.00
SS4	1976(7)	—	—	—	18.50
SS5	1977(8)	6,000	Y20,21,A18,18,26,33,34,35	—	13.50
SS6	1977(7)	—	—	—	16.50

PROOF SETS

STANDARD METALS

KM#	Date	Mintage	Identification	Issue Price	Mkt. Val.
101	1950(8)	—	Y#13-16, Two each	—	250.00
102	1950(4)	400	Y#13-16	—	110.00
103	1974(4)	—	Y29-32	—	—

MONGOLIA

The Mongolian People's Republic, a landlocked country in central Asia between the Soviet Union and the People's Republic of China, has an area of 604,000 sq. mi. (1,565,000 sq. km.) and a population of 1.4 million. Capital: Ulaanbaatar. Animal herds and flocks are the chief economic asset. Wool, cattle, butter, meat and hides are exported.

Mongolia (often referred to as Outer Mongolia), one of the world's oldest countries, attained its greatest power in the 13th century when Genghis Khan and his successors conquered all of China and extended their influence westward as far as Hungary and Poland. The empire dissolved in later centuries and in 1691 was brought under suzerainty of the Manchus, who had conquered China in 1644. After the Chinese republican movement led by Sun Yat-sen overthrew the Manchus and set up the Chinese Republic in 1911, Mongolia, with the support of Russia, proclaimed its independence from China and, on March 13, 1921, established the Mongolian People's Republic.

MONETARY SYSTEM

100 Mongo = 1 Tukhrik

MONGO

COPPER

Y#	Date	Year	Mintage	Fine	VF	XF
1	(1925)	15	—	5.00	7.00	10.00

ALUMINUM-BRONZE

Y#	Date	Year	Mintage	Fine	VF	XF
10	(1937)	27	—	3.00	3.50	5.00

Y#	Date	Year	Mintage	Fine	VF	XF
16	(1945)	35	—	2.00	3.00	6.00

ALUMINUM

Y#	Date	Year	Mintage	VF	XF	Unc
22	1959	—	—	.75	1.25	2.00

Y#	Date	Year	Mintage	VF	XF	Unc
28	1970	—	—	.75	1.00	1.50

2 MONGO

COPPER

Y#	Date	Year	Mintage	Fine	VF	XF
2	(1925)	15	—	5.00	8.00	10.00

ALUMINUM-BRONZE

Y#	Date	Year	Mintage	Fine	VF	XF
11	(1937)	27	—	2.50	3.50	5.00

Y#	Date	Year	Mintage	Fine	VF	XF
17	(1945)	17	—	1.00	2.00	3.00

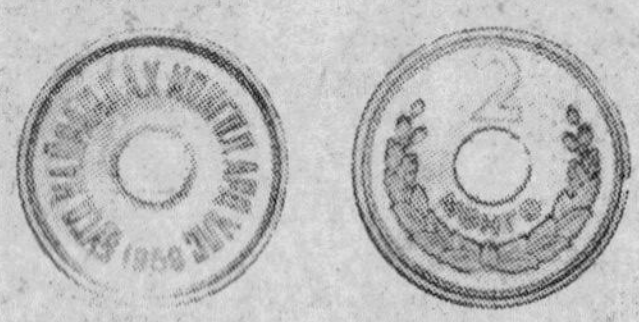

ALUMINUM

Y#	Date	Year	Mintage	VF	XF	Unc
23	1959	—	—	1.00	1.50	2.50

Y#	Date	Year	Mintage	VF	XF	Unc
29	1970	—	—	1.00	2.00	3.00

5 MONGO

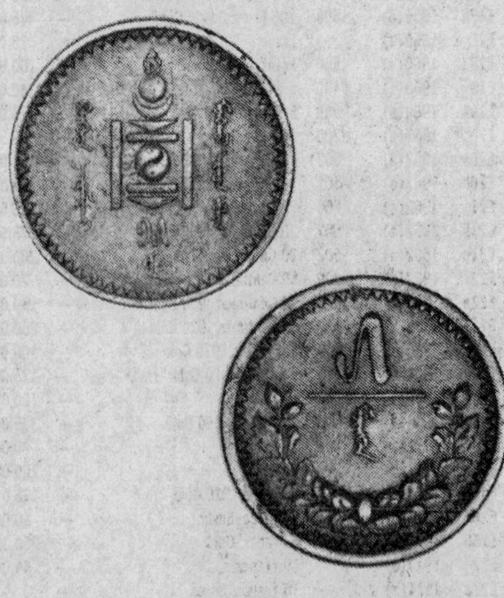

COPPER

Y#	Date	Year	Mintage	Fine	VF	XF
3	(1925)	15	—	6.00	12.00	15.00

ALUMINUM-BRONZE

Y#	Date	Year	Mintage	Fine	VF	XF
12	(1937)	27	—	2.75	3.50	5.00

Y#	Date	Year	Mintage	Fine	VF	XF
18	1945	35	—	2.00	3.00	4.00

ALUMINUM

Y#	Date	Year	Mintage	VF	XF	Unc
24	1959	—	—	1.00	1.50	2.50

Y#	Date	Year	Mintage	VF	XF	Unc
30	1970	—	—	1.00	2.00	3.00

10 MONGO

1.7996 gm., .500 SILVER, .0289 oz ASW

Y#	Date	Year	Mintage	Fine	VF	XF
4	(1925)	15	1.500	3.00	5.00	8.00

COPPER-NICKEL

Y#	Date	Year	Mintage	Fine	VF	XF
13	(1937)	27	—	2.00	3.50	6.00

Y#	Date	Year	Mintage	Fine	VF	XF
19	(1945)	35	—	2.00	3.50	5.00

ALUMINUM

Y#	Date	Year	Mintage	VF	XF	Unc
25	1959	—	—	1.50	3.00	5.00

COPPER-NICKEL

Y#	Date	Year	Mintage	VF	XF	Unc
31	1970	—	—	1.50	2.50	4.00

15 MONGO

2.6994 gm., .500 SILVER, .0433 oz ASW

Y#	Date	Year	Mintage	Fine	VF	XF
5	(1925)	15	.417	3.00	5.00	8.50

COPPER-NICKEL

Y#	Date	Year	Mintage	Fine	VF	XF
14	(1937)	27	—	2.00	3.00	5.00

Y#	Date	Year	Mintage	Fine	VF	XF
20	(1945)	35	—	2.25	2.75	4.00

ALUMINUM

Y#	Date	Year	Mintage	VF	XF	Unc
26	1959	—	—	1.00	2.00	3.50

COPPER-NICKEL

Y#	Date	Year	Mintage	VF	XF	Unc
32	1970	—	—	1.00	2.00	3.00

20 MONGO

3.5992 gm., .500 SILVER, .0578 oz ASW

Y#	Date	Year	Mintage	Fine	VF	XF
6	(1925)	15	1.625	4.00	7.00	10.00

COPPER-NICKEL

Y#	Date	Year	Mintage	Fine	VF	XF
15	(1937)	27	—	3.00	5.00	7.00

Y#	Date	Year	Mintage	Fine	VF	XF
21	(1945)	35	—	2.00	3.00	4.00

ALUMINUM

Y#	Date	Year	Mintage	VF	XF	Unc
27	1959	—	—	1.50	2.50	3.50

COPPER-NICKEL

Y#	Date	Year	Mintage	VF	XF	Unc
33	1970	—	—	1.00	2.00	3.00

50 MONGO

9.9979 gm., .900 SILVER, .2893 oz ASW

Y#	Date	Year	Mintage	Fine	VF	XF
7	(1925)	15	.920	9.00	11.00	13.50

COPPER-NICKEL

Y#	Date	Year	Mintage	VF	XF	Unc
34	1970	—	—	1.50	2.50	6.00

TUKHRIK

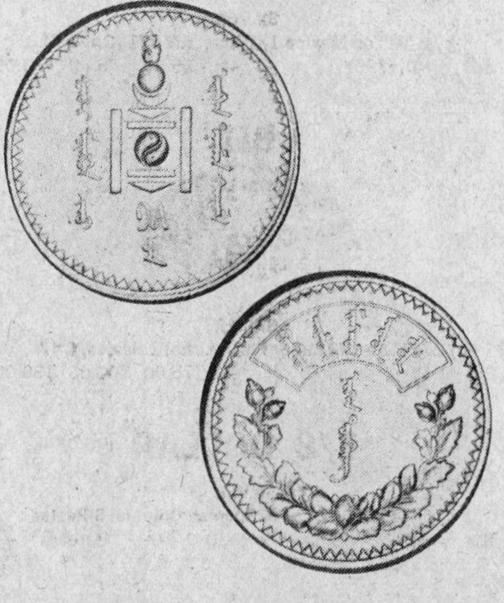

19.9957 gm., .900 SILVER, .5786 oz ASW

Y#	Date	Year	Mintage	Fine	VF	XF
8	(1925)	15	.400	17.50	22.50	30.00

ALUMINUM-BRONZE

50th Anniversary of Republic

Y#	Date	Year	Mintage	VF	XF	Unc
35	1971	—	—	8.00	10.00	15.00

COPPER-NICKEL

Y#	Date	Year	Mintage	VF	XF	Unc
35a	1971	—	—	8.00	10.00	20.00

10 TUKHRIK

COPPER-NICKEL

State Bank

Y#	Date	Year	Mintage	VF	XF	Unc
36	1975	—	—	—	—	—

25 TUKHRIK

.925 SILVER
Conservation Series

Y#	Date	Mintage	VF	XF	Unc
37	1976	3,500	BV	BV	25.00
	1976	—	—	Proof	30.00

50 TUKHRIK

.925 SILVER
Conservation Series

Y#	Date	Mintage	VF	XF	Unc
38	1976	3,500	BV	BV	40.00
	1976	—	—	Proof	50.00

750 TUKHRIK

.900 GOLD
Conservation Series

Y#	Date	Mintage	VF	XF	Unc
39	1976	751 pcs.	—	625.00	650.00
	1976	—	—	Proof	800.00

GOLD MINE INGOTS

NOTE: For silver coins with a circled small Russian eagle obverse and a circled fineness and weight in Russian reverse, see Gold Mine Ingots under Russia. These ingots were not intended for use in Mongolia.

Listings For

MONTENEGRO: refer to Yugoslavia

MONTSERRAT

Montserrat, a British crown colony located in the Lesser Antilles of the West Indies 27 miles (43 km.) southwest of Antigua, has an area of 39.5 sq. mi. (102.3 sq. km.) and a population of 13,000. Capital: Plymouth. The island - actually a range of volcanic peaks rising from the Caribbean - exports cotton, limes and vegetables.

Columbus discovered Montserrat in 1493 and named it after Monserrado, a mountain in Spain. It was colonized by the English in 1632 and, except for brief periods of French occupancy in 1667 and 1782-83, has remained a British possession from that time. Until becoming a separate colony in 1956, Montserrat was a presidency of the Leeward Islands.

RULERS
British

MONETARY SYSTEM

1740-1787
10 Bits = 1 Dollar
1787-1798
11 Bits = 1 Dollar
1798-1840
12 Bits = 1 Dollar

1-1/2 PENCE

BLACK DOG

BILLON
c/s: "M" on Cayenne 2 Sous, C#1.

C#	Date	Mintage	VG	Fine	VF
1	ND	—	12.50	25.00	50.00

1/2 BIT

SILVER
c/s: "M" on 1/4 cut of Spanish Colonial 2 Reales.

C#	Date	Mintage	VG	Fine	VF
5	ND	—	—	Rare	—

SILVER
c/s: "M" on Mexico 1/2 Real, KM#71 (C#73.5).

C#	Date	Mintage	VG	Fine	VF
5.1	ND(1790)	—	25.00	45.00	70.00

BIT

SILVER
c/s: "M" on 1/2 cut of Peru (Lima) 2 Reales, C#74.

C#	Date	Mintage	VG	Fine	VF
6	ND	—	75.00	100.00	130.00

1/8 DOLLAR

SILVER
c/s: "M" on 1/8 cut of Spanish Colonial 8 Reales

C#	Date	Mintage	VG	Fine	VF
8	ND	—	—	Rare	—

1/4 DOLLAR

SILVER
c/s: Cross on obv. and "M"s on rev. of 1/4 cut of Spanish Colonial 8 Reales.

C#	Date	Mintage	VG	Fine	VF
10	ND	—	75.00	100.00	130.00

c/s: Cross, crescent & star on Mexico 2 Reales
KM#86 (C#15).

C#	Date	Mintage	VG	Fine	VF
11.1	ND(1747-60)	—	250.00	300.00	400.00

c/s: Cross, crescent & star on Mexico 2 Reales
KM#88 (C#38).

C#	Date	Mintage	VG	Fine	VF
11.2	ND(1722-89)	—	150.00	200.00	300.00

DOLLAR

SILVER
c/s: Three crosses on Spanish Colonial 8 Reales

C#	Date	Mintage	VG	Fine	VF
13	ND	—	—	Rare	—

MODERN COINAGE

4 DOLLARS

COPPER-NICKEL
F.A.O. Issue

Y#	Date	Mintage	VF	XF	Unc
6*	1970	.020	—	5.00	7.50
	1970	2,000	—	Proof	50.00

NOTE: *This number refers to Yeomans East Caribbean Territories listings, where seven companion 4 dollar issues are listed.

MOROCCO

The Kingdom of Morocco, situated on the northwest corner of Africa south of Spain, has an area of 171,953 sq. mi. (44,356 sq. km.) and a population of 18.6 million. Capital: Rabat. The economy is essentially agricultural. Phosphates, fresh and preserved vegetables, canned fish, and raw materials are exported.

Morocco's strategic position at the gateway to western Europe has been the principal determinant of its violent, frequently unfortunate history. Time and again the fertile plain between the rugged Atlas Mountains and the sea has echoed the battle's trumpet as Phoenicians, Romans, Vandals, Visigoths, Byzantine Greeks and Islamic Arabs successively conquered and occupied the land. Modern Morocco is a remnant of an early empire formed by the Arabs at the close of the 7th century which encompassed all of northwest Africa and most of the Iberian Peninsula. During the 17th and 18th centuries, while under the control of native dynasties, it was the headquarters of the famous Sale pirates. Morocco's strategic position involved it in the competition of 19th century European powers for political influence in Africa, and resulted in the division of Morocco into French and Spanish spheres of interest which were established as protectorates in 1912. Morocco became independent on March 2, 1956, after France agreed to end its protectorate. Spain signed similar agreements on April 7 of the same year.

RULERS:

Muhammed XVI
AH1171-1205/AD1757-1790
Muhammed El-Yazid
AH1204-1206/AD1790-1792
El Hisham
AH1206-1209/AD1792-1795
Sulaiman II
AH1209-1238/AD1795-1822
Abd Al-Rahman II
AH1238-1276/AD1822-1859
Muhammad XVII
AH1276-1290/AD1859-1873
Mulai Hasan III
AH1290-1311/AD1873-1894
Abd Al-Aziz
AH1311-1325/AD1894-1908
Hafiz
AH1325-1330/AD1908-1912
Yusuf
AH1330-1346
Muhammad V
AH1346-1380/AD1927-1961
Hasan II
AH1380-/AD1961—

EARLY COINAGE

Prior to the introduction of modern machine-struck coinage in Morocco in AH1299(-1882AD), a variety of primitive cast bronze coins and crudely hammered silver and gold were in circulation, together with considerable quantities of foreign coin.

The cast bronze were produced in several denominations, multiples of the basic unit, the Falus. The size of the coins is variable, and the distinction of the various denominations is not always clear, particularly on the issues of Sulaiman. The early types are varied, but beginning about AH1218, the reverse bears the seal of Solomon, and the obverse contains the date and/or mint. The date is inscribed in European numerals, the mint, when present, is written out in Arabic script. Many of the issues are quite barbarous, with illegible dates and mints, and occasionally light in weight. These barbarous issues may have been contemporary counterfeits, and are of little numismatic value. The bronze pieces were cast in trees, and occasionally, entire or partial 'trees' are found on the market.

The silver and gold coins usually have the mint name on one side and the date on the other. The silver unit was the dirham of about 2.7 grams (but only about 2.0 grams from circa AH 1266-78), and the gold unit was the benduqi of about 3.25 grams. There were no fixed rates of exchange between coins of different metals.

Prices are for specimens with clearly legible dates and mint names (if any). Illegible, barbarous, and defectively produced pieces are worth much less.

MINTS

Fz = Fez (Fas) فاس

Rb = Rabat (Rabat al-Fath) رباط

Te = Tetuan تطوان

Mr = Marrakesh مراكس

(NM) = No mint name on coin.

Some of the earlier coins (Sulayman and Abd al-Rahman) were struck at several additional mints: Al-Araisha, Miknasa, Al-Suweira, and Tanja (Tangiers).

The following coins are listed by Craig's numbers, and are therefore divided by reign. However, all of the coins are anonymous, and the distinction by reign is purely artificial. There is much variation within each type, and several of the subtypes overlap more than one reign. The coinage of Sulayman and Abd al-Rahman are listed only by type (dates through AH 1276 inclusive); those of Muhammad IV (beginning AH 1277 inclusive) and Hasan I are broken down by mint and date. However, the date listings for these two rulers are believed to be very incomplete.

1/2 FALUS (ZELAGH)

BRONZE, 13-14mm
Rev: Flower design.

C#	Date	Good	VG	Fine	VF
120	ND	2.00	3.50	6.00	10.00
	Rev: Date.				
121	AH1245	2.50	4.50	7.50	12.50

FALUS

BRONZE, 16-18mm
Sulayman

C#	Date	Good	VG	Fine	VF
95	AH1209-38	1.50	2.50	4.00	6.50

NOTE: Many varieties exist.

Obv: Mint name above date.

C#	Date	Good	VG	Fine	VF
122	AH1240-76	1.00	2.00	3.00	5.00

NOTE: Many varieties exist.

 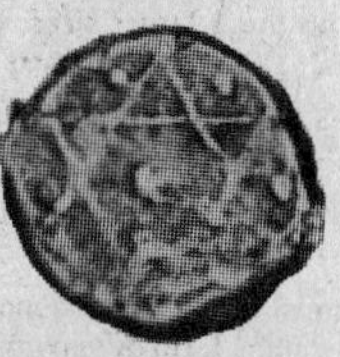

Muhammad IV - early types

C#	Date	Good	VG	Fine	VF
160	AH1277(NM)	1.00	2.00	3.00	5.00
	1278(NM)	1.00	2.00	3.00	5.00
	1279 Te	1.25	2.50	4.00	6.50
	1280	1.00	2.00	3.00	5.00
	1281(NM)	1.25	2.50	4.00	6.50

NOTE: Many varieties exist.

Reform type

C#	Date	Good	VG	Fine	VF
160a	AH1283 Fz	2.00	3.50	5.50	9.00
	1283 Mr	3.00	5.00	8.00	13.50
	1284 Fz	2.00	3.50	5.00	8.00
	1285 Fz	2.00	3.50	5.00	8.00
	1286 Fz	2.00	3.50	5.00	8.00
	1289 Fz	2.50	4.00	6.00	10.00

2 FALUS

BRONZE, 20-24mm
Sulaymen

C#	Date	Good	VG	Fine	VF
96	AH1209-38	3.00	5.00	7.50	12.50

Abd al-Rahman

C#	Date	Good	VG	Fine	VF
126	AH1240-76	1.15	1.60	2.50	4.00

NOTE: Many varieties exist.

Muhammad IV - early types

C#	Date	Good	VG	Fine	VF
163	AH1277 Te	1.25	2.50	4.00	6.50
	1277(NM)	1.00	2.00	3.00	5.00
	1278 Fz	1.50	2.75	4.50	7.50
	1278 Te	1.25	2.50	4.00	6.50
	1278(NM)	1.00	2.00	3.00	5.00
	1279 Fz	1.50	2.75	4.50	7.50
	1279(NM)	1.25	2.50	4.00	6.50
	1280(NM)	1.50	2.75	4.50	7.50
	1281 Fz	1.50	2.75	4.50	7.50
	1281 Te	1.50	2.75	4.50	7.50
	1281(NM)	1.50	2.50	3.50	6.00

NOTE: 1281 Fz found also with retrograde '2' in date.

Reform type

C#	Date	Good	VG	Fine	VF
163a	AH1283 Fz	2.50	4.50	6.50	11.00
	1283 Mr	2.75	5.00	7.50	12.50
	1284 Fz	2.00	4.00	6.00	10.00
	1285 Fz	2.50	4.50	6.50	11.00
	1285 Mr	3.00	5.00	7.50	12.50
	1286 Fz	2.00	4.00	6.00	10.00
	1287 Fz	3.00	5.00	7.50	12.50
	1288 Fz	2.00	4.00	6.00	10.00
	1288 Mr	3.00	5.00	7.50	12.50
	1289 Fz	3.00	5.00	7.50	12.50
	1290 Fz	3.00	5.00	7.50	12.50

Hasan I

C#	Date	Good	VG	Fine	VF
182	AH1295 uncertain mint	—	—	—	—

NOTE: All known specimens appear to be counterfeits.

3 FALUS

BRONZE, 27-30mm
Salayman

C#	Date	Good	VG	Fine	VF
97	AH1212-17	6.00	10.00	15.00	25.00

26-30mm
Abd al-Rahman

C#	Date	Good	VG	Fine	VF
128	AH1264-69	2.50	4.50	7.50	12.50

Muhammad IV - Reform types only

C#	Date	Good	VG	Fine	VF
166	AH1283 Fz	1.75	3.25	5.00	8.00
	1283 Mr	2.00	3.50	5.50	9.00
	1284 Fz	1.50	3.00	4.50	7.50
	1284 Mr	1.25	2.25	3.50	6.00

C#	Date	Good	VG	Fine	VF
	1285 Fz	1.50	2.75	4.00	6.50
	1285 Mr	1.50	2.75	4.00	6.50
	1286/5	1.75	3.25	5.00	8.00
	1286 Fz	1.00	1.75	2.75	4.50
	1286 Mr	1.00	1.75	2.75	4.50
	1287 Fz	2.00	3.50	5.50	9.00
	1287 Mr	2.00	3.50	5.50	9.00
	1288/7 Fz	2.25	4.00	6.00	10.00
	1288 Fz	.75	1.50	2.50	4.00
	1288 Mr	1.00	1.75	3.00	5.00
	1289/79	1.20	2.00	3.50	6.00
	1289/8 Mr	1.20	2.00	3.50	6.00
	1289 Fz	1.00	1.75	3.00	5.00
	1289 Mr	1.50	2.75	4.00	6.50
	1290 Fz	1.00	1.75	3.00	5.00

NOTE: AH1280 Fz is a poorly engraved 1284 Fz.

Hasan I

C#	Date	Good	VG	Fine	VF
183	AH1291 Fz	5.00	8.00	12.50	20.00
	1295 Fz	3.50	6.50	10.00	16.50

C#	Date	Good	VG	Fine	VF
—	Ah1311Fz	—	—	—	

1/4 DIRHAM (MAZUNA)

SILVER, 0.65 gm., 13mm

Muhammad IV

C#	Date	Good	VG	Fine	VF
170	AH1284 Fz	4.00	6.50	10.00	16.50
	1284 Mr	4.00	6.50	10.00	16.50
	1286 Fz	4.00	6.50	10.00	16.50
	1288 Fz	3.50	6.00	9.00	15.00

1/2 DIRHAM

SILVER, 15-18mm, 1.3-1.4 gm.

C#	Date	Good	VG	Fine	VF
	Sulaiman				
105	AH1211-15	5.00	8.50	13.50	21.50
	Abd al-Rahman				
135	AH1241-64	3.50	6.00	9.00	15.00
	Muhammad IV				
175	AH1283 Fz	3.00	5.50	8.50	13.50
	1284 Fz	3.00	5.50	8.50	13.50
	1284 Mr	4.00	7.00	11.00	18.50
	1284 Rb	4.25	8.00	12.50	20.00
	1286 Fz	3.00	5.50	8.50	13.50
	1288 Fz	3.00	5.50	8.50	13.50
	Hasan I				
186	AH1299 Fz	6.00	11.50	18.50	30.00

DIRHAM

SILVER, 17-20mm, 2.7 gm.

C#	Date	Good	VG	Fine	VF
	Sulaiman				
108	AH1218-37	4.00	7.00	11.00	18.50
	Abd al-Rahman				
140	AH1240-52	4.00	7.00	11.00	18.50
	Reduced standard, 2.0 gm.				
140a	AH1266-76	3.25	6.00	9.00	15.00
	Muhammad IV, light standard, 2.0 gm.				
176	AH1277 Fz	4.50	8.00	12.50	20.00
	1278 Fz	4.50	8.00	12.50	20.00

Heavy standard restored, 2.7 gm.

C#	Date	Good	VG	Fine	VF
176a	AH1283 Fz	4.00	7.00	11.00	18.50
	1284 Fz	3.25	6.00	10.00	16.50
	1284 Mr	3.75	7.00	11.00	18.50
	1284 Rb	3.75	7.00	11.00	18.50
	1285 Fz	4.00	7.00	11.00	18.50
	1286 Fz	3.25	6.00	10.00	16.50
	1288 Rb	4.00	7.00	11.00	18.50

Hasan I

C#	Date	Good	VG	Fine	VF
187	AH1291 Fz	8.50	15.00	22.50	37.50

1/2 BENDUQI

GOLD, 1.6-1.7 gm.

C#	Date	VG	Fine	VF	XF
145	AH1248	50.00	65.00	85.00	120.00
	1249	50.00	65.00	85.00	120.00

BENDUQI (MATBUU)

GOLD, 3.2-3.3 gm.

C#	Date	VG	Fine	VF	XF
	Salaiman				
115	AH1209-38	100.00	130.00	170.00	240.00
	Abd al-Rahman				
150	AH1243-73	100.00	130.00	170.00	240.00

MONETARY REFORM

MINTMARKS:

Paris (a) - privy marks only

Paris (Pa) بباريز

Poissy (Py): Inscribed "Pariṣ" but with thunderbolt privy mark.

Berlin (Be) برلين

Birmingham (Bh) بانغلند

London (Ln) [illegible]

Fez (Fz) بقاس

NOTE: Above forms of the mint names are shown as they appear on the coins, not in standard Arabic script.

MONETARY SYSTEM:
(Until 1921)

50 Mazunas = 1 Dirham
10 Dirhams = 1 Rial

NOTES:

Various copper and silver coins dated AH1297-1309 are believed to be patterns. Copper coins similar to Y#14-17, but without denomination on reverse, are patterns. On the silver coins the denominations are written in words and each series has its own characteristic names: Y#4-8 (1299-1314) Denomination in Shar'I Dirhams.

Y#9-13 (1313-1319) Denomination in 'Preferred' Dirhams.

Y#18-22 (1320-1323) Denomination in fractions of a Rial, but on the 3 larger sizes, the equivalent is given in "Urti parts", 1 Rial = 20 Urti parts.

Y#23-25 (1329) Denomination in Dirhams and in fraction of a Rial.

Y#30-33 (1331-1336) Denomination in Yusuti or "Treasury" Dirhams.

On most of the larger denomination, the denomination is given in the form of a rhymed couplet.

1/2 MAZUNA

BRONZE

Y#	Date	Mintage	Fine	VF	XF	Unc
C1	AH1310 Fz	—	115.00	175.00	250.00	500.00

NOTE: Some authorities consider Y#C1 to be a Mazuna.

MAZUNA

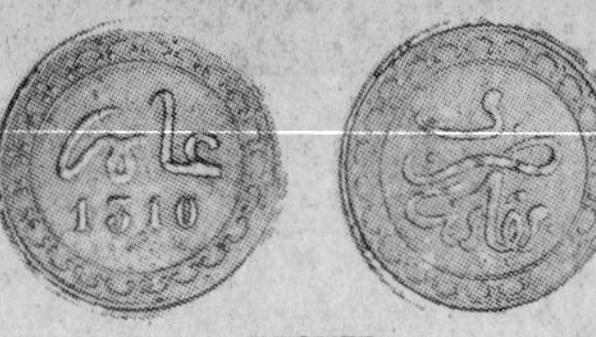

BRONZE

Y#	Date	Mintage	Fine	VF	XF	Unc
B1	AH1310 Fz	—	85.00	135.00	185.00	400.00

NOTE: Some authorities regard Y#B1 as a 2 Mazuna.

Y#	Date	Mintage	Fine	VF	XF	Unc
14	AH1320 Be	5 pcs.	—	Proof	—	
	1320 Bh	—	1.75	3.00	5.50	20.00
	1320 Fz	—	10.00	22.50	40.00	80.00
	1321 Bh	—	2.50	5.00	9.00	25.00

NOTE: 5 million examples of 1320 Pa were struck and melted, but at least one specimen is known to exist.

Y#	Date	Mintage	Fine	VF	XF	Unc
26	AH1330 Pa	1.850	3.50	5.50	8.00	20.00

2 MAZUNAS

BRONZE

Y#	Date	Mintage	Fine	VF	XF	Unc
15	AH1320 Be	5 pcs.	—	Proof	—	
	1320 Bh	1.450	1.75	3.00	4.25	15.00
	1320 Bh	—	—	Proof	60.00	120.00
	1320 Fz	—	5.00	10.00	20.00	40.00
	1321 Bh	Inc. w/1320 Bh	1.75	3.00	4.25	10.00
	1321 Pa	6.500	1.75	3.00	4.50	10.00
	1322 Fz	—	7.50	15.00	25.00	50.00
	1323 Fz	—	6.50	12.50	22.50	45.00

Y#	Date	Mintage	Fine	VF	XF	Unc
27	AH1330 Pa	2.790	1.50	5.00	10.00	

NOTE: Coins reportedly dated 1331 Pa probably bore date 1330.

2-1/2 MAZUNAS

BRONZE

Y#	Date	Mintage	Fine	VF	XF	Unc
1	AH1310 Fz	—	75.00	125.00	175.00	400.00

NOTE: Some authorities consider Y#1 to be a 3 Mazuna.

5 MAZUNAS

BRONZE

Y#	Date	Mintage	Fine	VF	XF	Unc
2	AH1310 Fz	—	35.00	65.00	100.00	200.00

Y#	Date	Mintage	Fine	VF	XF	Unc
16	AH1320 Be	5 pcs.	—	Proof	—	—
	1320 Bh	3.120	1.00	3.00	4.00	10.00
	1320 Bh	—	—	Proof	50.00	100.00
	1320 Fz	—	9.00	18.50	35.00	70.00
	1321 Bh	Inc. w/1320 Bh				
			1.00	2.00	3.50	7.00
	1321 Fz	—	Reported, not confirmed			
	1321 Pa	7.950	1.25	3.00	5.00	10.00
	1322 Fz	—	10.00	20.00	30.00	60.00

NOTE: Berlin reports nearly 800,000 pcs. in1904AD (t none have been verified.

Y#	Date	Mintage	Fine	VF	XF	Unc
28	AH1330 Pa	3.180	1.00	2.00	4.00	15.00
	1340 Pa	2.000	1.00	2.00	4.00	15.00
	1340 Py	2.010	1.75	3.50	5.00	15.00

10 MAZUNAS

BRONZE

Y#	Date	Mintage	Fine	VF	XF	Unc
3	AH1310 Fz	—	40.00	65.00	85.00	200.00
	1311 Fz	—	Reported, not confirmed			

Y#	Date	Mintage	Fine	VF	XF	Unc
17	1320 Bh	1.560	1.00	2.00	3.25	7.00
	1320 Be	2.400	1.25	2.50	4.00	8.00
	1320 Fz	—	7.00	15.00	30.00	60.00
	1321 Bh	Inc. w/1320 Bh				
			1.00	2.00	3.25	7.00
	1321 Be	2.600	1.25	2.50	4.00	8.00
	1321 Fz	—	7.00	15.00	30.00	60.00
	1323 Fz	—	10.00	20.00	40.00	80.00

Y#	Date	Mintage	Fine	VF	XF	Unc
29	AH1330 Pa	1.500	.75	1.50	3.00	15.00
	1340 Pa	1.000	.75	1.50	3.00	15.00
	1340 Py	1.000	1.25	2.50	4.50	15.00

1/2 DIRHAM
(=1/20 RIAL)

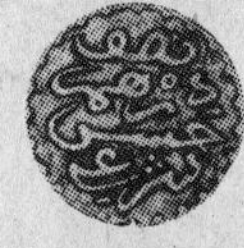

1.4558 gm., .835 SILVER, 15mm, .0391 oz ASW

Y#	Date	Mintage	Fine	VF	XF	Unc
4	AH1299 Pa	2.200	1.25	2.00	3.50	7.50
	1309 Pa	1.700	1.65	2.75	4.50	7.00
	1310 Pa	1.700	1.35	2.25	4.00	7.00
	1311 Pa	1.700	1.50	2.50	4.00	7.00
	1312 Pa	1.700	1.50	2.50	4.00	7.00
	1313 Pa	1.700	1.50	2.50	4.00	7.00
	1314 Pa	1.700	3.00	5.00	7.50	12.50

Y#	Date	Mintage	Fine	VF	XF	Unc
9	AH1313 Be	.560	7.50	12.50	17.50	22.50
	1314 Pa	2.200	2.50	4.00	6.00	10.00
	1315 Pa	1.190	2.50	4.00	6.00	10.00
	1316 Pa	2.280	2.50	4.00	6.00	10.00
	1317 Pa	1.700	2.00	4.00	6.00	20.00
	1318 Pa	.570	4.00	8.00	12.50	17.50
	1319 Pa	—	2.50	5.00	7.50	11.50

1.2500 gm., .835 SILVER, .0336 oz ASW

Y#	Date	Mintage	Fine	VF	XF	Unc
18	AH1320 Ln	.600	1.25	2.50	5.00	20.00
	1320 Pa	2.400	1.50	3.00	6.00	20.00
	1321 Ln	Inc. w/1320 Ln				
			1.50	2.50	5.00	20.00

DIRHAM
(=1/10 RIAL)

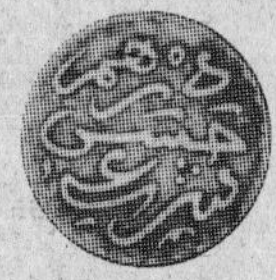

2.9116 gm., .835 SILVER, .0782 oz ASW

Y#	Date	Mintage	Fine	VF	XF	Unc
5	AH1299 Pa	6.800	2.75	4.00	7.50	15.00
	1309 Pa	1.700	2.75	4.00	7.50	15.00
	1310 Pa	1.800	2.75	4.00	7.50	15.00
	1311 Pa	.800	2.75	4.00	7.50	15.00
	1312 Pa	.800	2.75	4.00	7.50	15.00
	1313 Pa	.800	2.75	4.00	7.50	15.00
	1314					
		Inc. w/Y10	10.00	15.00	22.50	35.00

Y#	Date	Mintage	Fine	VF	XF	Unc
10	AH1313 Be	.430	3.00	5.00	9.00	16.50
	1314 Pa	1.400	2.75	4.50	8.50	15.00
	1315 Pa	.860	2.75	4.50	8.50	15.00
	1316 Pa	.860	2.75	4.50	8.50	15.00
	1317 Pa	.860	2.75	4.50	8.50	15.00
	1318 Pa	.290	2.75	4.50	8.50	15.00
	1319 Pa	—	Reported, Not Confirmed			

2.5000 gm., .835 SILVER, .0671 oz ASW

Y#	Date	Mintage	Fine	VF	XF	Unc
19	AH1320 Ln	3.700	2.50	4.50	8.50	25.00
	1321 Ln	I.A.	2.50	4.50	8.50	25.00

Y#	Date	Mintage	Fine	VF	XF	Unc
30	AH1331 Pa	.500	22.50	40.00	65.00	125.00

2-1/2 DIRHAMS
(=1/4 RIAL)

7.2790 gm., .835 SILVER, .1954 oz ASW

Y#	Date	Mintage	Fine	VF	XF	Unc
6	AH1299 Pa	2.100	7.00	10.00	13.50	20.00
	1299 Pa	—	—	—	Proof	80.00
	1309 Pa	.700	7.00	12.50	16.50	23.50
	1310 Pa	.400	7.00	10.00	13.50	20.00
	1311 Pa	.800	7.50	11.00	15.00	21.50
	1312 Pa	.300	7.50	11.00	15.00	21.50
	1313 Pa	.300	7.50	11.00	15.00	21.50
	1314 Pa	—	13.50	17.50	22.50	30.00

Y#	Date	Mintage	Fine	VF	XF	Unc
11	AH1313 Be	.220	12.50	17.50	23.50	35.00
	1314 Pa	1.036	6.00	7.50	10.00	13.50
	1315 Be	.640	6.00	7.50	11.00	15.00
	1315 Pa	.340	6.00	7.50	11.00	15.00
	1316 Pa	.400	6.00	7.50	11.00	15.00
	1317 Pa	.340	6.00	7.50	11.00	15.00
	1318 Be	.150	20.00	27.50	36.50	50.00
	1318 Pa	.110	12.50	17.50	23.50	35.00

6.2500 gm., .835 SILVER, .1678 OZ ASW

Y#	Date	Mintage	Fine	VF	XF	Unc
20	AH1320 Ln	4.900	5.00	7.00	11.50	20.00
	1320 Be	.380	6.00	12.50	20.00	40.00
	1320 Pa	.640	5.50	11.00	17.50	35.00
	1321 Ln	Inc. w/1320 Ln				
			5.00	7.00	11.50	20.00
	1321 Be	4.450	5.00	7.00	11.50	20.00
	1321 Pa	—	—	—	—	—

Y#	Date	Mintage	Fine	VF	XF	Unc
23	AH1329 Pa	3.130	5.00	8.50	15.00	30.00

Y#	Date	Mintage	Fine	VF	XF	Unc
31	AH1331 Pa	2.500	22.50	40.00	65.00	125.00

5 DIRHAMS

(=1/2 RIAL)

14.5580 gm., .835 SILVER, .3908 oz ASW

Y#	Date	Mintage	Fine	VF	XF	Unc
7	AH1299 Pa	1.400	BV	12.50	15.00	20.00
	1309 Pa	.280	BV	12.50	15.00	30.00
	1310 Pa	.170	BV	12.50	15.00	25.00
	1311 Pa	.170	BV	12.50	15.00	27.50
	1312 Pa	.170	BV	12.50	15.00	27.50
	1313 Pa	.170	BV	12.50	15.00	25.00
	1314 Pa	Inc. w/Y12	BV	13.50	22.50	35.00

Y#	Date	Mintage	Fine	VF	XF	Unc
12	AH1313 Be	.110	15.00	22.50	35.00	60.00
	1314 Pa	.517	BV	13.50	20.00	55.00
	1315 Be	.360	BV	15.00	17.50	55.00
	1315 Pa	.160	BV	15.00	17.50	55.00
	1316 Pa	.220	BV	15.00	20.00	55.00
	1317 Pa	.170	BV	15.00	17.50	60.00
	1318 Be	.070	15.00	20.00	30.00	55.00
	1318 Pa	.071	12.50	17.50	25.00	55.00

12.5000 gm., .835 SILVER, .3356 oz ASW

Y#	Date	Mintage	Fine	VF	XF	Unc
21	AH1320 Be	2.510	—	100.00	—	—
	1320 Ln	—	BV	10.00	13.50	40.00
	1321 Ln	—	BV	10.00	13.50	40.00
	1321 Ln	—	—	—	Proof	350.00
	1321 Pa	1.800	BV	10.00	12.50	40.00
	1322 Pa	.540	BV	10.00	15.00	45.00
	1323 Pa	1.090	BV	10.00	15.00	45.00

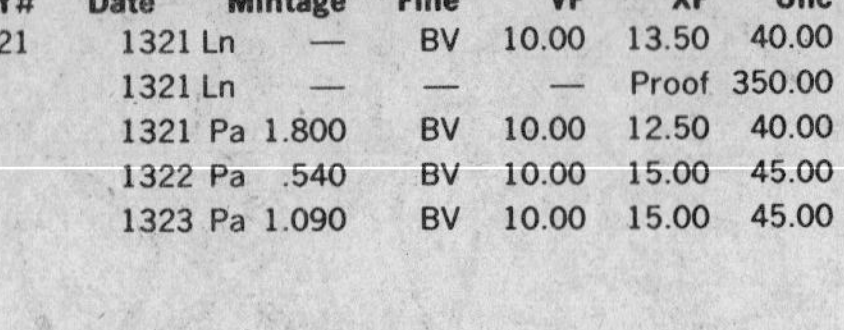

Y#	Date	Mintage	Fine	VF	XF	Unc
24	AH1329 Pa	4.660	BV	10.00	15.00	30.00

Y#	Date	Mintage	Fine	VF	XF	Unc
32	AH1331 Pa	1.500	BV	10.00	13.50	42.50
	1336 Pa	11.500	BV	10.00	12.50	40.00

10 DIRHAMS (RIAL)

29.1160 gm., .900 SILVER, .8425 oz ASW

Y#	Date	Mintage	Fine	VF	XF	Unc
8	AH1299 Pa	.870	27.50	30.00	40.00	60.00

Y#	Date	Mintage	Fine	VF	XF	Unc
13	AH1313 Be	.050	35.00	60.00	125.00	250.00
	1313 Be	—	—	—	Proof	Rare

25.0000 gm., .900 SILVER, .7234 oz ASW

Y#	Date	Mintage	Fine	VF	XF	Unc
22	AH1320 Ln	.330	BV	25.00	32.50	45.00
	1321 Pa	.300	BV	27.50	35.00	60.00

Y#	Date	Mintage	Fine	VF	XF	Unc
25	AH1329 Pa	7.040	BV	25.00	32.50	45.00

Y#	Date	Mintage	Fine	VF	XF	Unc
33	AH1331 Pa	7.000	BV	25.00	30.00	35.00
	1336 Pa	2.600	BV	25.00	30.00	37.50

DECIMAL COINAGE

(FRENCH CURRENCY SYSTEM)

100 Centimes = 1 Franc

100 Francs = 1 Dirham

NOTE: Y46-51 were struck for more than 20 years without change of date, until a new currency was introduced in 1974. Final mintage statistics are not yet available.

25 CENTIMES

COPPER-NICKEL

Y#	Date	Mintage	Fine	VF	XF	Unc
34	ND (1921) Pa w/o privy marks	13.000	.25	.50	1.00	2.50

Rev: Thunderbolt above CENTIMES.

Y#	Date	Mintage	Fine	VF	XF	Unc
	ND (1924) Py	6.020	.75	1.50	3.00	6.50

Rev: Privy marks to left and right of CENTIMES.

Y#	Date	Mintage	Fine	VF	XF	Unc
	ND(1924) Py w/thunderbolt and torch	Inc. Ab.	.75	1.50	3.50	7.00

50 CENTIMES

NICKEL

Y#	Date	Mintage	Fine	VF	XF	Unc
35	ND(1921)Pa w/o privy marks	11.000	.30	.60	1.50	4.00
	ND(1924) Py w/thunderbolt privy mark at lower rev.	3.000	.75	1.50	3.50	6.50

ALUMINUM-BRONZE

Y#	Date	Year	Mintage	VF	XF	Unc
40	AH1364(a)		24.000	.10	.20	.50	2.00

FRANC

NICKEL

Y#	Date	Mintage	Fine	VF	XF	Unc
36	ND(1921)Pa w/o privy marks	13.510	.35	.75	1.75	4.00
	ND(1924) Py w/thunderbolt privy mark below 1 on rev.	3.000	.35	1.25	2.75	6.00

ALUMINUM-BRONZE

Y#	Date	Year	Mintage	VF	XF	Unc
41	AH1364(a)	1945	12.000	.25	.60	2.50

ALUMINUM

Y#	Date	Year	Mintage	VF	XF	Unc
46	AH1370(a)	1951	—	—	.10	.20

2 FRANCS

ALUMINUM-BRONZE

Y#	Date	Year	Mintage	VF	XF	Unc
42	AH1364(a)	1945	12.000	.40	.85	2.00

ALUMINUM

Y#	Date	Year	Mintage	VF	XF	Unc
47	AH1370(a)	1951	—	.10	.15	.25

5 FRANCS

5.0000 gm., .680 SILVER, .1093 oz ASW

Y#	Date	Mintage	Fine	VF	XF	Unc
37	AH1347(a)	4.000	BV	3.50	5.00	10.00
	1352(a)	5.000	BV	3.50	4.50	8.50

ALUMINUM-BRONZE

Y#	Date	Mintage	Fine	VF	XF	Unc
43	AH1365(a)	20.000	.15	.35	.60	1.50

ALUMINUM

Y#	Date	Mintage	Fine	VF	XF	Unc
48	AH1370(a)	—	—	.10	.20	.35

10 FRANCS

10.0000 gm., .680 SILVER, .2186 oz ASW

Y#	Date	Mintage	Fine	VF	XF	Unc
38	AH1347(a)	1.600	BV	6.50	8.50	12.50
	1352(a)	2.9000	BV	6.50	8.00	10.00

COPPER-NICKEL

Y#	Date	Mintage	Fine	VF	XF	Unc
44	AH1366(a)	20.000	.35	.75	1.00	1.50

ALUMINUM-BRONZE

Y#	Date	Mintage	Fine	VF	XF	Unc
49	AH1371(a)	—	—	.10	.20	.35

20 FRANCS

20.0000 gm., .680 SILVER, .4372 oz ASW

Y#	Date	Mintage	Fine	VF	XF	Unc
39	AH1347(a)	—	BV	13.50	18.50	30.00
	1352(a)	2.000	BV	13.50	15.00	25.00

COPPER-NICKEL

Y#	Date	Mintage	Fine	VF	XF	Unc
45	AH1366(a)	6.000	.25	.50	1.00	2.00

ALUMINUM-BRONZE

Y#	Date	Mintage	Fine	VF	XF	Unc
50	AH1371(a)	—	.10	.25	.40	.60

50 FRANCS

ALUMINUM-BRONZE

Y#	Date	Mintage	Fine	VF	XF	Unc
51	AH1371(a)	—	.25	.50	.55	.75

100 FRANCS

4.5000 gm., .720 SILVER, .1041 oz ASW

Y#	Date	Year	Mintage	VF	XF	Unc
A54	AH1370(a)	1950	10.000	—	—	300.00

NOTE: Most were remelted.

Y#	Date	Year	Mintage	VF	XF	Unc
52	AH1372(a)	1953	5.000	BV	BV	3.50

DIRHAM

(=100 FRANCS)

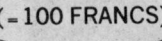

6.0000 gm., .720 SILVER, .1389 oz ASW

Y#	Date	Year	Mintage	VF	XF	Unc
55	AH1380(a)	1960	30.600	BV	BV	5.00

NICKEL

Y#	Date	Year	Mintage	VF	XF	Unc
56	AH1384(a)	1965	35.000	—	.75	1.00
	1388(a)	1968	—	.40	.50	.75
	(1389(a)	1969	—	—	.40	.75

200 FRANCS

9.0000 gm., .720 SILVER, .2083 oz ASW

Y#	Date	Year	Mintage	VF	XF	Unc
53	AH1372(a)	1953	9.200	BV	BV	6.50

500 FRANCS

22.5000 gm., .900 SILVER, .6511 oz ASW

Y#	Date	Year	Mintage	VF	XF	Unc
54	AH1376(a)	1956	2.000	BV	BV	20.00

5 DIRHAM

(=500 FRANCS)

11.7500 gm., .720 SILVER, .2720 oz ASW

Y#	Date	Year	Mintage	VF	XF	Unc
57	AH1384(a)	1965	2.000	BV	BV	8.50

MONETARY REFORM

(1974-)

100 Santimat = 1 Dirham

SANTIM

ALUMINUM

Y#	Date	Year	Mintage	VF	XF	Unc
58	AH1394	1974	10.000	—	—	.10
	1394	1974	.020	—	Proof	1.00
	1395	1975	1.700	—	—	.10

.917 GOLD (OMS)

Y#	Date	Year	Mintage	VF	XF	Unc
58a	AH1394	1974	30 pcs.	—	Proof	—

5 SANTIMAT

BRASS
F.A.O. Issue

Y#	Date	Year	Mintage	VF	XF	Unc
59	AH1394	1974	45.000	—	—	.15
	1394	1974	.020	—	Proof	2.00
	1395	1975	11.000	—	—	.15

.917 GOLD (OMS)

Y#	Date	Year	Mintage	VF	XF	Unc
59a	AH1394	1974	30 pcs.	—	Proof	—

10 SANTIMAT

BRASS
F.A.O. Issue

Y#	Date	Year	Mintage	VF	XF	Unc
60	AH1394	1974	60.000	—	.10	.20
	1394	1974	.020	—	Proof	3.00
	1395	1975	10.900	—	.10	.20

.917 GOLD (OMS)

Y#	Date	Year	Mintage	VF	XF	Unc
60a	AH1394(a)	1974	30 pcs.	—	Proof	—

20 SANTIMAT

BRASS

Y#	Date	Year	Mintage	VF	XF	Unc
61	AH1394	1974	25.000	—	.15	.35
	1394	1974	—	—	Proof	4.00
	1395	1975	10.700	—	.15	.35

.917 GOLD (OMS)

Y#	Date	Year	Mintage	VF	XF	Unc
61a	AH1394	1974	30 pcs.	—	Proof	—

50 SANTIMAT

COPPER-NICKEL

Y#	Date	Year	Mintage	VF	XF	Unc
62	AH1394	1974	35.000	—	.25	.50
	1394	1974	.020	—	Proof	5.00

.917 GOLD (OMS)

Y#	Date	Year	Mintage	VF	XF	Unc
62a	AH1394	1974	30 pcs.	—	Proof	—

DIRHAM

COPPER-NICKEL

Y#	Date	Year	Mintage	VF	XF	Unc
63	AH1394	1974	20.000	.40	.55	.75
	1394	1974	.020	—	Proof	8.00

.917 GOLD (OMS)

Y#	Date	Year	Mintage	VF	XF	Unc
63a	AH1394	1974	30 pcs.	—	Proof	—

5 DIRHAMS

COPPER-NICKEL
FAO Issue: World Food Conference

Y#	Date	Year	Mintage	VF	XF	Unc
64	AH1395	1975	.500	—	—	3.50
	1395	1975	.020	—	Proof	10.00

50 DIRHAMS

35.5000 gm., .925 SILVER, 1.0558 oz ASW
20th Year of Independence.

Y#	Date	Year	Mintage	VF	XF	Unc
65	AH1395	1975				
	1395	1975	.010	—	Proof	50.00

International Women's Year
Obv: Similar to Y#65.

Y#	Date	Year	Mintage	VF	XF	Unc
67	AH1395	1975	—	—	—	—
	1395	1975	.010	—	Proof	45.00

1st Anniversary of the Green March
Obv: Similar to Y#65.

Y#	Date	Year	Mintage	VF	XF	Unc
68	AH1395	1976	.010	—	Proof	45.00
	1397	1977	—	—	—	45.00
	1398	1978	—	—	—	45.00

35,0000 gm.
Obv: Similar to y#65

Y#	Date	Year	Mintage	VF	XF	Unc
—	AH1399	1979	—	—	Proof	45.00

Obv: Similar to y#65

Y#	Date	Year	Mintage	VF	XF	Unc
—	AH1399	1979	—	—	Proof	45.00

250 DIRHAMS

6.4500 gm., .900 GOLD, .1867 oz AGW
Birthday of King Hassan

Y#	Date	Year	Mintage	VF	XF	Unc
66	AH1395	1975	5,000	—	125.00	150.00
	1395	1975	1,020	—	Proof	175.00
	1397	1977	.015	—	125.00	150.00
	1397	1977	2,000	—	Proof	150.00

500 DIRHAMS

12.9000 gm., .900 GOLD, .3733 oz AGW

Y#	Date	Year	Mintage	VF	XF	Unc
—	AH1399	1979	—	—	Proof	250.00

NCLT ISSUES

PATTERNS

KM#	Date	Mintage	Identification	Mkt.Val.
1	AH1301Fz	—	5 Mazunas, Copper	—
XC1	AH1306 Fz	—	1/2 Mazuna, Bronze	—
XB1	AH1306 Fz	—	1 Mazuna, Bronze	—

KM#	Date	Mintage	Identification	Mkt.Val.
X1	AH1306 Fz	—	2-1/2 Mazunas, Bronze	—
X2	AH1306 Fz	—	5 Mazunas, Bronze	—
X3	AH1306	—	10 Mazunas, Bronze	—

ESSAIS (E)

Standard metals unless otherwise noted

Y#	Date	Mintage	Identification	Issue Price	Mkt Val.
E24	AH1329(Pa)	—	5 Dirhams	—	80.00
E26	AH1330(Pa)	—	1 Mazuna	—	50.00
E15	AH1330(Pa)	—	2 Mazunas	—	55.00
E16	AH1330(Pa)	—	5 Mazunas	—	60.00
E17	AH1330(Pa)	—	10 Mazunas	—	65.00
—	AH1331(Pa)	—	5 Dirhams, Nickel	—	75.00
—	AH1331(Pa)	—	5 Dirhams, Aluminum-Bronze	—	75.00
E32a	AH1331(Pa)	—	5 Dirhams, Aluminum	—	60.00
E32b	AH1331(Pa)	—	5 Dirhams, Nickel	—	60.00
E36	ND(Py)	—	1 Franc	—	75.00
E35	ND(Py)	—	50 Centimes	—	70.00
E34	ND(Py)	—	25 Centimes	—	65.00
E29	AH1340(Py)	—	10 Mazunas	—	60.00
E28	AH1340(Py)	—	5 Mazunas	—	55.00
—	AH1347(Pa)	—	10 Francs	—	100.00
—	AH1347(Pa)	—	10 Francs, w/o ESSAI	—	100.00
E38	AH1347(Pa)	—	10 Francs	—	125.00
—	AH1347(Pa)	—	20 Francs	—	125.00
—	AH1347(Pa)	—	20 Francs, w/o ESSAI	—	125.00
E39	AH1347(Pa)	—	20 Francs	—	150.00
E37	AH1347(Pa)	—	5 Francs	—	100.00
E40	AH1361(a)	—	50 Centimes	—	30.00
E41	AH1361(a)	—	1 Franc	—	35.00
E42	AH1361(a)	—	2 Francs	—	40.00
E40	AH1365(a)	—	50 Centimes	—	16.50
E41	AH1365(a)	—	1 Franc	—	18.50
E42	AH1365(a)	—	2 Francs	—	21.50
E43	AH1365(a)	1,100	5 Francs	—	25.00
E44	AH1366(a)	1,100	10 Francs	—	21.50
E45	AH1366(a)	1,100	20 Francs	—	25.00
E46	AH1370(a)	1,100	1 Franc	—	16.50
E47	AH1370(a)	1,100	2 Francs	—	18.50
E48	AH1370(a)	1,100	5 Francs	—	21.50
—	AH1370(a)	1,100	100 Francs, .720 Silver	—	50.00
E49	AH1371(a)	1,100	10 Francs	—	16.50
E50	AH1371(a)	1,100	20 Francs	—	18.50
E51	AH1371(a)	1,100	50 Francs	—	21.50
E52	AH1372(a)	1,100	100 Francs	—	60.00
E53	AH1372(a)	1,100	200 Francs	—	70.00

PIEFORTS (P)

PIEFORTS WITH ESSAI (PE)

(DOUBLE THICKNESS)
Standard metals unless otherwise noted

Y#	Date	Mintage	Identification	Issue Price	Mkt Val.
PE40	AH1361(a)	—	50 Centimes	—	90.00
PE41	AH1361(a)	—	1 Franc	—	100.00
PE42	AH1361(a)	—	2 Francs	—	110.00
PE40	AH1364(a)	104	50 Centimes	—	75.00
PE41	AH1364(a)	104	1 Franc	—	80.00
PE42	AH1364(a)	104	2 Francs	—	85.00
PE43	AH1365(a)	104	5 Francs	—	80.00
PE44	AH1366(a)	104	10 Francs	—	85.00
PE45	AH1366(a)	104	20 Francs	—	90.00
PE46	AH1370(a)	104	1 Franc	—	70.00

Y#	Date	Mintage	Identification	Issue Price	Mkt Val.
PE47	AH1370(a)	104	2 Francs	—	75.00
PE48	AH1370(a)	104	5 Francs	—	80.00
—	AH1370(a)	104	100 Francs, .720 Silver	—	120.00
PE49	AH1371(a)	104	10 Francs	—	70.00
PE50	AH1371(a)	104	20 Francs	—	75.00
PE51	AH1371(a)	104	50 Francs	—	80.00
PE52	AH1372(a)	104	100 Francs	—	85.00
PE53	AH1372(a)	104	200 Francs	—	90.00

MINT SETS

(Fleur de Coin)

KM#	Date	Mintage	Identification	Issue Price	Mkt. Val.
S1	1951-65(8)	—	Y46-51,56,57	—	17.50

PROOF SETS

STANDARD METALS

KM#	Date	Mintage	Identification	Issue Price	Mkt. Val.
101	1974(7)	.020	Y58-64	20.00	30.00
103	1974(6)	30	Y58a-63a	—	—

MOZAMBIQUE

The People's Republic of Mozambique, a former overseas province of Portugal stretching for 1,430 miles (2,301 km.) along the southeast coast of Africa, has an area of 303,769 sq. mi. (786,772 sq. km.) and a population of 9.1 million, 99 percent of whom are native Africans of the Bantu tribes. Capital: Maputo. Agriculture is the chief industry. Cashew nuts, cotton, sugar, copra and tea are exported.

Vasco de Gama explored all the coast of Mozambique in 1498 and found Arab trading posts already established along the coast. Portuguese settlement dates from the establishment of the trading post of Mozambique in 1505. Within five years Portugal absorbed all the former Arab sultanates along the east African coast. The area was organized as a colony in 1907 and became an overseas province in 1952. In Sept. of 1974, after more than a decade of guerrilla warfare with the forces of the Mozambique Liberation Front, Portugal agreed to the independence of Mozambique, effective June 25, 1975.

Maria Theresa talers and other foreign coins stamped with PM or with crowned PM served as an emergency coinage from about 1888 to 1895.

RULERS

Portuguese, until 1975

MINTMARKS

R - Rio

MONETARY SYSTEM

2880 Reis = 6 Cruzados = 1 Onca

REIS

COPPER

C#	Date	Mintage	Fine	VF	XF
57	1853	.100	4.00	8.00	13.50

II (2) REIS

COPPER

C#	Date	Mintage	Fine	VF	XF
58	1853	.100	5.00	10.00	15.00

NOTE: The V Reis, X Reis and XX Reis pieces dated 1853 were issued for circulation in Mozambique. These are also attributed to Portugal and will be found under their appropriate listings.

20 REIS

COPPER

C#	Date	Mintage	Fine	VF	XF
51	1813R	—	7.50	15.00	25.00
	1815R	—	5.00	12.50	22.50

NOTE: The above coins also circulated in St. Thomas and Prince Islands.

C#	Date	Mintage	Fine	VF	XF
54	1819 Rio	—	4.50	10.00	18.00
	1820 Rio	—	7.50	15.00	25.00
	1825	—	5.00	11.50	20.00

NOTE: For coins with c/s '10' refer to Brazil listings. The above coins also circulated in St. Thomas and Prince Islands.

C#	Date	Mintage	Fine	VF	XF
59	1840	.040	6.50	12.50	20.00

40 REIS

COPPER

C#	Date	Mintage	Fine	VF	XF
52	1813 Rio	—	12.50	20.00	35.00
	1815 Rio	—	12.50	20.00	35.00

NOTE: The above coins also circulated in St. Thomas and Prince Islands.

C#	Date	Mintage	Fine	VF	XF
55	1819 Rio	—	7.50	15.00	25.00
	1820 Rio	—	5.00	10.00	15.00
	1821 Bahia	—	7.50	15.00	25.00
	1821 Lisbon	—	4.50	9.00	13.50
	1822	—	6.00	11.50	16.50
	1825	—	6.00	11.50	16.50

NOTE: The difference between the Bahia and Lisbon coins is slight. The crown on the Bahia issue being rounder, touches the outer rim while the Lisbon issue has approximately 2mm between the crown and rim.

NOTE: For coins with c/s '20' refer to Brazil listings. The above coins also circulated in St. Thomas and Prince Islands.

C#	Date	Mintage	Fine	VF	XF
60	1840	.020	6.00	11.50	18.50

80 REIS

COPPER

C#	Date	Mintage	Fine	VF	XF
53	1813R	—	15.00	22.50	40.00

NOTE: The above coins also circulated in St. Thomas and Prince Islands.

C#	Date	Mintage	Fine	VF	XF
56	1819 Rio	—	12.50	20.00	35.00
	1820 Rio	—	10.00	15.00	22.50
	1825	—	8.00	12.50	20.00

NOTE: The above coins also circulated in St. Thomas and Prince Islands.

C#	Date	Mintage	Fine	VF	XF
61	1840	.010	7.50	15.00	25.00

ONCA

SILVER
Small date, lettering.

C#	Date	Mintage	Fine	VF	XF
62	1843	—	25.00	40.00	75.00

Large date, lettering.

C#	Date	Mintage	Fine	VF	XF
62.1	1845	—	35.00	55.00	100.00
	1847	—	50.00	75.00	150.00

1-1/4 MATICAES

GOLD, Rectangular, 11x17mm

C#	Date	Mintage	Fine	VF	XF
65	ND(1835)	—	600.00	900.00	1300.

C#65 with c/s: Rosette

C#	Date	Mintage	Fine	VF	XF
65.1	ND(1851)	—	450.00	700.00	950.00

2-1/2 MATICAES

GOLD, 11X25mm

C#	Date	Mintage	Fine	VF	XF
66	ND(1835)	—	500.00	800.00	1150.

C#66 with c/s: Rosette

C#	Date	Mintage	Fine	VF	XF
66.1	ND(1851)	—	400.00	650.00	850.00

COUNTERSTAMP ISSUES

Decree of May 28, 1767

This decree stated that all crown-sized coins were to be marked with a MR monogram and a 4. There are no known specimens listed in numismatic literature that tell of examples with the 4. The MR appears almost exclusively on Spanish Colonial Pillar dollars. Occasionally it appears on cob pieces and European coins. This counterstamp was to circulate for a longer period than any other Mozambique counterstamp.

8 REALES

SILVER
c/s: MR on Spanish Colonial 'cob' 8 Reales

KM#	Date	Mintage	VG	Fine	VF
4	ND	—	—	Rare	—

c/s: MR on Mexico City 8 Reales, KM#104.

KM#	Date	Mintage	VG	Fine	VF
5	(1747-1760)	—	—	—	—

c/s: MR on Mexico City 8 Reales, KM#105.

KM#	Date	Mintage	VG	Fine	VF
6	(1760-?)	—	—	—	—

Decree of March 31, 1887

This decree ordained that all foreign silver coinage circulating in Mozambique was to be counterstamped with a PM (Provincia de Mocambique) within a circle followed later by a crowned P.M. within a circle countermark. These coins were eventually to be replaced or exchanged by current Portuguese coinage upon their entry into the public treasury. The following list is a basic guide. Caution should be exercised as counterfeits exist. Grades noted are for the basic coin as the countermark is normally found in better condition than the coin bearing it.

1/2 RUPEE

.917 SILVER
c/s: PM on India 1/2 Rupee of Victoria.

Y#	Date	Mintage	Fine	VF	XF
6	—	—	15.00	25.00	35.00

c/s: Crowned PM on India 1/2 Rupee of Victoria.

Y#	Date	Mintage	Fine	VF	XF
—		—	15.00	25.00	35.00

(RUPEE)

.917 SILVER
c/s: PM on India Rupee of William IV.

Y#	Date	Mintage	Fine	VF	XF
C1	1835	—	115.00	125.00	135.00

c/s: Crowned PM on India Rupee of Victoria.

Y#	Date	Mintage	Fine	VF	XF
A1	—	—	15.00	25.00	35.00

c/s: Crowned PM on German East Africa Rupie, Y#4.

Y#	Date	Mintage	Fine	VF	XF
—	—	—	55.00	80.00	135.00

(THALER)

.833 SILVER
c/s: PM on Austrian Maria Theresa Thaler

Y#	Date	Mintage	Fine	VF	XF
D1	(1887)	—	40.00	50.00	100.00

c/s: Crowned PM on Austrian Maria Theresa Thaler

Y#	Date	Mintage	VG	Fine	VF
B1	(1887)	—	35.00	45.00	55.00

NOTE: Other 1/2 Rupee, Rupee and Thaler size coins exist with either style counterstamp. Rupees of German East Africa, Mombasa and Portuguese India are valued at 50 per cent above prices listed.

PRIVATE ISSUES

Companhia Do Nyassa

10 REIS

COPPER

KM#	Date	Mintage	VF	XF	Unc
1	1894H	—	85.00	125.00	120.00

20 REIS

COPPER

KM#	Date	Mintage	VF	XF	Unc
2	1894H	—	90.00	135.00	120.00

500 REIS

SILVER

KM#	Date	Mintage	VF	XF	Unc
3	1894H	—	150.00	200.00	275.00

NOTE: The above issues were produced at the Birmingham mint being struck to match the standards of the coins circulating in Portugal.

DECIMAL COINAGE

100 Centavos = 1 Escudo

10 CENTAVOS

BRONZE

Y#	Date	Mintage	VF	XF	Unc
1	1936	2.000	1.25	2.50	6.50
11	1942	2.000	.75	1.25	3.50

Y#	Date	Mintage	VF	XF	Unc
24	1960	3.750	—	.15	.40
	1961	10.300	—	.10	.40

20 CENTAVOS

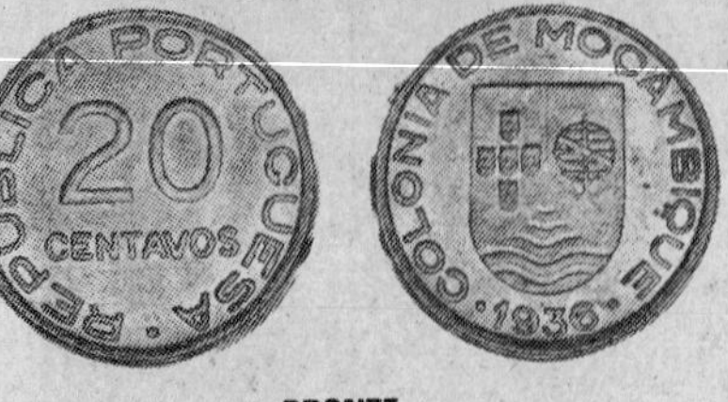

BRONZE

Y#	Date	Mintage	VF	XF	Unc
2	1936	2.500	1.50	2.25	6.75

Y#	Date	Mintage	VF	XF	Unc
12	1941	2.000	1.00	2.00	20.00

Y#	Date	Mintage	VF	XF	Unc
15	1949	8.000	.50	1.00	1.75
	1950	12.500	.50	.75	1.50

Y#	Date	Mintage	VF	XF	Unc
25	1961	12.500	—	.15	1.00

Reduced size, 16mm

Y#	Date	Mintage	VF	XF	Unc
25a	1973	1.798	—	.15	1.00
	1974	13.044	—	—	.25

50 CENTAVOS

COPPER-NICKEL

Y#	Date	Mintage	VF	XF	Unc
3	1936	2.500	1.50	2.25	12.50

BRONZE

Y#	Date	Mintage	VF	XF	Unc
13	1945	2.500	.75	1.75	3.00

NICKEL-BRONZE

Y#	Date	Mintage	VF	XF	Unc
16	1950	20.000	.50	1.00	1.50
	1951	16.000	.50	1.00	1.50

BRONZE

Y#	Date	Mintage	VF	XF	Unc
18	1953	5.010	—	.20	1.00
	1957	24.990	—	.10	.50

Y#	Date	Mintage	VF	XF	Unc
Y18a	1973	6.841	—	—	.50
	1974	23.810	—	—	.50
—	1975	—	—	—	—

ESCUDO

COPPER-NICKEL

Y#	Date	Mintage	VF	XF	Unc
4	1936	2.000	2.00	3.75	20.00

BRONZE

Y#	Date	Mintage	VF	XF	Unc
14	1945	2.000	1.50	3.00	5.00

NICKEL-BRONZE

Y#	Date	Mintage	VF	XF	Unc
17	1950	10.000	1.00	1.75	2.50
	1951	10.000	1.00	1.75	2.50

BRONZE

Y#	Date	Mintage	VF	XF	Unc
19	1953	2.013	.50	.75	1.75
	1957	2.987	.35	.50	1.25
	1962	.600	.50	.75	2.00
	1963	3.258	.10	.35	1.00
	1965	5.000	.10	.35	1.00
	1968	4.500	.10	.35	1.00
	1969	1.642	.15	.50	1.25
	1973	.501	.25	.40	1.00
	1974	25.281	—	.25	.75

2-1/2 ESCUDOS

3.5000 gm., .650 SILVER, .0731 oz ASW

Y#	Date	Mintage	VF	XF	Unc
5	1935	1.200	2.50	3.50	10.00

Y#	Date	Mintage	VF	XF	Unc
8	1938	1.000	2.50	3.50	6.50
	1942	1.200	2.50	3.50	6.00
	1948	—	Reported, Not Confirmed		
	1950	4.000	2.25	2.75	5.00
	1951	4.000	2.25	2.75	5.00

COPPER-NICKEL

Y#	Date	Mintage	VF	XF	Unc
20	1952	4.000	.15	.25	.75
	1953	4.000	.15	.25	.75
	1954	4.000	.15	.25	.75
	1955	4.000	.15	.25	.75
	1965	8.000	.15	.25	.75
	1973	1.767	.15	.25	.75

5 ESCUDOS

7.0000 gm., .650 SILVER, .1463 oz ASW

Y#	Date	Mintage	VF	XF	Unc
6	1935	1.000	BV	4.50	15.00

Y#	Date	Mintage	VF	XF	Unc
9	1938	.800	4.50	6.00	10.00
	1949	8.000	BV	5.00	10.00

3.5000 gm., .650 SILVER, .0731 oz ASW

Y#	Date	Mintage	VF	XF	Unc
21	1960	8.000	BV	2.25	3.00

COPPER-NICKEL

Y#	Date	Mintage	VF	XF	Unc
21a	1971	8.000	.25	.50	1.00
	1973	3.352	.25	.50	1.00

10 ESCUDOS

12.5000 gm., .835 SILVER, .3356 oz ASW

Y#	Date	Mintage	VF	XF	Unc
7	1936	.497	12.00	15.00	20.00

Y#	Date	Mintage	VF	XF	Unc
10	1938	.530	10.00	15.00	25.00

7.0000 gm., .720 SILVER, .1620 oz ASW

Y#	Date	Mintage	VF	XF	Unc
22	1952	1.503	BV	5.00	7.00
	1954	1.335	BV	5.00	7.00
	1955	1.162	BV	5.00	7.00
	1960	2.000	BV	5.00	6.00

5.0000 gm., .680 SILVER, .1093 oz ASW

Y#	Date	Mintage	VF	XF	Unc
22b	1966	.500	3.50	4.50	7.50

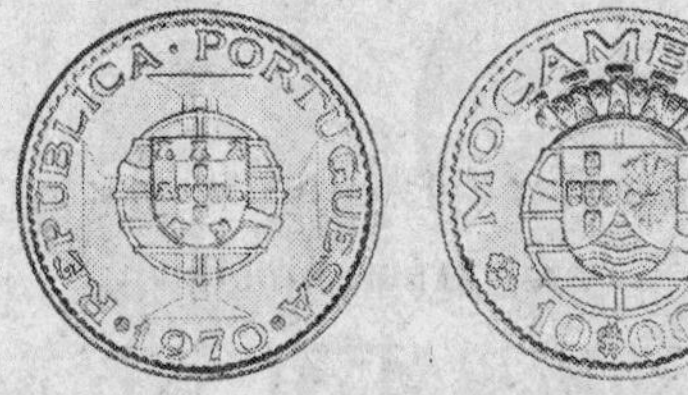

COPPER-NICKEL

Y#	Date	Mintage	VF	XF	Unc
22a	1968	5.000	1.25	2.75	4.00
	1970	4.000	.75	1.00	1.75
	1974	3.366	.75	1.00	1.75

20 ESCUDOS

10.0000 gm., .720 SILVER, .2315 oz ASW

Y#	Date	Mintage	VF	XF	Unc
23	1952	1.004	BV	7.50	8.50
	1955	.996	BV	7.50	8.50
	1960	2.000	BV	7.00	8.00

10.0000 gm., .680 SILVER, .2186 oz ASW

Y#	Date	Mintage	VF	XF	Unc
23a	1966	.250	6.75	8.00	10.00

NICKEL

Y#	Date	Mintage	VF	XF	Unc
26	1971	2.000	1.00	1.50	3.00
	1972	1.158	1.00	1.50	3.00
	1973	—	1.00	1.50	3.00

MONETARY REFORM

100 Centimos = 1 Metica

CENTIMO

ALUMINUM

Y#	Date	Mintage	VF	XF	Unc
—	1975	15.050	—	—	—

2 CENTIMOS

COPPER

Y#	Date	Mintage	VF	XF	Unc
—	1975	8.242	—	—	—

5 CENTIMOS

COPPER

Y#	Date	Mintage	VF	XF	Unc
—	1975	14.898	—	—	—

10 CENTIMOS

COPPER

Y#	Date	Mintage	VF	XF	Unc
—	1975	18.000	—	—	—

20 CENTIMOS

COPPER-NICKEL

Y#	Date	Mintage	VF	XF	Unc
—	1975	8.050	—	—	—

50 CENTIMOS

COPPER-NICKEL

Y#	Date	Mintage	VF	XF	Unc
—	1975	3.050	—	—	—

METICA

COPPER-NICKEL

Y#	Date	Mintage	VF	XF	Unc
27	1975	2.550	—	—	—

2-1/2 METICAS

COPPER-NICKEL

Y#	Date	Mintage	VF	XF	Unc
—	1975	1.500	—	—	—

NCLT ISSUES

PROVAS (Pr)

STANDARD METALS
Stamped 'PROVA' in field

Y#	Date	Mintage	Identification	Issue Price	Mkt Val.
Pr1	1936	—	10 Centavos	—	20.00
Pr2	1936	—	20 Centavos	—	20.00
Pr3	1936	—	50 Centavos	—	30.00
Pr4	1936	—	1 Escudo	—	30.00

Y#	Date	Mintage	Identification	Issue Price	Mkt Val.
Pr5	1935	—	2-1/2 Escudos	—	45.00
Pr6	1935	—	5 Escudos	—	50.00
Pr7	1936	—	10 Escudos	—	60.00
Pr8	1938	—	2-1/2 Escudos	—	45.00
Pr8	1942	—	2-1/2 Escudos	—	45.00
Pr8	1948	—	2-1/2 Escudos	—	—
Pr8	1950	—	2-1/2 Escudos	—	45.00
Pr8	1951	—	2-1/2 Escudos	—	45.00
Pr9	1938	—	5 Escudos	—	45.00
Pr9	1949	—	5 Escudos	—	45.00
Pr9	1951	—	5 Escudos	—	—
Pr9	1952	—	5 Escudos	—	—
Pr10	1938	—	10 Escudos	—	50.00
Pr11	1942	—	10 Centavos	—	20.00
Pr12	1941	—	20 Centavos	—	20.00
Pr13	1945	—	50 Centavos	—	20.00
Pr14	1945	—	1 Escudo	—	20.00
Pr15	1949	—	20 Centavos	—	20.00
Pr15	1949	—	20 Centavos	—	20.00
Pr16	1950	—	50 Centavos	—	20.00
Pr16	1951	—	50 Centavos	—	20.00
Pr17	1950	—	1 Escudo	—	20.00
Pr17	1951	—	1 Escudo	—	20.00
Pr18	1953	—	50 Centavos	—	20.00
Pr18	1957	—	50 Centavos	—	20.00
Pr18a	1973	—	50 Centavos	—	30.00
Pr18a	1974	—	50 Centavos	—	30.00
Pr19	1953	—	1 Escudo	—	20.00
Pr19	1957	—	1 Escudo	—	20.00
Pr19	1962	—	1 Escudo	—	20.00
Pr19	1963	—	1 Escudo	—	20.00
Pr19	1965	—	1 Escudo	—	20.00
Pr19	1968	—	1 Escudo	—	20.00
Pr19	1969	—	1 Escudo	—	20.00
Pr19	1973	—	1 Escudo	—	20.00
Pr19	1974	—	1 Escudo	—	20.00
Pr20	1952	—	2-1/2 Escudos	—	30.00
Pr20	1953	—	2-1/2 Escudos	—	30.00
Pr20	1954	—	2-1/2 Escudos	—	30.00
Pr20	1955	—	2-1/2 Escudos	—	30.00
Pr20	1965	—	2-1/2 Escudos	—	30.00
Pr20	1973	—	2-1/2 Escudos	—	30.00
Pr21	1960	—	5 Escudos	—	45.00
Pr21a	1971	—	5 Escudos	—	30.00
Pr21a	1973	—	5 Escudos	—	30.00
Pr22	1952	—	10 Escudos	—	45.00
Pr22	1954	—	10 Escudos	—	45.00
Pr22	1955	—	10 Escudos	—	45.00
Pr22	1960	—	10 Escudos	—	45.00
Pr22	1966	—	10 Escudos	—	45.00
Pr22a	1968	—	10 Escudos	—	30.00
Pr22a	1970	—	10 Escudos	—	30.00
Pr23	1952	—	20 Escudos	—	45.00
Pr23	1955	—	20 Escudos	—	45.00
Pr23	1960	—	20 Escudos	—	45.00
Pr23	1966	—	20 Escudos	—	45.00
Pr23a	1968	—	20 Escudos	—	30.00
Pr23a	1969	—	20 Escudos	—	30.00
Pr23a	1970	—	20 Escudos	—	30.00
Pr24	1960	—	10 Centavos	—	20.00
Pr24	1961	—	10 Centavos	—	20.00
Pr25	1961	—	20 Centavos	—	20.00
Pr25a	1973	—	20 Centavos	—	20.00
Pr25a	1974	—	20 Centavos	—	20.00
Pr26	1971	—	20 Escudos	—	25.00
Pr26	1972	—	20 Escudos	—	25.00
Pr26	1973	—	20 Escudos	—	25.00

LISTINGS FOR

MUKALLA: refer to Yemen Democratic Republic

MUSCAT & OMAN: refer to Oman

NEJD: refer to Saudi Arabia

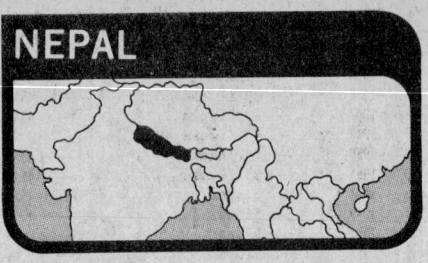

NEPAL

The Kingdom of Nepal, the world's only Hindu kingdom, is a landlocked country located in central Asia along the southern slopes of the Himalayan Mountains. It has an area of 56,136 sq. mi. (145,391 sq. km.) and a population of 13.4 million. Capital: Katmandu. Nepal has substantial deposits of coal, copper, iron, and cobalt but they are largely unexploited. Agriculture is the principal economic activity. Livestock, rice, timber and jute are exported.

Prithvi Narayan Shah, ruler of the principality of Gurkha, formed Nepal from a number of independent mountain states in the latter half of the 18th century. After his death a period of political instability ensued which lasted until the 1840's when the Rana family reduced the monarch to a figurehead and established itself as hereditary Prime Ministers. A popular revolution (1950-51) toppled the Rana family and reconstituted the power in the throne. In 1959 King Mahendra declared Nepal a constitutional monarchy. A new constitution promulgated in 1962 instituted a system of panchavat (village council) democracy from the village to the national levels.

DATING
Saka Era (SE)

Until 1911 AD, Nepalese coins are dated from the Saka Era which began in 78 AD. To arrive at the AD date, add 78 to the date of the coin. These listings have the letters 'SE' before the date.

Vikrama Samvat Era (VS)

Commencing 1911 AD, Nepalese coins are dated from the Vikrama Samvat Era which dates from 57 BC. To arrive at the AD date, subtract 57 from the date of the coin. These listings have the letters (VS) before the date.

RULERS

Prithvi Narayan Saha Deva

पृथ्वी नारायण साह देव

In Gorkha: Saka 1664-1690
1742-1768AD
In Kathmandu: Saka 1690-1696
(1768-1775AD)

Queen of Prithvi Narayan

Narindra Lakshmi Devi

नरिंद्र लक्ष्मी देवी

Pratap Simha Saha Deva

प्रताप सिंह साह देव

Saka 1696-1699 (1775-1777AD)

Queen of Pratap Simha:

Rajendra Lakshmi Devi

राजेन्द्र लक्ष्मी देवी

Rana Bahadur Saha Deva

रण वहादू साह देवः

Saka 1699-1720 (1777-1799AD)

Queens of Rana Bahadur:

Raja Rajesvari Devi

राज राज्येश्वरी देवी

Amara Rajesvari Devi

अमर राज्येश्वरी देवी

Suvarna Prabha Devi

सुवर्ण प्रभा देवी

Mahamahesvari Devi

महामाहेश्वरी देवी

Lalita Tripura Sundari Devi

ललित त्रिपुर सुन्दरी देवी

Girvan Yuddha Vikrama Saha Deva

गीर्वाण युद्ध विक्रम साहदेव

Saka 1720-1738 (1799-1816AD)

Queens of Girvan Yuddha Vikrama:

Siddhi Lakshmi Devi

सिद्धि लक्ष्मी देवी

Goraksha Rajya Lakshmi Devi

गोरक्ष राज्य लक्ष्मी देवी

Rajendra Vikrama Saha Deva

राजेन्द्र विक्रम साहदेव

Saka 1738-1769 (1816-1847 AD)

Queens of Rajendra Vikrama:

(Samrajya) Lakshmi Devi

साम्राज्य लक्ष्मी देवी

Rajya Lakshmi Devi

राज्य लक्ष्मी देवी

Surendra Vikrama Saha Deva

सुरेन्द्र बिक्रम साहदेव

Saka 1769-1803 (1847-1881 AD)

Obv. and rev. border of dots.

C#	Date	Year	Good	VG	Fine	VF
146.1	SE1787	(1865)	3.00	5.00	7.50	10.00

Rev: Legend 9 characters

C#	Date	Year	Good	VG	Fine	VF
146.2	SE1787	(1865)	1.50	2.00	3.50	5.00
	1788	(1866)	1.50	2.00	3.50	5.00
	1789	(1867)	1.50	2.00	3.50	5.00
	1790	(1868)	1.50	2.00	3.50	5.00
	1791	(1869)	1.50	2.00	3.50	5.00
	1792	(1870)	1.50	2.00	3.50	5.00
	1793	(1871)	1.50	2.00	3.50	5.00
	1794	(1872)	1.50	2.00	3.50	5.00
	1796	(1874)	1.50	2.00	3.50	5.00
	1797	(1875)	1.50	2.00	3.50	5.00
	1798	(1876)	1.50	2.00	3.50	5.00
	1799	(1877)	1.50	2.00	3.50	5.00
	1802	(1880)	1.50	2.00	3.50	5.00

Obv: Trident. Rev: Inscription in 4 lines.

Y#	Date	Year	Good	VG	Fine	VF
3	SE1810	(1888)	—	—	Rare	—

Obv: Crossed khukris, circular legends, border of flowers

Y#	Date	Year	Good	VG	Fine	VF
3.1	VS1945	(1888)	—	—	Rare	—

Obv: With 2 footprints above kukhris

Y#	Date	Year	Good	VG	Fine	VF
3.2	VS1945	(1888)	3.00	5.00	8.50	13.50

Obv. and rev. border of XXX's

Y#	Date	Year	Good	VG	Fine	VF
3.3	VS1948	(1891)	1.00	1.50	2.50	4.00
	1949	(1892)	2.00	3.00	5.00	8.00

Circular legends, border of crescents.

Y#	Date	Year	Good	VG	Fine	VF
3.4	VS1949	(1892)	1.00	1.50	2.50	4.00
	1950	(1893)	1.00	1.50	2.50	4.00
	1951	(1894)	1.25	1.75	3.00	5.00

Legends within wreaths

Y#	Date	Year	Good	VG	Fine	VF
A3	VS1949	(1892)	1.00	1.50	2.50	4.00
	1950	(1893)	1.00	1.50	2.50	4.00
	1951	(1894)	1.00	1.50	2.50	4.00
	1952	(1895)	1.00	1.50	2.50	4.00
	1953	(1896)	1.00	1.50	2.50	4.00
	1954	(1897)	1.00	1.50	2.50	4.00
	1955	(1898)	1.00	1.50	2.50	4.00
	1956	(1899)	1.00	1.50	2.50	4.00
	1957	(1900)	1.00	1.50	2.50	4.00
	1959	(1902)	1.00	1.50	2.50	4.00
	1960	(1903)	1.00	1.50	2.50	4.00
	1961	(1904)	1.00	1.50	2.50	4.00
	1962	(1905)	1.00	1.50	2.50	4.00
	1963	(1906)	1.00	1.50	2.50	4.00
	1964	(1907)	1.00	1.50	2.50	4.00

Legends within squares

Y#	Date	Year	Good	VG	Fine	VF
B3	VS1959	(1902)	1.00	1.50	2.25	3.50
	1962	(1905)	1.00	1.50	2.25	3.50
	1963	(1906)	1.00	1.50	2.25	3.50
	1964	(1907)	1.00	1.50	2.25	3.50
	1965	(1908)	1.00	1.50	2.25	3.50
	1966	(1909)	1.00	1.50	2.25	3.50
	1967	(1910)	1.00	1.50	2.25	3.50
	1968	(1911)	1.00	1.50	2.25	3.50

Legend within square/circle

Y#	Date	Year	Good	VG	Fine	VF
C3	VS1959	(1902)	7.50	12.50	20.00	33.50

Y#	Date	Year	Fine	VF	XF	Unc
7	VS1964	(1907)	5.50	9.00	15.00	22.50
	1968	(1911)	8.50	13.50	20.00	30.00

Y#	Date	Year	Good	VG	Fine	VF
27	VS1968	(1911)	2.00	3.00	4.50	7.50
	1969	(1912)	1.00	1.50	2.25	3.50
	1970	(1913)	1.00	1.50	2.25	3.50
	1971	(1914)	1.00	1.50	2.25	3.50
	1972	(1915)	1.00	1.50	2.25	3.50
	1973	(1916)	1.00	1.50	2.25	3.50
	1974	(1917)	1.00	1.50	2.25	3.50
	1975	(1918)	1.00	1.50	2.25	3.50
	1976	(1919)	1.00	1.50	2.25	3.50
	1977	(1920)	1.00	1.50	2.25	3.50

Y#	Date	Year	Fine	VF	XF	Unc
—	VS1975	(1918)	—	—	37.50	50.00

NOTE: The above issue is believed to be a pattern.

Crude, hand struck

Y#	Date	Year	Good	VG	Fine	VF
29	VS1978	(1921)	2.00	3.00	4.50	7.50
	1979	(1922)	2.00	3.00	4.50	7.50
	1980	(1923)	4.00	5.00	7.50	12.50
	1981	(1924)	4.00	5.00	7.50	12.50
	1982	(1925)	4.00	5.00	7.50	12.50
	1983	(1926)	4.00	5.00	7.50	12.50

Machine struck, 3.75 gm.

Y#	Date	Year	Fine	VF	XF	Unc
29.1	VS1975	(1918)	1.25	1.75	3.00	6.00
	1976	(1919)	1.25	1.75	3.00	6.00
	1977	(1920)	1.25	1.75	3.00	6.00
	1977 error, inverted date					
		(1920)	3.00	4.50	7.50	15.00
	1978	(1921)	1.25	1.75	3.00	6.00
	1979	(1922)	1.25	1.75	3.00	6.00
	1980	(1923)	1.50	3.00	5.00	10.00
	1981	(1924)	1.50	3.00	5.00	10.00
	1982	(1925)	1.25	1.75	3.00	6.00
	1984	(1927)	1.25	1.75	3.00	6.00

Y#	Date	Year	Fine	VF	XF	Unc
29.2	VS1985	(1928)	1.25	1.75	3.00	6.00
	1986	(1929)	1.25	1.75	3.00	6.00
	1987	(1930)	1.25	1.75	3.00	6.00

1/16 MOHAR
(2 Paisa)

SILVER

C#	Date	Year	VG	Fine	VF	XF
3	ND	(1768-74)	—	—	Rare	—
29	ND	(1774-77)	—	—	Rare	—

C#	Date	Year	VG	Fine	VF	XF
54	ND	(1777-99)	7.50	11.50	16.50	22.50

Obv: Die of 1 Paisa used in error.

C#	Date	Year	VG	Fine	VF	XF
54.1	ND	(1777-99)	—	—	Rare	—

SILVER, .35 gm.

C#	Date	VG	Fine	VF	XF
76.3	ND (1799-1816)	7.50	11.50	16.50	22.50

NOTE: Three varieties exist.

C#	Date	VG	Fine	VF	XF
94	ND (1816-1847)	5.00	8.50	12.00	16.50
150	ND (1847-1881)	6.00	10.00	13.50	18.50

Y#	Date	Year	Fine	VF	XF	Unc
11	ND (1881-1911)		6.00	10.00	13.50	20.00

NOTE: Five varieties exist.

2 PAISA (Dak)

(1/16 Mohar)

COPPER

Rev. legend: 12 characters

C#	Date	Year	Good	VG	Fine	VF
147	SE1787	(1865)	30.00	50.00	85.00	125.00

Rev. legend: 9 characters

C#	Date	Year	Good	VG	Fine	VF
147.1	SE1788	(1866)	2.00	3.50	5.00	10.00
	1790	(1868)	1.50	2.50	3.50	6.00
	1791	(1869)	1.50	2.50	3.50	6.00
	1796	(1874)	1.75	3.00	4.00	8.00
	1798	(1876)	1.75	3.00	4.00	8.00
	1802	(1880)	—	—	Rare	—

NOTE: Varieties exist.

Circular legends

Y#	Date	Year	Good	VG	Fine	VF
4	VS1948	(1891)	2.00	3.00	5.00	8.00
	1949	(1892)	2.50	3.50	5.00	8.00
	1950	(1893)	2.50	3.50	5.00	8.00

Legends within square/circle

Y#	Date	Year	Good	VG	Fine	VF
B4	1959	(1902)	2.50	4.50	8.50	15.00

Y#	Date	Year	Fine	VF	XF	Unc
8	VS1964	(1907)	8.50	13.50	20.00	30.00
	1968	(1911)	9.00	15.00	22.50	35.00

Crude struck

Y#	Date	Year	Good	VG	Fine	VF
30	VS1978	(1921)	1.00	2.00	3.50	6.00
	1979	(1922)	1.00	2.00	3.50	6.00
	1980	(1923)	1.00	2.00	3.50	6.00
	1981	(1924)	1.00	2.00	3.50	6.00
	1982	(1925)	1.00	2.00	3.50	6.00
	1983	(1926)	1.00	2.00	3.50	6.00
	1984	(1927)	1.00	2.00	3.50	6.00
	1985	(1928)	1.00	2.00	3.50	6.00
	1986	(1929)	1.50	2.50	4.00	7.00
	1987	(1930)	1.50	2.50	4.00	7.00
	1988	(1931)	2.00	3.00	5.00	8.50

Machine struck, 7.50 gm.

Y#	Date	Year	VG	Fine	VF	XF
30.1	VS1976	(1919)	1.00	2.00	3.00	5.00
	1977	(1920)	1.00	2.00	3.00	5.00
	1977 inverted date	(1920)	3.50	5.00	8.50	13.50

Reduced weight, 5.00 gm.

Y#	Date	Year	VG	Fine	VF	XF
30.2	VS1978	(1921)	1.00	2.00	3.00	4.50
	1979	(1922)	1.00	2.00	3.00	4.50
	1980	(1923)	1.00	2.00	3.00	4.50
	1981	(1924)	1.00	2.00	3.00	4.50
	1982	(1925)	1.00	2.00	3.00	4.50
	1983	(1926)	1.00	2.00	3.00	4.50
	1984	(1927)	1.00	2.00	3.00	4.50
	1991	(1934)	1.50	2.50	4.00	6.00

1/8 MOHAR

(4 Paisa)

SILVER, 0.7 gm.

C#	Date	Year	VG	Fine	VF	XF
4	ND	(1768-74)	Reported, not confirmed			
30	ND	(1774-77)	—	—	Rare	—
55	ND	(1777-99)	6.00	9.00	13.50	18.50

Obv: SHRI above sword.

C#	Date	Year	VG	Fine	VF	XF
76.4	ND (1799-1816)		6.00	10.00	13.50	18.50

Obv: Umbrella above sword.

C#	Date	Year	VG	Fine	VF	XF
76.4a	ND (1799-1816)		6.00	10.00	13.50	18.50

Obv: Wreath over sword.

C#	Date	Year	VG	Fine	VF	XF
76.4b	ND (1799-1816)		6.00	10.00	13.50	18.50

Obv: SHRI above sword.

C#	Date	Year	VG	Fine	VF	XF
95	ND (1816-1847)		3.00	5.00	8.50	13.50

Obv: Umbrella above sword.

C#	Date	Year	VG	Fine	VF	XF
95.1	ND (1816-1847)		3.00	5.00	8.50	13.50

C#	Date	Year	VG	Fine	VF	XF
151	ND (1847-1881)		5.00	8.50	12.50	17.50

12.5-15.5mm

Y#	Date	Year	Fine	VF	XF	Unc
12	ND (1881-1911)		7.50	12.50	18.50	27.50

5 PAISA

COPPER

Crude struck

Y#	Date	Year	Good	VG	Fine	VF
31	VS1978	(1921)	1.75	3.00	5.00	7.50
	1979	(1922)	1.75	3.00	5.00	7.50
	1980	(1923)	1.75	3.00	5.00	7.50
	1981	(1924)	1.75	3.00	5.00	7.50
	1982	(1925)	1.75	3.00	5.00	7.50
	1983	(1926)	1.75	3.00	5.00	7.50
	1984	(1927)	1.75	3.00	5.00	7.50
	1985	(1928)	1.75	3.00	5.00	7.50
	1986	(1929)	1.75	3.00	5.00	7.50
	1987	(1930)	1.75	3.00	5.00	7.50
	1988	(1931)	6.00	10.00	14.00	20.00

Machine struck, 18 gm.

Y#	Date	Year	VG	Fine	VF	XF
31.1	VS1975	(1918)	—	—	Rare	—
	1976	(1919)	6.00	10.00	14.00	20.00
	1977	(1920)	1.25	2.25	3.50	6.00
	1977 inverted date	(1920)	3.00	5.00	8.50	12.50

Reduced weight, 14 gm.

Y#	Date	Year	VG	Fine	VF	XF
31.2	VS1978	(1921)	1.25	2.25	3.50	5.00
	1979	(1922)	1.25	2.25	3.50	5.00
	1980	(1923)	1.25	2.25	3.50	5.00
	1981	(1924)	1.25	2.25	3.50	5.00
	1982	(1925)	1.25	2.25	3.50	5.00
	1983	(1926)	1.25	2.25	3.50	5.00
	1984	(1927)	1.25	2.25	3.50	5.00
	1991	(1934)	—	—	Rare	—

1/4 MOHAR

(Suki)

SILVER, 1.4 gm.

Queen Narindra Laksmi Devi

C#	Date	Year	VG	Fine	VF	XF
22	ND	—	—	—	Rare	—
23	SE1690	(1768)	10.00	13.50	18.50	25.00
	1691	(1769)	—	—	Rare	—
	1692	(1770)	10.00	13.50	18.50	25.00

Queen Rajendra Laksmi Devi

C#	Date	Year	VG	Fine	VF	XF
42	SE1696	(1774)	7.00	10.00	15.00	22.50

C#	Date	Year	VG	Fine	VF	XF
42	1697	(1775)	7.00	10.00	15.00	22.50
	1698	(1776)	7.00	10.00	15.00	22.50
	1699	(1777)	7.00	10.00	15.00	22.50

C#	Date	Year	VG	Fine	VF	XF
42.1	SE1700	(1778)	7.00	10.00	15.00	22.50

Rana Bahadur

C#	Date	Year	VG	Fine	VF	XF
56	SE1707	(1785)	8.50	12.50	18.50	25.00
	1708	(1786)	7.00	10.00	15.00	22.50
	1712	(1790)	8.50	12.50	18.50	25.00

Queen Raja Rajeshvari Devi

C#	Date	Year	VG	Fine	VF	XF
72	SE1711	(1789)	7.00	10.00	15.00	22.50
	1712	(1790)	5.00	8.50	12.50	17.50
	1716	(1794)	5.00	8.50	12.50	17.50
	1722	(1800)	7.00	10.00	15.00	22.50
	1723	(1801)	7.00	10.00	15.00	22.50
	1724	(1802)	7.00	10.00	15.00	22.50

Queen Suvarna Prabla Devi

C#	Date	Year	VG	Fine	VF	XF
74	SE1723	(1801)	5.50	9.00	13.50	20.00

Queen Lalita Tripura Sundari Devi

C#	Date	Year	VG	Fine	VF	XF
75	SE1728	(1806)	10.00	13.50	18.50	25.00
	1729	(1807)	10.00	13.50	18.50	25.00
	1738	(1816)	7.00	10.00	15.00	22.50
	1741	(1819)	5.00	8.50	12.50	18.50
	1744	(1822)	10.00	13.50	18.50	25.00

Queen Siddhi Laksmi Devi

C#	Date	Year	VG	Fine	VF	XF
90	SE1730	(1808)	10.00	13.50	18.50	25.00
	1733	(1733)	10.00	13.50	20.00	27.50
	1735	(1735)	10.00	13.50	18.50	25.00

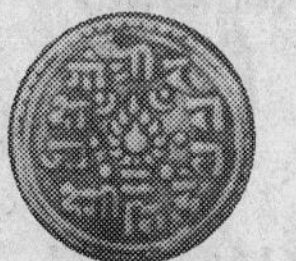

Queen Goraksha Rajya Laksmi Devi

C#	Date	Year	VG	Fine	VF	XF
91	SE1738	(1816)	12.50	17.50	25.00	35.00

Queen Samrajya Laksmi Devi

C#	Date	Year	VG	Fine	VF	XF
125	SE1745	(1823)	8.50	12.50	18.50	25.00
	1746	(1824)	5.00	8.50	12.50	18.50
	1753	(1831)	5.00	8.50	12.50	18.50
	1755	(1833)	5.00	8.50	12.50	18.50

C#	Date	Year	VG	Fine	VF	XF
125.1	SE1746	(1824)	5.00	8.50	12.50	18.50
	1759	(1837)	5.00	8.50	12.50	18.50

Obv: Wreath over vase.

C#	Date	Year	VG	Fine	VF	XF
125.2	SE1746	(1824)	5.00	8.50	12.50	18.50
	1753	(1831)	5.00	8.50	12.50	18.50
	1759	(1837)	5.00	8.50	12.50	18.50

Queen Rajya Laksmi Devi

C#	Date	Year	VG	Fine	VF	XF
140	SE1764	(1842)	8.50	12.50	18.50	25.00
	1766	(1844)	8.50	12.50	18.50	25.00
	1767	(1845)	8.50	12.50	18.50	25.00

Struck with gold dies

C#	Date	Year	VG	Fine	VF	XF
140.1	SE1764	(1842)	11.50	17.50	25.00	35.00

Queen Trailokyaraja Laksmi Devi

C#	Date	Year	VG	Fine	VF	XF
169	SE1769	(1847)	9.00	13.50	20.00	30.00
	1770	(1848)	9.00	13.50	20.00	30.00
	1772	(1850)	11.50	15.00	22.50	32.50

Queen Sura Raja Laksmi Devi

C#	Date	Year	VG	Fine	VF	XF
176	SE1769	(1847)	9.00	13.50	20.00	30.00
	1770	(1848)	9.00	13.50	20.00	30.00
	1772	(1850)	9.00	13.50	20.00	30.00
	1775	(1853)	9.00	13.50	20.00	30.00
	1776	(1854)	9.00	13.50	20.00	30.00
	1777	(1855)	9.00	13.50	20.00	30.00
	1782	(1860)	9.00	13.50	20.00	30.00
	1787	(1865)	9.00	13.50	20.00	30.00
	1788	(1866)	9.00	13.50	20.00	30.00

Queen Deva Raja Laksmi Devi

C#	Date	Year	VG	Fine	VF	XF
186	SE1769	(1847)	9.00	13.50	20.00	30.00
	1770	(1848)	9.00	13.50	20.00	30.00
	1773	(1851)	9.00	13.50	20.00	30.00
	1775	(1853)	9.00	13.50	20.00	30.00
	1776	(1854)	9.00	13.50	20.00	30.00

Queen Punyakumari Raja Laksmi Devi

C#	Date	Year	VG	Fine	VF	XF
193	SE1802	(1880)	15.00	25.00	35.00	50.00

Obv: Moon and spiral sun
Rev: With two moons

C#	Date	Year	VG	Fine	VF	XF
13	SE1804	(1882)	4.50	7.00	10.00	15.00
	1808	(1886)	10.00	17.50	25.00	35.00

Rev: With moon and spiral sun

C#	Date	Year	VG	Fine	VF	XF
13.1	SE1816	(1894)	2.50	3.50	5.00	7.00
	1817	(1895)	2.50	3.50	5.00	7.00

Obv: Moon and dot for sun

C#	Date	Year	VG	Fine	VF	XF
13.2	SE1827	(1905)	2.50	3.50	5.00	7.00

Machine struck

C#	Date	Year	VG	Fine	VF	XF
13.3	SE1833	(1911)	2.50	3.50	5.00	7.00
	1833	(1911)	—	—	Proof	25.00

C#	Date	Year	VG	Fine	VF	XF
32	VS1969	(1912)	2.50	3.50	5.00	7.00
	1970	(1913)	2.50	3.50	5.00	7.00

1/2 MOHAR
(Suka)

SILVER, 2.77 gm.

C#	Date	Year	VG	Fine	VF	XF
6	SE1693	(1771)	—	—	Rare	—

C#	Date	Year	VG	Fine	VF	XF
32	SE1697	(1775)	11.50	17.50	25.00	35.00

C#	Date	Year	VG	Fine	VF	XF
59	SE1701	(1779)	6.00	10.00	15.00	20.00
	1712	(1790)	4.50	7.50	12.50	17.50

C#	Date	Year	VG	Fine	VF	XF
77.2	SE1721	(1799)	7.50	12.50	20.00	30.00
	1728	(1806)	7.50	12.50	20.00	30.00
	1729	(1807)	7.50	12.50	20.00	30.00
	1730	(1808)	5.00	8.50	15.00	22.50
	1733	(1811)	7.50	12.50	20.00	30.00

Mule, Obv. of C#98. Rev. of C#77.2.

C#	Date	Year	VG	Fine	VF	XF
77.2a	SE1730	(1808)	15.00	25.00	40.00	60.00

C#	Date	Year	VG	Fine	VF	XF
98	SE1738	(1816)	3.50	6.50	10.00	15.00
	1744	(1822)	7.50	12.50	20.00	30.00
	1746	(1824)	4.50	7.50	12.50	17.50

Obv: 4 line legend

C#	Date	Year	VG	Fine	VF	XF
98.1	SE1746	(1824)	3.50	6.50	10.00	15.00
	1753	(1831)	3.50	6.50	10.00	15.00
	1755	(1833)	3.50	6.50	10.00	15.00
	1757	(1835)	3.50	6.50	10.00	15.00
	1759	(1837)	3.50	6.50	10.00	15.00
	1762	(1840)	3.50	7.50	12.00	16.50
	1764	(1842)	3.50	7.50	12.00	16.50
	1765	(1843)	3.50	7.50	12.00	16.50
	1766	(1844)	3.50	7.50	12.00	16.50

C#	Date	Year	VG	Fine	VF	XF
153	SE1769	(1847)	5.00	8.50	13.50	20.00
	1770	(1848)	5.00	8.50	13.50	20.00
	1771	(1849)	5.00	8.50	13.50	20.00
	1772	(1850)	5.00	8.50	13.50	20.00
	1775	(1853)	6.00	10.00	15.00	22.50
	1776	(1854)	6.00	10.00	15.00	22.50
	1787	(1865)	5.00	8.50	13.50	20.00
	1790	(1868)	—	—	Rare	—
	1802	(1880)	5.00	8.50	13.50	20.00

Y#	Date	Year	VG	Fine	VF	XF
14	SE1803	(1881)	3.00	5.00	7.00	10.00
	1804	(1882)	6.00	10.00	14.00	20.00

Obv: Legend modified

Y#	Date	Year	VG	Fine	VF	XF
14.1	SE1805	(1883)	3.00	5.00	7.00	10.00

Machine struck with plain edge

Y#	Date	Year	Fine	VF	XF	Unc
14.2	SE1816	(1894)	3.00	5.00	7.00	10.00
	1817	(1895)	3.00	5.00	7.00	10.00

NOTE: Many varieties exist.

Y#	Date	Year	Fine	VF	XF	Unc
14.3	SE1826	(1904)	3.00	5.00	7.00	10.00
	1827	(1905)	3.00	5.00	7.00	10.00
	1829	(1907)	3.50	5.50	8.50	11.50

Machine struck with milled edge

Y#	Date	Year	Fine	VF	XF	Unc
14a	SE1832	(1910)	—	—	Rare	—
	1833	(1911)	2.75	3.50	5.00	7.00
	1833	(1911)	—	—	Proof	35.00

Queen Laksmi Divyeswari

Y#	Date	Year	Fine	VF	XF	Unc
A26	VS1971	(1914)	4.00	6.00	9.00	13.50

Y#	Date	Year	Fine	VF	XF	Unc
33	VS1968	(1911)	2.75	3.50	5.00	7.00
	1970	(1913)	2.75	3.50	5.00	7.00

3/4 MOHAR

SILVER

C#	Date	Year	VG	Fine	VF	XF
77.5	SE1727	(1805)	35.00	45.00	65.00	90.00

MOHAR

SILVER, 5.6 gm.

C#	Date	Year	VG	Fine	VF	XF
7	SE1676	(1754)	6.50	10.00	15.00	20.00
	1678	(1756)	6.50	10.00	15.00	20.00
	1682	(1760)	9.00	15.00	20.00	30.00
	1683	(1761)	9.00	15.00	20.00	30.00
	1690	(1768)	5.00	7.00	10.00	13.50
	1691	(1769)	5.00	7.00	10.00	13.50
	1692	(1770)	5.00	7.00	10.00	13.50
	1693	(1771)	5.00	7.00	10.00	13.50
	1694	(1772)	5.00	7.00	10.00	13.50
	1695	(1773)	5.00	7.00	10.00	13.50
	1696	(1774)	5.00	7.00	10.00	13.50

NOTE: Several varieties exist for SE1676 dated coin.

Rev: Different

C#	Date	Year	VG	Fine	VF	XF
7.1	SE1685	(1763)	10.00	15.00	21.50	30.00

C#	Date	Year	VG	Fine	VF	XF
33	SE1696	(1774)	5.00	7.00	10.00	13.50
	1697	(1775)	5.00	7.00	10.00	13.50
	1698	(1776)	5.00	7.00	10.00	13.50
	1699	(1777)	6.50	10.00	15.00	20.00

Rev: Different

C#	Date	Year	VG	Fine	VF	XF
33.1	SE1697	(1775)	5.50	7.00	9.00	12.50
	1698	(1776)	5.50	7.50	9.00	12.50
	1699	(1777)	7.00	10.00	12.50	15.00

C#	Date	Year	VG	Fine	VF	XF
61	SE1699	(1777)	5.50	7.00	9.00	12.50
	1700	(1778)	5.50	7.00	9.00	12.50
	1701	(1779)	10.00	15.00	20.00	25.00
	1702	(1780)	5.50	7.00	9.00	12.50
	1703	(1781)	5.50	7.00	9.00	12.50
	1704	(1782)	5.50	7.00	9.00	12.50
	1705	(1783)	5.50	7.00	9.00	12.50
	1706	(1784)	5.50	7.00	9.00	12.50
	1707	(1785)	5.50	7.00	9.00	12.50
	1708	(1786)	5.50	7.00	9.00	12.50
	1709	(1787)	5.50	7.00	9.00	12.50
	1710	(1788)	5.50	7.00	9.00	12.50
	1711	(1789)	5.50	7.00	9.00	12.50

27MM

C#	Date	Year	VG	Fine	VF	XF
61.1	SE1711	(1789)	5.50	7.00	9.00	12.50
	1712	(1790)	5.50	7.00	9.00	12.50
	1713	(1791)	5.50	7.00	9.00	12.50
	1714	(1792)	5.50	7.00	9.00	12.50
	1716	(1794)	5.50	7.00	9.00	12.50
	1717	(1795)	5.50	7.00	9.00	12.50
	1718	(1796)	5.50	7.00	9.00	12.50
	1719	(1797)	5.50	7.00	9.00	12.50
	1720	(1798)	5.50	7.00	9.00	12.50

Obv: 2 Shri's above square

C#	Date	Year	VG	Fine	VF	XF
78	SE1720	(1798)	10.00	13.50	17.50	23.50

Obv: 3 Shri's above square

C#	Date	Year	VG	Fine	VF	XF
78.1	SE1721	(1799)	5.50	7.00	9.00	11.50
	1722	(1800)	5.50	7.00	9.00	11.50
	1723	(1801)	5.50	7.00	9.00	11.50
	1724	(1802)	5.50	7.00	9.00	11.50
	1725	(1803)	5.50	7.00	9.00	11.50
	1728	(1806)	5.50	7.00	9.00	11.50
	1729	(1807)	5.50	7.00	9.00	11.50
	1730	(1808)	5.50	7.00	9.00	11.50

C#	Date	Year	VG	Fine	VF	XF
78.1	1731	(1809)	5.50	7.00	9.00	11.50
	1732	(1810)	5.50	7.00	9.00	11.50
	1733	(1811)	5.50	7.00	9.00	11.50
	1734	(1812)	5.50	7.00	9.00	11.50
	1735	(1813)	5.50	7.00	9.00	11.50
	1736	(1814)	5.50	7.00	9.00	11.50
	1737	(1815)	5.50	7.00	9.00	11.50
	1738	(1816)	5.50	7.00	9.00	11.50

C#	Date	Year	VG	Fine	VF	XF
99	SE1738	(1816)	5.50	7.00	9.00	11.50
	1739	(1817)	5.50	7.00	9.00	11.50
	1740	(1818)	5.50	7.00	9.00	11.50
	1741	(1819)	5.50	7.00	9.00	11.50
	1742	(1820)	5.50	7.00	9.00	11.50
	1743	(1821)	5.50	7.00	9.00	11.50
	1744	(1822)	5.50	7.00	9.00	11.50
	1745	(1823)	5.50	7.00	9.00	11.50
	1746	(1824)	5.50	7.00	9.00	11.50
	1747	(1825)	5.50	7.00	9.00	11.50
	1748	(1826)	5.50	7.00	9.00	11.50
	1749	(1827)	5.50	7.00	9.00	11.50
	1750	(1828)	5.50	7.00	9.00	11.50
	1751	(1829)	5.50	7.00	9.00	11.50
	1752	(1830)	5.50	7.00	9.00	11.50
	1753	(1831)	5.50	7.00	9.00	11.50
	1754	(1832)	5.50	7.00	9.00	11.50
	1755	(1833)	5.50	7.00	9.00	11.50
	1756	(1834)	5.50	7.00	9.00	11.50
	1757	(1835)	5.50	7.00	9.00	11.50
	1758	(1836)	5.50	7.00	9.00	11.50
	1759	(1837)	5.50	7.00	9.00	11.50
	1760	(1838)	5.50	7.00	9.00	11.50
	1761	(1839)	7.00	10.00	13.50	17.50
	1761	(1840)	7.00	10.00	13.50	17.50
	1764	(1842)	5.50	7.00	9.00	11.50
	1766	(1844)	5.50	7.00	9.00	11.50
	1767	(1845)	5.50	7.00	9.00	11.50
	1768	(1846)	5.50	7.00	9.00	11.50
	1769	(1847)	7.00	10.00	13.50	17.50

Obv: "Sri 3" above.

C#	Date	Year	VG	Fine	VF	XF
99	SE1740	(1818)	7.00	10.00	13.50	17.50

Obv: Ornamentation reversed.

C#	Date	Year	VG	Fine	VF	XF
99.2	SE1762	(1840)	7.00	10.00	13.50	17.50

C#	Date	Year	VG	Fine	VF	XF
154	SE1769	(1847)	5.50	7.00	9.00	11.50
	1770	(1848)	5.50	7.00	9.00	11.50
	1771	(1849)	5.50	7.00	9.00	11.50
	1772	(1850)	5.50	7.00	9.00	11.50
	1773	(1851)	5.50	7.00	9.00	11.50
	1774	(1852)	7.00	10.00	13.50	17.50
	1775	(1853)	5.50	7.00	9.00	11.50
	1776	(1854)	5.50	7.00	9.00	11.50
	1777	(1855)	5.50	7.00	9.00	11.50
	1778	(1856)	5.50	7.00	9.00	11.50
	1779	(1857)	5.50	7.00	9.00	11.50
	1780	(1858)	5.50	7.00	9.00	11.50
	1781	(1859)	5.50	7.00	9.00	11.50
	1782	(1860)	5.50	7.00	9.00	11.50
	1785	(1863)	7.00	10.00	13.50	17.50
	1786	(1864)	7.00	10.00	13.50	17.50
	1787	(1865)	7.00	10.00	13.50	17.50
	1788	(1866)	7.00	10.00	13.50	17.50
	1789	(1867)	7.00	10.00	13.50	17.50
	1790	(1868)	7.00	10.00	13.50	17.50
	1791	(1869)	7.00	10.00	13.50	17.50
	1792	(1870)	7.00	10.00	13.50	17.50
	1793	(1871)	7.00	10.00	13.50	17.50
	1794	(1872)	7.00	10.00	13.50	17.50
	1796	(1874)	7.00	10.00	13.50	17.50
	1797	(1875)	7.00	10.00	13.50	17.50

C#	Date	Year	VG	Fine	VF	XF
154	1800	(1878)	5.50	7.00	9.00	11.50
	1801	(1879)	5.50	7.00	9.00	11.50
	1802	(1880)	5.50	7.00	9.00	11.50
	1803	(1881)	7.00	10.00	13.50	17.50

Machine struck, plain edge

C#	Date	Year	VG	Fine	VF	XF
154a	SE1786	(1864)	12.50	15.00	20.00	27.50
	1787	(1865)	7.50	10.00	15.00	22.50
	1788	(1866)	12.50	15.00	20.00	27.50
	1789	(1867)	12.50	15.00	20.00	27.50

Struck using gold dies.

C#	Date	Year	VG	Fine	VF	XF
154b	SE1801	(1879)	12.50	15.00	20.00	27.50

Handstruck

Y#	Date	Year	VG	Fine	VF	XF
15	SE1803	(1881)	5.50	7.00	9.00	11.50
	1804	(1882)	5.50	7.00	9.00	11.50

Machine struck, plain edge

Y#	Date	Year	Fine	VF	XF	Unc
15.1	SE1804	(1882)	5.50	6.50	8.00	10.00
	1805	(1883)	5.50	6.50	8.00	10.00
	1806	(1884)	5.50	6.50	8.00	10.00
	1807	(1885)	5.50	6.50	8.00	10.00
	1808	(1886)	5.50	6.50	8.00	10.00
	1809	(1887)	5.50	6.50	8.00	10.00
	1810	(1888)	5.50	6.50	8.00	10.00
	1811	(1889)	7.00	10.00	15.50	25.00
	1816	(1894)	5.50	6.50	8.00	10.00
	1817	(1895)	5.50	6.50	8.00	10.00
	1818	(1896)	5.50	6.50	8.00	10.00
	1819	(1897)	5.50	6.50	8.00	10.00
	1820	(1898)	5.50	6.50	8.00	10.00
	1821	(1899)	5.50	6.50	8.00	10.00
	1822	(1900)	5.50	6.50	8.00	10.00
	1823	(1901)	5.50	6.50	8.00	10.00
	1824	(1902)	5.50	6.50	8.00	10.00
	1825	(1903)	5.50	6.50	8.00	10.00
	1826	(1904)	5.50	6.50	8.00	10.00
	1827	(1905)	5.50	6.50	8.00	10.00

Machine struck, milled edge

Y#	Date	Year	Fine	VF	XF	Unc
15.2	SE1826	(1904)	5.50	6.50	8.00	10.00
	1827	(1905)	5.50	6.50	8.00	10.00
	1828	(1906)	5.50	6.50	8.00	10.00
	1829	(1907)	5.50	6.50	8.00	10.00
	1830	(1908)	5.50	6.50	8.00	10.00
	1831	(1909)	5.50	6.50	8.00	10.00
	1832	(1910)	5.50	6.50	8.00	10.00
	1833	(1911)	—	25.00	35.00	50.00

NOTE: The date 1833 was only issued in presentation sets.

Rev: Gold die, in error.

Y#	Date	Year	Fine	VF	XF	Unc
15.3	SE1825	(1903)	10.00	15.00	25.00	32.50

Queen Laksmi Divyeswari

Y#	Date	Year	Fine	VF	XF	Unc
B26	VS1971	(1914)	5.50	7.00	9.00	11.50

Y#	Date	Year	Fine	VF	XF	Unc
34	VS1968	(1911)	5.50	6.50	8.00	10.00
	1969	(1912)	5.50	6.50	8.00	10.00
	1971	(1914)	5.50	6.50	8.00	10.00

1- 1/2 MOHARS

SILVER, 8.4 gm.

C#	Date	Year	VG	Fine	VF	XF
79	SE1725	(1803)	15.00	25.00	35.00	50.00
	1726	(1804)	15.00	25.00	35.00	50.00

C#	Date	Year	VG	Fine	VF	XF
79.1	SE1727	(1805)	30.00	50.00	75.00	100.00

NOTE: The date 1787 in actuality was struck on an incorrect flan and for that reason is not listed.

2 MOHARS

SILVER, 11.2 gm.

C#	Date	Year	VG	Fine	VF	XF
8	SE1693	(1771)	45.00	75.00	110.00	150.00
34	SE1696	(1774)	20.00	30.00	40.00	55.00

C#	Date	Year	VG	Fine	VF	XF
63	SE1703	(1781)	20.00	30.00	40.00	55.00
	1705	(1783)	20.00	30.00	40.00	55.00

27MM

C#	Date	Year	VG	Fine	VF	XF
63.1	SE1712	(1790)	15.00	20.00	25.00	32.50
	1719	(1797)	20.00	30.00	40.00	55.00
100	SE1738	(1816)	17.50	27.50	37.50	50.00
	1740	(1818)	17.50	27.50	37.50	50.00
	1742	(1820)	17.50	27.50	37.50	50.00
	1743	(1821)	17.50	27.50	37.50	50.00
	1753	(1831)	17.50	27.50	37.50	50.00
	1757	(1835)	17.50	27.50	37.50	50.00
	1764	(1842)	17.50	27.50	37.50	50.00
155	SE1769	(1847)	12.50	18.50	27.50	40.00
	1770	(1848)	12.50	18.50	27.50	40.00
	1771	(1849)	12.50	18.50	27.50	40.00
	1772	(1850)	12.50	18.50	27.50	40.00
	1777	(1855)	12.50	17.50	27.50	40.00
	1796	(1874)	12.50	18.50	27.50	40.00
	1797	(1875)	12.50	18.50	27.50	40.00
	1801	(1879)	11.50	13.50	18.50	25.00
	1802	(1880)	12.50	18.50	27.50	40.00

Machine struck, milled edge

C#	Date	Year	VG	Fine	VF	XF
155.1	SE1786	(1864)	—	—	Rare	—

26mm
Struck with regualr gold dies

C#	Date	Year	VG	Fine	VF	XF
155.5	SE1801	(1879)	11.50	13.50	18.50	25.00

28mm

C#	Date	Year	VG	Fine	VF	XF
155.6	SE1801	(1879)	11.50	15.00	20.00	28.50

27mm
Machine struck with plain edge

Y#	Date	Year	Fine	VF	XF	Unc
16	SE1804	(1882)	17.50	27.50	40.00	55.00
	1811	(1889)	17.50	27.50	40.00	55.00
	1817	(1895)	11.50	13.50	18.50	27.50

Machine struck using gold dies, plain edge.

Y#	Date	Year	Fine	VF	XF	Unc
16.1	SE1821	(1899)	11.50	13.50	17.50	25.00

Y#	Date	Year	Fine	VF	XF	Unc
16.2	SE1829	(1907)	13.50	20.00	27.50	37.50
	1831	(1909)	11.50	14.00	16.50	20.00

Machine struck, 29mm

Y#	Date	Year	Fine	VF	XF	Unc
16a	SE1832	(1910)	11.50	14.00	16.50	20.00
	1833	(1911)	11.50	13.00	15.00	18.50

Y#	Date	Year	Fine	VF	XF	Unc
35	VS1968	(1911)	11.50	13.50	17.50	25.00
	1969	(1912)	11.50	13.00	15.00	18.50
	1970	(1913)	11.50	13.00	15.00	18.50
	1971	(1914)	11.50	13.00	15.00	18.50
	1972	(1915)	11.50	13.00	15.00	18.50
	1973	(1916)	13.50	20.00	28.50	40.00
	1974	(1917)	11.50	13.00	15.00	18.50
	1975	(1918)	11.50	13.00	15.00	18.50
	1976	(1919)	11.50	13.00	15.00	18.50
	1977	(1920)	11.50	13.00	15.00	18.50
	1978	(1921)	11.50	13.00	15.00	18.50
	1979	(1922)	11.50	13.00	15.00	18.50
	1980	(1923)	11.50	13.00	15.00	18.50
	1982	(1925)	11.50	13.00	15.00	18.50
	1983	(1926)	11.50	13.00	15.00	18.50
	1984	(1927)	11.50	13.00	15.00	18.50
	1985	(1928)	11.50	13.00	15.00	18.50
	1986	(1929)	11.50	13.00	15.00	18.50
	1987	(1930)	11.50	13.00	15.00	18.50
	1988	(1931)	11.50	13.00	15.00	18.50
	1989	(1932)	11.50	13.50	17.50	25.00

3 MOHARS

SILVER, 16.8 gm.

C#	Date	Year	VG	Fine	VF	XF
79.5	SE1725	(1803)	100.00	150.00	200.00	275.00
79.6	SE1726	(1804)	100.00	150.00	200.00	275.00

4 MOHARS

SILVER, 22.4 gm.

C#	Date	Year	VG	Fine	VF	XF
156	SE1769	(1847)	—	—	Rare	—

Y#	Date	Year	Fine	VF	XF	Unc
17	SE1817	(1895)	45.00	75.00	100.00	150.00

Y#	Date	Year	Fine	VF	XF	Unc
17.1	SE1833	(1911)	35.00	50.00	75.00	125.00

Y#	Date	Year	Fine	VF	XF	Unc
36	VS1971	(1914)	27.50	40.00	55.00	75.00

GOLD COINAGE

Nepalese gold coinage until recently did not carry any denominations and was traded for silver, etc. at the local bullion exchange rate. The four basic denominations used in the following listing are as follows:

MOHAR
5.6 Gm. Multiples and Fractions
TOLA
12.48 Gm. Multiples and Fractions
RUPEE
11.66 Gm. Multiples and Fractions
10 Gm. Reduced Weight
(Commencing 1966)
MULTIPLES AND FRACTIONS

NOTE: Many of the gold and silver issues were struck from the same dies.

1/128 MOHAR
(Dam)

GOLD, Uniface, .043 gm.
Similar to Silver 1/128 Mohar, C#11.

C#	Date	Year	VG	Fine	VF	XF
9	ND	(1768-74)	—	—	Rare	—
35	ND	(1774-77)	—	—	Rare	—
64	ND	(1777-99)	10.00	13.50	17.50	23.50
80	ND	(1799-1816)	10.00	13.50	18.50	25.00
101	ND	(1816-1847)	10.00	13.50	18.50	25.00

Actual Size 2 X Actual Size

C#	Date	Year	VG	Fine	VF	XF
157	ND	(1847-1881)	10.00	13.50	18.50	25.00

With 5 characters around sword
Similar to 1/64 Mohar, Y#A18.1

Y#	Date	Year	Fine	VF	XF	Unc
18	ND	(1881-1911)	10.00	13.50	18.50	25.00

Four characters about sword
Similar to 1/64 Mohar, Y#A18.

Y#	Date	Year	Fine	VF	XF	Unc
18.1	ND	(1881-1911)	10.00	13.50	18.50	25.00

Actual Size 2 X Actual Size

With circle around characters

Y#	Date	Year	Fine	VF	XF	Unc
18.2	ND	(1881-1911)	10.00	13.50	18.50	25.00

Actual Size 2 X Actual Size

With 2 characters under sword

Y#	Date	Year	Fine	VF	XF	Unc
18.3	ND	(1881-1911)	10.00	13.50	18.50	25.00

Y#	Date	Year	Fine	VF	XF	Unc
A37	ND	(1911-1950)	—	—	Rare	—

1/64 MOHAR
(2 Dam)

Actual Size 2 X Actual Size

GOLD, Uniface, 0.87 gm.
Obv: 4 characters around sword

Y#	Date	Year	Fine	VF	XF	Unc
A18	ND	(1881-1911)	13.50	17.50	22.50	30.00

Actual Size 2 X Actual Size

Obv: 5 characters around sword

Y#	Date	Year	Fine	VF	XF	Unc
A18.1	ND	(1881-1911)	13.50	17.50	22.50	30.00

1/32 MOHAR
(Paisa)

GOLD, Uniface, .175 gm.

C#	Date	Year	VG	Fine	VF	XF
10	ND	(1768-74)	—	—	Rare	—
65	ND	(1777-99)	13.50	18.50	23.50	30.00
81	ND	(1799-1816)	13.50	18.50	23.50	30.00
103	ND	(1816-1847)	13.50	18.50	23.50	30.00
157.5	ND	(1847-1881)	13.50	18.50	23.50	30.00

With 5 characters around sword

Y#	Date	Year	Fine	VF	XF	Unc
19	ND	(1881-1911)	13.50	18.50	23.50	30.00

With 4 characters around sword

Y#	Date	Year	Fine	VF	XF	Unc
19.1	ND	(1881-1911)	13.50	18.50	23.50	30.00
C37	ND	(1911-1950)	15.00	22.50	28.50	35.00

1/16 MOHAR
(Adhani)

GOLD

C#	Date	Year	Good	VG	Fine	VF
11	ND	(1768-74)	—	—	Rare	—
36	ND	(1774-77)	—	—	Rare	—
66	ND	(1777-99)	15.00	22.50	28.50	35.00

GOLD, 0.35 gm.

C#	Date	Year	VG	Fine	VF	XF
82	ND	(1799-1816)	13.50	18.50	23.50	30.00

NOTE: Three varieties exist.

C#	Date	Year	VG	Fine	VF	XF
104	ND	(1816-1847)	13.50	18.50	23.50	30.00
158	ND	(1847-1881)	13.50	18.50	23.50	30.00

Y#	Date	Year	Fine	VF	XF	Unc
20	ND	(1881-1911)	13.50	18.50	23.50	30.00
20.1	SE(18)33	(1911)	15.00	22.50	28.50	35.00

Y#	Date	Year	Fine	VF	XF	Unc
D37	VS(19)77	(1920)	20.00	28.50	40.00	50.00

1/8 MOHAR
(Ani)

GOLD

C#	Date	Year	Good	VG	Fine	VF
12	ND	(1768-74)	—	—	Rare	—

C#	Date	Year	Good	VG	Fine	VF
37	ND	(1774-77)	—	—	Rare	—

C#	Date	Year	Good	VG	Fine	VF
67	ND	(1777-99)	20.00	28.50	40.00	50.00

GOLD, 0.70 gm.
5 characters around sword

C#	Date	Year	VG	Fine	VF	XF
83	ND	(1799-1816)	22.50	28.50	35.00	45.00

4 characters around sword

C#	Date	Year	VG	Fine	VF	XF
83.1	ND	(1799-1816)	22.50	28.50	35.00	45.00

NOTE: Two other varieties exist.

C#	Date	Year	VG	Fine	VF	XF
105	ND	(1816-1847)	22.50	28.50	35.00	45.00

NOTE: 3 varieties exist.

C#	Date	Year	VG	Fine	VF	XF
159	ND	(1847-1881)	22.50	28.50	35.00	45.00

Y#	Date	Year	Fine	VF	XF	Unc
21	ND	(1881-1911)	22.50	28.50	35.00	45.00

NOTE: 3 varieties exist.

Y#	Date	Year	Fine	VF	XF	Unc
21.1	SE(18)33	(1911)	22.50	28.50	35.00	45.00

Y#	Date	Year	Fine	VF	XF	Unc
E37	VS(19)76	(1919)	35.00	40.00	50.00	75.00

1/4 MOHAR
(SUKI)

GOLD, 1.40 gm.

Queen Narindra Laksmi Devi

C#	Date	Year	Good	VG	Fine	VF
26	SE1693	(1771)	—	—	Rare	—

Queen Rajendra Laksmi Devi

C#	Date	Year	Good	VG	Fine	VF
46	SE1698	(1776)	—	—	Rare	—
46.1	SE1700	(1778)	40.00	50.00	65.00	85.00

Rana Bahadur

C#	Date	Year	Good	VG	Fine	VF
68	SE1712	(1790)	40.00	55.00	70.00	90.00

Queen Rajeshuari Devi

C#	Date	Year	Good	VG	Fine	VF
72.5	SE1716	(1794)	40.00	50.00	65.00	85.00
	1723	(1801)	40.00	50.00	70.00	90.00
	1724	(1802)	40.00	50.00	70.00	90.00

Queen Subharna Prabha Devi

C#	Date	Year	Good	VG	Fine	VF
74.5	SE1723	(1801)	40.00	50.00	70.00	90.00

Queen Amara Rajesvari Devi

C#	Date	Year	Good	VG	Fine	VF
73.5	SE1724	(1802)	60.00	70.00	85.00	100.00

Queen Lalita Tripura Sundari Devi

C#	Date	Year	VG	Fine	VF	XF
75.5	SE1728	(1806)	40.00	50.00	65.00	85.00
	1729	(1807)	40.00	50.00	65.00	85.00
	1741	(1819)	40.00	50.00	65.00	85.00

Queen Siddhi Laksmi Devi

C#	Date	Year	VG	Fine	VF	XF
90.5	SE1730	(1808)	40.00	50.00	65.00	85.00
	1732	(1810)	40.00	50.00	65.00	85.00
	1733	(1811)	40.00	50.00	65.00	85.00
	1736	(1814)	40.00	50.00	65.00	85.00

Queen Samrajya Laksmi Devi

C#	Date	Year	VG	Fine	VF	XF
135	SE1746	(1824)	40.00	50.00	65.00	85.00
	1757	(1835)	40.00	50.00	65.00	85.00
	1758	(1836)	40.00	50.00	65.00	85.00
	1759	(1837)	40.00	50.00	65.00	85.00

Queen Rajya Laksmi Devi

C#	Date	Year	VG	Fine	VF	XF
143	SE1764	(1842)	40.00	50.00	65.00	85.00

Queen Sura Raja Laksmi Devi

C#	Date	Year	VG	Fine	VF	XF
178	SE1769	(1847)	40.00	50.00	65.00	85.00
	1787	(1868)	40.00	50.00	65.00	85.00
	1790	(1868)	40.00	50.00	65.00	85.00

Queen Deva Raja Laksmi Deva

C#	Date	Year	VG	Fine	VF	XF
188	SE1770	(1848)	40.00	50.00	65.00	85.00

Queen Punyakumari Raja Laksmi Devi

C#	Date	Year	VG	Fine	VF	XF
196	SE1802	(1880)	55.00	75.00	100.00	135.00

Y#	Date	Year	Fine	VF	XF	Unc
22	SE1808	(1886)	40.00	50.00	60.00	75.00
	1811	(1889)	40.00	50.00	60.00	75.00
	1817	(1895)	40.00	50.00	60.00	75.00
	1823	(1901)	40.00	50.00	60.00	75.00
	1829	(1907)	40.00	50.00	60.00	75.00
	1833	(1911)	40.00	50.00	60.00	75.00

1/2 MOHAR
(Suka)

GOLD, 2.8 gm.

C#	Date	Year	Good	VG	Fine	VF
14	SE1693	(1771)	—	—	Rare	—
38	SE1697	(1775)	—	—	Rare	—
69	SE1701	(1779)	65.00	75.00	85.00	100.00
	1712	(1790)	65.00	75.00	85.00	100.00

C#	Date	Year	VG	Fine	VF	XF
85	SE1721	(1799)	70.00	80.00	100.00	125.00
	1728	(1806)	70.00	80.00	100.00	125.00
	1729	(1807)	70.00	80.00	100.00	125.00

C#	Date	Year	VG	Fine	VF	XF
85.1	SE1732	(1810)	70.00	80.00	100.00	125.00
	1733	(1811)	70.00	80.00	100.00	125.00
	1736	(1814)	70.00	80.00	100.00	125.00

C#	Date	Year	VG	Fine	VF	XF
107	SE1741	(1819)	70.00	80.00	100.00	125.00
	1744	(1822)	65.00	75.00	85.00	100.00
	1746	(1824)	65.00	75.00	85.00	100.00
	1753	(1831)	65.00	75.00	85.00	100.00
	1757	(1835)	65.00	75.00	85.00	100.00
	1758	(1836)	65.00	75.00	85.00	100.00
	1764	(1842)	65.00	75.00	85.00	100.00
	1766	(1844)	65.00	75.00	85.00	100.00
161	SE1769	(1847)	65.00	75.00	85.00	100.00
	1770	(1848)	65.00	75.00	85.00	100.00
	1790	(1868)	65.00	75.00	85.00	100.00
	1802	(1880)	65.00	75.00	85.00	100.00

Y#	Date	Year	Fine	VF	XF	Unc
23	SE1805	(1883)	65.00	75.00	85.00	100.00
	1817	(1895)	65.00	75.00	85.00	100.00
	1823	(1901)	65.00	75.00	85.00	100.00
	1829	(1907)	65.00	75.00	85.00	100.00
	1833	(1911)	65.00	75.00	85.00	100.00

Y#	Date	Year	Mintage	VF	XF	Unc
37	VS1969	(1912)	—	—	—	—

MOHAR

GOLD, 5.60 gm.

C#	Date	Year	VG	Fine	VF	XF
15	SE1693	(1771)	—	—	Rare	—
	1694	(1772)	—	—	Rare	—
	1695	(1773)	—	—	Rare	—
39	SE1698	(1776)	—	—	Rare	—
70	SE1700	(1778)	115.00	125.00	145.00	165.00
	1702	(1780)	115.00	125.00	145.00	165.00
	1703	(1781)	115.00	125.00	145.00	165.00
	1705	(1783)	115.00	125.00	145.00	165.00
	1706	(1784)	115.00	125.00	145.00	165.00
	1708	(1786)	115.00	125.00	145.00	165.00
	1709	(1787)	115.00	125.00	145.00	165.00
70.1	SE1716	(1794)	115.00	125.00	145.00	165.00
	1719	(1797)	115.00	125.00	145.00	165.00
	1720	(1798)	115.00	125.00	145.00	165.00
86	SE1721	(1799)	115.00	125.00	140.00	165.00
	1723	(1801)	115.00	125.00	140.00	165.00
	1724	(1802)	115.00	125.00	140.00	165.00
	1733	(1811)	115.00	125.00	140.00	165.00
108	SE1738	(1816)	115.00	125.00	140.00	165.00
108.1	SE1741	(1819)	115.00	125.00	140.00	165.00
	1746	(1824)	115.00	125.00	140.00	165.00
	1758	(1836)	115.00	125.00	140.00	165.00
	1760	(1838)	115.00	125.00	140.00	165.00
	1764	(1842)	115.00	125.00	140.00	165.00
	1766	(1844)	115.00	125.00	140.00	165.00

C#	Date	Year	VG	Fine	VF	XF
108.1	1768	(1846)	115.00	125.00	140.00	165.00
162	SE1769	(1847)	115.00	125.00	145.00	175.00
	1791	(1869)	115.00	125.00	145.00	175.00
	1794	(1872)	115.00	125.00	145.00	175.00
	1802	(1880)	115.00	125.00	145.00	175.00

Y#	Date	Year	Fine	VF	XF	Unc
24	SE1804	(1882)	115.00	125.00	145.00	175.00
	1805	(1883)	115.00	125.00	145.00	175.00
	1809	(1887)	115.00	125.00	145.00	175.00
	1817	(1895)	115.00	125.00	140.00	165.00
	1820	(1898)	115.00	125.00	140.00	165.00
	1823	(1901)	115.00	125.00	140.00	165.00
	1825	(1903)	115.00	125.00	140.00	165.00
	1826	(1904)	115.00	125.00	140.00	165.00
	1827	(1905)	115.00	125.00	140.00	165.00

With milled edge

Y#	Date	Year	Fine	VF	XF	Unc
24.1	SE1828	(1906)	115.00	125.00	140.00	165.00
	1829	(1907)	115.00	125.00	140.00	165.00
	1831	(1909)	115.00	125.00	140.00	165.00
	1833	(1911)	115.00	125.00	140.00	165.00
24.2	VS1949	(1892)	115.00	125.00	145.00	175.00

Y#	Date	Year	Fine	VF	XF	Unc
38	VS1969	(1912)	115.00	125.00	140.00	165.00
	1975	(1918)	115.00	125.00	140.00	165.00
	1978	(1921)	115.00	125.00	140.00	165.00
	1979	(1922)	115.00	125.00	140.00	165.00
	1981	(1924)	115.00	125.00	140.00	165.00
	1983	(1926)	115.00	125.00	140.00	165.00
	1985	(1928)	115.00	125.00	140.00	165.00
	1986	(1929)	115.00	125.00	140.00	165.00
	1987	(1930)	115.00	125.00	140.00	165.00
	1989	(1932)	115.00	125.00	140.00	165.00
	1990	(1933)	115.00	125.00	140.00	165.00
	1991	(1934)	115.00	125.00	140.00	165.00
	1998	(1941)	115.00	125.00	140.00	165.00
	1999	(1942)	115.00	125.00	140.00	165.00
	2000	(1943)	115.00	125.00	140.00	165.00
	2003	(1946)	115.00	125.00	140.00	165.00
	2005	(1948)	115.00	125.00	140.00	165.00

Queen Laksmi Divyesvari

Y#	Date	Year	Fine	VF	XF	Unc
C26	VS1971	(1914)	115.00	125.00	145.00	175.00

1/2 BAKLA RUPEE

GOLD, 6.24 gm.

C#	Date	Year	VG	Fine	VF	XF
154.3	SE1773	(1851)	125.00	135.00	160.00	200.00
	1786	(1864)	125.00	135.00	160.00	200.00
	1787	(1865)	125.00	135.00	160.00	200.00

Y#	Date	Year	Fine	VF	XF	Unc
A24	SE1805	(1883)	125.00	135.00	160.00	200.00
	1806	(1884)	125.00	135.00	160.00	200.00
	1807	(1885)	125.00	135.00	160.00	200.00
	1808	(1886)	125.00	135.00	160.00	200.00
	1809	(1887)	125.00	135.00	160.00	200.00
	1810	(1888)	125.00	135.00	160.00	200.00
	1811	(1889)	125.00	135.00	160.00	200.00
	1812	(1890)	125.00	135.00	160.00	200.00
	1813	(1891)	125.00	135.00	160.00	200.00
	1814	(1892)	125.00	135.00	160.00	200.00
	1815	(1893)	125.00	135.00	160.00	200.00
	1816	(1894)	125.00	135.00	160.00	200.00
	1817	(1895)	125.00	135.00	160.00	200.00
	1818	(1896)	125.00	135.00	160.00	200.00
	1819	(1897)	125.00	135.00	160.00	200.00
	1820	(1898)	125.00	135.00	160.00	200.00
	1821	(1899)	125.00	135.00	160.00	200.00
	1822	(1900)	125.00	135.00	160.00	200.00
	1823	(1901)	125.00	135.00	160.00	200.00
	1824	(1902)	125.00	135.00	160.00	200.00
	1825	(1903)	125.00	135.00	160.00	200.00
	1826	(1904)	125.00	135.00	160.00	200.00

1-1/2 MOHARS

GOLD, 8.4 gm.

C#	Date	Year	VG	Fine	VF	XF
87	SE1726	(1804)	180.00	210.00	250.00	300.00
	1728	(1806)	180.00	210.00	250.00	300.00

C#	Date	Year	VG	Fine	VF	XF
87	1729	(1807)	180.00	210.00	250.00	300.00

Rev: Hexagon

C#	Date	Year	VG	Fine	VF	XF
87a	SE1736	(1814)	180.00	210.00	250.00	300.00

2 MOHARS

GOLD, 11.2 gm.

C#	Date	Year	VG	Fine	VF	XF
16	SE1693	(1771)	—	—	Rare	—
	1695	(1773)	—	—	Rare	—
	1696	(1774)	—	—	Rare	—

C#	Date	Year	VG	Fine	VF	XF
40	SE1696	(1774)	—	—	Rare	—

GOLD, 11.2 gm.

C#	Date	Year	VG	Fine	VF	XF
88	SE1721	(1799)	240.00	265.00	300.00	375.00
	1733	(1811)	240.00	265.00	300.00	375.00

C#	Date	Year	VG	Fine	VF	XF
109	SE1738	(1816)	240.00	265.00	300.00	375.00
	1741	(1819)	240.00	265.00	300.00	375.00
	1746	(1824)	240.00	265.00	300.00	375.00
	1757	(1835)	240.00	265.00	300.00	375.00
	1768	(1846)	240.00	265.00	300.00	375.00

RUPEE

GOLD, 12.48 gm.

Queen Goraksha Rajya Laksmi Devi

C#	Date	Year	VG	Fine	VF	XF
91.5	SE1735	(1813)	—	—	Rare	—

Queen Samrajya Laksmi Devi

C#	Date	Year	VG	Fine	VF	XF
138	SE1759	(1837)	—	—	Rare	—

Queen Trailokya Raja Laksmi Devi

C#	Date	Year	VG	Fine	VF	XF
173	SE1769	(1847)	—	—	Rare	—
	1771	(1849)	285.00	350.00	425.00	500.00

BAKLA RUPEE

GOLD

C#	Date	Year	VG	Fine	VF	XF
163	SE1769	(1847)	235.00	250.00	285.00	325.00
	1773	(1851)	235.00	250.00	285.00	325.00
	1774	(1852)	235.00	250.00	285.00	325.00
	1778	(1856)	235.00	250.00	285.00	325.00
	1780	(1858)	235.00	250.00	285.00	325.00
	1786	(1864)	235.00	250.00	285.00	325.00
	1787	(1865)	235.00	250.00	285.00	325.00
	1791	(1869)	235.00	250.00	285.00	325.00
	1793	(1871)	235.00	250.00	275.00	300.00
	1794	(1872)	235.00	250.00	285.00	325.00
	1802	(1880)	235.00	250.00	285.00	325.00

With oblique edge milling

Y#	Date	Year	Fine	VF	XF	Unc
25	SE1803	(1881)	235.00	250.00	275.00	325.00
	1805	(1883)	235.00	250.00	275.00	325.00
	1805	(1889)	235.00	250.00	275.00	325.00

With vertical edge milling

Y#	Date	Year	Fine	VF	XF	Unc
25.1	SE1804	(1882)	235.00	250.00	275.00	325.00

With plain edge

Y#	Date	Year	Fine	VF	XF	Unc
25.2	SE1807	(1885)	235.00	250.00	275.00	325.00
	1817	(1895)	235.00	250.00	275.00	325.00
	1820	(1898)	235.00	250.00	275.00	300.00
	1823	(1901)	235.00	250.00	275.00	300.00
	1824	(1902)	235.00	250.00	275.00	325.00
	1825	(1903)	235.00	250.00	275.00	300.00
	1826	(1904)	235.00	250.00	275.00	300.00

With vertical edge milling

Y#	Date	Year	Fine	VF	XF	Unc
25.3	SE1828	(1906)	235.00	250.00	275.00	300.00
	1829	(1907)	235.00	250.00	285.00	325.00
	1831	(1909)	235.00	250.00	275.00	300.00
	1832	(1910)	235.00	250.00	275.00	300.00
	1833	(1911)	235.00	250.00	275.00	300.00

With plain edge

Y#	Date	Year	Fine	VF	XF	Unc
25.4	VS1947	(1890)	235.00	250.00	285.00	325.00

With oblique edge milling

Y#	Date	Year	Fine	VF	XF	Unc
25.5	VS1949	(1892)	235.00	250.00	285.00	325.00

Y#	Date	Year	Fine	VF	XF	Unc
39	VS1969	(1912)	235.00	250.00	275.00	300.00
	1974	(1917)	235.00	250.00	285.00	325.00
	1975	(1918)	235.00	250.00	275.00	300.00
	1976	(1919)	235.00	250.00	275.00	300.00
	1977	(1920)	235.00	250.00	275.00	300.00
	1978	(1921)	235.00	250.00	275.00	300.00
	1979	(1922)	235.00	250.00	275.00	300.00
	1980	(1923)	235.00	250.00	275.00	300.00
	1981	(1924)	235.00	250.00	275.00	300.00
	1982	(1925)	235.00	250.00	275.00	300.00
	1983	(1926)	235.00	250.00	275.00	300.00
	1984	(1927)	235.00	250.00	275.00	300.00
	1985	(1928)	235.00	250.00	275.00	300.00
	1986	(1929)	235.00	250.00	275.00	300.00
	1987	(1930)	235.00	250.00	275.00	300.00
	1988	(1931)	235.00	250.00	275.00	300.00
	1989	(1932)	235.00	250.00	275.00	300.00
	1990	(1933)	235.00	250.00	275.00	300.00
	1991	(1934)	235.00	250.00	275.00	300.00
	1998	(1941)	235.00	250.00	275.00	300.00
	1999	(1942)	235.00	250.00	275.00	300.00
39	2000	(1943)	235.00	250.00	275.00	300.00
	2003	(1946)	235.00	250.00	275.00	300.00
	2005	(1948)	235.00	250.00	275.00	300.00

2 RUPEES

GOLD, 23.32 gm.

C#	Date	Year	Mintage	Fine	VF	XF
17	SE1693	(1771)	—	—	Rare	—
41	SE1698	(1776)	—	—	Rare	—
71	SE1718	(1796)	—	—	Rare	—

C#	Date	Year	VG	Fine	VF	XF
89	SE1721	(1799)	—	—	Rare	—
110	SE1762	(1840)	—	—	Rare	—

C#	Date	Year	Fine	VF	XF	Unc
164	SE1769	(1847)	450.00	525.00	650.00	800.00
	1771	(1849)	450.00	525.00	650.00	800.00
	1794	(1872)	450.00	525.00	650.00	800.00

With oblique edge milling

Y#	Date	Year	Fine	VF	XF	Unc
26	SE1811	(1889)	450.00	550.00	650.00	750.00

Rev. die of Silver 2 Rupees, Y#17.

Y#	Date	Year	Fine	VF	XF	Unc
26.1	SE1817	(1895)	450.00	550.00	650.00	750.00

With plain edge

Y#	Date	Year	Fine	VF	XF	Unc
26.2	SE1817	(1895)	450.00	550.00	650.00	750.00
	1825	(1902)	450.00	550.00	650.00	750.00

With milled edge, 27mm

Y#	Date	Year	Fine	VF	XF	Unc
26.3	SE1829	(1907)	450.00	525.00	600.00	700.00

With milled edge, 29mm

Y#	Date	Year	Fine	VF	XF	Unc
26.4	SE1833	(1911)	450.00	525.00	575.00	650.00

DECIMAL COINAGE

MONETARY SYSTEM

100 Paisa = 1 Rupee

1/4 PAISA

COPPER

Y#	Date	Year	Fine	VF	XF	Unc
A42	VS2000	(1943)	15.00	25.00	30.00	40.00

1/2 PAISA

COPPER

Y#	Date	Year	Mintage	VF	XF	Unc
B42	VS2004	(1947)	—	25.00	30.00	40.00

PAISA

COPPER

Y#	Date	Year	Fine	VF	XF	Unc
40	VS1990	(1933)	1.00	2.00	3.00	5.00
	1991	(1934)	1.00	2.00	3.00	5.00
	1992	(1935)	1.00	2.00	3.00	5.00
	1993	(1936)	1.00	2.00	3.00	5.00
	1994	(1937)	1.00	2.00	3.00	5.00
	1995	(1938)	1.00	2.00	3.00	5.00
	1996	(1939)	1.00	2.00	3.00	5.00
	1997	(1940)	1.00	2.00	3.00	5.00
43	VS2005	(1948)	.75	1.25	1.75	2.50

BRASS

Y#	Date	Year	Fine	VF	XF	Unc
43a	VS2001	(1944)	.30	.50	.75	1.00
	2003	(1946)	.30	.50	.75	1.00
	2004	(1947)	3.00	5.00	7.00	10.00
	2005	(1948)	.30	.50	.75	1.00
	2006	(1949)	.60	1.00	1.25	1.75

18mm

Y#	Date	Year	Fine	VF	XF	Unc
58	VS2010	(1953)	9.00	15.00	20.00	25.00
	2011	(1954)	—	—	Rare	—
	2012	(1955) Restrike		1.00	1.50	2.00

17.5mm

Y#	Date	Year	Fine	VF	XF	Unc
58.1	VS2012	(1955)	1.25	2.00	2.50	3.50

Mahendra Coronation

Y#	Date	Year	Fine	VF	XF	Unc
66	VS2013	(1956)	.30	.50	.75	1.00

Denomination with shading

Y#	Date	Year	Fine	VF	XF	Unc
78	VS2014	(1957)	.10	.15	.25	.40
	2015	(1958)	.10	.15	.25	.40

Y#	Date	Year	Fine	VF	XF	Unc
78	2018	(1961)	.10	.15	.25	.40
	2019	(1962)	.10	.15	.25	.50
	2020	(1963)	.10	.15	.25	.50

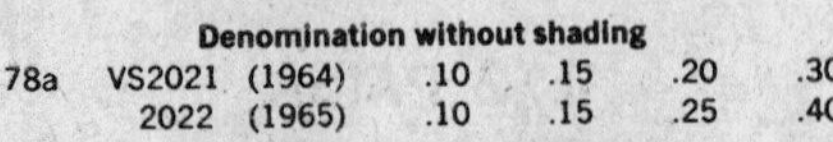

Denomination without shading

Y#	Date	Year	Fine	VF	XF	Unc
78a	VS2021	(1964)	.10	.15	.20	.30
	2022	(1965)	.10	.15	.25	.40

ALUMIÑUM

Y#	Date	Year	Mintage	VF	XF	Unc
90	VS2023	(1966)	—	.10	.15	.25
	2025	(1968)	—	.10	.15	.25
	2026	(1969)	—	.10	.15	.25
	2027	(1970)	2,187	Proof Only		3.50
	2028	(1971)	—	.10	.15	.25
	2028	(1971)	2,380	—	Proof	3.50

Y#	Date	Year	Mintage	VF	XF	Unc
99	VS2028	(1972)	.010	.30	.60	1.00
	2029	(1972)	3.036	.10	.15	.25
	2029	(1972)	3,943	—	Proof	3.00
	2030	(1973)	1.279	.10	.15	.25
	2030	(1973)	8,891	—	Proof	1.50
	2031	(1974)	.430	—	—	—
	2031	(1974)	.011	—	Proof	1.00
	2032	(1975)	.324	.10	.15	.25
	2032	(1975)	—	—	Proof	1.00
	2033	(1976)	.217	—	.10	.25
	2034	(1977)	.823	.10	.15	.25
	2035	(1978)	.075	.10	.15	.25

Virendra Coronation

Y#	Date	Year	Mintage	VF	XF	Unc
109	VS2031	(1974)	.075	.10	.15	.25

2 PAISA

COPPER

Y#	Date	Year	VG	Fine	VF	XF
41	VS1992	(1935)	3.00	5.00	8.50	13.50

COPPER, 27mm

Y#	Date	Year	Fine	VF	XF	Unc
A41	VS1992	(1935)	2.50	4.00	6.50	10.00
	1993	(1936)	1.25	2.00	3.00	5.00
	1994	(1937)	1.25	2.00	3.00	5.00
	1995	(1938)	1.25	2.00	3.00	5.00
	1996	(1939)	1.25	2.00	3.00	5.00
	1997	(1940)	2.50	4.00	6.50	10.00

25mm

Y#	Date	Year	Fine	VF	XF	Unc
A41a	VS1992	(1935)	.60	1.00	1.75	3.00
	1994	(1937)	.50	.75	1.50	2.50
	1995	(1938)	2.00	3.50	5.00	7.50
	1996	(1939)	.30	.50	1.00	1.50
	1997	(1940)	.50	.75	1.50	2.50
	1998	(1941)	.50	.75	1.50	2.50
	1999	(1942)	.50	.75	1.50	2.50

23mm

Y#	Date	Year	Fine	VF	XF	Unc
44	VS1999	(1942)	.30	.50	1.00	2.00
	2000	(1943)	.30	.50	1.00	2.00
	2003	(1945)	.30	.50	1.00	2.00
	2005	(1948)	3.00	5.00	7.00	10.00

BRASS

Y#	Date	Year	Fine	VF	XF	Unc
44a	VS1999	(1942)	.30	.50	1.00	2.00
	2000	(1943)	.30	.50	1.00	2.00
	2001	(1944)	.30	.50	1.00	2.00
	2005	(1948)	1.75	3.00	5.00	7.50
	2008	(1951)	.30	.50	1.00	2.00
	2009	(1952)	.30	.50	1.00	2.00
	2010	(1953)	.30	.50	1.00	2.00

21mm

Y#	Date	Year	Fine	VF	XF	Unc
59	VS2010	(1953)	12.50	20.00	37.50	60.00
	2011	(1954)	—	—	Rare	—
	2011	(1954)		Restrike	1.50	2.50

20mm

Y#	Date	Year	Fine	VF	XF	Unc
59a	VS2012	(1955)	.30	.50	.75	1.50
	2013	(1956)	.30	.50	.75	1.50
	2014	(1957)	.30	.50	.75	1.50

Mahendra Coronation

Y#	Date	Year	Fine	VF	XF	Unc
67	VS2013	(1956)	.30	.50	.75	1.00

Denomination with shading

Y#	Date	Year	Fine	VF	XF	Unc
79	VS2014	(1957)	.10	.15	.25	.40
	2015	(1958)	.10	.15	.25	.40
	2016	(1959)	.10	.15	.25	.40
	2018	(1961)	.10	.15	.25	.40
	2019	(1962)	.10	.15	.25	.40
	2020	(1963)	.10	.15	.25	.40

Denomination without shading

Y#	Date	Year	Fine	VF	XF	Unc
79a	VS2021	(1964)	.10	.15	.20	.35
	2022	(1965)	.10	.15	.25	.50
	2023	(1966)	.10	.15	.25	.50

ALUMINUM

Y#	Date	Year	Mintage	VF	XF	Unc
91	VS2023	(1966)	—	.10	.15	.25
	2024	(1967)	—	.10	.15	.25
	2025	(1968)	—	.10	.15	.25
	2026	(1969)	—	.10	.15	.25
	2027	(1970)	—	.10	.15	.25
	2027	(1970)	2,187	—	Proof	4.00
	2028	(1971)	—	.10	.15	.25
	2028	(1971)	2,380	—	Proof	4.00

Y#	Date	Year	Mintage	VF	XF	Unc
100	VS2028	(1972)	8,319	.50	.75	1.25
	2029	(1972)	5.206	.10	.15	.25
	2029	(1972)	3,943	—	Proof	3.50
	2030	(1973)	2.563	.10	.15	.25
	2030	(1973)	8,891	—	Proof	2.00
	2031	(1974)	.011	Proof only		1.25
	2032	(1975)	—	Proof only		—
	2033	(1976)	.072	.10	.15	.30
	2035	(1978)	—	.10	.15	.30

4 PAISA

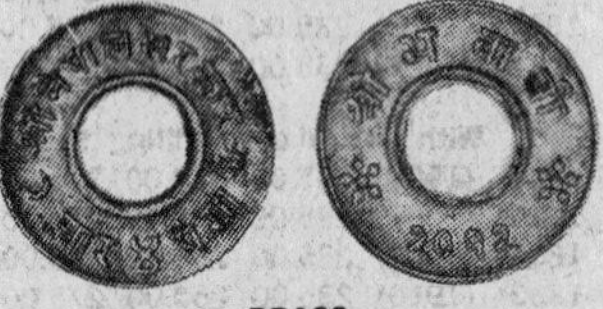

BRASS

Y#	Date	Year	Fine	VF	XF	Unc
61	VS2012	(1955)	1.00	1.75	3.00	5.00

5 PAISA

COPPER

Y#	Date	Year	Fine	VF	XF	Unc
42	VS1992	(1935)	1.75	3.00	4.50	6.50
	1993	(1936)	1.75	3.00	4.50	6.50
	1994	(1937)	1.75	3.00	4.50	6.50
	1995	(1938)	1.25	2.00	3.00	5.00
	1996	(1939)	1.75	3.00	4.50	6.50
	1997	(1940)	1.75	3.00	4.50	6.50
	1998	(1941)	1.75	3.00	4.50	6.50

COPPER-NICKEL

Y#	Date	Year	Fine	VF	XF	Unc
45	VS2000	(1943)	.65	1.00	1.50	2.50
	2009	(1952)	1.75	3.00	5.00	8.50
	2010	(1953)	1.25	2.00	3.00	5.00

NOTE: The original issues were struck in German silver (copper-nickel-zinc) while restrikes were struck in copper-nickel.

BRONZE, 3.89 gm.

Y#	Date	Year	Fine	VF	XF	Unc
62	VS2010	(1953)	2.75	4.50	7.00	10.00
	2011	(1954)	.65	1.00	2.75	5.00
	2012	(1955)	.30	.50	.75	1.00
	2013	(1956)	.30	.50	.75	1.00
	2014	(1957)	.30	.50	.75	1.00

COPPER-NICKEL, 4.04 gm. (OMS?)

Y#	Date	Year	Fine	VF	XF	Unc
62a	VS2014	(1957)	—	—	—	—

BRONZE
Mahendra Coronation

Y#	Date	Year	Fine	VF	XF	Unc
68	VS2013	(1956)	.35	.60	1.00	1.50

22mm
Denomination with shading

Y#	Date	Year	Fine	VF	XF	Unc
80	VS2014	(1957)	.10	.20	.30	.75
	2015	(1958)	.10	.20	.30	.75
	2016	(1959)	.10	.30	.50	1.00
	2017	(1960)	.10	.20	.30	.75
	2018	(1961)	.10	.20	.30	.75
	2019	(1962)	.10	.20	.30	.75
	2020	(1963)	.10	.20	.30	.75

ALUMINUM BRONZE, 22mm
Denomination without shading

Y#	Date	Year	Fine	VF	XF	Unc
80a	VS2021	(1964)	.60	1.00	1.50	2.50

BRONZE, 20.5mm

Y#	Date	Year	Fine	VF	XF	Unc
80b	VS2021	(1964)	.10	.15	.25	.50
	2022	(1965)	.10	.15	.30	.60
	2023	(1966)	.10	.15	.30	.60

ALUMINUM

Y#	Date	Year	Mintage	VF	XF	Unc
92	VS2023	(1966)	—	.15	.25	.50
	2024	(1967)	—	.10	.20	.35
	2025	(1968)	—	.10	.20	.35
	2026	(1969)	—	.10	.20	.25
	2027	(1970)	—	.10	.20	.35
	2027	(1970)	2,187	—	Proof	4.50
	2028	(1971)	—	.10	.20	.35
	2028	(1971)	2,380	—	Proof	4.50

Y#	Date	Year	Mintage	VF	XF	Unc
101	VS2028	(1972)	3.700	.10	.20	.35
	2029	(1972)	23.578	.10	.20	.35
	2029	(1972)	3,943	—	Proof	4.00
	2030	(1973)	12.320	.10	.20	.35
	2030	(1973)	8,891	—	Proof	2.25
	2031	(1974)	15.730	.10	.20	.35
	2031	(1974)	.011	—	Proof	1.50
	2032	(1975)	19.747	.10	.20	.35
	2032	(1975)	—	—	Proof	—
	2033	(1976)	29.619	.10	.20	.30
	2034	(1977)	28.046	.10	.20	.30
	2035	(1978)	—	.10	.20	.30

F.A.O. Issue

Y#	Date	Year	Mintage	VF	XF	Unc
107	VS2031	(1974)	4.584	—	.10	.15

Virendra Coronation

Y#	Date	Year	Mintage	VF	XF	Unc
110	VS2031	(1974)	2.869	—	.25	.50

1/16 RUPEE

SILVER

Y#	Date	Year	Fine	VF	XF	Unc
A45	VS(19)96	(1939)	12.50	20.00	32.50	50.00

10 PAISA

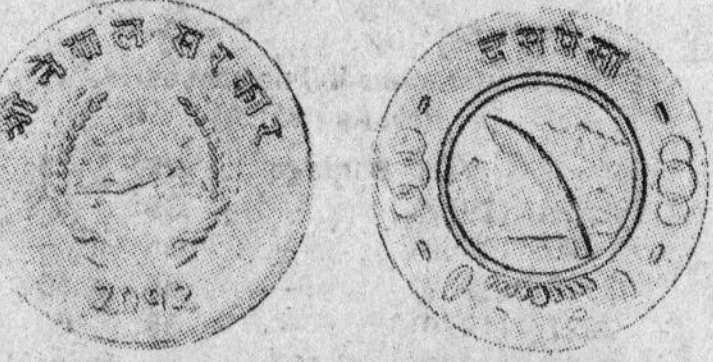

BRONZE

Y#	Date	Year	Fine	VF	XF	Unc
63	VS2010	(1953)	2.75	4.50	7.00	10.00
	2011	(1954)	.15	.25	.50	1.00
	2012	(1955)	.15	.25	.50	1.00

Mahendra Coronation

Y#	Date	Year	Fine	VF	XF	Unc
69	VS2013	(1956)	.30	.50	.75	1.50

25mm
Numeral with shading

Y#	Date	Year	Fine	VF	XF	Unc
81	VS2014	(1957)	2.75	4.50	7.00	10.00
81	2015	(1958)	.15	.25	.50	.75
	2016	(1959)	3.00	5.00	7.00	10.00
	2018	(1961)	.15	.25	.50	.75
	2019	(1962)	.15	.25	.50	.75
	2020	(1963)	.15	.25	.50	.75

ALUMINUM-BRONZE, 24.5mm
Numeral without shading

Y#	Date	Year	Fine	VF	XF	Unc
81a	VS2021	(1964)	.75	1.25	2.00	3.00

BRONZE, 25mm
Modified design

Y#	Date	Year	Fine	VF	XF	Unc
81b	VS2021	(1964)	.10	.15	.25	.50
	2022	(1965)	.10	.15	.25	.50
	2023	(1966)	.10	.15	.25	.50

BRASS

Y#	Date	Year	Mintage	VF	XF	Unc
93	VS2023	(1966)	—	.15	.25	.50
	2024	(1967)	—	.15	.25	.50
	2025	(1968)	—	.10	.20	.35
	2026	(1969)	—	.10	.20	.35
	2027	(1970)	—	.10	.20	.35
	2027	(1970)	2,187	—	Proof	5.00
	2028	(1971)	—	.10	.20	.35
	2028	(1971)	2,380	—	Proof	5.00

F.A.O. Issue

Y#	Date	Year	Mintage	VF	XF	Unc
98	VS2028	(1971)	2.017	.10	.15	.20

Y#	Date	Year	Mintage	VF	XF	Unc
102	VS2028	(1972)	—	1.00	1.75	2.50

Y#	Date	Year	Mintage	VF	XF	Unc
106	VS2029	(1972)	3.297	.15	.25	.40
	2029	(1972)	3,943	—	Proof	4.50
	2030	(1973)	5.670	.15	.25	.40
	2030	(1973)	8,891	—	Proof	2.50
	2031	(1974)	.011		Proof only	—
	2032	(1975)	—		Proof only	—

ALUMINUM
Virendra Coronation

Y#	Date	Year	Mintage	VF	XF	Unc
111	VS2031	(1974)	.192	.10	.20	.35

BRASS
F.A.O. Issue and International Women's Year

Y#	Date	Year	Mintage	VF	XF	Unc
122	VS2032	(1975)	2.500	.10	.15	.25

F.A.O. Issue

125	VS2033	(1976)	10.000	.10	.15	.25

1/6 RUPEE

GOLD
Mahendra Coronation

Y#	Date	Year	Fine	VF	XF	Unc
73	VS2013	(1956)	45.00	50.00	57.50	70.00

1/5 RUPEE

GOLD

—	VS2010	(1953)	—	—	—	—

NOTE: The above are believed to be restrikes.

2.33 gm.

85	VS2012	(1955)	45.00	50.00	60.00	75.00

20 PAISA

SILVER

46	VS1989	(1932)	3.00	4.00	5.00	6.50
	1991	(1934)	2.75	3.50	4.50	6.00
	1992	(1935)	2.75	3.50	4.50	6.00
	1993	(1936)	2.75	3.50	4.50	6.00
	1994	(1937)	4.50	6.50	10.00	15.00
	1995	(1938)	2.75	3.50	4.50	6.00
	1996	(1939)	2.75	3.50	4.50	6.00
	1997	(1940)	2.75	3.50	4.50	6.00
	1998	(1941)	2.75	3.50	4.50	6.00
	1999	(1942)	2.75	3.50	4.50	6.00
	2000	(1943)	2.75	3.50	4.50	6.00
	2001	(1944)	2.75	3.50	4.50	6.00
	2003	(1945)	2.75	3.50	4.50	6.00
	2004	(1947)	2.75	3.50	4.50	6.00
46.1	VS1989	(1932)	2.75	4.00	6.00	8.50

***NOTE:** The date SE1989 is given in different style characters.

2.2161 gm., .333 SILVER, .0237 oz ASW

46a	VS2006	(1949)	.75	1.00	1.25	1.75
	2009	(1952)	.75	1.00	1.50	2.50
	2010	(1953)	.75	1.00	1.50	2.50

COPPER-NICKEL

64	VS2010	(1953)	13.50	21.50	30.00	40.00
	2011	(1954)	—	—	Rare	—

BRASS
F.A.O. Issue

Y#	Date	Year	Mintage	VF	XF	Unc
126	VS2035	(1978)	—	.35	.75	1.00

25 PAISA

COPPER-NICKEL

Y#	Date	Year	Fine	VF	XF	Unc
65	VS2010	(1953)	2.00	3.50	4.50	6.00
	2011	(1954)	2.00	3.50	4.50	6.00
	2012	(1955)	1.25	2.00	2.50	3.50
	2014	(1957)	1.25	2.00	2.50	3.50

Mahendra Coronation

70	VS2013	(1956)	.30	.50	.70	1.00

Obv: 4 characters in line above trident
Rev: Small character at bottom (outer circle)

82	VS2015	(1958)	1.50	2.50	4.00	6.00
	2018	(1961)	.25	.40	.60	.80
	2020	(1963)	.25	.40	.60	.80
	2022	(1965)	2.00	3.50	6.00	9.00

Obv: As Y#82
Rev: Large different character at bottom

82.1	VS2021	(1964)	.30	.50	.70	1.00
	2022	(1965)	.30	.50	.70	1.00
	2023	(1966)	.30	.50	.70	1.00

Obv: 5 characters in line above trident
Rev: As Y#82.1

Y#	Date	Year	Mintage	VF	XF	Unc
82a	VS2024	(1967)	—	.35	.50	.75
	2025	(1968)	—	.35	.50	.75
	2026	(1969)	—	.35	.50	.75
	2027	(1970)	—	.35	.50	.75
	2027	(1970)	2,187	—	Proof	6.50
	2028	(1971)	—	.35	.50	.75
	2028	(1971)	2,380	—	Proof	6.50

103	VS2028	(1972)	5,691	.75	1.00	1.50
	2029	(1972)	3,943	—	Proof	5.50
	2030	(1973)	8.676	.30	.40	.50
	2030	(1973)	8,891	—	Proof	2.75
	2031	(1974)	1.172	.35	.50	.75
	2031	(1974)	.011	—	Proof	2.00
	2032	(1975)	4.584	.30	.40	.50
	2032	(1975)	—	—	Proof	—
	2033	(1976)	1.837	.30	.40	.50
	2034	(1977)	—	.30	.40	.50
	2035	(1978)	—	.30	.40	.50

Virendra Coronation

112	VS2031	(1974)	.431	.35	.50	.75

1/4 RUPEE

GOLD, 2.91 gm.

Obv: trident in center

Y#	Date	Year	Fine	VF	XF	Unc
50	VS1995	(1938)	80.00	100.00	125.00	150.00
86	VS2010	(1953)	—	—	—	—
	2012	(1955)	60.00	70.00	80.00	100.00

NOTE: Coins dated SE2010 are believed to be restrikes.

Reduced weight, 2.5 gm.

Y#	Date	Year	Mintage	VF	XF	Unc
—	VS2026	(1969)	—	—	Rare	—
—	VS2028	(1971)	*4 pcs.	—	Rare	—
	2030	(1973)	—	65.00	75.00	90.00
	2031	(1974)	—	65.00	75.00	90.00

Virenda Coronation

116	VS2031	1974	—	65.00	80.00	100.00

50 PAISA

5.5403 gm., .800 SILVER, .1425 oz ASW

Y#	Date	Year	Fine	VF	XF	Unc
47	VS1989	(1932)	5.50	6.50	8.00	10.00
	1991	(1934)	4.50	5.50	7.00	10.00
	1992	(1935)	4.50	5.50	7.00	10.00
	1993	(1936)	4.50	5.50	7.00	10.00
	1994	(1937)	4.50	5.50	7.00	10.00
	1995	(1938)	4.50	5.50	7.00	10.00
	1996	(1939)	4.50	5.50	7.00	10.00
	1997	(1940)	4.50	5.50	7.00	10.00
	1998	(1941)	4.50	5.50	7.00	10.00
	1999	(1942)	4.50	5.50	7.00	10.00
	2000	(1943)	4.50	5.50	7.00	10.00
	2001	(1944)	4.50	5.50	7.00	10.00
	2003	(1946)	4.50	5.50	7.00	10.00
	2004	(1947)	4.50	5.50	7.50	11.50
	2005	(1948)	4.50	5.50	7.00	10.00

47.1	VS1989	(1932)	4.50	5.50	7.00	9.00

NOTE: The date is given in different characters.

5.5403 gm., .333 SILVER, .0593 oz ASW
Obv: 4 dots around trident

47.2	VS2005	(1948)	45.00	75.00	100.00	125.00

Obv: No dots around trident

47a	VS2006	(1949)	1.50	2.00	2.75	4.50
	2007	(1950)	1.50	2.00	2.75	4.50
	2009	(1952)	1.50	2.00	2.75	4.50
	2010	(1953)	1.50	2.00	2.75	4.50

Jnanendra

Y#	Date	Year	Mintage	VF	XF	Unc
54	VS2007	(1950)	26 pcs.	—	Rare	—

COPPER-NICKEL

Y#	Date	Year	Fine	VF	XF	Unc
56	VS2010	(1953)	.50	1.00	2.00	3.00
	2011	(1954)	.35	.75	1.50	2.00

Queen Ratna Rajya Lakshmi

Y#	Date	Year	Mintage	VF	XF	Unc
A65	VS2012	(1955)	—	—	Rare	—

Mahendra Coronation

Y#	Date	Year	Fine	VF	XF	Unc
71	VS2013	(1956)	.35	.75	1.00	1.50

25mm

Rev: Small character at bottom (outer circle).

Y#	Date	Year	Fine	VF	XF	Unc
83	VS2011	(1954)	.50	1.00	1.50	3.00
	2012	(1955)	.25	.50	.75	1.00
	2013	(1956)	.25	.50	1.00	2.00
	2014	(1957)	.25	.50	1.00	2.00
	2015	(1958)	.25	.50	1.00	2.00
	2016	(1959)	.25	.50	1.00	2.00
	2017	(1960)	.25	.30	.75	1.25
	2018	(1961)	.25	.50	1.00	2.00
	2020	(1963)	.25	.30	.75	1.50

Rev: Large different character at bottom

Y#	Date	Year	Fine	VF	XF	Unc
83.1	VS2021	(1964)	.25	.35	.50	.75
	2022	(1965)	.25	.50	.75	1.50
	2023	(1966)	.25	.50	.75	1.00

Reduced size, 23.5mm

Obv: 4 characters in line above trident

Y#	Date	Year	Fine	VF	XF	Unc
83a	VS2023	(1966)	.25	.50	.75	1.50

Obv: 5 characters in line above trident

Y#	Date	Year	Mintage	VF	XF	Unc
83a.1	VS2025	(1968)	—	.30	.50	1.00
	2026	(1969)	—	.30	.50	.85
	2027	(1970)	2,187	Proof only		8.50
	2028	(1971)	2,380	Proof only		8.00

Y#	Date	Year	Mintage	VF	XF	Unc
104	VS2028	(1972)	5,343	1.00	1.50	2.00
	2029	(1972)	.347	.35	.50	.90
	2029	(1972)	3,943	—	Proof	6.50
	2030	(1973)	.998	.35	.50	.90
	2030	(1973)	8,891	—	Proof	3.00
	2031	(1974)	—	1.00	1.50	2.00
	2031	(1974)	.011	—	Proof	2.25
	2032	(1975)	.227	.35	.50	.90
	2032	(1975)	—	—	Proof	—
	2033	(1976)	3.446	.35	.50	.75
	2034	(1977)	—	.35	.50	.75
	2035	(1978)	—	.35	.50	.75

Virendra Coronation

Y#	Date	Year	Mintage	VF	XF	Unc
113	VS2031	(1974)	.136	.50	.75	1.25

1/2 RUPEE

GOLD

Y#	Date	Mintage	VF	XF	Unc
51	VS1995	—	120.00	135.00	160.00
	1996	—	120.00	135.00	160.00
	1997	—	120.00	135.00	160.00
	1998	—	120.00	135.00	160.00
	1999	—	120.00	135.00	160.00
	2000	—	120.00	135.00	160.00
	2001	—	120.00	135.00	160.00
	2002	—	120.00	135.00	160.00
	2003	—	120.00	135.00	160.00
	2004	—	120.00	135.00	160.00
	2005	—	120.00	135.00	160.00

Portrait type, 5.8 gm.

Y#	Date	Year	Mintage	VF	XF	Unc
—	VS2010	(1953)	—	—	—	—

NOTE: The above are believed to be restrikes.

Queen Ratna Rajya Laksmi Devi

Y#	Date	Year	Mintage	VF	XF	Unc
—	VS2012	(1955)	—	—	—	—

Mahendra Coronation

Y#	Date	Year	Mintage	VF	XF	Unc
76	VS2013	(1956)	—	120.00	135.00	160.00
87	VS2012	(1955)	—	120.00	135.00	160.00
	2019	(1962)	—	120.00	135.00	160.00

5.0 gm.

Y#	Date	Year	Mintage	VF	XF	Unc
—	VS2026	(1969)	—	—	Rare	—
—	VS2028	(1971)	*4 pcs.	—	Rare	—
	2030	(1973)	—	110.00	125.00	150.00
	2031	(1974)	—	110.00	125.00	150.00

Virenda Coronation

Y#	Date	Year	Mintage	VF	XF	Unc
117	VS2031	1974	—	—	125.00	150.00

RUPEE

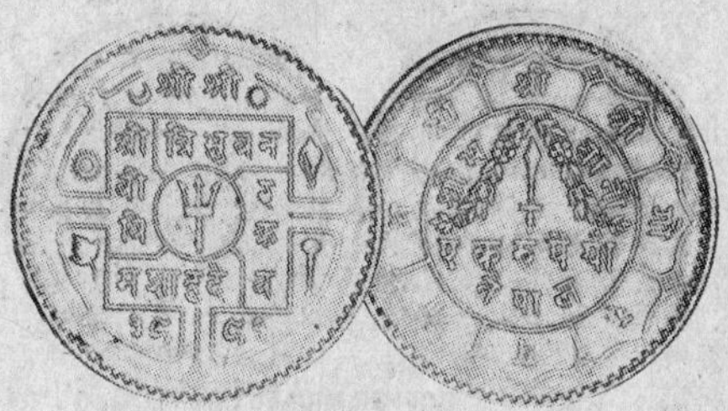

11.0806 gm., .800 SILVER, .2850 oz ASW

Y#	Date	Year	Fine	VF	XF	Unc
48	VS1989	(1932)	9.00	11.50	14.50	20.00
	1991	(1934)	9.00	11.00	13.00	16.50
	1992	(1935)	9.00	11.00	13.00	16.50
	1993	(1936)	9.00	11.00	13.00	16.50
	1994	(1937)	9.00	11.00	13.00	16.50
	1995	(1938)	9.00	11.00	13.00	16.50
	1996	(1939)	9.00	11.00	13.00	16.50
	1997	(1940)	9.00	11.00	13.00	16.50
	1998	(1941)	9.00	11.00	13.00	16.50
	1999	(1942)	9.00	11.00	13.00	16.50
	2000	(1943)	9.00	11.00	13.00	16.50
	2001	(1944)	9.00	11.00	13.00	16.50
	2003	(1946)	9.00	11.50	14.50	20.00
	2005	(1948)	9.00	11.00	13.00	16.50

Y#	Date	Year	Fine	VF	XF	Unc
48.1	VS1989	(1932)	9.00	11.00	12.50	15.00

NOTE: The date is given in different characters.

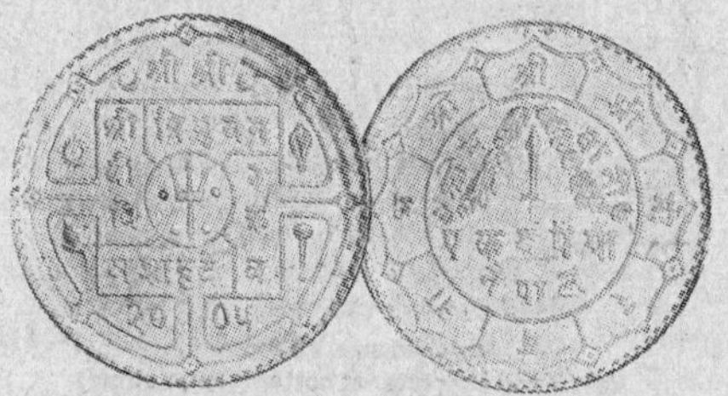

11.0806 gm., .333 SILVER, .1186 oz ASW

Obv: 4 dots around trident

Y#	Date	Year	Fine	VF	XF	Unc
48a	VS2005	(1948)	5.00	7.50	10.00	13.50

Obv: No dots around trident

Y#	Date	Year	Fine	VF	XF	Unc
48a.1	VS2006	(1949)	3.50	4.00	5.00	6.50
	2007	(1950)	3.50	4.00	5.00	6.50
	2008	(1951)	3.50	4.00	5.00	6.50
	2009	(1951)	3.50	4.00	5.00	6.50
	2010	(1952)	3.50	4.00	5.00	6.50

Jnanendra

Y#	Date	Year	Fine	VF	XF	Unc
55	VS2007	(1950)	4.50	6.50	9.00	12.50

COPPER-NICKEL
Equal denticles at rim

Y#	Date	Year	Fine	VF	XF	Unc
57	VS2010	(1953)	.75	1.25	2.00	3.50
	2011	(1954)	.75	1.25	2.00	3.50

Unequal denticles at rim

Y#	Date	Year	Fine	VF	XF	Unc
57.1	VS2011	(1954)	.75	1.25	2.00	3.50

GOLD, 11.66 gm.

Y#	Date	Year	Mintage	VF	XF	Unc
—	VS2010	(1953)	—	—	—	—

Ratna Rajya Laksmi Devi

Y#	Date	Year	Mintage	VF	XF	Unc
—	VS2012	(1955)	—	—	—	—

COPPER-NICKEL
29.6mm

Y#	Date	Year	Fine	VF	XF	Unc
84	VS2011	(1954)	1.25	2.25	3.50	5.00
	2012	(1955)	1.00	1.75	2.50	4.00

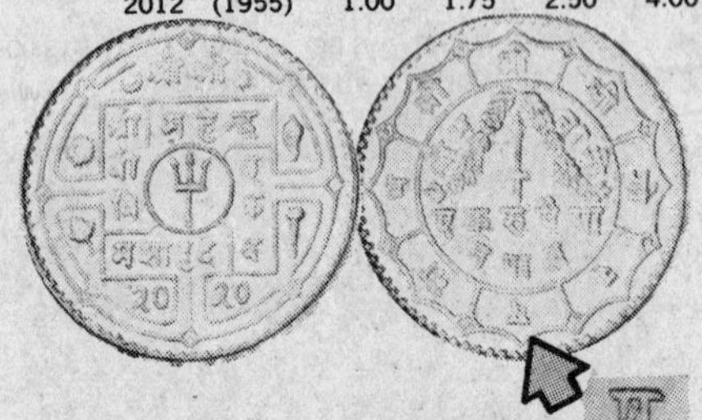

Reduced size, 28.8mm.
Rev: Small character at bottom (outer circle)

Y#	Date	Year	Fine	VF	XF	Unc
84a	VS2012	(1955)	.50	.85	1.25	1.75
	2013	(1956)	.50	.85	1.25	1.75
	2014	(1957)	.50	.85	1.25	1.75
	2015	(1958)	.50	.85	1.25	1.75
	2016	(1959)	.50	.85	1.25	1.75
	2018	(1961)	.50	.85	1.25	1.75
	2020	(1963)	.50	.85	1.25	1.75

Rev: Large character at bottom

Y#	Date	Year	Fine	VF	XF	Unc
84a.1	VS2021	(1964)	.50	.75	1.00	1.50
	2022	(1965)	.50	1.00	1.50	2.50
	2023	(1966)	4.50	7.50	10.00	15.00

Reduced size, 27mm
Obv: 4 characters in line above trident

Y#	Date	Year	Fine	VF	XF	Unc
84a.2	VS2023	(1966)	.75	1.00	1.35	2.00

Obv: 5 characters in line above trident

Y#	Date	Year	Mintage	VF	XF	Unc
84a.3	VS2025	(1968)	—	1.00	1.50	2.00
	2026	(1969)	—	1.00	1.40	2.00
	2027	(1970)	2,187	Proof Only		12.50
	2028	(1971)	2,380	Proof Only		11.50

GOLD

Y#	Date	Year	Mintage	VF	XF	Unc
88	VS2012	(1955)	—	235.00	260.00	300.00
	2019	(1962)	—	235.00	260.00	300.00

COPPER-NICKEL
Mahendra Coronation

Y#	Date	Year				
72	VS2013	(1956)	.75	1.25	1.75	2.50

GOLD
Mahendra Coronation

Y#	Date	Year	Mintage	VF	XF	Unc
77	VS2013	(1956)	—	235.00	260.00	300.00

10 gm.

Y#	Date	Year	Mintage	VF	XF	Unc
—	VS2026	(1969)	—	—	Rare	—

Y#	Date	Year	Mintage	VF	XF	Unc
—	VS2028	(1971)	*4 pcs.	—	Rare	—
	2030	(1973)	—	225.00	260.00	300.00
	2031	(1974)	—	225.00	260.00	300.00

COPPER-NICKEL

Y#	Date	Year	Mintage	VF	XF	Unc
105	VS2028	(1972)	5,030	2.00	3.00	4.00
	2029	(1972)	.022	1.00	1.50	2.25
	2029	(1972)	3,943	—	Proof	7.50
	2030	(1973)	5,667	2.00	3.00	4.00
	2030	(1973)	8,891	—	Proof	3.50
	2031	(1974)	.011	Proof Only		2.50
	2032	(1975)	—		Proof	—
	2033	(1976)	—	1.00	1.50	2.25
	2034	(1977)	—	1.00	1.50	2.25

Virendra Coronation

Y#	Date	Year	Mintage	VF	XF	Unc
114	VS2031	(1974)	—	1.00	1.50	1.75

GOLD
Virendra Coronation

Y#	Date	Year	Mintage	VF	XF	Unc
118	VS2031	1974	—	225.00	260.00	300.00

COPPER-NICKEL
F.A.O. Issue And International Women's Year

Y#	Date	Year	Mintage	VF	XF	Unc
123	VS2032	1975	1.500	.75	1.00	1.50

BAKLA RUPEE

GOLD
Obv: Trident in center.

Y#	Date	Year	Fine	VF	XF	Unc
52	VS1992	(1935)	235.00	250.00	285.00	325.00

2 RUPEES

GOLD
Obv: Trident in center.

Y#	Date	Year	Fine	VF	XF	Unc
53	VS2005	(1948)	450.00	500.00	550.00	650.00
89	VS2012	(1955)	450.00	500.00	550.00	625.00

10 RUPEES

15.4000 gms., .600 SILVER, .2971 oz ASW
F.A.O. Issue

Y#	Date	Year	Mintage	VF	XF	Unc
97	VS2025	(1968)	.539	BV	BV	10.00

8.0000 gms., .600 SILVER, .1543 oz ASW
F.A.O. Issue

Y#	Date	Year	Mintage	VF	XF	Unc
108	VS2031	(1974)	.039	BV	5.50	6.50

20 RUPEES

15.0000 gms., .500 SILVER, .2411 oz ASW
F.A.O. Issue and International Women's Year

Y#	Date	Year	Mintage	VF	XF	Unc
124	VS2032	(1975)	.050	BV	BV	7.50

25 RUPEES

17.0000 gms., .600 SILVER, .3280 oz ASW
Virendra Coronation

Y#	Date	Year	Mintage	VF	XF	Unc
115	VS2031	(1974)	.075	—	—	10.00

25.3100 gms., .500 SILVER, .4069 oz ASW
Conservation Series

Y#	Date	Year	Mintage	VF	XF	Unc
119	VS2031	(1974)	6,103	BV	BV	25.00
	28.2800 gms., .925 SILVER, .8411 oz ASW					
119a	VS2031	(1974)	.030	—	Proof	30.00
	2032	(1975)	9,394	—	Proof	30.00
	5th Anniversary of Coronation					
—	—	(1979)	—	—	Proof	50.00

50 RUPEES

31.6500 gms., .500 SILVER, .5088 oz ASW
Conservation Series
Rev: Similar to 25 Rupees, Y#119.

Y#	Date	Year	Mintage	VF	XF	Unc
120	VS2031	(1974)	—	BV	BV	30.00
	2032	(1975)	6,097	—	—	35.00
	35.0000 gms., .925 SILVER, 1.0410 oz ASW					
120a	VS2031	(1974)	.030	—	Proof	40.00
	2032	(1975)	9,079	—	Proof	50.00

1000 RUPEES

33.4400 gms., .900 GOLD, .9677 oz AGW
Conservation Series

Y#	Date	Year	Mintage	VF	XF	Unc
121	VS2031	(1974)	.010	—	—	650.00
	2031	(1974)	3,000	—	Proof	750.00
	2032	(1975)	2,574	—	Proof	750.00
	.500 GOLD					
	5th Anniversary of Coronation					
127	VS2036	(1979)	250 pcs.	—	Proof	300.00

TOKEN ISSUES

12 PAISA

IRON

KM#	Date	VG	Fine	VF	XF
1	ND	12.50	20.00	27.50	40.00

14 PAISA

IRON

KM#	Date	VG	Fine	VF	XF
2	ND	12.50	20.00	27.50	40.00

16 PAISA

BRASS

KM#	Date	Year	VG	Fine	VF
A4	1824	(1902)	—	20.00	27.50

NCLT ISSUES

MINT SETS

KM#	Date	Mintage	Identification	Issue Price	Mkt. Val.
S1	1932(3)	—	—	—	—
S2	1949(3)	—	Y46a,47,48 restrikes	—	8.00
S3	1955(3)	—	Y45(2000),58,59a(2012)	.85	1.50
S4	1956(7)	—	Y66-72	—	13.50
S5	1957(4)	—	Y56(2011)57,64(2010),65(2018)	.05	4.00
S6	1957(6)	—	YA41.1(1996),62(2014),63(2011) 2 Pcs. Each	.85	1.50
S7	1964(7)	—	Y78a,79A,80A,81A,82B,83B,84A	—	10.00
S8	1964(7)	—	Y78A,79A,80B,81B,82B,83B,84A,	—	5.00
S9	1965(7)	—	Y78a,79a(2022),80a,81a,82b 83b,84c(2021)	2.75	5.50
S10	1972(7)	—	Y99-105	—	7.00
S11	1974(7)	—	Y109-115	—	15.00
S12	1974(2)	—	Y119,120	32.50	32.50
S13	1975(5)	—	Y111-115	—	—
S14	1976(7)	—	Y90-93,82b,83a,84b	—	—

PROOF SETS

STANDARD METALS

KM#	Date	Mintage	Identification	Issue Price	Mkt. Val.
101	1911	—	Copper, Silver	—	—
102	1911	—	Gold	—	—
103	1970(7)	2,187	Y90-93,82a,83a,84a	10.00	40.00
104	1971(7)	2,380	Y90-93,82a,83a,84a	10.00	38.00
105	1972(7)	3,943	Y#99- 105	10.00	20.00
106	1973(7)	8,891	Y99-101,103-106	10.00	11.50
107	1974(7)	10,543	Y99-105	10.00	10.00
108	1974(2)	30,000	Y119a,120a	50.00	75.00
109	1979(7)	1,000	—	62.00	—

NETHERLANDS

The Kingdom of the Netherlands, a country of western Europe fronting on the North Sea and bordered by Belgium and Germany, has an area of 14,103 sq. mi. (36,526 sq. km.) and a population of 14.1 million. Capital: Amsterdam, but the seat of government is at The Hague. The economy is based on dairy farming and a variety of industrial activities. Chemicals, yarns and fabrics, and meat products are exported.

After being a part of Charlemagne's empire in the 8th and 9th centuries, the Netherlands came under control of Burgundy and the Austrian Hapsburgs, and finally was subjected to Spanish dominion in the 16th century. Led by William of Orange, the Dutch revolted against Spain in 1568. The seven northern provinces formed the Union of Utrecht and declared their independence, 1581, becoming the Republic of the United Netherlands. In the following century, the 'Golden Age' of Dutch history, the Netherlands became a great sea and colonial power, a patron of the arts and a refuge for the persecuted. In 1814, all the provinces of Holland and Belgium were merged into the Kingdom of the United Netherlands under William I. The Belgians withdrew in 1830 to form their own kingdom, the last substantial change in the configuration of European Netherlands.

WORLD WAR II COINAGE

Coinage of the Netherlands Homeland Types - Y#36, Y#34, Y#43, Y#44 and Y#46 - were minted by U.S. mints in the name of the government in exile and its remaining Curacao and Surinam Colonies during the years 1941-45. The Curacao and Surinam strikings, distinguished by the presence of a palm tree in combination with a mintmark (P-Philadelphia; D-Denver; S-San Francisco) flanking the date, are incorporated under those titles in this volume. Pieces of this period struck in the name of the homeland bear an acorn and mintmark and are incorporated in the following tabulation.

NOTE: Excepting the World War II issues struck at U.S. mints, all of the modern coins were struck at the Utrecht Mint and bear the caduceus mintmark of that facility. They also bear the mintmaster's marks as follow: Halberd - 1909, Sea Horse - 1909-33, Dr. C. Hoitsema; Grapes - 1933-42, Dr. W. J. Van Herteren; Fish - 1945-69, Dr. J.W. A. Van Hengel; Cock - 1969-present, Dr. M. Van Den Brandhof.

RULERS

United Netherlands (1543-1795)

BATAVIAN REPUBLIC
(French domination) 1795-1806

KINGDOM OF HOLLAND
(French protectorate)
Louis Napoleon 1806-1810

FRENCH ANNEXATION
Napoleon I 1810-1814

KINGDOM OF THE NETHERLANDS
William I, 1815-1840
William II, 1840-1849
William III, 1849-1890
Wilhelmina I, 1890-1948
Juliana I, 1948-

PRIVY MARKS

Date	Privy Mark
Harderwijk (Gelderland)	
1758-1776	Tree
1782-1806	Ear of corn
Dordrecht (Holland)	
1600-1806	Rosette
1795-1806	None
Enkhuizen (Holland)	
1761-1771	Ship
1791-1796	Rosette
1796-1803	Star
Hoorn (Holland)	
1751-1761	Rooster
1781-1791	Rosette
1803-1809	Star
Kampen (Overissel)	
1795-1807	Eagle
Medemblik (West Friesland)	
1771-1781	Ship
Middelburg (Zeeland)	
1601-1799	Castle
Utrecht (Utrecht)	
1738-1805	Shield
Utrecht	
1806-present	Caduceus

B - Brussels (Belgium), 1821-1830
P - Philadelphia, 1941-1945
D - Denver, 1943-1945
S - San Francisco, 1944-1945

MINTMARKS

Date	Privy Mark
Brussels Mint	
1821-1830	Palm branch
U. S. Mints	
1941-1945	Palm tree
Utrecht Mint	
1806-1810	Bee
1810-1813	Mast
1815-1816	Cloverleaf
1817	Child in swaddling clothes
1818-1840	Torch
1839-1846	Fleur de lis
1846-1874	Sword
1874	Sword in Scabbard
1875-1887	Broadaxe
1888-1909	Halberd
1909-1933	Seahorse
1933-1942	Grapes
1943-1945	Acorn
1945-1969	Fish
1969-1979	Cock
1980—	Cock and Star (Temporal)

NOTE: A star adjoining the privy mark indicates that the piece was struck at the beginning of the term of office of a successor.

MONETARY SYSTEM

4 Duits = 1 Stuiver (stiver)
6 Stuivers = 1 Schelling
20 Stuivers = 1 Gulden (guilder or florin)
50 Stuivers = 1 Rijksdaalder (silver ducat)
60 Stuivers = 1 Ducaton (silver rider)
14 Gulden = 1 Golden Rider

COMMENCING 1815
100 Cents = 1 Gulden
2-1/2 Gulden = 1 Rijksdaalder

UNITED NETHERLANDS

GELDERLAND

(Ducatus Gelriae)

Gelderland (Ducatus Gelriae): Gelder, a former duchy, was merged with the Hapsburg dominions in the Netherlands until the revolt of the Low Countries resulted in its partition. In 1579 the greater part of Gelder, comprising the quarters of Nijmegen, Arnhem, and Zutphen, became the province of Gelderland in the Dutch republic.

DUIT

COPPER
Obv: D/GEL/RIE over date in baroque cartouche.
Rev: Crowned arms.

C#	Date	Mintage	VG	Fine	VF	XF
A2b	1758	—	5.00	10.00	17.50	25.00
	1759	—	5.00	10.00	17.50	25.00
	1760	—	5.00	10.00	17.50	25.00
	1761	—	3.00	7.50	11.50	15.00
	1762	—	3.00	7.50	11.50	15.00
	1763	—	3.00	7.50	11.50	15.00
	1764	—	2.50	5.50	10.00	14.00
	1765	—	2.50	5.50	10.00	14.00
	1766	—	2.50	5.50	10.00	14.00
	1767	—	2.50	5.50	10.00	14.00
	1768	—	2.50	5.50	10.00	14.00

SILVER (OMS)

C#	Date	Mintage	VG	Fine	VF	XF
A2f	1759	—	40.00	60.00	75.00	125.00
	1761	—	40.00	60.00	75.00	125.00
	1762	—	40.00	60.00	75.00	125.00
	1765	—	40.00	60.00	75.00	125.00

GOLD (OMS)

C#	Date	Mintage	VG	Fine	VF	XF
A2e	1759	—	—	—	—	—
	1761	—	—	—	—	—
	1762	—	—	—	—	—

COPPER

C#	Date	Mintage	VG	Fine	VF	XF
A2c	1783	—	2.50	5.50	10.00	14.00
	1784	—	2.50	5.50	10.00	14.00
	1785	—	2.50	5.50	10.00	14.00
	1786	—	3.00	7.00	11.50	15.00
	1787	—	2.50	5.50	10.00	14.00
	1788	—	2.50	5.50	10.00	14.00

C#	Date	Mintage	VG	Fine	VF	XF
A2d	1788	—	2.50	5.50	10.00	14.00
	1793	—	2.50	5.50	10.00	14.00
	1794	—	2.50	5.50	10.00	14.00

STUIVER

(=bezemstuiver)

.583 SILVER
Obv: GEL/RIA over date.
Rev: Bundle of arrows divide 1 S.

C#	Date	Mintage	VG	Fine	VF	XF
A4	1759	—	12.50	20.00	30.00	45.00
	1760	—	12.50	20.00	30.00	45.00
	1761	—	12.50	20.00	30.00	45.00
	1764	—	12.50	20.00	30.00	45.00
	1765	—	12.50	20.00	30.00	45.00
	1766	—	12.50	20.00	30.00	45.00

GOLD (OMS)

C#	Date	Mintage	VG	Fine	VF	XF
A4b	1759	—	—	—	Rare	—
	1760	—	—	—	Rare	—
	1761	—	—	—	Rare	—

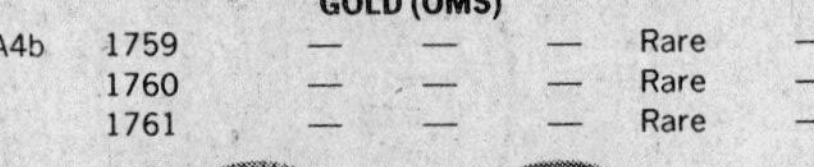

.333 SILVER

C#	Date	Mintage	VG	Fine	VF	XF
A4a	1785	.043	10.00	16.50	30.00	50.00

2 STUIVER

(=double Wapenstuiver)

.583 SILVER

C#	Date	Mintage	VG	Fine	VF	XF
A7	1785	—	2.50	4.50	10.00	15.00

Obv: Rosettes to either side of mintmark.

C#	Date	Mintage	VG	Fine	VF	XF
A8	1786	—	2.00	4.00	10.00	12.50
	1789	—	2.00	4.00	9.00	12.00
	1792	—	2.00	4.00	9.00	12.00

10 STUIVERS
(= 1/2 Gulden)

.920 SILVER
Obv: Crowned arms divide value; date over crown.
Rev: Standing figure holding pole with liberty cap, leaning on Bible on column.

C#	Date	Mintage	VG	Fine	VF	XF
A12a	1759	—	45.00	75.00	125.00	175.00
	1760	—	45.00	75.00	125.00	175.00
	1761	—	45.00	75.00	125.00	175.00
	1762	—	45.00	75.00	125.00	175.00
	1764	—	45.00	75.00	125.00	175.00
	1765	—	45.00	75.00	125.00	175.00

GOLD (OMS)

C#	Date	Mintage	VG	Fine	VF	XF
A12b	1761	—	—	—	—	—

GULDEN

.920 SILVER
Obv: Crowned arms, value, legend.
Rev: Standing figure holding pole with liberty cap leaning on Bible on column; leg: HAC NITIMVR

C#	Date	Mintage	VG	Fine	VF	XF
A13a	1760	—	22.50	32.50	60.00	85.00
	1762	—	20.00	30.00	50.00	70.00
	1763/56	—	—	—	—	—
	1763	—	20.00	30.00	50.00	70.00
	1764/3	—	22.50	35.00	70.00	100.00
	1764	—	22.50	35.00	70.00	100.00
	1765	—	22.50	35.00	70.00	100.00
	1786	—	22.50	35.00	70.00	100.00
	1786/65	—	40.00	65.00	100.00	135.00
	1794	—	22.50	32.50	60.00	75.00

3 GULDEN

.920 SILVER
Obv: Crowned arms, value, legend.
Rev: Standing figure holding pole with liberty cap, leaning on Bible on column; leg: HAC NITIMVR

C#	Date	Mintage	VG	Fine	VF	XF
A14	1764	.232	100.00	150.00	275.00	350.00
	1786	.128	100.00	150.00	325.00	375.00

1/2 DUCATON
(= Half Silver Rider)

.941 SILVER
Obv: Knight on galloping horse,
leg: BEL.PRO D GEL & C Z MONO. ARG. CONFOE.
Rev: Arms, legend around, date in cartouche.
Flowered edge.

C#	Date	Mintage	VG	Fine	VF	XF
A21	1761	—	150.00	350.00	525.00	700.00
	1762	—	150.00	350.00	525.00	700.00
	1764/63	—	150.00	350.00	525.00	700.00
	1764	—	100.00	275.00	325.00	550.00
	1765	—	100.00	275.00	325.00	550.00

Corded edge.

C#	Date	Mintage	VG	Fine	VF	XF
A21.1	1761	—	150.00	350.00	525.00	700.00
	1766	—	100.00	275.00	325.00	500.00
	1767	—	100.00	275.00	325.00	500.00
	1769	—	150.00	350.00	525.00	700.00
	1773	.104	100.00	275.00	325.00	550.00
	1774	—	200.00	500.00	750.00	1000.
	1775	—	100.00	275.00	325.00	550.00
	1785	Inc.w/A22	150.00	350.00	525.00	700.00
	1790	Inc.w/A22	100.00	275.00	325.00	550.00

1/2 RIJKSDAALDER
(= 1/2 Silver Ducat)

.873 SILVER
Obv: Knight standing holding crowned arms.
Rev: Crowned arms divide date.

C#	Date	Mintage	VG	Fine	VF	XF
A17	1762	—	150.00	325.00	450.00	600.00
	1763	—	150.00	325.00	450.00	600.00
A17	1764	—	150.00	325.00	450.00	600.00
	1765	—	150.00	325.00	450.00	600.00

RIJKSDAALDER
(= Silver Ducat)

.873 SILVER
Obv: Knight standing, small arms,
leg: MO.ARG.PRO.CONFOE.BELG.D.GEL.C.Z.
Rev: Arms, date, legend.

C#	Date	Mintage	VG	Fine	VF	XF
A18	1760	—	150.00	350.00	475.00	600.00
	1761	—	150.00	350.00	475.00	600.00
	1762	—	150.00	350.00	475.00	600.00
	1763	—	150.00	350.00	475.00	600.00
	1764	—	150.00	350.00	475.00	600.00
	1766	—	150.00	350.00	475.00	600.00
	1767	—	150.00	350.00	475.00	600.00
	1768	—	150.00	350.00	475.00	600.00
	1771	—	225.00	450.00	650.00	850.00
	1773	—	125.00	275.00	375.00	475.00
	1774	—	125.00	275.00	375.00	475.00
	1775	—	125.00	275.00	375.00	475.00
	1785	.039	100.00	225.00	300.00	400.00

DUCATON
(= Silver Rider)

.941 SILVER
Obv: Knight on galloping horse,
leg: MO NO ARG PRO CONFOE BELG.O GEL C Z.
Rev: Arms in circle of beads, date, mintmark.

C#	Date	Mintage	VG	Fine	VF	XF
A22	1759	—	150.00	350.00	500.00	700.00
	1760	—	150.00	350.00	500.00	700.00
	1761	—	150.00	350.00	500.00	700.00
	1764	—	125.00	325.00	450.00	600.00
	1765	—	125.00	325.00	450.00	600.00
	1766	—	125.00	325.00	450.00	600.00
	1767	—	100.00	250.00	350.00	500.00
	1773	—	100.00	250.00	350.00	500.00
	1774	—	100.00	250.00	350.00	500.00
	1775	—	100.00	250.00	350.00	500.00
	1785	.046	75.00	150.00	250.00	325.00
	1789	.367	75.00	150.00	250.00	325.00
	1790	Inc. Ab.	75.00	150.00	225.00	300.00
	1791	Inc. Ab.	75.00	150.00	250.00	325.00
	1792	Inc. Ab.	75.00	150.00	250.00	325.00

TRADE COINS

DUCAT

.986 GOLD
Obv: Standing knight, date,
leg: CONCORDIA RES.PAR.CRES.D.G.8C C.Z.
Rev: Legend on tablet.

C#	Date	Mintage	VG	Fine	VF	XF
A25	1758	—	175.00	275.00	375.00	500.00
	1759	—	175.00	275.00	375.00	500.00
	1760	—	175.00	275.00	375.00	500.00
	1761	—	175.00	275.00	375.00	500.00
	1762	—	175.00	275.00	375.00	500.00
	1763	—	175.00	275.00	375.00	500.00
	1766	—	175.00	275.00	375.00	500.00
	1767	—	175.00	275.00	375.00	500.00
	1769	—	175.00	300.00	450.00	600.00
	1786	.064	225.00	375.00	575.00	725.00
	1791	.036	175.00	300.00	450.00	600.00
	1792	Inc. Ab.	225.00	375.00	575.00	725.00

2 DUCATS

GOLD
Obv: Standing knight divides date.
Rev: Legend in ornamental tablet.

C#	Date	Mintage	VG	Fine	VF	XF
A26	1759	—	550.00	750.00	1000.	1500.
	1760	—	550.00	750.00	1000.	1500.
	1761	—	800.00	1500.	2500.	4000.

7 GULDEN

GOLD
Obv: Mounted knight, holding sword, over arms.
Rev: Crowned arms divide value; date above.

C#	Date	Mintage	VG	Fine	VF	XF
A27	1760	—	250.00	475.00	850.00	1250.
	1761	—	750.00	1150.	1750.	2500.
	1762	—	250.00	475.00	850.00	1250.

14 GULDEN

GOLD
Obv: Mounted knight, holding sword, over arms.
Rev: Crowned arms divide value; date above.

C#	Date	Mintage	VG	Fine	VF	XF
A28	1760	—	375.00	500.00	1000.	1500.
	1762	—	375.00	500.00	1000.	1500.

GRONINGEN
(Groningen and Ommeland)

The province of Groningen is located in northern Netherlands and is drained by numerous rivers and canals.

The early history of Groningen is chiefly one of conflict between the city and the surrounding districts known as the Ommelanden. The city remained loyal to the Spanish king while the surrounding area supported the revolt against Spain.

After 1594 Groningen and Ommelanden were united into one republic but it was not until 1795 that they were merged into one province.

DUIT

COPPER
Obv: GRON/EN/OMMEL over date.
Rev: Crowned arms in branches.
Small letters

C#	Date	Mintage	VG	Fine	VF	XF
B1	1770	—	10.00	37.50	55.00	75.00

Large letters

C#	Date	Mintage	VG	Fine	VF	XF
B2	1770	—	8.50	15.00	45.00	65.00
	1771	—	8.50	15.00	45.00	65.00
	1772	—	8.50	15.00	45.00	65.00

STUIVER

.583 SILVER
Obv: GRON/EN/OML over date.
Rev: Bundle of arrows divide 1 S.

C#	Date	Mintage	VG	Fine	VF	XF
B4	1765	—	25.00	45.00	75.00	100.00
	1766	—	25.00	45.00	75.00	100.00

GOLD (OMS)

C#	Date	Mintage	VG	Fine	VF	XF
B4a	1765	—	—	—	Rare	—

7 GULDEN

GOLD
Obv: Mounted knight, holding sword, over arms.
Rev: Crowned arms divide value; date above.

C#	Date	Mintage	VG	Fine	VF	XF
B27	1761	—	275.00	750.00	1000.	1250.

14 GULDEN

GOLD
Obv: Mounted knight holding sword, over arms.
Rev: Crowned arms divide value; date above.

C#	Date	Mintage	VG	Fine	VF	XF
B28	1761	—	500.00	1200.	1500.	1750.

HOLLAND
(Hollandia)

Holland, a Dutch maritime province fronting on the North Sea, is the most important region of the Netherlands, a leader in maritime activities and in efficient agriculture. During the period of Spanish domination, Holland was the bulwark of the Protestant faith in the Netherlands and the focus of the resistance to Spanish tyranny.

DUIT

COPPER
Rev: Rampant lion holding pole with hat at top, in fence.
Obv: HOL/LAN/DIA, date.

C#	Date	Mintage	VG	Fine	VF	XF
C2	1765	—	2.50	7.50	20.00	25.00
	1766	—	3.00	10.00	25.00	35.00

C#	Date	Mintage	VG	Fine	VF	XF
C2	1769	—	2.50	7.50	20.00	25.00
	1780	—	2.50	7.50	20.00	25.00

STUIVER

.583 SILVER
Rev: HOL/LAN/DIA over date.
Rev: Bundle of arrows divide 1 S.

C#	Date	Mintage	VG	Fine	VF	XF
C4	1760	—	5.00	10.00	20.00	30.00
	1764	—	5.00	10.00	20.00	30.00

GOLD (OMS)

C#	Date	Mintage	VG	Fine	VF	XF
C4a	1760	—	100.00	250.00	400.00	500.00
	1761	—	100.00	250.00	400.00	500.00
	1762	—	100.00	250.00	400.00	500.00
	1763	—	100.00	250.00	400.00	500.00
	1764	—	100.00	250.00	400.00	500.00
	1765	—	100.00	250.00	400.00	500.00
	1766	—	100.00	250.00	400.00	500.00
	1773	—	100.00	250.00	400.00	500.00

2 STUIVER

(= Double Wapenstuiver)

.583 SILVER
Obv: Hol/Lan/Dia over date.
Rev: Crowned arms divide value.

C#	Date	Mintage	VG	Fine	VF	XF
C8	1760	—	5.00	7.00	10.00	15.00
	1761	—	4.00	5.00	8.00	11.50
	1762	—	5.00	7.00	10.00	15.00
	1763	—	4.00	5.50	8.00	11.50
	1764/3	—	—	—	—	—
	1764	—	4.00	5.50	8.00	11.50
	1765/1	—	—	—	—	—
	1765	—	4.00	5.50	8.00	11.50
	1766/1	—	—	—	—	—
	1766/4	—	—	—	—	—
	1766	—	4.00	5.50	8.00	11.50
	1767/6	—	—	—	—	—
	1767	—	4.00	5.50	8.00	11.50
	1768/1	—	—	—	—	—
	1768	—	4.00	5.50	8.00	11.50
	1769	—	4.00	5.50	8.00	11.50
	1770	—	4.00	5.50	8.00	11.50
	1771	—	4.00	5.50	8.00	11.50
	1772	—	4.00	5.50	8.00	11.50
	1773	—	4.00	5.50	8.00	11.50
	1774	—	4.00	5.50	8.00	11.50
	1775	—	4.00	5.50	8.00	11.50
	1776	—	4.00	5.50	8.00	11.50
	1777	—	4.00	5.50	8.00	11.50
	1778	—	4.00	5.50	8.00	11.50
	1779	—	4.00	5.50	8.00	11.50
	1780	—	4.00	5.50	8.00	11.50
	1784/80	—	5.00	7.00	10.00	15.00
	1784	—	4.00	5.50	8.00	11.50
	1787	—	4.00	5.50	8.00	11.50
	1788	—	4.00	5.50	8.00	11.50
	1789	—	4.00	5.50	8.00	11.50
	1790	—	4.00	5.50	8.00	11.50
	1791	—	4.00	5.50	8.00	11.50
	1792	—	4.00	5.50	8.00	11.50
	1793	—	4.00	5.50	8.00	11.50

GOLD (OMS)

C#	Date	Mintage	VG	Fine	VF	XF
C8a	1760	—	250.00	450.00	650.00	800.00
	1761	—	250.00	450.00	650.00	800.00
	1762	—	250.00	450.00	650.00	800.00
	1763	—	250.00	450.00	650.00	800.00
	1766	—	250.00	450.00	650.00	800.00

1/4 GULDEN

(5 Stuivers)

.920 Silver
Obv: Crowned arms divide date.
Rev: Standing figure holding pole with liberty cap, leaning on Bible on column.

C#	Date	Mintage	VG	Fine	VF	XF
C10	1759	—	15.00	30.00	45.00	60.00

GOLD

C#	Date	Mintage	VG	Fine	VF	XF
C10a	1759	—	400.00	1000.	1600.	2000.

6 STUIVERS

(= Scheepjesschelling)

.583 SILVER
Obv: Crowned arms divide value; date over crown.
Rev: Ship sailing to right.

C#	Date	Mintage	VG	Fine	VF	XF
C11	1761	—	10.00	20.00	30.00	40.00

GOLD (OMS)

C#	Date	Mintage	VG	Fine	VF	XF
C11a	1760	—	750.00	1100.	1500.	1750.
	1761	—	750.00	1100.	1500.	1750.
	1762	—	750.00	1100.	1500.	1750.
	1763	—	750.00	1100.	1500.	1750.
	1764	—	750.00	1100.	1500.	1750.
	1765	—	750.00	1100.	1500.	1750.
	1766/4	—	900.00	1500.	2000.	2250.
	1766	—	750.00	1100.	1500.	1750.
	1767	—	750.00	1100.	1500.	1750.
	1768	—	750.00	1100.	1500.	1750.
	1769	—	750.00	1100.	1500.	1750.
	1770	—	750.00	1100.	1500.	1750.
	1771	—	750.00	1100.	1500.	1750.
	1772	—	750.00	1100.	1500.	1750.
	1773	—	750.00	1100.	1500.	1750.
	1774	—	750.00	1100.	1500.	1750.
	1775	—	750.00	1100.	1500.	1750.
	1776	—	750.00	1100.	1500.	1750.
	1777	—	750.00	1100.	1500.	1750.
	1778	—	750.00	1100.	1500.	1750.
	1779	—	750.00	1100.	1500.	1750.
	1780	—	750.00	1100.	1500.	1750.
	1781	—	750.00	1100.	1500.	1750.
	1782	—	750.00	1100.	1500.	1750.
	1783	—	750.00	1100.	1500.	1750.
	1784	—	750.00	1100.	1500.	1750.
	1789	—	750.00	1100.	1500.	1750.
	1790	—	750.00	1100.	1500.	1750.
	1791	—	750.00	1100.	1500.	1750.
	1792	—	750.00	1100.	1500.	1750.
	1793	—	750.00	1100.	1500.	1750.

1/2 GULDEN

(= 10 Stuivers)

.920 SILVER
Obv: Crowned arms divide value; date over crown.
Rev: Standing figure holding pole with liberty cap, leaning on Bible on column.

C#	Date	Mintage	VG	Fine	VF	XF
C12	1761	—	40.00	70.00	90.00	125.00
	1762	—	40.00	75.00	100.00	150.00

GULDEN

.920 SILVER

C#	Date	Mintage	VG	Fine	VF	XF
C13	1762	—	32.50	45.00	60.00	75.00
	1763	—	32.50	45.00	60.00	75.00
	1764	—	32.50	45.00	60.00	75.00
	1765	—	32.50	45.00	60.00	75.00
	1790	—	20.00	30.00	40.00	65.00
	1791	—	20.00	30.00	40.00	65.00
	1792	—	20.00	30.00	40.00	65.00
	1793	—	20.00	30.00	40.00	65.00
	1794	—	20.00	30.00	40.00	65.00

3 GULDEN

.920 SILVER
Obv: Arms, value, legend. Rev: Standing figure holding pole with liberty cap, leaning on Bible on column; leg: HAC NITIMVR HANC TVEMVR.

C#	Date	Mintage	VG	Fine	VF	XF
C14	1763	—	90.00	130.00	200.00	275.00
	1764	—	90.00	130.00	200.00	275.00
	1791	.276	90.00	130.00	200.00	275.00
	1792	Inc. Ab.	110.00	175.00	225.00	325.00
	1793	—	90.00	130.00	200.00	275.00
	1794	—	90.00	130.00	200.00	275.00

1/2 DUCATON

(= Half Silver Rider)

.941 SILVER
Obv: Knight on galloping horse, small arms below, leg: MO NO ARG CONFOE BELG PRO HOL.
Rev: Arms, legend.

C#	Date	Mintage	VG	Fine	VF	XF
C21	1765	—	100.00	160.00	225.00	300.00
	1766	—	100.00	160.00	225.00	300.00
	1767	—	100.00	160.00	225.00	300.00
	1770	—	100.00	160.00	225.00	300.00
	1771	—	110.00	180.00	250.00	325.00
	1772	—	100.00	160.00	225.00	300.00
	1773	—	110.00	180.00	250.00	325.00
	1774	—	100.00	160.00	225.00	300.00
	1775	—	100.00	160.00	225.00	300.00
	1776	—	100.00	160.00	225.00	300.00
	1777	—	100.00	160.00	225.00	300.00
	1780/76	—	110.00	180.00	250.00	325.00
	1780	Inc. w/C22	100.00	160.00	225.00	300.00
	1788	Inc.w/C22	100.00	160.00	225.00	300.00
	1789	Inc. Ab.	110.00	180.00	250.00	325.00
	1790	Inc.w/C22	100.00	160.00	225.00	300.00
	1792	Inc. Ab.	100.00	160.00	225.00	300.00

RIJKSDAALDER

(SILVER DUCAT)

.941 SILVER
Obv: Knight standing holding crowned arms.
Rev: Crowned arms divide date.

C#	Date	Mintage	VG	Fine	VF	XF
C18	1762	—	125.00	225.00	300.00	400.00
	1763	—	125.00	225.00	300.00	400.00
	1767	—	125.00	225.00	300.00	400.00
	1771	—	200.00	400.00	575.00	750.00
	1772	—	135.00	240.00	400.00	550.00

DUCATON

(= Silver Rider)

.941 SILVER
Obv: Knight on galloping horse, small arms below, leg: MO NO ARG CONFOE BELG PRO HOL.
Rev: Arms, legend.

C#	Date	Mintage	VG	Fine	VF	XF
C22	1760	—	75.00	125.00	180.00	225.00
	1761	—	75.00	125.00	180.00	225.00
	1762	—	75.00	125.00	180.00	225.00
	1765	—	100.00	160.00	225.00	300.00
	1766	—	75.00	125.00	180.00	225.00
	1767	—	100.00	160.00	225.00	300.00
	1770	—	75.00	125.00	180.00	225.00
	1771	—	125.00	225.00	300.00	400.00
	1772	—	75.00	125.00	180.00	225.00
	1773	—	75.00	125.00	180.00	225.00
	1774	—	75.00	125.00	180.00	225.00
	1775	—	100.00	160.00	225.00	300.00
	1777	—	—	—	Rare	—
	1779	.090	100.00	160.00	225.00	300.00
	1780	Inc. Ab.	90.00	155.00	225.00	275.00
	1784	.031	125.00	225.00	300.00	400.00
	1788	.076	100.00	160.00	225.00	300.00
	1789	Inc. Ab.	100.00	160.00	225.00	300.00
	1790	.096	90.00	140.00	200.00	250.00
	1791	Inc. Ab.	90.00	140.00	200.00	250.00
	1792/1	—	—	200.00	300.00	350.00
	1792	Inc. Ab.	90.00	140.00	200.00	250.00
	1793	.050	75.00	125.00	180.00	225.00

TRADE COINS

DUCAT

.986 GOLD
Obv: Knight standing, leg: CONCORDIA.RES.PAR.CRES.HOL.
Rev: Legend on tablet.

C#	Date	Mintage	VG	Fine	VF	XF
C25	1760	—	100.00	175.00	250.00	350.00
	1761	—	100.00	175.00	250.00	350.00
	1762	—	100.00	175.00	250.00	350.00
	1763	—	100.00	175.00	250.00	350.00
	1764	—	100.00	175.00	250.00	350.00
	1765	—	100.00	175.00	250.00	350.00
	1766	—	100.00	175.00	250.00	350.00
	1767	—	100.00	175.00	250.00	350.00
	1768	—	100.00	175.00	250.00	350.00
	1769	—	100.00	175.00	250.00	350.00
	1770	—	100.00	175.00	250.00	350.00
	1771	—	100.00	175.00	250.00	350.00
	1772	—	100.00	175.00	250.00	350.00
	1773	—	100.00	175.00	250.00	350.00
	1774	—	100.00	175.00	250.00	350.00
	1775	—	100.00	175.00	250.00	350.00
	1776	—	80.00	140.00	200.00	300.00
	1777	—	80.00	140.00	200.00	300.00
	1778	—	80.00	140.00	200.00	300.00
	1779	—	80.00	140.00	200.00	300.00
	1780	—	80.00	140.00	200.00	300.00
	1781	—	80.00	140.00	200.00	300.00
	1782	—	80.00	140.00	200.00	300.00
	1783	—	80.00	140.00	200.00	300.00
	1784	—	80.00	140.00	200.00	300.00

C#	Date	Mintage	VG	Fine	VF	XF
C25	1790	—	125.00	200.00	300.00	400.00
	1791	—	125.00	200.00	300.00	400.00

2 DUCATS

.986 GOLD
Obv: Standing knight, date,
leg: CONCORDIA RES.PAR.CRES.HOL.
Rev: Legend on tablet.

C#	Date	Mintage	VG	Fine	VF	XF
C26	1760	—	350.00	750.00	1250.	1750.
	1761	—	350.00	750.00	1250.	1750.
	1762	—	350.00	750.00	1250.	1750.
	1763	—	350.00	750.00	1250.	1750.
	1764	—	350.00	750.00	1250.	1750.
	1765	—	350.00	750.00	1250.	1750.
	1766	—	350.00	750.00	1250.	1750.
	1767	—	350.00	750.00	1250.	1750.
	1768	—	350.00	750.00	1250.	1750.
	1769	—	350.00	750.00	1250.	1750.
	1770	—	350.00	750.00	1250.	1750.
	1771	—	350.00	750.00	1250.	1750.
	1772	—	350.00	750.00	1250.	1750.
	1773	—	350.00	750.00	1250.	1750.
	1774	—	350.00	750.00	1250.	1750.
	1776	—	350.00	750.00	1250.	1750.
	1777	—	350.00	750.00	1250.	1750.
	1778	—	350.00	750.00	1250.	1750.
	1779	—	350.00	750.00	1250.	1750.
	1780	—	350.00	750.00	1250.	1750.
	1781	—	350.00	750.00	1250.	1750.
	1782	—	350.00	750.00	1250.	1750.
	1783	—	350.00	750.00	1250.	1750.
	1784	—	350.00	750.00	1250.	1750.
	1785	—	350.00	750.00	1250.	1750.
	1787	—	350.00	750.00	1250.	1750.
	1790	—	400.00	900.00	1500.	2000.
	1791	—	350.00	750.00	1250.	1750.
	1793	—	350.00	750.00	1250.	1750.

7 GULDEN

GOLD
Obv: Mounted knight, holding sword, over arms.
Rev: Crowned arms divide value; date above.

C#	Date	Mintage	VG	Fine	VF	XF
C27	1760	—	175.00	500.00	800.00	1000.
	1761	—	225.00	625.00	950.00	1200.
	1762	—	200.00	600.00	900.00	1100.
	1763	—	175.00	500.00	800.00	1000.

14 GULDEN

GOLD
Obv: Mounted knight, holding sword, over arms.
Rev: Crowned arms divide value; date above.

C#	Date	Mintage	VG	Fine	VF	XF
C28	1760	—	500.00	1200.	1500.	1750.
	1761	—	500.00	1200.	1500.	1750.
	1762	—	500.00	1200.	1500.	1750.
	1763	—	500.00	1200.	1500.	1750.

OVERYSSEL

Overyssel is a province in northeastern Netherlands whose name means 'beyond the Issel', a tributary of the Rhine. Originally known as the lordship of Oversticht it was a part of the holdings of the bishops of Utrecht. It was sold to Charles V in 1527 and made a part of the Hapsburg domain. Three of its cities - Kampen, Deventer and Zwolle were important Hanseatic towns of the medieval period.

DUIT

COPPER
Obv: OVER/YSSEL over date.
Rev: Crowned arms.

C#	Date	Mintage	VG	Fine	VF	XF
E2	1764	—	3.75	8.00	15.00	20.00
	1765	—	3.75	8.00	15.00	20.00
	1767	—	3.75	8.00	15.00	20.00
	1768	—	3.75	8.00	15.00	20.00
	1769	—	3.75	8.00	15.00	20.00

Obv: OVER/YSSEL over date; head in sprays below.

C#	Date	Mintage	VG	Fine	VF	XF
E2b	1766	—	6.50	12.50	20.00	32.50

SILVER (OMS)

C#	Date	Mintage	VG	Fine	VF	XF
E2c	1769	—	—	—	—	—
	1770	—	—	—	—	—

STUIVER

.583 SILVER
Obv: TRANS/ISALA/NIA over date.
Rev: Bundle of arrows divide 1 S rose mintmark.

C#	Date	Mintage	VG	Fine	VF	XF
E4	1765	—	10.00	20.00	35.00	45.00
	1766	—	10.00	20.00	35.00	45.00
	1767	—	10.00	20.00	35.00	45.00
	1769	—	10.00	20.00	35.00	45.00

GULDEN

.920 SILVER
Obv: Crowned arms divide value; date over crown.
Rev: Standing figure holding pole with liberty cap, leaning on Bible on column.
Eagle mintmark.

C#	Date	Mintage	VG	Fine	VF	XF
E13.1	1763	—	35.00	65.00	90.00	125.00
	1764	—	35.00	65.00	90.00	125.00

Half eagle mintmark.

C#	Date	Mintage	VG	Fine	VF	XF
E13.2	1763	—	75.00	125.00	175.00	250.00

3 dots mintmark.

C#	Date	Mintage	VG	Fine	VF	XF
E13.3	1764	—	35.00	65.00	90.00	125.00
	1765	—	30.00	55.00	70.00	115.00

RIJKSDAALDER

(Silver Ducat)

.873 SILVER
Obv: Knight standing holding crowned arms.
Rev: Crowned arms divide date.
Eagle mintmark.

C#	Date	Mintage	VG	Fine	VF	XF
E18	1764	—	150.00	325.00	450.00	600.00
	1767	—	225.00	450.00	650.00	850.00

DUCATON

(= SILVER RIDER)

.941 SILVER
Obv: Mounted knight, holding sword, over arms.
Rev: Crowned arms with lion supporters; date in

C#	Date	Mintage	VG	Fine	VF	XF
E22	1764	—	375.00	750.00	1000.	1500.

TRADE COINS

7 GULDEN

GOLD
Obv: Mounted knight, holding sword, over arms.
Rev: Crowned arms divide value; date above.

C#	Date	Mintage	VG	Fine	VF	XF
E27	1760	—	275.00	500.00	750.00	1000.
	1761	—	275.00	500.00	750.00	1000.
	1762	—	400.00	650.00	1000.	1250.
	1763	—	275.00	500.00	750.00	1000.

14 GULDEN

GOLD
Obv: Mounted knight, holding sword, over arms.
Rev: Crowned arms divide value; date above.

C#	Date	Mintage	VG	Fine	VF	XF
E28	1760	—	375.00	500.00	1000.	1500.
	1761	—	600.00	950.00	1250.	1750.
	1763	—	375.00	500.00	1000.	1500.

UTRECHT

Trajectum

Utrecht (Trajectum), the smallest Netherlands province, represents the bulk of a see founded in 722. It was one of the seven provinces which signed the union of Utrecht against Spain, a treaty regarded as the foundation of the later kingdom of the Netherlands.

DUIT

COPPER
Obv: STAD UTRECHT over date. Rev: Crowned arm with lion supporters; arabesque in exergue.

C#	Date	Mintage	VG	Fine	VF	XF
F2	1758	—	2.50	5.50	10.00	15.00
	1759	—	2.50	5.50	10.00	15.00
	1760	—	3.00	7.00	11.50	16.50
	1761	—	3.00	7.00	11.50	16.50
	1762	—	2.50	5.50	10.00	15.00
	1763	—	3.00	7.00	11.50	16.50
	1764	—	2.50	5.50	10.00	15.00
F2	1765	—	3.00	7.00	11.50	16.50
	1766	—	2.50	5.50	10.00	15.00
	1767	—	3.00	7.00	11.50	16.50
	1768	—	2.50	5.50	10.00	15.00
	1780	—	3.00	7.50	12.50	17.50
	1783	—	2.50	5.50	10.00	15.00
	1784	—	2.50	5.50	10.00	15.00
	1785	—	3.00	7.00	11.50	16.50
	1786	—	2.50	5.50	10.00	15.00
	1787	—	2.50	5.50	10.00	15.00
	1788	—	3.00	7.00	11.50	16.50
	1789	—	3.00	7.00	11.50	16.50
	1790	—	3.00	7.00	11.50	16.50
	1791	—	3.00	7.00	11.50	16.50
	1792	—	3.00	7.00	11.50	16.50
	1793	—	3.00	7.00	11.50	16.50
	1794	—	3.00	7.00	11.50	16.50

SILVER (OMS)

C#	Date	Mintage	VG	Fine	VF	XF
F2a	1758	—	30.00	50.00	75.00	125.00
	1760	—	30.00	50.00	75.00	125.00
	1761	—	30.00	50.00	75.00	125.00
	1762	—	30.00	50.00	75.00	125.00
	1763	—	30.00	50.00	75.00	125.00
	1765	—	30.00	50.00	75.00	125.00
	1767	—	30.00	50.00	75.00	125.00
	1769	—	30.00	50.00	75.00	125.00
	1770	—	30.00	50.00	75.00	125.00
	1772	—	30.00	50.00	75.00	125.00
	1773	—	30.00	50.00	75.00	125.00
	1774	—	30.00	50.00	75.00	125.00
	1775	—	30.00	50.00	75.00	125.00
	1776	—	30.00	50.00	75.00	125.00
	1777	—	30.00	50.00	75.00	125.00
	1778	—	30.00	50.00	75.00	125.00
	1779	—	30.00	50.00	75.00	125.00
	1780	—	30.00	50.00	75.00	125.00
	1781	—	30.00	50.00	75.00	125.00
	1782	—	30.00	50.00	75.00	125.00
	1783	—	30.00	50.00	75.00	125.00
	1784	—	30.00	50.00	75.00	125.00
	1786	—	30.00	50.00	75.00	125.00
	1787	—	30.00	50.00	75.00	125.00
	1788	—	30.00	50.00	75.00	125.00
	1789	—	30.00	50.00	75.00	125.00
	1790	—	30.00	50.00	75.00	125.00
	1791	—	30.00	50.00	75.00	125.00
	1792	—	30.00	50.00	75.00	125.00
	1793	—	30.00	50.00	75.00	125.00
	1794	—	30.00	50.00	75.00	125.00

GOLD (OMS)

C#	Date	Mintage	VG	Fine	VF	XF
F2b	1758	—	300.00	500.00	750.00	1000.
	1760	—	300.00	500.00	750.00	1000.
	1763	—	300.00	500.00	750.00	1000.
	1764	—	300.00	500.00	750.00	1000.
	1765	—	300.00	500.00	750.00	1000.
	1767	—	300.00	500.00	750.00	1000.
	1768	—	300.00	500.00	750.00	1000.
	1784	—	300.00	500.00	750.00	1000.
	1788	—	300.00	500.00	750.00	1000.
	1791	—	300.00	500.00	750.00	1000.
	1792	—	300.00	500.00	750.00	1000.
	1793	—	300.00	500.00	750.00	1000.
	1794	—	300.00	500.00	750.00	1000.

STUIVER

.583 SILVER
Obv: TRA/IEC/TUM over date.
Rev: Bundle of arrows divide 1 S.

C#	Date	Mintage	VG	Fine	VF	XF
F4	1760	—	10.00	16.50	25.00	35.00
	1765	—	10.00	16.50	25.00	35.00

GOLD (OMS)

C#	Date	Mintage	VG	Fine	VF	XF
F4a	1760	—	100.00	250.00	400.00	500.00
	1762	—	100.00	250.00	400.00	500.00
	1763	—	100.00	250.00	400.00	500.00
	1764	—	100.00	250.00	400.00	500.00
	1765	—	100.00	250.00	400.00	500.00
	1766	—	100.00	250.00	400.00	500.00
	1767	—	100.00	250.00	400.00	500.00
	1769	—	100.00	250.00	400.00	500.00
	1772	—	100.00	250.00	400.00	500.00
	1777	—	100.00	250.00	400.00	500.00
	1778	—	100.00	250.00	400.00	500.00
	1779	—	100.00	250.00	400.00	500.00
	1780	—	100.00	250.00	400.00	500.00
	1781	—	100.00	250.00	400.00	500.00
	1782	—	100.00	250.00	400.00	500.00
	1786	—	100.00	250.00	400.00	500.00
	1787	—	100.00	250.00	400.00	500.00
	1788	—	100.00	250.00	400.00	500.00
	1789	—	100.00	250.00	400.00	500.00

2 STUIVERS

(= Double Wapenstuiver)

.583 SILVER
Obv: TRA/IEC/TUM over date.
Rev: Crowned arms divide value.

C#	Date	Mintage	VG	Fine	VF	XF
F8	1784	—	5.00	6.50	10.00	15.00
	1785	—	5.00	6.50	10.00	15.00
	1786	—	5.00	6.50	10.00	15.00
	1787	—	5.00	6.50	10.00	15.00
	1788	—	5.00	6.50	10.00	15.00
	1789	—	5.00	6.50	10.00	13.50
	1790	—	5.00	6.50	10.00	13.50
	1791	—	5.00	6.50	10.00	13.50
	1792	—	5.00	6.50	10.00	13.50
	1793	—	5.00	6.50	10.00	13.50
	1794	—	5.00	6.50	10.00	13.50

NOTE: Varieties exist for the 1786 date. Nickel coins were struck at Birmingham in the period 1834-1866.

GOLD (OMS)

C#	Date	Mintage	VG	Fine	VF	XF
F8a	1790	—	—	—	—	—
	1791	—	—	—	—	—
	1793	—	—	—	—	—
	1794	—	—	—	—	—

6 STUIVERS

(= Scheepjesschelling)

.583 SILVER

C#	Date	Mintage	VG	Fine	VF	XF
F11	1764	.034	15.00	30.00	45.00	60.00
	1785	—	22.50	45.00	70.00	100.00
	1786	—	25.00	45.00	80.00	125.00
	1787	—	30.00	50.00	80.00	125.00
	1788	—	30.00	50.00	80.00	125.00
	1789	—	30.00	50.00	80.00	125.00
	1794	345 pcs.	125.00	250.00	400.00	500.00

GOLD (OMS)

C#	Date	Mintage	VG	Fine	VF	XF
F11a	1760	—	400.00	750.00	1000.	1400.
	1763	—	400.00	750.00	1000.	1400.
	1764	—	400.00	750.00	1000.	1400.
	1769	—	400.00	750.00	1000.	1400.
	1772	—	400.00	750.00	1000.	1400.
	1775	—	400.00	750.00	1000.	1400.
	1786	—	400.00	750.00	1000.	1400.
	1787	—	400.00	750.00	1000.	1400.
	1788	—	400.00	750.00	1000.	1400.
	1789	—	400.00	750.00	1000.	1400.
	1794	—	400.00	750.00	1000.	1400.

X (10) STUIVERS

(= 1/2 Gulden)

.920 SILVER
Obv: Arms, value, legend. Rev: Standing figure holding pole with liberty cap, leaning on Bible on column, leg: HAC NITIMVR HANC TVEMVR.

C#	Date	Mintage	VG	Fine	VF	XF
F12	1759	—	22.50	37.50	50.00	75.00
	1760	—	22.50	37.50	50.00	75.00
	1761	—	22.50	37.50	50.00	75.00
	1762	—	22.50	37.50	50.00	75.00
	1763	—	22.50	37.50	50.00	75.00
	1764	—	22.50	37.50	50.00	75.00
	1765	—	22.50	37.50	50.00	75.00
	1766	—	22.50	37.50	50.00	75.00
	1767	—	22.50	37.50	50.00	75.00
	1768	—	25.00	40.00	85.00	125.00
	1769	560 pcs.	75.00	150.00	175.00	350.00
	1770	—	75.00	150.00	175.00	350.00
	1771	—	32.50	55.00	80.00	125.00
	1772	—	32.50	55.00	80.00	125.00
	1773	—	32.50	55.00	80.00	125.00
	1774	—	32.50	55.00	80.00	125.00
	1775	—	32.50	55.00	80.00	125.00
	1776	—	32.50	55.00	80.00	125.00
	1778	—	32.50	55.00	80.00	125.00
	1779	—	32.50	55.00	80.00	125.00
	1780	—	32.50	55.00	80.00	125.00
	1781	—	32.50	55.00	80.00	125.00
	1782	—	32.50	55.00	80.00	125.00
	1783	—	25.00	40.00	65.00	100.00
	1784	—	25.00	40.00	65.00	100.00
	1785	—	25.00	40.00	65.00	100.00
	1786	—	25.00	40.00	65.00	100.00
	1787	—	25.00	40.00	65.00	100.00
	1788	—	25.00	40.00	65.00	100.00
	1789	—	25.00	40.00	65.00	100.00
	1790	—	25.00	40.00	65.00	100.00
	1791	—	22.50	37.50	50.00	75.00
	1792	—	22.50	37.50	50.00	75.00
	1793	—	22.50	37.50	50.00	75.00
	1794	—	22.50	37.50	50.00	75.00

GOLD (OMS)

C#	Date	Mintage	VG	Fine	VF	XF
F12a	1760	—	—	1350.	2000.	2500.
	1764	—	—	1350.	2000.	2500.
	1773	—	—	1350.	2000.	2500.
	1774/3	—	—	1350.	2000.	2500.
	1776	—	—	1350.	2000.	2500.
	1780	—	—	1350.	2000.	2500.
	1784	—	—	1350.	2000.	2500.
	1786	—	—	1350.	2000.	2500.
	1787	—	—	1350.	2000.	2500.
	1790	—	—	1350.	2000.	2500.
	1791	—	—	1350.	2000.	2500.
	1792	—	—	1350.	2000.	2500.
	1793	—	—	1350.	2000.	2500.
	1794	—	—	2000.	2500.	3000.

GULDEN

.920 SILVER

C#	Date	Mintage	VG	Fine	VF	XF
F13	1760	—	35.00	60.00	85.00	110.00
	1762	—	20.00	35.00	55.00	80.00
	1763	—	20.00	35.00	55.00	80.00
	1764	—	25.00	50.00	65.00	100.00
	1765	—	75.00	110.00	160.00	200.00
	1775	—	75.00	110.00	160.00	200.00
	1776	—	20.00	35.00	55.00	80.00
	1780	—	20.00	35.00	55.00	80.00
	1781	—	20.00	35.00	55.00	80.00
	1782	—	20.00	35.00	55.00	80.00
	1784	—	75.00	100.00	150.00	200.00
	1785	—	20.00	35.00	50.00	75.00
	1786	—	17.50	35.00	50.00	65.00
	1787	—	75.00	110.00	160.00	200.00
	1788	—	75.00	110.00	160.00	200.00
	1789	—	20.00	35.00	55.00	70.00
	1790	—	20.00	35.00	55.00	70.00
	1791	—	17.50	30.00	45.00	65.00
	1792	—	17.50	30.00	45.00	65.00
	1793	—	17.50	30.00	45.00	65.00
	1794	—	17.50	30.00	45.00	65.00

GOLD (OMS)

C#	Date	Mintage	VG	Fine	VF	XF
F13a	1794	—	—	—	—	—

3 GULDEN

.920 SILVER

C#	Date	Mintage	VG	Fine	VF	XF
F14	1763	—	75.00	110.00	150.00	250.00
	1764	—	75.00	110.00	150.00	250.00
	1785	.234	75.00	110.00	150.00	250.00
	1786	Inc. Ab.	75.00	110.00	150.00	250.00
	1791	.062	75.00	110.00	150.00	250.00
	1792/1	.147	75.00	110.00	150.00	250.00
	1792	Inc. Ab.	75.00	110.00	150.00	250.00
	1793	1.692	75.00	110.00	150.00	250.00
	1794	1.713	75.00	110.00	150.00	250.00

1/2 RIJKSDAALDER

(= 1/2 Silver Ducat)

.873 SILVER
Obv: Standing knight, small arms, leg: MO NO ARG PRO CONFOE; BELG; TRAI.
Rev: Arms, date, legend.

C#	Date	Mintage	VG	Fine	VF	XF
F17	1761	—	125.00	250.00	350.00	450.00
	1762	—	125.00	250.00	350.00	450.00
	1763	—	125.00	250.00	350.00	450.00
	1764	—	125.00	250.00	350.00	450.00
	1765	—	125.00	250.00	350.00	450.00
	1766	—	125.00	250.00	350.00	450.00
	1767	—	125.00	250.00	350.00	450.00
	1768	—	125.00	250.00	350.00	450.00
	1769	—	125.00	250.00	350.00	450.00
	1770	—	125.00	250.00	350.00	450.00
	1771	—	125.00	250.00	350.00	450.00
	1773	—	125.00	250.00	350.00	450.00
	1774	—	125.00	250.00	350.00	450.00
	1775	—	125.00	250.00	350.00	450.00
	1776	—	125.00	250.00	350.00	450.00
	1781	—	125.00	250.00	350.00	450.00
	1783	—	125.00	250.00	350.00	450.00

1/2 DUCATON

(= 1/2 Silver Rider)

.941 SILVER
Obv: Knight on galloping horse, leg: MO NO ARG CON FOE BELG PRO TRAI around.
Rev: Arms, date, legend.

C#	Date	Mintage	VG	Fine	VF	XF
F21	1761	—	100.00	200.00	300.00	400.00
	1762	—	100.00	200.00	300.00	400.00
	1763/2	—	100.00	200.00	300.00	400.00
	1763	—	100.00	200.00	300.00	400.00
	1764	—	100.00	175.00	250.00	350.00
	1765	—	100.00	175.00	250.00	350.00
	1766	—	100.00	175.00	250.00	350.00
	1767	—	100.00	175.00	250.00	350.00
	1768	—	100.00	175.00	250.00	350.00
	1769	—	100.00	175.00	250.00	350.00
	1770	—	100.00	175.00	250.00	350.00
	1771	—	100.00	175.00	250.00	350.00
	1772	—	100.00	175.00	250.00	350.00
	1773	—	100.00	175.00	250.00	350.00
	1774	—	100.00	175.00	250.00	350.00
	1775	—	100.00	175.00	250.00	350.00
	1776	—	100.00	175.00	250.00	350.00
	1778	—	110.00	175.00	250.00	350.00
	1779	—	100.00	175.00	250.00	350.00
	1780	—	100.00	175.00	250.00	350.00
	1781	—	100.00	175.00	250.00	350.00
	1782	—	100.00	175.00	250.00	350.00
	1783	—	100.00	175.00	250.00	350.00
	1784	Inc. F22	100.00	175.00	250.00	350.00
	1785	Inc. Ab.	100.00	175.00	250.00	300.00
	1786/5	—	100.00	175.00	250.00	350.00
	1786	Inc. Ab.	100.00	175.00	250.00	350.00
	1787	Inc. F22	100.00	175.00	250.00	350.00
	1788	Inc. Ab.	100.00	175.00	250.00	350.00
	1789	Inc. Ab.	100.00	175.00	250.00	350.00
	1790	—	100.00	175.00	250.00	350.00
	1791	—	100.00	175.00	250.00	350.00
	1792	—	100.00	175.00	250.00	350.00
	1793	—	100.00	175.00	250.00	350.00

C#	Date	Mintage	VG	Fine	VF	XF
F21	1794/2	—	100.00	175.00	250.00	350.00
	1794	—	100.00	175.00	250.00	350.00

GOLD (OMS)

C#	Date	Mintage	VG	Fine	VF	XF
F21a	1774	—	—	—	—	—
	1794	—	—	—	—	—

RIJKSDAALDER

(= Silver Ducat)

.873 SILVER
Obv: Standing knight, small arms, leg: MO NO ARG PRO CONFOE; BELG; TRAI.
Rev: Arms, date, legend.

C#	Date	Mintage	VG	Fine	VF	XF
F18	1758	—	100.00	170.00	250.00	350.00
	1760	—	100.00	170.00	250.00	350.00
	1761	—	150.00	300.00	400.00	600.00
	1762	—	125.00	225.00	325.00	500.00
	1763	—	100.00	170.00	250.00	350.00
	1764	—	100.00	170.00	250.00	350.00
	1765	—	100.00	170.00	250.00	350.00
	1766	—	100.00	170.00	250.00	350.00
	1767	—	100.00	170.00	250.00	350.00
	1768	—	Reported, not confirmed			
	1769	—	125.00	200.00	275.00	375.00
	1770	—	125.00	200.00	275.00	375.00
	1771	—	100.00	170.00	250.00	350.00
	1772	—	100.00	170.00	250.00	350.00
	1773	—	100.00	170.00	250.00	350.00
	1774	—	100.00	170.00	250.00	350.00
	1775	—	100.00	170.00	250.00	350.00
	1776	—	100.00	170.00	250.00	350.00
	1779	.356	110.00	175.00	250.00	350.00
	1780	.723	100.00	170.00	250.00	300.00
	1781	Inc. Ab.	100.00	170.00	250.00	300.00
	1782	Inc. Ab.	100.00	170.00	250.00	300.00
	1783	1.425	100.00	170.00	250.00	300.00
	1784	1.214	100.00	160.00	225.00	275.00
	1785	Inc. Ab.	100.00	160.00	225.00	275.00
	1786	Inc. Ab.	100.00	160.00	225.00	275.00
	1787	.546	100.00	160.00	225.00	275.00
	1788	Inc. Ab.	100.00	160.00	225.00	275.00
	1789	1.156	125.00	200.00	275.00	375.00
	1790	Inc. Ab.	100.00	160.00	225.00	275.00
	1791	Inc. Ab.	90.00	135.00	180.00	225.00
	1792	.019	110.00	185.00	250.00	350.00
	1793	.182	90.00	140.00	200.00	250.00
	1794	Inc. Ab.	90.00	140.00	200.00	250.00

DUCATON

(= Silver Rider)

.941 SILVER

C#	Date	Mintage	VG	Fine	VF	XF
F22	1760	—	85.00	150.00	200.00	250.00
	1761	—	100.00	175.00	250.00	350.00
	1762/61	—	125.00	225.00	325.00	425.00
	1762	—	95.00	160.00	225.00	300.00
	1763	705 pcs.	200.00	500.00	750.00	1000.
	1765	—	95.00	160.00	225.00	300.00
F22	1766	—	95.00	160.00	225.00	300.00
	1767	—	95.00	160.00	225.00	300.00
	1768	—	95.00	160.00	225.00	300.00
	1769	—	85.00	150.00	200.00	275.00
	1770	—	85.00	150.00	200.00	275.00
	1771	—	85.00	150.00	200.00	275.00
	1772	—	85.00	150.00	200.00	275.00
	1773	—	85.00	150.00	200.00	275.00
	1774	—	95.00	160.00	225.00	300.00
	1775	—	85.00	150.00	200.00	275.00
	1776	—	85.00	150.00	200.00	275.00
	1778	.020	90.00	150.00	200.00	275.00
	1779	Inc. Ab.	125.00	225.00	325.00	450.00
	1780	Inc. Ab.	90.00	150.00	200.00	275.00
	1781	.086	90.00	150.00	200.00	275.00
	1782	Inc. Ab.	100.00	160.00	225.00	300.00
	1783	.152	150.00	275.00	375.00	475.00
	1784	Inc. Ab.	100.00	180.00	250.00	325.00
	1785	Inc. Ab.	100.00	175.00	250.00	325.00
	1786	.270	100.00	160.00	225.00	275.00
	1787	Inc. Ab.	100.00	160.00	225.00	275.00
	1788	.055	100.00	160.00	225.00	275.00
	1789	.118	100.00	160.00	225.00	275.00
	1790	Inc. Ab.	125.00	200.00	350.00	450.00
	1791	.124	100.00	160.00	225.00	275.00
	1792	1,060	100.00	160.00	225.00	275.00
	1793	.052	100.00	160.00	225.00	275.00
	1794	Inc. Ab.	100.00	160.00	225.00	275.00

TRADE COINS

DUCAT

.986 GOLD

C#	Date	Mintage	VG	Fine	VF	XF
F25	1760	—	100.00	200.00	275.00	400.00
	1761	—	100.00	200.00	275.00	400.00
	1762	—	100.00	200.00	275.00	400.00
	1763	—	100.00	200.00	275.00	400.00
	1764	—	100.00	200.00	275.00	400.00
	1766	—	100.00	200.00	275.00	400.00
	1767	—	250.00	450.00	650.00	950.00
	1768	—	100.00	200.00	275.00	400.00
	1769	—	100.00	200.00	275.00	400.00
	1770	—	100.00	200.00	275.00	400.00
	1772	—	200.00	250.00	450.00	600.00
	1773	—	200.00	250.00	450.00	600.00
	1774	—	100.00	200.00	275.00	400.00
	1775	—	200.00	250.00	450.00	600.00
	1776	—	200.00	250.00	450.00	600.00
	1777	—	100.00	200.00	275.00	400.00
	1778	—	100.00	200.00	275.00	400.00
	1779	—	100.00	200.00	275.00	400.00
	1780	—	100.00	200.00	275.00	400.00
	1781	—	100.00	200.00	275.00	400.00
	1782	—	175.00	225.00	400.00	550.00
	1783	—	175.00	225.00	400.00	550.00
	1784	—	100.00	200.00	275.00	400.00
	1785	—	100.00	200.00	275.00	400.00
	1786	—	100.00	200.00	275.00	400.00
	1787	—	250.00	475.00	675.00	950.00
	1788	—	100.00	200.00	275.00	400.00
	1789	—	100.00	200.00	275.00	400.00
	1790	—	100.00	200.00	275.00	400.00
	1791	—	100.00	200.00	275.00	400.00
	1792	—	120.00	225.00	300.00	450.00
	1793	—	120.00	225.00	300.00	450.00
	1794	—	100.00	200.00	275.00	400.00

2 DUCATS

.986 GOLD

C#	Date	Mintage	VG	Fine	VF	XF
F26	1760	—	500.00	800.00	1250.	1500.
	1761	—	500.00	800.00	1250.	1500.
	1762	—	500.00	800.00	1250.	1500.
	1763	—	500.00	800.00	1250.	1500.
F26	1764	—	500.00	800.00	1250.	1500.
	1765	—	500.00	800.00	1250.	1500.
	1768	—	500.00	800.00	1250.	1500.
	1769	—	500.00	800.00	1250.	1500.
	1771	—	800.00	1350.	1750.	2000.
	1774	—	800.00	1350.	1750.	2000.
	1775	—	800.00	1350.	1750.	2000.
	1776	—	800.00	1350.	1750.	2000.
	1778	—	500.00	800.00	1250.	1500.
	1779	—	400.00	550.00	850.00	1500.
	1780	—	800.00	1350.	1750.	2000.
	1781	—	500.00	800.00	1250.	1500.
	1782	—	500.00	800.00	1250.	1500.
	1783	—	500.00	800.00	1250.	1500.
	1784	—	500.00	800.00	1250.	1500.
	1785	—	500.00	800.00	1250.	1500.
	1786	—	500.00	800.00	1250.	1500.
	1787	—	500.00	800.00	1250.	1500.
	1788	—	500.00	800.00	1250.	1500.
	1789	—	500.00	800.00	1250.	1500.
	1790	—	800.00	1350.	1750.	2000.
	1791	—	500.00	800.00	1250.	1500.
	1792	—	500.00	800.00	1250.	1500.
	1793	—	500.00	800.00	1250.	1500.
	1794	—	500.00	800.00	1250.	1500.

7 GULDEN

GOLD
Obv: Mounted knight, holding sword, over arms.
Rev: Crowned arms divide value; date above.

C#	Date	Mintage	VG	Fine	VF	XF
F27	1760	—	200.00	500.00	750.00	1000.
	1761	—	200.00	500.00	750.00	1000.
	1762	—	200.00	500.00	750.00	1000.
	1763	—	200.00	500.00	750.00	1000.

14 GULDEN

GOLD
Obv: Mounted knight, holding sword, over arms.
Rev: Crowned arms divide value; date above.

C#	Date	Mintage	VG	Fine	VF	XF
F28	1760	—	250.00	600.00	1000.	1500.
	1761	—	250.00	600.00	1000.	1500.
	1763	—	250.00	600.00	1000.	1500.

WEST FRIESLAND

West Frisia

West Friesland (West Frisia), also known as North Holland, is part of the province of Holland, and is not associated with the province of Friesland.

DUIT

COPPER
Obv: WEST FRISIA over date.
Rev: Crowned arms in sprays.

C#	Date	Mintage	VG	Fine	VF	XF
G2c	1765	—	3.75	8.00	15.00	20.00
	1769	—	3.75	8.00	15.00	20.00
	1778 R	—	5.00	9.00	15.00	20.00

GOLD (OMS)

C#	Date	Mintage	VG	Fine	VF	XF
G2d	1778	—	—	—	—	—

COPPER
Rev. leg: WEST/FRI/SIA

C#	Date	Mintage	VG	Fine	VF	XF
G2b	1780 R	—	3.75	8.00	13.50	17.50

STUIVER

.583 SILVER
Obv: WEST/FRI/SIE over date.
Rev: Bundle of arrows divide 1 S.
Rooster mintmark.

C#	Date	Mintage	VG	Fine	VF	XF
G4	1760	—	5.00	10.00	17.50	25.00

Ship mintmark.

C#	Date	Mintage	VG	Fine	VF	XF
G4.1	1764	—	5.00	10.00	17.50	25.00
	1765	—	5.00	10.00	17.50	25.00
	1766	—	5.00	10.00	17.50	25.00

GOLD (OMS)

C#	Date	Mintage	VG	Fine	VF	XF
G4a	1760	—	100.00	250.00	400.00	500.00
	1779	—	100.00	250.00	400.00	500.00
	1780/1775	—	175.00	350.00	500.00	600.00

2 STUIVER

(= Double Wapenstuiver)

.583 SILVER
Obv: Arms, value. Rev. leg: WEST FRISIAE, date.

C#	Date	Mintage	VG	Fine	VF	XF
G8	1761	—	2.50	4.00	8.00	13.50
	1762	—	2.50	4.00	8.00	13.50
	1765	—	2.50	4.00	8.00	13.50
	1766	—	2.50	4.00	8.00	13.50
	1767/6	—	6.00	7.50	15.00	20.00
	1767	—	2.50	4.00	8.00	13.50
	1768	—	2.50	4.00	8.00	13.50
	1769/8	—	6.00	7.50	15.00	20.00
	1769	—	2.50	4.00	8.00	13.50
	1770/68	—	6.00	7.50	15.00	20.00
	1770	—	2.50	4.00	8.00	13.50
	1771	—	2.50	4.00	8.00	13.50
	1772	—	2.50	4.00	8.00	13.50
	1773	—	2.50	4.00	8.00	13.50
	1774	—	2.50	4.00	8.00	13.50
	1775/4	—	6.00	7.50	15.00	20.00
	1775	—	2.50	4.00	8.00	13.50
	1776/5	—	6.00	7.50	15.00	20.00
	1776	—	2.50	4.00	8.00	13.50
	1777	—	2.50	4.00	8.00	13.50
	1778	—	2.50	4.00	8.00	13.50
	1779	—	2.50	4.00	8.00	13.50
	Rosette mintmark					
G8.1	1784/0	—	2.50	4.00	8.00	13.50
	1784 R	—	2.50	4.00	8.00	13.50
	1785 R	—	2.50	4.00	8.00	13.50
	1786/5	—	2.50	4.00	8.00	13.50
	1786 R	—	2.50	4.00	8.00	13.50
	1787 R	—	2.50	4.00	8.00	13.50
	1788/7 R	—	6.00	7.50	15.00	20.00
	1788 R	—	2.50	4.00	8.00	13.50
	1789 R	—	2.50	4.00	8.00	13.50
	1790/80 R	—	6.00	7.50	15.00	20.00
	1790 R	—	2.50	4.00	8.00	13.50
	1791/0 R	—	6.00	7.50	15.00	20.00
	1791/3 R	—	6.00	7.50	15.00	20.00
	1791 R	—	2.50	4.00	8.00	13.50
	1792 R	—	2.50	4.00	8.00	13.50
	1794 R	—	2.50	4.00	8.00	13.50

6 STUIVERS

(= Scheepjesschilling)

.583 SILVER
Obv: Crowned arms divide value; date over crown.
Rev: Ship sailing to right.
Rooster mintmark.

C#	Date	Mintage	VG	Fine	VF	XF
G11	1760	—	10.00	20.00	30.00	40.00
	1761	—	10.00	20.00	30.00	40.00
	Ship mintmark.					
G11.1	1762/0	—	12.50	25.00	40.00	50.00
	1762	—	10.00	20.00	30.00	40.00
	1765	—	10.00	20.00	30.00	40.00
	1767/6	—	12.50	25.00	40.00	50.00
	1767	—	10.00	20.00	30.00	40.00
	1771	—	10.00	20.00	30.00	40.00

X (10) STUIVERS

(= 1/2 Gulden)

.920 SILVER
Obv: Female standing leaning on altar,
leg: HAC NITIMVR HANC TVEMVR.
Rev: Arms, value, date, legend.

C#	Date	Mintage	VG	Fine	VF	XF
G12	1780	—	150.00	350.00	450.00	550.00
	1785	—	150.00	350.00	450.00	550.00
	1786	—	150.00	350.00	450.00	550.00

GULDEN

.920 SILVER
Obv: Crowned arms divide value.
Rev: Standing figure holding pole with liberty cap, leaning on Bible on column; date in exergue.
Ship mintmark.

C#	Date	Mintage	VG	Fine	VF	XF
G13	1762	—	20.00	35.00	45.00	55.00
	1763	—	20.00	35.00	45.00	55.00
	1764	—	20.00	35.00	45.00	55.00
	1765	—	25.00	40.00	55.00	75.00
	1767	—	50.00	85.00	130.00	175.00

W/o mintmark.

C#	Date	Mintage	VG	Fine	VF	XF
G13.1	1778/67	—	50.00	85.00	130.00	175.00
	1785	—	20.00	35.00	45.00	55.00
	1791/85	—	25.00	40.00	55.00	75.00
	1791	—	20.00	35.00	45.00	55.00
	1792/1	—	25.00	40.00	55.00	75.00
	1792	—	20.00	35.00	45.00	55.00
	1793	—	20.00	35.00	45.00	55.00
	1794	—	20.00	35.00	45.00	55.00

3 GULDEN

.920 SILVER
Ship mintmark.

C#	Date	Mintage	VG	Fine	VF	XF
G14	1761	—	75.00	100.00	150.00	250.00
	1763	—	75.00	100.00	150.00	250.00
	1764	—	75.00	100.00	150.00	250.00
	1767	—	175.00	250.00	400.00	600.00
	W/o mintmark.					
G14.1	1781	.068	90.00	150.00	200.00	275.00
	1785/1	.019	200.00	375.00	550.00	725.00
	1786/64	.419	110.00	225.00	250.00	325.00
	1786	Inc. Ab.	90.00	140.00	175.00	250.00
	1791/86	5.554	150.00	300.00	400.00	550.00
	1791	Inc. Ab.	75.00	100.00	150.00	225.00
	1792	Inc. Ab.	90.00	130.00	175.00	225.00
	1793/85	—	100.00	160.00	200.00	275.00
	1793/92	—	100.00	160.00	200.00	275.00
	1793	Inc. Ab.	75.00	100.00	150.00	225.00
	1794	Inc. Ab.	75.00	100.00	150.00	225.00

1/2 DUCATON

(= 1/2 Silver Rider)

.941 SILVER
Obv: Knight on galloping horse,
leg: MO NO ARG CONFOE BELG: WESTF.
Rev: Arms, date.
Ship mintmark.

C#	Date	Mintage	VG	Fine	VF	XF
G21	1762/1	—	150.00	250.00	325.00	400.00
	1762	—	90.00	150.00	200.00	250.00
	1764	—	90.00	150.00	200.00	250.00
	1765	—	90.00	150.00	200.00	250.00
	1766	—	90.00	150.00	200.00	250.00
	1767	—	90.00	150.00	200.00	250.00
	1768/67	—	150.00	250.00	325.00	400.00
	1768	—	90.00	150.00	200.00	250.00
	1770	—	90.00	150.00	200.00	250.00
	1771	—	90.00	150.00	200.00	250.00
	1772	—	90.00	150.00	200.00	250.00
	1773	—	90.00	150.00	200.00	250.00
	1774	—	90.00	150.00	200.00	250.00
	1775	—	90.00	150.00	200.00	250.00
	1776	—	90.00	150.00	200.00	250.00
	1778	—	90.00	150.00	200.00	250.00
	1779	—	90.00	150.00	200.00	250.00
	1780	—	90.00	150.00	200.00	250.00
	W/o mintmark.					
G21.1	1781/76	—	150.00	250.00	300.00	400.00

C#	Date	Mintage	VG	Fine	VF	XF
G21.1	1781	—	90.00	150.00	200.00	250.00
	1782	—	90.00	150.00	200.00	250.00
	1784	—	90.00	150.00	200.00	250.00
	1785	—	90.00	150.00	200.00	250.00
	1786	Inc.w/G22	90.00	150.00	200.00	250.00
	1788/6	—	225.00	375.00	550.00	700.00
	1788	Inc. Ab.	150.00	250.00	325.00	400.00
	1790/80	I.A.	225.00	375.00	550.00	700.00
	1790	Inc. Ab.	90.00	150.00	200.00	300.00
	1791	Inc. Ab.	90.00	150.00	200.00	250.00
	1792	Inc. Ab.	90.00	150.00	200.00	250.00
	1794	Inc. Ab.	150.00	250.00	325.00	400.00

RIJKSDAALDER

(= Silver Ducat)

.873 SILVER
Obv: Knight standing, small arms,
leg: MO NO ARG PRO CONFOE: BELG: WESTFRI.
Rev: Arms, date, legend.
Ship mintmark

C#	Date	Mintage	VG	Fine	VF	XF
G18	1761	—	90.00	160.00	225.00	275.00
	1762/1	—	105.00	200.00	275.00	375.00
	1762	—	90.00	160.00	225.00	275.00
	1763	—	80.00	150.00	200.00	250.00
	1764	—	90.00	160.00	225.00	275.00
	1765	—	105.00	225.00	325.00	400.00
	1767	—	90.00	160.00	225.00	275.00
	1770	—	90.00	160.00	225.00	275.00
	1771/61	—	100.00	225.00	325.00	400.00
	1771	—	90.00	160.00	225.00	275.00
	1772/71	—	100.00	225.00	325.00	400.00
	1772	—	100.00	225.00	325.00	400.00
	1773	—	80.00	150.00	200.00	250.00
	1774	—	100.00	225.00	325.00	400.00
	1775	—	80.00	150.00	200.00	250.00
	1776	—	80.00	150.00	200.00	250.00
	W/o mintmark.					
G18.1	1781	1.488	80.00	150.00	200.00	250.00
	1782	2.017	80.00	150.00	200.00	250.00
	1784/74	I.A.	90.00	155.00	200.00	275.00
	1785/4	—	105.00	225.00	325.00	400.00
	1784	Inc. Ab.	80.00	150.00	200.00	250.00
	1787	1.010	105.00	225.00	325.00	400.00
	1789/7	Inc. Ab.	90.00	225.00	325.00	400.00
	1789	Inc. Ab.	80.00	150.00	200.00	250.00
	1790	Inc. Ab.	90.00	160.00	225.00	275.00
	1791	Inc. Ab.	90.00	160.00	225.00	275.00
	1792	.690	80.00	150.00	200.00	250.00
	1793	Inc. Ab.	80.00	150.00	200.00	250.00
	1794	Inc. Ab.	80.00	150.00	200.00	250.00

DUCATON

(= Silver Rider)

.941 SILVER
Obv: Knight on galloping horse, arms below,
leg: MO: NO ARG PRO CONFOE: BELG. WESTF.
Rev: Arms, date, legend.
Ship mintmark.

C#	Date	Mintage	VG	Fine	VF	XF
G22	1762	—	125.00	200.00	275.00	375.00
	1765/62	—	125.00	200.00	275.00	375.00
	1765	—	110.00	190.00	250.00	300.00
	1766	—	110.00	190.00	250.00	300.00
	1767/6	—	110.00	190.00	250.00	300.00
	1767	—	110.00	190.00	250.00	300.00
	1768	—	75.00	110.00	160.00	200.00
	1770	—	75.00	110.00	160.00	200.00
	1771	—	75.00	110.00	160.00	200.00
	1772	—	75.00	110.00	160.00	200.00
	1773	—	75.00	110.00	160.00	200.00
	1774	—	75.00	110.00	160.00	200.00
	1775	—	110.00	190.00	250.00	300.00
	1778	.230	75.00	110.00	160.00	200.00
	1779	Inc. Ab.	75.00	110.00	160.00	200.00
	1780/76	I.A.	125.00	200.00	250.00	375.00
	1780/79 S/B		125.00	200.00	250.00	400.00
	1780	Inc. Ab.	75.00	110.00	160.00	200.00
	W/o mintmark.					
G22.1	1781	.538	90.00	135.00	180.00	225.00
	1782	Inc. Ab.	75.00	125.00	165.00	225.00
	1783	Inc. Ab.	75.00	125.00	165.00	225.00
	1784	Inc. Ab.	75.00	125.00	165.00	225.00
	1785	Inc. Ab.	90.00	135.00	180.00	225.00
	1786	Inc. Ab.	110.00	190.00	250.00	300.00
	1788	—	200.00	350.00	475.00	675.00
	1789	.275	90.00	135.00	180.00	225.00
	1790/66	I.A.	150.00	275.00	350.00	450.00
	1790/80	I.A.	125.00	200.00	275.00	375.00
	1790/89	I.A.	200.00	350.00	475.00	675.00
	1790	Inc. Ab.	90.00	135.00	180.00	225.00
	1791/0	Inc. Ab.	125.00	200.00	275.00	375.00

C#	Date	Mintage	VG	Fine	VF	XF
G22.1	1791	Inc. Ab.	90.00	135.00	180.00	225.00
	1792/1	—	125.00	200.00	275.00	375.00
	1792	—	90.00	135.00	180.00	225.00
	1793/2	—	125.00	200.00	275.00	375.00
	1793	—	90.00	135.00	180.00	225.00

TRADE COINS

DUCAT

.986 GOLD
Obv: Standing knight, date, leg: CONCORDIA RES. PAR. CRES. WESTF.
Rev: Legend on tablet.

C#	Date	Mintage	VG	Fine	VF	XF
G25	1760	—	150.00	225.00	350.00	500.00
	1761	—	150.00	225.00	350.00	500.00
	1762	—	150.00	225.00	350.00	500.00
	1775	—	150.00	225.00	350.00	500.00
	1776	—	150.00	225.00	350.00	500.00
	1777	—	150.00	225.00	350.00	500.00
	1778	—	150.00	225.00	350.00	500.00
	1780	—	150.00	225.00	350.00	500.00
	1783	.013	250.00	375.00	550.00	750.00
	1784	Inc. Ab.	225.00	350.00	500.00	700.00
	1785	Inc. Ab.	225.00	350.00	500.00	700.00
	1786	Inc. Ab.	250.00	375.00	550.00	750.00

2 DUCATS

.986 GOLD
Obv: Standing knight, date, leg: CONCORDIA RES. PAR. CRES. WESTFRI.
Rev: Legend on tablet.

C#	Date	Mintage	VG	Fine	VF	XF
G26	1761	—	500.00	800.00	1250.	1500.
	1778	—	500.00	800.00	1250.	1500.
	1779	—	500.00	800.00	1250.	1500.
	1780	—	400.00	600.00	1000.	1350.

7 GULDEN

GOLD
Obv: Mounted knight, holding sword, over arms.
Rev: Crowned arms divide value; date above.

C#	Date	Mintage	VG	Fine	VF	XF
G27	1760	—	275.00	500.00	750.00	1000.
	1761 Rooster	—	275.00	500.00	750.00	1000.
	1761 Ship	—	400.00	650.00	1000.	1250.
	1762	—	400.00	650.00	1000.	1250.
	1763	—	275.00	500.00	750.00	1000.

14 GULDEN

GOLD
Obv: Mounted knight, holding sword, over arms.
Rev: Crowned arms divide value; date above.

C#	Date	Mintage	VG	Fine	VF	XF
G28	1760	—	375.00	600.00	1000.	1500.
	1761	—	375.00	600.00	1000.	1500.
	1762	—	375.00	600.00	1000.	1500.
	1763	—	375.00	600.00	1000.	1500.

ZEELAND

Zelandia

Zeeland (Zelandia), the southernmost maritime province of the Netherlands, consists of a strip of the Flanders mainland and six islands.

DUIT

COPPER
Obv: ZEE/LAN/DIA over date.
Rev: Crowned arms.

C#	Date	Mintage	VG	Fine	VF	XF
H2	1761	—	3.00	6.50	11.50	17.50
	1762	—	3.00	6.50	11.50	17.50
	1763	—	3.00	6.50	11.50	17.50
	1764	—	3.00	6.50	11.50	17.50
	1765	—	3.00	6.50	11.50	17.50
	1766	—	3.00	6.50	11.50	17.50

C#	Date	Mintage	VG	Fine	VF	XF
H2a	1766	—	5.00	10.00	16.50	22.50
	1767	—	5.00	10.00	16.50	22.50
	1768	—	5.00	10.00	17.50	25.00
	1769	—	5.00	10.00	17.50	25.00
	1770	—	3.75	8.00	15.00	20.00
	1772	—	3.75	8.00	15.00	20.00
	1776	—	5.00	10.00	17.50	25.00
	1777	—	3.75	8.00	15.00	20.00
	1778	—	3.75	8.00	15.00	20.00
	1779	—	3.75	8.00	15.00	20.00
	1780	—	3.00	6.50	11.50	17.50
	1781	—	3.75	8.00	15.00	20.00
	1782	—	3.00	6.50	11.50	17.50
	1783	—	3.00	6.50	11.50	17.50
	1784	—	3.00	6.50	11.50	17.50
	1785	—	3.00	6.50	11.50	17.50
	1786	—	3.00	6.50	11.50	17.50
	1787	—	2.50	5.00	10.00	15.00
	1788	—	2.50	5.00	10.00	15.00
	1789	—	3.75	8.00	15.00	20.00
	1790	—	2.50	5.00	10.00	15.00
	1791	—	2.50	5.00	10.00	15.00
	1792	—	2.50	5.00	10.00	15.00

SILVER (OMS)

C#	Date	Mintage	VG	Fine	VF	XF
H2c	1761	—	—	—	—	—
	1769	—	—	—	—	—

COPPER

C#	Date	Mintage	VG	Fine	VF	XF
H2b	1792	—	3.00	6.50	11.50	17.50
	1793	—	2.50	5.00	10.00	15.00
	1794	—	3.75	8.00	15.00	20.00
	1795	—	5.00	10.00	17.50	22.50
	1796	—	5.00	10.00	17.50	22.50
	1797/6	—	10.00	20.00	30.00	45.00
	1797	—	5.00	11.50	20.00	30.00

STUIVER

Bezem Stuiver

.583 SILVER

C#	Date	Mintage	VG	Fine	VF	XF
H4	1760	—	10.00	16.50	27.50	40.00
	1761	—	10.00	16.50	27.50	40.00
	1762	—	10.00	16.50	27.50	40.00
	1763	—	10.00	16.50	27.50	40.00
	1764	—	10.00	16.50	27.50	40.00
	1765	—	10.00	16.50	27.50	40.00
	1791	—	10.00	16.50	20.00	25.00

2 STUIVERS

.583 SILVER
Obv: ZEE/LAN/DIA over date.
Rev: Crowned arms divide value.

C#	Date	Mintage	VG	Fine	VF	XF
H7	1765	—	10.00	16.50	20.00	25.00

6 STUIVERS

(= Scheepjesschelling)

.583 SILVER

C#	Date	Mintage	VG	Fine	VF	XF
H11	1760	—	15.00	22.50	30.00	40.00
	1761	—	15.00	22.50	30.00	40.00
	1762	—	15.00	22.50	30.00	40.00
	1763	—	15.00	22.50	30.00	40.00
	1765	—	10.00	17.50	25.00	35.00
	1766	—	15.00	22.50	30.00	40.00
	1767	—	15.00	22.50	30.00	40.00
	1768/7	—	17.50	30.00	40.00	50.00
	1768	—	15.00	22.50	30.00	40.00
	1769	—	15.00	22.50	30.00	40.00
	1770	—	10.00	17.50	25.00	35.00
	1771	—	15.00	22.50	35.00	40.00
	1772	—	15.00	22.50	30.00	40.00
	1773	—	10.00	17.50	25.00	35.00
	1774	—	15.00	22.50	30.00	40.00
	1775	—	10.00	17.50	25.00	35.00
	1776	—	10.00	17.50	25.00	35.00
	1777	—	100.00	150.00	200.00	275.00
	1778/7	—	22.50	35.00	50.00	75.00
	1778	—	15.00	22.50	30.00	40.00
	1779	—	15.00	22.50	30.00	40.00
	1780/70	—	15.00	25.00	35.00	45.00
	1780	—	15.00	22.50	30.00	40.00
	1785	—	15.00	22.50	30.00	40.00
	1788	—	10.00	17.50	25.00	35.00
	1790	—	10.00	17.50	25.00	35.00
	1791	—	10.00	17.50	25.00	35.00
	1792	—	10.00	17.50	25.00	35.00
	1793	—	10.00	17.50	25.00	35.00

GULDEN

.920 SILVER
Obv: Crowned arms divide value.
Rev: Standing figure holding pole with liberty cap, leaning on column; date in exergue.

C#	Date	Mintage	VG	Fine	VF	XF
H13	1763	—	135.00	375.00	500.00	600.00
	1764	—	135.00	375.00	500.00	600.00

GOLD (OMS)

C#	Date	Mintage	VG	Fine	VF	XF
H13a	1765	—	—	—	—	—

1/8 RIJKSDAALDER

(= 1/8 Silver Ducat)

.873 SILVER, 21.5mm
Obv: Knight standing, small arms, leg: MO NO ARG PRO CONFOE BELG CO ZEL.
Rev: Arms, legend, date.

C#	Date	Mintage	VG	Fine	VF	XF
H15	1762	—	27.50	55.00	80.00	120.00
	1763	—	27.50	55.00	80.00	120.00
	1764	—	22.50	37.50	55.00	80.00
	1765	—	22.50	37.50	55.00	80.00
	1766	—	19.50	27.50	40.00	55.00
	1767	—	19.50	27.50	40.00	55.00
	1768	—	19.50	27.50	40.00	55.00
	1769	—	19.50	27.50	40.00	55.00
	1770	—	19.50	27.50	40.00	55.00
	1771	—	19.50	27.50	40.00	55.00
	1772	—	19.50	27.50	40.00	55.00
	1773	—	19.50	27.50	40.00	55.00
	1774	—	19.50	27.50	40.00	55.00
	1775	—	19.50	27.50	40.00	55.00
	1776	—	19.50	27.50	40.00	55.00
	1777	3.081	32.50	60.00	85.00	120.00
	1778	1.605	32.50	60.00	85.00	120.00
	1779	Inc. Ab.	32.50	60.00	85.00	120.00
	1780	Inc. Ab.	25.00	45.00	65.00	100.00
	1781	1.433	25.00	45.00	65.00	100.00
	1782	Inc. Ab.	25.00	45.00	65.00	100.00
	1784	Inc. Ab.	25.00	45.00	65.00	100.00
	1785/3	—	32.50	60.00	85.00	120.00
	1785	Inc. Ab.	25.00	45.00	65.00	100.00
	1786	Inc. Ab.	25.00	45.00	65.00	100.00
	1787	.097	25.00	45.00	65.00	100.00
	1788/6	—	—	75.00	100.00	165.00
	1788/7	—	32.50	60.00	85.00	120.00
	1788	Inc. Ab.	25.00	40.00	65.00	100.00
	1790	1.290	22.50	37.50	55.00	80.00
	1791	Inc. Ab.	22.50	37.50	55.00	80.00
	1792	Inc. Ab.	22.50	37.50	55.00	80.00
	1793	—	22.50	37.50	55.00	80.00

GOLD (OMS)

C#	Date	Mintage	VG	Fine	VF	XF
H15a	1773	—	1200.	2000.	2500.	3000.
	1774	—	1200.	2000.	2500.	3000.
	1775	—	1200.	2000.	2500.	3000.
	1778	—	1200.	2000.	2500.	3000.
	1779	—	1200.	2000.	2500.	3000.
	1780	—	1200.	2000.	2500.	3000.
	1782	—	—	—	Rare	—
	1784	—	1200.	2000.	2500.	3000.
	1787	—	1200.	2000.	2500.	3000.
	1788	—	1200.	2000.	2500.	3000.
	1790	—	1200.	2000.	2500.	3000.

1/4 RIJKSDAALDER

(= 1/4 Silver Ducat)

.873 SILVER, 27mm
Obv: Knight standing, small arms, leg: MO NO ARG PRO CONFOE BELG CO ZEL.
Rev: Arms, legend, date.

C#	Date	Mintage	VG	Fine	VF	XF
H16	1762	—	75.00	120.00	170.00	225.00

C#	Date	Mintage	VG	Fine	VF	XF
H16	1763	—	75.00	120.00	170.00	225.00
	1764	—	50.00	75.00	125.00	175.00
	1765	—	50.00	75.00	125.00	175.00
	1766	—	50.00	75.00	125.00	175.00
	1767	—	50.00	75.00	125.00	175.00
	1768	—	50.00	75.00	125.00	175.00
	1769	—	50.00	75.00	125.00	175.00
	1770	—	50.00	75.00	125.00	175.00
	1771	—	50.00	75.00	125.00	175.00
	1772	—	50.00	75.00	125.00	175.00
	1773	—	50.00	75.00	125.00	175.00
	1774	—	50.00	75.00	125.00	175.00
	1775	—	50.00	75.00	125.00	175.00
	1776	—	50.00	75.00	125.00	175.00
	1777	Inc. w/H15	75.00	120.00	170.00	225.00
	1778	Inc.w/H15	75.00	120.00	170.00	225.00
	1779	Inc. Ab.	75.00	120.00	170.00	225.00
	1780	Inc. Ab.	75.00	120.00	170.00	225.00
	1781	Inc.w/H15	75.00	120.00	170.00	225.00
	1782	Inc. Ab.	75.00	120.00	170.00	225.00
	1785	Inc. Ab.	75.00	120.00	170.00	225.00
	1786	Inc. Ab.	75.00	120.00	170.00	225.00
	1787	Inc.w/H15	75.00	120.00	170.00	225.00
	1788/7	—	90.00	150.00	200.00	250.00
	1788	Inc. Ab.	90.00	150.00	190.00	250.00
	1791	Inc.w/H15	75.00	120.00	170.00	225.00
	1792	Inc. Ab.	50.00	100.00	150.00	190.00
	1793	—	50.00	100.00	150.00	190.00

GOLD (OMS)

C#	Date	Mintage	VG	Fine	VF	XF
H16a	1773	—	1500.	2750.	4000.	5000.
	1775	—	1500.	2750.	4000.	5000.
	1776	—	1500.	2750.	4000.	5000.
	1778	—	1500.	2750.	4000.	5000.
	1779	—	1500.	2750.	4000.	5000.
	1780	—	1500.	2750.	4000.	5000.
	1787	—	1500.	2750.	4000.	5000.

1/2 RIJKSDAALDER

(= 1/2 Silver Ducat)

.873 SILVER, 33mm.
Obv: Knight standing, small arms,
leg: MO NO ARG PRO CONFOE BELG CO ZEL.
Rev: Arms, legend, date.

C#	Date	Mintage	VG	Fine	VF	XF
H17	1760	—	100.00	165.00	225.00	275.00
	1761	—	90.00	135.00	180.00	225.00
	1762	—	90.00	135.00	180.00	225.00
	1763/2	—	100.00	165.00	225.00	275.00
	1763	—	90.00	135.00	180.00	225.00
	1764	—	90.00	135.00	180.00	225.00
	1765	—	90.00	135.00	180.00	225.00
	1766	—	90.00	135.00	180.00	225.00
	1767	—	90.00	135.00	180.00	225.00
	1768	—	90.00	135.00	180.00	225.00
	1769	—	90.00	135.00	180.00	225.00
	1770	—	90.00	135.00	180.00	225.00
	1771	—	90.00	135.00	180.00	225.00
	1772	—	90.00	135.00	180.00	225.00
	1773	—	90.00	135.00	180.00	225.00
	1774	—	90.00	135.00	180.00	225.00
	1775	—	90.00	135.00	180.00	225.00
	1776	—	90.00	135.00	180.00	225.00
	1777	Inc. w/H15	90.00	135.00	190.00	250.00
	1778	Inc.w/H15	90.00	135.00	190.00	250.00
	1779	Inc. Ab.	90.00	135.00	190.00	250.00
	1780	Inc. Ab.	90.00	135.00	190.00	250.00
	1781	Inc.w/H15	90.00	135.00	190.00	250.00
	1782	Inc. Ab.	90.00	135.00	190.00	250.00
	1786	Inc. Ab.	90.00	135.00	190.00	250.00
	1787	Inc.w/H15	100.00	165.00	225.00	275.00
	1788	Inc. Ab.	100.00	165.00	225.00	275.00
	1792	Inc.w/H15	90.00	135.00	190.00	250.00
	1793	—	90.00	135.00	190.00	250.00

GOLD (OMS)

C#	Date	Mintage	VG	Fine	VF	XF
H17a	1773	—	—	—	—	—
	1775	—	—	—	—	—

1/2 DUCATON

1/2 Silver Rider

.941 SILVER

C#	Date	Mintage	VG	Fine	VF	XF
H21	1766	—	110.00	150.00	250.00	325.00
	1767	—	110.00	150.00	250.00	325.00
	1768	—	135.00	175.00	300.00	425.00
	1768	—	110.00	150.00	250.00	325.00
	1769	—	110.00	150.00	250.00	325.00
	1771	—	100.00	190.00	225.00	300.00
	1772	—	100.00	190.00	275.00	350.00
	1773	—	100.00	190.00	250.00	300.00
	1775	—	100.00	190.00	225.00	300.00
	1785	.146	110.00	150.00	250.00	325.00
	1790	.339	100.00	150.00	225.00	300.00
	1792	.339	100.00	190.00	225.00	300.00
	1793	.128	100.00	190.00	225.00	300.00

RIJKSDAALDER

(= Silver Ducat)

.873 SILVER

C#	Date	Mintage	VG	Fine	VF	XF
H18	1760	—	100.00	165.00	225.00	300.00
	1761	—	100.00	165.00	225.00	300.00
	1762	—	75.00	120.00	165.00	225.00
	1763	—	75.00	120.00	165.00	225.00
	1764	—	75.00	120.00	165.00	225.00
	1765	—	75.00	120.00	165.00	225.00
	1766	—	75.00	120.00	165.00	225.00
	1767	—	65.00	100.00	135.00	185.00
	1768	—	65.00	100.00	135.00	185.00
	1769	—	65.00	100.00	135.00	185.00
	1770	—	65.00	100.00	135.00	185.00
	1771	—	50.00	80.00	120.00	175.00
	1772	—	65.00	100.00	135.00	185.00
	1773	—	75.00	120.00	165.00	225.00
	1774	—	50.00	80.00	120.00	175.00
	1775	—	50.00	80.00	120.00	175.00
	1776	—	50.00	80.00	120.00	175.00

C#	Date	Mintage	VG	Fine	VF	XF
H18	1777	Inc. w/H15	50.00	80.00	120.00	165.00
	1778	Inc.w/H15	40.00	70.00	120.00	160.00
	1779	Inc. Ab.	40.00	70.00	120.00	160.00
	1780	Inc. Ab.	37.50	60.00	100.00	150.00
	1781	Inc.w/H15	50.00	80.00	120.00	175.00
	1782	Inc. Ab.	50.00	80.00	120.00	175.00
	1784	Inc. Ab.	100.00	165.00	225.00	300.00
	1784	Inc. Ab.	75.00	120.00	165.00	225.00
	1785	Inc. Ab.	65.00	100.00	135.00	190.00
	1786	Inc. Ab.	75.00	120.00	165.00	225.00
	1787	Inc.w/H15	50.00	80.00	120.00	165.00
	1788	Inc. Ab.	50.00	80.00	120.00	165.00
	1789/8	—	50.00	80.00	120.00	165.00
	1789	Inc. Ab.	50.00	80.00	120.00	165.00
	1790	Inc.w/H15	50.00	80.00	120.00	165.00
	1791	Inc. Ab.	50.00	80.00	120.00	165.00
	1792	2.389	50.00	100.00	135.00	180.00
	1793	Inc. Ab.	50.00	80.00	120.00	165.00
	1794	Inc. Ab.	100.00	165.00	225.00	300.00
	1794	Inc. Ab.	110.00	180.00	250.00	325.00

GOLD (OMS)
Thick planchet, 36.60GR.

C#	Date	Mintage	VG	Fine	VF	XF
H18a	1764	—	—	—	—	—
	1777	—	—	—	—	—

Thin planchet, 22.70GR.

C#	Date	Mintage	VG	Fine	VF	XF
H18a.1	1792	—	—	—	—	—

DUCATON

(= Silver Rider)

.941 SILVER
Obv: Knight on galloping horse, small arms below,
leg: MO NO ARG PRO CONFOE BELG COM ZEEL.
Rev: Arms, date, legend.

C#	Date	Mintage	VG	Fine	VF	XF
H22	1760/50	—	75.00	110.00	160.00	275.00
	1760	—	75.00	110.00	160.00	275.00
	1761	—	75.00	110.00	160.00	275.00
	1761	—	75.00	110.00	160.00	275.00
	1762	—	75.00	110.00	160.00	275.00
	1763	—	75.00	110.00	160.00	275.00
	1765	—	75.00	110.00	160.00	275.00
	1766/5	—	—	275.00	300.00	375.00
	1766	—	75.00	110.00	160.00	225.00
	1767/6	—	—	275.00	300.00	375.00
	1767	—	75.00	110.00	160.00	225.00
	1768	—	—	—	—	—
	1769	—	—	—	—	—
	1771	—	—	—	—	—
	1772	—	75.00	110.00	160.00	225.00
	1773	—	75.00	110.00	160.00	225.00
	1774	—	75.00	110.00	160.00	225.00
	1775	—	75.00	110.00	160.00	225.00
	1776	—	75.00	110.00	160.00	225.00
	1785/75	—	110.00	190.00	275.00	300.00
	1785	Inc. w/H21	75.00	130.00	170.00	205.00
	1789	Inc. Ab.	75.00	110.00	160.00	225.00
	1790/89	Inc. Ab.	110.00	190.00	275.00	325.00
	1790	Inc. Ab.	90.00	130.00	175.00	225.00
	1791	Inc. Ab.	90.00	130.00	170.00	225.00
	1792/1	—	100.00	250.00	325.00	400.00
	1792	Inc. Ab.	90.00	130.00	170.00	225.00
	1793	Inc. Ab.	90.00	130.00	170.00	225.00

TRADE COINS

DUCAT

GOLD
Obv: Standing knight divides date.
Rev: Legend in ornamental tablet.

C#	Date	Mintage	VG	Fine	VF	XF
H25	1760	—	250.00	500.00	750.00	1000.
	1761	—	250.00	500.00	750.00	1000.
	1762	—	250.00	500.00	750.00	1000.
	1763	—	250.00	500.00	750.00	1000.

7 GULDEN

GOLD
Obv: Mounted knight, holding sword, over arms.
Rev: Crowned arms divide value, date above.

C#	Date	Mintage	VG	Fine	VF	XF
H27	1760	—	350.00	500.00	850.00	1100.
	1761	—	350.00	500.00	850.00	1100.
	1762	—	500.00	800.00	1250.	1500.
	1763	—	350.00	500.00	850.00	1100.
	1764	—	350.00	500.00	850.00	1100.

14 GULDEN

GOLD

Obv: Mounted knight, holding sword, over arms.
Rev: Crowned arms divide value, date above.

C#	Date	Mintage	VG	Fine	VF	XF
H28	1760	—	375.00	600.00	1000.	1500.
	1761	—	375.00	600.00	1000.	1500.
	1762	—	375.00	600.00	1000.	1500.
	1763	—	375.00	600.00	1000.	1500.
	1764	—	375.00	600.00	1000.	1500.

SIEGE COINAGE

MAASTRICHT

Maastricht, capital of the province of Limberg in the Netherlands, was the seat of a bishop from 382 to 721. Once part of the Frankish realm, it was ruled by the dukes of Brabant and the prince-bishops of Liege after 1673. It was taken by the French in 1673, 1748, and 1794. The Austrian defenders under the Prince of Hesse issued an emergency coinage for Maastricht during the 1794 siege.

5 STIVERS

BRONZE - UNIFACE
Similar to 50 Stivers, C#3.

C#	Date	Mintage	VG	Fine	VF
1	1794	—	225.00	350.00	450.00

50 STIVERS

SILVER - UNIFACE

C#	Date	Mintage	VG	Fine	VF
3	1794	—	750.00	1175.	1500.

100 STIVERS

SILVER

C#	Date	Mintage	VG	Fine	VF
5	1794	—	1350.	2000.	3000.

C#	Date	Mintage	VG	Fine	VF
6	1794	—	950.00	1350.	1950.
		BRONZE			
2	1794	—	175.00	300.00	500.00

SILVER - UNIFACE

C#	Date	Mintage	VG	Fine	VF
7	1794	—	250.00	400.00	600.00

COUNTERSTAMP ISSUES

50 STIVERS

SILVER
c/s: 1794, star and 50 St. on 1/2 Ecu of Louis XV.

C#	Date	Mintage	VG	Fine	VF
3a	1794	—	—	—	—

100 STIVERS

SILVER
c/s: 1794, star and 100 St. on Ecu of Louis XVI, C#78.

C#	Date	Mintage	VG	Fine	VF
7a	1794	—	—	—	—

BATAVIAN REPUBLIC

Prior to 1806, the Netherlands was a confederation of seven provinces, each producing coins similar in design but differing in the coat of arms or inscription. Generally the coins of each province contained an abbreviation of the name of the province somewhere in the inscription. Under the Batavian Republic, the following abbreviations were used.

MINTMARKS

G, GEL - Gelderland
HOL, HOLL - Holland
TRANSI - Overijsel
TRA, TRAI, TRAIECTUM - Utrecht
WESTF, WESTRI - Westfriesland
ZEL, ZEELANDIA - Zeeland

DUIT

COPPER

ZEELAND (ZEELANDIA, ZEL)

C#	Date	Mintage	Fine	VF	XF	Unc
H31	1795/4	—	20.00	30.00	40.00	50.00
	1795	—	10.00	17.50	25.00	32.50
	1796/66	—	20.00	30.00	40.00	50.00
	1796	—	10.00	17.50	25.00	32.50
	1797/69	—	30.00	40.00	50.00	65.00
	1797/6	—	20.00	30.00	40.00	50.00
	1797	—	17.50	25.00	30.00	37.50

2 STUIVERS

.558 SILVER

UTRECHT (TRAIECTUM, TRA, TRAI)

C#	Date	Mintage	Fine	VF	XF	Unc
F33	1796	2,110	155.00	225.00	275.00	350.00
	1797	—	300.00	400.00	450.00	500.00
	1799	4,070	125.00	170.00	200.00	250.00

2-1/2 STUIVERS
(of 1/8 Livre Copper)

COPPER

ZEELAND (ZEELANDIA, ZEL)

C#	Date	Mintage	Fine	VF	XF	Unc
H32	1795	—	1750.	2500.	3000.	3500.

10 STUIVERS

.912 SILVER

UTRECHT (TRAIECTUM, TRA, TRAI)

C#	Date	Mintage	Fine	VF	XF	Unc
F34	1795	—	125.00	175.00	250.00	325.00
	1796	796 pcs.	250.00	375.00	500.00	625.00

1/2 GULDEN

.912 SILVER

WEST FRIESLAND (WESTF, WESTRI)

C#	Date	Mintage	Fine	VF	XF	Unc
G34	1796	—	225.00	350.00	425.00	500.00

GULDEN

.912 SILVER

GELDERLAND (G, GEL)

C#	Date	Mintage	Fine	VF	XF	Unc
A35	1795	.790	85.00	125.00	150.00	175.00
	1796/5	.042	200.00	300.00	350.00	400.00
	1796	Inc. Ab.	175.00	250.00	300.00	350.00

C#	Date	Year	Mintage	Fine	VF	XF
A35a	1798	AN 7	—	200.00	250.00	325.00

NOTE: The above is considered a pattern by some experts.

HOLLAND (HOL, HOLL)

C#	Date	Mintage	Fine	VF	XF	Unc
C35	1795	.732	50.00	75.00	125.00	175.00
	1800	.040	125.00	200.00	250.00	300.00
		Denomination: GL				
C35a	1797	.230	125.00	200.00	250.00	300.00
	1797 HOLL/WESTF					
		Inc. Ab.	200.00	350.00	425.00	500.00

OVERIJSEL (TRANSI)

C#	Date	Mintage	Fine	VF	XF	Unc
E35	1795	.615	65.00	85.00	125.00	150.00
	1796	Inc. Ab.	135.00	200.00	250.00	300.00

UTRECHT (TRAIECTUM, TRA, TRAI)

C#	Date	Mintage	Fine	VF	XF	Unc
F35	1795	—	250.00	375.00	425.00	500.00
	1798	.016	200.00	300.00	375.00	450.00
	1799	.038	125.00	200.00	250.00	300.00

WEST FRIESLAND (WESTF, WESTRI)

C#	Date	Mintage	Fine	VF	XF	Unc
G35	1795	—	250.00	375.00	425.00	500.00
	1796 decorated altar, w/o garland					
		—	150.00	225.00	275.00	325.00
	1796 round altar, w/garland					
		—	200.00	300.00	350.00	400.00

1/2 DUCATON

.935 SILVER

UTRECHT (TRAIECTUM, TRA, TRAI)

C#	Date	Mintage	Fine	VF	XF	Unc
F38	1796	—	1000.	1500.	2000.	2500.
	1798	—	1000.	1500.	2000.	2500.

RIJKSDAALDER

.868 SILVER

GELDERLAND (G, GEL)

C#	Date	Mintage	Fine	VF	XF	Unc
A37	1795	5,000	1150.	1500.	1900.	2250.
	1797	.019	750.00	1000.	1250.	1500.
	1800	.254	700.00	950.00	1150.	1350.
	1801	Inc. Ab.	700.00	950.00	1150.	1350.
	1802	Inc. Ab.	700.00	950.00	1150.	1350.

HOLLAND (HOL, HOLL)

C#	Date	Mintage	Fine	VF	XF	Unc
C37	1796	2.668	425.00	625.00	750.00	875.00
	1797/6	Inc. Ab.	1750.	2750.	3250.	3750.
	1798	Inc. Ab.	750.00	1000.	1250.	1500.
	1799	Inc. Ab.	1750.	2000.	2500.	3750.
	1800	Inc. Ab.	325.00	500.00	625.00	750.00
	1801/0	I.A.	375.00	625.00	750.00	875.00
	1801	Inc. Ab.	325.00	500.00	625.00	750.00
	1802	Inc. Ab.	325.00	500.00	625.00	750.00
	1806	Inc. Ab.	1750.	2750.	3250.	3750.

OVERIJSEL (TRANSI)

C#	Date	Mintage	Fine	VF	XF	Unc
E37	1795	.049	1250.	2000.	2500.	3000.
	1796	Inc. Ab.	625.00	1000.	1250.	1500.

UTRECHT (TRAIECTUM, TRA, TRAI)

C#	Date	Mintage	Fine	VF	XF	Unc
F37	1795	6.283	750.00	1000.	1200.	1400.
	1796	Inc. Ab.	190.00	300.00	350.00	400.00
	1797	Inc. Ab.	750.00	1000.	1200.	1400.
	1798	Inc. Ab.	750.00	1000.	1200.	1400.
	1799	Inc. Ab.	200.00	325.00	375.00	450.00
	1800	Inc. Ab.	160.00	225.00	275.00	350.00
	1800 sm. 8	I.A.	160.00	225.00	275.00	350.00
	1801	Inc. Ab.	160.00	225.00	275.00	350.00
	1801 w/small 8-0	Inc. Ab.	175.00	250.00	300.00	375.00
	1802	Inc. Ab.	200.00	325.00	375.00	450.00
	1803 long sword	Inc. Ab.	160.00	225.00	275.00	350.00
	1803 short sword	Inc. Ab.	—	—	—	—
	1804	Inc. Ab.	160.00	225.00	275.00	350.00
	1805/1797	I.A.	175.00	250.00	300.00	375.00
	1805	Inc. Ab.	160.00	225.00	275.00	350.00

WEST FRIESLAND (WESTF, WESTRI)

C#	Date	Mintage	Fine	VF	XF	Unc
G37	1795	—	625.00	875.00	1000.	1250.
	1796	—	625.00	875.00	1000.	1250.

ZEELAND (ZELANDIA, ZEL)

C#	Date	Mintage	Fine	VF	XF	Unc
H37	1795	—	135.00	190.00	225.00	275.00
	1796	—	750.00	875.00	1000.	1250.
	1798/6	.099	150.00	200.00	250.00	300.00
	1798/7	I.A.	175.00	225.00	275.00	325.00
	1798	Inc. Ab.	150.00	200.00	250.00	300.00

3 GULDEN

.915 SILVER

GELDERLAND (G, GEL)

C#	Date	Mintage	Fine	VF	XF	Unc
A36	1795	.178	250.00	375.00	500.00	625.00
	1796/5	.045	400.00	625.00	750.00	875.00
A36	1796	Inc. Ab.	400.00	625.00	750.00	875.00

HOLLAND (HOL, HOLL)

C#	Date	Mintage	Fine	VF	XF	Unc
C36	1795/3	1.084	150.00	225.00	275.00	325.00
	1795	Inc. Ab.	150.00	200.00	250.00	300.00
	1796	Inc. Ab.	150.00	250.00	300.00	375.00
	1797	Inc. Ab.	150.00	225.00	275.00	325.00
	1798	Inc. Ab.	250.00	375.00	425.00	500.00
	1800	Inc. Ab.	250.00	375.00	425.00	500.00
	1801	Inc. Ab.	250.00	375.00	425.00	500.00

UTRECHT (TRAIECTUM, TRA, TRAI)

C#	Date	Mintage	Fine	VF	XF	Unc
F36	1795	1.713	150.00	225.00	275.00	325.00
	1796	Inc. Ab.	150.00	250.00	300.00	375.00

WEST FRIESLAND (WESTF, WESTRI)

C#	Date	Mintage	Fine	VF	XF	Unc
G36	1795	—	150.00	225.00	275.00	325.00
	1796/5	—	300.00	425.00	500.00	625.00
	1796	—	300.00	425.00	500.00	625.00

DUCATON

.935 SILVER

UTRECHT (TRAIECTUM, TRA, TRAI)

C#	Date	Mintage	Fine	VF	XF	Unc
F39	1796	435 pcs.	1750.	2500.	3000.	3500.
	1798	360 pcs.	1750.	2500.	3000.	3500.

TRADE COINS

DUCAT

.983 GOLD

GELDERLAND (G, GEL)

C#	Date	Mintage	Fine	VF	XF	Unc
A40	1795	.045	375.00	650.00	775.00	850.00
	1796	—	1500.	2500.	3000.	3500.
	1797	420 pcs.	1500.	2500.	3000.	3500.
	1800	1.297	375.00	700.00	800.00	900.00
	1801	Inc. Ab.	300.00	500.00	550.00	625.00
	1802	Inc. Ab.	300.00	500.00	550.00	625.00
	1803	—	1750.	2750.	3250.	3750.

HOLLAND (HOL, HOLL)

C#	Date	Mintage	Fine	VF	XF	Unc
C40	1795 w/o star	—	175.00	300.00	350.00	400.00
	1796 w/o star	—	175.00	300.00	350.00	400.00
	1796 w/star	—	500.00	750.00	875.00	1000.
	1797 w/o star	—	1250.	2000.	2500.	3000.
	1797 w/star	—	1250.	2000.	2500.	3000.
	1798 w/o star	6,930	1250.	2000.	2500.	3000.
	1799 w/o star	6,370	1250.	2000.	2500.	3000.
	1800 w/o star	—	200.00	375.00	425.00	450.00
	1800 w/star	—	500.00	750.00	875.00	1000.
C40	1801 w/o star	—	175.00	300.00	350.00	400.00
	1801 w/star	—	500.00	750.00	875.00	1000.
	1802 w/o star	—	175.00	300.00	350.00	400.00
	1802 w/star	—	500.00	750.00	875.00	1000.
	1803 w/o star	—	200.00	375.00	500.00	625.00
	1804 w/o star	—	200.00	375.00	500.00	625.00
	1805 w/o star	—	750.00	1250.	1500.	1750.

NOTE: Coins with the star were struck at the Enkhuizen Mint with a total mintage of 630,455. Coins without the star were struck at the Dordrecht Mint with a total mintage of 2,861,825.

UTRECHT (TRAIECTUM, TRA, TRAI)

C#	Date	Mintage	Fine	VF	XF	Unc
F40	1795	—	150.00	250.00	300.00	350.00
	1796	—	200.00	375.00	400.00	450.00
	1797	—	325.00	450.00	500.00	550.00
	1798	—	325.00	450.00	500.00	550.00
	1799	—	325.00	450.00	500.00	550.00
	1800	1.400	135.00	225.00	275.00	325.00
	1801	.960	135.00	225.00	275.00	325.00
	1802	1.705	135.00	225.00	275.00	325.00
	1803	2.089	135.00	225.00	275.00	325.00
	1804/3	.870	200.00	375.00	400.00	450.00
	1804	Inc. Ab.	150.00	250.00	300.00	350.00
	1805	1.300	125.00	225.00	275.00	325.00

2 DUCAT

.983 GOLD

HOLLAND (HOL, HOLL)

C#	Date	Mintage	Fine	VF	XF	Unc
C41	1795	—	2350.	3250.	3750.	4500.
	1802	—	2350.	3250.	3750.	4500.

UTRECHT (TRAIECTUM, TRA, TRAI)

C#	Date	Mintage	Fine	VF	XF	Unc
F41	1795	1 known	—	—	—	—
	1796	—	2250.	3250.	3750.	4500.
	1797	—	2500.	3500.	4000.	4750.
	1798	—	2250.	3250.	3750.	4500.
	1799	—	1750.	2750.	3250.	3750.
	1800	.350	1000.	1600.	1850.	2150.
	1801	.215	1000.	1600.	1850.	2150.
	1802	.115	1250.	2500.	3000.	3500.
	1803	.365	1000.	1600.	1850.	2150.
	1804	.250	1000.	1600.	1850.	2150.
	1805	.301	1000.	1600.	1850.	2150.

KINGDOM OF HOLLAND

10 STUIVERS

SILVER

C#	Date	Mintage	Fine	VF	XF	Unc
51	1808	—	—	Rare	—	—
	1809	—	750.00	1150.	1600.	2150.

FLORIN

SILVER

C#	Date	Mintage	Fine	VF	XF	Unc
51a	1807	—	750.00	1750.	2500.	3000.

GULDEN

SILVER

C#	Date	Mintage	Fine	VF	XF	Unc
52	1808	—	750.00	1150.	1600.	2150.
	1809	—	750.00	1150.	1600.	2150.
	1810	—	750.00	1150.	1600.	2150.

2-1/2 GULDEN

SILVER

C#	Date	Mintage	Fine	VF	XF	Unc
53	1808	—	2000.	3500.	4500.	5500.

50 STUIVERS

SILVER

C#	Date	Mintage	Fine	VF	XF	Unc
54	1807	300 pcs.	2000.	3750.	4500.	5500.
	1808	2.466	425.00	625.00	750.00	875.00

RIJKSDAALDER

.868 SILVER

C#	Date	Mintage	Fine	VF	XF	Unc
55	1806	.580	250.00	400.00	500.00	625.00
	1807	.151	300.00	475.00	550.00	675.00
	1808	.343	250.00	400.00	500.00	625.00

SILVER

C#	Date	Mintage	Fine	VF	XF	Unc
56	1809	—	2000.	3500.	4500.	5500.

C#	Date	Mintage	Fine	VF	XF	Unc
57	1809	—	2500.	4000.	5000.	6000.

10 GULDEN

.983 GOLD

C#	Date	Mintage	Fine	VF	XF	Unc
62	1808	—	1250.	2500.	3500.	5000.
	1810	—	1250.	2500.	3500.	5000.

20 GULDEN

.983 GOLD

C#	Date	Mintage	Fine	VF	XF	Unc
63	1808	—	3250.	6000.	8000.	9000.
	1810	—	3250.	6000.	8000.	9000.

TRADE COINS

DUCAT

.983 GOLD

HOLLAND (HOL, HOLL)

C#	Date	Mintage	Fine	VF	XF	Unc
58	1806	526 pcs.	875.00	1250.	1500.	2000.

UTRECHT (TRAIECTUM, TRA, TRAI)

C#	Date	Mintage	Fine	VF	XF	Unc
58a	1806 w/small letters	.794	225.00	350.00	475.00	600.00
	1806 w/large letters	1,300	225.00	350.00	475.00	600.00
	1807 w/small letters; normal 7 in date	.622	225.00	350.00	475.00	600.00
	1807 w/larger letters; fancy 7 in date	1.940	225.00	350.00	475.00	600.00
	1808/7	.037	325.00	500.00	625.00	750.00

C#	Date	Mintage	Fine	VF	XF	Unc
	1808	Inc. Ab.	250.00	450.00	550.00	675.00

C#	Date	Mintage	Fine	VF	XF	Unc
60	1808	.283	750.00	1250.	1500.	1750.
	1809	Inc. Ab.	750.00	1250.	1500.	1750.

C#	Date	Mintage	Fine	VF	XF	Unc
61	1809	2.371	625.00	1000.	1150.	1250.
	1810	Inc. Ab.	625.00	1000.	1150.	1250.

2 DUCATS

.983 GOLD

C#	Date	Mintage	Fine	VF	XF	Unc
59	1806	.199	900.00	1350.	1600.	1850.
	1807	.156	900.00	1350.	1600.	1850.
	1808	—	900.00	1350.	1600.	1850.

FRENCH ANNEXATION

From 1810 to 1814, the Netherlands were a part of France. During this period, homeland type coins were not minted. Regular French coins were struck at the Utrecht mint at this time, and are identified by the fish and mast privy marks. These coins are listed under France.

KINGDOM OF THE NETHERLANDS

1/2 CENT

COPPER

C#	Date	Mintage	Fine	VF	XF	Unc
71	1818	—	—	Rare	—	—
	1819	.144	275.00	350.00	500.00	600.00
	1821	3.500	35.00	60.00	90.00	120.00
	1821B	.271	200.00	350.00	500.00	600.00
	1822	9.888	35.00	60.00	90.00	120.00
	1822B	3.969	60.00	110.00	150.00	250.00
	1823	10.000	35.00	60.00	90.00	120.00
	1823B	13.228	60.00	110.00	150.00	175.00
	1824	2.402	75.00	125.00	175.00	200.00
	1824B	3.430	100.00	150.00	200.00	275.00
	1826	—	200.00	275.00	375.00	450.00
	1826B	2.076	60.00	110.00	150.00	200.00
	1827	4.574	35.00	60.00	90.00	120.00
	1827B	3.337	60.00	110.00	150.00	200.00
	1828	1.358	35.00	60.00	90.00	120.00
	1828B	4.034	60.00	110.00	150.00	200.00
	1829	3.347	35.00	60.00	90.00	120.00
	1831	3.850	35.00	60.00	90.00	120.00
	1832	10.328	35.00	60.00	90.00	120.00
	1833	.150	1000.	1200.	1500.	2000.
	1837	2.602	35.00	60.00	90.00	120.00

GOLD (OMS)

C#	Date	Mintage	Fine	VF	XF	Unc
71a	1819	—	—	—	Rare	—
	1822	—	—	—	Rare	—
	1824	—	—	—	Rare	—

COPPER

C#	Date	Mintage	Fine	VF	XF	Unc
86	1841	2.600	45.00	75.00	100.00	125.00
	1843	3.120	35.00	60.00	90.00	110.00
	1846	.600	45.00	75.00	100.00	125.00
	1847	2.000	35.00	60.00	90.00	110.00

Y#	Date	Mintage	Fine	VF	XF	Unc
1	1850	2.000	30.00	45.00	55.00	75.00
	1851	2.051	30.00	45.00	55.00	75.00
	1852	2.028	60.00	90.00	125.00	200.00
	1853	2.000	30.00	50.00	60.00	80.00
	1854	3.000	25.00	35.00	55.00	75.00
	1855	.999	225.00	300.00	375.00	450.00
	1857	4.155	25.00	35.00	55.00	75.00
	1859	4.052	25.00	35.00	55.00	75.00
	1861	1.446	35.00	60.00	75.00	100.00
	1862	2.026	25.00	35.00	55.00	75.00
	1863	2.428	25.00	35.00	55.00	75.00
	1864	2.016	25.00	35.00	55.00	75.00
	1865	2.006	25.00	35.00	55.00	75.00
	1867	2.008	25.00	35.00	55.00	75.00
	1869	2.014	25.00	35.00	55.00	75.00
	1870	2.004	25.00	35.00	55.00	75.00
	1872	2.026	25.00	35.00	55.00	75.00
	1873	2.026	25.00	35.00	55.00	75.00
	1875	2.026	25.00	35.00	55.00	75.00
	1876	2.020	25.00	35.00	55.00	75.00
	1877	1.400	35.00	60.00	75.00	100.00

SILVER (OMS)

Y#	Date	Mintage	Fine	VF	XF	Unc
1a	1872	—	—	—	Rare	—

GOLD (OMS)

Y#	Date	Mintage	Fine	VF	XF	Unc
1b	1872	—	—	—	Rare	—

BRONZE

Obv: 17 small shields in field, leg: KONINGRIJK.....

Y#	Date	Mintage	Fine	VF	XF	Unc
3	1878	4.000	10.00	20.00	25.00	30.00
	1883	.800	125.00	225.00	300.00	375.00
	1884	17.200	7.50	15.00	20.00	25.00
	1885	7.800	7.50	15.00	20.00	25.00
	1886	2.200	60.00	100.00	150.00	200.00
	1891	5.000	10.00	15.00	20.00	25.00
	1894	5.000	10.00	15.00	20.00	25.00
	1898	2.000	35.00	75.00	100.00	125.00
	1900	3.000	15.00	25.00	30.00	35.00
	1901	6.000	5.00	10.00	15.00	20.00

GOLD (OMS)

Y#	Date	Mintage	Fine	VF	XF	Unc
3a	1884	—	—	—	Rare	—

Obv: 15 large shields in field around larger lion, smaller date and legend. Rev: CENT in larger letters.

Y#	Date	Mintage	Fine	VF	XF	Unc
3c	1903	10.000	2.00	4.00	6.00	12.50
	1906	10.000	2.00	4.00	6.00	12.50

GOLD (OMS)

Y#	Date	Mintage	Fine	VF	XF	Unc
3d	1903	—	—	—	Rare	—

BRONZE

Y#	Date	Mintage	Fine	VF	XF	Unc
35	1909	5.000	2.00	4.00	5.00	7.50
	1911	5.000	2.00	4.00	5.00	7.50
	1912	5.000	2.00	4.00	5.00	7.50
	1914	5.000	2.00	4.00	5.00	7.50
	1915	2.500	10.00	15.00	20.00	25.00
	1916	4.000	2.00	4.00	5.00	7.50
	1917	5.000	2.00	4.00	5.00	7.50
	1921	1.500	15.00	20.00	25.00	30.00
	1922	2.500	10.00	15.00	20.00	25.00
	1928	4.000	2.00	4.00	5.00	7.50
	1930	6.000	2.00	4.00	5.00	7.50
	1934	5.000	1.00	2.00	3.00	5.00
	1936	5.000	1.00	2.00	3.00	5.00
	1937	1.600	2.00	4.00	5.00	7.50
	1938	8.400	1.00	2.00	3.00	5.00
	1940	6.000	1.00	2.00	3.00	5.00

SILVER (OMS)

Y#	Date	Mintage	Fine	VF	XF	Unc
35a	1911	—	—	—	Rare	—

CENT

COPPER

C#	Date	Mintage	Fine	VF	XF	Unc
72	1817	—	—	Rare	—	—
	1818	—	—	Rare	—	—
	1819	.165	175.00	350.00	400.00	500.00
	1821	10.325	20.00	40.00	60.00	125.00
	1821B	.113	225.00	350.00	400.00	500.00
	1822	18.462	20.00	40.00	60.00	125.00
	1822B	6.718	30.00	50.00	100.00	150.00
	1823	22.300	20.00	40.00	60.00	125.00
	1823B	11.272	25.00	45.00	75.00	150.00
	1824	5.450	20.00	40.00	60.00	100.00
	1824B	.144	250.00	375.00	425.00	500.00
	1826	4.600	20.00	40.00	60.00	100.00
	1826B	7.824	25.00	45.00	75.00	150.00
	1827	27.450	15.00	30.00	55.00	100.00
	1827B	20.966	15.00	30.00	55.00	100.00
	1828	8.261	20.00	40.00	60.00	100.00
	1828B	7.608	25.00	45.00	75.00	150.00
	1830	1.750	30.00	50.00	100.00	150.00
	1831	4.161	20.00	40.00	60.00	100.00
	1837	5.203	15.00	30.00	55.00	100.00

SILVER (OMS)

C#	Date	Mintage	Fine	VF	XF	Unc
72a	1823	—	—	—	Rare	—

GOLD (OMS)

C#	Date	Mintage	Fine	VF	XF	Unc
72b	1823	—	—	—	Rare	—
—	1826	—	—	—	Rare	—
—	1827	—	—	—	Rare	—

BRONZE

Y#	Date	Mintage	Fine	VF	XF	Unc
2	1860	2.032	15.00	30.00	50.00	100.00
	1861	2.050	15.00	30.00	50.00	100.00
	1862	2.026	15.00	30.00	50.00	100.00
	1863	10.246	8.00	12.50	20.00	40.00
	1864	2.026	15.00	30.00	50.00	100.00
	1870	4.010	10.00	15.00	25.00	50.00
	1873	3.026	12.00	20.00	35.00	60.00
	1875	3.015	12.00	20.00	35.00	60.00
	1876	13.047	8.00	12.50	20.00	40.00
	1877	11.026	8.00	12.50	20.00	40.00

SILVER (OMS)

Y#	Date	Mintage	Fine	VF	XF	Unc
2a	1875	—	—	—	Rare	—
—	1876	—	—	—	Rare	—

GOLD (OMS)

Y#	Date	Mintage	Fine	VF	XF	Unc
26	1875	—	—	—	Rare	—
—	1876	—	—	—	Rare	—
—	1877	—	—	—	Rare	—

BRONZE

Obv: 15 small shields in field, leg: KONINGRIJK

Y#	Date	Mintage	Fine	VF	XF	Unc
4	1877	6.100	7.50	12.50	25.00	40.00
	1878	53.900	1.00	2.00	10.00	15.00
	1880	20.000	2.00	4.00	8.00	20.00
	1881	10.000	3.00	5.00	10.00	20.00
	1882	5.000	5.00	10.00	15.00	30.00
	1883	15.000	1.00	3.00	10.00	15.00
	1884	10.000	2.00	4.00	10.00	15.00
	1892	5.000	5.00	12.00	15.00	20.00
	1896	3.000	12.00	25.00	35.00	50.00
	1897	2.500	15.00	25.00	35.00	50.00
	1898	5.000	4.00	10.00	15.00	25.00
	1899	5.100	4.00	10.00	15.00	25.00
	1900	12.400	2.00	4.00	10.00	15.00
4d	1884	—	—	—	Rare	—

Obv: 15 large shields in field, leg: KONINKRIJK

Y#	Date	Mintage	Fine	VF	XF	Unc
4a	1901	10.000	2.00	4.00	7.50	15.00

10 large shields in field, leg: KONINGRIJK.

Y#	Date	Mintage	Fine	VF	XF	Unc
4b	1901	10.000	2.00	4.00	7.50	15.00

Obv: 15 medium shields in field, leg: KONINGRIJK.

Y#	Date	Mintage	Fine	VF	XF	Unc
4c	1902	10.000	2.00	4.00	7.50	15.00
	1904	15.000	2.00	4.00	7.50	15.00
	1905	10.000	2.00	4.00	7.50	15.00
	1906	9.000	2.00	4.00	7.50	15.00
	1907	6.000	30.00	50.00	75.00	125.00

GOLD (OMS)

Y#	Date	Mintage	Fine	VF	XF	Unc
4e	1902	—	—	—	Rare	—

BRONZE

Y#	Date	Mintage	Fine	VF	XF	Unc
36	1913	5.000	10.00	20.00	30.00	50.00
	1914	9.000	1.00	1.50	2.50	6.00
	1915	10.800	1.00	1.50	2.50	6.00
	1916	21.700	1.00	1.50	2.50	6.00
	1917	20.000	1.00	1.50	2.50	6.00
	1918	10.000	1.00	1.50	2.50	6.00
	1919	6.000	2.00	4.00	6.50	12.00
	1920	11.400	1.00	1.50	2.50	6.00
	1921	12.600	1.00	1.50	2.50	6.00
	1922	20.000	1.00	1.50	2.50	6.00
	1924	1.400	40.00	75.00	100.00	150.00
	1925	18.600	1.00	1.50	2.50	6.00
	1926	10.000	1.00	1.50	2.50	6.00
	1927	10.000	1.00	1.50	2.50	6.00
	1928	10.000	1.00	1.50	2.50	6.00
	1929	20.000	1.00	1.50	2.50	6.00
	1930	10.000	1.00	1.50	2.50	6.00
	1931	3.400	20.00	35.00	45.00	60.00
	1937	10.000	1.00	1.50	2.50	4.00
	1938	16.600	1.00	1.50	2.50	4.00
	1939	22.000	1.00	1.50	2.50	4.00
	1940	24.600	1.00	1.50	2.50	4.00
	1941	66.600	1.00	1.50	2.50	4.00

NOTE: For similar coins dated 1942P see Curacao; 1943P, 1957-1960 see Surinam.

ZINC

Y#	Date	Mintage	Fine	VF	XF	Unc
48	1941	31.800	3.00	6.00	12.00	20.00
	1942	241.000	.20	.50	1.00	2.00
	1943	71.000	.25	.50	1.00	2.00
	1944	29.600	3.00	6.00	12.00	20.00

BRONZE

Y#	Date	Mintage	Fine	VF	XF	Unc
53	1948	130.400	.25	.75	1.75	2.50
	1948	—	—	—	Proof	125.00

Y#	Date	Mintage	Fine	VF	XF	Unc
57	1950	91.000	—	.25	.75	1.25
	1950	—	—	—	Proof	22.50
	1951	45.800	—	.25	.75	1.25
	1951	—	—	—	Proof	22.50
	1952	68.000	—	.10	.75	1.25
	1952	—	—	—	Proof	22.50
	1953	54.000	—	.10	.75	1.25
	1953	—	—	—	Proof	22.50
	1954	54.000	—	.10	.75	1.25
	1954	—	—	—	Proof	22.50
	1955	52.000	—	.10	.75	1.25
	1955	—	—	—	Proof	22.50
	1956	34.800	—	.10	.75	1.25
	1956	—	—	—	Proof	22.50
	1957	48.000	—	.10	.75	1.25
	1957	—	—	—	Proof	22.50
	1958	34.000	—	.10	.75	1.25
	1958	—	—	—	Proof	22.50
	1959	36.000	—	.10	.75	1.25
	1959	—	—	—	Proof	22.50

Y#	Date	Mintage	Fine	VF	XF	Unc
57	1960	40.000	—	.10	.75	1.25
	1960	—	—	—	Proof	22.50
	1961	52.000	—	—	.40	1.00
	1961	—	—	—	Proof	22.50
	1962	57.000	—	—	.40	1.00
	1962	—	—	—	Proof	22.50
	1963	70.000	—	—	.40	1.00
	1963	—	—	—	Proof	22.50
	1964	73.000	—	—	.40	1.00
	1964	—	—	—	Proof	22.50
	1965	91.000	—	—	.40	1.00
	1965	—	—	—	Proof	22.50
	1966 large date	104.000	—	—	.25	.50
	1966 large date		—	—	Proof	22.50
	1966 small date	Inc. Ab.	—	—	.25	.50
	1966 small date		—	—	Proof	22.50
	1967	140.000	—	—	.25	.50
	1967	—	—	—	Proof	22.50
	1968	28.000	—	—	.25	.50
	1968	—	—	—	Proof	22.50
	1969 w/fish privy mark	50.000	—	—	.25	.50
	1969 w/fish privy mark	—	—	—	Proof	25.00
	1969 w/cock privy mark	50.000	—	—	.25	.50
	1969 w/cock privy mark	—	—	—	Proof	25.00
	1970	100.000	—	—	—	.25
	1970	—	—	—	Proof	22.50
	1971	70.000	—	—	—	.25
	1972	40.000	—	—	—	.25
	1973	34.000	—	—	—	.25
	1974	46.000	—	—	—	.25
	1975	25.000	—	—	—	.25
	1976	15.000	—	—	—	.25
	1977	15.000	—	—	—	.25
	1978	15.000	—	—	—	—
	1979	15.000	—	—	—	—
	1980w/cock & star privy mark	—	—	—	—	—

2-1/2 CENTS

BRONZE

Obv: 17 small shields in field, leg: KONINGRIJK.

Y#	Date	Mintage	Fine	VF	XF	Unc
5	1877	4.000	6.00	15.00	25.00	50.00
	1880	4.000	6.00	15.00	25.00	50.00
	1881	4.000	6.00	15.00	25.00	50.00
	1883	.400	40.00	75.00	100.00	125.00
	1884	3.600	6.00	15.00	25.00	50.00
	1886	2.000	15.00	30.00	50.00	75.00
	1890	2.000	17.50	35.00	50.00	80.00
	1894	1.000	75.00	100.00	140.00	200.00
	1898	1.600	30.00	50.00	70.00	125.00

GOLD (OMS)

Y#	Date	Mintage	Fine	VF	XF	Unc
5a	1884	—	—	—	Rare	—

BRONZE

Obv: 15 large shields in field.

Y#	Date	Mintage	Fine	VF	XF	Unc
5c	1903	4.000	5.00	10.00	15.00	20.00
	1904	4.000	5.00	10.00	15.00	20.00
	1905	4.000	5.00	10.00	15.00	20.00
	1906	8.000	5.00	10.00	15.00	20.00

GOLD (OMS)

Y#	Date	Mintage	Fine	VF	XF	Unc
5d	1903	—	—	—	Rare	—

BRONZE

Y#	Date	Mintage	Fine	VF	XF	Unc
37	1912	2.000	15.00	25.00	35.00	45.00
	1913	4.000	5.00	10.00	15.00	20.00
	1914	2.000	15.00	25.00	35.00	50.00
	1915	3.000	8.00	15.00	20.00	35.00
	1916	8.000	4.00	8.00	12.50	17.50
	1918	4.000	5.00	10.00	15.00	20.00
	1919	2.000	15.00	25.00	35.00	50.00

Y#	Date	Mintage	Fine	VF	XF	Unc
37	1929	8.000	4.00	8.00	12.50	20.00
	1941	19.800	2.50	4.00	8.00	12.50

ZINC

Y#	Date	Mintage	Fine	VF	XF	Unc
49	1941	27.600	5.00	10.00	15.00	25.00
	1942	.200	—	—	Rare	—

5 CENTS

.569 SILVER

C#	Date	Mintage	Fine	VF	XF	Unc
73	1818	2,500	1000.	1500.	1750.	3000.
	1819	3,000	1000.	1500.	1750.	3000.
	1822	.047	450.00	750.00	1100.	1500.0
	1825B	.900	75.00	125.00	200.00	300.00
	1826B	1.021	75.00	125.00	200.00	300.00
	1827	.534	75.00	125.00	200.00	300.00
	1827B	.284	80.00	130.00	225.00	325.00
	1828B	.397	80.00	130.00	225.00	325.00

GOLD (OMS)

C#	Date	Mintage	Fine	VF	XF	Unc
73a	1818	—	—	—	Rare	—
—	1822	—	—	—	Rare	—

.640 SILVER

C#	Date	Mintage	Fine	VF	XF	Unc
87	1848	100 pcs.	—	—	Rare	—

GOLD (OMS)

C#	Date	Mintage	Fine	VF	XF	Unc
87a	1848	—	—	—	Rare	—

.6850 gm., .640 SILVER, .0141 oz ASW

Y#	Date	Mintage	Fine	VF	XF	Unc
6	1850	3.037	7.50	12.50	20.00	30.00
	1853	.011	500.00	750.00	1000.	1500.
	1855	.515	10.00	17.50	25.00	35.00
	1859	.400	10.00	17.50	25.00	35.00
	1862. w/dot after date	.400	10.00	17.50	25.00	35.00
	1862 w/o dot after date	Inc. Ab.	10.00	17.50	25.00	35.00
	1863	.640	10.00	17.50	25.00	35.00
	1868	.200	75.00	125.00	175.00	225.00
	1869	.500	10.00	17.50	25.00	35.00
	1876	.200	20.00	35.00	50.00	75.00
	1879	.200	20.00	35.00	50.00	75.00
	1887	.100	40.00	75.00	100.00	125.00

NOTE: Varieties exist for 1850 dated coins.

GOLD (OMS)

Y#	Date	Mintage	Fine	VF	XF	Unc
6a	1879	—	—	—	Rare	—

COPPER-NICKEL

Y#	Date	Mintage	Fine	VF	XF	Unc
33	1907	6.000	15.00	25.00	35.00	55.00
	1908	4.000	15.00	25.00	35.00	55.00
	1909	4.000	85.00	125.00	150.00	175.00

Y#	Date	Mintage	Fine	VF	XF	Unc
34	1913	6.000	10.00	15.00	20.00	27.50
	1914	7.400	10.00	15.00	20.00	27.50
	1923	10.000	10.00	15.00	20.00	27.50
	1929	8.000	10.00	15.00	20.00	27.50
	1932	2.000	25.00	45.00	60.00	75.00

Y#	Date	Mintage	Fine	VF	XF	Unc
34	1933	1.400	75.00	100.00	125.00	150.00
	1934	2.600	20.00	30.00	35.00	45.00
	1936	2.600	20.00	30.00	35.00	45.00
	1938	4.200	10.00	15.00	20.00	27.50
	1939	4.600	10.00	15.00	20.00	27.50
	1940	7.200	10.00	15.00	20.00	27.50

NOTE: For a similar coin dated 1943, see Curacao.

ZINC

Y#	Date	Mintage	Fine	VF	XF	Unc
50	1941	32.200	5.00	12.50	17.50	25.00
	1942	11.800	10.00	20.00	30.00	35.00
	1943	7.000	17.50	30.00	35.00	50.00

BRONZE

Y#	Date	Mintage	Fine	VF	XF	Unc
54	1948	23.600	.25	1.00	2.00	3.00
	1948	—	—	—	Proof	150.00

Y#	Date	Mintage	Fine	VF	XF	Unc
58	1950	20.000	—	.25	1.00	1.75
	1950	—	—	—	Proof	25.00
	1951	16.200	—	.25	1.00	1.75
	1951	—	—	—	Proof	25.00
	1952	14.400	—	.25	1.00	1.75
	1952	—	—	—	Proof	25.00
	1953	12.000	—	.25	1.00	1.75
	1953	—	—	—	Proof	25.00
	1954	14.000	—	.25	1.00	1.75
	1954	—	—	—	Proof	25.00
	1955	11.400	—	.25	1.00	1.75
	1955	—	—	—	Proof	25.00
	1956	7.400	—	.25	1.00	1.75
	1956	—	—	—	Proof	25.00
	1957	16.000	—	.25	1.00	1.75
	1957	—	—	—	Proof	25.00
	1958	9.000	—	.25	1.00	1.75
	1958	—	—	—	Proof	25.00
	1960	11.000	—	.25	1.00	1.75
	1960	—	—	—	Proof	25.00
	1961	12.000	—	—	.75	1.25
	1961	—	—	—	Proof	25.00
	1962	15.000	—	—	.75	1.25
	1962	—	—	—	Proof	25.00
	1963	18.000	—	—	.75	1.25
	1963	—	—	—	Proof	25.00
	1964	21.000	—	—	.75	1.25
	1964	—	—	—	Proof	25.00
	1965	28.000	—	—	.75	1.25
	1965	—	—	—	Proof	25.00
	1966	22.000	—	—	.25	.50
	1966	—	—	—	Proof	25.00
	1967 w/leaves far from rim	32.000	—	—	.25	.50
	1967 w/leaves far from rim	—	—	—	Proof	25.00
	1967 w/leaves touching rim	Inc. Ab.	—	—	.25	.50
	1967 w/leaves touching rim	—	—	—	Proof	27.50
	1969 w/fish privy mark	5.000	—	—	.25	.50
	1969 w/fish privy mark	—	—	—	Proof	27.50
	1969 w/cock privy mark	11.000	—	—	.25	.50
	1969 w/cock privy mark	—	—	—	Proof	27.50
	1970	22.000	—	—	.25	.50
	1970	—	—	—	Proof	25.00
	1970 w/date close to rim	Inc. Ab.	—	—	—	.50
	1970 w/date close to rim	—	—	—	Proof	25.00
	1971	25.000	—	—	—	.25
	1972	25.000	—	—	—	.25
	1973	22.000	—	—	—	.25
	1974	20.000	—	—	—	.25
	1975	46.000	—	—	—	.25
	1976	50.000	—	—	—	.25
	1977	50.000	—	—	—	.25
	1978	60.000	—	—	—	.25
	1979	80.000	—	—	—	.25
	1980 w/cock & star privy mark	—	—	—	—	.25

10 CENTS

.569 SILVER

C#	Date	Mintage	Fine	VF	XF	Unc
74	1818	60 pcs.	1250.	2000.	2500.	3000.
	1819	.025	750.00	1350.	1750.	2000.
	1822	.113	625.00	875.00	1250.	1500.
	1823B	.178	250.00	425.00	625.00	750.00
	1825	.972	75.00	125.00	150.00	175.00
	1825B	1.727	50.00	75.00	110.00	150.00
	1826	2.138	50.00	75.00	110.00	150.00
	1826B	1.430	50.00	75.00	110.00	150.00
	1827	5.895	35.00	60.00	110.00	150.00
	1827B	1.711	50.00	75.00	110.00	150.00
	1828	2.036	50.00	75.00	110.00	150.00
	1828B	1.168	50.00	75.00	110.00	150.00

GOLD (OMS)

C#	Date	Mintage	Fine	VF	XF	Unc
74a	1822	—	—	—	Rare	—

1.4000 gm., .640 SILVER, .0288 oz ASW

C#	Date	Mintage	Fine	VF	XF	Unc
88	1848	6.859	35.00	125.00	175.00	225.00
	1849. w/dot after date	4.051	35.00	100.00	150.00	200.00
	1849 w/o dot after date	Inc. Ab.	85.00	150.00	200.00	250.00

Y#	Date	Mintage	Fine	VF	XF	Unc
7	1849	6.204	35.00	100.00	140.00	175.00
	1850	7.270	35.00	100.00	140.00	175.00
	1853	1.104	85.00	135.00	200.00	250.00
	1855	.745	110.00	175.00	250.00	325.00
	1855 w/low 5	Inc. Ab.	115.00	175.00	250.00	325.00
	1856	1.000	35.00	100.00	140.00	175.00
	1859	1.000	35.00	100.00	140.00	175.00
	1862	.800	110.00	175.00	250.00	325.00
	1863	1.240	35.00	100.00	140.00	175.00
	1868	.200	175.00	375.00	500.00	625.00
	1869	1.000	35.00	100.00	140.00	175.00
	1871	1.000	35.00	100.00	140.00	175.00
	1873	1.000	35.00	100.00	140.00	175.00
	1874 w/sword privy mark	.800	125.00	175.00	250.00	325.00
	1874 w/sword in scabbard privy mark	.200	125.00	175.00	250.00	325.00
	1876	1.000	30.00	85.00	125.00	160.00
	1877	1.000	30.00	85.00	125.00	160.00
	1878	1.000	30.00	85.00	125.00	160.00
	1879	1.000	30.00	85.00	125.00	160.00
	1880	1.000	30.00	85.00	125.00	160.00
	1881	2.000	30.00	85.00	125.00	160.00
	1882	2.000	30.00	85.00	125.00	160.00
	1884	1.000	30.00	85.00	125.00	160.00
	1885	2.000	30.00	85.00	125.00	160.00
	1887	1.600	30.00	85.00	125.00	160.00
	1889	2.800	20.00	60.00	100.00	125.00
	1890	2.600	20.00	60.00	100.00	125.00

GOLD (OMS)

Y#	Date	Mintage	Fine	VF	XF	Unc
7a	1884	—	—	—	Rare	—
—	1885	—	—	—	Rare	—

1.4000 gm., .640 SILVER, .0288 oz ASW

Y#	Date	Mintage	Fine	VF	XF	Unc
20	1892	2.000	22.50	60.00	85.00	125.00
	1893	2.000	22.50	60.00	85.00	125.00
	1894	1.500	22.50	60.00	85.00	125.00
	1895	1.000	25.00	75.00	100.00	135.00
	1896	2.000	22.50	60.00	85.00	125.00
	1897	7.850	20.00	50.00	75.00	100.00

Y#	Date	Mintage	Fine	VF	XF	Unc
23	1898	2.000	30.00	85.00	125.00	175.00
	1901	2.000	30.00	85.00	125.00	175.00

Y#	Date	Mintage	Fine	VF	XF	Unc
23a	1903	6.000	20.00	50.00	85.00	125.00

Y#	Date	Mintage	Fine	VF	XF	Unc
23b	1904	3.000	25.00	60.00	100.00	125.00
	1905	2.000	30.00	85.00	125.00	160.00
	1906	4.000	20.00	50.00	75.00	100.00

Y#	Date	Mintage	Fine	VF	XF	Unc
39	1910	2.250	60.00	125.00	175.00	250.00
	1911	4.000	22.50	60.00	100.00	125.00
	1912	4.000	22.50	60.00	100.00	125.00
	1913	5.000	17.50	40.00	60.00	75.00
	1914	9.000	7.50	20.00	35.00	55.00
	1915	5.000	7.50	20.00	35.00	55.00
	1916	5.000	7.50	20.00	35.00	55.00
	1917	10.000	7.50	20.00	35.00	55.00
	1918	20.000	7.50	20.00	35.00	55.00
	1919	10.000	7.50	20.00	35.00	55.00
	1921	5.000	7.50	20.00	35.00	55.00
	1925	5.000	7.50	20.00	35.00	55.00

GOLD (OMS)

Y#	Date	Mintage	Fine	VF	XF	Unc
39a	1910	—	—	—	Rare	—

1.4000 gm., .640 SILVER, .0288 oz ASW

Y#	Date	Mintage	Fine	VF	XF	Unc
43	1926	2.700	12.50	25.00	35.00	50.00
	1927	2.300	12.50	25.00	35.00	50.00
	1928	10.000	4.00	10.00	17.50	25.00
	1930	5.000	4.00	10.00	17.50	25.00
	1934	2.000	12.50	25.00	35.00	50.00
	1935	8.000	4.00	7.50	12.50	17.50
	1936	15.000	1.50	3.75	6.00	10.00
	1937	18.600	1.50	3.75	6.00	10.00
	1938	21.400	1.50	3.75	6.00	10.00
	1939	20.000	1.50	3.75	6.00	10.00
	1941	43.000	1.50	3.75	6.00	10.00
	1943P w/acorn privy mark	Inc. Be.	10.00	15.00	20.00	25.00
	1944P	120.000	2.00	3.75	5.00	6.25
	1944D	25.400	2000.	3000.	4000.	5000.
	1944S	64.040	5.00	12.50	20.00	27.50
	1945P	90.560	325.00	750.00	875.00	1000.

NOTE: For similar coins dated 1941P-1943P with palm tree privy mark, see Curacao and Surinam.

ZINC

Y#	Date	Mintage	Fine	VF	XF	Unc
51	1941	29.800	2.50	6.25	10.00	15.00
	1942	95.600	1.25	2.50	5.00	10.00
	1943	29.000	2.50	6.25	10.00	15.00

NICKEL

Y#	Date	Mintage	Fine	VF	XF	Unc
55	1948	69.200	.25	.75	1.50	2.50
	1948	—	—	—	Proof	175.00

Y#	Date	Mintage	Fine	VF	XF	Unc
59	1950	56.600	—	.25	1.00	1.75
	1950	—	—	—	Proof	27.50
	1951	54.200	—	.25	1.00	1.75
	1951	—	—	—	Proof	27.50
	1954	8.200	—	.25	1.00	1.75
	1954	—	—	—	Proof	27.50
	1955	18.200	—	.25	1.00	1.75
	1955	—	—	—	Proof	27.50
	1956	12.000	—	.25	1.00	1.75
	1956	—	—	—	Proof	27.50
	1957	18.600	—	.25	1.00	1.75
	1957	—	—	—	Proof	27.50
	1958	34.000	—	.25	1.00	1.75
	1958	—	—	—	Proof	27.50
	1959	44.000	—	.25	1.00	1.75
	1959	—	—	—	Proof	27.50
	1960	12.000	—	.25	1.00	1.75
	1960	—	—	—	Proof	27.50
	1961	25.000	—	—	.75	1.25
	1961	—	—	—	Proof	27.50
	1962	30.000	—	—	.75	1.25
	1962	—	—	—	Proof	27.50
	1963	35.000	—	—	.75	1.25
	1963	—	—	—	Proof	27.50
	1964	41.000	—	—	.75	1.25
	1964	—	—	—	Proof	27.50
	1965	59.000	—	—	.75	1.25
	1965	—	—	—	Proof	27.50
	1966	44.000	—	—	.25	.50
	1966	—	—	—	Proof	27.50
	1967	39.000	—	—	.25	.50
	1967	—	—	—	Proof	27.50
	1968	42.000	—	—	.25	.50
	1968	—	—	—	Proof	27.50
	1969 w/fish privy mark					
		28.000	—	—	.25	.50
	1969 w/fish privy mark					
		—	—	—	Proof	30.00
	1969 w/cock privy mark					
		24.000	—	—	.25	.50
	1969 w/fish privy mark					
		—	—	—	Proof	30.00
	1970	50.000	—	—	.25	.50
	1970	—	—	—	Proof	27.50
	1971	55.000	—	—	—	.25
	1972	60.000	—	—	—	.25
	1973	90.000	—	—	—	.25
	1974	75.000	—	—	—	.25
	1975	110.000	—	—	—	.25
	1976	85.000	—	—	—	.25
	1977	100.000	—	—	—	.25
	1978	110.000	—	—	—	.25
	1979	120.000	—	—	—	.25

25 CENTS

.569 SILVER

C#	Date	Mintage	Fine	VF	XF	Unc
75	1817	—	—	—	Rare	—
	1818	—	—	—	Rare	—
	1819	.013	500.00	875.00	1250.	1750.
	1822	.116	375.00	625.00	875.00	1125.
	1823B	1.334	75.00	125.00	175.00	225.00
	1824B	6.033	35.00	75.00	125.00	175.00
	1825	10.311	35.00	75.00	125.00	175.00
	1825B	2.608	75.00	125.00	175.00	225.00
	1826	12.282	35.00	75.00	125.00	175.00
	1826B	7.299	35.00	75.00	125.00	175.00
	1827B	1.822	75.00	125.00	175.00	225.00
	1828B	.334	375.00	625.00	875.00	1150.
	1829	.106	375.00	625.00	875.00	1150.
	1829B	1.256	75.00	125.00	175.00	225.00
	1830	1.534	75.00	125.00	175.00	225.00
	1830B	.902	75.00	125.00	175.00	225.00

.640 SILVER

C#	Date	Mintage	Fine	VF	XF	Unc
89	1848	10.730	30.00	75.00	135.00	200.00
	1849	8.059	30.00	75.00	125.00	175.00

Y#	Date	Mintage	Fine	VF	XF	Unc
8	1849	Inc. Ab.	300.00	625.00	750.00	875.00
	1850	2.207	300.00	500.00	625.00	750.00
	1853	7,974	375.00	625.00	1000.	1250.
	1887	.100	300.00	625.00	750.00	875.00
	1889	.200	200.00	375.00	500.00	625.00
	1890. w/dot after date					
		.600	200.00	375.00	500.00	625.00
	1890 w/o dot after date					
		Inc. Ab.	250.00	425.00	550.00	700.00

GOLD (oms)

Y#	Date	Mintage	Fine	VF	XF	Unc
8a	1849	—	—	—	Rare	—

3.5750 gm., .640 SILVER, .0736 oz ASW

Y#	Date	Mintage	Fine	VF	XF	Unc
21	1891	—	—	—	Rare	—
	1892	.800	35.00	100.00	150.00	200.00
	1893	.800	35.00	100.00	150.00	200.00
	1894	1.000	35.00	100.00	150.00	200.00
	1895	1.200	35.00	100.00	150.00	200.00
	1895 w/slanted mintmark					
		Inc. Ab.	75.00	175.00	250.00	325.00
	1896	.600	75.00	175.00	250.00	325.00
	1897	3.100	30.00	75.00	110.00	150.00

Y#	Date	Mintage	Fine	VF	XF	Unc
24	1898	.400	300.00	750.00	1000.	1350.
	1901	1.600	30.00	75.00	125.00	175.00
	1901 w/bust with wider neck					
		Inc. Ab.	150.00	300.00	450.00	600.00
	1902	1.200	30.00	75.00	125.00	175.00
	1903	1.200	30.00	75.00	125.00	175.00
	1904	1.600	30.00	75.00	125.00	175.00
	1905	1.200	30.00	75.00	125.00	175.00
	1906	2.000	30.00	75.00	125.00	175.00

GOLD (OMS)

Y#	Date	Mintage	Fine	VF	XF	Unc
24a	1903	—	—	—	Rare	—

3.5750 gm., .640 SILVER, .0736 oz ASW

Y#	Date	Mintage	Fine	VF	XF	Unc
40	1910	.880	60.00	150.00	250.00	375.00
	1911	1.600	30.00	75.00	110.00	150.00
	1912	1.600	30.00	75.00	110.00	150.00
	1913	1.200	30.00	75.00	110.00	150.00
	1914	5.600	17.50	35.00	75.00	110.00
	1915	2.000	17.50	35.00	75.00	110.00
	1916	2.000	17.50	35.00	75.00	110.00
	1917	4.000	17.50	35.00	75.00	110.00
	1918	6.000	17.50	35.00	75.00	110.00
	1919	4.000	17.50	35.00	75.00	110.00
	1925	2.000	17.50	35.00	75.00	110.00

Y#	Date	Mintage	Fine	VF	XF	Unc
44	1926	2.000	15.00	30.00	50.00	75.00
	1928	8.000	5.00	15.00	20.00	25.00
	1939	4.000	4.00	7.50	10.00	15.00
	1940	9.000	4.00	7.50	10.00	15.00
	1941	40.000	2.50	5.00	7.50	12.50
	1943P w/acorn privy mark					
		Inc. Be.	5.00	10.00	15.00	20.00
	1944P w/acorn privy mark					
		40.000	2.50	6.00	10.00	12.50
	1945P w/acorn privy mark					
		92.000	75.00	200.00	325.00	400.00

NOTE: For similar coins dated 1941P and 1943P with palm tree privy mark, see Curacao.

ZINC

Y#	Date	Mintage	Fine	VF	XF	Unc
52	1941	34.600	2.50	7.50	12.50	15.00
	1942	27.800	2.50	7.50	12.50	15.00
	1943	13.600	10.00	17.50	25.00	30.00

NICKEL

Y#	Date	Mintage	Fine	VF	XF	Unc
56	1948	27.400	.50	1.00	2.00	3.00
	1948	—	—	—	Proof	200.00

Y#	Date	Mintage	Fine	VF	XF	Unc
60	1950	43.000	—	.50	1.50	2.50
	1950	—	—	—	Proof	30.00
	1951	33.200	—	.50	1.50	2.50
	1951	—	—	—	Proof	30.00
	1954	6.400	—	.50	1.50	2.50
	1954	—	—	—	Proof	30.00
	1955	10.000	—	.50	1.50	2.50
	1955	—	—	—	Proof	30.00
	1956	8.000	—	.50	1.50	2.50
	1956	—	—	—	Proof	30.00
	1957	8.000	—	.50	1.50	2.50
	1957	—	—	—	Proof	30.00
	1958	15.000	—	.50	1.50	2.50
	1958	—	—	—	Proof	30.00
	1960	9.000	—	.50	1.50	2.50
	1960	—	—	—	Proof	30.00
	1961	6.000	—	.50	1.50	2.50
	1961	—	—	—	Proof	30.00
	1962	12.000	—	.50	1.50	2.50
	1962	—	—	—	Proof	30.00
	1963	18.000	—	—	1.00	1.75
	1963	—	—	—	Proof	30.00
	1964	25.000	—	—	1.00	1.75
	1964	—	—	—	Proof	30.00
	1965	18.000	—	—	1.00	1.75
	1965	—	—	—	Proof	30.00
	1966	25.000	—	—	1.00	1.75
	1966	—	—	—	Proof	30.00
	1967	18.000	—	—	1.00	1.75
	1967	—	—	—	Proof	30.00
	1968	26.000	—	—	1.00	1.75
	1968	—	—	—	Proof	30.00

Y#	Date	Mintage	Fine	VF	XF	Unc
60	1969 w/fish privy mark	14.000	—	—	1.00	1.75
	1969 w/fish privy mark	—	—	—	Proof	35.00
	1969 w/cock privy mark	21.000	—	—	1.00	1.75
	1969 w/cock privy mark	—	—	—	Proof	35.00
	1970	39.000	—	—	1.00	1.75
	1970	—	—	—	Proof	30.00
	1971	40.000	—	—	—	.50
	1972	50.000	—	—	—	.50
	1973	45.000	—	—	—	.50
	1974	10.000	—	—	—	.50
	1975	25.000	—	—	—	.50
	1976	64.000	—	—	—	.50
	1977	55.000	—	—	—	.50
	1978	35.000	—	—	—	.50
	1979	45.000	—	—	—	—

1/2 GULDEN

.893 SILVER

C#	Date	Mintage	Fine	VF	XF	Unc
76	1818	.051	375.00	800.00	1250.	1750.
	1819	.043	375.00	800.00	1250.	1750.
	1822 w/engraver's name below bust	.119	350.00	750.00	1150.	1350.
	1822 w/o engraver's name	Inc. Ab.	700.00	875.00	1350.	1900.
	1829B	.180	350.00	750.00	1000.	1250.
	1830B	.100	350.00	750.00	1000.	1250.

.945 SILVER

C#	Date	Mintage	Fine	VF	XF	Unc
90	1846	—	1250.	2000.	3750.	5000.
	1847	1.111	75.00	250.00	325.00	425.00
	1848	4.050	45.00	150.00	200.00	250.00

Y#	Date	Mintage	Fine	VF	XF	Unc
9	1850	—	1500.	2500.	3500.	4500.
	1853/43	1.711	500.00	1000.	1250.	1500.
	1857	3.606	30.00	75.00	150.00	200.00
	1858	7.604	30.00	60.00	125.00	175.00
	1859	3.001	30.00	75.00	150.00	200.00
	1860	6.603	30.00	60.00	125.00	175.00
	1861	6.001	30.00	60.00	125.00	175.00
	1862	4.002	30.00	60.00	125.00	175.00
	1863	5.152	30.00	60.00	125.00	175.00
	1864	4.001	30.00	60.00	125.00	175.00
	1866	1.402	40.00	125.00	200.00	225.00
	1868 w/open 8	4.004	30.00	60.00	125.00	175.00
	1868 w/closed 8	Inc. Ab.	30.00	60.00	125.00	175.00

GOLD (OMS)

Y#	Date	Mintage	Fine	VF	XF	Unc
9a	1868/58	—	—	—	Rare	—

5.0000 gm., .945 SILVER, .1519 oz ASW

Y#	Date	Mintage	Fine	VF	XF	Unc
25	1898	2.000	35.00	75.00	150.00	200.00

GOLD (OMS)

Y#	Date	Mintage	Fine	VF	XF	Unc
25b	1898	—	—	—	Rare	—

5.0000 gm., .945 SILVER, .1519 oz ASW
Rev: Without 50 C. under shield

Y#	Date	Mintage	Fine	VF	XF	Unc
25a	1904	1.000	60.00	110.00	150.00	200.00
	1905	4.000	20.00	40.00	85.00	125.00
	1906	1.000	60.00	110.00	150.00	200.00
	1907	3.300	20.00	40.00	85.00	125.00
	1908	4.000	20.00	40.00	85.00	125.00
	1909	3.000	20.00	40.00	85.00	125.00

GOLD (OMS)

Y#	Date	Mintage	Fine	VF	XF	Unc
25c	1905	—	—	—	Rare	—

5.0000 gm., .945 SILVER, .1519 oz ASW

Y#	Date	Mintage	Fine	VF	XF	Unc
41	1910	4.000	25.00	50.00	75.00	100.00
	1912	4.000	25.00	50.00	75.00	100.00
	1913	8.000	17.50	35.00	60.00	75.00
	1919	8.000	17.50	35.00	60.00	75.00

3.0000gm., .720 SILVER, .0694oz ASW

Y#	Date	Mintage	Fine	VF	XF	Unc
45	1921	5.000	5.00	10.00	17.50	25.00
	1922	11.240	5.00	7.50	12.50	17.50
	1928	5.000	5.00	10.00	17.50	25.00
	1929	9.500	5.00	7.50	12.50	17.50
	1930	18.500	5.00	7.50	10.00	12.50

GULDEN

.893 SILVER

C#	Date	Mintage	Fine	VF	XF	Unc
77	1818	.043	1000.	1500.	2000.	2500.
	1819	.252	450.00	750.00	1000.	1250.
	1820	.543	300.00	450.00	550.00	675.00
	1821	1.239	300.00	400.00	500.00	625.00
	1822	.080	1250.	2000.	2500.	3000.
	1823	.732	300.00	450.00	550.00	675.00
	1823B	.025	1000.	1500.	2000.	2500.
	1824	1.096	300.00	400.00	500.00	625.00
	1824 w/dash between crown and shield	Inc. Ab.	300.00	450.00	550.00	675.00
	1828	.062	1000.	1500.	1750.	2000.
	1829B	.383	625.00	875.00	1100.	1350.
	1831/21	.120	625.00	875.00	1100.	1350.
	1831	Inc. Ab.	625.00	875.00	1100.	1350.
	1832/21	1.362	300.00	450.00	550.00	675.00
	1832/23	I.A.	300.00	450.00	550.00	675.00
	1832/24	I.A.	300.00	450.00	550.00	675.00
	1832/24 w/dash between crown and shield	Inc. Ab.	300.00	450.00	550.00	675.00
	1832	Inc. Ab.	300.00	450.00	550.00	675.00
	1837	.383	300.00	450.00	550.00	675.00

GOLD (oms)

C#	Date	Mintage	Fine	VF	XF	Unc
77a	1820	—	—	—	Rare	—
—	1821	—	—	—	Rare	—

.945 SILVER

C#	Date	Mintage	Fine	VF	XF	Unc
80	1840	.099	125.00	250.00	425.00	600.00

C#	Date	Mintage	Fine	VF	XF	Unc
91	1840	2 pcs.	—	—	Rare	—
	1842	.661	200.00	500.00	625.00	750.00
	1842 w/shorter bust	Inc. Ab.	425.00	750.00	1000.	1250.
	1843	1.720	150.00	325.00	450.00	550.00
	1844	1.575	150.00	325.00	450.00	550.00
	1845	3.803	35.00	125.00	200.00	275.00
	1845 w/dash between crown and shield	.221	125.00	250.00	350.00	450.00
	1846 w/Fleur de lis privy mark	.901	50.00	125.00	200.00	275.00
	1846 w/sword privy mark	3.772	32.50	85.00	150.00	200.00
	1847	8.280	30.00	75.00	125.00	175.00
	1848	13.615	30.00	75.00	125.00	175.00
	1849	.650	125.00	250.00	375.00	500.00

Y#	Date	Mintage	Fine	VF	XF	Unc
10	1850	10 pcs.	—	—	Rare	—
	1851	2.125	75.00	125.00	200.00	250.00
	1853/0	.652	500.00	625.00	750.00	875.00
	1853/1	Inc. Ab.	500.00	625.00	750.00	875.00
	1853	Inc. Ab.	400.00	500.00	625.00	750.00
	1854	4.511	50.00	100.00	150.00	200.00
	1855	5.133	50.00	100.00	150.00	200.00
	1856	4.955	50.00	100.00	150.00	200.00
	1857	2.125	50.00	100.00	150.00	200.00
	1858	4.199	30.00	65.00	125.00	175.00
	1859	2.717	50.00	100.00	150.00	200.00
	1860	4.036	30.00	65.00	125.00	175.00
	1861	5.079	30.00	65.00	125.00	175.00
	1863	7.986	30.00	65.00	125.00	175.00
	1864	3.600	30.00	65.00	125.00	175.00
	1865	6.402	30.00	65.00	125.00	175.00
	1866	1.002	60.00	125.00	175.00	225.00
	1867	—	—	—	Rare	—

GOLD (oms)

Y#	Date	Mintage	Fine	VF	XF	Unc
10a	1867	—	—	—	Rare	—

10.0000 gm., .945 SILVER, .3038 oz ASW

Y#	Date	Mintage	Fine	VF	XF	Unc
22	1892	3.500	17.50	40.00	100.00	125.00
	1896	.100	300.00	500.00	675.00	800.00
	1897	2.500	17.50	50.00	125.00	175.00

Y#	Date	Mintage	Fine	VF	XF	Unc
26	1898	2.000	60.00	100.00	200.00	300.00
	1901	2.000	60.00	100.00	200.00	300.00
	GOLD (oms)					
26b	1898	—	—	—	Rare	—

10.0000 gm., .945 SILVER, .3038 oz ASW
Rev: Without 100 C. under shield

Y#	Date	Mintage	Fine	VF	XF	Unc
26a	1904	2.000	35.00	75.00	125.00	175.00
	1905	1.000	60.00	125.00	200.00	300.00
	1906	.500	425.00	625.00	750.00	875.00
	1907	5.100	30.00	60.00	110.00	150.00
	1908	4.700	30.00	60.00	110.00	150.00
	1909	2.000	35.00	75.00	125.00	175.00

Y#	Date	Mintage	Fine	VF	XF	Unc
42	1910	1.000	125.00	200.00	300.00	400.00
	1911	2.000	150.00	300.00	500.00	625.00
	1912	3.000	25.00	50.00	85.00	125.00
	1913	8.000	25.00	50.00	85.00	125.00
	1914	15.785	20.00	35.00	75.00	100.00
	1915	14.215	20.00	35.00	75.00	100.00
	1916	5.000	35.00	85.00	125.00	175.00
	1917	2.300	35.00	85.00	125.00	175.00

10.0000 gm., .720 SILVER, .2315 oz ASW

Y#	Date	Mintage	Fine	VF	XF	Unc
46	1922	9.550	10.00	20.00	30.00	40.00
	1923	8.050	10.00	20.00	30.00	40.00
	1924	8.000	10.00	20.00	30.00	40.00
	1928	6.150	7.50	17.50	25.00	35.00
	1929	32.350	BV	7.50	15.00	25.00
	1930	13.500	BV	7.50	15.00	25.00
	1931	38.100	BV	7.50	15.00	25.00
	1938	5.000	12.50	22.50	30.00	40.00
	1939	14.200	BV	7.50	12.50	17.50
	1940	21.300	BV	7.50	12.50	17.50
	1944P w/acorn privy mark					
		105.125	30.00	75.00	110.00	135.00
	1944P w/acorn privy mark, leg. further under T					
		Inc. Ab.	125.00	250.00	375.00	450.00
	1945P w/acorn privy mark					
		25.375	750.00	1500.	2000.	2500.

NOTE: For similar coins dated 1943D with palm tree privy mark, see Netherlands East Indies.

6.5000 gm., .720 SILVER, .1504 oz ASW

Y#	Date	Mintage	Fine	VF	XF	Unc
61	1954	6.600	BV	BV	7.50	10.00
	1954	—	—	—	Proof	80.00
	1955	37.500	BV	BV	6.00	7.50
	1955	—	—	—	Proof	80.00
	1956	38.900	BV	BV	6.00	7.50
	1956	—	—	—	Proof	80.00
	1957	27.000	BV	BV	6.00	7.50
	1957	—	—	—	Proof	80.00
	1958	30.000	BV	BV	6.00	7.50
	1958	—	—	—	Proof	80.00
	1963	5.000	BV	5.00	7.50	10.00
	1963	—	—	—	Proof	80.00
	1964	9.000	BV	BV	6.00	7.50
	1964	—	—	—	Proof	80.00
	1965	21.000	BV	BV	4.50	6.00
	1965	—	—	—	Proof	80.00
	1966	5.000	BV	BV	4.50	6.00
	1966	—	—	—	Proof	80.00
	1967	7.000	BV	BV	4.50	6.00
	1967	—	—	—	Proof	80.00
	NICKEL					
61a	1967	31.000	—	.50	.65	1.25
	1967	—	—	—	Proof	80.00
	1968	61.000	—	.50	.65	1.25
	1969 fish	27.500	—	.50	.65	1.25
	1969 fish	—	—	—	Proof	90.00
	1969 cock					
		15.500	—	.50	.65	.75
	1969 cock	—	—	—	Proof	90.00
	1970	18.000	—	.50	.65	.75
	1970	—	—	—	Proof	80.00
	1971	50.000	—	.50	.65	.75
	1972	60.000	—	.50	.65	.75
	1973	27.000	—	.50	.65	.75
	1975	9.000	—	.50	.65	.75
	1976	32.000	—	.50	.65	.75
	1977	38.000	—	.50	.65	.75
	1978	30.000	—	.50	.65	.75
	1979	25.000	—	—	—	—
	Investiture Of New Queen					
67	1980	—	—	—	—	—

RIJKSDAALDER

.868 SILVER

C#	Date	Mintage	Fine	VF	XF	Unc
78	1815	12 pcs.	—	—	Rare	—
	1816	.174	1250.	1600.	2000.	2500.
	GOLD (oms)					
78a	1814	—	—	—	Rare	—
—	1816	—	—	—	Rare	—

2-1/2 GULDEN

25.0000 gm., .945 SILVER, .7596 oz ASW

C#	Date	Mintage	Fine	VF	XF	Unc
81	1840	.044	325.00	450.00	850.00	1250.
	GOLD (oms)					
81a	1840	2pcs.	—	—	Rare	—

25.0000 gm., .945 SILVER, .7596 oz ASW

C#	Date	Mintage	Fine	VF	XF	Unc
92	1841	.054	875.00	1500.	1750.	2000.
	1842	1.010	150.00	250.00	375.00	500.00
	1843	.643	250.00	400.00	550.00	700.00
	1844	.279	400.00	625.00	750.00	875.00
	1845	3.270	35.00	100.00	200.00	300.00
	1845 w/dash between crown and shield					
		.504	110.00	200.00	300.00	400.00
	1845 w/dot on band of privy mark					
		.154	110.00	200.00	300.00	400.00
	1846 w/Fleur de lis privy mark					
		3.630	35.00	75.00	175.00	225.00
	1846 w/sword privy mark					
		—	50.00	100.00	200.00	250.00
	1847	9.465	35.00	75.00	175.00	225.00
	1848	8.333	35.00	75.00	175.00	225.00
	1849	2.049	75.00	175.00	275.00	375.00

Y#	Date	Mintage	Fine	VF	XF	Unc
11	1849	.439	200.00	375.00	500.00	625.00
	1850	5.008	35.00	75.00	125.00	200.00
	1851	3.647	35.00	75.00	125.00	200.00
	1852	4.547	35.00	75.00	125.00	200.00
	1853/2	.234	300.00	400.00	550.00	700.00
	1853	Inc. Ab.	250.00	375.00	500.00	625.00
	1854/2	4.335	200.00	300.00	350.00	425.00
	1854	Inc. Ab.	35.00	75.00	125.00	200.00
	1855	2.082	35.00	75.00	125.00	200.00
	1856	.909	150.00	200.00	300.00	375.00
	1857	3.353	35.00	75.00	125.00	200.00
	1858	8.357	35.00	75.00	125.00	200.00
	1859	4.307	35.00	75.00	125.00	200.00
	1860	.847	150.00	200.00	300.00	375.00
	1861	.876	150.00	200.00	300.00	375.00
	1862	3.304	35.00	75.00	125.00	200.00
	1863	.051	1000.	1500.	2000.	2500.
	1864	2.034	35.00	75.00	100.00	150.00
	1865	2.288	35.00	75.00	100.00	150.00
	1866	3.563	35.00	75.00	100.00	150.00
	1867	4.949	35.00	55.00	85.00	125.00
	1868	4.040	35.00	55.00	85.00	125.00

Y#	Date	Mintage	Fine	VF	XF	Unc
11	1869	5.046	35.00	55.00	85.00	125.00
	1870	6.640	30.00	45.00	85.00	125.00
	1871	6.875	30.00	45.00	85.00	125.00
	1872	13.416	30.00	45.00	85.00	125.00
	1873	5.515	30.00	45.00	85.00	125.00
	1874 w/sword privy mark					
		3.040	30.00	45.00	85.00	125.00
	1874 w/sword in scabbard privy mark					
		9.756	30.00	45.00	85.00	125.00

GOLD (oms)

Y#	Date	Mintage	Fine	VF	XF	Unc
11a	1874w/sword in scabbard privy mark					
		—	—	—	Rare	—

25.0000 gm., .945 SILVER, .7596 oz ASW

Y#	Date	Mintage	Fine	VF	XF	Unc
27	1898	.100	325.00	450.00	750.00	900.00

GOLD (oms)

Y#	Date	Mintage	Fine	VF	XF	Unc
27a	1898	—	—	—	Rare	—

25.0000 gm., .720 SILVER, .5787 oz ASW

Y#	Date	Mintage	Fine	VF	XF	Unc
47	1929	4.400	BV	15.00	25.00	35.00
	1930	11.600	BV	12.50	17.50	25.00
	1931	4.400	BV	12.50	17.50	25.00
	1932	6.320	BV	12.50	17.50	25.00
	1932 w/deep hair lines					
		Inc. Ab.	250.00	375.00	425.00	500.00
	1933	3.560	10.00	20.00	30.00	35.00
	1937	4.000	10.00	15.00	22.50	30.00
	1938	2.000	20.00	30.00	40.00	50.00
	1938 w/deep hair lines					
		Inc. Ab.	200.00	350.00	400.00	450.00
	1939	3.760	10.00	15.00	22.50	30.00
	1940	4.640	60.00	125.00	150.00	175.00

For similar coins dated 1943D with palm tree privy mark, see Netherlands East Indies.

15.0000 gm., .720 SILVER, .3472 oz ASW

Y#	Date	Mintage	Fine	VF	XF	Unc
62	1959	7.200	BV	BV	12.00	15.00
	1959	—	—	—	Proof	100.00
	1960	12.800	BV	BV	BV	12.50
	1960	—	—	—	Proof	100.00
	1961	10.000	BV	BV	BV	12.50
	1961	—	—	—	Proof	100.00
	1962	5.000	BV	BV	BV	12.50
	1962	—	—	—	Proof	100.00
	1963	4.000	BV	BV	12.00	15.00
	1963	—	—	—	Proof	100.00
	1964	2.800	BV	12.50	17.50	25.00
	1964	—	—	—	Proof	100.00
	1966	5.000	BV	BV	BV	12.50
	1966	—	—	—	Proof	100.00

NICKEL

Y#	Date	Mintage	Fine	VF	XF	Unc
62a	1969 w/fish privy mark					
		1.200	—	2.00	3.00	4.00
	1969 w/fish privy mark					
		—	—	—	Proof	100.00
	1969 w/cock privy mark					
		15.600	—	—	1.25	1.75
	1969 w/cock privy mark					
		—	BV	BV	BV	100.00
	1970	22.000	—	—	1.25	1.75
	1970	—	—	—	Proof	100.00
	1971	8.000	—	—	1.25	1.75
	1972	20.000	—	—	1.25	1.75
	1978	5.000	—	—	1.25	1.75
	1980 w/cock and star privy mark					
		—	—	—	—	—

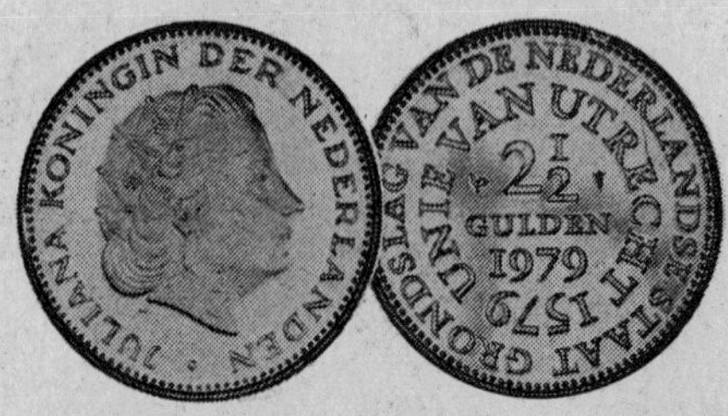

400th anniversary of the union of utrecht

Y#	Date	Mintage	Fine	VF	XF	Unc
66	1979	15.000	—	—	1.25	1.75

Investiture Of New Queen

Y#	Date	Mintage	Fine	VF	XF	Unc
68	1980	—	—	—	—	—

3 GULDEN

.893 SILVER

C#	Date	Mintage	Fine	VF	XF	Unc
79	1817	12 pcs.	—	—	Rare	—
	1818	.116	750.00	1000.	1250.	1500.
	1819/8	.151	1250.	1650.	2000.	2500.
	1819	Inc. Ab.	750.00	1000.	1250.	1500.
	1820	.713	750.00	1000.	1250.	1500.
	1821	.277	750.00	1000.	1250.	1500.
	1821 w/o engraver's name.					
		Inc. Ab.	875.00	1250.	1500.	1750.
	1822	.296	1250.	3000.	4000.	5000.
	1822 w/o engraver's name.					
	—	inc.ab.	1250.	3000.	4000.	5000.
	1823	.255	875.00	1250.	1500.	1750.
	1823B	.014	5000.	7500.	10,000.	12,500.
	1824	.644	750.00	1000.	1250.	1500.
	1824 w/dash between crown and shield					
		Inc. Ab.	750.00	1000.	1250.	1500.
	1830/20	.246	750.00	1000.	1250.	1500.
	1830/24	I.A.	750.00	1000.	1250.	1500.
	1830/24 w/dash between crown and shield					
		Inc. Ab.	750.00	1000.	1250.	1500.
	1830	Inc. Ab.	750.00	1000.	1250.	1500.
	1831/24	.117	750.00	1000.	1250.	1500.
	1831/24 w/dash between crown and shield					
		Inc. Ab.	750.00	1000.	1250.	1500.
	1831	Inc. Ab.	750.00	1000.	1250.	1500.
	1832/21	.371	750.00	1000.	1250.	1500.
	1832/22	I.A.	750.00	1000.	1250.	1500.
	1832/23	I.A.	750.00	1000.	1250.	1500.
	1832/24	I.A.	750.00	1000.	1250.	1500.
	1832/24 w/dash between crown and shield					
		Inc. Ab.	750.00	1000.	1250.	1500.
	1832	Inc. Ab.	750.00	1000.	1250.	1500.

GOLD (oms)

C#	Date	Mintage	Fine	VF	XF	Unc
79a	1823	—	—	—	Rare	—

5 GULDEN

.900 GOLD

C#	Date	Mintage	Fine	VF	XF	Unc
82	1826B	.843	625.00	1100.	1250.	1350.
	1827	.518	750.00	1250.	1350.	1500.
	1827B	1.629	625.00	1100.	1250.	1350.

Obv: Bust to right. Rev: Crowned arms.

C#	Date	Mintage	Fine	VF	XF	Unc
93	1843	1,595	1500.	2500.	3250.	3750.

Obv: Bust to right. Rev: Crowned arms within branches.

C#	Date	Mintage	Fine	VF	XF	Unc
—	1848	—	1750.	3000.	3500.	4000.

Y#	Date	Mintage	Fine	VF	XF	Unc
12	1850	—	1500.	2750.	3250.	3750.
	1851	.010	625.00	1500.	2000.	2500.

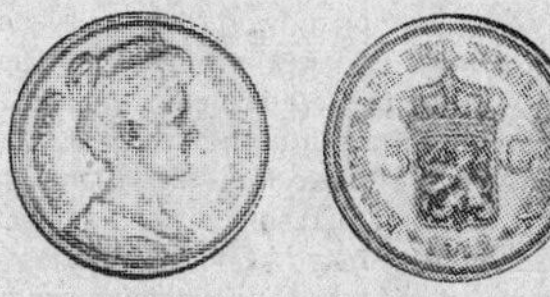

Y#	Date	Mintage	Fine	VF	XF	Unc
31	1912	1.000	200.00	450.00	550.00	650.00
	1912	120pcs.	—	—	Proof	—

10 GULDEN

6.7290 gm., .900 GOLD, .1947 oz AGW

C#	Date	Mintage	Fine	VF	XF	Unc
83	1818	—	2500.	4000.	4500.	5000.
	1819	.107	1250.	2250.	3000.	3750.
	1820	.033	1250.	2250.	3000.	3750.
	1822	.048	1250.	2250.	3000.	3750.
	1823	.266	750.00	1350.	1600.	1850.
	1824	.336	750.00	1350.	1600.	1850.
	1824B	3.735	750.00	1350.	1600.	1850.
	1825	.228	750.00	1350.	1600.	1850.
	1825B	3.821	750.00	1350.	1600.	1850.
	1826	—	2500.	4000.	4500.	5000.
	1826B	.079	1250.	2250.	3000.	3750.
	1827	.134	1000.	1750.	2000.	2250.
	1828	.015	2000.	3500.	4000.	4500.
	1828B	.562	750.00	1350.	1600.	1850.
	1829	9,484	1250.	2250.	3000.	3750.
	1829B	.084	1250.	2250.	3000.	3750.
	1830	.568	750.00	1350.	1600.	1850.
	1831/0	.099	1250.	2250.	3000.	3750.
	1831	Inc. Ab.	750.00	1350.	1600.	1850.
	1832/1	1.372	1250.	2250.	3000.	3750.
	1832	Inc. Ab.	750.00	1350.	1600.	1850.
	1833	.721	750.00	1350.	1600.	1850.
	1837	.458	750.00	1350.	1600.	1850.
	1839	.326	750.00	1350.	1600.	1850.
	1840	2.760	750.00	1350.	1600.	1850.

C#	Date	Mintage	Fine	VF	XF	Unc
94	1842	860 pcs.	2000.	3500.	4500.	5500.

Obv: Bust to right. Rev: Crowned arms within branches.

C#	Date	Mintage	Fine	VF	XF	Unc
	1848	—	2250.	4000.	5000.	6000.

Y#	Date	Mintage	Fine	VF	XF	Unc
13	1850	—	2000.	3500.	4000.	4500.
	1851	.010	875.00	2000.	2500.	3000.

Y#	Date	Mintage	Fine	VF	XF	Unc
B16	1875	4.110	BV	BV	BV	130.00

Y#	Date	Mintage	Fine	VF	XF	Unc
A16	1876	1.581	BV	BV	BV	130.00
	1877	1.108	BV	BV	BV	130.00
	1879/7	.581	425.00	1150.	1350.	1500.
	1879	Inc. Ab.	BV	130.00	150.00	175.00
	1880	.050	175.00	400.00	450.00	500.00
	1885	.067	150.00	375.00	425.00	450.00
	1886	.054	175.00	450.00	550.00	625.00
	1887	.041	175.00	450.00	550.00	625.00
	1888	.036	500.00	1150.	1350.	1600.
	1889	.205	130.00	200.00	225.00	250.00

Y#	Date	Mintage	Fine	VF	XF	Unc
28	1892	61 pcs.	3000.	5000.	7500.	10,000.
	1895	149 pcs.	2500.	4000.	6000.	7500.
	1897	.454	175.00	275.00	325.00	400.00

Y#	Date	Mintage	Fine	VF	XF	Unc
29	1898	.099	625.00	1150.	1400.	1500.

Y#	Date	Mintage	Fine	VF	XF	Unc
30	1911	.775	BV	130.00	140.00	150.00
	1912	3.000	BV	BV	BV	130.00
	1913	1.133	BV	BV	BV	130.00
	1917	4.000	BV	BV	BV	130.00

Y#	Date	Mintage	Fine	VF	XF	Unc
32	1925	2.000	BV	BV	BV	130.00
	1926	2.500	BV	BV	130.00	150.00
	1927	1.000	BV	BV	BV	140.00
	1932	4.324	BV	BV	BV	130.00
	1933	2.462	BV	BV	BV	130.00

25.0000 gm., .720 SILVER, .5787 oz ASW
25th Anniversary of Liberation

Y#	Date	Mintage	Fine	VF	XF	Unc
64	1970	6.000	BV	10.00	12.50	15.00
	1970	.020		Proof-like	50.00	60.00
	1970	40 pcs.	—	—	Proof	300.00

25th Anniversary of Reign

Y#	Date	Mintage	Fine	VF	XF	Unc
65	1973	4.500	BV	8.75	10.00	12.00
	1973	.106	—	—	Proof	50.00

20 GULDEN

.900 GOLD
Obv: Bust to right. Rev: Crowned arms within branches.

C#	Date	Mintage	Fine	VF	XF	Unc
—	1848	—	2000.	5000.	6250.	7500.

Y#	Date	Mintage	Fine	VF	XF	Unc
14	1850	—	2000.	5000.	6250.	7500.
	1851	2,500	1500.	2750.	3500.	4000.
	1853	136 pcs.	2000.	5000.	6250.	7500.

TRADE COINS

DUCAT

3.4940 gm., .983 GOLD, .1104 oz AGW

C#	Date	Mintage	Fine	VF	XF	Unc
84	1814	2.930	250.00	400.00	500.00	625.00
	1815	.673	250.00	400.00	500.00	625.00
	1815 cloverleaf					
		.614	225.00	425.00	500.00	625.00
	1816	.221	300.00	500.00	625.00	750.00

C#	Date	Mintage	Fine	VF	XF	Unc
85	1817	.495	425.00	750.00	875.00	1000.
	1818	2.902	175.00	300.00	350.00	400.00
	1819	.111	225.00	425.00	475.00	550.00
	1820	.010	400.00	625.00	700.00	800.00
	1821	.015	400.00	625.00	700.00	800.00
	1822	.012	400.00	625.00	700.00	800.00
	1824B	8,000	700.00	1000.	1100.	1250.
	1825	.119	225.00	400.00	450.00	500.00
	1825B	.056	400.00	600.00	675.00	800.00
	1827	.488	175.00	300.00	350.00	400.00
	1827B	.027	450.00	675.00	800.00	925.00
	1828/7	1.922	200.00	375.00	475.00	675.00
	1828	Inc. Ab.	350.00	550.00	625.00	750.00
	1828B	.534	225.00	400.00	450.00	500.00
	1829/8	.247	400.00	600.00	675.00	800.00
	1829B	Inc. Ab.	400.00	600.00	675.00	800.00
	1829	1.303	175.00	300.00	350.00	400.00
	1830	2.000	175.00	300.00	350.00	400.00
	1830B	.011	600.00	875.00	1000.	1100.
	1831	1.411	175.00	300.00	350.00	400.00
	1832	1.000	225.00	400.00	450.00	500.00
	1833	.597	225.00	400.00	450.00	500.00
	1834	.150	400.00	625.00	700.00	800.00
	1835	.650	400.00	625.00	700.00	800.00
	1836/5	.536	225.00	425.00	450.00	500.00
	1836	Inc. Ab.	225.00	400.00	450.00	500.00
	1837	1.400	225.00	400.00	450.00	500.00
	1838	1.200	225.00	400.00	450.00	500.00
	1839	1.501	225.00	400.00	450.00	500.00
	1840 w/torch privy mark					
		—	225.00	400.00	450.00	500.00
	1840 w/Fleur de lis privy mark					
		.103	225.00	400.00	500.00	625.00
95	1841 w/torch privy mark					
		3.904	225.00	400.00	500.00	625.00
	1841 w/Fleur de lis privy mark					
		.096	225.00	400.00	500.00	625.00

Y#	Date	Mintage	Fine	VF	XF	Unc
15	1849	.014	150.00	275.00	325.00	400.00
	1872	.030	150.00	275.00	325.00	400.00
	1873	.040	150.00	275.00	325.00	400.00
	1874	.044	150.00	275.00	325.00	400.00
	1876	.044	150.00	275.00	325.00	400.00
	1877	.015	250.00	400.00	450.00	500.00
	1878	.087	150.00	275.00	325.00	400.00
	1879	.020	425.00	750.00	875.00	1000.
	1880	.025	425.00	750.00	875.00	1000.
	1885	.081	425.00	750.00	875.00	1000.
	1894	.030	200.00	375.00	450.00	550.00
	1895/55	.058	175.00	350.00	425.00	500.00
	1895/59	I.A.	175.00	350.00	425.00	500.00
	1895	Inc. Ab.	175.00	350.00	425.00	500.00
	1899	.061	175.00	350.00	425.00	500.00
	1901	.029	200.00	375.00	450.00	550.00
	1903	.091	175.00	350.00	425.00	500.00
	1905	.088	175.00	350.00	425.00	500.00
	1906	.029	200.00	375.00	450.00	550.00
	1908	.091	175.00	350.00	425.00	500.00
	1909 halberd with star privy mark					
		.106	175.00	350.00	425.00	500.00
	1909 w/sea horse privy mark					
		.030	200.00	375.00	450.00	550.00
	1910	.421	175.00	300.00	375.00	450.00
	1912	.148	175.00	300.00	375.00	450.00
	1913	.205	175.00	300.00	375.00	450.00
	1914	.247	175.00	300.00	375.00	450.00
	1916	.117	175.00	300.00	375.00	450.00
	1917	.217	60.00	100.00	125.00	150.00
	1920	.293	60.00	100.00	125.00	150.00
	1921	.409	50.00	75.00	100.00	125.00
	1922	.050	200.00	350.00	400.00	450.00
	1923	.107	100.00	200.00	250.00	300.00
	1924	.084	100.00	200.00	250.00	300.00
	1925	.573	50.00	85.00	110.00	125.00
	1926	.191	75.00	125.00	150.00	175.00
	1927	.654	35.00	40.00	50.00	60.00
	1928	.572	35.00	40.00	50.00	60.00
	1932	.088	125.00	225.00	300.00	375.00

Y#	Date	Mintage	Fine	VF	XF	Unc
15	1937	.117	75.00	150.00	175.00	200.00
63	1960	3,605	550.00	1000.	1200.	1400.
	1972	.029	75.00	100.00	150.00	175.00
	1974	.087	BV	BV	BV	80.00
	1974metal struck					
		2,000	—	—	400.00	500.00
	1975	.205	BV	BV	BV	75.00
	1976	*.038	100.00	150.00	175.00	200.00
	1978	.029	BV	BV	BV	85.00

NOTE: The above coins (Y#63) were struck at Utrecht Mint on special order.

***NOTE: Of the original 37,844 pieces struck, 32,000 were melted.**

2 DUCATS

.983 GOLD

	Date	Mintage	Fine	VF	XF	Unc
16	1854	—	—	—	Rare	—
	1867	—	—	—	Rare	—

NCLT ISSUES

FLEUR DE COIN SETS

KM#	Date	Mintage	Identification	Issue Price	Mkt. Val.
S1	1971(5)	—	Y57-61a		15.00
S2	1972(5)	—	Y57-61a	—	7.50
S3	1973(5)	—	Y57-61a	—	7.50
S4	1974(4)	—	Y57-60	—	7.50
S5	1975(6)	12,000	*Y57-61a	—	7.50
S6	1976(5)	15,000	Y57-61a	—	12.00
S7	1977(5)	17,000	Y57-61a	—	12.00
S8	1978(6)	21,500	Y57-62a	6.50	12.00
S9	1979(6)	35,000	Y57-61a,66	6.50	10.00

***NOTE:** Set also includes 1973 25 cents.

PROOF SETS

STANDARD METALS

KM#	Date	Mintage	Identification	Issue Price	Mkt. Val.
101	1948(4)	50	Y53-56 w/proef	—	900.00
102	1948(4)	—	Y53-56	—	125.00
103	1949(4)	—	Y53-56	—	Rare
104	1950(4)	—	Y57-60 w/proef	—	900.00
105	1950(4)	—	Y57-60	—	175.00
106	1951(4)	—	Y57-60	—	125.00
107	1952(2)	—	Y57,58	—	75.00
108	1953(2)	—	Y57,58	—	75.00
109	1954(5)	—	Y57-61	—	250.00
110	1955(5)	—	Y57-61	—	250.00
111	1956(5)	—	Y57-61	—	250.00
112	1957(5)	—	Y57-61	—	250.00
113	1958(5)	—	Y57-61	—	250.00
114	1959(3)	—	Y57,59,62	—	125.00
115	1960(5)	—	Y57-60,62	—	250.00
116	1961(5)	—	Y57-60,62	—	250.00
117	1962(5)	40	Y57-60,62	—	250.00
118	1963(6)	40	Y57-62	—	300.00
119	1964(6)	40	Y57-62	—	300.00
120	1965(5)	—	Y57-61	—	250.00
121	1966(6)	—	Y57-62	—	300.00
122	1967(5)	—	Y57-60,61a	—	250.00
123	1968(3)	—	Y57,59,60	—	125.00
124	1968(6) Fish	—	Y57-60,61a,62a	—	300.00
125	1969(6) Cock	—	Y57-60,61a,62a	—	300.00
126	1970(6)	—	Y57-60,61a,62a	—	275.00

NOTE: After 1970 no proof sets were struck for collectors. Approximately 60 sets per year have been struck and presented to various officials, etc.

NETHERLANDS-ANTILLES

The Netherlands Antilles, an autonomous part of the Netherlands realm, comprise two groups of islands in the West Indies: Aruba, Bonaire and Curacao and their dependencies near the Venezuelan coast and St. Eustatius, Saba, and the southern part of St. Martin (St. Maarten) southeast of Puerto Rico. The island group has an area of 394 sq. mi. (1,020 sq. km.) and a population of 240,000. Capital: Willemstad. Chief industries are the refining of crude oil and tourism. Petroleum products and phosphates are exported.

On Dec. 15, 1954, the Netherlands Antilles were given complete domestic autonomy and granted equality within the Kingdom with Surinam and the Netherlands.

WEST INDIES

The Director of the West Indian Colonies went to the lawmakers of the Netherlands in 1792 in an effort to get coins made for the West Indies that would carry some distinctive mark as those of the East Indies did. Legislation was passed on Dec. 31, 1793 that such coins should be made to the standard of the Netherlands. The 1/4 Gulden was included in the series and the letter W below the arms was to be the distinctive mark. Some of the production was sent to the Dutch Settlement on the Gold Coast in Africa.

RULERS

Dutch

MONETARY SYSTEM

20 Stuiver = 1 Gulden

2 STUIVER

SILVER

C#	Date	Mintage	Fine	VF	XF	Unc
1	1794	.030	125.00	175.00	350.00	575.00

1/4 GULDEN

SILVER

C#	Date	Mintage	Fine	VF	XF	Unc
2	1794	.020	110.00	150.00	175.00	200.00

GULDEN

SILVER, 10.6 gm.

C#	Date	Mintage	Fine	VF	XF	Unc
3	1794	.014	350.00	550.00	625.00	700.00

3 GULDEN

SILVER

C#	Date	Mintage	Fine	VF	XF	Unc
4	1794	1,226	3750.	6250.	7500.	8750.

NCLT ISSUES

PIEFORTS (P)

KM#	Date	Mintage	Identification	Mkt.Val.
P1	1794	—	1 Gulden, Silver, 20 gm., C#3	—
P2	1794	—	1 Gulden, Silver, 31 gm., C#3	—

SAINT EUSTATIUS

St. Eustatius (Sint Eustatius, 'Statia'), a Netherlands West Indian island located in the Leeward Islands of the Lesser Antilles nine miles northwest of St. Kitts, has an area of 12 sq. mi. and a population of about 2,000. Politically, it is part of Curacao. Capital: Willemstad, on Curacao. The chief industries are farming, fishing, and tourism.

Between 1630 and 1640 the Dutch seized Curacao, Saba, St. Martin and St. Eustatius, all valuable as trading and smuggling depots. The territorial acquisitions were confirmed to the Dutch by the treaty of Munster in 1648. Under the guidance of merchants from Flushing, St. Eustatius became a prosperous entrepot of neutral trade. On Feb. 3, 1781, British Admiral George Rodney, acting under orders, captured the island and confiscated much valuable booty. Before passing permanently into Dutch hands, St. Eustatius was attacked or captured several times by the French and English, and was in English hands during the Napoleonic Wars from 1810 to 1814.

RULERS

Dutch

MONETARY SYSTEM

6 Stuivers = 1 Reaal

COUNTERMARKS

'SE' incuse countermark on French Guiana 2 Sous coins were official.

These were followed by raised 'SE' counterstamps on a variety of worn billon & silver coins generally thought to be forgeries.

From 1809 all coins had to be revalidated with a 'P' countermark. Both raised and incuse 'SE' varieties as well as unmarked coins were revalidated.

STUIVER

BILLON
c/s: Incuse 'SE' on French Guiana 2 Sous, C#1.

C#	Date	Mintage	VG	Fine	VF
1	ND(1797)	—	75.00	100.00	140.00

COPPER
c/s: Raised 'SE'

C#	Date	Mintage	VG	Fine	VF
1a	ND(1797-1809)	—	65.00	90.00	120.00

BILLON

C#	Date	Mintage	VG	Fine	VF
16	ND(1797-1809)	—	65.00	90.00	120.00

SILVER

C#	Date	Mintage	VG	Fine	VF
1c	ND(1797-1809)	—	150.00	200.00	250.00

VARIOUS METALS
c/s: 'P' revalidation on older 'SE'

C#	Date	Mintage	VG	Fine	VF
8	ND(1809-1812)	—	45.00	65.00	85.00

c/s: 'P' in circle of dots on worn silver coins

C#	Date	Mintage	VG	Fine	VF
11	ND(1810-1812)	—	—	Rare	—

SAINT MARTIN

St. Martin (Sint Maarten), the only island in the Antilles owned by two European powers (France and the Netherlands), is located in the Leeward Islands of the Lesser Antilles five miles south of the British island of Anguilla. The French northern section of the island (St. Martin) is a dependency of the French Department of Guadeloupe. It has an area of 20 sq. mi. and a population of about 8,000. Capital: Basse-Terre, on the island of that name. The Dutch southern section of the island (Sint Maarten) has an area of 17 sq. mi. and a population of about 2,500. Capital: Willemstad, on Curacao. The chief industries are farming, fishing, and tourism. Salt, horses, and mules are exported.

Although nominally a Spnaish possession at the time, St. Martin was occupied by French freebooters in 1638, but when Spain relinquished claim to the island in 1648 it was peaceably divided between France and Holland in recognition of the merchant communities already established on the island by nationals of both powers. St. Martin has remained under dual French-Dutch ownership to the present time, except for a period during the Napoleonic Wars when the British seized and occupied it.

MONETARY SYSTEM

6 Stuivers = 1 Reaal
20 Stuivers = 1 Gulden
12 (later 15) Reaals = 1 Peso

COUNTERMARK ISSUES

2 STUIVERS

BILLON
c/s: 'StM' in beaded circle on French Guiana 2 Sous.

C#	Date	Mintage	VG	Fine	VF
1b	ND(1798)	—	30.00	50.00	65.00

SILVER
c/s: 'StM' in beaded circle.

C#	Date	Mintage	VG	Fine	VF
8	ND(1798)	—	120.00	160.00	200.00

BILLON
c/s: 'StM' in beaded circle plus incuse 'M' on French Guiana 2 Sous.

C#	Date	Mintage	VG	Fine	VF
1d	ND(1820)	—	120.00	150.00	180.00

c/s: Incuse Fleur-de-Lys on French Guiana 2 sous.

C#	Date	Mintage	VG	Fine	VF
1e	ND(1805)	—	35.00	55.00	75.00

SILVER
c/s: Raised Fleur-de-Lis

C#	Date	Mintage	VG	Fine	VF
1f	ND(1805)	—	50.00	75.00	100.00

c/s: Additional M incuse on French Guiana, 2 Sous.

C#	Date	Mintage	VG	Fine	VF
1g	ND(1820)	—	—	—	—

c/s: Incuse M on French Guiana, 2 Sous.

C#	Date	Mintage	VG	Fine	VF
1h	ND(1820)	—	—	—	—

CUT & COUNTERSTAMPED

18 STUIVERS

SILVER
c/s: 'CC' and bundle of arrows & 18 on edge on 1/4 cut of Spanish or Spanish Colonial 8 Reales.

C#	Date	Mintage	VG	Fine	VF
12	ND(1797)	—	—	Rare	—

c/s: Bundle of arrows and '18' on edge on 1/4 cut of Spanish or Spanish Colonial 8 Reales.

C#	Date	Mintage	VG	Fine	VF
13	ND(1797-98)	—	2000.	3000.	4000.

c/s: St. Martin & arrows on 1/5 cut of Spanish or Spanish Colonial 8 Reales.

C#	Date	Mintage	VG	Fine	VF
11	ND(1809)	—	200.00	350.00	500.00

CURACAO

The island of Curacao, an autonomous part of the Kingdom of the Netherlands located in the Caribbean Sea 40 miles off the coast of Venezuela, has an area of 173 sq. mi. and a population of 150,000. Capital: Willemstad. The chief industry is the refining of crude oil imported from Venezuela and Colombia. Petroleum products, salt, phosphates and cattle are exported.

Curacao was discovered by Spanish navigator Alonso de Ojeda about 1499 and was settled by Spain in 1527. The Dutch West India Company took the island from Spain in 1634 and administered it until 1787, when it was surrendered to the crown. The Dutch held it thereafter except for two periods during the Napoleonic Wars, 1798 and 1806-14, when it was occupied by the British. During World War II, CURACAO refined 60 percent of the oil used by the Allies; the refineries were protected by U.S. troops after Germany invaded Holland in 1940.

During their occupation of the Napoleonic period, the British created an emergency coinage for Curacao by cutting the Spanish dollar into five equal segments and countermarking each piece with a rosette indent.

BATAVIAN REPUBLIC

MONETARY SYSTEM

1799-1803

1 Cent (U.S.) = 2-1/2 Stuivers
6 Stuivers = 1 Reaal
12 Realen = 1 Peso
20 Stuivers = 1 Gulden
20 Gulden = 8 Pesos = 1 Johannes (1/2 Dobra)

CENT

COPPER
c/s: Circular CURACAO on U.S. large cent.

KM#	Date	Mintage	VG	Fine	VF
1	ND	—	260.00	300.00	400.00

7 STUIVERS

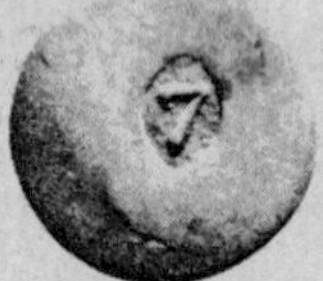

SILVER, 2-2.35 gm.
c/s: 7 in oval indent on French Livre

2	ND 1798	—	20.00	30.00	40.00

c/s: 7 in oval indent on Spanish Colonial 1 Real

	ND 1798	—	25.00	40.00	55.00

9 STUIVERS

SILVER
c/s: 9 in oval indent on Spanish Colonial 1 Real.

3	ND 1801	—	60.00	75.00	85.00

note: The above coins along with similar coins bearing the numbers 3, 5, 14-18 are of questionable origin. Thus, they are not listed in Craig. Pridmore states these as unattributable.

3 REALEN

SILVER
c/s: Five-petalled rosace in circle on 1/4 cut of Spanish or Spanish Colonial 8 Reales

C#	Date	Mintage	VG	Fine	VF	XF
1	ND(c.1810)	.030	75.00	200.00	375.00	425.00

8 PESOS

GOLD
Brazilian 1/2 Dobra, C#52, countermarked: GI, L, MH and B at edges. With GH in center. Rev: Countermark W.

1.5	ND(1799)	—	—	Rare	—

BRITISH OCCUPATION

1807-1816

MONETARY SYSTEM

1807-1825

15 Reales = 1 Peso
6 Stuivers = 1 Reaal
27 Gulden = 6 Pesos = 1 Johannes

Commencing 1838

100 Cents = 1 Gulden

3 REALEN

SILVER
Reconstructed 5 segments
c/s: Five-petalled rosace in circle on 1/5 cut of Spanish or Spanish Colonial 8 reales

NOTE: This replaced C#1.

C#	Date	Mintage	VG	Fine	VF	XF
3	ND(1814)	.040	75.00	200.00	375.00	425.00

3-1/2 REALEN

SILVER
c/s: Additional 21 Stuivers in oval indent on C#1.

2	ND(1814)	—	250.00	625.00	1000.	1250.

22 GULDEN

GOLD
c/s: 22 in square on Brazilian 1/2 dobra 22 in square.

4	ND	—	Rare	1100.00	—

NETHERLANDS RESTORED

1816

STUIVER

.300 SILVER

C#	Date	Mintage	Fine	VF	XF	Unc
8	1822	.529	125.00	175.00	200.00	250.00

NOTE: Struck also in 1840-41, circulating at that time as a 2 Cent piece.

1/4 REAAL

SILVER

1821	Unique?	—	—	—	—

REAAL

SILVER
4 acorns

C#	Date	Mintage	Fine	VF	XF	Unc
9	1821	.121	200.00	400.00	500.00	625.00
		7 acorns				
9.1	1821	Inc. Ab.	200.00	400.00	500.00	625.00
		8 acorns				
9.2	1821	Inc. Ab.	200.00	350.00	450.00	550.00
		9 acorns				
9.3	1821	Inc. Ab.	200.00	400.00	500.00	625.00
		12 acorns				
9.4	1821	Inc. Ab.	200.00	400.00	500.00	625.00

1/4 GUILDER

SILVER
Reconstructed 4 segments
c/s: C in oval indent on 1/4 cut of Netherlands 1 Gulden.

C#	Date	Mintage	VG	Fine	VF	XF
7	ND(1838)	.024	100.00	300.00	500.00	625.00

3 REALEN

SILVER
Reconstructed 5 segments
c/s: 3 in circle on 1/5 cut of Spanish or Colonial 8 Reales.

5	ND(1818)	.078	50.00	150.00	300.00	350.00

c/s: 3 in dentilated circle on 1/5 cut of Spanish or Colonial 8 Reales.

5a	ND(1819-25)	—	60.00	80.00	100.00

5 REALEN

SILVER
c/s: 5 in circle on 1/3 cut of Spanish or Colonial 8 Reales.

6	ND(1818)	3,000	1000.	3000.	5000.	6250.

MODERN COINAGE

100 Cents = 1 Gulden

CENT

BRONZE

Y#	Date	Mintage	Fine	VF	XF	Unc
Y36b	1942P	2.500	10.00	15.00	22.50	30.00

NOTE: This coin was also circulated in Surinam. For similar coins dated 1943P & 1957-1960, see Surinam.

Y#	Date	Mintage	Fine	VF	XF	Unc
3	1944D	3.000	.50	1.50	2.00	2.50
	1947	1.500	.50	1.50	2.00	2.50
	1947	80 pcs.	—	—	Proof	15.00

2-1/2 CENTS

BRONZE

Y#	Date	Mintage	Fine	VF	XF	Unc
4	1944D	1.000	1.00	2.00	3.00	4.00
	1947	.500	1.50	2.50	4.00	5.00
	1947	80 pcs.	—	—	Proof	20.00
	1948	1.000	1.00	2.00	3.00	4.00
	1948	75 pcs.	—	—	Proof	20.00

5 CENTS

COPPER-NICKEL

Y#	Date	Mintage	Fine	VF	XF	Unc
34a	1943	8.595	10.00	12.00	14.00	20.00

NOTE: The above piece does not bear either a palm tree or a mint mark, but it was struck expressly for use in Curacao and Surinam. This homeland type of Y#34 was last issued in the Netherlands in 1940.

Y#	Date	Mintage	Fine	VF	XF	Unc
9	1948	1.000	3.75	7.50	10.00	12.50
	1948	75 pcs.	—	—	Proof	40.00

1/10 GUILDER

1.4000 gm., .640 SILVER, .0288 oz ASW

Y#	Date	Mintage	Fine	VF	XF	Unc
1	1901	.300	30.00	60.00	75.00	85.00
	1901	40 pcs.	—	—	Proof	100.00

Y#	Date	Mintage	Fine	VF	XF	Unc
5	1944D	1.500	1.25	3.00	5.00	7.50
	1947	1.000	1.25	3.00	5.00	7.50
	1947	80 pcs.	—	—	Proof	40.00

Y#	Date	Mintage	Fine	VF	XF	Unc
8	1948	1.000	1.25	3.00	5.00	7.50
	1948	75 pcs.	—	—	Proof	75.00

10 CENTS

1.4000 gm., .640 SILVER, .0288 oz ASW

Y#	Date	Mintage	Fine	VF	XF	Unc
43a	1941P	.800	7.50	12.50	17.50	25.00
	1943P	4.500	3.75	10.00	15.00	20.00

NOTE: Both these coins were also circulated in Surinam. for coins dated 1942P, see Surinam.

1/4 GUILDER

3.5800 gm., .640 SILVER, .0736 oz ASW

Y#	Date	Mintage	Fine	VF	XF	Unc
2	1900	.480	30.00	60.00	75.00	85.00
	1900	40 pcs.	—	—	Proof	125.00

Y#	Date	Mintage	Fine	VF	XF	Unc
6	1944D	1.500	2.25	3.75	7.50	10.00
	1947	1.000	2.25	3.75	7.50	10.00
	1947	80 pcs.	—	—	Proof	55.00

25 CENTS

3.5800 gm., .640 SILVER, .0736 oz ASW

Y#	Date	Mintage	Fine	VF	XF	Unc
44a	1941P	1.100	10.00	15.00	20.00	25.00
	1943P	2.500	5.00	10.00	15.00	20.00

NOTE: Both these coins were also circulated in Surinam. For similar coins dated 1943, 1944 & 1945-P with acorn mintmark see Netherlands.

GULDEN

10.0000 gm., .720 SILVER, .2315 oz ASW

Y#	Date	Mintage	Fine	VF	XF	Unc
7	1944D	.500	10.00	30.00	50.00	65.00

2-1/2 GULDEN

25.0000 gm., .720 SILVER, .5787 oz ASW

Y#	Date	Mintage	Fine	VF	XF	Unc
10	1944D	.200	BV	17.50	20.00	22.50

NCLT ISSUES

PROOF SETS

STANDARD METALS

KM#	Date	Mintage	Identification	Issue Price	Mkt. Val.
101	1901(2)	40	Y1(1901), Y2(1900)	—	200.00
102	1947(4)	80	Y3-6	—	125.00
103	1948(3)	75	Y4, 8, 9	—	125.00

NETHERLANDS ANTILLES

RULERS

Juliana, 1948 -

MINTMARKS

Utrecht - privy marks only

FM - Franklin Mint, U.S.A.*

***NOTE:** During 1975-77 the Franklin Mint produced coinage in up to 3 different qualities. Qualities of issue are designated in ( ) after each date and are defined as follows:

(M) MATTE - Normal circulation strike or a dull finish produced by sandblasting special uncirculated (polish finish) or proof quality dies.

(U) SPECIAL UNCIRCULATED - Polished or proof-like in appearance without any frosted features.

(P) PROOF - The highest quality obtainable having mirror-like fields and frosted features.

MONETARY SYSTEM

100 Cents = 1 Gulden

CENT

BRONZE

Y#	Date	Mintage	Fine	VF	XF	Unc
1	1952 fish	1.000	.50	1.25	1.75	2.50
	1952	100 pcs.	—	—	Proof	75.00
	1954	1.000	.50	1.25	1.75	2.50
	1954	200 pcs.	—	—	Proof	20.00
	1957	1.000	.50	1.25	1.75	2.50
	1957	250 pcs.	—	—	Proof	20.00
	1959	1.000	.50	1.25	1.75	2.50

Y#	Date	Mintage	Fine	VF	XF	Unc
1	1959	250 pcs.	—	—	Proof	20.00
	1960	300 pcs.	—	—	Proof	20.00
	1961	1.000	.50	1.25	1.75	2.50
	1963	1.000	.50	1.25	1.75	2.50
	1963	—	—	—	Proof	—
	1964	—	—	—	Proof	—
	1965	1.200	.50	1.25	1.75	40.00
	1965	—	—	—	Proof	—
	1967 (2 varieties)					
		.850	.50	1.25	1.75	2.50
	1967	—	—	—	Proof	—
	1968					
		.900	.50	1.25	1.75	2.50
	1968 star & fish					
		.700	2.50	5.00	7.50	10.00
	1970 cock	.200	3.00	6.25	7.50	10.00
	1970	—	—	—	Proof	—

Y#	Date	Mintage	Fine	VF	XF	Unc
8	1970 cock	1.200	.10	.25	.50	.75
	1970	—	—	—	Proof	—
	1971	3.000	.10	.25	.50	.75
	1971	—	—	—	Proof	—
	1972	1.000	.10	.25	.50	.75
	1973	3.000	.10	.25	.50	.75
	1973	—	—	—	Proof	—
	1974	3.000	.10	.25	.50	.75
	1974	—	—	—	Proof	—
	1975	2.000	.10	.25	.50	.75
	1975	—	—	—	Proof	—
	1976	2.600	—	.10	.25	.50
	1977	4.000	—	—	.25	.50
	1978	2.000	—	—	.25	.50

ALUMINUM

Y#	Date	Mintage	Fine	VF	XF	Unc
8a	1979	7.500	—	—	.10	.25

2-1/2 CENTS

BRONZE

Y#	Date	Mintage	Fine	VF	XF	Unc
2	1956 fish	.400	1.00	2.50	3.75	5.00
	1956	500 pcs.	—	—	Proof	20.00
	1959	1.000	1.00	2.50	3.75	5.00
	1959	250 pcs.	—	—	Proof	25.00
	1965	.500	1.00	2.50	3.75	5.00
	1965	—	—	—	Proof	—
	1965 star & fish					
		.150	5.00	7.50	10.00	12.50

Y#	Date	Mintage	Fine	VF	XF	Unc
9	1970 cock	.500	.25	.30	.75	1.00
	1970	—	—	—	Proof	—
	1971	3.000	.25	.30	.75	1.00
	1971	—	—	—	Proof	—
	1973	1.000	.25	.30	.75	1.00
	1973	—	—	—	Proof	—
	1974	1.000	.25	.30	.75	1.00
	1974	—	—	—	Proof	—
	1975	1.000	.25	.30	.75	1.00
	1976	.600	.25	.30	.75	1.00
	1977	1.000	.25	.30	.75	1.00
	1978	1.500	.25	.30	.75	1.00

ALUMINUM

Y#	Date	Mintage	Fine	VF	XF	Unc
9a	1979	2.000	—	.10	.25	.50

5 CENTS

COPPER-NICKEL

Y#	Date	Mintage	Fine	VF	XF	Unc
3	1957	.500	1.75	3.75	5.00	7.50
	1957	250 pcs.	—	—	Proof	25.00
	1962	.250	3.75	7.50	10.00	12.50
	1962	200 pcs.	—	—	Proof	25.00
	1963	.400	1.75	3.75	5.00	7.50
	1963	—	—	—	Proof	—
	1965	.500	1.75	3.75	5.00	7.50
	1965	—	—	—	Proof	—
	1967	.600	1.75	3.75	5.00	7.50
	1967	—	—	—	Proof	—
	1970	.450	1.75	3.75	5.00	7.50
	1970	—	—	—	Proof	—

Y#	Date	Mintage	Fine	VF	XF	Unc
10	1971	2.000	—	.25	.50	.75
	1971	—	—	—	Proof	—
	1974	.500	—	.25	.50	.75
	1974	—	—	—	Proof	—
	1975	2.000	—	.25	.50	.75
	1975	—	—	—	Proof	—
	1976	1.500	—	.25	.50	.75
	1977	1.000	—	.25	.50	.75
	1978	1.500	—	.25	.50	.75
	1979	1.500	—	.10	.35	.75

1/10 GULDEN

1.4000 gm., .640 SILVER, .0288 oz ASW

Y#	Date	Mintage	Fine	VF	XF	Unc
4	1954	.200	1.75	3.75	5.00	7.50
	1954	200 pcs.	—	—	Proof	30.00
	1956	.250	1.75	3.75	5.00	7.50
	1956	500 pcs.	—	—	Proof	30.00
	1957	.250	1.75	3.75	5.00	7.50
	1957	250 pcs.	—	—	Proof	35.00
	1959	.250	1.75	3.75	5.00	7.50
	1959	250 pcs.	—	—	Proof	30.00
	1960	.400	1.25	3.00	4.00	5.00
	1960	300 pcs.	—	—	Proof	25.00
	1962	.400	1.25	3.00	4.00	5.00
	1962	200 pcs.	—	—	Proof	30.00
	1963	.900	1.25	3.00	4.00	5.00
	1963	—	—	—	Proof	—
	1966					
		1.000	1.25	3.00	4.00	5.00
	1966 star & fish					
		.200	3.00	7.50	10.00	12.50
	1970 cock	.300	3.00	7.50	10.00	12.50
	1970	—	—	—	Proof	—

10 CENTS

NICKEL

Y#	Date	Mintage	Fine	VF	XF	Unc
11	1970	1.000	—	.25	.75	1.25
	1970	—	—	—	Proof	—
	1971	3.000	—	.25	.75	1.25
	1971	—	—	—	Proof	—
	1974	1.000	—	.25	.75	1.25
	1974	—	—	—	Proof	—
	1975	1.500	—	.25	.75	1.25
	1975	—	—	—	Proof	—
	1976	2.000	—	.25	.75	1.25
	1977	1.000	—	.25	.75	1.25
	1978	1.500	—	.25	.75	1.25
	1979	1.500	—	.25	.50	1.00

1/4 G - 25 CENTS

3.5800 gm., .640 SILVER .0736 oz ASW

Y#	Date	Mintage	Fine	VF	XF	Unc
5	1954 fish	.200	2.50	5.00	7.50	10.00
	1954	200 pcs.	—	—	Proof	40.00
	1956	.200	2.50	5.00	7.50	10.00
	1956	500 pcs.	—	—	Proof	40.00
	1957	.200	2.50	5.00	7.50	10.00
	1957	250 pcs.	—	—	Proof	45.00
	1960	.240	2.50	5.00	7.50	10.00
	1960	300 pcs.	—	—	Proof	30.00
	1962	.240	2.50	5.00	7.50	10.00
	1962	200 pcs.	—	—	Proof	35.00
	1963	.300	2.50	5.00	7.50	10.00
	1963	—	—	—	Proof	—
	1965	.500	2.50	5.00	7.50	10.00
	1965	—	—	—	Proof	—
	1967	.310	2.50	5.00	7.50	10.00
	1967	—	—	—	Proof	—
	1967 star & fish					
		.200	3.00	7.50	10.00	12.50
	1970 cock	.150	3.00	7.50	10.00	12.50
	1970	—	—	—	Proof	—

25 CENTS

NICKEL

Y#	Date	Mintage	Fine	VF	XF	Unc
12	1970	.750	.50	.75	1.25	1.75
	1970	—	—	—	Proof	—
	1971	3.000	.50	.75	1.25	1.75
	1971	—	—	—	Proof	—
	1975	1.000	.50	.75	1.25	1.75
	1975	—	—	—	Proof	—
	1976	1.000	.50	.75	1.25	1.75
	1977	1.000	.50	.75	1.25	1.75
	1978	1.000	.50	.75	1.25	1.75
	1979	1.000	—	.50	1.00	2.00

GULDEN

10.0000 gm., .720 SILVER .2315 oz ASW

Y#	Date	Mintage	Fine	VF	XF	Unc
6	1952 fish	1.000	BV	7.00	9.00	12.00
	1952	100 pcs.	—	—	Proof	150.00
	1963	.100	7.50	12.00	17.50	20.00
	1963	—	—	—	Proof	—
	1964					
		.300	BV	7.00	9.00	12.00
	1964 star & fish					
		.200	7.00	10.00	12.50	15.00
	1964	—	—	—	Proof	—
	1970 cock	.050	12.50	30.00	35.00	45.00
	1970	—	—	—	Proof	—

NICKEL

Y#	Date	Mintage	Fine	VF	XF	Unc
13	1970	.500	1.50	2.50	4.00	5.00
	1970	—	—	—	Proof	—
	1971	3.000	1.50	2.00	3.00	3.75
	1971	—	—	—	Proof	—

Y#	Date	Mintage	Fine	VF	XF	Unc
	1978	.500	1.50	2.00	3.00	3.75
	1979	.500	—	1.00	1.50	3.00

2-1/2 GULDEN

25.0000 gm., .720 SILVER, .5787 oz ASW

Y#	Date	Mintage	Fine	VF	XF	Unc
7	1964	.200	BV	BV	17.50	20.00
	1964	—	—	—	Proof	—

NICKEL

Y#	Date	Mintage	Fine	VF	XF	Unc
19	1978	.100	—	3.75	5.00	7.50
	1979	.200	—	1.50	3.00	5.00

10 GULDEN

25.0000 gm., .720 SILVER, .5787 oz ASW
150th Anniversary of Bank

Y#	Date	Mintage	Fine	VF	XF	Unc
20	1978	.035	BV	BV	BV	17.50
	1978	.014	—	—	Proof	30.00

25 GULDEN

42.1100 gm., .925 SILVER 1.2524 oz ASW
25th Anniversary of Reign

Y#	Date	Mintage	Fine	VF	XF	Unc
14	1973	.040	BV	BV	BV	40.00
	1973	.020	—	—	Proof	85.00

U.S. Bicentennial

Y#	Date	Mintage	Fine	VF	XF	Unc
15	1976FM(m)					
		200 pcs.	—	—	—	—
	1976FM (u)	9,225	BV	BV	40.00	50.00
	1976FM(P)	.013	—	—	Proof	40.00

Stuyvesant

Y#	Date	Mintage	Fine	VF	XF	Unc
17	1977FM(U)	2,000	—	—	45.00	60.00

42.1100 gm., .925 SILVER 1.2524 oz ASW
International Year Of The Child

Y#	Date	Mintage	Fine	VF	XF	Unc
22	1979	.025	—	—	Proof	—

50 GULDEN

3.3600 gm., .900 GOLD, .0972 oz AGW
75th Anniversary of the Royal Covenant

Y#	Date	Mintage	Fine	VF	XF	Unc
23	1979	.011	—	—	—	—
	1979	.064	—	—	Proof	—

100 GULDEN

6.7200 gm., .900 GOLD .1944 oz AGW
150th Anniversary of Bank

Y#	Date	Mintage	Fine	VF	XF	Unc
21	1978	.027	BV	BV	130.00	150.00
	1978	.024	—	—	Proof	150.00

200 GULDEN

7.9500 gm., .900 GOLD .2300 oz AGW
U.S. Bicentennial

Y#	Date	Mintage	Fine	VF	XF	Unc
16	1976FM(m)					
		100 pcs.	—	—	—	—
	1976FM(u)	5,626	BV	BV	150.00	165.00
	1976FM(P)	.015	—	—	Proof	200.00

Peter Stuyvesant

Y#	Date	Mintage	Fine	VF	XF	Unc
18	1977FM(M)	1,000	—	—	175.00	225.00
	1977FM(U)					
		654 pcs.	—	—	200.00	275.00
	1977FM(P)	6,878	—	—	Proof	225.00

NCLT ISSUES

PROOF SETS
STANDARD METALS

KM#	Date	Mintage	Identification	Issue Price	Mkt. Val.
101	1952(2)	100	Y1,6	—	225.00
102	1954(3)	200	Y1,4,5	—	90.00
103	1956(3)	500	Y2,4,5	—	90.00
104	1957(4)	250	Y1,3,4,5	—	120.00
105	1959(3)	250	Y1,2,4	—	75.00
106	1960(3)	300	Y1,4,5	—	65.00
107	1962(3)	200	Y3-5	—	70.00
108	1963(5)	—	Y1,3-6	—	90.00
109	1964(3)	—	Y1,6,7	—	—
110	1965(4)	—	Y1,2,3,5	—	—
111	1967(3)	—	Y1,3,5	—	—
112	1970(10)	—	Y1,3-6,8,9,11-13	—	—
113	1971(6)	—	Y8-13	—	—
114	1973(3)	—	Y8,9,14	—	—
115	1974(4)	—	Y8-11	—	—
116	1975(4)	—	Y8,10-12	—	240.00
117	1976(2)	.013	Y15,16	187.50	145.00
118	1979 (7)	—	Y8a,9a,10-13,19	—	—

Listings For

NETHERLANDS EAST INDIES: refer to Indonesia

NEW BRUNSWICK: refer to Canada

NEVIS

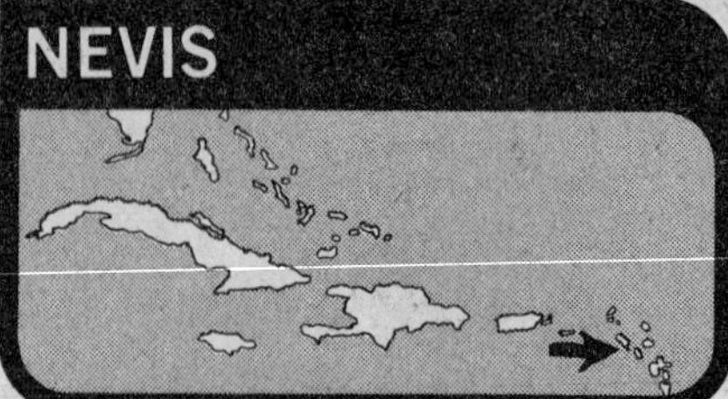

Nevis, a component of one of the West Indies Associated States, is located in the Leeward Islands and has an area of 50 sq. mi. (105 sq. km.) and a population of about 12,000. Charleston is the chief town and port. Sea-island cotton is the chief crop, and some sugar is raised.

Nevis was discovered by Columbus in 1493. It was first colonized by the English in 1628. Admiral De Grasse captured the island for France in 1782, but it was restored to Britain the following year. Alexander Hamilton, first Secretary of the Treasury, was born on Nevis in 1757.

RULERS

British

MONETARY SYSTEM

72 Black Dogs = 1 Dollar

BLACK DOG

BILLON
c/s: 'NEVIS' on French Guiana 2 Sous

C#	Date	Mintage	Good	VG	Fine
1	ND(1801)	—	50.00	75.00	125.00

4 BLACK DOGS

SILVER
c/s: 'NEVIS' over incuse '4'

C#	Date	Mintage	Good	VG	Fine
2	ND	—	115.00	175.00	275.00

6 BLACK DOGS

SILVER
c/s: 'NEVIS' over incuse '6'

C#	Date	Mintage	Good	VG	Fine
3	ND	—	120.00	175.00	275.00

7 BLACK DOGS

SILVER
c/s: 'NEVIS' over incuse '7'

C#	Date	Mintage	Good	VG	Fine
4	ND	—	115.00	175.00	275.00

9 BLACK DOGS

SILVER
c/s: 'NEVIS' over incuse '9'

C#	Date	Mintage	Good	VG	Fine
5	ND	—	115.00	175.00	275.00

NEW CALEDONIA

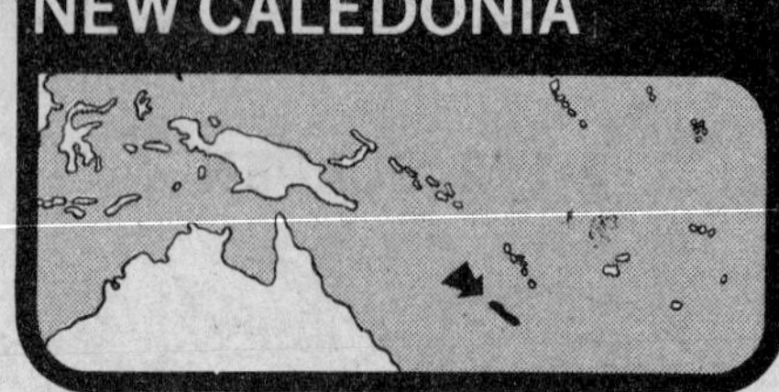

The French Overseas Territory of New Caledonia, a group of about 25 islands in the South Pacific, is situated about 750 miles (1,207 km.) east of Australia. The territory, which includes the dependencies of Ile des Pins, Loyalty Islands, Ile Huon, Isles Belep, Isles Chesterfield, and Ile Walpole, has a total land area of 7,366 sq. mi. (19,079 sq. km.) and a population of 134,000. Capital: Noumea. The islands are rich in minerals; New Caledonia has the world's largest known deposit of nickel. Nickel, nickel castings, coffee and copra are exported.

British navigator Capt. James Cook discovered New Caledonia in 1774. The French took possession in 1853, and established a penal colony on the island in 1854. The European population of the colony remained disproportionately convict until 1894. New Caledonia became an overseas territory within the French Community in 1946, and in 1958 and 1972 chose to remain affiliated with France.

MINTMARKS

(a) - Paris, privy marks only

MONETARY SYSTEM

100 Centimes = 1 Franc

50 CENTIMES

ALUMINUM

Y#	Date	Mintage	VF	XF	Unc
1	1949(a)	1.000	.25	.50	1.00

FRANC

ALUMINUM

Y#	Date	Mintage	VF	XF	Unc
2	1949(a)	4.000	—	.25	.90

Y#	Date	Mintage	VF	XF	Unc
A5	1971(a)	1.000	.10	.30	.75

Obv: I.E.O.M. added

Y#	Date	Mintage	VF	XF	Unc
A5a	1972(a)	.600	—	.15	.35
	1973(a)	1.000	—	.15	.40
	1977(a)	—	—	—	.30
	1979(a)	—	—	—	—

2 FRANCS

ALUMINUM

Y#	Date	Mintage	VF	XF	Unc
3	1949(a)	3.000	.10	.60	1.75

Y#	Date	Mintage	VF	XF	Unc
B5	1971(a)	1.000	.15	.60	1.25

Obv: I.E.O.M. added

Y#	Date	Mintage	VF	XF	Unc
B5a	1973(a)	.400	.05	.50	.70
	1977(a)	—	—	—	.40
	1979(a)	—	—	—	—

5 FRANCS

ALUMINUM

Y#	Date	Mintage	VF	XF	Unc
4	1952(a)	4.000	.15	.90	2.00
	1979(a)	—	—	—	—

10 FRANCS

NICKEL

Y#	Date	Mintage	VF	XF	Unc
5	1967(a)	.400	.40	.80	2.00
	1970(a)	1.000	.40	.65	1.00
	1972(a)	—	.40	.65	1.00

Obv: I.E.O.M. added

Y#	Date	Mintage	VF	XF	Unc
5a	1972(a)	.600	.45	.65	1.00
	1973(a)	.400	.45	.65	1.00
	1979(a)	—	—	—	—

20 FRANCS

NICKEL

Y#	Date	Mintage	VF	XF	Unc
6	1967(a)	.300	.75	1.25	2.75
	1970(a)	1.200	.50	1.00	2.00

Obv: I.E.O.M. added

Y#	Date	Mintage	VF	XF	Unc
6a	1972(a)	.700	.55	1.00	2.00
	1979(a)	—	—	—	—

50 FRANCS

NICKEL

Y#	Date	Mintage	VF	XF	Unc
7	1967(a)	.700	.90	1.75	3.00

Obv: I.E.O.M. added
Rev: Similar to Y#7

Y#	Date	Mintage	VF	XF	Unc
7a	1972(a)	.300	1.00	2.00	3.00
	1979(a)	—	—	—	—

100 FRANCS

NICKEL-BRONZE

Y#	Date	Mintage	VF	XF	Unc
8	1976(a)	2.000	1.50	2.50	3.50
	1979(a)	—	—	—	—

NCLT ISSUES

ESSAIS (E)

Standard metals unless otherwise noted

Y#	Date	Mintage	Identification	Issue Price	Mkt Val.
—	1948(a)	1,100	50 Centimes, Incuse Design	—	20.00
—	1948(a)	1,100	50 Centimes, Raised Design	—	20.00
—	1948(a)	1,100	1 Franc, Incuse Design	—	22.50
—	1948(a)	1,100	1 Franc, Raised Design	—	22.50
—	1948(a)	1,100	2 Francs, Incuse Design	—	25.00
—	1948(a)	1,100	2 Francs, Raised Design	—	25.00
E1a	1949(a)	2,000	50 Centimes, Copper-Nickel	—	14.00
E2a	1949(a)	2,000	1 Franc, Copper-Nickel	—	15.00
E3a	1949(a)	2,000	2 Francs, Copper-Nickel	—	18.00
E4	1952(a)	1,200	5 Francs	—	25.00
E5	1967(a)	1,700	10 Francs	—	18.00
E6	1967(a)	1,700	20 Francs	—	22.50
E7	1967(a)	1,700	50 Francs	—	20.00
E8	1976(a)	—	100 Francs	—	—

PIEFORTS (P)

Y#	Date	Mintage	Identification	Issue Price	Mkt Val.
PA5a	1979(a)	—	1 Franc	—	—
PA5b	1979(a)	250	1 Franc, .925 Silver	—	—
PA5c	1979(a)	200	1 Franc, .920 Gold	—	—
PB5a	1979(a)	—	2 Francs	—	—
PB5b	1979(a)	250	2 Francs, .925 Silver	—	—
PB5c	1979(a)	200	2 Francs, .920 Gold	—	—
P4	1979(a)	—	5 Francs	—	—
P4a	1979(a)	250	5 Francs, .925 Silver	—	—
P4b	1979(a)	200	5 Francs, .920 Gold	—	—
P5a	1979(a)	—	10 Francs	—	—
P5b	1979(a)	250	10 Francs, .925 Silver	—	—
P5c	1979(a)	200	10 Francs, .920 Gold	—	—
P6a	1979(a)	—	20 Francs	—	—
P6b	1979(a)	250	20 Francs, .925 Silver	—	—
P6c	1979(a)	200	20 Francs, .920 Gold	—	—
P7a	1979(a)	—	50 Francs	—	—
P7b	1979(a)	250	50 Francs, .925 Silver	—	—
P7c	1979(a)	250	50 Francs, .920 Gold	—	—
P8	1979(a)	—	100 Francs	—	—
P8a	1979(a)	350	100 Francs, .925 Silver	—	—
P8b	1979(a)	250	100 Francs, .920 Gold	—	—

PIEFORTS with ESSAI (PE)

(DOUBLE THICKNESS)

Standard metals unless otherwise noted

Y#	Date	Mintage	Identification	Issue Price	Mkt Val.
PE1	1949(a)	104	50 Centimes	—	100.00
PE2	1949(a)	104	1 Franc	—	115.00
PE3	1949(a)	104	2 Francs	—	125.00
PE4	1952(a)	104	5 Francs	—	150.00
P5	1967(a)	500	10 Francs	—	40.00
P5b	1967(a)	50	10 Francs, .950 Silver	—	200.00
P5c	1967(a)	20	10 Francs, .920 Gold	—	800.00
P6	1967(a)	500	20 Francs	—	45.00
P6b	1967(a)	50	20 Francs, .950 Silver	—	215.00
P6c	1967(a)	20	20 Francs, .920 Gold	—	1000.
P7	1967(a)	500	50 Francs	—	50.00
P7b	1967(a)	50	50 Francs, .950 Silver	—	250.00
P7c	1967(a)	20	50 Francs, .920 Gold	—	1350.

FLEUR DE COIN SETS

STANDARD METALS

KM#	Date	Mintage	Identification	Issue Price	Mkt. Val.
1	1967(a) (3)	2,200	Y5-7	10.00	15.00

NOTE: This set issued with New Hebrides and French Polynesia 1967 set.

Listings For

NEW FOUNDLAND: refer to Canada

NEW GUINEA: refer to Papua New Guinea

NEW HEBRIDES

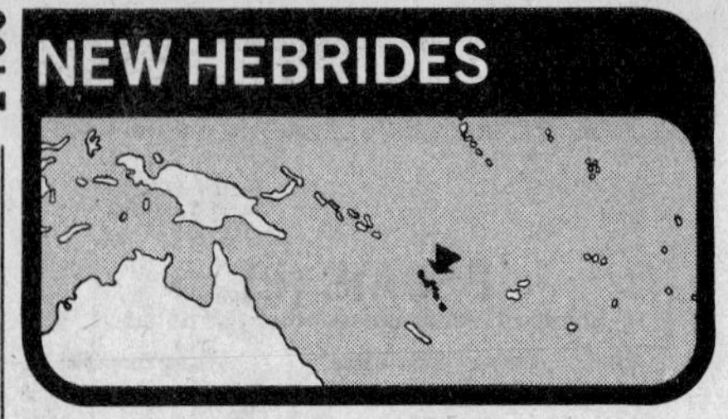

New Hebrides Condominium, a group of islands located in the South Pacific 500 miles (800 km.) west of Fiji, are under the joint sovereignty of Great Britain and France. The islands have an area of 5,700 sq. mi. (14,763 sq. km.) and a population of 93,000, mainly Melanesians of mixed blood. Capital: Port-Vila. The volcanic and coral islands, while malarial and subject to frequent earthquakes, are extremely fertile, and produce copra, coffee, tropical fruits and timber for export.

The New Hebrides were discovered by Portuguese navigator Pedro de Quiros in 1606, visited by French explorer Bougainville in 1768, and named by British navigator Capt. James Cook in 1774. Ships of all nations converged on the islands to trade for sandalwood, prompting France and Britain to relinquish their individual claims and declare the islands a neutral zone in 1878. The New Hebrides were placed under the control of a mixed Anglo-French commission of naval officers during the native uprisings of 1887, and established as a condominium under the joint sovereignty of France and Great Britain in 1906.

MINTMARKS

(a) - Paris, privy marks only

MONETARY SYSTEM

100 Centimes = 1 Franc

FRANC

NICKEL-BRASS

Y#	Date	Mintage	VF	XF	Unc
4	1970(a)	.435	.15	.30	.60

Obv: I.E.O.M. added

Y#	Date	Mintage	VF	XF	Unc
4a	1975(a)	.350	—	.20	.40
	1979(a)	—	—	—	—

2 FRANCS

NICKEL-BRASS

Y#	Date	Mintage	VF	XF	Unc
5	1970(a)	.264	.60	1.00	1.50

Obv: I.E.O.M. added

Y#	Date	Mintage	VF	XF	Unc
5a	1973(a)	.200	.10	.25	.40
	1975(a)	.300	.10	.25	.40
	1979(a)	—	—	—	—

5 FRANCS

NICKEL-BRASS

Y#	Date	Mintage	VF	XF	Unc
6	1970(a)	.375	.50	.75	1.25

Obv: I.E.O.M. added

Y#	Date	Mintage	VF	XF	Unc
6a	1975(a)	.350	.25	.50	.75
	1979(a)	—	—	—	—

10 FRANCS

NICKEL

Y#	Date	Mintage	VF	XF	Unc
1	1967(a)	.250	.25	.40	1.00
	1970(a)	.400	.25	.40	1.00

Obv: I.E.O.M. added

Y#	Date	Mintage	VF	XF	Unc
1a	1973(a)	.200	.25	.40	1.00
	1975(a)	.300	.25	.40	1.00
	1979(a)	—	—	—	—

20 FRANCS

NICKEL

Y#	Date	Mintage	VF	XF	Unc
2	1967(a)	.250	.50	.75	1.75
	1970(a)	.300	.50	.75	1.75

Obv: I.E.O.M. added

Y#	Date	Mintage	VF	XF	Unc
2a	1973(a)	.200	.50	.75	1.75
	1975(a)	.150	Reported, Not Confirmed		
	1979(a)	—	—	—	—

50 FRANCS

NICKEL

Y#	Date	Mintage	VF	XF	Unc
7	1972(a)	.200	1.25	2.00	3.00
	1979(a)	—	—	—	—

100 FRANCS

25.0000 gm., .835 SILVER, .6712 oz ASW

Y#	Date	Mintage	VF	XF	Unc
3	1966(a)	.200	BV	20.00	22.50
	1979(a)	—	—	—	—

NCLT ISSUES

ESSAIS (E)

Standard metals unless otherwise noted

Y#	Date	Mintage	Identification	Issue Price	Mkt Val.
E3	1966(a)	3,000	100 Francs	—	40.00
E1	1967(a)	1,700	10 Francs	—	15.00
E2	1967(a)	1,700	20 Francs	—	18.50
E4	1970(a)	1,700	1 Franc	—	13.50
E5	1970(a)	1,700	2 Francs	—	15.00
E6	1970(a)	1,700	5 Francs	—	17.50
E7	1972(a)	1,300	50 Francs	—	20.00

PIEFORTS (P)

PIEFORTS WITH ESSAI (PE)

(DOUBLE THICKNESS)

Standard metals unless otherwise noted

Y#	Date	Mintage	Identification	Issue Price	Mkt Val.
P3	1966(a)	500	100 Francs	—	100.00
P3b	1966(a)	50	100 Francs, .920 Gold	—	1000.
P1	1967(a)	500	10 Francs	—	30.00
P1b	1967(a)	50	10 Francs, .950 Silver	—	110.00
P1c	1967(a)	20	10 Francs, .920 Gold	—	500.00
P2	1967(a)	500	20 Francs	—	35.00

Y#	Date	Mintage	Identification	Issue Price	Mkt Val.
P2b	1967(a)	50	20 Francs, .950 Silver	—	120.00
P2c	1967(a)	20	20 Francs, .920 Gold	—	700.00
P3	1974(a)	—	100 Francs	—	—
P3a	1974(a)	500	100 Francs, .925 Silver	—	—
P3b	1974(a)	250	100 Francs, .920 Gold	—	—
P4a	1979(a)	—	1 Franc	—	—
P4b	1979(a)	250	1 Franc, .925 Silver	—	—
P4c	1979(a)	200	1 Franc, .920 Gold	—	—
P5a	1979(a)	—	2 Francs	—	—
P5b	1979(a)	250	2 Francs, .925 Silver	—	—
P5c	1979(a)	200	2 Francs, .920 Gold	—	—
P6a	1979(a)	—	5 Francs	—	—
P6b	1979(a)	250	5 Francs, .925 Silver	—	—
P6c	1979(a)	200	5 Francs, .920 Gold	—	—
P1a	1979(a)	—	10 Francs	—	—
P1b	1979(a)	250	10 Francs, .925 Silver	—	—
P1c	1979(a)	200	10 Francs, .920 Gold	—	—
P2a	1979(a)	—	20 Francs	—	—
P2b	1979(a)	250	20 Francs, .925 Silver	—	—
P2c	1979(a)	200	20 Francs, .920 Gold	—	—
P7	1979(a)	—	50 Francs	—	—
P7a	1979(a)	250	50 Francs, .925 Silver	—	—
P7b	1979(a)	200	50 Francs, .920 Gold	—	—

FLEUR DE COIN SETS

STANDARD METALS

KM#	Date	Mintage	Identification	Issue Price	Mkt. Val.
1	1967(3)	2,200	Y1-3	10.00	40.00*

NOTE: These sets were issued with New Caledonia and French Polynesia 1967 sets.

*New Herbrides Y#1-3 only.

NEW ZEALAND

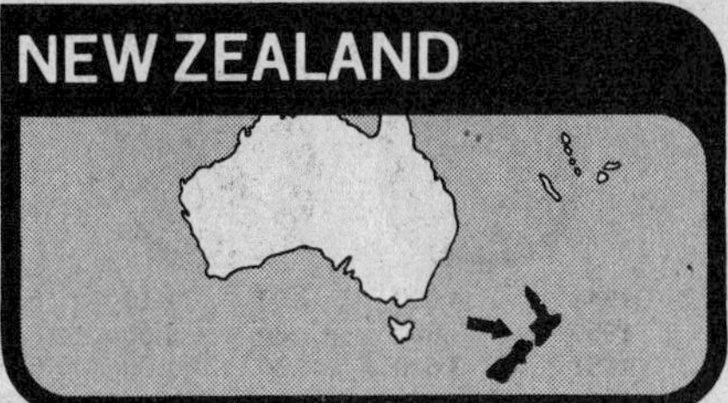

New Zealand, a parliamentary state located in the Southwestern Pacific 1,250 miles (2,011 km.) east of Australia, has an area of 103,736 sq. mi. (268,675 sq. km.) and a population of 3.1 million. Capital: Wellington. Wool, meat, dairy products and some manufactured items are exported.

New Zealand was discovered and named by Dutch navigator Abel Tasman in 1642, and explored by British navigator Capt. James Cook who surveyed it in 1769 and annexed the land to Great Britain. The British government disavowed the annexation and for the next 70 years the only white settlers to arrive were adventurers attracted by the prospects of lumbering, sealing and whaling. Great Britain annexed the land in 1840 by treaty with the native chiefs and made it a dependency of New South Wales. The colony was granted self-government in 1852, a ministerial form of government in 1856, and full dominion status on Sept. 26, 1907. Full internal and external autonomy, which New Zealand had in effect possessed for many years, was formally extended in 1947. New Zealand is a member of the Commonwealth of Nations. The Queen of England is Chief of State.

A decimal standard currency was adopted in 1967.

RULERS

British

MONETARY SYSTEM

12 Pence = 1 Shilling
2 Shillings = 1 Florin
2 Shillings & 6 Pence = Half Crown
5 Shillings = 1 Crown
20 Shillings = 1 Pound
2 Dollars = 1 Pound

TRADESMEN'S TOKENS

Because of a shortage of British money, New Zealand merchant tokens were issued beginning in 1857. There were some 147 varieties issued in ten cities, although the majority were issued in Auckland, Christchurch, Wellington, and Dunedin. Issuance was discontinued in 1881, but they continued to circulate until 1897 when British copper and silver and Australian gold became plentiful. Almost all tokens bear the name of the city and the issuing merchant, but few have a stated value so the user had to rely on size and weight - a very irregular standard to determine value. All tokens are of copper or bronze. These can be found listed in "THE COINS AND TOKENS OF BRITISH OCEANIA" by Robert L. Clarke and "AUSTRALASIAN TOKENS AND COINS" by Dr. Andrews.

1/2 PENNY

BRONZE

Y#	Date	Mintage	VF	XF	Unc
7	1940	3.432	.85	3.00	10.00
	1940	—	—	Proof	150.00
	1941	.960	.85	3.00	12.00
	1942	1.960	.85	3.00	15.00
	1944	2.035	.70	2.50	10.00
	1945	1.516	.75	2.25	10.00
	1946	3.120	.75	2.25	10.00
	1947	2.726	.70	2.25	10.00

Y#	Date	Mintage	VF	XF	Unc
20	1949	1.766	.65	2.00	7.00
	1949	—	—	Proof	150.00
	1950	1.426	.65	1.75	5.00
	1951	2.342	.65	1.75	5.00
	1952	2.400	.50	1.75	5.00
	150.00	—	—	Proof	150.00

Obv: w/o strap

Y#	Date	Mintage	VF	XF	Unc
28	1953	.720	2.00	3.00	10.00
	1953	—	—	Proof	10.00
	1954	.240	3.00	6.00	12.50
	1954	—	—	Proof	150.00
	1955	.240	3.00	6.00	12.50
	1955	—	—	Proof	150.00
	1956 w/strap				
		1.200	.50	1.50	4.00
	1957	1.440	.25	1.15	3.00
	1957	—	—	Proof	150.00
	1958	1.920	.30	1.15	3.00
	1959	1.920	.25	.50	2.00
	1960	2.400	—	.60	2.00
	1960	—	—	Proof	150.00
	1961	2.880	—	.35	1.00
	1962	2.880	—	.30	1.00
	1962	—	—	Proof	150.00
	1963	1.680	—	.25	1.00
	1963	—	—	Proof	150.00
	1964	2.885	—	.50	1.00
	1965	5.177	—	.50	1.00
	1965	—	—	Proof	2.50

PENNY

BRONZE

Y#	Date	Mintage	VF	XF	Unc
8	1940	5.424	.50	2.25	10.00
	1940	—	—	Proof	150.00
	1941	1.200	1.00	7.50	15.00
	1942	3.120	.50	7.00	15.00
	1943	8.400	.85	4.00	10.00
	1944	3.696	.85	3.00	10.00
	1944	—	—	Proof	150.00
	1945	4.764	.60	2.50	10.00
	1946	6.720	.60	1.65	10.00

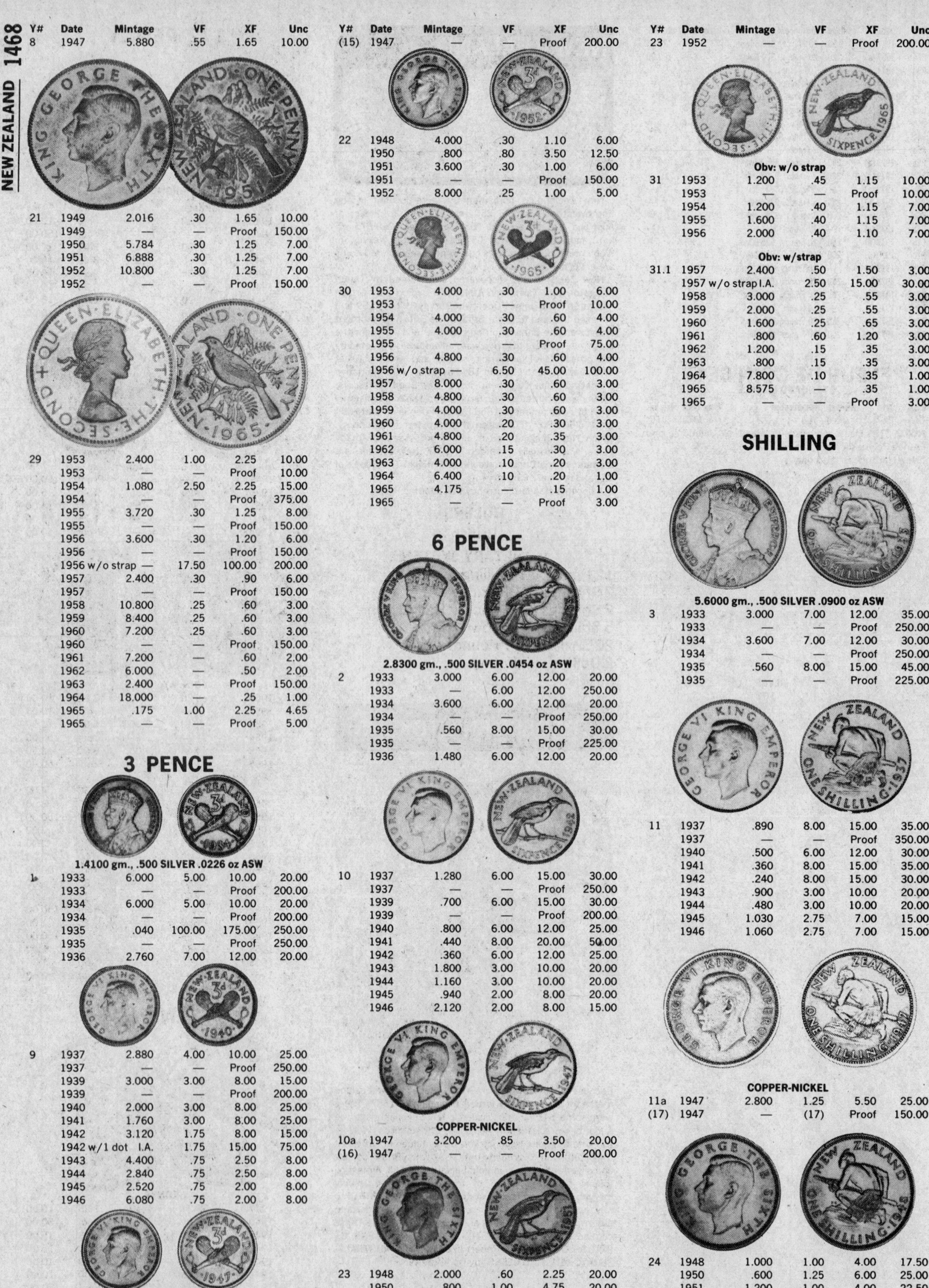

Y#	Date	Mintage	VF	XF	Unc
8	1947	5.880	.55	1.65	10.00
21	1949	2.016	.30	1.65	10.00
	1949	—	—	Proof	150.00
	1950	5.784	.30	1.25	7.00
	1951	6.888	.30	1.25	7.00
	1952	10.800	.30	1.25	7.00
	1952	—	—	Proof	150.00
29	1953	2.400	1.00	2.25	10.00
	1953	—	—	Proof	10.00
	1954	1.080	2.50	2.25	15.00
	1954	—	—	Proof	375.00
	1955	3.720	.30	1.25	8.00
	1955	—	—	Proof	150.00
	1956	3.600	.30	1.20	6.00
	1956	—	—	Proof	150.00
	1956 w/o strap	—	17.50	100.00	200.00
	1957	2.400	.30	.90	6.00
	1957	—	—	Proof	150.00
	1958	10.800	.25	.60	3.00
	1959	8.400	.25	.60	3.00
	1960	7.200	.25	.60	3.00
	1960	—	—	Proof	150.00
	1961	7.200	—	.60	2.00
	1962	6.000	—	.50	2.00
	1963	2.400	—	Proof	150.00
	1964	18.000	—	.25	1.00
	1965	.175	1.00	2.25	4.65
	1965	—	—	Proof	5.00

3 PENCE

1.4100 gm., .500 SILVER .0226 oz ASW

Y#	Date	Mintage	VF	XF	Unc
1	1933	6.000	5.00	10.00	20.00
	1933	—	—	Proof	200.00
	1934	6.000	5.00	10.00	20.00
	1934	—	—	Proof	200.00
	1935	.040	100.00	175.00	250.00
	1935	—	—	Proof	250.00
	1936	2.760	7.00	12.00	20.00
9	1937	2.880	4.00	10.00	25.00
	1937	—	—	Proof	250.00
	1939	3.000	3.00	8.00	15.00
	1939	—	—	Proof	200.00
	1940	2.000	3.00	8.00	25.00
	1941	1.760	3.00	8.00	25.00
	1942	3.120	1.75	8.00	15.00
	1942 w/1 dot	I.A.	1.75	15.00	75.00
	1943	4.400	.75	2.50	8.00
	1944	2.840	.75	2.50	8.00
	1945	2.520	.75	2.00	8.00
	1946	6.080	.75	2.00	8.00

COPPER-NICKEL

Y#	Date	Mintage	VF	XF	Unc
9a	1947	6.400	.30	2.00	8.00
(15)	1947	—	—	Proof	200.00
22	1948	4.000	.30	1.10	6.00
	1950	.800	.80	3.50	12.50
	1951	3.600	.30	1.00	6.00
	1951	—	—	Proof	150.00
	1952	8.000	.25	1.00	5.00
30	1953	4.000	.30	1.00	6.00
	1953	—	—	Proof	10.00
	1954	4.000	.30	.60	4.00
	1955	4.000	.30	.60	4.00
	1955	—	—	Proof	75.00
	1956	4.800	.30	.60	4.00
	1956 w/o strap	—	6.50	45.00	100.00
	1957	8.000	.30	.60	3.00
	1958	4.800	.30	.60	3.00
	1959	4.000	.30	.60	3.00
	1960	4.000	.20	.30	3.00
	1961	4.800	.20	.35	3.00
	1962	6.000	.15	.30	3.00
	1963	4.000	.10	.20	3.00
	1964	6.400	.10	.20	1.00
	1965	4.175	—	.15	1.00
	1965	—	—	Proof	3.00

6 PENCE

2.8300 gm., .500 SILVER .0454 oz ASW

Y#	Date	Mintage	VF	XF	Unc
2	1933	3.000	6.00	12.00	20.00
	1933	—	6.00	12.00	250.00
	1934	3.600	6.00	12.00	20.00
	1934	—	—	Proof	250.00
	1935	.560	8.00	15.00	30.00
	1935	—	—	Proof	225.00
	1936	1.480	6.00	12.00	20.00
10	1937	1.280	6.00	15.00	30.00
	1937	—	—	Proof	250.00
	1939	.700	6.00	15.00	30.00
	1939	—	—	Proof	200.00
	1940	.800	6.00	12.00	25.00
	1941	.440	8.00	20.00	50.00
	1942	.360	6.00	12.00	25.00
	1943	1.800	3.00	10.00	20.00
	1944	1.160	3.00	10.00	20.00
	1945	.940	2.00	8.00	20.00
	1946	2.120	2.00	8.00	15.00

COPPER-NICKEL

Y#	Date	Mintage	VF	XF	Unc
10a	1947	3.200	.85	3.50	20.00
(16)	1947	—	—	Proof	200.00
23	1948	2.000	.60	2.25	20.00
	1950	.800	1.00	4.75	20.00
	1951	1.800	.60	2.25	10.00
	1952	3.200	.50	1.20	15.00
23	1952	—	—	Proof	200.00

Obv: w/o strap

Y#	Date	Mintage	VF	XF	Unc
31	1953	1.200	.45	1.15	10.00
	1953	—	—	Proof	10.00
	1954	1.200	.40	1.15	7.00
	1955	1.600	.40	1.15	7.00
	1956	2.000	.40	1.10	7.00

Obv: w/strap

Y#	Date	Mintage	VF	XF	Unc
31.1	1957	2.400	.50	1.50	3.00
	1957 w/o strap	I.A.	2.50	15.00	30.00
	1958	3.000	.25	.55	3.00
	1959	2.000	.25	.55	3.00
	1960	1.600	.25	.65	3.00
	1961	.800	.60	1.20	3.00
	1962	1.200	.15	.35	3.00
	1963	.800	.15	.35	3.00
	1964	7.800	.10	.35	1.00
	1965	8.575	—	.35	1.00
	1965	—	—	Proof	3.00

SHILLING

5.6000 gm., .500 SILVER .0900 oz ASW

Y#	Date	Mintage	VF	XF	Unc
3	1933	3.000	7.00	12.00	35.00
	1933	—	—	Proof	250.00
	1934	3.600	7.00	12.00	30.00
	1934	—	—	Proof	250.00
	1935	.560	8.00	15.00	45.00
	1935	—	—	Proof	225.00
11	1937	.890	8.00	15.00	35.00
	1937	—	—	Proof	350.00
	1940	.500	6.00	12.00	30.00
	1941	.360	8.00	15.00	35.00
	1942	.240	8.00	15.00	30.00
	1943	.900	3.00	10.00	20.00
	1944	.480	3.00	10.00	20.00
	1945	1.030	2.75	7.00	15.00
	1946	1.060	2.75	7.00	15.00

COPPER-NICKEL

Y#	Date	Mintage	VF	XF	Unc
11a	1947	2.800	1.25	5.50	25.00
(17)	1947	—	(17)	Proof	150.00
24	1948	1.000	1.00	4.00	17.50
	1950	.600	1.25	6.00	25.00
	1951	1.200	1.00	4.00	22.50
	1952	.600	1.10	4.50	12.50
	1952	—	—	Proof	150.00

Obv: w/o strap

Y#	Date	Mintage	VF	XF	Unc
32	1953	.200	1.10	6.00	15.00
	1953	—	—	Proof	15.00
	1955	.200	1.50	6.00	15.00

Obv: w/strap

Y#	Date	Mintage	VF	XF	Unc
32.1	1955	—	—	Proof	150.00
	1956	.800	.65	4.00	10.00
	1957	.800	.50	4.00	10.00
	1957	—	—	Proof	150.00
	1958	1.000	.40	4.00	10.00
	1959	.600	.40	4.00	10.00
	1960	.600	.40	1.10	4.00
	1961	.400	.35	.90	4.00
	1962	1.000	.30	.60	4.00
	1963	.600	.35	.85	4.00
	1964	3.400	.30	.60	1.20
	1965	4.475	.30	.60	1.00
	1965	.040	—	Proof	3.50

FLORIN

11.3100 gm., .500 SILVER .1818 oz ASW

Y#	Date	Mintage	VF	XF	Unc
4	1933	2.100	10.00	20.00	50.00
	1933	—	10.00	20.00	275.00
	1934	2.850	10.00	20.00	50.00
	1934	—	—	Proof	275.00
	1935	.755	12.00	40.00	80.00
	1935	—	—	Proof	225.00
	1936	.150	20.00	75.00	300.00

Y#	Date	Mintage	VF	XF	Unc
12	1937	1.190	10.00	30.00	80.00
	1937	—	—	Proof	400.00
	1940	.500	20.00	75.00	150.00
	1941	.820	8.00	16.00	25.00
	1942	.150	10.00	25.00	60.00
	1943	1.400	8.00	16.00	25.00
	1944	.140	12.00	50.00	150.00
	1945	.515	8.00	25.00	50.00
	1946	1.200	8.00	25.00	50.00
	1946 flatback	—	10.00	35.00	85.00

COPPER-NICKEL

Y#	Date	Mintage	VF	XF	Unc
12a	1947	2.500	4.75	15.00	75.00
(18)	1947	—	(18)	Proof	400.00

Y#	Date	Mintage	VF	XF	Unc
25	1948	1.750	2.00	8.75	40.00
	1949	3.500	1.75	7.75	35.00
	1950	3.500	.90	3.50	15.00
	1951	1.000	.90	3.50	15.00

Obv: w/o strap

Y#	Date	Mintage	VF	XF	Unc
33	1953	.250	2.00	5.75	25.00
	1953	—	—	Proof	20.00

Obv: W/strap

Y#	Date	Mintage	VF	XF	Unc
33.1	1961	1.500	1.00	2.00	4.00
	1962	1.500	1.00	2.00	4.00
	1963	.100	4.00	8.00	12.00
	1964	7.000	.35	.50	2.00
	1965	9.425	.35	.50	2.00
	1965	.040	—	Proof	4.00

1/2 CROWN

14.1400 gm., .500 SILVER, .2273 oz ASW

Y#	Date	Mintage	VF	XF	Unc
5	1933	2.000	10.00	22.50	80.00
	1933	—	10.00	Proof	375.00
	1934	2.720	10.00	22.50	80.00
	1934	—	—	Proof	375.00
	1935	.612	8.50	60.00	200.00
	1935	—	—	Proof	300.00

Y#	Date	Mintage	VF	XF	Unc
13	1937	.672	10.00	20.00	50.00
	1937	—	—	Proof	450.00
	1941	.776	8.00	16.00	35.00
	1942	.240	10.00	25.00	60.00
	1943	1.120	8.00	16.00	35.00
	1944	.180	15.00	30.00	150.00
	1945	.420	10.00	18.50	45.00
	1946	.960	8.00	18.50	45.00

New Zealand Centennial

Y#	Date	Mintage	VF	XF	Unc
14	1940	.101	18.50	22.50	35.00
	1940	—	—	Proof	250.00

COPPER-NICKEL

Y#	Date	Mintage	VF	XF	Unc
13a	1947	1.600	5.00	25.00	85.00
(19)	1947	—	(19)	Proof	400.00

Y#	Date	Mintage	VF	XF	Unc
26	1948	1.400	2.50	10.00	35.00
	1949	2.800	3.00	12.50	38.50
	1950	3.600	1.50	8.00	15.00
	1951	1.200	1.50	8.00	15.00

Y#	Date	Mintage	VF	XF	Unc
34	1953	.120	2.25	8.00	25.00
	1953	—	—	Proof	25.00
	1961	.080	3.00	5.00	10.00
	1962	.600	1.25	2.25	3.50
	1963	.400	1.25	2.25	3.50
	1965	.175	1.00	2.50	5.00
	1965	.040	—	Proof	7.50

CROWN

.500 SILVER
Waitangi

Y#	Date	Mintage	VF	XF	Unc
6	1935	764 Pcs.	1600.	2000.	2600.
		364 Pcs.	—	Proof	3000.

28.2800 gm., .500 SILVER .4546 oz ASW
Proposed Royal Visit

Y#	Date	Mintage	VF	XF	Unc
27	1949	.200	15.00	20.00	25.00
	1949	25 pcs.	—	Proof	1000.

COPPER-NICKEL
Queen Elizabeth II Coronation

Y#	Date	Mintage	VF	XF	Unc
35	1953	.250	12.00	15.00	18.00
	1953	—	—	Proof	45.00

DECIMAL COINAGE

100 Cents = 1 Dollar

CENT

BRONZE

Y#	Date	Mintage	VF	XF	Unc
36	1967	120.250	—	.15	.20
	1967	.050	—	Proof	1.10
	1968	.035	—	.30	.90
	1968	.040	—	Proof	1.15
	1969	.050	—	.20	1.00
	1969	.050	—	Proof	1.10
	1970	10.090	—	.15	.20
	1970	.020	—	Proof	1.10
	1971	10.015	—	.15	.20
	1971	5,000	—	Proof	8.75
	1972	10.055	—	.15	.20
	1972	8,045	—	Proof	2.75
	1973	15.055	—	.15	.20
	1973	8,000	—	Proof	2.75
	1974	35.035	—	.15	.20
	1974	8,000	—	Proof	2.75
	1975	60.015	—	.15	.20
	1975	—	—	Proof	2.75
	1976	20.016	—	.10	.15
	1976	.011	—	Proof	2.75
	1977	.020	.25	1.00	4.00
	1978	—	—	—	—
	1978	.015	—	Proof	—
	1979	—	—	—	—
	1979	.016	—	Proof	—

2 CENTS

BRONZE

Y#	Date	Mintage	VF	XF	Unc
37	1967	75.250	—	.15	.30
	1967	.050	—	Proof	1.35
	1968	.035		.50	.90
	1968	.040	—	Proof	1.45
	1969	20.560	—	.15	.30
	1969	.050	—	Proof	1.35
	1970	.030	—	.15	.50
	1970	.020	—	Proof	8.75
	1971	15.065	—	.15	.30
	1971	5,000	—	Proof	2.75
	1972	17.525	—	.15	.30
	1972	8,045	—	Proof	2.75
	1973	38.565	—	.15	.30
	1973	8,000	—	Proof	2.75
	1974	50.015	—	.15	.30
	1974	8,000	—	Proof	2.75
	1975	20.015	—	.15	.30
	1975	—	—	Proof	2.75
	1976	15.016	—	.10	.15
	1976	.011	—	Proof	2.75
	1977	20.020	—	.10	.15
	1978	—	—	—	—
	1978	.015	—	Proof	—
	1979	—	—	—	—
	1979	.016	—	Proof	—

Y#	Date	Mintage	VF	XF	Unc
37a	ND(1967) Muled with obv. of Bahamas 5 Cent Y#2				
		—	15.00	20.00	30.00

5 CENTS

COPPER-NICKEL

Y#	Date	Mintage	VF	XF	Unc
38	1967	26.250	—	.65	.90
	1967	.050	—	Proof	1.50
	1968	.035	—	.15	.35
	1968	.040	—	Proof	1.50
	1969	10.310	—	.15	.35
	1969	.050	—	Proof	10.00
	1970	11.182	—	.15	.35
	1970	.020	—	Proof	3.75
	1971	11.535	—	.15	.30
	1971	5,000	—	Proof	3.75
	1972	20.015	—	.75	1.50
	1972	8,045	—	Proof	3.75
	1973	4.039	—	.15	.35
	1973	8,000	—	Proof	3.75
	1974	18.015	—	.15	.30
	1974	8,000	—	Proof	3.75
	1975	32.015	—	.15	.35
	1975	—	—	Proof	3.75
	1976	.016	.75	1.50	6.00
	1976	.011	—	Proof	3.75
	1977	.020	.50	1.00	4.00
	1978	—	—	—	—
	1978	.015	—	Proof	—
	1979	—	—	—	—
	1979	.016	—	Proof	—

10 CENTS

COPPER-NICKEL

Y#	Date	Mintage	VF	XF	Unc
39	1967	17.250	.15	.25	.40
	1967	.050	—	Proof	1.50
	1968	.035	.25	.55	1.15
	1968	.040	—	Proof	2.75
	1969	3.050	.15	.25	.90
	1969	.050	—	Proof	2.50

Y#	Date	Mintage	VF	XF	Unc
39a	1970	2.076	.15	.25	.75
	1970	.020	—	Proof	1.50
	1971	2.823	.15	.25	.40
	1971	5,000	—	Proof	10.00
	1972	2.039	.15	.25	.40
	1972	8,045	—	Proof	4.25
	1973	3.525	.15	.25	.40
	1973	8,000	—	Proof	4.25
	1974	4.619	.15	.25	.40
	1974	8,000	—	Proof	6.50
	1975	7.015	.15	.25	.40
	1975	—	—	Proof	6.00
	1976	5.016	.15	.25	.40
	1976	.011	—	Proof	6.00
	1977	5.020	.15	.20	.25
	1978	—	—	—	—
	1978	.015	—	Proof	—
	1979	—	—	—	—
	1979	.016	—	Proof	—

20 CENTS

COPPER-NICKEL

Y#	Date	Mintage	VF	XF	Unc
40	1967	13.250	.20	.45	.65
	1967	.050	—	Proof	2.75
	1968	.035	.50	1.00	2.00
	1968	.040	—	Proof	4.00
	1969	2.550	.20	.45	.65

Y#	Date	Mintage	VF	XF	Unc
40	1969	.050	—	Proof	2.75
	1970	.030	.50	1.00	2.00
	1970	.020	—	Proof	2.75
	1971	1.615	.20	.45	.75
	1971	5,000	—	Proof	15.00
	1972	1.531	.20	.45	.65
	1972	8,045	—	Proof	4.00
	1973	3.043	.20	.45	.65
	1973	8,000	—	Proof	4.00
	1974	4.527	.20	.45	.65
	1974	8,000	—	Proof	9.00
	1975	5.015	.20	.45	.65
	1975	—	—	Proof	5.50
	1976	7.516	.20	.45	.75
	1976	.011	—	Proof	5.50
	1977	7.520	—	.30	.40
	1978	—	—	—	.40
	1978	.015	—	Proof	—
	1979	—	—	—	—
	1979	.016	—	Proof	—

50 CENTS

COPPER-NICKEL

Y#	Date	Mintage	VF	XF	Unc
41	1967	10.250	—	.75	1.75
	1967	.050	—	Proof	3.50
	1968	.035	—	1.15	2.30
	1968	.040	—	Proof	4.00
	1970	.030	—	.75	1.15
	1970	.050	—	Proof	3.50
	1971	1.138	—	.75	1.25
	1971	5,000	—	Proof	25.00
	1972	1.423	—	.75	1.15
	1972	8,045	—	Proof	6.00
	1973	2.523	—	.75	1.15
	1973	8,000	—	Proof	6.00
	1974	1.215	—	.75	1.15
	1974	8,000	—	Proof	10.00
	1975	3.815	—	.75	1.25
	1976	2.016	—	.75	1.15
	1977	2.020	—	.65	1.00
	1978	—	—	—	.75
	1978	.015	—	Proof	—
	1979	—	—	—	—
	1979	.016	—	Proof	—

Captain Cook's Voyage 200th Anniversary
Similar to Y#41
Edge inscribed COOK BI-CENTENARY 1769-1969

Y#	Date	Mintage	VF	XF	Unc
43	1969	.050	2.00	4.00	6.00
	1969	—	—	Proof	10.00

DOLLAR

COPPER-NICKEL
Decimalization Commemorative, Lettered Edge

Y#	Date	Mintage	VF	XF	Unc
42	1967	.200	1.25	2.00	4.50
	1967	.040	—	Proof	10.00

Regular Issue, Reeded Edge

Y#	Date	Mintage	VF	XF	Unc
42a	1971	.030	1.50	2.75	6.00
	1971	—	—	Proof	65.00
	1972	.030	1.50	2.25	6.00
	1972	—	—	Proof	37.50
	1973	—	1.50	2.25	5.00
	1973	—	—	Proof	25.00
	1975	.056	1.50	2.25	4.00
	1975	.010	—	Proof	20.00
	1976	.020	—	2.00	3.00
	1976	.011	—	Proof	20.00

200th Anniversary Captain Cook's Voyage
Obv: Similar to Y#42.

Y#	Date	Mintage	VF	XF	Unc
44	1969	.400	1.25	2.00	5.00
	1969	—	—	Proof	9.00

Royal Visit
Obv: Similar to Y#42.

Y#	Date	Mintage	VF	XF	Unc
45	1970	.720	1.25	2.00	5.00
	1970	—	—	Proof	9.00

Cook Islands
Obv: Similar to Y#42.

Y#	Date	Mintage	VF	XF	Unc
46	1970	.025	10.00	15.00	30.00
	1970	5,030	—	Proof	100.00

Commonwealth Games
Obv: Similar to Y#42.

Y#	Date	Mintage	VF	XF	Unc
47	1974	.500	1.50	2.25	4.00

.925 SILVER

Y#	Date	Mintage	VF	XF	Unc
47a	1974	.010	—	Proof	65.00

COPPER-NICKEL
New Zealand Day
Obv: Similar to Y#42.

Y#	Date	Mintage	VF	XF	Unc
48	1974	.050	6.00	8.00	10.00

.925 SILVER

Y#	Date	Mintage	VF	XF	Unc
48a	1974	5,000	—	Proof	200.00

COPPER-NICKEL
Waitangi Day

Y#	Date	Mintage	VF	XF	Unc
49	1977	.070	—	—	8.00

.925 SILVER

Y#	Date	Mintage	VF	XF	Unc
49a	1977	.015	—	Proof	60.00

COPPER-NICKEL
25th Anniversary of Coronation

Y#	Date	Mintage	VF	XF	Unc
50	1978	.123	—	—	6.00
		.925 SILVER			
50a	1978	.033	—	Proof	45.00

COPPER-NICKEL
Obv: New effigy of Queen Elizabeth II.
Rev: Similar to Y#42.

Y#	Date	Mintage	VF	XF	Unc
51	1979	.085	—	—	4.00

27.0000 gm., .925 SILVER .8030 oz ASW

Y#	Date	Mintage	VF	XF	Unc
51a	1979	.019	—	Proof	45.00

NCLT ISSUES

MINT SETS

KM#	Date	Mintage	Identification	Issue Price	Mkt. Val.
S1	1965(7)	75,000	Y28-34	—	10.00
		Above are described as 'Selected Sets'.			
S1a	1965(7)	100,000	Y28-34	—	6.50
		Above are described as 'Uncirculated Sets'.			
S2	1967(7)	250,000	Y36-42	4.50	10.00
S4	1968(6)	35,000	Y36-41	2.15	10.00
S5	1969(7)	50,000	Y36-40,43,44	3.25	10.00
S7	1970(7)	30,000	Y36-38,39a,40-42,45	3.50	10.00
S10	1971(7)	15,000	Y36-41,42a	3.50	10.00
S12	1972(7)	15,000	Y36-41,42a	3.50	10.00
S14	1973(7)	15,000	Y36-41,42a	3.50	10.00
S17	1974(7)	15,000	Y36-38,39a,40,41,47	4.35	10.00
S20	1975(7)	15,000	Y36-41,42A	4.50	8.00
S22	1976(7)	16,000	Y36-38,39a,40,41,42a	—	8.00
S23	1977(7)	20,000	—	—	12.00
S24	1978(7)	23,000	Y36-38,39a,40,41,50	—	10.00
S25	1979(7)	25,000	Y36-38,39 A,40,41,51	5.50	7.00
S26	1980	—	—	—	—

PROOF SETS
STANDARD METALS

KM#	Date	Mintage	Identification	Issue Price	Mkt. Val.
101	1933(5)	20 Pcs.	Y1-5	—	3,000.
102	1934(5)	20 Pcs.	Y1-5	—	3,000.
103	1935(6)	364 Pcs.	Y1-6	—	4000.
104	1937(5)	200	Y9-13	—	2,200.
105	1947(5)	20 Pcs.	Y15-19	—	1,250.
106	1953(8)	7,000	Y28-35	—	65.00
107	1954(4)	—	Y28-31	—	—
108	1964(3)	—	Y31-33	—	950.00
109	1965(7)	25,000	Y28-34	—	13.50
110	1967(7)	50,000	Y36-42	10.00	15.00
111	1968(6)	40,000	Y36-41	7.00	8.50
112	1969(7)	50,000	Y36-40,43,44	7.00	15.00
113	1970(7)	20,000	Y36-38,39a,40-42,45	7.00	15.00
114	1971(7)	5,000	Y36-41,42a	15.00	175.00
115	1972(7)	8,045	Y36-41,42a	16.00	65.00
116	1973(7)	8,000	Y36-41,42a	16.00	40.00
117	1974(7)	8,000	Y36-41,47a	14.00	75.00
118	1975(7)	10,000	Y36-41,42a	14.00	32.50
119	1976(7)	11,000	Y36-38,39a,40,41,42a	15.00	30.00
120	1977(7)	12,000	Y36-38,39a,40,41,49a	19.50	75.00
121	1978(7)	15,000	Y36-38,39a,40,41,50a	20.00	55.00
122	1979(7)	16,000	Y36-38,39a,40,41,51a	22.00	55.00

NICARAGUA

The Republic of Nicaragua, situated in Central America between Honduras and Costa Rica, has an area of 57,143 sq. mi. (147,888 sq. km.) and a population of 21 million. Capital: Managua. Agriculture, mining (gold and silver) and hardwood logging are the principal industries. Cotton, meat, coffee and sugar are exported.

Columbus sighted the coast of Nicaragua in 1502 during the course of his last voyage of discovery. It was first visited in 1522 by conquistadores from Panama, under command of Gonzalez Davola. After the first settlements were established in 1524 at Granada and Leon. Nicaragua was incorporated, for administrative purpose, in the Captaincy General of Guatemala, which included every Central American state but Panama. The Captaincy General declared its independence from Spain on Sept. 15, 1821. The next year Nicaragua united with the Mexican Empire of Agustin de Iturbide, then in 1823 with the Central American Republic. When the federation was dissolved, Nicaragua declared itself an independent republic in 1838.

MINTMARKS

H - Heaton, Birmingham

MONETARY SYSTEM

(Until 1912)
100 Centavos = 1 Peso
Commencing 1912
100 Centavos = 1 Cordoba

1/2 CENTAVO

BRONZE

Y#	Date	Mintage	Fine	VF	XF	Unc
10	1912H	.900	1.00	2.00	11.00	17.00
	1912H	—	—	Proof	—	75.00
	1915H	.320	3.50	5.50	12.50	25.00
	1916H	.720	2.50	3.50	13.00	20.00
	1917	.720	2.50	3.50	13.00	20.00
	1922	.400	1.50	3.00	12.00	25.00
	1924	.400	1.50	3.00	12.00	25.00
	1934	.500	.50	.75	4.50	12.50
	1936	.600	.50	.75	3.50	12.50
	1937	1.000	.40	.60	3.00	12.50

CENTAVO

COPPER-NICKEL

Y#	Date	Mintage	Fine	VF	XF	Unc
1	1878	.500	4.00	8.00	20.00	40.00

BRONZE

Y#	Date	Mintage	Fine	VF	XF	Unc
11	1912H	.450	1.00	2.50	10.75	17.50
	1912H	—	—	Proof	—	75.00
	1914H	.300	8.50	15.00	30.00	60.00
	1915H	.500	3.00	6.00	15.00	25.00
	1916H	.450	2.00	4.50	11.00	17.50
	1917	.450	2.00	4.50	11.00	17.50
	1919	.750	1.50	4.00	11.00	17.50
	1920	.700	1.00	3.00	10.00	17.50
	1922	.500	1.00	3.00	10.00	17.50
	1924	.300	1.00	3.25	10.00	17.50

Y#	Date	Mintage	Fine	VF	XF	Unc
11	1927	.250	2.00	8.00	15.00	25.00
	1928	.500	.75	2.00	7.00	12.00
	1929	.500	.50	1.50	7.00	12.00
	1930	.250	2.00	8.00	15.00	30.00
	1934	.500	1.25	3.00	6.00	10.00
	1935	.500	1.25	3.00	6.00	10.00
	1936	.500	1.25	3.00	6.00	10.00
	1937	1.000	.40	1.00	2.50	8.00
	1938	2.000	.20	.40	1.50	8.00
	1940	2.000	.20	.40	1.50	8.00

BRASS

Y#	Date	Mintage	Fine	VF	XF	Unc
21	1943	1.000	.50	1.50	3.00	5.00

5 CENTAVOS

1.2500 gm., .800 SILVER, .0322 oz ASW

Y#	Date	Mintage	Fine	VF	XF	Unc
4	1880H	.250	5.00	12.00	35.00	70.00

Y#	Date	Mintage	Fine	VF	XF	Unc
7	1887H	1.000	4.00	8.00	25.00	50.00

COPPER-NICKEL

Y#	Date	Mintage	Fine	VF	XF	Unc
2	1898	2.000	1.00	2.00	4.00	25.00

Y#	Date	Mintage	Fine	VF	XF	Unc
3	1899	2.000	1.00	2.00	4.00	12.50

Y#	Date	Mintage	Fine	VF	XF	Unc
12	1912H	.460	2.00	8.00	15.00	35.00
	1912H	—	—	—	Proof	150.00
	1914H	.300	3.50	10.00	20.00	35.00
	1915H	.160	2.00	3.50	12.50	27.50
	1919	.100	4.00	7.00	15.00	35.00
	1920	.150	2.00	3.50	12.00	28.00
	1927	.100	2.00	3.50	12.00	20.00
	1928	.100	2.00	3.50	12.00	20.00
	1929	.100	2.00	3.50	12.00	20.00
	1930	.100	2.00	3.50	12.00	18.00
	1934	.200	1.00	2.00	4.00	9.00
	1935	.200	1.00	2.00	4.00	9.00
	1936	.300	.50	1.00	1.75	7.50
	1937	.300	.50	1.00	1.75	7.50
	1938	.800	.50	1.00	1.50	4.00
	1940	.800	.50	1.00	1.50	4.00

BRASS
Reeded edge

Y#	Date	Mintage	Fine	VF	XF	Unc
22	1943	2.000	.50	1.00	1.50	3.00

Plain edge

Y#	Date	Mintage	Fine	VF	XF	Unc
22a	1943	Inc. Ab.	—	—	—	—

COPPER-NICKEL
B.N.N. on edge

Y#	Date	Mintage	Fine	VF	XF	Unc
17	1946	4.000	.10	.15	.30	1.00
	1952	4.000	.10	.15	.25	.35
	1954	4.000	.10	.15	.25	.30
	1956	5.000	.10	.15	.25	.50

B.C.N. on edge

Y#	Date	Mintage	Fine	VF	XF	Unc
17a	1962	3.000	.05	.10	.15	.20
	1964	4.000	.05	.10	.15	.20
	1965	10.000	.05	.10	.15	.20

Reeded edge

Y#	Date	Mintage	Fine	VF	XF	Unc
17b	1972	.020	—	—	Proof	2.50

NICKEL CLAD STEEL

Y#	Date	Mintage	Fine	VF	XF	Unc
17c	1972	10.000	—	—	.15	.25

ALUMINUM
F.A.O. Issue

Y#	Date	Mintage	Fine	VF	XF	Unc
27	1974	2.000	—	—	.10	.15
26	1974	16.200	—	—	.10	.15

10 CENTAVOS

2.5000 gm., .800 SILVER, .0643 oz ASW

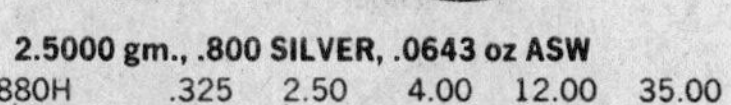

Y#	Date	Mintage	Fine	VF	XF	Unc
5	1880H	.325	2.50	4.00	12.00	35.00

Y#	Date	Mintage	Fine	VF	XF	Unc
8	1887H	1.500	2.00	3.00	5.00	10.00

Y#	Date	Mintage	Fine	VF	XF	Unc
13	1912H	.230	BV	2.50	5.00	15.00
	1912H	—	—	—	Proof	250.00
	1914H	.220	BV	2.50	5.00	15.00
	1927	.500	BV	2.00	3.00	7.00
	1928	1.000	BV	BV	2.00	5.00
	1930	.150	2.00	3.00	4.50	8.00
	1935	.250	BV	2.00	3.00	4.50
	1936	.250	BV	2.00	3.00	4.00

COPPER-NICKEL
B.N.N. on edge

Y#	Date	Mintage	Fine	VF	XF	Unc
18	1939	2.500	.50	1.00	1.50	3.00
	1946	2.000	.25	.50	.75	2.00
	1950	2.000	.25	.50	.75	1.00
	1952	1.500	.25	.50	.75	1.00
	1954	3.000	.05	.10	.15	.35
	1956	5.000	.05	.10	.15	.35

BRASS
Reeded edge

Y#	Date	Mintage	Fine	VF	XF	Unc
23	1943	2.000	.50	1.25	2.00	4.00

COPPER-NICKEL
B.C.N. on edge

Y#	Date	Mintage	Fine	VF	XF	Unc
18a	1962	4.000	.05	.10	.15	.25
	1964	4.000	.05	.10	.15	.25
	1965	12.000	.05	.10	.15	.20

Reeded edge

Y#	Date	Mintage	Fine	VF	XF	Unc
18b	1972	.020	—	—	Proof	2.50

NICKEL CLAD STEEL

Y#	Date	Mintage	Fine	VF	XF	Unc
18c	1972	10.000	—	.20	.25	.30

ALUMINUM
F.A.O. Issue

Y#	Date	Mintage	Fine	VF	XF	Unc
28	1974	2.000	—	—	.10	.25
A26	1974	20.000	—	—	.10	.25

COPPER-NICKEL

Y#	Date	Mintage	Fine	VF	XF	Unc
A26a	1978	—	—	—	—	.25

20 CENTAVOS

5.0000gm., .800 SILVER, .1286 oz ASW

Y#	Date	Mintage	Fine	VF	XF	Unc
6	1880H	.175	6.00	12.50	40.00	100.00

Y#	Date	Mintage	Fine	VF	XF	Unc
9	1887H	1.000	4.00	6.00	10.00	20.00

25 CENTAVOS

6.2500 gm., .800 SILVER, .1607 oz ASW

Y#	Date	Mintage	Fine	VF	XF	Unc
14	1912H	.320	BV	5.00	7.50	15.00
	1912H	—	—	—	Proof	300.00
	1914H	.100	BV	6.00	10.00	25.00
	1928	.200	BV	5.00	7.00	12.00
	1929	.020	5.00	9.00	13.50	32.50
	1930	.020	6.00	11.00	15.00	35.00
	1936	.100	BV	5.00	7.00	12.00

COPPER-NICKEL
B.N.N. on edge

Y#	Date	Mintage	Fine	VF	XF	Unc
19	1939	1.000	.50	1.00	1.25	3.00
	1946	1.000	.25	.40	.75	1.50
	1950	1.000	.20	.40	.75	1.25
	1952	1.000	.20	.40	.75	1.25
	1954	2.000	.05	.10	.15	.50
	1956	3.000	.05	.10	.15	.40

BRASS
Reeded edge

Y#	Date	Mintage	Fine	VF	XF	Unc
24	1943	1.000	1.00	1.50	3.50	10.00

COPPER-NICKEL
B.C.N. on edge

Y#	Date	Mintage	Fine	VF	XF	Unc
19a	1964	3.000	.05	.10	.25	.60
	1965	4.400	.05	.10	.15	.35

Reeded edge

Y#	Date	Mintage	Fine	VF	XF	Unc
19b	1972	4.000	—	—	.15	.35
	1972	.020	—	—	Proof	2.50
	1974	6.000	—	—	—	.35

50 CENTAVOS

12.5000 gm., .800 SILVER, .3215 oz ASW

Y#	Date	Mintage	Fine	VF	XF	Unc
15	1912H	.260	10.00	12.50	20.00	65.00
	1912H	—	—	—	Proof	400.00
	1929	.020	12.50	17.50	35.00	75.00

COPPER-NICKEL
B.N.N. on edge

Y#	Date	Mintage	Fine	VF	XF	Unc
20	1939	1.000	1.25	3.30	6.00	10.00
	1946	.500	.50	1.00	2.50	5.00
	1950	.500	.50	1.00	2.50	5.00
	1952	1.000	.25	.50	1.50	3.00
	1954	2.000	.10	.25	.50	1.50
	1956	2.000	.10	.25	.50	1.50

B.C.N. on edge

Y#	Date	Mintage	Fine	VF	XF	Unc
20a	1965	.600	1.25	3.50	6.00	10.00

Reeded edge

Y#	Date	Mintage	Fine	VF	XF	Unc
20b	1972	.020	—	—	Proof	2.50
	1974	2.000	—	—	—	1.25

UN (1) CORDOBA

25.0000 gm., .900 SILVER, .7234 oz ASW

Y#	Date	Mintage	Fine	VF	XF	Unc
16	1912H	.035	25.00	50.00	85.00	375.00
	1912H	—	—	—	Proof	750.00

COPPER-NICKEL
Reeded edge

Y#	Date	Mintage	Fine	VF	XF	Unc
25	1972	20.000	—	.20	.35	.75
	1972	—	—	—	Proof	5.00

20 CORDOBAS

5.0300 gm., .925 SILVER, .1496 oz ASW
Earthquake Relief Issue

Y#	Date	Mintage	VF	XF	Unc
30	1975	850 pcs.	5.00	7.50	10.00
	1975	—	—	Proof	12.50

50 CORDOBAS

.900 GOLD
Ruben Dario

Y#	Date	Mintage	VF	XF	Unc
29	1967	500 pcs.	—	Proof	400.00

12.5700 gm., .925 SILVER, .3738 oz ASW
U.S. Bicentennial

Y#	Date	Mintage	VF	XF	Unc
31	1975	1,200	BV	12.50	15.00
	1975	—	—	Proof	25.00

Earthquake Relief Issue

Y#	Date	Mintage	VF	XF	Unc
A31	1975	—	BV	12.00	14.00
	1975	—	—	Proof	20.00

100 CORDOBAS

23.2500 gm., .925 SILVER, .6915 oz ASW
U.S. Bicentennial

Y#	Date	Mintage	VF	XF	Unc
32	1975	1,400	BV	22.50	27.50
	1975	—	—	Proof	35.00

Earthquake Relief Issue

Y#	Date	Mintage	VF	XF	Unc
A32	1975	—	BV	21.50	25.00
	1975	—	—	Proof	32.50

200 CORDOBAS

2.1000 gm., .900 GOLD, .0608 oz AGW
U.S. Bicentennial

Y#	Date	Mintage	VF	XF	Unc
33	1975	200 pcs.	—	40.00	45.00
	1975	—	—	Proof	55.00

500 CORDOBAS

5.4000 gm., .900 GOLD, .1563 oz AGW
U.S. Bicentennial

Y#	Date	Mintage	VF	XF	Unc
34	1975	200 pcs.	—	110.00	125.00
	1975	—	—	Proof	150.00

Earthquake Relief Issue

Y#	Date	Mintage	VF	XF	Unc
A34	1975	—	—	110.00	125.00
	1975	—	—	Proof	150.00

1000 CORDOBAS

9.6000 gm., .900 GOLD, .2778 oz AGW
U.S. Bicentennial

Y#	Date	Mintage	VF	XF	Unc
35	1975	3,200	BV	180.00	200.00
	1975	—	—	Proof	250.00

2000 CORDOBAS

17.2800 gm., .900 GOLD, .5000 oz AGW
U.S. Bicentennial

Y#	Date	Mintage	VF	XF	Unc
36	1975	200 pcs.	325.00	335.00	350.00
	1975	—	—	Proof	400.00

NCLT ISSUES

MINT SETS

KM#	Date	Mintage	Identification	Issue Price	Mkt. Val.
S1	1975(5)	—	Y33,34,A34,35,36	—	845.00

PROOF SETS

STANDARD METALS

KM#	Date	Mintage	Identification	Issue Price	Mkt. Val.
101	1912(7)	—	Y10-16	—	—
102	1972(5)	20,000	Y17b-20b,25	8.00	15.00
103	1975(7)	—	Y30-36	—	925.00
104	1975(3)	—	—	—	—
105	1975(3)	—	A31,A32,A34	—	200.00

NOTE: A 1912 presentation set has been reported in gold.

NIGER

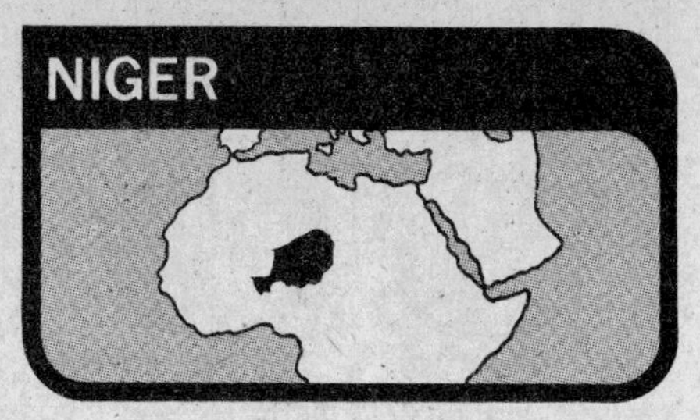

The Republic of Niger, located in West Africa's Sahara region 1,000 miles (1,609 km.) from the Mediterranean shore, has an area of 489,000 sq. mi. (1,267 sq. km.) and a population of 4.5 million. Capital: Niamey. The economy is based on subsistence agriculture and livestock raising. Peanuts, peanut oil, and livestock are exported.

Although four-fifths of Niger is arid desert, it was, some 6,000 years ago inhabited and an important economic crossroads. Its modern history began in the 19th century with the beginning of contacts with British and German explorers searching for the mouth of the Niger River. Niger was incorporated into French West Africa in 1896, but it was 1922 before all native resistance was quelled and Niger became a French colony. In 1958 the voters approved the new French Constitution and elected to become an autonomous republic within the French Community. On Aug. 3, 1960, Niger withdrew from the Community and procalimed its independence.

10 FRANCS

3.2000 gm., .900 GOLD, .0926 oz AGW
Similar to 25 Francs, H#5.

H#	Date	Mintage	XF	Unc	Proof
4	1960	1,000	—	—	75.00

H#	Date	Mintage	XF	Unc	Proof
9	1968	—	—	—	75.00

SILVER
Similar to 50 Francs, H#11.

H#	Date	Mintage	XF	Unc	Proof
	1968	—	—	—	30.00

25 FRANCS

8.0000 gm., .900 GOLD, .2315 oz AGW

H#	Date	Mintage	XF	Unc	Proof
5	1960	1,000	—	—	165.00

H#	Date	Mintage	XF	Unc	Proof
10	1968	—	—	—	165.00

50 FRANCS

16.0000 gm., .900 GOLD, .4630 oz AGW
Similar to 25 Francs, H#5.

H#	Date	Mintage	XF	Unc	Proof
6	1960	1,000	—	—	325.00
11	1968	—	—	—	325.00

100 FRANCS

32.0000 gm., .900 GOLD, .9260 oz AGW
Similar to 25 Francs, H#5.

H#	Date	Mintage	XF	Unc	Proof
7	1960	1,000	—	—	625.00
12	1968	—	—	—	625.00

500 FRANCS

10.0000 gm., .900 SILVER, .2893 oz ASW

H#	Date	Mintage	XF	Unc	Proof
1	1960	—	—	—	25.00

NOTE: Refer to ESSAIS in NCLT section.

1000 FRANCS

20.0000 gm., .900 SILVER, .5787 oz ASW
Rev: Similar to 500 Francs, H#1.

H#	Date	Mintage	XF	Unc	Proof
2	1960	—	—	—	50.00

NOTE: Refer to ESSAIS in NCLT section.

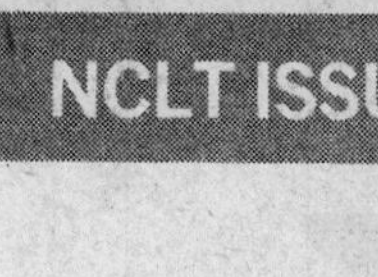

NCLT ISSUES

ESSAIS (E)

Standard metals unless otherwise noted.

KM#	Date	Mintage	Identification	Issue Price	Mkt. Val.
EH1	1960	1,000	500 Francs	—	25.00
EH2	1960	1,000	1000 Francs	—	35.00

PROOF SETS

STANDARD METALS

KM#	Date	Mintage	Identification	Issue Price	Mkt. Val.
101	1960(4)	1,000	H4-7	—	1150.
102	1968(4)	—	H9-12	—	1150.

NIGERIA

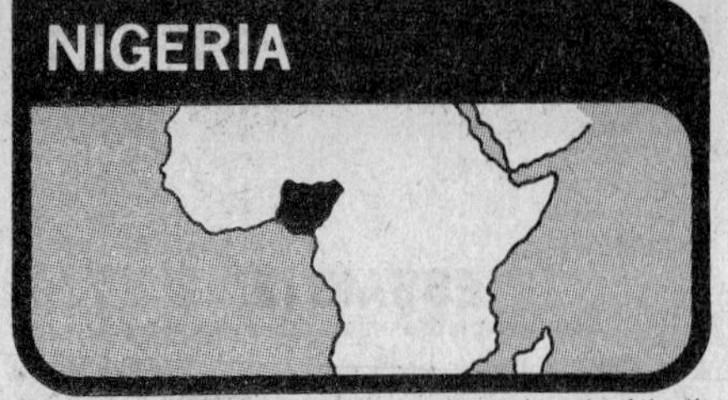

The Federal Republic of Nigeria, situated on the Atlantic coast of Africa between Benin and Cameroon, has an area of 356,699 sq. mi. (924,625 sq. km.) and a population of 79.8 million. Capital: Lagos. The economy is based on petroleum and agriculture. Crude oil, cocoa, tobacco and tin are exported.

Following the Napoleonic Wars, the British expanded their trade with the interior of Nigeria. British claims to a sphere of influence in that area were recognized by the Berlin Conference of 1885, and in the following year the Royal Niger Company was chartered. Direct British control of the territory was initiated in 1900, and in 1914 the amalgamation of Northern and Southern Nigeria into the Colony and Protectorate of Nigeria was effected. In 1960, following a number of territorial and constitutional changes, Nigeria was granted independence within the British Commonwealth as a federation of the Northern, Western and Eastern regions. Nigeria altered its political relationship with Great Britain on Oct. 1, 1963, by proclaiming itself a republic. It did, however, elect to remain a member of the Commonwealth of Nations. The Supreme Commander of Armed Forces is the Head of the Federal Military Government.

On May 30, 1967, the Eastern Region of the republic - an area occupied principally by the proud and resourceful Ibo tribe - seceded from Nigeria and proclaimed itself the independent Republic of Biafra. Civil war erupted and raged for 31 months. Casualties, including civilian, were about two million, the majority succumbing to malnutrition and disease. Biafra surrendered to the federal government on January 15, 1970.

RULERS

Elizabeth II, 1952-1963

MONETARY SYSTEM

12 Pence = 1 Shilling
20 Shillings = 1 Pound

1/2 PENNY

BRONZE

Y#	Date	Mintage	VF	XF	Unc
1	1959	78.919	—	—	.40
	1959	6,031	—	Proof	2.00

PENNY

BRONZE

Y#	Date	Mintage	VF	XF	Unc
2	1959	314.474	—	—	.20
	1959	6,031	—	Proof	2.50
	1961	—	Reported, Not Confirmed		

3 PENCE

NICKEL-BRASS

Y#	Date	Mintage	VF	XF	Unc
3	1959	143.000	—	.15	.50
	1959	6,031	—	Proof	3.50

6 PENCE

COPPER-NICKEL

Y#	Date	Mintage	VF	XF	Unc
4	1959	38.000	.20	.35	.75
	1959	6,031	—	Proof	5.00

SHILLING

COPPER-NICKEL

Y#	Date	Mintage	VF	XF	Unc
5	1959	450.000	.50	.75	2.00
	1959	6,031	—	Proof	6.50
	1961	162.944	.60	1.00	3.00
	1962	77.056	.60	1.00	3.50

2 SHILLINGS

COPPER-NICKEL
Reeded edge

Y#	Date	Mintage	VF	XF	Unc
6	1959	30.000	.40	.60	1.75
	1959	6,031	—	Proof	9.00
	Security edge				
6a	1959	Inc. Ab.	.40	.60	1.75

DECIMAL COINAGE

100 Kobo = 1 Naira
(10 Shillings)

1/2 KOBO

BRONZE

Y#	Date	Mintage	VF	XF	Unc
7	1973	166.618	.10	.30	.60
	1973	.010	—	Proof	2.00

KOBO

BRONZE

Y#	Date	Mintage	VF	XF	Unc
8	1973	552.800	.15	.35	.75
	1973	.010	—	Proof	3.00
	1974	—	—	—	—

5 KOBO

COPPER-NICKEL

Y#	Date	Mintage	VF	XF	Unc
9	1973	96.920	.25	.50	1.00
	1973	.010	—	Proof	4.00
	1974	—	—	—	—
	1976	—	—	—	—

10 KOBO

COPPER-NICKEL

Y#	Date	Mintage	VF	XF	Unc
10	1973	247.370	.35	.75	1.50
	1973	.010	—	Proof	6.00
	1974	—	—	.25	.75
	1976	—	—	.25	.75

25 KOBO

COPPER-NICKEL

Y#	Date	Mintage	VF	XF	Unc
11	1973	4.616	.65	1.25	2.25
	1973	.010	—	Proof	10.00
	1975	—	1.00	1.75	3.00

NCLT ISSUES

ESSAIS

Standard metals unless otherwise noted.

KM#	Date	Mintage	Identification	Mkt.Val.
E1	1962	—	1 Shilling, Trial	80.00

PROOF SETS

STANDARD METALS

KM#	Date	Mintage	Identification	Issue Price	Mkt. Val.
101	1959(6)	1,031	Y1-6, red case, originals	—	35.00
102	1959(6)	5,000	Y1-6, blue case, restrikes	—	15.00
103	1973(5)	10,200	Y7-11	14.70	22.50

BIAFRA

MONETARY SYSTEM

12 Pence = 1 Shilling

3 PENCE

ALUMINUM

Y#	Date	Mintage	VF	XF	Unc
1	1969	—	5.00	9.00	20.00

SHILLING

ALUMINUM

Y#	Date	Mintage	VF	XF	Unc
2	1969	—	1.00	2.50	5.00

2-1/2 SHILLINGS

ALUMINUM

Y#	Date	Mintage	VF	XF	Unc
3	1969	—	1.50	3.50	7.50

POUND

SILVER

H#	Date	Mintage	XF	Unc	Proof
7	1969	—	—	—	—
	1969	—	—	—	17.50

3.9940 gm., .916 GOLD, .1177 oz AGW
2nd Anniversary of Independence
Similar to 25 Pounds, FR#1.

Fr#	Date	Mintage	XF	Unc	Proof
5	1969	3,000	—	—	150.00

2 POUNDS

7.9881 gm., .916 GOLD, .2354 oz AGW
2nd Anniversary of Independence
Similar to 25 Pounds, Fr#1.

Fr#	Date	Mintage	XF	Unc	Proof
4	1969	3,000	—	—	175.00

5 POUNDS

15.9761 gm., .916 GOLD, .4709 oz AGW
2nd Anniversary of Independence
Similar to 25 Pounds, Fr#1.

Fr#	Date	Mintage	XF	Unc	Proof
3	1969	3,000	—	—	325.00

10 POUNDS

39.9403 gm., .916 GOLD, 1.1771 oz AGW
2nd Anniversary of Independence
Similar to 25 Pounds, Fr#1.

Fr#	Date	Mintage	XF	Unc	Proof
2	1969	3,000	—	—	775.00

25 POUNDS

79.8805 gm., .916 GOLD, 2.3543 oz AGW
2nd Anniversary of Independence

Fr#	Date	Mintage	XF	Unc	Proof
1	1969	3,000	—	—	1550.

NCLT ISSUES

PROOF SETS

STANDARD METALS

KM#	Date	Mintage	Identification	Issue Price	Mkt. Val.
101	1969(5)	3,000	Fr1-5	464.00	2975.

Listings For

NORTH KOREA: refer to Korea

NORTH VIETNAM: refer to Vietnam

NORWAY

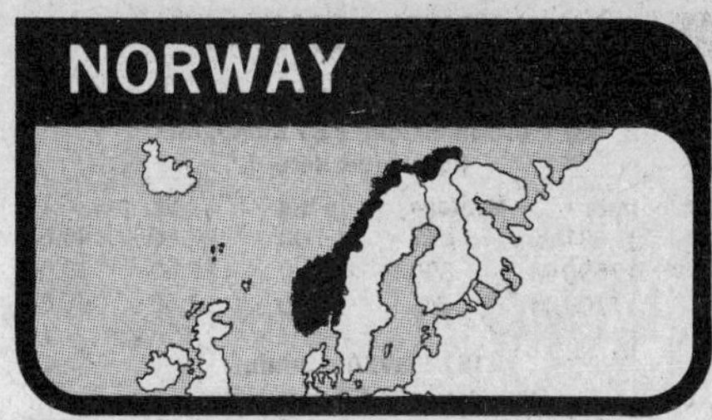

The Kingdom of Norway, a constitutional monarchy located in northwestern Europe, has an area of 150,000 sq. mi. (388,500 sq. km.), including the island territories of Spitzbergen (Svalbard) and Jan Mayen, and a population of 4 million. Capital: Oslo. The diversified economic base of Norway includes shipping, fishing, forestry, agriculture, and manufacturing. Nonferrous metals, paper and paperboard, paper pulp, iron, and steel are exported.

A United Norwegian kingdom was established in the 9th century, the era of the indomitable Norse Vikings who ranged far and wide, visiting the coasts of northwestern Europe, the Mediterranean, Greenland and North America. In the 13th century the Norse kingdom was united briefly with Sweden, then passed, through the Union of Kalmar, 1397, to the rule of Denmark which was maintained until 1814. In 1814 Norway fell again under the rule of Sweden. The union of sailors and peasants with aristocratic landowners and tenant sharecroppers was not a congenial one, but it lasted until 1905 when the Norwegian Parliament arranged a peaceful separation and invited a Danish prince (King Haakon VII) to occupy the throne of an independent Kingdom of Norway.

RULERS

Christian VII, 1766-1808
Frederik VI, 1808-1814
Carl XIII, 1814-1818
Carl XIV, 1818-1844
Oscar I, 1844-1859
Carl XV, 1859-1872
Oscar II, 1872-1905
Haakon VII, 1905-1957
Olav V, 1957-

MONETARY SYSTEM

Until 1873
120 Skilling = 1 Speciedaler
(Rigsdaler Specie)

1/2 SKILLING

COPPER

C#	Date	Mintage	Fine	VF	XF
71	1839	.613	10.00	17.50	35.00
	1840	2.558	3.75	6.75	15.00
	1841	1.629	5.50	10.00	18.00
	Rev: Star under hammers				
	1841	Inc. Ab.	4.50	7.50	16.50

Y#	Date	Mintage	VF	XF	Unc
1	1863	.480	22.50	35.00	70.00

Y#	Date	Mintage	VF	XF	Unc
2	1867	3.600	2.50	4.00	12.50

SKILLING

.250 SILVER, 14mm.
Obv: Crowned double C7 monogram.
Rev: Value, date.

C#	Date	Mintage	Fine	VF	XF
12	1768TL	.697	15.00	27.50	45.00
	1769IHM	.890	12.00	22.50	35.00
	1770IHM	.448	15.00	27.50	45.00

.187 SILVER, 15mm.
Obv: Crowned C7 monogram.

C#	Date	Mintage	Fine	VF	XF
14	1779HIAB	.845	10.00	20.00	30.00
	1780HIAB	1.152	10.00	20.00	30.00

COPPER, 25mm.
Rev: 5-petalled rosettes, by '1' and below date.

C#	Date	Mintage	Fine	VF	XF
51	1809	.346	10.00	20.00	45.00

Rev: 8-petalled rosettes, by '1' and below date.

C#	Date	Mintage	Fine	VF	XF
51.1	1809	Inc. Ab.	10.00	20.00	45.00

Rev: Ovals by '1' and below date.

C#	Date	Mintage	Fine	VF	XF
51.2	1809	Inc. Ab.	10.00	20.00	45.00

C#	Date	Mintage	Fine	VF	XF
52	1812	5.453	3.00	6.00	12.00
	*1812 w/o crossed hammers under date				
		Inc. Ab.	50.00	75.00	125.00

*Beware of removed mintmark or altered coin.

C#	Date	Mintage	Fine	VF	XF
61	1816	1.659	12.50	20.00	55.00

C#	Date	Mintage	Fine	VF	XF
72	1819	3.817	7.50	22.50	45.00
	1820	Inc. Ab.	7.50	22.50	45.00
	1824	6,000	90.00	140.00	275.00
	1825	—	100.00	200.00	350.00
	1827	.034	100.00	200.00	350.00
	1828	.038	200.00	350.00	500.00
	1831	1.440	90.00	130.00	225.00
	1832	Inc. Ab.	80.00	120.00	200.00
	1833	.126	80.00	120.00	200.00
	1834	Unknown	900.00	1200.	2000.

Y#	Date	Mintage	VF	XF	Unc
3	1870	1.200	5.00	12.50	30.00

2 SKILLING

.344 SILVER

C#	Date	Mintage	Fine	VF	XF
16	1778HIAB	.580	5.00	10.00	20.00
	1779HIAB	3.533	5.00	10.00	20.00
	1780HIAB	7.200	5.00	10.00	20.00
	1781HIAB R in Norway inverted				
		—	10.00	20.00	40.00
	1781HIAB	4.296	5.00	10.00	20.00
	1782HIAB	7.891	5.00	10.00	20.00
16	1783HIAB	7.896	5.00	10.00	20.00
	1784HIAB	7.891	5.00	10.00	20.00
	1785HIAB	3.531	5.00	10.00	20.00
	1786HIAB	6.341	5.00	10.00	20.00
	1787HIAB	3.862	5.00	10.00	20.00
	1788HIAB	1.841	5.00	10.00	20.00

.250 SILVER

C#	Date	Mintage	Fine	VF	XF
18	1800IGM	2.419	5.00	10.00	20.00
	1801IGM	1.109	5.00	10.00	20.00
	1802IGM	2.854	5.00	10.00	20.00
	1803IGM	2.419	5.00	10.00	20.00
	1804IGM	3.634	5.00	10.00	20.00
	1805IGM	2.412	5.00	10.00	20.00
	1807IGP	3.507	5.00	10.00	20.00

COPPER
Rev: 8-petalled rosettes by '2' and below date.

C#	Date	Mintage	Fine	VF	XF
53	1810	3.449	5.00	10.00	20.00

Rev: Cross

C#	Date	Mintage	Fine	VF	XF
53.1	1810	Inc. Ab.	4.50	9.00	17.50
	1811	1.191	5.50	11.00	22.50

C#	Date	Mintage	Fine	VF	XF
73	1822	.963	17.50	35.00	60.00
	1823 (error) 3 in date upside down				
		—	—	Rare	—
	1824	.549	17.50	35.00	60.00
	1825	.510	25.00	45.00	75.00
	1827	.288	25.00	45.00	75.00
	1828	.453	20.00	40.00	70.00
	1831	.723	20.00	40.00	70.00
	1832	Inc. Ab.	20.00	40.00	70.00
	1833	.060	20.00	40.00	70.00
	1834	.880	50.00	75.00	150.00

.250 SILVER, 17mm.

C#	Date	Mintage	Fine	VF	XF
78	1825	.240	22.50	40.00	65.00
93	1842	1.500	4.00	9.00	15.00
	1843	Inc. Ab.	6.00	12.50	22.50

Y#	Date	Mintage	VF	XF	Unc
4	1870	.900	6.00	10.00	20.00

Rev: Rosettes

Y#	Date	Mintage	VF	XF	Unc
4.1	1871	2.040	6.00	10.00	20.00

Rev: Stars

Y#	Date	Mintage	VF	XF	Unc
4.2	1871	Inc. Ab.	6.00	10.00	20.00

3 SKILLING

.250 SILVER

Y#	Date	Mintage	VF	XF	Unc
5	1868	.499	10.00	17.50	35.00

Rev: Rosettes

Y#	Date	Mintage	VF	XF	Unc
5.1	1869	.703	10.00	17.50	35.00

Rev: Stars

Y#	Date	Mintage	VF	XF	Unc
5.2	1869	Inc. Ab.	10.00	17.50	35.00

Rev: Rosettes

Y#	Date	Mintage	VF	XF	Unc
11	1872	1.080	7.50	15.00	30.00

Rev: Stars

Y#	Date	Mintage	VF	XF	Unc
11.1	1872	Inc. Ab.	7.50	15.00	30.00
	1873	.600	7.50	15.00	30.00

4 SKILLING

.562 SILVER, 18mm, 1.53 gm.
Obv: Crowned C7 monogram. Rev: Oval 3-fold arms.

C#	Date	Mintage	Fine	VF	XF
20	1778HIAB	.162	30.00	60.00	100.00

.312 SILVER, 2.75 gm.

C#	Date	Mintage	Fine	VF	XF
20a	1788HIAB	.375	22.50	40.00	70.00

COPPER
Rev: Rosettes by '4' and below date.

C#	Date	Mintage	Fine	VF	XF
54	1809	.251	35.00	70.00	125.00

Rev: Stars by '4' and below date.

C#	Date	Mintage	Fine	VF	XF
54.1	1809				
		Inc. Ab.	35.00	70.00	125.00

.250 SILVER

C#	Date	Mintage	Fine	VF	XF
58	1809 IGP Rev. with legend SKILLE:				
		2.228	8.00	16.00	35.00
58.1	1809 IGP Rev. with leg: SKILLE-				
		inc. Ab.	10.00	20.00	40.00

C#	Date	Mintage	Fine	VF	XF
79	1825 JMK	.333	15.00	30.00	50.00

C#	Date	Mintage	Fine	VF	XF
94	1842	.750	10.00	25.00	60.00

Y#	Date	Mintage	VF	XF	Unc
6	1871	.559	15.00	30.00	50.00

6 SKILLING

COPPER
Obv: Crowned shield. Rev: Value.

C#	Date	Mintage	Fine	VF	XF
55	1813	—	12.50	22.50	40.00

8 SKILLING

.562 SILVER
Obv: Crowned C7 monogram. Rev: Value, date.

C#	Date	Mintage	Fine	VF	XF
22	1773IHM	.549	25.00	45.00	85.00
	1774IHM	.414	25.00	45.00	85.00
	1775IHM	.144	27.50	60.00	100.00

Rev: Crowned oval 3-fold arms.

C#	Date	Mintage	Fine	VF	XF
24	1778HIAB	.922	15.00	32.50	60.00
	1779HIAB	1.315	15.00	32.50	60.00
	1780HIAB	.680	15.00	32.50	60.00
	1781HIAB	.890	15.00	32.50	60.00
	1782HIAB	1.027	15.00	32.50	60.00
	1783HIAB	1.032	15.00	32.50	60.00
	1784HIAB	.959	15.00	32.50	60.00
	1785HIAB	1.105	15.00	32.50	60.00
	1786HIAB	2,700	—	Rare	—
	1787HIAB	3,800	80.00	150.00	250.00
	1788HIAB	.197	35.00	60.00	120.00
	1789HIAB	.012	80.00	150.00	250.00
	1790HIAB	7,800	—	Rare	—
	1791HIAB	6,700	80.00	150.00	250.00
	1792HIAB	6,000	—	Rare	—
	1793HIAB	5,700	80.00	150.00	250.00
	1794HIAB	6,600	80.00	150.00	250.00
	1795HIAB	.020	80.00	150.00	250.00

.375 SILVER

C#	Date	Mintage	Fine	VF	XF
59	1809IGP	1.349	10.00	17.50	35.00

.500 SILVER

C#	Date	Mintage	Fine	VF	XF
67	1817IGP	.241	25.00	45.00	90.00
80	1819IGP	.101	30.00	50.00	100.00

.875 SILVER

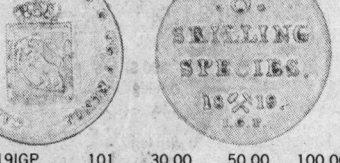

C#	Date	Mintage	Fine	VF	XF
87	1825	.016	30.00	60.00	120.00
	1827/5	.014	30.00	60.00	120.00

1/15 SPECIE DALER

.500 SILVER
Obv: Value, crowned oval arms. Rev: Value, date.

C#	Date	Mintage	Fine	VF	XF
26	1795HIAB	.144	12.50	27.50	45.00
	1796HIAB	.312	20.00	40.00	65.00
	1796IGM	Inc. Ab.	30.00	60.00	100.00

C#	Date	Mintage	Fine	VF	XF
26	1797IGM	.312	20.00	40.00	65.00
	1798IGM	.312	20.00	40.00	65.00
	1799IGM	.403	20.00	40.00	65.00
	1800IGM	.319	12.50	27.50	45.00
	1801IGM	.382	12.50	27.50	45.00
	1802IGM	.149	12.50	27.50	45.00

12 SKILLING

COPPER
Obv: Crowned shield. Rev: Value.

C#	Date	Mintage	Fine	VF	XF
56	1813	—	8.00	15.00	25.00

.875 SILVER
Plain border

C#	Date	Mintage	Fine	VF	XF
101	1845	.631	17.50	30.00	50.00
	1846	.250	17.50	30.00	60.00
	1847	.256	17.50	30.00	60.00
	1848/18	.316	—	—	—
	1848	Inc. Ab.	25.00	40.00	65.00

Beaded border

C#	Date	Mintage	Fine	VF	XF
101.1	1850 with legend V KONGE				
		.287	17.50	30.00	60.00
	1850 with legend V. KONGE				
		Inc. Ab.	17.50	30.00	60.00
	1852	.313	22.50	37.50	65.00
	1853	.360	17.50	30.00	60.00
	1854	.301	17.50	30.00	60.00
	1855	.450	17.50	30.00	60.00
	1856/5	.812	—	—	—
	1856	Inc. Ab.	15.00	25.00	45.00

Small head

Y#	Date	Mintage	VF	XF	Unc
7	1861	2,500	550.00	900.00	1500.
	1862	Unknown	550.00	900.00	1500.

Large head

Y#	Date	Mintage	VF	XF	Unc
7a	1865	.152	150.00	225.00	350.00

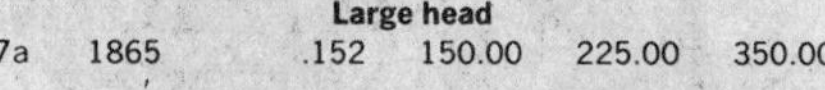

Y#	Date	Mintage	VF	XF	Unc
12	1873	.490	110.00	150.00	225.00

24 SKILLING

.562 SILVER

C#	Date	Mintage	Fine	VF	XF
28	1767TL	—	190.00	375.00	575.00

C#	Date	Mintage	Fine	VF	XF
30	1772IHM	.299	55.00	100.00	175.00
	1773IHM	1.035	40.00	75.00	115.00
	1774IHM	.283	45.00	90.00	150.00
	1775IHM	4,000	—	Rare	—
	1783HIAB	.016	100.00	175.00	300.00
	1788HIAB	.064	100.00	175.00	300.00

.687 SILVER

C#	Date	Mintage	Fine	VF	XF
81	1819IGP	.050	75.00	125.00	200.00

.875 SILVER

C#	Date	Mintage	Fine	VF	XF
81a	1823IGP	.125	175.00	250.00	400.00
	1824JMK	7,800	200.00	275.00	450.00

C#	Date	Mintage	Fine	VF	XF
88	1825	4,600	175.00	300.00	450.00
	1827/5	.027	125.00	250.00	375.00
	1827	Inc. Ab.	125.00	250.00	375.00
	1830	5,800	200.00	375.00	550.00
	1831/0	2,400	—	Rare	—
	1833	Unknown	250.00	450.00	700.00
	1834	Unknown	250.00	450.00	700.00
	1835	2,500	225.00	400.00	600.00
	1836	2,500	225.00	400.00	600.00

Plain border

C#	Date	Mintage	Fine	VF	XF
102.	1845	.359	20.00	40.00	80.00
	1846	.383	20.00	40.00	80.00
	1847	.217	20.00	40.00	80.00
	1848	.150	25.00	50.00	100.00

Beaded border

C#	Date	Mintage	Fine	VF	XF
102.1	1850	.102	25.00	50.00	100.00
	1852	.254	20.00	40.00	80.00
	1853	.327	20.00	40.00	80.00
	1854	.212	25.00	50.00	100.00
	1855	.204	20.00	40.00	80.00

Small head

Y#	Date	Mintage	VF	XF	Unc
8	1861	13 pcs.	—	Rare	—
	1862	1,200	600.00	1000.	1500.

Large head

Y#	Date	Mintage	VF	XF	Unc
8a	1865	.079	125.00	250.00	450.00

1/5 SPECIE DALER

.687 SILVER

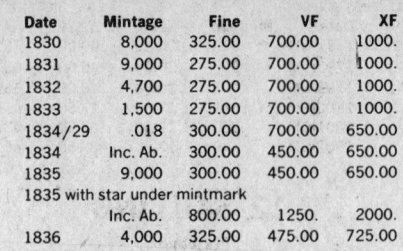

C#	Date	Mintage	Fine	VF	XF
32	1796HIAB	.081	150.00	300.00	450.00
	1796IGM	Inc. Ab.	40.00	70.00	100.00
	1797IGM	.192	40.00	70.00	100.00
	1798IGM	.189	40.00	70.00	100.00
	1799IGM	.158	40.00	70.00	100.00
	1800IGM	.125	40.00	70.00	100.00
	1801IGM	.163	40.00	70.00	100.00
	1803IGM	.092	40.00	70.00	100.00

1/3 SPECIE DALER

.875 SILVER

C#	Date	Mintage	Fine	VF	XF
34	1795HIAB	.015	150.00	325.00	500.00
	1796HIAB	.144	60.00	125.00	200.00
	1796IGM	Inc. Ab.	125.00	200.00	300.00
	1797IGM	.135	60.00	125.00	200.00
	1798IGM	.105	60.00	125.00	200.00
	1799IGM	.090	125.00	200.00	300.00
	1800IGM	.068	60.00	125.00	200.00
	1801IGM	.108	60.00	125.00	200.00
	1802IGM	.065	90.00	150.00	250.00
	1803IGM	.024	125.00	200.00	300.00
	Obv: Bust right without bow, P.G. below portrait.				
34.1	1803IGM	Inc. Ab.	200.00	400.00	600.00

1/2 SPECIE DALER

.875 SILVER

Obv: Crowned double C7 monogram. Rev: Crowned oval 3-fold arms.

C#	Date	Mintage	Fine	VF	XF
36	1776HIAB	.060	90.00	170.00	250.00
	1777HIAB	.031	100.00	175.00	275.00
	1778HIAB	.027	100.00	175.00	275.00
	1779HIAB	.012	—	—	—

C#	Date	Mintage	Fine	VF	XF
83	1819	.010	175.00	250.00	400.00
	1821	.069	160.00	225.00	375.00
	1823/1	6,100	450.00	650.00	900.00
	1824/1	.033	160.00	225.00	375.00
	1824	Inc. Ab.	160.00	275.00	400.00

C#	Date	Mintage	Fine	VF	XF
89	1827 SKI:	.070	160.00	225.00	375.00
	1827. SKI.	I.A.	160.00	225.00	375.00
	1829	5,100	225.00	325.00	500.00
89	1830	8,000	325.00	700.00	1000.
	1831	9,000	275.00	700.00	1000.
	1832	4,700	275.00	700.00	1000.
	1833	1,500	275.00	700.00	1000.
	1834/29	.018	300.00	700.00	650.00
	1834	Inc. Ab.	300.00	450.00	650.00
	1835	9,000	300.00	450.00	650.00
	1835 with star under mintmark				
		Inc. Ab.	800.00	1250.	2000.
	1836	4,000	325.00	475.00	725.00

C#	Date	Mintage	Fine	VF	XF
95	1844	.231	175.00	250.00	350.00

C#	Date	Mintage	Fine	VF	XF
103	1846	.146	150.00	200.00	325.00
	1847	.047	150.00	200.00	325.00
	1848	.015	150.00	250.00	400.00
	1849	.142	150.00	200.00	325.00
	1850	Inc. Ab.	150.00	200.00	325.00
	1855	.010	250.00	375.00	550.00

Y#	Date	Mintage	VF	XF	Unc
9	1861	500 pcs.	—	Rare	—
	1861 with B under bust				
		13 pcs.	—	Rare	—
	1862	.064	350.00	550.00	825.00
9a	1865	700 pcs.	2000.	3000.	4500.
13	1873	4,200	2000.	3000.	4000.

2/3 SPECIE DALER

.875 SILVER

Obv: Bust right. Rev: Crowned arms, value 2/3.

C#	Date	Mintage	Fine	VF	XF
36	1795HIAB	7,500	165.00	325.00	500.00
	1796HIAB	.093	135.00	250.00	425.00
	Rev: Value, 2 above 3.				
—	1795HIAB	Inc. Ab.	160.00	325.00	475.00
	1796HIAB	Inc. Ab.	—	—	—

SPECIE DALER

.875 SILVER

Obv: Crowned double C7 monogram. Rev: Lion shield.

C#	Date	Mintage	Fine	VF	XF
40	1767TL	.054	1150.	1850.	2800.
	1768TL	.047	1050.	1700.	2800.

C#	Date	Mintage	Fine	VF	XF
41	1776HIAB	.206	150.00	275.00	425.00
	1777HIAB	.127	160.00	275.00	475.00
	1778HIAB	.138	175.00	300.00	500.00
	1779HIAB	.064	190.00	350.00	525.00
	1781HIAB	.084	225.00	375.00	625.00
	1785HIAB	.043	250.00	425.00	700.00

C#	Date	Mintage	Fine	VF	XF
44	1791HIAB	.055	325.00	575.00	1000.
	1791HIAB B under bust				
		Inc. Ab.	—	Unique	—
	1791HIAB H under bust				
		Inc. Ab.	—	Unique	—
	1792HIAB	.050	275.00	525.00	800.00

NOTE: Varieties exist.

Obv: Different hairdo, w/o ribbon.

C#	Date	Mintage	Fine	VF	XF
44.1	1792HIAB SI under bust				
		Inc. Ab.	575.00	1150.	1700.
	1793HIAB	.064	450.00	875.00	1250.
	1794HIAB	.037	450.00	875.00	1250.
	1795HIAB	.096	325.00	600.00	950.00

C#	Date	Mintage	Fine	VF	XF
84	1819IGP	.024	275.00	550.00	900.00
	1821IGP	.101	250.00	525.00	800.00
	1823IGP	.016	600.00	950.00	1200.
	1824/1JMK	.121	250.00	425.00	650.00
	1824JMK	Inc. Ab.	250.00	425.00	650.00

C#	Date	Mintage	Fine	VF	XF
90	1826	.025	400.00	600.00	900.00
	1826 with initial M				
		Inc. Ab.	—	Rare	—
	1827/6	.132	400.00	550.00	850.00
	1827	Inc. Ab.	400.00	550.00	850.00
	1829/7	.016	450.00	625.00	950.00
	1829	Inc. Ab.	450.00	625.00	950.00
	1830	.026	450.00	625.00	950.00
	1831	.031	450.00	625.00	950.00
	1832	.024	450.00	625.00	950.00
	1833	2,732	1750.	2500.	4000.
	1834	.103	400.00	550.00	850.00
	1835	.040	400.00	550.00	850.00
	1835 with star under mintmark				
		Inc. Ab.	500.00	650.00	1150.
	1836	.052	650.00	950.00	1400.

C#	Date	Mintage	Fine	VF	XF
96	1844	.302	300.00	450.00	675.00

Rev: Similar to C#96.

C#	Date	Mintage	Fine	VF	XF
104	1846	.067	275.00	400.00	650.00
	1847	.140	275.00	400.00	650.00
	1848	.081	275.00	400.00	650.00
	1849	.114	275.00	400.00	650.00
	1850	.124	275.00	400.00	650.00
	1855	.148	275.00	400.00	650.00
	1856	.114	275.00	400.00	650.00
	1857	.160	325.00	450.00	750.00

Rev: Similar to C#96.

Y#	Date	Mintage	VF	XF	Unc
10	1861	.044	750.00	1150.	1450.
	1861 with B under bust				
		13 pcs.	—	Rare	—
	1862	.062	600.00	800.00	1250.

Large head
Rev: Similar to C#96.

Y#	Date	Mintage	VF	XF	Unc
10a	1864	.130	575.00	950.00	1350.
	1865	.086	575.00	950.00	1350.
	1867	.030	1000.	1250.	1900.
	1868	.114	850.00	1150.	1500.
	1869	.057	950.00	1150.	1750.

RIGSDALER

.875 SILVER
Obv: Armored bust right. Rev: Lion in double legend.

C#	Date	Mintage	VG	Fine	VF
43	1788	—	1200.	2250.	3250.

TRADE COINS

PIASTRE

SILVER
Obv: Crowned arms. Rev: Crowned globes between crowned pillars.

C#	Date	Mintage	VG	Fine	VF
39	1777	—	2000.	2500.	3200.

DECIMAL COINAGE

100 Ore = 1 Krone (30 Skilling)

ORE

BRONZE

Y#	Date	Mintage	VF	XF	Unc
19	1876	8.000	5.00	15.00	25.00
	1877	2.166	17.50	32.50	50.00
	1878	1.834	30.00	50.00	90.00
	1884	3.378	6.00	15.00	25.00
	1885	.622	100.00	150.00	225.00
	1889	3.000	6.00	15.00	30.00
	1891	3.000	6.00	15.00	30.00
	1893	3.000	6.00	15.00	30.00
	1897	3.000	6.00	15.00	30.00
	1899	4.500	4.00	8.00	22.50
	1902	4.500	4.00	8.00	22.50

Y#	Date	Mintage	VF	XF	Unc
30	1906	3.000	6.00	12.00	17.50
	1907	2.550	8.00	15.00	20.00

Y#	Date	Mintage	VF	XF	Unc
35	1908	1.450	15.00	22.50	35.00
	1910	2.480	2.50	6.00	17.50
	1911	3.270	2.50	5.00	17.50
	1912	2.850	2.50	6.00	17.50
	1913	2.840	2.50	6.00	17.50
	1914	5.020	2.50	5.00	17.50
	1915	1.540	8.00	20.00	35.00
	1921	3.805	15.00	25.00	40.00
	1922	Inc. Ab.	2.75	10.00	16.50
	1923	.770	10.00	15.00	27.50
	1925	3.000	1.00	5.00	12.50
	1926	2.200	1.00	5.00	12.50
	1927	.800	8.00	12.50	22.50
	1928	3.000	.75	3.00	8.00
	1929	4.990	.75	3.00	8.00
	1930	2.010	.75	3.00	8.00
	1931	2.000	.75	3.00	8.00
	1932	2.500	.75	3.00	8.00
	1933	2.000	.75	3.00	8.00
	1934	2.000	.75	3.00	8.00
	1935	5.495	.50	1.00	4.00
	1936	6.855	.50	1.00	4.00
	1937	6.020	.50	1.00	4.00
	1938	4.920	.50	1.00	4.00
	1939	2.500	.50	1.00	4.00
	1940	5.010	.50	1.00	4.00
	1941	12.260	.50	1.00	4.00
	1946	2.200	.25	.75	2.50
	1947	4.870	.25	.75	2.50
	1948	9.405	.25	.75	2.50
	1949	2.785	1.00	2.00	5.00
	1950	5.730	.25	.75	2.50
	1951	16.670	.25	.75	2.50
	1952	Inc. Ab.	.25	.75	2.50

IRON

Y#	Date	Mintage	VF	XF	Unc
35a	1918	6.000	6.00	12.00	25.00
	1919	12.930	3.00	7.00	17.50
	1920	4.445	6.00	12.00	25.00
	1921	2.270	30.00	50.00	80.00

World War II German Occupation

Y#	Date	Mintage	VF	XF	Unc
53	1941	13.410	.50	1.50	3.50
	1942	37.710	.50	1.50	3.50
	1943	33.030	.50	1.50	3.50
	1944	8.820	.50	1.50	3.50
	1945	1.740	3.25	5.00	10.00

BRONZE

Y#	Date	Mintage	VF	XF	Unc
59	1952	Inc. Y35	.25	.75	2.50
	1953	7.440	.25	.75	2.50
	1954	7.650	.25	.75	2.50
	1955	8.635	.25	.75	2.50
	1956	11.705	.25	.75	2.50
	1957	15.750	.25	.75	2.50

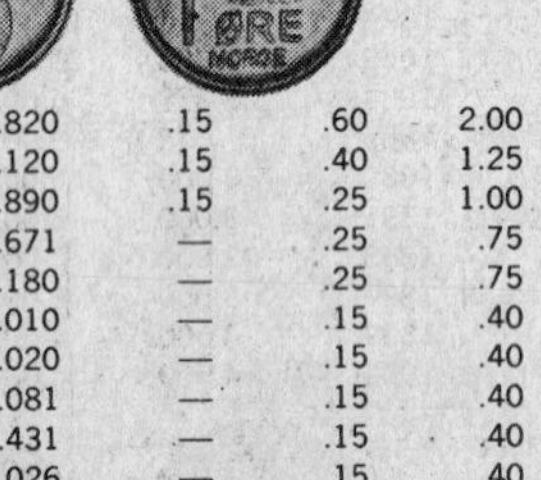

Y#	Date	Mintage	VF	XF	Unc
66	1958	2.820	.15	.60	2.00
	1959	9.120	.15	.40	1.25
	1960	7.890	.15	.25	1.00
	1961	5.671	—	.25	.75
	1962	12.180	—	.25	.75
	1963	8.010	—	.15	.40
	1964	11.020	—	.15	.40
	1965	8.081	—	.15	.40
	1966	12.431	—	.15	.40
	1967	13.026	—	.15	.40
	1968	.126	.35	1.00	2.50
	1969	6.291	—	.15	.25
	1970	6.608	—	.15	.25
	1971	18.966	—	.15	.25
	1972	21.103	—	.15	.25

2 ORE

BRONZE

Y#	Date	Mintage	VF	XF	Unc
20	1876 large date	1.774	5.00	10.00	20.00
	1876 small date	Inc. Ab.	5.00	10.00	20.00
	1877	1.976	4.00	9.00	20.00
	1884	1.000	7.50	15.00	25.00
	1889	1.000	3.50	6.00	17.50
	1891	1.000	3.50	6.00	17.50
	1893	1.000	3.50	6.00	17.50
	1897	1.000	3.50	6.00	17.50
	1899	1.000	3.00	5.00	15.00
	1902	1.005	3.00	5.00	12.00

Y#	Date	Mintage	VF	XF	Unc
31	1906	.500	6.00	15.00	30.00
	1907	.980	3.00	7.50	20.00

Y#	Date	Mintage	VF	XF	Unc
36	1909	.520	6.00	10.00	25.00
	1910	.500	6.00	15.00	35.00
	1911	.195	6.00	15.00	35.00
	1912	.805	6.00	15.00	35.00
36	1913	2.010	2.00	6.00	17.50
	1914	2.990	2.00	6.00	17.50
	1915	Inc. Ab.	4.00	10.00	25.00
	1921	2.073	1.00	5.00	15.00
	1922	2.288	1.00	4.00	15.00
	1923	.745	1.50	6.00	15.00
	1928	2.250	1.00	3.00	9.00
	1929	.750	1.00	3.00	9.00
	1931	1.570	1.00	3.00	9.00
	1932	.630	4.00	10.00	25.00
	1933	.750	1.50	4.00	9.00
	1934	.500	1.50	4.00	9.00
	1935	2.223	.50	1.00	4.50
	1936	4.533	.50	1.00	4.50
	1937	3.790	.50	1.00	4.50
	1938	3.765	.50	1.00	4.50
	1939	4.420	.50	1.00	4.50
	1940	2.655	.50	1.00	4.50
	1946	1.575	.25	.75	2.50
	1947	4.679	.25	.75	2.50
	1948	1.003	1.00	2.00	4.00
	1949	1.455	.25	.75	2.50
	1950	5.790	.25	.75	2.50
	1951	1.054	.25	.75	2.50
	1952	Inc. Ab.	.25	.75	2.50

IRON

Y#	Date	Mintage	VF	XF	Unc
36a	1917	.720	75.00	125.00	200.00
	1918	1.280	40.00	60.00	125.00
	1919	3.365	7.50	15.00	25.00
	1920	2.635	10.00	20.00	35.00

World War II German Occupation

Y#	Date	Mintage	VF	XF	Unc
54	1943	6.575	.60	1.50	3.75
	1944	9.805	.60	1.50	3.75
	1945	2.520	.75	1.75	4.00

BRONZE

Y#	Date	Mintage	VF	XF	Unc
60	1952	Inc. Ab.	.25	.75	2.50
	1953	6.705	.25	.75	2.50
	1954	2.805	.25	.75	2.50
	1955	3.600	.25	.75	2.50
	1956	6.780	.25	.75	2.50
	1957	6.090	.25	.75	2.50

Rev: Small lettering

Y#	Date	Mintage	VF	XF	Unc
67	1958	2.700	1.00	2.00	4.00

Rev: Large lettering

Y#	Date	Mintage	VF	XF	Unc
67a	1959	4.125	.50	1.50	5.00
	1960	3.735	.15	.25	1.00
	1961	4.477	.15	.25	1.00
	1962	6.205	—	.25	1.00
	1963	4.840	—	.25	1.00
	1964	7.250	—	.15	.60
	1965	6.241	—	.15	.60
	1966	10.485	—	.15	.60
	1967	11.993	—	.15	.60
	1968	3.467	—	295.00	360.00
	1969	.316	.15	.40	1.25
	1970	6.794	—	—	.40
	1971	15.462	—	—	.40
	1972	15.898	—	—	.40

5 ORE

BRONZE

Y#	Date	Mintage	VF	XF	Unc
21	1875	.354	25.00	40.00	75.00
	1876	1.647	6.00	15.00	30.00
	1878	.500	15.00	25.00	45.00
	1896	1.000	6.00	15.00	30.00
	1899	.700	6.00	15.00	30.00
	1902	.705	6.00	15.00	30.00

Y#	Date	Mintage	VF	XF	Unc
32	1907	.200	6.00	17.50	35.00

Y#	Date	Mintage	VF	XF	Unc
37	1908	.600	20.00	40.00	75.00
	1911	.480	3.00	10.00	30.00
	1912	.520	4.00	12.00	35.00
	1913	1.000	1.50	6.00	25.00
	1914	1.000	1.50	6.00	25.00
	1915	Inc. Ab.	10.00	20.00	50.00
	1916	.300	7.00	15.00	35.00
	1921	.683	2.00	5.00	30.00
	1922	2.296	2.00	5.00	30.00
	1923	.456	2.50	10.00	35.00
	1928	.848	1.00	6.00	15.00
	1929	.452	2.50	8.00	20.00
	1930	1.292	1.00	4.00	15.00
	1931	.808	1.00	4.00	15.00
	1932	.500	3.00	10.00	20.00
	1933	.300	5.00	15.00	30.00
	1935	.496	1.50	5.00	15.00
	1936	.760	1.00	4.00	15.00
	1937	1.552	.75	1.50	7.00
	1938	1.332	.75	1.50	7.00
	1939	1.370	.75	1.50	7.00
	1940	2.554	.50	1.00	5.00
	1941	3.576	.50	1.00	5.00
	1951	8.128	.50	1.00	5.00
	1952	Inc. Ab.	2.00	5.00	10.00

IRON

Y#	Date	Mintage	VF	XF	Unc
37a	1917	1.700	37.50	60.00	80.00
	1918/7	.432	125.00	200.00	300.00
	1918	Inc. Ab.	125.00	200.00	300.00
	1919	3.464	25.00	40.00	60.00
	1920	1.629	40.00	65.00	90.00

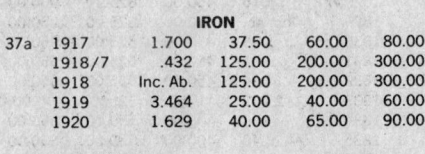

World War II German Occupation

Y#	Date	Mintage	VF	XF	Unc
55	1941	6.608	1.00	3.00	10.00
	1942	10.312	1.00	3.00	8.00
	1943	6.184	2.00	5.00	15.00
	1944	4.256	2.00	5.00	15.00
	1945	.408	75.00	125.00	200.00

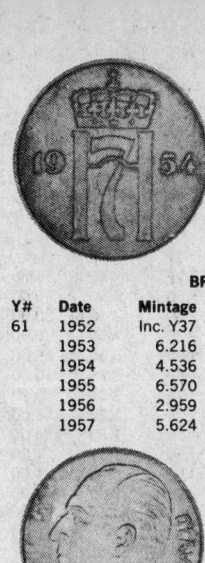

BRONZE

Y#	Date	Mintage	VF	XF	Unc
61	1952	Inc. Y37	.30	.75	3.00
	1953	6.216	.30	.75	3.00
	1954	4.536	.30	.75	3.00
	1955	6.570	.30	.75	3.00
	1956	2.959	.30	.75	3.00
	1957	5.624	.25	.75	3.00

Y#	Date	Mintage	VF	XF	Unc
68	1958	2.205	1.00	3.00	6.00
	1959	3.208	.15	.45	1.75
	1960	5.519	.45	1.00	1.75
	1961	4.554	.15	.45	2.25
	1962	7.764	—	.30	1.00
	1963	3.204	.15	.60	2.25
	1964	6.108	—	.30	1.00
	1965	6.841	—	.15	.50
	1966	8.415	—	.15	.50
	1967	9.071	—	.20	.45
	1968	4.286	—	.15	.40
	1969	4.328	—	.15	.30
	1970	7.351	—	.15	.30
	1971	13.450	—	.15	.30
	1972	19.002	—	.15	.30
	1973	9.584	—	.15	.20

Y#	Date	Mintage	VF	XF	Unc
76	1973	52.886	—	—	.10
	1974	37.150	—	—	.10
	1975	32.479	—	—	.10
	1976	24.233	—	—	.15
	1977	29.645	—	—	.15
	1978	13.838	—	—	—
	1979	—	—	—	—

10 ORE

(=3 Skilling)

.400 SILVER

Y#	Date	Mintage	VF	XF	Unc
14	1874	2.000	25.00	50.00	75.00
	1875	.996	45.00	80.00	150.00

Y#	Date	Mintage	VF	XF	Unc
22	1875	1.008	70.00	125.00	200.00
	1876	1.992	17.50	30.00	60.00
	1877	.588	70.00	100.00	175.00
	1878	.612	45.00	65.00	125.00
	1880	.600	30.00	50.00	100.00
	1882	.760	30.00	50.00	100.00
	1883	1.250	20.00	40.00	70.00
	1888	.500	25.00	45.00	80.00
	1889	.750	20.00	35.00	60.00
	1890	1.000	15.00	30.00	55.00
	1892	2.000	12.00	25.00	50.00
	1894	1.500	12.00	25.00	50.00
	1897	1.500	10.00	20.00	40.00
	1898	2.000	10.00	20.00	40.00
	1899	2.500	10.00	20.00	40.00
	1901	2.021	10.00	20.00	40.00
	1903	1.501	10.00	20.00	40.00

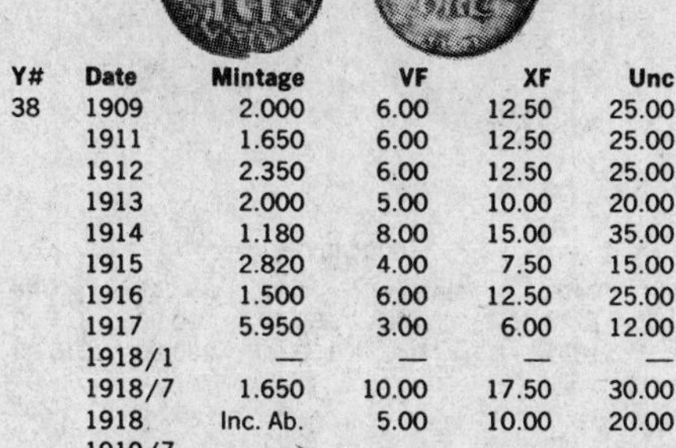

Y#	Date	Mintage	VF	XF	Unc
38	1909	2.000	6.00	12.50	25.00
	1911	1.650	6.00	12.50	25.00
	1912	2.350	6.00	12.50	25.00
	1913	2.000	5.00	10.00	20.00
	1914	1.180	8.00	15.00	35.00
	1915	2.820	4.00	7.50	15.00
	1916	1.500	6.00	12.50	25.00
	1917	5.950	3.00	6.00	12.00
	1918/1	—	—	—	—
	1918/7	1.650	10.00	17.50	30.00
	1918	Inc. Ab.	5.00	10.00	20.00
	1919/7	—	—	—	—
	1919	7.800	3.00	6.00	12.00

COPPER-NICKEL

Y#	Date	Mintage	VF	XF	Unc
46	1920	2.535	10.00	17.50	30.00
	1921	6.465	7.00	12.00	20.00
	1922	3.965	7.00	12.00	20.00
	1923	7.135	15.00	25.00	35.00

Y#	Date	Mintage	VF	XF	Unc
49	1924	12.079	.50	4.50	20.00
	1925	7.051	.50	4.50	20.00
	1926	11.764	.50	4.50	20.00
	1927	.527	6.00	12.00	30.00
	1937	.500	2.00	4.00	10.00
	1938	3.413	.50	1.00	5.00
	1939	1.538	.50	1.00	5.00
	1940	4.800	.50	1.00	5.00
	1941	10.150	.25	.75	4.00
	1945	1.719	.25	.75	5.00
	1946	3.723	.25	.75	3.00
	1947	7.257	.25	.75	2.00
	1948	3.105	.25	.75	2.00
	1949	11.546	.25	.60	1.50
	1951	5.150	.25	.60	1.50

NICKEL-BRASS
World War II Government in exile.

Y#	Date	Mintage	VF	XF	Unc
49a	1942	*6.000	50.00	75.00	125.00

NOTE: All Melted Down Except For 9,667.

ZINC
World War II Nazi Occupation

Y#	Date	Mintage	VF	XF	Unc
56	1941	15.310	1.00	3.00	8.00
	1942	50.388	1.00	2.00	4.50
	1943	13.378	1.00	3.00	8.00
	1944	3.549	6.00	12.00	25.00
	1945	5.646	5.00	10.00	17.50

COPPER-NICKEL

Y#	Date	Mintage	VF	XF	Unc
62	1951	17.400	.15	.45	1.50
	1952	Inc. Ab.	.15	.45	1.50
	1953	7.700	.15	.45	1.50
	1954	10.105	.15	.45	1.50
	1955	9.830	.15	.45	1.50
	1956	10.066	.15	.45	1.50
	1957	22.900	.15	.45	1.50

Rev: Small lettering

Y#	Date	Mintage	VF	XF	Unc
69	1958	1.425	.30	1.00	3.00

Rev: Large lettering

Y#	Date	Mintage	VF	XF	Unc
69a	1959	2.500	.15	.45	1.25
	1960	12.490	.15	.30	.75
	1961	10.386	.15	.30	.75
	1962	16.210	—	.15	.75
	1963	17.560	—	.15	.40
	1964	9.781	—	.15	.40
	1965	10.561	—	.15	.40
	1966	16.610	—	.15	.40
	1967	18.243	—	.15	.40
	1968	24.698	—	.15	.40
	1969	27.157	—	.15	.30
	1970	.639	—	.50	2.00
	1971	8.904	—	—	.45
	1972	24.834	—	—	.30
	1973	22.301	—	—	.20

Y#	Date	Mintage	VF	XF	Unc
77	1974	30.995	—	—	.15
	1975	21.845	—	—	.15
	1976	42.403	—	—	.15
	1977	40.238	—	—	.15
	1978	37.395	—	—	—
	1979	—	—	—	—

25 ORE

.600 SILVER

Y#	Date	Mintage	VF	XF	Unc
23	1876	3.200	20.00	40.00	75.00

Y#	Date	Mintage	VF	XF	Unc
24	1896	.400	25.00	50.00	75.00
	1898	.400	30.00	60.00	100.00
	1899	.600	20.00	35.00	70.00
	1900	.400	20.00	35.00	70.00
	1901	.607	20.00	35.00	70.00
	1902	.612	20.00	35.00	70.00
	1904	.600	20.00	35.00	70.00

Y#	Date	Mintage	VF	XF	Unc
39	1909	.600	17.50	30.00	55.00
	1911	.400	25.00	40.00	70.00
	1912	.200	75.00	125.00	175.00
	1913	.400	20.00	35.00	60.00
	1914	.400	20.00	35.00	60.00
	1915	1.032	15.00	25.00	45.00
	1916	.368	30.00	50.00	75.00
	1917	.400	30.00	50.00	75.00
	1918	.800	10.00	20.00	35.00
	1919	1.600	6.00	10.00	20.00

COPPER-NICKEL

Y#	Date	Mintage	VF	XF	Unc
47	1921	4.800	7.50	15.00	30.00
	1922	4.200	7.50	15.00	30.00
	1923	5.200	22.50	35.00	60.00

Y#	Date	Mintage	VF	XF	Unc
47a	1921	Inc. Y47	2.50	7.50	25.00
	1922	Inc. Y47	2.50	7.50	25.00
	1923	Inc. Y47	2.50	7.50	20.00

Y#	Date	Mintage	VF	XF	Unc
50	1924	4.000	1.20	2.00	20.00
	1927	6.200	1.20	2.50	20.00
	1929	.800	2.25	6.00	25.00
	1939	1.220	.45	1.25	7.00
	1940	1.160	.45	1.25	7.00
	1946	1.850	.45	1.25	3.00
	1947	2.592	.45	1.25	3.00
	1949	2.602	.45	1.25	3.00
	1950	2.800	.45	1.25	3.00

NICKEL-BRASS
World War II Government in exile.

Y#	Date	Mintage	VF	XF	Unc
50a	1942	*2.400	50.00	75.00	125.00

***NOTE:** All melted down except for 10,300 pieces.

ZINC
World War II German Occupation

Y#	Date	Mintage	VF	XF	Unc
57	1943	14.105	2.25	4.00	8.00
	1944	3.031	2.70	5.00	12.00
	1945	3.010	4.50	10.00	20.00

COOPER-NICKEL

Y#	Date	Mintage	VF	XF	Unc
63	1952	4.060	.15	.50	2.00
	1953	3.320	.15	.50	2.00
	1954	3.140	.15	.50	2.00
	1955	2.000	.15	.50	2.00
	1956	3.980	.15	.50	2.00
	1957	7.660	.15	.50	2.00

Y#	Date	Mintage	VF	XF	Unc
70	1958	1.316	—	.65	2.00
	1959	1.184	—	.65	2.00
	1960	3.964	—	.45	1.00
	1961	4.656	—	.45	1.00
	1962	6.304	—	.45	1.00
	1963	3.640	—	.45	1.00
	1964	4.953	—	.15	.50
	1965	2.798	—	.15	.50
	1966	6.075	—	.15	.50
	1967	6.641	.15	.20	.50
	1968	4.963	.10	.15	.30
	1969	12.427	—	.15	.40
	1970	1.545	.10	.30	.90
	1971	5.247	—	.10	.30
	1972	7.929	—	.10	.30
	1973	8.516	—	.10	.30

Y#	Date	Mintage	VF	XF	Unc
78	1974	8.048	—	—	.25
	1975	15.595	—	—	.15
	1976	24.721	—	—	.15
	1977	20.769	—	—	.15
	1978	11.259	—	—	—
	1979	—	—	—	—

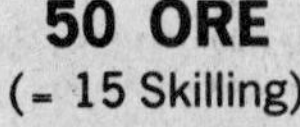

50 ORE
(= 15 Skilling)

.600 SILVER

Y#	Date	Mintage	VF	XF	Unc
15	1874	.160	150.00	200.00	375.00
	1875	.640	150.00	200.00	375.00

Rev: '15 SK.' removed.

Y#	Date	Mintage	VF	XF	Unc
25	1877	.800	35.00	80.00	150.00
	1880	.120	150.00	300.00	400.00
	1885	.100	150.00	300.00	400.00
	1887	.200	70.00	125.00	225.00
	1888	.100	125.00	175.00	300.00
	1889	.200	35.00	75.00	175.00
	1891	.400	30.00	60.00	150.00
	1893	.600	25.00	55.00	150.00
	1895	.200	30.00	60.00	150.00
	1896	.500	25.00	55.00	140.00
	1897	.200	40.00	75.00	175.00
	1898	.300	20.00	60.00	125.00
	1899	.200	20.00	60.00	125.00
	1900	.300	20.00	60.00	125.00
	1901	.404	20.00	60.00	125.00
	1902	.301	20.00	60.00	125.00
	1904	.101	150.00	250.00	400.00

Y#	Date	Mintage	VF	XF	Unc
40	1909	.200	35.00	60.00	110.00
	1911	.200	35.00	60.00	110.00
	1912	.200	60.00	125.00	200.00
	1913	.200	35.00	60.00	110.00
	1914	.800	10.00	20.00	40.00
	1915	.300	30.00	60.00	80.00
	1916	.700	10.00	20.00	40.00
	1918	3.090	6.00	10.00	20.00
	1919	1.219	6.00	10.00	20.00

COPPER-NICKEL

Y#	Date	Mintage	VF	XF	Unc
48	1920	1.236	60.00	90.00	135.00
	1921	7.345	12.50	20.00	30.00
	1922	3.000	12.50	20.00	30.00
	1923	4.540	120.00	150.00	200.00

Y#	Date	Mintage	VF	XF	Unc
48a	1920	Inc. Y48	50.00	90.00	150.00
	1921	Inc. Y48	3.00	6.00	25.00
	1922	Inc. Y48	3.00	6.00	25.00
	1923	Inc. Y48	3.00	6.00	25.00

Y#	Date	Mintage	VF	XF	Unc
51	1926	2.000	2.50	7.50	20.00
	1927	2.502	2.50	7.50	20.00
	1928	1.458	2.50	7.50	20.00
	1929	.600	3.00	6.00	25.00
	1939	.900	1.50	3.75	10.00
	1940	2.193	.75	2.25	6.00
	1941	2.373	.75	2.25	6.00
	1945	1.354	.75	1.50	4.00
	1946	1.533	.50	1.00	4.00
	1947	2.465	.50	1.00	4.00
	1948	5.911	.50	1.00	4.00
	1949	1.030	.50	1.00	4.00

NICKEL-BRASS
World War II Government in exile.

Y#	Date	Mintage	VF	XF	Unc
51a	1942	*1.600	50.00	75.00	125.00

***NOTE:** All melted down except for 9,238.

ZINC
World War II Nazi Occupation

Y#	Date	Mintage	VF	XF	Unc
58	1941	7.761	3.75	7.50	20.00
	1942	7.606	3.75	7.50	15.00
	1943	3.349	25.00	40.00	70.00
	1944	1.542	15.00	30.00	40.00
	1945	.226	200.00	350.00	500.00

COOPER-NICKEL

Y#	Date	Mintage	VF	XF	Unc
64	1953	2.370	.45	1.25	4.00
	1954	.230	1.25	2.00	8.00
	1955	1.930	.30	.60	2.50
	1956	1.630	.30	.60	2.50
	1957	1.800	.30	.60	2.50

Y#	Date	Mintage	VF	XF	Unc
71	1958	1.560	.45	1.00	5.00
	1959	.340	.75	2.00	10.00
	1960	1.584	.15	.30	1.00
	1961	2.425	.15	.30	1.00
	1962	3.064	.15	.30	1.00
	1963	2.168	.15	.30	1.00
	1964	2.692	.15	.30	1.00
	1965	1.248	—	.15	.90
	1966	4.262	—	.15	.60
	1967	4.001	—	.15	.60
	1968	5.431	—	.15	.45
	1969	7.591	—	.15	.45
	1970	.481	—	.50	2.00
	1971	2.489	—	.15	.45
	1972	4.453	—	.15	.45
	1973	3.317	—	.15	.45

Y#	Date	Mintage	VF	XF	Unc
79	1974	8.494	—	—	.40
	1975	10.123	—	—	.35
	1976	15.177	—	—	.35
	1977	18.349	—	—	.35
	1978	15.305	—	—	.35
	1979	—	—	—	—

KRONE

(= 30 Skilling)

.800 SILVER

Y#	Date	Mintage	VF	XF	Unc
16	1875	.600	200.00	300.00	450.00

Y#	Date	Mintage	VF	XF	Unc
26	1877	1.000	40.00	100.00	225.00
	1878	.060	350.00	500.00	1000.
	1879	.140	100.00	175.00	325.00
	1881	.080	100.00	175.00	325.00
	1882	.120	100.00	175.00	325.00
	1885	.100	100.00	175.00	325.00
	1887	.100	100.00	175.00	325.00
	1888	.075	100.00	175.00	325.00
	1889	.200	50.00	110.00	200.00
	1890	.200	50.00	110.00	200.00
	1892	.150	60.00	125.00	225.00
	1893	.100	60.00	125.00	225.00
	1894	.100	40.00	100.00	200.00
	1895	.100	40.00	100.00	200.00
	1897	.250	40.00	100.00	200.00
	1898	.150	40.00	100.00	200.00
	1900	.250	35.00	75.00	150.00
	1901	.152	35.00	75.00	150.00
	1904	.100	100.00	175.00	325.00

Y#	Date	Mintage	VF	XF	Unc
41	1908 crossed hammers on shield				
		.180	40.00	70.00	120.00
	1908 crossed hammers off shield				
		.170	40.00	70.00	120.00
	1910	.100	75.00	150.00	300.00
	1912	.200	60.00	110.00	225.00
	1913	.230	50.00	75.00	125.00
	1914	.602	20.00	45.00	75.00
	1915	.498	20.00	45.00	75.00
	1916	.400	25.00	50.00	90.00
	1917	.600	20.00	40.00	75.00

COPPER-NICKEL

Y#	Date	Mintage	VF	XF	Unc
52	1925	8.686	1.50	6.00	25.00
	1926	1.939	1.50	6.00	25.00
	1927	1.000	1.50	6.00	25.00
	1936	.700	3.00	7.50	25.00
	1937	1.000	2.25	5.00	25.00
	1938	.926	2.00	3.50	20.00
	1939	2.253	1.00	2.00	15.00
	1940	3.890	1.00	2.00	15.00
	1946	5.499	.70	2.00	6.00
	1947	.802	1.20	3.00	15.00
	1949	7.846	.60	1.50	5.00
	1950	9.942	.60	1.50	5.00
	1951	4.761	.60	1.50	5.00

Y#	Date	Mintage	VF	XF	Unc
65	1951	3.819	.50	1.25	5.00
	1953	1.465	.45	1.00	3.00
	1954	3.045	.45	.75	2.50
	1955	1.970	.45	.75	2.50
	1956	4.300	.45	.75	2.50
	1957	7.630	.45	.75	2.50

Y#	Date	Mintage	VF	XF	Unc
72	1958	.540	.60	5.00	15.00
	1959	4.450	—	3.00	7.00
	1960	1.790	—	1.00	5.00
	1961	3.934	—	1.00	5.00
	1962	6.015	—	1.00	5.00
	1963	4.677	—	.75	3.00
	1964	3.469	—	.45	2.00
	1965	3.222	—	.45	2.00
	1966	3.084	—	.45	1.00
	1967	6.680	—	.25	.45
	1968	6.149	—	.25	.45
	1969	5.186	—	.25	.45
	1970	8.637	—	.25	.45
	1971	10.258	—	.25	.45
	1972	13.197	—	.25	.45
	1973	9.140	—	.25	.45

Y#	Date	Mintage	VF	XF	Unc
80	1974	16.537	—	.25	.75
	1975	26.044	—	.25	.45
	1976	35.927	—	.25	.45
	1977	24.797	—	.25	.45
	1978	23.036	—	—	—
	1979	—	—	—	—

2 KRONER

.800 SILVER

Y#	Date	Mintage	VF	XF	Unc
27	1878	.300	60.00	200.00	350.00
	1885	.025	350.00	600.00	1200.
	1887	.025	350.00	600.00	1200.
	1888	.025	350.00	600.00	1200.
	1890	.100	75.00	150.00	300.00
	1892	.050	125.00	200.00	350.00
	1893	.075	75.00	150.00	300.00
	1894	.075	75.00	150.00	300.00
	1897	.050	80.00	165.00	325.00
	1898	.050	80.00	165.00	325.00
	1900	.125	50.00	135.00	200.00
	1902	.153	50.00	135.00	200.00
	1904	.076	100.00	175.00	300.00

Norway Independence
Obv: Large shield.

Y#	Date	Mintage	VF	XF	Unc
33	1906	.100	25.00	40.00	70.00

Obv: Smaller shield.

Y#	Date	Mintage	VF	XF	Unc
33a	1907	.055	50.00	75.00	120.00

Border Watch
Rev: Crossed rifles.

Y#	Date	Mintage	VF	XF	Unc
34	1907	.028	175.00	225.00	300.00

Y#	Date	Mintage	VF	XF	Unc
42	1908	.200	35.00	60.00	120.00
	1910	.150	60.00	100.00	150.00
	1912	.150	45.00	70.00	125.00
	1913	.270	30.00	50.00	80.00
	1914	.255	30.00	50.00	80.00
	1915	.225	30.00	50.00	80.00
	1916	.250	75.00	120.00	175.00
	1917	.378	17.50	35.00	60.00

Constitution Centennial

Y#	Date	Mintage	VF	XF	Unc
45	1914	.226	15.00	25.00	45.00

5 KRONER

COPPER-NICKEL

Y#	Date	Mintage	VF	XF	Unc
73	1963	7.074	1.25	2.00	10.00
	1964	7.346	—	1.50	5.00
	1965	2.233	—	2.00	8.00
	1966	2.502	—	2.00	8.00
	1967	.583	—	2.00	9.00
	1968	1.813	—	1.50	5.00
	1969	2.404	—	1.50	5.00
	1970	.202	—	4.00	8.00
	1971	.178	—	4.00	8.00
	1972	2.281	—	1.25	1.50
	1973	2.778	—	1.25	1.50

Y#	Date	Mintage	VF	XF	Unc
81	1974	1.983	—	1.00	1.25
	1975	2.946	—	1.00	1.25
	1976	9.056	—	1.00	1.25
	1977	4.443	—	1.00	1.25
	1978	5.853	—	—	—
	1979	—	—	—	—

100th Anniversary of Krone System

Y#	Date	Mintage	VF	XF	Unc
82	1975	1.192	—	1.25	3.00

150th Anniversary Emmigration to America

Y#	Date	Mintage	VF	XF	Unc
83	1975	1.223	—	1.25	3.00

350th Anniversary of Norwegian Army

Y#	Date	Mintage	VF	XF	Unc
84	1978	2.990	—	1.25	2.50

10 KRONER
(= 2-1/2 Speciedaler)

.900 GOLD

Y#	Date	Mintage	VF	XF	Unc
17	1874	.024	800.00	1100.	1400.

Y#	Date	Mintage	VF	XF	Unc
28	1877	.020	750.00	1000.	1250.
	1902	.025	400.00	650.00	900.00

Y#	Date	Mintage	VF	XF	Unc
43	1910	.053	300.00	400.00	500.00

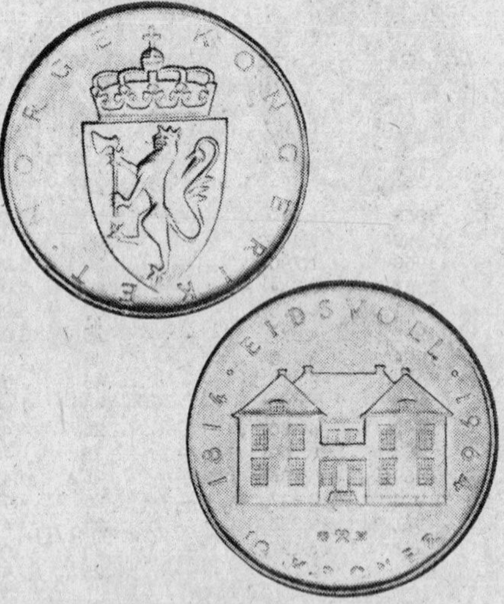

21.0000 gm. .900 SILVER, .6077 oz ASW
Constitution Sesquicentennial

Y#	Date	Mintage	VF	XF	Unc
74	1964	1.026	Bv	Bv	20.00

Reeded edge

Y#	Date	Mintage	VF	XF	Unc
74a	1964	.382	—	—	—

20 KRONER
(= 5 Speciedaler)

.900 GOLD

Y#	Date	Mintage	VF	XF	Unc
18	1874	.198	300.00	500.00	700.00
	1875	.105	300.00	500.00	700.00
29	1876	.109	375.00	475.00	650.00
	1877	.038	375.00	450.00	600.00
	1878	.139	375.00	450.00	600.00
	1879	.046	375.00	450.00	600.00
	1883	.036	2000.	3000.	4000.
	1886	.101	375.00	450.00	600.00
	1902	.050	375.00	450.00	600.00

Y#	Date	Mintage	VF	XF	Unc
44	1910	.250	250.00	350.00	450.00

25 KRONER

29.0000 gm. .875 SILVER, .8159 oz ASW
25th Anniversary of Liberation

Y#	Date	Mintage	VF	XF	Unc
75	1970	1.204	Bv	Bv	25.00

50 KRONER

27.0000 gm. .925 SILVER, .8030 oz ASW
75th Birthday of King Olav V

Y#	Date	Mintage	VF	XF	Unc
85	1978	.800	Bv	Bv	25.00

200 KRONER

.625 SILVER
35th Anniversary of Liberation

Y#	Date	Mintage	VF	XF	Unc
86	1980	—	—	—	—

NCLT ISSUES

MINT SETS

KM#	Date	Mintage	Identification	Issue Price	Mkt. Val.
S1	1963(8)	370	Y66,67a,68,69a,70-73	—	100.00
S2	1964(8)	1,260	Y66,67a,68,69a,70-73	—	50.00
S3	1965(8)	1,800	Y66,67a,68,69a,70-73	—	80.00
S4	1966(8)	1,400	Y66,67a,68,69a,70-73	—	90.00
S5	1967(8)	2,490	Y66,67a,68,69a,70-73	—	80.00
S6	1968(8)	3,467	Y66,67a,68,69a,70-73	—	425.00
S7	1969(8)	10,590	Y66,67a,68,69a,70-73	—	20.00
S8	1970(8)	9,316	Y66,67a,68,69a,70-73	—	35.00
S9	1971(8)	6,065	Y66,67a,68,69a,70-73	—	35.00
S10	1972(8)	12,984	Y66,67a,68,69a,70-73	—	15.00
S11	1973(7)	20.175	Y68,69a,70-73	—	9.00
S12	1974(6)	39.970	Y76-81	—	6.00
S13	1975(6)	35,494	Y76-81	5.00	12.00
S14	1976(6)	30,000	Y76-81	5.00	6.00
S15	1977(6)	30,000	Y76-81	—	7.50
S16	1978(6)	30,000	Y76-81, sandhill case	—	7.50
S17	1978(6)	5,000	Y76-81, plastic case	—	10.00
S18	1979(6)	—	Y76-81	—	10.00

PATTERNS

KM#	Date	Mintage	Identification	Mkt.Val.
1	1958	6	1 Ore	—

Listings For

NOVA SCOTIA: refer to Canada

OMAN

The Sultanate of Oman (formerly Muscat and Oman), an independent monarchy located in the southeastern part of the Arabian Peninsula, has an area of 115,800 sq. mi. (300,000 sq. km.) and a population of 820,000. Capital: Muscat. The economy is based on agriculture, herding and petroleum. Petroleum products, dates, fish and hides are exported.

The first European contact with Muscat and Oman was made by the Portuguese who captured Muscat, the capital and chief port, in 1508. They occupied the city, utilizing it as a naval base and factory and holding it against land and sea attacks by Arabs and Persians until finally ejected by local Arabs in 1650. It was next occupied by the Persians who maintained control until 1741, when it was taken by Ahmed ibn Sa'id of the present ruling family. Muscat and Oman was the most powerful state in Arabia during the first half of the 19th century, until weakened by the persistent attack of interior nomadic tribes. British influence, initiated by the signing of a treaty of friendship with the Sultanate in 1798, remains a dominant fact of the civil and military phases of the government, although Britain recognizes the Sultanate as a sovereign state and there is no colonial relationship between them.

Sultan Said bin Taimur was overthrown by his son, Qabus bin Said, on July 23, 1970. The new sultan changed the nation's name to Sultanate of Oman.

MUSCAT & OMAN

RULERS

Fessul Bin Turkee,
AH1285-1332 (AD1888-1913)
Sa'id Bin Taimur,
AH1351-1390 (AD1932-1970)
Qabus Bin Sa'id, AH1390- (AD1970-)

MONETARY SYSTEM

(Until 1970)
4 Baisa = 1 Anna
64 Baisa = 1 Rupee
200 Baisa = 1 Riyal
(Commencing 1970)
1000 Baisa = 1 Riyal

1/12 ANNA

COPPER

Y#	Date	Mintage	VG	Fine	VF	XF
1	AH1311	—	25.00	35.00	60.00	100.00

1/4 ANNA

COPPER

Y#	Date	Mintage	Good	VG	Fine	VF
2	AH1311	—	6.00	10.00	15.00	25.00

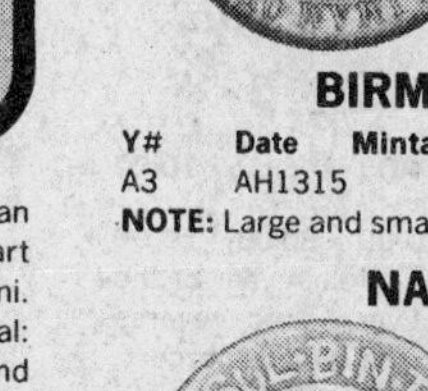

BIRMINGHAM MINT

Y#	Date	Mintage	Good	VG	Fine	VF
A3	AH1315	—	.20	.50	.75	1.25

NOTE: Large and small inscriptions.

NATIVE ISSUES

Y#	Date	Mintage	Good	VG	Fine	VF
3	AH1312	—	2.00	3.25	5.00	8.50

Y#	Date	Mintage	Good	VG	Fine	VF
3.1	AH1312	—	2.50	4.25	6.00	10.00

Y#	Date	Mintage	Good	VG	Fine	VF
3.2	AH1312	—	—	—	—	—
	1313	—	2.50	4.25	6.00	10.00

Y#	Date	Mintage	Good	VG	Fine	VF
3.3	AH1313	—	2.50	4.25	6.00	10.00

Y#	Date	Mintage	Good	VG	Fine	VF
3.4	AH1314	—	3.00	5.00	7.00	12.50

Y#	Date	Mintage	Good	VG	Fine	VF
3.5	AH1315	—	2.00	3.25	5.00	8.50

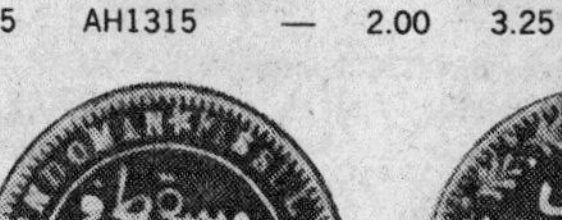

3.6 AH5131 error with date retrograde

Y#	Date	Mintage	Good	VG	Fine	VF
3.6		—	—	—	—	—

Y#	Date	Mintage	Good	VG	Fine	VF
3.7	AH1316	—	2.50	4.00	6.00	10.00
3.8	AH1316	—	12.50	20.00	30.00	50.00

NOTE: There are numerous varieties of each year of the native issues, varying in both obverse and reverse legends, in the presence or absence of wreath borders, etc.

COUNTERSTAMP ISSUES

1/4 ANNA

COPPER

c/s: ST in Arabic on 1/4 Anna, Y#3.

Y#	Date	Mintage	Good	VG	Fine	VF
A4	ND(1311-18)	—	15.00	25.00	40.00	60.00

MONETARY REFORM

2 BAISA

COPPER-NICKEL

Y#	Date	Mintage	Fine	VF	XF	Unc
7	AH1365	—	.50	.75	1.00	2.00
	1365	—	—	—	Proof	4.00

NOTE: Coins of AH1365 have the monetary unit spelled BAIZA; on all other coins it is spelled BAISA.

NOTE: Most of the proof issues of the AH1359 and 1365 dated coins of Muscat & Oman now on the market are probably later restrikes produced by the Bombay Mint.

BRONZE

Y#	Date	Mintage	Fine	VF	XF	Unc
18	AH1390	2.000	—	.15	.25	.40
	1390	—	—	—	Proof	1.50

3 BAISA

BRONZE, 20mm

Y#	Date	Mintage	Fine	VF	XF	Unc
13	AH1378	8.000	.50	.75	1.25	2.00

Size reduced, 18mm

Y#	Date	Mintage	Fine	VF	XF	Unc
14	AH1380	10.000	.35	.50	.60	.75
	1381	Inc. Ab.	.25	.35	.60	1.00

5 BAISA

COPPER-NICKEL

Y#	Date	Mintage	Fine	VF	XF	Unc
8	AH1365	—	1.00	1.25	1.50	2.00
	1365	—	—	—	Proof	5.00

Y#	Date	Mintage	Fine	VF	XF	Unc
16	AH1380	5.000	.40	.60	1.00	1.50
	1381	Inc. Ab.	.40	.60	1.00	1.50

BRONZE

Y#	Date	Mintage	Fine	VF	XF	Unc
19	AH1390	2.000	—	.10	.15	.25
	1390	—	—	—	Proof	2.00

10 BAISA

COPPER-NICKEL

Y#	Date	Mintage	Fine	VF	XF	Unc
4	AH1359	—	2.50	3.25	4.00	5.00
	1359	—	—	—	Proof	7.50

Struck for use in Dhofar province.

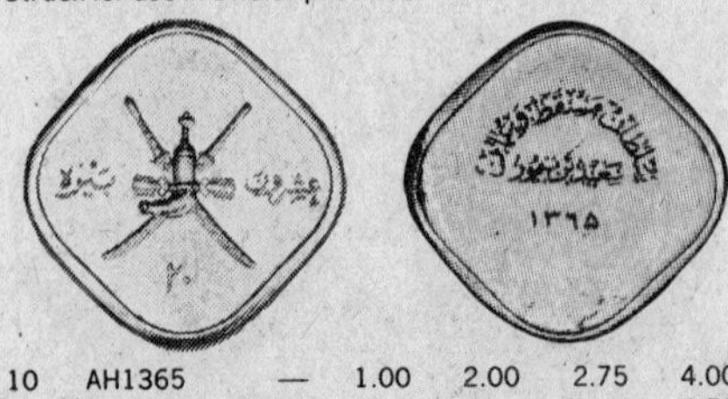

BRONZE

Y#	Date	Mintage	Fine	VF	XF	Unc
20	AH1390	2.000	—	.15	.20	.35
	1390	—	—	—	Proof	2.00

20 BAISA

COPPER-NICKEL

Y#	Date	Mintage	Fine	VF	XF	Unc
5	AH1359	—	3.00	5.00	7.50	10.50
	1359	—	—	—	Proof	13.50

Struck for use in Dhofar province.

Y#	Date	Mintage	Fine	VF	XF	Unc
10	AH1365	—	1.00	2.00	2.75	4.00
	1365	—	—	—	Proof	6.50

Mule: Obv. of Y#5 with the rev. of Y#10.

Y#	Date	Mintage	Fine	VF	XF	Unc
A11	AH1359/1365	—	—	—	—	17.50

25 BAISA

COPPER-NICKEL

Y#	Date	Mintage	Fine	VF	XF	Unc
21	AH1390	—	—	.15	.30	.50
	1390	—	—	—	Proof	2.50

.916 GOLD

Y#	Date	Mintage	Fine	VF	XF	Unc
21a	AH1390	350 pcs.	—	—	Proof	100.00

NOTE: An issue of 250 circulation strikes and 50 proof strikes of Y#21a, 22a, and 23a in gold, and bearing the date AH1392, were reported to have been struck by the Royal Mint in 1973, but no specimens of this issue bearing the date AH1392 have yet been reported.

50 BAISA

COPPER-NICKEL

Y#	Date	Mintage	Fine	VF	XF	Unc
6	AH1359	—	4.50	6.50	8.50	12.50
	1359	—	—	—	Proof	16.50

Struck for use in Dhofar province.

Y#	Date	Mintage	Fine	VF	XF	Unc
22	AH1390	1.600	—	.30	.50	.75
	1390	—	—	—	Proof	4.00

.916 GOLD

Y#	Date	Mintage	Fine	VF	XF	Unc
22a	AH1390	350 pcs.	—	—	Proof	125.00

See note after Y21a.

100 BAISA

COPPER-NICKEL

Y#	Date	Mintage	Fine	VF	XF	Unc
23	AH1390	1.000	—	.40	.60	1.00
	1390	—	—	—	Proof	5.00

.916 GOLD

Y#	Date	Mintage	Fine	VF	XF	Unc
23a	AH1390	350 pcs.	—	—	Proof	150.00

See note after Y21a.

1/2 DHOFARI RIYAL

SILVER

Y#	Date	Mintage	Fine	VF	XF	Unc
11	AH1367	—	12.50	15.00	20.00	27.50
	1367	—	—	—	Proof	40.00

1/2 SAIDI RIYAL

.500 SILVER

Y#	Date	Mintage	Fine	VF	XF	Unc
15	AH1380	.396	3.00	3.50	4.75	7.50
	1381	.454	3.00	3.50	4.75	6.50

.916 GOLD, 33mm, 25.6gm.

15a	AH1381	100 pcs.	—	—	Proof	550.00
	1382	100 pcs.	—	—	Proof	550.00
	1390	350 pcs.	—	—	Proof	500.00

An additional 224 proof pieces are reported to have been struck in gold bearing the date AH1391, but none have yet been observed.

SAIDI RIYAL

SILVER

12	AH1378	1.400	BV	BV	15.00	22.50

NOTE: According to mint reports 1,000,000 pcs. were struck in 1958-59 in .833 silver, plus 400,000 in 1963-64 in .500 silver, all of the same weight and all dated AH1378.

.916 GOLD 33.7mm, 46.65 gm.

12a	AH1378	100 pcs.	—	—	Proof	1000.
	1390	350 pcs.	—	—	Proof	900.00

An additional 224 proof pieces are reported struck in gold with date AH1391, but none have been seen to date.

15 SAIDI RIYALS

.916 GOLD, 7.99 gm.

17	AH1381	2,100	BV	160.00	170.00	200.00

An additional 460 pieces reported struck in 1971 and 1972, bearing the date AH1391.

NCLT ISSUES

MINT SETS

KM#	Date	Mintage	Identification	Issue Price	Mkt. Val.
S1	AH1390(6)	5,500	Y18-Y23	—	3.50

PROOF SETS

STANDARD METALS

KM#	Date	Mintage	Identification	Issue Price	Mkt. Val.
101	AH1359,65,67	(6)	Y4,5,6,7,8,11	—	75.00
102	AH1359,65,67	(6)	Y4,6,7,8,10,11	—	70.00
103	AH1390(6)	2,102	Y18-23	11.00	16.50

NOTE: Sets of 5 coins comprising Y4,6,7,8 and 10 or A11 have been marketed in recent years. They are Bombay mint restrikes.

NOTE: A series of 3 silver and 4 gold coins were produced in 1971/1391 and are inscribed STATE OF OMAN (Dawlat Uman) (H8-H14, and sets H15-H17). These were issued by the exile government of Imam Ghalib ibn Ali in Dammam, Saudi Arabia, and distributed from a post box in Amman, Jordan. The Imamate had enjoyed effective autonomy in the interior of Oman from 1920-54, at which time the Sultan resumed direct control. Imamist forces in Oman were finally driven out in 1959. The Imam has been in exile since 1955.

OMAN, SULTANATE

5 BAIZA

BRONZE

Y#	Date	Year	Mintage	VF	XF	Unc
8	AH1395	(1975)	2.000	—	.10	.25

10 BAIZA

BRONZE
F.A.O. Issue

1	AH1395	(1975)	3.000	—	.15	.30

9	AH1395	(1975)	1.000	—	.15	.30

25 BAIZA

.917 GOLD, 18mm, 5.96 gm.

2	AH1394	—	250 pcs.	—	—	—

NOTE: Struck for presentation purposes.

COPPER-NICKEL

10	AH1395	(1975)	2.000	—	.25	.50

.917 GOLD
Similar to 10 Baiza, y#9.

11	AH1395	(1975)	250 pcs.	—	—	—

50 BAIZA

.917 GOLD, 24mm, 12.89 gm.

3	AH1394	—	250 pcs.	—	—	—

NOTE: Struck for presentation purposes.

COPPER-NICKEL

Y#	Date	Year	Mintage	VF	XF	Unc
12	AH1395	(1975)	2.000	—	.35	.75

.917 GOLD
Similar to 10 Baiza, y#9.

13	AH1395	(1975)	250 pcs.	—	—	—

100 BAIZA

.917 GOLD, 28.5mm, 22.74 gm.

4	AH1394	(1974)	250 pcs.	—	—	—
	1395	(1975)	250 pcs.	—	—	—

NOTE: Struck for presentation purposes.

1/2 OMANI RIAL

.917 GOLD, 33mm, 25.6 gm.

5	AH1394	—	250 pcs.	—	—	—

NOTE: Struck for presentation purposes.

COPPER-NICKEL
F.A.O. Issue

17	A1398	1978	.015	—	2.00	3.50

OMANI RIAL

.917 GOLD, 38.7mm, 46.65 gm.

Y#	Date	Year	Mintage	VF	XF	Unc
6	AH1394	—	250 pcs.	—	Proof	325.00

NOTE: Struck for presentation purposes.

15.000 gm., .500 SILVER, .2412 oz ASW
F.A.O. Issue

Y#	Date	Year	Mintage	VF	XF	Unc
18	AH1398	1978	.015	—	7.50	10.00

2-1/2 OMANI RIALS

28.5000 gm., .925 SILVER, .8476 oz ASW
Conservation Series

Y#	Date	Year	Mintage	VF	XF	Unc
14	AH1397	(1977)	—	—	25.00	30.00
	1397	(1977)	.010	—	Proof	35.00

5 OMANI RIALS

35.4000 gm., .925 SILVER, 1.0529 oz ASW
Conservation Series
Obv Similar to 2-1/2 Omani Rials, y#14.

Y#	Date	Year	Mintage	VF	XF	Unc
15	AH1397	(1977)	—	—	31.00	40.00
	1397	(1977)	.010	—	Proof	50.00

15 OMANI RIALS

.917 GOLD, 22mm, 7.99 gm.

Y#	Date	Year	Mintage	VF	XF	Unc
7	AH1394	—	300 pcs.	—	—	

NOTE: Struck for presentation purposes.

75 OMANI RIALS

.900 GOLD
Conservation Series

Y#	Date	Year	Mintage	VF	XF	Unc
16	AH1397	(1977)	.010	BV	BV	650.00
	1397	(1977)	1,000	—	Proof	800.00

NCLT ISSUES

PROOF SETS

STANDARD METALS UNLESS OTHERWISE NOTED

KM#	Date	Mintage	Identification	Issue Price	Mkt. Val.
101	1977(3)	—	Y14-16	780.00	875.00
102	1977(2)	—	Y14,15	60.00	75.00

PAKISTAN

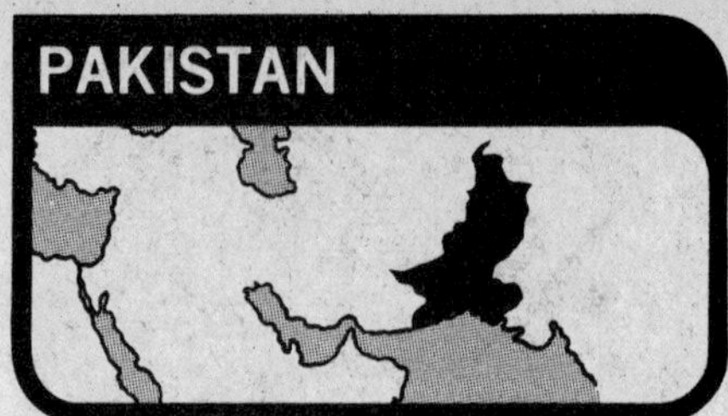

The Islamic Republic of Pakistan, located on the Indian sub-continent between India and Afghanistan, has an area of 307,374 sq. mi. (796,095 sq. km.) and a population of 74 million. Capital: Islamabad. Pakistan is mainly an agricultural land. Yarn, cotton, rice, and leather are exported.

Afghan and Turkish intrusions into northern India between the 11th and 18th centuries resulted in large numbers of Indians being converted to Islam. The idea of a separate Moslem state independent of Hindu India developed in the 1930's and was agreed to by Britain in 1946. The Islamic majority areas of India, consisting of the separate geographic entities known as East and West Pakistan, achieved self-government as Pakistan, with dominion status in the British Commonwealth, when the British withdrew from India on Aug. 14, 1947, and became a republic in 1956. When a basic constitutional crisis initiated by the election of Dec. 1, 1970 - the first direct general election in Pakistani history - could not be resolved by the leaders of East and West Pakistan, the East Pakistanis seceded from the Islamic Republic of Pakistan (March 26, 1971) and formed the independent People's Republic of Bangladesh.

MONETARY SYSTEM

3 Pies = 1 Pice
4 Pice = 1 Anna
16 Annas = 1 Rupee

PIE

BRONZE

Y#	Date	Mintage	Fine	VF	XF	Unc
8	1951	2.950	.10	.20	.30	.50
	1951	—	—	—	Proof	1.50
	1953	.110	.10	.40	.60	1.00
	1953	—	—	—	Proof	1.00
	1955	.211	.10	.40	.60	1.00
	1956	3.390	.10	.15	.25	.35

PICE

BRONZE

Y#	Date	Mintage	Fine	VF	XF	Unc
1	1948	101.070	.10	.15	.20	.40
	1948	—	—	—	Proof	1.50
	1949	25.740	.10	.15	.20	.35
	1951	14.050	.10	.15	.20	.40
	1952	41.680	.10	.15	.20	.35

NICKEL-BRASS

Y#	Date	Mintage	Fine	VF	XF	Unc
9	1953	47.540	.10	.15	.20	.25
	1953	—	—	—	Proof	1.25
	1955	31.280	.10	.15	.20	.25
	1956	9.710	.15	.20	.25	.35
	1957	57.790	.10	.15	.20	.25
	1958	52.470	.10	.15	.20	.25
	1959	41.620	.10	.15	.20	.25

1/2 ANNA

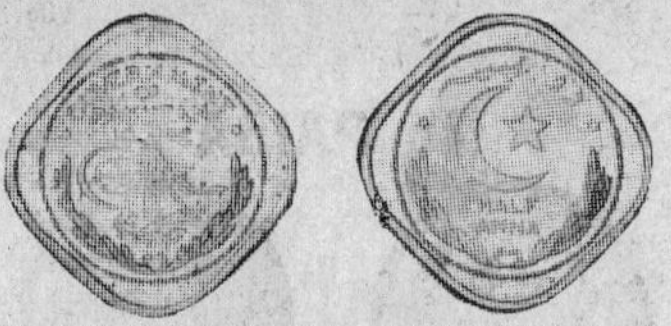

COPPER-NICKEL

Y#	Date	Mintage	Fine	VF	XF	Unc
2	1948	73.920	.10	.15	.20	.25
	1948	—	—	—	Proof	1.50
	1949 dot after date	—				
		16.940	.20	.25	.35	.50
	1951	75.360	.10	.15	.20	.25

NICKEL-BRASS

Y#	Date	Mintage	Fine	VF	XF	Unc
10	1953	8.350	.10	.20	.25	.35
	1953	—	—	—	Proof	1.25
	1955	17.310	.10	.15	.20	.30
	1958	38.250	.10	.15	.20	.25

ANNA

COPPER-NICKEL

Y#	Date	Mintage	Fine	VF	XF	Unc
3	1948	73.460	.10	.20	.30	.40
	1948	—	—	—	Proof	1.50
	1949	11.140	.10	.20	.25	.35
	1949 dot after date	—				
		Inc. w/Y#3a	.15	.25	.30	.40
	1951	40.800	.10	.20	.25	.35
	1952	15.430	.10	.20	.25	.35

Y#	Date	Mintage	Fine	VF	XF	Unc
3a	1950	94.830	2.00	3.75	5.50	8.50

Y#	Date	Mintage	Fine	VF	XF	Unc
11	1953	9.350	.10	.15	.20	.30
	1953	—	—	—	Proof	1.50
	1954	35.360	.10	.15	.20	.25
	1955	6.230	.10	.15	.20	.30
	1956	4.580	.10	.15	.20	.35
	1957	12.500	.10	.15	.20	.25
	1958	44.320	.10	.15	.20	.25

2 ANNAS

COPPER-NICKEL

Y#	Date	Mintage	Fine	VF	XF	Unc
4	1948	55.930	.15	.25	.35	.60
	1948	—	—	—	Proof	1.50
	1949	19.720	.15	.25	.35	.60
	1949 dot after date	—				
4		Inc. w/Y#4a	.20	.30	.40	.75
	1951	33.130	.15	.25	.35	.60

Y#	Date	Mintage	Fine	VF	XF	Unc
4a	1950	21.190	3.50	5.00	7.00	11.50

Y#	Date	Mintage	Fine	VF	XF	Unc
12	1953	7.910	.10	.15	.20	.50
	1953	—	—	—	Proof	1.50
	1954	5.740	.10	.15	.20	.50
	1955	6.230	.10	.15	.20	.50
	1956	1.370	.10	.20	.35	.75
	1957	2.570	.10	.15	.30	.60
	1958	6.200	.10	.15	.20	.50
	1959	8.010	.10	.15	.20	.50

1/4 RUPEE

NICKEL

Y#	Date	Mintage	Fine	VF	XF	Unc
5	1948	52.680	.20	.30	.40	.65
	1948	—	—	—	Proof	2.00
	1949	46.000	.20	.30	.35	.40
	1951	19.120	.20	.30	.35	.40

Y#	Date	Mintage	Fine	VF	XF	Unc
5a	1950	19.400	11.50	16.50	30.00	50.00

1/2 RUPEE

NICKEL

Y#	Date	Mintage	Fine	VF	XF	Unc
6	1948	33.260	.40	.60	.75	1.00
	1948	—	—	—	Proof	1.90
	1949	20.300	.40	.60	.75	1.00
	1951	11.430	.40	.60	.75	1.00

RUPEE

NICKEL

Y#	Date	Mintage	Fine	VF	XF	Unc
7	1948	46.200	.75	1.25	2.00	3.00
	1948	—	—	—	Proof	4.50
	1949	37.100	.75	1.25	2.00	3.00

DECIMAL COINAGE

100 Paisa (Pice) = 1 Rupee

PICE

BRONZE

Y#	Date	Mintage	Fine	VF	XF	Unc
13	1961	74.910	.10	.20	.25	.35

PAISA

BRONZE

Y#	Date	Mintage	Fine	VF	XF	Unc
13a	1961	134.650	—	.10	.15	.20
	1961	—	—	—	Proof	1.50
	1962	149.380	—	.10	.15	.20
	1963	127.810	—	.10	.15	.20

Y#	Date	Mintage	Fine	VF	XF	Unc
18	1964	39.890	.10	.25	.50	1.00
	1964	—	—	—	Proof	1.50
	1965	69.660	.10	.25	.50	1.00

NICKEL-BRASS

Y#	Date	Mintage	Fine	VF	XF	Unc
18a	1965	32.950	—	.10	.15	.20
	1966	179.370	—	.10	.15	.20

ALUMINUM

Y#	Date	Mintage	Fine	VF	XF	Unc
22	1967	170.070	—	—	.10	.15
	1968	—	—	—	.10	.15
	1969	—	—	—	.10	.15
	1970	204.606	—	—	.10	.15
	1971	191.880	—	—	.10	.15
	1972	108.510	—	—	.10	.15
	1973	Inc. Ab.	—	—	.10	.15

F.A.O. Issue

Y#	Date	Mintage	Fine	VF	XF	Unc
26	1974	14.230	—	—	—	.10
	1975	43.000	—	—	—	.10
	1976	49.180	—	—	—	.10
	1977	62.750	—	—	—	.10
	1978	19.990	—	—	—	.10
	1979	—	—	—	—	.10

2 PAISA

BRONZE

Y#	Date	Mintage	Fine	VF	XF	Unc
19	1964	67.660	.10	.15	.20	.25
	1964	—	—	.15	Proof	1.50
	1965	27.880	.10	.15	.20	.25
	1966	50.590	.10	.15	.20	.25

ALUMINUM

Y#	Date	Mintage	Fine	VF	XF	Unc
23	1966	11.940	.10	.15	.20	.25
	1967	73.970	—	.10	.15	.20
	1968	—	—	.10	.15	.20

Y#	Date	Mintage	Fine	VF	XF	Unc
19a	1968	—	—	—	.10	.15
	1969	—	—	—	.10	.15
	1970	24.401	—	—	.10	.15
	1971	10.140	—	—	.10	.15
	1972	4.040	—	.10	.15	.25
	1974	3.600	—	.10	.15	.25

F.A.O. Issue

Y#	Date	Mintage	Fine	VF	XF	Unc
27	1974	3.600	—	—	.10	.15
	1975	4.020	—	—	.10	.15
	1976	5.750	—	—	.10	.15

5 PICE

NICKEL-BRASS

Y#	Date	Mintage	Fine	VF	XF	Unc
14	1961	40.050	—	.10	.15	.20
	1961	—	—	—	Proof	1.50

5 PAISA

NICKEL-BRASS

Y#	Date	Mintage	Fine	VF	XF	Unc
14a	1961	40.790	—	—	.10	.20
	1961	—	—	—	Proof	1.50
	1962	48.200	—	—	.10	.20
	1963	45.020	—	—	.10	.20

Y#	Date	Mintage	Fine	VF	XF	Unc
20	1964	82.730	—	—	.10	.15
	1965	72.570	—	—	.10	.15
	1966	32.900	—	—	.10	.15
	1967	24.470	—	—	.10	.15
	1968	—	—	.10	.15	.30
	1969	5.690	—	.10	.15	.30
	1970	24.655	—	—	.10	.25
	1971	23.860	—	—	.10	.25
	1972	40.345	—	—	.10	.25
	1973	Inc. Ab.	—	—	.10	.25
	1974	7.695	—	—	.15	.25

ALUMINUM
F.A.O. Issue

Y#	Date	Mintage	Fine	VF	XF	Unc
28	1974	23.395	—	—	.10	.25
	1975	50.030	—	—	.10	.25
	1976	58.255	—	—	.10	.25
	1977	32.840	—	—	.10	.15
	1978	64.635	—	—	.10	.15
	1979	—	—	—	.10	.15

10 PICE

COPPER-NICKEL

Y#	Date	Mintage	Fine	VF	XF	Unc
15	1961	22.230	.10	.15	.25	.35

10 PAISA

COPPER-NICKEL

Y#	Date	Mintage	Fine	VF	XF	Unc
15a	1961	31.090	—	—	.15	.35
	1961	—	—	—	Proof	2.00
	1962	29.440	—	—	.15	.35
	1963	19.760	—	—	.15	.35

Y#	Date	Mintage	Fine	VF	XF	Unc
21	1964	52.580	—	—	.10	.25
	1965	51.540	—	—	.10	.25
	1966	—	—	—	.10	.25
	1967	16.430	—	—	.10	.25
	1968	—	—	—	.10	.25

Reduced size

Y#	Date	Mintage	Fine	VF	XF	Unc
21a	1969	—	—	—	.10	.25
	1970	30.250	—	—	.10	.25
	1971	26.270	—	—	.10	.25
	1972	24.845	—	—	.10	.25
	1973	Inc. Ab.	—	—	.10	.25
	1974	4.780	—	—	.10	.25

ALUMINUM
F.A.O. Issue

Y#	Date	Mintage	Fine	VF	XF	Unc
29	1974	18.640	—	—	.10	.25
	1975	28.875	—	—	.10	.25
	1976	43.755	—	—	.10	.25
	1977	29.045	—	—	.10	.20

Y#	Date	Mintage	Fine	VF	XF	Unc
29	1978	29.325	—	—	.10	.20
	1979	—	—	—	.10	.20

25 PAISA

NICKEL

Y#	Date	Mintage	Fine	VF	XF	Unc
16	1963	16.900	.10	.15	.20	.25
	1964	7.990	.10	.15	.25	.35
	1965	9.290	.10	.15	.25	.35
	1966	6.650	.10	.15	.25	.35
	1967	3.740	.10	.15	.25	.35

COPPER-NICKEL

Y#	Date	Mintage	Fine	VF	XF	Unc
24	1967	(?)5.500	.10	.15	.20	.30
	1968	(?)5.500	.10	.15	.20	.30
	1969	—	.10	.15	.20	.30
	1970	30.392	—	.10	.15	.25
	1971	12.664	—	.10	.15	.25
	1972	10.824	—	.10	.15	.25
	1973	—	—	.10	.15	—
	1974	9.756	—	.10	.15	.25

Y#	Date	Mintage	Fine	VF	XF	Unc
30	1975	14.264	—	.10	.15	.25
	1976	20.440	—	.10	.15	.25
	1977	—	—	.10	.15	.25
	1978	—	—	.10	.15	.25
	1979	—	—	.10	.15	.25

50 PAISA

NICKEL

Y#	Date	Mintage	Fine	VF	XF	Unc
17	1963	8.110	.10	.20	.30	.50
	1964	4.580	.15	.25	.40	.60
	1965	8.980	.10	.20	.30	.50
	1966	2.860	.15	.25	.50	1.00
	1968	—	.10	.20	.30	.50
	1969	—	.10	.20	.30	.50

COPPER-NICKEL

Y#	Date	Mintage	Fine	VF	XF	Unc
25	1969	—	.10	.20	.30	.70
	1970	—	.10	.15	.25	.50
	1971	4.670	.10	.15	.25	.50
	1972	4.900	.10	.15	.25	.50
	1974	1.128	.15	.20	.30	.70

Y#	Date	Mintage	Fine	VF	XF	Unc
31	1975	9.180	.10	.15	.25	.50

Y#	Date	Mintage	Fine	VF	XF	Unc
31	1976	—	.10	.15	.25	.50
	1977	—	.10	.15	.25	.50
	1978	—	—	.15	.25	.50
	1979	—	—	.15	.25	.50

Mohammad Ali Jinnah

Y#	Date	Mintage	Fine	VF	XF	Unc
35	1976	20.000	.10	.15	.25	.50

RUPEE

COPPER-NICKEL
Islamic Summit Minar

Y#	Date	Mintage	Fine	VF	XF	Unc
38	1977	20.000	—	.35	.60	1.00

Allama Mohammad Iqbal

Y#	Date	Mintage	Fine	VF	XF	Unc
41	1977	—	—	.35	.60	1.00

100 RUPEES

28.2500 gm., .925 SILVER, .8402 oz ASW
Conservation Series

Y#	Date	Mintage	Fine	VF	XF	Unc
32	1976	—	BV	BV	BV	30.00
	1976	—	—	—	Proof	35.00

Mohammad Ali Jinnah

Y#	Date	Mintage	Fine	VF	XF	Unc
36	1976	.050	BV	BV	BV	30.00
	1976	2,000	—	—	Proof	35.00

Islamic Summit Minar

Y#	Date	Mintage	Fine	VF	XF	Unc
39	1977	.050	BV	BV	BV	30.00
	1977	—	—	—	Proof	35.00

Allama Mohammad Iqbal

Y#	Date	Mintage	Fine	VF	XF	Unc
42	1977	—	BV	BV	BV	30.00
	1977	—	—	—	Proof	35.00

150 RUPEES

35.0000 gm., .925 SILVER, 1.0409 oz ASW
Conservation Series
Obv: Similar to 100 Rupees, Y#32.

Y#	Date	Mintage	Fine	VF	XF	Unc
33	1976	—	BV	BV	BV	40.00
	1976	—	—	—	Proof	50.00

500 RUPEES

4.5000 gm., .916 GOLD, .1325 oz AGW
Mohammad Ali Jinnah

Y#	Date	Mintage	Fine	VF	XF	Unc
37	1976	.025	BV	BV	BV	90.00
	1976	100 pcs.	—	—	Proof	95.00

Allama Mohammad Iqbal

Y#	Date	Mintage	Fine	VF	XF	Unc
43	1977	—	BV	BV	BV	90.00
	1977	—	—	—	Proof	95.00

1000 RUPEES

9.0000 gm., .916 GOLD, .2650 oz AGW
Islamic Summit Minar

Y#	Date	Mintage	Fine	VF	XF	Unc
40	1977	.025	BV	BV	BV	180.00
	1977	—	—	—	Proof	190.00

3000 RUPEES

.900 GOLD

Conservation Series

Y#	Date	Mintage	Fine	VF	XF	Unc
34	1976	699pcs.	BV	BV	BV	650.00
	1976	237pcs.	—	—	Proof	800.00

NCLT ISSUES

MINT SETS

KM#	Date	Mintage	Identification	Issue Price	Mkt. Val.
S1	1976(2)	—	Y36-37	63.00	120.00
S2	1976(2)	—	Y32-33	—	70.00
S3	1977(2)	—	Y39-40	—	210.00

PROOF SETS

STANDARD METALS

KM#	Date	Mintage	Identification	Issue Price	Mkt. Val.
101	1948(7)	5,000	Y1-7	4.00	15.00
102	1953(5)	—	Y8-12	2.00	6.50
103	1961(3)	—	Y13a,14A,15A	1.00	5.00
104	1976(2)	—	Y36-37	90.50	130.00
105	1976(2)	—	Y32-33	—	75.00
106	1977(2)	—	Y39-40	—	225.00

MIXED DATE SETS

KM#	Date	Mintage	Identification	Issue Price	Mkt. Val.
4	1948/51/53(8)	—	Y5-12	4.00	8.00
5	1948/61(6)	—	Y5-7,13a,14a,15a	2.00	6.00
6	1948/64(7)	—	Y7,16-21	2.00	6.00
7	1948/74(7)	—	Y7,24-29	2.00	6.00
8	1948/75(7)	—	Y7,26-31	—	—

NOTE: Restrikes have been issued for most of these sets.

Listings For

PALESTINE: refer to Israel

PANAMA

The Republic of Panama, a Central American country situated between Costa Rica and Colombia, has an area of 29,209 sq. mi. (75,635 sq. km.) and a population of 1.8 million. Capital: Panama City. The Panama Canal is the country's biggest asset; servicing world related transit trade and international commerce. Bananas, refined petroleum, sugar and shrimp are exported.

Panama was visited by Christopher Columbus in 1502 during his fourth voyage to America, and explored by Vasco de Balboa in 1513. Panama City, founded in 1519, was a primary transshipment center for treasure and supplies to and from Spain's American colonies. Panama declared its independence in 1821 and joined the confederation of Greater Colombia. In 1903, after Colombia rejected a treaty enabling the United States to build a canal across the Isthmus, Panama with the support of the United States proclaimed its independence from Colombia and became a sovereign republic.

The 1904 2-1/2 centesimos known as the 'Panama Pill' or 'Panama Pearl' is one of the world's smaller silver coins and a favorite with collectors.

MINTMARKS

FM - Franklin Mint, U.S.A.*

***NOTE:** During 1975-77 the Franklin Mint produced coinage in up to 3 different qualities. Qualities of issue are designated in ( ) after each date and are defined as follows:

(M) MATTE - Normal circulation strike or a dull finish produced by sandblasting special uncirculated (polish finish) or proof quality dies.

(U) SPECIAL UNCIRCULATED - Polished or proof-like in appearance without any frosted features.

(P) PROOF - The highest quality obtainable having mirror-like fields and frosted features.

MONETARY SYSTEM

100 Centesimos = 1 Balboa

1/2 CENTESIMO

COPPER-NICKEL

Y#	Date	Mintage	VF	XF	Unc
1	1907	1.000	2.50	3.50	6.00
	1907	—	—	Proof	—

CENTESIMO

BRONZE

Y#	Date	Mintage	VF	XF	Unc
10	1935	.200	5.00	7.50	37.50
	1937	.200	3.00	5.00	32.50

50th Anniversary of the Republic

Y#	Date	Mintage	VF	XF	Unc
17	1953	1.500	.15	.30	2.50

Y#	Date	Mintage	VF	XF	Unc
22	1961	2.500	—	.10	.60
	1962	2.000	—	.10	.60
	1962	*25 pcs.	—	—	—
	1966	3.000	.10	.15	.25
	1966	.013	—	Proof	1.50
	1967	7.600	.10	.15	.25
	1967	.020	—	Proof	1.25
	1968	25.000	.10	.15	.25
	1968	.023	—	Proof	1.25
	1969	.014	—	Proof	2.25
	1970	9,528	—	Proof	2.50
	1971	.011	—	Proof	2.50
	1972	.013	—	Proof	2.50
	1973	.017	—	Proof	2.00
	1974	*10.000	.10	.15	.25
	1974	*.018	—	Proof	1.25
	1975	10.000	.10	.15	.25
	1977	—	.10	.15	.25

*1974 circulation coins struck at West Point and proof coins at San Francisco.

Y#	Date	Mintage	VF	XF	Unc
33	1975FM(M)	.125	.10	.25	1.00
	1975FM(U)	1,410	—	—	2.50
	1975FM(P)	.041	—	Proof	2.00
	1976FM(M)	.063	.50	1.00	2.00
	1976FM(P)	.012	—	Proof	2.00
	1977FM(M)	.063	.50	1.00	2.00
	1977FM(P)	9,548	—	Proof	2.00
	1979FM(M)	—	.50	1.00	2.00
	1979FM(P)	—	—	Proof	2.00
	1980FM	—	—	—	—
	1980FM(P)	—	—	Proof	5.00
	75th Anniversary of Independence				
45	1978FM(U)	.050	—	—	.75
	1978FM(P)	.011	—	Proof	2.00

1-1/4 CENTESIMOS

BRONZE

Y#	Date	Mintage	VF	XF	Unc
11	1940	1.600	1.50	2.50	8.50

2-1/2 CENTESIMOS

1.2500 gm., .900 SILVER, .0362 oz ASW

Y#	Date	Mintage	VF	XF	Unc
5	1904	.400	14.00	17.50	27.50
	1904	—	—	Proof	—

NOTE: The above piece is popularly referred to as the 'Panama Pill' or 'Panama Pearl'.

COPPER-NICKEL

Rev. leg: DOS Y MEDIOS

Y#	Date	Mintage	VF	XF	Unc
2	1907	.800	3.00	8.00	45.00

Rev. leg: DOS Y MEDIO

Y#	Date	Mintage	VF	XF	Unc
2a	1916	.800	3.00	9.00	45.00

Y#	Date	Mintage	VF	XF	Unc
3	1929	1.000	4.00	12.00	125.00
	1929	—	—	Proof	—
12	1940	1.200	1.00	2.00	7.50

COPPER-NICKEL CLAD COPPER
F.A.O. Issue

Y#	Date	Mintage	VF	XF	Unc
31	1973	2.000	—	—	.20
	1975	1.000	—	—	.20

Y#	Date	Mintage	VF	XF	Unc
34	1975FM(M)	.050	.35	.60	2.00
	1975FM(U)	1,410	—	1.75	3.00
	1975FM(P)	.041	—	Proof	5.00
	1976FM(M)	.025	.60	1.00	1.50
	1976FM(P)	.024	—	Proof	3.00
	1977FM(M)	.025	.60	1.00	1.50
	1977FM(P)	9,548	—	Proof	3.50
	1979FM(M)	—	.60	1.00	1.50
	1979FM(P)	—	—	Proof	3.50
	1980FM	—	—	—	—
34a	1980FM(P)	—	—	Proof	6.00

75th Anniversary of Independence

Y#	Date	Mintage	VF	XF	Unc
46	1978FM(U)	.040	—	—	1.00
	1978FM(P)	.011	—	Proof	3.00

5 CENTESIMOS

2.5000 gm., .900 SILVER, .0723 ASW

Y#	Date	Mintage	VF	XF	Unc
6	1904	1.500	7.50	12.50	35.00
	1904	—	—	Proof	—
	1916	.100	185.00	225.00	350.00

COPPER-NICKEL

Y#	Date	Mintage	VF	XF	Unc
4	1929	.500	4.50	7.50	45.00
	1932	.332	4.50	8.50	50.00

Y#	Date	Mintage	VF	XF	Unc
23	1961	1.000	.50	1.25	6.00
23a	1962	2.600	.10	.20	.60
	1962	*25 pcs.	—	Proof	—
	1966	4.900	.10	.20	.30
	1966	.013	—	Proof	2.00
	1967	2.600	.10	.25	.50
	1967	.020	—	Proof	1.75
	1968	6.000	.10	.20	.30
	1968	.023	—	Proof	1.75
	1969	.014	—	Proof	2.25
	1970	5.000	.10	.20	.30
	1970	9,528	—	Proof	2.50
	1971	.011	—	Proof	3.00
	1972	.013	—	Proof	3.25
	1973	5.000	.10	.15	.25
	1973	.017	—	Proof	1.75
	1974	.019	—	Proof	3.00
	1975	5.000	.10	.15	.40

NOTE: The 1962 & 1966 strikes are normally sharper in detail. The stars on the reverse above the eagle are flat while previous dates are raised.

Y#	Date	Mintage	VF	XF	Unc
35	1975FM(M)	.015	.75	1.00	2.00
	1975FM(U)	1,410	—	2.50	4.00
	1975FM(P)	.041	—	Proof	2.00
	1976FM(M)	.013	.75	1.25	2.00
	1976FM(P)	.012	—	Proof	2.00
	1977FM(M)	.013	.75	1.25	2.00
	1977FM(P)	9,548	—	Proof	2.00
	1979FM(M)	—	.75	1.25	2.00
	1979FM(P)	—	—	Proof	2.00
	1980FM	—	—	—	—
35a	1980FM(P)	—	—	Proof	7.00

COPPER-NICKEL CLAD COPPER
75th Anniversary of Independence

Y#	Date	Mintage	VF	XF	Unc
47	1978FM(U)	.030	—	—	1.00
	1978FM(P)	.011	—	Proof	2.00

10 CENTESIMOS

5.0000 gm., .900 SILVER, .1447 oz ASW

Y#	Date	Mintage	VF	XF	Unc
7	1904	1.100	15.00	25.00	75.00
	1904	—	—	Proof	850.00

1/10 BALBOA

2.5000 gm., .900 SILVER, .0723 oz ASW

Y#	Date	Mintage	VF	XF	Unc
13	1930	.500	2.50	5.00	25.00
	1930	—	—	Proof	—
	1931	.200	4.00	7.50	60.00
13	1932	.150	5.00	9.00	85.00
	1933	.100	8.50	17.50	120.00
	1934	.075	10.00	20.00	200.00
	1947	1.000	BV	BV	6.00
	1962	5.000	BV	BV	2.25
	1962	*25 pcs.	—	Proof	—

NOTE: Coins dated 1962 vary somewhat in detail from those of 1930-1947.

50th Anniversary of the Republic

Y#	Date	Mintage	VF	XF	Unc
18	1953	3.300	BV	BV	2.50
24	1961	2.500	BV	BV	2.25

COPPER-NICKEL CLAD COPPER

Y#	Date	Mintage	VF	XF	Unc
13a	1966TI	6.955	.25	.35	.75
	1966TII	1.000	.35	.50	3.00
	1966	.013	—	Proof	2.50
	1967	.020	—	Proof	4.00
	1968	5.000	.20	.30	.50
	1968	.023	—	Proof	2.25
	1969	.014	—	Proof	4.00
	1970	7.500	.15	.25	.40
	1970	9,528	—	Proof	3.00
	1971	.011	—	Proof	4.00
	1972	.013	—	Proof	4.50
	1973	10.000	.15	.20	.30
	1973	.017	—	Proof	2.50
	1974	.018	—	Proof	4.50
	1975	.500	.25	.50	1.00

NOTE: The 1966 exists in two varieties, Type I is similar to the 1962 strike and Type II is similar to the 1947 strikes.

10 CENTESIMOS

COPPER-NICKEL CLAD COPPER

Y#	Date	Mintage	VF	XF	Unc
36	1975FM(M)	.013	.85	1.50	2.50
	1975FM(U)	1,410	—	3.00	5.00
	1975FM(P)	.041	—	Proof	2.00
	1976FM(M)	6,250	.85	1.50	2.50
	1976FM(P)	.012	—	Proof	2.00
	1977FM(M)	6,250	.85	1.50	2.50
	1977FM(P)	9,548	—	Proof	2.00
	1979FM(M)	—	.85	1.50	2.50
	1979FM(P)	—	—	Proof	2.00
	1980FM	—	—	—	—
	1980FM(P)	—	—	Proof	8.00

75th Anniversary of Independence

Y#	Date	Mintage	VF	XF	Unc
48	1978FM(U)	.020	—	—	1.25
	1978FM(P)	.011	—	Proof	2.00

25 CENTESIMOS

12.5000 gm., .900 SILVER, .3617 oz ASW

Y#	Date	Mintage	VF	XF	Unc
8	1904	1.600	20.00	35.00	90.00
	1904	—	—	Proof	1200.

1/4 BALBOA

6.2500 gm., .900 SILVER, .1809 oz ASW

Y#	Date	Mintage	VF	XF	Unc
14	1930	.400	5.00	12.50	50.00
	1930	—	—	Proof	—
	1931	.048	40.00	160.00	1200.
	1932	.126	5.00	20.00	100.00
	1933	.120	5.00	20.00	125.00
	1934	.090	7.50	25.00	150.00
	1947	.700	BV	BV	15.00
	1962	4.000	BV	BV	5.50
	1962	25 pcs.	—	Proof	—

NOTE: Coins dated 1962 vary somewhat in detail from those of 1930-1947.

50th Anniversary of the Republic

Y#	Date	Mintage	VF	XF	Unc
19	1953	1.200	BV	6.50	12.50

Y#	Date	Mintage	VF	XF	Unc
25	1961	2.000	BV	BV	5.50

COPPER-NICKEL CLAD COPPER

Y#	Date	Mintage	VF	XF	Unc
14a	1966	7.400	.35	.50	.90
	1966	.013	—	Proof	3.50
	1967	.020	—	Proof	5.00
	1968	1.200	.35	.60	1.25
	1968	.023	—	Proof	2.50
	1969	.014	—	Proof	5.00
	1970	2.000	.35	.50	1.00
	1970	9,528	—	Proof	3.50
	1971	.011	—	Proof	5.00
	1972	.013	—	Proof	5.00
	1973	.800	.40	1.00	1.50
	1973	.017	—	Proof	3.00
	1974	.018	—	Proof	5.00
	1975	1.500	.35	.50	.75

25 CENTESIMOS

COPPER-NICKEL CLAD COPPER

Y#	Date	Mintage	VF	XF	Unc
37	1975FM(M)	5,000	1.00	1.75	3.00
	1975FM(U)	1,410	—	3.00	5.00
	1975FM(P)	.041	—	Proof	3.00
	1976FM(M)	2,500	—	1.50	2.50
	1976FM(P)	.012	—	Proof	2.50

Y#	Date	Mintage	VF	XF	Unc
37	1977FM(M)	2,500	—	1.50	2.50
	1977FM(P)	9,548	—	Proof	2.50
	1979FM(M)	—	—	1.50	2.50
	1979FM(P)	—	—	Proof	2.50
	1980FM	—	—	—	—
37a	1980FM(P)	—	—	Proof	9.00

75th Anniversary of Independence

Y#	Date	Mintage	VF	XF	Unc
49	1978FM(M)	8,000	—	—	2.00
	1978FM(P)	.011	—	Proof	2.50

50 CENTESIMOS

25.0000 gm., .900 SILVER, .7235 oz ASW

Y#	Date	Mintage	VF	XF	Unc
9	1904	1.800	30.00	45.00	110.00
	1904	—	—	Proof	2000.
	1905	1.000	50.00	75.00	175.00

1/2 BALBOA

12.5000 gm., .900 SILVER, .3617 oz ASW

Y#	Date	Mintage	VF	XF	Unc
15	1930	.300	BV	10.00	100.00
	1930	—	—	Proof	—
	1932	.063	10.00	35.00	400.00
	1933	.120	BV	27.50	300.00
	1934	.090	10.00	30.00	350.00
	1947	.450	BV	BV	35.00
	1962	.700	BV	BV	11.00
	1962	25 pcs.	—	Proof	—

NOTE: Coins dated 1962 vary somewhat in detail from those of 1930-1947.

50th Anniversary of the Republic

Y#	Date	Mintage	VF	XF	Unc
20	1953	.600	BV	BV	12.00

Y#	Date	Mintage	VF	XF	Unc
26	1961	.350	BV	BV	12.00

12.5000 gm., .400 CLAD SILVER, .1608 oz ASW

Error: Type II helmet rim incomplete

Y#	Date	Mintage	VF	XF	Unc
26v	1966	1.000	2.00	2.50	7.50

Normal helmet

Y#	Date	Mintage	VF	XF	Unc
15a	1966 type I				
		Inc. Ab.	BV	BV	4.75
	1966	.013	—	Proof	5.00
	1967	.300	BV	BV	4.75
	1967	.020	—	Proof	4.50
	1968	1.000	BV	BV	4.75
	1968	.023	—	Proof	4.75
	1969	.014	—	Proof	7.50
	1970	.610	BV	BV	4.75
	1970	9,528	—	Proof	5.00
	1971	.011	—	Proof	7.50
	1972	.013	—	Proof	7.50

COPPER-NICKEL CLAD COPPER

Y#	Date	Mintage	VF	XF	Unc
15b	1973	1.000	1.00	1.25	1.50
	1973	.017	—	Proof	4.00
	1974	.018	—	Proof	7.50
	1975	1.200	.75	1.25	1.50

50 CENTESIMOS

COPPER-NICKEL CLAD COPPER

Y#	Date	Mintage	VF	XF	Unc
38	1975FM(M)	2,000	1.00	1.75	3.00
	1975FM(U)	1,410	—	4.50	7.50
	1975FM(P)	.041	—	Proof	5.00
	1976FM(M)	1,250	.85	1.50	2.50
	1976FM(P)	.012	—	Proof	5.00
	1977FM(M)	1,250	.85	1.50	2.50
	1977FM(P)	9,548	—	Proof	5.00
	1979FM(M)	—	.85	1.50	2.50
	1979FM(P)	—	—	Proof	5.00
	1980FM	—	—	—	—
38a	1980FM(P)	—	—	Proof	12.00

75th Anniversary of Independence

Y#	Date	Mintage	VF	XF	Unc
50	1978FM(U)	8,000	—	—	2.00
	1978FM(P)	.011	—	Proof	5.00

BALBOA

26.7300 gm., .900 SILVER, .7735 oz ASW

Y#	Date	Mintage	VF	XF	Unc
16	1931	.200	BV	BV	35.00
	1931	—	—	Proof	—
	1934	.225	BV	BV	35.00
	1947	.500	BV	BV	24.00

50th Anniversary of the Republic

Y#	Date	Mintage	VF	XF	Unc
21	1953	.050	BV	BV	25.00

Y#	Date	Mintage	VF	XF	Unc
27	1966	.240	—	—	23.00

Y#	Date	Mintage	VF	XF	Unc
27	1966	.013	—	Proof	25.00
	1967	.020	—	Proof	23.00
	1968	.023	—	Proof	23.00
	1969	.014	—	Proof	23.00
	1970	.013	—	Proof	30.00
	1971	.018	—	Proof	23.00
	1972	.023	—	Proof	23.00
	1973	.030	—	Proof	23.00
	1974	.030	—	Proof	23.00

COPPER-NICKEL CLAD COPPER

Y#	Date	Mintage	VF	XF	Unc
39	1975FM(M)	4,035	3.00	5.00	8.00
	1975FM(U)	1,410	—	9.00	15.00
	1976FM(M)	625 pcs.	55.00	90.00	150.00
	1977FM(M)	625 pcs.	55.00	90.00	150.00
	1979FM(M)	—	55.00	90.00	150.00
	1980FM	—	—	—	—

Error: Counage struck at Royal Canadian Mint with .925 silver fineness on rev.

Y#	Date	Mintage	VF	XF	Unc
39b	1975	*.010	—	40.00	60.00
	1976	*.012	—	35.00	50.00

*Note e stimated number remelted were 1975 - 4,000 1976 - 5,000.

26.7300 gm., .925 SILVER, .7950 oz ASW

Y#	Date	Mintage	VF	XF	Unc
39a	1975FM(P)	.045	—	Proof	24.00
	1976FM(P)	.014	—	Proof	24.00
	1977FM(P)	.011	—	Proof	24.00
	1979FM(P)	—	—	Proof	24.00

20.7400 gm., .500 SILVER, .3334 oz ASW

Y#	Date	Mintage	VF	XF	Unc
39c	1980FM(P)	—	—	Proof	18.00

COPPER-NICKEL CLAD COPPER
75th Anniversary of Independence

Y#	Date	Mintage	VF	XF	Unc
51	1978FM(U)	4,000	—	—	8.00

.925 SILVER

Y#	Date	Mintage	VF	XF	Unc
51a	1978FM(P)	.013	—	Proof	24.00

5 BALBOAS

35.1200 gm., .925 SILVER, 1.0446 oz ASW
11th Central American and Caribbean Games

Y#	Date	Mintage	VF	XF	Unc
28	1970FM(M)	.666	BV	BV	35.00
	1970FM(P)	.059	—	Proof	35.00

F.A.O. Issue
Obv: Similar to Y#28.

Y#	Date	Mintage	VF	XF	Unc
32	1972	.070	BV	BV	35.00
	1972	.010	—	Proof	40.00

COPPER-NICKEL CLAD COPPER
Obv: Similar to Y#28.

Y#	Date	Mintage	VF	XF	Unc
40	1975FM(M)	5,125	—	12.50	17.50
	1975FM(U)	1,410	—	45.00	75.00
	1976FM(M)	125 pcs.	90.00	150.00	250.00
	1977FM(M)	600pcs.	90.00	150.00	250.00
	1979FM(M)	—	90.00	150.00	250.00
	1980FM	—	—	—	—

Error coinage struck at Royal Canadian Mint with .925 silver fineness on rev.

Y#	Date	Mintage	VF	XF	Unc
40b	1975	*4,000	—	85.00	125.00
	1976	*5,000	—	55.00	90.00

*Note Estimated number remelted were 1975 - 3,200 1976 - 3,800.

35.1200 gm., .925 SILVER, 1.0446 oz ASW

Y#	Date	Mintage	VF	XF	Unc
40a	1975FM(P)	.041	—	Proof	31.00
	1976FM(P)	.012	—	Proof	31.00
	1977FM(P)	9,548	—	Proof	31.00
	1979FM(P)	—	—	Proof	31.00
40c	1980FM(P)	—	—	Proof	25.00

23.3300 gm., .500 SILVER, .3751 oz ASW
75th Anniversary of Independence

Y#	Date	Mintage	VF	XF	Unc
52	1978FM(U)	2,000	—	—	55.00

35.1200 gm., .925 SILVER, 1.0446 oz ASW

Y#	Date	Mintage	VF	XF	Unc
52a	1978FM(P)	.011	—	Proof	31.00

Panama Canal Treaty Implementation
Obv: Similar to y#28.

Y#	Date	Mintage	VF	XF	Unc
59	1979FM(P)	.050	—	Proof	50.00

10 BALBOAS

42.4800 gm., .925 SILVER, 1.2635 oz ASW
Panama Canal Treaty Ratification
Rev: Similar to 5 Balboas, Y#28.

Y#	Date	Mintage	VF	XF	Unc
55	1978FM	.012	—	Proof	40.00

NICKEL

Y#	Date	Mintage	VF	XF	Unc
55a	1978	.300	—	—	—

42.4800 gm., .925 SILVER, 1.2635 oz ASW
Panama Canal Treaty Implementation
Panamanian flag in map of Panama below.

Y#	Date	Mintage	VF	XF	Unc
60	1979FM(P)	—	—	Proof	50.00

20 BALBOAS

129.5900 gm., .925 SILVER, 3.8544 oz ASW
150th Anniversary of Central American Independence
Obv: Similar to 5 Balboas, Y#28.

Y#	Date	Mintage	VF	XF	Unc
29	1971FM(M)	.069	BV	BV	115.00
	1971FM(P)	.040	—	Proof	125.00

Actual size of this and following Panama listings - Y29, Y30 and Y44 - is 61mm.

Regular Issue, Simon Bolivar
Obv: Similar to 5 Balboas, Y#28.

Y#	Date	Mintage	VF	XF	Unc
30	1972FM(M)	.037	BV	BV	115.00
	1972FM(P)	.048	—	Proof	115.00
	1973FM(M)	.094	BV	BV	115.00
	1973FM(P)	.074	—	Proof	115.00
	1974FM(M)	.099	BV	BV	115.00
	1974FM(P)	.161	—	Proof	115.00
	1975FM(M)	2,500	BV	BV	115.00
	1975FM(P)	.062	—	Proof	115.00
	1976FM(M)	2,500	BV	BV	115.00
	1976FM(P)	.022	—	Proof	115.00

Obv: Similar to 5 Balboas, Y#28.

Y#	Date	Mintage	VF	XF	Unc
44	1977FM(M)	2,500	—	BV	115.00
	1977FM(U)	2,879	—	BV	115.00
	1977FM(P)	.024	—	Proof	115.00
	1979FM(P)	—	—	Proof	115.00

75th Anniversary of Independence
Rev: Similar to Y#44.

Y#	Date	Mintage	VF	XF	Unc
53	1978FM(U)	2,500	BV	BV	115.00
	1978FM(P)	.023	—	Proof	115.00

119.8800 gm., .500 SILVER, 1.9273 oz ASW
150th Anniversary of Simon Bolivar

Y#	Date	Mintage	VF	XF	Unc
63	1980FM(P)	—	—	Proof	200.00

75 BALBOAS

10.6000 gm., .500 GOLD, .1704 oz agw
75th Anniversary of Independence

Y#	Date	Mintage	VF	XF	Unc
54	1978FM(U)	410 pcs.	—	—	150.00
	1978FM(P)	9,161	—	Proof	125.00

100 BALBOAS

8.1600 gm., .900 GOLD, .2361 oz AGW
500th Anniversary of Balboa

Y#	Date	Mintage	VF	XF	Unc
41	1975FM(U)	*.044	BV	BV	155.00
	1975FM(P)	.075	—	Proof	165.00
	1976FM(M)	50 pcs.	—	—	—
	1976FM(U)	3,013	BV	153.00	225.00
	1976FM(P)	.011	—	Proof	165.00
	1977FM(M)	50 pcs.	—	—	—
	1977FM(U)	324 pcs.	153.00	200.00	300.00
	1977FM(P)	5,092	—	Proof	165.00

Dove - Orchid

Y#	Date	Mintage	VF	XF	Unc
56	1978FM(U)	300 pcs.	—	—	350.00
	1978FM(P)	6,086	—	Proof	175.00

Golden Turtle

Y#	Date	Mintage	VF	XF	Unc
62	1979FM(P)	—	—	Proof	200.00

Golden Condor

Y#	Date	Mintage	VF	XF	Unc
64	1980FM(P)	—	—	Proof	325.00

150 BALBOAS

93.0000 gm., 1.000 PLATINUM, 2.9903 oz APW
150th Anniversary Pan-American Congress

Y#	Date	Mintage	VF	XF	Unc
43	1976FM(M)	30 pcs.	—	BV	2100.
	1976FM(U)	510 pcs.	—	BV	2100.
	1976FM(P)	.013	—	Proof	2100.

200 BALBOAS

9.5000 gm., .980 PLATINUM, .2994 oz APW

Panama Canal Treaties

Y#	Date	Mintage	VF	XF	Unc
61	1979FM(P)	—	—	Proof	430.00

500 BALBOAS

41.7000 gm., .900 GOLD, 1.2067 oz AGW
500th Anniversary of Balboa

Y#	Date	Mintage	VF	XF	Unc
42	1975FM(M)	10 pcs.	—	—	—
	1975FM(U)	1,496	—	BV	785.00
	1975FM(P)	9,824	—	Proof	785.00
	1976FM(M)	10 pcs.	—	—	—
	1976FM(U)	160 pcs.	—	BV	800.00
	1976FM(P)	2,669	—	Proof	785.00
	1977FM(M)	10 pcs.	—	—	—
	1977FM(U)	59 pcs.	—	—	1050.
	1977FM(P)	1,980	—	Proof	785.00

30th Anniversary of Organization of American States
Obv: Similar to Y#42.

Y#	Date	Mintage	VF	XF	Unc
	1978FM(M)	10 pcs.	—	—	—
	1978FM(U)	106 pcs.	—	—	—
	1978FM(P)	2,009	—	Proof	785.00

Golden Jaguar
Obv: Similar to Y#42.

Y#	Date	Mintage	VF	XF	Unc
58	1979FM(P)	5,000		Proof only	785.00

PALO SECO

Palo Seco Leper Colony was established in Balboa, Canal Zone in 1907. It is known today as Palo Seco Hospital. The original issue of tokens totaled $1,800.00 of which $1,492.75 was destroyed on November 28, 1955. The issue was backed by United States Currency and was replaced by United States silver coinage.

Leprosarium Token Coinage

CENT

COPPER

KM#	Date	Mintage	Good	VG	Fine
1	ND(1919)	—	—	Rare	—

5 CENTS

BRASS

KM#	Date	Mintage	Good	VG	Fine
2	ND(1919)	—	—	Rare	—

10 CENTS

ALUMINUM

KM#	Date	Mintage	Good	VG	Fine
3	ND(1919)	—	—	Rare	—

25 CENTS

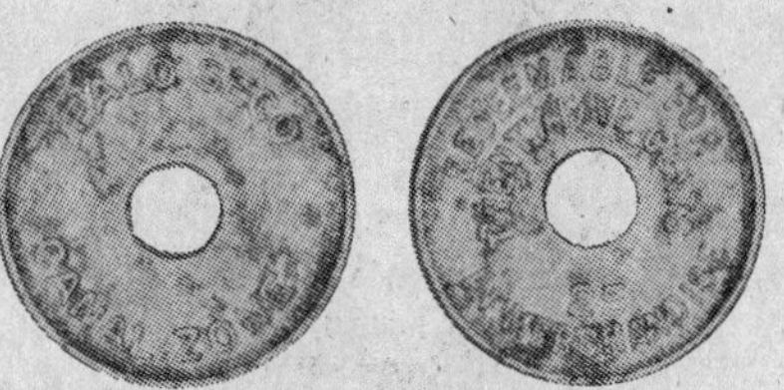

ALUMINUM

KM#	Date	Mintage	Good	VG	Fine
4	ND(1919)	—	—	Rare	—

50 CENTS

ALUMINUM

KM#	Date	Mintage	Good	VG	Fine
5	ND(1919)	—	—	Rare	—

DOLLAR

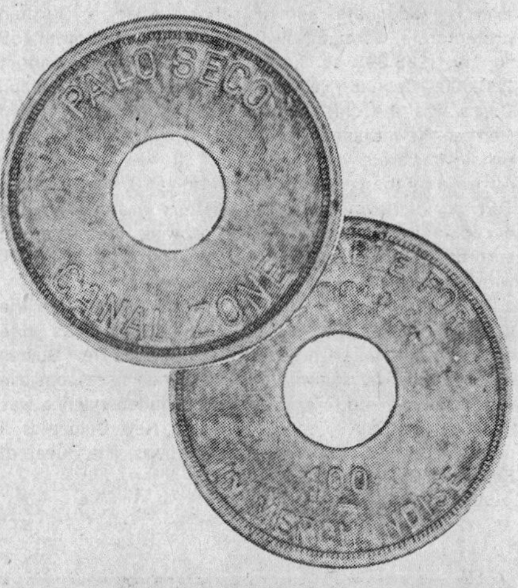

ALUMINUM

KM#	Date	Mintage	Good	VG	Fine
6	ND(1919)	—	—	Rare	—

NCLT ISSUES

MINT SETS
STANDARD METALS

KM#	Date	Mintage	Identification	Issue Price	Mkt. Val.
S1	1975(8)	1,410	Y34-40	25.00	200.00

PROOF SETS
STANDARD METALS

KM#	Date	Mintage	Identification	Issue Price	Mkt. Val.
101	1962(5)	25	Y13-15,22,23a	—	—
102	1966(6)	12,701	Y13a-15a,22,23a,27	15.25	40.00
103	1967(6)	19,983	As Above	15.25	40.00
104	1968(6)	23,210	As Above	15.25	36.00
105	1969(6)	14,000	As Above	15.25	44.00
106	1970(6)	9,528	As Above	15.25	47.00
107	1971(6)	10,696	As Above	15.25	45.00
108	1972(6)	13,322	As Above	15.50	46.00
109	1973(6)	16,946	Y13a-14a,15b,22,23a,27	17.50	37.00
110	1974(6)	17,521	As Above	17.50	45.00
111	1975(9)	37,041	Y30,34-38,39a-40a,41	130.00	340.00
112	1975(8)	4,057	Y34-41	50.00	225.00
113	1976(9)	10,610	Y33-38,39a,40a,30	102.00	186.50
114	1976(8)	1,792	Y33-38,39a,40a	50.00	71.50
115	1976(2)	11,479	Y30,34	51.00	118.00
116	1977(9)	8,093	Y33-38,39a,40a,44	100.00	187.00
117	1977(8)	1,455	Y33-38,39a,40a	50.00	72.00
118	1978(9)	9,667	Y45-50,51a,52a,53	110.00	186.50
119	1978(8)	1,122	45-50,51a,52a	—	71.50
120	1979(9)	—	Y33-38,39a,40a,44	132.00	187.00
121	1979(8)	—	Y33-38,39a,40a	60.00	72.00
122	1979(2)	—	Y59,60	125.00	100.00
123	1980(9)	—	Y33-38,39a,40a,20Balboa	287.00	290.00
124	1980(8)	—	Y33-38,39a,40a	87.00	90.00

PAPUA NEW GUINEA

Papua New Guinea, an independent member of the British Commonwealth, occupies the eastern half of the island of New Guinea. It lies north of Australia near the equator and borders on West Irian. The country, which includes nearby Bismark archipelago, Buka and Bougainville, has an area of 178,260 sq. mi. (461,691 sq. km.) and a population of 2.8 million who are divided into more than 1,000 seperate tribes speaking more than 700 mutually unintelligible languages. Capital: Port Moresby. The economy is agricultural, and exports copra, rubber, cocoa, coffee, tea, gold and copper.

In 1884 Germany annexed the area known as German New Guinea (also Neu Guinea or Kaiser Wilhelmsland) comprising the northern section of eastern New Guinea, and granted its administration and development to the Neu-Guinea Compagnie. Administration reverted to Germany in 1889 following the failure of the company to exercise adequate administration. While a German protectorate, German New Guinea had an area of 92,159 sq. mi. (238,692 sq. km.) and a population of about 250,000. Capital: Hebertshohe, later named Rabaul. Copra was the chief crop. Australian troops occupied German New Guinea in Aug. 1914, shortly after Great Britain declared war on Germany. It was mandated to Australia by the League of Nations in 1920, known as the Territory of New Guinea. The territory was invaded and occupied by Japan in 1942. Following the Japanese surrender, it came under U.N. trusteeship, Dec. 13, 1946, with Australia as the administering power.

The Papua and New Guinea act, 1949, provided for the government of Papua and New Guinea as one administrative unit. On Dec. 1, 1973, Papua New Guinea became selfgoverning with Australia retaining responsibility for defense and foreign affairs. Full independence was achieved on Sept. 16, 1975. Papua New Guinea is a member of the Commonwealth of Nations. The Queen of England is Chief of State.

GERMAN NEW GUINEA

RULERS

German, 1884-1918

MINTMARKS

A - Berlin

MONETARY SYSTEM

100 Pfennig = 1 Mark

PFENNIG

COPPER

Y#	Date	Mintage	VF	XF	Unc
1	1894A	.033	35.00	60.00	100.00
	1894A	—	—	Proof	100.00

2 PFENNIG

COPPER

Y#	Date	Mintage	VF	XF	Unc
2	1894A	.017	40.00	100.00	150.00
	1894A	—	—	Proof	225.00

10 PFENNIG

COPPER

Y#	Date	Mintage	VF	XF	Unc
3	1894A	.024	45.00	75.00	125.00
	1894A	—	—	Proof	225.00

1/2 MARK

2.7780 gm., .900 SILVER, .0804 oz ASW

Y#	Date	Mintage	VF	XF	Unc
4	1894A	.016	100.00	175.00	250.00
	1894A	—	—	Proof	400.00

MARK

5.5560 gm., .900 SILVER, .1608 oz ASW

Y#	Date	Mintage	VF	XF	Unc
5	1894A	.033	100.00	175.00	275.00
	1894A	—	—	Proof	400.00

2 MARK

11.1110 gm., .900 SILVER, .3215 oz ASW

Y#	Date	Mintage	VF	XF	Unc
6	1894A	.013	125.00	200.00	375.00
	1894A	—	—	Proof	550.00

5 MARK

27.7780 gm., .900 SILVER, .8039 oz ASW

Y#	Date	Mintage	VF	XF	Unc
7	1894A	.019	550.00	800.00	1250.
	1894A	—	—	Proof	2200.

10 MARK

3.9820 gm., .900 SILVER, .1152 oz ASW

Y#	Date	Mintage	VF	XF	Unc
8	1895A	2,000	—	4500.	6000.
	1895A	—	—	Proof	8000.

20 MARK

7.9650 gm., .900 GOLD, .2305 oz AGW

Y#	Date	Mintage	VF	XF	Unc
9	1895A	1,500	—	5000.	7000.
	1895A	—	—	Proof	8000.

NCLT ISSUES

PROOF SETS

STANDARD METALS

KM#	Date	Mintage	Identification	Issue Price	Mkt. Val.
	1894(7)	—	Y1-7	—	4500.

NEW GUINEA

New Guinea, the world's largest island after Greenland, was discovered by Spanish navigator Jorge de Menezes, who landed on the northwest shore in 1527. European interests, attracted by exaggerated estimates of the resources of the area, resulted in the island being claimed in whole or part by Spain, the Netherlands, Great Britain and Germany.

RULERS

British, 1910

1952

MONETARY SYSTEM

12 Pence 1 Shilling

20 Shillings 1 Pound

1/2 PENNY

COPPER-NICKEL

Y#	Date	Mintage	VF	XF	Unc
1	1929	—	350.00	450.00	600.00
	1929	—	—	Proof	650.00

NICKEL

Y#	Date	Mintage	VF	XF	Unc
1a	1929	20 pcs.	—	Proof	550.00

PENNY

COPPER-NICKEL

Y#	Date	Mintage	VF	XF	Unc
2	1929	—	350.00	450.00	600.00
	1929	—	—	Proof	650.00

NICKEL

Y#	Date	Mintage	VF	XF	Unc
2a	1929	20 pcs.	—	Proof	550.00

BRONZE

Y#	Date	Mintage	VF	XF	Unc
6	1936	.360	1.00	2.00	3.00
7	1938	.360	3.00	5.00	12.50
	1944	.240	1.50	3.00	6.00

3 PENCE

COPPER-NICKEL

Y#	Date	Mintage	VF	XF	Unc
3	1935	1.200	4.00	6.50	15.00
	1935	—	—	Proof	135.00

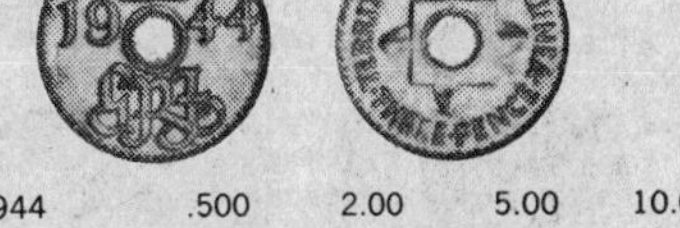

Y#	Date	Mintage	VF	XF	Unc
8	1944	.500	2.00	5.00	10.00

6 PENCE

COPPER-NICKEL

Y#	Date	Mintage	VF	XF	Unc
4	1935	2.000	4.50	7.50	17.50
	1935	—	—	Proof	150.00

Y#	Date	Mintage	VF	XF	Unc
9	1943	.130	5.00	8.00	15.00

SHILLING

.925 SILVER

Y#	Date	Mintage	VF	XF	Unc
5	1935	2.100	BV	5.00	6.50
	1936	1.360	BV	5.00	6.50
10	1938	3.400	BV	5.00	6.50
	1945	2.000	BV	5.00	6.50

NCLT ISSUES

PROOF SETS

STANDARD METALS

KM#	Date	Mintage	Identification	Issue Price	Mkt. Val.
101	1929(2)	—	Y1,2	—	1200.
102	1929(2)	20	Y1a,2a	—	1000.

PAPUA NEW GUINEA

Papua (formerly British New Guinea), situated in the southeastern part of the island of New Guinea, has an area of 90,540 sq. mi. (234,499 sq. km.) and a population of 740,000. It was temporarily annexed by Queensland in 1883 and by the British Crown in 1888. Papua came under control of the Australian Commonwealth in 1901 and became the Territory of Papua in 1906. Japan invaded New Guinea and Papua early in 1942, but Australian control was restored before the end of the year in Papua and in 1945 in New Guinea.

MINTMARKS

FM - Franklin Mint, U.S.A.*

***NOTE:** During 1975-77 the Franklin Mint produced coinage in up to 3 different qualities. Qualities of issue are designated in ( ) after each date and are defined as follows:

(M) MATTE - Normal circulation strike or a dull finish produced by sandblasting special uncirculated (polish finish) or proof quality dies.

(U) SPECIAL UNCIRCULATED - Polished or proof-like in appearance without any frosted features.

(P) PROOF - The highest quality obtainable having mirror-like fields and frosted features.

MONETARY SYSTEM

100 Toea = 1 Kina

TOEA

BRONZE

Y#	Date	Mintage	VF	XF	Unc
1	1975	14.400	—	.10	.15
	1975FM(M)	.083	—	.10	.15
	1975FM(U)	4,134	—	.50	1.00
	1975FM(P)	.067	—	Proof	1.00
	1976	5.100	—	—	.10
	1976FM(M)	.084	—	—	.10
	1976FM(U)	976 pcs.	—	.75	1.50
	1976FM(P)	.016	—	Proof	1.00
	1977FM(M)	.084	—	—	.10
	1977FM(U)	603 pcs.	—	—	2.00
	1977FM(P)	7,721	—	Proof	1.50
	1978FM(M)	.083	—	—	—
	1978FM(U)	777 pcs.	—	—	—
	1978FM(P)	5,540	—	Proof	2.00
	1979FM(U)	—	—	—	—
	1979FM(P)	—	—	Proof	1.50

2 TOEA

BRONZE

Y#	Date	Mintage	VF	XF	Unc
2	1975	11.400	.10	.15	.25
	1975FM(M)	.042	.10	.15	.25
	1975FM(U)	4,134	—	.75	1.50
	1975FM(P)	.067	—	Proof	1.25
	1976	5.100	—	—	.15
	1976FM(M)	.042	—	.10	.15
	1976FM(U)	976 pcs.	—	1.25	2.50
	1976FM(P)	.016	—	Proof	1.25
	1977FM(M)	.042	—	—	.15
	1977FM(U)	603 pcs.	—	—	3.00
	1977FM(P)	7,721	—	Proof	2.50
	1978FM(M)	.042	—	—	—
	1978FM(U)	777 pcs.	—	—	—
	1978FM(P)	5,540	—	Proof	3.00
	1979FM(U)	—	—	—	—
	1979FM(P)	—	—	Proof	2.50

5 TOEA

COPPER-NICKEL

Y#	Date	Mintage	VF	XF	Unc
3	1975	11.000	.15	.25	.40
	1975FM(M)	.017	.15	.25	.50
	1975FM(U)	4,134	—	1.00	1.75
	1975FM(P)	.067	—	Proof	1.50
	1976	24.000	.15	.25	.50
	1976FM(M)	.017	.15	.25	.50
	1976FM(U)	976 pcs.	—	2.00	3.50
	1976FM(P)	.016	—	Proof	1.50
	1977FM(M)	.017	—	—	.55
	1977FM(U)	603 pcs.	—	—	3.50
	1977FM(P)	7,721	—	Proof	2.50
	1978FM(M)	.017	—	—	—
	1978FM(U)	777 pcs.	—	—	—
	1978FM(P)	5,540	—	Proof	3.00
	1979FM(U)	—	—	—	—
	1979FM(P)	—	—	Proof	2.50

10 TOEA

COPPER-NICKEL

Y#	Date	Mintage	VF	XF	Unc
4	1975	8.600	.20	.30	.60
	1975FM(M)	8,300	.25	.50	1.00
	1975FM(U)	4,134	—	1.50	2.25
	1975FM(P)	.067	—	Proof	2.00
	1976FM(M)	8,300	.25	.50	1.00
	1976FM(U)	976 pcs.	—	3.00	5.00
	1976FM(P)	.016	—	Proof	2.00
	1977FM(M)	8,300	—	—	1.00
	1977FM(U)	603 pcs.	—	—	2.00
	1977FM(P)	7,721	—	Proof	3.00
	1978FM(M)	8,300	—	—	—
	1978FM(U)	777 pcs.	—	—	—
	1978FM(P)	5,540	—	Proof	4.00
	1979FM(U)	—	—	—	—
	1979FM(P)	—	—	Proof	3.00

20 TOEA

COPPER-NICKEL

Y#	Date	Mintage	VF	XF	Unc
5	1975	15.500	.50	.70	1.00
	1975FM(M)	4,150	2.00	3.00	5.00
	1975FM(U)	4,134	2.00	3.00	5.00
	1975FM(P)	.067	—	Proof	3.00
	1976FM(M)	4,150	2.00	3.00	5.00
	1976FM(U)	976 pcs.	—	5.00	7.00
	1976FM(P)	.016	—	Proof	3.00
	1977FM(M)	4,150	—	—	3.00
	1977FM(U)	603 pcs.	—	—	4.00
	1977FM(P)	7,721	—	Proof	4.25
	1978FM(M)	4,150	—	—	—
	1978FM(U)	777 pcs.	—	—	—
	1978FM(P)	5,540	—	Proof	5.00
	1979FM(U)	—	—	—	—
	1979FM(P)	—	—	Proof	4.25

KINA

COPPER-NICKEL

Y#	Date	Mintage	VF	XF	Unc
6	1975	2.000	1.50	2.00	2.50
	1975FM(M)	829 pcs.	—	15.00	25.00
	1975FM(U)	4,134	3.50	6.00	10.00
	1975FM(P)	.067	—	Proof	4.00
	1976FM(M)	829 pcs.	10.00	15.00	25.00
	1976FM(U)	976 pcs.	—	13.50	22.50
	1976FM(P)	.016	—	Proof	4.00
	1977FM(M)	829 pcs.	—	—	20.00
	1977FM(U)	603 pcs.	—	—	22.50
	1977FM(P)	7,721	—	Proof	12.50
	1978FM(M)	829 pcs.	—	—	—
	1978FM(U)	777 pcs.	—	—	—
	1978FM(P)	5,540	—	Proof	15.00
	1979FM(U)	—	—	—	—
	1979FM(P)	—	—	Proof	12.50

5 KINA

COPPER-NICKEL

Y#	Date	Mintage	VF	XF	Unc
7	1975FM(M)	166 pcs.	90.00	150.00	225.00
	1975FM(U)	4,134	—	30.00	50.00
	1976FM(M)	166 pcs.	90.00	150.00	225.00
	1976FM(U)	976 pcs.	—	30.00	60.00
	1977FM(M)	166 pcs.	—	—	225.00
	1977FM(U)	603 pcs.	—	—	70.00
	1978FM(M)	166pcs.	—	—	—
	1978FM(U)	777pcs.	—	—	—
	1979FM(U)	—	—	—	—
	25.9000 gm., .500 SILVER, .4164 oz ASW				
7a	1975FM(P)	.067	—	Proof	20.00
	1976FM(P)	.016	—	Proof	20.00
	1977FM(P)	7,721	—	Proof	30.00
	1978FM(P)	5,540	—	Proof	20.00
	1979FM(P)	—	—	Proof	20.00

10 KINA

COPPER-NICKEL

Y#	Date	Mintage	VF	XF	Unc
8	1975FM(M)	82 pcs.	175.00	225.00	300.00
	1975FM(U)	4,134	—	—	—
	1976FM(M)	82 pcs.	150.00	200.00	275.00
	1976FM(U)	976 pcs.	—	40.00	65.00
	1978FM(M)	168pcs.	—	—	—
	1978FM(U)	777pcs.	—	—	—
	1979FM(U)	—	—	—	—
	40.5000 gm., .925 SILVER, 1.2046 oz ASW				
8a	1975FM(P)	.079	—	Proof	50.00
	1976FM(P)	.021	—	Proof	50.00
	1978FM(P)	7,352	—	Proof	50.00
	1979FM(P)	—	—	Proof	50.00

COPPER-NICKEL
Silver Jubilee

Y#	Date	Mintage	VF	XF	Unc
11	1977FM(M)	82 pcs.	—	—	250.00
	1977FM(U)	603 pcs.	—	—	75.00
	40.5000 gm., .925 SILVER, 1.2046 oz ASW				
11a	1977FM(P)	.014	—	Proof	70.00

100 KINA

Y#	Date	Mintage	VF	XF	Unc
	9.5700 gm., .900 GOLD, .2769 oz AGW				
9	1975FM(M)	100 pcs.	200.00	300.00	500.00
	1975FM(U)	8,081	BV	BV	180.00
	1975FM(P)	.018	—	Proof	165.00

Y#	Date	Mintage	VF	XF	Unc
	1st Anniversary of Independence				
10	1976FM(M)	100 pcs.	200.00	300.00	500.00
	1976FM(U)	250 pcs.	BV	225.00	300.00
	1976FM(P)	8,020	—	Proof	185.00

Y#	Date	Mintage	VF	XF	Unc
12	1977FM(M)	100 pcs.	BV	275.00	475.00
	1977FM(U)	362 pcs.	BV	BV	275.00
	1977FM(P)	3,460	—	Proof	225.00

Y#	Date	Mintage	VF	XF	Unc
13	1978FM(M)	200pcs.	—	BV	225.00
	1978FM(U)	200pcs.	—	—	—
	1978FM(P)	4,751	—	Proof	200.00

Y#	Date	Mintage	VF	XF	Unc
14	1979FM(P)	—	—	Proof	250.00

NCLT ISSUES

SPECIMEN SET
STANDARD METALS

KM#	Date	Mintage	Identification	Issue Price	Mkt. Val.
S1	1975FM(8)	4,134	Y1-8	30.00	35.00
S2	1976FM(8)	976	Y1-8	30.00	125.00
S3	1977FM(8)	603	Y1-7,11	30.00	150.00
S4	1978FM(8)	777	—	30.00	—
S5	1979FM(8)	—	Y1-8	31.00	—

PROOF SETS
STANDARD METALS

KM#	Date	Mintage	Identification	Issue Price	Mkt. Val.
101	1975FM(8)	42,340	Y1-6,7a,8a	60.00	80.00
102	1976FM(8)	16,323	Y1-6,7a,8a	60.00	80.00
103	1977FM(8)	7,721	Y1-6,7a,11a	60.00	125.00
104	1978FM(8)	5,540	Y1-6,7a,8a	70.00	100.00
105	1979FM(8)	—	Y1-6,7a,8a	72.00	90.00

PARAGUAY

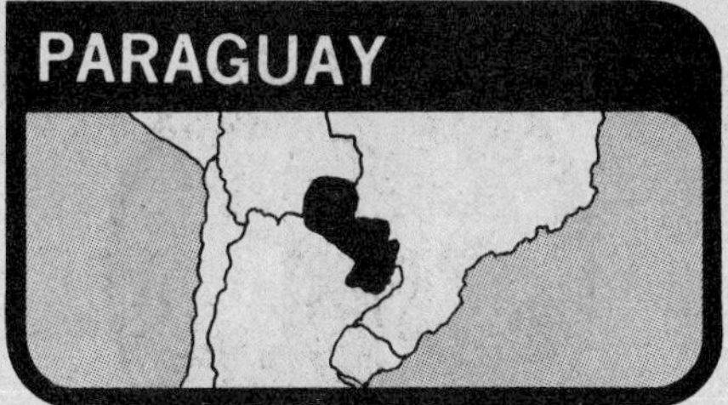

The Republic of Paraguay, a landlocked country in the heart of South America surrounded by Argentina, Bolivia and Brazil, has an area of 157,047 sq. mi. (406,750 sq. km.) and a population of 2.6 million, 95 percent of whom are of mixed Spanish and Indian descent. Capital: Asuncion. The country is predominantly agrarian, with no important mineral deposits or oil reserves. Meat, timber, oilseeds, tobacco and cotton account for 70 percent of Paraguay's export revenue.

Paraguay was first visited by Alejo Garcia, a shipwrecked Spaniard, in 1520. The interior was explored by Sebastian Cabot in 1526 and 1529, when he sailed up the Parana and Paraguay rivers. Asuncion, which would become the center of a province embracing much of southern South America, was established by the Spanish explorer Juan de Salazar on Aug. 15, 1537. For a century and a half the history of Paraguay was largely the history of the agricultural colonies established by the Jesuits in the south and east to Christianize the Indians. In 1811, following the outbreak of the South American wars of independence, Paraguayan patriots overthrew the local Spanish authorities and proclaimed their country's independence.

MONETARY SYSTEM

100 Centesimos = 1 Peso

1/12 REAL

COPPER

Y#	Date	Mintage	Fine	VF	XF	Unc
1	1845	3.168	11.50	20.00	45.00	—
	Crude issue struck at Asuncian Mint					
1.1	1845	—	—	—	35.00	—

DECIMAL COINAGE

100 Centavos (Centesimos)
= 1 Peso

CENTESIMO

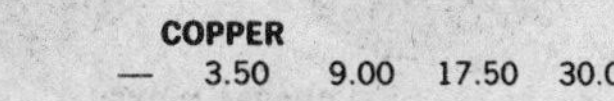

COPPER

Y#	Date	Mintage	Fine	VF	XF	Unc
2	1870	—	3.50	9.00	17.50	30.00

2 CENTESIMOS

COPPER

Y#	Date	Mintage	Fine	VF	XF	Unc
3	1870	—	4.00	10.00	20.00	37.50

4 CENTESIMOS

COPPER
Rev: SHAW to right of date (Birmingham Mint)

Y#	Date	Mintage	Fine	VF	XF	Unc
4	1870	—	5.00	15.00	25.00	50.00

Crude issue struck at Asuncion without Saez to right of date and without ribbon bow on wreath.

Y#	Date	Mintage	Fine	VF	XF	Unc
4a	1870	—	15.00	50.00	90.00	—

5 CENTAVOS

COPPER-NICKEL

Y#	Date	Mintage	Fine	VF	XF	Unc
6	1900	.400	1.00	3.00	4.00	8.50
	1903	.600	.75	3.00	3.50	10.00

Y#	Date	Mintage	Fine	VF	XF	Unc
9	1908	.400	5.00	13.50	27.50	60.00

10 CENTAVOS

COPPER-NICKEL

Y#	Date	Mintage	Fine	VF	XF	Unc
7	1900	.800	1.50	3.50	5.00	11.50
	1903	1.200	.90	3.00	4.25	9.00

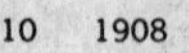

Y#	Date	Mintage	Fine	VF	XF	Unc
10	1908	.800	9.00	25.00	35.00	70.00

20 CENTAVOS

COPPER-NICKEL

Y#	Date	Mintage	Fine	VF	XF	Unc
8	1900	.500	1.75	3.50	5.00	12.00
	1903	.750	1.25	3.00	4.50	10.00

Y#	Date	Mintage	Fine	VF	XF	Unc
11	1908	1.000	4.00	8.00	17.50	35.00

50 CENTAVOS

COPPER-NICKEL

Y#	Date	Mintage	Fine	VF	XF	Unc
12	1925	4.000	.75	1.50	2.50	6.00

ALUMINUM

Y#	Date	Mintage	Fine	VF	XF	Unc
17	1938	.400	.90	1.25	2.00	4.50

PESO

.750 SILVER

Y#	Date	Mintage	Fine	VF	XF	Unc
5	1889	.600*	50.00	75.00	160.00	275.00

*Unknown quantity melted.

COPPER-NICKEL

Y#	Date	Mintage	Fine	VF	XF	Unc
13	1925	3.500	.50	1.25	2.00	5.50

ALUMINUM

Y#	Date	Mintage	Fine	VF	XF	Unc
18	1938	—	.50	1.25	2.00	3.00

2 PESOS

COPPER-NICKEL

Y#	Date	Mintage	Fine	VF	XF	Unc
14	1925	2.500	.60	1.50	2.50	5.00

ALUMINUM

Y#	Date	Mintage	Fine	VF	XF	Unc
19	1938	—	.60	1.50	2.50	6.00

5 PESOS

COPPER-NICKEL

Y#	Date	Mintage	Fine	VF	XF	Unc
15	1939	4.000	1.25	4.00	6.50	12.00

10 PESOS

COPPER-NICKEL

Y#	Date	Mintage	Fine	VF	XF	Unc
16	1939	4.000	1.00	3.00	5.00	8.00

NEW COINAGE

100 Centimos = 1 Guarani

CENTIMO

ALUMINUM-BRONZE

Y#	Date	Mintage	Fine	VF	XF	Unc
20	1944	3.500	—	.50	.65	1.25
	1948	2.000	—	.15	.35	1.00
	1950	1.096	—	.10	.20	.50

5 CENTIMOS

ALUMINUM-BRONZE

Y#	Date	Mintage	Fine	VF	XF	Unc
21	1944	2.195	—	.30	.50	1.15
	1947	13.111	—	.30	.35	.50

10 CENTIMOS

ALUMINUM-BRONZE

Y#	Date	Mintage	Fine	VF	XF	Unc
22	1944	.975	.75	1.00	1.25	3.00
	1947	6.656	—	.30	.50	.75

Y#	Date	Mintage	Fine	VF	XF	Unc
25	1953	5.000	—	—	.10	.20

15 CENTIMOS

ALUMINUM-BRONZE

Y#	Date	Mintage	Fine	VF	XF	Unc
26	1953	5.000	—	—	.15	.50

25 CENTIMOS

ALUMINUM-BRONZE

Y#	Date	Mintage	Fine	VF	XF	Unc
23	1944	.700	.50	2.00	3.50	6.50
	1948	.600	—	.40	1.00	3.00
	1951	1.000	—	.30	.60	1.00

Y#	Date	Mintage	Fine	VF	XF	Unc
27	1953	2.000	—	.15	.25	.75

50 CENTIMOS

ALUMINUM-BRONZE

Y#	Date	Mintage	Fine	VF	XF	Unc
24	1944	2.485	—	.75	1.50	5.00
	1951	2.893	—	.50	1.00	2.00

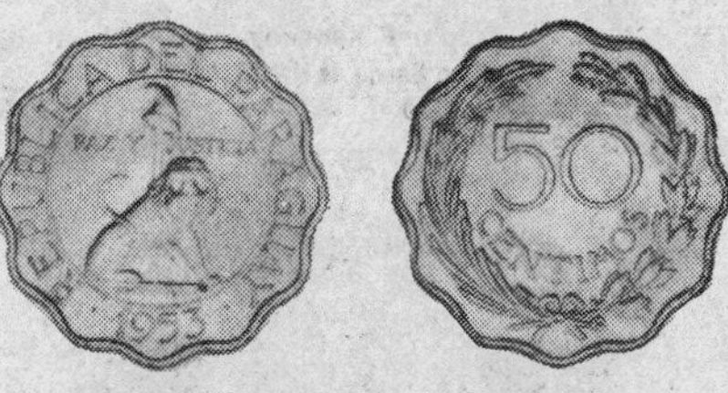

Y#	Date	Mintage	Fine	VF	XF	Unc
28	1953	3.000	—	.15	.25	.50

GUARANI

STAINLESS STEEL

Y#	Date	Mintage	Fine	VF	XF	Unc
31	1974	10.000	—	—	—	.10
	1975	10.000	—	—	—	.10
	1976	12.000	—	—	—	.10

F.A.O. Issue

Y#	Date	Mintage	Fine	VF	XF	Unc
35	1978	15.000	—	—	—	.10

5 GUARANIES

STAINLESS STEEL

Y#	Date	Mintage	Fine	VF	XF	Unc
32	1974	7.500	—	.10	.20	.25
	1975	7.500	—	.10	.20	.25

F.A.O. Issue

Y#	Date	Mintage	Fine	VF	XF	Unc
36	1978	10.000	—	—	—	.10

10 GUARANIES

STAINLESS STEEL

Y#	Date	Mintage	Fine	VF	XF	Unc
33	1974	10.000	—	.15	.25	.40
	1975	10.000	—	.15	.25	.50
33	1976	10.000	—	.15	.25	.50

F.A.O. Issue

Y#	Date	Mintage	Fine	VF	XF	Unc
37	1978	15.000	—	—	—	.10

50 GUARANIES

STAINLESS STEEL

Y#	Date	Mintage	Fine	VF	XF	Unc
34	1974	7.500	—	.50	.75	1.25
	1975	7.500	—	.50	1.25	1.50

150 GUARANIES

25.0000 gm., 1.000 SILVER, .8038 oz ASW
General A. Stroessner
Rev: Similar to H#2.

H#	Date	Mintage	XF	Unc	Proof
1	1972	.010	—	—	25.00

Munich Olympics

H#	Date	Mintage	XF	Unc	Proof
2	1972	.010	—	—	25.00

Munich Olympics
Obv: Broad jumper. Rev: Same as H#2.

H#	Date	Mintage	XF	Unc	Proof
3	1972	.010	—	—	25.00

Munich Olympics
Obv: Relay runner. Rev: Same as H#2.

H#	Date	Mintage	XF	Unc	Proof
4	1972	.010	—	—	25.00

Munich Olympics
Rev: Same as H#2.

H#	Date	Mintage	XF	Unc	Proof
5	1972	.010	—	—	25.00

Munich Olympics
Obv: Pole vaulter. Rev: Same as H#2.

H#	Date	Mintage	XF	Unc	Proof
6	1972	.010	—	—	25.00

Munich Olympics
Rev: Same as H#2.

H#	Date	Mintage	XF	Unc	Proof
7	1972	.010	—	—	25.00

Estigarriba
Obv: Head. Rev: Similar to H#20.

H#	Date	Mintage	XF	Unc	Proof
9	1973	.010	—	—	25.00

Mariscal Francisco Solano Lopez
Rev: Similar to H#20.

H#	Date	Mintage	XF	Unc	Proof
10	1973	.010	—	—	25.00

Diaz
Obv: Head. Rev: Similar to H#20.

H#	Date	Mintage	XF	Unc	Proof
11	1973	.010	—	—	25.00

General Bernardino Caballero
Rev: Similar to H#20.

H#	Date	Mintage	XF	Unc	Proof
12	1973	.010	—	—	25.00

Teotihucana Culture
Rev: Similar to H#20.

H#	Date	Mintage	XF	Unc	Proof
13	1973	.010	—	—	25.00

Huasteca Culture
Rev: Similar to H#20.

H#	Date	Mintage	XF	Unc	Proof
14	1973	.010	—	—	25.00

Mixteca Culture
Rev: Similar to H#20.

H#	Date	Mintage	XF	Unc	Proof
15	1973	.010	—	—	25.00

Veracruz Ceramica
Rev: Similar to H#20.

H#	Date	Mintage	XF	Unc	Proof
16	1973	.010	—	—	25.00

Veracruz Culture
Rev: Similar to H#20.

H#	Date	Mintage	XF	Unc	Proof
17	1973	.010	—	—	25.00

Albrecht Durer
Rev: Similar to H#20.

H#	Date	Mintage	XF	Unc	Proof
18	1973	.010	—	—	25.00

Johann Wolfgang Goethe
Obv: Head. Rev: Similar to H#20.

H#	Date	Mintage	XF	Unc	Proof
19	1973	.010	—	—	25.00

Abraham Lincoln

H#	Date	Mintage	XF	Unc	Proof
20	1974	.010	—	—	25.00

Ludwig von Beethoven
Obv: Head. Rev: Same as H#20.

H#	Date	Mintage	XF	Unc	Proof
21	1974	.010	—	—	25.00

Otto von Bismarck
Rev: Same as H#20.

H#	Date	Mintage	XF	Unc	Proof
22	1974	.010	—	—	25.00

Albert Einstein
Rev: Same as H#20.

H#	Date	Mintage	XF	Unc	Proof
23	1974	.010	—	—	25.00

Garibaldi
Obv: Head. Rev: Same as H#20.

H#	Date	Mintage	XF	Unc	Proof
24	1974	.010	—	—	25.00

Alessandro Manzoni
Obv: Head. Rev: Same as H#20.

H#	Date	Mintage	XF	Unc	Proof
25	1974	.010	—	—	25.00

William Tell
Obv: Head. Rev: Same as H#20.

H#	Date	Mintage	XF	Unc	Proof
26	1974	.010	—	—	25.00

John F. Kennedy
Rev: Same as H#20.

H#	Date	Mintage	XF	Unc	Proof
27	1974	.010	—	—	25.00

Konrad Adenauer
Rev: Same as H#20.

H#	Date	Mintage	XF	Unc	Proof
28	1974	.010	—	—	25.00

Winston Churchill
Obv: Head. Rev: Same as H#20.

H#	Date	Mintage	XF	Unc	Proof
29	1974	.010	—	—	25.00

Pope John XXIII
Rev: Same as H#20.

H#	Date	Mintage	XF	Unc	Proof
30	1974	.010	—	—	25.00

Pope Paul VI
Obv: Head. Rev: Same as H#20.

H#	Date	Mintage	XF	Unc	Proof
31	1974	.010	—	—	25.00

Parliament of Paraguay
Rev: Similar to H#20.

H#	Date	Mintage	XF	Unc	Proof
32	1974	.010	—	—	25.00

H#	Date	Mintage	XF	Unc	Proof
Apollo II					
33	1975	.010	—	—	25.00
Apollo 15					
34	1975	.010	—	—	25.00
Friendship Bridge. Obv: Bridge. Rev: Same as H#20.					
127	1975	—	—	—	25.00
St. Trinidad Church. Obv: Church. Rev: Same as H#20.					
128	1975	—	—	—	25.00
Humaite. Obv: Humaite ruins. Rev: Same as H#20.					
129	1975	—	—	—	25.00

300 GUARANIES

26.7300 gm., .720 SILVER, .6188 oz ASW
War Centennial

Y#	Date	Mintage	Fine	VF	XF	Unc
29	1968	.250	BV	BV	BV	18.50

1500 GUARANIES

10.7000 gm., .900 GOLD, .3096 oz AGW
General A. Stroessner
Obv: Head. Rev: Similar to 150 Guaranies, H#20.

H#	Date	Mintage	XF	Unc	Proof
65	1972	1,500	—	—	200.00
Munich Olympics. Obv: Similar to 150 Guaranies, H#2. Rev: Similar to 150 guaranies, H#20.					
36	1972	1,500	—	—	200.00
Munich Olympics. Obv: Broad jumper. Rev: Similar to 150 Guaranies, H#20.					
37	1972	1,500	—	—	200.00
Munich Olympics. Obv: Relay runner. Rev: Similar to 150 Guaranies, H#20.					
38	1972	1,500	—	—	200.00
Munich Olympics. Obv: Similar to 150 Guaranies, H#5. Rev: Similar to 150 Guaranies, H#20.					
39	1972	1,500	—	—	200.00
Munich Olympics. Obv: Pole vaulter. Rev: Similar to 150 Guaranies, H#20.					
40	1972	1,500	—	—	200.00
Munich Olympics. Obv: Similar to 150 Guaranies, H#7. Rev: Similar to 150 Guaranies, H#20.					
41	1972	1,500	—	—	200.00
Estigarribia. Obv: Head. Rev: Similar to 150 Guaranies, H#20.					
42	1973	1,500	—	—	200.00
Mariscal Francisco Solano Lopez. Obv: Similar to 150 Guaranies, H#10. Rev: Similar to 150 Guaranies, H#20.					
43	1973	1,500	—	—	200.00
Diaz. Obv: Head. Rev: Similar to 150 Guaranies, H#20.					
44	1973	1,500	—	—	200.00
General Bernardino Caballero. Obv: Similar to 150 Guaranies, H#12. Rev: Similar to 150 Guaranies, H#20.					
45	1973	1,500	—	—	200.00
Teotihucana Culture. Obv: Similar to 150 Guaranies, H#13. Rev: Similar to 150 Guaranies, H#20.					
46	1973	1,500	—	—	200.00
Huasteca Culture. Obv: Similar to 150 Guaranies, H#14. Rev: Similar to 150 Guaranies, H#20.					
47	1973	1,500	—	—	200.00
Mixteca Culture. Obv: Similar to 150 Guaranies, H#15. Rev: Similar to 150 Guaranies, H#20.					
48	1973	1,500	—	—	200.00
Veracruz Ceramica. Obv: Similar to 150 Guaranies, H#16. Rev: Similar to 150 Guaranies, H#20.					
49	1973	1,500	—	—	200.00
Veracruz Culture. Obv: Similar to 150 Guaranies, H#17. Rev: Similar to 150 Guaranies, H#20.					
50	1973	1,500	—	—	200.00
Albrecht Durer. Obv: Similar to 150 Guaranies, H#18. Rev: Similar to 150 Guaranies, H#20.					
51	1973	1,500	—	—	200.00
Johann Wolfgang Goethe. Obv: Head. Rev: Similar to 150 Guaranies, H#20.					
52	1973	1,500	—	—	200.00
Abraham Lincoln. Obv: Similar to 150 Guaranies, H#20. Rev: Similar to 150 Guaranies, H#20.					
53	1974	1,500	—	—	200.00
Ludwig von Beethoven. Obv: Head. Rev: Similar to 150 Guaranies, H#20.					
54	1974	1,500	—	—	200.00
Otto von Bismarck. Obv: Similar to 150 Guaranies, H#22. Rev: Similar to 150 Guaranies, H#20.					
55	1974	1,500	—	—	200.00
Albert Einstein. Obv: Similar to 150 Guaranies, H#23. Rev: Similar to 150 Guaranies, H#20.					
56	1974	1,500	—	—	200.00
Garibaldi. Obv: Head. Rev: Similar to 150 Guaranies, H#20.					
57	1974	1,500	—	—	200.00
Alessandro Manzoni. Obv: Similar to 4500 Guaranies, H#117. Rev: Similar to 150 Guaranies, H#20.					
58	1974	1,500	—	—	200.00
William Tell. Obv: Head. Rev: Similar to 150 Guaranies, H#20.					
59	1974	1,500	—	—	200.00
John F. Kennedy. Obv: Similar to 150 Guaranies, H#27. Rev: Similar to 150 Guaranies, H#20.					
60	1974	1,500	—	—	200.00
Konrad Adenauer. Obv: Similar to 150 Guaranies, H#28. Rev: Similar to 150 Guaranies, H#20.					
61	1974	1,500	—	—	200.00
Winston Churchill. Obv: Head. Rev: Similar to 150 Guaranies, H#20.					
62	1974	1,500	—	—	200.00
Pope John XXIII. Obv: Similar to 150 Guaranies, H#30. Rev: Similar to 150 Guaranies, H#20.					
63	1974	1,500	—	—	200.00
Pope Paul VI. Obv: Head. Rev: Similar to 150 Guaranies, H#20.					
64	1974	1,500	—	—	200.00

3000 GUARANIES

21.3000 gm., .900 GOLD, .6164 oz AGW
General A. Stroessner Commemorative

H#	Date	Mintage	XF	Unc	Proof
94a	1972	1,500	—	—	400.00

H#	Date	Mintage	XF	Unc	Proof
Munich Olympics. Rev: Similar to 150 Guaranies, H#20.					
66	1972	1,500	—	—	400.00
Munich Olympics. Obv: Broad jumper. Rev: Similar to 150 Guaranies, H#20.					
67	1972	1,500	—	—	400.00
Munich Olympics. Obv: Relay runner. Rev: Similar to 150 Guaranies, H#20.					
68	1972	1,500	—	—	400.00
Munich Olympics. Obv: Similar to 150 Guaranies, H#5. Rev: Similar to 150 Guaranies, H#20.					
69	1972	1,500	—	—	400.00
Munich Olympics. Obv: Pole vaulter. Rev: Similar to 150 Guaranies, H#20.					
70	1972	1,500	—	—	400.00
Munich Olympics. Obv: Similar to 150 Guaranies, H#7. Rev: Similar to 150 Guaranies, H#20.					
71	1972	1,500	—	—	400.00
Estigarribia. Obv: Head. Rev: Similar to 150 Guaranies, H#20.					
72	1973	1,500	—	—	400.00
Mariscal Francisco Solano Lopez. Obv: Similar to 150 Guaranies, H#10. Rev: Similar to 150 Guaranies, H#20.					
73	1973	1,500	—	—	400.00
Diaz. Obv: Head. Rev: Similar to 150 Guaranies, H#20.					
74	1973	1,500	—	—	400.00
General Bernardino Caballero. Obv: Similar to 150 Guaranies, H#12. Rev: Similar to 150 Guaranies, H#20.					
75	1973	1,500	—	—	400.00

Teotihucana Culture
Obv: Similar to 150 Guaranies, H#13.

Rev: Similar to 150 Guaranies, H#20.

H#	Date	Mintage	XF	Unc	Proof
76	1973	1,500	—	—	400.00

Huasteca Culture
Obv: Similar to 150 Guaranies, H#14.
Rev: Similar to 150 Guaranies, H#20.

77 1973 1,500 — — 400.00

Mixteca Culture
Obv: Similar to 150 Guaranies, H#15.
Rev: Similar to 150 Guaranies, H#20.

78 1973 1,500 — — 400.00

Veracruz Ceramica
Obv: Similar to 150 Guaranies, H#16.
Rev: Similar to 150 Guaranies, H#20.

79 1973 1,500 — — 400.00

Veracruz Culture
Obv: Similar to 150 Guaranies, H#17.
Rev: Similar to 150 Guaranies, H#20.

80 1973 1,500 — — 400.00

Albrecht Durer
Obv: Similar to 150 Guaranies, H#18.
Rev: Similar to 150 Guaranies, H#20.

81 1973 1,500 — — 400.00

Johann Wolfgang Goethe
Obv: Head. Rev: Similar to 150 Guaranies, H#20.

82 1973 1,500 — — 400.00

Abraham Lincoln
Obv: Similar to 150 Guaranies, H#20.
Rev: Similar to 150 Guaranies, H#20.

83 1974 1,500 — — 400.00

Ludwig von Beethoven
Obv: Head. Rev: Similar to 150 Guaranies, H#20.

84 1974 1,500 — — 400.00

Otto von Bismarck
Obv: Similar to 150 Guaranies, H#22.
Rev: Similar to 150 Guaranies, H#20.

85 1974 1,500 — — 400.00

Albert Einstein
Obv: Similar to 150 Guaranies, H#23.
Rev: Similar to 150 Guaranies, H#20.

86 1974 1,500 — — 400.00

Garibaldi
Obv: Head. Rev: Similar to 150 Guaranies, H#20.

87 1974 1,500 — — 400.00

Alessandro Manzoni
Obv: Similar to 4500 Guaranies, H#117.
Rev: Similar to 150 Guaranies, H#20.

88 1974 1,500 — — 400.00

William Tell
Obv: Head. Rev: Similar to 150 Guaranies, H#20.

89 1974 1,500 — — 400.00

John F. Kennedy
Obv: Similar to 150 Guaranies, H#27.
Rev: Similar to 150 Guaranies, H#20.

90 1974 1,500 — — 400.00

Konrad Adenauer
Obv: Similar to 150 Guaranies, H#28.
Rev: Similar to 150 Guaranies, H#20.

91 1974 1,500 — — 400.00

Winston Churchill
Obv: Head. Rev: Similar to 150 Guaranies, H#20.

92 1974 1,500 — — 400.00

Pope John XXIII
Obv: Similar to 150 Guaranies, H#30.
Rev: Similar to 150 Guaranies, H#20.

93 1974 1,500 — — 400.00

Pope Paul VI
Obv: Head. Rev: Similar to 150 Guaranies, H#20.

94 1974 1,500 — — 400.00

4500 GUARANIES

31.9000 gm., .900 GOLD, .9231 oz AGW
General A. Stroessner
Similar to 3000 Guaranies, H#94a.

124 1972 1,500 — — 600.00

Munich Olympics
Rev: Similar to 150 Guaranies, H#20.

H#	Date	Mintage	XF	Unc	Proof
95	1972	1,500	—	—	600.00

Munich Olympics
Obv: Broad jumper. Rev: Similar to 150 Guaranies, H#20.

96 1972 1,500 — — 600.00

Munich Olympics
Obv: Relay runner. Rev: Similar to 150 Guaranies, H#20.

97 1972 1,500 — — 600.00

Munich Olympics
Obv: Similar to 150 Guaranies, H#5.
Rev: Similar to 150 Guaranies, H#20.

98 1972 1,500 — — 600.00

Munich Olympics
Obv: Pole vaulter. Rev: Similar to 150 Guaranies, H#20.

99 1972 1,500 — — 600.00

Munich Olympics
Obv: Similar to 150 Guaranies, H#7.
Rev: Similar to 150 Guaranies, H#20.

100 1972 1,500 — — 600.00

Estigarribia
Obv: Head. Rev: Same as H#117.

101 1973 1,500 — — 600.00

Mariscal Francisco Solano Lopez
Obv: Similar to 150 Guaranies, H#10.
Rev: Same as H#117.

102 1973 1,500 — — 600.00

Diaz
Obv: Head. Rev: Same as H#117.

103 1973 1,500 — — 600.00

General Bernardino Caballero
Obv: Similar to 150 Guaranies, H#12.
Rev: Same as H#117.

104 1973 1,500 — — 600.00

Teotihucana Culture
Obv: Similar to 150 Guaranies, H#13.
Rev: Same as H#117.

105 1973 1,500 — — 600.00

Huasteca Culture
Obv: Similar to 150 Guaranies, H#14.
Rev: Same as H#117.

106 1973 1,500 — — 600.00

Mixteca Culture
Obv: Similar to 150 Guaranies, H#15.
Rev: Same as H#117.

107 1973 1,500 — — 600.00

Veracruz Ceramica
Obv: Similar to 150 Guaranies, H#16.
Rev: Same as H#117.

108 1973 1,500 — — 600.00

Veracruz Culture
Obv: Similar to 150 Guaranies, H#17.
Rev: Same as H#117.

109 1973 1,500 — — 600.00

Albrecht Durer
Obv: Similar to 150 Guaranies, H#18.
Rev: Same as H#117.

110 1973 1,500 — — 600.00

Johann Wolfgang Goethe
Obv: Head. Rev: Same as H#117.

111 1973 1,500 — — 600.00

Ludwig von Beethoven
Obv: Head. Rev: Same as H#117.

113 1973 1,500 — — 600.00

Otto von Bismarck
Obv: Similar to 150 Guaranies, H#22.

Rev: Same as H#117.

H#	Date	Mintage	XF	Unc	Proof
114	1973	1,500	—	—	600.00

Garibaldi
Obv: Head. Rev: Same as H#117.

116 1973 1,500 — — 600.00

Alessandro Manzoni

117 1973 1,500 — — 600.00

Abraham Lincoln
Obv: Similar to 150 Guaranies, H#20.
Rev: Similar to H#117.

112 1974 1,500 — — 600.00

Albert Einstein
Obv: Similar to 150 Guaranies, H#23.
Rev: Similar to H#117.

115 1974 1,500 — — 600.00

William Tell
Obv: Head. Rev: Similar to H#117.

118 1974 1,500 — — 600.00

John F. Kennedy
Obv: Similar to 150 Guaranies, H#27.
Rev: Similar to H#117.

119 1974 1,500 — — 600.00

Konrad Adenauer
Obv: Similar to 150 Guaranies, H#28.
Rev: Similar to H#117.

120 1974 1,500 — — 600.00

Winston Churchill
Obv: Head. Rev: Similar to H#117.

121 1974 1,500 — — 600.00

Pope John XXIII
Obv: Similar to 150 Guaranies, H#30.
Rev: Similar to H#117.

122 1974 1,500 — — 600.00

Pope Paul VI
Obv: Head. Rev: Similar to H#117.

123 1974 1,500 — — 600.00

10,000 GUARANIES

46.0100 gm., .900 GOLD, 1.3315 oz AGW

Y-30 1968 *50 pcs. 900.00

***NOTE:** These coins were struck for presentation.

NCLT ISSUES

PROOF SETS

STANDARD METALS

KM#	Date	Mintage	Identification	Issue Price	Mkt. Val.
201	1973-74 (96)	1,500	H9-32,42-65,72—94,101-123	—	28,200.
202	1972 (26)	1,500	H2-7,36-41,66-71 94a,95-100,124	—	8350.

KM#	Date	Mintage	Identification	Issue Price	Mkt. Val.
203	1972(5)	10,000	H2-6	142.50	125.00

Listings For

PERSIA: refer to Iran

PERU

The Republic of Peru, located on the Pacific coast of South America, has an area of 496,222 sq. mi. (1,285,209 sq. km.) and a population of 16 million. Capital: Lima. The diversified economy includes mining, fishing and agriculture. Fish meal, copper, sugar, zinc and iron ore are exported.

Once part of the great Inca Empire that reached from northern Ecuador to central Chile, Peru was conquered in 1531-33 by Francisco Pizarro. Desirable as the richest of the Spanish viceroyalties, it was torn by warfare between avaricious Spaniards until the arrival in 1569 of Francisco de Toledo, who initiated 2 1/2 centuries of efficient colonial rule which made Lima the most aristocratic colonial capital and the stronghold of Spain's American possessions. Jose de San Martin of Argentina proclaimed Peru's independence on July 28, 1821; Simon Bolivar of Venezuela secured it in Dec. of 1824 when he defeated the last Spanish army in South America. After several futile attempts to re-establish its South American empire, Spain recognized Peru's independence in 1879.

Andres de Santa Cruz, whose mother was a high ranking Inca, was the best of Bolivia's early presidents, and temporarily united Peru and Bolivia 1836-39, thus realizing his dream of a Peru/Bolivian confederation. Peru was divided into two republics: North Peru, numismatically identified as Nor-Peruano, remained independent; South Peru, numismatically identified as Sud Peruano, entered into a confederation with Bolivia. Peruvian resistance and Chilean intervention finally broke up the confederation, sending Santa Cruz into European exile. A succession of military strongman presidents ruled Peru until Marshall Casilla revitalized Peruvian politics in the mid-19TH century and repulsed the attempt, by Spain, to reclaim its one time colony. Subsequent loss of southern territory to Chile in the War of the Pacific, 1879-81, and gradually increasing rejection of foreign economic domination, combined with inflation, have affected the country numismatically.

DATING

Peruvian 5, 10 and 20 centavos, issued from 1918-1944, bear the dates written in Spanish. The following table translates those written dates into numerals:

1918 - UN MIL NOVECIENTOS DIECIOCHO
1919 - UN MIL NOVECIENTOS DIECINUEVE
1920 - UN MIL NOVECIENTOS VEINTE
1921 - UN MIL NOVECIENTOS VEINTIUNO
1923 - UN MIL NOVECIENTOS VEINTITRES
1926 - UN MIL NOVECIENTOS VEINTISEIS
1934 - UN MIL NOVECIENTOS TREINTICUATRO
1935 - UN MIL NOVECIENTOS TREINTICINCO
1937 - UN MIL NOVECIENTOS TREINTISIETE
1939 - UN MIL NOVECIENTOS TREINTINUEVE
1940 - UN MIL NOVECIENTOS CUARENTA
1941 - UN MIL NOVECIENTOS CUARENTIUNO

U. S. Mints

1942 - MIL NOVECIENTOS CUARENTA Y DOS

Lima Mint

1942 - MIL NOVECIENTOS CUARENTIDOS
1943 - MIL NOVECIENTOS CUARENTA Y TRES

U. S. Mints

1944 - MIL NOVECIENTOS CUARENTA Y CUATRO

Lima Mint

1944 - MIL NOVECIENTOS CUARENTICUATRO

MINT ASSAYER'S INITIALS

The letter(s) following the dates of Peruvian coins are the assayer's initials appearing on the coins. They generally appear at the 11 o'clock position on the Colonial coinage and at the 5 o'clock position along the rim on the obverse or reverse on the Republican coinage.

COLONIAL COINAGE

RULERS

Spanish, until 1822

MINTMARKS

AREQUIPA, AREQ = Arequipa
AYACUCHO = Ayacucho
(B) = Brussels
Cuzco (monogram), Cuzco, Co. Cuzco
L, LIMAE (monogram), Lima (monogram), LIMA = Lima
(L) = London
Pasco (monogram), Pasco, Paz, Po = Pasco
P = Philadelphia
S = San Francisco

NOTE: The LIMAE monogram appears in three forms. The early LM monogram form looks like a dotted L with M. The later LIMAE monogram has all the letters of LIMAE more readily distinguishable. The third form appears as an M monogram during early Republican issues.

COLONIAL COINAGE

RULERS

Spanish, until 1822

MONETARY SYSTEM

16 Reales = 1 Escudo = 2 Pesos

1/4 REAL

.8500 gm., .903 SILVER, .0247 oz ASW

MINTMARK: L

Obv. leg: CAROLUS IIII..., bust.
Rev. leg: HISPAN. ET IND. REX, arms.

C#	Date	Mintage	Fine	VF	XF
70	1792IJ	—	20.00	36.50	60.00
	1793IJ	—	45.00	75.00	100.00
	1794IJ	—	60.00	85.00	135.00
	1795IJ	—	20.00	36.50	60.00
	Obv: L-Castle-1/4. Rev Lion.				
78	1793	—	25.00	37.50	70.00
	1794	—	—	Rare	—
	1796	—	12.50	20.00	40.00
	1797	—	12.50	20.00	40.00
	1798	—	12.50	20.00	40.00
	1799	—	12.50	20.00	40.00
	1800	—	12.50	20.00	40.00
	1801	—	12.50	20.00	40.00
	1802	—	12.50	20.00	40.00
	1803	—	12.50	20.00	40.00
	1804	—	12.50	20.00	40.00
	1805	—	12.50	20.00	40.00
	1806	—	12.50	20.00	40.00
	1807	—	12.50	20.00	40.00
	1808	—	12.50	20.00	40.00
	Similar to C#78.				
91	1809	—	45.00	65.00	80.00
	1810	—	10.00	20.00	35.00
	1811	—	13.50	30.00	45.00
	1812	—	13.50	30.00	45.00
	1813	—	10.00	20.00	35.00
	1814	—	10.00	20.00	35.00
	1815	—	15.00	30.00	45.00
	1816	—	10.00	22.50	35.00
	1817	—	10.00	22.50	35.00
	1818	—	10.00	22.50	35.00
	1819	—	10.00	22.50	35.00
	1820	—	10.00	22.50	35.00
	1821	—	10.00	22.50	35.00
	1823	—	75.00	100.00	150.00
	1825	—	75.00	100.00	150.00

1/2 REAL

1.6500 gm., .903 SILVER, .0479 oz ASW

MINTMARK: LIMAE (monogram)

Obv. leg: CAR. III..., arms. Rev: Pillars.

C#	Date	Mintage	Fine	VF	XF
31	1760JM	—	12.50	27.50	45.00
	1761JM	—	10.00	22.50	40.00
	1762JM	—	9.00	17.50	35.00
	1763JM	—	9.00	17.50	35.00
	1764JM	—	9.00	17.50	35.00
	1765JM	—	9.00	17.50	35.00

C#	Date	Mintage	Fine	VF	XF
31	1766JM	—	15.00	35.00	50.00
	1767JM	—	9.00	17.50	35.00
	1768JM	—	9.00	17.50	35.00
	1769JM	—	9.00	17.50	35.00
	1770JM	—	9.00	17.50	35.00
	1771JM	—	10.00	20.00	37.50
	1772JM	—	50.00	75.00	100.00

Obv. leg: CAROLUS III..., bust. Rev: Arms, pillars.

C#	Date	Mintage	Fine	VF	XF
41	1772JM	—	12.50	27.50	45.00
	1773JM	—	6.00	13.50	25.00
	1773MJ	—	7.50	15.00	30.00
	1774MJ	—	6.00	12.50	22.50
	1775MJ	—	6.00	12.50	22.50
	1776MJ	—	5.00	10.00	20.00
	1777MJ	—	5.00	10.00	20.00
	1778MJ	—	5.00	10.00	20.00
	1779MJ	—	5.00	10.00	20.00
	1780MJ	—	6.00	13.50	25.00
	1780MI	—	12.50	27.50	45.00
	1781MI	—	6.00	13.50	25.00
	1782MI	—	6.00	12.50	22.50
	1783MI	—	5.00	10.00	20.00
	1784MI	—	6.00	12.50	22.50
	1785MI	—	6.00	12.50	22.50
	1786MI	—	6.00	12.50	22.50
	1787MI	—	7.00	13.50	25.00
	1787IJ	—	15.00	35.00	50.00
	1788IJ	—	6.00	12.50	22.50
	1789IJ	—	10.00	20.00	37.50

Obv. leg: CAROLUS IV..., bust of Charles III.

C#	Date	Mintage	Fine	VF	XF
65	1789IJ	—	10.00	18.50	30.00
	1790IJ	—	10.00	18.50	30.00
	1791IJ	—	7.50	12.50	25.00

Obv. leg: CAROLUS IIII, bust. Rev: Arms, pillars.

C#	Date	Mintage	Fine	VF	XF
72	1791IJ	—	32.50	45.00	70.00
	1792IJ	—	6.00	9.00	20.00
	1793IJ	—	6.00	10.00	20.00
	1794IJ	—	6.00	9.00	20.00
	1795IJ	—	6.00	10.00	20.00
	1796IJ	—	6.00	9.00	20.00
	1797IJ	—	6.00	10.00	22.50
	1798IJ	—	6.00	10.00	22.50
	1799IJ	—	6.00	9.00	20.00
	1800IJ	—	6.00	10.00	20.00
	1801IJ	—	6.00	10.00	22.50
	1802IJ	—	6.00	10.00	22.50
	1803IJ	—	9.00	15.00	30.00
	1803JP	—	6.00	9.00	20.00
	1804JP	—	6.00	9.00	20.00
	1805JP	—	6.00	10.00	22.50
	1805IJ	—	18.50	35.00	50.00
	1806JP	—	6.00	10.00	22.50
	1807JP	—	6.00	9.00	20.00
	1808JP	—	6.00	10.00	20.00

Obv. leg: FERDND. VII..., Lima bust.

C#	Date	Mintage	Fine	VF	XF
92	1808JP	—	18.50	40.00	70.00

Obv. leg: FERDIN. VII.

C#	Date	Mintage	Fine	VF	XF
92.1	1809JP	—	22.50	37.50	75.00
	1810JP	—	12.50	22.50	55.00
	1811JP	—	12.50	22.50	55.00

Similar to C#92.2, standard bust.

C#	Date	Mintage	Fine	VF	XF
97	1811JP	—	10.00	20.00	45.00
	1812JP	—	5.00	10.00	15.00
	1813JP	—	5.00	10.00	15.00
	1814JP	—	7.00	13.50	30.00
	1815JP	—	5.00	10.00	15.00
	1816JP	—	5.00	10.00	15.00
	1817JP	—	5.00	10.00	15.00
	1818JP	—	5.00	10.00	15.00
	1819JP	—	5.00	10.00	15.00
	1820JP	—	5.00	10.00	15.00
	1821JP	—	5.00	10.00	20.00

REAL

3.2500 GM., .903 SILVER, .0944 oz ASW

MINTMARK: LIMAE (monogram)

Obv. leg: CAR. III..., arms. Rev: Pillars.

C#	Date	Mintage	Fine	VF	XF
32	1760JM	—	11.50	22.50	50.00
	1761JM	—	11.50	22.50	50.00
	1762JM	—	11.50	22.50	50.00
	1763JM	—	11.50	25.00	50.00
	1764JM	—	11.50	22.50	50.00
	1765JM	—	11.50	22.50	50.00
	1766JM	—	13.50	30.00	55.00
	1767JM	—	11.50	22.50	50.00
	1768JM	—	11.50	22.50	50.00
	1769JM	—	11.50	22.50	50.00
	1770JM	—	11.50	22.50	50.00
	1771JM	—	11.50	22.50	50.00
	1772JM	—	60.00	80.00	150.00

Obv. leg: CAROLUS III.

C#	Date	Mintage	Fine	VF	XF
42	1772JM	—	9.00	15.00	37.50
	1773JM	—	13.50	30.00	55.00
	1773MJ	—	7.50	13.50	30.00
	1774MJ	—	6.00	10.00	25.00
	1775MJ	—	6.00	10.00	25.00
	1776MJ	—	5.00	10.00	22.50
	1777MJ	—	5.00	10.00	22.50
	1778MJ	—	5.00	10.00	22.50
	1779MJ	—	5.00	10.00	22.50
	1780MJ	—	6.00	10.00	22.50
	1780MI	—	10.00	20.00	45.00
	1781MI	—	6.00	10.00	22.50
	1782MI	—	6.00	10.00	22.50
	1782JM	—	6.00	10.00	22.50
	1783MI	—	6.00	10.00	22.50
	1784MI	—	6.00	10.00	22.50
	1785MI	—	6.00	10.00	20.00
	1786MI	—	6.00	10.00	22.50
	1787MI	—	6.00	10.00	22.50
	1787IJ	—	27.50	42.50	75.00
	1788IJ	—	6.00	10.00	22.50
	1789IJ	—	10.00	20.00	45.00

Obv. leg: CAROLUS IV..., bust of Charles III. Rev: Arms, pillars.

C#	Date	Mintage	Fine	VF	XF
66	1789IJ	—	10.00	25.00	50.00
	1790IJ	—	8.00	18.00	40.00
	1791IJ	—	8.00	18.00	40.00

Obv. leg: CAROLUS IIII..., bust of Charles IV.

C#	Date	Mintage	Fine	VF	XF
73	1791IJ	—	6.00	15.00	32.50
	1792IJ	—	5.00	10.00	25.00
	1793IJ	—	5.00	10.00	25.00
	1794IJ	—	5.00	10.00	20.00
	1795IJ	—	5.00	10.00	20.00
	1796IJ	—	5.00	10.00	20.00
	1797IJ	—	5.00	10.00	20.00
	1798IJ	—	5.00	10.00	20.00
	1799IJ	—	6.50	15.00	30.00
	1800IJ	—	5.00	10.00	20.00
	1800JP	—	50.00	90.00	150.00
	1801IJ	—	4.50	9.00	20.00
	1802IJ	—	12.00	20.00	32.50
	1803IJ	—	10.00	25.00	50.00
	1803JP	—	8.00	18.00	50.00
	1804IJ	—	10.00	25.00	50.00
	1804JP	—	10.00	25.00	50.00
	1805JP	—	8.00	18.00	50.00
	1806JP	—	4.50	9.00	25.00
	1807JP	—	4.50	9.00	20.00
	1808JP	—	20.00	50.00	70.00

Obv. leg: FERDIN VII..., Lima bust.

C#	Date	Mintage	Fine	VF	XF
93	1809JP	—	Reported, not confirmed		
	1810JP	—	9.00	15.00	36.50
	1811JP	—	9.00	15.00	37.50

Obv. leg: FERDIN. VII..., standard bust.

C#	Date	Mintage	Fine	VF	XF
98	1811JP	—	20.00	36.50	65.00
	1812JP	—	4.50	7.50	16.00
	1813JP	—	4.50	7.50	18.00
	1814JP	—	3.50	6.50	15.00
	1815JP	—	6.00	8.00	18.00
	1816JP	—	3.50	6.50	15.00
	1817JP	—	3.50	6.50	15.00
	1818JP	—	3.50	6.50	15.00
	1819JP	—	3.50	6.50	15.00
	1820JP	—	3.50	6.50	15.00
	1821JP	—	3.50	6.50	15.00
	1823JP	—	13.50	30.00	55.00

MINTMARK: CUZCO (monogram)

C#	Date	Mintage	Fine	VF	XF
98a	1824T	—	28.50	55.00	100.00

2 REALES

6.5000 gm., .903 SILVER, .1887 oz ASW

MINTMARK: LIMAE (monogram)

Obv. leg: CAR. III..., arms. Rev: Pillars, date.

C#	Date	Mintage	Fine	VF	XF
33	1760JM	—	17.50	35.00	65.00
	1761JM	—	17.50	35.00	65.00
	1762JM	—	17.50	35.00	65.00
	1763JM	—	17.50	35.00	65.00
	1764JM	—	17.50	35.00	65.00
	1765JM	—	17.50	40.00	65.00
	1766/5JM	—	75.00	110.00	150.00

C#	Date	Mintage	Fine	VF	XF
33	1766JM	—	60.00	90.00	125.00
	1767JM	—	27.50	55.00	80.00
	1768JM	—	55.00	80.00	125.00
	1769JM	—	25.00	60.00	80.00
	1770JM	—	27.50	60.00	80.00
	1771JM	—	27.50	60.00	80.00
	1772JM	—	27.50	60.00	80.00

Obv. leg: CAROLUS III..., bust. Rev: Arms, pillars.

C#	Date	Mintage	Fine	VF	XF
43	1772JM	—	6.00	7.50	15.00
	1773JM	—	6.00	7.50	15.00
	1774MJ	—	7.50	15.00	30.00
	1775MJ	—	7.50	15.00	30.00
	1776MJ	—	6.00	9.00	22.50
	1777MJ	—	6.00	9.00	22.50
	1778MJ	—	9.00	15.00	35.00
	1779MJ	—	6.00	10.00	27.50
	1780MJ	—	6.00	10.00	27.50
	1780MI	—	15.00	30.00	55.00
	1781MI	—	9.00	18.00	37.50
	1782MI	—	6.00	10.00	25.00
	1783MI	—	6.00	10.00	25.00
	1784MI	—	6.00	10.00	25.00
	1785MI	—	6.00	10.00	25.00
	1786MI	—	6.00	10.00	25.00
	1787MI	—	6.00	10.00	25.00
	1787IJ	—	35.00	55.00	100.00
	1788MI	—	35.00	55.00	100.00
	1788IJ	—	9.00	15.00	37.50
	1789IJ	—	6.00	9.00	12.00

Obv. leg: CAROLUS IV...., bust of CARLOS III. Rev. leg: 2R.

C#	Date	Mintage	Fine	VF	XF
67	1789IJ	—	8.00	15.00	35.00
	1790IJ	—	8.00	15.00	35.00
	1791IJ	—	10.00	20.00	42.50

Rev. leg: R2

C#	Date	Mintage	Fine	VF	XF
67.1	1789IJ	—	35.00	50.00	125.00
	1790IJ	—	35.00	50.00	125.00

Obv. leg: CAROLUS IIII, bust of Charles IV.

C#	Date	Mintage	Fine	VF	XF
74	1791IJ	—	8.00	15.00	35.00
	1792IJ	—	6.00	9.00	20.00
	1793IJ	—	6.00	9.00	18.00
	1794IJ	—	6.00	9.00	18.00
	1795IJ	—	6.00	9.00	18.00
	1796IJ	—	6.00	9.00	18.00
	1797IJ	—	6.00	9.00	18.00
	1798IJ	—	6.00	9.00	18.00
	1799IJ	—	6.00	9.00	18.00
	1800IJ	—	7.50	10.00	20.00
	1801IJ	—	7.50	10.00	20.00
	1802IJ	—	6.00	9.00	18.00
	1803IJ	—	12.50	30.00	50.00
	1803JP	—	6.00	9.00	20.00
	1804IJ	—	9.00	18.00	37.50
	1804JP	—	6.00	9.00	18.00
	1805JP	—	6.00	7.50	15.00
	1806JP	—	6.00	9.00	18.00
	1807JP	—	6.00	9.00	20.00
	1808JP	—	6.00	10.00	20.00

Obv. leg: FERDND. VII..., Lima bust.

C#	Date	Mintage	Fine	VF	XF
94	1808JP	—	18.00	35.00	60.00
	1809JP	—	—	Rare	—

Obv. leg: FERDIN. VII..., Lima bust.

C#	Date	Mintage	Fine	VF	XF
94.1	1808JP	—	6.00	15.00	27.50
	1809JP	—	6.00	15.00	27.50
	1810JP	—	7.50	10.00	20.00
	1811JP	—	18.00	30.00	50.00

Obv. leg: FERDIN. VII..., standard bust.

C#	Date	Mintage	Fine	VF	XF
99	1811JP	—	10.00	20.00	50.00
	1812JP	—	5.75	7.50	10.00
	1813JP	—	5.75	7.50	10.00

C#	Date	Mintage	Fine	VF	XF
99	1814JP	—	5.75	8.00	18.00
	1815JP	—	5.75	9.00	18.00
	1816JP	—	5.75	7.50	10.00
	1817JP	—	5.75	7.50	10.00
	1818JP	—	5.75	7.50	10.00
	1819JP	—	5.75	7.50	10.00
	1820JP	—	5.75	7.50	10.00
	1821JP	—	5.75	7.50	10.00
	1823JP	—	7.50	10.00	16.00
99b	1826IR	—	115.00	175.00	275.00

NOTE: C#99b was struck in Callao by Royalists prior to final capitulation on January 22, 1826.

MINTMARK: CUZCO (monogram)

C#	Date	Mintage	Fine	VF	XF
99a	1824T	—	80.00	150.00	225.00

4 REALES

13.0000 gm., .903 SILVER, .3774 oz ASW

MINTMARK: LIMAE (monogram)

Obv. leg: CAROLUS III...

C#	Date	Mintage	Fine	VF	XF
34	1760JM	—	150.00	200.00	450.00
	1761JM	—	120.00	175.00	400.00
	1762JM	—	100.00	150.00	375.00
	1763JM	—	350.00	500.00	1000.
	1764JM	—	80.00	150.00	325.00
	1765JM	—	200.00	300.00	700.00
	1766JM	—	120.00	175.00	500.00
	1767JM	—	80.00	150.00	500.00
	1768JM	—	80.00	150.00	325.00
	1769JM	—	80.00	150.00	325.00
	1770JM	—	135.00	200.00	450.00
	1771JM	—	80.00	150.00	325.00
	1772JM	—	45.00	75.00	140.00

Obv. leg: CAROLUS III..., bust. Rev: Arms, pillars.

C#	Date	Mintage	Fine	VF	XF
44	1772JM	—	200.00	300.00	750.00
	1773JM	—	55.00	100.00	225.00
	1773MJ	—	55.00	100.00	225.00
	1774MJ	—	50.00	80.00	150.00
	1775MJ	—	50.00	80.00	150.00
	1775MJ legend 'GARTIA' (error)	—	300.00	425.00	850.00
	1776MJ	—	50.00	90.00	180.00
	1777MJ	—	37.50	70.00	120.00
	1778MJ	—	30.00	90.00	180.00
	1779MJ	—	20.00	45.00	90.00
	1780MJ	—	20.00	45.00	90.00
	1780MI	—	45.00	90.00	180.00
	1781MI	—	20.00	45.00	90.00
	1782MI	—	45.00	90.00	180.00
	1783MI	—	37.50	65.00	120.00
	1784MI	—	45.00	90.00	180.00
	1785MI	—	45.00	90.00	180.00
	1786MI	—	45.00	90.00	180.00
	1787MI	—	45.00	90.00	180.00
	1787IJ	—	37.50	65.00	120.00
	1788IJ	—	45.00	90.00	180.00
	1789IJ	—	45.00	90.00	180.00

LIMA MINT

Obv. leg: CAROLUS IV..., bust of Charles III.

C#	Date	Mintage	Fine	VF	XF
68	1789IJ	—	30.00	60.00	120.00
	1790IJ	—	45.00	70.00	125.00
	1791IJ	—	45.00	70.00	125.00

Obv. leg: CAROLUS IIII...

C#	Date	Mintage	Fine	VF	XF
75	1791IJ	—	22.50	45.00	90.00
	1791JP	—	75.00	120.00	250.00
	1792IJ	—	25.00	50.00	90.00
	1793IJ	—	60.00	80.00	135.00
	1794IJ	—	22.50	45.00	90.00
	1795IJ	—	32.50	55.00	100.00
	1796IJ	—	20.00	45.00	90.00
	1797IJ	—	22.50	45.00	90.00
	1798IJ	—	22.50	45.00	90.00
	1799IJ	—	22.50	45.00	90.00
	1800IJ	—	15.00	37.50	65.00
	1801IJ	—	18.00	40.00	75.00
	1802IJ	—	20.00	45.00	90.00
	1803IJ	—	70.00	100.00	200.00
	1803JP	—	45.00	65.00	120.00
	1804JP	—	22.50	45.00	90.00
	1805JP	—	20.00	45.00	90.00
	1806JP	—	20.00	45.00	90.00
	1807JP	—	22.50	50.00	90.00
	1808JP	—	42.50	65.00	120.00

Obv. leg: FERDND. VII..., Lima bust.

C#	Date	Mintage	Fine	VF	XF
95	1808JP	—	80.00	125.00	250.00

Obv. leg: FERDIN. VII..., Lima bust.
Rev: Similar to C#75.

C#	Date	Mintage	Fine	VF	XF
95.1	1810JP	—	65.00	100.00	155.00
	1811JP	—	65.00	100.00	155.00

Obv. leg: FERDIN. VII..., standard bust.

C#	Date	Mintage	Fine	VF	XF
100	1811JP	—	—	Rare	—
	1812JP	—	20.00	45.00	75.00
	1813JP	—	70.00	120.00	225.00
	1814JP	—	70.00	120.00	225.00
	1815JP	—	55.00	90.00	150.00
	1816JP	—	15.00	37.50	70.00
	1817JP	—	15.00	37.50	70.00
	1818JP	—	15.00	37.50	70.00
	1819JP	—	15.00	37.50	70.00
	1820JP	—	12.00	24.00	55.00
	1821JP	—	15.00	37.50	70.00

8 REALES

25.0000 gm., .903 SILVER, .7259 oz ASW

MINTMARK: LIMAE (monogram)

C#	Date	Mintage	Fine	VF	XF
35	1760JM	—	225.00	350.00	675.00
	1761JM	—	70.00	110.00	200.00
	1762JM	—	70.00	110.00	200.00
	1763JM	—	70.00	110.00	200.00
	1764JM	—	70.00	110.00	180.00
	1765JM	—	70.00	110.00	180.00
	1766JM	—	65.00	100.00	170.00
	1767JM	—	65.00	100.00	170.00
	1768JM	—	65.00	100.00	170.00
	1769JM	—	65.00	100.00	170.00
	1770JM	—	65.00	100.00	170.00
	1771JM	—	70.00	110.00	180.00
	1772JM	—	85.00	170.00	275.00

Obv. leg: CAROLUS III...

C#	Date	Mintage	Fine	VF	XF
45	1772JM	—	18.00	42.50	70.00
	1773JM	—	22.50	36.00	60.00
	1773MJ	—	50.00	75.00	100.00
	1774/3MJ	—	50.00	75.00	100.00
	1774JM	—	50.00	75.00	100.00
	1774MJ	—	22.50	40.00	60.00
	1775MJ	—	22.50	40.00	55.00
	1776MJ	—	22.50	40.00	60.00
	1777MJ	—	22.50	45.00	75.00
	1778NF	—	22.50	45.00	75.00
	1779MJ	—	22.50	45.00	75.00
	1780MJ	—	22.50	45.00	75.00
	1780MI	—	60.00	100.00	150.00
	1781MI	—	22.50	45.00	75.00
	1782MI	—	22.50	45.00	75.00
	1783MI	—	22.50	40.00	60.00

C#	Date	Mintage	Fine	VF	XF
45	1784MI	—	22.50	45.00	75.00
	1785MI	—	22.50	45.00	75.00
	1786MI	—	22.50	45.00	75.00
	1787MI	—	22.50	45.00	75.00
	1787/6MI	—	37.50	60.00	100.00
	1787IJ	—	60.00	100.00	150.00
	1788IJ	—	22.50	45.00	75.00
	1789IJ	—	60.00	90.00	140.00

Obv. leg: CAROLUS IV..., bust of Charles III.

C#	Date	Mintage	Fine	VF	XF
69	1789IJ	—	50.00	100.00	200.00
	1790IJ	—	40.00	80.00	100.00
	1791IJ	—	40.00	80.00	100.00

Obv. leg: CAROLUS IIII..., bust of Charles IV.
Rev: Similar to C#45.

C#	Date	Mintage	Fine	VF	XF
76	1791IJ	—	25.00	55.00	80.00
	1792IJ	—	22.50	37.50	70.00
	1793IJ	—	22.50	30.00	45.00
	1794IJ	—	22.50	30.00	45.00
	1795IJ	—	22.50	37.50	75.00
	1796IJ	—	22.50	30.00	45.00
	1797IJ	—	22.50	30.00	45.00
	1798IJ	—	22.50	30.00	45.00
	1799IJ	—	22.50	30.00	45.00
	1800IJ	—	22.50	30.00	45.00
	1801IJ	—	22.50	30.00	45.00
	1802IJ	—	22.50	30.00	45.00
	1803IJ	—	30.00	70.00	90.00
	1803JP	—	22.50	30.00	45.00
	1804JP	—	22.50	30.00	45.00
	1805JP	—	22.50	30.00	45.00
	1806JP	—	22.50	30.00	45.00
	1807JP	—	22.50	30.00	45.00
	1808JP	—	22.50	30.00	45.00

Obv. leg: FERDND. VII..., imaginary bust.

C#	Date	Mintage	Fine	VF	XF
96	1808JP	—	200.00	275.00	425.00
	1809JP	—	37.50	67.50	90.00

Obv. leg: FERDIN. VII...., imaginary bust.
Rev: Similar to C#45.

C#	Date	Mintage	Fine	VF	XF
96.1	1809JP	—	22.50	36.50	100.00
	1810JP	—	22.50	24.00	75.00
	1811JP	—	22.50	24.00	75.00

Obv. leg: FERDIN. VII..., standard bust.
Rev: Similar to C#45.

C#	Date	Mintage	Fine	VF	XF
101	1811JP	—	75.00	100.00	150.00
	1812JP	—	22.50	25.00	45.00
	1813JP	—	22.50	25.00	40.00
	1814JP	—	22.50	25.00	42.50
101	1815JP	—	22.50	25.00	42.50
	1816JP	—	22.50	25.00	42.50
	1817JP	—	22.50	27.50	50.00
	1818JP	—	22.50	25.00	45.00
	1819JP	—	22.50	25.00	45.00
	1820JP	—	22.50	25.00	45.00
	1821JP	—	22.50	25.00	52.50
	1822JP	—	400.00	500.00	750.00
	1823JP	—	150.00	200.00	325.00
	1824JP	—	300.00	400.00	600.00
	1824JM	—	120.00	175.00	300.00

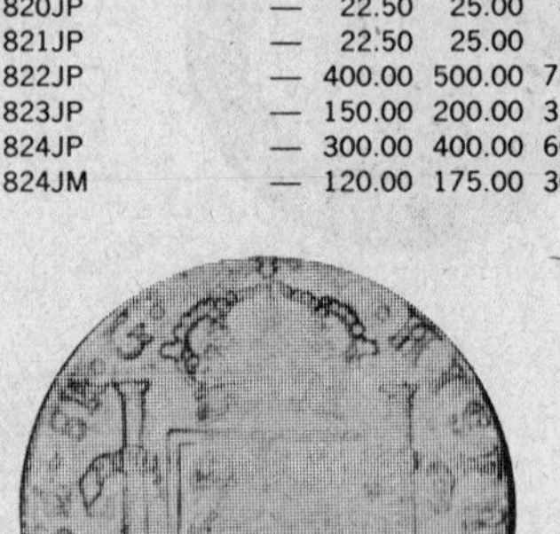

MINTMARK: CUZCO (monogram)

Obv: Similar to C#101.

C#	Date	Mintage	Fine	VF	XF
101a	1824T	—	80.00	90.00	150.00
	1824G	—	145.00	180.00	325.00

1/2 ESCUDO

1.6875 gm., .875 GOLD, .0475 oz AGW

MINTMARK: LIMAE (monogram)

C#	Date	Mintage	Fine	VF	XF
115	1815JP	—	400.00	500.00	900.00
	1816JP	—	450.00	550.00	950.00
	1817JP	—	400.00	500.00	900.00
	1818JP	—	450.00	550.00	950.00
	1819JP	—	475.00	675.00	1000.
	1820JP	—	400.00	500.00	900.00
	1821JP	—	500.00	675.00	1000.

ESCUDO

3.3750 gm., .875 GOLD, .0949 oz AGW

MINTMARK: LIMAE (monogram)

Obv. leg: CAROLUS III, bust. Rev: Arms.

C#	Date	Mintage	Fine	VF	XF
51	1761JM	—	155.00	250.00	500.00
	1762JM	—	140.00	250.00	625.00
	1766JM	—	125.00	250.00	500.00

Obv. leg: CAR. III..., young bust.
Rev. leg: IN UTROQ FELIX, arms.

C#	Date	Mintage	Fine	VF	XF
55	1767JM	—	90.00	155.00	250.00
	1768JM	—	100.00	175.00	325.00
	1769JM	—	90.00	155.00	250.00
	1770JM	—	90.00	155.00	250.00
	1771JM	—	90.00	155.00	250.00

Obv: Older, standard bust Charles III.
Rev: Arms, order chain.

C#	Date	Mintage	Fine	VF	XF
59	1772JM	—	100.00	190.00	325.00
	1773MJ	—	90.00	155.00	225.00
	1774MJ	—	90.00	155.00	225.00
	1775MJ	—	75.00	140.00	190.00
	1776MJ	—	75.00	140.00	190.00
	1777MJ	—	90.00	155.00	225.00
	1778MJ	—	75.00	140.00	190.00
	1779MJ	—	75.00	140.00	190.00
	1780MJ	—	90.00	155.00	225.00
	1781HI	—	75.00	140.00	190.00
	1782MI	—	75.00	140.00	190.00
	1783MI	—	75.00	140.00	190.00
	1784MI	—	75.00	140.00	190.00
	1785MI	—	65.00	100.00	155.00
	1786MI	—	65.00	100.00	155.00
	1787MI	—	65.00	100.00	155.00
	1788IJ	—	65.00	100.00	155.00
	1789IJ	—	125.00	250.00	375.00

Obv. leg: CAROL. IV..., bust of Charles III.

C#	Date	Mintage	Fine	VF	XF
81	1789IJ	—	125.00	250.00	375.00
	1790IJ	—	125.00	250.00	375.00
	1791IJ	—	125.00	250.00	375.00

Obv. leg: CAROL. IIII..., bust of Charles IV.

C#	Date	Mintage	Fine	VF	XF
85	1789IJ	—	125.00	170.00	275.00
	1790IJ	—	110.00	150.00	225.00
	1791IJ	—	100.00	125.00	170.00
	1792IJ	—	100.00	125.00	190.00
	1793IJ	—	75.00	90.00	125.00
	1794IJ	—	75.00	90.00	125.00
	1795IJ	—	75.00	90.00	125.00
	1796IJ	—	75.00	90.00	125.00
	1797IJ	—	75.00	90.00	125.00
	1798IJ	—	75.00	90.00	125.00
	1799IJ	—	75.00	90.00	125.00
	1800IJ	—	75.00	90.00	125.00
	1801IJ	—	75.00	90.00	125.00
	1802IJ	—	75.00	90.00	125.00
	1803IJ	—	75.00	90.00	125.00
	1803JP	—	75.00	90.00	125.00
	1804JP	—	75.00	90.00	125.00
	1805JP	—	75.00	90.00	125.00
	1806JP	—	75.00	90.00	125.00
	1807JP	—	75.00	90.00	125.00
	1808JP	—	75.00	90.00	125.00

Obv. leg: FERDIN. VII..., uniformed Lima bust.

C#	Date	Mintage	Fine	VF	XF
105	1809JP	—	—	—	—
	1810JP	—	100.00	175.00	375.00
	1811JP	—	375.00	500.00	825.00
	1812JP	—	180.00	250.00	500.00

Obv. leg: FERDIN. VII..., standard bust.

C#	Date	Mintage	Fine	VF	XF
110	1812JP	—	150.00	200.00	450.00
	1813JF	—	180.00	250.00	450.00
	1814JP	—	200.00	300.00	600.00

Obv. leg: FERDIN. VII..., laureate undraped bust.

C#	Date	Mintage	Fine	VF	XF
116	1814JP	—	80.00	150.00	300.00
	1815JP	—	65.00	100.00	200.00
	1816JP	—	65.00	100.00	200.00
	1817JP	—	65.00	100.00	200.00
	1818JP	—	65.00	100.00	200.00
	1819JP	—	80.00	135.00	300.00
	1820JP	—	65.00	75.00	145.00
	1821JP	—	75.00	125.00	275.00

2 ESCUDOS

6.7500 gm., .875 GOLD, .1899 oz AGW

MINTMARK: LIMAE (monogram)

Obv. leg: CAROLUS III.., bust. Rev: Arms.

C#	Date	Mintage	Fine	VF	XF
52	1761JM	—	300.00	400.00	900.00
	1762JM	—	200.00	300.00	800.00

Obv: Young, standard bust of Charles III.
Rev. leg: IN UTROQ FELIX, arms.

C#	Date	Mintage	Fine	VF	XF
56	1763JM	—	400.00	700.00	1200.
	1765JM	—	200.00	350.00	675.00
	1766JM	—	200.00	300.00	625.00
	1767JM	—	200.00	300.00	600.00
	1768JM	—	200.00	300.00	625.00
	1769JM	—	350.00	500.00	1000.
	1770JM	—	400.00	600.00	1000.
	1771JM	—	400.00	600.00	1000.

Obv: Older, standard bust of Charles III.
Rev: Arms, order chain.

C#	Date	Mintage	Fine	VF	XF
60	1772JM	—	350.00	500.00	1000.
	1773MJ	—	300.00	425.00	800.00
	1774MJ	—	425.00	600.00	1000.
	1776MJ	—	300.00	425.00	800.00
	1777MJ	—	250.00	375.00	700.00
	1778MJ	—	225.00	350.00	675.00
	1779MJ	—	225.00	350.00	675.00
	1780MJ	—	225.00	350.00	675.00
	1780MI	—	125.00	200.00	300.00
	1781MI	—	150.00	225.00	500.00
	1782MI	—	150.00	225.00	500.00
	1783MI	—	150.00	225.00	500.00
	1784MI	—	600.00	1200.	1750.
	1785MI	—	600.00	1200.	1750.
	1787MI	—	450.00	600.00	1500.

C#	Date	Mintage	Fine	VF	XF
60	1787IJ	—	175.00	250.00	500.00
	1788IJ	—	175.00	250.00	500.00
	1789IJ	—	200.00	300.00	600.00

Obv. leg: CAROL IV..., bust of Charles III.

C#	Date	Mintage	Fine	VF	XF
82	1789IJ	—	325.00	400.00	500.00
	1790IJ	—	275.00	375.00	500.00
	1791IJ	—	300.00	400.00	600.00

Obv. leg: CAROL IIII, bust of Charles IV.

C#	Date	Mintage	Fine	VF	XF
86	1792IJ	—	200.00	300.00	400.00
	1793IJ	—	180.00	225.00	375.00
	1794IJ	—	375.00	425.00	600.00
	1796IJ	—	400.00	525.00	725.00
	1797IJ	—	180.00	225.00	350.00
	1799IJ	—	180.00	225.00	350.00
	1800IJ	—	250.00	300.00	450.00
	1804JP	—	180.00	225.00	350.00
	1805JP	—	250.00	300.00	450.00
	1806JP	—	250.00	300.00	450.00
	1808PJ	—	300.00	400.00	525.00

Obv. leg: FERDIN. VII..., uniformed Lima bust.

C#	Date	Mintage	Fine	VF	XF
106	1809JP	—	275.00	375.00	600.00
	1810JP	—	250.00	350.00	600.00
	1811JP	—	250.00	325.00	500.00

Obv. leg: FERDIN. VII..., standard bust.

C#	Date	Mintage	Fine	VF	XF
111	1812JP	—	200.00	275.00	475.00
	1813JP	—	200.00	275.00	475.00

Obv. leg: FERDIN. VII..., laureate undraped bust

C#	Date	Mintage	Fine	VF	XF
117	1814JP	—	250.00	300.00	525.00
	1815JP	—	180.00	250.00	450.00
	1816JP	—	180.00	250.00	450.00
	1817JP	—	200.00	250.00	450.00
	1818JP	—	135.00	180.00	375.00
	1819JP	—	135.00	180.00	375.00
	1820JP	—	160.00	200.00	400.00
	1821JP	—	150.00	200.00	375.00

4 ESCUDOS

13.5000 gm., .875 GOLD, .3798 oz AGW

MINTMARK: LIMAE (monogram)

Obv. leg: CAROLUS III..., bust.
Rev: Arms, order chain.

C#	Date	Mintage	Fine	VF	XF
53	1761JM	—	1250.	2000.	3000.
	1762JM	—	1250.	2000.	3000.

Obv: Young, standard bust of Charles III. Rev: Arms.

C#	Date	Mintage	Fine	VF	XF
57	1764JM	—	600.00	900.00	1600.
	1765JM	—	600.00	900.00	1600.
	1768JM	—	450.00	750.00	1450.
	1769JM	—	750.00	1200.	2000.
	1770JM	—	750.00	1200.	2000.
	1771JM	—	750.00	1200.	2000.

Obv: Older, standard bust of Charles III.

C#	Date	Mintage	Fine	VF	XF
61	1772JM	—	600.00	1200.	2000.
	1773JM	—	400.00	700.00	1350.
	1774MJ	—	400.00	700.00	1350.
	1776MJ	—	400.00	700.00	1350.
	1777MJ	—	400.00	700.00	1350.
	1778MJ	—	400.00	700.00	1350.
	1779MJ	—	400.00	700.00	1350.
	1780MI	—	450.00	750.00	1400.
	1781MI	—	450.00	800.00	1500.
	1782MI	—	400.00	700.00	1350.
	1783MI	—	400.00	700.00	1350.
	1784MI	—	400.00	700.00	1350.
	1785MI	—	400.00	700.00	1350.
	1786MI	—	400.00	700.00	1350.
	1787MI	—	800.00	1200.	2000.
	1787IJ	—	400.00	700.00	1350.
	1788IJ	—	400.00	600.00	1200.
	1789IJ	—	400.00	700.00	1350.

Obv. leg: CAROL. IV..., bust of Charles III.
Rev: Arms, order chain.

C#	Date	Mintage	Fine	VF	XF
83	1789IJ	—	800.00	1000.	1600.
	1790IJ	—	800.00	1000.	1600.
	1791IJ	—	800.00	1000.	1600.

Obv. leg: CAROL. IV..., bust of Charles IV.

C#	Date	Mintage	Fine	VF	XF
87	1791IJ	—	800.00	1000.	1600.
	1792IJ	—	800.00	1000.	1600.
	1793IJ	—	600.00	800.00	1000.
	1794IJ	—	600.00	800.00	1000.
	1795IJ	—	600.00	800.00	1000.
	1796IJ	—	600.00	800.00	1000.
	1797IJ	—	600.00	800.00	1000.
	1798IJ	—	600.00	800.00	1000.
	1799IJ	—	600.00	800.00	1000.
	1800IJ	—	600.00	800.00	1000.
	1801IJ	—	600.00	800.00	1000.
	1804JP	—	600.00	800.00	1000.
	1805JP	—	600.00	800.00	1000.
	1806JP	—	600.00	800.00	1000.
	1807JP	—	600.00	800.00	1000.

Obv. leg: FERDIN. VII...

C#	Date	Mintage	Fine	VF	XF
107	1809JP	—	1500.	1800.	3600.
	1810JP	—	1000.	1500.	2500.

Obv: Laureate, draped bust of Ferdinand VII.

C#	Date	Mintage	Fine	VF	XF
112	1812JP	—	1200.	1800.	2700.

Obv: Smaller bust of Ferdinand VII.

C#	Date	Mintage	Fine	VF	XF
112a	1812JP	—	900.00	1200.	2250.
	1813JP	—	1200.	1500.	2400.

Obv: Laureate, undraped bust of Ferdinand VII.

C#	Date	Mintage	Fine	VF	XF
118	1814JP	—	750.00	1100.	1950.
	1815JP	—	525.00	750.00	1350.
	1816JP	—	750.00	1100.	1950.
	1817JP	—	1350.	1800.	3000.
	1818JP	—	750.00	1200.	1800.
	1819JP	—	825.00	1100.	2000.
	1820JP	—	825.00	1100.	2000.
	1821JP	—	825.00	1100.	2000.

8 ESCUDOS

27.0000 gm., .875 GOLD, .7596 oz AGW

MINTMARK: LIMAE (monogram)

Obv. leg: CAROLUS III....

C#	Date	Mintage	Fine	VF	XF
54	1761JM	—	900.00	1750.	4000.
	1762JM	—	850.00	1600.	3000.

Obv: Young, standard bust of Charles III.

C#	Date	Mintage	Fine	VF	XF
58	1763JM	—	850.00	1600.	3250.
	1764JM	—	850.00	1600.	3250.
	1765JM	—	850.00	1600.	3250.
	1766JM	—	850.00	1600.	3250.
	1767JM	—	850.00	1600.	3250.
	1768JM	—	1000.	2000.	6000.
	1769JM	—	1000.	1750.	3750.
	1770JM	—	850.00	1600.	3250.
	1771JM	—	850.00	1600.	3250.
	1772JM	—	1000.	2000.	3000.

Obv. Small bust of Charles III.

C#	Date	Mintage	Fine	VF	XF
58.1	1768JM	—	1000.	2000.	5000.

Obv: Older, standard bust of Charles III.

C#	Date	Mintage	Fine	VF	XF
62	1772JM	—	800.00	1200.	3000.
	1772JM assayer's initials inverted				
		—	600.00	1000.	2000.
	1773JM	—	600.00	1000.	2000.
	1773MJ	—	600.00	1000.	2000.
	1774MJ	—	600.00	1000.	1800.
	1775MJ	—	600.00	1000.	1800.
	1776MJ	—	750.00	1200.	2250.
	1777MJ	—	550.00	1000.	1800.
	1778MJ	—	550.00	1000.	1800.
	1779MJ	—	550.00	1000.	1800.
	1780MI	—	550.00	1000.	1800.
	1781MI	—	550.00	1000.	1800.
	1782MI	—	550.00	1000.	1800.
	1783MI	—	550.00	1000.	1800.
	1784MI	—	550.00	1000.	1800.
	1785MI	—	750.00	1200.	2500.
	1786MI	—	550.00	1000.	1800.
	1787MI	—	650.00	1000.	1800.
	1787IJ	—	650.00	1000.	1800.
	1788IJ	—	650.00	1000.	1800.
	1789IJ	—	650.00	1000.	1800.

Obv. leg: CAROL. IV..., bust of Charles III.

C#	Date	Mintage	Fine	VF	XF
84	1789IJ	—	500.00	700.00	1200.
	1790IJ	—	500.00	700.00	1000.
	1791IJ	—	500.00	700.00	1200.

Obv. leg: CAROL. IIII, bust of Charles IV.
Rev: Similar to C#58.

C#	Date	Mintage	Fine	VF	XF
88	1792IJ	—	500.00	650.00	1000.
	1793IJ	—	500.00	650.00	1000.
	1794IJ	—	500.00	600.00	950.00
	1795IJ	—	500.00	600.00	950.00
	1796IJ	—	500.00	650.00	1000.
	1797IJ	—	500.00	600.00	950.00
	1797JI	—	1500.	2000.	3000.
	1798IJ	—	500.00	600.00	950.00
	1799IJ	—	500.00	600.00	950.00
	1800IJ	—	500.00	650.00	1000.
	1801IJ	—	500.00	650.00	1000.
	1802IJ	—	500.00	650.00	1000.
	1803IJ	—	500.00	650.00	1000.
	1803JP	—	550.00	750.00	1400.
	1804IJ	—	500.00	650.00	1000.
	1804JP	—	500.00	600.00	950.00
	1805JP	—	500.00	650.00	1000.
	1806JP	—	500.00	650.00	1000.
	1807JP	—	500.00	650.00	1000.
	1808JP	—	500.00	700.00	1200.

Obv: Local, uniformed bust of Ferdinand VII.
Rev: Similar to C#88.

C#	Date	Mintage	Fine	VF	XF
108	1808JP	—	1300.	2400.	4500.
	1809JP	—	800.00	1200.	1750.
	1810JP	—	750.00	1000.	1650.
	1811JP	—	800.00	1200.	1750.
	1812JP	—	1000.	2000.	3000.
	Obv: Larger bust of Ferdinand VII.				
108.1	1811JP	—	1500.	2500.	5000.
	1812JP	—	800.00	1200.	1750.
	Obv: Laureate draped bust of Ferdinand VII. Rev: Arms, order chain.				
113	1812JP	—	500.00	800.00	1400.
	1814JP	—	2000.	3750.	6750.
	1815JP	—	3600.	5000.	10,000.

Obv: Smaller bust of Ferdinand VII.
Rev: Similar to C#88.

C#	Date	Mintage	Fine	VF	XF
113a	1813JP	—	1000.	2600.	3600.
	Obv: Similar to C#119.1. Rev: Similar to C#88.				
119	1814JP	—	500.00	600.00	1200.
	1815JP	—	500.00	600.00	1200.
	1816JP	—	500.00	600.00	1200.
	1817JP	—	500.00	600.00	1200.
	1818JP	—	500.00	600.00	1200.
	1819JP	—	500.00	600.00	1200.
	1820JP	—	500.00	600.00	1200.
	1821JP	—	550.00	750.00	1300.

MINTMARK: CUZCO (monogram)

C#	Date	Mintage	Fine	VF	XF
119.1	1824G	—	1000.	2000.	3000.

PROVISIONAL COINAGE

1/4 REAL

COPPER

C#	Date	Mintage	Fine	VF	XF
121	1822	—	5.50	8.50	15.00
	1823	—	7.00	10.00	17.50

OCTAVO DE (1/8) PESO

(= 1 REAL)

COPPER

C#	Date	Mintage	Fine	VF	XF
122	1823	—	4.50	6.50	12.50
	1823V	—	—	—	—

QUARTO DE (1/4) PESO

(= 2 REALES)

COPPER
Rev. denomination: QUARTO DE PESO

C#	Date	Mintage	Fine	VF	XF
123	1823	—	3.50	5.00	10.00
	1823V	—	—	—	—
	Rev. denomination: 1/4 de Peso				
123.1	1823	2 known	—	Rare	—

REGULAR COINAGE

1/4 REAL

.8500 gm., .903 SILVER, .0247 oz ASW

LIMA MINT

C#	Date	Mintage	Fine	VF	XF
127.1	1826	—	5.50	9.00	13.50
	1827	—	5.00	8.00	12.50
	1828	—	7.00	10.00	15.00
	1829/8	—	7.00	10.00	15.00
	1830/28	—	6.00	9.00	13.00
	1831/0	—	6.00	8.00	12.50
	1831	—	7.00	10.00	15.00
	1832	—	6.00	8.00	12.00
	1833	—	6.00	8.00	12.00
	1834	—	6.00	7.00	11.00
	1835	—	10.00	15.00	20.00
	1836	—	7.00	11.00	15.00
	1837	—	7.50	11.50	15.00
	1839	—	10.00	15.00	20.00
	1840	—	4.50	7.50	11.00
	1841/0	—	6.00	10.00	15.00
	1841	—	5.00	8.00	11.50
	1842	—	5.00	7.50	10.00
	1843	—	5.00	8.00	11.50
	1844	—	10.00	15.00	20.00
	1845	—	4.00	6.00	9.50
	1846/3	—	4.50	6.50	10.00
	1847	—	4.00	6.00	9.00
	1848	—	4.00	6.00	8.50
	1849/8	—	5.00	6.50	10.00
	1849	—	4.00	6.00	9.00
	1850	—	6.00	8.50	12.50
127.1	1851/31	—	3.50	5.00	8.00
	1851	—	3.50	5.00	8.00
	1853/1	—	5.00	7.00	10.00
	1855	—	2.00	3.50	6.00
	1856	—	3.00	5.00	8.50

AREQUIPA MINT

C#	Date	Mintage	Fine	VF	XF
127.2	1839	—	80.00	125.00	180.00

1/2 REAL

1.6500 gm., .903 SILVER, .0479 oz ASW

MINTMARK: LIMAE (monogram)

C#	Date	Mintage	Fine	VF	XF
128.1	1826JM	—	7.00	10.00	17.50
	1827JM	—	6.50	9.00	15.00
	1828JM	—	5.50	8.00	13.50
	1829/8JM	—	9.00	12.50	19.00
	1830JM	—	5.00	8.00	13.00
	1831MM	—	8.00	11.00	16.00
	1832MM	—	5.00	7.50	12.50
	1833MM	—	5.00	7.00	11.50
	1834MM	—	5.50	8.00	15.00
	1835MM	—	5.50	8.00	15.00
	1835MT	—	13.00	17.50	30.00
	1836MT	—	9.00	12.50	20.00
	1837TM	—	9.00	12.50	20.00
	1837M	—	13.00	17.50	30.00
	1838M	—	14.00	19.00	30.00
	1838MT	—	14.00	19.00	30.00
	1839MB	—	7.00	11.00	17.00
	1840M	—	—	—	—
	1840MB	—	7.00	10.00	15.00
128.1a	1840MB	—	7.00	10.00	15.00
	1841/0MB	—	7.00	10.00	15.00
	Obv. leg: REPUBLICA PERUANA				
—	1842MB	—	Reported, not confirmed		

Obv. leg: REP. PERUANA 10D. 20G

C#	Date	Mintage	Fine	VF	XF
128.1b	1841MB	—	—	—	—
	1842MB	—	20.00	30.00	40.00
	1843MB	—	9.00	13.00	20.00
	1843MMB	—	9.00	13.00	20.00
	1845MB	—	11.00	16.00	25.00
	1846MB	—	12.50	15.00	20.00
	1847MB	—	13.00	18.00	32.50
	1849MB	—	9.00	20.00	30.00
	1850MB	—	7.00	10.00	16.00

Size reduced to 16mm

C#	Date	Mintage	Fine	VF	XF
128.1c	1850MB	—	20.00	25.00	35.00
	1851MB	—	9.00	12.50	20.00
	1852MB	—	9.00	12.50	20.00
	1853MB	—	9.50	14.00	21.00
	1854MB	—	7.50	11.50	17.50
	1855/4MB	—	12.00	15.00	25.00
	1855MB	—	8.00	12.00	18.00
	1856MB	—	7.00	10.00	15.00

MINTMARK: CUZCO (monogram)

C#	Date	Mintage	Fine	VF	XF
128.3	1827GM	—	30.00	45.00	65.00
	1828G	—	30.00	45.00	70.00
	1829/8G	—	30.00	45.00	65.00
	1829G	—	35.00	50.00	75.00
	1830/28	—	25.00	40.00	55.00
	1830G	—	35.00	50.00	75.00
	1831G	—	20.00	30.00	45.00
	1835B	—	13.50	22.50	33.50

MINTMARK: CUZCO

C#	Date	Mintage	Fine	VF	XF
128.4	1833B	—	6.50	9.50	14.00
	1834B	—	7.50	11.00	16.50

AREQUIPA MINT (AREQ.)

Obv. leg: REPUB. PERUANA

C#	Date	Mintage	Fine	VF	XF
128.2	1836M	—	17.00	25.00	37.50

REAL

3.2500 gm., .903 SILVER, .0944 oz ASW

MINTMARK: LIMAE (monogram)

Obv. leg: REPUB. PERUANA

C#	Date	Mintage	Fine	VF	XF
129.1	1826JM	—	6.50	11.00	15.00
	1827JM	—	5.50	9.00	12.00
	1828JM	—	5.50	10.00	12.00
	1829JM	—	10.00	15.00	20.00
	1830JM	—	6.00	10.00	14.00
	1831JM	—	12.50	17.50	27.50
	1831MM	—	11.00	16.50	25.00
	1832MM	—	9.00	14.00	20.00
	1833/2MM	—	10.00	15.00	25.00
	1834MM	—	8.00	12.00	17.50
	1835/3	—	17.50	22.50	35.00
	1836MT	—	12.50	17.50	27.50
	1839MB	—	6.50	10.00	13.00
	1840MB	—	7.00	10.50	14.00

Obv. leg: REP. PERUANA 10D 20G

C#	Date	Mintage	Fine	VF	XF
129.2	1842MB	—	7.00	11.00	15.00
	1843MB	—	7.00	11.00	15.00
	1846MB	—	12.00	17.50	27.00
	1847/6MB	—	15.00	22.00	32.00
	1849MB	—	10.00	15.00	25.00
	1850MB	—	9.00	14.00	18.00
	1851MB	—	8.50	11.50	17.50
	1855MB	—	12.50	18.50	25.00
	1856MB	—	10.00	15.00	20.00

MINTMARK: CUZco (monogram)

Obv. leg: REPUB. PERUANA

C#	Date	Mintage	Fine	VF	XF
129.3	1826GM	—	25.00	40.00	65.00
	1827GM	—	25.00	40.00	65.00
	1828G	—	25.00	40.00	65.00
	1829G	—	22.50	25.00	60.00
	1830G	—	17.50	30.00	45.00
	1831G	—	17.50	25.00	45.00

MINTMARK: CUZCO

C#	Date	Mintage	Fine	VF	XF
129.4	1834B	—	35.00	60.00	80.00

2 REALES

6.5000 gm., .903 SILVER, .1887 oz ASW

MINTMARK: LIMAE (monogram)

Obv. leg: REPUB. PERUANA

C#	Date	Mintage	Fine	VF	XF
130.1	1825JM	—	15.00	25.00	35.00
	1826JM	—	5.50	6.00	10.00
	1827JM	—	5.50	6.00	10.00
	1828JM	—	5.50	6.00	8.00
	1829JM	—	—	Rare	—
	1830/29JM	—	10.00	20.00	35.00
	1830JM	—	5.50	6.00	12.50
	1831MM	—	7.00	10.00	20.00
	1832/1MM	—	10.00	15.00	30.00
	1832MM	—	5.50	8.00	15.00
	1833MM	—	8.00	12.50	25.00
	1834MM	—	6.50	10.00	17.50
	1836MT	—	15.00	22.50	35.00
	1839MB	—	11.50	15.00	25.00
	1840MB	—	7.00	11.00	20.00

Obv. leg: REP. over REPUB.

C#	Date	Mintage	Fine	VF	XF
130.1b	1841/0MB	—	17.50	30.00	40.00

Obv. leg: REP. PERUANA 10D 20G

C#	Date	Mintage	Fine	VF	XF
130.1a	1840MB	—	20.00	30.00	40.00
130.1a	1841MB	—	14.00	22.00	35.00
	1842MB	—	8.00	12.50	22.50
	1843MB	—	8.00	12.00	22.50
	1845MB	—	13.50	18.50	32.50
	1846MB	—	14.00	20.00	35.00
	1848MB	—	10.00	15.00	22.50
	1849MB	—	10.00	15.00	22.50
	1850MB with tassel on Liberty cap				
		—	14.00	20.00	30.00
	1850MB w/o tassel on Liberty cap				
		—	14.00	20.00	30.00
	1851MB	—	14.00	20.00	30.00
	1854MB	—	10.00	15.00	22.50
	1855MB	—	11.50	16.50	25.00
	1856MB	—	14.00	20.00	32.50

MINTMARK: CUZco (monogram)

Obv. leg: REPUB. PERUANA

C#	Date	Mintage	Fine	VF	XF
130.3	1827GM	—	20.00	30.00	45.00
	1828G	—	25.00	40.00	60.00
	1829G	—	25.00	40.00	60.00
	1830G	—	35.00	55.00	80.00
	1831G	—	20.00	35.00	45.00
	1835B	—	10.00	15.00	25.00

PASCO MINT

Obv. leg: REPUB. PERUANA

C#	Date	Mintage	Fine	VF	XF
130.4	1843M	—	—	Rare	—

4 REALES

13.0000 gm., .903 SILVER, .3775 oz ASW

MINTMARK: LIMAE (monogram)

Obv. leg: REPUB. PERUANA

C#	Date	Mintage	Fine	VF	XF
131.1a	1840MB	—	40.00	65.00	100.00
	1842MB	—	26.50	40.00	60.00
	1843/2MB	—	14.00	20.00	30.00
	1843MB	—	14.00	20.00	30.00
	1845MB	—	14.00	20.00	30.00
	1846MB	—	14.00	20.00	30.00
	1847MB	—	—	Rare	—
	1848MB	—	11.50	17.50	30.00
	1849MB	—	11.50	17.50	30.00
	1850MB	—	15.00	21.50	32.50
	1851MB	—	11.50	17.50	30.00
	1854MB	—	12.00	15.00	30.00
	1855/4MB	—	12.00	15.00	30.00
	1855MB	—	12.00	15.00	30.00
	1856MB	—	—	Rare	—

MINTMARK: CUZco (monogram)

C#	Date	Mintage	Fine	VF	XF
131.3	1835B	—	12.00	14.00	17.50
	1836B	—	12.00	14.00	17.50
	1838B	—	—	Rare	—

NOTE: There are many die varieties of 1835 and 1836.

MINTMARK: AREQ.

Obv. leg: REPUB PERUANA

C#	Date	Mintage	Fine	VF	XF
131.2	1836M	—	75.00	110.00	160.00
	1839MV	—	55.00	75.00	100.00
	1840MV	—	75.00	100.00	150.00

MINTMARK: PASCO

Rev: Similar to C#131.1a.

C#	Date	Mintage	Fine	VF	XF
131.4b	1844M	—	15.00	30.00	55.00

Obv. leg: REPUB. PERUANA. 10DS20GS

C#	Date	Mintage	Fine	VF	XF
131.4d	1855	—	40.00	65.00	100.00

Obv. leg: REPUBLICA PERUANA

C#	Date	Mintage	Fine	VF	XF
131.4	1844M	—	20.00	35.00	60.00
	1845M	—	—	Rare	—

Obv. leg: REP. PERUANA 10D 20G

C#	Date	Mintage	Fine	VF	XF
131.4c	1855M	—	35.00	55.00	85.00

Obv. leg: REP. PERUANA, B in wreath 10D 20G

C#	Date	Mintage	Fine	VF	XF
131.4f	1855M	—	40.00	70.00	100.00

Obv. leg: REP. PERUANA

C#	Date	Mintage	Fine	VF	XF
131.4g	1856Z	—	55.00	90.00	130.00
	1857Z	—	40.00	65.00	100.00

Assayer's initial Z in circle.

C#	Date	Mintage	Fine	VF	XF
131.4h	1856	—	—	Rare	—
	1857	—	15.00	30.00	70.00

Obv. leg: REP. PERUANA.

C#	Date	Mintage	Fine	VF	XF
131.4i	1857AF	—	—	Rare	—
	1857	—	40.00	65.00	100.00

MINTMARK: PAZCO (monogram)

Obv. leg: REPUB. PERUANA, 10DS20GS

C#	Date	Mintage	Fine	VF	XF
131.4a	1843M	—	30.00	50.00	80.00

Obv. leg: REP. PERUANA 10DS20GS

C#	Date	Mintage	Fine	VF	XF
131.4e	1844M	—	45.00	70.00	110.00

8 REALES

25.0000 gm., .903 SILVER, .7259 oz ASW

MINTMARK: LIMAE (monogram)

Peru Libre Type

C#	Date	Mintage	Fine	VF	XF
125	1822JP	—	50.00	85.00	140.00
	1823JP	—	55.00	90.00	150.00

ROYALIST ISSUES

c/s: Crown over 1824 on C#125.

C#	Date	Mintage	Fine	VF	XF
125a	1822JP	—	110.00	155.00	225.00
	1823JP	—	90.00	120.00	190.00

REGULAR COINAGE RESUMED

Obv. leg: REPUB. PERUANA

C#	Date	Mintage	Fine	VF	XF
132.1	1825JM	—	22.00	27.50	50.00
	1826JM	—	22.00	25.00	45.00
	1827JM	—	22.00	27.50	50.00
	1828JM	—	26.50	40.00	60.00

Obv: Larger sprays around arms.
Rev: Liberty and shield enlarged.

C#	Date	Mintage	Fine	VF	XF
132.1a	1828JM	—	22.00	32.50	55.00
	1829JM	—	22.00	32.50	55.00
	1830JM	—	22.00	32.50	55.00
	1831JM	—	40.00	60.00	80.00
	1831MM	—	22.00	30.00	50.00
	1832MM	—	22.00	30.00	50.00

C#	Date	Mintage	Fine	VF	XF
132.1a	1833MM	—	22.00	25.00	37.50
	1833MM Por al Union	—	—	Rare	—
	1834MM	—	22.00	25.00	37.50
	1835MM	—	22.00	25.00	37.50
	1835MM Por al Union	—	—	Rare	—
	1835MT	—	22.00	25.00	37.50
	1836MM	—	37.50	65.00	100.00
	1836MT	—	22.00	22.50	35.00
	1836TM	—	25.00	37.50	65.00
	1837TM	—	22.00	35.00	60.00
	1838MB	—	35.00	65.00	90.00
	1839MB	—	22.00	25.00	40.00
	1840MB	—	22.00	25.00	40.00

Obv. leg: REP. PERUANA 10DS20GS

C#	Date	Mintage	Fine	VF	XF
132.1b	1840MB	—	25.00	37.50	60.00
	1841MB	—	22.00	27.50	50.00

Obv. leg: REPUB. PERUANA 10DS20GS
Rev: Redesigned liberty and shield.

C#	Date	Mintage	Fine	VF	XF
132.1c	1841MB	—	—	Rare	—
	1842MB	—	22.00	27.50	65.00
	1843MB	—	22.00	27.50	65.00
	1844MB	—	30.00	50.00	90.00
	1845MB	—	22.00	27.50	65.00
	1846MB	—	22.00	27.50	65.00
	1847/6MB	—	22.00	30.00	70.00
	1847MB	—	25.00	45.00	90.00
	1848/7MB	—	22.00	27.50	65.00
	1848MB	—	22.00	27.50	65.00
	1849MB	—	—	Rare	—
	1850MB ornamented edge				
		—	30.00	45.00	100.00
	1850MB reeded edge	—	25.00	40.00	85.00
	1851MB	—	25.00	40.00	85.00
	1852MB	—	30.00	50.00	90.00
	1853MB	—	35.00	60.00	100.00

Obv. leg: REPUBLICA PERUANA

C#	Date	Mintage	Fine	VF	XF
132.1d	1853MB	—	70.00	100.00	140.00

Obv. leg: REPUB. PERUANA

C#	Date	Mintage	Fine	VF	XF
132.1e	1854MB	—	120.00	175.00	250.00
	1855MB	—	22.00	27.50	45.00

MINTMARK: CUZco (monogram)

C#	Date	Mintage	Fine	VF	XF
132.3	1826GM	—	55.00	80.00	125.00
	1826G	—	35.00	50.00	70.00
	1827GM	—	22.00	35.00	50.00
	1827G	—	60.00	100.00	150.00
	1828G	—	35.00	50.00	70.00
	1828GM	—	60.00	100.00	150.00
	1829G	—	22.00	35.00	50.00
	1829G REPMB	—	—	Rare	—

MINTMARK: CUZCO

C#	Date	Mintage	Fine	VF	XF
132.3b	1830G	—	22.00	30.00	50.00
	1831G	—	22.00	30.00	45.00
	1832B	—	22.00	30.00	45.00
	1833B	—	22.00	30.00	45.00
	1833BoAr	—	22.00	30.00	55.00
	1834B	—	45.00	70.00	100.00
	1834BOAR	—	22.00	30.00	45.00

MINTMARK: CUZco (monogram)

C#	Date	Mintage	Fine	VF	XF
132.3c	1835B	—	50.00	75.00	110.00
	1836B	—	—	Rare	—

Obv. leg: 10DS20GS

C#	Date	Mintage	Fine	VF	XF
132.3a	1840A	—	35.00	50.00	70.00

MINTMARK: AREQ.

C#	Date	Mintage	Fine	VF	XF
132.2	1839MV	—	—	Rare	—
	1840MV	—	—	Rare	—

Obv. leg: REPUB. PERUANA 10DS20GS

C#	Date	Mintage	Fine	VF	XF
132.2a	1841M	—	—	Rare	—

NOTE: Sold for $2750.00 in V.G. 3-30-73.

PASCO MINT

Obv. leg: REPUB. PERUANA

C#	Date	Mintage	Fine	VF	XF
132.4	1836MO	—	—	Rare	—
132.4a	1857Z/0	—	—	Rare	—
	1857Z/0 PRO LA UNION		—	Rare	—

1/2 ESCUDO

1.6875 gm., .875 GOLD, .0475 oz AGW

MINTMARK: LIMAE (monogram)

C#	Date	Mintage	VF	XF	Unc
141.1	1826JM	—	100.00	140.00	175.00
	1827JM	—	100.00	140.00	175.00
	1828JM	—	60.00	90.00	120.00
	1829JM	—	60.00	90.00	120.00
	1833MM	—	55.00	85.00	110.00
	1836TM	—	100.00	140.00	175.00
	1839MB	—	55.00	85.00	110.00
	1840MB	—	85.00	110.00	140.00
	1841MB	—	55.00	85.00	110.00
	1842MB	—	55.00	85.00	110.00
	1850MB	—	55.00	85.00	110.00
	1856MB	—	60.00	90.00	120.00

MINTMARK: CUZCO

C#	Date	Mintage	VF	XF	Unc
141.3	1826GM	—	70.00	100.00	150.00

ESCUDO

3.3750 gm., .875 GOLD, .0949 oz AGW

MINTMARK: LIMAE (monogram)

Obv. leg: REPUBLICA PERUANA

C#	Date	Mintage	VF	XF	Unc
142.1	1826JM	—	90.00	130.00	170.00
	1827JM	—	150.00	200.00	250.00
	1828/7JM	—	120.00	160.00	200.00
	1828JM	—	80.00	120.00	160.00
	1829JM	—	150.00	200.00	250.00
	1833MM	—	80.00	120.00	160.00

Obv. leg: REPUB. PERUANA

C#	Date	Mintage	VF	XF	Unc
142.1a	1855MB	—	80.00	120.00	160.00

MINTMARK: CUZCO

C#	Date	Mintage	VF	XF	Unc
142.3	1826GM	—	150.00	200.00	300.00
	1830G	—	100.00	150.00	200.00

MINTMARK: CUZco (monogram)

C#	Date	Mintage	VF	XF	Unc
142.3a	1840A	—	100.00	150.00	200.00
	1845A	—	100.00	150.00	200.00
	1846A	—	100.00	150.00	200.00

2 ESCUDOS

6.7500 gm., .875 GOLD, .1899 oz AGW

MINTMARK: LIMAE (monogram)

Obv. leg: REPUBLICA PERUANA

C#	Date	Mintage	VF	XF	Unc
143.1	1828JM	—	125.00	150.00	350.00
	1829JM	—	125.00	150.00	350.00

Obv. leg: REPUB. PERUANA

C#	Date	Mintage	VF	XF	Unc
143.1a	1850MB	—	125.00	150.00	350.00
	1851MB	—	125.00	150.00	350.00
	1853MB	—	125.00	140.00	350.00
	1854MB	—	125.00	140.00	350.00
	1855MB	—	125.00	140.00	350.00

4 ESCUDOS

13.5000 gm., .875 GOLD, .3798 oz AGW

MINTMARK: LIMA

C#	Date	Mintage	VF	XF	Unc
144.1	1828JM	—	—	Rare	—

MINTMARK: LIMAE (monogram)

C#	Date	Mintage	VF	XF	Unc
144.1a	1850MB	—	250.00	350.00	500.00
	1853MB	—	500.00	700.00	1000.
	1854MB	—	350.00	500.00	650.00

Obv. leg: REPUB. PERUANA

C#	Date	Mintage	VF	XF	Unc
144.1b	1855MB	—	350.00	500.00	650.00

8 ESCUDOS

27.0000 gm., .875 GOLD, .7596 oz AGW

MINTMARK: LIMAE (monogram)

Obv. leg: REPUBLICA PERUANA

C#	Date	Mintage	VF	XF	Unc
145.1	1826JM	—	500.00	750.00	1100.
	1827JM	—	500.00	750.00	1100.
	1828JM	—	500.00	750.00	1100.
	1829/8JM	—	500.00	750.00	1100.
	1829JM	—	500.00	750.00	1100.
	1833MM	—	500.00	750.00	1100.
	1840MB	—	750.00	1000.	1500.

Small legends

C#	Date	Mintage	VF	XF	Unc
145.1a	1854 MB small letters		500.00	750.00	1100.
	1855 MB small letters		500.00	750.00	1100.

Obv. leg: REPUB. PERUANA

C#	Date	Mintage	VF	XF	Unc
145.1b	1855MB	—	500.00	750.00	1100.

MINTMARK: CUZCO

Rev: Similar to C#145.1

C#	Date	Mintage	VF	XF	Unc
145.3	1826GM	—	500.00	650.00	1000.
	1827G	—	500.00	650.00	1000.
	1828G	—	500.00	650.00	1000.
	1829G	—	500.00	650.00	1000.
	1830G	—	500.00	650.00	1000.
	1831G	—	500.00	650.00	1000.
	1832VOARSH	—	500.00	650.00	1000.
	1833BoAr	—	500.00	650.00	1000.
	1834BoAr	—	500.00	650.00	1000.

MINTMARK: CUZco (monogram)

C#	Date	Mintage	VF	XF	Unc
145.3a	1835B	—	500.00	600.00	900.00
	1836B	—	—	—	—
	1839A	—	750.00	1000.	1250.
	1840A	—	500.00	600.00	1200.
	1843A	—	500.00	600.00	1200.
	1844A	—	500.00	600.00	1200.
	1845A	—	500.00	600.00	1200.
	1855A	—	Reported, not confirmed		

NORTH PERU

1/2 REAL

1.6500 gm., .903 SILVER, .0479 oz ASW

LIMA MINT

Obv. leg: EST NOR-PERUANO

C#	Date	Mintage	Fine	VF	XF
147	1836TM	—	60.00	90.00	130.00
	1837TM	—	50.00	75.00	120.00
	1837MT	—	65.00	100.00	140.00
	1837M	—	50.00	75.00	120.00
	1838M	—	60.00	90.00	130.00
	1838MB	—	60.00	90.00	130.00
	1839MB	—	Reported, not confirmed		

Obv. leg: REP NOR-PERUANA

C#	Date	Mintage	Fine	VF	XF
147a	1839MB	—	90.00	140.00	200.00

REAL

3.2500 gm., .903 SILVER, .0944 oz ASW

Obv. leg: EST NOR-PERUANO

C#	Date	Mintage	Fine	VF	XF
148	1838MB	—	115.00	225.00	400.00

2 REALES

6.5000 gm., .903 SILVER, .1887 oz ASW

Obv. leg: EST. NOR-PERUANA

C#	Date	Mintage	Fine	VF	XF
149	1837JM	—	—	—	—

8 REALES

25.0000 gm., .903 SILVER, .7259 oz ASW

Obv. leg: EST. NOR-PERUANO

C#	Date	Mintage	Fine	VF	XF
151	1836TM	—	22.00	35.00	50.00
	1837TM	—	22.00	30.00	45.00
	1837MT	—	—	Rare	—
	1837M	—	25.00	40.00	60.00
	1838M	—	22.00	30.00	55.00
	1838TM	—	Reported, not confirmed		
	1838MB	—	22.00	27.50	40.00
	1839MB	—	25.00	35.00	55.00

Obv. leg: REP. NOR-PERUANA

C#	Date	Mintage	Fine	VF	XF
151a	1839MB	—	—	Rare	—

ESCUDO

3.3750 gm., .875 GOLD, .0949 oz AGW

Obv. leg: EST. NOR-PERUANO

C#	Date	Mintage	VF	XF	Unc
152	1838M	—	400.00	500.00	750.00

2 ESCUDOS

6.7500 gm., .875 GOLD, .1899 oz AGW

Obv. leg: ESTADO NOR PERUANO

C#	Date	Mintage	VF	XF	Unc
153	1838M	—	500.00	750.00	1000.

4 ESCUDOS

13.5000 gm., .875 GOLD, .3798 oz AGW

Obv. leg: ESTADO NOR PERUANO

C#	Date	Mintage	VF	XF	Unc
154	1838M	—	—	Rare	—

8 ESCUDOS

27.0000 gm., .875 GOLD, .7596 oz AGW

Obv. leg: ESTADO NOR PERUANO

C#	Date	Mintage	VF	XF	Unc
155	1836TM	—	—	Rare	—
	1838M	—	1650.	2000.	2750.

SOUTH PERU

1/2 REAL

1.6500 gm., .903 SILVER, .0479 oz ASW

CUZCO MINT

Obv. leg: ESTADO. SUD-PERUANO

C#	Date	Mintage	Fine	VF	XF
176	1837B	—	16.00	25.00	40.00

AREQUIPA MINT

Obv. leg: REPUB. SUD PERUANA

C#	Date	Mintage	Fine	VF	XF
171	1837	—	16.50	25.00	40.00
	1838	—	—	Rare	—

2 REALES

6.5000 gm., .903 SILVER, .1887 oz ASW

Obv. leg: REPUB. SUD-PERUANA

C#	Date	Mintage	Fine	VF	XF
178	1837BA	—	8.00	15.00	30.00

AREQUIPA MINT

Obv. leg: REPUB SUD-PERUANA

C#	Date	Mintage	Fine	VF	XF
173	1838	—	15.00	20.00	40.00

4 REALES

13.0000 gm., .903 SILVER, .3775 oz ASW
Obv. leg: REPUB. SUD-PERUANA

C#	Date	Mintage	Fine	VF	XF
174	1838MV	—	22.50	35.00	60.00

8 REALES

25.0000 gm., .903 SILVER, .7259 oz ASW

CUZCO MINT

Obv. leg: REPUB. SUD-PERUANA/written CUZCO FEDERACION

C#	Date	Mintage	Fine	VF	XF
180	1837BA	—	45.00	65.00	85.00

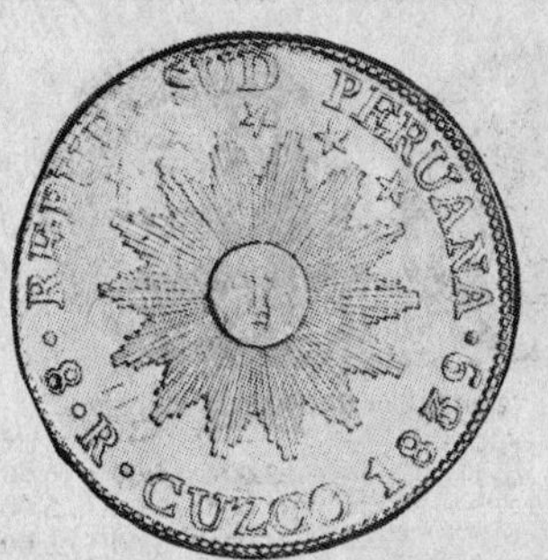

Obv. leg: REPUB. SUD-PERUANA/CONFEDERACION

C#	Date	Mintage	Fine	VF	XF
180a	1837BA	—	45.00	60.00	85.00
	1837MS	—	65.00	95.00	120.00
	1838BA	—	30.00	45.00	75.00
	1838MS	—	30.00	45.00	75.00
	1839MS	—	75.00	125.00	250.00

AREQUIPA MINT

Obv. leg: REPUB. SUD-PERUANA/written AREQ.

C#	Date	Mintage	Fine	VF	XF
175	1838MV	—	750.00	1000.	1500.
	1839MV	—	—	Rare	—

1/2 ESCUDO

1.6875 gm., .875 GOLD, .0475 oz AGW

CUZCO MINT

Obv. leg: REPUB. SUD PERUANA CUZ.

C#	Date	Mintage	VF	XF	Unc
181	1838MS	—	175.00	225.00	300.00

ESCUDO

3.3750 gm., .875 GOLD, .0949 oz AGW
Obv. leg: REPUB. SUD PERUANA

C#	Date	Mintage	VF	XF	Unc
182	1838MS	—	125.00	165.00	225.00

8 ESCUDOS

27.0000 gm., .875 GOLD, .7596 oz AGW
Obv. leg: ESTADO SUD PERUANO/written CUZCO

C#	Date	Mintage	VF	XF	Unc
183	1837BA	—	1350.	2000.	2500.

Obv. leg: REPUB SUD PERUANA/CONFEDERACION

C#	Date	Mintage	VF	XF	Unc
184	1837BA	—	1000.	1500.	2250.
	1838MS	—	1350.	2000.	2750.

TRANSITIONAL COINAGE

Issued during the changeover to the decimal system.

MEDIO (1/2) REAL

.750 SILVER

Y#	Date	Mintage	VF	XF	Unc
1	1858MB	—	15.00	25.00	50.00

Y#	Date	Mintage	VF	XF	Unc
3	1859Y.B.	—	35.00	50.00	100.00
	1860Y.B	—	22.50	45.00	70.00
	1861Y.B.	—	50.00	75.00	150.00

Many die varieties exist.

REAL

.750 SLVER

Y#	Date	Mintage	VF	XF	Unc
4	1859Y.B.	—	12.50	17.50	22.50
	1860Y.B	—	4.00	6.00	15.00
	1861Y.B.	—	15.00	20.00	35.00

Many die varieties exist.

25 CENTAVOS

.750 SILVER

Y#	Date	Mintage	VF	XF	Unc
5	1859Y.B	—	—	—	—
	1859/8Y.B	—	25.00	35.00	75.00

Die varieties exist.

50 CENTIMOS

.750 SILVER

Y#	Date	Mintage	VF	XF	Unc
2	1858MB	—	15.00	22.50	35.00
	1858MB	—	—	Proof	—

50 CENTAVOS

.750 SILVER

Y#	Date	Mintage	VF	XF	Unc
6	1858MB short hair	—	35.00	50.00	75.00
	1858Y.B. long hair	—	30.00	40.00	60.00
	1859Y.B.	—	25.00	35.00	50.00

Die varieties exist.

4 ESCUDOS

13.5000 gm., .875 GOLD, .3798 oz AGW
Rev: Seated Patria

Y#	Date	Mintage	VF	XF	Unc
7	1863Y.B	—	—	Rare	—

8 ESCUDOS

27.0000 gm., .875 GOLD, .7596 oz AGW

Y#	Date	Mintage	VF	XF	Unc
8	1862Y.B	—	700.00	850.00	1250.
	1863/2Y.B	—	500.00	600.00	800.00
	1863Y.B	—	500.00	600.00	800.00

DECIMAL COINAGE

100 Centavos (10 Dineros) = 1 Sol
10 Soles = 1 Libra

CENTAVO

COPPER-NICKEL

Y#	Date	Mintage	VF	XF	Unc
9	1863	1.000	2.00	3.00	10.00
	1864	Inc. Ab.	3.00	4.00	12.00

BRONZE

Y#	Date	Mintage	VF	XF	Unc
9a	1875	—	2.00	3.00	5.00
	1876	—	1.50	2.50	4.00
	1877	—	6.00	7.50	10.00
	1878	—	20.00	24.00	30.00

Sharper diework

Y#	Date	Mintage	VF	XF	Unc
9a.1	1919 (Phila.)	4.000	1.00	2.00	3.50

Thick planchet

Y#	Date	Mintage	VF	XF	Unc
11	1901	.600	1.00	1.50	3.00
	1904	1.000	20.00	25.00	40.00
	1933	.275	3.00	4.00	6.00
	1934	1.185	1.50	2.00	3.50
	1935	1.105	1.50	2.00	3.50
	1936	.565	3.00	4.00	7.00
	1937/6	.735	2.00	3.00	4.00
	1937	Inc. Ab.	1.50	2.00	3.00
	1938	.340	1.50	2.00	3.00
	1939	1.225	3.00	4.50	6.00
	1940	1.250	1.00	1.50	2.00
	1941	2.593	.50	1.00	1.50

Y#	Date	Mintage	VF	XF	Unc
12	1909	—	15.00	20.00	35.00
	1915	.250	6.00	8.00	10.00
	1916	.360	2.00	3.00	5.00
	1917	.830	2.00	3.00	5.00
	1917R	—	—	—	—
	1918	Inc. Ab.	2.00	3.00	5.00
	1918R	—	—	—	—
	1920R	.360	3.00	4.50	7.50
	1933R	Inc. Y#11	1.50	2.00	3.00
	1934	—	15.00	17.00	22.50
	1935R	—	15.00	17.00	22.50
	1936R	Inc. Y#11	3.50	5.00	7.50
	1937R	Inc. Y#11	3.50	5.00	7.50
	1939R	—	15.00	17.00	22.50

Thin Planchet
Rev: CENTAVO in straight line.

Y#	Date	Mintage	VF	XF	Unc
11a	1941	Inc. Y#11	1.00	1.50	2.00
	1942	2.865	1.00	1.50	2.00
	1943	— Reported, Not Confirmed			
	1944	—	15.00	20.00	25.00

Rev: CENTAVO is curved.

Y#	Date	Mintage	VF	XF	Unc
12a	1941	Inc. Y#11	2.00	3.00	5.00
	1942	Inc. Y#11a	1.00	2.00	3.00
	1943	—	6.00	12.50	25.00
	1944	2.490	.50	1.00	1.50
	1945	2.157	.50	1.00	1.50
	1946	3.198	.50	1.00	1.50
	1947	2.976	.50	1.00	1.50
	1948	3.195	.50	1.00	1.50
	1949	1.104	.50	1.00	1.50

ZINC

Y#	Date	Mintage	VF	XF	Unc
12b	1949	—	—	—	—

Error: Y#12a struck on reduced size planchet, 2 Centavos, Y#42.

Y#	Date	Mintage	VF	XF	Unc
12b.1	1949	—	—	—	—

Y#	Date	Mintage	VF	XF	Unc
41	1950	3.196	.50	1.00	2.00
	1951	3.289	.15	.25	.40
	1952	3.050	.50	.75	1.00
	1953	3.260	.50	.75	1.00
	1954	3.215	1.50	2.00	3.50
	1955	3.400	.50	1.00	1.50
	1956	2.500	.50	1.00	1.50
	1957	4.400	.50	1.00	1.50
	1958	2.600	.50	1.00	1.50
	1959	3.200	.50	1.00	1.50
	1960/50	3.060	.50	1.00	1.50
	1961/51	2.600	.50	1.00	1.50
	1962/52	2.600	1.00	2.00	3.00
	1962	Inc. Ab.	.50	1.00	2.00
	1963	2.400	.50	1.00	2.00
	1965	.360	.50	2.00	4.00

Copper plated examples of type dated 1951 exist.

2 CENTAVOS

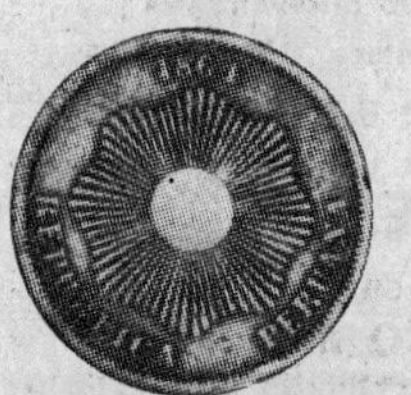

COPPER-NICKEL

Y#	Date	Mintage	VF	XF	Unc
10	1863	1.000	5.00	10.00	25.00
	1864	Inc. Ab.	5.00	15.00	30.00

COPPER or BRONZE

Y#	Date	Mintage	VF	XF	Unc
10a	1864	—	—	—	—
	1876	—	2.00	4.00	6.50
	1877	—	1.00	3.00	5.00
	1878	—	1.00	3.00	5.00
	1879	—	2.00	6.00	10.00
	1895	—	1.00	2.00	3.00

Sharper diework

Y#	Date	Mintage	VF	XF	Unc
10a.1	1919	3.000	.35	.75	2.00

Thick planchet

Y#	Date	Mintage	VF	XF	Unc
13	1917C	.073	5.00	8.00	12.50
	1918/17	—	2.50	4.50	7.00
	1918	—	10.00	12.50	15.00
	1920	.328	.75	1.00	1.50
	1933	.285	.75	1.00	1.50
	1933C	—	—	—	—
	1934	.973	.50	.75	1.00
	1934C	—	—	—	—
	1935	.950	.50	.75	1.00
	1935C	—	—	—	—
	1936C	.763	.50	.75	1.00
	1937	.963	.50	.75	1.00
	1937C	—	—	—	—

Y#	Date	Mintage	VF	XF	Unc
13	1938C	.428	.50	.75	1.00
	1939C	.783	.50	.75	1.00
	1940C	.565	.50	.75	1.00
	1941/33C	.870	—	—	—
	1941/38C	I.A.	—	—	—
	1941C	Inc. Ab.	6.00	12.50	20.00

Thin planchet

Y#	Date	Mintage	VF	XF	Unc
13a	1941	Inc. Ab.	.75	1.00	1.50
	1942	4.418	.75	1.00	1.50
	1943	1.829	2.00	3.00	4.50
	1944	2.068	2.00	3.00	4.50
	1945	2.288	2.00	3.00	4.50
	1946	2.121	.75	.80	1.00
	1947	1.280	.75	.80	1.00
	1948	1.518	.75	.80	1.00
	1949	.938	.75	.80	1.00

19mm

Y#	Date	Mintage	VF	XF	Unc
13a.1	1949	—	Reported, not confirmed		

ZINC

Y#	Date	Mintage	VF	XF	Unc
42	1950	1.702	.50	.75	1.00
	1951	3.289	.50	.75	1.00
	1952	1.155	.50	.75	2.00
	1953	1.150	.50	.75	1.00
	1954	—	—	Rare	—
	1955	1.185	.50	.75	1.00
	1956	.400	1.00	1.50	2.00
	1957	.520	2.00	3.00	5.00
	1958	.200	2.00	4.00	8.00

Copper plated examples of type dated 1951 exist.

1/2 DINERO

1.2500 gm., .900 SILVER, .0362 oz ASW

LIMA MINT

Y#	Date	Mintage	VF	XF	Unc
14	1863Y.B	—	3.00	4.00	5.00
	1864Y.B	—	3.00	4.00	5.00
	1890T.F.	.870	7.50	10.00	12.50
	1891T.F.	.160	10.00	15.00	25.00
	1892T.F.	.228	5.00	10.00	20.00
	1893T.F.	—	75.00	100.00	—
	1895T.F.	.422	3.00	5.00	7.50
	1896T.F.	.456	4.50	6.50	12.50
	1896F.	Inc. Ab.	4.00	5.50	8.00
	1897J.F.	.320	2.50	3.50	5.00
	1897V.N.	Inc. Ab.	20.00	30.00	50.00
	1898V.N.	.600	2.00	3.00	4.50
	1898J.F.	Inc. Ab.	2.00	3.00	4.50
	1899/8J.F.	.500	2.00	3.00	4.50
	1899J.F.	Inc. Ab.	2.00	3.00	4.50
	1900/1890J.F.	.400	2.00	3.00	4.50
	1900J.F.	Inc. Ab.	2.00	3.00	4.50
	1901/1891J.F.	.500	—	—	—
	1901J.F.	Inc. Ab.	3.00	3.75	5.25
	1902J.F.	.616	2.00	2.50	3.50
	1903/1803J.F.	1.798	2.00	2.50	3.50
	1903/897J.F.	I.A.	2.25	3.00	4.50
	1903J.F.	Inc. Ab.	2.00	2.50	3.50
	1904/1894J.F.	.723	—	—	—
	1904J.F.	Inc. Ab.	1.50	2.00	2.50
	1905/3J.F.	1.400	—	—	—
	1905J.F.	Inc. Ab.	1.50	2.00	2.50
	1906J.F.	.900	1.50	2.00	2.50
	1907F.G.	.600	1.50	2.50	3.50
	1908/7F.G.	.200	10.00	15.00	25.00
	1908F.G.	Inc. Ab.	2.00	3.00	4.50
	1909/7F.G.	—	13.50	18.50	25.00
	1909F.G.	—	11.50	15.00	20.00
	1910F.G.	.640	1.50	2.50	3.50
	1911F.G.	.460	2.50	4.00	6.50
	1912F.G.	.120	3.50	5.00	7.50
	1913F.G.	.480	1.50	2.50	3.50
	1914F.G.	—	1.50	2.50	3.50
	1916F.G.	.860	1.50	2.50	3.50
	1916F.G.(error FERUANA)	Inc. Ab.	—	—	—
	1917F.G.	.140	2.50	3.50	5.00

R.B. designer's initials, left on obverse of 1863 and 1864 issues.

CUZCO MINT

Y#	Date	Mintage	VF	XF	Unc
14a	1885J.M.	—	—	Rare	—

1/2 REAL

1.2500 gm., .900 SILVER, .0362 oz ASW

AYACUCHO MINT

Y#	Date	Mintage	VF	XF	Unc
28	1882L.M.	—	200.00	300.00	500.00

5 CENTAVOS

COPPER-NICKEL

Y#	Date	Mintage	VF	XF	Unc
25	1879	12.000	2.00	3.00	8.00
	1880	2.000	2.50	4.00	10.00

Date is spelled out.

Y#	Date	Mintage	VF	XF	Unc
31	1918	4.000	2.00	2.50	3.00
	1919	10.000	1.50	1.75	2.00
	1923	2.000	2.00	2.50	3.00
	1926	4.000	2.50	3.00	5.00
	1934	4.000	2.00	2.50	3.00
	1935	4.000	1.50	1.75	2.00
	1937	2.000	2.00	2.50	3.00
	1939	2.000	1.50	1.75	2.00
	1940	2.000	1.50	1.75	2.00
	1941	2.000	1.50	1.75	2.00

COPPER-ZINC

Y#	Date	Mintage	VF	XF	Unc
31a	1942	4.000	2.00	3.00	4.00
	1942	4.000	2.00	3.00	4.00
	1943	4.000	2.00	3.00	4.00
	1943	4.000	2.00	3.00	4.00
	1944	4.000	2.00	3.00	4.00

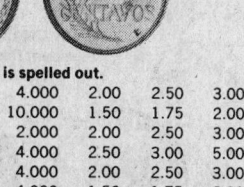

LIMA MINT

Y#	Date	Mintage	VF	XF	Unc
31a.1	1944	1.106	3.00	3.75	5.25

Thick planchet

Y#	Date	Mintage	VF	XF	Unc
38	1945	2.768	.75	1.00	1.50
	1946/5	4.270	—	—	—
	1946	Inc. Ab.	.75	1.00	1.50
	1947	7.683	.75	1.00	1.50
	1948	6.711	.50	.75	1.00
	1949/8	5.550	—	—	—
	1949	Inc. Ab.	.50	.75	1.00
	1950	7.933	.25	.50	.75
	1951	8.064	.25	.50	.75

Thin planchet

Y#	Date	Mintage	VF	XF	Unc
38a	1951	Inc. Ab.	.25	.50	1.00
	1952	7.840	.25	.50	1.00
	1953	6.976	.25	.50	1.00
	1954	6.244	.20	.40	1.00
	1955	8.064	.20	.40	.50
	1956	16.200	—	—	.50
	1957	16.000	—	—	.25
	1958	4.600	—	—	.35
	1959	8.300	—	—	.35
	1960	9.900	—	—	.25
	1961	10.200	—	—	.25
	1962	11.064	—	—	.25
	1963	12.012	—	—	.25
	1964/3	12.304	—	—	—
	1964	Inc. Ab.	—	—	.25
	1965	12.500	—	—	.25

ALUMINUM-BRONZE
Castilla

Y#	Date	Mintage	VF	XF	Unc
45	1954	2.080	2.50	5.00	7.50

BRASS
400th Anniversary of Lima Mint

Y#	Date	Mintage	VF	XF	Unc
53	1965	.712	—	.10	.25
	1965	—	—	Proof	—

Reeded edge

Y#	Date	Mintage	VF	XF	Unc
64	1966	14.620	—	—	.10
	1966	1.000	—	Proof	—
	1967	14.088	—	—	.15
	1968	17.880	—	—	.15

Plain edge

Y#	Date	Mintage	VF	XF	Unc
64a	1969	17.880	—	—	.10
	1970	—	—	—	—
	1971	24.320	—	—	.10
	1972	24.342	—	—	.10
	1973	25.074	—	—	.10
	1974	—	—	—	.10
	1975	—	—	—	.10

DINERO

2.5000 gm., .900 SILVER, .0723 oz ASW

LIMA MINT

Y#	Date	Mintage	VF	XF	Unc
15	1863Y.B	—	1.75	5.00	7.50
	1864/3 R.	—	10.00	20.00	30.00
	1864Y.B	—	3.00	5.00	7.50
	1865Y.B	—	8.00	15.00	25.00
	1866Y.B	—	2.25	3.00	5.00
	1867Y.B	—	—	—	—
	1870/69Y.J./Y.B.	—	—	—	—
	1870Y.J	—	3.00	5.00	7.50
	1870Y.J/B	—	3.00	5.00	7.50
	1872Y.J	—	—	Rare	—
	1874Y.J	—	4.00	6.00	9.00
	1875Y.J	—	3.00	4.00	6.50
	1877Y.J.	—	4.50	6.50	15.00
	1888T.F.	.010	—	Rare	—
	1890T.F.	.400	2.25	3.00	5.00
	1891T.F.	.060	10.00	12.50	15.00
	1892T.F.	.069	10.00	12.50	15.00
	1893T.F.	.023	15.00	17.50	20.00
	1894/3T.F.	—	30.00	50.00	100.00
	1894T.F.	—	—	Rare	—

Y#	Date	Mintage	VF	XF	Unc
	1895T.F.	.090	10.00	12.00	15.00
	1896T.F.	.534	10.00	13.50	17.50
	1896F.	Inc. Ab.	2.25	3.00	5.00
	1897J.F.	.511	2.25	3.00	5.00
	1897V.N.	Inc. Ab.	2.25	3.00	5.00
	1898/7J.F.	.200	3.00	5.00	7.50
	1898J.F.	Inc. Ab.	3.00	5.00	7.50
	1900/98J.F.	.550	3.00	5.00	8.50
	1900/1890J.F.	Inc. Ab.	3.00	5.00	8.50
	1900J.F.	Inc. Ab.	2.25	3.00	5.00
	1902J.F.	.375	2.25	3.00	5.00
	1903J.F.	.887	2.25	3.00	5.00
	1904J.F.	.380	2.25	3.00	5.00
	1905J.F.	.700	2.25	3.00	5.00
	1906J.F.	.826	2.25	3.00	5.00
	1907F.G./J.F.	.500	4.00	6.00	10.00
	1907F.G.	Inc. Ab.	2.25	3.00	5.00
	1908F.G./J.F.	.200	3.00	5.00	8.50
	1908F.G.	Inc. Ab.	2.25	3.00	5.00
	1909F.G.	—	17.50	20.00	30.00
	1910F.G./J.F.	.210	3.00	5.00	8.50
	1910F.G.	Inc. Ab.	2.25	3.00	5.00
	1911F.G.	.200	3.00	5.00	7.50
	1912F.G.	.400	3.00	5.00	7.50
	1913F.G.	.360	2.25	3.00	4.00
	1916F.G. large date	.430	2.25	3.00	4.00
	1919F.G. small date	Inc. Ab.	2.25	3.00	4.00

CUZCO MINT

Y#	Date	Mintage	VF	XF	Unc
15a	1886	—	100.00	150.00	200.00

10 CENTAVOS

COPPER-NICKEL

Y#	Date	Mintage	VF	XF	Unc
26	1879	3.005	3.00	9.00	20.00
	1880	4.000	2.00	7.00	15.00

Y#	Date	Mintage	VF	XF	Unc
32	1918	3.000	.75	1.00	1.50
	1919	2.500	.75	1.00	1.50
	1920	3.080	.50	.75	1.00
	1921	6.920	.50	.75	1.00
	1926	3.000	.50	.75	1.00
	1935	1.000	1.00	1.50	2.00
	1937	1.000	1.00	1.50	2.00
	1939	2.000	.50	.75	1.00
	1940	2.000	.50	.75	1.00
	1941	2.000	.50	.75	1.00

BRASS
Date is spelled out.

Y#	Date	Mintage	VF	XF	Unc
32a	1942	2.000	2.00	3.00	5.00
	1942	2.000	7.00	10.00	20.00
	1943	2.000	2.00	3.00	5.00
	1943	2.000	2.00	3.00	5.00
	1944	2.000	2.00	3.00	5.00

LIMA MINT

Date is spelled out.

Y#	Date	Mintage	VF	XF	Unc
32a.1	1942	—	10.00	15.00	25.00
	1944	—	7.00	10.00	20.00

Thick planchet

Y#	Date	Mintage	VF	XF	Unc
39	1945	2.810	.50	.75	1.00
	1946/5	4.863	.50	.75	1.00
	1946	Inc. Ab.	.35	.50	.75
	1947	6.806	.35	.50	.75
	1948	5.771	.35	.50	.75
	1949	4.730	.35	.50	.75
	1950	5.298	.35	.50	.75
	1951	7.324	12.50	15.00	25.00

Thin Planchet, 1.3mm

Y#	Date	Mintage	VF	XF	Unc
39a	1951	Inc. Ab.	.15	.20	.35
	1952	6.694	.15	.20	.35
	1953	5.668	—	—	.25
	1954	7.786	—	—	.25
	1955	6.690	—	—	.25
	1956	8.410	—	—	.25
	1957	8.420	—	—	.25
	1958	10.380	—	—	.25
	1959	8.300	—	—	.25
	1960	12.600	—	—	.25
	1961	12.700	—	—	.15
	1962	14.598	—	—	.15
	1963	16.100	—	—	.15
	1964	16.504	—	—	.15
	1965	17.808	—	—	.15

ALUMINUM-BRONZE
President Castilla

Y#	Date	Mintage	VF	XF	Unc
46	1954	1.818	5.00	7.00	10.00

BRASS
400th Anniversary of Lima Mint

Y#	Date	Mintage	VF	XF	Unc
54	1965	.572	.20	.25	.35
	1965	—	—	Proof	—

Reeded edge

Y#	Date	Mintage	VF	XF	Unc
65	1966	14.930	.20	.25	.35
	1966	1,000	—	Proof	—
	1967	19.330	.20	.25	.35
	1968	24.390	.20	.25	.35

Plain edge

Y#	Date	Mintage	VF	XF	Unc
65a	1969	24.390	—	—	.15
	1970	29.110	—	—	.15
	1971	30.590	—	—	.15
	1972	34.442	—	—	.15
	1973	33.864	—	—	.15
	1974	—	—	—	.15
	1975	10.430	—	—	.15

Y#	Date	Mintage	VF	XF	Unc
78	1975	—	—	—	—

1/5 SOL

5.0000 gm., .900 SILVER, .1447 oz ASW

LIMA MINT

Y#	Date	Mintage	VF	XF	Unc
16	1863Y.B	—	4.50	8.00	15.00
	1864/3Y.B.	—	10.00	20.00	50.00
	1864Y.B	—	4.50	6.00	8.00
	1864Y.B.D.D.	—	—	Rare	—
	1865/4Y.B	—	—	—	—
	1865Y.B	—	4.50	6.00	8.00
	1866/5Y.B.	—	—	—	—
	1866Y.B	—	4.50	6.00	8.00
	1867Y.B	—	4.50	6.00	8.00
	1869Y.B	—	10.00	15.00	25.00
	1874Y.J	—	4.50	6.00	12.50
	1875/65Y.J.	—	—	—	—
	1875Y.J	—	5.00	7.00	15.00
	1888T.F.	.550	5.00	7.00	10.00
	1889T.F.	—	—	Rare	—
	1890/88T.F.	.085	—	—	—
	1890T.F.	Inc. Ab.	10.00	13.00	17.50
	1891T.F.	.064	10.00	13.00	17.50
	1892T.F.	.128	6.00	9.00	12.50
	1893T.F.J.R.	.049	10.00	13.00	17.50
	1895T.F.J.R.	I.A.	20.00	25.00	55.00
	1896T.F.J.R.	.586	4.50	6.00	8.00
	1896.F.J.R.	I.A.	4.50	6.00	14.00
	1897J.F.	—	4.50	6.00	8.00
	1897J.F./J.R	.745	4.50	6.00	8.00
	1897V.N.	Inc. Ab.	4.50	6.00	10.00
	1898J.F.	.350	4.50	6.00	7.50
	1899J.F.	.700	4.50	6.00	7.50
	1900/800J.F.	.750	4.50	6.00	7.50
	1900/800J.F./J.R.	Inc. Ab.	4.50	6.00	7.50
	1900J.F.	Inc. Ab.	4.50	6.00	7.50
	1901J.F.	.638	4.50	6.00	7.50
	1903/1J.F.	.702	4.50	6.00	7.50
	1903/13F.F.	I.A.	4.50	6.00	8.00
	1903J.F.	Inc. Ab.	4.50	6.00	7.50
	1906J.F.	.660	BV	4.50	6.00
	1907J.F.	1.370	4.50	6.00	8.50
	1907F.G.	Inc. Ab.	BV	4.50	6.00
	1908/7F.G.	.560	4.50	5.00	7.00
	1908F.G.	Inc. Ab.	BV	4.50	6.00
	1909F.G.	.042	6.50	8.00	10.00
	1910F.G.	.165	BV	4.50	6.00
	1911F.G.	.250	BV	4.50	6.50
	1911F.G.R	—	BV	4.50	6.50
	1912F.G.	.300	BV	4.50	6.50
	1912F.G.R	—	BV	4.50	6.50
	1913F.G.	.223	5.00	10.00	25.00
	1913F.G.R	—	5.00	10.00	25.00
	1914F.G.	.010	30.00	35.00	45.00
	1915F.G.	—	125.00	150.00	175.00
	1916F.G.	—	—	—	—
	1916F.G.R	.425	BV	4.50	6.00
	1917F.G.R	.020	50.00	60.00	75.00

AREQUIPA MINT

Y#	Date	Mintage	VF	XF	Unc
16a	1885A.C.	—	—	Rare	—

PESETA

5.0000 gm., .900 SILVER, .1447 oz ASW

Y#	Date	Mintage	VF	XF	Unc
29	1880B.F.	—	5.00	7.00	20.00

20 CENTAVOS

COPPER-NICKEL

Y#	Date	Mintage	VF	XF	Unc
27	1879	.498	8.00	12.50	18.50

Date is spelled out.

Y#	Date	Mintage	VF	XF	Unc
33	1918	2.500	.75	1.00	1.50
	1919	1.250	.75	1.00	1.50
	1920	1.464	.75	1.00	1.50
	1921	8.536	.50	1.00	1.50
	1926	2.500	.75	1.00	1.50
	1940	1.000	.75	1.00	1.50
	1941	1.000	.75	1.00	1.50

BRASS
Date is spelled out.

Y#	Date	Mintage	VF	XF	Unc
33a	1942	.500	2.00	3.00	5.00
	1942	.500	5.25	7.50	15.00
	1943	.500	2.00	3.00	5.00
	1943	.500	2.00	3.00	5.00
	1944	.500	3.00	4.50	7.50

Thick planchet

Y#	Date	Mintage	VF	XF	Unc
40	1942	.300	3.00	6.00	10.00
	1943	1.900	.50	.75	1.00
	1944	2.963	.50	.75	1.00
	1945	3.043	.50	.75	1.00
	1946/5	3.410	.65	.90	1.25
	1946	Inc. Ab.	.50	.75	1.00
	1947	4.307	.50	.75	1.00
	1948	3.578	.50	.75	1.00
	1949/8	2.709	.65	.80	1.00
	1949	Inc. Ab.	.50	.60	.75
	1950	2.427	.50	.60	.75
	1951	2.941	7.50	12.50	25.00

Obv: Large Head, Divided Legend.

Y#	Date	Mintage	VF	XF	Unc
40.1	1943	—	—	—	—

Obv: Small Head, Continuous Legend.

Y#	Date	Mintage	VF	XF	Unc
40.2	1945	—	—	—	—

Obv:Large Head W/AFPon truncation, continuous legend.

Y#	Date	Mintage	VF	XF	Unc
40.3	1947	—	—	—	—

Thin Planchet, 1.3mm

Y#	Date	Mintage	VF	XF	Unc
40a	1951	Inc. Ab.	.40	.60	1.25
	1952	4.410	.40	.60	1.25
	1953	2.615	.40	.60	1.25
	1954	1.816	4.00	6.00	8.00
	1955lg.date	4.050	.10	.15	.25
	1955sm.date	I.A.	.10	.15	.25
	1956	3.760	.10	.15	.25
	1957	3.680	.10	.15	.25
	1958	3.100	.10	.15	.25
	1959	5.450	.10	.15	.25
	1960	6.750	.10	.15	.20
	1961	6.800	.10	.15	.20
40a	1962	7.357	.10	.15	.20
	1963	8.843	.10	.15	.20
	1964	9.550	.10	.15	.20
	1965	—	.10	.15	.20

ALUMINUM-BRONZE
Castilla

Y#	Date	Mintage	VF	XF	Unc
47	1954	.799	7.50	10.00	15.00

BRASS

Y#	Date	Mintage	VF	XF	Unc
79	1975	—	—	.10	.20

25 CENTAVOS

BRASS
400th Anniversary of Lima Mint

Y#	Date	Mintage	VF	XF	Unc
55	1965	1.113	.10	.15	.25
	1965	—	—	Proof	—

Reeded edge

Y#	Date	Mintage	VF	XF	Unc
66	1966	9.300	.10	.15	.25
	1966	1,000	—	Proof	—
	1967	8.150	.10	.15	.25
	1968	7.440	.10	.15	.25

Plain edge

Y#	Date	Mintage	VF	XF	Unc
66a	1969	7.440	.10	.15	.25
	1970	6.341	.10	.15	.25
	1971	3.196	.10	.15	.25
	1972	5.523	.10	.15	.25
	1973 lg. arms	7.492	.10	.15	.25
	1973 sm. arms	I.A.	.10	.15	.25
	1974	—	.10	.15	.25
	1975	—	.10	.15	.25

1/2 SOL

12.5000 gm., .900 SILVER, .3617 oz ASW

LIMA MINT

Y#	Date	Mintage	VF	XF	Unc
17	1864Y.B RB	—	11.00	15.00	25.00
	1865Y.B RB	—	11.00	12.00	15.00
	1907F.G.JR	1.000	BV	BV	12.00
	1908/7F.G.Jr	.030	55.00	80.00	125.00
17	1908F.G.JR	Inc. Ab.	45.00	65.00	100.00
	1914F.G.JR	.173	11.00	15.00	25.00
	1915F.G.JR	.570	11.00	12.00	20.00
	1916F.G.	.384	11.00	12.00	15.00
	1916F.G.JR	—	11.00	12.00	15.00
	1917F.G.JR	.178	BV	11.00	12.50

12.5000 gm., .500 SILVER, .2009 oz ASW

Y#	Date	Mintage	VF	XF	Unc
34	1922 LIBERTAD incuse	.465	BV	6.00	10.00
	1922 LIBERTAD in relief	Inc. Ab.	BV	6.00	10.00
	1923 round top 3	2.520	BV	6.00	10.00
	1923 flat top 3	I.A.	BV	6.00	10.00
	1924	.238	7.50	10.00	15.00
	1926	.694	7.50	10.00	15.00
	1927	2.640	BV	6.00	10.00
	1928	3.028	BV	6.00	10.00
	1929	3.068	BV	6.00	10.00
	1935	2.653	BV	6.00	10.00

BRASS

Y#	Date	Mintage	VF	XF	Unc
43	1935(L)	10.000	.50	.60	.75
	1941(L)	4.000	.50	.60	.75
	1942(p)	4.000	3.00	4.00	6.75
	1942S	1.668	3.00	4.00	6.75
	1943S	6.332	3.00	4.00	6.75
	1943(p)	4.000	3.00	4.00	6.75
	1944(p)	Inc. Ab.	3.00	4.00	6.75
	1945(P)	4.000	3.00	4.00	6.75
	1946/5	3.744	.65	.90	1.25
	1946	Inc. Ab.	.50	.60	.75
	1947	6.066	.50	.60	.75
	1948	3.324	.50	.60	.75
	1949/8	.420	.65	.90	1.25
	1949	Inc. Ab.	.50	.75	1.00
	1950	.091	.75	1.00	1.50
	1951/8	.930	.60	.75	.90
	1951	Inc. Ab.	.50	.60	.75
	1952	.935	.50	.60	.75
	1953	.817	.50	.60	.75
	1954	.637	.50	.60	.75
	1955	1.383	.25	.30	.50
	1956	2.309	.25	.30	.50
	1957	2.700	.25	.30	.50
	1958	2.691	.25	.30	.50
	1959	3.609	.25	.30	.50
	1960	5.600	.25	.30	.35
	1961	4.400	.15	.20	.35
	1962	3.540	.15	.20	.35
	1963	4.345	.15	.20	.35
	1964	5.315	.15	.20	.35
	1965	—	.10	.15	.25

400th Anniversary Of Lima Mint

Y#	Date	Mintage	VF	XF	Unc
56	1965	.971	.15	.20	.35
	1965	—	—	Proof	—

Y#	Date	Mintage	VF	XF	Unc
67	1966	13.720	.10	.20	.40
	1966	1,000	—	Proof	—
	1967	15.500	.10	.20	.35
	1968	13.890	.10	.20	.40
	1969	13.890	.10	.20	.40
	1970	11.901	.10	.20	.40
	1971	7.524	.15	.20	.40
	1972	19.441	.10	.20	.40
	1973 lg. arms	14.951	.10	.20	.40
	1973 sm. arms	I.A.	.10	.20	.40
	1974	—	.10	.20	.40
	1975	—	.10	.20	.40

Y#	Date	Mintage	VF	XF	Unc
80	1975	—	.10	.20	.30
	1976	369.828	.10	.20	.30

9.3500 gm., .900 GOLD, .2706 oz AGW
150th Anniversary Battle of Ayacucho

Y#	Date	Mintage	VF	XF	Unc
84	1976	.010	175.00	200.00	250.00

SOL

25.0000 gm., .900 SILVER, 37.5mm .7234 oz ASW

LIMA MINT

Type I

Obv: Small wreath above shield has ribbon ties.
Rev: Shield below liberty's hand is tilted.
Santiago issues have LIMA on the coin.

Y#	Date	Mintage	VF	XF	Unc
18.1	1864/54Y.B.	—	BV	22.00	25.00
	1864Y.B.	—	—	Rare	—
	1865/55Y.B.	—	BV	22.00	25.00
	1865Y.B.	—	—	Rare	—
	1866/56Y.B.	—	BV	22.00	25.00
	1866Y.B.	—	—	Rare	—
	1867/57Y.B.	—	BV	22.00	25.00
	1867Y.B.	—	BV	22.00	25.00
	1868/58Y.B.	—	BV	22.00	25.00

Obv: Derteneo on bottom row of coins falling from cornucopia.

Y#	Date	Mintage	VF	XF	Unc
18.1a	1864/54Y.B.	—	—	Rare	—

Type II

Y#	Date	Mintage	VF	XF	Unc
18.2	1868Y.B. Arabic 1	—	BV	22.00	25.00
	1868Y.B. Roman 1	—	—	Rare	—
	1869Y.B.	—	BV	22.00	25.00
	1870Y.J.	—	BV	22.00	25.00
	1871Y.J.	—	BV	22.00	25.00
	1872Y.J.	—	BV	22.00	25.00
	1873Y.J.	—	50.00	75.00	100.00
	1874Y.J.	—	BV	22.00	25.00
	1875Y.J.	—	BV	22.00	25.00

SANTIAGO MINT

Y#	Date	Mintage	VF	XF	Unc
18.2a	1873L.D. Arabic 1	—	BV	22.50	30.00
	1873L.D./backwards D. Arabic 1	—	—	Rare	—
	1873L.D. Roman 1	—	30.00	45.00	60.00

Type III

Letters R.B. on stems flanking date.

Y#	Date	Mintage	VF	XF	Unc
18.3	1879Y.J.	—	25.00	30.00	40.00
	1880Y.J.	—	60.00	70.00	85.00

Letters R.B. on ribbon of wreath, 3 olives in bunch.

Y#	Date	Mintage	VF	XF	Unc
18.3a	1880Y.J.	—	—	Rare	—

No extra letters, 2 olives in bunch.

Y#	Date	Mintage	VF	XF	Unc
18.3b	1880Y.J.	—	—	Rare	—

Type IV

Y#	Date	Mintage	VF	XF	Unc
18.4	1881B.F.	—	—	—	—

Rev: Letters R.L. on base of column.

Y#	Date	Mintage	VF	XF	Unc
18.4a	1881B.F.	—	—	—	—

Type V

B.F. on reverse

Y#	Date	Mintage	VF	XF	Unc
18.5	1881B.F.	—	22.00	30.00	45.00

R.B. on reverse

Y#	Date	Mintage	VF	XF	Unc
18.5a	1881B.F.	—	22.00	30.00	45.00
	1882B.F.	—	20.00	30.00	45.00

F.D. on reverse.

Y#	Date	Mintage	VF	XF	Unc
18.5b	1881b.f.	—	22.00	25.00	30.00
	1882b.f.	—	22.00	25.00	30.00

Type VI

F.D. on reverse.

Y#	Date	Mintage	VF	XF	Unc
18.6	1882.N.	—	BV	22.00	25.00

Type VII

B.F. on reverse.

Y#	Date	Mintage	VF	XF	Unc
18.7	1883.N.	—	BV	22.00	25.00

F.D. on reverse.

Y#	Date	Mintage	VF	XF	Unc
18.7a	1883F.N.	—	BV	22.00	25.00
	1884B.D.	—	BV	22.00	25.00

Type VIII

F.D. on reverse.

Y#	Date	Mintage	VF	XF	Unc
18.8	1884R.D.	—	BV	22.00	25.00

Type IX

No extra initials.

Y#	Date	Mintage	VF	XF	Unc
18.9	1884R.D.	—	—	—	—

Type X

Y#	Date	Mintage	VF	XF	Unc
18.10	1885R.D.	—	BV	22.00	25.00
	1885/T.D./B.D.	—	BV	22.00	25.00
	1885T.D.	—	BV	22.00	25.00
	1886/5T.F.	—	BV	22.00	25.00
	1886T.F.	—	BV	22.00	25.00
	1887T.F./B.F.	—	BV	22.00	25.00
	1887T.F.	—	BV	22.00	25.00

Type XI

Rev: Shield below Liberty's hand is tilted.
UN SOL is in a straight line.

Y#	Date	Mintage	VF	XF	Unc
18.11	1888T.F./B.F.	3.150	BV	22.00	25.00
	1888T.F.	—	BV	22.00	25.00
	1889T.F./B.F.	2.840	BV	22.00	25.00
	1889T.F.	—	BV	22.00	25.00
	1890/80T.F./B.F.	2.300	—	Rare	—
	1890T.F./B.F.	I.A.	BV	22.00	25.00
	1890T.F.	Inc. Ab.	BV	22.00	25.00
	1891T.F./B.F.	2.980	BV	22.00	25.00
	1891T.F.	Inc. Ab.	BV	22.00	25.00
	1892T.F./B.F.	2.270	BV	22.00	25.00
	1892T.F.	Inc. Ab.	BV	22.00	25.00

Type XII

Legends have smaller lettering, 37mm.

Y#	Date	Mintage	VF	XF	Unc
18.12	1393T.F. Error date	—	65.00	90.00	125.00
	1893T.F.	—	BV	22.00	25.00
	1894T.F.	4.358	BV	22.00	25.00
	1895T.F.	4.111	BV	22.00	25.00
	1896T.F.	2.511	BV	22.00	25.00
	1896F.	Inc. Ab.	BV	22.00	25.00
	1897J.F.	.234	22.00	30.00	50.00
	1914F.G.	.620	BV	22.00	25.00
	1915F.G.	1.736	BV	22.00	25.00

Rev: LIBERTAD incuse, 36.5mm.

Y#	Date	Mintage	VF	XF	Unc
18.12a	1916F.G.	1.927	BV	22.00	25.00

Type XIII

Rev: LIBERTAD in relief.

Y#	Date	Mintage	VF	XF	Unc
18.13	1916F.G.	Inc. Ab.	BV	BV	22.00

Y#	Date	Mintage	VF	XF	Unc
23	1910	—	22.00	30.00	50.00

25.000 gm., .500 SILVER, .4019 oz ASW

Obv: Fineness omitted. Rev: LIBERTAD in relief.

Y#	Date	Mintage	VF	XF	Unc
35.1	1923	1,400	65.00	75.00	100.00

Rev: LIBERTAD incuse.

Y#	Date	Mintage	VF	XF	Unc
35.2	1923	3,600	75.00	90.00	125.00

.500 SILVER

PHILADELPHIA MINT

Small letters

Y#	Date	Mintage	VF	XF	Unc
36.1	1923(P)	*2.369	BV	BV	12.00
	1924(P)	*3.113	BV	BV	12.00
	1925(P)	*1.291	BV	BV	12.00
	1926(P)	*2.157	BV	BV	12.00

***NOTE:** The Philadelphia and Lima strikings may be distinguished by the fact that the letters in the legends are smaller on those pieces produced at Philadelphia. All bear the name of the Lima Mint.

LIMA MINT

Large letters

Y#	Date	Mintage	VF	XF	Unc
36.2	1924	.096	45.00	55.00	65.00
	1925	1.005	BV	12.00	15.00
	1930	.076	BV	BV	12.00
	1931	.024	12.50	15.00	17.50
	1933	5,000	20.00	30.00	40.00
	1934	2.855	BV	BV	14.00
	1935	.695	15.00	17.00	20.00

BRASS

Y#	Date	Mintage	VF	XF	Unc
44	1943	10.000	2.00	3.00	4.00
	1944	Inc. Ab.	2.00	3.00	4.00
	1945	—	2.00	3.00	4.00
	1946	1.752	1.00	2.00	3.00
	1947	3.302	1.00	2.00	3.00
	1948	1.992	1.00	2.00	3.00
	1949/8	Inc. Ab.	1.25	2.50	3.50
	1949	.751	1.00	2.00	3.00
	1950	1.249	4.00	6.00	12.00
	1951	2.094	.50	1.00	2.00
	1952	2.037	.50	1.00	1.50
	1953	1.243	.50	1.25	3.00
	1954	1.220	.85	1.00	1.75
	1955	1.323	.50	1.00	1.50
	1956	3.450	.50	1.00	1.50
	1957	3.086	.50	1.00	1.50
	1958	3.390	.50	1.00	1.50
	1959	4.975	.50	1.00	1.50
	1960	5.800	.25	.35	.50
	1961	5.200	.25	.35	.50
	1962	5.102	.25	.35	.50
	1963	5.499	.25	.35	.50
	1964	5.888	.25	.35	.50
	1965	5.504	.20	.25	.35

400th Anniversary Of Lima Mint

Y#	Date	Mintage	VF	XF	Unc
57	1965	3.103	—	—	.60
	1965	—	—	Proof	—

Y#	Date	Mintage	VF	XF	Unc
68	1966	16.410	—	—	.50
	1966	1,000	—	Proof	—
	1967	13.920	—	—	.50
	1968	12.260	—	—	.50
	1969	12.260	—	—	.50
	1970	12.336	—	—	.50
	1971	11.927	—	—	.50
	1972	3.945	—	—	.50
	1973	12.856	—	—	.50
	1974	—	—	—	.50
	1975	—	—	—	.50

21mm

Y#	Date	Mintage	VF	XF	Unc
81	1975	Inc. Ab.	—	—	.25
	1976	112.560	—	—	.40

17mm

Y#	Date	Mintage	VF	XF	Unc
81a	1978	—	—	—	.20

23.4000 gm., .900 GOLD, .6772 oz AGW
150th Anniversary Battle of Ayacucho

Y#	Date	Mintage	VF	XF	Unc
85	1976	.010	450.00	475.00	550.00

5 PESETAS

25.0000 gm., .900 SILVER, .7234 oz ASW

LIMA MINT

Obv: B under wreath.

Y#	Date	Mintage	VF	XF	Unc
30.1	1880B.F.	—	25.00	40.00	75.00

w/o b. under wreath

Y#	Date	Mintage	VF	XF	Unc
30.2	1880B.F.	—	25.00	40.00	75.00

AYACUCHO MINT

Rev: Similar to Y#30.1.

Y#	Date	Mintage	VF	XF	Unc
30a	1881B.	—	350.00	450.00	750.00
	1882L.M.	—	90.00	135.00	450.00

5 SOLES

8.0645 gm., .900 gold, .2334 oz AGW

Y#	Date	Mintage	VF	XF	Unc
A19	1863Y.B.	—	150.00	175.00	350.00

2.3404 gm., .900 GOLD, .0677 oz AGW

Y#	Date	Mintage	VF	XF	Unc
24	1910	—	50.00	75.00	100.00

LIMA MINT

Y#	Date	Mintage	VF	XF	Unc
48	1956	4,510	BV	45.00	50.00
	1957	2,146	BV	45.00	50.00
	1958	3,325 Reported, Not Confirmed			
	1959	1,536	45.00	47.50	60.00
	1960	8,133	BV	45.00	45.00
	1961	1,154	45.00	47.50	60.00
	1962	1,550	45.00	47.50	60.00
	1963	3,945	BV	45.00	50.00
	1964	2,063	BV	45.00	55.00
	1965	.014	BV	BV	45.00
	1966	4,738	BV	45.00	50.00
	1967	3,651	BV	44.00	50.00
	1968	129 pcs. Reported, Not Confirmed			
	1969	127 pcs.	225.00	300.00	400.00

COPPER-NICKEL

Y#	Date	Mintage	VF	XF	Unc
69	1969	10.000	—	—	1.00

150th Anniversary Of Independence

Y#	Date	Mintage	VF	XF	Unc
71	1971	3.480	—	—	1.75

Regular Issue

Y#	Date	Mintage	VF	XF	Unc
74	1972	2.068	—	—	.75
	1973	.475	—	—	.75
	1974	—	—	—	.75
	1975	—	—	—	.75

Y#	Date	Mintage	VF	XF	Unc
82	1975	—	—	—	.75
	1976	17.016	—	—	.75
	1977	—	—	.50	1.00

BRASS

Y#	Date	Mintage	VF	XF	Unc
86	1978	—	—	.25	.50
	1979	—	—	.25	.50

10 SOLES

16.1290 gm., .900 GOLD

Y#	Date	Mintage	VF	XF	Unc
B19	1863YB	—	135.00	175.00	400.00

LIMA MINT

4.6807 gm., .900 GOLD, .1354 oz AGW

Y#	Date	Mintage	VF	XF	Unc
49	1956	5,410	BV	BV	90.00
	1957	1,300	BV	90.00	100.00
	1958	3,325	Reported, not confirmed		
	1959	1,103	BV	BV	90.00
	1960	7,178	BV	BV	90.00
	1961	1,634	BV	90.00	100.00
	1962	1,676	BV	90.00	100.00
	1963	3,372	BV	BV	90.00
	1964	1,554	BV	BV	90.00
	1965	.014	BV	BV	90.00
	1966	2,601	BV	BV	90.00
	1967	3,002	BV	BV	90.00
	1968	100 Pcs.	BV	BV	90.00
	1969	100 Pcs.	BV	BV	90.00

COPPER-NICKEL

Y#	Date	Mintage	VF	XF	Unc
70	1969	15.000	—	—	1.75

150th Anniversary Of Independence

Y#	Date	Mintage	VF	XF	Unc
72	1971	2.460	—	—	2.75

Y#	Date	Mintage	VF	XF	Unc
75	1972	2.235	—	—	1.25
	1973	1.765	—	—	1.25
	1974	—	—	—	1.25
	1975	—	—	—	1.25

BRASS

Y#	Date	Mintage	VF	XF	Unc
75a	1978	—	—	.75	1.50
	1979	—	—	—	—

20 SOLES

32.2581 gm., .900 GOLD, .9334 oz AGW

Y#	Date	Mintage	VF	XF	Unc
19	1863YB	—	BV	610.00	700.00

LIMA MINT

9.3614 gm., .900 GOLD, .2709 oz AGW

Y#	Date	Mintage	VF	XF	Unc
50	1950	1,800	BV	180.00	250.00
	1951	9,264	BV	BV	180.00
	1952	1,424	BV	180.00	200.00
	1953	1,435	BV	180.00	200.00
	1954	1,732	BV	180.00	200.00
	1955	1,971	BV	180.00	200.00
	1956	1,201	BV	180.00	200.00
	1957	.011	BV	BV	180.00
	1958	.011	Reported, not confirmed		

Y#	Date	Mintage	VF	XF	Unc
50	1959	.012	BV	BV	180.00
	1960	7,753	BV	BV	180.00
	1961	1,825	BV	180.00	200.00
	1962	2,282	BV	BV	180.00
	1963	3,892	BV	BV	180.00
	1964	1,302	BV	180.00	200.00
	1965	.012	BV	BV	180.00
	1966	4,001	BV	BV	180.00
	1967	5,003	BV	BV	180.00
	1968	640 pcs.	180.00	BV	275.00
	1969	640 pcs.	180.00	BV	275.00

8.0000 gm., .900 SILVER, .2315 oz ASW
400th Anniversary Of Lima Mint

Y#	Date	Mintage	VF	XF	Unc
58	1965	.150	BV	BV	7.00

1866 Peru-Spain Naval Battle

Y#	Date	Mintage	VF	XF	Unc
61	1966	4,001	8.50	12.50	32.50

50 SOLES

33.4363 gm., .900 GOLD, .9675 oz AGW

Y#	Date	Mintage	VF	XF	Unc
37	1930	5,584	628.00	750.00	1000.
	1931	5,538	628.00	750.00	1000.
	1967	.010	BV	BV	630.00
	1968	300 pcs.	628.00	650.00	900.00
	1969	300 pcs.	628.00	650.00	900.00

23.4056 gm., .900 GOLD, .6772 oz AGW

LIMA MINT

Y#	Date	Mintage	VF	XF	Unc
51	1950	1,927	BV	400.00	600.00
	1951	5,292	BV	BV	440.00
	1952	1,201	BV	450.00	650.00
	1953	1,464	BV	450.00	650.00
	1954	1,839	BV	450.00	650.00
	1955	1,898	BV	450.00	650.00
	1956	.011	BV	BV	450.00
	1957	.011	BV	BV	450.00
	1958	.011	BV	BV	450.00
	1959	5,734	BV	BV	450.00

Y#	Date	Mintage	VF	XF	Unc
51	1960	2,139	BV	BV	450.00
	1961	1,110	BV	450.00	650.00
	1962	3,319	BV	BV	450.00
	1963	3,089	BV	BV	450.00
	1964	2,425	BV	BV	450.00
	1965	.023	BV	BV	450.00
	1966	3,409	BV	BV	450.00
	1967	5,805	BV	BV	450.00
	1968	443 pcs.	500.00	650.00	800.00
	1969	443 pcs.	500.00	650.00	800.00
	1970	553 pcs.	Reported, not confirmed		

400th Anniversary Of Lima Mint

59	1965	.017	BV	500.00	350.00

Peru-Spain Naval Battle

62	1966	6,409	BV	600.00	750.00

22.0000 gm., .800 SILVER, .5659 oz ASW
150th Anniversary of Independence

73	1971	.100	BV	17.00	20.00

100 SOLES

46.8071 gm., .900 GOLD, 1.3544 oz AGW

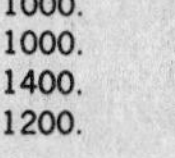

LIMA MINT

52	1950	1,176	BV	900.00	1000.
	1951	8,241	BV	900.00	1000.
	1952	126 pcs.	900.00	1000.	1400.
	1953	498 pcs.	900.00	1000.	1200.

Y#	Date	Mintage	VF	XF	Unc
52	1954	1,808	BV	900.00	1000.
	1955	901 pcs.	900.00	1000.	1100.
	1956	1,159	BV	900.00	1000.
	1957	550 pcs.	900.00	1000.	1200.
	1958	101 pcs.	900.00	1000.	1400.
	1959	4,710	BV	900.00	1000.
	1960	2,207	BV	900.00	1000.
	1961	6,982	BV	900.00	1000.
	1962	9,678	BV	900.00	1000.
	1963	7,342	BV	900.00	1000.
	1964	.011	BV	900.00	1000.
	1965	.023	BV	900.00	1000.
	1966	3,409	BV	900.00	1000.
	1967	6,431	BV	900.00	1000.
	1968	540 pcs.	900.00	1000.	1200.
	1969	540 pcs.	900.00	1000.	1200.
	1970	425 pcs.	900.00	1000.	1100.

60	1965	.027	BV	1000.	1400.

1866 Peru-Spain Naval Battle

63	1966	6,253	BV	900.00	1000.

22.0000 gm., .800 SILVER, .5659 oz ASW
Centennial Peru-Japan Trade Relations

76	1973	.375	BV	17.00	20.00

200 SOLES

22.0000 gm., .800 SILVER, .5659 oz ASW
Aviation Heroes

Y#	Date	Mintage	VF	XF	Unc
77	1974	.025	BV	17.00	20.00
	1975	.090	BV	17.00	20.00
	1976	.025	BV	17.00	20.00
	1977	3,000	17.00	20.00	30.00

400 SOLES

27.5500 gm., .900 SILVER, .7973 oz ASW
150th Anniversary Battle of Ayacucho
Obv: Similar to 200 Soles, Y#77.

83	1976	—	BV	BV	25.00

1000 SOLES

.500 SILVER
Battle of Iquique
Similar to 5000 Soles, Y#88.

87	1979	—	—	—	—

COPPER-NICKEL
National Congress

95	1979	—	—	—	—

15.5500 gm., .500 SILVER, .2500 oz ASW

95a	1979	.200	—	7.50	9.00

5000 SOLES

33.4500 gm., .925 SILVER, .9949 oz ASW
Battle of Iquique

Y#	Date	Mintage	VF	XF	Unc
88	1979	—	—	—	40.00

50,000 SOLES

16.9700 gm., .917 GOLD, .5004 oz AGW
Alfonso Urgarte

Y#	Date	Mintage	VF	XF	Unc
89	1979	—	BV	325.00	350.00

Elias Aguirre

Y#	Date	Mintage	VF	XF	Unc
90	1979	—	BV	325.00	350.00

F. Garcia Calderon

Y#	Date	Mintage	VF	XF	Unc
91	1979	—	BV	325.00	350.00

100,000 SOLES

33.9000 gm., .917 GOLD, .9995 oz AGW
Francisco Bolognese

Y#	Date	Mintage	VF	XF	Unc
92	1979	—	BV	650.00	700.00

Andres A. Caceras
Obv: Similar To Y#92.

Y#	Date	Mintage	VF	XF	Unc
93	1979	—	BV	650.00	700.00

Miguel Grau
Obv: Similar To Y#92.

Y#	Date	Mintage	VF	XF	Unc
94	1979	—	BV	650.00	700.00

TRADE COINAGE

1/5 LIBRA (POUND)

1.5976 gm., .917 GOLD, .0471 oz AGW

LIMA MINT

Y#	Date	Mintage	VF	XF	Unc
20	1905ROZF	.045	BV	BV	35.00
	1905GOZF	Inc. Ab.	BV	BV	35.00
	1906GOZF	.106	BV	BV	35.00
	1907GOZF	.031	BV	BV	35.00
	1907GOZG	—	BV	35.00	40.00
	1908	—	Reported, not confirmed		
	1909	—	Reported, not confirmed		
	1910GOZG	—	BV	BV	35.00
	1911GOZF	.062	BV	BV	35.00
	1911GOZG	—	BV	BV	35.00
	1912GOZG	—	BV	35.00	40.00
	1912POZG	—	BV	35.00	40.00
	1913POZG	.060	BV	BV	35.00
	1914POZG	.025	BV	32.50	40.00
	1914PBLG	Inc. Ab.	BV	35.00	42.50
	1915	.010	BV	35.00	42.50
	1916	.013	Reported, not confirmed		
	1917	3,896	BV	32.50	40.00
	1918	.016	BV	35.00	42.50
	1919	.010	BV	35.00	42.50
	1920	.072	BV	BV	35.00
	1921	—	Reported, not confirmed		
	1922	8,110	BV	32.50	40.00
	1923	.027	BV	BV	35.00
	1924	—	BV	BV	35.00
	1925	.020	BV	BV	35.00
	1926	.011	BV	32.50	40.00
	1927	.014	BV	32.50	40.00
20	1928	9,322	BV	32.50	40.00
	1929	8,971	BV	32.50	40.00
	1930	9,991	BV	35.00	42.50
	1931	8,722	Reported, not confirmed		
	1932	8,430	Reported, not confirmed		
	1946	.010	Reported, not confirmed		
	1947	.010	Reported, not confirmed		
	1948	.015	Reported, not confirmed		
	1949	.011	Reported, not confirmed		
	1951BBR	4,637	Reported, not confirmed		
	1952BBR	6,337	Reported, not confirmed		
	1953BBR	9,821	BV	BV	35.00
	1954	9,473	Reported, not confirmed		
	1955ZBR	.010	BV	BV	35.00
	1956ZBR	8,116	Reported, not confirmed		
	1957ZBR	6,345	Reported, not confirmed		
	1958ZBR	5,098	35.00	40.00	45.00
	1959ZBR	6,308	35.00	40.00	45.00
	1960ZBR	6,083	35.00	40.00	45.00
	1961ZBR	.012	35.00	40.00	45.00
	1962ZBR	5,431	35.00	40.00	45.00
	1963ZBR	.011	BV	40.00	45.00
	1964ZBR	.025	BV	BV	35.00
	1965ZBR	.019	BV	BV	35.00
	1966ZBR	.060	BV	BV	35.00
	1967BBR	9,914	BV	32.50	40.00
	1968BBR	4,781	40.00	50.00	60.00
	1968BBB	Inc. Ab.	50.00	60.00	75.00
	1969BBB	.015	BV	BV	35.00

1/2 LIBRA (POUND)

3.9940 gm., .917 GOLD, .1177 oz AGW

Y#	Date	Mintage	VF	XF	Unc
21	1902ROZF	7,800	BV	BV	80.00
	1903ROZF	7,245	BV	BV	80.00
	1904ROZF	8,360	BV	BV	80.00
	1905ROZF	8,010	BV	BV	80.00
	1905GOZF	Inc. Ab.	BV	BV	80.00
	1906GOZF	9,176	BV	BV	80.00
	1907GOZF	.010	BV	BV	80.00
	1907GOZG	—	BV	BV	80.00
	1908GOZG	8,180	BV	BV	80.00
	1909GOZG	6,799	Reported, not confirmed		
	1910GOZG	4,221	Reported, not confirmed		
	1911GOZG	.014	Reported, not confirmed		
	1912GOZG	.016	Reported, not confirmed		
	1912POZG	—	Reported, not confirmed		
	1913POZG	.020	BV	BV	80.00
	1914PBLG	—	Reported, not confirmed		
	1915	—	Reported, not confirmed		
	1916	1,900	Reported, not confirmed		
	1917	8,133	Reported, not confirmed		
	1918	8,800	Reported, not confirmed		
	1919	8,765	Reported, not confirmed		
	1925	—	Reported, not confirmed		
	1926	—	Reported, not confirmed		
	1927	—	Reported, not confirmed		
	1928	—	Reported, not confirmed		
	1930	1,889	Reported, not confirmed		
	1940	—	Reported, not confirmed		
	1941	—	Reported, not confirmed		
	1946	7,750	Reported, not confirmed		
	1947	3,146	Reported, not confirmed		
	1948	.012	Reported, not confirmed		
	1949	.020	Reported, not confirmed		
	1950	5,890	Reported, not confirmed		
	1951	.018	Reported, not confirmed		
	1952BBR	8,345	Reported, not confirmed		
	1953BBR	9,210	BV	BV	80.00
	1954ZBR	9,220	Reported, not confirmed		
	1955ZBR	.014	BV	BV	80.00
	1956ZBR	7,385	Reported, not confirmed		
	1957ZBR	8,472	Reported, not confirmed		
	1958ZBR	.011	Reported, not confirmed		
	1959ZBR	5,236	Reported, not confirmed		
	1960ZBR	.016	Reported, not confirmed		
	1961ZBR	752 pcs.	80.00	90.00	125.00
	1962ZBR	4,286	BV	BV	80.00
	1963ZBR	908 pcs.	80.00	90.00	125.00
	1964ZBR	.010	BV	BV	80.00
	1965ZBR	5,490	BV	BV	80.00
	1966ZBR	.044	BV	BV	80.00
	1967ZBR	—	—	—	—
	1968BBB	.014	BV	BV	80.00
	1968PBB	Inc. Ab.	BV	BV	80.00
	1969BBB	4,400	BV	BV	80.00

LIBRA (POUND)

7.9881 gm., .917 GOLD, .2354 oz AGW

Y#	Date	Mintage	VF	XF	Unc
22	1898ROZF	—	BV	BV	155.00
	1899ROZF	—	BV	BV	155.00
	1900ROZF	.064	BV	BV	155.00
	1901ROZF	.081	BV	BV	155.00
	1902ROZF	.089	BV	BV	155.00
	1903ROZF	.100	BV	BV	155.00
	1904ROZF	.033	BV	BV	155.00
	1905ROZF	.141	BV	BV	155.00
	1905GOZF	—	BV	BV	155.00
	1906GOZF	.201	BV	BV	155.00
	1907GOZF	.123	BV	BV	155.00
	1907GOZG	Inc. Ab.	BV	BV	155.00
	1908GOZG	.036	BV	BV	155.00
	1909GOZG	.052	BV	BV	155.00
	1910GOZG	.047	BV	BV	155.00
	1911GOZG	.042	BV	BV	155.00
	1912GOZG	.054	BV	BV	155.00
	1912POZG	Inc. Ab.	BV	BV	155.00
	1913POZG	—	BV	BV	155.00
	1914POZG	—	BV	BV	155.00
	1914PBLG	.119	BV	BV	155.00
	1915PVG	.091	BV	BV	155.00
	1915	Inc. Ab.	BV	BV	155.00
	1916	.582	BV	BV	155.00
	1917	1.928	BV	BV	155.00
	1918	.600	BV	BV	155.00
	1919	Inc. Ab.	BV	BV	155.00
	1920	.152	BV	BV	155.00
	1921	Inc. Ab.	BV	BV	155.00
	1922	.013	BV	BV	155.00
	1923	.015	BV	BV	155.00
	1924	8,113	BV	155.00	200.00
	1925	9,068	BV	155.00	200.00
	1926	4,596	BV	155.00	200.00
	1927	8,360	BV	155.00	200.00
	1928	2,184	BV	155.00	225.00
	1929	3,119	BV	155.00	225.00
	1930	1,050	BV	155.00	250.00
	1931	—	Reported, not confirmed		
	1932	—	Reported, not confirmed		
	1940	—	Reported, not confirmed		
	1951	—	Reported, not confirmed		
	1959ZBR	605 pcs.	BV	155.00	250.00
	1961ZBR	402 pcs.	BV	165.00	250.00
	1962ZBR	6,203	BV	155.00	200.00
	1963ZBR	302 pcs.	155.00	175.00	300.00
	1964ZBR	.013	BV	BV	155.00
	1965ZBR	9,917	BV	155.00	175.00
	1966ZBR	.039	BV	BV	155.00
	1967BBR	2,002	BV	155.00	200.00
	1968BBR	7,307	BV	155.00	200.00
	1969BBB	7,307	BV	155.00	200.00

NCLT ISSUES

PATTERNS

KM#	Date	Mintage	Identification	Mkt.Val.
1	1855	—	1 Centavo, Copper, Sunface	—
2	1855	—	2 Centavos, Copper, Sunface	—
3	1855	—	20 Centavos, Silver, Standing Patria	—

KM#	Date	Mintage	Identification	Mkt.Val.
4	1855	—	2 Pesos, .900 Gold	—

KM#	Date	Mintage	Identification	Mkt.Val.
5	1855	—	5 Pesos, .900 Gold	—

KM#	Date	Mintage	Identification	Mkt.Val.
6	1855	—	10 Pesos, .900 Gold	—

KM#	Date	Mintage	Identification	Mkt.Val.
7	1855	—	20 Pesos, .900 Gold	—

NOTE: KM#4-7 were the first foreign gold coins struck at the Philadelphia Mint.

KM#	Date	Mintage	Identification	Mkt.Val.
8	1863	—	1/2 Sol, .900 Silver	—
9	1863	—	Sol, .900 Silver	—

MINT SETS

PROOF SETS

STANDARD METALS

KM#	Date	Mintage	Identification	Issue Price	Mkt. Val.
101	1965(5)	—	Y53-57	—	—
102	1966(5)	1,000*	Y64-68	—	—

***Estimated mintage.**

PHILIPPINES

The Republic of the Philippines, an archipelago in the western Pacific 500 miles (805 km.) from the southeast coast of Asia, has an area of 115,707 sq. mi. (299,679 sq. km.) and a population of 42.5 million. Capital: Manila. The economy of the 7,000—island group is based on agriculture, forestry and fishing. Timber, coconut products, sugar and hemp are exported.

Migration to the Philippines began about 30,000 years ago when land bridges connected the islands with Borneo and Sumatra. Ferdinand Magellan claimed the islands for Spain in 1521. The first permanent settlement was established by Miguel de Legazpi at Cebu in April of 1565; Manila was established in 1572. A British expedition captured Manila and occupied the Spanish colony in Oct. of 1762, but it was returned to Spain by the treaty of Paris, 1763. Spain held the Philippines amid a growing movement of Filipino nationalism until 1898 when they were ceded to the United States at the end of the Spanish- American War. The Philippines became a self-governing commonwealth of the United States in 1935, and attained independence as the Republic of the Philippines on July 4, 1946.

RULERS

Spanish until 1898

MINTMARKS

D - Denver, 1944-1945
(Lt) - Llantrisant
M, MA - Manila
S - San Francisco, 1903-1947
SGV - Madrid
(Sh) - Sherritt
(US) - United States
FM - Franklin Mint, U.S.A.*
(VDM) - Vereinigte Deutsche Metall Werks; Altona, W. Germany

***NOTE:** During 1975-77 the Franklin Mint produced coinage in up to 3 different qualities. Qualities of issue are designated in ( ) after each date and are defined as follows:

(M) MATTE - Normal circulation strike or a dull finish produced by sandblasting special uncirculated (polish finish) or proof quality dies.

(U) SPECIAL UNCIRCULATED - Polished or proof-like in appearance without any frosted features.

(P) PROOF - The highest quality obtainable having mirror-like fields and frosted features.

MONETARY SYSTEM

8 Octavos = 4 Quartos = 1 Real
8 Reales = 1 Peso

BARILLA

COPPER

C#	Date	Mintage	Good	VG	Fine	VF
1	1766	—	250.00	400.00	500.00	650.00

OCTAVO

COPPER

MINTMARK: M

Obv: Lion and globes. Rev: Spanish arms.

C#	Date	Mintage	Good	VG	Fine	VF
2	1773M	—	250.00	400.00	500.00	650.00
	1782M	—	250.00	400.00	500.00	650.00
	1783M	—	250.00	400.00	500.00	650.00

C#	Date	Mintage	Good	VG	Fine	VF
11	1798F	—	250.00	400.00	500.00	650.00
	1805F	—	75.00	100.00	130.00	200.00
	1806F	—	75.00	100.00	130.00	200.00

C#	Date	Mintage	Fine	VF	XF	Unc
21	1820F	—	30.00	50.00	75.00	150.00
	1829F	—	—	—	Rare	—
	1830F	—	45.00	75.00	100.00	200.00

QUARTO

COPPER

MINTMARK: M

C#	Date	Mintage	Good	VG	Fine	VF
3	1771M dot	—	75.00	100.00	130.00	200.00
	1773M	—	75.00	100.00	130.00	200.00
	1774M	2 known	300.00	350.00	400.00	600.00
	1782M	—	250.00	300.00	400.00	650.00
	1783M	—	65.00	90.00	120.00	175.00

C#	Date	Mintage	Good	VG	Fine	VF
12	1798F	—	20.00	25.00	35.00	60.00
	1799F	—	150.00	200.00	250.00	300.00
	1805F	—	17.50	25.00	35.00	60.00
	1806F	—	17.50	25.00	35.00	60.00
	1807F	—	17.50	25.00	35.00	60.00

C#	Date	Mintage	VG	Fine	VF	XF
22	1817F	—	150.00	200.00	250.00	350.00
	1820F	—	25.00	40.00	60.00	90.00
	1821F	—	25.00	40.00	65.00	90.00
	1822F	—	—	—	Rare	—
	1823F	—	35.00	65.00	90.00	140.00
	1824F	—	—	—	Rare	—
	1826F	—	25.00	40.00	65.00	85.00
	1827F	—	—	—	Rare	—
	1828F	—	20.00	35.00	50.00	65.00
	1829F	—	18.50	30.00	40.00	55.00
	1830F	—	18.50	30.00	40.00	55.00
—	1831F	—	250.00	300.00	350.00	500.00
—	1833F	—	250.00	300.00	350.00	500.00

C#	Date	Mintage	Good	VG	Fine	VF
24	1822F	—	70.00	95.00	130.00	200.00
	1823F	—	25.00	40.00	60.00	100.00
	1824F	—	150.00	200.00	250.00	400.00

MINTMARK: MA

C#	Date	Mintage	Good	VG	Fine	VF
27	1834F	—	22.50	30.00	40.00	65.00

C#	Date	Mintage	Good	VG	Fine	VF
51	1835F	—	150.00	200.00	275.00	350.00

2 QUARTOS

COPPER

MINTMARK: MA

C#	Date	Mintage	Good	VG	Fine	VF
28	1834F	—	250.00	300.00	350.00	450.00

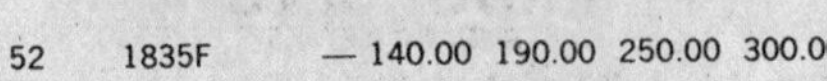

C#	Date	Mintage	Good	VG	Fine	VF
52	1835F	—	140.00	190.00	250.00	300.00

4 QUARTOS

COPPER

MINTMARK: MA

C#	Date	Mintage	Good	VG	Fine	VF
29	1834F	—	200.00	350.00	450.00	700.00

C#	Date	Mintage	Good	VG	Fine	VF
53	1835F	—	150.00	200.00	275.00	350.00

1/4 REAL

SILVER

C#	Date	Mintage	VG	Fine	VF	XF
6	ND(1788-90)	—	25.00	35.00	50.00	75.00

NOTE: Attribution of the above 1/4 Real to the Philippines is questionable.

COUNTERSTAMP ISSUES

(8 REALES)

MANILA 1828

SILVER

Type I

Obv: MANILA 1828 within serrated circle.
Rev. leg: HABILITADO POR EL REY N.S.D. FERN. VII. around crowned Spanish royal arms.

This counterstamp was inaugurated on October 13, 1828 by the Captain-General of the Philippines. The outer serrated border was intended to obliterate the legends on the foreign dollars being overstruck. This failed to work satisfactorily and the legend and serrated border were later removed.

c/s: MANILA 1828 on Bolivia 8 Reales, C#47.

C#	Date	Year	Mintage	VG	Fine	VF
39.1	1828	(1808-25)	—	200.00	250.00	300.00

c/s: MANILA 1828 on Mexico 8 Reales, KM#376 (Y#S19).

C#	Date	Year	Mintage	VG	Fine	VF
39.2	1828	(1823-5)	—	200.00	275.00	350.00

c/s: MANILA 1828 on Mexico 8 Reales, KM#377 (Y#S25).

C#	Date	Year	Mintage	VG	Fine	VF
39.3	1828	(1824-8)	—	175.00	225.00	300.00

c/s: MANILA 1828 on Peru (Lima) 8 Reales, C#101.

C#	Date	Year	Mintage	VG	Fine	VF
39.4	1828	(1810-24)	—	150.00	200.00	275.00

c/s: MANILA 1828 on Peru (Lima) 8 Reales, C#125.

C#	Date	Year	Mintage	VG	Fine	VF
39.5	1828	(1822-3)	—	150.00	200.00	275.00

c/s: MANILA 1828 on Peru (Lima) 8 Reales, C#132.1.

39.6 1828 (1825-8) — 135.00 175.00 250.00

c/s: MANILA 1828 on Peru (Lima) 8 Reales, C#132.1a.

39.7 1828 (1828) — 135.00 175.00 250.00

c/s: MANILA 1828 on Peru (Cuzco) 8 Reales, C#132.3.

39.8 1828 (1826-28) — — — —

NOTE: Other coin types may exist with this particular counterstamp.

MANILA 1828

SILVER

TYPE II

Obv: MANILA 1828. Rev: Crowned Spanish royal arms without legends and serrated circles.

c/s: MANILA 1828 on Bolivia 8 Reales, C#47.

39a.1 1828 (1808-25) — 125.00 150.00 200.00

c/s: MANILA 1828 on Mexico 8 Reales, KM#376 (Y#S19).

39a.2 1828 (1823-5) — 135.00 185.00 235.00

c/s: MANILA 1828 on Mexico 8 Reales, KM#377 (Y#S25).

39a.3 1828 (1824-8) — 125.00 150.00 200.00

c/s: MANILA 1828 on Peru 8 Reales, C#101.

39a.4 1828 (1810-24) — 100.00 135.00 200.00

c/s: MANILA 1828 on Peru 8 Reales, C#125.

39a.5 1828 (1822-3) — 100.00 135.00 200.00

c/s: MANILA 1828 on Peru 8 Reales, C#132-1.

39a.6 1828 (1825-8) — 85.00 130.00 200.00

c/s: MANILA 1828 on Peru 8 Reales, C#132-1a.

39a.7 1828 (1828) — 85.00 130.00 200.00

NOTE: Other coin types may exist with this particular counterstamp.

(8 ESCUDOS)

MANILA 1829

GOLD

Type III

c/s: MANILA 1829. Rev: Crowned Spanish royal arms on Mexico, 8 Escudos, KM#383 (Y#S31).

40 1829 (1825JM) Unique — — —

NOTE: The above is in the collection of Fabrica Nacional de Moneda Y Timbre de Madrid (Spain).

(8 REALES)

MANILA 1830

SILVER

Type IV

c/s: MANILA 1830 within serrated circle. Rev. legend: HABILITADO POR EL REY N.S.D.FERN.VII. around crowned Spanish royal arms on Bolivia 8 Sueldos, C#55.

C#	Date	Year	Mintage	VG	Fine	VF
41.1	1830	(1827-30)	—	—	—	2500.

c/s: MANILA 1830 on Mexico 8 Reales, KM#376 (Y#S19).

41.2 1830 (1823-5) — — — 2500.

c/s: MANILA 1830 on Mexico 8 Reales, KM#377 (Y#S25).

41.3 1830 (1824-30) — — — 2500.

NOTE: Other coin types may exist with this particular counterstamp.

FERDINAND VII

SILVER

Type V

Actual size 9-10mm

This countermark was introduced by decree of October 27, 1832 due to the problems encountered with the larger countermarks of 1828-1830. Pierced or holed coins were declared non valid but later were countermarked over the hole with Type V or Type VI and circulated freely. The latter types may be countermarked on both sides over the hole and are very scarce. This countermark was retired in 1834 after the death of Ferdinand VII and replaced with a new die of Isabel II, Type VI. Coins with the Type V countermark dated after 1834 can be considered counterfeit.

(REAL)

SILVER

c/s: F.7.o on Mexico 1 Real.

A42 ND — — — Rare —

(2 REALES)

SILVER

c/s: F.7.o on Mexico 2 Reales, KM#372 (Y#S23).

B42a ND (1825-34) — 85.00 120.00 150.00

c/s: F.7.o on Peru 2 Reales, C#130.

B42b ND (1825-34) — 85.00 120.00 150.00

(4 REALES)

SILVER

c/s: F.7.o on Mexico 4 Reales.

C42 ND — — 300.00 500.00 700.00

(8 REALES)

SILVER

c/s: F.7.o on Argentina 8 Reales, C#15.

42a.1 ND (1813-5) — 85.00 150.00 200.00

c/s: F.7.o on Argentina 8 Soles, C#20.

42a.2 ND (1815) — 85.00 150.00 200.00

c/s: F.7.o on Argentina 8 Reales, C#26.

42a.3 ND (1826-34) — 100.00 165.00 225.00

c/s: F.7.o on Bolivia 8 Reales, C#18.

42b.1 ND (1773-89) — 120.00 165.00 225.00

c/s: F.7.o on Bolivia 8 Reales, C#27.

42b.2 ND (1789-91) — 120.00 165.00 225.00

c/s: F.7.o on Bolivia 8 Reales, C#37.

42b.3 ND (1791-1808) — 120.00 165.00 225.00

c/s: F.7.o on Bolivia 8 Reales, C#47.

42b.4 ND (1808-25) — 120.00 165.00 225.00

c/s: F.7.o on Bolivia 8 Sueldos, C#55.

42b.5 ND (1827-34) — 35.00 45.00 60.00

c/s: F.7.o on Brazil 960 Reis, C#94.

42c.1 ND (1809-18) — 175.00 400.00 700.00

c/s: F.7.o on Brazil 960 Reis, C#117.

42c.2 ND (1818-22) — 175.00 400.00 700.00

c/s: F.7.o on Brazil 960 Reis, C#138.

42c.3 ND (1823-7) — 175.00 400.00 700.00

c/s: F.7.o on Chile 1 Peso, C#86.

42d ND (1817-34) — 50.00 60.00 80.00

c/s: F.7.o on Guatemala 8 Reales, C#95.

C#	Date	Year	Mintage	VG	Fine	VF
42e	ND	(1824-34)	—	60.00	80.00	110.00

c/s: F.7.o on Mexico 8 Reales, KM#105 (C#35).

42f.1 ND (1760-71) — — Rare 2000.

c/s: F.7.o on Mexico 8 Reales, KM#106 (C#40).

42f.2 ND (1772-89) — 120.00 180.00 250.00

c/s: F.7.o on Mexico 8 Reales, KM#107 (C#73).

42f.3 ND (1789-90FM) — 135.00 200.00 250.00

c/s: F.7.o on Mexico 8 Reales, KM#108 (C#75).

42f.4 ND (1790FM) — 150.00 225.00 275.00

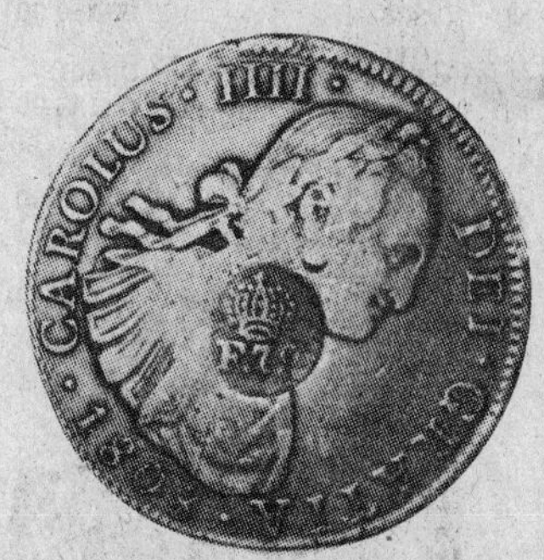

c/s: F.7.o on Mexico 8 Reales, KM#109 (C#81).

42f.5 ND (1791-1808) — 120.00 180.00 250.00

c/s: F.7.o on Mexico 8 Reales, KM#110 (C#111).

42f.6 ND (1808-11) — 120.00 180.00 250.00

c/s: F.7.o on Mexico 8 Reales, KM#111 (C#121).

42f.7 ND (1811-21) — 120.00 180.00 250.00

c/s: F.7.o on Mexico 8 Reales, KM#304 (C#184).

42f.8 ND (1822JM) — 90.00 120.00 200.00

c/s: F.7.o on Mexico 8 Reales, KM#305 (C#185).

42f.9 ND (1822JM) — 100.00 130.00 180.00

c/s: F.7.o on Mexico 8 Reales, KM#306 (C#185).

42f.10 ND (1822JM) - 100.00 130.00 180.00

c/s: F.7.o on Mexico 8 Reales, KM#307 (C#185).

42f.11 ND (1822JM) — 90.00 120.00 150.00

c/s: F.7.o on Mexico 8 Reales, KM#308 (C#185).

42f.12 ND (1822JM) — 90.00 120.00 150.00

c/s: F.7.o on Mexico 8 Reales, KM#309 (C#185).

42f.13 ND (1822JM) — — Rare —

c/s: F.7.o on Mexico 8 Reales, KM#310 (C#185).

42f.14 ND (1822-3JM) — 75.00 100.00 125.00

C#	Date	Year	Mintage	VG	Fine	VF
c/s: F.7.o on Mexico 8 Reales, KM#376 (Y#S19).						
42f.15	ND	(1823-5)	—	110.00	145.00	190.00
c/s: F.7.o on Mexico 8 Reales, KM#377 (Y#S25).						
42f.16	ND	(1824-34)	—	22.50	30.00	40.00
c/s: F.7.o on Peru 8 Reales, C#45.						
42g.1	ND	(1772-89)	—	125.00	175.00	225.00
c/s: F.7.o on Peru 8 Reales, C#69.						
42g.2	ND	(1789-91)	—	140.00	200.00	250.00
c/s: F.7.o on Peru 8 Reales, C#76.						
42g.3	ND	(1791-1808)	—	100.00	130.00	180.00
c/s: F.7.o on Peru 8 Reales, C#96.						
42g.4	ND	(1808-11)	—	120.00	150.00	200.00
c/s: F.7.o on Peru 8 Reales, C#101.						
42g.5	ND	(1810-24)	—	110.00	145.00	190.00
c/s: F.7.o on Peru 8 Reales, C#125.						
42g.6	ND	(1822-3)	—	60.00	75.00	90.00

C#	Date	Year	Mintage	VG	Fine	VF
c/s: F.7.o on Peru 8 Reales, C#125a.						
42g.7	ND	(1824)	—	125.00	175.00	250.00
c/s: F.7.o on Peru 8 Reales, C#132-1.						
42g.8	ND	(1825-8)	—	25.00	45.00	65.00

C#	Date	Year	Mintage	VG	Fine	VF
c/s: F.7.o on Peru 8 Reales, C#132-1a.						
42g.9	ND	(1828-34)	—	22.50	35.00	45.00

8 ESCUDOS

GOLD

C#	Date	Year	Mintage	VG	Fine	VF
c/s: F.7.o on Chile 8 Escudos, C#92.						
42h.1	Nd	1822FD	—	5000.	6000.	7000.
c/s: F.7.o on Mexico 8 Escudos, KM#383.4.						
42H.2	Nd	1829LF	—	—	—	Unique

NOTE: Other coin types may exist with this particular counterstamp.

ISABEL II

SILVER

Type VI

This countermark was introduced after the death of Ferdinand VII on December 20, 1834. It exists with several varieties of crowns. Counterstamping of foreign coins was halted in Manila by the edict of March 31, 1837 after Spain had recognized the independence of Mexico, Peru, Colombia, Bolivia, Chile and other former colonies in Central and South America. Coins with the Type VI countermarked after 1837 can be considered counterfeit.

(REAL)

SILVER

C#	Date	Year	Mintage	VG	Fine	VF
c/s: Y.II on Mexico Real.						
A54	ND	—	—	—	Rare	—

(2 REALES)

SILVER

C#	Date	Year	Mintage	VG	Fine	VF
c/s: Y.II on Mexico 2 Reales, KM#372 (Y#S23).						
B54a	ND	(1825-37)	—	85.00	120.00	150.00

C#	Date	Year	Mintage	VG	Fine	VF
c/s: Y.II on Peru 2 Reales, C#130.						
B54b	ND	(1825-37)	—	85.00	120.00	150.00

(4 REALES)

SILVER

C#	Date	Year	Mintage	VG	Fine	VF
c/s: Y.II. on Mexico 4 Reales.						
C54	ND	—	—	400.00	500.00	700.00

(8 REALES)

SILVER

C#	Date	Year	Mintage	VG	Fine	VF
c/s: Y.II. on Argentina 8 Reales, C#15.						
54a.1	ND	(1813-5)	—	85.00	150.00	200.00
c/s: Y.II. on Argentina 8 Soles, C#20.						
54a.2	ND	(1815)	—	85.00	150.00	200.00
c/s: Y.II. on Argentina 8 Reales, C#26.						
54a.3	ND	(1826-37)	—	100.00	165.00	225.00
c/s: Y.II. on Bolivia 8 Reales, C#18.						
54b.1	ND	(1773-89)	—	120.00	165.00	225.00
c/s: Y.II. on Bolivia 8 Reales, C#27.						
54b.2	ND	(1789-91)	—	120.00	165.00	225.00
c/s: Y.II. on Bolivia 8 Reales, C#37.						
54b.3	ND	(1791-1808)	—	120.00	165.00	225.00
c/s: Y.II. on Bolivia 8 Reales, C#47.						
54b.4	ND	(1808-25)	—	120.00	165.00	225.00
c/s: Y.II. on Bolivia 8 Sueldos, C#55.						
54b.5	ND	(1827-37)	—	27.50	35.00	45.00
c/s: Y.II. on Brazil 960 Reis, C#94.						
54c.1	ND	(1809-18)	—	175.00	225.00	300.00
c/s: Y.II. on Brazil 960 Reis, C#117.						
54c.2	ND	(1818-22)	—	175.00	225.00	300.00
c/s: Y.II. on Brazil 960 Reis, C#138.						
54c.3	ND	(1823-30)	—	175.00	225.00	300.00
c/s: Y.II. on Brazil 960 Reis, C#182.						
54c.4	ND	(1832-4)	—	—	Rare	—
c/s: Y.II. on Brazil 1200 Reis, C#187.						
54c.5	ND	(1834-7)	—	200.00	275.00	350.00
c/s: Y.II. on Chile 1 Peso, C#86.						
54d	ND	(1817-34)	—	50.00	60.00	80.00
c/s: Y.II. on Guatemala 8 Reales, C#95.						
54e	ND	(1824-37)	—	60.00	80.00	110.00
c/s: Y.II. on Mexico 8 Reales, KM#104 (C#17).						
54f.1	ND	(1747-60)	—	—	Rare	—
c/s: Y.II. on Mexico 8 Reales, KM#105 (C#35).						
54f.2	ND	(1760-71)	—	—	Rare	—
c/s: Y.II. on Mexico 8 Reales, KM#106 (C#40).						
54f.3	ND	(1772-89)	—	120.00	180.00	250.00
c/s: Y.II. on Mexico 8 Reales, KM#107 (C#73).						
54f.4	ND	(1789-90FM)	—	135.00	200.00	250.00
c/s: Y.II. on Mexico 8 Reales, KM#108 (C#75).						
54f.5	ND	(1790FM)	—	150.00	225.00	275.00
c/s: Y.II. on Mexico 8 Reales, KM#109 (C#81).						
54f.6	ND	(1791-1808)	—	120.00	180.00	250.00
c/s: Y.II. on Mexico 8 Reales, KM#110 (C#111).						
54f.7	ND	(1808-11)	—	120.00	180.00	250.00
c/s: Y.II. on Mexico 8 Reales, KM#111 (C#121).						
54f.8	ND	(1811-21)	—	120.00	180.00	250.00

C#	Date	Year	Mintage	VG	Fine	VF
c/s: Y.II. on Mexico 8 Reales, KM#304 (C#184).						
54f.9	ND	(1822JM)	—	90.00	120.00	150.00
c/s: Y.II. on Mexico 8 Reales, KM#305 (C#185).						
54f.10	ND	(1822JM)	—	100.00	130.00	180.00
c/s: Y.II. on Mexico 8 Reales, KM#306 (C#185).						
54f.11	ND	(1822JM)	—	100.00	130.00	180.00
c/s: Y.II. on Mexico 8 Reales, KM#307 (C#185).						
54f.12	ND	(1822JM)	—	90.00	120.00	150.00
c/s: Y.II. on Mexico 8 Reales, KM#308 (C#185).						
54f.13	ND	(1822JM)	—	90.00	120.00	150.00
c/s: Y.II. on Mexico 8 Reales, KM#309 (C#185).						
54f.14	ND	(1822JM)	—	—	Rare	—
c/s: Y.II. on Mexico 8 Reales, KM#310 (C#185).						
54f.15	ND	(1822-3JM)	—	75.00	100.00	125.00
c/s: Y.II. on Mexico 8 Reales, KM#376 (Y#S19).						
54f.16	ND	(1823-4)	—	110.00	145.00	190.00
c/s: Y.II. on Mexico 8 Reales, KM#377 (Y#S25).						
54f.17	ND	(1824-37)	—	22.50	30.00	40.00
c/s: Y.II. on Peru 8 Reales, C#45.						
54g.1	ND	(1772-89)	—	125.00	175.00	225.00
c/s: Y.II. on Peru 8 Reales, C#69.						
54g.2	ND	(1789-91)	—	140.00	200.00	250.00
c/s: Y.II. on Peru 8 Reales, C#76.						
54g.3	ND	(1791-1808)	—	100.00	130.00	180.00
c/s: Y.II. on Peru 8 Reales, C#96.						
54g.4	ND	(1808-11)	—	120.00	150.00	200.00

c/s: Y.II. on Peru 8 Reales, C#101.

C#	Date	Year	Mintage	VG	Fine	VF
54g.5	ND	(1810-24)	—	110.00	140.00	185.00

c/s: Y.II. on Peru 8 Reales, C#125.

54g.6	ND	(1822-3)	—	60.00	75.00	90.00

c/s: Y.II. on Peru 8 Reales, C#125a.

54g.7	ND	(1824)	—	125.00	175.00	250.00

c/s: Y.II. on Peru 8 Reales, C#132-1.

54g.8	ND	(1825-8)	—	30.00	40.00	60.00

c/s: Y.II. on Peru 8 Reales, C#132-1a.

54g.9	ND	(1828-37)	—	25.00	30.00	45.00

c/s: Y.II. on Colombia 8 Reales, C#126.

54H	ND	(1834-6)	—	60.00	80.00	110.00

1 ESCUDO

GOLD

c/s y.ii. on Colombia 1 Escudo, c#132.a.

54i	Nd	1827FM	—	—	Unique	—

8 ESCUDO

GOLD

c/s y.ii. on Colombia 8 Escudos, c#135.

54J	Nd	1826JF	—	5000.	6000.	7000

NOTE: The above counterstamps have been reported on other coins, (i.e. U.S. 1/2 Dollar, Dollar, and Spanish 20 Reales). Coins bearing both Type V or Type VI countermarks with other countermarks are considered rare. Certain holed or pierced coins are sometimes found with an additional set of counterstamps usually struck on both sides over the hole to approve it for normal circulation.

DECIMAL COINAGE

1861-1897

CENTAVO

COPPER, 25mm.
Obv: Boy head of Alfonso XIII of Spain.
Rev: Crowned arms between branches.

KM#	Date	Mintage	VF	XF	Unc
5	1894	—	—	4000.	5000.

2 CENTAVOS

COPPER, 30mm.
Obv: Boy head of Alfonso XIII of Spain.
Rev: Crowned arms between branches.

6	1894	—	—	6500.	8000.

10 CENTIMOS

2.5960 gm., .900 SILVER, .0751 oz ASW

Y#	Date	Mintage	Fine	VF	XF	Unc
3	1864	4.586	90.00	175.00	400.00	1200.
	1865	.082	50.00	75.00	150.00	750.00
	1866	.039	65.00	100.00	175.00	750.00
	1867/6	.124	30.00	75.00	350.00	750.00
	1867	Inc. Ab.	25.00	40.00	100.00	750.00
	1868	*.139	15.00	20.00	30.00	150.00

NOTE: An additional 450,000 pieces were struck between 1870-74, all dated 1868.

2.5960 gm., .835 SILVER, .0697 oz ASW

Y#	Date	Mintage	Fine	VF	XF	Unc
9	1880	.015	200.00	300.00	400.00	1500.
	1881/0	.624	25.00	30.00	75.00	200.00
	1881	Inc. Ab.	8.50	25.00	70.00	150.00
	1882/1	.525	10.00	25.00	75.00	200.00
	1882	Inc. Ab.	10.00	25.00	70.00	150.00
	1883/1	.983	100.00	140.00	200.00	275.00
	1883/2	Inc. Ab.	15.00	30.00	75.00	200.00
	1883	Inc. Ab.	8.50	25.00	70.00	150.00
	1884	.010	200.00	300.00	600.00	1500.
	1885	*5.625	4.00	6.00	8.00	40.00

***NOTE:** An additional 5,432,614 pieces were struck between 1886-1898, all dated 1885.

20 CENTIMOS

5.1920 gm., .900 SILVER, .1502 oz ASW

Y#	Date	Mintage	Fine	VF	XF	Unc
4	1864	.067	50.00	100.00	150.00	1000.
	1865	.239	20.00	40.00	100.00	1000.
	1866/5	.134	40.00	60.00	100.00	1000.
	1866	Inc. Ab.	40.00	90.00	125.00	1000.
	1867	.138	25.00	50.00	100.00	1000.
	1868	*.418	8.00	15.00	25.00	200.00

***NOTE:** An additional 708,400 pieces were struck between 1869-1874, all dated 1868.

5.1920 gm., .835 SILVER, .1394 oz ASW

Y#	Date	Mintage	Fine	VF	XF	Unc
10	1880	.070	50.00	85.00	125.00	600.00
	1881/0	1.029	25.00	35.00	60.00	250.00
	1881	Inc. Ab.	15.00	25.00	45.00	250.00
	1882/1	.968	20.00	35.00	75.00	350.00
	1882	Inc. Ab.	20.00	45.00	95.00	350.00
	1883/2	1.972	15.00	25.00	50.00	250.00
	1883/horizontal 8 Inc. Ab.		—	—	—	—
	1883	Inc. Ab.	15.00	25.00	45.00	250.00
	1884	.859	40.00	75.00	150.00	450.00
	1885	*1.344	6.00	9.00	15.00	50.00

***NOTE:** An additional 4,092,205 pieces were struck between 1886-1898, all dated 1885.

50 CENTIMOS

12.9800 gm., .900 SILVER, .3756 oz ASW

Y#	Date	Mintage	Fine	VF	XF	Unc
5	1865	.081	65.00	90.00	125.00	1000.
	1866	7,442	250.00	400.00	600.00	3000.
	1867	6,870	200.00	300.00	500.00	3000.
	1868/58	*.423	15.00	30.00	100.00	350.00
	1868	Inc. Ab.	15.00	25.00	75.00	300.00

***NOTE:** An additional 200,800 pieces were struck between 1869-1874, all dated 1868.

12.9800 gm., .835 SILVER, .3485 oz ASW

Y#	Date	Mintage	Fine	VF	XF	Unc
11	1880	.127	80.00	200.00	350.00	2000.
	1881	2.480	15.00	30.00	40.00	300.00
	1882/0	1.890	15.00	45.00	60.00	350.00
	1882/1	Inc. Ab.	15.00	45.00	60.00	350.00
	1882	Inc. Ab.	15.00	40.00	60.00	350.00
	1883	2.221	15.00	30.00	40.00	300.00
	1884	.023	80.00	200.00	350.00	2000.
	1885	*22.700	11.00	16.00	25.00	50.00

***NOTE:** An additional 22,649,115 pieces were struck between 1886-1898, all dated 1885.

PESO

1.6915 gm., .875 GOLD, .0476 oz AGW

Y#	Date	Mintage	Fine	VF	XF	Unc
6	1861/0	.237	75.00	120.00	225.00	350.00
	1861	Inc. Ab.	65.00	100.00	175.00	275.00
	1862/1	.143	75.00	100.00	225.00	350.00
	1862	Inc. Ab.	65.00	100.00	175.00	275.00
	1863/2	.236	85.00	135.00	190.00	325.00
	1863	Inc. Ab.	70.00	110.00	150.00	250.00
	1864/0	.274	90.00	145.00	225.00	350.00
	1864	Inc. Ab.	75.00	120.00	175.00	275.00
	1865	.189	65.00	100.00	175.00	275.00
	1866	.077	130.00	175.00	450.00	1000.
	1867	.012	325.00	700.00	1000.	2500.
	1868/6	*.028	75.00	90.00	225.00	350.00
	1868/7	Inc. Ab.	75.00	90.00	225.00	350.00
	1868	Inc. Ab.	65.00	90.00	150.00	250.00

***NOTE:** An additional 372,724 pieces were struck between 1869-1874, all dated 1868.

25.0000 gm., .900 SILVER, .7234 oz ASW

Y#	Date	Mintage	Fine	VF	XF	Unc
13	1897 SGV	6.000	25.00	40.00	60.00	150.00

2 PESOS

3.3830 gm., .875 GOLD, .0952 oz AGW

Y#	Date	Mintage	Fine	VF	XF	Unc
7	1861/0	.265	75.00	130.00	190.00	300.00
	1861	Inc. Ab.	75.00	130.00	170.00	250.00
	1862/1	.237	85.00	130.00	190.00	300.00
	1862	Inc. Ab.	75.00	130.00	170.00	250.00
	1863/2	.176	85.00	130.00	190.00	300.00

Y#	Date	Mintage	Fine	VF	XF	Unc
	1863	Inc. Ab.	75.00	130.00	170.00	250.00
	1864/0	.181	85.00	130.00	190.00	300.00
	1864/3	Inc. Ab.	85.00	130.00	190.00	300.00
	1864	Inc. Ab.	75.00	130.00	170.00	250.00
	1865	.034	250.00	500.00	600.00	1000.
	1866/5	.016	700.00	1000.	2000.	3000.
	1866	Inc. Ab.	700.00	1000.	2000.	3000.
	1868	*.048	70.00	120.00	160.00	250.00

NOTE: An additional 304,691 pieces were struck between 1869-1873, all dated 1868.

4 PESOS

6.7661 gm., .875 GOLD, .1903 oz AGW

Y#	Date	Mintage	Fine	VF	XF	Unc
8	1861	.183	125.00	225.00	300.00	400.00
	1862/1	.507	125.00	200.00	250.00	350.00
	1862	Inc. Ab.	125.00	200.00	250.00	350.00
	1863	.475	125.00	200.00	250.00	350.00
	1864	.461	125.00	200.00	250.00	350.00
	1865	.241	125.00	250.00	300.00	400.00
	1866/65	.044	425.00	650.00	1200.	2500.
	1866	Inc. Ab.	400.00	600.00	1200.	2500.
	1867	1,530	8000.	12,000.	16,000.	25,000.
	1868	.036	125.00	150.00	200.00	325.00

NOTE: 1,521,505 were struck between 1869-1873, all dated 1868.

Y#	Date	Mintage	Fine	VF	XF	Unc
12	1880	—	—	Rare	—	—
	1881	—	—	7000.	8000.	12,000.
	1882	—	750.00	1000.	1500.	1800.
	1883	—	—	Reported, not confirmed		
	1884	—	—	Reported, not confirmed		
	1885	—	6000.	7000.	8000.	12,000.

Revolutionary Issues

CENTAVO

COPPER
Obv: Helmeted head right, legend.
Rev: Sun in triangle, legend.

KM#	Date	Mintage	Fine	VF	XF
1	1899	—	—	Rare	—

Similar but with 'M' c/s behind head.

KM#	Date	Mintage	Fine	VF	XF
2	1899	—	—	Rare	—

2 CENTAVOS

COPPER

KM#	Date	Mintage	Fine	VF	XF
3	1899	—	—	—	9000.

Obv: Sun, stars in triangle, legend.
Rev: 2 between 2 circles in wreath.

KM#	Date	Mintage	Fine	VF	XF
4	1899	—	—	—	9000.

MONETARY REFORM

1903-1967
100 Centavos = 1 Peso

1/2 CENTAVO

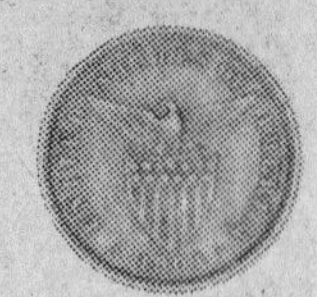

BRONZE

Y#	Date	Mintage	Fine	VF	XF	Unc
14	1903	12.084	.50	1.00	2.00	10.00
	1903	2,558	—	—	Proof	25.00
	1904	5.654	.50	1.25	2.50	12.00
	1904	1,355	—	—	Proof	28.00
	1905	471 pcs.	—	Proof only		55.00
	1906	500 pcs.	—	Proof only		45.00
	1908	500 pcs.	—	Proof only		45.00

CENTAVO

BRONZE

Y#	Date	Mintage	Fine	VF	XF	Unc
15	1903	10.790	.50	1.50	3.00	8.50
	1903	2,558	—	—	Proof	25.00
	1904	17.040	.50	1.50	3.00	9.00
	1904	1,355	—	—	Proof	28.00
	1905	10.000	.50	1.00	2.50	9.00
	1905	471 pcs.	—	—	Proof	60.00
	1906	500 pcs.	—	Proof only		50.00
	1908	500 pcs.	—	Proof only		50.00
	1908S	2.187	2.00	3.50	5.00	25.00
	1909S	1.738	5.00	8.00	14.00	50.00
	1910S	2.700	2.50	3.50	4.50	25.00
	1911S	4.803	1.00	2.00	4.50	20.00
	1912S	3.000	1.25	2.50	5.00	30.00
	1913S	5.000	1.25	2.25	4.50	20.00
	1914S	5.000	1.00	2.25	4.50	12.50
	1915S	2.500	17.50	25.00	40.00	85.00
	1916S	4.330	10.00	15.00	25.00	65.00
	1917/6S	7.070	11.00	12.00	20.00	45.00
	1917S	Inc. Ab.	1.00	2.00	3.50	10.00
	1918S	11.660	1.00	2.00	3.00	8.50
	1918S large S	—	7.50	12.50	25.00	100.00
	1919S	4.540	—	2.50	3.50	10.00
	1920S	2.500	3.00	5.50	15.00	50.00
	1920M	3.552	2.00	3.50	5.00	10.00
	1921M	7.283	.75	1.50	3.00	9.00
	1922M	3.519	.75	1.50	3.00	9.00
	1925M	9.332	.25	1.00	2.50	8.00
	1926M	9.000	.25	1.00	2.50	8.00
	1927M	9.270	.25	1.00	2.50	10.00
	1928M	9.150	.25	1.00	2.50	10.00
	1929M	5.657	1.00	2.00	4.00	10.00
	1930M	5.577	1.00	2.00	3.00	10.00
	1931M	5.659	1.00	2.00	3.50	10.00
	1932M	4.000	1.25	2.50	6.00	20.00
	1933M	8.393	.50	1.00	4.00	10.00
	1934M	3.179	2.00	5.00	7.00	20.00
	1936M	17.455	.75	1.75	3.00	10.00

Commonwealth

Y#	Date	Mintage	Fine	VF	XF	Unc
29	1937M	15.790	.25	1.00	2.50	10.00
	1938M	10.000	.25	1.00	1.25	10.00
	1939M	6.500	.25	1.00	2.50	10.00
	1940M	4.000	.25	1.00	1.25	10.00
	1941M	5.000	.50	2.00	2.50	10.00
	1944S	58.000	.10	.20	.25	1.00

Republic

Y#	Date	Mintage	Fine	VF	XF	Unc
36	1958	20.000	—	—	.10	.25
	1960	40.000	—	—	.05	.15
	1962	30.000	—	—	.05	.15
	1963	130.000	—	—	.05	.15

5 CENTAVOS

COPPER-NICKEL

Y#	Date	Mintage	Fine	VF	XF	Unc
16	1903	8.910	.50	1.00	2.25	10.00
	1903	2,558	—	—	Proof	30.00
	1904	1.075	.60	1.50	3.00	15.00
	1904	1,355	—	—	Proof	35.00
	1905	471 pcs.	—	Proof only		85.00
	1906	500 pcs.	—	Proof only		80.00
	1908	500 pcs.	—	Proof only		80.00
	1916S	.300	12.50	20.00	35.00	120.00
	1917S	2.300	1.00	2.50	6.50	40.00
	1918/7S/S	2.780	—	—	—	—
	1918S	Inc. Ab.	1.00	3.00	6.50	40.00
	1919S	1.220	1.25	4.50	9.00	40.00
	1920M	1.421	2.25	5.00	10.00	40.00
	1921M	2.132	2.00	5.00	9.00	40.00
	1925M	1.000	2.00	5.00	8.50	40.00
	1926M	1.200	2.00	4.50	8.50	40.00
	1927M	1.000	1.25	3.50	7.50	40.00
	1928M	1.000	1.25	4.00	8.50	40.00

Obv. muled to rev. of 20 Centavos, Y#23.

Y#	Date	Mintage	Fine	VF	XF	Unc
16a	1918S	—	75.00	150.00	300.00	1000.

Y#	Date	Mintage	Fine	VF	XF	Unc
17	1930M	2.905	1.25	2.50	3.50	25.00
	1931M	3.477	1.00	2.25	3.50	25.00
	1932M	3.956	1.00	2.25	3.50	25.00
	1934M	2.154	1.25	3.25	6.00	30.00
	1935M	2.754	1.00	2.75	5.00	25.00

Commonwealth

Y#	Date	Mintage	Fine	VF	XF	Unc
30	1937M	2.494	1.00	1.50	3.00	15.00
	1938M	4.000	1.00	1.50	2.50	15.00
	1941M	2.750	1.25	2.50	4.00	11.00

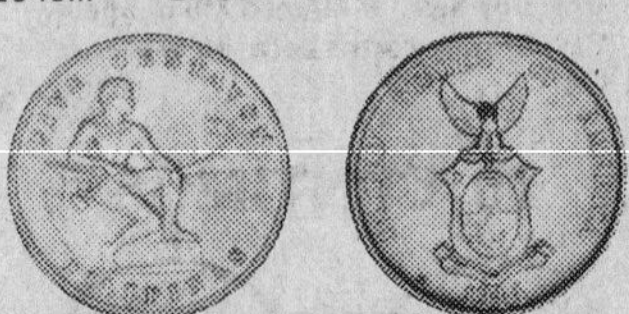

COPPER-NICKEL-ZINC

Y#	Date	Mintage	Fine	VF	XF	Unc
30a	1944	21.198	.10	.15	.35	1.25
	1944S	14.040	—	.10	.25	.75
	1945S	72.796	—	.10	.20	.60

BRASS
Republic

Y#	Date	Mintage	Fine	VF	XF	Unc
37	1958	10.000	—	—	.10	.25

Y#	Date	Mintage	Fine	VF	XF	Unc
	1959	10.000	—	—	.10	.25
	1960	40.000	—	—	.10	.15
	1962	40.000	—	—	.10	.20
	1963	50.000	—	—	.10	.15
	1964	100.000	—	—	—	.10
	1966	10.000	—	—	.10	.25

10 CENTAVOS

2.6924 gm., .900 SILVER, .0779 oz ASW

Y#	Date	Mintage	Fine	VF	XF	Unc
18	1903	5.103	2.25	2.50	3.50	15.00
	1903	2,558	—	—	Proof	35.00
	1903S	1.200	12.50	15.00	22.50	100.00
	1904	.011	11.50	13.50	20.00	40.00
	1904	1,355	—	—	Proof	45.00
	1904S	5.040	2.25	2.50	4.00	25.00
	1905	471 pcs.	—		Proof only	95.00
	1906	500 pcs.	—		Proof only	90.00

2.0000 gm., .750 SILVER, .0482 oz ASW

Y#	Date	Mintage	Fine	VF	XF	Unc
22	1907	1.501	1.50	3.00	5.00	40.00
	1907S	4.930	1.50	2.50	3.00	25.00
	1908	500 pcs.	—		Proof only	90.00
	1908S	3.364	1.50	1.75	3.00	25.00
	1909S	.312	10.00	20.00	30.00	125.00
	1910S	5-10 pcs.	Unknown In Any Collection			
	1911S	1.101	1.50	3.50	8.00	40.00
	1912S	1.010	1.50	4.00	8.00	40.00
	1913S	1.361	1.50	4.50	8.50	40.00
	1914S	1.180	2.50	4.50	10.00	50.00
	1915S	.450	7.00	12.50	20.00	125.00
	1917S	5.991	1.50	1.75	2.50	15.00
	1918S	8.420	1.50	1.75	2.50	15.00
	1919S	1.630	1.50	1.75	3.00	15.00
	1920	.520	5.00	7.00	12.50	40.00
	1921	3.863	1.50	1.75	2.50	15.00
	1929M	1.000	1.50	2.00	4.00	15.00
	1935M	1.280	1.50	1.75	3.00	15.00

Commonwealth

Y#	Date	Mintage	Fine	VF	XF	Unc
31	1937M	3.500	BV	1.50	2.00	10.00
	1938M	3.750	BV	1.50	1.75	10.00
	1941M	2.500	BV	1.50	2.00	12.00
	1944D	31.592	BV	BV	1.50	2.00
	1945D	137.208	BV	BV	1.50	2.00

NICKEL-BRASS
Republic

Y#	Date	Mintage	Fine	VF	XF	Unc
38	1958	10.000	—	.10	.15	.25
	1960	70.000	—	.10	.15	.20
	1962	50.000	—	.10	.15	.20
	1963	50.000	—	.10	.15	.20
	1964	100.000	—	—	.10	.20
	1966	110.000	—	—	.10	.20

20 CENTAVOS

5.3849 gm., .900 SILVER, .1558 oz ASW

Y#	Date	Mintage	Fine	VF	XF	Unc
19	1903	5.353	BV	4.50	5.00	15.00
	1903	2,558	—	—	Proof	40.00
	1903S	.150	12.50	15.00	25.00	75.00
	1904	.011	12.50	15.00	25.00	50.00

Y#	Date	Mintage	Fine	VF	XF	Unc
19	1904	1,355	—	—	Proof	50.00
	1904S	2.060	BV	4.50	5.00	20.00
	1905	471 pcs.	—		Proof only	100.00
	1905S	.420	10.00	12.50	25.00	75.00
	1906	500 pcs.	—		Proof only	85.00

4.0000 gm., .750 SILVER, .0965 oz ASW

Y#	Date	Mintage	Fine	VF	XF	Unc
23	1907	1.251	3.00	5.00	7.50	35.00
	1907S	3.165	2.75	3.00	5.00	30.00
	1908	500 pcs.	—		Proof only	125.00
	1908S	1.535	3.00	4.00	5.50	30.00
	1909S	.450	5.00	10.00	25.00	120.00
	1910S	.500	5.00	10.00	25.00	150.00
	1911S	.505	5.00	10.00	25.00	70.00
	1912S	.750	3.50	9.00	12.50	70.00
	1913S/S	.949	7.50	10.00	15.00	75.00
	1913S	Inc. Ab.	3.00	8.50	12.50	75.00
	1914S	.795	3.00	7.50	12.50	75.00
	1915S	.655	3.50	7.00	20.00	80.00
	1916S	1.435	3.00	4.00	10.00	75.00
	1917S	3.151	BV	2.75	4.00	30.00
	1918S	5.560	BV	2.75	4.00	30.00
	1919S	.850	1.25	3.25	5.00	35.00
	1920	—	—	—	—	—
	1920M	1.046	3.50	5.50	10.00	60.00
	1921M	1.843	BV	2.75	4.00	30.00
	1929M	1.970	BV	2.75	4.00	30.00

Obv. muled to rev. of 5 Centavos, Y#16.

Y#	Date	Mintage	Fine	VF	XF	Unc
23a	1928/7M	.100	6.00	10.00	50.00	200.00

Commonwealth

Y#	Date	Mintage	Fine	VF	XF	Unc
32	1937M	2.665	BV	2.75	4.00	9.00
	1938M	3.000	BV	2.75	3.50	7.00
	1941M	1.500	BV	2.75	4.00	9.00
	1944D	28.596	BV	BV	BV	3.00
	1945D	82.804	BV	BV	BV	3.00

25 CENTAVOS

NICKEL-BRASS
Republic

Y#	Date	Mintage	Fine	VF	XF	Unc
39	1958	10.000	—	.20	.25	.50
	1960	10.000	—	.20	.30	.50
	1962	40.000	—	.15	.25	.50
	1964	49.800	—	.15	.20	.35
	1966 Royal Mint, 8 smoke rings from volcano	50.000	—	.15	.20	.40
	1966 VEREINIGTE DEUTSCHE METALLWERKE, 6 smoke rings rings	40.000	—	.15	.20	.40

50 CENTAVOS

13.4784 gm., .900 SILVER, .3900 oz ASW

Y#	Date	Mintage	Fine	VF	XF	Unc
20	1903	3.102	12.00	15.00	18.00	35.00
	1903	2,558	—	—	Proof	65.00
	1904	.011	20.00	25.00	30.00	80.00
	1904	1,355	—	—	Proof	95.00
	1904S	2.160	12.00	15.00	18.00	75.00
	1905	471 pcs.	—		Proof Only	175.00
	1905S	.852	12.00	15.00	25.00	75.00
	1906	500 pcs.	—		Proof Only	150.00

10.0000 gm., .750 SILVER, .2411 oz ASW

Y#	Date	Mintage	Fine	VF	XF	Unc
24	1907	1.201	7.50	10.00	20.00	45.00
	1907S	2.112	7.50	12.00	20.00	40.00
	1908	500 pcs.	—		Proof Only	150.00
	1908S	1.601	7.50	12.00	18.00	35.00
	1909S	.528	7.50	12.00	25.00	60.00
	1917S	.674	7.50	12.00	20.00	50.00
	1918S	2.202	7.50	12.00	20.00	25.00
	1919S	1.200	7.50	12.00	20.00	25.00
	1920M	.420	7.50	12.00	20.00	25.00
	1921M	2.317	7.50	12.00	20.00	25.00

Establishment of the Commonwealth

Y#	Date	Mintage	Fine	VF	XF	Unc
26	1936	.020	15.00	27.50	40.00	60.00

Y#	Date	Mintage	Fine	VF	XF	Unc
33	1944S	19.187	BV	8.00	10.00	12.00
	1945S	18.120	BV	8.00	10.00	12.00

General Douglas Mac Arthur

Y#	Date	Mintage	Fine	VF	XF	Unc
34	1947S	.200	BV	8.00	12.00	15.00

NICKEL-BRASS
Republic

Y#	Date	Mintage	Fine	VF	XF	Unc
40	1958	5.000	.25	.35	.50	1.00
	1964	25.000	.25	.30	.40	.50

1/2 PESO

12.5000 gm., .900 SILVER, .3617 oz ASW
Dr. Jose Rizal

Y#	Date	Mintage	Fine	VF	XF	Unc
41	1961	.100	BV	11.00	12.50	16.00

PESO

26.9568 gm., .900 SILVER, .7800 oz ASW

Y#	Date	Mintage	Fine	VF	XF	Unc
21	1903	2.791	23.00	25.00	30.00	45.00
	1903	2,558	—	—	Proof	120.00
	1903S	11.361	23.00	25.00	30.00	40.00
	1904	.011	50.00	75.00	120.00	150.00
	1904	1,355	—	—	Proof	190.00
	1904S	6.600	23.00	25.00	30.00	40.00
	1905	471 pcs.	—		Proof Only	275.00
	1905S	6.056	23.00	25.00	30.00	45.00
	1906	500 pcs.	—		Proof Only	225.00
	1906S	.201	150.00	175.00	250.00	525.00

20.0000 gm., .800 SILVER, .5144 oz ASW

Y#	Date	Mintage	Fine	VF	XF	Unc
25	1907S	10.276	BV	15.00	20.00	35.00
	1908	500 pcs.	—		Proof Only	225.00
	1908S	20.955	BV	15.00	20.00	35.00
	1909S	7.578	BV	15.00	20.00	35.00
25	1910S	3.154	BV	15.00	20.00	55.00
	1911S	.463	18.00	25.00	35.00	120.00
	1912S	.680	18.00	25.00	35.00	120.00

Establishment of the Commonwealth
Presidents Roosevelt And Quezon

Y#	Date	Mintage	Fine	VF	XF	Unc
27	1936	.010	50.00	65.00	90.00	150.00

Establishment of the Commonwealth
Governor General Murphy And President Quezon
Obv: Similar to Y#27.

Y#	Date	Mintage	Fine	VF	XF	Unc
28	1936	.010	50.00	65.00	90.00	150.00

General Douglas Mac Arthur

Y#	Date	Mintage	Fine	VF	XF	Unc
35	1947S	.100	BV	15.00	20.00	32.00

Dr. Jose Rizal

Y#	Date	Mintage	Fine	VF	XF	Unc
42	1961	.100	BV	20.00	25.00	35.00

Andres Bonifacio

Y#	Date	Mintage	Fine	VF	XF	Unc
43	1963	.100	BV	20.00	25.00	35.00

Apolinario Mabini
Obv: Similar to Y#43.

Y#	Date	Mintage	Fine	VF	XF	Unc
44	1964	.100	BV	20.00	25.00	35.00

25th Anniversary of Bataan Day
Obv: Similar to Y#42.

Y#	Date	Mintage	Fine	VF	XF	Unc
45	1967	.100	BV	20.00	25.00	35.00

NOTE: These coins are "proof-like" issues.

MONETARY REFORM

Commencing 1967

100 Sentimos = 1 Piso

SENTIMO

ALUMINUM

Y#	Date	Mintage	VF	XF	Unc
46	1967	10.000	—	—	.10
	1968	27.940	—	—	.10
	1969	12.060	—	—	.10
	1974	165.000	—	—	.10
	1974	.010	—	Proof	7.50

Y#	Date	Mintage	VF	XF	Unc
55	1975	9.241	—	—	.10
	1975FM(M)	.108	—	—	.10
	1975FM(U)	5,875	—	1.25	2.00
	1975FM(P)	.037	—	Proof	1.50
	1975 Lt	—	—	—	.10
	1975(US)	105.000	—	—	.10
	1976FM(M)	.010	—	—	.10
	1976FM(U)	1,826	—	1.00	2.50
	1976FM(P)	9,901	—	Proof	2.00
	1976	10.000	—	—	.20
	1976(US)	108.000	—	—	.20
	1977FM(M)	.010	—	—	1.00
	1977FM(U)	354 pcs.	—	—	4.00
	1977FM(P)	4,822	—	Proof	2.00
	1978FM(m)	.010	—	—	1.00
	1978FM(P)	4,792	—	Proof	2.00

Rev: Redesigned seal

Y#	Date	Mintage	VF	XF	Unc
55a	1979FM(U)	—	—	—	2.00
	1979FM(P)	—	—	Proof	2.00

5 SENTIMOS

BRASS

Y#	Date	Mintage	VF	XF	Unc
47	1967	40.000	—	—	.15
	1968	50.000	—	—	.15
	1970	5.000	—	—	.15
	1972	71.744	—	—	.10
	1974	90.025	—	—	.10
	1974	.010	—	Proof	10.00

Y#	Date	Mintage	VF	XF	Unc
56	1975	9.995	—	—	.10
	1975FM(M)	.104	—	—	.10
	1975FM(U)	5,875	—	1.50	2.50
	1975FM(P)	.037	—	Proof	2.00
	1975(US)	90.035	—	—	.10
	1975 US	.010	—	Proof	2.50
	1975 Lt	—	—	—	.10
	1976FM(M)	.010	—	—	.10
	1976FM(U)	1,826	—	4.50	5.50
	1976FM(P)	9,901	—	Proof	3.50
	1976	10.000	—	—	.10
	1976(US)	98.938	—	—	.10
	1977FM(M)	.010	—	—	1.50
	1977FM(U)	354 pcs.	—	—	5.00
	1977FM(P)	4,822	—	Proof	4.00
	1978FM(m)	.010	—	—	1.50
	1978FM(P)	4,792	—	Proof	4.00

Rev: Redesigned seal

Y#	Date	Mintage	VF	XF	Unc
56a	1979FM(U)	—	—	—	2.00
	1979FM(P)	—	—	Proof	4.00

10 SENTIMOS

COPPER-NICKEL

Y#	Date	Mintage	VF	XF	Unc
48	1967	50.000	—	—	.25
	1968	60.000	—	—	.20
	1969	40.000	—	—	.20
	1970	50.000	—	—	.20
	1971	80.000	—	—	.15
	1972	121.390	—	—	.15
	1974	60.208	—	—	.15
	1974	.010	—	Proof	12.50

Y#	Date	Mintage	VF	XF	Unc
57	1975	10.000	—	—	.15
	1975FM(M)	.104	—	—	.15
	1975FM(U)	5,875	—	1.75	3.00
	1975FM(P)	.037	—	Proof	3.50
	1975(VDM)	—	—	—	.15
	1975(US)	60.000	—	—	.15
	1976FM(M)	.010	—	—	.15
	1976FM(U)	1,826	—	6.00	7.50
	1976FM(P)	9,901	—	Proof	5.00
	1976	10.000	—	—	.15
	1976(US)	50.010	—	—	.15
	1977FM(M)	.010	—	—	2.50
	1977FM(U)	354 pcs.	—	—	6.50
	1977FM(P)	4,822	—	Proof	5.00
	1978FM(m)	.010	—	—	2.50
	1978FM(P)	4,792	—	Proof	5.00

Rev: Redesigned seal

Y#	Date	Mintage	VF	XF	Unc
57a	1979FM(U)	—	—	—	2.50
	1979FM(P)	—	—	Proof	5.00

25 SENTIMOS

COPPER-NICKEL
Republic

Y#	Date	Mintage	VF	XF	Unc
49	1967	40.000	—	.10	.30
	1968	10.000	—	.10	.35
	1969	10.000	—	.10	.35
	1970	40.000	—	.10	.30
	1971	60.000	—	.10	.30
	1972	59.572	—	.10	.30
	1974	10.000	—	.15	.40
	1974	.010	—	Proof	15.00

Y#	Date	Mintage	VF	XF	Unc
58	1975	10.000	—	.10	.30
	1975FM(M)	.104	—	.10	.30
	1975FM(U)	5,875	—	2.50	4.00
	1975FM(P)	.037	—	Proof	5.00
	1975(US)	10.000	—	.10	.30
	1975(VDM)	—	—	.10	.30
	1976FM(M)	.010	—	.10	.30
	1976FM(U)	1,826	—	7.50	10.00
	1976FM(P)	9,901	—	Proof	7.50
	1976	10.000	—	.10	.30
	1976(US)	10.010	—	.10	.30
	1977FM(M)	.010	—	.10	4.00
	1977FM(U)	354 pcs.	—	—	9.00
	1977FM(P)	4,822	—	Proof	12.50
	1978FM(m)	.010	—	—	4.00
	1978FM(P)	4,792	—	Proof	12.50

Rev: Redesigned seal

Y#	Date	Mintage	VF	XF	Unc
58a	1979FM(U)	—	—	—	4.00
	1979FM(P)	—	—	Proof	12.50

50 SENTIMOS

COPPER-NICKEL-ZINC

Y#	Date	Mintage	VF	XF	Unc
50	1967	20.000	.10	.35	.60
	1971	10.000	.10	.20	.55
	1972 w/serif on 2	20.517	.10	.20	.50
	1972 w/plain 2	—	—	—	—
	1974	5.004	.10	.25	.75
	1974	.010	—	Proof	25.00
	1975	5.714	.10	.25	.75

PISO

26.7500 gm., .900 SILVER, .7741 oz ASW
Centennial Birth of Aguinaldo

Y#	Date	Mintage	VF	XF	Unc
51	1969	.100	25.00	27.50	35.00

NOTE: These coins are 'proof-like' issues.

NICKEL
Pope Paul VI Visit

Y#	Date	Mintage	VF	XF	Unc
52	1970	.070	.75	1.25	2.50

26.7500 gm., .900 SILVER, .7741 oz ASW

Y#	Date	Mintage	VF	XF	Unc
52a	1970	.030	25.00	27.50	35.00

19.3000 gm., .917 GOLD, .5691 oz AGW

Y#	Date	Mintage	VF	XF	Unc
52b	1970	1,000	370.00	550.00	750.00

COPPER-NICKEL
Regular Issue

Y#	Date	Mintage	VF	XF	Unc
53	1972	121.821	.20	.35	1.00
	1974	45.631	.20	.35	1.00
	1974	.010	—	Proof	50.00

Y#	Date	Mintage	VF	XF	Unc
59	1975	10.000	.25	.40	1.00
	1975FM(M)	.104	.25	.40	1.00
	1975FM(U)	5,877	—	—	6.00
	1975FM(P)	.037	—	Proof	5.00
	1975(VDM)	—	.20	.35	.75

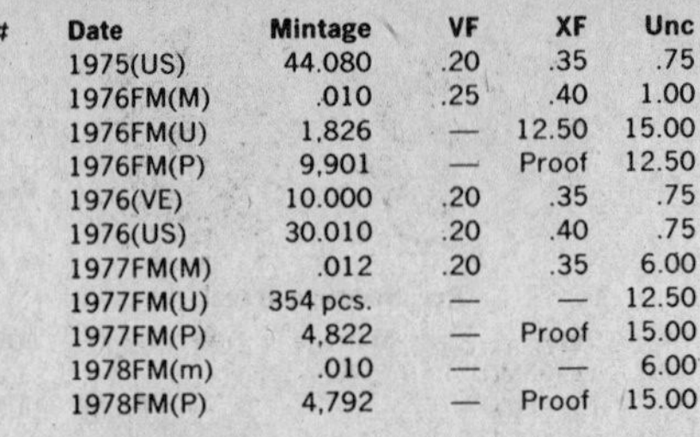

Y#	Date	Mintage	VF	XF	Unc
	1975(US)	44.080	.20	.35	.75
	1976FM(M)	.010	.25	.40	1.00
	1976FM(U)	1,826	—	12.50	15.00
	1976FM(P)	9,901	—	Proof	12.50
	1976(VE)	10.000	.20	.35	.75
	1976(US)	30.010	.20	.40	.75
	1977FM(M)	.012	.20	.35	6.00
	1977FM(U)	354 pcs.	—	—	12.50
	1977FM(P)	4,822	—	Proof	15.00
	1978FM(m)	.010	—	—	6.00
	1978FM(P)	4,792	—	Proof	15.00

Rev. motto below shield: ISANG BANSA ISANG DIWA

Y#	Date	Mintage	VF	XF	Unc
59a	1979FM(U)	—	—	—	6.00
	1979FM(P)	—	—	Proof	15.00

5 PISO

NICKEL

Y#	Date	Mintage	VF	XF	Unc
60	1975FM(M)	3,850	15.00	25.00	45.00
	1975FM(U)	7,875	—	25.00	45.00
	1975FM(P)	.039	—	Proof	15.00
	1975(Sh)	20.000	1.00	1.50	2.50
	1976FM(M)	.010	5.00	10.00	15.00
	1976FM(U)	1,826	—	—	35.00
	1976FM(P)	9,901	—	Proof	17.50
	1976(SH)	10.000	1.00	1.25	2.00
	1977FM(M)	.010	3.50	6.00	10.00
	1977FM(U)	354 pcs.	—	—	20.00
	1977FM(P)	4,822	—	Proof	20.00
	1978FM(m)	.010	—	—	10.00
	1978FM(P)	4,792	—	Proof	20.00

Obv. motto below shield: ISANG BANSA ISANG DIWA

Y#	Date	Mintage	VF	XF	Unc
60a	1979FM(U)	—	—	—	10.00
	1979FM(P)	—	—	Proof	20.00

25 PISO

26.4000 gm., .900 SILVER, .7640 oz ASW
25th Anniversary of Bank

Y#	Date	Mintage	VF	XF	Unc
54	1974	.100	23.00	30.00	35.00

27.0000 gm., .500 SILVER, .4341 oz ASW
Emilio Aguinaldo
Obv: Similar to Y#54.

Y#	Date	Mintage	VF	XF	Unc
61	1975FM(M)	.010	13.00	24.00	25.00
	1975FM(U)	5,875	13.00	24.00	25.00
	1975FM(P)	.037	—	Proof	25.00

F.A.O. Issue
Obv: Similar to Y#54.

Y#	Date	Mintage	VF	XF	Unc
64	1976	.022	13.00	20.00	25.00
	1976FM(M)	.022	13.00	20.00	25.00
	1976FM(U)	1,826	15.00	45.00	60.00
	1976FM(P)	9,901	—	Proof	32.00

Banawie Rice Terraces
Obv: Similar to Y#54.

Y#	Date	Mintage	VF	XF	Unc
67	1977FM(M)	.010	13.00	18.00	25.00
	1977FM(U)	354 pcs.	20.00	30.00	45.00
	1977FM(P)	4,822	—	Proof	35.00

100th Anniversary of Birth of Quezon
Obv: Similar to Y#54.

Y#	Date	Mintage	VF	XF	Unc
70	1978FM(m)	.010	BV	13.00	20.00

Y#	Date	Mintage	VF	XF	Unc
70	1978FM(P)	9,930	—	Proof	35.00

UN Conference on Trade and Development

Y#	Date	Mintage	VF	XF	Unc
73	1979FM	—	BV	13.00	20.00
	1979FM(p)	—	—	Proof	35.00

50 PISO

28.0000 gm., .925 SILVER, .8328 oz ASW

Y#	Date	Mintage	VF	XF	Unc
62	1975FM(M)	.010	BV	25.00	40.00
	1975FM(U)	7,875	BV	25.00	40.00
	1975FM(P)	.054	—	Proof	40.00

I.M.F. Meeting

Y#	Date	Mintage	VF	XF	Unc
65	1976	.012	BV	25.00	40.00
	1976	5,477	—	Proof	55.00
	1976FM(M)	.010	BV	25.00	40.00
	1976FM(U)	1,826	30.00	60.00	75.00
	1976FM(P)	.015	—	Proof	40.00

Inauguration of New Mint Facilities
Obv: Similar to Y#62.

Y#	Date	Mintage	VF	XF	Unc
68	1977FM(M)	.010	BV	25.00	40.00
	1977FM(U)	354 pcs.	25.00	50.00	95.00
	1977FM(P)	6,704	—	Proof	55.00

100th Anniversary of Birth of Quezon
Obv: Similar to Y#62.

Y#	Date	Mintage	VF	XF	Unc
71	1978FM(m)	.010	BV	25.00	37.00
	1978FM(p)	9,969	—	Proof	60.00

International Year of the Child

Y#	Date	Mintage	VF	XF	Unc
74	1979FM	—	BV	25.00	45.00
	1979FM(p)	—	—	Proof	70.00

1000 PISO

9.9500 gm., .900 GOLD, .2879 oz AGW
3rd Anniversary of the New Society

Y#	Date	Mintage	VF	XF	Unc
63	1975	.023	190.00	220.00	235.00
	1975	.013	—	Proof	250.00

1500 PISO

20.5500 gm., .900 GOLD, .5947 oz AGW
I.M.F. Meeting

Y#	Date	Mintage	VF	XF	Unc
66	1976	5,500	BV	400.00	425.00
	1976	6,500	—	Proof	450.00

Security Printing & Mint

Y#	Date	Mintage	VF	XF	Unc
72	1977	3,000	BV	400.00	425.00
	1977	3,000	—	Proof	450.00

5000 PISO

68.7400 gm., .900 GOLD, 1.9893 oz AGW
5th Anniversary of the New Society

Y#	Date	Mintage	VF	XF	Unc
69	1977FM(U)	100 pcs.	BV	1300.	1500.
	1977FM(P)	3,832	—	Proof	1300.

NCLT ISSUES

MINT SETS

KM#	Date	Mintage	Identification	Issue Price	Mkt. Val.
S1	1936(3)	—	Y26-28	—	360.00
S2	1947(2)	—	Y34-35	—	47.00
S3	1958(5)	—	Y36-40	—	2.50
S4	1970(2)	—	Y52,52a	—	37.50
S5	1975(8)	5,877	Y55-62	33.50	150.00

KM#	Date	Mintage	Identification	Issue Price	Mkt. Val.
S6	1976(8)	1,826	Y55-60,64,65	—	175.00
S7	1977(8)	354	Y55-60,67,68	—	200.00
S8	1978(8)	—	Y55-60,70,71	—	80.00
S9	1979(8)	—	Y55a-60a,73,74	—	90.00

PROOF SETS

STANDARD METALS

KM#	Date	Mintage	Identification	Issue Price	Mkt. Val.
101	1903(7)	2,558	Y14-21	—	300.00
102	1904(7)	1,355	Y14-21	—	450.00
103	1905(7)	471	Y14-21	—	825.00
104	1906(7)	500	Y14-21	—	700.00
105	1908(7)	500	Y14-16, 22-25	—	750.00
106	1974(6)	*10,000	Y46-50,53	—	125.00
107	1975(8)	36,516	Y55-62	67.00	100.00
108	1976(8)	9,901	Y55-60,64,65	67.00	120.00
109	1977(8)	4,822	Y55-60,67,68	70.00	150.00
110	1978(8)	4,792	Y55-60,70,71	70.00	155.00
111	1978(2)	3,911	Y70-71	46.00	130.00
112	1979(8)	—	Y55a-60a,73,74	68.00	160.00
113	1979(2)	—	Y73,74	47.50	100.00

NOTE: The 1974 proof set was not released to the general public. Almost the entire issue is in Manila.

CULION LEPER COLONY

Leprosarium Coinage

The Culion Leper Colony was established around 1903 on the island of Culion about 150 miles southeast of Manila by the Commission of Public Health. The first issue of coins valid only in the colony was produced by a private firm, Frank & Company. Later issues were struck at the Manila mint.

MINTMARKS:

PM = Philippine Mint at Manila

MONETARY SYSTEM:

100 Centavos = 1 Peso

1/2 CENTAVO

ALUMINUM

KM#	Date	Mintage	VF	XF	Unc
1	1913	.017	1.00	1.50	2.50

NOTE: Some authorities doubt that this coin circulated.

CENTAVO

ALUMINUM

KM#	Date	Mintage	Good	VG	Fine
2	1913	.033	12.50	25.00	35.00

COPPER-NICKEL

As below, but 1st die; better strike.

KM#	Date	Mintage	Good	VG	Fine
3	1927PM	.030	4.00	8.50	15.00

2nd die, poor strike.

KM#	Date	Mintage	Good	VG	Fine
4	1927PM	Inc. Ab.	5.00	10.00	20.00

Obv: Bust of Rizal in circle.
Rev: PHILIPPINE HEALTH SERVICE/ LEPER COIN ONE CENTAVO.

KM#	Date	Mintage	
5	1930	—	Reported, Not Confirmed

5 CENTAVOS

ALUMINUM
Similar to 1 Centavo, KM#1

KM#	Date	Mintage	Good	VG	Fine
6	1913	6,600	10.00	20.00	35.00

COPPER-NICKEL

KM#	Date	Mintage	Good	VG	Fine
7	1927	.016	4.00	6.00	10.00

10 CENTAVOS

ALUMINUM
Similar to 1 Centavo, KM#1

KM#	Date	Mintage	Good	VG	Fine
8	1913	6,600	3.50	6.00	10.00

Similar to 1 Peso, KM#15

KM#	Date	Mintage	Good	VG	Fine
9	1920	.020	2.50	4.50	8.00

COPPER-NICKEL

KM#	Date	Mintage	VG	Fine	VF
10	1930	.017	1.50	3.00	6.00

NOTE: One pattern exists in copper, but it has not been authenticated.

20 CENTAVOS

ALUMINUM
Similar to 1 Centavo, KM#1

KM#	Date	Mintage	Good	VG	Fine
11	1913	.010	4.00	8.00	15.00

Similar to 1 Peso, KM#15

KM#	Date	Mintage	Good	VG	Fine
12	1920	.010	2.50	5.00	10.00

COPPER-NICKEL
Obv: CULION LEPER COLONY 20/CENTAVOS/PHILIPPINE ISLANDS.
Rev: A caduceus and PHILIPPINE HEALTH SERVICE.

KM#	Date	Mintage	VG	Fine	VF
13	1922PM	.010	2.00	4.00	7.50

PESO

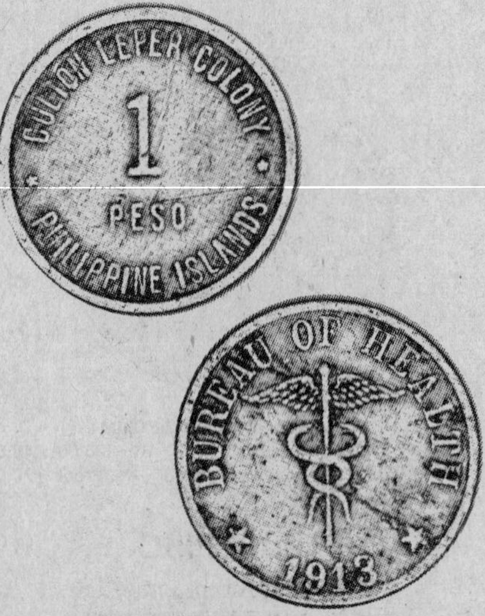

ALUMINUM

KM#	Date	Mintage	Good	VG	Fine
14	1913	8,600	2.00	3.50	7.50

NOTE: This coins exists with thick and thin planchets.

Obv: Similar to KM#14

KM#	Date	Mintage	VG	Fine	VF
15	1920	4,000	2.50	4.00	7.00

COPPER-NICKEL
Obv: Similar to KM#14

KM#	Date	Mintage	VG	Fine	VF
16	1922PM	8,280	2.50	5.00	7.50

Similar to KM#16, but caduceus has curved wings.

KM#	Date	Mintage	VG	Fine	VF
17	1922PM	Inc. Ab.	14.00	18.50	25.00

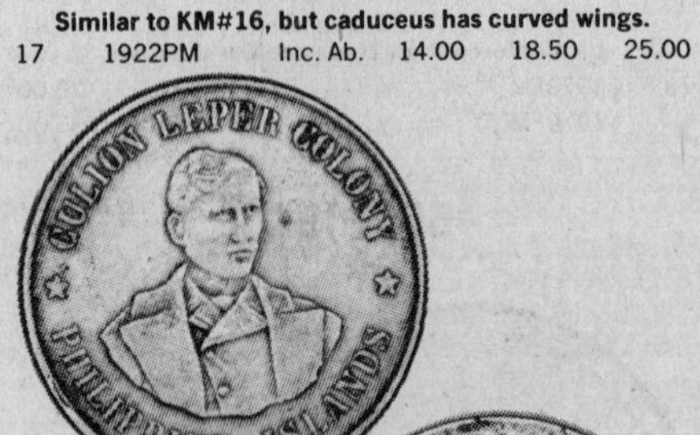

KM#	Date	Mintage	Fine	VF	XF
18	1925	.020	3.00	5.00	7.50

POLAND

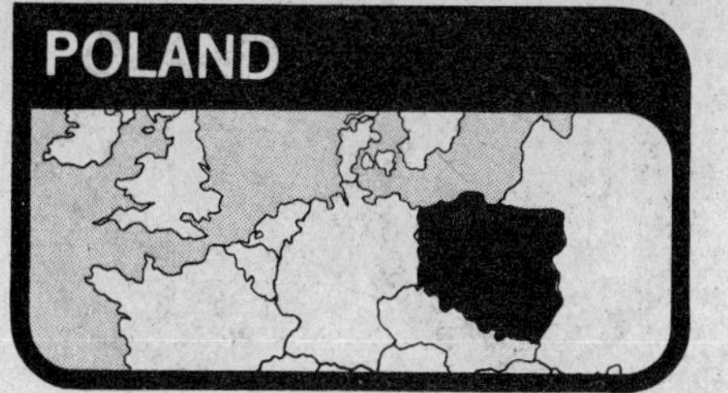

The Polish People's Republic, located in central Europe, has an area of 120,700 sq. mi. (312,612 sq. km.) and a population of 35 million. Capital: Warsaw. The economy is essentially agricultural, but industrial activity provides the products for foreign trade. Machinery, coal, coke, iron, steel and transport equipment are exported.

Poland, which began as a Slavic duchy in the 10th century and reached its peak of power between the 14th and 16th centuries, has had a turbulent history of invasion, occupation or partition by Mongols, Turkey, Hungary, Sweden, Austria, Prussia and Russia.

The first partition took place in 1772. Prussia took Polish Pomerania. Russia took part of the eastern provinces. Austria took Galicia, in which lay the fortress city of Cracow (Krakow). The second partition occurred in 1793 when Russia took another slice of the eastern provinces and Prussia took what remained of western Poland. The third partition, 1795, literally removed Poland from the map. Russia took what was left of the eastern provinces. Prussia seized most of central Poland, including Warsaw. Austria took what was left of the south. Napoleon restored to Poland much of the territory lost to Prussia and Austria, but after his defeat another partition returned the Duchy of Warsaw to Prussia, made Cracow into a tiny republic, and declared what remained to be the Kingdom of Poland under the czar and in permanent union with Russia.

Poland re-emerged as an independent state recognized by the Treaty of Versailles on June 28, 1919, and maintained its independence until 1939 when it was invaded by, and partitioned between, Germany and Russia. Poland's present boundaries were determined by the U.S.-British- Russian agreement of Aug. 16, 1945. The Polish Communist- Socialist faction won a decisive victory at the polls in 1947 and established a 'people's republic' of the Soviet type in 1952.

RULERS

Stanislaus Augustus, 1764-1795
Friedrich August I, King of Saxony,
As Grand Duke, 1807-1814
Alexander I, Czar of Russia,
As King, 1815-1825
Nicholas (Mikolay) I, Czar of Russia,
As King, 1825-1855

MINTMARKS

MV,MW - Warsaw Mint
FF - Stuttgart Germany 1916-1917
(w) Arrow-Warsaw 1925-39
Other letters appearing with date denote the Mint Master at the time the coin was struck.

MINTMASTER'S INITIALS

AP - Anton Partenstein (Warsaw Mint, 1765-74)
EB - Ephraim Brenn (Warsaw Mint, 1774-92)
FH - Frederick Hunger (Warsaw Mint, 1765-67)
G - Peter Michael Gartenberg (Krakow and Warsaw 1765-72)
IB - Jacob Benik (Warsaw Mint, 1811-27)
IP - Jerzy (George) Pusch (Warsaw Mint, 1834-43)
IS - Justin Schroder (Warsaw Mint, 1768-74)
US - John Stockmann (Warsaw Mint, 1810-11)
KG - Carl Gronau (Warsaw Mint, 1829-34)

MONETARY SYSTEM

(Until 1815)
1 Solidus = 1 Schilling
3 Solidi = 2 Poltura = 1 Grosz
3 Poltura = 1-1/2 Grosze = 1 Polturak
6 Groszy = 1 Szostak
18 Groszy = 1 Tympf
30 Groszy = 4 Silbergroschen
= 1 Zloty
1 Talara = 1 Zloty
6 Zlotych = 1 Reichsthaler
8 Zlotych = 1 Speciesthaler
5 Speciesthaler = 1 August D'or
3 Ducats = 1 Stanislaus D'or

(Commencing 1815)
30 Groszy = 15 Russian Kopeks
= 1 Zloty
10 Zlotych = 1-1/2 Rubles

Kingdom

SOLIDUS

COPPER
Obv: Crowned SAR monogram. Rev: Value.

C#	Date	Mintage	VG	Fine	VF
33	1766G	—	35.00	65.00	90.00
	1767G	—	2.25	3.50	5.50
	1768G sm. letters		2.25	3.50	5.50
	1768 lg. letters		—	—	—
	1768	—	35.00	65.00	90.00
	1776EB	—	5.00	8.50	12.50
	1792MV	—	12.50	20.00	32.50

NOTE: Varieties exist.

C#	Date	Mintage	VG	Fine	VF
33a	ND G sm.monogram		35.00	65.00	90.00
	ND G lg. monogram		35.00	65.00	90.00

POL (1/2) GROSZ

COPPER
Obv: Crowned SAR monogram. Rev: Value.

C#	Date	Mintage	VG	Fine	VF
34	1765G	—	35.00	65.00	90.00
	1766G	—	2.25	3.50	5.50
	1767G	—	2.25	3.50	5.50
	1768G sm.monogram		2.25	3.50	5.50
	1768G lg.monogram		2.25	3.50	5.50
	1775EB	—	2.25	3.50	5.50
	1776EB	—	4.00	6.50	9.50
	1777EB	—	7.50	12.50	17.50
	1780EB	—	5.00	8.50	12.50
	1781EB	—	7.50	12.50	17.50
	1782EB	—	5.00	8.50	12.50

Similar to C#34 but value POL GROSZA, leg: Z/MIEDZI KRAIOW

C#	Date	Mintage	VG	Fine	VF
35	1792MV	—	25.00	40.00	60.00

GROSZ

COPPER
Obv: Bust right. Rev: Arms.

C#	Date	Mintage	VG	Fine	VF
36	1765	—	—	—	—

Obv: SAR monogram.
Rev: Crowned arms within branches.

C#	Date	Mintage	VG	Fine	VF
38	1765G	—	2.00	3.00	5.00
	1766G	—	2.00	3.00	4.50
	1767G	—	2.00	3.00	4.50
	1768G	—	2.00	3.00	4.50
	1769G	—	2.00	3.00	4.50
	1770G	—	2.00	3.00	4.50
	1771G	—	2.00	3.00	4.50
	1772G	—	2.00	3.00	4.50
	1772AP	—	55.00	85.00	120.00
	1773AP	—	2.00	3.00	4.50
	1774AP	—	4.00	6.50	9.00
	1774EB	—	2.00	3.00	4.50
	1775EB	—	2.00	3.00	4.50
	1776AP	—	15.00	25.00	40.00
	1776EB	—	2.00	3.00	4.50
	1777AP	—	20.00	40.00	57.50
	1777EB	—	2.00	3.00	4.50
	1778EB	—	2.00	3.00	4.50
	1779EB	—	2.00	3.00	4.50
	1780EB	—	2.00	3.00	4.50
	1781EB	—	2.00	3.00	4.50
	1782EB	—	2.00	3.00	4.50
	1783EB	—	2.00	3.00	4.50
	1784EB	—	2.00	3.00	4.50
	1785EB	—	2.00	3.00	4.50
	1786EB	—	2.50	4.00	6.50
	1787EB	—	2.00	3.00	4.50
	1788EB	—	2.00	3.00	4.50
	1789EB	—	2.00	3.00	4.50
	1790EB	—	2.00	3.00	4.50
	1791EB	—	2.00	3.00	4.50
	1791MV	—	4.00	6.50	9.00
	1792EB	—	2.00	3.00	4.50
	1792MV	—	2.00	3.00	4.50
	1793MV	—	2.00	3.00	4.50
	1794MV	—	2.00	3.00	4.50
	1795MV	—	15.00	25.00	37.50

NOTE: Varieties exist.

MINING GROSZ

COPPER
Obv: Bust right. Rev: Crowned arms within wreath, leg: MIEDZI KRAJOWEY.

C#	Date	Mintage	VG	Fine	VF
39	1786	—	10.00	15.00	27.50
	1787	—	10.00	15.00	27.50
	1788	—	6.00	9.00	13.50

3 GROSZY

COPPER
Obv: Bust right. Rev: Crowned arms within branches, value: GROSSUS POLON: TRIPLEX

C#	Date	Mintage	VG	Fine	VF
41	1765g	—	4.50	6.75	10.00
	1766g	—	4.50	6.75	10.00

Obv: Head right

C#	Date	Mintage	VG	Fine	VF
41a	1766G	—	2.25	3.50	5.50
	1767G	—	2.25	3.50	5.50
	1768G	—	2.25	3.50	5.50
	1769G	—	2.25	3.50	5.50
	1770G	—	2.25	3.50	5.50
	1771G	—	2.25	3.50	5.50
	1772G	—	2.25	3.50	5.50
	1772AP	—	2.25	3.50	5.50
	1773AP	—	2.25	3.50	5.50
	1774AP	—	2.25	3.50	5.50
	1775EB	—	2.25	3.50	5.50
	1776EB	—	2.25	3.50	5.50
	1777EB	—	2.25	3.50	5.50
	1778EB	—	2.25	3.50	5.50
	1779EB	—	2.25	3.50	5.50
	1780EB	—	2.25	3.50	5.50
	1781EB	—	2.25	3.50	5.50
	1782EB	—	2.75	4.50	7.50
	1783EB	—	2.25	3.50	5.50
	1784EB	—	2.25	3.50	5.50
	1785EB	—	2.75	4.50	7.50
	1786EB	—	2.75	4.50	7.50
	1787EB	—	2.25	3.50	5.50
	1788EB	—	2.25	3.50	5.50
	1789EB	—	2.25	3.50	5.50
	1790EB	—	2.25	3.50	5.50
	1791EB	—	2.25	3.50	5.50
	1792EB	—	2.25	3.50	5.50
	1792MV	—	2.25	3.50	5.50
	1793MV	—	2.25	3.50	5.50
	1794MV	—	2.25	3.50	5.50

NOTE: Varieties exist.

3 MINING GROSZY

COPPER
Obv: Head right. Rev: Arms, leg: ZMIEDZI KRAIOWEY.

C#	Date	Mintage	VG	Fine	VF
43	1786EB	—	4.50	7.25	10.00
	1787EB	—	7.50	11.25	17.50
	1788EB	—	7.50	11.25	17.50
	1791EB	—	7.50	11.25	17.50
	1793MN	—	—	—	—
	1794MW	—	7.50	11.25	17.50
	1795MW	—	7.50	11.25	17.50

6 GROSZY

BILLON
Obv: Arms. Rev: Value.

C#	Date	Mintage	VG	Fine	VF
46	1794	—	3.50	5.00	7.50
	1795	—	3.50	5.00	7.50

GROSCHEN

(= 7-1/2 Groszy)

1.9900 gm., .3668 SILVER, .0234 oz ASW
Obv: SAR in square. Rev: 320 EX....

on tablet.

C#	Date	Mintage	VG	Fine	VF
47	1766	—	35.00	65.00	90.00
	1766FS	—	8.00	12.50	17.50
	1767	—	35.00	65.00	90.00
	1767FS	—	3.00	4.50	7.50
	1768	—	—	—	—
	1768FS	—	3.00	4.50	7.50
	1768IS	—	55.00	85.00	120.00
	1772AP	—	22.50	40.00	60.00
	1773AP	—	3.00	4.50	7.50
	1774AP	—	3.00	4.50	7.50
	1775EB	—	3.00	4.50	7.50
	1776EB	—	3.00	4.50	7.50
	1777EB	—	3.00	4.50	7.50
	1778EB	—	5.00	8.50	12.50
	1779EB	—	3.00	4.50	7.50
	1780EB	—	5.00	8.50	12.50
	1781EB	—	5.00	8.50	12.50
	1782EB	—	3.00	4.50	7.50

10 GROSZY

2.4900. gm., .3734 SILVER, .0299 oz ASW
Obv: Crowned arms. Rev: Value, date.

C#	Date	Mintage	VG	Fine	VF
48	1787	—	3.00	4.50	7.50
	1788	—	3.00	4.50	7.50
	1789	—	3.00	4.50	7.50
	1790	—	3.00	4.50	7.50
	1791	—	3.00	4.50	7.50
	1792MV	—	10.00	17.50	27.50
	1792MW	—	3.00	4.50	7.50
	1793MW	—	3.00	4.50	7.50
	1794MW	—	3.00	4.50	7.50
	1795MW	—	10.00	17.50	27.50

2 GROSCHEN

(= 15 Groszy)

3.3400 gm., .5868 SILVER, .0630 oz ASW

C#	Date	Mintage	VG	Fine	VF
49	1766FS	—	2.50	3.50	5.50
	1767FS	—	2.50	3.50	5.50
	1768IS	—	2.50	3.50	5.50
	1769IS	—	2.50	3.50	5.50
	1770IS	—	2.50	3.50	5.50
	1771IS	—	2.50	3.50	5.50
	1772IS	—	2.50	3.50	5.50
	1772A.P	—	2.50	3.50	5.50
	1773A.P	—	2.50	3.50	5.50
	1773PA	—	12.50	22.50	35.00
	1774A.P	—	2.50	3.50	5.50
	1775A.P	—	55.00	85.00	120.50
	1775EB	—	2.50	3.50	5.50
	1776EB	—	5.00	8.50	12.50
	1777EB	—	5.00	8.50	12.50
	1778EB	—	5.00	8.50	12.50
	1779EB	—	5.00	8.50	12.50
	1780EB	—	5.00	8.50	12.50
	1781EB	—	8.50	12.50	17.50
	1782EB	—	5.00	8.50	12.50
	1785EB	—	2.50	3.50	5.50
	1786EB	—	2.50	3.50	5.50

4 GROSCHEN

(= 1 Zloty)

5.3100 gm., .5499 SILVER, .0938 oz ASW

C#	Date	Mintage	Fine	VF	XF
50	1766FS	—	9.50	13.50	20.00
	1767FS	—	9.50	13.50	20.00
	1768IS	—	10.00	17.50	27.50
	1769IS	—	30.00	55.00	75.00
	1771IS	—	9.50	13.50	20.00
	1772IS	—	9.00	12.00	15.00
	1773IS	—	65.00	100.50	150.00
	1774IS	—	10.00	17.50	27.50
	1775EB	—	10.00	17.50	27.50
	1776EB	—	10.00	17.50	27.50
	1777EB	—	10.00	17.50	27.50
	1778EB	—	10.00	17.50	27.50
	1779EB	—	10.00	17.50	27.50
	1780EB	—	10.00	17.50	27.50
	1781EB	—	15.00	25.00	35.00
	1782EB	—	10.00	17.50	27.50

Obv: Head with braid.

C#	Date	Mintage	Fine	VF	XF
—	1783EB	—	15.00	25.00	35.00
	1784EB	—	15.00	25.00	35.00
	1785EB	—	9.50	13.50	20.00

Obv: Head with two braids.

C#	Date	Mintage	Fine	VF	XF
—	1786	—	10.00	13.50	20.00

Obv: Head right. Rev: Arms with pointed shield, leg: 83 1/2 EX.....

C#	Date	Mintage	Fine	VF	XF
51	1787	—	6.00	10.00	15.00
	1788	—	6.00	10.00	15.00
	1789	—	6.00	10.00	15.00
	1790	—	6.00	10.00	15.00
	1791	—	6.00	10.00	15.00
	1793	—	6.00	10.00	15.00

Obv: Head right. Rev: Arms with pointed shield, leg: 84 1/2 EX....

C#	Date	Mintage	Fine	VF	XF
52	1792MV	—	6.00	10.00	15.00
	1793MV	—	6.00	10.00	15.00
	1794MV	—	10.00	13.50	20.00
	1795MV	—	20.00	35.00	55.00

8 GROSCHEN

(2 ZLOTYCH)

9.3500 gm., .6267 SILVER, .1884 .OZ ASW

C#	Date	Mintage	Fine	VF	XF
53	1766FS	—	10.00	13.50	20.00
	1767FS	—	10.00	13.50	20.00
	1768FS	—	10.00	13.50	20.00
	1769IS	—	20.00	35.00	55.00
	1770IS	—	10.00	13.50	20.00
	1771IS	—	10.00	13.50	20.00
	1772AP	—	10.00	13.50	20.00
	1772IS	—	10.00	13.50	20.00
	1773AP	—	10.00	17.50	27.50
	1774AP	—	10.00	13.50	20.00
	1774EB	—	10.00	17.50	27.50
	1775EB	—	10.00	13.50	20.00
	1776EB	—	10.00	13.50	20.00
	1777EB	—	10.00	13.50	20.00
	1778EB	—	10.00	13.50	20.00
	1779EB	—	10.00	13.50	20.00
	1780EB	—	10.00	13.50	20.00
	1781EB	—	10.00	13.50	20.00
	1782EB	—	10.00	13.50	20.00

NOTE: Varieties exist.

Obv: Head with braid.

C#	Date	Mintage	Fine	VF	XF
—	1783	—	10.00	13.50	20.00
	1784	—	10.00	13.50	20.00
	1785	—	10.00	17.50	27.50

Obv: Braid behind head.

C#	Date	Mintage	Fine	VF	XF
—	1783	—	150.00	250.00	350.00

C#	Date	Mintage	Fine	VF	XF
54	1787	—	7.50	12.50	17.50
	1788	—	7.50	12.50	17.50
	1789	—	7.50	12.50	17.50
	1790	—	7.50	12.50	17.50
	1791	—	7.50	12.50	17.50
	1792	—	7.50	12.50	17.50
	1792MV	—	7.50	12.50	17.50
	1793MV	—	7.50	12.50	17.50
	1794MV	—	7.50	12.50	17.50

Rev. leg: 42 1/2 EX.....

C#	Date	Mintage	Fine	VF	XF
55	1794MV	—	20.00	35.00	55.00
	1795MV	—	10.00	17.50	27.50

4 ZLOTYCH

14.0300 gm., .833 SILVER, .3758 oz ASW
Obv: Head right. Rev: Crowned arms within wreath, leg: XX EX.....

C#	Date	Mintage	Fine	VF	XF
56	1767FS	—	55.00	85.00	120.00
	1768IS	—	20.00	30.00	45.00
	1768IS with hairband	—	20.00	30.00	45.00
	1772AP	—	20.00	30.00	45.00
	1773AP	—	20.00	30.00	45.00
	1774AP	—	20.00	30.00	45.00
	1775EB	—	20.00	30.00	45.00
	1776EB	—	20.00	30.00	45.00
	1777EB	—	20.00	30.00	45.00
	1778EB	—	20.00	30.00	45.00
	1779EB	—	20.00	30.00	45.00
	1780EB	—	20.00	30.00	45.00
	1781EB	—	20.00	30.00	45.00
	1782EB	—	20.00	30.00	45.00

NOTE: Varieties exist.

Same as C#56 but Klippe

C#	Date	Mintage	Fine	VF	XF
—	1780EB	—	600.00	750.00	1000.

Similar to C#56 but head with braid.

C#	Date	Mintage	Fine	VF	XF
—	1783EB	—	20.00	30.00	45.00
	1784EB	—	20.00	30.00	45.00

Obv: Head right. Rev: Arms with pointed shield, leg: 20 7/8 EX.....

C#	Date	Mintage	Fine	VF	XF
57	1788	—	35.00	65.00	90.00
	1792MV	—	150.00	225.00	300.00

6 ZLOTYCH

SILVER

C#	Date	Mintage	Fine	VF	XF
58	1794	—	55.00	85.00	120.00
	1795	—	70.00	100.00	135.00

8 ZLOTYCH

28.0600 gm., .833 SILVER, .7495 oz ASW
Obv: Bust right. Rev: Crowned round arms, leg: X EX....

C#	Date	Mintage	Fine	VF	XF
62	1766	—	100.00	160.00	250.00

C#	Date	Mintage	Fine	VF	XF
63	1768IS	—	50.00	75.00	100.00
	1769IS	—	—	—	—
	1770IS	—	50.00	75.00	100.00
	1772AP	—	50.00	75.00	100.00
	1772IS	—	50.00	75.00	100.00
	1773AP	—	50.00	75.00	100.00
	1774AP	—	50.00	75.00	100.00
	1775EB	—	50.00	75.00	100.00
	1776EB	—	50.00	75.00	100.00
	1777EB	—	50.00	75.00	100.00
	1778EB	—	50.00	75.00	100.00
	1779EB	—	50.00	75.00	100.00
	1780EB	—	50.00	75.00	100.00
	1781EB	—	50.00	75.00	100.00
	1782EB	—	50.00	75.00	100.00

Obv: Head with braid

C#	Date	Mintage	Fine	VF	XF
—	1783EB	—	50.00	75.00	100.00
	1784EB	—	50.00	75.00	100.00
	1785EB	—	50.00	75.00	100.00

Rev. leg: 10 7/16 EX.....

C#	Date	Mintage	Fine	VF	XF
64	1788	—	75.00	100.00	150.00
	1792MV	—	160.00	225.00	300.00

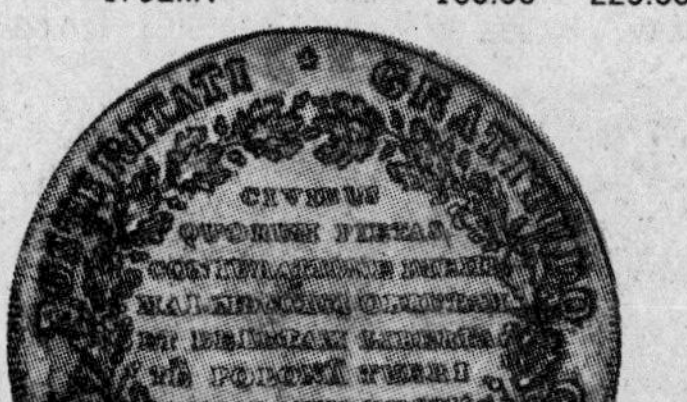

Convention of Targowitz
Obv: 10 7/16 EX...., GRATITUDO...., 9 lines in wreath. Rev: Value, DECRETO....

C#	Date	Mintage	Fine	VF	XF
65	1793	—	165.00	250.00	350.00

TRADE COINS

DUCAT

GOLD
Obv: Bust. Rev: Arms.

C#	Date	Mintage	Fine	VF	XF
66	1765FS	—	950.00	1450.	2150.

Obv: Crowned SAR monogram within star.
Rev: Crowned arms, MON AUR POLONIC.

C#	Date	Mintage	Fine	VF	XF
67	1766FS	—	900.00	1350.	2000.

Obv: Head right. Rev: MON. AUR. POLON on tablet.

C#	Date	Mintage	Fine	VF	XF
68	1766FS	—	900.00	1350.	2000.

C#	Date	Mintage	Fine	VF	XF
69	1766	—	500.00	775.00	1150.
	1766FS	—	550.00	775.00	1150.
	1767	—	550.00	775.00	1150.
	1767FS	—	550.00	775.00	1150.
	1768FS	—	550.00	775.00	1150.
	1770IS	—	550.00	775.00	1150.
	1771IS	—	550.00	775.00	1150.
	1772AP	—	550.00	775.00	1150.
	1772IS	—	550.00	775.00	1150.

C#	Date	Mintage	Fine	VF	XF
70	1772AP	—	450.00	675.00	1000.
	1773AP	—	450.00	675.00	1000.
	1774AP	—	450.00	675.00	1000.
	1774EB	—	—	—	—
	1775EB	—	450.00	675.00	1000.
	1776EB	—	450.00	675.00	1000.
	1777EB	—	450.00	675.00	1000.
	1778EB	—	—	—	—
	1779EB	—	450.00	675.00	1000.

COPPER

C#	Date	Mintage	Fine	VF	XF
70a	1772AP	—	—	—	—

.986 GOLD

C#	Date	Mintage	Fine	VF	XF
71	1779EB	—	—	—	—
	1780EB	—	400.00	600.00	900.00
	1781EB	—	400.00	600.00	900.00
	1782EB	—	400.00	600.00	900.00
	1783EB	—	400.00	600.00	900.00
	1792EB	—	400.00	600.00	900.00
	1792MV	—	400.00	600.00	900.00
	1793MV	—	400.00	600.00	900.00
	1794MV	—	400.00	600.00	900.00
	1795MV	—	400.00	600.00	900.00

Obv: Different hairstyle.

C#	Date	Mintage	Fine	VF	XF
71.1	1784EB	—	400.00	600.00	900.00
	1785EB	—	400.00	600.00	900.00
	1786EB	—	400.00	600.00	900.00
	1787EB	—	400.00	600.00	900.00
	1788EB	—	400.00	600.00	900.00
	1789EB	—	400.00	600.00	900.00
	1790EB	—	400.00	600.00	900.00
	1791EB	—	400.00	600.00	900.00

COPPER

C#	Date	Mintage	Fine	VF	XF
71a	1794MV	—	—	—	—

1-1/2 DUCATS

.986 GOLD

C#	Date	Mintage	Fine	VF	XF
72	1794	—	800.00	1200.	1800.

3 DUCATS

.986 GOLD

C#	Date	Mintage	Fine	VF	XF
73	1794	—	1750.	2600.	4000.

Grand Duchy of Warsaw

GROSZ

COPPER

C#	Date	Mintage	Fine	VF	XF
81	1810IS	.743	3.50	4.50	8.50
	1811IS	4.358	3.50	4.50	8.50
	1811IB	Inc. Ab.	3.50	4.50	8.50
	1812IB	6.346	3.50	4.50	8.50
	1814IB	3.072	3.50	4.50	8.50

3 GROSZY

COPPER

C#	Date	Mintage	Fine	VF	XF
82	1810IS	1.008	3.50	6.00	12.50
	1811IS	5.479	3.50	6.00	12.50
	1811IB	Inc. Ab.	3.50	6.00	12.50
	1812IB	6.816	3.50	6.00	12.50
	1813IB	1.139	3.50	6.00	12.50
	1814IB	3.427	3.50	6.00	12.50

5 GROSZY

2.2000 gm., .195 SILVER, .0138 oz ASW

C#	Date	Mintage	Fine	VF	XF
83	1811IS	11.595	4.00	6.00	10.00
	1811IB	—	4.00	6.00	10.00
	1812IB	3.405	4.00	8.00	12.50

10 GROSZY

2.9900 gm., .194 SILVER, .0186 oz ASW

C#	Date	Mintage	Fine	VF	XF
84	1810IS	—	10.00	17.50	25.00
	1812IB	.906	5.00	7.00	15.00
	1813IB	3.549	5.00	7.00	12.50

1/6 TALARA

4.98 gm., .532 SILVER, .0852 oz ASW

C#	Date	Mintage	Fine	VF	XF
85	1811IS	.113	15.00	18.00	21.50
	1812IB	.223	15.00	18.00	21.50
	1813IB	.106	25.00	50.00	60.00
	1814IB	1.492	15.00	18.00	21.50

1/3 TALARA

8.66 gm., .624 SILVER, .1739 oz ASW

C#	Date	Mintage	Fine	VF	XF
86	1810IS	.123	20.00	40.00	60.00
	1811IS	.993	20.00	25.00	45.00
	1812IB	2.804	20.00	25.00	35.00
	1813IB	1.966	20.00	25.00	40.00
	1814IB	8.611	20.00	25.00	30.00

TALAR

22.92 gm., .718 SILVER, .5295 oz ASW

C#	Date	Mintage	Fine	VF	XF
87	1811IB	4,488	150.00	175.00	200.00
	1812IB	.036	150.00	175.00	200.00
	1814IB	.014	150.00	175.00	200.00

TRADE COINS

DUCAT

3.64 gm., .986 GOLD, .1103 oz AGW

C#	Date	Mintage	Fine	VF	XF
88	1812IB	8,456	400.00	500.00	650.00
	1813IB	3,000	775.00	950.00	1200.

Congress Kingdom of Poland

MONETARY SYSTEM

30 Groszy = 15 Russian Kopeks
= 1 Zloty
10 Zlotych = 1-1/2 Rubles

GROSZ

COPPER

C#	Date	Mintage	Fine	VF	XF
93	1815IB	N	6.50	11.50	20.00
	1816IB	1.873	3.00	7.50	15.00
	1817IB	3.092	3.00	7.50	15.00
	1818IB	1.035	3.00	7.50	15.00
	1818	Inc. Ab.	6.50	11.50	20.00
	1819IB	Inc. Bl.	4.00	9.00	17.50
	1820IB	.372	3.00	7.50	15.00
	1821IB	.571	3.00	7.50	15.00
	1822IB	Inc.C#94	7.50	17.50	32.50
	1824IB	N	5.50	13.50	25.00

C#	Date	Mintage	Fine	VF	XF
105	1828FH	1.190	3.00	7.50	15.00
	1829FH	.931	3.00	7.50	15.00
	1830FH	1.569	3.00	7.50	15.00
	1830KG	Inc. Ab.	3.00	7.50	15.00
	1831KG	.353	3.00	7.50	15.00
	1832KG	1.559	3.00	7.50	15.00
	1833KG	.375	3.00	7.50	15.00
	1834KG	.427	3.00	7.50	15.00
	1834IP	Inc. Ab.	3.00	7.50	15.00
	1835IB	.541	3.00	7.50	15.00

Rev: INSC.Z MIEDZI KRALOWEY translates as "mining coin".

C#	Date	Mintage	Fine	VF	XF
94	1822IB	2.721	3.00	7.50	15.00
	1823IB	5.046	3.00	7.50	15.00
	1824IB	5.413	3.00	7.50	15.00
	1825IB	3.204	3.00	7.50	15.00
	1826IB	—	5.50	12.50	23.50

C#	Date	Mintage	Fine	VF	XF
106	1835MW	Inc.C#105	3.00	7.50	15.00
	1836MW	.839	3.00	7.50	15.00
	1837MW	1.016	3.00	7.50	15.00
	1837WM	Inc. Ab.	—	Rare	—

C#	Date	Mintage	Fine	VF	XF
106	1838MW	.487	3.00	7.50	15.00
	1839MW	.670	3.00	7.50	15.00
	1840MW	12.106	2.75	6.00	12.50
	1841MW	N	—	Rare	—
	Rev: Without wreath				
106a	1840	Inc. Ab.	12.50	17.50	25.00
	Rev: JEDEN or IEDEN above value.				
107	1840MW	Inc. Ab.	5.00	10.00	20.00
	1841MW	—	5.50	12.50	23.50

3 GROSZE

COPPER
No collar

C#	Date	Mintage	Fine	VF	XF
95	1815IB	N	—	Rare	—
	1816IB	N	—	Rare	—
	1817IB	.843	4.00	10.00	20.00
	1818IB	.158	8.00	22.50	40.00
	Reeded, struck in collar				
	1818IB	—	—	Rare	—
	1819IB	.187	4.00	11.50	20.00
	1820IB	.089	4.00	11.50	20.00
	Rev. inscription: Z MIEDZI KRAIOWEY				
108	1826IB	.557	5.00	7.00	12.50
	1827IB	Inc. Ab.	5.00	7.00	12.50
	1827FH	N	—	Rare	—

Rev. inscription: 3/GROSZE/POLSKI

C#	Date	Mintage	Fine	VF	XF
109	1827FH	.495	5.00	11.50	22.50
	1828FH	1.159	4.00	10.00	20.00
	1829FH	1.057	4.00	10.00	20.00
	1830FH	.891	4.00	10.00	20.00
	1830KG	Inc. Ab.	12.50	35.00	75.00
	1831FH	—	40.00	65.00	90.00
	1831KG	1.541	4.00	10.00	20.00
	1832FH	.030	20.00	65.00	125.00
	1832KG	Inc. Ab.	4.00	10.00	20.00
	1833KG	.515	4.00	10.00	20.00
	1834KG	.346	4.00	10.00	20.00
	1834IP	Inc. Ab.	4.00	10.00	20.00
	1835IP	.185	8.50	18.50	35.00
	Rev: Wreath surrounding value				
110	1835MW	Inc.C#109	4.00	11.50	20.00
	1836MW	.267	4.00	11.50	20.00
	1837MW	.398	4.00	11.50	20.00
	1838MW	.288	4.00	11.50	20.00
	1839MW	.333	4.00	11.50	20.00

Obv: Eagle's heads larger, shield smaller.

C#	Date	Mintage	Fine	VF	XF
110.1	1840MW	4.032	4.00	10.00	20.00
	1840WW	Inc. Ab.	4.00	10.00	20.00
	1841MW	Inc. Ab.	5.00	11.50	22.00

Insurrection Of 1830-31

C#	Date	Mintage	Fine	VF	XF
120	1831K.G.	1.112	6.00	12.50	20.00

5 GROSZY

1.4500 gm., .192 SILVER, .0090 oz ASW
Obv: Eagle's wings smaller. Rev: Value: 5 GROSZY.
Smooth edge

C#	Date	Mintage	Fine	VF	XF
96	1816IB	2.700	4.00	10.00	20.00

Reeded edge

C#	Date	Mintage	Fine	VF	XF
96.1	1817IB	—	—	Rare	—

Obv: Redesigned shield

C#	Date	Mintage	Fine	VF	XF
96.2	1818IB	3.056	4.00	10.00	20.00
	1819IB	5.552	4.00	10.00	20.00
	1820IB	3.475	4.00	10.00	20.00
	1821IB	1.651	4.00	10.00	20.00
	1822IB	1.282	4.00	10.00	20.00
	1823IB	2.098	4.00	10.00	20.00
	1824IB	.235	8.00	22.50	45.00
	1825IB	.351	4.00	10.00	20.00
111	1826IB	2.079	4.00	10.00	20.00
	1827IB	1.904	4.00	10.00	20.00
	1827FH	Inc. Ab.	4.00	10.00	20.00
	1828FH	.402	4.00	10.00	20.00
	1829FH	.714	4.00	10.00	20.00
	1829KG	N	—	Rare	—
	1830FH	.571	4.00	10.00	20.00
	1831KG	.154	6.00	13.50	25.00
	1832KG	Inc. Ab.	—	Rare	—

C#	Date	Mintage	Fine	VF	XF
111a	1836MW	.159	4.00	10.00	20.00
	1838MW	.085	4.00	10.00	20.00
	1839MW	.380	4.00	10.00	20.00
	1840MW	7.081	2.00	6.00	10.00
	1841MW	—	—	Rare	—

Obv: Similar to 25 Zlotych, C#118.

C#	Date	Mintage	Fine	VF	XF
112	1841	—	—	Rare	—

10 GROSZY

2.9000 gm., .192 SILVER, .0180 oz ASW
Obv: Eagle

C#	Date	Mintage	Fine	VF	XF
97	1816IB	.750	4.00	—	20.00
	1820IB	.799	9.00	17.50	35.00
	1821IB	.707	4.00	10.00	20.00
	1822IB	1.238	4.00	10.00	20.00
	1823IB	.262	6.00	12.50	25.00
	1825IB	.750	10.00	17.50	37.50
113	1826IB	.750	4.00	10.00	20.00
	1827IB	.737	4.00	10.00	20.00
	1827FH	Inc. Ab.	6.50	12.50	25.00
	1828FH	.529	4.00	10.00	20.00
	1830FH	.145	5.50	12.50	25.00
	1830KG	Inc. Ab.	4.00	10.00	20.00
	1831KG	4.530	5.50	12.50	25.00
	1832KG	N	—	Rare	—
	1833KG	N	—	Rare	—

Insurrection Of 1830-31

C#	Date	Mintage	Fine	VF	XF
121	1831KG	6.038	5.00	11.50	20.00

C#	Date	Mintage	Fine	VF	XF
113a	1835MW	.859	4.00	10.00	20.00
	1836MW	1.733	4.00	10.00	20.00
	1837MW	.767	4.00	10.00	20.00
	1838MW	1.829	4.00	10.00	20.00
	1839MW	.060	4.00	10.00	20.00
	1840MW	63.349	2.00	3.00	6.00
	1840WW	Inc. Ab.	4.00	10.00	20.00

ZLOTY

4.5400 gm., .866 SILVER, .2530 oz ASW
Obv: Large bust. Rev: Eagle, lettered edge.

C#	Date	Mintage	Fine	VF	XF
98	1818IB	2.523	10.00	20.00	40.00
	1818IB struck in collar				
		—		Rare	—
	1819IB	1.208	10.00	20.00	40.00
	1819IB struck in collar				
98		—	—	Rare	—

Obv: Smaller bust.

C#	Date	Mintage	Fine	VF	XF
98a	1818IB	Inc. Ab.	—	Rare	—
	1822IB	.286	10.00	20.00	40.00
	1823IB	.052	10.00	20.00	40.00
	1824IB	.119	10.00	20.00	40.00
	1825IB	.140	10.00	20.00	40.00

Obv: Large head. Rev: Value.

C#	Date	Mintage	Fine	VF	XF
114	1827IB	.106	10.00	20.00	35.00
	1828FH	.192	10.00	20.00	35.00
	1829FH	.124	10.00	20.00	35.00
	1830FH	.611	10.00	20.00	35.00
	1831KG	1.112	10.00	20.00	35.00
	1832KG	Inc. Ab.	10.00	20.00	35.00

Obv: Small head

C#	Date	Mintage	Fine	VF	XF
114.1	1831KG	Inc. Ab.	—	Rare	—
	1832KG	Inc. Ab.	10.00	20.00	35.00
	1833KG	.041	11.00	25.00	37.50
	1834KG	.201	11.00	25.00	37.50
	1834IP	Inc. Ab.	10.00	20.00	35.00

Insurrection of 1830-31
Obv: Shield

C#	Date	Mintage	Fine	VF	XF
122	1831KG	—	10.00	15.00	25.00

ZLOTY-15 KOPEKS

3.0700 gm., .870 SILVER, .0858 oz ASW

C#	Date	Mintage	Fine	VF	XF
129	1832 НГ	.049	8.00	12.50	15.00
	1833 НГ	.650	8.00	12.50	15.00
	1834 НГ	.030	10.00	20.00	25.00
	1834 МШ	.240	—	Rare	—
	1835 НГ	.150	8.00	12.50	16.50
	1835 МШ	2.190	8.00	12.50	16.50
	1836 НГ	1.450	8.00	12.50	15.00
	1836 МШ	3.340	8.00	12.50	15.00
	1837 НГ	.080	8.00	16.50	22.00
	1837 МШ	2.980	8.00	12.50	15.00
	1838 НГ	1.410	8.00	12.50	15.00
	1838 МШ	3.720	8.00	12.50	15.00
	1839 НГ	1.510	8.00	12.50	15.00
	1839 МШ	3.580	8.00	12.50	15.00
	1840 НГ	1.060	8.00	12.50	15.00
	1840 МШ	.490	8.00	12.50	15.00
	1841 НГ	1.060	—	Rare	—
	1841 МШ	1.320	8.00	12.50	15.00

NOTE: Varieties exist.

40 GROSZY-20 KOPEKS

4.0500 gm., .888 SILVER, .1157 oz ASW

C#	Date	Mintage	Fine	VF	XF
130	1842 МШ	.200	15.00	18.50	20.00
	1843 МШ	.110	15.00	18.50	20.00
	1844 МШ	—	15.00	18.50	20.00
	1845 МШ	.250	15.00	18.50	20.00
	1846 МШ	—	—	Rare	—
	1848 МШ	.110	15.00	18.50	20.00
	1850 МШ	1.520	15.00	18.50	20.00

50 GROSZY-25 KOPEKS

5.2500 gm., .857 SILVER, .1446 oz ASW

C#	Date	Mintage	Fine	VF	XF
131	1842 МШ	.056	15.00	20.00	25.00
	1843 МШ	.027	15.00	20.00	25.00
	1844 МШ	—	20.00	25.00	35.00
	1845 МШ	.052	15.00	20.00	25.00
131	1846 МШ	.560	15.00	20.00	25.00
	1847 МШ	.480	15.00	20.00	25.00
	1848 МШ	.190	15.00	20.00	25.00
	1850 МШ	.150	15.00	20.00	25.00

2 ZLOTE

9.0800 gm., .868 SILVER, .4360 oz ASW
Obv: Large head. Rev: Eagle. Lettered edge.

C#	Date	Mintage	Fine	VF	XF
99	1816IB	1.393	15.00	25.00	50.00
	1817IB	1.084	15.00	25.00	50.00
	1818IB	1.311	15.00	25.00	50.00
	1819IB	1.241	15.00	25.00	50.00
	1820IB	1.970	15.00	25.00	50.00

Obv: Medium head. Struck in collar, reeded edge.

C#	Date	Mintage	Fine	VF	XF
99a	1819IB	—	—	Rare	—
	1820IB	Inc. Ab.	13.50	22.50	40.00
	1821IB	1.000	13.50	22.50	40.00
	1822IB	.093	13.50	22.50	40.00
	1823IB	.450	13.50	22.50	40.00
	1824IB	.350	13.50	22.50	40.00
	1825IB	.230	13.50	22.50	40.00

Obv: Laureated head

C#	Date	Mintage	Fine	VF	XF
115	1826IB	.065	30.00	50.00	75.00
	1828FH	.119	13.50	22.50	40.00
	1830FH	.356	13.50	22,50	40.00

Insurrection Of 1830-31

C#	Date	Mintage	Fine	VF	XF
123	1831KG	.171	20.00	25.00	35.00

2 ZLOTE-30 KOPEKS

6.1600 gm., .868 SILVER, .1591 oz ASW

C#	Date	Mintage	Fine	VF	XF
132	1834 МШ	.210	15.00	22.50	35.00
	1835 МШ	20.020	12.50	17.50	25.00
	1836 МШ	23.640	12.50	17.50	25.00
	1837 МШ	13.890	12.50	17.50	25.00
	1838 МШ	17.430	12.50	17.50	25.00
	1839 МШ	18.310	12.50	17.50	25.00
	1840 МШ	2.760	12.50	17.50	25.00
	1841 МШ	11.350	12.50	17.50	25.00

5 ZLOTYCH

15.5900 gm., .868 SILVER, .4360 oz ASW

C#	Date	Mintage	Fine	VF	XF
100	1816IB	.971	40.00	65.00	100.00
	1817IB	2.585	40.00	65.00	100.00
	1818IB	.201	40.00	65.00	100.00

Reeded edge, no collar.

C#	Date	Mintage	Fine	VF	XF
116	1829FH	1.234	25.00	45.00	75.00
	1830FH	.287	25.00	45.00	75.00
	1830KG	Inc. Ab.	25.00	45.00	75.00
	1831KG	.311	25.00	45.00	75.00
	1831KG w/collar				
		—	—	Rare	—
	1832KG	.639	25.00	45.00	75.00
	1833KG	.445	25.00	45.00	75.00
	1834KG	—	25.00	45.00	75.00
	1834IP	—	25.00	45.00	75.00

Insurrection of 1830-31

C#	Date	Mintage	Fine	VF	XF
124	1831	.023	25.00	45.00	75.00

5 ZLOTYCH-3/4 RUBLE

15.5100 gm., .868 SILVER, .4337 oz ASW

C#	Date	Mintage	Fine	VF	XF
133	1833 НГ	.260	13.50	25.00	40.00
	1834 НГ	.210	13.50	25.00	40.00
	1834 МШ	.086	15.00	27.50	50.00
	1835 НГ	.110	13.50	25.00	40.00
	1835 МШ	.540	13.50	25.00	40.00
	1836 НГ	.078	13.50	25.00	40.00
	1836 МШ	1.200	13.50	25.00	40.00
	1837 НГ	.260	13.50	25.00	40.00
	1837 МШ	1.000	13.50	25.00	40.00
	1838 НГ	.012	—	Rare	—
	1838 МШ	2.000	13.50	17.50	25.00
	1839 НГ	—	—	Rare	—
	1839 МШ	2.690	13.50	17.50	25.00
	1840 НГ	.002	—	Rare	—
	1840 МШ	2.480	13.50	17.50	25.00
	1841 НГ	—	—	Rare	—
	1841 МШ	1.270	13.50	25.00	40.00

10 ZLOTYCH

31.2000 gm., .868 SILVER, .8723 oz ASW

C#	Date	Mintage	Fine	VF	XF
101	1820IB	534 pcs.	225.00	350.00	450.00
	1821IB	1,195	200.00	300.00	375.00
	1822IB	233 pcs.	275.00	400.00	550.00

C#	Date	Mintage	Fine	VF	XF
101.1	1823IB	1,124	200.00	300.00	375.00
	1824IB	513 pcs.	225.00	350.00	450.00
	1825IB	—	225.00	350.00	450.00

Obv: Laureated head

C#	Date	Mintage	Fine	VF	XF
117	1827IB	123 pcs.	—	Rare	—
	1827FH	Inc. Ab.	400.00	750.00	1250.

10 ZLOTYCH
1-1/2 RUBLES

31.0700 gm., .868 SILVER, .8672 oz ASW

C#	Date	Mintage	Fine	VF	XF
134	1833 НГ	.130	27.50	35.00	60.00
	1834 НГ	.064	27.50	35.00	65.00
	1835 НГ	.260	27.50	35.00	60.00
	1835 МШ	.003	27.50	35.00	65.00
	1836 НГ	.130	27.50	35.00	60.00
	1836 МШ	.220	27.50	35.00	60.00
	1837 НГ	.034	30.00	40.00	70.00
	1837 МШ	.190	27.50	35.00	60.00
	1838 НГ	—	—	Rare	—
	1838 МШ	.010	—	Rare	—
	1839 НГ	.007	—	Rare	—
	1839 МШ	.002	35.00	50.00	90.00
	1840 НГ	.002	—	Rare	—
	1840 МШ	.003	27.50	35.00	65.00
	1841 НГ	—	—	Rare	—
	1841 МШ	.037	27.50	35.00	60.00

20 ZLOTYCH-3 RUBLES

3.8900 gm., .915 GOLD, .1144 oz AGW

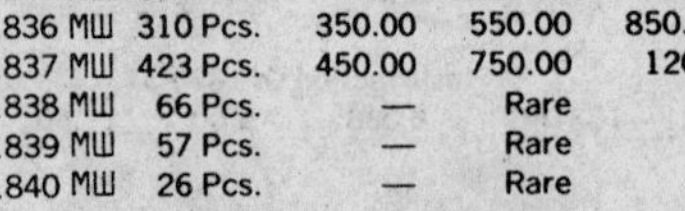

C#	Date	Mintage	Fine	VF	XF
136	1834 МШ	243 Pcs.	400.00	650.00	1000.
	1835 МШ	350 Pcs.	400.00	650.00	1000.
	1836 МШ	310 Pcs.	350.00	550.00	850.00
	1837 МШ	423 Pcs.	450.00	750.00	1200.
	1838 МШ	66 Pcs.	—	Rare	—
	1839 МШ	57 Pcs.	—	Rare	—
	1840 МШ	26 Pcs.	—	Rare	—

With ПД on obverse, СПБ on reverse

C#	Date	Mintage	Fine	VF	XF
136.1	1834 СПБ	.077	125.00	200.00	275.00
	1835 СПБ	.052	125.00	200.00	275.00
	1836 СПБ	.010	125.00	200.00	275.00
	1837 СПБ	.030	125.00	200.00	275.00
	1838 СПБ	.017	125.00	200.00	275.00
	1839 СПБ	.010	125.00	200.00	275.00

C#	Date	Mintage	Fine	VF	XF
136.2	1840 СПБ	5,000	300.00	450.00	650.00
	1841 СПБ	—	—	Rare	—

25 ZLOTYCH

4.8900 gm., .916 GOLD, .1443 oz AGW

102	1817IB	.096	200.00	275.00	400.00
	1818IB	.055	200.00	275.00	400.00
	1819IB	.032	200.00	300.00	400.00

Struck in collar

102a	1818IB	—	—	Rare	—
	1822IB	1,124	400.00	575.00	800.00
	1823IB	479 pcs.	400.00	525.00	825.00
	1824IB	612 pcs.	300.00	425.00	600.00
	1825IB	1,021	300.00	425.00	600.00

118	1828FH	241 pcs.	400.00	575.00	800.00
	1829FH	1,501	300.00	425.00	600.00
	1832KG	304 pcs.	400.00	575.00	800.00
	1833KG	424 pcs.	300.00	425.00	600.00

50 ZLOTYCH

9.7800 gm., .916 GOLD, .289 oz AGW

103	1817IB	.017	300.00	375.00	500.00
	1818IB	.050	300.00	375.00	500.00
	1819IB	.020	400.00	550.00	800.00

Obv: Small head

103a	1819IB	Inc. Ab.	400.00	550.00	800.00
	1820IB	7,098	300.00	375.00	500.00
	1821IB	2,638	400.00	550.00	800.00
	1822IB	1,610	300.00	375.00	500.00
	1823IB	251 pcs.	400.00	550.00	800.00

119	1827FH	237 pcs.	—	Rare	—
	1829FH	1,890	400.00	550.00	750.00

TRADE COINS

DUCAT

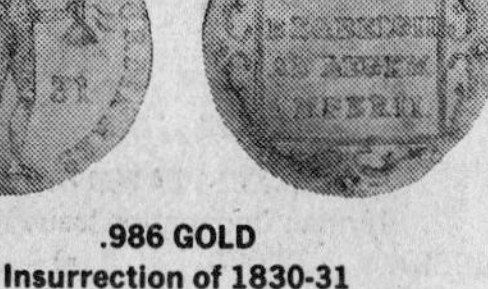

.986 GOLD
Insurrection of 1830-31

Obv: Small eagle to right of head of standing knight.

C#	Date	Mintage	Fine	VF	XF
125	1831	.156	200.00	275.00	350.00

World War I Occupation Coinage

Germany released a 1, 2 and 3 Kopek coinage series in 1916 which circulated during their occupation of Poland. They will be found listed as Germany A18, B18 and C18.

German-Austrian Regency

(100 Fenigow = 1 Marka

FENIG

IRON

Y#	Date	Mintage	VF	XF	Unc
4	1918FF	51.484	6.00	11.50	18.50

5 FENIGOW

IRON

5	1917FF	18.700	1.75	2.00	3.50
	1917FF	—	—	Proof	80.00
	1918FF	22.690	1.75	2.00	3.50

Obv: German Y#21. Rev: Muling of Y#6.

5.1	1917FF	—	100.00	150.00	200.00

10 FENIGOW

IRON

6	1917FF obverse inscription touches edge				
		33.000	15.00	20.00	25.00
	1917FF	—	—	Proof	85.00
	1917FF obverse inscription away from edge				
		—	1.50	3.00	7.00
	1918FF obverse inscription touches edge				
		14.990	1.50	3.00	7.00
	1918FF obverse inscription away from edge				
		—	1.50	3.00	7.00

ZINC

6a	1917FF	—	40.00	50.00	70.00

Mule, obv. of German 10 Pfennig, Y#22.
Rev. of Poland 10 Fenigow, Y#6.

6.1	1917FF	—	100.00	150.00	200.00

20 FENIGOW

IRON

7	1917FF	1.900	4.00	5.00	6.00
	1918FF	19.260	2.00	3.00	4.00

ZINC

Y#	Date	Mintage	VF	XF	Unc
7a	1917FF	—	—	—	—

REPUBLIC ISSUES

100 Groszy = 1 Zloty

GROSZ

BRASS

8	1923	30.000	.50	.75	1.50

BRONZE

8a	1925(w)	40.000	.50	.75	1.50
	1927(w)	17.000	.50	.75	1.50
	1928(w)	13.600	.50	.75	1.50
	1930(w)	22.500	.50	.75	1.50
	1931(w)	9.000	1.00	1.25	1.50
	1932(w)	12.000	.50	.75	1.50
	1933(w)	7.000	.50	.75	1.50
	1934(w)	5.900	1.00	1.25	2.50
	1935(w)	7.300	1.50	1.75	3.00
	1936(w)	12.600	.50	.75	1.50
	1937(w)	17.370	.50	.75	1.50
	1938(w)	20.530	.50	.75	1.50
	1939(w)	12.000	.50	.75	1.50

Rev: 21.V below GROSZ, 1.5 gm.

8a.1	1925(w)	1,000	3.50	6.00	10.00

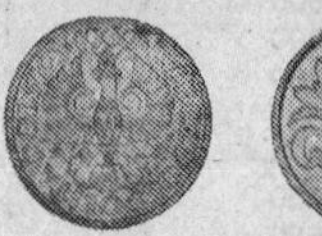

ZINC
German Occupation Issue W W II

34	1939	33.909	1.00	1.25	1.75

ALUMINUM

39	1949	400.116	.05	.10	.15

2 GROSZE

YELLOW BRONZE

9	1923	20.500	.60	1.00	3.00

BRONZE

9a	1923	Inc. Ab.	.40	.60	1.75
	1925(w)	39.000	.40	.60	1.75
	1927(w)	15.300	.40	.60	1.75
	1928(w)	13.400	.40	.60	1.75
	1930(w)	20.000	.40	.60	1.75
	1931(w)	9.500	.40	.60	1.75
	1932(w)	6.500	.40	.60	1.75
	1933(w)	7.000	1.50	1.75	2.50
	1934(w)	9.350	.40	.60	1.50
	1935(w)	5.800	.40	.75	1.75
	1936(w)	5.800	.40	.60	1.50
	1937(w)	17.360	.40	.60	1.50
	1938(w)	20.530	.40	.60	1.50
	1939(w)	12.000	.40	.60	1.50

Rev: 27x26 below GROSZE, 2.47 gm.

Y#	Date	Mintage	VF	XF	Unc
9a.1	1926	600 pcs.	8.00	13.50	22.50

ALUMINUM

Y#	Date	Mintage	VF	XF	Unc
40	1949	300.106	.05	.10	.25

5 GROSZY

YELLOW-BRONZE

Y#	Date	Mintage	VF	XF	Unc
10	1923	32.150	1.25	1.75	4.00

BRONZE

Y#	Date	Mintage	VF	XF	Unc
10a	1923	350 pcs.	.20	.40	1.50
	1925(w)	45.500	.40	.50	3.00
	1928(w)	8.900	.40	.50	3.00
	1930(w)	14.200	.40	.60	3.00
	1931(w)	1.500	.40	.60	3.00
	1934(w)	.420	1.50	2.00	5.00
	1935(w)	4.660	.40	.60	1.75
	1936(w)	4.660	.40	.60	1.75
	1937(w)	9.050	.40	.60	1.75
	1938(w)	17.300	.40	.60	1.75
	1939(w)	10.000	.40	.60	1.75

Rev: 12/IV SW 24 below GROSZY, 3 gm.

Y#	Date	Mintage	VF	XF	Unc
10a.1	1923	500 pcs.	6.00	10.00	18.00

2nd Polish Numismatic and Medallographic Society Meeting At Posen On June 3, 1929

Y#	Date	Mintage	VF	XF	Unc
	1929(w)	45 pcs.	60.00	75.00	150.00

ZINC
German Occupation Issue W W II

Y#	Date	Mintage	VF	XF	Unc
35	1939	15.324	3.50	4.00	5.00

BRONZE

Y#	Date	Mintage	VF	XF	Unc
41	1949	300.000	.70	.80	1.00

ALUMINUM

Y#	Date	Mintage	VF	XF	Unc
41a	1949	200.000	.75	.85	1.00

Y#	Date	Mintage	VF	XF	Unc
A46	1958	53.521	.05	.10	.20
	1959	28.563	.05	.10	.15
	1960	12.246	.05	.10	.20
	1961	29.502	.05	.10	.20
	1962	90.257	.05	.10	.15
	1963	20.878	.05	.10	.15
	1965MW	5.050	.05	.10	.20
	1967MW	10.056	.05	.10	.20
	1968MW	10.196	.05	.10	.20
	1970MW	20.095	.10	.15	.20
	1971MW	20.220	.10	.15	.20
	1971	—	.10	.15	.20
	1972	10.000	.10	.15	.20

10 GROSZY

NICKEL

Y#	Date	Mintage	VF	XF	Unc
11	1923	100.200	.45	.80	1.25

ZINC
German Occupation Issue W W II

Y#	Date	Mintage	VF	XF	Unc
36	1923	42.175	.20	.30	1.50

Above piece actually struck in 1941-44.

COPPER-NICKEL

Y#	Date	Mintage	VF	XF	Unc
42	1949	200.000	.40	.60	1.00

ALUMINUM

Y#	Date	Mintage	VF	XF	Unc
42a	1949	31.047	.20	.30	.60

Y#	Date	Mintage	VF	XF	Unc
AA47	1961	73.400	.05	.10	.25
	1962	25.362	.05	.10	.25
	1963	40.434	.05	.10	.25
	1965	50.521	.05	.10	.15
	1965MW	—	.05	.10	.25
	1966MW	70.749	.05	.10	.25
	1967MW	62.059	.05	.10	.25
	1968	62.204	.05	.10	.15
	1968MW	—	.05	.10	.25
	1969	71.566	.05	.10	.25
	1969MW	—	.05	.10	.25
	1970MW	38.844	.05	.10	.25
	1971MW	50.140	.05	.10	.25
	1972	60.000	.05	.10	.25
	1972MW	Inc. Ab.	.05	.10	.25
	1973MW	8.000	.05	.10	.25
	1974	50.000	—	—	.20
	1974MW	Inc. Ab.	—	—	.20
	1975	50.000	—	—	.15
	1975MW	Inc. Ab.	—	—	.15
	1976MW	—	—	—	.10
	1977MW	—	—	—	.10
	1978MW	—	—	—	—

20 GROSZY

NICKEL

Y#	Date	Mintage	VF	XF	Unc
12	1923	150.000	.75	1.25	2.00

ZINC
German Occupation Issue W W II

Y#	Date	Mintage	VF	XF	Unc
37	1923	40.025	.25	.50	1.50

Above piece actually struck in 1941-44.

COPPER-NICKEL

Y#	Date	Mintage	VF	XF	Unc
43	1949	133.383	.60	.75	1.00

ALUMINUM

Y#	Date	Mintage	VF	XF	Unc
43a	1949	197.472	.30	.50	.65

Y#	Date	Mintage	VF	XF	Unc
A47	1957	3.940	.05	.15	.35
	1961	53.108	.05	.15	.35
	1962	19.140	.05	.15	.35
	1963	41.217	.05	.15	.35
	1965MW	32.022	.05	.15	.25
	1966MW	23.860	.05	.15	.35
	1967MW	29.099	.05	.15	.35
	1968MW	29.191	.05	.15	.35
	1969	40.227	.05	.15	.35
	1969MW	—	.05	.15	.35
	1970MW	20.028	.05	.15	.35
	1971MW	20.000	.05	.15	.35
	1972	60.000	.05	.15	.35
	1972MW	—	.05	.15	.35
	1973	50.000	—	—	.15
	1973MW	15.000	—	—	.15
	1975MW	50.000	—	—	—
	1976MW lg. date	—	—	—	.10
	1976MW sm. date	—	—	—	—
	1977MW	—	—	—	—

50 GROSZY

NICKEL

Y#	Date	Mintage	VF	XF	Unc
13	1923	101.200	1.00	1.25	3.00

NICKEL PLATED IRON
German Occupation Issue W W II

Y#	Date	Mintage	VF	XF	Unc
38	1938	32.000	2.00	3.50	4.50

COPPER-NICKEL

Y#	Date	Mintage	VF	XF	Unc
44	1949	109.000	1.00	1.50	2.25

ALUMINUM

Y#	Date	Mintage	VF	XF	Unc
44a	1949	59.393	.40	.50	.75

Y#	Date	Mintage	VF	XF	Unc
48	1957	91.316	.15	.30	.50
	1965MW	22.090	.15	.30	.50
	1967MW	2.065	.15	.30	.50
	1968MW	2.027	.15	.30	.60
	1970MW	3.273	.15	.30	.60
	1971MW	7.000	.15	.30	.60
	1972MW	10.000	.15	.30	.60
	1973MW	39.000	.10	.25	.50
	1974	33.000	.10	.25	.50
	1974MW	—	.10	.25	.50
	1975	25.000	.10	.25	.40
	1975MW	—	.10	.20	.40
	1976	—	.10	.20	.40
	1977MW	—	—	—	—

ZLOTY

5.0000 gm., .750 SILVER, .1206 oz ASW

Y#	Date	Mintage	VF	XF	Unc
15	1924 (Paris) torches at sides of date				
		16.000	BV	4.00	7.00
	1925 (London) dot after date				
		24.000	BV	4.00	7.00

NICKEL

Y#	Date	Mintage	VF	XF	Unc
14	1929	32.000	1.00	1.75	5.00

COPPER-NICKEL

Y#	Date	Mintage	VF	XF	Unc
45	1949	87.053	2.00	2.50	3.00

ALUMINUM

Y#	Date	Mintage	VF	XF	Unc
45a	1949	43.000	.20	1.00	1.25

Y#	Date	Mintage	VF	XF	Unc
49	1957	58.631	.25	.35	.75
	1965	15.015	.25	.35	.75
	1965MW	—	.25	.35	.75

Y#	Date	Mintage	VF	XF	Unc
49	1966MW	18.185	.25	.35	.75
	1967MW	1.002	.25	.35	.75
	1968MW	1.176	.25	.35	.75
	1969MW	3.024	.20	.30	.60
	1970MW	6.016	.20	.30	.60
	1971	6.110	.15	.25	.50
	1971MW	—	.20	.30	.60
	1972	7.000	.15	.25	.50
	1972MW	—	.20	.30	.60
	1973MW	15.000	.10	.25	.50
	1974MW	42.000	.10	.25	.50
	1975	—	.15	.30	.60
	1975MW	25.000	.10	.20	.40
	1976	—	.15	.25	.50
	1977MW	—	.10	.15	.25
	1978MW	—	.10	.15	.25

2 ZLOTE

10.0000 gm., .750 SILVER, .2411 oz ASW

Y#	Date	Mintage	VF	XF	Unc
16	1924 (Paris) torches at sides of date				
		8.200	BV	9.00	20.00
	1924H Birmingham				
		1.200	25.00	40.00	60.00
	1924 (Philadelphia) no torches				
		.800	17.50	20.00	40.00
	1925 (London) dot after date				
		11.000	BV	12.50	17.50
	1925(Philadelphia)				
		5.200	30.00	45.00	65.00

4.400 gm., .750 SILVER, .1061 .OZ ASW

Y#	Date	Mintage	VF	XF	Unc
20	1932	15.700	BV	4.00	10.00
	1933	9.250	BV	4.00	10.00
	1934	.250	BV	4.00	10.00

Y#	Date	Mintage	VF	XF	Unc
27	1934	10.425	BV	6.50	20.00
	1936	.075	BV	4.00	10.00

Y#	Date	Mintage	VF	XF	Unc
30	1936	3.918	BV	4.00	8.00

ALUMINUM

Y#	Date	Mintage	VF	XF	Unc
46	1958	83.640	.50	.60	.75
	1959	7.170	.50	.60	.75
	1960	36.131	.20	.40	.75
	1970	2.014	.20	.40	.75
	1971	3.050	.20	.40	.75
	1971MW	—	.20	.40	.75
	1972	5.000	.20	.40	.75

Y#	Date	Mintage	VF	XF	Unc
46	1972MW	—	.20	.40	.75
	1973MW	10.000	.20	.35	.65
	1974	—	.15	.35	.65
	1974MW	46.000	.15	.30	.60

BRASS, 21mm

Y#	Date	Mintage	VF	XF	Unc
80	1975	25.000	—	—	1.25
	1976	—	—	—	.50
	1977	—	—	—	.50
	1978	—	—	—	.50
	1978MW	—	—	—	.50
	1979MW	—	—	—	.40

5 ZLOTYCH

25.0000 gm., .900 SILVER, .7234 oz ASW

Y#	Date	Mintage	XF	Unc	Proof
17	1925	1,000	200.00	300.00	400.00
	Without mintmark				
	1925	1,000	200.00	300.00	400.00

18.0000 gm., .750 SILVER, .434 oz ASW

Y#	Date	Mintage	VF	XF	Unc
18	1928 (Warsaw) conjoined arrow and 'K' mintmark				
		7.260	20.00	30.00	50.00
	1928 error 'SUPRMA' edge inscription				
		Inc. Ab.	75.00	100.00	225.00
	1928 (London) no mintmark				
		4.300	20.00	30.00	50.00
	1930	5.900	22.50	35.00	60.00
	1931	2.200	25.00	45.00	70.00
	1932	3.100	65.00	100.00	175.00

1830 Revolution Commemorative

Y#	Date	Mintage	VF	XF	Unc
19	1930	1.000	20.00	30.00	55.00

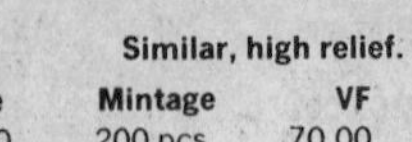

Similar, high relief.

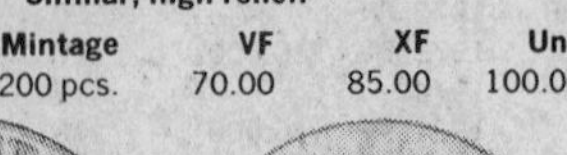

Y#	Date	Mintage	VF	XF	Unc
19	1930	200 pcs.	70.00	85.00	100.00

11.0000 gm., .750 SILVER, .2652 oz ASW

Y#	Date	Mintage	VF	XF	Unc
21	1932(Warsaw)				
		1.000	BV	8.50	13.50
	1932 (London) no mintmark				
		3.000	BV	8.50	13.50
	1933	11.000	BV	8.00	13.50
	1934	.250	BV	8.50	13.50

Rifle Corps Aug. 6, 1914

Y#	Date	Mintage	VF	XF	Unc
25	1934	.300	BV	10.00	20.00

Y#	Date	Mintage	VF	XF	Unc
28	1934	6.510	BV	8.50	13.50
	1935	1.800	BV	8.50	13.50
	1936	1.000	BV	8.50	13.50
	1938	.289	BV	8.50	15.00

Y#	Date	Mintage	VF	XF	Unc
31	1936	1.800	BV	10.00	15.00

ALUMINUM

Y#	Date	Mintage	VF	XF	Unc
47	1958	1.328	10.00	14.00	20.00
	1959	56.811	.50	.75	1.25
	1960	16.301	.50	.75	1.00
	1971MW	1.000	.40	.70	.85
	1972	3.000	.40	.70	.85
	1973MW	—	.35	.70	.85
	1974	—	.35	.65	.90
	1974MW	—	.30	.65	.85
	1976	—	.30	.60	.80

BRASS, 24mm

Y#	Date	Mintage	VF	XF	Unc
81	1975	—	.75	.85	1.25
	1976	—	.65	.75	1.00

Y#	Date	Mintage	VF	XF	Unc
81	1977	—	.65	.75	1.00

10 ZLOTYCH

3.2258 gm., .900 GOLD, .0933 oz AGW
Boleslaus I

Y#	Date	Mintage	VF	XF	Unc
32	1925	.050	BV	65.00	75.00

22.0000 .GM., .750 SILVER, .5305 oz ASW

Y#	Date	Mintage	VF	XF	Unc
22	1932(Warsaw)				
		3.100	BV	17.00	20.00
	1932 (London) no mintmark				
		6.000	BV	17.00	20.00
	1933	3.400	BV	17.00	20.00
	1933	—	—	Proof	—

250th Anniversary Relief Of Vienna
Obv: Similar to Y#22.

Y#	Date	Mintage	VF	XF	Unc
23	1933	.300	BV	22.50	45.00
	1933	—	—	Proof	—

1863 Insurrection
Obv: Similar to Y#22.

Y#	Date	Mintage	VF	XF	Unc
24	1933	.300	BV	22.50	45.00
	1933	—	—	Proof	—

Rifle Corps Aug. 6, 1914

Y#	Date	Mintage	VF	XF	Unc
26	1934	.300	BV	17.50	30.00

Obv: Similar to Y#26.

Y#	Date	Mintage	VF	XF	Unc
29	1934	.200	25.00	30.00	40.00
	1935	1.670	BV	17.00	20.00
	1936	2.130	BV	17.00	20.00
	1937	.908	BV	17.00	20.00
	1938	.234	BV	17.00	25.00
	1939	—	BV	17.00	20.00

COPPER-NICKEL
Tadeusz Kosciuszko

Y#	Date	Mintage	VF	XF	Unc
50	1959	13.107	.60	1.00	1.75
	1960	27.551	.75	1.00	2.50
	1966	4.157	.60	1.00	1.75
	1966MW	—	.60	1.00	1.75

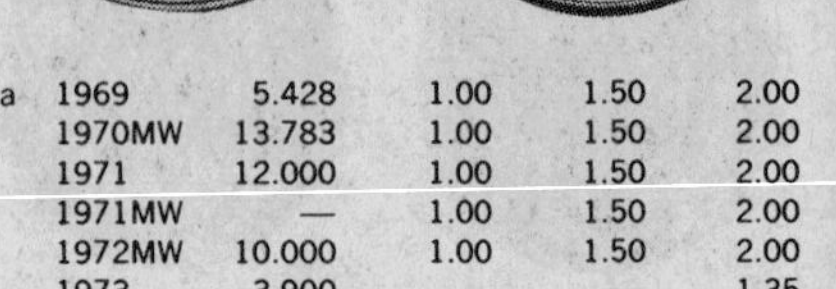

Y#	Date	Mintage	VF	XF	Unc
50a	1969	5.428	1.00	1.50	2.00
	1970MW	13.783	1.00	1.50	2.00
	1971	12.000	1.00	1.50	2.00
	1971MW	—	1.00	1.50	2.00
	1972MW	10.000	1.00	1.50	2.00
	1973	3.900	—	—	1.35

Mikolaj Kopernik

Y#	Date	Mintage	VF	XF	Unc
51	1959	12.559	1.50	2.00	3.00
	1965MW	3.000	1.50	2.00	3.00

Y#	Date	Mintage	VF	XF	Unc
51a	1967MW	2.128	.75	1.25	2.00
	1968	9.389	.75	1.25	2.00
	1969MW	8.612	.75	1.25	2.00

600th Anniversary Of Jagiello University
Legends raised

52	1964	2.612	.60	1.50	2.50

Legends incuse

52a	1964	2.610	.60	1.00	2.50

700th Anniversary Of Warsaw

54	1965	3.492	.60	1.00	2.50

700th Anniversary Of Warsaw

55	1965	2.000	.60	1.00	2.50

200th Anniversary Of Warsaw Mint

56	1966	.102	2.50	3.00	3.50

The above piece comes with two varieties of inscriptions.

General Swierczewski

Y#	Date	Mintage	VF	XF	Unc
58	1967MW	2.000	1.00	1.65	2.00

Marie Curie Centennial

59	1967MW	2.000	.50	.80	2.00

25th Anniversary Peoples Army

60	1968MW	2.000	.50	.80	2.00

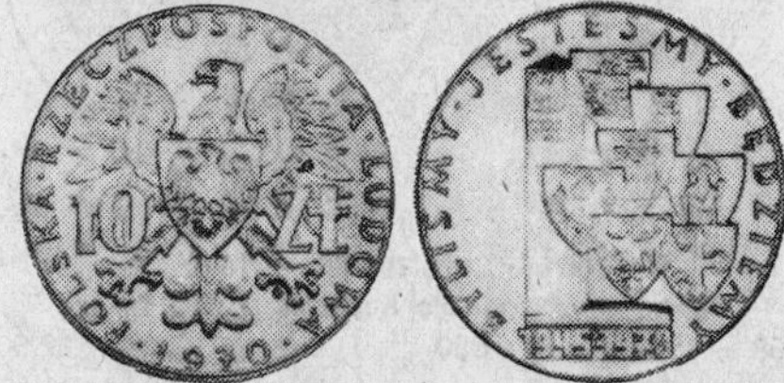

25th Anniversary Peoples Republic

61	1969MW	2.000	.50	.80	2.00

25th Anniversary Provincial Annexations

62	1970MW	2.000	.50	.80	2.00

F. A. O. Issue

63	1971MW	2.000	.50	.80	2.00

Battle Of Upper Silesia 50th Anniversary

64	1971MW	2.000	.50	.80	2.00

50th Anniversary Gdynia Seaport

Y#	Date	Mintage	VF	XF	Unc
65	1972MW	2.001	.50	.80	2.00

Boleslaw Prus

73	1975MW	35.000	.65	1.50	2.00
	1976MW	—	—	—	—

Adam Mickiewicz

74	1975MW	35.000	.65	1.50	2.00
	1976MW	—	—	—	—

20 ZLOTYCH

6.4516 gm., .900 GOLD, .1867 oz AGW
Boleslaus I

33	1925	.027	BV	125.00	150.00

COPPER-NICKEL

67	1973	25.000	.75	1.50	2.50
	1974	12.000	—	—	—
	1976	—	—	—	—

Marceli Nowotko

69	1974MW	10.000	—	—	—
	1975	10.000	.75	1.00	2.00
	1976	—	—	—	—
	1976MW	—	—	—	—

25th Anniversary Comcon

Y#	Date	Mintage	VF	XF	Unc
70	1974MW	2.000	.75	1.00	2.00

International Woman's Year

Y#	Date	Mintage	VF	XF	Unc
75	1975	1.900	1.75	2.50	2.00
	1975MW	—	1.75	2.50	2.00

Maria Konopnicka

Y#	Date	Mintage	VF	XF	Unc
95	1978	—	—	—	2.50

First Polish Cosmonaut

Y#	Date	Mintage	VF	XF	Unc
97	1978MW	—	—	—	2.50

Year of the Child

Y#	Date	Mintage	VF	XF	Unc
99	1979MW	—	—	—	2.50

50 ZLOTYCH

12.6400 gm., .750 SILVER, .3048 .OZ ASW
Fryderyk Chopin

Y#	Date	Mintage	VF	XF	Unc
66	1972	.050	BV	10.00	12.50
	1974	.010	BV	10.00	12.50

COPPER-NICKEL
Prince Mieszko I

Y#	Date	Mintage	VF	XF	Unc
100	1979	—	—	—	—

100 ZLOTYCH

20.1000 gm., .900 SILVER, .5816 oz ASW
Polish Millenium

Y#	Date	Mintage	VF	XF	Unc
57	1966	.198	BV	BV	17.50

16.5000 gm., .625 SILVER, .3316 oz ASW
Mikolaj Kopernik

Y#	Date	Mintage	VF	XF	Unc
68	1973	.050	BV	10.00	12.50
	1974	—	BV	10.00	11.50

Maria Sklodowska Curie

Y#	Date	Mintage	VF	XF	Unc
71	1974	.050	BV	10.00	12.50

Royal Castle In Warsaw

Y#	Date	Mintage	VF	XF	Unc
76	1975	.100	BV	10.00	13.00

Ignacy Jan Paderewski

Y#	Date	Mintage	VF	XF	Unc
77	1975	.060	BV	10.00	14.00

Helena Modrzejewska

Y#	Date	Mintage	VF	XF	Unc
78	1975	.060	BV	10.00	14.00

Tadeusz Kosciuszko

Y#	Date	Mintage	VF	XF	Unc
82	1976	.100	BV	10.00	14.00

Kazimierz Pulaski

Y#	Date	Mintage	VF	XF	Unc
84	1976	.100	BV	10.00	12.00

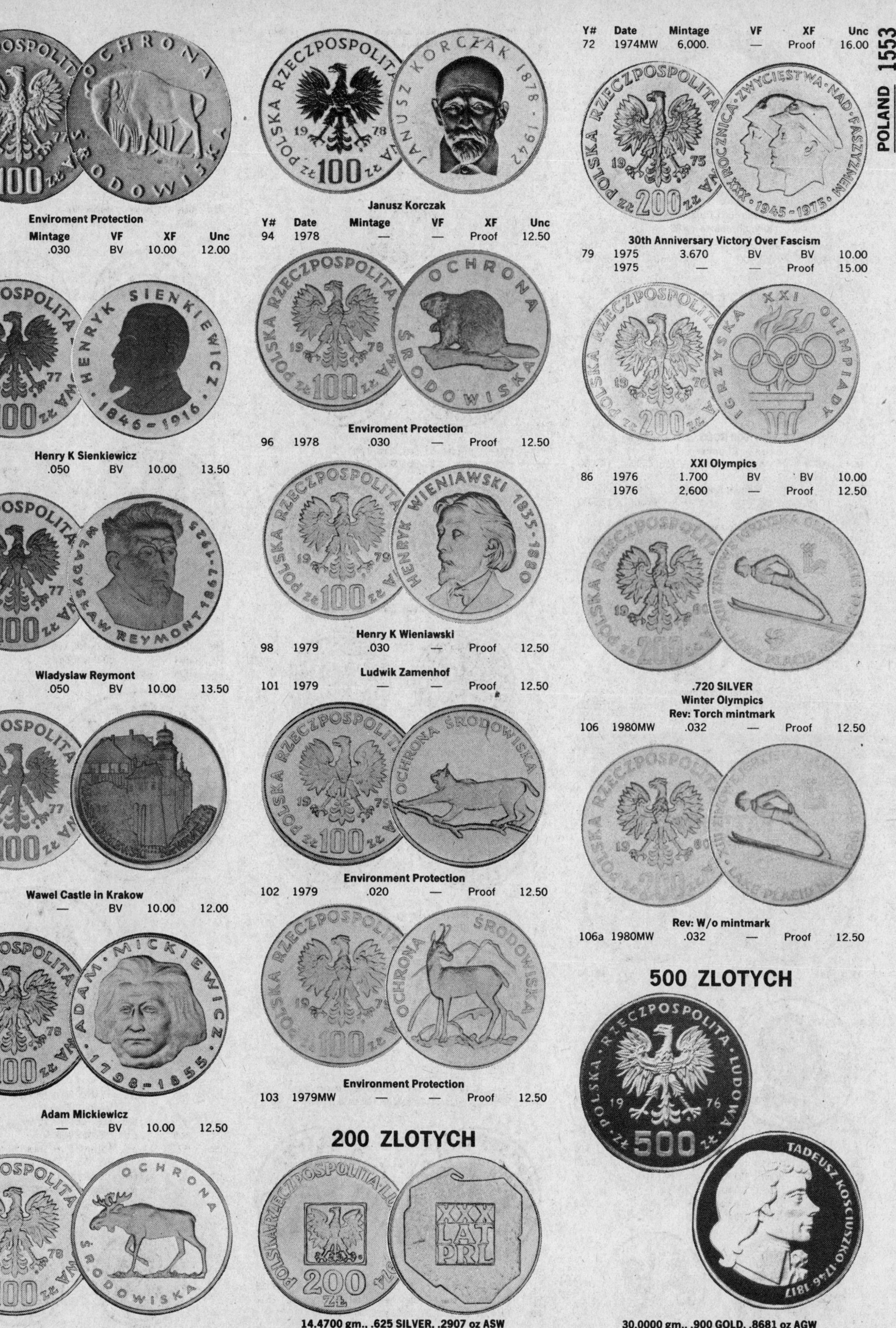

Enviroment Protection

Y#	Date	Mintage	VF	XF	Unc
87	1977	.030	BV	10.00	12.00

Henry K Sienkiewicz

Y#	Date	Mintage	VF	XF	Unc
88	1977	.050	BV	10.00	13.50

Wladyslaw Reymont

Y#	Date	Mintage	VF	XF	Unc
89	1977	.050	BV	10.00	13.50

Wawel Castle in Krakow

Y#	Date	Mintage	VF	XF	Unc
91	1978	—	BV	10.00	12.00

Adam Mickiewicz

Y#	Date	Mintage	VF	XF	Unc
92	1978	—	BV	10.00	12.50

Environment Protection

Y#	Date	Mintage	VF	XF	Unc
93	1978	—	BV	10.00	12.50

Janusz Korczak

Y#	Date	Mintage	VF	XF	Unc
94	1978	—	—	Proof	12.50

Enviroment Protection

Y#	Date	Mintage	VF	XF	Unc
96	1978	.030	—	Proof	12.50

Henry K Wieniawski

Y#	Date	Mintage	VF	XF	Unc
98	1979	.030	—	Proof	12.50

Ludwik Zamenhof

Y#	Date	Mintage	VF	XF	Unc
101	1979	—	—	Proof	12.50

Environment Protection

Y#	Date	Mintage	VF	XF	Unc
102	1979	.020	—	Proof	12.50

Environment Protection

Y#	Date	Mintage	VF	XF	Unc
103	1979MW	—	—	Proof	12.50

200 ZLOTYCH

14.4700 gm., .625 SILVER, .2907 oz ASW
30th Anniversary Polish People's Republic

Y#	Date	Mintage	VF	XF	Unc
72	1974MW	13.600	BV	BV	9.00
72	1974MW	6,000.	—	Proof	16.00

30th Anniversary Victory Over Fascism

Y#	Date	Mintage	VF	XF	Unc
79	1975	3.670	BV	BV	10.00
	1975	—	—	Proof	15.00

XXI Olympics

Y#	Date	Mintage	VF	XF	Unc
86	1976	1.700	BV	BV	10.00
	1976	2,600	—	Proof	12.50

.720 SILVER
Winter Olympics
Rev: Torch mintmark

Y#	Date	Mintage	VF	XF	Unc
106	1980MW	.032	—	Proof	12.50

Rev: W/o mintmark

Y#	Date	Mintage	VF	XF	Unc
106a	1980MW	.032	—	Proof	12.50

500 ZLOTYCH

30.0000 gm., .900 GOLD, .8681 oz AGW
Tadeusz Kosciuszko

Y#	Date	Mintage	VF	XF	Unc
83	1976	3,000	BV	600.00	650.00

Kazimierz Pulaski
Rev: Similar to Y#83

Y#	Date	Mintage	VF	XF	Unc
85	1976	3,000	BV	600.00	650.00

2000 ZLOTYCH

8.0000 gm., .900 GOLD, .2315 oz AGW

Y#	Date	Mintage	VF	XF	Unc
		Chopin			
90	1977	4,000	—Proof Only		165.00
		Mikolaj Kopernik			
104	1979	—	—	Proof	165.00
		Maria Sklodowska Curie			
105	1979	—	—	Proof	165.00
		Winter Olympics			
107	1980MW	7,500	—	Proof	165.00

NCLT ISSUES

PATTERNS

KM#	Date	Mintage	Identification	Mkt.Val.
1	1919	—	50 Groszy, Nickel	—
2	1922	60 pcs.	100 Marek, Copper, 8.84 gm.	175.00
2a	1922	100 pcs.	100 Marek, Bronze, 8.84 gm.	80.00
2b	1922	10 pcs.	100 Marek, Brass, 8.84 gm.	—
2c	1922	4 pcs.	100 Marek, Tin, 4.57 gm.	—
2d	1922	50 pcs.	100 Marek, Silver, 8.80 gm.	175.00
2e	1922	3 Pcs.	100 Marek, Gold	—
3	1923	120 pcs.	50 Marek, Brass, 5.13 gm.	80.00

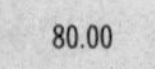

KM#	Date	Mintage	Identification	Mkt.Val.
3a	1923	12 pcs.	50 Marek, Silver, 5.25 gm.	—
3b	1923	—	50 Marek, Gold	—
4	1923	30 pcs.	1 Grosz, Bronze, 5.13 gm.	50.00

KM#	Date	Mintage	Identification	Mkt.Val.
5	1923	125 pcs.	2 Grosze, Bronze, 1.56 gm.	50.00
5a	1923	—	2 Grosze, Gold	—
6	1923	10 pcs.	5 Groszy, Brass, 3 gm.	—
6a	1923	100 pcs.	5 Groszy, Silver, 3.29 gm.	80.00
7	1923	3 pcs.	5 Groszy, Brass	125.00
8	1923	30 pcs.	20 Groszy, Brass, 4.52 gm.	60.00
9	1923	30 pcs.	50 Groszy, Brass	—
8a	1924	10 pcs.	20 Groszy, Nickel, 3 gm.	—

KM#	Date	Mintage	Identification	Mkt.Val.
10	1924	15 pcs.	1 Zloty, Silver, ESSAI on reverse, 5 gm.	—
10a	1924	8 pcs.	1 Zloty, Silver H mintmark on reverse	—

KM#	Date	Mintage	Identification	Mkt.Val.
11	1924r	40 pcs.	2 Zlote, Brass, 9.65 gm.	175.00
11a	1924r	100 pcs.	2 Zlote, Silver, rotated dies, 10 gm.	65.00
11b	1924r,	15 pcs.	2 Zlote, Silver, ESSAI on reverse, Paris Mint	—
11c	1924r	60 pcs.	2 Zlote, Silver, H mintmark	140.00
11d	1924r	10 pcs.	2 Zlote, Silver, Warsaw Mint	—

KM#	Date	Mintage	Identification	Mkt.Val.
12	1924	3 pcs.	2 Zlote, Silver, larger eagle	—

KM#	Date	Mintage	Identification	Mkt.Val.
13	1924	120 pcs.	20 Zlotych, Bronze, 3.95 gm.	100.00
13a	1924	10 pcs.	20 Zlotych, Silver, 5.69 gm.	225.00
13b	1924	10 pcs.	20 Zlotych, Gold	—

KM#	Date	Mintage	Identification	Mkt.Val.
14	1924	105 pcs.	50 Zlotych, Copper, 10.42 gm.	100.00
14a	1924	2 pcs.	50 Zlotych, Lead, 7.8 gm.	—
14b	1924	2 pcs.	50 Zlotych, Aluminum, 2.8 gm.	—
14c	1924	—	50 Zlotych, Gold	—
5c	1925	15 pcs.	5 Groszy, Bronze	—

KM#	Date	Mintage	Identification	Mkt.Val.
15	1925	60 pcs.	5 Zlotych, Brass, 100 pearls in circle on reverse, 21.5 gm.	250.00
15a	1925	1,000	5 Zlotych, Silver, 25 gm.	425.00
15b	1925	2 pcs.	5 Zlotych, Gold	—
15c	1925	100 pcs.	5 Zlotych, Silver, SW and WG monograms and 3/V, 25 gm.	600.00
15d	1925	2 pcs.	5 Zlotych, Gold	—
15c	1925	100 pcs.	5 Zlotych, Tombak, 81 pearls in circle, 21.32 gm.	250.00

KM#	Date	Mintage	Identification	Mkt.Val.
16	1925	154 pcs.	10 Zlotych, Bronze, 3.27 gm.	80.00

KM#	Date	Mintage	Identification	Mkt.Val.
17	1925	100 pcs.	10 Zlotych, Bronze, 3.31 gm.	90.00
17a	1925	50 pcs.	10 Zlotych, Silver, 4.37 gm.	125.00
17b	1925	—	10 Zlotych, Gold	—

KM#	Date	Mintage	Identification	Mkt.Val.
18	1925	105 pcs.	20 Zlotych, Bronze, 5.39 gm.	90.00
18a	1925	10 pcs.	20 Zlotych, Copper, 5.39 gm.	150.00
18b	1925	12 pcs.	20 Zlotych, Silver, 4.32 gm.	200.00
18c	1925	5 pcs.	20 Zlotych, Gold	—

KM#	Date	Mintage	Identification	Mkt.Val.
19	1925	35 pcs.	20 Zlotych, Bronze, 3.27 gm.	100.00
19a	1925	20 pcs.	20 Zlotych, Nickel, 3.5 gm.	100.00
19b	1925	900 pcs.	20 Zlotych, Gold, 6.451 gm.	250.00

KM#	Date	Mintage	Identification	Mkt.Val.
20	1925	100 pcs.	100 Zlotych, Bronze, 3.5 gm., Kopernik Commemorative	90.00
20a	1925	50 pcs.	100 Zlotych, Silver, 4.15 gm.	175.00
20b	1925	—	100 Zlotych, Gold	—

KM#	Date	Mintage	Identification	Mkt.Val.
22	1926	20 pcs.	2 Grosze, Nickel, 2.47 gm.	—
22a	1926	100 pcs.	2 Grosze, Silver, 2.29 gm.	80.00
4a	1927	100 pcs.	1 Grosz, Silver, 5.25 gm.	—
4b	1927	6 pcs.	1 Grosz, Gold	—
11c	1927r	100 pcs.	2 Zlote, Silver, Warsaw Mint	65.00

KM#	Date	Mintage	Identification	Mkt.Val.
23	1928	—	1 Zloty, Copper, 6.81 gm.	—
23a	1928	105 pcs.	1 Zloty, Bronze, 7.02 gm.	—
23b	1928	30 pcs.	1 Zloty, Nickel, 6.98 gm.	—

KM#	Date	Mintage	Identification	Mkt.Val.
24	1928	2 pcs.	1 Zloty, Copper, 6.98 gm.	—
24a	1928	125 pcs.	1 Zloty, Bronze, 6.9 gm.	55.00
24b	1928	8 pcs.	1 Zloty, Tombak, 6 gm.	—
24c	1928	15 pcs.	1 Zloty, Nickel, 7.07 gm.	—

KM#	Date	Mintage	Identification	Mkt.Val.
15f	1928	20 pcs.	5 Zlotych, Tombak, denticals instead of dots	450.00

KM#	Date	Mintage	Identification	Mkt.Val.
25	1929	10 pcs.	1 Zloty, Aluminum, 2.28 gm.	—
25a	1929	12 pcs.	1 Zloty, Bronze, 4.87 gm.	—

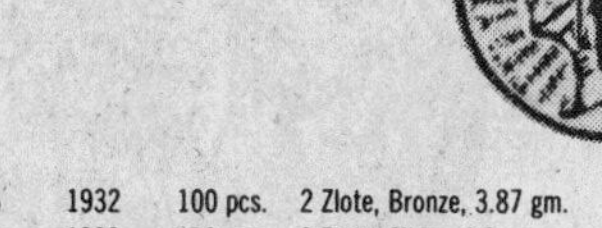

KM#	Date	Mintage	Identification	Mkt.Val.
26	1932	100 pcs.	2 Zlote, Bronze, 3.87 gm.	65.00
26a	1932	110 pcs.	2 Zlote, Silver, 4.4 gm.	60.00

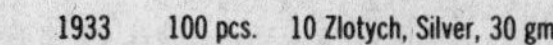

KM#	Date	Mintage	Identification	Mkt.Val.
27	1933	100 pcs.	10 Zlotych, Silver, 30 gm.	150.00

KM#	Date	Mintage	Identification	Mkt.Val.
28	1933	100 pcs.	10 Zlotych, Silver, 30 gm.	375.00

KM#	Date	Mintage	Identification	Mkt.Val.
29	1934	300 pcs.	10 Zlotych, Silver, 42 gm.	650.00

KM#	Date	Mintage	Identification	Mkt.Val.
30	1936	200 pcs.	5 Zlotych, Bronze, 17.46 gm.	300.00
30a	1936	200 pcs.	5 Zlotych, Silver, 20 gm.	600.00

KM#	Date	Mintage	Identification	Mkt.Val.
31	1958	5 pcs.	10 Zlotych, Aluminum	—

KM#	Date	Mintage	Identification	Mkt.Val.
32	1958	5 pcs.	10 Zlotych, Copper-Nickel	—

KM#	Date	Mintage	Identification	Mkt.Val.
33	1959	10 pcs.	10 Zlotych, Aluminum	35.00
32a	1960	10 pcs.	10 Zlotych, Aluminum	75.00
33a	1965	5 pcs.	10 Zlotych, Aluminum	—
33b	1967	17 pcs.	10 Zlotych, Aluminum, 28mm	—
33c	1968	10 pcs.	10 Zlotych, Aluminum, 28mm	—
33d	1970	5 pcs.	10 Zlotych, Aluminum, 28mm	—

KM#	Date	Mintage	Identification	Mkt.Val.
34	1974	20 pcs.	100 Zlotych, .625 Silver	—
35	1974	15,000	200 Zlotych, .625 Silver	8.00

PROBAS (Pr)

In Poland rejected coin designs are often minted in numbers from a few to many thousands for sale to collectors. These coins have the word PROBA on them. For more information see "An Illustrated Catalogue of Polish Coins 1916-1976", by Czeslaw Kaminski, published in Warsaw in 1977.

Standard metals unless otherwise stated.

KM#	Date	Mintage	Identification	Issue Price	Mkt. Val.
—	1925	25,000	100 Zlotych	—	—
—	1925	25,000	100 Zlotych, edge inscription: SALUS REIPUBLICAE SUPREMA LEX	—	—
Pr16	1927	100 pcs.	2 Zlote	—	65.00

KM#	Date	Mintage	Identification	Issue Price	Mkt. Val.
Pr17	1927	10 pcs.	2 Zlote, Bronze	—	—

KM#	Date	Mintage	Identification	Issue Price	Mkt. Val.
Pr18	1927	81 pcs.	5 Zlotych	—	225.00
—	1928	2 pcs.	1 Zloty, Copper	—	—
—	1928	2 pcs.	1 Zloty, Tombak	—	—
—	1928	25 pcs.	1 Zloty, Nickel	—	—

KM#	Date	Mintage	Identification	Issue Price	Mkt. Val.
—	1928	110 pcs.	1 Zloty, Nickel	—	50.00
—	1929	115 pcs.	1 Zloty	—	55.00
Pr19	1930	20 pcs.	5 Zlotych, Bronze	—	150.00
—	1932	100 pcs.	1 Zloty, Bronze	—	60.00
—	1932	120 pcs.	1 Zloty, Silver	—	75.00

KM#	Date	Mintage	Identification	Issue Price	Mkt. Val.
Pr22	1932	100 pcs.	10 Zlotych, 22 gm.	—	145.00
Pr22	1932	10 pcs.	10 Zlotych, Bronze	—	—
Pr22	1932	100 pcs.	10 Zlotych, 19.7 gm.	—	110.00
Pr21	1933	100 pcs.	5 Zlotych, Bronze	—	85.00
Pr21	1933	100 pcs.	5 Zlotych	—	100.00

KM#	Date	Mintage	Identification	Issue Price	Mkt. Val.
Pr23	1933	100 pcs.	10 Zlotych	—	175.00
Pr24	1933	100 pcs.	10 Zlotych	—	200.00

KM#	Date	Mintage	Identification	Issue Price	Mkt. Val.
Pr25	1934	100 pcs.	5 Zlotych, Bronze	—	85.00
Pr25a	1934	100 pcs.	5 Zlotych	—	100.00

KM#	Date	Mintage	Identification	Issue Price	Mkt. Val.
—	1934	2 pcs.	10 Zlotych, Aluminum, 22mm	—	125.00
—	1934	130 pcs.	10 Zlotych, Iron-Plated Nickel, 22mm	—	100.00
—	1934	3 pcs.	10 Zlotych, Tombak, 34mm	—	250.00

KM#	Date	Mintage	Identification	Issue Price	Mkt. Val.
—	1934	100 pcs.	10 Zlotych, 22 gm.	—	250.00
—	1934	3 pcs.	10 Zlotych, 15 gm.	—	350.00
Pr30	1936	100 pcs.	2 Zlote	—	60.00
Pr31	1936	110 pcs.	5 Zlotych	—	150.00
—	1980	3,500	200 Zlotych, .720 Silver	—	—
Pr11	1938	100 pcs.	10 Groszy, Bronze	—	90.00

KM#	Date	Mintage	Identification	Issue Price	Mkt. Val.
—	1938	100 pcs.	20 Groszy, Nickeled Iron	—	60.00
Pr38	1938	120 pcs.	50 Groszy, 23mm	—	50.00
Pr38	1938	10 pcs.	50 Groszy, Aluminum	—	—
Pr38	1938	100 pcs.	50 Groszy, 24.5mm	—	60.00
Pr13	1938	Unique	50 Groszy, Bronze	—	—

KM#	Date	Mintage	Identification	Issue Price	Mkt. Val.
—	1938	3 pcs.	50 Groszy, Aluminum	—	—
—	1938	200 pcs.	50 Groszy, Iron-Plated Nickel	—	35.00
Pr34	1939	200 pcs.	Grosz	—	35.00

KM#	Date	Mintage	Identification	Issue Price	Mkt. Val.
—	1939	200 pcs.	2 Grosze, Zinc	—	35.00
Pr35	1939	200 pcs.	5 Groszy	—	35.00

KM#	Date	Mintage	Identification	Issue Price	Mkt. Val.
Pr39	1949	100 pcs.	Grosz, Brass	—	—
Pr39	1949	500 pcs.	Grosz, Nickel	—	—

KM#	Date	Mintage	Identification	Issue Price	Mkt. Val.
Pr40	1949	100 pcs.	2 Grosze, Brass	—	35.00
Pr40	1949	500 pcs.	2 Grosze, Nickel	—	—

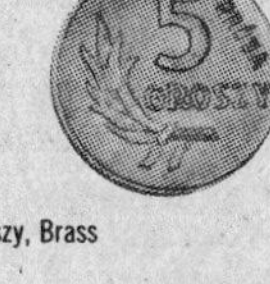

KM#	Date	Mintage	Identification	Issue Price	Mkt. Val.
Pr41	1949	100 pcs.	5 Groszy, Brass	—	60.00

KM#	Date	Mintage	Identification	Issue Price	Mkt. Val.
Pr41	1949	500 pcs.	5 Groszy, Nickel	—	—
Pr42	1949	100 pcs.	10 Groszy, Brass	—	—
Pr42	1949	500 pcs.	10 Groszy, Nickel	—	—
Pr43	1949	100 pcs.	20 Groszy, Brass	—	—
Pr43	1949	500 pcs.	20 Groszy, Nickel	—	—
Pr44	1949	100 pcs.	50 Groszy, Brass	—	—
Pr44	1949	20 pcs.	50 Groszy, Tombak	—	—
Pr44	1949	500 pcs.	50 Groszy, Nickel	—	—
Pr45	1949	100 pcs.	1 Zloty, Brass	—	60.00
Pr45	1949	500 pcs.	1 Zloty, Nickel	—	—
Pr43	1957	100 pcs.	20 Groszy, Brass	—	—

KM#	Date	Mintage	Identification	Issue Price	Mkt. Val.
Pr44	1957	100 pcs.	50 Groszy, Brass	—	—
Pr44	1957	500 pcs.	50 Groszy, Nickel	—	16.50

KM#	Date	Mintage	Identification	Issue Price	Mkt. Val.
Pr45	1957	100 pcs.	1 Zloty, Brass	—	60.00
Pr45	1957	500 pcs.	1 Zloty, Nickel	—	17.50
Pr45	1957	5 pcs.	1 Zloty, Copper-Nickel	—	—

KM#	Date	Mintage	Identification	Issue Price	Mkt. Val.
—	1958	212 pcs.	50 Groszy, Aluminum	—	30.00
—	1958	500 pcs.	50 Groszy, Nickel	—	—

KM#	Date	Mintage	Identification	Issue Price	Mkt. Val.
—	1958	245 pcs.	50 Groszy, Aluminum	—	30.00
—	1958	500 pcs.	50 Groszy, Nickel	—	—

KM#	Date	Mintage	Identification	Issue Price	Mkt. Val.
—	1958	198 pcs.	50 Groszy, Aluminum	—	30.00
—	1958	500 pcs.	50 Groszy, Nickel	—	—

KM#	Date	Mintage	Identification	Issue Price	Mkt. Val.
—	1958	234 pcs.	1 Zloty, Aluminum	—	35.00
—	1958	500 pcs.	1 Zloty, Nickel	—	—

KM#	Date	Mintage	Identification	Issue Price	Mkt. Val.
—	1958	235 pcs.	1 Zloty, Aluminum	—	35.00
—	1958	500 pcs.	1 Zloty, Nickel	—	—

KM#	Date	Mintage	Identification	Issue Price	Mkt. Val.
—	1958	211 pcs.	1 Zloty, Aluminum	—	35.00
—	1958	500 pcs.	1 Zloty, Nickel	—	—

KM#	Date	Mintage	Identification	Issue Price	Mkt. Val.
—	1958	210 pcs.	1 Zloty, Aluminum, Low Relief	—	35.00
—	1958	53 pcs.	1 Zloty, Aluminum, High Relief	—	150.00
—	1958	500 pcs.	1 Zloty, Nickel	—	—
Pr46	1958	100 pcs.	2 Zlote, Brass	—	60.00

KM#	Date	Mintage	Identification	Issue Price	Mkt. Val.
—	1958	5 pcs.	5 Zlotych, Brass	—	—
—	1958	20 pcs.	5 Zlotych, Aluminum	—	60.00
—	1958	500 pcs.	5 Zlotych, Nickel	—	60.00

KM#	Date	Mintage	Identification	Issue Price	Mkt. Val.
—	1958	10 pcs.	10 Zlotych, Aluminum	—	—
—	1958	5 pcs.	10 Zlotych, Brass	—	—
—	1958	5 pcs.	10 Zlotych, Copper-Nickel	—	—

KM#	Date	Mintage	Identification	Issue Price	Mkt. Val.
Pr46	1959	500 pcs.	2 Zlote, Nickel	—	—

KM#	Date	Mintage	Identification	Issue Price	Mkt. Val.
Pr47	1959	100 pcs.	5 Zlotych, Brass	—	67.50
Pr47a	1959	500 pcs.	5 Zlotych, Nickel	—	50.00

KM#	Date	Mintage	Identification	Issue Price	Mkt. Val.
—	1959	500 pcs.	5 Zlotych, Nickel	—	60.00

KM#	Date	Mintage	Identification	Issue Price	Mkt. Val.
—	1959	500 pcs.	5 Zlotych, Nickel	—	60.00

KM#	Date	Mintage	Identification	Issue Price	Mkt. Val.
—	1959	500 pcs.	10 Zlotych, Nickel	—	50.00
—	1960	500 pcs.	5 Zlotych, Nickel	—	60.00

KM#	Date	Mintage	Identification	Issue Price	Mkt. Val.
—	1960	500 pcs.	10 Zlotych, Nickel	—	65.00

KM#	Date	Mintage	Identification	Issue Price	Mkt. Val.
—	1960	500 pcs.	10 Zlotych, Nickel	—	55.00

KM#	Date	Mintage	Identification	Issue Price	Mkt. Val.
—	1960	500 pcs.	10 Zlotych, Nickel	—	50.00

KM#	Date	Mintage	Identification	Issue Price	Mkt. Val.
—	1960	10 pcs.	100 Zlotych, Copper-Nickel	—	—
—	1960	20 pcs.	100 Zlotych, .750 Silver	—	—
—	1960	500 pcs.	100 Zlotych, Nickel	—	35.00
—	1960	500 pcs.	100 Zlotych, Nickel	—	—

KM#	Date	Mintage	Identification	Issue Price	Mkt. Val.
—	1960	12 pcs.	100 Zlotych, .750 Silver	—	—
—	1960	14 pcs.	100 Zlotych, .700 Silver	—	—
—	1960	20 pcs.	100 Zlotych, Copper-Nickel	—	—
—	1960	500 pcs.	100 Zlotych, Nickel	—	—
—	1960	20 pcs.	100 Zlotych, .500 Silver	—	—

KM#	Date	Mintage	Identification	Issue Price	Mkt. Val.
—	1960	13 pcs.	100 Zlotych, .750 Silver	—	—
—	1960	500 pcs.	100 Zlotych, Nickel	—	—

KM#	Date	Mintage	Identification	Issue Price	Mkt. Val.
—	1960	5 pcs.	100 Zlotych, .750 Silver	—	—
—	1960	500 pcs.	100 Zlotych, Nickel	—	—

KM#	Date	Mintage	Identification	Issue Price	Mkt. Val.
—	1960	29 pcs.	100 Zlotych, .700 Silver	—	35.00
—	1960	500 pcs.	100 Zlotych, Nickel	—	—

KM#	Date	Mintage	Identification	Issue Price	Mkt. Val.
—	1960	12 pcs.	100 Zlotych, .750 Silver	—	35.00
—	1960	500 pcs.	100 Zlotych, Nickel	—	—

KM#	Date	Mintage	Identification	Issue Price	Mkt. Val.
—	1960	6 pcs.	100 Zlotych, .750 Silver	—	—
—	1960	500 pcs.	100 Zlotych, Nickel	—	—

KM#	Date	Mintage	Identification	Issue Price	Mkt. Val.
PrAA47	1962	500 pcs.	10 Groszy, Nickel	—	—

KM#	Date	Mintage	Identification	Issue Price	Mkt. Val.
PrA46	1963	500 pcs.	5 Groszy, Nickel	—	—

KM#	Date	Mintage	Identification	Issue Price	Mkt. Val.
PrA47	1963	500 pcs.	20 Groszy, Nickel	—	—

KM#	Date	Mintage	Identification	Issue Price	Mkt. Val.
Pr52	1964	125 pcs.	10 Zlotych, Raised Legend	—	60.00
Pr52	1964	500 pcs.	10 Zlotych, Nickel	—	25.00
Pr52a	1964	125 pcs.	10 Zlotych, Incuse Legend	—	60.00
Pr52a	1964	5 pcs.	10 Zlotych, Tombak	—	85.00
Pr52a	1964	500 pcs.	10 Zlotych, Nickel	—	35.00

KM#	Date	Mintage	Identification	Issue Price	Mkt. Val.
—	1964	.020	10 Zlotych, Copper-Nickel	—	8.00
—	1964	500 pcs.	10 Zlotych, Nickel	—	35.00

KM#	Date	Mintage	Identification	Issue Price	Mkt. Val.
—	1964	10 pcs.	10 Zlotych, Copper-Nickel	—	—
—	1964	500 pcs.	10 Zlotych, Nickel	—	35.00

KM#	Date	Mintage	Identification	Issue Price	Mkt. Val.
—	1964	10 pcs.	10 Zlotych, Copper-Nickel	—	—

KM#	Date	Mintage	Identification	Issue Price	Mkt. Val.
—	1964	10 pcs.	10 Zlotych, Copper-Nickel	—	—

KM#	Date	Mintage	Identification	Issue Price	Mkt. Val.
—	1964	20 pcs.	10 Zlotych, Copper-Nickel	—	—
—	1964	500 pcs.	10 Zlotych, Nickel	—	35.00

KM#	Date	Mintage	Identification	Issue Price	Mkt. Val.
—	1964	10 pcs.	10 Zlotych, Copper-Nickel	—	—

KM#	Date	Mintage	Identification	Issue Price	Mkt. Val.
—	1964	10 pcs.	10 Zlotych, Copper-Nickel	—	—
—	1964	500 pcs.	10 Zlotych, Nickel	—	35.00

KM#	Date	Mintage	Identification	Issue Price	Mkt. Val.
—	1964	10 pcs.	10 Zlotych, Copper-Nickel	—	—

KM#	Date	Mintage	Identification	Issue Price	Mkt. Val.
—	1964	20 pcs.	10 Zlotych, Copper-Nickel	—	—
—	1964	500 pcs.	10 Zlotych, Nickel	—	35.00

KM#	Date	Mintage	Identification	Issue Price	Mkt. Val.
—	1964	20 pcs.	20 Zlotych, Copper-Nickel	—	—
—	1964	500 pcs.	20 Zlotych, Nickel	—	—

KM#	Date	Mintage	Identification	Issue Price	Mkt. Val.
—	1964	20 pcs.	20 Zlotych, Copper-Nickel	—	—

KM#	Date	Mintage	Identification	Issue Price	Mkt. Val.
—	1964	20 pcs.	20 Zlotych, Copper-Nickel	—	—
—	1964	500 Pcs.	20 Zlotych, Nickel	—	35.00

KM#	Date	Mintage	Identification	Issue Price	Mkt. Val.
—	1964	20 pcs.	20 Zlotych, Copper-Nickel	—	—
—	1964	500 pcs.	20 Zlotych, Nickel	—	35.00

KM#	Date	Mintage	Identification	Issue Price	Mkt. Val.
—	1964	20 pcs.	20 Zlotych, Copper-Nickel	—	—

KM#	Date	Mintage	Identification	Issue Price	Mkt. Val.
—	1964	500 pcs.	20 Zlotych, Nickel	—	35.00
Pr54	1965	20 pcs.	10 Zlotych	—	—
Pr54	1965	500 pcs.	10 Zlotych, Nickel	—	35.00

KM#	Date	Mintage	Identification	Issue Price	Mkt. Val.
—	1965	20 pcs.	10 Zlotych, Copper-Nickel	—	—
—	1965	500 pcs.	10 Zlotych, Nickel	—	35.00

KM#	Date	Mintage	Identification	Issue Price	Mkt. Val.
—	1965	.030	10 Zlotych, Copper-Nickel	—	8.50
—	1965	500 pcs.	10 Zlotych, Nickel	—	35.00

KM#	Date	Mintage	Identification	Issue Price	Mkt. Val.
—	1965	.031	10 Zlotych, Copper-Nickel	—	8.50
—	1965	500 pcs.	10 Zlotych, Nickel	—	35.00
Pr55	1965	20 pcs.	10 Zlotych	—	—
Pr55	1965	500 pcs.	10 Zlotych, Nickel	—	35.00
Pr50a	1966	25 pcs.	10 Zlotych, Copper-Nickel	—	55.00
Pr50a	1966	500 pcs.	10 Zlotych, Nickel	—	55.00
Pr56	1966	500 pcs.	10 Zlotych, Nickel	—	35.00
—	1966	10 pcs.	100 Zlotych, Copper-Nickel	—	—
—	1966	10 pcs.	100 Zlotych, .750 Silver	—	40.00
Pr57	1966	500 pcs.	100 Zlotych, Nickel	—	—
—	1966	500 pcs.	100 Zlotych, Nickel	—	35.00
—	1966	.030	100 Zlotych, .900 Silver	—	20.00
Pr51a	1967	500 pcs.	10 Zlotych, Nickel	—	25.00

KM#	Date	Mintage	Identification	Issue Price	Mkt. Val.
Pr58	1967	10 pcs.	10 Zlotych, Plain Edge	—	—
Pr58	1967	10 pcs.	10 Zlotych, Milled Edge	—	—
Pr58	1967	500 pcs.	10 Zlotych, Nickel	—	35.00

KM#	Date	Mintage	Identification	Issue Price	Mkt. Val.
—	1967	20 pcs.	10 Zlotych, Copper-Nickel	—	—
—	1967	500 pcs.	10 Zlotych, Nickel	—	35.00
Pr59	1967	16 pcs.	10 Zlotych, Reeded Edge	—	—
Pr59	1967	10 pcs.	10 Zlotych, Plain Edge	—	—
Pr59	1967	500 pcs.	10 Zlotych, Nickel	—	35.00

KM#	Date	Mintage	Identification	Issue Price	Mkt. Val.
—	1967	25 pcs.	10 Zlotych, Copper-Nickel	—	—
—	1967	500 pcs.	10 Zlotych, Nickel	—	35.00

KM#	Date	Mintage	Identification	Issue Price	Mkt. Val.
—	1967	40 pcs.	10 Zlotych, Copper-Nickel	—	—
—	1967	500 pcs.	10 Zlotych, Nickel	—	35.00
Pr60	1968	20 pcs.	10 Zlotych	—	—
Pr60	1968	500 pcs.	10 Zlotych, Nickel	—	35.00
—	1969	20 pcs.	10 Zlotych, Gold	—	—
Pr61	1969	20 pcs.	10 Zlotych	—	—
Pr61	1969	20 pcs.	10 Zlotych, Gold	—	—
Pr61	1969	500 pcs.	10 Zlotych, Nickel	—	—
Pr61	1969	20 pcs.	10 Zlotych	—	—
Pr61	1969	500 pcs.	10 Zlotych, Nickel	—	—

KM#	Date	Mintage	Identification	Issue Price	Mkt. Val.
—	1969	20 pcs.	10 Zlotych, Copper-Nickel	—	—
—	1969	500 pcs.	10 Zlotych, Nickel	—	35.00

KM#	Date	Mintage	Identification	Issue Price	Mkt. Val.
—	1969	20 pcs.	10 Zlotych, Copper-Nickel	—	—
—	1969	500 pcs.	10 Zlotych, Nickel	—	35.00

KM#	Date	Mintage	Identification	Issue Price	Mkt. Val.
—	1970	20 pcs.	10 Zlotych, Copper-Nickel	—	—
—	1970	500 pcs.	10 Zlotych, Nickel	—	35.00
Pr62	1970	20 pcs.	10 Zlotych	—	—

KM#	Date	Mintage	Identification	Issue Price	Mkt. Val.
Pr62	1970	300 pcs.	10 Zlotych, Silver	—	50.00
Pr62	1970	500 pcs.	10 Zlotych, Nickel	—	35.00
Pr63	1971	20 pcs.	10 Zlotych	—	—
Pr63	1971	500 pcs.	10 Zlotych, Nickel	—	—

—	1971	.051	10 Zlotych, Copper-Nickel	—	8.50
—	1971	500 pcs.	10 Zlotych, Nickel	—	35.00

—	1971	.052	10 Zlotych, Copper-Nickel	—	8.50
—	1971	500 pcs.	10 Zlotych, Nickel	—	35.00
Pr64	1971	20 pcs.	10 Zlotych	—	—
Pr64	1971	500 pcs.	10 Zlotych, Nickel	—	35.00

—	1971	20 pcs.	10 Zlotych, Copper-Nickel	—	—
—	1971	500 pcs.	10 Zlotych, Nickel	—	35.00

—	1972	20 pcs.	10 Zlotych, Copper-Nickel	—	—
—	1972	500 pcs.	10 Zlotych, Nickel	—	21.00
Pr65	1972	20 pcs.	10 Zlotych	—	—
Pr65	1972	500 pcs.	10 Zlotych, Nickel	—	21.00
Pr66	1972	20 pcs.	50 Zlotych	—	16.50
Pr66	1972	500 pcs.	50 Zlotych, Nickel	—	75.00

—	1972	.015	50 Zlotych, .750 Silver	—	125.00
—	1972	500 pcs.	50 Zlotych, Nickel	—	30.00

—	1973	20 pcs.	10 Zlotych, Copper-Nickel	—	—
—	1973	500 pcs.	10 Zlotych, Nickel	—	—

KM#	Date	Mintage	Identification	Issue Price	Mkt. Val.
—	1973	10 pcs.	10 Zlotych, Copper-Nickel	—	—
—	1973	500 pcs.	10 Zlotych, Nickel	—	—
Pr67	1973	20 pcs.	20 Zlotych, Plain Edge	—	35.00
Pr67	1973	20 pcs.	20 Zlotych, Milled Edge	—	35.00
Pr67	1973	500 pcs.	20 Zlotych, Nickel	—	—

—	1973	20 pcs.	20 Zlotych, Copper-Nickel	—	—
—	1973	500 pcs.	20 Zlotych, Nickel	—	—
Pr68	1973	20 pcs.	100 Zlotych	—	—
Pr68	1973	500 pcs.	100 Zlotych, Nickel	—	35.00

—	1973	500 pcs.	100 Zlotych, .625 Silver	—	30.00
—	1973	500 pcs.	100 Zlotych, Nickel	—	35.00

—	1973	1222 pcs.	100 Zlotych, .625 Silver	—	250.00
—	1973	500 pcs.	100 Zlotych, Nickel	—	35.00

KM#	Date	Mintage	Identification	Issue Price	Mkt. Val.
—	1974	40 pcs.	10 Zlotych, Copper-Nickel	—	—
—	1974	500 pcs.	10 Zlotych, Nickel	—	—
Pr74	1974	40 pcs.	10 Zlotych, Copper-Nickel	—	—
Pr74	1974	500 pcs.	10 Zlotych, Nickel	—	—
Pr69	1974	20 pcs.	20 Zlotych	—	—
Pr69	1974	500 pcs.	20 Zlotych, Nickel	—	—

—	1974	20 pcs.	20 Zlotych, Copper-Nickel	—	—
—	1974	500 pcs.	20 Zlotych, Nickel	—	—

—	1974	20 pcs.	20 Zlotych, Copper-Nickel	—	—
—	1974	500 pcs.	20 Zlotych, Nickel	—	—

—	1974	20 pcs.	20 Zlotych, Copper-Nickel	—	—
—	1974	500 pcs.	20 Zlotych, Nickel	—	—

—	1974	20 pcs.	20 Zlotych, Copper-Nickel	—	—
—	1974	500 pcs.	20 Zlotych, Nickel	—	—
Pr70	1974	20 pcs.	20 Zlotych	—	—
Pr70	1974	500 pcs.	20 Zlotych, Nickel	—	—
Pr76	1974	20 pcs.	100 Zlotych	—	—
Pr76	1974	500 pcs.	100 Zlotych, Nickel	—	—

KM#	Date	Mintage	Identification	Issue Price	Mkt. Val.
—	1974	.030	100 Zlotych	—	20.00
—	1974	500 pcs.	100 Zlotych, Nickel	—	—
P72	1974	10 pcs.	100 Zlotych, .625 Silver	—	20.00
P72	1974	500 pcs.	100 Zlotych, Nickel	—	—

KM#	Date	Mintage	Identification	Issue Price	Mkt. Val.
—	1974	.010	100 Zlotych, .625 Silver	—	—
—	1974	500 pcs.	100 Zlotych, Nickel	—	—
Pr72	1974	20 pcs.	200 Zlotych	—	20.00
Pr72	1974	500 pcs.	200 Zlotych, Nickel	—	—
Pr73	1975	40 pcs.	10 Zlotych	—	—
Pr73	1975	500 pcs.	10 Zlotych, Nickel	—	—
Pr75	1975	20 pcs.	20 Zlotych	—	—
Pr75	1975	500 pcs.	20 Zlotych, Nickel	—	—

KM#	Date	Mintage	Identification	Issue Price	Mkt. Val.
—	1975	20 pcs.	20 Zlotych, Copper-Nickel	—	—
—	1975	500 pcs.	20 Zlotych, Nickel	—	—
Pr78	1975	20 pcs.	100 Zlotych	—	—
Pr78	1975	500 pcs.	100 Zlotych, Nickel	—	—

KM#	Date	Mintage	Identification	Issue Price	Mkt. Val.
—	1975	20 pcs.	100 Zlotych, .625 Silver	—	—

KM#	Date	Mintage	Identification	Issue Price	Mkt. Val.
—	1975	500 pcs.	100 Zlotych, Nickel	—	—
Pr77	1975	20 pcs.	100 Zlotych	—	—
Pr77	1975	500 pcs.	100 Zlotych, Nickel	—	—

KM#	Date	Mintage	Identification	Issue Price	Mkt. Val.
—	1975	20 pcs.	100 Zlotych, .625 Silver	—	—
—	1975	500 pcs.	100 Zlotych, Nickel	—	—

KM#	Date	Mintage	Identification	Issue Price	Mkt. Val.
—	1975	20 pcs.	200 Zlotych, .750 Silver	—	25.00
—	1975	500 pcs.	200 Zlotych, Nickel	—	—

KM#	Date	Mintage	Identification	Issue Price	Mkt. Val.
—	1975	20 pcs.	200 Zlotych, .750 Silver	—	25.00
—	1975	500 pcs.	200 Zlotych, Nickel	—	—
Pr79	1975	20 pcs.	200 Zlotych	—	—
Pr79	1975	500 pcs.	200 Zlotych, Nickel	—	—
Pr82	1976	20 pcs.	100 Zlotych	—	17.50
Pr82	1976	500 pcs.	100 Zlotych, Nickel	—	—

KM#	Date	Mintage	Identification	Issue Price	Mkt. Val.
—	1976	20 pcs.	100 Zlotych, .625 Silver	—	—
—	1976	500 pcs.	100 Zlotych, Nickel	—	—
Pr84	1976	20 pcs.	100 Zlotych	—	17.50
Pr84	1976	500 pcs.	100 Zlotych, Nickel	—	—

KM#	Date	Mintage	Identification	Issue Price	Mkt. Val.
—	1976	20 pcs.	100 Zlotych, .625 Silver	—	—
—	1976	500 pcs.	100 Zlotych, Nickel	—	—
Pr86	1976	5,000	200 Zlotych	—	—
Pr86	1976	500 pcs.	200 Zlotych, Nickel	—	—

KM#	Date	Mintage	Identification	Issue Price	Mkt. Val.
—	1976	5,000	200 Zlotych, .625 Silver	—	—
—	1976	500 pcs.	200 Zlotych, Nickel	—	—
Pr83	1976	300 pcs.	500 Zlotych	—	—
Pr83	1976	500 pcs.	500 Zlotych, Nickel	—	—

KM#	Date	Mintage	Identification	Issue Price	Mkt. Val.
—	1976	500 pcs.	500 Zlotych, Nickel	—	—
Pr85	1976	300 pcs.	500 Zlotych	—	—
Pr85	1976	500 pcs.	500 Zlotych, Nickel	—	—

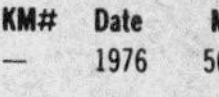
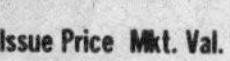

KM#	Date	Mintage	Identification	Issue Price	Mkt. Val.
—	1976	500 pcs.	500 Zlotych, Nickel	—	—

KM#	Date	Mintage	Identification	Issue Price	Mkt. Val.
Pr88	1977	3,000	100 Zlotych	—	20.00

KM#	Date	Mintage	Identification	Issue Price	Mkt. Val.
Pr89	1977	—	100 Zlotych, .625 Silver	—	20.00

KM#	Date	Mintage	Identification	Issue Price	Mkt. Val.
	1977	5,000	100 Zlotych	—	20.00

KM#	Date	Mintage	Identification	Issue Price	Mkt. Val.
	1978	3,000	100 Zlotych	—	—

KM#	Date	Mintage	Identification	Issue Price	Mkt. Val.
	1978	3,000	100 Zlotych	—	20.00

KM#	Date	Mintage	Identification	Issue Price	Mkt. Val.
	1978	3,000	100 Zlotych	—	20.00

KM#	Date	Mintage	Identification	Issue Price	Mkt. Val.
—	1978	3,000	100 Zlotych	—	20.00

KM#	Date	Mintage	Identification	Issue Price	Mkt. Val.
	1978	3,000	100 Zlotych	—	—

KM#	Date	Mintage	Identification	Issue Price	Mkt. Val.
—	1979	3,000	100 Zlotych	—	20.00

KM#	Date	Mintage	Identification	Issue Price	Mkt. Val.
—	1979	4,000	100 Zlotych	—	20.00

KM#	Date	Mintage	Identification	Issue Price	Mkt. Val.
—	1979	3,500	100 Zlotych	—	21.50

KM#	Date	Mintage	Identification	Issue Price	Mkt. Val.
—	1980	3,500	200 Zlotych, .720 Silver	—	—

COURLAND

Part of Latvian S.S.R. Courland was at one time the property of the Livonian Order of Knights. When the Livonian Order was dissolved in 1561 the then Master of the Order, Gotthard Kettler was made duke of Courland. When the Kettler line became extinct in 1737 Courland was awarded to Ernst Johann Biron, chief advisor and lover of Empress Anna of Russia. After her death he was exiled but returned in 1763. He abdicated in favor of his son Peter in 1769.

RULERS

Carl of Saxony - Poland, 1759-1762
Ernst Johann Biron, 1762-1769
Peter Biron, 1769-1795

SOLIDUS

COPPER
Obv: Bust of Carl right.
Rev: 2 crowned shields of arms.

C#	Date	Mintage	VG	Fine	VF	XF
1	1762	—	15.00	25.00	40.00	65.00
	Obv: Crowned E J monogram.					
9	1763	—	10.00	15.00	25.00	40.00

C#	Date	Mintage	VG	Fine	VF	XF
10	1764	—	15.00	25.00	40.00	65.00

GROSSUS (GROSZ)

BILLON
Obv: Bust of Carl.
Rev: 2 crowned shields of arms.

C#	Date	Mintage	VG	Fine	VF	XF
3	1762	—	20.00	35.00	55.00	85.00
	Obv: Crowned E J monogram.					
13	1763	—	15.00	25.00	40.00	65.00
	1764	—	15.00	25.00	40.00	65.00
	1765	—	15.00	25.00	40.00	65.00

3 GROSZY

BILLON
Obv: Bust of Ernst Johann.
Rev: 2 crowned shields of arms.

C#	Date	Mintage	VG	Fine	VF	XF
15	1763	—	22.50	37.50	60.00	100.00
	1764	—	22.50	37.50	60.00	100.00

6 GROSZY

BILLON
Obv: Bust of Carl.

Rev: 2 crowned shields of arms.

C#	Date	Mintage	VG	Fine	VF	XF
5	1762	—	27.50	45.00	65.00	100.00

Obv: Bust of Ernst Johann.

C#	Date	Mintage	VG	Fine	VF	XF
17	1763	—	27.50	45.00	65.00	100.00
	1764	—	27.50	45.00	65.00	100.00
	1765	—	27.50	45.00	65.00	100.00

THALER

SILVER

Obv: Head right. Rev: Crowned double arms.

C#	Date	Mintage	Fine	VF	XF
23	1780	—	250.00	400.00	600.00

TRADE COINS

DUCAT

GOLD

Obv: Bust of Ernst Johann.

Rev: 2 crowned shields of arms.

C#	Date	Mintage	VG	Fine	VF	XF
20	1764	—	750.00	1000.	1500.	2250.

Obv: Head right. Rev: Crowned double arms.

C#	Date	Mintage	Fine	VF	XF
25	1780	—	1000.	1500.	2250.

DANZIG

A seaport on the nothern coast of Poland giving access to the Baltic Sea. An important port from early times. Has at different times belonged to the Teutonic Knights, Pomerania, Russia, and Prussia. Danzig was a free city from 1919 to 1939 during which most of its modern coinage was made.

RULERS

Stanislaus August (of Poland), 1764-1772
Friedrich Wilhelm II (of Prussia), 1786-1797
Friedrich Wilhelm III (Of Prussia) 1797-1840
Marshal Lefebvre (As Duke) 1807-1814

MINTMARKS

A - Berlin
M - Milan

MONETARY SYSTEM

3 Schilling = 1 Groschen

SOLIDUS

COPPER

Obv: Crowned SAR monogram and date. Rev: Value.

C#	Date	Mintage	VG	Fine	VF
9	1765	—	5.00	8.50	12.50
	1766	—	5.00	8.50	12.50
14	1793	—	—	Rare	—

SCHILLING

COPPER

Obv: Crowned FW monogram.

Rev: Value and date.

C#	Date	Mintage	VG	Fine	VF
15	1801A	—	5.00	8.50	12.50

C#	Date	Mintage	VG	Fine	VF
16	1808M	—	5.00	8.50	13.50
	1812M	—	5.00	8.50	13.50

Rev: Date, value

C#	Date	Mintage	VG	Fine	VF
16a	1808M	—	7.50	15.00	21.50

EIN (1) GROSCHEN

COPPER

C#	Date	Mintage	VG	Fine	VF
17	1809M	—	6.00	9.00	14.00
	1812M	—	6.00	9.00	14.00

3 GROSZE

BILLON

Obv: Crowned SAR monogram and date.

Rev: Crowned and supported arms with value.

C#	Date	Mintage	VG	Fine	VF
10	1765	—	7.50	11.50	15.00
	1766	—	7.50	11.50	15.00

6 GROSZY

BILLON

Obv: Crowned bust right.

Rev: Supported arms, value above.

C#	Date	Mintage	VG	Fine	VF
11	1764	—	10.00	15.00	25.00
	1765	—	10.00	15.00	25.00

60 GROSZY

SILVER

Obv: Crowned bust right.

Rev: Supported arms over value.

C#	Date	Mintage	Fine	VF	XF
12	1764	—	150.00	200.00	275.00
	1767	—	150.00	200.00	275.00

TRADE COINS

DUCAT

GOLD

Obv: Crowned bust right.

Rev: Supported arms.

C#	Date	Mintage	Fine	VF	XF
13	1765	—	—	Rare	—

DECIMAL COINAGE

(Until 1923)
100 Pfennig = 1 Mark
(Commencing 1923)
100 Pfennig = 1 Gulden

PFENNIG

BRONZE

Y#	Date	Mintage	VF	XF	Unc
3	1923	4.000	2.00	2.50	7.50
	1923	—	—	Proof	30.00
	1926	1.500	2.25	3.50	10.00
	1929	1.000	2.50	4.00	12.50
	1930	2.000	2.00	3.00	10.00
	1937	3.000	2.00	2.50	6.50

2 PFENNIG

BRONZE

Y#	Date	Mintage	VF	XF	Unc
4	1923	1.000	2.00	3.00	8.00
	1923	—	—	Proof	35.00
	1926	1.750	2.00	2.50	6.50
	1937	.500	2.50	3.50	11.00

5 PFENNIG

COPPER-NICKEL

Y#	Date	Mintage	VF	XF	Unc
5	1923	3.000	2.00	2.50	7.00
	1923	—	—	Proof	40.00
	1928	1.000	3.00	3.50	8.00

ALUMINUM-BRONZE

Y#	Date	Mintage	VF	XF	Unc
13	1932	4.000	2.00	3.00	6.00

10 PFENNIG

ZINC

Notgeld Issue

Y#	Date	Mintage	VF	XF	Unc
1	1920	1.000	15.00	20.00	37.50

NOTE: Many die varieties exist.

COPPER-NICKEL

Y#	Date	Mintage	VF	XF	Unc
6	1923	5.000	2.00	3.50	7.50
	1923	—	—	Proof	50.00

ALUMINUM-BRONZE

Y#	Date	Mintage	VF	XF	Unc
14	1932	5.000	2.00	3.00	7.00

1/2 GULDEN

.750 SILVER

Y#	Date	Mintage	VF	XF	Unc
7	1923	1.000	8.50	15.00	25.00
	1923	—	—	Proof	65.00
	1927	.400	15.00	25.00	45.00

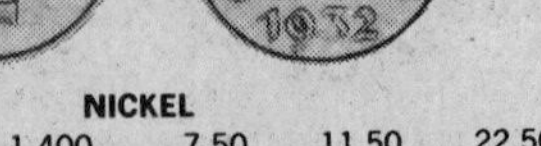
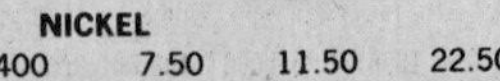

NICKEL

Y#	Date	Mintage	VF	XF	Unc
15	1932	1.400	7.50	11.50	22.50

GULDEN

.750 SILVER

Y#	Date	Mintage	VF	XF	Unc
8	1923	3.500	12.50	17.50	32.50
	1923	—	—	Proof	80.00

NICKEL

Y#	Date	Mintage	VF	XF	Unc
16	1932	2.500	10.00	15.00	27.50

2 GULDEN

.750 SILVER

Y#	Date	Mintage	VF	XF	Unc
9	1923	1.250	30.00	45.00	70.00
	1923	—	—	Proof	110.00

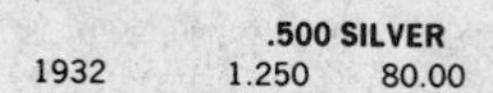

.500 SILVER

Y#	Date	Mintage	VF	XF	Unc
17	1932	1.250	80.00	125.00	175.00

5 GULDEN

.750 SILVER

Y#	Date	Mintage	VF	XF	Unc
10	1923	.700	75.00	110.00	165.00
	1923	—	—	Proof	300.00
	1927	.160	135.00	200.00	275.00
	1927	—	—	Proof	1000.

.500 SILVER

Y#	Date	Mintage	VF	XF	Unc
18	1932	.430	200.00	300.00	450.00

Y#	Date	Mintage	VF	XF	Unc
19	1932	.430	225.00	350.00	500.00

NICKEL

Y#	Date	Mintage	VF	XF	Unc
20	1935	.800	125.00	175.00	250.00

10 GULDEN

NICKEL

Y#	Date	Mintage	VF	XF	Unc
21	1935	.380	250.00	400.00	550.00

25 GULDEN

.916 GOLD

Obv: Arms between two columns

Y#	Date	Mintage	VF	XF	Unc
11	1923	200 pcs.	—	—	2000.
	1923	800 pcs.	—	Proof	2800.

NOTE: This issue was presented to members of the Senate.

Obv: No columns between lions.

Y#	Date	Mintage	VF	XF	Unc
12	1930	*4,000	—	7500.	10,000.

NOTE: Not released for circulation; a few were given in presentation cases on September 1, 1939.

NCLT ISSUES

PATTERNS

KM#	Date	Mintage	Identification	Mkt.Val.
1	1920	.124	10 Pfennig, Zinc, Y#2	225.00

PROOF SETS

STANDARD METALS

KM#	Date	Mintage	Identification	Issue Price	Mkt. Val.
101	1923(8)	—	Y3-10	—	700.00

EAST PRUSSIA

An area on the southeastern coast of the Baltic Sea. Part of the area is in present day Poland and part in the U.S.S.R. A possession of Prussia from 1525 until 1945. Coinage for the area made by the Prussian kings except for brief occupation by Russia from 1756-1762 when Russia produced special coin types for the area.

RULERS

Friedrich II, 1740-1786
Freidrich Wilhelm II of Prussia 1786-1797
Friedrich Wilhelm III (Of Prussia) 1797-1840

MINTMARKS

A- Berlin
G- Glatz, Silesia

SCHILLING

COPPER

Obv: Crowned FW monogram.
Rev: Value and date.

C#	Date	Mintage	VG	Fine	VF	XF
50	1790E	—	5.00	7.50	12.50	20.00
	1790.E.	—	5.00	7.50	12.50	20.00
	1791E	—	5.00	7.50	12.50	20.00
	1791.E.	—	5.00	7.50	12.50	20.00
	1792E	—	5.00	7.50	12.50	20.00
	1792.E.	—	5.00	7.50	12.50	20.00
	1793E	—	5.00	7.50	12.50	20.00
	1793.E.	—	5.00	7.50	12.50	20.00
	1794E	—	5.00	7.50	12.50	20.00
	1794.E.	—	5.00	7.50	12.50	20.00
	1795.E.	—	5.00	7.50	12.50	20.00
	1796.E.	—	5.00	7.50	12.50	20.00
	1797E large rosettes					
		—	5.00	7.50	12.50	20.00
	1797E small rosettes					
		—	5.00	7.50	12.50	20.00
	1797.E.	—	5.00	7.50	12.50	20.00

BILLON

C#	Date	Mintage	VG	Fine	VF	XF
51	1788E	—	6.00	10.00	15.00	25.00

COPPER

C#	Date	Mintage	Fine	VF	XF
53	1804A	—	3.25	6.00	11.00
	1805A	—	3.25	6.00	10.00
	1806A	—	3.25	6.00	11.00

C#	Date	Mintage	Fine	VF	XF
54	1810A	—	3.25	6.00	11.00

SOLIDUS

BILLON
Obv: Crowned FR monogram; E below.
Rev: Value and date.

C#	Date	Mintage	VG	Fine	VF	XF
6	1764E	—	3.75	6.00	10.00	15.00

Obv: Crowned FR monogram divides date.
Rev: Value with E below.

C#	Date	Mintage	VG	Fine	VF	XF
6a	1766E	—	3.75	6.00	10.00	15.00
	1767E	—	3.75	6.00	10.00	15.00
	1768E	—	3.75	6.00	10.00	15.00
	1769E	—	3.75	6.00	10.00	15.00
	1771E	—	3.75	6.00	10.00	15.00

Obv: Small crown over FR monogram; E below
Rev: Value in large letters over date.

C#	Date	Mintage	VG	Fine	VF	XF
6b	1775E	—	3.75	6.00	10.00	15.00
	1777E	—	3.75	6.00	10.00	15.00
	1779E	—	3.75	6.00	10.00	15.00
	1780E	—	3.75	6.00	10.00	15.00
	1781E	—	3.75	6.00	10.00	15.00
	1782E	—	3.75	6.00	10.00	15.00
	1783E	—	3.75	6.00	10.00	15.00
	1785E	—	3.75	6.00	10.00	15.00
	1786E	—	3.75	6.00	10.00	15.00

Obv: Crowned FR monogram; A below.

C#	Date	Mintage	VG	Fine	VF	XF
6c	1776A	—	3.75	6.00	10.00	15.00

1/2 GROSCHEN

COPPER

C#	Date	Mintage	Fine	VF	XF
56	1811A	—	4.00	7.00	12.00

GROSCHEN

BILLON
Obv: Crowned eagle; E below.
Rev: Value and date.

C#	Date	Mintage	VG	Fine	VF	XF
8	1764E	—	5.00	7.50	12.50	20.00
	1769E	—	5.00	7.50	12.50	20.00
	1770E	—	5.00	7.50	12.50	20.00

Obv: Crowned flying eagle; E below.

C#	Date	Mintage	VG	Fine	VF	XF
10	1771E	—	5.00	7.50	12.50	20.00
	1772E	—	5.00	7.50	12.50	20.00
	1778E	—	5.00	7.50	12.50	20.00
	1779E	—	5.00	7.50	12.50	20.00
	1780E	—	5.00	7.50	12.50	20.00
	1781E	—	5.00	7.50	12.50	20.00
	1782E	—	5.00	7.50	12.50	20.00
	1783E	—	5.00	7.50	12.50	20.00
	1785E	—	5.00	7.50	12.50	20.00
	1786E	—	5.00	7.50	12.50	20.00

Obv: Crowned flying eagle; A below.

C#	Date	Mintage	VG	Fine	VF	XF
10a	1776A	—	5.00	7.50	12.50	20.00

Obv: Bust of Friedrich Wilhelm right.
Rev: Crowned arms divide value and date.

C#	Date	Mintage	VG	Fine	VF	XF
52	1787E	—	5.00	7.50	12.50	20.00
	1788E	—	5.00	7.50	12.50	20.00
	1790E	—	5.00	7.50	12.50	20.00
	1791E	—	5.00	7.50	12.50	20.00
	1792E	—	5.00	7.50	12.50	20.00
	1793E	—	5.00	7.50	12.50	20.00
	1794E	—	5.00	7.50	12.50	20.00
	1795E	—	5.00	7.50	12.50	20.00
	1796E	—	5.00	7.50	12.50	20.00
	1797E	—	5.00	7.50	12.50	20.00
	1798E	—	5.00	7.50	12.50	20.00

COPPER

C#	Date	Mintage	Fine	VF	XF
58	1810	—	4.00	8.00	14.00
	1811A	—	4.00	8.00	14.00

2 GROSCHEN (GROSSUS)

BILLON
Obv: Crowned eagle; E below.
Rev: Value and date.

C#	Date	Mintage	VG	Fine	VF	XF
12	1764E	—	6.00	10.00	15.00	25.00
	1768E	—	6.00	10.00	15.00	25.00

Obv: Crowned flying eagle; E below.

C#	Date	Mintage	VG	Fine	VF	XF
14	1773E	—	6.50	10.00	15.00	25.00

3 GROSCHEN

BILLON
Obv: Bare head of Friedrich right.
Rev: Crowned eagle; date above; value below.

C#	Date	Mintage	VG	Fine	VF	XF
17	1765E	—	10.00	15.00	25.00	40.00

Obv: Crowned head of Friedrich right.

C#	Date	Mintage	VG	Fine	VF	XF
18	1765E	—	7.50	12.50	20.00	35.00
	1766E	—	7.50	12.50	20.00	35.00
	1767E	—	7.50	12.50	20.00	35.00

Obv: Laureate head of Friedrich right.
Rev: Crowned flying eagle; E value and date below.

C#	Date	Mintage	VG	Fine	VF	XF
21	1771E	—	6.00	10.00	15.00	25.00
	1772E	—	6.00	10.00	15.00	25.00
	1773E	—	6.00	10.00	15.00	25.00
	1774E	—	6.00	10.00	15.00	25.00
	1775E	—	6.00	10.00	15.00	25.00
	1776E	—	6.00	10.00	15.00	25.00
	1777E	—	6.00	10.00	15.00	25.00
	1778E	—	6.00	10.00	15.00	25.00
	1779E	—	6.00	10.00	15.00	25.00
	1780E	—	6.00	10.00	15.00	25.00
	1781E	—	6.00	10.00	15.00	25.00
	1782E	—	6.00	10.00	15.00	25.00
	1783E	—	6.00	10.00	15.00	25.00
	1784E	—	6.00	10.00	15.00	25.00
	1785E	—	6.00	10.00	15.00	25.00
	1786E	—	6.00	10.00	15.00	25.00

C#	Date	Mintage	Fine	VF	XF
60	1800A	—	8.00	12.00	20.00
	1801A	—	8.00	12.00	20.00
	1802A	—	8.00	12.00	20.00
	1803A	—	8.00	12.00	20.00
	1805A	—	8.00	12.00	20.00
	1806A	—	8.00	12.00	20.00
	1807A	—	8.00	12.00	20.00
60a	1807G	—	8.00	12.00	20.00
	1808G	—	8.00	12.00	20.00

6 GROSZY

BILLON
Obv: Small crowned head of Friedrich right.
Rev: Crowned eagle; date above; value and mint below.

C#	Date	Mintage	VG	Fine	VF	XF
28	1764E	—	7.50	12.50	20.00	35.00
	1770E	—	7.50	12.50	20.00	35.00

Obv: Large crowned head of Friedrich right.

C#	Date	Mintage	VG	Fine	VF	XF
28a	1771E	—	7.50	12.50	20.00	35.00
	1772E	—	7.50	12.50	20.00	35.00
	1773E	—	7.50	12.50	20.00	35.00
	1774E	—	7.50	12.50	20.00	35.00
	1775E	—	7.50	12.50	20.00	35.00
	1776E	—	7.50	12.50	20.00	35.00
	1777E	—	7.50	12.50	20.00	35.00
	1778E	—	7.50	12.50	20.00	35.00
	1779E	—	7.50	12.50	20.00	35.00
	1780E	—	7.50	12.50	20.00	35.00
	1781E	—	7.50	12.50	20.00	35.00

Obv: Old head of Friedrich right.

C#	Date	Mintage	VG	Fine	VF	XF
29	1782E	—	7.50	12.50	20.00	35.00
	1783E	—	7.50	12.50	20.00	35.00
	1784E	—	7.50	12.50	20.00	35.00

18 GROSZY

BILLON

C#	Date	Mintage	VG	Fine	VF	XF
32	1764E	—	10.00	15.00	25.00	40.00
	1765E	—	10.00	15.00	25.00	40.00

GALICIA AND LODOMERIA

Ancient principality that is part of modern Poland and U.S.S.R. became part of Poland in 1386 and was passed to Austria in the first partition of Poland in 1772. Coins were made at Oswiecim for the area with special Austrian types in the 1770's and 1790's.

MINTMARKS

A - Vienna
S - Schmollnitz

MINMASTERS INITIALS

A, Fa - F. A Ycherau
C, Ic - J. A. Cronberg

MONETARY SYSTEM

6 Schillings (Solidi) = 2 Grosze
= 1 Kreuzer

SCHILLING

COPPER
Obv: Crowned arms.
Rev: Value over date, S below.

C#	Date	Mintage	Fine	VF	XF
1	1774	—	6.00	10.00	15.00

GROSSUS

COPPER

C#	Date	Mintage	Fine	VF	XF
4	1794	—	10.00	15.00	35.00

III GROSSI

COPPER

C#	Date	Mintage	Fine	VF	XF
5	1794	—	10.00	15.00	25.00

VI GROSSI

BILLON
Obv: Crowned arms over crossed banners.
Rev: Value and date over branches.

C#	Date	Mintage	VG	Fine	VF
6	1794	—	—	Rare	—

c#4, 5, and 6 used by the Austrian army fighting Kosciuzko.

15 KREUZER

SILVER
Obv: Veiled head over branches.
Rev: Crowned arms and value within garlands over branches.

C#	Date	Mintage	Fine	VF	XF
2	1775C-A	—	10.00	15.00	25.00
	1776C-A	—	10.00	15.00	25.00
	1777C-A	—	10.00	15.00	25.00

30 KREUZER

SILVER
Obv: Veiled head over branches.
Rev: Crowned arms supported by griffons; value in garland below.

C#	Date	Mintage	Fine	VF	XF
3	1775IC-FA	—	15.00	25.00	40.00
	1776IC-FA	—	15.00	25.00	40.00
	1777IC-FA	—	15.00	25.00	40.00

KRAKOW

A city in southern Poland, the third largest in the country formed an independent republic in 1815 that lasted until 1846 at which time the city reverted to Austria. Coins made for the republic in 1835.

MONETARY SYSTEM

30 Groszy = 1 Zloty

5 GROSZY

BILLON

C#	Date	Mintage	Fine	VF	XF
11	1835	—	10.00	13.50	20.00

10 GROSZY

SILVER

C#	Date	Mintage	Fine	VF	XF
12	1835	—	12.50	17.50	25.00

ZLOTY

SILVER

C#	Date	Mintage	Fine	VF	XF
13	1835	—	25.00	30.00	37.50

LODZ GHETTO

A major industrial city in western Poland before World War ii. Site of the first wartime ghetto under German occupation (May,1940) and also the last ghetto to close during the war (August,1944). Coins were made in 1942 and 1943.

1942-1944
MONETARY SYSTEM

100 Pfennig = 1 Mark

NOTE: This series has seen very little circulation, but are commonly found in conditions from slightly to badly corroded. the badly corroded specimens have the appearance of zinc.

10 PFENNIG

ALUMINUM-MAGNESIUM

KM#	Date	Mintage	VG	Fine	VF	XF
1	1942	*.100	35.00	50.00	65.00	100.00

NOTE: Most were destroyed or remelted as the design was too similar to regular German coinage.

KM#	Date	Mintage	VG	Fine	VF	XF
5	1942	—	35.00	50.00	65.00	125.00

5 MARK

ALUMINUM

KM#	Date	Mintage	VG	Fine	VF	XF
2	1943	.600	—	10.00	15.00	25.00

10 MARK

ALUMINUM

KM#	Date	Mintage	VG	Fine	VF	XF
3	1943	.100	—	10.00	15.00	25.00

20 MARK

ALUMINUM

KM#	Date	Mintage	VG	Fine	VF	XF
4	1943	—	—	125.00	135.00	175.00

POMERANIA

RULERS

Gustav iv Adolf, King of Sweden, 1792-1809

Pomerania (Pommern, Pomorze), a stretch of land on the Baltic Sea between the Vistula and the Oder Rivers, was included in the territory of Mieszko I, Poland's first historical ruler. It passed to Brandenburg in 1637, and in 1648 was divided with Sweden; the northern part remained Swedish until 1815. In 1945 virtually all of historic Pomerania became part of Poland.

3 PFENNIGE

COPPER

Obv: Crowned griffin. Rev: Value, date below.

C#	Date	Mintage	VG	Fine	VF
29	1806	—	5.00	10.00	17.50
—	1808	—	5.00	10.00	17.50

POSEN

One of the oldest cities in Poland. An active member of Hanseatic League. Given to Prussia in 1793. Became part of the Grand Duchy of Warsaw. Returned to Prussia after the Congress of Vienna (1815). A special coin issue was made for Posen by Prussia immediately after repossession.

RULERS

Friedrich Wilhelm III (Of Prussia) 1797-1840

MINTMARKS

A- Berlin
B- Breslau

GROSCHEN

COPPER

C#	Date	Mintage	Fine	VF	XF
1	1816A	—	5.00	6.50	9.00
	1816B	—	5.00	6.50	9.00
	1817A	—	5.00	6.50	10.00

3 GROSCHEN

COPPER

C#	Date	Mintage	Fine	VF	XF
2	1816A	—	7.00	10.00	14.00
	1817A	—	7.00	10.00	15.00

SOUTH PRUSSIA

South Prussia (Borussia Meridionalis) consisted of the central provinces of Prussian Poland between West Prussia and Silesia taken by Prussia in the second and third partitions of Poland. With the territory seized by Austria in the third partition, it formed the Grand Duchy of Warsaw created by Napoleon in 1807. The duchy was occupied by Russia after Napoleon's Russian defeat.

SOLIDUS

COPPER

Obv: FWR monogram. Rev: Value.

C#	Date	Mintage	Fine	VF	XF
1	1796B	—	3.00	6.00	10.00
	1796E	—	3.00	6.00	10.00
	1797B	—	3.00	6.00	10.00
	1797E	—	3.00	6.00	10.00

1/2 GROSSUS

COPPER

Obv: Monogram. Rev: 'REGNI BORUSS'.

C#	Date	Mintage	Fine	VF	XF
2	1796B	—	4.00	10.00	15.00

Rev: 'BORUSS: MERID:'

C#	Date	Mintage	Fine	VF	XF
	1796B	—	4.00	8.00	12.50
	1796E	—	4.00	8.00	12.50
	1797B	—	4.00	8.00	12.50
	1797E	—	4.00	8.00	12.50

GROSSUS

COPPER

Obv: Head right. Rev: Eagle in wreath.

C#	Date	Mintage	Fine	VF	XF
3	1796B	—	8.00	12.50	15.00
	1796E	—	10.00	15.00	20.00
	1797B	—	8.00	12.50	15.00
	1797E	—	8.00	12.50	15.00
	1798E	—	8.00	12.50	15.00

3 GROSSUS

COPPER

Rev: 'GROSSUS BORUSSIAE TRIPLEX'

C#	Date	Mintage	Fine	VF	XF
4	1796A	—	12.50	15.00	20.00

Rev: 'GROSSUS BORUSS MERID. TRIPLEX'

C#	Date	Mintage	Fine	VF	XF
4a	1796B	—	12.50	15.00	22.50
	1796E	—	12.50	15.00	22.50
	1797A	—	12.50	15.00	22.50
	1797B	—	12.50	15.00	22.50
	1797E	—	12.50	15.00	22.50

ZAMOSC

MONETARY SYSTEM

30 Groszy = 1 Zloty

6 GROSZY

BRONZE

C#	Date	Mintage	Fine	VF	XF
1	1813	1,330	200.00	275.00	400.00

10 GROSZY

BILLON

C#	Date	Mintage	Fine	VF	XF
6	1831	—	175.00	250.00	350.00

2 ZLOTY

SILVER

C#	Date	Mintage	Fine	VF	XF
2	1813	7,930	90.00	125.00	200.00

Obv: Legend in 4 lines

C#	Date	Mintage	Fine	VF	XF
2a	1813	Inc. Ab.	225.00	300.00	400.00

PORTUGAL

The Portuguese Republic, located in the western part of the Iberian Peninsula in southwestern Europe, has an area of 35,510 sq. mi. (56,461 sq. km.) and a population of 9.6 million. Capital: Lisbon. Portugal's economy is based on agriculture and a small but expanding industrial sector. Textiles, machinery, chemicals, wine and cork are exported.

After centuries of domination by Romans, Visigoths and Moors, Portugal emerged in the 13th century as an independent kingdom financially and philosophically prepared for the great period of exploration that would follow. Attuned to the inspiration of Prince Henry the Navigator (1394-1460), Portugal's daring explorers of the 14th and 15th centuries roamed the world's oceans from Brazil to Japan in an unprecendented burst of energy and endeavor that culminated in 1494 with Portugal laying claim to half the transoceanic world. Unfortunately for the fortunes of the tiny kingdom, the Portuguese proved to be inept colonizers. Less than a century after Portugal laid claim to half the world, English, French and Dutch trading companies had seized the lion's share of the world's colonies and commerce, and Portugal's place as an imperial power was lost forever. The monarchy was overthrown in 1910 and a republic established.

On April 25, 1974, the government of Portugal was seized by a military junta which reached agreements providing for independence for the Portuguese overseas provinces of Portuguese Guinea (Guinea-Bissau), Mozambique, Cape Verde Islands, Angola, and St. Thomas and Prince Islands (Sao Tome and Principe).

RULERS

Maria I and Pedro III, 1777-1786
Maria I, 1786-1799
Joao, As Prince Regent, 1799-1816
Joao, As King (Joao VI), 1816-1826
Pedro IV, 1826-1828
Miguel, 1828-1834
Maria II, 1834-1853
Pedro V, 1853-1861
Luiz I, 1861-1889
Carlos I, 1889-1908
Manuel II, 1908-1910
Republic, 1910 To Date

MINTMARKS

No Mintmark - Lisbon
A - Paris (1891-1892, Copper Only)

MONETARY SYSTEM

(1826-1836)

7500 Reis = 1 Peca (1826-1836)

Beginning in 1836 all coins were expressed in terms of Reis and arranged in a decimal sequence, (until 1910).

(Commencing 1836)

20 Reis = 1 Vintem
100 Reis = 1 Tostao
480 Reis = 24 Vintens = 1 Cruzado
1600 Reis = 1 Escudo
6400 Reis = 4 Escudos = 1 Peca

(Commencing 1910)

100 Centavos = 1 Escudo

III (3) REIS

COPPER

Obv. leg: MARIA I ET PETRUS III..., arms. Rev: PORTUGAL, etc., value in wreath.

C#	Date	Mintage	VG	Fine	VF
17	1777	—	3.00	6.00	12.50
	1778	—	—	Rare	—

C#	Date	Mintage	VG	Fine	VF
32	1797	—	4.00	7.50	15.00
	1799	—	—	Rare	—

Obv: JOANNES, etc. around shield. Rev: Legend around wreath, date and denomination within.

C#	Date	Mintage	Fine	VF	XF
48	1804	.123	5.00	8.00	15.00

Obv: Crowned arms. Rev: Value and date in branches.

C#	Date	Mintage	Fine	VF	XF
65	1818	—	15.00	40.00	75.00

V (5) REIS

COPPER

Obv. leg: MARIA I ET PETRUS III..., arms. Rev: PORTUGAL, etc., value in wreath.

C#	Date	Mintage	VG	Fine	VF
18	1777	—	5.00	12.50	25.00
	1778	—	3.00	8.00	17.50
	1779	—	10.00	25.00	50.00
	1782	—	4.00	10.00	20.00
	1785	—	2.00	5.00	10.00

C#	Date	Mintage	VG	Fine	VF
33	1791	—	8.00	16.50	25.00
	1792	—	4.00	8.00	12.50
	1797	—	2.00	4.00	6.00
	1798	—	—	Rare	—
	1799	—	1.50	3.00	4.50

Obv. leg: JOANNES..., arms. Rev. leg. ends: PRINCEPS.

C#	Date	Mintage	Fine	VF	XF
49	1800	—	12.50	20.00	32.50
	1801	—	17.50	25.00	55.00

Mule. Obv. of C#49. Rev. of C#33.

C#	Date	Mintage	Fine	VF	XF
49a	1799	—	12.50	20.00	32.50

Rev. leg. ends: REGENS.

C#	Date	Mintage	Fine	VF	XF
49b	1804	—	Reported, Not Confirmed		
49c	1812	.399	1.25	3.00	6.50
	1813	.539	1.50	3.50	8.00
	1814	.448	2.50	5.50	10.00

Mule: Obv. of C#33, rev. of C#49c.

C#	Date	Mintage	Fine	VF	XF
49d	1812	—	7.50	13.50	22.50

Obv: Arms, JOANNES VI. Rev: PORTUGALIAE... REX, value in wreath.

C#	Date	Mintage	Fine	VF	XF
66	1818	—	15.00	40.00	75.00
	1819	.011	6.00	12.50	20.00
	1820	—	5.00	10.00	16.50
	1823	.032	6.00	12.50	20.00
	1824	.098	4.00	8.00	12.50

Obv. leg: MICHAEL I DEI GRATIA, crowned arms. Rev: Leg. around wreath, value within, date below.

C#	Date	Mintage	Fine	VF	XF
88	1829	.037	2.50	5.00	8.00

Titles of Maria II

C#	Date	Mintage	Fine	VF	XF
99	1830	—	1.00	3.50	5.50

(Struck at London.)

Titles of Maria II
Obv: Square shield.

C#	Date	Mintage	Fine	VF	XF
99a	1833	—	45.00	75.00	110.00

(Struck at Porto.)

C#	Date	Mintage	Fine	VF	XF
99b	1836	5,593	12.50	20.00	30.00

X (10) REIS

COPPER
Obv. leg: MARIA I ET PETRUS III..., arms.
Rev: PORTUGAL, etc., value in wreath.

C#	Date	Mintage	VG	Fine	VF
19	1777	—	4.00	10.00	22.50
	1778	—	3.00	8.00	17.50
	1779	—	15.00	30.00	70.00
19a	1782	—	2.00	5.00	10.00
	1785	—	1.50	3.00	8.00

C#	Date	Mintage	VG	Fine	VF
34	1791	—	5.00	10.00	15.00
	1792	—	3.50	5.00	8.00
34a	1797	—	2.00	4.00	6.00
	1799	—	1.50	3.00	4.50

Obv. leg: JOANNES..., arms.
Rev. leg. ends: PRINCEPS.

C#	Date	Mintage	Fine	VF	XF
50	1800	—	8.00	15.00	27.50

Rev. leg. ends: REGENS.

C#	Date	Mintage	Fine	VF	XF
50a	1803	—	—	Rare	—

C#	Date	Mintage	Fine	VF	XF
50b	1812	.332	1.25	3.00	6.50
	1813	.276	1.25	3.00	6.50

Obv. leg: JOANNES VI..., arms.

Rev. leg: PORTUGALIAE... REX, value in wreath.

C#	Date	Mintage	Fine	VF	XF
67	1818	—	20.00	30.00	45.00
	1819	.806	1.25	2.50	4.00
	1820	6,773	12.50	20.00	30.00
	1822	.021	14.00	25.00	37.50
	1823	.044	8.50	14.00	22.50
	1824	.064	4.00	8.00	12.50
	1825	—	Reported, Not Confirmed		

C#	Date	Mintage	Fine	VF	XF
89	1829	.056	3.00	6.00	10.00
	1831	.345	2.00	3.50	6.00
	1833	.070	8.00	14.00	20.00

Titles of Maria II

C#	Date	Mintage	Fine	VF	XF
100	1830	—	1.25	4.50	9.00

(Struck at London.)

Similar to 5 Reis, C#99b.

C#	Date	Mintage	Fine	VF	XF
100a	1833	—	40.00	70.00	100.00

(Struck at Porto.)

C#	Date	Mintage	Fine	VF	XF
100b	1835	.287	5.00	10.00	15.00
	1836	.227	3.00	5.00	8.00
	1837	.360	12.50	20.00	32.50
	1838	.645	3.00	5.00	8.00
	1839	.469	3.00	5.00	8.00

20 REIS (VINTEM)

COPPER, 34mm
Obv. leg: JOANNES..., arms.
Rev. leg: PORTUGALIAE..., date, value within wreath.

C#	Date	Mintage	Fine	VF	XF
51	1800	—	12.50	22.50	37.50
	1801	—	Reported, Not Confirmed		

Large planchet, 37mm.

C#	Date	Mintage	Fine	VF	XF
51a	1800	—	15.00	25.00	40.00

SILVER
Obv: Globe. Rev: Cross with rosettes in angles.

C#	Date	Mintage	Fine	VF	XF
53	ND(1799-1816)		3.00	5.00	7.50

BRONZE
Titles of Maria II

C#	Date	Mintage	Fine	VF	XF
102	1833	—	18.50	27.50	55.00

(Struck at Porto.)

40 REIS (PATACO)

BRONZE

C#	Date	Mintage	Fine	VF	XF
52	1811	.163	30.00	45.00	80.00

NOTE: There are 5 edge varieties of this date.

C#	Date	Mintage	Fine	VF	XF
52a	1812	1.384	3.50	7.50	35.00
	1813	1.762	2.50	5.00	30.00
	1814	.542	6.00	8.00	45.00
	1815	.118	40.00	60.00	100.00
	1817	—	Reported, Not Confirmed		
68	1819	.422	10.00	25.00	50.00

C#	Date	Mintage	Fine	VF	XF
68a	1820	1.579	2.00	5.00	30.00
	1821	1.575	2.00	5.00	30.00
	1822	2.370	2.00	5.00	30.00
	1823	2.621	2.00	5.00	30.00
	1824	3.051	2.00	5.00	30.00
	1825	1.124	2.50	6.00	32.50

Similar to C#52.

C#	Date	Mintage	Fine	VF	XF
68b	1821	—	25.00	50.00	75.00
	1823	—	20.00	40.00	65.00

Rev: Similar to C#52.

C#	Date	Mintage	Fine	VF	XF
81	1826	1.253	10.00	20.00	60.00
	1827	1.447	5.00	10.00	30.00
	1828	1.378	5.00	10.00	30.00

C#	Date	Mintage	Fine	VF	XF
90	1828	1.378	8.50	15.00	35.00
	1829 two varieties of shield				
		1.678	3.00	6.50	30.00
	1830	1.783	2.00	5.00	30.00
	1831	1.391	2.00	5.00	30.00
	1832	1.780	2.00	5.00	30.00
	1833	1.631	2.00	3.50	30.00
	1834	—	Reported, Not Confirmed		

NOTE: The Pataco of 1828 with oval shield (C#90) is believed to be a pattern.

Titles Of Maria II
Similar to 20 Reis, C#102, shield flared outward at upper corners, value in wreath.

C#	Date	Mintage	Fine	VF	XF
103	1833	—	20.00	30.00	60.00

(Struck at Porto.)

Shield with right-angle upper corners.

C#	Date	Mintage	Fine	VF	XF
103a	1833	—	2.00	5.00	30.00
	1834	—	2.00	5.00	30.00
	1847	—	25.00	40.00	50.00

The 1833-34 coins were struck at Lisbon, the 1847 at Porto.

XXXX (= 50 REIS)

SILVER
Obv. leg: MARIA I ET PETRUS III...., crown.
Rev. leg: IN HOC..., cross.

C#	Date	Mintage	Fine	VF	XF
20	ND	—	5.00	10.00	25.00

Obv. leg: MARIA I D.G. ...

C#	Date	Mintage	Fine	VF	XF
35	ND	—	5.00	10.00	25.00

NOTE: 2 varieties are known.

XXXX (= 1/2 TOSTAO)

NOTE: Despite marking "XXXX" (=40), the half Tostao circulated at a value of 50 Reis.

SILVER
Obv. leg: JOANNES.... ET ALG.... Rev: IN HOC ..., cross.

C#	Date	Mintage	Fine	VF	XF
54	ND	—	5.00	10.00	20.00

Obv. leg. ends: P. REGENS.

C#	Date	Mintage	Fine	VF	XF
54a	ND	—	5.00	10.00	20.00
69	ND	—	5.00	10.00	20.00

Obv. leg: MICHAEL I.... REX, crowned value.
Rev. leg: IN HOC..., cross.

C#	Date	Mintage	Fine	VF	XF
91	ND	—	12.00	20.00	30.00

3 VINTENS (=60 REIS)

SILVER, 1.83 gm.
Obv. leg: MARIA I ET PETRUS III..., arms.
Rev. leg: IN HOC..., cross.

C#	Date	Mintage	Fine	VF	XF
21	ND	—	6.00	12.00	20.00

Obv. leg: MARIA I D.G. POR..., arms.

C#	Date	Mintage	Fine	VF	XF
36	ND	—	5.00	10.00	17.50

SILVER
Obv. leg: JOANNES.... ET ALG., arms.
Rev. leg: IN HOC..., cross.

C#	Date	Mintage	Fine	VF	XF
55	ND	—	6.00	12.00	20.00

Obv. leg. ends: P. REGENS.

C#	Date	Mintage	Fine	VF	XF
55a	ND	—	6.00	12.00	20.00

Obv: Crowned arms over globe.

C#	Date	Mintage	Fine	VF	XF
70	ND	—	6.00	12.00	20.00

Obv. leg: PETRUS IV.... REX, arms.

C#	Date	Mintage	Fine	VF	XF
82	ND	—	50.00	100.00	150.00

Obv. leg: MICHAEL I..., crowned arms.

C#	Date	Mintage	Fine	VF	XF
92	ND	—	7.50	15.00	25.00

LXXX (= 100 REIS)

SILVER
Obv. leg: MARIA I ET PETRUS III..., crown.
Rev. leg: IN HOC..., cross.

C#	Date	Mintage	Fine	VF	XF
22	ND	—	10.00	20.00	30.00

Obv. leg: MARIA I D.G. ...., crown.

C#	Date	Mintage	Fine	VF	XF
37	ND	—	10.00	17.50	25.00

NOTE: 2 varieties are known.

TOSTAO ("LXXX")

NOTE: Worth 100 Reis, though marked LXXX = 80 Reis.

SILVER
Obv. leg: JOANNES ... ET. ELG.
Rev. leg: IN HOC..., cross.

C#	Date	Mintage	Fine	VF	XF
56	ND	—	10.00	20.00	35.00

Obv. leg. ends: P. REGENS

C#	Date	Mintage	Fine	VF	XF
56a	ND	—	10.00	17.50	25.00

Similar to 1/2 Tostao, C#69.

C#	Date	Mintage	Fine	VF	XF
71	ND	—	10.00	20.00	35.00

Obv. leg: PETRUS IV .... REX, crowned arms.

C#	Date	Mintage	Fine	VF	XF
83	ND	—	125.00	175.00	225.00

Obv. leg: MICHAEL I ..., crowned arms.

C#	Date	Mintage	Fine	VF	XF
93	ND	—	20.00	30.00	50.00

6 VINTENS (120 REIS)

SILVER, 3.67 gm.
Obv. leg: MARIA I ET PETRUS III ..., arms.
Rev. leg: IN HOC ..., cross.

C#	Date	Mintage	Fine	VF	XF
23	ND	—	6.00	12.00	20.00

Obv. leg: MARIA I D.G. ..., crown.

C#	Date	Mintage	Fine	VF	XF
38	ND	—	6.00	12.00	17.50

C#	Date	Mintage	Fine	VF	XF
72	ND	—	8.00	15.00	25.00

Obv. leg: PETRUS IV .... REX, crowned arms.

C#	Date	Mintage	Fine	VF	XF
84	ND	—	100.00	150.00	200.00

Obv. leg: MICHAEL I ...., crowned arms.

C#	Date	Mintage	Fine	VF	XF
94	ND	—	15.00	25.00	40.00

12 VINTENS
(200 = 240 Reis)

SILVER

C#	Date	Mintage	Fine	VF	XF
24	1778	—	125.00	200.00	400.00
	1779	—	65.00	100.00	175.00
	1780	—	12.00	20.00	35.00
	1781	—	15.00	25.00	40.00
	1782	—	12.00	20.00	35.00
	1784	—	20.00	40.00	65.00
	1785	—	50.00	80.00	125.00
	1786	—	200.00	500.00	800.00

Obv. leg: MARIA I D.G. ...., crown.

C#	Date	Mintage	Fine	VF	XF
39	1786	—	400.00	750.00	1750.
	1788	—	200.00	375.00	800.00
	1791	—	1000.	2000.	6000.
	1792	—	500.00	1000.	2000.
39a	1793	—	35.00	90.00	175.00
	1794	—	250.00	500.00	1200.
	1795	—	—	Rare	—
	1797	—	—	Rare	—
	1798	—	125.00	250.00	600.00
	1799	—	100.00	200.00	450.00

Obv. leg: JOANNES .... P. REGENS., arms.

C#	Date	Mintage	Fine	VF	XF
58	1806	—	100.00	200.00	300.00
	1807	—	Reported, Not Confirmed		
	1808	—	40.00	65.00	90.00
	1809	.022	50.00	90.00	150.00
	1816	—	125.00	175.00	225.00

C#	Date	Mintage	Fine	VF	XF
73	1818	.021	40.00	75.00	110.00
	1819	.024	50.00	100.00	150.00
	1820	2,818	45.00	85.00	125.00
	1821	2,293	125.00	225.00	350.00
	1822	6,483	60.00	120.00	180.00

Obv. leg: MICHAEL I ..., crowned arms.

C#	Date	Mintage	Fine	VF	XF
95	1829	3,584	30.00	60.00	90.00
	1830	6,594	40.00	80.00	125.00

CRUZADO NOVO
(400 = 480 Reis)

SILVER
Obv. leg: MARIA I ET PETRUS III ...., arms.
Rev. leg: IN HOC ...., cross.

C#	Date	Mintage	Fine	VF	XF
25	1778	—	450.00	1000.	2000.
	1779	—	150.00	250.00	400.00
	1780	—	50.00	75.00	125.00
	1781	—	50.00	75.00	125.00
	1782	—	40.00	65.00	100.00
25a	1784	—	100.00	150.00	225.00
	1785	—	300.00	600.00	1200.

Obv. leg: MARIA I D.G. ...., crown.

C#	Date	Mintage	Fine	VF	XF
40	1786	—	1750.	3500.	7000.
	1788	—	800.00	1750.	3500.
	1792	—	400.00	800.00	1750.
	1793	—	40.00	65.00	125.00
	1794	—	200.00	400.00	900.00
	1795	—	50.00	75.00	140.00
	1796	—	60.00	85.00	175.00
	1797	—	50.00	75.00	140.00
	1798	—	40.00	65.00	125.00
	1799	—	200.00	375.00	800.00

Obv. leg. ends: ET. ALG.
Rev: Similar to C#59a.

C#	Date	Mintage	Fine	VF	XF
59	1799	.725	25.00	40.00	65.00
	1800	.438	40.00	65.00	100.00
	1801	.196	150.00	250.00	350.00
	1802	—	—	Rare	—

Obv. leg. ends: P.REGENS

C#	Date	Mintage	Fine	VF	XF
59a	1802	—	40.00	65.00	100.00
	1805	—	30.00	45.00	65.00
	1807	—	20.00	30.00	50.00
	1808	—	20.00	30.00	50.00
	1809	—	20.00	30.00	50.00
	1810	—	20.00	30.00	50.00
	1811	—	20.00	30.00	50.00
	1812	—	20.00	30.00	50.00
	1813	—	20.00	30.00	50.00
	1814	—	20.00	30.00	50.00
	1815	—	20.00	30.00	50.00
	1816	—	20.00	30.00	50.00
	1816	VINECS (error for VINCES)			
		—	50.00	75.00	100.00

C#	Date	Mintage	Fine	VF	XF
74	1818	2.337	25.00	35.00	60.00
	1819	1.432	20.00	30.00	50.00
	1820	1.845	20.00	30.00	50.00
	1821	1.937	20.00	30.00	50.00
	1822	.568	25.00	35.00	60.00
	1823	.667	25.00	35.00	60.00
	1825	.028	55.00	100.00	150.00

Obv. leg: PETRUS IV .... REX., arms.

C#	Date	Mintage	Fine	VF	XF
85	1826	.257	50.00	80.00	120.00
	1827	—	None Known To Have Survived		

Rev: Similar to C#59a.

C#	Date	Mintage	Fine	VF	XF
96	1828	.135	75.00	125.00	200.00
	1829	.022	—	Rare	—
	1830	.029	85.00	140.00	225.00
	1831	.065	65.00	110.00	165.00
	1832	.108	60.00	100.00	150.00
	1833	.798	60.00	100.00	150.00
	1834	—	Reported, Not Confirmed		

Obv. leg: *MARIA II.... REGINA*, arms.

C#	Date	Mintage	Fine	VF	XF
106	1833	—	—	Rare	—

(Struck in Porto.)

Obv. leg: Stars removed (Lisbon issues).
Rev: Similar to C#59a.

C#	Date	Mintage	Fine	VF	XF
106a	1833	.798	30.00	45.00	75.00
	1834	1.864	20.00	30.00	50.00
	1835	3.433	20.00	30.00	50.00
	1836	.829	25.00	40.00	70.00
	1837	.194	150.00	275.00	400.00

GOLD COINAGE

NOTE: The primary denomination was the Peca, weighing 14.34 gm., tariffed at 6400 Reis until 1825, and at 7500 Reis after 1826. The weight was not changed.

PINTO (480 REIS)
INSCRIBED "400" REIS

1.0720 gm., .917 GOLD, .0316 oz AGW
Obv. leg: MARIA I / ET P. III, in crowned wreath.
Rev. leg: IN HOC ...., cross.

C#	Date	Mintage	Fine	VF	XF
26	1777	—	325.00	650.00	900.00
	1778	—	175.00	350.00	500.00
	1780	—	175.00	350.00	500.00
	1783	—	200.00	425.00	600.00
	1784	—	200.00	425.00	600.00
	1785	—	325.00	650.00	900.00

Obv: Crowned MARIA I.

C#	Date	Mintage	Fine	VF	XF
41	1787	—	100.00	200.00	300.00
	1790	—	75.00	125.00	200.00
	1795	—	100.00	150.00	275.00
	1796	—	150.00	350.00	500.00

Obv: JOANNES P.R. in crowned wreath.

C#	Date	Mintage	Fine	VF	XF
60	1807	8,857	125.00	200.00	325.00

Obv: JOAN VI in crowned wreath.

C#	Date	Mintage	Fine	VF	XF
75	1818	4,401	125.00	200.00	325.00
	1819	1,387	140.00	225.00	350.00
	1820	200 Pcs.	400.00	650.00	850.00
	1821	266 Pcs.	400.00	650.00	850.00

1/2 ESCUDO (800 REIS)

1.7875 gm., .917 GOLD, .0527 oz AGW
Rev: Arms.

C#	Date	Mintage	Fine	VF	XF
27	1777	—	225.00	450.00	600.00
	1778	—	150.00	275.00	400.00
	1780	—	175.00	350.00	500.00
	1784	—	125.00	250.00	400.00

Obv. leg: MARIA I D.G. PORT ..., bust with widow's veil.

C#	Date	Mintage	Fine	VF	XF
42	1787	—	350.00	700.00	1000.
	1788	—	400.00	800.00	1200.

Obv: Bust with jeweled hairdress.

C#	Date	Mintage	Fine	VF	XF
42a	1789	—	100.00	200.00	300.00
	1792	—	150.00	275.00	400.00
	1796	—	100.00	225.00	300.00

Obv. leg: JOANNES D.G. PORT. ET ALG. P. REGENS., bust.

C#	Date	Mintage	Fine	VF	XF
61	1805	3,278	200.00	325.00	425.00
	1806	—	200.00	325.00	425.00
	1807	5,253	200.00	325.00	425.00

Obv. leg: JOANNES VI D.G. PORT... Rev: Arms.

C#	Date	Mintage	Fine	VF	XF
76	1818	270 pcs.	600.00	1000.	1250.
	1819	5,536	125.00	175.00	250.00
	1820	82 pcs.	—	Rare	—
	1821	286 pcs.	500.00	750.00	1000.

QUARTINHO (1200 REIS)
INSCRIBED "1000" REIS

2.6800 gm., .917 GOLD, .0790 oz AGW
Obv. leg: MARIA I ET PETRUS III ..., ornate arms.
Rev. leg: IN HOC ...., cross.

C#	Date	Mintage	Fine	VF	XF
28	1777	—	325.00	650.00	900.00
	1778	—	225.00	450.00	600.00
	1779	—	225.00	450.00	600.00
	1784	—	250.00	500.00	700.00

Obv. leg: MARIA I D. G. PORT ..., crowned arms.

C#	Date	Mintage	Fine	VF	XF
43	1787	—	700.00	1400.	2000.
	1789	—	275.00	550.00	800.00
	1792	—	250.00	500.00	750.00
	1800	—	1500.	2750.	4000.

Similar to 1/2 Tostao, C#69.

C#	Date	Mintage	Fine	VF	XF
77	1818	3,144	225.00	300.00	500.00
	1819	1,247	450.00	600.00	800.00
	1820	270 pcs.	—	Rare	—
	1821	275 pcs.	500.00	700.00	900.00

ESCUDO (1600 REIS)

3.5750 gm., .917 GOLD, .1054 oz AGW
Obv. leg: MARIA I ET PETRUS III., busts.
Rev: Arms.

C#	Date	Mintage	Fine	VF	XF
29	1777	—	300.00	600.00	900.00
	1778	—	200.00	350.00	500.00
	1779	—	200.00	350.00	500.00
	1781	—	350.00	700.00	1000.
	1784	—	200.00	350.00	500.00

C#	Date	Mintage	Fine	VF	XF
29	1785	—	325.00	650.00	950.00

Obv. leg: MARIA I D. G. PORT...., bust with widow's veil.

C#	Date	Mintage	Fine	VF	XF
44	1787	—	250.00	525.00	750.00
	1788	—	275.00	575.00	800.00

Obv: Bust with jeweled hairdress.

C#	Date	Mintage	Fine	VF	XF
44a	1789	—	375.00	750.00	1250.
	1790	—	200.00	375.00	750.00
	1791	—	375.00	750.00	1250.
	1792	—	175.00	350.00	500.00
	1794	—	200.00	425.00	600.00
	1796	—	200.00	425.00	600.00

Obv. leg: JOANNES D.G. PORT ET ALG. P. REGENS, bust.

C#	Date	Mintage	Fine	VF	XF
62	1805	—	—	Rare	—
	1807	800 pcs.	—	Rare	—

Obv. leg: JOANNES VI D.G. PORT .... REX, bust.

C#	Date	Mintage	Fine	VF	XF
78	1818	1,804	225.00	300.00	500.00
	1819	1,523	450.00	600.00	850.00
	1821	270 pcs.	550.00	750.00	1000.

2 ESCUDOS

7.1500 gm., .917 GOLD, .2107 oz AGW

C#	Date	Mintage	Fine	VF	XF
30	1778	—	700.00	900.00	1200.
	1784	—	900.00	1200.	1500.

C#	Date	Mintage	Fine	VF	XF
45	1789	—	700.00	900.00	1200.

1/2 PECA (3200 REIS)
REVALUED TO 3750 REIS IN 1826

.917 GOLD
Obv. leg: JOANNES D.G. PORT ET ALG. P. REGENS, bust.

C#	Date	Mintage	Fine	VF	XF
63	1805	74 pcs.	—	Rare	—
63a	1807	483 pcs.	—	Rare	—

C#	Date	Mintage	Fine	VF	XF
79	1818	100 pcs.	—	Rare	—
	1819	1,700	700.00	1000.	1500.
	1820	242 pcs.	—	Rare	—
	1821	196 pcs.	—	Rare	—
	1822	.014	450.00	600.00	1000.
	1823	—	—	Rare	—

C#	Date	Mintage	Fine	VF	XF
86	1827	1,713	1250.	1800.	2500.

C#	Date	Mintage	Fine	VF	XF
97	1828	242 pcs.	—	Rare	—

C#	Date	Mintage	Fine	VF	XF
97a	1830	525 pcs.	—	Rare	—
	1831	225 pcs.	—	Rare	—

4 ESCUDOS

14.3000 gm., .917 GOLD, .4215 oz. AGW
Obv: Busts right, leg: MARIA I ET PETRUS III.
Rev: Arms.

C#	Date	Mintage	Fine	VF	XF
31	1777	—	1200.	2500.	5000.
	1778	—	650.00	900.00	1200.
	1779	—	650.00	900.00	1200.
	1780	—	650.00	900.00	1200.
	1781	—	650.00	900.00	1200.
31a	1782	—	650.00	900.00	1200.
	1783	—	650.00	900.00	1200.
	1784	—	650.00	900.00	1200.
	1785	—	650.00	900.00	1200.

Obv: Bust right with widow's veil, legend separated after D.G.

C#	Date	Mintage	Fine	VF	XF
46.1	1786	—	1250.	2500.	5000.

Obv: Smaller letters in legend separated by head after PORT.

C#	Date	Mintage	Fine	VF	XF
46.2	1786	—	1000.	2000.	4000.

Obv: Large letters in legend.

C#	Date	Mintage	Fine	VF	XF
46.3	1787	—	700.00	1500.	3000.

Obv: Bust right with jeweled hairdress.

C#	Date	Mintage	Fine	VF	XF
46a	1789	—	600.00	800.00	1200.
	1791	—	600.00	800.00	1200.
	1792	—	600.00	800.00	1200.
	1793	—	700.00	900.00	1500.
	1796	—	700.00	900.00	1500.
	1797	—	800.00	1000.	1750.
	1798	—	800.00	1000.	1750.
	1799	—	700.00	900.00	1500.

PECA (6400 REIS)
REVALUED TO 7500 REIS IN 1826

.917 GOLD
Obv: JOANNES D.G. PORT ET ALG. P. REGENS, bust

C#	Date	Mintage	Fine	VF	XF
64	1802	.030	1000.	1500.	2000.

Modified design

C#	Date	Mintage	Fine	VF	XF
64a	1804	476 pcs.	—	Rare	—
	1805	.027	600.00	800.00	1000.
	1806	.041	500.00	700.00	900.00
	1807	.036	500.00	700.00	900.00
	1808	.027	500.00	700.00	900.00
	1809	.013	700.00	900.00	1100
	1812	.025	500.00	700.00	900.00
	1813	5,590	—	Rare	—
	1814	21 pcs.	—	Rare	—
	1815	305 pcs.	1800.	2500.	3000.
	1816	—	—	Rare	—
	1817	620 pcs.	Reported, Not Confirmed		

NOTE: Similar pieces with "R" after date were struck in Rio de Janeiro and are found listed under Brazil.

C#	Date	Mintage	Fine	VF	XF
80	1818	291 pcs.	—	Rare	—
	1819	1,727	800.00	1200.	1500.
	1820	1,687	800.00	1200.	1500.
	1821	391 pcs.	1500.	2000.	3000.
	1822	.030	450.00	600.00	850.00
	1823	.027	450.00	600.00	850.00
	1824	1,553	850.00	1250.	1500.

NOTE: Similar pieces with "R" after date were struck in Rio de Janeiro and are listed under Brazil.

C#	Date	Mintage	Fine	VF	XF
87	1826	10,883	1100.	1600.	2000.
	1828	1,255	1400.	2000.	2500.

NOTE: Similar pieces dated 1826 with square shield on reverse are patterns.

Similar to C#98a.

C#	Date	Mintage	Fine	VF	XF
98	1828	Inc. Ab.	—	Rare	—

Modified design

C#	Date	Mintage	Fine	VF	XF
98a	1830	2,274	1100.	1600.	2000.
	1831	1,618	1200.	1800.	2200.

Obv: Bare head of queen

C#	Date	Mintage	Fine	VF	XF
112	1833	1,265	—	Rare	—

C#	Date	Mintage	Fine	VF	XF
112a	1833	—	—	Rare	—
	1834	.032	1000.	1500.	1750.

Obv. legend continuous

C#	Date	Mintage	Fine	VF	XF
112b	1835	2,989	1200.	1800.	2200.

COUNTERMARK ISSUES

40 REIS

COPPER

c/s: GCP in a circle on 40 Reis, C#103a.

C#	Date	Mintage	VG	Fine	VF
103b	1833	—	15.00	25.00	50.00
	1847	—	5.00	7.50	15.00

c/s: With dot added below GCP on 40 Reis, C#103a.

C#	Date	Mintage	VG	Fine	VF
103c	1847	—	6.50	10.00	17.50

870 REIS

In 1834, the Portuguese government ordered that the countermarking of all Spanish and Spanish American 8 Reales in circulation with the crowned arms of Portugal, to indicate a revaluation to 870 reis.

SILVER

C#	Date	Mintage	VG	Fine	VF
	c/s: On Bolivia (Potosi) 8 Reales, C#18.				
113.1	ND(1773-89)	—	120.00	180.00	240.00
	c/s: On Bolivia (Potosi) 8 Reales, C#27.				
113.2	ND(1789-91)	—	120.00	180.00	240.00
	c/s: On Bolivia (Potosi) 8 Reales, C#37.				
113.3	ND(1791-1808)	—	70.00	100.00	135.00
	c/s: On Bolivia (Potosi) 8 Reales, C#47.				
113.4	ND(1808-25)	—	70.00	100.00	135.00
	c/s: On Brazil 960 Reis, C#117.				
113.5	ND(1818-22)	—	120.00	180.00	240.00
	c/s: On Chile 8 Reales, C#61.				
113.6	ND(1791-1808)	—	240.00	350.00	550.00
	c/s: On Guatemala 8 Reales, C#72.				
113.7	ND(1808-22)	—	180.00	240.00	325.00

C#	Date	Mintage	VG	Fine	VF
	c/s: On Mexico 8 Reales, KM#103 (C#8).				
113.8	ND(1732-47)	—	180.00	240.00	325.00
	c/s: On Mexico 8 Reales, KM#104 (C#17).				
113.9	ND(1747-60)	—	150.00	200.00	375.00
	c/s: On Mexico 8 Reales, KM#105 (C#35).				
113.10	ND(1760-72)	—	150.00	200.00	375.00
	c/s: On Mexico 8 Reales, KM#106 (C#40).				
113.11	ND(1772-89)	—	60.00	90.00	120.00
	c/s: On Mexico 8 Reales, KM#107 (C#73).				
113.12	ND(1789-90)	—	75.00	100.00	150.00
	c/s: On Mexico 8 Reales, KM#109 (C#81).				
113.13	ND(1791-1808)	—	60.00	90.00	120.00
	c/s: On Mexico 8 Reales, KM#110 (C#111).				
113.14	ND(1808-11)	—	60.00	90.00	120.00
	c/s: On Mexico 8 Reales, KM#111 (C#121).				
113.15	ND(1811-21)	—	60.00	90.00	120.00
	c/s: On Mexico (Durango) 8 Reales KM#111.2 (C#121).				
113.16	ND(1812-22)	—	250.00	375.00	550.00
	c/s: On Mexico (Guadalajara) 8 Reales, KM#111.3 (C#121).				
113.17	ND(1812-22)	—	90.00	130.00	200.00
	c/s: On Mexico (Guanajuato) 8 Reales, KM#111.4 (C#121).				
113.18	ND(1812-22)	—	90.00	130.00	200.00

C#	Date	Mintage	VG	Fine	VF
	c/s: On Mexico (Zacatecas) 8 Reales, KM#111.5 (C#121).				
113.19	ND(1813-22)	—	60.00	90.00	120.00
	c/s: On Peru (Lima) 8 Reales, C#69.				
113.20	ND(1789-91)	—	75.00	100.00	135.00
	c/s: On Peru (Lima) 8 Reales, C#76.				
113.21	ND(1791-1808)	—	60.00	90.00	120.00

C#	Date	Mintage	VG	Fine	VF
	c/s: On Peru (Lima) 8 Reales, C#96.				
113.22	ND(1808-11)	—	60.00	90.00	120.00
	c/s: On Peru (Lima) 8 Reales, C#101.				
113.33	ND(1810-24)	—	60.00	90.00	120.00
	c/s: On Spain (Cadiz), C#136.				
113.34	ND(1810-15)	—	90.00	130.00	200.00
	c/s: On Spain (Madrid) 8 Reales, C#71.				
113.35	ND(1789-1808)	—	90.00	130.00	200.00

C#	Date	Mintage	VG	Fine	VF
	c/s: On Spain (Madrid) 20 Reales, C#92.				
113.36	ND(1808-13)	—	90.00	130.00	200.00
	c/s: On Spain (Madrid) 8 Reales, C#136.				
113.37	ND(1812-33)	—	75.00	100.00	135.00
	c/s: On Spain (Seville) 8 Reales, C#40.				
113.38	ND(1772-88)	—	240.00	350.00	550.00
	c/s: On Spain (Seville) 8 Reales, C#71.				
113.39	ND(1788-1808)	—	160.00	210.00	275.00
	c/s: On Spain (Seville) 8 Reales, C#136.				
113.40	ND(1809-30)	—	75.00	100.00	135.00
	c/s: On Spain (Valencia) 8 Reales, C#136a.				
113.41	ND(1809-11)	—	120.00	180.00	240.00

30,000 REIS

In 1847, the same countermark was applied to the Dobrao of John V, indicating a revaluation from 20,000 to 30,000 Reis.

GOLD

c/s: Crowned arms on 20,000 Reis of John V.

C#	Date	Mintage	Fine	VF	XF
115	1724-27	(1847)	2000.	2500.	3500.

DECIMAL CURRENCY

New denominations, all expressed in terms of Reis, were introduced by Maria II in 1836, to bring Portugal's currency into decimal form. Some of the coins retained old names, as follows:

1000 Reis Silver - Coroa

100 Reis Silver - Tostao

NOTE: The diameter of the new copper coins, first minted by Maria II in 1837, was smaller than the earlier coinage, but the weight was unaltered. However, in 1882, Luis I reduced the size and weight of the copper currency.

3 REIS

COPPER

Y#	Date	Mintage	VF	XF	Unc
1	1868	.100	3.50	6.00	12.50
	1874	.280	3.50	6.00	12.50
	1875	1.200	3.50	7.50	15.00

5 REIS

COPPER

C#	Date	Mintage	Fine	VF	XF
99c	1840	.174	7.50	16.00	30.00
	1843	—	20.00	40.00	75.00
	1848	.147	7.50	16.00	30.00
	1850	.130	7.50	16.00	30.00
	1852	.292	7.50	16.00	30.00
	1853	.063	7.50	16.00	30.00

Y#	Date	Mintage	VF	XF	Unc
2	1867	.737	4.00	7.50	12.50

Y#	Date	Mintage	VF	XF	Unc
2	1868	.740	4.00	7.50	12.50
	1871	.340	25.00	50.00	90.00
	1872	.700	4.00	7.50	12.50
	1873	.600	20.00	32.50	60.00
	1874	1.080	2.00	5.00	10.00
	1875	2.200	2.00	5.00	10.00
	1876	.320	17.50	30.00	55.00
	1877	.620	17.50	30.00	55.00
	1878	Inc. Ab.	2.00	5.00	10.00
	1879	.332	6.00	15.00	25.00
	1882	—	Reported, Not Confirmed		

BRONZE

Y#	Date	Mintage	VF	XF	Unc
5	1882	5.200	1.25	3.00	6.00
	1883	4.700	1.25	3.00	6.00
	1884	1.730	1.50	3.50	7.00
	1885	3.200	1.25	3.00	6.00
	1886	4.170	1.75	4.00	8.00

Y#	Date	Mintage	VF	XF	Unc
15	1890	.430	1.50	2.50	5.00
	1891	Inc. Ab.	1.00	2.50	5.00
	1892/1	—	—	—	—
	1892	1.510	.75	1.50	4.50
	1893	.280	.75	1.50	4.50
	1897	1.120	1.25	3.00	6.00
	1898	.790	.75	1.50	4.50
	1899	1.220	.75	1.50	4.50
	1900	1.110	1.25	3.00	6.00
	1901	1.070	1.50	3.50	7.50
	1904	.720	1.00	2.50	5.00
	1905	1.340	.75	1.50	4.50
	1906	1.260	.75	1.50	4.50

Y#	Date	Mintage	VF	XF	Unc
28	1910	1.000	.75	1.50	4.50

10 REIS

COPPER

Obv: Plain shield, struck in collared dies.

C#	Date	Mintage	Fine	VF	XF
100c	1837	—	15.00	30.00	50.00
	1838	—	8.00	16.00	35.00
	1839	—	8.00	16.00	35.00

Obv: Ornate shield

C#	Date	Mintage	Fine	VF	XF
100d	1840	.392	8.00	16.00	35.00
	1841	.476	8.00	16.00	35.00
	1842	1.131	8.00	16.00	35.00
	1843	.837	8.00	16.00	35.00
	1844	.620	8.00	16.00	35.00
	1845	.545	8.00	16.00	35.00
	1846	1.166	8.00	16.00	35.00
	1847	.057	25.00	50.00	80.00
	1850	.443	8.00	16.00	35.00
	1851	1,236	8.00	16.00	35.00
	1852	.558	8.00	16.00	35.00
	1853	.046	8.00	16.00	35.00

Y#	Date	Mintage	Fine	VF	XF
3	1867	.300	4.00	6.50	12.50
	1868	.450	15.00	25.00	45.00
	1870	Inc. Ab.	60.00	100.00	150.00
	1871	.360	10.00	17.50	30.00
	1873	2.000	2.50	5.00	10.00
	1874	.220	50.00	75.00	125.00
	1878	—	Reported, Not Confirmed		

BRONZE

Y#	Date	Mintage	VF	XF	Unc
6	1882	14.795	2.00	5.00	10.00
	1883	Inc. Ab.	2.00	5.00	10.00
	1884	10.190	2.00	5.00	10.00
	1885	8.100	2.00	5.00	10.00
	1886	3.915	2.50	7.50	15.00

Y#	Date	Mintage	VF	XF	Unc
16	1891	3.445	2.00	5.00	10.00
	1891A	.895	2.50	7.50	15.00
	1892	10.300	2.00	5.00	10.00
	1892A	5.769	2.00	5.00	10.00

20 REIS

COPPER

C#	Date	Mintage	Fine	VF	XF
101	1847	2.484	6.00	15.00	40.00
	1848	.861	6.00	15.00	40.00
	1849	2.269	6.00	15.00	40.00
	1850	1.803	6.00	15.00	40.00
	1851	.850	6.00	15.00	40.00
	1852	1.215	6.00	15.00	40.00
	1853	.791	6.00	15.00	40.00

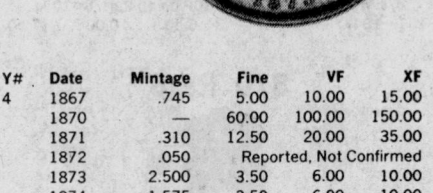

Y#	Date	Mintage	Fine	VF	XF
4	1867	.745	5.00	10.00	15.00
	1870	—	60.00	100.00	150.00
	1871	.310	12.50	20.00	35.00
	1872	.050	Reported, Not Confirmed		
	1873	2.500	3.50	6.00	10.00
	1874	1.575	3.50	6.00	10.00

BRONZE

Y#	Date	Mintage	VF	XF	Unc
7	1882	17.735	2.00	10.00	20.00
	1883	Inc. Ab.	2.00	10.00	20.00
	1884	17.200	2.00	10.00	20.00
	1885	18.492	2.00	10.00	20.00
	1886	4.572	2.00	10.00	20.00

Y#	Date	Mintage	VF	XF	Unc
17	1891	3.282	2.00	10.00	20.00
	1891A	6.016	2.00	10.00	20.00
	1892	15.411	2.00	10.00	20.00
	1892A	.658	2.00	10.00	20.00

40 REIS

Refer to earlier listings for 40 Reis of Maria II dated 1847 (C#103a-c).

50 REIS

1.2500 gm., .917 SILVER, .0368 oz ASW

C#	Date	Mintage	Fine	VF	XF
116	1855	.041	17.50	30.00	50.00
	1861	.800	3.50	5.00	7.50

Y#	Date	Mintage	Fine	VF	XF
8	1862	.017	7.50	15.00	30.00
	1863	.215	3.50	7.50	15.00
	1864	.050	10.00	20.00	40.00
	1868	—	Reported, Not Confirmed		
	1874	.060	7.50	15.00	35.00
	1875	Inc. Ab.	45.00	75.00	100.00
	1876	.100	3.50	7.00	15.00
	1877	.100	3.50	7.00	15.00
	1879	.080	3.50	7.00	15.00
	1880	.320	3.50	7.00	15.00
	1886	.100	3.50	7.00	15.00
	1887	Inc. Ab.	25.00	45.00	70.00
	1888	Inc. Be.	—	Rare	—
	1889	1.000	2.00	4.00	7.00

Y#	Date	Mintage	Fine	VF	XF
20	1893	.620	2.50	5.50	12.50

COPPER-NICKEL

Y#	Date	Mintage	VF	XF	Unc
18	1900	8.000	.85	1.50	3.00

100 REIS

2.5000 gm., .917 SILVER, .0737 oz ASW

Obv: Young head

C#	Date	Mintage	Fine	VF	XF
104a	1838	1,544	40.00	100.00	200.00
	1842	—	Reported, Not Confirmed		
	1843	—	10.00	20.00	40.00
	1848	—	Reported, Not Confirmed		

Obv: Mature head

C#	Date	Mintage	Fine	VF	XF
104b	1851	—	6.00	15.00	30.00

Obv: Older head

C#	Date	Mintage	Fine	VF	XF
104c	1853	—	5.00	12.50	25.00

C#	Date	Mintage	Fine	VF	XF
117	1854	.422	6.50	12.50	25.00

Obv: Young head

C#	Date	Mintage	Fine	VF	XF
117a	1857	.043	50.00	100.00	200.00
	1858	—	50.00	100.00	200.00
	1859	.455	5.00	10.00	20.00
	1860	—	Reported, Not Confirmed		
	1861	.762	5.00	10.00	20.00

Y#	Date	Mintage	Fine	VF	XF
9	1864	.160	17.50	40.00	80.00
	1865	.100	12.50	30.00	60.00
	1866	.010	125.00	200.00	300.00
	1869	.010	125.00	200.00	300.00
	1871	.060	20.00	40.00	80.00
	1872	.060	15.00	30.00	60.00
	1873	—	Reported, Not Confirmed		
	1874	.170	10.00	20.00	40.00
	1875	.130	7.50	15.00	30.00

Y#	Date	Mintage	Fine	VF	XF
9	1876	.220	3.50	7.50	15.00
	1877	.120	8.00	20.00	40.00
	1878	.030	15.00	30.00	60.00
	1879	.560	3.50	7.50	15.00
	1880	.440	3.00	6.00	12.00
	1881	Inc. Ab.	75.00	150.00	225.00
	1886	.360	2.50	5.00	10.00
	1888	.500	2.50	5.00	10.00
	1889	1.500	2.50	5.00	10.00

Y#	Date	Mintage	Fine	VF	XF
21	1890	.700	8.00	15.00	22.50
	1891	.270	8.00	20.00	40.00
	1893	11.050	3.50	7.00	14.00
	1894	Inc. Ab.	50.00	100.00	150.00
	1895	—	Reported, Not Confirmed		
	1898	.930	3.50	7.00	14.00

COPPER-NICKEL

Y#	Date	Mintage	VF	XF	Unc
19	1900	16.000	1.00	1.75	4.00

.835 SILVER

Y#	Date	Mintage	Fine	VF	XF
29	1909	6.363	3.00	5.00	7.50
	1910	Inc. Ab.	2.50	4.00	6.00

200 REIS

5.0000 gm., .917 SILVER, .1474 oz ASW

Obv: Young head

C#	Date	Mintage	Fine	VF	XF
105a	1838	2,177	30.00	60.00	150.00
	1841	272 pcs.	50.00	100.00	200.00
	1842	—	Reported, Not Confirmed		
	1843	1,181	10.00	25.00	75.00
	1846	—	Reported, Not Confirmed		
	1848	—	Reported, Not Confirmed		

C#	Date	Mintage	Fine	VF	XF
118	1854	.292	5.00	10.00	30.00
	1855	.056	5.00	10.00	30.00

C#	Date	Mintage	Fine	VF	XF
118a	1858	.280	5.00	10.00	30.00
	1859	—	Reported, Not Confirmed		
	1860	—	5.00	10.00	30.00
	1861	.202	50.00	100.00	200.00

Y#	Date	Mintage	Fine	VF	XF
10	1862	.694	15.00	40.00	80.00
	1863	.345	12.00	30.00	60.00
	1865	.050	25.00	60.00	120.00

Second bust

Similar to 100 Reis, Y#9.

Y#	Date	Mintage	Fine	VF	XF
10a	1866	.010	125.00	225.00	600.00
	1867	.010	80.00	150.00	400.00
	1868	5,000	80.00	150.00	400.00
	1871	.075	25.00	50.00	100.00
	1872	.070	35.00	60.00	120.00
	1875	.070	20.00	35.00	80.00
	1876	.080	125.00	225.00	500.00
	1877	.030	35.00	60.00	150.00
	1878	.020	80.00	150.00	400.00
	1879	5,000	125.00	225.00	600.00
	1880	.150	12.50	20.00	35.00
	1886	.340	6.00	10.00	25.00
	1887	3.600	4.50	6.00	16.00
	1888	.700	6.00	10.00	20.00

Y#	Date	Mintage	Fine	VF	XF
22	1891	2.365	4.50	6.00	10.00
	1892	2.450	4.50	6.00	12.00
	1893	1.220	12.50	20.00	30.00
	1893/2	Inc. Ab.	12.50	20.00	35.00
	1901	.205	80.00	125.00	175.00
	1903	.200	12.50	20.00	40.00

400th Anniversary Discovery of India

Y#	Date	Mintage	Fine	VF	XF
25	1898	.250	4.50	7.50	10.00

5.0000 gm., .835 SILVER, .1342 oz ASW

Y#	Date	Mintage	Fine	VF	XF
30	1909	7.650	Bv	Bv	5.00

500 REIS

12.5000 gm., .917 SILVER, .3684 oz ASW

C#	Date	Mintage	Fine	VF	XF
107a	1837	1,266	225.00	450.00	800.00
	1838	2,645	200.00	400.00	700.00
	1839	2,084	200.00	400.00	700.00
	1841	.022	12.50	25.00	45.00
	1842	.135	12.50	25.00	45.00
	1843	.105	30.00	60.00	100.00
	1844	4,265	35.00	75.00	125.00
	1845	—	45.00	90.00	150.00
	1846	.074	12.50	25.00	40.00
	1847	.775	12.50	25.00	40.00
	1848	.024	30.00	60.00	100.00

C#	Date	Mintage	Fine	VF	XF
107a	1849	.059	15.00	30.00	50.00
	1850	.041	30.00	60.00	100.00
	1851	.091	12.50	25.00	40.00
	1853	.022	75.00	150.00	250.00

Obv. leg: PETRUS.V..., young head.

C#	Date	Mintage	Fine	VF	XF
119	1854	.592	12.50	35.00	60.00
119a	1855	1.210	7.50	15.00	30.00
	1856	1.478	7.00	15.00	30.00
119b	1857	1.950	15.00	40.00	80.00
	1858	3.091	7.00	15.00	30.00
	1859	2.660	12.50	15.00	30.00

Y#	Date	Mintage	Fine	VF	XF
11	1863	.148	12.50	20.00	60.00
	1864	.341	12.50	20.00	60.00
	1865	.406	12.50	20.00	60.00
	1866	.378	12.50	20.00	60.00
	1867	.458	12.50	20.00	60.00
	1868	.388	12.50	20.00	60.00
	1870	.314	12.50	15.00	20.00
	1871	.228	12.50	15.00	20.00
	1872	.576	175.00	300.00	450.00
	1875	.140	12.50	15.00	20.00
	1876	.280	100.00	175.00	250.00
	1877	.050	30.00	60.00	120.00
	1879	.688	BV	12.50	20.00
	1886	.300	BV	12.50	15.00
	1887	.432	BV	12.50	15.00
	1888	2.740	BV	12.50	15.00
	1889	.960	BV	12.50	15.00

Y#	Date	Mintage	Fine	VF	XF
23	1891	12.476	BV	12.50	15.00
	1892/1	Inc. Ab.	—	—	—
	1892	4.716	BV	12.50	15.00
	1893	1.494	BV	12.50	15.00
	1894	.254	300.00	500.00	700.00
	1895	.216	25.00	50.00	100.00
	1896	3.520	BV	12.50	15.00
	1898	1.000	BV	12.50	15.00
	1899	3.100	BV	12.50	15.00
	1900	.200	100.00	150.00	225.00
	1901	1.050	15.00	25.00	50.00
	1903	.920	BV	12.50	15.00
	1904	—	Reported, Not Confirmed		
	1906	—	15.00	25.00	50.00
	1907	.384	BV	12.50	15.00
	1908	1.840	BV	12.50	15.00

400th Anniversary Discovery of India

Y#	Date	Mintage	Fine	VF	XF
26	1898	.300	12.50	15.00	20.00

Y#	Date	Mintage	Fine	VF	XF
31	1908	2.500	BV	12.50	15.00
	1909	1.513	12.50	15.00	22.50

Peninsular War Centennial

Y#	Date	Mintage	Fine	VF	XF
32	1910	.200	20.00	35.00	50.00

Marquis De Pombal

Y#	Date	Mintage	Fine	VF	XF
34	1910	.400	12.50	17.50	27.50

1000 REIS

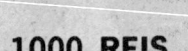

29.6000 gm., .917 SILVER, .8727 oz ASW

C#	Date	Mintage	Fine	VF	XF
108a	1837	2,295	100.00	150.00	250.00
	1838	3,959	80.00	130.00	200.00
	1842	—	—	—	3000.
	1843	—	Reported, Not Confirmed		
	1844	—	75.00	100.00	150.00
	1845	10,724	75.00	100.00	150.00

2.3900 gm., .917 GOLD, .0704 oz AGW

C#	Date	Mintage	Fine	VF	XF
109	1851	.012	50.00	75.00	100.00

1.7735 gm., .917 GOLD, .0523 oz AGW
Obv: Boy head

C#	Date	Mintage	Fine	VF	XF
120	1855	6,100	65.00	100.00	135.00

25.0000 gm., .917 SILVER, .7368 oz ASW
400th Anniversary Discovery Of India

Y#	Date	Mintage	Fine	VF	XF
27	1898	.300	22.50	27.50	35.00

Y#	Date	Mintage	Fine	VF	XF
24	1899	1.500	22.50	25.00	32.50
	1900	Inc. Ab.	800.00	1200.	2000.

Peninsular War Centennial

Y#	Date	Mintage	Fine	VF	XF
33	1910	.200	30.00	40.00	55.00

2000 REIS

3.5470 gm., .917 GOLD, .1045 oz AGW
Obv: Boy head

C#	Date	Mintage	Fine	VF	XF
121	1856	.038	70.00	85.00	125.00
	1857	.044	70.00	85.00	125.00

Obv: Young head

C#	Date	Mintage	Fine	VF	XF
121a	1858	.013	70.00	85.00	125.00
	1859	.016	70.00	85.00	125.00
	1860	.053	70.00	85.00	125.00

Rev: Arms in spray.

Y#	Date	Mintage	Fine	VF	XF
A12	1864	.101	70.00	80.00	125.00
	1865	.095	70.00	80.00	125.00
	1866	.086	70.00	80.00	125.00

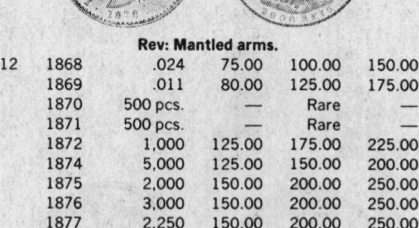

Rev: Mantled arms.

Y#	Date	Mintage	Fine	VF	XF
12	1868	.024	75.00	100.00	150.00
	1869	.011	80.00	125.00	175.00
	1870	500 pcs.	—	Rare	—
	1871	500 pcs.	—	Rare	—
	1872	1,000	125.00	175.00	225.00
	1874	5,000	125.00	150.00	200.00
	1875	2,000	150.00	200.00	250.00
	1876	3,000	150.00	200.00	250.00
	1877	2,250	150.00	200.00	250.00
	1878	.022	75.00	100.00	150.00
	1881	1,000	150.00	175.00	225.00
	1888	500 pcs.	—	Rare	—

2500 REIS

4.7800 gm., .917 GOLD, .1409 oz AGW
Obv: Young head

C#	Date	Mintage	Fine	VF	XF
110a	1838	1,114	150.00	225.00	300.00

C#	Date	Mintage	Fine	VF	XF
110b	1851	.058	100.00	125.00	175.00

C#	Date	Mintage	Fine	VF	XF
110c	1853	1,010	175.00	275.00	400.00

5000 REIS

9.5600 gm., .917 GOLD, .2818 oz AGW
Obv: Young head

C#	Date	Mintage	Fine	VF	XF
111a	1838	2,410	225.00	275.00	350.00
111a	1845	401 pcs.	300.00	350.00	450.00
	1851	.057	200.00	250.00	300.00

8.8675 gm., .917 GOLD, .2613 oz AGW
Obv: Young head

C#	Date	Mintage	Fine	VF	XF
122	1860	.052	170.00	200.00	250.00
	1861	.081	170.00	200.00	250.00

Rev: Arms in spray

Y#	Date	Mintage	Fine	VF	XF
A13	1862	.116	175.00	200.00	275.00
	1863	.038	175.00	200.00	275.00

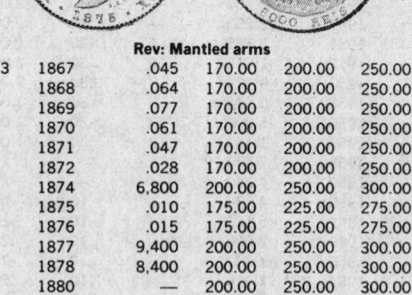

Rev: Mantled arms

Y#	Date	Mintage	Fine	VF	XF
13	1867	.045	170.00	200.00	250.00
	1868	.064	170.00	200.00	250.00
	1869	.077	170.00	200.00	250.00
	1870	.061	170.00	200.00	250.00
	1871	.047	170.00	200.00	250.00
	1872	.028	170.00	200.00	250.00
	1874	6,800	200.00	250.00	300.00
	1875	.010	175.00	225.00	275.00
	1876	.015	175.00	225.00	275.00
	1877	9,400	200.00	250.00	300.00
	1878	8,400	200.00	250.00	300.00
	1880	—	200.00	250.00	300.00
	1883	.023	175.00	225.00	275.00
	1886	.027	175.00	225.00	275.00
	1887	.044	175.00	225.00	275.00
	1888	4,800	200.00	250.00	300.00
	1889	9,000	200.00	250.00	300.00

10,000 REIS

17.7350 gm., .917 GOLD, .5227 oz AGW

Y#	Date	Mintage	Fine	VF	XF
14	1878	.023	340.00	375.00	450.00
	1879	.036	340.00	375.00	450.00
	1880	.030	340.00	375.00	450.00
	1881	.019	340.00	375.00	450.00
	1882	.015	340.00	375.00	450.00
	1883	8,500	400.00	450.00	500.00
	1884	.013	340.00	375.00	450.00
	1885	.021	340.00	375.00	450.00
	1886	1,800	400.00	450.00	500.00
	1888	7,000	400.00	450.00	500.00
	1889	4,400	375.00	425.00	475.00

REPUBLIC

100 Centavos = 1 Escudo

CENTAVO

BRONZE

Y#	Date	Mintage	VF	XF	Unc
36	1917	12.260	.30	.75	1.25
	1918	13.280	.30	.75	1.25
36	1919	12.535	.30	.75	1.25
	1920	—	.40	1.00	2.00
	1921	4.949	1.50	2.00	5.00
	1922	Inc. Ab.	—	Rare	—

2 CENTAVOS

IRON

Y#	Date	Mintage	VF	XF	Unc
35	1918	.170	30.00	45.00	75.00

BRONZE

Y#	Date	Mintage	VF	XF	Unc
37	1918	4.295	.25	.75	1.50
	1920	10.103	.25	.75	1.25
	1921	.679	6.00	10.00	15.00

4 CENTAVOS

COPPER NICKEL

Y#	Date	Mintage	VF	XF	Unc
42	1917	4.961	.25	.75	2.00
	1919	10.067	.25	.75	1.50

5 CENTAVOS

BRONZE

Y#	Date	Mintage	VF	XF	Unc
38	1920	.114	6.00	10.00	15.00
	1921	5.916	.40	1.00	10.00
	1922	Inc. Ab.	45.00	60.00	85.00

Y#	Date	Mintage	VF	XF	Unc
39	1924	6.480	.25	.75	10.00
	1925	7.260	2.00	2.50	5.00
	1927	26.320	.20	.50	10.00

10 CENTAVOS

2.5000 gm., .835 SILVER, .0671 oz ASW

Y#	Date	Mintage	VF	XF	Unc
48	1915	3.418	2.00	3.50	5.00

COPPER-NICKEL

Y#	Date	Mintage	VF	XF	Unc
43	1920	1.120	.30	.65	1.50
	1921	1.285	.30	.65	1.50

BRONZE

Y#	Date	Mintage	VF	XF	Unc
40	1924	1.210	2.00	3.50	6.00
	1925	9.090	.30	.60	1.75
	1926	26.250	.30	.60	1.75
	1930	1.730	15.00	25.00	35.00
	1938	2.000	5.00	10.00	20.00
	1940	3.384	2.00	3.50	6.00

Y#	Date	Mintage	VF	XF	Unc
60	1942	1.035	.30	.50	2.00
	1943	18.765	.10	.15	.45
	1944	5.090	.10	.15	.50
	1945	8.090	.10	.15	.50
	1946	7.740	.10	.15	.50
	1947	9.283	.10	.15	.50
	1948	5.900	.10	.15	.50
	1949	15.240	.10	.20	.40
	1950	8.860	—	.10	.40
	1951	5.040	—	.10	.40
	1952	4.960	—	.10	.30
	1953	7.548	.10	.20	.30
	1954	2.452	—	.10	.30
	1955	10.000	—	.10	.20
	1956	3.336	—	.10	.25
	1957	6.654	—	.10	.20
	1958	7.320	—	.10	.20
	1959	7.140	—	.10	.20
	1960	15.055	—	.10	.20
	1961	5.020	—	.10	.20
	1962	14.980	—	.10	.20
	1963	5.393	—	—	.15
	1964	10.257	—	—	.15
	1965	15.550	—	—	.15
	1966	10.800	—	—	.15
	1967	12.713	—	—	.20
	1968	21.415	—	—	.20
	1969	3.871	—	—	.15

ALUMINUM

Y#	Date	Mintage	VF	XF	Unc
71	1970	—	—	—	.10
	1971	24.693	—	—	.10
	1972	3.227	—	—	.10
	1973	4.239	—	—	.10
	1974	17.043	—	—	.10
	1975	Inc. Ab.	—	—	.10
	1976	19.906	—	—	.10
	1977	—	—	—	.10

20 CENTAVOS

5.0000 gm., .835 SILVER, .1342 oz ASW

Y#	Date	Mintage	VF	XF	Unc
49	1913	.540	6.00	10.00	15.00
	1916	.706	6.00	10.00	15.00

COPPER-NICKEL

Y#	Date	Mintage	VF	XF	Unc
44	1920	1.568	.50	1.25	3.00
	1921	3.030	.50	1.25	3.00
44	1922	.580	150.00	200.00	350.00

BRONZE

Y#	Date	Mintage	VF	XF	Unc
41	1924	6.220	.50	1.25	3.00
	1925	10.560	.50	1.25	3.00

Y#	Date	Mintage	VF	XF	Unc
61	1942	Inc. Bl.	.10	.30	2.00
	1943	1.170	—	.30	2.00
	1944	7.290	—	.30	2.00
	1945	7.553	—	.30	2.00
	1948	2.750	—	.30	2.00
	1949	12.250	—	.30	2.00
	1951	3.185	—	.30	2.00
	1952	1.815	.10	.30	2.00
	1953	9.426	—	.30	2.00
	1955	5.574	—	.30	1.00
	1956	5.000	—	.30	1.00
	1957	1.450	.10	.30	1.00
	1958	7.470	—	—	.25
	1959	4.780	—	—	.25
	1960	4.790	—	.10	.25
	1961	5.180	—	.10	.25
	1962	2.500	—	.10	.25
	1963	7.990	—	.10	.20
	1964	7.010	—	.10	.20
	1965	7.365	—	.10	.20
	1966	8.075	—	.10	.20
	1967	9.220	—	.10	.25
	1968	10.372	—	.10	.25
	1969	8.657	—	.10	.20

Y#	Date	Mintage	VF	XF	Unc
72	1969	5.000	—	—	.15
	1970	20.000	—	—	.15
	1971	1.973	—	—	.15
	1972	3.274	—	—	.10
	1973	10.787	—	—	.10
	1974	26.975	—	—	.15

50 CENTAVOS

12.5000 gm., .835 SILVER, .3356 oz ASW

Y#	Date	Mintage	VF	XF	Unc
50	1912	1.695	BV	10.00	12.50
	1913	4.443	BV	10.00	12.50
	1914	4.992	BV	10.00	12.50
	1916	5.080	BV	10.00	12.50

ALUMINUM-BRONZE

Y#	Date	Mintage	VF	XF	Unc
45	1924	.810	20.00	30.00	50.00
	1925	—	250.00	350.00	500.00
	1926	11.340	.30	.75	2.00

COPPER-NICKEL

Y#	Date	Mintage	VF	XF	Unc
54	1927	3.330	.35	1.00	3.00
	1928	6.823	.30	1.00	3.00
	1929	9.779	.30	1.00	3.00
	1930	1.116	.50	1.00	3.00
	1931	7.127	.30	1.00	3.00
	1935	.902	2.00	6.00	15.00
	1938	.923	.65	1.00	3.00
	1940	2.000	.10	.30	.85
	1944	2.974	.10	.30	.85
	1945	5.700	—	.15	.50
	1946	4.334	—	.15	.50
	1947	6.998	—	.15	.50
	1951	4.610	—	.15	.50
	1952	2.421	—	.15	.50
	1953	2.369	—	.15	.50
	1955	3.057	—	.15	.50
	1956	3.003	—	.15	.50
	1957	3.940	—	.15	.50
	1958	2.687	—	.15	.50
	1959	4.027	—	.15	.50
	1960	2.592	—	.10	.50
	1961	3.324	—	.10	.50
	1962	6.678	—	.10	.35
	1963	2.346	—	.10	.35
	1964	7.654	—	.10	.35
	1965	3.366	—	.10	.35
	1966	6.634	—	.10	.35
	1967	9.589	—	.10	.35
	1968	1.411	—	.10	.35

BRONZE

Y#	Date	Mintage	VF	XF	Unc
73	1969	3.480	—	.10	.15
	1970	18.800	—	.10	.15
	1971	14.684	—	.10	.15
	1972	6.559	—	.10	.15
	1973	40.558	—	.10	.15
	1974	37.429	—	.10	.15
	1975	2.372	—	.10	.15
	1976	23.734	—	.10	.15
	1977	—	—	.10	.15
	1978	—	—	.10	.15
	1979	—	—	—	—

ESCUDO

25.0000 gm., .835 SILVER, .6711 oz ASW
October 5, 1910, Birth Of The Republic

Y#	Date	Mintage	VF	XF	Unc
47	1910	*1.000	25.00	30.00	35.00

***NOTE:** Struck in 1914.

Y#	Date	Mintage	VF	XF	Unc
51	1915	1.818	22.50	25.00	30.00
	1916	1.405	22.50	25.00	30.00

ALUMINUM-BRONZE

Y#	Date	Mintage	VF	XF	Unc
46	1924	2.709	.75	2.00	5.00
	1926	2.346	20.00	35.00	50.00

COPPER-NICKEL

Y#	Date	Mintage	VF	XF	Unc
55	1927	1.917	.50	1.50	10.00
	1928	7.462	.40	1.50	10.00
	1929	1.617	.50	1.50	10.00
	1930	1.911	.50	3.00	25.00
	1931	2.039	4.00	6.00	25.00
	1935	—	15.00	25.00	100.00
	1939	.304	6.00	10.00	30.00
	1940	1.259	.50	1.00	4.00
	1944	.993	4.00	6.00	15.00
	1945	Inc. Ab.	.85	1.65	3.25
	1946	2.507	.10	.30	2.00
	1951	2.500	.10	.25	2.00
	1952	2.500	.10	.25	3.00
	1957	1.656	.25	.35	.50
	1958	1.447	.10	.15	.65
	1959	1.908	.10	.15	.50
	1960	1.107	.10	.15	.50
	1961	2.505	.20	.30	.40
	1962	2.757	.10	.15	.40
	1964	1.611	.10	.15	.40
	1965	1.683	.10	.15	.40
	1966	2.607	.10	.15	.40
	1968	4.099	.10	.15	.40

BRONZE

Y#	Date	Mintage	VF	XF	Unc
74	1969	3.020	.10	.15	.25
	1970	10.032	.10	.15	.20
	1971	9.246	.10	.15	.20
	1972	1.277	.10	.15	.25
	1973	12.452	.10	.15	.20

Y#	Date	Mintage	VF	XF	Unc
74	1974	21.023	.10	.15	.20
	1975	1.121	.10	.15	.25
	1976	7.353	.10	.15	.25
	1979	—	—	—	—

2-1/2 ESCUDOS

3.5000 gm., .650 SILVER, .0731 oz ASW

Y#	Date	Mintage	VF	XF	Unc
57	1932	2.592	4.00	6.00	12.00
	1933	2.457	4.00	6.00	12.00
	1937	1.000	40.00	60.00	100.00
	1940	2.763	3.00	5.00	8.00
	1942	3.847	BV	2.50	4.00
	1943	8.302	BV	2.50	4.00
	1944	9.134	BV	2.50	4.00
	1945	6.316	BV	2.50	4.00
	1946	3.208	BV	2.50	4.00
	1947	2.610	BV	2.50	4.00
	1948	1.818	4.00	6.00	10.00
	1951	4.000	BV	2.50	4.00

COPPER-NICKEL

Y#	Date	Mintage	VF	XF	Unc
67	1963	12.711	.15	.20	.50
	1964	17.948	.15	.20	.35
	1965	19.512	.15	.20	.35
	1966	3.828	.15	.20	.35
	1967	5.545	.15	.20	.35
	1968	6.087	.15	.20	.35
	1969	10.368	.15	.20	.40
	1970	2.400	.15	.20	.35
	1971	6.791	.15	.20	.35
	1972	2.316	.15	.20	.35
	1973	9.489	.15	.20	.35
	1974	22.913	.10	.20	.35
	1975	15.284	.10	.20	.35
	1976	14.763	.10	.20	.40
	1977	—	.10	.20	.40
	1978	—	.10	.20	.40
	1979	—	.10	.20	.40

100th Anniversary Death of Alexandre Herculano

Y#	Date	Mintage	VF	XF	Unc
82	1977	6.000	—	—	—

5 ESCUDOS

7.0000 gm., .650 SILVER, .1463 oz ASW

Y#	Date	Mintage	VF	XF	Unc
58	1932	.800	6.50	10.00	25.00
	1933	6.717	4.50	6.00	15.00
	1934	1.012	4.50	6.00	15.00
	1937	1.500	15.00	25.00	75.00
	1940	.578	4.50	6.00	10.00
	1942	2.051	BV	4.50	6.50
	1943	1.354	BV	4.50	6.50
	1946	.404	BV	4.50	6.50
	1947	2.420	BV	4.50	6.50
	1948	2.018	BV	4.50	6.50
	1951	.966	BV	4.50	6.50

500th Anniversary Death Of Prince Henry The Navigator

Y#	Date	Mintage	VF	XF	Unc
64	1960	.800	4.50	5.50	7.50

COPPER-NICKEL

Y#	Date	Mintage	VF	XF	Unc
68	1963	2.200	.25	.35	.60
	1964	4.268	.25	.35	.60
	1965	7.294	.25	.35	.50
	1966	8.120	.25	.35	.50
	1967	9.459	.25	.35	.50
	1968	3.681	.25	.35	.50
	1969	4.977	.25	.35	.60
	1970	1.200	.25	.35	.75
	1971	3.380	.25	.35	.50
	1973	2.836	.25	.35	.50
	1974	4.810	.20	.35	.50
	1975	Inc. Ab.	.20	.30	.50
	1976	12.814	.20	.30	.50
	1977	—	.20	.30	.60
	1979	—	—	—	.60

100th Anniversary Death of Alexandre Herculano

Y#	Date	Mintage	VF	XF	Unc
83	1977	6.000	—	—	—

10 ESCUDOS

12.5000 gm., .835 SILVER, .3356 oz ASW
Battle of Ourique

Y#	Date	Mintage	VF	XF	Unc
56	1928	.200	15.00	20.00	25.00

Y#	Date	Mintage	VF	XF	Unc
59	1932	3.220	10.00	12.50	25.00
	1933	1.780	17.50	22.50	50.00
	1934	.400	10.00	15.00	35.00
	1937	.500	30.00	50.00	125.00
	1940	1.200	10.00	12.50	25.00
	1942	.186	75.00	100.00	200.00
	1948	.507	10.00	12.50	17.50

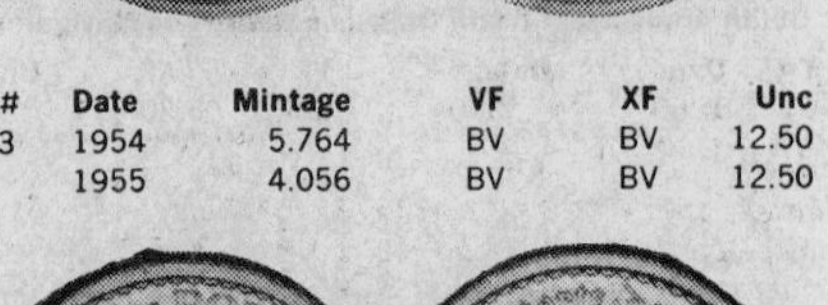

Y#	Date	Mintage	VF	XF	Unc
63	1954	5.764	BV	BV	12.50
	1955	4.056	BV	BV	12.50

12.5000 gm., .650 SILVER, .2612 oz ASW
500th Anniversary Death of Prince Henry the Navigator

Y#	Date	Mintage	VF	XF	Unc
65	1960	.200	8.00	10.00	15.00

COPPER-NICKEL-CLAD-NICKEL

Y#	Date	Mintage	VF	XF	Unc
A68	1971	3.937	.45	.65	1.00
	1972	1.570	.45	.75	1.00
	1973	3.427	.45	.75	1.00
	1974	4.043	.45	.75	1.00

20 ESCUDOS

21.0000 gm., .800 SILVER, .5401 oz ASW
25th Anniversary of Financial Reform

Y#	Date	Mintage	VF	XF	Unc
62	1953	1.000	BV	16.50	20.00

500th Anniversary Death of Prince Henry the Navigator

Y#	Date	Mintage	VF	XF	Unc
66	1960	.200	BV	17.50	45.00

10.0000 gm., .650 SILVER, .2090 oz ASW
Salazar Bridge

Y#	Date	Mintage	VF	XF	Unc
69	1966	.200	BV	BV	7.50

25 ESCUDOS

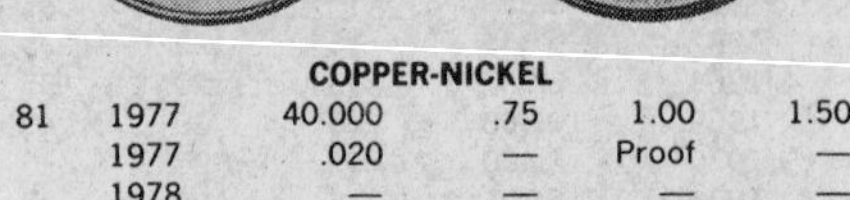

COPPER-NICKEL

Y#	Date	Mintage	VF	XF	Unc
81	1977	40.000	.75	1.00	1.50
	1977	.020	—	Proof	—
	1978	—	—	—	—

100th Anniversary Death of Alexandre Herculano

Y#	Date	Mintage	VF	XF	Unc
84	1977	6.000	—	—	—
81a	1980	—	—	—	—

50 ESCUDOS

18.0300 gm., .650 SILVER, .3768 oz ASW
500th Anniversary Cabral's Birth

Y#	Date	Mintage	VF	XF	Unc
70	1968	1.000	BV	BV	11.50

500th Anniversary Vasco Da Gama's Birth

Y#	Date	Mintage	VF	XF	Unc
75	1969	1.000	BV	BV	11.50

Centennial Marshal Carmona's Birth

Y#	Date	Mintage	VF	XF	Unc
76	1969	.500	BV	BV	12.50

125th Anniversary Bank of Portugal

Y#	Date	Mintage	VF	XF	Unc
77	1971	.500	BV	BV	12.50

400th Anniversary of Publication 'Os Lusiadas'

Y#	Date	Mintage	VF	XF	Unc
78	1972	1.000	BV	BV	12.50

100 ESCUDOS

18.0000 gm., .650 SILVER, .3762 oz ASW
1974 Revolution

79	1974	.900	BV	BV	12.50
	1974	5,775	—	Proof	—

250 ESCUDOS

24.0000 gm., .900 SILVER, .6945 oz ASW
1974 Revolution

80	1974	.900	BV	BV	22.50
	1974	1,350	—	Proof	—

NCLT ISSUES

PATTERNS

KM#	Date	Mintage	Identification	Mkt.Val.
1	1836	—	100 Reis, .917 Silver, C#104	350.00
2	1836	—	200 Reis, .917 Silver, C#105	500.00
3	1836	—	500 Reis, .917 Silver, C#107	600.00
4	1836	—	1000 Reis, .917 Silver, C#108	1000
5	1836	—	2500 Reis, .917 Gold, C#110	—
6	1836	—	5000 Reis, .917 Gold, C#111	—
7	1879	2 pcs.	1000 Reis, .917 Gold	—

PROVAS (Pr)

STANDARD METALS
Stamped 'PROVA' in field

Y#	Date	Mintage	Identification	Issue Price	Mkt Val.
Pr58	1943	—	5 Escudos	—	45.00
Pr60	1943	—	10 Centavos	—	25.00
Pr61	1943	—	20 Centavos	—	25.00
Pr64	1960	—	5 Escudos	—	22.50
Pr65	1960	—	10 Escudos	—	25.00
Pr66	1960	—	20 Escudos	—	35.00
Pr67	1966	—	2-1/2 Escudos	—	40.00
Pr68	1966	—	5 Escudos	—	35.00
Pr70	1968	—	50 Escudos	—	35.00
Pr75	1969	—	50 Escudos	—	35.00
Pr76	1969	—	50 Escudos	—	35.00
Pr77	1971	—	50 Escudos	—	35.00
Pr78	1972	—	50 Escudos	—	35.00

MINT SETS

KM#	Date	Mintage	Identification	Issue Price	Mkt. Val.
S1	1960(3)	—	Y64-66	—	—

Listings For

PORTUGUESE GUINEA: refer to Guinea-Bissau

PORTUGUESE INDIA: refer to Indian Enclaves

PRINCE EDWARD ISLAND: refer to Canada

The Commonwealth of Puerto Rico, the easternmost island of the Greater Antilles in the West Indies, has an area of 3,435 sq. mi. (8,897 sq. km.) and a population of 3 million. Capital: San Juan. The commonwealth has its own constitution and elects its own governor. Its people are citizens of the United States, liable to the draft -- but not to federal taxation. The chief industries of Puerto Rico are manufacturing, agriculture, and tourism. Manufactured goods, cement, dairy and livestock products, sugar, rum, and coffee are exported, mainly to the United States.

Puerto Rico ('Rich Port') was discovered by Columbus who landed on the island and took possession for Spain on Oct. 19, 1493 -- the only time Columbus set foot on the soil of what is now the United States. The first settlement, Caparra, was established by Ponce de Leon in 1508. The early years of the colony were not promising. Considerable gold was found, but the supply was soon exhausted. Efforts to enslave the Indians caused violent reprisals. Hurricanes destroyed crops and homes. French, Dutch, and English freebooters burned the towns. Puerto Rico remained a Spanish possession until 1898, when it was ceded to the United States following the Spanish-American War. Puerto Ricans were granted a measure of self-government and U.S. citizenship in 1917. Effective July 25, 1952, a Congressional resolution elevated Puerto Rico to the status of a free commonwealth associated with the United States.

RULERS

Spanish until 1898

MONETARY SYSTEM

100 Centavos = 1 Peso

COUNTERSTAMP ISSUES

In 1884 a large number of holed coins were counterstamped at Puerto Rico's seven customs houses to legitimatize them with a device very similar to a Fleur-de-Lys. These coins were redeemed in 1894.

5 CENTIMOS

BRONZE
c/s: Lys on Spanish 5 Centimos, Y#69.

KM#	Date	Year	Good	VG	Fine	VF
1	ND	(1877-79)	60.00	100.00	150.00	225.00

10 CENTIMOS

BRONZE
c/s: Lys on Spanish 5 Centimos, Y#69.

2	ND	(1877-79)	60.00	100.00	150.00	225.00

1/5 DOLLAR

SILVER
c/s: Lys on U.S. 20 Cent piece, Y#28.

3	ND	(1875-78)	200.00	325.00	450.00	650.00

1/4 DOLLAR

SILVER
c/s: Lys on U.S. Quarter, Y#31.

KM#	Date	Year	Good	VG	Fine	VF
4	ND	(1866-91)	60.00	100.00	125.00	175.00
	c/s: Lys on Spanish or Colonial 2 Reales, C#33.					
5	ND	(1759-71)	60.00	100.00	150.00	225.00

1/2 DOLLAR

SILVER
c/s: Lys on U.S. Half Dollar, Y#37.

KM#	Date	Year	Good	VG	Fine	VF
6	ND	(1839-66)	60.00	100.00	150.00	225.00

c/s: Lys on Spanish or Colonial 4 Reales, C#36.

KM#	Date	Year	Good	VG	Fine	VF
7	ND	(1791-1808)	150.00	250.00	300.00	450.00

DOLLAR

SILVER
c/s: Lys on U.S. bust type Dollar, C#34a.

KM#	Date	Year	Good	VG	Fine	VF
8	ND	(1798-1803)	90.00	150.00	200.00	300.00
	c/s: Lys on U.S. Trade Dollar, Y#44.					
9	ND	(1873-85)	125.00	200.00	250.00	375.00

c/s: Lys on Spanish or Colonial 8 Reales, C#45.

KM#	Date	Year	Good	VG	Fine	VF
10	ND	(1772-89)	100.00	175.00	250.00	375.00

REGULAR ISSUES

5 CENTAVOS

.900 SILVER

Y#	Date	Mintage	Fine	VF	XF	Unc
1	1896	.600	17.50	25.00	50.00	100.00

10 CENTAVOS

.900 SILVER

Y#	Date	Mintage	Fine	VF	XF	Unc
2	1896	.700	25.00	40.00	100.00	275.00

20 CENTAVOS

.900 SILVER

Y#	Date	Mintage	Fine	VF	XF	Unc
3	1895	3.350	30.00	50.00	75.00	225.00

40 CENTAVOS

.900 SILVER

Y#	Date	Mintage	Fine	VF	XF	Unc
4	1896	.725	150.00	250.00	450.00	1200.

PESO

.900 SILVER

Y#	Date	Mintage	Fine	VF	XF	Unc
5	1895	8.500	275.00	450.00	750.00	1500.

NCLT ISSUES

ESSAIS

STANDARD METALS unless otherwise noted.

Y#	Date	Mintage	Identification	Issue Price	Mkt Val.
PE1	1898	6	20 Centavos	—	1500.

VIEQUE

(CRAB ISLAND)

Vieque (or Crab Island), located to the east of Puerto Rico, is the largest of the Commonwealth's major offshore islands. The others are Culebra, a naval station to the east, and Mona to the west.

c/s: 12 rayed sunburst

COPPER
c/s: On Nova Constellatio Cent

C#	Date	Mintage	Good	VG	Fine
1.1	ND 1783	—	50.00	75.00	125.00
	ND 1785	—	50.00	75.00	125.00

SILVER
c/s: On Danish West Indies 2 Skilling, C#12.

C#	Date	Mintage	Good	VG	Fine
1.2	ND 1837	—	40.00	55.00	85.00
	c/s: On Danish West Indies 2 Skilling, C#18.				
1.3	ND 1848	—	40.00	55.00	85.00
	c/s: On Danish West Indies 10 Skilling, C#16.				
1.4	ND 1845	—	45.00	65.00	95.00
	c/s: On Danish West Indies 20 Skilling, C#17.				
1.5	ND 1840	—	50.00	75.00	125.00

c/s: On Danish 18th century silver coin.

C#	Date	Mintage	Good	VG	Fine
1.6	ND	—	50.00	85.00	110.00

c/s: On Spain 2 Reales, C#134.

C#	Date	Mintage	Good	VG	Fine
1.7	ND 1825	—	85.00	125.00	150.00

c/s: V in 12 rayed sunburst

c/s: On 1/2 cut of Spanish-American 2 Reales

C#	Date	Mintage	Good	VG	Fine
2.1	ND	—	100.00	135.00	175.00

QATAR

The State of Qatar, a Persian Gulf shaikhdom between Bahrain and Trucial Oman, has an area of 4,000 sq. mi. (10,360 sq. km.) and a population of 165,000. Capital: Doha. Oil is the chief industry and export.

Qatar was under Turkish control from 1872 until the beginning of World War I when the Ottoman Turks evacuated the Qatar Peninsula. In 1916 Shaikh Abdullah placed Qatar under the protection of Great Britain and gave Britain responsibility for its defense and foreign relations. Qatar joined with Dubai in a Monetary Union and issued coins and paper money in 1966 and 1969. When Britain announced in 1968 that it would end treaty relationships with the Persian Gulf shaikhdoms in 1971, this union was dissolved, Qatar joined Bahrain and the seven trucial shaikhdoms (the latter now called the United Arab Emirates) in an effort to form a union of Arab emirates. However the nine shaikhdoms were unable to agree on terms of union, and Qatar declared its independence as the State of Qatar on Sept. 3, 1971.

MONETARY SYSTEM

100 Dirhem = 1 Riyal

DIRHEM

BRONZE

Y#	Date	Year	Mintage	VF	XF	Unc
1	AH1393	1973	.500	—	.10	.15

5 DIRHEMS

BRONZE

Y#	Date	Year	Mintage	VF	XF	Unc
2	AH1393	1973	1.000	.10	.15	.25

10 DIRHEMS

BRONZE

Y#	Date	Year	Mintage	VF	XF	Unc
3	AH1392	1972	1.500	.20	.30	.40
	1393	1973	1.500	.20	.30	.40

25 DIRHEMS

COPPER-NICKEL

Y#	Date	Year	Mintage	VF	XF	Unc
4	AH1393	1973	1.500	.25	.35	.60
	1396	1976	2.000	.25	.35	.60

50 DIRHEMS

COPPER-NICKEL

Y#	Date	Year	Mintage	VF	XF	Unc
5	AH1393	1973	1.500	.40	.65	1.00

QATAR & DUBAI

The State of Qatar, which occupies the Qatar Peninsula jutting into the Persian Gulf from eastern Saudi Arabia, has an area of 4,000 sq. mi. (10,360 sq. km.) and a population of 165,000. Capital: Doha. The traditional occupations of pearling, fishing, and herding have been replaced in economic by petroleum-related industries. Crude oil, petroleum products, and tomatoes are exported.

Dubai is one of the seven emirates comprising the United Arab Emirates (formerly Trucial States) located along the southern shore of the Persian Gulf. It has a population of about 60,000. Capital (of the United Arab Emirates): Abu Dhabi.

Qatar, which initiated protective treaty relations with Great Britain in 1820, achieved independence on Sept. 3, 1971, upon withdrawal of the British military presence from the Persian Gulf, and replaced its special treaty arrangement with Britain with a treaty of general friendship. Dubai attained independence on Dec. 1, 1971, upon termination of Britain's protective treaty with the trucial Shaikhdoms, and on Dec. 2, 1971, entered into the union of the United Arab Emirates.

Despite the fact that the sultanate of Qatar and the Shaikhdom of Dubai were merged under a monetary union, the two territories were governed independently from each other. Qatar now uses its own currency while Dubai uses the United Arab Emirates currency and coins.

MONETARY SYSTEM

100 Dirhem = 1 Riyal

DIRHEM

BRONZE

Y#	Date	Year	Mintage	VF	XF	Unc
1	AH1386	1966	1.000	.10	.20	.30

5 DIRHEMS

BRONZE

Y#	Date	Year	Mintage	VF	XF	Unc
2	AH1386	1966	2.000	.10	.20	.35
	1389	1969	2.000	.10	.20	.35

10 DIRHEMS

BRONZE

Y#	Date	Year	Mintage	VF	XF	Unc
3	AH1386	1966	2.000	.20	.30	.50

25 DIRHEMS

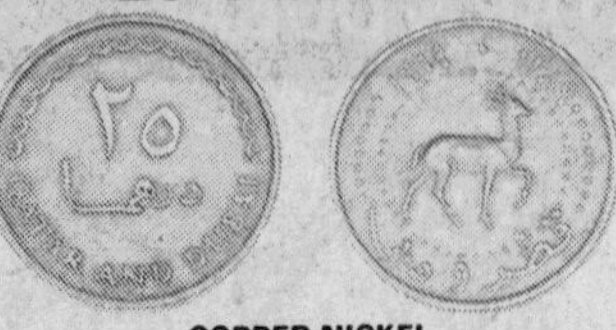

COPPER-NICKEL

Y#	Date	Year	Mintage	VF	XF	Unc
4	AH1386	1966	2.000	.25	.50	1.00
	1389	1969	2.000	.25	.50	1.00

50 DIRHEMS

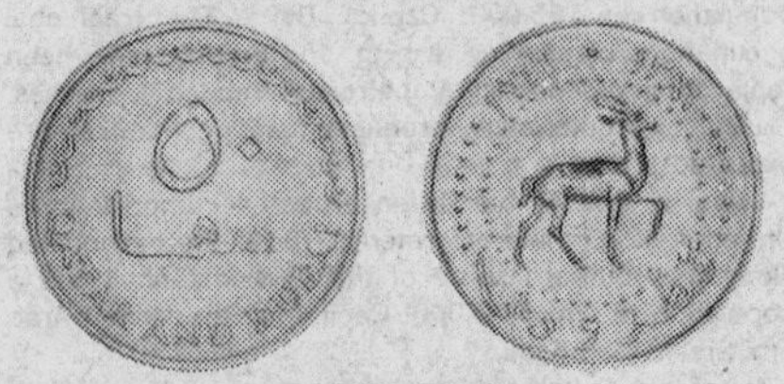

COPPER-NICKEL

Y#	Date	Year	Mintage	VF	XF	Unc
5	AH1386	1966	2.000	.40	.75	1.25

Listings For

QUAITI: refer to Yemen Democratic Republic

RAS AL KHAIMA: refer to United Arab Emirates

REUNION

The Department of Reunion, an overseas department of France located in the Indian Ocean 400 miles (640 km.) east of Madagascar, has an area of 970 sq. mi. (2,512 sq. km.) and a population of 490,000. Capital: Saint-Denis. The island's volcanic soil is extremely fertile. Sugar, vanilla, coffee and rum are exported.

Although first visited by Portuguese navigators in the 16th century, Reunion was uninhabited when claimed for France by Capt. Goubert in 1638. It was first colonized as Isle de Bourbon by the French in 1662 as a layover station for ships rounding the Cape of Good Hope to India. It was renamed Reunion in 1793. The island remained in French possession except for the period of 1810-15, when it was occupied by the British. Reunion became an overseas department of France in 1946, and in 1958 voted to continue that status within the new French Union.

During the first half of the 19th century, Reunion was officially known as Isle de Bonaparte (1801-14) and Isle de Bourbon (1814-48). Reunion coinage of those periods is so designated.

ISLE DE BOURBON

The Restoration of the House of Bourbon in France caused the name of the Reunion Island to be changed to Isle de Bourbon from 1814-1848.

RULERS

Louis XVIII, 1814-1828

MONETARY SYSTEM

100 Centimes = 1 Franc

10 CENTIMES

BILLON

C#	Date	Mintage	VG	Fine	VF	XF
21	1816A	.150	15.00	35.00	60.00	100.00

REUNION

TOKEN ISSUES

MONETARY SYSTEM

100 Centimes = 1 Franc

5 CENTIMES

ALUMINUM
Bank Token (Demonetized 1941)

Y#	Date	Mintage	Fine	VF	XF	Unc
3	1920	—	15.00	25.00	50.00	90.00

10 CENTIMES

ALUMINUM
Bank Token (Demonetized 1941)

Y#	Date	Mintage	Fine	VF	XF	Unc
4	1920	—	22.00	30.00	65.00	115.00

25 CENTIMES

ALUMINUM
Bank Token (Demonetized 1941)

Y#	Date	Mintage	Fine	VF	XF	Unc
5	1920	—	30.00	45.00	75.00	150.00

50 CENTIMES

COPPER-NICKEL

Y#	Date	Mintage	Fine	VF	XF	Unc
1	1896	1.000	20.00	40.00	90.00	200.00

ALUMINUM
Bank Token (Demonetized 1952)

Y#	Date	Mintage	Fine	VF	XF	Unc
6	1941	Reported, not confirmed				

FRANC

COPPER-NICKEL

Y#	Date	Mintage	Fine	VF	XF	Unc
2	1896	.500	40.00	65.00	150.00	200.00

ALUMINUM
Bank Token (Demonetized 1952)

Y#	Date	Mintage	VF	XF	Unc
7	1941	—	Reported, Not Confirmed		

REGULAR COINAGE

MINTMARKS

(a) - Paris, privy marks only

FRANC

ALUMINUM

Y#	Date	Mintage	VF	XF	Unc
8	1948(a)	3.000	.30	.50	1.25
	1964(a)	1.000	.20	.30	1.00
	1968(a)	.450	.30	.50	2.50
	1969(a)	.500	.20	.30	2.00

Y#	Date	Mintage	VF	XF	Unc
	1971(a)	.800	.20	.30	1.75
	1973(a)	.500	.20	.30	2.00
		Thinner Planchet			
8.1	1969(a)	Inc. Ab.	.50	.90	2.50

Mule, French Colonial obv. with rev. of Y#8.

Y#	Date	Mintage	VF	XF	Unc
8.2	1948(A)	Inc. Ab.	—	—	—

2 FRANCS

ALUMINUM

Y#	Date	Mintage	VF	XF	Unc
9	1948(a)	2.000	.50	.75	1.50
	1968(a)	.100	1.75	3.00	7.00
	1969(a)	.150	1.00	2.00	5.00
	1970(a)	.300	.50	1.00	2.50
	1971(a)	.300	.50	1.00	2.50
	1973(a)	.500	.50	1.00	2.50

5 FRANCS

ALUMINUM

Y#	Date	Mintage	VF	XF	Unc
10	1955(a)	3.000	.30	.50	1.25
	1969(a)	.100	2.00	3.50	7.00
	1970(a)	.200	1.00	2.00	5.00
	1971(a)	.100	1.00	2.00	5.00
	1972(a)	.300	.60	1.00	2.00
	1973(a)	.250	.60	1.00	2.00

10 FRANCS

ALUMINUM-BRONZE

Y#	Date	Mintage	VF	XF	Unc
11	1955(a)	1.500	.30	.50	1.25
	1962(a)	.700	1.00	2.00	5.00
	1964(a)	1.000	.30	.50	1.00
	1969(a)	.300	.75	1.25	4.00
	1970(a)	.300	.75	1.25	4.00
	1971(a)	.200	1.00	2.00	6.00
	1972(a)	.400	.75	1.25	4.00
	1973(a)	.700	.50	1.00	2.00

20 FRANCS

ALUMINUM-BRONZE

Y#	Date	Mintage	VF	XF	Unc
12	1955(a)	1.250	.45	.75	1.50
12	1960(a)	.100	2.00	4.00	9.00
	1961(a)	.300	1.50	3.00	5.00
	1962(a)	.190	2.00	3.50	5.50
	1964(a)	.750	.60	1.00	2.00
2.00	3.50	5.50	2.00	3.50	5.50
2.00	3.50	5.50	2.00	3.50	5.50
2.00	3.50	5.50	2.00	3.50	5.50
	1972(a)	.300	1.00	1.75	2.50
	1973(a)	.550	.50	1.00	1.75

50 FRANCS

NICKEL

Y#	Date	Mintage	VF	XF	Unc
13	1962(a)	1.000	1.00	1.75	3.50
	1964(a)	.500	1.25	2.00	4.00
	1969(a)	.100	2.00	3.50	6.00
	1970a	1.00	2.00	3.50	6.00
	1973(a)	.350	1.00	1.75	3.00

100 FRANCS

NICKEL

Y#	Date	Mintage	VF	XF	Unc
14	1964(a)	2.000	.60	1.00	3.00
	1969(a)	.200	1.50	2.50	5.00
	1970(a)	.150	1.50	2.50	5.00
	1971(a)	.100	2.00	4.50	11.00
	1972(a)	.400	1.00	1.50	3.75
	1973(a)	.200	2.00	4.00	5.50

NCLT ISSUES

ESSAIS (E)

Standard metals unless otherwise noted

Y#	Date	Mintage	Identification	Issue Price	Mkt Val.
E1	1896	—	50 Centimes	—	200.00
E2	1896	—	1 Franc	—	350.00
E8a	1948(a)	2,000	1 Franc, Copper-Nickel	—	15.00
E9a	1948(a)	2,000	2 Francs, Copper-Nickel	—	18.00
E10	1955(a)	1,200	5 Francs	—	18.00
E11	1955(a)	1,200	10 Francs	—	21.00
E12	1955(a)	1,200	20 Francs	—	25.00
E13	1962(a)	1,200	50 Francs	—	30.00
E14	1964(a)	2,000	100 Francs	—	22.00

PIEFORTS (P)

PIEFORTS with ESSAI (PE)

(DOUBLE THICKNESS)

Standard metals unless otherwise noted

Y#	Date	Mintage	Identification	Issue Price	Mkt Val.
PE1	1896	—	50 Centimes	—	250.00
PE2	1896	—	1 Franc	—	350.00
Pe8	1948(a)	104	1 Franc	—	75.00
Pe9	1948(a)	104	2 Francs	—	85.00
Pe10	1955(a)	104	5 Francs	—	90.00
Pe11	1955(a)	104	10 Francs	—	95.00
Pe12	1955(a)	104	20 Francs	—	100.00

FLEUR DE COIN SETS

STANDARD METALS

KM#	Date	Mintage	Identification	Issue Price	Mkt. Val.
1	1964(5)	—	Y8, 11-14	—	13.00

Listings For
REUNION & MAURITIUS Joint Coinage: refer to Mauritius and Reunion

ROMANIA

The Socialist Republic of Romania, a Balkan country in southeast Europe, has an area of 91,699 sq. mi. (237,499 sq. km.) and a population of 21.7 million. Capital: Bucharest. The economy is predominantly agricultural; heavy industry and oil have become increasingly important since 1959. Machinery, foodstuffs, raw minerals and petroleum products are exported.

Romania, the ancient Roman province of Dacia, endured wave after wave of barbarian conquest and foreign domination before it declared its independence (of Turkey) in 1877. In 1881 it became a monarchy under Carol I, changing to a constitutional monarchy with a bicameral legislature in 1888. The government was reorganized along Fascist lines in 1940, and in the following year Romania joined Germany's attack on the Soviet Union. The country was subsequently occupied by the Russian Army which actively supported the program and goals of the Romanian Communists. A plebiscite on Nov. 19, 1946, installed a Communist-dominated government and prompted the abdication of King Michael. Romania became a 'people's republic' on Dec. 30, 1947.

RULERS

Carol I (as Prince), 1866-81 (as King), 1881-1914
Ferdinand I, 1914-1927
Mihai I, 1927-1930
Carol II, 1930-1940
Mihai I, 1940-1947

MINTMARKS

(a) - Paris, privy marks only
(b) - Brussels, privy marks only
B - Bucharest (1879-1885)
C - Bucharest
H - Heaton
J - Hamburg
KN - Kings Norton
(p) - Thunderbolt - Poissy
V - Vienna
W - Watt (James Watt & Co.)
Huguenin - Le Locole

MONETARY SYSTEM

100 Bani = 1 Leu

BANU

COPPER

Y#	Date	Mintage	VF	XF	Unc
1	1867H	5.000	5.00	7.50	11.50
	1867H	Inc.Ab.	—	Proof	—
	1867W	Inc. Ab.	5.00	7.50	11.50

BAN

COPPER

Y#	Date	Mintage	VF	XF	Unc
29	1900(b)	20.000	.75	1.00	3.00

ALUMINUM-BRONZE
Currency Revaluation

Obv: No star at top of arms.

Y#	Date	Mintage	VF	XF	Unc
96	1952	—	.15	.25	.40

Obv: Star at top of arms.

Y#	Date	Mintage	VF	XF	Unc
96a	1953	—	.10	.20	.30
	1954	—	.10	.20	.30

2 BANI

COPPER

Y#	Date	Mintage	VF	XF	Unc
2	1867HEATON	10.000	3.00	5.00	10.00
	1867HEATON	Inc.Ab.	—	Proof	—
	1867W	Inc. Ab.	3.00	5.00	10.00

Obv leg: CAROL I DOMNUL (Prince)

Y#	Date	Mintage	VF	XF	Unc
11	1879B	—	5.00	7.00	12.50
	1880/79B	—	10.00	25.00	45.00
	1880B	—	5.00	7.00	12.50
	1881B	—	5.00	7.00	15.00

Obv. leg: CAROL I REGE (King)

Y#	Date	Mintage	VF	XF	Unc
17	1882B	—	2.50	4.00	10.00

Rev: ROMANIA added above shield.

Y#	Date	Mintage	VF	XF	Unc
30	1900(b)	20.000	.75	1.00	5.00

3 BANI

ALUMINUM-BRONZE
Obv: No star at top of arms.

Y#	Date	Mintage	VF	XF	Unc
97	1952	—	.50	.60	.75

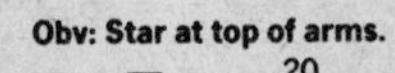

Obv: Star at top of arms.

Y#	Date	Mintage	VF	XF	Unc
97a	1953	—	.20	.30	.50

5 BANI

COPPER

Y#	Date	Mintage	VF	XF	Unc
3	1867WATT	25.000	2.25	3.50	10.00
	1867H	Inc. Ab.	2.25	3.50	10.00

Obv. leg: CAROL I REGE (King)

Y#	Date	Mintage	VF	XF	Unc
18	1882B	5.000	1.50	3.00	10.00
	1883B	3.000	1.50	3.00	10.00
	1884B	8.400	1.50	3.00	10.00
	1885B	3.600	1.75	3.50	11.00

COPPER-NICKEL

Y#	Date	Mintage	VF	XF	Unc
31	1900	20.000	.50	1.00	2.50

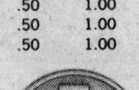

Y#	Date	Mintage	VF	XF	Unc
34	1905	25.000	.50	1.00	3.00
	1906	24.000	.50	1.00	3.00
	1906J	25.000	.50	1.00	3.00

ALUMINUM-BRONZE
Currency Revaluation
Obv: No star at top of arms.

Y#	Date	Mintage	VF	XF	Unc
98	1952	—	.40	.60	.90

Obv: Star at top of arms.

Y#	Date	Mintage	VF	XF	Unc
98a	1953	—	.50	.75	1.00
	1954	—	.50	.75	1.00
	1955	—	.50	.75	1.00
	1956	—	.45	.60	.90
	1957	—	.45	.60	.90

NICKEL-CLAD STEEL
Obv: RPR on ribbon in arms.

Y#	Date	Mintage	VF	XF	Unc
102	1963	—	—	.15	.30

Obv: ROMANIA on ribbon in arms.

Y#	Date	Mintage	VF	XF	Unc
107	1966	—	—	.10	.20

ALUMINUM

Y#	Date	Mintage	VF	XF	Unc
107a	1975	—	—	—	.20

10 BANI

COPPER

Y#	Date	Mintage	VF	XF	Unc
4	1867WATT	25.000	1.50	3.00	8.00
	1867HEATON Inc. Ab.		1.50	3.00	8.00
	1867HEATON Inc.Ab.			Proof	

COPPER-NICKEL

Y#	Date	Mintage	VF	XF	Unc
32	1900	15.000	.50	1.00	3.00

Y#	Date	Mintage	VF	XF	Unc
35	1905	17.500	.50	1.00	3.00
	1906	17.000	.50	1.00	3.00
	1906J	17.000	.50	1.00	3.00

Currency Revaluation
Obv: No star at top of arms.

Y#	Date	Mintage	VF	XF	Unc
99	1952	—	.40	.50	.75

Obv: Star at top of arms, leg: ROMANA.

Y#	Date	Mintage	VF	XF	Unc
99a	1953	—	.20	.40	.75
	1954	—	.20	.40	.70
	1955	—	.20	.40	.65

Obv. leg: ROMINA

Y#	Date	Mintage	VF	XF	Unc
99b	1955	—	.20	.30	.50
	1956	—	.20	.30	.50

15 BANI

NICKEL-CLAD STEEL

Y#	Date	Mintage	VF	XF	Unc
103	1960	—	.20	.30	.50

Y#	Date	Mintage	VF	XF	Unc
108	1966	—	.10	.20	.40

ALUMINUM

Y#	Date	Mintage	VF	XF	Unc
108a	1975	—	—	—	—

20 BANI

COPPER-NICKEL

Y#	Date	Mintage	VF	XF	Unc
33	1900	2.500	3.25	5.00	10.00

Y#	Date	Mintage	VF	XF	Unc
36	1905	2.500	.75	2.00	7.50
	1906	3.000	.75	2.00	7.50
	1906J	2.500	.75	2.00	7.50

25 BANI

ALUMINUM

Y#	Date	Mintage	VF	XF	Unc
47	1921	30.000	1.00	3.00	6.00

COPPER-NICKEL
Currency Revaluation
Obv: No star at top of arms.

Y#	Date	Mintage	VF	XF	Unc
100	1952	—	.50	.75	1.25

Obv: Star at top of arms, leg: ROMNA.

Y#	Date	Mintage	VF	XF	Unc
100a	1953	—	.40	.60	1.00
	1954	—	.40	.60	1.00
	1955	—	Reported, not confirmed		

Obv. leg: ROMINA.

Y#	Date	Mintage	VF	XF	Unc
100b	1955	—	.30	.50	1.00

NICKEL-CLAD STEEL

Y#	Date	Mintage	VF	XF	Unc
104	1960	—	.30	.40	.60

Y#	Date	Mintage	VF	XF	Unc
109	1966	—	.15	.25	.65

50 BANI

2.5000 gm., .835 SILVER, .0671 oz ASW

Y#	Date	Mintage	VF	XF	Unc
8	1873	4.800	3.00	5.00	10.00
	1876	2.117	3.50	6.00	12.00

Y#	Date	Mintage	VF	XF	Unc
13	1881V	1.000	2.25	3.50	10.00

Rev: Large letters.

Y#	Date	Mintage	VF	XF	Unc
19	1884B	1.000	4.50	7.00	11.00
	1885B	.200	6.00	10.00	20.00

Rev: Small letters.

Y#	Date	Mintage	VF	XF	Unc
24	1894	.600	3.50	6.00	15.00
	1900	3.800	3.00	5.00	7.50
	1901	.190	4.50	7.50	20.00

Y#	Date	Mintage	VF	XF	Unc
44	1910	3.600	2.00	2.50	4.00
	1911	3.000	2.00	2.50	4.00
	1912	1.800	2.00	3.00	5.00
	1914	1.600	2.00	3.00	5.00

ALUMINUM

Y#	Date	Mintage	VF	XF	Unc
48	1921	20.000	1.00	3.00	5.00

BRASS

August 1947 Coinage Reform

Y#	Date	Mintage	VF	XF	Unc
88	1947	13.200	1.75	2.50	4.50

COPPER-NICKEL
Currency Revaluation

Y#	Date	Mintage	VF	XF	Unc
101	1955	—	1.25	1.50	1.75
	1956	—	.75	.90	1.50

LEU

5.0000 gm., .835 SILVER, .1342 oz ASW

Y#	Date	Mintage	VF	XF	Unc
6	1870C	.400	12.50	18.50	30.00
	1870B	Inc. Ab.	15.00	22.50	40.00

Y#	Date	Mintage	VF	XF	Unc
9	1873(b)	4.443	BV	4.50	10.00
	1874(b)	4.511	4.25	6.00	11.50
	1876(b)	.225	5.00	8.50	20.00

Obv. leg: CAROL I DOMNUL (Prince).

Y#	Date	Mintage	VF	XF	Unc
14	1881V	1.800	BV	4.50	10.00

Obv. leg: CAROL I REGE (King).

Y#	Date	Mintage	VF	XF	Unc
20	1884B	1.000	BV	5.00	20.00
	1885B	.400	6.00	10.00	30.00

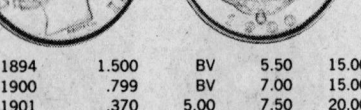

Y#	Date	Mintage	VF	XF	Unc
25	1894	1.500	BV	5.50	15.00
	1900	.799	BV	7.00	15.00
	1901	.370	5.00	7.50	20.00

40th Anniversary of Reign

Y#	Date	Mintage	VF	XF	Unc
37	1906	2.500	8.00	12.50	25.00

Y#	Date	Mintage	VF	XF	Unc
45	1910	4.600	BV	4.50	7.50
	1911	2.573	BV	6.00	10.00
	1912	3.540	BV	4.50	7.50
	1914	4.283	BV	4.50	7.50

COPPER-NICKEL

Y#	Date	Mintage	VF	XF	Unc
49	1924	100.000	.50	1.00	2.00
	1924(p)	100.006	.50	1.00	2.00

NICKEL-BRASS

Y#	Date	Mintage	VF	XF	Unc
57	1938	27.900	.20	.30	.50
	1939	—	.20	.30	.50
	1940		.20	.30	.50
	1941	—	.20	.30	.50

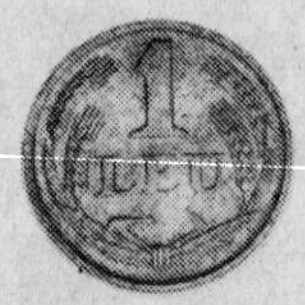

BRASS
August 1947 Coinage Reform

Y#	Date	Mintage	VF	XF	Unc
89	1947	88.341	1.75	2.50	3.50

ALUMINUM-BRONZE
People's Republic

Y#	Date	Mintage	VF	XF	Unc
92	1949	—	1.50	1.75	2.25
	1950	—	1.50	1.75	2.25
	1951	—	1.50	1.75	2.25

ALUMINUM

Y#	Date	Mintage	VF	XF	Unc
92a	1951	—	2.00	2.50	3.50
	1952	—	2.00	2.50	3.50

NICKEL-CLAD STEEL
Currency Revaluation

Y#	Date	Mintage	VF	XF	Unc
105	1963	—	.50	.70	.90

Y#	Date	Mintage	VF	XF	Unc
110	1966	—	.25	.50	.75

2 LEI

10.000 gm., .835 SILVER, .2684 oz ASW

Y#	Date	Mintage	VF	XF	Unc
10	1872(b)	.262	8.50	12.50	25.00
	1873(b)	1.745	BV	10.00	20.00
	1874(b)	.425	35.00	75.00	125.00
	1875(b)	3.092	BV	8.50	15.00
	1876(b)	.653	8.25	10.00	22.50

Y#	Date	Mintage	VF	XF	Unc
15	1881V	1.150	8.50	12.50	25.00

Y#	Date	Mintage	VF	XF	Unc
26	1894	.600	8.50	12.50	25.00
	1900	.087	12.50	22.50	45.00
	1901	.012	20.00	35.00	60.00

Y#	Date	Mintage	VF	XF	Unc
46	1910	1.800	BV	8.50	10.00
	1911	1.000	BV	8.50	10.00
	1912	1.500	BV	8.50	10.00
	1914	2.452	BV	8.50	10.00

COPPER-NICKEL

Y#	Date	Mintage	VF	XF	Unc
50	1924	50.000	.50	1.00	4.00
	1924(p)	50.000	.50	1.00	4.00

ZINC

Y#	Date	Mintage	VF	XF	Unc
73	1941	99.592	.75	1.25	2.50

BRONZE
August 1947 Coinage Reform

Y#	Date	Mintage	VF	XF	Unc
90	1947	40.000	1.75	2.50	3.50

ALUMINUM-BRONZE
People's Republic

Y#	Date	Mintage	VF	XF	Unc
93	1950	—	1.75	2.25	3.00
	1951	—	1.75	2.25	3.00

ALUMINUM

Y#	Date	Mintage	VF	XF	Unc
93a	1951	—	2.50	3.00	4.00
	1952	—	2.50	3.00	4.00

3 LEI

NICKEL-CLAD STEEL

Y#	Date	Mintage	VF	XF	Unc
106	1963	—	.50	.75	1.25

Y#	Date	Mintage	VF	XF	Unc
111	1966	—	.40	.70	1.00

5 LEI

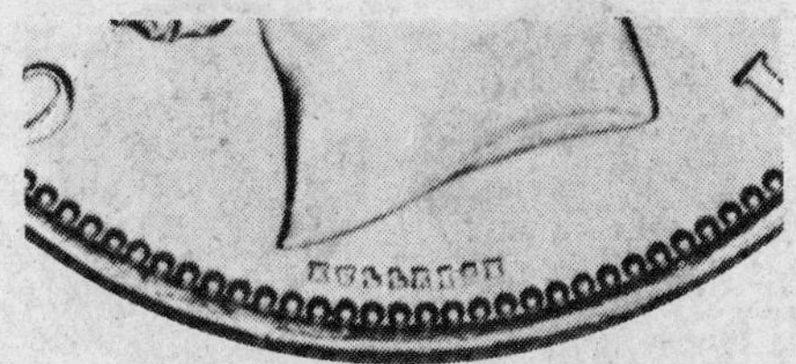

25.0000 gm., .900 SILVER, .7234 oz ASW

Y#	Date	Mintage	VF	XF	Unc
16	1880B name near rim				
		1.800	25.00	50.00	100.00

Y#	Date	Mintage	VF	XF	Unc
16	1880B name near neck				
		Inc. Ab.	25.00	50.00	100.00
	1881B	4.000	22.50	40.00	100.00

Y#	Date	Mintage	VF	XF	Unc
27	1881B	2.400	30.00	60.00	120.00

Lettered Edge
Obv: Similar to Y#27.

Y#	Date	Mintage	VF	XF	Unc
23	1881B	1.100	25.00	50.00	100.00
	1882B	Inc. Ab.	25.00	50.00	100.00
	1883B	2.300	22.50	45.00	90.00
	1884B	.300	35.00	75.00	125.00
	1885B	.040	40.00	85.00	165.00

Reeded Edge

Y#	Date	Mintage	VF	XF	Unc
23a	1901B	.082	35.00	75.00	125.00

40th Anniversary of Reign

Y#	Date	Mintage	VF	XF	Unc
38	1906	.200	45.00	80.00	180.00

NICKEL-BRASS

Y#	Date	Mintage	VF	XF	Unc
55	1930H	15.000	1.50	3.00	5.00
	1930KN	15.000	1.50	3.00	5.00
	1930A	30.000	1.25	2.50	4.50

ZINC

Y#	Date	Mintage	VF	XF	Unc
74	1942	139.900	1.00	1.50	2.00

ALUMINUM
August 1947 Coinage Reform

Y#	Date	Mintage	VF	XF	Unc
91	1947	56.000	2.50	5.00	10.00

People's Republic

Y#	Date	Mintage	VF	XF	Unc
94	1948	—	1.75	2.50	4.00
	1949	—	1.75	2.50	4.00
	1950	—	1.75	2.50	4.00
	1951	—	1.75	2.50	4.00

Y#	Date	Mintage	VF	XF	Unc
112	1978	—	—	—	—

10 LEI

NICKEL-BRASS

Y#	Date	Mintage	VF	XF	Unc
58	1930	15.000	.75	1.50	3.00
	1930A	30.000	.50	1.00	2.00
	1930H	7.500	1.25	4.00	7.50
	1930KN	7.500	1.25	4.00	7.50

12-1/2 LEI

.900 GOLD

Carol I - 40th Anniversary of Reign

Y#	Date	Mintage	VF	XF	Unc
39	1906	.032	80.00	140.00	200.00

20 LEI

6.4516 gm., .900 GOLD, .1867 oz AGW
Obv. leg: CAROL I DOMNULU (Prince), light beard.

5	1868	100 pcs.	850.00	1000.	1250.

Obv. leg: CAROL I DOMNUL (Prince), heavy beard.

7	1870C	—	135.00	225.00	350.00

Obv. leg: CAROL I REGE (King).

28	1883B	—	125.00	135.00	165.00
	1890B	—	125.00	135.00	165.00

40th Anniversary of Reign

41	1906	.015	135.00	165.00	225.00

Ferdinand I Coronation
Obv: Laureated head left over date.
Rev: Crowned and supported arms over value.

Fr#	Date	Mintage	VF	XF	Unc
10	1922	.300	180.00	250.00	375.00

NICKEL-BRASS

Y#	Date	Mintage	VF	XF	Unc
56	1930 London	42.000	3.00	5.00	9.00
	1930H	5.000	4.50	10.00	25.00
	1930KN	5.000	4.50	10.00	25.00

59	1930	6.750	1.00	1.50	5.00
	1930(a)	17.505	.75	1.00	4.00
	1930H	4.370	1.25	2.25	6.00
	1930KN	4.380	1.25	2.25	6.00

6.4516 gm., .900 GOLD, .1867 oz AGW
Centennial Birth Of Carol I

65	1939(arms)	—	150.00	185.00	250.00

Y#	Date	Mintage	VF	XF	Unc
66	1939(eagle)	—	150.00	185.00	250.00

Carol II 10th Anniversary

71	1940	—	160.00	225.00	275.00

72	1940	—	160.00	225.00	275.00

ZINC

75	1942	30.500	1.50	3.00	6.00
	1943	26.925	2.25	4.00	8.00
	1944	18.213	3.00	4.50	9.00

6.5500 gm., .900 GOLD, .1895 oz AGW
Romanian Kings

Fr#	Date	Mintage	VF	XF	Unc
21	1944	74.480	125.00	135.00	150.00

ALUMINUM
People's Republic

Y#	Date	Mintage	VF	XF	Unc
95	1951	—	15.00	25.00	45.00

25 LEI

8.0645 gm., .900 GOLD, .2333 oz AGW
Carol I 40th Anniversary of Reign

40	1906	.024	175.00	250.00	350.00

Ferdinand I Coronation

Fr#	Date	Mintage	VF	XF	Unc
12	1922	.150	BV	165.00	200.00

50 LEI

16.1290 gm., .900 GOLD, .4667 oz AGW
Carol I 40th Anniversary of Reign

Y#	Date	Mintage	VF	XF	Unc
43	1906	.028	BV	325.00	375.00

Ferdinand I Coronation

Fr#	Date	Mintage	VF	XF	Unc
11	1922	.105	BV	325.00	350.00

NICKEL

Y#	Date	Mintage	VF	XF	Unc
60	1937	*12.000	2.50	4.50	7.50
	1938	*8.000	7.50	15.00	25.00

*NOTE: 16.731 melted.

100 LEI

32.2580 gm., .900 GOLD, .9335 oz AGW
Carol I 40th Anniversary of Reign

Y#	Date	Mintage	VF	XF	Unc
42	1906	3,000	1000.	2000.	3000.

Ferdinand I Coronation

Fr#	Date	Mintage	VF	XF	Unc
9	1922	.030	625.00	1000.	1750.

12.0000 gm., .500 SILVER, .1929 oz ASW

Y#	Date	Mintage	VF	XF	Unc
62	1932(a)	2.000	12.50	20.00	35.00
	1932	16.400	9.00	15.00	25.00

NICKEL

Y#	Date	Mintage	VF	XF	Unc
61	1936	*16.750	2.50	5.00	8.50
	1938	*3.250	8.50	17.50	32.50

***NOTE:** 17.030 melted.

32.2580 gm. .900 GOLD, .9335 oz AGW

Centennial Birth Of Carol I

Y#	Date	Mintage	VF	XF	Unc
67	1939(Arms)	—	650.00	800.00	1200.
68	1939(Eagle)		625.00	750.00	1150.

Carol II 10th Anniversary
Obv: Ornamented.

Y#	Date	Mintage	VF	XF	Unc
A71	1940	—	1200.	2000.	5000.

Obv: Plain.

Y#	Date	Mintage	VF	XF	Unc
A72	1940	—	1000.	1800.	4500.

NICKEL-CLAD STEEL

Y#	Date	Mintage	VF	XF	Unc
76	1943	40.590	1.50	2.00	5.00
	1944	21.289	1.50	3.00	5.00

200 LEI

6.0000 gm., .500 SILVER, .0964 oz ASW

Y#	Date	Mintage	VF	XF	Unc
77	1942	27.000	3.00	4.00	6.00

BRASS

Y#	Date	Mintage	VF	XF	Unc
81	1945	1.399	3.00	4.00	6.00

250 LEI

13.5000 gm., .750 SILVER, .3255 oz ASW

Y#	Date	Mintage	VF	XF	Unc
63	1935	4.500	10.00	20.00	37.50

12.0000 gm., .750 SILVER, .2893 oz ASW

Y#	Date	Mintage	VF	XF	Unc
64	1939	—	9.00	11.00	15.00
	1940	—	9.00	11.00	14.00

Lettered edge: NIHIL SINE DEO

Y#	Date	Mintage	VF	XF	Unc
78	1941(p)	8.600	BV	9.00	11.00

Lettered edge: TOTUL PENTRU TARA

Y#	Date	Mintage	VF	XF	Unc
78a	1941	Inc. Ab.	15.00	22.50	30.00

NOTE: Counterfeits exist.

500 LEI

24.9000 gm., .750 SILVER, .6004 oz ASW

Y#	Date	Mintage	VF	XF	Unc
79	1941	.803	BV	18.00	22.50

11.9000 gm., .500 SILVER, .1913 oz ASW

Y#	Date	Mintage	VF	XF	Unc
80	1944	9.700	BV	6.00	7.50

BRASS

Y#	Date	Mintage	VF	XF	Unc
82	1945	3.422	3.50	4.50	6.00

ALUMINUM

Y#	Date	Mintage	VF	XF	Unc
83	1946	5.823	2.50	5.50	12.50

2000 LEI

SILVER PLATED BRASS

Y#	Date	Mintage	VF	XF	Unc
84	1946	24.600	2.25	3.00	4.00

10,000 LEI

BRASS

Y#	Date	Mintage	VF	XF	Unc
85	1947	11.850	3.00	6.00	12.50

25,000 LEI

12.3000 gm., .500 SILVER, .1977 oz ASW

Y#	Date	Mintage	VF	XF	Unc
86	1946	2.372	6.00	7.50	10.00

100,000 LEI

25.0000 gm., .500 SILVER, .4019 oz ASW

Y#	Date	Mintage	VF	XF	Unc
87	1946	2.000	BV	12.50	15.00

NCLT ISSUES

MEDALLIC ISSUES

NOTE: The medals listed below were issued with the commemorative gold coins listed earlier in this section. These are referred to as Galbeni.

GOLD, 42gm., 41mm

KM#	Date	Mintage	VF	XF	Unc
M1	1939	—	—	—	800.00

KM#	Date	Mintage	VF	XF	Unc
M2	1939	—	—	—	800.00

Carol II 10th Anniversary

KM#	Date	Mintage	VF	XF	Unc
M3	1940	—	—	—	—

KM#	Date	Mintage	VF	XF	Unc
M4	1940	—	—	—	—

PATTERNS

KM#	Date	Mintage	Identification	Mkt.Val.
1	1867	—	20 Lei, Gold, Y#5	1000.
2	1868	—	20 Lei, Gold	—
3	1870	—	20 Lei, Gold	—
4	1883	—	20 Lei, Gold	—

KM#	Date	Mintage	Identification	Mkt.Val.
5	1888	500	1 Bani, Gilt Bronze	100.00
6	1888(b)	100	1 Ban, Copper, Y#A17	—
7	1890	—	20 Lei, Gold	—

KM#	Date	Mintage	Identification	Mkt.Val.
8	1905	—	5 Bani, Gold	600.00
9	1905	—	5 Bani, Gold, hole punched out	—
10	1905	—	10 Bani, Gold	800.00
11	1905	—	10 Bani, Gold, hole punched out	—
12	1905	—	10 Bani, Gold	—

KM#	Date	Mintage	Identification	Mkt.Val.
13	1905	—	20 Bani, Gold	—
14	1905	—	20 Bani, Gold, hole punched out	900.00
15	1906	—	1 Lei, Gold	—
16	1906	—	20 Lei, Gold	—
17	1906	—	25 Lei, Gold	—
18	1906	—	50 Lei, Gold	—
19	1906	—	100 Lei, Gold	—
20	1922	—	50 Bani, Aluminum	—
21	1922	—	20 Lei, Gold	—
22	1922	—	25 Lei, Gold	—
23	1922	—	50 Lei, Gold	—
24	1922	—	100 Lei, Gold	—
25	1930	—	20 Lei, Gold, plain obverse	—
26	1930	—	20 Lei, Gold, ornamented obverse	—
27	1930	—	100 Lei, Gold, plain obverse	—
28	1930	—	100 Lei, Gold, ornamented obverse	—
29	1931	—	20 Lei, Gold, plain obverse	—
30	1931	—	20 Lei, Gold, ornamented obverse	—
31	1931	—	100 Lei, Gold, plain obverse	—
32	1931	—	100 Lei, Gold, ornmented obverse	—
33	1932	—	20 Lei, Gold, plain obverse	—
34	1932	—	20 Lei, Gold, ornamented obverse	—
35	1932	—	100 Lei, Gold, plain obverse	—
36	1932	—	100 Lei, Gold, ornamented obverse	—
37	1933	—	20 Lei, Gold, plain obverse	—
38	1933	—	20 Lei, Gold, ornamented obverse	—
39	1933	—	100 Lei, Gold, plain obverse	—
40	1933	—	100 Lei, Gold, ornamented obverse	—
41	1934	—	20 Lei, Gold, plain obverse	—
42	1934	—	20 Lei, Gold, ornamented obverse	—
43	1934	—	100 Lei, Gold, plain obverse	—
44	1934	—	100 Lei, Gold, ornamented obverse	—
45	1935	—	20 Lei, Gold, plain obverse	—
46	1935	—	20 Lei, Gold, ornamented obverse	—
47	1935	—	100 Lei, Gold, plain obverse	—
48	1935	—	100 Lei, Gold, ornamented obverse	—
49	1935	—	200 Lei, Silver	250.00
50	1936	—	20 Lei, Gold, plain obverse	—
51	1936	—	20 Lei, Gold, ornamented obverse	—
52	1936	—	100 Lei, Gold, plain obverse	—
53	1936	—	100 Lei, Gold, ornamented obverse	—
54	1937	—	20 Lei, Gold, plain obverse	—
55	1937	—	20 Lei, Gold, ornamented obverse	—
56	1937	—	100 Lei, Gold, plain obverse	—
57	1937	—	100 Lei, Gold, ornamented obverse	—
58	1938	—	20 Lei, Gold, plain obverse	—
59	1938	—	20 Lei, Gold, ornamented obverse	—

KM#	Date	Mintage	Identification	Mkt.Val.
60	1938	—	100 Lei, Gold, plain obverse	—
61	1938	—	100 Lei, Gold, ornamented obverse	—
62	1939	—	20 Lei, Gold, plain obverse	—
63	1939	—	20 Lei, Gold, ornamented obverse	—
64	1939	—	20 Lei, Gold, arms reverse	—
65	1939	—	20 Lei, Gold, eagle reverse	—
66	1939	—	100 Lei, Gold, plain obverse	—
67	1939	—	100 Lei, Gold, ornamented obverse	—
68	1939	—	100 Lei, Gold, bust obverse	—
69	1940	—	20 Lei, Gold, plain obverse	—
70	1940	—	20 Lei, Gold, ornamented obverse	—
71	1940	—	100 Lei, Gold, plain obverse	—
72	1940	—	100 Lei, Gold, ornamented obverse	—
73	1944	—	20 Lei, Gold, three busts to left	—
74	1945	—	100 Lei, Nickel-Clad Steel	125.00

MOLDAVIA AND WALLACHIA

The 2 principalities that constitute most of modern Romania. A vassal state of the Turks for 300 years. As a Russian-Turkish buffer state it was occupied by Russia from 1768 to 1774. During this period a special coinage was made for the area using the copper from captured Turkish cannons.

PARA/3 DENGI

BRONZE

C#	Date	Mintage	Fine	VF	XF
2	1772	—	25.00	40.00	65.00
	1773	—	25.00	40.00	65.00
	1774	Unique	—	—	—

2 PARA/3 KOPECK

BRONZE

C#	Date	Mintage	Fine	VF	XF
3	1772	—	20.00	32.50	50.00
	1773	—	20.00	32.50	50.00
	1774	—	20.00	32.50	50.00

NCLT ISSUES

PATTERNS

KM#	Date	Mintage	Identification	Mkt.Val.
1	1771	—	1 Para/3 Dengi, Bronze, C#1, double eagle	250.00
2	1771	—	1 Para/3 Dengi, Bronze, C#1a, E monograms	250.00
3	1771	—	1 Para/3 Dengi, Bronze, C#1b, value in exerque	250.00
4	1771	—	1 Para/3 Dengi, Bronze, crowned local arms, value in square, C#2	200.00

KM#	Date	Mintage	Identification	Mkt.Val.
5	1771	—	5 Kopecks, Bronze, with lines	275.00
6	1771	—	5 Kopecks, Bronze, w/o lines on obverse and reverse	275.00

a map of
RUSSIA: Its Mints and Dependencies
Kolpino
Sestroretsk
St. Petersburg
Warsaw
Moscow
Nizhny-Novgorod
Annensk
Ekaterinburg
Feodosia
Armavir
Kolyvan-Suzun
Khiwarizm
Khuqand
Bukhara
—KEY—
Krim
Russia
Russian Caucasia
Russian Turkestan
Siberia
Tannu-Tuva

The Union of Soviet Socialist Republics, which occupies the northern part of Asia and the eastern half of Europe, has an area of 8,649,490 sq. mi. (22,402,076 sq. km.) and a population of 258.9 million. Capital: Moscow. The Soviet Union, the world's second ranking industrial power, exports machinery, iron and steel, crude oil, timber and nonferrous metals.

The first Russian dynasty was founded in Novgorod by the Viking Rurik in 862 A.D. Under Yaroslav the Wise (1019-54) the subsequent Kievan state became one of the great commercial and cultural centers of Europe before falling to the Mongols of the Batu Khan, 13th century, who ruled Russia until late in the 15th century when Ivan III threw off the Mongol yoke. The Russian Empire was enlarged, solidified and Westernized during the reigns of Ivan the Terrible, Peter the Great and Catherine the Great, and by 1881 extended to the Pacific and into Central Asia. Modern Russian history began in March of 1917 when Tsar Nicholas II abdicated under pressure and was replaced by a provisional government composed of both radical and conservative elements. This government rapidly lost ground to the Bolshevik wing of the Socialist Democratic Labor Party which attained power following the Bolshevik Revolution which began on Nov. 7, 1917. The Union of Soviet Socialist Republics was established as a federation under the premiership of Lenin on Dec. 30, 1922.

RULERS

Peter III, 1762
Catherine II, 1762-1796
Paul I, 1796-1801
Alexander I, 1801-1825
Nicholas I, 1825-1855
Alexander II, 1855-1881
Alexander III, 1881-1894
Nicholas II, 1894-1917

MINTMARKS

АМ - Anninsk
ЕМ - Ekaterinburg
ТМ - Feodesia, Crimea
ИМ - Ichora
КМ - Kolpina (Ichora), 1810
КМ - Kolyvan, 1767-1830
(later Souzan)
ММ ММД - Moscow
БМ - St. Petersburg
СМ - St. Petersburg (gold)
СП - St. Petersburg
СПБ - St. Petersburg
СПМ St. Petersburg (Ichora)
СМ - Sestroretsk, 1763-1767
СМ - Souzan (Kolyvan), 1831-
ВМ - Warsaw
МШ - Warsaw
Star (on rim) - Paris
2 Stars (on rim) - Brussels

MINTMASTER'S INITIALS

EKATERINBURG MINT

Initials	Years	Mintmaster
НМ	1810-21	Nicholai Mundt
ИФ	1811	Ivan Felkner
ФГ	1811-23	Granz German
ПГ	1823-25	Peter Gramatchikov
ИШ	1825	Ivan Shevkunov
ИК	1825-30	Ivan Kolovov
ФХ	1830-37	Fedor Chwochinski
КТ	1837	Konstantin Tomson
НА	1837-39	Nicholai Alexiev

ICHORA and KOLPINA MINTS

Initials	Years	Mintmaster
МК	1810-11	Mikhail Kleiner
ПС	1811-14	Paul Stupitzin
ЯБ	1820-21	Jacob Wilson

KOLYVAN and SOUZAN MINTS

Initials	Years	Mintmaster
ПБ	1810-11	Peter Beresowski
АМ	1812-17	Alexei Malejew
ДБ	1817-18	Dmitri Bichto
АД	1818-21	Alexander Deichmann
АМ	1821-30	Andrei Mevius

MOSCOW MINT

Initials	Years	Mintmaster
А	1751	Afonasiev
ІШ	1752-53	Ilya Shagin
Е	1752-69	Igor Ivanov
ЕІ	1762-69	Igor Ivanov
ІП	1753-54	I.Plavilshchikov
МБ	1754-57	M.Bobrovshchikov
ДМ	1762-70	Daniel Mochalkin
АШ	1766-68	Alexei Schneze
СА	1774-75	Stepan Afonasiev

ST. PETERSBURG MINT

Initials	Years	Mintmaster
ІМ	1751-58	Ivan Markov
ЯІ	1752-66	Yakov Ivanov
ЯИ	1752-66	Yakov Ivanov
НК	1758-63	Nazar Kutuzov
СА	1764-70	Stepan Afonasiev
АШ	1766-72	Alexei Schneze
ЕІ	1767-68	Igor Ivanov
ЯЧ	1770-76	Yakov Chernishev
ЭЛ	1773-79	Fedor Lesnikov
ИЗ	1780-83	Ivan Zaitsev
АГ	1781	Avraam Hutseus
ММ	1783-84	Mikhail Mikhailov
ЯА	1785-93	Yakov Afonasiev
АК	1793-95	Andrei Kutzberg
ІС	1796	Ivan Sabelnikov
ГЛ	1797	Gregory Lvov
ФЦ	1797-1801	Fedor Tsetreus
МБ	1798-99	M. Bobrovshchikov
ОМ	1798-1801	Ossip Medzher
АИ	1799-1800	Alexei Ivanov
АИ	1801-03	Alexander Ivanov
ФГ	1803-17	Fedor Hellman
ХЛ	1804-05	Christopher Leo
МК	1808-09	Mikhail Kleiner
МФ	1812-22	Mikhail Fedorov
ПС	1811-25	Paul Stupitzin
ПД	1820-38	Paul Danilov
НГ	1825-42	Nicholai Grachev
АЧ	1839-43	Alexei Chadov
КБ	1844-46	Constantine Butenev
АГ	1846-57	Alexander Gertov
ПА	1847-52	Paul Alexiev
НІ	1848-77	Nicholai Iossa
ФБ	1856-61	Fedor Blum
ПФ	1858-62	Paul Follendorf
МИ	1861-63	Mikhail Ivanov
АБ	1863	Alexander Belezerov
АС	1864-65	Aggei Swetchin
НФ	1864-82	Nicholai Follendorf
СШ	1865-66	Sergei Shostak
ДС	1882-83	Dmitri Sabaniev
АГ	1883-99	Appolon Grasgov
ЭБ	1899-1913	Elikum Babayontz
ФЗ	1899-01	Felix Zaleman
АР	1901-05	Alexander Redko
ВС	1913-17	Victor Smirnov

MONETARY SYSTEM

1/4 Kopek = Polushka ПОЛУШКА
1/2 Kopek = Denga, Denezhka
ДЕНГА ДЕНЕЖКА
Kopek КОПЬИКА
(2, 3 & 4) Kopeks = КОЛЬИКИ
(5 and up) Kopeks = КОЛЬЕКЪ
10 Kopeks = Grivna, Grivennik
ГРИВГА ГРИЕЕННИКЪ
25 Kopeks = Polupoltina, Polupoltinnik
Polupoltinnik
ПОЛПОЛСИНА
ПОЛУПОЛТИННИКЪ
50 Kopeks = Poltina, Poltinnik
ПОЛТИНА ПОЛТИННКЪ
100 Kopeks = Rouble, Ruble
РУБЛЪ
10 Roubles = Imperial
10 Roubles = Chervonetz

NOTE: Mintage figures for years after 1885 are for fiscal years and may or may not reflect actual rarity, the commemorative and 1917 silver figures being exceptions.

NOTE: The letter N in the mintage column indicates that the coin is a novodel (restrike).

NOTE: For gold or silver coins with Kopek and Zlotych denominations see Poland.

POLUSHKA (1/4 KOPEK)

COPPER

C#	Date	Mintage	VG	Fine	VF	XF
MINT: ANNINSK АМ						
55.1	1789	—	—	—	—	—
MINT: ANNINSK (no mintmark)						
55.2	1789	—	15.00	30.00	50.00	90.00
	1793	.079	20.00	40.00	75.00	125.00
	1795	.062	20.00	40.00	75.00	125.00
MINT: EKATERINBURG ЕМ						
55.3	1766	3.107	6.00	12.00	25.00	50.00
	1767	4.311	6.00	12.00	25.00	50.00
	1768	5.684	6.00	12.00	25.00	50.00
	1769	3.778	6.00	12.00	25.00	50.00
	1770/69	6.040	7.50	15.00	30.00	60.00
	1770	Inc. Ab.	6.00	12.00	25.00	50.00
	1771	4.470	6.00	12.00	25.00	50.00
	1772	.960	6.00	12.00	25.00	50.00
	1773	.198	100.00	200.00	300.00	500.00
	1775	.378	60.00	100.00	150.00	275.00
	1786	.450	6.00	12.00	25.00	50.00
	1789	2.037	6.00	12.00	25.00	50.00
	1790	1.019	6.00	12.00	25.00	50.00
	1794	.009	60.00	100.00	150.00	275.00
	1795	.071	6.00	12.00	25.00	50.00
	1796	.261	20.00	40.00	75.00	125.00
MINT: KOLYVAN КМ						
55.4	1783	—	15.00	30.00	50.00	90.00
	1784	—	15.00	30.00	50.00	90.00
	1785	—	15.00	30.00	50.00	90.00
	1786	—	40.00	80.00	150.00	275.00
	1787	—	30.00	60.00	100.00	175.00
	1788	—	30.00	60.00	100.00	175.00
	1789	—	30.00	60.00	100.00	175.00
	1790	—	30.00	60.00	100.00	175.00
	1791	—	60.00	100.00	150.00	275.00
	1792	—	20.00	40.00	75.00	125.00
	1793	—	20.00	40.00	75.00	125.00
	1794	—	60.00	100.00	150.00	275.00
	1795	—	30.00	60.00	100.00	175.00

C#	Date	Mintage	VG	Fine	VF	XF
MINT: ANNINSK АМ						
92.1	1797	—	8.50	17.00	35.00	70.00
	1798	—	8.50	17.50	35.00	70.00
MINT: EKATERINBURG ЕМ						
92.2	1797	—	7.50	15.00	30.00	60.00
	1798	1.510	7.50	15.00	30.00	60.00
	1799	.011	—	—	Rare	—
	1800	—	75.00	150.00	250.00	500.00
	1801	—	—	—	Rare	—
MINT: KOLYVAN КМ						
92.3	1797	—	37.50	75.00	150.00	250.00
	1798	—	37.50	75.00	150.00	250.00
	1799	—	37.50	75.00	150.00	250.00

C#	Date	Mintage	VG	Fine	VF	XF
MINT: EKATERINBURG ЕМ						
111.1	1803	.012	20.00	37.50	75.00	150.00
	1804	20 pcs.	—	—	Rare	—
	1805	.025	15.00	30.00	60.00	120.00
	1808	—	37.50	75.00	150.00	300.00
	1810	—	30.00	65.00	125.00	250.00
MINT: KOLYVAN КМ						
111.2	1804	—	25.00	50.00	100.00	200.00
	1805	—	25.00	50.00	100.00	200.00
	1807	—	25.00	50.00	100.00	200.00

MINT: EKATERINBURG ЕМ

C#	Date	Mintage	VG	Fine	VF	XF
142.1	1840	10.972	3.00	6.00	12.00	24.00
	1841	3.230	3.00	6.00	12.00	24.00
	1842	3.600	3.00	6.00	12.00	24.00
	1843	1.664	3.00	6.00	12.00	30.00

MINT: ST. PETERSBURG СПМ

C#	Date	Mintage	VG	Fine	VF	XF
142.2	1840	6.400	4.00	7.50	15.00	30.00
	1841	6.400	3.00	6.00	12.00	24.00
	1842	12.800	3.00	6.00	12.00	24.00

MINT: SOUZAN СМ

C#	Date	Mintage	VG	Fine	VF	XF
142.3	1839	.450	12.50	25.00	50.00	100.00
	1840	2.572	4.00	7.50	15.00	30.00
	1841	3.572	4.00	7.50	15.00	30.00
	1842	3.960	4.00	7.50	15.00	30.00
	1843	2.006	4.00	7.50	15.00	30.00
	1844	3.400	4.00	7.50	15.00	30.00
	1845	3.000	4.00	7.50	15.00	30.00
	1846	3.000	4.00	7.50	15.00	30.00

MINT: EKATERINBURG ЕМ

C#	Date	Mintage	VG	Fine	VF	XF
147.1	1849	—	—	—	Rare	—
	1850	5.184	1.50	3.00	6.00	12.00
	1851	7.776	1.50	3.00	6.00	12.00
	1852	1.177	1.50	3.00	6.00	12.00
	1853	5.382	1.50	3.00	6.00	12.00
	1854	4.540	1.50	3.00	6.00	12.00
	1855	6.442	5.00	10.00	15.00	30.00

MINT: ST. PETERSBURG СПМ

C#	Date	Mintage	VG	Fine	VF	XF
147.2	1849	—	—	—	Rare	—

MINT: WARSAW ВМ

C#	Date	Mintage	VG	Fine	VF	XF
147.3	1850	—	7.50	12.00	25.00	50.00
	1851	.080	7.50	12.00	25.00	50.00
	1852	.080	7.50	12.00	25.00	50.00
	1853	.040	7.50	12.00	25.00	50.00

MINT: EKATERINBURG ЕМ

Plain border

Y#	Date	Mintage	Fine	VF	XF	Unc
1.1	1855	Inc.C147.1	2.50	5.00	10.00	25.00
	1856	6.000	2.50	5.00	10.00	25.00
	1857	6.000	2.50	5.00	10.00	25.00
	1858	6.969	2.50	5.00	10.00	25.00
	1859	3.833	2.50	5.00	10.00	25.00

MINT: WARSAW МШ

Y#	Date	Mintage	Fine	VF	XF	Unc
1.2	1855	.200	7.50	15.00	30.00	60.00
	1860	—	7.50	15.00	30.00	60.00

MINT: EKATERINBURG ЕМ

Toothed border

Y#	Date	Mintage	Fine	VF	XF	Unc
1.3	1858	—	—	—	Rare	—
	1859	—	2.50	5.00	10.00	25.00
	1860	—	—	—	Rare	—
	1861	.192	3.50	7.50	15.00	35.00
	1862	.992	2.50	5.00	10.00	25.00
	1863	.300	6.00	12.50	25.00	50.00
	1864	.403	5.00	10.00	20.00	45.00
	1865	.121	2.50	5.00	10.00	25.00
	1866	.326	2.50	5.00	10.00	25.00
	1867	.832	12.50	25.00	50.00	100.00

MINT: WARSAW МШ

Y#	Date	Mintage	Fine	VF	XF	Unc
1.4	1861	.400	3.50	7.50	15.00	35.00

MINT: EKATERINBURG ЕМ

Y#	Date	Mintage	Fine	VF	XF	Unc
7.1	1867	Inc. Ab.	10.00	17.00	35.00	75.00
	1868	.700	2.50	5.00	10.00	20.00
	1869	.615	2.50	5.00	10.00	20.00
	1870	.435	2.50	5.00	10.00	20.00
	1871	.155	3.00	6.00	12.00	25.00
	1872	.540	2.50	5.00	10.00	20.00
	1873	.822	2.50	5.00	10.00	20.00
	1874	.340	2.50	5.00	10.00	20.00
	1875	.300	1.25	2.50	5.00	10.00
	1876	—	—	—	Rare	—

MINT: ST. PETERSBURG СПБ

Y#	Date	Mintage	Fine	VF	XF	Unc
7.2	1867	24 pcs.	5.00	10.00	20.00	40.00
	1868	.060	3.00	6.00	12.00	25.00
	1869	.092	3.00	6.00	12.00	25.00
	1870	.020	3.50	7.50	15.00	30.00
	1871	—	—	—	Rare	—
	1876	.800	1.25	2.50	5.00	10.00
	1877	.720	1.25	2.50	5.00	10.00
	1878	1.100	1.25	2.50	5.00	10.00
	1879	.280	1.25	2.50	5.00	10.00
	1880	.180	1.75	3.50	7.50	15.00
	1881	.060	1.75	3.50	7.50	15.00

MINT: ST. PETERSBURG СПБ

Y#	Date	Mintage	Fine	VF	XF	Unc
29	1881	.200	2.50	5.00	10.00	20.00
	1882	.060	2.50	5.00	10.00	20.00
	1883	.240	1.50	3.00	6.00	12.00
	1884	.140	2.50	5.00	10.00	20.00
	1885	.480	1.50	3.00	6.00	12.00
	1886	1.060	1.00	2.50	5.00	10.00
	1887	1.000	1.00	2.50	5.00	10.00
	1888	.200	1.50	3.00	6.00	12.00
	1889	.181	2.50	5.00	10.00	20.00
	1890	Inc. Ab.	1.50	3.00	6.00	12.00
	1891	.400	1.50	3.00	6.00	12.00
	1892	.918	1.25	2.50	5.00	10.00
	1893	.740	1.25	2.50	5.00	10.00

MINT: ST. PETERSBURG СПБ

Y#	Date	Mintage	Fine	VF	XF	Unc
47	1894	—	6.00	12.50	25.00	50.00
	1895	.060	2.50	5.00	10.00	20.00
	1896	5.960	1.25	2.50	5.00	10.00
	1897	3.040	1.25	2.50	5.00	10.00
	1898	8.000	1.00	1.75	3.50	7.00
	1899	8.000	1.00	1.75	3.50	7.00
	1900	4.000	1.00	1.75	3.50	7.00
	1909	2.000	1.50	3.00	6.00	12.00
	1910	8.000	5.00	10.00	20.00	40.00

MINT: ST. PETERSBURG (no mintmark)

Y#	Date	Mintage	Fine	VF	XF	Unc
	1915	.500	3.75	7.50	15.00	30.00
	1916	1.200	—	—	Rare	—

DENGA (1/2 KOPEK)

COPPER

No mintmark

C#	Date	Mintage	VG	Fine	VF	XF
40	1762 plain edge		—	—	Rare	—
	1762 reeded edge		—	—	Rare	—

MINT: ANNINSK (no mintmark)

C#	Date	Mintage	VG	Fine	VF	XF
56.1	1788	—	10.00	20.00	35.00	70.00
	1789	—	10.00	20.00	35.00	70.00
	1790	—	20.00	40.00	75.00	125.00
	1791	.088	30.00	60.00	100.00	175.00
	1792	.059	30.00	60.00	100.00	175.00
	1793	.015	150.00	300.00	500.00	800.00
56.1	1794	—	75.00	150.00	250.00	400.00

MINT: EKATERINBURG ЕМ

C#	Date	Mintage	VG	Fine	VF	XF
56.2	1764EM	—	200.00	300.00	500.00	800.00
	1766EM	2.841	5.00	10.00	17.50	35.00
	1767EM	2.623	5.00	10.00	17.50	35.00
	1768EM	2.422	5.00	10.00	17.50	35.00
	1769EM	1.450	5.00	10.00	17.50	35.00
	1770EM	4.020	5.00	10.00	17.50	35.00
	1771EM	2.910	5.00	10.00	17.50	35.00
	1772EM	1.160	5.00	10.00	17.50	35.00
	1773EM	.451	5.00	10.00	17.50	35.00
	1774EM	.020	100.00	150.00	250.00	400.00
	1775EM	.508	5.00	10.00	17.50	35.00
	1786EM	.573	5.00	10.00	17.50	35.00
	1789EM	2.009	5.00	10.00	17.50	35.00
	1790EM	1.235	5.00	10.00	17.50	35.00
	1793EM	.933	5.00	10.00	17.50	35.00
	1794EM	.797	5.00	10.00	17.50	35.00
	1795EM	3.199	5.00	10.00	17.50	35.00
	1796EM	—	5.00	10.00	17.50	35.00

MINT: FEODESIA ТМ

C#	Date	Mintage	VG	Fine	VF	XF
56.3	1787TM	—	—	—	—	—

MINT: KOLYVAN КМ

C#	Date	Mintage	VG	Fine	VF	XF
56.4	1783	—	8.00	15.00	25.00	50.00
	1784	—	8.00	15.00	25.00	50.00
	1785	—	8.00	15.00	25.00	50.00
	1786	—	8.00	15.00	25.00	50.00
	1787	—	8.00	15.00	25.00	50.00
	1788	—	8.00	15.00	25.00	50.00
	1789	—	60.00	100.00	150.00	275.00
	1790	—	8.00	15.00	25.00	50.00
	1791	—	8.00	15.00	25.00	50.00
	1792	—	8.00	15.00	25.00	50.00
	1793	—	8.00	15.00	25.00	50.00
	1794	—	8.00	15.00	25.00	50.00
	1795	—	8.00	15.00	25.00	50.00

MINT: ST. PETERSBURG (no mintmark)

C#	Date	Mintage	VG	Fine	VF	XF
56.5	1763	—	—	—	Rare	—

MINT: ANNINSK АМ

C#	Date	Mintage	VG	Fine	VF	XF
93.1	1797	—	10.00	20.00	40.00	80.00
	1798	—	11.00	22.50	45.00	90.00

MINT: EKATERINBURG ЕМ

C#	Date	Mintage	VG	Fine	VF	XF
93.2	1797	.130	6.50	12.50	25.00	50.00
	1798	5.194	6.00	12.50	25.00	50.00
	1799	7,000	6.00	12.50	25.00	50.00
	1800	—	—	—	Rare	—
	1801	.026	12.50	25.00	50.00	100.00

MINT: KOLYVAN КМ

C#	Date	Mintage	VG	Fine	VF	XF
93.3	1797	—	15.00	30.00	60.00	100.00
	1798KM	—	15.00	30.00	60.00	100.00
	1799	—	12.00	22.50	45.00	90.00
	1800	—	13.50	26.50	55.00	95.00

MINT: EKATERINBURG ЕМ

C#	Date	Mintage	VG	Fine	VF	XF
112.1	1804	20 pcs.	—	—	Rare	—
	1805	.040	35.00	70.00	140.00	225.00
	1808	—	—	—	Rare	—
	1810	—	—	—	Rare	—

MINT: KOLYVAN КМ

C#	Date	Mintage	VG	Fine	VF	XF
112.2	1804	—	50.00	100.00	200.00	350.00
	1805	—	50.00	100.00	200.00	350.00
	1807	—	50.00	100.00	200.00	350.00
	1810	—	—	—	Rare	—

MINT: EKATERINBURG EM

Obv: Type 1 eagle

C#	Date	Mintage	VG	Fine	VF	XF
116.1	1810 HM	.036	—	—	Rare	—

MINT: KOLYVAN KM

Obv: Type 2 eagle

C#	Date	Mintage	VG	Fine	VF	XF
116.2	1811 ПБ	—	5.00	10.00	20.00	40.00

MINT: EKATERINBURG EM

Obv: Type 3 eagle

C#	Date	Mintage	VG	Fine	VF	XF
116.3	1811 HM	.099	3.75	7.50	15.00	30.00
	1813 HM	.024	5.00	9.00	17.50	35.00
	1815 HM	.059	5.00	9.00	17.50	35.00
	1818 HM	23.410	4.00	7.50	12.50	25.00
	1819 HM	1.360	4.00	7.50	12.50	25.00
	1822 ФГ	—	—	—	Rare	—
	1825 ИК	.555	4.00	7.50	2.50	25.00

MINT: ICHORA ИМ

C#	Date	Mintage	VG	Fine	VF	XF
116.4	1810 ФГ	.026	—	—	Rare	—
	1810 MK	Inc. Ab.	3.75	7.50	15.00	30.00
	1811 MK	.160	3.00	6.00	12.50	25.00
	1812 ПС	.510	4.00	7.50	15.00	30.00
	1813 ПС	1.220	3.50	6.50	12.50	25.00
	1814 ПС	2.250	—	—	Rare	—
	1814 СП	Inc. Ab.	4.00	7.50	15.00	30.00

MINT: KOLYVAN KM

C#	Date	Mintage	VG	Fine	VF	XF
116.5	1812 AM	—	5.00	9.00	17.50	35.00
	1813 AM	—	5.00	9.00	17.50	35.00
	1814 AM	—	5.00	9.00	17.50	35.00
	1815 AM	—	5.00	9.00	17.50	35.00
	1816 AM	—	5.00	9.00	17.50	35.00
	1817 AM	—	5.00	9.00	17.50	35.00

MINT: ST. PETERSBURG СПБ

C#	Date	Mintage	VG	Fine	VF	XF
116.6	1810 ФГ	—	6.00	12.50	25.00	50.00
	1811 MK	.075	3.00	6.00	12.50	25.00
	1812 ПС	—	—	—	Rare	—

MINT: EKATERINBURG EM

Similar to C#116.3

C#	Date	Mintage	VG	Fine	VF	XF
135.1	1827 ИК	2.165	3.50	6.50	12.50	25.00
	1828 ИК	—	3.50	6.50	12.50	25.00

MINT: ST. PETERSBURG СПБ

C#	Date	Mintage	VG	Fine	VF	XF
135.2	1828	—	—	—	Rare	—

MINT: EKATERINBURG EM

C#	Date	Mintage	VG	Fine	VF	XF
143.1	1840	10.999	2.00	4.00	8.00	15.00
	1841	3.384	2.00	4.00	8.00	15.00
	1842	3.600	2.00	4.00	8.00	15.00
	1843	2.580	2.00	4.00	8.00	15.00

MINT: ST. PETERSBURG СПБ

C#	Date	Mintage	VG	Fine	VF	XF
143.2	1840	—	7.00	12.50	25.00	50.00

MINT: ST. PETERSBURG СПМ

C#	Date	Mintage	VG	Fine	VF	XF
143.3	1840	6.400	2.00	4.00	8.00	15.00
	1841	6.400	2.00	4.00	8.00	15.00
	1842	12.800	2.00	4.00	8.00	15.00

MINT: SOUZAN CM

C#	Date	Mintage	VG	Fine	VF	XF
143.4	1839	.454	5.00	10.00	20.00	40.00
143.4	1840	2.560	2.50	5.00	10.00	20.00
	1841	3.542	2.50	5.00	10.00	20.00
	1842	4.000	2.50	5.00	10.00	20.00
	1843	2.000	2.50	5.00	10.00	20.00
	1844	3.400	2.50	5.00	10.00	20.00
	1845	3.000	2.50	5.00	10.00	20.00
	1846	3.000	2.50	5.00	10.00	20.00
	1847	2.532	4.00	7.50	15.00	30.00

MINT: WARSAW МШ

C#	Date	Mintage	VG	Fine	VF	XF
143.5	1848	.087	—	—	Rare	—
	1849	50 pcs.	—	—	Rare	—

MINT: EKATERINBURG EM

C#	Date	Mintage	VG	Fine	VF	XF
148.1	1849	—	—	—	Rare	—
	1850	3.561	1.00	2.00	4.00	8.00
	1851	6.425	1.00	2.00	4.00	8.00
	1852	14.672	1.00	2.00	4.00	8.00
	1853	12.243	1.00	2.00	4.00	8.00
	1854	13.753	1.00	2.00	4.00	8.00
	1855	Inc. in Y2	2.00	4.00	7.50	15.00

MINT: ST. PETERSBURG СПМ

C#	Date	Mintage	VG	Fine	VF	XF
148.2	1849	—	—	—	Rare	—

MINT: WARSAW BM

C#	Date	Mintage	VG	Fine	VF	XF
148.3	1850	1.840	2.00	4.50	9.00	17.50
	1851	1.200	2.00	4.50	9.00	17.50
	1852	1.210	2.00	4.50	9.00	17.50
	1853	.804	2.00	4.50	9.00	17.50
	1854	.352	2.00	4.50	9.00	17.50
	1855	Inc. In Y2	7.00	12.50	25.00	50.00

MINT: EKATERINBURG EM

Plain border

Y#	Date	Mintage	Fine	VF	XF	Unc
2.1	1855	20.510	2.00	4.00	8.00	16.00
	1856	6.000	2.00	4.00	8.00	16.00
	1857	6.000	2.00	4.00	8.00	16.00
	1858	11.147	2.00	4.00	8.00	16.00
	1859	5.871	2.00	4.00	8.00	16.00

MINT: WARSAW BM

Y#	Date	Mintage	Fine	VF	XF	Unc
2.2	1855	6.380	5.00	10.00	20.00	40.00
	1856	4.452	5.00	10.00	20.00	40.00
	1857	1.908	5.00	10.00	20.00	40.00
	1858	.311	3.50	6.50	12.50	25.00
	1859	3.718	5.00	10.00	20.00	40.00
	1860	1.860	3.50	6.50	12.50	25.00

MINT: EKATERINBURG EM

Toothed border

Y#	Date	Mintage	Fine	VF	XF	Unc
2.3	1859	—	2.50	5.00	10.00	20.00
	1860	2.838	2.50	5.00	10.00	20.00
	1861	2.276	2.50	5.00	10.00	20.00
	1862	3.072	2.50	5.00	10.00	20.00
	1863	1.011	2.50	5.00	10.00	20.00
	1864	.560	4.00	7.50	15.00	30.00
	1865	.560	—	—	Rare	—
	1866	.332	5.00	10.00	20.00	40.00
	1867	.390	10.00	20.00	40.00	75.00

MINT: WARSAW BM

Y#	Date	Mintage	Fine	VF	XF	Unc
2.4	1861	1.564	4.00	7.50	15.00	30.00
	1862	1.035	4.00	7.50	15.00	30.00
	1863	2.400	6.00	12.50	25.00	50.00

MINT: EKATERINBURG EM

Y#	Date	Mintage	Fine	VF	XF	Unc
8.1	1867	Inc. Ab.	6.50	12.50	25.00	50.00
8.1	1868	1.190	1.50	3.00	6.00	12.00
	1869	.592	1.50	3.00	6.00	12.00
	1870	.510	2.00	4.00	7.50	15.00
	1871	.222	1.50	3.00	6.00	12.00
	1872	.365	1.50	3.00	6.00	12.00
	1873	.962	1.50	3.00	6.00	12.00
	1874	.365	1.50	3.00	6.00	12.00
	1875	.321	3.50	6.50	12.50	25.00
	1876	Inc. Ab.	—	—	Rare	—

MINT: ST. PETERSBURG СПБ

Y#	Date	Mintage	Fine	VF	XF	Unc
8.2	1867	—	5.00	10.00	20.00	45.00
	1868	.060	3.00	6.00	12.00	25.00
	1869	.145	2.00	4.50	9.00	17.50
	1870	.025	5.00	10.00	20.00	40.00
	1871	—	—	—	Rare	—
	1876	.770	1.00	2.25	4.50	9.00
	1877	1.290	1.00	2.25	4.50	9.00
	1878	1.120	1.00	2.25	4.50	9.00
	1879	.740	1.00	2.25	4.50	9.00
	1880	1.260	1.00	2.25	4.50	9.00
	1881	.420	1.00	2.25	4.50	9.00

MINT: ST. PETERSBURG СПБ

Y#	Date	Mintage	Fine	VF	XF	Unc
30	1881	.440	2.00	4.00	8.00	16.00
	1882	.350	1.00	2.25	4.50	9.00
	1883	.540	1.00	2.25	4.50	9.00
	1884	.550	1.00	2.25	4.50	9.00
	1885	.680	1.00	2.25	4.50	9.00
	1886	.560	1.00	2.25	4.50	9.00
	1887	.600	1.00	2.25	4.50	9.00
	1888	.610	1.00	2.25	4.50	9.00
	1889	4.650	1.00	2.00	4.00	7.50
	1890	2.040	1.00	2.00	4.00	7.50
	1892	2.271	1.00	2.00	4.00	7.50
	1893	3.900	1.00	2.00	4.00	7.50
	1894	—	1.00	2.00	4.00	7.50

MINT: ST. PETERSBURG СПБ

Y#	Date	Mintage	Fine	VF	XF	Unc
48.1	1894	—	5.00	10.00	20.00	40.00
	1895	2.992	1.00	2.00	4.00	8.00
	1896	1.340	1.00	2.00	4.00	8.00
	1897	60.000	.65	1.25	2.50	5.00
	1898	76.000	.65	1.25	2.50	5.00
	1899	76.000	.65	1.25	2.50	5.00
	1900	36.000	.65	1.25	2.50	5.00
	1908	8.000	.65	1.25	2.50	5.00
	1909	49.500	.50	1.00	2.00	4.00
	1910	24.000	.65	1.25	2.50	5.00
	1911	35.800	.65	1.25	2.50	5.00
	1912	28.000	.65	1.25	2.50	5.00
	1913	50.000	.65	1.25	2.50	5.00
	1914	14.000	.75	1.50	3.00	6.00

MINT: ST. PETERSBURG (no mintmark)

Y#	Date	Mintage	Fine	VF	XF	Unc
48.2	1915	12.000	1.00	2.00	4.00	7.00
	1916	9.400	1.00	2.00	4.00	7.00

KOPEK

COPPER

NO MINTMARK

C#	Date	Mintage	VG	Fine	VF	XF
41	1762 reeded edge	—	100.00	150.00	250.00	500.00
	1762 grilled edge	—	100.00	150.00	250.00	500.00

MINT: UNKNOWN (no mintmark)

C#	Date	Mintage	VG	Fine	VF	XF
57.1	1788	—	8.00	15.00	30.00	60.00
	1795	.132	15.00	25.00	50.00	100.00

MINT: EKATERINBURG ЕМ

C#	Date	Mintage	VG	Fine	VF	XF
57.2	1763	.050	—	—	Rare	—
	1789	6.343	5.00	10.00	20.00	40.00
	1790	1.862	5.00	10.00	20.00	40.00
	1791	—	5.00	10.00	20.00	40.00
	1793	—	—	—	Rare	—
	1794	.756	5.00	10.00	20.00	40.00
	1795	2.286	5.00	10.00	20.00	40.00
	1796	.523	8.00	15.00	30.00	60.00

MINT: FEODESIA ТМ

C#	Date	Mintage	VG	Fine	VF	XF
57.3	1787	—	—	—	Rare	—

MINT: MOSCOW ММ

C#	Date	Mintage	VG	Fine	VF	XF
57.4	1763	—	12.00	20.00	40.00	75.00
	1764	—	60.00	125.00	200.00	350.00
	1766	—	30.00	60.00	100.00	175.00
	1767	—	100.00	200.00	300.00	500.00
	1788	—	12.00	20.00	40.00	75.00
	1795	—	40.00	75.00	150.00	275.00

MINT: ST. PETERSBURG СПМ

C#	Date	Mintage	VG	Fine	VF	XF
57.5	1764	—	100.00	200.00	300.00	500.00
	1766	—	50.00	100.00	150.00	275.00
	1767	—	100.00	200.00	300.00	500.00

MINT: ANNINSK АМ

C#	Date	Mintage	VG	Fine	VF	XF
94.1	1797	—	6.00	12.00	25.00	50.00

COPPER

MINT: EKATERINBURG ЕМ

C#	Date	Mintage	VG	Fine	VF	XF
94.2	1797	.523	3.00	6.50	12.50	25.00
	1798	19.243	3.00	6.50	12.50	25.00
	1799	23.789	3.00	6.50	12.50	25.00
	1800	9.493	3.00	6.50	12.50	25.00
	1801	1.708	4.00	7.50	15.00	30.00

MINT: KOLYVAN КМ

C#	Date	Mintage	VG	Fine	VF	XF
94.3	1797	—	12.50	25.00	40.00	80.00
	1798	—	12.50	25.00	40.00	80.00
	1799	—	12.50	25.00	40.00	80.00

MINT: EKATERINBURG ЕМ

C#	Date	Mintage	VG	Fine	VF	XF
113.1	1804	20 pcs.	—	—	Rare	—
	1805	.114	20.00	35.00	75.00	150.00
	1807	—	25.00	50.00	100.00	200.00

MINT: KOLYVAN КМ

C#	Date	Mintage	VG	Fine	VF	XF
113.2	1804	—	25.00	50.00	100.00	200.00
	1805	—	25.00	50.00	100.00	200.00
	1807	—	25.00	50.00	100.00	200.00

MINT: EKATERINBURG ЕМ

Obv: Type 1 eagle

C#	Date	Mintage	VG	Fine	VF	XF
117.1	1810 НМ	.510	—	—	Rare	—

MINT: KOLYVAN КМ

Obv: Type 2 eagle

C#	Date	Mintage	VG	Fine	VF	XF
117.2	1810	—	—	—	Rare	—
	1811 ПБ	—	—	—	Rare	—

MINT: EKATERINBURG ЕМ

Obv: Type 3 eagle

C#	Date	Mintage	VG	Fine	VF	XF
117.3	1810 НМ	—	—	—	Rare	—
	1811 НМ	1.420	1.50	3.00	6.00	10.00
	1813 НМ	.030	—	—	Rare	—
	1815 НМ	.031	—	—	Rare	—
	1818 НМ	55.750	2.50	5.00	10.00	20.00
	1819 НМ	35.030	2.50	5.00	10.00	20.00
	1821 НМ	10.160	2.50	5.00	10.00	20.00
	1822 ФГ	10.265	2.50	5.00	10.00	20.00
	1823 ФГ	10.350	2.50	5.00	10.00	20.00
	1824 ПГ	—	2.50	5.00	10.00	20.00
	1825 ИК	—	2.50	5.00	10.00	20.00

MINT: ICHORA ИМ

C#	Date	Mintage	VG	Fine	VF	XF
117.4	1811 МК	.490	2.50	5.00	10.00	25.00
	1812 ПС	1.040	2.50	5.00	10.00	20.00
	1813 ПС	1.980	2.50	5.00	10.00	20.00
	1814 ПС	3.740	2.50	5.00	10.00	20.00

MINT: KOLYVAN КМ

C#	Date	Mintage	VG	Fine	VF	XF
117.5	1810 ПБ	—	—	—	Rare	—
	1811 ПБ	—	1.50	3.00	6.00	10.00
	1812 АМ	—	4.00	10.00	20.00	40.00
	1813 АМ	—	5.00	10.00	20.00	40.00
	1814 АМ	—	5.00	10.00	20.00	40.00
	1815 АМ	—	3.50	7.50	15.00	30.00
	1816 АМ	—	5.00	10.00	20.00	40.00
	1817 АМ	—	5.00	10.00	20.00	40.00
	1818 АД	—	3.50	7.50	15.00	30.00
	1818 ДБ	—	2.50	5.00	10.00	20.00
	1819 АД	—	3.50	7.50	15.00	30.00
	1820 АД	—	2.50	5.00	10.00	20.00
	1821 АМ	—	2.50	5.00	10.00	20.00
	1822 АМ	—	3.50	7.50	15.00	30.00
	1823 АМ	—	3.50	7.50	15.00	30.00
	1824 АМ	—	3.50	7.50	15.00	30.00
	1825 АМ	—	3.50	7.50	15.00	30.00

MINT: ST. PETERSBURG СПБ

C#	Date	Mintage	VG	Fine	VF	XF
117.6	1810 ФГ	.093	—	—	Rare	—
	1810 МК	I.A.	2.00	4.50	9.00	17.00
	1810 МК	.260	1.50	3.00	6.00	10.00

MINT: EKATERINBURG ЕМ

Similar to C#117.3

C#	Date	Mintage	VG	Fine	VF	XF
136.1	1827 ИК	2.646	3.50	7.50	15.00	30.00
	1828 ИК	43.015	3.50	7.50	15.00	30.00
	1829 ИК	48.266	2.50	5.00	10.00	20.00
	1830 ИК	2.100	2.50	5.00	10.00	20.00

MINT: KOLYVAN КМ

C#	Date	Mintage	VG	Fine	VF	XF
136.2	1826 АМ	6.250	3.50	7.50	15.00	30.00
	1827 АМ	6.250	3.50	7.50	15.00	30.00
	1828 АМ	5.000	3.50	7.50	15.00	30.00
	1829 АМ	5.000	3.50	7.50	15.00	30.00
	1830 АМ	5.000	3.50	7.50	15.00	30.00

MINT: ST. PETERSBURG СПБ

C#	Date	Mintage	VG	Fine	VF	XF
136.3	1828	—	—	—	Rare	—

MINT: EKATERINBURG ЕМ

C#	Date	Mintage	VG	Fine	VF	XF
138.1	1830 ФХ	—	—	—	Rare	—
	1831 ФХ	13.050	3.50	6.50	12.50	25.00
	1832 ФХ	3.400	3.50	6.50	12.50	25.00
	1833 ФХ	2.882	3.50	6.50	12.50	25.00
	1834 ФХ	5.020	3.50	6.50	12.50	25.00
	1835 ФХ	6.570	3.50	6.50	12.50	25.00
	1836 ФХ	2.100	3.50	6.50	12.50	25.00
	1837 КТ	4.890	3.50	6.50	12.50	25.00
	1837 НА	I.A.	4.50	6.50	12.50	25.00
	1838 НА	1.043	—	—	Rare	—

MINT: ST. PETERSBURG СПБ

C#	Date	Mintage	VG	Fine	VF	XF
138.2	1830	29 pcs.	—	—	Rare	—

MINT: SOUZAN СМ

C#	Date	Mintage	VG	Fine	VF	XF
138.3	1831	2.000	4.50	7.50	15.00	30.00
	1832	2.000	4.50	7.50	15.00	30.00
	1833	.045	4.50	7.50	15.00	30.00
	1834	2.000	4.50	7.50	15.00	30.00
	1835	2.000	4.50	7.50	15.00	30.00
	1836	.100	4.50	7.50	15.00	30.00
	1837	1.000	3.50	7.50	15.00	30.00
	1838	1.800	3.50	7.50	15.00	30.00
	1839	.020	—	—	Rare	—

MINT: EKATERINBURG ЕМ

C#	Date	Mintage	VG	Fine	VF	XF
144.1	1840	20.778	1.25	2.50	5.00	10.00
	1841	19.341	1.25	2.50	5.00	10.00
	1842	13.581	1.25	2.50	5.00	10.00
	1843	12.520	1.25	2.50	5.00	10.00
	1844	—	1.25	2.50	5.00	10.00

MINT: ST. PETERSBURG СПБ

C#	Date	Mintage	VG	Fine	VF	XF
144.2	1840	11.200	—	—	Rare	—

MINT: ST. PETERSBURG СПМ

C#	Date	Mintage	VG	Fine	VF	XF
144.3	1840	Inc. Ab.	1.25	2.50	5.00	10.00
	1841	11.200	1.25	2.50	5.00	10.00
	1842	11.200	1.25	2.50	5.00	10.00
	1843	11.200	1.25	2.50	5.00	10.00

MINT: SOUZAN СМ

C#	Date	Mintage	VG	Fine	VF	XF
144.4	1839	.795	2.50	5.00	10.00	20.00
	1840	4.500	1.75	3.50	7.00	14.00
	1841	6.120	1.75	3.50	7.00	14.00
	1842	7.002	1.75	3.50	7.00	14.00
	1843	3.498	1.75	3.50	7.00	14.00
	1844	5.250	1.75	3.50	7.00	14.00
	1845	5.250	1.75	3.50	7.00	14.00
	1846	5.250	1.75	3.50	7.00	14.00
	1847	2.368	5.00	10.00	20.00	40.00

MINT: EKATERINBURG ЕМ

C#	Date	Mintage	VG	Fine	VF	XF
149.1	1849	—	—	—	Rare	—
	1850	1.843	1.00	2.00	4.00	7.50
	1851	4.790	1.00	2.00	4.00	7.50
	1852	14.006	1.00	2.00	4.00	7.50
	1853	21.328	1.00	2.00	4.00	7.50
	1854	22.396	1.00	2.00	4.00	7.50
	1855	—	2.50	5.00	10.00	20.00

MINT: ST. PETERSBURG СПМ

C#	Date	Mintage	VG	Fine	VF	XF
149.2	1849	50 pcs.	—	—	Rare	—

MINT: WARSAW BM

C#	Date	Mintage	VG	Fine	VF	XF
149.3	1850	—	4.00	7.50	15.00	30.00
	1851	.797	2.50	5.00	10.00	20.00
	1852	.311	2.50	5.00	10.00	20.00
	1853	.391	2.50	5.00	10.00	20.00
	1855	—	2.50	5.00	10.00	20.00

MINT: WARSAW BM

Obv: Crowned tall A. Rev: Large date. Plain border.

Y#	Date	Mintage	Fine	VF	XF	Unc
3.1	1855	3.533	2.00	4.00	12.00	25.00
	1856	3.316	2.00	4.00	12.00	25.00
	1858	1.525	2.00	4.00	12.00	25.00
	1859	3.019	2.00	4.00	12.00	25.00
	1860	3.765	2.00	4.00	12.00	25.00

MINT: EKATERINBURG ДЛ

Obv: Crowned small A

Y#	Date	Mintage	Fine	VF	XF	Unc
3.2	1855	24.593	1.00	2.50	5.00	10.00
	1856	10.641	1.00	2.50	5.00	10.00
	1857	5.659	1.00	2.50	5.00	10.00
	1858	13.731	1.00	2.50	5.00	10.00
	1859	11.059	1.00	2.50	5.00	10.00

MINT: EKATERINBURG ДЛ

Toothed border.

Y#	Date	Mintage	Fine	VF	XF	Unc
3.3	1859	—	1.00	2.00	4.00	8.00
	1860	8.305	1.00	2.00	4.00	8.00
	1861	10.129	1.00	2.00	4.00	8.00
	1862	10.164	1.00	2.00	4.00	8.00
	1863	6.544	1.00	2.00	4.00	8.00
	1864	4.400	1.00	2.00	4.00	8.00
	1865	14.230	1.00	2.00	4.00	8.00
	1866	12.304	1.00	2.00	4.00	8.00
	1867	5.851	6.50	12.50	25.00	50.00

MINT: WARSAW MINT BM

Obv: Crowned tall A

Y#	Date	Mintage	Fine	VF	XF	Unc
3.4	1861	1.800	2.50	5.00	10.00	20.00
	1862	2.099	2.50	5.00	10.00	20.00
	1863	2.854	2.50	5.00	10.00	20.00
	1864	1.045	2.50	5.00	10.00	20.00

MINT: EKATERINBURG EM

Y#	Date	Mintage	Fine	VF	XF	Unc
9.1	1867	Inc. Ab.	4.00	7.50	15.00	30.00
	1868	6.305	.75	2.00	5.00	12.00
	1869	10.230	.75	2.00	5.00	12.00
9.1	1870	9.875	.75	2.00	5.00	12.00
	1871	2.880	1.50	2.00	6.00	12.00
	1872	5.712	.75	1.50	4.00	10.00
	1873	5.212	.75	1.50	4.00	10.00
	1874	5.012	.75	1.50	4.00	10.00
	1875	6.437	.75	1.50	4.00	10.00
	1876	1.755	5.00	10.00	20.00	40.00

MINT: ST. PETERSBURG СПБ

Y#	Date	Mintage	Fine	VF	XF	Unc
9.2	1867	—	2.50	5.00	10.00	20.00
	1868	.750	1.50	3.00	6.00	12.00
	1869	.739	1.50	3.00	6.00	12.00
	1870	1.143	1.50	3.00	6.00	12.00
	1871	Inc. 1870	—	—	Rare	—
	1876	2.930	.75	1.50	3.00	8.00
	1877	7.065	.75	1.50	3.00	8.00
	1878	8.241	.75	1.50	3.00	8.00
	1879	9.045	.75	1.50	3.00	8.00
	1880	7.730	.75	1.50	3.00	8.00
	1881	8.415	.75	1.50	3.00	8.00
	1882	5.685	.75	1.50	3.00	8.00
	1883	7.830	.75	1.50	3.00	8.00
	1884	2.500	.75	1.50	3.00	8.00
	1885	3.400	.75	1.50	3.00	8.00
	1886	3.210	.75	1.50	3.00	8.00
	1887	6.000	.60	1.25	3.00	8.00
	1888	6.000	.60	1.25	3.00	8.00
	1889	9.000	.60	1.25	3.00	8.00
	1890	6.905	.60	1.25	3.00	8.00
	1891	10.875	.50	1.00	2.00	5.00
	1892	5.640	.50	1.00	2.00	5.00
	1893	13.395	.50	1.00	2.00	5.00
	1894	15.490	.50	1.00	2.00	5.00
	1895	18.200	.35	.75	1.50	4.50
	1896	22.960	.35	.75	1.50	4.50
	1897	30.000	.35	.75	1.50	4.50
	1898	50.000	.35	.75	1.50	4.50
	1899	50.000	.35	.75	1.50	4.50
	1900	30.000	.35	.75	1.50	4.50
	1901	30.000	.35	.75	1.50	4.50
	1902	20.000	2.50	5.00	10.00	20.00
	1903	74.400	.35	.75	1.50	4.50
	1904	30.600	.35	.75	1.50	4.50
	1905	23.000	.35	.75	1.50	4.50
	1906	20.000	.35	.75	1.50	4.50
	1907	20.000	.35	.75	1.50	4.50
	1908	40.000	.35	.75	1.50	4.50
	1909	27.500	.35	.75	1.50	4.50
	1910	36.500	.35	.75	1.50	4.50
	1911	38.150	.35	.75	1.50	4.50
	1912	31.850	.35	.75	1.50	4.50
	1913	61.500	.35	.75	1.50	4.50
	1914	32.500	.35	.75	1.50	4.50

MINT: ST. PETERSBURG (no mintmark)

Y#	Date	Mintage	Fine	VF	XF	Unc
9.3	1915	58.000	.35	.75	1.50	4.50
	1916	46.500	.35	.75	1.50	4.50

2 KOPEKS

COPPER

MINT: UNKNOWN (no mintmark)

C#	Date	Mintage	VG	Fine	VF	XF
42	1762 large 2	—	50.00	75.00	150.00	250.00
	1762 small 2	—	50.00	75.00	150.00	250.00

MINT: UNKNOWN - NO MINTMARK

C#	Date	Mintage	VG	Fine	VF	XF
58.1	1763	—	30.00	60.00	100.00	175.00
	1766	—	15.00	30.00	50.00	100.00

MINT: ANNINSK AM

C#	Date	Mintage	VG	Fine	VF	XF
58.2	1789	—	15.00	30.00	50.00	100.00
	1790	—	65.00	125.00	200.00	350.00
	1791	.333	65.00	125.00	200.00	350.00
	1793	.154	100.00	150.00	250.00	400.00
	1794	—	60.00	100.00	150.00	275.00
	1795	.056	100.00	150.00	250.00	350.00
	1796	—	65.00	125.00	200.00	350.00

MINT: EKATERINBURG ДЛ

C#	Date	Mintage	VG	Fine	VF	XF
58.3	1763	1.765	5.00	10.00	20.00	40.00
	1764	3.357	5.00	10.00	17.50	35.00
	1765	1.715	5.00	10.00	17.50	35.00
	1766	1.662	5.00	10.00	17.50	35.00
	1767	1.294	5.00	10.00	17.50	35.00
	1768	.911	5.00	10.00	17.50	35.00
	1769	1.588	5.00	10.00	17.50	35.00
	1770	5.311	5.00	10.00	17.50	35.00
	1771	1.944	5.00	10.00	17.50	35.00
	1772	2.433	5.00	10.00	17.50	35.00
	1773	3.225	5.00	10.00	17.50	35.00
	1774	.645	12.00	25.00	50.00	100.00
	1775	1.476	5.00	10.00	17.50	35.00
	1776	1.332	5.00	10.00	17.50	35.00
	1777	1.596	5.00	10.00	17.50	35.00
	1778	1.291	5.00	10.00	17.50	35.00
	1779	.073	15.00	30.00	50.00	100.00
	1789	2.878	5.00	10.00	17.50	35.00
	1790	4.765	5.00	10.00	17.50	35.00
	1791	.371	5.00	10.00	17.50	35.00
	1793	—	100.00	150.00	250.00	400.00
	1795	1.546	5.00	10.00	17.50	35.00
	1796	.620	5.00	10.00	17.50	35.00

MINT: FEODESIA TM

C#	Date	Mintage	VG	Fine	VF	XF
58.4	1787	—	—	—	—	—
	1788	.060	400.00	700.00	1000.	1300.

MINT: MOSCOW MM

C#	Date	Mintage	VG	Fine	VF	XF
58.5	1763	—	8.00	15.00	25.00	50.00
	1764	—	5.00	10.00	20.00	40.00
	1765	—	5.00	10.00	20.00	40.00
	1766	—	5.00	10.00	20.00	40.00
	1767	—	60.00	100.00	150.00	275.00
	1788	—	5.00	10.00	20.00	40.00
	1789	—	400.00	700.00	1000.	1300.
	1795	—	60.00	100.00	150.00	275.00

MINT: ST. PETERSBURG СПМ

C#	Date	Mintage	VG	Fine	VF	XF
58.6	1763	—	8.00	15.00	25.00	50.00
	1764	—	5.00	10.00	20.00	40.00
	1765	—	5.00	10.00	20.00	40.00
	1766	—	5.00	10.00	20.00	40.00
	1767	—	30.00	60.00	100.00	175.00
	1788	—	5.00	10.00	20.00	40.00

MINT UNKNOWN: NO MINTMARK

C#	Date	Mintage	VG	Fine	VF	XF
95.1	1797	—	15.00	30.00	60.00	120.00

MINT: ANNINSK АМ

C#	Date	Mintage	VG	Fine	VF	XF
95.2	1797	—	7.50	15.00	30.00	60.00
	1798	—	7.50	15.00	30.00	60.00

MINT: EKATERINBURG ЕМ

C#	Date	Mintage	VG	Fine	VF	XF
95.3	1797	4.914	4.00	8.00	16.00	32.00
	1798	56.528	4.00	8.00	16.00	32.00
	1799	55.641	4.00	8.00	16.00	32.00
	1800	28.156	4.00	8.00	16.00	32.00
	1801	27.380	4.00	8.00	16.00	32.00

MINT: KOLYVAN КМ

C#	Date	Mintage	VG	Fine	VF	XF
95.4	1797	—	6.00	12.00	25.00	50.00
	1798	—	6.00	12.00	25.00	50.00
	1799	—	18.00	37.50	75.00	150.00
	1800	—	10.00	20.00	40.00	80.00
	1801	—	10.00	20.00	40.00	80.00

MINT: EKATERINBURG ЕМ

C#	Date	Mintage	VG	Fine	VF	XF
114.1	1802	45.798	9.00	18.00	37.50	75.00
	1803	.298	—	—	Rare	—
	1804	—	—	—	Rare	—

MINT: KOLYVAN КМ

C#	Date	Mintage	VG	Fine	VF	XF
114.2	1804	—	—	—	Rare	—
	1805	—	—	—	Rare	—
	1807	—	—	—	Rare	—

MINT: EKATERINBURG ЕМ

Obv: Type 1 eagle

C#	Date	Mintage	VG	Fine	VF	XF
118.1	1810 НМ	79.364	4.00	7.50	15.00	30.00

MINT: KOLYVAN КМ

Obv: Type 2 eagle

C#	Date	Mintage	VG	Fine	VF	XF
118.2	1810	—	5.00	10.00	20.00	40.00
	1810 ПБ	—	5.00	10.00	20.00	40.00
	1811 ПБ	—	5.00	10.00	20.00	40.00
	1812	—	5.00	10.00	20.00	40.00

MINT: EKATERINBURG ЕМ

Obv: Type 3 eagle

C#	Date	Mintage	VG	Fine	VF	XF
118.3	1810 НМ	129.000	1.00	2.00	4.00	7.50
	1811 НМ	I.A.	1.00	2.00	4.00	7.50
	1812 НМ	132.085	1.00	2.00	4.00	7.50
	1813 НМ	64.980	1.00	2.00	4.00	7.50
	1814 НМ	110.000	1.00	2.00	4.00	7.50
	1815 НМ	44.970	1.00	2.00	4.00	7.50
	1816 НМ	64.150	1.00	2.00	4.00	7.50
	1817 НМ	75.000	1.00	2.00	4.00	7.50
	1818 НМ	60.625	1.00	2.00	4.00	7.50
	1818 ФГ	I.A.	1.00	2.00	4.00	7.50
	1819 НМ	100.468	1.00	2.00	4.00	7.50
	1820 НМ	75.180	1.00	2.00	4.00	7.50
	1821 НМ	55.170	1.00	2.00	4.00	7.50
	1821 ФГ	I.A.	1.00	2.00	4.00	7.50
	1822 ФГ	44.867	1.00	2.00	4.00	7.50
	1823 ФГ	44.935	1.00	2.00	4.00	7.50
	1823 ПГ	I.A.	—	—	Rare	—
	1824 ПГ	36.600	1.00	2.00	4.00	7.50
	1825 ПГ	73.856	1.00	2.00	4.00	7.50
	1825 ИШ	I.A.	1.00	2.00	4.00	7.50
	1825 ИК	I.A.	1.00	2.00	4.00	7.50

MINT: ICHORA ИМ

C#	Date	Mintage	VG	Fine	VF	XF
118.4	1810 МК	—	1.00	2.00	4.00	7.50
	1811 ПС	I.A.	1.00	2.00	4.00	7.50
	1811 МК	—	1.00	2.00	4.00	7.50
	1812 ПС	—	1.00	2.00	4.00	7.50
	1813 ПС	—	1.00	2.00	4.00	7.50
	1814 ПС	—	1.00	2.00	4.00	7.50
	1814	—	4.00	7.50	15.00	30.00

MINT: KOLYVAN КМ

C#	Date	Mintage	VG	Fine	VF	XF
118.5	1810 МК	—	7.50	15.00	30.00	60.00
	1811 ПБ	—	1.00	2.00	4.00	7.50
	1812 АМ	—	1.00	2.00	4.00	7.50
	1813 АМ	—	1.00	2.00	4.00	7.50
	1814 АМ	—	1.00	2.00	4.00	7.50
	1815 АМ	—	1.00	2.00	4.00	7.50
	1816 АМ	—	1.00	2.00	4.00	7.50
	1817 АМ	—	1.00	2.00	4.00	7.50
	1817 АБ	—	1.00	2.00	4.00	7.50
	1818 АА	—	—	—	Rare	—
	1818 АБ	—	1.00	2.00	4.00	7.50
	1819 АД	—	1.00	2.00	4.00	7.50
	1820 АД	—	1.00	2.00	4.00	7.50
	1821 АД	—	1.00	2.00	4.00	7.50
	1821 АМ	—	1.00	2.00	4.00	7.50
	1822 АМ	—	1.00	2.00	4.00	7.50
	1823 АМ	—	1.00	2.00	4.00	7.50
	1824 АМ	—	1.00	2.00	4.00	7.50
	1825 АМ	—	1.00	2.00	4.00	7.50

MINT: ST. PETERSBURG СПБ

C#	Date	Mintage	VG	Fine	VF	XF
118.6	1810 ФГ	—	1.00	2.00	4.00	7.50
	1810 МК	—	1.00	2.00	4.00	7.50
	1810 ПС	—	2.00	4.00	7.50	15.00
118.6	1811 МК	—	1.00	2.00	4.00	7.50
	1811 ПС	—	1.00	2.00	4.00	7.50
	1812 ПС	—	1.00	2.00	4.00	7.50
	1813 ПС	—	1.00	2.00	4.00	7.50
	1814 ПС	—	4.00	7.50	15.00	30.00
	1818	—	—	—	Rare	—

MINT: EKATERINBURG ЕМ

Similar to C#118.3

C#	Date	Mintage	VG	Fine	VF	XF
137.1	1826 ИК	50.450	2.50	5.00	10.00	20.00
	1827 ИК	34.065	2.50	5.00	10.00	20.00
	1828 ИК	14.475	2.50	5.00	10.00	20.00
	1829 ИК	13.789	3.00	6.50	12.50	25.00
	1830 ИК	15.450	3.50	7.50	15.00	30.00

MINT: KOLYVAN КМ

C#	Date	Mintage	VG	Fine	VF	XF
137.2	1826 АМ	9.375	2.50	5.00	10.00	20.00
	1827 АМ	Inc. w/1826	2.50	5.00	10.00	20.00
	1828 АМ	15.000	3.00	6.50	12.50	25.00
	1829 АМ	15.000	3.50	7.50	15.00	30.00
	1830 АМ	15.000	4.50	9.00	17.50	35.00

MINT: ST. PETERSBURG СПБ

C#	Date	Mintage	VG	Fine	VF	XF
137.3	1828	—	—	—	Rare	—

MINT: EKATERINBURG ЕМ

C#	Date	Mintage	VG	Fine	VF	XF
139.1	1830 ФХ	—	—	—	Rare	—
	1831 ФХ	—	—	—	Rare	—
	1833 ФХ	.260	3.00	6.00	12.50	25.00
	1837 НА	16.845	3.00	6.00	12.50	25.00
	1838 НА	6.623	3.00	6.00	12.50	25.00
	1839 НА	8.250	3.00	6.00	12.50	25.00

MINT: ST. PETERSBURG СПБ

C#	Date	Mintage	VG	Fine	VF	XF
139.2	1830	29 pcs.	—	—	Rare	—

MINT: SOUZAN СМ

C#	Date	Mintage	VG	Fine	VF	XF
139.3	1831	1.500	3.00	6.00	12.50	25.00
	1832	1.500	3.00	6.00	12.50	25.00
	1833	.539	3.00	6.00	12.50	25.00
	1834	1.500	3.00	6.00	12.50	25.00
	1835	1.500	3.00	6.00	12.50	25.00
	1836	1.350	3.00	6.00	12.50	25.00
	1837	1.000	3.00	6.00	12.50	25.00
	1838	10.500	3.00	6.00	12.50	25.00
	1839	7.072	3.00	6.00	12.50	25.00

MINT: EKATERINBURG ЕМ

C#	Date	Mintage	VG	Fine	VF	XF
145.1	1840	20.778	1.50	3.00	6.00	12.00
	1841	14.998	1.50	3.00	6.00	12.00
	1842	12.450	1.50	3.00	6.00	12.00
	1843	11.020	1.50	3.00	6.00	12.00
	1844	5.500	1.50	3.00	6.00	12.00

MINT: ST. PETERSBURG СПБ

C#	Date	Mintage	VG	Fine	VF	XF
145.2	1840	—	6.50	12.50	25.00	50.00
	1841	—	—	—	Rare	—

MINT: ST. PETERSBURG СПМ

C#	Date	Mintage	VG	Fine	VF	XF
145.3	1840	4.800	1.50	3.00	6.00	12.00
	1841	4.800	1.50	3.00	6.00	12.00
	1842	4.800	1.50	3.00	6.00	12.00
	1843	4.800	1.50	3.00	6.00	12.00

MINT: SOUZAN СМ

C#	Date	Mintage	VG	Fine	VF	XF
145.4	1839	.340	4.00	7.50	15.00	30.00
	1840	—	—	—	Rare	—
	1840	1.929	2.50	5.00	10.00	20.00
	1841	2.636	2.50	5.00	10.00	20.00
	1842	3.000	3.00	5.00	10.00	20.00
	1843	1.500	3.00	5.00	10.00	20.00

C#	Date	Mintage	VG	Fine	VF	XF
145.4	1845	2.250	2.50	5.00	10.00	20.00
	1846	2.250	2.50	5.00	10.00	20.00
	1847	2.209	2.50	5.00	10.00	20.00

MINT: WARSAW МШ

C#	Date	Mintage	VG	Fine	VF	XF
145.5	1848	.031	—	—	Rare	—

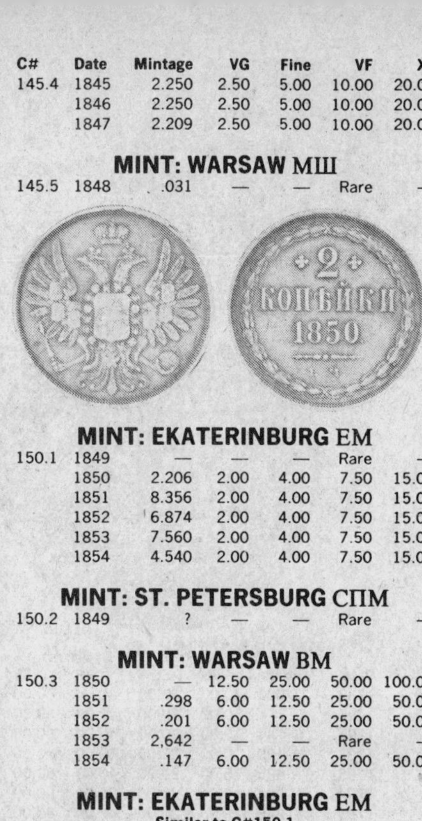

MINT: EKATERINBURG EM

C#	Date	Mintage	VG	Fine	VF	XF
150.1	1849	—	—	—	Rare	—
	1850	2.206	2.00	4.00	7.50	15.00
	1851	8.356	2.00	4.00	7.50	15.00
	1852	6.874	2.00	4.00	7.50	15.00
	1853	7.560	2.00	4.00	7.50	15.00
	1854	4.540	2.00	4.00	7.50	15.00

MINT: ST. PETERSBURG СПМ

C#	Date	Mintage	VG	Fine	VF	XF
150.2	1849	?	—	—	Rare	—

MINT: WARSAW BM

C#	Date	Mintage	VG	Fine	VF	XF
150.3	1850	—	12.50	25.00	50.00	100.00
	1851	.298	6.00	12.50	25.00	50.00
	1852	.201	6.00	12.50	25.00	50.00
	1853	2,642	—	—	Rare	—
	1854	.147	6.00	12.50	25.00	50.00

MINT: EKATERINBURG EM

Similar to C#150.1

Y#	Date	Mintage	Fine	VF	XF	Unc
4.1	1855	8.586	1.50	3.00	6.00	15.00
	1856	9.167	1.50	3.00	6.00	15.00
	1857	3.359	1.50	3.00	6.00	15.00
	1858	10.028	1.50	3.00	6.00	15.00
	1859	14.772	1.50	3.00	6.00	15.00

MINT: WARSAW BM

Y#	Date	Mintage	Fine	VF	XF	Unc
4.2	1855	1.162	4.00	7.50	15.00	40.00
	1856	1.190	4.00	7.50	15.00	40.00
	1858	.879	4.00	7.50	15.00	40.00
	1859	1.565	4.00	7.50	15.00	40.00
	1860	1.604	4.00	7.50	15.00	40.00

MINT: EKATERINBURG EM

Obv: Ribbons added to crown.

Y#	Date	Mintage	Fine	VF	XF	Unc
4a.1	1859	—	1.50	3.00	6.00	15.00
	1860	19.239	1.50	3.00	6.00	15.00
	1861	18.547	1.50	3.00	6.00	15.00
	1862	16.889	1.50	3.00	6.00	15.00
	1863	21.703	1.50	3.00	6.00	15.00
	1864	14.175	1.50	3.00	6.00	15.00
	1865	26.920	1.50	3.00	6.00	15.00
	1866	21.889	1.50	3.00	6.00	15.00
	1867	8.970	2.50	5.00	10.00	25.00

MINT: WARSAW BM

Y#	Date	Mintage	Fine	VF	XF	Unc
4a.2	1860	—	4.00	7.50	15.00	40.00
	1861	.900	4.00	7.50	15.00	40.00
	1862	.966	4.00	7.50	15.00	40.00
	1863	1.733	4.00	7.50	15.00	40.00

MINT: EKATERINBURG EM

Y#	Date	Mintage	Fine	VF	XF	Unc
10.1	1867	.150	5.00	10.00	20.00	40.00
	1868	18.200	1.00	2.00	4.00	10.00
	1869	22.173	1.00	2.00	4.00	10.00
	1870	21.883	1.00	2.00	4.00	10.00
10.1	1871	7.057	1.00	2.00	4.00	10.00
	1872	12.733	1.00	2.00	4.00	10.00
	1873	7.363	1.00	2.00	4.00	10.00
	1874	8.551	1.00	2.00	4.00	10.00
	1875	10.451	1.00	2.00	4.00	10.00
	1876	2.905	1.00	2.00	4.00	10.00

MINT: ST. PETERSBURG СПБ

Y#	Date	Mintage	Fine	VF	XF	Unc
10.2	1867	—	3.50	7.50	15.00	30.00
	1868	.658	1.50	3.00	6.00	15.00
	1869	.642	1.50	3.00	6.00	15.00
	1870	.231	2.00	4.00	8.00	20.00
	1871	—	—	—	Rare	—
	1876	3.240	1.00	2.00	4.00	10.00
	1877	5.010	1.00	2.00	4.00	10.00
	1878	8.092	1.00	2.00	4.00	10.00
	1879	7.380	1.00	2.00	4.00	10.00
	1880	6.525	1.00	2.00	4.00	10.00
	1881	7.299	1.00	2.00	4.00	10.00
	1882	4.477	.75	1.50	3.00	8.00
	1883	6.230	.75	1.50	3.00	8.00
	1884	2.625	.75	1.50	3.00	8.00
	1885	3.070	.75	1.50	3.00	8.00
	1886	3.122	.75	1.50	3.00	8.00
	1887	1.725	.75	1.50	3.00	8.00
	1888	1.822	.75	1.50	3.00	8.00
	1889	2.812	.75	1.50	3.00	8.00
	1890	2.537	.75	1.50	3.00	8.00
	1891	2.787	.75	1.50	3.00	8.00
	1892	.917	2.00	4.00	8.00	20.00
	1893	10.295	.75	1.50	3.00	8.00
	1894	8.600	.75	1.50	3.00	8.00
	1895	9.122	.65	1.25	2.50	6.00
	1896	14.675	.65	1.25	2.50	6.00
	1897	9.500	.65	1.25	2.50	6.00
	1898	17.500	.65	1.25	2.50	6.00
	1899	17.500	.65	1.25	2.50	6.00
	1900	20.500	.65	1.25	2.50	6.00
	1901	20.000	.65	1.25	2.50	6.00
	1902	10.000	.65	1.25	2.50	6.00
	1903	29.200	.65	1.25	2.50	6.00
	1904	13.300	.65	1.25	2.50	6.00
	1905	15.000	.65	1.25	2.50	6.00
	1906	6.250	.65	1.25	2.50	6.00
	1907	7.500	.65	1.25	2.50	6.00
	1908	19.000	.50	1.00	2.00	5.00
	1909	16.250	.50	1.00	2.00	5.00
	1910	12.000	.50	1.00	2.00	5.00
	1911	17.200	.50	1.00	2.00	5.00
	1912	17.000	.50	1.00	2.00	5.00
	1913	26.000	.50	1.00	2.00	5.00
	1914	20.000	.50	1.00	2.00	5.00

MINT: ST. PETERSBURG (no mintmark)

Y#	Date	Mintage	Fine	VF	XF	Unc
10.3	1915	33.750	.50	1.00	2.00	5.00
	1916	31.500	.50	1.00	2.00	5.00

3 KOPEKS

COPPER

MINT: EKATERINBURG

C#	Date	Mintage	VG	Fine	VF	XF
146.1	1840	5.230	3.00	6.50	12.50	25.00
	1841	13.420	3.00	6.50	12.50	25.00
	1842	13.700	3.00	6.50	12.50	25.00
	1843	14.578	3.00	6.50	12.50	25.00
	1844	4.840	3.00	6.50	12.50	25.00

MINT: ST. PETERSBURG

C#	Date	Mintage	VG	Fine	VF	XF
146.2	1840	—	—	—	Rare	—

MINT: ST. PETERSBURG

C#	Date	Mintage	VG	Fine	VF	XF
146.3	1840	2.133	3.00	6.50	12.50	25.00
	1841	2.133	3.00	6.50	12.50	25.00
	1842	2.133	3.00	6.50	12.50	25.00
	1843	2.133	3.00	6.50	12.50	25.00

MINT: SOUZAN

C#	Date	Mintage	VG	Fine	VF	XF
146.4	1839	.141	6.50	12.50	25.00	50.00
	1840	.827	4.00	7.50	15.00	30.00
	1841	1.171	4.00	7.50	15.00	30.00
	1842	1.360	4.00	7.50	15.00	30.00
	1843	.668	4.00	7.50	15.00	30.00
	1844	1.000	4.00	7.50	15.00	30.00
	1845	1.000	4.00	7.50	15.00	30.00
	1846	1.000	4.00	7.50	15.00	30.00
	1847	1.000	4.00	7.50	15.00	30.00

MINT: WARSAW

C#	Date	Mintage	VG	Fine	VF	XF
	1848	.011	—	—	Rare	—

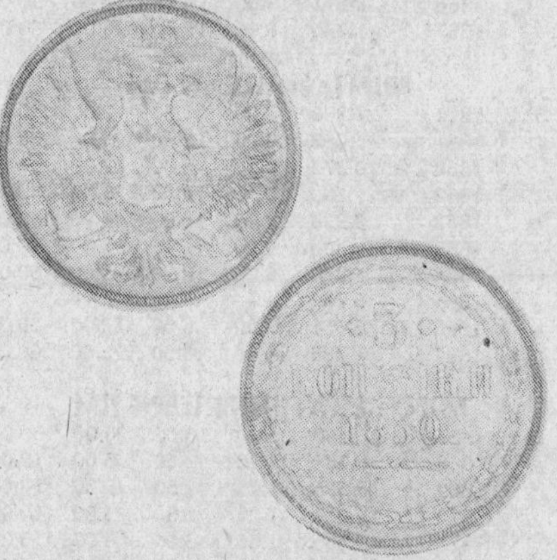

MINT: EKATERINBURG

Obv: First variety - six coats of arms.

C#	Date	Mintage	VG	Fine	VF	XF
151.1	1849	—	—	—	Rare	—
	1850	.184	2.00	4.00	7.50	15.00
	1851	3.448	2.00	4.00	7.50	15.00
	1852	5.444	2.00	4.00	7.50	15.00
	1853	3.720	2.00	4.00	7.50	15.00
	1854	1.351	2.00	4.00	7.50	15.00

MINT: ST. PETERSBURG

C#	Date	Mintage	VG	Fine	VF	XF
151.2	1849	—	—	—	Rare	—

MINT: WARSAW

C#	Date	Mintage	VG	Fine	VF	XF
151.3	1850	—	4.00	7.50	15.00	30.00
	1851	.100	4.00	7.50	15.00	30.00
	1852	.010	4.00	7.50	15.00	30.00
	1853	.089	4.00	7.50	15.00	30.00
	1854	.160	4.00	7.50	15.00	30.00

MINT: EKATERINBURG

Similar to C#151.1

Y#	Date	Mintage	Fine	VF	XF	Unc
5.1	1855	2.835	2.50	5.00	10.00	25.00
	1856	6.700	2.50	5.00	10.00	25.00
5.2	1857	4.725	2.50	5.00	10.00	25.00
	1858	10.662	2.50	5.00	10.00	25.00
	1859	15.821	2.50	5.00	10.00	25.00
	1860	14.009	2.50	5.00	10.00	25.00

MINT: WARSAW

Y#	Date	Mintage	Fine	VF	XF	Unc
5.2	1856	.416	5.00	10.00	20.00	50.00
	1857	.021	12.50	25.00	50.00	125.00
	1858	10.662	2.50	5.00	10.00	25.00
	1858	.711	5.00	10.00	20.00	50.00
	1859	15.821	2.50	5.00	10.00	25.00
	1859	.400	7.50	15.00	30.00	75.00
	1860	.400	7.50	15.00	30.00	75.00
	1860	14.009	2.50	5.00	10.00	25.00

MINT: EKATERINBURG ЕМ

Obv: Second variety - eight coats of arms.

Y#	Date	Mintage	Fine	VF	XF	Unc
5a.1	1859	—	2.50	5.00	10.00	25.00
	1860	14.010	3.00	6.00	12.00	30.00
	1861	7.738	3.00	6.00	12.00	30.00
	1862	10.377	3.00	6.00	12.00	30.00
	1863	3.938	3.00	6.00	12.00	30.00
	1864	.370	6.00	12.50	25.00	60.00
	1865	5.740	—	—	Rare	—
	1866	6.611	3.00	6.00	12.00	30.00
	1867	1.785	6.00	12.50	25.00	60.00

MINT: WARSAW ВМ

Y#	Date	Mintage	Fine	VF	XF	Unc
5a.2	1861	7.738	3.00	6.00	12.00	30.00
	1861	.283	6.00	12.50	25.00	60.00
	1862	10.377	3.00	6.00	12.00	30.00
	1862	.200	6.00	12.50	25.00	60.00
	1863	3.938	3.00	6.00	12.00	30.00
	1863	.400	9.00	17.50	35.00	80.00
	1864	.370	6.00	12.50	25.00	60.00
	1865	5.740	—	—	Rare	—
	1866	6.611	3.00	6.00	12.00	30.00
	1867	1.785	6.00	12.50	25.00	60.00

MINT: EKATERINBURG ЕМ

Y#	Date	Mintage	Fine	VF	XF	Unc
11.1	1867	.160	5.00	10.00	20.00	50.00
	1868	6.058	1.25	2.50	5.00	12.00
	1869	5.525	1.25	2.50	5.00	12.00
	1870	5.017	1.25	2.50	5.00	12.00
	1871	1.585	1.50	3.00	6.00	15.00
	1872	3.017	1.50	3.00	6.00	15.00
	1873	4.704	1.50	3.00	6.00	15.00
	1874	4.419	1.50	3.00	6.00	15.00
	1875	3.595	1.50	3.00	6.00	15.00
	1876	.890	2.00	4.00	8.00	20.00

MINT: ST. PETERSBURG СПБ

Y#	Date	Mintage	Fine	VF	XF	Unc
11.2	1867	—	4.00	7.50	15.00	40.00
	1868	.909	2.50	5.00	10.00	25.00
	1869	5.525	1.25	2.50	5.00	12.00
	1869	.723	2.50	5.00	10.00	25.00
	1870	5.017	1.25	2.50	5.00	12.00
	1870	.079	7.50	15.00	30.00	80.00
	1871	1.585	1.50	3.00	6.00	15.00
	1871	Inc. Ab.	—	—	Rare	—
	1872	3.017	1.50	3.00	6.00	15.00
	1873	4.704	1.50	3.00	6.00	15.00
	1874	4.419	1.50	3.00	6.00	15.00
	1875	3.595	1.50	3.00	6.00	15.00
	1876	.890	2.00	4.00	8.00	20.00
	1876	4.863	1.25	2.50	5.00	12.00
	1877	5.901	1.25	2.50	5.00	12.00
	1878	6.355	1.25	2.50	5.00	12.00
	1879	7.355	1.25	2.50	5.00	12.00
	1880	6.773	1.25	2.50	5.00	12.00
	1881	6.141	1.25	2.50	5.00	12.00
	1882	4.280	1.50	3.00	6.00	15.00
	1883	1.060	1.50	3.00	6.00	15.00
11.2	1884	2.975	1.50	3.00	6.00	15.00
	1891	1.983	4.00	8.00	16.00	40.00
	1892	.648	4.00	8.00	16.00	40.00
	1893	6.365	1.50	3.00	6.00	15.00
	1894	4.803	1.50	3.00	6.00	15.00
	1895	5.416	.75	1.50	3.00	7.50
	1896	7.923	.75	1.50	3.00	7.50
	1897	6.666	.75	1.50	3.00	7.50
	1898	11.666	.75	1.50	3.00	7.50
	1899	11.666	.75	1.50	3.00	7.50
	1900	16.666	.75	1.50	3.00	7.50
	1901	10.000	.75	1.50	3.00	7.50
	1902	3.333	.75	1.50	3.00	7.50
	1903	11.400	.75	1.50	3.00	7.50
	1904	6.933	1.00	1.75	3.50	8.50
	1905	3.333	1.00	1.75	3.50	8.50
	1906	5.666	1.00	1.75	3.50	8.50
	1907	2.500	1.00	1.75	3.50	8.50
	1908	12.666	.75	1.50	3.00	7.50
	1909	6.733	.75	1.50	3.00	7.50
	1910	6.666	.75	1.50	3.00	7.50
	1911	9.466	.75	1.50	3.00	7.50
	1912	8.533	.75	1.50	3.00	7.50
	1913	15.333	.75	1.50	3.00	7.50
	1914	8.166	.75	1.50	3.00	7.50

MINT: ST. PETERSBURG (NO MINTMARK)

Y#	Date	Mintage	Fine	VF	XF	Unc
11.3	1915	19.833	.75	1.50	3.00	7.50
	1916	25.666	1.00	1.75	3.50	8.50

4 KOPEKS

COPPER

MINT: EKATERINBURG (NO MINTMARK)

Lettered edge.

C#	Date	Mintage	VG	Fine	VF	XF
43.1	1762	—	30.00	50.00	100.00	200.00

MINT: MOSCOW - NO MINTMARK

Grilled edge.

C#	Date	Mintage	VG	Fine	VF	XF
43.2	1762	—	25.00	45.00	90.00	190.00

MINT: SESTRORETSK (NO MINTMARK)

Reeded edge

C#	Date	Mintage	VG	Fine	VF	XF
43.3	1762	—	25.00	45.00	90.00	190.00

5 KOPEKS

COPPER

MINT: UNKNOWN - NO MINTMARK

C#	Date	Mintage	VG	Fine	VF	XF
59.1	1763	—	—	—	Rare	—
	1764	—	Reported, not confirmed			
	1765	—	100.00	200.00	300.00	500.00
	1791	—	100.00	200.00	400.00	700.00
	1793	—	—	—	Rare	—
	1796	—	200.00	300.00	500.00	800.00

MINT: ANNINSK АМ

C#	Date	Mintage	VG	Fine	VF	XF
59.2	1789	8.000	10.00	20.00	40.00	80.00
	1790	—	10.00	20.00	40.00	80.00
	1791	—	10.00	20.00	40.00	80.00
	1792	8.190	10.00	20.00	40.00	80.00
	1793	7.426	10.00	20.00	40.00	80.00
	1794	7.364	10.00	20.00	40.00	80.00
	1795	9.948	10.00	20.00	40.00	80.00
	1796	6.728	10.00	20.00	40.00	80.00

MINT: EKATERINBURG ЕМ

C#	Date	Mintage	VG	Fine	VF	XF
59.3	1763	40.398	6.00	10.00	20.00	40.00
	1764	35.824	6.00	10.00	20.00	40.00
	1765	41.109	6.00	10.00	20.00	40.00
	1766	26.562	6.00	10.00	20.00	40.00
	1767	37.020	6.00	10.00	20.00	40.00
	1768	28.542	6.00	10.00	20.00	40.00
	1769	39.441	6.00	10.00	20.00	40.00
	1770	48.480	6.00	10.00	20.00	40.00
	1771	57.053	6.00	10.00	20.00	40.00
	1772	46.266	6.00	10.00	20.00	40.00
	1773	38.829	6.00	10.00	20.00	40.00
	1774	14.535	6.00	10.00	20.00	40.00
	1775	30.487	6.00	10.00	20.00	40.00
	1776	21.454	6.00	10.00	20.00	40.00
	1777	37.429	6.00	10.00	20.00	40.00
	1778	47.142	6.00	10.00	20.00	40.00
	1779	39.732	6.00	10.00	20.00	40.00
	1780	51.007	6.00	10.00	20.00	40.00
	1781	43.401	6.00	10.00	20.00	40.00
	1782	36.175	6.00	10.00	20.00	40.00
	1783	30.156	6.00	10.00	20.00	40.00
	1784	36.059	6.00	10.00	20.00	40.00
	1785	43.070	6.00	10.00	20.00	40.00
	1786	30.377	6.00	10.00	20.00	40.00
	1787	19.088	6.00	10.00	20.00	40.00
	1788	49.141	6.00	10.00	20.00	40.00
	1789	25.841	6.00	10.00	20.00	40.00
	1790	39.995	6.00	10.00	20.00	40.00
	1791	23.739	6.00	10.00	20.00	40.00
	1792	26.177	6.00	10.00	20.00	40.00
	1793	22.736	6.00	10.00	20.00	40.00
	1794	20.950	6.00	10.00	20.00	40.00
	1795	15.531	6.00	10.00	20.00	40.00
	1796	1.949	6.00	10.00	20.00	40.00

MINT: FEODESIA СМ

C#	Date	Mintage	VG	Fine	VF	XF
59.4	1787	.460	200.00	300.00	500.00	800.00
	1788	.539	100.00	200.00	300.00	500.00

MINT: KOLYVAN КМ

C#	Date	Mintage	VG	Fine	VF	XF
59.5	1781	—	10.00	20.00	40.00	80.00
	1782	6.014	10.00	20.00	40.00	80.00
	1783	3.046	10.00	20.00	40.00	80.00
	1784	4.619	10.00	20.00	40.00	80.00
	1785	5.577	10.00	20.00	40.00	80.00
	1786	3.820	10.00	20.00	40.00	80.00
	1787	2.911	10.00	20.00	40.00	80.00
	1788	3.354	10.00	20.00	40.00	80.00
	1789	2.310	10.00	20.00	40.00	80.00
	1790	4.000	10.00	20.00	40.00	80.00
	1791	4.000	10.00	20.00	40.00	80.00
	1792	4.000	10.00	20.00	40.00	80.00
	1793	4.000	10.00	20.00	40.00	80.00
	1794	4.000	10.00	20.00	40.00	80.00
	1795	4.000	10.00	20.00	40.00	80.00
	1796	3.020	10.00	20.00	40.00	80.00

MINT: MOSCOW ММД

C#	Date	Mintage	VG	Fine	VF	XF
59.6	1763	17.729	10.00	20.00	40.00	80.00
	1764	9.480	10.00	20.00	40.00	80.00
	1765	5.224	10.00	20.00	40.00	80.00
	1766	7.538	10.00	20.00	40.00	80.00
	1767	—	20.00	40.00	80.00	150.00
	1768	—	10.00	20.00	40.00	80.00
	1788	—	10.00	20.00	40.00	80.00
	1789	—	300.00	500.00	750.00	1000.
	1795	—	300.00	500.00	750.00	1000.

MINT: ST. PETERSBURG СПМ

C#	Date	Mintage	VG	Fine	VF	XF
59.7	1763	13.428	10.00	20.00	40.00	80.00
	1764	3.073	20.00	40.00	80.00	150.00
	1765	2.374	10.00	20.00	40.00	80.00
	1766	3.719	10.00	20.00	40.00	80.00
	1767	—	20.00	40.00	80.00	150.00
	1788	—	10.00	20.00	40.00	80.00

MINT: SESTRORETSK СМ

C#	Date	Mintage	VG	Fine	VF	XF
59.8	1763	2.491	20.00	40.00	80.00	150.00
	1764	—	20.00	40.00	80.00	150.00
	1765	.663	20.00	40.00	80.00	150.00
	1766	.200	20.00	40.00	80.00	150.00
	1767	—	20.00	40.00	80.00	150.00

SILVER

MINT: ST. PETERSBURG СМ

C#	Date	Mintage	VG	Fine	VF	XF
96.1	1797 ФЦ	.014	20.00	40.00	75.00	150.00
	1798 МБ	.114	12.00	22.50	50.00	100.00
	1800 ОМ	—	—	—	Rare	—
	1801 АИ	.010	15.00	32.50	65.00	110.00
	1801 ФЧ	Inc. Ab.	—	—	Rare	—

MINT: ST. PETERSBURG СП

C#	Date	Mintage	VG	Fine	VF	XF
96.2	1798 ОМ	Inc. Ab.	15.00	32.50	65.00	110.00

COPPER

MINT: EKATERINBURG ЕМ

C#	Date	Mintage	VG	Fine	VF	XF
115.1	1802	12.592	9.00	17.50	30.00	50.00
	1803	31.819	9.00	17.50	30.00	50.00
	1804	26.267	9.00	17.50	30.00	50.00
	1805	16.518	10.00	20.00	40.00	80.00
	1806	38.415	10.00	20.00	40.00	80.00
	1807	10.666	10.00	20.00	40.00	80.00
	1808	10.000	10.00	20.00	40.00	80.00
	1809	10.140	10.00	20.00	40.00	80.00
	1810	15.801	10.00	20.00	40.00	80.00

MINT: KOLPINA КМ

C#	Date	Mintage	VG	Fine	VF	XF
115.2	1810	—	20.00	40.00	80.00	160.00

MINT: KOLYVAN КМ

C#	Date	Mintage	VG	Fine	VF	XF
115.3	1802	4.000	15.00	30.00	60.00	120.00
	1803	3.600	15.00	30.00	60.00	120.00
	1804	4.000	15.00	30.00	60.00	120.00
	1805	5.000	15.00	30.00	60.00	120.00
115.3	1806	5.000	15.00	30.00	60.00	120.00
	1807	5.000	15.00	30.00	60.00	120.00
	1808	5.000	15.00	30.00	60.00	120.00
	1809	5.000	15.00	30.00	60.00	120.00

1.0366 gm., .868 SILVER, .0289 oz ASW

MINT: ST. PETERSBURG СПБ

C#	Date	Mintage	VG	Fine	VF	XF
126	1810 ФГ	—	—	—	Rare	—
	1811 ФГ	.080	10.00	20.00	40.00	80.00
	1811	Inc. Ab.	—	—	Rare	—
	1812 МФ	—	—	—	Rare	—
	1813 ПС	.620	2.50	5.00	10.00	20.00
	1814 ПС	1.300	2.50	5.00	10.00	20.00
	1814 МФ	Inc. Ab.	2.50	5.00	10.00	20.00
	1815 МФ	3.000	2.50	5.00	10.00	20.00
	1815	Inc. Ab.	—	—	Rare	—
	1816 МФ	1.040	2.50	5.00	10.00	20.00
	1816 ПС	Inc. Ab.	2.50	5.00	10.00	20.00
	1817 ПС	.120	7.50	15.00	30.00	60.00
	1818 ПС	.340	2.50	5.00	10.00	20.00
	1819 ПС	.920	2.50	5.00	10.00	20.00
	1820 ПС	.460	2.50	5.00	10.00	20.00
	1820 ПД	Inc. Ab.	2.50	5.00	10.00	20.00
	1821 ПД	2.000	2.50	5.00	10.00	20.00
	1822 ПД	1.060	2.50	5.00	10.00	20.00
	1823 ПД	2.300	2.50	5.00	10.00	20.00
	1824 ПД	1.740	2.50	5.00	10.00	20.00
	1825 ПД	1.160	2.50	5.00	10.00	20.00
	1825 НГ	Inc. Ab.	—	—	Rare	—

MINT: ST. PETERSBURG СПБ

C#	Date	Mintage	VG	Fine	VF	XF
152.3	1826 НГ	1.340	4.00	7.50	15.00	30.00

MINT: ST. PETERSBURG СПБ

C#	Date	Mintage	VG	Fine	VF	XF
156	1826 НГ	Inc. Ab.	4.00	7.50	15.00	30.00
	1827 НГ	1.769	4.00	7.50	15.00	30.00
	1828 НГ	.060	6.50	12.50	25.00	50.00
	1829 НГ	.080	6.50	12.50	25.00	50.00
	1830 НГ	1.500	4.00	7.50	15.00	30.00
	1831 НГ	.520	4.00	7.50	15.00	30.00

COPPER

MINT: EKATERINBURG ЕМ

C#	Date	Mintage	VG	Fine	VF	XF
140.1	1830 ФХ	—	—	—	Rare	—
	1831 ФХ	41.140	3.50	6.50	12.50	25.00
	1831	—	5.00	10.00	20.00	40.00
	1832 ФХ	30.080	3.50	6.50	12.50	25.00
	1833 ФХ	14.332	3.50	6.50	12.50	25.00
	1837 ФХ	41.795	3.50	6.50	12.50	25.00
	1835 ФХ	41.795	3.50	6.50	12.50	25.00
	1836 ФХ	31.331	3.50	6.50	12.50	25.00
	1837/6 НА	—	—	—	—	—
	1837 ФХ	19.745	5.00	10.00	20.00	40.00
	1837 КТ	Inc. Ab.	3.50	6.50	12.50	25.00
	1837 НА	Inc. Ab.	3.50	6.50	12.50	25.00
	1838 НА	24.430	3.50	6.50	12.50	25.00
	1839 НА	1.400	5.00	10.00	20.00	40.00

MINT: ST. PETERSBURG СПБ

C#	Date	Mintage	VG	Fine	VF	XF
140.2	1830	25 pcs.	—	—	Rare	—

MINT: SOUZAN СМ

C#	Date	Mintage	VG	Fine	VF	XF
140.3	1831	5.900	4.00	7.50	15.00	30.00
	1832	5.900	4.00	7.50	15.00	30.00
	1833	6.295	4.00	7.50	15.00	30.00
	1834	5.900	4.00	7.50	15.00	30.00
	1835	5.000	4.00	7.50	15.00	30.00
	1836	5.240	4.00	7.50	15.00	30.00
	1837	5.200	4.00	7.50	15.00	30.00
	1838	1.420	4.00	7.50	15.00	30.00
	1839	1.400	10.00	20.00	37.50	75.00

1.0366 gm., .868 SILVER, .0289 oz ASW

MINT: ST. PETERSBURG СПБ

C#	Date	Mintage	VG	Fine	VF	XF
163	1832 НГ	.224	1.25	2.50	5.00	10.00
	1833 НГ	1.030	1.25	2.50	5.00	10.00
	1834 НГ	.780	1.25	2.50	5.00	10.00
	1835 НГ	1.010	1.25	2.50	5.00	10.00
	1836 НГ	.900	1.25	2.50	5.00	10.00
	1837 НГ	1.140	1.25	2.50	5.00	10.00
	1838 НГ	2.400	1.25	2.50	5.00	10.00
	1839 НГ	1,002	—	—	Rare	—
	1840 НГ	.420	1.25	2.50	5.00	10.00
	1841 НГ	.100	1.50	3.00	6.00	12.00
	1842 АЧ	.100	1.50	3.00	6.00	12.00
	1843 АЧ	.400	1.25	2.50	5.00	10.00
	1844 КБ	.401	1.25	2.50	5.00	10.00
	1845 КБ	1.740	1.25	2.50	5.00	10.00
	1846 ПА	.280	1.25	2.50	5.00	10.00
	1847 ПА	1.010	1.25	2.50	5.00	10.00
	1848 НI	1.000	1.25	2.50	5.00	10.00
	1849 ПА	1.020	1.25	2.50	5.00	10.00
	1850 ПА	1.300	1.25	2.50	5.00	10.00
	1851 ПА	1.000	1.25	2.50	5.00	10.00
	1852 ПА	.900	1.25	2.50	5.00	10.00
	1852 НI	Inc. Ab.	6.50	12.50	25.00	50.00
	1853 НI	.900	1.25	2.50	5.00	10.00
	1854 НI	.500	1.25	2.50	5.00	10.00

COPPER

MINT: EKATERINBURG ЕМ

Obv: Six coats of arms.

C#	Date	Mintage	Fine	VF	XF	Unc
152.1	1849	—	—	—	Rare	—
	1850	.373	4.00	7.50	15.00	40.00
	1851	2.240	4.00	7.50	15.00	40.00
	1852	3.960	4.00	7.50	15.00	40.00
	1853	1.478	—	—	Rare	—
	1854	.355	4.00	7.50	15.00	40.00

MINT: ST. PETERSBURG СПМ

C#	Date	Mintage	Fine	VF	XF	Unc
152.2	1849	—	—	—	Rare	—

MINT: WARSAW ВМ

C#	Date	Mintage	Fine	VF	XF	Unc
152.4	1850	—	15.00	25.00	50.00	125.00
	1851	.024	15.00	25.00	50.00	125.00
	1852	.016	15.00	25.00	50.00	125.00
	1853	.040	15.00	25.00	50.00	125.00

MINT: EKATERINBURG ЕМ

Y#	Date	Mintage	Fine	VF	XF	Unc
6.1	1855	.740	3.00	6.00	12.00	30.00
	1856	5.145	2.00	4.00	8.00	20.00
	1857	8.675	2.00	4.00	8.00	20.00
	1858	19.560	2.00	4.00	7.50	18.00
	1859	19.441	2.00	4.00	7.50	18.00

MINT: WARSAW ВМ

Y#	Date	Mintage	Fine	VF	XF	Unc
6.2	1856	.040	10.00	20.00	40.00	100.00

1.0366 gm., .750 SILVER, .0250 oz ASW

MINT: EKATERINBURG ЕМ

Obv: Eight coats of arms.

Y#	Date	Mintage	Fine	VF	XF	Unc
6a	1858	—	—	—	Rare	—
	1859	Inc. Ab.	2.50	5.00	10.00	25.00
	1860	25.260	2.50	5.00	10.00	25.00
	1861	28.021	2.50	5.00	10.00	25.00
	1862	22.055	2.50	5.00	10.00	25.00
	1863	22.510	2.50	5.00	10.00	25.00
	1864	26.042	2.50	5.00	10.00	25.00
	1865	38.930	2.50	5.00	10.00	25.00
	1866	24.767	2.50	5.00	10.00	25.00
	1867	11.697	6.50	12.50	25.00	60.00

1.0366 gm., .868 SILVER, .0289 oz ASW

MINT: ST. PETERSBURG СПБ

Y#	Date	Mintage	Fine	VF	XF	Unc
13	1855 НІ	.640	3.00	6.00	12.00	25.00
	1856 ФБ	.680	3.00	6.00	12.00	25.00
	1857 ФБ	.080	4.00	7.50	15.00	35.00
	1858 ФБ	.040	5.00	10.00	20.00	50.00

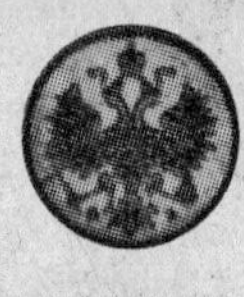

MINT: ST. PETERSBURG СПБ

Obv: Ribbons added to crown.

Y#	Date	Mintage	Fine	VF	XF	Unc
19.1	1859	.120	—	—	Rare	—
	1859 ФБ	I.A.	4.00	8.00	16.00	40.00
	1860 ФБ	.020	6.50	12.50	25.00	60.00

1.0366 gm., .750 SILVER, .0250 oz ASW

MINT: ST. PETERSBURG СПБ

Obv: Redesigned eagle, engrailed edge.

Y#	Date	Mintage	Fine	VF	XF	Unc
19.2	1860 ФБ	.180	2.00	4.00	8.00	20.00
	1861 ФБ	.320	2.00	4.00	8.00	20.00
	1861 МИ	I.A.	7.50	15.00	30.00	75.00
	1861	—	—	—	Rare	—
	1862 МИ	.400	2.00	4.00	7.50	17.50
	1863 АБ	.200	2.00	4.00	7.50	17.50
	1864 АБ	.240	2.00	4.00	7.50	17.50
	1865 НФ	.190	2.00	4.00	7.50	17.50
	1866 НФ	.200	2.00	4.00	7.50	17.50
19.2	1866 НІ	I.A.	7.50	15.00	30.00	75.00

.8998 gm., .500 SILVER, .0144 oz ASW

MINT: ST. PETERSBURG СПБ

Reeded edge

Y#	Date	Mintage	Fine	VF	XF	Unc
19a.1	1867 НІ	.180	1.75	3.50	7.50	17.50
	1868 НІ	.240	1.75	3.50	7.50	17.50
	1869 НІ	.170	1.75	3.50	7.50	17.50
	1870 НІ	.220	1.75	3.50	7.50	17.50
	1871 НІ	.200	1.75	3.50	7.50	17.50
	1872 НІ	.180	1.75	3.50	7.50	17.50
	1873 НІ	.160	1.75	3.50	7.50	17.50
	1874 НІ	.200	1.75	3.50	7.50	17.50
	1875 НІ	.200	1.75	3.50	7.50	17.50
	1876 НІ	.240	1.75	3.50	7.50	17.50
	1877 НІ	.200	1.75	3.50	7.50	17.50
	1877 НФ	I.A.	5.00	10.00	20.00	50.00
	1878 НФ	.220	1.75	3.50	7.50	17.50
	1878 НІ	I.A.	7.50	15.00	30.00	75.00
	1879 НФ	.140	1.75	3.50	7.50	17.50
	1880 НФ	.240	1.75	3.50	7.50	17.50
	1881 НФ	.200	1.75	3.50	7.50	17.50
	1882 НФ	1.760	1.00	2.00	4.00	10.00
	1883 АС	1.000	1.50	3.00	6.00	15.00
	1883 АГ	I.A.	1.50	3.00	6.00	15.00
	1884 АГ	3.460	1.00	2.00	4.00	10.00
	1885 АГ	1.700	1.00	2.00	4.00	10.00
	1886 АГ	2.000	1.00	2.00	4.00	10.00
	1887 АГ	3.000	1.00	2.00	4.00	10.00
	1888 АГ	4.000	1.00	2.00	4.00	10.00
	1889 АГ	3.500	1.00	2.00	4.00	10.00
	1890 АГ	8.000	1.00	2.00	4.00	10.00
	1891 АГ	2.000	1.00	2.00	4.00	10.00
	1892 АГ	8.000	1.00	2.00	4.00	10.00
	1893 АГ	2.000	1.00	2.00	4.00	10.00
	1897 АГ	2.000	1.25	2.50	5.00	12.50
	1898 АГ	3.980	1.25	2.50	5.00	12.50
	1899 АГ	4.605	1.25	2.50	5.00	12.50
	1899 ЭБ	I.A.	1.50	3.00	6.00	15.00
	1900 ФЗ	5.205	1.25	2.50	5.00	12.50
	1901 ФЗ	5.790	1.25	2.50	5.00	12.50
	1901 АР	I.A.	1.50	3.00	6.00	15.00
	1902 АР	6.000	1.25	2.50	5.00	12.50
	1903 АР	9.000	1.25	2.50	5.00	12.50
	1904 АР	10 pcs.	—	—	Rare	—
	1905 АР	10.000	1.25	2.50	5.00	12.50
	1906 ЭБ	4.000	1.25	2.50	5.00	12.50
	1908 ЭБ	.400	1.50	3.00	6.00	15.00
	1909 ЭБ	3.100	1.25	2.50	5.00	12.50
	1910 ЭБ	2.500	1.25	2.50	5.00	12.50
	1911 ЭБ	2.700	1.25	2.50	5.00	12.50
	1912 ЭБ	3.000	1.25	2.50	5.00	12.50
	1913 ЭБ	1.300	1.25	2.50	5.00	12.50
	1913 ВС	I.A.	1.25	2.50	5.00	12.50
	1914 ВС	I.A.	1.25	2.50	5.00	12.50

MINT: ST. PETERSBURG (NO MINTMARK)

Y#	Date	Mintage	Fine	VF	XF	Unc
19a.2	1915 ВС	3.000	1.25	2.50	5.00	12.50

COPPER

MINT: EKATERINBURG ЕМ

Y#	Date	Mintage	Fine	VF	XF	Unc
12.1	1867	1.459	4.00	7.50	15.00	40.00
	1868	23.018	2.00	4.00	8.00	20.00
	1869	20.277	2.50	5.00	10.00	25.00
	1870	21.158	2.50	5.00	10.00	25.00
	1871	6.304	3.00	6.00	12.00	30.00
	1872	11.890	2.50	5.00	10.00	25.00
	1873	13.052	2.50	5.00	10.00	25.00
	1874	12.878	2.50	5.00	10.00	25.00
	1875	19.623	2.50	5.00	10.00	25.00
	1876	5.329	2.50	5.00	10.00	25.00

MINT: OSAKA, JAPAN (NO MINTMARK)

Y#	Date	Mintage	Fine	VF	XF	Unc
12.2	1916	8.000	—	—	Rare	—

MINT: ST. PETERSBURG СПБ

Y#	Date	Mintage	Fine	VF	XF	Unc
12.3	1867	—	4.00	7.50	15.00	40.00
	1868	.821	3.00	6.00	12.00	30.00
	1869	.942	2.00	4.00	8.00	30.00
	1870	.028	5.00	10.00	20.00	50.00
	1871	—	—	—	Rare	—
	1876	4.655	2.50	5.00	10.00	25.00
	1877	7.184	2.50	5.00	10.00	25.00
	1878	12.542	2.50	5.00	10.00	25.00
	1879	14.652	2.50	5.00	10.00	25.00
	1880	6.773	2.50	5.00	10.00	25.00
	1881	13.824	2.50	5.00	10.00	25.00
	1911	3.800	5.00	10.00	20.00	50.00
	1912	2.700	7.50	15.00	30.00	75.00

MINT: ST. PETERSBURG (NO MINTMARK)

Y#	Date	Mintage	Fine	VF	XF	Unc
12.4	1917	—		—	Rare	—

10 KOPEKS

COPPER

MINT: UNKNOWN - NO MINTMARK

C#	Date	Mintage	VG	Fine	VF	XF
44	1762	—	40.00	75.00	150.00	300.00

.750 SILVER

MINT: MOSCOW - NO MINTMARK

C#	Date	Mintage	VG	Fine	VF	XF
61.1	1764	.340	10.00	20.00	35.00	75.00
	1765	.050	7.00	15.00	30.00	60.00

MINT: ST. PETERSBURG СПБ

C#	Date	Mintage	VG	Fine	VF	XF
61.2	1764	—	20.00	40.00	70.00	125.00
	1765	.070	10.00	20.00	35.00	75.00

MINT: MOSCOW - NO MINTMARK

C#	Date	Mintage	VG	Fine	VF	XF
61a.1	1766	.041	20.00	40.00	70.00	125.00

MINT: MOSCOW ММД

C#	Date	Mintage	VG	Fine	VF	XF
61a.2	1767	.050	10.00	20.00	35.00	75.00
	1768	.075	20.00	40.00	70.00	125.00
	1769	.100	20.00	40.00	70.00	125.00
	1770	.170	10.00	20.00	35.00	75.00
	1771	.260	10.00	20.00	35.00	75.00
	1774	.107	10.00	20.00	35.00	75.00
	1775	.250	7.00	15.00	30.00	60.00

MINT: ST. PETERSBURG СПБ

C#	Date	Mintage	VG	Fine	VF	XF
61a.3	1766	.460	7.00	15.00	30.00	60.00
	1767	.550	7.00	15.00	30.00	60.00
	1768	.674	7.00	15.00	30.00	60.00
	1769	2.550	7.00	15.00	30.00	60.00
	1770	1.640	7.00	15.00	30.00	60.00
	1771	1.939	7.00	15.00	30.00	60.00
	1772	.510	7.00	15.00	30.00	60.00
	1773	.205	7.00	15.00	30.00	60.00
	1774	—	10.00	20.00	40.00	75.00
	1775	.285	10.00	20.00	40.00	75.00
	1776	.066	20.00	40.00	75.00	125.00

MINT: ST. PETERSBURG СПБ

C#	Date	Mintage	VG	Fine	VF	XF
61b	1777	—	30.00	50.00	100.00	175.00
	1778	.540	7.00	15.00	30.00	60.00
	1779	1.376	7.00	15.00	30.00	60.00
	1780	.142	40.00	75.00	125.00	200.00
	1781	—	7.00	15.00	30.00	60.00
	1782	.714	100.00	150.00	300.00	500.00

MINT: ST. PETERSBURG СПБ

Obv: Old bust.

C#	Date	Mintage	VG	Fine	VF	XF
61c	1783	—	7.00	15.00	30.00	60.00
	1784	3.863	7.00	15.00	30.00	60.00
	1785	3.274	7.00	15.00	30.00	60.00
	1786	—	7.00	15.00	30.00	60.00
	1787	2.000	7.00	15.00	30.00	60.00
	1788	3.067	7.00	15.00	30.00	60.00
	1789	.500	7.00	15.00	30.00	60.00
	1790	2.529	7.00	15.00	30.00	60.00
	1791	1.730	7.00	15.00	30.00	60.00
	1792	2.000	10.00	20.00	35.00	75.00
	1793	.840	20.00	40.00	70.00	125.00
	1794	2.030	7.00	15.00	30.00	60.00
	1795	1.230	7.00	15.00	30.00	60.00
	1796	1.321	7.00	15.00	30.00	60.00

SILVER

MINT: ST. PETERSBURG СМ

C#	Date	Mintage	VG	Fine	VF	XF
97.1	1797 ФЦ	.048	30.00	65.00	125.00	250.00
	1798 МБ	.170	20.00	40.00	75.00	150.00
	1799 МБ	.680	20.00	40.00	75.00	150.00
	1801 АИ	.010	25.00	50.00	100.00	200.00
	1801 ФЦ	I.A.	—	—	Rare	—

MINT: ST. PETERSBURG СП

C#	Date	Mintage	VG	Fine	VF	XF
97.2	1798 ОМ	I.A.	20.00	40.00	75.00	150.00

2.0732 gm., .868 SILVER, .0578 oz ASW

MINT: ST. PETERSBURG СПБ

C#	Date	Mintage	VG	Fine	VF	XF
119	1802 АИ	.190	25.00	50.00	100.00	200.00
	1803 АИ	.040	—	—	Rare	—
	1804 ФГ	.380	25.00	50.00	100.00	200.00
	1805 ФГ	.112	25.00	50.00	100.00	200.00

MINT: ST. PETERSBURG СПБ

C#	Date	Mintage	VG	Fine	VF	XF
119a	1808 ФГ	—	—	—	Rare	—
	1809 МК	.035	30.00	60.00	120.00	240.00
	1810 ФГ	.077	25.00	50.00	100.00	200.00

MINT: ST. PETERSBURG СПБ

C#	Date	Mintage	VG	Fine	VF	XF
127	1810 ФГ	—	6.50	12.50	25.00	50.00
	1811 ФГ	.930	2.50	5.00	10.00	20.00
	1812 МФ	—	—	—	Rare	—
	1813 ПС	1.010	2.50	5.00	10.00	20.00
	1814 ПС	2.120	2.50	5.00	10.00	20.00
	1814 СП	I.A.	2.50	5.00	10.00	20.00
	1814 МФ	I.A.	2.50	5.00	10.00	20.00
	1815 МФ	2.000	2.50	5.00	10.00	20.00
	1816 МФ	.250	5.00	10.00	20.00	40.00
	1816 ПС	I.A.	2.50	5.00	10.00	20.00
	1817 ПС	.160	2.50	5.00	10.00	20.00
	1818 ПС	.630	2.50	5.00	10.00	20.00
	1819 ПС	1.520	2.50	5.00	10.00	20.00
	1820 ПС	.520	2.50	5.00	10.00	20.00
	1820 ПД	I.A.	2.50	5.00	10.00	20.00
	1821 ПД	2.250	2.50	5.00	10.00	20.00
	1822 ПД	2.070	2.50	5.00	10.00	20.00
	1823 ПД	3.850	2.50	5.00	10.00	20.00
	1824 ПД	1.330	2.50	5.00	10.00	20.00
	1825 ПД	1.350	2.50	5.00	10.00	20.00
	1825 НГ	I.A.	5.00	10.00	20.00	40.00

MINT: ST. PETERSBURG СПБ

C#	Date	Mintage	VG	Fine	VF	XF
152	1826 НГ	2.050	6.50	12.50	25.00	50.00

MINT: ST. PETERSBURG СПБ

C#	Date	Mintage	VG	Fine	VF	XF
157	1826 НГ	I.A.	3.50	6.50	12.50	25.00
	1827 НГ	1.290	4.00	9.00	17.50	35.00
	1828 НГ	.370	4.00	9.00	17.50	35.00
	1829 НГ	.040	6.50	12.50	25.00	50.00
	1830 НГ	.500	4.00	9.00	17.50	35.00
	1831 НГ	.450	4.00	9.00	17.50	35.00

COPPER

MINT: EKATERINBURG ЕМ

C#	Date	Mintage	VG	Fine	VF	XF
141.1	1830 ФХ	—	—	—	Rare	—
	1830	—	—	—	Rare	—
	1831 ФХ	2.640	7.50	15.00	30.00	60.00
	1832 ФХ	7.620	7.50	15.00	30.00	60.00
	1833 ФХ	6.968	7.50	15.00	30.00	60.00
	1834 ФХ	9.133	7.50	15.00	30.00	60.00
	1835 ФХ	5.175	7.50	15.00	30.00	60.00
	1836 ФХ	7.240	7.50	15.00	30.00	60.00
	1837 ФХ	9.728	7.50	15.00	30.00	60.00
	1837 КТ ФХ	—	—	—	—	—
	1837 КТ	I.A.	7.50	15.00	30.00	60.00
	1837 НА	I.A.	7.50	15.00	30.00	60.00
	1838 НА	5.470	7.50	15.00	30.00	60.00
	1839 НА	.350	8.50	17.50	35.00	70.00

MINT: ST. PETERSBURG СПБ

C#	Date	Mintage	VG	Fine	VF	XF
141.2	1830	25 pcs.	—	—	Rare	—

MINT: MOSCOW СМ

C#	Date	Mintage	VG	Fine	VF	XF
141.3	1831	.510	8.50	17.50	35.00	70.00
	1832	.510	8.50	17.50	35.00	70.00
	1833	.700	8.50	17.50	35.00	70.00
	1834	.510	8.50	17.50	35.00	70.00
	1835	.500	8.50	17.50	35.00	70.00
	1836	.600	8.50	17.50	35.00	70.00
	1837	.500	8.50	17.50	35.00	70.00
	1838	.350	8.50	17.50	35.00	70.00
	1839	.350	12.50	25.00	50.00	100.00

.868 SILVER, 2.07 gms.

MINT: ST. PETERSBURG СПБ

C#	Date	Mintage	VG	Fine	VF	XF
164.1	1832 НГ	.103	6.50	12.50	25.00	50.00
	1833 НГ	.880	2.25	4.50	9.00	17.50
	1834 НГ	.400	2.25	4.50	9.00	17.50
	1835 НГ	.940	2.25	4.50	9.00	17.50
	1836 НГ	.490	2.25	4.50	9.00	17.50
	1837 НГ	2.360	2.25	4.50	9.00	17.50
	1838 НГ	.500	2.25	4.50	9.00	17.50
	1839 НГ	2.410	2.25	4.50	9.00	17.50
	1840 НГ	.190	2.25	4.50	9.00	17.50
	1841 НГ	.500	2.25	4.50	9.00	17.50
	1842 АЧ	.300	2.25	4.50	9.00	17.50
	1843 АЧ	.180	2.25	4.50	9.00	17.50
	1844 КБ	.460	2.25	4.50	9.00	17.50
	1845 КБ	2.440	2.25	4.50	9.00	17.50
	1846 ПА	.810	2.25	4.50	9.00	17.50
	1847 ПА	3.180	2.25	4.50	9.00	17.50
	1848 НI	1.860	2.25	4.50	9.00	17.50
	1849 ПА	3.110	2.25	4.50	9.00	17.50
	1850 ПА	2.450	2.25	4.50	9.00	17.50
	1851 ПА	1.500	2.25	4.50	9.00	17.50
	1852 ПА	1.350	2.25	4.50	9.00	17.50
	1852 НI	I.A.	5.00	10.00	20.00	40.00
	1853 НI	1.350	2.25	4.50	9.00	17.50
	1854 НI	1.000	2.25	4.50	9.00	17.50

MINT: WARSAW МШ

C#	Date	Mintage	VG	Fine	VF	XF
164.2	1854	—	—	—	Rare	—

MINT: ST. PETERSBURG СПБ

Y#	Date	Mintage	Fine	VF	XF	Unc
14.1	1855 НI	3.201	5.00	10.00	20.00	50.00
	1856 ФБ	1.940	5.00	10.00	20.00	50.00
	1857 ФБ	3.110	5.00	10.00	20.00	50.00
	1858 ФБ	2.600	5.00	10.00	20.00	50.00

MINT: WARSAW МШ

Y#	Date	Mintage	Fine	VF	XF	Unc
14.2	1855	.103	—	—	Rare	—

2.0732 gm., .750 SILVER, .0499 oz ASW

MINT: ST. PETERSBURG СПБ

Type 1, engrailed edge.

Y#	Date	Mintage	Fine	VF	XF	Unc
20.1	1859 ФБ	3.920	3.00	6.50	12.50	25.00
	1860 ФБ	.580	4.50	9.00	17.50	35.00

MINT: ST. PETERSBURG СПБ

Type 2, eagle redesigned.

Y#	Date	Mintage	Fine	VF	XF	Unc
20.2	1860 ФБ	2.810	1.50	2.50	5.00	12.00
	1861 ФБ	5.660	1.50	2.50	5.00	12.00
	1861 МИ	I.A.	5.00	10.00	20.00	50.00
	1861	19.300	1.50	3.00	6.00	15.00
	1862 МИ	I.A.	1.50	2.50	5.00	12.00
	1863 АБ	5.750	1.50	2.50	5.00	12.00
	1864 НФ	3.740	1.50	2.50	5.00	12.00
	1865 НФ	3.886	1.50	2.50	5.00	12.00
	1866 НФ	2.532	1.50	3.00	6.00	12.00
	1866 НI	I.A.	2.00	4.00	8.00	16.00

1.7996 gm., .500 SILVER, .0289 oz ASW

MINT: OSAKA, JAPAN (NO MINTMARK)

Y#	Date	Mintage	Fine	VF	XF	Unc
20a.1	1916	70.001	1.00	1.25	2.00	3.00

MINT: ST. PETERSBURG СПБ

Reeded edge

Y#	Date	Mintage	Fine	VF	XF	Unc
20a.2	1867 HI	6.445	1.00	2.00	4.00	10.00
	1868 HI	4.740	1.00	2.00	4.00	10.00
	1869 HI	3.710	1.00	2.00	4.00	10.00
	1870 HI	3.310	1.00	2.00	4.00	10.00
	1871 HI	4.194	1.00	2.00	4.00	10.00
	1872 HI	2.130	1.00	2.00	4.00	10.00
	1873 HI	2.620	1.00	2.00	4.00	10.00
	1874 HI	2.520	1.00	2.00	4.00	10.00
	1875 HI	3.590	1.00	2.00	4.00	10.00
	1876 HI	4.900	1.00	2.00	4.00	10.00
	1877 HI	2.000	1.00	2.00	4.00	10.00
	1877 НФ	I.A.	1.25	2.50	5.00	12.00
	1878 НФ	6.920	1.00	2.00	4.00	10.00
	1878 HI	I.A.	1.25	2.50	5.00	12.00
	1879 НФ	6.890	1.00	2.00	4.00	10.00
	1880 НФ	6.740	1.00	2.00	4.00	10.00
	1881 НФ	2.950	1.00	2.00	4.00	10.00
	1882 НФ	.920	1.00	2.00	4.00	10.00
	1883 ДС	1.520	1.00	2.00	4.00	10.00
	1883 АГ	I.A.	1.00	2.00	4.00	10.00
	1884 АГ	1.710	1.00	2.00	4.00	10.00
	1885 АГ	1.300	1.00	2.00	4.00	10.00
	1886 АГ	2.000	1.00	2.00	4.00	10.00
	1887 АГ	4.000	1.00	2.00	4.00	10.00
	1888 АГ	2.000	1.00	2.00	4.00	10.00
	1889 АГ	5.000	1.00	2.00	4.00	10.00
	1890 АГ	3.750	1.00	2.00	4.00	10.00
	1891 АГ	3.240	1.00	2.00	4.00	10.00
	1893 АГ	4.250	1.00	2.00	4.00	10.00
	1894 АГ	4.000	1.00	2.00	4.00	10.00
	1895 АГ	1.000	1.00	2.00	4.00	10.00
	1896 АГ	2.010	1.00	2.00	4.00	10.00
	1897 АГ	3.150	1.50	3.00	6.00	15.00
	1898 АГ	6.610	1.00	1.50	2.50	6.00
	1899 АГ	14.000	1.00	1.50	2.50	6.00
	1899 ЭБ	I.A.	1.00	1.50	2.50	6.00
	1900 ФЗ	14.000	1.00	1.50	2.00	5.00
	1901 ФЗ	15.000	1.00	1.50	2.00	5.00
	1901 АР	I.A.	1.00	1.50	2.50	6.00
	1902 АР	17.000	1.00	1.50	2.00	5.00
	1903 АР	28.500	1.00	1.50	2.00	5.00
	1904 АР	20.000	1.00	1.50	2.00	5.00
	1905 АР	25.000	1.00	1.50	2.00	5.00
	1906 ЭБ	17.500	1.00	1.50	2.00	5.00
	1907 ЭБ	20.000	1.00	1.50	2.00	5.00
	1908 ЭБ	8.210	1.00	1.50	2.00	5.00
	1909 ЭБ	25.290	1.00	1.50	2.00	5.00
	1910 ЭБ	20.000	1.00	1.50	2.00	5.00
	1911 ЭБ	19.180	1.00	1.50	2.00	4.00
	1912 ЭБ	20.000	1.00	1.50	2.00	4.00
	1913 ЭБ	7.250	1.00	1.50	2.00	4.00
	1913 ВС	I.A.	1.00	1.50	2.00	4.00
	1914 ВС	51.250	1.00	1.50	2.00	4.00

MINT: ST. PETERSBURG (NO MINTMARK)

Y#	Date	Mintage	Fine	VF	XF	Unc
20a.3	1915 ВС	82.500	1.00	1.50	1.75	2.50
	1916 ВС	121.500	1.00	1.50	1.75	2.50
	1917 ВС	17.600	10.00	20.00	30.00	60.00

15 KOPEKS

.750 SILVER

MINT: MOSCOW ММД

C#	Date	Mintage	VG	Fine	VF	XF
62.1	1764	.667	12.00	20.00	40.00	75.00
	1765	.427	12.00	20.00	40.00	75.00
	1766	.469	12.00	20.00	40.00	75.00

MINT: ST. PETERSBURG СПБ

C#	Date	Mintage	VG	Fine	VF	XF
62.2	1763	—	100.00	150.00	300.00	500.00

MINT: MOSCOW ММД

C#	Date	Mintage	VG	Fine	VF	XF
62a	1767	.427	15.00	30.00	50.00	90.00
	1768	.210	25.00	40.00	75.00	125.00
	1769	.153	12.00	20.00	40.00	75.00
	1770	.757	12.00	20.00	40.00	75.00
	1771	.987	12.00	20.00	40.00	75.00
62a	1774	.057	15.00	30.00	50.00	90.00
	1775	.359	12.00	20.00	40.00	75.00

MINT: ST. PETERSBURG СПБ

C#	Date	Mintage	VG	Fine	VF	XF
62b	1778	.800	12.00	20.00	40.00	75.00
	1779	1.420	12.00	20.00	40.00	75.00
	1781	—	12.00	20.00	40.00	75.00
	1782	.445	—	—	—	500.00

MINT: ST. PETERSBURG СПБ

C#	Date	Mintage	VG	Fine	VF	XF
62c	1783	—	12.00	20.00	40.00	75.00
	1784	2.168	12.00	20.00	40.00	75.00
	1785	2.500	12.00	20.00	40.00	75.00
	1786	—	12.00	20.00	40.00	75.00
	1787	3.200	12.00	20.00	40.00	75.00
	1788	1.634	15.00	30.00	50.00	90.00
	1789	1.200	12.00	20.00	40.00	75.00
	1790	2.024	15.00	30.00	50.00	90.00
	1791	.960	15.00	30.00	50.00	90.00
	1792	1.400	25.00	40.00	75.00	125.00
	1793	.440	100.00	150.00	300.00	500.00
	1794	.200	25.00	40.00	75.00	125.00

For similar coins not listed here refer to Poland.

3.1097 gm., .750 SILVER, .0750 oz ASW

MINT: ST. PETERSBURG СПБ

Engrailed edge

Y#	Date	Mintage	Fine	VF	XF	Unc
21	1860 ФБ	4.480	BV	2.25	4.00	10.00
	1861 ФБ	10.120	BV	2.25	4.00	10.00
	1861 МИ	I.A.	2.50	5.00	10.00	20.00
	1861	13.300	BV	2.25	4.00	10.00
	1862 МИ	10.000	BV	2.25	4.00	10.00
	1863 АБ	9.960	BV	2.25	4.00	10.00
	1864 НФ	10.715	BV	2.25	4.00	10.00
	1865 НФ	10.703	BV	2.25	4.00	10.00
	1866 НФ	6.329	BV	2.25	4.00	10.00
	1866 HI	I.A.	BV	2.25	4.00	10.00

2.6994 gm., .500 SILVER, .0434 oz ASW

MINT: OSAKA, JAPAN (NO MINTMARK)

Reeded edge

Y#	Date	Mintage	Fine	VF	XF	Unc
21a.1	1916	96.666	BV	BV	1.50	3.00

MINT: ST. PETERSBURG СПБ

Y#	Date	Mintage	Fine	VF	XF	Unc
21a.2	1867 HIK	8.720	BV	2.00	4.00	10.00
	1868 HIK	7.460	BV	2.00	4.00	10.00
	1869 HIK	8.120	BV	2.00	4.00	10.00
	1870 HIK	9.380	BV	2.00	4.00	10.00
	1871 HIK	9.460	BV	2.00	4.00	10.00
	1872 HIK	5.880	BV	2.00	4.00	10.00
	1873 HIK	7.960	BV	2.00	4.00	10.00
	1874 HIK	6.960	BV	2.00	4.00	10.00
	1875 HIK	7.480	BV	2.00	4.00	10.00
	1876 HIK	9.760	BV	2.00	4.00	10.00
	1877 HIK	4.360	BV	2.00	4.00	10.00
	1877 НФ	I.A.	BV	2.00	4.00	10.00
	1878 НФ	11.155	BV	2.00	4.00	10.00
	1879 НФ	12.504	BV	2.00	4.00	10.00
	1880 НФ	11.655	BV	2.00	4.00	10.00
	1881 НФ	4.900	BV	2.00	4.00	10.00
	1882 НФ	1.470	BV	2.00	4.00	10.00
	1882 ДС	Inc. Ab.	2.00	4.00	8.00	20.00
	1883 ДС	4.020	BV	2.00	4.00	10.00
	1883 АГ	I.A.	BV	2.00	4.00	10.00
	1884 АГ	2.520	BV	2.00	4.00	10.00
	1885 АГ	1.420	BV	2.00	4.00	10.00
	1886 АГ	1.840	BV	2.00	4.00	10.00
	1887 АГ	3.000	BV	2.00	4.00	10.00
	1888 АГ	—	2.00	4.00	7.50	18.00
	1889 АГ	2.835	BV	1.50	3.00	8.00
	1890 АГ	3.500	BV	1.50	3.00	8.00
	1891 АГ	4.710	BV	1.50	3.00	8.00
	1893 АГ	6.500	BV	1.50	3.00	8.00
	1896 АГ	3.160	BV	1.50	2.50	7.00
	1897 АГ	I.A.	BV	1.50	2.50	7.00
	1898 АГ	3.000	BV	1.50	2.00	6.00
	1899 АГ	12.665	BV	1.50	2.00	5.00
21a.2	1899 ЭБ	I.A.	BV	2.00	4.00	10.00
	1900 ФЗ	12.665	BV	1.50	1.75	5.00
	1901 ФЗ	6.670	BV	1.50	2.50	6.00
	1901 АР	I.A.	BV	1.50	2.50	6.00
	1902 АР	28.666	BV	1.50	2.00	5.00
	1903 АР	16.666	BV	1.50	2.00	5.00
	1904 АР	15.600	BV	1.50	2.00	5.00
	1905 АР	24.000	BV	1.50	2.00	5.00
	1906 ЭБ	23.333	BV	1.50	2.00	5.00
	1907 ЭБ	30.000	BV	1.50	2.00	5.00
	1908 ЭБ	29.000	BV	1.50	2.00	5.00
	1909 ЭБ	21.666	BV	1.50	2.00	5.00
	1911 ЭБ	6.313	BV	1.50	2.00	5.00
	1912 ЭБ	13.333	.75	1.25	1.50	4.00
	1912 ВС	Inc. Ab.	BV	2.50	5.00	12.00
	1913 ЭБ	5.300	BV	1.50	2.00	4.00
	1913 ВС	I.A.	BV	1.50	2.00	4.00
	1914 ВС	43.366	BV	1.50	2.00	3.50

MINT: ST. PETERSBURG (NO MINTMARK)

Y#	Date	Mintage	Fine	VF	XF	Unc
21a.3	1915 ВС	59.333	BV	1.50	2.00	3.00
	1916 ВС	96.773	BV	1.50	2.00	2.50
	1917 ВС	14.320	10.00	20.00	30.00	60.00

20 KOPEKS

.750 SILVER

MINT: MOSCOW ММД

C#	Date	Mintage	VG	Fine	VF	XF
63.1	1764	.520	12.00	25.00	45.00	80.00
	1765	—	12.00	25.00	45.00	80.00

MINT: ST. PETERSBURG СПБ

C#	Date	Mintage	VG	Fine	VF	XF
63.2	1763	—	100.00	150.00	300.00	500.00
	1764	—	50.00	100.00	200.00	400.00
	1765	.115	12.00	25.00	45.00	80.00

MINT: MOSCOW ММД

C#	Date	Mintage	VG	Fine	VF	XF
63a.1	1766	.555	20.00	40.00	75.00	125.00
	1767	.235	12.00	25.00	45.00	80.00
	1768	.220	30.00	50.00	100.00	175.00
	1769	.020	30.00	50.00	100.00	175.00
	1770	.160	30.00	50.00	100.00	175.00
	1775	.015	20.00	35.00	60.00	100.00

MINT: ST. PETERSBURG СПБ

C#	Date	Mintage	VG	Fine	VF	XF
63a.2	1766	.525	12.00	25.00	45.00	80.00
	1767	.245	20.00	40.00	75.00	125.00
	1768	.350	12.00	25.00	45.00	80.00
	1769	1.075	12.00	25.00	45.00	80.00
	1770	.785	12.00	25.00	45.00	80.00
	1771	2.105	12.00	25.00	45.00	80.00
	1772	.870	12.00	25.00	45.00	80.00
	1773	.290	12.00	25.00	45.00	80.00
	1774	—	12.00	25.00	45.00	80.00
	1775	.290	12.00	25.00	45.00	80.00
	1776	.223	12.00	25.00	45.00	80.00

MINT: ST. PETERSBURG СПБ

C#	Date	Mintage	VG	Fine	VF	XF
63b	1778	.630	12.00	25.00	45.00	80.00
	1779	.535	12.00	25.00	45.00	80.00
	1781	—	20.00	35.00	60.00	100.00

MINT: ST. PETERSBURG СПБ

C#	Date	Mintage	VG	Fine	VF	XF
63c	1783	.389	12.00	25.00	45.00	80.00
	1784	2.080	12.00	25.00	45.00	80.00
	1785	1.887	12.00	25.00	45.00	80.00
	1786	—	12.00	25.00	45.00	80.00
	1787	1.000	12.00	25.00	45.00	80.00
	1788	2.376	12.00	25.00	45.00	80.00
	1789	.250	12.00	25.00	45.00	80.00
	1790	2.870	20.00	35.00	60.00	100.00
	1791	1.600	20.00	35.00	60.00	100.00
	1792	1.510	12.00	25.00	45.00	80.00
	1793	.685	30.00	50.00	100.00	175.00

4.1463 gm., .868 SILVER, .1157 oz ASW

MINT: ST. PETERSBURG СПБ

C#	Date	Mintage	VG	Fine	VF	XF
128	1810 ФГ	.250	4.00	7.50	15.00	30.00
	1811 ФГ	1.969	3.50	5.00	9.00	18.00
	1813 ПС	1.900	3.50	5.00	9.00	18.00
	1814 ПС	1.850	3.50	5.00	9.00	18.00
	1814 МФ	I.A.	3.50	5.00	9.00	18.00
	1815 МФ	1.025	3.50	5.00	9.00	18.00
	1816 МФ	.115	10.00	20.00	35.00	70.00
	1816 ПС	I.A.	3.50	5.00	9.00	18.00
	1817 ПС	1.545	3.50	5.00	9.00	18.00
	1818 ПС	2.000	3.50	5.00	9.00	18.00
	1819 ПС	1.705	3.50	5.00	9.00	18.00
	1820 ПС	1.895	3.50	5.00	9.00	18.00
	1820 ПД	I.A.	3.50	5.00	9.00	18.00
	1821 ПД	3.025	3.50	5.00	9.00	18.00
	1822 ПД	2.100	3.50	5.00	9.00	18.00
	1823 ПД	7.075	3.50	5.00	9.00	18.00
	1823	1 Known	—	—	Rare	—
	1824 ПД	1.750	3.50	5.00	9.00	18.00
	1825 ПД	1.375	3.50	5.00	9.00	18.00
	1825 НГ	I.A.	—	—	Rare	—

MINT: ST. PETERSBURG СПБ

Similar to C#128.

C#	Date	Mintage	VG	Fine	VF	XF
153	1826 НГ	2.815	5.00	10.00	20.00	40.00

MINT: ST. PETERSBURG СПБ

Obv: Eagle with wings pointed down.

C#	Date	Mintage	VG	Fine	VF	XF
158	1826 НГ	I.A.	4.50	9.00	17.50	35.00
	1827 НГ	.465	4.50	9.00	17.50	35.00
	1828 НГ	.050	7.50	15.00	30.00	60.00
	1829 НГ	.250	4.50	9.00	17.50	35.00
	1831 НГ	1.185	4.50	9.00	17.50	35.00
	1831	.385	4.50	9.00	17.50	35.00

MINT: ST. PETERSBURG СПБ

Obv: Variety I eagle.

C#	Date	Mintage	VG	Fine	VF	XF
165	1832 НГ	.097	3.50	5.00	10.00	20.00
	1833 НГ	.435	3.50	5.00	7.50	15.00
	1834 НГ	.320	3.50	5.00	7.50	15.00
	1835 НГ	.500	3.50	5.00	7.50	15.00
	1836 НГ	1.280	3.50	5.00	7.50	15.00
	1837 НГ	1.300	3.50	5.00	7.50	15.00
	1838 НГ	1.645	3.50	5.00	7.50	15.00
	1839 НГ	4.030	3.50	5.00	7.50	15.00
	1840 НГ	2.075	3.50	5.00	7.50	15.00
	1841 НГ	.025	6.50	12.50	25.00	50.00
	1842 АЧ	—	—	—	Rare	—
	1843 АЧ	—	—	—	Rare	—
	1844 КБ	—	—	—	Rare	—
	1845 КБ	.105	3.50	5.00	7.50	15.00
	1846 ПА	.630	3.50	5.00	7.50	15.00
	1847 ПА	3.922	3.50	5.00	7.50	15.00
	1848 НІ	2.165	3.50	5.00	7.50	15.00
	1849 ПА	3.250	3.50	5.00	7.50	15.00
	1850 ПА	3.075	3.50	5.00	7.50	15.00
	1851 ПА	2.000	3.50	5.00	7.50	15.00
	1852 НІ	1.800	3.50	5.00	7.50	15.00
	1852 ПА	I.A.	10.00	12.50	25.00	50.00
	1853 НІ	1.800	3.50	5.00	7.50	15.00
	1854 НІ	.990	3.50	5.00	7.50	15.00

MINT: ST. PETERSBURG СПБ

Y#	Date	Mintage	Fine	VF	XF	Unc
15	1855 НІ	3.090	6.50	12.50	25.00	60.00
	1856 ФБ	3.240	6.50	12.50	25.00	60.00
	1857 ФБ	4.275	6.50	12.50	25.00	60.00
	1858 ФБ	4.150	6.50	12.50	25.00	60.00

4.1463 gm., .750 SILVER, .0999 oz ASW

MINT: ST. PETERSBURG СПБ

Engrailed edge

Y#	Date	Mintage	Fine	VF	XF	Unc
22	1859 ФБ	3.960	3.50	6.50	12.50	25.00
	1860 ФБ	1.070	3.50	6.50	12.50	25.00

MINT: ST. PETERSBURG СПБ

Obv: Eagle redesigned.

Y#	Date	Mintage	Fine	VF	XF	Unc
22.1	1860 ФБ	14.440	BV	3.00	5.00	12.00
	1861 ФБ	19.500	BV	3.00	5.00	12.00
	1861 МИ	I.A.	9.00	17.50	35.00	70.00
	1861	19.000	BV	3.00	5.00	12.00
	1862 МИ	19.500	BV	3.00	5.00	12.00
	1863 АБ	19.230	BV	3.00	5.00	12.00
	1864 НФ	20.060	BV	3.00	5.00	12.00
	1865 НФ	20.047	BV	3.00	5.00	12.00
	1866 НФ	10.067	BV	3.00	5.00	12.00
	1866 НІ	Inc. Ab.	BV	3.00	5.00	12.00

3.5992 gm., .500 SILVER, .0579 oz ASW

MINT: ST. PETERSBURG СПБ

Reeded edge

Y#	Date	Mintage	Fine	VF	XF	Unc
22a.1	1867 НІ	15.355	BV	2.00	4.00	10.00
	1868 НІ	11.975	BV	2.00	4.00	10.00
	1869 НІ	17.017	BV	2.00	4.00	10.00
	1870 НІ	16.255	BV	2.00	4.00	10.00
	1871 НІ	18.860	BV	2.00	4.00	10.00
	1872 НІ	11.980	BV	2.00	4.00	10.00
	1873 НІ	15.185	BV	2.00	4.00	10.00
	1874 НІ	14.850	BV	2.00	4.00	10.00
	1875 НІ	15.545	BV	2.00	4.00	10.00
	1876 НІ	16.250	BV	2.00	4.00	10.00
	1877 НІ	6.950	BV	2.00	4.00	10.00
	1877 НФ	I.A.	BV	2.50	5.00	12.00
	1878 НФ	25.335	BV	2.00	4.00	10.00
	1878 НІ	I.A.	—	—	Rare	—
	1879 НФ	23.070	BV	2.00	4.00	10.00
	1880/70	—	—	—	—	—
	1880 НФ	22.605	BV	2.00	4.00	10.00
	1881 НФ	9.350	BV	2.00	4.00	10.00
	1882 НФ	3.535	BV	2.00	4.00	10.00
	1883 ДС	4.270	BV	2.00	4.00	10.00
	1883 АГ	I.A.	BV	2.00	4.00	10.00
	1884 АГ	2.595	BV	2.00	4.00	10.00
	1885 АГ	1.610	BV	2.00	4.00	10.00
	1886 АГ	2.625	BV	2.00	4.00	10.00
	1887 АГ	2.500	BV	2.00	4.00	10.00
	1888 АГ	3.035	BV	2.00	4.00	10.00
	1889 АГ	1.963	BV	1.75	3.50	9.00
	1890 АГ	3.500	BV	1.75	3.50	9.00
	1891 АГ	6.105	BV	1.75	3.50	9.00
	1893 АГ	7.500	BV	1.75	3.50	9.00
	1901 ФЗ	7.750	BV	1.75	2.50	5.00
	1901 АР	I.A.	BV	2.50	5.00	12.00
	1902 АР	10.000	BV	2.00	3.00	8.00
	1903 АР	I.A.	BV	2.00	3.00	8.00
	1904 АР	13.000	BV	1.75	2.50	5.00
	1905 АР	11.000	BV	1.75	2.50	5.00
	1906 ЭБ	15.000	BV	1.75	2.50	5.00
	1907 ЭБ	20.000	BV	1.75	2.50	5.00
	1908 ЭБ	5.000	BV	1.75	2.50	5.00
	1909 ЭБ	18.875	BV	1.75	2.50	5.00
	1910 ЭБ	11.000	BV	1.75	2.50	5.00
	1911 ЭБ	7.100	BV	1.75	2.50	5.00
	1912 ЭБ	15.000	BV	1.75	2.50	5.00
	1912 ВС	I.A.	3.00	6.50	12.50	25.00
	1913 ЭБ	4.250	BV	1.75	2.25	4.00
	1913 ВС	I.A.	BV	1.75	2.25	4.00
	1914 ВС	52.750	BV	1.75	2.25	4.00

MINT: ST. PETERSBURG (no mintmark)

Y#	Date	Mintage	Fine	VF	XF	Unc
22a.2	1915 ВС	105.500	BV	1.75	2.25	4.00
	1916 ВС	131.670	BV	1.75	2.25	4.00
	1917 ВС	3.500	10.00	20.00	40.00	75.00

POLUPOLTINIK

SILVER

MINT: ST. PETERSBURG СМ

C#	Date	Mintage	VG	Fine	VF	XF
98.1	1797 ФЦ	.028	30.00	60.00	120.00	250.00
	1797 МБ	—	—	—	Rare	—
	1798 МБ	.088	27.00	55.00	110.00	225.00
	1798 ФЦ	I.A.		—	Rare	—
	1799 МБ	.440	27.00	55.00	110.00	225.00
	1799 ФЦ	I.A.	27.00	55.00	110.00	225.00
	1800 ОМ	8,003	—	—	Rare	—
	1801 АИ	.068	27.00	55.00	110.00	225.00
	1801 ОЦ	I.A.	—	—	Rare	—

MINT: ST. PETERSBURG СП

C#	Date	Mintage	VG	Fine	VF	XF
98.2	1798 ОМ	I.A.	27.00	55.00	110.00	225.00
	1800 ОМ	I.A.	—	—	Rare	—

.868 SILVER, 4.146 gms.

MINT: ST. PETERSBURG СПБ

C#	Date	Mintage	VG	Fine	VF	XF
121	1802 АИ	.324	50.00	100.00	175.00	250.00
	1803 АИ	.152	60.00	110.00	200.00	275.00
	1803 ФГ	I.A.	—	—	Rare	—
	1804 ФГ	.168	50.00	100.00	175.00	250.00
	1805 ФГ	.137	60.00	110.00	200.00	275.00

MINT: ST. PETERSBURG СПБ

C#	Date	Mintage	VG	Fine	VF	XF
121a	1808 ФГ	—	—	—	Rare	—
	1809 МК	.040	60.00	125.00	200.00	275.00
	1809 ФГ	I.A.	—	—	Rare	—
	1810 ФГ	.066	60.00	125.00	200.00	275.00

25 KOPEKS

.750 SILVER

MINT: MOSCOW ММД

C#	Date	Mintage	VG	Fine	VF	XF
65	1764 ЕІ	.112	12.00	25.00	45.00	80.00
	1765 ЕІ	.912	20.00	35.00	60.00	100.00
	1766 ЕІ	.832	20.00	35.00	60.00	100.00

MINT: MOSCOW ММД

C#	Date	Mintage	VG	Fine	VF	XF
65a	1767 ЕІ	1.668	12.00	25.00	45.00	80.00
	1768 ЕІ	.484	20.00	35.00	60.00	100.00
	1769 ЕІ	.460	20.00	35.00	60.00	100.00
	1770 ЕІ	.780	30.00	50.00	100.00	175.00
	1770 ДМ	.352	12.00	25.00	45.00	80.00
	1774 СА	1.400	30.00	50.00	100.00	175.00
	1774 СА-ІП	—	—	—	—	—
	1775 СА	.132	20.00	35.00	60.00	100.00

MINT: ST. PETERSBURG СПБ

C#	Date	Mintage	VG	Fine	VF	XF
65b	1779	—	50.00	100.00	200.00	400.00
	1779 ЕЛ	.394	12.00	25.00	45.00	80.00
	1781 АГ	.336	12.00	25.00	45.00	80.00

MINT: ST. PETERSBURG СПБ

C#	Date	Mintage	VG	Fine	VF	XF
65c	1783 MM	—	20.00	35.00	60.00	100.00
	1784 MM	.441	12.00	25.00	45.00	80.00
	1785 ЯА	.605	12.00	25.00	45.00	80.00
	1786 ЯА	—	20.00	35.00	60.00	100.00
	1787 ЯА	.800	12.00	25.00	45.00	80.00
	1788 ЯА	1.706	20.00	35.00	60.00	100.00
	1789 ЯА	.800	20.00	35.00	60.00	100.00
	1790 ЯА	.412	20.00	35.00	60.00	100.00
	1791 ЯА	.704	20.00	35.00	60.00	100.00
	1792 ЯА	1.404	20.00	35.00	60.00	100.00
	1793 ЯА	.368	30.00	50.00	100.00	175.00
	1794 AK	1.016	20.00	35.00	60.00	100.00
	1795 AK	.464	20.00	35.00	60.00	100.00
	1796 IC					
		.745	12.00	25.00	45.00	80.00

5.1830 gm., .868 SILVER, .1446 oz ASW

MINT: ST. PETERSBURG СПБ

C#	Date	Mintage	VG	Fine	VF	XF
159	1827 НГ	1.860	5.00	10.00	20.00	40.00
	1828 НГ	.320	5.00	10.00	20.00	40.00
	1829 НГ	1.200	4.50	9.00	17.50	35.00
	1830 НГ	1.160	4.50	9.00	17.50	35.00
	1831 НГ	.484	4.50	9.00	17.50	35.00

For similar coins not listed here refer to Poland.

MINT: ST. PETERSBURG СПБ

Obv: Variety I eagle.

C#	Date	Mintage	VG	Fine	VF	XF
166	1832 НГ	.308	BV	5.00	10.00	20.00
	1833 НГ	.260	BV	5.00	10.00	20.00
	1834 НГ	.260	BV	5.00	10.00	20.00
	1835 НГ	.356	BV	5.00	10.00	20.00
	1836 НГ	1.072	BV	5.00	10.00	20.00
	1837 НГ	1.144	BV	5.00	10.00	20.00
	1838 НГ	2.672	BV	5.00	10.00	20.00
	1839 НГ	2.738	BV	5.00	10.00	20.00
	1840 НГ	.604	BV	5.00	10.00	20.00
	1841 НГ	.020	—	—	Rare	—
	1842 АЧ	—	—	—	Rare	—
	1843 АЧ	—	—	—	Rare	—
	1844 КБ	.020	—	—	Rare	—
	1845 КБ	.568	BV	4.50	9.00	18.00
	1846 ПА	.576	BV	4.50	9.00	18.00
	1847 ПА	4.824	BV	4.50	9.00	18.00
	1848 HI	2.636	BV	4.50	9.00	18.00
	1849 ПА	3.440	BV	4.50	9.00	18.00
	1850 ПА	3.740	BV	4.50	9.00	18.00
	1851 ПА	2.400	BV	4.50	9.00	18.00
	1852 ПА	2.160	BV	4.50	9.00	18.00
	1852 HI	I.A.	—	—	Rare	—
	1853 HI	2.160	BV	4.50	9.00	18.00
	1854 HI	1.148	BV	4.50	9.00	18.00

MINT: ST. PETERSBURG СПБ

Y#	Date	Mintage	Fine	VF	XF	Unc
16.1	1855 HI	10.396	4.50	7.50	15.00	30.00
	1856 ФБ	4.444	4.50	7.50	15.00	30.00
	1857 ФБ	5.420	4.50	7.50	15.00	30.00
	1858 ФБ	5.528	4.50	7.50	15.00	30.00
	1858	Inc. Ab.	—	—	Rare	—

MINT: WARSAW МШ

Y#	Date	Mintage	Fine	VF	XF	Unc
16.2	1857	.032	12.50	25.00	50.00	100.00

MINT: ST. PETERSBURG СПБ

Obv: Eagle redesigned

Y#	Date	Mintage	Fine	VF	XF	Unc
23	1859 ФБ	4.400	BV	5.00	10.00	25.00
	1860 ФБ	1.052	BV	5.00	10.00	25.00
	1861 ФБ	.116	BV	5.00	10.00	25.00
	1861 МИ	Inc. Ab.	6.00	12.50	25.00	60.00
	1862 МИ	.036	5.00	10.00	20.00	50.00
	1863 АБ	.036	5.00	10.00	20.00	50.00
	1864 НФ	.068	5.00	10.00	20.00	50.00
	1865 НФ	.016	5.00	10.00	20.00	50.00
	1866 НФ	.036	5.00	10.00	20.00	50.00
	1866 HI	I.A.	5.00	10.00	20.00	50.00
	1867 HI	.048	5.00	10.00	20.00	50.00
	1868 HI	.040	5.00	10.00	20.00	50.00
	1869 HI	.020	5.00	10.00	20.00	50.00
	1870 HI	.044	5.00	10.00	20.00	50.00
	1871 HI	.014	5.00	10.00	20.00	50.00
	1872 HI	.044	5.00	10.00	20.00	50.00
	1873 HI	.036	5.00	10.00	20.00	50.00
	1874 HI	.032	5.00	10.00	20.00	50.00
	1875 HI	.024	5.00	10.00	20.00	50.00
	1876 HI	.040	5.00	10.00	20.00	50.00
	1877 HI	1.776	BV	4.50	8.00	20.00
	1877	Inc. Ab.	—	—	Rare	—
	1877 НФ	I.A.	BV	4.50	8.00	20.00
	1878 НФ	1.768	BV	4.50	8.00	20.00
	1879 НФ	.032	7.50	15.00	30.00	70.00
	1880 НФ	.072	7.50	15.00	30.00	70.00
	1881 НФ	2,001	15.00	30.00	60.00	150.00
	1882 НФ	2,007	15.00	30.00	60.00	150.00
	1883 ДС	2,008	15.00	30.00	60.00	150.00
	1883 АГ	Inc. Ab.	20.00	40.00	75.00	200.00
	1884 АГ	2,004	17.50	35.00	70.00	175.00
	1885 АГ	1,001	17.50	35.00	70.00	175.00

4.9990 gm., .900 SILVER, .1446 oz ASW

MINT: ST. PETERSBURG (NO MINTMARK)

Y#	Date	Mintage	Fine	VF	XF	Unc
44	1886 АГ	4,058	25.00	50.00	100.00	250.00
	1887 АГ	.028	22.00	45.00	90.00	200.00
	1888 АГ	4,007	27.00	55.00	110.00	275.00
	1889 АГ	1,002	27.00	55.00	110.00	275.00
	1890 АГ	2,006	27.00	55.00	110.00	275.00
	1891 АГ	.024	22.00	45.00	90.00	200.00
	1892 АГ	4,006	25.00	50.00	100.00	250.00
	1893 АГ	8,008	25.00	50.00	100.00	250.00
	1894 АГ	—	22.00	45.00	90.00	200.00

MINT: ST. PETERSBURG (NO MINTMARK)

Y#	Date	Mintage	Fine	VF	XF	Unc
57	1895	2.660	15.00	30.00	60.00	95.00
	1896	25.932	7.50	12.50	20.00	40.00
	1900	.584	20.00	40.00	80.00	150.00
	1901	*150 pcs.	40.00	75.00	170.00	300.00

30 KOPEKS

Refer to Poland

POLTINA (1/2 RUBLE)

MINT: MOSCOW ММД

Obv: Bust of Peter right.
Rev: Crowned double eagle with arms.

C#	Date	Mintage	VG	Fine	VF	XF
46.1	1762 ДМ	—	75.00	225.00	375.00	750.00

MINT: ST. PETERSBURG СПБ

C#	Date	Mintage	VG	Fine	VF	XF
46.2	1762 НК	—	75.00	225.00	375.00	750.00

MINT: MOSCOW ММД

C#	Date	Mintage	VG	Fine	VF	XF
66.1	1762 ДМ	.014	50.00	100.00	200.00	400.00
	1763 EI	.049	50.00	100.00	200.00	400.00

MINT: ST. PETERSBURG СПБ

C#	Date	Mintage	VG	Fine	VF	XF
66.2	1762 НК	.148	50.00	100.00	200.00	400.00
	1763 НК	.252	35.00	65.00	125.00	200.00
	1763 ЯР	I.A.	35.00	65.00	125.00	200.00
	1764 ЯР	.543	35.00	65.00	125.00	200.00
	1764 СА	I.A.	35.00	65.00	125.00	200.00
	1765 ЯР	.332	35.00	65.00	125.00	200.00
	1765 СА	I.A.	35.00	65.00	125.00	200.00

MINT: ST. PETERSBURG СПБ

C#	Date	Mintage	VG	Fine	VF	XF
66a	1766 ЯР	.093	50.00	100.00	200.00	400.00
	1766 АШ	I.A.	35.00	65.00	125.00	200.00
	1767 АШ	.052	35.00	65.00	125.00	200.00
	1767	—	100.00	200.00	300.00	500.00
	1768 АШ	.046	35.00	65.00	125.00	200.00
	1768 СА	I.A.	50.00	100.00	200.00	400.00
	1769 СА	.100	35.00	65.00	125.00	200.00
	1771 ЯЧ	.025	50.00	100.00	200.00	400.00
	1772 АШ	.029	50.00	100.00	200.00	400.00
	1773 ЯЧ	.041	35.00	65.00	125.00	200.00
	1773 ФЛ	I.A.	100.00	200.00	300.00	500.00
	1774 ФЛ					
		550 pcs.	50.00	100.00	200.00	400.00
	1775 ФЛ	.091	50.00	100.00	200.00	400.00
	1776 ЯЧ	.067	50.00	100.00	200.00	400.00

MINT: ST. PETERSBURG СПБ

C#	Date	Mintage	VG	Fine	VF	XF
66b	1777 ФЛ	—	35.00	65.00	125.00	200.00
	1778 ФЛ	—	35.00	65.00	125.00	200.00
	1779 ФЛ	.155	100.00	200.00	300.00	500.00

MINT: ST. PETERSBURG СПБ

C#	Date	Mintage	VG	Fine	VF	XF
66c	1785 ЯА	.035	35.00	65.00	125.00	200.00
	1787 ЯА	.057	35.00	65.00	125.00	200.00

C#	Date	Mintage	VG	Fine	VF	XF
66c	1791 ЯА	.094	35.00	65.00	125.00	200.00
	1794 АК	.072	35.00	65.00	125.00	200.00
	1795 АК	.148	35.00	65.00	125.00	200.00
	1796 IC	.270	35.00	65.00	125.00	200.00

.917 GOLD

MINT: ST. PETERSBURG (NO MINTMARK)

C#	Date	Mintage	Fine	VF	XF	Unc
75	1777	—	125.00	175.00	225.00	300.00
	1778	—	175.00	225.00	275.00	375.00

SILVER

MINT: ST. PETERSBURG СП

C#	Date	Mintage	VG	Fine	VF	XF
99.1	1797 ФЦ	.214	50.00	100.00	200.00	350.00
	1798 МБ	.284	40.00	75.00	150.00	275.00
	1799 МБ	.348	40.00	75.00	150.00	275.00
	1799 ФЦ	I.A.	50.00	100.00	200.00	350.00
	1800 ОМ	.330	40.00	75.00	150.00	275.00
	1800 МБ	I.A.	—	—	Rare	—
	1801 ОМ	.172	40.00	75.00	150.00	275.00
	1801 ФЦ	I.A.	40.00	75.00	150.00	275.00

MINT: ST. PETERSBURG СП

C#	Date	Mintage	VG	Fine	VF	XF
99.2	1798 ОМ	I.A.	—	—	Rare	—

9.9980 gm., .868 SILVER, .2790 oz ASW

MINT: ST. PETERSBURG СПБ

C#	Date	Mintage	VG	Fine	VF	XF
123	1802 АИ	.104	20.00	40.00	70.00	130.00
	1803 АИ	.242	30.00	60.00	100.00	175.00
	1804 ФГ	.230	30.00	60.00	100.00	175.00
	1805 ФГ	.315	35.00	70.00	120.00	220.00

MINT: ST. PETERSBURG СПБ

C#	Date	Mintage	VG	Fine	VF	XF
123a	1809 МК	.011	50.00	100.00	200.00	400.00
	1810 ФГ	.079	30.00	60.00	100.00	200.00

MINT: ST. PETERSBURG СПБ

C#	Date	Mintage	VG	Fine	VF	XF
129	1810 ФГ	I.A.	15.00	25.00	50.00	100.00
	1811 ФГ	.090	15.00	25.00	50.00	100.00
	1812 МФ	.045	12.50	20.00	40.00	80.00
	1813 ПС	.580	10.00	20.00	40.00	80.00
	1814 ПС	.662	15.00	25.00	50.00	100.00
129	1814 МФ	I.A.	12.50	20.00	40.00	80.00
	1815 МФ	1.700	12.50	20.00	40.00	80.00
	1816 МФ	.270	15.00	25.00	50.00	100.00
	1816 ПС	I.A.	12.50	20.00	40.00	80.00
	1817 ПС	2.820	12.50	20.00	40.00	80.00
	1818 ПС	4.250	12.50	20.00	40.00	80.00
	1819 ПС	2.430	12.50	20.00	40.00	80.00
	1819	Inc. Ab.	—	—	Rare	—
	1820 ПС	1.356	12.50	20.00	40.00	80.00
	1820 ПД	I.A.	—	—	Rare	—
	1821 ПД	.480	12.50	20.00	40.00	80.00
	1822 ПД	.090	12.50	20.00	40.00	80.00
	1823 ПД	.200	12.50	22.00	45.00	90.00
	1824 ПД	.320	12.50	22.00	45.00	90.00
	1825 ПД	.152	12.50	22.00	45.00	90.00
	1826 НГ	.210	15.00	25.00	50.00	100.00

MINT: ST. PETERSBURG СПБ

C#	Date	Mintage	VG	Fine	VF	XF
160	1826 НГ	Inc. Ab.	20.00	40.00	80.00	160.00
	1827 НГ	.164	20.00	40.00	80.00	160.00
	1828 НГ	.274	20.00	40.00	80.00	160.00
	1829 НГ	.880	20.00	40.00	80.00	160.00
	1830 НГ	.290	20.00	40.00	80.00	160.00
	1831 НГ	.140	20.00	40.00	80.00	160.00

MINT: ST. PETERSBURG СПБ

Variety I eagle

C#	Date	Mintage	VG	Fine	VF	XF
167.1	1832 НГ	.050	17.50	30.00	60.00	120.00
	1833 НГ	.082	12.50	20.00	40.00	80.00
	1834 НГ	.046	12.50	20.00	40.00	80.00
	1835 НГ	.020	12.50	20.00	40.00	80.00
	1836 НГ	.140	12.50	20.00	40.00	80.00
	1837 НГ	.104	8.50	10.00	20.00	40.00
	1838 НГ	.004	10.00	15.00	30.00	60.00
	1839 НГ	1.830	8.50	10.00	20.00	40.00
	1840 НГ	.960	8.50	10.00	20.00	40.00
	1841 НГ	.001	10.00	15.00	30.00	60.00
	1842 АЧ	.214	8.50	10.00	20.00	40.00
	1843 АЧ	—	—	—	Rare	—
	1844 КБ	.347	8.50	10.00	20.00	40.00
	1845 КБ	2.008	8.50	10.00	20.00	40.00
	1846 ПА	.460	8.50	10.00	20.00	40.00
	1847 ПА	.615	8.50	10.00	20.00	40.00
	1848 HI	1.560	8.50	10.00	20.00	40.00
	1849 ПА	.450	8.50	10.00	20.00	40.00
	1850 ПА	.530	8.50	10.00	20.00	40.00
	1851 ПА	.800	8.50	10.00	20.00	40.00
	1852 ПА	.720	8.50	10.00	20.00	40.00
	1852 HI	I.A.	10.00	15.00	30.00	60.00
	1853 HI	.720	8.50	10.00	20.00	40.00
	1854 HI	.440	8.50	10.00	20.00	40.00

MINT: WARSAW МШ

C#	Date	Mintage	VG	Fine	VF	XF
167.2	1842	.076	15.00	25.00	50.00	100.00
	1843	.022	15.00	25.00	50.00	100.00
	1844	.116	15.00	25.00	50.00	100.00
	1845	.137	15.00	25.00	50.00	100.00
	1846	.308	15.00	25.00	50.00	100.00
	1847	.783	15.00	25.00	50.00	100.00

MINT: ST. PETERSBURG СПБ

Y#	Date	Mintage	Fine	VF	XF	Unc
17	1855 HI	.714	15.00	25.00	50.00	125.00
	1856 ФБ	.450	15.00	25.00	50.00	125.00
	1857 ФБ	1.650	15.00	25.00	50.00	125.00
	1858 ФБ	1.112	15.00	25.00	50.00	125.00

MINT: ST. PETERSBURG СПБ

Variety II eagle

Y#	Date	Mintage	Fine	VF	XF	Unc
24	1859 ФГ	1.392	11.00	16.00	32.00	75.00
	1860 ФГ	.192	11.00	16.00	32.00	75.00
	1861 ФГ	.064	11.00	16.00	32.00	75.00
	1861 МИ	I.A.	—	—	Rare	—
	1862 МИ	.024	10.00	15.00	30.00	70.00
	1863 АБ	.022	10.00	15.00	30.00	70.00
	1864 НФ	.034	10.00	15.00	30.00	70.00
	1865 НФ	.024	10.00	15.00	30.00	70.00
	1866 НФ	.022	10.00	15.00	30.00	70.00
	1866 HI	I.A.	12.50	20.00	40.00	100.00
	1867 HI	.026	10.00	15.00	30.00	75.00
	1868 HI	.030	10.00	15.00	30.00	75.00
	1869 HI	.020	12.50	20.00	40.00	100.00
	1870 HI	.006	15.00	25.00	50.00	125.00
	1871 HI	.020	10.00	15.00	30.00	75.00
	1872 HI	.022	10.00	15.00	30.00	75.00
	1873 HI	.036	10.00	15.00	30.00	75.00
	1874 HI	.016	10.00	15.00	30.00	75.00
	1875 HI	.014	10.00	15.00	30.00	75.00
	1876 HI	.024	10.00	15.00	30.00	75.00
	1876	Inc. Ab.	15.00	25.00	50.00	125.00
	1877 HI	1.034	8.50	10.00	15.00	30.00
	1877 НФ	I.A.	15.00	25.00	50.00	125.00
	1878 НФ	.778	8.50	10.00	15.00	30.00
	1879 НФ	.014	12.50	20.00	40.00	100.00
	1880 НФ	.042	10.00	15.00	30.00	75.00
	1881 НФ	.001	20.00	40.00	80.00	200.00
	1882 НФ	.001	20.00	40.00	80.00	200.00
	1883 ДС	.001	20.00	40.00	80.00	200.00
	1883 АГ	I.A.	20.00	40.00	80.00	200.00
	1884 АГ	.001	20.00	40.00	80.00	200.00
	1885 АГ	511 pcs.	30.00	60.00	120.00	300.00

50 KOPEKS

9.9980 gm., .900 SILVER, .2893 oz ASW

MINT: ST. PETERSBURG (NO MINTMARK)

Y#	Date	Mintage	Fine	VF	XF	Unc
45	1886 АГ	.002	15.00	30.00	60.00	150.00
	1887 АГ	.026	20.00	40.00	80.00	200.00
	1888 АГ	.002	15.00	30.00	60.00	150.00
	1889 АГ	.001	20.00	40.00	80.00	200.00
	1890 АГ	.002	15.00	30.00	60.00	150.00
	1891 АГ	.024	20.00	40.00	80.00	200.00
	1892 АГ	.002	15.00	30.00	60.00	150.00
	1893 АГ	.004	15.00	30.00	60.00	150.00
	1894 АГ	—	15.00	30.00	60.00	150.00

MINT: PARIS - MINTMARK - Star on rim

Y#	Date	Mintage	Fine	VF	XF	Unc
58.1	1896	.244	9.00	12.50	25.00	60.00
	1897	46.755	BV	12.50	25.00	60.00
	1899	10.000	BV	12.50	25.00	60.00

MINT: ST. PETERSBURG (NO MINTMARK)

Y#	Date	Mintage	Fine	VF	XF	Unc
58.2	1895 АГ	5.400	15.00	30.00	60.00	150.00
	1896 АГ	17.402	BV	12.50	25.00	60.00
	1898 АГ	—	—	—	Rare	—

Y#	Date	Mintage	Fine	VF	XF	Unc
58.2	1899 ЗБ	15.442	BV	12.50	25.00	60.00
	1899 ФЗ	I.A.	BV	12.50	25.00	60.00
	1899 АГ	I.A.	BV	12.50	25.00	60.00
	1900 ФЗ	3.360	BV	12.50	25.00	60.00
	1901 АР	.412	BV	10.00	20.00	50.00
	1901 ФЗ	I.A.	BV	10.00	20.00	50.00
	1902 АР	.036	12.50	25.00	50.00	125.00
	1903 АР	19 pcs.	—	—	Rare	—
	1904 АР	.004	30.00	60.00	120.00	300.00
	1906 ЗБ	.010	25.00	50.00	100.00	250.00
	1907 ЗБ	.200	12.50	25.00	50.00	125.00
	1908 ЗБ	.040	12.50	25.00	50.00	125.00
	1909 ЗБ	.050	12.50	25.00	50.00	125.00
	1910 ЗБ	.150	12.50	25.00	50.00	125.00
	1911 ЗБ	.800	BV	10.00	15.00	40.00
	1912 ЗБ	7.085	BV	10.00	15.00	40.00
	1913 ЗБ	6.420	—	—	Rare	—
	1913 ВС	I.A.	BV	10.00	15.00	40.00
	1914 ВС	1.200	BV	12.00	20.00	50.00

75 KOPEKS

Refer to Poland

ROUBLE

.750 SILVER

MINT: MOSCOW ММД

C#	Date	Mintage	VG	Fine	VF	XF
47.1	1762 АМ	—	60.00	175.00	275.00	550.00

MINT: ST. PETERSBURG СПБ

C#	Date	Mintage	VG	Fine	VF	XF
47.2	1762 НК	—	50.00	150.00	250.00	500.00

MINT: MOSCOW ММД

C#	Date	Mintage	VG	Fine	VF	XF
67.1	1762 ДМ	.406	75.00	150.00	300.00	500.00
	1763 ЕІ	.095	75.00	150.00	300.00	500.00
	176463 ЕІ	.264	30.00	60.00	100.00	175.00
	176563 ЕІ	.121	75.00	150.00	300.00	500.00

MINT: ST. PETERSBURG СПБ

C#	Date	Mintage	VG	Fine	VF	XF
67.2	1762 НК	1.459	30.00	60.00	100.00	175.00
	1763 НК	1.817	30.00	60.00	100.00	175.00
	1763 Ян	I.A.	75.00	150.00	300.00	500.00
	1764 Ян	3.016	40.00	80.00	125.00	200.00
	1764 СА	I.A.	40.00	80.00	125.00	200.00
	1765 Ян	2.782	30.00	60.00	100.00	175.00
	1765 СА	I.A.	30.00	60.00	100.00	175.00

MINT: MOSCOW ММД

Rev: Similar to C#67.1.

C#	Date	Mintage	VG	Fine	VF	XF
67a.1	1766 АШ	—	200.00	400.00	600.00	1000.
	1767 ЕІ	.025	75.00	150.00	300.00	500.00
	1768 АШ	.491	100.00	200.00	400.00	700.00
	1768 ЕААР	I.A.	40.00	80.00	125.00	200.00
	1769 ЕІ	.277	75.00	150.00	300.00	500.00
	1770 ДМ	.080	100.00	200.00	400.00	700.00
	1775 СА	1.648	75.00	150.00	300.00	500.00

MINT: ST. PETERSBURG СПБ

C#	Date	Mintage	VG	Fine	VF	XF
67a.2	1766 ЯІ	1.682	30.00	60.00	100.00	175.00
	1766 АШ	I.A.	30.00	60.00	100.00	175.00
	1767 АШ	1.210	30.00	60.00	100.00	175.00
	1767 ЕІ	I.A.	75.00	150.00	300.00	500.00
	1768 ЕІ	1.028	75.00	150.00	300.00	500.00
	1768 АШ	I.A.	75.00	150.00	300.00	500.00
	1768 СА	I.A.	30.00	60.00	100.00	175.00
	1769 СА	2.200	30.00	60.00	100.00	175.00
	1770 СА	1.198	100.00	200.00	400.00	700.00
	1770 ЯЧ	I.A.	30.00	60.00	100.00	175.00
	1771 ЯЧ	1.025	30.00	60.00	100.00	175.00
	1771 АШ	I.A.	30.00	60.00	100.00	175.00
	1772 ЯЧ	1.050	30.00	60.00	100.00	175.00
	1772 АШ	I.A.	30.00	60.00	100.00	175.00
	1773 ЯЧ	2.378	75.00	150.00	300.00	500.00
	1773 ФЛ	I.A.	40.00	80.00	125.00	200.00
	1774 ФЛ	2.770	30.00	60.00	100.00	175.00
	1775 ФЛ	I.A.	30.00	60.00	100.00	175.00
	1775 ЯЧ	I.A.	40.00	80.00	125.00	200.00
	1776 ЯЧ	2.625	30.00	60.00	100.00	175.00

MINT: ST. PETERSBURG СПБ

Rev: Similar to C#67.

C#	Date	Mintage	VG	Fine	VF	XF
67b	1777	—	100.00	200.00	400.00	700.00
	1777 ФЛ	2.000	30.00	60.00	100.00	175.00
	1778 ФЛ	1.700	30.00	60.00	100.00	175.00
	1779 ФЛ	.413	30.00	60.00	100.00	175.00
	1780 ИЗ	2.866	40.00	80.00	125.00	200.00
	1781 ИЗ	2.283	40.00	80.00	125.00	200.00
	1782 ИЗ	1.200	40.00	80.00	125.00	200.00

MINT: ST. PETERSBURG СПБ

C#	Date	Mintage	VG	Fine	VF	XF
67c	1783 ИЗ	1.880	40.00	80.00	125.00	200.00
	1783 ММ	I.A.	100.00	200.00	400.00	700.00
	1784 ММ	.144	75.00	150.00	300.00	500.00
	1785 ЯА	.139	40.00	80.00	125.00	200.00
	1786 ЯА	2.600	40.00	80.00	125.00	200.00
	1787 ЯА	.900	40.00	80.00	125.00	200.00
	1788 ЯА	1.475	40.00	80.00	125.00	200.00
	1789 ЯА	.500	40.00	80.00	125.00	200.00
	1790 ЯА	.239	40.00	80.00	125.00	200.00
	1791 ЯА	.274	40.00	80.00	125.00	200.00

C#	Date	Mintage	VG	Fine	VF	XF
	1792 ЯА	1.509	40.00	80.00	125.00	200.00
	1793 ЯА	1.124	40.00	80.00	125.00	200.00
	1793 АК	I.A.	40.00	80.00	125.00	200.00
	1794 АК	.895	40.00	80.00	125.00	200.00
	1795 АК	.677	40.00	80.00	125.00	200.00
	1795 ІС	I.A.	75.00	150.00	300.00	500.00
	1796 ІС	.954	40.00	80.00	125.00	200.00

.917 GOLD

MINT: ST. PETERSBURG

C#	Date	Mintage	Fine	VF	XF	Unc
76	1779	—	135.00	200.00	275.00	400.00

SILVER

MINT: ST. PETERSBURG БМ

"Albertus Rouble"

C#	Date	Mintage	VG	Fine	VF	XF
100	1796	—	275.00	500.00	750.00	1250.

MINT: ST. PETERSBURG СМ

40mm

C#	Date	Mintage	VG	Fine	VF	XF
101	1797 ФЦ	.920	75.00	150.00	250.00	500.00

MINT: ST. PETERSBURG

Smaller planchet, 38mm.

C#	Date	Mintage	VG	Fine	VF	XF
101a	1798 МБ	3.279	25.00	50.00	100.00	200.00
	1798 ОМ	I.A.	—	—	Rare	—
	1799 МБ	3.124	25.00	50.00	100.00	200.00
	1799 ФЦ	I.A.	25.00	50.00	100.00	200.00
	1799 АИ	I.A.	—	—	Rare	—
	1800 ОМ	1.870	25.00	50.00	100.00	200.00
	1800 АИ	I.A.	—	—	Rare	—
	1801 АИ	3.143	25.00	50.00	100.00	200.00
	1801 ФЦ	I.A.	25.00	50.00	100.00	200.00
	1801 ОМ	I.A.	—	—	Rare	—

20.7300 gm., .868 SILVER, .5785 oz ASW

MINT: ST. PETERSBURG СПБ

C#	Date	Mintage	VG	Fine	VF	XF
125	1802 АИ	5.360	22.00	45.00	90.00	180.00
	1803 АИ	2.429	22.00	45.00	90.00	180.00
	1803 ФГ	I.A.	45.00	90.00	180.00	360.00
	1804 ФГ	4.355	22.00	45.00	90.00	180.00
	1805 ФГ	2.020	22.00	45.00	90.00	180.00

MINT: ST. PETERSBURG СПБ

C#	Date	Mintage	VG	Fine	VF	XF
125a	1807 ФГ	.533	45.00	70.00	140.00	280.00
	1808 ФГ	1.701	35.00	60.00	120.00	240.00
	1808 МК	I.A.	35.00	60.00	120.00	240.00
	1809 МК	2.177	35.00	60.00	120.00	240.00
	1809 ФГ	I.A.	35.00	60.00	120.00	240.00
	1810 ФГ	1.682	35.00	60.00	120.00	240.00

MINT: ST. PETERSBURG СПБ

C#	Date	Mintage	VG	Fine	VF	XF
130	1810 ФГ	I.A.	—	—	Rare	—
	1811 ФГ	2.675	17.50	30.00	50.00	100.00
	1812 МФ	4.076	17.50	22.50	40.00	80.00
	1813 ПС	5.210	17.50	22.50	40.00	80.00
	1814 МФ	3.600	17.50	30.00	50.00	100.00
	1814 ПС	I.A.	—	—	—	—
	1814	Inc. Ab.	17.50	22.50	40.00	80.00
	1815 МФ	4.750	17.50	22.50	40.00	80.00
	1816 МФ	1.782	17.50	22.50	40.00	80.00
	1816 ПС	Inc. Ab.	17.50	25.00	50.00	100.00
	1817 ПС	11.775	17.50	22.50	40.00	80.00
	1818 ПС	16.275	17.50	22.50	40.00	80.00
	1818 СП	Inc. Ab.	17.50	22.50	40.00	80.00
	1818	Inc. Ab.	17.50	22.50	40.00	80.00
	1819 ПС	6.355	17.50	22.50	40.00	80.00
	1820 ПА	1.962	17.50	22.50	40.00	80.00
	1820 ПС	Inc. Ab.	—	—	Rare	—
	1821 ПД	.840	17.50	22.50	40.00	80.00
	1822 ПД	3.120	17.50	22.50	40.00	80.00
	1823 ПД	2.955	17.50	22.50	40.00	80.00
	1824/3	—		—	—	—
	1824 ПД	2.035	17.50	22.50	40.00	80.00
	1825 ПД	1.461	17.50	22.50	40.00	80.00
	1825 НГ	Inc. Ab.	17.50	22.50	40.00	80.00

MINT: ST. PETERSBURG СПБ

C#	Date	Mintage	VG	Fine	VF	XF
155	1826 НГ	.730	17.50	30.00	50.00	100.00

MINT: ST. PETERSBURG СПБ

C#	Date	Mintage	VG	Fine	VF	XF
161	1826 НГ	Inc. Ab.	17.50	30.00	50.00	100.00
	1827 НГ	.584	17.50	30.00	50.00	100.00
	1828 НГ	2.530	17.50	30.00	50.00	100.00
	1829 НГ	5.510	17.50	30.00	50.00	100.00
	1830 НГ	6.010	17.50	30.00	50.00	100.00
	1831 НГ	3.670	17.50	30.00	50.00	100.00

MINT: ST. PETERSBURG СПБ

C#	Date	Mintage	VG	Fine	VF	XF
168.1	1832 НГ	1.941	17.50	20.00	35.00	75.00
	1833 НГ	1.711	17.50	20.00	35.00	75.00
	1834 НГ	2.270	17.50	20.00	35.00	75.00
	1835 НГ	.243	17.50	20.00	35.00	75.00
	1836 НГ	1.101	17.50	20.00	35.00	75.00
	1837 НГ	1.477	17.50	20.00	35.00	75.00
	1838 НГ	.232	17.50	20.00	35.00	75.00
	1839 НГ	.035	—	—	Rare	—
	1840 НГ	2.627	17.50	20.00	35.00	75.00
	1841 НГ	6.155	17.50	20.00	35.00	75.00
	1842 АЧ	4.965	17.50	20.00	35.00	75.00
	1843 АЧ	5.320	17.50	20.00	35.00	75.00
	1844 КБ	2.923	17.50	20.00	35.00	75.00
	1845 КБ	.682	17.50	20.00	35.00	75.00
	1846 ПА	3.523	17.50	20.00	35.00	75.00
	1847 ПА	.562	17.50	20.00	35.00	75.00
	1848 НІ	1.542	17.50	20.00	35.00	75.00
	1849 ПА	1.708	17.50	20.00	35.00	75.00

C#	Date	Mintage	VG	Fine	VF	XF
168.1	1850 ПА	1.600	17.50	20.00	35.00	75.00
	1851 ПА	2.400	17.50	20.00	35.00	75.00
	1852 ПА	2.560	17.50	20.00	35.00	75.00
	1852 НІ	I.A.	—	—	Rare	—
	1853 НІ	2.160	17.50	20.00	35.00	75.00
	1854 НІ	3.070	17.50	20.00	35.00	75.00

MINT: WARSAW МШ

C#	Date	Mintage	VG	Fine	VF	XF
168.2	1842	.257	—	—	Rare	—
	1943	.267	17.50	22.50	40.00	80.00
	1844	2.364	17.50	22.50	40.00	80.00
	1845	.345	17.50	22.50	40.00	80.00
	1846	.5111	17.50	22.50	40.00	80.00
	1847	.987	17.50	22.50	40.00	80.00

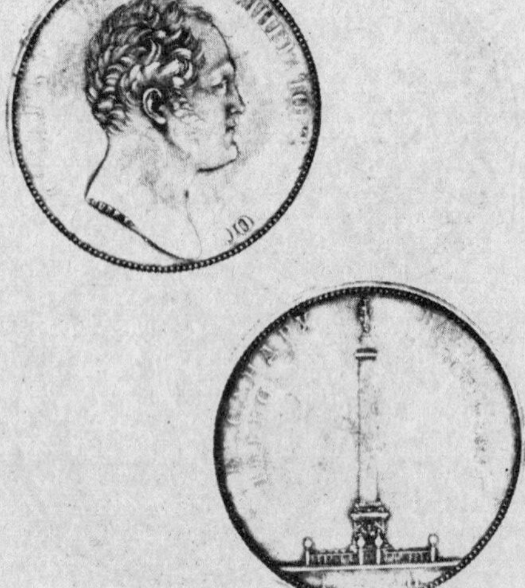

MINT: ST. PETERSBURG СПБ

Alexander I Monument

C#	Date	Mintage	VG	Fine	VF	XF
169	1834	.015	50.00	100.00	175.00	350.00

MINT: ST. PETERSBURG СПБ

Battle of Borodino Memorial

C#	Date	Mintage	VG	Fine	VF	XF
170	1839 НГ	.160	65.00	125.00	250.00	550.00

NOTE: The 1841 marriage Rouble is a medal.

MINT: ST. PETERSBURG СПБ

Y#	Date	Mintage	Fine	VF	XF	Unc
18	1855 НІ	1.060	20.00	40.00	75.00	180.00
	1856 МБ	1.388	20.00	40.00	75.00	180.00
	1857 МБ	.250	20.00	40.00	80.00	200.00
	1858 МБ	.570	20.00	40.00	80.00	200.00

MINT: ST. PETERSBURG (NO MINTMARK)

Nicholas I Memorial Commemorative

Y#	Date	Mintage	Fine	VF	XF	Unc
28	1859	.050	50.00	100.00	175.00	350.00

MINT: ST. PETERSBURG СПБ

Y#	Date	Mintage	Fine	VF	XF	Unc
25	1859 МБ	.014	30.00	60.00	120.00	280.00
	1860 МБ	.018	25.00	50.00	100.00	250.00
	1861 МБ	.076	20.00	35.00	70.00	180.00
	1861 МИ	I.A.	37.50	75.00	150.00	350.00
	1862 МИ	.022	35.00	70.00	140.00	320.00
	1863 АБ	.005	37.50	75.00	150.00	350.00
	1864 НФ	.114	17.50	20.00	40.00	100.00
	1865 НФ	.115	17.50	20.00	40.00	100.00
	1866 НІ	.110	17.50	20.00	40.00	100.00
	1866 НФ	I.A.	17.50	25.00	50.00	125.00
	1867 НІ	.425	17.50	22.50	35.00	75.00
	1868 НІ	.775	17.50	22.50	35.00	75.00
	1869 НІ	.285	17.50	22.50	35.00	75.00
	1870 НІ	.386	17.50	22.50	35.00	75.00
	1871 НІ	.884	17.50	22.50	35.00	75.00
	1872 НІ	.978	17.50	22.50	35.00	75.00
	1873 НІ	.673	17.50	22.50	35.00	75.00
	1874 НІ	.648	17.50	22.50	35.00	75.00
	1875 НІ	.687	17.50	22.50	35.00	75.00

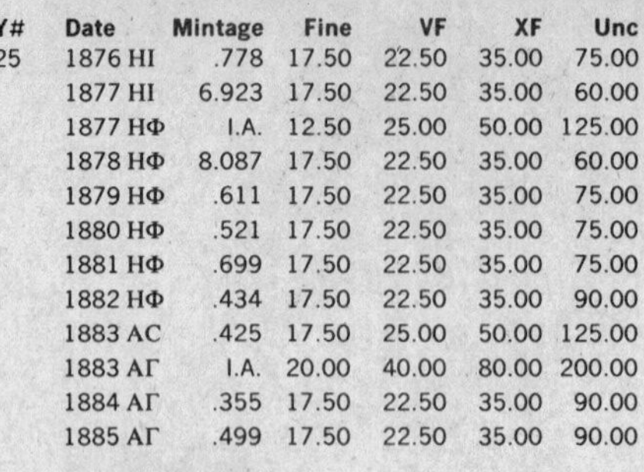

Y#	Date	Mintage	Fine	VF	XF	Unc
25	1876 НІ	.778	17.50	22.50	35.00	75.00
	1877 НІ	6.923	17.50	22.50	35.00	60.00
	1877 НФ	I.A.	12.50	25.00	50.00	125.00
	1878 НФ	8.087	17.50	22.50	35.00	60.00
	1879 НФ	.611	17.50	22.50	35.00	75.00
	1880 НФ	.521	17.50	22.50	35.00	75.00
	1881 НФ	.699	17.50	22.50	35.00	75.00
	1882 НФ	.434	17.50	22.50	35.00	90.00
	1883 АС	.425	17.50	25.00	50.00	125.00
	1883 АГ	I.A.	20.00	40.00	80.00	200.00
	1884 АГ	.355	17.50	22.50	35.00	90.00
	1885 АГ	.499	17.50	22.50	35.00	90.00

MINT: ST. PETERSBURG (NO MINTMARK)

Alexander III Coronation

Y#	Date	Mintage	Fine	VF	XF	Unc
43	1883	.279	25.00	50.00	100.00	225.00

.900 SILVER, 19.996 gms.

MINT: ST. PETERSBURG (NO MINTMARK)

Mintmaster's initials and stars found on edge.

Y#	Date	Mintage	Fine	VF	XF	Unc
46	1886 АГ	.487	20.00	40.00	80.00	200.00
	1887 АГ	.490	20.00	40.00	80.00	200.00
	1888 АГ	.498	20.00	40.00	80.00	200.00
	1889 АГ	.001	50.00	100.00	200.00	500.00
	1890 АГ	.090	25.00	50.00	100.00	250.00
	1891 АГ	1.117	20.00	40.00	80.00	200.00
	1892 АГ	2.131	20.00	40.00	80.00	200.00
	1893 АГ	1.845	20.00	40.00	80.00	200.00
	1894 АГ	1.503	25.00	50.00	100.00	250.00

MINT: BRUSSELS - MINTMARK - 2 Stars on rim

Y#	Date	Mintage	Fine	VF	XF	Unc
59.1	1897	26.000	BV	17.50	30.00	75.00
	1898	14.000	BV	17.50	30.00	75.00
	1899	10.000	BV	17.50	30.00	75.00

MINT: PARIS - MINTMARK - Star on rim

Y#	Date	Mintage	Fine	VF	XF	Unc
59.2	1896	12.000	BV	17.50	30.00	75.00
	1898	5.000	BV	17.50	30.00	75.00

MINT: ST. PETERSBURG (NO MINTMARK)

Y#	Date	Mintage	Fine	VF	XF	Unc
59.3	1895 АГ	1.240	17.50	25.00	50.00	120.00
	1896 АГ	12.540	BV	17.50	30.00	75.00
	1897 АГ	18.515	BV	17.50	30.00	75.00
	1898 АГ	18.725	BV	17.50	30.00	75.00
	1899 ЗБ	6.502	20.00	17.50	30.00	75.00
	1899 ФЗ	I.A.	BV	17.50	30.00	75.00
	1899 I3 (Error)	Inc. Ab.	—	—	Rare	—
	1900 ФЗ	11.484	BV	17.50	30.00	75.00
	1901 ФЗ	2.608	BV	17.50	30.00	75.00
	1901 AP*	I.A.	17.50	25.00	40.00	90.00
	1902 AH	.140	20.00	35.00	60.00	150.00
	1903 AP	.055	50.00	100.00	200.00	500.00
	1904 AP	.012	50.00	100.00	200.00	500.00
	1905 AP	.020	50.00	100.00	200.00	500.00
	1906 ЗБ	.045	50.00	100.00	200.00	500.00
	1907 ЗБ	.400	BV	20.00	40.00	100.00
	1908 ЗБ	.130	20.00	35.00	60.00	150.00
	1909 ЗБ	.050	50.00	100.00	200.00	500.00
	1910 ЗБ	.075	30.00	60.00	120.00	300.00
	1911 ЗБ	.129	25.00	50.00	100.00	250.00
	1912 ЗБ	2.111	BV	17.50	25.00	60.00
	1913 ЗБ	.022	65.00	125.00	250.00	550.00
	1913 BC	I.A.	65.00	125.00	250.00	550.00
	1914 BC	.536	37.50	75.00	150.00	300.00
	1915 BC	*5,000	37.50	75.00	150.00	300.00

NOTE: Varieties exist with plain edge. These are mint errors and rare.

MINT: ST. PETERSBURG (NO MINTMARK)

Nicholas II Coronation

Y#	Date	Mintage	Fine	VF	XF	Unc
60	1896	.190	20.00	35.00	70.00	150.00

MINT: ST. PETERSBURG (NO MINTMARK)

Alexander II Memorial

Y#	Date	Mintage	Fine	VF	XF	Unc
61	1898 АГ	*5,000	100.00	200.00	450.00	900.00

MINT: ST. PETERSBURG (NO MINTMARK)

Napoleon Defeat Centennial

Y#	Date	Mintage	Fine	VF	XF	Unc
68	1912 ЗБ	.046	50.00	100.00	200.00	350.00

MINT: ST. PETERSBURG (NO MINTMARK)

Alexander III Memorial

Y#	Date	Mintage	Fine	VF	XF	Unc
69	1912 ЗБ	*2,400	250.00	500.00	1000.	1700.

MINT: ST. PETERSBURG (NO MINTMARK)

300th Anniversary Romanov Dynasty

Y#	Date	Mintage	Fine	VF	XF	Unc
70	1913 BC	1.500	BV	17.50	25.00	50.00

MINT: ST. PETERSBURG (NO MINTMARK)

200th Anniversary Battle of Gangut

Y#	Date	Mintage	Fine	VF	XF	Unc
71	1914 BC	*	—	700.00	1400.	2300.

***NOTE:** Only 317 pieces were issued.

1-1/2 ROUBLES

For similar coins not listed here refer to Poland.

SILVER

MINT: ST. PETERSBURG (NO MINTMARK)

C#	Date	Mintage	VG	Fine	VF	XF
172	1835	36 pcs.	—	3000.	5000.	8000.
	1836	50 pcs.	—	3000.	5000.	8000.

NOTE: The above coins were struck as presentation pieces.

.868 SILVER

MINT: ST. PETERSBURG СПБ

Battle of Borodino Memorial

C#	Date	Mintage	VG	Fine	VF	XF
173	1839	6,000	—	700.00	1000.	1600.

2 ROUBLES

.917 GOLD

MINT: ST. PETERSBURG СПБ

C#	Date	Mintage	Fine	VF	XF	Unc
77	1766	—	250.00	400.00	550.00	700.00

MINT: ST. PETERSBURG СПБ

C#	Date	Mintage	Fine	VF	XF	Unc
77c	1785	—	275.00	450.00	600.00	800.00

3 ROUBLES

PLATINUM

NOTE: The low mintage figures incorporated in the following listings of Russian platinum issues are not necessarily reflective of relative scarcity as many of the issues were restruck at later dates, using original dies in unrecorded quantities.

MINT: ST. PETERSBURG СПБ

C#	Date	Mintage	Fine	VF	XF
177	1828	.020	200.00	250.00	300.00
	1829	.043	200.00	250.00	300.00
	1830	.106	200.00	250.00	300.00
	1831	.086	200.00	250.00	300.00
	1832	.065	200.00	250.00	300.00
	1833	.084	200.00	250.00	300.00
	1834	.090	200.00	250.00	300.00
	1835	.138	200.00	250.00	300.00
	1836	.043	200.00	250.00	300.00
	1837	.046	200.00	250.00	300.00
	1838	.048	200.00	250.00	300.00
	1839	2 pcs.	—	Rare	—
	1840	1 pc.	—	Rare	—
	1841	.016	200.00	250.00	300.00
	1842	.146	200.00	250.00	300.00
	1843	.172	200.00	250.00	300.00
	1844	.214	200.00	250.00	300.00
	1845	.050	200.00	250.00	300.00

For similar coins not listed here refer to Poland.

.917 GOLD, 3.926 gms.

MINT: ST. PETERSBURG СПБ

Y#	Date	Mintage	VF	XF	Unc
26	1869 НІ	.143	300.00	475.00	700.00
	1870 НІ	.200	300.00	475.00	700.00
	1871 НІ	.200	300.00	475.00	700.00
	1872 НІ	.100	300.00	475.00	700.00
	1873 НІ	.077	300.00	475.00	700.00
	1874 НІ	.270	300.00	475.00	700.00
	1875 НІ	.100	300.00	475.00	700.00
	1876 НІ	.063	300.00	475.00	700.00
	1877 НІ	.050	300.00	475.00	700.00
	1877 НФ	I.A.	300.00	475.00	700.00
	1878 НФ	.194	300.00	475.00	700.00
	1879 НФ	5 pcs.	—	Rare	—
	1880 НФ	.100	300.00	475.00	700.00
	1881 НФ	.048	300.00	475.00	700.00
	1882 НФ	6 pcs.	—	Rare	—
	1883 ДС	9,000	300.00	475.00	700.00
	1883 АГ	I.A.	—	Rare	—
	1884 АГ	.047	300.00	475.00	700.00
	1885 АГ	.029	300.00	475.00	700.00

5 ROUBLES

.917 GOLD

MINT: ST. PETERSBURG СПБ

C#	Date	Mintage	Fine	VF	XF	Unc
49	1762	—	500.00	750.00	1250.	2000.

MINT: MOSCOW ММД

C#	Date	Mintage	Fine	VF	XF	Unc
78.1	1763	—	—	—	Rare	—

MINT: ST. PETERSBURG СПБ

C#	Date	Mintage	Fine	VF	XF	Unc
78.2	1762	.020	325.00	500.00	650.00	800.00
	1763	7,515	—	—	Rare	—
	1764	.024	325.00	500.00	650.00	800.00
	1765	.051	275.00	400.00	550.00	700.00

MINT: ST. PETERSBURG СПБ

Mature bust.

C#	Date	Mintage	Fine	VF	XF	Unc
78a	1766	.034	275.00	400.00	550.00	700.00
	1767	.090	275.00	400.00	550.00	700.00
	1768	.020	275.00	400.00	550.00	700.00
	1769	.016	275.00	400.00	550.00	700.00
	1770	.016	325.00	500.00	650.00	800.00
	1771	.012	275.00	400.00	550.00	700.00
	1772	.014	275.00	400.00	550.00	700.00
	1773	.016	275.00	400.00	550.00	700.00
	1774	.015	275.00	400.00	550.00	700.00
	1775	.010	325.00	500.00	650.00	800.00
	1776	.020	275.00	400.00	550.00	700.00
	1777	—	—	—	Rare	—

MINT: ST. PETERSBURG СПБ

C#	Date	Mintage	Fine	VF	XF	Unc
78b	1778	.024	325.00	500.00	650.00	800.00
	1780	.026	275.00	400.00	550.00	700.00
	1781	.063	275.00	400.00	550.00	700.00
	1782	.039	—	400.00	550.00	700.00

MINT: ST. PETERSBURG СПБ

C#	Date	Mintage	Fine	VF	XF	Unc
78c	1783	.033	275.00	400.00	550.00	700.00
	1784	3,000	450.00	650.00	800.00	1000.
	1785	.047	275.00	400.00	550.00	700.00
	1786	.074	275.00	400.00	550.00	700.00
	1788	.012	450.00	650.00	800.00	1000.
	1789	.012	450.00	650.00	800.00	1000.
	1790	.020	325.00	500.00	650.00	800.00
	1791	.048	275.00	400.00	550.00	700.00
	1792	.067	275.00	400.00	550.00	700.00
	1794	.045	275.00	400.00	550.00	700.00
	1795	6,906	325.00	500.00	650.00	800.00
	1796	.020	275.00	400.00	550.00	700.00

.986 GOLD

MINT: ST. PETERSBURG СМ

C#	Date	Mintage	VF	XF	Unc
104.1	1798 ФЦ	.157	700.00	1000.	1350.
	1798 ОГ	I.A.	700.00	1000.	1350.
	1799 АИ	.107	700.00	1000.	1350.
	1800 ОМ	.065	700.00	1000.	1350.
	1801 АИ	.180	700.00	1000.	1350.

MINT: ST. PETERSBURG СП

C#	Date	Mintage	VF	XF	Unc
104.2	1800 ОМ	Inc. Ab.	700.00	1000.	1350.

MINT: ST. PETERSBURG СПБ

C#	Date	Mintage	VF	XF	Unc
131	1802	15 pcs.	—	Rare	—
	1803 ХЛ	6 pcs.	—	Rare	—
	1804 ХЛ	.040	700.00	1000.	1350.
	1805 ХЛ	.008	700.00	1000.	1350.

6.5440 gm., .917 GOLD, .1929 oz AGW

MINT: ST. PETERSBURG СПБ

C#	Date	Mintage	VF	XF	Unc
132	1817 ФГ	.710	200.00	325.00	475.00
	1818 МФ	1.520	200.00	325.00	475.00
	1819 МФ	.963	200.00	325.00	475.00
	1822 МФ	—	200.00	325.00	475.00
	1823 ПС	.444	200.00	325.00	475.00
	1824 ПС	.276	200.00	325.00	475.00
	1825 ПС	.101	—	Rare	—
	1825 ПД	I.A.	200.00	325.00	475.00

MINT: ST. PETERSBURG СПБ

Similar to C#132.

C#	Date	Mintage	VF	XF	Unc
174	1826 ПД	.212	200.00	325.00	475.00
	1827 ПД	—	—	Rare	—
	1828 ПД	.604	200.00	325.00	475.00
	1829 ПД	.732	200.00	325.00	475.00
	1830 ПД	.490	200.00	325.00	475.00
	1831 ПД	.845	200.00	325.00	475.00

MINT: ST. PETERSBURG СПБ

Discovery of Gold at Kolyvan Mines

C#	Date	Mintage	VF	XF	Unc
176	1832 ПД	1,000	1500.	2000.	—

MINT: ST. PETERSBURG СПБ

C#	Date	Mintage	VF	XF	Unc
175.1	1832 ПД	.480	125.00	150.00	225.00
	1833 ПД	.829	125.00	150.00	225.00
	1834 ПД	1.350	125.00	150.00	225.00
	1835 ПД	1.440	125.00	150.00	225.00
	1835	Inc. Ab.	—	Rare	—
	1836 ПД	.953	125.00	150.00	225.00
	1837 ПД	.048	125.00	150.00	225.00
	1838 ПД	.301	125.00	150.00	225.00
	1839 АЧ	1.609	125.00	150.00	225.00
	1840 АЧ	1.277	125.00	150.00	225.00
	1841 АЧ	1.668	125.00	150.00	225.00
	1842 АЧ	2.180	125.00	150.00	225.00
	1843 АЧ	1.852	125.00	150.00	225.00
	1844 КБ	2.364	125.00	150.00	225.00
	1845 КБ	2.841	125.00	150.00	225.00
	1846 АГ	3.442	125.00	150.00	225.00

MINT: WARSAW МШ

C#	Date	Mintage	VF	XF	Unc
175.2	1842	695 pcs.	1000.	1500.	—
	1846	62 pcs.	1500.	2000.	—
	1848	485 pcs.	—	—	—
	1849	133 pcs.	1000.	1500.	—

MINT: ST. PETERSBURG СПБ

Different eagle

C#	Date	Mintage	VF	XF	Unc
175.3	1846 АГ	Inc. 1846	125.00	150.00	225.00
	1847 АГ	3.900	125.00	150.00	225.00
	1848 АГ	2.900	125.00	150.00	225.00
	1849 АГ	3.100	125.00	150.00	225.00
	1850 АГ	3.900	125.00	150.00	225.00
	1851 АГ	3.400	125.00	150.00	225.00
	1852 АГ	3.900	125.00	150.00	225.00
	1853 АГ	3.900	125.00	150.00	225.00
	1854 АГ	3.900	125.00	150.00	225.00

MINT: ST. PETERSBURG СПБ

Y#	Date	Mintage	VF	XF	Unc
A26	1855 АГ	3.900	125.00	150.00	225.00
	1856 АГ	3.800	125.00	150.00	225.00
	1857 АГ	4.500	125.00	150.00	225.00
	1858 ПФ	3.500	125.00	150.00	225.00

MINT: ST. PETERSBURG СПБ

Y#	Date	Mintage	VF	XF	Unc
B26	1859 ПФ	3.900	125.00	150.00	225.00
	1860 ПФ	3.600	100.00	140.00	200.00
	1860 ПФ	3.500	125.00	150.00	225.00
	1862 ПФ	6.354	125.00	150.00	225.00
	1863 МИ	7.200	125.00	150.00	225.00
	1864 АС	3.900	125.00	150.00	225.00
	1865 АС	3.901	125.00	150.00	225.00
	1865 СШ	I.A.	125.00	150.00	225.00
	1866 СШ	3.900	140.00	175.00	225.00
	1866 HI	I.A.	140.00	150.00	225.00
	1867 HI	3.494	140.00	150.00	225.00
	1868 HI	3.400	140.00	150.00	225.00
	1869 HI	3.900	140.00	150.00	225.00
	1870 HI	5.000	140.00	150.00	225.00
	1871 HI	8.000	140.00	150.00	225.00
	1872 HI	2.400	140.00	150.00	225.00
	1873 HI	3.000	140.00	150.00	225.00
	1874 HI	4.800	140.00	150.00	225.00
	1875 HI	4.000	140.00	150.00	225.00
	1876 HI	6.000	140.00	150.00	225.00
	1877 HI	6.600	140.00	150.00	225.00
	1877 НФ	I.A.	140.00	150.00	225.00
	1878 НФ	6.800	140.00	150.00	225.00
	1879 НФ	7.225	140.00	150.00	225.00
	1880 НФ	6.200	140.00	150.00	225.00
B26	1881 НФ	5.500	140.00	150.00	225.00
	1882 НФ	4.547	140.00	150.00	225.00
	1883 ДС	5.632	140.00	150.00	225.00
	1883 АГ	I.A.	140.00	150.00	225.00
	1884 АГ	4.801	140.00	150.00	225.00
	1885 АГ	5.343	140.00	150.00	225.00

6.4516 gm., .900 GOLD, .1867 oz AGW

MINT: ST. PETERSBURG (NO MINTMARK)

Y#	Date	Mintage	VF	XF	Unc
42	1886 АГ	.351	BV	125.00	150.00
	1887 АГ	3.261	BV	125.00	150.00
	1888 АГ	5.257	BV	135.00	175.00
	1889 АГ	4.200	BV	135.00	160.00
	1890 АГ	5.600	BV	125.00	150.00
	1891 АГ	.541	BV	125.00	150.00
	1892 АГ	.128	BV	125.00	150.00
	1893 АГ	.598	BV	125.00	150.00
	1894 АГ	.598	BV	125.00	150.00

MINT: ST. PETERSBURG

Y#	Date	Mintage	VF	XF	Unc
A61	1895 АГ	36 pcs.	—	—	7500.
	1896 АГ	33 pcs.	—	—	7500.

4.3013 gm., .900 GOLD, .1244 oz AGW

MINT: ST. PETERSBURG

Y#	Date	Mintage	VF	XF	Unc
62	1897 АГ	5.372	BV	80.00	90.00
	1898 АГ	52.378	BV	80.00	90.00
	1899 ЭБ	20.400	BV	80.00	90.00
	1899 ФЗ	I.A.	BV	80.00	90.00
	1900 ФЗ	31.077	BV	80.00	90.00
	1901 ФЗ	7.500	BV	80.00	90.00
	1901 АР	I.A.	BV	80.00	90.00
	1902 АР	6.240	BV	80.00	90.00
	1903 АР	5.148	BV	80.00	90.00
	1904 АР	2.016	BV	80.00	90.00
	1906 ЭБ	10 pcs.	—	Rare	—
	1907 ЭБ	109 pcs.	—	Rare	—
	1909 ЭБ	—	BV	80.00	90.00
	1910 ЭБ	.200	BV	80.00	100.00
	1911 ЭБ	.100	BV	80.00	100.00

6 ROUBLES

PLATINUM

MINT: ST. PETERSBURG СПБ

C#	Date	Mintage	VF	XF	Unc
178	1829	828 pcs.	3000.	4000.	5000.
	1830	8,610	3000.	4000.	5000.
	1831	2,784	3000.	4000.	5000.
	1832	1,502	3000.	4000.	5000.
	1833	302 pcs.	3000.	4000.	5000.
	1834	11 pcs.	3000.	4000.	5000.
	1835	107 pcs.	3000.	4000.	5000.
	1836	11 pcs.	3000.	4000.	5000.
	1837	253 pcs.	3000.	4000.	5000.
	1838	12 pcs.	3000.	4000.	5000.
	1839	2 pcs.	—	Rare	—
	1840	1 pc.	—	Rare	—
	1841	170 pcs.	3000.	4000.	5000.
	1842	121 pcs.	3000.	4000.	5000.
	1843	127 pcs.	3000.	4000.	5000.
	1844	4 pcs.	3000.	4000.	5000.
	1845	2 pcs.	3000.	4000.	5000.

7-1/2 ROUBLES

6.4516 gm., .900 GOLD, .1867 oz AGW

MINT: ST. PETERSBURG

Y#	Date	Mintage	VF	XF	Unc
63	1897 АГ	16.829	125.00	150.00	200.00

10 ROUBLES

.917 GOLD

MINT: ST. PETERSBURG

C#	Date	Mintage	Fine	VF	XF	Unc
49	1762	—	850.00	1250.	2000.	3000.

MINT: MOSCOW ММД

C#	Date	Mintage	Fine	VF	XF	Unc
79.1	1762	.032	550.00	800.00	1000.	1500.
	1763	—	—	—	Rare	—

MINT: ST. PETERSBURG СПБ

C#	Date	Mintage	Fine	VF	XF	Unc
79.2	1762	Inc. Ab.	325.00	500.00	650.00	800.00
	1763	.021	325.00	500.00	650.00	800.00
	1764	.030	300.00	450.00	600.00	750.00
	1765	.032	300.00	450.00	600.00	750.00

MINT: ST. PETERSBURG СПБ

C#	Date	Mintage	Fine	VF	XF	Unc
79a	1766	.159	300.00	450.00	600.00	750.00
	1767	.092	300.00	450.00	600.00	750.00
	1768	.050	300.00	450.00	600.00	750.00
	1769	.080	300.00	450.00	600.00	750.00
	1770	.010	325.00	500.00	650.00	800.00
	1771	.031	300.00	450.00	600.00	750.00

C#	Date	Mintage	Fine	VF	XF	Unc
79a	1772	.051	300.00	450.00	600.00	750.00
	1773	.054	300.00	450.00	600.00	750.00
	1774	.053	300.00	450.00	600.00	750.00
	1775	.050	300.00	450.00	600.00	750.00
	1776	.068	300.00	450.00	600.00	750.00

MINT: ST. PETERSBURG СПБ

C#	Date	Mintage	Fine	VF	XF	Unc
79b	1777	.015	325.00	500.00	650.00	800.00
	1778	.084	300.00	450.00	600.00	750.00
	1779	.015	300.00	450.00	600.00	750.00
	1780	.072	300.00	450.00	600.00	750.00
	1781	.023	300.00	450.00	600.00	750.00
	1782	4,000	425.00	600.00	750.00	950.00

MINT: ST. PETERSBURG СПБ

Older bust.

C#	Date	Mintage	Fine	VF	XF	Unc
79c	1783	.026	300.00	450.00	600.00	750.00
	1785	.020	300.00	450.00	600.00	750.00
	1786	Inc. Ab.	325.00	500.00	650.00	800.00
	1795	2,300	—	—	—	—
	1796	Inc. Ab.	—	—	—	—

.986 GOLD

MINT: ST. PETERSBURG СПБ

C#	Date	Mintage	VF	XF	Unc
133	1802	.074	3000.	3500.	4000.
	1802 АИ	I.A.	3000.	3500.	4000.
	1804 ХЛ	.072	3000.	3500.	4000.
	1805 ХЛ	.055	3000.	3500.	4000.

12.9039 gm., .900 GOLD, .3734 oz AGW

MINT: ST. PETERSBURG (NO MINTMARK)

Y#	Date	Mintage	VF	XF	Unc
A42	1886 АГ	.057	250.00	325.00	450.00
	1887 АГ	.475	250.00	325.00	450.00
	1888 АГ	.022	250.00	325.00	450.00
	1889 АГ	.343	250.00	325.00	450.00
	1890 АГ	.015	250.00	325.00	450.00
	1891 АГ	.003	250.00	325.00	450.00
	1892 АГ	.008	250.00	325.00	450.00
	1893 АГ	.001	250.00	325.00	450.00
	1894 АГ	.001	250.00	325.00	450.00

MINT: ST. PETERSBURG

Y#	Date	Mintage	VF	XF	Unc
A63	1895 АГ	5.000	—	—	7500.
	1896 АГ	125 pcs.	—	—	7500.
	1897 АГ	—	—	—	7500.

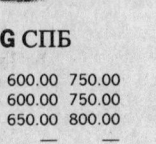

8.6026 gm., .900 GOLD, .2489 oz AGW

MINT: ST. PETERSBURG

Y#	Date	Mintage	VF	XF	Unc
64	1898 АГ	.200	BV	165.00	175.00
	1899 АГ	27.600	BV	165.00	175.00
	1899 ФЗ	I.A.	BV	165.00	175.00
	1899 ЭБ	I.A.	BV	165.00	175.00
	1900 ФЗ	6.021	165.00	200.00	225.00
	1901 ФЗ	2.380	BV	165.00	175.00
	1901 АР	I.A.	BV	165.00	175.00
	1902 АР	2.019	BV	165.00	175.00
	1903 АР	2.817	BV	165.00	175.00
	1904 АР	1.024	BV	165.00	175.00
	1906 ЭБ	10 pcs.	—	2000.	4000.
	1909 ЭБ	.050	BV	165.00	175.00
	1910 ЭБ	.050	BV	165.00	175.00
	1911 ЭБ	.050	BV	165.00	175.00

12 ROUBLES

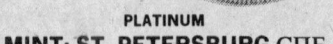

PLATINUM

MINT: ST. PETERSBURG СПБ

C#	Date	Mintage	VF	XF	Unc
179	1830	119 pcs.	5000.	7500.	10,000.
	1831	1,463	5000.	7500.	10,000.
	1832	1,102	5000.	7500.	10,000.
	1833	255 pcs.	5000.	7500.	10,000.
	1834	11 pcs.	5000.	7500.	10,000.
	1835	127 pcs.	5000.	7500.	10,000.
	1836	11 pcs.	—	Rare	—
	1837	53 pcs.	5000.	7500.	10,000.
	1838	12 pcs.	—	Rare	—
	1839	2 pcs.	—	Rare	—
	1840	1 pc.	—	Rare	—
	1841	75 pcs.	5000.	7500.	10,000.
	1842	115 pcs.	5000.	7500.	10,000.
	1843	122 pcs.	5000.	7500.	10,000.
	1844	4 pcs.	—	Rare	—
	1845	2 pcs.	5000.	7500.	10,000.

15 ROUBLES

12.9039 gm., .900 GOLD, .3734 oz AGW

MINT: ST. PETERSBURG

Y#	Date	Mintage	VF	XF	Unc
65	1897 АГ	11.900	BV	250.00	275.00

25 ROUBLES

.917 GOLD

MINT: ST. PETERSBURG СПБ

C#	Date	Mintage	VF	XF	Unc
27	1876	100 pcs.	—	—	8500.

.900 GOLD, 12.904 gms.

MINT: ST. PETERSBURG

Y#	Date	Mintage	VF	XF	Unc
A65	1896	300 pcs.	—	—	9000.
	1908	175 pcs.	—	—	9000.

37-1/2 ROUBLES

.900 GOLD, 32.260 gms.

MINT: ST. PETERSBURG

Y#	Date	Mintage	VF	XF	Unc
B65	1902	225 pcs.	—	—	10,000.

TRADE COINS

DUCAT

.986 GOLD

MINT: ST. PETERSBURG СПБ

C#	Date	Mintage	Fine	VF	XF	Unc
51	1762	—	750.00	1000.	1500.	2250.

MINT: ST. PETERSBURG СПБ

C#	Date	Mintage	Fine	VF	XF	Unc
80	1763	.050	300.00	500.00	700.00	1000.

MINT: ST. PETERSBURG СПБ

Mature bust.

C#	Date	Mintage	Fine	VF	XF	Unc
80a	1766	.023	300.00	500.00	700.00	1000.

MINT: ST. PETERSBURG СПБ

C#	Date	Mintage	Fine	VF	XF	Unc
80c	1796	.040	375.00	600.00	800.00	1200.

.986 GOLD

MINT: ST. PETERSBURG СМ

C#	Date	Mintage	VF	XF	Unc
102	1796 БМ	2,500	1750.	2000.	2500.

MINT: ST. PETERSBURG СМ

C#	Date	Mintage	VF	XF	Unc
103	1797 ГЛ	.137	1100.	1300.	1500.

GOLD MINE INGOTS

During the late 19th and early 20th century, Russian law provided that gold mine owners who supplied gold to the mints should receive back whatever silver was recovered during refining of the gold. The silver was returned in the form of circular ingots of various weights which resembled coins. These pieces have often been erroneously described as Russian trade coins for use in Mongolia, China and Turkestan.

NOTE: Both the Doyla and the Zolotnik are weights, not denominations.

96 Doli (Dolya) = 1 Zolotnik

1 Zolotnik = 4.27 Grams

24 DOLYA

.990 SILVER

KM#	Date	Mintage	VF	XF	Unc
1	ND	—	200.00	225.00	275.00

ZOLOTNIK

.990 SILVER

KM#	Date	Mintage	VF	XF	Unc
2	ND	—	200.00	225.00	275.00

3 ZOLOTNIKS

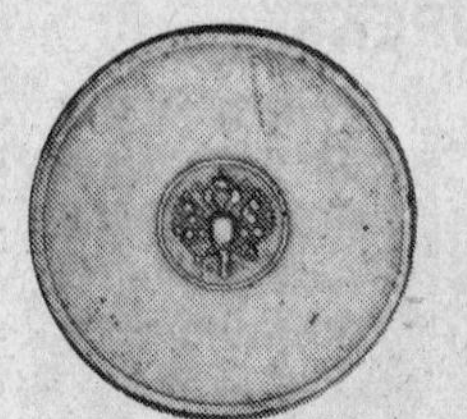

.990 SILVER

KM#	Date	Mintage	VF	XF	Unc
3	ND	—	200.00	225.00	275.00

10 ZOLOTNIKS

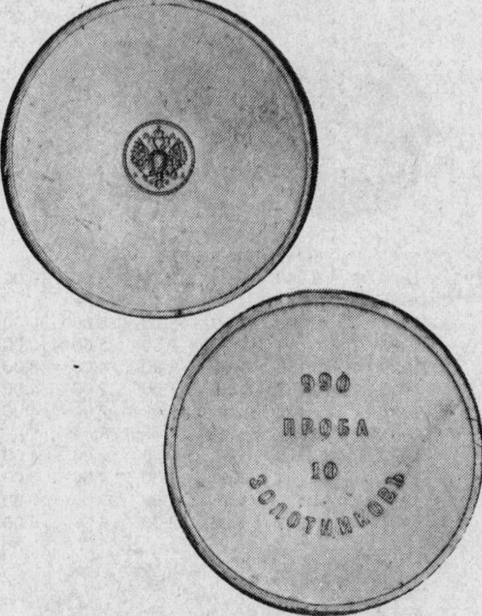

.990 SILVER

KM#	Date	Mintage	VF	XF	Unc
4	ND	—	225.00	275.00	325.00

RUSSIA-U.S.S.R.

100 Kopecks = 1 Rouble

1/2 KOPEK

COPPER

Y#	Date	Mintage	Fine	VF	XF	Unc
75	1925	45.380	3.00	6.00	12.00	25.00
	1927	—	3.00	6.00	12.00	25.00
	1928	—	4.00	8.00	16.00	35.00

KOPEK

BRONZE

Y#	Date	Mintage	Fine	VF	XF	Unc
76	1924 reeded edge					
76		176.511	1.50	3.00	7.00	15.00
	1924 plain edge					
		Inc. Ab.	25.00	50.00	100.00	200.00
	1925	Inc. Ab.	50.00	100.00	200.00	400.00

ALUMINUM-BRONZE

Y#	Date	Mintage	Fine	VF	XF	Unc
91	1926	87.915	.60	1.25	2.50	5.00
	1927	—	.75	1.50	3.00	6.00
	1928	—	.75	1.50	3.00	6.00
	1929	95.950	1.00	2.00	4.00	7.50
	1930	85.351	1.00	2.00	4.00	7.50
	1931	106.100	.60	1.25	2.50	5.00
	1932	56.900	.60	1.25	2.50	5.00
	1933	111.256	.60	1.25	2.50	5.00
	1934	100.245	.60	1.25	2.50	5.00
	1935	66.405	1.00	2.00	4.00	7.50

Y#	Date	Mintage	Fine	VF	XF	Unc
98	1935	Inc. Ab.	1.00	2.00	4.00	7.50
	1936	132.204	.75	1.50	3.00	6.00

Y#	Date	Mintage	Fine	VF	XF	Unc
105	1937	—	.25	.50	.75	1.50
	1938	—	.25	.50	.75	1.50
	1939	—	.25	.50	.75	1.50
	1940	—	.25	.50	.75	1.50
	1941	—	.25	.60	1.00	1.75
	1945	—	1.50	3.00	6.00	10.00
	1946	—	1.00	2.00	4.00	7.50

Y#	Date	Mintage	Fine	VF	XF	Unc
112	1948	—	.50	1.00	2.00	5.00
	1949	—	.50	1.00	2.00	5.00
	1950	—	1.50	3.00	6.00	12.00
	1951	—	1.50	3.00	6.00	12.00
	1952	—	.30	.75	1.50	3.00
	1953	—	.30	.75	1.50	3.00
	1954	—	.30	.75	1.50	3.00
	1955	—	.30	.75	1.50	3.00
	1956	—	.30	.75	1.50	3.00

Y#	Date	Mintage	Fine	VF	XF	Unc
119	1957	—	.30	.75	1.50	3.00

BRASS

Y#	Date	Mintage	Fine	VF	XF	Unc
126	1961	—	—	.10	.25	.45
	1962	—	—	.10	.25	.45
	1963	—	—	.10	.25	.45
	1964	—	—	.10	.25	.45
	1965	—	—	.10	.25	.45
	1966	—	—	.10	.25	.45
	1967	—	—	.10	.25	.45
	1968	—	—	.10	.25	.45
	1969	—	—	.10	.25	.45
	1970	—	—	.10	.25	.45
	1971	—	—	.10	.25	.45
	1972	—	—	.10	.25	.45
	1973	—	—	.10	.25	.45
	1974	—	—	.10	.25	.45
	1975	—	—	.10	.25	.45
	1976	—	—	.10	.25	.45
	1977	—	—	.10	.25	.45
	1978	—	—	.10	.25	.45
	1979	—	—	.10	.25	.45

2 KOPEKS

COPPER

Y#	Date	Mintage	Fine	VF	XF	Unc
77	1924 reeded edge					
		119.995	2.00	5.00	10.00	15.00
	1924 plain edge		25.00	50.00	100.00	200.00
	1925	Inc. Ab.	50.00	100.00	200.00	400.00

ALUMINUM-BRONZE

Y#	Date	Mintage	Fine	VF	XF	Unc
92	1926	105.052	.25	.75	1.25	2.50
	1927	—	50.00	75.00	150.00	250.00
	1928	—	.25	.75	1.50	3.00
	1929	80.000	.50	1.00	2.00	4.00
	1930	134.185	.25	.75	1.50	3.00
	1931	99.522	.25	.75	1.50	3.00
	1932	39.572	.25	.75	1.50	3.00
	1933	54.873	.25	.75	1.50	3.00
	1934	61.574	.25	.75	1.50	3.00
	1935	81.121	.25	.75	1.50	3.00

Y#	Date	Mintage	Fine	VF	XF	Unc
99	1935	—	1.00	2.50	5.00	9.00
	1936	94.353	.75	1.50	3.00	5.00

Y#	Date	Mintage	Fine	VF	XF	Unc
106	1937	—	.25	.75	1.25	2.50
	1938	—	.25	.75	1.25	2.50
	1939	—	.25	.75	1.25	2.50
	1940	—	.25	.75	1.25	2.50
	1941	—	.25	.75	1.25	2.50
	1945	—	1.25	2.50	5.00	10.00
	1946	—	.75	1.50	3.00	5.00

Y#	Date	Mintage	Fine	VF	XF	Unc
113	1948	—	.25	.75	1.25	2.50
	1949	—	.25	.75	1.25	2.50
	1950	—	.25	.75	1.25	2.50
	1951	—	1.25	2.50	5.00	10.00
	1952	—	.25	.75	1.50	3.00
	1953	—	.20	.50	1.00	2.00
	1954	—	.20	.50	1.00	2.00
	1955	—	.20	.50	1.00	2.00
	1956	—	.20	.50	1.00	2.00

Y#	Date	Mintage	Fine	VF	XF	Unc
120	1957	—	.20	.50	1.00	2.00

BRASS

Y#	Date	Mintage	Fine	VF	XF	Unc
127	1961	—	—	.10	.25	.50
	1962	—	—	.10	.25	.50
	1963	—	—	.10	.25	.50
	1964	—	—	.10	.25	.50
	1965	—	—	.10	.25	.50
127	1966	—	—	.10	.25	.50
	1967	—	—	.10	.25	.50
	1968	—	—	.10	.25	.50
	1969	—	—	.10	.25	.50
	1970	—	—	.10	.25	.50
	1971	—	—	.10	.25	.50
	1972	—	—	.10	.25	.50
	1973	—	—	.10	.25	.50
	1974	—	—	.10	.25	.50
	1975	—	—	.10	.25	.50
	1976	—	—	.10	.25	.50
	1977	—	—	.10	.25	.50
	1978	—		.10	.25	.50
	1979	—	—	.10	.25	.50

3 KOPEKS

BRONZE

Y#	Date	Mintage	Fine	VF	XF	Unc
78	1924 reeded edge					
		101.282	50.00	75.00	150.00	250.00
	1924 plain edge					
		Inc. Ab.	2.00	5.00	10.00	20.00

ALUMINUM-BRONZE

Y#	Date	Mintage	Fine	VF	XF	Unc
93	1926	19.940	1.25	2.50	5.00	10.00
	1926 (obv. of Y100)		—	—	Rare	—
	1927	—	7.50	15.00	25.00	50.00
	1928	—	1.25	2.50	5.00	10.00
	1929	50.150	1.00	2.00	4.00	8.00
	1930	74.158	.50	1.00	2.00	4.00
	1931	121.168	.50	1.00	2.00	4.00
	1931 w/o CCCP obv.		—	—	Rare	—
	1932	37.718	.50	1.00	2.00	4.00
	1933	44.764	1.00	2.00	4.00	8.00
	1934	44.528	1.25	2.50	5.00	10.00
	1935	58.302	1.00	2.00	4.00	8.00

Y#	Date	Mintage	Fine	VF	XF	Unc
100	1935	—	1.25	2.50	5.00	10.00
	1936	62.757	.75	1.50	3.00	6.00

Y#	Date	Mintage	Fine	VF	XF	Unc
107	1937	—	.50	1.00	2.00	4.00
	1938	—	.50	1.00	2.00	4.00
	1939	—	.75	1.50	3.00	6.00
	1940	—	.50	1.00	1.50	3.00
	1941	—	.50	1.00	2.00	4.00
	1943	—	.50	1.00	2.00	4.00
	1945	—	1.25	2.50	5.00	10.00
	1946	—	.50	1.00	2.00	4.00

Y#	Date	Mintage	Fine	VF	XF	Unc
114	1948	—	.50	1.25	2.50	5.00
114	1949	—	.50	1.00	2.00	4.00
	1950	—	.50	1.00	2.00	4.00
	1951	—	1.25	2.50	5.00	10.00
	1952	—	.50	1.00	2.00	4.00
	1953	—	.50	1.00	2.00	4.00
	1954	—	.50	1.00	2.00	4.00
	1955	—	.50	1.00	2.00	4.00
	1956	—	.50	1.00	2.00	4.00

Y#	Date	Mintage	Fine	VF	XF	Unc
121	1957	—	.30	.75	1.50	3.00

BRASS

Y#	Date	Mintage	Fine	VF	XF	Unc
128	1961	—	—	.10	.25	.60
	1962	—	—	.10	.25	.60
	1965	—	—	.10	.25	.60
	1966	—	—	.10	.25	.60
	1967	—	—	.10	.25	.60
	1968	—	—	.10	.25	.60
	1969	—	—	.10	.25	.60
	1970	—	—	.10	.25	.60
	1971	—	—	.10	.25	.60
	1972	—	—	.10	.25	.60
	1973	—	—	.10	.25	.60
	1974	—	—	.10	.25	.60
	1975	—	—	.10	.25	.60
	1976	—	—	.10	.25	.60
	1977	—	—	.10	.25	.60
	1978	—	—	.10	.25	.60
	1979	—	—	.10	.25	.60

5 KOPEKS

COPPER

Y#	Date	Mintage	Fine	VF	XF	Unc
79	1924 reeded edge					
		88.510	50.00	75.00	150.00	250.00
	1924 plain edge		BV			
		Inc. Ab.	3.00	7.50	15.00	30.00

ALUMINUM-BRONZE

Y#	Date	Mintage	Fine	VF	XF	Unc
94	1926	14.697	BV	2.00	4.50	9.00
	1927	—	BV	7.50	15.00	30.00
	1928	—	.50	1.25	2.50	5.00
	1929	20.220	BV	1.50	3.00	6.00
	1930	44.490	.50	1.25	2.50	5.00
	1931	89.540	.50	1.25	2.50	5.00
	1932	65.100	.50	1.25	2.50	5.00
	1933	18.134	2.50	5.00	10.00	20.00
	1934	5.354	1.00	2.25	4.50	9.00
	1935	11.735	1.00	1.75	3.50	7.50

Y#	Date	Mintage	Fine	VF	XF	Unc
101	1935	—	3.00	6.00	10.00	20.00
	1936	5.241	3.00	6.00	10.00	20.00

Y#	Date	Mintage	Fine	VF	XF	Unc
108	1937	—	.50	1.25	2.50	5.00
	1938	—	.50	1.25	2.50	5.00
	1939	—	.50	1.00	2.00	4.00
	1940	—	.50	.75	1.50	3.00
	1941	—	.50	1.25	2.50	5.00
	1943	—	.50	1.00	2.00	4.00
	1945	—	2.00	3.50	7.50	15.00
	1946	—	.50	1.00	2.00	4.00

Y#	Date	Mintage	Fine	VF	XF	Unc
115	1948	—	.50	1.00	2.00	4.00
	1949	—	.50	1.25	2.50	5.00
	1950	—	.50	1.00	2.00	4.00
	1951	—	1.25	2.50	5.00	10.00
	1952	—	.50	1.00	2.00	4.00
	1953	—	.50	1.00	2.00	4.00
	1954	—	.50	1.00	2.00	4.00
	1955	—	.50	1.00	2.00	4.00
	1956	—	.50	1.00	2.00	4.00

Y#	Date	Mintage	Fine	VF	XF	Unc
122	1957	—	.50	.75	1.50	3.00

Y#	Date	Mintage	Fine	VF	XF	Unc
129	1961	—	—	.15	.30	.75
	1962	—	—	.15	.30	.75
	1965	—	—	.15	.30	.75
	1966	—	—	.15	.30	.75
	1967	—	—	.15	.30	.75
	1968	—	—	.15	.30	.75
	1969	—	—	.15	.30	.75
	1970	—	—	.15	.30	.75
	1971	—	—	.15	.30	.75
	1972	—	—	.15	.30	.75
	1973	—	—	.15	.30	.75
	1974	—	—	.15	.30	.75
	1975	—	—	.15	.30	.75
	1976	—	—	.15	.30	.75
	1978	—	—	.15	.30	.75
	1979	—	—	.15	.30	.75

10 KOPEKS

1.8000 gm., .500 SILVER, .0289 oz ASW

Y#	Date	Mintage	Fine	VF	XF	Unc
80	1921	.950	7.50	15.00	35.00	70.00
	1921	—	—	—	Proof	75.00
	1922	18.640	1.00	2.00	4.00	7.50
	1922	—	—	—	Proof	65.00
	1923	33.424	BV	1.25	2.50	5.00
	1923	—	—	—	Proof	55.00

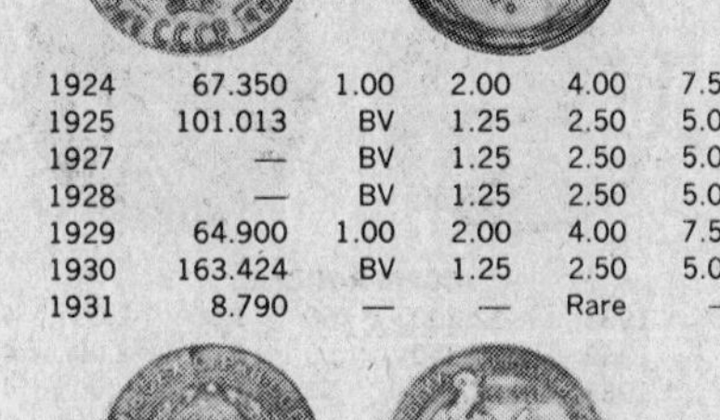

Y#	Date	Mintage	Fine	VF	XF	Unc
86	1924	67.350	1.00	2.00	4.00	7.50
	1925	101.013	BV	1.25	2.50	5.00
	1927	—	BV	1.25	2.50	5.00
	1928	—	BV	1.25	2.50	5.00
	1929	64.900	1.00	2.00	4.00	7.50
	1930	163.424	BV	1.25	2.50	5.00
	1931	8.790	—	—	Rare	—

COPPER-NICKEL

Y#	Date	Mintage	Fine	VF	XF	Unc
95	1931	122.511	.50	.75	1.50	3.00
	1932	171.641	.50	.75	1.50	3.00
	1933	163.124	.50	.75	1.50	3.00
	1934	104.058	.50	1.25	2.50	5.00

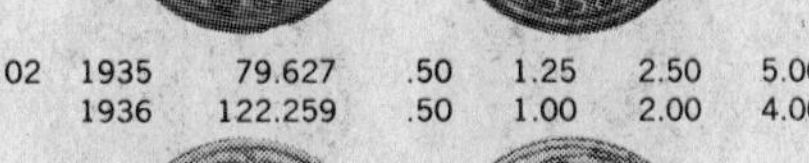

Y#	Date	Mintage	Fine	VF	XF	Unc
102	1935	79.627	.50	1.25	2.50	5.00
	1936	122.259	.50	1.00	2.00	4.00

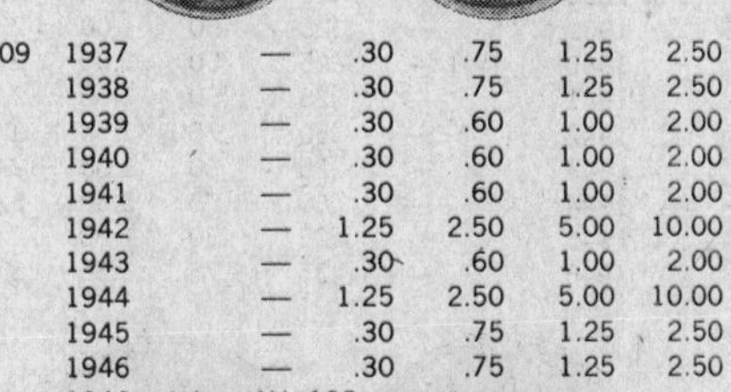

Y#	Date	Mintage	Fine	VF	XF	Unc
109	1937	—	.30	.75	1.25	2.50
	1938	—	.30	.75	1.25	2.50
	1939	—	.30	.60	1.00	2.00
	1940	—	.30	.60	1.00	2.00
	1941	—	.30	.60	1.00	2.00
	1942	—	1.25	2.50	5.00	10.00
	1943	—	.30	.60	1.00	2.00
	1944	—	1.25	2.50	5.00	10.00
	1945	—	.30	.75	1.25	2.50
	1946	—	.30	.75	1.25	2.50
	1946 w/obv. of Y#102					
		—	—	—	Rare	—

8 and 7 ribbons on wreath

Y#	Date	Mintage	Fine	VF	XF	Unc
116	1948	—	.25	.50	1.00	2.00
	1949	—	.25	.50	1.00	2.00
	1950	—	1.00	2.00	4.00	7.50
	1951	—	1.25	2.50	5.00	10.00
	1952	—	.25	.50	1.00	2.00
	1953	—	.25	.50	1.00	2.00
	1954	—	.25	.50	1.00	2.00
	1955	—	.25	.35	.75	1.50
	1956	—	.25	.50	1.00	2.00
	1956 (rev. of Y#123)					
		—	50.00	75.00	150.00	250.00

7 and 7 ribbons on wreath

Y#	Date	Mintage	Fine	VF	XF	Unc
123	1957 (rev. of Y#116)					
		—	50.00	75.00	150.00	250.00
	1957	—	.25	.50	1.00	2.00

COPPER-NICKEL-ZINC

Y#	Date	Mintage	Fine	VF	XF	Unc
130	1961	—	—	.15	.30	.75
	1962	—	—	.10	.25	.50
	1965	—	—	.10	.25	.50
	1966	—	—	.10	.25	.50
	1967	—	—	.10	.25	.50
	1968	—	—	.10	.25	.50
	1969	—	—	.10	.25	.50
	1970	—	—	.10	.25	.50
	1971	—	—	.10	.25	.50
	1972	—	—	.10	.25	.50
	1973	—	—	.10	.25	.50
	1974	—	—	.10	.25	.50
	1975	—	—	.10	.25	.50
	1976	—	—	.10	.25	.50
	1977	—	—	.10	.25	.50
	1978	—	—	.10	.25	.50
	1978	—	—	.10	.25	.50

50th Anniversary 1917 Revolution

Y#	Date	Mintage	Fine	VF	XF	Unc
136	1967	—	—	.15	.30	.75

15 KOPEKS

2.7000 gm., .500 SILVER, .0434 oz ASW

Y#	Date	Mintage	Fine	VF	XF	Unc
81	1921	.933	10.00	15.00	35.00	70.00
	1921	—	—	—	Proof	85.00
	1922	13.633	1.50	2.50	5.00	10.00
	1922	—	—	—	Proof	70.00
	1923	28.503	BV	1.50	2.50	5.00
	1923	—	—	—	Proof	60.00

Y#	Date	Mintage	Fine	VF	XF	Unc
87	1924	72.426	BV	1.50	2.50	5.00
	1925	112.708	BV	1.50	2.00	4.00
	1927	—	BV	1.50	2.00	4.00
	1928	—	BV	1.50	2.00	4.00
	1929	46.400	BV	1.50	2.00	4.00
	1930	79.867	BV	1.50	2.00	4.00
	1931	5.099	—	—	Rare	—

COPPER-NICKEL

Y#	Date	Mintage	Fine	VF	XF	Unc
96	1931	75.859	.50	1.00	1.75	3.50
	1932	136.045	.50	1.00	1.75	3.50
	1933	127.590	.50	1.00	1.75	3.50
	1934	58.367	.50	1.00	2.50	5.00

Y#	Date	Mintage	Fine	VF	XF	Unc
103	1935	51.308	.50	1.00	1.75	3.50
	1936	52.183	.35	.75	1.50	3.00

Y#	Date	Mintage	Fine	VF	XF	Unc
110	1937	—	.35	.75	1.50	3.00
	1938	—	.25	.50	1.00	2.00
	1939	—	.25	.50	1.00	2.00
	1940	—	.25	.50	1.00	2.00
	1941	—	.25	.50	1.00	2.00
	1942	—	1.25	2.50	5.00	10.00
	1943	—	.35	.75	1.25	2.50
	1944	—	.50	1.00	2.00	3.50
	1945	—	.50	1.25	2.50	5.00
	1946	—	.35	.75	1.50	3.00

Y#	Date	Mintage	Fine	VF	XF	Unc
117	1948	—	.25	.50	1.00	2.00
	1949	—	.35	.75	1.50	3.00
	1950	—	.25	.50	1.00	2.00
	1951	—	1.25	2.50	5.00	10.00
	1952	—	.25	.50	1.00	2.00
	1953	—	.25	.50	1.00	2.00
	1954	—	.25	.50	1.00	2.00
	1955	—	.25	.50	1.00	2.00
	1956	—	.25	.50	1.00	2.00

Y#	Date	Mintage	Fine	VF	XF	Unc
124	1957	—	.25	.50	1.00	2.00

COPPER-NICKEL-ZINC

Y#	Date	Mintage	Fine	VF	XF	Unc
131	1961	—	—	.20	.35	.75
	1962	—	—	.20	.35	1.00
	1965	—	—	.20	.35	.75
	1966	—	—	.20	.35	.75
	1967	—	—	.20	.35	.75
	1968	—	—	.20	.35	.75
	1969	—	—	.20	.35	.75
	1970	—	—	.20	.35	.75
	1971	—	—	.20	.35	.75
	1972	—	—	.20	.35	.75
	1973	—	—	.20	.35	.75
	1974	—	—	.20	.35	.75
	1975	—	—	.20	.35	.75
	1976	—	—	.20	.35	.75
	1977	—	—	.20	.35	.75
	1978	—	—	.20	.35	.75
	1979	—	—	.20	.35	.75

50th Anniversary 1917 Revolution

Y#	Date	Mintage	Fine	VF	XF	Unc
137	1967	—	—	.25	.50	1.00

20 KOPEKS

3.6000 gm., .500 SILVER, .0578 oz ASW

Y#	Date	Mintage	Fine	VF	XF	Unc
82	1921	.825	11.00	15.00	35.00	70.00
	1921	—	—	—	Proof	95.00
	1922	14.220	1.75	3.00	6.00	12.00
	1922	—	—	—	Proof	85.00
82	1923	27.580	BV	1.75	3.00	6.00
	1923	—	—	—	Proof	75.00

Y#	Date	Mintage	Fine	VF	XF	Unc
88	1924	93.810	BV	1.75	3.00	6.00
	1925	135.188	BV	1.75	3.00	6.00
	1927	—	BV	2.00	4.00	10.00
	1928	—	BV	1.75	3.00	6.00
	1929	67.250	BV	1.75	3.00	6.00
	1930	125.658	BV	1.75	3.00	6.00
	1931	9.530	—	—	Rare	—

COPPER-NICKEL

Y#	Date	Mintage	Fine	VF	XF	Unc
97	1931	82.200	.50	1.00	2.00	4.00
	1932	175.350	.50	1.00	2.00	4.00
	1933	143.927	.50	1.00	2.00	4.00
	1934	70.420	—	—	Rare	—

Y#	Date	Mintage	Fine	VF	XF	Unc
104	1935	125.165	.75	1.25	2.50	5.00
	1936	52.968	.50	1.00	2.00	4.00

Y#	Date	Mintage	Fine	VF	XF	Unc
111	1937	—	.25	.50	1.00	2.00
	1938	—	.25	.50	1.00	2.00
	1939	—	.25	.50	1.00	2.00
	1940	—	.25	.50	1.00	2.00
	1941	—	.25	.50	1.00	2.00
	1942	—	.50	.75	1.50	3.00
	1943	—	.25	.50	1.00	2.00
	1944	—	.60	1.25	2.50	5.00
	1945	—	.25	.50	1.00	2.00
	1946	—	.35	.75	1.50	3.00

Y#	Date	Mintage	Fine	VF	XF	Unc
118	1948	—	.35	.75	1.50	3.00
	1949	—	.35	.75	1.50	3.00
	1950	—	1.25	2.50	5.00	10.00
	1951	—	1.25	2.50	5.00	10.00
	1952	—	.25	.50	1.00	2.00
	1953	—	.25	.50	1.00	2.00
	1954	—	.25	.50	1.00	2.00
	1955	—	.25	.50	1.00	2.00
	1956	—	.25	.50	1.00	2.00

Y#	Date	Mintage	Fine	VF	XF	Unc
125	1957	—	.25	.50	1.00	2.00

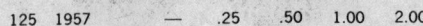

COPPER-NICKEL-ZINC

Y#	Date	Mintage	Fine	VF	XF	Unc
132	1961	—	.10	.25	.50	1.00
	1962	—	.10	.35	.75	1.50
	1965	—	.10	.25	.50	1.00
	1966	—	.10	.25	.50	1.00
	1967	—	.10	.25	.50	1.00
	1968	—	.10	.25	.50	1.00
	1969	—	.10	.25	.50	1.00
	1970	—	.10	.25	.50	1.00
	1971	—	.10	.25	.50	1.00
	1972	—	.10	.25	.50	1.00
	1973	—	.10	.25	.50	1.00
	1974	—	.10	.25	.50	1.00
	1975	—	.10	.25	.50	1.00
	1976	—	.10	.25	.50	1.00
	1977	—	.10	.25	.50	1.00
	1978	—	.10	.20	.35	.60
	1979	—	.10	.20	.35	.60

50th Anniversary 1917 Revolution

Y#	Date	Mintage	Fine	VF	XF	Unc
138	1967	—	.20	.35	.75	1.50

50 KOPEKS

9.9980 gm., .900 SILVER, .2893 oz ASW
Mint master's initials on edge

Y#	Date	Mintage	Fine	VF	XF	Unc
83	1921 АГ	1.400	BV	9.00	12.00	20.00
	1921 АГ	—	—	—	Proof	75.00
	1922 АГ	8.224	10.00	15.00	30.00	60.00
	1922 АГ	—	—	—	Proof	100.00
	1922 ПЛ	I.A.	BV	9.00	12.00	22.50
	1922 ПЛ	—	—	—	Proof	75.00

Y#	Date	Mintage	Fine	VF	XF	Unc
89	1924 ПЛ	26.559	BV	9.00	11.00	15.00
	1924 ПЛ	Inc. Ab.	—	—	Proof	75.00
	1924 ФР	40.000	BV	9.00	11.00	15.00
	1924 ФР	Inc. Ab.	—	—	Proof	75.00
	1925 ПЛ	43.557	BV	9.00	11.00	15.00
	1925 ПЛ	Inc. Ab.	—	—	Proof	75.00
	1926 ПЛ	24.374	BV	9.00	11.00	16.00
	1926 ПЛ	Inc. Ab.	—	—	Proof	75.00
	1927 ПЛ	—	BV	9.00	11.00	20.00
	1927 ПЛ	—	—	—	Proof	75.00

COPPER-NICKEL-ZINC
Plain edge

Y#	Date	Mintage	Fine	VF	XF	Unc
133	1961	—	.25	.75	1.50	3.00

Lettered edge

Y#	Date	Mintage	Fine	VF	XF	Unc
133a	1964	—	.20	.35	.75	1.50
	1965	—	.20	.35	.75	1.50
	1966	—	.20	.35	.75	1.50
	1967	—	.20	.35	.75	1.50
	1968	—	.20	.35	.75	1.50
	1969	—	.20	.35	.75	1.50
	1970	—	.20	.35	.75	1.50
	1971	—	.20	.35	.75	1.50
	1972	—	.20	.35	.75	1.50
	1973	—	.20	.35	.75	1.50
	1974	—	.20	.35	.75	1.50
	1975	—	.20	.35	.75	1.50
	1976	—	.20	.35	.75	1.50
	1977	—	.20	.35	.75	1.50
	1978	—	.20	.35	.75	1.50
	1979	—	.20	.35	.75	1.50

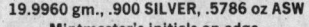

50th Anniversary 1917 Revolution

139	1967	—	.25	.50	1.00	2.00

ROUBLE

19.9960 gm., .900 SILVER, .5786 oz ASW
Mintmaster's initials on edge.

84	1921 АГ	1.000	17.50	20.00	30.00	45.00
	1921 АГ	—	—	—	Proof	100.00
	1922 АГ	2.050	22.50	35.00	50.00	110.00
	1922 АГ	—	—	—	Proof	150.00
	1922 ПЛ	I.A.	22.50	35.00	50.00	110.00
	1922 ПЛ	—	—	—	Proof	150.00

Y#	Date	Mintage	Fine	VF	XF	Unc
90	1924 ПЛ	12.998	17.50	20.00	25.00	35.00
	1924 ПЛ	—	—	—	Proof	175.00

COPPER-NICKEL-ZINC
Plain edge

134	1961	—	.50	1.25	2.50	5.00

Lettered edge

134a	1964	—	.50	1.00	2.00	4.00
	1965	—	.50	1.25	2.50	5.00
	1966	—	.50	1.00	2.00	4.00
	1967	—	.50	1.00	2.00	4.00
	1968	—	.50	1.00	2.00	4.00
	1969	—	.50	1.00	2.00	4.00
	1970	—	.50	1.00	2.00	4.00
	1971	—	.50	1.00	2.00	4.00
	1972	—	.50	1.00	2.00	4.00
	1973	—	.50	1.00	2.00	4.00
	1974	—	.50	1.00	2.00	4.00
	1975	—	.50	1.00	2.00	4.00
	1976	—	.50	1.00	2.00	4.00
	1977	—	.50	1.00	2.00	4.00
	1978	—	.50	1.00	2.00	4.00
	1979	—	.50	1.00	2.00	4.00

20th Anniversary End Of World War II

135	1965	—	.75	1.25	2.50	5.00

50th Anniversary of 1917 Revolution

140	1967	—	.50	1.00	2.00	4.00

Lenin Birth Centennial

Y#	Date	Mintage	Fine	VF	XF	Unc
141	1970	—	.50	1.00	2.00	4.00

30th Anniversary of World War II Victory

142	1975 date on edge		.50	1.00	2.00	4.00

60th Anniversary of Revolution

143	1977	—	.50	1.25	2.50	5.00

1980 Olympics

144	1977	—	.50	1.25	2.50	5.00

1980 Olympics

153	1978	—	.50	1.25	2.50	5.00

1980 Olympics

—	1979	—	.75	2.00	3.00	6.50

1980 Olympics

Y#	Date	Mintage	Fine	VF	XF	Unc
—	1979	—	.75	2.00	3.00	6.50

COPPER-NICKEL
1980 Olympics

Y#	Date	Mintage	Fine	VF	XF	Unc
—	1980	—	—	—	—	—

1980 Olympics

Y#	Date	Mintage	Fine	VF	XF	Unc
—	1980	—	—	—	—	—

5 ROUBLES

16.6700 gm., .900 SILVER, .4824 oz ASW
1980 Olympics
Rev: City view of Kiev.

Y#	Date	Mintage	Fine	VF	XF	Unc
145	1977	.450	BV	BV	Bv	15.00
	1977	Inc. Ab.	—	—	Proof	20.00

1980 Olympics
Rev: City view of Leningrad.

Y#	Date	Mintage	Fine	VF	XF	Unc
146	1977	.450	BV	BV	Bv	15.00
	1977	Inc. Ab.	—	—	Proof	20.00

1980 Olympics
Rev: City view of Minsk.

Y#	Date	Mintage	Fine	VF	XF	Unc
147	1977	.450	BV	BV	Bv	15.00
	1977	Inc. Ab.	—	—	Proof	20.00

1980 Olympics
Rev: City view of Tallinn.

Y#	Date	Mintage	Fine	VF	XF	Unc
148	1977	.450	BV	BV	Bv	15.00
	1977	Inc. Ab.	—	—	Proof	20.00

1980 Olympics

Y#	Date	Mintage	Fine	VF	XF	Unc
154	1978	—	BV	BV	Bv	15.00
	1978	—	—	—	Proof	20.00

1980 Olympics

Y#	Date	Mintage	Fine	VF	XF	Unc
155	1978	—	BV	BV	Bv	15.00
	1978	—	—	—	Proof	20.00

1980 Olympics

Y#	Date	Mintage	Fine	VF	XF	Unc
156	1978	.450	BV	BV	Bv	15.00
	1978	Inc. Ab.	—	—	Proof	20.00

1980 Olympics

Y#	Date	Mintage	Fine	VF	XF	Unc
157	1978	Inc. Ab.	BV	BV	Bv	15.00
	1978	Inc. Ab.	—	—	Proof	20.00

1980 Olympics

Y#	Date	Mintage	Fine	VF	XF	Unc
—	1979	—	BV	BV	Bv	15.00
	1979	—	—	—	Proof	20.00

1980 Olympics

Y#	Date	Mintage	Fine	VF	XF	Unc
—	1979	—	BV	BV	Bv	15.00
	1979	—	—	—	Proof	—

10 ROUBLES
(Chervonetz)

8.6026 gm., .900 GOLD, .2489 oz AGW
Mint master's initials on edge

Y#	Date	Mintage	Fine	VF	XF	Unc
85	1923 ПЛ	2.751	—	—	250.00	325.00
	1925	.600	—	—	Unique	—
	1975	.250	BV	BV	Bv	165.00
	1976	—	BV	BV	Bv	165.00
	1977	—	BV	BV	Bv	165.00
	1978	.300	BV	BV	Bv	165.00
	1979	.750	BV	BV	Bv	165.00

33.3000 gm., .900 SILVER, .9636 oz ASW
1980 Olympics
Rev: City view of Moscow.

Y#	Date	Mintage	Fine	VF	XF	Unc
149	1977	.450	BV	BV	Bv	30.00
	1977	Inc. Ab.	—	—	Proof	35.00

1980 Olympics
Rev: Map of Soviet Union.

Y#	Date	Mintage	Fine	VF	XF	Unc
150	1977	.450	BV	BV	Bv	30.00
	1977	Inc. Ab.	—	—	Proof	35.00

1980 Olympics

Y#	Date	Mintage	Fine	VF	XF	Unc
158	1978	—	BV	BV	BV	30.00
	1978	—	—	—	Proof	35.00

1980 Olympics

Y#	Date	Mintage	Fine	VF	XF	Unc
159	1978	—	BV	BF	BV	30.00
	1978	—	—	—	Proof	35.00

1980 Olympics

Y#	Date	Mintage	Fine	VF	XF	Unc
160	1978	—	BV	BV	Bs	30.00
	1978	—	—	—	Proof	35.00

1980 Olympics
Obv: Similar to Y#155

Y#	Date	Mintage	Fine	VF	XF	Unc
161	1978	—	BV	BV	BV	30.00
	1978	—	—	—	Proof	35.00

1980 Olympics
Obv: Similar to Y#155

Y#	Date	Mintage	Fine	VF	XF	Unc
—	1979	.450	BV	BV	BV	30.00
	1979	Inc. Ab.	—	—	Proof	35.00

1980 Olympics
Obv: Similar to Y#155

Y#	Date	Mintage	Fine	VF	XF	Unc
—	1979	Inc. Ab.	BV	BV	Bv	30.00
	1979	Inc. Ab.	—	—	Proof	35.00

1980 Olympics
Obv: Similar to Y#155.

Y#	Date	Mintage	Fine	VF	XF	Unc
—	1979	—	BV	BV	BV	30.00
	1979	—	—	—	Proof	35.00

1980 Olympics
Obv: Similar to Y#155.

Y#	Date	Mintage	Fine	VF	XF	Unc
—	1979	—	BV	BV	BV	30.00
	1979	—	—	—	Proof	35.00

1980 Olympics
Obv: Similar to Y#155.

Y#	Date	Mintage	Fine	VF	XF	Unc
—	1979	—	BV	BV	BV	30.00
	1979	—	—	—	Proof	35.00

100 ROUBLES

17.2800 gm., .900 GOLD, .500 oz AGW
1980 Olympics

Y#	Date	Mintage	Fine	VF	XF	Unc
151	1977	.130	BV	BV	BV	325.00
	1977	Inc. Ab.	—	—	Proof	375.00

1980 Olympics

Y#	Date	Mintage	Fine	VF	XF	Unc
—	1977	—	BV	BV	BV	325.00
	1977	—	—	—	Proof	375.00

1980 Olympics

Y#	Date	Mintage	Fine	VF	XF	Unc
162	1978	.130	BV	BV	BV	325.00
	1978	Inc. Ab.	—	—	Proof	375.00

1980 Olympics

Y#	Date	Mintage	Fine	VF	XF	Unc
163	1978	.130	BV	BV	BV	325.00
	1978	Inc. Ab.	—	—	Proof	375.00

1980 Olympics

Y#	Date	Mintage	Fine	VF	XF	Unc
—	1979	.130	BV	BV	BV	325.00
	1979	Inc. Ab.	—	—	Proof	375.00

150 ROUBLES

15.5400 gm., .999 PLATINUM, .4991 oz APW
1980 Olympics

Y#	Date	Mintage	Fine	VF	XF	Unc
152	1977	—	—	—	—	400.00
	1977	—	—	—	Proof	450.00

1980 Olympics

Y#	Date	Mintage	Fine	VF	XF	Unc
164	1978	.040	—	—	—	400.00
	1978	Inc. Ab.	—	—	Proof	450.00

1980 Olympics
Obv: Similar to 100 Roubles, Y# . Rev: Ancient wrestlers.

Y#	Date	Mintage	Fine	VF	XF	Unc
—	1979	—	—	—	—	400.00

1980 Olympics

Y#	Date	Mintage	Fine	VF	XF	Unc
—	1979	—	—	—	—	400.00
	1979	—	—	—	Proof	450.00

NCLT ISSUES

NOVODELS

KM#	Date	Identification	Mkt.Val.
N1	1762 СПБ ЯИ	Ruble, Silver, eagle rev., plain edge	—
N2	1762 СПБ СЪ	Ruble, Silver, monogram rev., Petersburg lettered edge	—
N3	1762 СПБ СЪ	Ruble, Silver, overstruck on Elizabeth Ruble, Petersburg lettered edge	—
N4	1762 СПБ СЪ	Ruble, Silver, diagonal reeded edge	—
N5	1762 СПБ СЪ	Ruble, Silver, plain edge	—
N6	1762 СПБ СЪ	Ruble, Silver, dot-dash edge	—
N7	1762 СПБ	Ruble, Silver, plain edge	—
N8	1762 СПБ	Ducat, Gold, w/o dot after date, plain edge	—
N9	1763	Kopeck, Copper, plain edge	—
N10	1763	Kopeck, Copper, large crown, tread edge	—
N11	1763 СПБ	5 Rubles, Gold, small letters on rev., diagonal reeded edge	—
N12	1764 СПБ	10 Kopecks, Silver, plain edge	—
N13	1765	Polushka, Copper, diagonal reeded edge	—
N15	1765 EM	Polushka, Copper, diagonal reeded edge	—

KM#	Date	Identification	Mkt.Val.
N16	1765 EM	Denga, Copper, diagonal reeded edge	—

KM#	Date	Identification	Mkt.Val.
N17	1765	Denga, Copper, diagonal reeded edge	—
N18	1765 EM	Kopeck, Copper, diagonal reeded edge	—
N19	1765 EM	Kopeck, Copper, tread edge	—
N20	1765	Kopeck, Copper, small date, diagonal reeded edge	—
N21	1765	Kopeck, Copper, tread edge	—
N22	1765	Kopeck, Copper, plain edge	—
N23	1765 EM	2 Kopecks, Copper, tread edge	—
N24	1765	2 Kopecks, Copper, value above St. George, reverse diagonal reeded edge	—
N25	1765	2 Kopecks, Copper, tread edge	—

KM#	Date	Identification	Mkt.Val.
N26	1765	2 Kopecks, Copper, diagonal reeded edge	—

KM#	Date	Identification	Mkt.Val.
N27	1765 EM	5 Kopecks, Copper, tread edge	—

KM#	Date	Identification	Mkt.Val.
N28	1765 EM	5 Kopecks, Copper, cross hatched edge	—
N29	1765 EM	5 Kopecks, Copper, tread edge	—
N30	1765	5 Kopecks, Copper, diagonal reeded edge	—
N31	1765	5 Kopecks, Copper, tread edge	—
N32	1766 СПБ	2 Rubles, Gold, diagonal reeded edge	—

KM#	Date	Identification	Mkt.Val.
N33	1767	5 Kopecks, Copper, small mintmark, plain edge	—
N34	1767	5 Kopecks, Copper, small mintmark, tread edge	—
N35	1768 СПБ	10 Kopecks, Silver, plain edge	—
N36	1768 СПБ	20 Kopecks, Silver, plain edge	—
N37	1768	20 Kopecks, Silver, no MM, plain edge	—
N38	1768 СПБ	1/2 Ruble, Silver, plain edge	—
N39	1769	Polushka, Copper, plain edge	—
N40	1769	Polushka, Copper, diagonal reeded edge	—
N41	1771	Denga, Copper, plain edge	—
N42	1774 СПБ	10 Roubles, Gold, large letters in inscription, diagonal reeded edge	—
N43	1776 СПМ	2 Kopecks, Copper, tread edge	—
N44	1776 СПБ	10 Kopecks, Silver, diagonal reeded edge	—
N45	1776 СПБ	20 Kopecks, Silver, plain edge	—
N46	1776 СПБ	Ruble, Silver, short legend, plain edge	—
N47	1777 СПБ	15 Kopecks, Silver, new portrait, plain edge	—
N48	1777 СПБ	20 Kopecks, Silver, old type, plain edge	—
N49	1777 СПБ	25 Kopecks, Silver, old type, plain edge	—
N50	1777 СПБ	1/2 Ruble, Silver, old obv., diagonal reeded edge	—
N51	1777 СПБ	Ruble, Silver, oldest portrait, plain edge	—
N52	1777 СПБ	5 Rubles, Gold, earlier portrait, diagonal reeded edge	—
N53	1777 СПБ	10 Roubles, Gold, earlier portrait, diagonal reeded edge	—
N54	1778 СПБ	1/2 Ruble, Silver, higher relief portrait, plain edge	—
N55	1778	1/2 Ruble, Gold, thick flan, plain edge	—
N56	1779 СПБ	15 Kopecks, Silver, higher relief, plain edge	—
N57	1779 СПБ	1/4 Ruble, Silver, higher relief, plain edge	—
N58	1780 СПБ	15 Kopecks, Silver, legend ends on bust, diagonal reeded edge	—
N59	1780 СПБ	15 Kopecks, Silver, legend off bust, plain edge	—

KM#	Date	Identification	Mkt.Val.
N60	1780 СПБ ИЗ	1/2 Ruble, Silver, diagonal reeded edge	—
N61	1780 СПБ	Ruble, Silver, oldest portrait, plain edge	—
N62	1781 КМ	Polushka, Copper, diagonal reeded edge	—
N63	1781 КМ	Denga, Copper, diagonal reeded edge	—

KM#	Date	Identification	Mkt.Val.
N64	1781 КМ	5 Kopecks, Copper, diagonal reeded edge	—
N65	1781 СПМ	5 Kopecks, Copper, plain edge	—
N66	1781 СПМ	5 Kopecks, Copper, tread edge	—
N67	1781 СПБ	10 Kopecks, Silver, younger portrait, plain edge	—
N68	1781 СПБ	10 Kopecks, Silver, younger portrait, diagonal reeded edge	—
N69	1781 СПБ	15 Kopecks, Silver, higher relief, plain edge	—
N70	1781 СПБ	20 Kopecks, Silver, leg. ends ВСЕРОСС, plain edge	—
N71	1781 СПБ	1/4 Ruble, Silver, Wide MM, plain edge	—
N72	1781 СПБ	Ruble, Silver, higher relief, diagonal reeded edge	—
N73	1781 СПБ	Ruble, Silver, oldest portrait, diagonal reeded edge	—
N74	1782 КМ	Polushka, Copper, diagonal reeded edge	—
N75	1782 КМ	Denga, Copper, diagonal reeded edge	—

KM#	Date	Identification	Mkt.Val.
N76	1782 КМ	5 Kopecks, Copper, diagonal reeded edge	—
N77	1782 СПБ	10 Kopecks, Silver, large head, plain edge	—
N78	1782 СПБ	10 Kopecks, Silver, small head, plain edge	—
N79	1782 СПБ	10 Kopecks, Silver, younger portrait, plain edge	—

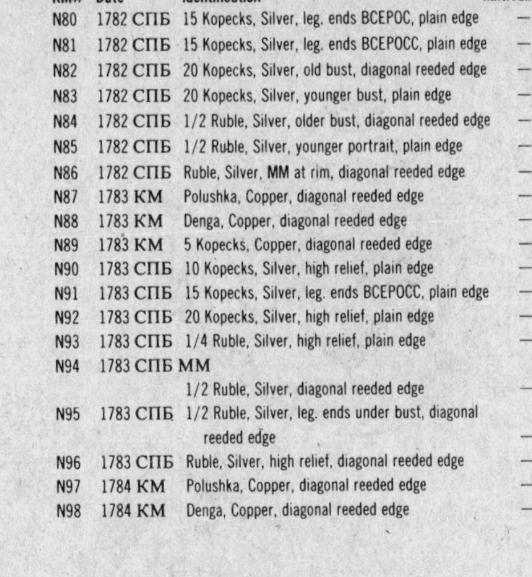

KM#	Date	Identification	Mkt.Val.
N80	1782 СПБ	15 Kopecks, Silver, leg. ends ВСЕРОС, plain edge	—
N81	1782 СПБ	15 Kopecks, Silver, leg. ends ВСЕРОСС, plain edge	—
N82	1782 СПБ	20 Kopecks, Silver, old bust, diagonal reeded edge	—
N83	1782 СПБ	20 Kopecks, Silver, younger bust, plain edge	—
N84	1782 СПБ	1/2 Ruble, Silver, older bust, diagonal reeded edge	—
N85	1782 СПБ	1/2 Ruble, Silver, younger portrait, plain edge	—
N86	1782 СПБ	Ruble, Silver, MM at rim, diagonal reeded edge	—
N87	1783 КМ	Polushka, Copper, diagonal reeded edge	—
N88	1783 КМ	Denga, Copper, diagonal reeded edge	—
N89	1783 КМ	5 Kopecks, Copper, diagonal reeded edge	—
N90	1783 СПБ	10 Kopecks, Silver, high relief, plain edge	—
N91	1783 СПБ	15 Kopecks, Silver, leg. ends ВСЕРОСС, plain edge	—
N92	1783 СПБ	20 Kopecks, Silver, high relief, plain edge	—
N93	1783 СПБ	1/4 Ruble, Silver, high relief, plain edge	—
N94	1783 СПБ ММ	1/2 Ruble, Silver, diagonal reeded edge	—
N95	1783 СПБ	1/2 Ruble, Silver, leg. ends under bust, diagonal reeded edge	—
N96	1783 СПБ	Ruble, Silver, high relief, diagonal reeded edge	—
N97	1784 КМ	Polushka, Copper, diagonal reeded edge	—
N98	1784 КМ	Denga, Copper, diagonal reeded edge	—

KM#	Date	Identification	Mkt.Val.
N99	1784 КМ	5 Kopecks, Copper, diagonal reeded edge	—
N100	1784 СПБ	10 Kopecks, Silver, plain edge	—
N101	1784 СПБ	15 Kopecks, Silver, plain edge	—
N102	1784 СПБ	20 Kopecks, Silver, high relief, plain edge	—
N103	1784 СПБ ЯА	1/4 Ruble, Silver, plain edge	—
N104	1784 СПБ СА	1/2 Ruble, Silver, diagonal reeded edge	—
N105	1784 СПБ IC	Ruble, Silver, diagonal reeded edge	—
N106	1785 КМ	Poluska, Copper, diagonal reeded edge	—
N107	1785 КМ	Denga, Copper, diagonal reeded edge	—
N108	1785 КМ	5 Kopecks, Copper, diagonal reeded edge	—
N109	1785 СПБ	10 Kopecks, Silver, plain edge	—
N110	1785 СПБ	15 Kopecks, Silver, divided date, plain edge	—
N111	1785 СПБ	20 Kopecks, Silver, high relief, plain edge	—
N112	1785 СПБ	1/4 Ruble, Silver, high relief, plain edge	—
N113	1785 СПБ	1/2 Ruble, Silver, high relief, diagonal reeded edge	—
N114	1785 СПБ	Ruble, Silver, high relief, diagonal reeded edge	—

KM#	Date	Identification	Mkt.Val.
N115	1786 КМ	Polushka, Copper, diagonal reeded edge	—
N116	1786 КМ	Denga, Copper, diagonal reeded edge	—

KM#	Date	Identification	Mkt.Val.
N117	1786 КМ	5 Kopecks, Copper, diagonal reeded edge	—
N118	1786 СПБ	10 Kopecks, Silver, plain edge	—
N119	1786 СПБ	15 Kopecks, Silver, leg. ends ВСЕРОСС, plain edge	—
N120	1786 СПБ	20 Kopecks, Silver, plain edge	—
N121	1786 СПБ	1/4 Ruble, Silver, plain edge	—
N122	1786 СПБ ЯА	1/2 Ruble, Silver, broad portrait, diagonal reeded edge	—
N123	1786 СПБ	1/2 Ruble, Silver, narrow portrait, diagonal reeded edge	—
N124	1786 СПБ	Ruble, Silver, high relief, plain edge	

KM#	Date	Identification	Mkt.Val.
N125	1787 КМ	5 Kopecks, Copper, diagonal reeded edge	—
N126	1787 СПБ	15 Kopecks, Silver, leg. ends ВСЕРОСС, plain edge	—
N127	1787 СПБ	20 Kopecks, Silver, plain edge	—
N128	1787 СПБ	1/4 Ruble, Silver, small planchet, plain edge	—
N129	1787 СПБ	1/4 Ruble, Silvered Copper, plain edge	—
N130	1787 СПБ	1/2 Ruble, Silver, high relief, diagonal reeded edge	—
N131	1787 СПБ	Ruble, Silver, high relief, plain edge	—
N132	1788	Polushka, Copper, plain edge	—
N133	1788	Polushka, Copper, diagonal reeded edge	—
N134	1788	Denga, Copper, plain edge	—
N135	1788	Denga, Copper, diagonal reeded edge	—

KM#	Date	Identification	Mkt.Val.
N136	1788	Kopeck, Copper, plain edge	—
N137	1788	Kopeck, Copper, tread edge	—

KM#	Date	Identification	Mkt.Val.
N138	1788 КМ	5 Kopecks, Copper, diagonal reeded edge	—
N139	1788 СПБ	10 Kopecks, Silver, plain edge	—
N140	1788 СПБ	1/4 Ruble, Silver, plain edge	—
N141	1788 СПБ ЯА	1/2 Ruble, Silver, narrow portrait, diagonal reeded edge	—
N142	1788 СПБ	1/2 Ruble, Silver, broad portrait, diagonal reeded edge	—
N143	1788 СПБ	Ruble, Silver, diagonal reeded edge	—
N144	1788 СПБ	5 Rubles, Gold, end of inscription high, diagonal reeded edge	—

KM#	Date	Identification	Mkt.Val.
N145	1789 КМ	5 Kopecks, Copper, diagonal reeded edge	—
N146	1789 СПБ АК	Ruble, Silver, diagonal reeded edge	—
N147	1789 СПБ	Ruble, Silver, ТIВАНОВЪ under bust, diagonal reeded edge	—

KM#	Date	Identification	Mkt.Val.
N148	1790 КМ	5 Kopecks, Copper, diagonal reeded edge	—
N149	1790 СПБ	15 Kopecks, Silver, plain edge	—
N150	1790 СПБ	20 Kopecks, Silver, plain edge	—
N151	1790 СПБ	Ruble, Silver, high relief, plain edge	—
N152	1791 КМ	Polushka, Copper, diagonal reeded edge	—
N153	1791 КМ	Denga, Copper, diagonal reeded edge	—

KM#	Date	Identification	Mkt.Val.
N154	1791 КМ	5 Kopecks, Copper, small mintmark, diagonal reeded edge	—
N155	1791 СПБ	10 Kopecks, Silver, plain edge	—
N156	1791 СПБ	15 Kopecks, Silver, dot at end of legend, plain edge	—
N157	1791 СПБ	15 Kopecks, Silver, w/o dot at end of legend, plain edge	—
N158	1791 СПБ	20 Kopecks, Silver, plain edge	—
N159	1791 СПБ	1/4 Ruble, Silver, plain edge	—
N160	1791 СПБ	1/2 Ruble, Silver, high relief, diagonal reeded edge	—
N161	1791 СПБ	Ruble, Silver, ТIВАНОВЪ under bust, plain edge	—
N162	1791 СПБ	Ruble, Silver, high relief, diagonal reeded edge	—

KM#	Date	Identification	Mkt.Val.
N163	1792 КМ	5 Kopecks, Copper, diagonal reeded edge	—
N164	1792 СПБ	10 Kopecks, Silver, plain edge	—
N165	1792 СПБ	15 Kopecks, Silver, leg. ends ВСЕРОСС, plain edge	—
N166	1792 СПБ	20 Kopecks, Silver, plain edge	—
N167	1792 СПБ	1/4 Ruble, Silver, plain edge	—
N168	1792 СПБ ЯА	1/2 Ruble, Silver, diagonal reeded edge	—
N169	1792 СПБ	1/2 Ruble, Silver, high relief, diagonal reeded edge	—
N170	1792 СПБ	Ruble, Silver, diagonal reeded edge	—
N171	1792 СПБ	Ruble, Silver, ТIВАНОВЪ under bust diagonal reeded edge	—

KM#	Date	Identification	Mkt.Val.
N172	1793 КМ	5 Kopecks, Copper, diagonal reeded edge	—
N173	1793 СПБ	10 Kopecks, Silver, Plain Edge	—
N174	1793 СПБ	15 Kopecks, Silver, leg. ends ВСЕРОСС, plain edge	—
N175	1793 СПБ	20 Kopecks, Silver, plain edge	—
N176	1793 СПБ	1/4 Ruble, Silver, plain edge	—
N177	1793 СПБ АК	1/2 Ruble, Silver, diagonal reeded edge	—
N178	1793 СПБ	1/2 Ruble, Silver, dot ends legend, diagonal reeded edge	—
N179	1793 СПБ	Ruble, Silver, value between .S, diagonal	

KM#	Date	Identification	Mkt.Val.
N179		reeded edge	—
N180	1794 KM	5 Kopecks, Copper, diagonal reeded edge	—
N181	1794 СПБ	10 Kopecks, Silver, plain edge	—
N182	1794 СПБ	15 Kopecks, Silver, leg. ends ВСЕРОСС, plain edge	—
N183	1794 СПБ	20 Kopecks, Silver, leg. ends at bust, diagonal reeded edge	—
N184	1794 СПБ	20 Kopecks, Silver, legend ends under bust, plain edge	—
N185	1794 СПБ	1/4 Ruble, Silver, plain edge	—
N186	1794 СПБ	1/2 Ruble, Silver, narrow portrait, diagonal reeded edge	—
N187	1794 СПБ	Ruble, Silver, diagonal reeded edge	—
N188	1794 СПБ	5 Rubles, Gold, small letters in inscription, diagonal reeded edge	—
N189	1795 KM	5 Kopecks, Copper, diagonal reeded edge	—
N190	1795 СПБ	10 Kopecks, Silver, plain edge	—
N191	1795 СПБ	20 Kopecks, Silver, diagonal reeded edge	—
N192	1795 СПБ АК	1/4 Ruble, Silver, diagonal reeded edge	—
N193	1795 СПБ	1/2 Ruble, Silver, no dot at end of legend, plain edge	—
N194	1795 СПБ	1/2 Ruble, Silver, high relief, diagonal reeded edge	—
N195	1795 СПБ	Ruble, Silver, diagonal reeded edge	—
N196	1795 СПБ	Ruble, Silver, ТIВАНОВЪ under bust diagonal reeded edge	—

KM#	Date	Identification	Mkt.Val.
N197	1796 KM	5 Kopecks, Copper, diagonal reeded edge	—
N198	1796 СПБ	10 Kopecks, Silver, plain edge	—
N199	1796 СПБ	20 Kopecks, Silver, dot at end of legend, diagonal reeded edge	—
N200	1796 СПБ	20 Kopecks, Silver, plain edge	—
N201	1796 СПБ	1/4 Ruble, Silver, plain edge	—
N202	1796 СПБ	1/2 Ruble, Silver, high relief, diagonal reeded edge	—
N203	1796 БМ	Albertus Ruble, Silver, CM/ФА, plain edge	—
N204	1796 БМ	Albertus Ruble, Silver, CM/OM, plain edge	—
N205	1796 БМ	Albertus Ruble, Silver, diagonal reeded edge	—
N206	1796 СПБ	10 Rubles, Gold, large mint letters, diagonal reeded edge	—
N207	1796 СПБ	Ducat, Gold, Youthful portrait, thick flan, diagonal reeded edge	—
N208	1796 БМ	Ducat, Gold, diagonal reeded edge	—
N209	1796	Ducat, Gold, thick planchet, diagonal reeded edge	—
N210	1797 EM	Polushka, Copper, large value, diagonal reeded edge	—

KM#	Date	Identification	Mkt.Val.
N211	1797 KM	Polushka, Copper, small mintmark, diagonal reeded edge	—
N212	1797	Polushka, Copper, diagonal reeded edge	250.00
N213	1797 EM	Denga, Copper, reverse diagonal reeded edge	—
N214	1797 EM	Denga, Copper, diagonal reeded edge	—
N215	1797 KM	Denga, Copper, small mintmark, diagonal reeded edge	—
N216	1797	Denga, Copper, diagonal reeded edge	—
N217	1797 EM	Kopeck, Copper, diagonal reeded edge	—
N218	1797 KM	Kopeck, Copper, diagonal reeded edge	—
N219	1797	Kopeck, Copper, diagonal reeded edge	—
N220	1797 EM	2 Kopecks, Copper, small mintmark, diagonal reeded edge	—
N221	1797 KM	2 Kopecks, Copper, diagonal reeded edge	—
N222	1797	2 Kopecks, Copper, wide date, diagonal reeded edge	—

KM#	Date	Identification	Mkt.Val.
N223	1797	2 Kopecks, Copper, narrow date, diagonal reeded edge	—
N224	1797 МБ	5 Kopecks, Silver, plain edge	—
N225	1797 МБ	1/4 Ruble, Silver, plain edge	—
N226	1797 ФЦ	1/4 Ruble, Silver, plain edge	—
N227	1797 МБ	1/2 Ruble, Silver, plain edge	—
N228	1797 МБ	Ruble, Silver, dot after date, plain edge	—
N229	1797 CM	Ducat, Gold, no MM., diagonal reeded edge	—
N230	1798 KM	Polushka, Copper, small mintmark, diagonal reeded edge	—
N231	1798KM	Denga, Copper, small mintmark, diagonal reeded edge	—
N232	1798	Denga, Copper, diagonal reeded edge	—
N233	1798 KM	Kopeck, Copper, small mintmark, diagonal reeded edge	—
N234	1798	Kopeck, Copper, diagonal reeded edge	—
N235	1798 KM	2 Kopecks, Copper, reverse diagonal reeded edge	—
N236	1798 CM ФЦ	1/2 Ruble, Silver, diagonal reeded edge	—
N237	1798 CM АИ	Ruble, Silver, dot after date, diagonal reeded edge	—
N238	1799	Polushka, Copper, diagonal reeded edge	250.00
N239	1799 KM	Polushka, Copper, small mintmark, diagonal reeded edge	—
N240	1799 KM	Denga, Copper, small mintmark, diagonal reeded edge	—
N241	1799	Denga, Copper, diagonal reeded edge	—

KM#	Date	Identification	Mkt.Val.
N242	1799 KM	Kopeck, Copper, small mintmark, diagonal reeded edge	—
N243	1799	Kopeck, Copper, diagonal reeded edge	—
N244	1799 KM	2 Kopecks, Copper, small mintmark, reverse diagonal reeded edge	—
N245	1799	2 Kopecks, Copper, diagonal reeded edge	—
N246	1799 CM МБ	5 Kopecks, Silver, diagonal reeded edge	—
N247	1799 CM	1/2 Ruble, Silver, Value...ИНА, diagonal reeded edge	—
N248	1799 CM	Ruble, Silver, diagonal reeded edge	—
N249	1800 KM	Polushka, Copper, diagonal reeded edge	250.00
N250	1800 KM	Denga, Copper, diagonal reeded edge	—
N251	1800	Denga, Copper, diagonal reeded edge	—
N252	1800 KM	Kopeck, Copper, diagonal reeded edge	—
N253	1800	Kopeck, Copper, diagonal reeded edge	—
N254	1800 EM	2 Kopecks, Copper, plain edge	—
N255	1800 KM	2 Kopecks, Copper, small mintmark, diagonal reeded edge	—
N256	1800	2 Kopecks, Copper, diagonal reeded edge	—
N257	1800 CM	10 Kopecks, Copper, plain edge	—
N258	1800 CM АИ	1/4 Ruble, Silver, plain edge	—
N259	1801 KM	Polushka, Copper, diagonal reeded edge	1000.
N260	1801 KM	Denga, Copper, diagonal reeded edge	—
N261	1801	Denga, Copper, diagonal reeded edge	—
N262	1801 KM	Kopeck, Copper, reverse diagonal reeded edge	—
N263	1801 KM	2 Kopecks, Copper, diagonal reeded edge	—
N264	1801	2 Kopecks, Copper, diagonal reeded edge	—
N265	1801 CM	10 Kopecks, Silver, diagonal reeded edge	—
N266	1801 CM	Ruble, Silver, diagonal reeded edge	

KM#	Date	Identification	Mkt.Val.
N267	1802 EM	Polushka, Copper, mintmark below eagle, diagonal reeded edge	150.00
N268	1802 EM	Polushka, Copper, mintmark below eagle, plain edge	—
N269	1802 EM	Polushka, Copper, high relief, diagonal reeded edge	—
N270	1802 EM	Polushka, Copper, mintmark below date, plain edge	—
N271	1802 EM	Polushka, Copper, low relief, diagonal reeded edge	—
N272	1802 EM	Polushka, Copper, obv. struck with Denga die, diagonal reeded edge	—
N273	1802 KM	Polushka, Copper w/outer ring, diagonal reeded edge	250.00

KM#	Date	Identification	Mkt.Val.
N274	1802 KM	Polushka, Copper, w/o outer ring, diagonal reeded edgd	—

KM#	Date	Identification	Mkt.Val.
N275	1802 EM	Denga, Copper, high relief, diagonal reeded edge	—
N276	1802 EM	Denga, Copper, low relief, diagonal reeded edge	—
N277	1802 EM	Denga, Copper, low relief, plain edge	—

KM#	Date	Identification	Mkt.Val.
N278	1802 KM	Denga, Copper, w/outer ring, diagonal reeded edge	—
N279	1802 KM	Denga, Copper, w/o outer ring, diagonal reeded edge	—
N280	1802	Denga, Copper, diagonal reeded edge	—

KM#	Date	Identification	Mkt.Val.
N281	1802	Denga, Copper, plain edge	—

KM#	Date	Identification	Mkt.Val.
N282	1802 EM	Kopeck, Copper, high relief, diagonal reeded edge	—
N283	1802 EM	Kopeck, Copper, low relief, diagonal reeded edge	—
N284	1802 KM	Kopeck, Copper, w/outer ring, diagonal reeded edge	—

KM#	Date	Identification	Mkt.Val.
N285	1802 KM	Kopeck, Copper, w/o outer ring, diagonal reeded edge	—
N286	1802	Kopeck, Copper, diagonal reeded edge	—
N287	1802	Kopeck, Copper, plain edge	—
N288	1802 EM	2 Kopecks, Copper, mintmark below eagle, diagonal reeded edge	—
N289	1802 EM	2 Kopecks, Copper, mintmark below eagle, plain edge	—

KM#	Date	Identification	Mkt.Val.
N290	1802 EM	2 Kopecks, Copper, high relief, diagonal reeded edge	—
N291	1802 EM	2 Kopecks, Copper, low relief, diagonal reeded edge	—
N292	1802 EM	2 Kopecks, Copper, low relief, diagonal reeded edge	—
N293	1802 KM	2 Kopecks, Copper, w/outer ring, diagonal reeded edge	—

KM#	Date	Identification	Mkt.Val.
N294	1802 KM	2 Kopecks, Copper, w/o outer ring, diagonal reeded edge	—
N295	1802 EM	5 Kopecks, Copper, mintmark below eagle, diagonal reeded edge	—
N296	1802 EM	5 Kopecks, Copper, high relief, diagonal reeded edge	—
N297	1802 EM	5 Kopecks, Copper, low relief, diagonal reeded edge	—
N298	1802 KM	5 Kopecks, Copper w/outer ring, diagonal reeded edge	—
N299	1802 KM	5 Kopecks, Copper, w/o outer ring, diagonal reeded edge	—
N300	1802 СПБ ФГ	10 Kopecks, Silver, diagonal reeded edge	—
N301	1802 СПБ	1/4 Ruble, Silver, plain edge	—
N302	1802 СПБ	1/4 Ruble, Copper, plain edge	—
N303	1802 СПБ	Ruble, Silver, plain edge	—
N304	1802 СПБ	Ruble, Silver, diagonal reeded edge	—
N305	1802 СПБ ХЛ	10 Rubles, Gold, diagonal reeded edge	—
N306	1802 СПБ АИ	10 Rubles, Gold, double weight, diagonal reeded edge	—
N307	1803 KM	Polushka, Copper, diagonal reeded edge	150.00
N308	1803 KM	Denga, Copper, diagonal reeded edge	—
N309	1803 KM	Kopeck, Copper, diagonal reeded edge	—
N310	1803 KM	2 Kopecks, Copper, diagonal reeded edge	—
N311	1803 KM	5 Kopecks, Copper, diagonal reeded edge	—
N312	1803 СПБ ФГ	10 Kopecks, Silver, plain edge	—
N313	1803 СПБ АИ	1/4 Ruble, Silver, plain edge	—
N314	1803 СПБ ФГ	1/4 Ruble, Silver, plain edge	—
N315	1803 СПБ АИ	Ruble, Silver, plain edge	—
N316	1803 СПБ ФГ	Ruble, Silver, incuse edge lettering, lettered edge	—
N317	1803 СПБ ХЛ	5 Rubles, Gold, diagonal reeded edge	—

KM#	Date	Identification	Mkt.Val.
N318	1803 СПБ ХЛ	10 Roubles, Gold, diagonal reeded edge	—
N319	1804 KM	Polushka, Copper, diagonal reeded edge	—
N320	1804 KM	Denga, Copper, diagonal reeded edge	—
N321	1804 KM	Kopeck, Copper, diagonal reeded edge	—
N322	1804 KM	2 Kopecks, Copper, diagonal reeded edge	—
N323	1804 KM	5 Kopecks, Copper, diagonal reeded edge	—
N324	1805 KM	Polushka, Copper, diagonal reeded edge	—
N325	1805 KM	Denga, Copper, diagonal reeded edge	—
N326	1805 KM	Kopeck, Copper, diagonal reeded edge	—
N327	1805 KM	2 Kopecks, Copper, diagonal reeded edge	—
N328	1805 KM	5 Kopecks, Copper, diagonal reeded edge	—
N329	1806 KM	Polushka, Copper, w/o outer ring, diagonal reeded edge	—
N330	1806 KM	Denga, Copper, diagonal reeded edge	—
N331	1806 KM	Kopeck, Copper, diagonal reeded edge	—
N332	1806 KM	2 Kopecks, Copper, diagonal reeded edge	—
N333	1806 KM	5 Kopecks, Copper, diagonal reeded edge	—
N334	1807 KM	Polushka, Copper, w/o outer ring, diagonal reeded edge	—
N335	1807 KM	Denga, Copper, diagonal reeded edge	—
N336	1807 KM	Kopeck, Copper, diagonal reeded edge	—
N337	1807 KM	2 Kopecks, Copper, diagonal reeded edge	—
N338	1807 KM	5 Kopecks, Copper, diagonal reeded edge	—
N339	1808 KM	Polushka, Copper, w/o outer ring, diagonal reeded edge	150.00
N340	1808 KM	Denga, Copper, diagonal reeded edge	—
N341	1808 KM	Kopeck, Copper, diagonal reeded edge	—
N342	1808 KM	2 Kopecks, Copper, diagonal reeded edge	—
N343	1808 KM	5 Kopecks, Copper, diagonal reeded edge	—
N344	1808 СПБ ФГ	1/4 Ruble, Silver, plain edge	—
N345	1809 KM	Polushka, Copper, w/o outer ring, diagonal reeded edge	150.00
N346	1809 KM	Denga, Copper, diagonal reeded edge	—
N347	1809 KM	Kopeck, Copper, diagonal reeded edge	—
N348	1809 KM	2 Kopecks, Copper, diagonal reeded edge	—
N349	1809 KM	5 Kopecks, Copper, diagonal reeded edge	—
N350	1809 СПБ ФГ	10 Kopecks, Silver, plain edge	—
N351	1809 СПБ	10 Kopecks, Silver, plain edge	—
N352	1809 СПБ	1/2 Ruble, Silver, plain edge	—
N353	1809 СПБ ХЛ	10 Roubles, Gold, diagonal reeded edge	—
N354	1810 KM	Polushka, Copper, diagonal reeded edge	150.00
N355	1810 KM	Denga, Copper, diagonal reeded edge	—
N356	1810 KM	Kopeck, Copper, diagonal reeded edge	—
N357	1810 KM	2 Kopecks, Copper, diagonal reeded edge	—
N358	1810 KM	5 Kopecks, Copper, diagonal reeded edge	—

New Standard

KM#	Date	Identification	Mkt.Val.
N359	1810 EM HM	Denga, Copper, curved date, plain edge	—
N360	1810 EM	Denga, Copper, no initials, plain edge	—
N361	1810 KM ПБ	Denga, Copper, plain edge	—
N362	1810 EM HM	Kopeck, Copper, curved date, plain edge	—
N363	1810 KM ПБ	Kopeck, Copper, no initials, plain edge	—
N364	1810 EM HM	2 Kopecks, Copper, curved date, plain edge	—
N365	1810 EM HM	2 Kopecks, Copper, small initials, plain edge	—
N366	1810 KM	2 Kopecks, Copper, plain edge	—
N367	1810 KM ПБ	2 Kopecks, Copper, small eagle, plain edge	—
N368	1810 СПБ ФГ	2 Kopecks, Copper, plain edge	—
N369	1810 СПБ МК	10 Kopecks, Silver, old type, plain edge	—
N370	1810 СПБ ФГ	1/4 Ruble, Silver, old type, plain edge	—
N371	1810 СПБ ФГ	Ruble, Silver, old type, plain edge	—
N372	1810 СПБ ФГ	10 Kopecks, Silver, new type, plain edge	—
N373	1810 СПБ	1/2 Ruble, Silver, plain edge	—
N374	1811 KM ПБ	Denga, Copper, wings far from rim, plain edge	—
N375	1811 СПБ МК	Denga, Copper, plain edge	—
N376	1811 KM ПБ	Kopeck, Copper, plain edge	—
N377	1811 СПБ ПС	Kopeck, Copper, plain edge	—
N378	1811 EM ИФ	2 Kopecks, Copper, diagonal reeded edge	—
N379	1811 KM ПБ	2 Kopecks, Copper, small eagle, plain edge	—
N380	1811 СПБ ФГ	5 Kopecks, Silver, plain edge	—
N381	1811 СПБ ФГ	10 Kopecks, Silver, broad crown, plain edge	—
N382	1811 СПБ ФГ	1/2 Ruble, Silver, tapered crown, plain edge	—
N383	1813 СПБ ПС	10 Kopecks, Silver, broad crown, plain edge	—

KM#	Date	Identification	Mkt.Val.
N384	1813 СПБ	1/2 Ruble, Silver, plain edge	—
N385	1814 СПБ ПС	Denga, Copper, plain edge	—
N386	1814 СПБ ПС	Kopeck, Copper, plain edge	—
N387	1814 СПБ	5 Kopecks, Silver, tapered crown, plain edge	—
N388	1814 СПБ	20 Kopecks, Silver, plain edge	—
N389	1814 СПБ	1/2 Ruble, Silver, plain edge	—
N390	1815 СПБ	20 Kopecks, Silver, open 2 in value, plain edge	—
N391	1815 СПБ	1/2 Ruble, Silver, tapered crown, plain edge	—
N392	1815 СПБ	Ruble, Silver, plain edge	—
N393	1816 СПБ	5 Kopecks, Silver, large crown, plain edge	—
N394	1816 СПБ	20 Kopecks, Silver, large crown, plain edge	—
N395	1816 СПБ	1/2 Ruble, Silver, tapered crown, plain edge	—
N396	1817СПБ	1/2 Ruble, Silver, tapered crown, plain edge	—
N397	1818 KM AM	Kopeck, Copper, plain edge	—
N398	1818 KM АД	2 Kopecks, Copper, plain edge	—
N399	1818 СПБ	1/2 Ruble, Silver, tapered crown, plain edge	—
N400	1819 KM АД	Kopeck, Copper, plain edge	—
N401	1819 KM ДБ	2 Kopecks, Copper, plain edge	—
N402	1819 СПБ	10 Kopecks, Silver, tapered crown, plain edge	—
N403	1819 СПБ	1/2 Ruble, Silver, tapered crown, plain edge	—
N404	1819 СПБ	Ruble, Silver, plain edge	—
N405	1820 KM АД	Kopeck, Copper, plain edge	—
N406	1820 СПБ	5 Kopecks, Silver, broad crown, plain edge	—
N407	1821KM АД	Kopeck, Copper, plain edge	—
N408	1821 СПБ	5 Kopecks, Silver, plain edge	—
N409	1821 СПБ	Ruble, Silver, plain edge	—
N410	1823 KM AM	Denga, Copper, plain edge	—
N411	1825 СПБ	20 Kopecks, Silver, tapered crown, plain edge	—
N412	1826 СПБ	20 Kopecks, Silver, open 2 in value, plain edge	—
N413	1826 СПБ	20 Kopecks, Silver, new type, large crown, plain edge	—
N414	1826 СПБ ПД	1/2 Ruble, Silver, new type, lettered edge	—
N415	1830 EM	Kopeck, Copper, plain edge	—
N416	1830 EM	2 Kopecks, Copper, plain edge	—
N417	1830 EM	5 Kopecks, Copper, plain edge	—
N418	1830 EM	10 Kopecks, Copper, no initials, plain edge	—
N419	1831 CM	Kopeck, Copper, plain edge	—
N420	1831 CM	2 Kopecks, Copper, plain edge	—
N421	1831 CM	5 Kopecks, Copper, plain edge	—
N422	1831 CM	10 Kopecks, Copper, plain edge	—
N423	1832 CM	Kopeck, Copper, plain edge	—
N424	1832 CM	2 Kopecks, Copper, plain edge	—
N425	1832 CM	5 Kopecks, Copper, plain edge	—
N426	1832 CM	10 Kopecks, Copper, plain edge	—
N427	1833 CM	Kopeck, Copper, plain edge	—
N428	1833 CM	2 Kopecks, Copper, plain edge	—
N429	1833 CM	5 Kopecks, Copper, plain edge	—
N430	1833 CM	10 Kopecks, Copper, plain edge	—
N431	1833 СПБ НГ	3/4 Ruble, Silver, St. George w,mantle, plain edge	—
N432	1834 CM	Kopeck, Copper, plain edge	—
N433	1834 CM	2 Kopecks, Copper, plain edge	—
N434	1834 CM	5 Kopecks, Copper, plain edge	—
N435	1834 CM	10 Kopecks, Copper, plain edge	—
N436	1835 CM	Kopeck, Copper, plain edge	—
N437	1835 CM	2 Kopecks, Copper, plain edge	—

KM#	Date	Identification	Mkt.Val.
N438	1835 CM	5 Kopecks, Copper, plain edge	—
N439	1835 CM	10 Kopecks, Copper, plain edge	—

KM#	Date	Identification	Mkt.Val.
N440	1836 CM	Kopeck, Copper, plain edge	—
N441	1836 CM	2 Kopecks, Copper, plain edge	—
N442	1836 CM	5 Kopecks, Copper, plain edge	—
N443	1836 CM	10 Kopecks, Copper, plain edge	—
N444	1837 CM	Kopeck, Copper, plain edge	—
N445	1837 CM	2 Kopecks, Copper, plain edge	—
N446	1837 CM	5 Kopecks, Copper, plain edge	—
N447	1837 CM	10 Kopecks, Copper, plain edge	—
N448	1838 CM	Kopeck, Copper, plain edge	—
N449	1838 CM	2 Kopecks, Copper, plain edge	—
N450	1838 CM	5 Kopecks, Copper, plain edge	—
N451	1838 CM	10 Kopecks, Copper, plain edge	—
N452	1839 CM	Kopeck, Copper, plain edge	—
N453	1839 CM	2 Kopecks, Copper, plain edge	—
N454	1839 CM	5 Kopecks, Copper, plain edge	—
N455	1839 CM	10 Kopecks, Copper, plain edge	—
		New Standard	
N456	1839 CM	Polushka, Copper, plain edge	—
N457	1839 CM	Denga, Copper, plain edge	—
N458	1839 CM	Kopeck, Copper, plain edge	—
N459	1839 CM	2 Kopecks, Copper, plain edge	—
N460	1839 CM	3 Kopecks, Copper, plain edge	—
N461	1840 CM	Polushka, Copper, plain edge	—
N462	1840 CM	Denga, Copper, plain edge	—
N463	1840	Denga, Copper, plain edge	—
N464	1840 CM	Kopeck, Copper, plain edge	—
N465	1840	Kopeck, Copper, plain edge	—
N466	1840 CM	2 Kopecks, Copper, plain edge	—
N467	1840	2 Kopecks, Copper, plain edge	—
N468	1840 CM	3 Kopecks, Copper, plain edge	—
N469	1840	3 Kopecks, Copper, plain edge	—
N470	1840	25 Kopecks, Silver, lis missing on sceptre, plain edge	—
N471	1840	Ruble, Silver, St. George w/mantle, plain edge	—
N472	1841 CM	Polushka, Copper, plain edge	—
N473	1841 CM	Denga, Copper, plain edge	—
N474	1841 CM	Kopeck, Copper, plain edge	—
N475	1841 CM	2 Kopecks, Copper, plain edge	—
N476	1841 CM	3 Kopecks, Copper, plain edge	—
N477	1842 CM	Polushka, Copper, plain edge	—
N478	1842 CM	Denga, Copper, plain edge	—
N479	1842 CM	Kopeck, Copper, plain edge	—
N480	1842 CM	2 Kopecks, Copper, plain edge	—
N481	1842 CM	3 Kopecks, Copper, plain edge	—
N482	1842 НГ	10 Kopecks, Silver, plain edge	—
N483	1842 АЧ	1/2 Ruble, Silver, large center tail feather, plain edge	—
N484	1842 НГ	1/2 Ruble, Silver, plain edge	—
N485	1842 НГ	Ruble, Silver, St. Geroge w/mantle, plain edge	—
N486	1843 CM	Polushka, Copper, plain edge	—
N487	1843 CM	Denga, Copper, plain edge	—
N488	1843 CM	Kopeck, Copper, plain edge	—
N489	1843 CM	2 Kopecks, Copper, plain edge	—
N490	1843 CM	3 Kopecks, Copper, plain edge	—
N491	1844 CM	Polushka, Copper, plain edge	—
N492	1844 CM	Denga, Copper, plain edge	—
N493	1844 CM	Kopeck, Copper, plain edge	—
N494	1844 CM	2 Kopecks, Copper, plain edge	—
N495	1844 CM	3 Kopecks, Copper, plain edge	—
N496	1845 CM	Polushka, Copper, plain edge	—
N497	1845 CM	Denga, Copper, plain edge	—
N498	1845 CM	Kopeck, Copper, plain edge	—
N499	1845 CM	2 Kopecks, Copper, plain edge	—
N500	1845 CM	3 Kopecks, Copper, plain edge	—
N501	1846 CM	Polushka, Copper, plain edge	—
N502	1846 CM	Denga, Copper, plain edge	—
N503	1846 CM	Kopeck, Copper, plain edge	—
N504	1846 CM	2 Kopecks, Copper, plain edge	—
N505	1846 CM	3 Kopecks, Copper, plain edge	—
N506	1846 СПБ	1/2 Ruble, Silver, wave-shaped tail feathers, plain edge	—
N507	1847 CM	Denga, Copper, plain edge	—
N508	1847 CM	Kopeck, Copper, plain edge	—
N509	1847 CM	2 Kopecks, Copper, plain edge	—
N510	1847 CM	3 Kopecks, Copper, plain edge	—
		New Standard	
N511	1849 EM	3 Kopecks, Copper, small 3, plain edge	—
N512	1852 ПА	Ruble, Silver, St. George w/mantle, plain edge	—
N513	1855 EM	2 Kopecks, Copper, small 2, plain edge	—
N514	1857 EM	Denga, Copper, plain edge	—
N515	1859 EM	2 Kopecks, Copper, small 2, plain edge	—
N516	1859 EM	3 Kopecks, Copper, small 3, plain edge	—
N517	1859 EM	5 Kopecks, Copper, small 5, plain edge	—
N518	1860	20 Kopecks, Silver, old type large shield, plain edge	—
N519	1860	1/2 Ruble, Silver, new type short shield, lettered edge	—
N520	1860	1/2 Ruble, Silver, new type tall shield, plain edge	—
N521	1861	5 Kopecks, Silver, no MM., plain edge	—

NCLT ISSUES

PATTERNS

KM#	Date	Mintage	Identification	Mkt.Val.
1	1827	—	3 Kopeks, Copper, C#137.5	—
2	1840	—	Polushka (1/4 Kopek) Copper, C#142	350.00
3	1958	—	1 Kopek, Aluminum-Bronze, Y119	200.00
4	1958	—	2 Kopeks, Aluminum-Bronze, Y120	200.00
5	1958	—	3 Kopeks, Aluminum-Bronze, Y121	200.00
6	1958	—	5 Kopeks, Aluminum-Bronze, Y122	200.00
7	1958	—	10 Kopeks, Copper-Nickel, Y123	300.00
8	1958	—	15 Kopeks, Copper-Nickel, Y124	300.00
9	1958	—	20 Kopeks, Copper-Nickel, Y125	300.00
10	1958	—	2 Ruble, Copper-Nickel, Y126	300.00
11	1958	—	5 Ruble, Copper-Nickel, Y127	300.00

MINT SETS

KM#	Date	Mintage	Identification	Issue Price	Mkt. Val.
S1	1957(4)	—	Y122-125	2.25	8.00
S2	1961(9)	—	Y126-134	4.50	8.00
S3	1962(7)	—	Y126-132	2.25	6.50
S4	1964(4)	—	Y126,127,133a,134a	2.55	7.50
S5	1965(9)	—	Y126-132,133a,134a	4.50	8.00
S6	1966(9)	—	Y126-132,133a,134a	4.50	9.00
S7	1967(9)	—	Y126-132,133a,134a	4.50	8.50
S8	1967(5)	—	Y136-140	6.00	8.50
S9	1968(9)	—	Y126-132,133a,134a And Mint Token.	6.00	8.00
S10	1969(9)	—	Same As Above	7.00	9.00
S11	1970(9)	—	Same As Above	11.00	15.00
S12	1971(9)	—	Y126-132,133a,134a	6.00	9.00
S13	1972(9)	10,000	Same As Above	7.00	8.50
S14	1973(9)	8,000	Same As Above	11.00	15.00
S15	1974(9)	27,500	Same As Above, But Square Mint Token.	11.00	15.00
S16	1975(9)	27,500	Same As 8	11.00	15.00
S17	1976(9)	55,000	Same As 15	—	15.00
S18	1977(9)	58,750	—	—	15.00
S19	1978(9)	60,000	Y126-132,133a,134a	—	15.00
S20	1979(9)	—	Y126-132,133a,134a	19.00	—

RUSSIAN CAUCASIA

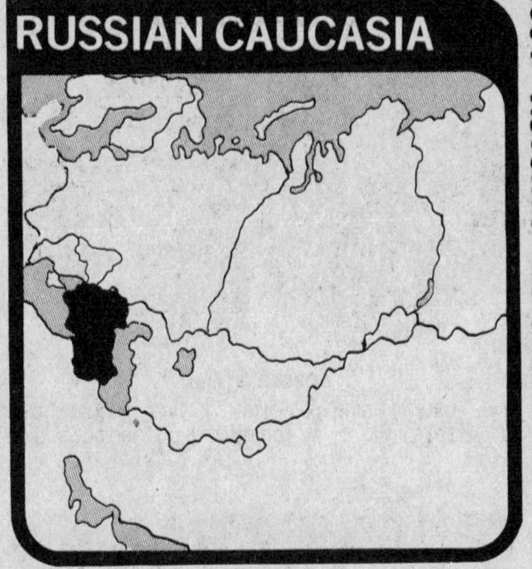

Russian Caucasia, a natural area in Russia located between the Black and Caspian seas, was a region of mystery and myth to the Ancient Greeks. It was there that Prometheus was bound for the eagle's torment and the Argonauts sought the golden fleece. For more than a thousand years Caucasia was the refuge for wave after wave of migrating peoples. Greeks, Romans, Persians, Turks, Huns, Mongols and finally the Russians invaded the treeless steppes and wooded highlands of this range-flanked granite bridge between Europe and Asia. Russian aggression, heroically resisted by the independent mountain races, began early in the 18th century and continued until the last opposition was stifled. The several states of Caucasia made a futile attempt to establish an independent federated republic during the Russian February Revolution of 1917, but were quickly reconquered after the triumph of Bolshevism over the Kerensky administration.

The following areas of Russian Caucasia were coin—issuing entities of interest to numismatics:

ARMAVIR

Armavir is a trading town located in the center of the province of Armavir in northern Russian Caucasia.

LOCAL CURRENCY UNDER THE WHITE RUSSIANS

ROUBLE

COPPER, 26mm.
Reeded edge, thin planchet, monogram under tail.

Y#	Date	Mintage	Fine	VF	XF	Unc
1.1	1918	—	75.00	150.00	250.00	400.00

3 ROUBLES

COPPER, 28mm
Monogram under tail, reeded edge.

Y#	Date	Mintage	Fine	VF	XF	Unc
2.1	1918	—	50.00	100.00	175.00	275.00

Monogram under claw.

Y#	Date	Mintage	Fine	VF	XF	Unc
2.2	1918	—	50.00	100.00	175.00	275.00

5 ROUBLES

COPPER, 31mm

Y#	Date	Mintage	Fine	VF	XF	Unc
3	1918	—	100.00	175.00	300.00	500.00

NCLT ISSUES

PATTERNS

KM#	Date	Mintage	Identification	Mkt.Val.
1	1918	—	1 Rouble, Copper, 28mm, reeded edge, thin planchet, Y1.2	—
2	1918	—	1 Rouble, Copper, 28mm, plain edge, thin planchet, Y1.3	—
3	1918	—	1 Rouble, Copper, 28mm, plain edge, thick planchet, Y1.4	—
4	1918	—	3 Roubles, Copper, 31mm, monogram under tail, Y2.3	400.00
5	1918	—	3 Roubles, Silver, Y2.4	—
6	1918	—	5 Roubles, Aluminum, Y3a	—

ARMENIA

Armenia, a mountainous, sub-tropical Soviet Socialist Republic bounded on the north by Georgia, on the east by Azerbaijan, on the south by Iran, and on the west by Turkey, was a formidable power during the century prior to the birth of Christ when the Armenian king ruled from the capital city of Antioch. Thereafter Armenia was conquered and ruled by a series of aggressor states, chiefly Rome, Persia and Turkey. Russia appeared in the region in 1801, and brought it under Russian control in 1828. In 1938 Armenia became a constituent republic of the U.S.S.R.

Coins of Iravan Yerevan are listed under Iran. A 5 Ruble piece dated 1920 purports to be an issue of the Ephemeral Armenian Republic. It is believed to be a fantasy.

AZERBAIJAN

During the 18th century, a number of independent Khanates arose in what is now Soviet Azerbaijan. three of these khanates struck coins in the 19th century and are listed individually: Karabagh, Sheki and Shemakha. Coins of Iranian Azerbaijan (Maragheh, Tabriz, Khuy, Saujbulagh, Ardabil and Urumi) are of ordinary Iranian type, and are listed under Iran. A 5 ruble piece dated 1920 of the Azerbaijan Republic is believed to be a fantasy.

DAGHESTAN

(DAGESTAN)

Dagestan is a mountainous S.S.R. bounded on the north by Chechno-Ingush, on the south by Azerbaijan, on the east by the Caspian Sea, and on the west by Georgia. The republic was created in 1921 from the former province of Dagestan.

RULERS

Emir Uzun-Hayir (Uzun-Kheir)
AH1338-1339/AD1919-20

2-1/2 TOMAN

A 2-1/2 toman coin was reportedly struck, but no specimens are known.

5 TOMAN

BRASS

Y#	Date	Mintage	Fine	VF	XF
2	AH1338	—	—	—	—

10 TOMAN

BRASS

Y#	Date	Mintage	Fine	VF	XF
3	AH1338	—	—	—	—

COPPER
Struck over Russia 2 Kopek, Y#10.

Y#	Date	Mintage	Fine	VF	XF
3a	AH1338	—	—	—	—

GEORGIA

Georgia is a S.S.R. and former kingdom bounded on the north by the Russian Soviet Federated Socialist Republic, on the south by Armenia and Turkey, on the east by Azerbaijan, and on the west by the Black Sea. After centuries of rule by Turkey or Persia, Georgia became a vassal of Russia in 1783. It came under direct rule in September, 1801. Russia recognized Georgia's independence in 1920, invaded the country in 1921, and made it a direct member of the U.S.S.R. in 1936. Soviet dictator Joseph Stalin was a native son of Georgia.

LOCAL ISSUES

RULERS

Erekle II,
AH1176-1213/AD1762-1798
Giorgi XII,
AH1213-1215/AD1798-1800
David, Regent
AH1215-1216/AD1801

ANONYMOUS ISSUES

Struck under the authority of Alexander I (1801-25) and Nicholas I (1825-55) of Russia at the Tiflis (Tbilisi) Mint.

MONETARY SYSTEM

200 Dinars = 1 Abaze

DATING

The dates are shown in a quantitive manner ex. 1000 plus 800 plus 10 plus 9 = 1819.

NOTE: The fine style 1 and 2 Abaze coins of 1828 are patterns, struck at St. Petersburg.

5 (DINARS) = PULI

(= 1/2 Kopek)

COPPER, 20mm

C#	Date	Mintage	VG	Fine	VF	XF
81	1804	4,000	—	—	Rare	—
	1805	Inc. Ab.	50.00	100.00	175.00	275.00
	1806	.015	50.00	100.00	175.00	275.00

10 (DINARS) = 2 PULI

(= Kopek)

COPPER, 24mm

C#	Date	Mintage	VG	Fine	VF	XF
82	1804	3,000	—	—	Rare	—
	1805	Inc. Ab.	60.00	120.00	200.00	325.00
	1806	.034	60.00	120.00	200.00	325.00
	1808	.012	60.00	120.00	200.00	325.00
	1810	.050	60.00	120.00	200.00	325.00

20 (DINARS) = BISTI

(= 2 Kopeks)

COPPER, 30mm

C#	Date	Mintage	VG	Fine	VF	XF
83	1804	1,000	—	—	Rare	—
	1805	Inc. Ab.	62.50	125.00	175.00	275.00
	1806	.025	62.50	125.00	175.00	275.00
	1808	.020	62.50	125.00	175.00	275.00
	1810	.315	62.50	125.00	175.00	275.00

1/2 ABAZI (= 100 DINARS)

(= 10 Kopeks)

.917 SILVER, 16mm

C#	Date	Mintage	VG	Fine	VF	XF
84	1804II.3	5,000	—	—	Rare	—
	1805II.3	Inc. Ab.	25.00	50.00	100.00	200.00
	1810AT	398 pcs.	—	—	Rare	—
	1813AT	2,000	—	—	Rare	—
	1820AT	4,000	30.00	60.00	110.00	225.00
	1821AT	Inc. Ab.	25.00	50.00	100.00	200.00
	1822AK	1,000	25.00	50.00	100.00	200.00
	1823AK	4,000	25.00	50.00	100.00	200.00
	1824AK	4,000	25.00	50.00	100.00	200.00
	1826AT	5,000	25.00	50.00	100.00	200.00
	1827AT	7,000	25.00	50.00	100.00	200.00
	1828AT	.016	25.00	50.00	100.00	200.00
	1831AT	—	25.00	50.00	100.00	225.00
	1832BK	—	25.00	50.00	100.00	200.00
	1833BK	—	25.00	50.00	95.00	200.00

ABAZI (= 200 DINARS)

(= 20 Kopeks)

SILVER, 19mm

C#	Date	Mintage	VG	Fine	VF	XF
85	1804II.3	—	—	—	Rare	—
	1805II.3	.019	13.50	27.50	40.00	60.00
	1806II.3	.023	12.50	25.00	50.00	75.00
	1806AK	Inc. Ab.	13.50	27.50	40.00	60.00
	1807AK	9,000	13.50	27.50	40.00	60.00
	1808AK	.014	13.50	27.50	40.00	60.00
	1809AK	.017	13.50	27.50	40.00	60.00
	1810AT	4,000	25.00	50.00	75.00	110.00
	1811AT	1,000	—	—	Rare	—
	1812AT	9,000	12.50	25.00	50.00	75.00
	1813AT	7,000	12.50	25.00	50.00	75.00
	1814AT	3,000	13.50	27.50	40.00	60.00
	1815AT	3,000	20.00	40.00	60.00	90.00
	1816AT	.012	13.50	27.50	40.00	60.00
	1818AT	8,000	13.50	27.50	40.00	60.00
	1819AT	.010	13.50	27.50	40.00	60.00
	1820AT	.012	13.50	27.50	40.00	60.00
	1821AT	.014	13.50	27.50	40.00	60.00
	1822AT	5,000	15.00	30.00	50.00	75.00
	1822AK	Inc. Ab.	13.50	27.50	40.00	60.00
	1823AK	5,000	13.50	27.50	40.00	60.00
	1824AK	5,000	13.50	27.50	40.00	60.00
	1826AT	5,000	13.50	27.50	40.00	60.00
	1828AT	—	—	—	Rare	—
	1828ESSAI	—	—	—	Rare	—
	1830AT	—	13.50	27.50	40.00	60.00
	1831AT	—	13.50	27.50	40.00	60.00

2 ABAZI (=400 DINARS)

(= 40 Kopeks)

.917 SILVER, 23mm

C#	Date	Mintage	VG	Fine	VF	XF
86	1804II.3	.033	—	—	Rare	—
	1805II.3	Inc. Ab.	15.00	30.00	50.00	75.00
	1806AK	.042	15.00	30.00	50.00	75.00
	1807AK	.071	15.00	30.00	50.00	75.00
	1807AT	Inc. Ab.	30.00	60.00	90.00	150.00
	1808AK	.065	15.00	30.00	50.00	75.00
	1809AK	.086	15.00	30.00	50.00	75.00
	1810AK	.020	17.50	35.00	55.00	85.00
	1811AT	.005	20.00	40.00	60.00	90.00
	1812AT	.059	15.00	30.00	50.00	75.00
	1813AT	.048	15.00	30.00	50.00	75.00
	1814AT	.020	15.00	30.00	50.00	75.00
	1815AT	.021	15.00	30.00	50.00	75.00
	1816AT	.079	15.00	30.00	50.00	75.00
	1818AT	.085	15.00	30.00	50.00	75.00
	1819AT	.105	15.00	30.00	50.00	75.00
	1820AT	.112	15.00	30.00	50.00	75.00
	1821AT	.075	15.00	30.00	50.00	75.00
	1822AT	.024	22.50	45.00	65.00	100.00
	1822AK	Inc. Ab.	15.00	30.00	50.00	75.00
	1823AK	.039	15.00	30.00	50.00	75.00
	1824AK	.032	15.00	30.00	50.00	75.00
	1826AT	.075	15.00	30.00	50.00	75.00
	1827AT	.172	15.00	30.00	50.00	75.00
	1828AT	.126	15.00	30.00	50.00	75.00
	1828 ESSAI	—	—	—	Rare	—
	1829AT	.213	15.00	30.00	50.00	75.00
	1830AT	.273	15.00	30.00	50.00	75.00
	1831AT	.338	15.00	30.00	50.00	75.00
	1831BK	Inc. Ab.	15.00	30.00	50.00	75.00
	1832BK	.210	15.00	30.00	50.00	75.00
	1833BK	.114	15.00	30.00	50.00	75.00

NCLT ISSUES

PATTERNS

KM#	Date	Mintage	Identification	Mkt.Val.
1	1804	—	1 Abazi, Silver, 20 Dinars error, C85	—

KARABAGH

Former khanate in Azerbaijan. Principal mint in modern town of Shusha (then Panahabad). Broke away from Persia in second half of 1700's. Absorbed by Russia in 1819.

RULERS

Ibrahim Khan
Mahdi Quli Khan Muzatfar

MONETARY SYSTEM

Derived From The Safavid Persian System
1 Bisti = 20 Dinars
1 Abbasi = 200 Dinars

MINT: Panahabad (=shusha). The silver abbasi of Karabagh circulated widely in Iran, where it came to be known as a "Panabadi", a term later used for the half Kran in Iran.

All coins are anonymous except KM#5, which is in the name of Fath'ali Shah of Iran.

1/2 BISTI

COPPER, 20-22mm

KM#	Date	Good	VG	Fine	VF
1		7.50	15.00	20.00	30.00

ABBASI

SILVER, 21-24mm
In the name of Fath'ali Shah

KM#	Date	Good	VG	Fine	VF
5	AH1216	10.00	20.00	30.00	45.00

Obv: Mint. Rev: Russian crown and branches.

KM#	Date	Good	VG	Fine	VF
6	AH1222	10.00	20.00	32.50	50.00

Obv: Kalimah. Rev: Mint and date.

KM#	Date	Good	VG	Fine	VF
7	AH1221	6.50	13.50	25.00	40.00

Obv: Date and unread inscription. Rev: Mint.
(Date sometimes also on reverse.)

KM#	Date	Good	VG	Fine	VF
8	AH1228-1237	—	10.00	20.00	30.00

NOTE: The above listing of types is incomplete. In addition, more dates of the listed type likely exist.

SCHAMAKHI

Schamakhi is a former khanate located in Azerbaijan. It was under Persian rule throughout much of its history until liberated by the Russians who annexed the khanate in 1813.

MONETARY SYSTEM

1 Bisti = 20 Dinars
1 Abbasi = 200 Dinars

LOCAL KHANATE

Annexed To Russia In 1813

ABBASI

SILVER, 2.0-2.3 gm.

KM#	Date	Good	VG	Fine	VF
51	AH1227-35	12.50	25.00	45.00	70.00

SHEKI

Sheki, a former khanate in Russian Caucasia, was occupied by Russia in 1807 and annexed in 1819.

MONETARY SYSTEM

1 Bisti = 20 Dinars
1 Abbasi = 200 Dinars

MINT: NUKHA

Coins Struck Under Russian Occupation, 1807-1819.
Annexed To Russia In 1819.

BISTI

COPPER, 30-34mm
Obv: Crowned date. Rev: Mint name.

KM#	Date	Good	VG	Fine	VF
5,7, &10	AH1221-33	25.00	45.00	75.00	140.00

1/2 ABBASI

SILVER, 1.1-1.2 gm.

KM#	Date	Good	VG	Fine	VF
21	AH1231-32	25.00	50.00	100.00	165.00

ABBASI

SILVER, 2.1-2.3 gm.

KM#	Date	Good	VG	Fine	VF
23	AH1232	25.00	50.00	100.00	165.00

KRIM

The Crimea (ancient Tauris or Tauric Chersonese, Turkish Kirim or Krim, Russian Krym) is a peninsula of southern Russia extending into the Black Sea southwest of the Sea of Azov.

In ancient times, the Crimea was inhabited by the Goths and Scythinians, was colonized by the Greeks, and ranked, in part, as a tributary state of Rome. During the succeeding centuries, the Crimea was overrun by the Goths, the Huns, the Khazars, the Byzantine Greeks, the Kipchak Turks, and the Tatars of Batu Khan who founded the Tatar khanate in Russia known as the empire of the Golden Horde. After the destruction of the Golden Horde by Tamerlane (Timur) in 1395, the Crimean Tatars founded an independent khanate under Haji Ghirai which reigned first at Solkhat (Eski Kirim or Stary Krym). The Crimean khans ruled as tributary princes of the Ottoman empire from 1478 to 1777, when they became dependent upon Russia.

Catherine II annexed the Crimea to Russia on April 26, 1783, and after a period as the Tavrida province, it was made an autonomous republic of the Russian federation in 1921. The Tatars, however, remained fiercely nationalistic and during World War II collaborated with the German-Rumanian occupation force. Upon Russian reconquest of the Crimea in May, 1944, the entire Tatar population was deported to Russia and Siberia. The autonomous Crimean republic was dissolved and reconstituted as a region of the Russian Soviet Federated Socialist Republic. On Feb. 14, 1954, this region was transferred to the Ukrainian Soviet Socialist Republic, becoming its southernmost province.

KHANATE ISSUES

RULERS

Shahin Giray bin Ahmad Giray,
AH1191-1197/AD1777-1783

IMPERIAL ISSUES

RULERS

Catherine II, 1783-1796

MINTMARKS

TM - Feodosia Mint

2 KOPECKS

SILVER
Obv: Crowned E II monogram, date.
Rev: 2, 2 dots, T.M.

C#	Date	Mintage	Fine	VF	XF
7	1787	—	—	Rare	—

5 KOPECKS

SILVER
Obv: Crowned E II monogram, date.
Rev: 5, 5 dots, T.M.

C#	Date	Mintage	Fine	VF	XF
8	1787	—	—	Rare	—

10 KOPECKS

SILVER
Obv: Crowned E II monogram, date.
Rev: 10, 10 dots, T.M.

C#	Date	Mintage	Fine	VF	XF
9	1787	—	—	Rare	—

20 KOPECKS

SILVER
Obv: Crowned E II monogram, date.
Rev: 20, 20 dots, T.M.

C#	Date	Mintage	Fine	VF	XF
10	1787	—	—	Rare	—

SIBERIA

Siberia, the vast expanse that is most of Asiatic Russia covers 4,950,000 square miles and has a population of about 35,090,000 (1974 est.). Siberia which means Sleeping Land in the Tatar language reaches from the Ural Mountains in the west to the Pacific Ocean in the east and from the Arctic Ocean in the north to the borders of China in the south. It is composed of 3 major regions: the Lena River Basin; the Central Siberian Plateau (reaching to 5,581 ft.) and the West Siberian Plain. Siberia is probably best known for its severe winters with temperatures of -90F being recorded. Leading industries are mining and forestry.

Siberia was tribal in nature until 1581 when an expedition from Russia made up of Cossacks overthrew the Sibir khanate. In the next 3 centuries explorers and traders explored throughout Siberia. Under the czars it became a place to send criminals and political dissidents, a purpose it serves to this day. With the construction of the Trans-Siberian Railroad, (1891-1905) migration began from the West and settlements grew along the railroad right-of-way.

The Siberian coinage of Catherine the Great was inaugurated because of a coin shortage. A mint was established at Kolyvan-Voskressensk in the mining areas of the Altai Mountains. Men and machinery were sent from the Ekaterinburg Mint to get the new mint started. The normal Russian copper denominations were used plus the addition of a copper 10 kopeck piece. The regular series runs from 1766 to 1781 but there are known pieces dated 1763 and 1764.

MINTMARKS

KM - Kolyvan

MONETARY SYSTEM

100 Kopecks = 1 Rouble

POLUSHKA

COPPER

C#	Date	Mintage	VG	Fine	VF	XF
1	1766	—	300.00	500.00	700.00	1000.
	1767KM	—	90.00	150.00	225.00	325.00
	1768KM	—	90.00	150.00	225.00	325.00
	1769KM	—	90.00	150.00	225.00	325.00
	1770KM	—	60.00	100.00	160.00	225.00
	1771KM	—	60.00	100.00	160.00	225.00
	1772KM	—	60.00	100.00	160.00	225.00
	1773KM	—	90.00	150.00	225.00	325.00
	1774KM	—	90.00	150.00	225.00	325.00
	1775KM	—	90.00	150.00	225.00	325.00
	1776KM	—	90.00	150.00	225.00	325.00
	1777KM	—	90.00	150.00	225.00	325.00
	1778KM	—	90.00	150.00	225.00	325.00
	1779KM	—	90.00	150.00	225.00	325.00

DENGA

COPPER

C#	Date	Mintage	VG	Fine	VF	XF
2	1764	—	—	—	Rare	—
	1766	—	—	—	Rare	—
	1767KM	—	50.00	90.00	125.00	200.00
	1768KM	—	30.00	50.00	80.00	125.00
	1769KM	—	30.00	50.00	80.00	125.00
	1770KM	—	30.00	50.00	80.00	125.00
	1771KM	—	30.00	50.00	80.00	125.00
	1772KM	—	30.00	50.00	80.00	125.00
	1773KM	—	30.00	50.00	80.00	125.00
	1774KM	—	30.00	50.00	80.00	125.00
	1775KM	—	30.00	50.00	80.00	125.00
	1776KM	—	50.00	90.00	125.00	200.00
	1777KM	—	50.00	90.00	125.00	200.00
	1778KM	—	50.00	90.00	125.00	200.00
	1779KM	—	50.00	90.00	125.00	200.00

KOPECK

COPPER

C#	Date	Mintage	VG	Fine	VF	XF
3	1764	—	—	—	Rare	—
	1766	—	100.00	175.00	250.00	350.00
	1767	—	100.00	175.00	250.00	350.00
	1767KM	—	100.00	175.00	250.00	350.00
	1768KM	—	25.00	40.00	60.00	95.00
	1769KM	—	25.00	40.00	60.00	95.00
	1770KM	—	25.00	40.00	60.00	95.00
	1771KM	—	25.00	40.00	60.00	95.00
	1772KM	—	25.00	40.00	60.00	95.00
	1773KM	—	25.00	40.00	60.00	95.00
	1774KM	—	25.00	40.00	60.00	95.00
	1775KM	—	25.00	40.00	60.00	95.00
	1776KM	—	25.00	40.00	60.00	95.00
	1777KM	—	25.00	40.00	60.00	95.00
	1778KM	—	25.00	40.00	60.00	95.00
	1779KM	—	25.00	40.00	60.00	95.00

2 KOPECKS

COPPER

C#	Date	Mintage	VG	Fine	VF	XF
4	1764	—	—	—	Rare	—
	1766	—	100.00	175.00	250.00	400.00
	1767	—	60.00	100.00	150.00	250.00
	1767KM	—	40.00	65.00	100.00	150.00
	1768KM	—	25.00	40.00	60.00	90.00
	1769KM	—	25.00	40.00	60.00	90.00
	1770KM	—	25.00	40.00	60.00	90.00
	1771KM	—	25.00	40.00	60.00	90.00
	1772KM	—	25.00	40.00	60.00	90.00
	1773KM	—	25.00	40.00	60.00	90.00
	1774KM	—	25.00	40.00	60.00	90.00
	1775KM	—	25.00	40.00	60.00	90.00
	1776KM	—	25.00	40.00	60.00	90.00
	1777KM	—	25.00	40.00	60.00	90.00
	1778KM	—	25.00	40.00	60.00	90.00
	1779KM	—	25.00	40.00	60.00	90.00

5 KOPECKS

COPPER

C#	Date	Mintage	VG	Fine	VF	XF
5	1763	—	—	—	Rare	—
	1764	—	—	—	Rare	—
	1766	—	—	—	Rare	—
	1767	—	75.00	125.00	200.00	350.00
	1767KM	—	75.00	125.00	200.00	350.00
	1768KM	—	25.00	40.00	65.00	100.00
	1769KM	—	25.00	40.00	65.00	100.00
	1770KM	—	25.00	40.00	65.00	100.00
	1771KM	—	25.00	40.00	65.00	100.00
	1772KM	—	25.00	40.00	65.00	100.00
	1773KM	—	25.00	40.00	65.00	100.00
	1774KM	—	25.00	40.00	65.00	100.00
	1775KM	—	25.00	40.00	65.00	100.00
	1776KM	—	25.00	40.00	65.00	100.00
	1777KM	—	25.00	40.00	65.00	100.00
	1778KM	—	25.00	40.00	65.00	100.00
	1779KM	—	25.00	40.00	65.00	100.00
	1780KM	—	65.00	100.00	150.00	250.00

10 KOPECKS

COPPER

C#	Date	Mintage	VG	Fine	VF	XF
6	1763	—	—	—	Rare	—
	1764	—	—	—	Rare	—
	1766	—	100.00	200.00	300.00	500.00
	1767	—	65.00	100.00	150.00	275.00
	1767KM	—	100.00	150.00	250.00	400.00
	1768KM	—	40.00	65.00	100.00	175.00
	1769KM	—	40.00	65.00	100.00	175.00
	1770KM	—	40.00	65.00	100.00	175.00
	1771KM	—	40.00	65.00	100.00	175.00
	1772KM	—	40.00	65.00	100.00	175.00
	1773KM	—	40.00	65.00	100.00	175.00
	1774KM	—	40.00	65.00	100.00	175.00
	1775KM	—	40.00	65.00	100.00	175.00
	1776KM	—	40.00	65.00	100.00	175.00

C#	Date	Mintage	VG	Fine	VF	XF
6	1777KM	—	40.00	65.00	100.00	175.00
	1778KM	—	40.00	65.00	100.00	175.00
	1779KM	—	40.00	65.00	100.00	175.00
	1780KM	—	40.00	65.00	100.00	175.00
	1781KM	—	100.00	150.00	250.00	400.00

NCLT ISSUES

NOVODELS

COPPER

With close oblique edge milling unless otherwise noted.

KM#	Date	Mintage	Identification	Mkt.Val.
N1	1763	Unique	10 Kopecks, lettered edge	—
N2	1764	—*	Polushka, C1	500.00

KM#	Date	Mintage	Identification	Mkt.Val.
N3	1764	—	Denga, C2	—

KM#	Date	Mintage	Identification	Mkt.Val.
N4	1764	—	Kopeck, C3	—
N5	1764	—	Kopeck, C4, tread edge	—

KM#	Date	Mintage	Identification	Mkt.Val.
N6	1764	—	2 Kopecks, C4	—
N7	1764	—	2 Kopecks, C4, lettered edge	—
N8	1764	—	2 Kopecks, C4, tread edge	—

KM#	Date	Mintage	Identification	Mkt.Val.
N9	1764	—	5 Kopecks, C5, large edge lettering	—
N10	1764	—	5 Kopecks, C5, small edge lettering	—
N11	1764	—	5 Kopecks, C5	—

KM#	Date	Mintage	Identification	Mkt.Val.
N12	1764	—	10 Kopecks, C6, large edge lettering	—
N13	1764	—	10 Kopecks, C6, small edge lettering	—
N14	1764	—	10 Kopecks, C6	—
N15	1764	—	10 Kopecks, C6, tread edge	—
N16	1764	—	10 Kopecks, EII monogram, silver, plain edge	—
N17	1764	—	10 Kopecks, EII monogram, silver oblique milling	—

KM#	Date	Mintage	Identification	Mkt.Val.
N18	1764	—	10 Kopecks, silver	—
N19	1764	—	15 Kopecks, silver, plain edge	—
N20	1764	—	15 Kopecks, silver, oblique milling	—
N21	1764	—	15 Kopecks, portrait	—
N22	1764	—	20 Kopecks, EII monogram, silver plain edge	—
N23	1764	—	20 Kopecks, EII monogram, silver oblique milling	—
N24	1764	—	20 Kopecks, silver	—
N25	1766	—	Polushka, C1	—
N26	1766KM	—	Polushka, C1	500.00
N27	1766	—	Denga, C2	—
N28	1766KM	—	Denga, C2	250.00
N29	1766	—	Kopeck, C3	—
N30	1766KM	—	Kopeck, C3	200.00
N31	1766	—	2 Kopecks, C4, lettered edge	—
N32	1766KM	—	2 Kopecks, C4	150.00
N33	1766	—	5 Kopecks, C5, lettered edge	—
N34	1766KM	—	5 Kopecks, C5	250.00
N35	1766	—	10 Kopecks, C6, lettered edge	—
N36	1766KM	—	10 Kopecks, C6	200.00
N37	1767KM	—	Polushka, C1	—
N38	1767KM	—	Denga, C2	—
N39	1767KM	—	Kopeck, C3	—
N40	1767KM	—	2 Kopecks, C4	—
N41	1767KM	—	5 Kopecks, C5	—
N42	1767KM	—	10 Kopecks, C6	—
N43	1768KM	—	Polushka, C1	—
N44	1768KM	—	Denga, C2	—
N45	1768KM	—	Kopeck, C3	—
N46	1768KM	—	2 Kopecks, C4	—
N47	1768KM	—	5 Kopecks, C5	—
N48	1768KM	—	10 Kopecks, C6	—
N49	1769KM	—	Polushka, C1	—
N50	1769KM	—	Denga, C2	—
N51	1769KM	—	Kopeck, C3	—
N52	1769KM	—	5 Kopecks, C5	—
N53	1769KM	—	10 Kopecks, C6	—
N54	1770KM	—	Polushka, C1	—
N55	1770KM	—	Denga, C2	—
N56	1770KM	—	Kopeck, C3	—
N57	1770KM	—	2 Kopecks, C4	—
N58	1770KM	—	5 Kopecks, C5	—

KM#	Date	Mintage	Identification	Mkt.Val.
N59	1770KM	—	10 Kopecks, C6	—
N60	1771KM	—	Polushka, C1	—
N61	1771KM	—	Denga, C2	—
N62	1771KM	—	Kopeck, C3	—
N63	1771KM	—	2 Kopecks, C4	—
N64	1771KM	—	5 Kopecks, C5	—
N65	1771KM	—	10 Kopecks, C6	—
N66	1772KM	—	Polushka, C1	—
N67	1772KM	—	Denga, C2	—
N68	1772KM	—	Kopeck, C3	—
N69	1772KM	—	2 Kopecks, C4	—
N70	1772KM	—	5 Kopecks, C5	—
N71	1772KM	—	10 Kopecks, C6	—
N72	1773KM	—	Polushka, C1	—
N73	1773KM	—	Denga, C2	—
N74	1773KM	—	Kopeck, C3	—
N75	1773KM	—	2 Kopecks, C4	—
N76	1773KM	—	5 Kopecks, C5	—
N77	1773KM	—	10 Kopecks, C6	—
N78	1774KM	—	Polushka, C1	—
N79	1774KM	—	Denga, C2	—
N80	1774KM	—	Kopeck, C3	—
N81	1774KM	—	2 Kopecks, C4	—
N82	1774KM	—	5 Kopecks, C5	—
N83	1774KM	—	10 Kopecks, C6	—
N84	1775KM	—	Polushka, C1	—
N85	1775KM	—	Denga, C2	—
N86	1775KM	—	Kopeck, C3	—
N87	1775KM	—	2 Kopecks, C4	—
N88	1775KM	—	5 Kopecks, C5	—
N89	1775KM	—	10 Kopecks, C6	—
N90	1776KM	—	Polushka, C1	—
N91	1776KM	—	Denga, C2	—
N92	1776KM	—	Kopeck, C3	—
N93	1776KM	—	2 Kopecks, C4	—
N94	1776KM	—	5 Kopecks, C5	—
N95	1776KM	—	10 Kopecks, C6	—
N96	1777KM	—	Polushka, C1	—
N97	1777KM	—	Denga, C2	—
N98	1777KM	—	Kopeck, C3	—
N99	1777KM	—	2 Kopecks, C4	—
N100	1777KM	—	5 Kopecks, C5	—
N101	1777KM	—	10 Kopecks, C6	—
N102	1778KM	—	Polushka, C1	—
N103	1778KM	—	Denga, C2	—
N104	1778KM	—	Kopeck, C3	—
N105	1778KM	—	2 Kopecks, C4	—
N106	1778KM	—	5 Kopecks, C5	—

KM#	Date	Mintage	Identification	Mkt.Val.
N107	1778KM	—	10 Kopecks, C6	—
N108	1779KM	—	Polushka, C1	—
N109	1779KM	—	Denga, C2	—
N110	1779KM	—	Kopeck, C3	—
N111	1779KM	—	2 Kopecks, C4	—
N112	1779KM	—	5 Kopecks, C5	—
N113	1779KM	—	10 Kopecks, C6	—
N114	1780KM	—	Polushka, C1	500.00
N115	1780KM	—	Denga, C2	200.00
N116	1780KM	—	Kopeck, C3	250.00
N117	1780KM	—	2 Kopecks, C4	150.00
N118	1780KM	—	5 Kopecks, C5	—
N119	1780KM	—	10 Kopecks, C6	—

TANNU TUVA

The Tannu-Tuva People's Republic (Tuva), an autonomous part of the Union of Soviet Socialist Republics located in central Asia on the northwest border of Outer Mongolia, has an area of 64,000 sq. mi. (165,760 sq. km.) and a population of about 175,000. Capital: Kyzyl. The economy is based on herding, forestry and mining.

As Urianghi, Tuva was part of Outer Mongolia of the Chinese Empire when tsarist Russia, after fomenting a separatist movement, extended its protection to the mountainous country in 1914. Tuva declared its independence as the Tannu-Tuva People's Republic in 1921 under the auspices of the Tuva people's Revolutionary Party. In 1926, following Russia's successful mediation of the resultant Tuvinian-Mongolian territorial dispute, Tannu—Tuva and Outer Mongolia formally recognized each other's independence. The Tannu-Tuva People's Republic became an autonomous region of the U.S.S.R. on Oct. 13, 1944.

MONETARY SYSTEM

100 Kopejek (Kopeks) = 1 Aksha

KOPEJEK

ALUMINUM-BRONZE

Y#	Date	Mintage	VG	Fine	VF	XF
1	1934	—	17.50	25.00	35.00	60.00

2 KOPEJEK

ALUMINUM-BRONZE

Y#	Date	Mintage	VG	Fine	VF	XF
2	1934	—	20.00	27.50	40.00	65.00

3 KOPEJEK

ALUMINUM-BRONZE

Y#	Date	Mintage	VG	Fine	VF	XF
3	1934	—	17.50	25.00	35.00	60.00

5 KOPEJEK

ALUMINUM-BRONZE

Y#	Date	Mintage	VG	Fine	VF	XF
4	1934	—	20.00	27.50	40.00	65.00

10 KOPEJEK

COPPER-NICKEL

Y#	Date	Mintage	VG	Fine	VF	XF
5	1934	—	20.00	27.50	40.00	65.00

15 KOPEJEK

COPPER-NICKEL

Y#	Date	Mintage	VG	Fine	VF	XF
6	1934	—	20.00	27.50	40.00	65.00

20 KOPEJEK

COPPER-NICKEL

Y#	Date	Mintage	VG	Fine	VF	XF
7	1934	—	20.00	27.50	40.00	65.00

RUSSIAN TURKESTAN

Turkestan is the name conventionally used to designate the extensive area of desert plains and low plateaus in central Asia lying between Siberia on the north, Chinese Sinkiang and Afghanistan on the south, the Caspian Sea on the west, and Mongolia and the Gobi desert on the east. The region was occupied by Turkic nomads in the 11th century. They did not form a state and except for a few oasis cities, were relatively undisturbed by successive invasions by Mongols. Gradually, separate independent Islamic emirates developed around the cities of Bukhara, Khiva and Khoqand. The eastern part of Turkestan, (Chinese Sinkiang) fell to the Chinese Communists in Oct. of 1949. The domination of Russia over most of the Turkic peoples of Asia began late in the 15th century when Ivan III brought the Mongol occupation of Russia to an end. By 1900 the whole of central Asia to the borders of China, Afghanistan and Persia had come under Russian suzerainty. Western Turkestan was established as an autonomous Soviet Socialist Republic in 1920. J. V. Stalin, then People's Commissar of Nationalities, objected to the formation of a single Turkish nation within the U.S.S.R. and effected the partition of the republic into the several Soviet Socialist republics of Uzbekistan, Turkmenistan, (Kazakhstan), Kirghizstan and Tajikistan.

NOTE: The numerals '0' and '5' have variant forms in Russian Turkestan:

0 O instead of ♦

5 ں or ں instead of ٥ ٥

Note that the circle is used for 'zero', not for 'five' in Turkestan.

EMIRATE OF BUKHARA

Bukhara, a city and former emirate in southern Russian Turkestan, formed part (Sogdiana) of the Seleucid empire after the conquest of Alexander the Great. It became virtually a Russian vassal in 1868 as a consequence of the Czarist invasion of 1866, following which it gradually became a part of Russian Turkestan.

Independent Until AH 1284/AD 1868
Russian Vassal
AH1284-1336/AD1868-1917
Independent AH1336-38/AD1917-20
Later Part Of Soviet Union

Haidar Tora

(Abu'l-Ghazi)
AH1171-1200/AD1758-1785
(Amir Said Mir Haidar)
AH 1215-42/AD 1800-26

MINTMARKS

Bukhara

بخارا

FALUS

COPPER 15mm
Legends, both sides.

C#	Date	Good	VG	Fine	VF
48	AH1232	3.00	5.00	10.00	20.00

18-19mm
Legends within Greek border

C#	Date	Good	VG	Fine	VF
51	AH1221	3.50	6.50	12.50	25.00
	1228	3.50	6.50	12.50	25.00
	1229	3.50	6.50	12.50	25.00
	1241	3.50	6.50	12.50	25.00
	1242	3.50	6.50	12.50	25.00

Obv: Fish.

C#	Date	Good	VG	Fine	VF
—	AH1241	—	7.50	15.00	30.00

2 FILUS

SILVER

C#	Date	VG	Fine	VF	XF
—	AH1227	—	15.00	25.00	50.00
	1228	—	15.00	25.00	50.00

TENGA

SILVER, 2.5-3 gm.

C#	Date	VG	Fine	VF	XF
55	AH1216	8.00	15.00	25.00	45.00
	1217	8.00	15.00	25.00	45.00
	1223/17	8.00	15.00	25.00	45.00
	1226	8.00	15.00	25.00	45.00
	1230/31	8.00	15.00	25.00	45.00
	1231/16	8.00	15.00	25.00	45.00
	1232/1	8.00	15.00	25.00	45.00
	1233/18	8.00	15.00	25.00	45.00
	1234	8.00	15.00	25.00	45.00
	1235	8.00	15.00	25.00	45.00
	1236	8.00	15.00	25.00	45.00

TILLA

GOLD
In his own name
Obv: Teardrop and date. Rev: Circle.

C#	Date	VG	Fine	VF	XF
61	AH1215/AHAD	75.00	100.00	150.00	175.00
	1215	75.00	100.00	150.00	175.00
	1216	75.00	100.00	150.00	175.00
	1217/6	75.00	100.00	150.00	175.00
	1218	75.00	100.00	150.00	175.00
	1219	75.00	100.00	150.00	175.00
	1220/16	75.00	100.00	150.00	175.00
	Rev: Octagon.				
62	AH1221	—	75.00	125.00	250.00
	1222	—	75.00	125.00	250.00
	1225	—	75.00	125.00	250.00
	1226	—	75.00	125.00	250.00
	1229	—	75.00	125.00	250.00
	Obv: Teardrop. Rev: Circle.				
61.1	AH1225	75.00	100.00	150.00	175.00
	In name of Ma'Sum Ibn Danyal				
	Obv: Teardrop border				
65	AH1230/29	75.00	100.00	150.00	175.00
	1230	75.00	100.00	150.00	175.00
	1231	75.00	100.00	150.00	175.00
	1233/1023(sic)	75.00	100.00	150.00	175.00
	1233/2	75.00	100.00	150.00	175.00
	1234	75.00	100.00	150.00	175.00

C#	Date	VG	Fine	VF	XF
65a	AH1233	70.00	100.00	140.00	170.00
	1234	70.00	100.00	140.00	170.00
	1235	70.00	100.00	140.00	170.00
	1236/5	70.00	100.00	140.00	170.00

C#	Date	VG	Fine	VF	XF
65a	1236	70.00	100.00	140.00	170.00
	1239/40	70.00	100.00	140.00	170.00

C#	Date	VG	Fine	VF	XF
65a.1	AH1236	70.00	100.00	140.00	170.00

Hussain Sayyid
AH1242/AD1826

TENGA

SILVER

C#	Date	VG	Fine	VF	XF
70	AH1241-42	20.00	50.00	75.00	100.00

Nasrullah
AH 1242-77/AD 1826-60

FILUS

BRASS

C#	Date	VG	Fine	VF	XF
—	AH1244	10.00	20.00	35.00	70.00

TENGA

SILVER
Legends of Haidar Tora

C#	Date	VG	Fine	VF	XF
72	AH1244-5	—	Reported, not confirmed		

In name of Ma'sum

C#	Date	VG	Fine	VF	XF
75	AH1242	8.50	15.00	30.00	45.00
	1244	8.50	15.00	30.00	45.00
	1245	8.50	15.00	30.00	45.00
	1247	8.50	15.00	30.00	45.00
	1248	8.50	15.00	30.00	45.00
	1249	8.50	15.00	30.00	45.00
	1255	8.50	15.00	30.00	45.00
	1257	8.50	15.00	30.00	45.00
	1258	8.50	15.00	30.00	45.00
	1263	8.50	15.00	30.00	45.00
	1265	8.50	15.00	30.00	45.00
	1267	8.50	15.00	30.00	45.00
	1269	8.50	15.00	30.00	45.00
	1271	8.50	15.00	30.00	45.00
	1273	8.50	15.00	30.00	45.00
	1275	8.50	15.00	30.00	45.00
	1276	8.50	15.00	30.00	45.00
	1277	8.50	15.00	30.00	45.00

TILLA

GOLD

C#	Date	VG	Fine	VF	XF
85	AH1243/42	75.00	100.00	150.00	165.00
	1243	75.00	100.00	150.00	165.00
	1244/5	75.00	100.00	150.00	165.00
	1244	75.00	100.00	150.00	165.00
	1246	75.00	100.00	150.00	165.00
	1247/4	75.00	100.00	150.00	165.00
	1248	75.00	100.00	150.00	165.00
	1254	75.00	100.00	150.00	165.00
	1255/4	75.00	100.00	150.00	165.00
	1255	75.00	100.00	150.00	165.00
	1256/4	75.00	100.00	150.00	165.00
	1256/5	75.00	100.00	150.00	165.00
	1256	75.00	100.00	150.00	165.00
	1257/8	75.00	100.00	150.00	165.00
	1257	75.00	100.00	150.00	165.00
	1264	75.00	100.00	150.00	165.00
	1265/6	75.00	100.00	150.00	165.00
	1272/5	75.00	100.00	150.00	165.00
	1273	75.00	100.00	150.00	165.00

Muzaffar Al-Din
AH 1277-1303/AD 1860-1885
Became Russian Vassal In 1284/1868,
But no change in his coinage

FALUS

COPPER OR BRASS

C#	Date	Good	VG	Fine	VF
90	AH1277	5.00	8.50	15.00	22.50
	1281	5.00	8.50	15.00	22.50
	1284	5.00	8.50	15.00	22.50
	1285	5.00	8.50	15.00	22.50

TENGA

SILVER

C#	Date	VG	Fine	VF	XF
91	AH1278	8.00	13.50	20.00	30.00
	1279	8.00	13.50	20.00	30.00
	1281	8.00	13.50	20.00	30.00
	1282	8.00	13.50	20.00	30.00
	1283	8.00	13.50	20.00	30.00
	1284	8.00	13.50	20.00	30.00
	1285	8.00	13.50	20.00	30.00
	1293/83	8.00	13.50	20.00	30.00
	1293	8.00	13.50	20.00	30.00
	1294/6	8.00	13.50	20.00	30.00
	1294	8.00	13.50	20.00	30.00
	1296	8.00	13.50	20.00	30.00
	1297/8	8.00	13.50	20.00	30.00
	1297	8.00	13.50	20.00	30.00
	1298	8.00	13.50	20.00	30.00
	1299/8	8.00	13.50	20.00	30.00
	1299/—	8.00	13.50	20.00	30.00
	1299	8.00	13.50	20.00	30.00
	1300	8.00	13.50	20.00	30.00
	1301/299	8.00	13.50	20.00	30.00
	1301	8.00	13.50	20.00	30.00

TILLA

GOLD

C#	Date	VG	Fine	VF	XF
95	AH1278	55.00	75.00	100.00	135.00
	1279	55.00	75.00	100.00	135.00
	1283	55.00	75.00	100.00	135.00
	1284	55.00	75.00	100.00	135.00
	1285	55.00	75.00	100.00	135.00
	1289	55.00	75.00	100.00	135.00
	1291	55.00	75.00	100.00	135.00
	1294	55.00	75.00	100.00	135.00
	1296/300	55.00	75.00	100.00	135.00
	1296	55.00	75.00	100.00	135.00
	1297	55.00	75.00	100.00	135.00

Sayyid Abdul Ahad
AH 1303-1329/AD 1885-1911

FALUS

BRONZE or BRASS, 15mm

Y#	Date	VG	Fine	VF	XF
1	AH1322	8.50	16.50	25.00	45.00
	1324	8.50	16.50	25.00	45.00

TENGA

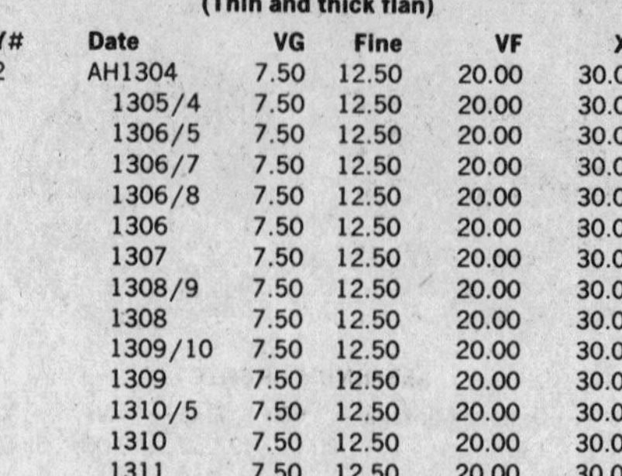

SILVER
(Thin and thick flan)

Y#	Date	VG	Fine	VF	XF
2	AH1304	7.50	12.50	20.00	30.00
	1305/4	7.50	12.50	20.00	30.00
	1306/5	7.50	12.50	20.00	30.00
	1306/7	7.50	12.50	20.00	30.00
	1306/8	7.50	12.50	20.00	30.00
	1306	7.50	12.50	20.00	30.00
	1307	7.50	12.50	20.00	30.00
	1308/9	7.50	12.50	20.00	30.00
	1308	7.50	12.50	20.00	30.00
	1309/10	7.50	12.50	20.00	30.00
	1309	7.50	12.50	20.00	30.00
	1310/5	7.50	12.50	20.00	30.00
	1310	7.50	12.50	20.00	30.00
	1311	7.50	12.50	20.00	30.00
	1315	7.50	12.50	20.00	30.00
	1319	7.50	12.50	20.00	30.00
	1320	7.50	12.50	20.00	30.00
	1322	7.50	12.50	20.00	30.00

TILLA

GOLD 21-23mm

Y#	Date	VG	Fine	VF	XF
3	AH1306	55.00	75.00	100.00	130.00
	1315	55.00	75.00	100.00	130.00
	1319	55.00	75.00	100.00	130.00
	1327	55.00	75.00	100.00	130.00
	1329	55.00	75.00	100.00	130.00

Alim Ibn Sayyid Mir Amin
AH 1329-1338/AD 1911-1920
Independent after 1336/1917

FALUS

COPPER
Rev: "2" in circle.

Y#	Date	VG	Fine	VF	XF
4	AH1332	5.00	8.50	15.00	22.50
	1334	7.50	12.00	—	25.00

Date range 1331-36 reported, but unconfirmed.

Rev: 32 in a circle

Y#	Date	VG	Fine	VF	XF
4.1	AH1323	5.00	8.50	15.00	30.00
	1324	5.00	8.50	15.00	30.00
	1326	5.00	8.50	15.00	30.00
	1329	5.00	8.50	15.00	30.00
	1330	5.00	8.50	15.00	30.00
	1332	5.00	8.50	15.00	30.00
	1333	5.00	8.50	15.00	30.00

4 FALUS

COPPER

Y#	Date	VG	Fine	VF	XF
5	AH1334	6.00	10.00	16.50	25.00

TENGA

BRONZE

Y#	Date	VG	Fine	VF	XF
6	AH1336	15.00	25.00	37.50	65.00

18-19mm

Y#	Date	VG	Fine	VF	XF
6a	AH1336	15.00	25.00	35.00	60.00
	1337	15.00	25.00	35.00	60.00

2 TENGA

BRONZE or BRASS

Y#	Date	VG	Fine	VF	XF
7	AH1336	15.00	25.00	35.00	55.00
	1337	15.00	25.00	35.00	55.00

Y#	Date	VG	Fine	VF	XF
7.1	AH1336	20.00	30.00	50.00	75.00
	1337	20.00	30.00	50.00	75.00

3 TENGA

BRONZE or BRASS

Y#	Date	VG	Fine	VF	XF
8	AH1336	15.00	25.00	35.00	50.00
	1337	15.00	25.00	35.00	50.00

4 TENGA

BRONZE or BRASS

Y#	Date	VG	Fine	VF	XF
9	AH1336	25.00	45.00	65.00	90.00

5 TENGA

BRONZE or BRASS

Y#	Date	VG	Fine	VF	XF
10	AH1336	22.50	35.00	50.00	75.00
	1337	22.50	35.00	50.00	75.00

10 TENGA

BRONZE or BRASS

Y#	Date	VG	Fine	VF	XF
11	AH1337	10.00	17.50	30.00	50.00
	1338	10.00	17.50	30.00	50.00

20 TENGA

BRONZE or BRASS

Y#	Date	VG	Fine	VF	XF
12	AH1336	22.50	35.00	50.00	75.00
	1337	22.50	35.00	50.00	75.00

KHANATE OF KHIVA

KHWAREZM

Khiva, a present town and once a great kingdom under the names of Chorasmia, Khwarezm and Urgenj, is located in Russian Turkestan east of the Caspian Sea and south of the Aral Sea. Russia established relations with Khiva in the 17th century, occupied it in 1873, and annexed it in 1875.

Independent until AH1290/AD1873
Under Russia, AH1290-1337/ AD1873-1918
Regained Independence, AH1337-38/AD1918-20

Muhammad Rahim

AH122x-1241

TENGA

SILVER

C#	Date	VG	Fine	VF	XF
—	AH1232	12.50	25.00	40.00	75.00
	1235	12.50	25.00	40.00	75.00

Allah Quli

AH 1241-58/AD 1825-42

TENGA

SILVER, Vars.

C#	Date	VG	Fine	VF	XF
50	AH1247-48	12.50	25.00	40.00	75.00
	1248	12.50	25.00	40.00	75.00
	1258	12.50	25.00	40.00	75.00

Muhammad Amin

AH1261-71/AD1845-55

TENGA

SILVER

C#	Date	VG	Fine	VF	XF
—	AH1262	12.50	25.00	40.00	75.00
	1263	12.50	25.00	40.00	75.00
	1264	12.50	25.00	40.00	75.00
	1265	12.50	25.00	40.00	75.00
	1266	12.50	25.00	40.00	75.00
	1267	12.50	25.00	40.00	75.00
	1268	12.50	25.00	40.00	75.00
	1269	12.50	25.00	40.00	75.00

1/2 TILLA

GOLD

C#	Date	Mintage	VG	Fine	VF	XF
65	AH1261	—	—	—	250.00	400.00
	1265	—	—	—	250.00	400.00
	1271	—	—	—	250.00	400.00

Sayyid Muhammad Khan

AH 1272-82/AD 1856-65

FALUS

COPPER

Y#	Date	VG	Fine	VF	XF
1	AH1272	20.00	35.00	50.00	75.00
	1274	20.00	35.00	50.00	75.00
	1275	20.00	35.00	50.00	75.00
	1277	20.00	35.00	50.00	75.00
	1278	20.00	35.00	50.00	75.00
	1279	20.00	35.00	50.00	75.00
	1280	20.00	35.00	50.00	75.00

TENGA

SILVER

Type I - Obv: Date in center. Rev: Ornamented.

Y#	Date	VG	Fine	VF	XF
2	AH1273	10.00	25.00	40.00	60.00
	1274	10.00	25.00	40.00	60.00
	1275	10.00	25.00	40.00	60.00
	1276	10.00	25.00	40.00	60.00
	1277	10.00	25.00	40.00	60.00
	1278	10.00	25.00	40.00	60.00
	1279	10.00	25.00	40.00	60.00
	1280	10.00	25.00	40.00	60.00
	1281	10.00	25.00	40.00	60.00

Type II - Plain posthumous issue.

Y#	Date	VG	Fine	VF	XF
2.1	AH1282	8.00	20.00	30.00	45.00
	1283	8.00	20.00	30.00	45.00
	1284/3	8.00	20.00	30.00	45.00
	1284	8.00	20.00	30.00	45.00
	1285	8.00	20.00	30.00	45.00
	1287	8.00	20.00	30.00	45.00
	1288	8.00	20.00	30.00	45.00
	1305	10.00	25.00	40.00	60.00

TILLA

GOLD

Y#	Date	VG	Fine	VF	XF
—	AH1276	—	—	—	—

Sayyid Muhammad Rahim
AH1282-1289/AD1865-1872

FALUS

COPPER,17mm

Y#	Date	VG	Fine	VF	XF
3	AH1290	12.50	25.00	50.00	75.00
	1308	12.50	25.00	50.00	75.00
	1310	12.50	25.00	50.00	75.00
	1311	12.50	25.00	50.00	75.00

TENGA

SILVER

Y#	Date	VG	Fine	VF	XF
6	AH1294	10.00	20.00	40.00	60.00
	1301	10.00	20.00	40.00	60.00
	1303	10.00	20.00	40.00	60.00
	1305	10.00	20.00	40.00	60.00
	1306	10.00	20.00	40.00	60.00
	1307	10.00	20.00	40.00	60.00
	1308	10.00	20.00	40.00	60.00
	1311	10.00	20.00	40.00	60.00
	1312	10.00	20.00	40.00	60.00

2-1/2 TENGA

COPPER,26mm

Y#	Date	VG	Fine	VF	XF
4	AH1303	—	25.00	32.50	—

5 TENGA

COPPER,30mm

Y#	Date	VG	Fine	VF	XF
5	AH1303	—	30.00	37.50	—

TILLA

GOLD

Y#	Date	VG	Fine	VF	XF
7	AH1277	90.00	125.00	250.00	400.00

Sayyid Abdullah Khan And Junaid Khan
AH1337-38/AD1918-20

TENGA

SILVER

Y#	Date	VG	Fine	VF	XF
8	AH1337	—	—	Rare	—

2-1/2 TENGA

COPPER,21-23mm

Y#	Date	VG	Fine	VF	XF
9	AH1337	27.50	37.50	50.00	90.00

5 TENGA

COPPER

Y#	Date	VG	Fine	VF	XF
10	AH1337	37.50	52.50	70.00	110.00

KHWAREZM SOVIET PEOPLE'S REPUBLIC

KHIVA
AH 1338-43/AD 1920-24

20 ROUBLES

BRONZE or BRASS

Y#	Date	VG	Fine	VF	XF
1	AH1338	22.50	30.00	40.00	65.00
	1339	20.00	30.00	40.00	65.00
	1340	20.00	30.00	40.00	65.00

25 ROUBLES

BRONZE or BRASS

Y#	Date	VG	Fine	VF	XF
2	AH1339	17.50	30.00	40.00	65.00

100 ROUBLES

BRONZE or BRASS

Y#	Date	VG	Fine	VF	XF
3	AH1339	17.50	25.00	32.50	55.00

500 ROUBLES

BRONZE or BRASS, 25mm

Y#	Date	VG	Fine	VF	XF
4	AH1339	50.00	75.00	200.00	275.00

19mm

Y#	Date	VG	Fine	VF	XF
4a	AH1339	20.00	30.00	40.00	65.00
4a	1340	20.00	30.00	40.00	65.00

KHANATE OF KHOQAND

Khoqand, a town and former khanate in eastern Russian Turkestan, was a powerful state in the 18th century. Russian superiority in the area was recognized following the holy war of 1875. Annexation followed in 1876.

NOTE: The numerals '0' and '5' have variant forms in Russian Turkestan:

Note that the circle is used for 'zero', not for 'five' in Turkestan.

Independent until AH 1283/AD 1866
Russian Vassal AH1283-93/
AD1866-76
Annexed To Russia, 1875-76

MINTS

Until AH1257, the coinage of Khoqand was struck at two mints.

Fergana(Fa) فرغانه

Khoqand(Kd) خوقند

Muhammad Ali Khan
AH 1238-56/AD 1822-40

PUL

COPPER

C#	Date	VG	Fine	VF	XF
60	AH1249 KD	6.00	12.50	20.00	35.00

C#	Date	VG	Fine	VF	XF
63	AH1252(Fa)	15.00	35.00	50.00	70.00

TENGA

SILVER

C#	Date	VG	Fine	VF	XF
65	AH1241	10.00	22.50	37.50	55.00
	1243	10.00	22.50	37.50	55.00
	1244	10.00	22.50	37.50	55.00

Obv: Teardrop border. Rev: Hexagon.

C#	Date	VG	Fine	VF	XF
66	AH1245	15.00	25.00	40.00	65.00

TILLA

GOLD

C#	Date	VG	Fine	VF	XF
67	AH1247(Fa)	—	—	—	—

C#	Date	VG	Fine	VF	XF
68	AH1252	75.00	100.00	150.00	250.00
	1254	75.00	100.00	150.00	250.00
	1255	75.00	100.00	150.00	250.00
	1256	75.00	100.00	150.00	250.00
	1257	75.00	100.00	150.00	250.00

Sher Ali
AH 1258-61/AD 1842-45

FALUS

COPPER

C#	Date	VG	Fine	VF	XF
—	AH1259	—	—	—	—

TILLA

GOLD

C#	Date	VG	Fine	VF	XF
78	AH1259/8	80.00	100.00	135.00	175.00
	1259	80.00	100.00	135.00	175.00
	1260	80.00	100.00	135.00	175.00

Muhammad Khudayar Khan

2nd Reign

AH 1261-75/AD 1845-58

PUL

COPPER

C#	Date	VG	Fine	VF	XF
87	AH 1265	8.00	14.00	23.50	35.00
	1269	8.00	14.00	23.50	35.00

TENGA

SILVER

C#	Date	VG	Fine	VF	XF
95	AH1266/8	25.00	50.00	65.00	80.00
	1266	25.00	50.00	65.00	80.00
	1269	25.00	50.00	65.00	80.00
	1270	25.00	50.00	65.00	80.00
	1271	25.00	50.00	65.00	80.00
	1272	25.00	50.00	65.00	80.00
	1273	25.00	50.00	65.00	80.00
	1274	25.00	50.00	65.00	80.00
	1275	25.00	50.00	65.00	80.00

TILLA

GOLD

C#	Date	VG	Fine	VF	XF
100	AH1260	75.00	100.00	150.00	250.00
	1261/4	75.00	100.00	150.00	250.00
	1261	75.00	100.00	150.00	250.00
	1262/1	75.00	100.00	150.00	250.00
	1263	75.00	100.00	150.00	250.00
	1264	75.00	100.00	150.00	250.00
	1265	75.00	100.00	150.00	250.00
	1266	75.00	100.00	150.00	250.00
	1270	75.00	100.00	150.00	250.00
	1272	75.00	100.00	150.00	250.00
	1273	75.00	100.00	150.00	250.00
	1274	75.00	100.00	150.00	250.00
	1275	75.00	100.00	150.00	250.00

Muhammad Fulad, Rebel

AH 1275-90/AD 1858-73

TENGA

SILVER

C#	Date	VG	Fine	VF	XF
105	AH1292	15.00	25.00	40.00	60.00

TILLA

GOLD

C#	Date	VG	Fine	VF	XF
110	AH1275-90	60.00	80.00	100.00	125.00

Malla Khan

AH 1275-78/AD 1858-62

PUL

COPPER, square

C#	Date	VG	Fine	VF	XF
112	AH1277	10.00	20.00	32.50	60.00

TENGA

SILVER

C#	Date	VG	Fine	VF	XF
115	AH1275	27.50	55.00	70.00	85.00
	1276	27.50	55.00	70.00	85.00
	1277	27.50	55.00	70.00	85.00

TILLA

GOLD

C#	Date	VG	Fine	VF	XF
118	AH1275	70.00	90.00	115.00	150.00
	1276	70.00	90.00	115.00	150.00
	1277	70.00	90.00	115.00	150.00
	1278	70.00	90.00	115.00	150.00

Shah Murad

AH 1278-79/AD 1862

TILLA

GOLD

C#	Date	VG	Fine	VF	XF
128	AH1278	100.00	125.00	150.00	175.00

Muhammad Khudayar Khan

3rd Reign

AH 1279-80/AD 1862-63

TENGA

SILVER

Obv. & rev: Teardrop borders.

C#	Date	VG	Fine	VF	XF
130	AH1279	30.00	60.00	100.00	150.00

TILLA

GOLD

C#	Date	VG	Fine	VF	XF
135	Dates unknown	75.00	95.00	115.00	125.00

Sayyid Sultan

AH 1280-82/AD 1863-65

TENGA

SILVER

Sayyid Sultan Muhammad Bahadur Khan

C#	Date	VG	Fine	VF	XF
140	AH1280	40.00	75.00	125.00	175.00
	1281	40.00	75.00	125.00	175.00

TILLA

GOLD

C#	Date	VG	Fine	VF	XF
145	AH1280	100.00	115.00	140.00	165.00
	1281	100.00	115.00	140.00	165.00

Muhammad Khudayar Khan

4th Reign

AH 1282-92/AD 1865-75

PUL

COPPER

C#	Date	VG	Fine	VF	XF
148	AH1287	6.00	13.50	26.50	37.50

TENGA

SILVER

C#	Date	VG	Fine	VF	XF
151	AH1282	25.00	50.00	75.00	100.00
	1284	25.00	50.00	75.00	100.00
	1285	25.00	50.00	75.00	100.00
	1286	25.00	50.00	75.00	100.00
	1287	25.00	50.00	75.00	100.00
	1289	25.00	50.00	75.00	100.00

TILLA

GOLD

C#	Date	VG	Fine	VF	XF
155	AH1282	70.00	80.00	100.00	140.00
	1283	70.00	80.00	100.00	140.00
	1285	70.00	80.00	100.00	140.00

Nasir al din

AH1292-1293

TILLA

GOLD

C#	Date	VG	Fine	VF	XF
—	AH1292	—	—	—	—

RWANDA

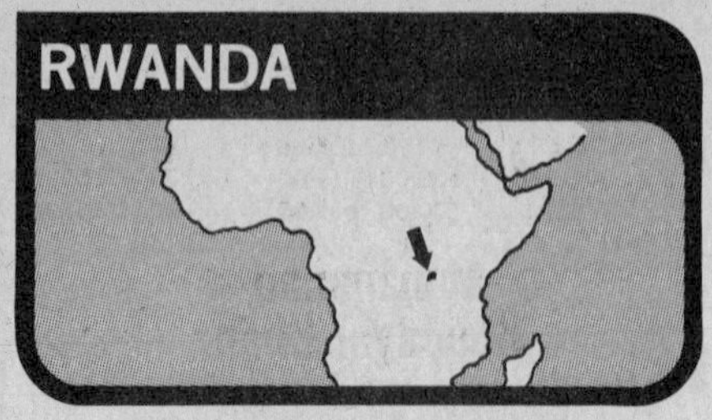

The Republic of Rwanda, located in central Africa between the Republic of the Congo and Tanzania, has an area of 10,169 sq. mi. (26,338 sq. km.) and a population of 4.2 million. Capital: Kigali. The economy is based on agriculture and mining. Coffee and tin are exported.

German lieutenant Count von Goetzen was the first European to visit Rwanda, 1894. Four years later the court of the Mwami (the Tutsi king of Rwanda) willingly permitted the kingdom to become a protectorate of Germany. In 1916, during the African campaigns of World War I, Belgian troops from Congo occupied Rwanda. After the war it, together with Burundi, became a Belgian League of Nations mandate under the name of the Territory of Ruanda-Urundi. Following World War II, Ruanda-Urundi became a Belgian administered U.N. trust territory. The Tutsi monarchy was deposed by the U.N. supervised election of 1961, after which Belgium granted Rwanda internal autonomy. On July 1, 1962, the U.N. terminated the Belgian trusteeship and granted full independence to both Rwanda and Burundi.

NOTE: For earlier coinage see Belgian Congo, and Rwanda and Burundi.

MINTMARKS

(a) - Paris, privy marks only
(b) - Brussels, privy marks only

MONETARY SYSTEM

100 Centimes = 1 Franc

1/2 FRANC

ALUMINUM

Y#	Date	Mintage	VF	XF	Unc
5	1970	5.000	—	.10	.40

FRANC

COPPER-NICKEL

Y#	Date	Mintage	VF	XF	Unc
1	1964(b)	3.000	.10	.30	.60
	1965(b)	4.500	.10	.25	.40

ALUMINUM

Y#	Date	Mintage	VF	XF	Unc
6	1969	5.000	—	.10	.25

Y#	Date	Mintage	VF	XF	Unc
8	1974	13.000	—	—	.25

2 FRANCS

ALUMINUM
F.A.O. Issue

Y#	Date	Mintage	VF	XF	Unc
4	1970	5.000	.10	.20	.50

5 FRANCS

BRONZE

Y#	Date	Mintage	VF	XF	Unc
2	1964(b)	4.000	.10	.30	.60
	1965(b)	3.000	.10	.40	.75

Y#	Date	Mintage	VF	XF	Unc
9	1974	7.000	—	—	.75

10 FRANCS

3.7000 gm., .900 GOLD, .1085 oz AGW

Fr#	Date	Mintage	VF	XF	Unc
4	1961	10,000	BV	BV	75.00
	1961	—	—	Proof	125.00

COPPER-NICKEL

Y#	Date	Mintage	VF	XF	Unc
3	1964(b)	6.000	.25	.75	1.25

Y#	Date	Mintage	VF	XF	Unc
10	1974	6.000	—	—	1.25

20 FRANCS

BRASS

Y#	Date	Mintage	VF	XF	Unc
11	1977(a)	—	—	—	1.00

25 FRANCS

7.5000 gm., .900 GOLD, .2170 oz AGW
Similar to 10 Francs, FR#4.

Fr#	Date	Mintage	VF	XF	Unc
3	1961	4,000	—	Proof	150.00

50 FRANCS

15.0000 gm., .900 GOLD, .4340 oz AGW
Similar to 10 Francs, FR#4.

Fr#	Date	Mintage	VF	XF	Unc
2	1961	3,000	—	Proof	300.00

BRASS

Y#	Date	Mintage	VF	XF	Unc
12	1977(a)	—	—	—	1.25

100 FRANCS

30.0000 gm., .900 GOLD, .8681 oz AGW
Similar to 10 Francs, FR#4.

Fr#	Date	Mintage	VF	XF	Unc
1	1961	3,000	—	Proof	575.00

200 FRANCS

18.6200 gm., .800 SILVER, .4789 oz ASW
F.A.O. Issue

Y#	Date	Mintage	VF	XF	Unc
7	1972	.030	BV	BV	15.00

NCLT ISSUES

ESSAIS

Standard metals unless otherwise noted

KM#	Date	Mintage	Identification	Issue Price	Mkt. Val.
E2	1964	—	5 Francs	—	—

PROOF SETS

STANDARD METALS

101	1961(4)	3,000	FR#1-4	—	1150.

RWANDA & BURUNDI

Rwanda-Burundi, a Belgian League of Nations mandate and United Nations trust territory comprising the provinces of Rwanda and Burundi of the former colony of German East Africa, was located in central Africa between the present Republic of the Congo, Uganda and mainland Tanzania. The mandate-trust territory had an area of 20,916 sq. mi. (54,272 sq. km.) and a population of 4.3 million.

For specific statistics and history of Rwanda and of Burundi see individual entries.

When Rwanda and Burundi were formed into a mandate for administration by Belgium, their names were changed to Ruanda and Urundi and they were organized as an integral part of the Belgian Congo. During the mandate-trust territory period, they utilized the coinage of the Belgian Congo, which from 1954 through 1960 carried the appropriate dual identification. After the Belgian Congo acquired independence as the Republic of the Congo, the provinces of Ruanda and Urundi reverted to their former names of Rwanda and Burundi and utilized a common currency issued by a Central Bank (B.E.R.B.) established for that purpose until the time when, as independent republics, each issued its own national coinage.

NOTE: For earlier coinage see Belgian Congo.

FRANC

BRASS

Y#	Date	Mintage	VF	XF	Unc
1	1960	2.000	.50	.75	1.25
	1961	16.000	.45	.70	1.00
	1964	3.000	.50	.75	1.25

NOTE: For later coinage see individual listings under Rwanda and Burundi.

COPPER-NICKEL
Obv. mule of Belgian, 1 Franc Y#57.
Rev. of Rwanda and Burundi Y#1.

Y#	Date	Mintage	VF	XF	Unc
1a	1961	*50 pcs.	—	—	—

Listings For

SAARLAND: refer to Germany/West

SAINT BARTHOLOMEW

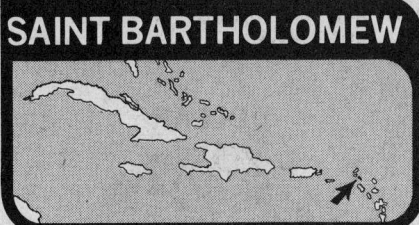

St. Bartholomew (St. Barthelemy, St. Barts), a French island possession located in the Leeward Islands of the West Indies about 15 miles northwest of Guadeloupe, of which it is a dependency, has an area of 10 sq. mi. (26 sq. km.) and a population of about 3,000. Capital: Basse-Terre, on the island of that name. The treeless island produces sugar, bananas, and rum.

St. Bartholomew was occupied by France in 1648 and sold to Sweden in 1784. In 1877 it was reacquired, by purchase, by France.

The coins issued under Sweden for St. Bartholomew -- crown-countermarked U.S. coins, Cayenne sous, Swedish and Polish billon -- have been extensively counterfeited.

RULERS

French, until 1784, 1877—
Swedish, 1784-1877

MONETARY SYSTEM

6 Stivers = 1 Real
11 Reales = 1 Dollar

COUNTERSTAMP ISSUES

CENT

COPPER
c/s: Crown on U.S. Large Cent, C#16.

C#	Date	Mintage	VG	Fine	VF
1	ND	—	150.00	225.00	350.00

2 SOU

BILLON
c/s: Crown on Cayenne 2 Sou, C#1.

C#	Date	Mintage	VG	Fine	VF
2	ND	—	125.00	200.00	275.00

STIVER

SILVER
c/s: Crown on Curacao Stiver, C#8.

C#	Date	Mintage	VG	Fine	VF
11	ND	—	100.00	150.00	200.00

3 STIVERS

SILVER
c/s: Crowned 3/M on Spanish Colonial 1/2 Real.

C#	Date	Mintage	VG	Fine	VF
23	ND(1808)	—	150.00	200.00	250.00

4 STIVERS

SILVER
c/s: Crowned 4/M on Spanish Colonial 1/2 Real.

C#	Date	Mintage	VG	Fine	VF
24	ND(1808)	—	150.00	200.00	250.00

REAL

SILVER
c/s: Crown on Spanish Colonial 1 Real.

C#	Date	Mintage	VG	Fine	VF
11	ND	—	100.00	170.00	250.00

7 STIVERS

SILVER
c/s: Crowned 7/M on Spanish Colonial 1 Real.

C#	Date	Mintage	VG	Fine	VF
25	ND(1808)	—	150.00	200.00	250.00

9 STIVERS

SILVER
c/s: Crowned 9/M on Spanish Colonial 1 Real.

C#	Date	Mintage	VG	Fine	VF
26.1	ND(1808)	—	175.00	225.00	275.00

c/s: Crowned 9/M on Spanish 2 Reales.

C#	Date	Mintage	VG	Fine	VF
26.2	ND(1808)	—	175.00	225.00	275.00

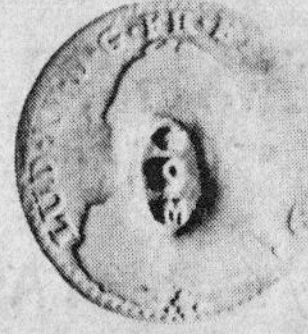

c/s: Crowned 9/M on France 1/10 Ecu, C#39.

C#	Date	Mintage	VG	Fine	VF
26.3	ND(1808)	—	175.00	225.00	275.00

14 STIVERS

SILVER
c/s: Crowned 14/M on Spanish Colonial 2 Reales.

C#	Date	Mintage	VG	Fine	VF
27	ND(1808)	—	175.00	225.00	275.00

2 REALES

SILVER
c/s: Crown on Spanish Colonial 2 Reales.

C#	Date	Mintage	VG	Fine	VF
11	ND	—	150.00	200.00	250.00

18 STIVERS

SILVER
c/s: Crowned 18/M on Spanish Colonial 2 Reales.

C#	Date	Mintage	VG	Fine	VF
28	ND(1808)	—	175.00	225.00	275.00

SAINT CROIX

St. Croix, which has an area of 82 sq. mi. (212 sq. km.), is with St. Thomas and St. John one of the three principal islands of the more than 50 islands comprising the Virgin Islands of the United States, which are located in the western part of the Virgin Islands east of Puerto Rico and at the western end of the Lesser Antilles. Capital: Charlotte Amalie, on St. Thomas. Politically, the Virgin Islands of the United States are an unincorporated territory administered by the Interior Dept. The inhabitants, who have been citizens of the United States since 1927, have an elected governor, and one delegate to the U.S. House of Representatives who may vote in committee but not on the House floor. Tourism is the largest industry. Watch movements, jewelry, rum, wool, textiles, thermometers, and bay rum are exported.

The Virgin Islands were discovered by Columbus during his second voyage to America in 1493. St. Thomas was colonized by Denmark in 1666, and the entire Danish island group was under the control of the Danish West Indies Company until 1755, when the group was purchased by Frederick V of Denmark and made a royal colony. England occupied the Danish West Indies, during the Napoleonic Wars, in 1801 and again from 1807 to 1815, after which they were restored to Denmark. The United States purchased the Danish West Indies for defense purposes on March 31, 1917, for $25,000,000.

RULERS

Danish, until 1800,
1802-06, 1816-1917
British 1801, 1807-1815

COUNTERSTAMP ISSUES

1798-1813

1/4 DOLLAR

SILVER

c/s: StC on Mexico 2 Reales, KM#90 (C#71).

KM#	Date	Mintage	VG	Fine	VF
1	ND(1790)	—	150.00	200.00	275.00

c/s: StC on Mexico 2 Reales, KM#91 (C#79).

KM#	Date	Mintage	VG	Fine	VF
2	ND(1792-1808)	—	150.00	200.00	275.00

1/2 DOLLAR

SILVER

c/s: StC on Bolivia (Potosi) 4 Reales, C#36.

KM#	Date	Mintage	VG	Fine	VF
3	ND(1791-1809)	—	150.00	250.00	325.00

DOLLAR

SILVER

c/s: StC on Mexico 8 Reales, KM#109 (C#81).

KM#	Date	Mintage	VG	Fine	VF
4	ND(1791-1808)	—	150.00	250.00	325.00

c/s: StC on Mexico 8 Reales, KM#110 (C#111).

KM#	Date	Mintage	VG	Fine	VF
5	ND(1808-11)	—	150.00	250.00	325.00

Listings For

ST. EUSTATIUS: refer to Netherlands Antilles

ST. HELENA

The Colony of St. Helena, a British colony located about 1,150 miles (1,850 km.) from the west coast of Africa, has an area of 47 sq. mi. (122 sq. km.) and a population of 5,000. Capital: Jamestown. Flax, lace, and rope are produced for export. Ascension and Tristan da Cunha are dependencies of St. Helena.

The island was discovered and named by the Portuguese navigator Joao de Nova Castella in 1502. The Portuguese imported livestock, fruit trees, and vegetables but established no permanent settlement. The Dutch occupied the island temporarily, 1645-51. The original European settlement was founded by representatives of the British East India Company sent to annex the island after the departure of the Dutch. The Dutch returned and captured St. Helena from the British on New Year's Day, 1673, but were in turn ejected by a British force under Sir Richard Munden. Thereafter St. Helena was the undisputed possession of Great Britain. The island served as the place of exile for Napoleon, several Zulu chiefs, and an ex-sultan of Zanzibar.

RULERS

British

MONETARY SYSTEM

12 Pence = 1 Shilling

MINTMARKS

PM - Popjoy Mint

HALF PENNY

COPPER

C#	Date	Mintage	VF	XF	Unc
1	1821	—	7.50	15.00	30.00
	1821	—	—	Proof	80.00
	BRONZE				
1a	1821	—	—	Proof	90.00
	GILT BRONZE				
1b	1821	—	—	Proof	250.00

TRADESMANS' TOKEN

HALF PENNY

Solomon, Dickson And Taylor

KM#	Date	Mintage	Fine	VF	XF
1	ND	—	5.00	10.00	18.50

DECIMAL COINAGE

100 Pence = 1 Pound

25 PENCE

COPPER NICKEL
St. Helena Tercentenary

Y#	Date	Mintage	VF	XF	Unc
1	1973	.100	.75	1.10	1.75
	28.2800 gm., .925 SILVER, .8411 oz ASW				
1a	1973	.010	—	Proof	27.50

COPPER-NICKEL
Queen's Silver Jubilee

Y#	Date	Mintage	VF	XF	Unc
2	1977	.050	1.00	1.50	2.00
	28.2800 gm., .925 SILVER, .8411 oz ASW				
2a	1977	.025	—	Proof	30.00

CROWN

COPPER-NICKEL
25th Anniversary of Coronation
Obv: Similar to 25 Pence, Y#1.

Y#	Date	Mintage	VF	XF	Unc
3	1978PM	—	.85	1.25	2.00
	28.2800 gm., .925 SILVER, .8411 oz ASW				
3a	1978PM	.070	—	—	27.50
	1978PM	.025	—	Proof	35.00

ST. KITTS

St. Kitts (St. Christopher), a West Indian island located in the Leeward Islands southeast of Puerto Rico, is the principal component of a British associated state composed of the islands of St. Kitts, Nevis, and Anguilla. The associated state has an area of 118 sq. mi. (306 sq. km.) and a population of 65,000. Capital: Basseterre, on St. Kitts. The islands export sugar, molasses, rum, cotton, and coconuts.

St. Kitts was discovered by Columbus in 1493 and was settled by Thomas Warner, an Englishman, in 1623. The island was ceded to the British by the Treaty of Utrecht, 1713. France protested British occupancy, and on three occasions between 1666 and 1782 seized the island and held it for short periods. In early 1967 St. Kitts was united politically with Nevis and Anguilla to form a self-governing British associated state. In June 1967 Anguilla declared its independence of the federated state, and in Feb. 1969 unilaterally severed all ties with Britain and established the Republic of Anguilla. Britain refused to accept the unilateral movement and installed a commissioner to govern Anguilla, which remains a nominal part of the associated state. The political status of the three islands will be decided in the near future by a referendum.

From approximately 1750-1830, billon 2 sous of the French colony of Cayenne were countermarked 'SK' and used on St. Kitts. They were valued at 1-1/3 Pence.

RULERS

British

MONETARY SYSTEM

19th Century

108 Pence = 9 Shillings =
12 Bits = 1 Dollar

20th Century

100 Cents = 1 Dollar

NOTE: The grades shown describe the condition of the counterstamp, not the coin itself, which is typically well worn.

COUNTERSTAMP ISSUES

1-1/2 PENCE
"Black Dog"

BILLON
c/s: 'S' on French Colonies 24 Deniers, C#6.

C#	Date	Mintage	VG	Fine	VF
1	(1801)	—	40.00	50.00	65.00

2-1/4 PENCE

BILLON
c/s: S.K. on French Guyana 2 Sous, C#1.

C#	Date	Mintage	VG	Fine	VF
2	(1809-1812?)	—	40.00	50.00	65.00

1/8 DOLLAR

SILVER
c/s: 'S' on cut 1/8 section of Spanish 8 Reales.

C#	Date	Mintage	VG	Fine	VF
4	(1801)	—	300.00	400.00	500.00

1/4 DOLLAR

SILVER
c/s: 'S' on 1/4 section of Spanish 8 Reales.

C#	Date	Mintage	VG	Fine	VF
5	(1801)	—	300.00	400.00	500.00

1/2 DOLLAR

SILVER
c/s: 'S' on 1/2 section of Spanish 8 Reales.

C#	Date	Mintage	VG	Fine	VF
6	(1801)	—	300.00	400.00	500.00

MODERN COINAGE

4 DOLLARS

COPPER-NICKEL
F.A.O. Issue

Y#	Date	Mintage	VF	XF	Unc
3*	1970	.020	3.50	5.00	7.50
	1970	2,000	—	Proof	50.00

*This number refers to Yeoman's East Caribbean Territories listings, where seven companion 4-dollar issues are listed. Issued under authority of the East Caribbean Territories.

ST. LUCIA

Saint Lucia, an independent island nation located in the Windward Islands of the West Indies between St. Vincent and Martinique, has an area of 238 sq. mi. (616 sq. km.) and a population of 112,000. Capital: Castries. The economy is agricultural. Bananas, copra, cocoa, sugar and logwood are exported.

Saint Lucia was discovered by Columbus in 1502. The first attempts at settlement undertaken by the British in 1605 and 1638 were frustrated by sickness and the determined hostility of the fierce Carib inhabitants. The French settled it in 1650 and made a treaty with the natives. Until 1814, when the island became a definite British possession, it was the scene of a continuous conflict between the British and French which saw the island change hands on at least 14 occasions. In 1967, under the West Indies Act, Saint Lucia was established as a British associated state, self-governing in internal affairs. Complete independence was attained on February 22, 1979. Saint Lucia is a member of the Commonwealth of Nations. The Queen of England is Chief of State.

RULERS

British

MONETARY SYSTEM

12 Deniers = 1 Sou
15 Sous = 1 Escalin
20 Sous = 1 Livre
6 Black Dogs = 4 Stampees
= 1 Bit = 9 Pence

COUNTERSTAMP ISSUES OF 1798

2 ESCALINS

SILVER
c/s: 'SL' monogram on 1/6 cut of Spanish or Spanish Colonial 8 Reales

C#	Date	Mintage	VG	Fine	VF
11	ND(1798)	—	—	Rare	—

3 ESCALINS

SILVER, 6.4gm.
c/s: 3 'SL' monogram on 1/4 cut of Spanish or Spanish Colonial 8 Reales.

C#	Date	Mintage	VG	Fine	VF
13	ND(1798)	—	100.00	150.00	190.00

4 ESCALINS

SILVER
c/s: 3 'SL' monogram on 1/3 cut of Spanish or Spanish Colonial 8 Reales.

C#	Date	Mintage	VG	Fine	VF
14	ND(1798)	—	100.00	150.00	200.00

6 ESCALINS

SILVER
c/s: 2 'SL' monogram on 1/2 cut of Spanish or Spanish Colonial 8 Reales.

C#	Date	Mintage	VG	Fine	VF
15	ND(1798)	—	100.00	150.00	200.00

COUNTERSTAMP ISSUES OF 1811

3 STAMPEES

SILVER
c/s: Circle with crenalated edges on 1/4 cut of Spanish or Spanish Colonial 2 Reales.

C#	Date	Mintage	VG	Fine	VF
31	ND(1811)	—	25.00	50.00	100.00

ESCALIN

SILVER, 2gm.
c/s: Circle on 1/3 cut of Spanish or Spanish Colonial 2 Reales.

C#	Date	Mintage	VG	Fine	VF
34	ND(1811)	—	25.00	45.00	65.00

1-1/2 ESCALINS

SILVER
c/s: Two circles on 1/4 cut of Spanish or Spanish Colonial 4 Reales.

C#	Date	Mintage	VG	Fine	VF
36	ND(1811)	—	30.00	60.00	100.00

2 ESCALINS

SILVER, 4gm.
c/s: Three circles on 1/3 cut of Spanish or Spanish Colonial 4 Reales.

C#	Date	Mintage	VG	Fine	VF
38	ND(1811)	—	30.00	60.00	100.00

COUNTERSTAMP ISSUES OF 1813

2 LIVRES, 5 SOUS

SILVER, 5.3gm.
c/s: 'S:Lucie' on 1/3 outer cut of Spanish or Spanish Colonial 8 Reales.

C#	Date	Mintage	VG	Fine	VF
44	ND(1813)	—	40.00	70.00	115.00

6 LIVRES, 15 SOUS

SILVER, 15gm
c/s: 'S:Lucie' on 1/3 center cut of Spanish or Spanish Colonial 8 Reales.

C#	Date	Mintage	VG	Fine	VF
46	ND(1813)	—	100.00	160.00	200.00

NOTE: There are no known genuine examples existing today of any other similar varieties cut from Spanish or Spanish Colonial 2 and 4 Reales with this counterstamp.

MODERN COINAGE

4 DOLLARS

COPPER-NICKEL
F.A.O. Issue

Y#	Date	Mintage	VF	XF	Unc
7*	1970	.020	3.50	5.00	7.50
	1970	2,000	—	Proof	50.00

*This refers to Yeoman's East Caribbean Territories listings, where seven companion 4 dollar issues are listed.

Listings For

ST. MARTIN: refer to Netherlands Antilles

ST. PIERRE & MIQUELON

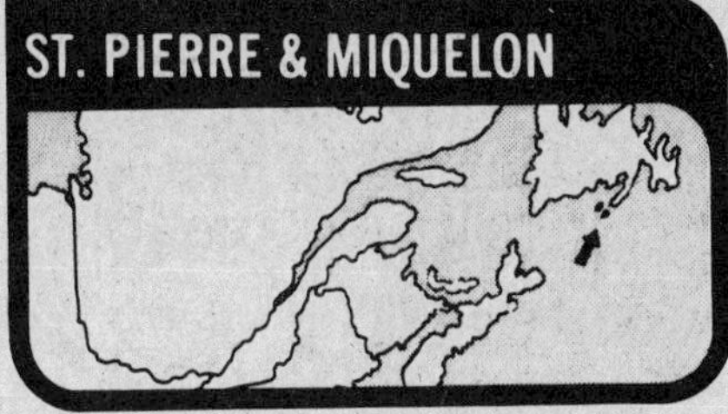

The Territory of St. Pierre and Miquelon, a French overseas territory located 10 miles (16 km.) off the south coast of Newfoundland, has an area of 93 sq. mi. (241 sq. km.) and a population of 5,000. Capital: St. Pierre. The economy of the barren archipelago is based on cod fishing and fur farming. Fish and fish products, and mink and silver fox pelts are exported.

The islands, occupied by the French in 1604, were captured by the British in 1702 and held until 1763 when they were returned to the possession of France and employed as a fishing station. They passed between France and England on six more occasions between 1778 and 1814 when they were awarded permanently to France by the Treaty of Paris. The rugged, soil-poor granite islands, which will support only evergreen shrubs, are all that remain to France of her extensive colonies in North America. In 1958 St. Pierre and Miquelon voted in favor of the new constitution of the Fifth Republic of France, thereby choosing to remain within the new French Community.

RULERS

French

MINTMARKS

(a) - Paris, privy marks only

MONETARY SYSTEM

100 Centimes = 1 Franc

FRANC

ALUMINUM

Y#	Date	Mintage	VF	XF	Unc
1	1948(a)	.600	.75	1.50	4.00

2 FRANCS

ALUMINUM

Y#	Date	Mintage	VF	XF	Unc
2	1948(a)	.300	1.00	2.00	5.00

NCLT ISSUES

ESSAIS (E)

Standard metals unless otherwise noted

Y#	Date	Mintage	Identification	Issue Price	Mkt Val.
E1a	1948(a)	2,000	1 Franc, Copper-Nickel	—	17.50
E2a	1948(a)	2,000	2 Francs, Copper-Nickel	—	20.00

PIEFORTS (P)

PIEFORTS WITH ESSAI (PE)

(DOUBLE THICKNESS)

Standard metals unless otherwise noted

Y#	Date	Mintage	Identification	Issue Price	Mkt Val.
PE1	1948(a)	104	1 Franc	—	100.00
PE2	1948(a)	104	2 Francs	—	110.00

ST. THOMAS & PRINCE

The Democratic Republic of Sao Tome and Principe (formerly the Portuguese overseas province of St. Thomas and Prince Islands) is located in the Gulf of Guinea 150 miles (241 km.) off the west African coast. It has an area of 372 sq. mi. (963 sq. km.) and a population of 79,000. Capital: Sao Tome. The economy of the islands is based on cocoa, copra and coffee.

St. Thomas and St. Prince were uninhabited when discovered by Portuguese navigators Joao de Santarem and Pedro de Escobar in 1470. After the failure of their initial settlement, 1485, the Portuguese successfully colonized St. Thomas with a colony of prisoners and exiled Jews, 1493. An initial prosperity based on the sugar trade gave way to a time of misfortune, 1567-1709, that saw the colony attacked and occupied or plundered by the French and Dutch; ravaged by the slave revolt of 1595; and finally rendered destitute by the transfer of the world sugar trade to Brazil. In the late 1800s, the colony turned from the production of sugar to cocoa, the basis of its present prosperity.

The islands were designated a Portuguese overseas province in 1951. On April 25, 1974, the government of Portugal was seized by a military junta which reached agreements providing for independence for the Portuguese overseas provinces of Portuguese Guinea (Guinea-Bissau), Mozambique, Cape Verde Islands, Angola, and St. Thomas and Prince Islands. The Democratic Republic of Sao Tome and Principe was declared on July 12, 1975.

RULERS

Portuguese, until 1975

MONETARY SYSTEM

100 Centavos = 1 Escudo

10 CENTAVOS

NICKEL-BRONZE

Y#	Date	Mintage	VF	XF	Unc
1	1929	.500	2.50	5.00	8.00

BRONZE

Y#	Date	Mintage	VF	XF	Unc
15	1962	.500	.10	.25	1.00

ALUMINUM

Y#	Date	Mintage	VF	XF	Unc
15a	1971	1.000	.10	.25	.50

20 CENTAVOS

NICKEL-BRONZE

Y#	Date	Mintage	VF	XF	Unc
2	1929	.250	2.50	6.00	12.00

BRONZE

18mm

Y#	Date	Mintage	VF	XF	Unc
16	1962	.250	.20	.50	1.00

16mm

Y#	Date	Mintage	VF	XF	Unc
16a	1971	.750	—	.10	.15

50 CENTAVOS

NICKEL-BRONZE

Y#	Date	Mintage	Fine	VF	XF
3	1928	—	4.00	10.00	15.00
	1929	.400	4.00	10.00	15.00

Y#	Date	Mintage	VF	XF	Unc
5	1948	.080	3.50	7.00	35.00

COPPER-NICKEL

Y#	Date	Mintage	VF	XF	Unc
10	1951	.050	5.00	8.00	35.00

BRONZE

20mm

Y#	Date	Mintage	VF	XF	Unc
17	1962	.480	.25	.50	1.00

22mm

Y#	Date	Mintage	VF	XF	Unc
17a	1971	.600	—	.15	.25

ESCUDO

COPPER-NICKEL

Y#	Date	Mintage	Fine	VF	XF
4	1939	.100	1.50	3.50	6.00

NICKEL-BRONZE

Y#	Date	Mintage	VF	XF	Unc
6	1948	.060	3.00	7.00	40.00

COPPER-NICKEL

Y#	Date	Mintage	VF	XF	Unc
11	1951	.018	20.00	50.00	125.00

BRONZE

Y#	Date	Mintage	VF	XF	Unc
18	1962	.160	.50	1.00	2.00
	1971	.350	.15	.40	.85

2-1/2 ESCUDOS

3.5000 gm., .650 SILVER, .1462 oz ASW

Y#	Date	Mintage	Fine	VF	XF
7	1939	.080	6.00	10.00	15.00
	1948	.120	6.00	10.00	15.00

Y#	Date	Mintage	VF	XF	Unc
12	1951	.060	3.50	10.00	25.00

COPPER-NICKEL

Y#	Date	Mintage	VF	XF	Unc
19	1962	.140	.50	1.50	2.00
	1971	.250	.20	.30	.60

5 ESCUDOS

7.0000 gm., .650 SILVER, .1462 oz ASW

Y#	Date	Mintage	Fine	VF	XF
8	1939	.060	4.75	7.00	10.00
8	1948	.100	4.50	6.00	8.00

25mm

Y#	Date	Mintage	VF	XF	Unc
13	1951	.070	5.00	15.00	30.00

22mm

Y#	Date	Mintage	VF	XF	Unc
20	1962	.090	BV	BV	6.00

COPPER-NICKEL
24.3mm

Y#	Date	Mintage	VF	XF	Unc
20a	1971	.160	.35	.60	.90

10 ESCUDOS

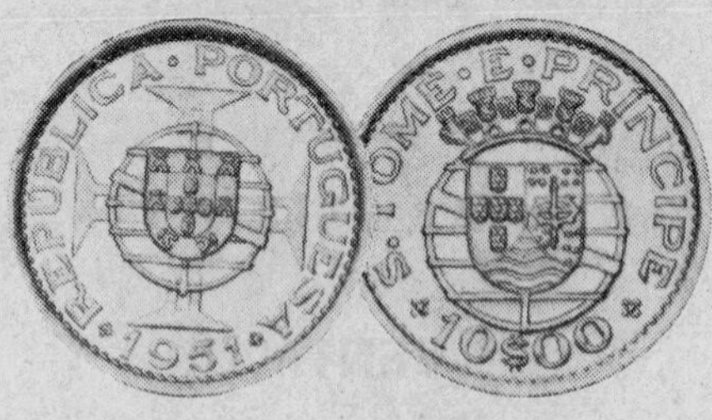

12.5000 gm., .835 SILVER, .3356 oz ASW

Y#	Date	Mintage	Fine	VF	XF
9	1939	.040	17.50	27.50	80.00

12.5000 gm., .720 SILVER, .2778 oz ASW

Y#	Date	Mintage	Fine	VF	XF
14	1951	.040	8.50	15.00	30.00

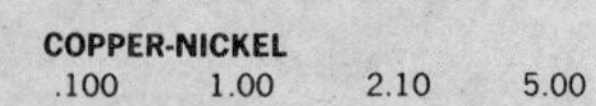

COPPER-NICKEL

Y#	Date	Mintage	VF	XF	Unc
A21	1971	.100	1.00	2.10	5.00

20 ESCUDOS

NICKEL

Y#	Date	Mintage	VF	XF	Unc
B21	1971	.060	2.00	3.00	4.50

50 ESCUDOS

18.0000 gm., .650 SILVER, .3762 oz ASW
500th Anniversary of Discovery

Y#	Date	Mintage	VF	XF	Unc
21	1970	1.000	BV	BV	12.50

DECIMAL COINAGE

100 Centimos = 1 Dobra

50 CENTIMOS

BRASS
F.A.O. Issue

Y#	Date	Mintage	VF	XF	Unc
22	1977	2.000	—	.10	.15
	1977	2,500	—	Proof	—

DOBRA

BRASS
F.A.O. Issue

Y#	Date	Mintage	VF	XF	Unc
23	1977	1.500	.10	.15	.25
	1977	2,500	—	Proof	—

2 DOBRAS

COPPER-NICKEL
F.A.O. Issue

Y#	Date	Mintage	VF	XF	Unc
24	1977	1.000	.20	.30	.50
	1977	2,500	—	Proof	—

5 DOBRAS

COPPER-NICKEL
F.A.O. Issue

Y#	Date	Mintage	VF	XF	Unc
25	1977	.750	.30	.50	.75
	1977	2,500	—	Proof	—

10 DOBRAS

COPPER-NICKEL
F.A.O. Issue

Y#	Date	Mintage	VF	XF	Unc
26	1977	.300	.60	1.00	1.50
	1977	2,500	—	Proof	—

20 DOBRAS

COPPER-NICKEL
F.A.O. Issue

Y#	Date	Mintage	VF	XF	Unc
27	1977	.500	1.00	1.50	2.50
	1977	2,500	—	Proof	—

250 DOBRAS

17.4000 gm., .925 SILVER, .5175 oz ASW
World Population

Y#	Date	Mintage	VF	XF	Unc
—	1977	—	—	—	—
	1977	—	—	Proof	—

World Friendship
Obv: Similar to above.

Y#	Date	Mintage	VF	XF	Unc
—	1977	—	—	—	—
	1977	—	—	Proof	—

Folklore
Obv: Similar to above.

Y#	Date	Mintage	VF	XF	Unc
—	1977	—	—	—	—
	1977	—	—	Proof	—

World Unity

Y#	Date	Mintage	VF	XF	Unc
—	1977	—	—	—	—
	1977	—	—	Proof	—

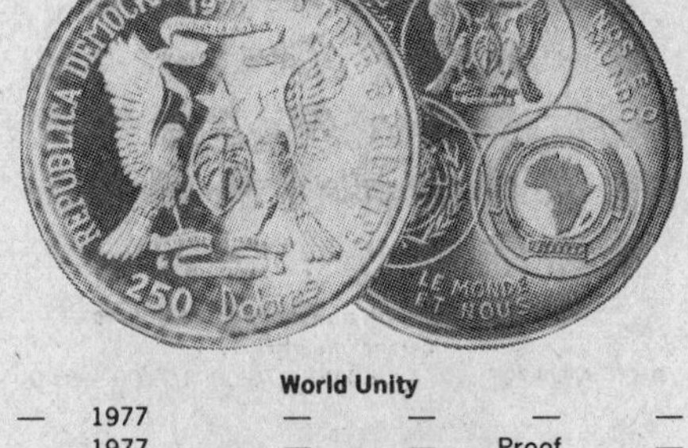

Mother and Child
Obv: Similar to above.

Y#	Date	Mintage	VF	XF	Unc
—	1977	—	—	—	—
	1977	—	—	Proof	—

2500 DOBRAS

6.4800 gm., .900 GOLD, .1875 oz AGW
World Friendship
Obv: Arms, date above, denomination below.

Y#	Date	Mintage	VF	XF	Unc
—	1977	—	—	—	—

World Population

Y#	Date	Mintage	VF	XF	Unc
—	1977	—	—	—	—

Folklore
Rev: Group of dancers and musicians.

Y#	Date	Mintage	VF	XF	Unc
—	1977	—	—	—	—

World Unity
Rev: Three interlocking circles: coat of arms, UN symbol and map of Africa between wheat.

Y#	Date	Mintage	VF	XF	Unc
—	1977	—	—	—	—

Mother and Child
Rev: Mother carrying child in back sling.

Y#	Date	Mintage	VF	XF	Unc
—	1977	—	—	—	—

NCLT ISSUES

PROVAS (Pr)

STANDARD METALS
Stamped 'PROVA' in field

Y#	Date	Mintage	Identification	Issue Price	Mkt Val.
Pr1	1929	—	10 Centavos	—	40.00
Pr2	1929	—	20 Centavos	—	40.00
Pr3	1928	—	20 Centavos	—	50.00
Pr3	1929	—	20 Centavos	—	50.00
Pr4	1939	—	1 Escudo	—	50.00
Pr5	1948	—	50 Centavos	—	55.00
Pr6	1948	—	1 Escudo	—	55.00
Pr7	1939	—	2-1/2 Escudos	—	75.00
Pr7	1948	—	2-1/2 Escudos	—	50.00
Pr8	1939	—	5 Escudos	—	60.00
Pr8	1948	—	5 Escudos	—	55.00
Pr9	1939	—	10 Escudos	—	150.00
Pr10	1951	—	50 Centavos	—	45.00
Pr11	1951	—	1 Escudo	—	175.00
Pr12	1951	—	2-1/2 Escudos	—	45.00
Pr13	1951	—	5 Escudos	—	65.00
Pr14	1951	—	10 Escudos	—	100.00
Pr15	1962	—	10 Centavos	—	20.00
Pr15a	1971	—	10 Centavos	—	20.00
Pr16	1962	—	20 Centavos	—	20.00
Pr16a	1971	—	20 Centavos	—	20.00
Pr17	1962	—	50 Centavos	—	20.00
Pr17a	1971	—	50 Centavos	—	20.00
Pr18	1962	—	1 Escudo	—	20.00
Pr18	1971	—	1 Escudo	—	20.00
Pr19	1962	—	2-1/2 Escudos	—	30.00
Pr19	1971	—	2-1/2 Escudos	—	30.00
Pr20	1962	—	5 Escudos	—	45.00
Pr20a	1971	—	5 Escudos	—	30.00
PrA21	1971	—	10 Escudos	—	30.00
Pr21	1971	—	20 Escudos	—	30.00
Pr21	1970	—	50 Escudos	—	45.00
Pr27	1970	—	50 Escudos	—	50.00

SAINT VINCENT

St. Vincent and the Grenadines, consisting of the island of St. Vincent and the northern Grenadines (a string of islets stretching southward from St. Vincent), is located in the Windward Islands of the West Indies, west of Barbados and south of St. Lucia. The tiny nation has an area of 150 sq. mi. (389 sq. km.) and a population of 100,000. Capital: Kingstown. Arrowroot, cotton, sugar, molasses, rum, and cocoa are exported. Tourism is a principal industry.

St. Vincent was discovered by Columbus on Jan. 22, 1498, but was left undisturbed for more than a century. The British began colonization early in the 18th century against bitter and prolonged Carib resistance. The island was taken by the French in 1779, but was restored to the British in 1783, at the end of the American Revolution. St. Vincent and the northern Grenadines became a British Associated State in Oct. 1969. Independence under the name of St. Vincent and the Grenadines was attained at midnight of Oct. 26, 1979. The new nation chose to become a member of the Commonwealth of Nations with the Queen of England as Chief of State.

RULERS

British

MONETARY SYSTEM

6 Black Dogs = 4 Stampees
= 1 Bit = 9 Pence

1797-1811

8 Shillings, 3 Pence = 11 Bits
= 1 Dollar

Commencing 1811

9 Shillings = 12 Bits = 1 Dollar

Commencing 1979

100 Cents = 1 Dollar

COUNTERSTAMP ISSUES

BLACK DOG

BILLON

c/s: 'SV' monogram on French Colonial coin

C#	Date	Mintage	Good	VG	Fine	VF
3	ND(1797)	—	12.50	25.00	50.00	75.00

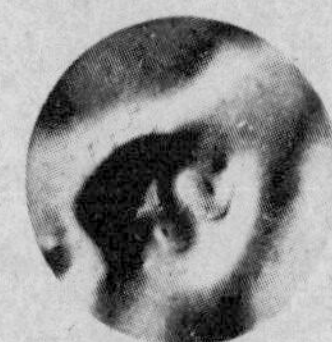

c/s: intaglio 'S'

C#	Date	Mintage	Good	VG	Fine	VF
12	ND(1814)	—	12.50	25.00	50.00	75.00

STAMPEE

BILLON

c/s: 'SV' monogram on French Colonial coin bearing a crowned 'C' c/s.

C#	Date	Mintage	Good	VG	Fine	VF
4	ND(1797)	—	12.50	25.00	50.00	75.00

c/s: intaglio 'S' on French Colonial coin bearing a crowned 'C' c/s.

C#	Date	Mintage	Good	VG	Fine	VF
13	ND(1814)	—	12.50	25.00	50.00	75.00

1/4 DOLLAR

SILVER

c/s: 'SV' monogram on 1/4 cut of Spanish or Spanish Colonial 8 Reales.

C#	Date	Mintage	Good	VG	Fine	VF
9	ND(1797)	—	50.00	75.00	90.00	120.00

1/2 DOLLAR

SILVER, 9.4gm

c/s: 'SV' monogram on 1/3 cut of Spanish or Spanish Colonial 8 Reales.

C#	Date	Mintage	Good	VG	Fine	VF
10	ND(1797)	—	50.00	75.00	100.00	135.00

10.25 gm.

Similar to C#10 with plug added to adjust to correct weight.

C#	Date	Mintage	Good	VG	Fine	VF
10a	ND(1797)	—	50.00	75.00	100.00	135.00

IV - 1/2 BITS

SILVER

c/s: S/IV 1/2/B on Spanish or Spanish Colonial 2 Reales.

C#	Date	Mintage	Good	VG	Fine	VF
15	ND(1811-14)	—	100.00	200.00	300.00	350.00

VI BITS

SILVER

c/s: S/VI on 23mm center disk cut from Spanish or Spanish Colonial 8 Reales (C#17).

C#	Date	Mintage	Good	VG	Fine	VF
16	ND(1811-14)	—	75.00	125.00	175.00	200.00

IX BITS

SILVER

c/s: S/IX on Spanish or Spanish American 4 Reales.

C#	Date	Mintage	Good	VG	Fine	VF
16.5	ND(1811-14)	—	750.00	1000.	1300.	1500.

XII BITS

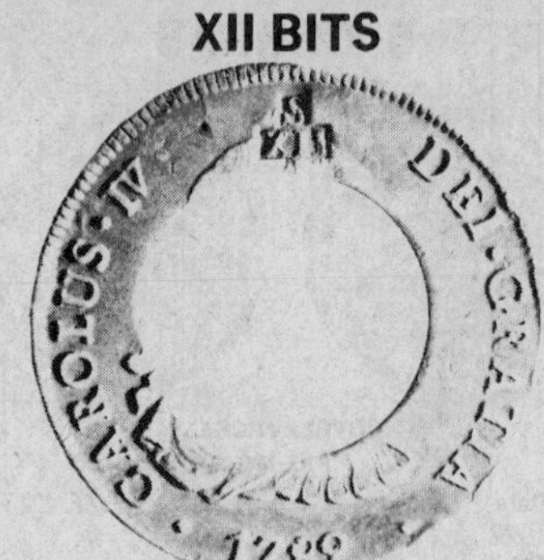

SILVER

c/s: S/XII on holed Spanish or Spanish Colonial 8 Reales.

C#	Date	Mintage	Good	VG	Fine	VF
17	ND(1811-14)	—	500.00	750.00	1000.	1200.

NOTE: Refer to VI bits, C#16.

66 SHILLINGS

GOLD

c/s: 'S' (3 times) and 'IS' on the plug of a Brazil or Portuguese 6400 Reis ('Joe') with plug added to adjust to correct weight.

C#	Date	Mintage	Good	VG	Fine	VF
21	ND(1798)	—	—	—	Rare	—

c/s: 'S' (3 times) and 'GH' similar to C#21.

C#	Date	Mintage	Good	VG	Fine	VF
22	ND(1798)	—	—	—	Rare	—

MODERN COINAGE

4 DOLLARS

COPPER-NICKEL

F.A.O. Issue

Y#	Date	Mintage	VF	XF	Unc
8*	1970	.020	3.50	5.00	7.50
	1970	2,000	—	Proof	50.00

*This number refers to Yeoman's East Caribbean Territories listings, where seven companion 4-dollar issues are listed.

Listings For

SAMOA: refer to Western Samoa

SAN MARINO

The Republic of San Marino, the oldest and smallest republic in the world, is located in north central Italy entirely surrounded by the Province of Emilia- Romagna. It has an area of 24 sq. mi. (62 sq. km.) and a population of 20,000. Capital: San Marino. The principal economic activities are farming, livestock raising, cheesemaking, tourism and light manufacturing. Building stone, lime, wheat, hides and baked goods are exported. The government derives most of its revenue from the sale of postage stamps for philatelic purpose.

According to tradition, San Marino was founded about 350 AD by a Christian stonecutter as a refuge against religious persecution. While gradually acquiring the institutions of an independent state, it avoided the fractional fights of the middle ages and, except for a brief period in fief to Cesare Borgia, retained its freedom despite attacks on its sovereignty by the Papacy, the lords of Rimini, Napoleon and Mussolini. In 1862 San Marino established a customs union with, and put itself under the protection of, Italy. A Communist-Socialist coalition controlled the Government for 12 years after World War II. The Christian Democratic Party has been the core of Government since 1957.

San Marino has its own coinage, but Italian and Vatican City coins and currency are in general use.

MINTMARKS

M - Milan
R - Rome

MONETARY SYSTEM

100 Centesimi = 1 Lira

5 CENTESIMI

COPPER

Y#	Date	Mintage	Fine	VF	XF	Unc
1	1864M	.280	3.00	5.00	11.00	30.00
	1869M	.600	3.00	5.00	9.00	17.50
	1894R	.600	3.00	5.00	8.00	16.50

BRONZE

Y#	Date	Mintage	Fine	VF	XF	Unc
14	1935R	.400	1.50	2.00	3.50	6.00
	1936R	.400	1.50	2.00	3.50	6.00
	1937R	.400	1.50	2.00	3.50	6.00
	1938R	.200	1.50	2.00	3.50	6.00

10 CENTESIMI

COPPER

Y#	Date	Mintage	Fine	VF	XF	Unc
2	1875M	.150	4.00	8.00	15.00	30.00
	1893R	.150	4.00	6.50	10.00	20.00
	1894R	.150	4.00	6.50	10.00	20.00

BRONZE

Y#	Date	Mintage	Fine	VF	XF	Unc
15	1935R	.300	2.00	3.00	4.50	8.00
	1936R	.300	2.00	3.00	4.50	8.00
	1937R	.300	2.00	3.00	4.50	8.00
	1938R	.400	2.00	3.00	4.50	8.00

50 CENTESIMI

2.5000 gm., .835 SILVER, .0671 oz ASW

Y#	Date	Mintage	Fine	VF	XF	Unc
3	1898R	.040	15.00	20.00	35.00	45.00

LIRA

5.0000 gm., .835 SILVER, .1342 oz ASW

Y#	Date	Mintage	Fine	VF	XF	Unc
4	1898R	.020	17.50	25.00	37.50	60.00
	1906R	.030	15.00	20.00	35.00	60.00

ALUMINUM

Y#	Date	Mintage	VF	XF	Unc
16	1972	.291	—	—	.15
24	1973	.291	—	—	.15
32	1974	.276	—	—	.15
42	1975	.291	—	—	.15
51	1976	.195	—	—	.15

F.A.O. Issue

Y#	Date	Mintage	VF	XF	Unc
60	1977	1.250	—	—	.20
73	1978	—	—	—	.20
86	1979	—	—	—	—

2 LIRE

10.0000 gm., .835 SILVER, .2684 oz ASW

Y#	Date	Mintage	Fine	VF	XF	Unc
5	1898R	.010	25.00	35.00	50.00	100.00
	1906R	.015	25.00	35.00	50.00	100.00

ALUMINUM

Y#	Date	Mintage	VF	XF	Unc
17	1972	.291	—	—	.20
25	1973	.291	—	—	.20
33	1974	.276	—	—	.20
43	1975	.291	—	—	.20
52	1976	.195	—	—	.20

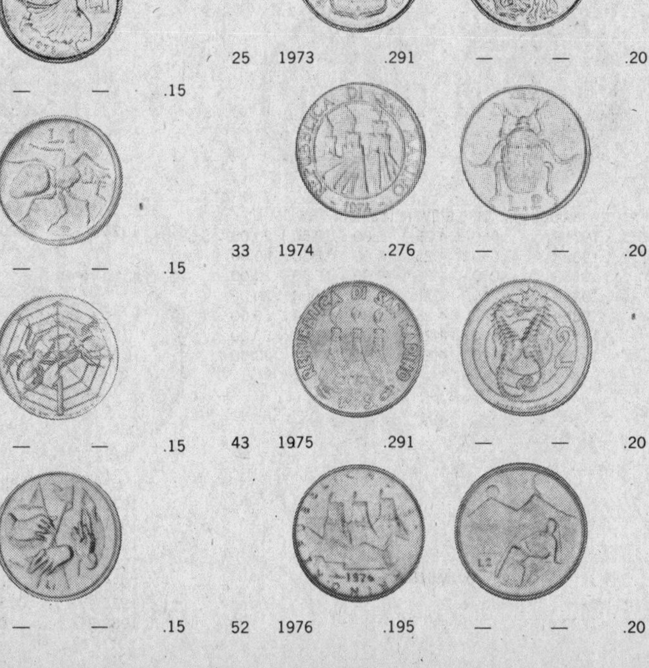

Y#	Date	Mintage	VF	XF	Unc
61	1977	—	—	—	.20
74	1978	—	—	—	.20
87	1979	—	—	—	—

5 LIRE

25.0000 .GM., .900 SILVER, .7234 oz ASW

Y#	Date	Mintage	Fine	VF	XF	Unc
6	1898R	.018	100.00	175.00	250.00	400.00

5.0000 gm., .835 SILVER, .1342 oz ASW

Y#	Date	Mintage	Fine	VF	XF	Unc
9	1931R	.050	4.25	6.00	12.50	20.00
	1932R	.050	4.25	6.00	12.50	20.00
	1933R	.050	4.25	6.00	12.50	20.00
	1935R	.200	4.25	6.00	12.50	20.00
	1936R	Inc. Ab.	4.25	6.00	12.00	20.00
	1937R	.100	4.25	6.00	12.00	20.00
	1938R	.120	4.25	6.00	12.00	20.00

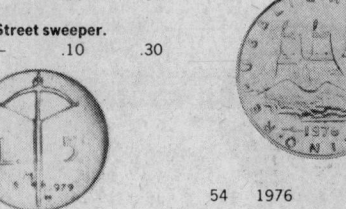

ALUMINUM

Y#	Date	Mintage	VF	XF	Unc
18	1972	.291	—	—	.30
26	1973	.291	—	—	.30

Y#	Date	Mintage	VF	XF	Unc
34	1974	.276	—	—	.30

Y#	Date	Mintage	VF	XF	Unc
44	1975	.291	—	—	.30

F.A.O. Issue

Y#	Date	Mintage	VF	XF	Unc
53	1976	.791	—	.10	.25
62	1977	—	—	.10	.30

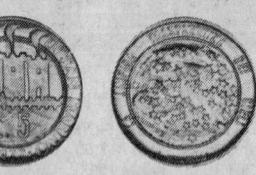

Obv: Similar to Y#62. Rev: Street sweeper.

Y#	Date	Mintage	VF	XF	Unc
75	1978	—	—	.10	.30
88	1979	—	—	—	—

10 LIRE

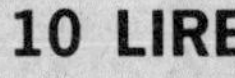

3.2258 gm., .900 GOLD, .0933 oz AGW

Y#	Date	Mintage	VF	XF	Unc
12	1925R	.020	500.00	700.00	1000.

10.0000 gm., .835 SILVER, .2684 oz ASW

Y#	Date	Mintage	VF	XF	Unc
10	1931R	.025	8.50	15.00	25.00
	1932R	.025	8.50	15.00	25.00
	1933R	.025	8.50	15.00	25.00
	1935R	.030	8.50	15.00	25.00
	1936R	Inc. Ab.	10.00	20.00	27.50
	1937R	.015	8.50	15.00	25.00
	1938R	.010	15.00	25.00	30.00

ALUMINUM

Y#	Date	Mintage	VF	XF	Unc
19	1972	.291	—	.15	.40
27	1973	.291	—	.15	.40

F.A.O. Issue

Y#	Date	Mintage	VF	XF	Unc
35	1974	1.270	—	.15	.25

Y#	Date	Mintage	VF	XF	Unc
45	1975	.291	—	.15	.40

Y#	Date	Mintage	VF	XF	Unc
54	1976	.195	—	.15	.40

Y#	Date	Mintage	VF	XF	Unc
63	1977	—	—	.15	.40

Y#	Date	Mintage	VF	XF	Unc
76	1978	—	—	.15	.40
89	1979	—	—	—	—

20 LIRE

6.4516 gm., .900 GOLD, .1867 oz AGW

Y#	Date	Mintage	VF	XF	Unc
13	1925R	9,334	750.00	1000.	1500.

15.0000 gm., .800 SILVER, .3858 oz ASW

Y#	Date	Mintage	VF	XF	Unc
11	1931R	.010	50.00	100.00	175.00
	1932R	.010	50.00	100.00	175.00
	1933R	.010	50.00	100.00	175.00
	1935R	.010	50.00	100.00	175.00
	1936R	Inc. Ab.	65.00	100.00	175.00

20.0000 gm., .600 SILVER, .3858 oz ASW

Y#	Date	Mintage	VF	XF	Unc
11a	1935R	Inc. Ab.	75.00	250.00	325.00
	1937R	5,100	55.00	250.00	325.00
	1938R	2,500	150.00	300.00	600.00

ALUMINUM-BRONZE

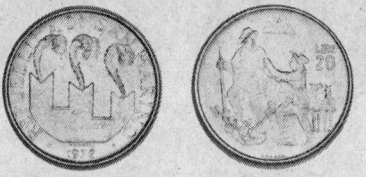

Y#	Date	Mintage	VF	XF	Unc
20	1972	.291	.10	.25	.50
28	1973	.291	.10	.25	.50

Y#	Date	Mintage	VF	XF	Unc
36	1974	.276	.10	.25	.50

F.A.O. Issue

Y#	Date	Mintage	VF	XF	Unc
46	1975	1.291	.10	.25	.50

Y#	Date	Mintage	VF	XF	Unc
55	1976	.195	.10	.25	.50

Y#	Date	Mintage	VF	XF	Unc
64	1977	—	.10	.25	.50

Y#	Date	Mintage	VF	XF	Unc
77	1978	—	.10	.25	.50

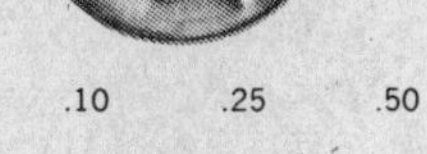

Y#	Date	Mintage	VF	XF	Unc
90	1979	—	—	—	—

50 LIRE

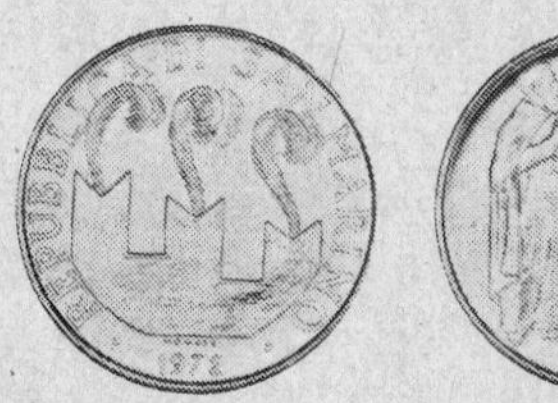

STEEL

Y#	Date	Mintage	Fine	VF	XF	Unc
21	1972	.291	.15	.25	.50	1.00

Y#	Date	Mintage	Fine	VF	XF	Unc
29	1973	.291	.15	.25	.50	1.00

Y#	Date	Mintage	Fine	VF	XF	Unc
37	1974	.276	.15	.25	.50	1.00

Y#	Date	Mintage	Fine	VF	XF	Unc
47	1975	.831	.15	.25	.50	1.00

Y#	Date	Mintage	Fine	VF	XF	Unc
56	1976	.195	.15	.25	.50	1.00

Y#	Date	Mintage	Fine	VF	XF	Unc
65	1977	—	.15	.25	.50	1.00

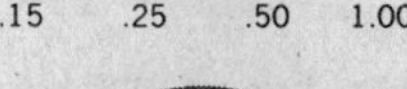

Y#	Date	Mintage	Fine	VF	XF	Unc
78	1978	—	.15	.25	.50	1.00

Y#	Date	Mintage	Fine	VF	XF	Unc
91	1979	—	.15	.25	.50	1.00

100 LIRE

STEEL

Y#	Date	Mintage	Fine	VF	XF	Unc
22	1972	.291	.25	.35	.60	1.25

Y#	Date	Mintage	Fine	VF	XF	Unc
30	1973	.291	.25	.35	.60	1.25
38	1974	.276	.25	.35	.60	1.25
48	1975	.821	.25	.35	.60	1.25
57	1976	1.853	.25	.35	.60	1.00
66	1977	—	.25	.35	.60	1.25
67	1977	—	.25	.35	.60	1.25

F.A.O. Issue

Y#	Date	Mintage	Fine	VF	XF	Unc
79	1978	.878	—	.40	.60	1.00

Y#	Date	Mintage	Fine	VF	XF	Unc
92	1979	—	—	.40	.60	1.00

200 LIRE

ALUMINUM BRONZE

Y#	Date	Mintage	VF	XF	Unc
80	1978	—	—	—	—

F.A.O. Issue

Y#	Date	Mintage	VF	XF	Unc
93	1979	—	—	—	—

500 LIRE

11.0000 gm., .835 SILVER, .2953 oz ASW

Y#	Date	Mintage	VF	XF	Unc
23	1972	.291	BV	10.00	15.00
31	1973	.291	BV	9.00	12.00
39	1974	.276	BV	9.00	12.00

Y#	Date	Mintage	VF	XF	Unc
49	1975	.291	BV	9.00	12.00

Numismatic Agency Opening

Y#	Date	Mintage	VF	XF	Unc
50	1975	.200	—	—	75.00
58	1976	.390	—	—	75.00

Social Security

Y#	Date	Mintage	VF	XF	Unc
59	1976	—	—	—	75.00
68	1977	—	—	—	75.00
81	1978	—	—	—	—
94	1979	—	—	—	—

1000 LIRE

14.6000 gm., .835 SILVER, .3919 oz ASW
Brunelleschi

Y#	Date	Mintage	VF	XF	Unc
69	1977	.180	BV	12.50	15.00

Tolstoy

Y#	Date	Mintage	VF	XF	Unc
82	1978	.100	BV	12.00	15.00

14.55 gm.
European Unity

Y#	Date	Mintage	VF	XF	Unc
95	1979	—	—	—	—

14.6 gm.
Obv: Similar to Y#59. Rev: Portrait of a hermit.

Y#	Date	Mintage	VF	XF	Unc
—	1980	—	—	—	—

SCUDO

3.0000 gm., .916 GOLD, .0883 oz AGW

Y#	Date	Mintage	XF	Unc	Proof
40	1974	.060	—	—	60.00
A41	1975	.040	—	—	60.00

Y#	Date	Mintage	XF	Unc	Proof
A60	1976	.090	—	—	80.00

Democrazia

Y#	Date	Mintage	XF	Unc	Proof
70	1977	.030	—	—	60.00

Miss Liberta

Y#	Date	Mintage	XF	Unc	Proof
75	1978	—	—	—	—

Peace

Y#	Date	Mintage	XF	Unc	Proof
96	1979	—	—	—	—

2 SCUDI

6.0000 gm., .916 GOLD, .1767 oz AGW

Y#	Date	Mintage	XF	Unc	Proof
83	1974	.060	—	—	120.00

Y#	Date	Mintage	XF	Unc	Proof
B41	1975	.080	—	—	120.00

Y#	Date	Mintage	XF	Unc	Proof
B60	1976	.118	—	—	135.00

Democrazia

Y#	Date	Mintage	XF	Unc	Proof
71	1977	.030	—	—	120.00

Miss Liberta

Y#	Date	Mintage	XF	Unc	Proof
84	1978	—	—	—	—

Peace

Y#	Date	Mintage	XF	Unc	Proof
97	1979	—	—	—	—

5 SCUDI

15.0000 gm., .916 GOLD, .4418 oz AGW

Y#	Date	Mintage	XF	Unc	Proof
C60	1976	.015	—	—	800.00

Democrazia

Y#	Date	Mintage	XF	Unc	Proof
72	1977	—	—	—	425.00

10 SCUDI

30.0000 gm., .916 gold, .8836 oz AGW

Y#	Date	Mintage	XF	Unc	Proof
85	1978	—	—	—	—

NCLT ISSUES

MINT SETS

KM#	Date	Mintage	Identification	Issue Price	Mkt. Val.
S1	1972(8)	—	Y16-23	5.00	16.00
S2	1973(8)	—	Y24-31	6.00	16.00
S3	1974(8)	60,000	Y32-39	9.00	13.00
S4	1975(8)	—	Y42-49	6.50	25.00
S5	1976(8)	—	Y51-58	6.00	72.50
S6	1977(8)	—	Y60-65,67,68	—	12.50
S7	1978(9)	—	Y73-82	—	—
S8	1979(9)	—	Y86-95	—	—
S9	1980(9)	—	—	—	—

PROOF SETS

STANDARD METALS

KM#	Date	Mintage	Identification	Issue Price	Mkt. Val.
101	1974(2)	60,000	Y40,41	—	160.00
102	1975(2)	90,000	YA41,42	—	100.00
103	1976(2)	40,000	Y59,60	—	100.00
104	1977(2)	30,000	Y70,71	—	95.00

SANTO DOMINGO

Santo Domingo was the name commonly applied to the entire West Indian island of Hispaniola; also to the eastern two thirds of the island while under Spanish control.

Before the European discovery and conquest of the New World, Hispaniola was known to its native inhabitants as Quisqueya, Bohio or Haiti. Columbus discovered Quisqueya in 1492 and named it La Isla Espanola or 'Spanish Island'. The first European settlement in the new world was established on the north side of the island by Columbus in 1493; Spain utilized it as a springboard for Spanish conquest in the Caribbean. The western third of Hispaniola, which the French called Saint-Domingue, was ceded to France by Spain in 1697. It became Haiti in 1804 as a consequence of the slave revolts of 1791-1804. In 1822, on the eve of declaring its independence from Spain, Santo Domingo (eastern Hispaniola) was seized by Haiti. Not until 1844, after a successful rebellion against the Haitians, did the Spanish portion (calling itself the Dominican Republic) attain freedom. The Republic voluntarily returned to Spanish dominion in 1861 but reclaimed its independence in 1863.

TOWN OF LE CAP

(OLD CAP FRANCOIS)

Port city on the northern coast of Haiti, which is western third of Santo Domingo.

Under a French edict of July 13, 1781 various Spanish-American and other circulating silver coins were to be counterstamped with a crowned anchor and C for the island. These were made at the capitol and the pieces given values of 1 Escalin and 1/2 Escalin. Copper coins were counterstamped L.C.

FRENCH OCCUPATION

MONETARY SYSTEM

15 Sols = 1 Escalin (1 Real)

SOL

BRONZE

c/s: L.C. in rectangle on English 1/2 Penny token of 1792.

C#	Date	Mintage	VG	Fine	VF
3a	ND(1802-09)	—	20.00	35.00	75.00

c/s: S D in rectangle on French Sol, C#73.

C#	Date	Mintage	VG	Fine	VF
41	ND(1802-09)	—	75.00	120.00	185.00

SILVER

Ring substituted for crown on anchor.

C#	Date	Mintage	VG	Fine	VF
8a	ND	—	50.00	75.00	115.00

1/2 ESCALIN

SILVER

c/s: C and anchor on Potosi minor cob.

C#	Date	Mintage	VG	Fine	VF
8	ND(1780-1802)	—	40.00	65.00	100.00

ESCALIN

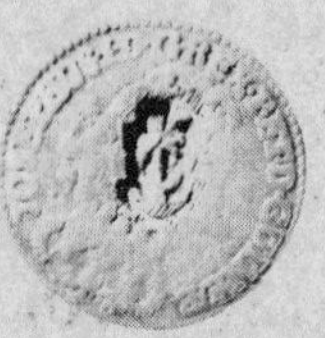

SILVER

c/s: C and anchor on Angola 2 Macutas.

C#	Date	Mintage	VG	Fine	VF
—	ND(1780-1802)	—	50.00	75.00	115.00

Counterstamp Issues of the Napoleonic Occupation

SOL

BRONZE

c/s: N over SD on French copper coin.

C#	Date	Mintage	VG	Fine	VF
42	ND(1802-09)	—	50.00	75.00	115.00

c/s: Crowned N on English 1/2 Penny, C#20.

C#	Date	Mintage	VG	Fine	VF
44	ND(1802-09)	—	65.00	110.00	165.00

Coinage Of Toussaint

RULERS

Toussaint L'ouverture, 1798-1802

MONETARY SYSTEM

15 Sols (Sous) = 1 Escalin (Real)

DEMY (1/2) ESCALIN

SILVER

Similar to 1 Escalin, C#32.

C#	Date	Mintage	VG	Fine	VF
31	ND(1802)	—	120.00	225.00	400.00

UN (1) ESCALIN

SILVER

C#	Date	Mintage	VG	Fine	VF
32	ND(1802)	—	100.00	200.00	350.00

DEUX (2) ESCALIN

SILVER

C#	Date	Mintage	VG	Fine	VF
33	ND(1802)	—	100.00	225.00	450.00

SPANISH OCCUPATION

RULER

Ferdinand VII, 1808-1822

MONETARY SYSTEM

16 Reales = 1 Escudo

1/4 REAL

COPPER

C#	Date	Mintage	VG	Fine	VF
48	ND	—	75.00	125.00	175.00

C#	Date	Mintage	VG	Fine	VF
51	ND	—	15.00	25.00	35.00

2/4 REAL

COPPER

C#	Date	Mintage	VG	Fine	VF
49	ND	—	80.00	110.00	150.00

REAL

SILVER

C#	Date	Mintage	VG	Fine	VF
55	ND	—	70.00	90.00	135.00

2 REALES

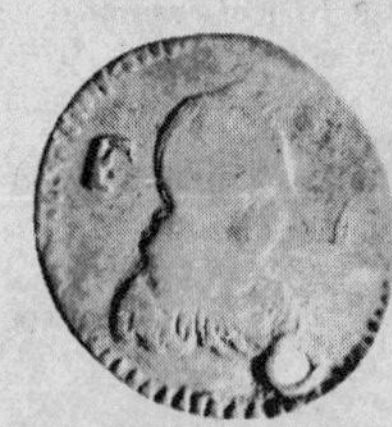

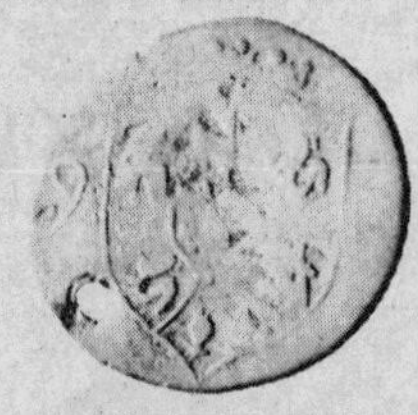

SILVER

C#	Date	Mintage	VG	Fine	VF
56	ND	—	80.00	110.00	150.00

Spanish Counterstamp Issues

REAL

.903 SILVER

c/s: Crowned F.7o on Mexico 1 Real, KM#75.

C#	Date	Mintage	Good	VG	Fine
61	ND(1732-47)	—	40.00	65.00	100.00

8 REALES

.903 SILVER

c/s: Crowned F.7o on Mexico 8 Reales, KM#109 (C#81).

C#	Date	Mintage	Good	VG	Fine
64	ND(1791-1808)	—	750.00	1000.	—

SAUDI ARABIA

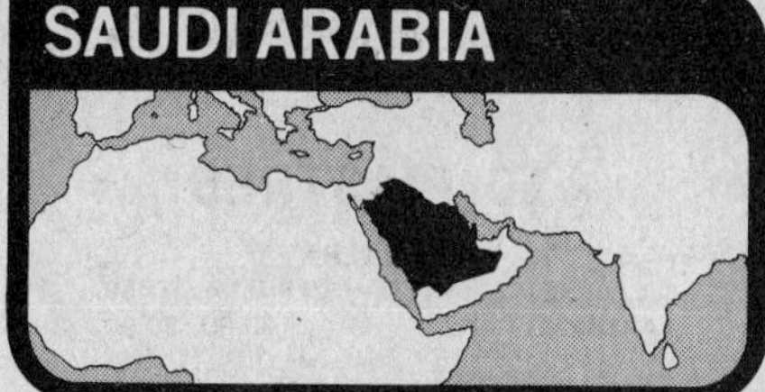

The Kingdom of Saudi Arabia, an independent and absolute hereditary monarchy comprising the former sultanate of Nejd, the old kingdom of Hejaz, Asir and El Jasa, occupies four-fifths of the Arabian peninsula. The kingdom has an area of 873,000 sq. mi. (2,261,060 sq. km.) and a population of 5.6 million. Capital: Riyadh. The economy is based on oil, which provides 85 percent of Saudi Arabia's revenue.

Mohammed united the Arabs in the 7th century and his followers founded a great empire with its capital at Medina. The Turks established nominal rule over much of Arabia in the 16th and 17th centuries, and in the 18th century divided it into principalities.

The Kingdom of Saudi Arabia was created by King Ibn-Saud (1882-1953), a descendant of earlier Wahabi rulers of the Arabian peninsula. In 1901 he seized Riyadh, capital of the Sultanate of Nejd, and in 1905 established himself as Sultan. In 1913 he captured the Turkish province of Hasa; took the Hejaz in 1925 and by 1926 most of Asir. In 1932 he combined Nejd and Hejaz into the single kingdom of Saudi Arabia. Asir was incorporated into the kingdom a year later.

The following areas of Saudi Arabia were coin-issuing entities of interest to numismatics:

MECCA

Mecca, the metropolis of Islam and the capital of Hejaz, is located inland from the Red Sea due east of the port of Jidda. A center of non-political commercial, cultural and religious activities, Mecca remained virtually independent until 1259 when Egypt established an effective sovereignty over the Hejaz. Two centuries of Egyptian rule were followed by four centuries of Turkish rule which lasted until the Arab revolts of 1916 and the peace treaties of World War I, which extinguished all Turkish pretensions to sovereignty over any part of the Arabian peninsula.

RULERS

Sharifs of Mecca

Ghalib b. Ma'Sud, AH1219-1229

Yahya b. Surer, AH1230-1240

Abdul Muttalib and Ibn Awn, AH1240-1248

1/2 MAHMUDI

COPPER

MINT: MECCA

C#	Date	Mintage	Good	VG	Fine
50	AH1240	—	40.00	80.00	120.00

MAHMUDI

COPPER

C#	Date	Mintage	Good	VG	Fine
51	AH1219	—	60.00	110.00	150.00

C#	Date	Mintage	Good	VG	Fine
52	AH1220	—	50.00	80.00	125.00
	1221	—	50.00	80.00	125.00
	1222	—	50.00	80.00	125.00

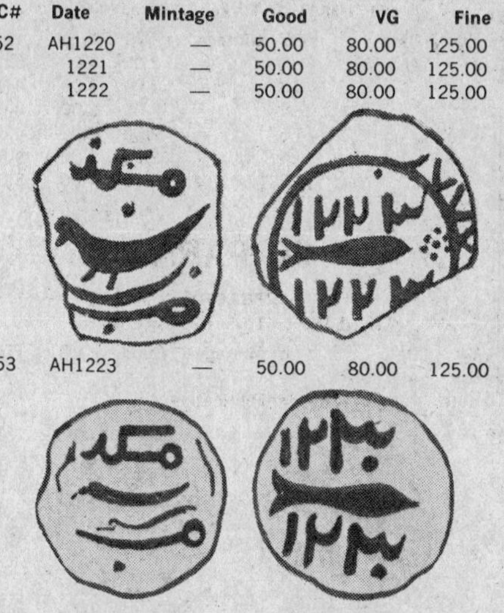

C#	Date	Mintage	Good	VG	Fine
53	AH1223	—	50.00	80.00	125.00
54	AH1230	—	60.00	100.00	140.00

HEJAZ

Hejaz, a province of Saudi Arabia and a former vilayet of the Ottoman empire, occupies an 800-mile long (1,287 km.) coastal strip between Nejd and the Red Sea. The province was a Turkish dependency until freed in World War I. Husian ibn Ali, amir of Mecca, opposed the Turkish control and, with the aid of Lawrence of Arabia, wrested much of Hejaz from the Turks and in 1916 assumed the title of King of Hejaz. Ibn Saud of Nejd conquered Hejaz in 1925, and in 1926 combined it and Nejd into a single kingdom.

RULERS

Al Husain Ibn Ali

AH1334-42/AD1916-24

Ibn Saud (of Nejd)

AH1342/AD1924

MONETARY SYSTEM

40 Para = 1 Piastre (Ghirsh)

20 Piastres = 1 Riyal

100 Piastres = 1 Dinar

COUNTERSTAMP ISSUES

Maria Theresa Thalers, as well as many Turkish and Egyptian coins, are found counterstamped "Al-Hijaz." The countermark occurs in various sizes and styles of lettering. The mark was first applied during 1916, and is reckoned by some authorities to have been used as late as 1923.

الحجاز

Type A

الحجاز

Type B

NOTE: Caution should be excercised in the purchase of any of the Hejaz countermarked coins. The authenticity of most of the pieces on the market today is the subject of controversy, particularly pieces other than the Maria Theresa Thaler, the Turkish 20 Piastres and 10 Piastres of AH1327, and the Turkish 20 and 40 Para nickel pieces (#'s 2,3,10,11,and 12 below). Also,the large-size countermark on crown size pieces is not believed to be original. Any coin dating after 1923 with the countermark is most doubtful.

10 PARA

BILLON

c/s: 'HEJAZ' on Turkey 10 Para, C#266.

Y#	Date	Year	Mintage	Good	VG	Fine
4	AH1255*	1-5	—	—	—	5.00

***note:** Possibly A Recent Fabrication.

NICKEL

Listings For

SARAWAK: refer to Malaysia

c/s: 'HEJAZ' on Turkey 10 Para, Y#44.

Y#	Date	Year	Mintage	VG	Fine	VF
1	AH1327	2	—	2.00	4.00	6.00
		3	—	2.00	3.00	4.00
		4	—	2.00	3.00	4.00
		5	—	2.00	3.00	4.00
		6	—	2.00	3.00	4.00
		7	—	3.00	4.00	5.00

20 PARA

BILLON

c/s: 'HEJAZ' on Turkey 20 Para, C#267.

Y#	Date	Year	Mintage	Good	VG	Fine
5	AH1255*	—	—	—	—	5.00

note: Possibly A Recent Fabrication.

NICKEL

c/s: 'HEJAZ' on Turkey 20 Para, Y#45.

Y#	Date	Year	Mintage	VG	Fine	VF
2	AH1327	2	—	2.00	3.00	6.00
		3	—	1.00	2.00	4.00
		4	—	1.00	2.00	4.00
		5	—	1.00	2.00	4.00
		6	—	1.00	2.00	4.00

40 PARA

NICKEL

c/s: 'HEJAZ' on Turkey 40 Para, Y#46.

Y#	Date	Year	Mintage	VG	Fine	VF
3	AH1327	3	—	2.00	3.00	4.00
		4	—	1.00	2.00	3.00
		5	—	1.00	2.00	3.00

COPPER-NICKEL

c/s: 'HEJAZ' on Turkey 40 Para, Y#46a.

Y#	Date	Year	Mintage	VG	Fine	VF
3.1	AH1327	8	—	1.00	2.00	4.00
		9	—	2.00	4.00	7.50

c/s: 'HEJAZ' on Turkey 40 Para, Y#58.

Y#	Date	Year	Mintage	VG	Fine	VF
3.2	AH1336	4	—	2.50	5.00	10.00

2 PIASTRES

SILVER

c/s: 'HEJAZ' on Turkey 2 Piastres, Y#48.

Y#	Date	Year	Mintage	VG	Fine	VF
8	AH1327	—	—	—	—	—

c/s: 'HEJAZ' on Turkey 2 Piastres, Y#A50.

Y#	Date	Year	Mintage	VG	Fine	VF
8.1	AH1327	—	—	20.00	27.50	40.00

c/s: 'HEJAZ' on Egypt 2 Guerche, Y#30.

Y#	Date	Year	Mintage	VG	Fine	VF
8.2	AH1327	—	—	—	—	—

NOTE: The above coins are all controversial.

5 PIASTRES

SILVER

c/s: 'HEJAZ' on Turkey 5 Piastres, Y#49.

Y#	Date	Year	Mintage	VG	Fine	VF
9	AH1327	1-7	—	15.00	30.00	50.00

c/s: 'HEJAZ' on Turkey 5 Piastres, Y#B50.

Y#	Date	Year	Mintage	VG	Fine	VF
9.1	AH1327	7-9	—	20.00	40.00	60.00

c/s: 'HEJAZ' on Egypt 5 Guerche, Y#31.

Y#	Date	Year	Mintage	VG	Fine	VF
9.2	AH1327	2H-6H	—	20.00	40.00	60.00

10 PIASTRES

SILVER

c/s: 'HEJAZ' on Turkey 10 Piastres, Y#50.

Y#	Date	Year	Mintage	VG	Fine	VF
10	AH1327	1-7	—	30.00	60.00	80.00

c/s: 'HEJAZ' on Turkey 10 Piastres, Y#C50.

Y#	Date	Year	Mintage	VG	Fine	VF
10.1	AH1327	7-10	—	50.00	100.00	140.00

c/s: 'HEJAZ' on Egypt 10 Guerche, Y#32.

Y#	Date	Year	Mintage	VG	Fine	VF
10.2	AH1327	—	—	35.00	70.00	100.00

20 PIASTRES

SILVER

c/s: 'HEJAZ' on Egypt 20 Guerche, Y#33.

Y#	Date	Year	Mintage	VG	Fine	VF
11	AH1327	2H-6H	—	50.00	75.00	100.00

c/s: 'HEJAZ' on Turkey 20 Piastres, Y#51.

Y#	Date	Year	Mintage	VG	Fine	VF
11.1	AH1327	8-10	—	40.00	60.00	75.00

c/s: 'HEJAZ' on Austria M.T. Thaler, Y#55.

Y#	Date	Year	Mintage	VG	Fine	VF
12	1780 (restrike)		—	25.00	35.00	50.00

REGULAR COINAGE

NOTE: All the regular coins of Hejaz bear the accessional date 1334 of Al-Husayn ibn Ali, plus the regnal year. Many of the bronze coins occur with a light silver wash.

1/8 PIASTRE

BRONZE

Y#	Date	Year	Mintage	Fine	VF	XF
16	AH1334	5	—	15.00	20.00	25.00

1/4 PIASTRE

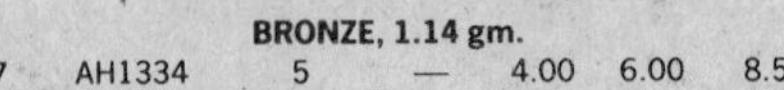

BRONZE, 1.14 gm.

Y#	Date	Year	Mintage	Fine	VF	XF
17	AH1334	5	—	4.00	6.00	8.50

Y#	Date	Year	Mintage	Fine	VF	XF
20	AH1334	8	—	6.00	7.50	14.00

1/2 PIASTRE

BRONZE

Y#	Date	Year	Mintage	Fine	VF	XF
18	AH1334	5	—	4.50	7.50	10.00

Similar to 1/4 Piastre, Y#20.

Y#	Date	Year	Mintage	Fine	VF	XF
21	AH1334	8	—	—	Rare	—

PIASTRE

BRONZE

Y#	Date	Year	Mintage	Fine	VF	XF
19	AH1334	5	—	6.50	11.00	16.50

Y#	Date	Year	Mintage	Fine	VF	XF
22	AH1334	8	—	6.00	10.00	15.00

5 PIASTRES

SILVER

Y#	Date	Year	Mintage	Fine	VF	XF
23	AH1334	8	—	25.00	40.00	60.00

10 PIASTRES

SILVER

Y#	Date	Year	Mintage	Fine	VF	XF
24	AH1334	8	—	80.00	130.00	175.00

20 PIASTRES

(= 1 Ryal)

SILVER

Y#	Date	Year	Mintage	Fine	VF	XF
25	AH1334	8	—	25.00	40.00	70.00
	—	9	—	40.00	60.00	100.00

DINAR HASHIMI

GOLD

26	AH1334	8	—	100.00	150.00	225.00

NEJD

Nejd, a province of Saudi Arabia which may be described as an open steppe, occupies the core of the Arabian peninsula. The province became a nominal dependency of the Turkish empire in 1871 and a sultanate of King Ibn-Saud in 1906.

RULERS

Ibn Sa'ud,
AH1322-1373/AD1905-1953
(In all of Hejaz after 1926, in all Saudi Arabia after 1932).

MONETARY SYSTEM

40 Para = 1 Piastre (Ghrish)
20 Piastres = 1 Riyal
100 Piastres = 1 Dinar

COUNTERSTAMP ISSUES

Maria Theresa Thalers were countermarked "NEJD" between 1916-1923.

NOTE: Other Turkish and Egyptian coins are reported with the Nejd cmk., but their legitimacy remains a matter of controversy. They are listed here, but should be regarded with caution. Indian Rupees cmk.'d 'NEJD' are rather dubious. Coins bearing both the Nejd and Hejaz countermarks are of very questionable legitimacy.

10 PARA

BILLON
c/s: 'NEJD' on Turkey 10 Para, C#266.

Y#	Date	Year	Mintage	Good	VG	Fine
A1	AH1255*	1-5	—	—	—	6.00

note: Possibly A Recent Fabrication.

20 PARA

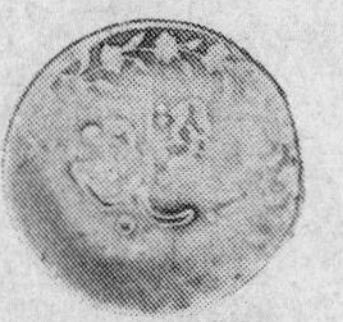

BILLON
c/s: 'NEJD' on Turkey 20 Para, C#267.

B1	AH1255*	1-5	—	—	—	6.00

***note:** Possibly A Recent Fabrication.

5 PIASTRES

SILVER
c/s: 'NEJD' on Egypt 5 Guerche, Y#31.

Y#	Date	Year	Mintage	VG	Fine	VF
1	AH1327	2H-6H	—	25.00	45.00	60.00
	c/s: 'NEJD' on Egypt 5 Guerche, Y#40.					
1.1	AH1335	1916	—	20.00	40.00	60.00
		1917	—	20.00	40.00	60.00
		1917H	—	20.00	40.00	60.00
	c/s: 'NEJD' on Turkey 5 Piastres, Y#49.					
1.2	AH1327	1-7	—	20.00	35.00	50.00
	c/s: 'NEJD' on Turkey 5 Piastres, Y#B50.					
1.3	AH1327	7-9	—	20.00	35.00	50.00

RUPEE

SILVER
c/s: 'NEJD' on India Rupee, C#303.

2a	1835	—	—	30.00	45.00	60.00
	c/s: 'NEJD' on India Rupee, Y#4.					
2a.1	1840	—	—	25.00	35.00	50.00
	c/s: 'NEJD' on India Rupee, Y#4a.					
2a.2	1840	—	—	25.00	35.00	50.00
	c/s: 'NEJD' on India Rupee, Y#12.					
2a.3	1862-76	—	—	25.00	35.00	45.00

NOTE: The above coins are all controversial.

10 PIASTRES

SILVER
c/s: 'NEJD' on Egypt 10 Guerche, Y#21.

Y#	Date	Year	Mintage	VG	Fine	VF
2	AH1293	10-33H	—	60.00	80.00	110.00
	c/s: 'NEJD' on Turkey 10 Piastres, Y#50.					
2.1	AH1327	1-7	—	50.00	70.00	95.00
	c/s: 'NEJD' on Turkey 10 Piastres, Y#C50.					
2.2	AH1327	7-10	—	50.00	75.00	100.00

20 PIASTRES

SILVER
c/s: 'NEJD' on Egypt 20 Guerche, Y#33.

3	AH1327	2H-6H	—	50.00	70.00	95.00
	c/s: 'NEJD' on Turkey 20 Piastres, Y#51.					
3.1	AH1327	8-10	—	45.00	65.00	85.00

c/s: 'NEJD' on Austria M.T. Thaler, Y#55.

3a	1780	—	—	35.00	45.00	60.00

ROYAL TITLES
APPEARING ON COINS

AH1344 (AD1926)
King of Hejaz and Sultan of Nejd

AH1346-48 (AD1928-30)
King of Hejaz and Nejd and Dependencies

AH1356 (AD1937) and later
King of the Kingdom of Saudi Arabia

SAUDI ARABIA

RULERS

Abd Al-Aziz Ibn Sa'ud
AH1344-1373 (AD1926-1953)
Sa'ud Ibn Abdul Aziz
AH1373-1383 (AD1953-1964)
Faisal, AH1383-1395 (AD1964-1975)
Khaled, AH1395- (1975-)

MONETARY SYSTEM

5 Halala = 1 Ghirsh
20 Ghirsh = 1 Riyal
40 Riyals = 1 Guinea

INTERIM COINAGE

Struck at occupied Mecca, Hejaz Mint by Ibn Sa'ud while establishing his kingdom.

1/4 GHIRSH

COPPER

Y#	Date	Mintage	Fine	VF	XF
1	AH1343	—	4.00	8.00	12.00

Several varieties exist, including plain and reeded edge.

1/2 GHIRSH

COPPER

Y#	Date	Mintage	Fine	VF	XF
2	AH1343	—	3.00	6.00	11.00

Several varieties exist, including plain and reeded edge.

Y#	Date	Mintage	Fine	VF	XF
A3	AH1344, yr. 2	—	1.50	3.00	8.00

REGULAR COINAGE

NOTE: Copper-nickel, reeded-edge coins dated 1356 and silver coins dated AH1354 were struck at Philadelphia between 1944-1949.

HALALA

BRONZE

Y#	Date	Mintage	VF	XF	Unc
30	AH1383	5.000	.05	.10	.20
	1392	5,000	—	—	—

1/4 GHIRSH

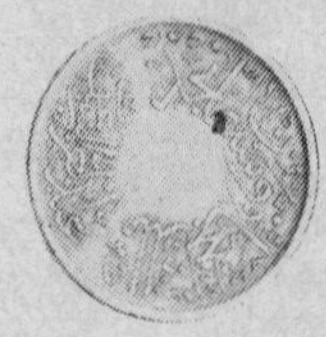 

COPPER NICKEL

Y#	Date	Mintage	Fine	VF	XF
3	AH1344	—	2.50	5.00	10.00

Y#	Date	Mintage	Fine	VF	XF
6	AH1346	—	2.50	5.00	10.00

Y#	Date	Mintage	Fine	VF	XF
6a	AH1348	—	2.50	5.00	10.00

Plain edge

Y#	Date	Mintage	Fine	VF	XF
9	AH1356	—	2.00	4.00	8.00

Reeded edge

Y#	Date	Mintage	Fine	VF	XF
9a	AH1356	21.500	.25	.30	.75

Struck in 1947 (AH1366-67) at Philadelphia.

٦٥ '65' COUNTERSTAMP

The following pieces are counterstamped examples of earlier types bearing the Arabic numerals "65". They were counterstamped in a move to break money changers' monopoly on small coins in 1365 A.H. (1946 A.D.) These counterstamps vary and are found with the Arabic numbers raised in a circle and incuse, the latter being scarcer.

c/s: '65' on 1/4 Ghirsh, Y#3.

Y#	Date	Mintage	VG	Fine	VF
A21.1	AH1344	—	4.00	7.50	10.00

c/s: '65' on 1/4 Ghirsh, Y#6.

Y#	Date	Mintage	VG	Fine	VF
A21.2	AH1346	—	4.00	7.50	10.00

c/s: '65' on 1/4 Ghirsh, Y#6a.

Y#	Date	Mintage	VG	Fine	VF
A21.3	AH1348	—	4.00	7.50	10.00

Plain edge
c/s: '65' on 1/4 Ghirsh, Y#9.

Y#	Date	Mintage	VG	Fine	VF
A21.4	AH1356	—	2.00	4.00	8.00

1/2 GHIRSH

COPPER NICKEL

Y#	Date	Mintage	Fine	VF	XF
4	AH1344	—	3.00	6.00	12.00

Y#	Date	Mintage	Fine	VF	XF
7	AH1346	—	2.50	5.00	10.00

Y#	Date	Mintage	Fine	VF	XF
7a	AH1348	—	3.00	7.50	15.00

Plain edge

Y#	Date	Mintage	Fine	VF	XF
10	AH1356	—	2.00	5.00	10.00

Reeded edge

Y#	Date	Mintage	Fine	VF	XF
10a	AH1356	10.850	.25	.35	1.00

Struck in 1947 (AH1366-67) at Philadelphia.

٦٥ '65' COUNTERSTAMP

c/s: '65' on 1/2 Ghirsh, Y#4.

Y#	Date	Mintage	VG	Fine	VF
B21.1	AH1344	—	3.50	7.50	15.00

 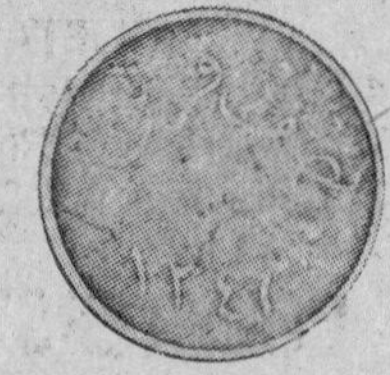

c/s: '65' on 1/2 Ghirsh, Y#7.

Y#	Date	Mintage	VG	Fine	VF
B21.2	AH1346	—	3.00	7.00	14.00

c/s: '65' on 1/2 Ghirsh, Y#7a.

Y#	Date	Mintage	VG	Fine	VF
B21.3	AH1348	—	4.00	8.00	16.00

Plain edge
c/s: '65' on 1/2 Ghirsh, Y#10.

Y#	Date	Mintage	VG	Fine	VF
B21.4	AH1356	—	2.25	5.00	10.00

GHIRSH

COPPER NICKEL

Y#	Date	Mintage	Fine	VF	XF
5	AH1344	—	3.50	7.00	12.00

Y#	Date	Mintage	Fine	VF	XF
8	AH1346	—	3.00	6.00	10.00

Y#	Date	Mintage	Fine	VF	XF
8a	AH1348	—	4.50	9.00	14.00

Plain edge

Y#	Date	Mintage	Fine	VF	XF
11	AH1356	—	1.50	3.00	5.00

Reeded edge

Y#	Date	Mintage	Fine	VF	XF
11a	AH1356	7.150	.30	.50	.85

Struck in 1947 (AH1366-67) at Philadelphia.

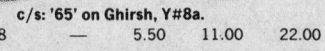

٦٥ '65' COUNTERSTAMP

See note under 1/4 Ghirsh.

c/s: '65' on Ghirsh, Y#5.

Y#	Date	Mintage	VG	Fine	VF
C21.1	AH1344	—	4.50	9.00	18.00

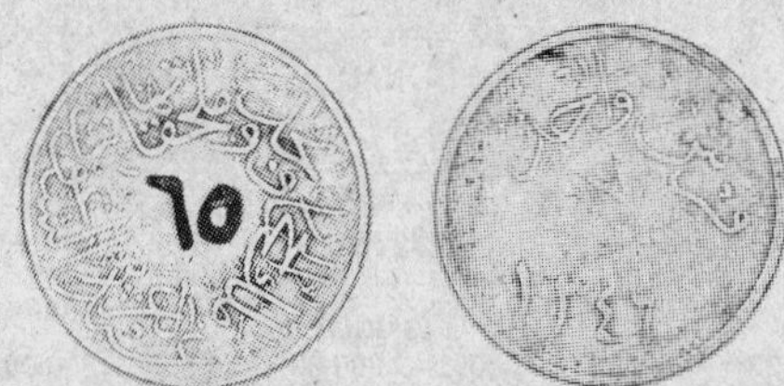

c/s: '65' on Ghirsh, Y#8.

Y#	Date	Mintage	VG	Fine	VF
C21.2	AH1346	—	4.00	8.00	16.00

c/s: '65' on Ghirsh, Y#8a.

Y#	Date	Mintage	VG	Fine	VF
C21.3	AH1348	—	5.50	11.00	22.00

Plain edge
c/s: '65' on Ghirsh, Y#11.

Y#	Date	Mintage	VG	Fine	VF
C21.4	AH1356	—	2.50	5.00	10.00

Y#	Date	Mintage	VF	XF	Unc
A23	AH1376	10.000	.15	.20	.35
	1378	50.000	.15	.20	.25

5 HALALA (= 1 GHIRSH)

COPPER-NICKEL

Y#	Date	Mintage	VF	XF	Unc
32	AH1392	130.00	.10	.20	.50

F.A.O. Issue

Y#	Date	Mintage	VF	XF	Unc
42	AH1398	1.000	—	.20	.50

2 GHIRSH

COPPER-NICKEL

Y#	Date	Mintage	VF	XF	Unc
24	AH1376	50.000	.20	.30	.45
	1379	28.110	.20	.30	.40

10 HALALA

COPPER-NICKEL

Y#	Date	Mintage	VF	XF	Unc
33	AH1392	55.000	.20	.25	.50
	1396	20.000	—	.25	.50

F.A.O. Issue

Y#	Date	Mintage	VF	XF	Unc
43	AH1398	1.000	—	.30	.75

4 GHIRSH

COPPER-NICKEL

Y#	Date	Mintage	VF	XF	Unc
25	AH1376	49.100	.25	.45	1.00
	1378	10.000	.25	.45	.75

1/4 RIYAL

2.9160 gm., .917 SILVER, .0859 oz ASW

Y#	Date	Mintage	Fine	VF	XF
12	AH1346	.400	20.00	45.00	65.00
	1346	—	—	Proof	—
	1348	.200	30.00	55.00	90.00

Y#	Date	Mintage	VF	XF	Unc
18	AH1354	3.000	2.50	3.00	4.00
	1354	—	—	Proof	2.00

Y#	Date	Mintage	VF	XF	Unc
26	AH1374	4.000	BV	BV	2.50

25 HALALA

COPPER-NICKEL
Denomination in masculine gender

Y#	Date	Mintage	VF	XF	Unc
34	AH1392	48.465	1.00	1.50	2.00

Denomination in feminine gender

Y#	Date	Mintage	VF	XF	Unc
34a	AH1392	Inc. Ab.	.20	.30	.50

F.A.O. Issue

Y#	Date	Year	Mintage	VF	XF	Unc
A31	AH1393	1973	.200	.40	.50	.75

Y#	Date	Year	Mintage	VF	XF	Unc
39	AH1397	1977	—	—	.50	.75

1/2 RIYAL

5.8319 gm., .917 SILVER, .1719 oz ASW

Y#	Date	Mintage	Fine	VF	XF
13	AH1346	.200	45.00	75.00	110.00
	1346	—	—	Proof	Rare
	1348	.100	55.00	90.00	130.00

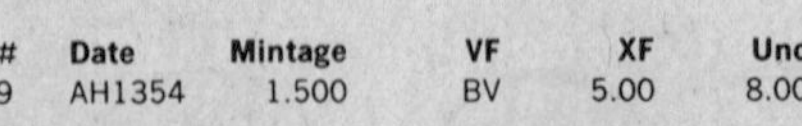

Y#	Date	Mintage	VF	XF	Unc
19	AH1354	1.500	BV	5.00	8.00

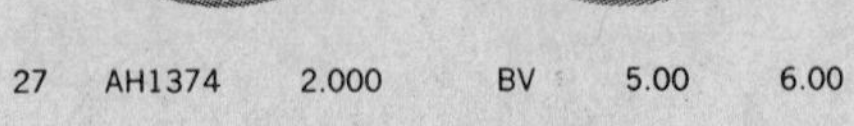

Y#	Date	Mintage	VF	XF	Unc
27	AH1374	2.000	BV	5.00	6.00

50 HALALA

COPPER-NICKEL
F.A.O. Issue

Y#	Date	Year	Mintage	VF	XF	Unc
31	AH1392	1972	.500	.65	1.00	1.25

Y#	Date	Mintage	VF	XF	Unc
35	AH1392	10.000	.40	.50	1.00
	1396	6.000	—	.50	1.00

Y#	Date	Year	Mintage	VF	XF	Unc
40	AH1397	1977	—	—	.50	1.00

RIYAL

11.6638 gm., .917 SILVER, .3437 oz ASW

Y#	Date	Mintage	Fine	VF	XF
14	AH1346	.800	32.00	40.00	50.00
	1346	—	—	Proof	—
	1348	.400	48.00	60.00	80.00

Y#	Date	Mintage	VF	XF	Unc
20	AH1354	80.500	BV	11.00	15.00
	1354	—	—	Proof	—
	1367	Inc. Ab.	BV	10.00	12.00
	1370	—	BV	10.00	12.00

Y#	Date	Mintage	VF	XF	Unc
28	AH1374	48.000	BV	10.00	12.00

COPPER-NICKEL
F.A.O. Issue

Y#	Date	Mintage	VF	XF	Unc
44	1978	.250	—	—	—

100 HALALA

COPPER-NICKEL

Y#	Date	Year	Mintage	VF	XF	Unc
36	AH1396	(1976)	—	—	1.00	1.50

F.A.O. Issue

Y#	Date	Year	Mintage	VF	XF	Unc
41	AH1398	1978	—	—	.50	1.00

TRADE COINAGE

SOVEREIGN
(POUND)

7.9881 gm., .917 GOLD, .2354 oz AGW

Y#	Date	Mintage	VF	XF	Unc
21	ND(1947)	.121	325.00	350.00	375.00

NOTE: This Sovereign was struck at the Philadelphia Mint for the Aramco Oil Co.

GUINEA

GOLD

Y#	Date	Mintage	VF	XF	Unc
23	AH1370		BV	155.00	175.00
29	AH1377	1.579	155.00	175.00	225.00

4 SOVEREIGNS
(POUNDS)

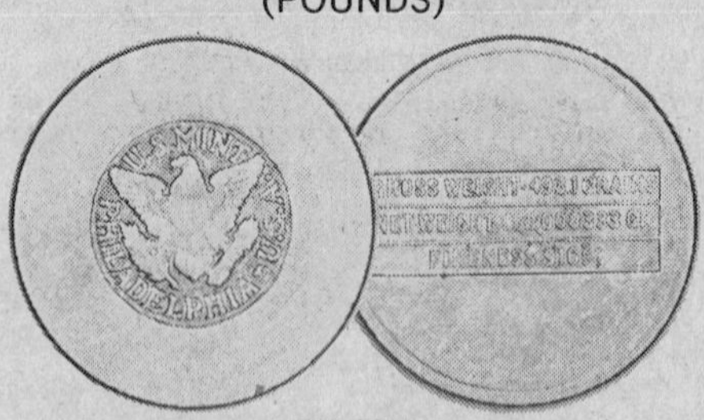

.917 GOLD

Y#	Date	Mintage	VF	XF	Unc
22	ND(1945)	.091	600.00	700.00	800.00

NOTE: The 4 Sovereign was struck at the Philadelphia Mint for the Aramco Oil Co. (Most of these coins were melted into bullion.)

SENEGAL

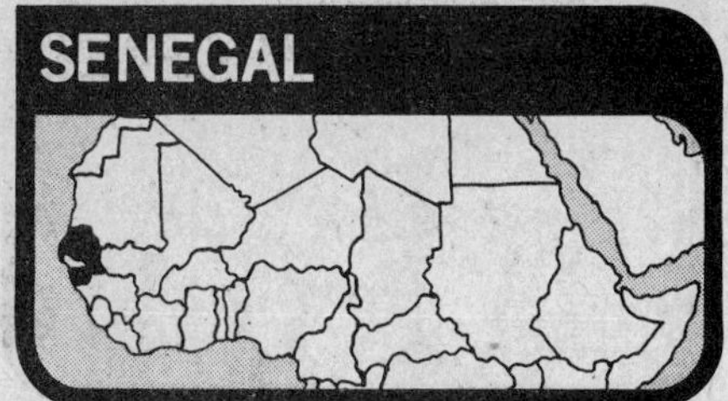

The Republic of Senegal, located on the bulge of West Africa between Mauritania and Guinea-Bissau, has an area of 76,124 sq. mi. (197,160 sq. km.) and a population of 5.4 million. Capital: Dakar. The economy is primarily agricultural. Peanuts and products, phosphates, and canned fish are exported.

An abundance of megalithic remains indicates that Senegal was inhabited in prehistoric times. The Portuguese had some trading stations on the banks of the Senegal River in the 15th century. French commercial establishments date from the 17th century. The French gradually acquired control over the interior regions, which were administered as a protectorate until 1920, and as a colony thereafter. After the 1958 French constitutional referendum, Senegal became a member of the French Community with virtual autonomy. In 1959 Senegal and the French Soudan merged to form the Mali Federation, which became fully independent on June 20, 1960. (April 4, the date the transfer of power agreement was signed with France, is celebrated as Senegal's independence day.) The federation broke up on Aug. 20, 1960, when Senegal seceded and proclaimed the Republic of Senegal. Soudan became the Republic of Mali a month later.

Senegal is a member of a monetary union of autonomous republics called the Monetary Union of West African States (Union Monetaire Quest-Africaine). The other members are Ivory Coast, Benin, Upper Volta, Niger, Mauritania and Togo. Mali was a member, but seceded in 1962. Some of the member countries have issued coinage in addition to the common currency issued by the Monetary Union of West African States.

10 FRANCS

3.2000 gm., .900 GOLD, .0926 oz AGW
Anniversary of Independence

H#	Date	Mintage	XF	Unc	Proof
1	1968	—	—	—	65.00

25 FRANCS

8.0000 gm., .900 GOLD, .2315 oz AGW
Anniversary of Independence

H#	Date	Mintage	XF	Unc	Proof
2	1968	—	—	—	150.00

50 FRANCS

16.0000 gm., .900 GOLD, .4630 oz AGW
Anniversary of Independence

H#	Date	Mintage	XF	Unc	Proof
3	1968	—	—	—	300.00

28.2800 gm., .925 SILVER, .8411 oz ASW
25th Anniversary of Eurafrique Program

H#	Date	Mintage	XF	Unc	Proof
6	1975	1,968	—	60.00	—
	1975	—	—	—	75.00

100 FRANCS

32.0000 gm., .900 GOLD, .9260 oz AGW
Anniversary of Independence

H#	Date	Mintage	XF	Unc	Proof
4	1968	—	—	—	600.00

150 FRANCS

79.9400 gm., .925 SILVER, 2.3776 oz ASW
25th Anniversary of Eurafrique Program

H#	Date	Mintage	XF	Unc	Proof
7	1975	1,075	—	160.00	—
	1975	—	—	—	175.00

250 FRANCS

3.9800 gm., .916 GOLD, .1172 oz AGW
25th Anniversary of Eurafrique Program

H#	Date	Mintage	XF	Unc	Proof
9	1975	1,000	—	100.00	—
	1975	—	—	—	100.00

500 FRANCS

7.9600 gm., .916 GOLD, .2344 oz AGW
25th Anniversary of Eurafrique Program

H#	Date	Mintage	XF	Unc	Proof
10	1975	500 pcs.	—	175.00	—
	1975	—	—	—	175.00

1000 FRANCS

15.9500 gm., .916 GOLD, .4697 oz AGW
25th Anniversary of Eurafrique Program

H#	Date	Mintage	XF	Unc	Proof
11	1975	217 pcs.	—	325.00	—
	1975	—	—	—	325.00

2500 FRANCS

39.9300 gm., .916 GOLD, 1.1760 oz AGW
25th Anniversary of Eurafrique Program

H#	Date	Mintage	XF	Unc	Proof
12	1975	195 pcs.	—	800.00	—
	1975	—	—	—	800.00

TOKEN ISSUES

Senegal
CHAMBER OF COMMERCE

5 CENTIMES

ALUMINUM

KM#	Date	Mintage	Fine	VF	XF
1	1920	—	2.00	3.50	6.00

Dakar
CHAMBER OF COMMERCE

5 CENTIMES

ALUMINUM

KM#	Date	Mintage	Fine	VF	XF
2	1920	—	1.50	3.00	5.00

10 CENTIMES

ALUMINUM

KM#	Date	Mintage	Fine	VF	XF
3	1920	—	1.25	2.50	4.50

BRASS

KM#	Date	Mintage	Fine	VF	XF
4	1920	—	2.00	3.50	6.00

25 CENTIMES

ALUMINUM

KM#	Date	Mintage	Fine	VF	XF
5	1920	—	2.00	3.50	6.00

50 CENTIMES

ALUMINUM

KM#	Date	Mintage	Fine	VF	XF
6	1920	—	2.50	4.25	7.50

Kayes
CHAMBER OF COMMERCE

5 CENTIMES

ALUMINUM

KM#	Date	Mintage	Fine	VF	XF
7	1920	—	3.00	5.00	8.00

10 CENTIMES

ALUMINUM

KM#	Date	Mintage	Fine	VF	XF
8	1920	—	3.00	5.00	8.00

25 CENTIMES

ALUMINUM

KM#	Date	Mintage	Fine	VF	XF
9	1920	—	3.50	6.00	10.00

COPPER-NICKEL

KM#	Date	Mintage	Fine	VF	XF
10	1920	—	3.50	6.00	10.00

50 CENTIMES

ALUMINUM

KM#	Date	Mintage	Fine	VF	XF
11	1920	—	3.50	6.00	10.00

Rufisque
CHAMBER OF COMMERCE

5 CENTIMES

ALUMINUM

KM#	Date	Mintage	Fine	VF	XF
12	1920	—	2.50	4.50	6.50

10 CENTIMES

ALUMINUM

KM#	Date	Mintage	Fine	VF	XF
13	1920	—	2.50	4.50	6.50

25 CENTIMES

ALUMINUM

KM#	Date	Mintage	Fine	VF	XF
14	1920	—	2.50	4.50	6.50

50 CENTIMES

ALUMINUM

KM#	Date	Mintage	Fine	VF	XF
15	1920	—	3.00	5.00	8.00

BRASS

KM#	Date	Mintage	Fine	VF	XF
16	1920	—	3.00	5.00	8.00

Ziguinchor
CHAMBER OF COMMERCE

50 CENTIMES

BRASS

KM#	Date	Mintage	Fine	VF	XF
17	1921	—	3.00	5.00	8.00

FRANC

BRASS

KM#	Date	Mintage	Fine	VF	XF
18	1921	—	3.00	5.00	8.00

ALUMINUM

KM#	Date	Mintage	Fine	VF	XF
19	1921	—	2.25	4.00	6.00

NOTE: For further listings of private token issues refer to MONNAIES ET BILLETS DE NECESSITE 1914-1931 by Argus Thimonier, and CATALOGUE OF FRENCH EMERGENCY TOKENS OF 1914-1922 by Robert Lamb.

NCLT ISSUES

ESSAIS (E)
Standard metals unless otherwise noted

Y#	Date	Mintage	Identification	Issue Price	Mkt Val.
E10	1920	—	25 Centimes, Kayes	—	35.00
E17	1921	—	50 Centimes, Zinguinchor	—	35.00
E18	1921	—	1 Franc, Zinguinchor	—	35.00

MINT SETS

KM#	Date	Mintage	Identification	Issue Price	Mkt. Val.
S1	1975(4)	195	H9-12	—	1400.

PROOF SETS
STANDARD METALS

KM#	Date	Mintage	Identification	Issue Price	Mkt. Val.
101	1968(4)	—	H1-4	—	1100.
102	1975(2)	—	H6-7	—	—

Listings For
SERBIA: REFER TO Yugoslavia

SEYCHELLES

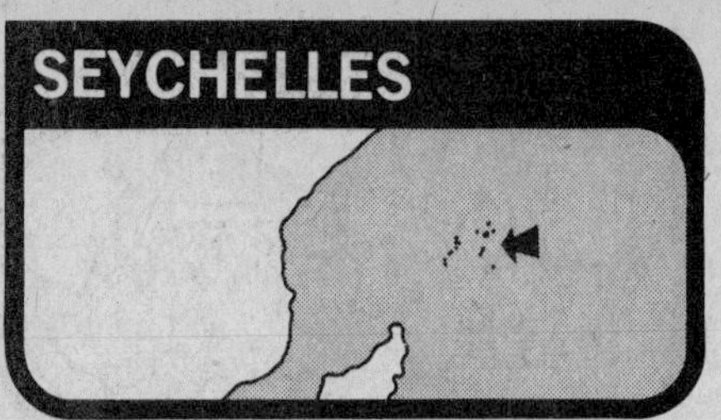

The Republic of Seychelles, an archipelago of 85 granite and coral islands situated in the Indian Ocean 600 miles (965 km.) northeast of Madagascar, has an area of 171 sq. mi. (443 sq. km.) and a population of 60,000. Among these islands are the Aldabra Islands, the Farquhar Group, and Ile Desroches, which the United Kingdom ceded to the Seychelles upon its independence. Capital: Victoria, on Mahe. The economy is based on fishing, a plantation system of agriculture, and tourism. Copra, cinnamon and vanilla are exported.

Although the Seychelles are marked on Portuguese charts of the early 16th century, the first recorded visit to the islands, by an English ship, occurred in 1609. The Seychelles were annexed to France by Captain Lazare Picault in 1743 and permanently settled in 1768, with the intention of establishing spice plantations to compete with the Dutch monopoly of the spice trade. British troops seized the islands in 1810, during the Napoleonic Wars; they were formally ceded to Britain by the Treaty of Paris, 1814. The Seychelles were a dependency of Mauritius until Aug. 31, 1903, when they became a seperate British Crown Colony. The colony was granted limited internal self-government in 1970, and attained independence on June 28, 1976, becoming Britain's last African possession to do so. Seychelles is a member of the Commonwealth of Nations. The president is the Head of State and of Government.

RULERS
British

MONETARY SYSTEM
100 Cents = 1 Rupee

CENT

BRONZE

Y#	Date	Mintage	VF	XF	Unc
5	1948	.300	.25	.50	1.00
	1948	—	—	Proof	40.00

Y#	Date	Mintage	VF	XF	Unc
14	1959	.030	.75	1.50	2.75
	1961	.030	.50	1.00	1.50
	1963	.040	.50	1.00	1.75
	1965	.020	1.50	1.75	3.50
	1969	*5,000	—	—	3.50
	1969	—	—	Proof	5.00

*Latest reports indicate only 5,000 circulation strikes have been released to date in addition to proof issues.

ALUMINUM
F.A.O. Issue

Y#	Date	Mintage	VF	XF	Unc
17	1972	2.350	—	—	.15

Declaration of Independence

Y#	Date	Mintage	VF	XF	Unc
21	1976	.109	—	—	.15
	1976	8,500	—	Proof	2.00

Y#	Date	Mintage	VF	XF	Unc
31	1977	—	—	—	.15

2 CENTS

BRONZE

Y#	Date	Mintage	VF	XF	Unc
6	1948	.350	.35	.60	1.00
	1948	—	—	Proof	45.00

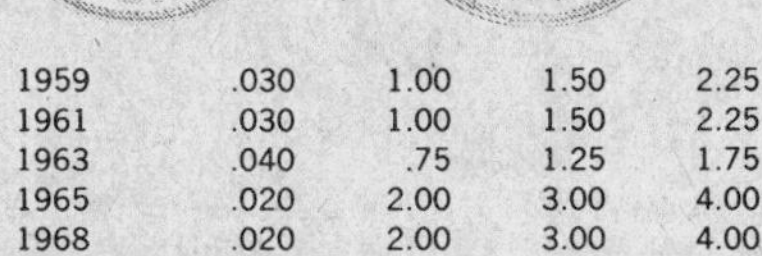

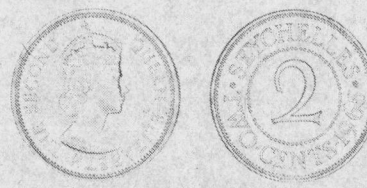

Y#	Date	Mintage	VF	XF	Unc
15	1959	.030	1.00	1.50	2.25
	1961	.030	1.00	1.50	2.25
	1963	.040	.75	1.25	1.75
	1965	.020	2.00	3.00	4.00
	1968	.020	2.00	3.00	4.00
	1969	5,000	— Proof only		6.00

5 CENTS

BRONZE

Y#	Date	Mintage	VF	XF	Unc
7	1948	.300	.40	.80	1.25
	1948	—	—	Proof	55.00

Y#	Date	Mintage	VF	XF	Unc
16	1964	.020	1.00	1.75	3.50
	1965	.040	1.00	1.50	3.00
	1967	.020	1.00	1.75	3.50
	1968	.040	.75	1.25	3.00
	1969	.100	.30	.45	.85
	1969	—	—	Proof	3.00
	1971	.025	.30	1.50	3.00

ALUMINUM
F.A.O. Issue

Y#	Date	Mintage	VF	XF	Unc
18	1972	2.200	—	—	.15
	1975	1.200	—	—	.15

Declaration of Independence

Y#	Date	Mintage	VF	XF	Unc
22	1976	.209	—	—	.20
	1976	8,500	—	Proof	2.00

F.A.O. Issue

Y#	Date	Mintage	VF	XF	Unc
32	1977	—	—	—	—

10 CENTS

COPPER-NICKEL

Y#	Date	Mintage	VF	XF	Unc
1	1939	.036	3.25	10.00	35.00
	1939	—	—	Proof	75.00
	1943	.036	3.25	10.00	22.50
	1944	.036	3.25	10.00	35.00
	1944	—	—	Proof	60.00

Y#	Date	Mintage	VF	XF	Unc
8	1951	.036	2.50	4.00	5.00

NICKEL-BRASS

Y#	Date	Mintage	VF	XF	Unc
10	1953	.130	.45	.75	1.00
	1953	—	—	Proof	60.00
	1965	.040	1.00	1.50	3.50
	1967	.020	2.00	3.00	5.50
	1968	.050	.75	1.25	2.50
	1969	.060	.75	1.00	1.50
	1969	—	—	Proof	3.50
	1970	.075	.50	1.00	1.50
	1971	.100	.50	.75	1.00
	1972	.120	.30	.50	.75
	1973	.100	—	.25	.75
	1974	.100	—	.25	.50

Declaration of Independence

Y#	Date	Mintage	VF	XF	Unc
23	1976	.209	—	—	.40
	1976	8,500	—	Proof	2.50

F.A.O. Issue

Y#	Date	Mintage	VF	XF	Unc
33	1977	—	—	—	.25

25 CENTS

2.9200 gm., .500 SILVER .0469 oz ASW

Y#	Date	Mintage	VF	XF	Unc
2	1939	.036	5.00	12.50	50.00
	1939	—	—	Proof	85.00
	1943	.036	5.00	12.50	30.00
	1944	.036	5.00	12.50	30.00

COPPER-NICKEL

Y#	Date	Mintage	VF	XF	Unc
9	1951	.036	1.50	4.00	17.50

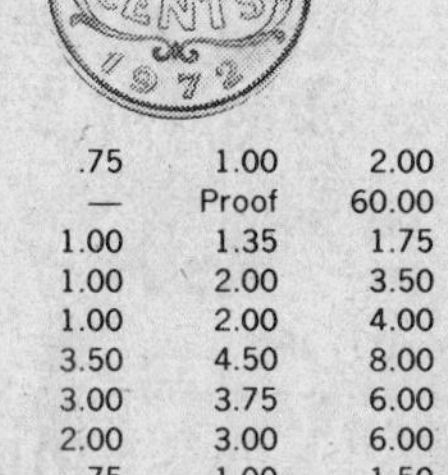

Y#	Date	Mintage	VF	XF	Unc
11	1954	.124	.75	1.00	2.00
	1954	—	—	Proof	60.00
	1960	.040	1.00	1.35	1.75
	1964	.040	1.00	2.00	3.50
	1965	.040	1.00	2.00	4.00
	1966	.010	3.50	4.50	8.00
	1967	.020	3.00	3.75	6.00
	1968	.020	2.00	3.00	6.00
	1969	.100	.75	1.00	1.50
	1969	—	—	Proof	4.00
	1970	.040	1.50	1.75	3.00
	1972	.120	.50	.75	1.00
	1973	.100	.50	.75	1.00
	1974	.100	.50	.75	1.00

Declaration of Independence

Y#	Date	Mintage	VF	XF	Unc
24	1976	.209	—	—	.60
	1976	8,500	—	Proof	3.00

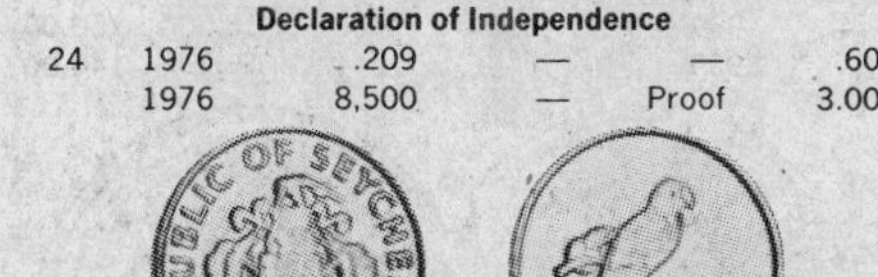

Y#	Date	Mintage	VF	XF	Unc
34	1977	—	—	—	.75

1/2 RUPEE

5.8300 gm., .500 SILVER .0937 oz ASW

Y#	Date	Mintage	VF	XF	Unc
3	1939	.036	8.00	17.50	75.00
	1939	—	—	Proof	125.00

COPPER-NICKEL

Y#	Date	Mintage	VF	XF	Unc
12	1954	.072	1.00	2.00	3.50
	1954	—	—	Proof	65.00
	1960	.060	.50	1.00	2.50

Y#	Date	Mintage	VF	XF	Unc
12	1960	—	—	Proof	65.00
	1966	.015	3.00	5.00	7.50
	1967	.020	2.75	4.00	6.00
	1968	.020	2.75	4.00	6.00
	1969	.060	.75	1.00	1.75
	1969	—	—	Proof	4.25
	1970	.050	.75	1.00	2.00
	1971	.100	.75	.90	1.25
	1972	.120	.75	.90	1.25
	1974	.100	—	—	1.00

50 CENTS

COPPER-NICKEL
Declaration of Independence

Y#	Date	Mintage	VF	XF	Unc
25	1976	.209	—	—	.75
	1976	8,500	—	Proof	5.00

Y#	Date	Mintage	VF	XF	Unc
35	1977	—	—	—	.75

RUPEE

11.6600 gm., .500 SILVER .1874 oz ASW

Y#	Date	Mintage	VF	XF	Unc
4	1939	.090	7.00	15.00	50.00
	1939	—	—	Proof	140.00

COPPER-NICKEL

Y#	Date	Mintage	VF	XF	Unc
13	1954	.150	1.00	2.00	3.25
	1954	—	—	Proof	70.00
	1960	.060	.90	1.75	3.00
	1966	.045	1.25	2.25	4.00
	1967	.010	4.00	6.00	9.00
	1968	.040	2.50	3.25	4.75
	1969	.050	1.25	1.75	2.75
	1969	—	—	Proof	5.00
	1970	.050	1.25	1.75	2.75
	1971	.100	.75	1.50	2.50
	1972	.120	.75	1.50	2.50
	1974	.100	—	—	1.50

Declaration of Independence

Y#	Date	Mintage	VF	XF	Unc
26	1976	.259	—	—	1.25
26	1976	8,500	—	Proof	8.00
36	1977	—	—	—	1.25

5 RUPEES

COPPER-NICKEL

Y#	Date	Mintage	VF	XF	Unc
19	1972	.220	2.25	2.50	3.00

.925 SILVER

Y#	Date	Mintage	VF	XF	Unc
19a	1972	2,500	—	Proof	65.00
	1974	4,581	—	Proof	45.00

COPPER-NICKEL
Declaration of Independence

Y#	Date	Mintage	VF	XF	Unc
27	1976	.050	1.00	1.50	2.00

.925 SILVER

Y#	Date	Mintage	VF	XF	Unc
27a	1976	8,500	—	Proof	17.50

COPPER-NICKEL

Y#	Date	Mintage	VF	XF	Unc
37	1977	—	—	1.50	2.00

10 RUPEES

COPPER-NICKEL

Y#	Date	Mintage	VF	XF	Unc
20	1974	—	—	3.00	5.00

28.2800 gm., .925 SILVER .8411 oz ASW

Y#	Date	Mintage	VF	XF	Unc
20a	1974	.025	—	Proof	27.50

COPPER-NICKEL
Declaration of Independence

Y#	Date	Mintage	VF	XF	Unc
28	1976	.050	—	—	3.00

28.2800 gm., .925 SILVER .8411 oz ASW

Y#	Date	Mintage	VF	XF	Unc
28a	1976	.029	—	Proof	27.50

COPPER-NICKEL
F.A.O. Issue

Y#	Date	Mintage	VF	XF	Unc
38	1977	—	—	Proof	3.50

25 RUPEES

28.5000 gm., .500 SILVER .4581 oz ASW
Queen's Silver Jubilee

Y#	Date	Mintage	VF	XF	Unc
30	1977	—	—	Proof	15.00

28.5000 gm., .925 SILVER .8476 oz ASW

Y#	Date	Mintage	VF	XF	Unc
30a	1977	.015	—	Proof	27.50

50 RUPEES

28.2800 gm., .925 SILVER .8411 oz ASW
Conservation Series

Y#	Date	Mintage	VF	XF	Unc
39	1978	—	BV	BV	25.00
	1978	—	—	Proof	30.00

100 RUPEES

35.0000 gm., .925 SILVER, 1.0409 oz ASW
Conservation Series
Obv: Similar to 50 Rupees, Y#39.

Y#	Date	Mintage	VF	XF	Unc
40	1978	—	BV	BV	40.00
	1978	—	—	Proof	50.00

1000 RUPEES

15.9800 gm., .916 GOLD .4706 oz AGW
Obv: President Mancham. Rev: Tortoise, date, value.

Y#	Date	Mintage	VF	XF	Unc
29	1976	5,000	BV	BV	325.00
	1976	1,000	—	Proof	425.00

1500 RUPEES

.900 GOLD
Conservation Series

Y#	Date	Mintage	VF	XF	Unc
41	1978	—	BV	BV	650.00
	1978	—	—	Proof	800.00

NCLT ISSUES

MINT SETS

KM#	Date	Mintage	Identification	Issue Price	Mkt. Val.
S1	1972(7)	—	Y10-13,17-19	—	9.00
S2	1974(5)	—	—	—	7.00
S3	1976(8)	—	Y21-28	—	7.00

PROOF SETS

STANDARD METALS

KM#	Date	Mintage	Identification	Issue Price	Mkt. Val.
1	1969(7)	5,000	Y10-16	8.40	22.50
2	1974(2)	5,000	Y19a,20A	37.00	70.00
3	450.00	1,000	Y21-27,28a,29	375.00	400.00
4	1976(8)	7,500	Y21-27,28a	42.50	55.00

Listings For

SHARJAH: refer to United Arab Emirates

SIAM: refer to Thailand

SIERRA LEONE

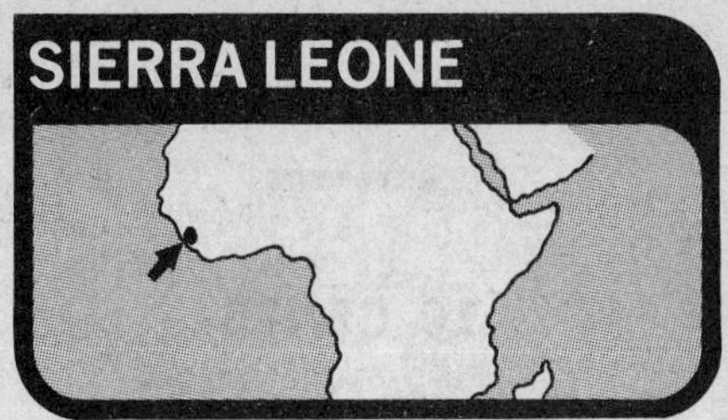

The Republic of Sierra Leone, a British Commonwealth nation located in western Africa between Guinea and Liberia, has an area of 27,925 sq. mi. (72,325 sq. km.) and a population of 3.3 million. Capital: Freetown. The economy is predominantly agricultural but mining contributes significantly to export revenues. Diamonds, iron ore, palm kernels, cocoa, and coffee are exported.

The coast of Sierra Leone was first visited by Portuguese and British slavers in the 15th and 16th centuries. The first settlement, at Freetown, 1787, was established as a refuge for freed slaves within the British Empire, runaway slaves from the United States and Negroes discharged from the British armed forces. The first settlers were virtually wiped out by tribal attacks and disease. The colony was re-established under the auspices of the Sierra Leone Company and transferred to the British Crown in 1807. The interior region was secured and established as a protectorate in 1896. Sierra Leone became independent within the Commonwealth on April 27, 1961, and adopted a republican constitution ten years later. It is a member of the Commonwealth of Nations. The president is Chief of State and Head of Government.

NOTE: Also see British West Africa.

RULERS

British, until 1971

MONETARY SYSTEM

(Until 1906)
100 Cents = 50 Pence = 1 Dollar
(Until 1960)
12 Pence = 1 Shilling
(Commencing 1960)
100 Cents = 1 Leone

SIERRA LEONE COMPANY

CENT

BRONZE

C#	Date	Mintage	Fine	VF	XF
1	1791	—	15.00	20.00	30.00
	1791	—	—	Proof	85.00

GILT BRONZE

C#	Date	Mintage	Fine	VF	XF
1a	1791	—	— Proof only		175.00
	1796	—	20.00	25.00	35.00

PENNY

BRONZE, 32mm

C#	Date	Mintage	Fine	VF	XF
2	1791	—	15.00	20.00	30.00
	1791	—	—	Proof	95.00

30mm

C#	Date	Mintage	Fine	VF	XF
2.1	1791	—	—	Proof only	125.00
			GILT BRONZE		
2a	1791	—	—	Proof only	175.00

10 CENTS

.902 SILVER

C#	Date	Mintage	Fine	VF	XF
3	1791	—	30.00	60.00	100.00
	1791	—	—	Proof	400.00
	1796	—	35.00	65.00	110.00
	1796	—	—	Proof	450.00
	1805	—	40.00	75.00	130.00
			COPPER		
3a	1791	—	—	Proof only	150.00
			GILT COPPER		
3b	1791	—	—	Proof only	400.00
	1796	—	—	Proof only	400.00

20 CENTS

.902 SILVER

C#	Date	Mintage	Fine	VF	XF
4	1791	—	60.00	225.00	400.00
	1791	—	—	Proof	550.00
			COPPER		
4a	1791	—	—	Proof only	225.00
			GILT COPPER		
4b	1791	—	—	Proof only	850.00

50 CENTS

.902 SILVER

C#	Date	Mintage	Fine	VF	XF
5	1791	—	100.00	250.00	300.00
	1791	—	—	Proof	1200.
			COPPER		
5a	1791	—	—	Proof only	300.00
			GILT COPPER		
5b	1791	—	—	Proof only	1100.

100 CENTS

.902 SILVER

C#	Date	Mintage	Fine	VF	XF
6a	1791	—	275.00	375.00	500.00
	1791	—	—	Proof	3000.
			COPPER		
6b	1791	—	—	Proof only	650.00
			GILT COPPER		
6c	1791	—	—	Proof only	2600.

DOLLAR

.902 SILVER

C#	Date	Mintage	Fine	VF	XF
6	1791	—	1500.	—	—
	1791	—	—	Proof	—
			COPPER		
6d	1791	—	—	Proof only	—
			GILT COPPER		
6e	1791	—	—	Proof only	—

COUNTERSTAMP ISSUES

1/4 DOLLAR

.903 SILVER
c/s: Crowned WR on one quarter cut of a Spanish or Colonial 8 Reales.

C#	Date	Mintage	Fine	VF	XF
11	ND	—	75.00	100.00	125.00

1/2 DOLLAR

.903 SILVER
c/s: Crowned WR on Spanish or Colonial 4 Reales.

C#	Date	Mintage	Fine	VF	XF
12	ND	—	60.00	80.00	100.00

SIERRA LEONE

1/2 CENT

BRONZE

Y#	Date	Mintage	VF	XF	Unc
1	1964	.600	.05	.10	.20
	1964	—	—	Proof	1.25
			.925 SILVER		
1a	1964	22 pcs.	—	Proof	—

CENT

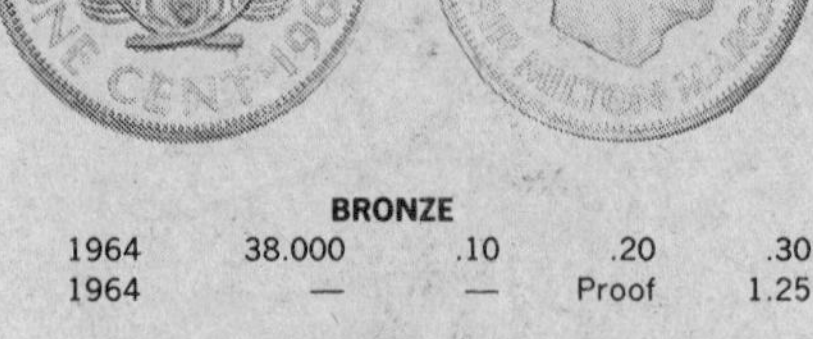

BRONZE

Y#	Date	Mintage	VF	XF	Unc
2	1964	38.000	.10	.20	.30
	1964	—	—	Proof	1.25
			.925 SILVER		
2a	1964	22 pcs.	—	Proof	—

5 CENTS

COPPER-NICKEL

Y#	Date	Mintage	VF	XF	Unc
3	1964	.900	.15	.25	.50
	1964	—	—	Proof	2.00
			.925 SILVER		
3a	1964	22 pcs.	—	Proof	—

10 CENTS

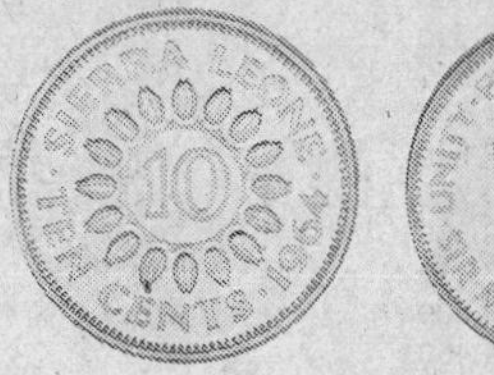

COPPER-NICKEL

Y#	Date	Mintage	VF	XF	Unc
4	1964	24.000	.25	.40	.60
	1964	—	—	Proof	2.50

.925 SILVER

Y#	Date	Mintage	VF	XF	Unc
4a	1964	22 pcs.	—	Proof	—

20 CENTS

COPPER-NICKEL

Y#	Date	Mintage	VF	XF	Unc
5	1964	11.000	.35	.55	.85
	1964	—	—	Proof	4.00

.925 SILVER

Y#	Date	Mintage	VF	XF	Unc
5a	1964	22 pcs.	—	Proof	—

50 CENTS

COPPER-NICKEL

Y#	Date	Mintage	VF	XF	Unc
11	1972	1.000	.80	1.25	2.50
	1972	2,000	—	Proof	5.00

LEONE

COPPER-NICKEL

Y#	Date	Mintage	VF	XF	Unc
6	1964	.010		Proof Only	10.00

.925 SILVER

Y#	Date	Mintage	VF	XF	Unc
6a	1964	12 pcs.	—	Proof	—

.916 GOLD

Y#	Date	Mintage	VF	XF	Unc
6b	1964	10 pcs.	—	Proof	1575.

COPPER NICKEL
10th Anniversary of Bank

Y#	Date	Mintage	VF	XF	Unc
12	1974	.103	—	—	3.00

28.2800 gm., .925 SILVER, .8411 oz ASW

Y#	Date	Mintage	VF	XF	Unc
12a	1974	.040	—	Proof	27.50

2 LEONES

COPPER-NICKEL
F.A.O. Issue

Y#	Date	Mintage	VF	XF	Unc
13	1976	.020	—	—	4.00

1/4 GOLDE

13.6360 gm., .900 GOLD, .3946 oz AGW
5th Anniversary of Independence

Y#	Date	Mintage	VF	XF	Unc
7	1966	5,000	BV	BV	300.00

.916 GOLD

Y#	Date	Mintage	VF	XF	Unc
7a	1966	600 pcs.	—	Proof	350.00

PALLADIUM

Y#	Date	Mintage	VF	XF	Unc
7b	1966	100 pcs.	—	Proof	—

1/2 GOLDE

27.2730 gm., .900 GOLD, .7891 oz AGW
5th Anniversary of Independence

Y#	Date	Mintage	VF	XF	Unc
8	1966	2,500	BV	BV	550.00

.916 GOLD

Y#	Date	Mintage	VF	XF	Unc
8a	1966	600 pcs.	—	Proof	650.00

PALLADIUM

Y#	Date	Mintage	VF	XF	Unc
8b	1966	100 pcs.	—	Proof	—

GOLDE

54.5450 gm., .900 GOLD, 1.5783 oz AGW
5th Anniversary of Independence

Y#	Date	Mintage	VF	XF	Unc
9	1966	1,500	BV	BV	1100.

.916 GOLD

Y#	Date	Mintage	VF	XF	Unc
9a	1966	400 pcs.	—	Proof	1250.

PALLADIUM

Y#	Date	Mintage	VF	XF	Unc
9b	1966	100 pcs.	—	Proof	—

PLATINUM

Y#	Date	Mintage	VF	XF	Unc
9c	1966	—	—	Proof	—

10 GOLDE

57.6000 gm., .916 GOLD, 1.6965 oz AGW
70th Birthday Dr. Siaka Stevens

Y#	Date	Mintage	VF	XF	Unc
—	1975	916 pcs.	—	—	—
	1975	600 pcs.	—	Proof	1250.

NCLT ISSUES

MINT SETS

KM#	Date	Mintage	Identification	Issue Price	Mkt. Val.
S1	1966(3)	—	Y7-9	—	950.00

PROOF SETS

Standard metals unless otherwise noted

KM#	Date	Mintage	Identification	Issue Price	Mkt. Val.
101	1964(6)	10,000	Y1-6	—	20.00
102	1964(6)	12	Y1a-5a,6b	—	—
103	1964(6)	10	Y1a-6a	—	—
104	1966(3)	400	Y7-9	—	1950.
105	1972(2)	1,000	Y11 (2 pcs. with 50 cent banknote (0 serials) in plush case.	—	50.00

SINGAPORE

The Republic of Singapore, a British Commonwealth nation situated at the southern tip of the Malay peninsula, has an area of 233 sq. mi. (603 sq. km.) and a population of 2.2 million. Capital: Singapore. The economy is based on entrepot trade, manufacturing and oil. Rubber, petroleum products, machinery and spices are exported.

Singapore's modern history - it was an important shipping center in the 14th century before the rise of Malacca and Penang - began in 1819 when Sir Thomas Stamford Raffles, an agent for the British East India Company, founded the town of Singapore. By 1825 its trade exceeded that of Malacca and Penang combined. The opening of the Suez Canal (1869) and the demand for rubber and tin created by the automobile and packaging industries combined to make Singapore one of the major ports of the world. In 1826 Singapore, Penang and Malacca were combined to form the Straits Settlements, which was made a Crown Colony in 1867. Singapore became a separate Crown Colony in 1946 when the Straits Settlements was dissolved. It joined in the formation of Malaysia in 1963, but broke away on Aug. 9, 1965, to become an independent republic. Singapore is a member of the Commonwealth of Nations. The president is Chief of State. The prime minister is Head of Government.

NOTE: For earlier coinage see Straits Settlements, Malaya, Malaya and British Borneo, and Malaysia.

MONETARY SYSTEM

100 Cents = 1 Dollar

CENT

BRONZE

Y#	Date	Mintage	VF	XF	Unc
1	1967	7.500	—	—	.15
	1967	2,000	—	Proof	3.50
	1968	2.696	—	—	.15
	1968	5,000	—	Proof	2.75
	1969	7.220	—	—	.15
	1969	3,000	—	Proof	4.50
	1970	1.402	—	—	.15
	1971	9.731	—	—	.10
	1972	1.655	—	—	.15
	1972	749 pcs.	—	Proof	25.00
	1973	6.767	—	—	.10
	1973	1,000	—	Proof	14.00
	1974	100.870	—	—	.10
	1974	1,500	—	Proof	9.00
	1975	24.226	—	—	.10
	1975	3,000	—	Proof	7.50
	1976	Inc. Ab.	—	—	.50
	1976	3,500	—	Proof	2.75

COPPER-CLAD STEEL

Y#	Date	Mintage	VF	XF	Unc
1a	1976	16.165	—	—	.10
	1977	13.940	—	—	.10
	1977	3,500	—	Proof	2.75
	1978	5.931	—	—	.10
	1978	—	—	Proof	—
	1979	—	—	—	.10
	1979	—	—	Proof	—

5 CENTS

COPPER-NICKEL

Y#	Date	Mintage	VF	XF	Unc
2	1967	28.000	—	—	.20
	1967	2,000	—	Proof	4.50
	1968	4.217	—	—	.20
	1968	5,000	—	Proof	3.50
2	1969	14.778	—	—	.20
	1969	3,000	—	Proof	5.00
	1970	3.065	—	—	.20
	1971	13.202	—	—	.20
	1972	9.817	—	—	.20
	1972	749 pcs.	—	Proof	27.50
	1973	3.013	—	—	.15
	1973	1,000	—	Proof	12.50
	1974	28.262	—	—	.20
	1974	1,500	—	Proof	10.00
	1975	1.729	—	—	.15
	1975	3,000	—	Proof	8.00
	1976	15.541	—	—	.15
	1976	3,500	—	Proof	4.00
	1977	9.956	—	—	.15
	1977	3,500	—	Proof	4.00
	1978	5.956	—	—	.20
	1978	—	—	Proof	—
	1979	—	—	—	.20
	1979	—	—	Proof	—
	1980	—	—	—	.20
	1980	—	—	Proof	—

ALUMINUM
F.A.O. Issue

Y#	Date	Mintage	VF	XF	Unc
8	1971	3.049	—	—	.20

10 CENTS

COPPER-NICKEL

Y#	Date	Mintage	VF	XF	Unc
3	1967	40.000	.15	.20	.30
	1967	2,000	—	Proof	5.00
	1968	36.261	.15	.20	.35
	1968	5,000	—	Proof	4.00
	1969	25.000	.15	.20	.30
	1969	3,000	—	Proof	6.00
	1970	21.304	—	.15	.25
	1971	33.041	.10	.15	.25
	1972	2.675	—	.15	.35
	1972	749 pcs.	—	Proof	30.00
	1973	6.027	—	.15	.25
	1973	1,000	—	Proof	15.00
	1974	40.904	—	.15	.25
	1974	1,500	—	Proof	11.50
	1975	.828	—	.15	.25
	1975	3,000	—	Proof	8.00
	1976	29.718	—	.15	.25
	1976	3,500	—	Proof	5.00
	1977	11.776	—	.15	.25
	1977	3,500	—	Proof	5.00
	1978	5.936	—	—	.25
	1978	—	—	Proof	—
	1979	—	—	—	.25
	1979	—	—	Proof	—
	1980	—	—	—	.25
	1980	—	—	Proof	—

20 CENTS

COPPER-NICKEL

Y#	Date	Mintage	VF	XF	Unc
4	1967	36.500	.20	.25	.40
	1967	2,000	—	Proof	6.00
	1968	10.934	.20	.25	.40
	1968	5,000	—	Proof	5.00
	1969	8.460	.10	.20	.40
	1969	3,000	—	Proof	7.50
	1970	3.25	.10	.20	.40
	1971	1.732	.10	.20	.35
	1972	9.107	.15	.20	.40
	1972	749 pcs.	—	Proof	35.00
4	1973	9.589	.15	.20	.35
	1973	1,000	—	Proof	17.50
	1974	20.510	—	.20	.30
	1974	1,500	—	Proof	13.50
	1975	1.546	—	.20	.30
	1975	3,000	—	Proof	9.00
	1976	19.760	.15	.20	.30
	1976	3,500	—	Proof	8.00
	1977	7.074	—	.20	.30
	1977	3,500	—	Proof	8.00
	1978	4.450	—	—	.30
	1978	—	—	Proof	—
	1979	—	—	—	.30
	1979	—	—	Proof	—

50 CENTS

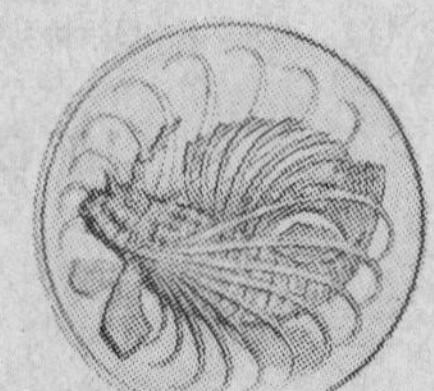

COPPER-NICKEL

Y#	Date	Mintage	VF	XF	Unc
5	1967	11.000	.35	.50	1.00
	1967	2,000	—	Proof	7.50
	1968	3.189	.30	.45	.80
	1968	5,000	—	Proof	6.50
	1969	2.008	.35	.50	.75
	1969	3,000	—	Proof	11.50
	1970	3.102	.30	.40	.75
	1971	3.933	.40	.50	.80
	1972	5.427	.35	.50	.80
	1972	749 pcs.	—	Proof	40.00
	1973	4.474	.35	.50	.75
	1973	1,000	—	Proof	20.00
	1974	47.899	.30	.40	.70
	1974	1,500	—	Proof	17.00
	1975	1.432	.30	.40	.60
	1975	3,000	—	Proof	10.00
	1976	5.728	.30	.40	.60
	1976	3,500	—	Proof	10.00
	1977	6.953	.30	.40	.60
	1977	3,500	—	Proof	10.00
	1978	3.934	—	—	.60
	1978	—	—	Proof	—
	1979	—	—	—	.60
	1979	—	—	Proof	—

DOLLAR

COPPER-NICKEL

Y#	Date	Mintage	VF	XF	Unc
6	1967	3.000	.50	.75	2.00
	1967	2,000	—	Proof	23.50
	1968	2.194	.50	.75	2.00
	1968	5,000	—	Proof	20.00
	1969	1.871	.50	.75	2.00
	1969	3,000	—	Proof	32.50
	1970	.560	.60	.80	2.50
	1971	.900	.55	.75	2.00
	1972	.458	.55	.75	2.00
	1972	749 pcs.	—	Proof	65.00
	1973	.359	.55	.75	2.50
	1973	1,000	—	Proof	35.00
	1974	.821	.55	.80	1.90
	1974	1,500	—	Proof	22.50
	1975	.430	.55	.80	1.90

Y#	Date	Mintage	VF	XF	Unc
6	1975	3,000	—	Proof	17.50
	1976	.165	.50	.70	1.60
	1976	3,500	—	Proof	15.00
	1977	.132	.50	.70	1.40
	1977	3,500	—	Proof	15.00
	1978	.037	—	—	—
	1978	—	—	Proof	—
	1979	—	—	—	—
		18.0500 gm., .925 SILVER, .5368 oz ASW			
6a	1975	3,000	—	Proof	40.00
	1976	.010	—	Proof	20.00
	1977	.010	—	Proof	20.00
	1978	.010	—	Proof	20.00
	1979	8,000	—	Proof	25.00

5 DOLLARS

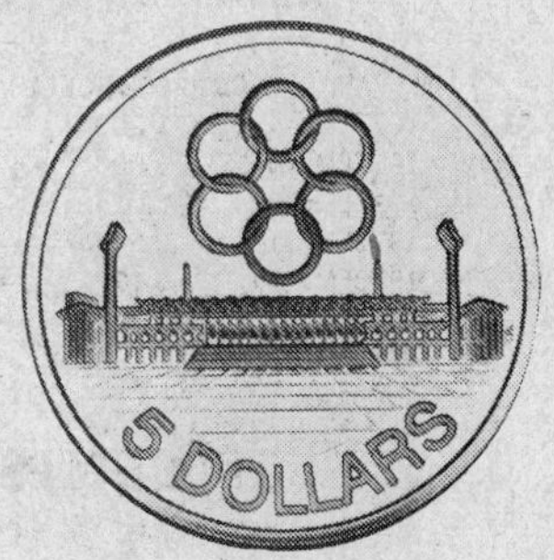

25.0000 gm., .500 SILVER, .4019 oz ASW
7th South East Asia Peninsular Games

Y#	Date	Mintage	VF	XF	Unc
10	1973	.249	BV	BV	12.50
	1973	5,300	—	Proof	45.00

10 DOLLARS

30.4500 gm., .900 SILVER, .8811 oz ASW
Obv. leg: SINGAPORE inverted.

Y#	Date	Mintage	VF	XF	Unc
9	1972	.080	BV	BV	30.00
	1972	3,000	—	Proof	80.00

Rev: Similar to Y#9.

Y#	Date	Mintage	VF	XF	Unc
9a	1973	.080	BV	BV	27.50
	1973	5,000	—	Proof	40.00
	1974	.100	BV	BV	27.50
	1974	6,000	—	Proof	35.00

30.4500 gm., .500 SILVER, .4895 oz ASW
10th Anniversary of Independence

Y#	Date	Mintage	VF	XF	Unc
11	1975	.200	BV	BV	15.00
	1975	.010	—	Proof	25.00

Rev: Similar to Y#11.

Y#	Date	Mintage	VF	XF	Unc
15	1976	.150	BV	BV	15.00
	1976	.010	—	Proof	25.00
	1977	.150	BV	BV	15.00
	1977	.010	—	Proof	25.00

Asean 10th Anniversary

Y#	Date	Mintage	VF	XF	Unc
16	1977	.200	BV	BV	15.00
	1977	.010	—	Proof	25.00

Obv: Similar to Y#15.
Communications Satellites

Y#	Date	Mintage	VF	XF	Unc
17	1978	.167	BV	BV	15.00
	1978	.010	—	Proof	25.00
	1979	.168	BV	BV	15.00
	1979	9,000	—	Proof	25.00
		NICKEL			
17a	1980	.120	—	—	—

50 DOLLARS

.500 SILVER
Financial Center

Y#	Date	Mintage	VF	XF	Unc
18	1980	—	—	—	—

100 DOLLARS

6.9119 gm., .900 GOLD, .2000 oz AGW
10th Anniversary of Independence

Y#	Date	Mintage	VF	XF	Unc
12	1975	.100	BV	BV	135.00
	1975	3,000	—	Proof	175.00

150 DOLLARS

24.8830 gm., .920 GOLD, .7360 oz AGW

Y#	Date	Mintage	VF	XF	Unc
7	1969	.198	BV	BV	500.00
	1969	500 pcs.	—	Proof	750.00

250 DOLLARS

17.2797 gm., .900 GOLD, .5000 oz AGW
10th Anniversary of Independence

Y#	Date	Mintage	VF	XF	Unc
13	1975	.030	BV	BV	325.00
	1975	2,000	—	Proof	400.00

500 DOLLARS

34.5594 gm., .900 GOLD, 1.0000 oz AGW
10th Anniversary of Independence
Obv: Similar to 250 dollars, Y#13.

Y#	Date	Mintage	VF	XF	Unc
14	1975	.030	BV	BV	650.00
	1975	2,000	—	Proof	750.00

NCLT ISSUES

MINT SETS

KM#	Date	Mintage	Identification	Issue Price	Mkt. Val.
S1	1967(6)	8,000	Y1-6	1.50	8.00
S2	1968(6)	16,000	Y1-6	1.50	6.00
S3	1969(6)	14,000	Y1-6	1.50	6.00
S4	1970(6)	13,000	Y1-6	1.50	15.00
S5	1970(6)*	27,000	Y1-6	1.75	13.00
S7	1972(6)	13,000	Y1-6	3.00	7.00
S8	1973(6)	15,000	Y1-6	2.00	6.00
S9	1974(6)	20,000	Y1-6	2.00	4.50
S10	1975(6)	30,000	Y1-6	*12.00	4.50
S11	1975(3)	30,000	Y12-14	—	1100.
S12	1976(6)	35,000	Y1a,2-6	2.00	3.00
S13	1977(6)	40,000	Y1a,2-6	2.00	3.00
S14	1978(6)	55,000	Y1a,2-6	—	—
S15	1979(6)	65,000	Y1a,2-6	—	—

*Issued only in package of 3 sets plus Y#11, each set in plastic wallet for Expo '70 Osaka Japan.

PROOF SETS
STANDARD METALS

KM#	Date	Mintage	Identification	Issue Price	Mkt. Val.
101	1967(6)	2,000	Y1-6	25.00	42.00
102	1968(6)	5,000	Y1-6	25.00	45.00
103	1969(6)	3,000	Y1-6	25.00	120.00
104	1972(6)	749	Y1-6	25.00	260.00
105	1973(6)	1,000	Y1a,2-6	31.70	90.00
106	1974(6)	1,500	Y1-6	34.00	75.00
107	1975(6)	3,000	Y1-6a	35.00	62.00
108	1976(6)	3,500	Y1a,2-6a	37.00	45.00
109	1977(6)	3,500	Y1a,2-6a	—	45.00
110	1978(6)	4,000	Y1a,2-6a	—	—
111	1979 7	3,500	Y1a,2-5, 6a,17	51.00	—

SOLOMON ISLANDS

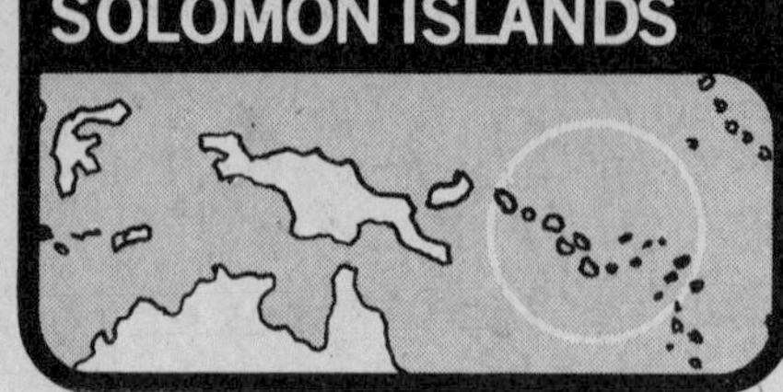

The Solomon Islands, located in the southwest Pacific east of Papua New Guinea, has an area of 11,500 sq. mi. (29,785 sq. km.) and a population of 200,000. Capital: Honiara. The most important islands of the Solomon chain are Guadalcanal (scene of some of the fiercest fighting of World War II), Malaitia, New Georgia, Florida, Vella Lavella, Choiseul, Rendova, San Cristobal, the Lord Howe group, the Santa Cruz islands, and the Duff group. Copra is the only important cash crop but it is hoped that timber will become an economic factor.

The Solomon Islands were discovered by Spanish navigator Alvaro de Mendana in 1567, and in 1569 he made an unsuccessful attempt to colonize them. European knowledge of the group would not be completed until the end of the 18th century. Germany declared a protectorate over the northern Solomons in 1885. The British protectorate over the southern Solomons was established in 1893. In 1899 Germany transferred its claim to all Solomon Islands except Buka and Bougainville to Great Britain in exchange for recognition of German claims in western Samoa. Australia occupied the two German islands in 1914, and administered them after 1920.

The Japanese invaded the Solomons during 1942-43, but were driven out by an American counteroffensive after a series of bloody clashes.

Following World War II, the islands returned to the status of a British protectorate. In 1976 the protectorate was abolished, and the Solomons became a self-governing dependency. Full independence was achieved on July 7, 1978. Solomon Islands is a member of the Commonwealth of Nations. The Queen of England is Chief of State.

RULERS

British

MINTMARKS

FM - Franklin Mint, U.S.A.*

NOTE: During 1977 the Franklin Mint produced coinage in up to 3 different qualities. Qualities of issue are designated in ( ) after each date and are defined as follows:

(M) MATTE - Normal circulation strike or a dull finish produced by sandblasting special uncirculated (polish finish) or proof quality dies.

(U) - SPECIAL UNCIRCULATED - Polished or proof-like in appearance without any frosted features.

(P) PROOF - The highest quality obtainable having mirror-like fields and frosted features.

MONETARY SYSTEM

100 Cents = 1 Dollar

CENT

BRONZE
F.A.O. Issue

Y#	Date	Mintage	VF	XF	Unc
1	1977	1.800	—	—	.15
	1977FM(M)	6,000	—	.45	.75
	1977FM(P)	.014	—	Proof	1.50
	1978FM(U)	6,544	—	—	.40
	1978FM(P)	5,122	—	Proof	—
	1979FM(U)	—	—	—	—
	1979FM(P)	—	—	Proof	—

2 CENTS

BRONZE

Y#	Date	Mintage	VF	XF	Unc
2	1977	2.400	—	.10	.20
	1977FM(M)	6,000	—	.75	1.25
	1977FM(P)	.014	—	Proof	2.00
	1978FM(U)	6,544	—	—	—
	1978FM(P)	5,122	—	Proof	—
	1979FM(U)	—	—	—	—
	1979FM(P)	—	—	Proof	—

5 CENTS

COPPER-NICKEL

Y#	Date	Mintage	VF	XF	Unc
3	1977	1.200	—	.15	.25
	1977FM(M)	6,000	—	1.25	2.00
	1977FM(P)	.014	—	Proof	2.50
	1978FM(U)	6,544	—	—	—
	1978FM(P)	5,122	—	Proof	—
	1979FM(U)	—	—	—	—
	1979FM(P)	—	—	Proof	—

10 CENTS

COPPER-NICKEL

Y#	Date	Mintage	VF	XF	Unc
4	1977	3.600	.15	.20	.30
	1977FM(M)	6,000	—	1.50	2.50
	1977FM(P)	.014	—	Proof	3.50
	1978FM(U)	6,544	—	—	—
	1978FM(P)	5,122	—	Proof	—
	1979FM(U)	—	—	—	—
	1979FM(P)	—	—	Proof	—

20 CENTS

COPPER-NICKEL

Y#	Date	Mintage	VF	XF	Unc
5	1977	3.300	.25	.30	.40
	1977FM(M)	5,000	—	2.00	3.50
	1977FM(P)	.014	—	Proof	5.00
	1978FM(U)	5,544	—	—	—
	1978FM(P)	5,122	—	Proof	—
	1979FM(U)	—	—	—	—
	1979FM(P)	—	—	Proof	—

DOLLAR

COPPER-NICKEL

Y#	Date	Mintage	VF	XF	Unc
6	1977	1.500	1.25	1.50	1.75
	1977FM(M)	3,000	—	4.50	7.50
	1977FM(P)	.014	—	Proof	10.00
	1978FM(U)	3,544	—	—	—
	1978FM(P)	5,122	—	Proof	—
	1979FMu	—	—	—	—
	1979FM(P)	—	—	Proof	—

5 DOLLARS

28.2800 gm., .925 SILVER, .8411 oz ASW

Y#	Date	Mintage	VF	XF	Unc
7	1977FM(M)	200 pcs.	—	90.00	125.00
	1977FM(P)	.015	—	Proof	30.00
	1978FM(P)	5,148	—	Proof	—
	1979FM(P)	—	—	Proof	—

COPPER-NICKEL

Y#	Date	Mintage	VF	XF	Unc
7a	1978FM(U)	744pcs.	—	—	22.50
	1979FM(U)	—	—	—	—

27.2800 gm., .925 SILVER, .8113 oz ASW
Coronation Jubilee
Obv: Similar to Y#7.

Y#	Date	Mintage	VF	XF	Unc
8	1978FM(P)	8,886	—	Proof	25.00

10 DOLLARS

COPPER-NICKEL

Y#	Date	Mintage	VF	XF	Unc
10	1979FM(U)	—	—	—	—

40.5000 gm., .925 SILVER, 1.2045 oz ASW

Y#	Date	Mintage	VF	XF	Unc
10a	1979FM(P)	—	—	Proof	50.00

100 DOLLARS

9.3700 gm., .900 GOLD, .2711 oz AGW
Attainment of Sovereignty

Y#	Date	Mintage	VF	XF	Unc
9	1978FM(M)	50 pcs.	—	—	—
—	1978FM(U)	213pcs.	—	—	—
—	1978FM(P)	3,159	—	Proof	—

NCLT ISSUES

MINT SETS

KM#	Date	Mintage	Identification	Issue Price	Mkt. Val.
S1	1978(7)	—	Y1-6,7a	22.00	—
S2	1979(8)	—	Y1-6,7a,10	31.00	—

PROOF SETS

STANDARD METALS

KM#	Date	Mintage	Identification	Issue Price	Mkt. Val.
101	1977(7)	72,748	Y1-7	40.00	55.00
102	1978(7)	—	Y1-7	45.00	—
103	1979(8)	—	Y1-7,10a	77.00	—

SOMALIA

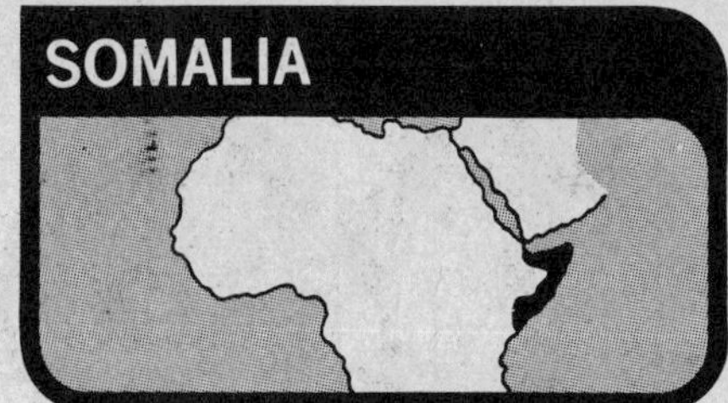

The Somali Democratic Republic, comprising the former British Somaliland Protectorate and Italian Somaliland, is located on the coast of the eastern projection of the African continent commonly referred to as the Horn. It has an area of 246,155 sq. mi. (627,541 sq. km.) and a population of 3.4 million. Capital: Mogadishu. The economy is pastoral and agricultural. Livestock, bananas and hides are exported.

The area of the British Somaliland Protectorate was known to the Egyptains at least 1,500 years B.C., and was occupied by the Arabs and Portuguese before British sea captains obtained trading and anchorage rights in 1827. The land of sandy clay and sporadic rainfall acquired a strategic importance with the opening of the Suez Canal in 1869. After negotiating treaties with the tribes, Britain declared the area a protectorate in 1888. Italy acquired Italian Somaliland in 1895 by purchase from the sultan of Zanzibar. Britain occupied Italian Somaliland in 1941 and administered it until April 1, 1950, when it was returned to Italy as a U.N. trusteeship. The British Somaliland protectorate became independent on July 1, 1960. Five days later it joined with Italian Somaliland to form the Somali Republic. The country is presently under a revolutionary military regime installed Oct. 21, 1969.

ITALIAN SOMALILAND

RULERS

Vittorio Emanuele III, 1900-1946

MINT MARKS

R- Rome

MONETARY SYSTEM

100 Bese = 1 Rupia

BESA

BRONZE

Y#	Date	Mintage	Fine	VF	XF
1	1909R	2.000	7.50	15.00	27.50
	1910R	.500	7.50	15.00	27.50
	1913R	.200	8.50	17.50	30.00
	1921R	.500	8.50	17.50	30.00

2 BESE

BRONZE

Y#	Date	Mintage	Fine	VF	XF
2	1909R	.500	10.00	20.00	32.50
	1910R	.250	10.00	20.00	32.50
	1913R	.300	10.00	20.00	42.50
	1921R	.600	10.00	20.00	42.50
	1923R	1.500	10.00	20.00	42.50
	1924R	Inc. Ab.	10.00	20.00	42.50

4 BESE

BRONZE

Y#	Date	Mintage	Fine	VF	XF
3	1909R	.250	12.50	25.00	50.00
	1910R	.250	12.50	25.00	50.00
	1913R	.050	15.00	30.00	65.00
	1921R	.200	12.50	25.00	50.00
	1923R	1.000	12.50	25.00	50.00
	1924R	Inc. Ab.	12.50	25.00	50.00

1/4 RUPIA

2.9160 gm., .917 SILVER, .0859 oz ASW

Y#	Date	Mintage	VF	XF	Unc
4	1910R	.400	25.00	50.00	75.00
	1913R	.100	25.00	60.00	100.00

1/2 RUPIA

5.8319 gm., .917 SILVER, .1719 oz ASW

Y#	Date	Mintage	Fine	VF	XF	Unc
5	1910R	.400	15.00	30.00	60.00	85.00
	1912R	.100	15.00	30.00	60.00	85.00
	1913R	.100	15.00	30.00	60.00	85.00
	1915R	.050	35.00	70.00	135.00	180.00
	1919R	.200	15.00	30.00	60.00	85.00

RUPIA

11.6638 gm., .917 SILVER, .3437 oz ASW

Y#	Date	Mintage	VF	XF	Unc
6	1910R	.300	40.00	85.00	130.00
	1912R	.600	40.00	85.00	130.00
	1913R	.300	40.00	85.00	130.00
	1914R	.300	40.00	85.00	130.00
	1915R	.250	40.00	85.00	130.00
	1919R	.400	40.00	85.00	130.00
	1920R	1.300	500.00	1000.	1500.
	1921	.940	1100.	1700.	2500.

NEW COINAGE

100 Centesimi = 1 Lira

5 LIRE

6.0000 gm., .835 SILVER, .1611 oz ASW

Y#	Date	Mintage	VF	XF	Unc
7	1925	.400	50.00	100.00	175.00

10 LIRE

12.0000 gm., .835 SILVER, .3221 oz ASW

Y#	Date	Mintage	VF	XF	Unc
8	1925	.100	75.00	135.00	225.00

SOMALIA

MONETARY SYSTEM

100 Centesimi = 1 Somalo =
1 Scellino = 1 Shilling

CENTESIMO

COPPER

Y#	Date	Year	Mintage	VF	XF	Unc
1	AH1369	1950	4.000	.15	.25	.50

5 CENTESIMI

COPPER

Y#	Date	Year	Mintage	VF	XF	Unc
2	AH1369	1950	6.800	.20	.40	.75

BRASS

Y#	Date	Mintage	VF	XF	Unc
6	1967	10.000	—	.10	.15
	1975	—	.10	.15	.20

10 CENTESIMI

COPPER

Y#	Date	Year	Mintage	VF	XF	Unc
3	AH1369	1950	7.400	.30	.65	1.25

BRASS

Y#	Date	Mintage	VF	XF	Unc
7	1967	6.600	.10	.20	.30
	1975	—	.10	.20	.35

50 CENTESIMI

3.8000 gm., .250 SILVER, .0305 oz ASW

Y#	Date	Year	Mintage	VF	XF	Unc
4	AH1369	1950	1.800	2.75	4.00	5.50

COPPER-NICKEL

Y#	Date	Mintage	VF	XF	Unc
8	1967	5.100	.25	.35	.75
	1975	—	.25	.35	.75

SOMALO

7.6000 gm., .250 SILVER, .0610 oz ASW

Y#	Date	Year	Mintage	VF	XF	Unc
5	AH1369	1950	11.480	2.00	3.75	5.00

SCELLINO

SCHILLING

COPPER-NICKEL

Y#	Date	Mintage	VF	XF	Unc
9	1967	8.150	.35	.75	1.25

5 SHILLINGS

COPPER-NICKEL
F.A.O. Issue

Y#	Date	Mintage	VF	XF	Unc
10	1970	.100	—	3.00	3.50
	1970	1,000		Proof	40.00

20 SHILLINGS

2.8000 gm., .900 GOLD, .0810 oz AGW
5th Anniversary of Independence

Fr#	Date	Mintage	XF	Unc	Proof
5	1965	—	—	—	65.00

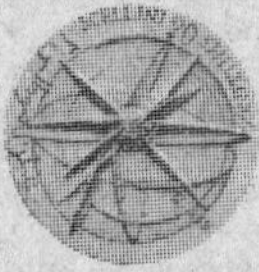

10th Anniversary of Independence

Fr#	Date	Mintage	XF	Unc	Proof
10	1970	8,000	—	—	65.00

50 SHILLINGS

7.0000 gm., .900 GOLD, .2025 oz AGW
5th Anniversary of Independence

Fr#	Date	Mintage	XF	Unc	Proof
4	1965	—	—	—	150.00

10th Anniversary of Independence

Fr#	Date	Mintage	XF	Unc	Proof
9	1970	8,000	—	—	150.00

1st Anniversary of the 1969 Revolution

Fr#	Date	Mintage	XF	Unc	Proof
13	1970	—	—	—	150.00

100 SHILLINGS

14.0000 gm., .900 GOLD, .4051 oz AGW
5th Anniversary of Independence

Fr#	Date	Mintage	XF	Unc	Proof
3	1965	—	—	—	275.00

10th Anniversary of Independence

Fr#	Date	Mintage	XF	Unc	Proof
8	1970	8,000	—	—	275.00

1st Anniversary of the 1969 Revolution

Fr#	Date	Mintage	XF	Unc	Proof
12	1970	—	—	—	275.00

200 SHILLINGS

28.0000 gm., .900 GOLD, .8102 oz AGW
5th Anniversary of Independence

Fr#	Date	Mintage	XF	Unc	Proof
2	1965	—	—	—	550.00

10th Anniversary of Independence

Fr#	Date	Mintage	XF	Unc	Proof
7	1970	8,000	—	—	550.00

1st Anniversary of the 1969 Revolution

Fr#	Date	Mintage	XF	Unc	Proof
11	1970	—	—	—	550.00

500 SHILLINGS

70.0000 gm., .900 GOLD, 2.0257 oz AGW
5th Anniversary of Independence

Fr#	Date	Mintage	XF	Unc	Proof
1	1965	—	—	—	1350.

10th Anniversary of Independence

Fr#	Date	Mintage	XF	Unc	Proof
6	1970	8,000	—	—	1350.

DECIMAL COINAGE

100 Senti = 1 Shilin

5 SENTI

ALUMINUM
F.A.O. Issue

Y#	Date	Mintage	VF	XF	Unc
11	1976	11.000	—	.10	.25

10 SENTI

ALUMINUM
F.A.O. Issue

Y#	Date	Mintage	VF	XF	Unc
12	1976	20.500	.10	.20	.50

50 SENTI

COPPER-NICKEL
F.A.O. Issue

Y#	Date	Mintage	VF	XF	Unc
13	1976	5.040	.15	.30	.75

SHILIN

COPPER-NICKEL
F.A.O. Issue

Y#	Date	Mintage	VF	XF	Unc
14	1976	10.020	.20	.40	1.00

NCLT ISSUES

PROOF SETS
STANDARD METALS

KM#	Date	Mintage	Identification	Issue Price	Mkt. Val.
101	1965(5)	6,325	Fr1-5	—	2300.
102	1970(5)	8,000	Fr6-10	334.95	2300.
103	1970(3)	14,500	Fr11-13	—	950.00

Listings For
SOMALILAND: refer to Djibouti

SOUTH AFRICA

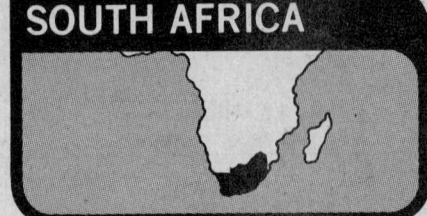

The Republic of South Africa, located at the southern tip of Africa, has an area, including the enclave of Walvis Bay, of 472,359 sq. mi. (1,233,404 sq. km.) and a population of 26.1 million. Capital: Administrative, Pretoria; Legislative, Cape Town; Judicial, Bloemfontein. Manufacturing, mining and agriculture are the principal industries. Exports include wool, diamonds, gold, and metallic ores.

Portuguese navigator Bartholomew Diaz became the first European to sight the region of South Africa when he rounded the Cape of Good Hope in 1488, but throughout the 16th century the only white men to come ashore were the survivors of ships wrecked while attempting the stormy Cape passage. The first permanent settlement was established by Jan van Riebeeck of the Dutch East India Company in 1652. In subsequent decades additional Dutch and Germans and Huguenot refugees from France settled in the Cape area to form the Afrikaner segment of today's population.

Great Britain captured the Cape colony in 1795, and again in 1806, receiving permanent title in 1814. To escape British political rule and cultural dominance, many Afrikaner farmers (Boers) migrated northward (the Great Trek) beginning in 1836, and established the independent Boer republics of the Transvaal (the South African Republic, Zuid Afrikaansche Republic) in 1852, and the Orange Free State in 1854. British political intrigues against the two republics, coupled with the discovery of diamonds and gold in the Boer- settled regions, led to the bitter Boer Wars (1880-81, 1899-1902) and the incorporation of the Boer republics into the British Empire.

On May 31, 1910, the two former Boer republics (Transvaal and Orange Free State) were joined with the British colonies of Cape of Good Hope and Natal to form the Union of South Africa, a dominion of the British Empire. In 1934 the Union achieved status as a sovereign state within the British Empire.

Political integration of the various colonies did not still the conflict between the Afrikaners and the English-speaking groups, which continued to have a significant impact on political developments. A resurgence of Afrikaner nationalism in the 1940's and 1950's led to a referendum in the white community authorizing the relinquishment of dominion status and the establishment of a republic. The decision took effect on May 31, 1961. The Republic of South Africa withdrew from the British Commonwealth in Oct. 1961.

South African coins and currency bear inscriptions in both Afrikaans and English.

RULERS

British until 1961

MONETARY SYSTEM

(Until 1961)

12 Pence = 1 Shilling
2 Shillings = 1 Florin
20 Shillings = 1 Pound

(Commencing 1961)

100 Cents = 1 Rand

CAPE OF GOOD HOPE

Cape of Good Hope, the largest of the four provinces of the Republic of South Africa, has an area of 278,380 sq. mi. (721,001 sq. km.) and a population of 4.3 million. Capital: Cape Town. The colony of Cape of Good Hope was founded by the Dutch in 1652 and was occupied by the British in 1795-1803 and 1806-14. The Dutch ceded it to the British in 1814. It was united for administrative purpose with Natal, 1843-56; annexed British Kaffraria in 1865 and British Becchuanaland in 1895; and administered Basutoland (now Lesotho), 1871-84. Cape Colony attained internal self-government in 1872, and joined the Union of South Africa in 1910. An extensive token series exists. One penny patterns are known for 1889.

RULERS

British, 1814-1910
South Africa, 1910-

MONETARY SYSTEM

12 Pence = 1 Shilling
20 Shillings = 1 Pound

NCLT ISSUES

PATTERNS

KM#	Date	Mintage	Identification	Mkt.Val.
7	1889	—	1 Penny, Bronze, 'I' of 'BRITANNIAR' above hair ribbon	175.00
8	1889	—	1 Penny, Silver	1000.
9	1889	—	1 Penny, Nickel, 'I' of 'BRITANNIAR' above hair ribbon	300.00
10	1889	—	1 Penny, Bronze	125.00
11	1889	—	1 Penny, Nickel	325.00
12	1889	—	1 Penny, Aluminum	750.00
13	1889	—	1 Penny, Tin	750.00

GRIQUATOWN

Griquatown is located in the Griqualand West region of northern Cape Hope Province, 90 miles west of Kimberley. Griqualand West occupies an area of 15,400 sq. mi. (50,500 sq. km.) north of the Orange River and west of Orange Free State. It is dry desert country, noted for its diamond fields. Chief town: Kimberley. Following the discovery of diamonds in 1867, a bitter dispute over possession erupted between the British and Orange Free State. Britain annexed the territory in 1871. It was joined to Cape Colony in 1880. The only actual coinage for the area was commissioned by Rev. John Campbell and produced by Thomas Halliday. The coins were produced in 1815-16, but are undated. They were eventually retired from circulation and melted. In 1890, two pattern types were struck by Otto Nolte & Co. of Berlin for advertising purpose.

RULERS

British until 1910
South Africa, 1910-

MONETARY SYSTEM

12 Pence = 1 Shilling
20 Shillings = 1 Pound

1/4 PENNY

COPPER

KM#	Date	Mintage	XF	Unc	Proof
1	ND(1815-16)	—	375.00	550.00	1200.

1/2 PENNY

COPPER

KM#	Date	Mintage	XF	Unc	Proof
2	ND(1815-16)	—	400.00	600.00	925.00

5 PENCE

SILVER
Obv: Dove. Rev: IIIII.

KM#	Date	Mintage	XF	Unc	Proof
4	ND(1815-16)	—	750.00	1100.	1200.

10 PENCE

SILVER

KM#	Date	Mintage	XF	Unc	Proof
5	ND(1815-16)	—	850.00	1200.	2100.

NCLT ISSUES

PATTERNS

KM#	Date	Mintage	Identification	Issue Price	Mkt. Val.
3	1890	—	1 Penny, Copper	—	150.00
6	ND	—	1 Penny, Copper	—	150.00

ORANGE FREE STATE

Orange Free State, a province of the Republic of South Africa bounded by Natal and Lesotho on the east, Cape Province on the south and west, and the Transvaal on the north, has an area of 49,866 sq. mi. (129,152 sq. km.) and a population of 1.8 million. Capital: Bloemfontein. The first settlements in the Orange region were established 1810-20, but general occupancy began with the great trek of the Boers in 1836. The British annexed it in 1848, then withdrew their sovereignty and recognized the independence of the Boer state, 1854. It joined Transvaal In the Boer War of 1899-1902, after which it was annexed by Britain and established as the Orange River Colony, May 28, 1900. It attained internal self- government in 1907 and joined the Union of South Africa in 1910. A series of patterns was struck by Otto Nolte & Co. of Berlin, but no regular-issue coins were produced. Tokens are known.

RULERS

British, 1848-1854, 1900-1910
South Africa, 1910-

MONETARY SYSTEM

12 Pence = 1 Shilling
20 Shillings = 1 Kroon

NCLT ISSUES

PATTERNS

KM#	Date	Mintage	Identification	Issue Price	Mkt. Val.
14	1874	—	1 Penny, Bronze	—	225.00
15	1874	—	1 Penny, Bronze, double thickness	—	475.00
16	1874	—	1 Penny, Bronze, triple thickness	—	600.00
17	1887	—	1 Kroon, Silver	—	5000.
18	1887	—	1 Kroon, Lead	—	Rare
19	1887	—	1 Kroon, Silver w/o 'LLC' and 'ESSAY'	—	Rare

KM#	Date	Mintage	Identification	Issue Price	Mkt. Val.
20	1888	—	1 Penny, Bronze	—	175.00
21	1888	—	1 Penny, Nickel	—	300.00
22	1888	—	1 Penny, Bronze, value larger	—	225.00
23	1888	—	1 Penny, Nickel	—	325.00
24	1888	—	1 Penny, Bronze	—	175.00
25	1888	—	1 Penny, Bronze, double thickness	—	225.00
26	1888	—	1 Penny, Bronze, triple thickness	—	600.00
27	1888	—	1 Penny, Silver	—	Rare
28	1888	—	1 Penny, Nickel	—	300.00
29	1888	—	1 Penny, Aluminum	—	400.00

ZUID AFRIKAANSCHE REPUBLIC

MONETARY SYSTEM

12 Pence = 1 Shilling
20 Shillings = 1 Pond

PENNY

BRONZE

Y#	Date	Mintage	VF	XF	Unc
1	1892	.028	8.00	15.00	30.00
	1892	*8-10 pcs.	—	Proof	3500.
	1893	.055	110.00	150.00	225.00
	1894	.011	5.00	10.00	30.00
	1898	.263	8.00	10.00	20.00

3 PENCE

1.4138 gm., .925 SILVER, .0420 oz ASW

Y#	Date	Mintage	VF	XF	Unc
2	1892	.024	15.00	30.00	60.00
	1892	*35-40 pcs.	—	Proof	450.00
	1893	.135	10.50	37.50	60.00
	1894	.104	12.00	25.00	90.00
	1895	.113	12.00	25.00	60.00
	1896	.166	8.00	15.00	32.50
	1897	.201	8.00	15.00	32.50

6 PENCE

2.8276 gm., .925 SILVER, .0841 oz ASW

Y#	Date	Mintage	VF	XF	Unc
3	1892	.028	25.00	40.00	75.00
	1892	*40-50 pcs.	—	Proof	300.00
	1893	.096	15.00	30.00	100.00
	1894	.168	10.00	20.00	90.00
	1895	.179	13.00	25.00	90.00
	1896	.205	7.00	15.00	30.00
	1896	1 known	—	Proof	—
	1897	.220	7.00	15.00	30.00
	1897	1 known	—	Proof	—

SHILLING

5.6555 gm., .925 SILVER, .1682 oz ASW

Y#	Date	Mintage	VF	XF	Unc
4	1892	.130	25.00	60.00	100.00
	1892	*40-50 pcs.	—	Proof	450.00
	1893	.137	50.00	175.00	500.00
	1894	.366	20.00	50.00	175.00
	1895	.327	20.00	40.00	250.00
	1896	.437	20.00	75.00	350.00
	1897	.397	15.00	30.00	40.00

2 SHILLINGS

11.3100 gm., .925 SILVER, .3364 oz ASW

Y#	Date	Mintage	VF	XF	Unc
5	1892	.055	40.00	100.00	220.00
	1892	*50-60 pcs.	—	Proof	450.00
	1893	.106	100.00	225.00	400.00
	1894	.173	25.00	60.00	200.00
	1895	.150	25.00	60.00	200.00
	1896	.353	20.00	40.00	60.00
	1897	.148	20.00	40.00	65.00

2-1/2 SHILLINGS

14.1380 gm., .925 SILVER, .4205 oz ASW

Y#	Date	Mintage	VF	XF	Unc
6	1892	.163	45.00	100.00	300.00
	1892	*50-60 pcs.	—	Proof	700.00
	1893	.135	100.00	225.00	500.00
	1894	.135	30.00	80.00	250.00
	1895	.182	30.00	80.00	300.00
	1896	.285	20.00	45.00	65.00
	1897	.149	20.00	45.00	70.00

5 SHILLINGS

28.2759 gm., .925 SILVER, .8410 oz ASW
Single shaft wagon tongue.

Y#	Date	Mintage	VF	XF	Unc
7	1892	.014	175.00	300.00	700.00

Double shaft wagon tongue

Y#	Date	Mintage	VF	XF	Unc
7a	1892	4,327	250.00	350.00	900.00
	1892	*25-30 pcs.	—	Proof	2000.

Beware of counterfeit double shafts. Aside from there being two shafts on the wagon in the coat of arms (reverse), the two wheels of the wagon must be the same size. On single shaft crowns, the rear wheel is noticeably larger than the front wheel.

Single shaft wagon tongue

Double shaft wagon tongue

1/2 POND

3.9940 gm., .916 GOLD, .1176 oz AGW
Rev: Double shaft wagon tongue

Y#	Date	Mintage	VF	XF	Unc
8a	1892	.010	225.00	275.00	400.00
	1892	*20-25 pcs.	—	Proof	4500.

Rev: Single shaft wagon tongue

Y#	Date	Mintage	VF	XF	Unc
8	1892	Unique	—	Rare	—
	1893	Inc. Bl.	1800.	3000.	4500.
	1894	.039	200.00	250.00	600.00
	1895	.135	200.00	250.00	500.00
	1896	.104	200.00	250.00	500.00
	1897	.075	200.00	250.00	500.00

EEN (1) POND

7.9880 gm., .916 GOLD, .2353 oz AGW
Coarse beard

Y#	Date	Mintage	VF	XF	Unc
A1	1874	837 pcs.	9500.	13,500.	18,000.

Fine beard

Y#	Date	Mintage	VF	XF	Unc
A1.1	1874	Inc. Ab.	7000.	10,000.	12,000.

Rev: Double shaft wagon tongue

Y#	Date	Mintage	VF	XF	Unc
9a	1892	.016	300.00	350.00	500.00
	1892	*12-15 pcs.	—	Proof	4500.

Rev: Single shaft wagon tongue

Y#	Date	Mintage	VF	XF	Unc
9	1892	Inc. Bl.	1000.	2000.	3500.
	1893	.062	200.00	250.00	450.00
	1894	.318	200.00	250.00	375.00
	1895	.336	200.00	250.00	400.00
	1896	.235	200.00	250.00	400.00
	1897	.311	200.00	250.00	400.00
	1898	.137	200.00	250.00	375.00
	1898/stamped 99				
		130 pcs.	7500.	9000.	10,000.
	1898/stamped 9		—	Unique	—
	1900	.788	200.00	250.00	375.00

.999 GOLD
'VELD' Boer War Siege Issue

Y#	Date	Mintage	VF	XF	Unc
10	1902	986 pcs.	3750.	4500.	7500.

NCLT ISSUES

PATTERNS

KM#	Date	Mintage	Identification	Issue Price	Mkt. Val.
30	1874	—	1 Penny, Bronze	—	175.00
31	1874	—	1 Penny, double thickness	—	300.00
32	1874	—	1 Penny, triple thickness	—	600.00
33	1874	—	1 Penny, Bronze	—	175.00
34	1874	—	2 Pence, Bronze	—	175.00
35	1874	—	Half Crown, Gilt Bronze milled edge	—	3500.
36	1874	—	Half Crown, Silver, milled edge	—	3500.
37	1874	—	Half Crown, Silver, plain edge	—	3500.
38	1874	—	Half Crown, Aluminum, milled edge	—	3000.
39	1874	—	Half Crown, Aluminum, plain edge	—	2000.

KM#	Date	Mintage	Identification	Issue Price	Mkt. Val.
40	1874	—	Crown, Gilt Bronze, milled edge	—	3500.
41	1874	—	Crown, Gilt Bronze, plain edge	—	Rare
42	1874	—	Crown, Aluminum, milled edge	—	3000.
43	1874	—	Crown, Gilt Copper, milled edge	—	—
44	1874	—	Crown, Gilt Copper, plain edge	—	—
45	1874	—	Crown, Silver, milled edge	—	5000.
46	1874	—	Crown, Silver, plain edge	—	—
47	1874	—	Crown, Aluminum, milled edge	—	2500.
48	1874	—	1 Pond, Bronze, short beard	—	1000.
49	1874	—	1 Pond, Bronze, longer beard	—	Rare
50	1874	—	1 Pond, Aluminum, longer beard	—	1500.

KM#	Date	Mintage	Identification	Issue Price	Mkt. Val.
51	1890	—	1 Penny, Bronze	—	175.00

PROOF SETS

STANDARD METALS

KM#	Date	Mintage	Identification	Issue Price	Mkt. Val.
101	1892(9)	—	Y1-9	—	20,000.

UNION OF SOUTH AFRICA

MONETARY SYSTEM

12 Pence = 1 Shilling
2 Shillings = 1 Florin
20 Shillings = 1 Pound

1/4 PENNY FARTHING

BRONZE
Rev. denomination: '1/4 PENNY 1/4'

Y#	Date	Mintage	VF	XF	Unc
11	1923	.033	10.00	17.50	20.00
	1923	1,402	—	Proof	50.00
	1924	.095	6.00	11.50	15.00

Rev. denomination: '1/4 PENNY'

Y#	Date	Mintage	VF	XF	Unc
11a	1926	16 pcs.	—	Proof only	10,000.
	1928	.064	5.00	9.00	15.00
	1930	6,560	150.00	250.00	350.00
	1930	14 pcs.	—	Proof	500.00
	1931	.154	4.50	7.00	10.00

Rev. denomination: '1/4 D'

Y#	Date	Mintage	VF	XF	Unc
23	1931	Inc. Ab.	25.00	35.00	45.00
	1931	62 pcs.	—	Proof	250.00
	1932	.105	4.00	6.00	8.00
	1932	12 pcs.	—	Proof	400.00
	1933	76 pcs.	—	—	2000.
	1933	20 pcs.	—	Proof	2500.
	1934	52 pcs.	—	—	2000.
	1934	24 pcs.	—	Proof	2500.
	1935	.061	4.00	6.00	8.00
	1935	20 pcs.	—	Proof	450.00
	1936	43 pcs.	—	—	3000.
	1936	40 pcs.	—	Proof	4000.

Y#	Date	Mintage	VF	XF	Unc
31	1937	.038	4.00	10.00	15.00
	1937	116 pcs.	—	Proof	100.00
	1938	.051	3.00	7.00	10.00
	1938	44 pcs.	—	Proof	450.00
	1939	.102	2.00	6.00	8.00
	1939	30 pcs.	—	Proof	550.00
	1941	.091	2.00	6.00	8.00

Y#	Date	Mintage	VF	XF	Unc
31	1942	3.756	1.00	2.00	3.00
	1943	9.918	1.00	2.00	3.00
	1943	104 pcs.	—	Proof	50.00
	1944	4.468	1.00	2.00	3.00
	1944	150 pcs.	—	Proof	40.00
	1945	5.297	1.00	2.00	3.00
	1945	150 pcs.	—	Proof	40.00
	1946	4.378	1.00	2.00	3.00
	1946	150 pcs.	—	Proof	40.00
	1947	3.895	1.00	2.00	3.00
	1947	2,600	—	Proof	15.00

Y#	Date	Mintage	VF	XF	Unc
40	1948	2.415	1.00	2.00	3.00
	1948	1,120	—	Proof	10.00
	1949	3.568	1.00	2.00	3.00
	1949	800 pcs.	—	Proof	16.00
	1950	8.694	1.00	2.00	3.00
	1950	500 pcs.	—	Proof	16.00

Rev. legend reversed: SUID AFRIKA-SOUTH AFRICA

Y#	Date	Mintage	VF	XF	Unc
49	1951	3.511	1.00	2.00	3.00
	1951	2,000	—	Proof	10.00
	1952	2.804	1.00	2.00	3.00
	1952	15,500	—	Proof	5.00

Y#	Date	Mintage	VF	XF	Unc
59	1953	9.633	.50	.75	1.00
	1953	5,000	—	Proof	5.00
	1954	6.568	.50	.75	1.00
	1954	3,150	—	Proof	7.00
	1955	11.798	.50	.75	1.00
	1955	2,850	—	Proof	7.00
	1956	1.287	.50	1.50	2.00
	1956	1,700	—	Proof	5.00
	1957	3.056	.50	1.50	2.00
	1957	1,130	—	Proof	8.00
	1958	5.452	.50	1.50	2.00
	1958	985 pcs.	—	Proof	10.00
	1959	1.567	.50	1.50	2.00
	1959	950 pcs.	—	Proof	10.00
	1960	1.023	.50	1.50	2.00
	1960	3,360	—	Proof	5.00

1/2 PENNY

BRONZE
Rev. denomination: '1/2 PENNY 1/2'

Y#	Date	Mintage	VF	XF	Unc
12	1923	.012	75.00	125.00	150.00
	1923	1,402	—	Proof	200.00
	1924	.064	30.00	60.00	100.00
	1925	.069	30.00	60.00	100.00
	1926	.065	30.00	60.00	120.00
	1926	16 pcs.	—	Proof	Rare

Rev. denomination: '1/2 PENNY'

Y#	Date	Mintage	VF	XF	Unc
12a	1928	.105	20.00	50.00	75.00
	1929	.272	20.00	50.00	75.00
	1930	.147	20.00	50.00	75.00
	1930	14 pcs.	—	Proof	500.00
	1930 no star after date				
		Inc. Ab.	30.00	60.00	120.00
	1931	.145	20.00	50.00	75.00

Rev. denomination: '1/2 D'

Y#	Date	Mintage	VF	XF	Unc
24	1931	62 pcs.	—	Proof only	1500.
	1932	.106	20.00	40.00	65.00
	1932	12 pcs.	—	Proof	500.00
	1933	.063	30.00	60.00	120.00
	1933	20 pcs.	—	Proof	500.00
	1934	.326	15.00	30.00	40.00
	1934	24 pcs.	—	Proof	500.00
	1935	.405	15.00	30.00	40.00
	1935	20 pcs.	—	Proof	500.00
	1936	.407	15.00	30.00	40.00
	1936	40 pcs.	—	Proof	300.00

Y#	Date	Mintage	VF	XF	Unc
32	1937	.638	4.00	12.00	18.00
	1937	116 pcs.	—	Proof	100.00
	1938	.560	4.00	12.00	18.00
	1938	44 pcs.	—	Proof	150.00
	1939	.271	6.00	14.00	20.00
	1939	30 pcs.	—	Proof	350.00
	1940	1.535	2.00	7.00	10.00
	1941	2.053	2.00	7.00	10.00
	1942	8.382	2.00	7.00	10.00
	1943	5.135	2.00	7.00	10.00
	1943	104 pcs.	—	Proof	75.00
	1944	3.920	2.00	7.00	10.00
	1944	150 pcs.	—	Proof	55.00
	1945	2.357	2.00	7.00	10.00
	1945	150 pcs.	—	Proof	55.00
	1946	1.022	2.00	7.00	10.00
	1946	150 pcs.	—	Proof	55.00
	1947	.258	5.00	12.00	18.00
	1947	2,600	—	Proof	30.00

Y#	Date	Mintage	VF	XF	Unc
41	1948	.685	2.00	4.00	6.00
	1948	1,120	—	Proof	20.00
	1949	1.850	2.00	3.00	4.00
	1949	800 pcs.	—	Proof	25.00
	1950	2.186	2.00	3.00	4.00
	1950	500 pcs.	—	Proof	20.00
	1951	3.746	2.00	3.00	4.00
	1951	2,000	—	Proof	10.00
	1952	4.174	2.00	3.00	4.00
	1952	.016	—	Proof	5.00

Y#	Date	Mintage	VF	XF	Unc
60	1953	5.572	.20	.30	3.00
	1953	5,000	—	Proof	6.00
	1954	.101	5.00	12.00	15.00
	1954	3,150	—	Proof	25.00
	1955	3.774	.50	2.00	3.00
	1955	2,850	—	Proof	6.00
	1956	1.305	.50	2.00	3.00
	1956	1,700	—	Proof	8.00
	1957	2.025	.50	2.00	3.00
	1957	1,130	—	Proof	8.00
	1958	2.171	.50	2.00	3.00
	1958	985 pcs.	—	Proof	10.00
	1959	2.397	.50	2.00	3.00
	1959	900 pcs.	—	Proof	11.00
	1960	2.552	.50	2.00	3.00
	1960	3,360	—	Proof	7.50

PENNY

BRONZE
Rev. denomination: '1 PENNY 1'

Y#	Date	Mintage	VF	XF	Unc
13	1923	.091	10.00	30.00	50.00
	1923	1,402	—	Proof	60.00
	1924	.134	10.00	40.00	60.00

Rev. denomination: 'PENNY'

Y#	Date	Mintage	VF	XF	Unc
13a	1926	.393	10.00	30.00	80.00
	1926	16 pcs.	—	Proof	Rare
	1927	.285	10.00	30.00	70.00
	1928	.386	10.00	30.00	70.00
	1929	1.093	10.00	20.00	30.00
	1930	.754	10.00	20.00	35.00
	1930	14 pcs.	—	Proof	600.00

Rev. denomination: '1 D.'

Y#	Date	Mintage	VF	XF	Unc
25	1931	.248	10.00	35.00	60.00
	1931	62 pcs.	—	Proof	200.00
	1932	.260	10.00	35.00	50.00
	1932	12 pcs.	—	Proof	700.00
	1933	.225	10.00	35.00	50.00
	1933	20 pcs.	—	Proof	600.00
	1933 w/o star after date				
		Inc. Ab.	12.50	25.00	40.00
	1934	2.090	5.00	10.00	20.00
	1934	24 pcs.	—	Proof	600.00
	1935	2.295	5.00	10.00	20.00
	1935	20 pcs.	—	Proof	600.00
	1936	1.819	5.00	10.00	20.00
	1936	40 pcs.	—	Proof	350.00

Y#	Date	Mintage	VF	XF	Unc
33	1937	3.281	3.00	6.00	13.00
	1937	116 pcs.	—	Proof	150.00
	1938	1.840	3.00	6.00	13.00
	1938	44 pcs.	—	Proof	250.00

Y#	Date	Mintage	VF	XF	Unc
33	1939	1.506	4.00	14.00	18.00
	1939	30 pcs.	—	Proof	500.00
	1940	3.592	2.00	6.00	8.00
	1940 w/o star after date		5.00	7.00	15.00
	1941	7.871	1.50	3.00	8.00
	1942	14.428	1.50	3.00	8.00
	1943	4.010	1.50	3.00	8.00
	1943	104 pcs.	—	Proof	125.00
	1944	6.425	1.50	3.00	7.00
	1944	150 pcs.	—	Proof	75.00
	1945	4.810	1.00	2.00	4.00
	1945	150 pcs.	—	Proof	75.00
	1946	2.605	2.00	5.00	7.00
	1946	150 pcs.	—	Proof	75.00
	1947	.135	6.00	18.00	25.00
	1947	2,600	—	Proof	40.00

Y#	Date	Mintage	VF	XF	Unc
42	1948	2.398	1.00	2.00	5.00
	1948	1,120	—	Proof	25.00
	1948 star after date	Inc. Ab.	1.00	2.00	5.00
	1949	3.634	.50	2.00	3.00
	1949	800 pcs.	—	Proof	30.00
	1950	4.890	1.00	2.00	5.00
	1950	500 pcs.	—	Proof	30.00

Rev. leg: 'SUID AFRIKA-SOUTH AFRICA'

Y#	Date	Mintage	VF	XF	Unc
50	1951	3.787	2.00	3.00	6.00
	1951	2,000	—	Proof	10.00
	1952	12.674	1.00	2.00	5.00
	1952	.016	—	Proof	6.00

Y#	Date	Mintage	VF	XF	Unc
61	1953	5.491	.50	2.00	4.00
	1953	5,000	—	Proof	7.00
	1954	6.665	.50	2.00	4.00
	1954	3,150	—	Proof	7.00
	1955	6.508	.50	2.00	3.00
	1955	2,850	—	Proof	7.00
	1956	4.390	.50	2.00	3.00
	1956	1,700	—	Proof	8.00
	1957	3.973	.50	2.00	3.00
	1957	1,130	—	Proof	8.00
	1958	5.311	.50	2.00	3.00
	1958	985 pcs.	—	Proof	10.00
	1959	5.066	.50	2.00	3.00
	1959	900 pcs.	—	Proof	12.00
	1960	5.106	.50	2.00	4.00
	1960	3,360	—	Proof	7.00

3 PENCE

1.4100 gm., .800 SILVER, .0362 oz ASW

Y#	Date	Mintage	VF	XF	Unc
15	1923	.303	10.00	30.00	40.00
	1923	1,402	—	Proof	60.00
	1924	.501	15.00	25.00	50.00
	1925	Inc. Bl	35.00	100.00	185.00

Rev. denomination: 3 PENCE

Y#	Date	Mintage	VF	XF	Unc
17	1925	.358	20.00	50.00	100.00
	1926	1.572	5.00	20.00	35.00
	1926	16 pcs.	—	Proof	Rare
	1927	2.285	5.00	20.00	35.00
	1928	.919	12.00	25.00	60.00
	1929	1.948	5.00	20.00	45.00
	1930	.981	5.00	20.00	45.00
	1930	14 pcs.	—	Proof	900.00

Rev. denomination: 3D

Y#	Date	Mintage	VF	XF	Unc
26	1931	128 pcs.	—	Rare	—
	1931	62 pcs.	—	Proof	3500.
	1932	2.622	5.00	20.00	30.00
	1932	12 pcs.	—	Proof	800.00
	1933	5.135	5.00	20.00	30.00
	1933	20 pcs.	—	Proof	750.00
	1934	2.357	5.00	20.00	30.00
	1934	24 pcs.	—	Proof	750.00
	1935	1.655	5.00	20.00	30.00
	1935	20 pcs.	—	Proof	750.00
	1936	1.095	2.00	15.00	30.00
	1936	40 pcs.	—	Proof	500.00

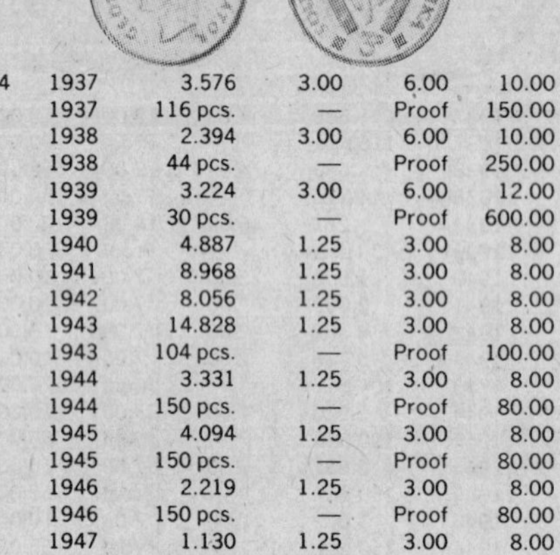

Y#	Date	Mintage	VF	XF	Unc
34	1937	3.576	3.00	6.00	10.00
	1937	116 pcs.	—	Proof	150.00
	1938	2.394	3.00	6.00	10.00
	1938	44 pcs.	—	Proof	250.00
	1939	3.224	3.00	6.00	12.00
	1939	30 pcs.	—	Proof	600.00
	1940	4.887	1.25	3.00	8.00
	1941	8.968	1.25	3.00	8.00
	1942	8.056	1.25	3.00	8.00
	1943	14.828	1.25	3.00	8.00
	1943	104 pcs.	—	Proof	100.00
	1944	3.331	1.25	3.00	8.00
	1944	150 pcs.	—	Proof	80.00
	1945	4.094	1.25	3.00	8.00
	1945	150 pcs.	—	Proof	80.00
	1946	2.219	1.25	3.00	8.00
	1946	150 pcs.	—	Proof	80.00
	1947	1.130	1.25	3.00	8.00
	1947	2,600	—	Proof	20.00

New obverse legend

Y#	Date	Mintage	VF	XF	Unc
43	1948	2.721	2.00	4.00	6.00
	1948	1,120	—	Proof	20.00
	1949	1.905	2.00	4.00	6.00
	1949	800 pcs.	—	Proof	25.00
	1950	4.096	2.00	3.00	5.00
	1950	500 pcs.	—	Proof	20.00

1.4100 gm., .500 SILVER, .0226 oz ASW
Modified rev. design

Y#	Date	Mintage	VF	XF	Unc
43a	1951	6.325	2.00	3.00	5.00
	1951	2,000	—	Proof	12.00
	1952	13.072	2.00	3.00	5.00
	1952	.016	—	Proof	7.00

Y#	Date	Mintage	VF	XF	Unc
62	1953	5.488	1.00	2.00	4.00
	1953	5,000	—	Proof	7.50
	1954	3.901	1.00	2.00	4.00
	1954	3,150	—	Proof	7.50
	1955	4.723	1.00	2.00	4.00
	1955	2,850	—	Proof	8.00
	1956	6.191	1.00	2.00	4.00
	1956	1,700	—	Proof	8.00
	1957	1.894	1.00	2.00	4.00
	1957	1,130	—	Proof	8.00
62	1958	3.228	1.00	2.00	4.00
	1958	985 pcs.	—	Proof	10.00
	1959	2.553	1.00	2.00	4.00
	1959	900 pcs.	—	Proof	20.00
	1960	.021	5.00	10.00	12.00
	1960	3,360	—	Proof	15.00

6 PENCE

2.8300 gm., .800 SILVER, .0727 oz ASW

Y#	Date	Mintage	VF	XF	Unc
16	1923	.209	10.00	30.00	50.00
	1923	1,402	—	Proof	90.00
	1924	.326	10.00	40.00	60.00

Rev. denomination: 6 PENCE

Y#	Date	Mintage	VF	XF	Unc
18	1925	.079	30.00	80.00	100.00
	1926	.722	10.00	30.00	45.00
	1926	16 pcs.	—	Proof	Rare
	1927	1.548	10.00	30.00	45.00
	1929	.784	10.00	30.00	45.00
	1930	.448	20.00	40.00	60.00
	1930	14 pcs.	—	Proof	1000.

Rev. denomination: 6 D

Y#	Date	Mintage	VF	XF	Unc
27	1931	4,805	100.00	300.00	550.00
	1931	62 pcs.	—	Proof	1000.
	1932	1.525	10.00	25.00	35.00
	1932	12 pcs.	—	Proof	1000.
	1933	2.819	10.00	25.00	35.00
	1933	20 pcs.	—	Proof	900.00
	1934	1.519	10.00	25.00	40.00
	1934	24 pcs.	—	Proof	900.00
	1935	.573	10.00	25.00	100.00
	1935	20 pcs.	—	Proof	800.00
	1936	.627	10.00	25.00	40.00
	1936	40 pcs.	—	Proof	650.00

Y#	Date	Mintage	VF	XF	Unc
35	1937	1.696	3.00	10.00	25.00
	1937	116 pcs.	—	Proof	200.00
	1938	1.725	3.00	10.00	25.00
	1938	44 pcs.	—	Proof	300.00
	1939	30 pcs.		Proof only	3000.
	1940	1.629	2.50	8.00	15.00
	1941	2.263	2.50	8.00	15.00
	1942	4.936	2.50	8.00	15.00
	1943	3.776	2.50	8.00	15.00
	1943	104 pcs.	—	Proof	130.00
	1944	.228	12.00	24.00	35.00
	1944	150 pcs.	—	Proof	100.00
	1945	.420	8.00	15.00	30.00
	1945	150 pcs.	—	Proof	100.00
	1946	.291	8.00	15.00	35.00
	1946	150 pcs.	—	Proof	100.00
	1947	.579	3.00	6.00	10.00
	1947	2,600	—	Proof	25.00

Y#	Date	Mintage	VF	XF	Unc
44	1948	2.267	2.50	4.00	8.00
	1948	1,120	—	Proof	30.00
	1949	.197	10.00	18.00	25.00
	1949	800 pcs.	—	Proof	45.00

Y#	Date	Mintage	VF	XF	Unc
44	1950	2.122	2.50	4.00	8.00
	1950	500 pcs.	—	Proof	25.00

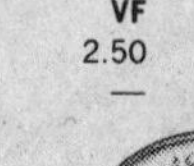

2.8300 gm., .500 SILVER, .0454 oz ASW

Y#	Date	Mintage	VF	XF	Unc
51	1951	2.604	2.00	4.00	6.00
	1951	2,000	—	Proof	15.00
	1952	4.281	1.50	3.00	5.00
	1952	.016	—	Proof	10.00

Y#	Date	Mintage	VF	XF	Unc
63	1953	2.501	1.50	3.00	5.00
	1953	5,000	—	Proof	10.00
	1954	2.200	1.50	3.00	5.00
	1954	3,150	—	Proof	10.00
	1955	1.972	1.50	3.00	5.00
	1955	2,850	—	Proof	10.00
	1956	1.774	1.50	3.00	5.00
	1956	1,700	—	Proof	15.00
	1957	3.290	1.50	3.00	5.00
	1957	1,130	—	Proof	15.00
	1958	1.174	1.50	3.00	5.00
	1958	985 pcs.	—	Proof	18.00
	1959	.262	4.00	6.00	10.00
	1959	900 pcs.	—	Proof	20.00
	1960	1.590	1.50	3.00	5.00
	1960	3,360	—	Proof	10.00

SHILLING

5.6600 gm., .800 SILVER, .1455 oz ASW
Rev. denomination: 1 SHILLING 1

Y#	Date	Mintage	VF	XF	Unc
19	1923	.809	20.00	50.00	75.00
	1923	1,402	—	Proof	100.00
	1924	1.269	25.00	40.00	70.00

Rev. denomination: SHILLING

Y#	Date	Mintage	VF	XF	Unc
19a	1926	.238	75.00	150.00	500.00
	1926	16 pcs.	—	Proof	Rare
	1927	.488	50.00	80.00	250.00
	1928	.889	25.00	50.00	150.00
	1929	.926	20.00	50.00	100.00
	1930	.422	35.00	75.00	130.00
	1930	14 pcs.	—	Proof	1300.

Y#	Date	Mintage	VF	XF	Unc
28	1931	6,603	200.00	400.00	800.00
	1931	62 pcs.	—	Proof	1250.
	1932	2.537	10.00	35.00	55.00
	1932	12 pcs.	—	Proof	1400.
	1933	1.463	10.00	35.00	55.00
	1933	20 pcs.	—	Proof	1200.
	1934	.821	10.00	37.00	55.00
	1934	24 pcs.	—	Proof	1200.
	1935	.685	10.00	37.00	55.00
	1935	20 pcs.	—	Proof	1200.
	1936	.693	10.00	37.00	55.00
28	1936	40 pcs.	—	Proof	750.00

Y#	Date	Mintage	VF	XF	Unc
36	1937	1.194	5.00	18.00	25.00
	1937	116 pcs.	—	Proof	250.00
	1938	1.160	5.00	18.00	28.00
	1938	44 pcs.	—	Proof	500.00
	1939	30 pcs.		Proof only	3500.
	1940	1.365	5.00	10.00	15.00
	1941	1.826	5.00	10.00	15.00
	1942	3.867	5.00	10.00	15.00
	1943	4.188	4.00	8.00	10.00
	1943	104 pcs.	—	Proof	200.00
	1944	.049	24.00	50.00	120.00
	1944	150 pcs.	—	Proof	200.00
	1945	.054	24.00	50.00	100.00
	1945	150 pcs.	—	Proof	200.00
	1946	.027	30.00	75.00	100.00
	1946	150 pcs.	—	Proof	200.00
	1947	9,784	20.00	65.00	80.00
	1947	2,600	—	Proof	100.00

Y#	Date	Mintage	VF	XF	Unc
45	1948	6,094	35.00	50.00	60.00
	1948	1,120	—	Proof	75.00
	1949	800 pcs.		Proof only	400.00
	1950	1.704	4.50	7.00	12.50
	1950	500 pcs.	—	Proof	60.00

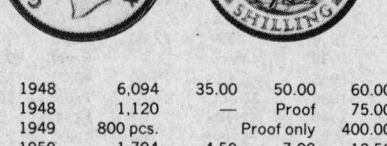

5.6600 gm., .500 SILVER, .0909 oz ASW
Rev. denomination: 1 S.

Y#	Date	Mintage	VF	XF	Unc
45a	1951	2.407	2.75	4.50	9.00
	1951	2,000	—	Proof	16.00
	1952	1.935	2.75	6.00	8.00
	1952	.016	—	Proof	10.00

Y#	Date	Mintage	VF	XF	Unc
64	1953	2.677	2.75	4.00	8.00
	1953	5,000	—	Proof	15.00
	1954	3.579	2.75	4.00	8.00
	1954	3,150	—	Proof	15.00
	1955	2.209	2.75	4.00	8.00
	1955	2,850	—	Proof	15.00
	1956	2.143	2.75	4.00	8.00
	1956	1,700	—	Proof	20.00
	1957	.792	3.00	8.00	15.00
	1957	1,130	—	Proof	30.00
	1958	4.068	2.75	4.00	8.00
	1958	985 pcs.	—	Proof	30.00
	1959	.205	5.00	10.00	20.00
	1959	900 pcs.	—	Proof	40.00
	1960	2.190	2.75	4.00	8.00
	1960	3,360	—	Proof	12.00

FLORIN

11.3100 gm., .800 SILVER, .2909 oz ASW

Y#	Date	Mintage	VF	XF	Unc
20	1923	.696	30.00	60.00	80.00
	1923	1,402	—	Proof	125.00
	1924	1.513	25.00	70.00	100.00
	1925	.050	450.00	1000.	2000.
	1926	.324	20.00	100.00	350.00
	1926	16 pcs.	—	Proof	Rare
	1927	.399	20.00	100.00	350.00
	1928	1.092	15.00	60.00	90.00
	1929	.648	12.00	45.00	90.00
	1930	.267	20.00	60.00	125.00
	1930	14 pcs.	—	Proof	1600.

2 SHILLINGS

11.3100 gm., .800 SILVER, .2909 oz ASW
Rev. denomination: 2 SHILLINGS

Y#	Date	Mintage	VF	XF	Unc
29	1931	445 pcs.	675.00	1300.	1600.
	1931	62 pcs.	—	Proof	2500.
	1932	1.315	15.00	35.00	50.00
	1932	12 pcs.	—	Proof	1800.
	1933	.891	45.00	65.00	85.00
	1933	20 pcs.	—	Proof	1800.
	1934	.559	20.00	50.00	75.00
	1934	24 pcs.	—	Proof	1800.
	1935	.554	20.00	50.00	75.00
	1935	20 pcs.	—	Proof	1600.
	1936	.669	20.00	50.00	75.00
	1936	40 pcs.	—	Proof	900.00

Y#	Date	Mintage	VF	XF	Unc
37	1937	1.495	9.00	20.00	25.00
	1937	116 pcs.	—	Proof	300.00
	1938	.214	15.00	40.00	60.00
	1938	44 pcs.	—	Proof	800.00
	1939	.279	15.00	40.00	60.00
	1939	30 pcs.	—	Proof	900.00
	1940	2.600	BV	13.00	25.00
	1941	1.764	BV	12.00	25.00
	1942	2.847	BV	10.00	25.00
	1943	3.124	BV	10.00	25.00
	1943	104 pcs.	—	Proof	250.00
	1944	.225	15.00	35.00	50.00
	1944	150 pcs.	—	Proof	200.00
	1945	.473	12.00	25.00	40.00
	1945	150 pcs.	—	Proof	200.00
	1946	.014	35.00	60.00	100.00
	1946	150 pcs.	—	Proof	300.00
	1947	5,492	35.00	75.00	100.00
	1947	2,600	—	Proof	150.00

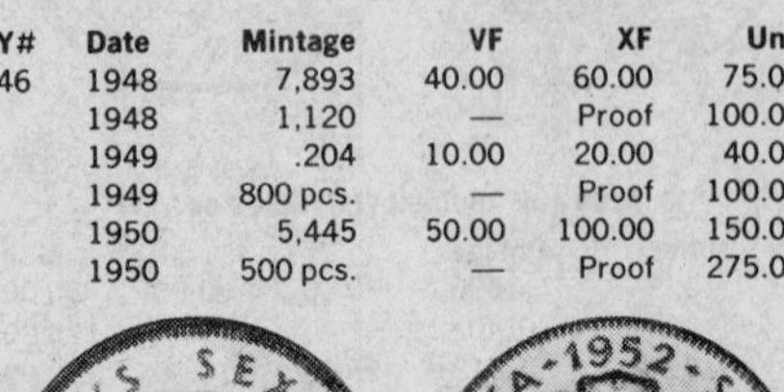

Y#	Date	Mintage	VF	XF	Unc
46	1948	7,893	40.00	60.00	75.00
	1948	1,120	—	Proof	100.00
	1949	.204	10.00	20.00	40.00
	1949	800 pcs.	—	Proof	100.00
	1950	5,445	50.00	100.00	150.00
	1950	500 pcs.	—	Proof	275.00

11.3100 gm., .500 SILVER, .1818 oz ASW
Rev. denomination: 2 S

Y#	Date	Mintage	VF	XF	Unc
52	1951	.732	5.50	7.50	15.00
	1951	2,000	—	Proof	25.00
	1952	3.585	BV	6.00	10.00
	1952	.016	—	Proof	15.00

Y#	Date	Mintage	VF	XF	Unc
65	1953	3.279	BV	8.00	12.00
	1953	5,000	—	Proof	18.00
	1954	5.869	BV	6.00	8.00
	1954	3,150	—	Proof	18.00
	1955	3.748	BV	6.00	12.00
	1955	2,850	—	Proof	18.00
	1956	2.551	BV	6.00	12.00
	1956	1,700	—	Proof	25.00
	1957	2.508	BV	6.00	12.00
	1957	1,130	—	Proof	40.00
	1958	2.821	BV	6.00	12.00
	1958	985 pcs.	—	Proof	40.00
	1959	1.220	BV	6.00	12.00
	1959	900 pcs.	—	Proof	45.00
	1960	1.954	BV	6.00	12.00
	1960	3,360	—	Proof	15.00

2-1/2 SHILLINGS

14.1400 gm., .800 SILVER, .3637 oz ASW
Rev. leg: ZUID-AFRICA,
denomination 2-1/2 SHILLINGS 2-1/2

Y#	Date	Mintage	VF	XF	Unc
21	1923	1.228	20.00	35.00	70.00
	1923	1,402	—	Proof	150.00
	1924	2.556	25.00	50.00	80.00
	1925	.460	50.00	100.00	350.00

Rev. denomination 2-1/2 SHILLINGS

Y#	Date	Mintage	VF	XF	Unc
21a	1926	.205	75.00	150.00	350.00
	1926	16 pcs.	—	Proof	Rare
	1927	.194	75.00	120.00	350.00
	1928	.984	25.00	70.00	100.00
	1929	.617	25.00	55.00	100.00
	1930	.324	25.00	60.00	100.00
	1930	14 pcs.	—	Proof	1700.

Rev. leg: SUID. AFRICA

Y#	Date	Mintage	VF	XF	Unc
30	1931	852 pcs.	—	Rare	1500.
	1931	62 pcs.	—	Proof	2000.
	1932	1.029	15.00	35.00	50.00
	1932	12 pcs.	—	Proof	2200.
	1933	.136	45.00	120.00	300.00
	1933	20 pcs.	—	Proof	2500.
	1934	.416	20.00	50.00	75.00
	1934	24 pcs.	—	Proof	2500.
	1935	.345	20.00	50.00	75.00
	1935	20 pcs.	—	Proof	2000.
	1936	.553	20.00	50.00	75.00
	1936	40 pcs.	—	Proof	1100.

Y#	Date	Mintage	VF	XF	Unc
38	1937	1.154	11.00	20.00	30.00
	1937	116 pcs.	—	Proof	375.00
	1938	.534	12.00	30.00	40.00
	1938	44 pcs.	—	Proof	800.00
	1939	.133	15.00	40.00	60.00
	1939	30 pcs.	—	Proof	1000.
	1940	2.976	BV	12.00	15.00
	1941	1.988	BV	12.00	22.00
	1942	3.180	BV	12.00	15.00
	1943	2.098	BV	12.00	15.00
	1943	104 pcs.	—	Proof	300.00
	1944	1.361	BV	10.00	20.00
	1944	150 pcs.	—	Proof	250.00
	1945	.183	20.00	50.00	70.00
	1945	150 pcs.	—	Proof	250.00
	1946	.011	75.00	100.00	125.00
	1946	150 pcs.	—	Proof	300.00
	1947	6,182	50.00	60.00	75.00
	1947	2,600	—	Proof	100.00

Y#	Date	Mintage	VF	XF	Unc
47	1948	2,720	75.00	100.00	150.00
	1948	1,120	—	Proof	200.00
	1949	2,691	75.00	100.00	150.00
	1949	800 pcs.	—	Proof	250.00
	1950	5,576	75.00	100.00	150.00
	1950	500 pcs.	—	Proof	350.00

14.1400 gm., .500 SILVER, .2273 oz ASW
Rev: Denomination 2-1/2 S

Y#	Date	Mintage	VF	XF	Unc
47a	1951	.785	7.50	10.00	15.00
	1951	2,000	—	Proof	25.00
	1952	2.011	7.00	9.00	12.00
	1952	.016	—	Proof	20.00

Y#	Date	Mintage	VF	XF	Unc
66	1953	2.519	BV	7.50	10.00
	1953	5,000	—	Proof	20.00
	1954	4.252	12.50	15.00	18.00
	1954	3,150	—	Proof	25.00
	1955	3.866	BV	7.00	18.00
	1955	2,850	—	Proof	25.00
	1956	2.438	BV	7.00	18.00
	1956	1,700	—	Proof	35.00
	1957	2.138	BV	7.00	15.00
	1957	1,130	—	Proof	40.00
	1958	2.261	BV	7.00	18.00
	1958	985 pcs.	—	Proof	50.00
	1959	.047	7.50	15.00	30.00
	1959	900 pcs.	—	Proof	50.00
	1960	.016	7.50	15.00	20.00
	1960	3,360	—	Proof	25.00

5 SHILLINGS

28.2800 gm., .800 SILVER, .7274 oz ASW
Royal Visit

Y#	Date	Mintage	VF	XF	Unc
39	1947	.306	BV	22.00	25.00
	1947	3,000	—	Proof	50.00

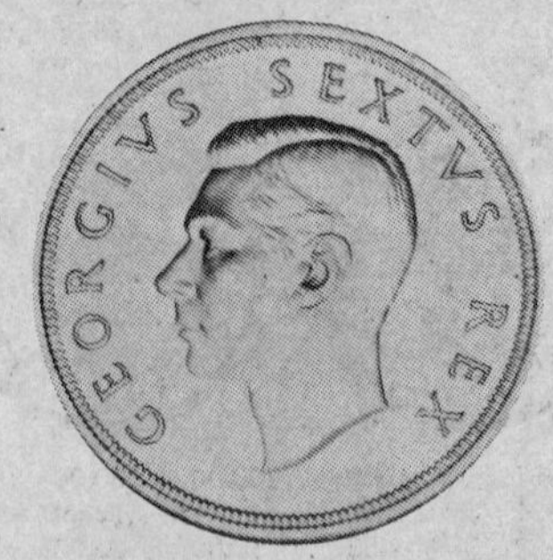

Rev: Similar to 5 Shillings Y#39

Y#	Date	Mintage	VF	XF	Unc
48	1948	.782	BV	22.00	25.00
	1948	.010	—	Proof	30.00
	1949	.538	BV	22.00	25.00
	1949	2,000	—	Proof	35.00
	1950	.084	22.00	25.00	35.00
	1950	1,200	—	Proof	100.00

28.2800 gm., .500 SILVER, .4546 oz ASW
Obv: Similar to Y#48.
Rev. denomination 5 S.

Y#	Date	Mintage	VF	XF	Unc
53	1951	.367	BV	14.00	20.00
	1951	2,000	—	Proof	35.00

300th Anniversary Founding of Capetown
Obv: Similar to Y#48.

Y#	Date	Mintage	VF	XF	Unc
56	1952	1.726	BV	14.00	17.50
	1952	.016	—	Proof	20.00

Y#	Date	Mintage	VF	XF	Unc
67	1953	.263	BV	14.00	18.00
	1953	8,000	—	Proof	25.00
	1954	.017	20.00	30.00	50.00
	1954	3,890	—	Proof	60.00
	1955	.045	14.00	17.50	25.00
	1955	2,250	—	Proof	40.00
	1956	.104	BV	14.00	20.00
	1956	2,200	—	Proof	35.00
	1957	.157	BV	14.00	20.00
	1957	1,600	—	Proof	50.00
	1958	.236	BV	14.00	17.50
	1958	1,500	—	Proof	65.00
	1959	6,139	150.00	200.00	300.00
	1959	2,200	—	Proof	350.00

50th Anniversary

Y#	Date	Mintage	VF	XF	Unc
70	1960	.422	BV	14.00	17.50
	1960	.022	—	Proof	25.00

NOTE: Many varieties exist.

1/2 SOVEREIGN

3.9940 gm., .917 GOLD, .1177 oz AGW
British type with Pretoria Mintmark: SA

Y#	Date	Mintage	VF	XF	Unc
A21	1923	655 pcs.		Proof only	1450.
	1925	.947	BV	80.00	90.00
	1926	.808	BV	80.00	90.00

NOTE: All gold 1923-32 is extensively counterfeited.

1/2 POUND

3.9940 gm., .917 GOLD, .1177 oz AGW
Similar to 1 Pound, Y#58.

Y#	Date	Mintage	VF	XF	Unc
57	1952	.016	BV	80.00	90.00
	1952	.012	—	Proof	120.00

Y#	Date	Mintage	VF	XF	Unc
68	1953	4,000	—	Proof only	125.00
	1954	1,225	—	Proof only	150.00
	1955	900 pcs.	—	Proof only	210.00
	1956	508 pcs.	—	Proof only	475.00
	1957	560 pcs.	—	Proof only	450.00
	1958	515 pcs.	—	Proof only	475.00
	1959	1,130	150.00	275.00	350.00
	1959	630 pcs.	—	Proof	400.00
	1960	3,002	80.00	100.00	150.00
	1960	1,950	—	Proof	180.00

SOVEREIGN

7.9881 gm., .917 GOLD, .2354 oz AGW
British type with Pretoria Mintmark: SA

Y#	Date	Mintage	VF	XF	Unc
22	1923	719 pcs.	400.00	600.00	1200.
	1923	655 pcs.	—	Proof	1450.
	1924	3,184	5000.	6000.	8000.
	1925	6.086	BV	BV	160.00
	1926	11.108	BV	BV	160.00
22	1927	16.380	BV	BV	160.00
	1928	18.235	BV	BV	160.00
	1929	12.024	BV	BV	160.00
	1930	10.028	BV	BV	160.00
	1931	8.512	BV	BV	160.00
	1932	1.067	BV	BV	175.00

NOTE: All gold 1923-32 is extensively counterfeited.

POUND

.917 GOLD

Y#	Date	Mintage	VF	XF	Unc
58	1952	.017	BV	BV	160.00
	1952	.012	—	Proof	175.00

Y#	Date	Mintage	VF	XF	Unc
69	1953	4,000	—	Proof only	175.00
	1954	1,225	—	Proof only	200.00
	1955	900 pcs.	—	Proof only	250.00
	1956	508 pcs.	—	Proof only	500.00
	1957	560 pcs.	—	Proof only	450.00
	1958	515 pcs.	—	Proof only	500.00
	1959	1,132	175.00	275.00	350.00
	1959	630 pcs.	—	Proof	400.00
	1960	3,111	160.00	175.00	200.00
	1960	1,950	—	Proof	225.00

REPUBLIC

DECIMAL COINAGE

100 Cents = 1 Rand

1/2 CENT

BRASS

Y#	Date	Mintage	VF	XF	Unc
71	1961	39.196	.30	.80	1.00
	1961	7,530	—	Proof	4.00
	1962	17.899	.30	.40	.50
	1962	3,844	—	Proof	4.00
	1963	11.615	.30	.80	1.00
	1963	4,025	—	Proof	4.00
	1964	9.274	.30	.80	1.00
	1964	.016	—	Proof	4.00

BRONZE
Bilingual

Y#	Date	Mintage	VF	XF	Unc
95	1970	*57.721	—	—	.10
	1970	.010	—	Proof	1.00
	1971	.020	—	—	.10
	1971	.012	—	Proof	1.00
	1972	.020	—	—	.10
	1972	.010	—	Proof	1.00
	1973	17.464	—	—	.10
	1973	.011	—	Proof	1.00
	1974	.509	—	—	.10
	1974	.015	—	Proof	1.00
	1975	10.760	—	—	.10
	1975	.018	—	Proof	.50

Y#	Date	Mintage	VF	XF	Unc
95	1977	10.000	—	—	.10
	1977	.019	—	Proof	.50
	1978	.017		in sets only	—

***NOTE:** Coins dated 1970 were also minted in 1971, 1972 and 1973.

Similar to 1 Cent, Y#106.

Y#	Date	Mintage	VF	XF	Unc
105	1976	9.762	—	—	.10
	1976	.021	—	Proof	.50

Y#	Date	Mintage	VF	XF	Unc
112	1979	—	—	Proof	.10
	1979	—	—	Proof	1.00

CENT

BRASS

Y#	Date	Mintage	VF	XF	Unc
72	1961	52.274	—	.10	1.50
	1961	7,530	—	Proof	4.50
	1962	21.933	—	.10	1.50
	1962	3,844	—	Proof	4.50
	1963	9.085	—	.10	2.00
	1963	4,025	—	Proof	4.50
	1964	14.281	—	.10	1.50
	1964	.016	—	Proof	3.00

BRONZE
English legend

Y#	Date	Mintage	VF	XF	Unc
80	1965	.026	.50	1.00	3.00
	1965	.025	—	Proof	.75
	1966	50.157	—	.05	.10
	1967	21.114	—	.05	.10
	1969	10.196	—	.05	.10

Afrikaans legend

Y#	Date	Mintage	VF	XF	Unc
80a	1965	1,031	30.00	60.00	120.00
	1966	50.182	—	.05	.15
	1966	.025	—	Proof	.75
	1967	21.139	—	.05	.10
	1967	.025	—	Proof	.75
	1969	10.208	—	.05	.10
	1969	.012	—	Proof	1.00

Charles Swart
English legend

Y#	Date	Mintage	VF	XF	Unc
88	1968	6.025	—	.05	.10
	1968	.025	—	Proof	1.00

Afrikaans legend

Y#	Date	Mintage	VF	XF	Unc
88a	1968	6.000	—	.05	.10

Bilingual

Y#	Date	Mintage	VF	XF	Unc
96	1970	37.082	—	—	.10
	1970	.010	—	Proof	1.00
	1971	34.065	—	—	.15
	1971	.012	—	Proof	1.00
	1972	35.672	—	—	.10
	1972	.010	—	Proof	1.00
	1973	1.770	—	—	.10
	1973	.011	—	Proof	1.00
	1974	54.954	—	—	.10
	1974	.015	—	Proof	1.00
	1975	63.752	—	—	—
	1975	.018	—	Proof	1.00
	1977	72.463	—	—	.10
	1977	.019	—	Proof	.75
	1978	74.811	—	—	.10
	1978	.017	—	Proof	1.00

Y#	Date	Mintage	VF	XF	Unc
106	1976	91.860	—	—	.10
	1976	.021	—	Proof	.75

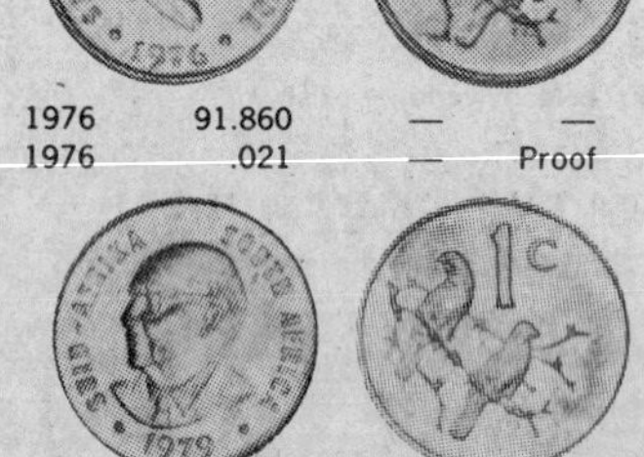

Y#	Date	Mintage	VF	XF	Unc
113	1979	—	—	Proof	.10
	1979	—	—	Proof	1.00

2 CENTS

BRONZE
English legend

Y#	Date	Mintage	VF	XF	Unc
81	1965	29.887	—	.05	.15
	1965	85 pcs.	—	Proof	50.00
	1966	9.292	—	.05	.15
	1966	.025	—	Proof	1.00
	1967	11.887	—	.05	.15
	1967	.025	—	Proof	1.00
	1969	5.829	—	.05	.15
	1969	.012	—	Proof	1.50

Afrikaans legend

Y#	Date	Mintage	VF	XF	Unc
81a	1965	29.912	—	.05	.15
	1965	.025	—	Proof	1.00
	1966	9.267	—	.05	.15
	1967	11.862	—	.05	.15
	1969	5.817	—	.05	.15

Charles Swart
English legend

Y#	Date	Mintage	VF	XF	Unc
89	1968	5.500	—	.05	.15

Afrikaans legend

Y#	Date	Mintage	VF	XF	Unc
89a	1968	5.525	—	.05	.15
	1968	.025	—	Proof	1.00

Bilingual

Y#	Date	Mintage	VF	XF	Unc
97	1970	35.227	—	—	.15
	1970	.010	—	Proof	1.00
	1971	24.105	—	—	.15
	1971	.012	—	Proof	1.00
	1972	7.314	—	—	.15
	1972	.010	—	Proof	1.00
	1973	18.696	—	—	.15
	1973	.011	—	Proof	1.00
	1974	25.315	—	—	.15
	1974	.015	—	Proof	1.00
	1975	25.000	—	—	—
	1975	.018	—	Proof	1.00
	1977	45.135	—	—	.15
	1977	.019	—	Proof	1.00
	1978	50.544	—	—	.15
	1978	.017	—	Proof	1.00

Y#	Date	Mintage	VF	XF	Unc
107	1976	51.474	—	—	.15
	1976	.021	—	Proof	1.00

Y#	Date	Mintage	VF	XF	Unc
117	1979	—	—	—	.25
	1979	—	—	Proof	1.00

2-1/2 CENTS

1.4100 gm., .500 SILVER, .0226 oz ASW

Y#	Date	Mintage	VF	XF	Unc
73	1961	.299	1.50	2.50	4.50
	1961	7,530	—	Proof	9.00
	1962	.013	5.00	10.00	13.00
	1962	3,844	—	Proof	18.00
	1963	.037	4.00	7.00	10.00
	1963	4,025	—	Proof	14.00
	1964	.030	4.00	8.00	11.00
	1964	.016	—	Proof	14.00

5 CENTS

2.8300 gm., .500 SILVER, .0454 oz ASW

Y#	Date	Mintage	VF	XF	Unc
74	1961	1.486	BV	BV	2.00
	1961	7,530	—	Proof	5.00
	1962	4.192	BV	BV	1.50

Y#	Date	Mintage	VF	XF	Unc
74	1962	3,844	—	Proof	5.00
	1963	8.058	BV	BV	1.50
	1963	4,025	—	Proof	5.00
	1964	3.583	BV	BV	1.50
	1964	.016	—	Proof	4.00

NICKEL
English legend

Y#	Date	Mintage	VF	XF	Unc
82	1965	32.715	—	.10	.35
	1965	.025	—	Proof	1.00
	1966	4.101	—	.10	.35
	1967	4.590	—	.10	.35
	1969	5.020	—	.10	.35

Afrikaans legend

Y#	Date	Mintage	VF	XF	Unc
82a	1965	32.690	—	.10	.35
	1965	85 pcs.	—	Proof	50.00
	1966	4.126	—	.10	.35
	1966	.025	—	Proof	1.00
	1967	4.615	—	.10	.35
	1967	.025	—	Proof	1.00
	1969	5.020	—	.10	.35
	1969	.012	—	Proof	1.00

Charles Swart
English legend

Y#	Date	Mintage	VF	XF	Unc
90	1968	6.025	—	.10	.35
	1968	.025	—	Proof	1.00

Afrikaans legend

Y#	Date	Mintage	VF	XF	Unc
90a	1968	6.000	—	.10	.35

Bilingual

Y#	Date	Mintage	VF	XF	Unc
98	1970	6.662	—	—	.35
	1970	.010	—	Proof	1.50
	1971	20.341	—	—	.35
	1971	.012	—	Proof	1.50
	1972	3.126	—	—	.35
	1972	.010	—	Proof	1.50
	1973	17.103	—	—	.35
	1973	.011	—	Proof	1.50
	1974	19.993	—	—	.35
	1974	.015	—	Proof	1.00
	1975	22.000	—	—	.20
	1975	.018	—	Proof	1.00
	1977	51.748	—	—	.15
	1977	.019	—	Proof	1.00
	1978	25.659	—	—	.15
	1978	.017	—	Proof	1.00

Y#	Date	Mintage	VF	XF	Unc
108	1976	48.991	—	—	.15
	1976	.021	—	Proof	1.00

Y#	Date	Mintage	VF	XF	Unc
115	1979	—	—	—	.15
	1979	—	—	Proof	1.00

10 CENTS

5.6600 gm., .500 SILVER, .0909 oz ASW

Y#	Date	Mintage	VF	XF	Unc
75	1961	1.143	BV	2.75	4.00
	1961	7,530	—	Proof	7.00
	1962	2.451	BV	2.75	4.00
	1962	3,844	—	Proof	7.00
	1963	3.331	BV	2.75	4.00
	1963	4,025	—	Proof	7.00
	1964	4.169	BV	2.75	4.00
	1964	.016	—	Proof	5.00

NICKEL
English legend

Y#	Date	Mintage	VF	XF	Unc
83	1965	29.210	—	.15	.50
	1965	85 pcs.	—	Proof	50.00
	1966	3.710	—	.15	.50
	1966	.025	—	Proof	1.50
	1967	.075	—	—	1.00
	1967	.025	—	Proof	4.50
	1969	.558	—	.15	.50
	1969	.012	—	Proof	4.00

Afrikaans legend

Y#	Date	Mintage	VF	XF	Unc
83a	1965	29.235	—	.15	.50
	1965	.025	—	Proof	1.50
	1966	3.685	—	.15	.50
	1967	.050	.35	.75	1.50
	1969	.558	—	.15	.50

Charles Swart
English legend

Y#	Date	Mintage	VF	XF	Unc
91	1968	.050	.30	.60	1.00

Afrikaans legend

Y#	Date	Mintage	VF	XF	Unc
91a	1968	.075	.35	.75	3.00
	1968	.025	—	Proof	5.00

Bilingual

Y#	Date	Mintage	VF	XF	Unc
99	1970	7.608	—	—	.35
	1970	.010	—	Proof	3.00
	1971	6.452	—	—	.35
	1971	.012	—	Proof	3.00
	1972	10.038	—	—	.25
	1972	.010	—	Proof	3.00
	1973	1.770	—	—	.25
	1973	.011	—	Proof	3.00
	1974	9.912	—	—	.25
	1974	.015	—	Proof	3.00
	1975	13.006	—	—	.25
	1975	.018	—	Proof	3.00
	1977	28.870	—	—	.25
	1977	.019	—	Proof	1.00
	1978	25.026	—	—	.25
	1978	.017	—	Proof	1.00

Similar to 1 Cent, Y#106.

Y#	Date	Mintage	VF	XF	Unc
109	1976	30.986	—	—	.25
	1976	.021	—	Proof	2.00

Obv.: Similar to 5 Cents, Y# 115. Rev.: Similar to Y# 99.

Y#	Date	Mintage	VF	XF	Unc
116	1979	—	—	—	.25
	1979	—	—	Proof	2.00

20 CENTS

11.3100 gm., .500 SILVER, .1818 oz ASW

Y#	Date	Mintage	VF	XF	Unc
76	1961	2.962	BV	5.50	6.50
	1961	7,530	—	Proof	7.50
	1962	3.572	BV	5.50	6.50
	1962	3,844	—	Proof	7.50
	1963	4.384	BV	5.50	6.50
	1963	4,025	—	Proof	7.50
	1964	4.351	BV	5.50	6.50
	1964	.016	—	Proof	7.50

NICKEL
English legend

Y#	Date	Mintage	VF	XF	Unc
84	1965	29.235	—	.30	.75
	1965	.025	—	Proof	2.00
	1966	4.049	—	.30	.75
	1967	.058	—	—	1.50
	1969	9,952	—	—	15.00

Afrikaans legend

Y#	Date	Mintage	VF	XF	Unc
84a	1965	29.210	—	.30	.75
	1965	85 pcs.	—	Proof	50.00
	1966	4.074	—	.30	.75
	1966	.025	—	Proof	3.00

Y#	Date	Mintage	VF	XF	Unc
84a	1967	.083	—	—	1.50
	1967	.025	—	Proof	6.00
	1969	.021	—	—	10.00
	1969	.012	—	Proof	15.00

Charles Swart
English legend

Y#	Date	Mintage	VF	XF	Unc
92	1968	.075	—	—	3.00
	1968	.025	—	Proof	7.00

Afrikaans legend

Y#	Date	Mintage	VF	XF	Unc
92a	1968	.050	—	—	3.00

Bilingual

Y#	Date	Mintage	VF	XF	Unc
100	1970	.024	3.00	5.00	10.00
	1970	.010	—	Proof	15.00
	1971	5.905	—	—	.75
	1971	.012	—	Proof	6.00
	1972	9.079	—	—	.75
	1972	.010	—	Proof	6.00
	1973	.031	—	—	8.00
	1973	.011	—	Proof	10.00
	1974	2.451	—	—	.75
	1974	.015	—	Proof	5.00
	1975	13.000	—	—	.75
	1975	.018	—	Proof	3.00
	1977	30.669	—	.25	.40
	1977	.019	—	Proof	2.00
	1978	10.067	—	—	.40
	1978	.017	—	Proof	2.50

Y#	Date	Mintage	VF	XF	Unc
110	1976	18.826	—	.25	.40
	1976	.021	—	Proof	3.00

Obv.: Similar to 5 Cents, Y#115. Rev.: Similar to Y#100.

Y#	Date	Mintage	VF	XF	Unc
117	1979	—	—	—	.30
	1979	—	—	Proof	2.50

50 CENTS

28.2800 gm., .500 SILVER, .4546 oz ASW

Y#	Date	Mintage	VF	XF	Unc
77	1961	.055	BV	17.50	20.00
	1961	.020	—	Proof	25.00
	1962	.024	BV	17.50	25.00
	1962	6,024	—	Proof	35.00
	1963*	.158	BV	15.00	17.50
	1963	.010	—	Proof	22.50
	1964	.127	BV	15.00	17.50
	1964	.025	—	Proof	22.50

*2 varieties, narrow, high relief and wide, low letters.

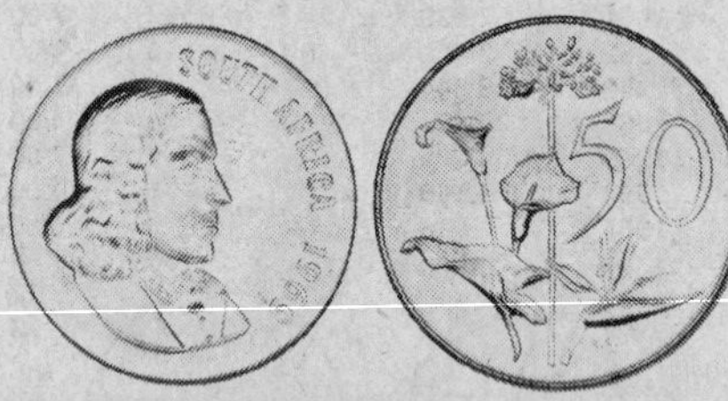

NICKEL
English legend

Y#	Date	Mintage	VF	XF	Unc
85	1965	Est. 30 pcs.	600.00	800.00	1500.
	1965	85 pcs.	—	Proof	70.00
	1966	8.081	—	.75	1.50
	1966	.025	—	Proof	4.00
	1967	.077		In sets only	2.25
	1967	.025	—	Proof	6.00
	1969	7,968		In sets only	10.00
	1969	.012	—	Proof	6.00

Afrikaans legend

Y#	Date	Mintage	VF	XF	Unc
85a	1965	.028	3.00	4.00	5.00
	1965	.025	—	Proof	10.00
	1966	8.056	—	.75	1.00
	1967	.052		In sets only	6.00
	1969	7,968		In sets only	20.00

Charles Swart
English legend

Y#	Date	Mintage	VF	XF	Unc
93	1968	.750	.50	.75	1.50

Afrikaans legend

Y#	Date	Mintage	VF	XF	Unc
93a	1968	.775	.50	.75	1.50
	1968	.025	—	Proof	10.00

Bilingual

Y#	Date	Mintage	VF	XF	Unc
101	1970	4.108	—	—	1.00
	1970	.010	—	Proof	4.00
	1971	5.074	—	—	1.00
	1971	.012	—	Proof	4.00
	1972	.781	.50	.75	1.50
	1972	.010	—	Proof	4.00
	1973	1.054	—	—	1.00
	1973	.011	—	Proof	4.00
	1974	1.957	—	—	1.00
	1974	.015	—	Proof	4.00
	1975	4.906	—	—	1.00
	1975	.018	—	Proof	4.00
	1977	10.215	—	.75	1.00
	1977	.019	—	Proof	3.00
	1978	5.088	—	—	.75
	1978	.017	—	Proof	3.00

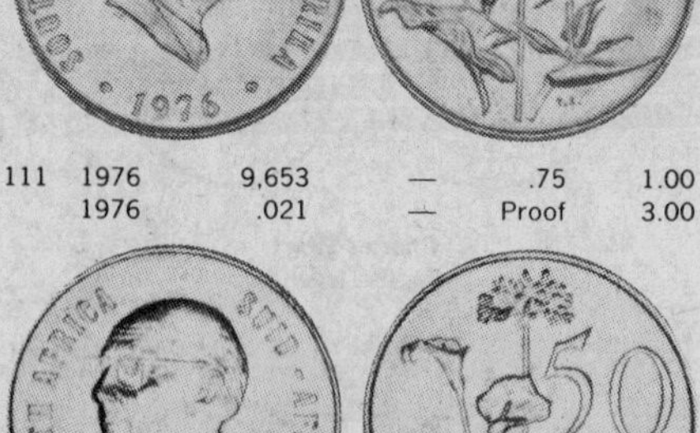

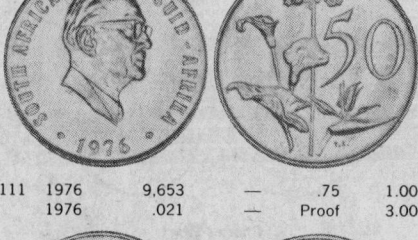

Y#	Date	Mintage	VF	XF	Unc
111	1976	9,653	—	.75	1.00
	1976	.021	—	Proof	3.00

Y#	Date	Mintage	VF	XF	Unc
118	1979	—	—	—	.75
	1979	—	—	Proof	3.00

RAND

3.9940 gm., .917 GOLD, .1177 oz AGW

Y#	Date	Mintage	VF	XF	Unc
78	1961	8,178	BV	BV	80.00
	1961	3,932	—	Proof	110.00
	1962	6,299	BV	BV	80.00
	1962	2,344	—	Proof	130.00
	1963	6,531	BV	BV	80.00
	1963	2,508	—	Proof	100.00
	1964	9,866	BV	BV	80.00
	1964	4,000	—	Proof	115.00
	1965	.016	BV	BV	80.00
	1965	6,024	—	Proof	100.00
	1966	.021	BV	BV	80.00
	1966	.011	—	Proof	100.00
	1967	.021	BV	BV	80.00
	1967	.011	—	Proof	100.00
	1968	.020	BV	BV	80.00
	1968	.011	—	Proof	100.00
	1969	.018	BV	BV	80.00
	1969	8,000	—	Proof	100.00
	1970	.017	BV	BV	80.00
	1970	6,000	—	Proof	100.00
	1971	.018	BV	BV	80.00
	1971	7,650	—	Proof	100.00
	1972	.020	BV	BV	80.00
	1972	7,500	—	Proof	100.00

Y#	Date	Mintage	VF	XF	Unc
78	1973	.027	BV	BV	80.00
	1973	.013	—	Proof	100.00
	1974	.039	BV	BV	80.00
	1974	.017	—	Proof	100.00
	1975	.042	BV	BV	80.00
	1975	.020	—	Proof	100.00
	1976	.012	BV	BV	80.00
	1976	.020	—	Proof	100.00
	1977	.027	BV	BV	80.00
	1977	.012	—	P/L	—
	1977	.020	—	Proof	100.00
	1978	.021	—	—	80.00
	1978	.013	—	Proof	100.00

15.0000 gm., .800 SILVER, .3858 oz ASW

English legend

Y#	Date	Mintage	VF	XF	Unc
86	1965	.027	12.00	15.00	17.50
	1965	.025	—	Proof	20.00
	1966	1.434	BV	BV	12.00
	1966	20 pcs.	—	Proof	2500.
	1968	.075		In sets only	12.00
	1968	.025	—	Proof	15.00

Afrikaans legend

Rev: Similar to 1 Rand Y#86

Y#	Date	Mintage	VF	XF	Unc
86a	1965	85 pcs.		V.I.P. Proof	1000.
	1966	1.459	BV	BV	12.00
	1966	.025	—	Proof	12.00
	1968	.050		In sets only	15.00
	1968	20 pcs.	—	Proof	2500.

Verwoerd

English legend

Rev: Similar to 1 Rand Y#86

Y#	Date	Mintage	VF	XF	Unc
87	1967	1.544	BV	BV	12.00
	1967	20 pcs.	—	Proof	2500.

Afrikaans legend

Rev: Similar to 1 Rand Y#86

Y#	Date	Mintage	VF	XF	Unc
87a	1967	1.569	BV	BV	12.00
	1967	.025	—	Proof	15.00

Dr. T. E. Donges

English legend

Y#	Date	Mintage	VF	XF	Unc
94	1969	.506	BV	BV	12.00
	1969	20 pcs.	—	Proof	2500.

Afrikaans legend

Rev: Similar to 1 Rand Y#94

Y#	Date	Mintage	VF	XF	Unc
94a	1969	.517	BV	BV	12.00
	1969	.012	—	Proof	17.50

Bilingual

Y#	Date	Mintage	VF	XF	Unc
102	1970	.024	BV	BV	12.00
	1970	.010	—	Proof	15.00
	1971	.032	BV	BV	12.00
	1971	.012	—	Proof	15.00
	1972	.030	BV	BV	12.00
	1972	.010	—	Proof	15.00
	1973	.031	BV	BV	12.00
	1973	.011	—	Proof	15.00
	1975	.038	BV	BV	12.00
	1975	.018	—	Proof	15.00
	1976	.041	BV	BV	12.00
	1976	.021	—	Proof	15.00
	1977	.019	—	Proof	15.00
	1978	—	—	—	—

.800 SILVER

Y#	Date	Mintage	VF	XF	Unc
103	1974	.035	BV	BV	12.00
	1974	.015	—	Proof	17.50
	1977	.019	—	Proof	15.00
	1978	.019	—	Proof	15.00

NICKEL

Y#	Date	Mintage	VF	XF	Unc
112	1977	29.871	.50	1.00	2.50

Y#	Date	Mintage	VF	XF	Unc
119	1979	—	—	—	2.50
	1979	—	—	Proof	5.00

2 RAND

7.9881 gm., .917 GOLD, .2354 oz AGW

Y#	Date	Mintage	VF	XF	Unc
79	1961	6,946	BV	BV	160.00
	1961	3,932	—	Proof	175.00
	1962	.012	BV	BV	160.00
	1962	2,344	—	Proof	200.00
	1963	5,687	BV	BV	160.00
	1963	2,508	—	Proof	175.00
	1964	7,994	BV	BV	160.00
	1964	4,000	—	Proof	175.00
	1965	.016	BV	BV	160.00
	1965	6,109	—	Proof	175.00
	1966	.021	BV	BV	160.00
	1966	.011	—	Proof	175.00
	1967	.021	BV	BV	160.00
	1967	.011	—	Proof	175.00
	1968	.021	BV	BV	160.00
	1968	.011	—	Proof	175.00
	1969	.018	BV	BV	160.00
	1969	8,000	—	Proof	175.00
	1970	.010	BV	BV	160.00
	1970	6,000	—	Proof	175.00
	1971	.010	BV	BV	160.00
	1971	7,650	—	Proof	175.00
	1972	.010	BV	BV	160.00
	1972	7,500	—	Proof	175.00

Y#	Date	Mintage	VF	XF	Unc
	1973	.010	BV	BV	160.00
	1973	.013	—	Proof	175.00
	1974	.029	BV	BV	160.00
	1974	.017	—	Proof	175.00
	1975	.032	BV	BV	160.00
	1975	.020	—	Proof	175.00
	1976	.012	BV	BV	160.00
	1976	.026	—	Proof	175.00
	1977	—	BV	BV	160.00
	1977	.012	—	P/L	—
	1977	.020	—	Proof	175.00
	1978	.011	—	P/L	160.00
	1978	.019	—	Proof	175.00

TRADE COINS

KRUGERRAND

33.9305 gm., .917 GOLD, 1.0000 oz AGW

These pieces contain one Troy ounce of gold and uncirculated specimens are sold slightly above the current market value of gold.

Y#	Date	Mintage	VF	XF	Unc
104	1967	.050	BV	BV	650.00
	1967	—	—	Proof	*—
	1968	.030	BV	BV	650.00
	1968 with frosted bust and frosted reverse				
		Inc. Ab	—	1250.	2000.
	1968	—	—	Proof	*—
	1969	.020	BV	BV	650.00
	1969	—	—	Proof	*—

***NOTE:** In 1967-1969 superior quality specimens exhibiting proof-like surfaces are known. In addition, the following varieties are known: 1968 with normal mirror like obverse and reverse; 1968 with mirror like obverse and frosted reverse; 1969 with normal mirror like obverse and reverse; and 1969 with frosted bust and reverse frosted.

Y#	Date	Mintage	XF	Unc	Proof
104	1970	.211	BV	650.00	—
	1970	.010	—	Proof	750.00
	1971	.550	BV	650.00	—
	1971	6,000	—	—	750.00
	1972	.544	BV	650.00	—
	1972	6,625	—	—	750.00
	1973	.859	BV	650.00	—
	1973	.010	—	—	700.00
	1974	3.203	BV	650.00	—
	1974	6,352	—	—	700.00
	1975	5.581	BV	650.00	—
	1975	5,600	—	—	750.00
	1976	—	BV	650.00	—
	1976	6,000	—	—	750.00
	1977 188 serrations on edge				
		8,500	—	—	—
	1977 220 serrations on edge				
		—	BV	650.00	750.00
	1978	—	—	P/L	—
	1978	—	—	—	—

NCLT ISSUES

SPECIAL SELECTS (S/S)

Special selects are crowns struck specially using buffed up proof dies. Their appearance is prooflike but with magnification one can usually see raised hair lines on the surface of the field caused by the buffing operation of the already polished dies used for striking proof quality coins.

Y#	Date	Mintage	Identification	Issue Price	Mkt Val.
48	1948	10,000	5 Shillings, KGVI	—	25.00
	1949	2,000	5 Shillings, KGVI	—	37.50
	1950	1,200	5 Shillings, KGVI	—	75.00
53	1951	1,483	5 Shillings, KGVI	—	35.00
56	1952	12,000	5 Shillings, Capetown	—	20.00
67	1953	8,000	5 Shillings, QEII	—	20.00
	1954	3,890	5 Shillings, QEII	—	55.00
	1955	2,230	5 Shillings, QEII	—	30.00
	1956	2,200	5 Shillings, QEII	—	30.00
	1957	1,600	5 Shillings, QEII	—	40.00
67	1958	1,500	5 Shillings, QEII	—	35.00
	1959	2,200	5 Shillings, QEII	—	300.00
70	1960	22,367	5 Shillings, 50th Anniversary	—	17.50
77	1961	19,956	50 Cents, van Riebeeck	—	15.00
	1962	6,024	50 Cents, van Riebeeck	—	25.00
	1963	10,227	50 Cents, van Riebeeck	—	15.00
	1964	25,000	50 Cents, van Riebeeck	—	15.00

MINT SETS

KM#	Date	Mintage	Identification	Issue Price	Mkt. Val.
77	1964(7)	—	Y71-77	—	—
S1	1967(7)	50,000	Y80-85,87,(English)	7.50	9.00
S2	1967(7)	50,000	Y80a-85a,87a(Afrikaans)	7.50	15.00
S3	1968(7)	50,000	Y86,88-93(English)	7.50	9.00
S4	1968(7)	50,000	Y86a,88a-93a(Afrikaans)	7.50	9.00
S5	1969(7)	5,000	Y80-85,94(English)	7.50	35.00
S6	1969(7)	5,000	Y80a-85a,94a(Afrikaans)	7.50	50.00
S7	1970(8)	14,000	Y95-102	7.50	25.00
S8	1971(8)	20,000	Y95-102	7.50	25.00
S9	1972(8)	20,000	Y95-102	7.50	25.00
S10	1973(8)	20,000	Y95-102	7.50	22.50
S11	1974(8)	20,000	Y95-101,103	7.50	12.50
S12	1975(8)	20,000	Y95-101,102	7.50	16.00
S13	1976(8)	20,000	Y102,105-111	5.65	16.00
S14	1977(8)	20,000	Y105-111,Nickel 1 Rand	—	14.00

PROOF SETS

STANDARD METALS

KM#	Date	Mintage	Identification	Issue Price	Mkt. Val.
102	1923(10)	655	Y11-13,15,16,19-22,A21	—	3735.
103	1923(8)	747	Y11-13,15,16,19-21	—	835.00
104	1926(8)	16	Y11A,12,13A,17-18,19A,20,21A		
105	1930(8)	14	Y11A-13A,17-18		
			19A,20,21A	—	8000.
106	1931(8)	62	Y23-30	—	12,000.
107	1932(8)	12	Y23-30	—	8500.
108	1933(8)	20	Y23-30	—	10,750.
109	1934(8)	24	Y23-30	—	10,750.
110	1935(8)	20	Y23-30	—	7900.
111	1936(8)	40	Y23-30	—	8500.
112	1937(8)	116	Y31-38	—	1600.
113	1938(8)	500.	Y31-38	—	3500.
114	1939(8)	30	Y31-38	—	10,000.
115	1943(8)	104	Y31-38	—	1200.
116	1944(8)	150	Y31-38	—	1000.
117	1945(8)	150	Y31-38	—	1000.
118	1946(8)	150	Y31-38	—	1150.
119	1947(9)	2,600	Y31-39	—	525.00
120	1948(9)	1,120	Y40-48	—	500.00
121	1949(9)	800	Y40-48	—	925.00
122	1950(9)	500	Y40-48	—	900.00
123	1951(9)	2,000	Y41,43A,45A,47A,49-53	—	150.00
124	1952(11)	12,000	Y41,43A,45A,47A,49-52,56-58	—	375.00
125	1952(9)	3,500	Y41,43A,45A,47A,49-52,56	—	100.00
126	1953(11)	3,000	Y59-69	29.40	400.00
127	1953(9)	2,000	Y59-67	4.35	100.00
128	1953(2)	1,000	Y68,69	25.20	300.00
129	1954(11)	875	Y59-69	29.40	525.00
130	1954(9)	2,275	Y59-67	4.35	175.00
131	1954(2)	350	Y68,69	25.20	350.00
132	1955(11)	600	Y59-69	29.40	575.00
133	1955(9)	2,250	Y59-67	4.35	135.00
134	1955(2)	300	Y68,69	25.20	450.00
135	1956(11)	350	Y59-69	29.40	1100.
136	1956(9)	1,350	Y59-67	4.35	150.00
137	1956(2)	158	Y68,69	25.20	975.00
138	1957(11)	380	Y59-69	29.40	1100.
139	1957(9)	750	Y59-67	4.35	200.00
140	1957(2)	180	Y68,69	25.20	900.00
141	1958(11)	360	Y59-69	29.40	1200.
142	1958(9)	625	Y59-67	4.35	250.00
143	1958(2)	155	Y68,69	25.20	975.00
144	1959(11)	390	Y59-69	29.40	1350.
145	1959(9)	560	Y59-67	4.35	550.00
146	1959(2)	240	Y68,69	25.20	800.00
147	1960(11)	1,500	Y59-66,68-69,70	29.40	525.00
148	1960(9)	1,860	Y59-66,70	4.35	120.00
149	1960(2)	450	Y68,69	25.20	400.00
150	1961(9)	3,139	Y71-79	—	340.00
151	1961(7)	4,391	Y71-77	—	60.00
152	1961(2)	793	Y78,79	—	285.00
153	1962(9)	1,544	Y71-79	—	400.00
154	1962(7)	2,300	Y71-77	—	80.00
155	1962(2)	800	Y78,79	—	325.00
156	1963(9)	1,500	Y71-79	—	350.00
157	1963(7)	2,525	Y71,77	—	65.00
158	1963(2)	1,008	Y78,79	—	275.00
159	1964(9)	2,000	Y71-79	—	345.00
160	1964(7)	16,948	Y71-77	—	60.00
161	1964(2)	1,000	Y78-79	—	290.00
162	1965(9)	5,099	Y78,79,80,81a,82,		
			83a,84,85a,86	23.50	310.00
163	1965(9)	85	Y78,79,80,81,82a,83,84a,		
			85,86a,V.I.P.	—	1500.
164	1965(7)	19,889	Y80,81a,82,83a,		
			84,85a,86	5.00	35.00
165	1965(2)	925	Y78,79	18.15	275.00
166	1966(9)	10,000	78-79,80A,81,82A,83,84A,85,86A	24.10	300.00
167	1966(7)	15,000	80A,81,82A,83,84A,85,86A	5.00	25.00
168	1966(2)	1,000	Y78,79	18.15	275.00
169	1967(9)	10,000	Y80a,81,82a,83		
			84a,85,87a,78,79	24.10	310.00
170	1967(7)	15,000	Y80A,81,82A,83,84A,85,87A	5.00	35.00
171	1967(2)	1,000	Y78,79	18.15	275.00
172	1968(9)	10,000	Y86,88a,89,90a,91		
			92a,93,78,79	35.00	300.00
173	1968(7)	15,000	Y86,88,89,90		
			91A,92,93A	16.00	32.00
174	1968(2)	1,000	Y78,79	28.00	275.00
175	1969(9)	7,000	Y80a,81,82a,83		
			84a,85,94a,78,79	34.85	320.00
176	1969(7)	5,000	Y80a,81,82a,83		
			84a,85,94a	13.95	45.00
177	1969(2)	1,000	Y78,79	27.85	275.00
178	1970(10)	6,000	Y95-102,78,79	35.05	315.00
179	1970(8)	4,000	Y95-102	14.00	40.00
180	1970(2)	1,000	Y78,79	28.05	275.00
181	1971(10)	7,000	Y95-102,78-79	35.00	300.00
182	1971(8)	5,000	Y95-102	14.00	30.00
183	1971(2)	650	Y78,79	28.00	275.00
184	1972(10)	6,000	Y95-102,78-79	32.80	300.00
185	1972(8)	4,000	Y95-102	13.10	30.00
186	1972(2)	1,500	Y78,79	26.25	275.00
187	1973(10)	6,850	Y95-102,78-79	32.00	300.00
188	1973(8)	4,000	Y95-102	12.80	30.00
189	1973(2)	6,088	Y78,79	25.60	275.00
190	1974(10)	11,000	Y95-101,103,78,79	52.50	300.00
191	1974(8)	4,000	Y95-101,103	15.00	30.00
192	1974(2)	5,600	Y78,79	45.00	275.00
193	1975(10)	12,500	Y95-101,103,78,79	116.40	300.00
194	1975(8)	5,512	Y95-101,102	14.55	30.00
195	1975(2)	7,000	Y78-79	101.85	275.00
196	1976(10)	14,000	Y78-79,102,105-111	92.00	300.00
197	1976(8)	7,000	Y102,105-111	11.50	30.00
198	1976(2)	12,000	Y78-79	80.50	275.00
199	1977(10)	12,000	Y78-79,102,105-111	92.00	300.00
200	1977(8)	7,000	Y102,105-111	11.50	30.00
201	1977(2)	8,500	Y78-79	80.50	275.00
202	1978 10		Y95-101,103,78-79	—	300.00
203	1978 8	—	Y95-101	—	25.00
204	1978 2	—	Y78-79	—	275.00
205	1979 8	—	Y112-119	—	16.00

Listings For

SOUTH ARABIA: refer to Yemen Democratic Republic

SOUTH KOREA: refer to Korea/South

SOUTH VIETNAM: refer to Vietnam/South

SOUTHERN RHODESIA: refer to Zimbabwe

SOVIET CENTRAL ASIA: refer to Russian Turkestan

SPAIN

The Spanish State, forming the greater part of the Iberian Peninsula of southwest Europe, has an area of 195,988 sq. mi. (507,606 sq. km.) and a population of 36.4 million including the Balearic and the Canary Islands. Capital: Madrid. The economy is based on agriculture, industry and tourism. Machinery, fruit, vegetables and chemicals are exported.

It isn't known when man first came to the Iberian peninsula - the Altamira caves off the Cantabrian coast approximately 50 miles west of Santander were fashioned in Palaeolithic times. Spain was a battleground for centuries before it became a united nation, fought for by Phoenicians, Carthaginians, Greeks, Celts, Romans, Vandals, Visigoths and Moors. Ferdinand and Isabella destroyed the last Moorish stronghold in 1492, freeing the national energy and resources for the era of discovery and colonization that would make Spain the most powerful country in Europe during the 16th century. After the destruction of the Spanish Armada, 1588, Spain never again played a major role in European politics. Napoleonic France ruled Spain between 1808 and 1814. The monarchy was restored in 1814 and continued, interrupted by the short-lived republic of 1873-74, until the exile of Alfonso XIII in 1931 when the Second Republic was established.

The monarchy was reconstituted in 1947 under the regency of General Francisco Franco; the king designate to be crowned after Franco's death. Franco died on Nov. 30, 1975. Two days after his passing, Juan Carlos de Borbon, the grandson of Alfonso XIII, was proclaimed King of Spain.

RULERS

Carlos III, 1759-1788
Carlos IV, 1788-1808
Jose Napoleon, 1808-1813
Ferdinand VII, 1808-1833 (in exile until 1814)
Isabel II, 1833-1868
1st Republic
Amadeo I, 1871-1873
Regency
Alfonso XII, 1875-1885
Alfonso XIII, 1886-1931
2nd Republic and Civil War
Francisco Franco, 1937-1975
Juan Carlos I, 1975 —

NOTE: From 1868 to the present time, two dates may be found on most Spanish coinage. The larger date is the year of authorization and the smaller date incused on the six pointed-star found on most types is the year of issue. The latter appears in parentheses in these listings.

MINTMARKS

(Until 1851)

B, BA - Barcelona
Bo - Bilbao
C - Catalonia
Crowned C - Cadiz
J, JA - Jubia
Crowned M - Madrid
P,P.P., P.L., PA - Pamplona
Sr - Santander
Aqueduct - Segovia
S, S/L - Seville
V, VAL - Valencia

(After 1851)

3-Pointed star - Segovia
4-Pointed star - Jubia
6-Pointed star - Madrid
7-Pointed star - Seville
8-Pointed star - Barcelona

Other letters after date are initials of mint officials.

MONETARY SYSTEM

34 Maravedi = 1 Real (of Silver)

NOTE: The early coinage of Spain is listed by denomination based on a system of 16 Reales de Plata (silver) = 1 Escudo. However, in the Constitutional period of 1820-23 a concurrent system was introduced in which 20 Reales de Vellon (billon) = 8 Reales de Plata. This system does not necessarily refer to the composition of the coin itself. To avoid confusion we have listed the coins using the value as it appears on each coin, ignoring the monetary base.

MARAVEDI

COPPER

MADRID MINT - Crowned M

Obv: Head of Charles III right.
Rev: Arms in angles of cross.

C#	Date	Mintage	Fine	VF	XF
26.1	1770	—	55.00	110.00	250.00
	1771	—	80.00	120.00	300.00

SEGOVIA MINT - Aqueduct

C#	Date	Mintage	Fine	VF	XF
26.2	1772	—	15.00	30.00	55.00
	1773	—	10.00	25.00	60.00
	1774	—	15.00	30.00	55.00
	1775	—	25.00	55.00	120.00
	1789	— Reported, Not Confirmed			

C#	Date	Mintage	Fine	VF	XF
59	1791	—	30.00	60.00	110.00
	1793	—	15.00	25.00	45.00
	1799	—	25.00	50.00	80.00
	1802	—	25.00	50.00	85.00

JUBIA MINT - J, JA

Obv: Head of Ferdinand right.
Rev: Arms in angles of cross.

C#	Date	Mintage	Fine	VF	XF
112	1824	—	17.50	20.00	30.00

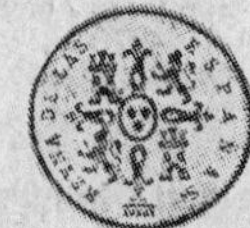

C#	Date	Mintage	Fine	VF	XF
167.1	1842	—	17.50	42.50	75.00
	1843	—	125.00	225.00	300.00

MADRID MINT - Crowned M

C#	Date	Mintage	Fine	VF	XF
167.2	1842 DG	—	150.00	200.00	250.00

SEGOVIA MINT - Aqueduct

C#	Date	Mintage	Fine	VF	XF
167.3	1842	—	13.50	27.50	50.00

2 MARAVEDIS

COPPER

MADRID MINT (Md)

C#	Date	Mintage	Fine	VF	XF
27.1	1770	—	30.00	75.00	150.00
	1771	—	35.00	85.00	190.00

SEGOVIA MINT - Aqueduct

C#	Date	Mintage	Fine	VF	XF
27.2	1772	—	8.00	15.00	25.00
	1773	—	10.00	20.00	35.00
	1774	—	7.00	12.00	25.00
	1775	—	7.00	12.00	25.00
	1776	—	10.00	20.00	40.00
	1777	—	5.00	8.00	18.00
	1778	—	8.00	15.00	25.00
	1779	—	8.00	15.00	25.00
27.2	1780	—	8.00	15.00	25.00
	1781	—	8.00	15.00	25.00
	1782	—	80.00	150.00	275.00
	1783	—	15.00	25.00	45.00
	1784	—	10.00	20.00	35.00
	1785	—	8.00	15.00	25.00
	1786	—	10.00	20.00	35.00
	1787	—	7.00	12.50	20.00
	1788	—	7.00	12.50	20.00

C#	Date	Mintage	Fine	VF	XF
60	1788	—	15.00	25.00	45.00
	1789	—	12.50	22.50	40.00
	1790	—	12.50	22.50	40.00
	1791	—	12.50	22.50	40.00
	1792	—	8.00	15.00	25.00
	1793	—	5.00	10.00	15.00
	1794	—	4.00	7.50	12.50
	1795	—	10.00	18.00	30.00
	1796	—	5.00	10.00	15.00
	1797	—	4.00	7.50	12.50
	1798	—	4.00	7.50	12.50
	1799	—	4.00	7.50	12.50
	1800	—	4.00	7.50	12.50
	1801	—	4.00	7.50	12.50
	1802	—	7.00	12.00	20.00
	1803	—	4.00	7.50	12.50
	1804	—	12.50	20.00	35.00
	1805	—	4.00	7.50	12.50
	1806	—	12.50	22.50	37.00
	1807	—	4.00	7.50	12.50
	1808	—	4.00	7.50	12.50

JUBIA MINT - J, JA

C#	Date	Mintage	Fine	VF	XF
106	1812	—	10.00	20.00	30.00
	1813	—	7.00	12.50	22.50
	1814	—	7.00	11.50	20.00
	1815	—	7.00	11.50	20.00
	1816	—	5.00	10.00	15.00
	1817	—	7.00	11.50	25.00

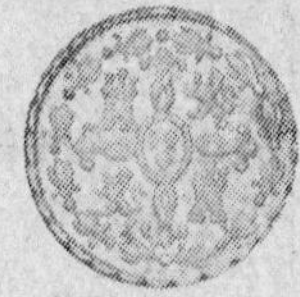

SEGOVIA MINT - Aqueduct

C#	Date	Mintage	Fine	VF	XF
116	1816	—	7.00	12.50	25.00
	1817	—	5.00	9.00	18.50
	1818	—	5.00	8.50	18.50
	1819	—	5.00	8.50	18.50
	1820	—	5.00	7.00	15.00
	1824	—	3.50	6.50	10.00
	1825	—	3.50	6.50	10.00
	1826	—	3.50	6.50	10.00
	1827	—	3.50	6.50	10.00
	1828	—	3.50	6.50	10.00
	1829	—	3.50	6.50	10.00
	1830	—	3.50	6.50	10.00
	1831	—	3.50	6.50	10.00
	1832	—	3.50	6.50	10.00
	1833	—	3.50	6.50	10.00

Obv. leg: FERDIN. IIV. (error).

C#	Date	Mintage	Fine	VF	XF
116a	1832	—	—	—	—

JUBIA MINT - J, JA

Thin laureate bust

C#	Date	Mintage	Fine	VF	XF
109	1817	—	6.00	11.50	22.50
	1818	—	5.00	10.00	20.00
	1819	—	5.00	10.00	20.00
	1820	—	5.00	10.00	20.00
	1821	—	27.50	40.00	70.00

Large bare head

C#	Date	Mintage	Fine	VF	XF
113	1824	—	6.00	11.50	22.50
	1826	—	5.00	10.00	20.00
	1827	—	7.50	13.50	27.50

BARCELONA MINT - B, BA

C#	Date	Mintage	Fine	VF	XF
168.1	1855	—	20.00	40.00	65.00
	1858	—	22.50	30.00	50.00

JUBIA MINT - J, JA

C#	Date	Mintage	Fine	VF	XF
168.2	1838	—	22.50	50.00	85.00
	1840	—	50.00	125.00	180.00
	1841	—	70.00	150.00	225.00
	1842	—	70.00	150.00	250.00
	1844	—	50.00	125.00	200.00
	1848	—	7.75	12.50	20.00
	1849	—	5.00	11.50	20.00

MADRID MINT - Crowned M

C#	Date	Mintage	Fine	VF	XF
168.3	1837 DG	—	150.00	275.00	500.00

SEGOVIA MINT - Aqueduct

C#	Date	Mintage	Fine	VF	XF
168.4	1836	—	12.50	25.00	50.00
	1837	—	12.50	20.00	40.00
	1838	—	3.50	7.50	12.50
	1839	—	3.75	7.50	17.50
	1840	—	3.50	7.50	17.50
	1841	—	3.50	7.50	17.50
	1842	—	3.50	7.50	17.50
	1843	—	3.50	7.50	17.50
	1844	—	3.50	7.50	12.50
	1845	—	3.50	7.50	12.50
	1846	—	3.50	7.50	12.50
	1847	—	3.50	7.50	12.50
	1848	—	3.50	7.00	12.50
	1849	—	3.50	7.00	12.50
	1850	—	3.50	7.00	12.50

4 MARAVEDIS

COPPER

MADRID MINT - Crowned M

C#	Date	Mintage	Fine	VF	XF
28.1	1770	—	80.00	170.00	250.00
	1771	—	100.00	180.00	300.00

SEGOVIA MINT - Aqueduct

C#	Date	Mintage	Fine	VF	XF
28.2	1772	—	10.00	18.50	28.50
	1773	—	7.00	12.50	20.00
	1774	—	5.00	8.00	15.00
	1775	—	4.00	7.50	12.50
	1776	—	8.00	15.00	20.00
	1777	—	6.00	11.50	18.50
	1778	—	6.00	11.50	18.50
	1779	—	6.00	11.50	18.50
	1780	—	6.00	11.50	18.50
	1781	—	6.00	11.50	18.50
	1782	—	6.00	11.50	18.50
	1783	—	15.00	25.00	45.00
	1784	—	10.00	18.00	30.00
	1785	—	6.00	11.50	18.50
	1786	—	8.00	15.00	22.50
	1787	—	6.00	11.50	18.50
	1788	—	6.00	11.50	18.50

C#	Date	Mintage	Fine	VF	XF
61	1788	—	30.00	50.00	90.00
	1789	—	20.00	40.00	75.00
	1790	—	18.50	35.00	65.00
	1791	—	15.00	25.00	45.00
	1792	—	10.00	18.50	30.00
	1793	—	9.00	16.50	25.00
	1794	—	8.00	14.00	20.00
	1795	—	9.00	16.50	25.00

C#	Date	Mintage	Fine	VF	XF
61	1796	—	8.00	14.00	20.00
	1797	—	9.00	16.50	25.00
	1798	—	8.00	14.00	20.00
	1799	—	9.00	16.50	25.00
	1800	—	9.00	16.50	25.00
	1801	—	4.00	7.00	12.50
	1802	—	4.00	7.00	12.50
	1803	—	4.00	7.00	12.50
	1804	—	8.00	14.00	25.00
	1805	—	8.00	14.00	25.00
	1806	—	8.00	14.00	25.00
	1807	—	7.00	12.50	20.00
	1808	—	4.00	7.00	12.50

JUBIA MINT - J, JA

Similar to 2 Maravedis, C#106.

C#	Date	Mintage	Fine	VF	XF
107	1812	—	4.50	9.00	20.00
	1813	—	4.50	9.00	17.50
	1814	—	3.50	8.00	17.50
	1815	—	4.50	10.00	17.50
	1816	—	3.50	10.00	17.50
117.1	1817	—	4.50	10.00	20.00
	1818	—	6.50	12.50	25.00

SEGOVIA MINT - Aqueduct

C#	Date	Mintage	Fine	VF	XF
117.2	1816	—	4.00	8.00	17.50
	1818	—	6.50	12.50	25.00
	1819	—	4.00	10.00	20.00
	1820	—	4.00	8.00	17.50
	1823	—	3.50	8.00	15.00
	1824	—	3.50	8.50	14.00
	1825	—	3.50	8.00	15.00
	1826	—	3.50	8.00	15.00
	1827	—	3.50	8.00	15.00
	1828	—	3.50	7.50	12.50
	1829	—	3.50	7.50	12.50
	1830	—	3.50	5.00	7.50
	1831	—	3.50	7.50	12.50
	1832	—	3.50	8.00	14.00
	1833	—	3.50	7.50	12.50

JUBIA MINT - J, JA

Small head
Similar to 2 Maravedis, C#109.

C#	Date	Mintage	Fine	VF	XF
110.1	1817	—	4.50	8.50	18.50
	1819	—	6.00	12.50	25.00
	1820	—	4.50	8.50	18.50

SEGOVIA MINT - AQUEDUCT

C#	Date	Mintage	Fine	VF	XF
110.2	1817	—	4.50	8.50	18.50

JUBIA MINT - J, JA

Large head

C#	Date	Mintage	Fine	VF	XF
114	1824	—	3.00	6.50	13.50
	1825	—	10.00	22.50	45.00
	1826	—	3.00	6.00	12.50
	1827	—	4.50	9.00	15.00
161.1	1835	—	15.00	27.50	50.00
	1836	—	10.00	20.00	45.00

MADRID MINT - Crowned M

C#	Date	Mintage	Fine	VF	XF
161.2	1836 DG	—	175.00	375.00	500.00

SEGOVIA MINT - Aqueduct

C#	Date	Mintage	Fine	VF	XF
161.3	1835	—	12.00	25.00	45.00
	1836	—	8.00	15.00	25.00

BARCELONA MINT - B, BA

C#	Date	Mintage	Fine	VF	XF
169.1	1853	—	75.00	175.00	225.00
	1855	—	50.00	90.00	150.00

JUBIA MINT - J, JA

C#	Date	Mintage	Fine	VF	XF
169.2	1837	—	10.00	20.00	40.00
	1840	—	40.00	100.00	150.00
	1841	—	10.00	20.00	40.00
	1842	—	10.00	25.00	40.00
	1843	—	10.00	20.00	35.00
	1844	—	10.00	25.00	40.00
	1845	—	7.50	14.00	25.00
	1846	—	10.00	20.00	35.00
	1847	—	6.00	20.00	40.00
	1848	—	7.50	15.00	25.00
	1849	—	10.00	20.00	40.00
	1850	—	6.75	15.00	25.00

SEGOVIA MINT - Aqueduct

C#	Date	Mintage	Fine	VF	XF
169.3	1837	—	6.00	15.00	30.00
	1838	—	6.00	15.00	30.00
	1839	—	15.00	30.00	50.00
	1840	—	6.00	20.00	35.00
	1841	—	15.00	25.00	50.00
	1842	—	5.00	15.00	25.00
	1843	—	10.00	20.00	35.00
	1844	—	5.00	14.00	25.00
	1845	—	5.00	14.00	25.00
	1846	—	5.00	14.00	25.00
	1847	—	6.50	15.00	30.00
	1848	—	6.00	15.00	30.00
	1849	—	5.00	15.00	25.00
	1850	—	10.00	27.50	50.00

8 MARAVEDIS

COPPER

MADRID MINT - Crowned M

C#	Date	Mintage	Fine	VF	XF
29.1	1770	—	70.00	130.00	250.00
	1771	—	80.00	150.00	275.00

SEGOVIA MINT - Aqueduct

C#	Date	Mintage	Fine	VF	XF
29.2	1772	—	10.00	18.50	30.00
	1773	—	8.00	14.00	20.00
	1774	—	10.00	16.50	25.00
	1775	—	8.00	14.00	20.00
	1776	—	10.00	18.50	30.00
	1777	—	5.00	10.00	18.50
	1778	—	5.00	10.00	18.50
	1779	—	5.00	10.00	18.50
	1780	—	5.00	10.00	18.50
	1781	—	5.00	10.00	18.50
	1782	—	5.00	10.00	18.50
	1783	—	30.00	55.00	120.00
	1784	—	15.00	25.00	40.00
	1785	—	5.00	10.00	18.50
	1786	—	7.00	12.50	20.00
	1787	—	5.00	10.00	18.50
	1788	—	4.00	7.00	11.50

C#	Date	Mintage	Fine	VF	XF
62	1788	—	10.00	18.50	30.00
	1789	—	18.50	35.00	75.00
	1790	—	18.50	35.00	75.00
	1791	—	15.00	25.00	40.00
	1792	—	25.00	50.00	110.00
	1793	—	10.00	18.50	30.00
	1794	—	6.00	11.50	18.50
	1795	—	6.00	12.50	20.00
	1796	—	5.00	10.00	18.50
	1797	—	5.00	10.00	18.50
	1798	—	5.00	10.00	18.50

C#	Date	Mintage	Fine	VF	XF
62	1799	—	7.00	12.50	20.00
	1800	—	7.00	13.50	20.00
	1801	—	5.00	10.00	18.50
	1802	—	5.00	10.00	18.50
	1803	—	5.00	10.00	18.50
	1804	—	6.00	11.50	20.00
	1805	—	5.00	10.00	18.50
	1806	—	6.00	11.50	20.00
	1807	—	5.00	10.00	18.50
	1808	—	4.00	7.00	12.50

C#	Date	Mintage	Fine	VF	XF
82	1809	—	15.00	25.00	35.00
	1810	—	12.50	20.00	30.00
	1811	—	12.50	20.00	30.00
	1812	—	12.50	20.00	30.00
	1813	—	15.00	25.00	35.00

JUBIA MINT - J, JA

C#	Date	Mintage	Fine	VF	XF
108	1811	—	25.00	55.00	100.00
	1812	—	17.50	32.50	65.00
	1813	—	7.00	13.50	25.00
	1814	—	7.00	13.50	25.00
	1815	—	7.00	13.50	25.00
	1816	—	5.00	10.00	20.00
	1817	—	6.00	12.50	25.00

SEGOVIA MINT - AQUEDUCT

C#	Date	Mintage	Fine	VF	XF
118	1815	—	7.50	15.00	30.00
	1816	—	5.00	10.00	25.00
	1817	—	5.00	10.00	20.00
	1818	—	5.00	10.00	20.00
	1819	—	3.50	7.50	12.50
	1820	—	5.00	11.00	20.00
	1821	—	10.00	22.50	40.00
	1822	—	10.00	22.50	40.00
	1823	—	5.00	10.00	20.00
	1824	—	4.00	8.00	15.00
	1825	—	4.50	8.00	17.50
	1826	—	4.50	8.00	15.00
	1827	—	5.00	12.50	18.50
	1828	—	10.00	20.00	40.00
	1829	—	4.00	8.00	15.00
	1830	—	5.00	10.00	15.00
	1831	—	3.50	7.00	12.50
	1832	—	3.50	6.00	11.50
	1833	—	3.50	6.00	11.50

JUBIA MINT - J, JA

C#	Date	Mintage	Fine	VF	XF
111	1817	—	4.00	8.50	20.00
	1818	—	3.50	6.50	12.50
111	1819	—	3.50	6.50	12.50
	1820	—	3.50	6.50	12.50
	1821	—	3.00	6.00	12.00

Obv: Bust, leg: FERN 7o POR LA....

C#	Date	Mintage	Fine	VF	XF
115	1822	—	9.00	15.00	30.00
	1823	—	6.50	10.00	16.50

Obv: Value omitted

C#	Date	Mintage	Fine	VF	XF
115a	1823	—	9.00	15.00	30.00

Obv: Bust, leg: FERDIN.VII D.G.HISP.REX.

C#	Date	Mintage	Fine	VF	XF
114.5	1823	—	8.00	14.00	25.00
	1824	—	8.00	13.50	20.00
	1825	—	8.00	13.50	20.00
	1826	—	7.50	10.00	15.00
	1827	—	7.00	10.00	18.50

SEGOVIA MINT - Aqueduct

C#	Date	Mintage	Fine	VF	XF
114.7	1823	—	6.50	10.00	18.50

PAMPLONA MINT - P, P.P., P.L., PA

Obv: Bust, leg: FERDIN.VII.D.G. HISP.REX.

C#	Date	Mintage	Fine	VF	XF
118a	1823	—	15.00	25.00	50.00

JUBIA MINT - J, JA

C#	Date	Mintage	Fine	VF	XF
162.1	1835	—	7.50	16.50	35.00
	1836	—	9.00	25.00	45.00

MADRID MINT - Crowned M

C#	Date	Mintage	Fine	VF	XF
162.2	1835 DG	—	75.00	150.00	225.00

SEGOVIA MINT - Aqueduct

C#	Date	Mintage	Fine	VF	XF
162.3	1835	—	6.75	20.00	35.00
	1836	—	5.00	14.00	25.00

CAST BELL METAL

PAMPLONA MINT - P, P.P., P.L., PA

C#	Date	Mintage	VG	Fine	VF
170a.1	1837	—	15.00	40.00	65.00

Mintmark within oval

C#	Date	Mintage	VG	Fine	VF
170a.2	1837	—	15.00	25.00	45.00

COPPER

BARCELONA MINT - B, BA

C#	Date	Mintage	Fine	VF	XF
170.1	1853	—	45.00	65.00	125.00
	1854	*	375.00	550.00	750.00
	1855	—	45.00	100.00	175.00
	1858	—	10.00	25.00	45.00

*NOTE: Only counterfeits seen.

JUBIA MINT - J, JA

C#	Date	Mintage	Fine	VF	XF
170.2	1837	—	4.50	12.50	25.00
	1838	—	5.75	15.00	35.00
	1839	—	12.50	25.00	60.00
	1840	—	14.00	32.50	70.00
	1841	—	6.00	15.00	30.00
	1842	—	5.00	13.00	25.00
	1843	—	4.00	12.50	25.00
	1844	—	5.00	12.50	32.50
	1845	—	4.75	12.50	17.50
	1846	—	6.75	17.50	40.00
	1847	—	15.00	35.00	75.00
	1848	—	4.50	12.50	16.50
	1849	—	12.00	18.50	30.00
	1850	—	5.00	12.50	22.50

SEGOVIA MINT - Aqueduct

C#	Date	Mintage	Fine	VF	XF
170.3	1837	—	6.00	13.50	25.00
	1838	—	6.00	13.50	25.00
	1839	—	6.00	13.50	25.00
	1840	—	6.00	13.50	27.50
	1841	—	4.50	12.50	25.00
	1842	—	5.00	13.50	25.00
	1843	—	4.00	12.50	25.00
	1844	—	5.00	12.50	17.50
	1845	—	4.50	12.50	22.50
	1846	—	4.50	12.50	25.00
	1847	—	9.00	17.50	30.00
	1848	—	12.50	18.50	37.50
	1849	—	5.00	12.50	25.00
	1850	—	10.00	25.00	60.00

1/2 REAL

1.6900 gm., .903 SILVER, .0490 oz ASW

MADRID MINT - Crowned M

Obv: Crowned arms.
Rev: Arms in angles of cross.

C#	Date	Mintage	Fine	VF	XF
31.1	1760 JP	—	20.00	35.00	60.00
	1761 JP	—	12.50	20.00	35.00
	1762 JP	—	12.50	20.00	35.00
	1764 JP	—	15.00	25.00	35.00
	1765 PJ	—	12.50	20.00	40.00
	1766 PJ	—	15.00	25.00	35.00
	1769 PJ	—	20.00	35.00	60.00
	1770 PJ	—	20.00	35.00	60.00
	1771 P	—	18.50	35.00	55.00

SEVILLE MINT - S, S/L

C#	Date	Mintage	Fine	VF	XF
31.2	1760 JV	—	20.00	35.00	60.00
	1761 JV	—	18.50	30.00	55.00
	1762 VC	—	40.00	75.00	110.00
	1769 CF	—	30.00	55.00	100.00
	1770 CF	—	20.00	35.00	60.00

MADRID MINT - Crowned M

Obv: Bust of Charles III right.
Rev: Crowned arms.

C#	Date	Mintage	Fine	VF	XF
36.1	1772 PJ	—	30.00	55.00	100.00
	1773 PJ	—	20.00	35.00	60.00
	1774 PJ	—	18.50	30.00	55.00
	1775 PJ	—	15.00	25.00	45.00
	1777 PJ	—	15.00	25.00	45.00
	1778 PJ	—	25.00	40.00	75.00
	1779 PJ	—	15.00	25.00	45.00
	1780 PJ	—	10.00	18.50	30.00
	1781 PJ	—	15.00	25.00	45.00
	1782 JD	—	25.00	40.00	75.00
	1783 JD	—	18.50	30.00	55.00
	1784 JD	—	15.00	25.00	45.00
	1785 DV	—	10.00	18.50	30.00
	1786 DV	—	18.50	35.00	55.00
	1788 M	—	8.00	15.00	25.00

SEVILLE MINT - S, S/L

C#	Date	Mintage	Fine	VF	XF
36.2	1772 CF	—	30.00	55.00	100.00
	1773 CF	—	10.00	18.50	30.00
	1774 CF	—	10.00	18.50	30.00
	1775 CF	—	20.00	35.00	60.00
	1776 CF	—	15.00	25.00	45.00
	1778 CF	—	18.50	30.00	55.00
	1779 CF	—	30.00	55.00	100.00
	1780 CF	—	25.00	40.00	75.00
	1783 CF	—	35.00	60.00	110.00
	1788 C	—	10.00	18.50	30.00

MADRID MINT - Crowned M

Obv: Bust of Charles IV right.
Rev: Crowned arms.

C#	Date	Mintage	Fine	VF	XF
66.1	1789 MF	—	25.00	40.00	75.00
	1790 MF	—	18.50	35.00	55.00
	1791 MF	—	19.00	37.50	60.00
	1793 MF	—	9.00	16.50	28.50
	1795 MF	—	32.50	60.00	100.00
	1796 MF	—	32.50	60.00	100.00
	1797 MF	—	32.50	60.00	100.00
	1798 MF	—	18.50	35.00	65.00
	1799 FA	—	18.50	35.00	55.00

C#	Date	Mintage	Fine	VF	XF
66.1	1799 MF	—	20.00	38.00	60.00
	1800 FA	—	18.50	35.00	65.00
	1802 FA	—	25.00	40.00	75.00
	1803 FA	—	10.00	18.50	30.00
	1804 FA	—	18.50	35.00	55.00
	1808 AI	—	25.00	40.00	75.00
	1808 FA	—	35.00	60.00	110.00

SEVILLE MINT - S, S/L

C#	Date	Mintage	Fine	VF	XF
66.2	1793 CN	—	32.50	60.00	100.00
	1796 CN	—	15.00	25.00	45.00
	1798 CN	—	40.00	75.00	120.00
	1799 CN	—	32.50	60.00	100.00
	1800 CN	—	40.00	75.00	120.00
	1802 CN	—	30.00	55.00	100.00
	1805 CN	—	40.00	75.00	120.00
	1807 CN	—	25.00	40.00	75.00

CADIZ MINT - Crowned C

C#	Date	Mintage	Fine	VF	XF
132.1	1814 CI	—	10.00	22.50	40.00
	1814 CJ	—	10.00	22.50	40.00

MADRID MINT - Crowned M

C#	Date	Mintage	Fine	VF	XF
132.2	1815 GJ	—	12.50	27.50	55.00
	1816 GJ	—	8.50	20.00	35.00
	1817 GJ	—	9.00	20.00	40.00
	1818 GJ	—	8.50	17.50	37.50
	1819 GJ	—	9.00	20.00	40.00
	1820 GJ	—	12.50	20.00	50.00
	1824 AJ	—	20.00	35.00	70.00
	1826 AJ	—	12.50	25.00	50.00
	1828 AJ	—	15.00	25.00	55.00
	1830 AJ	—	7.50	17.50	35.00
	1831 AJ	—	17.50	35.00	65.00
	1832 AJ	—	9.00	20.00	40.00
	1833 AJ	—	5.00	15.00	35.00
	1833 JI	—	20.00	30.00	65.00

SEVILLE MINT - S, S/L

C#	Date	Mintage	Fine	VF	XF
132.3	1825 JB	—	7.00	12.50	25.00
	1831 JB	—	7.00	12.50	25.00
	1832 JB	—	4.00	15.00	35.00
	1833 JB	—	5.00	15.00	35.00

CATALONIA MINT - C

Small draped bust

C#	Date	Mintage	Fine	VF	XF
132a.1	1812 SF	—	18.50	30.00	60.00
	1813 SF	—	18.50	30.00	60.00
	1814 SF	—	22.50	35.00	65.00

MADRID MINT - Crowned M

C#	Date	Mintage	Fine	VF	XF
132a.2	1813 IJ	—	12.50	25.00	50.00
	1813 GJ	—	10.00	20.00	40.00
	1814 GJ	—	15.00	25.00	55.00

REAL

3.3800 gm., .917 SILVER, .0995 oz ASW

MADRID MINT - Crowned M

Obv: Crowned arms.
Rev: Arms of Castile and Leon.

C#	Date	Mintage	Fine	VF	XF
32.1	1759 JP	—	32.50	60.00	100.00
	1759 J	—	100.00	150.00	200.00
	1760 JP	—	32.50	60.00	100.00
	1761 JP	—	25.00	40.00	75.00
	1762 JP	—	25.00	40.00	75.00
	1764 JP	—	25.00	40.00	75.00
	1765 PJ	—	25.00	40.00	75.00
	1766 PJ	—	12.50	20.00	40.00
	1768 PJ	—	25.00	40.00	75.00
	1769 PJ	—	25.00	40.00	75.00
	1770 PJ	—	25.00	40.00	75.00
	1771 PJ	—	25.00	40.00	75.00

SEVILLE MINT - S, S/L

C#	Date	Mintage	Fine	VF	XF
32.2	1760 JV	—	32.50	60.00	100.00
	1761 JV	—	18.50	35.00	65.00
	1762 VC	—	50.00	80.00	125.00
	1768 CF	—	60.00	90.00	150.00
	1770 CF	—	25.00	40.00	75.00

MADRID MINT - Crowned M

Obv: Bust of Charles III right.
Rev: Crowned arms.

C#	Date	Mintage	Fine	VF	XF
37.1	1772 PJ	—	50.00	80.00	125.00
	1773 PJ	—	25.00	40.00	75.00
	1774 PJ	—	25.00	40.00	75.00
	1775 PJ	—	25.00	40.00	75.00
	1777 PJ	—	25.00	40.00	75.00
37.1	1778 PJ	—	18.50	37.50	65.00
	1779 PJ	—	25.00	40.00	75.00
	1780 PJ	—	25.00	40.00	75.00
	1781 PJ	—	25.00	40.00	75.00
	1782 PJ	—	25.00	40.00	75.00
	1782 JD	—	60.00	100.00	150.00
	1783 JD	—	25.00	40.00	75.00
	1784 JD	—	25.00	40.00	75.00
	1785 JD	—	25.00	40.00	75.00
	1785 DV	—	25.00	40.00	75.00
	1786 DV	—	25.00	40.00	75.00
	1787 DV	—	60.00	100.00	150.00
	1788 DV	—	60.00	100.00	150.00
	1788 M	—	18.50	37.50	65.00

SEVILLE MINT - S, S/L

C#	Date	Mintage	Fine	VF	XF
37.2	1772 CF	—	20.00	37.50	60.00
	1773 CF	—	18.50	35.00	55.00
	1774 CF	—	18.50	37.50	65.00
	1775 CF	—	32.50	60.00	100.00
	1776 CF	—	32.50	60.00	100.00
	1777 CF	—	32.50	60.00	100.00
	1778 CF	—	32.50	60.00	100.00
	1779 CF	—	25.00	40.00	75.00
	1780 CF	—	30.00	55.00	100.00
	1783 CF	—	32.50	60.00	100.00
	1788 C	—	15.00	25.00	45.00

MADRID MINT - Crowned M

Obv: Bust of Charles IV right.

C#	Date	Mintage	Fine	VF	XF
68.1	1788 MF	—	70.00	120.00	200.00
	1789 MF	—	70.00	120.00	200.00
	1790 MF	—	70.00	120.00	200.00
	1791 MF	—	70.00	120.00	200.00
	1793 MF	—	15.00	25.00	45.00
	1794 MF	—	30.00	55.00	100.00
	1795 MF	—	30.00	55.00	100.00
	1796 MF	—	30.00	55.00	100.00
	1797 MF	—	18.50	35.00	55.00
	1799 MF	—	18.50	35.00	55.00
	1800 FA	—	32.50	60.00	100.00
	1801 FA	—	20.00	37.50	60.00
	1802 FA	—	32.50	60.00	100.00
	1803 FA	—	15.00	25.00	45.00
	1805 FA	—	18.50	37.50	65.00
	1807 FA	—	15.00	25.00	45.00
	1807 AI	—	50.00	80.00	125.00
	1808 AI	—	20.00	37.50	60.00

SEVILLE MINT - S, S/L

C#	Date	Mintage	Fine	VF	XF
68.2	1793 CN	—	50.00	80.00	125.00
	1794 CN	—	45.00	85.00	130.00
	1796 CN	—	60.00	100.00	150.00
	1798 CN	—	60.00	100.00	150.00
	1799 CN	—	60.00	100.00	150.00
	1802 CN	—	60.00	100.00	150.00
	1807 CN	—	40.00	75.00	120.00

CATALONIA MINT - C

Obv: Large laureate bust

C#	Date	Mintage	Fine	VF	XF
133.1	1811 SF	—	15.00	25.00	50.00
	1814 SF	—	32.50	65.00	115.00

CADIZ MINT - Crowned C

C#	Date	Mintage	Fine	VF	XF
133.2	1813 CJ	—	18.50	27.50	55.00

MADRID MINT - Crowned M

C#	Date	Mintage	Fine	VF	XF
133.3	1815 GJ	—	16.50	32.50	55.00
	1816 GJ	—	16.50	30.00	55.00
	1817 GJ	—	16.50	25.00	50.00
	1819 GJ	—	20.00	27.50	50.00
	1820 GJ	—	18.50	25.00	60.00
	1824 AJ	—	30.00	55.00	90.00
	1826 AJ	—	20.00	40.00	70.00
	1828 AJ	—	20.00	40.00	70.00
	1830 AJ	—	8.00	18.50	35.00
	1831 AJ	—	10.00	22.50	50.00
	1832 AJ	—	7.50	15.00	40.00
	1833 AJ	—	20.00	30.00	60.00
	1833 JI	—	22.50	38.50	70.00
	1833 JJ	—	12.50	22.50	50.00

SEVILLE MINT - S, S/L

C#	Date	Mintage	Fine	VF	XF
133.4	1830 JB	—	10.00	22.50	50.00
	1831 JB	—	8.50	20.00	50.00
	1832 JB	—	12.50	22.50	50.00
	1833 JB	—	11.50	20.00	45.00

CATALONIA MINT - C

Obv: Small draped bust

C#	Date	Mintage	Fine	VF	XF
133a.1	1811 SF	—	25.00	37.50	55.00

MADRID MINT - Crowned M

C#	Date	Mintage	Fine	VF	XF
133a.2	1813 IJ	—	40.00	50.00	85.00
	1814 IJ	—	30.00	45.00	75.00
	1814 GJ	—	18.50	30.00	50.00
171.1	1837 CL	—	32.50	55.00	115.00
	1838 CL	—	7.50	12.50	25.00
	1838 DG	—	50.00	70.00	115.00
	1839 CL	—	16.50	35.00	65.00
	1840 CL	—	30.00	60.00	115.00
	1841 CL	—	57.50	115.00	225.00
	1842 CL	—	20.00	45.00	90.00
	1843 CL	—	32.50	60.00	115.00
	1844 CL	—	16.50	35.00	70.00
	1845 CL	—	7.00	12.50	27.50
	1847 CL	—	6.50	10.00	25.00
	1848 CL	—	6.50	10.00	25.00
	1849 CL	—	7.00	12.50	32.50

SEVILLE MINT - S, S/L

C#	Date	Mintage	Fine	VF	XF
171.2	1840 RD	—	25.00	55.00	115.00
	1844 RD	—	16.50	35.00	70.00
	1845 RD	—	12.50	32.50	65.00
	1850 RD	—	8.00	14.00	32.50
	1851 RD	—	7.50	12.50	30.00
	1852 RD	—	7.00	12.50	25.00

2 REALES

6.7700 gm., .903 SILVER, .1965 oz ASW

MADRID MINT - Crowned M

Obv: Crowned arms.
Rev: Arms of Castile and Leon.

C#	Date	Mintage	Fine	VF	XF
33.1	1759 J	—	25.00	40.00	75.00
	1759 JP	—	12.50	20.00	40.00
	1760 JP	—	10.00	18.50	30.00
	1761 JP	—	12.50	20.00	40.00
	1762 JP	—	12.50	20.00	40.00
	1763 JP	—	12.50	20.00	40.00
	1764 PJ	—	15.00	25.00	45.00
	1765 PJ	—	12.50	20.00	40.00
	1766 PJ	—	12.50	20.00	40.00
	1767 PJ	—	25.00	40.00	75.00
	1768 PJ	—	18.50	35.00	55.00
	1769 PJ	—	20.00	37.50	60.00
	1770 PJ	—	30.00	55.00	100.00
	1771 PJ	—	30.00	55.00	100.00

SEVILLE MINT - S, S/L

C#	Date	Mintage	Fine	VF	XF
33.2	1760 JV	—	12.50	20.00	40.00
	1761 JV	—	12.50	20.00	40.00
	1762 JV	—	12.50	20.00	40.00
	1766 VC	—	125.00	225.00	325.00
	1768 CF	—	30.00	55.00	100.00
	1769 CF	—	20.00	37.50	60.00
	1770 CF	—	25.00	40.00	75.00
	1771 CF	—	18.50	35.00	55.00

MADRID MINT - Crowned M

Obv: Bust of Charles III right.
Rev: Crowned arms.

C#	Date	Mintage	Fine	VF	XF
38.1	1772 PJ	—	18.50	35.00	55.00
	1773 PJ	—	20.00	37.50	60.00
	1774 PJ	—	12.50	20.00	40.00
	1775 PJ	—	12.50	20.00	40.00
	1776 PJ	—	10.00	18.50	30.00
	1777 PJ	—	10.00	18.50	30.00
	1778 PJ	—	10.00	18.50	30.00
	1779 PJ	—	10.00	18.50	30.00
	1780 PJ	—	10.00	18.50	30.00
	1781 PJ	—	10.00	18.50	30.00
	1782 PJ	—	12.50	20.00	40.00
	1782 JD	—	18.50	37.50	65.00
	1783 PJ	—	18.50	37.50	65.00

C#	Date	Mintage	Fine	VF	XF
38.1	1783 JP	—	32.50	60.00	100.00
	1783 JD	—	50.00	80.00	125.00
	1784 JD	—	18.50	35.00	55.00
	1785 JD	—	25.00	40.00	75.00
	1785 DV	—	12.50	20.00	40.00
	1786 DV	—	10.00	18.50	30.00
	1787 DV	—	10.00	18.50	30.00
	1788 M	—	10.00	18.50	30.00
	1788 MF	—	32.50	60.00	100.00
	1788 DV	—	110.00	150.00	200.00

SEVILLE MINT - S, S/L

C#	Date	Mintage	Fine	VF	XF
38.2	1773 CF	—	20.00	37.50	60.00
	1774 CF	—	18.50	35.00	55.00
	1775 CF	—	18.50	35.00	55.00
	1776 CF	—	12.50	20.00	40.00
	1777 CF	—	12.50	20.00	40.00
	1778 CF	—	12.50	20.00	40.00
	1779 CF	—	12.50	20.00	40.00
	1780 CF	—	12.50	20.00	40.00
	1782 CF	—	50.00	80.00	125.00
	1788 C	—	10.00	18.50	30.00

MADRID MINT - Crowned M

Obv: Bust of Charles IV right.

C#	Date	Mintage	Fine	VF	XF
69.1	1788 MF	—	50.00	80.00	125.00
	1789 MF	—	10.00	18.50	30.00
	1790 MF	—	10.00	18.50	30.00
	1791 MF	—	10.00	18.50	30.00
	1792 MF	—	10.00	18.50	30.00
	1793 MF	—	10.00	18.50	30.00
	1794 MF	—	10.00	18.50	30.00
	1795 MF	—	10.00	18.50	30.00
	1796 MF	—	10.00	18.50	30.00
	1797 MF	—	10.00	18.50	30.00
	1798 MF	—	10.00	18.50	30.00
	1799 MF	—	10.00	18.50	30.00
	1800 MF	—	10.00	18.50	30.00
	1800 FA	—	30.00	55.00	100.00
	1801 FA	—	10.00	18.50	30.00
	1802 FA	—	10.00	18.50	30.00
	1803 FA	—	10.00	18.50	30.00
	1804 FA	—	10.00	18.50	30.00
	1805 FA	—	10.00	18.50	30.00
	1806 FA	—	10.00	18.50	30.00
	1807 FA	—	10.00	18.50	30.00
	1807 AI	—	15.00	25.00	45.00
	1808 FA	—	10.00	18.50	30.00
	1808 IG	—	15.00	25.00	45.00
	1808 AI	—	6.00	11.50	18.50

SEVILLE MINT - S, S/L

C#	Date	Mintage	Fine	VF	XF
69.2	1793 CN	—	10.00	18.50	30.00
	1795 CN	—	10.00	18.50	30.00
	1796 CN	—	10.00	18.50	30.00
	1797 CN	—	10.00	18.50	30.00
	1798 CN	—	10.00	18.50	30.00
	1799 CN	—	10.00	18.50	30.00
	1800 CN	—	10.00	18.50	30.00
	1801 CN	—	10.00	18.50	30.00
	1802 CN	—	10.00	18.50	30.00
	1803 CN	—	10.00	18.50	30.00
	1804 CN	—	10.00	18.50	30.00
	1805 CN	—	10.00	18.50	30.00
	1806 CN	—	10.00	18.50	30.00
	1807 CN	—	10.00	18.50	30.00
	1808 CN	—	10.00	18.50	30.00

CATALONIA MINT - C

C#	Date	Mintage	Fine	VF	XF
134.1	1812 SF	—	60.00	100.00	175.00
	1813 SF	—	8.50	17.50	27.50
	1814 SF	—	12.50	25.00	50.00

CADIZ MINT - Crowned C

C#	Date	Mintage	Fine	VF	XF
134.2	1810 CI	—	6.50	12.50	27.50
	1810 small 'C' with mintmark				
		—	12.50	25.00	50.00
	1811 CI	—	7.50	15.00	27.50
	1812 CI	—	6.50	12.50	25.00

MADRID MINT - Crowned M

C#	Date	Mintage	Fine	VF	XF
134.3	1814 GJ	—	8.50	16.50	27.50
	1815 GJ	—	8.50	16.50	30.00
	1816 GJ	—	8.50	18.50	30.00
	1817 GJ	—	8.50	16.50	27.50
	1818 GJ	—	12.50	25.00	40.00
	1819 GJ	—	12.50	25.00	45.00
	1820 GJ	—	8.50	16.50	27.50
	1821 AJ	—	15.00	30.00	45.00
	1822 AJ	—	32.50	40.00	65.00
	1823 AJ	—	7.50	17.50	27.50
	1824 AJ	—	7.50	17.50	27.50
	1825 AJ	—	7.50	17.50	30.00
	1826 AJ	—	7.50	16.50	30.00
	1827 AJ	—	7.50	18.50	40.00
	1828 AJ	—	7.50	16.50	30.00
	1829 AJ	—	7.50	16.50	30.00
	1830 AJ	—	7.50	16.50	25.00
	1831 AJ	—	7.50	17.50	30.00
	1832 AJ	—	7.50	16.50	30.00
	1833 AJ	—	8.00	20.00	30.00

SEVILLE MINT - S, S/L

C#	Date	Mintage	Fine	VF	XF
134.4	1815 CJ	—	12.50	25.00	40.00
	1820 CJ	—	7.50	16.50	30.00
	1821 CJ	—	7.50	9.00	18.50
	1823 CJ	—	7.50	17.50	27.50
	1824 J	—	30.00	40.00	60.00
	1824 JB	—	7.50	17.50	30.00
	1825 JB	—	7.50	17.50	30.00
	1826 JB	—	7.50	16.50	30.00
	1827 JB	—	7.50	16.50	30.00
	1828 JB	—	7.50	17.50	30.00
	1829 JB	—	7.50	16.50	25.00
	1830 JB	—	7.50	20.00	30.00
	1831 JB	—	7.50	16.50	25.00
	1832 JB	—	7.50	16.50	30.00
	1833 JB	—	8.50	25.00	40.00

BARCELONA MINT - B, BA

Obv: Bare head of Ferdinand right.
Rev: Crowned arms.

C#	Date	Mintage	Fine	VF	XF
134a.1	1812 SF	—	125.00	190.00	325.00

CATALONIA MINT - C

C#	Date	Mintage	Fine	VF	XF
134a.2	1810 FS	—	11.50	22.50	45.00
	1810 SF	—	35.00	60.00	90.00
	1811 SF	—	8.00	17.50	35.00
	1811 FS	—	12.50	22.50	40.00

MADRID MINT - Crowned M

C#	Date	Mintage	Fine	VF	XF
134a.3	1812 IJ	—	12.50	20.00	40.00
	1813 IJ	—	7.50	16.50	30.00
	1813 IG	—	20.00	30.00	50.00
	1813 GJ	—	8.00	17.50	30.00
	1814 GJ	—	20.00	35.00	55.00

VALENCIA MINT - V, VAL.

C#	Date	Mintage	Fine	VF	XF
134a.4	1811 GS	—	65.00	110.00	175.00
	1812 GS	—	80.00	115.00	225.00

MADRID MINT - Crowned M

Obv: Young head of Isabella right.
Rev: Crowned arms in collar of The Golden Fleece.

C#	Date	Mintage	Fine	VF	XF
163.1	1836 CR	—	32.50	55.00	90.00
	1836 DG	—	175.00	250.00	375.00
	1837 CR	—	18.50	45.00	70.00
	1838 CR	—	70.00	160.00	250.00
	1839 CL	—	60.00	115.00	175.00
	1841 CL	—	20.00	45.00	75.00
	1842 CL	—	100.00	250.00	350.00
	1843 CL	—	20.00	50.00	90.00

SEVILLE MINT - S, S/L

C#	Date	Mintage	Fine	VF	XF
163.2	1836 DR	—	40.00	60.00	125.00
	1839 RD	—	18.50	45.00	100.00
	1840 RD	—	35.00	70.00	125.00

MADRID MINT - Crowned M

C#	Date	Mintage	Fine	VF	XF
172.1	1844 CL	—	12.50	35.00	60.00
	1845 CL	—	12.50	30.00	50.00
	1847 CL	—	9.00	22.50	40.00
	1848 CL	—	12.50	30.00	55.00
	1849 CL	—	9.00	22.50	40.00

SEVILLE MINT - S, S/L

C#	Date	Mintage	Fine	VF	XF
172.2	1845 RD	—	30.00	60.00	125.00
	1848 RD	—	18.50	40.00	75.00
	1850/45 RD	—	—	—	—
	1850 RD	—	11.50	17.50	45.00
	1851 RD	—	9.00	22.50	40.00

4 REALES

13.5400 gm., .917 SILVER, .3931 oz ASW

MADRID MINT - Crowned M

Obv: Crowned arms.
Rev: Arms of Castile and Leon.

C#	Date	Mintage	Fine	VF	XF
34.1	1760 JP	—	450.00	550.00	1200.
	1761 JP	—	30.00	55.00	120.00

SEVILLE MINT - S, S/L

C#	Date	Mintage	Fine	VF	XF
34.2	1761 JV	—	40.00	80.00	150.00

MADRID MINT - Crowned M

Obv: Bust of Charles III right.
Rev: Crowned arms.

C#	Date	Mintage	Fine	VF	XF
39.1	1772 PJ	—	100.00	200.00	400.00
	1773 PJ	—	50.00	90.00	175.00
	1774 PJ	—	300.00	500.00	1000.
	1775 PJ	—	25.00	60.00	110.00
	1776 PJ	—	30.00	55.00	120.00
	1777 PJ	—	30.00	55.00	120.00
	1778 PJ	—	25.00	50.00	110.00
	1779 PJ	—	30.00	55.00	120.00
	1780 PJ	—	30.00	55.00	120.00
	1781 PJ	—	30.00	55.00	120.00
	1782 PJ	—	50.00	90.00	175.00
	1782 JD	—	50.00	90.00	175.00
	1784 JD	—	275.00	400.00	1000.
	1788 MF	—	30.00	55.00	120.00
	1788 M	—	70.00	150.00	300.00

SEVILLE MINT - S, S/L

C#	Date	Mintage	Fine	VF	XF
39.2	1772 CF	—	100.00	200.00	400.00
	1773 CF	—	50.00	90.00	175.00
	1774 VF	—	50.00	90.00	175.00
	1775 CF	—	100.00	200.00	400.00
	1776 CF	—	200.00	350.00	700.00
	1777 CF	—	50.00	90.00	175.00
	1778 CF	—	100.00	200.00	400.00
	1779 CF	—	50.00	90.00	175.00
	1780 CF	—	50.00	90.00	175.00
	1781 CF	—	100.00	200.00	350.00
	1782 CF	—	120.00	250.00	550.00
	1788 C	—	50.00	90.00	175.00

MADRID MINT - Crowned M

C#	Date	Mintage	Fine	VF	XF
70.1	1788 MF	—	700.00	900.00	1750.
	1789 MF	—	120.00	180.00	300.00
	1790 MF	—	700.00	900.00	1750.
	1791 MF	—	25.00	50.00	110.00
	1792 MF	—	15.00	30.00	75.00
	1793 MF	—	15.00	30.00	75.00
	1794 MF	—	15.00	30.00	75.00
	1795 MF	—	25.00	50.00	110.00
	1796 MF	—	25.00	50.00	110.00
	1797 MF	—	100.00	150.00	250.00
	1804 FA	—	30.00	55.00	120.00
	1805 FA	—	25.00	55.00	120.00
	1806 FA	—	120.00	200.00	300.00
	1808 AI	—	60.00	110.00	200.00
	1808 FA	—	50.00	100.00	200.00

SEVILLE MINT - S, S/L

C#	Date	Mintage	Fine	VF	XF
70.2	1803 CN	—	50.00	90.00	175.00
	1807 CN	—	60.00	110.00	200.00

CATALONIA MINT - C

C#	Date	Mintage	Fine	VF	XF
135a.1	1809 MP	—	125.00	225.00	450.00
	1809 SF	—	150.00	250.00	450.00
	1810 SF	—	200.00	325.00	575.00
	1814 SF	—	325.00	525.00	700.00

VALENCIA MINT - V, VAL.

C#	Date	Mintage	Fine	VF	XF
135a.2	1809 SG	—	110.00	150.00	250.00
	1810 SG	—	40.00	80.00	200.00
	1811 SG	—	35.00	70.00	125.00

CATALONIA MINT - C

C#	Date	Mintage	Fine	VF	XF
135.1	1811 SF	—	115.00	175.00	350.00
	1812 SF	—	175.00	300.00	525.00
	1813 SF	—	500.00	950.00	1800.

CADIZ MINT - Crowned C

C#	Date	Mintage	Fine	VF	XF
135.2	1812 CJ	—	30.00	50.00	70.00
	1812 CI	—	40.00	55.00	100.00

MADRID MINT - Crowned M

C#	Date	Mintage	Fine	VF	XF
135.3	1814 GJ	—	175.00	275.00	500.00
	1815 GJ	—	13.50	30.00	55.00
	1816 GJ	—	35.00	55.00	90.00
	1817 GJ	—	25.00	45.00	70.00
	1818 GJ	—	40.00	60.00	100.00
	1819 GJ	—	125.00	200.00	400.00
	1822 SR	—	55.00	85.00	160.00
	1824 AJ	—	22.50	40.00	60.00
	1830 AJ	—	20.00	40.00	65.00

SEVILLE MINT - S, S/L

C#	Date	Mintage	Fine	VF	XF
135.4	1818 CJ	—	30.00	55.00	90.00
	1818 J	—	40.00	70.00	110.00
	1819 CJ	—	30.00	55.00	80.00
	1820 CJ	—	30.00	55.00	80.00
	1824 J	—	40.00	70.00	150.00
	1824 JB	—	25.00	40.00	65.00
	1825 JB	—	12.50	30.00	55.00
	1826 JB	—	25.00	40.00	60.00
	1828 JB	—	35.00	60.00	100.00
	1830 JB	—	20.00	40.00	65.00
	1832 JB	—	15.00	30.00	60.00
	1833 JB	—	25.00	45.00	70.00

MADRID MINT - Crowned M

Obv. leg: FERDINANDOS

C#	Date	Mintage	Fine	VF	XF
135b	1813 IJ	—	125.00	250.00	425.00
	1813 GJ	—	175.00	300.00	550.00
	1814 GJ	—	175.00	300.00	550.00
164.1	1834 CR	—	45.00	100.00	175.00
	1834 DG	—	175.00	400.00	750.00
	1835 CR	—	15.00	35.00	60.00
	1836 CR	—	15.00	30.00	60.00

SEVILLE MINT - S, S/L

C#	Date	Mintage	Fine	VF	XF
164.2	1835 DR	—	25.00	55.00	75.00
	1836 DR	—	25.00	60.00	100.00

BARCELONA MINT - B, BA

C#	Date	Mintage	Fine	VF	XF
173a	1836 PS	—	40.00	80.00	175.00
	1837 PS	—	40.00	85.00	160.00
	1837 RS	—	13.50	30.00	65.00

C#	Date	Mintage	Fine	VF	XF
173.1	1837 PJ	—	15.00	32.50	60.00
	1838 PS	—	25.00	50.00	90.00
	1839 PS	—	125.00	275.00	525.00
	1840 PS	—	25.00	55.00	100.00
	1841 PS	—	12.50	25.00	55.00
	1842 CC	—	18.50	35.00	65.00
	1843 CC	—	75.00	125.00	250.00
	1843 PS	—	75.00	125.00	275.00
	1844 PS	—	17.50	35.00	75.00
	1845 PS	—	25.00	55.00	125.00
	1846 PS	—	55.00	100.00	250.00
	1847 PS	—	40.00	80.00	150.00

MADRID MINT - Crowned M

C#	Date	Mintage	Fine	VF	XF
173.2	1837 CR	—	20.00	40.00	65.00
	1838 CL	—	40.00	85.00	175.00
	1839 CL	—	10.00	25.00	55.00
	1840 CL	—	50.00	100.00	175.00
	1841 CL	—	50.00	100.00	175.00
	1842 CL	—	60.00	115.00	200.00
	1843 CL	—	50.00	100.00	175.00
	1844 CL	—	60.00	120.00	200.00
	1845 CL	—	60.00	125.00	225.00
	1846 CL	—	35.00	60.00	125.00
	1847 CL	—	18.50	40.00	75.00
	1848 CL	—	10.00	20.00	45.00
	1848 DG	—	175.00	400.00	650.00
	1849 CL	—	10.00	20.00	45.00

SEVILLE MINT - S, S/L

C#	Date	Mintage	Fine	VF	XF
173.3	1837 DR	—	27.50	60.00	100.00
	1838 DR	—	40.00	85.00	175.00
	1838 RD	—	32.50	85.00	160.00
	1839 DR	—	40.00	80.00	175.00
	1839 RD	—	40.00	85.00	200.00
	1840 RD	—	75.00	130.00	275.00
	1841 RD	—	35.00	75.00	150.00
	1842 RD	—	32.50	70.00	150.00
	1843 RD	—	12.50	30.00	60.00
	1844 RD	—	80.00	185.00	375.00
	1845 RD	—	80.00	160.00	350.00

8 REALES

27.0700 gm., .903 SILVER, .7859 oz ASW

MADRID MINT - Crowned M

Obv: Crowned arms.
Rev: Arms of Castile and Leon.

C#	Date	Mintage	Fine	VF	XF
35.1	1762 JP	—	250.00	375.00	750.00

SEVILLE MINT - S, S/L

C#	Date	Mintage	Fine	VF	XF
35.2	1762 JV	—	300.00	450.00	850.00

MADRID MINT - Crowned M

Obv: Bust of Charles III right.
Rev: Crowned arms.

C#	Date	Mintage	Fine	VF	XF
40.1	1772 PJ	—	500.00	700.00	1200.
	1773 PJ	—	750.00	1000.	1600.
	1774 PJ	—	600.00	900.00	1400.
	1775 PJ	—	700.00	1000.	1600.
	1777 PJ	—	500.00	800.00	1300.
	1782 PJ	—	600.00	900.00	1500.
	1788 M	—	600.00	900.00	1500.

SEVILLE MINT - S, S/L

C#	Date	Mintage	Fine	VF	XF
40.2	1772 CF	—	500.00	700.00	1200.
	1773 CF	—	500.00	700.00	1200.
	1774 CF	—	500.00	800.00	1300.
	1775 CF	—	600.00	800.00	1400.
	1776 CF	—	450.00	700.00	1200.
	1777 CF	—	500.00	800.00	1300.
	1778 CF	—	500.00	800.00	1300.
	1779 CF	—	550.00	850.00	1400.
	1788 C	—	600.00	900.00	1500.

MADRID MINT - Crowned M

Obv: Bust of Charles IV right.

C#	Date	Mintage	Fine	VF	XF
71.1	1788 MF	—	1800.	2500.	3000.
	1789 MF	—	1200.	1500.	2100.
	1796 MF	—	2200.	2800.	3200.
	1797 MF	—	1200.	1500.	2000.
	1798 MF	—	900.00	1200.	1500.
	1802 MF	—	350.00	600.00	800.00
	1802 FA	—	250.00	400.00	500.00
	1803 FA	—	300.00	450.00	550.00
	1805 FA	—	180.00	250.00	350.00
	1808 FA	—	300.00	500.00	600.00
	1808 AI	—	350.00	600.00	800.00
	1808 IG	—	500.00	750.00	1100.

SEVILLE MINT - S, S/L

C#	Date	Mintage	Fine	VF	XF
71.2	1788 C	—	1000.	1300.	1900.
	1789 C	—	700.00	1000.	1700.
	1790 C	—	900.00	1200.	1700.
	1791 C	—	900.00	1200.	1700.
	1792 C	—	500.00	800.00	1100.
	1792 CN	—	300.00	500.00	700.00
	1793 CN	—	700.00	1000.	1400.
	1795 CN	—	350.00	600.00	1000.
	1796 CN	—	700.00	1000.	1400.
	1797 CN	—	2500.	3500.	5000.
	1798 CN	—	300.00	500.00	700.00
	1799 CN	—	850.00	1100.	1600.
	1800 CN	—	850.00	1100.	1600.
	1802 CN	—	300.00	500.00	600.00
	1803 CN	—	300.00	500.00	650.00

MADRID MINT - Crowned M

C#	Date	Mintage	Fine	VF	XF
93	1809 IG	—	80.00	200.00	350.00
	1810 JG	—	1050.	2500.	3250.

SEVILLE MINT - S, S/L

C#	Date	Mintage	Fine	VF	XF
136b	1808 CN	—	60.00	100.00	175.00
	1809 CN	—	60.00	90.00	150.00

MADRID MINT - Crowned M

Rev: Similar to C#136b.

C#	Date	Mintage	Fine	VF	XF
136c	1812 IJ	—	250.00	325.00	500.00
	1813 IJ	—	225.00	275.00	400.00
	1813 IG	—	200.00	250.00	350.00
	1813 GJ	—	225.00	300.00	450.00

CATALONIA MINT - C

Rev: Similar to C#136b.

C#	Date	Mintage	Fine	VF	XF
136a.1	1809 MP	—	325.00	475.00	775.00
	1809 SF	—	250.00	400.00	625.00
	1810 SF	—	300.00	425.00	725.00

VALENCIA MINT - V, VAL.

C#	Date	Mintage	Fine	VF	XF
136a.2	1811 GS	—	250.00	425.00	650.00
	1811 SG	—	225.00	275.00	450.00

CATALONIA MINT - C

Rev: Similar to C#136b.

C#	Date	Mintage	Fine	VF	XF
136.1	1811 SF	—	400.00	600.00	750.00
	1812 SF	—	400.00	525.00	700.00
	1813 SF	—	400.00	525.00	700.00
	1814 SF	—	400.00	625.00	850.00

CADIZ MINT - Crowned C

C#	Date	Mintage	Fine	VF	XF
136.2	1810 CI	—	475.00	700.00	900.00
	1811 CI	—	200.00	275.00	425.00
	1811 CJ	—	275.00	325.00	500.00
	1812 CJ	—	200.00	275.00	425.00
	1813 CJ	—	110.00	150.00	275.00
	1814 CJ	—	70.00	100.00	175.00
	1815 CJ	—	700.00	1000.	2100.

MADRID MINT - Crowned M

C#	Date	Mintage	Fine	VF	XF
136.3	1814 GJ	—	70.00	100.00	175.00
	1815 GJ	—	55.00	75.00	140.00
	1816 GJ	—	50.00	70.00	110.00
	1817 GJ	—	70.00	90.00	175.00
	1818 GJ	—	65.00	85.00	175.00
	1823 AJ	—	475.00	625.00	950.00
	1824 AJ	—	500.00	600.00	900.00
	1825 AJ	—	475.00	650.00	900.00
	1830 AJ	—	600.00	825.00	1150.

SEVILLE MINT - S, S/L

C#	Date	Mintage	Fine	VF	XF
136.4	1809 CN	—	250.00	325.00	500.00
	1810 CN	—	550.00	900.00	1250.
136.4	1812 CN	—	725.00	1150.	1600.
	1814 CJ	—	250.00	300.00	525.00
	1815 CJ	—	60.00	80.00	140.00
	1816 CJ	—	60.00	85.00	140.00
	1817 CJ	—	55.00	70.00	110.00
	1818 CJ	—	50.00	75.00	110.00
	1819 CJ	—	90.00	115.00	225.00
	1820 CJ	—	55.00	70.00	125.00

1/2 ESCUDO

1.6900 gm., .917 GOLD, .0498 oz AGW

MADRID MINT - Crowned M

C#	Date	Mintage	Fine	VF	XF
41.1	1759 J*	—	300.00	450.00	600.00
	1759 JP	—	100.00	200.00	350.00
	1760 JP	—	100.00	200.00	350.00
	1761 JP	—	100.00	200.00	350.00
	1762 JP	—	100.00	200.00	350.00
	1763 JP	—	100.00	250.00	450.00
	1764 JP	—	100.00	200.00	350.00
	1765 PJ	—	100.00	200.00	350.00
	1766 PJ	—	175.00	300.00	500.00
	1767 PJ	—	100.00	200.00	350.00
	1768 PJ	—	250.00	400.00	550.00
	1769 PJ	—	100.00	250.00	400.00
	1770 PJ	—	100.00	250.00	400.00
	1771 PJ	—	250.00	400.00	600.00

SEVILLE MINT - S, S/L

C#	Date	Mintage	Fine	VF	XF
41.2	1759 JV	—	300.00	450.00	650.00
	1760 JV	—	150.00	275.00	400.00
	1761 JV	—	200.00	350.00	500.00
	1762 JV	—	350.00	500.00	800.00
	1764 VC	—	300.00	450.00	650.00
	1765 VC	—	300.00	450.00	650.00
	1766 VC	—	500.00	900.00	1500.
	1767 VC	—	250.00	400.00	550.00
	1767 CF	—	500.00	800.00	1400.
	1768 CF	—	400.00	600.00	1000.
	1769 CF	—	500.00	900.00	1600.
	1770 CF	—	400.00	600.00	1000.
	1771 CF	—	400.00	600.00	1100.

1.6900 gm., .900 GOLD, .0486 oz AGW

MADRID MINT - Crowned M

Obv: Older bust of Charles III right.
Rev: Crowned arms in collar of The Golden Fleece.

C#	Date	Mintage	Fine	VF	XF
51.1	1772 PJ	—	700.00	1800.	3000.
	1773 PJ	—	75.00	150.00	300.00
	1774 PJ	—	75.00	150.00	300.00
	1775 PJ	—	75.00	150.00	300.00
	1776 PJ	—	100.00	200.00	350.00
	1777 PJ	—	100.00	200.00	350.00
	1778 PJ	—	75.00	150.00	300.00
	1779 PJ	—	150.00	250.00	400.00
	1781 PJ	—	500.00	1000.	1800.
	1783 JD	—	50.00	150.00	300.00
	1784 JD	—	75.00	150.00	300.00
	1785 DV	—	300.00	500.00	900.00

1.6900 gm., .875 GOLD, .0475 oz AGW

C#	Date	Mintage	Fine	VF	XF
51.1a	1786 DV	—	50.00	150.00	250.00
	1787 DV	—	75.00	150.00	300.00
	1788 DV	—	2000	4500	6000
	1788 M	—	50.00	100.00	250.00

SEVILLE MINT - S, S/L

C#	Date	Mintage	Fine	VF	XF
51.2	1773 CF	—	300.00	500.00	800.00
	1774 CF	—	350.00	600.00	1000.
	1775 CF	—	250.00	400.00	600.00
	1776 CF	—	500.00	750.00	1200.
	1777 CF	—	250.00	400.00	600.00
	1778 CF	—	200.00	350.00	500.00
	1779 CF	—	250.00	400.00	600.00
	1781 CF	—	350.00	600.00	1200.
	1782 CF	—	500.00	900.00	1600.
	1783 CF	—	500.00	1000.	1800.

1.6900 gm., .875 GOLD, .0475 oz AGW

C#	Date	Mintage	Fine	VF	XF
51.2a	1786 C	—	1500.	3000.	5000.
	1788 C	—	75.00	150.00	300.00

MADRID MINT - Crowned M

Obv: Bust of Charles IV right.

C#	Date	Mintage	Fine	VF	XF
72	1788 MF	—	1800.	2500.	3500.
	1789 MF	—	1000.	1700.	2500.
	1790 MF	—	1400.	1800.	2500.
	1791 MF	—	1400.	1800.	2500.
	1792 MF	—	1600.	2000.	2800.
	1793 MF	—	1500.	1800.	2500.
	1794 MF	—	1500.	2000.	2800.
	1795 MF	—	1700.	2200.	3000.
	1796 MF	—	1300.	1700.	2500.

Obv: Laureate head of Ferdinand right.
Rev: Crowned oval arms.

C#	Date	Mintage	Fine	VF	XF
141	1817 GJ	—	BV	60.00	90.00

ESCUDO

3.3800 gm., .900 GOLD, .0978 oz AGW

MADRID MINT - Crowned M

Obv: Bust of Charles III right.
Rev: Crowned arms in collar of The Golden Fleece.

C#	Date	Mintage	Fine	VF	XF
52.1	1772 PJ	—	600.00	900.00	1700.
	1779 PJ	—	90.00	135.00	200.00
	1780 PJ	—	90.00	135.00	200.00
	1781 PJ	—	90.00	135.00	200.00
	1782 JD	—	100.00	200.00	300.00
	1784 JD	—	75.00	150.00	300.00
	1785 DV	—	75.00	150.00	300.00

3.3800 gm., .875 GOLD, .0951 oz AGW

C#	Date	Mintage	Fine	VF	XF
52.1a	1787 DV	—	75.00	150.00	300.00
	1788 DV	—	75.00	125.00	200.00
	1788 M	—	75.00	150.00	300.00

3.3800 gm., .900 GOLD, .0978 oz AGW

SEVILLE MINT - S, S/L

C#	Date	Mintage	Fine	VF	XF
52.2	1773 CF	—	75.00	150.00	300.00
	1774 CF	—	75.00	150.00	300.00
	1779 CF	—	75.00	150.00	300.00
	1780 CF	—	75.00	150.00	300.00
	1781 CF	—	75.00	150.00	300.00
52.2a	1784 V	—	100.00	200.00	350.00
	1785 C	—	100.00	200.00	350.00
	1787 CM	—	100.00	200.00	300.00

MADRID MINT - Crowned M

C#	Date	Mintage	Fine	VF	XF
73	1788 MF	—	750.00	900.00	1600.
	1789 MF	—	150.00	300.00	600.00
	1790 MF	—	75.00	150.00	250.00
	1791 MF	—	75.00	150.00	250.00
	1792 MF	—	75.00	150.00	250.00
	1793 MF	—	75.00	150.00	250.00
	1794 MF	—	75.00	150.00	250.00
	1796 MF	—	75.00	150.00	250.00
	1797 MF	—	75.00	150.00	250.00
	1798 MF	—	75.00	150.00	250.00
	1799 MF	—	75.00	150.00	250.00
	1799 FA	—	100.00	200.00	350.00
	1801 FA	—	75.00	150.00	250.00
	1807 FA	—	75.00	150.00	250.00

Similar to 1/2 Escudo, C#141.

C#	Date	Mintage	Fine	VF	XF
142	1817 GJ	—	250.00	325.00	650.00

2 ESCUDOS

6.7700 gm., .900 GOLD, .1959 oz AGW

MADRID MINT - Crowned M

Obv: Bust of Charles III right.
Rev: Crowned arms in collar of The Golden Fleece.

C#	Date	Mintage	Fine	VF	XF
53.1	1772 PJ	—	150.00	225.00	300.00
	1773 PJ	—	150.00	200.00	275.00
	1774 PJ	—	175.00	250.00	450.00
	1775 PJ	—	150.00	225.00	300.00
53.1	1776 PJ	—	150.00	200.00	300.00
	1777 PJ	—	150.00	200.00	300.00
	1778 PJ	—	150.00	225.00	300.00
	1779 PJ	—	150.00	250.00	450.00
	1780 PJ	—	150.00	225.00	300.00
	1781 PJ	—	140.00	200.00	275.00
	1784 JD	—	1000.	1500.	3000.
	1785 DV	—	2500.	5000.	9000.

6.7700 gm., .875 GOLD, .1905 oz AGW

C#	Date	Mintage	Fine	VF	XF
53.1a	1786 DV	—	200.00	400.00	750.00
	1787 DV	—	800.00	1300	2500
	1788 M	—	140 00	200.00	300.00

6.7700 gm., .900 GOLD, .1959 oz AGW

SEVILLE MINT - S, S/L

C#	Date	Mintage	Fine	VF	XF
53.2	1773 CF	—	150.00	225.00	300.00
	1774 CF	—	150.00	225.00	300.00
	1775 CF	—	150.00	225.00	300.00
	1776 CF	—	150.00	225.00	300.00
	1777 CF	—	300.00	500.00	1000.
	1779 CF	—	200.00	400.00	750.00

6.7700 gm., .875 GOLD, .1905 oz AGW

C#	Date	Mintage	Fine	VF	XF
53.2a	1787 CM	—	150.00	250.00	450.00
	1788 C	—	150.00	250.00	450.00

MADRID MINT - Crowned M

C#	Date	Mintage	Fine	VF	XF
74.1	1788 MF	—	600.00	800.00	1200.
	1789 MF	—	200.00	250.00	350.00
	1790 MF	—	150.00	225.00	300.00
	1791 MF	—	2000.	2500.	3500.
	1792 MF	—	450.00	600.00	750.00
	1793 MF	—	150.00	225.00	300.00
	1794 MF	—	150.00	225.00	300.00
	1795 MF	—	150.00	225.00	300.00
	1796 MF	—	150.00	225.00	300.00
	1797 MF	—	150.00	225.00	300.00
	1798 MF	—	150.00	225.00	300.00
	1799 MF	—	200.00	275.00	350.00
	1800 MF	—	150.00	225.00	300.00
	1800 FA	—	300.00	400.00	500.00
	1801 MF	—	250.00	300.00	375.00
	1801 FM	—	200.00	275.00	350.00
	1801 FA	—	150.00	225.00	300.00
	1802 FA	—	200.00	275.00	350.00
	1803 FA	—	150.00	225.00	300.00
	1804 FA	—	150.00	225.00	300.00
	1805 FA	—	150.00	225.00	300.00
	1806 FA	—	200.00	275.00	350.00
	1807 FA	—	275.00	350.00	450.00
	1807 AI	—	200.00	275.00	350.00
	1808 AI	—	150.00	225.00	300.00

SEVILLE MINT - S, S/L

C#	Date	Mintage	Fine	VF	XF
74.2	1790 C	—	600.00	750.00	1200.
	1791 C	—	250.00	300.00	450.00
	1791 CN	—	750.00	850.00	1400.
	1793 CN	—	250.00	350.00	450.00
	1794 CN	—	200.00	250.00	350.00
	1795 CN	—	200.00	250.00	350.00
	1796 CN	—	200.00	275.00	350.00
	1797 CN	—	150.00	225.00	300.00
	1798 CN	—	150.00	225.00	300.00
	1799 CN	—	200.00	275.00	350.00
	1800 CN	—	200.00	275.00	350.00
	1801 CN	—	250.00	300.00	375.00
	1802 CN	—	150.00	225.00	300.00
	1803 CN	—	200.00	275.00	350.00
	1804 CN	—	200.00	275.00	350.00
	1805 CN	—	600.00	750.00	1200.
	1806 CN	—	200.00	275.00	350.00
	1807 CN	—	275.00	350.00	450.00
	1808 CN	—	250.00	300.00	375.00

CADIZ MINT - Crowned C

Obv: Laureate uniformed bust of Ferdinand right.
Rev: Crowned arms in collar of The Golden Fleece.

C#	Date	Mintage	Fine	VF	XF
143.1	1811 CI	—	325.00	450.00	700.00

MADRID MINT - Crowned M

C#	Date	Mintage	Fine	VF	XF
143.2	1813 IG	—	350.00	475.00	700.00
	1813 IJ	—	160.00	225.00	375.00
	1813 GJ	—	150.00	200.00	300.00
	1814 GJ	—	140.00	200.00	400.00

SEVILLE MINT - S, S/L

C#	Date	Mintage	Fine	VF	XF
143.3	1808 CN	—	150.00	200.00	300.00
	1809 CN	—	150.00	200.00	300.00

CATALONIA MINT - C

Obv: Laureate head of Ferdinand right.

C#	Date	Mintage	Fine	VF	XF
143a.1	1811 SF	—	275.00	375.00	650.00
	1812 SF	—	350.00	475.00	725.00
	1813 SF	—	300.00	375.00	675.00

CADIZ MINT - Crowned C

C#	Date	Mintage	Fine	VF	XF
143a.2	1812 CI	—	150.00	200.00	300.00
	1813 CI	—	150.00	200.00	300.00

MADRID MINT - Crowned M

C#	Date	Mintage	Fine	VF	XF
143a.3	1812 IJ	—	250.00	400.00	475.00
	1814 GJ	—	150.00	200.00	250.00
	1815 GJ	—	200.00	275.00	500.00
	1816 GJ	—	200.00	275.00	500.00
	1817 GJ	—	175.00	250.00	400.00
	1818 GJ	—	160.00	225.00	350.00
	1819 GJ	—	150.00	200.00	275.00
	1820 CJ	—	150.00	200.00	250.00
	1822 AJ	—	375.00	475.00	700.00
	1823 AJ	—	225.00	325.00	550.00
	1824 AJ	—	150.00	200.00	250.00
	1825 AJ	—	150.00	200.00	250.00
	1826 AJ	—	150.00	200.00	250.00
	1827 AJ	—	150.00	200.00	300.00
	1828 AJ	—	225.00	275.00	525.00
	1829 AJ	—	150.00	200.00	275.00
	1830 AJ	—	150.00	200.00	275.00
	1831 AJ	—	150.00	200.00	275.00
	1832 AJ	—	160.00	225.00	300.00
	1833 AJ	—	160.00	325.00	450.00

SEVILLE MINT - S, S/L

C#	Date	Mintage	Fine	VF	XF
143a.4	1815 CJ	—	150.00	200.00	300.00
	1816 CJ	—	150.00	200.00	250.00
	1817 CJ	—	150.00	200.00	250.00
	1818 CJ	—	150.00	200.00	275.00
	1819 CJ	—	150.00	200.00	275.00
	1820 CJ	—	150.00	200.00	275.00
	1821 CJ	—	150.00	200.00	275.00
	1824 JB	—	150.00	200.00	275.00
	1825 JB	—	150.00	200.00	275.00
	1826 JB	—	150.00	200.00	275.00
	1827 JB	—	150.00	200.00	300.00
	1828 JB	—	150.00	200.00	300.00
	1829 JB	—	150.00	200.00	300.00
	1830 JB	—	150.00	200.00	300.00
	1831 JB	—	150.00	200.00	300.00
	1832 JB	—	150.00	200.00	250.00
	1833 JB	—	160.00	250.00	275.00

CADIZ MINT - Crowned C

Obv: Bare head

C#	Date	Mintage	Fine	VF	XF
143a.5	1811 CI	—	325.00	425.00	700.00

SEVILLE MINT - S, S/L

C#	Date	Mintage	Fine	VF	XF
143a.6	1809 CN	—	150.00	225.00	400.00

CATALONIA MINT - C

Obv: Bare head, military bust.

C#	Date	Mintage	Fine	VF	XF
143a.7	1814 SF	—	400.00	525.00	800.00

CADIZ MINT - Crowned C

C#	Date	Mintage	Fine	VF	XF
143a.8	1811 CI	—	80.00	155.00	275.00
	1812 CJ	—	90.00	160.00	275.00
	1813 CJ	—	85.00	150.00	275.00
	1814 CJ	—	90.00	160.00	325.00

4 ESCUDOS

13.5400 gm., .917 GOLD, .3992 oz AGW

MADRID MINT - Crowned M

Obv: Bust of Charles III right.
Rev: Crowned arms in collar of The Golden Fleece.

C#	Date	Mintage	Fine	VF	XF
45	1761 JP	—	800.00	1500.	2500.

13.5400 gm., .900 GOLD, .3918 oz AGW

C#	Date	Mintage	Fine	VF	XF
54.1	1772 PJ	—	250.00	400.00	750.00
	1773 PJ	—	250.00	350.00	650.00
	1774 PJ	—	250.00	400.00	750.00
	1775 PJ	—	250.00	400.00	800.00
	1777 PJ	—	250.00	350.00	650.00
	1778 PJ	—	250.00	350.00	650.00
	1779 PJ	—	250.00	400.00	800.00
	1780 PJ	—	250.00	400.00	800.00
	1781 PJ	—	250.00	400.00	800.00
	1782 PJ	—	300.00	450.00	850.00
	1782 JD	—	350.00	600.00	1100.
	1783 JD	—	250.00	400.00	800.00
	1785 DV	—	250.00	400.00	800.00

13.5400 gm., .875 GOLD, .3809 oz AGW

C#	Date	Mintage	Fine	VF	XF
54.1a	1786 BV	—	250.00	350.00	700.00
	1787 DV	—	250.00	400.00	800.00
	1788 M	—	500.00	750.00	1500.

13.5400 gm., .900 GOLD, .3918 oz AGW

SEVILLE MINT - S, S/L

C#	Date	Mintage	Fine	VF	XF
54.2	1772 CF	—	400.00	600.00	1500.
	1773 CF	—	350.00	600.00	1100.
	1774 CF	—	250.00	500.00	1000.
	1775 CF	—	250.00	450.00	900.00
	1776 CF	—	250.00	400.00	800.00
	1777 CF	—	250.00	400.00	800.00
	1779 CF	—	250.00	400.00	750.00
	1781 CF	—	250.00	450.00	850.00
	1784 C	—	300.00	550.00	1100.
	1784 V	—	1200.	1800.	3200.
	1785 C	—	450.00	700.00	1400.

13.5400 gm., .875 GOLD, .3809 oz AGW

C#	Date	Mintage	Fine	VF	XF
54.2a	1786 C	—	250.00	350.00	700.00
	1787 CM	—	250.00	500.00	1000.
	1788 C	—	250.00	500.00	1000.

MADRID MINT - Crowned M

Obv: Bust of Charles IV right.
Rev: Crowned arms in collar of The Golden Fleece.

C#	Date	Mintage	Fine	VF	XF
75.1	1788 MF	—	1500.	2000.	3000.
	1789 MF	—	1800.	2500.	3500.
	1790 MF	—	300.00	500.00	900.00
	1791 MF	—	250.00	450.00	800.00
	1792 MF	—	250.00	450.00	800.00
	1794 MF	—	250.00	450.00	800.00
	1795 MF	—	250.00	450.00	800.00
	1796 MF	—	250.00	450.00	800.00
	1801 MF	—	400.00	600.00	1100.
	1801 FA	—	350.00	500.00	850.00
	1803 FA	—	400.00	600.00	1000.

SEVILLE MINT - S, S/L

C#	Date	Mintage	Fine	VF	XF
75.2	1801 C	—	1800.	3000.	4000.
	1808 C	—	1800.	2500.	3500.

MADRID MINT - Crowned M

Similar to 2 Escudos, C#143a.

C#	Date	Mintage	Fine	VF	XF
144	1814 GJ	—	200.00	325.00	650.00
	1815 GJ	—	250.00	300.00	600.00
	1816 GJ	—	250.00	300.00	600.00
	1818 GJ	—	250.00	325.00	650.00
	1819 GJ	—	165.00	300.00	500.00
	1820 GJ	—	150.00	250.00	375.00
	1824 AI	—	700.00	1400.	2600.

8 ESCUDOS

27.0700 gm., .917 GOLD, .7982 oz AGW

MADRID MINT - Crowned M

Obv: Young bust of Charles III right.
Rev: Crowned arms in collar of The Golden Fleece.

C#	Date	Mintage	Fine	VF	XF
47	1760 JP	—	3500.	10,000.	20,000.

SEVILLE MINT - S, S/L

C#	Date	Mintage	Fine	VF	XF
55.1	1762 JV	—	10,000.	16,000.	40,000.

27.0700 gm., .900 GOLD, .7834 oz AGW

MADRID MINT - Crowned M

Obv: Older bust of Charles III right.

C#	Date	Mintage	Fine	VF	XF
55.2	1771 JP	—	5000.	12,000.	30,000.
	1772 PJ	—	1800.	2700.	5500.
	1773 PJ	—	1000.	2500.	4500.
	1774 PJ	—	1500.	2400.	4500.
	1775 PJ	—	1500.	2700.	5000.
	1776 PJ	—	1500.	2300.	4000.
	1776 FA	—	2000.	3000.	5500.
	1777 PJ	—	1800.	2500.	5000.
	1778 PJ	—	2000.	3000.	5500.
	1779 PJ	—	2700.	5500.	7500.
	1783 JD	—	2500.	3500.	6000.
	1784 JD	—	2500.	3500.	6000.

27.0700 gm., .875 GOLD, .7616 oz AGW

C#	Date	Mintage	Fine	VF	XF
55.2a	1786 DV	—	2000.	3000.	5500.
	1788 M	—	2700.	5500.	7500.

27.0700 gm., .900 GOLD, .7834 oz AGW

SEVILLE MINT - S, S/L

C#	Date	Mintage	Fine	VF	XF
55.3	1772 CF	—	2000.	3000.	6000.
	1773 CF	—	1500.	2700.	5000.
	1774 CF	—	2000.	3000.	5500.
	1775 CF	—	1800.	2300.	4000.
	1776 CF	—	1800.	2500.	5000.
	1779 CF	—	2500.	4000.	6000.
	1784 C	—	2500.	3500.	6000.

27.0700 gm., .875 GOLD, .7616 oz AGW

C#	Date	Mintage	Fine	VF	XF
55.3a	1786 C	—	1400.	2200.	4400.
	1787 CM	—	1400.	2200.	4400.
	1788 C	—	1400.	2200.	4400.

MADRID MINT - Crowned M

Obv: Bust of Charles IV right.

C#	Date	Mintage	Fine	VF	XF
76.1	1788 MF	—	10,000.	12,000.	15,000.
	1789 MF	—	6000.	12,000.	17,000.
	1790 MF	—	3500.	6000.	7500.
	1802 FA	—	1200.	1600.	3000.
	1803 FA	—	3500.	5000.	7000.
	1805 FA	—	3500.	4500.	6000.

SEVILLE MINT - S, S/L

C#	Date	Mintage	Fine	VF	XF
76.2	1790 C	—	4000.	7500.	9000.
	1791 C	—	4000.	7500.	9000.

CADIZ MINT - Crowned C

Obv: Laureate uniformed bust of Ferdinand right.

C#	Date	Mintage	Fine	VF	XF
145	1811 CI	—	1100.	2250.	3000.

CATALONIA MINT - C

Obv: Laureate head.

C#	Date	Mintage	Fine	VF	XF
145a.1	1813 SF	—	3500.	6500.	8500.
	1814 SF	—	3400.	6500.	8500.

MADRID MINT - Crowned M

C#	Date	Mintage	Fine	VF	XF
145a.2	1814 GJ	—	1550.	3000.	4000.
	1816 GJ	—	1600.	3000.	4000.
	1817 GJ	—	1350.	3000.	4000.
	1819 GJ	—	1500.	3000.	4000.
	1820 GJ	—	600.00	1200.	1600.

DE VELLON ISSUES

REAL

1.3500 gm., .875 SILVER, .0392 oz ASW

MADRID MINT - Crowned M

C#	Date	Mintage	Fine	VF	XF
88	1812 AJ	—	30.00	50.00	75.00
	1813 RN	—	50.00	80.00	110.00

2 REALES

2.7050 gm., .903 SILVER, .0787 oz ASW

MADRID MINT - Crowned M

C#	Date	Mintage	Fine	VF	XF
89	1811 AI	—	35.00	70.00	110.00
	1812 AI	—	100.00	150.00	225.00
	1812 RN	—	80.00	135.00	200.00
	1813 RN	—	200.00	300.00	400.00

4 REALES

5.4100 gm., .903 SILVER, .1573 oz ASW

MADRID MINT - Crowned M

C#	Date	Mintage	Fine	VF	XF
90.1	1808 AI	—	55.00	125.00	200.00
	1809 AI	—	13.50	30.00	50.00
	1810 AI	—	11.50	27.50	45.00
	1811 AI	—	11.50	25.00	40.00
	1811 RS	—	45.00	70.00	90.00
	1812 AI	—	11.50	27.50	45.00
	1812 RS	—	45.00	70.00	90.00
	1812 RN	—	17.50	32.50	45.00
	1813 RN	—	13.50	30.00	40.00

SEVILLE MINT - S, S/L

C#	Date	Mintage	Fine	VF	XF
90.2	1810 LA	—	60.00	125.00	175.00
	1812 LA	—	20.00	40.00	70.00

BARCELONA MINT - B, BA

C#	Date	Mintage	Fine	VF	XF
137.5	1822 SP	—	17.50	30.00	50.00
	1823 SP	—	20.00	30.00	50.00

MADRID MINT - Crowned M

C#	Date	Mintage	Fine	VF	XF
137.6	1822 SR	—	10.00	22.50	40.00
	1823 SR	—	30.00	45.00	60.00

SEVILLE MINT - S, S/L

C#	Date	Mintage	Fine	VF	XF
137.7	1823 RD	—	20.00	35.00	50.00

VALENCIA MINT - V, VAL.

Obv: Small bare head bust of Ferdinand right.

C#	Date	Mintage	Fine	VF	XF
137.1	1823 R Spanish arms	—	27.50	40.00	60.00

10 REALES DE VELLON

13.5400 gm., .903 SILVER, .3931 oz ASW

MADRID MINT - Crowned M

C#	Date	Mintage	Fine	VF	XF
91	1809 AI	—	275.00	450.00	625.00
	1810 AI	—	200.00	350.00	500.00
	1811 AI	—	100.00	200.00	325.00
	1812 AI	—	100.00	200.00	325.00
	1812 RN	—	90.00	200.00	300.00
	1813 RN	—	115.00	275.00	375.00

BILBAO MINT - Bo

C#	Date	Mintage	Fine	VF	XF
138.1	1821 UG	—	25.00	40.00	75.00

MADRID MINT - Crowned M

C#	Date	Mintage	Fine	VF	XF
138.2	1821 SR	—	7.00	18.50	40.00

SANTANDER MINT - Sr

C#	Date	Mintage	Fine	VF	XF
138.3	1821 LT	—	50.00	75.00	150.00

SEVILLE MINT - S, S/L

C#	Date	Mintage	Fine	VF	XF
138.4	1821 RD	—	27.50	50.00	85.00

MADRID MINT - Crowned M

C#	Date	Mintage	Fine	VF	XF
174.1	1840 CL	—	175.00	350.00	650.00
	1840 DG	—	325.00	1000.	1550.
	1841 CL	—	175.00	350.00	650.00
	1842 CL	—	100.00	250.00	425.00
	1843 CL	—	125.00	300.00	525.00
	1844 CL	—	100.00	225.00	375.00
	1845 CL	—	100.00	225.00	400.00

SEVILLE MINT - S, S/L

C#	Date	Mintage	Fine	VF	XF
174.2	1841 RD	—	175.00	350.00	650.00
	1842 RD	—	125.00	300.00	550.00
	1843 RD	—	100.00	200.00	325.00

20 REALES DE VELLON

27.0800 gm., .903 SILVER, .7863 oz ASW

BARCELONA MINT - B, BA

C#	Date	Mintage	Fine	VF	XF
92.1	1811	—	125.00	200.00	475.00
	1812	—	125.00	225.00	500.00

MADRID MINT - Crowned M

C#	Date	Mintage	Fine	VF	XF
92.2	1808 AI	—	160.00	275.00	550.00
	1809 AI	—	50.00	80.00	140.00
	1810 IA	—	850.00	1750.	2800.
	1810 AI	—	50.00	80.00	125.00
	1811 AI	—	50.00	80.00	140.00
	1812 AI	—	85.00	175.00	425.00
	1813 RN	—	225.00	450.00	675.00

SEVILLE MINT - S, S/L

C#	Date	Mintage	Fine	VF	XF
92.3	1812 LA	—	225.00	375.00	725.00

BARCELONA MINT - B, BA

C#	Date	Mintage	Fine	VF	XF
139.1	1822 SP	—	400.00	550.00	800.00
	1823 SP	—	80.00	115.00	200.00

MADRID MINT - Crowned M

C#	Date	Mintage	Fine	VF	XF
139.2	1821 SR	—	550.00	900.00	1250.
	1822 SR	—	75.00	100.00	180.00
	1823 SR	—	80.00	115.00	250.00

SEVILLE MINT - S, S/L

C#	Date	Mintage	Fine	VF	XF
139.3	1822 RD	—	75.00	125.00	200.00
	1823 RD	—	115.00	150.00	275.00

MADRID MINT - Crowned M

C#	Date	Mintage	Fine	VF	XF
140	1833 DG	—	—	—	—

Obv. leg. ends: DIOS

Rev: Similar to C#140.

C#	Date	Mintage	Fine	VF	XF
165	1834 DG	—	900.00	2100.	3750.
	1834 NC	4,769	475.00	950.00	1450.
	1835 CR	.013	325.00	775.00	1200.
	1836 CR	.048	350.00	800.00	1450.

C#	Date	Mintage	Fine	VF	XF
175.1	1837 CR	.115	150.00	375.00	675.00
	1838 CL	.231	150.00	350.00	650.00
	1839 CL	.074	275.00	1350.	2000.
	1840 CL	6,012	375.00	1500.	2400.
	1847 DG	—	825.00	2000.	3250.
	1848 CL	.067	125.00	275.00	500.00
	1849 CL	.120	150.00	325.00	650.00
	1850 DG	—	900.00	2200.	4000.

SEVILLE MINT - S, S/L

C#	Date	Mintage	Fine	VF	XF
175.2	1842 RD	.012	450.00	900.00	1500.

80 REALES

6.7700 gm., .875 GOLD, .1905 oz AGW

MADRID MINT - Crowned M

C#	Date	Mintage	Fine	VF	XF
94	1809 AI	—	170.00	325.00	575.00
	1810 AI	—	300.00	425.00	850.00

C#	Date	Mintage	Fine	VF	XF
94a	1811 AI	—	150.00	325.00	625.00
	1812 AI	—	200.00	375.00	725.00
	1813 RN	—	250.00	400.00	850.00

BARCELONA MINT - B, BA

Obv: Old bare head of Ferdinand right.
Rev: Crowned arms in collar of the Golden Fleece.

C#	Date	Mintage	Fine	VF	XF
146.1	1822 SP	—	300.00	400.00	675.00
	1823 SP	—	150.00	225.00	300.00

MADRID MINT - Crowned M

C#	Date	Mintage	Fine	VF	XF
146.2	1822 SR	—	150.00	225.00	300.00
	1823 SR	—	120.00	175.00	350.00

SEVILLE MINT - S, S/L

C#	Date	Mintage	Fine	VF	XF
146.3	1823 RD	—	325.00	425.00	700.00

BARCELONA MINT - B, BA

Obv. leg. ends: DIOS

C#	Date	Mintage	Fine	VF	XF
166.1	1836 PS	—	450.00	625.00	1150.

MADRID MINT - Crowned M

C#	Date	Mintage	Fine	VF	XF
166.2	1834 CR	—	150.00	200.00	300.00
	1835 CR	—	150.00	200.00	325.00
	1836 CL	—	150.00	200.00	350.00
	1836 CR	—	175.00	350.00	700.00

SEVILLE MINT - S, S/L

C#	Date	Mintage	Fine	VF	XF
166.3	1835 DR	—	150.00	225.00	425.00
	1835 RD	—	150.00	300.00	525.00
	1836 DR	—	150.00	275.00	525.00
	1837 DR	—	175.00	350.00	600.00

BARCELONA MINT - B, BA

C#	Date	Mintage	Fine	VF	XF
176.1	1836 PS	—	375.00	525.00	1200.
	1838 PS	—	250.00	400.00	600.00
	1839 PS CONSTITUCION	—	150.00	350.00	500.00
	1839 PS CONST	—	150.00	350.00	500.00
	1840 PS	—	160.00	200.00	325.00
	1841 PS	—	150.00	200.00	350.00
	1842 CC	—	160.00	200.00	350.00
	1842 PS	—	650.00	1250.	2250.
	1843 CC	—	550.00	900.00	1500.
	1843 PS	—	550.00	900.00	1500.
	1844 PS	—	150.00	200.00	300.00
	1845 PS	—	150.00	200.00	300.00
	1846 PS	—	150.00	200.00	325.00
	1847 PS	—	160.00	225.00	475.00
	1848 PS	—	150.00	200.00	325.00

MADRID MINT - Crowned M

C#	Date	Mintage	Fine	VF	XF
176.2	1834 CR	—	150.00	175.00	300.00
	1835 CR	—	150.00	175.00	300.00
	1836 CL	—	200.00	250.00	475.00
	1836 CR	—	225.00	450.00	900.00
	1837 CR	—	350.00	675.00	1150.
	1838 CL	—	150.00	225.00	325.00
	1839 CL	—	175.00	250.00	450.00
	1840 CL	—	200.00	275.00	525.00
	1841 CL	—	150.00	200.00	350.00
	1842 CL	—	150.00	200.00	350.00
	1843 CL	—	150.00	200.00	300.00
	1844 CL	—	150.00	200.00	325.00
	1845 CL	—	165.00	250.00	375.00
	1846 CL	—	165.00	275.00	500.00
	1847 CL	—	150.00	225.00	350.00
	1848 CL	—	150.00	200.00	350.00
	1849 CL	—	225.00	375.00	650.00

SEVILLE MINT - S, S/L

C#	Date	Mintage	Fine	VF	XF
176.3	1835 DR	—	175.00	275.00	450.00
	1835 RD	—	150.00	250.00	375.00
	1836 DR	—	170.00	375.00	700.00
	1837 DR	—	225.00	450.00	900.00
	1838 DR	—	150.00	200.00	350.00
	1838 RD	—	150.00	200.00	300.00
	1839 RD	—	180.00	200.00	350.00
	1840 RD	—	225.00	300.00	500.00
	1841 RD	—	100.00	200.00	325.00
	1842 RD	—	150.00	300.00	500.00
	1843 RD	—	165.00	225.00	325.00
	1844 RD	—	150.00	300.00	575.00
	1845 RD	—	150.00	200.00	325.00
	1846 RD	—	150.00	300.00	475.00
	1847 RD	—	225.00	500.00	725.00
	1848 RD	—	150.00	225.00	375.00

BARCELONA MINT - B, BA

Obv. leg. ends: CONSTITUCION

C#	Date	Mintage	Fine	VF	XF
176a	1837 PS	—	375.00	550.00	1000.
	1838 PS	—	150.00	275.00	500.00

160 REALES

13.5400 gm., .875 GOLD, .3809 oz AGW

MADRID MINT - Crowned M

Similar to 80 Reales, C#146.

C#	Date	Mintage	Fine	VF	XF
147	1822 SR	—	550.00	900.00	1150.

320 REALES

27.0700 gm., .875 GOLD, .7616 oz AGW

MADRID MINT - Crowned M

C#	Date	Mintage	Fine	VF	XF
95	1810 AI	—	4200.	5250.	7500.
	1810 RS	—	3500.	5250.	6750.
	1812 RS	—	3150.	5200.	6500.

Similar to 80 Reales, C#146.

C#	Date	Mintage	Fine	VF	XF
148	1822 SR	—	650.00	1200.	1700.
	1823 SR	—	1100.	1750.	2750.

DECIMAL COINAGE

10 Decimos = 1 Real
100 Centimos = 1 Real

1/20 REAL

COPPER

SEGOVIA MINT - 3-pointed star

Y#	Date	Mintage	Fine	VF	XF
15	1852	—	12.50	27.50	55.00
	1853	—	5.75	12.50	22.50

5 CENTIMOS

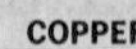

COPPER

SEGOVIA MINT - 3-pointed star

Y#	Date	Mintage	Fine	VF	XF
24	1854	—	10.00	90.00	175.00
	1855	—	4.00	7.50	18.50
	1856	—	4.25	9.00	25.00
	1857	—	4.25	9.00	25.00
	1858	—	15.00	30.00	70.00
	1859	—	2.75	4.50	11.50
	1860	—	4.25	9.00	22.50
	1861	—	4.25	9.00	22.50
	1862	—	4.25	9.00	22.50
	1863	—	4.25	9.00	22.50
	1864	—	11.50	30.00	60.00

1/10 REAL

COPPER

SEGOVIA MINT - 3-pointed star

Y#	Date	Mintage	Fine	VF	XF
16	1850	—	5.25	10.00	18.50
	1851	—	18.50	40.00	70.00
	1852	—	3.50	7.00	15.00
	1853	—	2.50	5.00	12.50

10 CENTIMOS

COPPER

SEGOVIA MINT - 3-pointed star

Y#	Date	Mintage	Fine	VF	XF
25	1854	—	50.00	90.00	175.00
	1855	—	3.75	6.00	13.50
	1856	—	6.75	12.50	25.00
	1857	—	3.50	6.00	12.50
	1858	—	5.00	8.50	17.50
	1859	—	3.50	6.00	12.50
	1860	—	3.50	6.00	12.50
	1861	—	3.50	6.00	12.50
	1862	—	6.75	11.50	30.00
	1863	—	6.75	11.50	30.00
	1864	—	18.50	32.50	70.00

1/5 REAL

COPPER

SEGOVIA MINT - 3-pointed star

Y#	Date	Mintage	Fine	VF	XF
17	1853	—	12.50	25.00	50.00

25 CENTIMOS

COPPER

BARCELONA MINT - 8-pointed star

Y#	Date	Mintage	Fine	VF	XF
26.1	1863	—	100.00	130.00	325.00
	1864	—	25.00	50.00	100.00

SEGOVIA MINT - 3-pointed star

Y#	Date	Mintage	Fine	VF	XF
26.2	1854	—	6.50	10.00	17.50
	1855	—	8.50	16.50	32.50
	1856	—	11.50	16.50	45.00
	1857	—	5.00	10.00	20.00
	1858	—	8.50	15.00	30.00
	1859	—	8.50	15.00	35.00
	1860	—	6.50	10.00	20.00
	1861	—	5.00	8.50	20.00
	1862	—	5.00	8.50	20.00
	1863	—	16.00	32.50	70.00
	1864	—	7.75	12.50	25.00

1/2 REAL

COPPER

JUBIA MINT - 4-pointed star

Similar to 1/5 Real, Y#17.

Y#	Date	Mintage	Fine	VF	XF
18.1	1850	—	28.50	60.00	125.00

MADRID MINT - 6-pointed star

Y#	Date	Mintage	Fine	VF	XF
18.2	1848 DG	—	110.00	150.00	225.00
	1848	—	10.00	20.00	40.00

SEGOVIA MINT - 3-pointed star

Y#	Date	Mintage	Fine	VF	XF
18.3	1848	—	11.50	20.00	40.00
	1849	—	15.00	30.00	55.00
	1850	—	17.50	30.00	50.00
	1851	—	17.50	30.00	50.00
	1852	—	17.50	30.00	50.00
	1853	—	10.00	18.50	35.00

REAL

1.3146 gm., .900 SILVER, .0380 oz ASW

BARCELONA MINT - 8-pointed star

Y#	Date	Mintage	Fine	VF	XF
19.1	1852	—	7.50	15.00	45.00
	1853	—	6.50	12.50	20.00
	1854	—	9.00	17.50	32.50
	1855	—	6.75	12.50	25.00

MADRID MINT - 6-pointed star

Y#	Date	Mintage	Fine	VF	XF
19.2	1852	—	6.50	13.50	22.50
	1853	—	7.50	15.00	30.00
	1854	—	25.00	55.00	100.00
	1855	—	25.00	45.00	90.00

SEVILLE MINT - 7-pointed star

Y#	Date	Mintage	Fine	VF	XF
19.3	1850	—	12.50	27.50	70.00
	1851	—	12.50	27.50	70.00
	1852	—	6.50	12.50	20.00
	1853	—	7.50	10.00	17.50
	1854	—	10.00	20.00	45.00
	1855	—	6.75	13.50	32.50

BARCELONA MINT - 8-pointed star

Y#	Date	Mintage	Fine	VF	XF
27.1	1857	—	6.50	12.50	25.00
	1858	—	9.00	20.00	35.00
	1859	—	18.50	40.00	75.00
	1860	—	7.00	13.50	25.00
	1861	—	7.00	13.50	25.00
	1862	—	10.00	20.00	50.00
	1863	—	12.50	22.50	45.00
	1864	—	15.00	35.00	65.00

MADRID MINT - 6-pointed star

Y#	Date	Mintage	Fine	VF	XF
27.2	1857	—	6.50	12.50	25.00
	1858	—	20.00	35.00	70.00
	1859	—	6.50	12.50	20.00
	1860	—	7.00	13.50	25.00
	1861	—	8.50	17.50	35.00
	1862	—	9.00	20.00	40.00
	1863	—	7.50	16.00	40.00
	1864	—	12.50	22.50	45.00

SEVILLE MINT - 7-pointed star

Y#	Date	Mintage	Fine	VF	XF
27.3	1857	—	30.00	65.00	150.00
	1858	—	35.00	75.00	150.00
	1859	—	15.00	35.00	70.00
	1860	—	7.00	13.50	25.00
	1861	—	40.00	70.00	125.00
	1862	—	9.00	20.00	40.00
	1863	—	8.50	17.50	40.00
	1864	—	12.50	22.50	45.00

2 REALES

2.6291 gm., .900 SILVER, .0761 oz ASW

BARCELONA MINT - 8-pointed star

Y#	Date	Mintage	Fine	VF	XF
20.1	1852	—	11.50	35.00	60.00
	1853	—	9.00	20.00	40.00
	1854	—	13.50	27.50	60.00
	1855	—	11.50	27.50	55.00

MADRID MINT - 6-pointed star

Y#	Date	Mintage	Fine	VF	XF
20.2	1851	—	18.00	45.00	75.00
	1852	—	7.50	18.50	45.00
	1853	—	25.00	45.00	80.00
	1854	—	11.50	20.00	50.00
	1855	—	8.50	18.50	40.00

SEVILLE MINT - 7-pointed star

Y#	Date	Mintage	Fine	VF	XF
20.3	1850	—	35.00	60.00	90.00
	1851	—	11.50	22.50	50.00
	1852	—	5.50	15.00	30.00
	1853	—	5.00	8.50	25.00
	1854	—	7.50	17.50	40.00
	1855	—	8.50	18.50	40.00

BARCELONA MINT - 8-pointed star

Y#	Date	Mintage	Fine	VF	XF
28.1	1857	—	3.75	10.00	30.00
	1858	—	37.50	80.00	130.00
	1860	—	13.50	30.00	60.00
	1861	—	27.50	40.00	65.00
	1863	—	35.00	70.00	135.00

MADRID MINT - 6-pointed star

Y#	Date	Mintage	Fine	VF	XF
28.2	1857	—	12.50	35.00	70.00
	1859	—	3.75	15.00	30.00
	1860	—	25.00	60.00	125.00
	1861	—	7.50	15.00	30.00
	1862	—	5.00	10.00	30.00
	1863	—	13.50	30.00	60.00
	1864	—	40.00	100.00	200.00

SEVILLE MINT - 7-pointed star

Y#	Date	Mintage	Fine	VF	XF
28.3	1857	—	13.50	35.00	70.00
	1858	—	12.50	55.00	100.00
	1859	—	22.50	70.00	110.00
	1860	—	12.50	30.00	60.00
	1861	—	7.50	18.50	35.00
	1862	—	7.50	15.00	30.00
	1863	—	6.75	15.00	22.50
	1864	—	20.00	45.00	75.00

4 REALES

5.2582 gm., .900 SILVER, .1521 oz ASW

BARCELONA MINT - 8-pointed star

Y#	Date	Mintage	Fine	VF	XF
21.1	1852	—	16.50	27.50	55.00
	1853	—	22.50	45.00	100.00
	1854	—	10.00	15.00	40.00
	1855	—	11.50	25.00	50.00

MADRID MINT - 6-pointed star

Y#	Date	Mintage	Fine	VF	XF
21.2	1852	—	11.50	20.00	40.00
	1853	—	35.00	75.00	150.00
	1854	—	12.50	30.00	45.00

Y#	Date	Mintage	Fine	VF	XF
21.2	1855	—	22.50	50.00	90.00

SEVILLE MINT - 7-pointed star

Y#	Date	Mintage	Fine	VF	XF
21.3	1852	—	35.00	75.00	150.00
	1853	—	6.75	15.00	30.00
	1854	—	6.75	11.50	25.00
	1855	—	6.75	11.50	30.00

BARCELONA MINT - 8-pointed star

Y#	Date	Mintage	Fine	VF	XF
29.1	1857	—	32.50	55.00	100.00
	1858	—	11.50	30.00	55.00
	1859	—	17.50	32.50	65.00
	1860	—	11.50	20.00	60.00
	1861	—	11.50	30.00	55.00
	1862	—	125.00	225.00	425.00
	1864	—	13.50	32.50	65.00

MADRID MINT - 6-pointed star

Y#	Date	Mintage	Fine	VF	XF
29.2	1856	—	55.00	85.00	125.00
	1857	—	11.50	20.00	45.00
	1858	—	6.50	16.50	32.50
	1859	—	7.50	16.50	32.50
	1860	—	65.00	125.00	225.00
	1861	—	10.00	25.00	40.00
	1862	—	6.50	16.50	32.50
	1863	—	6.00	11.50	27.50
	1864	—	22.50	55.00	125.00

SEVILLE MINT - 7-pointed star

Y#	Date	Mintage	Fine	VF	XF
29.3	1857	—	70.00	200.00	300.00
	1858	—	100.00	250.00	350.00
	1859	—	75.00	225.00	300.00
	1860	—	12.50	35.00	65.00
	1861	—	20.00	45.00	90.00
	1862	—	10.00	20.00	40.00
	1863	—	11.50	20.00	40.00
	1864	—	10.00	20.00	40.00

10 REALES

13.1455 gm., .900 SILVER, .3804 oz ASW

BARCELONA MINT - 8-pointed star

Similar to 4 Reales, Y#21.

Y#	Date	Mintage	Fine	VF	XF
22.1	1851	—	275.00	675.00	1000.
	1852	—	35.00	85.00	150.00
	1853	—	18.50	45.00	70.00
	1854	—	18.50	45.00	70.00
	1855	—	45.00	100.00	200.00

MADRID MINT - 6-pointed star

Y#	Date	Mintage	Fine	VF	XF
22.2	1851	—	45.00	90.00	200.00
	1852	—	18.50	45.00	70.00
	1853	—	18.50	45.00	70.00
	1854	—	22.50	45.00	75.00
	1855	—	65.00	100.00	175.00

SEVILLE MINT - 7-pointed star

Y#	Date	Mintage	Fine	VF	XF
22.3	1851	—	75.00	175.00	325.00
	1852	—	18.50	45.00	70.00
	1853	—	16.50	35.00	60.00
	1854	—	18.50	40.00	75.00
	1855	—	12.50	35.00	70.00
	1856	—	150.00	275.00	500.00

BARCELONA MINT - 8-pointed star

Y#	Date	Mintage	Fine	VF	XF
30.1	1859	—	35.00	55.00	125.00
	1860	—	15.00	32.50	75.00
	1861	—	16.50	45.00	70.00
	1862	—	35.00	55.00	125.00
	1863	—	35.00	55.00	100.00
	1864	—	80.00	150.00	300.00

MADRID MINT - 6-pointed star

Y#	Date	Mintage	Fine	VF	XF
30.2	1857	—	55.00	90.00	225.00
	1858	—	22.50	55.00	125.00
	1859	—	22.50	55.00	125.00
	1860	—	30.00	50.00	100.00
	1861	—	35.00	60.00	125.00
	1862	—	12.50	25.00	50.00
	1863	—	12.50	25.00	50.00
	1864	—	12.50	26.50	55.00
	1865	—	45.00	85.00	175.00

SEVILLE MINT - 7-pointed star

Y#	Date	Mintage	Fine	VF	XF
30.3	1857	—	35.00	60.00	125.00
	1858	—	15.00	32.50	70.00
	1859	—	35.00	60.00	125.00
	1860	—	200.00	300.00	475.00
	1861	—	22.50	45.00	90.00
	1863	—	60.00	125.00	225.00
	1864	—	60.00	150.00	275.00

20 REALES

26.2910 gm., .900 SILVER, .7607 oz ASW

MADRID MINT - 6-pointed star

Rev: Similar to C#140.

Y#	Date	Mintage	Fine	VF	XF
13.1	1850 CL	.126	40.00	75.00	200.00
	1850 DG	—	1000.	1500.	3250.

SEVILLE MINT - 7-pointed star

Y#	Date	Mintage	Fine	VF	XF
13.2	1850 RD	—	225.00	500.00	850.00

BARCELONA MINT - 8-pointed star

Y#	Date	Mintage	Fine	VF	XF
23.1	1850	—	350.00	550.00	900.00
	1851	1.055	125.00	200.00	375.00
	1852	1.053	200.00	300.00	475.00

MADRID MINT - 6-pointed star

Y#	Date	Mintage	Fine	VF	XF
23.2	1850	.500	35.00	65.00	100.00
	1851	Inc. Ab.	35.00	65.00	100.00
	1852	Inc. Ab.	32.50	65.00	100.00
	1854	1.355	32.50	60.00	100.00
	1855	1.229	42.50	70.00	110.00

SEVILLE MINT - 7-pointed star

Y#	Date	Mintage	Fine	VF	XF
23.3	1850	—	200.00	300.00	600.00
	1851	Inc. Ab.	45.00	65.00	100.00
	1852	Inc. Ab.	55.00	125.00	225.00
	1854	Inc. Ab.	42.50	70.00	110.00
	1855	Inc. Ab.	35.00	70.00	125.00

BARCELONA MINT - 8-pointed star

Rev: Similar to Y#23.1

Y#	Date	Mintage	Fine	VF	XF
31.1	1857	.713	225.00	325.00	600.00
	1859	.880	500.00	625.00	1000.
	1862	1.594	525.00	700.00	1100.
	1863	.520	625.00	950.00	1500.

MADRID MINT - 6-pointed star

Y#	Date	Mintage	Fine	VF	XF
31.2	1856	1.021	27.50	55.00	100.00
	1857	Inc. Ab.	30.00	60.00	100.00
	1858	1.626	30.00	60.00	100.00
	1859	Inc. Ab.	30.00	60.00	100.00
	1860	.941	25.00	60.00	100.00
	1861	1.352	35.00	60.00	125.00
	1862	Inc. Ab.	35.00	60.00	100.00
	1863	Inc. Ab.	125.00	160.00	300.00
	1864	2.776	45.00	75.00	175.00

SEVILLE MINT - 7-pointed star

Y#	Date	Mintage	Fine	VF	XF
31.3	1856	Inc. Ab.	90.00	175.00	350.00
	1857	Inc. Ab.	40.00	65.00	100.00
	1858	Inc. Ab.	55.00	100.00	200.00
	1859	Inc. Ab.	125.00	200.00	450.00
	1860	Inc. Ab.	60.00	80.00	125.00
	1861	Inc. Ab.	175.00	300.00	550.00
	1862	Inc. Ab.	125.00	175.00	375.00
	1863	Inc. Ab.	125.00	225.00	375.00

1.6674 gm., .900 GOLD, .0482 oz AGW

MADRID MINT - 6-pointed star

Similar to 40 Reales, Y#33.

Y#	Date	Mintage	Fine	VF	XF
32	1857	—	450.00	675.00	1100.
	1861	—	175.00	275.00	575.00
	1862	—	175.00	250.00	425.00
	1863	—	350.00	525.00	950.00

40 REALES

3.3349 gm., .900 GOLD, .0965 oz AGW

BARCELONA MINT - 8-pointed star

Y#	Date	Mintage	Fine	VF	XF
33.1	1863	—	100.00	175.00	300.00
	1864	—	110.00	175.00	300.00

MADRID MINT - 6-pointed star

Y#	Date	Mintage	Fine	VF	XF
33.2	1861	—	200.00	400.00	800.00
	1862	—	100.00	150.00	275.00
	1863	—	110.00	175.00	300.00

Obv: Draped bust of Isabel II left.
Rev: Crowned draped arms.

Y#	Date	Mintage	Fine	VF	XF
A35.1	1864	—	85.00	150.00	225.00

SEVILLE MINT - 7-pointed star

Y#	Date	Mintage	Fine	VF	XF
A35.2	1864	—	325.00	650.00	1100.

100 REALES

8.3371 gm., .900 GOLD, .2412 oz AGW

BARCELONA MINT - 8-pointed star

Y#	Date	Mintage	Fine	VF	XF
A23.1	1850 SM	—	1200.	2000.	3000.

MADRID MINT - 6-pointed star

Y#	Date	Mintage	Fine	VF	XF
A23.2	1850 CL	—	125.00	250.00	400.00
	1850 DG	—	850.00	1400.	1900.
	1851 CL	—	1100.	1650.	2500.

SEVILLE MINT - 7-pointed star

Y#	Date	Mintage	Fine	VF	XF
A23.3	1850 RD	—	625.00	1100.	1550.

BARCELONA MINT - 8-pointed star

Y#	Date	Mintage	Fine	VF	XF
B23.1	1851	—	850.00	1300.	1600.
	1854	—	175.00	250.00	450.00
	1855	—	175.00	350.00	600.00

MADRID MINT - 6-pointed star

Y#	Date	Mintage	Fine	VF	XF
B23.2	1851	—	850.00	1300.	1600.
	1852	—	850.00	1300.	1600.
	1854	—	175.00	350.00	525.00
	1855	—	200.00	450.00	675.00

SEVILLE MINT - 7-pointed star

Y#	Date	Mintage	Fine	VF	XF
B23.3	1852	—	2200.	3000.	4000.
	1854	—	175.00	325.00	525.00
	1855	—	185.00	350.00	550.00

BARCELONA MINT - 8-pointed star

Similar to 2 Reales, C#33.

Y#	Date	Mintage	Fine	VF	XF
35.1	1856	—	575.00	825.00	1400.
	1857	—	175.00	250.00	400.00
	1858	—	175.00	250.00	350.00
	1859	—	175.00	250.00	350.00
	1860	—	175.00	225.00	300.00
	1861	—	600.00	1250.	2000.
	1862	—	200.00	350.00	575.00

MADRID MINT - 6-pointed star

Y#	Date	Mintage	Fine	VF	XF
35.2	1856	—	175.00	250.00	375.00
	1857	—	225.00	450.00	675.00
	1858	—	175.00	250.00	300.00
	1859	—	175.00	250.00	400.00
	1860	—	175.00	225.00	275.00
	1861	—	175.00	225.00	275.00
	1862	—	155.00	175.00	300.00

SEVILLE MINT - 7-pointed star

Y#	Date	Mintage	Fine	VF	XF
35.3	1856	—	425.00	950.00	1500.
	1857	—	200.00	250.00	300.00
	1858	—	175.00	250.00	375.00
	1859	—	175.00	250.00	325.00
	1860	—	175.00	250.00	375.00
	1861	—	175.00	250.00	300.00
	1862	—	165.00	275.00	350.00

MADRID MINT - 6-pointed star

Rev: Crowned and mantled rectangluar arms.

Y#	Date	Mintage	Fine	VF	XF
B35.1	1863	—	175.00	250.00	300.00
	1864	—	175.00	250.00	325.00

SEVILLE MINT - 7-pointed star

Y#	Date	Mintage	Fine	VF	XF
B35.2	1863	—	325.00	575.00	800.00
	1864	—	375.00	525.00	900.00

SECOND DECIMAL COINAGE

100 Centimos = 1 Escudo

NOTE: For similar coins, but with denominations expressed Cs. de Peso, see Philippines.

1/2 CENTIMO

COPPER

BARCELONA MINT - 8-pointed star

Y#	Date	Mintage	Fine	VF	XF
36.1	1866 OM	—	11.50	22.50	45.00
	1867 OM	—	5.00	8.50	17.50
	1868 OM	—	5.00	8.50	20.00

JUBIA MINT - 4-pointed star

Y#	Date	Mintage	Fine	VF	XF
36.2	1866 OM	—	6.00	13.00	27.50
	1867 OM	—	5.00	10.00	20.00
	1868 OM	—	5.00	8.50	15.00

MADRID MINT - 6-pointed star

Y#	Date	Mintage	Fine	VF	XF
36.3	1865	—	200.00	375.00	525.00
	1867 OM	—	11.50	27.50	60.00

SEGOVIA MINT - 3-pointed star

Y#	Date	Mintage	Fine	VF	XF
36.4	1866 OM	—	5.00	11.50	22.50
	1867 OM	—	4.50	7.50	17.50
	1868 OM	—	5.00	12.50	25.00

SEVILLE MINT - 7-pointed star

Y#	Date	Mintage	Fine	VF	XF
36.5	1867 OM	—	15.00	27.50	60.00
	1868 OM	—	7.50	16.50	35.00

CENTIMO

COPPER

BARCELONA MINT - 8-pointed star

Y#	Date	Mintage	Fine	VF	XF
37.1	1866	—	16.50	32.50	55.00
	1866 OM	—	4.50	9.00	22.50
	1867 OM	—	4.50	8.50	16.50
	1868 OM	—	4.00	6.00	13.50

JUBIA MINT - 4-pointed star

Y#	Date	Mintage	Fine	VF	XF
37.2	1866	—	22.50	40.00	80.00
	1866 OM	—	12.50	22.50	50.00
	1867 OM	—	6.50	16.50	32.50
	1868 OM	—	4.50	11.50	18.50

MADRID MINT - 6-pointed star

Y#	Date	Mintage	Fine	VF	XF
37.3	1865	—	150.00	300.00	450.00

SEGOVIA MINT - 3-pointed star

Y#	Date	Mintage	Fine	VF	XF
37.4	1866	—	16.50	32.50	60.00
	1866 OM	—	15.00	27.50	60.00
	1867	—	35.00	70.00	150.00
	1867 OM	—	4.50	8.00	16.50
	1868 OM	—	10.00	16.50	30.00

SEVILLE MINT - 7-pointed star

Y#	Date	Mintage	Fine	VF	XF
37.5	1867 OM	—	4.50	10.00	20.00
	1868 OM	—	4.50	13.50	25.00

2-1/2 CENTIMOS

COPPER

BARCELONA MINT - 8-pointed star

Y#	Date	Mintage	Fine	VF	XF
38.1	1866	—	11.50	22.50	45.00
	1866 OM	—	11.50	22.50	45.00
	1867 OM	—	5.50	11.50	20.00
	1868 OM	—	5.00	7.50	17.50

JUBIA MINT - 4-pointed star

Y#	Date	Mintage	Fine	VF	XF
38.2	1866 OM	—	22.50	40.00	80.00
	1867 OM	—	6.50	12.50	20.00
	1868 OM	—	5.00	7.50	17.50

MADRID MINT - 6-pointed star

Y#	Date	Mintage	Fine	VF	XF
38.3	1865	—	150.00	225.00	350.00
	1867 OM	—	22.50	45.00	85.00

SEGOVIA MINT - 3-pointed star

Y#	Date	Mintage	Fine	VF	XF
38.4	1866 OM	—	55.00	80.00	150.00
	1867 OM	—	5.50	10.00	20.00
	1868 OM	—	5.50	10.00	20.00

SEVILLE MINT - 7-pointed star

Y#	Date	Mintage	Fine	VF	XF
38.5	1867 OM	—	5.50	10.00	20.00
	1868 OM	—	11.50	22.50	50.00

5 CENTIMOS

COPPER

BARCELONA MINT - 8-pointed star

Y#	Date	Mintage	Fine	VF	XF
39.1	1866	—	50.00	85.00	150.00
	1866 OM	—	20.00	40.00	85.00
	1867 OM	—	5.50	8.50	17.50
	1868 OM	—	5.50	7.75	15.00

JUBIA MINT - 4-pointed star

Y#	Date	Mintage	Fine	VF	XF
39.2	1866	—	16.50	35.00	70.00
	1867 OM	—	5.50	8.50	17.50
	1868 OM	—	6.75	12.50	27.50

MADRID MINT - 6-pointed star

Y#	Date	Mintage	Fine	VF	XF
39.3	1865	—	100.00	200.00	300.00

SEGOVIA MINT - 3-pointed star

Y#	Date	Mintage	Fine	VF	XF
39.4	1866 OM	—	7.00	14.00	25.00
	1867 OM	—	7.00	12.50	27.50
	1868 OM	—	5.50	8.50	18.50

SEVILLE MINT - 7-pointed star

Y#	Date	Mintage	Fine	VF	XF
39.5	1867 OM	—	11.50	20.00	45.00
	1868 OM	—	5.50	8.50	18.50

10 CENTIMOS

1.2980 gm., .810 SILVER, .0338 oz ASW

MADRID MINT - 6-pointed star

Similar to 20 Centimos, Y#41.

Y#	Date	Mintage	Fine	VF	XF
40.1	1865	—	12.50	20.00	45.00
	1866	—	18.50	40.00	80.00
	1868 (68)	—	12.50	22.50	50.00

SEVILLE MINT - 7-pointed star

Y#	Date	Mintage	Fine	VF	XF
40	1864	—	32.50	55.00	125.00

Y#	Date	Mintage	Fine	VF	XF
40	1865	—	15.00	27.50	55.00
	1866	—	15.00	27.50	60.00
	1868	—	32.50	55.00	100.00

20 CENTIMOS

2.5960 gm., .810 SILVER, .0676 oz ASW

MADRID MINT - 6-pointed star

Y#	Date	Mintage	Fine	VF	XF
41.1	1864	—	15.00	30.00	60.00
	1865	—	12.50	22.50	45.00
	1866	—	15.00	27.50	45.00
	1867	—	12.50	20.00	40.00
	1868 (68)	—	9.00	15.00	27.50

SEVILLE MINT - 7-pointed star

Y#	Date	Mintage	Fine	VF	XF
41.2	1864	—	15.00	30.00	60.00
	1865	—	12.50	20.00	40.00
	1866	—	22.50	40.00	75.00

40 CENTIMOS

5.1920 gm., .810 SILVER, .1352 oz ASW

BARCELONA MINT - 8-pointed star

Y#	Date	Mintage	Fine	VF	XF
42.1	1865	—	27.50	50.00	90.00

MADRID MINT - 6-pointed star

Y#	Date	Mintage	Fine	VF	XF
42.2	1864	—	11.50	22.50	45.00
	1865	—	8.00	15.00	27.50
	1866	—	8.00	13.50	25.00
	1867	—	8.75	12.50	27.50
	1868 (68)	—	9.00	13.00	25.00

SEVILLE MINT - 7-pointed star

Y#	Date	Mintage	Fine	VF	XF
42.3	1864	—	50.00	80.00	140.00
	1865	—	11.50	22.50	45.00
	1866	—	8.50	17.50	37.50

ESCUDO

12.9800 gm., .900 SILVER, .3756 oz ASW

MADRID MINT - 6-pointed star

Y#	Date	Mintage	Fine	VF	XF
43.1	1864	—	50.00	90.00	150.00
	1865	—	45.00	70.00	150.00
	1866	—	22.50	40.00	90.00
	1867	—	15.00	27.50	50.00
	1868 (68)	—	11.50	22.50	45.00

SEVILLE MINT - 7-pointed star

Y#	Date	Mintage	Fine	VF	XF
43.2	1864	—	40.00	65.00	125.00
	1866	—	70.00	115.00	225.00

2 ESCUDOS

25.9600 gm., .900 SILVER, .7512 oz ASW

MADRID MINT - 6-pointed star

Obv: Head of Isabel II right.
Rev: Crowned arms between pillars.

Y#	Date	Mintage	Fine	VF	XF
44	1865	—	375.00	575.00	875.00
	1866	—	375.00	650.00	1050.
	1867	4.234	50.00	70.00	125.00
	1868 68)	2.225	50.00	70.00	150.00

1.6774 gm., .900 GOLD, .0485 oz AGW

Y#	Date	Mintage	VF	XF	Unc
45	1865	—	150.00	200.00	300.00
	1867	—	500.00	875.00	1200.
	1868 (68)	—	300.00	500.00	750.00

4 ESCUDOS

3.3548 gm., .900 GOLD, .0971 oz AGW

MADRID MINT - 6-pointed star

Y#	Date	Mintage	VF	XF	Unc
46.1	1865	—	175.00	225.00	300.00
	1866	—	175.00	225.00	325.00
	1867	—	175.00	275.00	325.00
	1868 (68)	—	175.00	275.00	325.00

SEVILLE MINT - 7-pointed star

Y#	Date	Mintage	VF	XF	Unc
46.2	1865	—	400.00	625.00	850.00
	1866	—	400.00	600.00	850.00

10 ESCUDOS

8.3870 gm., .900 GOLD, .2427 oz AGW

MADRID MINT - 6-pointed star

Y#	Date	Mintage	VF	XF	Unc
47.1	1866	—	450.00	825.00	1250.
	1867	—	225.00	400.00	650.00
	1868 (68)	—	175.00	200.00	350.00
	1868 (73)	—	—	Rare	—

SEVILLE MINT - 7-pointed star

Y#	Date	Mintage	VF	XF	Unc
47.2	1865	—	800.00	1400.	2000.

THIRD DECIMAL COINAGE

100 Centimos = 1 Peseta

CENTIMO

COPPER

BARCELONA MINT - 8-pointed star

Y#	Date	Mintage	VF	XF	Unc
51	1870	169.891	.60	1.00	3.00

BRONZE

MADRID MINT - 6-pointed star

Y#	Date	Mintage	VF	XF	Unc
96	1906(6) SLV	7.500	.50	2.00	4.00
	1906 SMV	Inc. Ab.	150.00	300.00	650.00

Y#	Date	Mintage	VF	XF	Unc
98	1911(1) PCV	1.462	15.00	30.00	75.00
	1912(2) PCV	2.109	1.00	3.50	10.00
	1913(3) PCV	1.429	2.25	5.00	12.50

2 CENTIMOS

COPPER

BARCELONA MINT - 8-pointed star

Y#	Date	Mintage	VF	XF	Unc
52	1870	115.869	.50	1.00	3.00

BRONZE

MADRID MINT - 6-pointed star

Y#	Date	Mintage	VF	XF	Unc
97	1904(04) SMV	10.000	.50	1.00	4.00
	1905(05) SMV	5.000	.50	2.00	5.00

Y#	Date	Mintage	VF	XF	Unc
99	1911(11) PCV	2.284	.25	2.50	6.00
	1912(12) PCV	5.216	.75	2.25	5.25

25 MILESIMAS DE ESCUDO

BRONZE

SEGOVIA MINT - 3-pointed star

Y#	Date	Mintage	Fine	VF	XF
A50	1868	—	60.00	80.00	115.00

5 CENTIMOS

COPPER

BARCELONA MINT - 8-pointed star

Y#	Date	Mintage	VF	XF	Unc
53	1870	287.381	.50	2.75	20.00

BRONZE

Y#	Date	Mintage	VF	XF	Unc
69	1877	34.376	1.00	5.00	37.50
	1878	67.954	2.00	11.50	45.00
	1879	54.994	1.00	5.00	20.00

IRON

MADRID MINT - 6-pointed star

Y#	Date	Mintage	VF	XF	Unc
103	1937	—	.50	1.00	2.00
	1938	—	100.00	175.00	275.00

ALUMINUM

Y#	Date	Mintage	VF	XF	Unc
110	1940	175.000	.20	1.00	6.00
	1941	202.107	.15	.25	3.00
	1945	221.500	.15	.25	2.50
	1953	31.573	.80	2.00	6.50

10 CENTIMOS

COPPER

BARCELONA MINT - 8-pointed star

Y#	Date	Mintage	VF	XF	Unc
54.1	1869	—	—	Rare	—
54.2	1870	170.088	.90	5.00	30.00

BRONZE

Y#	Date	Mintage	VF	XF	Unc
70	1877	29.567	15.00	35.00	70.00
	1878	68.740	10.00	30.00	65.00
	1879	56.313	20.00	40.00	80.00

ALUMINUM

MADRID MINT - 6-pointed star

Y#	Date	Mintage	VF	XF	Unc
111	1937	—	—	Rare	—
	1940	225.000	.50	.90	5.50
	1941	247.981	.15	.90	4.00
	1945	250.000	.40	.90	2.25
	1953	865.850	.40	.90	4.00

Y#	Date	Mintage	VF	XF	Unc
121	1959	900.000	—	—	.10
	1959	.100	—	Proof	2.00

20 CENTIMOS

1.0000 gm., .835 SILVER, .0268 oz ASW

MADRID MINT - 6-pointed star

Similar to 50 Centimos, Y#56.

Y#	Date	Mintage	VF	XF	Unc
55	1869(69) SNM	91 pcs.	3000.	3750.	7000.
	1870(70) SNM	5,000	600.00	1000.	1650.

25 CENTIMOS

NICKEL-BRASS

MADRID MINT - 6-pointed star

Y#	Date	Mintage	VF	XF	Unc
100	1925 PCS	8.001	.50	.75	4.00

COPPER-NICKEL

Y#	Date	Mintage	VF	XF	Unc
101	1927 PCS	12.000	.20	.50	3.00

NICKEL-BRONZE

Y#	Date	Mintage	VF	XF	Unc
107	1934	12.272	1.75	2.50	9.00

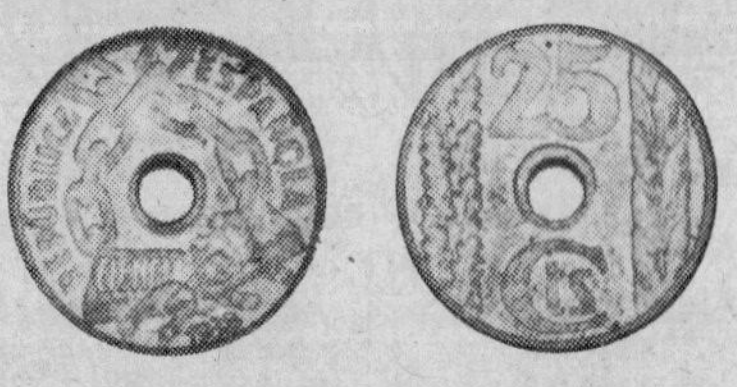

COPPER

Y#	Date	Mintage	VF	XF	Unc
104	1938	45.500	2.00	7.00	15.00

COPPER-NICKEL

VIENNA MINT

Y#	Date	Mintage	VF	XF	Unc
109	1937Bg	42.000	.50	.75	2.00

50 CENTIMOS

2.5000 gm., .835 SILVER, .0671 oz ASW

MADRID MINT - 6-pointed star

Y#	Date	Mintage	VF	XF	Unc
56	1869(69) SNM	.453	100.00	175.00	425.00
	1870(70) SNM	.540	125.00	250.00	800.00

Y#	Date	Mintage	VF	XF	Unc
A76	1880(80) MSM	2.787	7.00	15.00	60.00
	1881(81) MSM	5.647	7.00	15.00	60.00
	1885(85) MSM	—	20.00	40.00	90.00
	1885(86) MSM	1.468	7.00	15.00	60.00

Y#	Date	Mintage	VF	XF	Unc
79	1889(89) MPM	.537	25.00	75.00	200.00
	1892(89)	—	—	—	—
	1892(92) PGM	3.954	5.00	15.00	30.00
	1892(22) PGM	—	30.00	80.00	125.00
	1892(82) PGM	—	30.00	90.00	150.00
	1892(G2) PGM	—	30.00	125.00	200.00

Y#	Date	Mintage	VF	XF	Unc
83	1894(94) PGV	1.109	15.00	40.00	90.00

Y#	Date	Mintage	VF	XF	Unc
87	1896(96) PGV	.297	35.00	90.00	210.00
	1900(00) SMV	2.128	7.50	15.00	30.00

Y#	Date	Mintage	VF	XF	Unc
92	1904(04) SMV	4.851	2.00	6.00	20.00
	1904(10) PCV	1.303	2.00	6.00	20.00

Y#	Date	Mintage	VF	XF	Unc
93	1910(10) PCV	4.526	7.50	10.00	25.00

Y#	Date	Mintage	VF	XF	Unc
102	1926 PCS	4.000	2.50	5.50	10.00

COPPER

Y#	Date	Mintage	VF	XF	Unc
105	1937(34)	—	1.25	2.00	3.00
	1937(36)	—	1.25	2.00	3.00
	1937 no stars	—	4.00	8.00	15.00

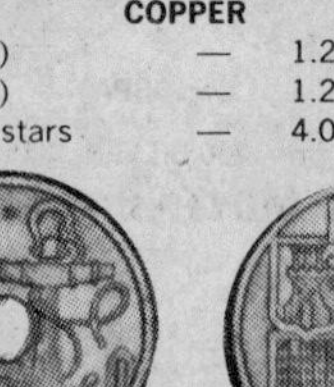

COPPER-NICKEL

Rev: Arrows pointing down

Y#	Date	Mintage	VF	XF	Unc
115	1949(51)	.990	3.00	5.00	15.00

Rev: Arrows pointing up

Y#	Date	Mintage	VF	XF	Unc
116	1949(51)	8.010	.20	1.75	7.00

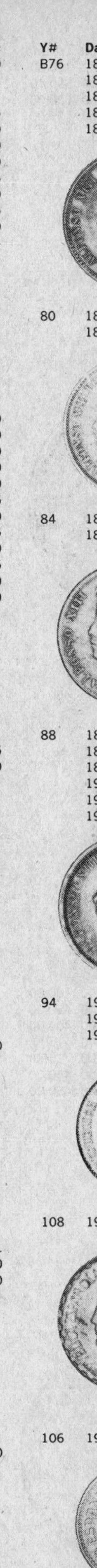

Y#	Date	Mintage	VF	XF	Unc
116	1949(E51)	5,000	—	350.00	600.00

To commemorate a numismatic exposition December 2, 1951 an E replaces the 19 on the lower star.

Y#	Date	Mintage	VF	XF	Unc
	1949(52)	18.567	.15	.50	.75
	1949(53)	17.500	.15	1.00	5.50
	1949(54)	37.000	.15	1.00	4.50
	1949(56)	38.000	.15	.90	3.50
	1949(62)	31.000	.15	.50	.75
	1963(63)	4.000	.15	1.00	4.50
	1963(64)	20.000	.15	.50	.75
	1963(65)	14.000	.10	.75	1.00
	1963(66)	—	—	—	—

ALUMINUM

Y#	Date	Mintage	VF	XF	Unc
124	1966(67)	80.000	.10	.75	1.00
	1966(68)	100.000	.10	.25	.40
	1966(69)	50.000	.10	.75	1.00
	1966(70)	.023	3.50	8.00	15.00
	1966(71)	83.000	.10	.25	.40
	1966(72)	—	—	—	.65
	1966(72)	.030	—	Proof	2.00
	1966(73)	—	—	—	.65
	1966(73)	.030	—	Proof	2.00
	1966(74)	—	—	—	.65
	1966(74)	—	—	Proof	2.00
	1966(75)	.025	—	Proof	2.00

Y#	Date	Mintage	VF	XF	Unc
126	1975(76)	4.060	—	—	.15
	1975(76)	—	—	Proof	2.00

PESETA

5.0000 gm., .835 SILVER, .1342 oz ASW

MADRID MINT - 6-pointed star

Obv. leg: GOBIERNO PROVISIONAL

Y#	Date	Mintage	VF	XF	Unc
A55	1869(69) SNM	7.000	75.00	200.00	500.00

Obv. leg: ESPANA

Y#	Date	Mintage	VF	XF	Unc
58	1869(69) SNM	.367	275.00	875.00	2500.
	1870(70) SNM	3,865	35.00	150.00	650.00
	1870(73) DEM	5.165	35.00	150.00	650.00

Y#	Date	Mintage	VF	XF	Unc
B75	1876(76) DEM	4.427	35.00	150.00	650.00

Y#	Date	Mintage	VF	XF	Unc
B76	1881(81) MSM	.799	275.00	875.00	2500.
	1882(82) MSM	3.506	100.00	250.00	575.00
	1883(83) MSM	8.440	100.00	250.00	575.00
	1884(84) MSM	5,839	1000.	2000.	6000.
	1885(85) MSM	3.336	100.00	200.00	650.00
	1885(86) MSM	3.954	75.00	175.00	575.00

Y#	Date	Mintage	VF	XF	Unc
80	1889(89) MPM	.760	200.00	400.00	1000.
	1891(91) PGM	4.948	40.00	100.00	350.00

Y#	Date	Mintage	VF	XF	Unc
84	1893(93) PGL	1.958	75.00	200.00	500.00
	1894(94) PGV	1.044	150.00	300.00	825.00

Y#	Date	Mintage	VF	XF	Unc
88	1896(96) PGV	6.412	15.00	35.00	100.00
	1897(97) SGV	—	55.00	90.00	175.00
	1899(99) SGV	7.472	15.00	35.00	100.00
	1900(00) SMV	18.650	15.00	30.00	75.00
	1901(01) SMV	8.449	15.00	35.00	100.00
	1902(02) SMV	2.599	15.00	35.00	100.00

Y#	Date	Mintage	VF	XF	Unc
94	1903(03) SMV	10.602	20.00	40.00	90.00
	1904(04) SMV	5.294	30.00	50.00	100.00
	1905(05) SMV	.492	20.00	75.00	225.00

Y#	Date	Mintage	VF	XF	Unc
108	1933(3-4)	2.000	4.00	8.00	15.00

BRASS

Y#	Date	Mintage	VF	XF	Unc
106	1937	—	.60	1.00	3.00

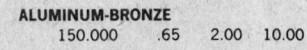

ALUMINUM-BRONZE

Y#	Date	Mintage	VF	XF	Unc
112	1944	150.000	.65	2.00	10.00

Y#	Date	Mintage	VF	XF	Unc
113	1947(48)	15.000	.50	2.00	10.00
	1947(49)	27.600	.40	1.00	4.00
	1947(50)	4.000	1.00	4.00	20.00
	1947(51)	9.185	.75	3.00	10.00
	1949(E51)	5,000	—	400.00	700.00

To commemorate a numismatic exposition December 2, 1951 an E replaces 19 on the lower star.

Y#	Date	Mintage	VF	XF	Unc
	1947(52)	19.195	—	.50	1.00
	1947(53)	34.000	—	.50	1.00
	1947(54)	50.000	—	.50	1.00
	1947(56)	—	30.00	65.00	150.00
	1953(54)	40.272	—	.50	1.50
	1953(56)	118.000	—	.25	.75
	1953(60)	45.160	—	.20	.75
	1953(61)	25.830	—	.25	.90
	1953(62)	66.252	—	.20	.75
	1953(63)	37.000	—	.25	1.50
	1963(63)	36.000	—	.25	1.50
	1963(64)	80.000	—	.20	.30
	1963(65)	70.000	—	.35	.75
	1963(66)	63.000	—	.20	.75
	1963(67)	11.300	—	.25	2.00

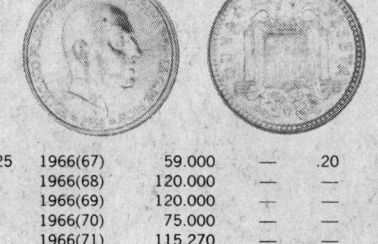

Y#	Date	Mintage	VF	XF	Unc
125	1966(67)	59.000	—	.20	.25
	1966(68)	120.000	—	—	.50
	1966(69)	120.000	—	—	.50
	1966(70)	75.000	—	—	.50
	1966(71)	115.270	—	—	.50
	1966(72)	106.000	—	—	.50
	1966(72)	.030	—	Proof	3.00
	1966(73)	152.000	—	—	.50
	1966(73)	.030	—	Proof	3.00
	1966(74)	Inc. Ab.	—	—	.20
	1966(74)	—	—	Proof	3.00
	1966(75)	227.580	—	—	—
	1966(75)	.025	—	Proof	2.00

Y#	Date	Mintage	VF	XF	Unc
127	1975(76)	170.380	—	—	.25
	1975(76)	—	—	Proof	2.00
	1975(77)	—	—	—	.25
	1975(77)	—	—	Proof	2.00
	1975(78)	—	—	—	—
	1975(78)	—	—	Proof	1.50
	1975 (79)	—	—	—	—
	1975(79)	—	—	Proof	1.00
	1975(80)	—	—	—	—
	1975(80)	—	—	Proof	1.00

2 PESETAS

10.0000 gm., .835 SILVER, .2685 oz ASW

MADRID MINT - 6-pointed star

Y#	Date	Mintage	VF	XF	Unc
59	1869(68) SNM	—	150.00	250.00	725.00
	1869(69) SNM	3.270	35.00	100.00	400.00
	1870(70) SNM	1.504	40.00	125.00	450.00
	1870(73) DEM	11.880	30.00	75.00	200.00
	1870(74) DEM	14.893	30.00	75.00	200.00
	1870(75) DEM	4.997	40.00	85.00	300.00

NOTE: Former Y#62, 2 Pesetas, 1873 Cartagena Mint,

Cantonal issue similar to Y#64, 10 Reales and Y#63, 5 Pesetas is thought to be a fantasy struck later for collectors.

Y#	Date	Mintage	VF	XF	Unc
C76	1879(79) EMM	5.578	30.00	75.00	325.00
	1881(81) MSM	3.639	25.00	65.00	300.00
	1882(82)MSM	20.343	20.00	40.00	275.00
	1882(82) PGM	Inc. Ab.	30.00	90.00	300.00
	1883(83) MSM	3.318	20.00	65.00	375.00
	1884(84) MSM	2.839	25.00	80.00	450.00

Y#	Date	Mintage	VF	XF	Unc
81	1889(89) MPM	.559	100.00	250.00	600.00
	1891(91) PGM	.093	250.00	500.00	1000.
	1892(92) PGM	1.379	30.00	75.00	350.00

Y#	Date	Mintage	VF	XF	Unc
85	1894(94) PGV	.279	200.00	400.00	900.00

Y#	Date	Mintage	VF	XF	Unc
95	1905(05) SMV	3.589	10.00	35.00	55.00

10 REALES/(2-1/2 Pesetas)

12.5000 gm., .835 SILVER, .3356 oz ASW

CARTAGENA MINT

Y#	Date	Mintage	VF	XF	Unc
64	1873	—	150.00	350.00	475.00

2-1/2 PESETAS

ALUMINUM-BRONZE

MADRID MINT - 6-pointed star

Y#	Date	Mintage	VF	XF	Unc
114	1953(54)	22.729	.25	1.25	6.00
	1953(56)	30.322	.25	1.00	1.50

Y#	Date	Mintage	VF	XF	Unc
114	1953(68)	1,000	200.00	500.00	700.00
	1953(69)	2,000	100.00	600.00	800.00
	1953(70)	6,800	40.00	75.00	120.00
	1953(71)	10,000	25.00	45.00	75.00

5 PESETAS

25.0000 gm., .900 SILVER, .7234 oz ASW

MADRID MINT - 6-pointed star

Y#	Date	Mintage	VF	XF	Unc
60	1869(69) SNM	100 Pcs.	—	Rare	—
	1870(70) SNM	5.923	25.00	60.00	450.00

Rev: Similar to Y#60.

Y#	Date	Mintage	VF	XF	Unc
61	1871 SDM	13.641	22.50	35.00	100.00
	1871(71)SDM	Inc. Ab.	75.00	200.00	450.00
	1871(71) MSD	Inc. Ab.	100.00	175.00	400.00
	1871(73) DEM	2.870	250.00	650.00	1500.
	1871(73) SDM	Inc. Ab.	250.00	650.00	1500.
	1871(74) DEM	5.075	75.00	200.00	450.00
	1871(75) DEM	3.000	75.00	200.00	450.00

CARTAGENA MINT

Y#	Date	Mintage	VF	XF	Unc
63	1873	—	140.00	200.00	240.00

MADRID MINT - 6-pointed star

Rev: Similar to Y#60.

Y#	Date	Mintage	VF	XF	Unc
74	1875(75) DEM	8.641	30.00	90.00	400.00
	1876(76) DEM	8.548	30.00	90.00	400.00

Y#	Date	Mintage	VF	XF	Unc
75	1877(77) DEM	6.987	30.00	90.00	400.00
	1878(78) DEM	5.000	30.00	90.00	400.00
	1878(78) EMM	4.147	25.00	85.00	375.00
	1879(79) EMM	1.634	75.00	200.00	700.00
	1881(81) MSM	.699	100.00	350.00	1000.

Rev: Similar to Y#75

Y#	Date	Mintage	VF	XF	Unc
76	1882/1 MSM	—	17.50	75.00	150.00
	1882(81)	—	30.00	100.00	300.00
	1882(82) MSM	1.662	22.50	45.00	75.00
	1883(83) MSM	5.507	22.50	60.00	400.00
	1884(84) MSM	5.848	22.50	60.00	400.00
	1885(85) MSM	3.144	30.00	100.00	450.00
	1885(86) MSM	1.951	100.00	225.00	550.00
	1885(87) MSM	9.000	30.00	100.00	275.00
	1885(87) MPM	2.803	50.00	135.00	525.00
	1885(87) PGL	Inc. Ab.	200.00	525.00	525.00

Rev: Similar to Y#75

Y#	Date	Mintage	VF	XF	Unc
82	1888(88)MSM	—	200.00	600.00	1500.
	1888(88) MPM	10.644	6.50	27.50	55.00
	1889(89) MPM	4.681	25.00	75.00	285.00
	1889(89) MSM	Inc. Ab.	25.00	75.00	285.00
	1890(90) MPM	4.275	22.50	70.00	275.00
	1890(90) PGM	3.000	22.50	80.00	300.00
	1891(91) PGM	11.660	25.00	70.00	250.00
	1891(91) PGL	Inc. Ab.	25.00	70.00	250.00
	1892(92) PGM	8.294	25.00	80.00	300.00

Rev: Similar to Y#75

Y#	Date	Mintage	VF	XF	Unc
86	1892(92) PGM	Inc. Ab.	35.00	100.00	250.00
	1893(93) PGL	2.500	30.00	90.00	250.00
	1893(93) PGV	.518	125.00	200.00	850.00
	1894(94) PGV	3.871	30.00	100.00	275.00

Rev: Similar to Y#75

Y#	Date	Mintage	VF	XF	Unc
89	1896(96) PGV	4.272	30.00	90.00	250.00
	1897(97) SGV	6.733	30.00	85.00	225.00
	1898(98) SGV	39.977	25.00	75.00	200.00
	1899(99) SGV	13.930	25.00	75.00	150.00

NOTE: All other date and Mintmaster's or Assayer's initial combinations of crowns of this era are contemporary counterfeits.

NICKEL

Y#	Date	Mintage	VF	XF	Unc
117	1949(49)	.612	1.15	3.25	6.50
	1949(50)	21.000	.35	.75	1.75
	1949(51)	.145	40.00	100.00	200.00
	1949(E51)	6,000	600.00	900.00	1500.

To commemorate a numismatic exposition December 2, 1951, an E replaces the 19 on the lower star.

COPPER-NICKEL

Y#	Date	Mintage	VF	XF	Unc
118	1957(58)	13.000	.20	.50	1.50
	1957(BA)	.043	30.00	60.00	150.00
	To commemorate the 1958 Barcelona Exposition-,BA replaces the star on left side of reverse.				
	1957(59)	107.000	—	.25	.75
	1957(60)	26.000	.20	.30	1.00
	1957(61)	78.992	—	.25	1.00
	1957(62)	40.963	—	.50	1.00
	1957(63)	50.000	—	.50	1.25
	1957(64)	51.000	—	5.00	30.00
	1957(65)	25.000	—	.75	1.75
	1957(66)	28.000	—	.75	3.00
	1957(67)	30.000	—	.75	2.00
	1957(68)	60.000	—	—	1.50
	1957(69)	40.000	—	—	1.75
	1957(70)	43.000	—	—	1.75
	1957(71)	77.000	—	—	2.00
	1957(72)	70.000	—	—	.50
	1957(72)	.030	—	Proof	3.00
	1957(73)	—	—	—	3.00
	1957(73)	.030	—	Proof	4.00
	1957(74)	—	—	—	.50
	1957(74)	—	—	Proof	3.00
	1957(75)	139.047	—	—	.35
	1957(75)	.025	—	Proof	3.00

Y#	Date	Mintage	VF	XF	Unc
128	1975(76)	156.658	—	—	.75
	1975(76)	—	—	Proof	2.50
	1975(77)	—	—	—	.75
	1975(77)	—	—	Proof	2.00
	1975(78)	—	—	—	.75
	1975(78)	—	—	Proof	2.00
	1975(79)	—	—	—	.50
	1975(79)	—	—	Proof	1.75
	1975(80)	—	—	—	.50
	1975(80)	—	—	Proof	1.50

10 PESETAS

3.2258 gm., .900 GOLD, .0933 oz AGW

MADRID MINT - 6-pointed star

Similar to 25 Pesetas, Y#78.

Y#	Date	Mintage	VF	XF	Unc
77	1878(78) EMM	.091	500.00	600.00	750.00
	1879(79) EMM	.033	2500.	3000.	3750.
	1878(61) DEM	496	1000.	1200.	1500.
	1878(62) DEM	.018	100.00	125.00	175.00

NOTE: The above two coins were restruck by the Spanish Mint from original dies in 1961 and 1962 and are considered official restrike issues.

20 PESETAS

6.4516 gm., .900 GOLD, .1867 oz AGW

MADRID MINT - 6-pointed star

Y#	Date	Mintage	VF	XF	Unc
A82	1889(89) MPM	.875	400.00	500.00	675.00
	1890(90) MPM	2.344	200.00	300.00	375.00
	1887(61) PGV	800	750.00	900.00	1200.
	1887(62) PGV	.011	200.00	275.00	325.00

NOTE: For above two coins dated (61) & (62) see note after 10 Pesetas, Y#77.

Obv: Child head of Alfonso right.
Rev: Crowned and mantled arms.

Y#	Date	Mintage	VF	XF	Unc
A86	1892(92) PGM	2.430	3250.	3750.	5000.

Y#	Date	Mintage	VF	XF	Unc
A89	1899(99) SMV	2.086	450.00	550.00	650.00
	1896(61) MPM	900	900.00	1100.	1300.
	1896(62) MPM	.012	250.00	270.00	325.00

NOTE: For above two coins dated (61) & (62) see note after 10 Pesetas, Y#77.

Obv: Uniformed bust of Alfonso right.

Y#	Date	Mintage	VF	XF	Unc
91	1904(04) SMV	3,814	3000.	3500.	4000.

25 PESETAS

8.0645 gm., .900 GOLD, .2333 oz AGW

MADRID MINT - 6-pointed star

Obv: Bust of King Amadeo I to right.
Rev: Crowned, draped arms.

Fr#	Date	Mintage	VF	XF	Unc
192	1871(75)SDM	25 pcs.	—	Rare	—

Y#	Date	Mintage	VF	XF	Unc
78	1876(76) DEM	1.281	275.00	300.00	400.00
	1877(77) DEM	10.048	275.00	300.00	400.00
	1878(78) DEM	5.192	275.00	300.00	400.00
	1878(78) EMM	3.000	275.00	300.00	400.00
	1879(79) EMM	3.478	275.00	300.00	400.00
	1880(80) MSM	6.863	275.00	300.00	400.00
	1876(61) DEM	300	1000.	1400.	2000.
	1876(62) DEM	6,000	350.00	450.00	575.00

NOTE: For above two coins dated (61) & (62) see note after 10 Pesetas, Y#77.

Y#	Date	Mintage	VF	XF	Unc
A78	1881(81) MSM	4.366	275.00	300.00	375.00
	1882(82) MSM	.414	800.00	1000.	1800.
	1883(83) MSM	.669	800.00	1000.	1800.
	1884(84) MSM	1.033	600.00	750.00	1000.
	1885(85) MSM	.503	3000.	3500.	4000.
	1885(86) MSM	.491	4500.	5500.	6500.

COPPER-NICKEL

Y#	Date	Mintage	VF	XF	Unc
119	1957(58)	8.635	.50	1.00	1.50
	1957(BA)	.043	60.00	75.00	150.00

NOTE: To commemorate the 1958 Barcelona Exposition, BA replaces the star on left side of reverse.

Y#	Date	Mintage	VF	XF	Unc
	1957(59)	42.185	.40	.60	1.25
	1957(61)	24.120	—	.75	3.00
	1957(63)	—	—	.50	1.50
	1957(64)	42.200	.20	.50	1.50
	1957(65)	20.000	—	.50	1.75
	1957(66)	15.000	—	.50	2.25

Y#	Date	Mintage	VF	XF	Unc
119	1957(67)	20.000	—	.50	1.75
	1957(68)	30.000	—	.50	1.50
	1957(69)	24.000	—	.50	1.50
	1957(70)	25.000	—	.25	.50
	1957(71)	7.800	—	.25	.50
	1957(72)	—	—	—	.50
	1957(72)	.030	—	Proof	3.00
	1957(73)	—	—	—	.50
	1957(73)	.030	—	Proof	3.00
	1957(74)	—	—	—	.50
	1957(74)	—	—	Proof	3.00
	1957(75)	10.270	—	—	.50
	1957(75)	.025	—	Proof	3.00

Y#	Date	Mintage	VF	XF	Unc
129	1975(76)	35.333	—	—	1.75
	1975(76)	—	—	Proof	2.50
	1975(77)	—	—	—	1.75
	1975(77)	—	—	Proof	—
	1975(80)	—	—	—	1.50
	1975(80)	—	—	Proof	2.50

50 PESETAS

COPPER-NICKEL

MADRID MINT - 6-pointed star

Y#	Date	Mintage	VF	XF	Unc
120	1957(58)	21.471	.50	1.00	3.00
	1957(BA)	.043	60.00	75.00	150.00

NOTE: To commemorate the 1958 Barcelona Exposition, BA replaces the star on left side of reverse.

Y#	Date	Mintage	VF	XF	Unc
	1957(59)	28.000	1.00	1.50	4.00
	1957(60)	24.800	1.00	1.50	4.00
	1957(61)	—	1.00	1.50	4.00
	1957(64)	—	—	1.50	4.00
	1957(65)	—	—	1.50	4.00
	1957(67)	.850	3.50	6.50	12.50
	1957(68)	1,000	475.00	575.00	750.00
	1957(69)	1,200	375.00	450.00	600.00
	1957(70)	.019	60.00	75.00	150.00
	1957(71)	4.400	—	—	3.00
	1957(72)	—	—	—	1.75
	1957(72)	.030	—	Proof	4.00
	1957(73)	—	—	—	5.00
	1957(73)	.030	—	Proof	4.00
	1957(74)	—	—	—	5.00
	1957(74)	—	—	Proof	4.00
	1957(75)	—	—	—	3.00
	1957(75)	.025	—	Proof	3.00

Y#	Date	Mintage	VF	XF	Unc
130	1975(76)	4.000	—	—	1.50
	1975(76)	—	—	Proof	3.00
	1975(80)	—	—	—	1.00
	1975(80)	—	—	Proof	2.50

100 PESETAS

32.2581 gm., .900 GOLD, .9334 oz AGW

MADRID MINT - 6-pointed star

Provisional Government

Obv: Hispania standing.

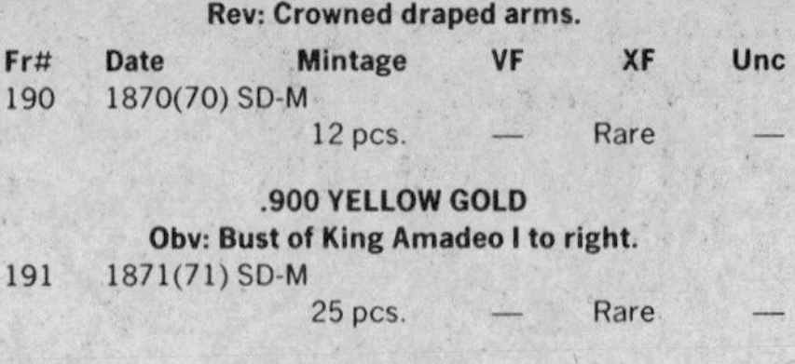

Rev: Crowned draped arms.

Fr#	Date	Mintage	VF	XF	Unc
190	1870(70) SD-M				
		12 pcs.	—	Rare	—

.900 YELLOW GOLD

Obv: Bust of King Amadeo I to right.

Fr#	Date	Mintage	VF	XF	Unc
191	1871(71) SD-M				
		25 pcs.	—	Rare	—

.900 RED GOLD

Fr#	Date	Mintage	VF	XF	Unc
	1871(71) SD-M				
		50 pcs.	—	Rare	—

Y#	Date	Mintage	VF	XF	Unc
90	1897(97)SGV	.150	2500.	2750.	3250.
	1897(61)SGV	810 pcs.	1300.	1500.	2000.
	1897(62)SGV	.006	650.00	1000.	1500.

NOTE: The above two coins were restruck by the Spanish Mint from original dies in 1961 and 1962 and are considered official restrike issues.

.800 SILVER

Y#	Date	Mintage	VF	XF	Unc
122	1966(66)	35.000	4.00	5.00	6.75
	1966(67)	15.000	4.00	5.75	8.00
	1966(68)	24.000	4.00	5.00	6.00
	1966(69) 69 with straight 9 in star				
		1.000	85.00	150.00	250.00
	1966(69) 69 with curved 9 in star				
		Inc. Ab.	55.00	80.00	110.00
	1966(70)	Inc. Ab.	7.50	12.50	20.00

COPPER-NICKEL

Y#	Date	Mintage	VF	XF	Unc
131	1975(76)	4.000	—	—	—
	1975(76)	—	—	Proof	3.00

PRETENDER ISSUES

Charles V

(1835-1840)

Charles V, brother of Ferdinand VII, claimed the throne upon the death of his brother, but Isabella II became the ruler. Charles V fled to Portugal and set up, what he called, the true monarchy of Spain.

8 MARAVEDIS

COPPER

SEGOVIA MINT - Aqueduct

C#	Date	Mintage	Fine	VF	XF
154	1837	—	175.00	350.00	525.00

c/s: CAB/BER/A on 8 Maravedi of Ferdinand VII.

C#	Date	Mintage	Fine	VF	XF
153	(1833-40)	—	75.00	150.00	275.00

6 CUARTOS

COPPER

BERGA MINT - BREGE, BGA

Obv: Crude laureated head right, date below.

Rev: Crowned Catalonian arms within legend.

C#	Date	Mintage	VG	Fine	VF
153	1840	—	100.00	175.00	375.00

Rev: Crowned Spanish arms within legend.

C#	Date	Mintage	VG	Fine	VF
	1840	—	300.00	400.00	500.00

2 REALES

2.6291 gm., .903 SILVER, .0761 oz ASW

SEGOVIA MINT - Aqueduct

C#	Date	Mintage	VG	Fine	VF
157	1837	—	150.00	225.00	600.00

BERGA MINT - BREGE, BGA

C#	Date	Mintage	VG	Fine	VF
156	1838	—	150.00	225.00	600.00

Charles VII

(1872-75)

A grandson of Charles V who claimed the throne and maintained a court and government in exile. All Charles VII pieces were made at the Brussells Mint.

5 CENTIMOS

COPPER

Obv: Laureated head right.

Rev: Crowned arms divide crowned monograms in inner circle, date below.

Y#	Date	Mintage	VF	XF	Unc
66	1875	.050	30.00	45.00	65.00

10 CENTIMOS

COPPER

Obv: Laureated head right.

Rev: Crowned arms divide crowned monograms in inner circle, date below.

Y#	Date	Mintage	VF	XF	Unc
67	1875	.100	25.00	37.50	60.00

50 CENTIMOS

2.0875 gm., .835 SILVER, .0671 oz ASW

Obv: Crowned C7 monogram over date.

Rev: Crowned arms in sprays, value below.

KM#	Date	Mintage	VF	XF	Unc
A68	1876	—	450.00	525.00	750.00

5 PESETAS

25.0000 gm., .900 SILVER, .7234 oz ASW

Reeded edge

KM#	Date	Mintage	VF	XF	Unc
68	1874	—	—	—	—
	1875	—	—	—	—

Piedfort (double thickenss)

KM#	Date	Mintage	VF	XF	Unc
68a	1874	—	—	—	—

Plain edge

KM#	Date	Mintage	VF	XF	Unc
68b	1874	—	—	—	—

Triple piedfort

KM#	Date	Mintage	VF	XF	Unc
68c	1874	—	—	—	—

BRONZE

KM#	Date	Mintage	VF	XF	Unc
68d	1874	—	—	—	—
	1875	—	—	—	—

SILVER

Obv: Laureated head right, date below.

Rev: Crowned arms divide value.

Plain edge

KM#	Date	Mintage	VF	XF	Unc
A68	1874	—	350.00	500.00	600.00

Piedfort (double thickenss)

KM#	Date	Mintage	VF	XF	Unc
A68a	1874	—	—	—	—

Reeded edge

KM#	Date	Mintage	VF	XF	Unc
A68b	1874	—	—	—	—

BRONZE - Obv. only

KM#	Date	Mintage	VF	XF	Unc
A68c	1874	—	—	—	—

BRONZE - Rev. only

KM#	Date	Mintage	VF	XF	Unc
A68d	1874	—	—	—	—

SILVER

Obv: Laureated head right, date below.

Rev: Crowned arms divide value, date below.

KM#	Date	Mintage	VF	XF	Unc
B68	1874	—	—	—	—

BRONZE

KM#	Date	Mintage	VF	XF	Unc
B68a	1874	—	225.00	300.00	400.00

Piedfort (double thickness)

KM#	Date	Mintage	VF	XF	Unc
B68b	1874	—	250.00	375.00	450.00

TIN

KM#	Date	Mintage	VF	XF	Unc
B68c	1874	—	—	—	—

1.6129 gm., .900 GOLD, .0467 oz AGW

KM#	Date	Mintage	VF	XF	Unc
B68d	1874	—	—	—	—

SILVER, 25.5gm.

Obv: Laureated head right, date below.

Rev: Crowned arms on sprays divide crowned monograms, value below. Reeded edge.

KM#	Date	Mintage	VF	XF	Unc
C68	1885	—	—	—	—

The private patterns of Charles VII, were of a purely political-speculative nature.

NCLT ISSUES

MINT SETS

KM#	Date	Mintage	Identification	Issue Price	Mkt. Val.
S1	1949(E51)(3)				
		5,000	Y113,116,117	—	3000.
S2	1958Ba(3)	—	Y118-120	—	350.00
S3	1968(8)	2,000	Y118-121,124,125	3.60	1900.
S4	1969(8)	1,000	Y118-121,124,125	3.60	1900.
S5	1970(8)	9,000	Y118-121,124,125	3.60	425.00
S6	1971(8)	8,000	Y118-121,124,125	3.60	200.00

PROOF SETS

STANDARD METALS

NOTE: The following sets contain 10 Centimos, Y121 dated 1959.Other denominations have the date in the stars.

KM#	Date	Mintage	Identification	Issue Price	Mkt. Val.
101	1972(6)	23,000	Y118-121,124,125	10.00	24.00
102	1973(6)	28,500	Y118-121,124,125	10.00	60.00
103	1974(6)	24,680	Y118-121,124,125	10.00	70.00
104	1975(6)	29,000*	Y118-121,124,125	10.00	35.00
	*Estimated				
105	1976(6)	39,600	Y126-131	7.50	15.00
106	1980(4)	—	Y127-129,130	—	—

SPAIN — Local

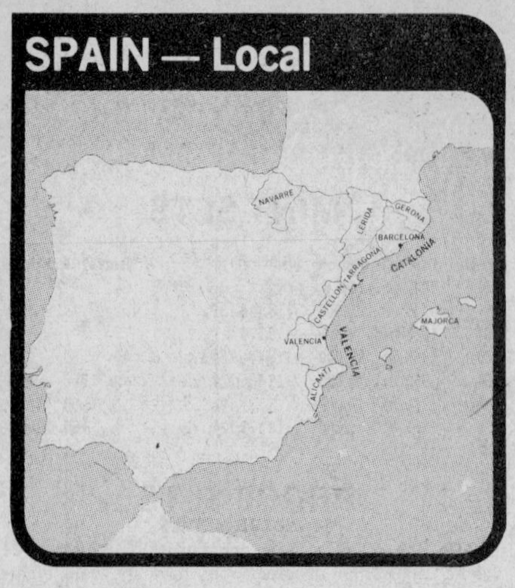

The following cities and provinces of Spain were coin-issuing entities:

BALEARIC ISLANDS

(MAJORCA)

The Balearic Islands, an archipelago located in the Mediterranean Sea off the east coast of Spain including Majorca, Minorca, Cabrera, Ibiza, Formentera and a number of islets.

Majorca, largest of the Balearic Islands is famous for its 1,000-year-old olive trees.

RULERS

Ferdinand (Fernando) VII 1808-33

MONETARY SYSTEM

12 Dineros = 6 Doblers = 1 Sueldo (Sou)
30 Sueldos = 1 Duro

12 DINEROS

COPPER

C#	Date	Mintage	VG	Fine	VF	XF
L51	1811	—	20.00	50.00	100.00	200.00
	1812 (DEI GRATIA)		6.50	12.50	25.00	50.00
	1812 (DEI GRAT)		10.00	20.00	40.00	80.00

30 SUELDOS (SOUS)

SILVER
Obv: Rulers name, value and date incuse.
Rev: Incuse crowned arms.

C#	Date	Mintage	VG	Fine	VF	XF
L7	1808	—	85.00	175.00	200.00	275.00
	1808 (value and date in depression)	—	70.00	100.00	150.00	225.00

C#	Date	Mintage	VG	Fine	VF	XF
L52	1808	—	275.00	325.00	500.00	750.00

Obv: Similar to C#L52.

C#	Date	Mintage	VG	Fine	VF	XF
L52a	1808 w/FER. VII		125.00	175.00	250.00	350.00

Similar to C#L53a w/o FRo. VII.

C#	Date	Mintage	VG	Fine	VF	XF
L53	1821	—	450.00	700.00	950.00	1200.

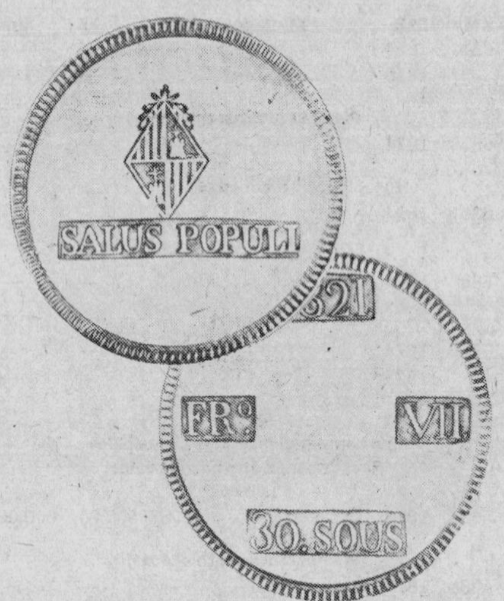

C#	Date	Mintage	VG	Fine	VF	XF
L53a	1821W/Fro. Vii	—	50.00	80.00	120.00	150.00

5 PESETAS

SILVER
Obv: Name and date in wreath.
Rev: Arms and value in circle.

C#	Date	Mintage	VG	Fine	VF	XF
L9	1823	—	70.00	100.00	150.00	225.00
	1823 (legend ends EYND instead of CONST.)	—	125.00	175.00	250.00	350.00

BARCELONA

Barcelona, a maritime province in north-east Spain and it's provincal capital city of Barcelona. The city of Barcelona is a major port and commercial center.

RULERS

Joseph (Jose) Napoleon 1808-14
Ferdinand (Fernando) VII, Restored 1814-33

MONETARY SYSTEM

4 Quartos = 1 Sueldo
6 Sueldos = 1 Peseta

1/2 QUARTO

COPPER
Similar to 4 Quartos, C#L14.

C#	Date	Mintage	Good	VG	Fine	VF
L11	ND(1811)Ba	—	8.50	17.50	35.00	70.00

QUARTO

COPPER
Similar to 4 Quartos, C#L14.

C#	Date	Mintage	Good	VG	Fine	VF
L12	1808Ba	—	8.50	15.00	30.00	60.00
	1809Ba	—	4.00	7.50	17.50	35.00
	1810Ba	—	4.00	7.50	17.50	35.00
	1811Ba	—	10.00	20.00	40.00	80.00
	1812Ba	—	3.75	7.50	15.00	30.00
	1813Ba	—	10.00	20.00	40.00	80.00

2 QUARTOS

COPPER
Similar to 4 Quartos, C#L14.

C#	Date	Mintage	Good	VG	Fine	VF
L13	1808Ba	—	4.00	7.50	15.00	30.00
	1809Ba	—	3.00	5.00	10.00	20.00
	1810Ba	—	3.50	5.50	12.50	25.00
	1813Ba	—	6.00	10.00	25.00	50.00
	1814Ba	—	4.00	7.50	15.00	30.00

3 QUARTOS

COPPER

C#	Date	Mintage	Good	VG	Fine	VF
L21	1823	—	2.00	3.50	7.50	15.00

4 QUARTOS

COPPER

C#	Date	Mintage	Good	VG	Fine	VF
L14	1808Ba	—	8.00	20.00	25.00	40.00
	1809Ba	—	6.00	15.00	20.00	30.00
	1810Ba	—	3.00	7.00	10.00	16.50
	1811Ba	—	4.00	8.50	12.50	20.00
	1812Ba	—	3.00	7.00	9.00	15.00

Obv. leg: widely spaced.

C#	Date	Mintage	Good	VG	Fine	VF
L14b	1813Ba	—	5.00	12.50	17.50	27.50
	1814Ba	—	7.50	15.00	25.00	40.00

CAST COPPER

C#	Date	Mintage	Good	VG	Fine	VF
L14a	1808Ba	—	6.00	10.00	12.50	20.00
	1809Ba	—	3.00	9.00	11.50	18.50
	1810Ba	—	2.00	6.50	8.50	13.50
	1811Ba	—	4.00	8.50	12.50	20.00
	1812Ba	—	3.00	7.50	10.00	16.50
L14c	1813Ba	—	4.00	8.50	12.50	20.00
	1814Ba	—	4.00	8.50	12.50	20.00

6 QUARTOS

COPPER

C#	Date	Mintage	Good	VG	Fine	VF
L22	1823Ba	—	6.00	10.00	20.00	40.00

PESETA

SILVER

C#	Date	Mintage	VG	Fine	VF	XF
L15	1809Ba	—	6.00	12.50	25.00	40.00
	1810Ba	—	6.00	12.50	22.50	37.50
	1811Ba	—	6.00	12.50	22.50	37.50
	1812Ba	—	7.50	17.50	25.00	45.00
	1813Ba	—	8.00	20.00	30.00	55.00
	1814Ba	—	10.00	27.50	50.00	85.00

2-1/2 PESETAS

SILVER

C#	Date	Mintage	VG	Fine	VF	XF
L16	1808Ba	—	75.00	130.00	175.00	250.00
	1809Ba	—	75.00	130.00	175.00	250.00
	1810Ba	—	100.00	200.00	300.00	450.00
	1814Ba	—	125.00	250.00	400.00	650.00

5 PESETAS

SILVER

C#	Date	Mintage	VG	Fine	VF	XF
L17	1808Ba	—	100.00	200.00	300.00	700.00
	1809Ba	—	75.00	125.00	200.00	400.00
	1810Ba	—	75.00	125.00	225.00	450.00
	1811Ba	—	85.00	150.00	275.00	600.00
	1812Ba	—	90.00	175.00	275.00	700.00
	1813Ba	—	175.00	400.00	600.00	900.00
	1814Ba	—	400.00	800.00	1350.	2200.

20 PESETAS

GOLD

C#	Date	Mintage	VG	Fine	VF	XF
L18	1812Ba	—	350.00	550.00	900.00	1500.
	1813Ba	—	450.00	750.00	1200.	2000.
	1814Ba	—	500.00	850.00	1350.	2250.

CATALONIA

Catalonia, a triangular territory forming the north-east corner of the Iberian Peninsula, was formerly a province of Spain and also formerly a principality of Aragon. In 1833 the region was divided into four provinces, Barcelona, Gerona, Lerida and Tarragona.

RULERS

Ferdinand (Fernando) VII 1808-33
Isabel II 1833-68

MONETARY SYSTEM:

12 Ardites (Dineros) = 8 Ochavos = 4 Quartos = 1 Sueldo;
6 Sueldos = 1 Peseta;
5 Pesetas = 1 Duro.

OCHAVO

COPPER

C#	Date	Mintage	Good	VG	Fine	VF
L34	1813	—	6.00	11.50	18.50	37.50

QUARTO

COPPER
Obv: Crowned spade Catalonian arms.
Rev: Crowned Spanish arms.

C#	Date	Mintage	Good	VG	Fine	VF
L35	1813	—	5.00	10.00	15.00	25.00

QUARTO/Y MEDIO

(1-1/2 Quartos)

COPPER
Obv: Crowned round Catalonian arms.
Rev: Crowned oval Spanish arms.

C#	Date	Mintage	Good	VG	Fine	VF
L36	1811	—	6.00	12.50	25.00	45.00
	1812	—	15.00	35.00	55.00	85.00
	1813	—	3.00	6.50	10.00	17.50

II QUARTOS

COPPER
Obv: Crowned lozenge Catalonian arms in branches.
Rev: Crowned Spanish arms.

C#	Date	Mintage	Good	VG	Fine	VF
L37	1813	—	3.00	7.50	15.00	25.00
	1814	—	3.00	7.50	15.00	25.00

III QUARTOS

COPPER

C#	Date	Mintage	Good	VG	Fine	VF
L38	1810	—	3.00	7.50	15.00	27.50
	1811	—	2.00	5.00	10.00	17.50
	1812	—	2.00	5.00	10.00	17.50
	1813	—	2.00	4.75	8.00	12.50
	1814	—	2.00	4.00	7.00	11.50

C#	Date	Mintage	VG	Fine	VF	XF
L40a	1836C III (CAT HAL)					
		—	35.00	75.00	150.00	300.00
	1836 III (CAT ALUNA)					
		—	20.00	45.00	90.00	150.00
	1836C 3	—	5.00	10.00	15.00	30.00
	1837C	—	3.00	6.50	11.50	22.50
	1838C	—	4.00	7.50	11.50	22.50
	1839C	—	4.00	9.00	15.00	30.00
	1840C	—	10.00	22.50	40.00	65.00
	1841C	—	5.00	9.00	15.00	25.00
	1842C	—	15.00	30.00	50.00	75.00
	1843C	—	20.00	35.00	60.00	80.00
	1844C	—	5.00	9.00	15.00	26.50
	1845C	—	15.00	30.00	60.00	100.00
	1846C	—	7.50	12.50	22.50	35.00

VI QUARTOS

COPPER
Similar to C# L40.3

C#	Date	Mintage	Good	VG	Fine	VF
L39	1810	—	5.00	11.50	20.00	35.00
	1811	—	4.00	8.00	13.50	25.00
	1812	—	3.00	6.00	12.50	27.50
	1813	—	3.00	6.00	12.50	27.50
	1814	—	8.00	15.00	27.50	40.00

C#	Date	Mintage	VG	Fine	VF	XF
L40.3	1836C VI	—	60.00	125.00	250.00	475.00
	1836C 6	—	5.00	12.50	25.00	55.00
	1837C	—	3.00	7.50	17.50	40.00
	1838C	—	3.00	7.50	17.50	40.00
	1839C	—	7.50	16.50	35.00	80.00
	1840C	—	8.50	20.00	50.00	85.00
	1841C	—	4.00	8.50	15.00	40.00
	1842C	—	100.00	225.00	375.00	625.00
	1843C	—	30.00	70.00	125.00	300.00
	1844C	—	6.00	12.50	25.00	75.00
	1845C	—	6.00	12.50	25.00	75.00
	1846C	—	4.00	7.50	20.00	60.00
	1847C	—	25.00	55.00	90.00	150.00
	1848C	—	25.00	55.00	90.00	150.00

PESETA

SILVER

C#	Date	Mintage	VG	Fine	VF	XF
L40.7	1836C PS	—	16.50	31.50	62.50	125.00
	1837C	—	17.50	35.00	70.00	140.00

GERONA

Gerona, a maritime frontier province in the extreme north-east corner of Spain and it's provincal capital city of Gerona. The city of Gerona is the ancient city of Gerunda where St. Paul and St. James known as Santiago, patron saint of Spain and one of the twelve apostles, first rested when they came to Spain.

RULERS

Ferdinand (Fernando) VII 1808-33

MONETARY SYSTEM

12 Ardites (Dineros) = 8 Ochavos =
4 Quartos = 1 Sueldo
6 Sueldos = 1 Peseta
5 Pesetas = 1 Duro

DURO

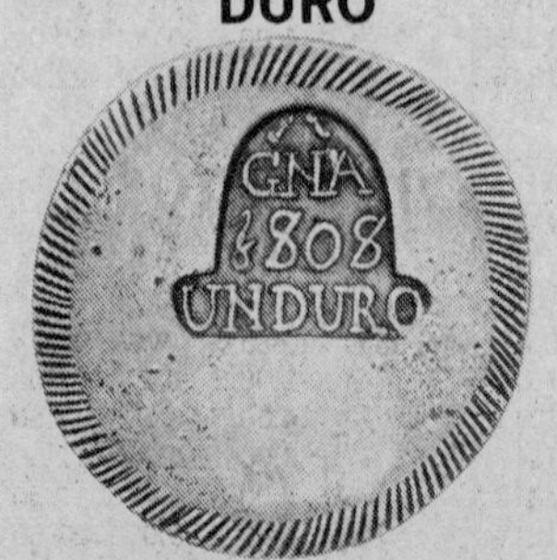

SILVER

C#	Date	Mintage	VG	Fine	VF	XF
L41	1808	—	60.00	100.00	175.00	350.00

COPPER

C#	Date	Mintage	VG	Fine	VF	XF
L41a	1809	—	75.00	125.00	200.00	400.00

5 PESETAS

SILVER
Obv: Crude bust of Ferdinand right.
Rev: Crowned arms divide value.

C#	Date	Mintage	VG	Fine	VF	XF
L42	1809	—	1000.	1750.	3000.	4500.

LERIDA

Lerida, a frontier province of northern Spain and it's provincal capital city of Lerida. The province is bounded on the north by France and on the east by Barcelona and Gerona.

RULERS

Ferdinand VII 1808-33

MONETARY SYSTEM:

12 Ardites (Dineros) = 8 Ochavos =
4 Quartos = 1 Sueldo
6 Sueldos = 1 Peseta
5 Pesetas = 1 Duro

5 PESETAS

SILVER
Similar to Balearic Islands 30 Sueldos, C#L7.

C#	Date	Mintage	VG	Fine	VF	XF
L45	1809	—	1100.	1750.	3000.	5000.

C#	Date	Mintage	VG	Fine	VF	XF
L46	1809	—	1000.	1650.	2750.	4500.

NAVARRE

Navarre; a frontier province of northern Spain and a former kingdom which included part of the south-west corner of France. The Kingdom of Navarre was ultimately divided and absorbed by France and Spain.

RULERS

Carlos VI (= III in Spain)
1759-1788
Carlos VII (= IV in Spain)
1788-1808
Ferdinand (Fernando) III
(= VII in Spain) 1808-1833

1/2 MARAVEDI

COPPER
Similar to 6 Maravedi, C#L92.

C#	Date	Mintage	VG	Fine	VF	XF
L81	1818PP	—	6.00	15.00	25.00	40.00
	1819PP	—	10.00	17.50	35.00	60.00

C#	Date	Mintage	VG	Fine	VF	XF
L82	1831PP	—	10.00	22.50	17.50	45.00
	1381PP(error)	—	75.00	125.00	175.00	250.00
	1832PP	—	75.00	125.00	175.00	250.00

MARAVEDI

COPPER
Obv: CAR VI monogram. Rev: Arms.

C#	Date	Mintage	VG	Fine	VF	XF
L71	ND P	—	10.00	12.50	20.00	35.00

C#	Date	Mintage	VG	Fine	VF	XF
L83	1818PP	—	7.50	15.00	22.50	40.00
	1824Ja	—	7.00	15.00	20.00	35.00
	1825PP	—	4.75	10.00	17.50	30.00
	1826PP	—	4.50	10.00	17.50	30.00

Similar to 6 Maravedi, C#92a.

C#	Date	Mintage	VG	Fine	VF	XF
L83a	1818PP	—	6.00	13.50	20.00	30.00
	1819PP	—	6.00	13.50	20.00	30.00
	1820PP	—	8.50	16.50	25.00	35.00

Similar to 1/2 Maravedi, C#L82.

C#	Date	Mintage	VG	Fine	VF	XF
L84	1829PP	—	5.50	10.00	16.50	25.00
	1830PP	—	5.00	10.00	16.50	25.00
	1831PP	—	6.00	11.50	18.50	30.00
	1832PP	—	5.00	10.00	18.50	30.00
	1833PP	—	8.50	15.00	27.50	40.00

3 MARAVEDIS

COPPER
Similar to 6 Maravedi, C#L92a.

C#	Date	Mintage	VG	Fine	VF	XF
L89	1818PP	—	13.50	30.00	55.00	75.00
	1819PP	—	5.50	11.50	25.00	45.00
	1820PP	—	5.00	10.00	20.00	40.00
	1825PP	—	5.00	12.50	22.50	45.00
	1826PP	—	4.50	8.50	17.50	35.00

Similar to 6 Maravedi, C#L92b.

C#	Date	Mintage	VG	Fine	VF	XF
L89a	1818PP	—	6.50	15.00	30.00	45.00
	1819PP	—	6.00	14.00	25.00	35.00

Similar to 1/2 Maravedi, C#L82.

C#	Date	Mintage	VG	Fine	VF	XF
L90	1829PP	—	3.75	8.00	16.50	25.00
	1830PP	—	3.75	8.50	16.50	25.00
	1831PP	—	4.50	10.00	20.00	45.00
	1832PP	—	3.50	7.50	16.50	25.00
	1833PP	—	3.75	7.50	16.50	25.00

QUARTO

COPPER, octagonal
Similar to 2 Maravedi, C#L71.

C#	Date	Mintage	VG	Fine	VF	XF
L72	1784P	—	10.00	18.50	35.00	55.00
	1788P	—	15.00	20.00	37.50	65.00

Obv: CAR VII monogram. Rev: Arms.

C#	Date	Mintage	VG	Fine	VF	XF
L78	1789P	—	5.00	7.00	12.00	20.00

6 MARAVEDIS

COPPER

Obv: Young bust, bare head. Rev: Arms.

L92	1818PP	—	15.00	35.00	60.00	100.00

Obv: Laureate bust.

L92a	1818PP	—	12.50	27.50	50.00	100.00
	1819PP	—	12.50	27.50	50.00	100.00
	1820PP	—	20.00	50.00	75.00	125.00

TARRAGONA

Tarragona, a maritime province in north east Spain, south of Barcelona and Lerida, and it's provincal capital city of Tarragona. The province produces excellent wines; the city is a flourishing seaport.

RULERS

Ferdinand (Fernando) III
(=vii in Spain) 1808-33)

5 PESETAS

SILVER

L96	1809	—	55.00	90.00	150.00	250.00

TORTOSA

Tortosa, a fortified city of Spain, is in Tarragona province.

RULERS

Fernando VII 1808-1833

DURO (= 5 PESETAS)

SILVER, uniface

Obv: 4 c/s: tower, 1, Duro & TOR . SA.

L100	ND (1808-9)	—	—	—	Rare	—

VALENCIA

Valencia, a maritime province of eastern Spain and the capital city of Valencia. Once a former kingdom, Valencia included the present provinces of Castellon de la Plana and Alicante.

RULERS

Ferdinand (Fernando) VII 1808-33

2 REALES DE VELLON

(= 1 Real)

SILVER

Similar to 4 Reales, C#L106.

C#	Date	Mintage	VG	Fine	VF	XF
L103	1809	—	16.50	31.50	62.50	125.00

4 REALES DE VELLON

(= 2 Reales)

SILVER

L106	1823LL	—	10.00	18.50	37.50	75.00

NOTE: The 4 Reales de Vellon circulated as a regular issue 2 Reales while the 2 Reales de Vellon circulated as a regular 1 Real.

With the loss of her American empire, Spain drifted into chaotic times. Stung by their defeats in Cuba, the army blamed the socialists for what they considered to be mismanagement at home. Additional political complications were derived from the successful Russian Revolution which gave impetus to an already thriving socialist party and trade union movement. Finally, King Alphonso XIII committed the fatal mistake of encouraging a reckless general to start a campaign in Morocco that ended in the virtual extermination of the Spanish army. Fearing that the inevitable parliamentary investigation would incriminate the crown, he offered no objection when General Primo de Rivera seized the government and established himself as dictator in 1926. Rivera fell from power in 1930, and the government was taken over by an alliance of liberals and Socialists who tried to separate the Church and State, take the army out of politics, and introduce effective labor and agrarian reforms despite numerous strikes and street riots. The election of 1936 brought to power a coalition of Socialists, Liberals and Communists, to the dismay of the traditionalists and landowners.

A number of right-wing generals, including the young and clever Francisco Franco, began preparations for a military coup which erupted into a civil war in July of 1936. The destructive conflict, in which more than a million died, lasted three years. During the struggle, areas under control of both the Nationalist (rebels) and the Republican (Loyalists) issued coinages that circulated to whatever extent the political and military situation permitted. The war ended in defeat for the Loyalists when Madrid fell to Franco on March 28, 1939.

During the Spanish Civil War (1936-1939) a great many coins and tokens were minted in the provincial districts. The coins are grouped here under the heading of the district in which they most commonly circulated.

REPUBLICAN ZONE

ARENYS DE MAR

A resort village on the Mediterranean shore that is 20 miles north of Barcelona. One of the villages in the area of operations of General Mola at the beginning of the war.

50 CENTIMOS

ALUMINUM, 21mm

Uniface, arms of Arenys divides value.

KM#	Date	Mintage	Fine	VF	XF	Unc
1	ND(1937)	6,000	10.00	20.00	40.00	80.00

PESETA

ALUMINUM, 29mm

Uniface, arms of Arenys divides value.

2	ND(1937)	3,500	12.50	25.00	50.00	100.00

ASTURIAS AND LEON

Asturias is a province on the northern coast of Spain with the province of Leon just to its south. The councils of these adjoining provinces decided to mint coins in 1937 for use in the area due to lack of other circulating coins in the north.

50 CENTIMOS

COPPER-NICKEL, 21mm
GIJON MINT
Obv: Tools and machinery parts.
Rev: Value over date.

KM#	Date	Mintage	Fine	VF	XF	Unc
1	1937	.200	3.50	6.50	12.50	25.00

PESETA

COPPER, 23mm
GUERNICA MINT

KM#	Date	Mintage	Fine	VF	XF	Unc
2	1937	.100	2.50	5.00	10.00	20.00

2 PESETAS

COPPER-NICKEL, 27mm
GIJON MINT

KM#	Date	Mintage	Fine	VF	XF	Unc
3	1937	.400	1.25	2.50	5.00	10.00

EUZKADI

Viscayan Republic

Euzkadi or the Viscayan Republic was located in north central Spain adjoining the southeast corner of France. It was made up of 4 provinces -Bilbao, Guipuzcoa, Navarre, and Vitoria. These Basque provinces declared autonomy on October 8, 1936. The 2 nickel coins were made in Brussels, Belgium and saw some circulation before the end of the Republic on June 18, 1937.

PESETA

NICKEL, 22mm
BRUSSELS MINT

KM#	Date	Mintage	Fine	VF	XF	Unc
1	1937	7.000	.75	1.50	3.00	6.00

2 PESETAS

NICKEL, 26mm
BRUSSELS MINT

KM#	Date	Mintage	Fine	VF	XF	Unc
2	1937	6.000	1.00	2.00	4.00	8.00

IBI

A village north and west of Alicante on the east coast of Spain. The isolation of the area in comparison with other contending areas made the maintaining of this area during the war very diffcult.

25 CENTIMOS

COPPER, 24mm

KM#	Date	Mintage	Fine	VF	XF	Unc
1	1937	.030	3.50	6.50	12.50	25.00

Obv: Map in field.

KM#	Date	Mintage	Fine	VF	XF	Unc
1a	1937	7,000	5.00	10.00	20.00	40.00

PESETA

NICKEL-BRASS, 24mm

KM#	Date	Mintage	Fine	VF	XF	Unc
2	1937	5,000	7.50	15.00	30.00	60.00

L'AMETLLA DEL VALLES

A town in the province of Tarragona in northeastern Spain. The town adopted the name L'Ametlla del Valles in 1933. Before that the name was La Ametlla. Undated coins of 3 denominations were made in 1937.

25 CENTIMOS

BRASS, 25mm

KM#	Date	Mintage	Fine	VF	XF	Unc
1	ND1937	.050	2.50	5.00	10.00	20.00

50 CENTIMOS

ALUMINUM, 20mm

KM#	Date	Mintage	Fine	VF	XF	Unc
2	ND(1937)	3,000	10.00	20.00	40.00	80.00

Obv: No legend.

KM#	Date	Mintage	Fine	VF	XF	Unc
2a	ND(1937)	.030	3.50	6.50	12.50	25.00

PESETA

ALUMINUM, 26mm

KM#	Date	Mintage	Fine	VF	XF	Unc
3	ND(1937)	3,000	10.00	18.50	37.50	75.00

Obv: No legend.

KM#	Date	Mintage	Fine	VF	XF	Unc
3a	ND(1937)	.030	3.50	6.50	12.50	25.00

MENORCA

Menorca is the smaller of the 2 major islands in the Balearic Islands. A serious coin and supply shortage developed during the war because of the isolation of the island from the mainland.5 denominations with a lighthouse as the major feature were minted in 1937.

5 CENTIMOS

BRASS, 14mm

KM#	Date	Mintage	Fine	VF	XF	Unc
1	1937	.042	2.50	5.00	10.00	20.00

10 CENTIMOS

BRASS, 16mm

KM#	Date	Mintage	Fine	VF	XF	Unc
2	1937	.032	2.00	3.75	7.50	15.00

25 CENTIMOS

BRASS, 18mm

KM#	Date	Mintage	Fine	VF	XF	Unc
3	1937	.038	1.25	2.50	5.00	10.00

PESETA

BRASS, 20mm

KM#	Date	Mintage	Fine	VF	XF	Unc
4	1937	.037	1.25	2.50	5.00	10.00

2-1/2 PESETAS

BRASS, 22mm

KM#	Date	Mintage	Fine	VF	XF	Unc
5	1937	.024	3.50	6.50	12.50	25.00

NULLES

Nulles is a mountian village in the province of Tarragona.The mountainous terrain of the area isolated the village from friendly forces and normal commerce. Therefore, in 1937, an undated series of 5 denominations were issued.

5 CENTIMOS

ZINC, octagonal, 23mm
Uniface, similar to 10 Centimos, KM#2.

KM#	Date	Mintage	Fine	VF	XF	Unc
1	ND(1937)	5,000	16.50	27.50	45.00	75.00

10 CENTIMOS

ZINC, uniface, 21mm

KM#	Date	Mintage	Fine	VF	XF	Unc
2	ND(1937)	3,000	27.50	45.00	75.00	175.00

25 CENTIMOS

BRASS, square, 20mm
Uniface, similar to 10 Centimos, KM#2.

KM#	Date	Mintage	Fine	VF	XF	Unc
3	ND(1937)	5,000	16.50	27.50	45.00	75.00

50 CENTIMOS

BRASS, octagonal, 22mm
Uniface, similar to 10 Centimos, KM#2.

KM#	Date	Mintage	Fine	VF	XF	Unc
4	ND(1937)	1,000	30.00	50.00	85.00	140.00

PESETA

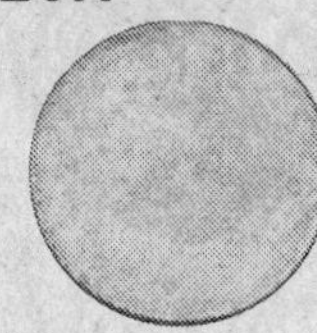

BRASS, uniface, 22mm

KM#	Date	Mintage	Fine	VF	XF	Unc
5	ND(1937)	5,000	16.50	27.50	45.00	75.00

OLOT

A village in the province of Gerona in northeastern Spain near the French border. The village council authorized 2 denominations of coins on September 24,1937.

10 CENTIMOS

IRON
Obv: Arms of Orlot in circle.
Rev: Caduceus and Mercury hat divide value.

KM#	Date	Mintage	Fine	VF	XF	Unc
1	1937	.025	10.00	18.50	35.00	70.00

15 CENTIMOS

IRON
Obv: Arms of Orlot in circle.
Rev: Factory scene over value.

KM#	Date	Mintage	Fine	VF	XF	Unc
2	1937	100pcs.	100.00	175.00	300.00	500.00

NOTE: The above is considered a pattern.

SANTANDER, PALENCIA & BURGOS

Three provinces in northern Spain with Santander being the northern-most on the Spainsh coast. The three provinces met in council and issued two denominations of coins for use in the provinces.

50 CENTIMOS

COPPER-NICKEL, 20mm
Obv: Man working at anvil, dates in exergue.
Rev: Value in branches.

KM#	Date	Mintage	Fine	VF	XF	Unc
1	1937	.100	1.25	2.50	5.00	10.00
	Letters PR in legend					
1a	1937	.010	5.00	10.00	20.00	40.00

PESETA

COPPER-NICKEL, 23mm

KM#	Date	Mintage	Fine	VF	XF	Unc
2	1937	.300	1.25	2.50	5.00	10.00

SEGARRA DE GAIA

A village in the southern part of the province of Tarragona.A single denomination of coin was authorized in 1937.

PESETA

COPPER-NICKEL, 23mm
Uniface, value over bars of Aragon in circle.

KM#	Date	Mintage	Fine	VF	XF	Unc
1	1937	5,000	6.00	10.00	18.50	30.00
	COPPER, 23mm **Uniface**					
1a	1937	.020	3.50	6.50	12.50	25.00
	ALUMINUM, 24mm, stamped **Uniface, 5 line inscription**					
2	1937	.030	5.00	10.00	20.00	40.00

NATIONALIST ZONE

ARAHAL

A town 30 miles southeast of Seville. Issued three undated types of coins in 1936.

50 CENTIMOS

BRASS, 19mm
Uniface, legend incuse with value in center.

KM#	Date	Mintage	Fine	VF	XF	Unc
1	ND(1936)	3,000	11.50	18.50	30.00	50.00

PESETA

BRASS, 25mm
Uniface, legend incuse with value in center.

KM#	Date	Mintage	Fine	VF	XF	Unc
2	ND(1936)	.010	3.50	6.50	12.50	25.00

2 PESETAS

BRASS, 30mm
Uniface, legend incuse with value in center.

KM#	Date	Mintage	Fine	VF	XF	Unc
3	ND(1936)	.010	3.50	6.50	12.50	25.00

CAZALLA DE SIERRA

A town 43 miles north of Seville that issued a 10 centimos in brass in 1936 (undated).

10 CENTIMOS

BRASS
Obv: 6 line inscription, arms of Cazalla to right.
Rev: 5 line inscription, olive branch to left.

KM#	Date	Mintage	Fine	VF	XF	Unc
1	ND(1936)	.010	3.75	7.50	15.00	30.00

LORA DEL RIO

A town 35 miles northeast of Seville. Issued an undated 25 centimos in 1936.

25 CENTIMOS

BRASS
Obv: 5 line inscription, wheat ear to right.
Rev: Crowned arms of Lora del Rio on cross.

KM#	Date	Mintage	Fine	VF	XF	Unc
1	ND(1936)	1,500	18.50	30.00	50.00	85.00

MARCHENA

A village 12 miles east of Marchena. It was the last issuer in Seville province. Two values of undated coins were produced in 1936.

25 CENTIMOS

BRASS
Uniface, vale above '25 C' in center, 'MARCHENA' below.
Value as 25C

KM#	Date	Mintage	Fine	VF	XF	Unc
1	ND(1936)	5,000	11.50	18.50	30.00	50.00
	Value as 0.25C, uniface.					
1a	ND(1936)	500pcs.	27.50	45.00	75.00	125.00

PUEBLA DE CAZALIA

A village only a few miles from Cazalla de la Sierra and some 65 miles from the Portuguese frontier. Undated coins of two values were issued in 1936.

10 CENTIMOS

BRASS, 23mm
Obv: Bundle of arrows to left of 3 line inscription.
Rev: Value in circle.

KM#	Date	Mintage	Fine	VF	XF	Unc
1	ND(1936)	1,500	17.50	27.50	45.00	75.00

There are several vàrieties.

25 CENTIMOS

BRASS, 25mm
Obv: Bundle of arrows to left of 3 line inscription.
Rev: Value in circle.

KM#	Date	Mintage	Fine	VF	XF	Unc
2	ND(1936)	5,000	11.50	18.50	30.00	50.00

There are several varieties.

SPITZBERGEN

Spitzbergen (Svalbard), a Norwegian territory, is a group of mountainous islands in the Arctic Ocean 360 miles (579 km.) north of Norway. The islands have an area of 23,957 sq. mi. (62,050 sq. km.) and a population of about 4,000. West Spitzbergen, the largest island, is the seat of administration. Sealing and fishing are economically important. Despite rich carboniferous and tertiary coal deposits, coal mining, which was started on a commercial scale by the Arctic Coal Co. of Boston, Mass. in 1904, produces only small quantities.

Spitzbergen was probably discovered in 1194, but modern knowledge of it dates from its discovery by William Barents in 1596. Quarrels among the various nationalities involved in the whaling industry, which was set up in 1611, resulted in a de facto division of the coast, but despite diverse interests in, and claims to the islands by British, Dutch, Norwegians, Swedes, Danes, Russians and Americans, the question of sovereignty was not resolved until 1920, when a treaty agreed to by the claimants awarded the islands to Norway.

In 1932, the Russian mining company 'Arktikugol' began operations in the islands. The tokens listed here were minted in Leningrad for use by the company in Spitzbergen.

RULERS

Norwegian, 1920 -

TOKEN ISSUES

10 KOPEKS

ALUMINUM-BRONZE

KM#	Date	Mintage	Fine	VF	XF	Unc
1	1946	—	13.50	17.50	35.00	50.00

15 KOPEKS

ALUMINUM-BRONZE

KM#	Date	Mintage	Fine	VF	XF	Unc
2	1946	—	13.50	17.50	35.00	50.00

20 KOPEKS

COPPER-NICKEL

KM#	Date	Mintage	Fine	VF	XF	Unc
3	1946	—	15.00	20.00	40.00	60.00

50 KOPEKS

COPPER-NICKEL

KM#	Date	Mintage	Fine	VF	XF	Unc
4	1946	—	15.00	20.00	40.00	60.00

SRI LANKA

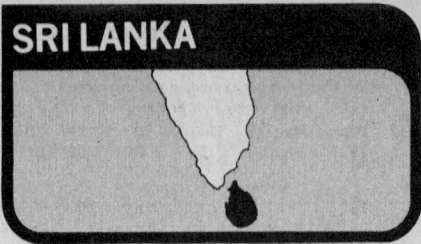

The Republic of Sri Lanka (formerly Ceylon), situated in the Indian Ocean 18 miles (29 km.) southeast of India, has an area of 25,332 sq. mi. (65,610 sq. km.) and a population of 14 million. Capital: Colombo. The economy is chiefly agricultural. Tea, coconut products and rubber are exported.

The earliest known inhabitants of Ceylon, the Veddahs, were subjugated by the Sinhalese from northern India in the 6th century B.C. Sinhalese rule was maintained until 1408, after which the island was controlled by China for 30 years. The Portuguese came to Ceylon in 1505 and maintained control of the coastal area for 150 years. They were supplanted by the Dutch in 1658, who were in turn supplanted by the British who seized the island in 1796, and made it a Crown Colony in 1802. Constitutional changes in 1931 and 1946 granted the Ceylonese a measure of autonomy and a parliamentary form of government. Ceylon became a self-governing dominion of the British Commonwealth on Feb. 4, 1948. On May 22, 1972, the Ceylonese adopted a new Constitution which declared Ceylon to be the Republic of Sri Lanka - 'Resplendent Island'. Sri Lanka is a member of the Commonwealth of Nations. The president is Chief of State. The prime minister is Head of Government.

RULERS

Dutch, until 1796
British, 1796-1972

CEYLON

Netherlands United East India Company

MONETARY SYSTEM

4 Duits = 1 Stuiver
4 Stuivers = 1 Fanam
9-1/2 Stuivers = 1 Larin
12 Fanams = 1 Rixdollar

1/8 DUIT

TIN
Obv: 17/47 around central depression.
Rev: Value.

C#	Date	Mintage	Good	VG	Fine	VF
1	1747	—	—	—	Rare	—

DUIT

TIN, 15-16gm.
Obv: C over VOC monogram and date.
Rev: Bird on tree divides dates.

C#	Date	Mintage	Good	VG	Fine	VF
2	1782	—	40.00	75.00	125.00	200.00

Lighter weight, 9-11 gm.

C#	Date	Mintage	Good	VG	Fine	VF
2a	1785	—	35.00	65.00	100.00	150.00
	1786	—	35.00	65.00	100.00	150.00

LEAD
Obv: C over VOC monogram.
Rev: Value 1 DT and date.

C#	Date	Mintage	Good	VG	Fine	VF
4	1789	—	30.00	50.00	85.00	125.00
	1790	—	30.00	50.00	85.00	125.00
	1791	—	—	—	Rare	—

Value stated 1 DUIT.

C#	Date	Mintage	Good	VG	Fine	VF
4a	1792	—	25.00	45.00	75.00	100.00
	1793	—	—	—	Rare	—

1/4 STUIVER

COPPER
Obv: C over VOC monogram.
Rev: Value.

C#	Date	Mintage	Good	VG	Fine	VF
3	ND (1783)	—	10.00	20.00	40.00	65.00

STUIVER

COPPER
Obv: C over VOC monogram.

C#	Date	Mintage	Good	VG	Fine	VF
5	1783	—	5.00	10.00	20.00	35.00
	1784	—	7.50	15.00	27.50	45.00
	1785	—	5.00	10.00	20.00	35.00
	1786	—	5.00	10.00	20.00	35.00
	1787	—	6.50	12.50	22.50	40.00
	1788	—	7.50	15.00	27.50	45.00
	1789	—	5.00	10.00	20.00	35.00
	1790	—	5.00	10.00	20.00	35.00
	1791	—	5.00	10.00	20.00	35.00
	1792	—	6.50	12.50	22.50	40.00
	1793	—	7.50	15.00	27.50	45.00
	1794	—	6.50	12.50	22.50	40.00
	1795	—	7.50	15.00	27.50	45.00

NOTE: Varieties exist.

JAFFNA MINT
Obv: I(J) over VOC monogram and value.
Rev: Date, value in Tamil.

C#	Date	Mintage	Good	VG	Fine	VF
6	1783	—	—	—	Rare	—
	1788	—	—	—	Rare	—
	1790	—	—	—	Rare	—
	1791	—	—	—	Rare	—
	1792	—	—	—	Rare	—

GALLE MINT
Obv: G over VOC monogram.
Rev: Value in Sinhalese.

C#	Date	Mintage	Good	VG	Fine	VF
7	1783	—	10.00	20.00	40.00	65.00
	1787	—	10.00	20.00	40.00	65.00
	1788	—	10.00	20.00	40.00	65.00
	1789	—	10.00	20.00	40.00	65.00
	1790	—	10.00	20.00	40.00	65.00
	1792	—	10.00	20.00	40.00	65.00
	1793	—	10.00	20.00	40.00	65.00

NOTE: Varieties exist.

TRINCOMALEE MINT
Obv: T over VOC monogram.
Rev: Value and date.

C#	Date	Mintage	Good	VG	Fine	VF
8	1789	—	10.00	20.00	40.00	65.00
	1790	—	10.00	20.00	40.00	65.00
	1791	—	10.00	20.00	40.00	65.00
	1792	—	10.00	20.00	40.00	65.00
	1793	—	10.00	20.00	40.00	65.00

2 STUIVER

COPPER

JAFFNA MINT
Obv: I(J) over VOC monogram and value.
Rev: Date, value in Tamil.

C#	Date	Mintage	Good	VG	Fine	VF
9	1783	—	15.00	50.00	85.00	125.00
	1784	—	25.00	60.00	100.00	150.00
	1786	—	—	—	Rare	—
	1787	—	—	—	Rare	—
	1788	—	15.00	50.00	85.00	125.00
	1792	—	15.00	50.00	85.00	125.00
	1793	—	25.00	60.00	100.00	150.00

NOTE: Varieties exist.

TIN

C#	Date	Mintage	Good	VG	Fine	VF
9a	1783	—	—	—	Rare	—

COPPER

GALLE MINT

Obv: G over VOC monogram.

C#	Date	Mintage	Good	VG	Fine	VF
10	1783	—	10.00	30.00	50.00	85.00
	1787	—	10.00	30.00	50.00	85.00
	1788	—	10.00	30.00	50.00	85.00
	1789	—	10.00	30.00	50.00	85.00
	1790	—	10.00	30.00	50.00	85.00
	1791	—	10.00	30.00	50.00	85.00
	1792	—	10.00	30.00	50.00	85.00

NOTE: Varieties exist.

4-3/4 STUIVER

COPPER

Bonk (bar), 58 to 105mm in length.
4-3/4 ST and C over VOC monogram in stamps at ends.

C#	Date	Mintage	Good	VG	Fine	VF
14	ND (1785)	—	115.00	250.00	350.00	500.00

RUPEE

SILVER

COLOMBO MINT

Obv: Corrupted Arabic-Malay legend.
Rev: Same with date.

C#	Date	Mintage	Good	VG	Fine	VF
18	1784	.122	50.00	135.00	175.00	225.00
	1786	1,636	50.00	125.00	155.00	200.00
	1787	.020	50.00	135.00	175.00	225.00

TUTICORIN MINT

C#	Date	Mintage	Good	VG	Fine	VF
18.1	1788	.066	50.00	125.00	155.00	200.00
	1789	.038	50.00	125.00	155.00	200.00

British Colonial Issues

MINTMARKS

H - Heaton, Birmingham
B - Bombay

MONETARY SYSTEM

4 Pies = 1 Stiver
4 Stivers = 1 Fanam
12 Fanams = 1 Rixdoller = 1 Rupee
2 Rupees = 3 Shillings
1-1/2 Shillings

1/4 PICE

1/256 RIXDALLER

COPPER

Obv: C.G., date. Rev: Value.

C#	Date	Mintage	Fine	VF	XF	Unc
27.5	1813	—	—	—	—	—

1/192 RIXDOLLAR

COPPER

C#	Date	Mintage	Fine	VF	XF	Unc
25	1802	3.600	3.50	8.00	20.00	50.00
	1802	—	—	—	Proof	100.00
	1802	—	—		Gilt Proof	90.00
25a	1804	—	—		Proof only	125.00
	1804	—	—		Gilt Proof	100.00

1/96 RIXDOLLAR

COPPER

C#	Date	Mintage	Fine	VF	XF	Unc
26	1802	1.800	4.00	6.50	16.50	40.00
	1802	—	—	—	Proof	125.00
	1802	—	—		Gilt Proof	110.00

1/2 STIVER

COPPER

C#	Date	Mintage	Fine	VF	XF	Unc
28	1815	2.400	4.00	10.00	25.00	60.00
	1815	—	—	—	Proof	135.00

1/48 RUPEE

COPPER dump

Rev: Elephant faces left

C#	Date	Mintage	VG	Fine	VF	XF
22	1801	—	4.50	7.50	15.00	30.00
	1802	—	4.50	7.50	15.00	30.00
	1803	—	4.50	7.50	15.00	30.00
	1811	—	6.00	10.00	20.00	40.00
	1812	—	6.00	10.00	17.50	35.00
	1813	—	8.00	12.50	20.00	40.00
	1814	—	8.00	12.50	20.00	40.00
	1815	—	8.00	12.50	20.00	40.00
	1816	—	8.50	14.00	22.50	45.00

Obv: Two parallel lines under 48

C#	Date	Mintage	VG	Fine	VF	XF
22.1	1802	—	13.50	18.50	25.00	50.00

Rev: Elephant faces right.

C#	Date	Mintage	VG	Fine	VF	XF
22.2	1803	—	—	—	Unique	—

1/48 RIXDOLLAR

COPPER

C#	Date	Mintage	Fine	VF	XF	Unc
27	1802	2.700	6.00	10.00	25.00	60.00
	1802	—	—	—	Proof	150.00
	1802	—	—		Gilt Proof	125.00
27a	1803	—	—	—	Proof	200.00
	1804	—	—	—	Proof	200.00
	1804	—	—		Gilt Proof	150.00

STIVER

COPPER

C#	Date	Mintage	Fine	VF	XF	Unc
29	1815	2.800	4.00	8.00	20.00	50.00
	1815	—	—	—	Proof	90.00

1/24 RUPEE

COPPER dump

Rev: Elephant faces left

C#	Date	Mintage	VG	Fine	VF	XF
23	1801	—	10.00	22.50	35.00	50.00
	1802	—	7.00	18.50	40.00	50.00
	1803	—	6.00	17.50	30.00	40.00
	1805	—	13.50	18.50	45.00	55.00
	1811	—	7.00	16.50	30.00	40.00
	1812	—	7.00	18.50	30.00	40.00
	1813	—	7.00	18.50	35.00	45.00
	1814	—	12.50	23.50	32.50	45.00
	1815	—	12.50	21.50	45.00	55.00
	1816	—	19.00	50.00	75.00	90.00

Obv: Two parallel lines under 24

C#	Date	Mintage	VG	Fine	VF	XF
23.1	1802	—	55.00	120.00	300.00	325.00

Rev: Elephant faces right.

C#	Date	Mintage	VG	Fine	VF	XF
23a	1803	—	50.00	120.00	160.00	200.00

2 STIVERS

COPPER

Obv: W/o rose below bust.

C#	Date	Mintage	Fine	VF	XF	Unc
30	1815	1.920	5.00	12.50	30.00	75.00
	1815	—	—	—	Proof	150.00

Obv: W/rose below bust

C#	Date	Mintage	Fine	VF	XF	Unc
30.1	1815	—	—		Proof only	175.00

1/12 RUPEE

COPPER dump

Rev: Elephant faces left.

C#	Date	Mintage	VG	Fine	VF	XF
24	1801	—	10.00	25.00	32.50	50.00
	1802	—	8.00	16.50	25.00	40.00
	1803	—	8.00	16.50	25.00	40.00
	1804	—	12.50	25.00	35.00	60.00
	1805	—	12.50	25.00	35.00	60.00
	1811	—	9.00	22.50	35.00	50.00
	1812	—	9.00	22.50	35.00	50.00
	1813	—	9.00	30.00	45.00	65.00
	1814	—	9.00	27.50	45.00	65.00
	1815	—	9.00	22.50	35.00	60.00

Obv: Two parallel lines under 12

C#	Date	Mintage	VG	Fine	VF	XF
24.1	1802	Unique	—	—	—	—

Rev: Elephant faces right.

C#	Date	Mintage	VG	Fine	VF	XF
24a	1803	—	85.00	300.00	350.00	400.00

FANAM TOKEN

.833 SILVER

Obv: Circular legends, FANAM. Rev: TOKEN.

C#	Date	Mintage	VG	Fine	VF	XF
34	ND(1814-15)	2.095	5.00	9.50	17.50	35.00

1/3 RIXDOLLAR

SILVER dump
Crown countermark on Madras Arcot 1/4 Rupee

37.5	ND(1823)	.260	18.50	37.50	75.00	10.00

24 STIVERS

.892 SILVER

31	1803	—	27.50	55.00	90.00	150.00
	1804	—	22.50	45.00	75.00	125.00
	1805	—	37.50	75.00	120.00	200.00
	1808	—	17.50	35.00	60.00	100.00
	1809	—	20.00	40.00	65.00	110.00

48 STIVERS

.892 SILVER

32	1803	—	25.00	50.00	100.00	160.00
	1804	—	25.00	50.00	100.00	160.00
	1805	—	25.00	50.00	100.00	160.00
	1808	—	25.00	50.00	100.00	160.00
	1809	—	20.00	40.00	80.00	145.00

Rev: Elephant faces right.

32a	1803	—	85.00	125.00	175.00	250.00

RIX DOLLAR

.892 SILVER

C#	Date	Mintage	Fine	VF	XF	Unc
38	1821	.400	18.50	37.50	75.00	125.00
	1821	—	—	—	Proof	200.00

1-1/3 RIXDOLLAR
(16 Fanams)

SILVER dump
c/s: Crown on Madras Arcot Rupee

C#	Date	Mintage	VG	Fine	VF	XF
37.6	ND(1823)	.282	75.00	150.00	250.00	325.00

96 STIVERS

.833 SILVER

33	1803	—	—	—	—	—
	1808	—	37.50	75.00	125.00	200.00
	1809	—	45.00	90.00	150.00	250.00

COLONIAL COINAGE
4 Farthings = 1 Penny

1/4 FARTHINGS

COPPER and BRONZE

NOTE: From 1839 through 1868 homeland type 1/4 Farthings were issued by Great Britain for circulation in Ceylon. These are listed under Great Britain.

1/2 FARTHINGS

COPPER and BRONZE

NOTE: From 1828 through 1868 homeland type 1/2 Farthings were issued by Great Britain for circulation in Ceylon. These are listed under Great Britain.

1-1/2 PENCE

SILVER

NOTE: From 1834 through 1870 homeland type 1 1/2 Pence were issued by Great Britain for circulation in Ceylon and Jamaica. These are listed under Great Britain.

DECIMAL COINAGE
100 Cents = 1 Rupee

1/4 CENT

COPPER

Y#	Date	Mintage	Fine	VF	XF	Unc
4	1870	.200	2.50	5.00	10.00	20.00
	1870	—	—	—	Proof	75.00
	1890	.200	2.50	5.00	10.00	20.00
	1890	—	—	—	Proof	75.00
	1891	—	—		Proof only	150.00
	1892	—	—		Proof only	150.00
	1898	.160	3.50	6.50	12.50	25.00
	1898	—	—	—	Proof	75.00
	1899	—	—		Proof only	150.00
	1901	.216	2.50	5.00	10.00	20.00
	1901	—	—	—	Proof	75.00
			SILVER (OMS)			
4a	1870	—	—		Proof only	250.00
	1891	—	—		Proof only	250.00
	1898	—	—		Proof only	250.00
			GOLD (OMS)			
4b	1870	—	—		Proof only	600.00
	1891	—	—		Proof only	600.00
	1904	—	—		Proof only	600.00

COPPER

11	1904	.103	4.00	7.50	15.00	30.00
	1904	—	—	—	Proof	100.00

1/2 CENT

COPPER

Y#	Date	Mintage	Fine	VF	XF	Unc
5	1870	3.040	2.50	5.00	10.00	20.00
	1870	—	—	—	Proof	75.00
	1890	.400	5.00	10.00	20.00	40.00
	1890	—	—	—	Proof	85.00
	1891	1.000	2.50	5.00	10.00	20.00
	1891	—	—	—	Proof	75.00
	1892	—	—		Proof only	150.00
	1895	4.040	2.50	5.00	10.00	20.00
	1895	—	—	—	Proof	75.00
	1898	4.000	2.50	5.00	10.00	20.00
	1898	—	—	—	Proof	75.00
	1901	2.020	2.50	5.00	10.00	20.00
			SILVER (OMS)			
5a	1870	—	—		Proof only	250.00
	1891	—	—		Proof only	250.00
	1895	—	—		Proof only	250.00
	1898	—	—		Proof only	250.00
			GOLD (OMS)			
5b	1870	—	—		Proof only	600.00
	1891	—	—		Proof only	600.00
	1895	—	—		Proof only	600.00

COPPER

12	1904	2.012	1.75	3.75	7.50	15.00
	1904	—	—	—	Proof	75.00
	1905	1.000	1.75	3.75	7.50	15.00
	1905	—	—	—	Proof	75.00
	1906	3.056	1.75	3.75	7.50	15.00
	1906	—	—	—	Proof	75.00
	1908	1.000	1.75	3.75	7.50	15.00
	1908	—	—	—	Proof	75.00
	1909	3.000	1.75	3.75	7.50	15.00
	1909	—	—	—	Proof	75.00
	1910	—	—		Proof only	150.00

18	1912	5.008	1.25	2.50	5.00	10.00
	1912	—	—	—	Proof	75.00
	1914	2.000	1.25	2.50	5.00	10.00
	1914	—	—	—	Proof	75.00
	1917	2.000	1.25	2.50	5.00	10.00
	1917	—	—	—	Proof	75.00
	1926	10.000	.75	1.50	3.00	6.00

24	1937	3.026	.65	1.25	2.50	5.00
	1940	5.080	.65	1.25	2.50	5.00

CENT

COPPER

6	1870	7.055	1.75	3.75	7.50	15.00
	1870	—	—	—	Proof	75.00
	1890	4.940	1.75	3.75	7.50	15.00
	1890	—	—	—	Proof	75.00
	1891	1.328	2.75	5.50	11.50	22.50
	1891	—	—	—	Proof	75.00
	1892	5.000	1.75	3.75	7.50	15.00
	1892	—	—	—	Proof	75.00

Y#	Date	Mintage	Fine	VF	XF	Unc
6	1898	—	—		Proof only	175.00
	1900	1.000	3.50	6.50	12.50	25.00
	1901	1.014	3.50	6.50	12.50	25.00

SILVER (OMS)

Y#	Date	Mintage	Fine	VF	XF	Unc
6a	1870	—	—		Proof only	250.00
	1891	—	—		Proof only	250.00
	1892	—	—		Proof only	250.00

GOLD (OMS)

Y#	Date	Mintage	Fine	VF	XF	Unc
6b	1870	—	—		Proof only	600.00
	1891	—	—		Proof only	600.00

COPPER

Y#	Date	Mintage	Fine	VF	XF	Unc
13	1904	2.529	1.25	2.50	5.00	10.00
	1904	—	—	—	Proof	75.00
	1905	1.509	1.25	2.50	5.00	10.00
	1905	—	—	—	Proof	75.00
	1906	1.751	1.25	2.50	5.00	10.00
	1906	—	—	—	Proof	75.00
	1908	—	1.25	2.50	5.00	10.00
	1908	—	—	—	Proof	75.00
	1909	2.500	1.25	2.50	5.00	10.00
	1909	—	—	—	Proof	75.00
	1910	8.236	1.25	2.50	5.00	10.00
	1910	—	1.25	2.50	5.00	75.00

Y#	Date	Mintage	Fine	VF	XF	Unc
19	1912	5.855	.75	1.50	3.00	6.00
	1912	—	—	—	Proof	75.00
	1914	6.000	.75	1.50	3.00	6.00
	1914	—	—	—	Proof	75.00
	1917	1.000	1.00	2.00	4.00	8.00
	1917	—	—	—	Proof	75.00
	1920	2.000	.75	1.50	3.00	6.00
	1920	—	—	—	Proof	75.00
	1922	2.930	.75	1.50	3.00	6.00
	1922	—	—	—	Proof	75.00
	1923	12.110	.75	1.50	3.00	6.00
	1923	—	—	—	Proof	75.00
	1925	7.490	.50	1.00	2.00	4.00
	1925	—	—	—	Proof	75.00
	1926	7.500	.50	1.00	2.00	4.00
	1926	—	—	—	Proof	75.00
	1928	5.000	.50	1.00	2.00	4.00
	1928	—	—	—	Proof	75.00
	1929	7.522	.50	1.00	2.00	4.00
	1929	—	—	—	Proof	75.00

Y#	Date	Mintage	Fine	VF	XF	Unc
25	1937	4.538	.50	1.00	2.00	4.00
	1940	10.190	.50	1.00	2.00	4.00
	1940	—	—	—	Proof	75.00
	1942	20.780	.50	1.00	2.00	4.00

BRONZE

Y#	Date	Mintage	Fine	VF	XF	Unc
25a	1942	Inc. Ab.	.25	.50	1.00	2.00
(26)	1942	—	—	—	Proof	50.00
	1943	43.705	.15	.35	.75	1.50
	1945	34.100	.15	.35	.75	1.50
	1945*	—	—	—	Proof	25.00

***NOTE:** These were restruck in quantity.

ALUMINUM
Independent

Y#	Date	Mintage	Fine	VF	XF	Unc
43	1963	33.000	—	—	—	.10
	1965	12.000	—	—	.10	.15
	1967	10.000	—	—	.10	.15
	1968	22.500	—	—	—	.10
	1969	20.000	—	—	—	.10
	1970	15.000	—	—	.10	.15
	1971	55.000	—	—	—	.10
	1971	—	—	—	Proof	.50

2 CENTS

NICKEL-BRASS

Y#	Date	Mintage	Fine	VF	XF	Unc
27	1944	30.165	.10	.25	.50	1.00

Obv: EMPEROR OF INDIA dropped

Y#	Date	Mintage	Fine	VF	XF	Unc
34	1951	15.000	.10	.25	.50	1.00
	1951	—	—	—	Proof	20.00
	1951	—	—		Proof restrike	5.00

Y#	Date	Mintage	Fine	VF	XF	Unc
39	1955	37.131	.10	.25	.50	1.00
	1957	38.200	.10	.25	.50	1.00
	1957	—	—	—	Proof	40.00

ALUMINUM
Independent

Y#	Date	Mintage	Fine	VF	XF	Unc
44	1963	26.000	—	—	.10	.15
	1965	7.000	—	—	.10	.15
	1967	15.000	—	—	.10	.15
	1968	15.000	—	—	.10	.15
	1969	—	—	—	.10	.15
	1970	13.000	—	—	.10	.15
	1971	45.000	—	—	.10	.15
	1971	—	—	—	Proof	.75

5 CENTS

COPPER

Y#	Date	Mintage	Fine	VF	XF	Unc
7	1870	7.009	5.00	12.50	25.00	60.00
	1870	—	—	—	Proof	100.00
	1890	1.001	6.00	15.00	30.00	75.00
	1890	—	—	—	Proof	125.00
	1891	—	—		Proof only	200.00
	1892	1.000	6.00	15.00	30.00	75.00
	1892	—	—	—	Proof	125.00
	1904	*4-8 pcs.	—		Proof only	3500.

SILVER (OMS)

Y#	Date	Mintage	Fine	VF	XF	Unc
7a	1891	—	—		Proof only	350.00
	1892	—	—		Proof only	350.00

GOLD (OMS)

Y#	Date	Mintage	Fine	VF	XF	Unc
7b	1891	—	—		Proof only	750.00

COPPER-NICKEL

Y#	Date	Mintage	Fine	VF	XF	Unc
14	1909	2.000	1.25	2.50	5.00	12.00
	1910	4.000	1.00	2.00	4.00	10.00

Y#	Date	Mintage	Fine	VF	XF	Unc
20	1912H	4.000	.65	1.25	2.50	6.00
	1920	6.000	.50	1.00	2.00	5.00
	1926	3.000	.65	1.35	2.75	6.50

NICKEL-BRASS

Y#	Date	Mintage	Fine	VF	XF	Unc
28	1942	12.752	.35	.75	1.50	4.00
	1942	—	—	—	Proof	60.00
	1943	Inc. Ab.	.35	.75	1.50	4.00
	1943	—	—	—	Proof	60.00

Thin Planchet

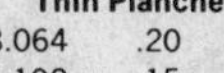

Y#	Date	Mintage	Fine	VF	XF	Unc
28a	1944	18.064	.20	.35	.70	1.75
	1945	31.192	.15	.30	.60	1.50
	1945	—	—	—	Proof	80.00

Obv: EMPEROR OF INDIA dropped

Y#	Date	Mintage	Fine	VF	XF	Unc
35	1951	—	—	—	Proof	20.00
	1951	—	—		Proof restrike	5.00

Independent

Y#	Date	Mintage	Fine	VF	XF	Unc
45	1963	16.000	—	—	.10	.15
	1965	9.000	—	—	.10	.15
	1968	12.000	—	—	.10	.15
	1968	—	—	—	Proof	2.50
	1969	7.500	—	—	.10	.15
	1970	7.000	—	—	.10	.15
	1971	32.000	—	—	.10	.15
	1971	—	—	—	Proof	1.00

10 CENTS

1.1664 gm., .800 SILVER, .0300 oz ASW

Y#	Date	Mintage	Fine	VF	XF	Unc
8	1892	2.500	2.00	5.00	12.00	30.00
	1892	—	—	—	Proof	100.00
	1893	2.500	2.00	5.00	12.00	30.00
	1893	—	—	—	Proof	100.00
	1894	3.000	2.00	5.00	12.00	30.00
	1894	—	—	—	Proof	100.00
	1897	1.500	2.00	5.00	12.00	30.00
	1899	1.000	2.00	5.00	12.00	30.00
	1900	1.000	2.00	5.00	12.00	30.00

Y#	Date	Mintage	Fine	VF	XF	Unc
15	1902	1.000	2.00	5.00	12.00	30.00
	1902	—	—	—	Proof	100.00
	1903	1.000	2.00	5.00	12.00	30.00
	1903	—	—	—	Proof	100.00
	1907	.500	3.25	8.00	20.00	50.00
	1908	1.500	2.00	5.00	12.00	30.00
	1909	1.000	2.00	5.00	12.00	30.00
	1910	2.000	2.00	5.00	12.00	30.00

Y#	Date	Mintage	Fine	VF	XF	Unc
21	1911	1.000	1.00	2.00	5.00	12.00
	1912	1.000	1.00	2.00	5.00	12.00
	1913	2.000	1.00	2.00	5.00	12.00
	1914	2.000	1.00	2.00	5.00	12.00
	1914	—	—	—	Proof	100.00
	1917	.879	1.25	3.25	8.00	20.00
	1917	—	—	—	Proof	100.00

1.1664 gm., .550 SILVER, .0206 oz ASW

Y#	Date	Mintage	Fine	VF	XF	Unc
21a	1919B	.750	2.00	5.00	12.00	30.00
	1919B	—	—	—	Proof	100.00
	1920B	3.059	1.25	3.25	8.00	20.00
	1920B	—	—	—	Proof	100.00
	1921B	1.583	.80	2.00	5.00	12.00
	1921B	—	—	—	Proof	100.00
	1922	.282	2.00	5.00	12.00	30.00
	1922	—	—	—	Proof	100.00
	1924	1.508	.75	1.75	4.50	11.00
	1924	—	—	—	Proof	100.00
	1925	1.500	.75	1.75	4.50	11.00
	1925	—	—	—	Proof	100.00
	1926	1.500	.75	1.75	4.50	11.00
	1926	—	—	—	Proof	100.00
	1927	1.500	.75	1.75	4.50	11.00
	1927	—	—	—	Proof	100.00
	1928	1.500	.75	1.75	4.50	11.00
	1928	—	—	—	Proof	100.00

Y#	Date	Mintage	Fine	VF	XF	Unc
32	1941	16.271	.65	1.00	2.50	6.00

NICKEL-BRASS

Y#	Date	Mintage	Fine	VF	XF	Unc
29	1944	30.500	.25	.50	1.00	2.50

Obv: EMPEROR OF INDIA dropped

Y#	Date	Mintage	Fine	VF	XF	Unc
36	1951	34.760	.10	.20	.40	1.00
36	1951	—	—	—	Proof	20.00
	1951	—	—	Proof restrike		5.00

Independent

Y#	Date	Mintage	Fine	VF	XF	Unc
46	1963	14.000	—	—	.15	.20
	1965	3.000	—	—	.15	.20
	1969	8.000	—	—	.15	.20
	1970	—	—	—	.15	.20
	1971	29.000	—	—	.15	.20
	1971	—	—	—	Proof	1.50

25 CENTS

2.9160 gm., .800 SILVER, .0750 oz ASW

Y#	Date	Mintage	Fine	VF	XF	Unc
9	1892	.500	6.50	12.50	25.00	50.00
	1892	—	—	—	Proof	100.00
	1893	1.500	4.50	8.50	17.50	35.00
	1893	—	—	—	Proof	100.00
	1895	1.200	4.50	8.50	17.50	35.00
	1899	.600	6.50	12.50	25.00	50.00
	1900	.400	6.50	12.50	25.00	50.00

Y#	Date	Mintage	Fine	VF	XF	Unc
16	1902	.400	3.75	7.50	15.00	30.00
	1902	—	—	—	Proof	100.00
	1903	.400	3.75	7.50	15.00	30.00
	1903	—	—	—	Proof	100.00
	1907	.120	5.00	10.00	20.00	40.00
	1908	.400	3.75	7.50	15.00	30.00
	1909	.400	3.75	7.50	15.00	30.00
	1910	.800	3.25	6.50	12.50	25.00

Y#	Date	Mintage	Fine	VF	XF	Unc
22	1911	.400	3.75	7.50	15.00	30.00
	1911	—	—	—	Proof	100.00
	1913	1.200	2.50	5.00	10.00	20.00
	1913	—	—	—	Proof	100.00
	1914	.400	3.75	7.50	15.00	30.00
	1914	—	—	—	Proof	100.00
	1917	.300	5.00	10.00	20.00	40.00
	1917	—	—	—	Proof	100.00

2.9160 gm., .550 SILVER, .0516 oz ASW

Y#	Date	Mintage	Fine	VF	XF	Unc
22a	1919B	1.400	1.75	3.75	7.50	15.00
	1919B	—	—	—	Proof	100.00
	1920B	1.600	1.75	3.75	7.50	15.00
	1920B	—	—	—	Proof	100.00
	1921B	.600	3.75	7.50	15.00	30.00
	1921B	—	—	—	Proof	100.00
	1922	1.211	1.75	3.75	7.50	15.00
	1922	—	—	—	Proof	100.00
	1925	1.004	1.75	3.75	7.50	15.00
	1925	—	—	—	Proof	100.00
	1926	1.000	1.75	3.75	7.50	15.00
	1926	—	—	—	Proof	100.00

NICKEL-BRASS

Y#	Date	Mintage	Fine	VF	XF	Unc
30	1943	13.920	.25	.50	1.00	2.50

Obv. leg: w/o EMPEROR OF INDIA.

Y#	Date	Mintage	Fine	VF	XF	Unc
37	1951	25.940	.10	.30	.60	1.50
	1951	—	—	—	Proof	20.00
	1951	—	—	Proof restrike		5.00

COPPER-NICKEL
Independent

Y#	Date	Mintage	Fine	VF	XF	Unc
47	1963	30.000	—	.10	.20	.40
	1965	8.000	.10	.15	.25	.50
	1968	—	.10	.15	.25	.50
	1969	—	.10	.15	.25	.50
	1970	—	.10	.15	.25	.50
	1971	24.000	—	.10	.15	.30
	1971	—	—	—	Proof	2.25

50 CENTS

5.8319 gm., .800 SILVER, .1500 oz ASW

Y#	Date	Mintage	Fine	VF	XF	Unc
10	1892	.250	11.50	21.50	42.50	85.00
	1892	—	—	—	Proof	150.00
	1893	.750	8.50	16.50	32.50	65.00
	1893	—	—	—	Proof	150.00
	1895	.450	10.00	20.00	40.00	80.00
	1899	.100	11.50	22.50	45.00	90.00
	1900	.200	11.50	21.50	42.50	85.00

Y#	Date	Mintage	Fine	VF	XF	Unc
17	1902	.200	10.00	20.00	40.00	80.00
	1902	—	—	—	Proof	125.00
	1903	.800	6.50	12.50	25.00	50.00
	1903	—	—	—	Proof	125.00
	1910	.200	10.00	20.00	40.00	80.00

Y#	Date	Mintage	Fine	VF	XF	Unc
23	1913	.400	10.00	20.00	40.00	80.00
	1913	—	—	—	Proof	125.00
	1914	.200	12.50	25.00	50.00	100.00
	1914	—	—	—	Proof	125.00
	1917	1.073	BV	6.50	12.50	25.00
	1917	—	—	—	Proof	125.00

5.8319 gm., .550 SILVER, .1031 oz ASW

Y#	Date	Mintage	Fine	VF	XF	Unc
23a	1919B	.750	BV	5.00	10.00	20.00
	1919B	—	—	—	Proof	100.00
	1920B	.800	BV	5.00	10.00	20.00
	1920B	—	—	—	Proof	100.00
	1921B	.800	BV	5.00	10.00	20.00
	1921B	—	—	—	Proof	100.00
	1922	1.040	BV	5.00	10.00	20.00
	1922	—	—	—	Proof	100.00
	1924	1.010	BV	5.00	10.00	20.00
	1924	—	—	—	Proof	100.00
	1925	.500	BV	5.00	10.00	20.00
	1925	—	—	—	Proof	100.00
	1926	.500	BV	5.00	10.00	20.00
	1926	—	—	—	Proof	100.00
	1927	.500	BV	5.00	10.00	20.00
	1927	—	—	—	Proof	100.00

Y#	Date	Mintage	Fine	VF	XF	Unc
	1928	.500	BV	5.00	10.00	20.00
	1928	—	—	—	Proof	100.00
	1929	.500	BV	5.00	10.00	20.00
	1929	—	—	—	Proof	100.00

33	1942	.662	4.50	8.50	17.50	35.00

NICKEL BRASS

31	1943	8.600	.35	.75	1.50	3.00
	1943	6 known	—	—	Proof	—

Obv: EMPEROR OF INDIA dropped

38	1951	19.980	.20	.35	.75	1.50
	1951	—	—	—	Proof	20.00
	1951	—	—	Proof restrike		5.00

COPPER-NICKEL
Independent

48	1963	15.000	.10	.20	.35	.75
	1965	7.000	.10	.20	.35	.75
	1968	—	.10	.20	.35	.75
	1969	—	.10	.20	.35	.75
	1970	—	.10	.20	.35	.75
	1971	4.000	.10	.20	.35	.75
	1971	—	—	—	Proof	3.25
	1972	8.000	.10	.20	.35	.75

RUPEE

COPPER-NICKEL
2500 Years of Buddhism

40	1957	2.000	.35	.75	1.25	2.50
	1957	1,800	—	—	Proof	25.00

Independent

Y#	Date	Mintage	Fine	VF	XF	Unc
49	1963	20.000	.15	.25	.50	1.00
	1965	5.000	.15	.25	.50	1.00
	1969	2.500	.15	.25	.50	1.25
	1970	—	—	.25	.50	1.50
	1971	5.000	—	.25	.50	1.25
	1971	—	—	—	Proof	4.25
	1972	7.000	—	.25	.50	1.00

2 RUPEES

COPPER-NICKEL
Independent
F.A.O. Issue

50	1968	.500	.35	.75	1.50	3.00

5 RUPEES

28.2757 gm., .925 SILVER, .8409 oz ASW
2500 Years of Buddhism

41	1957	.500	BV	BV	25.00	32.50
	1957	1,800	—	—	Proof	275.00

NCLT ISSUES

PATTERNS

KM#	Date	Mintage	Identification	Mkt.Val.
1	1812	—	Rix Dollar, Silver, C35	2500.
2	1812	—	2 Rix Dollars, Silver	2500.
3	1815	—	Rix Dollar, Silver, C35	500.00

PROOF SETS
STANDARD METALS

KM#	Date	Mintage	Identification	Issue Price	Mkt. Val.
101	1951(6)	150*	Y26,34-38	—	30.00
			*Restrikes Exist.		
102	1957(2)	400	Y40,41	—	60.00
103	1957(4)	700	Double set of KM102	—	120.00
104	1971(7)	20,000	Y43-49	—	20.00

SRI LANKA

100 Cents = 1 Rupee

CENT

ALUMINUM

Y#	Date	Mintage	VF	XF	Unc
1	1975	34.000	—	.10	.20
	1975	1,431	—	Proof	2.00
	1978	1.000	—	—	.25
	1978	—	—	Proof	2.00

2 CENTS

ALUMINUM

2	1975	41.500	—	—	.25
	1975	1,431	—	Proof	3.00
	1978	1.000	—	—	.25
	1978	—	—	Proof	3.00

5 CENTS

NICKEL-BRASS

3	1975	19.584	—	.10	.25
	1975	1,431	—	Proof	3.00

ALUMINUM

3a	1978	30.000	—	—	.25
	1978	—	—	Proof	3.00

10 CENTS

NICKEL-BRASS

4	1975	10.800	—	.10	.25
	1975	1,431	—	Proof	3.00

ALUMINUM

4a	1978	30.000	—	—	.25
	1978	—	—	Proof	3.00

25 CENTS

COPPER-NICKEL

Y#	Date	Mintage	VF	XF	Unc
5	1975	36.000	—	.10	.25
	1975	1,431	—	Proof	3.00
	1978	1.000	—	—	.35
	1978	—	—	Proof	3.00

50 CENTS

COPPER-NICKEL

Y#	Date	Mintage	VF	XF	Unc
6	1972	11.000	.15	.30	.60
	1975	34.000	.15	.30	.60
	1975	1,431	—	Proof	3.00
	1978	1.000	—	—	.50
	1978	—	—	Proof	4.00

RUPEE

COPPER-NICKEL

Y#	Date	Mintage	VF	XF	Unc
7	1972	5.000	.25	.50	1.00
	1975	31.000	.25	.50	1.00
	1975	1,431	—	Proof	5.00
	1978	3.000	—	—	1.00
	1978	—	—	Proof	5.00

Inauguration of President

Y#	Date	Mintage	VF	XF	Unc
10	1978	2.000	—	.50	1.00
	1978	—	—	Proof	7.00

2 RUPEES

COPPER-NICKEL
Non-Aligned Nations Conference

Y#	Date	Mintage	VF	XF	Unc
8	1976	2.000	.55	.90	1.50
	1976	1,000	—	Proof	6.00

5 RUPEES

NICKEL
Non-Aligned Nations Conference

Y#	Date	Mintage	VF	XF	Unc
9	1976	1.000	1.00	2.00	3.50
	1976	1,000	—	Proof	10.00

NCLT ISSUES

PROOF SETS

KM#	Date	Mintage	Identification	Issue Price	Mkt. Val.
101	1978 (7)	20,000	Y1-2,3a-4a,5-7	26.00	30.00

Listings For
Straits Settlements refer to Malaysia

The Democratic Republic of the Sudan, located in northeast Africa on the Red Sea between the United Arab Republic and Ethiopia, has an area of 967,500 sq. mi. (2,505,813 sq. km.) and a population of 17.2 million. Capital: Khartoum. Agriculture and livestock raising are the chief occupations. Cotton, gum arabic and peanuts are exported.

The Sudan, site of the powerful Nubian kingdom of Roman times, was a collection of small independent states from the 14th century until 1820-22 when it was conquered and united by Mohammed Ali, Pasha of Egypt. Egyptian forces were driven from the area during the Mahdist revolt, 1881-98, but the Sudan was retaken by Anglo-Egyptian expeditions, 1896-98, and established as an Anglo-Egyptian condominium in 1899. Britain supplied the administrative apparatus and personnel, but the appearance of joint Anglo—Egyptian administration was continued until Jan. 9, 1954, when the first Sudanese self-government parliament was inaugurated. The Sudan achieved independence on Jan. 1, 1956 with the consent of the British and Egyptian government.

RULERS

Mohammed Ahmed (The Mahdi),
AH1298-1302 = 1881-1885AD
Abdullah Ibn Mohammed (The Khalifa)
AH1302-1316 = 1885-1898AD

MONETARY SYSTEM

40 Para = 1 Ghirsh = Piastre

MOHAMMED AHMED (The Mahdi)

(Khartoum Mint)

Translation of Arabic legends on Mahdi coinage:

بامر المهدی **by order of the Mahdi (in Tughra)**

ضرب **Struck**

فی **In (at)**

الهجرة **Hejira**

١٣٠٢ **1302**

سنة **Sanat(year)**

10 PIASTRES

SILVER

Y#	Date	Year	Mintage	Fine	VF	XF
1	AH1302	5	—	—	Rare	—

20 PIASTRES

SILVER

Y#	Date	Year	Mintage	Fine	VF	XF
2	AH1302	5	—	200.00	350.00	450.00

100 PIASTRES

GOLD

Y#	Date	Year	Mintage	Fine	VF	XF
3*	AH1255	2	—	275.00	350.00	600.00

*Coin struck by the Mahdi which is a copy of Egyptian coin under Turkish Sultan. This issue is more crude than the Egyptian type and has crude edge milling. Coin states "Struck in Cairo" however struck in the Sudan about 1302 A.H.

ABDULLAH IBN MOHAMMED

(the Khalifa)

OMDURMAN MINT

مقبول - **Accepted (money) i.e., legal (Tughra) - 'Maqbul'**

سنة ٥ - **Sanat (year) 5**

سنة ٤ - **Sanat (year) 4**

سنة ١١ - **Sanat 11 (year)**

ضرب - **Struck - 'Duriba'**

في - **At**

ام درمان - **Omdurman**

١٣٠٤ - **1304(A.H.)**

١٣٠٩ - **1309(A.H.)**

٢٠ - **20**

ش - قرش - **Guresh - Piastres**

عملة جديدة - **New coinage (in tughra) - 'Umla Jadida'**

جيد - **Good - 'Jayyid'**

عز نصره - **May his victory be glorified- 'Azza Nasruhu'**

ش ٢٠ - **20 Piastres**

NOTE: The coins of the Khalifa have been reordered in this edition by Yeoman #'s rather than by metallic composition. Except for the 10 Para (Y4), which is of copper (more or less pure), the remaining coins (Y6-32a) show the following progressive debasement: debasement:

AH Year Metallic Composition
- 1304 - Silver
- 1309 - Debased Silver
- 1310 - Debased Silver, Silver—Washed Copper, Billon
- 1311 - Billon, Silver-Washed Copper, Copper
- 1312 - Billon, Silver-Washed Copper, Copper
- 1315 - Copper, Sometimes Silver-Washed.

NOTE: The metal is not indicated beneath the photos, as usual, because each type occurs in a range of debasements. Different degrees of debasement do not constitute definable subtypes.

10 PARA

25mm

Y#	Date	Year	Mintage	VG	Fine	VF
4	AH1308	6	—	—	—	—

NOTE: Probably a pattern.

PIASTRE

(GHIRSH)

Plain borders, 18mm

Y#	Date	Year	Mintage	VG	Fine	VF
9	AH1304	1	—	60.00	100.00	150.00
	1311	9	—	40.00	65.00	100.00
	1311	11	—	40.00	65.00	100.00

2 PIASTRES

Plain borders, 18mm

Y#	Date	Year	Mintage	VG	Fine	VF
10	AH1310	8	—	65.00	100.00	150.00
	1311	9	—	65.00	100.00	150.00
	1311	11	—	65.00	100.00	150.00

Wreath borders, 17mm

Y#	Date	Year	Mintage	VG	Fine	VF
27	AH1311	11	—	30.00	35.00	40.00

Borders of crescents, stars and roses.

Y#	Date	Year	Mintage	VG	Fine	VF
15	AH1312	—	—	25.00	40.00	65.00

2-1/2 PIASTRES

"UMLA JADIDA" below Toughra, 18mm.
Border of crescents, stars, circles:

Y#	Date	Year	Mintage	VG	Fine	VF
16	AH1312	—	—	25.00	35.00	45.00

NOTE: Y#16 differs from Y#15 by the presence of the "shadda" which looks like the letter W, after the numeral "2" on the reverse.

"MAQBUL" below Toughra.
Border of crescents, stars, circles:

Y#	Date	Year	Mintage	VG	Fine	VF
16.1	AH1312	—	—	35.00	50.00	75.00

Border of crescents only

Y#	Date	Year	Mintage	VG	Fine	VF
22	AH1312	—	—	30.00	45.00	65.00

4 PIASTRES

Plain borders, 25mm

Y#	Date	Year	Mintage	VG	Fine	VF
11	AH1310	8	—	175.00	250.00	325.00

5 PIASTRES

Border of double crescents, 23-24mm

Y#	Date	Year	Mintage	VG	Fine	VF
6	AH1304	4	—	35.00	55.00	80.00
	1304	5	—	25.00	40.00	65.00
	1311	11	—	15.00	27.50	40.00

Plain borders, 21-22mm

Y#	Date	Year	Mintage	VG	Fine	VF
12	AH1310	8	—	45.00	75.00	125.00

Borders of crescents and stars.

Y#	Date	Year	Mintage	VG	Fine	VF
17	AH1311	—	—	22.50	35.00	50.00

Borders of crescents only

Y#	Date	Year	Mintage	VG	Fine	VF
23	AH1311	—	—	40.00	60.00	100.00

10 PIASTRES

Borders of double crescents,27mm

Y#	Date	Year	Mintage	VG	Fine	VF
7	AH1304	4	—	70.00	125.00	175.00
	1311	11	—	50.00	100.00	150.00

Plain borders

Y#	Date	Year	Mintage	VG	Fine	VF
13	AH1310	8	—	45.00	140.00	200.00

Wreath borders

Y#	Date	Year	Mintage	VG	Fine	VF
30	AH1310	8	—	65.00	110.00	150.00

20 PIASTRES

Borders of double crescents, 33-35mm

Y#	Date	Year	Mintage	VG	Fine	VF
8	AH1304	4	—	15.00	25.00	40.00
	1304	5 on obv., 1 on rev.				
			—	15.00	25.00	40.00
	1309	5 on obv., 1 on rev.				
			—	12.50	22.50	35.00

Borders of crescents, stars & roses

Y#	Date	Year	Mintage	VG	Fine	VF
19	AH1310	10	—	10.00	15.00	25.00
	1311	—	—	10.00	15.00	25.00
	1311	9	—	10.00	15.00	25.00
	1311	11	—	10.00	15.00	25.00
	1312	12	—	10.00	15.00	25.00
	1312	—	—	10.00	15.00	25.00

Borders of crescents only.
Rev: W/o 'AZZA NASRUHU'

Y#	Date	Year	Mintage	VG	Fine	VF
24	AH1311	11	—	15.00	25.00	40.00
	1312	12	—	15.00	25.00	40.00

Borders of crescents only.
Rev: W/ 'AZZA NASRUHU'

Y#	Date	Year	Mintage	VG	Fine	VF
25	AH1302	9	—	17.50	30.00	50.00
	1312	12	—	12.50	20.00	30.00

NOTE: The date 1302 on the year 9 is in error for 1312, and is not to be confused with the Mahdi crown, Y#2.

AH1315, R.Y. 8

AH1312, R.Y. 12
Rev: Wreath borders w/spears below.

Y#	Date	Year	Mintage	VG	Fine	VF
31	AH1310	8	—	11.50	17.50	27.50
	1311	11	—	15.00	25.00	40.00
	1312	12	—	8.00	12.50	20.00
	1315	8	—	7.00	11.50	18.50

NOTE: Many minor variants of this type exist.

Obv. & rev: Wreath with spears below.

Y#	Date	Year	Mintage	VG	Fine	VF
31.1	AH1310	8	—	25.00	35.00	50.00

AH1312, R.Y. 12
Wreath borders. Obv: Spears below.

Y#	Date	Year	Mintage	VG	Fine	VF
32	AH1312*	12	—	5.00	6.50	10.00
	1313	13	—	10.00	14.00	20.00
	1315	8	—	8.00	12.50	17.50
	1315	12	—	8.00	12.50	17.50

***NOTE:** A contemporary counterfeit by mint employee exists.

Wreath borders. No spears on either side.

Y#	Date	Year	Mintage	VG	Fine	VF
32.1	AH1310	8	—	10.00	15.00	25.00
	AH1315	12	—	10.00	15.00	25.00

REPUBLIC

10 Millim (Milliemes) - 1 Ghirsh (Piastre)

MILLIM

BRONZE

Y#	Date	Year	Mintage	VF	XF	Unc
34	AH1376	1956	5.000	—	.10	.20
	1379	1960	1.300	—	—	.20
	1387	1967	—	—	—	.15
	1387	1967	7,834	—	Proof	.50
	1388	1968	—	—	—	.15
	1388	1968	5,251	—	Proof	.75
	1389	1969	—	—	—	.15
	1389	1969	2,149	—	Proof	1.25

NOTE: Except for the proof sets, mintage figures have not generally been made available since 1967.Existence of circulation strikes of Y34-40 of years 1967, 68, 69 are uncertain.

Rev: New Arabic legends

Y#	Date	Year	Mintage	VF	XF	Unc
A43	AH1390	1970	1,646	—	Proof	2.50
	1391	1971	1,772	—	Proof	2.50

NOTE: Existence of circulation strikes of Y#A43-Y#H43 dated 1970 or 1971 is uncertain, despite unconfirmed reports of their existence.

2 MILLIM

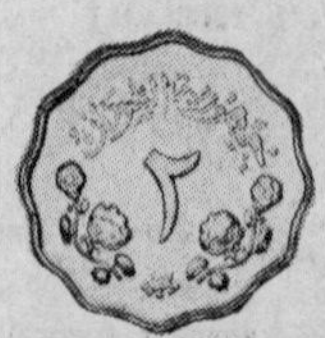

BRONZE

Y#	Date	Year	Mintage	VF	XF	Unc
35	AH1376	1956	5.000	—	.15	.35
	1387	1967	—	—	.10	.20
	1387	1967	7,834	—	Proof	.75
	1388	1968	—	—	.10	.20
	1388	1968	5,251	—	Proof	1.00
	1389	1969	—	—	.10	.20
	1389	1969	2,149	—	Proof	1.50

Y#	Date	Year	Mintage	VF	XF	Unc
B43	AH1390	1970	1,646	—	Proof	2.50
	1391	1971	1,772	—	Proof	2.50

5 MILLIM

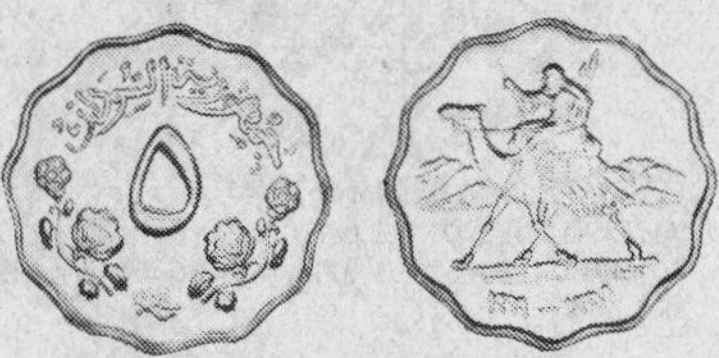

BRONZE

Y#	Date	Year	Mintage	VF	XF	Unc
36	AH1376	1956	30.000	.10	.25	.50
	1382	1962	6.000	.10	.20	.40
	1386	1966	4.000	—	.10	.25
	1387	1967	4.000	—	.10	.25
	1387	1967	7,834	—	Proof	1.00
	1388	1968	—	—	.10	.25
	1388	1968	5,251	—	Proof	1.25
	1389	1969	—	—	.10	.25
	1389	1969	2,149	—	Proof	1.75

Y#	Date	Year	Mintage	VF	XF	Unc
C43	AH1390	1970	—	.25	.50	1.00
	1390	1970	1,646	—	Proof	2.50
	1391	1971	3.000	.25	.50	1.00
	1391	1971	1,772	—	Proof	2.50

Anniversary of Revolution

Y#	Date	Year	Mintage	VF	XF	Unc
43	AH1391	1971	.500	—	.10	.30

F.A.O.Issue

Y#	Date	Year	Mintage	VF	XF	Unc
48	AH1392	1972	6.000	—	.10	.20
	1393	1973	9.000	—	.10	.25

BRASS

Y#	Date	Year	Mintage	VF	XF	Unc
50	AH1395	1975	1.132	—	.10	.25

F.A.O. Issue

Y#	Date	Year	Mintage	VF	XF	Unc
58	AH1396	1976	3.000	—	.10	.20

10 MILLIM

BRONZE

Y#	Date	Year	Mintage	VF	XF	Unc
37	AH1376	1956	15.00	.15	.30	.60
	1380	1960	12.250	—	.15	.30
	1381	1962 high date	—	—	.15	.30
	1381	1962 low date	—	—	.15	.30
	1386	1966	1.000	—	.15	.40
	1387	1967	1.000	—	.15	.30
	1387	1967	7,834	—	Proof	1.25
	1388	1968	—	—	.15	.30
	1388	1968	5,251	—	Proof	1.50
	1389	1969	—	—	.15	.30
	1389	1969	2,149	—	Proof	2.00

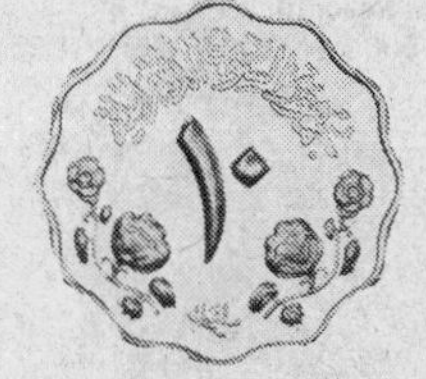

Y#	Date	Year	Mintage	VF	XF	Unc
D43	AH1390	1970	—	—	—	—
	1390	1970	1,646	—	Proof	2.50
	1391	1971	3.000	—	.35	1.00
	1391	1971	1,772	—	Proof	2.50

Anniversary of Revolution

Y#	Date	Year	Mintage	VF	XF	Unc
44	AH1391	1971	.500	—	.15	.35

Y#	Date	Year	Mintage	VF	XF	Unc
51	AH1392	1972	6.500	—	.15	.50

BRASS

Y#	Date	Year	Mintage	VF	XF	Unc
51a	AH1395	1975	8.200	—	.15	.35

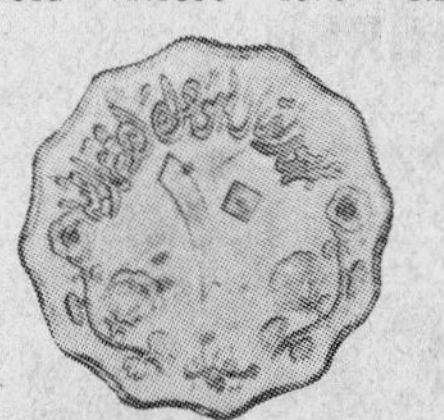

F.A.O. Issue

Y#	Date	Year	Mintage	VF	XF	Unc
59	AH1396	1976	3.000	—	.15	.25

20th Anniversary of Independence

Y#	Date	Year	Mintage	VF	XF	Unc
63	AH1396	1976	.350	—	.15	.35

2 GHIRSH

COPPER-NICKEL 17.5mm

Y#	Date	Year	Mintage	VF	XF	Unc
38	AH1376	1956	5.000	.15	.35	5.00

20mm

Y#	Date	Year	Mintage	VF	XF	Unc
38a	AH1382	1963	1.250	.15	.35	.75
	1387	1967	—	.15	.35	.75
	1387	1967	7,834	—	Proof	1.50
	1388	1968	—	.15	.35	.75
	1388	1968	5,251	—	Proof	1.75
	1389	1969	—	.15	.35	.75
	1389	1969	2,149	—	Proof	2.50

Y#	Date	Year	Mintage	VF	XF	Unc
E43	AH1390	1970	—	.30	.60	1.25
	1390	1970	1,646	—	Proof	2.50
	1391	1971	1,772	—	Proof	2.50

Anniversary of Revolution

Y#	Date	Year	Mintage	VF	XF	Unc
45	AH1391	1971	.500	.10	.20	.40

Y#	Date	Year	Mintage	VF	XF	Unc
52	AH1395	1975	—	.10	.20	.40

F.A.O. Issue

Y#	Date	Year	Mintage	VF	XF	Unc
60	AH1396	1976	.500	.10	.20	.40

20th Anniversary of Independence

Y#	Date	Year	Mintage	VF	XF	Unc
64	AH1396	1976	—	.10	.20	.40

5 GHIRSH

COPPER-NICKEL

Y#	Date	Year	Mintage	VF	XF	Unc
39	AH1376	1956	40.000	.20	.30	.75
	1387	1967	—	.20	.30	.60

Y#	Date	Year	Mintage	VF	XF	Unc
39	1387	1967	7,834	—	Proof	2.00
	1388	1968	—	.20	.30	.60
	1388	1968	5,251	—	Proof	2.25
	1389	1969	—	.20	.30	.60
	1389	1969	2,149	—	Proof	3.00

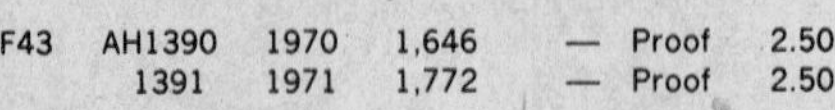

Y#	Date	Year	Mintage	VF	XF	Unc
F43	AH1390	1970	1,646	—	Proof	2.50
	1391	1971	1,772	—	Proof	2.50

Anniversary of Revolution

Y#	Date	Year	Mintage	VF	XF	Unc
46	AH1391	1971	.500	.20	.30	.60

Y#	Date	Year	Mintage	VF	XF	Unc
53	AH1395	1975	—	.20	.30	.60

F.A.O. Issue

Y#	Date	Year	Mintage	VF	XF	Unc
61	AH1396	1976	.500	—	.25	.50

20th Anniversary of Independence

Y#	Date	Year	Mintage	VF	XF	Unc
65	AH1396	1976	—	—	.50	1.00

10 GHIRSH

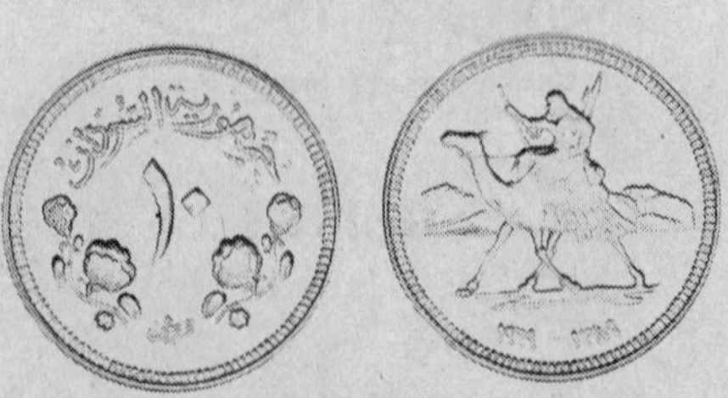

COPPER-NICKEL

Y#	Date	Year	Mintage	VF	XF	Unc
40	AH1376	1956	15.000	.35	.75	1.25
	1387	1967	—	.30	.60	1.00
	1387	1967	7,834	—	Proof	2.50
	1388	1968	—	.30	.60	1.00
	1388	1968	5,251	—	Proof	3.25
	1389	1969	—	.30	.60	1.00
	1389	1969	2,149	—	Proof	4.00

Y#	Date	Year	Mintage	VF	XF	Unc
G43	AH1390	1970	—	.60	1.25	2.00
	1390	1970	1,646	—	Proof	3.50
	1391	1970	.385	.60	1.25	2.00
	1391	1971	1,772	—	Proof	3.50

Anniversary of Revolution

Y#	Date	Year	Mintage	VF	XF	Unc
47	AH1391	1971	.500	.35	.75	1.25

Y#	Date	Year	Mintage	VF	XF	Unc
54	AH1395	1975	—	.35	.75	1.25

F.A.O. Issue

Y#	Date	Year	Mintage	VF	XF	Unc
62	AH1396	1976	.500	.25	.50	1.00

20th Anniversary of Independence

Y#	Date	Year	Mintage	VF	XF	Unc
66	AH1396	1976	—	.25	.50	1.00

20 GHIRSH

COPPER-NICKEL

Y#	Date	Year	Mintage	VF	XF	Unc
41	AH1387	1967	7,834	Proof only		4.00
	1388	1968	5,251	Proof only		4.75
	1389	1969	2,149	Proof only		18.50

Rev: Similar to Y#41.

Y#	Date	Year	Mintage	VF	XF	Unc
H43	AH1390	1970	1,646	Proof only		20.00
	1391	1971	1,772	Proof only		20.00

25 GHIRSH

COPPER-NICKEL
F.A.O. Issue

Y#	Date	Year	Mintage	VF	XF	Unc
42	AH1388	1968	.024	Proof only		10.00

50 GHIRSH

COPPER-NICKEL
F.A.O. Issue

Y#	Date	Year	Mintage	VF	XF	Unc
49	AH1392	1972	1.000	1.75	2.50	4.00

NOTE: An additional 30,000 specimens, dated 1976, are reported to have been struck.

Establishment of Arab Cooperative

Y#	Date	Year	Mintage	VF	XF	Unc
67	AH1396	1976	—	—	2.00	3.50

8th Anniversary of 1969 Revolt
F.A.O. Issue

Y#	Date	Year	Mintage	VF	XF	Unc
68	AH1397	1977	.100	—	2.00	3.50

POUND

Rural Women and F.A.O. Issue

Y#	Date	Year	Mintage	VF	XF	Unc
69	AH1398	1978	.010	—	2.00	3.50

2-1/2 POUNDS

28.9000 gm., .925 SILVER, .8596 oz ASW
Conservation Series

Y#	Date	Year	Mintage	VF	XF	Unc
55	AH1396	1976	—	BV	BV	26.00
	1396	1976	—	—	Proof	26.00

5 POUNDS

35.0000 gm., .925 SILVER, 1.0410 oz ASW
Conservation Series
Obv: Similar to 2-1/2 Pounds, Y#55.

Y#	Date	Year	Mintage	VF	XF	Unc
56	AH1396	1976	—	BV	BV	32.00
	1396	1976	—	—	Proof	50.00

17.5000 gm., .925 SILVER, .5205 oz ASW
Khartoum Meeting of O.A.U.

Y#	Date	Year	Mintage	VF	XF	Unc
70	AH1398	1978	.030	—	—	15.00
	1398	1978	.015	—	Proof	20.00
	New Islamic Century					
74	AH1400	1979	—	—	—	—
	1400	1979	—	—	Proof	—

10 POUNDS

35.0000 gm., .925 SILVER, 1.0410 oz ASW
Khartoum Meeting of O.A.U.

Y#	Date	Year	Mintage	VF	XF	Unc
71	AH1398	1978	.030	BV	BV	32.00
	1398	1978	.015	—	Proof	35.00
	New Islamic Century					
75	AH1488	1979	—	—	—	—
	1400	1979	—	—	Proof	—

25 POUNDS

8.2500 gm., .917 GOLD, .2432 oz AGW
Khartoum Meeting of O.A.U.

Y#	Date	Year	Mintage	VF	XF	Unc
72	AH1398	1978	.030	—	—	158.00
	1398	1978	.015	—	Proof	165.00
	New Islamic Century					
76	AH1400	1979	—	—	—	—
	1400	1979	—	—	Proof	—

50 POUNDS

17.5000 gm., .917 GOLD, .5160 oz AGW
Khartoum Meeting of O.A.U.

Y#	Date	Year	Mintage	VF	XF	Unc
73	AH1398	1978	.030	—	—	335.00
	1398	1978	.015	—	Proof	340.00
	New Islamic Century					
77	AH1400	1979	—	—	—	—
	1400	1979	—	—	Proof	—

100 POUNDS

.900 GOLD
Conservation Series

Y#	Date	Year	Mintage	VF	XF	Unc
57	AH1396	1976	BV	BV	BV	650.00
	1396	1976	—	—	Proof	800.00

NCLT ISSUES

PROOF SETS
STANDARD METALS

KM#	Date	Mintage	Identification	Issue Price	Mkt. Val.
101	1967(8)	7,834	Y34-37,38a-41	15.25	13.50
102	1968(8)	5,251	Y34-37,38a-41	15.25	16.50
103	1969(8)	2,149	Y34-37,38a-41	15.25	34.50
104	1970(8)	1,646	YA43-H43	15.25	38.50
105	1971(8)	1,772	YA43-H43	15.25	38.50

1970 and 1971 coins in sets are all same design as 10 Ghirsh, Y G43.

DARFUR

The province of Darfur makes up most of the western border of the Republic of Sudan. Darfur had been an independent kingdom until taken over by Egypt in 1874. While the British were involved in subduing the eastern Sudan, Ali Dinar established the sultanate of Darfur. His coins copied the type of 20 para of Mohammed ii of Egypt. The mint was located at Al Fasher (the capitol of the province) and was active from 1908 to 1914 with most of the coins bearing a 1327 (1909AD) DATE.

PIASTRE

BILLON, 25mm

AL-FASHER MINT

KM#	Date	Mintage	VG	Fine	VF
1	AH1327	—	40.00	60.00	80.00

NOTE: Very crudely struck.

The Republic of Surinam also known as Dutch Guiana, located on the north central coast of South America between Guyana and French Guiana has an area of 63,251 sq. mi. 181,455 sq. km. and a population of 385,000. Capital: Paramaribo. The country is rich in minerals and forests, and self-sufficient in rice, the staple food crop. The mining, processing and exporting of bauxite is the principal economic activity.

Lieutenants of Amerigo Vespucci sighted the Guiana Coast in 1499. Spanish explorers of the 16th century, disappointed at finding no gold, departed leaving the area to be settled by the British in 1652. The colony prospered and the Netherlands acquired it in 1667 in exchange for the Dutch rights in Nieuw Nederland (state of New York). During the European wars of the 18th and 19th centuries, which were fought in part in the New World, Surinam was occupied by the British from 1799-1814. Surinam became an autonomous part of the Kingdom of the Netherlands on Dec. 29, 1954. Full independence was achieved on Nov. 25, 1975.

World War II Coinage

The 1942-43 issues following are homeland coinage types of the Netherlands - Y#36, Y#43 and Y#44 - were executed expressly for use in Surinam. Related issues produced for use in both Curacao and Surinam are listed under Curacao. They are distinguished by the presence of a palm tree (acorn on Homeland issues) and a mintmark (P-Philadelphia, D-Denver, S-San Francisco) flanking the date. Also see the Netherlands for similar issues.

RULERS

Dutch, until 1975

MONETARY SYSTEM

100 Cents = 1 Gulden

MINTMARKS

P - Philadelphia, U.S.A.
(u) - Utrecht (privy marks only)

CENT

BRASS

Y#	Date	Mintage	Fine	VF	XF	Unc
36a	1943P palm					
		4.000	2.25	6.00	12.00	24.00

BRONZE

Y#	Date	Mintage	Fine	VF	XF	Unc
36b	1957(u)	1.200	1.75	3.00	5.00	7.50
	1959(u)	1.800	1.75	3.00	5.00	7.50
	1960(u)	1.200	1.75	3.00	5.00	7.50

NOTE: For similar coins dated 1942P see Curacao.

Y#	Date	Mintage	Fine	VF	XF	Unc
2	1962(u)	6.000	.25	.35	.50	.75
	1962(u)S650 pcs.		—	—	Proof	15.00
	1966(u)	9.500	—	.25	.35	.50
	1966(u)	—	—	—	Proof	70.00
	1970(u)	5.000	—	.25	.35	.50
	1972(u)	6.000	—	.25	.35	.50
	ALUMINUM					
2a	1974(u)	1.000	—	.10	.25	.35
2a	1975(u)	1.000	—	.10	.25	.35
	1976(u)	3.000	—	.10	.25	.35
	1977(u)	10.000	—	.10	.25	.35
	1978(u)	6.000	—	.10	.25	.35
	1979 (u)	8.000	—	.10	.25	.35

5 CENT

For a 5 cent coin dated 1943 see Curacao.

NICKEL-BRASS

Y#	Date	Mintage	Fine	VF	XF	Unc
3	1962(u)	2.200	.25	.50	.75	1.25
	1962(u)S650 pcs.		—	—	Proof	17.50
	1966(u) w/privy marks					
		1.800	.25	.50	.75	1.25
	1966(u)	—	—	—	Proof	75.00
	1966 w/o privy marks					
		.400	3.75	6.25	8.75	12.50
	1971(u)	.500	—	.35	.65	1.00
	1972(u)	1.500	—	.35	.65	1.00
	Medal struck					
3e	1966(u)	—	20.00	30.00	35.00	40.00
	ALUMINUM					
3a	1976(u)	5.500	—	.25	.50	.75
	1978(u)	3.000	—	.25	.50	.75
	1979 (u)	2.000	—	—	.25	.50

10 CENT

1.4000 gm., .640 SILVER, .0288 oz ASW

Y#	Date	Mintage	Fine	VF	XF	Unc
43a	1942P palm					
		1.500	8.50	15.00	25.00	35.00

For similar coins dated 1941P and 1943P see Curacao.

COPPER-NICKEL

Y#	Date	Mintage	Fine	VF	XF	Unc
4	1962(u)	3.000	.40	.65	1.10	1.50
	1962(u)S650 pcs.		—	—	Proof	20.00
	1966(u)	2.500	—	.50	.75	1.00
	1966(u)	—	—	—	Proof	80.00
	1971(u)	.500	—	.25	.50	.75
	1972(u)	1.500	—	.25	.50	.75
	1974(u)	1.500	—	.25	.50	.75
	1976(u)	5.000	—	.25	.50	.75
	1978(u)	2.000	—	.25	.50	.75
	1979 (u)	2.000	—	—	.25	.50

25 CENT

COPPER-NICKEL

Y#	Date	Mintage	Fine	VF	XF	Unc
5	1962(u)	2.300	.75	1.25	1.75	2.50
	1962(u)S650 pcs.		—	—	Proof	22.50
	1966(u)	2.300	—	1.00	1.50	2.00
	1966(u)	—	—	—	Proof	90.00
	1972(u)	1.800	—	.65	.90	1.25
	1974(u)	1.500	—	.65	.90	1.25
	1976(u)	5.000	—	.65	.90	1.25
	1979 (u)	2.000	—	—	.50	.75

GULDEN

10.0000 gm., .720 SILVER, .2315 oz ASW

Y#	Date	Mintage	Fine	VF	XF	Unc
6	1962(u)	.150	BV	10.00	15.00	20.00
	1962(u)S650 pcs.		—	—	Proof	35.00
	1966(u)	*.100	50.00	150.00	200.00	250.00
	1966(u)	—	—	—	Proof	125.00

*Never officially released to circulation.

10 GULDEN

16.0000 gm., .925 SILVER, .4759 oz ASW
1st Anniversary of Independence

Y#	Date	Mintage	Fine	VF	XF	Unc
7	1976(u)	.100	BV	BV	BV	14.50
	1976(u)F	5,711	—	—	Proof	27.50

25 GULDEN

26.0000 gm., .925 SILVER, .7733 oz ASW
1st Anniversary of Independence

Y#	Date	Mintage	Fine	VF	XF	Unc
8	1976(u)	.075	BV	BV	27.50	35.00
	1976(u)F	5,503	—	—	Proof	50.00

100 GULDEN

6.7200 gm., .900 GOLD, .1945 oz ASW
1st Anniversary of Independence

Y#	Date	Mintage	Fine	VF	XF	Unc
9	1976(u)	.020	BV	BV	BV	126.50
	1976(u)F	4,749	—	—	Proof	150.00

NOTE: 900 pieces have been reported struck in 'rose' gold.

NCLT ISSUES

PROOF SETS

STANDARD METALS

KM#	Date	Mintage	Identification	Issue Price	Mkt. Val.
101	1962(5)	650	Y2-6	—	110.00
102	1966(5)	—	Y2-6	—	530.00
103	1976(3)	—	Y7-9	145.00	225.00
104	1976(2)	—	Y7-8	50.00	75.00

SWAZILAND

The Kingdom of Swaziland, located in south-eastern Africa, has an area of 6,705 sq. mi. (17,365 sq. km.) and a population of 494,000. Capital: Mbabane (administrative); Lobamba (legislative). The diversified economy includes mining, agriculture, and light industry. Asbestos, iron ore, wood pulp, and sugar are exported.

The people of the present Swazi nation established themselves in an area including what is now Swaziland in the early 1800s. The first Swazi contact with the British came early in the reign of the extremely able Swazi leader Mswati when he asked the British for aid against Zulu raids into Swaziland. The British and Transvaal responded by guaranteeing the independence of Swaziland, 1881. South Africa assumed the power of protection and adminstration in 1894 and Swaziland continued under this administration until the conquest of the Transvaal during the Anglo-Boer War, when administration was transferred to the British government. After World War II, Britain began to prepare Swaziland for independence, which was achieved on Sept. 6, 1968. The Kingdom is a member of the Commonwealth of Nations. The king of Swaziland is Chief of State. The prime minister is Head of Government.

RULERS

Sobhuza II, 1968-

MONETARY SYSTEM

100 Cents = 1 Luhlanga
25 Luhlanga = 1 Lilangeni
(Plural - Emalangeni)

CENT

BRONZE

Y#	Date	Mintage	VF	XF	Unc
1	1974	6.002	—	—	.15
	1974	.013	—	Proof	1.00
	1979	—	—	—	.15
	1979	.010	—	Proof	1.00

F.A.O. Issue

Y#	Date	Mintage	VF	XF	Unc
13	1975	2.500	—	—	.15

2 CENTS

BRONZE

Y#	Date	Mintage	VF	XF	Unc
2	1974	2.252	—	—	.20
	1974	.013	—	Proof	1.00
	1979	—	—	.10	.20
	1979	.010	—	Proof	1.50

F.A.O. Issue

Y#	Date	Mintage	VF	XF	Unc
14	1975	1.500	—	.10	.20

5 CENTS

2.5000 gm., .800 SILVER, .0643 oz ASW

KM#	Date	Mintage	XF	Unc	Proof
1	1968	.010	—	—	6.50

COPPER-NICKEL

Y#	Date	Mintage	VF	XF	Unc
3	1974	1.252	—	.15	.30
	1974	.013	—	Proof	2.00
	1975	1.500	—	.15	.30
	1979	—	—	.15	.30
	1979	.010	—	Proof	3.00

10 CENTS

4.0000 gm., .800 SILVER, .1209 oz ASW

KM#	Date	Mintage	XF	Unc	Proof
2	1968	.010	—	—	7.50

COPPER-NICKEL

Y#	Date	Mintage	VF	XF	Unc
4	1974	.752	.25	.35	.50
	1974	.013	—	Proof	2.00
	1979	—	—	.20	.50
	1979	—	—	Proof	4.00

F.A.O. Issue

Y#	Date	Mintage	VF	XF	Unc
15	1975	1.500	.25	.35	.75

20 CENTS

6.0000 gm., .800 SILVER, .1543 oz ASW

KM#	Date	Mintage	XF	Unc	Proof
3	1968	.010	—	—	8.50

COPPER-NICKEL

Y#	Date	Mintage	VF	XF	Unc
5	1974	.502	.50	.75	1.00
	1974	.013	—	Proof	3.00
	1975	1.000	.50	.75	1.00
	1979	—	—	.50	1.00
	1979	.010	—	Proof	6.00

50 CENTS

9.5000 gm., .800 SILVER, .2444 oz ASW

KM#	Date	Mintage	XF	Unc	Proof
4	1968	.010	—	—	10.00

COPPER-NICKEL

Y#	Date	Mintage	VF	XF	Unc
6	1974	.252	1.00	1.75	2.50
	1974	.013	—	Proof	4.50
	1975	.500	1.00	1.75	2.50
	1979	—	—	1.00	2.50
	1979	.010	—	Proof	9.00

LUHLANGA

15.0000 gm., .800 SILVER .3858 oz ASW

KM#	Date	Mintage	XF	Unc	Proof
5	1968	.010	—	—	15.00

LILANGENI

28.3500 gm., .917 GOLD, 8359 oz AGW

KM#	Date	Mintage	XF	Unc	Proof
6	1968	*2,000	—	—	550.00

***NOTE:** Approximately 1,450 melted.

COPPER-NICKEL

Y#	Date	Mintage	VF	XF	Unc
7	1974	.127	2.00	3.00	4.50
	1974	.013	—	Proof	6.50
	1979	—	—	2.00	4.50
	1979	.010	—	Proof	12.00

F.A.O. Issue And International Women's Year

16	1975	.100	2.00	3.00	5.00

F.A.O. Issue

17	1976	.100	2.00	3.50	5.00

5 EMALANGENI

10.3000 gm., .925 SILVER, .3063 oz ASW
H. M. 75th Anniversary

KM#	Date	Mintage	XF	Unc	Proof
7	1974	—	—	—	20.00

5.5600 gm., .900 GOLD, .1609 oz AGW
H. M. 75th Anniversary

Y#	Date	Mintage	XF	Unc	Proof
8	1974	.060	—	—	110.00

7-1/2 EMALANGENI

16.2000 gm., .925 SILVER, .4818 oz ASW

KM#	Date	Mintage	XF	Unc	Proof
8	1974	—	—	—	30.00

10 EMALANGENI

11.1200 gm., .900 GOLD, .3218 oz AGW
H. M. 75th Anniversary

Y#	Date	Mintage	XF	Unc	Proof
9	1974	.040	—	—	225.00

25.5000 gm., .925 SILVER, .7584 oz ASW
H. M. 75th Birthday
Obv: Similar to 25 Emalangeni, Y#11.

KM#	Date	Mintage	XF	Unc	Proof
10	1975	—	—	28.00	—
	1975	—	—	—	35.00

15 EMALANGENI

32.6000 gm., .925 SILVER, .9696 oz ASW
H.M. 75th Anniversary and Independence
Obv: Similar to 25 Emalangeni, Y#11.

9	1974	—	—	—	50.00

NOTE: Stamped serial number of issue on reverse.

20 EMALANGENI

22.2300 gm., .900 GOLD, .6433 oz AGW
H. M. 75th Anniversary and UNICEF
Obv: Similar to 7-1/2 Emalengeni, KM#8.

Y#	Date	Mintage	XF	Unc	Proof
10	1974	.025	—	—	450.00

25 EMALANGENI

27.7800 gm., .900 GOLD, .8039 oz AGW
H. M. 75th Anniversary

11	1974	.015	—	—	550.00

50 EMALANGENI

4.3100 gm., .900 GOLD, .1247 oz AGW
H. M. 75th Birthday

11	1975	.025	BV	100.00	
	1975	Inc.Ab.			125.00

100 EMALANGENI

8.6400 gm., .900 GOLD, .2500 oz AGW
H. M. 75th Birthday

KM#	Date	Mintage	XF	Unc	Proof
12	1975	.025	—	200.00	—
	1975	Inc. Ab.	—	—	240.00

NCLT ISSUES

MINT SETS

KM#	Date	Mintage	Identification	Issue Price	Mkt. Val.
S1	1974(7)	—	Y1-7	10.00	10.00
	1975 3	—	Km10-12	—	328.00

PROOF SETS

STANDARD METALS

101	1968(5)	10,000	KM1-5	25.80	47.50
102	1974(7)	20,000	Y1-7	18.00	20.00
103	1974(3)	—	KM7-9	70.00	100.00
104	1974(4)	—	Y8-11	745.00	1335.
105	1975(2)	25,000	KM11-12	252.00	365.00
	1975 3	—	Km10-12	—	400.00
106	1979(7)	10,000	Y1-7	34.00	36.50

SWEDEN

The Kingdom of Sweden, a limited constitutional monarchy located in northern Europe between Norway and Finland, has an area of 173,000 sq. mi. (448,068 sq. km.) and a population of 8.2 million. Capital: Stockholm. Mining, lumbering and a specialized machine industry dominate the economy. Machinery, paper, iron and steel, motor vehicles and wood pulp are exported.

Sweden was founded as a Christian stronghold by Olaf Skottkonung late in the 10th century. After conquering Finland late in the 13th century, Sweden, together with Norway, came under the rule of Denmark, 1397-1523, in an association known as the Union of Kalmar. Modern Sweden had its beginning in 1523 when Gustavus Vasa drove the Danes out of Sweden and was himself chosen king. Under Gustavus Adolphus II and Charles XII, Sweden was one of the great powers of 17th century Europe - until Charles invaded Russia, 1708, and was defeated at the Battle of Pultowa in June, 1709. Early in the 18th century, a coalition of Russia, Poland and Denmark took away Sweden's Baltic empire and in 1809 Sweden was forced to cede Finland to Russia. Norway was ceded to Sweden by the Treaty of Kiel in January, 1814. The Norwegians resisted for a time but later signed the Act of Union at the Convention of Moss in August, 1814. The Union was dissolved in 1905 and Norway became independent. A new constitution which took effect on Jan. 1, 1975, restricts the function of the king to a ceremonial role.

RULERS

Gustaf III, 1771-1792
Gustaf IV Adolph, 1792-1809
Carl XIII, 1809-1818
Carl XIV Johan, 1818-1844
Oscar I, 1844-1859
Carl XV, 1859-1872
Oscar II, 1872-1907
Gustaf V, 1907-1950
Gustaf VI, 1950-1973
Carl XVI Gustaf, 1973 -

MONETARY SYSTEM

(1704-1798)

8 Ore = 1 Mark
32 Ore = 1 Daler
96 Ore S(ilver) M(oney) = 1 Riksdaler
= 3 Daler S(ilver) M(oney)
= 9 Daler K(opper) M(oney)

(1798-1830)

48 Skilling = 1 Riksdaler Species
2 Riksdaler (Speciesdaler) = 1 Ducat

(1830-1855)

32 Skilling Banco = 1 Riksdaler Riksgalds
12 Riksdaler Riksgalds = 3 Riksdaler Species

(1855-1873)

100 Ore = 4 Riksdaler Riksmynt
4 Riksdaler Riksmynt = 1 Riksdaler Species

(Commencing 1873)

100 Ore = 1 Riksdaler Riksmynt = 1 Krona

MINTMASTER'S INITIALS

AG,G - Alexander Grandinson
Cb - Christopher Borg
EB - Emil Brusewitz
G - Alf Grabe
LB - Lars Bergencreutz
OL - Olof Lidiin
ST,T - Sebastian Tham
TS - Torsten Swensson
U - Benkt Ulvfot
W - Karl-August Wallroth

OR - K.M.

COPPER, 24mm

C#	Date	Mintage	VG	Fine	VF	XF
51	1772	.662	5.00	10.00	20.00	60.00
	1778	.576	6.00	12.00	25.00	70.00
	27-34mm thick planchet					
	1772	—	300.00	600.00	1200.	2000.

OR - S.M.

COPPER
Obv: Crowned G III monogram. Rev: Crossed arrows dividing value, crown above, date below.

C#	Date	Mintage	VG	Fine	VF	XF
53	1778	.192	25.00	70.00	125.00	250.00

Space between the top crown and monogram G.

C#	Date	Mintage	VG	Fine	VF	XF
53.1	1778	Inc. Ab.	25.00	70.00	125.00	250.00

2 OR S.M.

COPPER
Obv: Similar to 1 OR S.M., C#53 but G III S.G-V.R. Rev: Similar to 1 OR S.M., C#53.

C#	Date	Mintage	VG	Fine	VF	XF
55	1777 small date					
		1.031	20.00	50.00	100.00	300.00
	1777 large date					
		Inc. Ab.	20.00	50.00	100.00	300.00

1/24 RIKSDALER

SILVER
Obv: Same as C#61a. Rev: Similar to C#61a but with 4 O - S.M. divided by crowned arms.

C#	Date	Mintage	VG	Fine	VF	XF
61	1777	1.217	5.00	15.00	35.00	90.00

C#	Date	Mintage	VG	Fine	VF	XF
61a	1778	1.354	3.00	10.00	25.00	60.00
	1779	1.456	3.00	10.00	25.00	60.00
	1780/79	.549	4.00	12.00	30.00	70.00
	1780	Inc. Ab.	4.00	12.00	30.00	70.00
	1783/80	.268	5.00	15.00	35.00	90.00
	1783	Inc. Ab.	5.00	15.00	35.00	90.00

1/12 RIKSDALER

SILVER
8 O - S.M. divided by crowned arms.

C#	Date	Mintage	VG	Fine	VF	XF
62	1777	.896	10.00	30.00	60.00	100.00

C#	Date	Mintage	VG	Fine	VF	XF
62a	1778	.718	7.00	20.00	40.00	75.00
	1779	.889	7.00	20.00	40.00	75.00

16 ORE

SILVER

C#	Date	Mintage	VG	Fine	VF	XF
64	1773 7 seraphs					
		.201	12.00	40.00	80.00	250.00
	1773 9 seraphs					
		Inc. Ab.	10.00	30.00	70.00	200.00
	1774	.152	10.00	30.00	70.00	200.00

1/6 RIKSDALER

SILVER
Obv: Same as C#66a. Rev: Similar to C#66a but with 16 OR - S.M. divided by crowned arms.

C#	Date	Mintage	VG	Fine	VF	XF
66	1776	.068	20.00	50.00	100.00	200.00
	1777	.834	10.00	25.00	50.00	100.00

C#	Date	Mintage	VG	Fine	VF	XF
66a	1778	.978	7.00	20.00	40.00	80.00
	1779	1.027	7.00	20.00	40.00	80.00
	1781/79	.179	20.00	40.00	80.00	175.00

C#	Date	Mintage	VG	Fine	VF	XF
66a	1781	Inc. Ab.	20.00	40.00	80.00	175.00
	1783	.414	7.00	20.00	40.00	80.00
	1784	.388	7.00	20.00	40.00	80.00
	1785	.252	10.00	25.00	50.00	100.00
	1786	.791	7.00	20.00	40.00	80.00
	1787	.026	30.00	80.00	175.00	350.00
	1788	.742	7.00	20.00	40.00	80.00
	1789	.209	10.00	25.00	50.00	100.00
	1790	.399	7.00	20.00	40.00	80.00

1/3 RIKSDALER

SILVER
Obv: Same as C#67a. Rev: Similar to C#67a but with 1 D - S.M. divided by crowned arms.

C#	Date	Mintage	VG	Fine	VF	XF
67	1776	.097	15.00	40.00	80.00	175.00
	1777	.665	12.00	30.00	70.00	150.00

C#	Date	Mintage	VG	Fine	VF	XF
67a	1778	.610	10.00	25.00	50.00	100.00
	1779	.228	10.00	25.00	50.00	100.00
	1780/79	.282	10.00	25.00	50.00	100.00
	1780	Inc. Ab.	10.00	25.00	50.00	100.00
	1781	.017	50.00	125.00	275.00	500.00
	1782	.116	12.00	30.00	70.00	150.00
	1783/2	.707	10.00	25.00	50.00	100.00
	1783	Inc. Ab.	10.00	25.00	50.00	100.00
	1784	.514	10.00	25.00	50.00	100.00
	1785	.197	10.00	25.00	50.00	100.00
	1786	.051	20.00	50.00	100.00	200.00
	1787	.461	10.00	25.00	50.00	100.00
	1788	.071	12.00	30.00	70.00	150.00
	1789	.641	10.00	25.00	50.00	100.00

2/3 RIKSDALER

SILVER
Obv: Similar to 1/3 Riksdaler, C#67a.
Rev: Similar to 1/3 Riksdaler, C#67a, but with 2 D - S.M. divided by crowned arms.

C#	Date	Mintage	VG	Fine	VF	XF
68	1776	.152	30.00	70.00	140.00	275.00
	1777	.088	35.00	80.00	150.00	300.00

Obv: Same as C#68. Rev: Similar to C#68 but without 2 D - S.M.

C#	Date	Mintage	VG	Fine	VF	XF
68a	1778	.043	40.00	100.00	200.00	400.00
	1779	.152	30.00	75.00	150.00	300.00
	1780/79	.011	50.00	125.00	250.00	500.00
	1780	Inc. Ab.	50.00	125.00	250.00	500.00

1 RIKSDALER

SILVER
Obv: Same as C#69a. Rev: 3 D - S.M. divided by crowned arms.

C#	Date	Mintage	VG	Fine	VF	XF
69	1771	—	150.00	350.00	700.00	1200.
	1772	.051	125.00	300.00	600.00	1000.
	1773	.038	125.00	300.00	600.00	1000.
	1774	.709	100.00	225.00	400.00	800.00
	1775	—	100.00	250.00	500.00	900.00

C#	Date	Mintage	VG	Fine	VF	XF
69a	1775	.035	45.00	100.00	220.00	350.00
	1776/5	1.461	40.00	90.00	175.00	300.00
	1776	Inc. Ab.	40.00	90.00	175.00	300.00
	1777	.289	50.00	110.00	220.00	350.00

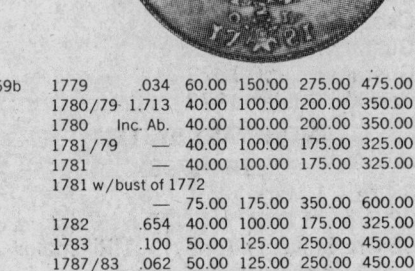

C#	Date	Mintage	VG	Fine	VF	XF
69b	1779	.034	60.00	150.00	275.00	475.00
	1780/79	1.713	40.00	100.00	200.00	350.00
	1780	Inc. Ab.	40.00	100.00	200.00	350.00
	1781/79	—	40.00	100.00	175.00	325.00
	1781	—	40.00	100.00	175.00	325.00
	1781 w/bust of 1772					
		—	75.00	175.00	350.00	600.00
	1782	.654	40.00	100.00	175.00	325.00
	1783	.100	50.00	125.00	250.00	450.00
	1787/83	.062	50.00	125.00	250.00	450.00
	1787	Inc. Ab.	50.00	125.00	250.00	450.00
	1788	.151	40.00	100.00	200.00	350.00
	1790	.636	40.00	110.00	220.00	350.00
	1791	.921	40.00	110.00	220.00	350.00
	1792	—	50.00	120.00	240.00	400.00

MONETARY REFORM

1/12 SKILLING

COPPER

C#	Date	Mintage	VG	Fine	VF	XF
78	1802	2.039	.50	1.00	2.00	6.00
	1803	1.008	.75	1.50	3.00	9.00
	1805	2.526	.50	1.00	2.00	6.00
	1808	3.476	.50	1.00	2.00	6.00

C#	Date	Mintage	VG	Fine	VF	XF
100	1812	2.880	.50	1.00	4.00	8.00

C#	Date	Mintage	VG	Fine	VF	XF
120	1825 with reeded edge					
		.576	2.00	4.00	10.00	20.00
	1825 with plain edge					
		—	2.50	7.50	15.00	30.00

1/6 SKILLING

COPPER

C#	Date	Mintage	VG	Fine	VF	XF
121	1830 reeded edge					
		2.544	.50	1.25	2.50	6.00
	1830 plain edge					
		Inc. Ab.	1.00	2.00	4.00	9.00
	1831	Inc. Ab.	2.00	4.00	8.50	17.50

Draped bust, with pearl edge.

C#	Date	Mintage	VG	Fine	VF	XF
125	1832	.912	3.00	7.50	15.00	30.00
	1832 with plain edge					
		Inc. Ab.	1.00	2.50	5.00	12.00

Obv: Naked bust, with pearl edge.

C#	Date	Mintage	VG	Fine	VF	XF
125a	1832	Inc. Ab.	6.00	15.00	25.00	50.00

C#	Date	Mintage	VG	Fine	VF	XF
129	1835	.538	1.00	2.00	4.00	10.00
	1836/5	1.498	1.00	2.00	4.00	10.00
	1836	Inc. Ab.	.75	1.50	4.00	10.00
	1838	.427	1.50	3.00	6.00	15.00
	1839	.827	.75	1.50	4.00	10.00
	1840/35	.860	1.00	2.00	4.00	10.00
	1840	Inc. Ab.	.75	1.50	4.00	10.00
	1843/35	.865	1.00	2.50	5.00	12.50
	1843	Inc. Ab.	1.50	3.00	6.00	15.00
	1844	.071	9.00	20.00	40.00	85.00

C#	Date	Mintage	VG	Fine	VF	XF
160	1844	.291	1.00	2.00	4.00	7.50
	1845	.092	2.50	5.00	10.00	20.00
	1846	.067	3.00	6.00	12.50	25.00
	1847	.823	1.00	2.00	4.00	7.50
	1849	.537	1.00	2.00	4.00	7.50
	1850	.407	1.00	2.50	4.50	8.50
	1851	.486	1.00	2.00	4.00	7.50
	1852	.462	1.00	2.00	4.00	7.50
	1853	.126	2.00	4.50	9.00	17.50
	1854	.422	1.00	2.00	4.00	7.50
	1855	.311	1.00	2.00	4.00	7.50

1/4 SKILLING

COPPER

C#	Date	Mintage	VG	Fine	VF	XF
75	1799	.096*	1.00	2.50	5.00	17.50
	1800	4.932*	1.00	2.50	5.00	17.50

***NOTE:** Reports give mintage figures of 96,000 for 1799 and 4,391,616 for 1800, the latter is believed to include both dates.

C#	Date	Mintage	VG	Fine	VF	XF
79	1802	3.383	.75	1.50	3.00	10.00
	1803	3.217	.75	1.50	3.00	10.00
	1805	5.189	.75	1.50	3.00	10.00
	1806	8.141	.75	1.50	3.00	10.00
	1807	.641	.75	1.50	3.00	10.00
	1808 with narrow crown					
		7.480	1.00	2.00	4.00	12.50
	1808 with wider crown					
		Inc. Ab.	.75	1.50	3.00	10.00

C#	Date	Mintage	VG	Fine	VF	XF
101	1817	1.152	5.00	15.00	30.00	75.00

C#	Date	Mintage	VG	Fine	VF	XF
122	1819	2.500	.75	1.50	4.00	12.50
	1820	2.652	.75	1.50	4.00	12.50
	1821	.768	.75	1.50	4.00	12.50
	1824 space between crown & monogram					
		2.496	.75	1.50	4.00	20.00
	1824 crown touches monogram					
		Inc. Ab.	1.50	5.00	10.00	25.00
	1825 open 4 in denomination					
		3.200	.75	1.50	4.00	12.50
	1825 closed 4 in denomination					
		Inc. Ab.	.75	1.50	4.00	12.50
	1827 open 4 in denomination					
		4.320	.75	1.50	4.00	12.50
	1827 closed 4 in denomination					
		Inc. Ab.	.75	1.50	4.00	12.50
	1828	.905	.75	1.50	4.00	12.50
	1829	1.080	.75	1.50	4.00	12.50
	1830	2.560	.75	1.50	4.00	12.50

C#	Date	Mintage	VG	Fine	VF	XF
126	1832	.160	15.00	35.00	65.00	100.00
	1833/2	.096	10.00	20.00	35.00	55.00

1/3 SKILLING

COPPER

C#	Date	Mintage	VG	Fine	VF	XF
130	1835	.483	2.50	5.50	12.50	30.00
	1836	.985	1.00	2.50	5.00	12.50
	1837	1.096	1.00	2.50	5.00	12.50
	1839	.921	1.00	2.50	5.00	12.50
	1840	.692	1.00	3.00	6.50	15.00
	1841	.013	25.00	55.00	100.00	200.00
	1842	.612	1.00	2.50	5.00	12.50
	1843	.593	1.50	3.00	6.50	15.00

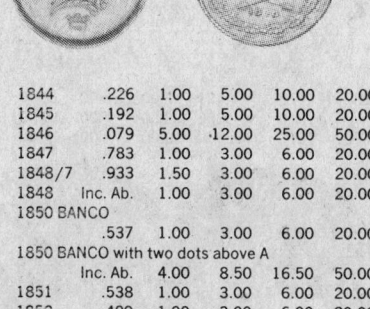

C#	Date	Mintage	VG	Fine	VF	XF
161	1844	.226	1.00	5.00	10.00	20.00
	1845	.192	1.00	5.00	10.00	20.00
	1846	.079	5.00	12.00	25.00	50.00
	1847	.783	1.00	3.00	6.00	20.00
	1848/7	.933	1.50	3.00	6.00	20.00
	1848	Inc. Ab.	1.00	3.00	6.00	20.00
	1850 BANCO					
		.537	1.00	3.00	6.00	20.00
	1850 BANCO with two dots above A					
		Inc. Ab.	4.00	8.50	16.50	50.00
	1851	.538	1.00	3.00	6.00	20.00
	1852	.489	1.00	3.00	6.00	20.00
	1853	.070	5.00	15.00	25.00	50.00
	1854	.495	1.00	3.00	6.00	20.00
	1855	.377	1.00	3.00	6.00	20.00

1/2 SKILLING

COPPER
King's Visit to Avesta
Obv: Crowned G above 3 crowns.
Rev: Crossed arrows separate date 'D-JULI', crown above, 1794 below.

C#	Date	Mintage	VG	Fine	VF	XF
80	1794 with square edge milling					
		—	32.50	75.00	150.00	300.00
	1794 with diagonal edge milling					
		—	25.00	50.00	100.00	200.00
	1794 with plain edge					
		—	—	55.00	120.00	225.00

C#	Date	Mintage	VG	Fine	VF	XF
76	1799	.763	1.25	2.50	5.00	18.50
	1800	3.624	1.25	2.50	5.00	18.50
	1801	3.203	1.25	2.50	5.00	18.50
	1802	1.188	1.25	2.50	5.00	18.50

C#	Date	Mintage	VG	Fine	VF	XF
81	1802	*2.340	1.00	2.50	5.00	12.50
	1803	*5.048	1.00	2.50	5.00	12.50
	1804	(.595)	50.00	125.00	250.00	450.00
	1805	*.173	1.25	2.50	5.00	18.50
	1807	1.950	1.25	2.50	5.00	15.00
	1809	4.845	1.50	3.00	6.00	18.50

***NOTE:** Struck over 18th century 1 ore - worth 50 per cent to 100 per cent more if earlier date visible.

C#	Date	Mintage	VG	Fine	VF	XF
102	1815	1.421	2.00	6.00	12.00	25.00
	1816	.566	2.50	7.00	15.00	35.00
	1817	Inc. Ab.	3.00	8.00	17.50	40.00

C#	Date	Mintage	VG	Fine	VF	XF
123	1819	1.264	1.25	3.00	6.00	25.00
	1820	1.296	1.25	3.00	6.00	25.00
	1821	1.840	1.25	3.00	6.00	25.00
	1822	.944	1.25	3.00	6.00	25.00
	1824	.640	1.25	3.00	6.00	25.00
	1825	.816	2.50	8.00	15.00	40.00
	1827(Skil--Ling)					
		.800	1.25	3.00	6.00	25.00
	1827(Skil Ling)					
			3.00	7.50	15.00	45.00
	1828	1.872	1.25	3.00	6.00	25.00
	1829	.822	1.25	3.00	6.00	25.00
	1830	.394	1.50	3.00	6.00	25.00

C#	Date	Mintage	VG	Fine	VF	XF
127	1832	.288	10.00	20.00	35.00	70.00
	1833	3 pcs.	—	—	Rare	—

2/3 SKILLING

COPPER

C#	Date	Mintage	VG	Fine	VF	XF
131	1835	.198	3.00	8.00	17.50	45.00
	1836	.928	1.50	5.00	10.00	30.00
	1837	1.026	1.50	5.00	10.00	30.00
	1839	.654	1.50	5.00	10.00	30.00
	1840	.646	1.50	5.00	10.00	30.00
	1842	.526	1.50	5.00	10.00	30.00
	1843	.626	1.50	5.00	10.00	30.00

C#	Date	Mintage	VG	Fine	VF	XF
162	1844	.266	2.50	8.00	15.00	35.00
	1845/4	.495	2.50	8.00	15.00	35.00
	1845	Inc. Ab.	2.50	8.00	15.00	35.00

Redesigned smaller head

C#	Date	Mintage	VG	Fine	VF	XF
	1845/4	Inc. Ab.	6.00	17.50	30.00	60.00
165	1845	Inc. Ab.	6.00	17.50	30.00	60.00
	1846/4	.123	2.00	8.00	15.00	30.00
	1846	Inc. Ab.	2.00	8.00	15.00	30.00
	1847	.089	1.50	8.00	15.00	30.00
	1849/4	.219	1.50	6.00	12.50	25.00
	1849	Inc. Ab.	1.50	6.00	12.50	25.00
	1850	.329	1.50	6.00	12.50	25.00
	1851	.467	1.50	6.00	12.50	25.00
	1852	.297	1.50	6.00	12.50	25.00
	1853	.052	12.00	30.00	60.00	120.00
	1854	.408	1.50	5.00	10.00	22.50
	1855	.506	1.50	5.00	10.00	22.50

SKILLING

COPPER
Similar to 1/2 Skilling, C#81.

C#	Date	Mintage	VG	Fine	VF	XF
82	1802	—	1.75	3.50	7.50	27.50
	1803	—	3.25	7.50	15.00	45.00
	1805	—	1.75	3.50	7.50	27.50

NOTE: Struck over 18th century 2 Ore - worth 50 per cent to 100 per cent more if earlier date visible.

C#	Date	Mintage	VG	Fine	VF	XF
103	1812	.480	3.50	10.00	20.00	45.00
	1814	.730	3.50	10.00	20.00	45.00
	1815	Inc. Ab.	3.50	10.00	20.00	45.00
	1816	.230	5.00	15.00	25.00	60.00
	1817	.202	6.00	20.00	35.00	70.00

C#	Date	Mintage	VG	Fine	VF	XF
124	1819	1.176	3.00	6.00	15.00	35.00
	1820 with oblique milling					
		1.376	3.00	6.00	15.00	35.00
	1820 with square milling					
		Inc. Ab.	6.00	12.50	30.00	85.00
	1821	.704	3.00	6.00	15.00	35.00
	1822	.520	3.00	6.00	15.00	35.00
	1825	.472	3.00	6.00	15.00	35.00
	1827	.504	3.00	6.00	15.00	35.00
	1828	.664	3.00	6.00	15.00	35.00
	1829	.816	3.00	6.00	15.00	35.00
	1830	.220	3.50	7.50	17.50	40.00

Obv: Large head of Charles XIV John right.
Rev: Value among 3 crowns over palms and date.

C#	Date	Mintage	VG	Fine	VF	XF
128	1832	8,000	60.00	120.00	225.00	325.00

C#	Date	Mintage	VG	Fine	VF	XF
132	1835 with wide wreath					
		.186	65.00	150.00	350.00	700.00
	1835 with narrow wreath					
		Inc. Ab.	4.00	12.50	25.00	60.00
	1836/5	.651	3.00	10.00	20.00	50.00
	1836	Inc. Ab.	3.00	10.00	20.00	50.00
	1837	.628	3.00	10.00	20.00	50.00
	1838	.140	4.00	12.50	25.00	60.00
	1839	.360	3.00	10.00	20.00	50.00
	1840	.278	3.00	10.00	20.00	50.00
	1842	.499	3.00	10.00	20.00	50.00
	1843	.361	3.00	10.00	20.00	50.00

Large head of Oscar I.

C#	Date	Mintage	VG	Fine	VF	XF
163	1844	.093	4.00	12.50	25.00	60.00
	1845/4	.097	4.00	12.50	25.00	60.00

C#	Date	Mintage	VG	Fine	VF	XF
163	1845	Inc. Ab.	4.00	12.50	25.00	60.00

Redesigned, smaller head.

C#	Date	Mintage	VG	Fine	VF	XF
166	1847	.150	2.50	8.00	17.50	40.00
	1849	.306	2.50	7.00	15.00	35.00
	1850	.137	2.50	8.00	17.50	40.00
	1851	.151	2.50	8.00	17.50	40.00
	1852	.154	2.50	8.00	17.50	40.00
	1853	.031	10.00	30.00	60.00	120.00
	1854	.064	4.00	10.00	20.00	45.00
	1855	.040	5.00	15.00	30.00	75.00

2 SKILLING

COPPER

C#	Date	Mintage	VG	Fine	VF	XF
133	1835	.079	17.50	40.00	80.00	200.00
	1836 with wide wreath					
		.583	250.00	600.00	900.00	1600.
	1836 with narrow wreath					
		Inc. Ab.	6.00	17.50	35.00	80.00
	1837	.388	8.00	20.00	45.00	120.00
	1839	.270	8.00	20.00	45.00	120.00
	1840	.069	8.00	20.00	45.00	120.00
	1841	.093	8.00	20.00	45.00	120.00
	1842	.123	8.00	20.00	45.00	120.00
	1843	.162	8.00	20.00	45.00	120.00

C#	Date	Mintage	VG	Fine	VF	XF
164	1844	.089	10.00	25.00	50.00	130.00
	1845	.120	10.00	25.00	50.00	130.00

Smaller head

C#	Date	Mintage	VG	Fine	VF	XF
167	1845	Inc. Ab.	12.00	30.00	55.00	130.00
	1846	.056	8.00	20.00	45.00	110.00
	1847	.115	7.00	17.50	40.00	100.00
	1849	.138	7.00	17.50	40.00	100.00
	1850	.081	7.00	17.50	40.00	100.00
	1851	.083	7.00	17.50	40.00	100.00
	1852	.061	7.00	17.50	40.00	100.00
	1853	.023	20.00	45.00	90.00	175.00
	1854	.038	7.00	17.50	40.00	100.00
	1855	.011	25.00	60.00	120.00	175.00

4 SKILLING

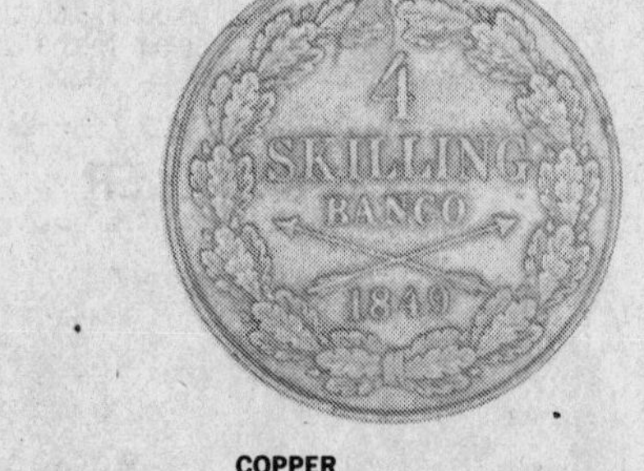

COPPER

C#	Date	Mintage	VG	Fine	VF	XF
168	1849	.444	8.00	17.50	35.00	80.00
	1850	.170	10.00	20.00	40.00	100.00
	1851	.038	12.00	25.00	60.00	120.00
	1852	.038	15.00	30.00	65.00	130.00
	1855	.074	15.00	30.00	65.00	130.00
	1855 with value and BANCO larger					
		Inc. Ab.	13.50	27.50	80.00	200.00

1/32 RIKSDALER

.750 SILVER

C#	Date	Mintage	VG	Fine	VF	XF
171	1851	Unique	—	—	—	—
	1852/1AG	.480	1.50	4.00	8.50	20.00
	1852AG	Inc. Ab.	1.00	4.00	8.50	20.00
	1853AG with small AG					
		.775	1.00	4.00	8.50	20.00
	1853AG with large AG					
		Inc. Ab.	1.50	4.00	8.50	20.00

1/24 RIKSDALER

.382 SILVER

C#	Date	Mintage	VG	Fine	VF	XF
105	1810OL	.742	6.00	15.00	25.00	45.00
	1811OL	.378	6.00	15.00	25.00	45.00
	1812OL	.537	6.00	15.00	25.00	45.00
	1813OL	.444	6.00	15.00	25.00	45.00
	1814OL	.101	10.00	25.00	35.00	60.00
	1816OL	.160	8.00	20.00	30.00	55.00

1/16 RIKSDALER

.750 SILVER

C#	Date	Mintage	VG	Fine	VF	XF
144	1835CB	.433	6.00	15.00	30.00	50.00
	1836/5CB	.088	6.00	15.00	30.00	50.00
	1836CB	Inc. Ab.	6.00	15.00	30.00	50.00

C#	Date	Mintage	VG	Fine	VF	XF
173	1845AG	4,185	75.00	150.00	250.00	375.00
	1846/5AG	.034	35.00	75.00	150.00	250.00
	1846AG	Inc. Ab.	35.00	75.00	150.00	250.00
	1848AG	4.173	2.50	5.00	10.00	20.00
	1849AG	1.006	—	—	Rare	—
	1850AG	Inc. Ab.	3.00	6.00	12.00	25.00
	1851AG	.847	3.00	6.00	12.00	25.00
	1852AG	.934	3.00	6.00	12.00	25.00
	1855AG	.830	3.00	6.00	12.00	25.00

1/12 RIKSDALER

.507 SILVER
Obv: Crowned linked CC monogram.
Rev: Crowned arms.

C#	Date	Mintage	VG	Fine	VF	XF
106	1811OL	.735	20.00	40.00	80.00	150.00

.750 SILVER

C#	Date	Mintage	VG	Fine	VF	XF
145	1831CB	.212	8.00	20.00	40.00	70.00
	1832/1CB	1.463	8.00	20.00	40.00	70.00
	1832CB	Inc. Ab.	8.00	20.00	40.00	70.00
	1833CB	Inc. Ab.	8.00	20.00	40.00	70.00
	1833/1CB	.157	8.00	20.00	40.00	70.00

1/8 RIKSDALER

.750 SILVER

C#	Date	Mintage	VG	Fine	VF	XF
146	1830 CB plain edge					
		1.796	25.00	60.00	100.00	175.00

C#	Date	Mintage	VG	Fine	VF	XF
146	1830 CB stars & flowers on edge					
		Inc. Ab.	35.00	80.00	175.00	300.00
	1831CB	1.324	7.50	15.00	35.00	60.00
	1832CB	2.829	7.50	15.00	35.00	60.00
	1833CB	1.032	7.50	15.00	35.00	60.00
	1834CB	.103	20.00	50.00	90.00	150.00
	1835CB	.103	20.00	50.00	90.00	150.00
	1836CB	2,026	50.00	125.00	225.00	350.00
	1837CB	7,000	50.00	125.00	225.00	350.00

Obv: Head of Oscar right.
Rev: Crowned arms in order collar.

C#	Date	Mintage	VG	Fine	VF	XF
175	1852AG	.046	100.00	250.00	500.00	1000.

1/6 RIKSDALER

.691 SILVER
Obv: Bust with flowing hair right.
Rev: Crowned arms within wreath dividing value.

C#	Date	Mintage	VG	Fine	VF	XF
85	1799	.103	50.00	120.00	200.00	375.00

C#	Date	Mintage	VG	Fine	VF	XF
86	1800	.106	15.00	30.00	60.00	125.00
	1801	.420	10.00	20.00	40.00	85.00
	1802	1.254	7.50	15.00	30.00	60.00
	1803	2.341	7.50	15.00	30.00	60.00
	1804	2.156	7.50	15.00	30.00	60.00
	1805	.978	7.50	15.00	30.00	60.00
	1806	.341	8.50	17.50	35.00	70.00
	1807	.909	7.50	15.00	30.00	60.00
	1808	943	7.50	15.00	30.00	60.00
	1809	.707	8.50	17.50	35.00	75.00

Obv: Head of Charles XIII right.
Rev: Crowned arms in order collar.

C#	Date	Mintage	VG	Fine	VF	XF
107	1809OL	—	60.00	140.00	250.00	500.00
	1810OL	.297	25.00	55.00	110.00	225.00
	1814OL	.199	25.00	55.00	110.00	225.00
	1814/0OL	I.A.	25.00	55.00	110.00	225.00

Obv: With NORR in legends

C#	Date	Mintage	VG	Fine	VF	XF
107a	1815OL	.059	75.00	175.00	325.00	650.00
	1817OL	.091	75.00	175.00	325.00	650.00

Obv: Large head of Charles XIV John right.

C#	Date	Mintage	VG	Fine	VF	XF
135	1819OL	.052	75.00	150.00	225.00	450.00
	1826CB	1,974	150.00	350.00	600.00	800.00

C#	Date	Mintage	VG	Fine	VF	XF
140	1827	Unique	—	—	—	—
	1828CB with edge inscription					
		1,024	225.00	500.00	700.00	1000.
	1828CB without edge inscription					
		Inc. Ab.	225.00	500.00	700.00	1000.
	1829CB	2,039	40.00	80.00	125.00	225.00

1/4 RIKSDALER

.750 SILVER

C#	Date	Mintage	VG	Fine	VF	XF
147	1830CB	.704	25.00	50.00	100.00	150.00
	1830CB with plain edge					
		Inc. Ab.	30.00	70.00	125.00	175.00
	1831CB	2.470	20.00	50.00	75.00	125.00
	1832CB	.522	20.00	50.00	90.00	160.00
	1833CB	.063	30.00	75.00	140.00	200.00
	1834/3 CB	.953	25.00	50.00	75.00	125.00
	1834CB	Inc. Ab.	20.00	50.00	75.00	125.00
	1836CB	2,766	150.00	275.00	400.00	700.00

C#	Date	Mintage	VG	Fine	VF	XF
177	1846/4AG	.221	30.00	60.00	125.00	225.00
	1848/4AG	.130	30.00	60.00	125.00	225.00
	1848AG	I.A.	30.00	60.00	125.00	225.00
	1852AG	—	—	—	Rare	—

1/3 RIKSDALER

.878 SILVER

C#	Date	Mintage	VG	Fine	VF	XF
87	1798	.070	175.00	350.00	650.00	1000.

Obv: Military bust right.

C#	Date	Mintage	VG	Fine	VF	XF
88	1799	.070	100.00	225.00	400.00	700.00
	1800	.113	120.00	225.00	400.00	600.00

Obv: Head of Charles XIII right.
Rev: Crowned arms in order collar.

C#	Date	Mintage	VG	Fine	VF	XF
108	1813OL	.063	100.00	200.00	325.00	600.00
	1814OL	.033	125.00	225.00	350.00	650.00

C#	Date	Mintage	VG	Fine	VF	XF
141	1827CB	—	—	—	Rare	—
	1828CB w/edge inscription					
		.061	60.00	120.00	200.00	300.00
	1828CB w/o edge inscription					
		Inc. Ab.	75.00	150.00	250.00	350.00
	1829CB w/edge inscription					
		.109	60.00	120.00	200.00	300.00
	1829CB w/o edge inscription					
		Inc. Ab.	75.00	150.00	250.00	350.00

1/2 RIKSDALER

.750 SILVER

C#	Date	Mintage	VG	Fine	VF	XF
148	1831CB	.270	35.00	80.00	150.00	275.00
	1831 CB plain edge					
		Inc. Ab.	50.00	100.00	175.00	300.00
	1832CB	.142	75.00	150.00	250.00	400.00
	1833/31CB	.191	50.00	100.00	175.00	300.00
	1833CB	Inc. Ab.	50.00	100.00	175.00	300.00
	1836/1CB	2,482	125.00	275.00	450.00	800.00
	1836CB	Inc. Ab.	125.00	275.00	450.00	800.00
	1838CB	—	—	—	Rare	—

Similar to 1 Riksdaler Specie, C#181.

C#	Date	Mintage	VG	Fine	VF	XF
179	1845AG	.022	60.00	125.00	200.00	350.00
	1846/5AG	.082	60.00	125.00	200.00	350.00
	1846AG	Inc. Ab.	60.00	125.00	200.00	350.00
	1848/7AG	.074	60.00	125.00	200.00	350.00
	1848AG	Inc. Ab.	60.00	125.00	200.00	350.00
	1852AG	1,104	—	—	Rare	—

RIKSDALER

SILVER

C#	Date	Mintage	VG	Fine	VF	XF
89	1792	.076	80.00	175.00	350.00	600.00
	1793	.262	60.00	125.00	225.00	400.00
	1794	.278	60.00	125.00	225.00	400.00
	1795	.266	60.00	125.00	225.00	400.00

C#	Date	Mintage	VG	Fine	VF	XF
89.2	1796	.225	60.00	125.00	225.00	400.00
	1797	.155	75.00	150.00	250.00	450.00

C#	Date	Mintage	VG	Fine	VF	XF
90	1801	.091	60.00	125.00	225.00	400.00
	1805	.150	60.00	125.00	225.00	400.00
	1806	.205	60.00	125.00	225.00	400.00
	1807	.037	60.00	125.00	250.00	500.00

C#	Date	Mintage	VG	Fine	VF	XF
110	1812OL	.043	125.00	250.00	500.00	800.00
	1814/2OL	6,600	150.00	275.00	550.00	900.00
	1814OL	Inc. Ab.	150.00	275.00	550.00	900.00

Obv: NORR added to legend

C#	Date	Mintage	VG	Fine	VF	XF
110a	1814OL	Inc. Ab.	350.00	800.00	1400.	2200.
	1815OL	.066	100.00	225.00	450.00	800.00
	1816/5OL	.012	125.00	250.00	475.00	850.00
	1816OL	Inc. Ab.	125.00	250.00	475.00	850.00
	1817OL	9,895	150.00	300.00	600.00	900.00
	1818OL	.015	175.00	325.00	625.00	1000.

C#	Date	Mintage	VG	Fine	VF	XF
138	1818OL	Inc. Ab.	100.00	250.00	500.00	900.00
	1819OL	.014	150.00	350.00	600.00	1000.
	1819LB	Inc. Ab.	125.00	300.00	550.00	950.00
	1820LB	.011	175.00	375.00	700.00	1100.
	1820LB with bust of Karl XIII					
		—	600.00	1200.	2500.	4000.
	1821LB	.029	100.00	200.00	350.00	600.00
	1822CB	.034	100.00	200.00	375.00	700.00
	1823CB with large bust					
		.026	100.00	200.00	375.00	700.00
	1823CB with small bust					
		Inc. Ab.	100.00	200.00	375.00	700.00
	1824CB	.053	100.00	200.00	350.00	600.00
	1825CB	.020	100.00	200.00	375.00	700.00
	1826CB	7,538	100.00	250.00	450.00	750.00
	1827CB	.017	100.00	200.00	375.00	700.00

Obv: Similar to C#143.2.
Rev: With 7 angel heads around arms.

C#	Date	Mintage	VG	Fine	VF	XF
143.1	1827CB	—	350.00	800.00	1500.	2750.

Rev: With 9 angel heads around arms.

C#	Date	Mintage	VG	Fine	VF	XF
143.2	1827CB	610 pcs.	750.00	1500.	2500.	4000.
	1829CB	409 pcs.	1000.	2000.	3000.	—

300 Years of Political and Religious Freedom

C#	Date	Mintage	VG	Fine	VF	XF
139	1825CB	7,339	100.00	200.00	450.00	800.00

.750 SILVER

C#	Date	Mintage	VG	Fine	VF	XF
149	1831CB	.047	75.00	150.00	250.00	450.00
	1832/1CB	2,100	300.00	700.00	1200.	2200.
	1832CB	Inc. Ab.	300.00	700.00	1200.	2200.
	1833/1CB	.039	75.00	150.00	250.00	450.00
	1833CB	Inc. Ab.	75.00	150.00	250.00	450.00
	1834/1CB	.068	65.00	125.00	225.00	450.00
	1834CB	Inc. Ab.	65.00	125.00	225.00	450.00
	1834 CB plain edge					
		Inc. Ab.	75.00	150.00	250.00	400.00
	1835CB	.331	65.00	125.00	225.00	450.00
	1836CB	.093	65.00	125.00	225.00	450.00
	1837CB	.177	65.00	125.00	225.00	450.00
	1838AG	.834	65.00	125.00	225.00	450.00
	1839AG	.212	65.00	125.00	225.00	450.00
	1840AG	.068	125.00	250.00	500.00	750.00
	1841AG	.549	65.00	125.00	225.00	450.00
	1842AG	.288	75.00	150.00	250.00	500.00

Rev: Different arms

C#	Date	Mintage	VG	Fine	VF	XF
149	1842AG	Inc. Ab.	75.00	140.00	250.00	350.00
	1843/2AG	I.A.	—	Rare	—	

C#	Date	Mintage	Fine	VF	XF	Unc
180	1844 AG	.088	135.00	250.00	450.00	750.00
	1845AG with large head					
		.043	150.00	275.00	475.00	800.00

C#	Date	Mintage	Fine	VF	XF	Unc
181	1845AG with small head					
		Inc. Ab.	200.00	300.00	450.00	750.00
	1846AG obv. GOTH.					
		.111	120.00	200.00	350.00	650.00
	1846AG obv. GOTH no period					
		Inc. Ab.	120.00	200.00	350.00	650.00
	1847AG	.060	120.00	200.00	350.00	650.00
	1848AG	.185	120.00	200.00	350.00	650.00
	1850AG	.070	120.00	200.00	350.00	650.00
	1851AG	.122	120.00	200.00	350.00	650.00
	1852AG	.054	120.00	200.00	350.00	650.00
	1853ag goth small date					
		.109	120.00	200.00	350.00	650.00
	1853AG GOTH no period small date					
		Inc. Ab.	120.00	200.00	350.00	650.00
	1853 large date					
		Inc. Ab.	120.00	200.00	350.00	650.00
	1854AG	.034	120.00	200.00	350.00	650.00
	1855AG small date					
		.161	120.00	200.00	350.00	650.00
	1855AG large date					
		Inc. Ab.	120.00	200.00	350.00	650.00

MONETARY REFORM

400 Ore 4 riksdaler riksmynt

1 Riksdaler Specie

1/2 ORE

BRONZE

C#	Date	Mintage	VG	Fine	VF	XF
185	1856	.026	25.00	45.00	90.00	175.00
	1857	1.312	1.00	2.00	4.00	8.00
	1858/7	1.849	1.50	2.50	6.00	15.00
	1858	Inc. Ab.	1.00	2.00	4.00	8.00

Y#	Date	Mintage	VG	Fine	VF	XF
1	1867 lg.dt.	.064	3.00	6.00	12.50	25.00
	1867 small date					
		Inc. Ab.	3.50	7.50	15.00	35.00

ORE

BRONZE

C#	Date	Mintage	Fine	VF	XF	Unc
186	1856	.024	45.00	90.00	175.00	375.00
	1857	1.596	3.00	5.00	10.00	20.00
	1858/7	6.290	5.00	7.50	15.00	35.00
	1858L.A.	Inc. Ab.	2.00	4.00	8.00	20.00
	1858L.A	Inc. Ab.	2.00	4.00	8.00	20.00
	1858 LA	Inc. Ab.	2.00	4.00	8.00	20.00

Y#	Date	Mintage	Fine	VF	XF	Unc
2	1860	.046	20.00	45.00	90.00	175.00
	1861	.300	5.00	10.00	20.00	45.00
	1862	.079	10.00	17.50	30.00	60.00
	1863	.450	5.00	10.00	20.00	45.00
	1864L.A.	1.848	2.00	4.00	8.00	20.00
	1864LA	Inc. Ab.	2.00	4.00	8.00	20.00
	1865/4	.561	5.00	10.00	20.00	45.00
	1865	Inc. Ab.	3.50	7.00	15.00	30.00
	1866	.327	4.00	8.00	15.00	35.00
	1867	.956	2.00	3.50	7.00	17.50
	1870	1.079	2.00	3.50	7.00	17.50
	1871L.A.	1.063	2.00	3.50	7.00	17.50
	1871LA	Inc. Ab.	2.00	3.50	7.00	17.50
	1872L.A.	1.897	2.00	3.50	7.00	17.50
	1872LA.	Inc. Ab.	2.00	3.50	7.00	17.50
	1872LA	Inc. Ab.	2.00	3.50	7.00	17.50

Y#	Date	Mintage	Fine	VF	XF	Unc
11	1873LA	1.867	6.00	12.00	20.00	40.00
	1873L.A.	Inc. Ab.	6.00	12.00	20.00	40.00
	1873LA.	Inc. Ab.	6.00	12.00	20.00	40.00
	1873 SVFRIGES error					
		Inc. Ab.	60.00	90.00	150.00	225.00

2 ORE

BRONZE

C#	Date	Mintage	Fine	VF	XF	Unc
187	1856	.022	60.00	125.00	225.00	450.00
	1857 long beard					
		1.121	5.00	10.00	20.00	50.00
	1857 short beard					
		Inc. Ab.	5.00	10.00	20.00	50.00
	1858/7	2.831	7.50	12.50	30.00	75.00
	1858	Inc. Ab.	4.00	8.00	20.00	45.00

Y#	Date	Mintage	Fine	VF	XF	Unc
3	1860	.197	20.00	45.00	90.00	200.00
	1861	1.626	4.00	8.00	15.00	40.00
	1862	.213	12.50	22.50	45.00	100.00
	1863/2	1.621	4.00	7.50	15.00	30.00
	1863	Inc. Ab.	4.00	7.50	15.00	30.00
	1864	.600	4.00	7.50	15.00	30.00
	1865	.629	4.00	7.50	15.00	30.00
	1866/5	.400	5.00	10.00	20.00	45.00
	1866	Inc. Ab.	5.00	10.00	20.00	45.00
	1867L.A.	.428	5.00	10.00	20.00	45.00
	1867LA	Inc. Ab.	5.00	10.00	20.00	45.00
	1871/61	.718	4.50	9.00	17.50	37.50
	1871	Inc. Ab.	3.50	7.50	15.00	30.00
	1872	1.647	2.50	5.00	12.50	30.00

Y#	Date	Mintage	Fine	VF	XF	Unc
12	1873	1.294	12.50	25.00	45.00	90.00

5 ORE

BRONZE

C#	Date	Mintage	Fine	VF	XF	Unc
188	1857 small L.A					
		.731	8.00	15.00	40.00	90.00
	1857 large L.A					
		Inc. Ab.	8.00	15.00	40.00	90.00
	1857 curved top 5					
		Inc. Ab.	40.00	75.00	150.00	350.00
	1858/7	1.193	8.00	15.00	40.00	90.00
	1858	Inc. Ab.	8.00	15.00	40.00	90.00

Y#	Date	Mintage	Fine	VF	XF	Unc
4	1860/57	.067	40.00	75.00	150.00	300.00
4	1860	Inc. Ab.	40.00	75.00	150.00	300.00
	1861/57	.343	12.50	25.00	45.00	90.00
	1861	Inc. Ab.	12.50	25.00	45.00	90.00
	1862 star	.136	15.00	30.00	55.00	110.00
	1862 rose	Inc. Ab.	55.00	90.00	200.00	400.00
	1863/2	.633	10.00	20.00	40.00	75.00
	1863	Inc. Ab.	10.00	20.00	40.00	75.00
	1864/2	.264	10.00	20.00	40.00	75.00
	1864	Inc. Ab.	10.00	20.00	40.00	75.00
	1865	.104	12.50	25.00	45.00	90.00
	1866/5	Inc.Ab.	12.50	25.00	45.00	90.00
	1866	Inc. Ab.	25.00	45.00	90.00	200.00
	1867/6	.741	8.00	15.00	30.00	65.00
	1867	Inc. Ab.	8.00	15.00	30.00	65.00
	1872	.620	7.50	14.00	25.00	60.00

Y#	Date	Mintage	Fine	VF	XF	Unc
13	1873/2	.783	25.00	50.00	100.00	200.00
	1873 no dots above "O" in GOTH					
		Inc. Ab.	22.50	45.00	90.00	175.00
	1873 dots above "O" in GOTH					
		Inc. Ab.	22.50	45.00	90.00	175.00

10 ORE

.750 SILVER

C#	Date	Mintage	Fine	VF	XF	Unc
192	1855AG with small AG					
		1.359	30.00	60.00	130.00	200.00
	1855AG with larger AG					
		Inc. Ab.	30.00	60.00	130.00	200.00
	1855G with long beard					
		Inc. Ab.	7.50	12.50	22.50	55.00
	1855G with shorter beard					
		Inc. Ab.	7.50	12.50	22.50	55.00
	1855T	Inc. Ab.	8.50	15.00	25.00	60.00
	1857ST	1.007	6.00	12.50	22.50	55.00
	1858/7	.354	10.00	17.50	27.50	65.00
	1858ST	Inc. Ab.	8.50	15.00	25.00	60.00
	1859/7	1.684	8.50	15.00	25.00	60.00
	1859ST	Inc. Ab.	6.00	12.50	22.50	55.00

Y#	Date	Mintage	Fine	VF	XF	Unc
5	1861ST	.579	8.50	17.50	40.00	75.00
	1862ST	Inc. Ab.	750.00	1250.	2000.	2750.
	1863ST	.449	15.00	25.00	45.00	90.00
	1864ST	Inc. Ab.	8.50	15.00	25.00	60.00
	1865ST	.560	8.50	15.00	25.00	60.00
	1867ST	.609	8.50	15.00	25.00	60.00
	1869ST	.210	10.00	20.00	35.00	75.00
	1870ST	.384	6.00	12.50	22.50	55.00
	1871ST	1.162	5.00	10.00	20.00	50.00

Y#	Date	Mintage	Fine	VF	XF	Unc
17	1872ST	.120	45.00	75.00	110.00	200.00
	1873ST	.635	40.00	65.00	100.00	175.00
	1873 (error) inverted V in SVERIGES					
		Inc. Ab.	60.00	90.00	150.00	275.00
	1873 ST SVF.RIGES					
		Inc. Ab.	—	—	Rare	—

25 ORE

.750 SILVER

C#	Date	Mintage	Fine	VF	XF	Unc
193	1855ST	.437	10.00	20.00	40.00	90.00
	1856ST	1.763	8.00	15.00	30.00	75.00
	1857/6	.434	25.00	55.00	100.00	200.00
	1857ST	Inc. Ab.	25.00	55.00	100.00	200.00
	1858/7	1.183	25.00	55.00	100.00	200.00
	1858ST	Inc. Ab.	25.00	55.00	100.00	200.00
	1859/7	Inc. Ab.	15.00	25.00	55.00	100.00
	1859ST	Inc. Ab.	8.00	15.00	30.00	75.00

Y#	Date	Mintage	Fine	VF	XF	Unc
6	1862ST	1.762	1000.	1500.	2000.	3000.
	1864/2	.266	20.00	30.00	60.00	150.00
	1864ST	Inc. Ab.	20.00	30.00	60.00	150.00
	1865ST	.400	20.00	30.00	60.00	150.00
	1866ST	.039	20.00	30.00	60.00	150.00
	1867/6	.198	20.00	30.00	60.00	150.00
	1867ST	Inc. Ab.	20.00	30.00	60.00	150.00
	1871/61	.660	15.00	25.00	55.00	100.00
	1871ST	Inc. Ab.	15.00	25.00	55.00	100.00

50 ORE

.750 SILVER

C#	Date	Mintage	Fine	VF	XF	Unc
194	1857 ST	.492	65.00	125.00	225.00	375.00

Y#	Date	Mintage	Fine	VF	XF	Unc
7	1862ST	2,319	1250.	1750.	2500.	4000.

RIKSDALER RIKSMYNT

.750 SILVER
Obv: Short goatee

C#	Date	Mintage	Fine	VF	XF	Unc
195	1857 ST	.645	65.00	125.00	200.00	375.00

Obv: Long goatee

C#	Date	Mintage	Fine	VF	XF	Unc
195a	1857 ST	Inc. Ab.	65.00	125.00	200.00	375.00

Y#	Date	Mintage	Fine	VF	XF	Unc
8	1860st	.125	100.00	150.00	250.00	450.00
	1861/0ST	.158	100.00	150.00	250.00	450.00
	1861ST	Inc. Ab.	100.00	150.00	250.00	450.00
	1862ST	—	1250.	1750.	2500.	3250.
	1864ST	.085	110.00	175.00	250.00	450.00
	1864ST w/out edge lettering					
		Inc. Ab.	125.00	200.00	300.00	500.00
	1865ST	.059	150.00	250.00	400.00	650.00
	1867ST	.106	110.00	175.00	250.00	450.00
	1871/61ST	.208	80.00	125.00	250.00	350.00

Y#	Date	Mintage	Fine	VF	XF	Unc
8	1871ST	Inc. Ab.	80.00	125.00	250.00	350.00

Obv: Deepened hairlines

Y#	Date	Mintage	Fine	VF	XF	Unc
18	1873ST	Inc. Ab.	375.00	600.00	1000.	1500.

2 RIKSDALER RIKSMYNT

SILVER

C#	Date	Mintage	Fine	VF	XF	Unc
196	1857 ST	.288	175.00	300.00	475.00	800.00

Y#	Date	Mintage	Fine	VF	XF	Unc
9	1862ST	640 pcs.	1000.	1500.	2250.	3000.
	1864/2ST	.038	225.00	400.00	700.00	1000.
	1864ST	Inc. Ab.	225.00	400.00	700.00	1000.
	1871ST with small date and large head					
		.019	225.00	400.00	700.00	1000.

Y#	Date	Mintage	Fine	VF	XF	Unc
9.1	1871ST with large date and small head					
		Inc. Ab.	225.00	400.00	700.00	1000.

RIKSDALER SPECIES

(= 4 Riksdaler Riksmynt)

SILVER
Obv: Bust right with short goatee.
Rev: Crowned, supported arms.

C#	Date	Mintage	Fine	VF	XF	Unc
197	1855ST	2,117	—	—	Rare	—
	1856ST	Inc. Be.	400.00	600.00	1000.	1500.
	1857ST	Inc. Be.	125.00	200.00	400.00	600.00

C#	Date	Mintage	Fine	VF	XF	Unc
197a	1856ST	.776	100.00	175.00	350.00	650.00
	1857ST	.483	125.00	250.00	400.00	700.00
	1859ST	.101	150.00	275.00	450.00	750.00

Y#	Date	Mintage	Fine	VF	XF	Unc
10	1861ST	.207	125.00	200.00	325.00	550.00
	1862ST, L.A., edge lettering large & small					
		.943	100.00	175.00	300.00	650.00
	1862ST L A					
		Inc. Ab.	100.00	175.00	300.00	500.00
	1862ST, without engraver's initials					
		Inc. Ab.	125.00	200.00	400.00	600.00
	1862ST, without edge lettering					
		Inc. Ab.	125.00	225.00	450.00	700.00
	1863ST	.268	125.00	200.00	325.00	550.00
	1864ST	.535	100.00	175.00	300.00	500.00
	1865ST	.107	125.00	200.00	325.00	550.00
	1866ST	.041	140.00	225.00	375.00	650.00
	1866 without edge lettering					
		Inc. Ab.	150.00	250.00	450.00	700.00
	1867ST	.064	140.00	225.00	375.00	650.00
	1868ST	.120	140.00	225.00	375.00	650.00
	1869ST	.314	100.00	150.00	300.00	500.00
	1870ST	.161	100.00	150.00	300.00	500.00
	1871ST	.260	100.00	150.00	300.00	500.00

MONETARY REFORM

100 Ore = 1 Krona

DATE VARIETIES

1916 short tailed 6

1936 long tailed 6

ORE

BRONZE
Obv: Monogram type, small lettering.

Y#	Date	Mintage	Fine	VF	XF	Unc
14	1874	2.370	4.00	7.00	20.00	40.00
	1875	2.829	5.00	8.00	25.00	50.00
	1876	1.889	25.00	40.00	75.00	150.00
	1877	1.590	17.50	25.00	45.00	90.00

Obv: Large lettering

Y#	Date	Mintage	Fine	VF	XF	Unc
14a	1877	Inc. Ab.	17.50	25.00	45.00	90.00
	1878	1.570	15.00	20.00	40.00	75.00
	1879	1.630	7.50	12.50	20.00	50.00

Obv: Legend lengthened

Y#	Date	Mintage	Fine	VF	XF	Unc
14b	1879	Inc. Ab.	150.00	225.00	375.00	600.00
	1880	1.713	20.00	30.00	40.00	90.00
	1881	1.984	6.00	10.00	15.00	45.00
	1882	2.587	3.50	6.00	10.00	25.00
	1883	2.587	3.50	6.00	10.00	25.00
	1884	2.626	3.50	6.00	10.00	25.00
	1885	2.464	3.50	6.00	10.00	25.00
	1886	1.234	10.00	15.00	25.00	60.00
	1888	1.738	6.00	10.00	15.00	35.00
	1889	1.189	10.00	15.00	22.50	50.00
	1890	1.949	2.50	5.00	10.00	22.50
	1891	2.723	2.00	4.00	8.00	20.00
	1892	.280	40.00	60.00	100.00	175.00
	1893	2.145	2.00	4.00	8.00	20.00
	1894	.589	30.00	45.00	75.00	125.00
	1895	2.012	2.00	3.00	6.00	15.00
	1896	.145	3.00	5.00	10.00	25.00
	1897	2.544	.75	1.50	3.50	12.50
	1898	2.959	.75	1.50	3.50	12.50
	1899	2.821	.75	1.50	3.50	12.50
	1900	2.929	.75	1.50	3.50	12.50
	1901	3.075	.75	1.50	3.50	12.50
	1902	2.685	.75	1.50	3.50	12.50
	1903	2.666	.75	1.50	3.50	12.50
	1904	2.033	.75	1.50	3.50	12.50
	1905	3.556	.75	1.50	3.50	12.50

Y#	Date	Mintage	Fine	VF	XF	Unc
32	1906	1.783	5.00	10.00	17.50	30.00
	1907	8.251	.30	.75	1.50	6.00

Obv: Small cross

Y#	Date	Mintage	Fine	VF	XF	Unc
44	1909	3.810	10.00	17.50	35.00	150.00

Obv: Large cross

Y#	Date	Mintage	Fine	VF	XF	Unc
	1909	Inc. Ab.	2.50	6.00	10.00	45.00
	1910	1.583	2.50	6.00	15.00	60.00
	1911	3.150	.75	1.50	4.00	20.00
	1912	3.170	1.00	2.00	5.00	25.00
	1913/12	3.197	3.50	6.50	10.00	20.00
	1913	Inc. Ab.	.50	1.00	3.00	17.50
	1914 with open 4					
		2.214	45.00	65.00	125.00	250.00
	1914 with closed 4					
		Inc. Ab.	1.25	2.50	7.50	35.00
	1915	4.471	.25	.75	2.00	8.00
	1916 with short 6					
		7.620	.25	.75	2.00	7.50
	1916 with long 6					
		Inc. Ab.	.30	.85	2.50	10.00
	1920	5.548	.25	.50	1.50	5.00
	1921	7.442	.25	.50	1.50	5.00
	1922	1.165	2.50	4.50	7.50	30.00
	1923	4.512	.50	1.00	2.50	10.00
	1924	2.579	.25	.50	2.00	8.00
	1925	4.715	.25	.50	1.00	3.50
	1926	7.739	.25	.50	1.00	3.50
	1927	3.602	.25	.50	1.00	3.50
	1928	2.381	.50	1.00	2.00	7.00
	1929	6.091	.25	.50	1.00	3.00
	1930	5.477	.25	.50	1.00	3.00
	1931	5.680	.25	.50	1.00	3.00
	1932	3.339	.30	.75	1.75	6.00
	1933	3.427	.30	.75	2.00	8.00
	1934	6.121	.25	.40	.75	2.50
	1935	4.600	.25	.40	.75	2.50
	1936 with long 6					
		6.116	.40	.75	1.50	4.50
	1936 with short 6					
		Inc. Ab.	.25	.40	.75	2.50
	1937	7.738	.25	.30	.75	2.00
	1938	6.993	.20	.30	1.00	3.50
	1939	6.562	.20	.30	.75	2.50
	1940	4.060	.20	.30	.75	2.00
	1941	11.599	.20	.30	.50	2.00
	1942	3.992	.20	.30	.75	2.50
	1950	22.421	—	.10	.40	1.00

IRON
World War I Issues
Similar to Y#44.

Y#	Date	Mintage	Fine	VF	XF	Unc
52	1917	8.128	1.50	3.00	7.50	20.00
	1918	9.706	2.00	4.00	10.00	25.00
	1919	7.170	3.00	6.00	15.00	30.00

World War II Issues
Similar to Y#44.

Y#	Date	Mintage	Fine	VF	XF	Unc
69	1942	10.053	—	.30	.75	2.00
	1943	10.714	—	.50	1.25	5.50
	1944	8.699	—	.30	1.00	5.00
	1945	9.527	—	.50	1.25	5.00
	1946	6.611	—	.20	2.75	6.50
	1947	14.245	—	.20	.75	2.00
	1948	15.442	—	.20	.75	2.00
	1949	11.779	—	.20	1.00	2.50
	1950	14.432	—	.20	.75	2.00

BRONZE

Y#	Date	Mintage	Fine	VF	XF	Unc
72	1952TS	3.819	—	.50	1.00	3.00
	1953TS	22.636	—	—	.50	2.00
	1954TS	15.492	—	—	.50	2.50
	1955TS	24.008	—	—	.25	1.75
	1956TS	20.792	—	—	.25	1.50
	1957TS	21.019	—	—	.25	1.50
	1958TS	20.220	—	—	.50	1.75
	1959TS	14.028	—	—	.25	1.50
	1959 5'9	Inc. Ab.	—	5.75	9.00	18.00
	1960TS	21.840	—	—	.25	1.25
	1961TS	15.208	—	—	.20	1.50
	1961U	Inc. Ab.	—	—	.50	2.00
	1962U	20.875	—	—	.20	1.50
	1963U	26.070	—	—	—	.65
	1964U	19.290	—	—	—	.35
	1965U	22.335	—	—	—	.25
	1966U	24.093	—	—	—	.25
	1967U	29.738	—	—	—	.20
	1968U	21.693	—	—	—	.20
	1969U	20.198	—	—	—	.25
	1970U	42.800	—	—	—	.15
	1971U	18.680	—	—	—	.15

2 ORE

BRONZE
Obv: Small lettering

Y#	Date	Mintage	Fine	VF	XF	Unc
15	1874	1.914	1.00	4.00	10.00	55.00
	1875/74	2.441	6.00	15.00	35.00	75.00
	1875	Inc. Ab.	1.00	4.00	10.00	55.00
	1876/5	1.402	40.00	60.00	125.00	300.00
	1876	Inc. Ab.	4.00	10.00	35.00	90.00
	1877	1.015	4.00	10.00	35.00	90.00
	1878	.865	45.00	75.00	150.00	350.00

Obv: Large lettering

Y#	Date	Mintage	Fine	VF	XF	Unc
15a	1877	Inc. Ab.	5.00	15.00	40.00	110.00
	1878	Inc. Ab.	5.00	15.00	40.00	90.00
	1879	.935	1.50	5.00	15.00	65.00
	1880	.825	4.00	8.00	22.50	75.00
	1881	1.244	1.00	4.00	12.50	45.00
	1882	1.777	1.00	3.00	10.00	40.00
	1883	1.483	1.00	3.00	10.00	40.00
	1884 with open 4					
		1.316	1.00	3.00	10.00	40.00
	1884 with closed 4					
		Inc. Ab.	8.00	15.00	35.00	100.00
	1885	.615	2.50	6.00	15.00	50.00
	1886	1.241	1.50	3.00	10.00	40.00
	1888	.865	1.50	4.00	15.00	60.00
	1889	.589	1.00	3.00	12.00	45.00
	1890	.912	.75	2.50	7.50	35.00
	1891	.942	.75	2.50	7.50	35.00
	1892	.688	.75	2.50	7.50	35.00
	1893	.558	.75	2.50	7.50	35.00
	1894 with open 4					
		.586	.75	2.50	7.50	35.00
	1894 with closed 4					
		Inc. Ab.	8.50	15.00	35.00	100.00
	1895	.781	.75	2.50	7.50	35.00
	1896	.908	.75	2.50	7.50	35.00
	1897	1.300	.75	1.50	4.00	20.00
	1898	1.527	.75	1.50	4.00	20.00
	1899	2.170	.75	2.00	5.00	20.00
	1900 with oval OO					
		.688	.75	2.00	5.00	20.00
	1900 with round OO					
		Inc. Ab.	40.00	60.00	125.00	250.00
	1901	1.420	.75	1.50	4.00	20.00
	1902	2.040	.75	1.50	4.50	20.00
	1904	.698	.75	1.50	4.50	20.00
	1905	1.430	.50	1.00	3.50	20.00

Obv: New leg: SVERIGES VAL

Y#	Date	Mintage	Fine	VF	XF	Unc
33	1906/5	.994	12.50	20.00	50.00	125.00
	1906	Inc. Ab.	2.00	4.00	10.00	40.00
	1907	3.810	.35	1.00	3.50	12.50

Y#	Date	Mintage	Fine	VF	XF	Unc
45	1909	1.580	1.00	2.50	7.50	30.00
	1910	.809	2.00	5.00	20.00	75.00
	1912	.446	2.50	6.00	25.00	90.00
	1913	.806	1.00	2.50	7.50	45.00
	1914	1.200	.75	2.50	7.50	45.00
	1915	.814	.75	2.50	7.50	45.00
	1916/5	2.820	4.00	8.00	17.50	55.00
	1916 with short 6					
		Inc. Ab.	.75	2.00	5.00	25.00
	1916 with long 6					
45		Inc. Ab.	.75	2.00	5.00	25.00
	1919	1.203	.35	1.50	4.00	22.50
	1920	3.465	.30	.60	2.50	15.00
	1921	2.958	.30	.60	3.00	15.00
	1922	.932	1.00	3.50	15.00	45.00
	1923	.769	2.50	6.00	17.50	50.00
	1924	1.283	.35	.75	3.00	17.50
	1925	3.903	.30	.60	2.50	12.50
	1926	3.579	.30	.60	2.00	12.50
	1927	2.190	.20	.60	3.50	17.50
	1928	.832	.50	1.00	4.00	25.00
	1929	2.384	.20	.60	2.50	12.50
	1930	2.590	.20	.60	2.50	12.50
	1931	2.296	.20	.50	2.50	12.50
	1932	1.179	.50	.75	6.00	25.00
	1933	1.721	.20	.60	5.00	17.50
	1934	1.795	.10	.40	2.00	12.50
	1935	3.678	.10	.40	1.50	10.00
	1936 with short 6					
		2.244	.10	.40	4.00	20.00
	1936 with long 6					
		Inc. Ab.	1.00	1.50	5.00	12.50
	1937	2.981	.10	.40	2.00	10.00
	1938	3.225	.10	.40	1.50	6.00
	1939	4.014	.10	.30	1.00	6.00
	1940 with round O					
		3.305	.10	.40	1.50	6.00
	1941	7.337	.10	.30	1.00	4.00
	1942	1.614	.50	1.00	2.00	15.00
	1950	5.823	—	.10	.50	3.00

IRON
World War I Issues
Similar to Y#45.

Y#	Date	Mintage	Fine	VF	XF	Unc
53	1917	4.576	2.50	5.00	10.00	25.00
	1918	4.982	4.00	8.00	15.00	40.00
	1919	2.923	8.00	15.00	25.00	55.00
	1920	1 Pc.	—	—	—	—

World War II Issues
Similar to Y#45.

Y#	Date	Mintage	Fine	VF	XF	Unc
70	1942	9.343	—	.30	1.50	6.00
	1943	6.999	—	.30	2.00	7.50
	1944	6.126	—	.30	2.00	7.50
	1945	4.773	—	.40	2.00	8.50
	1946	5.854	—	.40	2.00	7.00
	1947	9.536	—	.30	1.00	4.00
	1948	11.424	—	.30	1.50	4.00
	1949long 9					
		10.600	—	.20	1.00	3.50
	1949 short 9	I.A.	—	.20	1.00	3.50
	1950	13.323	—	.20	1.00	3.50

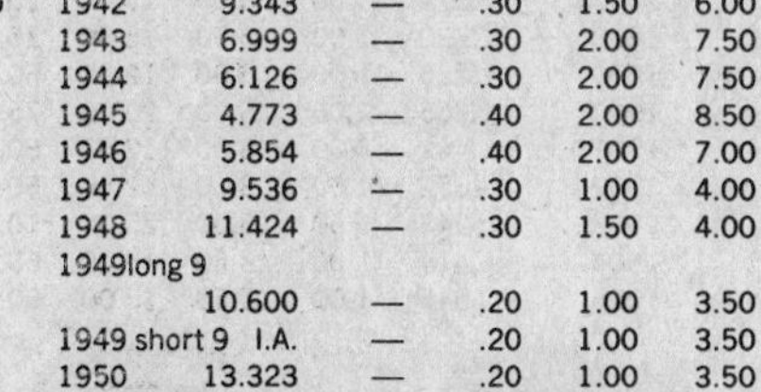

BRONZE

Y#	Date	Mintage	Fine	VF	XF	Unc
73	1952TS	3.011	—	.50	1.00	4.50
	1953TS	15.620	—	—	.60	3.50
	1954TS	12.706	—	—	.60	3.50
	1955TS	10.342	—	—	.60	3.50
	1956TS	13.890	—	—	.30	2.50
	1957TS	9.991	—	—	.30	2.50
	1958TS	10.106	—	—	.20	1.50
	1959TS	11.572	—	—	.50	2.50
	1960TS	11.093	—	—	.30	1.50
	1961TS	10.750	—	—	.30	2.00
	1961U	Inc. Ab.	—	2.50	5.00	17.50
	1962U	9.570	—	—	.30	1.25
	1963U	13.340	—	—	.30	1.25
	1964U	20.610	—	—	.20	.50
	1965U	23.144	—	—	.20	.50
	1966U	18.153	—	—	—	.50
	1967U	23.931	—	—	—	.30
	1968U	26.240	—	—	—	.20
	1969U	16.843	—	—	—	.20
	1970U	32.850	—	—	—	.15
	1971U	19.400	—	—	—	.15

5 ORE

Obv: Small lettering.

Y#	Date	Mintage	Fine	VF	XF	Unc
16	1874	.866	2.50	9.00	40.00	150.00
	1875/4	1.234	10.00	22.50	65.00	175.00
	1875	Inc. Ab.	2.00	7.50	35.00	125.00
	1876	.609	3.00	10.00	40.00	125.00
	1877	.514	15.00	45.00	150.00	450.00
	1878	.364	2.00	8.50	35.00	150.00
	1879	.350	12.50	30.00	125.00	300.00
	1880/70	.403	12.50	25.00	90.00	275.00
	1880	Inc. Ab.	12.00	25.00	90.00	250.00
	1881	.625	2.50	7.50	25.00	125.00
	1882/1	.825	22.50	50.00	175.00	400.00
	1882	Inc. Ab.	2.00	6.00	25.00	110.00
	1883	.578	2.00	6.00	22.50	100.00
	1884	.784	2.00	6.00	22.50	100.00
	1885	.282	3.50	12.00	30.00	125.00
	1886	.269	3.50	12.00	30.00	125.00
	1887	.251	4.00	12.50	35.00	150.00
	1888	.214	4.00	12.50	35.00	150.00
	1889	.220	4.00	10.00	30.00	100.00

Obv: Large lettering.

Y#	Date	Mintage	Fine	VF	XF	Unc
16a	1888	Inc. Ab.	75.00	125.00	175.00	300.00
	1889	Inc. Ab.	3.00	7.50	22.50	110.00
	1890	.339	3.00	7.50	22.50	110.00
	1891/81	.374	2.00	7.00	22.50	100.00
	1891	Inc. Ab.	1.75	5.00	20.00	100.00
	1892	.585	1.50	5.00	20.00	100.00
	1895	.529	1.50	5.00	20.00	100.00
	1896	.309	1.75	6.00	25.00	110.00
	1897	.570	1.00	3.50	15.00	75.00
	1898	.720	1.00	3.50	15.00	75.00
	1899	1.225	1.00	3.00	12.50	60.00
	1900	.365	2.00	5.00	20.00	75.00
	1901	.442	1.00	3.00	12.50	60.00
	1902	.652	1.00	3.00	12.50	60.00
	1903	.243	1.50	6.00	25.00	110.00
	1904	.414	1.00	3.50	15.00	60.00
	1905	.545	1.00	3.50	15.00	60.00

Obv. leg: SVERIGES VAL

Y#	Date	Mintage	Fine	VF	XF	Unc
34	1906	.565	1.50	3.00	12.50	50.00
	1907	1.953	.50	1.50	6.00	25.00

Y#	Date	Mintage	Fine	VF	XF	Unc
46	1909 with small cross	.917	1.50	7.50	20.00	75.00
	1909 with large cross	Inc. Ab.	10.00	30.00	90.00	250.00
	1910	.031	150.00	250.00	600.00	1250.
	1911	.778	1.50	4.00	22.50	110.00
	1912	.547	2.00	6.00	25.00	110.00
	1913	.762	1.00	4.00	22.50	110.00
	1914	.400	1.50	6.00	50.00	175.00
	1915	1.123	.50	2.50	17.50	60.00
	1916/5	.955	20.00	35.00	90.00	200.00
	1916 with short 6	Inc. Ab.	.50	2.50	17.50	60.00
	1916 with long 6	Inc. Ab.	.50	2.50	20.00	60.00
	1919	1.129	.50	2.00	12.50	50.00
	1920	2.360	.30	1.00	7.50	30.00
	1921	1.879	.30	1.00	7.50	30.00
	1922	.763	.50	2.00	15.00	75.00
	1923	.506	1.50	5.00	35.00	150.00
	1924	.900	.40	1.50	12.50	60.00
	1925	1.944	.30	1.50	5.00	40.00
	1926	1.742	.30	1.50	5.00	40.00
	1927	.036	100.00	200.00	400.00	1000.
	1928	.988	.30	1.50	6.00	30.00
	1929	1.670	.30	1.50	6.00	30.00
	1930	1.716	.30	1.50	6.00	30.00
	1931	1.131	.20	1.00	6.00	30.00
	1932	1.165	.20	1.00	6.00	30.00
	1933	.574	.20	1.00	20.00	90.00
	1934	1.710	.20	1.00	8.50	20.00
	1935	1.682	.20	.75	4.00	15.00
	1936 with short 6	1.626	.20	.75	7.50	20.00
	1936 with long 6	Inc. Ab.	.40	2.00	9.00	25.00
	1937	2.637	.20	.60	5.00	15.00
	1938	2.354	.20	.40	2.00	12.50
	1939	2.592	.20	.40	2.00	12.50
	1940	2.730	.20	.40	2.00	12.50
	1940 serif 4	Inc. Ab.	2.00	4.00	7.50	20.00
	1941	2.055	.20	.30	1.50	8.00
	1942	.395	1.50	2.50	12.50	45.00
	1950	12.560	—	.20	1.00	2.00

IRON
World War I Issues
Similar to Y#46.

Y#	Date	Mintage	Fine	VF	XF	Unc
54	1917	2.953	7.50	12.50	30.00	60.00
	1918	2.458	17.50	25.00	45.00	80.00
	1919	2.302	17.50	25.00	40.00	75.00

World War II Issues
similar to y#46.

Y#	Date	Mintage	Fine	VF	XF	Unc
71	1942	4.343	.20	.30	4.00	15.00
	1943	5.570	—	1.00	6.00	20.00
	1944	4.562	—	.50	2.50	20.00
	1945	3.771	—	.60	5.00	20.00
	1946	2.575	—	.75	4.50	20.00
	1947	6.035	—	.50	3.00	10.00
	1948	6.250	—	.40	3.00	10.00
	1949	7.840	—	.40	2.50	10.00
	1950	5.290	—	.30	2.00	10.00

BRONZE

Y#	Date	Mintage	Fine	VF	XF	Unc
74	1952TS	3.065	—	—	2.00	8.00
	1953TS	12.330	—	—	1.00	7.50
	1954TS	9.700	—	—	1.00	7.50
	1955TS	6.000	—	—	.75	7.50
	1956TS	8.000	—	—	.75	7.50
	1957TS	6.280	—	—	.75	7.50
	1958TS	9.500	—	—	.50	7.50
	1959TS	8.971	—	—	.50	7.50
	1960TS	8.585	—	—	.30	4.00
	1961TS	7.718	—	—	.40	4.50
	1961U	Inc. Ab.	—	—	1.00	12.50
	1962U	22.306	—	—	.20	1.50
	1963U	17.207	—	—	.20	1.50
	1964U	10.601	—	—	.30	2.00
	1964U 50 in crown	Inc. Ab.	2.50	4.50	7.50	12.50
	1965U	22.985	—	—	—	.50
	1966U	18.140	—	—	—	.50
	1967U	20.776	—	—	—	.50
	1968U	28.270	—	—	—	.25
	1969U	26.887	—	—	—	.25
	1970U	30.320	—	—	—	.25
	1971U	17.060	—	—	—	.25

Y#	Date	Mintage	Fine	VF	XF	Unc
88	1972U	61.886	—	—	—	.10
	1973U	67.865	—	—	—	.10

Y#	Date	Mintage	Fine	VF	XF	Unc
91	1976	9.345	—	—	—	.10
	1977	31.037	—	—	—	.10
91	1978	—	—	—	—	.10
	1979	—	—	—	—	—

10 ORE

1.4500 gm., .400 SILVER, .0186 oz ASW
Obv: Small lettering

Y#	Date	Mintage	Fine	VF	XF	Unc
19	1874ST	2.875	12.00	17.50	40.00	100.00
	1875/74	1.503	55.00	80.00	135.00	300.00
	1875ST	Inc. Ab.	50.00	75.00	125.00	275.00
	1876/5	1.814	16.00	25.00	65.00	130.00
	1876ST	Inc. Ab.	12.50	20.00	55.00	120.00

Obv: Large lettering

Y#	Date	Mintage	Fine	VF	XF	Unc
27	1880EB	.851	25.00	45.00	75.00	150.00
	1881EB	.763	25.00	45.00	75.00	150.00
	1882/1EB	.735	40.00	60.00	100.00	200.00
	1882EB	Inc. Ab.	40.00	60.00	100.00	200.00
	1883EB	.694	22.50	40.00	60.00	125.00
	1884EB	1.560	6.00	12.50	30.00	90.00
	1887E.B.	1.513	6.00	12.50	30.00	90.00
	1890EB	.921	6.00	12.50	30.00	90.00
	1891EB	.827	6.00	12.50	30.00	90.00
	1892EB	1.215	2.50	6.00	22.50	60.00
	1894EB	1.733	1.25	4.00	12.50	30.00
	1896EB	2.084	1.25	4.00	12.50	30.00
	1897EB	.819	2.00	6.00	15.00	45.00
	1898EB	2.087	1.00	3.00	12.50	30.00
	1899EB	2.041	1.00	3.00	12.50	30.00
	1900EB	1.173	1.00	3.00	12.50	30.00
	1902EB	1.946	1.00	3.00	12.50	30.00
	1903EB	1.509	1.00	3.00	12.50	30.00
	1904EB	3.280	.75	2.00	7.50	22.50

Obv: New leg: SVERIGES VAL

Y#	Date	Mintage	Fine	VF	XF	Unc
35	1907EB	7.320	.60	1.50	5.00	15.00

Y#	Date	Mintage	Fine	VF	XF	Unc
47	1909W	1.610	3.50	6.50	20.00	65.00
	1911W	3.181	.75	3.00	9.00	35.00
	1913W	1.581	1.50	6.00	17.50	45.00
	1914W	1.571	1.00	4.00	12.50	35.00
	1915W	1.547	1.00	4.00	12.50	35.00
	1916/5W	3.035	12.50	22.50	45.00	110.00
	1916W	Inc. Ab.	1.00	3.00	10.00	35.00
	1917W	4.996	BV	1.50	4.00	15.00
	1918W	4.114	BV	1.50	4.00	15.00
	1919W	5.740	BV	1.50	4.00	15.00
	1927W	2.510	BV	1.00	4.00	20.00
	1928G	2.901	BV	1.00	4.00	20.00
	1929G	5.506	BV	1.00	3.00	15.00
	1930G	3.222	BV	1.00	3.00	15.00
	1931G	4.272	BV	.75	2.00	12.50
	1933G	1.948	BV	.75	5.00	20.00
	1934G	4.059	BV	.60	1.00	6.00
	1935G	2.426	BV	.60	1.00	6.00
	1936G with short 6	5.097	2.50	7.00	15.00	60.00
	1936G with long 6	Inc. Ab.	BV	.60	1.00	6.00
	1937G	5.117	BV	.60	1.00	7.00
	1938G	7.428	BV	.60	1.00	7.00
	1939G	2.021	BV	.75	2.50	10.00
	1940G	3.017	BV	.60	1.00	4.00
	1941G	9.106	BV	.60	1.00	4.00
	1942G	3.692	BV	.60	1.00	4.00

NICKEL-BRONZE

Y#	Date	Mintage	Fine	VF	XF	Unc
55	1920W	3.612	.50	2.00	8.00	32.50
	1921W	2.270	.50	2.00	8.00	32.50
	1923W	2.144	1.00	3.50	10.00	40.00
	1924W	1.600	1.00	6.00	15.00	75.00
	1925W	1.472	1.00	6.00	15.00	75.00
	1940G	3.374	.20	.50	2.50	15.00
	1941	.816	.60	2.00	7.50	35.00
70	1946TS	4.117	.10	.30	1.50	5.00
	1947TS	4.133	.10	.30	1.50	5.00

1.4400 gm., .400 SILVER, .0185 oz ASW

Y#	Date	Mintage	Fine	VF	XF	Unc
64	1942G	1.600	BV	BV	1.50	6.00
	1943G	7.661	BV	BV	1.00	4.00
	1944G	12.277	BV	BV	.75	2.50
	1945G	11.703	BV	BV	.75	2.50
	1945TS	Inc. Ab.	BV	BV	1.50	6.00
	1945ts/g	Inc.Ab.	BV	BV	2.50	8.50
	1946/5 with open 6	3.576	4.50	7.50	12.50	27.50
	1946TS with open 6	Inc. Ab.	BV	BV	1.50	5.00
	1947TS	7.293	BV	BV	1.00	2.50
	1948TS	10.419	BV	BV	.75	2.50
	1949TS	12.044	BV	BV	BV	2.00
	1950TS	31.824	BV	BV	BV	1.50

Y#	Date	Mintage	Fine	VF	XF	Unc
75	1952TS	4.660	BV	BV	.75	4.50
	1953TS	28.484	BV	BV	BV	3.00
	1954TS	15.913	BV	BV	BV	5.00
	1955TS	16.687	BV	BV	BV	5.00
	1956TS	21.986	BV	BV	BV	2.00
	1957TS	21.294	BV	BV	BV	2.00
	1958TS	19.605	BV	BV	BV	2.00
	1959TS	18.523	BV	BV	BV	2.50
	1960TS	16.610	BV	BV	BV	1.75
	1961TS	17.626	BV	BV	BV	2.00
	1961U	Inc. Ab.	BV	BV	BV	2.50
	1962U	7.119	BV	BV	BV	2.00

COPPER-NICKEL

Y#	Date	Mintage	Fine	VF	XF	Unc
83	1962U	8.814	—	—	.20	2.50
	1963U	28.170	—	.10	.20	1.00
	1964U	35.550	—	—	.10	.75
	1965U	21.781	—	—	.10	.50
	1966U	27.060	—	—	.10	.50
	1967U	18.245	—	—	.10	.40
	1968U	55.490	—	.10	.20	.30
	1969U	55.880	—	—	—	.30
	1970U	61.280	—	—	—	.30
	1971U	30.120	—	—	—	.30
	1972U	36.750	—	—	—	.20
	1973U	152.184	—	—	—	.10

Y#	Date	Mintage	Fine	VF	XF	Unc
92	1976(U)	9.041	—	—	—	.10
	1977(U)	44.517	—	—	—	.10
	1978(U)	—	—	—	—	.10
	1979(U)	—	—	—	—	—

25 ORE

2.4200 gm., .600 SILVER, .0467 oz ASW
Obv: Small lettering

Y#	Date	Mintage	Fine	VF	XF	Unc
20	1874ST	2.100	15.00	25.00	55.00	150.00
	1875/4	1.131	40.00	65.00	110.00	350.00
	1875ST	Inc. Ab.	35.00	60.00	100.00	325.00
	1876/5	2.125	20.00	25.00	65.00	200.00
	1876ST	Inc. Ab.	15.00	20.00	55.00	150.00
	1877EB	.894	15.00	25.00	60.00	175.00
	1878/7	.859	60.00	100.00	175.00	500.00
	1878EB	Inc. Ab.	60.00	100.00	175.00	500.00

Obv: Large lettering

Y#	Date	Mintage	Fine	VF	XF	Unc
28	1880EB	1.180	6.00	15.00	50.00	150.00
	1881EB with large thick cross	1.392	4.00	8.00	30.00	100.00
	1883EB	1.100	3.00	7.50	22.50	90.00
	1885EB	1.168	3.50	8.00	30.00	100.00
	1889EB	.422	6.00	10.00	45.00	150.00
	1890EB	.469	6.00	10.00	30.00	100.00
	1896EB	.794	2.00	5.00	20.00	70.00
	1897EB	1.097	1.50	3.00	10.00	45.00
	1898EB	1.458	1.50	3.00	10.00	45.00
	1899EB	1.458	1.50	3.00	10.00	45.00
	1902EB	1.250	1.50	3.00	10.00	45.00
	1904EB	.693	1.50	3.00	10.00	45.00
	1905EB	.732	1.50	3.00	10.00	45.00

Obv: New leg: SVERIGES VAL

Y#	Date	Mintage	Fine	VF	XF	Unc
36	1907EB	3.223	BV	2.00	6.00	20.00

Y#	Date	Mintage	Fine	VF	XF	Unc
48	1910W with small cross	2.044	17.50	25.00	40.00	100.00
	1910W with large cross	Inc. Ab.	BV	2.00	10.00	40.00
	1912W	1.014	2.00	4.00	20.00	60.00
	1914W	3.719	BV	2.50	10.00	30.00
	1916W	1.270	BV	4.00	17.50	55.00
	1917W	1.657	BV	2.00	10.00	35.00
	1918W	2.365	BV	2.00	10.00	35.00
	1919W	3.205	BV	2.00	8.00	25.00
	1927W	1.688	BV	2.50	8.00	27.50
	1928G	.836	2.00	4.00	17.50	45.00
	1929G	1.125	BV	2.00	8.00	27.50
	1930G	3.490	BV	1.50	3.00	12.50
	1931G	1.392	BV	1.50	3.00	12.50
	1932G	1.133	BV	1.50	3.00	12.50
	1933G	.964	BV	2.00	10.00	35.00
	1934G	1.404	BV	BV	2.00	10.00
	1936G	1.852	BV	BV	2.00	10.00
	1937G	3.290	BV	BV	BV	6.00
	1938G	3.679	BV	BV	BV	6.00
	1939G	2.136	BV	BV	BV	6.00
	1940G	2.302	BV	BV	BV	6.00
	1941G	1.960	BV	BV	BV	6.00

NICKEL-BRONZE
Similar to 10 Ore, Y#55.

Y#	Date	Mintage	Fine	VF	XF	Unc
56	1921W	1.355	2.00	4.50	25.00	90.00
	1940G	2.333	.40	1.00	2.00	25.00
	1941G	1.057	.40	1.00	2.00	25.00
	1946TS	2.066	.20	.40	1.50	5.00
	1947TS	1.594	.20	.50	1.50	5.00

2.3200 gm., .400 SILVER, .0298 oz ASW

Y#	Date	Mintage	Fine	VF	XF	Unc
65	1943G	9.855	BV	BV	1.00	6.00
	1944G	9.532	BV	BV	1.00	6.00
	1945G	5.363	BV	BV	1.50	6.00
	1945TS	Inc. Ab.	BV	2.00	4.25	6.00
	1945G/TS	I.A.	BV	BV	2.00	6.00
	1946TS	2.250	BV	BV	2.00	10.00
	1947TS	5.633	BV	BV	1.00	4.00
	1948TS	3.191	BV	BV	1.00	4.00
	1949TS	5.812	BV	BV	1.00	4.00
	1950TS	12.059	BV	BV	1.00	2.00

Y#	Date	Mintage	Fine	VF	XF	Unc
76	1952TS	2.114	BV	BV	1.25	10.00
	1953TS	18.177	BV	BV	BV	5.00
	1954TS	9.492	BV	BV	BV	5.00
	1955TS	7.633	BV	BV	BV	5.00
	1956TS	10.931	BV	BV	BV	5.00
	1957TS	12.500	BV	BV	BV	5.00
	1958TS	6.884	BV	BV	BV	5.00
	1959TS	4.772	BV	BV	BV	2.00
	1960TS	1.000	BV	BV	BV	4.50
	1961TS	11.755	BV	BV	BV	2.00

COPPER-NICKEL

Y#	Date	Mintage	Fine	VF	XF	Unc
84	1962U	4.426	—	—	.40	2.50
	1963U	26.710	—	—	.30	1.00
	1964U	17.230	—	—	.30	1.00
	1965U	6.960	—	—	.20	.50
	1966U	12.932	—	—	.20	.50
	1967U	28.050	—	—	.10	.30
	1968U	14.370	—	—	.10	.40
	1969U	20.214	—	—	—	.30
	1970U	24.260	—	—	—	.30
	1971U	10.060	—	—	—	.30
	1972U	13.270	—	—	—	.15
	1973U	128.506	—	—	—	.15

Y#	Date	Mintage	Fine	VF	XF	Unc
93	1976(U)	6.085	—	—	—	.15
	1977(U)	5.509	—	—	—	.15
	1978(U)	—	—	—	—	.15
	1979(U)	—	—	—	—	—

50 ORE

5.0000 gm., .600 SILVER, .0965 oz ASW

Y#	Date	Mintage	Fine	VF	XF	Unc
21	1875ST	1.908	7.50	20.00	75.00	225.00
	1877EB	.149	60.00	100.00	275.00	750.00
	1878EB	.319	12.50	40.00	150.00	400.00
	1880EB	.188	25.00	65.00	200.00	500.00
	1881EB	.268	17.50	45.00	165.00	400.00
	1883EB	.770	6.00	17.50	60.00	200.00
	1898EB	.505	5.00	12.50	45.00	150.00
	1899EB	.720	5.00	12.50	45.00	140.00

Obv: New leg: SVERIGES VAL

Y#	Date	Mintage	Fine	VF	XF	Unc
37	1906EB	.319	4.00	12.50	40.00	125.00
	1907EB	.803	3.00	8.00	25.00	90.00

Y#	Date	Mintage	Fine	VF	XF	Unc
49	1911W	.473	3.00	10.00	40.00	125.00
	1912W	.483	3.00	10.00	40.00	125.00
	1914W	.378	3.00	10.00	40.00	125.00
	1916/5 W	.537	27.50	35.00	60.00	150.00
	1916W	Inc. Ab.	3.00	10.00	40.00	125.00

Y#	Date	Mintage	Fine	VF	XF	Unc
49	1919W	.458	3.00	8.00	32.00	100.00
	1927W	.672	BV	3.00	20.00	60.00
	1928G	1.135	BV	3.00	15.00	40.00
	1929G	.471	BV	3.00	25.00	55.00
	1930G	.548	BV	3.00	20.00	50.00
	1931G	.671	BV	BV	10.00	35.00
	1933G	.548	BV	3.00	12.50	40.00
	1934G	.613	BV	BV	10.00	30.00
	1935G	.691	BV	BV	10.00	30.00
	1936G with short 6					
		.823	BV	BV	10.00	30.00
	1936G with long 6					
		Inc. Ab.	3.00	8.00	25.00	100.00
	1938G	.442	BV	BV	10.00	30.00
	1939G	.922	BV	BV	4.00	17.50

NICKEL-BRONZE
Similar to 10 Ore, Y#55.

Y#	Date	Mintage	Fine	VF	XF	Unc
57	1920W	.480	1.00	4.00	45.00	150.00
	1921W	.215	7.00	17.50	100.00	250.00
	1924W	.645	1.00	4.50	45.00	175.00
	1940G	1.341	.30	.50	2.00	35.00
	1946TS	1.426	.30	.60	2.00	17.50
	1947TS	1.032	.30	.60	2.00	17.50

4.8000 gm., .400 SILVER, .0617 oz ASW

Y#	Date	Mintage	Fine	VF	XF	Unc
66	1943G	.785	2.50	5.00	12.50	65.00
	1944G	1.540	BV	BV	2.00	10.00
	1945G	2.585	BV	BV	2.00	10.00
	1946TS	1.091	BV	BV	3.00	17.50
	1947TS	1.771	BV	BV	2.00	10.00
	1948TS	1.731	BV	BV	2.00	10.00
	1949TS	1.883	BV	BV	2.00	8.00
	1950TS	3.354	BV	BV	2.00	6.00

Y#	Date	Mintage	Fine	VF	XF	Unc
77	1952TS	.466	BV	BV	4.00	25.00
	1953TS	4.396	BV	BV	3.00	20.00
	1954TS	5.779	BV	BV	3.00	20.00
	1955TS	2.700	BV	BV	3.50	25.00
	1956TS	7.057	BV	BV	2.50	20.00
	1957TS	2.405	BV	BV	3.50	25.00
	1958TS	1.660	BV	BV	3.50	25.00
	1961TS	2.775	BV	BV	2.00	15.00

COPPER-NICKEL

Y#	Date	Mintage	Fine	VF	XF	Unc
85	1962U	1.400	—	—	1.00	10.00
	1963U	5.808	—	—	.75	4.00
	1964U	5.324	—	—	.75	4.00
	1965U	7.322	—	—	.30	1.50
	1966U	5.440	—	—	.30	1.00
	1967U	7.890	—	—	.20	1.00
	1968U	7.600	—	—	.10	.75
	1969U	7.265	—	—	.10	.75
	1970U	10.350	—	—	—	.50
	1971U	5.420	—	—	—	.50
	1972U	7.390	—	—	—	.30
	1973U	89.263	—	—	—	.30

Y#	Date	Mintage	Fine	VF	XF	Unc
94	1976	5.621	—	—	—	.35
	1977	10.360	—	—	—	.30
	1978	—	—	—	—	.30
	1979	—	—	—	—	—

KRONA

7.5000 gm., .800 SILVER, .1929 oz ASW

Y#	Date	Mintage	Fine	VF	XF	Unc
22	1875ST	3.531	6.00	25.00	90.00	275.00
	1876/5ST	2.510	15.00	30.00	150.00	425.00
	1876ST	Inc. Ab.	6.00	25.00	100.00	325.00

Obv: OCH replaces O in royal title.

Y#	Date	Mintage	Fine	VF	XF	Unc
22a	1877EB	.554	10.00	30.00	150.00	500.00
	1879EB	.077	45.00	75.00	450.00	1200.
	1880EB	.177	15.00	40.00	200.00	550.00
	1881EB	.619	10.00	40.00	175.00	500.00
	1883EB	.205	15.00	45.00	200.00	650.00
	1884EB	.382	10.00	30.00	175.00	500.00
	1887EB	.058	50.00	125.00	450.00	1200.
	1888EB	.062	50.00	125.00	450.00	1200.
	1889EB	.425	8.00	30.00	150.00	450.00

Obv: No initials below bust.

Y#	Date	Mintage	Fine	VF	XF	Unc
29	1890EB	.593	6.00	25.00	100.00	300.00
	1897EB	.735	6.00	15.00	60.00	150.00
	1898EB	1.860	BV	12.00	50.00	150.00
	1901/898EB	.271	15.00	30.00	140.00	275.00
	1901EB	Inc. Ab.	6.00	20.00	75.00	175.00
	1903EB	.473	6.00	15.00	45.00	150.00
	1904EB	.564	6.00	12.00	40.00	150.00

Obv: New leg: SVERIGES KONUNG

Y#	Date	Mintage	Fine	VF	XF	Unc
38	1906EB	.427	6.00	12.00	45.00	150.00
	1907EB	1.058	6.00	10.00	30.00	120.00

Y#	Date	Mintage	Fine	VF	XF	Unc
50	1910W	.643	BV	6.00	40.00	90.00
	1912W	.303	6.00	15.00	100.00	175.00
	1913W	.353	6.00	10.00	60.00	150.00
	1914W	.622	BV	6.00	40.00	90.00
	1915w	1.416	BV	6.00	25.00	75.00
	1916/5W	1.139	8.00	15.00	75.00	200.00
	1916W	Inc. Ab.	BV	6.00	30.00	80.00
	1918W	.258	8.00	20.00	100.00	250.00
	1923W	.746	BV	6.00	20.00	60.00
	1924W with dots in date					
		2.066	BV	BV	15.00	45.00
	1924W without dots in date					
		Inc. Ab.	BV	BV	15.00	45.00
	1925W	.370	BV	6.00	50.00	125.00
	1926W	.465	BV	BV	25.00	60.00
	1927G	.401	BV	BV	40.00	60.00
	1928G	.739	BV	BV	20.00	65.00
	1929G	1.346	BV	BV	15.00	35.00

Y#	Date	Mintage	Fine	VF	XF	Unc
50	1930G	1.744	BV	BV	7.50	30.00
	1931G	1.008	BV	BV	6.00	25.00
	1932G	1.036	BV	BV	6.00	25.00
	1933G	1.045	BV	BV	6.00	20.00
	1934G	.586	BV	BV	15.00	45.00
	1935G	1.604	BV	BV	BV	10.00
	1936/5 G	3.222	BV	BV	BV	10.00
	1936G	Inc. Ab.	BV	BV	BV	10.00
	1937G	2.667	BV	BV	BV	10.00
	1938G	1.911	BV	BV	BV	10.00
	1939G	7.589	BV	BV	BV	7.50
	1940G	6.917	BV	BV	BV	7.50
	1941/4G	2.183	BV	BV	6.00	12.50
	1941G	Inc. Ab.	BV	BV	BV	8.00
	1942G	.240	45.00	65.00	125.00	200.00

7.0000 gm. .400 SILVER, .0900 oz ASW

Y#	Date	Mintage	Fine	VF	XF	Unc
67	1942G	5.650	BV	BV	3.00	15.00
	1943G	7.916	BV	BV	3.00	15.00
	1944G	6.943	BV	BV	3.00	8.00
	1945G	7.631	BV	BV	3.00	8.00
	1945TS	Inc. Ab.	BV	BV	5.00	15.00
	1945TS/G	I.A.	BV	BV	3.00	15.00
	1946TS	19.247	BV	BV	3.00	6.00
	1947TS	9.129	BV	BV	3.00	6.00
	1948TS	10.431	BV	BV	3.00	6.00
	1949TS	8.228	BV	BV	3.00	6.00
	1950TS	5.310	BV	BV	3.00	6.00

Y#	Date	Mintage	Fine	VF	XF	Unc
78	1952TS	1.102	BV	BV	5.00	25.00
	1953TS	3.306	BV	BV	BV	22.50
	1954TS	6.461	BV	BV	BV	20.00
	1955TS	4.141	BV	BV	BV	25.00
	1956TS	6.227	BV	BV	BV	20.00
	1957TS	3.544	BV	BV	BV	12.00
	1958TS	1.439	BV	BV	10.00	35.00
	1959TS	1.187	BV	3.00	14.00	60.00
	1960TS	4.085	BV	BV	BV	10.00
	1961TS	7.506	BV	BV	BV	10.00
	1961U	Inc. Ab.	BV	BV	BV	15.00
	1962U	6.589	BV	BV	BV	8.00
	1963U	14.228	BV	BV	BV	5.00
	1964U	15.973	BV	BV	BV	3.00
	1965U	18.639	BV	BV	BV	2.75
	1966U	19.456	BV	BV	BV	2.75
	1967U	20.176	BV	BV	BV	2.75
	1968U	12.286	BV	BV	BV	2.75

CLAD COPPER-NICKEL

Y#	Date	Mintage	Fine	VF	XF	Unc
78a	1968U	5.117	—	—	.35	1.25
	1969U	32.090	—	—	.35	1.50
	1970U	26.620	—	—	.25	.60
	1971U	18.390	—	—	.25	.60
	1972U	21.940	—	—	—	.30
	1973U	156.393	—	—	—	.25

Y#	Date	Mintage	Fine	VF	XF	Unc
95	1976(U)	9.213	—	—	—	.45
	1977(U)	80.478	—	—	—	.35
	1978(U)	—	—	—	—	.35

Y#	Date	Mintage	Fine	VF	XF	Unc
95	1979(U)	—	—	—	—	—

2 KRONOR

15.0000 gm., .800 SILVER, .3858 oz ASW

Y#	Date	Mintage	Fine	VF	XF	Unc
23	1876EB wide date, 6mm wide, large E.B.					
		.370	600.00	1250.	2500.	5000.
	1876EB wide date, small E.B.					
		Inc. Ab.	300.00	750.00	1250.	2500.
	1876EB smaller date, 5mm wide					
		Inc. Ab.	17.50	45.00	300.00	750.00
	1877EB	.168	20.00	60.00	325.00	800.00
	1878EB	.193	20.00	50.00	325.00	800.00
	1880/76EB	.128	—	—	—	—
	1880EB	Inc. Ab.	30.00	80.00	600.00	1700.

Obv: OCH replaces O in royal title.

Y#	Date	Mintage	Fine	VF	XF	Unc
23a	1878EB	.022	600.00	1000.	1750.	4000.
	1880EB	.065	25.00	75.00	375.00	1400.

Obv: No initials below bust.

Y#	Date	Mintage	Fine	VF	XF	Unc
30	1890EB	.072	20.00	65.00	450.00	800.00
	1892EB	.087	20.00	60.00	450.00	800.00
	1893EB	.049	45.00	100.00	500.00	1000.
	1897EB	.207	12.00	25.00	125.00	325.00
	1898EB	.141	12.00	27.50	135.00	325.00
	1900EB	.131	15.00	30.00	150.00	350.00
	1903EB	.064	50.00	75.00	375.00	750.00
	1904EB	.175	12.00	25.00	125.00	300.00

Silver Jubilee

Y#	Date	Mintage	Fine	VF	XF	Unc
31	1897EB	.246	12.50	20.00	30.00	40.00

Obv: New leg: SVERIGES KONUNG

Y#	Date	Mintage	Fine	VF	XF	Unc
39	1906EB	.112	17.50	30.00	90.00	225.00
	1907EB	.301	15.00	25.00	65.00	150.00

Golden Wedding Anniversary

Y#	Date	Mintage	Fine	VF	XF	Unc
40	1907EB	.251	BV	12.50	17.50	35.00

Y#	Date	Mintage	Fine	VF	XF	Unc
51	1910W	.375	12.50	20.00	50.00	100.00
	1910W mintmaster's initial further away from date					
		Inc. Ab.	30.00	90.00	250.00	600.00
	1912W	.157	15.00	35.00	75.00	225.00
	1913W	.305	12.50	20.00	50.00	100.00
	1914W	.192	12.50	20.00	65.00	150.00
	1915W	.156	12.50	20.00	65.00	150.00
	1922W	.202	BV	12.50	35.00	75.00
	1924W	.199	BV	12.50	40.00	90.00
	1926W	.222	BV	12.50	30.00	65.00
	1928G	.160	BV	15.00	50.00	100.00
	1929g	.184	BV	12.50	35.00	75.00
	1930G	.178	BV	12.50	30.00	60.00
	1931G	.211	BV	BV	12.50	25.00
	1934G	.273	BV	BV	12.50	20.00
	1935G	.211	BV	BV	12.50	20.00
	1936G	.491	BV	BV	12.50	17.50
	1937G	.130	12.50	15.00	25.00	65.00
	1938G	.639	BV	BV	12.50	15.00
	1939G	1.200	BV	BV	12.50	15.00
	1940G	.518	BV	BV	12.50	15.00
	1940G serif 4					
		Inc. Ab.	BV	12.50	15.00	25.00

400th Anniversary of Political Liberty

Y#	Date	Mintage	Fine	VF	XF	Unc
58	1921W	.265	BV	12.50	15.00	25.00

300th Anniversary Death of Gustaf II Adolf

Y#	Date	Mintage	Fine	VF	XF	Unc
59	1932G	.254	BV	12.50	15.00	25.00

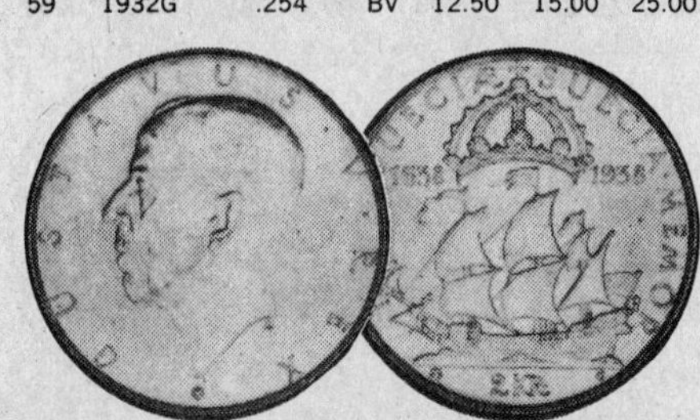

300th Anniversary Settlement of Delaware

Y#	Date	Mintage	Fine	VF	XF	Unc
61	1938G	.509	BV	12.50	15.00	20.00

14.0000 gm., .400 SILVER, .1800 oz ASW

Y#	Date	Mintage	Fine	VF	XF	Unc
68	1942G	.200	BV	BV	6.00	17.50
	1943G	.272	7.50	12.50	17.50	60.00
	1944G	.627	BV	BV	5.50	8.00
	1945G	.970	BV	BV	5.50	8.00
	1945TS	Inc. Ab.	BV	BV	6.00	15.00
	1945TS/G	I.A.	BV	BV	5.50	10.00
	1946TS	.978	BV	BV	5.50	8.00
	1947TS	1.466	BV	BV	5.50	8.00
	1948TS	.282	BV	BV	6.00	15.00
	1949TS	.332	BV	BV	6.00	12.50
	1950/1TS	3.727	BV	BV	5.50	7.50
	1950TS	Inc. Ab.	BV	BV	5.50	7.50

Y#	Date	Mintage	Fine	VF	XF	Unc
79	1952TS	.520	BV	5.50	7.50	15.00
	1953TS	1.009	BV	BV	5.50	8.00
	1954TS	2.301	BV	BV	5.50	6.50
	1955TS	1.138	BV	BV	6.00	10.00
	1956TS	1.709	BV	BV	5.50	8.00
	1957TS	.689	BV	BV	6.00	10.00
	1958TS	.777	BV	BV	5.50	6.50
	1959TS	.909	BV	BV	6.00	15.00
	1961TS	.534	BV	BV	6.00	15.00
	1963U	1.469	BV	BV	BV	6.00
	1964U	1.213	BV	BV	BV	6.00
	1965U	1.190	BV	BV	BV	6.00
	1966U	.989	BV	BV	BV	6.00

COPPER-NICKEL

Y#	Date	Mintage	Fine	VF	XF	Unc
79a	1968U	1.171	—	—	—	.75
	1969U	1.148	—	—	—	.75
	1970U	1.160	—	—	—	.65
	1971U	1.213	—	—	—	1.00

5 KRONOR

2.2402 gm., .900 GOLD, .0648 oz AGW

Y#	Date	Mintage	VF	XF	Unc
24	1881EB	.065	125.00	200.00	250.00
	1882EB	.030	300.00	400.00	600.00
	1883EB	.028	200.00	350.00	425.00
	1886/3EB	.042	150.00	225.00	450.00
	1886EB	Inc. Ab.	150.00	225.00	275.00
	1894EB	.051	125.00	200.00	250.00
	1899EB	.104	120.00	175.00	200.00

Obv: Larger head

Y#	Date	Mintage	VF	XF	Unc
24a	1901EB	.109	110.00	150.00	200.00

Y#	Date	Mintage	VF	XF	Unc
62	1920W	.103	110.00	175.00	225.00

25.0000 gm., SILVER, .7234 oz ASW
500th Anniversary of Riksdag

Y#	Date	Mintage	Fine	VF	XF	Unc
60	1935G	.664	BV	BV	22.50	25.00

18.0000 gm., .400 SILVER, .2315 oz ASW
70th Birthday of Gustaf VI Adolf

Y#	Date	Mintage	Fine	VF	XF	Unc
81	1952TS	.242	—	27.50	37.50	55.00

Regular issue

Y#	Date	Mintage	Fine	VF	XF	Unc
80	1954TS	1.510	BV	BV	BV	8.50
	1955TS	3.569	BV	BV	BV	7.50
	1971U	.356	BV	BV	BV	7.00

Constitution Sesquincentennial

Y#	Date	Mintage	Fine	VF	XF	Unc
82	1959TS	.504	BV	BV	8.00	20.00

80th Birthday of Gustaf VI Adolf

Y#	Date	Mintage	Fine	VF	XF	Unc
86	1962U	.250	12.50	35.00	55.00	85.00

Parliament Reform

Y#	Date	Mintage	Fine	VF	XF	Unc
87	1966U	1.024	BV	BV	BV	8.00

COPPER-NICKEL

Y#	Date	Mintage	Fine	VF	XF	Unc
89	1972U	.108	—	—	—	1.75
	1973(U)	1.247	—	—	—	2.50

Y#	Date	Mintage	Fine	VF	XF	Unc
96	1976(U)	4.611	—	—	—	2.00
	1977(U)	3.985	—	—	—	2.00
	1978(U)	—	—	—	—	2.00
	1979(U)	—	—	—	—	—

10 KRONOR

4.4803 gm., .900 GOLD, .1296 oz AGW

Y#	Date	Mintage	VF	XF	Unc
25	1873ST	.200	175.00	250.00	325.00
	1874/3ST	.261	125.00	200.00	250.00
	1874ST	Inc. Ab.	120.00	175.00	225.00
	1876ST	.102	125.00	200.00	250.00

Obv: OCH substituted for O. in royal title.

Y#	Date	Mintage	VF	XF	Unc
25a	1876EB	.068	250.00	400.00	525.00
	1877EB	.055	350.00	525.00	650.00
	1880EB	.027	350.00	525.00	650.00
	1883EB L.A.	.149	130.00	200.00	250.00
	1883LA	Inc. Ab.	150.00	225.00	275.00
	1883L.A. larger L.A.	Inc. Ab.	180.00	250.00	325.00
	1894EB	.036	180.00	250.00	325.00
	1895EB	.065	150.00	225.00	275.00

Obv: Larger head.

Y#	Date	Mintage	VF	XF	Unc
25b	1901EB	.213	110.00	160.00	200.00

18.0000 gm., .830 SILVER, .4803 oz ASW
90th Birthday of Gustaf VI Adolf

Y#	Date	Mintage	Fine	VF	XF	Unc
90	1972U	2.000	BV		BV	15.00

20 KRONOR

8.9606 gm., .900 GOLD, .2593 oz AGW
Obv: Head right. Rev: Crowned draped arms.

Y#	Date	Mintage	VF	XF	Unc
26	1873ST	.115	350.00	550.00	700.00
	1874ST	.240	325.00	475.00	600.00
	1875ST	.359	300.00	450.00	550.00
	1876/5ST	.026	1200.	1800.	2500.
	1876ST	Inc. Ab.	1200.	1800.	2500.

Rev: Arms wider

Y#	Date	Mintage	VF	XF	Unc
26c	1876EB	.173	325.00	475.00	600.00
	1877EB	.103	350.00	525.00	650.00

Obv: OCH substituted for O. in royal title.

Y#	Date	Mintage	VF	XF	Unc
26a	1877EB	.083	350.00	550.00	700.00
	1878/7EB	.245	350.00	525.00	650.00
	1878EB	Inc. Ab.	325.00	475.00	600.00
	1879EB	.075	800.00	1200.	1600.
	1880EB	.127	350.00	525.00	650.00
	1881EB	.047	1000.	1500.	2000.
	1884EB	.191	300.00	450.00	550.00
	1885EB	6,250	3000.	5000.	6000.
	1886EB	.173	325.00	475.00	600.00
	1887EB	.059	1000.	1500.	2000.
	1889EB	.202	300.00	450.00	550.00
	1890EB	.155	350.00	525.00	650.00
	1895EB	.135	350.00	525.00	650.00
	1898EB	.313	300.00	450.00	550.00
	1899EB	.261	300.00	450.00	550.00

Obv: Larger head.

Y#	Date	Mintage	VF	XF	Unc
26b	1900EB	.104	600.00	800.00	1000.
	1901EB	.227	350.00	525.00	650.00
	1902EB	.114	400.00	600.00	800.00

Y#	Date	Mintage	VF	XF	Unc
63	1925W	.387	750.00	1200.	1500.

50 KRONOR

27.0300 gm., .925 SILVER, .8039 oz ASW
Constitutional Reform

Y#	Date	Mintage	VF	XF	Unc
97	1975	.500	BV	BV	25.00

Wedding Commemorative
Obv: Facing heads of Queen Silvia and King Carl XVI.
Rev: Crowned and supported arms.

Y#	Date	Mintage	VF	XF	Unc
98	1976	4.109	BV	BV	25.00

TRADE COINS

DUCAT

.986 GOLD
Similar to 1/6 Riksdaler, C#66a.

C#	Date	Mintage	Fine	VF	XF
71	1771	—	—	Rare	—
	1772	4,536	1000.	2000.	3600.
	1773	3,636	1000.	2000.	3600.
	1774	6,827	800.00	1600.	3000.
	1775	4,088	1000.	2000.	3600.
	1776	.015	800.00	1600.	3000.
	1777	.010	800.00	1600.	3000.
	1778	—	1000.	2000.	3600.
	1779	4,496	1200.	2400.	4000.
	1780	2,585	—	Rare	—
	1781	6,096	800.00	1600.	3000.
	1782	.016	800.00	1600.	3000.
	1783	7,448	900.00	1800.	3200.
	1784	2,422	—	Rare	—
	1785	1,245	—	Rare	—
	1786	6,787	1000.	2000.	3600.
	1787	5,009	800.00	1600.	3000.
	1788	804 pcs.	—	Rare	—
	1789	8,198	800.00	1600.00	3000.
	1790	3,643	1300.	2600.	4500.
	1791	1,160	1200.	2400.	4000.
	1792	3,415	1200.	2400.	4000.

Obv: Similar to 1/6 Riksdaler, C#66a.
Rev: Crowned arms divide date, Smaland arms in exergue.

C#	Date	Mintage	Fine	VF	XF
72	1771	1,556	1800.	3600.	6000.
	1772	805 pcs.	3000.	6000.	10,000.
	1773	563 pcs.	—	Rare	—
	1774	824 pcs.	3000.	6000.	10,000.
	1776	382 pcs.	—	Rare	—
	1777	230 pcs.	—	Rare	—
	1778	4,075	—	Rare	—
	1779	800 pcs.	—	Rare	—
	1781	500 pcs.	—	Rare	—
	1782	300 pcs.	—	Rare	—
	1783	500 pcs.	3000.	6000.	10,000.
	1784	403 pcs.	—	Rare	—
	1785	160 pcs.	—	Rare	—
72	1786	690 pcs.	—	Rare	—

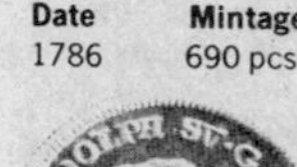

Obv: Bust right. Rev: Crowned arms within order collar.

C#	Date	Mintage	Fine	VF	XF
91	1793	1,528	1200.	2400.	4000.
	1794	1,440	1300.	2600.	4500.
	1795	4,071	1200.	2400.	4000.

Obv: Bust right with flowing hair.

C#	Date	Mintage	Fine	VF	XF
	1796	2,800	1200.	2400.	4000.
	1797	4,100	1200.	2400.	4000.
	1798	5,056	1500.	3000.	5000.

Rev: Crowned arms divide date, Smaland arms in exergue.

C#	Date	Mintage	Fine	VF	XF
92	1796	1,200	2500.	5000.	9000.

C#	Date	Mintage	Fine	VF	XF
93	1799	6,420	1100.	2200.	3600.
	1800	5,100	900.00	1800.	3000.
	1801	3,100	1100.	2200.	3600.
	1802	4,827	750.00	1500.	3000.
	1803	7,300	700.00	1400.	2400.
	1804	8,700	750.00	1500.	3000.
	1805	.013	700.00	1400.	2400.
	1806	.014	700.00	1400.	2400.
	1807	.011	700.00	1400.	2400.
	1808	.033	700.00	1400.	2400.
	1809	.021	700.00	1400.	2400.

Rev: Crowned arms divide date, Smaland arms in exergue.

C#	Date	Mintage	Fine	VF	XF
94	1801	900 pcs.	2200.	4500.	8000.

Rev: Dalarna arms in exergue.

C#	Date	Mintage	Fine	VF	XF
95	1804	1,254	1800.	3600.	6000.

Obv: Head left. Rev: Crowned arms within order collar.

C#	Date	Mintage	Fine	VF	XF
111	1810OL	.014	700.00	1400.	2400.
	1811OL	9,750	800.00	1600.	2600.
	1812OL	.016	700.00	1400.	2400.
	1813OL	.026	700.00	1400.	2400.

C#	Date	Mintage	Fine	VF	XF
111	1814OL	.022	700.00	1400.	2400.

C#	Date	Mintage	Fine	VF	XF
111a	1815OL	8,060	800.00	1600.	2600.
	1816OL	6,130	900.00	1800.	2800.
	1817OL	5,673	950.00	2000.	3000.

Darlarna Mines Commemorative
Rev: Crowned arms divide date, Dalarna arms in exergue.

C#	Date	Mintage	Fine	VF	XF
112	1810OL	1,322	1500.	3000.	5000.

Obv: Bust right. Rev: Crowned rectangular arms.

C#	Date	Mintage	Fine	VF	XF
150	1818OL	6,389	800.00	1600.	2400.
	1819OL	1,828	1800.	3000.	5000.
	1820LB	7,248	900.00	1800.	2600.
	1821LB	.019	750.00	1500.	2200.
	1822CB	5,222	900.00	1600.	2400.
	1823CB	3,155	1200.	2000.	2800.
	1824CB	3,370	1100.	1800.	2600.
	1825CB	8,127	750.00	1600.	2400.
	1826CB	4,126	950.00	1800.	2600.
	1827/6CB	4,579	750.00	1800.	2600.
	1827CB	Inc. Ab.	750.00	1800.	2600.
	1828CB	5,150	900.00	1600.	2400.
	1829CB	5,642	900.00	1600.	2400.

C#	Date	Mintage	Fine	VF	XF
151	1830CB	5,269	550.00	1100.	1800.
	1831CB	3,917	480.00	1400.	2200.
	1832CB	2,082	600.00	1200.	2000.
	1833CB	2,310	600.00	1200.	2000.
	1834CB	3,142	550.00	1100.	1800.
	1835CB	7,622	550.00	1100.	1800.
	1836CB	1,947	—	Rare	—
	1837CB	.013	450.00	1000.	1700.
	1838AG	.015	450.00	1000.	1700.
	1839AG	.010	450.00	1000.	1700.
	1840AG	1,840	2100.	3000.	5500.
	1841AG	.013	480.00	1000.	1700.
	1842AG	.030	450.00	1000.	1700.
	1843AG	.074	425.00	950.00	1500.

Obv: Large head of Oscar I right.

C#	Date	Mintage	Fine	VF	XF
198	1844AG	946 pcs.	—	Rare	—
	1845/4AG	.046	750.00	1500.	2200.

Obv: Smaller head.

C#	Date	Mintage	Fine	VF	XF
198a	1845/4AG	Inc. Ab.	750.00	1500.	2200.
	1845AG	Inc. Ab.	750.00	1500.	2200.
	1846AG	.022	400.00	800.00	1300.
	1847/4AG	.018	400.00	800.00	1300.
	1847AG	Inc. Ab.	400.00	800.00	1300.
	1848AG	.037	400.00	800.00	1300.
	1849/4AG	.014	400.00	800.00	1300.
	1849AG	Inc. Ab.	400.00	800.00	1300.
	1850AG	.020	400.00	800.00	1300.
	1851AG	.016	400.00	800.00	1300.
	1852AG	.027	400.00	800.00	1300.
	1853AG	.013	400.00	800.00	1300.
	1854AG small AG	.020	400.00	800.00	1300.
	1854AG large AG	Inc. Ab.	400.00	800.00	1300.
	1855AG	.018	400.00	800.00	1300.
	1856ST	.012	400.00	800.00	1300.
	1857ST small ST	.027	400.00	800.00	1300.
	1857ST large ST	Inc. Ab.	400.00	800.00	1300.
	1858ST	.041	400.00	800.00	1300.
	1859ST	.031	400.00	800.00	1300.

Obv: Head of Charles XV right.
Rev: Crowned and mantled arms.

C#	Date	Mintage	Fine	VF	XF
B10	1860ST	.058	400.00	800.00	1800.
	1861/60ST	.038	400.00	800.00	1800.
	1861ST	Inc. Ab.	400.00	800.00	1800.
	1862ST	.042	400.00	800.00	1800.
	1863ST	.037	400.00	800.00	1800.
	1864/63ST	.038	400.00	800.00	1800.
	1864ST small L.A.	Inc. Ab.	400.00	800.00	1800.
	1864ST larger L.A.	Inc. Ab.	400.00	800.00	1800.
	1865ST large year and ST	.039	400.00	800.00	1800.
	1865ST smaller year and ST	Inc. Ab.	400.00	800.00	1800.
	1866ST large ST	.032	400.00	800.00	1800.
	1866ST smaller ST	Inc. Ab.	400.00	800.00	1800.
	1867ST	.011	400.00	800.00	1800.
	1867TS	Inc. Ab.	2400.	3600.	4750.
	1868ST small ST	9,398	1200.	1800.	2400.
	1868ST larger ST	Inc. Ab.	1200.	1800.	2400.

CAROLIN-10 FRANCS

 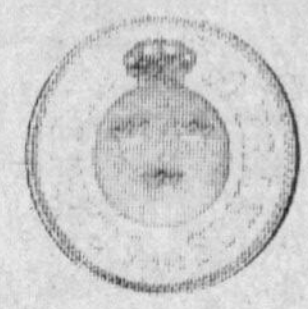

.900 GOLD

Y#	Date	Mintage	VF	XF	Unc
A10	1868 diamonds in crowned ring	.033	450.00	700.00	1000.
	1868	Inc. Ab.	450.00	700.00	1000.
	1869	.031	500.00	800.00	1200.
	1871	5,153	900.00	1300.	1800.
	1872	.012	800.00	1300.	1800.
	1872 larger portrait	Inc. Ab.	1400.	2000.	2800.

2 DUCAT

.986 GOLD
Obv: Bust right. Rev: Crowned draped arms.

C#	Date	Mintage	Fine	VF	XF
152	1830	2 pcs.	—	Rare	—
	1836CB	1,500	1500.	3500.	5200.
	1837CB	1,989	1500.	3500.	5200.
	1838AG	1,000	1500.	3500.	5400.
	1839AG	2,200	1500.	3400.	5000.
	1842AG	1,546	1500.	4000.	5600.
	1843AG	2,159	1500.	3200.	5000.

Obv: Head of Oscar right.
Rev: Crowned and mantled arms.

C#	Date	Mintage	Fine	VF	XF
199	1850AG	819 pcs.	2500.	4500.	6000.
	1852AG	386 pcs.	—	Rare	—
	1857ST	763 pcs.	2000.	3500.	5500.

4 DUCAT

.986 GOLD
Obv: Bust right. Rev: Crowned draped arms.

C#	Date	Mintage	Fine	VF	XF
153	1837CB	1,625	2500.	4000.	6000.
	1838AG	625 pcs.	2500.	4000.	6000.
	1839AG	2,000	2500.	4000.	6000.
	1841AG	2,084	2500.	4000.	6000.
	1843AG	4,405	2500.	4000.	6000.

Similar to 2 Ducat, C#199.

C#	Date	Mintage	Fine	VF	XF
200	1846AG	400 pcs.	3500.	4500.	6500.
	1850AG	507 pcs.	3000.	4000.	6000.
	1852AG	2 pcs.	—	Rare	—

NCLT ISSUES

MINT SETS

KM#	Date	Mintage	Identification	Issue Price	Mkt. Val.
S1	1948(5)	45*	Y64-66,57,68	—	125.00
S2	1950(8)	45*	Y44-46,57,64-66,68	—	95.00
S3	1953(8)	45*	Y72-79	—	75.00
S4	1954(9)	45*	Y72-80	—	95.00
*Estimated mintages.					
S5	1973(6)	—	Y88,83,85,78a,89	7.50	—
S6	1976(6)	—	Y91-96	7.50	—
S7	1978(6)	—	Y91-96	—	—

a map of the SWISS CANTONS

GERMANY
SCHAFFHAUSEN
THURGAU
BAZEL
AARGAU
ZURICH
SOLOTHURN
APPENZEL
FRANCE
ST. GALL
ZUG
LUZERN
Einsiedeln
AUSTRIA
NEUCHATEL
SCHWYZ
BERN
GLARUS
F
UNTERWALDEN
F
F
URI
FREYBURG
GRAUBUNDEN
(Grison)
VAUD
TICINO
GENEVA
Sitten
VALAIS
Bellinzona
ITALY

SWITZERLAND-CANTONS

In Switzerland, canton is the name given to each of the 22 states comprising the Swiss Federation. The origin of the cantons is rooted in the liberty-loving instincts of the peasants of Helvetia.

After the Romans departed Switzerland to defend Rome against the barbarians, Switzerland became, in the Middle Ages, a federation of fiefs of the Holy Roman Empire. In 888 it was again united by Rudolf of Burgundy, a minor despot, and for 150 years Switzerland had a king. Upon the death of the last Burgundian king, the kingdom crumbled into a loose collection of feudal fiefs ruled by bishops and ducal families who made their own laws and levied their own taxes. Eventually this division of rule by arbitrary despots became more than the freedom-loving and resourceful peasants could bear. The citizens living in the remote valleys of Uri, Schwyz (from which Switzerland received its name) and Unterwalden decided to liberate themselves from all feudal obligations and become free men.

On Aug. 1, 1291, the elders of these three small states met on a tiny heath known as the Rutli on the shores of the Lake of Lucerne and negotiated an 'eternal pact', which recognized their right to local self-government, and pledged one another assistance against any encroachment upon these rights. The pact was the beginning of the 'Everlasting League' and the foundation of the Swiss Confederation.

CANTONAL MINTMARKS OF SWITZERLAND

Mintmark	Canton	Mint
A.-B.	Geneva	Geneva 1847 (Auguste Bovet)
A.B.	Graubunden	Geneva 1842 (Antoine Bovy)
A-B	Graubunden	Private coiner 1836 (Antoine Bovy)
A-B	Graubunden	Geneva 1842 (Antoine Bovy)
B	Basel	Basel 1826 (Bel-Bessiere)
B	Fribourg	Fribourg 1830 (Bel-Bessiere)
B	Glarus	Unknown site 1806-1814
B	Graubunden	Bern 1820
B	Graubunden	Private coiner 1826
B	Luzern	Luzern 1807-1814 (Bruppacher)
B	Schwyz	Schwyz or Aargau 1810
B	Zurich	Zurich 1806-1813 (Bruckmann)
BEL	Basel	Basel 1826 (Bel-Bessiere)
BEL	Fribourg	Fribourg 1830-1846 (Bel-Bessiere)
BEL	Vaud	Lausanne 1826-1834 (Bel-Bessiere)
D	Zurich	Stuttgart 1842-1848
DB	Schwyz	Schwyz 1843-1846
F	Glarus	Unknown site 1806-1807
G	Geneva	Geneva An 8-13
H	Geneva	Geneva 1817 (Hoyer)
H	Schwyz	Schwyz or Aargau 1810-1811
HB	Graubunden	Private coiner 1836 (Bruppacher)
K	St. Gallen	St. Gallen 1807-1817 (Kukler)
M	Aargau	Aargau 1807-1808 (Meyer)
M	Schwyz	Aargau or Schwyz 1844
N	Graubunden	Bern 1825 (Nett
SIBER	Vaud	Lausanne 1845 (Siber)
Star	Ticino	Luzern 1813

AARGAU

ARGUA, ARGOVIE

Located in north central Switzerland. Was named after the river Aar. Was admitted to the Swiss Confederation in 1803.

MONETARY SYSTEM

10 Rappen = 4 Kreuzer = 1 Batzen
10 Batzen = 1 Frank

RAPPEN

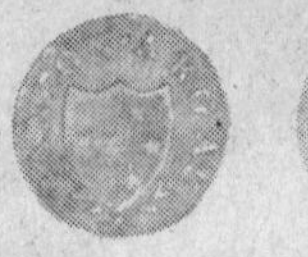

BILLON

C#	Date	Mintage	VG	Fine	VF	XF
1	1809	.044	6.00	12.00	20.00	30.00
	1810	.020	6.00	12.00	20.00	30.00
	1811	.039	5.00	10.00	14.00	20.00
	1816	—	5.00	10.00	14.00	20.00

2 RAPPEN

BILLON

C#	Date	Mintage	VG	Fine	VF	XF
2	1808	.092	5.00	7.00	12.00	20.00
	1811	—	8.00	14.00	20.00	30.00
	1812	—	5.00	7.00	12.00	20.00
	1813	—	5.00	7.00	12.00	20.00
	1814	—	5.00	7.00	12.00	20.00
	1816	—	5.00	7.00	12.00	20.00

2-1/2 RAPPEN

(= Ein (1) Kreuzer)

BILLON

C#	Date	Mintage	VG	Fine	VF	XF
11	1831	—	6.00	9.00	15.00	22.00

5 RAPPEN

BILLON

Similar to 2-1/2 Rappen, C#11.

C#	Date	Mintage	VG	Fine	VF	XF
12	1829	1,000	6.00	9.00	15.00	22.00
	1831	—	6.00	9.00	15.00	22.00

1/2 BATZEN

BILLON

Obv: Spade arms in branches.
Rev: Value and date.

C#	Date	Mintage	VG	Fine	VF	XF
3	1807	—	6.00	9.00	15.00	22.00
	1808	—	6.00	9.00	15.00	22.00
	1809	—	6.00	9.00	15.00	22.00
	1811	—	6.00	9.00	15.00	22.00
	1815	—	6.00	9.00	15.00	22.00

BATZEN

BILLON

Obv: Oval arms 'AARGAU'

C#	Date	Mintage	VG	Fine	VF	XF
4	1805	1,000	20.00	35.00	55.00	85.00
	1806	—	20.00	35.00	55.00	85.00

Obv: 'ARGAU'

C#	Date	Mintage	VG	Fine	VF	XF
4a	1808	—	40.00	65.00	90.00	135.00

Obv: Pointed arms

C#	Date	Mintage	VG	Fine	VF	XF
4b	1806	—	12.00	25.00	45.00	80.00

C#	Date	Mintage	VG	Fine	VF	XF
5	1807	.132	6.00	15.00	22.00	30.50
	1808	.184	6.00	15.00	22.00	30.50
	1809	.350	6.00	15.00	22.00	30.50
	1810	.215	6.00	15.00	22.00	30.50
	1811	.060	6.00	18.00	30.00	45.50
	1816	—	8.00	20.00	45.00	75.00

Rev: Beaded inner circle

C#	Date	Mintage	VG	Fine	VF	XF
13	1826	—	5.00	13.00	20.00	30.00

Rev: No inner circle

C#	Date	Mintage	VG	Fine	VF	XF
13.1	1826	—	15.00	45.00	80.00	115.00

5 BATZEN

SILVER

Rev: Letter M

C#	Date	Mintage	VG	Fine	VF	XF
5	1807M	250 pcs.	100.00	175.00	225.00	325.00
	1808M	.114	10.00	25.00	40.00	75.00

Rev: Without Letter M

C#	Date	Mintage	VG	Fine	VF	XF
5.1	1808	—	50.00	110.00	155.00	200.00
	1809	.084	10.00	25.00	40.00	70.00
	1810	.171	10.00	25.00	40.00	70.00
	1811	.065	10.00	25.00	40.00	70.00
	1812	.073	30.00	80.00	100.00	140.00
	1814	—	30.00	80.00	100.00	140.00
	1815	—	10.00	25.00	40.00	70.00

C#	Date	Mintage	VG	Fine	VF	XF
14	1826	.508	10.00	25.00	40.00	60.00

10 BATZEN

SILVER

Obv: With palm and laurel wreath flanking arms.

C#	Date	Mintage	VG	Fine	VF	XF
8	1808	3,884	35.00	90.00	150.00	275.00
	1809	9,842	30.00	90.00	150.00	275.00
	1818	3,223	35.00	90.00	175.00	350.00

Obv: Laurel branches both sides of arms.

C#	Date	Mintage	VG	Fine	VF	XF
8.1	1809	Inc. Ab.	75.00	200.00	400.00	550.00

20 BATZEN

SILVER

C#	Date	Mintage	VG	Fine	VF	XF
9	1809	.014	50.00	125.00	250.00	325.00

4 FRANK

SILVER

C#	Date	Mintage	VG	Fine	VF	XF
10	1812	2,527	100.00	300.00	600.00	950.00

NCLT ISSUES

PATTERNS

KM#	Date	Mintage	Identification	Mkt.Val.
X9	1809	80	20 Batzen, Silver	3000.

APPENZELL

Located in northeast Switzerland, completely surrounded by the canton of St. Gall. The name was derived from "Abbot's Cell." It was admitted to the Swiss Confederation in 1513.

MONETARY SYSTEM

4 Pfenning = 1 Kreuzer
10 Rappen = 4 Kreuzer = 1 Batzen
10 Batzen = 1 Franken

AUSSER RHODEN

PFENNIG

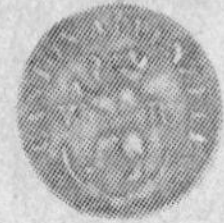

COPPER

C#	Date	Mintage	VG	Fine	VF	XF
1	1816	.066	25.00	75.00	120.00	175.00

KREUZER

BILLON

C#	Date	Mintage	VG	Fine	VF	XF
2	1813	.086	5.00	15.00	25.00	35.00

1/2 BATZEN

BILLON

C#	Date	Mintage	VG	Fine	VF	XF
3	1808	.073	6.00	20.00	30.00	45.00
	1809	.060	6.00	20.00	30.00	45.00
	1816	.081	6.00	20.00	30.00	45.00

BATZEN

BILLON

Obv: Arms in branches, date in exergue.
Rev: Value in wreath.

C#	Date	Mintage	VG	Fine	VF	XF
4	1808	.266	6.00	20.00	30.00	45.00
	1816	.203	6.00	20.00	30.00	45.00

1/2 FRANKEN

SILVER

C#	Date	Mintage	VG	Fine	VF	XF
5	1809	6,534	50.00	135.00	180.00	225.00

2 FRANKEN

SILVER

C#	Date	Mintage	VG	Fine	VF	XF
6	1812	1,861	50.00	135.00	200.00	275.00

4 FRANKEN

SILVER

C#	Date	Mintage	VG	Fine	VF	XF
7	1812	2,357	100.00	300.00	550.00	900.00

C#	Date	Mintage	VG	Fine	VF	XF
8	1816	1,850	100.00	300.00	550.00	900.00

BASEL

BASILEA

BISHOPRIC

A bishopric in northwest Switzerland, founded in the 5th century. The first coinage was c.1000AD. The bishopric was divided between France and Baden after secularization in 1801.

RULERS

Joseph Sigismund von Roggenbach, 1782-1793

MINTMASTER'S INITIALS

D-B - De Beyer
H - Haag
I-HH - Handmann
S - Johann Ulrich Samson

MONETARY SYSTEM

4 Kreuzer = 1 Batzen

1/2 BATZEN

BILLON

C#	Date	Mintage	VG	Fine	VF	XF
22	1787	—	6.00	15.00	20.00	30.00

BATZEN

BILLON
Obv: Crowned shield. Rev: Value, date within crossed branches.

C#	Date	Mintage	VG	Fine	VF	XF
23	1787	—	6.00	15.00	20.00	30.00

12 KREUZERS

SILVER
Obv: Head left. Rev: Double headed eagle, value on chest.

C#	Date	Mintage	VG	Fine	VF	XF
26	1786	—	10.00	25.00	50.00	80.00
	1787	—	10.00	25.00	50.00	80.00
	1788	—	10.00	25.00	50.00	80.00

24 KREUZERS

SILVER
Obv: Head left. Rev: Double headed eagle, value on chest.

C#	Date	Mintage	VG	Fine	VF	XF
28	1788	—	25.00	60.00	100.00	150.00

CITY

A city in northwest Switzerland was founded in 374 by the Roman Emperor Valentinian. It became a Burgundian Mint in the 10th century and obtained the mint right in 1373. It was admitted to the Swiss Confederation in 1501. Developed into a canton.

MONETARY SYSTEM

Until 1798
8 Rappen = 1 Batzen
30 Batzen = 2 Gulden = 1 Thaler

1/2 BATZEN

BILLON
Obv: Basel arms within cartouche.
Rev: Value, date within cartouche.

C#	Date	Mintage	VG	Fine	VF	XF
51	1762	—	4.00	10.00	17.50	25.00
	1763	—	4.00	10.00	17.50	25.00
	1765	—	4.00	10.00	17.50	25.00
	1794	—	4.00	10.00	20.00	30.00

BATZEN

BILLON
Obv: Basel arms within cartouche.
Rev: Value, date within cartouche.

C#	Date	Mintage	Fine	VF	XF
52	1762	—	—	—	—

Obv: Basel symbol within cartouche, legend.

C#	Date	Mintage	VG	Fine	VF	XF
53	1763	—	4.00	10.00	17.50	30.00
	1764	—	4.00	10.00	17.50	30.00
	1765	—	4.00	10.00	17.50	30.00

3 BATZEN

BILLON
Obv: Basel symbol within cartouche.
Rev: Value, date within cartouche.

C#	Date	Mintage	VG	Fine	VF	XF
56	1764	—	10.00	25.00	40.00	65.00
	1765	—	10.00	25.00	40.00	65.00

1/6 THALER

SILVER

C#	Date	Mintage	VG	Fine	VF	XF
58	1764	—	25.00	60.00	100.00	150.00
	1766	—	20.00	45.00	65.00	100.00

1/3 THALER

SILVER
Obv: Basilisk holding arms.
Rev: Value within branches.

C#	Date	Mintage	VG	Fine	VF	XF
60	1764	—	25.00	60.00	125.00	200.00
	1766	—	25.00	60.00	125.00	200.00

1/2 THALER

SILVER
Obv: Basilisk holding arms. Rev: Value within branches, date below.

C#	Date	Mintage	VG	Fine	VF	XF
64	1765H	—	50.00	100.00	200.00	300.00

Obv: City view, 8 shields above; Basilea and date in exergue.
Rev: Basilisk looking back holding oval arms.

C#	Date	Mintage	VG	Fine	VF	XF
66	1785	—	75.00	150.00	250.00	375.00
	1786	—	75.00	175.00	300.00	425.00

Obv: Oval arms within crossed branches.
Rev: Motto DOMINE CONSERVA NOS IN PACE, in oak wreath.

C#	Date	Mintage	VG	Fine	VF	XF
68	1797	—	75.00	175.00	300.00	425.00

THALER

SILVER
Obv: Basilisk holding cartouche shield.
Rev: Value within crossed branches, date below.

C#	Date	Mintage	VG	Fine	VF	XF
71	1765IH	—	100.00	200.00	375.00	600.00

C#	Date	Mintage	VG	Fine	VF	XF
72	1785	—	100.00	250.00	375.00	600.00

Rev: Similar to C#72.

C#	Date	Mintage	VG	Fine	VF	XF
73	1793	—	100.00	300.00	450.00	650.00

Obv: Similar to C#73.
Rev: Smaller legend, taller Basilisk facing left.

C#	Date	Mintage	VG	Fine	VF	XF
73.1	1793	—	125.00	350.00	500.00	700.00

Obv: Oval arms. Rev: DOMINE CONSERVA NOS IN PACE legend within branches.

C#	Date	Mintage	VG	Fine	VF	XF
74	1795	—	125.00	300.00	450.00	650.00
	1796	—	125.00	300.00	450.00	650.00

DUPLONE

.900 GOLD

C#	Date	Mintage	VG	Fine	VF	XF
92	1795	—	500.00	1600.	3000.	5000.

C#	Date	Mintage	VG	Fine	VF	XF
93	1795	—	300.00	750.00	1200.	2000.
	1796	—	350.00	1000.	2400.	4000.

GOLD GULDEN

.900 GOLD

C#	Date	Mintage	VG	Fine	VF	XF
90	ND(1790)	—	350.00	1000.	1600.	2800.

2 GOLD GULDEN

.900 GOLD

C#	Date	Mintage	VG	Fine	VF	XF
91	ND(1790)	—	500.00	1600.	3000.	5000.

CANTON

MONETARY SYSTEM

After 1803
10 Rappen = 1 Batzen
10 Batzen = 1 Frank

RAPPEN

BILLON

101	1810	—	2.50	5.00	6.50	12.00
	1818	—	2.50	5.00	6.50	12.00

2 RAPPEN

BILLON
Similar to 1 Rappen, C#101.

102	1810	—	2.50	5.00	8.50	12.50
	1818	—	2.50	5.00	8.50	12.50

5 RAPPEN

BILLON
Obv: Pointed arms

108	1826B	—	3.00	8.00	15.00	20.00

Obv. Oval arms

108a	1826 no line	15.00	40.00	60.00	90.00
	1826 exergue line	15.00	40.00	60.00	90.00

1/2 BATZEN

BILLON

103	1809	—	5.00	15.00	20.00	25.00

BATZEN

BILLON
Under the Republic
Obv: Arms in cartouche.
Rev: Value and date in branches.

C#	Date	Mintage	Fine	VF	XF
104	1805	—	30.00	45.00	60.00

As a Canton
Obv: Pointed arms.

C#	Date	Mintage	VG	Fine	VF	XF
104a	1805	—	12.00	30.00	45.00	60.00
	1806	—	8.00	20.00	35.00	55.00
	1809	—	5.00	12.00	20.00	25.00

C#	Date	Mintage	VG	Fine	VF	XF
104a	1810	—	5.00	12.00	20.00	25.00

Obv: Oval arms

109a	1826	—	20.00	50.00	65.00	85.00

Obv: Pointed arms

109	1826B	—	4.00	10.00	20.00	25.00

3 BATZEN

SILVER

105	1809	—	8.00	20.00	35.00	60.00
	1810	—	10.00	25.00	40.00	60.00

5 BATZEN

SILVER

106	1809	—	10.00	25.00	40.00	60.00
	1810	—	10.00	25.00	40.00	60.00

Rev: BATZEN

110	1826	—	8.00	22.50	35.00	60.00

Rev: BATZn

110	1826	—	10.00	25.00	40.00	60.00

TRADE COINS

1/4 DUCAT

.986 GOLD
Obv: Basilisk holding oval shield.
Rev: Value, plain rim.

C#	Date	Mintage	Fine	VF	XF
86	ND(1770)H	—	725.00	1200.	2000.

Obv: Larger shield.

86.1	ND(1780)S	—	—	—	—

1/2 DUCAT

.986 GOLD
Obv: Basilisk holding oval shield.
Rev: Value within crossed branches.

87	ND(1770)H	—	725.00	1200.	2000.

87.1	ND(1780)S	—	1000.	1400.	2400.

DUCAT

GOLD
Obv: Basilisk holding oval shield.
Rev: Legend and value within ornate circle.

87.5	ND (1775)	—	1000.	1400.	2400.

Rev: Different border around legend and value.

87.5a	ND (1780)	—	1000.	1600.	3000.

2 DUCATS

.986 GOLD

C#	Date	Mintage	Fine	VF	XF
88	ND (1795)	—	2000.	3000.	4750.

Obv: Draped oval arms. Rev: Value within crossed branches.

89	1795	—	—	—	—

NCLT ISSUES

PATTERNS

KM#	Date	Mintage	Identification	Mkt.Val.
1	ND(1762)	—	2 Thalers, Silver	Rare
2	1764	—	1/6 Thaler, Silver	Rare
3	1826	—	5 Batzen, Silver	—

BELLINZONA

Awarded to Uri, Schwyz and Unterwalden by the French king in 1503. It was the capitol of the short-lived Bellinzona Canton during the Helvetian Republic period. It became the joint capitol of Ticino Canton in 1803.

MONETARY SYSTEM

12 Denari = 3 Quattrino = 1 Soldo
20 Soldi = 1 Lira

These patterns were struck jointly by Uri, Schwyz and Unterwalden

QUATTRINO

COPPER
Obv: 3 shields. Rev: Value, date.

C#	Date	Mintage	Fine	VF	XF
1	1788	—	—	—	—

MEZZO (1/2) SOLDO

COPPER
Obv: 3 shields. Rev: Value, date within wreath.

2	1788	—	350.00	500.00	800.00

UN (1) SOLDO

COPPER
Obv: 3 shields. Rev: Value, date within branches.

3	1788	—	—	—	—

BERN

A city and canton in west central Switzerland. It was founded as a military post in 911 and became an imperial city with the mint right in 1218. It was admitted to the Swiss Confederation as a canton in 1353.

MINTMASTER'S INITIALS

D-B - De Beyer

MONETARY SYSTEM

Until 1798
8 Vierer = 4 Kreuzer = 1 Batzen
40 Batzen = 1 Thaler

VIERER

(= 1/2 Kreuzer)

BILLON
Obv: Bear coat of arms within circle.

Rev: Anchor cross within circle.

C#	Date	Mintage	VG	Fine	VF	XF
2a	1762	—	3.00	6.00	9.00	15.00
	1763	—	3.00	10.00	20.00	35.00
	1765	—	3.00	6.00	9.00	15.00
	1766	—	3.00	6.00	9.00	15.00
	1769	—	3.00	6.00	9.00	15.00
	1771	—	3.00	6.00	9.00	15.00
	1774	—	3.00	5.50	8.50	15.00
	1775	—	3.00	5.50	8.50	15.00
	1777	—	3.00	5.50	8.50	15.00
	1778	—	3.00	5.50	8.50	15.00
	1780	—	3.00	5.50	8.50	15.00
	1781	—	3.00	5.50	8.50	15.00
	1785	—	3.00	5.50	8.50	15.00
	1786	—	3.00	5.50	8.50	15.00
	1788	—	3.00	5.50	8.50	15.00
	1789	—	3.00	5.50	8.50	15.00
	1790	—	3.00	5.50	8.50	15.00
	1792	—	3.00	5.50	8.50	15.00
	1794	—	3.00	5.50	8.50	15.00
	1796	—	3.00	5.50	8.50	15.00
	1797	—	3.00	5.50	8.50	15.00

GOLD

C#	Date	Mintage	VG	Fine	VF	XF
2b	1766	—	—	—	—	—
	1777	—	—	—	—	—
	1781	—	—	—	—	—

KREUZER

BILLON
Obv: Coat of arms within circle.
Rev: Anchor cross within circle.

C#	Date	Mintage	VG	Fine	VF	XF
4a	1755	—	3.00	6.00	9.00	15.00
	1765	—	3.00	6.00	9.00	15.00
	1772	—	3.00	5.00	7.50	15.00
	1774	—	3.00	5.00	7.50	15.00
	1775	—	3.00	5.00	7.50	15.00
	1776	—	3.00	5.00	7.50	15.00
	1777	—	3.00	5.00	7.50	15.00
	1779	—	3.00	5.00	7.50	15.00
	1781	—	3.00	5.00	7.50	15.00
	1785	—	3.00	5.00	7.50	15.00
	1789	—	3.00	5.00	7.50	15.00
	1792	—	3.00	5.00	7.50	15.00
	1793	—	3.00	5.00	7.50	15.00
	1796	—	3.00	5.00	7.50	15.00
	1797	—	3.00	5.00	7.50	15.00

GOLD

C#	Date	Mintage	VG	Fine	VF	XF
4b	1781	—	—	—	—	—

COPPER
Thick Planchets

C#	Date	Mintage	VG	Fine	VF	XF
4c	1772	—	—	—	—	—

SILVER

C#	Date	Mintage	VG	Fine	VF	XF
4d	1772	—	—	—	—	—

1/2 BATZEN

BILLON

C#	Date	Mintage	VG	Fine	VF	XF
8	1753	—	3.00	6.50	10.00	16.00
	1754	—	3.00	6.50	10.00	16.00
	1755	—	3.00	6.50	10.00	20.00
	1770	—	3.00	6.50	10.00	16.00
	1771	—	3.00	5.50	8.50	15.00
	1772	—	3.00	5.50	8.50	15.00
	1774	—	3.00	5.50	8.50	15.00
	1775	—	3.00	5.50	8.50	15.00
	1776	—	3.00	6.50	8.50	15.00
	1777	—	2.00	6.50	10.00	20.00
	1778	—	2.00	6.50	10.00	15.00
	1784	—	3.00	5.50	8.50	15.00
	1785	—	3.00	5.50	8.50	15.00
	1788	—	3.00	5.50	8.50	15.00
	1794	—	3.00	5.50	8.50	15.00
	1796	—	3.00	5.50	8.50	15.00
	1798	—	3.00	5.50	8.50	15.00

2 KREUZER

BILLON
Obv: Coat of arms within circle.

Rev: Anchor cross within circle, value in center of cross.

C#	Date	Mintage	VG	Fine	VF	XF
9	1770	—	4.00	10.00	15.00	30.00

BATZEN

BILLON
Obv: Coat of arms within circle, value CR 4 below.
Rev: Anchor cross within circle.

C#	Date	Mintage	VG	Fine	VF	XF
11	1754	—	4.00	10.00	15.00	25.00
	1765	—	4.00	8.00	12.50	20.00
	1766	—	4.00	8.00	12.50	20.00
	1770	—	3.00	5.50	8.50	15.00
	1772	—	3.00	5.50	8.50	15.00
	1774	—	3.00	5.50	8.50	15.00
	1775	—	3.00	5.50	8.50	15.00
	1776	—	3.00	5.50	8.50	15.00
	1778	—	3.00	5.50	8.50	15.00
	1784	—	3.00	5.50	8.50	15.00
	1789	—	3.00	5.50	8.50	15.00
	1793	—	3.00	5.50	8.50	15.00
	1794	—	3.00	5.50	8.50	15.00
	1795	—	3.00	5.50	8.50	15.00
	1797	—	3.00	5.50	8.50	15.00
	1798	—	3.00	5.50	8.50	15.00

10 KREUZER

SILVER
Obv: Arms. Rev: Value, date in cartouche.

C#	Date	Mintage	VG	Fine	VF	XF
14	1755	—	6.00	15.00	25.00	40.00
	1756	—	6.00	15.00	25.00	40.00

Obv: Crowned round arms.
Rev: Similar to 1/4 Thaler, C#31a.

C#	Date	Mintage	VG	Fine	VF	XF
16	1759	—	6.00	15.00	25.00	40.00
	1764	—	6.00	15.00	25.00	40.00
	1765	—	6.00	15.00	25.00	40.00
	1776	—	6.00	15.00	25.00	40.00
	1777	—	6.00	15.00	25.00	40.00
	1778	—	6.00	15.00	25.00	40.00
	1787	—	6.00	15.00	25.00	40.00
	1790	—	6.00	15.00	25.00	40.00

GOLD

C#	Date	Mintage	VG	Fine	VF	XF
16b	1759	—	—	—	—	—

Obv: Similar to 1/4 Thaler, C#31a.

C#	Date	Mintage	VG	Fine	VF	XF
16a	1797	—	6.00	15.00	25.00	40.00

20 KREUZERS

SILVER

C#	Date	Mintage	VG	Fine	VF	XF
18	1755	—	8.00	25.00	45.00	65.00
	1756	—	8.00	25.00	45.00	65.00

GOLD

C#	Date	Mintage	VG	Fine	VF	XF
18a	1755	—	—	—	—	—

SILVER
Obv: Crowned round arms.
Rev: Similar to 1/4 Thaler, C#31a.

C#	Date	Mintage	VG	Fine	VF	XF
20	1758	—	8.00	25.00	45.00	65.00
	1759	—	8.00	25.00	45.00	65.00
	1764	—	8.00	25.00	45.00	65.00
	1776	—	7.00	25.00	45.00	65.00
	1777	—	7.00	25.00	45.00	65.00
	1787	—	7.00	25.00	45.00	65.00

Obv: Crowned oval arms.

C#	Date	Mintage	VG	Fine	VF	XF
20a	1797	—	7.00	15.00	35.00	55.00
	1798	—	7.00	15.00	35.00	55.00

1/4 THALER

SILVER

C#	Date	Mintage	VG	Fine	VF	XF
30	1757	—	15.00	35.00	75.00	140.00
	1758	—	15.00	35.00	75.00	140.00
	1759	—	15.00	35.00	75.00	140.00
	1760	—	15.00	35.00	75.00	140.00
	1773	—	15.00	35.00	75.00	140.00
	1774	—	15.00	35.00	75.00	140.00

C#	Date	Mintage	VG	Fine	VF	XF
31a	1797	—	15.00	35.00	75.00	140.00

1/2 THALER

SILVER

C#	Date	Mintage	VG	Fine	VF	XF
32	1796	—	30.00	50.00	125.00	170.00
	1797	—	30.00	50.00	125.00	170.00

Rev: Swiss stands on ledge.

C#	Date	Mintage	VG	Fine	VF	XF
32a	1797	—	30.00	50.00	125.00	170.00
	1798	—	200.00	800.00	1200.	1600.

THALER

SILVER

C#	Date	Mintage	VG	Fine	VF	XF
36	1795	—	75.00	200.00	300.00	450.00
	1796	—	75.00	200.00	300.00	450.00

C#	Date	Mintage	VG	Fine	VF	XF
36.1	1795	—	75.00	200.00	300.00	450.00

C#	Date	Mintage	VG	Fine	VF	XF
36a	1798	—	100.00	300.00	400.00	550.00

Narrower oval.

C#	Date	Mintage	VG	Fine	VF	XF
36a.1	1798	—	100.00	350.00	450.00	600.00

1/2 DUPLONE

.900 GOLD

C#	Date	Mintage	Fine	VF	XF
60	1797	—	600.00	1000.	1600.

DUPLONE

.900 GOLD

C#	Date	Mintage	Fine	VF	XF
58	1793	—	475.00	800.00	1200.
	1794	—	475.00	800.00	1200.
	1795	—	600.00	1000.	1400.

C#	Date	Mintage	Fine	VF	XF
58a	1796	—	475.00	800.00	1200.

C#	Date	Mintage	VG	Fine	VF	XF
61	1793	—	—	950.00	1600.	2800.

C#	Date	Mintage	Fine	VF	XF
61.1	1797	—	725.00	1200.	2000.
	1819	—	600.00	1100.	1850.
	1829	—	725.00	1200.	2000.

2 DUPLONES

.900 GOLD

C#	Date	Mintage	Fine	VF	XF
59	1793	—	850.00	1400.	2500.
	1794	—	950.00	1600.	3000.
	1795	—	850.00	1400.	2500.

C#	Date	Mintage	Fine	VF	XF
59a	1796	—	850.00	1400.	2500.

C#	Date	Mintage	Fine	VF	XF
62	1794	—	1400.	2400.	4000.
	1796	—	1300.	2200.	3600.
	1797	—	1400.	2400.	4000.
	1798	—	1700.	2800.	4800.

MONETARY REFORM

MONETARY SYSTEM

1803 Onward

10 Rappen = 1 Batzen

10 Batzen = 1 Frank

RAPPEN

BILLON

Obv: CANTON BERN

C#	Date	Mintage	VG	Fine	VF	XF
71	1811	—	3.00	5.00	10.00	18.00
	1829	—	3.00	5.00	10.00	18.00

Obv: REPUBL. BERN

C#	Date	Mintage	VG	Fine	VF	XF
71a	1818	—	3.00	6.00	12.00	20.00
	1819	—	3.00	5.00	10.00	18.00
	1836	—	3.00	5.00	10.00	18.00

2 RAPPEN

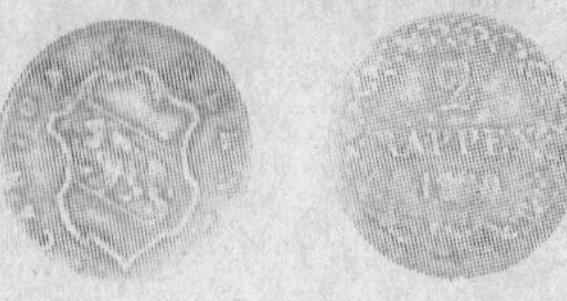

BILLON

C#	Date	Mintage	VG	Fine	VF	XF
73	1809	—	3.00	6.00	12.00	20.00

2-1/2 RAPPEN

BILLON

C#	Date	Mintage	VG	Fine	VF	XF
75	1811	.114	3.00	6.00	10.00	20.00
	1829	—	3.00	6.00	10.00	20.00

5 RAPPEN

BILLON

Beaded rim and quatrefoils

C#	Date	Mintage	VG	Fine	VF	XF
87	1826	—	3.00	5.00	7.50	15.00

Without beaded rim

C#	Date	Mintage	VG	Fine	VF	XF
87.1	1826	—	5.00	15.00	20.00	30.00

1/2 BATZEN

BILLON

C#	Date	Mintage	VG	Fine	VF	XF
77	1818	—	4.00	10.00	15.00	25.00
	1824	—	4.00	10.00	15.00	25.00

BATZEN

BILLON

C#	Date	Mintage	VG	Fine	VF	XF
79	1818	—	3.00	6.50	15.00	25.00
	1824	—	3.00	6.50	15.00	25.00

Obv: BATZ

C#	Date	Mintage	VG	Fine	VF	XF
88	1826	—	3.00	5.00	10.00	18.00

Obv: BAZ

C#	Date	Mintage	VG	Fine	VF	XF
88.1	1826	—	3.00	5.00	10.00	18.50

NOTE: These are found overstruck on 1/2 Batzen, C#8.

2-1/2 BATZEN

SILVER

Obv: BATZ

C#	Date	Mintage	VG	Fine	VF	XF
89	1826	—	4.00	10.00	15.00	25.00

Obv: BAZ

C#	Date	Mintage	VG	Fine	VF	XF
89.1	1826	—	6.00	15.00	27.50	45.00

5 BATZEN

SILVER

C#	Date	Mintage	VG	Fine	VF	XF
81	1808	—	10.00	25.00	40.00	60.00
	1810	—	10.00	25.00	40.00	60.00
	1811	—	25.00	65.00	110.00	220.00
	1818	—	12.00	30.00	45.00	70.00

Obv: BATZ

C#	Date	Mintage	VG	Fine	VF	XF
90	1826	—	8.00	20.00	32.00	50.00

Obv: BAZ

C#	Date	Mintage	VG	Fine	VF	XF
90.1	1826	—	10.00	25.00	40.00	70.00

C#	Date	Mintage	VG	Fine	VF	XF
90.2	1826	—	16.00	45.00	60.00	85.00

FRANK

SILVER

C#	Date	Mintage	VG	Fine	VF	XF
82	1811	.011	25.00	60.00	100.00	160.00

2 FRANKEN

SILVER

C#	Date	Mintage	VG	Fine	VF	XF
83	1835	—	50.00	150.00	200.00	275.00

4 FRANKEN

SILVER

C#	Date	Mintage	VG	Fine	VF	XF
85	1823	—	150.00	450.00	800.00	1200.

C#	Date	Mintage	VG	Fine	VF	XF
85.1	1835	—	150.00	350.00	600.00	900.00
91	1826	75 pcs.	—	—	—	8000.

COUNTERSTAMP ISSUES

40 BATZEN

NOTE: During the period 1816-1819 an estimated 660,000 French Ecus of Louis XV and Louis XVI 1726-1793 and 6 Livres dated 1793-1794 along with 40 Batzen and 4 Franken of the Helvetian Republic were counterstamped with a bear and 40 BZ. on shields.

Approximately ninety per cent of the counterstamped pieces were melted by 1851. It is estimated some 5,000 pieces or less still exist.

SILVER

c/s: On Louis XV Ecu, C#42.

C#	Date	Year	VG	Fine	VF	XF
34.1	ND	1726-41	125.00	200.00	375.00	800.00

c/s: On Louis XV Ecu, C#47.

C#	Date	Year	VG	Fine	VF	XF
34.2	ND	1740-71	100.00	200.00	375.00	800.00

c/s: On Louis XV Ecu, C#47a.

C#	Date	Year	VG	Fine	VF	XF
34.3	ND	1770-74	125.00	200.00	375.00	750.00

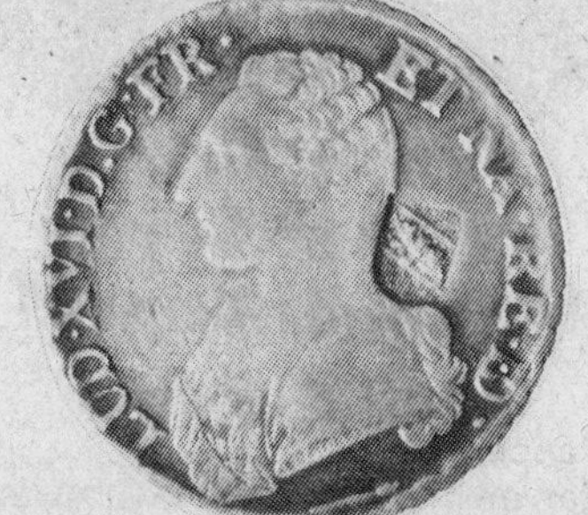

c/s: On France Louis XVI Ecu, C#78.

C#	Date	Year	VG	Fine	VF	XF
34.4	ND	1774-92	100.00	200.00	350.00	750.00

c/s: On France Louis XVI constitutional Ecu, C#93.

C#	Date	Year	VG	Fine	VF	XF
34.5	ND	1792-93	100.00	200.00	350.00	775.00

c/s: On France 6 Livres, C#123.

C#	Date	Year	VG	Fine	VF	XF
34.6	ND	1793-94	100.00	200.00	350.00	850.00

c/s: On Helvetia 40 Batzen, C#7.

34.7 ND 1798 Reported, not confirmed

c/s: On Helvetia 40 Batzen, C#7a.

34.8 ND 1798 Reported, not confirmed

c/s: On Helvetia 4 Franken, C#8.

34.9 ND 1799 Reported, not confirmed

c/s: On Helvetia 4 Franken, C#8a.

34.10 ND 1801 Reported, not confirmed

TRADE COINS

DUCAT

.986 GOLD

C#	Date	Mintage	VG	Fine	VF	XF
43	ND(1772)	—	600.00	1000.	2000.	3000.
	BILLON					
43c	ND(1772)	—	—	—	—	—

C#	Date	Mintage	VG	Fine	VF	XF
43a	1788	—	950.00	1600.	3000.	4000.

Obv: Pointed arms.
Rev: Legend in horizontal oval.

C#	Date	Mintage	VG	Fine	VF	XF
43b	1789	—	850.00	1400.	2400.	3000.

Obv: Oval arms. Rev: Value, date within wreath.

C#	Date	Mintage	VG	Fine	VF	XF
53	1793	—	—	—	—	—

Obv: Pointed arms.

C#	Date	Mintage	VG	Fine	VF	XF
53a	1794	—	475.00	800.00	1500.	2500.

2 DUCATS

.986 GOLD
Obv: 2 lions holding cap over arms.
Rev. leg: BENEDICTUS SIT IEUHOVA DEUS within cartouche.

C#	Date	Mintage	VG	Fine	VF	XF
45	1771	—	2000.	4000.	6500.	7500.

Obv: Shield shaped arms.

C#	Date	Mintage	VG	Fine	VF	XF
46	1788	—	—	—	—	—

Obv: Flat topped shield arms.
Rev: Legend in horizontal oval.

C#	Date	Mintage	VG	Fine	VF	XF
46a	1789	—	1800.	2400.	4000.	5000.

Obv: Pointed arms within crossed branches.
Rev: Value, date within wreath.

C#	Date	Mintage	VG	Fine	VF	XF
54	1796	—	800.00	2800.	4800.	5500.

3 DUCATS

.986 GOLD
Similar to 1/4 Thaler, C#30.

C#	Date	Mintage	VG	Fine	VF	XF
—	1757	—	—	—	—	—

Obv: Crowned oval arms within cartouche.
Rev. leg: BENEDICTUS SIT IEHOVA DEUS, value, date within cartouche.

C#	Date	Mintage	VG	Fine	VF	XF
47	1772	—	—	—	8000.	10,000.

4 DUCATS

.986 GOLD
Obv: Crowned pointed arms within crossed branches.

Rev: Value, date within wreath.

C#	Date	Mintage	VG	Fine	VF	XF
55	1796	—	3500.	6000.	8000.	10,000.
	1798	—	4500.	7500.	10,000.	12,000.

Obv: Similar to 6 Ducats, C#56.

C#	Date	Mintage	VG	Fine	VF	XF
55	1825	—	1400.	2900.	4500.	6000.

6 DUCATS

.986 GOLD

C#	Date	Mintage	VG	Fine	VF	XF
56	1796	—	—	—	—	—

8 DUCATS

.986 GOLD
Obv: Crowned pointed arms within crossed branches.
Rev: Value, date within wreath.

C#	Date	Mintage	VG	Fine	VF	XF
57	1796	—	5500.	9000.	12,000.	15,000.
	1798	—	—	—	—	—

NCLT ISSUES

PATTERNS

KM#	Date	Mintage	Identification	Mkt.Val.
1	ND(1772)	64 pcs.	10 Franken, Gold	—
2	1792	—	Kreuzer, Billon	Rare
3	1804	—	1 Batzen, Billon	—
4	1825	—	1 Batzen, Billon	—
5	1825	—	5 Batzen, Silver	—
6	1826	—	1 Thaler, Silver	—

KM#	Date	Mintage	Identification	Mkt.Val.
7	1838	100 pcs.	1 Cent, Copper with Silver center plug	—
7a	1838	Inc. Ab.	1 Cent, Silvered Copper	—

EINSIEDELN

An abbey in the canton of Schwyz. It was founded in 934 and produced few coins.

RULERS

Beatus Kuttel, Abbot, 1780-1808

DUCAT

.986 GOLD
Obv: Arms. Rev: Madonna.

C#	Date	Mintage	VG	Fine	VF	XF
3	1783	—	—	—	3500.	5000.

SILVER

C#	Date	Mintage	VG	Fine	VF	XF
3a	1783	—	—	Rare	—	—

FREYBURG

FRIBURG, FRIBOURG

A canton and city located in western Switzerland. The city was founded in 1178 and obtained the mint right in 1422. It joined the Swiss Confederation in 1481. During the Helvetian Republic period it was known as Sarine Et Broye but changed the name back to Freyburg in 1803.

MONETARY SYSTEM

Until 1798

16 Denier = 8 Vierer =
4 Kreuzer = 1 Batzen
56 Kreuzer = 8 Piecette = 1 Gulden
24 Piecette = 1 Thaler

DENIER

COPPER
Obv: Cross. Rev: Blank.

C#	Date	Mintage	VG	Fine	VF	XF
1	1735	—	3.00	7.50	12.00	18.00
	1745	—	5.00	10.00	15.00	25.00
	1763	—	3.00	7.50	12.00	18.00

VIERER

BILLON
Obv: Cartouche shield. Rev: Ornate anchor cross.

C#	Date	Mintage	VG	Fine	VF	XF
2a	1769	—	3.00	6.00	10.00	18.00
	1770	—	3.00	6.00	10.00	18.00
	1774	—	4.00	8.00	15.00	20.00
	1787	—	3.00	6.00	10.00	18.00
	1790	—	3.00	6.00	10.00	18.00

KREUZER

BILLON
Obv: Cartouche shield. Rev: Ornate anchor cross.

C#	Date	Mintage	VG	Fine	VF	XF
4	1732	—	5.00	10.00	15.00	23.00
	1736	—	5.00	10.00	15.00	23.00
	1737	—	3.00	5.00	7.50	12.00
	1738	—	3.00	5.00	7.50	12.00
	1741	—	3.00	5.00	7.50	12.00
	1761	—	4.00	8.00	12.50	18.00
	1769	—	3.00	7.00	9.00	15.00
	1770	—	3.00	7.00	9.00	15.00
	1772	—	3.00	5.00	7.50	12.00
	1774	—	3.00	5.00	7.50	12.00
	1787	—	3.00	5.00	8.50	14.00
	1789	—	3.00	5.00	7.50	12.00

SILVER

C#	Date	Mintage	VG	Fine	VF	XF
4a	1787	—	10.00	25.00	50.00	85.00

1/2 BATZEN

BILLON
Obv: Cartouche shield. Rev: Anchor cross.

C#	Date	Mintage	VG	Fine	VF	XF
6	1741	—	3.00	7.50	13.50	20.00
	1746	—	6.00	12.50	20.00	30.00
	1751	—	5.00	10.00	20.00	30.00
	1752	—	5.00	10.00	16.00	25.00
	1754	—	5.00	10.00	20.00	30.00
	1767	—	6.00	15.00	25.00	38.00
	1769	—	6.00	15.00	25.00	38.00
	1770	—	6.00	15.00	25.00	38.00
	1772	—	3.00	8.00	12.50	20.00
	1774	—	3.00	8.00	12.50	20.00
	1777	—	6.00	15.00	25.00	38.00
	1787	—	3.00	8.00	12.50	20.00
	1788	—	3.00	8.00	12.50	20.00
	1789	—	3.00	8.00	12.50	20.00
	1793	—	3.00	8.00	12.50	20.00
	1797	—	6.00	15.00	25.00	38.00
	1798	—	3.00	8.00	12.50	20.00

SILVER

C#	Date	Mintage	VG	Fine	VF	XF
6a	1774	—	—	—	—	—

GOLD

C#	Date	Mintage	VG	Fine	VF	XF
6b	1787	—	—	—	—	—

7 KREUZERS

SILVER
Similar to 28 Kreuzers, C#14.

C#	Date	Mintage	VG	Fine	VF	XF
10	1786	—	10.00	20.00	35.00	55.00
	1787	—	5.00	10.00	20.00	35.00
	1788	—	5.00	10.00	20.00	35.00
	1789	—	5.00	10.00	20.00	35.00
	1791	—	5.00	10.00	20.00	35.00
	1793	—	5.00	10.00	20.00	35.00
	1794	—	5.00	10.00	20.00	35.00
	1795	—	5.00	10.00	20.00	35.00
	1797	—	5.00	10.00	20.00	35.00

14 KREUZERS

SILVER
Similar to 28 Kreuzers, C#14.

C#	Date	Mintage	VG	Fine	VF	XF
12	1787	—	6.00	15.00	35.00	50.00
	1788	—	6.00	15.00	35.00	50.00
	1790	—	6.00	15.00	35.00	50.00
	1793	—	6.00	15.00	35.00	50.00
	1797	—	6.00	15.00	35.00	50.00
	1798	—	10.00	25.00	45.00	65.00

28 KREUZERS

SILVER

C#	Date	Mintage	VG	Fine	VF	XF
14	1793	—	20.00	50.00	100.00	185.00
	1798	—	25.00	60.00	125.00	210.00

56 KREUZERS

SILVER

C#	Date	Mintage	VG	Fine	VF	XF
16	1796	—	100.00	250.00	275.00	400.00
	1797	—	100.00	250.00	275.00	400.00

De Sarine Et Broye

42 KREUZERS

SILVER

C#	Date	Mintage	VG	Fine	VF	XF
21	1798	—	75.00	150.00	250.00	400.00

MONETARY REFORM

(After 1798)

10 Rappen = 1 Batzen
10 Batzen = 1 Frank

2-1/2 RAPPEN

BILLON
Obv: Arms, value below.
Rev: Cross in circle.

C#	Date	Mintage	VG	Fine	VF	XF
41	1827	—	3.00	5.00	7.50	12.00

Obv: Pointed arms.
Rev: Value and date in wreath.

C#	Date	Mintage	VG	Fine	VF	XF
41.5	1846BEL	—	2.00	5.00	7.50	12.00

5 RAPPEN

BILLON
Obv: Rectangular arms in corded circle, date below.
Rev: Value in octagon.

C#	Date	Mintage	VG	Fine	VF	XF
31	1806	—	4.00	15.00	20.00	28.00

Obv: Date

C#	Date	Mintage	VG	Fine	VF	XF
42	1827	—	3.00	8.00	14.00	23.00
	1828	—	3.00	8.00	14.00	23.00
	1829	—	3.00	8.00	14.00	23.00

Rev: Date

C#	Date	Mintage	VG	Fine	VF	XF
42a	1830BEL	—	3.00	7.00	11.00	15.00
	1831BEL	—	3.00	7.00	11.00	15.00

1/2 BATZEN

BILLON
Obv: Arms in circle, date below.
Rev: Value in branches.

C#	Date	Mintage	VG	Fine	VF	XF
32	1810	—	3.00	7.50	12.00	20.00
	1811	—	3.00	7.50	12.00	20.00

BATZEN

BILLON
Rev: Cross

C#	Date	Mintage	VG	Fine	VF	XF
33	1806	—	6.00	17.00	28.00	40.00

Rev. value: 1 BATZ. 10 RAP.

C#	Date	Mintage	VG	Fine	VF	XF
34	1810	—	6.00	17.00	28.00	40.00

Rev. value: 1 BATZEN/10

C#	Date	Mintage	VG	Fine	VF	XF
34a	1811	—	5.00	15.00	25.00	35.00

Rev. value: BAZ

C#	Date	Mintage	VG	Fine	VF	XF
43	1827	—	3.00	8.50	15.00	25.00
	1828	—	3.00	8.50	15.00	25.00

Rev. value: BATZ.

C#	Date	Mintage	VG	Fine	VF	XF
	1829	—	3.00	8.50	15.00	22.50

C#	Date	Mintage	VG	Fine	VF	XF
43a	1830B	—	3.00	8.50	15.00	22.50

5 BATZEN

SILVER

C#	Date	Mintage	VG	Fine	VF	XF
35	1811	—	8.00	20.00	40.00	65.00
	1814	—	8.00	20.00	40.00	65.00

Obv: Crowned oval arms in palm branches, value below.
Rev: Cross in quatrefoil.

C#	Date	Mintage	VG	Fine	VF	XF
44	1827	—	8.00	20.00	40.00	65.00
	1828	—	8.00	20.00	40.00	65.00
	1829	—	8.00	20.00	40.00	65.00

C#	Date	Mintage	VG	Fine	VF	XF
44a	1830	—	8.00	20.00	40.00	65.00

10 BATZEN

SILVER
Obv: Crowned oval arms in palm branches.
Rev: Knight with halberd holding shield, value below.

C#	Date	Mintage	VG	Fine	VF	XF
37	1811	4,907	40.00	100.00	200.00	300.00

Obv: Crowned oval arms within rectangular shield in palm and laurel branches.

C#	Date	Mintage	VG	Fine	VF	XF
—	1812	Inc. Ab.	40.00	100.00	200.00	300.00

4 FRANKEN

SILVER

C#	Date	Mintage	VG	Fine	VF	XF
39	1813	2,429	175.00	350.00	650.00	1000.

GENEVA

A canton and city in south western Switzerland. The city became a bishopric c.400 AD and was part of the Burgundian Kingdom for 500 years. They became completely independent in 1530. In 1798 they were occupied by France but became independent again in 1813. They joined the Swiss Confederation in 1815.

MINTMASTER'S INITIALS

A-B - Auguste Bovet
B - Binet
G - Girod
G - Gresset
H - Hoyer
I.G. - Jacques Gresset
J.G. - Jean Gresset
P.B. - Paul Binet
T.B. - Theodore Benneton
W - Charles Wielandy

MONETARY SYSTEM

Until 1794
12 Deniers = 4 Quarts = 1 Sol
12 Sols = 1 Florin
12 Florins, 9 Sols = 1 Thaler
35 Florins = 1 Pistole

6 DENIERS

BILLON
Obv: Round arms. Rev: Sun with beams.

C#	Date	Mintage	VG	Fine	VF	XF
2	1754	—	2.00	4.50	8.50	15.00
	1756	—	2.00	4.50	8.50	15.00
	1759	—	2.00	4.50	8.50	15.00
	1762	—	2.00	4.50	8.50	15.00
	1765	—	2.00	4.50	8.50	15.00
	1766	—	5.00	10.00	15.00	25.00
	1769	—	2.00	4.50	8.50	15.00
	1770	—	3.00	5.00	9.00	15.00
	1775	—	2.00	4.50	8.50	15.00
	1776	—	2.00	4.50	8.50	15.00
	1785	—	2.00	4.50	8.50	15.00
	1788	—	2.00	4.50	8.50	15.00

SILVER

C#	Date	Mintage	VG	Fine	VF	XF
2a	1750	—	20.00	50.00	75.00	115.00
	1754	—	20.00	50.00	75.00	115.00
	1759	—	20.00	50.00	75.00	115.00
	1776	—	20.00	50.00	75.00	115.00
	1785	—	20.00	50.00	75.00	115.00
	1788	—	20.00	50.00	75.00	115.00

GOLD

C#	Date	Mintage	VG	Fine	VF	XF
2b	1785	—	—	—	—	—
	1788	—	—	—	—	—

9 DENIERS

BILLON
Obv: Arms. Rev: Imperial eagle.

C#	Date	Mintage	VG	Fine	VF	XF
4	1753	—	3.00	5.00	10.00	18.00
	1763	—	3.00	5.00	10.00	18.00
	1775	—	3.00	5.00	10.00	18.00
	1785	—	3.00	5.00	10.00	18.00

SILVER

C#	Date	Mintage	VG	Fine	VF	XF
4a	1775	—	20.00	50.00	75.00	115.00
	1785	—	20.00	50.00	75.00	115.00

UN (1) SOL

BILLON

C#	Date	Mintage	VG	Fine	VF	XF
6	1785G	—	3.00	5.00	10.00	18.00
	1786G	—	3.00	5.00	10.00	18.00
	1788B	—	3.00	5.00	10.00	18.00

SILVER

C#	Date	Mintage	VG	Fine	VF	XF
6a	1785G	—	25.00	65.00	90.00	120.00
	1786	—	25.00	65.00	90.00	120.00
	1788	—	25.00	65.00	90.00	120.00

GOLD

C#	Date	Mintage	VG	Fine	VF	XF
6b	1786G	—	—	—	—	—

6 QUARTS

BILLON
Obv: Arms. Rev: Ornate cross within circle.

C#	Date	Mintage	VG	Fine	VF	XF
8	1722G	—	6.00	15.00	25.00	40.00
	1750G	—	6.00	12.50	20.00	30.00
	1763G	—	6.00	12.50	20.00	30.00
	1766G	—	6.00	12.50	20.00	30.00
	1775G	—	5.00	12.50	20.00	30.00
	1776G	—	5.00	12.50	20.00	30.00

SILVER

C#	Date	Mintage	VG	Fine	VF	XF
8a	1750G	—	20.00	50.00	75.00	115.00
	1763G	—	20.00	50.00	75.00	115.00
	1775G	—	20.00	50.00	75.00	115.00
	1776G	—	20.00	50.00	75.00	115.00

3 SOLS

BILLON
Obv: Arms. Rev: Anchor cross within cartouche, date at top.

C#	Date	Mintage	VG	Fine	VF	XF
10	1763GR	—	3.00	7.50	15.00	28.00
	1764GR	—	3.00	7.50	15.00	28.00
	1764	—	3.00	7.50	15.00	28.00
	1766	—	3.00	7.50	15.00	28.00
	1776 I-G	—	3.00	7.50	15.00	28.00

SILVER

C#	Date	Mintage	VG	Fine	VF	XF
10b	1763GR	—	25.00	60.00	90.00	120.00
	1766	—	25.00	60.00	90.00	120.00
	1776I-G	—	25.00	60.00	90.00	120.00

BILLON
Rev: Date at bottom.

C#	Date	Mintage	VG	Fine	VF	XF
10a	1791	—	3.00	7.50	15.00	25.00

SILVER

C#	Date	Mintage	VG	Fine	VF	XF
10c	1791	—	25.00	60.00	90.00	120.00

6 SOLS

BILLON
Obv: Arms.
Rev: Value in cartouche.

C#	Date	Mintage	VG	Fine	VF	XF
12	1765	—	6.00	15.00	25.00	40.00
	1765JG	—	6.00	15.00	25.00	40.00
	1776IG	—	6.00	15.00	25.00	40.00
	1791PB	—	6.00	15.00	25.00	40.00

SILVER

C#	Date	Mintage	VG	Fine	VF	XF
12a	1765	—	25.00	65.00	90.00	120.00
	1776IG	—	25.00	65.00	90.00	120.00
	1791PB	—	25.00	65.00	90.00	120.00

PISTOLE

.900 GOLD
Obv: Arms in cartouche. Rev: Imperial eagle.

C#	Date	Mintage	VG	Fine	VF	XF
22	1772	—	400.00	950.00	1600.	2900.

3 PISTOLES

.900 GOLD

C#	Date	Mintage	VG	Fine	VF	XF
23	1771	—	750.00	1800.	3000.	5000.

REVOLUTIONARY ISSUES

MONETARY SYSTEM

1794-1795
10 Decimes = 1 Genevoise
1795-1798
12 Deniers = 4 Quarts = 1 Sol
12 Sols = 1 Florin
12 Florins, 9 Sols = 1 Thaler
35 Florins = 1 Pistole

6 DENIERS

BILLON
Obv: Arms. Rev: Value within wreath.

C#	Date	Mintage	VG	Fine	VF	XF
31	1795	—	2.00	4.50	8.50	15.00

UN (1) SOL / SIX DENIERS

BILLON
Obv: Arms. Rev: Value I. SOL SIX D within wreath.

C#	Date	Mintage	VG	Fine	VF	XF
32	1795	—	5.00	12.50	20.00	30.00

Rev: Value UN SOL 6 D within wreath.

C#	Date	Mintage	VG	Fine	VF	XF
32.1	1795	—	5.00	12.50	20.00	30.00

SILVER

C#	Date	Mintage	VG	Fine	VF	XF
32a	1795	—	20.00	50.00	75.00	110.00

TROIS (3) SOLS

BILLON
Obv: Arms. Rev: Value within wreath.

C#	Date	Mintage	VG	Fine	VF	XF
35	1795	—	3.00	7.50	15.00	25.00
	1798	—	3.00	7.50	20.00	35.00

SILVER

C#	Date	Mintage	VG	Fine	VF	XF
35a	1798	—	22.00	50.00	75.00	110.00

6 SOLS

BILLON

C#	Date	Mintage	VG	Fine	VF	XF
37	1795TB	—	6.00	15.00	20.00	30.00
	1795	—	6.00	15.00	20.00	30.00
	1796	—	6.00	15.00	20.00	30.00
	1797	—	6.00	15.00	20.00	30.00

COPPER

C#	Date	Mintage	VG	Fine	VF	XF
37a	1795	—	8.00	20.00	30.00	45.00
	1796	—	8.00	20.00	30.00	45.00

SILVER

C#	Date	Mintage	VG	Fine	VF	XF
37b	1795	—	25.00	60.00	90.00	120.00
	1796	—	25.00	60.00	90.00	120.00

15 SOLS

SILVER

C#	Date	Mintage	VG	Fine	VF	XF
39	1794W	—	8.00	20.00	45.00	85.00
	1794	—	8.00	20.00	45.00	85.00

GOLD

C#	Date	Mintage	VG	Fine	VF	XF
39a	1794W	—	—	—	—	—

VI FLORINS

(= IV Sols = VI Deniers)

SILVER

C#	Date	Mintage	VG	Fine	VF	XF
41	1795W	—	20.00	50.00	100.00	165.00

GENEVOISE

(10 Decimes)

SILVER

C#	Date	Mintage	VG	Fine	VF	XF
43	1794 TB	.017	90.00	250.00	400.00	600.00

COPPER

C#	Date	Mintage	VG	Fine	VF	XF
43a	1794 TB	—	45.00	100.00	250.00	400.00

LEAD

C#	Date	Mintage	VG	Fine	VF	XF
43b	1794 TB	—	45.00	100.00	250.00	400.00

XII FLORINS / IX SOLS

SILVER

C#	Date	Mintage	VG	Fine	VF	XF
44	1795 TB	.021	65.00	150.00	275.00	450.00

Rev: Denomination in legend, IHS in sunburst.

C#	Date	Mintage	VG	Fine	VF	XF
44.1	1796	.012	65.00	150.00	275.00	450.00

MONETARY REFORM

1813-1838

12 Deniers = 4 Quarts = 1 Sol
12 Sols = 1 Florin
12 Florins, 9 Sols = 1 Thaler
35 Florins = 1 Pistole

6 DENIERS

BILLON
Rev: Value as 6 D.

C#	Date	Mintage	VG	Fine	VF	XF
51	1817	—	2.00	5.00	10.00	15.00

SILVER

C#	Date	Mintage	VG	Fine	VF	XF
51b	1817	—	18.00	40.00	60.00	100.00

BILLON

C#	Date	Mintage	VG	Fine	VF	XF
51a	1819	—	2.00	5.00	12.00	18.00
	1825	—	2.00	5.00	12.00	18.00
	1833	—	2.00	5.00	12.00	18.00

SILVER

C#	Date	Mintage	VG	Fine	VF	XF
51c	1819	—	18.00	40.00	60.00	100.00
	1825	—	18.00	40.00	60.00	100.00
	1833	—	18.00	40.00	60.00	100.00

SOL

BILLON

C#	Date	Mintage	VG	Fine	VF	XF
52	1817H	—	3.00	6.00	12.00	20.00
	1819	—	3.00	6.00	12.00	20.00

SILVER

C#	Date	Mintage	VG	Fine	VF	XF
52c	1817	—	20.00	50.00	75.00	110.00
	1819	—	20.00	50.00	75.00	110.00

BILLON

C#	Date	Mintage	VG	Fine	VF	XF
52a	1825	—	3.00	6.00	12.00	20.00
	1833	—	3.00	6.00	12.00	20.00

SILVER

C#	Date	Mintage	VG	Fine	VF	XF
52d	1825	—	20.00	50.00	75.00	110.00
	1833	—	20.00	50.00	75.00	110.00

1-1/2 SOL

BILLON
Rev: Value as UN/SOL/6 D

C#	Date	Mintage	VG	Fine	VF	XF
53	1817H	—	—	10.00	20.00	30.00

C#	Date	Mintage	VG	Fine	VF	XF
53a	1825	—	—	10.00	20.00	30.00

SILVER

C#	Date	Mintage	VG	Fine	VF	XF
53b	1825	—	25.00	60.00	90.00	120.00

DECIMAL SYSTEM

100 Centimes = 1 Franc

CENTIME

BILLON

C#	Date	Mintage	VG	Fine	VF	XF
63	1839	.325	2.00	5.00	10.00	18.00

SILVER

C#	Date	Mintage	VG	Fine	VF	XF
63a	1839	—	—	40.00	60.00	90.00

COPPER

C#	Date	Mintage	VG	Fine	VF	XF
61	1840	—	—	4.50	7.00	10.00
	1844	—	—	4.50	7.00	10.00
	1846	—	—	4.50	9.00	14.00

C#	Date	Mintage	VG	Fine	VF	XF
62	1847	—	—	5.00	9.00	12.00

SILVER

C#	Date	Mintage	VG	Fine	VF	XF
62a	1847	—	20.00	40.00	60.00	90.00

2 CENTIMES

BILLON

C#	Date	Mintage	VG	Fine	VF	XF
64	1839	.078	4.00	10.00	20.00	30.00

SILVER

C#	Date	Mintage	VG	Fine	VF	XF
64a	1839	—	20.00	50.00	70.00	100.00

4 CENTIMES

BILLON
Obv: Arms. Rev: Value over date.

C#	Date	Mintage	VG	Fine	VF	XF
65	1839	.331	4.00	10.00	20.00	35.00

SILVER

C#	Date	Mintage	VG	Fine	VF	XF
65a	1839	—	25.00	60.00	80.00	110.00

5 CENTIMES

BILLON

C#	Date	Mintage	VG	Fine	VF	XF
66	1840	.699	2.00	5.00	12.00	20.00

SILVER

C#	Date	Mintage	VG	Fine	VF	XF
66a	1840	—	12.00	30.00	60.00	90.00

BILLON

Rev: Arms on shield

C#	Date	Mintage	VG	Fine	VF	XF
69	1847A.-B.	I.A.	—	5.00	12.00	20.00

SILVER

C#	Date	Mintage	VG	Fine	VF	XF
69a	1847	—	12.00	30.00	60.00	90.00

10 CENTIMES

BILLON

C#	Date	Mintage	VG	Fine	VF	XF
67	1839	—	3.00	7.00	15.00	22.00
	1844	—	3.00	7.00	15.00	22.00

SILVER

C#	Date	Mintage	VG	Fine	VF	XF
67a	1839	—	12.00	30.00	50.00	75.00

BILLON

C#	Date	Mintage	VG	Fine	VF	XF
70	1847A.-B.	—	3.00	7.00	15.00	22.00

SILVER

C#	Date	Mintage	VG	Fine	VF	XF
70a	1847	—	12.00	30.00	50.00	75.00

25 CENTIMES

BILLON

C#	Date	Mintage	VG	Fine	VF	XF
68	1839	—	3.00	8.50	15.00	25.00
	1844	—	3.00	8.50	15.00	25.00

SILVER

C#	Date	Mintage	VG	Fine	VF	XF
68a	1839	—	15.00	35.00	65.00	95.00

BILLON

C#	Date	Mintage	VG	Fine	VF	XF
71	1847A.-B.	—	3.00	7.50	15.00	25.00

SILVER

C#	Date	Mintage	VG	Fine	VF	XF
71a	1847	—	15.00	35.00	65.00	95.00

5 FRANCS

SILVER

C#	Date	Mintage	VG	Fine	VF	XF
72	1848	1,176	50.00	100.00	250.00	350.00

10 FRANCS

SILVER

C#	Date	Mintage	VG	Fine	VF	XF
73	1848	385 pcs.	250.00	450.00	650.00	950.00
	1851	1,000	175.00	350.00	550.00	850.00

.750 GOLD

C#	Date	Mintage	VG	Fine	VF	XF
74	1848	336 pcs.	—	1000.	2000.	3000.

20 FRANCS

.750 GOLD

C#	Date	Mintage	VG	Fine	VF	XF
75	1848	3,421	—	800.00	1100.	2200.

NCLT ISSUES

PATTERNS

KM#	Date	Mintage	Identification	Mkt.Val.
1	1794TB	—	5 Centimes, silver	700.00
2	1794	—	XII Florins, copper	900.00

KM#	Date	Mintage	Identification	Mkt.Val.
3	1795	—	Decime, silver	750.00

KM#	Date	Mintage	Identification	Mkt.Val.
4	1795	—	XII Florins/IX Sols	—

GLARUS

A canton in eastern Switzerland. Independence was gained in c. 1390 but from 1798-1803 it was occupied by the French. They rejoined the Swiss Confederation in 1803.

MONETARY SYSTEM

3 Rappen = 1 Schilling
100 Rappen = 1 Frank

SCHILLING

BILLON
Obv: Arms, date in exergue. Rev: Value.

C#	Date	Mintage	VG	Fine	VF	XF
1	1806F	—	5.00	12.00	20.00	35.00
	1807F	—	5.00	17.00	25.00	40.00
	1808	—	5.00	12.00	20.00	35.00
	1809 draped shield					
		—	5.00	14.00	20.00	40.00
	1809 undraped shield					
		—	5.00	12.00	20.00	35.00
	1810	—	5.00	27.00	50.00	70.00
	1811	—	5.00	12.00	20.00	35.00
	1812	—	5.00	12.00	20.00	35.00
	1813	—	5.00	12.00	20.00	35.00

3 SCHILLING

BILLON
Obv: Arms, date in exergue. Rev: Value.

C#	Date	Mintage	VG	Fine	VF	XF
2	1806	.134	8.00	21.00	30.00	50.00
	1808	—	8.00	21.00	30.00	50.00
	1809	—	8.00	21.00	30.00	50.00
	1810	—	8.00	21.00	30.00	50.00
	1812	—	8.00	21.00	30.00	50.00
	1814	—	8.00	21.00	30.00	50.00

15 SCHILLING

SILVER
Obv: Arms, date in exergue. Rev: Value.

C#	Date	Mintage	VG	Fine	VF	XF
3	1806B	7,067	25.00	60.00	110.00	160.00
	1807B	Inc. Ab.	25.00	60.00	110.00	160.00
	1811B	Inc. Ab.	25.00	60.00	110.00	160.00
	1813B	Inc. Ab.	25.00	60.00	110.00	160.00
	1814B	Inc. Ab.	25.00	60.00	110.00	160.00

GRAUBUNDEN

The largest and most easterly of the Swiss cantons. The district was set up in the reign of Roman Emperor Augustus and was one of the various factions sparring for power in the 14th and 15th centuries. The name is derived from "Grey League." The first coins were issued in c. 1600. They joined the Swiss Confederation in 1803.

MINTMASTER'S INITIALS

A-B - Bouey
H.B. - Bruppacher

MONETARY REFORM

15 Rappen = 6 Bluzger = 1 Schweizer Batzen
10 Schweizer Batzen = 1 Frank
16 Franken = 1 Duplone

1/6 BATZEN

BILLON
Rev. value: 1/6 BATZEN

C#	Date	Mintage	VG	Fine	VF	XF
1	1807	.058	5.00	12.00	22.00	30.00
	1820	.480	5.00	12.00	25.00	35.00

Rev. value: 1/6 BAZEN

C#	Date	Mintage	VG	Fine	VF	XF
1a	1842A.B.	.172	5.00	12.00	20.00	30.00

1/2 BATZEN

BILLON
Rev. value: 1/2 BATZEN

C#	Date	Mintage	VG	Fine	VF	XF
2	1807	.075	6.00	15.00	30.00	50.00
	1812	.100	6.00	15.00	35.00	60.00
	1820B	.060	6.00	15.00	30.00	50.00

Rev. value: 1/2 BAZEN

C#	Date	Mintage	VG	Fine	VF	XF
3	1836A-B	.212	6.00	15.00	25.00	45.00
	1842A-B	.162	6.00	15.00	25.00	45.00

BATZEN

BILLON

Rev. value: 1 BATZEN

C#	Date	Mintage	VG	Fine	VF	XF
4	1807	.056	7.00	18.00	27.50	50.00
	1820B	.050	7.00	18.00	27.50	50.00
	1826B	.050	7.00	18.00	27.50	50.00

Rev. value: 1 BAZEN

C#	Date	Mintage	VG	Fine	VF	XF
5	1836	.099	10.00	30.00	40.00	60.00
	1836HB	Inc. Ab.	7.00	18.00	25.00	45.00
	1842A-B	.100	7.00	18.00	25.00	45.00

5 BATZEN

SILVER

C#	Date	Mintage	VG	Fine	VF	XF
6	1807	6,398	20.00	50.00	110.00	200.00
	1820	.016	20.00	50.00	110.00	200.00
	1826	—	20.00	50.00	110.00	200.00

10 BATZEN

SILVER

C#	Date	Mintage	VG	Fine	VF	XF
7	1825N	2,000	100.00	200.00	300.00	450.00

16 FRANKEN

.900 GOLD

C#	Date	Mintage	VG	Fine	VF	XF
8	1813	100 Pcs.	—	2000.	4000.	6000.

LUZERN

LUCERNE

A canton and city in central Switzerland. The city grew around the Benedictine Monastary which was founded in 750. They joined the Swiss Confederation as the 4th member in 1332. Few coins were issued before the 1500s.

MINTMASTER'S INITIALS

B, Br - Bruppacher
HL - Hedlinger
M - Meyer

MONETARY SYSTEM

Until 1798

240 Angster = 120 Rappen
= 40 Schillinge = 1 Gulden
10 Rappen = 1 Batzen
4 Kreuzer = 1 Batzen
10 Batzen = 1 Frank
40 Batzen = 3 Gulden = 1 Thaler
4 Franken = 1 Thaler
12 Gulden = 1 Duplone

ANGSTER

COPPER

C#	Date	Mintage	VG	Fine	VF	XF
1	1773	—	3.00	5.00	10.00	15.00

C#	Date	Mintage	VG	Fine	VF	XF
3	1775	—	2.00	4.50	6.50	10.00
	1790	—	2.00	4.50	6.50	10.00
	1804	—	3.00	6.00	10.00	15.00
	1811	—	2.00	4.00	6.50	10.00
	1823	—	2.00	4.00	6.50	10.00
	1832	—	2.00	4.00	6.50	10.00
	1834	—	2.00	4.00	6.50	10.00

SILVER

C#	Date	Mintage	VG	Fine	VF	XF
3a	1775	—	10.00	25.00	50.00	100.00
	1790	—	10.00	25.00	50.00	100.00

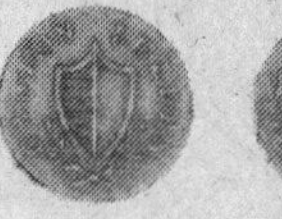

Obv. leg: CANTON LUZERN

C#	Date	Mintage	VG	Fine	VF	XF
6	1839	—	2.00	4.00	6.50	10.00
	1843	—	2.00	4.00	6.50	10.00

RAPPEN

COPPER

C#	Date	Mintage	VG	Fine	VF	XF
2	ND(1773)	—	2.00	3.25	6.00	9.00

Obv: Arms in cartouche.
Rev: Value as 1 RAPPEN in cartouche, date.

C#	Date	Mintage	VG	Fine	VF	XF
4	1774	—	2.00	4.50	6.50	10.00
	1787	—	2.00	4.50	6.50	10.00
	1789	—	2.00	4.50	6.50	10.00
	1795	—	2.00	4.50	6.50	10.00
	1796	—	2.00	4.50	6.50	10.00
	1804	—	2.00	4.50	6.50	10.00

SILVER

C#	Date	Mintage	VG	Fine	VF	XF
4a	1774	—	10.00	25.00	50.00	85.00
	1787	—	10.00	25.00	50.00	85.00

GOLD

C#	Date	Mintage	VG	Fine	VF	XF
4b	1774	—	—	—	—	—

Rev. value: 1 RAPEN in wreath.

C#	Date	Mintage	VG	Fine	VF	XF
4.1	1804	—	2.00	5.00	10.00	15.00

Rev. value: 1 RAPPEN or RAPEN

C#	Date	Mintage	VG	Fine	VF	XF
5	1831	—	2.00	5.00	7.50	12.00
5a	1834	—	2.00	5.00	7.50	12.00

Obv. leg: CANTON LUZERN, oak circle.

C#	Date	Mintage	VG	Fine	VF	XF
6	1839	—	2.00	5.00	7.50	12.00

Obv. leg: CANTON LUZERN, oak wreath.

C#	Date	Mintage	VG	Fine	VF	XF
7	1839	—	2.00	5.00	6.50	10.00
	1843	—	2.00	5.00	6.50	10.00
	1844	—	2.00	5.00	6.50	10.00
	1845	—	2.00	5.00	6.50	10.00
	1846	—	2.00	5.00	6.50	10.00

SCHILLING

BILLON

Obv: Arms in shield within circle.
Rev: Facing portrait of Saint Leodegari.

C#	Date	Mintage	VG	Fine	VF	XF
11	1794	—	2.00	5.50	8.50	16.00
	1795	—	2.00	5.50	8.50	16.00

COPPER

C#	Date	Mintage	VG	Fine	VF	XF
11a	1794	—	—	—	—	—

1/2 BATZEN

BILLON

Obv: Oval arms in cartouche.
Rev: Anchor cross within circle.

C#	Date	Mintage	VG	Fine	VF	XF
13	1795	—	2.00	5.50	12.00	25.00
	1796	—	2.00	5.50	12.00	25.00

C#	Date	Mintage	VG	Fine	VF	XF
28	1813	—	4.00	10.00	12.00	28.00

BATZEN

BILLON

Obv: Oval arms in cartouche within circle.
Rev: Anchor cross within circle.

C#	Date	Mintage	VG	Fine	VF	XF
14	1796	—	2.00	5.50	10.00	20.00
	1797	—	2.00	5.50	10.00	20.00

Obv. value: 1 BAZ. Rev: X RAPPEN.

C#	Date	Mintage	VG	Fine	VF	XF
30	1803	—	6.00	15.00	25.00	40.00

Obv: Oval arms between branches, 1 BAZ in exergue.
Rev: Value and date in oak wreath.

C#	Date	Mintage	VG	Fine	VF	XF
30a	1804	—	4.00	10.00	16.00	25.00
	1806	—	4.00	10.00	18.00	30.00

Obv: Garlands over oval arms, date in exergue.

C#	Date	Mintage	VG	Fine	VF	XF
31	1807	—	—	10.00	15.00	25.00
	1808	—	—	10.00	15.00	25.00
	1809	—	—	10.00	15.00	25.00
	1810	—	—	10.00	15.00	25.00
	1811	—	—	10.00	15.00	25.00

Obv. value: 1 BATZEN-10 RAPPEN

C#	Date	Mintage	VG	Fine	VF	XF
31b	1813	—	—	8.00	12.00	18.00

Obv: MONETA REIPUB.LUCERNENCIS

C#	Date	Mintage	VG	Fine	VF	XF
30b	1805	—	—	15.00	20.00	28.00

1/8 GULDEN

(5 Schillings)

SILVER

Similar to 40 Kreuzers, C#21.

C#	Date	Mintage	VG	Fine	VF	XF
16	1793	—	6.00	12.00	25.00	45.00

GOLD

C#	Date	Mintage	VG	Fine	VF	XF
16a	1793	—	—	—	—	—

1/4 GULDEN

(10 Schillings)

SILVER

Similar to 40 Kreuzers, C#21.

C#	Date	Mintage	VG	Fine	VF	XF
17	1793	—	6.00	15.00	35.00	60.00
	1796	—	6.00	15.00	35.00	60.00

2-1/2 BATZEN

SILVER
Obv: Date

C#	Date	Mintage	VG	Fine	VF	XF
33a	1815	—	6.00	15.00	30.00	45.00

Rev: Date

C#	Date	Mintage	VG	Fine	VF	XF
33	1815	—	10.00	25.00	45.00	75.00

20 KREUZERS

SILVER
Similar to 40 Kreuzers, C#21.

C#	Date	Mintage	VG	Fine	VF	XF
20	1793	—	8.00	20.00	40.00	70.00

C#	Date	Mintage	VG	Fine	VF	XF
20a	1795	—	8.00	20.00	40.00	70.00
	1796	—	8.00	20.00	40.00	70.00

5 BATZEN

SILVER
Rev. value: V BATZEN.

C#	Date	Mintage	VG	Fine	VF	XF
34	1806	—	8.00	20.00	35.00	60.00

Rev. value: 5 BATZ.

C#	Date	Mintage	VG	Fine	VF	XF
34a	1810	—	8.00	20.00	35.00	60.00
	1813	—	8.00	20.00	35.00	60.00
	1814	—	8.00	20.00	35.00	60.00

Obv: Date

C#	Date	Mintage	VG	Fine	VF	XF
34b	1815	—	8.00	20.00	35.00	60.00
	1816	—	8.00	20.00	35.00	60.00

40 KREUZERS

SILVER
Obv: Crowned arms in cartouche.
Rev: Double L monogram.

C#	Date	Mintage	VG	Fine	VF	XF
19	1782	—	50.00	100.00	160.00	250.00

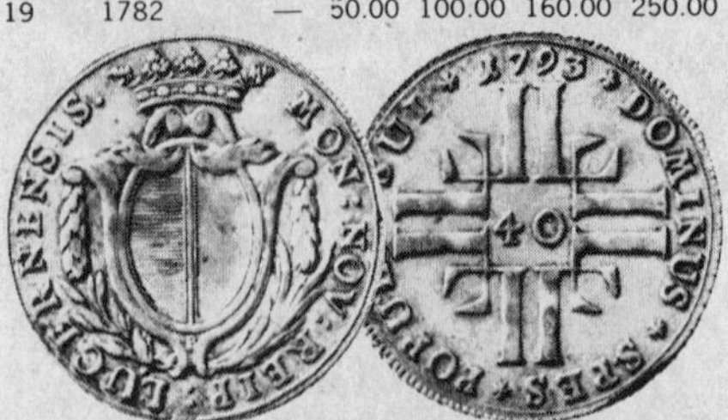

C#	Date	Mintage	VG	Fine	VF	XF
21	1793	—	20.00	50.00	110.00	200.00

C#	Date	Mintage	VG	Fine	VF	XF
21a	1796	—	25.00	60.00	125.00	215.00

10 BATZEN

SILVER

C#	Date	Mintage	VG	Fine	VF	XF
35	1811	—	75.00	180.00	250.00	350.00
	1812	—	30.00	65.00	150.00	230.00

20 BATZEN

SILVER

C#	Date	Mintage	VG	Fine	VF	XF
23	1795M	—	20.00	50.00	125.00	200.00

40 BATZEN

SILVER

C#	Date	Mintage	VG	Fine	VF	XF
24	1796	.012	80.00	200.00	350.00	650.00

C#	Date	Mintage	VG	Fine	VF	XF
37	1816	3,107	100.00	300.00	475.00	775.00
	1817	3,989	125.00	350.00	500.00	800.00

4 FRANKEN

SILVER

C#	Date	Mintage	VG	Fine	VF	XF
36	1813	—	75.00	180.00	350.00	600.00
	1814	.044	45.00	100.00	200.00	275.00

10 FRANKEN

GOLD

C#	Date	Mintage	VG	Fine	VF	XF
43	1804	—	—	600.00	800.00	1200.

20 FRANKEN

GOLD

C#	Date	Mintage	VG	Fine	VF	XF
44	1807B	—	—	1000.	2000.	3500.

12 MUNZGULDEN

GOLD

Fr#	Date	Mintage	Fine	VF	XF
275	1794B	—	600.00	1000.	1800.
	1796B	—	725.00	1200.	2000.

COPPER

Fr#	Date	Mintage	Fine	VF	XF
—	1796B	—	—	—	—

24 MUNZGULDEN

GOLD

Obv: Crowned and draped arms. Rev: Value, date.

Fr#	Date	Mintage	Fine	VF	XF
274	1794B	—	1100.	1800.	3000.
	1796M	—	850.00	1400.	2400.

NEUCHATEL

A canton on the west central border of Switzerland. The first coins (bracteates) were struck in the 11th century. They were under Prussian rule from 1707 to 1806. France occupied the canton from 1806-1815. They reverted to Prussia until 1857, when they became a full member of the Swiss Confederation.

RULERS

Friedrich Wilhelm II, Prussia, 1786-1797
Friedrich Wilhelm III (Prussia) 1797-1806
Alexandre Berthier, Prince, 1806-1814
Friedrich Wilhelm III, 1814-1840

MONETARY SYSTEM

4 Kreuzer = 1 Batzen
7 Kreuzer = 1 Piecette
21 Batzen = 1 Gulden
2 Gulden = 1 Thaler

1/2 KREUZER

BILLON

Obv: Crowned shield. Rev: Anchor cross.

C#	Date	Mintage	VG	Fine	VF	XF
10	1789	—	4.00	12.50	25.00	40.00
	1790	—	4.00	10.00	17.50	30.00
	1791	—	4.00	10.00	17.50	30.00
	1792	—	4.00	10.00	17.50	30.00
	1793	—	6.00	15.00	30.00	50.00
	1794	—	4.00	10.00	17.50	30.00
	1795	—	4.00	10.00	17.50	30.00
	1796	—	4.00	10.00	17.50	30.00
25	1802	—	6.00	16.00	35.00	55.00

KREUZER

BILLON

C#	Date	Mintage	VG	Fine	VF	XF
11	1789	—	10.00	25.00	40.00	65.00
	1790	—	4.00	10.00	17.50	30.00
	1791	—	4.00	10.00	17.50	30.00
	1792	—	4.00	10.00	17.50	30.00
	1794	—	4.00	10.00	17.50	30.00
27	1800	—	3.00	8.00	12.00	25.00
	1802	—	3.00	8.00	12.00	25.00
	1803	—	3.00	8.00	12.00	25.00
35	1807	—	2.00	6.50	10.00	18.00
35	1808	—	3.00	6.50	10.00	18.00

C#	Date	Mintage	VG	Fine	VF	XF
40	1817	.303	3.00	6.50	10.00	18.00
	1818	Inc. Ab.	4.00	10.00	15.00	25.00

1/2 BATZEN

BILLON

C#	Date	Mintage	VG	Fine	VF	XF
12	1789	—	5.00	12.00	18.50	28.00
	1790	—	5.00	12.00	18.50	28.00
	1791	—	5.00	12.00	18.50	28.00
	1792	—	5.00	12.00	18.50	28.00
	1793	—	5.00	12.00	18.50	28.00
	1794	—	5.00	12.00	18.50	28.00

SILVER

C#	Date	Mintage	VG	Fine	VF	XF
12a	1793	—	—	—	—	—

BILLON

Obv. leg: F.G.BOR.REX.PR......

C#	Date	Mintage	VG	Fine	VF	XF
28	1798	—	3.00	7.50	15.00	23.00
	1799	—	3.00	7.50	15.00	23.00
	1803	—	3.00	7.50	15.00	23.00

Obv. leg: F.W.III.BOR.REX.P......, large crowned wide shield.

C#	Date	Mintage	VG	Fine	VF	XF
28.1	1799	—	3.00	7.50	15.00	23.00
	1800	—	3.00	7.50	15.00	23.00
	1803	—	3.00	7.50	15.00	23.00

Obv: Crowned spade shaped shield.

C#	Date	Mintage	VG	Fine	VF	XF
28.2	1799	—	3.00	7.50	15.00	23.00
	1800	—	3.00	7.50	15.00	23.00

Rev. value: DEMI BATZ

C#	Date	Mintage	VG	Fine	VF	XF
36a	1807	—	3.00	9.50	18.00	25.00

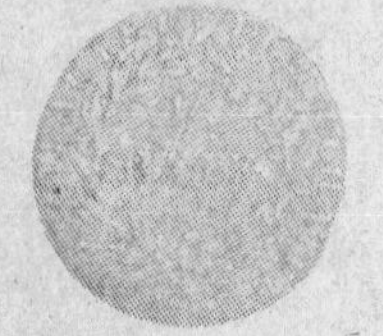

Rev. value: 1/2 BATZ

C#	Date	Mintage	VG	Fine	VF	XF
36	1807	—	3.00	7.00	14.00	20.00
	1808	—	3.00	7.00	14.00	20.00
	1809	—	3.00	8.50	18.00	28.00

4 KREUZER

BILLON

C#	Date	Mintage	VG	Fine	VF	XF
13	1790	—	5.00	12.00	18.00	28.00
	1791	—	5.00	12.00	18.00	28.00
	1792	—	5.00	12.50	24.50	36.00
	1793	—	5.00	12.00	18.00	28.00

Obv. leg: F.G.BOR.REX.PR.....

C#	Date	Mintage	VG	Fine	VF	XF
29	1798	—	4.00	10.00	16.00	25.00

Obv. leg: F W 111.BOR REX.P....

C#	Date	Mintage	VG	Fine	VF	XF
29.1	1799	—	4.00	10.00	16.00	25.00

Obv. and rev. with inner dotted circle.

C#	Date	Mintage	VG	Fine	VF	XF
29.2	1800	—	4.00	10.00	16.00	25.00

BATZEN

Rev. value: 1 BATZ

C#	Date	Mintage	VG	Fine	VF	XF
37	1806	—	6.00	15.00	20.00	30.00
	1807	—	4.00	9.50	15.00	22.00
	1808	—	4.00	9.50	15.00	22.00
	1809	—	4.00	9.50	15.00	22.00
	1810	—	6.00	15.00	20.00	30.00

Rev. value: UN BATZ

C#	Date	Mintage	VG	Fine	VF	XF
37a	1807	—	4.00	9.50	15.00	28.00
	1808	—	4.00	9.50	15.00	28.00

28 KREUZERS

SILVER

C#	Date	Mintage	VG	Fine	VF	XF
15	1793	7,887	25.00	65.00	125.00	200.00
	1796	Inc. Ab.	20.00	50.00	100.00	160.00

10-1/2 BATZEN

SILVER

C#	Date	Mintage	VG	Fine	VF	XF
17	1796	5,052	25.00	60.00	125.00	185.00

56 KREUZERS

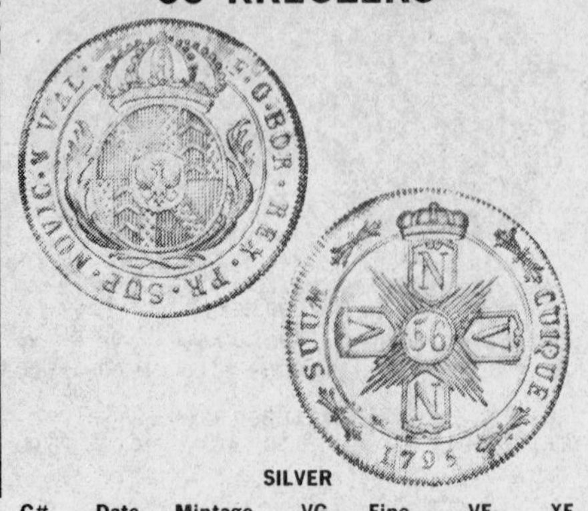

SILVER

C#	Date	Mintage	VG	Fine	VF	XF
19	1795	5,478	50.00	125.00	200.00	325.00

21 BATZEN

SILVER

C#	Date	Mintage	VG	Fine	VF	XF
21	1796	.023	100.00	225.00	350.00	500.00

C#	Date	Mintage	VG	Fine	VF	XF
32	1799	.036	75.00	175.00	275.00	425.00

Rev: UI in legend joined.

C#	Date	Mintage	VG	Fine	VF	XF
32.1	1799	Inc. Ab.	100.00	250.00	375.00	500.00

NCLT ISSUES

PATTERNS

KM#	Date	Mintage	Identification	Mkt.Val.
1	1814	—	2 Francs, Copper	—
2	1814	—	2 Francs, Silver	—

KM#	Date	Mintage	Identification	Mkt.Val.
3	181-.	—	5 Francs, Silver, PRIN.	—

KM#	Date	Mintage	Identification	Mkt.Val.
4	181-.	—	5 Francs, Silver, PRINCE (Restruck at end of 19th Century)	—

ST. GALL

(ST. GALLEN)

RULERS

Beda Angehrn Von Hagenwyl, Abbot, 1767-1796

MINTMASTER'S INITIALS

H - Haag
K - Kankler

MONETARY SYSTEM

4 Pfennig = 1 Kreuzer
4 Kreuzer = 1 Batzen
10 Batzen = 1 Frank

Abbey Coinage

An abbey in northeast Switzerland. Established in c. 720 they obtained the mint right in 947 but the first coins were not made until about 100 years later. The power of the abbey dwindled until the last Abbot resigned in 1805.

PFENNIG

BILLON

Obv: Bear left. Rev: Value in cartouche.

C#	Date	Mintage	VG	Fine	VF	XF
1	ND	—	—	—	—	—
	GOLD					
1a	ND	—	—	—	—	—

KREUZER

BILLON

Obv: Bear left. Rev: Value in cartouche, H mintmark.

C#	Date	Mintage	VG	Fine	VF	XF
2	ND	—	28.00	60.00	100.00	160.00
	Obv: Bear right. Rev: Value in curved line within cartouche.					
2a	ND	—	20.00	35.00	60.00	110.00

2 KREUZERS

(= 1/2 Batzen)

BILLON

Obv: Bear right. Rev: Value, date within crossed branches.

C#	Date	Mintage	VG	Fine	VF	XF
3	1780	—	8.00	17.50	35.00	60.00

4 KREUZERS

(= Batzen)

BILLON

Obv: Bear right. Rev: Value, date within crossed branches.

C#	Date	Mintage	VG	Fine	VF	XF
4	1780	—	6.00	15.00	30.00	50.00
	1782	—	8.00	22.50	40.00	60.00

5 KREUZERS

BILLON

Similar to 20 Kreuzers, C#10.

C#	Date	Mintage	VG	Fine	VF	XF
5	1774H	—	6.00	15.00	30.00	45.00
	1775	—	6.00	15.00	30.00	45.00

6 KREUZERS

BILLON

Obv: Crowned BAP monogram. Rev: Crowned draped arms.

C#	Date	Mintage	VG	Fine	VF	XF
6	ND H	—	—	—	—	—
	Date added.					
6a	1773H	—	12.00	35.00	70.00	100.00

10 KREUZERS

SILVER

Similar to 20 Kreuzers, C#10.

C#	Date	Mintage	VG	Fine	VF	XF
7	1774	—	20.00	50.00	75.00	125.00
	1775	—	12.00	30.00	60.00	90.00

12 KREUZERS

SILVER

Obv: Crowned BAP monogram. Rev: Crowned draped arms.

C#	Date	Mintage	VG	Fine	VF	XF
8	ND H	—	—	—	—	—
	COPPER					
8b	ND H	—	—	—	—	—

SILVER
Obv: Date

C#	Date	Mintage	VG	Fine	VF	XF
8a	1773H	—	30.00	80.00	125.00	180.00

Rev: Date

C#	Date	Mintage	VG	Fine	VF	XF
8a.1	1773H	—	25.00	60.00	120.00	150.00

15 KREUZERS

SILVER
Obv: MON. PRINCIP. TERRIT. GALLI, date, value.
Rev: Bear within branches.

C#	Date	Mintage	VG	Fine	VF	XF
9	1781	—	12.00	35.00	75.00	135.00

20 KREUZERS

SILVER

C#	Date	Mintage	VG	Fine	VF	XF
10	1774H	—	10.00	25.00	50.00	100.00

Similar to C#11a but different arms.

C#	Date	Mintage	VG	Fine	VF	XF
11	1777H	—	40.00	100.00	200.00	325.00
	1779	—	20.00	50.00	100.00	175.00

C#	Date	Mintage	VG	Fine	VF	XF
11a	1780B	—	10.00	25.00	50.00	90.00
	1780	—	10.00	25.00	50.00	90.00
	1783	—	12.00	35.00	70.00	125.00

30 KREUZERS

(= 1/2 Gulden)

SILVER
Obv: MON. PRINCIP. TERRIT. GALLI, date, value.
Rev: Bear within branches.

C#	Date	Mintage	VG	Fine	VF	XF
12	1781	—	25.00	60.00	125.00	185.00
	1796	—	25.00	60.00	125.00	185.00

1/2 TALER

SILVER

C#	Date	Mintage	VG	Fine	VF	XF
13	1776	—	50.00	100.00	200.00	300.00
	1777	—	50.00	100.00	200.00	300.00

C#	Date	Mintage	VG	Fine	VF	XF
13a	1780B	—	50.00	100.00	200.00	300.00
	1780	—	50.00	100.00	200.00	300.00
	1782	—	60.00	125.00	250.00	350.00

GULDEN

SILVER
Obv: MON. PRINCIP. TERRIT. GALLI, date, value.
Rev: Bear within branches.

C#	Date	Mintage	VG	Fine	VF	XF
13.5	1781	—	—	—	Rare	—

TALER

SILVER
Obv. and rev: Small legends.

C#	Date	Mintage	VG	Fine	VF	XF
14	1776V	—	100.00	250.00	450.00	700.00

Obv. and rev: Large legends.

C#	Date	Mintage	VG	Fine	VF	XF
14.1	1777H	—	100.00	250.00	450.00	700.00
	1779	—	1000.	2250.	3500.	4500.

C#	Date	Mintage	VG	Fine	VF	XF
14a	1780B	—	100.00	250.00	450.00	700.00

TRADE COINS

1/2 DUCAT

.986 GOLD
Obv: Crowned BAP monogram.
Rev: Crowned, draped arms.

C#	Date	Mintage	VG	Fine	VF	XF
14.5	1773	—	—	—	—	—

DUCAT

.986 GOLD
Obv: Crowned, draped arms. Rev: Seated abbot, bear to left, date in legend.

C#	Date	Mintage	VG	Fine	VF	XF
15	1773H	—	—	1800.	3000.	5000.

Obv: Wider draped on arms, date divided by arms.

C#	Date	Mintage	VG	Fine	VF	XF
15.1	1774	—	—	1400.	2400.	4000.

C#	Date	Mintage	VG	Fine	VF	XF
16	1781	—	—	1200.	2000.	3400.

City Coinage

A city located in northeast Switzerland which was built to protect the abbey. It became a free city in 1311 and gained independence from the Abbots in 1457. The first coins were struck in the 1400s and the last ones in 1790.

MINTMASTER'S INITIALS

H.G.Z.,Z - Hans Georg Zolli Kofer

2 KREUZERS

BILLON
Obv: Bear within circle. Rev: SOLI DEO GLORIA, date.

C#	Date	Mintage	VG	Fine	VF	XF
34	1766	—	3.00	8.00	15.00	25.00
	1767	—	3.00	8.00	15.00	25.00
	1768	—	6.00	15.00	32.50	55.00

3 KREUZERS

BILLON
Obv: Bear within circle. Rev: 3 in circle in center of floral cross within circle.

C#	Date	Mintage	VG	Fine	VF	XF
35	1790	—	3.00	8.00	15.00	25.00

6 KREUZERS

BILLON
Obv: Bear within circle. Rev: Value, date within crossed branches.

C#	Date	Mintage	VG	Fine	VF	XF
38	1786	—	4.00	10.00	25.00	45.00
	1790	—	3.00	8.00	20.00	40.00

15 KREUZERS

BILLON
Obv: Bear within circle. Rev: SOLI DEO GLORIA, date, value within cartouche.

C#	Date	Mintage	VG	Fine	VF	XF
39	1786	—	10.00	25.00	50.00	80.00
	1789	—	50.00	125.00	175.00	240.00

Cantonal Coinage

A canton in northeast Switzerland which completely surrounds the canton of Appenzell. It joined the Swiss Confederation in 1803.

PFENNIG

BILLON
Uniface, arms on concave planchet.

C#	Date	Mintage	VG	Fine	VF	XF
51	ND	.151	3.00	8.00	12.00	20.00

2 PFENNIG

BILLON

C#	Date	Mintage	VG	Fine	VF	XF
52	1808	—	8.00	20.00	40.00	75.00

1/2 KREUZER

BILLON

C#	Date	Mintage	VG	Fine	VF	XF
53	1808K	.111	3.00	8.00	12.00	20.00
	1809K	.118	3.00	8.00	12.00	20.00
	1810K	.101	3.00	8.00	12.00	20.00
	1811K	.099	3.00	8.00	12.00	20.00
	1812K	.175	3.00	8.00	12.00	20.00
	1813K	.149	3.00	8.00	12.00	20.00
	1814K	.114	3.00	8.00	12.00	20.00
	1815K	.136	3.00	8.00	12.00	20.00
	1816K	.238	3.00	8.00	12.00	20.00
	1817K	—	3.00	8.00	12.00	20.00

Rev. value: 2 PFENNIG

C#	Date	Mintage	VG	Fine	VF	XF
52	1808K	—	35.00	80.00	125.00	185.00

KREUZER

BILLON
Rev. value: 1/4 SCHWEIZ BASEN

C#	Date	Mintage	VG	Fine	VF	XF
54	1807K	.162	10.00	25.00	35.00	60.00
	1808K	.202	3.00	8.00	12.00	18.00

Rev. value: 1 KREUZER

C#	Date	Mintage	VG	Fine	VF	XF
55	1807	Inc. Ab.	10.00	25.00	35.00	50.00
	1809K	.160	2.00	5.50	6.00	11.00
	1810K	.146	2.00	5.50	6.00	11.00
	1811K	.106	2.00	5.50	6.00	11.00
	1812K	.135	2.00	5.50	6.00	11.00
	1813K	.102	2.00	5.50	6.00	11.00
	1815K	1.116	2.00	4.50	6.00	11.00
	1816K	.135	2.00	4.50	6.00	11.00

1/2 BATZEN

BILLON
Rev. value: 1/2 BAZEN

C#	Date	Mintage	VG	Fine	VF	XF
57	1807	.110	3.00	8.00	12.00	20.00
	1808K	.209	3.00	8.00	12.00	20.00
	1809K	.267	3.00	8.00	12.00	20.00
	1810K	.290	3.00	8.00	12.00	20.00
	1811K	.349	3.00	8.00	12.00	20.00
	1812K	.252	3.00	8.00	12.00	20.00
	1813K	.154	3.00	8.00	12.00	20.00
	1814K	.140	3.00	8.00	12.00	20.00
	1815K	.181	3.00	8.00	12.00	20.00
	1816K	.134	3.00	8.00	12.00	20.00
	1817K	—	8.00	18.00	28.00	35.00

Rev. value: 1/2 SCHWEIZER BAZEN

C#	Date	Mintage	VG	Fine	VF	XF
56	1807K	Inc. Ab.	3.00	8.00	12.00	20.00
	1808K	Inc. Ab.	3.00	8.00	12.00	20.00
	1809K	Inc. Ab.	3.00	8.00	12.00	20.00
	1810K	Inc. Ab.	3.00	8.00	12.00	20.00

NOTE: Some varieties of C#56 do not have the K mintmark.

BATZEN

BILLON
Rev. value: 1 SCHWIZER BAZEN

C#	Date	Mintage	VG	Fine	VF	XF
59	1807K	.063	6.00	15.00	20.00	30.00
	1808K	.133	4.00	10.00	15.00	20.00
	1809K	.187	4.00	10.00	15.00	23.00

Rev. value: 1 BAZEN

C#	Date	Mintage	VG	Fine	VF	XF
58	1807	Inc. Ab.	4.00	10.00	15.00	25.00

Obv: Date. Rev. value: 1 BATZEN.

C#	Date	Mintage	VG	Fine	VF	XF
60	1810K	.259	4.00	9.50	14.00	18.50
	1811K	.319	4.00	9.50	14.00	18.50
	1812K	.341	4.00	9.50	14.00	18.50
	1814K	.229	4.00	9.50	14.00	18.50
	1815K	1.008	4.00	9.50	14.00	18.50
	1816K	.068	4.00	9.50	14.00	18.50
	1817K	—	4.00	9.50	14.00	18.50

Many varieties of C#60 are known, including some without the K mintmark.

6 KREUZER

BILLON
Obv: Arms in oak branches.
Rev: Value and date in oak branches.

C#	Date	Mintage	VG	Fine	VF	XF
61	1807	4,510	30.00	75.00	100.00	[illegible]

5 BATZEN

SILVER
Obv: Date in exergue

C#	Date	Mintage	VG	Fine	VF	XF
63	1810K	—	10.00	25.00	35.00	55.00
	1811K	—	12.00	35.00	45.00	65.00
	1812K	—	18.00	45.00	60.00	80.00
	1813K	—	10.00	25.00	35.00	55.00

Obv: Date below wreath

C#	Date	Mintage	VG	Fine	VF	XF
63.1	1813K	—	12.00	30.00	50.00	80.00
	1814K	—	12.00	30.00	50.00	80.00
	1817K	—	12.00	35.00	60.00	85.00

Rev: Date

C#	Date	Mintage	VG	Fine	VF	XF
63.2	1817K	—	18.00	45.00	60.00	80.00

Rev. value: 1/2 SCHWEIZ FRANKEN

C#	Date	Mintage	VG	Fine	VF	XF
62	1810K	759 pcs.	100.00	250.00	600.00	1000.

SCHAFFHAUSEN

A canton located on the north central border of Switzerland. The first coins, which were issued in the 13th century were known as "Ram Bracteates." It joined the Swiss Confederation in 1501.

MONETARY SYSTEM

4 Kreuzer = 1 Batzen

KREUZER

BILLON
Obv: Arms in laurel branches.
Rev: Value and date in wreath.

C#	Date	Mintage	VG	Fine	VF	XF
1	1808	.216	16.00	35.00	50.00	85.00

1/2 BATZEN

BILLON
Rev. value: 1/2 SCHWEIZ BATZEN

C#	Date	Mintage	VG	Fine	VF	XF
2	1808	.080	6.00	15.00	35.00	50.00

Rev. value: 1/2 BATZEN

C#	Date	Mintage	VG	Fine	VF	XF
2.1	1809	.030	10.00	25.00	40.00	60.00

BATZEN

BILLON
Rev. value: 1 SCHWEIZER BATZEN

C#	Date	Mintage	VG	Fine	VF	XF
3	1808	.064	20.00	50.00	65.00	120.00

Rev. value: 1 BATZEN

C#	Date	Mintage	VG	Fine	VF	XF
3.1	1809	.015	10.00	25.00	40.00	60.00

SCHWYZ

SCHWYTZ, SUITENSIS

A canton in central Switzerland. In 1291 it became one of the three cantons that would ultimately become the Swiss Confederation and were known as the "Everlasting League." The first coinage was issued in 1624.

MINTMASTER'S INITIALS

S - Stedelin

MONETARY SYSTEM

UNTIL 1798

240 Angster = 120 Rappen
= 40 Schillinge = 1 Gulden
4 Kreuzer = 1 Batzen
40 Batzen = 3 Gulden = 1 Thaler
12 Gulden = 1 Duplone

ANGSTER

COPPER

C#	Date	Mintage	VG	Fine	VF	XF
1	1773	—	3.00	6.00	12.00	18.00
	1774	—	3.00	6.00	12.00	18.00
	1775	—	3.00	6.00	12.00	18.00
	1776	—	3.00	6.00	12.00	18.00
	1777	—	3.00	6.00	12.00	18.00
	1778	—	3.00	6.00	12.00	18.00
	1779	—	3.00	6.00	12.00	18.00
	1780	—	3.00	6.00	12.00	18.00

Obv: Oval arms within laurel branch.

Rev: Value 1 ANGSTER, date.

C#	Date	Mintage	VG	Fine	VF	XF
2	1781	—	3.00	6.00	12.00	18.00
	1782	—	6.00	15.00	25.00	40.00
	1791	—	3.00	6.00	12.00	18.00
	1792	—	3.00	6.00	12.00	18.00
	1797	—	3.00	6.00	12.00	18.00

Obv: Arms within cartouche.
Rev: Value within wreath.

C#	Date	Mintage	VG	Fine	VF	XF
2a	1797	—	3.00	6.00	10.00	12.50
	1798	—	3.00	6.00	10.00	12.50

RAPPEN

BILLON
Obv: Arms in cartouche between palm and laurel branches. Rev: Value, date within cartouche.

C#	Date	Mintage	VG	Fine	VF	XF
6	1776S	—	8.00	20.00	40.00	65.00

COPPER

C#	Date	Mintage	VG	Fine	VF	XF
3	1777S	—	3.00	6.00	10.00	12.00
	1778S	—	3.00	6.00	10.00	12.00
	1779S	—	3.00	6.00	10.00	12.00
	1780S	—	3.00	6.00	10.00	12.00
	1781S	—	3.00	6.00	10.00	12.00
	1782S	—	3.00	6.00	10.00	12.00

Rev: Wreath forms top of cartouche.

C#	Date	Mintage	VG	Fine	VF	XF
3a	1782	—	3.00	6.00	10.00	12.00
	1785	—	5.00	10.00	20.00	35.00
	1792	—	3.00	8.00	12.50	20.00
	1793	—	3.00	6.00	10.00	12.00
	1794	—	3.00	6.00	10.00	12.00
	1795	—	3.00	6.00	10.00	12.00
	1796	—	3.00	6.00	10.00	12.00
	1797	—	3.00	6.00	10.00	12.00
	1798	—	3.00	7.50	15.00	22.00

GOLD

C#	Date	Mintage	VG	Fine	VF	XF
3b	1793	—	—	—	—	—

EIN (1) GROSCHEN

BILLON
Obv: Round arms, hanging laurel garland.
Rev: Value date within wreath.

C#	Date	Mintage	VG	Fine	VF	XF
8	1791	—	40.00	100.00	150.00	225.00

Obv: Shield type arms, hanging laurel garland.
Rev: Leaves and flowers above value and date.

C#	Date	Mintage	VG	Fine	VF	XF
8a	1793	—	40.00	100.00	150.00	225.00

GOLD

C#	Date	Mintage	VG	Fine	VF	XF
8b	1793	—	—	—	—	—

5 SCHILLINGS

SILVER
Obv: Crowned oval arms between crossed branches.
Rev: Value 5 SCHILLING, date.

C#	Date	Mintage	VG	Fine	VF	XF
12	1785	—	25.00	50.00	100.00	165.00

Rev: Value V SCHILLING.

C#	Date	Mintage	VG	Fine	VF	XF
12a	1787	—	25.00	50.00	100.00	165.00

10 SCHILLINGS

SILVER
Obv: Crowned oval arms within crossed branches.
Rev: Value, date within wreath.

C#	Date	Mintage	VG	Fine	VF	XF
15	1786	—	50.00	100.00	150.00	225.00

1/2 GULDEN

(= 20 Schillings)

SILVER
Obv: Oval arms within cartouche, value below.
Rev: PAX OPTIMA RERUM, date within beaded wreath.

C#	Date	Mintage	VG	Fine	VF	XF
18	1785St	—	30.00	75.00	150.00	225.00

Obv: Crowned oval arms within crossed branches, value, 20 S. Rev: Cross with S, date.

C#	Date	Mintage	VG	Fine	VF	XF
19	1797	—	55.00	125.00	175.00	300.00

GULDEN

SILVER

C#	Date	Mintage	VG	Fine	VF	XF
23	1785	—	60.00	150.00	325.00	500.00

Obv: Arms within branches, value.
Rev: Cross with S.

C#	Date	Mintage	VG	Fine	VF	XF
24	1797S	—	100.00	250.00	400.00	600.00

TRADE COINS

DUCAT

.986 GOLD

C#	Date	Mintage	VG	Fine	VF	XF
29	ND(1779)	—	—	1800.	3000.	5000.
	1781	—	—	1200.	2000.	3400.

Obv: Leaves and flowers above legend.

C#	Date	Mintage	VG	Fine	VF	XF
29.1	1788	—	—	1200.	2000.	3400.
	1790	—	—	1200.	2000.	3400.

Obv: Lion holding shield of arms.
Rev: Motto and date in branches.

C#	Date	Mintage	VG	Fine	VF	XF
45	1844M	50 pcs.	—	2400.	3500.	4500.

MONETARY REFORM

2 Angster = 1 Rappen
10 Rappen = 1 Batzen
10 Batzen = 1 Frank
4 Franken = 1 Thaler

ANGSTER

COPPER

C#	Date	Mintage	VG	Fine	VF	XF
31	1810	—	2.00	6.00	8.00	12.00
	1811	—	2.00	6.00	8.00	12.00
	1812	—	2.00	6.00	8.00	12.00
	1813	—	3.00	10.00	12.00	14.00
	1814	—	3.00	8.00	10.00	12.00
	1815	—	4.00	10.00	12.00	14.00
	1816	—	2.00	6.00	8.00	12.00
	1821	—	4.00	10.00	12.00	14.00
	1827	—	4.00	10.00	12.00	14.00
	1838	—	4.00	10.00	12.00	14.00
	1843	—	2.00	6.00	8.00	12.00
	1845	—	2.00	6.00	8.00	12.00
	1846	—	2.00	6.00	8.00	12.00

RAPPEN

COPPER
Rev. value: 1 RAPEN

C#	Date	Mintage	VG	Fine	VF	XF
32	1811	—	2.00	6.00	8.50	12.00
	1812	—	2.00	6.00	8.50	12.00
	1815	—	2.00	6.00	8.50	12.00
	1845	—	2.00	6.00	8.50	12.00
	1846	—	2.00	6.00	8.50	12.00

Rev. value: 1 RAPPEN

C#	Date	Mintage	VG	Fine	VF	XF
33	1811	—	2.00	6.00	8.50	12.50
	1812	—	2.00	6.50	8.50	12.50

Reduced size, modified design

C#	Date	Mintage	VG	Fine	VF	XF
33.1	1815	—	2.00	6.00	8.50	12.50
	1816	—	2.00	6.00	8.50	12.50
	1843	—	2.00	6.00	8.50	12.50
	1844	—	3.00	8.00	12.00	16.50
	1845	—	2.00	6.00	8.50	12.50
	1846	—	2.00	6.00	8.50	12.50

2 RAPPEN

BILLON
Obv: Baroque shield

C#	Date	Mintage	VG	Fine	VF	XF
35	1811	—	2.00	6.00	8.00	12.00
	1812	—	2.00	6.00	8.00	12.50
	1813	—	2.00	6.00	8.00	12.50

NOTE: Varieties of these coins are known with value as: 2 RAPEN.

Obv: Pointed shield

C#	Date	Mintage	VG	Fine	VF	XF
35a	1811	—	2.00	6.00	8.50	12.50
	1812	—	2.00	6.00	8.50	12.50
	1813	—	2.00	6.00	8.50	12.50
	1814	—	2.00	6.00	8.00	12.50
	1815	—	2.00	6.00	8.00	12.50
	1842	—	5.00	12.00	20.00	30.00
	1843	—	2.00	6.00	8.00	12.50
	1843DB	—	2.00	6.00	8.00	12.50
	1844DB	—	2.00	6.00	8.00	12.50
	1845DB	—	2.00	6.00	8.00	12.50
	1846DB	—	2.00	6.00	8.00	12.50

See note above. Many varieties, including some with mintmark B.

2/3 BATZEN

BILLON

C#	Date	Mintage	VG	Fine	VF	XF
36	1810	—	10.00	25.00	45.00	65.00
	1811	—	10.00	25.00	45.00	65.00

Rev. value: 2/3 BATZEN

C#	Date	Mintage	VG	Fine	VF	XF
36a	1812	—	12.00	30.00	65.00	95.00

2 BATZEN

BILLON
Similar to 2/3 Batzen, C#36.

C#	Date	Mintage	VG	Fine	VF	XF
38	1810B	—	18.00	45.00	75.00	120.00

4 BATZEN

SILVER
Obv: Arms in laurel branches.
Rev: Value and date in wreath, legend around border.

C#	Date	Mintage	VG	Fine	VF	XF
40	1810H	—	50.00	150.00	250.00	350.00

C#	Date	Mintage	VG	Fine	VF	XF
40	1811H	—	50.00	150.00	250.00	350.00

Varieties are known with value as: 4 BATZ.

NOTE: For pattern issues struck under joint coinage of Uri, Schwyz and Unterwalden - see Uri.

SITTEN

A canton which was founded in 580 that comprises most of the canton of Valais. Sitten was a Burgundian Mint in the 9th century with the first Episcopal coinage being struck c. 1496. They joined the Swiss Confederation as Valais in 1815.

RULERS

Franz Friedrich am Buel, 1760-1780

MINTMASTER'S INITIALS

D-S - David Stedelin

KREUZER

BILLON

Obv: Arms with sword, miter, and crozier. Rev: Arms with eagle above.

C#	Date	Mintage	VG	Fine	VF	XF
11	1776	—	—	15.00	25.00	40.00

1/2 BATZEN

BILLON

Obv: Four fold arms. Rev: Arms divide date.

C#	Date	Mintage	VG	Fine	VF	XF
12	1776	—	—	15.00	25.00	40.00
	1777	—	—	15.00	25.00	40.00

BATZEN

BILLON

Obv: Four fold arms, sword, miter and crozier. Rev: Arms dividing date, leg: COM. ET. PRAEF. UTR. VALLE.

C#	Date	Mintage	VG	Fine	VF	XF
13	1776	—	—	20.00	35.00	55.00

Rev. leg: COM. ET. PRAEF. REIP. VALLES.

C#	Date	Mintage	VG	Fine	VF	XF
13a	1776	—	—	20.00	35.00	55.00
	1777	—	—	15.00	25.00	40.00
	1778	—	—	15.00	25.00	40.00

6 KREUZER

BILLON

C#	Date	Mintage	VG	Fine	VF	XF
14	1777	—	—	20.00	35.00	55.00

12 KREUZER

BILLON

C#	Date	Mintage	VG	Fine	VF	XF
15	1777	—	—	40.00	75.00	110.00

20 KREUZER

SILVER

Obv: Oval four fold arms with sword, miter and crozier. Rev: Madonna over arms divide date.

C#	Date	Mintage	VG	Fine	VF	XF
17	1777	—	—	50.00	100.00	150.00

SOLOTHURN

SOLODORNENSIS, SOLEURE

A canton in northwest Switzerland. Bracteates were struck in the 1300s even though the mint right was not officially granted until 1381. They joined the Swiss Confederation in 1481.

MINTMASTER'S INITIALS

T - Thiebaud

MONETARY SYSTEM

Until 1798

2 Vierer = 1 Kreuzer
4 Kreuzer = 1 Batzen
40 Batzen = 2 Gulden = 1 Thaler

VIERER

BILLON

Obv: Arms dividing SO, palm branch below. Rev: Anchor cross within circle, date.

C#	Date	Mintage	VG	Fine	VF	XF
5	1761	—	5.00	12.50	30.00	45.00
	1789	—	3.00	8.00	12.50	18.00
	1790	—	3.00	8.00	12.50	18.00
	1793	—	3.00	8.00	12.50	18.00
	1794	—	3.00	8.00	12.50	18.00
	1795	—	6.00	15.00	25.00	50.00
	1796	—	3.00	8.00	12.50	18.00
	1797	—	3.00	8.00	12.50	18.00
	1798	—	3.00	8.00	12.50	18.00

GOLD

C#	Date	Mintage	VG	Fine	VF	XF
5a	1761	—	—	—	—	—

KREUZER

BILLON

Obv: Arms dividing SO within circle. Rev: Anchor cross with ornamentation within circle.

C#	Date	Mintage	VG	Fine	VF	XF
6	1760	—	4.00	10.00	17.50	25.00
	1762	—	4.00	10.00	17.50	25.00
	1794	—	4.00	10.00	15.00	22.50
	1796	—	4.00	10.00	15.00	22.50
	1797	—	6.00	15.00	30.00	50.00
	1798	—	6.00	15.00	30.00	50.00

GOLD

C#	Date	Mintage	VG	Fine	VF	XF
6a	1760	—	—	—	—	—

2 KREUZERS

(= 1/2 Batzen)

BILLON

C#	Date	Mintage	VG	Fine	VF	XF
8	1760	—	4.00	10.00	17.50	27.50
	1761	—	4.00	10.00	17.50	27.50
	1762	—	4.00	10.00	17.50	27.50
	1787	—	4.00	10.00	17.50	27.50
	1793	—	3.00	8.50	15.00	22.00
	1794	—	3.00	8.50	15.00	22.00
	1795	—	3.00	8.50	15.00	22.00
	1796	—	3.00	8.50	15.00	22.00

SILVER

C#	Date	Mintage	VG	Fine	VF	XF
8a	1793	—	—	—	—	—

4 KREUZERS

BILLON

Obv: Arms between palm and laurel branches within circle. Rev: Similar to 10 Batzen, C#22b but S twines around cross.

C#	Date	Mintage	VG	Fine	VF	XF
10	1760	—	30.00	75.00	125.00	200.00

Obv: Arms dividing SO within circle. Rev: Cross with ornamentation.

C#	Date	Mintage	VG	Fine	VF	XF
11	1760	—	4.00	10.00	17.50	30.00
	1761	—	4.00	10.00	17.50	30.00
	1762	—	4.00	10.00	17.50	30.00

Obv: Arms similar to 20 Kreuzer, C#19. Rev: Flowered cross within circle.

C#	Date	Mintage	VG	Fine	VF	XF
12	1766	—	4.00	10.00	17.50	30.00
	1787	—	4.00	10.00	17.50	30.00
	1788	—	4.00	10.00	17.50	30.00
	1793	—	3.00	8.50	15.00	22.00
	1795	—	3.00	8.50	15.00	22.00
	1796	—	3.00	8.50	15.00	22.00
	1797	—	3.00	8.50	15.00	22.00

10 KREUZERS

SILVER

Similar to 20 Kreuzers, C#19.

C#	Date	Mintage	VG	Fine	VF	XF
16	1760	—	25.00	50.00	75.00	110.00

Similar to 20 Kreuzers C#19 but with wider arms and no branches.

C#	Date	Mintage	VG	Fine	VF	XF
16.1	1762	—	25.00	50.00	75.00	110.00

Similar to 20 Kreuzers, C#19a.

C#	Date	Mintage	VG	Fine	VF	XF
16a	1785	—	12.00	25.00	40.00	80.00

Similar to 10 Batzen, C#22b.

C#	Date	Mintage	VG	Fine	VF	XF
17	1787	—	12.00	25.00	40.00	80.00
	1794	—	10.00	20.00	35.00	60.00
	1795	—	10.00	20.00	35.00	60.00

20 KREUZERS

SILVER

C#	Date	Mintage	VG	Fine	VF	XF
19	1760	—	25.00	50.00	100.00	175.00

Wider arms and larger cross and S.

C#	Date	Mintage	VG	Fine	VF	XF
19.1	1763	—	25.00	50.00	100.00	175.00

C#	Date	Mintage	VG	Fine	VF	XF
19a	1785	—	25.00	30.00	45.00	85.00

Similar to 10 Batzen, C#22b.

C#	Date	Mintage	VG	Fine	VF	XF
20	1787	—	12.00	30.00	45.00	75.00
	1794	—	12.00	30.00	45.00	75.00
	1795	—	12.00	30.00	45.00	75.00

10 BATZEN

SILVER

Obv: Oval arms within branches. Rev: Similar to 20 Kreuzers, C#19 but larger cross and S.

C#	Date	Mintage	VG	Fine	VF	XF
22	1761	—	50.00	100.00	175.00	275.00

Similar to 10 Batzen, C#22.2, but with more ornate arms and fuller branches.

C#	Date	Mintage	VG	Fine	VF	XF
22.1	1763	—	50.00	100.00	175.00	275.00
	1766	—	100.00	200.00	300.00	425.00

C#	Date	Mintage	VG	Fine	VF	XF
22.2	1767	—	40.00	90.00	150.00	220.00

C#	Date	Mintage	VG	Fine	VF	XF
22a	1773	—	70.00	150.00	250.00	350.00
	1778	—	35.00	80.00	125.00	185.00
	1785	—	45.00	100.00	175.00	275.00

C#	Date	Mintage	VG	Fine	VF	XF
22b	1787	—	30.00	75.00	100.00	150.00
	1788	—	30.00	75.00	100.00	150.00
	1791	—	30.00	75.00	100.00	150.00
	1794	—	30.00	75.00	100.00	150.00

20 BATZEN

SILVER

C#	Date	Mintage	VG	Fine	VF	XF
25	1795	—	50.00	125.00	250.00	350.00
	1798	—	40.00	100.00	200.00	300.00

1/4 DUPLONE

.900 GOLD

C#	Date	Mintage	VG	Fine	VF	XF
31	1789	—	—	275.00	475.00	800.00

Rev: Date below saint.

C#	Date	Mintage	VG	Fine	VF	XF
31.1	1796	—	—	350.00	600.00	1000.

1/2 DUPLONE

.900 GOLD

C#	Date	Mintage	VG	Fine	VF	XF
33	1787	—	—	600.00	1000.	1600.

Rev: Date below saint.

C#	Date	Mintage	VG	Fine	VF	XF
33.1	1796	—	—	725.00	1200.	1800.

DUPLONE

.900 GOLD
Obv: Crowned arms. Rev: Standing saint.

C#	Date	Mintage	VG	Fine	VF	XF
34	1787	—	—	950.00	1600.	3000.

Rev: Date under saint.

C#	Date	Mintage	VG	Fine	VF	XF
34.1	1796	—	—	950.00	1600.	3000.
	1797	—	—	825.00	1400.	2400.
	1798	—	—	1200.	2000.	3400.

2 DUPLONES

.900 GOLD

C#	Date	Mintage	VG	Fine	VF	XF
35	1787	—	—	3000.	4750.	7000.

Rev: Date below saint.

C#	Date	Mintage	VG	Fine	VF	XF
35.1	1796	—	—	1900.	3200.	5200.
	1797	—	—	1400.	2400.	4000.
	1798	—	—	1800.	3000.	4800.

MONETARY REFORM

(Commencing 1804)
10 Rappen = 4 Kreuzer = 1 Batzen
10 Batzen = 1 Frank

RAPPEN

BILLON
Obv: Arms over branches.
Rev: Value and date in wreath.

C#	Date	Mintage	VG	Fine	VF	XF
41	1813	—	7.50	15.00	30.00	45.00

2-1/2 RAPPEN

BILLON
Obv: Arms in circle, value below.
Rev: Cross in circle, date below.

C#	Date	Mintage	VG	Fine	VF	XF
52	1830	—	3.00	8.00	12.00	20.00

KREUZER

BILLON
Obv: Arms over branches.
Rev: Value and date in wreath.

C#	Date	Mintage	VG	Fine	VF	XF
42	1813	—	5.00	10.00	15.00	30.00

5 RAPPEN

BILLON
Obv: Arms divide S O in circle, value below.
Rev: Ornamented cross in quatrefoil.

C#	Date	Mintage	VG	Fine	VF	XF
53	1826	—	6.00	15.00	30.00	45.00

BATZEN

BILLON
Rev. value: 1 BATZEN - X RAPPEN

C#	Date	Mintage	VG	Fine	VF	XF
44	1805	—	8.00	20.00	40.00	65.00

Rev. value: 1 BATZEN - 10

C#	Date	Mintage	VG	Fine	VF	XF
45	1807	—	20.00	50.00	80.00	125.00
	1808	—	6.00	15.00	25.00	40.00
	1809	—	6.00	15.00	25.00	40.00

Rev. value: 1 BATZEN

C#	Date	Mintage	VG	Fine	VF	XF
45a	1809	—	3.00	8.00	15.00	25.00
	1810	—	3.00	8.00	15.00	25.00
	1811	—	3.00	8.00	15.00	25.00

Obv. value: 1 BAZ

C#	Date	Mintage	VG	Fine	VF	XF
54	1826	—	3.00	8.00	15.00	25.00

Obv. value: 1 BATZ

C#	Date	Mintage	VG	Fine	VF	XF
54.1	1826	—	4.00	10.00	15.00	25.00

2-1/2 BATZEN

SILVER
Obv: Crowned oval arms in laurel branches, value below.
Rev: Cross in quatrefoil.

C#	Date	Mintage	VG	Fine	VF	XF
55	1826	—	6.00	15.00	30.00	45.00

5 BATZEN

SILVER
Rev. value: 5 BATZEN

C#	Date	Mintage	VG	Fine	VF	XF
46	1809	—	30.00	70.00	110.00	155.00
	1811	—	18.00	35.00	45.00	65.00

Obv. value: 5 BATZ

C#	Date	Mintage	VG	Fine	VF	XF
56	1826	—	10.00	25.00	40.00	60.00

Value as: 5 BAZ

C#	Date	Mintage	VG	Fine	VF	XF
56.1	1826	—	16.00	30.00	55.00	85.00

FRANK

SILVER

C#	Date	Mintage	VG	Fine	VF	XF
47	1812	2,000	60.00	140.00	250.00	375.00

4 FRANKEN

SILVER

C#	Date	Mintage	VG	Fine	VF	XF
48	1813	250 pcs.	125.00	350.00	650.00	1000.

8 FRANKEN

.900 GOLD
Obv: Crowned oval arms on spade shield in branches, date below.
Rev: Standing knight holding shield, value below.

C#	Date	Mintage	VG	Fine	VF	XF
49	1813	106 pcs.	—	2000.	4000.	6000.

16 FRANKEN

.900 GOLD
Obv: Crowned oval arms on spade shield in branches, date below.
Rev: Standing knight holding shield, value below.

C#	Date	Mintage	VG	Fine	VF	XF
50	1813	150 pcs.	—	2300.	4500.	6000.

32 FRANKEN

.900 GOLD
Obv: Crowned oval arms on spade shield in branches, date below.
Rev: Standing knight holding shield, value below.

C#	Date	Mintage	VG	Fine	VF	XF
51	1813	—	—	—	Rare	—

TRADE COINS

DUCAT

GOLD
Obv: Crowned oval arms between branches.
Rev: Standing saint.

C#	Date	Mintage	VG	Fine	VF	XF
32	1768	—	—	—	—	—

THURGAU

(THURGOVIE)

A canton in northeast Switzerland. They were ruled by the Swiss Confederates beginning c. 1460 until 1798. In 1803 they joined the Swiss Confederation.

MONETARY SYSTEM

4 Kreuzer = 1 Schweizer Batzen
10 Batzen = 1 Frank

1/2 KREUZER

BILLON
Obv: Arms in oak branches.
Rev: Value and date in wreath.

C#	Date	Mintage	VG	Fine	VF	XF
1	1808	.100	25.00	60.00	125.00	170.00

KREUZER

BILLON
Obv: Arms in oak branches.
Rev: Value and date in wreath.

C#	Date	Mintage	VG	Fine	VF	XF
2	1808	.099	5.00	12.00	20.00	35.00

1/2 BATZEN

BILLON
Obv: Arms in oak branches.
Rev: Value with SCHWEIZ added, date in wreath.

C#	Date	Mintage	VG	Fine	VF	XF
3	1808	.149	9.00	20.00	35.00	60.00

BATZEN

BILLON

C#	Date	Mintage	VG	Fine	VF	XF
4	1808	.232	9.00	20.00	35.00	80.00
	1809	Inc. Ab.	9.00	20.00	35.00	80.00

5 BATZEN

SILVER
Similar to 1 Batzen, C#4.

C#	Date	Mintage	VG	Fine	VF	XF
5	1808	2,580	—	200.00	300.00	450.00

TICINO

TESSIN

A canton in southeast Switzerland. They were previously known as the Lombard vassal state of Bellinzona. They joined the Swiss Confederation in 1803.

MONETARY SYSTEM

12 Denari = 1 Soldo
20 Soldi = 1 Franco

TRE (3) DENARI

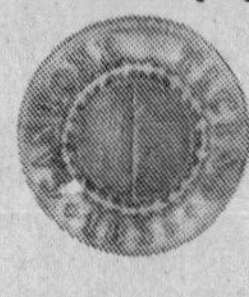

COPPER
Obv: Round arms

C#	Date	Mintage	VG	Fine	VF	XF
1	1814	.417	4.00	10.00	15.00	25.00
	1835	.598	4.00	10.00	15.00	25.00

Obv: Spade-shaped arms

C#	Date	Mintage	VG	Fine	VF	XF
1a	1841	.322	4.00	10.00	15.00	25.00

SEI (6) DENARI

COPPER

C#	Date	Mintage	VG	Fine	VF	XF
2	1813	.280	4.00	8.50	18.00	28.00
	1835	.364	4.00	10.00	18.00	28.00
	1841	.241	4.00	10.00	18.00	28.00

TRE (3) SOLDI

BILLON

C#	Date	Mintage	VG	Fine	VF	XF
3	1813 star	1.405	4.00	10.00	20.00	32.00
	1813 w/o star	—				
		Inc. Ab.	4.00	10.00	20.00	32.00
	1835	.323	4.00	10.00	20.00	32.00
	1838	.514	4.00	10.00	20.00	32.00
	1841	.243	4.00	10.00	20.00	32.00

1/4 FRANCO

SILVER
Similar to 1/2 Franco, C#5.

C#	Date	Mintage	VG	Fine	VF	XF
4	1835	.058	20.00	40.00	60.00	90.00

1/2 FRANCO

SILVER

C#	Date	Mintage	VG	Fine	VF	XF
5	1835	.044	25.00	60.00	85.00	120.00

FRANCO

SILVER

C#	Date	Mintage	VG	Fine	VF	XF
6	1813 star	5,920	50.00	150.00	250.00	375.00
	1813 w/o star	—				
		Inc. Ab.	50.00	150.00	250.00	375.00

2 FRANCHI

SILVER

C#	Date	Mintage	VG	Fine	VF	XF
7	1813 star	4,150	75.00	200.00	450.00	650.00
	1813 w/o star	—				
		Inc. Ab.	75.00	200.00	450.00	650.00

4 FRANCHI

SILVER

C#	Date	Mintage	VG	Fine	VF	XF
8	1814 star	7,921	100.00	250.00	500.00	800.00
	1814 w/o star	—				
		Inc. Ab.	100.00	250.00	500.00	800.00

NOTE: Coins of 3 Soldi, Franco, 2 Franchi and 4 Franchi with star mintmark were struck at Luzern. Those without star were coined at Bern.

UNTERWALDEN

SUBSILVANIA

A canton in central Switzerland which was one of the three original cantons which became the Swiss Confederation in 1291. It is made up of two half cantons - Nidwalden and Obwalden. They had their own coinage beginning in the 1500s.

MINTMASTER'S INITIALS

S - Samson

MONETARY SYSTEM

4 Kreuzer = 1 Batzen
10 Batzen = 1 Frank

NIDWALDEN

1/2 BATZEN

BILLON
**Obv: Spade arms in branches.
Rev: Value and date in wreath.**

C#	Date	Mintage	VG	Fine	VF	XF
11	1811	.012	10.00	30.00	45.00	80.00

BATZEN

BILLON
**Obv: Spade arms in branches.
Rev: Value stated as 1 BATZEN 10 RAPPEN, date in wreath.**

C#	Date	Mintage	VG	Fine	VF	XF
12	1811	.012	10.00	35.00	50.00	90.00

5 BATZEN

SILVER

C#	Date	Mintage	VG	Fine	VF	XF
13	1811	3,600	50.00	120.00	175.00	250.00

OBWALDEN

1/2 BATZEN

BILLON
**Obv: Oval arms in palm branches.
Rev: Value and date in wreath.**

C#	Date	Mintage	VG	Fine	VF	XF
21	1812	—	15.00	35.00	50.00	100.00

BATZEN

BILLON
**Obv: Spade arms in palm branches, date in exergue.
Rev: Value in wreath.**

C#	Date	Mintage	VG	Fine	VF	XF
22	1812	—	15.00	35.00	50.00	100.00

5 BATZEN

SILVER
**Obv: Spade arms in palm and laurel branches.
Rev: Value and date in wreath.**

C#	Date	Mintage	VG	Fine	VF	XF
23	1812	—	50.00	125.00	200.00	275.00

TRADE COINS

DUCAT

.986 GOLD
Obv: Arms. Rev: St. Nicholas v. der Flue kneeling.

C#	Date	Mintage	Fine	VF	XF
31	1774	—	—	Rare	—
32	1787	—	1000.	1750.	3000.
32a	1787 *Restrike	—	550.00	750.00	

NOTE: Restruck in 1887.

NOTE: For pattern issues struck under joint coinage of Uri, Schwyz and Unterwalden - see Uri.

URI

(URANIE)

A canton in central Switzerland. It is one of the three original cantons which became the Swiss Confederation in 1291. They had their own coinage from the early 1600s until 1811.

MONETARY SYSTEM

10 Rappen = 1 Batzen
10 Batzen = 1 Frank

RAPPEN

BILLON
**Obv: Arms in palm branches.
Rev: Value and date in beaded circle.**

C#	Date	Mintage	VG	Fine	VF	XF
11	1811	.019	30.00	70.00	100.00	150.00

1/2 BATZEN

BILLON
**Obv: Arms in palm and laurel branches.
Rev: Value and date in wreath.**

C#	Date	Mintage	VG	Fine	VF	XF
12	1811	.015	20.00	50.00	90.00	150.00

BATZEN

BILLON
Obv: Arms in palm and laurel branches, 10 RAP in exergue. Rev: Value and date in wreath.

C#	Date	Mintage	VG	Fine	VF	XF
13	1811	.020	20.00	50.00	90.00	150.00

2 BATZEN

SILVER

C#	Date	Mintage	VG	Fine	VF	XF
14	1811	4,995	35.00	75.00	100.00	150.00

4 BATZEN

SILVER

C#	Date	Mintage	VG	Fine	VF	XF
15	1811	3,510	50.00	100.00	150.00	275.00

NCLT ISSUES

PATTERNS

Joint coinage for Uri, Schwyz, Unterwalden

KM#	Date	Mintage	Identification	Mkt.Val.
1	1788	—	1 Quattrino, Copper	Rare
2	1788	—	1/2 Soldo, Copper	—
3	1788	—	1 Soldo, Copper	Rare

VAUD

WAADT

A canton in southwest Switzerland. They had possession of Bern from 1536 until 1798. They joined the Swiss Confederation in 1803.

MINTMASTER'S INITIALS

BEL - Bel Bessiere

MONETARY SYSTEM

10 Rappen = 1 Batz
10 Batz = 1 Franc
4 Francs = 1 Thaler

RAPPEN

BILLON

C#	Date	Mintage	VG	Fine	VF	XF
1	1804	.211	10.00	25.00	45.00	60.00
1a	1807	Inc. Ab.	6.00	15.00	30.00	40.00

2-1/2 RAPPEN

BILLON

Obv. value: 2-1/2 RAPPES

C#	Date	Mintage	VG	Fine	VF	XF
2	1809	.230	5.00	12.00	15.00	22.00
	Obv. value: 2-1/2 RAP.					
2a	1816	—	5.00	12.00	15.00	22.00

1/2 BATZEN

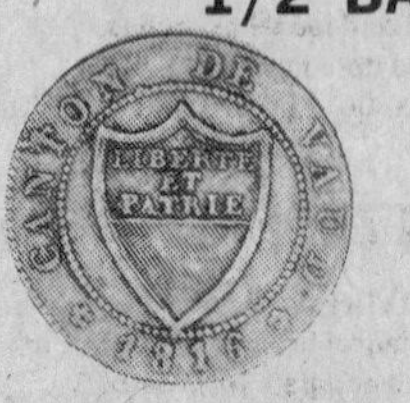

BILLON

C#	Date	Mintage	VG	Fine	VF	XF
3	1804	2.962	2.00	5.00	12.00	20.00
	1805	Inc. Ab.	2.00	5.00	12.00	20.00
	1806	Inc. Ab.	2.00	5.00	12.00	20.00
	1807	Inc. Ab.	2.00	5.00	12.00	20.00
	1808	Inc. Ab.	2.00	5.00	12.00	20.00
	1809	—	2.00	5.00	12.00	20.00
	1810	—	2.00	5.00	12.00	20.00
	1811	—	2.00	5.00	12.00	20.00
	1813	—	2.00	5.00	12.00	20.00
	1814	—	2.00	5.00	12.00	20.00
	1816	—	2.00	5.00	12.00	20.00
	1817	—	2.00	5.00	12.00	20.00
	1818	—	2.00	5.00	12.00	20.00
	1819	—	2.00	5.00	12.00	20.00

BATZEN

BILLON

Obv: No branches around arms, leg: CANTON DE VAUD.

C#	Date	Mintage	VG	Fine	VF	XF
4	1804	—	8.00	20.00	30.00	45.00

C#	Date	Mintage	VG	Fine	VF	XF
	1804	—	3.00	8.00	15.00	25.00
	1805	—	2.00	5.00	12.00	20.00
	1806	—	2.00	5.00	12.00	20.00
	1807	—	2.00	5.00	12.00	20.00
	1808	—	10.00	25.00	35.00	50.00
	1809	—	4.00	10.00	18.00	30.00
	1810	—	2.00	6.00	12.00	20.00
	1811	—	2.00	6.00	12.00	20.00
	1812	—	2.00	6.00	12.00	20.00
	1813	—	2.00	6.00	12.00	20.00
	1814	—	2.00	6.00	12.00	20.00
	1815	—	2.00	6.00	12.00	20.00
	1816	—	2.00	6.00	12.00	20.00
	1817	—	2.00	6.00	12.00	20.00
	1818	—	2.00	6.00	12.00	20.00
	1819	—	2.00	6.00	12.00	20.00
	1820	—	2.00	6.00	12.00	20.00

C#	Date	Mintage	VG	Fine	VF	XF
11	1826BEL	—	8.00	20.00	35.00	55.00
	1827BEL	—	2.00	5.00	12.00	20.00
	1828BEL	—	2.00	5.00	12.00	20.00
	1829BEL	—	2.00	5.00	12.00	20.00
	1830BEL	—	2.00	5.00	12.00	20.00
	1831BEL	—	2.00	5.00	12.00	20.00
	1832BEL	—	2.00	5.00	12.00	20.00
	1834BEL	—	3.00	7.50	15.00	27.50

5 BATZEN

SILVER

Obv. leg: CANTON DE VAUD

C#	Date	Mintage	VG	Fine	VF	XF
5	1804	1,692	50.00	100.00	175.00	275.00

C#	Date	Mintage	VG	Fine	VF	XF
5a	1805	—	20.00	45.00	75.00	120.00
	1806	—	20.00	45.00	75.00	120.00
	1807	—	6.00	15.00	25.00	45.00
	1810	—	6.00	15.00	25.00	45.00
	1811	—	6.00	15.00	25.00	45.00
	1812	—	6.00	15.00	25.00	45.00
	1813	—	6.00	15.00	25.00	45.00
	1814	—	10.00	25.00	40.00	75.00

C#	Date	Mintage	VG	Fine	VF	XF
12	1826	—	6.00	15.00	25.00	45.00
	1827BEL	—	6.00	15.00	25.00	45.00
	1828BEL	—	6.00	15.00	25.00	45.00
	1829BEL	—	6.00	15.00	25.00	45.00
	1830BEL	—	6.00	15.00	25.00	45.00
	1831BEL	—	6.00	15.00	25.00	45.00

FRANC

SILVER

C#	Date	Mintage	VG	Fine	VF	XF
13	1845	8,626	—	30.00	60.00	100.00

NOTE: This coin was struck to commemorate a Shooting Festival held on August 10, 1845. It had legal tender status.

10 BATZEN

SILVER

C#	Date	Mintage	VG	Fine	VF	XF
6	1804	1,234	100.00	250.00	350.00	500.00
	Obv. leg: CONFEDERATION SUISSE					
7	1810	1,234	50.00	130.00	175.00	225.00
	1811	2,963	50.00	130.00	175.00	225.00
7a	1823	6,198	50.00	130.00	175.00	225.00

20 BATZEN

SILVER

C#	Date	Mintage	VG	Fine	VF	XF
8	1810	6,590	50.00	100.00	150.00	300.00
	1811	Inc. Ab.	50.00	100.00	150.00	275.00

40 BATZEN

SILVER

C#	Date	Mintage	VG	Fine	VF	XF
10	1812	2,485	125.00	250.00	500.00	950.00

COUNTERSTAMP ISSUES

39 BATZEN

As in the canton of Bern, French Ecus dated 1726 to 1793 along with 6 Livres dated 1793-1794 were counterstamped and freely circulated. In Vaud, the counterstamp consisted of the arms of Vaud on one side and the new value as 39 BZ on the other.

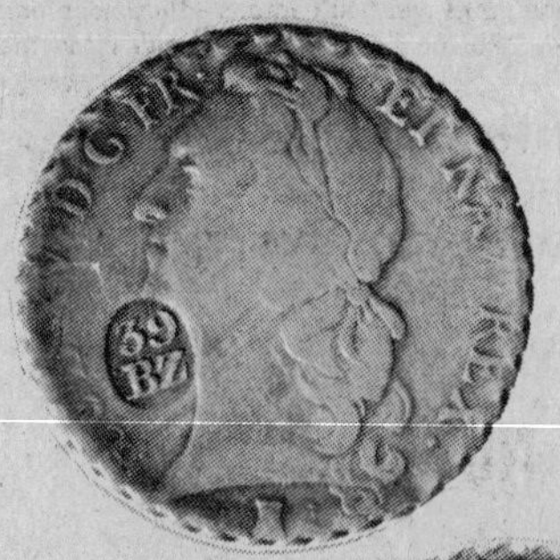

SILVER

c/s: On Louis XV Ecu, C#42.

C#	Date	Year	VG	Fine	VF	XF
9.1	ND	1726-41	500.00	1000.	1650.	2000.

c/s: On France Louis XV Ecu, C#47.

C#	Date	Year	VG	Fine	VF	XF
9.2	ND	1740-71	375.00	800.00	1200.	1600.

c/s: On France Louis XV Ecu, C#47a.

C#	Date	Year	VG	Fine	VF	XF
9.3	ND	1770-74	500.00	1000.	1650.	2000.

c/s: On France Louis XVI Ecu, C#78.

C#	Date	Year	VG	Fine	VF	XF
9.4	ND	1774-92	375.00	800.00	1200.	1600.

c/s: On France Louis XVI Constitutional Ecu, C#93.

C#	Date	Year	VG	Fine	VF	XF
9.5	ND	1792-93	375.00	800.00	1200.	1600.

c/s: On France 6 Livres, C#123.

C#	Date	Year	VG	Fine	VF	XF
9.6	ND	1793-94	375.00	800.00	1200.	1600.

NCLT ISSUES

PATTERNS

KM#	Date	Mintage	Identification	Mkt.Val.
1	1804	—	1/2 Batzen, Billon	—
2	1830	—	1/4 Franc, Silver	—

ZUG

(TUGIUM, TUGIENSIS)

A canton in central Switzerland. They joined the Swiss Confederation in 1352 and had their own coinage from 1564 to 1805.

MONETARY SYSTEM

12 Haller = 12 Angster = 3 Rappen
= 1 Schilling
2 Schilling = 1 Assis

ANGSTER

COPPER

C#	Date	Mintage	VG	Fine	VF	XF
1	1778	—	8.00	20.00	25.00	35.00
	1781	—	8.00	20.00	25.00	35.00
	1782	—	8.00	20.00	25.00	35.00
	1783	—	8.00	20.00	25.00	35.00
	1784	—	8.00	20.00	25.00	35.00
	1791	—	8.00	20.00	25.00	35.00
	1794	—	8.00	20.00	25.00	35.00
	1796	—	8.00	20.00	25.00	35.00
	1804	—	8.00	20.00	25.00	35.00

RAPPEN

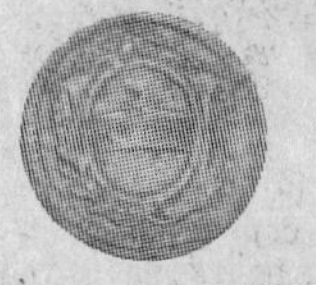

COPPER

C#	Date	Mintage	VG	Fine	VF	XF
2	1782	—	3.00	6.00	9.00	15.00
	1783	—	—	—	—	—
	1785	—	3.00	6.00	9.00	15.00
	1794	—	3.00	6.00	9.00	15.00
	1805	—	3.00	6.00	9.00	15.00

ZURICH

THICURINAE, THURICENSIS
TICURINAE, TURICENSIS

A canton in north central Switzerland. It was the mint for the dukes of Swabia in the 10th and 11th centuries. The mint right was obtained in 1238. The first coinage was Bracteates and the last coins were struck in 1848. They joined the Swiss Confederation in 1351.

MINTMASTER'S INITIALS

B - Bruckmann
V - Vorster

MONETARY SYSTEM

Until 1798
12 Haller = 4 Rappen = 1 Schilling
72 Schillinge = 2 Gulden = 1 Thaler

5 SCHILLINGS

SILVER
Obv: Lion holding sword beside oval arms.
Rev: Value V SCHILLING within laurel wreath.

C#	Date	Mintage	VG	Fine	VF	XF
12	1783	—	6.00	16.50	30.00	45.00
	1784	—	6.00	16.50	30.00	45.00

20 SCHILLINGS

SILVER
Similar to C#20a but arms between branches.

C#	Date	Mintage	VG	Fine	VF	XF
20	1773	—	50.00	125.00	175.00	250.00

C#	Date	Mintage	VG	Fine	VF	XF
20a	1774	—	15.00	35.00	60.00	100.00
	1776	—	15.00	35.00	60.00	100.00
	1779	—	20.00	50.00	80.00	140.00
	1780	—	15.00	40.00	80.00	135.00

Obv: Arms between branches, garland over face of arms. Rev: Value XX SCHILLING, date within laurel wreath.

C#	Date	Mintage	VG	Fine	VF	XF
21	1783	—	15.00	35.00	60.00	100.00
	1786	—	60.00	160.00	250.00	350.00
	1790	—	15.00	40.00	80.00	135.00
	1791	—	15.00	40.00	80.00	135.00
	1792	—	15.00	35.00	60.00	100.00
	1798	—	15.00	40.00	80.00	135.00

1/2 TALER

SILVER
Gessener Half-Taler

C#	Date	Mintage	VG	Fine	VF	XF
27	1773AV	—	300.00	800.00	1400.	2200.

C#	Date	Mintage	VG	Fine	VF	XF
25b	1773	—	75.00	175.00	300.00	450.00

Obv: Lion facing left. Rev: Similar to C#25b.

C#	Date	Mintage	VG	Fine	VF	XF
28	1773	—	75.00	175.00	300.00	450.00

C#	Date	Mintage	VG	Fine	VF	XF
28.1	1776	—	50.00	100.00	250.00	375.00

Obv: Liberty cap on arms.
Rev: Laurel wreath
around JUSTITIA ET CONCORDIA.

C#	Date	Mintage	VG	Fine	VF	XF
28a	1779	—	60.00	160.00	250.00	350.00

Obv: Two lions holding arms.

C#	Date	Mintage	VG	Fine	VF	XF
29	1780	—	50.00	125.00	250.00	350.00

NOTE: Varieties exist.

Similar to 1 Taler, C#38.

C#	Date	Mintage	VG	Fine	VF	XF
31	1783B	—	50.00	120.00	200.00	300.00
	1786B	*	50.00	100.00	200.00	300.00
	1788B	*	50.00	100.00	200.00	300.00
	1794B	*	50.00	100.00	200.00	300.00
	1798B	—	60.00	140.00	200.00	300.00

***NOTE:** Varieties exist.

TALER

SILVER
Gessener Taler
Obv: Similar to C#36.
Rev: Pedestal with flowers and branches.

C#	Date	Mintage	VG	Fine	VF	XF
35	1773	36 pcs.	1500.	3000.	6000.	10,000.

C#	Date	Mintage	VG	Fine	VF	XF
36	1773	—	100.00	300.00	500.00	800.00

C#	Date	Mintage	VG	Fine	VF	XF
36a	1776	—	50.00	150.00	350.00	550.00
	1777	—	50.00	150.00	350.00	550.00

NOTE: Varieties exist.

Obv: Similar to C#36a but liberty cap on arms.
Rev: Similar to C#36a but laurel wreath around JUSTITIA ET CONCORDIA.

C#	Date	Mintage	VG	Fine	VF	XF
36b	1779	—	100.00	250.00	450.00	850.00

NOTE: Varieties exist.

Obv: Two lions holding arms.
Rev: Similar to C#36a but fuller wreath and bows at top and bottom.

C#	Date	Mintage	VG	Fine	VF	XF
37	1780	—	60.00	135.00	350.00	575.00

C#	Date	Mintage	VG	Fine	VF	XF
38	1783	—	60.00	150.00	350.00	550.00
	1794	—	60.00	125.00	350.00	550.00
	1796	*	60.00	125.00	375.00	650.00

***NOTE:** Varieties exist.

C#	Date	Mintage	VG	Fine	VF	XF
39	1790	—	75.00	150.00	350.00	550.00

TRADE COINS

1/2 DUCAT

.986 GOLD
Obv: Similar to Ducat, C#43.

C#	Date	Mintage	Fine	VF	XF
42.3	1767	—	250.00	400.00	600.00

DUCAT

.986 GOLD

C#	Date	Mintage	Fine	VF	XF
43	1775	—	400.00	700.00	1200.

C#	Date	Mintage	Fine	VF	XF
60	1810B	—	400.00	550.00	850.00

2 DUCATS

.986 GOLD
Similar to Ducat, C#43.

C#	Date	Mintage	Fine	VF	XF
45	1776	—	825.00	1400.	2400.

MONETARY REFORM

Commencing 1803
3 Haller = 1 Rappen
4 Rappen = 1 Schilling
10 Schilling = 4 Batzen
160 Batzen = 1 Ducat

RAPPEN

BILLON

C#	Date	Mintage	VG	Fine	VF	XF
51	1842	—	1.50	3.00	5.50	10.00
	1844	—	1.50	3.00	5.50	10.00
	1845	—	1.50	3.00	5.50	10.00
	1846	—	2.50	6.50	10.00	15.00
	1848	—	1.50	3.00	5.50	10.00

3 HALLER

BILLON

C#	Date	Mintage	VG	Fine	VF	XF
4	ND	3.518	2.00	4.00	6.50	10.00

Error: HALER

C#	Date	Mintage	VG	Fine	VF	XF
4a	ND	Inc. Ab.	3.00	7.50	12.50	20.00

NOTE: These were struck from 1827-1841.

2 RAPPEN

BILLON

C#	Date	Mintage	VG	Fine	VF	XF
52	1842D	.460	2.00	4.50	6.50	10.00

10 SCHILLING

SILVER

C#	Date	Mintage	VG	Fine	VF	XF
55	ND(1806)	—	8.00	20.00	30.00	45.00
	1807B	—	4.00	10.00	20.00	35.00
	1808B	—	4.00	10.00	20.00	35.00
	1809B	—	4.00	10.00	20.00	35.00
	1810B	—	4.00	10.00	20.00	35.00
	1811B	—	4.00	10.00	20.00	35.00

8 BATZEN

SILVER

C#	Date	Mintage	VG	Fine	VF	XF
56	1810B	.108	16.00	40.00	70.00	130.00
	1814B	Inc. Ab.	20.00	50.00	90.00	150.00

10 BATZEN

SILVER

C#	Date	Mintage	VG	Fine	VF	XF
57	1812	.028	25.00	60.00	90.00	160.00

20 BATZEN

SILVER

C#	Date	Mintage	VG	Fine	VF	XF
58	1813	—	25.00	60.00	100.00	150.00
58a	1826	—	45.00	100.00	150.00	275.00

40 BATZEN

SILVER

C#	Date	Mintage	VG	Fine	VF	XF
59	1813	—	45.00	100.00	200.00	300.00

NCLT ISSUES

MEDALLIC ISSUES

(DUCAT)

.986 GOLD
Magister Zwingli

KM#	Date	Mintage	Fine	VF	XF
1	1810	—	—	—	—

PATTERNS

KM#	Date	Mintage	Identification	Mkt.Val.
1	1811	—	1/2 Kreuzer, Billon	—
2	1842	—	1 Kreuzer, Billon	—

SWITZERLAND

The Swiss Federation, located in central Europe north of Italy and south of Germany, has an area of 15,941 sq. mi. (41,290 sq. km.) and a population of 6.5 million. Capital: Bern. The economy centers about a well-developed manufacturing industry. Machinery, chemicals, watches and clocks, and textiles are exported.

Switzerland, the habitat of lake dwellers in prehistoric times, was peopled by the Celtic Helvetians when Julius Caesar made it a part of the Roman Empire in 58 B.C. After the decline of Rome, Switzerland was invaded by Teutonic tribes, who established small temporal holdings which in the Middle Ages, became a federation of fiefs of the Holy Roman Empire. As a nation, Switzerland originated in 1291 when the districts of Nidwalden, Schwyz and Uri united to defeat Austria and attain independence as the Swiss Confederation. After acquiring new cantons in the 14th century, Switzerland was made independent from the Holy Roman Empire by the 1648 Treaty of Westphalia. The revolutionary armies of Napoleonic France occupied Switzerland and set up the Helvetian Republic, 1798-1803. After the fall of Napoleon, the Congress of Vienna, 1815, recognized the independence of Switzerland and guaranteed its neutrality. The Swiss Constitutions of 1848 and 1874 established a union modeled upon that of the United States.

MINTMARKS

A - Paris
AB - Strasbourg
B - Bern
B. - Brussels 1874
BA - Basel
BB - Strasbourg
S - Solothurn

NOTE: The coinage of Switzerland has been struck at the Bern Mint since 1853 with but a few exceptions. All coins minted there carry a 'B' mintmark through 1969, except for the 2- Centime and 2-Franc values where the mintmark was discontinued after 1968. In 1968 and 1969 some issues were struck at both Bern (B) and in London (no mintmark).

MONETARY SYSTEM

10 Rappen = 1 Batzen
10 Batzen = 1 Franc
16 Franken = 1 Duplone

HELVETIAN REPUBLIC

RAPPEN

BILLON

C#	Date	Mintage	VG	Fine	VF	XF
1	1800	—	6.00	12.50	25.00	35.00
	1801	—	5.00	10.00	22.50	30.00
	1802	—	6.00	12.50	25.00	35.00

1/2 BATZEN

BILLON
Obv: Without number five.

C#	Date	Mintage	VG	Fine	VF	XF
2	1799	—		65.00	100.00	150.00

Rev: Number five.

C#	Date	Mintage	VG	Fine	VF	XF
2a	1799	—	6.00	12.50	25.00	47.00
	1800	—	6.00	15.00	40.00	65.00
	1802	—	6.00	15.00	40.00	65.00
	1803	—	6.00	15.00	40.00	65.00

BATZEN

Obv: Number ten.
BILLON

C#	Date	Mintage	VG	Fine	VF	XF
3	1799	—	20.00	45.00	90.00	130.00

Obv: Without number ten.

C#	Date	Mintage	VG	Fine	VF	XF
3a	1799B	—	10.00	25.00	50.00	80.00
	1799S	—	10.00	25.00	50.00	80.00
	1799	—	7.00	20.00	30.00	45.00
	1800	—	15.00	45.00	70.00	115.00
	1800B	—	5.00	10.00	20.00	30.00
	1801B	—	6.00	15.00	25.00	60.00
	1802B	—	6.00	15.00	25.00	60.00
	1803B	—	6.00	15.00	25.00	60.00

5 BATZEN

SILVER

C#	Date	Mintage	VG	Fine	VF	XF
4	1799B	—	20.00	45.00	80.00	135.00
	1799S	—	50.00	120.00	275.00	425.00
	1800B	—	30.00	80.00	145.00	210.00
	1802B	—	75.00	200.00	375.00	550.00

10 BATZEN

SILVER

C#	Date	Mintage	VG	Fine	VF	XF
5	1798B	—	75.00	200.00	400.00	600.00
	1799B	—	50.00	100.00	200.00	375.00
	1799S	—	75.00	200.00	375.00	550.00
	1801B	—	55.00	125.00	250.00	450.00

20 BATZEN

SILVER
Rev: Small leaves, narrow '20'.

C#	Date	Mintage	VG	Fine	VF	XF
6	1798S	—	100.00	225.00	375.00	600.00
	1799S	1 pc. known	—	Rare	—	

Rev: Large leaves, wide '20'.

C#	Date	Mintage	VG	Fine	VF	XF
6.1	1798S	—	100.00	225.00	375.00	600.00

40 BATZEN

SILVER
Rev: Similar to C#7.1.

C#	Date	Mintage	VG	Fine	VF	XF
7	1798S	—	100.00	250.00	550.00	950.00
	1798B	—	250.00	700.00	1200.	2000.
	1798BA	—	250.00	750.00	1400.	2300.

Obv: Soldier faces to left.

C#	Date	Mintage	VG	Fine	VF	XF
7.1	1798S	—	75.00	300.00	600.00	1000.

4 FRANKEN

SILVER

C#	Date	Mintage	VG	Fine	VF	XF
8	1799B	—	200.00	550.00	800.00	1200.

Obv: Similar to C#8.

C#	Date	Mintage	VG	Fine	VF	XF
8a	1801B	—	200.00	550.00	800.00	1200.

16 FRANKEN

.900 GOLD

C#	Date	Mintage	VG	Fine	VF	XF
9	1800B	—	500.00	1500.	2750.	4500.

32 FRANKEN

.900 GOLD

C#	Date	Mintage	VG	Fine	VF	XF
10	1800B	—	1000.	3000.	6000.	11,000.

NCLT ISSUES

PATTERNS

KM#	Date	Mintage	Identification	Mkt.Val.
1	ND	—	1 Kreuzer, Billon	—
2	1798	32	20 Batzen, Silver	800.00
3	1799	—	1 Rappen, Billon	—
4	1800	—	1 Rappen, Billon	—

SWITZERLAND (CONFOED. HELVETICA)

MONETARY SYSTEM

100 Centimes (Rappen) = 1 Franc

RAPPEN (CENTIME)

BRONZE

Y#	Date	Mintage	Fine	VF	XF	Unc
18	1850A	2.270	20.00	45.00	80.00	125.00
	1851A	2.730	15.00	30.00	45.00	100.00
	1853B with thick cross —					
		2.008	15.00	30.00	45.00	100.00
	1853B with thin cross —					
		Inc. Ab.	800.00	1600	2000	2500
	1855B	.500	100.00	200.00	300.00	450.00
	1856B	2.500	15.00	30.00	50.00	75.00
	1857B	1.587	12.50	25.00	40.00	65.00
	1863B	.501	70.00	100.00	140.00	200.00
	1864B	.501	80.00	110.00	150.00	210.00
	1866B	1.000	25.00	50.00	75.00	100.00
	1868B	2.000	10.00	17.50	25.00	45.00
	1870B	.500	30.00	60.00	100.00	140.00
	1872B	2.080	6.00	10.00	20.00	35.00
	1875B	.975	10.00	20.00	30.00	50.00
	1876B	1.000	10.00	20.00	30.00	50.00
	1877B	.923	8.00	15.00	20.00	32.00
	1878B	.981	8.00	15.00	20.00	32.00
	1879B	.998	8.00	15.00	20.00	32.00
	1880B	.992	10.00	20.00	30.00	50.00
	1882B	1.000	6.00	10.00	20.00	35.00
	1883B	1.000	6.00	10.00	20.00	35.00
	1884B	1.000	6.00	10.00	20.00	35.00
	1887B	1.504	4.00	8.00	12.00	20.00
	1889B	.500	12.00	20.00	35.00	60.00
	1890B	1.000	8.00	12.00	17.50	22.50
	1891B with thick cross —					
		2.000	8.00	12.00	17.50	22.50
	1891B with thin cross —					
		Inc. Ab.	8.00	12.00	17.50	22.50
	1892B	1.000	8.00	12.00	17.50	22.50
	1894B	1.000	8.00	12.00	17.50	22.50
	1895B	2.000	2.00	4.00	10.00	15.00
	1896B	36 pcs.	—	—	Rare	—
	1897B	.500	6.00	12.00	20.00	35.00
	1898B	1.500	2.00	4.00	10.00	15.00
	1899B	1.500	2.00	4.00	10.00	15.00
	1900B	2.000	2.00	4.00	10.00	15.00
	1902B	.950	20.00	35.00	50.00	75.00
	1903B	1.000	6.00	12.00	20.00	35.00
	1904B	1.000	6.00	12.00	20.00	35.00
	1905B	2.000	2.00	4.00	7.00	12.00
	1906B	1.000	6.00	12.00	20.00	35.00
	1907B	2.000	2.00	4.00	7.00	12.00
	1908B	3.000	4.00	6.00	8.00	11.00
	1909B	1.000	8.00	15.00	25.00	35.00
	1910B	.500	4.00	6.00	8.00	11.00
	1911B	.500	4.00	6.00	8.00	11.00
	1912B	2.000	.50	1.00	3.00	7.00
	1913B	3.000	.50	1.00	3.00	7.00

Y#	Date	Mintage	Fine	VF	XF	Unc
18	1914B	3.500	.50	1.00	3.00	7.00
	1915B	3.000	.50	1.00	3.00	7.00
	1917B	2.000	.50	1.00	3.00	7.00
	1918B	3.000	.50	1.00	3.00	7.00
	1919B	3.000	.50	1.00	3.00	7.00
	1920B	1.000	.50	1.00	3.00	7.00
	1921B	3.000	.50	1.00	3.00	7.00
	1924B	2.000	.50	1.00	3.00	7.00
	1925/4B	2.500	—	—	—	—
	1925B	Inc. Ab.	.50	1.00	3.00	7.00
	1926B	2.000	.50	1.00	3.00	7.00
	1927B	1.500	.50	1.00	3.00	7.00
	1928B	2.000	.50	1.00	3.00	7.00
	1929B	4.000	.50	1.00	2.00	4.00
	1930B	2.500	.50	1.00	2.00	4.00
	1931B	5.000	.50	1.00	2.00	4.00
	1932B	5.000	.50	1.00	2.00	4.00
	1933B	3.000	.50	1.00	2.00	4.00
	1934B	3.000	.50	1.00	2.00	4.00
	1936B	2.000	.50	1.00	2.00	4.00
	1937B	2.400	.50	1.00	2.00	4.00
	1938B	5.300	.50	1.00	2.00	4.00
	1939B	.010	10.00	15.00	20.00	35.00
	1940B	3.027	.50	1.00	2.00	4.00
	1941B	12.794	.20	.50	1.00	3.50

ZINC

Y#	Date	Mintage	Fine	VF	XF	Unc
18a	1942B	17.969	.50	.75	1.50	3.50
	1943B	8.647	.50	1.00	2.00	4.50
	1944B	11.825	.50	.75	1.50	3.50
	1945B	2.800	2.50	5.00	10.00	17.50
	1946B	12.063	.50	.75	1.50	5.00

BRONZE

Y#	Date	Mintage	Fine	VF	XF	Unc
54	1948B	10.500	—	.15	.40	.80
	1949B	11.100	—	.15	.40	.50
	1950B	3.610	—	.40	2.00	3.00
	1951B	22.624	—	.15	.40	.50
	1952B	11.520	—	.15	.25	.50
	1953B	5.947	—	.15	.40	1.00
	1954B	5.175	—	.15	.40	.50
	1955B	5.282	—	.25	.80	1.50
	1956B	4.960	—	.15	.40	1.00
	1957B	15.226	—	.10	.15	.40
	1958B	20.142	—	.10	.15	.50
	1959B	5.582	—	.15	.25	.80
	1962B	5.010	—	.15	.25	.80
	1963B	15.920	—	.10	.15	.40
	1966B	5.030	—	.10	.15	.40
	1967B	3.020	—	.10	.15	.40
	1968B	4.920	—	—	.10	.20
	1969	4.810	—	—	.10	.15
	1970	7.810	—	—	.10	.15
	1971	5.030	—	—	.10	.15
	1973	3.000	—	—	.10	.15
	1974	3.007	—	—	.10	.15
	1974	—	—	—	Proof	1.50
	1975	3.010	—	—	.10	.15
	1975	.010	—	—	Proof	1.50
	1976	3.005	—	—	.10	.15
	1976	—	—	—	Proof	—
	1977	—	—	—	.10	.15
	1977	—	—	—	Proof	1.50
	1978	—	—	—	.10	.15
	1978	—	—	—	Proof	1.50
	1979	—	—	—	.10	.15
	1979	—	—	—	Proof	1.50

2 RAPPEN

BRONZE

Y#	Date	Mintage	Fine	VF	XF	Unc
19	1850A	7.290	.75	3.50	7.50	20.00
	1851A	3.720	.75	3.50	7.50	20.00
	1866B	1.000	3.00	8.00	15.00	25.00
	1870B	.540	20.00	30.00	50.00	75.00
	1875B	.984	3.00	8.00	15.00	25.00
	1879B	.990	3.00	8.00	15.00	25.00
	1883B	1.000	1.00	4.00	6.00	12.00
	1886B	1.000	1.00	4.00	6.00	12.00
	1888B	.500	15.00	25.00	35.00	55.00
	1890B	1.000	1.00	4.00	6.00	12.00
	1893B	2.000	1.00	4.00	6.00	12.00
19	1896B	20 pcs.	—	—	Rare	—
	1897B	.487	10.00	20.00	30.00	45.00
	1898B	.500	10.00	20.00	30.00	45.00
	1899B	1.000	2.00	4.00	8.00	15.00
	1900B	1.000	2.00	4.00	8.00	15.00
	1902B	.500	10.00	20.00	30.00	45.00
	1903B	.500	10.00	20.00	30.00	45.00
	1904B	.500	10.00	20.00	30.00	45.00
	1906B	.500	10.00	20.00	30.00	45.00
	1907B	1.000	2.00	4.00	8.00	15.00
	1908B	1.000	2.00	4.00	8.00	15.00
	1909B	1.000	2.00	4.00	8.00	15.00
	1910B	.500	6.00	12.00	20.00	30.00
	1912B	1.000	1.00	2.00	4.00	10.00
	1913B	1.000	1.00	2.00	4.00	10.00
	1914B	1.000	1.00	2.00	4.00	10.00
	1915B	1.000	1.00	2.00	4.00	10.00
	1918B	1.000	1.00	2.00	4.00	10.00
	1919B	2.000	.50	1.00	3.00	5.00
	1920B	.500	3.50	7.50	12.50	20.00
	1925B	1.250	.50	1.00	3.50	5.00
	1926B	.750	2.50	6.00	10.00	20.00
	1927B	.500	3.50	7.50	12.50	20.00
	1928B	.500	3.50	7.50	12.50	20.00
	1929B	.750	1.00	2.00	5.00	10.00
	1930B	1.000	1.00	2.00	4.00	6.00
	1931B	1.288	1.00	2.00	4.00	6.00
	1932B	1.500	1.00	2.00	4.00	6.00
	1933B	1.000	1.00	2.00	4.00	6.00
	1934B	.500	2.50	6.00	10.00	20.00
	1936B	.500	2.50	6.00	10.00	20.00
	1937B	1.200	1.00	2.00	3.00	5.00
	1938B	1.369	1.00	2.00	3.00	5.00
	1941B	3.448	.50	1.00	1.50	3.00

ZINC

Y#	Date	Mintage	Fine	VF	XF	Unc
19a	1942B	8.954	.50	1.00	2.00	6.00
	1943B	4.499	1.00	2.00	4.00	7.50
	1944B	8.086	.50	1.00	2.00	6.00
	1945B	3.640	.50	1.50	3.00	12.00
	1946B	1.393	6.00	10.00	17.50	25.00

BRONZE

Y#	Date	Mintage	Fine	VF	XF	Unc
55	1948B	10.197	—	.15	.35	.50
	1951B	9.622	—	.15	.35	.50
	1952B	1.915	—	.15	.35	.50
	1953B	2.006	—	.15	.35	1.25
	1954B	2.539	—	.15	.35	.50
	1955B	2.493	—	.15	.35	.75
	1957B	8.099	—	.10	.15	.40
	1958B	6.078	—	.10	.15	.35
	1963B	10.065	—	.10	.15	.35
	1966B	2.510	—	.10	.15	.35
	1967B	1.510	—	.15	.35	.75
	1968B	2.860	—	.10	.15	.35
	1969	6.200	—	—	.10	.15
	1970	3.115	—	—	.10	.15
	1974	3.540	—	—	.10	.15
	1974	—	—	—	Proof	2.00

5 RAPPEN

BILLON

Y#	Date	Mintage	Fine	VF	XF	Unc
20	1850BB	7.970	3.00	4.50	20.00	45.00
	1850AB	Inc.Ab.	25.00	45.00	75.00	150.00
	1850	Inc. Ab.	150.00	250.00	325.00	750.00
	1851BB	12.042	100.00	150.00	275.00	475.00
	1872B	1.213	17.50	30.00	45.00	65.00
	1873B	1.622	12.50	20.00	30.00	55.00
	1874B	1.700	12.50	20.00	30.00	55.00
	1876B	.989	17.50	30.00	45.00	65.00
	1877B	.978	17.50	30.00	45.00	65.00

COPPER-NICKEL

Y#	Date	Mintage	Fine	VF	XF	Unc
23	1879B	1.000	10.00	15.00	25.00	70.00
	1880B	2.000	2.00	5.00	10.00	30.00
23	1881B	2.000	2.00	5.00	10.00	30.00
	1882B	3.000	2.00	5.00	10.00	30.00
	1883B	3.000	2.00	5.00	10.00	30.00
	1884B	2.000	2.00	5.00	10.00	30.00
	1885B	3.000	2.00	5.00	10.00	30.00
	1887B	.500	20.00	35.00	70.00	125.00
	1888B	1.500	2.00	5.00	10.00	30.00
	1889B	.500	20.00	35.00	70.00	125.00
	1890B	1.000	4.00	8.00	20.00	50.00
	1891B	1.000	4.00	8.00	20.00	50.00
	1892B	1.000	4.00	8.00	20.00	50.00
	1893B	2.000	1.00	2.50	10.00	25.00
	1894B	2.000	1.00	2.50	10.00	25.00
	1895B	2.000	1.00	2.50	10.00	25.00
	1896B	16 pcs.	—	—	Rare	—
	1897B	.500	4.00	8.00	20.00	50.00
	1898B	2.500	.50	1.00	8.00	25.00
	1899B	1.500	.50	1.00	8.00	25.00
	1900B	2.000	.50	1.00	8.00	25.00
	1901B	3.000	.50	1.00	8.00	25.00
	1902B	1.000	6.00	10.00	20.00	45.00
	1903B	2.000	.50	1.00	8.00	25.00
	1904B	1.000	6.00	10.00	20.00	45.00
	1905B	1.000	6.00	10.00	20.00	45.00
	1906B	3.000	.50	1.00	4.00	17.50
	1907B	5.000	.50	1.00	4.00	17.50
	1908B	3.000	.50	1.00	4.00	17.50
	1909B	2.000	.50	1.00	4.00	17.50
	1910B	1.000	.75	2.50	5.00	20.00
	1911B	2.000	.50	1.00	4.00	17.50
	1912B	3.000	.50	1.00	4.00	17.50
	1913B	3.000	.50	1.00	4.00	17.50
	1914B	3.000	.50	1.00	4.00	17.50
	1915B	3.000	.50	1.00	4.00	17.50
	1917B	1.000	.50	1.00	4.00	17.50

BRASS

Y#	Date	Mintage	Fine	VF	XF	Unc
23b	1918B	6.000	10.00	17.50	22.50	30.00

COPPER-NICKEL

Y#	Date	Mintage	Fine	VF	XF	Unc
23	1919B	6.000	.10	.20	1.50	5.00
	1920B	5.000	.10	.20	1.50	5.00
	1921B	3.000	.10	.25	1.50	5.00
	1922B	4.000	.10	.20	1.50	5.00
	1925B	3.000	.10	.20	1.50	5.00
	1926B	3.000	.10	.20	1.50	5.00
	1927B	2.000	.10	.20	1.50	5.00
	1928B	2.000	.10	.20	1.50	5.00
	1929B	2.000	.10	.20	1.50	5.00
	1930B	3.000	.10	.20	1.50	5.00
	1931B	5.037	.10	.20	1.50	5.00

NICKEL

Y#	Date	Mintage	Fine	VF	XF	Unc
23a	1932B	6.000	.10	.20	.50	4.00
	1933B	3.000	.10	.20	.50	4.00
	1934B	4.000	.10	.20	.50	4.00
	1936B	1.000	.10	.35	.50	4.00
	1937B	2.000	.10	.20	.50	4.00
	1938B	1.000	.10	.35	.50	4.00
	1939B	10.048	.10	.20	.50	4.00
	1940B	1.410	.10	.20	.50	4.00
	1941B	3.030	.25	.50	1.00	4.00

COPPER-NICKEL

Y#	Date	Mintage	Fine	VF	XF	Unc
23	1940B	1.416	—	.20	.80	5.00
	1942B	5.078	—	.10	.40	3.00
	1943B	6.591	—	.10	.40	3.00
	1944B	9.981	—	.10	.40	3.00
	1945B	.985	—	.20	.80	4.00
	1946B	6.179	—	.10	.40	3.00
	1947B	5.125	—	.10	.40	3.00
	1948B	4.710	—	.10	.40	3.00
	1949B	4.589	—	.10	.40	3.00
	1950B	.920	—	.20	.80	4.00
	1951B	2.141	—	.10	.40	2.50
	1952B	4.690	—	.10	.25	2.00
	1953B	9.131	—	.10	.25	1.00
	1954B	8.038	—	.10	.25	2.00
	1955B	19.943	—	.10	.15	1.20
	1957B	10.147	—	.10	.15	1.20
	1958B	10.217	—	.10	.15	1.20
	1959B	11.086	—	.10	.15	1.20
	1962B	23.840	—	.10	.15	.40
	1963B	29.730	—	.10	.15	.80
	1964B	17.080	—	.10	.15	.50
	1965B	1.430	—	.10	.25	1.20
	1966B	10.010	—	—	.10	.20
	1967B	13.010	—	—	.10	.20
	1968B	10.020	—	—	.10	.15
	1969B	32.990	—	—	.10	.15
	1970	34.800	—	—	.10	.15
	1971	40.020	—	—	.10	.15
	1974	30.002	—	—	.10	.15
	1974	—	—	—	Proof	2.75
	1975	34.005	—	—	.10	.15
	1975	.010	—	—	Proof	2.75
	1976	12.005	—	—	.10	.15

Y#	Date	Mintage	Fine	VF	XF	Unc
	1976	—	—	—	Proof	—
	1977	—	—	—	—	.10
	1977	—	—	—	Proof	2.75
	1978	—	—	—	—	.10
	1978	—	—	—	Proof	2.75
	1979	—	—	—	Proof	.10
	1979	—	—	—	Proof	2.75

10 RAPPEN

BILLON

Y#	Date	Mintage	Fine	VF	XF	Unc
21	1850BB	8.780	4.00	12.00	25.00	45.00
	1851BB	4.530	17.50	30.00	55.00	125.00
	1871B	.844	12.00	25.00	45.00	75.00
	1873B	1.398	10.00	20.00	30.00	50.00
	1875B	.174	150.00	250.00	450.00	750.00
	1876B	1.962	10.00	20.00	30.00	50.00

COPPER-NICKEL

Y#	Date	Mintage	Fine	VF	XF	Unc
24	1879B	1.000	4.00	8.00	25.00	55.00
	1880B	2.000	1.00	4.00	12.50	35.00
	1881B	3.000	1.00	4.00	12.50	35.00
	1882B	3.000	1.00	4.00	12.50	35.00
	1883B	2.000	1.00	4.00	12.50	35.00
	1884B	3.000	1.00	4.00	12.50	35.00
	1885B	3.000	1.00	4.00	12.50	35.00
	1894B	1.000	1.00	4.00	12.50	35.00
	1895B	2.000	1.00	4.00	12.50	35.00
	1896B	16 pcs.	—	—	Rare	—
	1897B	.500	2.00	6.00	20.00	45.00
	1898B	1.000	2.00	6.00	20.00	45.00
	1899B	.500	2.00	6.00	20.00	45.00
	1900B	1.500	2.00	4.00	12.50	30.00
	1901B	1.000	2.00	4.00	12.50	30.00
	1902B	1.000	2.00	4.00	12.50	30.00
	1903B	1.000	2.00	4.00	12.50	30.00
	1904B	1.000	2.00	4.00	12.50	30.00
	1906B	1.000	2.00	4.00	12.50	30.00
	1907B	2.000	.50	1.00	4.00	15.00
	1908B	2.000	.50	1.00	4.00	15.00
	1909B	2.000	.50	1.00	4.00	15.00
	1911B	1.000	.50	1.00	4.00	15.00
	1912B	1.500	.50	1.00	4.00	15.00
	1913B	2.000	.50	1.00	4.00	15.00
	1914B	2.000	.50	1.00	4.00	15.00
	1915B	1.200	.50	1.00	4.00	15.00

BRASS

Y#	Date	Mintage	Fine	VF	XF	Unc
24b	1918B	6.000	10.00	15.00	20.00	30.00
	1919B	3.000	35.00	50.00	65.00	100.00

COPPER-NICKEL

Y#	Date	Mintage	Fine	VF	XF	Unc
24	1919B	3.000	.10	.20	3.00	10.00
	1920B	3.500	.10	.20	2.00	10.00
	1921B	3.000	.10	.20	2.00	10.00
	1922B	2.000	.10	.20	2.00	10.00
	1924B	2.000	.10	.20	2.00	10.00
	1925B	3.000	.10	.20	2.00	10.00
	1926B	3.000	.10	.20	2.00	10.00
	1927B	2.000	.10	.20	2.00	10.00
	1928B	2.000	.10	.20	2.00	10.00
	1929B	2.000	.10	.20	2.00	10.00
	1930B	2.000	.10	.20	2.00	10.00
	1931B	2.244	.10	.20	.50	10.00

NICKEL

Y#	Date	Mintage	Fine	VF	XF	Unc
24a	1932B	3.500	.10	.20	.50	5.00
	1933B	2.000	.10	.20	.50	5.00
	1934B	3.000	.10	.20	.50	5.00
	1936B	1.500	.20	.50	1.50	5.00
	1937B	1.000	.20	.50	1.50	5.00
	1938B	1.000	.20	.50	1.50	5.00
	1939B	10.022	.10	.20	.50	5.00

COPPER-NICKEL

Y#	Date	Mintage	Fine	VF	XF	Unc
24	1940B	2.000	.10	.25	.50	5.00
	1942B	2.110	.10	.25	.50	5.00
	1943B	3.176	.10	.20	.50	5.00
	1944B	6.133	.10	.15	.50	5.00
	1945B	.993	.10	.50	1.00	5.00
	1946B	4.010	.10	.15	.50	4.00
	1947B	3.152	.10	.15	.50	4.00
24	1948B	1.000	.10	.50	1.00	4.00
	1949B	2.269	.10	.15	.50	4.00
	1950B	3.200	.10	.15	.25	3.50
	1951B	3.430	.10	.15	.25	3.50
	1952B	4.452	.10	.15	.25	3.50
	1953B	6.149	.10	.15	.25	3.50
	1954B	3.200	.10	.15	.25	3.50
	1955B	11.795	.10	.15	.25	3.50
	1957B	10.092	.10	.15	.25	3.50
	1958B	10.040	.10	.15	.25	3.50
	1959B	13.053	.10	.15	.25	3.50
	1960B	4.040	.10	.15	.25	3.50
	1961B	7.949	.10	.15	.20	1.50
	1962B	34.965	.10	.15	.20	1.00
	1964B	16.340	.10	.15	.20	1.00
	1965B	14.190	.10	.15	.20	1.00
	1966B	4.025	—	—	.10	.50
	1967B	10.000	—	—	.10	.50
	1968B	14.065	—	—	.10	.50
	1969B	28.855	—	—	.10	.50
	1970	40.020	—	—	.10	.50
	1972	7.877	—	—	.10	.50
	1973	30.350	—	—	.10	.25
	1974	30.007	—	—	.10	.25
	1974	—	—	—	Proof	3.50
	1975	25.003	—	—	.10	.25
	1975	.010	—	—	Proof	3.50
	1976	19.013	—	—	.10	.25
	1976	—	—	—	Proof	—
	1977	—	—	—	.10	.25
	1977	—	—	—	Proof	3.50
	1978	—	—	—	—	.25
	1978	—	—	—	Proof	3.50
	1979	—	—	—	—	.25
	1979	—	—	—	Proof	3.50

20 RAPPEN

BILLON

Y#	Date	Mintage	Fine	VF	XF	Unc
22	1850BB	5.390	3.50	8.00	25.00	50.00
	1851BB	6.160	40.00	65.00	100.00	200.00
	1858B	1.548	15.00	20.00	40.00	65.00
	1859B	2.776	8.00	15.00	25.00	45.00

NICKEL

Y#	Date	Mintage	Fine	VF	XF	Unc
25a	1881B	1.000	1.00	4.00	12.00	30.00
	1883B	2.500	.50	1.50	6.00	20.00
	1884B	4.000	.50	1.50	6.00	20.00
	1885B	3.000	.50	1.50	6.00	20.00
	1887B	.500	4.00	6.00	10.00	45.00
	1891B	1.000	.50	1.50	6.00	20.00
	1893B	1.000	.50	1.50	6.00	20.00
	1894B	1.000	.50	1.50	6.00	20.00
	1896B	1.000	.50	1.50	6.00	20.00
	1897B	.500	3.00	6.00	10.00	45.00
	1898B	.500	4.00	6.00	10.00	45.00
	1899B	.500	4.00	6.00	10.00	45.00
	1900B	1.000	.50	1.50	3.00	20.00
	1901B	1.000	.50	1.50	3.00	20.00
	1902B	1.000	.50	1.50	3.00	20.00
	1903B	1.000	.50	1.50	3.00	20.00
	1906B	1.000	.50	1.50	3.00	20.00
	1907B	1.000	.50	1.50	3.00	20.00
	1908B	1.500	.25	1.00	2.00	8.00
	1909B	2.000	.25	1.00	2.00	8.00
	1911B	1.000	.50	1.00	2.00	8.00
	1912B	2.000	.25	.50	2.00	8.00
	1913B	1.500	.25	.50	2.00	8.00
	1919B	1.500	.25	.50	2.00	8.00
	1920B	3.100	.15	.25	1.00	4.00
	1921B	2.500	.15	.25	1.00	4.00
	1924B	1.100	.25	.50	1.00	4.00
	1925B	1.500	.15	.35	1.00	4.00
	1926B	1.500	.15	.35	1.00	4.00
	1927B	.500	1.00	2.00	4.00	15.00
	1929B	2.000	.15	.25	.75	3.00
	1930B	2.000	.15	.25	.75	3.00
	1931B	2.250	.15	.25	.75	3.00
	1932B	2.000	.15	.25	.75	3.00
	1933B	1.500	.15	.40	1.00	3.00
25a	1934B	2.000	.15	.25	.75	3.00
	1936B	1.000	.15	.50	1.00	3.00
	1938B	2.805	.15	.25	.75	3.00

COPPER-NICKEL

Y#	Date	Mintage	Fine	VF	XF	Unc
25	1939B	8.100	.10	.15	.20	3.00
	1943B	10.173	.10	.15	.20	3.00
	1944B	7.139	.10	.15	.20	3.00
	1945B	1.992	.10	.15	.50	3.00
	1947B	5.131	—	.10	.15	2.00
	1950B	5.970	—	.10	.15	2.00
	1951B	3.640	—	.10	.25	2.00
	1952B	3.070	—	.10	.25	2.00
	1953B	6.958	—	.20	.15	2.00
	1954B	1.504	—	.10	.40	2.00
	1955B	9.104	—	.10	.15	2.00
	1956B	5.111	—	.10	.15	1.50
	1957B	2.535	—	.10	.15	1.50
	1958B	5.037	—	.10	.15	1.50
	1959B	10.136	—	.10	.15	1.00
	1960B	15.467	—	.10	.15	1.00
	1961B	8.234	—	.10	.15	1.00
	1962B	30.145	—	.10	.15	1.00
	1963B	9.020	—	.10	.15	1.00
	1964B	14.370	—	—	.10	1.00
	1965B	15.005	—	—	.10	1.00
	1966B	10.785	—	—	.10	.50
	1967B	8.995	—	—	.10	.50
	1968B	10.540	—	—	.10	.50
	1969B	39.875	—	—	.10	.50
	1970	45.605	—	—	.10	.20
	1971	25.160	—	—	.10	.20
	1974	30.025	—	—	.10	.20
	1974	—	—	—	Proof	4.50
	1975	50.060	—	—	.10	.20
	1975	.010	—	—	Proof	4.50
	1976	23.150	—	—	.10	.20
	1976	—	—	—	Proof	—
	1977	—	—	—	.10	.20
	1977	—	—	—	Proof	4.50
	1978	—	—	—	—	.20
	1978	—	—	—	Proof	4.50
	1979	—	—	—	—	.20
	1979	—	—	—	Proof	4.50

1/2 FRANC

2.5000 gm., .900 SILVER, .0723 oz ASW

Y#	Date	Mintage	Fine	VF	XF	Unc
26	1850A	4.500	50.00	80.00	125.00	200.00
	1851A	Inc. Ab.	50.00	80.00	125.00	200.00

2.5000 gm., .835 SILVER, .0671 oz ASW

Y#	Date	Mintage	Fine	VF	XF	Unc
30	1875B	1.000	40.00	65.00	100.00	175.00
	1877B	1.000	40.00	65.00	100.00	175.00
	1878B	1.000	40.00	65.00	100.00	175.00
	1879B	1.000	30.00	50.00	75.00	135.00
	1881B	1.000	10.00	20.00	35.00	80.00
	1882B	1.000	10.00	20.00	35.00	80.00
	1894A	.800	20.00	45.00	75.00	150.00
	1896B	28 pcs.	—	—	Rare	—
	1898B	1.600	2.25	5.00	20.00	50.00
	1899B	.400	4.00	8.00	30.00	60.00
	1900B	.400	10.00	20.00	35.00	80.00
	1901B	.200	25.00	45.00	75.00	200.00
	1903B	.800	2.25	4.00	12.00	45.00
	1904B	.400	4.00	8.00	30.00	75.00
	1905B	.600	2.25	4.00	12.00	45.00
	1906B	1.000	BV	2.50	7.50	35.00
	1907B	1.200	BV	2.50	7.50	35.00
	1908B	.800	BV	2.50	7.50	35.00
	1909B	1.000	BV	2.50	7.50	35.00
	1910B	1.000	BV	2.50	7.50	35.00
	1911B	—	BV	2.50	7.50	35.00
	1912B	—	BV	2.50	7.50	35.00

Y#	Date	Mintage	Fine	VF	XF	Unc
30	1913B	.800	BV	2.50	7.50	35.00
	1914B	2.000	BV	BV	4.00	12.00
	1916B	.800	BV	BV	5.00	20.00
	1920B	5.400	BV	BV	3.50	8.00
	1921B	6.000	BV	BV	3.50	8.00
	1928B	1.000	BV	BV	4.00	10.00
	1929B	2.000	BV	BV	4.00	10.00
	1931B	1.000	BV	BV	4.00	10.00
	1932B	1.000	BV	BV	4.00	10.00
	1934B	2.000	BV	BV	3.50	6.00
	1936B	.400	BV	BV	3.50	6.00
	1937B	1.000	BV	BV	3.50	6.00
	1939B	1.001	BV	BV	3.50	6.00
	1940B	2.002	BV	BV	2.25	4.00
	1941B	.200	BV	BV	3.00	7.50
	1942B	2.969	BV	BV	2.25	4.00
	1943B	4.572	BV	BV	2.25	4.00
	1944B	7.456	BV	BV	2.25	4.00
	1945B	4.928	BV	BV	2.25	4.00
	1946B	6.817	BV	BV	2.25	4.00
	1948B	6.113	BV	BV	2.25	4.00
	1950B	7.148	BV	BV	2.25	4.00
	1951B	8.530	BV	BV	BV	3.00
	1952B	14.023	BV	BV	BV	3.00
	1953B	3.567	BV	BV	BV	3.00
	1955B	1.320	BV	BV	BV	3.00
	1956B	4.250	BV	BV	BV	3.00
	1957B	12.085	BV	BV	BV	3.00
	1958B	11.558	BV	BV	BV	3.00
	1959B	12.581	BV	BV	BV	3.00
	1960B	14.528	BV	BV	BV	3.00
	1961B	6.906	BV	BV	BV	3.00
	1962B	18.272	BV	BV	BV	3.00
	1963B	25.168	BV	BV	BV	3.00
	1964B	22.720	BV	BV	BV	3.00
	1965B	17.920	BV	BV	BV	3.00
	1966B	10.008	BV	BV	BV	3.00
	1967B	16.096	BV	BV	BV	3.00

COPPER-NICKEL

Y#	Date	Mintage	Fine	VF	XF	Unc
30a	1968	20.000	.30	.35	.40	.50
	1968B	44.920	.30	.35	.40	.50
	1969	31.400	.30	.35	.40	.50
	1969B	51.704	.30	.35	.40	.50
	1970	52.620	.30	.35	.40	.50
	1971	34.472	.30	.35	.40	.50
	1972	9.996	.30	.35	.40	.50
	1973	5.000	.30	.35	.40	.50
	1974	45.006	.30	.35	.40	.50
	1974	—	—	—	Proof	5.00
	1975	27.234	.30	.35	.40	.50
	1975	.010	—	—	Proof	5.00
	1976	10.009	.30	.35	.40	.50
	1976	—	—	—	Proof	—
	1977	—	.30	.35	.40	.50
	1977	—	—	—	Proof	5.00
	1978	—	—	—	—	.50
	1978	—	—	—	Proof	5.00
	1979	—	—	—	—	.50
	1979	—	—	—	Proof	5.00

FRANC

5.0000 gm., .900 SILVER, .1447 oz ASW

Y#	Date	Mintage	Fine	VF	XF	Unc
27	1850A	5.750	60.00	100.00	125.00	225.00
	1851A	Inc. Ab.	60.00	100.00	125.00	225.00
	1857B	526 pcs.	—	—	Rare	—

5.0000 gm., .800 SILVER, .1286 oz ASW

Y#	Date	Mintage	Fine	VF	XF	Unc
27a	1860B	.515	75.00	125.00	200.00	600.00
	1861B	3.002	20.00	40.00	75.00	150.00

5.0000 gm., .835 SILVER, .1342 oz ASW

Y#	Date	Mintage	Fine	VF	XF	Unc
31	1875B	1.036	25.00	60.00	120.00	275.00
	1876B	2.500	4.50	10.00	60.00	175.00
	1877B	2.520	4.50	10.00	60.00	175.00
	1880B	.944	8.00	20.00	65.00	200.00
	1886B	1.000	4.50	6.50	30.00	90.00
	1887B	1.000	4.50	6.50	30.00	90.00

Y#	Date	Mintage	Fine	VF	XF	Unc
31	1894A	1.200	4.50	6.50	30.00	90.00
	1896B	28 pcs.	—	—	Rare	—
	1898B	.400	6.00	12.50	25.00	100.00
	1899B	.400	6.00	12.50	25.00	100.00
	1900B	.400	6.00	12.50	25.00	100.00
	1901B	.400	6.00	12.50	25.00	100.00
	1903B	1.000	BV	5.00	20.00	75.00
	1904B	.400	5.00	8.00	30.00	120.00
	1905B	.700	BV	5.00	20.00	75.00
	1906B	.700	BV	5.00	20.00	75.00
	1907B	.800	BV	5.00	20.00	75.00
	1908B	1.200	BV	5.00	20.00	60.00
	1909B	.900	BV	5.00	20.00	60.00
	1910B	1.000	BV	4.50	8.00	40.00
	1911B	1.200	BV	4.50	8.00	40.00
	1912B	1.200	BV	4.50	8.00	40.00
	1913B	1.200	BV	4.50	8.00	40.00
	1914B	4.200	BV	4.50	8.00	40.00
	1916B	1.000	BV	4.50	8.00	40.00
	1920B	3.300	BV	4.50	8.00	30.00
	1921B	3.800	BV	BV	6.00	12.50
	1928B	1.500	BV	BV	6.00	12.50
	1931B	1.000	BV	BV	6.00	12.50
	1932B	.500	BV	BV	7.50	25.00
	1934B	.500	BV	BV	7.50	25.00
	1936B	.500	BV	BV	7.50	25.00
	1937B	1.000	BV	BV	6.00	10.00
	1939B	2.106	BV	BV	6.00	10.00
	1940B	2.003	BV	BV	6.00	10.00
	1943B	3.526	BV	BV	4.25	5.00
	1944B	6.225	BV	BV	4.25	5.00
	1945B	7.794	BV	BV	4.25	5.00
	1946B	2.539	BV	BV	4.25	5.00
	1947B	.624	BV	BV	5.00	7.50
	1952B	2.853	BV	BV	4.25	5.00
	1953B	.786	BV	BV	4.25	5.00
	1955B	.194	BV	BV	8.00	12.00
	1956B	2.500	BV	BV	4.25	5.00
	1957B	6.420	BV	BV	4.25	5.00
	1958B	3.580	BV	BV	4.25	5.00
	1959B	1.859	BV	BV	4.25	5.00
	1960B	3.523	BV	BV	4.25	5.00
	1961B	6.549	BV	BV	4.25	5.00
	1962B	6.220	BV	BV	4.25	5.00
	1963B	13.476	BV	BV	4.25	5.00
	1964B	12.560	BV	BV	4.25	5.00
	1965B	5.032	BV	BV	4.25	5.00
	1966B	3.032	BV	BV	4.25	5.00
	1967B	2.088	BV	BV	4.25	5.00

COPPER-NICKEL

Y#	Date	Mintage	Fine	VF	XF	Unc
31a	1968	15.000	—	—	.75	1.00
	1968B	40.864	—	—	.75	1.00
	1969B	37.598	—	—	.75	1.00
	1970	24.240	—	—	.75	1.00
	1971	11.496	—	—	.75	1.00
	1973	5.000	—	—	1.00	1.50
	1974	15.012	—	—	.75	1.00
	1974	—	—	—	Proof	5.50
	1975	13.012	—	—	.75	1.00
	1975	.010	—	—	Proof	5.50
	1976	5.009	—	—	.75	1.00
	1976	—	—	—	Proof	—
	1977	—	—	—	.75	1.00
	1977	—	—	—	Proof	5.50
	1978	—	—	—	—	1.00
	1978	—	—	—	Proof	5.50
	1979	—	—	—	—	1.00
	1979	—	—	—	Proof	5.50

2 FRANCS

10.0000 gm., .900 SILVER, .2894 oz ASW

Y#	Date	Mintage	Fine	VF	XF	Unc
28	1850A	2.500	150.00	200.00	300.00	600.00
	1857B	622 pcs.	1500.	4000.	6000.	9000.

10.0000 gm., .800 SILVER, .2572 oz ASW

Y#	Date	Mintage	Fine	VF	XF	Unc
28a	1860B	2.001	50.00	80.00	175.00	250.00
	1862B	1.000	60.00	100.00	200.00	275.00
	1863B	.500	100.00	175.00	300.00	600.00

10.0000 gm., .835 SILVER, .2685 oz ASW

Y#	Date	Mintage	Fine	VF	XF	Unc
32	1874B	1.000	10.00	20.00	100.00	275.00
	1875B	.982	12.50	22.50	150.00	300.00
	1878B	1.500	8.50	12.00	70.00	250.00
	1879B	.518	12.50	25.00	80.00	300.00
	1886B	1.000	BV	8.50	20.00	135.00
	1894A	.700	BV	8.50	60.00	175.00
	1896B	20 pcs.	—	—	Rare	—
	1901B	.050	125.00	175.00	500.00	1750.
	1903B	.300	BV	8.50	35.00	80.00
	1904B	.200	BV	10.00	100.00	250.00
	1905B	.300	BV	8.50	25.00	75.00
	1906B	.400	BV	8.50	25.00	75.00
	1907B	.300	BV	8.50	25.00	75.00
	1908B	.200	BV	10.00	100.00	250.00
	1909B	.300	BV	8.50	20.00	75.00
	1910B	.250	BV	8.50	25.00	75.00
	1911B	.400	BV	8.50	12.50	60.00
	1912B	.400	BV	8.50	12.50	60.00
	1913B	.300	BV	8.50	12.50	60.00
	1914B	1.000	BV	BV	8.50	25.00
	1916B	.250	BV	8.50	25.00	75.00
	1920B	2.300	BV	BV	8.50	12.50
	1921B	2.000	BV	BV	8.50	12.50
	1922B	.400	BV	BV	15.00	50.00
	1928B	.750	BV	BV	8.50	12.50
	1931B	.500	BV	BV	8.50	20.00
	1932B	.250	BV	BV	30.00	60.00
	1936B	.250	BV	BV	30.00	60.00
	1937B	.250	BV	BV	30.00	60.00
	1939B	1.455	BV	BV	8.50	10.00
	1940B	2.502	BV	BV	8.50	10.00
	1941B	1.192	BV	BV	8.50	10.00
	1943B	2.089	BV	BV	8.50	10.00
	1944B	6.276	BV	BV	8.50	10.00
	1945B	1.134	BV	BV	8.50	10.00
	1946B	1.629	BV	BV	8.50	10.00
	1947B	.500	BV	BV	8.50	10.00
	1948B	.920	BV	BV	8.50	10.00
	1953B	.438	BV	BV	8.50	10.00
	1955B	1.032	BV	BV	8.50	10.00
	1957B	2.298	BV	BV	8.50	10.00
	1958B	.650	BV	BV	8.50	10.00
	1959B	2.905	BV	BV	8.50	10.00
	1960B	1.980	BV	BV	8.50	10.00
	1961B	4.653	BV	BV	8.50	10.00
	1963B	8.030	BV	BV	8.50	10.00
	1964B	4.558	BV	BV	8.50	10.00
	1965B	8.526	BV	BV	8.50	10.00
	1967B	4.132	BV	BV	8.50	10.00

COPPER-NICKEL

Y#	Date	Mintage	Fine	VF	XF	Unc
32a	1968	10.000	—	—	1.50	2.00
	1968B	31.588	—	—	1.50	2.00
	1969B	17.296	—	—	1.50	2.00
	1970	10.350	—	—	1.50	2.00
	1972	5.003	—	—	1.25	1.50
	1973	5.996	—	—	1.25	1.50
	1974	15.009	—	—	1.25	1.50
	1974	—	—	—	Proof	7.00
	1975	7.061	—	—	1.25	1.50
	1975	.010	—	—	Proof	7.00
	1976	5.011	—	—	1.25	1.50
	1976	—	—	—	Proof	—
	1977	—	—	—	1.25	1.50
	1977	—	—	—	Proof	7.00
	1978	—	—	—	—	1.50
	1978	—	—	—	Proof	7.00
	1979	—	—	—	—	1.50
	1979	—	—	—	Proof	7.00

5 FRANCS

25.0000 gm., .900 SILVER, .7234 oz ASW

Y#	Date	Mintage	Fine	VF	XF	Unc
29	1850A	.140	100.00	150.00	225.00	400.00
	1851A	.360	100.00	150.00	225.00	400.00
	1873B	.030	300.00	450.00	650.00	1200.
	1874B.	1.400	60.00	100.00	150.00	225.00
	1874B	.196	75.00	110.00	175.00	300.00

NOTE: The dot after the B is for Brussels. For coins dated 1855 see Shooting Talers.

Y#	Date	Mintage	Fine	VF	XF	Unc
33	1888B	.025	300.00	450.00	600.00	900.00
	1889B	.225	100.00	140.00	175.00	300.00
	1890B	.305	100.00	140.00	175.00	300.00
	1891B	.150	100.00	140.00	175.00	300.00
	1892B	.190	100.00	140.00	175.00	300.00
	1894B	.034	200.00	350.00	500.00	1000.
	1895B	.046	200.00	350.00	500.00	1000.
	1896B	2,000	—	—	Rare	—
	1900B	.033	225.00	375.00	600.00	1000.
	1904B	.040	200.00	350.00	500.00	1000.
	1907B	.277	100.00	140.00	175.00	300.00
	1908B	.200	100.00	140.00	175.00	300.00
	1909B	.120	100.00	150.00	200.00	325.00
	1912B	.011	1200.	1500.	2000.	2400.
	1916b	.022	—	—	Rare	—

Obv: Similar to Y#34a.

Y#	Date	Mintage	Fine	VF	XF	Unc
34	1922B	2.400	65.00	85.00	120.00	150.00
	1923B	11.300	50.00	75.00	100.00	135.00

Y#	Date	Mintage	Fine	VF	XF	Unc
34a	1924B	.182	100.00	175.00	250.00	400.00
(35)			65.00	85.00	125.00	175.00
	1926B	2.000	65.00	85.00	125.00	175.00
	1928B	.024	2000.	3500.	6000.	7500.

15.0000 gm., .835 SILVER, .4027 oz ASW

NOTE: The several varieties of number Y#36, the 1931 5 Francs, are distinguished by the relation of the edge lettering to the head of William Tell and in the amount of rotation of the reverse in relation to the obverse. Beginning above the head the normal sequence is:

a) PROVIDEBIT ********** *** DOMINUS

A fairly common variety shows the lettering:
b) ********** *** DOMINUS PROVIDEBIT

A somewhat rarer variety shows:
c) ********** PROVIDEBIT *** DOMINUS

The reverse of the regular issue is upset 180 degrees. There are varieties with:

d) The reverse rotated about 15 degrees to the left of the normal upset position.

e) The reverse rotated about 15 degrees to the right of the normal position.

Y#	Date	Mintage	Fine	VF	XF	Unc
36	1931B(a)	3.520	BV	BV	12.50	30.00
	1931B(b)	Inc. Ab.	—	—	—	—
	1931B(c)	Inc. Ab.	—	—	—	—
	1932B	10.580	BV	BV	BV	15.00
	1933B	5.900	BV	BV	12.50	15.00
	1935B	3.000	BV	BV	12.50	15.00
	1937B	.645	BV	BV	12.50	15.00
	1939B	2.197	BV	BV	12.50	15.00
	1940B	1.601	BV	BV	12.50	15.00
	1948B	.416	BV	BV	12.50	15.00
	1949B	.407	BV	BV	12.50	15.00
	1950B	.482	BV	BV	12.50	15.00
	1951B	1.196	BV	BV	12.50	15.00
	1952B	.155	25.00	45.00	70.00	120.00
	1953B	3.403	BV	BV	BV	15.00
	1954B	6.600	BV	BV	BV	15.00
	1965B	5.021	BV	BV	BV	15.00
	1966B	9.016	BV	BV	BV	15.00
	1967B	13.817	BV	BV	BV	15.00
	1968B	—	—	—	Rare	—
	1969B	8.637	BV	BV	BV	15.00

COPPER-NICKEL

Y#	Date	Mintage	Fine	VF	XF	Unc
36a	1968B	33.871	—	3.25	3.50	4.00
	1970	6.306	—	3.25	3.50	4.00
36a	1973	5.002	—	3.25	3.50	4.00
	1974	6.007	—	3.25	3.50	4.00
	1974	—	—	—	Proof	8.50
	1975	2.500	—	3.25	3.50	4.00
	1975	.010	—	—	Proof	8.50
	1976	1.500	—	3.25	3.50	4.00
	1977	—	—	3.25	3.50	4.00
	1978	.900	—	—	—	5.00
	1979	—	—	—	—	4.00

COMMEMORATIVE SERIES

5 FRANCS

15.0000 gm., .835 SILVER, .4027 oz ASW
Armament Fund

Y#	Date	Mintage	Fine	VF	XF	Unc
46	1936B	.200	BV	12.50	20.00	40.00

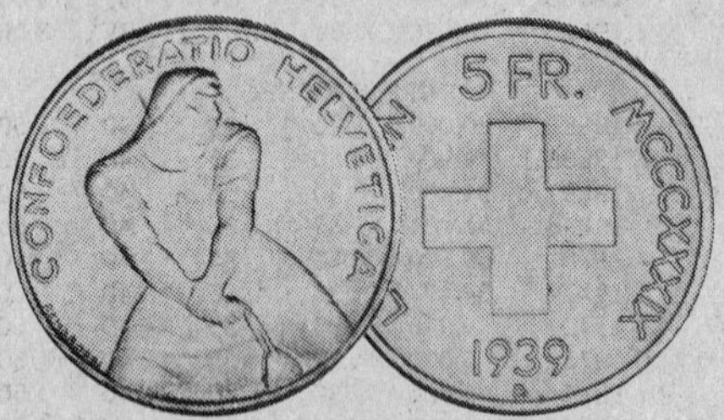

600th Anniversary Battle of Laupen

Y#	Date	Mintage	Fine	VF	XF	Unc
49	1939B	.031	65.00	100.00	150.00	350.00

Zurich Exposition

Y#	Date	Mintage	Fine	VF	XF	Unc
50	1939*	.060	12.50	20.00	45.00	75.00

*Minted at Huguenin, Le Locle.

650th Anniversary of Confederation

Y#	Date	Mintage	Fine	VF	XF	Unc
51	1941B	.100	12.50	15.00	40.00	65.00

500th Anniversary Battle of St. Jakob An Der Birs

Y#	Date	Mintage	Fine	VF	XF	Unc
52	1944B	.102	12.50	15.00	40.00	65.00

Swiss Confederation Centennial

Y#	Date	Mintage	Fine	VF	XF	Unc
53	1948B	.500	BV	BV	15.00	25.00

Red Cross Centennial

Y#	Date	Mintage	Fine	VF	XF	Unc
56	1963B	.623	BV	BV	12.50	17.50

COPPER-NICKEL

100th Anniversary of Constitution

Y#	Date	Mintage	Fine	VF	XF	Unc
57	1974	3.700	—	3.00	3.25	5.00
	1974	.130	—	—	Proof	15.00

European Monument Protection

Y#	Date	Mintage	Fine	VF	XF	Unc
58	1975	2.500	—	3.00	3.25	5.00
	1975	.060	—	—	Proof	15.00

Battle of Murten

Y#	Date	Mintage	Fine	VF	XF	Unc
59	1976	1.500	—	3.00	3.25	5.00
	1976	.100	—	—	Proof	15.00

Johann Heinrich Pestalozzi

Y#	Date	Mintage	Fine	VF	XF	Unc
60	1977	.800	—	3.00	3.25	5.00
	1977	.050	—	—	Proof	18.00

Henry Dunant

Y#	Date	Mintage	Fine	VF	XF	Unc
61	1978	.900	—	3.00	3.25	5.00
	1978	.060	—	—	Proof	15.00

Centennial of Birth of Albert Einstein

Y#	Date	Mintage	Fine	VF	XF	Unc
62	1979	.900	—	—	—	5.00
	1979	.035	—	—	Proof	—

Centennial of Birth of Albert Einstein

Y#	Date	Mintage	Fine	VF	XF	Unc
63	1979	.900	—	—	—	5.00
	1979	.035	—	—	Proof	—

10 FRANCS

3.2258 gm., .900 GOLD, .0933 oz AGW

Y#	Date	Mintage	Fine	VF	XF	Unc
42	1911B	.100	BV	BV	275.00	350.00
	1912B	.200	BV	BV	80.00	100.00
	1913B	.600	BV	BV	65.00	90.00
	1914B	.200	BV	BV	70.00	90.00
	1915B	.400	BV	BV	65.00	90.00
	1916B	.130	BV	BV	85.00	100.00
	1922B	1.020	37.50	40.00	70.00	90.00

20 FRANCS

6.4516 gm., .900 GOLD, .1867 oz AGW

Y#	Date	Mintage	Fine	VF	XF	Unc
40	1883	.250	BV	BV	125.00	150.00
	1886	.250	BV	BV	125.00	150.00
	1887B	176 pcs.	—	—	—	20,000.
	1888B	4,224	1000.	2500.	7000.	8500.
	1889B	.100	BV	BV	150.00	175.00
	1890B	.125	BV	BV	125.00	150.00
	1891B	.100	BV	BV	135.00	175.00
	1892B	.100	BV	BV	125.00	150.00
	1893B	.100	BV	BV	125.00	150.00
	1893B*	25 pcs.	—	—	—	15,000.
	1894B	.121	BV	BV	125.00	150.00
	1895B	.200	BV	BV	125.00	150.00
	1895B*	19 pcs.	—	—	—	15,000.

Edge: DOMINUS XXX PROVIDEBIT XXXXXXXXXX

Y#	Date	Mintage	Fine	VF	XF	Unc
40a	1896B	.400	BV	BV	125.00	135.00

Edge: DOMINUS XXX/XXXXXXXXXX PROVIDEBIT

***NOTE:** Struck of bright Valaisan gold from Gondo having a small cross punched in the center of the Swiss cross.

Y#	Date	Mintage	Fine	VF	XF	Unc
41	1897B	.400	BV	BV	125.00	135.00
	1897B*	29 pcs.	—	—	—	15,000.
	1898B	.400	BV	BV	125.00	135.00
	1899B	.300	BV	BV	125.00	135.00
	1900B	.400	BV	BV	125.00	135.00
	1901B	.500	BV	BV	125.00	135.00
	1902B	.600	BV	BV	125.00	135.00
	1903B	.200	BV	BV	125.00	135.00
	1904B	.100	BV	BV	175.00	200.00
	1905B	.100	BV	BV	175.00	200.00
	1906B	.100	BV	BV	125.00	150.00
	1907B	.150	BV	BV	125.00	135.00
	1908B	.355	BV	BV	125.00	135.00
	1909B	.400	BV	BV	125.00	135.00
	1910B	.375	BV	BV	125.00	135.00
	1911B	.350	BV	BV	125.00	135.00
	1912B	.450	BV	BV	125.00	135.00
	1913B	.700	BV	BV	125.00	135.00
	1914B	.700	BV	BV	125.00	135.00
	1915B	.750	BV	BV	125.00	135.00
	1916B	.300	BV	BV	125.00	135.00
	1922B	2.784	BV	BV	125.00	135.00
	1925B	.400	BV	BV	125.00	135.00
	1926B	.050	175.00	225.00	275.00	300.00
	1927B	5.015	BV	BV	125.00	135.00
	1930B	3.372	BV	BV	125.00	135.00
	1935B	.175	BV	BV	125.00	135.00

***NOTE:** Struck of bright Valaisan gold from Gondo having a small cross punched in the center of the Swiss cross.

Y#	Date	Mintage	Fine	VF	XF	Unc
	1935L-B	20.009	BV	BV	125.00	135.00

NOTE: The 1935L-B coin was struck in 1945, 1946 and 1947.

Edge: AD LEGEM ANNI MCMXXXI

Y#	Date	Mintage	Fine	VF	XF	Unc
41a	1947B	9.200	BV	BV	125.00	135.00
	1949B	10.000	BV	BV	125.00	135.00

100 FRANCS

32.2581 gm., .900 GOLD, .9334 oz AGW

Y#	Date	Mintage	Fine	VF	XF	Unc
43	1925B	5,000	1000.	2500.	6500.	8250.

SHOOTING TALERS

4 FRANCS

.880 SILVER
Chur In Graubunden

Y#	Date	Mintage	Fine	VF	XF	Unc
1S	1842	6,000	300.00	500.00	700.00	1000.

40 BATZEN

.900 SILVER
Glarus

Y#	Date	Mintage	Fine	VF	XF	Unc
2S	1847	3,200	500.00	1000.	2000.	2500.

5 FRANCS

Solothurn
Same as regular issue Y#29, edge is lettered:
EIDGEN FREISCHIESEN SOLOTHURN 1855*

Y#	Date	Mintage	Fine	VF	XF	Unc
3S	1855	3,000	500.00	1000.	2000.	2500.

Bern

Y#	Date	Mintage	Fine	VF	XF	Unc
4S	1857	5,195	150.00	225.00	300.00	450.00

Zurich

Y#	Date	Mintage	Fine	VF	XF	Unc
5S	1859	6,000	120.00	200.00	250.00	350.00

Stans In Nidwalden

Y#	Date	Mintage	Fine	VF	XF	Unc
6S	1861	6,000	75.00	125.00	200.00	275.00

La Chaux-De-Fonds In Neuchatel

Y#	Date	Mintage	Fine	VF	XF	Unc
7S	1863	6,000	120.00	150.00	200.00	300.00

Schaffhausen

Y#	Date	Mintage	Fine	VF	XF	Unc
8S	1865	.010	65.00	100.00	125.00	150.00

Schwyz

Y#	Date	Mintage	Fine	VF	XF	Unc
9S	1867	8,000	75.00	125.00	150.00	200.00

St. Gallen

Y#	Date	Mintage	Fine	VF	XF	Unc
12S	1874	.015	40.00	60.00	75.00	100.00

Fribourg

Y#	Date	Mintage	Fine	VF	XF	Unc
15S	1881	.030	30.00	45.00	60.00	100.00

Zug

Y#	Date	Mintage	Fine	VF	XF	Unc
10S	1869	6,000	90.00	125.00	150.00	200.00

Lausanne

Y#	Date	Mintage	Fine	VF	XF	Unc
13S	1876	.020	35.00	50.00	65.00	100.00

Lugano

Y#	Date	Mintage	Fine	VF	XF	Unc
16S	1883	.030	30.00	45.00	60.00	100.00

Zurich

Y#	Date	Mintage	Fine	VF	XF	Unc
11S	1872	.010	60.00	90.00	120.00	160.00

Basel

Y#	Date	Mintage	Fine	VF	XF	Unc
14S	1879	.030	30.00	45.00	60.00	100.00

Bern

Y#	Date	Mintage	Fine	VF	XF	Unc
17S	1885	.025	30.00	45.00	60.00	100.00

.835 SILVER
Fribourg

Y#	Date	Mintage	Fine	VF	XF	Unc
44	1934	.040	25.00	35.00	50.00	65.00

SILVER
Lucerne

Y#	Date	Mintage	Fine	VF	XF	Unc
47	1939	.040	25.00	35.00	50.00	65.00

100 FRANCS

25.9000 gm., .900 GOLD, .7494 oz AGW
Fribourg

Y#	Date	Mintage	Fine	VF	XF	Unc
45	1934	2,000	1000.	2000.	2600.	3100.

17.5000 gm., .900 GOLD, .5064 oz AGW
Lucerne

Y#	Date	Mintage	Fine	VF	XF	Unc
48	1939	6,000	350.00	600.00	800.00	1000.

NCLT ISSUES

PATTERNS

KM#	Date	Mintage	Identification	Mkt.Val.
1	1855	—	5 Francs, Silver	—
2	1860	—	2 Francs, Silver	—
3	1871	—	20 Francs, Gold	—
4	1871	—	20 Francs, Gold	—

KM#	Date	Mintage	Identification	Mkt.Val.
5	1873	—	20 Francs, Gold, w/mm.	—
5a	1873	—	20 Francs, Gold, w/o mm.	—

MINT SETS

KM#	Date	Mintage	Identification	Issue Price	Mkt. Val.
S1	1896(9)	—	Y18,19,23,24,25a,30-33	—	95,300.
S2	1970(9)	10,000	Y23-25,30a,31a,32a,36a, 54,55	6.40	15.00
S3	1971(5)	5,000	Y23,25,30a,31a,54	2.40	7.00
S4	1972(3)	5,000	Y24,30a,32a	2.40	7.00
S5	1973(6)	10,000	Y24,30a,31a,32a,36a,54	6.40	15.00
S6	1974(9)	10,000	Y23-25,30a,31a,32a,36a, 54,55	6.40	15.00
S7	1975(8)	10,000	Y23-25,30a,31a,32a,36a, 54	6.40	15.00
S8	1976(8)	10,000	Y23-25,30a,31a,32a,36a, 54	—	15.00
S9	1977(8)	10,000	Y23-25,30a,31a,32a,36a, 54	—	15.00
S10	1978(8)	10,000	Y23-25,30a,31a,32a,36a, 54	—	15.00
S..	1979(8)	—	Y23-25,30a-32a,36a,54	—	—

PROOF SETS

STANDARD METALS

KM#	Date	Mintage	Identification	Issue Price	Mkt. Val.
101	1974(9)	—	Y23-25,30a,31a,32a,36a, 54,55	12.80	350.00
102	1975(8)	10,000	Y23-25,30a,31a,32a,36a, 54	16.75	45.00
103	1976(8)	5,000	Y23-25,30a,31a,32a,36a, 54	—	75.00
104	1977(8)	7,000	Y23-25,30a,31a,32a,36a, 54	—	50.00
105	1978(8)	10,000	Y23-25,30a,31a,32a,36a, 54	—	45.00

SYRIA

The Syrian Arab Republic, located in the Near East at the eastern end of the Mediterranean Sea, has an area of 71,498 sq. mi. (185,182 sq. km.) and a population of 7.8 million. Capital: Greater Damascus. Agriculture and animal breeding are the chief industries. Cotton, crude oil and livestock are exported.

Ancient Syria, a land bridge connecting Europe, Africa and Asia, has spent much of its history in thrall to the conqueror's whim. Its subjection by Egypt about 1500 B.C. was followed by successive conquests by the Hebrews, Phoenicians, Babylonians, Assyrians, Persians, Macedonians, Romans, Byzantines and finally, in 636 A.D., by the Moslems. The Arabs made Damascus, one of the oldest continuously inhabited cities of the world, the trade center and capital of an empire stretching from India to Spain. In 1517, following the total destruction of Damascus by the Mongols of Tamerlane, Syria fell to the Ottoman Turks and remained a Turkish province until World War I. The League of Nations gave France a mandate to the Levant states of Syria and Lebanon in 1920. In 1930, following a series of uprisings, France recognized Syria as an independent republic, but still subject to the mandate. Lebanon became fully independent on Nov. 22, 1943, and Syria on Jan. 1, 1944.

MINTMARKS

(a) - Paris, privy marks only

MONETARY SYSTEM

100 Piastres = 1 Pound (Lira)

1/2 PIASTRE

COPPER-NICKEL

Y#	Date	Mintage	Fine	VF	XF	Unc
1	1921(a)	4.000	.60	1.25	3.50	8.50

NICKEL-BRASS

Y#	Date	Mintage	Fine	VF	XF	Unc
4	1935(a)	.600	1.00	2.00	4.00	15.00
	1936(a)	.800	.90	1.75	3.00	12.50

PIASTRE

NICKEL-BRASS

Y#	Date	Mintage	Fine	VF	XF	Unc
5	1929(a)	.750	.50	1.00	3.00	15.00
	1933(a)	.600	.75	1.50	4.00	17.50
	1935(a)	1.950	.35	.75	2.00	10.00
	1936(a)	1.400	.35	1.00	2.00	12.00

ZINC

Y#	Date	Mintage	Fine	VF	XF	Unc
5a	1940(a)	2.060	1.00	1.50	2.50	7.50

BRASS
World War II Provisional Issue

Y#	Date	Mintage	Fine	VF	XF	Unc
10	N.D.	—	.75	1.00	2.50	4.50

2 PIASTRES

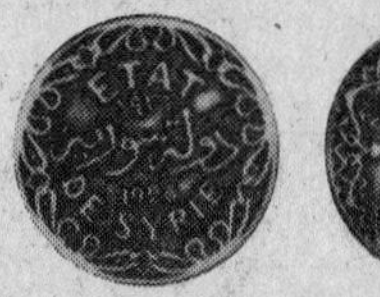

ALUMINUM-BRONZE

Y#	Date	Mintage	Fine	VF	XF	Unc
2	1926(a)	.600	5.00	8.00	20.00	40.00

2-1/2 PIASTRES

ALUMINUM-BRONZE

Y#	Date	Mintage	Fine	VF	XF	Unc
6	1940(a)	2.000	.35	.60	1.50	4.00

ALUMINUM
World War II Provisional Issue

Y#	Date	Mintage	Fine	VF	XF	Unc
11	N.D.	—	5.00	7.50	10.00	20.00

COPPER-NICKEL

Y#	Date	Year	Mintage	VF	XF	Unc
12	AH1367	1948	—	.30	.50	1.25
	1375	1956	5.000	.25	.40	.75

ALUMINUM-BRONZE

Y#	Date	Year	Mintage	VF	XF	Unc
21	.35	1960	1.100	—	.15	.35

Y#	Date	Year	Mintage	VF	XF	Unc
24	AH1382	1962	8.000	—	.10	.25
	1385	1965	8.000	—	.20	.50

Y#	Date	Year	Mintage	VF	XF	Unc
35	AH1393	1973	10.000	—	—	.25

5 PIASTRES

ALUMINUM-BRONZE

Y#	Date	Mintage	Fine	VF	XF	Unc
3	1926(a)	.300	.75	1.25	2.50	12.00
	1926 w/o privy marks					
		.400	.75	1.25	2.50	12.00
	1933(a)	1.200	.40	.85	3.00	10.00
	1935(a)	2.000	.35	.75	3.00	6.00
	1936(a)	.900	.50	1.00	4.00	9.00
	1940(a)	.500	.40	.85	1.50	9.00

COPPER-NICKEL

Y#	Date	Year	Mintage	VF	XF	Unc
13	AH1367	1948	—	.50	1.50	4.50
	1375	1956	4.000	.35	.60	1.00

ALUMINUM-BRONZE

Y#	Date	Year	Mintage	VF	XF	Unc
22	AH1380	1960	4.240	—	.15	.35

Y#	Date	Year	Mintage	VF	XF	Unc
25	AH1382	1962	7.000	—	.15	.30
	1385	1965	18.000	—	.15	.30

BRASS
F.A.O. Issue

Y#	Date	Year	Mintage	VF	XF	Unc
31	AH1391	1971	15.000	—	—	.25

Y#	Date	Year	Mintage	VF	XF	Unc
36	AH1394	1974	—	—	—	.25

F.A.O. Issue

Y#	Date	Year	Mintage	VF	XF	Unc
41	AH1396	1976	2.000	—	—	.15

10 PIASTRES

2.0000 gm., .680 SILVER .0437 oz ASW

Y#	Date	Mintage	Fine	VF	XF	Unc
7	1929	1.000	1.75	4.00	15.00	35.00

COPPER-NICKEL

Y#	Date	Year	Mintage	VF	XF	Unc
14	AH1367	1948	—	.60	1.25	4.00
	1375	1956	4.000	.40	.75	1.25

ALUMINUM-BRONZE

Y#	Date	Year	Mintage	VF	XF	Unc
23	AH1380	1960	2.800	.10	.20	.65

Y#	Date	Year	Mintage	VF	XF	Unc
26	AH1382	1962	6.000	—	.15	.40
	1385	1965	22.000	—	.15	.40

Y#	Date	Year	Mintage	VF	XF	Unc
37	AH1394	1974	—	—	.15	.30

BRASS
F.A.O. Issue

Y#	Date	Year	Mintage	VF	XF	Unc
42	AH1396	1976	.500	—	.15	.25

25 PIASTRES

5.0000 gm., .680 SILVER .1093 oz ASW

Y#	Date	Mintage	Fine	VF	XF	Unc
8	1929	1.000	4.00	5.00	10.00	25.00
	1933(a)	.500	4.00	6.00	12.50	35.00
	1936(a)	.897	3.50	5.00	11.50	27.50
	1937(a)	.393	4.00	8.00	15.00	35.00

2.5000 gm., .600 SILVER .0482 oz ASW

Y#	Date	Year	Mintage	VF	XF	Unc
15	AH1366	1947	6.300	2.50	4.50	12.50

Y#	Date	Year	Mintage	VF	XF	Unc
A19	AH1377	1958	2.300	1.50	2.00	

NICKEL

Y#	Date	Year	Mintage	VF	XF	Unc
27	AH1387	1968	15.000	.20	.30	.50

25th Anniversary Al-Ba'ath Party

32	AH1392	1972	—	.15	.25	.50

38	AH1394	1974	—	.10	.25	.50

F.A.O. Issue

43	AH1396	1976	1.000	.10	.20	.40

50 PIASTRES

10.0000 gm., .680 SILVER .2186 oz ASW

Y#	Date	Mintage	Fine	VF	XF	Unc
9	1929	.880	7.00	10.00	20.00	45.00
	1933(a)	.250	9.00	16.50	25.00	65.00
	1936(a)	.400	9.00	16.50	25.00	60.00
	1937(a)	Inc. Ab.	9.00	16.50	25.00	60.00

5.0000 gm., .600 SILVER .0965 oz ASW

Y#	Date	Year	Mintage	VF	XF	Unc
16	AH1366	1947	4.500	3.50	7.00	17.50

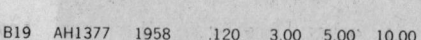

B19	AH1377	1958	.120	3.00	5.00	10.00

Y#	Date	Year	Mintage	VF	XF	Unc
20	AH1378	1959	1.500	3.00	4.50	7.50

NICKEL

28	AH1387	1968	10.000	.25	.50	.80

25th Anniversary Al-Ba'ath Party

33	AH1392	1972	—	.20	.30	.75

39	AH1394	1974	—	.20	.30	.75

F.A.O. Issue

44	AH1396	1976	1.000	.20	.40	.80

1/2 POUND

3.3793 gm., .900 GOLD, .0978 oz AGW

18	AH1369	1950	.100	BV	65.00	75.00

LIRA

10.0000 gm., .680 SILVER, .2186 oz ASW

17	AH1369	1950	7.000	BV	7.00	10.00

POUND

6.7586 gm., .900 GOLD .1956 oz AGW

19	AH1369	1950	.250	135.00	165.00	185.00

NICKEL

Y#	Date	Year	Mintage	VF	XF	Unc
29	AH1387	1968	10.000	.40	.70	1.10
	1391	1971	10.000	.40	.70	1.10

F.A.O. Issue

30	AH1388	1968	.500	.45	.80	1.30

25th Anniversary Al-Ba'ath Party

34	AH1392	1972	10.000	.50	1.00	1.50

40	AH1394	1974	—	.40	.70	1.25

F.A.O. Issue

45	AH1396	1976	.500	.40	.70	1.25

NCLT ISSUES

ESSAIS (E)

(Standard metals unless otherwise noted)

Y#	Date	Mintage	Identification	Issue Price	Mkt Val.
E2	1926(a)	—	2 Piastres	—	65.00
E3	1926(a)	—	5 Piastres	—	80.00

E5	1929(a)	—	Piastre	—	80.00
E7	1929(a)	64(?)	10 Piastres	—	225.00
E8	1929(a)	64(?)	25 Piastres	—	300.00
E9	1929(a)	64(?)	50 Piastres	—	375.00
—	AH1350(a)	—	50 Piastres	—	375.00
E4	1935(a)	—	1/2 Piastre	—	30.00

Listings For

TANNA-TUVA: refer to Russia

TANZANIA

The United Republic of Tanzania, located on the east coast of Africa between Kenya and Mozambique, consists of Tanganyika and the islands of Zanzibar and Pemba. It has an area of 363,950 sq. mi. (942,623 sq. km.) and a population of 16 million. Capital: Dar es Salaam (Haven of Peace). The chief exports are cotton, coffee, diamonds, sisal, cloves, petroleum products, and cashew nuts.

GERMAN EAST AFRICA

German East Africa (Tanganyika), located on the coast of east-central Africa between British East Africa (now Kenya) and Portuguese East Africa (now Mozambique), had an area of 362,284 sq. mi. (938,216 sq. km.) and a population of about 6 million. Capital: Dar es Salaam. Chief products prior to German control were ivory and slaves; after German control, sisal, coffee, and rubber. Germany acquired control of the area by treaties with coastal chiefs in 1884, established it as a protectorate in 1891, and proclaimed it the Colony of German East Africa in 1897. After World War I, Tanganyika was entrusted to Great Britain as a League of Nations mandate, and after World War II as a United Nations trust territory. Tanganyika became an independent nation within the British Commonwealth on Dec. 9, 1961.

RULERS

Wilhelm II, 1888-1918

MINT MARKS

A - Berlin
J - Hamburg
T - Tabora

MONETARY SYSTEM

(Until 1902)
64 Pesa = 1 Rupie
(Commencing 1902)
100 Heller = 1 Rupie

PESA

COPPER

Y#	Date	Mintage	VF	XF	Unc
1	1890	1.000	1.75	3.50	9.00
	1890	—	—	Proof	100.00
	1891	12.551	1.25	3.00	10.00
	1892	27.541	1.25	3.00	10.00

1/2 HELLER

BRONZE

Y#	Date	Mintage	VF	XF	Unc
6	1904A	1.201	2.00	4.50	8.00
	1905A	7.192	1.50	3.00	8.00
	1905J	4.000	1.50	3.00	8.00
	1906J	6.000	1.50	3.00	8.00

HELLER

BRONZE

Y#	Date	Mintage	VF	XF	Unc
7	1904A	10.256	1.00	2.00	10.00
	1904A	—	—	Proof	75.00
	1904J	2.500	1.00	2.00	10.00
	1905A	3.760	1.00	2.00	10.00
	1905A	—	—	Proof	75.00
	1905J	7.556	1.00	2.00	10.00
	1906A	3.004	1.00	2.00	10.00
	1906A	—	—	Proof	75.00
	1906J	1.962	1.25	2.50	12.00
	1907J	17.790	1.00	2.00	10.00
	1908J	12.205	1.00	2.00	10.00
	1909J	1.698	1.25	2.50	12.00
	1910J	5.096	1.00	2.00	10.00
	1910J	—	—	Proof	75.00
	1911J	6.420	1.00	2.00	10.00
	1911J	—	—	Proof	75.00
	1912J	7.012	1.00	2.00	10.00
	1912J	—	—	Proof	75.00
	1913A	—	1.00	2.00	10.00
	1913A	—	—	Proof	75.00
	1913J	5.186	1.00	2.00	10.00
	1913J	—	—	Proof	75.00

5 HELLER

BRONZE

Y#	Date	Mintage	VF	XF	Unc
8	1908J	.600	15.00	25.00	225.00
	1908J	—	—	Proof	250.00
	1909J	.756	15.00	25.00	225.00
	1909J	—	—	Proof	250.00

COPPER-NICKEL

Y#	Date	Mintage	VF	XF	Unc
11	1913A	—	3.00	6.50	25.00
	1913A	—	—	Proof	75.00
	1913J	1.000	3.00	6.50	25.00
	1913J	—	—	Proof	75.00
	1914J	1.000	3.00	6.50	25.00
	1914J	—	—	Proof	75.00

BRASS

1 1/2-2mm thick

Y#	Date	Mintage	VF	XF	Unc
9	1916T oval opening on crown				
		—	3.00	9.00	15.00

1mm or less thick

Y#	Date	Mintage	VF	XF	Unc
9.1	1916T horiz. opening on crown				
		—	3.00	9.00	15.00

10 HELLER

COPPER-NICKEL

Y#	Date	Mintage	VF	XF	Unc
12	1908J	2.000	7.50	15.00	50.00
	1908J	—	—	Proof	150.00
	1909J	Inc. Ab.	5.00	7.50	25.00
	1909J	—	—	Proof	100.00
	1910J	.500	3.00	6.50	25.00
	1910J	—	—	Proof	100.00
	1911A	—	3.00	6.50	25.00
	1911J	—	—	Proof	100.00
	1914J	.200	3.25	8.00	35.00
	1914J	—	—	Proof	100.00

20 HELLER

Obverse A
Large Crown

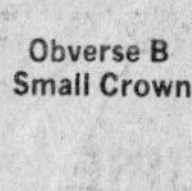

Obverse B
Small Crown

Reverse A
Curled Tip On Second L

Reverse B
Pointed Tips On L's

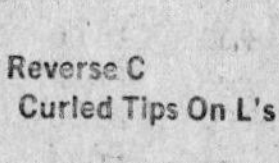

Reverse C
Curled Tips On L's

COPPER

Y#	Date	Mintage	VG	Fine	VF
10	1916T	Obv. A Rev. A	3.00	4.00	—
	1916T	Obv. A Rev. B	90.00	100.00	—
	1916T	Obv. B Rev. A	65.00	75.00	—
	1916T	Obv. B Rev. B	3.00	3.50	—
	1916T	Obv. A Rev. C	—	Rare	—
	1916T	Obv. B Rev. C	—	Rare	—

Total mintage: .3 million

BRASS

Y#	Date	Mintage	VG	Fine	VF
10a	1916T	Obv. A Rev. A	2.50	3.00	7.00
	1916T	Obv. A Rev. B	2.50	3.75	8.00
	1916T	Obv. B Rev. A	3.00	6.00	12.00
	1916T	Obv. B Rev. B	2.50	3.00	7.00
	1916T	Obv. A Rev. C	3.00	5.00	8.00
	1916T	Obv. B Rev. C	3.00	8.00	10.00

Total mintage: 1.6 million

1/4 RUPIE

2.9160 gm., .917 SILVER, .0859 oz ASW

Y#	Date	Mintage	VF	XF	Unc
2	1891	.077	5.50	12.50	45.00
	1891	—	—	Proof	150.00
	1898	.100	5.50	10.00	50.00
	1901	.350	4.50	8.00	50.00

Y#	Date	Mintage	VF	XF	Unc
13	1904A	.300	5.00	9.00	55.00
	1904A	—	—	Proof	135.00
	1906A	.300	5.00	9.00	55.00
	1906A	—	—	Proof	135.00
	1906J	.100	5.50	9.50	55.00
	1907J	.200	5.00	9.00	55.00
	1909A	.300	5.00	9.00	55.00
	1910J	.600	5.00	9.00	55.00
	1910J	—	—	Proof	135.00
	1912J	.400	5.00	9.00	55.00
	1912J	—	—	Proof	135.00
	1913A	.200	5.00	9.00	55.00
	1913A	—	—	Proof	135.00
	1913J	.400	5.00	9.00	55.00
	1913J	—	—	Proof	135.00
	1914J	.200	5.50	9.50	55.00

1/2 RUPIE

5.8319 gm., .917 SILVER, .1719 oz ASW

Y#	Date	Mintage	VF	XF	Unc
3	1891	.068	9.00	15.00	45.00
	1891	—	—	Proof	150.00
	1897	.075	9.00	15.00	50.00
	1901	.215	9.00	15.00	50.00

Y#	Date	Mintage	VF	XF	Unc
14	1904A	.400	8.00	15.00	75.00
	1904A	—	—	Proof	150.00
	1906A	.050	12.00	20.00	100.00
	1906A	—	—	Proof	150.00
	1906J	.050	12.00	20.00	100.00
	1907J	.140	8.00	15.00	75.00
	1907J	—	—	Proof	150.00
	1909A	.100	8.00	15.00	75.00
	1910J	.300	8.00	15.00	75.00
	1912J	.200	8.00	15.00	75.00
	1913A	.100	8.00	15.00	75.00
	1913J	.200	8.00	15.00	75.00
	1914J	.100	8.00	15.00	75.00

RUPIE

11.6638 gm., .917 SILVER, .3437 oz ASW

Y#	Date	Mintage	VF	XF	Unc
4	1890	.154	11.00	15.00	60.00
	1890	—	—	Proof	150.00
	1891	.126	11.00	15.00	60.00
	1891	—	—	Proof	150.00
	1892	.360	11.00	15.00	60.00
	1892	—	—	Proof	150.00
	1893	.142	12.00	17.50	100.00
	1894	.048	14.00	27.50	200.00
	1897	.244	11.00	15.00	100.00
	1898	.357	11.00	14.50	100.00
	1899	.227	11.00	15.00	100.00
	1900	.209	11.00	15.00	100.00
	1901	.319	11.00	14.50	100.00
	1902	.151	11.00	15.00	100.00

Y#	Date	Mintage	VF	XF	Unc
15	1904A	1.000	10.50	14.50	75.00
	1904A	—	—	Proof	150.00
	1905A	.300	11.00	15.00	75.00
	1905A	—	—	Proof	150.00
	1905J	1.000	10.50	14.50	75.00
	1905J	—	—	Proof	150.00
	1906A	.950	10.50	14.50	75.00
	1906J	.700	10.50	14.50	75.00
	1907J	.880	10.50	14.50	75.00
	1908J	.500	10.50	14.50	75.00
	1908J	—	—	Proof	150.00
	1909A	.200	11.00	15.00	75.00
	1910J	.270	10.50	15.00	75.00
	1911A	—	10.50	14.50	75.00
	1911A	—	—	Proof	150.00
	1911J	1.400	10.50	14.50	75.00
	1912J	.300	11.00	15.00	75.00
	1913A	—	11.00	15.00	75.00
	1913J	1.400	10.50	14.50	75.00
	1914J	.500	7.00	15.00	75.00

2 RUPIEN

.917 SILVER

Y#	Date	Mintage	VF	XF	Unc
5	1893	.033	225.00	325.00	750.00
	1893	—	—	Proof	1200.
	1894	.018	265.00	375.00	900.00

15 RUPIEN

7.1680 gm., .750 GOLD, .1728 oz AGW

Y#	Date	Mintage	VF	XF	Unc
16	1916T right arabesque ends under T of Ostafrika	9,803	650.00	700.00	1100.

Y#	Date	Mintage	VF	XF	Unc
16.1	1916T right arabesque ends under first A of Ostafrika	6,395	675.00	750.00	1150.

PEMBA

Pemba, located in the India Ocean, 22 miles (35km.) off the coast of Tanganyika, comprised a portion of British East Africa. It has an area of 380 sq. mi. (207 sq. km.) and is noted for their cloves. Chief city: Chake Chake.

Pemba, came under British control in 1890, On April 26, 1964, Tanganyika, Zanzibar and Pemba united to form the United Republic of Tanganyika and Zanzibar.

RUPEE

SILVER

NOTE: The authenticity of the countermarks attributed to Pemba has not been confirmed.

ZANZIBAR

The British Protectorate of Zanzibar and adjacent small islands, located in the Indian Ocean 22 miles (35 km.) off the coast of Tanganyika, comprised a portion of British East Africa. Zanzibar was also the name of a sultanate which included the Zanzibar and Kenya protectorates. Zanzibar has an area of 637 sq. mi. (1,651 sq. km.). Chief city: Zanzibar. The islands are noted for their cloves, of which Zanzibar is the world's foremost producer.

Zanzibar came under Portuguese control in 1503, was conquered by the Omani Arabs in 1698, became independent of Oman in 1860, and (with Pemba) came under British control in 1890. Britain granted the protectorate self-government in 1961, and independence within the British Commonwealth on Dec. 19, 1963. On April 26, 1964, Tanganyika and Zanzibar (with Pemba) united to form the United Republic of Tanganyika and Zanzibar. The name of the country, which remained within the British Commonwealth, was changed to Tanzania on Oct. 29, 1964.

Tanzania is a member of the Commonwealth of Nations. The president is Chief of State.

RULERS

Sultan Barghash Ibn Sa' Id, 1870-1888AD

Sultan Ali Bun Hamud, 1902-1911AD

MONETARY SYSTEM

64PYSA(Pice) = 1RUPEE
136 Pysa = 1 Ryal (To 1908)
100 Cents = 1 Rupee (To 1909)

PYSA

COPPER

Y#	Date	Mintage	Fine	VF	XF	Unc
1	AH1299	4.640	1.25	1.50	3.00	25.00
	1299	—	—	—	Proof	150.00

Y#	Date	Mintage	Fine	VF	XF	Unc
2	AH1304	18.680	1.50	1.75	4.00	40.00
	1304	—	—	—	Proof	250.00

RYAL

SILVER

Y#	Date	Mintage	Fine	VF	XF	Unc
5	AH1299	.060	125.00	200.00	275.00	500.00

5 RYALS

GOLD

Y#	Date	Mintage	Fine	VF	XF	Unc
7	AH1299	2,000	—	—	Rare	—

DECIMAL COINAGE

100 Cents = 1 Rupee

CENT

BRONZE

Y#	Date	Mintage	VF	XF	Unc
8	1908	1.000	—	200.00	300.00
	1908	—	—	Proof	400.00

10 CENTS

BRONZE

Y#	Date	Mintage	VF	XF	Unc
9	1908	.100	—	250.00	600.00
	1908	—	—	Proof	600.00

20 CENTS

NICKEL

Y#	Date	Mintage	VF	XF	Unc
10	1908	.100	—	450.00	750.00
	1908	—	—	Proof	750.00

NCLT ISSUES

PATTERNS

KM#	Date	Mintage	Identification	Mkt.Val.
1	AH1299	—	1/4 Ryal Silver	—
2	AH1299	—	1/2 Ryal Silver	—
3	AH1299	—	2 1/2 Ryal Gold	—

TANZANIA

MONETARY SYSTEM

100 Senti = 1 Shilingi

5 SENTI

BRONZE

Y#	Date	Mintage	VF	XF	Unc
1	1966	55.250	—	—	.15
	1966	5,500	—	Proof	2.50
	1971	5.000	—	—	.15
	1972	—	—	—	.15
	1973	20.000	—	—	.15
	1974	12.500	—	—	.15
	1975	—	—	—	.15
	1976	37.500	—	—	—

20 SENTI

NICKEL-BRASS

Y#	Date	Mintage	VF	XF	Unc
2	1966	26.500	—	.15	.30
	1966	5,500	—	Proof	3.00
	1970	5.000	—	.15	.30
	1973	20.100	—	.15	.30
	1975	—	—	.15	.30
	1976	10.000	—	—	—

50 SENTI

COPPER-NICKEL

Y#	Date	Mintage	VF	XF	Unc
3	1966	26.000	.15	.25	.50
	1966	5,500	—	Proof	3.00
	1970	10.000	.15	.25	.50
	1973	10.000	.15	.25	.50

SHILINGI

COPPER-NICKEL

Y#	Date	Mintage	VF	XF	Unc
4	1966	45.000	.40	.60	1.00
	1966	5,500	—	Proof	5.50
	1972	10.000	.25	.50	.85
	1974	15.000	.25	.50	1.00

5 SHILINGI

COPPER-NICKEL
F.A.O. Issue
10th Anniversary of Independence

Y#	Date	Mintage	VF	XF	Unc
5	1971	1.000	1.00	1.50	2.00

F.A.O. Issue
Rev: Similar to Y#5.

Y#	Date	Mintage	VF	XF	Unc
5a	1972	8.000	1.00	1.50	2.00
	1973	5.000	1.00	1.50	2.00

10th Anniversary Bank of Tanzania

Y#	Date	Mintage	VF	XF	Unc
9	1976	1.000	1.25	1.50	2.00
	1976	200 pcs.	—	Proof	—
	F.A.O. Issue				
10	1978	.050	—	—	—

25 SHILINGI

25.3100 gm., .500 SILVER, .4069 oz ASW
Conservation Series

Y#	Date	Mintage	VF	XF	Unc
6	1974	.065	BV	15.00	25.00
	28.2800 gm., .925 SILVER, .8411 oz ASW				
6a	1974	.033	—	Proof	30.00

50 SHILINGI

31.6500 gm., .500 SILVER, .5088 oz ASW
Conservation Series
Obv: Similar to 25 Shilingi, Y#6.

Y#	Date	Mintage	VF	XF	Unc
7	1974	.065	BV	22.50	40.00
	35.0000 gm., .925 SILVER, .OZ 1.0409 oz ASW				
7a	1974	.033	—	Proof	50.00

1500 SHILINGI

33.4370 gm., .900 GOLD, .9676 oz AGW
Conservation Series

Y#	Date	Mintage	VF	XF	Unc
8	1974	.013	BV	BV	650.00
	1974	3,050	—	Proof	800.00

NCLT ISSUES

PROOF SETS
STANDARD METALS

KM#	Date	Mintage	Identification	Issue Price	Mkt. Val.
1	1966(4)	5,500	Y1-4	10.50	11.50
2	1974(2)	30,000	Y6a,7a	50.00	75.00

Listings For

TARIM: refer to Yemen Democratic Republic

TCHAD: refer to Chad

THAILAND

The Kingdom of Thailand (formerly Siam), a constitutional monarchy located in the center of mainland Southeast Asia between Burma and Laos, has an area of 200,000 sq. mi. (517,000 sq. km.) and a population of 44 million. Capital: Bangkok. The economy is based on agriculture and mining. Rubber, rice, teakwood, tin and tungsten are exported.

The history of Thailand, the only country in South and Southeast Asia that was never colonized by a European power, dates from the 6th century A.D. when tribes of the Thai stock migrated into the area from the Asiatic continent, a process that accelerated with the Mongol invasion of China in the 13th century. After 400 years of sporadic warfare with the neighboring Burmese, King Taskin won the last battle in 1767. He founded a new capital, Dhonburi, on the west bank of Chao Praya River. King Rama I moved the capital to Bangkok in 1782, thus initiating the so-called Bangkok Period of Siamese coinage characterized by Pot Duang money (bullet coins) stamped with regal symbols.

The Thai were introduced to the Western world by the Portuguese, who were followed by the Dutch, British and French. Rama III of the present ruling dynasty negotiated a treaty of friendship and commerce with Britain in 1826, and in 1896 the independence of the kingdom was guaranteed by an Anglo-French accord. The absolute monarchy was changed into a constitutional monarchy in 1932.

RULERS

King Taskin, 1767-1782
Rama I (Phra Buddha Yot Fa), 1782-1809
Rama II (Phra Buddah Lot La), 1809-1824
Rama III (Phra Nang Klao), 1824-1851
Rama IV (Phra Chom Klao 'Mongkut'), 1851-1868
Rama V (Phra Maha Chulalongkorn), 1868-1910
Rama VI (Vajiravudh), 1910-1925
Rama VII (Prajadhipok), 1925-1935
Rama VIII (Ananda Mahidol), 1935-1946
Rama IX (Phumiphol Adulyadet), 1946

MONETARY SYSTEM

OLD CURRENCY SYSTEM

2 Solot = 1 Att
2 Sio = 1 Sik
2 Att = 1 Sio
2 Sik = 1 Fuang
2 Fuang = 1 Salung (not Sal'ung)
4 Salung = 1 Baht
4 Baht = 1 Tumlung
20 Tumlung = 1 Chang

UNITS OF OLD THAI CURRENCY

Chang	=	ชั่ง
Tamlung	=	ตำลึง
Salung	=	สลึง
Baht	=	บาท
Fueng	=	เฟื้อง
At	=	อัฐ
Solos	=	โสพส
Sik	=	ซีก
Siew	=	เสี้ยว

MINTMARKS

H-Heaton Birmingham

READING DATES & DENOMINATIONS

Typical BE Dating

1 2 3 8 1244

Typical CS Dating

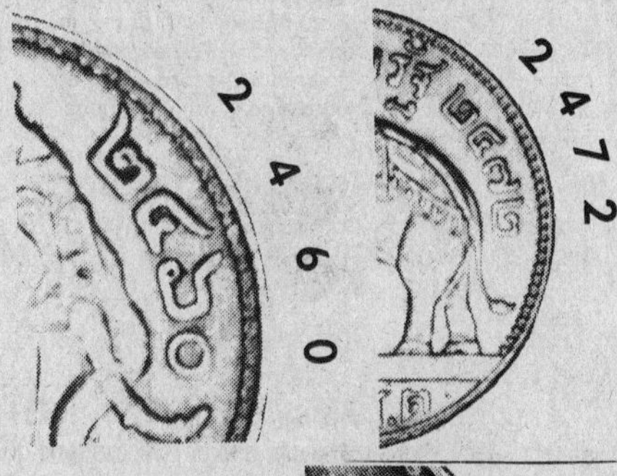

Denomination 2-1/2 (Satang)

Typical RS Dating

Date Conversion Tables:

B.E. date - 543 - A.D. date
Ex: 2516 - 543 - 1973

R.S. date and 1781 - A.D. date
Ex: 127 and 1781 - 1908

C.S. date and 638 - A.D. date
Ex 1238 and 638 - 1876

Primary denominations used were 1 Baht, 1/8 and 1/4 Baht up to the reign of Rama IV. Other denominations are much scarcer.

BULLET COINAGE

Gold and silver "bullet" coins have been a medium of exchange since medieval times. Interesting enough is the fact that a one Baht bullet made of gold will weigh the same as a one Baht bullet in silver. The reason for this is that Baht originally was a weight not a denomination. It was a coinage weight only until the time of Rama VII, (1925-1935) and now it is a weight and also a denomination. (As far as standard weight coins are concerned). Usually one gold Baht was equal to 16 silver Baht on an exchange basis.

Bullet Weights

Grams

BAHT	1/2 BAHT	1/4 BAHT	1/8 BAHT
15.4	7.7	3.85	1.92

1/16 BAHT	1/32 BAHT	1/64 BAHT
.96	.48	.24

Chopmarks exist on bullet coins as they do on many other coins that have traveled on their way through the Orient. One must be careful not to mistake a money changers' chopmark for the regular dynastic marks on the bullet. Some chopmarks are rather simple in design while others appear to be rather elaborate.

DYNASTIC MARKS

Chakra

The Chakra, symbol of the God Vishnu, is the mark of the Bangkok Dynasty. It varies slightly in design between issues being very ornate on ceremonial issues.

RAMA I
1782-1789

Tri

A trident, the symbol of the Hindu God, Siva, used as the first mark of Rama I.

Unalom

An ornamented conch shell, used as the second mark of Rama I.

RAMA II
1809-1824

Krut

A facing Krut, half man - half bird, used as the mark of Rama II.

RAMA III
(1824-1851)

Krut Sio

A Krut bird to left, used as the first mark of Rama III.

Prasat

A palace used as second mark of Rama III.

Dok Mai

A flower used as the third mark of Rama III.

Bai Matum

A Bale-Fruit Tree Used As The Fourth Mark Of Rama III.

Ruang Puang

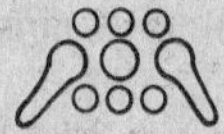

A beehive used as the fifth mark of Rama II.

Arrow Head

Similar to Dok Mai, having only one dot below the point used as the sixth mark of Rama III.

Chaleo

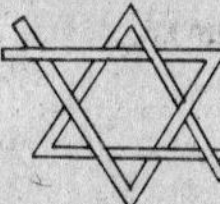

A symbol of varied meanings. In this instance it is believed to represent a charm to ward off evil spirits, found as a seventh mark on bullet coinage of Rama III.

RAMA IV
(1851-1861)

P'ra Tao

The Royal water pot used as the first mark of Rama IV.

Mongkut

The Siamese Royal Crown used as the second mark of Rama IV.

RAMA V
1868-1910

P'ra Kieo
1876

The Royal Coronet worn on the top knot of the Royal Princess on ceremonial occasions. First used on the occasion of the funeral of Princess Charoenkamol Suksawadi who died in 1874.

Cho Rampeuy
1880

The Thai flower used on a ceremonial issue along with an ornate crown of two vessels in memory of Somdet Phra Deb Sirindhra, the mother of Rama V and commemorating his age, dated C.S.1242.

MARKET VALUATIONS
market valuations are primarily based on the quality and condition of the countermarks found on Bullet Coinage.

SILVER POT DUANG
(Bullet Coins)

1/128 BAHT

SILVER, .12gm.

C#	Emperor	Mark	Fine	VF	XF
120	Rama IV	P'ra Tao	—	—	—

ATT (1/64 BAHT)

SILVER, .24gm.

C#	Emperor	Mark	Fine	VF	XF
121	Rama IV	P'ra Tao	18.50	30.00	45.00

PAI (1/32 BAHT)

SILVER, .48gm.

C#	Emperor	Mark	Fine	VF	XF
1	Rama I	Tri	9.00	15.00	22.50
8	Rama I	Unalom	9.00	15.00	22.50
42	Rama III	Prasat	9.00	15.00	22.50
51	Rama III	Dok Mai	9.00	15.00	22.50
61	Rama III	Bai Matum	9.00	15.00	22.50
71	Rama III	Ruang Puang	9.00	15.00	22.50
81	Rama III	Arrow Head	9.00	15.00	22.50
122	Rama IV	P'ra Tao	9.00	15.00	22.50

SIK (1/16 BAHT)

SILVER, .96gm.

C#	Emperor	Mark	Fine	VF	XF
2	Rama I	Tri	12.50	20.00	30.00
9	Rama I	Unalom	16.50	27.50	40.00
16	Rama II	Krut	20.00	35.00	50.00
43	Rama III	Prasat	6.00	10.00	15.00
52	Rama III	Dok Mai	3.50	6.00	10.00
62	Rama III	Bai Matum	5.00	8.00	12.00
72	Rama III	Ruang Puang	5.00	8.00	12.00
82	Rama III	Arrow Head	5.00	8.00	12.00
123	Rama IV	P'ra Tao	2.50	4.00	6.00
133	Rama IV	Mongkut	5.50	9.00	13.50

FUANG (1/8 BAHT)

SILVER, 1.92gm.

C#	Emperor	Mark	Fine	VF	XF
3	Rama I	Tri	15.00	25.00	37.50
10	Rama I	Unalom	15.00	25.00	37.50
17	Rama II	Krut	20.00	35.00	50.00
44	Rama III	Prasat	6.00	10.00	15.00
44.1	Rama III	Prasat and Unalom	25.00	40.00	60.00
44.2	Rama III	Prasat and Krut	25.00	40.00	60.00
53	Rama III	Dok Mai	5.00	8.00	12.00
63	Rama III	Bai Matum	3.00	5.00	7.50
73	Rama III	Ruang Puang	4.50	7.50	11.00
83	Rama III	Arrow Head	4.50	7.50	11.00
124	Rama IV	P'ra Tao	2.50	4.00	6.00
134	Rama IV	Mongkut	3.00	5.00	7.50

SALU'NG (1/4 BAHT)

SILVER, 3.85gm.

C#	Emperor	Mark	Fine	VF	XF
4	Rama I	Tri	11.50	18.50	27.50
11	Rama I	Unalom	15.00	25.00	37.50
18	Rama II	Krut	15.00	25.00	37.50
45	Rama III	Prasat	6.00	10.00	15.00
54	Rama III	Dok Mai	6.00	10.00	15.00
64	Rama III	Bai Matum	5.00	8.00	12.00
74	Rama III	Ruang Puang	5.50	9.00	13.50
84	Rama III	Arrow Head	5.50	9.00	13.50
125	Rama IV	P'ra Tao	3.50	5.00	7.50
135	Rama IV	Mongkut	3.50	4.50	6.50

2 SALU'NG (1/2 BAHT)

SILVER, 7.7gm.

C#	Emperor	Mark	Fine	VF	XF
5	Rama I	Tri	9.00	15.00	22.50
12	Rama I	Unalom	15.00	25.00	37.50
19	Rama II	Krut	18.50	30.00	45.00
46	Rama III	Prasat	7.50	12.50	18.50
55	Rama III	Dok Mai	18.50	30.00	45.00
65	Rama III	Bai Matum	12.50	20.00	30.00

C#	Emperor	Mark	Fine	VF	XF
136	Rama IV	Mongkut	7.50	13.50	20.00
136.1	Rama Iv	Monkut and Prasat	20.00	35.00	50.00

BAHT

SILVER, 15.4 gm.

C#	Emperor	Mark	Fine	VF	XF
1	Rama I	Tri	15.00	18.50	23.50

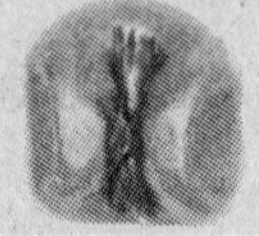

C#	Emperor	Mark	Fine	VF	XF
13	Rama I	Unalom	15.00	18.50	23.50

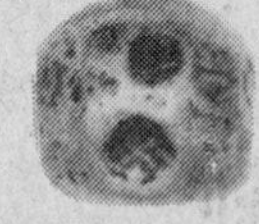

C#	Emperor	Mark	Fine	VF	XF
20	Rama II	Krut	15.00	18.50	23.50
39	Rama III	Chaleo	—	Rare	—
47	Rama III	Prasat	15.00	18.50	23.50
56	Rama III	Dok Mai	30.00	50.00	75.00
66	Rama III	Bai Matum	27.50	45.00	65.00
127	Rama IV	P'ra Tao	Reported, not confirmed		

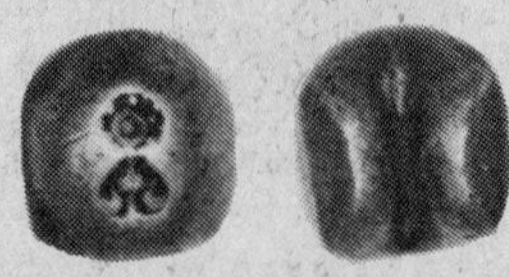

C#	Emperor	Mark	Fine	VF	XF
137	Rama IV	Mongkut	15.00	18.50	23.50
137.1	Rama IV	Monkut and Prasat	50.00	80.00	120.00

Death Of Princess Charoenkamol Suksawadi

C#	Emperor	Mark	Fine	VF	XF
177	Rama V	P'ra Kieo	—	Rare	—

1-1/2 BAHT

SILVER, 23.1 gm.

C#	Emperor	Mark	Fine	VF	XF
48	Rama III	Prasat	—	Rare	—

2 BAHT

SILVER, 30.8gm.

C#	Emperor	Mark	Fine	VF	XF
14	Rama I	Unalom	—	Rare	—
21	Rama II	Krut	—	Rare	—
49	Ramaiii	Prasat	—	Rare	—

c/s: with 8 dots in Chakra

C#	Emperor	Mark	Fine	VF	XF
138	Rama IV	Mongkut	75.00	125.00	185.00

c/s: with 6 blades in Chakra

C#	Emperor	Mark	Fine	VF	XF
138.1	Rama IV	Mongkut	200.00	350.00	475.00

c/s: with 8 blades in Chakra, elaborate design

C#	Emperor	Mark	Fine	VF	XF
138.2	Rama IV	Mongkut	90.00	150.00	225.00

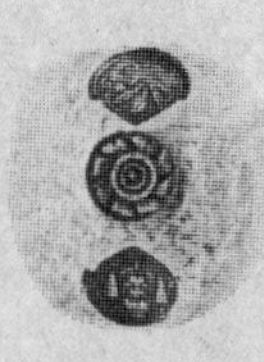

Somdet P'ra Deb Sirindhra

C#	Emperor	Mark	Fine	VF	XF
188	Rama V	Cho Rampeuy	350.00	425.00	500.00

2-1/2 BAHT

SILVER, 38.5gm.

C#	Emperor	Mark	Fine	VF	XF
31	Rama III	Krut Sio	300.00	500.00	750.00

NOTE: Two varieties exist.

TAMLUNG (4 BAHT)

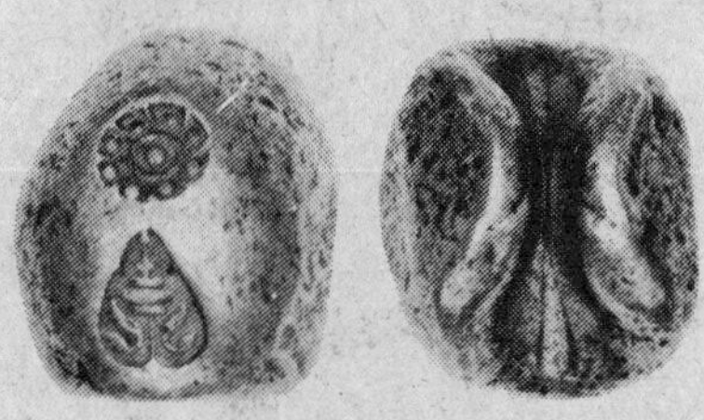

SILVER, 61.6gm.

c/s with 8 dots in chakra

C#	Emperor	Mark	Fine	VF	XF
139	Rama IV	Mongkut	135.00	225.00	335.00

c/s with 7 dots in chakra

C#	Emperor	Mark	Fine	VF	XF
139.1	Rama IV	Mongkut	135.00	225.00	325.00

Cremation of Somdet P'ra Deb Sirindhra

C#	Emperor	Mark	Fine	VF	XF
189	Rama V	Cho Rampeuy	350.00	450.00	550.00

4-1/2 BAHT

SILVER

C#	Emperor	Mark	Fine	VF	XF
32	Rama III	Krut Sio	950.00	1000.	1150.

8 BAHT

SILVER, 123.2gm.

C#	Emperor	Mark	Fine	VF	XF
33	Rama III	Krut Sio	950.00	1000.	1200.

2 1/2 TAMLUNG (10 BAHT)

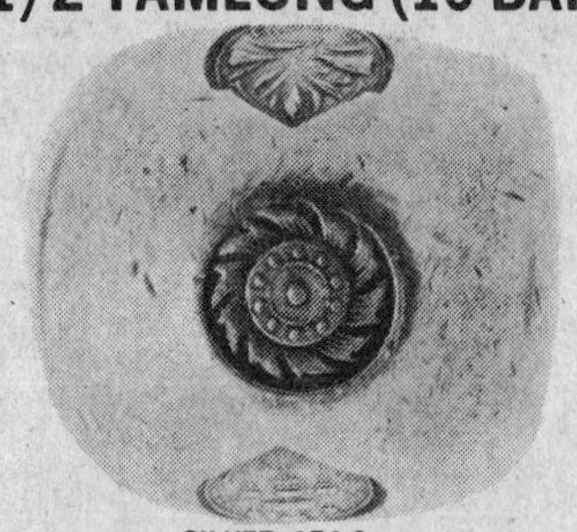

SILVER, 154.0gm.
Cremation of Somdet P'ra Deb Sirindhra

C#	Emperor	Mark	Fine	VF	XF
190	Rama V	Cho Rampeuy	600.00	750.00	900.00

5 TAMLUNG (20 BAHT)

SILVER, 308.0gm.
Cremation of Somdet P'ra Deb Sirindhra

C#	Date	Mintage	Fine	VF	XF
191	Rama V	Cho Rampeuy	1500.	1850.	2250.

10 TAMLUNG (40 BAHT)

SILVER, 616.0gm.
Cremation of Somdet P'ra Deb Sirindhra

C#	Emperor	Mark	Fine	VF	XF
192	Rama V	Cho Rampeuy	3000.	3750.	4500.

20 TAMLUNG (80 BAHT)

SILVER, 1,232gm.
Cremation of Somdet P'ra Deb Sirindhra

193	Rama V	Cho Rampeuy	6000.	7500.	9000.

140	Rama IV	Mongkut	6000.	7500.	9000.

GOLD POT DUANG

(Bullet Coins)

1/32 GOLD BAHT

GOLD, .48gm.

152	Rama IV	P'ra Tao	80.00	100.00	120.00

C#	Emperor	Mark	Fine	VF	XF
162	Rama IV	Mongkut	—	—	—

1/16 GOLD BAHT

GOLD, .96gm.

92	Rama III	Prasat	100.00	125.00	150.00
153	Rama IV	P'ra Tao	130.00	165.00	200.00
163	Rama IV	Mongkut	—	—	—

1/8 GOLD BAHT

GOLD, 1.96gm.

93	Rama III	Prasat	150.00	200.00	250.00
103	Rama III	Dok Mai	200.00	250.00	300.00
113	Rama III	Bai Matum	200.00	250.00	300.00
154	Rama IV	P'ra Tao	130.00	165.00	200.00

1/4 GOLD BAHT

GOLD, 3.85gm.

155	Rama IV	P'ra Tao	140.00	175.00	210.00
165	Rama IV	Mongkut	325.00	400.00	475.00

1/2 GOLD BAHT

GOLD, 7.7gm.

105	Rama III	Dok Mai	—	Rare	—
166	Rama IV	Mongkut	350.00	450.00	550.00

GOLD BAHT

GOLD, 15.4gm.

96	Rama III	Prasat	850.00	1100.	1350.
167	Rama IV	Mongkut	700.00	900.00	1150.

1-1/2 GOLD BAHT

GOLD, 23.1gm.

167.5	Rama IV	Mongkut	—	Rare	—

2 GOLD BAHT

GOLD, 30.8gm.

168	Rama IV	Mongkut	675.00	750.00	875.00

4 GOLD BAHT

GOLD, 61.6gm.

169	Rama IV	Mongkut	1350.	1500.	1750.

TRADE COINS

DOLLAR

SILVER
c/s: Chakra and Mongkut on Mexico 8 Reales, KM#377.

C#	Date	Year	VG	Fine	VF	XF
141.1	ND	(1824-57)	250.00	325.00	400.00	550.00

c/s: Chakra and Mongkut on Peru 8 Reales, Cr#132.

141.2	ND	(1825-55)	—	—	Rare	—

NOTE: Foreign trade brought in quantities of 8 Reales which were not widely accepted by the public. As a result, many were counterstamped with the royal marks: Chakra and Mongkut in the period 1858-1860, to guarantee their value. Today they are very scarce and have been counterfeited.

LOCAL ISSUES

The following tin coins were struck in 5 of the 7 districts formerly comprising the Kingdom of Patani, during the period of Thai Suzerainty (1832-1902).

JARING (JERING)

All coins of Jaring are uniface

One of the 7 provinces cut out of Patani State after the uprising of 1830/31. It lies on the east coast of the Malay peninsula. The uniface tin coins were made from 1845 to 1894.

PITIS

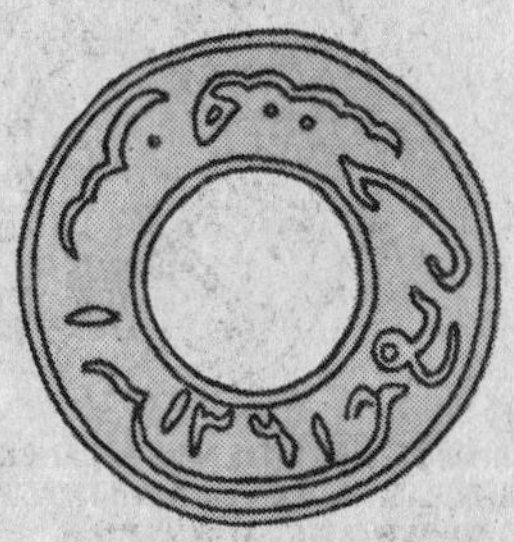

TIN
Arabic legend: INI PITIS JERING SANAT 1261

KM#	Date	Good	VG	Fine	VF
1	AH1261	10.00	15.00	21.50	32.50

Arabic legend: INI PITIS BALAD JARIN SANAT 1297

2	AH1297	10.00	15.00	21.50	32.50

Arabic legend: HADHA AL-DIWAN AL-RAJ AL-ADIL FI BALAD AL-JARIN 1302

3	AH1302	11.50	17.50	25.00	35.00
	1312	11.50	17.50	25.00	35.00

Crude imitation of KM#3

3a	ND	6.00	10.00	15.00	21.50

LEGEH (LIGEH, LIGOR, LANGKAT)

One of the inland provinces cut out of Patani State. Coins attributable to Legeh run from 1840 to 1893. Siam again assumed control in 1902.

PITIS

TIN
Obv: Arabic legend PITIS NEGERI LANGKAT DAR AL-SALAM. Rev: Arabic legend MALIK AL ADIL KHALIFAT AL-MU'MININ.

KM#	Date	Good	VG	Fine	VF
1	ND	13.50	20.00	27.50	35.00

NOTE: For a piece dated 1256, sometimes attributed to Legeh, see KM#4 of Kelantan (Malaysia).

Obv: Arabic legend AL-SULTAN AL-MUZAFFAR DAULAT LANGKAT KHALIFAT Rev: Arabic legend AL-SHAMAR WAL-QAMAR FI RABI AL-AWAL SANAT 1307

KM#	Date	Good	VG	Fine	VF
2	AH1307	7.50	12.50	18.50	26.50
	1313	— Reported, Not Confirmed			

PATANI

(PATTANI)

Patani (Pattani), a former Malay state in the Malay Peninsula, is a small province or 'changwat' of Thailand (Siam) on the eastern side of peninsula Thailand near the border of Malaya, has an area of 777 sq. mi. (2,012 sq. km. and a population of about 275,000. After the 1830/31 uprising it was one of 7 provinces administered by Siam through Malayan governors. Patani was the most prolific coin issuer of the Siamese period having made coins periodically from 1845 to 1891. Formerly ruled by a Moslem Rajah subject to Siam.

PITIS

TIN
Obv: Arabic INI PITIS BELANJA RAJA PATANI Rev: Arabic KHALIFAT AL-MU'MININ SANAT 1261

KM#	Date	Good	VG	Fine	VF
1	AH1261	7.50	12.50	18.50	26.50

Obv: Arabic AL-SULTAN AL-AZAM WA KHALIFAT AL-KARAM. Rev: Arabic AL-MALIK AL-BALAD AL-PATANI AL-IMAMI 1284

KM#	Date	Good	VG	Fine	VF
2	AH1284	7.50	12.50	18.50	26.50

Obv: Arabic AL-SULTAN AL-PATANI SANAT 1297 Rev: Arabic WA KHALIFAT AL-KARAM

KM#	Date	Good	VG	Fine	VF
3	AH1297	7.50	12.50	18.50	26.50

Obv: Arabic AL-MATSARAF FI BALAD AL-PATANIA SANAT 1301. Rev: Arabic ZARB FI HARAT AL-DAULAT AZZA NASRAHU

KM#	Date	Good	VG	Fine	VF
4	AH1301	12.50	18.50	25.00	35.00

Obv: Arabic AL-MATSARAF FI BALAD AL-PATANI SANAT 1309. Rev: Arabic INI PITIS BELANJA DI-DALAM NEGRI PATANI

KM#	Date	Good	VG	Fine	VF
5	AH1309	7.50	12.50	18.50	26.50

KUPANG

GOLD
Obv: Bull standing to left. Rev. Arabic leg: MAIIK AL-ADIL in 2 lines.

KM#	Date	Year	Fine	VF	XF	Unc
50	ND	(1800-50)	45.00	52.50	62.50	80.00

Obv: Bull standing to left. Rev. Arabic leg: AL-ADIL

KM#	Date	Year	Fine	VF	XF	Unc
51	ND	(1800-50)	45.00	52.50	62.50	80.00

Obv: Bull standing left Rev. Arabic leg: MALIK AL-ADIL in 3 lines.

KM#	Date	Year	Fine	VF	XF	Unc
52	ND	(1800-50)	45.00	52.50	62.50	80.00

Obv: Bull standing left. Rev. Arabic leg: ASMA ADIL.

KM#	Date	Year	Fine	VF	XF	Unc
53	ND	(1800-50)	45.00	52.50	62.50	80.00

Obv: Bull standing to right. Rev. Arabic leg: MALIK AL-ADIL in 2 lines.

KM#	Date	Year	Fine	VF	XF	Unc
54	ND	(1800-50)	60.00	85.00	110.00	140.00

Obv: 8-pointed star. Rev. Arabic leg: MALIK AL-ADIL.

KM#	Date	Year	Fine	VF	XF	Unc
55	ND	(1800-50)	50.00	60.00	75.00	100.00

Obv: 6-pointed star. Rev. Arabic leg: MALIK AL-ADIL.

KM#	Date	Year	Fine	VF	XF	Unc
56	ND	(1800-50)	45.00	52.50	62.50	80.00

Obv: 4-petalled flower. Rev. Arabic leg: MALIK AL-ADIL

KM#	Date	Year	Fine	VF	XF	Unc
57	ND	(1800-50)	50.00	60.00	70.00	90.00

Obv. Arabic leg: DAMA SHAH. Rev. Arabic leg: BINAQDI SAHIBI.

KM#	Date	Year	Fine	VF	XF	Unc
58	ND	(1800-50)	50.00	60.00	70.00	90.00

Obv. Arabic leg: SHAH ADIL. Rev. Arabic leg: MALIK AL-ADIL.

KM#	Date	Year	Fine	VF	XF	Unc
59	ND	(1800-50)	50.00	60.00	70.00	90.00

Obv. Arabic leg: AL-JULUS KELANTAN. Rev. Arabic leg: AL-MUTAWAKKILU ALA LIAH.

KM#	Date	Year	Fine	VF	XF	Unc
60	ND	(1800-50)	50.00	60.00	70.00	90.00

Obv. Arabic leg: AQAM'U'D-DIN. Rev. Arabic leg: MALIK AL-ADIL.

KM#	Date	Year	Fine	VF	XF	Unc
61	ND	(1800-50)	50.00	60.00	70.00	90.00

Obv. Arabic leg: SHAH ALAM. Rev. Arabic leg: MALIK AL-ADIL.

KM#	Date	Year	Fine	VF	XF	Unc
62	ND	(1800-50)	50.00	60.00	70.00	90.00

Obv. Arabic leg: SULTAN Rev. Arabic leg: MU'AZZAN SHAH

KM#	Date	Year	Fine	VF	XF	Unc
63	ND	(1800-50)	60.00	70.00	85.00	110.00

Obv. Arabic leg: SULTAN MUHAMMAD. Rev. Arabic leg: MU'AZZAM SHAH.

KM#	Date	Year	Fine	VF	XF	Unc
64	ND	(1800-50)	60.00	70.00	85.00	110.00

Obv. Arabic leg: AL-JULUS KELANTAN. Rev. Arabic leg: KHALIFATA'R-RAHMAN.

KM#	Date	Year	Fine	VF	XF	Unc
65	ND(1800-50)	—	40.00	50.00	60.00	90.00

REMAN (RHAMAN)

Another of the inland provinces cut from Patani State. Only a single type tin coin is presently known from Reman. This piece was minted about 1890.

PITIS

TIN
Uniface. Retrograde Arabic inscription: INI PITIS RAHMAN RAJA MELAYU

KM#	Date	Good	VG	Fine	VF
1	ND	12.50	18.50	25.00	35.00

SAI (SAIBURI, TELUBAN)

Sai is one of the provinces on the east coast of Malaya cut from the state of Patani. The tin Pitis of this province were made from c.1870 to 1891 and are distinctive in that they have a reverse that bears no legend. It carries only a decorative motif.

PITIS

TIN
Arabic inscription on obverse only: MALIK AL-ADIL FI BALAD AL-SAIWI 1290

KM#	Date	Good	VG	Fine	VF
1	AH1290	12.50	18.50	25.00	35.00

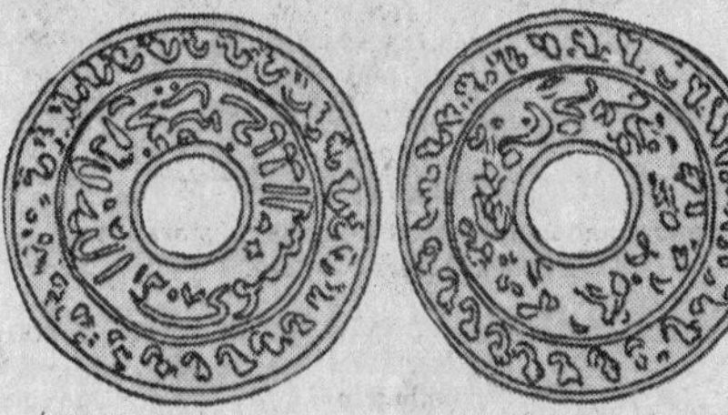

Arabic: AL-DAWLAT AL-KHAIRIYAT FI BALAD AL-SAIWI 1307

KM#	Date	Good	VG	Fine	VF
2	AH1307	12.50	18.50	25.00	35.00

NOTE: A number of Chinese token issues are tentatively assigned to the Patani state of Jala (Jalor).

REGULAR ISSUES

1/16 FUANG

(= 1 Solot)

TIN
Dark color and crude rims. Usually plain edge.

Y#	Date	Year	Mintage	Fine	VF	XF
5	ND	(1862)	—	2.00	4.00	6.00

NOTE: Rotated dies are common.

Y#	Date	Year	Mintage	Fine	VF	XF
16	ND	1868	—	9.50	17.50	25.00

1/2 ATT

(= 1 Solot)

COPPER

Y#	Date	Year	Mintage	VF	XF	Unc
17	CS1236	(1874)	—	1.50	3.00	6.00
	1244	(1882)	2.560	1.50	3.00	6.00

COPPER-NICKEL

Y#	Date	Year	Mintage	VF	XF	Unc
17a	CS1244	(1882)	—	125.00	150.00	225.00

BRONZE

Y#	Date	Year	Mintage	VF	XF	Unc
21	CS1249	(1887)	—	3.00	3.50	8.00
	RS109	(1890)	5.100	1.50	2.50	6.00
	118	(1899)	—	1.50	2.50	6.00
	124	(1905)	—	1.50	2.50	6.00

NOTE: These coins were also minted in RS114, RS115, RS121, and RS122. The last year had a mintage of 5,120,000. Coins with these dates have not been observed and were probably additional mintings of coins dated RS109 and RS118. Varieties exist.

1/8 FUANG

(= 1 Att)

TIN
Dark color, reeded edge.

Y#	Date	Year	Mintage	Fine	VF	XF
6	ND	(1862)	—	1.75	3.50	6.00

NOTE: Rotated dies are common. Contemporary counterfeits from Hong Kong were also widely distributed. They are somewhat more common in the higher grades.

ATT

(= 1/64 Baht)

COPPER

Y#	Date	Year	Mintage	VF	XF	Unc
18	CS1236	(1874)	—	2.00	3.00	7.00
	1238	(1876)	—	2.00	3.00	7.00
	1244	(1882)	15.300	2.00	3.00	7.00

BRONZE

Y#	Date	Year	Mintage	VF	XF	Unc
22	CS1249	(1887)	—	3.50	6.00	10.00
	RS109	(1890)	10.200	2.00	3.50	7.00
	114*	(1895)	5.100	2.00	3.50	7.00
	115	(1896)	—	2.00	3.50	7.00
	118	(1899)	—	2.00	3.50	7.00
	121	(1902)	—	2.00	3.50	7.00
	122*	(1903)	15.300	2.00	3.50	7.00
	124	(1905)	—	2.00	3.50	7.00

***NOTE:** RS114 and RS122 are found with two types of numerals large and small.

1/4 FUANG

(= 1/32 Baht = 1 Sio)

COPPER
Thick (2.5mm) planchet, crude with plain edge.

Y#	Date	Year	Mintage	Fine	VF	XF
1	ND	1865	—	15.00	22.50	35.00

NOTE: Rotated dies are common.

BRASS

Y#	Date	Year	Mintage	Fine	VF	XF
1a	ND	(1865)	—	20.00	35.00	50.00

COPPER
Thin (1.5mm) planchet

Y#	Date	Year	Mintage	Fine	VF	XF
3	ND	(1865)	—	20.00	35.00	50.00

BRASS

Y#	Date	Year	Mintage	Fine	VF	XF
3a	ND	(1865)	—	—	—	—

2 ATT

(= 1/32 Baht = 1 Sio)

COPPER

Y#	Date	Year	Mintage	VF	XF	Unc
19	CS1236	(1874)	—	3.50	6.00	12.50
	1238	(1876)	—	3.50	6.00	12.50
	1244	(1882)	10.200	3.50	6.00	12.50

BRONZE

Y#	Date	Year	Mintage	VF	XF	Unc
23	CS1249	(1887)	—	6.00	10.00	20.00
	RS109	(1890)	10.200	2.50	3.50	7.00
	114	(1895)	—	2.50	3.50	7.00
	115	(1896)	—	2.50	3.50	7.00
	118	(1899)	—	2.50	3.50	7.00
	119	(1900)	—	4.00	6.50	12.50
	121	(1902)	—	2.50	3.50	7.00
	122	(1903)	—	2.50	3.50	7.00
	124	(1905)	—	2.50	3.50	7.00

NOTE: Varieties exist.

1/2 FUANG

(= 1/16 Baht = 1 Sik)

COPPER
Thick (3mm) planchet. Crude, plain edges.

Y#	Date	Year	Mintage	Fine	VF	XF
2	ND	(1865)	—	10.00	15.00	25.00

BRASS

Y#	Date	Year	Mintage	Fine	VF	XF
2a	ND	(1865)	—	12.50	17.50	30.00

COPPER
Thin (1.5mm) planchet.

Y#	Date	Year	Mintage	Fine	VF	XF
4	ND	(1865)	—	10.00	20.00	40.00
		BRASS				
4a	ND	(1865)	—	17.50	30.00	50.00

NOTE: Rotated dies are common.

1/16 BAHT

(= 1 Sik)

SILVER
Thick Flan

Y#	Date	Year	Mintage	VF	XF	Unc
7.7	ND	(1860)	—	25.00	30.00	40.00
		Obv: Smaller crown, Rev: Larger elephant.				
7.1	ND	(1860)	—	35.00	50.00	75.00
		Thin Flan				
7.2	ND	(1864)	—	225.00	275.00	350.00

4 ATT

(= 1/16 Baht = 1 Sik)

COPPER

Y#	Date	Year	Mintage	VF	XF	Unc
20	CS1238	(1876)	—	17.50	30.00	50.00

NOTE: Beware of high quality fakes which rock when placed on a flat surface.

FUANG

(= 1/8 Baht)

SILVER
Thick Flan
Denomination indicated by number of stars on the edge: 8 stars = 1 Baht

Y#	Date	Year	Mintage	VF	XF	Unc
8	ND	(1860)	—	6.00	9.00	16.50
		Thin Flan				
8.1	ND	(1864)	—	275.00	325.00	400.00

Y#	Date	Year	Mintage	VF	XF	Unc
28	ND	(1868)	—	5.00	8.00	15.00

Y#	Date	Year	Mintage	VF	XF	Unc
32	ND (1876-1902)		—	3.50	4.50	6.50

Y#	Date	Year	Mintage	VF	XF	Unc
32a	RS121	(1902)	.380	2.50	4.00	5.50
	122	(1903)	.460	2.50	4.00	5.50
	123	(1904)	.310	2.50	4.00	5.50
	124	(1905)	.410	2.50	4.00	5.50
	125	(1906)	—	2.50	4.00	5.50
	126	(1907)	—	2.50	4.00	5.50
	127	(1908)	.480	2.50	4.00	5.50

SALUNG

(= 1/4 Baht)

SILVER
Thick Flan
Denomination indicated by number of stars on the edge; 8 stars = 1 Baht.

Y#	Date	Year	Mintage	VF	XF	Unc
9	ND	(1860)	—	15.00	35.00	60.00
		Thin Flan				
9.1	ND	(1864)	—	550.00	650.00	800.00

Y#	Date	Year	Mintage	VF	XF	Unc
29	ND	(1868)	—	15.00	25.00	45.00

Y#	Date	Year	Mintage	VF	XF	Unc
33	ND (1876-1902)		—	7.50	12.50	15.00

Y#	Date	Year	Mintage	VF	XF	Unc
33a	RS120	(1901)	—	6.00	6.00	12.00
	121	(1902)	.560	4.00	5.00	8.00
	122	(1903)	.340	4.00	5.00	8.00
	123	(1904)	.190	5.00	6.00	10.00
	125	(1906)	—	4.00	5.00	8.00
	126	(1907)	—	5.00	6.50	10.00
	127	(1908)	.270	4.00	5.00	8.00

2 SALUNG

(= 1/2 Baht)

SILVER
Thick Flan
Denomination indicated by number of stars on the edge; 8 stars = 1 Baht.

Y#	Date	Year	Mintage	VF	XF	Unc
10	ND	(1860)	—	55.00	85.00	120.00
		Thin Flan				
10.1	ND	(1864)	—	1350.	1650.	2000.

BAHT

SILVER
Thick Flan
Denomination indicated by number of stars at the edge; 8 stars = 1 Baht.

Y#	Date	Year	Mintage	VF	XF	Unc
11	ND	(1860)	—	20.00	40.00	80.00
		thin flan				
11.1	ND	1864	—	1850.	2350.	3000.

.937 GOLD
Design and diameter as 1/16 Tical, Y#7, but thinner planchet.

Fr#	Date	Mintage	VF	XF	Unc
23	ND (1864)	—	350.00	400.00	500.00

NOTE: These coins have a plain edge. Numerous counterfeits exist, many with reeded edge.

SILVER

Y#	Date	Year	Mintage	VF	XF	Unc
31	ND	(1868)	—	17.50	30.00	45.00

Y#	Date	Year	Mintage	VF	XF	Unc
34	ND (1876-1902)		—	BV	15.00	25.00

Y#	Date	Year	Mintage	VF	XF	Unc
34a	RS120	(1901) with flat bottom 0 in date				
			—	15.00	20.00	30.00
	120	(1901)	with normal 0 in date			
			—	100.00	135.00	200.00
	121	(1902)	4.070	15.00	20.00	35.00
	122	(1903)	19.150	BV	15.00	25.00

Y#	Date	Year	Mintage	VF	XF	Unc
34a	123	(1904)	4.790	BV	15.00	30.00
	124	(1905)	6.770	BV	15.00	30.00
	125	(1906)	—	BV	15.00	30.00
	126	(1907)	—	20.00	30.00	45.00

2 BAHT

SILVER
Thick Flan
Denomination indicated by number of stars on edge
16 stars - 2 Baht

12	ND	(1860)	—	200.00	275.00	650.00

Thin Flan

12.1	ND	(1864)	—	3750.	4250.	5000.

GOLD
Reeded edge, similar to 1 Fuang, Y#8.

13	ND	(1863)	2.000	400.00	550.00	700.00

Similar to 1 Fuang, Y#8, but thinner planchet.

Fr#	Date	Mintage	VF	XF	Unc
22	ND (1864)	—	400.00	550.00	700.00

Y#	Date	Year	Mintage	VF	XF	Unc
A34	ND	(1876)	—	150.00	185.00	250.00
	RS123	(1904)	—	—	—	—
	RS127	1908	—	700.00	800.00	900.00
	RS128	1909	—	650.00	750.00	850.00

NOTE: Original strikings of ND are of smaller dies than the silver issue Fuang, Y#32. Dated coins are gold strikings of larger Fuang silver dies.

Edge: Usually reeded. Larger elephant.

13a	ND	(1895)	—	400.00	550.00	700.00

4 BAHT

GOLD
Reeded edge. Obv: Four rays on left, five rays on right above crown.

14	ND	(1863)	—	500.00	700.00	1000.

Similar to 1 Sal'ung, Y#9, but thinner planchet.

Fr#	Date	Mintage	VF	XF	Unc
21	ND (1864)	—	700.00	825.00	1000.

NOTE: Counterfeits are common.

SILVER
Thick Flan

Y#	Date	Year	Mintage	VF	XF	Unc
A12	ND	(1860)	2000.	2750.	3000.	3500.

Thin Flan

A12.1	ND	(1864)	—	—	Rare	—

GOLD
Usually reeded edge. Obv: Five rays both sides.

14a	ND	(1895)	—	700.00	825.00	1000.

8 BAHT

GOLD
Usually reeded edge. Obv: Four rays, both sides above crown.

15	ND	(1863)	—	1000.	1350.	1800.

Fr#	Date	Mintage	VF	XF	Unc
20	ND (1864)	—	1350.	1600.	1850.

Usually reeded edge. Obv: Six rays, both sides.

Y#	Date	Year	Mintage	VF	XF	Unc
15a	ND	(1863)	—	1000.	1300.	1600.

16 BAHT

GOLD

Similar to 1 Baht, Y#11, but thinner planchet.

Fr#	Date	Mintage	VF	XF	Unc
19	ND(1864)	—	1700.	2000.	2500.

NOTE: Counterfeits are common.

32 BAHT

GOLD
Similar to 2 Baht, Y#12, but thinner planchet.

18	ND(1864)	—	4000.	4500.	5000.

PRESENTATION ISSUES

Bannakin (Royal Gift) Coins

1/8 BAHT

GOLD
Similar to 1/8 Baht, Y#8.
Obv: Larger crown.

KM#	Date	Year	Fine	VF	XF	Unc
10	ND	(1860)	—	—	Rare	—

SILVER
Milled edge

11	ND	(1860)	75.00	135.00	250.00	350.00

1/4 BAHT

SILVER
Milled Edge

12	ND	(1860)	—	—	Rare	—

1/2 BAHT

SILVER
Milled edge

13	ND	(1860)	—	—	Rare	—

1 BAHT

SILVER
Milled edge

14	ND	(1860)	250.00	400.00	550.00	700.00

DECIMAL COINAGE

100 Satang = 1 Baht
25 Satang = 1 Salung

1/2 SATANG

BRONZE

Y#	Date	Year	Mintage	VF	XF	Unc
50	BE2480	(1937)	—	.50	1.00	1.50

SATANG

BRONZE

35	RS127	(1908)	17.000	2.50	5.00	9.00
	128	(1909)	.150	3.50	7.00	15.00
	129	(1910)	9.000	1.50	3.50	6.00
	130	(1911)	30.000	1.50	3.50	6.00
	BE2456	(1913)	10.000	1.00	1.50	3.00
	2457	(1914)	1.000	2.00	4.00	8.00
	2458	(1915)	5.000	.75	1.00	1.50
	2461	(1918)	18.880	.65	1.25	1.50
	2462	(1919)	14.750	.65	1.00	1.50
	2463	(1920)	3.580	1.00	1.50	2.00

Y#	Date	Year	Mintage	VF	XF	Unc
35	2464	(1921)	11.400	10.00	15.00	25.00
	2466	(1923)	14.000	.75	1.00	1.50
	2467	(1924)	Inc. Ab.	1.00	1.50	2.00
	2469	(1926)	20.000	.50	.75	1.25
	2470	(1927)	—	.50	.75	1.00
	2472	(1929)	—	.50	1.00	1.25
	2478	(1935)	—	.50	.70	1.00
	2480	(1937)	—	.50	.70	.85

NOTE: Variations in lettering exist.

Y#	Date	Year	Mintage	VF	XF	Unc
51	BE2482	(1939)	24.400	1.50	3.00	4.00

Y#	Date	Year	Mintage	VF	XF	Unc
54	BE2484	(1941)	—	.50	1.25	2.00

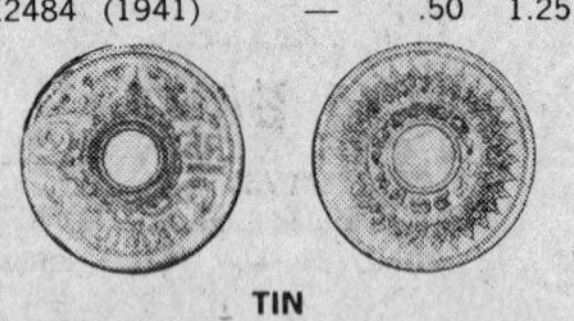

TIN

BE date & denomination in Thai numerals, no hole.

Y#	Date	Year	Mintage	VF	XF	Unc
57	BE2485	(1942)	1.560	.30	.40	.50

NOTE: Approximately 790,000 coins were restruck for circulation 1967-73.

BE date and denomination in Western numerals, no hole.

Y#	Date	Year	Mintage	VF	XF	Unc
60	BE2487	(1944)	—	.10	.20	.40

2-1/2 SATANG

COPPER-NICKEL

Y#	Date	Year	Mintage	VF	XF	Unc
24.	RS116H	(1897)	5.000	3.00	4.00	5.00

NOTE: Issued in 1898 although dated RS116 (1897).

5 SATANG

COPPER-NICKEL

Y#	Date	Year	Mintage	VF	XF	Unc
25	RS116H	(1897)	5.000	10.00	14.00	20.00

NOTE: Issued in 1898 although dated RS116 (1897).

NICKEL

Y#	Date	Year	Mintage	VF	XF	Unc
36	RS127	(1908)	7.000	3.00	4.00	6.00
	128	(1909)	4.000	3.50	4.50	7.00
	129	(1910)	4.000	1.50	2.00	5.00
	131	(1912)	2.000	1.50	2.50	6.00
	BE2456	(1913)	2.000	1.50	2.50	4.00
	2457	(1914)	2.000	1.50	2.50	4.00
	2461	(1918)	2.000	1.50	2.50	4.00
	2462	(1919)	4.000	1.00	2.00	4.00
	2463	(1920)	9.900	1.00	1.50	3.00
	2464	(1921)	Inc. Ab.	.60	1.00	2.00
	2469	(1926)	20.000	.60	1.00	2.00
	2478	(1935)	10.000	.50	1.00	2.00
	2480	(1937)	20.000	.60	1.25	2.00
	2482	(1939)	—Reported, not confirmed			

NOTE: Varieties in lettering in all Y#36 exist.

1.5000 gm., .650 SILVER, .0313 oz ASW

Y#	Date	Year	Mintage	VF	XF	Unc
55	BE2484	(1941)	—	2.00	3.00	4.50

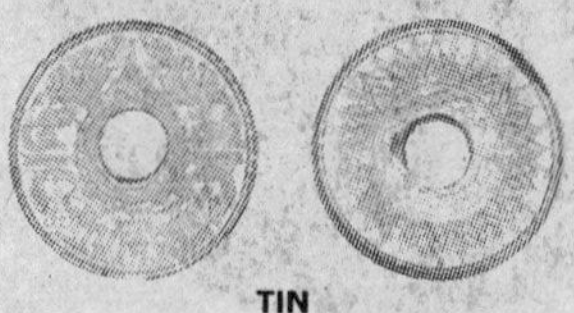

TIN

BE date and denomination in Thai numerals.

Y#	Date	Year	Mintage	VF	XF	Unc
58	BE2485	(1942)	—	.50	1.25	1.75

Thick (2.2mm) planchet.

BE date and denomination in Western numerals.

Y#	Date	Year	Mintage	VF	XF	Unc
61	BE2487	(1944)	—	.50	.85	1.75
	2488	(1945)	—	.45	.75	1.50

Thin (2.0mm) planchet.

Y#	Date	Year	Mintage	VF	XF	Unc
61a	BE2488	(1945)	—	.50	.85	1.50

Obv: King Ananda, child head.

Y#	Date	Year	Mintage	VF	XF	Unc
64	BE2489	(1946)	—	.50	.85	1.75

Obv: King Ananda, youth head.

Y#	Date	Year	Mintage	VF	XF	Unc
68	BE2489	(1946)	24.480	.15	.25	.40

Obv: King Phumiphol, one medal on uniform.

Y#	Date	Year	Mintage	VF	XF	Unc
72	BE2493	(1950)	*6.480	.50	1.00	1.50

*These coins were also struck 1954, 58, 59, and 73 and mintages are included here.

ALUMINUM-BRONZE

Y#	Date	Year	Mintage	VF	XF	Unc
72a	BE2493	(1950)	15.500	.25	.45	1.00

Obv: Smaller head, three medals on uniform.

Y#	Date	Year	Mintage	VF	XF	Unc
78	BE2500	(1957)	*40.100	—	.10	.25

*Current issues are minted without date change.

BRONZE

Y#	Date	Year	Mintage	VF	XF	Unc
78a	BE2500	(1957)	*6.240	.25	.75	1.25

TIN

Y#	Date	Year	Mintage	VF	XF	Unc
78b	BE2500	1957	—	1.75	3.00	5.00

NOTE: The above coins were struck to replace Y#72 in mint sets.

10 SATANG

COPPER-NICKEL

Y#	Date	Year	Mintage	VF	XF	Unc
26	RS116H	(1897)	3.800	20.00	25.00	35.00

NICKEL

Y#	Date	Year	Mintage	VF	XF	Unc
37	RS127	(1908)	7.000	1.50	2.50	5.00
	129	(1910)	5.000	1.50	2.50	5.00
	130	(1911)	.500	2.00	4.00	7.00
	131	(1912)	1.500	1.50	2.50	5.00
	BE2456	(1913)	1.000	1.25	2.00	4.00
	2457	(1914)	1.000	1.25	2.00	4.00
	2461	(1918)	.770	2.50	3.50	6.00
	2462	(1919)	2.000	1.25	1.50	2.00
	2463	(1920)	Inc. Ab.	1.25	1.50	2.00
	2464	(1921)	23.400	1.00	1.25	1.50
	2478	(1935)	5.000	1.00	1.25	1.50
	2480	(1937)	5.000	.75	1.00	1.25
	2482	(1939)	—Reported, not confirmed			

NOTE: Varieties in lettering of Y#37 exist.

2.5000 gm., .650 SILVER, .0522 oz ASW

Y#	Date	Year	Mintage	VF	XF	Unc
56	BE2484	(1941)	—	4.00	6.00	9.00

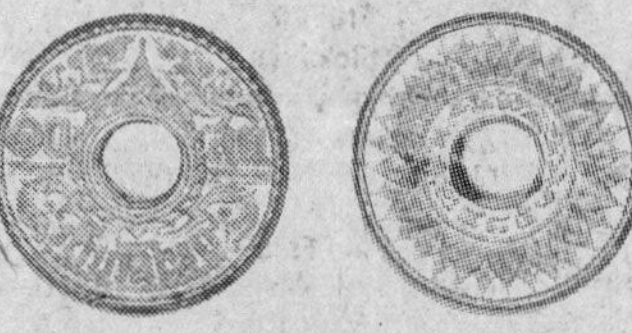

TIN

BE date and denomination in Thai numerals.

Y#	Date	Year	Mintage	VF	XF	Unc
59	BE2485	(1942)	.230	.50	1.75	2.25

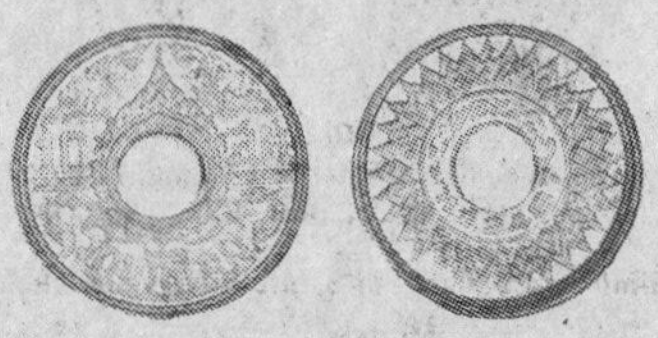

Thick (2.5mm) planchet.

BE date and denomination in Western numerals.

Y#	Date	Year	Mintage	VF	XF	Unc
62	BE2487	(1944)	—	.75	1.75	2.25

Thin (2.0mm) planchet.

Y#	Date	Year	Mintage	VF	XF	Unc
62a	BE2488	(1945)	—	.75	2.00	2.50

Obv: King Ananda, child head.

Y#	Date	Year	Mintage	VF	XF	Unc
65	BE2489	(1946)	—	.50	1.00	1.50

Obv: Youth head.

Y#	Date	Year	Mintage	VF	XF	Unc
69	BE2489	(1946)	40.470	.40	.75	1.00

Obv: King Phumiphol, one medal on uniform.

Y#	Date	Year	Mintage	VF	XF	Unc
73	BE2493	(1950)	*139.695	.40	1.00	1.25

*These coins were also struck in 1954-1973 and the mintages are also included here.

ALUMINUM-BRONZE

Y#	Date	Year	Mintage	VF	XF	Unc
73a	BE2493	(1950)	4.060	.75	1.50	2.25

Obv: Smaller head. Three medals on uniform.

Y#	Date	Year	Mintage	VF	XF	Unc
79	BE2500	(1957)	*50.550	.10	.25	.50

*Current issues are minted without date change.

BRONZE

Y#	Date	Year	Mintage	VF	XF	Unc
79a	BE2500	(1957)	*13.365	.25	.75	1.25

TIN

Y#	Date	Year	Mintage	VF	XF	Unc
79b	BE2500	(1957)	—	—	—	100.00

20 SATANG

COPPER-NICKEL

Y#	Date	Year	Mintage	VF	XF	Unc
27	RS116H	(1897)	3.120	12.00	16.00	25.00

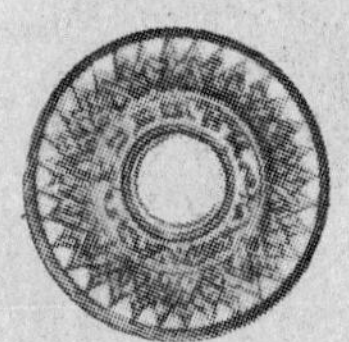

3.0000 gm., .650 SILVER, .0627 oz ASW
BE date and denomination in Thai numerals.

Y#	Date	Year	Mintage	VF	XF	Unc
A56	BE2484	1941	—	7.50	11.50	15.00
	BE2485	1942	—	7.50	11.50	15.00

TIN
BE date and denomination in Western numerals.

Y#	Date	Year	Mintage	VF	XF	Unc
63	BE2488	(1945)	—	1.00	2.25	3.00

SALUNG = 1/4 BAHT

3.7500 gm., .800 SILVER, .0965 oz ASW

Y#	Date	Year	Mintage	VF	XF	Unc
43	BE2458	(1915)	2.040	3.50	4.50	6.00
	2460	(1917)	1.100	3.50	4.50	6.00
	2461	(1918)	2.170	3.50	4.50	6.00
	2462	(1919)	7.860	3.50	4.50	6.00
	2462	(1919)	dot after legend			
			Inc. Ab.	35.00	45.00	60.00
	2467	(1924)	2.100	3.50	4.50	6.00
	2468	(1925)	—	3.50	4.50	6.00

25 SATANG = 1/4 BAHT

3.7500 gm., .650 SILVER, .0784 oz ASW

Y#	Date	Year	Mintage	VF	XF	Unc
48	BE2472	(1929)	—	3.50	5.00	8.00

TIN
Obv: King Ananda, child head.

Y#	Date	Year	Mintage	VF	XF	Unc
66	BE2489	(1946)	—	3.00	4.00	6.00

Obv: Youth head.

Y#	Date	Year	Mintage	VF	XF	Unc
70	BE2489	(1946)	*226.348	.20	.40	.75

*These coins were also struck 1954-64 and mintage figure is a total.

ALUMINUM-BRONZE
Obv: King Phumiphol, one medal on uniform.

Y#	Date	Year	Mintage	VF	XF	Unc
76	BE2493	1950	23.170	.75	1.75	3.00

Obv: Smaller head; three medals on uniform.

Y#	Date	Year	Mintage	VF	XF	Unc
80	BE2500	(1957)	*476.328	.10	.15	.25

*Current issues are minted without date change.

BRASS

Y#	Date	Year	Mintage	VF	XF	Unc
109	BE2520	(1977)	—	—	—	.15

2 SALUNG = 1/2 BAHT

7.5000 gm., .800 SILVER, .1929 oz ASW

Y#	Date	Year	Mintage	VF	XF	Unc
44	BE2458	(1915)	2.740	5.50	7.00	10.00
	2462	(1919)	3.230	5.50	7.00	10.00
	2462	(1919)	dot after legend			
			Inc. Ab.	6.50	10.00	20.00
	2463	(1920)	4.970	5.50	7.00	10.00
	2464	(1921)	—	5.50	7.00	10.00

50 SATANG = 1/2 BAHT

7.5000 gm., .650 SILVER, .1567 oz ASW

Y#	Date	Year	Mintage	VF	XF	Unc
49	BE2472	1929	17.008	7.50	12.50	20.00

TIN
Obv: King Ananda, child head.

Y#	Date	Year	Mintage	VF	XF	Unc
67	BE2489	(1946)	—	12.50	40.00	90.00

Obv: Youth head.

Y#	Date	Year	Mintage	VF	XF	Unc
71	BE2489	(1946)	*17.008	.75	1.00	1.50

*These coins were also minted in 1954-57 and mintage figure is a total.

ALUMINUM-BRONZE
Obv: King Phumiphol, one medal on uniform.

Y#	Date	Year	Mintage	VF	XF	Unc
77	BE2493	(1950)	20.710	.75	1.75	3.50

Obv: Smaller head; three medals on uniform.

Y#	Date	Year	Mintage	VF	XF	Unc
81	BE2500	(1957)	*272.384	.10	.15	.25

*Current issues are minted without date change.

BAHT

15.0000 gm., .900 SILVER, .4340 oz ASW

Y#	Date	Year	Mintage	VF	XF	Unc
39	RS127	(1908)	1.340	150.00	185.00	250.00

NOTE: Counterfeits are common.

Y#	Date	Year	Mintage	VF	XF	Unc
45	BE2456	(1913)	2.690	13.50	15.00	20.00
	2457	(1914)	.490	13.50	18.50	30.00
	2458	(1915)	5.000	13.50	15.00	20.00
	2459	(1916)	9.080	13.50	15.00	20.00
	2460	(1917)	14.340	13.50	15.00	20.00
	2461	(1918)	3.840	13.50	15.00	20.00

NOTE: BE2456 is often found weakly struck so it does appear similar to a counterfeit.

COPPER-NICKEL-SILVER-ZINC

Y#	Date	Year	Mintage	VF	XF	Unc
82	BE2500	(1957)	*3.143	.75	1.25	2.00

*These coins were minted in years 1958-60 and mintage figure is a total.

COPPER-NICKEL
King Phumiphol & Queen Sirikit

Y#	Date	Year	Mintage	VF	XF	Unc
83	BE2504	(1961)	4.610	.40	.75	1.25
84	BE2505	(1962)	*414.361	.10	.15	.25

*These coins were minted from 1962-73 and mintage figure is a total.

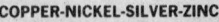

King's 36th Birthday

Y#	Date	Year	Mintage	VF	XF	Unc
85	ND	(1963)	3.000	.25	.75	1.25

Fifth Asian Games

Y#	Date	Year	Mintage	VF	XF	Unc
87	BE2509	1966	9.000	.25	.75	1.25

Sixth Asian Games

Y#	Date	Year	Mintage	VF	XF	Unc
91	BE2513	1970	9.000	.25	.75	1.25

F.A.O. Issue

Y#	Date	Year	Mintage	VF	XF	Unc
96	BE2515	(1972)	9.000	.20	.50	.85

Vajiralongk

Y#	Date	Year	Mintage	VF	XF	Unc
97	BE2515	(1972)	41.000	.15	.40	.65

25th Anniversary World Health Organization

Y#	Date	Year	Mintage	VF	XF	Unc
99	BE2516	1973	1.000	.25	.65	1.00

Y#	Date	Year	Mintage	VF	XF	Unc
100	BE2517	(1974)	175.127	.15	.40	.65

Eighth SEAP Games

Y#	Date	Year	Mintage	VF	XF	Unc
105	BE2518	1975	3.000	.25	.65	1.00

75th Birthday of Princess Mother

Y#	Date	Year	Mintage	VF	XF	Unc
107	BE2518	(1975)	9.000	.15	.40	.80

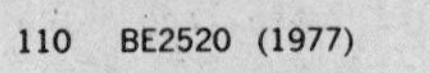
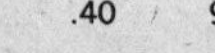

Y#	Date	Year	Mintage	VF	XF	Unc
110	BE2520	(1977)	—	.10	.20	.40

F.A.O. Issue

Y#	Date	Year	Mintage	VF	XF	Unc
112	BE2520	(1977)	9.000	.10	.20	.40

Princess' Graduation

Y#	Date	Year	Mintage	VF	XF	Unc
114	BE2520	(1977)	9.000	.10	.20	.40

Investiture of Princess Sirindhorn

Y#	Date	Year	Mintage	VF	XF	Unc
124	BE2520	(1977)	5.000	.10	.20	.40

Graduation of Crown Prince

Y#	Date	Year	Mintage	VF	XF	Unc
127	BE2521	(1978)	4.000	.10	.20	.40

Eighth Asian Games

Y#	Date	Year	Mintage	VF	XF	Unc
130	BE2521	1978	9.000	.10	.20	.40

2 BAHT

COPPER-NICKEL
Graduation of Princess Chulabhorn

Y#	Date	Year	Mintage	VF	XF	Unc
134	BE2522	(1979)	—	.20	.35	.75

5 BAHT

COPPER-NICKEL

Y#	Date	Year	Mintage	VF	XF	Unc
98	BE2515	(1972)	26.552	.40	.65	1.25

COPPER-NICKEL CLAD COPPER

Y#	Date	Year	Mintage	VF	XF	Unc
111	BE2520	(1977)	—	.40	.65	1.25

King's 50th Birthday
Obv: Legend reads "Prathet Thai."

120	BE2520	(1977)	5.000	.35	.60	1.00

Error: Obv. legend reads "Siam Minta."

121	BE2520	(1977)	—	1.00	2.00	4.00

Eighth Asian Games

131	BE2521	1978	1.000	.35	.60	1.00

Royal Cradle Ceremony

132	BE2522	(1979)	.500	.35	.60	1.00

10 BAHT

5.0000 gm., .800 SILVER, .1286 oz ASW
King Phumiphol 25th Anniversary of Reign

92	BE2514	(1971)	2.000	BV	4.00	5.50

NICKEL
Crown Prince Vajiralong Korn and Princess Soamsawali Wedding

Y#	Date	Year	Mintage	VF	XF	Unc
117	BE2520	(1977)	10.000	.65	1.00	1.50

Princess' Graduation

115	BE2520	(1977)	4.000	.65	1.00	1.50

COPPER-NICKEL
Graduation of Princess Chulabhorn

135	BE2522	(1979)	—	.65	1.00	1.50

20 BAHT

20.0000 gm., .750 SILVER, .4823 oz ASW
King Phumiphol 36th Birthday

86	ND	(1963)	2.000	BV	15.00	25.00

50 BAHT

25.0000 gm., .900 SILVER, .7234 oz ASW
20th Year Buddhist Fellowship

Y#	Date	Year	Mintage	VF	XF	Unc
95	BE2514	(1971)	.200	BV	22.00	30.00

Polished, high relief coin in case

95.1	BE2514	1971	.060	—	Proof	40.00

25.0000 gm., .400 SILVER, .3215 oz ASW
National Museum Centennial

101	BE2517	(1974)	.400	BV	10.00	20.00

28.2800 gm., .500 SILVER, .4546 oz ASW
Conservation Series

102	BE2517	1974	.019	BV	15.00	30.00

28.2800 gm., .925 SILVER, .8411 oz ASW

102a	BE2517	(1974)	.038	—	Proof	40.00

100 BAHT

35.0000 gm., .500 SILVER, .5627 oz ASW
Conservation Series
Obv: Similar to 50 Baht, Y#102.

Y#	Date	Year	Mintage	VF	XF	Unc
103	BE2517	(1974)	.019	BV	17.00	30.00
	35.0000 gm., .925 SILVER, 1.0409 oz ASW					
103a	BE2517	(1974)	.108	—	Proof	50.00

25.0000 gm., .500 SILVER, .4019 oz ASW
Ministry of Finance

Y#	Date	Year	Mintage	VF	XF	Unc
106	BE2518	(1975)	.200	BV	12.50	30.00

150 BAHT

3.7500 gm., .900 GOLD, .1085 oz AGW
Queen Sirikit 36th Birthday

Y#	Date	Year	Mintage	VF	XF	Unc
88	BE2511	(1968)	.200	BV	70.00	75.00

22.0000 gm., .925 SILVER, .6543 oz ASW
75th Birthday of Princess Mother

Y#	Date	Year	Mintage	VF	XF	Unc
108	BE2518	(1975)	.400	BV	20.00	27.50

F.A.O. Issue

Y#	Date	Year	Mintage	VF	XF	Unc
113	BE2520	(1977)	.100	BV	20.00	40.00

Crown Prince Vajiralong Korn and Princess Soamsawali Wedding

Y#	Date	Year	Mintage	VF	XF	Unc
118	BE2520	(1977)	.400	BV	20.00	30.00

Princess' Graduation

Y#	Date	Year	Mintage	VF	XF	Unc
116	BE2520	(1977)	.100	BV	20.00	40.00

Investiture of Princess Sirindhorn

Y#	Date	Year	Mintage	VF	XF	Unc
125	BE2520	1977	.050	BV	20.00	45.00

9th World Orchid Conference

Y#	Date	Year	Mintage	VF	XF	Unc
123	BE2521	1978	.050	BV	20.00	45.00

Graduation of Crown Prince

Y#	Date	Year	Mintage	VF	XF	Unc
128	BE2521	(1978)	.050	BV	20.00	45.00

200 BAHT

22.3900 gm., .925 SILVER, .6659 oz ASW
Royal Cradle Ceremony

Y#	Date	Year	Mintage	VF	XF	Unc
133	BE2522	(1979)	.050	BV	20.00	30.00

300 BAHT

7.5000 gm., .900 GOLD, .2170 oz AGW
Queen Sirikit 36th Birthday

Y#	Date	Year	Mintage	VF	XF	Unc
89	BE2511	(1968)	.100	BV	140.00	150.00

22.0000 gm., .925 SILVER, .6543 oz ASW
Graduation of Princess Chulabhorn

Y#	Date	Year	Mintage	VF	XF	Unc
136	BE2522	(1979)	.020	BV	20.00	30.00

400 BAHT

10.0000 gm., .900 GOLD, .2893 oz AGW
King Phumiphol 25th Anniversary of Reign

Y#	Date	Year	Mintage	VF	XF	Unc
93	BE2514	(1971)	.040	BV	188.00	200.00

600 BAHT

15.0000 gm., .900 GOLD, .4340 oz AGW
Queen Sirikit 36th Birthday

Y#	Date	Year	Mintage	VF	XF	Unc
90	BE2511	(1968)	.040	BV	285.00	300.00

800 BAHT

20.0000 gm., .900 GOLD, .5787 oz AGW
King Phumiphol 25th Anniversary of Reign

Y#	Date	Year	Mintage	VF	XF	Unc
94	BE2514	(1971)	.020	BV	375.00	380.00

2500 BAHT

33.4300 gm., .900 GOLD, .9674 oz ASW
Conservation Series

Y#	Date	Year	Mintage	VF	XF	Unc
104	BE2517	(1974)	.013	BV	630.00	650.00
	BE2517	(1974)	3,000	—	Proof	1000.

15.0000 gm., .900 GOLD, .4340 oz AGW
Crown Prince Vajiralong Korn and Princess Soamsawali Wedding
Obv: Portraits of Royal couple.

Y#	Date	Year	Mintage	VF	XF	Unc
119	BE2520	(1977)	.020	BV	285.00	300.00

Investiture of Princess Sirindhorn

Y#	Date	Year	Mintage	VF	XF	Unc
126	BE2520	(1977)	5,000	BV	285.00	325.00

3000 BAHT

15.0000 gm., .900 GOLD, .4340 oz AGW
Graduation of Crown Prince

Y#	Date	Year	Mintage	VF	XF	Unc
129	BE2521	(1978)	.010	BV	285.00	300.00

5000 BAHT

30.0000 gm., .900 GOLD, .8681 oz AGW
King's 50th Birthday

Y#	Date	Year	Mintage	VF	XF	Unc
122	BE2520	(1977)	5,000	BV	565.00	800.00

BULLION ISSUES

In 1943, the government of Thailand made an internal loan by virtue of the Royal Act of Internal Loan and a related Regulation of the Ministry of Finance, both dated 17th May, 1943.

Eight years later another Regulation of the Ministry of Finance dated 11th June, 1951 related to the actual redemption of the loan above mentioned was proclaimed with the following effect: -

Bond holders have the choice to be paid either in gold coins or gold bars or in other forms, all of which should bear the Garuda emblem and the specific inscription as to its weight and gold purity.

50 BAHT

8.6930 gm., .995 GOLD, .2781 oz AGW

KM#	Date	Mintage	VF	XF	Unc
1	ND(1951)	—	200.00	250.00	325.00

100 BAHT

17.3870 gm., .995 GOLD, .5562 oz AGW

KM#	Date	Mintage	VF	XF	Unc
2	ND(1951)	—	400.00	500.00	650.00

1000 BAHT

173.8790 gm., .995 GOLD, 5.5630 oz AGW

KM#	Date	Mintage	VF	XF	Unc
3	ND(1951)	—	4000.	5000.	6500.

NCLT ISSUES

MINT SETS

KM#	Date	Mintage	Identification	Issue Price	Mkt. Val.
S1	ND (1895)	(3) —	Y13-15	—	—
S2	Mixed	(32) —	Two Each Y57,70,72,73 78a,78-87,91	22.00	75.00
S3	Mixed	(8) —	Y83,85-87,91,92,95,97	11.00	75.00
S4	1975	(2) —	50 & 100 Baht, Y102-103	32.50	60.00

PROOF SETS
STANDARD METALS

KM#	Date	Mintage	Identification	Issue Price	Mkt. Val.
101	1968 (3)	—	Y88-90	—	450.00
102	1975 (2)	30,000	50 & 100 Baht Y102a-103a	50.00	80.00

Listings For
TIBET: refer to China
TIMOR: refer to Indonesia

The Republic of Togo (formerly part of German Togoland), situated on the Gulf of Guinea in West Africa between Ghana and Dahomey, has an area of 21,853 sq. mi. (56,600 sq. km.) and a population of 2.4 million. Capital: Lome. Agriculture and herding, the production of dye- woods, and the mining of phosphates and iron ore are the chief industries. Copra, phosphates and coffee are exported.

Although Brazilians were the first traders to settle in Togo, Germany achieved possession, in 1844, by inducing coastal chiefs to place their territories under German protection. The German protectorate was extended international recognition at the Berlin conference of 1885 and its ultimate boundaries delimited by treaties with France in 1897 and with Britain in 1904. Togoland was occupied by Anglo-French forces in 1914, subsequently becoming a League of Nations mandate and a U.N. trusteeship divided, for administrative purpose, between Great Britain and France. The British portion voted in 1957 for incorporation with Ghana. The French portion became the independent Republic of Togo on April 27, 1960.

RULERS
German, until 1914
Anglo - French, until 1957
French, until 1960

MINTMARKS
(a) - Paris, privy marks only

MONETARY SYSTEM
100 Centimes = 1 Franc

50 CENTIMES

ALUMINUM-BRONZE

Y#	Date	Mintage	VG	Fine	VF	XF
1	1924(a)	3.691	1.00	2.00	4.50	10.00
	1925a	2.064	1.00	2.00	6.00	12.00
	1926(a)	.445	2.50	5.00	12.00	22.00

FRANC

ALUMINUM-BRONZE

Y#	Date	Mintage	VG	Fine	VF	XF
2	1924(a)	3.472	1.00	2.00	5.00	10.00
	1925(a)	2.768	2.00	3.50	7.50	15.00

ALUMINUM

Y#	Date	Mintage	Fine	VF	XF	Unc
4	1948(a)	5.000	6.50	10.00	15.00	20.00

2 FRANCS

ALUMINUM-BRONZE

Y#	Date	Mintage	VG	Fine	VF	XF
3	1924(a)	.750	1.75	4.00	9.00	15.00
	1925(a)	.580	2.00	4.50	11.00	20.00

ALUMINUM

Y#	Date	Mintage	Fine	VF	XF	Unc
5	1948(a)	5.000	8.00	12.00	20.00	30.00

5 FRANCS

ALUMINUM-BRONZE

Y#	Date	Mintage	Fine	VF	XF	Unc
6	1956(a)	10.000	.50	1.00	2.00	4.00

NCLT ISSUES

ESSAIS (E)
Standard metals unless otherwise noted

Y#	Date	Mintage	Identification	Issue Price	Mkt Val.
E1	1924(a)	—	50 Centimes	—	85.00

Y#	Date	Mintage	Identification	Issue Price	Mkt Val.
E2	1924(a)	—	1 Franc	—	90.00
E3	1924(a)	—	2 Francs	—	100.00
E4a	1948(a)	2,000	1 Franc, Copper-Nickel	—	15.00
E5a	1948(a)	2,000	2 Francs, Copper-Nickel	—	18.50
E6	1956(a)	2,300	5 Francs	—	17.00
E7	1956(a)	2,300	10 Francs	—	25.00
E8	1956(a)	2,300	25 Francs	—	30.00

PIEFORTS (P)

PIEFORTS with ESSAI (PE)
(DOUBLE THICKNESS)
Standard metals unless otherwise noted

Y#	Date	Mintage	Identification	Issue Price	Mkt Val.
PE4	1948(a)	104	1 Franc	—	100.00
PE5	1948(a)	104	2 Francs	—	115.00

NOTE: For integrated coinage (1957) see French West Africa. Also see West African States and Ghana for later coinage.

TOKELAU ISLANDS

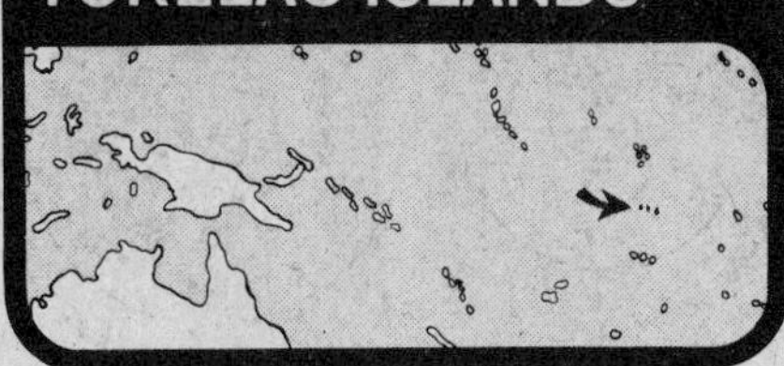

Tokelau or Union Islands, a New Zealand Territory located in the South Pacific 2,100 miles (3,379 km.) northeast of New Zealand and 300 miles (483 km.) north of Samoa, has an area of 3.95 sq. mi. (10.13 sq. km.) and a population of 1,574. Geographically, the group consists of four atolls - Atafu, Nukunono, Fakaofo and Swains - but the last belongs to American Samoa (and the United States claims the other three). The people are of Polynesian origin; Samoan is the official language. The islands are administered by the New Zealand Minister for Foreign Affairs; councils of family elders handle local government at the village level. The chief settlement is Fenuafala, on Fakaofo. It is connected by wireless with the offices of the New Zealand Administrative Center, located at Apia, Western Samoa. Subsistence farming and the production of copra for export are the main occupations. Revenue is also derived from the sale of postage stamps and, since 1978, coins.

Great Britain annexed the group of islands in 1889. They were added to the Gilbert and Ellice Islands colony in 1916. In 1926, they were brought under the jurisdiction of Western Samoa, which was held as a mandate of the League of Nations by New Zealand. They were declared a part of New Zealand in 1948.

Tokelau Islands issued its first coin in 1978, a "$1 Tahi Tala," Tokelauan for "One Dollar." The coin has a number of unusual features. The edge is inscribed, "Tokelau's First Coin." The obverse portrait of Queen Elizabeth II is identified by neither name nor title. The three dots of each such group comprising the obverse border symbolize the three principal atolls.

TALA

COPPER-NICKEL

Y#	Date	Mintage	VF	XF	Unc
1	1978	—	—	—	5.50

27.2500 gm., .925 SILVER, .8104 oz ASW

Y#	Date	Mintage	VF	XF	Unc
1a	1978	5,000	—	Proof	25.00

COPPER-NICKEL
Obv: Similar to Y#1.

Y#	Date	Mintage	VF	XF	Unc
2	1979	—	—	—	—

27.3000 gm., .925 SILVER, .8119 oz ASW

Y#	Date	Mintage	VF	XF	Unc
2a	1979	—	—	Proof	25.00

TONGA

The Kingdom of Tonga (or Friendly Islands), a member of the British Commonwealth, is an archipelago situated in the southern Pacific Ocean south of Western Samoa and east of Fiji comprising 150 islands. Tonga has an area of 269 sq. mi. (697 sq. km.) and a population of 98,000. Capital: Nuku'alofa. Primarily agricultural, the kingdom exports bananas and copra.

Dutch navigators Willem Schouten and Jacob Lemaire were the first Europeans to visit Tonga in 1616. They were followed by the noted Dutch explorer Abel Tasman who visited the Tongatapu group in 1643. No further European contact was made until 1773 when British navigator Capt. James Cook arrived and, impressed by the peaceful deportment of the natives, named the islands the Friendly Islands. Within a few years of Cook's visit, Tonga was embroiled in a civil war that lasted until the great chief Tauffahau, who reigned as George Tubou I (1845-93), was converted to Christianity and brought unity and peace to the islands. Tonga became a self-governing protectorate of Great Britain in 1900 and a fully independent state on June 4, 1970. The monarchy is a member of the Commonwealth of Nations. The monarch is Chief of State and Head of Government.

RULERS

Queen Salote, 1918-1965
King Taufa'Ahau, 1965—

MONETARY SYSTEM

16 Pounds = 1 Koula

1/4 KOULA

8.1250 gm., .916 GOLD, .2395 oz AGW

Y#	Date	Mintage	VF	XF	Unc
1	1962	—	BV	BV	160.00
	1962	6,300	—	Proof	175.00

PLATINUM

Y#	Date	Mintage	VF	XF	Unc
1a	—	—	—	Proof	1000.

1/2 KOULA

16.2500 gm., GOLD, .4789 oz AGW

Y#	Date	Mintage	VF	XF	Unc
2	1962	—	BV	BV	325.00
	1962	3,000	—	Proof	350.00

PLATINUM

Y#	Date	Mintage	VF	XF	Unc
2a	—	—	—	Proof	1500.

KOULA

32.5000 gm., .916 GOLD, .9278 oz AGW

Y#	Date	Mintage	VF	XF	Unc
3	1962	—	BV	BV	625.00
	1962	—	—	Proof	675.00

PLATINUM

Y#	Date	Mintage	VF	XF	Unc
3a	1962	—	—	Proof	2000.

DECIMAL COINAGE

100 Seniti = 1 Pa'anga
100 Pa'anga = 1 Hau

SENITI

BRONZE

Y#	Date	Mintage	VF	XF	Unc
4	1967	.500	—	.10	.15
	1967	—	—	Proof	2.00

Y#	Date	Mintage	VF	XF	Unc
18	1968	.500	—	.10	.15
	1968	—	—	Proof	2.00

BRASS

Y#	Date	Mintage	VF	XF	Unc
18a	1974	.500	—	.10	.15

BRONZE
F.A.O. Issue

Y#	Date	Mintage	VF	XF	Unc
26	1975	1.000	—	.10	.15
	1979	—	—	—	—

2 SENITI

BRONZE

Y#	Date	Mintage	VF	XF	Unc
5	1967	.500	—	.10	.20
	1967	—	—	Proof	2.50

Y#	Date	Mintage	VF	XF	Unc
19	1968	.200	—	.10	.20
	1968	—	—	Proof	2.50
	1974	.025	—	.10	.20

F.A.O. Issue

Y#	Date	Mintage	VF	XF	Unc
27	1975	.400	—	.10	.20
	1979	—	—	—	—

5 SENITI

COPPER-NICKEL

Y#	Date	Mintage	VF	XF	Unc
6	1967	.300	.10	.15	.40
	1967	—	—	Proof	3.00

Y#	Date	Mintage	VF	XF	Unc
20	1968	.100	.10	.15	.25
	1968	—	—	Proof	3.00
	1974	.075	.10	.15	.35

F.A.O. Issue

Y#	Date	Mintage	VF	XF	Unc
28	1975	.100	.10	.15	.40
	1977	.110	.10	.15	.40

10 SENITI

COPPER-NICKEL

Y#	Date	Mintage	VF	XF	Unc
7	1967	.300	.20	.35	.50
	1967	—	—	Proof	3.25

Y#	Date	Mintage	VF	XF	Unc
21	1968	.100	.20	.40	.60
	1968	—	—	Proof	3.50
	1974	.050	.25	.50	.75

F.A.O. Issue

Y#	Date	Mintage	VF	XF	Unc
29	1975	.075	.20	.35	.50
	1977	.025	.20	.30	.50

F.A.O. Issue

Y#	Date	Mintage	VF	XF	Unc
30	1975	.075	.35	.60	1.00
	1977	.025	.35	.60	1.00
	1979	—	—	—	—

20 SENITI

COPPER-NICKEL

Y#	Date	Mintage	VF	XF	Unc
8	1967	.150	.35	.60	.85
	1967	—	—	Proof	4.00

Y#	Date	Mintage	VF	XF	Unc
11	1967	.015	.75	1.25	2.00
	1967	—	—	Proof	3.00

c/s: 1918/TTIV/1968 on Y#11.

Y#	Date	Mintage	VF	XF	Unc
11a	1967	1,577	—	Proof only	7.50

Y#	Date	Mintage	VF	XF	Unc
22	1968	.035	.40	.70	1.00
	1968	—	—	Proof	4.00
	1974	.050	.35	.60	.85

50 SENITI

COPPER-NICKEL

Y#	Date	Mintage	VF	XF	Unc
9	1967	.075	.85	1.25	1.50
	1967	—	—	Proof	4.50

c/s: IN MEMORIAM/1965-1970 on Y#9.

Y#	Date	Mintage	VF	XF	Unc
9a	1967	—	—	—	2.50

Obv: Similar to Y#9.

Y#	Date	Mintage	VF	XF	Unc
12	1967	.015	1.50	2.25	3.50
	1967	—	—	Proof	4.00

c/s: 1918/TTIV/1968 on Y#12.

Y#	Date	Mintage	VF	XF	Unc
12a	1967	1,577	—	Proof only	7.50

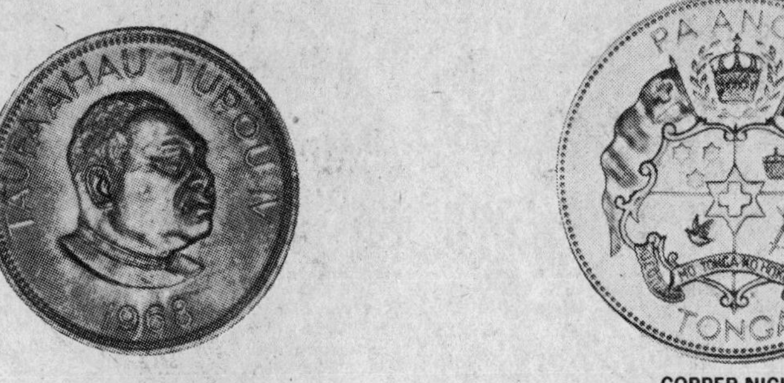

COPPER-NICKEL

Y#	Date	Mintage	VF	XF	Unc
10	1967	.078	2.00	3.00	4.50
	1967	—	—	Proof	15.00

c/s: IN MEMORIAM/1965-1970 on Y#10.

10a	1967	—	—	—	3.00

Obv: Similar to Y#10.

13	1967	Inc Y#10	1.50	2.50	6.00
	1967	—	—	Proof	7.00

c/s: 1918/TTIV/1968 on Y#13.

13a	1967	1,577	— Proof only		7.50

Obv: Similar to Y#9.

Y#	Date	Mintage	VF	XF	Unc
23	1968	.025	1.00	1.50	2.25
	1968	—	—	Proof	5.00

23a	1974	.050	1.00	1.25	1.75

F.A.O. Issue

31	1975	.040	1.00	1.25	1.50
	1977	.020	1.00	1.25	1.50

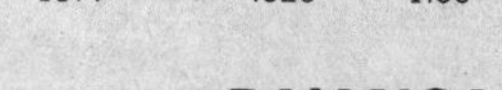

PA'ANGA

Obv: Similar to Y#10.

24	1968	.014	1.25	2.25	4.00
	1968	—	—	Proof	10.00
	1974	.010	1.25	2.25	3.50

c/s: OIL RIG 1969 OIL SEARCH on Y#13.

24a	1968	5,017	—	—	5.00

c/s: COMMONWEALTH MEMBER/1970 on Y#13.

Y#	Date	Mintage	VF	XF	Unc
24b	1968	3,000	—	—	4.00

c/s: INVESTITURE/1971 on Y#13.

24c	1968	3,000	—	—	4.00

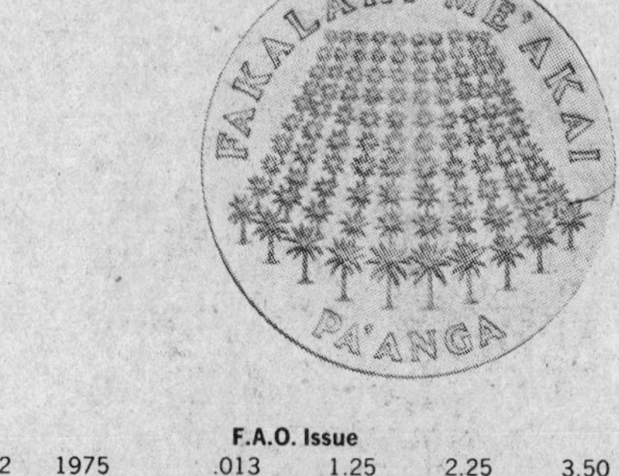

F.A.O. Issue

32	1975	.013	1.25	2.25	3.50

F.A.O. Issue

41	1977	.025	1.25	1.75	3.50

60th Birthday and F.A.O. Issue

Y#	Date	Mintage	VF	XF	Unc
42	1978	.010	—	—	—

1.000 SILVER

Y#	Date	Mintage	VF	XF	Unc
42a	1978	750 pcs.	— Proof only		—

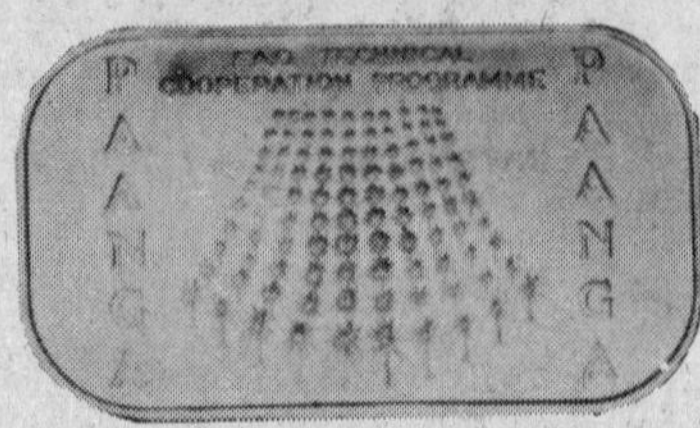

COPPER-NICKEL
F.A.O. Technical Cooperation Program

Y#	Date	Mintage	VF	XF	Unc
44	1979	.025	—	—	—

1.000 SILVER

Y#	Date	Mintage	VF	XF	Unc
44a	1979	850 pcs.	— Proof only		—

2 PA'ANGA

COPPER-NICKEL

Y#	Date	Mintage	VF	XF	Unc
14	1967	.010	3.00	4.00	9.00
	1967	—	—	Proof	12.00

c/s: 1918/TTIV/1968 on Y#14.

Y#	Date	Mintage	VF	XF	Unc
14a	1967	1,577	— Proof only		7.50

Obv: Similar to Y#14.

Y#	Date	Mintage	VF	XF	Unc
25	1968	.014	2.50	4.00	7.50
	1968	—	—	Proof	14.00
	1974	.010	2.50	4.00	5.50

c/s: OIL RIG 1969 OIL SEARCH on Y#25.

Y#	Date	Mintage	VF	XF	Unc
25a	1968	5,039	3.50	6.00	8.00

c/s: COMMONWEALTH MEMBER/1970 on Y#25.

Y#	Date	Mintage	VF	XF	Unc
25b	1968	3,006	—	—	6.00

c/s: INVESTITURE/1971 on Y#25.

Y#	Date	Mintage	VF	XF	Unc
25c	1968	3,000	—	—	6.00

F.A.O. Issue

Y#	Date	Mintage	VF	XF	Unc
33	1975	.013	—	3.50	5.00
	1976	—	—	—	—
	1977	.012	—	—	3.50

60th Birthday and F.A.O. Issue

Y#	Date	Mintage	VF	XF	Unc
43	1978	.010	—	—	—

1.000 SILVER

Y#	Date	Mintage	VF	XF	Unc
43a	1978	750 pcs.	— Proof only		—

COPPER-NICKEL
F.A.O. Issue - Sea Resource Management

Y#	Date	Mintage	VF	XF	Unc
45	1979	8,000	—	—	—

1.000 SILVER

Y#	Date	Mintage	VF	XF	Unc
45a	1979	850 pcs.	— Proof only		—

5 PA'ANGA

31.0000 gm., .999 SILVER, .9957 oz ASW
Constitution Centennial
Obv: Arms. Rev: King Tupou IV above document.

Y#	Date	Mintage	VF	XF	Unc
34	1975	2,118	—	—	—
	1975	418 pcs.	—	Proof	—

10 PA'ANGA

62.0000 gm., .999 SILVER, 1.9915 oz ASW
Constitution Centennial
Obv: Arms. Rev: King Tupou IV above palm trees.

Y#	Date	Mintage	VF	XF	Unc
35	1975	1,116	—	—	—
	1975	420 pcs.	—	Proof	—

20 PA'ANGA

140.0000 gm., .999 SILVER, 4.4971 oz ASW
Constitution Centennial
Obv: Arms. Rev: Busts of four monarchs.

Y#	Date	Mintage	VF	XF	Unc
36	1975	1,170	—	—	—
	1975	800 pcs.	—	Proof	—

25 PA'ANGA

5.0000 .GM., .916 GOLD, .1473 .OZ AGW
Constitution Centennial
Obv: Arms. Rev: King George Tupou I.

Y#	Date	Mintage	VF	XF	Unc
37	1975	405 pcs.	—	—	—
	1975	105 pcs.	—	Proof	—

50 PA'ANGA

10.0000 gm., .916 GOLD, .2947 oz AGW
Constitution Centennial
Obv: Arms. Rev: King George Tupou II.

Y#	Date	Mintage	VF	XF	Unc
38	1975	205 pcs.	—	—	—
	1975	105 pcs.	—	Proof	—

75 PA'ANGA

15.0000 gm., .916 GOLD, .4421 oz AGW
Constitution Centennial
Obv: Arms. Rev: Queen Salote Tupou III.

Y#	Date	Mintage	VF	XF	Unc
39	1975	204 pcs.	—	—	—
	1975	105 pcs.	—	Proof	—

100 PA'ANGA

20.0000 gm., .916 GOLD, .5894 oz AGW
Constitution Centennial
Obv: Arms. Rev: King Taufa'ahau Tupou IV.

Y#	Date	Mintage	VF	XF	Unc
40	1975	205 pcs.	—	—	—
	1975	105 pcs.	—	Proof	600.00

1/4 HAU

PALLADIUM

Y#	Date	Mintage	VF	XF	Unc
15	1967	1,700	—	—	135.00

c/s: 1918/TTIV/1968 on Y#15.

Y#	Date	Mintage	VF	XF	Unc
15a	1967	400 pcs.	—	—	—

1/2 HAU

PALLADIUM

Y#	Date	Mintage	VF	XF	Unc
16	1967	1,650	—	—	225.00

c/s: 1918/TTIV/1968 on Y#16a.

Y#	Date	Mintage	VF	XF	Unc
16a	1967	513 pcs.	—	—	—

HAU

PALLADIUM

Y#	Date	Mintage	VF	XF	Unc
17	1967	1,500	—	—	300.00

c/s: 1918/TTIV/1968 on Y#17.

Y#	Date	Mintage	VF	XF	Unc
17a	1967	400 pcs.	—	—	—

NCLT ISSUES

MINT SETS

KM#	Date	Mintage	Identification	Issue Price	Mkt. Val.
S1	1967(3)	1,500	Y7-9, palladium	207.00	750.00
S2	1970C/S(2)	10,000	Y9,10*	2.30	7.00
S3	1971C/S(2)	3,000	Y24,25*	4.80	10.00
S4	1974(8)	10,000	Y18a,19-22,	7.60	—
		—	23a,24,25	—	—
S5	1975(8)	—	Y26-33	7.75	—
S6	1975(4)	2,025	Y37-40	384.50	—
S7	1975(3)	11,000	Y34-36	59.60	—

***NOTE:** Countermarked 1967 coins.
**Countermarked 1968 coins.

PROOF SETS

STANDARD METALS

KM#	Date	Mintage	Identification	Issue Price	Mkt. Val.
101	1962(3)	250	Y1-3	—	750.00
102	1962(3)	25	Y1a-3a	—	—
103	1967(7)	5,000	Y4-10	15.00	28.00
104	1967(4)	1,923	Y11-14	17.25	30.00
105	1968(8)	2,500	Y18-25	22.50	32.50
106	1968C/S(4)	1,577	Y11-14*	22.80	35.00
107	1968C/S(3)	400	Y7-9*,Palladium	216.00	400.00
108	1969C/S(2)	10,000	Y24,25**,Gilded Copper-Nickel	13.68	20.00
109	1970C/S(2)	4,000	Y24,25**	13.68	20.00
110	1971C/S(2)	1,000	Y24,25**	13.40	20.00
111	1975(7)	—	Y34-40	—	—
112	1975(4)	975	Y37-40	537.89	—
113	1975(3)	4,000	Y34-36	81.95	—

***NOTE:** Countermarked 1967 coins.
**Countermarked 1968 coins.

Listings For

TONKIN: refer to Vietnam

TRINIDAD & TOBAGO

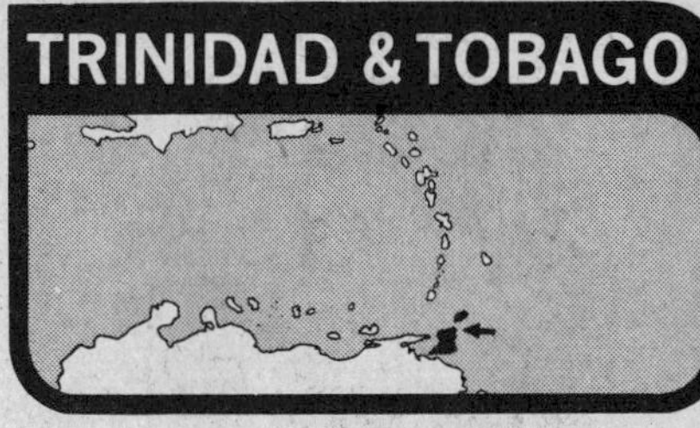

The Republic of Trinidad and Tobago, a member of the British Commonwealth situated 7 miles (11 km.) off the coast of Venezuela, has an area of 1,980 sq. mi. (5,128 sq. km.) and a population of 1.1 million. Capital: Port-of-Spain. The island of Trinidad contains the world's largest natural asphalt bog. Birds of Paradise live on little Tobago, the only place outside of their native New Guinea where they can be found in a wild state. Petroleum and petroleum products are the mainstay of the economy. Petroleum products, crude oil and sugar are exported.

Trinidad and Tobago were discovered by Columbus in 1498. Trinidad remained under Spanish rule from the time of its settlement in 1592 until its capture by the British in 1797. It was ceded to the British in 1802. Tobago was occupied at various times by the French, Dutch and English before being ceded to Britain in 1814. Trinidad and Tobago were merged into a single colony in 1888. The colony was part of the Federation of the West Indies until Aug. 31, 1962, when it became an independent member of the Commonwealth of Nations. A new constitution establishing a republican form of government was adopted on Aug. 1, 1976. Trinidad and Tobago is a member of the Commonwealth of Nations. The president is Chief of State. The prime minister is Head of Government.

RULERS

British, until 1976

TOBAGO

MONETARY SYSTEM

9 Pence = 1 Bit
11 Bits = 8 Shillings
3 Pence = 8 Reales

1-1/2 PENCE

BILLON
c/s: 'TB' on various French colonial coins

C#	Date	Mintage	VG	Fine	VF
5	ND(1798)	—	12.00	20.00	30.00

2-1/4 PENCE

BILLON or COPPER
c/s: 'TBO' on French colonial coins

C#	Date	Mintage	VG	Fine	VF
6	ND(1798)	—	20.00	30.00	40.00

1-1/2 BITS

SILVER
c/s: Script T with rays on center plug cut from Spanish or Spanish Colonial 8 Reales, C#12.

C#	Date	Mintage	VG	Fine	VF
11	ND(1798)	—	150.00	200.00	250.00

11 BITS

SILVER
Spanish or Spanish Colonial crenalated hole cut in 8 Reales.

C#	Date	Mintage	VG	Fine	VF
12	ND(1798)	—	400.00	500.00	550.00

NOTE: The plug was used for making the 1-1/2 Bits, C#11.

TRINIDAD

MONETARY SYSTEM

9 Bits or Shillings = 8 Reales

1/2 PENNY

COPPER
c/s: 'FD' on various types of half Penny size coins including French Colonial

C#	Date	Mintage	VG	Fine	VF
	ND(1854-74)	—	10.00	20.00	30.00

SHILLING

SILVER, 3gm
c/s: 'T' on 1/8 or 1/9 cut of Spanish or Spanish Colonial 8 Reales

C#	Date	Mintage	VG	Fine	VF
15	ND(1798-1801)	—	—	Rare	—

2.98 gm.
c/s: 'T' on center plug cut from Spanish or Spanish Colonial 8 Reales, (C#26).

C#	Date	Mintage	VG	Fine	VF
25	ND(1811)	25,000	45.00	65.00	85.00

9 SHILLINGS

SILVER
c/s: 'T' on holed Spanish or Spanish Colonial 8 Reales

C#	Date	Mintage	VG	Fine	VF
26	ND(1811)	25,000	250.00	325.00	375.00

Similar to C#26 but without 'T' c/s.

C#	Date	Mintage	VG	Fine	VF
26a	ND(1811)	Inc. Ab.	150.00	225.00	260.00

MODERN COINAGE

MINT MARKS

FM - Franklin Mint, U.S.A.*

***NOTE:** During 1975-1978 the Franklin Mint produced coinage in up to 3 different qualities. Qualities of issue are designated in ( ) after each date and are defined as follows:

(M) MATTE - Normal circulation strike or a dull finish produced by sandblasting special uncirculated (polish finish) or proof quality dies.

(U) SPECIAL UNCIRCULATED - Polished or proof-like in appearance without any frosted features.

(P) PROOF - The highest quality obtainable having mirror-like fields and frosted features.

MONETARY SYSTEM

100 Cents = 1 Dollar

CENT

BRONZE

Y#	Date	Mintage	VF	XF	Unc
1	1966	24.500	—	—	.15
	1966	8,000	—	Proof	2.50
	1967	4.000	—	—	.15
	1968	10.000	—	—	.15
	1970	5.000	—	—	.15
	1970	2,104	—	Proof	2.00
	1971	10.600	—	—	.15
	1971FM(M)	.286	—	.10	.20
	1971FM(P)	.012	—	Proof	1.75
	1972	16.500	—	—	.15
	1973	10.000	—	—	.15

10th Anniversary of Independence

Y#	Date	Mintage	VF	XF	Unc
9	1972	5.000	—	—	.20
	1972FM(M)	.125	—	—	.20
	1972FM(P)	.016	—	Proof	1.00

Y#	Date	Mintage	VF	XF	Unc
9a	1973FM(M)	.127	—	—	.15
	1973FM(P)	.020	—	Proof	1.00

Y#	Date	Mintage	VF	XF	Unc
17	1974FM(M)	.128	—	—	.10
	1974FM(P)	.014	—	Proof	1.00
	1975	10.000	—	—	.15
	1975FM(M)	.125	—	—	.10
	1975FM(U)	1,111	—	—	1.25
	1975FM(P)	.024	—	Proof	1.00
	1976	15.050	—	—	.10

Y#	Date	Mintage	VF	XF	Unc
17a	1976FM(M)	.150	—	—	.10
	1976FM(U)	582 pcs.	—	—	2.00
	1976FM(P)	.010	—	Proof	1.00
	1977FM(M)	.150	—	—	.10
	1977FM(U)	633 pcs.	—	1.25	2.00
	1977FM(P)	5,337	—	Proof	1.25
	1978FM(M)	.150	—	—	.10
	1978FM(U)	472 pcs.	—	—	—
	1978FM(P)	4,845	—	Proof	1.25
	1979FM(M)	.150	—	—	—
	1979FM(P)	3,270	—	Proof	1.25
	1980FM(M)	—	—	—	—
	1980FM(P)	—	—	Proof	1.25

5 CENTS

BRONZE

Y#	Date	Mintage	VF	XF	Unc
2	1966	7.500	—	—	.25
	1966	8,000	—	Proof	2.50
	1967	3.000	—	—	.25
	1970	2,104	—	Proof	4.00
	1971	2.400	—	—	.15
	1971FM(M)	.057	—	—	.15
	1971FM(P)	.012	—	Proof	2.00
	1972	2.250	—	—	.25
	1973FM(M)	.027	—	—	.25
	1973FM(P)	.020	—	Proof	1.25

10th Anniversary of Independence

Y#	Date	Mintage	VF	XF	Unc
10	1972	.015	—	.10	.35
	1972FM(M)	.025	—	.10	.25
	1972FM(P)	.016	—	Proof	1.25

Y#	Date	Mintage	VF	XF	Unc
18	1974FM(M)	.028	—	.10	.25
	1974FM(P)	.014	—	Proof	1.00
	1975	1.500	—	.10	.20
	1975FM(M)	.025	—	.10	.20
	1975FM(U)	1,111	—	1.00	1.75
	1975FM(P)	.024	—	Proof	1.00
	1976	7.500	—	—	.20

Y#	Date	Mintage	VF	XF	Unc
18a	1976FM(M)	.030	—	.10	.20
	1976FM(U)	582 pcs.	—	1.35	2.25
	1976FM(P)	.010	—	Proof	1.00
	1977FM(M)	.030	—	.10	.20
	1977FM(U)	633pcs.	—	1.50	2.50
	1977FM(P)	5,337	—	Proof	1.50
	1978FM(M)	.030	—	.10	.20
	1978FM(U)	472 pcs.	—	—	—
	1978FM(P)	4,845	—	Proof	1.50
	1979FM(M)	.030	—	—	—
	1979FM(P)	3,270	—	Proof	1.50
	1980FM(M)	—	—	—	—
	1980FM(P)	—	—	Proof	1.50

10 CENTS

COPPER-NICKEL

Y#	Date	Mintage	VF	XF	Unc
3	1966	7.800	—	—	.30
	1966	8,000	—	Proof	3.00
	1967	4.000	—	—	.35
	1970	2,104	—	Proof	5.00
	1971FM(M)	.029	.15	.20	.25
	1971FM(P)	.012	—	Proof	2.25
	1972	4.000	—	—	.40
	1973FM(M)	.014	.20	.30	.50
	1973FM(P)	.020	—	Proof	1.50

10th Anniversary of Independence

Y#	Date	Mintage	VF	XF	Unc
11	1972	.041	.15	.25	.40
	1972FM(M)	.013	.20	.35	.60
	1972FM(P)	.016	—	Proof	1.50

Y#	Date	Mintage	VF	XF	Unc
19	1974FM(M)	.016	.20	.30	.50
	1974FM(P)	.014	—	Proof	1.25
	1975	4.000	—	—	.40
	1975FM(M)	.013	.20	.30	.50
	1975FM(U)	1,111	—	1.25	2.00
	1975FM(P)	.024	—	Proof	1.00
	1976	14.720	—	—	.50

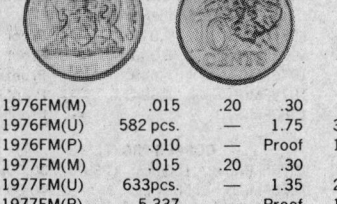

Y#	Date	Mintage	VF	XF	Unc
19a	1976FM(M)	.015	.20	.30	.50
	1976FM(U)	582 pcs.	—	1.75	3.00
	1976FM(P)	.010	—	Proof	1.25
	1977FM(M)	.015	.20	.30	.50
	1977FM(U)	633pcs.	—	1.35	2.25
	1977FM(P)	5,337	—	Proof	1.75
	1978FM(M)	.015	.20	.30	.50
	1978FM(U)	472 pcs.	—	—	—
	1978FM(P)	4,845	—	Proof	1.75
	1979FM(M)	.015	—	—	—
	1979FM(P)	3,270	—	Proof	1.75
	1980FM(M)	—	—	—	—
	1980FM(P)	—	—	Proof	1.75

25 CENTS

COPPER-NICKEL

Y#	Date	Mintage	VF	XF	Unc
4	1966	7.200	.25	.40	.60
	1966	8,000	—	Proof	4.00
	1967	1.800	.20	.30	.75
	1970	2,014	—	Proof	6.00
	1971	1.500	.20	.35	.60
	1971FM(M)	.011	.25	.40	.65
	1971FM(P)	.012	—	Proof	2.50
	1972	3.000	.20	.30	.50
	1973FM(M)	6,575	.50	.75	1.25
	1973FM(P)	.020	—	Proof	1.50

10th Anniversary of Independence

Y#	Date	Mintage	VF	XF	Unc
12	1972	.014	.30	.50	.75
	1972FM(M)	5,000	.60	.90	1.50
	1972FM(P)	.016	—	Proof	2.00

Y#	Date	Mintage	VF	XF	Unc
20	1974FM(M)	8,258	.50	.75	1.25
	1974FM(P)	.014	—	Proof	2.00
	1975	3.000	.20	.30	.50
	1975FM(M)	5,000	.60	1.00	1.50
	1975FM(U)	1,111	—	—	2.50
	1975FM(P)	.024	—	Proof	2.00
	1976	9.000	—	—	1.00

Y#	Date	Mintage	VF	XF	Unc
20a	1976FM(M)	6,000	.35	.60	1.00
	1976FM(U)	582 pcs.	1.50	2.50	4.00
	1976FM(P)	.010	—	Proof	2.50
	1977FM(M)	6,000	.35	.60	1.00
	1977FM(U)	633pcs.	—	2.00	3.50
	1977FM(P)	5,337	—	Proof	3.00
	1978FM(M)	6,000	.35	.60	1.00
	1978FM(U)	472 pcs.	—	—	—
	1978FM(P)	4,845	—	Proof	3.00
	1979FM(M)	6,000	—	—	—
	1979FM(P)	3,270	—	Proof	3.00
	1980FM(M)	—	—	—	—
	1980FM(P)	—	—	Proof	3.00

50 CENTS

COPPER-NICKEL

Y#	Date	Mintage	VF	XF	Unc
5	1966	.975	.50	.70	1.25
	1966	8,000	—	Proof	6.00
	1967	.750	.30	.50	1.25
	1970	2,104		Proof	10.00
	1971FM(M)	5,714	.75	1.25	2.00
	1971FM(P)	.012	—	Proof	3.00

10th Anniversary of Independence

Y#	Date	Mintage	VF	XF	Unc
13	1972	.375	.60	.90	1.50
	1972FM(M)	2,500	4.00	6.50	10.00
	1972FM(P)	.016	—	Proof	2.50

Y#	Date	Mintage	VF	XF	Unc
21	1973FM(M)	4,075	1.25	2.00	3.50
	1973FM(P)	.020	—	Proof	2.00
	1974FM(M)	5,758	.50	.75	1.25
	1974FM(P)	.014	—	Proof	2.75
	1975FM(M)	2,500	2.75	4.50	7.50
	1975FM(U)	1,111	—	2.00	3.50
	1975FM(P)	.024	—	Proof	1.25
	1976	.750	—	—	1.25

Y#	Date	Mintage	VF	XF	Unc
21a	1976FM(M)	3,000	2.50	4.00	6.50
	1976FM(U)	582 pcs.	—	3.50	5.50
	1976FM(P)	.010	—	Proof	3.50
	1977FM(M)	3,000	2.50	4.00	6.50
	1977FM(U)	633pcs.	—	3.00	5.00
	1977FM(P)	5,337	—	Proof	4.00
	1978FM(M)	3,000	2.50	4.00	6.50
	1978FM(U)	472 pcs.	—	—	—
	1978FM(P)	4,845	—	Proof	4.00

Y#	Date	Mintage	VF	XF	Unc
21a	1979FM(M)	3,000	—	—	—
	1979FM(P)	3,270	—	Proof	4.00
	1980FM(M)	—	—	—	—
	1980FM(P)	—	—	Proof	4.00

DOLLAR

NICKEL
F.A.O. Issue

Y#	Date	Mintage	VF	XF	Unc
7	1969	.250	1.50	3.00	6.00

COPPER-NICKEL

Y#	Date	Mintage	VF	XF	Unc
6	1970	2,014	—	Proof	25.00
	1971FM(M)	2,857	1.50	2.50	4.00
	1971FM(P)	.012	—	Proof	7.50

10th Anniversary of Independence

Y#	Date	Mintage	VF	XF	Unc
14	1972	9,700	2.00	3.50	6.00
	1972FM(M)	1,250	27.50	45.00	75.00
	1972FM(P)	.016	—	Proof	9.00

Rev: Similar to Y#14

Y#	Date	Mintage	VF	XF	Unc
22	1973FM(M)	2,825	2.00	3.00	5.00
	1973FM(P)	.020	—	Proof	4.00
	1974FM(M)	4,508	1.25	2.00	3.50
	1974FM(P)	.014	—	Proof	5.00
	1975FM(M)	1,250	10.00	16.50	27.50
	1975FM(U)	1,111	—	3.50	6.00
	1975FM(P)	.024	—	Proof	4.00

Rev: Similar to Y#14.

Y#	Date	Mintage	VF	XF	Unc
22a	1976FM(M)	1,500	9.00	15.00	25.00
	1976FM(U)	582 pcs.	—	13.50	20.00
	1976FM(P)	.010	—	Proof	6.00
	1977FM(M)	1,500	9.00	15.00	25.00
	1977FM(U)	633pcs.	—	12.50	20.00
	1977FM(P)	5,337	—	Proof	8.00
	1978FM(M)	1,500	9.00	15.00	25.00
	1978FM(U)	472 pcs.	—	—	—
	1978FM(P)	4,845	—	Proof	8.00
	1979FM(M)	1,500	—	—	—
	1979FM(P)	3,270	—	Proof	8.00
	1980FM(M)	—	—	—	—
	1980FM(P)	—	—	Proof	8.00

Copper-Nickel
2nd F.A.O. Issue
Similar to Y#7.

Y#	Date	Mintage	VF	XF	Unc
7a	1979FM(U)	—	—	—	—

5 DOLLARS

29.7000 gm., .925 SILVER, .8833 oz ASW

Y#	Date	Mintage	VF	XF	Unc
8	1971FM(M)	571 pcs.	40.00	65.00	110.00
	1971FM(P)	.011	—	Proof	30.00
	1973FM(M)	1,825	BV	BV	27.50
	1973FM(P)	.025	—	Proof	27.50
	1974FM(P)	.016	—	Proof	30.00
	1975FM(P)	.026	—	Proof	27.50

COPPER-NICKEL

Y#	Date	Mintage	VF	XF	Unc
8a	1974FM(M)	3,508	3.50	6.00	10.00
	1975FM(M)	250 pcs.	50.00	80.00	135.00
	1975FM(U)	1,111	—	12.50	20.00

29.7000 gm., .925 SILVER, .8833 oz ASW
10th Anniversary of Independence
Rev: Similar to Y#8.

Y#	Date	Mintage	VF	XF	Unc
15	1972	.010	BV	BV	30.00
	1972FM	250 pcs.	50.00	80.00	135.00
	1972FM	.019	—	Proof	27.50

Rev: Similar to Y#8.

Y#	Date	Mintage	VF	XF	Unc
8b	1976FM(P)	.011	—	Proof	27.50
	1977FM(P)	6,107	—	Proof	30.00
	1978FM(P)	5,460	—	Proof	30.00
	1979FM(P)	3,755	—	Proof	30.00
	1980FM(P)	—	—	Proof	30.00

COPPER-NICKEL

Y#	Date	Mintage	VF	XF	Unc
8c	1976FM(M)	300 pcs.	35.00	60.00	100.00
	1976FM(U)	582 pcs.	—	30.00	50.00
	1977FM(M)	300 pcs.	35.00	60.00	100.00
	1977FM(U)	633pcs.	—	25.00	40.00
	1978FM(M)	300 pcs.	35.00	60.00	100.00
	1978FM(U)	472 pcs.	—	40.00	60.00
	1979FM(M)	300pcs.	—	—	—
	1980FM(M)	—	—	—	—

10 DOLLARS

35.0000 gm., .925 SILVER, 1.0409 oz ASW
10th Anniversary of Independence
Obv: Similar to 5 Dollars, Y#15.

Y#	Date	Mintage	VF	XF	Unc
16	1972	—	—	—	40.00
	1972FM(M)	125 pcs.	175.00	275.00	450.00
	1972FM(P)	.026	—	Proof	32.00

Rev: Similar to Y#16.

Y#	Date	Mintage	VF	XF	Unc
23	1973FM(M)	1,700	BV	32.00	35.00
	1973FM(P)	.024	—	Proof	32.00
	1974FM(P)	.021	—	Proof	32.00
	1975FM(P)	.028	—	Proof	32.00

COPPER-NICKEL

Y#	Date	Mintage	VF	XF	Unc
23a	1974FM(M)	3,632	6.00	10.00	16.50
	1975FM(M)	125 pcs.	150.00	250.00	400.00
	1975FM(U)	1,111	—	13.50	22.50

35.0000 gm., .925 SILVER, 1.0409 oz ASW
Rev: Similar to Y#16.

Y#	Date	Mintage	VF	XF	Unc
23b	1976FM(P)	.013	—	Proof	35.00
	1977FM(P)	6,643	—	Proof	35.00
	1978FM(P)	7,449	—	Proof	35.00
	1979FM(P)	4,994	—	Proof	35.00
	1980FM(P)	—	—	Proof	35.00

COPPER-NICKEL

Y#	Date	Mintage	VF	XF	Unc
23c	1976FM(M)	150 pcs.	125.00	200.00	350.00
	1976FM(U)	582 pcs.	—	40.00	65.00
	1977FM(M)	150 pcs.	125.00	200.00	350.00
	1977FM(U)	633pcs.	—	35.00	55.00
	1978FM(M)	150 pcs.	125.00	200.00	350.00
	1978FM(U)	472 pcs.	—	45.00	75.00
	1979FM(M)	—	—	—	—
	1980FM(M)	—	—	—	65.00

100 DOLLARS

6.2100 gm., .500 GOLD, .0998 oz AGW

Y#	Date	Mintage	VF	XF	Unc
24	1976FM(M)	200 pcs.	—	—	—
	1976FM(P)	.029	—	Proof	75.00

NCLT ISSUES

MINT SETS

KM#	Date	Mintage	Identification	Issue Price	Mkt. Val.
S1	1973(8)	1,575	Y2-4,8,9a,21-23	24.00	35.00
S2	1974(8)	3,258	Y17-22,8a,23a	25.00	30.00
S3	1975(8)	1,111	Y17-22,8a,23a	27.50	40.00
S4	1976(8)	582	Y17a-22a,8c,23c	27.50	95.00
S5	1977(8)	632	Y17a-22a,8c,23c	27.50	85.00
S6	1978(8)	472	Y17a-22a,8c,23c	27.50	90.00
S7	1979(8)	—	Y17a-22a,8c,23c	28.50	50.00
S8	1980(8)	—	Y17a-22a,8c,23c	28.50	30.00

PROOF SETS

STANDARD METALS

KM#	Date	Mintage	Identification	Issue Price	Mkt. Val.
101	1966(5)	8,000	Y1-5	12.50	18.00
102	1970(6)	2,104	Y1-5,6	15.25	50.00
103	1971(7)	11,039	Y1-5,6,8	21.00	50.00
104	1971(6)	488	Y1-5,6	15.00	20.00
105	1972(8)	13,874	Y9-16	35.00	75.00
106	1972(7)	15,957	Y9-15	22.00	45.00
107	1973(8)	14,615	Y2-4,8,9a,21-23	35.00	70.00
108	1973(7)	5,050	Y2-4,8,9a,21-22	22.00	35.00
109	1974(8)	13,991	Y17-23,8	50.00	75.00
110	1975(8)	24,472	Y17-23,8	55.00	70.00
111	1976(8)	10,099	Y17a-22a,8b,23b	55.00	75.00
112	1977(8)	5,337	Y17a-22a,8b,23b	55.00	85.00
113	1978(8)	4,845	Y17a-22a,8b,23b	55.00	85.00
114	1979(8)	3,270	Y17a-22a,8b,23b	57.00	80.00
115	1980(8)	—	Y17a-22a,8b,23b	66.00	80.00

TRISTAN DA CUNHA

Tristan da Cunha is the principal island and group name of a small cluster of volcanic islands located in the South Atlantic midway between the Cape of Good Hope and South America, and 1,500 miles (2,414 km.) south-southwest of the British colony of St. Helena. The other islands are Inaccessible, Gough, and the three Nightingale Islands. The group, which comprises a dependency of St. Helena, has a total area of 40 sq. mi. (104 sq. km.) and a population of less than 300. There is a village of 60 houses called Edinburgh. Potatoes are the staple subsistence crop.

Tristan da Cunha was discovered in 1506 by Portuguese admiral Tristao da Cunha. Unsuccessful attempts to colonize the islands were made by the Dutch in 1656, but the first permanent inhabitant didn't arrive until 1810. During the exile of Napoleon on St. Helena, Britain placed a temporary garrison on Tristan da Cunha to prevent any attempt to rescue Napoleon from his island prison. The islands were formally annexed to Britain in 1816 and became a dependency of St. Helena in 1938.

RULERS

British

MINTMARKS

Pm - Pobjoy Mint

25 PENCE

COPPER-NICKEL
Queen's Silver Jubilee

Y#	Date	Mintage	VF	XF	Unc
1	1977	.050	1.00	1.50	2.50
	28.2800 gm., .925 SILVER, .8411 oz ASW				
1a	1977	.025	—	Proof	30.00

CROWN

COPPER-NICKEL
25th Anniversary of Coronation

Y#	Date	Mintage	VF	XF	Unc
2	1978PM	—	.85	1.25	2.50
	28.2800 gm., .925 SILVER, .8411 oz ASW				
2a	1978PM	.070	BV	BV	26.00
	1978PM	.025	—	Proof	30.00

TUNISIA-TUNIS

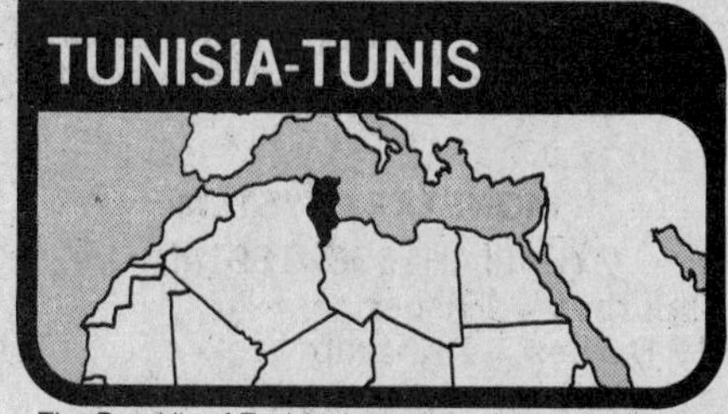

The Republic of Tunisia, located on the northern coast of Africa between Algeria and Libya, has an area of 63,378 sq. mi. (164,149 sq. km.) and a population of 6 million. Capital: Tunis. Agriculture is the backbone of the economy. Crude oil, phosphates, olive oil, and wine are exported.

Tunisia, settled by the Phoenicians in the 12th century B.C., was the center of the seafaring Carthaginian empire. After the total destruction of Carthage, Tunisia became part of Rome's African province. It remained a part of the Roman Empire (except for the 439-533 interval of Vandal conquest) until taken by the Arabs, 648, who administered it until the Turkish invasion of 1570. Under Turkish control, the public revenue was heavily dependent upon the piracy of Mediterranean shipping, an endeavor that wasn't abandoned until 1819 when a coalition of powers threatened appropriate reprisal. Deprived of its major source of income, Tunisia underwent a financial regression that ended in bankruptcy, enabling France to establish a protectorate over the country in 1881. National agitation and guerrilla fighting forced France to grant Tunisia internal autonomy in 1955 and to recognize Tunisian independence on March 20, 1956. Tunisia abolished the monarchy and established a republic on July 25, 1957.

TUNIS

OTTOMAN RULERS

Tunis, the capital and major seaport of Tunisia, existed in the Carthaginian era, but its importance dates only from the Moslem conquest, following which it became a major center of Arab power and prosperity. Spain seized it in 1535, lost it in 1564, retook it in 1573 and ceded it to the Turks in 1574. Thereafter the history of Tunis merged with that of Tunisia.

Mahmud II,
AH1223-1255/AD1808-1839
Abdul Mejid,
AH1255-1277/AD1839-1861
Abdul Aziz,
AH1277-1293/AD1861-1876
Muzad V, AH1293/AD1876
Abdul Hamid II
AH1293-1327/AH1876-1909

LOCAL RULERS

Muhammad Bey
AH1271-1276/1855-1859AD
Muhammad Al-Sadiq Bey
AH1276-1299/1859-1882AD
Ali Bey
AH1299-1320/1882-1902AD
Muhammad Al-Hadi Bey
AH1320-1324/1902-1906AD
Muhammad Al-Nasir Bey
AH1324-1340/1906-1922AD
Muhammad Al-Habib Bey
AH1340-1348/1922-1929AD
Ahmad Pasha Bey
AH1348-1361/1929-1942AD
Muhammad Al-Munsif Bey
AH1361-1362/1942-1943AD
Muhammad Al-Amin Bey
AH1362-1376/1943-1957AD

NOTE: All coins struck until AH1298 (=1881AD) bear the name of the Ottoman Sultan; the name of the Bey of Tunis was added in AH1272 (=1855AD). After 1298, when the French established their protectorate, only the Bey's name appears on the coin (until AH1376 = 1957).

MINTMARKS

TUNIS

With exceptions noted in their proper place, all coins were struck at Tunis prior to AH1308=1891AD. Thereafter, all coins were struck at Paris with mintmark A until 1928, symbols of the mint from 1929-1957.

MONETARY SYSTEM:

(Until AH1308=1891AD)

2 Burbes = 1 Asper
13 Burbes = 1 Kharub
16 Kharubs = 1 Piastre ('Sebili')

Mahmud II

AH1223-1255/1808-1839AD

ASPER

BILLON, 8mm (square), 0.2 gm.

C#	Date	Mintage	VG	Fine	VF
—	AH1228	—	—	—	—

KHARUB

BILLON, 14mm, 0.6-0.7 gm.

C#	Date	Mintage	VG	Fine	VF
70	AH1241	—	10.00	17.50	30.00
	1242	—	10.00	17.50	30.00
	1249	—	5.00	10.00	20.00
	1250	—	5.00	10.00	20.00
	1251	—	5.00	10.00	20.00
	1252	—	5.00	10.00	20.00
	1253	—	5.00	10.00	20.00
	1254	—	5.00	10.00	20.00
	1255	—	5.00	10.00	20.00

2 KHARUBS

BILLON, 16mm, 1.3 gm.

C#	Date	Mintage	VG	Fine	VF
72	AH1243	—	15.00	25.00	50.00
	1244	—	15.00	25.00	50.00

4 KHARUBS (1/4 PIASTRE)

BILLON, 21mm, 3.5 gm.

C#	Date	Mintage	VG	Fine	VF
66	AH1223	—	15.00	30.00	75.00
	1228	—	15.00	30.00	75.00
	1231	—	15.00	30.00	75.00

20mm, 2.5 gm.

C#	Date	Mintage	VG	Fine	VF
74	AH1240	—	10.00	30.00	60.00
	1242	—	10.00	30.00	60.00
	1243	—	10.00	30.00	60.00
	1246	—	10.00	30.00	60.00
	1249	—	10.00	30.00	60.00
	1250	—	10.00	30.00	60.00
	1252	—	10.00	30.00	60.00
	1253	—	10.00	30.00	60.00
	1254	—	10.00	30.00	60.00
	1255	—	10.00	30.00	60.00

8 KHARUBS (1/2 PIASTRE)

BILLON, 27mm, 7.5 gm.

C#	Date	Mintage	VG	Fine	VF
67	AH1228	—	20.00	45.00	95.00
	1231	—	20.00	45.00	95.00
	1232	—	20.00	45.00	95.00
	1233	—	20.00	45.00	95.00

26mm, 5.0 gm.

C#	Date	Mintage	VG	Fine	VF
76	AH1240	—	10.00	20.00	40.00
	1241	—	10.00	20.00	40.00
	1242	—	10.00	20.00	40.00
	1243	—	10.00	20.00	40.00
	1244	—	10.00	20.00	40.00
	1245	—	10.00	20.00	40.00
	1246	—	10.00	20.00	40.00
	1247	—	10.00	20.00	40.00
	1248	—	10.00	20.00	40.00
	1251	—	Reported, Not Confirmed		
	1252	—	10.00	20.00	40.00
	1253	—	10.00	20.00	40.00
	1254	—	10.00	20.00	40.00

PIASTRE

BILLON, 35mm, 16.0 gm.

C#	Date	Mintage	VG	Fine	VF
68	AH1225	—	20.00	40.00	80.00
	1226	—	20.00	40.00	80.00
	1227	—	20.00	40.00	80.00
	1228	—	20.00	40.00	80.00
	1229	—	20.00	40.00	80.00
	1230	—	20.00	40.00	80.00
	1231	—	20.00	40.00	80.00
	1232	—	20.00	40.00	80.00

32-33mm, 11.0-11.5 gm.

C#	Date	Mintage	VG	Fine	VF
78	AH1240	—	9.00	15.00	30.00
	1241	—	9.00	15.00	30.00
	1242	—	9.00	15.00	30.00
	1243	—	9.00	15.00	30.00
	1244	—	9.00	15.00	30.00
	1245	—	9.00	15.00	30.00
	1246	—	9.00	15.00	30.00
	1247	—	9.00	15.00	30.00
	1248	—	9.00	15.00	30.00
	1249	—	9.00	15.00	30.00
	1250	—	9.00	15.00	30.00
	1251	—	9.00	15.00	30.00
	1252	—	9.00	15.00	30.00
	1253	—	9.00	15.00	30.00
	1254	—	9.00	15.00	30.00
	1255	—	9.00	15.00	30.00

2 PIASTRES

BILLON, 39mm, 27.4 gm.

C#	Date	Mintage	VG	Fine	VF
69	AH1232	—	100.00	150.00	200.00

38mm, 23 gm.

C#	Date	Mintage	VG	Fine	VF
80	AH1244	—	60.00	100.00	150.00
	1245	—	60.00	100.00	150.00
	1246	—	60.00	100.00	150.00
	1248	—	75.00	110.00	175.00

SULTANI

GOLD, 20mm, 2.50 gm.

C#	Date	Mintage	VG	Fine	VF
—	AH1236	—	200.00	250.00	300.00

Sultan Abdul Mejid

AH1255-77 1839-61AD

Without the name of the Bey of Tunis

PRE-REFORM COINAGE

4 KHARUBS

BILLON, 20mm, 2.5 gm.

C#	Date	Mintage	VG	Fine	VF
86	AH1256	—	50.00	100.00	150.00

8 KHARUB

BILLON, 25mm, 5.0 gm.

C#	Date	Mintage	VG	Fine	VF
88	AH1256	—	50.00	100.00	150.00

PIASTRE

BILLON, 32mm, 11.0 gm.

C#	Date	Mintage	VG	Fine	VF
90	AH1255	—	50.00	85.00	125.00

REFORM COINAGE

After AH1263/1847AD

BURBE

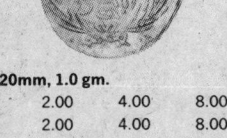

COPPER, 20mm, 1.0 gm.

C#	Date	Mintage	VG	Fine	VF
95	AH1263	—	2.00	4.00	8.00
	1264	—	2.00	4.00	8.00
	1265	—	2.00	4.00	8.00
	1266	—	2.00	4.00	8.00

ASPER

COPPER, 23mm, 2.0 gm.

C#	Date	Mintage	VG	Fine	VF
96	AH1263	—	3.00	5.50	10.00
	1264	—	3.00	5.50	10.00
	1265	—	3.00	5.50	10.00
	1266	—	3.00	5.50	10.00
	1267	—	3.00	5.50	10.00

3 ASPERS

COPPER, 24mm, 5.5 gm.

C#	Date	Mintage	VG	Fine	VF
97	AH1263	—	4.00	7.50	15.00
	1264	—	4.00	7.50	15.00
	1265	—	4.00	7.50	15.00
	1266	—	4.00	7.50	15.00
	1267	—	4.00	7.50	15.00
	1268	—	4.00	7.50	15.00
	1269	—	4.00	7.50	15.00

6 ASPERS

COPPER, 29mm, 11.5 gm.

C#	Date	Mintage	VG	Fine	VF
98	AH1263	—	1.75	3.50	6.00
	1264	—	1.75	3.50	6.00
	1265	—	1.25	2.50	5.00
	1266	—	1.25	2.50	5.00
	1267	—	1.25	2.50	5.00
	1268	—	1.25	2.50	5.00
	1269	—	1.25	2.50	5.00
	1270	—	2.00	4.00	8.00
	1271	—	2.00	4.00	8.00

KHARUB

COPPER

c/s: Arabic '1' on 6 Aspers, C#98.

C#	Date	Mintage	VG	Fine	VF
98a	AH1263-71	—	3.00	5.00	10.00

2 PIASTRES

SILVER, 28mm, 6.5 gm.

C#	Date	Mintage	VG	Fine	VF
101	AH1263	—	17.50	35.00	70.00
	1264	—	17.50	35.00	70.00

Modified design

C#	Date	Mintage	VG	Fine	VF
101a	AH1267	—	20.00	35.00	75.00

5 PIASTRES

SILVER, 33mm, 15.5 gm.

C#	Date	Mintage	VG	Fine	VF
102	AH1263	—	30.00	60.00	120.00
	1264	—	30.00	60.00	120.00

Modified design

C#	Date	Mintage	VG	Fine	VF
102a	AH1265	—	60.00	125.00	200.00
	1266	—	18.00	40.00	75.00
	1267	—	18.00	40.00	75.00
	1268	—	18.00	40.00	75.00
	1269	—	18.00	40.00	75.00
	1270	—	18.00	40.00	75.00
	1271	—	18.00	40.00	75.00

NOTE: Coins of 1/4, 1/2, and 1 Piastre dated AH1270 are patterns.

Sultan Abdul Mejid

With Muhammad Bey

AH1272-1276

NOTE: The copper coins of this series exhibit two major varieties of calligraphy, the first having thin, crude lettering, the second having thicker, more elegant lettering.

3 ASPERS

COPPER, 25mm, 5.8 gm.

C#	Date	Mintage	VG	Fine	VF
112	AH1272	—	7.50	15.00	30.00
	1273	—	7.50	15.00	30.00

Thicker legends

C#	Date	Mintage	VG	Fine	VF
112.1	AH1274	—	7.50	15.00	30.00

6 ASPERS

COPPER, 28mm, 11.6 gm.

C#	Date	Mintage	VG	Fine	VF
113	AH1272	—	4.50	8.00	15.00
	1273	—	4.50	8.00	15.00

Thicker legends

C#	Date	Mintage	VG	Fine	VF
113.1	AH1272	—	4.50	8.00	15.00
	1274	—	4.50	8.00	15.00

KHARUB

COPPER

c/s: Arabic '1' on 6 Aspers, C#113 and 113.1.

C#	Date	Mintage	VG	Fine	VF
113a	AH1272-4	—	4.00	7.50	15.00

13 ASPERS

COPPER, 34mm, 23 gm.

C#	Date	Mintage	VG	Fine	VF
114	AH1272	—	8.50	12.50	25.00
	1273	—	8.50	12.50	25.00

Thicker legends

C#	Date	Mintage	VG	Fine	VF
114.1	AH1273	—	8.50	12.50	25.00
	1274	—	8.50	12.50	25.00

2 KHARUBS

COPPER

c/s: Arabic '2' on 13 Aspers, C#114 and 114.1.

C#	Date	Mintage	VG	Fine	VF
114a	AH1272-4	—	6.00	10.00	20.00

34mm, 23 gm.

C#	Date	Mintage	VG	Fine	VF
115	AH1275	—	7.50	15.00	30.00
	1276	—	10.00	20.00	40.00

SILVER, 13mm, 0.4 gm.

C#	Date	Mintage	VG	Fine	VF
120	AH1273	—	6.00	12.00	25.00
	1274	—	6.00	12.00	25.00
	1275	—	6.00	12.00	25.00
	1276	—	6.00	12.00	25.00

4 KHARUBS

SILVER, 15mm, 0.8 gm.

C#	Date	Mintage	VG	Fine	VF
121	AH1274	—	15.00	25.00	50.00
	1275	—	15.00	25.00	50.00

8 KHARUBS

SILVER, 18mm, 1.45 gm.

C#	Date	Mintage	VG	Fine	VF
122	AH1274	—	15.00	30.00	60.00
	1275	—	15.00	30.00	60.00

PIASTRE

SILVER, 23mm, 3.1 gm.

C#	Date	Mintage	VG	Fine	VF
123	AH1272	—	15.00	25.00	50.00
	1273	—	15.00	25.00	50.00

2 PIASTRES

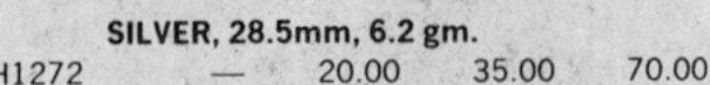

SILVER, 28.5mm, 6.2 gm.

C#	Date	Mintage	VG	Fine	VF
124	AH1272	—	20.00	35.00	70.00

3 PIASTRES

SILVER, 30mm, 9.3 gm.

C#	Date	Mintage	VG	Fine	VF
125	AH1272	—	35.00	65.00	125.00

4 PIASTRES

SILVER, 31mm, 12.5 gm.

C#	Date	Mintage	VG	Fine	VF
126	AH1272	—	50.00	100.00	175.00

5 PIASTRES

SILVER, 33mm, 16 gm.

C#	Date	Mintage	VG	Fine	VF
127	AH1272	—	50.00	100.00	150.00
	1273	—	50.00	100.00	150.00
	1274	—	50.00	100.00	150.00

.9800 gm., .900 GOLD, 12mm, .0284 oz AGW

C#	Date	Mintage	Fine	VF	XF
133	AH1272	—	30.00	40.00	80.00
	1274	—	30.00	40.00	80.00
	1275	—	30.00	40.00	80.00

10 PIASTRES

1.7700 gm., .900 GOLD, 18mm, .0512 oz AGW

C#	Date	Mintage	Fine	VF	XF
128	AH1272	—	50.00	75.00	150.00

1.9700 gm., .900 GOLD, .0570 oz AGW

C#	Date	Mintage	Fine	VF	XF
134	AH1272	—	45.00	60.00	120.00
	1274	—	45.00	60.00	120.00

20 PIASTRES

3.5500 gm., .900 GOLD, 21mm, .1027 oz AGW

C#	Date	Mintage	Fine	VF	XF
129	AH1272	—	75.00	125.00	250.00

25 PIASTRES

4.9200 gm., .900 GOLD, 20mm, .1424 oz AGW

C#	Date	Mintage	Fine	VF	XF
135	AH1273	—	95.00	125.00	250.00
	1274	—	95.00	125.00	250.00
	1275	—	95.00	125.00	250.00

40 PIASTRES

7.1000 gm., .900 GOLD, 26mm, .2055 oz AGW

C#	Date	Mintage	Fine	VF	XF
130	AH1272	—	155.00	175.00	300.00

50 PIASTRES

9.8400 gm., .900 GOLD, 26.5mm, .2847 oz AGW

C#	Date	Mintage	Fine	VF	XF
136	AH1272	—	190.00	225.00	350.00
	1273	—	190.00	225.00	350.00
	1274	—	190.00	225.00	350.00
	1275	—	190.00	225.00	350.00

80 PIASTRES

14.2100 gm., .900 GOLD, 31mm, .4112 oz AGW

C#	Date	Mintage	Fine	VF	XF
131	AH1272	—	300.00	500.00	900.00

100 PIASTRES

17.7100 gm., .900 GOLD, 33mm, .5125 oz AGW

C#	Date	Mintage	Fine	VF	XF
132	AH1272	—	335.00	400.00	800.00

19.6800 gm., .900 GOLD, 33mm, .5695 oz AGW

C#	Date	Mintage	Fine	VF	XF
137	AH1272	—	375.00	500.00	900.00
	1273	—	375.00	500.00	900.00
	1274	—	375.00	500.00	900.00

Sultan Abdul Mejid

With Muhammad al-Sadiq Bey
AH1276-1277

2 KHARUBS

COPPER, 34mm, 23 gm.

C#	Date	Mintage	Fine	VF	XF
	Thin legends				
140	AH1276	—	20.00	35.00	60.00
	Thick legends				
140.1	AH1276	—	18.50	30.00	60.00

8 KHARUBS

SILVER, 18mm, 1.60 gm.

C#	Date	Mintage	Fine	VF	XF
146	AH1277	—	100.00	200.00	350.00

PIASTRE

SILVER, 22mm, 3.2 gm.

C#	Date	Mintage	Fine	VF	XF
147	AH1278 (sic)	—	75.00	150.00	250.00

25 PIASTRES

GOLD, 20mm, 4.9 gm.

C#	Date	Mintage	Fine	VF	XF
155	AH1276	—	100.00	150.00	200.00

50 PIASTRES

GOLD, 26mm, 9.8 gm.

C#	Date	Mintage	Fine	VF	XF
156	AH1276	—	175.00	300.00	400.00

100 PIASTRES

GOLD, 33mm, 19.7 gm.

C#	Date	Mintage	Fine	VF	XF
157	AH1276	—	300.00	400.00	500.00

Sultan Abdul Aziz

With Muhammad al-Sadiq Bey
AH1277-1293

1/4 KHARUB

COPPER, 14mm, 0.9 gm.

C#	Date	Mintage	Fine	VF	XF
161	AH1281	3,200	3.00	6.00	12.00

18mm, 1.5 gm.

C#	Date	Mintage	Fine	VF	XF
170	AH1289	—	7.50	20.00	40.00

1/2 KHARUB

COPPER, 18mm, 1.8 gm.

C#	Date	Mintage	Fine	VF	XF
162	AH1281	3,200	1.00	2.00	4.00

25mm, 3.1 gm.

C#	Date	Mintage	Fine	VF	XF
171	AH1289	—	4.00	7.50	15.00

KHARUB

COPPER, 22mm, 3.7 gm.

C#	Date	Mintage	Fine	VF	XF
163	AH1281	5,600	1.00	2.00	4.00

28.5mm, 6.2 gm.

C#	Date	Mintage	Fine	VF	XF
172	AH1289	—	2.00	5.00	10.00
	1290	—	3.00	6.00	12.00

2 KHARUBS

COPPER, 27.5mm, 7.5 gm.

C#	Date	Mintage	Fine	VF	XF
164	AH1281	.012	1.25	3.00	6.00

31mm, 14.6 gm.

C#	Date	Mintage	Fine	VF	XF
169	AH1283	—	4.00	10.00	20.00
	1284	—	4.00	10.00	20.00

31mm, 12.5 gm.

C#	Date	Mintage	Fine	VF	XF
173	AH1289	—	3.00	6.00	12.50
	1290	—	5.00	8.00	17.50

4 KHARUBS

COPPER, 31mm, 15 gm.

C#	Date	Mintage	Fine	VF	XF
165	AH1281	.012	2.50	4.00	8.00
	1283	—	—	—	—

8 KHARUBS

COPPER, 34mm, 30 gm.

C#	Date	Mintage	Fine	VF	XF
166	AH1281	.010	3.50	8.50	18.50

NOTE: C#161-166 were struck at the Heaton Mint, Birmingham, and are relatively common in higher grades.

SILVER, 18mm, 1.6 gm.

C#	Date	Mintage	Fine	VF	XF
176	AH1281	—	25.00	50.00	100.00
	1282	—	25.00	50.00	100.00
	1283	—	25.00	50.00	100.00
	1284	—	25.00	50.00	100.00

C#	Date	Mintage	Fine	VF	XF
176	1285	—	25.00	50.00	100.00
	1287	—	25.00	50.00	100.00
	1288	—	25.00	50.00	100.00
	1289	—	25.00	50.00	100.00
	1290	—	25.00	50.00	100.00
	1291	—	25.00	50.00	100.00
	1292	—	25.00	50.00	100.00
	1293	—	25.00	50.00	100.00

PIASTRE

SILVER, 22.5mm, 3.2 gm.

C#	Date	Mintage	Fine	VF	XF
177	AH1279	—	15.00	25.00	40.00
	1281	—	15.00	25.00	40.00
	1282	—	15.00	25.00	40.00
	1284	—	15.00	25.00	40.00
	1287	—	10.00	20.00	40.00
	1288	—	10.00	20.00	40.00
	1289	—	8.00	15.00	40.00
	1290	—	10.00	20.00	40.00
	1291	—	8.00	15.00	35.00
	1292	—	8.00	15.00	35.00
	1293	—	10.00	20.00	40.00

c/s: Star on Piastre, C#177.

C#	Date	Mintage	Fine	VF	XF
177a	AH1279-93	—	10.00	15.00	30.00

2 PIASTRES

SILVER, 28mm, 6.4 gm.

C#	Date	Mintage	Fine	VF	XF
178	AH1281 Paris	—	—	Proof	250.00

NOTE: Without name of the Bey of Tunis - possibly a pattern.

27mm, 6.4 gm.

C#	Date	Mintage	Fine	VF	XF
178.5	AH1287	—	25.00	50.00	100.00
	1288	—	25.00	50.00	100.00
	1289	—	25.00	50.00	100.00
	1290	—	25.00	50.00	100.00
	1291	—	25.00	50.00	100.00
	1292	—	25.00	50.00	100.00
	1293	—	25.00	50.00	100.00

c/s: Star on 2 Piastres, C#178.5.

C#	Date	Mintage	Fine	VF	XF
178.5a	AH1287-93	—	10.00	25.00	50.00

3 PIASTRES

SILVER, 30mm, 9.6 gm.

C#	Date	Mintage	Fine	VF	XF
179	AH1288	—	35.00	60.00	100.00

4 PIASTRES

SILVER, 31mm, 11.9 gm.

C#	Date	Mintage	Fine	VF	XF
179.5	AH1288	—	25.00	50.00	100.00
	1290	—	25.00	50.00	100.00
	1291	—	25.00	50.00	100.00
	1292	—	25.00	50.00	100.00
	1293	—	25.00	50.00	100.00

c/s: Star on C#179.5.

C#	Date	Mintage	Fine	VF	XF
179.5a	AH1288-93	—	25.00	30.00	50.00

5 PIASTRES

.9800 gm., .900 GOLD, .0284 oz AGW

C#	Date	Mintage	Fine	VF	XF
181	AH1281	—	30.00	45.00	80.00

C#	Date	Mintage	Fine	VF	XF
181.1	AH1288	—	30.00	45.00	80.00
	1289	—	30.00	45.00	80.00
	1290	—	30.00	42.50	80.00
	1291	—	30.00	42.50	80.00
	1292	—	30.00	45.00	80.00

c/s: Star on C#181.

C#	Date	Mintage	Fine	VF	XF
181a	AH1281	—	35.00	55.00	100.00

c/s: Star on C#181.

C#	Date	Mintage	Fine	VF	XF
181.1a	AH1288	—	35.00	55.00	100.00
	1289	—	35.00	60.00	100.00
	1290	—	35.00	60.00	100.00
	1291	—	35.00	60.00	100.00
	1292	—	35.00	60.00	100.00

SILVER, 33mm, 16gm.

C#	Date	Mintage	Fine	VF	XF
180	AH1288	—	50.00	90.00	175.00
	1290	—	50.00	90.00	175.00
	1291	—	45.00	80.00	150.00
	1293	—	50.00	90.00	175.00

10 PIASTRES

1.9700 gm., .900 GOLD, .0570 oz AGW

C#	Date	Mintage	Fine	VF	XF
182	AH1280	—	60.00	80.00	120.00
	1281	—	62.50	80.00	120.00
	1284	—	60.00	80.00	120.00
	1287	—	60.00	80.00	120.00
182	1288	—	60.00	80.00	120.00

c/s: Star on C#182.

C#	Date	Mintage	Fine	VF	XF
182a	AH1280-8	—	70.00	85.00	125.00

25 PIASTRES

4.9200 gm., .900 GOLD, .1424 oz AGW

C#	Date	Mintage	Fine	VF	XF
183	AH1279	—	95.00	125.00	250.00
	1280	—	95.00	125.00	250.00
	1281	—	95.00	125.00	250.00
	1283	—	95.00	125.00	250.00
	1285	—	95.00	125.00	250.00
	1287	—	95.00	125.00	250.00
	1288	—	95.00	125.00	250.00
	1289	—	95.00	125.00	250.00
	1290	—	95.00	125.00	250.00
	1291	—	95.00	125.00	250.00

50 PIASTRES

9.8400 gm., .900 GOLD, .2847 oz AGW

C#	Date	Mintage	Fine	VF	XF
184	AH1280	—	190.00	225.00	350.00
	1281	—	190.00	225.00	350.00
	1286	—	190.00	225.00	350.00
	1288	—	190.00	225.00	350.00
	1293	—	190.00	225.00	350.00

100 PIASTRES

19.6800 gm., .900 GOLD, .5695 oz AGW

C#	Date	Mintage	Fine	VF	XF
185	AH1279	—	375.00	500.00	900.00
	1280	—	375.00	500.00	900.00
	1281	—	375.00	500.00	900.00
	1283	—	375.00	500.00	900.00
	1285	—	375.00	500.00	900.00

NOTE: C#178-185, dated AH1281, were all struck at Tunis, from dies produced at the Heaton mint, Birmingham - hence their obvious superiority.

Sultan Murad V

With Muhammad al-Sadiq Bey
AH1293

25 PIASTRES

4.9200 gm., .900 GOLD, 20mm, .1424 oz AGW

C#	Date	Mintage	Fine	VF	XF
190	AH1293	—	450.00	500.00	550.00

Sultan Abdul Hamid II

With Muhammad al-Sadiq Bey
AH1293-1299

2 KHARUBS

COPPER, 31mm, 12.5 gm.

C#	Date	Mintage	Fine	VF	XF
192	AH1293	—	20.00	40.00	75.00

8 KHARUBS

SILVER, 18mm, 1.5 gm.
Obv: With 'AL-GHAZI'

C#	Date	Mintage	Fine	VF	XF
193	AH1293	—	50.00	150.00	275.00
	1296	—	50.00	150.00	275.00
	1297	—	50.00	150.00	275.00
	1298	—	50.00	150.00	275.00

Obv: w/o "AL-Ghazi'

C#	Date	Mintage	Fine	VF	XF
193.1	AH1294	—	100.00	250.00	400.00

PIASTRE

SILVER, 22.5mm, 3.2 gm.
Obv: Without 'AL-GHAZI'

C#	Date	Mintage	Fine	VF	XF
194	AH1293	—	50.00	100.00	150.00
	1294	—	50.00	100.00	150.00

Obv: With 'AL-GHAZI' added.

C#	Date	Mintage	Fine	VF	XF
194a	AH1294	—	50.00	100.00	150.00
	1295	—	50.00	100.00	150.00
	1296	—	50.00	100.00	150.00
	1297	—	50.00	100.00	150.00
	1298	—	50.00	100.00	150.00

c/s: Star in circle on C#194.

C#	Date	Mintage	Fine	VF	XF
194b	AH1293-4	—	50.00	100.00	150.00

c/s: Star in circle on C#194a.

C#	Date	Mintage	Fine	VF	XF
194c	AH1294-8	—	50.00	100.00	150.00

2 PIASTRES

SILVER, 26.5mm, 6.4 gm.

C#	Date	Mintage	Fine	VF	XF
195	AH1293	—	50.00	100.00	150.00
	1294	—	50.00	100.00	150.00

Obv: With 'AL-GHAZI' added.

C#	Date	Mintage	Fine	VF	XF
195a	AH1294	—	50.00	100.00	150.00

c/s: Star in circle on C#195.

C#	Date	Mintage	Fine	VF	XF
195b	AH1293-4	—	50.00	100.00	150.00

c/s: Star in circle on C#195a.

C#	Date	Mintage	Fine	VF	XF
195c	AH1294	—	50.00	100.00	150.00

4 PIASTRES

SILVER, 31mm, 12.8 gm.
Obv: Without 'AL-GHAZI'

C#	Date	Mintage	Fine	VF	XF
196	AH1293	—	25.00	75.00	125.00
	1294	—	25.00	75.00	125.00

Obv: With 'AL-GHAZI' added.

C#	Date	Mintage	Fine	VF	XF
196a	AH1294	—	25.00	75.00	125.00
	1296	—	25.00	75.00	125.00

c/s: Star in circle on C#196.

C#	Date	Mintage	Fine	VF	XF
196b	AH1293-4	—	25.00	75.00	125.00

c/s: Star in circle on C#196a.

C#	Date	Mintage	Fine	VF	XF
196c	AH1294,6	—	25.00	75.00	125.00

5 PIASTRES

.9800 gm., .900 GOLD, 12.5mm, .0284 oz AGW

C#	Date	Mintage	Fine	VF	XF
197	AH1294	—	40.00	55.00	95.00

25 PIASTRES

4.9200 gm., .900 GOLD, 20mm, .1424 oz AGW

C#	Date	Mintage	Fine	VF	XF
200	AH1294	—	95.00	125.00	250.00
	1295	—	95.00	125.00	250.00
	1296	—	95.00	125.00	250.00
	1297	—	95.00	125.00	250.00

50 PIASTRES

9.8400 gm., .900 GOLD, 26mm, .2847 oz AGW

C#	Date	Mintage	Fine	VF	XF
201	AH1297	—	200.00	250.00	350.00

FRENCH PROTECTORATE

MINTMARKS

(a) - Paris, privy marks only
A - Paris

Muhammad Al-Sadiq Bey,

Alone: AH1298-99/AD1881-82

8 KHARUBS

SILVER, 18.5mm, 1.6 gm.

Y#	Date	Mintage	Fine	VF	XF
1	AH1299	—	60.00	150.00	200.00

PIASTRE

SILVER, 22.5mm, 3.2 gm.

Y#	Date	Mintage	Fine	VF	XF
2	AH1299	—	75.00	175.00	250.00

2 PIASTRES

SILVER, 26.5 mm, 6.4 gm.

Y#	Date	Mintage	Fine	VF	XF
3	AH1299	—	75.00	200.00	300.00

25 PIASTRES

4.9200 gm., GOLD, 20mm, .1424 oz AGW

Y#	Date	Mintage	Fine	VF	XF
4	AH1298	—	95.00	130.00	250.00
	1300	—	95.00	150.00	250.00

50 PIASTRES

9.8400 gm., .900 GOLD, 26mm, .2847 oz AGW

Y#	Date	Mintage	Fine	VF	XF
A4	AH1299	—	250.00	500.00	1000.

Ali Bey

AH1299-1320/AD1882-1902

8 KHARUBS

SILVER, 18mm, 1.6 gm.

Y#	Date	Mintage	Fine	VF	XF
5	AH1300	—	25.00	50.00	100.00
	1301	—	25.00	50.00	100.00
	1302	—	25.00	50.00	100.00
	1303	—	25.00	50.00	100.00
	1304	—	25.00	50.00	100.00
	1305	—	25.00	50.00	100.00
	1306	—	25.00	50.00	100.00
	1307	—	25.00	50.00	100.00
	1308	—	25.00	50.00	100.00

PIASTRE

SILVER, 22.5mm, 3.2 gm.

Y#	Date	Mintage	Fine	VF	XF
6	AH1300	—	30.00	60.00	120.00
	1301	—	30.00	60.00	120.00
	1302	—	30.00	60.00	120.00
	1303	—	30.00	60.00	120.00
	1304	—	30.00	60.00	120.00
	1305	—	30.00	60.00	120.00
	1306	—	30.00	60.00	120.00
	1307	—	30.00	60.00	120.00
	1308	—	30.00	60.00	120.00

2 PIASTRES

SILVER, 27mm, 6.4 gm.

Y#	Date	Mintage	Fine	VF	XF
7	AH1300	—	50.00	100.00	200.00
	1301	—	50.00	100.00	200.00
	1302	—	50.00	100.00	200.00
	1303	—	50.00	100.00	200.00
	1304	—	50.00	100.00	200.00
	1305	—	50.00	100.00	200.00
	1306	—	50.00	100.00	200.00
	1307	—	50.00	100.00	200.00
	1308	—	50.00	100.00	200.00

4 PIASTRES

SILVER, 31mm, 12.8 gm.

Y#	Date	Mintage	Fine	VF	XF
8	AH1300	—	50.00	100.00	200.00
	1301	—	50.00	100.00	200.00
	1302	—	50.00	100.00	200.00
	1303	—	50.00	100.00	200.00
	1304	—	50.00	100.00	200.00
	1305	—	50.00	100.00	200.00
	1306	—	50.00	100.00	200.00
	1307	—	50.00	100.00	200.00
	1308	—	50.00	100.00	200.00

25 PIASTRES

4.9200 gm., .900 GOLD, 20mm, .1424 oz AGW

Y#	Date	Mintage	Fine	VF	XF
9	AH1300	—	95.00	125.00	250.00
	1302	—	95.00	125.00	250.00

25 PIASTRES-15 FRANCS

4.8730 gm., .900 gold, .1410 oz AGW

Y#	Date	Mintage	Fine	VF	XF
10	AH1304	.080	95.00	125.00	200.00
	1308	Inc. Ab.	95.00	125.00	200.00

Modified design

Y#	Date	Mintage	Fine	VF	XF
10.1	AH1307A	.052	95.00	125.00	200.00
	1308A	.120	95.00	125.00	200.00

50 PIASTRES

4.8730 gm., .900 GOLD, .1410 oz AGW

Y#	Date	Mintage	Fine	VF	XF
A10	AH1304	—	100.00	150.00	250.00

100 PIASTRES

9.7460 gm., .900 GOLD, .2820 oz AGW

Y#	Date	Mintage	Fine	VF	XF
B10	AH1303	—	200.00	300.00	400.00

TUNISIA

DECIMAL SYSTEM

100 Centimes = 1 Franc

NOTE: The following coins all bear French inscriptions on one side, Arabic on the other, and usually have both AH and AD dates. They are struck in the name of the Tunisian Bey.

CENTIME

BRONZE
Ali

Y#	Date	Year	Mintage	VF	XF	Unc
11	AH1308	1891A	.500	3.00	6.00	14.00

2 CENTIMES

BRONZE
Ali

Y#	Date	Year	Mintage	VF	XF	Unc
12	AH1308	1891A	1.000	2.00	4.00	8.00

5 CENTIMES

BRONZE
Ali

Y#	Date	Year	Mintage	VF	XF	Unc
13	AH1308	1891A	4.300	2.00	7.00	15.00
	1308	1891A	—	—	Proof	35.00
	1309	1892A	1.192	2.00	7.00	15.00
	1310	1893A	1.008	2.00	7.00	15.00

Muhammad al-Hadi

Y#	Date	Year	Mintage	VF	XF	Unc
20	AH1321	1903A	.500	4.00	10.00	20.00
	1322	1904A	1.000	4.00	10.00	20.00

Muhammad al-Nasir

Y#	Date	Year	Mintage	VF	XF	Unc
27	AH1325	1907A	1.000	2.00	4.00	10.00
	1326	1908A	1.000	2.00	4.00	10.00
	1330	1912A	1.000	2.00	4.00	10.00
	1332	1914A	1.000	2.00	4.00	10.00
	1334	1916A	2.000	2.00	4.00	10.00
	1336	1917A	2.021	2.00	4.00	10.00

NICKEL BRONZE, 19mm.
Mohammed al-Nasir

Y#	Date	Year	Mintage	VF	XF	Unc
34	AH1337	1918(a)	1.549	.50	2.00	5.00
	1337	1919(a)	4.451	.50	2.00	5.00
	1338/7	1920(a)	2.206	—	—	—
	1338	1920(a)	Inc. Ab.	.50	2.00	5.00
	1339	1920(a)	Inc. Ab.	.50	2.00	5.00

Reduced Size (17mm)

Y#	Date	Year	Mintage	VF	XF	Unc
34a	AH1339	1920(a)	1.794	1.00	5.00	15.00

Ahmad

Y#	Date	Year	Mintage	VF	XF	Unc
46	AH1350	1931(a)	2.000	.50	1.00	4.00
	1352	1933(a)	1.000	.50	1.00	4.00
	1357	1938(a)	1.200	.50	1.00	5.00

10 CENTIMES

BRONZE
Ali

Y#	Date	Year	Mintage	VF	XF	Unc
14	AH1308	1891A	2.600	1.00	5.00	15.00
	1309	1892A	1.374	1.00	5.00	15.00
	1310	1893A	.026	8.00	15.00	30.00

Muhammad al-Hadi

Y#	Date	Year	Mintage	VF	XF	Unc
21	AH1321	1903A	.250	2.00	8.00	20.00
	1322	1904A	.500	2.00	8.00	20.00

Muhammad al-Nasir

Y#	Date	Year	Mintage	VF	XF	Unc
28	AH1325	1907A	.500	1.00	4.00	10.00
	1326	1908A	.500	1.00	4.00	10.00
	1329	1911A	.500	1.00	4.00	10.00
	1330	1912A	.500	1.00	4.00	10.00
	1332	1914A	.500	1.00	4.00	10.00
	1334	1916A	1.000	1.00	4.00	10.00
	1336	1917A	1.050	1.00	4.00	10.00

NICKEL-BRONZE
Muhammed al-Nasir

Y#	Date	Year	Mintage	VF	XF	Unc
35	AH1337	1918(a)	1.288	.30	.75	2.00
	1337	1919(a)	2.712	.30	.75	2.00
	1338	1920(a)	3.000	.30	.75	2.00

Muhammad al-Habib

Y#	Date	Year	Mintage	VF	XF	Unc
40	AH1345	1926(a)	1.000	.45	1.00	8.00

Ahmad

Y#	Date	Year	Mintage	VF	XF	Unc
47	AH1350	1931(a)	.750	.50	1.00	5.00
	1352	1933(a)	1.000	.50	1.00	5.00
	1357	1938(a)	1.200	.50	1.00	5.00

ZINC
Ahmad

Y#	Date	Year	Mintage	VF	XF	Unc
58	AH1360	1941(a)	5.000	.25	.75	3.00
	1361	1942(a)	10.000	.25	.75	3.00

Muhammad al Amin

Y#	Date	Year	Mintage	VF	XF	Unc
60	AH1364	1945(a)	10.000	20.00	40.00	75.00

NOTE: Most were probably melted.

20 CENTIMES

ZINC
Ahmad

Y#	Date	Year	Mintage	VF	XF	Unc
59	AH1361	1942(a)	5.000	1.50	2.50	10.00

Muhammad al-Amin

Y#	Date	Year	Mintage	VF	XF	Unc
61	AH1364	1945(a)	5.205	20.00	35.00	75.00

NOTE: A large quantity was remelted.

25 CENTIMES

NICKEL-BRONZE
Muhammad al-Nasir

Y#	Date	Year	Mintage	VF	XF	Unc
36	AH1337	1918(a)	—	.60	1.25	4.00
	1337	1919(a)	2.000	.30	1.00	4.00
	1338	1920(a)	2.000	.30	1.00	4.00

Ahmad

Y#	Date	Year	Mintage	VF	XF	Unc
48	AH1350	1931(a)	.300	.75	1.50	2.25
	1352	1933(a)	.400	.75	1.50	2.25
	1357	1938(a)	.480	.60	1.35	2.00

50 CENTIMES

2.5000 gm., .835 SILVER, .0671 oz ASW
Ali

NOTE: On this and all subsequent silver and gold issues, limited numbers were struck annually for presentation purposes, while circulation issues were only produced from time to time. The presentation pieces are listed as "NCLT" and not priced. They were not intended for circulation, but many did find their way into circulation. Similar strikes in years for which regular issues were produced cannot be distinguished from the ordinary strikes and are therefore not listed separately.

Y#	Date	Year	Mintage	VF	XF	Unc
15	AH1308	1891A	1.470	BV	5.00	25.00
	1309	1892A	1,000	—	—	—
	1310	1893A	1,000	—	—	—
	1311	1894A	1,000	—	—	—
	1313	1895A	1,000	—	—	—
	1314	1896A	1,000	—	—	—
	1315	1897A	1,000	—	—	—
	1316	1898A	1,000	—	—	—
	1317	1899A	1,000	—	—	—
	1318	1900A	1,000	—	—	—
	1319	1901A	1,000	—	—	—
	1320	1902A	1,000	—	—	—

Muhammad al-Hadi

Y#	Date	Year	Mintage	VF	XF	Unc
22	AH1321	1903A	1,003	—	—	—
	1322	1904A	1,003	—	—	—
	1323	1905A	1,003	—	—	—
	1324	1906A	1,003	—	—	—

Muhammad al-Nasir

Y#	Date	Year	Mintage	VF	XF	Unc
29	AH1325	1907A	.201	1.50	3.00	12.00
	1326	1908A	2,006	—	—	—
	1327	1909A	1,003	—	—	—

Y#	Date	Year	Mintage	VF	XF	Unc
29	1328	1910A	1,003	—	—	—
	1329	1911A	1,003	—	—	—
	1330	1912A	.201	1.25	3.00	—
	1331	1912A	—Reported, not confirmed			
	1331	1913A	1,003	—	—	—
	1332	1914A	.201	1.25	3.00	12.00
	1334	1915A	.707	1.00	2.00	8.00
	1334	1916A	3,614	1.00	2.00	8.00
	1335	1916A	Inc. Ab.	1.00	2.00	8.00
	1335	1917A	2.139	1.00	2.00	8.00
	1336	1917A	Inc. Ab.	1.00	2.00	8.00
	1337	1918A	1,003	—	—	—
	1338	1919A	1,003	—	—	—
	1339	1920A	1,003	—	—	—
	1340	1921A	1,003	—	—	—
	Muhammad al-Habib					
41	AH1341	1922A	1,003	—	—	—
	1342	1923A	2,009	—	—	—
	1343	1924A	1,003	—	—	—
	1344	1925A	1,003	—	—	—
	1345	1926A	1,003	—	—	—
	1346	1927A	1,003	—	—	—
	1347	1928A	1,003	—	—	—

ALUMINUM-BRONZE

Y#	Date	Year	Mintage	VF	XF	Unc
37	AH1340	1921(a)	4.000	.25	.60	2.00
	1345	1926(a)	1.000	.40	1.00	2.00
	1352	1933(a)	.500	.60	1.50	2.00
	1360	1941(a)	4.646	.25	.50	2.00
	1364	1945(a)	11.180	.25	.50	2.00

FRANC

5.0000 gm., .835 SILVER, .1342 oz ASW
Ali

Y#	Date	Year	Mintage	VF	XF	Unc
16	AH1308	1891A	1.575	5.00	10.00	20.00
	1309	1892A	1.575	5.00	10.00	20.00
	1310	1893A	700 pcs.	—	—	—
	1311	1894A	700 pcs.	—	—	—
	1313	1895A	700 pcs.	—	—	—
	1314	1896A	700 pcs.	—	—	—
	1315	1897A	700 pcs.	—	—	—
	1316	1898A	700 pcs.	—	—	—
	1317	1899A	700 pcs.	—	—	—
	1318	1900A	700 pcs.	—	—	—
	1319	1901A	700 pcs.	—	—	—
	1320	1902A	700 pcs.	—	—	—
	Muhammad al-Hadi					
23	AH1321	1903A	703 pcs.	—	—	—
	1322	1904A	.500	5.00	10.00	20.00
	1323	1905A	703 pcs.	—	—	—
	1324	1906A	703 pcs.	—	—	—

Muhammad al-Nasir

Y#	Date	Year	Mintage	VF	XF	Unc
30	AH1325	1907A	.301	5.00	8.00	12.00
	1326	1908A	.401	5.00	8.00	12.00
	1327	1909A	703 pcs.	—	—	—
	1328	1910A	703 pcs.	—	—	—
	1329	1911A	1.051	5.00	7.00	12.00
	1330	1912A	.501	5.00	8.00	12.00
	1331	1912A	—	5.00	9.00	12.00
	1331	1913A	703 pcs.	—	—	12.00
	1332	1914A	.201	5.00	10.00	15.00
	1333	1914A	I.A.	5.00	9.50	15.00
	1334	1915A	1.060	4.50	7.00	14.00
	1334	1916A	3.270	4.50	6.00	12.00
	1335	1916A	Inc. Ab.	4.50	7.00	14.00
	1335	1917A	1.628	4.50	6.00	12.00
	1336	1918A	.804	4.50	7.00	14.00
	1337	1918A	Inc. Ab.	4.50	7.00	14.00

Y#	Date	Year	Mintage	VF	XF	Unc
	1338	1919A	703 pcs.	—	—	—
	1339	1920A	703 pcs.	—	—	—
	1340	1921A	703 pcs.	—	—	—
	Muhammad al-Habib					
42	AH1341	1922A	703 pcs.	—	—	—
	1342	1923A	1,409	—	—	—
	1343	1924A	703 pcs.	—	—	—
	1344	1925A	703 pcs.	—	—	—
	1345	1926A	703 pcs.	—	—	—
	1346	1927A	703 pcs.	—	—	—
	1347	1928A	703 pcs.	—	—	—

ALUMINUM-BRONZE

Y#	Date	Year	Mintage	VF	XF	Unc
38	AH1340	1921(a)	5.000	.35	.70	3.00
	1344	1926(a)	1.000	.40	1.25	3.00
	1345	1926(a)	1.000	.40	1.25	3.00
	1360	1941(a)	6.612	.35	.50	3.00
	1364	1945(a)	10.699	.35	.45	3.00

2 FRANCS

10.0000 gm., .835 SILVER, .2685 oz ASW
Ali

Y#	Date	Year	Mintage	VF	XF	Unc
17	AH1308	1891A	.595	8.00	15.00	30.00
	1309	1892A	.432	8.00	15.00	30.00
	1310	1893A	300 pcs.	—	—	—
	1311	1894A	300 pcs.	—	—	—
	1313	1895A	300 pcs.	—	—	—
	1314	1896A	300 pcs.	—	—	—
	1315	1897A	300 pcs.	—	—	—
	1316	1898A	300 pcs.	—	—	—
	1317	1899A	300 pcs.	—	—	—
	1318	1900A	300 pcs.	—	—	—
	1319	1901A	300 pcs.	—	—	—
	1320	1902A	300 pcs.	—	—	—
	Muhammad al-Hadi					
24	AH1321	1903A	303 pcs.	—	—	—
	1322	1904A	.150	8.50	15.00	30.00
	1323	1905A	303 pcs.	—	—	—
	1324	1906A	303 pcs.	—	—	—

Muhammad al-Nasir

Y#	Date	Year	Mintage	VF	XF	Unc
31	AH1325	1907A	306 Pcs.	—	—	—
	1326	1908A	.101	8.50	16.50	25.00
	1327	1909A	303 pcs.	—	—	—
	1328	1910A	303 pcs.	—	—	—
	1329	1911A	.475	8.50	15.00	25.00
	1330	1912A	.200	8.50	15.00	25.00
	1331	1912A	—Reported, not confirmed			
	1331	1913A	303 pcs.	—	—	—
	1332	1914A	.100	8.50	15.00	25.00
	1333	1914A	I.A.	8.50	15.00	25.00
	1334	1915A	.408	8.50	15.00	25.00
	1334	1916A	1.000	8.50	15.00	25.00
	1335	1916A	Inc. Ab.	8.50	15.00	25.00
	1336	1917A	303 pcs.	—	—	—
	1337	1918A	303 pcs.	—	—	—
	1338	1919A	303 pcs.	—	—	—
	1339	1920A	303 pcs.	—	—	—
	1340	1921A	303 pcs.	—	—	—
	Muhammad al-Habib					
43	AH1341	1922A	303 pcs.	—	—	—
	1342	1923A	690 pcs.	—	—	—
	1343	1924A	303 pcs.	—	—	—

Y#	Date	Year	Mintage	VF	XF	Unc
43	1344	1925A	303 pcs.	—	—	—
	1345	1926A	303 pcs.	—	—	—
	1346	1927A	303 pcs.	—	—	—
	1347	1928A	303 pcs.	—	—	—

ALUMINUM-BRONZE

Y#	Date	Year	Mintage	VF	XF	Unc
39	AH1340	1921(a)	1.500	.85	1.75	3.00
	1343	1924(a)	.500	1.50	7.50	10.00
	1345	1926(a)	.500	1.50	3.50	5.00
	1360	1941(a)	1.976	.60	1.35	3.00
	1364	1945(a)	6.464	.50	1.00	3.00

5 FRANCS

5.0000 gm., .680 SILVER, .1093 oz ASW
Ahmad

Y#	Date	Mintage	Fine	VF	XF
51	AH1353(a)	2.000	3.50	5.00	10.00
	1355(a)	2.000	3.50	5.00	10.00

Y#	Date	Year	Mintage	VF	XF	Unc
54	AH1358(a)	1939	1.600	3.50	5.00	10.00

ALUMINUM-BRONZE
Muhammad al-Amin

Y#	Date	Year	Mintage	VF	XF	Unc
62	AH1365(a)	1946	10.000	1.25	2.00	10.00

COPPER-NICKEL

Y#	Date	Year	Mintage	VF	XF	Unc
63	AH1373(a)	1954	18.000	.25	.50	1.00
	1376(a)	1957	4.000	.25	.50	1.00

10 FRANCS

3.2258 gm., .900 GOLD, .0933 oz AGW
Ali

Y#	Date	Year	Mintage	VF	XF	Unc
18	AH1308	1891A	.400	60.00	75.00	100.00
	1309	1892A	80 pcs.	—	—	—
	1310	1893A	80 pcs.	—	—	—
	1311	1894A	80 pcs.	—	—	—
	1313	1895A	80 pcs.	—	—	—
	1314	1896A	80 pcs.	—	—	—

Y#	Date	Year	Mintage	VF	XF	Unc
	1315	1897A	80 pcs.	—	—	—
	1316	1898A	80 pcs.	—	—	—
	1317	1899A	80 pcs.	—	—	—
	1318	1900A	80 pcs.	—	—	—
	1319	1901A	80 pcs.	—	—	—
	1320	1902A	80 pcs.	—	—	—
	Muhammad al-Hadi					
25	AH1321	1903A	83 pcs.	—	—	—
	1322	1904A	83 pcs.	—	—	—
	1323	1905A	83 pcs.	—	—	—
	1324	1906A	83 pcs.	—	—	—
	Muhammad al-Nasir					
32	AH1325	1907A	36 pcs.	—	—	—
	1326	1908A	166 pcs.	—	—	—
	1327	1909A	83 pcs.	—	—	—
	1328	1910A	83 pcs.	—	—	—
	1329	1911A	83 pcs.	—	—	—
	1330	1912A	83 pcs.	—	—	—
	1331	1913A	83 pcs.	—	—	—
	1332	1914A	83 pcs.	—	—	—
	1334	1915A	83 pcs.	—	—	—
	1334	1916A	83 pcs.	—	—	—
	1336	1917A	83 pcs.	—	—	—
	1337	1918A	83 pcs.	—	—	—
	1338	1919A	83 pcs.	—	—	—
	1339	1920A	83 pcs.	—	—	—
	1340	1921A	83 pcs.	—	—	—
	Muhammad al-Habib Bey					
44	AH1341	1922A	83 pcs.	—	—	—
	1342	1923A	169 pcs.	—	—	—
	1343	1924A	83 pcs.	—	—	—
	1344	1925A	83 pcs.	—	—	—
	1345	1926A	83 pcs.	—	—	—
	1346	1927A	83 pcs.	—	—	—
	1347	1928A	83 pcs.	—	—	—

10.0000 gm., .680 SILVER, .2186 oz ASW
Ahmad

Y#	Date	Year	Mintage	VF	XF	Unc
49	AH1349	1930A	.060	30.00	45.00	75.00
	1350	1931A	1,103	—	—	—
	1351	1932A	.060	45.00	75.00	100.00
	1352	1933A	1,103	—	—	—
	1353	1934A	.030	30.00	45.00	75.00

Y#	Date	Mintage	Fine	VF	XF
52	AH1353(a)	1.501	6.75	8.50	20.00
	1354(a)	1,103	—	—	—
	1355(a)	2,006	—	—	—
	1356(a)	1,103	—	—	—

Y#	Date	Year	Mintage	VF	XF	Unc
55	AH1358	1939(a)	.501	6.75	8.50	15.00
	1359	1940a	—	—	—	—
	1360	1941a	1,163	—	—	—
	1361	1942(a)	1,103	—	—	—
	Muhammad al-Amin					
—	AH1363	1943	1,503	—	—	—
	1364	1944	2,206	—	—	—

NOTE: Similar pieces, such as Y55 but with large date replacing the denomination, were struck each year from 1945 to 1956 in silver in small quantities for presentation. They bear no denomination, and are properly classed as largesse medals. The pieces dated 1956 are of a different design. Likewise, Silver Medals Of 20 Franc size, such as Y56 were struck each year, 1945 to 1956, as presentation medals.

20 FRANCS

6.4516 gm., .900 GOLD, .1867 oz AGW
Ali

Y#	Date	Year	Mintage	VF	XF	Unc
19	AH1308	1891A	.400	125.00	140.00	175.00
	1309	1892A	.837	125.00	140.00	175.00
	1310	1892A	Inc. Ab.	125.00	140.00	175.00
	1310	1893A	.035	125.00	140.00	175.00
	1311	1894A	20 pcs.	—	—	—
	1313	1895A	20 pcs.	—	—	—
	1314	1896A	20 pcs.	—	—	—
	1315	1897A	.164	125.00	140.00	175.00
	1316	1898A	.150	125.00	140.00	175.00
	1316	1899A	.150	125.00	140.00	175.00
	1318	1900A	.150	125.00	140.00	175.00
	1319	1901A	.150	125.00	140.00	175.00
	1320	1902A	20 pcs.	—	—	—

Y#	Date	Year	Mintage	VF	XF	Unc
	Muhammad al-Hadi					
26	AH1321	1903A	.300	125.00	140.00	175.00
	1321	1904A	.600	125.00	140.00	175.00
	1322	1904A	Inc. Ab.	125.00	140.00	175.00
	1323	1905A	23 pcs.	—	—	—
	1324	1906A	23 pcs.	—	—	—
	Muhammad al-Nasir					
33	AH1325	1907A	26 pcs.	—	—	—
	1326	1908A	46 pcs.	—	—	—
	1327	1909A	23 pcs.	—	—	—
	1328	1910A	23 pcs.	—	—	—
	1329	1911A	23 pcs.	—	—	—
	1330	1912A	23 pcs.	—	—	—
	1331	1913A	23 pcs.	—	—	—
	1332	1914A	23 pcs.	—	—	—
	1334	1915A	23 pcs.	—	—	—
	1334	1916A	23 pcs.	—	—	—
	1336	1917A	23 pcs.	—	—	—
	1337	1918A	23 pcs.	—	—	—
	1338	1919A	23 pcs.	—	—	—
	1339	1920A	23 pcs.	—	—	—
	1340	1921A	23 pcs.	—	—	—
	Muhammad al-Habib					
45	AH1341	1922A	23 pcs.	—	—	—
	1342	1923A	49 pcs.	—	—	—
	1343	1924A	23 pcs.	—	—	—
	1344	1925A	23 pcs.	—	—	—
	1345	1926A	23 pcs.	—	—	—
	1346	1927A	23 pcs.	—	—	—
	1347	1928A	23 pcs.	—	—	—

20.0000 gm., .680 SILVER, .4372 oz ASW
Ahmad

Y#	Date	Year	Mintage	VF	XF	Unc
50	AH1349	1930(a)	.020	50.00	70.00	125.00
	1350	1931(a)	53 pcs.	—	—	—
	1351	1932(a)	.020	55.00	82.50	130.00
	1352	1933(a)	53 pcs.	—	—	—
	1353	1934(a)	9,500	47.50	65.00	125.00

Y#	Date	Mintage	VF	XF	Unc
53	AH1353(a)	1.250	13.00	18.00	35.00
	1354(a)	53 pcs.	—	—	—
	1355(a)	106 pcs.	—	—	—
	1356(a)	53 pcs.	—	—	—

Y#	Date	Year	Mintage	VF	XF	Unc
56	AH1358	1939(a)	.100	25.00	50.00	100.00
	1359	1940(a)	—	—	—	—
	1360	1941(a)	53 pcs.	—	—	—
	1361	1942(a)	53 pcs.	—	—	—
	Muhammad al-Amin					
—	AH1363	1943	103 pcs.	—	—	—
	1364	1944	106 pcs.	—	—	—

NOTE: For similar pieces with large date in place of denomination, see note after Y55 (10 Francs).

COPPER-NICKEL

Y#	Date	Year	Mintage	VF	XF	Unc
64	AH1370	1950(a)	10.000	.25	.40	1.00
	1376	1957(a)	4.000	.25	.40	1.00

50 FRANCS

COPPER-NICKEL
Muhammad al-Amin

Y#	Date	Year	Mintage	VF	XF	Unc
65	AH1370	1950(a)	5.000	.30	.50	1.00
	1376	1957(a)	.600	.30	.50	1.00

100 FRANCS

6.5500 gm., .900 GOLD, .1895 oz AGW
Ahmad

Y#	Date	Year	Mintage	VF	XF	Unc
57	AH1349	1930(a)	3,000	125.00	150.00	200.00
	1350	1931(a)	33 pcs.	—	—	—
	1351	1932(a)	3,000	125.00	150.00	200.00
	1352	1933(a)	33 pcs.	—	—	—
	1353	1934(a)	3,133	125.00	150.00	200.00
	1354	1935(a)	—	125.00	150.00	200.00
	1355	1936(a)	33 pcs.	—	—	—
	1356	1937(a)	33 pcs.	—	—	—

NOTE: From 1938-1956, similar pieces with large date in place of denomination, were struck each year for presentation purposes. They are, properly speaking, medals and bear no indication of value.

COPPER-NICKEL
Muhammad al-Amin

Y#	Date	Year	Mintage	VF	XF	Unc
66	AH1370	1950(a)	8.000	.50	1.00	5.00
	1376	1957(a)	1.000	.50	1.00	5.00

REPUBLIC

1000 Millim = 1 Dinar

NOTE: Nos. 67-73 were struck in Czechoslovakia, mint is unknown. Nos. 74-75 were struck at Paris and have the usual privy marks of that mint. Nos. 67-73 have frozen dates and are being restruck as needed.

MILLIM

ALUMINUM

Y#	Date	Mintage	VF	XF	Unc
67	1960	—	.05	.10	.25

2 MILLIM

ALUMINUM

Y#	Date	Mintage	VF	XF	Unc
68	1960	—	.05	.10	.25

5 MILLIM

ALUMINUM

Y#	Date	Mintage	VF	XF	Unc
69	1960	—	.05	.10	.25

10 MILLIM

BRASS

Y#	Date	Year	Mintage	VF	XF	Unc
70	AH1380	1960	—	.05	.10	.30

20 MILLIM

BRASS

Y#	Date	Year	Mintage	VF	XF	Unc
71	AH1380	1960	—	.30	.40	.50

50 MILLIM

BRASS

Y#	Date	Year	Mintage	VF	XF	Unc
72	AH1380	1960	—	.10	.35	.75

100 MILLIM

BRASS

Y#	Date	Year	Mintage	VF	XF	Unc
73	AH1380	1960	—	.25	.50	1.00

1/2 DINAR

NICKEL

Y#	Date	Mintage	VF	XF	Unc
74	1968(a)	.500	1.50	3.50	5.00

COPPER-NICKEL
F.A.O. Issue

Y#	Date	Mintage	VF	XF	Unc
77	1976	—	3.00	5.00	10.00

DINAR

21.1840 gm., .925 SILVER, .6300 oz ASW
Hannibal

H#	Date	Mintage	XF	Unc	Proof
8	1969FM	.035	—	—	25.00
	1969 NI	5,000	—	—	150.00

Masinissa
Obv: Similar to H#8.

H#	Date	Mintage	XF	Unc	Proof
9	1969FM	.035	—	—	25.00
	1969 NI	5,000	—	—	150.00

Jugurtha
Obv: Similar to H#8.

H#	Date	Mintage	XF	Unc	Proof
10	1969FM	.035	—	—	25.00
	1969 NI	5,000	—	—	150.00

Virgil
Obv: Similar to H#8.

H#	Date	Mintage	XF	Unc	Proof
11	1969FM	.035	—	—	25.00
	1969 NI	5,000	—	—	150.00

St. Augustine
Obv: Similar to H#8.

H#	Date	Mintage	XF	Unc	Proof
12	1969FM	.035	—	—	25.00
	1969 NI	5,000	—	—	150.00

Phoenician Ship
Obv: Similar to H#8.

H#	Date	Mintage	XF	Unc	Proof
13	1969FM	.035	—	—	25.00
	1969 NI	5,000	—	—	150.00

Neptune
Obv: Similar to H#8.

H#	Date	Mintage	XF	Unc	Proof
14	1969FM	.035	—	—	25.00
	1969 NI	5,000	—	—	150.00

Venus
Obv: Similar to H#8.

H#	Date	Mintage	XF	Unc	Proof
15	1969FM	.035	—	—	25.00
	1969 NI	5,000	—	—	150.00

Thysdrus-El Djem
Obv: Similar to H#8.

H#	Date	Mintage	XF	Unc	Proof
16	1969FM	.035	—	—	25.00
	1969 NI	5,000	—	—	150.00

Sbeitla-Sufetula
Obv: Similar to H#8.

H#	Date	Mintage	XF	Unc	Proof
17	1969FM	.035	—	—	25.00
	1969 NI	5,000	—	—	150.00

.680 SILVER
F.A.O. Issue

Y#	Date	Mintage	VF	XF	Unc
75	1970(a)	.100	2.50	5.00	10.00
	1970(a)	1,250	—	Proof	—

COPPER-NICKEL
F.A.O. Issue

Y#	Date	Mintage	VF	XF	Unc
78	1976	—	3.00	5.00	10.00

2 DINARS

3.8000 gm., .900 GOLD, .1099 oz AGW
Habib Bourguiba

Fr#	Date	Mintage	XF	Unc	Proof
5	1967	7,259	—	—	80.00

5 DINARS

9.5000 gm., .900 GOLD, .2749 oz AGW
Habib Bourguiba

Fr#	Date	Mintage	XF	Unc	Proof
4	1967	7,259	—	—	185.00

24.0000 gm., .680 SILVER, .5247 oz ASW
XX Anniversary of Independence

Y#	Date	Mintage	VF	XF	Unc
76	1976	.201	15.00	20.00	45.00
	1976	—	—	Proof	55.00

10 DINARS

19.0000 gm., .900 GOLD, .5498 oz AGW
Habib Bourguiba

Fr#	Date	Mintage	XF	Unc	Proof
3	1967	4,480	—	—	365.00

20 DINARS

38.0000 gm., .900 GOLD, 1.0996 oz AGW
Habib Bourguiba

Fr#	Date	Mintage	XF	Unc	Proof
2	1967	3,536	—	—	720.00

40 DINARS

76.0000 gm., .900 GOLD, 2.1991 oz AGW
Habib Bourguiba

Fr#	Date	Mintage	XF	Unc	Proof
1	1967	3,031	—	—	1450.

NCLT ISSUES

ESSAIS (E)

Standard metals unless otherwise noted

Y#	Date	Mintage	Identification	Issue Price	Mkt Val.
E34	1918(A)	—	5 Centimes	—	75.00
E34	1920(A)	—	5 Centimes	—	—
E35	1918(A)	—	10 Centimes	—	80.00
E36	1918(A)	—	25 Centimes	—	85.00
E37	1921 A	—	50 Centimes	—	90.00
E38	1921 A	—	Franc	—	95.00

Y#	Date	Mintage	Identification	Issue Price	Mkt Val.
E39a	1921 A	—	Franc, Aluminum	—	100.00
E42a	1928 A	—	Franc, Nickel-Bronze	—	75.00
E43a	1928A	—	2 Francs, Silver/Bronze	—	80.00
E49	1930(a)	—	10 Francs	—	80.00
E50	1930(a)	—	20 Francs	—	90.00
E57	1930(a)	—	100 Francs	—	100.00

NOTE: E49, 50 and 57 exist uniface.

Y#	Date	Mintage	Identification	Issue Price	Mkt Val.
E46	1931(a)	—	5 Centimes	—	65.00
E47	1931(a)	—	10 Centimes	—	70.00
E48	1931(a)	—	25 Centimes	—	75.00
E51	AH1353(a)	—	5 Francs	—	80.00
—	AH1353(a)	—	5 Francs	—	80.00
E49	AH1353(a)	—	10 Francs	—	90.00
E50	AH1353(a)	—	20 Francs	—	100.00
—	1938(a)	—	100 Francs, Gilt Bronze	—	100.00
—	1938(a)	—	100 Francs, Gold	—	—

NOTE: Refer to 100 Francs Y#57 on above.

Y#	Date	Mintage	Identification	Issue Price	Mkt Val.
E54	1939(a)	—	5 Francs	—	50.00
E55	1939(a)	—	10 Francs	—	55.00
E56	1939(a)	—	20 Francs	—	60.00
E59	1942(a)	—	20 Centimes	—	40.00
E60	1945(a)	1,100	10 Centimes	—	25.00
E61	1945(a)	1,100	20 Centimes	—	28.50
E62	1946(a)	1,100	5 Francs	—	30.00
E64	1950(a)	1,100	20 Francs	—	18.50
E65	1950(a)	1,100	50 Francs	—	21.50
E66	1950(a)	1,100	100 Francs	—	25.00
E63	1954(a)	1,100	5 Francs	—	16.50
E74	1968	—	1/2 Dinar	—	21.50
E75	1970	—	1 Dinar	—	30.00

PIEFORTS (P)

PIEFORTS with ESSAI (PE)

(Double Thickness)

Standard metals unless otherwise noted

PE60	1945(a)	104	10 Centimes	—	75.00
PE61	1945(a)	104	20 Centimes	—	80.00
PE37	1945(a)	104	50 Centimes	—	85.00
PE38	1945(a)	104	1 Franc	—	90.00

PE39	1945(a)	104	2 Francs	—	95.00
PE62	1946(a)	104	5 Francs	—	100.00
PE64	1950(a)	104	20 Francs	—	75.00
PE65	1950(a)	104	50 Francs	—	80.00
PE66	1950(a)	104	100 Francs	—	85.00
PE63	1954(a)	104	5 Francs	—	70.00
PE74	1968(a)	500	1/2 Dinar	—	30.00

PROOF SETS

STANDARD METALS

KM#	Date	Mintage	Identification	Issue Price	Mkt. Val.
101	1864(AH1281) (5)		C181-185	—	4200.
102	1967(5)	3,031	Fr#1-5	—	2800.
103	1969FM(10)	35,202	H8-17	77.00	250.00
	1969NI(10)	5,000	H8-17	—	1500.

TURKEY

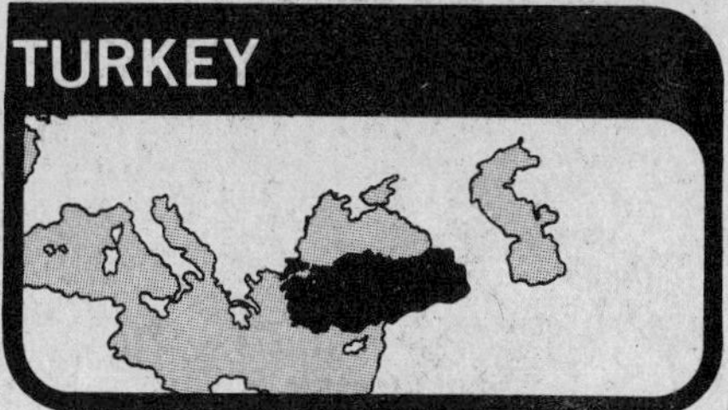

The Republic of Turkey, a parliamentary democracy of the Near East located partially in Europe and partially in Asia between the Black and the Mediterranean seas, has an area of 296,000 sq. mi. (766,640 sq. km.) and a population of 40 million. Capital: Ankara. Turkey exports cotton, hazelnuts, and tobacco, and enjoys a virtual monopoly in meerschaum.

The Ottoman Turks, a tribe from Central Asia, first appeared in the early 13th century, and by the 17th century had established the Ottoman Empire which stretched from the Persian Gulf to the southern frontier of Poland, and from the Caspian Sea to the Algerian plateau. The defeat of the Turkish navy by the Holy League in 1571, and of the Turkish forces besieging Vienna in 1683, began the steady decline of the Ottoman Empire which, accelerated by the rise of nationalism, contracted its European border, and by the end of World War I deprived it of its Arab lands. The present Turkish boundaries were largely fixed by the Treaty of Lausanne in 1923. The sultanate and caliphate, the political and spiritual ruling institutions of the old empire, were separated and the sultanate abolished in 1922. On Oct. 29, 1923, Turkey formally became a republic.

RULERS

Abdul Hamid I, AH1187-1203/ AD1774-1789
Selim III, AH1203-1222/ AD1789-1807
Mustafa IV, AH1222-1223/ AD1807-1808
Mahmud II, AH1223-1255 AD1808-1839
Abdulmejid, AH1255-1277/ AD1839-1861
Abdulaziz, AH1277-1293/ AD1861-1876
Murad V, AH1293/AD1876
Abdulhamid II, AH1293-1327/ AD1876-1909
Muhammad V, AH1327-1336/ AD1909-1918
Muhammad VI, AH1336-1341/ AD1918-1923
Republic, Since AH1341/AD1923

MINT

قسطنطنية

ISTANBUL (CONSTANTINOPLE)

NOTE: A number of special issues state that they were struck in other cities, including Bursa, Edirne, Kosova, Manastir, and Selanik, but these were actually struck at Istanbul, usually on the occasion of a Sultan's visit to that city.

MONETARY SYSTEM

3 Aspers (Akce) = 1 Para
40 Para = 1 Piastre (Kurus)
100 Piastres = 1 Turkish Pound (Lira)

This system has remained essentially unchanged since its introduction by Suleyman II in 1688, except that the Asper and Para have long since ceased to be coined. The Piastre, established as a crown-sized silver coin approximately equal to the French Ecu of Louis XIV, has shrunk to a tiny copper coin, worth about 1/15 of a U.S. Cent. Since the establishment of the Republic in 1923, the Turkish terms, Kurus and Lira, have replaced the European names Piastres and Turkish Pounds.

EMPIRE ISSUES

The silver currency of the reign of Mahmud II is characterized by frequent change of standard, so that the Piastre (Kurus), which began with 5.90 gr. of pure silver, had dropped to only 0.56 gr. in the lower denominations (token currency), and 0.94 gr. in the higher (actual currency). From time to time, the fineness, diameter, weight and type of the coins were changed, with the result that it is difficult, and not very meaningful, to attempt to trace individual denominations through the 32 years of his reign. For that reason, following Craig and others, the coins are grouped by standards of weight, fineness, or size. Changes in fineness, weight, and size are regularly indicated, as are distinguishing features whenever necessary for the proper indentification of coins. The various denominations have special names in Turkish, which are usually but not always expressions of multiples of the Para or Kurus (Piastre). These are as follows:

3 Akce (Asper) = 1 Para
Beslik (Besparalik) = 5 Para
Onluk = 10 Para
Yirmilik = 20 Para
Zolta = 30 Para
Kurus (Piastre) = 40 Para
Altmislik = 60 Para = 1 1/2 Piastres

Silver Coinage

Ikilik = 80 Para = 2 Piastres
Yuzluk = 100 Para = 2 1/2 Piastres
Ucluk = 120 Para = 3 Piastres
Beslik = 200 Para = 5 Piastres
Altilik = 240 Para = 6 Piastres

For sake of simplicity, all denominations, except the Asper, are given in terms of their equivalent in Para or Piastres.

NOTE: The tolerance on Mahmud's silver coinage was considerable, particularly on the smaller denominations; the weights given are approximate.

FIRST SERIES

0.465 SILVER, Yrs. 1-2

AKCE

0.10-0.12 gm., 9mm

C#	Date	Year	Mintage	VG	Fine	VF
171	AH1223	1	—	15.00	25.00	—
		2	—	15.00	25.00	—

PARA

0.32 gm., 14mm

C#	Date	Year	Mintage	VG	Fine	VF
172	AH1223	1	—	7.00	10.00	15.00
		2	—	7.00	10.00	15.00

5 PARA

1.5-1.6 gm., 19mm

C#	Date	Year	Mintage	VG	Fine	VF
173	AH1223	1	—	15.00	25.00	35.00
		2	—	15.00	25.00	35.00

10 PARA

2.8-3.1 gm., 23mm

C#	Date	Year	Mintage	VG	Fine	VF
174	AH1223	1*	—	11.50	17.50	22.50
		2	—	10.00	15.00	20.00

***NOTE:** Two obverse varieties exist.

PIASTRE

12-13 gm., 36mm

C#	Date	Year	Mintage	VG	Fine	VF
176	AH1223	1	—	100.00	150.00	250.00
		2	—	100.00	150.00	250.00

NOTE: Patterns were issued in similar style in denominations of 20, 30, 60, 80 and 100 Para.

SECOND SERIES

0.465 SILVER, Yrs. 2-14

AKCE = ASPER

0.10-0.12 gm., 11mm

C#	Date	Year	Mintage	VG	Fine	VF
171a	AH1223	5	—	3.00	4.50	7.50
		12	—	3.00	4.50	7.50

PARA

0.18-0.26 gm., 14mm

C#	Date	Year	Mintage	VG	Fine	VF
172a	AH1223	3	—	1.00	2.00	3.00
		4	—	1.00	2.00	3.00
		5	—	1.00	2.00	3.00
		6	—	1.00	2.00	3.00
		7	—	1.00	2.00	3.00
		8	—	1.00	2.00	3.00
		9	—	1.00	2.00	3.00
		10	—	1.00	2.00	3.00
		11	—	1.00	2.00	3.00
		12	—	1.00	2.00	3.00
		13	—	1.00	2.00	3.00
		14	—	1.00	2.00	3.00

5 PARA

1.01-1.2 gm., 18mm

C#	Date	Year	Mintage	VG	Fine	VF
173a	AH1223	3	—	10.00	15.00	25.00
		4	—	2.50	4.50	6.00
		5	—	2.50	4.50	6.00
		6	—	5.00	10.00	20.00
		7	—	5.00	10.00	20.00
		8	—	5.00	10.00	20.00
		9	—	5.00	10.00	20.00
		10	—	5.00	10.00	20.00
		11	—	5.00	10.00	20.00
		12	—	5.00	10.00	20.00
		13	—	5.00	10.00	20.00
		14	—	5.00	10.00	20.00

10 PARA

2.1-2.5 gm., 22mm

C#	Date	Year	Mintage	VG	Fine	VF
174a	AH1223	3	—	2.00	4.50	10.00
		4	—	2.00	4.50	10.00
		5	—	2.00	4.50	10.00
		6	—	2.00	4.50	10.00
		7	—	2.00	4.50	10.00
		8	—	2.00	4.50	10.00
		9	—	2.00	4.50	10.00
		10	—	2.00	4.50	10.00
		11	—	2.00	4.50	10.00
		12	—	2.00	4.50	10.00
		13	—	2.00	4.50	10.00
		14	—	2.00	4.50	10.00

PIASTRE

9.6 gm., 32mm

C#	Date	Year	Mintage	VG	Fine	VF
176a	AH1223	3	—	11.50	18.00	23.50
		4	—	10.00	15.00	21.50
		5	—	11.50	18.00	20.00
		6	—	11.50	18.00	20.00
		7	—	11.50	18.00	20.00
		8	—	11.50	18.00	20.00
		9	—	11.50	18.00	20.00
		10	—	11.50	18.00	20.00
		11	—	11.50	18.00	20.00
		12	—	10.00	15.00	21.50
		13	—	11.50	18.00	20.00

THIRD SERIES

0.730 SILVER, Yrs. 3-11

PIASTRE

4.6-5.2 gm., 28mm

C#	Date	Year	Mintage	VG	Fine	VF
181	AH1223	3	—	60.00	100.00	150.00

100 PARA(2 1/2 PIASTRES)

12.5 gm., 34-37mm

C#	Date	Year	Mintage	VG	Fine	VF
183	AH1223	2	—Reported, Not Confirmed			
		3	—	35.00	45.00	60.00
		4	—	25.00	35.00	50.00
		5	—	25.00	35.00	50.00
		6	—	27.50	40.00	55.00
		7	—	25.00	35.00	50.00
		8	—	30.00	40.00	55.00
		9	—	35.00	40.00	60.00
		10	—	50.00	75.00	100.00
		11	—	100.00	200.00	400.00

5 PIASTRES

24-26 gm., 40-41mm

C#	Date	Year	Mintage	VG	Fine	VF
184	AH1223	3	—	35.00	45.00	55.00
		4	—	30.00	40.00	50.00
		5	—	30.00	40.00	50.00
		6	—	30.00	40.00	50.00
		7	—	30.00	40.00	50.00
		8	—	40.00	50.00	70.00
		9	—	40.00	50.00	70.00
		10	—	75.00	100.00	200.00
		11	—	100.00	200.00	400.00

FOURTH SERIES

0.465 SILVER, Yrs. 14-15

PARA

0.15 gm., 13mm

C#	Date	Year	Mintage	VG	Fine	VF
172b	AH1223	14	—	2.50	4.00	6.50
		15	—	2.50	4.00	6.50

5 PARA

0.85 gm., 18mm

C#	Date	Year	Mintage	VG	Fine	VF
173b	AH1223	14	—	10.00	20.00	35.00

NOTE: Yr. 13 is reported.

10 PARA

1.6-1.8 gm., 22mm

C#	Date	Year	Mintage	VG	Fine	VF
174b	AH1223	14	—	10.00	25.00	40.00
		15	—	12.50	30.00	45.00

PIASTRE

5.5 gm., 32mm

C#	Date	Year	Mintage	VG	Fine	VF
176b	AH1223	14	—	25.00	35.00	50.00
		15	—	30.00	40.00	60.00

2 PIASTRES

11.5-13.4 gm., 34.37mm

C#	Date	Year	Mintage	VG	Fine	VF
190	AH1223	14	—	20.00	35.00	75.00

C#	Date	Year	Mintage	VG	Fine	VF
190		15	—	25.00	40.00	80.00

NOTE: Some coins have stars above and below regnal year box.

FIFTH SERIES

0.730 SILVER, Yrs. 15-16
Reeded edge on all but Para

PARA

0.14-0.17 gm., 13mm

C#	Date	Year	Mintage	VG	Fine	VF
172c	AH1223	15	—	3.00	6.00	8.00
		16	—	3.00	6.00	8.00

5 PARA

0.8 gm., 17mm

C#	Date	Year	Mintage	VG	Fine	VF
186	AH1223	15	—	15.00	20.00	35.00
		16	—	15.00	20.00	35.00
		18	—	15.00	20.00	35.00

10 PARA

1.6 gm., 20-21mm

C#	Date	Year	Mintage	VG	Fine	VF
174c	AH1223	15	—	10.00	15.00	20.00
		16	—	10.00	15.00	20.00
		18	—	10.00	15.00	20.00

PIASTRE

6 gm., 32mm

C#	Date	Year	Mintage	VG	Fine	VF
176c	AH1223	15	—	15.00	25.00	35.00
		16	—	15.00	25.00	35.00

2 PIASTRES

12-13 gm., 37mm

C#	Date	Year	Mintage	VG	Fine	VF
190a	AH1223	15	—	17.50	27.50	35.00
		16	—	20.00	30.00	40.00

SIXTH SERIES

0.600 SILVER, Yrs. 16-21

PARA

0.15-0.2 gm., 12mm

C#	Date	Year	Mintage	VG	Fine	VF
172d	AH1223	17	—	2.50	4.25	6.00
		18	—	2.50	4.25	6.00
		19	—	2.50	4.25	6.00
		20	—	2.50	4.25	6.00
		21	—	2.50	4.25	6.00

30 PARA

3.0-3.4 gm., 27-28mm

C#	Date	Year	Mintage	VG	Fine	VF
192	AH1223	17	—	6.50	10.00	15.00
		18	—	6.50	10.00	15.00
		19	—	6.50	10.00	15.00
		20	—	6.50	10.00	15.00
		21	—	8.00	12.50	16.50

NOTE: This coin occurs frequently in high grade.

60 PARA

5.6-6.2 gm., 33-35mm

C#	Date	Year	Mintage	VG	Fine	VF
193	AH1223	16	—	10.00	13.50	18.00
		17	—	9.00	12.50	16.00
		18	—	9.00	12.50	16.00
		19	—	9.00	12.50	16.00
		20	—	9.00	12.50	16.00
		21	—	9.00	12.50	16.00

NOTE: This coin occurs frequently in high grade.

SEVENTH SERIES

0.833 SILVER, Yrs. 21-22
Wavy borders

NOTE: A Para was struck in this series, in low grade silver .460, in the year 22, but is not distinguishable from yr. 22 pieces of the eighthseries C#172e.

20 PARA

0.8 gm., 17-18mm

C#	Date	Year	Mintage	VG	Fine	VF
194	AH1223	21	—	4.00	6.00	9.00
		22	—	5.00	7.00	11.00

NOTE: This coin occurs frequently in high grade, also with open and closed rosettes on obverse and reverse.

PIASTRE

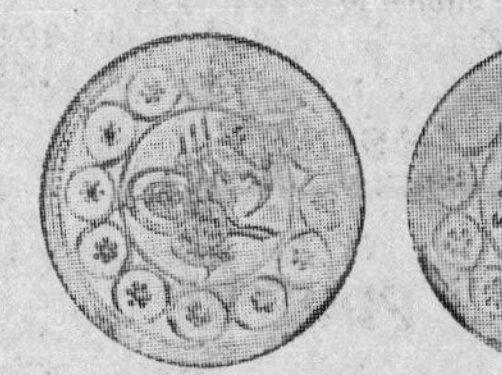

1.4-1.6 gm., 22mm

C#	Date	Year	Mintage	VG	Fine	VF
195	AH1223	21	—	5.00	6.50	11.00
		22	—	6.00	7.50	13.50

NOTE: This coin occurs frequently in high grade, also with open and closed rosettes on obverse and reverse

EIGHTH SERIES

0.220 SILVER, Yrs. 22-25

NOTE: Coins of the eighth series are readily distinguished from the ninth series, as they lack the large dot below the inner wreath that appears on the ninth series. In the eighth and ninth series, with the exception of the Para, all coins have the word "ADLI" (the Just) at right of the toughra, sometimes with vertical mark below. The Para Is distinguished only by date, however. Many coins are debased with a silver wash.

PARA

0.10 gm., 11mm

C#	Date	Year	Mintage	VG	Fine	VF
172e	AH1223	22	—	.65	1.60	2.50
		23	—	.65	1.60	2.50
		24	—	.65	1.60	2.50
		25	—	.90	2.00	3.50

10 PARA

0.8 gm., 17mm

C#	Date	Year	Mintage	VG	Fine	VF
197	AH1223	22	—	2.25	3.50	4.50
		23	—	2.75	3.75	5.00
		24	—	1.75	2.75	4.50
		25	—	2.25	3.50	5.00

20 PARA

1.4-1.8 gm., 21mm

C#	Date	Year	Mintage	VG	Fine	VF
198	AH1223	22	—	3.00	4.00	6.50
		23	—	2.00	3.00	5.00
		24	—	2.00	3.00	5.00
		25	—	2.00	3.50	5.00

PIASTRE

2.6-3.0 gm., 27-28mm

C#	Date	Year	Mintage	VG	Fine	VF
199	AH1223	22	—	2.75	4.50	6.25
		23	—	2.75	4.50	6.25
		24	—	2.75	4.50	6.25
		25	—	3.00	5.00	6.50

100 PARA (2 1/2 PIASTRES)

7.2-7.8 gm., 33mm

C#	Date	Year	Mintage	VG	Fine	VF
200	AH1223	22	—	4.75	7.50	11.00
		23	—	3.50	5.00	8.00
		24	—	3.50	5.00	8.00
		25	—	3.25	5.00	8.00

5 PIASTRES

15-16 gm., 39mm
Rev: Similar to 100 Para, C#200.

C#	Date	Year	Mintage	VG	Fine	VF
201	AH1223	22	—	4.25	6.50	12.50
		23	—	4.25	6.50	12.50
		24	—	4.25	6.50	12.50
		25	—	5.00	8.50	15.00

NINTH SERIES
0.170 SILVER, Yrs. 25-32

Large dot added beneath inner wreath on obverse and reverse except on 1 Para.

ACKE

0.04-0.07 gm.

C#	Date	Year	Mintage	VG	Fine	VF
171f	AH1223	25	—	4.00	6.00	10.00
		26	—	2.50	4.00	6.00
		27	—	2.50	4.00	6.00

PARA

0.08-0.15 gm., 9.5-12mm

C#	Date	Year	Mintage	VG	Fine	VF
172f	AH1223	26	—	1.00	1.50	2.75
		27	—	.75	1.25	2.00
		28	—	.75	1.25	2.00
		29	—	.75	1.25	2.00
		30	—	.75	1.25	2.00
		31	—	.75	1.25	2.00
		32	—	.75	1.25	2.00

10 PARA

0.5-0.75 gm., 17mm

C#	Date	Year	Mintage	VG	Fine	VF
197a	AH1223	25	—	2.00	3.00	5.00
		26	—	2.00	3.00	5.00
		27	—	2.00	3.00	5.00
		28	—	2.00	3.00	5.00
		29	—	2.00	3.00	5.00
		30	—	2.00	3.00	5.00
		31	—	2.00	3.00	5.00
		32	—	2.00	3.00	5.00

20 PARA

1.35-1.6 gm., 20-21mm

C#	Date	Year	Mintage	VG	Fine	VF
198a	AH1223	25	—	2.00	2.50	4.00
		26	—	2.00	2.50	4.00
		27	—	2.00	2.50	4.00
		28	—	2.00	2.50	4.00
		29	—	2.00	2.50	4.00
		30	—	2.00	2.50	4.00
		31	—	2.00	2.50	4.00
		32	—	2.00	2.50	4.00

NOTE: Years 26 and 31 are easily confused.

PIASTRE

2.6-3.0 gm., 27-28mm

C#	Date	Year	Mintage	VG	Fine	VF
199a	AH1223	25	—	3.50	5.00	8.00
		26	—	3.50	5.00	8.00

100 PARA(2 1/2 PIASTRES)

6.4-7.8 gm., 34-35mm

C#	Date	Year	Mintage	VG	Fine	VF
200a	AH1223	25	—	3.00	4.50	10.00
		26	—	3.00	4.50	10.00

5 PIASTRES

13-16 gm., 38-39mm
Obv: Similar to C#201.

C#	Date	Year	Mintage	VG	Fine	VF
201a	AH1223	25	—	4.00	7.00	12.50
		26	—	4.00	7.00	12.50

TENTH SERIES
0.435 SILVER, Yrs. 26-32

1-1/2 PIASTRE

2.6-3.0 gm., 28mm

C#	Date	Year	Mintage	VG	Fine	VF
206	AH1223	26	—	4.50	6.00	8.50
		27	—	3.50	5.00	7.00
		28	—	3.50	5.00	7.00
		29	—	3.50	5.00	7.00
		30	—	3.50	5.00	7.00
		31	—	3.50	5.00	7.00
		32	—	3.50	5.00	7.00

3 PIASTRES

5.6-6.2 gm., 33mm

C#	Date	Year	Mintage	VG	Fine	VF
207	AH1223	26	—	4.50	6.00	9.00
		27	—	4.50	6.00	9.00
		28	—	4.50	6.00	9.00
		29	—	4.50	6.00	9.00
		30	—	4.50	6.00	9.00
		31	—	4.50	6.00	9.00
		32	—	4.50	6.00	9.00

6 PIASTRES

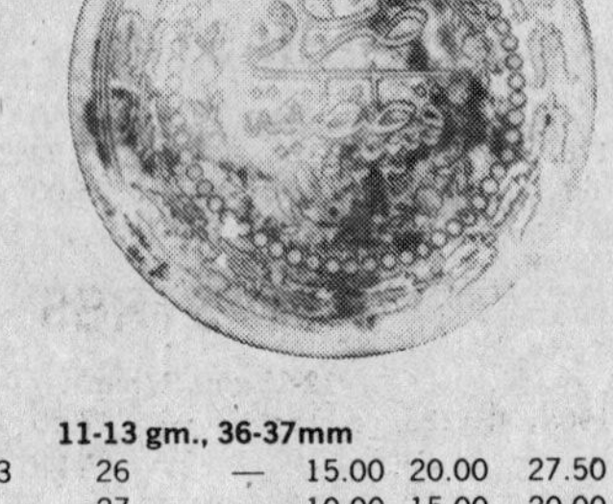

11-13 gm., 36-37mm

C#	Date	Year	Mintage	VG	Fine	VF
208	AH1223	26	—	15.00	20.00	27.50
		27	—	10.00	15.00	20.00
		28	—	10.00	15.00	20.00
		29	—	10.00	15.00	20.00
		30	—	10.00	15.00	20.00
		31	—	10.00	15.00	20.00
		32	—	10.00	15.00	20.00

Gold Coinage

The gold emissions of Mahmud II are characterized by several simultaneous series, each with its characteristic name. They are distinguished by weight and by special symbols, such as the ornament to right of the toughra, the border, and variations in design. These are indicated for each series, along with the weights and diameters of each denomination. Each series comprises several denominations, with the basic unit known as the Altin ('Gold Coin') or Tak ('Single'); other denominations include the Double (Cifte), Half (Yarim, or Nisfiye), and Quarter (Ceyrek, or Rubiye). Not all denominations were struck in every series. Some series can be divided into several subvarieties, which are listed separately below. Finally, a few coins were struck that do not fit into any of the series.

'BELOVED GOLD' SERIES
ZERI MAHBUB

Obverse of all denominations consists of a toughra, with mint name and date below on the 1 and 1/2 Zeri Mahbub only. The reverse of the 1 and 1/2 bears a four-line inscription; the reverse of the 1/4, the mint and date.

1/4 ALTIN

0.70-0.80 gm., 12-15mm

C#	Date	Year	Mintage	Fine	VF	XF
218	AH1223	1	—	40.00	50.00	60.00
		2	—	40.00	50.00	60.00
		3	—	30.00	40.00	50.00
		4	—	30.00	40.00	50.00
		5	—	30.00	40.00	50.00

1/2 ZERI MAHBUB

1.1-1.2 gm., 18mm

C#	Date	Year	Mintage	Fine	VF	XF
209	AH1223	1	—	50.00	70.00	90.00
		2	—	50.00	70.00	90.00
		3	—	50.00	70.00	90.00
		4	—	50.00	70.00	90.00
		5	—	50.00	70.00	90.00

ZERI MAHBUB

2.3-2.4 gm., 22mm

C#	Date	Year	Mintage	Fine	VF	XF
210	AH1223	1	—	75.00	100.00	150.00
		2	—	75.00	100.00	150.00
		3	—	Reported, not confirmed		
		4	—	Reported, not confirmed		
		5	—	75.00	100.00	150.00

SECOND VARIETY. Rose replaces lily on 1 and 1/2 Zeri Mahbub, branch with 2 roses replaces branch with one rose on the 1/4.

1/4 ZERI MAHBUB

0.75-0.79 gm., 14mm

C#	Date	Year	Mintage	Fine	VF	XF
218	AH1223	6	—	25.00	30.00	40.00
		7	—	25.00	30.00	40.00
		8	—	25.00	30.00	40.00
		9	—	25.00	30.00	40.00
		10	—	25.00	30.00	40.00
		11	—	27.50	35.00	45.00
		12	—	27.50	35.00	45.00
		13	—	27.50	35.00	45.00
		14	—	27.50	35.00	45.00

1/2 ZERI MAHBUB

1.1-1.2 gm., 18mm

C#	Date	Year	Mintage	Fine	VF	XF
209	AH1223	6	—	Reported, not confirmed		
		7	—	Reported, not confirmed		
		8	—	60.00	80.00	100.00
		9	—	Reported, not confirmed		
		10	—	Reported, not confirmed		
		11	—	Reported, not confirmed		
		12	—	60.00	80.00	100.00

ZERI MAHBUB

2.3-2.4 gm., 22mm

C#	Date	Year	Mintage	Fine	VF	XF
210	AH1223	6	—	75.00	85.00	110.00
		7	—	75.00	85.00	110.00
		8	—	75.00	85.00	110.00
		9	—	75.00	85.00	110.00
		10	—	75.00	85.00	110.00
		11	—	75.00	85.00	110.00
		12	—	75.00	85.00	110.00
		13	—	Reported, not confirmed		
		14	—	75.00	85.00	110.00
		15	—	75.00	85.00	110.00

RUMI SERIES.

Characterized by a flower to right of tughra and an ornamental border, consisting of a wavy line hexagon, on both sides.

1/2 RUMI ALTIN

1.2 gm., 19mm

C#	Date	Year	Mintage	Fine	VF	XF
212	AH1223	10	—	100.00	125.00	175.00
		11	—	100.00	125.00	175.00
		12	—	100.00	125.00	175.00
		13	—	100.00	125.00	175.00

RUMI ALTIN

2.4 gm., 22mm

C#	Date	Year	Mintage	Fine	VF	XF
213	AH1223	10	—	300.00	400.00	600.00

2 RUMI ALTIN

4.7-4.8 gm., 27mm

C#	Date	Year	Mintage	Fine	VF	XF
214	AH1223	8	—	100.00	125.00	175.00
		9	—	100.00	125.00	175.00
		10	—	100.00	125.00	175.00
		11	—	100.00	125.00	175.00
		12	—	100.00	125.00	175.00
		13	—	100.00	125.00	175.00
		22	—	125.00	150.00	200.00

NEW RUMI SERIES.

Similar to the Rumi series, except that the wavy borders are replaced by an inscription containing the name and titles of Mahmud II.

RUMI ALTIN

2.4 gm., 23mm

C#	Date	Year	Mintage	Fine	VF	XF
215	AH1223	9		Reported, not confirmed		
		10	—	70.00	90.00	100.00
		11	—	70.00	90.00	100.00
		12	—	70.00	90.00	100.00
		13	—	70.00	90.00	100.00
		14	—	70.00	90.00	100.00
		15	—	70.00	90.00	100.00

2 RUMI ALTIN

4.7-4.8 gm., 29mm

C#	Date	Year	Mintage	Fine	VF	XF
217	AH1223	9	—	100.00	150.00	200.00
		10	—	100.00	150.00	200.00
		11	—	100.00	150.00	200.00
		12	—	100.00	150.00	200.00

SURRE SERIES.

'SURRE' means a purse, the amount sent by the Sultan annually to the Hejaz for the holy cities. They were used by pilgrims to Mecca. They bear the mint name "Darulhilafe" in place of "Constantinople", with either of two epithets, el-Aliye (the Lofty) or es-Seniye (the Sublime) and are therefore known as Elaliye and Esseniye Altins, respectively.

ELALIYE SERIES.

1/4 SURRE ALTIN

0.48 gm., 13mm

C#	Date	Year	Mintage	Fine	VF	XF
219a	AH1223	15	—	35.00	60.00	80.00
		16	—	35.00	60.00	80.00

1/2 SURRE ALTIN

0.78 gm., 15-16mm

C#	Date	Year	Mintage	Fine	VF	XF
220a	AH1223	15	—	60.00	90.00	125.00
		16	—	60.00	90.00	125.00

SURRE ALTIN

1.56 gm., 20mm

C#	Date	Year	Mintage	Fine	VF	XF
221a	AH1223	15	—	85.00	110.00	150.00
		16	—	85.00	110.00	150.00

ESSENIYE SERIES.

1/4 SURRE ALTIN

0.48 gm., 13mm

C#	Date	Year	Mintage	Fine	VF	XF
219	AH1223	15	—	35.00	60.00	85.00

1/2 SURRE ALTIN

0.78 gm., 17mm

C#	Date	Year	Mintage	Fine	VF	XF
220	AH1223	15	—	75.00	100.00	125.00

SURRE ALTIN

C#	Date	Year	Mintage	Fine	VF	XF
221	AH1223	15	—	90.00	115.00	150.00

MISCELLANEOUS 1/4 ALTINS.

The following types do not fit into any of the recognized series.

1/4 ALTIN

0.58 gm., 14mm
Considered a 1/4 Zeri Mahbub.
With "AZZE NASARUH" above mint name.

C#	Date	Year	Mintage	Fine	VF	XF
218a	AH1223	13	—	40.00	50.00	60.00
		14	—	40.00	50.00	60.00
		15	—	40.00	50.00	60.00

NOTE: A number of 1/4 Altins were struck with year 21 (C# 218c) in England for the Ottoman government. They are best regarded as patterns.

ADLI SERIES.

Types as the Zeri Mahbub series, except that the word 'ADLI' replaces the flower to right of tughra.

1/4 ADLI ALTIN

0.4-0.45 gm., 12-13mm

C#	Date	Year	Mintage	Fine	VF	XF
219b	AH1223	16	—	30.00	40.00	55.00
		17	—	30.00	40.00	55.00

1/2 ADLI ALTIN

0.75-0.85 gm., 16mm

C#	Date	Year	Mintage	Fine	VF	XF
209a	AH1223	15	—	60.00	75.00	90.00
		16	—	Reported, not confirmed		
		17	—	60.00	75.00	90.00
		18	—	60.00	75.00	90.00
		19	—	60.00	75.00	90.00
		20	—	60.00	75.00	90.00
		21	—	60.00	75.00	90.00
		22	—	60.00	75.00	90.00
		23	—	60.00	75.00	90.00
		24	—	Reported, not confirmed		
		25	—	60.00	75.00	90.00
		26	—	Reported, not confirmed		
		27	—	60.00	75.00	90.00
		28	—	Reported, not confirmed		
		29	—	60.00	75.00	90.00
		30	—	60.00	75.00	90.00
		31	—	60.00	75.00	90.00

ADLI ALTIN

1.5-1.6 gm., 19mm

C#	Date	Year	Mintage	Fine	VF	XF
210a	AH1223	15	—	80.00	100.00	130.00
		17	—	80.00	100.00	130.00
		18	—	80.00	100.00	130.00
		19	—	80.00	100.00	130.00
		20	—	80.00	100.00	130.00

NEW ADLI SERIES.

Tughra on obverse, mint and date on reverse.Additional legends around, obverse and reverse.

1/4 NEW ADLI ALTIN

0.38-0.43 gm., 12-13mm

C#	Date	Year	Mintage	Fine	VF	XF
228	AH1223	15	—	25.00	30.00	40.00
		17	—	25.00	30.00	40.00
		18	—	25.00	30.00	40.00
		19	—	25.00	30.00	40.00
		20	—	25.00	30.00	40.00
		21	—	25.00	30.00	40.00
		22	—	25.00	30.00	40.00
		23	—	25.00	30.00	40.00
		24	—	35.00	40.00	50.00

1/2 NEW ADLI ALTIN

0.78 gm., 16mm

C#	Date	Year	Mintage	Fine	VF	XF
229	AH1223	16	—	40.00	50.00	70.00
		17	—	40.00	50.00	70.00
		18	—	40.00	50.00	70.00
		19	—	40.00	50.00	70.00
		20	—	40.00	50.00	70.00
		21	—Reported, not confirmed			

NEW ADLI ALTIN

1.58 gm., 19mm

C#	Date	Year	Mintage	Fine	VF	XF
230	AH1223	16	—	40.00	60.00	75.00
		17	—	40.00	60.00	75.00
		18	—	40.00	60.00	75.00
		19	—	40.00	60.00	75.00
		20	—	40.00	60.00	75.00
		21	—Reported, not confirmed			
		22	—Reported, not confirmed			

HAYRIYE SERIES.

Similar to the New Adli, but in place of the ring of legend around the edge, there are alternating ovals of inscription and branches.

1/2 HAYRIYE ALTIN

0.86 gm., 15mm

C#	Date	Year	Mintage	Fine	VF	XF
232	AH1223	21	—	35.00	45.00	60.00
		22	—	35.00	45.00	60.00
		23	—	35.00	45.00	60.00
		24	—	35.00	45.00	60.00
		25	—	35.00	45.00	60.00
		26	—	35.00	45.00	60.00

HAYRIYE ALTIN

1.73 gm., 20mm

C#	Date	Year	Mintage	Fine	VF	XF
233	AH1223	21	—	45.00	55.00	80.00
		22	—	45.00	55.00	80.00
		23	—	45.00	55.00	80.00
		24	—	45.00	55.00	80.00
		25	—	45.00	55.00	80.00
		26	—Reported, not confirmed			

2 HAYRIYE ALTIN

3.55 gm., 27mm

C#	Date	Year	Mintage	Fine	VF	XF
234	AH1223	21	—	110.00	150.00	200.00

"NEW" SERIES.

The Yeni or new series comprises but one denomination, distinguished by starlike wavy pattern around edge.

1/4 NEW ALTIN

YENI RUBIYE

0.26-0.31 gm., 12mm

C#	Date	Year	Mintage	Fine	VF	XF
237	AH1223	24	—	30.00	40.00	55.00
		25	—	30.00	40.00	55.00
		26	—	30.00	40.00	55.00
		27	—	30.00	40.00	55.00
		28	—	30.00	40.00	55.00
		29	—Reported, not confirmed			
		30	—	16.00	18.50	22.00

CEDID MAHMUDIYE SERIES.

Like the Hayriye, but ovals of inscription and branches replaced by a wreath design.

1/4 CEDID MAHMUDIYE

0.38-0.40 gm., 13mm

C#	Date	Year	Mintage	Fine	VF	XF
239	AH1223	26	—	25.00	35.00	45.00
		27	—	25.00	35.00	45.00
		28	—	25.00	35.00	45.00
		29	—	25.00	35.00	45.00
		30	—	25.00	35.00	45.00
		31	—	25.00	35.00	45.00
		32	—	25.00	35.00	45.00

1/2 CEDID MAHMUDIYE

0.76-0.80 gm., 15mm

C#	Date	Year	Mintage	Fine	VF	XF
240	AH1223	26	—	40.00	47.50	60.00
		27	—	40.00	47.50	60.00
		28	—	40.00	47.50	60.00
		29	—	40.00	47.50	60.00
		30	—	40.00	47.50	60.00
		31	—	40.00	47.50	60.00
		32	—	40.00	47.50	60.00

CEDID MAHMUDIYE

1.58-1.60 gm., 20mm

C#	Date	Year	Mintage	Fine	VF	XF
241	AH1223	26	—	60.00	70.00	85.00
		27	—	60.00	70.00	85.00
		28	—	60.00	70.00	85.00
		29	—	60.00	70.00	85.00
		30	—	60.00	70.00	85.00
		31	—	60.00	70.00	85.00
		32	—	60.00	70.00	85.00

EDIRNE HAYRIYESI SERIES.

Similar to the Hayriye, but with stars in place of branches and mint name "EDIRNE". Probably not struck at Edirne, but at Istanbul.

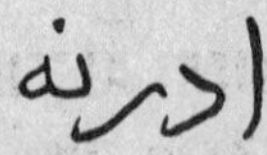

1/2 HAYRIYE ALTIN

0.88 gm., 16.5mm

C#	Date	Year	Mintage	Fine	VF	XF
232a	AH1223	24	—	100.00	145.00	200.00

1 HAYRIYE ALTIN

1.80 gm., 21mm

C#	Date	Year	Mintage	Fine	VF	XF
233a	AH1223	24	—	100.00	140.00	200.00

2 HAYRIYE ALTIN

3.55 gm., 27mm

C#	Date	Year	Mintage	Fine	VF	XF
234a	AH1223	24	—	225.00	275.00	350.00

PRE-REFORM COINAGE

OF ABDULMEJID

Standard, fineness, and denominations of the silver coinage similar to the ninth (for the 1, 10, and 20 Para) and tenth (for the 1-1/2, 3, and 6 Piastres) series of Muhmud II (C# 202-204, 206-208).

PARA

BILLON, 0.14-0.20 gm., 12mm

C#	Date	Year	Mintage	VG	Fine	VF
265	AH1255	1	—	1.50	2.25	3.00
		2	—	1.50	2.25	3.00
		3	—	1.50	2.25	3.00
		4	—	1.50	2.25	3.00
		5	—	1.50	2.25	3.00
		6	—	6.00	8.00	10.00

10 PARA

BILLON, 0.6-0.8 gm., 17mm

C#	Date	Year	Mintage	VG	Fine	VF
266	AH1255	1	—	2.00	3.00	4.00
266		2	—	2.00	3.00	4.00
		3	—	2.00	3.00	4.00
		4	—	2.00	3.00	4.00
		5	—	2.00	3.00	4.00

20 PARA

BILLON, 1.35-1.6 gm., 20mm

C#	Date	Year	Mintage	VG	Fine	VF
267	AH1255	1	—	.50	1.00	2.25
		2	—	1.50	2.50	3.75
		3	—	1.50	2.50	3.75
		4	—	1.50	2.50	3.75
		5	—	1.50	2.50	3.75

1-1/2 PIASTRES

SILVER, 2.6-3.0 gm., 27mm

C#	Date	Year	Mintage	VG	Fine	VF
269	AH1255	1	—	6.00	8.50	12.50
		2	—	5.00	6.50	11.00
		3	—	7.00	9.00	13.50
		4	—	5.00	6.50	11.00
		5	—	5.00	6.50	11.00

3 PIASTRES

SILVER, 5.6-6.2 gm., 33mm

C#	Date	Year	Mintage	VG	Fine	VF
270	AH1255	1	—	20.00	32.50	45.00
		2	—	45.00	75.00	100.00
		3	—	100.00	200.00	325.00
		4	—	100.00	200.00	325.00

6 PIASTRES

SILVER, 12.5-13 gm., 37mm

C#	Date	Year	Mintage	VG	Fine	VF
271	AH1255	1	—	22.50	35.00	50.00
		2	—	60.00	80.00	100.00

1/4 MEMDUHIYE ALTIN

GOLD, 0.38-0.40 gm., 13mm

C#	Date	Year	Mintage	Fine	VF	XF
273	AH1255	1	—	25.00	35.00	55.00
		2	—	25.00	35.00	55.00
		3	—	25.00	35.00	55.00
		4	—	25.00	35.00	55.00
		5	—	25.00	35.00	55.00

1/2 MEMDUHIYE ALTIN

GOLD, 0.78-0.80 gm., 15mm

C#	Date	Year	Mintage	Fine	VF	XF
274	AH1255	1	—	50.00	60.00	80.00
		2	—	50.00	60.00	80.00
		3	—	50.00	60.00	80.00
		4	—	50.00	60.00	80.00
		5	—	50.00	60.00	80.00

MEMDUHIYE ALTIN

GOLD, 1.58-1.60 gm., 20mm

C#	Date	Year	Mintage	Fine	VF	XF
275	AH1255	1	—	55.00	65.00	90.00
		2	—	55.00	65.00	90.00
		3	—	55.00	65.00	90.00
		4	—	55.00	65.00	90.00
		5	—	55.00	65.00	90.00

NOTE: The Memduhiye issue of Abdulmejid was of the same fineness, weight and diameter as the Mahmudiye issue of Mahmud II. Although officially valued at 20 Piastres, the actual value of the Memduhiye Altin varied with the relative prices of gold and silver.

1/2 ZERI MAHBUB

GOLD 0.80 gm., 15-16mm
Rev: Four-line inscription.

C#	Date	Year	Mintage	Fine	VF	XF
278	AH1255	1	—	60.00	75.00	100.00
		2	—	60.00	75.00	100.00
		3	—	60.00	75.00	100.00
		4	—	60.00	75.00	100.00
		5	—	60.00	75.00	100.00
		6	—	100.00	120.00	200.00

MODERN COINAGE

MONETARY SYSTEM

1844-1923

40 Para = 1 Piastre (Kurus)

100 Piastres = 1 Pound (Lira)

NOTE: The 20 Piastre coin was known as a Mecidi, after the name of Abdulmecid, who established the currency reform in 1844. The entire series is sometimes called Mecidiye coinage.

PARA

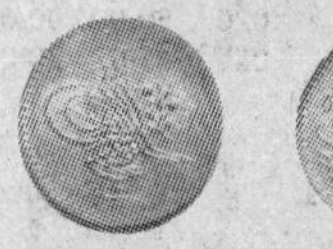

COPPER
Thick planchet, 1.0-1.1 gm.

C#	Date	Year	Mintage	Fine	VF	XF
282	AH1255	8	1.000	7.00	10.00	12.50
		9	.375	7.00	10.00	12.50
		10	1.250	7.00	10.00	12.50
		11	.165	7.00	10.00	12.50
		12	1.600	2.50	4.50	7.50
		13	.800	1.25	2.00	4.00
		14	.300	7.00	10.00	12.50
		15	.700	2.50	4.50	7.50
		16	3.400	2.50	4.50	7.50

Medium planchet, 0.8-0.9 gm.

C#	Date	Year	Mintage	Fine	VF	XF
282a	AH1255	16	Inc. Ab.	1.00	1.75	3.50
		17	.800	2.00	4.00	6.00
		18	4.500	1.50	2.50	5.00

Thin planchet, 0.5-0.6 gm.

C#	Date	Year	Mintage	Fine	VF	XF
282b	AH1255	18	Inc. Ab.	1.00	2.50	5.00
		19	2.500	.50	1.25	2.50
		21	2.000	10.00	15.00	20.00

NOTE: The thin planchet coin of "year 16" is actually year 19 with broken 9.

5 PARA

COPPER
Thick planchet, 4.9-6.8 gm.

C#	Date	Year	Mintage	Fine	VF	XF
283	AH1255	7	—	15.00	20.00	25.00
		8	1.000	2.00	5.00	8.50
		9	.300	10.00	15.00	17.50
		10	.800	3.00	5.00	8.00
		11	2.542	3.00	5.50	11.50
		12	3.680	1.25	2.00	5.00
		13	4.640	1.25	2.00	5.00
		14	3.400	1.25	2.00	5.00
		15	5.060	1.25	2.50	6.00

Medium planchet, 3.7-4.2 gm.

C#	Date	Year	Mintage	Fine	VF	XF
283a	AH1255	15	Inc. Ab.	4.00	8.00	15.00
		16	6.300	1.00	2.00	5.00
		17	6.500	1.00	2.00	5.00

Thin planchet, 2.5-3.3 gm.

C#	Date	Year	Mintage	Fine	VF	XF
283b	AH1255	18	2.000	2.75	5.00	11.00
		19	9.300	1.00	1.75	4.50
		20	10.060	1.00	1.75	4.50
		21	6.200	1.00	1.75	4.50

Y#	Date	Year	Mintage	Fine	VF	XF
1	AH1277	1	—	4.50	6.00	10.00

Y#	Date	Year	Mintage	Fine	VF	XF
4	AH1277	4	—	1.00	1.75	2.75

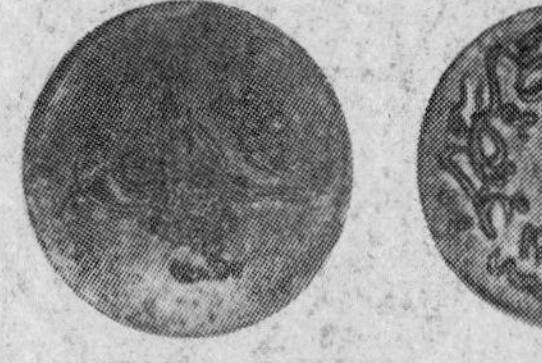

Y#	Date	Year	Mintage	Fine	VF	XF
23	AH1293	3	—	.50	1.00	2.50
		4	—	.50	1.00	2.50

1.0023 gm., .100 SILVER, .0032 oz ASW

Y#	Date	Year	Mintage	Fine	VF	XF
24	AH1293	25	—	.30	.50	1.25
		26	—	.30	.50	1.25
		27	—	.30	.50	1.25
		28	—	.30	.50	1.25
		30	—	3.50	7.50	12.50

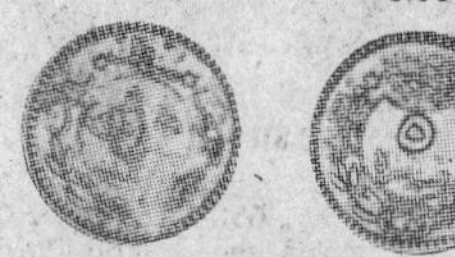

NICKEL
Obv: 'RESHAT' right of tughra

Y#	Date	Year	Mintage	Fine	VF	XF
43	AH1327	2	1.664	.75	1.25	3.25
		3	21.760	.25	.40	1.00
		4	21.392	.25	.40	1.00
		5	30.579	.25	.40	1.00
		6	15.751	.25	.40	1.00
		7	2.512	25.00	45.00	75.00

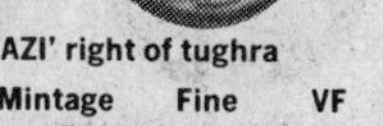

Obv: 'EL-GHAZI' right of tughra

Y#	Date	Year	Mintage	Fine	VF	XF
43a	AH1327	7	.740	10.00	15.00	20.00

10 PARA

COPPER
Thick planchet, 9.0-12.8 gm.

C#	Date	Year	Mintage	Fine	VF	XF
284	AH1255	15	.750	2.50	6.50	12.00

Medium planchet, 7.5-8.2 gm.

C#	Date	Year	Mintage	Fine	VF	XF
284a	AH1255	16	9.120	1.50	3.75	7.00
		17	9.110	1.50	3.75	7.00
		18	1.900	2.50	5.00	9.00

Thin planchet, 4.9-5.7 gm.

C#	Date	Year	Mintage	Fine	VF	XF
284b	AH1255	17	Inc. Ab.	5.00	6.50	9.00
		18	Inc. Ab.	2.50	5.00	9.00
		19	33.600	.75	2.00	5.00
		20	20.800	.75	2.00	5.00
		21	7.500	.75	2.00	5.00

Y#	Date	Year	Mintage	Fine	VF	XF
2	AH1277	1	—	1.75	3.00	7.50

Y#	Date	Year	Mintage	Fine	VF	XF
5	AH1277	4	—	.90	1.70	3.50

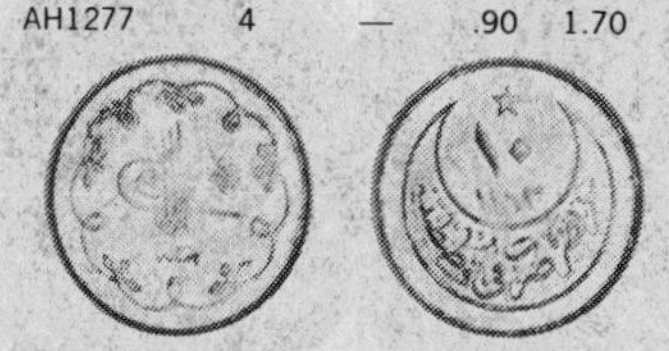

2.0046 gm., .100 SILVER, .0064 oz ASW

Y#	Date	Year	Mintage	Fine	VF	XF
25	AH1293	25	—	.25	.45	1.00
		26	—	.25	.45	1.00
		27	—	.25	.45	1.00
		28	—	.25	.45	1.00
		30	—	.60	1.50	2.50

Obv: Large Regnal year.

Y#	Date	Year	Mintage	Fine	VF	XF
25a	AH1293	27	—	—	—	—

NICKEL
Obv: 'RESHAT' at right of tughra

Y#	Date	Year	Mintage	Fine	VF	XF
44	AH1327	2	2.576	.50	1.00	2.50
		3	18.992	.20	.40	1.00
		4	18.576	.20	.40	1.00
		5	31.799	.20	.40	1.00
		6	17.024	.20	.40	1.00
		7	21.680	.65	1.50	3.50

Obv: 'EL GHAZI' at right of tughra

Y#	Date	Year	Mintage	Fine	VF	XF
44a	AH1327	7				
			Inc.w/Y#44	.40	.80	1.75
		8	7.590	.50	.90	2.00

20 PARA

COPPER
Thick planchet, 14-16 gm.

C#	Date	Year	Mintage	Fine	VF	XF
285	AH1255	16	4.350	2.50	5.00	9.00
		17	2.050	4.00	7.50	12.00

Thin planchet, 10-11 gm.

C#	Date	Year	Mintage	Fine	VF	XF
285a	AH1255	17	Inc. Ab.	2.00	4.50	8.50
		19	1.200	2.00	4.50	8.50
		20	3.000	2.00	4.50	8.50
		21	8.400	1.00	3.00	6.00

.830 SILVER

C#	Date	Year	Mintage	Fine	VF	XF
287	AH1255	9	.400	4.00	7.00	12.00
		10	.910	5.00	8.50	15.00
		11	.390	4.00	7.00	12.00
		12	.270	7.50	10.00	15.00
		13	.230	9.00	17.50	27.50
		14	.180	7.50	10.00	15.00
		15	.240	7.50	10.00	15.00
		16	.270	5.00	8.00	12.50
		17	.170	5.00	8.00	12.50
		18	.260	4.00	7.00	12.50
		19	.900	4.25	7.50	12.50
		20	.150	4.25	7.50	12.50
		21	.250	8.50	12.50	17.50
		22	.190	8.50	12.50	17.50
		23	.620	20.00	40.00	55.00

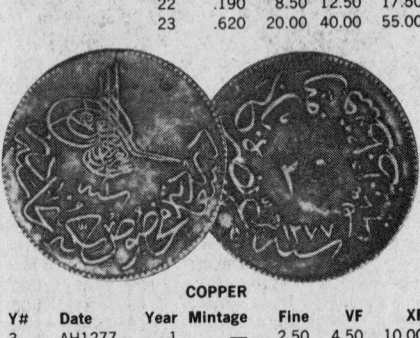

COPPER

Y#	Date	Year	Mintage	Fine	VF	XF
3	AH1277	1	—	2.50	4.50	10.00

Y#	Date	Year	Mintage	Fine	VF	XF
6	AH1277	4	—	.85	1.25	3.00

0.6013 gm., .830 SILVER, .0160 oz ASW

Y#	Date	Year	Mintage	Fine	VF	XF
8	AH1277	1	.420	3.00	5.00	10.00
		2	.850	3.00	5.00	10.00
		3	1.570	3.00	5.00	10.00
		4	.930	12.50	22.50	40.00
		5	.740	3.25	5.50	10.00
		6	.520	8.00	12.50	18.50
		7	.350	8.00	12.50	18.50

Y#	Date	Year	Mintage	Fine	VF	XF
26	AH1293	1	.110	35.00	65.00	100.00
		4	.050	50.00	75.00	125.00
F31	AH1293	8	.350	2.50	5.00	7.50

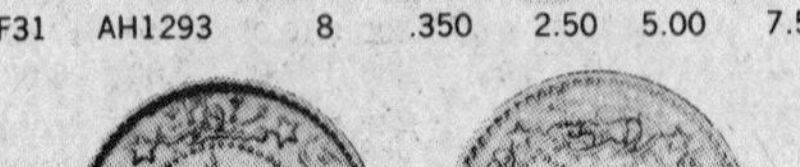

NICKEL
Obv: "Reshat" at right of tughra.

Y#	Date	Year	Mintage	Fine	VF	XF
45	AH1327	2	1.524	.50	1.00	2.25
		3	11.418	.20	.40	1.25
		4	10.848	.20	.40	1.25
		5	24.350	.20	.40	1.25
		6	20.663	.20	.40	1.25
		7	—	15.00	45.00	70.00

Obv: "El-Ghazi" at right of tughra

Y#	Date	Year	Mintage	Fine	VF	XF
45.1	AH1327	7	—	15.00	45.00	70.00

40 PARA = 1 PIASTRE

NOTE: The copper and nickel pieces of this denomination bear the value '40 Para', while the silver pieces, known as Piastres, bear no indication of their value.

COPPER

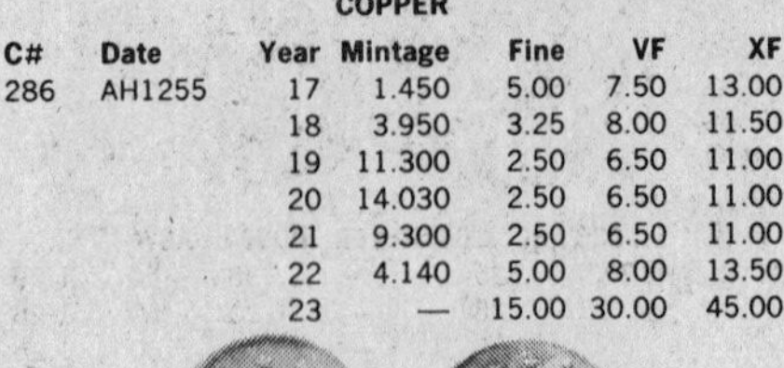

C#	Date	Year	Mintage	Fine	VF	XF
286	AH1255	17	1.450	5.00	7.50	13.00
		18	3.950	3.25	8.00	11.50
		19	11.300	2.50	6.50	11.00
		20	14.030	2.50	6.50	11.00
		21	9.300	2.50	6.50	11.00
		22	4.140	5.00	8.00	13.50
		23	—	15.00	30.00	45.00

.830 SILVER

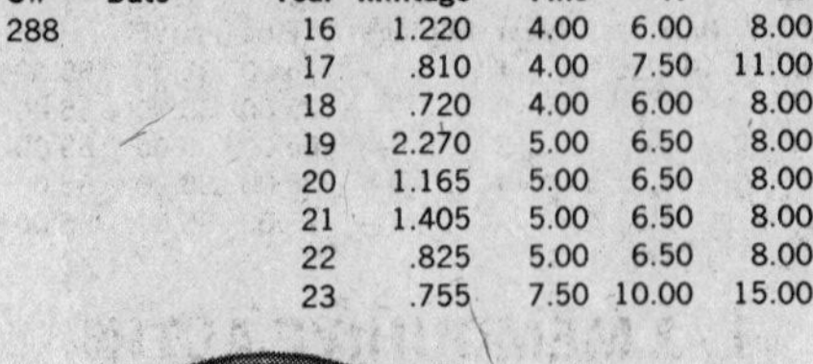

C#	Date	Year	Mintage	Fine	VF	XF
288	AH1255	6	—	10.00	12.50	25.00
		7	.650	5.00	7.00	10.00
		8	1.420	5.00	7.00	10.00
		9	.910	4.50	6.00	8.50
		10	.970	4.50	6.00	8.50
		11	1.040	4.50	6.00	8.50
		12	1.100	1.75	3.25	6.50
		13	.820	4.00	6.00	8.00
		14	.790	4.00	6.00	8.00
		15	.960	4.00	6.00	8.00
		16	1.220	4.00	6.00	8.00
		17	.810	4.00	7.50	11.00
		18	.720	4.00	6.00	8.00
		19	2.270	5.00	6.50	8.00
		20	1.165	5.00	6.50	8.00
		21	1.405	5.00	6.50	8.00
		22	.825	5.00	6.50	8.00
		23	.755	7.50	10.00	15.00

COPPER

Y#	Date	Year	Mintage	Fine	VF	XF
7	AH1277	4	—	1.75	3.00	10.00

1.2027 gm., .830 SILVER, .0321 oz ASW

Y#	Date	Year	Mintage	Fine	VF	XF
9	AH1277	1	.545	5.00	7.50	10.00
		2	2.245	5.00	7.50	10.00
		3	1.370	5.00	7.50	10.00
		4	.900	5.00	7.50	10.00
		5	.685	5.00	7.50	10.00
		7	.535	20.00	30.00	50.00

Obv: 'MURAD V' no flower right of tughra

Y#	Date	Year	Mintage	Fine	VF	XF
18	AH1293	1	—	100.00	150.00	225.00

Obv: 'ABDULHAMID II' flower right of tughra

Y#	Date	Year	Mintage	Fine	VF	XF
27	AH1293	1	.065	40.00	60.00	90.00
		2	.020	50.00	90.00	125.00
		4	.045	45.00	70.00	90.00

Obv: 'EL-GHAZI' to right of tughra

Y#	Date	Year	Mintage	Fine	VF	XF
32	AH1293	8	.210	1.25	3.00	6.00
		9	.600	.75	1.25	3.50
		11	8.830	.50	1.00	2.25
		13	.130	2.50	4.50	10.00
		16	4.000	.50	1.00	2.25
		17	6.440	.50	1.00	2.25
		18	.040	7.00	15.00	32.50
		19	3.070	.50	1.00	2.25
		20	4.122	.50	1.00	2.25
		21	.040	2.50	4.50	10.00
		22	3.979	.50	1.00	2.25
		23	3.760	.50	1.00	2.25
		24	2.041	.50	1.00	2.25
		25	.084	2.50	4.50	10.00
		26	.055	2.50	4.50	10.00
		27	9.945	.50	1.00	2.25
		28	16.139	.50	1.00	2.25
		29	7.076	.50	1.00	2.25
		30	.707	.50	1.00	2.25
		31	1.366	.50	1.00	2.25
		32	1.140	.50	1.00	2.25

Y#	Date	Year	Mintage	Fine	VF	XF
32		33	1.700	.50	1.00	2.25
		34	—	20.00	30.00	50.00

NICKEL
Obv: 'RESHAT' to right of tughra

Y#	Date	Year	Mintage	Fine	VF	XF
46	AH1327	3	1.992	.40	.75	2.00
		4	8.716	.30	.60	1.50
		5	9.248	.30	.60	1.50

COPPER-NICKEL

Y#	Date	Year	Mintage	Fine	VF	XF
46a	AH1327	8	16.339	.30	.60	1.60
		9	3.034	.75	1.50	3.50

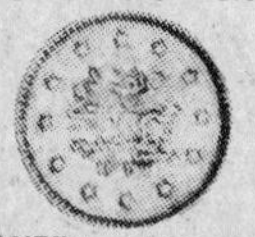

.830 SILVER

Y#	Date	Year	Mintage	Fine	VF	XF
47	AH1327	1	1.270	1.50	2.50	5.00
		2	8.770	.75	1.25	3.25
		3	.840	2.00	3.00	6.00

COPPER-NICKEL

Y#	Date	Year	Mintage	Fine	VF	XF
58	AH1336	4	6.520	1.50	2.00	2.50

2 PIASTRES

2.4055 gm., .830 SILVER, .0642 oz ASW

C#	Date	Year	Mintage	Fine	VF	XF
289	AH1255	7	1.035	1.75	3.00	7.50
		8	1.150	1.75	3.00	7.50
		9	.530	1.50	2.60	6.50
		10	.543	5.00	6.50	10.00
		11	.695	3.00	4.50	7.00
		12	.685	3.00	5.00	8.00
		13	.540	4.50	5.00	10.00
		14	.280	7.00	10.00	15.00
		15	.300	3.00	5.00	8.00
		16	.510	7.00	10.00	15.00
		19	.275	10.00	15.00	25.00
		20	.105	10.00	15.00	25.00

Y#	Date	Year	Mintage	Fine	VF	XF
10	AH1277	1	.055	22.50	32.50	50.00
		2	.065	30.00	50.00	75.00
		3	.235	17.50	27.50	50.00
		5	.135	35.00	55.00	90.00

Obv: Flower to right of tughra

Y#	Date	Year	Mintage	Fine	VF	XF
28	AH1293	1	.010	200.00	300.00	500.00

Obv: 'EL-GHAZI' to right of tughra

Y#	Date	Year	Mintage	Fine	VF	XF
33	AH1293	8	.103	1.50	2.75	4.50
		9	.605	1.00	1.85	3.25
		11	5.115	.75	1.50	2.75
		13	.030	6.00	12.50	20.00
		16	.980	.85	1.65	3.00
		17	3.736	.75	1.50	2.75
		18	.023	6.50	13.50	21.00
		19	3.507	.75	1.50	2.75
		20	2.420	.75	1.50	2.75
		21	.021	5.50	11.00	18.50
		22	2.980	.75	1.50	2.75
		23	3.139	.75	1.50	2.75
		24	1.490	.90	1.75	3.00
		25	.014	7.50	12.50	20.00
		26	.017	7.50	12.50	20.00
		27	4.689	.75	1.50	2.75
		28	7.567	.75	1.50	2.75
		29	7.775	.75	1.50	2.75
		30	1.366	.75	1.50	2.75
		31	3.014	.75	1.50	2.75
		32	1.625	.75	1.50	2.75
		33	2.173	.75	1.50	2.75
		34	—	11.50	17.50	22.50

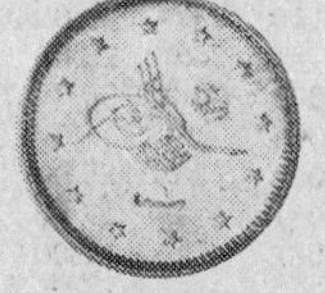

Obv: 'RESHAT' to right of tughra

Y#	Date	Year	Mintage	Fine	VF	XF
48	AH1327	1	5.157	1.00	1.60	2.50
		2	11.120	.80	1.25	2.50
		3	6.110	.80	1.25	2.50
		4	4.031	.90	1.40	2.50
		5	.301	5.00	12.50	20.00
		6	1.884	1.50	2.50	4.00

Obv: 'EL GHAZI' to right of tughra

Y#	Date	Year	Mintage	Fine	VF	XF
A50	AH1327	7	.017	25.00	40.00	50.00
		8	.398	30.00	40.00	60.00
		9	.008	100.00	125.00	200.00

Y#	Date	Year	Mintage	Fine	VF	XF
59	AH1336	1	.025	100.00	200.00	300.00
		2	.003	100.00	200.00	300.00

5 PIASTRES

6.0130 gm., .830 SILVER, .1605 oz ASW

C#	Date	Year	Mintage	Fine	VF	XF
290	AH1255	6	1.347	BV	6.50	10.00
		7	2.612	BV	6.50	10.00
		8	.362	BV	6.50	10.00
		9	.240	BV	6.50	10.00
		10	.252	BV	6.50	10.00
		11	.314	BV	6.50	10.00
		12	.452	BV	6.50	10.00
		13	.498	BV	6.50	10.00
		14	.354	BV	6.50	10.00
		15	.680	BV	6.50	10.00
		16	.972	BV	6.50	10.00
		17	.206	BV	6.50	10.00
		18	.218	BV	6.50	10.00
		19	.384	BV	6.50	10.00
		20	.310	BV	6.50	10.00

C#	Date	Year	Mintage	Fine	VF	XF
290		21	.324	BV	6.50	10.00
		22	.214	BV	6.50	10.00
		23	.120	8.50	12.50	20.00

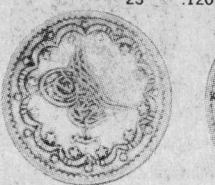

Y#	Date	Year	Mintage	Fine	VF	XF
11	AH1277	1	.016	BV	6.00	15.00
		2	.280	BV	6.00	15.00
		3	.288	BV	6.00	15.00
		4	.280	BV	6.00	15.00
		5	.242	BV	6.00	15.00
		6	.342	BV	6.00	15.00
		7	.248	BV	6.00	15.00
		8	.020	35.00	50.00	80.00
		9	.050	BV	6.00	15.00
		10	.230	BV	6.00	15.00
		11	.126	BV	6.00	15.00
		12	.186	BV	6.00	15.00
		13	.284	BV	6.00	15.00
		14	.202	BV	6.00	15.00
		15	.154	BV	6.00	15.00

Obv: 'MURAD V' no flower to right of tughra

Y#	Date	Year	Mintage	Fine	VF	XF
20	AH1293	1	—	100.00	150.00	250.00

Obv: 'ABDULHAMID II' flower right of tughra

Y#	Date	Year	Mintage	Fine	VF	XF
29	AH1293	1	.022	90.00	140.00	200.00
		2	.014	50.00	70.00	150.00
		3	.016	15.00	20.00	35.00
		4	.269	15.00	20.00	35.00

Obv: 'EL-GHAZI' to right of tughra

Y#	Date	Year	Mintage	Fine	VF	XF
34	AH1293	8	.082	8.00	11.00	17.50
		9	.614	BV	BV	7.50
		11	1.788	BV	BV	7.50
		12	1.880	BV	BV	7.50
		13	2.182	BV	BV	7.50
		14	.380	BV	BV	7.50
		15	.194	BV	BV	9.00
		16	.914	BV	BV	7.50
		17	1.237	BV	BV	7.50
		18	.012	25.00	35.00	55.00
		19	.031	10.00	15.00	30.00
		20	.162	7.50	12.00	20.00
		21	.018	20.00	30.00	50.00
		22	.008	20.00	30.00	50.00
		23	.007	20.00	30.00	50.00
		24	.126	BV	BV	10.00
		25	.013	20.00	30.00	50.00
		26	.008	20.00	30.00	50.00
		27	.016	20.00	30.00	50.00
		28	.006	20.00	30.00	50.00
		29	.007	20.00	30.00	50.00
		30	.038	BV	6.50	15.00
		31/30	—	13.00	25.00	35.00
		31	3.175	BV	7.00	15.00
		32	3.334	BV	BV	7.00
		33	.907	BV	BV	7.00
		34	—	50.00	65.00	90.00

Obv: 'RESHAT' to right of tughra

Y#	Date	Year	Mintage	Fine	VF	XF
49	AH1327	1	1.558	BV	BV	6.00
		2	1.886	BV	BV	6.00
		3	1.273	BV	BV	6.00
		4	1.635	BV	BV	6.00
		5	.194	BV	9.00	15.00
		6	.664	BV	BV	8.00
		7	.834	BV	6.50	10.00

Obv: 'EL GHAZI' to right of tughra

Y#	Date	Year	Mintage	Fine	VF	XF
B50	AH1327	7	Inc. Ab.	BV	7.00	10.00
		8	.648	7.00	10.00	16.50
		9	3,938	60.00	100.00	175.00

Y#	Date	Year	Mintage	Fine	VF	XF
60	AH1336	1	.010	100.00	150.00	200.00
		2	2,000	150.00	200.00	300.00

10 PIASTRES

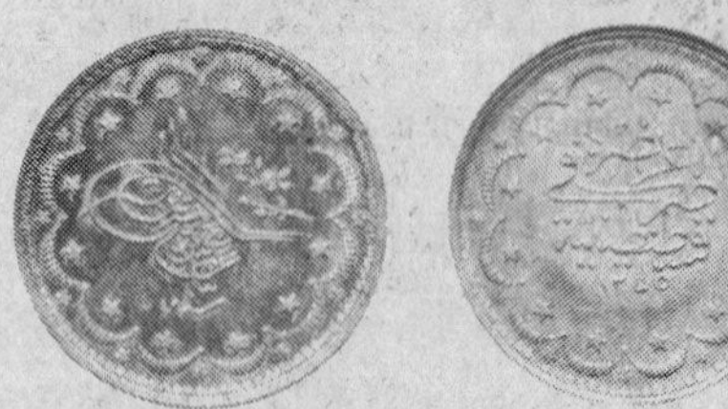

12.0270 gm., .830 SILVER, .6419 oz ASW

C#	Date	Year	Mintage	Fine	VF	XF
291	AH1255	6	.338	25.00	35.00	60.00
		7	.012	60.00	100.00	175.00
		13	—	—	Rare	—

Y#	Date	Year	Mintage	Fine	VF	XF
12	AH1277	1	—	35.00	75.00	150.00
		2	.280	75.00	135.00	225.00

Obv: Flower to right of tughra

Y#	Date	Year	Mintage	Fine	VF	XF
30	AH1293	1	.004	60.00	90.00	150.00
		3	.005	25.00	37.50	80.00

Obv: 'EL GHAZI' to right of tughra

Y#	Date	Year	Mintage	Fine	VF	XF
35	AH1293	12	—	35.00	55.00	85.00
		13	.161	10.00	20.00	30.00
		20	.034	30.00	45.00	70.00
		31	.051	35.00	55.00	85.00
		32	.595	BV	BV	20.00
		33	.273	BV	BV	15.00

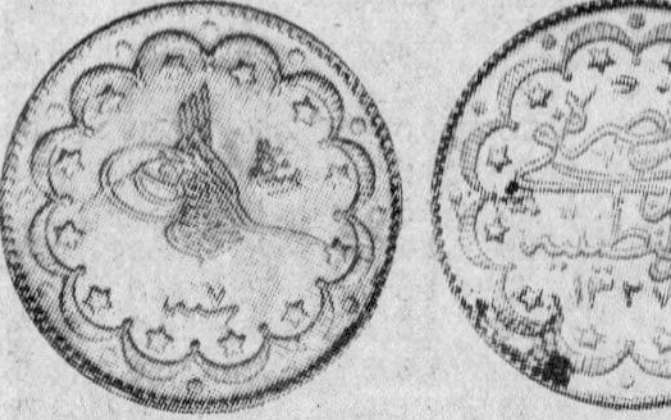

Obv: 'RESHAT' to right of tughra

Y#	Date	Year	Mintage	Fine	VF	XF
50	AH1327	1	.110	25.00	40.00	60.00
		2	Inc. Ab.	20.00	30.00	45.00
		3	8,000	200.00	350.00	550.00
		4	.096	BV	BV	17.50
		5	.034	15.00	25.00	40.00
		6	.081	BV	17.50	25.00
		7	.582	BV	15.00	19.00

Obv: 'EL-GHAZI' to right of tughra

Y#	Date	Year	Mintage	Fine	VF	XF
C50	AH1327	7	Inc. Ab.	BV	BV	12.50
		8	.408	BV	BV	14.00
		9	.299	BV	14.00	17.50
		10	.666	12.50	16.50	25.00

Y#	Date	Year	Mintage	Fine	VF	XF
61	AH1336	1	—	200.00	350.00	500.00
		2	1,000	400.00	600.00	800.00

20 PIASTRES

24.0550 gm., .830 SILVER, .6419 oz ASW

Rev: Small inscription.

C#	Date	Year	Mintage	Fine	VF	XF
292	AH1255	6	2.013	BV	BV	30.00
		7	.740	BV	BV	30.00
		8	1.671	BV	BV	30.00
		9	3.125	BV	BV	30.00
		10	1.020	BV	BV	30.00
		11	.815	BV	BV	30.00
		12	.684	BV	BV	30.00
		13	.485	BV	BV	30.00
		14	.633	BV	BV	30.00
		15	.797	BV	BV	30.00

Rev: Large inscription.

C#	Date	Year	Mintage	Fine	VF	XF
292.1	AH1255	15	Inc. Ab.	BV	BV	30.00
		16	.320	BV	BV	30.00
		17	.410	BV	BV	30.00
		18	.340	BV	35.00	60.00
		19	.201	35.00	55.00	100.00
		20	.103	BV	30.00	50.00
		21	.513	BV	30.00	50.00
		22	.624	BV	30.00	50.00
		23	.317	BV	30.00	50.00

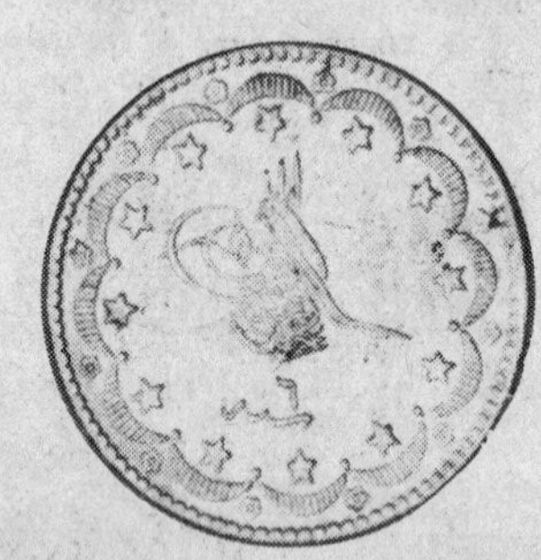

Rev: Similar to Y#22.

Y#	Date	Year	Mintage	Fine	VF	XF
13	AH1277	1	1.055	BV	BV	30.00
		2	3.106	BV	BV	30.00
		3	.257	BV	BV	30.00
		4	.234	25.00	45.00	70.00
		5	.387	BV	BV	30.00
		6	.314	BV	BV	30.00
		7	.640	BV	BV	30.00
		8	1.457	BV	BV	30.00
		9	.859	BV	BV	30.00
		10	.528	BV	BV	32.50
		11	.530	BV	BV	30.00
		12	.233	BV	BV	30.00
		13	.514	BV	BV	30.00
		14	.584	BV	BV	30.00
		15	4.034	BV	BV	30.00

Obv: 'MURAD V' no flower to right of tughra

Y#	Date	Year	Mintage	Fine	VF	XF
22	AH1293	1	—	30.00	60.00	120.00

NOTE: Beware of specimens of Y#31 altered to appear as a piece of Murad. The tughra is very different.

Obv: Flower to right of tughra.
Rev: Similar to Y#22.

Y#	Date	Year	Mintage	Fine	VF	XF
31	AH1293	1	1.274	15.00	20.00	32.50
		2	2.357	15.00	20.00	32.50
		3	5.940	15.00	20.00	32.50

Rev: Similar to Y#22.

Y#	Date	Year	Mintage	Fine	VF	XF
51	AH1327	8	.713	15.00	20.00	30.00
		9	5.962	15.00	20.00	30.00
		10	11.025	15.00	20.00	30.00

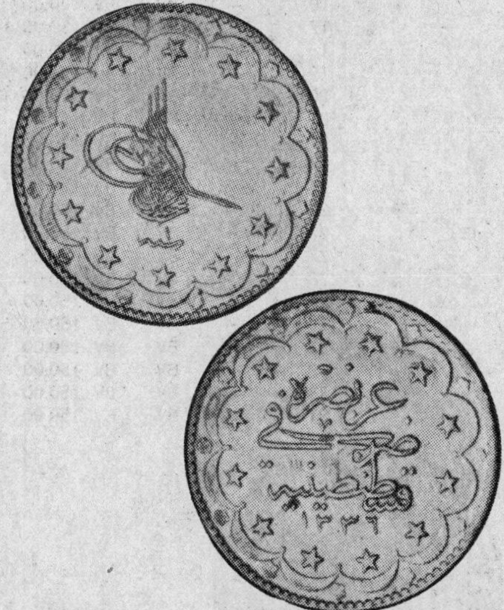

Y#	Date	Year	Mintage	Fine	VF	XF
62	AH1336	1	Inc. Ab.	60.00	100.00	165.00
		2	1,530	250.00	300.00	400.00

GOLD COINAGE

In the 23rd year of the reign of Abdulhamid II, two parallel series of gold coins were produced, regular mint issues and 'monnaies deluxe,' which were intended primarily for presentation and jewelry purposes. The 'monnaies de luxe' were struck to a slightly less weight and the same fineness as regular issues, but were broader and thinner, and from more ornate dies.

Coins are listed by type, followed by a list of reported years. Most of the reported years have never been confirmed and other years may also exist. Mintage figures are known for the 1293 and 1327 series, but are unreliable and of little utility.

Although some years are undoubtedly much rarer than others, there is at present no date collecting of Ottoman gold and therefore little justification for higher prices for rare dates.

There is no change in design in either the regular or de luxe series; only the toughra, accessional date and regnal year vary. The standard coins do not bear the denomination.

12-1/2 PIASTRES

.9020 gm., .917 GOLD, .0266 oz AGW

Monnaie de Luxe

Y#	Date	Year	Mintage	Fine	VF	XF
—	AH1293	25	—	45.00	50.00	60.00
		26	—	45.00	50.00	60.00
		27	—	45.00	50.00	60.00
		28	—	45.00	50.00	60.00
		29	—	45.00	50.00	60.00
		30	—	45.00	50.00	60.00
		31	—	45.00	50.00	60.00
		32	—	45.00	50.00	60.00

Monnaie de Luxe

Y#	Date	Year	Mintage	Fine	VF	XF
A40	AH1327	2	—	52.50	60.00	70.00
		3	—	52.50	60.00	70.00
		4	—	52.50	60.00	70.00
		5	—	52.50	60.00	70.00
		6	—	52.50	60.00	70.00

25 PIASTRES

1.8040 gm., .916 gold, .0532 oz AGW

C#	Date	Year	Mintage	Fine	VF	XF
295	AH1255	17	—	40.00	50.00	75.00
		18	—	40.00	50.00	75.00
		19	—	40.00	50.00	75.00
		20	—	40.00	50.00	75.00
		21	—	40.00	50.00	75.00
		22	—	40.00	50.00	75.00
		23	—	40.00	50.00	75.00

Y#	Date	Year	Mintage	Fine	VF	XF
16	AH1277	1	—	37.50	45.00	55.00
		2	—	37.50	45.00	55.00
		3	—	37.50	45.00	55.00
		4	—	37.50	45.00	55.00
		5	—	37.50	45.00	55.00
		6	—	37.50	45.00	55.00
		7	—	37.50	45.00	55.00
		9	—	37.50	45.00	55.00
		11	—	37.50	45.00	55.00
		12	—	37.50	45.00	55.00
		13	—	37.50	45.00	55.00
		15	—	37.50	45.00	55.00

Years 1-7,9,11-13,15 reported.

Obv: 'MURAD V' no flower to right of tughra

Y#	Date	Year	Mintage	Fine	VF	XF
A22	AH1293	1	—	200.00	250.00	300.00

Obv: 'ABDULHAMID II' flower to right of tughra

Y#	Date	Year	Mintage	Fine	VF	XF
A31	AH1293	3	—	70.00	80.00	100.00
		4	—	70.00	80.00	100.00
		6	—	70.00	80.00	100.00

Obv: 'EL GHAZI' to right of tughra

Y#	Date	Year	Mintage	Fine	VF	XF
36	AH1293	7	—	40.00	65.00	80.00
		8	—	40.00	65.00	80.00
		9	—	40.00	65.00	80.00
		10	—	40.00	65.00	80.00
		11	—	40.00	65.00	80.00
		12	—	40.00	65.00	80.00
		13	—	40.00	65.00	80.00
		14	—	40.00	65.00	80.00
		15	—	40.00	65.00	80.00
		16	—	40.00	65.00	80.00
		17	—	40.00	65.00	80.00
		18	—	40.00	65.00	80.00
		19	—	40.00	65.00	80.00
		20	—	40.00	65.00	80.00
		21	—	40.00	65.00	80.00
		22	—	40.00	65.00	80.00
		23	—	40.00	65.00	80.00
		24	—	40.00	65.00	80.00
		25	—	40.00	65.00	80.00
		26	—	40.00	65.00	80.00
		27	—	40.00	65.00	80.00
		28	—	40.00	65.00	80.00
		29	—	40.00	65.00	80.00

Y#	Date	Year	Mintage	Fine	VF	XF
36		30	—	40.00	65.00	80.00
		31	—	40.00	65.00	80.00
		32	—	40.00	65.00	80.00
		33	—	40.00	65.00	80.00
		34	—	40.00	65.00	80.00

Monnaie de Luxe

Y#	Date	Year	Mintage	Fine	VF	XF
B40	AH1293	23	—	50.00	60.00	70.00
		24	—	50.00	60.00	70.00
		25	—	50.00	60.00	70.00
		26	—	50.00	60.00	70.00
		27	—	50.00	60.00	70.00
		28	—	50.00	60.00	70.00
		29	—	50.00	60.00	70.00
		30	—	50.00	60.00	70.00
		31	—	50.00	60.00	70.00
		32	—	50.00	60.00	70.00
		33	—	50.00	60.00	70.00
		34	—	50.00	60.00	70.00

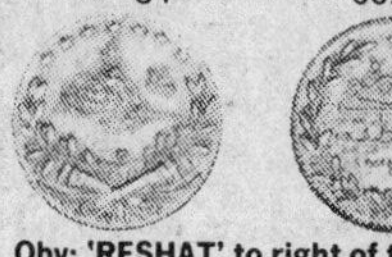

Obv: 'RESHAT' to right of tughra

Y#	Date	Year	Mintage	Fine	VF	XF
A51	AH1327	1	—	22.50	25.00	30.00
		2	—	22.50	25.00	30.00
		3	—	22.50	25.00	30.00
		4	—	22.50	25.00	30.00
		5	—	22.50	25.00	30.00
		6	—	22.50	25.00	30.00
		7	—	22.50	25.00	30.00

Obv: 'EL GHAZI' to right of tughra

Y#	Date	Year	Mintage	Fine	VF	XF
53	AH1327	7	—	BV	BV	45.00
		8	—	BV	BV	45.00
		9	—	BV	BV	45.00
		10	—	BV	BV	45.00

Years 7-10 reported.

Monnaie de Luxe
Obv: 'RESHAT' to right of tughra

Y#	Date	Year	Mintage	Fine	VF	XF
	AH1327	2	—	BV	BV	45.00
		3	—	BV	BV	45.00
		4	—	BV	BV	45.00
		5	—	BV	BV	45.00
		6	—	BV	BV	45.00

Monnaie de Luxe
Obv: 'EL GHAZI' to right of tughra

Y#	Date	Year	Mintage	Fine	VF	XF
—	AH1327	7	—	BV	BV	60.00
		8	—	BV	BV	60.00
		10	—	BV	BV	60.00

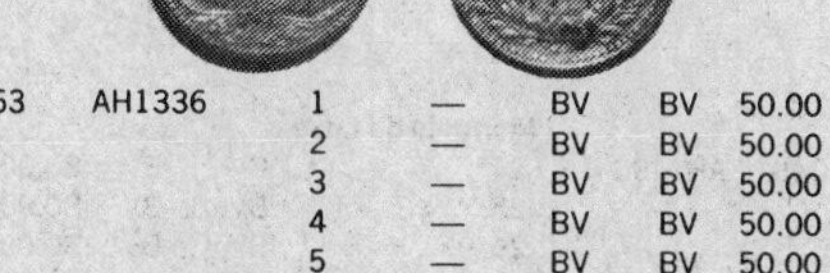

Y#	Date	Year	Mintage	Fine	VF	XF
63	AH1336	1	—	BV	BV	50.00
		2	—	BV	BV	50.00
		3	—	BV	BV	50.00
		4	—	BV	BV	50.00
		5	—	BV	BV	50.00

Monnaie de Luxe

Y#	Date	Year	Mintage	Fine	VF	XF
—	AH1336	2	—	BV	BV	60.00
		3	—	BV	BV	60.00

50 PIASTRES

3.6080 gm., .917 GOLD, .1064 oz AGW

C#	Date	Year	Mintage	Fine	VF	XF
296	AH1255	6	—	BV	BV	80.00
		7	—	BV	BV	80.00
		8	—	BV	BV	80.00
		9	—	BV	BV	80.00
		10	—	BV	BV	80.00
		11	—	BV	BV	80.00
		12	—	BV	BV	80.00
		13	—	BV	BV	80.00

C#	Date	Year	Mintage	Fine	VF	XF
296		15	—	BV	BV	80.00
		16	—	BV	BV	80.00
		17	—	BV	BV	80.00
		20	—	BV	BV	80.00
		22	—	BV	BV	80.00

Years 6-13, 15-17, 20, 22 reported.

Y#	Date	Year	Mintage	Fine	VF	XF
A16	AH1277	1	—	BV	BV	80.00
		2	—	BV	BV	80.00
		3	—	BV	BV	80.00
		7	—	BV	BV	80.00
		8	—	BV	BV	80.00
		9	—	BV	BV	80.00

Years 1, 2, 3, 7-9 reported.

Obv: 'MURAD V' no flower to right of tughra

Y#	Date	Year	Mintage	Fine	VF	XF
B22	AH1293	1	—	250.00	275.00	300.00

Obv: 'ABDULHAMID II' flower to right of tughra

Y#	Date	Year	Mintage	Fine	VF	XF
B31	AH1293	1	—	BV	BV	80.00
		2	—	BV	BV	80.00
		3	—	BV	BV	80.00
		6	—	BV	BV	80.00

Obv: ABDULHAMID II: 'EL GHAZI' to right of tughra

Y#	Date	Year	Mintage	Fine	VF	XF
37	AH1293	7	—	BV	BV	80.00
		8	—	BV	BV	80.00
		9	—	BV	BV	80.00
		10	—	BV	BV	80.00
		11	—	BV	BV	80.00
		12	—	BV	BV	80.00
		13	—	BV	BV	80.00
		14	—	BV	BV	80.00
		15	—	BV	BV	80.00
		16	—	BV	BV	80.00
		17	—	BV	BV	80.00
		18	—	BV	BV	80.00
		19	—	BV	BV	80.00
		20	—	BV	BV	80.00
		21	—	BV	BV	80.00
		22	—	BV	BV	80.00
		23	—	BV	BV	80.00
		24	—	BV	BV	80.00
		25	—	BV	BV	80.00
		26	—	BV	BV	80.00
		27	—	BV	BV	80.00
		28	—	BV	BV	80.00
		29	—	BV	BV	80.00
		30	—	BV	BV	80.00
		31	—	BV	BV	80.00
		32	—	BV	BV	80.00
		33	—	BV	BV	80.00
		34	—	BV	BV	80.00

Monnaie de Luxe

Y#	Date	Year	Mintage	Fine	VF	XF
C40	AH1293	24	—	BV	BV	80.00
		25	—	BV	BV	80.00
		26	—	BV	BV	80.00
		27	—	BV	BV	80.00
		28	—	BV	BV	80.00
		29	—	BV	BV	80.00
		30	—	BV	BV	80.00
		31	—	BV	BV	80.00
		32	—	BV	BV	80.00
		33	—	BV	BV	80.00
		34	—	BV	BV	80.00

Obv: 'RESHAT' to right of tughra

Y#	Date	Year	Mintage	Fine	VF	XF
B51	AH1327	1	—	BV	BV	80.00
		2	—	BV	BV	80.00
		3	—	BV	BV	80.00
		4	—	BV	BV	80.00
		5	—	BV	BV	80.00
		6	—	BV	BV	80.00

Obv: 'EL GHAZI' to right of tughra

Y#	Date	Year	Mintage	Fine	VF	XF
54	AH1327	7	—	BV	BV	80.00
		8	—	BV	BV	80.00
		9	—	BV	BV	80.00
		10	—	BV	BV	80.00

Monnaie de Luxe
Obv: 'RESHAT' to right of tughra

Y#	Date	Year	Mintage	Fine	VF	XF
—	AH1327	2	—	BV	BV	80.00
		3	—	BV	BV	80.00
		4	—	BV	BV	80.00
		5	—	BV	BV	80.00
		6	—	BV	BV	80.00

Monnaie de Luxe
Obv: 'EL GHAZI' to right of tughra

Y#	Date	Year	Mintage	Fine	VF	XF
—	AH1327	8	—	BV	75.00	80.00

Y#	Date	Year	Mintage	Fine	VF	XF
64	AH1336	1	—	BV	100.00	150.00
		2	—	BV	100.00	150.00

100 PIASTRES

7.2160 gm., .917 GOLD, .2128 oz AGW

C#	Date	Year	Mintage	Fine	VF	XF
297	AH1255	5	—	BV	BV	150.00
		6	—	BV	BV	150.00
		7	—	BV	BV	150.00
		8	—	BV	BV	150.00
		9	—	BV	BV	150.00
		10	—	BV	BV	150.00
		11	—	BV	BV	150.00
		12	—	BV	BV	150.00
		13	—	BV	BV	150.00
		14	—	BV	BV	150.00
		15	—	BV	BV	150.00
		16	—	BV	BV	150.00
		17	—	BV	BV	150.00
		18	—	BV	BV	150.00
		19	—	BV	BV	150.00
		20	—	BV	BV	150.00
		21	—	BV	BV	150.00
		22	—	BV	BV	150.00
		23	—	BV	BV	150.00

Y#	Date	Year	Mintage	Fine	VF	XF
17	AH1277	1	—	BV	BV	150.00
		2	—	BV	BV	150.00
		3	—	BV	BV	150.00
		4	—	BV	BV	150.00
		5	—	BV	BV	150.00
		6	—	BV	BV	150.00
		7	—	BV	BV	150.00
		8	—	BV	BV	150.00
		9	—	BV	BV	150.00
		10	—	BV	BV	150.00
		11	—	BV	BV	150.00
		12	—	BV	BV	150.00
		13	—	BV	BV	150.00
		14	—	BV	BV	150.00
		15	—	BV	BV	150.00

Obv: 'MURAD V' no flower to right of tughra

Y#	Date	Year	Mintage	Fine	VF	XF
C22	AH1293	1	—	200.00	225.00	250.00

Obv: 'ABDULHAMID II' flower to right of tughra

Y#	Date	Year	Mintage	Fine	VF	XF
C31	AH1293	1	—	BV	BV	150.00
		2	—	BV	BV	150.00
		3	—	BV	BV	150.00
		4	—	BV	BV	150.00
		6	—	BV	BV	150.00

Obv: 'EL GHAZI' to right of tughra

Y#	Date	Year	Mintage	Fine	VF	XF
38	AH1293	6	—	BV	BV	150.00
		7	—	BV	BV	150.00
		8	—	BV	BV	150.00
		9	—	BV	BV	150.00
		10	—	BV	BV	150.00
		11	—	BV	BV	150.00
		12	—	BV	BV	150.00
		13	—	BV	BV	150.00
		14	—	BV	BV	150.00
		15	—	BV	BV	150.00
		16	—	BV	BV	150.00
		17	—	BV	BV	150.00
		18	—	BV	BV	150.00
		19	—	BV	BV	150.00
		20	—	BV	BV	150.00
		21	—	BV	BV	150.00
		22	—	BV	BV	150.00
		23	—	BV	BV	150.00
		24	—	BV	BV	150.00
		25	—	BV	BV	150.00
		26	—	BV	BV	150.00
		27	—	BV	BV	150.00
		28	—	BV	BV	150.00
		29	—	BV	BV	150.00
		30	—	BV	BV	150.00
		31	—	BV	BV	150.00
		32	—	BV	BV	150.00
		33	—	BV	BV	150.00
		34	—	BV	BV	150.00

Monnaie de Luxe
Obv: 'EL GHAZI' to right of tughra

Y#	Date	Year	Mintage	Fine	VF	XF
D40	AH1293	24	—	BV	BV	150.00
		25	—	BV	BV	150.00
		26	—	BV	BV	150.00
		27	—	BV	BV	150.00
		28	—	BV	BV	150.00
		29	—	BV	BV	150.00
		30	—	BV	BV	150.00
		31	—	BV	BV	150.00
		32	—	BV	BV	150.00
		33	—	BV	BV	150.00
		34	—	BV	BV	150.00

Obv: 'RESHAT' to right of tughra

Y#	Date	Year	Mintage	Fine	VF	XF
C51	AH1327	1	—	BV	BV	150.00
		2	—	BV	BV	150.00
		3	—	BV	BV	150.00
		4	—	BV	BV	150.00
		5	—	BV	BV	150.00
		6	—	BV	BV	150.00
		7	—	BV	BV	150.00

Obv: 'EL GHAZI' to right of tughra

Y#	Date	Year	Mintage	Fine	VF	XF
55	AH1327	7	—	BV	BV	150.00
		8	—	BV	BV	150.00
		9	—	BV	BV	150.00
		10	—	BV	BV	150.00

Monnaie de Luxe
Obv: 'RESHAT' to right of tughra

Y#	Date	Year	Mintage	Fine	VF	XF
—	AH1327	1	—	BV	BV	150.00
		2	—	BV	BV	150.00
		3	—	BV	BV	150.00
		4	—	BV	BV	150.00
		5	—	BV	BV	150.00
		6	—	BV	BV	150.00

Monnaie de Luxe
Obv: 'EL GHAZI' to right of tughra

Y#	Date	Year	Mintage	Fine	VF	XF
—	AH1327	8	—	200.00	225.00	250.00

Y#	Date	Year	Mintage	Fine	VF	XF
65	AH1336	1	—	BV	BV	150.00
		2	—	BV	BV	150.00

Monnaie de Luxe

Y#	Date	Year	Mintage	Fine	VF	XF
—	AH1336	2	—	200.00	225.00	250.00
		3	—	200.00	225.00	250.00

250 PIASTRES

18.0400 gm., .917 GOLD, .5319 oz AGW

Y#	Date	Year	Mintage	Fine	VF	XF
298	AH1255	7	—	BV	BV	400.00
		9	—	BV	BV	400.00
		18	—	BV	BV	400.00
		22	—	BV	BV	400.00
A17	AH1277	1	—	BV	BV	400.00
		5	—	BV	BV	400.00
		7	—	BV	BV	400.00
		8	—	BV	BV	400.00
		9	—	BV	BV	400.00

Obv: 'ABDULHAMID II' flower to right of tughra

Y#	Date	Year	Mintage	Fine	VF	XF
D31	AH1293	1	—	900.00	1100.	1400.
		2	—	900.00	1100.	1400.

Years 1-2 reported.

Y#	Date	Year	Mintage	Fine	VF	XF
39	AH1293	7	—	BV	BV	400.00
		8	—	BV	BV	400.00
		9	—	BV	BV	400.00
		10	—	BV	BV	400.00
		11	—	BV	BV	400.00
		12	—	BV	BV	400.00
		13	—	BV	BV	400.00
		14	—	BV	BV	400.00
		15	—	BV	BV	400.00
		16	—	BV	BV	400.00
		17	—	BV	BV	400.00
		18	—	BV	BV	400.00
		19	—	BV	BV	400.00
		20	—	BV	BV	400.00
		21	—	BV	BV	400.00
		22	—	BV	BV	400.00
		23	—	BV	BV	400.00
		24	—	BV	BV	400.00
		25	—	BV	BV	400.00
		26	—	BV	BV	400.00
		27	—	BV	BV	400.00
		28	—	BV	BV	400.00
		29	—	BV	BV	400.00
		30	—	BV	BV	400.00
		31	—	BV	BV	400.00
		32	—	BV	BV	400.00

Monnaie de Luxe

Y#	Date	Year	Mintage	Fine	VF	XF
41	AH1293	24	—	BV	BV	400.00
		25	—	BV	BV	400.00
		26	—	BV	BV	400.00
		27	—	BV	BV	400.00
		28	—	BV	BV	400.00
		29	—	BV	BV	400.00
		30	—	BV	BV	400.00
		31	—	BV	BV	400.00
		32	—	BV	BV	400.00
		33	—	BV	BV	400.00

Obv: 'RESHAT' to right of tughra

Y#	Date	Year	Mintage	Fine	VF	XF
D51	AH1327	1	—	BV	BV	400.00
		2	—	BV	BV	400.00
		3	—	BV	BV	400.00
		4	—	BV	BV	400.00
		5	—	BV	BV	400.00
		6	—	BV	BV	400.00

Obv: 'EL GHAZI' to right of tughra

Y#	Date	Year	Mintage	Fine	VF	XF
56	AH1327	7	—	750.00	900.00	1200.

Monnaie de Luxe
Obv: 'RESHAT' to right of tughra

Y#	Date	Year	Mintage	Fine	VF	XF
—	AH1327	2	—	BV	BV	400.00
		3	—	BV	BV	400.00
		4	—	BV	BV	400.00
		5	—	BV	BV	400.00
		6	—	BV	BV	400.00

Monnaie de Luxe
Obv: 'EL GHAZI' to right of tughra

Y#	Date	Year	Mintage	Fine	VF	XF
—	AH1327	8	—	BV	BV	400.00
66	AH1336	1	—	1000.	1100.	1200.
		2	—	1000.	1100.	1200.
		3	—	1000.	1100.	1200.

Monnaie de Luxe

Y#	Date	Year	Mintage	Fine	VF	XF
—	AH1336	2	—	BV	BV	400.00
		3	—	BV	BV	400.00

500 PIASTRES

36.0800 gm., .917 GOLD, 1.0638 oz AGW

Y#	Date	Year	Mintage	Fine	VF	XF
299	AH1255	6	—	BV	900.00	1000.
		18	—	BV	900.00	1000.
		20	—	BV	900.00	1000.
		22	—	BV	900.00	1000.

Y#	Date	Year	Mintage	Fine	VF	XF
B17	AH1277	2	—	BV	900.00	1000.
		3	—	BV	900.00	1000.
		4	—	BV	900.00	1000.
		5	—	BV	900.00	1000.
		6	—	BV	900.00	1000.
		7	—	BV	900.00	1000.
		8	—	BV	900.00	1000.
		9	—	BV	900.00	1000.
		10	—	BV	900.00	1000.
		11	—	BV	900.00	1000.
		12	—	BV	900.00	1000.
		13	—	BV	900.00	1000.

Obv: Flower to right of tughra

Y#	Date	Year	Mintage	Fine	VF	XF
E31	AH1293	1	—	BV	900.00	1000.
		2	—	BV	900.00	1000.

Obv: 'EL GHAZI' to right of tughra

Y#	Date	Year	Mintage	Fine	VF	XF
40	AH1293	7	—	BV	900.00	1000.
		8	—	BV	900.00	1000.
		9	—	BV	900.00	1000.
		10	—	BV	900.00	1000.
		11	—	BV	900.00	1000.
		12	—	BV	900.00	1000.
		13	—	BV	900.00	1000.
		14	—	BV	900.00	1000.
		15	—	BV	900.00	1000.
		16	—	BV	900.00	1000.
		17	—	BV	900.00	1000.
		18	—	BV	900.00	1000.
		19	—	BV	900.00	1000.
		20	—	BV	900.00	1000.
		21	—	BV	900.00	1000.
		22	—	BV	900.00	1000.
		23	—	BV	900.00	1000.
		24	—	BV	900.00	1000.
		25	—	BV	900.00	1000.
		26	—	BV	900.00	1000.
		27	—	BV	900.00	1000.
		28	—	BV	900.00	1000.
		29	—	BV	900.00	1000.
		30	—	BV	900.00	1000.
		31	—	BV	900.00	1000.
		32	—	BV	900.00	1000.

Monnaie de Luxe

Y#	Date	Year	Mintage	Fine	VF	XF
42	AH1293	26	—	BV	900.00	1000.
		27	—	BV	900.00	1000.

Y#	Date	Year	Mintage	Fine	VF	XF
42		28	—	BV	900.00	1000.
		29	—	BV	900.00	1000.
		30	—	BV	900.00	1000.
		31	—	BV	900.00	1000.
		32	—	BV	900.00	1000.
		33	—	BV	900.00	1000.

Obv: 'RESHAT' to right of tughra

Y#	Date	Year	Mintage	Fine	VF	XF
E51	AH1327	1	—	1800.	2000.	2500.
		2	—	1800.	2000.	2500.
		3	—	1800.	2000.	2500.
		4	—	1800.	2000.	2500.
		5	—	1800.	2000.	2500.
		6	—	1800.	2000.	2500.

Obv: 'EL GHAZI' to right of tughra

Y#	Date	Year	Mintage	Fine	VF	XF
57	AH1327	10	—	2000.	2300.	2750.

Monnaie de Luxe
Obv: 'RESHAT' to right of tughra, similar to Y#42.

Y#	Date	Year	Mintage	Fine	VF	XF
—	AH1327	2	—	1880.	2000.	2500.
		3	—	1800.	2000.	2500.
		4	—	1800.	2000.	2500.
		5	—	1800.	2000.	2500.
		6	—	1800.	2000.	2500.

Monnaie de Luxe
Obv: 'EL GHAZI' to right of tughra

Y#	Date	Year	Mintage	Fine	VF	XF
—	AH1327	7	—	1800.	2000.	2500.
		8	—	1800.	2000.	2500.

Y#	Date	Year	Mintage	Fine	VF	XF
67	AH1336	1	—	BV	900.00	1000.
		2	—	BV	900.00	1000.
		3	—	BV	900.00	1000.

Monnaie de Luxe

Y#	Date	Year	Mintage	Fine	VF	XF
—	AH1336	1	—	1000.	1200.	1500.
		2	—	1000.	1200.	1500.
		3	—	1000.	1200.	1500.
		4	—	1000.	1200.	1500.

REPUBLIC

OLD MONETARY SYSTEM

100 PARA

ALUMINUM-BRONZE

Y#	Date	Mintage	Fine	VF	XF
68	AH1340	1.798	.25	.45	1.25
	1341	5.583	.25	.45	1.25
68a	AD1926	4.388	.25	.45	1.25
	1928	—	75.00	125.00	175.00

5 KURUS

ALUMINUM-BRONZE

Y#	Date	Mintage	Fine	VF	XF
69	AH1340	5.023	.30	.50	1.25
	1341	23.545	.30	.50	1.25
69a	AD1926	.356	.30	.50	1.25
	1928	—	75.00	125.00	175.00

10 KURUS

ALUMINUM-BRONZE

Y#	Date	Mintage	Fine	VF	XF
70	AH1340	4.836	.40	.85	2.00
	1341	14.223	.40	.85	2.00
70a	AD1926	.856	.40	.85	2.00
	1928	—	75.00	125.00	175.00

25 KURUS

NICKEL

Y#	Date	Mintage	Fine	VF	XF
71	AH1341	4.973	.75	1.25	3.00
71a	AD1926	.027	100.00	150.00	250.00
	1928	5.794	.80	1.50	3.25

GOLD COINS

The gold coins continued to be struck to the weights and finenesses of the old Ottoman system, but were tariffed at the going price of gold. The same continues to hold true today. Both regular and de luxe strikes were made.

25 PIASTRES

1.8040 gm., .917 GOLD, .0532 oz AGW

Y#	Date	Mintage	Fine	VF	XF
72	1926	4,539	50.00	60.00	75.00
	1927	.014	50.00	60.00	75.00
	1928	8,424	50.00	60.00	75.00
	1929	—	50.00	60.00	75.00

1.7540 gm., .917 GOLD, .0517 oz AGW
Monnaie de Luxe

Y#	Date	Mintage	Fine	VF	XF
77	1927	4,103	75.00	90.00	100.00
	1928	4,549	75.00	90.00	100.00

50 PIASTRES

3.6080 gm., .917 GOLD, .1064 oz AGW

Y#	Date	Mintage	Fine	VF	XF
73	1926	2,168	75.00	90.00	100.00
	1927	2,116	75.00	90.00	100.00
	1928	2,431	75.00	90.00	100.00
	1929	—	75.00	90.00	100.00

3.5080 gm., .917 GOLD, .1034 oz AGW
Monnaie de Luxe

Y#	Date	Mintage	Fine	VF	XF
78	1927	3,903	150.00	175.00	200.00
	1928	3,620	150.00	175.00	200.00

100 PIASTRES

7.2160 gm., .917 GOLD, .2128 oz AGW

Y#	Date	Mintage	Fine	VF	XF
74	1926	1,073	150.00	180.00	225.00
	1927	—	150.00	180.00	225.00
	1928	920 pcs.	150.00	180.00	225.00
	1929	—	150.00	180.00	225.00

7.0160 gm., .917 GOLD, .2069 oz AGW
Monnaie de Luxe

Y#	Date	Mintage	Fine	VF	XF
79	1927	8,676	225.00	275.00	300.00
	1928	6,092	225.00	275.00	300.00

250 PIASTRES

18.0400 gm., .917 GOLD, .5319 oz AGW

Y#	Date	Mintage	Fine	VF	XF
75	1926	604 Pcs.	400.00	500.00	750.00
	1927	886 Pcs.	400.00	500.00	750.00
	1928	110 Pcs.	400.00	500.00	750.00
	1929	—	400.00	500.00	750.00

17.5400 gm., .917 GOLD, .5172 oz AGW
Monnaie de Luxe
Obv: Similar to 500 Piastres, Y#81.

Y#	Date	Mintage	Fine	VF	XF
80	1927	7,411	500.00	600.00	850.00
	1928	5,045	500.00	600.00	850.00

500 PIASTRES

36.0800 gm., .917 GOLD, 1.0638 oz AGW

Y#	Date	Mintage	Fine	VF	XF
76	1925	226 Pcs.	1000.	1200.	1500.
	1926	2,268	1000.	1200.	1500.
	1927	4,011	1000.	1200.	1500.
76	1928	375 Pcs.	1000.	1200.	1500.
	1929	—	1000.	1200.	1500.

35.0800 gm., .917 GOLD, 1.0344 oz AGW
Monnaie de Luxe

Y#	Date	Mintage	Fine	VF	XF
81	1927	5,097	1200.	1400.	1650.
	1928	2,242	1200.	1400.	1650.

DECIMAL COINAGE

Western numerals and Latin alphabet

40 Para = 1 Kurus
100 Kurus = 1 Lira

10 PARA
(1/4 KURUS)

ALUMINUM-BRONZE

Y#	Date	Mintage	Fine	VF	XF
91	1936	—	—	Pattern	250.00
	1940	30.800	.20	.35	.75
	1941	22.400	.20	.35	.75
	1942	26.800	.20	.35	.75

1/2 KURUS
(= 20 PARA)

BRASS

Y#	Date	Mintage	Fine	VF	XF
A92	1948	150 pcs.	250.00	300.00	350.00

Not released to circulation.

KURUS

COPPER-NICKEL

Y#	Date	Mintage	Fine	VF	XF
87	1935	.784	.50	1.00	2.50
	1936	5.300	.25	.45	1.00
	1937	4.500	.25	.45	1.00

Y#	Date	Mintage	Fine	VF	XF
90	1938	16.400	.25	.50	1.00
	1939	21.600	.25	.50	1.00
	1940	8.800	.25	.60	1.20
	1941	6.700	.25	.60	1.20
	1942	10.800	.25	.50	1.00
	1943	4.000	.25	.60	1.20
	1944	6.000	.25	.60	1.20

BRASS

Y#	Date	Mintage	VF	XF	Unc
93	1947	.890	1.00	2.00	3.00
	1948	35.470	.15	.25	.70
	1949	29.530	.15	.25	.60
	1950	32.800	.15	.25	.60
	1951	6.310	.30	.50	1.50
154	1961	1.180	—	—	.15
(117)	1962	3.620	—	—	.15
	1963	1.085	—	—	.15

BRONZE

Y#	Date	Mintage	VF	XF	Unc
154a	1963	1.180	—	—	.15
(117a)	1964	2.520	—	—	.10
	1965	1.860	—	—	.10
	1966	1.820	—	—	.10
	1967	2.410	—	—	.10
	1968	1.040	—	—	.10
	1969	.900	—	—	.10
	1970	1.960	—	—	.10
	1971	2.940	—	—	.30
	1972	.720	—	—	.30
	1973	.540	—	—	.30
	1974	.510	—	—	.30

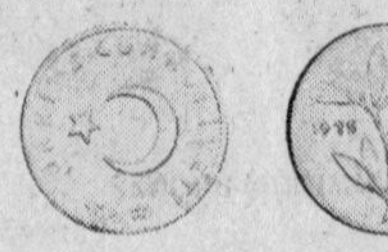

ALUMINUM

Y#	Date	Mintage	VF	XF	Unc
154c	1975	.690	—	—	.50
(117b)	1976	.200	—	—	.75
	1977	.110	—	—	.90

BRONZE
F.A.O. Issue

Y#	Date	Mintage	VF	XF	Unc
187	1979	.015	—	—	2.00
	1979	Inc. Ab.	—	Proof	3.00

ALUMINUM
F.A.O. Issue

Y#	Date	Mintage	VF	XF	Unc
187a	1979	.015	—	—	2.00
	1979	Inc. Ab.	—	Proof	3.00

2-1/2 KURUS

BRASS

Y#	Date	Mintage	VF	XF	Unc
94	1948	24.720	.25	.50	1.00
	1949	23.720	.25	.50	1.00
	1950	11.560	.25	.50	1.00
	1951	2.000	1.00	3.00	5.00

5 KURUS

COPPER-NICKEL

Y#	Date	Mintage	Fine	VF	XF
88	1935	.100	2.00	3.50	8.50
	1936	2.900	.25	.75	2.00
	1937	4.060	.25	.70	1.85
	1938	13.380	.20	.50	1.00
	1939	12.520	.20	.50	1.00
	1940	4.340	.20	.60	1.25
	1942	10.160	.20	.50	1.00
	1943	15.360	.20	.50	1.00

BRASS

Y#	Date	Mintage	VF	XF	Unc
95	1949	4.500	—	.15	.75
	1950	45.900	—	.15	.50
	1951	29.600	—	.15	.50
	1955	15.300	—	.15	.50
	1956	21.380	—	.15	.50
	1957	3.320	—	.15	.75

BRONZE, 2.5 gm.

Y#	Date	Mintage	VF	XF	Unc
155	1958	25.870	.25	.50	.75
(111)	1959	21.580	—	—	.15
	1960	17.150	—	—	.15
	1961	11.110	—	—	.10
	1962	15.280	—	—	.15
	1963	17.680	—	—	.10
	1964	18.190	—	—	.15
	1965	19.170	—	—	.10
	1966	19.840	—	—	.15
	1967	16.170	—	—	.15
	1968	26.050	—	—	.15

Reduced weight, 2.0 gm.

Y#	Date	Mintage	VF	XF	Unc
155a	1969	33.630	—	—	.15
(111a)	1970	29.360	—	—	.15
	1971	17.440	—	—	.15
	1972	22.670	—	—	.10
	1973	17.370	—	—	.15

1.35 gm.

Y#	Date	Mintage	VF	XF	Unc
155b	1974	13.540	—	—	.15

ALUMINUM

Y#	Date	Mintage	VF	XF	Unc
155c	1975	1.560	—	—	.20
(111b)	1976	1.321	—	—	.20
	1977	.308	—	—	.75

F.A.O. Issue

Y#	Date	Mintage	VF	XF	Unc
163	1975	1.019	—	—	.25
(126)					

F.A.O. Issue

Y#	Date	Mintage	VF	XF	Unc
172	1976	.017	—	—	.50

10 KURUS

COPPER-NICKEL

Y#	Date	Mintage	Fine	VF	XF
89	1935	.060	4.00	7.50	17.50
	1936	3.580	.30	.50	1.00
	1937	3.020	.30	.50	1.00
	1938	6.610	.30	.50	1.00
	1939	4.610	.30	.50	1.00
	1940	6.960	.30	.50	1.00

BRASS

Y#	Date	Mintage	VF	XF	Unc
96	1949	27.000	—	.15	.50
	1951	6.200	—	.15	.60
	1955	10.090	—	.15	.50
	1956	9.910	—	.15	.50

BRONZE, 4.0 gm.

Y#	Date	Mintage	VF	XF	Unc
156	1958	14.770	.10	.25	1.00
(112)	1959	11.160	—	.10	.20
	1960	9.450	—	.10	.20
	1961	5.370	—	.10	.20
	1962	9.250	—	.10	.20
	1963	10.390	—	.10	.20
	1964	9.890	—	.10	.20
	1965	10.480	—	.10	.20
	1966	12.200	—	.10	.20
	1967	11.410	—	.10	.20
	1968	1.862	—	.10	.20

Reduced weight, 3.5 gm.

Y#	Date	Mintage	VF	XF	Unc
156a	1969	21.190	—	—	.15
	1970	19.930	—	—	.15
	1971	14.780	—	—	.15
	1972	17.960	—	—	.15
	1973	11.930	—	—	.15

2.5 gm.

Y#	Date	Mintage	VF	XF	Unc
156c	1974	9.280	—	—	.20
(112b)					

ALUMINUM

Y#	Date	Mintage	VF	XF	Unc
156b	1975	2.165	—	—	.15

Y#	Date	Mintage	VF	XF	Unc
156b	1976	.559	—	—	.35
	1977	.308	—	.50	.75

BRONZE
F.A.O. Issue, 3.5 gm.

Y#	Date	Mintage	VF	XF	Unc
164	1971	.630	—	—	.15
(A118)	1972	.500	.15	.40	1.25
	1973	.010	1.00	2.50	7.50

F.A.O. Issue, 2.5 gm.

Y#	Date	Mintage	VF	XF	Unc
164a (A118a)	1974	.605	—	.25	.50

ALUMINUM
F.A.O. Issue

Y#	Date	Mintage	VF	XF	Unc
164b	1975	.517	—	—	.25
(118b)	1976	.738	—	—	—

F.A.O. Issue

Y#	Date	Mintage	VF	XF	Unc
173	1976	.017	—	.25	.50

25 KURUS

3.0000 gm., .830 SILVER, .0801 oz ASW

Y#	Date	Mintage	Fine	VF	XF
83	1935	.888	BV	4.00	7.50
	1936	10.576	BV	5.00	9.00
	1937	8.536	BV	5.00	9.00

NICKEL-BRONZE

Y#	Date	Mintage	VF	XF	Unc
92	1944	20.000	.20	.50	1.25
	1945	5.328	.20	.50	1.25
	1946	2.672	.40	.85	2.00

BRASS

Y#	Date	Mintage	VF	XF	Unc
97	1948	18.000	.15	.40	.65
	1949	21.000	.15	.40	.65
	1951	2.000	.20	.50	1.00
	1955	9.624	.15	.40	.65
	1956	14.376	.15	.40	.65

STAINLESS STEEL
Obv: Ground unbroken under woman's feet.

Y#	Date	Mintage	VF	XF	Unc
157 (113)	1959	21.864	.15	.25	.35

Obv: Uneven ground under woman's feet.

Y#	Date	Mintage	VF	XF	Unc
157b	1960	14.778	—	.15	.35
	1961	7.248	—	.15	.50
	1962	10.722	—	.15	.40
	1963	11.016	—	.15	.40
	1964	13.962	—	.15	.35
	1965	9.816	—	.15	.35
	1966	2.424	—	.15	.40

Reduced weight, 4 gm.

Y#	Date	Mintage	VF	XF	Unc
157a	1966	7.596	—	.15	.30
(113a)	1967	17.022	—	.10	.25
	1968	31.482	—	.10	.25
	1969	34.566	—	.10	.25
	1970	32.960	—	.10	.25
	1973	20.496	—	.10	.25
	1974	16.602	—	.10	.25
	1977	10.210	—	.10	.25
	1978	.185	—	.10	.25

50 KURUS

6.0000 gm., .830 SILVER, .1601 oz ASW

Y#	Date	Mintage	Fine	VF	XF
84	1935	.630	BV	7.00	10.00
	1936	5.082	BV	BV	7.00
	1937	4.270	BV	BV	7.00

4.0000 gm., .600 SILVER, .0772 oz ASW

Y#	Date	Mintage	VF	XF	Unc
98	1947	9.296	BV	BV	6.00
	1948	12.704	BV	BV	6.00

Without edge inscription.

Y#	Date	Mintage	VF	XF	Unc
98a	1947	Inc. Ab.	6.00	7.00	9.00
	1948	Inc. Ab.	6.00	7.00	9.00

STAINLESS STEEL

Y#	Date	Mintage	VF	XF	Unc
161	1971	16.756	—	.15	.40
(A113)	1972	22.152	—	.15	.40
	1973	18.928	—	.15	.40
	1974	14.480	—	.15	.35
	1975	27.714	—	.15	.35
	1976	27.476	—	.15	.35
	1977	13.976	—	—	—
	1979	150.220	—	—	—

F.A.O. Issue

Y#	Date	Mintage	VF	XF	Unc
178	1978	.010	—	—	—

F.A.O. Issue

Y#	Date	Mintage	VF	XF	Unc
188	1979	.010	—	—	—

100 KURUS (1 LIRA)

12.0000 gm., .830 SILVER, .3203 oz ASW

Y#	Date	Mintage	Fine	VF	XF
82.1	1934 high star	.718	12.50	22.50	35.00

Y#	Date	Mintage	Fine	VF	XF
82.2	1934 low star	Inc. Ab.	BV	BV	15.00

LIRA

12.0000 gm., .830 SILVER, .3203 oz ASW
Kemal Ataturk

Y#	Date	Mintage	Fine	VF	XF
85	1937	1.624	BV	BV	15.00
	1938	8.282	BV	15.00	30.00
	1939	.376	BV	BV	15.00

Ismet Inonu

Y#	Date	Mintage	Fine	VF	XF
86	1940	.253	BV	12.50	20.00
	1941	6.167	BV	BV	15.00

7.5000 gm., .600 SILVER, .1447 oz ASW

Y#	Date	Mintage	VF	XF	Unc
99	1947	11.104	BV	BV	8.00

Y#	Date	Mintage	VF	XF	Unc
	1948	16.896	BV	BV	6.00

Without edge inscription.

Y#	Date	Mintage	VF	XF	Unc
99a	1947	Inc. Ab.	7.00	8.50	12.00
	1948	Inc. Ab.	6.00	8.00	10.00

COPPER-NICKEL

Y#	Date	Mintage	VF	XF	Unc
158 (110)	1957	25.000	.60	1.00	3.00

STAINLESS STEEL

Y#	Date	Mintage	VF	XF	Unc
158a	1959	7.452	.20	.30	.60
(114)	1960	11.436	.20	.30	.60
	1961	2.100	.20	.30	.60
	1962	4.228	.20	.30	.60
	1963	4.316	.20	.30	.60
	1964	4.976	.20	.30	.60
	1965	5.348	.20	.30	.60
	1966	8.040	.20	.30	.60

Reduced weight, 7 gm.

Y#	Date	Mintage	VF	XF	Unc
158b	1967	10.444	—	.25	.50
(114a)	1968	12.728	—	.25	.50
	1969	6.612	—	.25	.50
	1970	8.652	—	.25	.50
	1971	10.504	—	.20	.40
	1972	26.512	—	.20	.40
	1973	12.596	—	.20	.40
	1974	11.596	—	.20	.40
	1975	20.348	—	.20	.40
	1976	23.144	—	.20	.40
	1977	28.300	—	.20	.40
	1978	22.156	—	.20	.40
	1979	—	—	.20	.40

F.A.O. Issue

Y#	Date	Mintage	VF	XF	Unc
179	1978	.010	—	—	—

F.A.O. Issue
Similar to 50 Kurus, Y#188.

Y#	Date	Mintage	VF	XF	Unc
189	1979	.010	—	—	—

2-1/2 LIRA

STAINLESS STEEL, 12 gm.

Y#	Date	Mintage	VF	XF	Unc
159	1960	4.015	.35	.60	1.00
(115)	1961	1.222	.35	.60	1.50
	1962	3.636	.35	.60	1.00
	1963	3.108	.35	.60	1.00
	1964	2.710	.35	.60	1.00
	1965	1.246	.35	.60	1.10
	1966	1.788	.35	.60	1.00
	1967	5.333	.35	.60	.75
	1968	2.707	.35	.60	.75

Reduced weight, 9 gm.

Y#	Date	Mintage	VF	XF	Unc
159b	1969	1.378	.15	.25	.50
(115a)	1970	3.777	.15	.25	.50
	1971	2.170	.15	.25	.50
	1972	9.147	.15	.25	.50
	1973	4.348	.15	.25	.60
	1974	3.816	.15	.25	.50
	1975	9.811	.15	.25	.50
	1976	3.952	.15	.25	.50
	1977	19.553	.15	.25	.50
	1978	15.738	.15	.25	.50
	1979	—	.15	.25	.50

F.A.O. Issue

Y#	Date	Mintage	VF	XF	Unc
165 (118)	1970	.200	—	—	1.00

STAINLESS STEEL
F.A.O. Issue

Y#	Date	Mintage	VF	XF	Unc
175	1977	.025	—	—	2.00

F.A.O. Issue

Y#	Date	Mintage	VF	XF	Unc
180	1978	.010	—	—	3.00

F.A.O. Issue

Y#	Date	Mintage	VF	XF	Unc
190	1979	.010	—	—	3.00

5 LIRA

STAINLESS STEEL

Y#	Date	Mintage	VF	XF	Unc
162	1974	2.842	.40	.75	1.00
(125)	1975	10.855	.40	.75	1.25
	1976	17.532	.35	.55	1.25
	1977	6.172	—	—	—
	1978	.076	—	—	—
	1979	40.271	—	—	—

International Women's Year and F.A.O. Issue

Y#	Date	Mintage	VF	XF	Unc
174	1976	.017	.35	.60	1.25

F.A.O. Issue

Y#	Date	Mintage	VF	XF	Unc
176	1977	.025	.50	1.00	1.50

F.A.O. Issue

Y#	Date	Mintage	VF	XF	Unc
181	1978	.010	.75	2.00	3.00

F.A.O. Issue

Y#	Date	Mintage	VF	XF	Unc
191	1979	.010	.75	2.00	3.00

10 LIRA

15.0000 gm., .830 SILVER, .4003 oz ASW

Y#	Date	Mintage	VF	XF	Unc
160 (116)	1960	8.000	BV	BV	15.00

NOTE: Counterfeits of Y#160 are common.

25 LIRA

.830 SILVER
50th Anniversary of National Assembly

Y#	Date	Mintage	VF	XF	Unc
166 (119)	1970	.023	BV	15.00	20.00

50 LIRA

.830 SILVER
900th Anniversary of Battle of Malazgirt

Y#	Date	Mintage	VF	XF	Unc
167	1971	.033	BV	BV	17.50
(120)	1971	Inc. Ab.	—	Proof	25.00

50th Anniversary of 30 August 1922 Victory

Y#	Date	Mintage	VF	XF	Unc
168	1972	.172	BV	BV	15.00
(121)	1972	—	—	Proof	18.00

19.0000 gm., .900 SILVER, .5498 oz ASW
50th Anniversary of Republic

Y#	Date	Mintage	VF	XF	Unc
169 (122)	1973	.070	BV	BV	20.00

F.A.O. Issue

Y#	Date	Mintage	VF	XF	Unc
177	1977	.025	BV	BV	20.00

100 LIRA

22.0000 gm., .900 SILVER, .6367 oz ASW
50th Anniversary of Republic

Y#	Date	Mintage	VF	XF	Unc
170 (123)	1973	.065	BV	BV	30.00

150 LIRA

8.9200 gm., .800 SILVER, .2295 oz ASW
World Cup Soccer Championship

Y#	Date	Mintage	VF	XF	Unc
185	1978	9,000	BV	BV	30.00
	1978	1,000	—	Proof	50.00

F.A.O. Issue

Y#	Date	Mintage	VF	XF	Unc
182	1978	.010	BV	BV	35.00
	1978	2,500	—	Proof	65.00

F.A.O. Issue

Y#	Date	Mintage	VF	XF	Unc
192	1979	.010	BV	BV	35.00
	1979	2,500	—	Proof	65.00

200 LIRA

9.0000 gm., .830 SILVER, .2402 oz ASW
Mevlana Celaleddin I-Rumi

Y#	Date	Mintage	VF	XF	Unc
186	1978	.011	BV	BV	30.00
	1978	1,000	—	Proof	50.00

500 LIRA

9.0000 gm., .917 GOLD, .2654 oz AGW
50th Anniversary of Republic

Y#	Date	Mintage	VF	XF	Unc
171 (124)	1973	.030	BV	BV	225.00

F.A.O. Issue

Y#	Date	Mintage	VF	XF	Unc
183	1978	900 pcs.	—	Proof	300.00
	1979	—	—	Proof	200.00

Mevlana Celaleddin I-Rumi

Y#	Date	Mintage	VF	XF	Unc
—	1978	900 pcs.	—	Proof	200.00

1000 LIRA

.917 GOLD

Y#	Date	Mintage	VF	XF	Unc
184	1978	450 pcs.	—	Proof	500.00
	1979	450 pcs.	—	Proof	500.00

Mevlana Celaleddin I-Rumi

Y#	Date	Mintage	VF	XF	Unc
—	1979	—	—	Proof	500.00

GOLD COINAGE

Since 1943, the Turkish government has issued regular and deluxe gold coins in five denominations corresponding to the traditional 25, 50, 100, 250, and 500 Piastres of the Ottoman period. The regular coins are all dated 1923, plus the year of the republic (e.g. 1923/40 - 1963), de luxe coins bear actual AD dates. For a few years, 1944—1950, the bust of Ismet Inonu replaced that of Kemal Ataturk.

25 PIASTRES

1.8041 gm., .917 GOLD, .0532 oz AGW
Ismet Inonu

Y#	Date	Mintage	VF	XF	Unc
A99	1923/20	Inc. Ab.	BV	40.00	60.00
	1923/22	3,228	BV	40.00	60.00
	1923/23	2,757	BV	40.00	60.00
	1923/24	.046	BV	40.00	60.00
	1923/25	.020	BV	45.00	60.00
	1923/26	.011	BV	40.00	60.00

Kemal Ataturk

Y#	Date	Mintage	VF	XF	Unc
134	1923/20	.014	BV	40.00	60.00
(100)	1923/27	.018	BV	40.00	600.00
	1923/28	.015	BV	40.00	60.00
	1923/29	.015	BV	40.00	60.00
	1923/30	.017	BV	40.00	60.00
	1923/31	.019	BV	40.00	60.00
	1923/32	5,455	50.00	55.00	75.00
	1923/33	.011	BV	40.00	60.00
	1923/34	.020	BV	40.00	60.00
	1923/35	.025	BV	40.00	60.00
	1923/36	.034	BV	40.00	60.00
	1923/37	.031	BV	40.00	60.00
	1923/38	.035	BV	40.00	60.00
	1923/39	.046	BV	40.00	60.00
	1923/40	.049	BV	40.00	60.00
	1923/41	.059	BV	40.00	60.00
	1923/42	.074	BV	40.00	60.00
	1923/43	.090	BV	40.00	60.00
	1923/44	.085	BV	40.00	60.00
	1923/45	.073	BV	40.00	60.00
	1923/46	.089	BV	40.00	60.00
	1923/47	.119	BV	40.00	60.00
	1923/48	.112	BV	40.00	60.00
	1923/49	.112	BV	40.00	60.00
	1923/50	.067	BV	40.00	60.00
	1923/51	.040	BV	40.00	60.00
	1923/52	.071	BV	40.00	50.00
	1923/53	.124	BV	40.00	50.00
	1923/54	196	BV	40.00	50.00
	1923/55	.112	BV	40.00	50.00
	1923/56	—	—	—	—

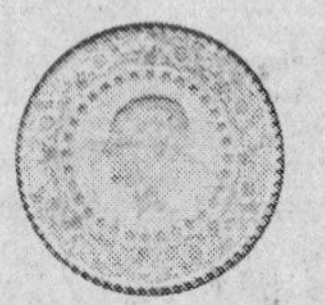
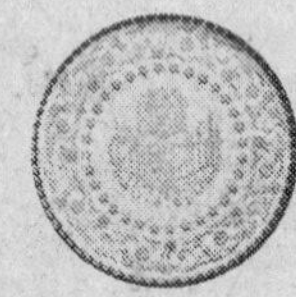

1.7540 gm., .917 GOLD, .0517 oz AGW
Monnaie de Luxe
Kemal Ataturk

Y#	Date	Mintage	VF	XF	Unc
144	1942	138 pcs.	80.00	90.00	130.00
	1943	386 pcs.	70.00	80.00	120.00
	1944	811 pcs.	60.00	75.00	115.00
	1946	235 pcs.	70.00	80.00	120.00
	1950	2,053	40.00	50.00	70.00
	1951	2,035	40.00	50.00	70.00
	1952	3,374	40.00	50.00	70.00
	1953	1,944	40.00	50.00	70.00
	1954	2,244	40.00	50.00	70.00
	1955	2,573	40.00	50.00	70.00
	1956	4,004	40.00	50.00	70.00
	1957	8,842	40.00	50.00	70.00
	1958	9,546	40.00	50.00	70.00
	1959	.017	BV	40.00	60.00
	1960	.019	BV	40.00	60.00
	1961	.035	BV	40.00	60.00
	1962	.031	BV	40.00	60.00
	1963	.047	BV	40.00	60.00
	1964	.057	BV	40.00	60.00
	1965	.078	BV	40.00	60.00
	1966	.106	BV	40.00	60.00
	1967	.114	BV	40.00	60.00
	1968	.152	BV	40.00	60.00
	1969	.163	BV	40.00	60.00
	1970	.224	BV	40.00	60.00
	1971	.306	BV	40.00	60.00
	1972	.271	BV	40.00	60.00
	1973	.162	BV	40.00	60.00
	1974	.141	BV	40.00	50.00
	1975	.202	BV	40.00	50.00
	1976	.583	BV	40.00	50.00
	1977	1.089	BV	40.00	50.00
	1978	.238	BV	40.00	50.00

Monnaie de Luxe
Ismet Inonu

Y#	Date	Mintage	VF	XF	Unc
144.1	1943	Inc. 1943 Ab.	—	—	—
	1944	Inc. 1944 Ab.	—	—	—
	1945	592 pcs.	85.00	95.00	120.00
	1946	Inc. 1946 Ab.	85.00	95.00	120.00
	1947	3,443	80.00	90.00	115.00
	1948	714 pcs.	85.00	95.00	125.00
	1949	552 pcs.	85.00	95.00	125.00

50 PIASTRES

3.6083 gm., .917 GOLD, .1064 oz AGW

Ismet Inonu

Y#	Date	Mintage	VF	XF	Unc
B99	1923/20	Inc. Ab.	BV	80.00	100.00
	1923/22	1,093	80.00	90.00	110.00
	1923/23	897 pcs.	90.00	100.00	120.00
	1923/24	.011	BV	80.00	100.00
	1923/25	3,004	80.00	90.00	110.00
	1923/26	817 pcs.	90.00	100.00	125.00
	1923/27	5,228	80.00	90.00	110.00

Kemal Ataturk

Y#	Date	Mintage	VF	XF	Unc
135	1923/20	.012	BV	80.00	100.00
(101)	1923/27	Inc. Ab.	BV	80.00	100.00
	1923/28	3,300	BV	80.00	100.00
	1923/29	6,384	BV	80.00	100.00
	1923/30	4,590	BV	80.00	100.00
	1923/31	9,068	BV	80.00	100.00
	1923/32	4,344	BV	80.00	100.00
	1923/33	3,958	BV	80.00	100.00
	1923/34	9,499	BV	80.00	100.00
	1923/35	9,307	BV	80.00	100.00
	1923/36	.012	BV	80.00	100.00
	1923/37	9,049	BV	80.00	100.00
	1923/38	9,854	BV	80.00	100.00
	1923/39	.011	BV	80.00	100.00
	1923/40	.013	BV	80.00	100.00
	1923/41	.013	BV	80.00	100.00
	1923/42	.018	BV	80.00	100.00
	1923/43	.026	BV	80.00	100.00
	1923/44	.026	BV	80.00	100.00
	1923/45	.025	BV	80.00	100.00
	1923/46	.028	BV	80.00	100.00
	1923/47	.038	BV	80.00	100.00
	1923/48	.035	BV	80.00	100.00
	1923/49	.028	BV	80.00	100.00
	1923/50	.016	BV	80.00	100.00
	1923/51	.008	BV	80.00	100.00
	1923/52	.014	BV	80.00	100.00
	1923/53	.028	BV	80.00	100.00
	1923/54	.054	BV	80.00	100.00
	1923/55	.016	BV	80.00	100.00

Monnaie de Luxe
Kemal Ataturk

Y#	Date	Mintage	VF	XF	Unc
145	1942	115 pcs.	90.00	100.00	120.00
	1943	91 pcs.	90.00	100.00	120.00
	1944	950 pcs.	80.00	90.00	110.00
	1946	565 pcs.	80.00	90.00	110.00
	1950	1,971	BV	80.00	100.00
	1951	1,780	BV	80.00	100.00
	1952	2,557	BV	80.00	100.00
	1953	2,392	BV	80.00	100.00
	1954	1,714	BV	80.00	100.00
	1955	4,143	BV	80.00	100.00
	1956	2,956	BV	80.00	100.00
	1957	6,855	BV	80.00	100.00
	1958	6,381	BV	80.00	100.00
	1959	.012	BV	80.00	100.00
	1960	.012	BV	80.00	100.00
	1961	.015	BV	80.00	100.00
	1962	.022	BV	80.00	100.00
	1963	.029	BV	80.00	100.00
	1964	.034	BV	80.00	100.00
	1965	.044	BV	80.00	100.00
	1966	.058	BV	80.00	100.00
	1967	.064	BV	80.00	100.00
	1968	.082	BV	80.00	100.00
	1969	.079	BV	80.00	100.00
	1970	.109	BV	80.00	100.00
	1971	.154	BV	80.00	100.00
	1972	.110	BV	80.00	100.00
	1973	.073	BV	80.00	100.00
	1974	.045	BV	80.00	100.00
	1975	.072	150.00	155.00	160.00
	1976	.196	150.00	155.00	160.00
	1977	.361	150.00	155.00	160.00
	1978	.161	150.00	155.00	160.00

Monnaie de Luxe
Ismet Inonu

Y#	Date	Mintage	VF	XF	Unc
145.1	1943	Inc. 1943 Ab.	—	—	—
	1944	Inc. 1944 Ab.	BV	125.00	175.00
	1945	515 pcs.	90.00	100.00	130.00
	1946	Inc. 1946 Ab.	85.00	135.00	200.00
	1947	3,481	80.00	90.00	110.00
	1948	773 pcs.	90.00	100.00	130.00
	1949	582 pcs.	90.00	100.00	130.00

100 PIASTRES

7.2160 gm., .917 GOLD, .2126 oz AGW
Ismet Inonu

Y#	Date	Mintage	VF	XF	Unc
C99	1923/20	Inc. Ab.	BV	155.00	180.00
	1923/22	3 pcs.	—	Rare	—
	1923/23	.381	BV	155.00	180.00
	1923/24	2,274	BV	155.00	180.00
	1923/25	.028	BV	155.00	180.00
	1923/26	2,097	BV	155.00	180.00
	1923/27	.017	BV	155.00	180.00

Kemal Ataturk

Y#	Date	Mintage	VF	XF	Unc
136	1923/20	.029	BV	155.00	180.00
(102)	1923/27	Inc. Ab.	BV	155.00	180.00
	1923/28	3 pcs.	—	Rare	—
	1923/29	2,111	BV	155.00	180.00
	1923/30	.013	BV	155.00	180.00
	1923/31	.109	BV	155.00	180.00
	1923/32	.134	BV	155.00	180.00
	1923/33	.216	BV	155.00	180.00
	1923/34	.463	BV	155.00	180.00
	1923/35	.405	BV	155.00	180.00
	1923/36	.025	BV	155.00	180.00
	1923/37	.131	BV	155.00	180.00
	1923/38	.159	BV	155.00	180.00
	1923/39	.085	BV	155.00	180.00
	1923/40	.010	BV	155.00	180.00
	1923/41	.164	BV	155.00	180.00
	1923/42	.063	BV	155.00	180.00
	1923/43	.056	BV	155.00	180.00
	1923/44	.198	BV	155.00	180.00
	1923/45	.176	BV	155.00	180.00
	1923/46	1.290	BV	155.00	180.00
	1923/47	.513	BV	155.00	180.00
	1923/48	600 pcs.	BV	155.00	180.00
	1923/49	1,300	BV	155.00	180.00
	1923/50	.047	BV	155.00	180.00
	1923/51	.240	BV	155.00	180.00
	1923/52	1.047	BV	155.00	180.00
	1923/53	.550	BV	155.00	180.00
	1923/54	.018	BV	155.00	185.00
	1923/55	.309	BV	155.00	180.00

7.0160 gm., .917 GOLD, .2069 oz AGW
Monnaie de Luxe
Kemal Ataturk

Y#	Date	Mintage	VF	XF	Unc
146	1942	8,659	BV	155.00	180.00
	1943	6,594	BV	155.00	180.00
	1944	7,160	BV	155.00	180.00
	1948	.014	BV	155.00	180.00
	1950	.025	BV	155.00	180.00
	1951	.035	BV	155.00	180.00
	1952	.041	BV	155.00	180.00
	1953	.032	BV	155.00	180.00
	1954	.024	BV	155.00	180.00
	1955	4,881	150.00	160.00	190.00
	1956	.011	BV	155.00	180.00
	1957	.049	55.00	60.00	70.00
	1958	.067	BV	155.00	180.00
	1959	.089	BV	155.00	180.00
	1960	.057	BV	155.00	180.00
	1961	.077	BV	155.00	180.00
	1962	.108	BV	155.00	180.00
	1963	.146	BV	155.00	180.00
	1964	.128	BV	155.00	180.00

Y#	Date	Mintage	VF	XF	Unc
146	1965	.157	BV	155.00	180.00
	1966	.190	BV	155.00	180.00
	1967	.177	BV	155.00	180.00
	1968	.143	BV	155.00	180.00
	1969	.206	BV	155.00	180.00
	1970	.253	BV	155.00	180.00
	1971	.293	BV	155.00	180.00
	1972	.222	BV	155.00	180.00
	1973	.140	BV	155.00	180.00
	1974	.082	BV	155.00	180.00
	1975	.142	BV	155.00	180.00
	1976	.265	BV	155.00	180.00
	1977	.277	BV	155.00	180.00
	1978	.086	BV	155.00	180.00

Monnaie de Luxe
Ismet Inonu

Y#	Date	Mintage	VF	XF	Unc
146.1	1943	Inc. 1943 Ab.	BV	160.00	180.00
	1944	Inc. 1944 Ab.	BV	160.00	180.00
	1945	2,202	160.00	170.00	200.00
	1946	8,863	150.00	160.00	190.00
	1947	.028	BV	160.00	180.00
	1948	Inc. 1948 Ab.	BV	160.00	180.00
	1949	6,578	150.00	160.00	190.00
	1950	Inc. 1950 Ab.	BV	155.00	185.00

250 PIASTRES

18.0400 gm., .917 GOLD, .5319 oz AGW
Ismet Inonu

Y#	Date	Mintage	VF	XF	Unc
D99	1923/20	Inc. Ab.	BV	375.00	450.00
	1923/23	.014	BV	375.00	450.00
	1923/24	60 pcs.	400.00	500.00	700.00

Kemal Ataturk

Y#	Date	Mintage	VF	XF	Unc
137	1923/20	.010	BV	375.00	450.00
(103)	1923/29	3 pcs.	—	Rare	—
	1923/30	130 pcs.	400.00	500.00	700.00
	1923/38	245 pcs.	550.00	600.00	700.00
	1923/39	389 pcs.	550.00	600.00	700.00
	1923/40	435 pcs.	550.00	600.00	700.00
	1923/41	349 pcs.	550.00	600.00	700.00
	1923/42	460 pcs.	550.00	600.00	700.00
	1923/43	1,008	500.00	550.00	650.00
	1923/44	712 pcs.	550.00	600.00	700.00
	1923/45	1,034	500.00	550.00	650.00
	1923/46	1,035	500.00	550.00	650.00
	1923/47	1,408	500.00	550.00	650.00
	1923/48	904 pcs.	550.00	600.00	700.00
	1923/49	1,066	500.00	550.00	650.00
	1923/50	975 pcs.	550.00	600.00	700.00
	1923/51	298 pcs.	550.00	600.00	700.00
	1923/52	610 pcs.	540.00	575.00	700.00
	1923/53	586 pcs.	540.00	575.00	700.00
	1923/54	289 pcs.	540.00	575.00	700.00
	1923/55	267 pcs.	540.00	575.00	700.00

17.5400 gm., .917 GOLD, .5172 oz AGW
Monnaie de Luxe
Kemal Ataturk

Y#	Date	Mintage	VF	XF	Unc
147	1942	.010	BV	375.00	500.00
	1943	.011	BV	375.00	500.00
	1944	.015	BV	375.00	500.00
	1946	.016	BV	375.00	500.00
	1947	.042	BV	375.00	500.00
	1948	.013	BV	375.00	500.00

Y#	Date	Mintage	VF	XF	Unc
147	1950	.045	BV	375.00	500.00
	1951	.041	BV	375.00	500.00
	1952	.059	BV	375.00	500.00
	1953	.045	BV	375.00	500.00
	1954	.040	BV	375.00	500.00
	1955	7,067	BV	375.00	500.00
	1956	.014	BV	375.00	500.00
	1957	.047	BV	375.00	500.00
	1958	.075	BV	375.00	500.00
	1959	.093	BV	375.00	500.00
	1960	.050	BV	375.00	500.00
	1961	.065	BV	375.00	500.00
	1962	.099	BV	375.00	500.00
	1963	.137	BV	375.00	500.00
	1964	.152	BV	375.00	500.00
	1965	.194	BV	375.00	500.00
	1966	.218	BV	375.00	500.00
	1967	.201	BV	375.00	500.00
	1968	.150	BV	375.00	500.00
	1969	.262	BV	375.00	500.00
	1970	.301	BV	375.00	500.00
	1971	.356	BV	375.00	500.00
	1972	.305	BV	375.00	500.00
	1973	.198	BV	375.00	500.00
	1974	.142	BV	375.00	500.00
	1975	.223	600.00	610.00	625.00
	1976	.345	600.00	610.00	625.00
	1977	.227	600.00	610.00	625.00
	1978	.311	600.00	610.00	625.00

Monnaie de Luxe
Ismet Inonu

Y#	Date	Mintage	VF	XF	Unc
147.1	1943	Inc. 1943 Ab.	BV	375.00	500.00
	1944	Inc. 1944 Ab.	BV	375.00	500.00
	1945	4,135	BV	375.00	500.00
	1946	Inc. 1946 Ab.	375.00	400.00	550.00
	1947	Inc. 1947 Ab.	BV	375.00	500.00
	1948	Inc. 1948 Ab.	BV	375.00	500.00
	1949	.011	BV	375.00	500.00
	1950	Inc. 1950 Ab.	BV	375.00	500.00

500 PIASTRES

36.0800 gm., .917 GOLD, 1.0638 oz AGW
Ismet Inonu

Y#	Date	Mintage	VF	XF	Unc
E99	1923/20	Inc. Ab.	BV	750.00	800.00
	1923/23	9,006	BV	750.00	800.00
	1923/24	7,923	BV	750.00	800.00
	1923/25	272 pcs.	750.00	775.00	825.00

Kemal Ataturk

Y#	Date	Mintage	VF	XF	Unc
138	1923/20	.012	BV	750.00	825.00
(104)	1923/27	615 pcs.	750.00	800.00	950.00
	1923/28	34 pcs.	775.00	850.00	1000.
	1923/29	137 pcs.	750.00	800.00	950.00
	1923/30	45 pcs.	775.00	850.00	1000.
	1923/31	100 pcs.	750.00	800.00	950.00
	1923/32	74 pcs.	750.00	800.00	950.00
	1923/33	268 pcs.	750.00	800.00	950.00
	1923/34	758 pcs.	750.00	800.00	950.00
	1923/35	1,586	750.00	800.00	950.00
	1923/36	765 pcs.	750.00	800.00	950.00
	1923/37	983 pcs.	750.00	800.00	950.00
	1923/38	1,738	750.00	800.00	950.00
	1923/39	2,629	750.00	800.00	950.00
	1923/40	2,763	750.00	800.00	950.00
	1923/41	3,440	750.00	800.00	950.00
	1923/42	3,335	750.00	800.00	950.00
	1923/43	4,914	750.00	800.00	950.00
	1923/44	4,308	750.00	800.00	950.00
	1923/45	3,488	750.00	800.00	950.00
	1923/46	5,636	750.00	800.00	950.00
	1923/47	7,588	750.00	800.00	950.00
	1923/48	6,060	750.00	800.00	950.00
	1923/49	4,235	BV	750.00	850.00
	1923/50	4,733	BV	750.00	850.00
	1923/51	2,757	BV	750.00	850.00
	1923/52	2,041	1100.	1200.	1300.
	1923/53	4,819	1100.	1200.	1300.
	1923/54	1,401	1100.	1200.	1300.
	1923/55	1,484	1100.	1200.	1300.

35.0800 gm., .917 GOLD, 1.0344 oz AGW
Monnaie de Luxe
Kemal Ataturk

Y#	Date	Mintage	VF	XF	Unc
148	1942	2,949	BV	750.00	850.00
	1943	1,210	BV	750.00	850.00
	1944	1,254	BV	750.00	850.00
	1947	3,699	BV	750.00	850.00
	1950	59 pcs.	750.00	800.00	900.00
	1951	21 pcs.	800.00	850.00	950.00
	1952	26 pcs.	800.00	850.00	950.00
	1953	35 pcs.	800.00	850.00	950.00
	1954	182 pcs.	750.00	800.00	900.00
	1955	14 pcs.	800.00	850.00	950.00
	1956	13 pcs.	800.00	850.00	950.00
	1957	68 pcs.	800.00	850.00	950.00
	1958	121 pcs.	750.00	800.00	900.00
	1959	294 pcs.	750.00	800.00	900.00
	1960	208 pcs.	750.00	800.00	900.00
	1961	619 pcs.	750.00	800.00	900.00
	1962	1,228	750.00	800.00	900.00
	1963	1,985	750.00	800.00	900.00
	1964	2,787	750.00	800.00	900.00
	1965	4,631	750.00	800.00	900.00
	1966	5,572	750.00	800.00	900.00
	1967	6,637	750.00	800.00	900.00
	1968	5,983	750.00	800.00	900.00
	1969	7,152	750.00	800.00	900.00
	1970	.011	BV	750.00	850.00
	1971	.015	BV	750.00	850.00
	1972	.015	BV	750.00	850.00
	1973	7,939	BV	750.00	850.00
	1974	5,412	BV	750.00	850.00
	1975	6,205	1350.	1400.	1450.
	1976	.011	1350.	1400.	1450.
	1977	6,931	1350.	1400.	1450.
	1978	5,740	1350.	1400.	1450.

Monnaie de Luxe
Ismet Inonu
Rev: Similar to Ataturk 500 Piastres.

Y#	Date	Mintage	VF	XF	Unc
148.1	1943	Inc. 1943 Ab.	BV	750.00	900.00
	1944	Inc. 1944 Ab.	BV	750.00	900.00
	1945	115 pcs.	750.00	800.00	1000.
	1946	298 pcs.	750.00	800.00	1000.
	1947	Inc. 1947 Ab.	BV	750.00	900.00
	1948	40 pcs.	750.00	800.00	900.00

NCLT ISSUES

CITY VISIT ISSUES

From time to time, certain cities of the Ottoman Empire were honored by having special coins struck at Istanbul, but with inscriptions stating that they were struck in the city of honor. These were produced on the occasion of the Sultan's visit to that city. The coins were struck in limited, but not small quantities, and were probably intended for distribution to the notables of the city and the Sultan's own followers. Because they were of the same size and type as the regular circulation issues struck at Istanbul, many specimens found their way into circulation and worn or mounted specimens are found today, although some have been preserved in XF or better condition. Mintage statistics are not known.

Issues of Abdulaziz's visit to Bursa

BURSA MINTMARK بروسه

PIASTRE

.830 SILVER

Y#	Date	Year	Mintage	VF	XF	Unc
9a	AH1277	1	.040	125.00	150.00	175.00

2 PIASTRES

.830 SILVER

Y#	Date	Year	Mintage	VF	XF	Unc
10a	AH1277	1	.040	125.00	150.00	175.00

5 PIASTRES

.830 SILVER

Y#	Date	Year	Mintage	VF	XF	Unc
11a	AH1277	1	.018	150.00	200.00	250.00

25 PIASTRES

.917 GOLD

Y#	Date	Year	Mintage	VF	XF	Unc
16a	AH1277	1	4,800	100.00	150.00	225.00

50 PIASTRES

.917 GOLD

Y#	Date	Year	Mintage	VF	XF	Unc
A16a	AH1277	1	2,476	125.00	200.00	275.00

100 PIASTRES

.917 GOLD

Y#	Date	Year	Mintage	VF	XF	Unc
17a	AH1277	1	9,737	135.00	215.00	300.00

Issues of Mohammed V's visit to Bursa

2 PIASTRES

.830 SILVER

Y#	Date	Year	Mintage	VF	XF	Unc
48a	AH1327	1	—	100.00	125.00	175.00

5 PIASTRES

.830 SILVER

Y#	Date	Year	Mintage	VF	XF	Unc
49a	AH1327	1	—	150.00	200.00	250.00

25 PIASTRES

.917 GOLD

Y#	Date	Year	Mintage	VF	XF	Unc
B51a	AH1327	1	—	135.00	215.00	300.00

50 PIASTRES

.917 GOLD

Y#	Date	Year	Mintage	VF	XF	Unc
50a	AH1327	1	—	100.00	175.00	275.00

100 PIASTRES

.917 GOLD

Y#	Date	Year	Mintage	VF	XF	Unc
C51a	AH1327	1	—	140.00	225.00	325.00

Issues of Abdulmecid's visit to Edirne

EDIRNE MINTMARK ادرنه

50 PIASTRES

.917 GOLD

C#	Date	Year	Mintage	VF	XF	Unc
296a	AH1255	8	.010	125.00	200.00	275.00

100 PIASTRES

.917 GOLD

C#	Date	Year	Mintage	VF	XF	Unc
297a	AH1255	8	.010	135.00	215.00	300.00

Issues of Mohammed V's Visit to Edirne

EDIRNE MINTMARK ادرنه

2 PIASTRES

.830 SILVER

Y#	Date	Year	Mintage	VF	XF	Unc
48b	AH1327	2	—	100.00	125.00	175.00

5 PIASTRES

.830 SILVER

Y#	Date	Year	Mintage	VF	XF	Unc
49b	AH1327	2	—	120.00	175.00	250.00

10 PIASTRES

.830 SILVER

Y#	Date	Year	Mintage	VF	XF	Unc
50b	AH1327	2	—	175.00	275.00	375.00

50 PIASTRES

.917 GOLD

Y#	Date	Year	Mintage	VF	XF	Unc
B51b	AH1327	2	—	100.00	150.00	225.00

100 PIASTRES

.917 GOLD

Y#	Date	Year	Mintage	VF	XF	Unc
C51b	AH1327	2	—	160.00	225.00	325.00

500 PIASTRES

.917 GOLD

Y#	Date	Year	Mintage	VF	XF	Unc
E51b	AH1327	2	—	1250.	2000.	3000.

Issues of Mohammed V's Visit to Kosova

KOSOVA MINTMARK قوصوه

2 PIASTRES

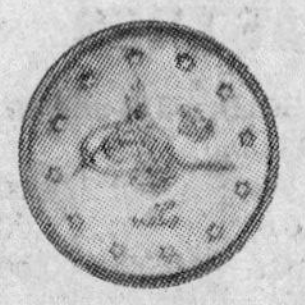
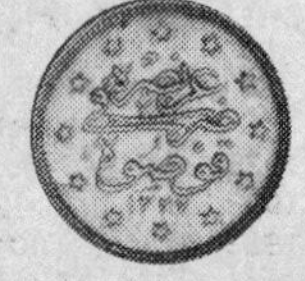

.830 SILVER

Y#	Date	Year	Mintage	VF	XF	Unc
48c	AH1327	3	.013	115.00	150.00	200.00

5 PIASTRES

.830 SILVER

Y#	Date	Year	Mintage	VF	XF	Unc
49c	AH1327	3	3,000	140.00	225.00	300.00

10 PIASTRES

.830 SILVER

Y#	Date	Year	Mintage	VF	XF	Unc
50c	AH1327	3	1,500	175.00	275.00	375.00

50 PIASTRES

.917 GOLD

Y#	Date	Year	Mintage	VF	XF	Unc
B51c	AH1327	3	—	175.00	275.00	400.00

100 PIASTRES

.917 GOLD

Y#	Date	Year	Mintage	VF	XF	Unc
C51c	AH1327	3	750 pcs.	200.00	325.00	475.00

500 PIASTRES

.917 GOLD

Y#	Date	Year	Mintage	VF	XF	Unc
E51c	AH1327	3	20 pcs.	2000.	3250.	4750.

Issues of Mohammed V's Visit to Manastir

MANASTIR MINTMARK مناستر

2 PIASTRES

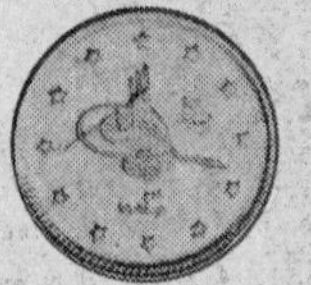

.830 SILVER

Y#	Date	Year	Mintage	VF	XF	Unc
48d	AH1327	3	.013	100.00	125.00	175.00

5 PIASTRES

.830 SILVER

Y#	Date	Year	Mintage	VF	XF	Unc
49d	AH1327	3	3,000	150.00	225.00	250.00

10 PIASTRES

.830 SILVER

Y#	Date	Year	Mintage	VF	XF	Unc
50d	AH1327	3	1,500	175.00	275.00	375.00

50 PIASTRES

.917 GOLD

Y#	Date	Year	Mintage	VF	XF	Unc
B51d	AH1327	3	1,200	135.00	215.00	300.00

100 PIASTRES

.917 GOLD

Y#	Date	Year	Mintage	VF	XF	Unc
C51d	AH1327	3	750 pcs.	175.00	275.00	400.00

500 PIASTRES

.917 GOLD

Y#	Date	Year	Mintage	VF	XF	Unc
E51d	AH1327	3	20 pcs.	1250.	2250.	3250.

Issues of Mohammed V's visit to Selanik Salonika

SALANIK MINTMARK سلانيك

2 PIASTRES

.830 SILVER

Y#	Date	Year	Mintage	VF	XF	Unc
48e	AH1327	3	.013	125.00	175.00	250.00

5 PIASTRES

.830 SILVER

Y#	Date	Year	Mintage	VF	XF	Unc
49e	AH1327	3	3,000	120.00	175.00	250.00

10 PIASTRES

.830 SILVER

Y#	Date	Year	Mintage	VF	XF	Unc
50e	AH1327	3	1,500	175.00	275.00	350.00

50 PIASTRES

.917 GOLD

Y#	Date	Year	Mintage	VF	XF	Unc
B51e	AH1327	3	1,200	135.00	215.00	300.00

100 PIASTRES

.917 GOLD

Y#	Date	Year	Mintage	VF	XF	Unc
C51e	AH1327	3	750 pcs.	150.00	250.00	350.00

500 PIASTRES

.917 GOLD

Y#	Date	Year	Mintage	VF	XF	Unc
E51e	AH1327	3	20 pcs.	1250.	2000.	3000.

MINT SETS

KM#	Date	Mintage	Identification	Issue Price	Mkt. Val.
S1	1962	—	Y111-115,116	—	Rare
S2	1964(6)	—	Y111-115,117a	—	6.00
S3	1965(6)	—	Y111-115,117a	—	6.00
S4	1966(6)	—	Y111-115,117a	—	6.00
S5	1968(6)	—	Y111-112,113a 114a,115,117a	—	6.00
S6	1969(6)	—	Y111a-115a,117a	—	4.00
S7	1970(6)	—	Y111a-115a,117a	—	3.00
S8	1971(6)	—	Y111a-115A, 117A	—	7.00
S9	1972(6)	—	Y111a-115a,117a	—	3.00
S10	1973(7)	—	Y111a-115a,117a,A113	—	4.00
S11	1974(8)	—	Y117a,111b,112b,113a,A113, 114a,115a,125	—	3.00
S12	1975(7)	—	Y117b,111c,A113,114a,115a, 125	—	2.50
S13	1976(7)	—	Y117b,111c,112c,A113,114a,115a, 127	—	2.00
S14	1977(8)	—	—	—	1.75

The Colony of the Turks and Caicos Islands, a British colony situated in the West Indies at the eastern end of the Bahama Islands, has an area of 166 sq. mi. (430 sq. km.) and a population of 6,000. Capital: Cockburn Town, on Grand Turk. The principal industry of the colony is the production of salt, which is gathered by raking. Salt, crayfish, and conch shells are exported.

The Turks and Caicos Islands were discovered by Juan Ponce de Leon in 1512, but were not settled until 1678 when Bermudians arrived to rake salt from the salt ponds. The British settlers were driven from the island by the Spanish in 1710, during the long War of the Spanish Succession. They returned and throughout the remaining years of the war repulsed repeated attacks by France and Spain. In 1799 the islands were granted representation in the Bahamian assembly, but in 1848, on petition of the inhabitants, they were made a separate colony under Jamaica. They were annexed by Jamaica in 1873 and remained a dependency until 1959 when they became a unit territory of the Federation of the West Indies. When the Federation was dissolved in 1962, the Turks and Caicos Islands became a separate Crown Colony.

RULERS

British

CROWN

COPPER-NICKEL

Y#	Date	Mintage	Fine	VF	XF	Unc
1	1969	.050	1.25	2.00	2.75	3.50
	1969	6,000	—	—	Proof	15.00

Y#	Date	Mintage	Fine	VF	XF	Unc
5	1975	—	1.25	2.00	2.50	3.00
	1975	—	—	—	Proof	7.50
	1976	1,960	1.25	2.00	2.50	3.00
	1976	—	—	—	Proof	7.50
	1977	—	—	—	Proof	—

5 CROWNS

24.2900 gm., .500 SILVER, .3905 oz ASW
Obv: Similar to Crown, Y#5.

Y#	Date	Mintage	Fine	VF	XF	Unc
6	1975	—	BV	12.00	14.00	16.00
	1975	—	—	—	Proof	20.00
	1976	1,760	BV	12.00	14.00	16.00
	1976	—	—	—	Proof	20.00
	1977	—	—	—	Proof	20.00

10 CROWNS

29.8000 gm., .925 SILVER, .8863 oz ASW
Obv: Similar to Crown, Y#5.

Y#	Date	Mintage	Fine	VF	XF	Unc
7	1975	1,665	BV	27.00	30.00	35.00
	1975	4,205	—	—	Proof	45.00

Obv: Similar to Crown, Y#5.

Y#	Date	Mintage	Fine	VF	XF	Unc
14	1976	4,185	BV	27.00	30.00	35.00
	1976	—	—	—	Proof	45.00
	1977	—	—	—	Proof	40.00

10th Anniversary of Prince Charles' Investiture

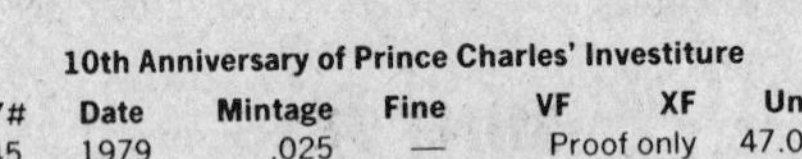

Y#	Date	Mintage	Fine	VF	XF	Unc
45	1979	.025	—	Proof only		47.00

20 CROWNS

38.8000 gm., .925 SILVER, 1.1540 oz ASW
Churchill Centenary

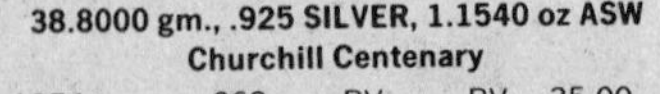

Y#	Date	Mintage	Fine	VF	XF	Unc
2	1974	.268	BV	BV	35.00	40.00
	1974	8,400*	—	—	Proof	45.00

NOTE: 4,100 ISSUED INDIVIDUALLY; **NOTE** 4,300 ISSUED IN Binational Sets With Cayman Islands 25 Dollars, Y#10.

Christopher Columbus
Obv: Similar to Crown, Y#5.

Y#	Date	Mintage	Fine	VF	XF	Unc
8	1975	5,305	BV	BV	35.00	47.50
	1975	4,039	—	—	Proof	50.00

U.S. Bicentennial
Obv: Similar to Crown, Y#5.

Y#	Date	Mintage	Fine	VF	XF	Unc
12	1976	2,523	BV	BV	35.00	40.00
	1976	6,425	—	—	Proof	48.00

Victoria Portraits
Obv: Similar to Crown, Y#5.

Y#	Date	Mintage	Fine	VF	XF	Unc
15	1976	.031	BV	BV	35.00	42.00
	1976	2,031	—	—	Proof	50.00

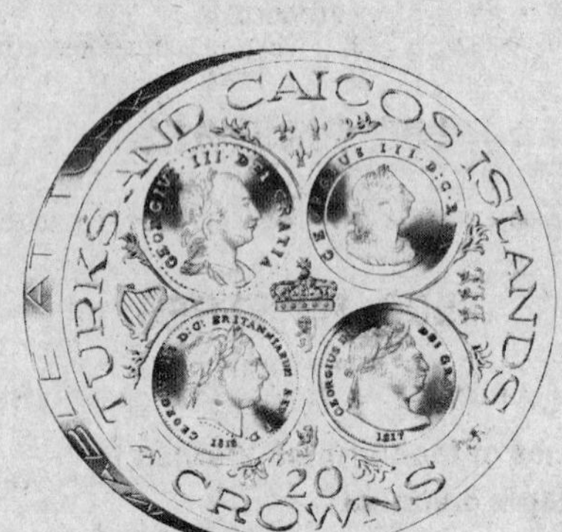

George III Portraits

Y#	Date	Mintage	Fine	VF	XF	Unc
20	1977	—	BV	BV	35.00	42.00
	1977	—	—	—	Proof	50.00

XI Commonwealth Games

Y#	Date	Mintage	Fine	VF	XF	Unc
23	1978	.010	BV	BV	35.00	40.00

25 CROWNS

3.1100 gm., .500 GOLD, .0500 oz AGW

Y#	Date	Mintage	Fine	VF	XF	Unc
9	1975	825 pcs.	BV	BV	35.00	75.00
	1975	3,367	—	—	Proof	50.00

19mm

Y#	Date	Mintage	Fine	VF	XF	Unc
9.1	1976	—	BV	BV	35.00	45.00
	1976	—	—	—	Proof	50.00
	1977	—	—	—	Proof	50.00

43.7500 gm., .925 SILVER, 1.3012 oz ASW
Queen's Silver Jubilee
Obv: Similar to Crown, Y#5.

Y#	Date	Mintage	Fine	VF	XF	Unc
18	1977	—	BV	BV	40.00	50.00
	1977	—	—	—	Proof	75.00

25th Anniversary of Coronation
Type I. Obv: Similar to 50 Crowns, Y#35.

Y#	Date	Mintage	Fine	VF	XF	Unc
25	1978	—	—		Proof only	50.00

Type II. Obv: Similar to 50 Crowns, Y#35.

Y#	Date	Mintage	Fine	VF	XF	Unc
26	1978	—	—		Proof only	50.00

Type III. Rev: Similar to 50 Crowns, Y#35.

Y#	Date	Mintage	Fine	VF	XF	Unc
27	1978	—	—		Proof only	50.00

Type IV. Obv: Similar to 50 Crowns, Y#35.

Y#	Date	Mintage	Fine	VF	XF	Unc
28	1978	—	—		Proof only	50.00

Type V. Obv: Similar to 50 Crowns, Y#35.

Y#	Date	Mintage	Fine	VF	XF	Unc
29	1978	—	—		Proof only	50.00

Type VI. Obv. & Rev: Similar to 50 Crowns, Y#40.

Y#	Date	Mintage	Fine	VF	XF	Unc
30	1978	—	—		Proof only	50.00

Type VII. Obv. & Rev: Similar to 50 Crowns, Y#41.

Y#	Date	Mintage	Fine	VF	XF	Unc
31	1978	—	—		Proof only	50.00

Type VIII. Obv. & Rev: Similar to 50 Crowns, Y#42.

Y#	Date	Mintage	Fine	VF	XF	Unc
32	1978	—	—		Proof only	50.00

Type IX. Obv. & Rev: Similar to 50 Crowns, Y#43.

Y#	Date	Mintage	Fine	VF	XF	Unc
33	1978	—	—		Proof only	50.00

Type X. Obv. & Rev: Similar to 50 Crowns, Y#44.

Y#	Date	Mintage	Fine	VF	XF	Unc
34	1978	—	—		Proof only	50.00

50 CROWNS

6.2200 gm., .500 GOLD, .1000 oz AGW
Churchill Centenary

Y#	Date	Mintage	Fine	VF	XF	Unc
3	1974	.030	BV	65.00	95.00	100.00
	1974	4,000	—	—	Proof	115.00

Christopher Columbus

Y#	Date	Mintage	Fine	VF	XF	Unc
10	1975	2,863	BV	65.00	110.00	150.00
	1975	2,847	—	—	Proof	125.00

U.S. Bicentennial

Y#	Date	Mintage	Fine	VF	XF	Unc
13	1976	3,796	BV	65.00	110.00	150.00
	1976	4,372	—	—	Proof	135.00

55.1800 gm., .925 SILVER, 1.6412 oz ASW

Queen Victoria
Obv: Similar to Crown, Y#5.

Y#	Date	Mintage	Fine	VF	XF	Unc
16	1976	4,000	BV	BV	55.00	65.00
	1976	4,939	—	—	Proof	80.00

9.0000 gm., .500 GOLD, .1447 oz AGW
Queen's Silver Jubilee
Obv: Similar to Crown, Y#5.

Y#	Date	Mintage	Fine	VF	XF	Unc
19	1977	—	BV	BV	95.00	100.00
	1977	—	—	—	Proof	120.00

55.1800 gm., .925 SILVER, 1.6412 oz ASW
George III Portraits
Obv: Similar to Crown, Y#5.

Y#	Date	Mintage	Fine	VF	XF	Unc
21	1977	—	BV	55.00	60.00	70.00
	1977	—	—	—	Proof	75.00

9.0000 gm., .500 GOLD, .1447 oz AGW
25th Anniversary of Coronation
Type I. Rev: Similar to 25 Crowns, Y#25.

Y#	Date	Mintage	Fine	VF	XF	Unc
35	1978	—	—		Proof only	110.00

Type II. Obv: Similar to Y#35.
Rev: Similar to 25 Crown, Y#26.

Y#	Date	Mintage	Fine	VF	XF	Unc
36	1978	—	—		Proof only	110.00

Type III. Obv: Similar to Y#35.
Rev: Similar to 25 Crown, Y#27.

Y#	Date	Mintage	Fine	VF	XF	Unc
37	1978	—	—		Proof only	110.00

Type IV. Obv: Similar to Y#35.
Rev: Similar to 25 Crown, Y#28.

Y#	Date	Mintage	Fine	VF	XF	Unc
38	1978	—	—		Proof only	110.00

Type V. Obv: Similar to Y#35.
Rev: Similar to 25 Crown, Y#29.

Y#	Date	Mintage	Fine	VF	XF	Unc
39	1978	—	—		Proof only	110.00

Type VI.

Y#	Date	Mintage	Fine	VF	XF	Unc
40	1978	—	—		Proof only	110.00

Type VII.

Y#	Date	Mintage	Fine	VF	XF	Unc
41	1978	—	—		Proof only	110.00

Type VIII.

Y#	Date	Mintage	Fine	VF	XF	Unc
42	1978	—	—		Proof only	110.00

Type IX.

Y#	Date	Mintage	Fine	VF	XF	Unc
43	1978	—	—		Proof only	110.00

Type X.

Y#	Date	Mintage	Fine	VF	XF	Unc
44	1978	—	—		Proof only	110.00

100 CROWNS

12.4400 gm., .500 GOLD, .2000 oz AGW
Churchill Centenary

Y#	Date	Mintage	VF	XF	Unc
4	1974	4,500	130.00	160.00	200.00
	1974	5,100	—	Proof	225.00

Y#	Date	Mintage	VF	XF	Unc
11	1975	2,580 pcs.	130.00	175.00	200.00
	1975	2,780	—	Proof	200.00

Victoria Portraits
Obv: Similar to 50 Crowns, Y#13

Y#	Date	Mintage	VF	XF	Unc
17	1976	600 pcs.	BV	190.00	200.00
	1976	3,570	—	Proof	225.00
		George III Portraits			
22	1977	—	BV	190.00	200.00
	1977	—	—	Proof	225.00
		XI Commonwealth Coins			
24	1978	5,000	BV	190.00	225.00

10th Anniversary of Prince Charles' Investiture

Y#	Date	Mintage	VF	XF	Unc
46	1979	.010	—	Proof only	225.00

NCLT ISSUES

MINT SETS

KM#	Date	Mintage	Identification	Issue Price	Mkt. Val.
S1	1975(7)	440	Y5-11	214.00	490.00

PROOF SETS

STANDARD METALS

KM#	Date	Mintage	Identification	Issue Price	Mkt. Val.
101	1974(2)	1,600	Y2,4	—	225.00
102	1975(7)	1,270	Y5-11	313.00	500.00
103	1976(4)	2,185	Y5,6,9.1,14	78.00	122.00
104	1976(3)	—	Y15-17	280.00	350.00
105	1976(2)	1,951	Y12,13	108.00	180.00
106	1977(4)	1,370	Y5-6,9a,14	87.50	115.00
107	1977(3)	—	Y20-22	280.00	350.00
108	1978(10)	—	Y25-34	560.00	500.00
109	1978(10)	—	Y35-44	1120.	1100.
110	1979(2)	—	Y45,46	227.50	270.00

TUVALU

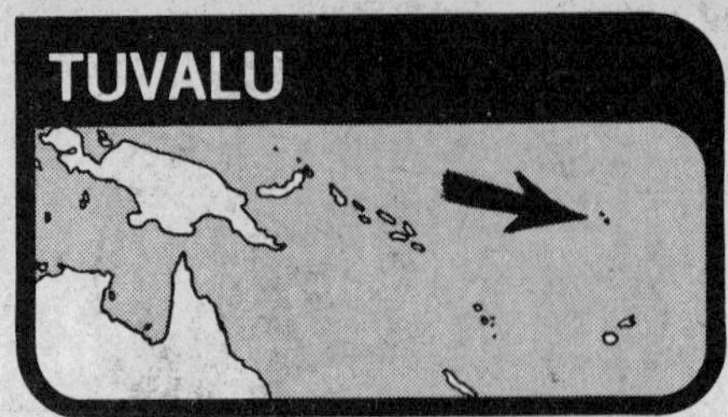

Tuvalu (formerly the Ellice or Lagoon Islands of the Gilbert and Ellice Islands), located in the South Pacific north of the Fiji Islands, has an area of 10 sq. mi. (26 sq. km.) and a population of 6,000. Capital: Funafuti. The independent state includes the islands of Nanumanga, Nanumea, Nui, Niutao, Viatupa, Funafuti, Nukufetau, Nukulailai and Nurakita. The latter four islands were claimed by the United States until relinquished by the Feb. 7, 1979, Treaty of Friendship signed by the United States and Tuvalu. The principal industries are copra production and phosphate mining.

The islands were discovered in 1764 by John Byron, a British navigator, and annexed by Britain in 1892. In 1915 they became part of the crown colony of the Gilbert and Ellice Islands. In 1974 the islanders voted to separate from the Gilberts, becoming on Jan. 1, 1976, the separate constitutional dependency of Tuvalu. Full independence was attained on Oct. 1, 1978. Tuvalu is a member of the Commonwealth of Nations. The Queen of England is Head of State.

RULERS

British

MONETARY SYSTEM

100 Cents = 1 Dollar

CENT

BRONZE

Y#	Date	Mintage	Fine	VF	XF	Unc
1	1976	.093	—	.05	.10	.15
	1976	.020	—	—	Proof	1.00

2 CENTS

BRONZE

Y#	Date	Mintage	Fine	VF	XF	Unc
2	1976	.051	.05	.10	.15	.25
	1976	.020	—	—	Proof	1.25

5 CENTS

COPPER-NICKEL

Y#	Date	Mintage	Fine	VF	XF	Unc
3	1976	.026	—	.10	.20	.35
	1976	.020	—	—	Proof	1.50

10 CENTS

COPPER-NICKEL

Y#	Date	Mintage	Fine	VF	XF	Unc
4	1976	.026	.15	.20	.30	.50
	1976	.020	—	—	Proof	2.00

20 CENTS

COPPER-NICKEL

Y#	Date	Mintage	Fine	VF	XF	Unc
5	1976	.036	.30	.35	.50	1.00
	1976	.020	—	—	Proof	2.50

50 CENTS

COPPER-NICKEL

Y#	Date	Mintage	Fine	VF	XF	Unc
6	1976	.019	.65	.75	1.00	1.75
	1976	.020	—	—	Proof.	3.00

DOLLAR

COPPER-NICKEL

Y#	Date	Mintage	Fine	VF	XF	Unc
7	1976	.021	1.25	1.50	2.00	3.50
	1976	.020	—	—	Proof	4.50

5 DOLLARS

28.2800 gm., .925 SILVER, .8411 oz ASW

Y#	Date	Mintage	XF	Unc	Proof
8	1976	.020	—	—	27.50

10 DOLLARS

35.0000 gm., .500 SILVER, .5627 oz ASW
First Anniversary of Independence

Y#	Date	Mintage	VF	XF	Unc
10	1979	5,000	—	—	20.00

35.0000 gm., .925 SILVER, 1.0409 oz ASW

Y#	Date	Mintage	VF	XF	Unc
10a	1979	2,500	—	Proof	40.00

50 DOLLARS

15.9800 gm., .917 GOLD, .4710 oz AGW
Obv: Similar to 5 Dollars, Y#8.

Y#	Date	Mintage	XF	Unc	Proof
9	1976	2,000	—	—	350.00

NCLT ISSUES

PROOF SETS

STANDARD METALS

KM#	Date	Mintage	Identification	Issue Price	Mkt. Val.
101	1976(7)	20,000	Y1-7	13.00	20.00

UGANDA

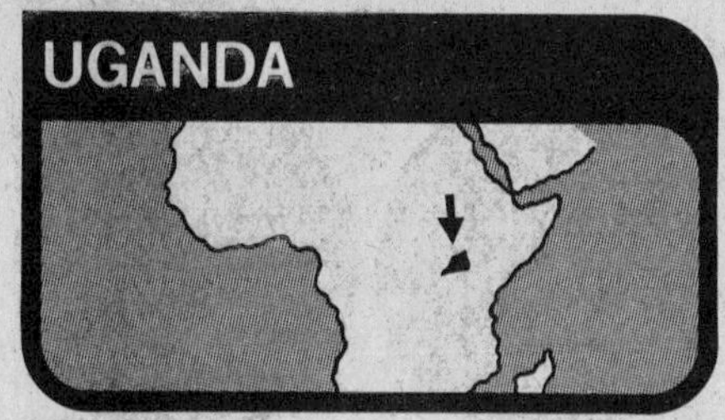

The Republic of Uganda, a former British protectorate located astride the equator in east-central Africa, has an area of 91,076 sq. mi. (235,885 sq. km.) and a population of 11.9 million. Capital: Kampala. Agriculture, including livestock, is the basis of the economy; there is some mining of copper, tin, gold and lead. Coffee, cotton, copper and tea are exported.

Uganda was first visited by Arab slavers in the 1830s. They were followed in the 1860s by British explorers searching for the headwaters of the Nile. The explorers, and the missionaries who followed them into the Lake Victoria region of south-central Africa in 1877-79, found well—developed African kingdoms dating back several centuries. In 1894 the local native Kingdom of Buganda was established as a British protectorate that was extended in 1896 to encompass an area substantially the same as the present Republic of Uganda. The protectorate was given a ministerial form of government in 1955, full internal self-government on March 1, 1962, and complete independence on Oct. 9, 1962. Uganda is a member of the Commonwealth of Nations. The president is Chief of State and Head of Government.

Uganda issued a set of ten silver and gold medal coins in 1969 to commemorate the July visit of Pope Paul. They were authorized to be legal tender but were not released because of their excessive intrinsic value.

NOTE: For earlier coinage see East Africa.

MONETARY SYSTEM

100 Cents = 1 Shilling

5 CENTS

BRONZE

Y#	Date	Mintage	VF	XF	Unc
1	1966	41.000	—	.10	.15
	1966	—	—	Proof	1.00
	1974	10.000	—	.10	.20
	1975	14.784	—	—	—
	1976	10.000	—	—	—

10 CENTS

BRONZE

Y#	Date	Mintage	VF	XF	Unc
2	1966	20.000	—	.15	.25
	1966	—	—	Proof	1.00
	1968	20.000	—	.15	.25
	1970	6.000	—	.15	.25
	1972	5.000	—	.15	.25
	1974	5.000	—	.15	.25
	1975	14.110	—	—	—
	1976	10.000	—	—	—

20 CENTS

BRONZE

Y#	Date	Mintage	VF	XF	Unc
3	1966	7.000	—	.20	.35
	1966	—	—	Proof	2.00
	1974	2.000	—	.25	.50

50 CENTS

COPPER-NICKEL

Y#	Date	Mintage	VF	XF	Unc
4	1966	16.000	—	.20	.50
	1966	—	—	Proof	2.00
	1970	3.000	—	.20	.50
	1974	10.000	—	.20	.50
	1976	10.000	—	—	—

SHILLING

COPPER-NICKEL

Y#	Date	Mintage	VF	XF	Unc
5	1966	24.500	.35	.65	1.00
	1966	—	—	Proof	2.00
	1968	10.000	.20	.50	1.00
	1972	—	—	—	—
	1975	15.540	—	—	—
	1976	10.000	—	—	—

2 SHILLINGS

COPPER-NICKEL

Y#	Date	Mintage	VF	XF	Unc
6	1966	4.000	.50	.90	1.50
	1966	—	—	Proof	3.00

4.0000 gm., 1.000 SILVER, .1286 oz ASW

H#	Date	Mintage	XF	Unc	Proof
3	1969	.018	—	—	12.50
	1970	—	—	—	12.50

5 SHILLINGS

COPPER-NICKEL
F.A.O. Issue

Y#	Date	Mintage	VF	XF	Unc
7	1968	.100	—	—	3.50
	1968	5,000	Proof	—	8.00

10.0000 gm., 1.000 SILVER, .3215 oz ASW

H#	Date	Mintage	XF	Unc	Proof
4	1969	.018	—	—	15.00
	1970	—	—	—	15.00

Y#	Date	Mintage	VF	XF	Unc
8	1972	8.000	—	—	—

NOTE: Not released for circulation.

10 SHILLINGS

20.0000 gm., 1.000 SILVER, .6430 oz ASW

H#	Date	Mintage	XF	Unc	Proof
5	1969	.018	—	—	22.50
	1970	—	—	—	22.50

20 SHILLINGS

40.0000 gm., 1.000 SILVER, 1.2861 oz ASW
Rev: Similar to 10 Shillings, H#5.

H#	Date	Mintage	XF	Unc	Proof
6	1969	.018	—	—	45.00
	1970	—	—	—	45.00

25 SHILLINGS

50.0000 gm., 1.000 SILVER, 1.6077 oz ASW
Rev: Similar to 10 Shillings, H#5.

H#	Date	Mintage	XF	Unc	Proof
7	1969	.018	—	—	50.00
	1970	—	—	—	50.00

30 SHILLINGS

60.0000 gm., 1.000 SILVER, 1.9292 oz ASW
Actual diameter - 60mm.
Rev: Similar to 10 Shillings, H#5.

H#	Date	Mintage	XF	Unc	Proof
8	1969	.018	—	—	60.00
	1970	—	—	—	60.00

50 SHILLINGS

6.9100 gm., .900 GOLD, .1999 oz AGW

Fr#	Date	Mintage	XF	Unc	Proof
4	1969	3,000	—	—	130.00
	1970	—	—	—	—

100 SHILLINGS

13.8200 gm., .900 GOLD, .3999 oz AGW

Fr#	Date	Mintage	XF	Unc	Proof
3	1969	3,000	—	—	260.00
	1970	—	—	—	—

500 SHILLINGS

69.1200 gm., .900 GOLD, 2.0002 oz AGW
Similar to 25 Shillings, H#7.

Fr#	Date	Mintage	XF	Unc	Proof
2	1969	3,000	—	—	1300.
	1970	—	—	—	—

1000 SHILLINGS

138.2400 gm., .900 GOLD, 4.0005 oz AGW

Fr#	Date	Mintage	XF	Unc	Proof
1	1969	3,000	—	—	2600.
	1970	—	—	—	—

NCLT ISSUES

PROOF SETS
STANDARD METALS

KM#	Date	Mintage	Identification	Issue Price	Mkt. Val.
101	1966(6)	8,250	Y1-6	7.75	12.00
102	1969(10)	3,000	H3-8,F1-4	790.00	4500.
103	1969(6)	15,000	H3-8	78.50	200.00
104	1970(10)	—	H3-8,F1-4	790.00	—
105	1970(6)	—	H3-8	78.50	200.00

Listings For

UMM AL QAIWAIN: refer to United Arab Emirates

UNITED ARAB EMIRATES

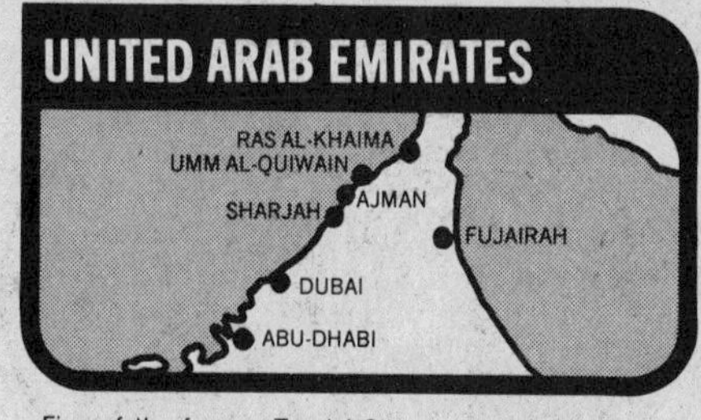

Five of the former Trucial States which comprise The United Arab Emirates, and which were formerly British treaty protectorates located along the southern shore of the Arabian Peninsula, have issued Non-Circulating Legal Tender Coins (NCLTs). They are Ajman, Fujairah, Ras alKhaimah, Sharjah and Umm Al-Quiwain. These coins have been declared legal tender by the issuing states but are not intended to circulate. No circulation strikes were minted, and none of the coins were available at face value.

AJMAN

Ajman is the smallest and poorest of the emirates in the United Arab Emirates. It has an estimated area of 100 sq. mi. (250 sq. km.) an a population of 6,000. Ajman's first act as an antonomous entity was a treaty with Great Britian in 1820. On December 2, 1971 Ajman became one of the six original members of the United Arab Emirates.

MONETARY SYSTEM

100 Dirhams = 1 Ryal

RIYAL

3.9000 gm., .640 SILVER, .0802 oz ASW

H#	Date	Year	Mintage	XF	Unc	Proof
1.1	AH1389	1969	.020	—	3.00	—
	Obv: Stamped Assay					
	AH1389	1969	1,250	—	—	12.00

Obv: Stamped Assay

H#	Date	Year	Mintage	XF	Unc	Proof
1.2	AH1390	1970	100 pcs.	—	—	40.00

2 RIYALS

6.5000 gm., .835 SILVER, .1745 oz ASW

H#	Date	Year	Mintage	XF	Unc	Proof
2.1	AH1389	1969	.020	—	5.50	—
	Obv: Stamped Assay					
	AH1389	1969	1,250	—	—	12.00

Obv: Stamped Assay

H#	Date	Year	Mintage	XF	Unc	Proof
2.2	AH1390	1970	100 pcs.	—	—	40.00

5 RIYALS

15.0000 gm., .835 SILVER, .4027 oz ASW

H#	Date	Year	Mintage	XF	Unc	Proof
3.1	AH1389	1969	.010	—	12.50	—
	Obv: Stamped Assay					
	AH1389	1969	1,250	—	—	15.00

Obv: Stamped Assay

H#	Date	Year	Mintage	XF	Unc	Proof
3.2	AH1390	1970	100 pcs.	—	—	75.00

H#	Date	Year	Mintage	XF	Unc	Proof
	Gamal Abdel Nassar					
12	AH1390	1970	5,000	—	—	12.50
	15.1000 gm., .925 SILVER, .4491 oz ASW					
	Rev: Dag Hammarskjold					
17	ND	(1970)	1,175	—	—	75.00
	Rev: Mahatma Gandhi					
18	ND	(1970)	1,175	—	—	75.00
	Rev: Martin Luther King					
19	ND	(1970)	1,175	—	—	75.00
	Rev: George C. Marshall					
20	ND	(1970)	1,175	—	—	75.00
	Rev: Bertrand A. Russell					
21	ND	(1970)	1,175	—	—	75.00
	Rev: Albert Schweitzer					
22	ND	(1970)	1,175	—	—	75.00
	Rev: Jan Palac					
23	ND	(1970)	1,175	—	—	75.00
	Rev: Albert J. Luthuli					
24	ND	(1970)	1,175	—	—	75.00

F.A.O. Issue

H#	Date	Year	Mintage	XF	Unc	Proof
26	AH1390	1970	2,000	—	—	20.00

NOTE: This issue is not recognized by the FAO.

Save Venice

H#	Date	Year	Mintage	XF	Unc	Proof
27	ND	(1971)	4,800	—	—	15.00

7-1/2 RIYALS

23.0000 gm., .925 SILVER, .6840 oz ASW

H#	Date	Year	Mintage	XF	Unc	Proof
5	AH1389	1970	4,350	—	22.00	—
	1389	1970	650 pcs.	—	—	100.00

H#	Date	Year	Mintage	XF	Unc	Proof
6	AH1389	1970	4,350	—	22.00	—
	1389	1970	650 pcs.	—	—	100.00

Rev: Same as H#6.

H#	Date	Year	Mintage	XF	Unc	Proof
7	AH1389	1970	4,350	—	22.00	—
	1389	1970	650 pcs.	—	—	100.00

23.0000 gm., .835 SILVER, .6175 oz ASW
Rev: Gamal Abdel Nassar

H#	Date	Year	Mintage	XF	Unc	Proof
13	AH1390	1970	6,000	—	—	20.00

10 RIYALS

29.0000 gm., .925 SILVER, .8625 oz ASW
Rev: Nikolai Lenin

H#	Date	Year	Mintage	XF	Unc	Proof
9.1	ND	(1970)	3,200	—	27.50	—
	Obv: Stamped Proof					
9.2	ND	(1970)	800 pcs.	—	—	100.00

25 RIYALS

5.1750 gm., .900 GOLD, .1497 oz AGW
Rev: Gamal Abdel Nassar

H#	Date	Year	Mintage	XF	Unc	Proof
15	AH1390	1970	1,100	—	—	100.00

NOTE: Some of these coins have a serial number on the obverse below the bust.

Rev: Dag Hammarskjold

H#	Date	Year	Mintage	XF	Unc	Proof
28	ND	(1970)	—	—	—	100.00

Rev: Mahatma Gandhi

H#	Date	Year	Mintage	XF	Unc	Proof
29	ND	(1970)	—	—	—	100.00

Rev: Martin Luther King

H#	Date	Year	Mintage	XF	Unc	Proof
30	ND	(1970)	—	—	—	100.00

Rev: George C. Marshall

H#	Date	Year	Mintage	XF	Unc	Proof
31	ND	(1970)	—	—	—	100.00

Rev: Bertrand A. Russell

H#	Date	Year	Mintage	XF	Unc	Proof
32	ND	(1970)	—	—	—	100.00

Rev: Albert Schweitzer

H#	Date	Year	Mintage	XF	Unc	Proof
33	ND	(1970)	—	—	—	100.00

Rev: Jan Palac

H#	Date	Year	Mintage	XF	Unc	Proof
34	ND	(1970)	—	—	—	100.00

Rev: Albert J. Luthuli

H#	Date	Year	Mintage	XF	Unc	Proof
35	ND	(1970)	—	—	—	100.00

Rev: Save Venice.

H#	Date	Year	Mintage	XF	Unc	Proof
36	ND	(1971)	—	—	—	100.00

50 RIYALS

10.3500 gm., .900 GOLD, .2995 oz AGW
Rev: Gamal Abdel Nassar
Design as 7.5 Riyals H#13.

H#	Date	Year	Mintage	XF	Unc	Proof
16	AH1390	1970	700 pcs.	—	—	200.00

NOTE: Some of these coins have a serial number below the bust on the obverse.

Rev: Save Venice

H#	Date	Year	Mintage	XF	Unc	Proof
39	ND	(1971)	—	—	—	200.00

75 RIYALS

15.5300 gm., .900 GOLD, .4494 oz AGW
Obv: Fish

H#	Date	Year	Mintage	XF	Unc	Proof
	AH1389	1970	—	—	—	300.00

100 RIYALS

20.7000 gm., .900 GOLD, .5990 oz AGW
Rev:Nikolai Lenin

H#	Date	Year	Mintage	XF	Unc	Proof
10	ND	(1970)	1,000	—	—	400.00

Rev: Save Venice

H#	Date	Year	Mintage	XF	Unc	Proof
40	ND	(1971)	—	—	—	400.00

NCLT ISSUES

MINT SETS

KM#	Date	Mintage	Identification	Issue Price	Mkt. Val.
11	1969(3)	1,200	Hu.1-3.1	11.22	20.00
12	1970(3)	4,350	H5-7	—	—

PROOF SETS
STANDARD METALS

KM#	Date	Mintage	Identification	Issue Price	Mkt. Val.
101	1970(8)	1,175	H17-24	—	600.00
102	1970(8)	—	H28-35	—	800.00
103	1970(4)	—	H12,13,15,16	—	325.00
104	1970(3)	100	H1.2-3.2	—	150.00
105	1970(3)	650	H5-7	19.50	300.00
106	1970(3)	—	H9.1,9.2,10	—	525.00
107	1970(2)	800	H9.2,10	—	500.00
108	1970(2)	5,000	H12,13	9.50	30.00
109	1971(4)	—	H27,36,39,40	—	700.00

FUJAIRAH

Fujairah is the only emirate of the United Arab Emirates that does not have territory on the Persian Gulf. It is on the eastern side of the "horn" of Oman. It has an estimated area of 450 sq. mi. (1200 sq. km.) and a population of 27,000.Fujairah has been, historically, a frequent rival of Sharjah.As recently as 1952 Great Britian recognized Fujairah as an autonomous state. An original member of the United Arab Emirates.

RIYAL

3.0000 gm., 1.000 SILVER, .0964 oz ASW
Obv: Arms.

H#	Date	Mintage	XF	Unc	Proof
1	1969	2,550	—	—	5.00
	1970	200 pcs.	—	—	—

2 RIYALS

6.0000 gm., 1.000 SILVER, .1929 oz ASW
Obv: Arms.

H#	Date	Mintage	XF	Unc	Proof
2	1969	2,650	—	—	7.00
	1970	200 pcs.	—	—	—

5 RIYALS

15.0000 gm., 1.000 SILVER, .4823 oz ASW
Obv: Arms.

H#	Date	Mintage	XF	Unc	Proof
3	1969	3,550	—	—	20.00
	1970	1,300	—	—	—

10 RIYALS

30.0000 gm., 1.000 SILVER, .9646 oz ASW

H#	Date	Mintage	XF	Unc	Proof
4	1969	4,500	—	—	30.00
	1970	500 pcs.	—	—	50.00

Obv: Similar to H#4.

H#	Date	Mintage	XF	Unc	Proof
5	1969	6,000	—	—	30.00
	1970	500 pcs.	—	—	50.00

Obv: Similar to H#4.

H#	Date	Mintage	XF	Unc	Proof
19	1970	1,750	—	—	30.00

Obv: Similar to H#4.

H#	Date	Mintage	XF	Unc	Proof
20	1970	300 pcs.	—	—	60.00

Obv: Similar to H#4.

H#	Date	Mintage	XF	Unc	Proof
21	1970	300 pcs.	—	—	60.00

Obv: Similar to H#4.

H#	Date	Mintage	XF	Unc	Proof
22	1971	400 pcs.	—	—	50.00

25 RIYALS

5.1800 gm., .900 GOLD, .1499 oz AGW

H#	Date	Mintage	XF	Unc	Proof
7	1969	5,000	—	—	100.00

50 RIYALS

10.3600 gm., .900 GOLD, .2998 oz 2998 oz AGW
Similar to 5 Riyals, H#3.

H#	Date	Mintage	XF	Unc	Proof
8	1969	5,000	—	—	200.00
	1970	400 pcs.	—	—	—

100 RIYALS

20.7300 gm., .900 GOLD, .5999 oz AGW

H#	Date	Mintage	XF	Unc	Proof
	Similar to 10 Riyals, H#4.				
9	1969	5,000	—	—	400.00
	Similar to 10 Riyals, H#5.				
10	1969	5,000	—	—	400.00
	Similar to 10 Riyals, H#19.				
23	1970	—	—	—	400.00
	Similar to 10 Riyals, H#20.				
24	1970	—	—	—	400.00
	Similar to 10 Riyals, H#21.				
—	1970	—	—	—	400.00
	Similar to 10 Riyals, H#22.				
25	1971	—	—	—	400.00

200 RIYALS

41.4600 gm., .900 GOLD, 1.1998 oz AGW
Obv: Arms.

H#	Date	Mintage	XF	Unc	Proof
11	1969	5,000	—	—	775.00

NOTE: The above pieces are serially numbered on the obverse.

NCLT ISSUES

PROOF SETS
STANDARD METALS

KM#	Date	Mintage	Identification	Issue Price	Mkt. Val.
101	Mixed 1969-71	(18)	—	—	—
102	Mixed 1969-71	(9)	H1-5,19-22	—	275.00
103	Mixed 1969-71	(8)	H4-5,19,22,9,10,23,25	—	—
104	1969(8)	—	H1-4,7-9,11	—	—
105	1969(5)	2,550	H1-5	40.00	90.00
106	1969(5)	5,000	H7-11	280.00	1875.
107	1969(4)	—	H1-4	—	—
108	1970(5)	200	H1-5	40.00	—

RAS AL KHAIMA

Ras Al Khaima is only one of the coins issuing emirates that was not one of the orginal member of the United Arab Emirates. It was a part of Sharjah. It has an estimated area of 650 sq. mi. (1700 sq. km.) and a population of 30,000. Ras Al Khaima is the only member of the United Arab Emirates that has agriculture as its principal industry.

MONETARY SYSTEM

100 Dirhams 1 Riyal

50 DIRHAMS

COPPER-NICKEL

H#	Date	Mintage	XF	Unc	Proof
28	1970	—	—	1.50	—

RIYAL

3.9000 gm., .640 SILVER, .0802 oz ASW

H#	Date	Mintage	XF	Unc	Proof
1	1969	1,500	—	6.00	—

2 RIYALS

6.5000 gm., .835 SILVER, .1745 oz ASW

H#	Date	Mintage	XF	Unc	Proof
2	1969	1,500	—	9.00	—

2 1/2 RIYALS

7.0000 gm,. .925 SILVER, .2081 oz ASW

H#	Date	Mintage	XF	Unc	Proof
29	1970	—	—	10.00	—

5 RIYALS

15.0000 gm., .835 SILVER, .4027 oz ASW

H#	Date	Mintage	XF	Unc	Proof
3	1969	1,500	—	12.50	—

7 1/2 RIYALS

22.3100 gm., .925 SILVER, .6635 oz ASW
Rev: Facing bust, Obv: Condor.

H#	Date	Mintage	XF	Unc	Proof
30	1970	—	—	20.00	—

H#	Date	Mintage	XF	Unc	Proof
5	ND(1970)	—	—	—	40.00
	Obv: Denominatuon. Rev: Foundation of Rome.				
17	1970	—	—	—	40.00
	Rev: Jules Rimet cup. Similar to 10 Riyals, h#6				
—	(1970)	—	—	—	40.00

10 RIYALS

29.9800 gm., .925 SILVER, .8916 oz ASW

H#	Date	Mintage	XF	Unc	Proof
31.1	1970	4,500	—	—	27.50

H#	Date	Mintage			Proof
31.2	1970	1,400	w/"PROOF"		45.00

Obv: Denomination.

H#	Date	Mintage	XF	Unc	Proof
6	1970	—	—	—	30.00

Obv: Denomination.

H#	Date	Mintage	XF	Unc	Proof
7	ND(1970)	—	—	—	30.00

Obv: Denomination. Rev: Augustus and 3 horses.

H#	Date	Mintage	XF	Unc	Proof
18	1970	—	—	—	30.00

15 RIYALS

44.8700 gm., .925 SILVER, 1.3345 oz ASW
Obv: Denomination.

H#	Date	Mintage	XF	Unc	Proof
8	ND(1970)	—	—	—	40.00

Obv: Denomination. Rev: RESPUBLICA.

H#	Date	Mintage	XF	Unc	Proof
19	1970	—	—	—	40.00

Obv: Denomination. Rev: Similar to 10 Riyals, H#6

H#	Date	Mintage	XF	Unc	Proof
—	(1970)	—	—	—	40.00

50 RIYALS

10.3500 gm., .900 GOLD, .2995 oz AGW
Obv: Denomination. Rev: Bust of Gigi Riva.

H#	Date	Mintage	XF	Unc	Proof
10	ND(1970)	—	—	—	200.00

Obv: Denomination. Rev: Kingdom of Italy.

H#	Date	Mintage	XF	Unc	Proof
21	1970	—	—	—	200.00

75 RIYALS

15.5300 gm., .900 GOLD, .4494 oz AGW
Obv: Denomination. Rev: Bust of Gianni Rivera.

H#	Date	Mintage	XF	Unc	Proof
11	ND(1970)	—	—	—	300.00

Obv: Denomination. Rev: Centennial of Rome as capitol.

H#	Date	Mintage	XF	Unc	Proof
22	1970	—	—	—	300.00

100 RIYALS

20.7000 gm., .900 GOLD, .5990 oz AGW
Similar to 10 Riyals, H#6.

H#	Date	Mintage	XF	Unc	Proof
12	(1970)	—	—	—	400.00

Obv: Denomination. Rev: WW I victory.

H#	Date	Mintage	XF	Unc	Proof
23	1970	—	—	—	400.00

150 RIYALS

31.0500 gm., .900 GOLD, .8985 oz AGW
Obv: Denomination. Rev: 1972 Olympics.

H#	Date	Mintage	XF	Unc	Proof
13	ND(1970)	—	—	—	600.00

Obv: Denomination. Rev: Standing Liberty.

H#	Date	Mintage	XF	Unc	Proof
24	1970	—	—	—	600.00

200 RIYALS

41.4000 gm., .900 GOLD, 1.1980 oz AGW
Similar to 15 Riyals, H#8.

H#	Date	Mintage	XF	Unc	Proof
14	1970	—	—	—	775.00

Obv: Denomination. Rev: Romulus and Remus.

H#	Date	Mintage	XF	Unc	Proof
25	1970	—	—	—	775.00

NCLT ISSUES

MINT SETS

KM#	Date	Mintage	Identification	Issue Price	Mkt. Val.
S1	1969(3)	1,500	H1-3	10.80	25.00

PROOF SETS

STANDARD METALS

Y#	Date	Mintage	Identification	Issue Price	Mkt Val.
101	(1970) (9)	—	H5-8,10-14	—	2400.
102	1970(8)	—	H17-19,21-25	—	2400.
103	(1970) (5)	2,000	H10-14	—	—
104	1970(5)	2,000	H21-25	—	2275.
105	(1970) (4)	2,000	H5-8	41.50	140.00
106	1970(3)	—	H17-19	—	100.00

SHARJAH

Sharjah is the only one of the emirates that shares boundaries with all of the others plus Oman. It has an area of 1,000 sq. mi. (2,600 sq. km.) and a population of 40,000. Sharjah was an important pirate base in the 18 th and early 19 th centuries. Most of the treaties and diplomatic relations were with Great Britian.

5 RUPEES

25.0000 gm., .720 SILVER, .5787 oz ASW

H#	Date	Mintage	XF	Unc	Proof
1	1964	—	BV	17.50	22.50
	1964 with PROOF below flags on reverse				
		—	—	—	—

RIYAL

3.0000 gm., .999 SILVER, .0963 oz ASW

H#	Date	Mintage	XF	Unc	Proof
2	1970	5,000	—	—	15.00

2 RIYALS

6.0000 gm., .999 SILVER, .1927 oz ASW

H#	Date	Mintage	XF	Unc	Proof
3	1970	5,000	—	—	12.50

5 RIYALS

15.0000 gm., .999 SILVER, .4818 oz ASW

H#	Date	Mintage	XF	Unc	Proof
4	1970	5,000	—	—	20.00

10 RIYALS

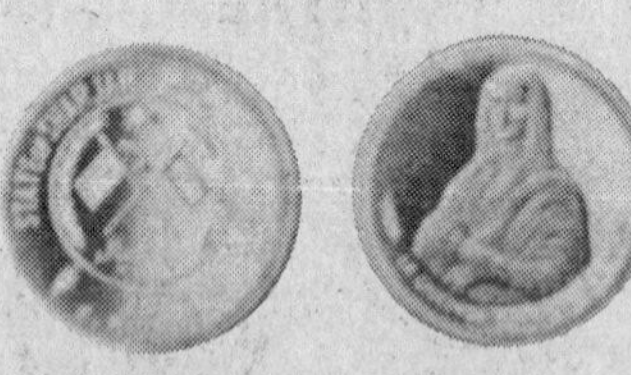

30.0000 gm., .999 SILVER, .9636 oz ASW
Obv: Similar to 1 Riyal, H#2.

H#	Date	Mintage	XF	Unc	Proof
5	1970	5,000	—	—	32.50

25 RIYALS

5.1800 gm., .900 gold, .1499 oz AGW

H#	Date	Mintage	XF	Unc	Proof
7	1970	5,000	—	—	100.00

50 RIYALS

10.3600 gm., .900 GOLD, .2998 oz AGW
Obv: Similar to 25 Riyals, H#7.

H#	Date	Mintage	XF	Unc	Proof
8	1970	5,000	—	—	200.00

100 RIYALS

20.7300 gm., .900 GOLD, .5999 oz AGW
Obv: Similar to 25 Riyals, H#7.

H#	Date	Mintage	XF	Unc	Proof
9	1970	5,000	—	—	400.00

Obv: Similar to 25 Riyals, H#7.

H#	Date	Mintage	XF	Unc	Proof
10	1970	5,000	—	—	400.00

200 RIYALS

41.4600 gm., .900 GOLD, 1.1998 oz AGW
Obv: Similar to 25 Riyals, H#7.

H#	Date	Mintage	XF	Unc	Proof
11	1970	5,000	—	—	775.00

NCLT ISSUES

PROOF SETS
STANDARD METALS

KM#	Date	Mintage	Identification	Issue Price	Mkt. Val.
101	1970(9)	5,000	H2-5,7-11	—	1950.
102	1970(5)	5,000	H7-11	—	1875.
103	1970(4)	5,000	H2-5	25.30	80.00

UMM AL QAIWAIN

This emirate is the second smallest, least developed and smallest in population. The area is 300 sq. mi. (800 sq.km.) and the population is 5,000. The first recognition by the West was in 1820. Most of the emirates is uninhabited desert. Native boat building is an important activity. One of The original member of the United Arab Emirates.

RIYAL

3.0000 gm., .999 SILVER, .0963 oz ASW

H#	Date	Year	Mintage	XF	Unc	Proof
1	AH1389	1970	1,000	—	—	10.00

2 RIYALS

6.0000 gm., .999 SILVER, .1927 oz ASW

H#	Date	Year	Mintage	XF	Unc	Proof
2	AH1389	1970	1,000	—	—	15.00

5 RIYALS

15.0000 gm., .999 SILVER, .4818 oz ASW

H#	Date	Year	Mintage	XF	Unc	Proof
3	AH1389	1970	1,000	—	—	21.00

10 RIYALS

30.0000 gm., .999 SILVER, .9636 oz ASW
Obv: Similar to 5 Riyals, H#3.

H#	Date	Year	Mintage	XF	Unc	Proof
4	AH1389	1970	5,000	—	—	40.00

25 RIYALS

5.1800 gm., .900 GOLD, .1499 oz AGW

H#	Date	Year	Mintage	XF	Unc	Proof
6	AH1389	1970	5,000	—	—	100.00

50 RIYALS

10.3600 gm., .900 GOLD, .2998 oz AGW

Obv: Similar to 25 Riyals, H#6.

H#	Date	Year	Mintage	XF	Unc	Proof
7	AH1389	1970	5,000	—	—	200.00

100 RIYALS

20.7300 gm., .900 GOLD, .5999 oz AGW
Obv: Similar to 25 Riyals, H#6.

8	AH1389	1970	5,000	—	—	400.00

200 RIYALS

41.4600 gm., .900 GOLD, 1.1998 oz AGW
Obv: Similar to 25 Riyals, H#6.

9	AH1389	1970	5,000	—	—	775.00

NCLT ISSUES

PROOF SETS

STANDARD METALS

KM#	Date	Mintage	Identification	Issue Price	Mkt. Val.
101	1970(4)	1,000	H1-4	26.30	85.00
102	1970(4)	5,000	H6-9	—	1475.

UNITED ARAB EMIRATES

RAS AL KHAIMAH
UMM AL-QUIWAIN
AJMAN
SHARJAH
FUJAIRAH
DUBAI
ABU-DHABI

The seven United-Arab Emirates (formerly known as the Trucial Shaikhdoms or States), located along the southern shore of the Persian Gulf, are comprised of the Shaikhdoms of Abu Dhabi, Dubai, Sharjah, Ajman, Umm al Quawain, Ras al Khaimah and Fujairah. They have a combined area of about 32,000 sq. mi. (82,880 sq. km.) and a population of about 760,000. Capital: Abu Zaby (Abu Dhabi). Since the oil strikes of 1958-60, the economy has centered about petroleum.

The Trucial States came under direct British influence in 1892 when the maritime truce treaty enacted after the suppression of pirate activity along the Trucial Coast was enlarged to enjoin the states from disposing of any territory, or entering into any foreign agreements, without British consent in return for British protection from external aggression. In March of 1971 Britain reaffirmed its decision to terminate its treaty relationships with the Trucial Shaikhdoms, whereupon the seven states joined with Bahrain and Qatar in an effort to form a union of Arab emirates under British protection. When the prospective members failed to agree on terms of union, Bahrain and Qatar declared their respective independence, Aug. and Sept. of 1971. Six of the shaikhdoms united to form the United Arab Emirates on Dec. 2, 1971. Ras al Khaimah joined a few weeks later.

MONETARY SYSTEM

100 Fils = 1 Dinar
1000 Fils = 1 Dirham

FIL

BRONZE
F.A.O. Issue

Y#	Date	Year	Mintage	VF	XF	Unc
1	AH1393	1973	4.000	.10	.15	.20
	1395	1975	—	—	—	—

5 FILS

BRONZE
F.A.O. Issue

2	AH1393	1973	8.200	.10	.15	.25

10 FILS

BRONZE

3	AH1393	1973	4.800	.15	.35	1.00

25 FILS

COPPER-NICKEL

Y#	Date	Year	Mintage	VF	XF	Unc
4	AH1393	1973	8.000	.25	.35	.50

50 FILS

COPPER-NICKEL

5	AH1393	1973	5.200	.35	.50	2.00

DINAR

COPPER-NICKEL

6	AH1393	1973	6.000	.50	.75	2.00

UNITED STATES

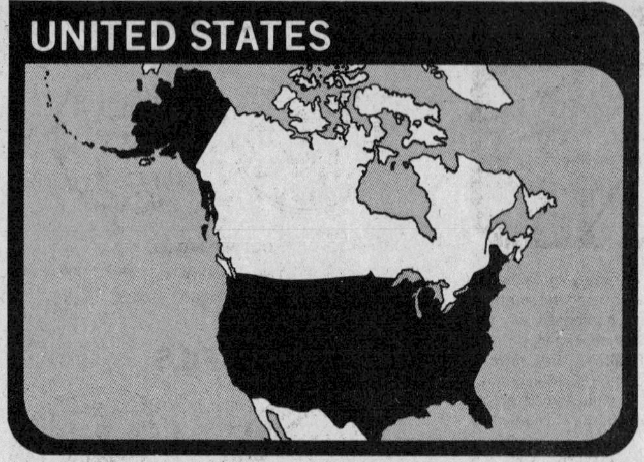

The United States of America as politically organized under the Article of Confederation consisted of the 13 original British-American colonies — New Hampshire, Massachusetts, Rhode Island, Connecticut, New York, New Jersey, Pennsylvania, Delaware, Virginia, North Carolina, South Carolina, Georgia and Maryland — clustered along the eastern seaboard of North America between the forests of Maine and the marshes of Georgia. Under the Articles of Confederation, the United States had no national capital; Philadelphia, where the "United States in Congress Assembled" met, was the "seat of the government." The population during this political phase of America's history (1781-1789) was about 3 million, most of whom lived on self-sufficient family farms. Fishing, lumbering and the production of grains for export were major economic endeavors. Rapid strides were also being made in industry and manufacturing; by 1775, the (then) colonies were accounting for one-seventh of the world's production of raw iron.

On the basis of the voyage of John Cabot to the North American mainland in 1497, England claimed the entire continent. The first permanent English settlement was established at Jamestown, Virginia, in 1607. France and Spain also claimed extensive territory in North America. At the end of the French and Indian Wars (1763), England acquired all of the territory east of the Mississippi River, including East and West Florida. From 1776 to 1781, the States were governed by the Continental Congress. From 1781 to 1789, they were organized under the Articles of Confederation, during which period the individual States had the right to issue money. Independence from Great Britain was attained by the American Revolution, 1775-1783. The Constitution which organized and governs the present United States was ratified on Nov. 21, 1788.

FUGIO CENTS

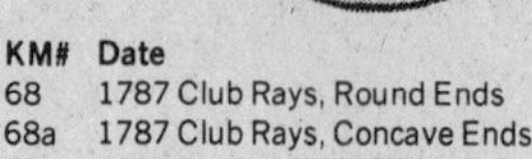

KM#	Date	VG	Fine	VF
68	1787 Club Rays, Round Ends	80.00	175.00	425.00
68a	1787 Club Rays, Concave Ends	800.00	1,500.	3,000.
68b	1787 Similar, FUCIO Error	900.00	1,700.	3,500.

KM#	Date	VG	Fine	VF
69	1787 Pointed Rays, UNITED above, STATES below	400.00	750.00	1,100.
69a	1787 Similar, UNITED STATES at sides of Ring	50.00	85.00	125.00
69b	1787 Similar, STATES UNITED at sides of Ring	55.00	100.00	150.00
69c	1787 Similar, 8-pointed Stars on Ring	75.00	115.00	165.00
69d	1787 Similar, Raised Rims on Ring, Large Lettering in Center	80.00	125.00	250.00
69e	1787 Obv: No Cinquefoils. Cross after Date. Rev: UNITED STATES	150.00	325.00	450.00
69f	1787 Same Obv., Rev: STATES UNITED	175.00	350.00	500.00
69g	1787 Same Obv., Rev: Raised Rims on Ring	—	—	2,000.

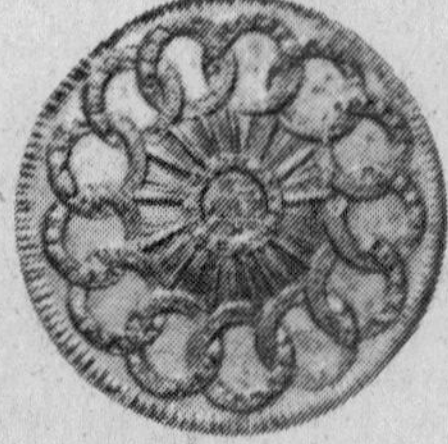

70 1787 Same Obv., Rev. with Rays and AMERICAN CONGRESS — Extremely Rare

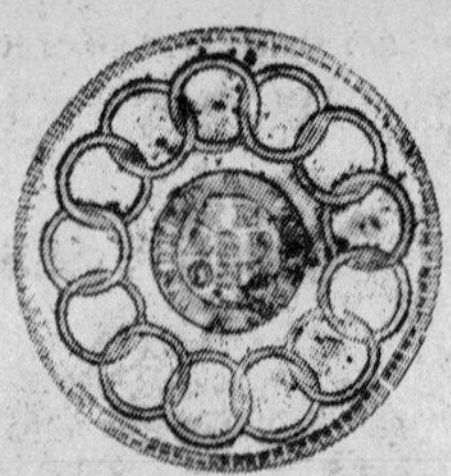

KM#	Date	Unc.
71	New Haven Restrikes (1858): Brass	225.00
	Copper	225.00
	Silver	400.00
	Gold	Extremely Rare

U. S. MINT ISSUES OF 1792

HALF DISME

KM#	Date	Good	Fine	VF
75	1792	1,000.	2,500.	3,500.
75a	1792 Copper (unique)			

DISME

76 1792 Silver (3 known)

76a 1792 Copper (2 reeded edge, about 10 plain edge)

SILVER CENTER CENT

77 1792 Silver Center (about 8 known)

77a 1792 No Silver Center (copper or billon, 4 known) (Offered in a 1974 fixed price list G-VG grade at $14,950.00)

BIRCH CENT

78 1792 Copper (known with plain and two types of lettered edges, about 15 known combined.)

78a 1792 "G.W. Pt." on reverse below wreath tie, White Metal (unique)

WRIGHT QUARTER

79 1792 Copper, Reeded Edge (2 known)

79b 1792 White Metal Die-Trial (unique)

REGULAR ISSUE U.S. COINS

HALF CENTS

Although it survived as a regular issue for 65 years, the half cent was never a popular issue with the public. In total face value less than $40,000 of half cents were issued from 1793 through 1857 when it was discontinued in accordance with an act dated February 21, 1857. In most years 100,000 or less examples were issued, and for 20 years, 1830 through 1849, excepting 1832-35, none were actually struck for circulation, while the coinage was suspended completely from 1812 through 1824, and in only two years did the production exceed one million examples ($5,000).

With approximately 85 percent of the production concentrated in no less than nine years — 1804, 1805, 1806, 1807, 1808, 1809, 1828, 1829 and 1835 — many half cent dates and varieties are extremely scarce. Authorized as a 132 grain issue by the original coinage law of 1792, the half cent's weight was reduced to 104 grains by a January 14, 1793 law before coinage commenced, and further to 84 grains by an act of March 3, 1795.

Date	Mintage	G-4	VG-8	F-12	VF-20	XF-40	MS-60
1793 Head L	35,334	1250.	1700.	2450.	3700.	6300.	—
1794 Head R	81,600	150.	200.	315.	700.	1325.	—
1795 Lettered Edge, Pole	25,600	125.	175.	325.	750.	1750.	—
1795 Plain Edge, No Pole	109,000	125.	165.	315.	700.	1325.	—
1795 Lettered Edge, Punctuated Date	Inc. Ab.	125.	175.	325.	750.	1750.	—
1795 Plain Edge, Punctuated Date	Inc. Ab.	125.	165.	315.	700.	1600.	—
1796 W/Pole	5,090	1750.	2450.	4000.	6300.	8000.	—
1796 No Pole	1,390	—	—	—	Rare	—	—
1797 Pl. Edge	119,215	125.	175.	315.	700.	1600.	—
1797 Let. Edge	Inc. Ab.	225.	350.	575.	1600.	2000.	—
1797 1 Above 1	Inc. Ab.	125.	175.	315.	700.	1600.	—

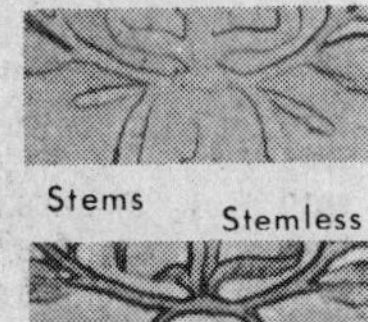
Stems Stemless

Draped Bust

Date	Mintage	G-4	VG-8	F-12	VF-20	XF-40	MS-60
1800	211,530	25.00	38.00	45.00	65.00	110.	—
1802/0 Rev. 1800	14,366	1750.	2500.	3500.	—	—	—
1802/0 Rev. 1802	Inc. Ab.	125.	200.	350.	750.	1800.	—
1803	97,900	20.00	38.00	45.00	50.00	110.	—
1804 Plain 4, Stemless Wreath	1,055,312	20.00	38.00	45.00	50.00	110.	490.
1804 Plain 4, Stems	Inc. Ab.	20.00	38.00	45.00	50.00	110.	—
1804 Cross 4, Stemless	Inc. Ab.	20.00	38.00	45.00	50.00	110.	—
1804 Cross 4, Stems	Inc. Ab.	20.00	38.00	45.00	50.00	110.	—
1804 Spiked Chin	Inc.Ab.	20.00	38.00	45.00	50.00	125.	—
1805 Small 5, Stemless	814,464	20.00	38.00	45.00	75.00	120.	—
1805 Small 5, Stems	Inc. Ab.	75.00	125.	350.	600.	—	—
1805 Large 5, Stems	Inc. Ab.	20.00	38.00	45.00	60.00	110.	—
1806 Small 6, Stems	356,000	30.00	45.00	85.00	150.	230.	—
1806 Small 6, Stemless	Inc. Ab.	20.00	38.00	45.00	55.00	110.	—
1806 Large 6, Stems	Inc. Ab.	20.00	38.00	45.00	55.00	105.	—
1807	476,000	20.00	38.00	45.00	70.00	130.	—
1808 Over 7	400,000	45.00	60.00	115.	225.	—	—
1808	Inc. Ab.	20.00	38.00	45.00	65.00	125.	490.

Turban Head

Date	Mintage	G-4	VG-8	F-12	VF-20	XF-40	MS-60
1809 Over 6	1,154,572	20.00	30.00	35.00	45.00	60.00	290.
1809	Inc. Ab.	20.00	30.00	35.00	45.00	60.00	300.
1810	215,000	20.00	35.00	45.00	75.00	90.00	400.
1811	63,140	65.00	80.00	150.	350.	800.	1250.
1811 Restrike, Reverse Of 1802, Uncirculated				—	—	—	2500.
1825	63,000	25.00	30.00	35.00	45.00	75.00	450.
1826	234,000	16.50	20.00	23.50	30.00	42.50	285.
1828 13 Stars	606,000	16.50	20.00	23.50	30.00	42.50	285.
1828 12 Stars	Inc. Ab.	16.50	20.00	25.00	40.00	60.00	400.
1829	487,000	16.50	20.00	23.50	30.00	42.50	285.
1831 Original	2,200	—	—	—	800.	1000.	2000.
1831 Restrike, Lg. Berries, Reverse Of 1836, Proof					—	—	1750.
1831 Restrike, Sm. Berries, Reverse Of 1852, Proof					—	—	3000.
1832	154,000	16.50	20.00	23.50	30.00	42.50	285.
1833	120,000	16.50	20.00	23.50	30.00	42.50	285.
1834	141,000	16.50	20.00	23.50	30.00	42.50	285.
1835	398,000	16.50	20.00	23.50	30.00	42.50	285.
1836 Original	—	—	Proof	Only	—	—	1400.
1836 Restrike, Reverse Of 1852, Proof Only					—	—	2500.

Braided Hair

Date	Mintage	G-4	VG-8	F-12	VF-20	XF-40	MS-60
1840 Original	—	—	—	Proof	Only	—	3500.
1840 Restrike	—	—	—	Proof	Only	—	3500.
1841 Original	—	—	—	Proof	Only	—	3500.
1841 Restrike	—	—	—	Proof	Only	—	3500.
1842 Original	—	—	—	Proof	Only	—	4000.
1842 Restrike	—	—	—	Proof	Only	—	3500.
1843 Original	—	—	—	Proof	Only	—	3600.
1843 Restrike	—	—	—	Proof	Only	—	3500.
1844 Original	—	—	—	Proof	Only	—	4000.
1844 Restrike	—	—	—	Proof	Only	—	3600.
1845 Original	—	—	—	Proof	Only	—	4500.
1845 Restrike	—	—	—	Proof	Only	—	3600.
1846 Original	—	—	—	Proof	Only	—	3600.
1846 Restrike	—	—	—	Proof	Only	—	3500.
1847 Original	—	—	—	Proof	Only	—	3600.
1847 Restrike	—	—	—	Proof	Only	—	3600.
1848 Original	—	—	—	Proof	Only	—	3600.
1848 Restrike	—	—	—	Proof	Only	—	3500.
1849 Original Small Date			—	Proof	Only	—	4500.
1849 Restrike Small Date			—	Proof	Only	—	3600.

NOTE: The so-called 'original' and 'restrike' half cent examples of the 1840-49 period were struck utilizing indistinguishable obverse dies, the distinction between the two versions being evidenced by the size of the berries on the reverse wreath. Relatively large berries are present on the originals, small on the restrikes.

Date	Mintage	G-4	VG-8	F-12	VF-20	XF-40	MS-60
1849 Lg. Date	39,864	25.00	30.00	35.00	45.00	58.00	375.
1850	39,812	25.00	30.00	35.00	45.00	68.00	375.
1851	147,672	22.00	30.00	35.00	45.00	59.00	285.
1852	—	—	—	Proof	Only	—	850.
1853	129,694	22.00	30.00	35.00	45.00	59.00	285.
1854	55,358	23.00	30.00	35.00	45.00	62.00	285.
1855	56,500	23.00	30.00	35.00	45.00	62.00	285.
1856	40,430	27.50	32.00	35.00	45.00	70.00	285.
1857	35,180	30.00	35.00	40.00	50.00	75.00	300.

NOTE: Brilliant original uncirculated half cent command substantially higher prices.

LARGE CENTS

The early years of our coinage found the mint concentrating on the minting of cents, the coin most needed for daily commercial transactions. Most mintages were substantial and varieties numerous. Like a number of coin issues which would follow, the original chain cent design was subjected to much criticism and abandoned in favor of the wreath reverse. Although the chain's 15 links were intended to represent the solidarity of the states then in the union, it was interpreted as representing the chains of bondage.

The large cent, at double the weight of the half cent, was subjected to the same weight changes as the latter, with mintages being produced in every year except 1815. The weight changes in both the cent and half cent during this period were necessitated by rising copper prices. The 1795 change was substantial enough to prevent the need for any more adjustments for more than 60 years, but ultimately the unprofitable nature of the large cent, coupled with its inconvenient, cumbersome size demanded the introduction of the small cent.

Flowing Hair

Date	Mintage	G-4	VG-8	F-12	VF-20	XF-40	MS-60
1793 Chain	36,103	1850.	2450.	3400.	7000.	14,000.	—
		Garrett Sale, Nov. 1979 MS-63 115,000.					
1793 Wreath	63,353	800.	1200.	1825.	3300.	7300.	—

Liberty Cap

Date	Mintage	G-4	VG-8	F-12	VF-20	XF-40	MS-60
1793 Cap	11,056	650.	950.	1750.	3500.	—	—
1794	918,521	90.00	120.	250.	425.	850.	—
1794 Head '93	Inc. Ab.	160.	285.	450.	850.	—	—
1795	501,500	90.00	110.	210.	410.	800.	—
1795 Lettered Edge, One Cent High In Wreath							
	37,000	100.	120.	250.	425.	800.	—
1796 Lib. Cap	109,825	100.	120.	250.	425.	850.	—

Draped Bust

Date	Mintage	G-4	VG-8	F-12	VF-20	XF-40	MS-60
1796	363,375	47.50	75.00	140.	285.	650.	—
1797	897,510	25.00	37.50	60.00	130.	350.	—

Stems

Stemless

Date	Mintage	G-4	VG-8	F-12	VF-20	XF-40	MS-60
1797 Stemless	Inc. Ab.	50.00	90.00	175.	325.	750.	—
1798	979,700	18.00	30.00	50.00	120.	300.	—
1798/97	Inc. Ab.	32.50	50.00	125.	250.	400.	—
1799	904,585	450.	850.	1650.	2650.	—	—
1800	2,822,175	17.50	20.00	45.00	100.	285.	—
1801	1,362,837	17.50	20.00	45.00	110.	290.	—
1801 3 Errors 1/000, One Stem, IINITED							
	Inc. Ab.	30.00	50.00	125.	300.	600.	—
1802	3,435,100	17.50	20.00	45.00	100.	275.	3300.
1803	2,471,353	17.50	20.00	45.00	100.	275.	3300.
1804	756,838	200.	230.	650.	1100.	2100.	—
1805	941,116	17.50	20.00	50.00	120.	300.	—
1806	348,000	25.00	40.00	65.00	150.	375.	—
1807	727,221	17.50	20.00	45.00	100.	275.	—

Turban Head

Date	Mintage	G-4	VG-8	F-12	VF-20	XF-40	MS-60
1808	1,109,000	24.00	35.00	75.00	175.	450.	—
1809	222,867	70.00	95.00	225.	400.	800.	—
1810	1,458,500	20.00	30.00	50.00	160.	450.	3300.
1811	218,025	45.00	60.00	100.	225.	500.	—
1812	1,075,500	20.00	30.00	50.00	160.	450.	3300.
1813	418,000	37.00	50.00	90.00	200.	450.	—
1814	357,830	20.00	30.00	50.00	150.	450.	3300.

Coronet Type

Date	Mintage	G-4	VG-8	F-12	VF-20	XF-40	MS-60
1816	2,820,982	8.00	9.00	17.50	32.00	60.00	275.
1817	3,948,400	7.00	8.00	12.00	22.50	45.00	250.
1817 15 Stars	Inc. Ab.	8.00	11.50	22.00	32.50	65.00	375.
1818	3,167,000	7.00	8.00	12.00	22.50	45.00	250.
1819	2,671,000	7.00	8.00	12.00	22.50	45.00	250.
1820	4,407,550	6.00	7.00	12.00	20.00	45.00	250.
1821	389,000	17.50	25.00	40.00	75.00	200.	—
1822	2,072,339	7.00	8.00	12.00	25.00	50.00	350.

Date	Mintage	G-4	VG-8	F-12	VF-20	XF-40	MS-60
1823	Inc. 1824	30.00	40.00	90.00	120.	650.	—
1823/22	Inc. 1824	20.00	30.00	60.00	150.	350.	1750.
1824	1,262,000	7.50	12.00	18.00	35.00	70.00	1000.
1824/22	Inc. Ab.	13.00	20.00	30.00	60.00	225.	1500.
1825	1,461,100	8.00	11.00	18.00	25.00	50.00	350.
1826	1,517,425	8.00	10.00	16.00	24.00	50.00	300.
1826/25	Inc. Ab.	12.50	20.00	30.00	60.00	150.	500.
1827	2,357,732	7.00	8.50	11.00	22.50	47.00	300.
1828	2,260,624	7.00	8.50	12.00	22.50	50.00	300.
1829	1,414,500	8.00	10.00	14.00	20.00	50.00	350.
1830	1,711,500	8.50	10.00	14.00	17.00	45.00	300.
1831	3,359,260	7.00	8.50	10.00	15.00	45.00	315.
1832	2,362,000	7.00	8.50	10.00	15.00	50.00	315.
1833	2,739,000	7.00	8.50	10.00	15.00	47.00	300.
1834	1,855,100	7.00	9.00	11.00	17.50	47.00	285.
1835	3,878,400	6.50	8.50	10.00	17.50	45.00	275.
1836	2,111,000	6.50	8.50	12.00	17.50	45.00	275.
1837	5,558,300	6.00	8.00	10.00	15.00	45.00	250.
1838	6,370,200	6.00	8.00	10.00	15.00	45.00	250.
1839	3,128,661	6.50	8.00	12.00	17.00	50.00	350.
1839/36	Inc. Ab.	85.00	125.	200.	350.	1000.	—

Braided Hair

Date	Mintage	G-4	VG-8	F-12	VF-20	XF-40	MS-60
1840	2,462,700	5.50	6.00	8.50	17.00	40.00	250.
1841	1,597,367	5.50	6.00	8.00	16.00	48.00	275.
1842	2,383,390	5.50	6.00	8.50	17.00	40.00	250.

Small Date

Large Date

Large cents of 1840 and 1842 are known with both small and large dates, with little differential in value.

Date	Mintage	G-4	VG-8	F-12	VF-20	XF-40	MS-60
1843	2,425,342	5.50	6.00	8.00	16.00	40.00	250.
1843 Obverse 1842 With Reverse Of 1844							
	Inc. Ab.	10.00	18.00	35.00	45.00	75.00	350.
1844	2,398,752	5.00	5.50	6.50	12.00	39.00	250.
1844/81	Inc. Ab.	6.00	7.25	9.50	15.00	40.00	300.
1845	3,894,804	5.00	5.50	6.50	12.00	38.00	250.
1846	4,120,800	5.00	5.50	6.50	12.00	38.00	250.
1847	6,183,669	5.00	5.50	6.50	12.00	40.00	250.
1848	6,415,799	5.00	5.50	6.50	12.00	40.00	250.
1849	4,178,500	5.00	5.50	6.50	12.00	40.00	275.
1850	4,426,844	5.00	5.50	6.50	12.50	42.00	275.
1851	9,889,707	5.00	5.50	6.50	12.50	40.00	275.
1851/81	Inc. Ab.	6.00	8.25	10.50	18.00	47.50	300.
1852	5,063,094	5.00	5.50	6.50	12.50	40.00	250.
1853	6,641,131	5.00	5.50	6.50	12.50	40.00	250.
1854	4,236,156	5.00	5.50	6.50	12.50	40.00	250.

Slanting 5's

Upright 5's

Large cents of 1855 and 1856 are known with both slanting and upright 5's, with little differential in value.

Date	Mintage	G-4	VG-8	F-12	VF-20	XF-40	MS-60
1855	1,574,829	5.00	5.50	6.50	12.50	40.00	250.
1856	2,690,463	5.00	5.50	6.50	12.50	40.00	250.
1857	333,456	20.00	25.00	32.00	42.00	65.00	300.

NOTE: Brilliant original uncirculated large cents command substantially higher prices.

FLYING EAGLE CENTS

The short lived Flying Eagle cent was conceived as the replacement for the large cent, offering the public a more convenient, cleaner and durable coin than the old coppers. It was made of an alloy of 88 percent copper and 12 percent nickel, its 72 grain weight being less than half that of its predecessor, and 12 grains less than the half cent. In the strictest sense the 1856 issue is a pattern, produced in large numbers so that the then proposed new issue could be offered in sample form to legislators, a substantial quantity of which were ultimately released to circulation.

Date	Mintage	G-4	VG-8	F-12	VF-20	XF-40	AU-50	MS-60	MS-65	Prf-65
1856	Est. 1,000	750.	850.	1100.	1450.	1650.	1850.	3200.	4200.	7500.
1857	17,450,000	7.00	8.50	11.00	23.00	55.00	150.	360.	1450.	6900.

Large Letters
AM Connected

Small Letters
AM Separated

Date	Mintage	G-4	VG-8	F-12	VF-20	XF-40	AU-50	MS-60	MS-65	Prf-65
1858LL	24,600,000	7.50	9.00	12.50	25.00	60.00	150.	360.	1450.	6900.
1858SL	Inc. Ab.	7.50	9.00	12.50	25.00	60.00	150.	360.	1450.	6900.

INDIAN HEAD CENTS

After just two years the flying eagle design on the small cent, which James B. Longacre had copied from the Gobrecht pattern dollars of 1836-39, was replaced by his Indian head design. Two major changes were instituted during the life of this type, the first being in 1860 when after one year of issue the laurel wreath reverse was replaced by an oak wreath and shield device, then in 1864 the metal composition in the cent was changed to bronze and the weight reduced to 48 grains in accordance with a law enacted on April 22, 1864, designed to halt the practice of hoarding which had set in as a result of the Civil War and which led to the Civil War token issues.

1859

1860-1909

Mintmark

COPPER-NICKEL

Date	Mintage	G-4	VG-8	F-12	VF-20	XF-40	AU-50	MS-60	MS-65	Prf-65
1859	36,400,000	5.00	6.00	9.00	20.00	55.00	120.	360.	1450.	6200.
1860	20,566,000	3.50	4.75	7.00	12.00	22.00	40.00	200.	650.	3250.
1861	10,100,000	8.00	10.00	16.50	23.00	40.00	75.00	300.	850.	3200.
1862	28,075,000	3.00	3.50	5.75	8.50	19.00	35.00	200.	650.	3150.
1863	49,840,000	2.75	3.50	4.75	7.50	17.00	31.00	125.	630.	350.
1864	13,740,000	7.00	8.00	12.50	18.00	32.00	45.00	250.	700.	3150.

BRONZE

Date	Mintage	G-4	VG-8	F-12	VF-20	XF-40	AU-50	MS-60	MS-65	Prf-65
1864	39,233,714	3.00	4.50	7.50	15.00	25.00	30.00	80.00	650.	3500.
1864L	Inc. Ab.	18.00	27.50	45.00	65.00	95.00	175.	350.	1200.	8000.

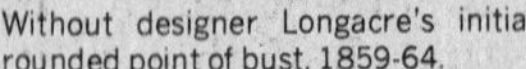
Without designer Longacre's initial rounded point of bust, 1859-64.

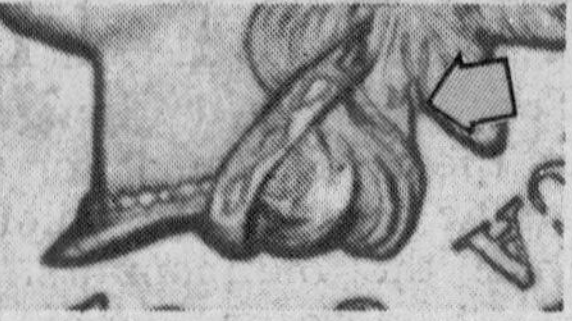
With designer Longacre's initial added, pointed bust, 1864-1909.

Date	Mintage	G-4	VG-8	F-12	VF-20	XF-40	AU-50	MS-60	MS-65	Prf-65
1865	35,429,286	2.75	3.25	6.50	14.00	22.50	30.00	70.00	600.	1000.
1866	9,826,500	16.00	19.00	28.00	45.00	70.00	90.00	250.	800.	950.
1867	9,821,000	16.00	19.00	28.00	45.00	70.00	90.00	250.	800.	950.
1868	10,266,500	16.00	19.00	28.00	45.00	70.00	90.00	250.	800.	950.
1869/8	6,420,000	65.00	90.00	195.	285.	400.	585.	1000.	4000.	—
1869	Inc. Ab.	24.00	32.00	57.00	80.00	110.	170.	400.	1000.	1100.
1870	5,275,000	19.00	28.00	50.00	70.00	110.	130.	225.	900.	1000.
1871	3,929,500	27.00	35.00	57.00	75.00	100.	135.	250.	950.	1000.
1872	4,042,000	33.00	40.00	70.00	95.00	130.	180.	350.	1100.	1100.
1873	11,676,500	7.00	8.50	16.00	25.00	42.00	60.00	150.	650.	850.
1874	14,187,500	7.00	8.50	14.50	24.00	40.00	55.00	150.	650.	850.
1875	13,528,000	7.00	8.50	14.50	25.00	41.00	60.00	125.	650.	850.
1876	7,944,000	10.50	13.00	22.50	30.00	50.00	70.00	180.	650.	850.
1877	852,500	250.	275.	300.	450.	600.	825.	1400.	4500.	6000.
1878	5,799,850	10.50	13.00	25.00	40.00	55.00	75.00	200.	750.	700.
1879	16,231,200	3.25	4.00	8.00	12.00	20.00	24.00	80.00	700.	700.
1880	38,964,955	1.25	2.00	4.00	5.75	15.00	20.00	75.00	600.	700.
1881	39,211,575	1.25	2.00	3.50	5.75	15.00	20.00	75.00	600.	700.
1882	38,581,100	1.25	2.00	3.50	5.75	15.00	20.00	75.00	600.	700.
1883	45,589,109	1.25	2.00	3.50	5.75	15.00	20.00	75.00	600.	700.
1884	23,261,742	2.00	3.00	6.50	10.00	18.00	30.00	80.00	650.	700.
1885	11,765,384	3.25	6.25	9.00	18.00	30.00	40.00	90.00	700.	700.
1886	17,654,290	2.25	3.25	6.50	10.00	25.00	35.00	80.00	750.	700.
1887	45,226,483	1.00	1.25	2.50	3.50	10.00	15.00	70.00	600.	700.
1888	37,494,414	1.00	1.25	2.50	3.50	10.00	15.00	70.00	600.	700.
1889	48,869,361	1.00	1.25	2.50	3.50	10.00	14.00	50.00	600.	700.
1890	57,182,854	.85	1.25	2.25	3.25	10.00	14.00	50.00	600.	700.
1891	47,072,350	.85	1.25	2.25	3.25	10.00	14.00	50.00	600.	700.
1892	37,649,832	.85	1.25	2.25	3.25	10.00	14.00	50.00	600.	400.
1893	46,642,195	.85	1.25	2.25	3.25	10.00	14.00	50.00	600.	400.
1894	16,752,132	1.75	4.00	7.00	10.00	19.00	27.00	70.00	650.	800.
1895	38,343,636	.85	1.00	1.75	3.75	7.50	14.00	50.00	500.	615.
1896	39,057,293	.85	1.00	1.75	3.75	7.50	14.00	50.00	500.	615.
1897	50,466,330	.85	1.00	1.50	3.00	7.50	14.00	50.00	500.	615.
1898	49,823,079	.85	1.00	1.50	3.00	7.50	14.00	50.00	500.	615.
1899	53,600,031	.85	1.00	1.50	3.00	7.50	14.00	50.00	500.	615.
1900	66,833,764	.80	.90	1.50	3.00	7.00	12.00	32.00	500.	615.
1901	79,611,143	.75	.85	1.50	2.75	7.00	12.00	32.00	500.	615.
1902	87,376,722	.75	.85	1.50	2.75	7.00	12.00	32.00	500.	615.
1903	85,094,493	.75	.85	1.50	2.75	7.00	12.00	32.00	500.	615.
1904	61,328,015	.75	.85	1.50	2.75	7.00	12.00	32.00	500.	615.
1905	80,719,163	.75	.85	1.50	2.75	7.00	12.00	32.00	500.	615.
1906	96,022,255	.75	.85	1.50	2.75	7.00	12.00	32.00	500.	615.
1907	108,138,618	.75	.85	1.50	2.75	7.00	12.00	32.00	500.	615.
1908	32,327,987	.75	.85	1.50	2.75	7.00	12.00	34.00	500.	700.
1908S	1,115,000	17.00	19.00	22.00	27.50	37.50	65.00	150.	600.	—
1909	14,370,645	1.00	1.50	2.00	3.00	8.00	15.00	60.00	600.	800.
1909S	309,000	75.00	90.00	110.	130.	165.	225.	380.	1200.	—

LINCOLN CENTS

On the occasion of the 100th anniversary of Abraham Lincoln's birth in 1909 the introduction of Victor D. Brenner's Lincoln cent ended the life of the Indian cent at 50 years. In another 50 years a new reverse featuring the Lincoln Memorial, engraved by Frank Gasparro, was mated to Brenner's obverse. In 1969 Mint artisans refurbished Brenner's Lincoln portrait which had deteriorated badly in 60 years of use.

Through the years the 95 percent copper, 5 percent tin and zinc cent alloy specified in the coinage law of April 22, 1864, was altered in its latter proportions, with tin being permanently eliminated after September 5, 1962. An order of the Secretary of the Treasury dated December 16, 1943, which carried through December 31, 1946, allowed the mint to produce its cents from salvaged shell cases. This action was taken after the zinc coated steel cent issue of 1943, which had lawful weights of both 41.5 and 42.5 grains, proved unsatisfactory.

1909-Date

V.D.B.

1909-1958

Mintmark

Date	Mintage	G-4	VG-8	F-12	VF-20	XF-40	AU-50	MS-60	MS-65	Prf-65
1909	72,702,618	.30	.40	.50	.60	1.25	4.00	10.00	35.00	375.
1909VDB	27,995,000	1.50	1.85	2.00	2.25	3.00	5.00	13.50	28.00	2300.
1909S	1,825,000	28.00	30.00	31.00	36.00	47.00	58.00	100.	200.	—
1909SVDB	484,000	210.	225.	250.	300.	330.	350.	450.	900.	—
1910	146,801,218	.15	.25	.35	.50	1.50	4.00	16.00	40.00	400.
1910S	6,045,000	5.50	6.00	7.50	9.00	12.00	24.00	65.00	190.	—
1911	101,177,787	.15	.30	.65	1.25	2.00	7.00	20.00	75.00	400.
1911D	12,672,000	2.50	3.50	4.50	9.00	17.50	36.00	70.00	200.	—
1911S	4,026,000	9.00	9.75	10.50	13.00	22.00	45.00	80.00	250.	—
1912	68,153,060	.25	.45	1.65	3.75	6.00	13.00	28.00	75.00	375.
1912D	10,411,000	2.50	3.00	4.50	10.00	20.00	40.00	75.00	200.	—
1912S	4,431,000	8.00	9.00	10.00	13.00	16.00	40.00	75.00	300.	—
1913	76,532,352	.15	.35	1.25	2.00	5.75	7.00	32.00	95.00	300.
1913D	15,804,000	1.35	1.75	3.75	7.50	17.50	38.00	70.00	250.	—
1913S	6,101,000	5.50	6.00	6.50	7.50	15.00	36.00	70.00	325.	—
1914	75,238,432	.20	.35	1.25	3.00	4.50	13.00	48.00	160.	400.
1914D	1,193,000	70.00	75.00	85.00	120.	225.	375.	850.	1250.	—
1914S	4,137,000	6.25	6.50	7.50	9.00	19.00	65.00	135.	1000.	—
1915	29,092,120	.50	1.00	4.25	9.00	25.00	35.00	110.	250.	450.
1915D	22,050,000	.50	.80	1.05	5.00	11.00	22.00	45.00	175.	—
1915S	4,833,000	5.25	5.50	6.25	7.75	16.00	38.00	90.00	250.	—
1916	131,833,677	.15	.20	.35	.75	3.00	6.00	13.00	75.00	500.
1916D	35,956,000	.25	.50	1.00	1.50	5.50	24.00	35.00	175.	—
1916S	22,510,000	.55	.70	1.25	1.50	5.50	22.00	45.00	190.	—
1917	196,429,785	.15	.20	.35	.60	2.00	5.00	15.00	60.00	—
1917D	55,120,000	.25	.45	.65	2.75	4.50	23.00	40.00	150.	—
1917S	32,620,000	.25	.45	.65	2.50	4.00	27.00	50.00	180.	—
1918	288,104,634	.15	.20	.35	.60	2.00	5.00	16.00	70.00	—
1918D	47,830,000	.25	.45	.60	2.25	5.00	25.00	45.00	190.	—
1918S	34,680,000	.25	.45	.60	2.25	5.00	22.00	55.00	250.	—
1919	392,021,000	.15	.20	.30	.50	1.75	5.00	11.00	50.00	—
1919D	57,154,000	.20	.30	.65	2.75	5.25	15.00	40.00	175.	—
1919S	139,760,000	.20	.30	.40	.75	2.00	13.00	35.00	150.	—
1920	310,165,000	.15	.20	.30	.50	1.75	5.00	12.00	45.00	—
1920D	49,280,000	.15	.20	.55	1.25	4.00	22.00	50.00	175.	—
1920S	46,220,000	.15	.20	.50	1.25	4.00	15.00	55.00	225.	—
1921	39,157,000	.20	.25	.50	1.00	4.25	12.00	45.00	150.	—
1921S	15,274,000	.60	.75	1.00	2.25	9.00	75.00	165.	450.	—
1922D	7,160,000	4.00	4.50	5.50	7.50	12.00	30.00	65.00	205.	—
1922	Inc. Ab.	120.	140.	180.	220.	380.	850.	2400.	8000.	—
1923	74,723,000	.15	.20	.35	.60	2.00	4.00	12.00	40.00	—
1923S	8,700,000	1.50	1.75	2.25	4.00	10.00	80.00	185.	600.	—
1924	75,178,000	.15	.20	.35	.60	3.50	10.00	40.00	150.	—
1924D	2,520,000	8.25	9.00	11.00	13.00	35.00	100.	250.	700.	—
1924S	11,696,000	.50	.75	1.00	2.25	6.50	40.00	125.	425.	—
1925	139,949,000	.15	.20	.35	.60	2.00	4.00	12.00	40.00	—
1925D	22,580,000	.25	.35	.55	1.10	4.00	15.00	45.00	170.	—
1925S	26,380,000	.15	.25	.40	1.00	3.00	14.00	55.00	225.	—
1926	157,088,000	.15	.20	.35	.50	2.00	4.00	12.00	40.00	—
1926D	28,020,000	.20	.25	.45	.80	3.00	23.00	45.00	250.	—
1926S	4,550,000	2.75	3.25	4.50	6.00	9.50	60.00	150.	450.	—
1927	144,440,000	.15	.20	.30	.40	2.00	4.00	10.00	40.00	—
1927D	27,170,000	.15	.20	.30	.40	2.50	14.00	35.00	160.	—
1927S	14,276,000	.25	.35	.50	1.65	4.00	25.00	60.00	210.	—
1928	134,116,000	.15	.20	.30	.40	1.50	4.00	9.00	35.00	—
1928D	31,170,000	.20	.25	.30	.60	1.50	12.00	22.00	120.	—
1928S	17,266,000	.25	.30	.35	.65	2.00	19.00	60.00	205.	—
1929	185,262,000	.15	.20	.30	.40	1.25	3.50	9.00	30.00	—
1929D	41,730,000	.15	.20	.30	.40	1.25	6.00	16.00	50.00	—
1929S	50,148,000	.15	.20	.30	.40	1.25	4.50	11.00	50.00	—
1930	157,415,000	.10	.15	.20	.30	1.00	3.00	10.00	30.00	—
1930D	40,100,000	.10	.15	.20	.40	1.00	5.00	10.00	35.00	—
1930S	24,286,000	.10	.15	.20	.40	1.00	3.50	12.00	40.00	—
1931	19,396,000	.20	.25	.30	.40	1.50	7.00	20.00	50.00	—
1931D	4,480,000	2.25	2.50	2.75	3.50	4.75	27.50	55.00	125.	—
1931S	866,000	25.00	26.00	27.50	29.00	32.00	40.00	60.00	115.	—
1932	9,062,000	1.25	1.50	1.75	2.00	2.75	7.50	19.00	50.00	—
1932D	10,500,000	.65	.75	1.25	2.00	2.50	7.50	18.00	40.00	—
1933	14,360,000	.50	.60	.70	.90	2.00	7.50	16.00	50.00	—
1933D	6,200,000	1.85	2.00	2.25	2.75	4.00	7.50	20.00	60.00	—
1934	219,080,000	.10	.15	.20	.30	.50	.75	1.50	7.00	—
1934D	28,446,000	.15	.20	.25	.30	1.00	7.00	18.00	35.00	—
1935	245,338,000	—	.10	.15	.20	.25	.50	1.25	2.50	—
1935D	47,000,000	.15	.20	.25	.30	.45	1.25	2.50	4.25	—
1935S	38,702,000	.15	.20	.25	.30	.45	2.50	4.00	9.75	—
1936	309,637,569	—	.10	.15	.20	.25	.50	1.25	2.00	400.
1936D	40,620,000	.15	.20	.25	.30	.35	.50	1.25	3.00	—
1936S	29,130,000	.15	.20	.25	.30	.35	.75	1.50	3.50	—
1937	309,179,320	—	—	.10	.15	.20	.50	1.00	2.25	175.
1937D	50,430,000	—	.10	.15	.20	.25	.55	1.35	3.25	—
1937S	34,500,000	—	.10	.15	.20	.25	.75	1.50	3.00	—
1938	156,696,734	—	—	—	.10	.15	.40	1.40	2.25	90.00
1938D	20,010,000	.15	.20	.25	.30	.50	.75	1.50	2.75	—
1938S	15,180,000	.20	.30	.40	.50	.60	1.00	2.40	4.00	—
1939	316,479,520	—	—	—	.10	.15	.35	1.00	1.75	65.00

Date	Mintage	G-4	VG-8	F-12	VF-20	XF-40	AU-50	MS-60	MS-65	Prf-65
1939D	15,160,000	.30	.35	.50	.60	.75	1.75	3.00	7.00	—
1939S	52,070,000	—	.10	.15	.20	.25	.90	1.75	3.00	—
1940	586,825,872	—	—	—	.10	.15	.35	1.00	1.75	45.00
1940D	81,390,000	—	—	—	.10	.15	.40	1.25	2.00	—
1940S	112,940,000	—	—	—	.10	.15	.30	.95	1.50	—
1941	887,039,100	—	—	—	.10	.15	.30	.80	1.50	45.00
1941D	128,700,000	—	—	—	.10	.15	1.00	2.50	3.50	—
1941S	92,360,000	—	—	—	.10	.15	1.25	3.50	6.50	—
1942	657,828,600	—	—	—	.10	.15	.25	.45	1.50	45.00
1942D	206,698,000	—	—	—	.10	.15	.25	.60	1.50	—
1942S	85,590,000	—	—	—	.15	.25	1.50	4.00	6.50	—

Date	Mintage	XF-40	MS-60	Prf-65
1943	684,628,670	.20	.60	—
1943D	217,660,000	.30	1.00	—
1943S	191,550,000	.30	1.75	—
1944	1,435,400,000	.10	.25	—
1944D	430,578,000	.10	.25	—
1944D, D/S	—	65.	200.	—
1944S	282,760,000	.15	.35	—
1945	1,040,515,000	.10	.30	—
1945D	226,268,000	.10	.70	—
1945S	181,770,000	.15	.50	—
1946	991,655,000	.10	.20	—
1946D	315,690,000	.10	.25	—
1946S	198,100,000	.15	.60	—
1947	190,555,000	.15	.60	—
1947D	194,750,000	.10	.30	—
1947S	99,000,000	.15	.75	—
1948	317,570,000	.10	.50	—
1948D	172,637,000	.10	.30	—
1948S	81,735,000	.15	.90	—
1949	217,775,000	.10	.75	—
1949D	153,132,000	.10	.60	—
1949S	64,290,000	.20	1.75	—
1950	272,686,386	.10	.40	39.00
1950D	334,950,000	.10	.30	—
1950S	118,505,000	.15	.60	—
1951	295,633,500	.10	1.25	15.00
1951D	625,355,000	.10	.25	—
1951S	136,010,000	.15	1.70	—
1952	186,856,980	.10	.60	12.00
1952D	746,130,000	.10	.25	—
1952S	137,800,004	.15	.90	—
1953	256,883,800	.10	.20	10.00
1953D	700,515,000	.10	.20	—
1953S	181,835,000	.15	.45	—
1954	71,873,350	.20	.45	6.50
1954D	251,552,500	.10	.25	—
1954S	96,190,000	.15	.35	—

Date				
1955 Double Die				
VF-20	XF-40	AU-50	MS-60	MS-65
310.	350.	400.	650.	1600.

Date	Mintage	XF-40	MS-60	Prf-65
1955	330,958,000	.10	.20	3.00
1955D	563,257,500	.10	.20	—
1955S	44,610,000	.35	.60	—

Date	Mintage	XF-40	MS-60	Prf-65
1956	421,414,384	—	.15	2.00
1956D	1,098,201,100	—	.15	—
1957	283,787,952	—	.15	2.00
1957D	1,051,342,000	—	.15	—
1958	253,400,652	—	.15	3.00
1958D	800,953,300	—	.15	—

LINCOLN MEMORIAL REVERSE INTRODUCED 1959

Date	Mintage	XF-40	MS-60	Prf-65
1959	610,864,291	—	.15	1.10
1959D	1,279,760,000	—	.15	—

Small Date

Large Date

Date	Mintage	XF-40	MS-60	Prf-65
1960SD	588,096,602	1.75	5.50	21.00
1960LD	Inc. Ab.	—	.10	1.10
1960D SD	1,580,884,000	.15	.30	—
1960D LD	Inc. Ab.	—	.15	—
1961	756,373,244	—	.10	.70
1961D	1,753,266,700	—	.10	—
1962	609,263,019	—	.10	.70
1962D	1,793,148,400	—	.10	—
1963	757,185,645	—	.10	.70
1963D	1,774,020,400	—	.10	—
1964	2,652,525,762	—	.10	.60
1964D	3,799,071,500	—	.10	—

Commencing 1965 - See Modern Singles - Page 1897

Large Date | Small Date

Date	MS-60	Prf-65
1970S LD	.15	.50
1970S SD	5.75	140.

Date	F-12	VF-20	XF-40	MS-60
1972 Double Die	—	—	150.	225.

TWO CENT

Authorized by the same law which provided for the change to a bronze composition for the cent, the two cent piece had a weight (96 grains) exactly twice that of the cent. It served to fill the vital need for small change in expediting the replacement of monetary substitutes then in circulation, but soon outlived its usefulness, and its issue was halted by the major revision in the nation's coinage laws instituted in 1873. This coin, at the instigation of the Reverend Mark R. Watkinson, with the support of Lincoln's Secrtary of the Treasury Salmon P. Chase, became the first to carry the motto "In God We Trust."

Date	Mintage	G-4	VG-8	F-12	VF-20	XF-40	AU-50	MS-60	MS-65	Prf-65
1864SM	19,847,500	40.00	50.00	65.00	90.00	150.	195.	425.	1500.	—
1864LM	Inc. Ab.	5.00	6.00	7.50	12.50	28.00	55.00	215.	1070.	2650.

SMALL MOTTO

LARGE MOTTO

Date	Mintage	G-4	VG-8	F-12	VF-20	XF-40	AU-50	MS-60	MS-65	Prf-65
1865	13,640,000	4.00	4.50	6.00	12.50	28.00	55.00	215.	1070.	2650.
1866	3,177,000	4.50	5.00	7.00	12.50	30.00	65.00	230.	1100.	2650.
1867	2,938,750	4.50	5.00	6.00	12.50	30.00	65.00	230.	1100.	2650.
1868	2,803,750	4.75	5.50	6.00	12.50	30.00	65.00	230.	1100.	2650.
1869	1,546,500	5.50	6.50	8.50	14.50	35.00	75.00	250.	1125.	2650.
1870	861,250	6.50	8.00	17.00	28.00	45.00	75.00	325.	1400.	2700.
1871	721,250	8.00	10.00	17.00	30.00	50.00	80.00	350.	1500.	3000.
1872	65,000	70.00	90.00	125.	175.	250.	350.	550.	1600.	3100.
1873	Est. 1100	—	—	Proof	Only	—	—	—	—	3500.
	Impaired Proof		495.	525.	550.	595.	675.	—	—	—

THREE CENT SILVER

The trime, as the silver three cent piece was originally known, was created as a direct result of a reduction in the nation's first class postage rates, from five to three cents in 1851, although the issue was actually conceived a year earlier as an exchange coin for the redemption of underweight foreign fractional silver coins which were then still recognized as legal tender in the U.S. It was also applied to the latter purpose, which is the reason why its content was specified as .750 fine silver in a 12 3/8 grain weight, the latter exactly proportionate with the .900 fine silver coins of the day.

Although the denomination seems today to be quite odd, it was a well conceived issue which gained immediate public popularity. During the first three years of issue it was produced at a then unbelievable rate of about a million examples per month (half dimes of the period were being produced at a rate of substantially less than a million pieces per year).

The silver content of the coin was raised to .900 fine and the weight reduced slightly to 11.52 grains by an act of March 3, 1853 (the coin had been authorized on the same date three years earlier), which brought it into conformity with the minor adjustments made in the weight of the nation's other silver coins by a law of February 21, 1853. The chaotic economic conditions brought on by the Civil War drove the coin out of circulation, and although it survived in limited issue qualities until the nation's coinage laws were rewritten in 1873, circulation quantities were not struck after 1862.

Mintmark

TYPE 1 - NO OUTLINES TO STAR

Date	Mintage	G-4	VG-8	F-12	VF-20	XF-40	AU-50	MS-60	MS-65	Prf-65
1851	5,447,400	8.00	9.50	12.00	20.00	45.00	95.00	440.	3465.	—
1851O	720,000	12.00	15.00	20.00	30.00	55.00	170.	600.	3550.	—
1852	18,663,500	8.00	9.50	12.00	20.00	45.00	95.00	440.	3465.	—
1853	11,400,000	8.00	9.50	12.00	20.00	45.00	95.00	440.	3465.	—

TYPE 2 - THREE OUTLINES TO STAR

Date	Mintage	G-4	VG-8	F-12	VF-20	XF-40	AU-50	MS-60	MS-65	Prf-65
1854	671,000	10.00	14.00	20.00	30.00	75.00	385.	820.	5350.	—
1855	139,000	15.00	20.00	32.50	50.00	140.	450.	900.	5500.	8100.
1856	1,458,000	9.50	12.50	20.00	30.00	75.00	385.	820.	5350.	8100.
1857	1,042,000	9.50	12.50	20.00	30.00	75.00	385.	820.	5350.	7900.
1858	1,604,000	9.50	12.50	20.00	30.00	75.00	385.	820.	7900.	6300.

TYPE 3 - TWO OUTLINES TO STAR

Date	Mintage	G-4	VG-8	F-12	VF-20	XF-40	AU-50	MS-60	MS-65	Prf-65
1859	365,000	12.50	15.00	20.00	30.00	55.00	95.00	440.	3465.	4725.
1860	287,000	12.50	15.00	20.00	30.00	55.00	95.00	440.	3465.	4725.
1861	498,000	12.50	15.00	20.00	30.00	55.00	95.00	440.	3465.	4725.
1862	343,550	12.50	15.00	20.00	30.00	55.00	95.00	440.	3465.	4725.
1863	21,460	—	—	—	—	275.	350.	500.	3700.	4725.
1864	12,470	—	—	—	—	285.	360.	525.	5000.	4725.
1865	8,500	—	—	—	—	295.	375.	575.	3700.	4725.
1866	22,725	—	—	—	—	275.	360.	525.	3550.	4725.
1867	4,625	—	—	—	—	325.	425.	575.	4000.	4725.
1868	4,100	—	—	—	—	325.	425.	575.	4000.	4725.
1869	5,100	—	—	—	—	295.	375.	575.	4000.	4725.
1870	4,000	—	—	—	—	325.	425.	575.	4000.	4725.
1871	4,360	—	—	—	—	325.	425.	575.	5800.	4725.
1872	1,950	—	—	—	—	325.	475.	675.	3465.	4725.
1873	600	—	—	Proof	Only	—	—	—	—	4725.
	Impaired Proof		175.	200.	275.	325.	—	—	—	4725.

THREE CENT NICKEL

Faced with the fact that the silver trime was not circulating, the Congress moved in an act dated March 3, 1865, to authorize the introduction of a nickel composition three cent piece. The series enjoyed an uneventful history stretching over 25 years, although the annual quantities of issue after 1874 were largely insignificant. When the series was closed out in 1889, the quantities produced in any of the last 13 years exceeded 41,200 only in 1881 when over a million examples were offered.

Nickel

Date	Mintage	G-4	VG-8	F-12	VF-20	XF-40	AU-50	MS-60	MS-65	Prf-65
1865	11,382,000	5.00	6.00	7.00	9.00	15.00	35.00	215.	1500.	5000.
1866	4,801,000	5.00	6.00	7.00	9.00	15.00	35.00	215.	1500.	2950.
1867	3,915,000	5.00	6.00	7.00	9.00	15.00	35.00	215.	1500.	2950.
1868	3,252,000	5.00	6.00	7.00	9.00	15.00	35.00	215.	1500.	2950.
1869	1,604,000	6.00	7.00	8.00	10.00	17.00	35.00	215.	1500.	2950.
1870	1,335,000	6.00	7.00	8.50	11.00	18.00	35.00	225.	1550.	2950.
1871	604,000	6.00	7.00	9.00	11.50	18.00	45.00	250.	1600.	2950.
1872	862,000	6.00	7.00	9.00	11.50	18.00	45.00	250.	1600.	2950.
1873	1,173,000	6.00	7.00	8.50	11.00	18.00	35.00	215.	1500.	2950.
1874	790,000	6.00	7.00	9.00	11.50	18.00	45.00	215.	1500.	2950.
1875	228,000	7.00	9.00	12.50	17.50	25.00	85.00	275.	1700.	2950.
1876	162,000	10.00	12.50	15.00	20.00	27.50	85.00	275.	1700.	3100.
1877	Est. 900	—	—	Proof	Only	—	—	—	—	5000.
	Impaired Proof		600.	650.	725.	850.	700.	—	—	—
1878	2,350	—	—	Proof	Only	—	—	—	—	3500.
	Impaired Proof		215.	235.	265.	295.	315.	—	—	—
1879	41,200	37.50	42.00	47.00	52.00	62.00	165.	400.	2300.	2950.
1880	24,955	45.00	50.00	55.00	70.00	80.00	165.	500.	2200.	2950.
1881	1,080,575	5.00	6.00	7.00	9.00	15.00	45.00	215.	2200.	2950.
1882	25,300	40.00	42.00	50.00	55.00	67.50	150.	500.	2200.	2950.
1883	10,609	75.00	87.00	105.	125.	150.	175.	500.	2200.	2950.
1884	5,642	140.	150.	165.	180.	200.	240.	600.	2300.	2950.
1885	4,790	200.	215.	235.	265.	295.	350.	625.	2400.	2950.
1886	4,290	—	—	Proof	Only	—	—	—	—	2950.
	Impaired Proof		190.	200.	225.	250.	265.	—	—	—
1887/6	7,961	—	—	Proof	Only	—	—	—	—	2950.
	Impaired Proof		200.	215.	235.	260.	275.	—	—	—
1887	Inc. Ab.	160.	170.	185.	200.	225.	275.	600.	2600.	3050.
1888	41,083	32.50	35.00	37.00	42.00	50.00	125.	425.	2400.	2950.
1889	21,561	40.00	42.00	50.00	55.00	67.50	135.	475.	2400.	2950.

HALF DIMES

These were the silver predecessors of today's nickel. The basic history of this series throughout its 80 year mintage closely parallels that of its sister fractional silver issues of the period, excepting the fact that its coinage was suspended during the years 1806 through 1828. Although the first issue is dated 1794, it was not produced until early the following year.

Originally authorized, like the nation's other silver coins, as a .8924 fine issue with a proportionate weight of 20.8 grains, the fineness was increased to .900 and the grain weight reduced to 20 5/8 by a January 18, 1837, law which similarly influenced the other denominations. The weight of the coin was reduced more substantially to 19.2 grains by the February 21, 1853, coinage law. To emphasize this change arrows were placed either side of the date on the affected 1853 coins, and all issues of 1854 and 1855. The half dime series was terminated as a result of the coinage law revisions of 1873, eight years after the first nickel five cent piece was issued.

Flowing Hair Half-Dimes

Date	Mintage	G-4	VG-8	F-12	VF-20	XF-40	MS-60
1794	86,416	800.	1000.	1325.	2000.	3850.	12,000.
1795	Inc. Ab.	800.	1000.	1325.	2000.	3150.	10,000.

Draped Bust Half-Dimes

Date	Mintage	G-4	VG-8	F-12	VF-20	XF-40	MS-60
1796	10,230	850.	950.	1550.	2200.	3900.	12,000.
1796 Likerty	Inc. Ab.	900.	1000.	1600.	2300.	4000.	—
1796/5	Inc. Ab.	1000.	1050.	1650.	2350.	4000.	13,000.
1797 13 Stars	44,527	875.	975.	1575.	2300.	4000.	12,000.
1797 15 Stars	Inc. Ab.	850.	950.	1550.	2200.	3900.	12,000.
1797 16 Stars	Inc. Ab.	850.	950.	1550.	2200.	3900.	12,000.

LIBEKTY

HERALDIC EAGLE INTRODUCED

Date	Mintage	G-4	VG-8	F-12	VF-20	XF-40	MS-60
1800	24,000	575.	675.	950.	1575.	3150.	10,750.
1800 Libekty	Inc. Ab.	575.	675.	950.	1575.	3150.	10,750.
1801	33,910	575.	675.	950.	1575.	3150.	10,750.
1802	13,010	2400.	3000.	7500.	12,000.	45,000.	—
1803	37,850	575.	675.	950.	1575.	3150.	10,750.
1805	15,600	575.	675.	950.	1575.	3150.	—

Liberty Cap Half-Dimes

Date	Mintage	G-4	VG-8	F-12	VF-20	XF-40	AU-50	MS-60	MS-65
1829	1,230,000	16.00	18.00	22.00	41.00	90.00	250.	630.	5675.
1830	1,240,000	16.00	18.00	22.00	41.00	90.00	250.	630.	5675.
1831	1,242,700	16.00	18.00	22.00	41.00	90.00	250.	630.	5675.
1832	965,000	16.00	18.00	22.00	41.00	90.00	250.	630.	5675.
1833	1,370,000	16.00	18.00	22.00	41.00	90.00	250.	630.	5675.
1834	1,480,000	16.00	18.00	22.00	41.00	90.00	250.	630.	5675.
1835 Large Date, Large 5C.	2,760,000	16.00	18.00	22.00	41.00	90.00	250.	630.	5675.
1835 Large Date, Small 5C.	Inc. Ab.	16.00	18.00	22.00	41.00	90.00	250.	630.	5675.
1835 Small Date, Large 5C.	Inc. Ab.	16.00	18.00	22.00	41.00	90.00	250.	630.	5675.
1835 Small Date, Small 5C.	Inc. Ab.	16.00	18.00	22.00	41.00	90.00	250.	630.	5675.
1836 Large 5C.	1,900,000	16.00	18.00	22.00	41.00	90.00	250.	630.	5675.
1836 small 5C.	I.A.	16.00	18.00	22.00	41.00	90.00	250.	630.	5675.
1837 Large 5C.	2,276,000	16.00	18.00	22.00	41.00	90.00	250.	630.	5675.
1837 small 5C.	I.A.	22.00	30.00	55.00	85.00	150.	300.	700.	6500.

MINTMARK ABOVE AND BELOW WREATH TIE

Liberty Seated Half-Dimes

WITHOUT STARS AROUND RIM

Date	Mintage	G-4	VG-8	F-12	VF-20	XF-40	MS-60
1837 Sm. Date	Inc. Ab.	50.00	65.00	80.00	130.	260.	1500.
1837 Lg. Date	Inc. Ab.	40.00	55.00	70.00	110.	240.	1375.
1838O	70,000	65.00	100.	200.	350.	650.	—

STARS ADDED AROUND RIM

Date	Mintage	G-4	VG-8	F-12	VF-20	XF-40	MS-60
1838	2,255,000	10.00	15.00	20.00	35.00	60.00	950.
1838 sm.stars	Inc. Ab.	20.00	30.00	50.00	80.00	200.	1200.
1839	1,069,150	10.00	15.00	20.00	35.00	60.00	950.
1839O	1,034,039	15.00	18.00	25.00	45.00	80.00	975.
1839O Rev. 1838O		75.00	100.	175.	250.	500.	—
1840	1,344,085	10.00	15.00	20.00	35.00	60.00	925.
1840O	935,000	15.00	20.00	30.00	50.00	85.00	1000.

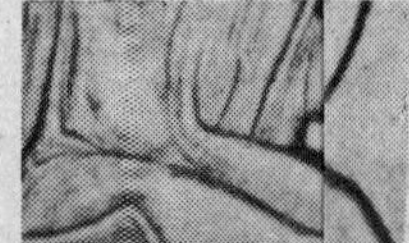

Without Drapy

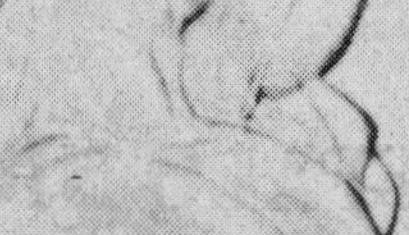

With Drapery

DRAPRY ADDED TO LIBERTY

Date	Mintage	G-4	VG-8	F-12	VF-20	XF-40	MS-60
1840	Inc. Ab.	35.00	50.00	80.00	200.	500.	1800.
1840O	Inc. Ab.	40.00	60.00	125.	250.	550.	—
1841	1,150,000	10.00	15.00	20.00	35.00	60.00	535.
1841O	815,000	12.00	18.00	25.00	40.00	70.00	650.
1842	815,000	10.00	15.00	20.00	35.00	60.00	535.
1842O	350,000	15.00	25.00	35.00	125.	250.	—
1843	1,165,000	10.00	15.00	20.00	35.00	60.00	535.
1844	430,000	10.00	15.00	20.00	35.00	60.00	535.

Date	Mintage	G-4	VG-8	F-12	VF-20	XF-40	MS-60
1844O	220,000	60.00	80.00	200.	350.	800.	—
1845	1,564,000	10.00	15.00	20.00	35.00	60.00	565.
1845/1845	Inc. Ab.	20.00	30.00	50.00	90.00	125.	550.
1846	27,000	125.	150.	275.	400.	800.	—
1847	1,274,000	10.00	15.00	20.00	35.00	60.00	535.
1848 Medium Date	668,000	10.00	15.00	20.00	35.00	60.00	535.
1848 Lg. Date	Inc. Ab.	15.00	20.00	30.00	60.00	85.00	550.
1848O	600,000	15.00	20.00	30.00	60.00	85.00	600.
1849/8	1,309,000	18.00	25.00	30.00	45.00	70.00	535.
1849/6	Inc. Ab.	12.00	18.00	25.00	40.00	65.00	550.
1849	Inc. Ab.	10.00	15.00	20.00	35.00	60.00	550.
1849O	140,000	25.00	35.00	65.00	250.	450.	—
1850	955,000	10.00	15.00	20.00	25.00	60.00	550.
1850O	690,000	15.00	20.00	30.00	45.00	85.00	600.
1851	781,000	10.00	15.00	20.00	25.00	60.00	550.
1851O	860,000	12.00	18.00	30.00	50.00	80.00	600.
1852	1,000,500	10.00	15.00	20.00	25.00	60.00	535.
1852O	260,000	30.00	35.00	60.00	95.00	200.	—
1853	135,000	15.00	25.00	50.00	75.00	125.	535.
1853O	160,000	115.	135.	250.	400.	800.	—

ARROWS AT DATE

Date	Mintage	G-4	VG-8	F-12	VF-20	XF-40	MS-60	Prf-65
1853	13,210,020	6.00	8.00	9.00	15.00	50.00	665.	6200.
1853O	2,200,000	6.00	8.00	10.00	16.00	55.00	675.	—
1854	5,740,000	6.00	8.00	9.00	15.00	50.00	665.	5800.
1854O	1,560,000	8.00	12.00	15.00	35.00	75.00	900.	—
1855	1,750,000	6.00	8.00	9.00	15.00	50.00	665.	5800.
1855O	600,000	15.00	20.00	30.00	50.00	85.00	1000.	—

ARROWS AT DATE REMOVED

Date	Mintage	G-4	VG-8	F-12	VF-20	XF-40	MS-60	Prf-65
1856	4,880,000	8.00	12.00	16.00	20.00	50.00	535.	7000.
1856O	1,100,000	10.00	15.00	20.00	30.00	60.00	550.	—
1857	7,280,000	8.00	12.00	16.00	20.00	50.00	535.	6400.
1857O	1,380,000	10.00	15.00	20.00	30.00	60.00	550.	—
1858	3,500,000	8.00	12.00	16.00	20.00	50.00	535.	4500.
1858 Inverted Date	Inc. Ab.	30.00	35.00	70.00	115.	150.	600.	—
1858 Double Date	Inc. Ab.	40.00	60.00	80.00	200.	325.	1200.	—
1858O	1,660,000	10.00	15.00	20.00	30.00	60.00	550.	—
1859	340,000	15.00	25.00	50.00	65.00	100.	535.	5800.
1859O	560,000	15.00	20.00	30.00	40.00	70.00	700.	—

TRANSITIONAL PATTERNS

Date	Mintage	G-4	VG-8	F-12	VF-20	XF-40	MS-60	Prf-65
1859 Obverse Of 1859, Reverse 1860					—	—	—	10,000.
1860 Obverse Of 1859, Reverse 1860					—	—	3000.	—

Mintmark

ONLY 1871-72

OBVERSE LEGEND REPLACES STARS

Date	Mintage	G-4	VG-8	F-12	VF-20	XF-40	MS-60	Prf-65
1860	799,000	8.00	12.00	20.00	25.00	50.00	400.	4000.
1860O	1,060,000	8.00	12.00	25.00	35.00	60.00	420.	—
1861	3,361,000	8.00	12.00	20.00	25.00	50.00	400.	4000.
1862	1,492,550	8.00	12.00	20.00	25.00	50.00	400.	4000.
1863	18,460	60.00	70.00	100.	150.	200.	700.	4000.
1863S	100,000	15.00	20.00	30.00	45.00	100.	900.	—
1864	48,470	225.	275.	350.	400.	500.	1200.	4200.
1864S	90,000	25.00	35.00	75.00	100.	165.	1200.	—
1865	13,500	100.	130.	175.	200.	275.	800.	4000.
1865S	120,000	15.00	20.00	30.00	65.00	100.	975.	—
1866	10,725	110.	140.	185.	225.	300.	800.	4000.
1866S	120,000	15.00	20.00	30.00	50.00	125.	950.	—
1867	8,625	150.	200.	250.	300.	400.	1000.	4000.
1867S	120,000	15.00	20.00	35.00	70.00	150.	900.	—
1868	89,200	20.00	30.00	40.00	75.00	150.	500.	2800.
1868S	280,000	9.00	15.00	18.00	30.00	60.00	450.	—
1869	208,600	10.00	15.00	25.00	35.00	65.00	420.	2800.
1869S	230,000	9.00	15.00	18.00	30.00	60.00	425.	—
1870	536,600	10.00	15.00	20.00	30.00	60.00	400.	4000.
1870S	Unique, 1 known in unc. private sale, apr.1980							$425,000.
1871	1,873,960	8.00	12.00	15.00	30.00	60.00	400.	4000.
1871S	161,000	15.00	30.00	50.00	75.00	125.	675.	—
1872	2,947,950	8.00	12.00	15.00	30.00	60.00	400.	4000.
1872S Mintmark In Wreath	837,000	10.00	15.00	20.00	30.00	50.00	400.	—
1872S Mintmark Below Wreath	Inc. Ab.	10.00	15.00	20.00	30.00	60.00	420.	—
1873	712,600	8.00	12.00	15.00	30.00	70.00	400.	4000.
1873S	324,000	10.00	15.00	20.00	30.00	60.00	450.	—

SHIELD NICKELS

Issue of the nickel was authorized by an act of May 16, 1866, as a companion coin to the nickel three cent piece authorized a little more than a year earlier. Originally approved as a substitute for the half dime during the period following the Civil War when specie payments were suspended, the issue ultimately brought on the demise of the silver coin. The shield nickel designs are the work of the Mint's chief engraver James B. Longacre.

Date	Mintage	G-4	VG-8	F-12	VF-20	XF-40	AU-50	MS-60	MS-65	Prf-65
1866	14,742,500	10.00	14.00	25.00	35.00	115.	150.	600.	4000.	8000.
1867 With Rays										
	2,019,000	12.00	15.00	27.00	40.00	125.	165.	600.	4000	10,500.
1867 Without Rays										
	28,890,500	7.50	9.00	12.50	17.50	30.00	45.00	270.	2000.	3200.
1868	28,817,000	7.50	9.00	12.50	17.50	30.00	45.00	270.	2000.	3200.
1869	16,395,000	7.50	9.00	12.50	17.50	30.00	45.00	275.	2000.	3200.
1870	4,806,000	10.00	11.50	14.50	20.00	35.00	50.00	275.	2000.	3200.
1871	561,000	33.00	38.00	43.00	55.00	85.00	110.	325.	2300.	3200.
1872	6,036,000	10.00	11.50	14.50	20.00	35.00	50.00	275.	2000.	3200.
1873	4,550,000	6.00	11.50	14.50	20.00	35.00	50.00	275.	2000.	3200.
1874	3,538,000	10.00	12.00	16.00	22.50	37.50	55.00	275.	2000.	3200.
1875	2,097,000	12.00	15.00	20.00	27.50	45.00	70.00	285.	2000.	3200.
1876	2,530,000	11.00	14.00	18.00	25.00	42.50	60.00	275.	2000.	3200.
1877	Est. 500	—	—	Proof	Only	—	—	—	—	9500.
	Impaired Proof		550.	585.	650.	700.	800.	—	—	—
1878	2,350	—	—	Proof	Only	—	—	—	—	6500.
	Impaired Proof		215.	235.	265.	295.	310.	—	—	—
1879	29,100	85.00	100.	120.	140.	160.	230.	375.	2800.	4000.
1880	19,995	90.00	105.	125.	145.	170.	235.	400.	2700.	4000.
1881	72,375	65.00	75.00	85.00	100.	120.	230.	350.	2700.	3200.
1882	11,476,600	7.50	9.00	12.50	17.50	30.00	45.00	270.	2000.	2650.
1883	1,456,919	10.00	11.00	12.50	17.50	30.00	45.00	270.	2000.	2650.

LIBERTY HEAD NICKELS

Charles E. Barber executed the designs for the Liberty nickel introduced in 1883. His initial design offered only the large "V" inside the wreath as an indication of denomination. This was too much for those of deceitful intent, who, finding the coin so similar in size to the half eagle, gave them a reeded edge and gold plating so that they might be passed on the unsuspecting as $5 instead of 5¢. This fault was quickly corrected with the addition of the word "CENTS" below the wreath in place of "E PLURIBUS UNUM," which was incorporated above the wreath.

The Liberty nickel series also encompasses one of the most famous American coins, the clandestine 1913 nickel made famous in nationwide numismatic promotions conducted by B. Max Mehl, in which he offered to pay $50 for specimens of the issue. Mehl never owned one of the coins, but knowing that the only five produced rested in collections he could make the offer without fear of its being accepted. The originals were produced in secrecy at the instigation of Samuel Brown, a one time mint employee, and they later passed into the possession of the rich eccentric Col. E. H. R Green, the son of Hetty Green.

Untold thousands of 1903, 1910 and 1912 Liberty nickels have been industriously altered with varying degrees of skill through the years by those who would pass them as authentic issues. Mehl was undoubtedly on the receiving end of many such specimens. One which was authentic was owned for some twenty-five years by coin dealer J. V. McDermott of Milwaukee, Wis., who offered his $900 purchase for display at coin events throughout the country. Following his death, the coin was sold to another dealer, Aubrey E. Bebee of Omaha, for $46,000.

Without Cents Mintmark With Cents

Date	Mintage	G-4	VG-8	F-12	VF-20	XF-40	AU-50	MS-60	MS-65	Prf-65
1883 NC	5,479,519	2.00	3.00	3.75	6.50	9.00	19.00	60.00	950.	3025.
1883 WC	16,032,983	6.00	8.50	17.50	24.00	39.00	50.00	300.	1550.	2000.
1884	11,273,942	7.00	8.75	18.50	25.00	40.00	55.00	310.	1700.	2100.
1885	1,476,490	160.	180.	265.	340.	400.	500.	1200.	4000.	4000.
1886	3,330,290	35.00	45.00	80.00	105.	155.	225.	500.	2300.	2600.
1887	15,263,652	4.00	5.50	14.00	22.00	36.00	50.00	300.	1600.	2000.
1888	10,720,483	6.00	10.00	17.50	28.00	44.00	60.00	310.	1650.	2000.
1889	15,881,361	4.00	5.50	14.00	22.00	36.00	45.00	300.	1600.	2000.
1890	16,259,272	4.00	5.50	14.00	22.00	36.00	45.00	300.	1650.	2000.
1891	16,834,350	3.75	5.50	14.00	22.00	36.00	45.00	300.	1600.	2000.
1892	11,699,642	4.50	7.00	16.00	25.00	42.00	54.00	300.	1650.	2000.
1893	13,370,195	4.25	6.00	15.00	23.00	37.50	50.00	300.	1700.	2000.
1894	5,413,132	7.00	9.50	19.50	30.00	55.00	65.00	310.	1800.	2100.
1895	9,979,884	5.50	6.50	16.00	26.00	39.00	50.00	215.	1575.	2100.
1896	8,842,920	5.75	7.00	17.50	28.00	42.00	55.00	225.	1650.	2100.
1897	20,428,735	1.00	2.00	5.50	9.00	28.00	40.00	215.	1500.	2000.
1898	12,532,087	1.25	2.25	5.75	9.75	29.50	42.00	255.	1550.	1750.
1899	26,029,031	.85	1.75	4.00	7.50	25.00	35.00	215.	1450.	2000.
1900	27,255,995	.75	1.25	3.50	7.00	25.00	35.00	215.	1450.	2000.
1901	26,480,213	.75	1.25	3.50	7.00	25.00	35.00	215.	1450.	2000.
1902	31,480,579	.75	1.15	3.25	6.50	24.00	32.00	215.	1450.	2000.
1903	28,006,725	.75	1.25	3.50	6.75	25.00	35.00	215.	1450.	2000.
1904	21,404,984	.80	1.30	3.75	7.50	26.00	36.00	215.	1450.	2000.
1905	29,827,276	.75	1.15	3.25	6.50	24.00	32.00	215.	1450.	2000.
1906	38,613,725	.65	.90	3.00	6.00	23.00	30.00	215.	1450.	2000.
1907	39,214,800	.65	.90	3.00	6.00	23.00	30.00	215.	1450.	2000.
1908	22,686,177	.75	1.10	3.50	7.00	25.00	35.00	215.	1450.	2000.
1909	11,590,526	.85	1.20	3.75	8.25	26.00	36.00	215.	1450.	2000.
1910	30,169,353	.65	.90	3.00	6.00	23.00	30.00	215.	1450.	2000.
1911	39,559,372	.65	.90	3.00	6.00	23.00	30.00	215.	1450.	2000.
1912	26,236,714	.70	1.10	3.25	6.50	24.00	32.00	215.	1450.	2000.
1912D	8,474,000	.95	1.50	5.50	13.50	50.00	80.00	450.	2100.	2000.
1912S	238,000	29.00	40.00	50.00	100.	195	260.	700.	2800.	—
1913	only	5	known,	last	sold	in	private	sale	at	$200,000.

Authentic

Altered Date

The above enlargements of the date areas of authentic ıd altered date 1913 Liberty Head nickels illustrate the normal differences in the coıguration of the 3.

BUFFALO NICKELS

The Buffalo or Indian head nckel designed by James E. Fraser features the pfile of an Indian head on the obverse and a likenes of the American bison Black Diamond from the Nw York Zoological Gardens on the reverse. Throug the years many Indians have claimed to havebeen one of the three models Fraser stated he ıed in forming the obverse design, who were chie John Tree, Iron Tail and Two Moon.

One of only five overdates among the U.S. 20th century coins is included in this series. It also includes a "D" over "S" mint mark variety, and one of the most popular mint error coins, the three-legged buffalo of 1937 from the Denver Mint. This error was created when the die was over polished in the area of the buffalo's front right leg, making it disappear. This error is easily faked, but there are several distinguishing marks on authentic specimens, including an irregular row of raised dots arching to the ground below the belly of the buffalo.

Date	Mintage	G-4	VG-8	F-12	VF-20	XF-40	AU-50	MS-60	MS-65	Prf-65
1930	22,849,000	.30	.50	.75	1.50	3.50	9.50	43.00	265.	—
1930S	5,435,000	.50	.60	1.00	1.75	6.50	18.00	72.00	440.	—
1931S	1,200,000	3.00	3.25	3.75	5.25	12.50	28.00	72.00	380.	—
1934	20,213,003	.30	.40	.60	1.50	3.50	11.00	55.00	150.	—
1934D	7,480,000	.45	.55	.85	1.50	4.00	25.00	100.	250.	—
1935	58,264,000	.30	.35	.40	.75	1.50	8.00	28.00	90.00	—
1935D	12,092,000	.35	.45	.60	1.75	2.50	22.00	95.00	440.	—
1935S	10,300,000	.35	.40	.50	1.00	2.00	13.00	60.00	105.	—
1936	119,001,420	.30	.35	.40	.75	1.50	8.50	35.00	85.00	4500.
1936D	24,814,000	..30	.40	.50	1.00	2.00	10.00	35.00	80.00	—
1936S	14,930,000	.30	.40	.50	1.00	1.75	12.00	32.00	80.00	—
1937	79,485,769	.30	.35	.40	.75	1.50	8.75	30.00	75.00	4500.
1937D	17,826,000	.30	.40	.55	1.00	1.75	9.50	30.00	75.00	—
1937D 3LEG	Inc. Ab.	180.	210.	240.	320.	380.	500.	800.	3800.	—

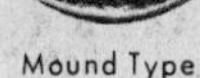

Mound Type

Line Type

Mintmark

Overdate — 18D/17

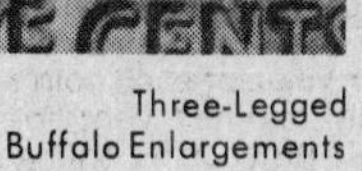

Three-Legged Buffalo Enlargements

Date	Mintage	G-4	VG-8	F-12	VF-20	XF-40	AU-50	MS-60	MS-65	Prf-65
1937S	5,635,000	.40	.45	.50	1.00	1.50	10.00	30.00	80.00	—
1938D	7,020,000	.40	.45	.55	1.00	1.50	7.50	27.50	75.00	—
1938D/S	Inc. Ab.	—	—	6.00	7.50	10.00	15.00	35.00	100.	—

MOUND TYPE

Date	Mintage	G-4	VG-8	F-12	VF-20	XF-40	AU-50	MS-60	MS-65	Prf-65
1913	30,993,520	2.50	3.00	4.00	6.75	11.00	20.00	65.00	500.	4950.
1913D	5,337,000	5.00	6.00	8.50	11.00	20.00	38.00	95.00	650.	—
1913S	2,105,000	8.00	9.50	13.00	21.00	38.00	60.00	160.	800.	—

LINE-TYPE

Date	Mintage	G-4	VG-8	F-12	VF-20	XF-40	AU-50	MS-60	MS-65	Prf-65
1913	29,858,700	3.00	3.50	4.50	6.50	12.00	17.00	53.00	260.	5000.
1913D	4,156,000	40.00	45.00	50.00	65.00	90.00	110.	190.	725.	—
1913S	1,209,000	60.00	65.00	80.00	95.00	115.	165.	315.	975.	—
1914	20,665,738	4.00	5.00	6.50	7.50	12.00	23.00	65.00	325.	4400.
1914D	3,912,000	25.00	30.00	42.00	55.00	95.00	145.	280.	1050.	—
1914S	3,470,000	4.00	5.00	12.00	15.00	35.00	45.00	140.	625.	—
1915	20,987,270	1.75	2.50	4.00	5.50	10.00	20.00	58.00	300.	4400.
1915D	7,569,500	6.00	6.50	12.00	30.00	50.00	70.00	175.	725.	—
1915S	1,505,000	9.50	12.00	20.00	46.00	80.00	115.	295.	1150.	—
1916	63,498,066	.60	.85	1.25	2.50	6.00	13.50	50.00	220.	4400.
1916/16	Inc. Ab.	—	100.	210.	280.	490.	700.	1125.	3350.	
1916D	13,333,000	4.25	5.50	9.00	18.00	40.00	65.00	180.	850.	—
1916S	11,860,000	3.00	4.00	6.50	15.00	40.00	65.00	180.	800.	—
1917	51,424,029	.75	1.00	1.50	3.00	10.00	20.00	55.00	265.	—
1917D	9,910,800	4.50	5.50	10.00	40.00	80.00	100.	280.	1100.	—
1917S	4,193,000	4.50	5.25	9.00	35.00	60.00	105.	310.	1300.	—
1918	32,086,314	.65	1.25	2.50	5.00	14.00	36.00	100.	500.	—
1918D/17	8,362,314	440.	510.	800.	1300.	2650.	5300	13,000	35,000.	—
1918D	Inc. Ab.	5.00	7.00	11.00	60.00	80.00	150.	400.	3400.	—
1918S	4,882,000	3.50	5.00	9.00	35.00	75.00	120.	325.	2000.	—
1919	60,868,000	.60	.75	1.00	3.00	7.50	15.00	48.00	250.	—
1919D	8,006,000	5.00	6.50	15.00	70.00	100.	175.	330.	3600.	—
1919S	7,521,000	3.00	5.00	10.00	45.00	75.00	125.	360.	2950.	—
1920	63,093,000	.50	.70	1.00	3.00	7.50	18.00	50.00	290.	—
1920D	9,418,000	3.00	4.75	9.00	50.00	95.00	165.	450.	3700.	—
1920S	9,689,000	2.00	3.00	7.00	25.00	80.00	115.	350.	4500.	—
1921	10,663,000	.80	1.00	2.50	6.00	16.00	40.00	100.	440.	—
1921S	1,557,000	12.00	16.00	30.00	75.00	195.	325.	630.	3000.	—
1923	35,715,000	.50	.75	1.00	3.00	7.50	18.00	50.00	265.	—
1923S	6,142,000	1.25	2.50	5.00	22.00	55.00	85.00	225.	3500.	—
1924	21,620,000	.35	.55	.65	3.00	9.00	20.00	65.00	330.	—
1924D	5,258,000	2.50	3.50	7.50	40.00	75.00	120.	325.	2300.	—
1924S	1,437,000	4.50	6.25	15.00	85.00	190.	360.	750.	1900.	—
1925	35,565,100	.40	.60	1.00	2.25	15.00	45.00	250.	100.	—
1925D	4,450,000	3.50	6.00	12.00	50.00	82.00	165.	415.	2600.	—
1925S	6,256,000	2.25	4.00	7.00	22.00	45.00	105.	330.	3000.	—
1926	44,693,000	.30	.40	.75	2.00	5.00	12.00	45.00	200.	—
1926D	5,638,000	2.00	4.00	8.50	35.00	45.00	90.00	120.	215.	—
1926S	970,000	5.25	8.00	13.00	55.00	180.	300.	695.	4300.	—
1927	37,981,000	.30	.40	.75	1.50	5.00	12.00	40.00	200.	—
1927D	5,730,000	1.00	1.25	2.75	10.00	38.00	58.00	130.	680.	—
1927S	3,430,000	.90	1.25	2.30	12.00	55.00	85.00	250.	1100.	—
1928	23,411,000	.30	.40	.75	2.00	3.75	13.00	42.00	215.	—
1928D	6,436,000	.75	.90	2.00	4.00	11.00	25.00	60.00	275.	—
1928S	6,936,000	.50	.70	1.25	2.50	10.00	30.00	110.	580.	—
1929	36,446,000	.30	.40	.75	1.50	3.50	8.50	40.00	190.	—
1929D	8,370,000	.75	.85	1.35	3.50	9.50	22.00	70.00	525.	—
1929S	7,754,000	.40	.50	.75	1.50	8.00	18.00	57.00	315.	—

JEFFERSON NICKELS

The design of this issue resulted from a public competition in which Felix Schlag bested some 390 artists for a $1,000 cash award. Although Schlag's obverse design was largely retained in the production design, a completely new reverse was prepared by the Mint's engraving staff. The design went unsigned for nearly 30 years, until a small "FS" was added below the bust in 1966, in tribute to the last private artist to conceive a regular issue U.S. coin design. The Bicentennial coin designs were the work of private artists, but they were special one year commemoratives.

During the war years, the nickel composition for the nickel was abandoned in favor of a copper-silver-manganese alloy containing 35 percent silver. By the early 60's the bullion value of these coins exceeded their face value. To distinguish these issues from the nickel version large mint marks were placed above the dome of Monticello on the reverse, including a "P" for Philadelphia, the only time the U. S. mother mint has placed a mint mark on her domestic issues. Mint engravers prepared new master dies, sharpening the features on this coin for the 1971 edition.

Mintmarks

Reverse 1938-42, 46-64

Obverse Since 1968

Date	Mintage	G-4	VG-8	F-12	VF-20	XF-40	MS-60	Prf-65
1938	19,515,365	—	.20	.25	.30	.50	1.00	75.00
1938D	5,376,000	1.10	1.25	1.50	1.75	2.35	7.00	—
1938S	4,105,000	2.15	2.25	2.50	2.75	3.25	6.50	—
1939	120,627,535	—	—	—	.20	.35	1.75	40.00
Doubled Monticello			7.50	10.00	25.00	50.00	200.	—
1939D	3,514,000	4.00	4.25	4.50	4.75	8.00	60.00	—
1939S	6,630,000	.50	.65	.75	1.00	2.00	50.00	—
1940	176,499,158	—	—	—	.15	.25	1.10	40.00
1940D	43,540,000	—	—	—	.20	.30	1.50	—
1940S	39,690,000	—	—	—	.25	.50	1.50	—
1941	203,283,720	—	—	—	—	.20	1.00	40.00
1941D	53,432,000	—	—	.15	.20	.35	2.00	—
1941S	43,445,000	—	—	—	.20	.35	2.50	—
1942	49,818,600	—	—	—	.20	.35	1.65	40.00
1942D	13,938,000	.20	.25	.30	.40	2.00	20.00	—

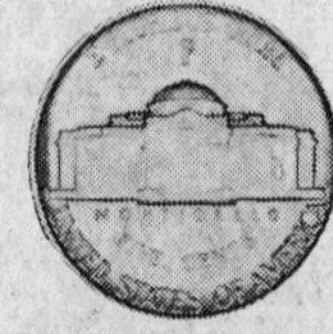

SILVER WARTIME NICKELS

NOTE: A $ .75 Numismatic value base has been assigned to wartime nickels, based on the $13.00 market price for one ounce of silver at the time these valuations were assigned. The bullion value of each coin's silver content increases or decreases approximately one-half cent for each 10-cent change in the bullion price, or 5.63-cents for each $1 change.

Date	Mintage	G-4	VG-8	F-12	VF-20	XF-40	MS-60	Prf-65
1942P	57,900,600	—	—	—	.75	3.00	16.00	470.
1942S	32,900,000	—	—	—	.75	1.50	11.00	—
1943P	271,165,000	—	—	—	.75	—	3.50	—
1943P 3/2	Inc. Ab.	70.00	75.00	85.00	125.	325.	650.	—
1943D	15,294,000	—	—	—	.75	1.50	6.00	—
1943S	104,060,000	—	—	—	.75	1.50	8.00	—
1944P	119,150,000	—	—	—	.75	1.50	5.50	—
1944D	32,309,000	—	—	—	.75	1.50	6.00	—
1944S	21,640,000	—	—	—	.75	1.50	6.00	—
1945P	119,408,100	—	—	—	.75	1.50	5.50	—
1945D	37,158,000	—	—	—	.75	1.50	4.00	—
1945S	58,939,000	—	—	—	.75	1.50	3.50	—

PRE-WAR COMPOSITION

Date	Mintage	G-4	VG-8	F-12	VF-20	XF-40	MS-60	Prf-65
1946	161,116,000	—	—	—	—	.15	1.00	—
1946D	45,292,200	—	—	—	—	.20	1.10	—
1946S	13,560,000	—	—	—	—	.40	1.00	—
1947	95,000,000	—	—	—	—	.15	.85	—
1947D	37,822,000	—	—	—	—	.30	1.35	—
1947S	24,720,000	—	—	—	.25	.40	1.00	—
1948	89,348,000	—	—	—	—	.15	1.00	—
1948D	44,734,000	—	—	—	—	.30	1.10	—
1948S	11,300,000	—	—	.20	.30	.50	1.35	—
1949	60,652,000	—	—	—	—	.15	1.00	—
1949D	36,498,000	—	—	—	.25	.30	1.00	—
1949D D/S	Inc. Ab.	—	—	20.00	30.00	65.00	280.	—
1949S	9,716,000	—	.25	.30	.40	.75	2.25	—
1950	9,847,386	—	.30	.40	.50	.90	2.25	35.00
1950D	2,630,030	—	7.50	7.75	8.00	8.25	12.00	—
1951	28,609,500	—	—	—	—	.35	1.25	18.00
1951D	20,460,000	—	—	—	—	.30	1.30	—
1951S	7,776,000	—	.35	.40	.50	.90	5.25	—
1952	64,069,980	—	—	—	—	.15	1.00	12.50
1952D	30,638,000	—	—	—	—	.65	2.00	—
1952S	20,572,000	—	—	—	—	.20	.60	—
1953	46,772,800	—	—	—	—	—	.30	8.50
1953D	59,878,600	—	—	—	—	—	.35	—
1953S	19,210,900	—	—	—	—	.20	.50	—
1954	47,917,350	—	—	—	—	—	.35	5.50
1954D	117,136,560	—	—	—	—	—	.35	—
1954S	29,384,000	—	—	—	—	—	.40	—
1954S S/D	Inc. Ab.	—	—	5.00	6.50	11.50	25.00	—
1955	8,266,200	—	.35	.40	.50	.60	1.00	3.25
1955D	74,464,100	—	—	—	—	—	.25	—
1956	35,885,384	—	—	—	—	—	.25	1.65
1956D	67,222,940	—	—	—	—	—	.20	—
1957	39,655,952	—	—	—	—	—	.25	1.25
1957D	136,828,900	—	—	—	—	—	.20	—
1958	17,963,652	—	—	—	.20	.25	.35	1.35
1958D	168,249,120	—	—	—	—	—	.20	—

Date	Mintage	MS-60	Proof	Date	Mintage	MS-60	Proof
1959	28,397,291	.25	1.10	1962	100,602,019	.15	.60
1959D	160,738,240	.15	—	1962D	280,195,720	.15	—
1960	57,107,602	.15	.85	1963	178,851,645	.15	.60
1960D	192,582,180	.15	—	1963D	276,829,460	.15	—
1961	76,668,244	.15	.60	1964	1,028,622,762	.15	.60
1961D	229,342,760	.15	—	1964D	1,787,297,160	.15	—

Commencing 1965 - See Modern Singles - Page 1897

DIMES

During the early years of U.S. coinage, the concentration on dime production was minimal, with only slightly more than a million pieces ($102,279.60) being struck up to 1820, as coins were issued in only 13 of 25 possible years. By the time the Liberty cap design was abandoned in 1837 the total had grown to only about 12.8 million pieces.

Draped Bust Dimes

Date	Mintage	G-4	VG-8	F-12	VF-20	XF-40	MS-60
1796	22,135	1150.	1400.	1950.	3150.	5200.	11,000
1797 13 Stars	25,261	1150.	1400.	1950.	3150.	5200.	10,500.
1797 16 Stars	Inc. Ab.	1150.	1400.	1950.	3150.	5200.	10,500.

HERALDIC EAGLE INTRODUCED

Date	Mintage	G-4	VG-8	F-12	VF-20	XF-40	MS-60
1798	27,550	500.	600.	975.	1375.	2200.	7000.
1798/97 13 Stars	Inc. Ab.	—	—	Rare	—	—	—
1798/97 16 Stars	Inc. Ab.	500.	600.	975.	1375.	2200.	6750
1798 Small 8	Inc. Ab.	—	—	Rare	—	—	—
1800	21,760	500.	600.	950.	1325.	2100.	6500.
1801	34,640	500.	600.	950.	1325.	2100.	6500
1802	10,975	500.	600.	1050.	1450.	2200.	7000.
1803	33,040	500.	600.	950.	1325.	2100.	7000
1804 13 Stars	8,265	850.	1050.	1650.	3000.	4000.	—
1804 14 Stars	Inc. Ab.	850.	1050.	1650.	3000.	4000.	—
1805 4 Berries	120,780	500.	600.	950.	1325.	2100.	6500.
1805 5 Berries	Inc. Ab.	500.	600.	950.	1325.	2100.	6500.
1807	165,000	500.	600.	950.	1325.	2100.	6500.

Liberty Cap Dimes

Date	Mintage	G-4	VG-8	F-12	VF-20	XF-40	MS-60
1809	51,065	47.50	67.50	90.00	160.	250.	4200.
1811/9	65,180	37.50	45.00	65.00	100.	225.	4000.
1814 Sm. Dt.	421,500	18.00	27.50	35.00	65.00	200.	2500.
1814 Lg. Dt.	Inc. Ab.	16.50	24.00	30.00	65.00	200.	2500.
1820 Lg. O	942,587	16.00	20.00	25.00	65.00	200.	2450.
1820 Sm. O	Inc. Ab.	16.00	20.00	25.00	65.00	200.	2500.
1821 Lg. Dt.	1,186,512	16.00	20.00	25.00	65.00	200.	2500.
1821 Sm. Dt.	Inc. Ab.	16.00	20.00	25.00	65.00	200.	2500.
1822	100,000	60.00	80.00	135.	225.	350.	4000.
1823/22 Lg.E'S	440,000	18.00	24.00	30.00	65.00	200.	2500.
1823/22 Sm.E'S	Inc. Ab.	18.00	24.00	30.00	65.00	200.	2500.
1824/22	Undetermined	19.50	27.50	35.00	65.00	210.	2500.
1825	510,000	16.00	20.00	25.00	60.00	200.	2450.
1827	1,215,000	16.00	20.00	25.00	60.00	200.	2450.
1828 Lg.Dt.	125,000	25.00	35.00	55.00	85.00	200.	3000.

COIN SIZE REDUCED SLIGHTLY

Date	Mintage	G-4	VG-8	F-12	VF-20	XF-40	MS-60
1828 Sm.Dt.	Inc. Ab.	18.00	25.00	30.00	65.00	175.	2250.
1829 Lg. 10C.	770,000	16.00	20.00	25.00	45.00	150.	2100.
1829 Med. 10C.	Inc. Ab.	12.50	15.00	18.00	42.00	140.	1900.
1829 Sm. 10C.	Inc. Ab.	12.50	15.00	18.00	42.00	140.	1900.
1830 Lg. 10C.	510,000	12.50	15.00	18.00	42.00	140.	2000.
1830 Sm. 10C.	Inc. Ab.	12.50	15.00	18.00	42.00	140.	2000.
1830/29	Inc. Ab.	—	75.00	125.	200.	300.	2500.
1831	771,350	12.50	15.00	18.00	42.00	140.	1900.
1832	522,500	12.50	15.00	18.00	42.00	140.	2150.

Date	Mintage	G-4	VG-8	F-12	VF-20	XF-40	MS-60
1833	485,000	12.50	15.00	18.00	42.00	140.	2100.
1833 High 3	Inc. Ab.	12.50	15.00	18.00	42.00	140.	2100.
1834 Lg. 4	635,000	12.50	15.00	18.00	42.00	140.	2000.
1834 Sm. 4	Inc. Ab.	12.50	15.00	18.00	42.00	140.	2000.
1835	1,410,000	12.50	15.00	18.00	42.00	140.	1825.
1836	1,190,000	12.50	15.00	18.00	42.00	140.	1825.
1837	1,042,000	12.50	15.00	18.00	42.00	140.	1825.

Date	Mintage	G-4	VG-8	F-12	VF-20	XF-40	MS-60
1849	839,000	8.00	10.00	25.00	45.00	70.00	725.
1849/8	Inc. Ab.	50.00	75.00	250.	400.	600.	—
1849O	300,000	15.00	20.00	35.00	150.	350.	—
1850	1,931,500	8.00	10.00	15.00	25.00	60.00	695.
1850O	510,000	12.00	16.00	30.00	75.00	125.	1000.
1851	1,026,500	8.00	10.00	15.00	30.00	65.00	695.
1851O	400,000	12.00	16.00	30.00	75.00	150.	1200.
1852	1,535,500	8.00	10.00	15.00	30.00	65.00	695.
1852O	430,000	15.00	20.00	40.00	85.00	175.	1500.
1853	95,000	30.00	40.00	55.00	100.	225.	1000.

LIBERTY SEATED DIMES

Introduction of the Liberty seated dime series, and half dimes, quarters and halves as well, followed on the heels of the enactment of a January 18, 1837, law which reduced its weight to 41.25 grains from 41.6, in conformity with a 3.5 grain weight reduction for the silver dollar standard. This change in the law also provided for the fineness of silver coins to be increased from .8924 to .900.

An act of February 21, 1853, reduced the weight of all fractional silver coins by nearly seven percent, to 38.4 grains for the dime, so that they could be maintained in circulation in the face of the growing disparity between the relative values of silver and gold brought on by the California gold discoveries. Arrows were placed either side of the date on most 1853, and all 1854 and 1855 issues to note this change. A similar step was taken twenty years later when the weight of the dime, and the quarter and half proportionately, was increased slightly to 38.58 grains.

MINTMARK ABOVE AND BELOW WREATH TIE

WITHOUT STARS AROUND RIM

Date	Mintage	G-4	VG-8	F-12	VF-20	XF-40	MS-60
1837 Sm.Date	Inc. Ab.	40.00	60.00	85.00	165.	350.	2500.
1837 Lg.Date	Inc. Ab.	40.00	60.00	85.00	165.	350.	2500.
1838O	406,034	45.00	80.00	125.	250.	550.	3500.

STARS ADDED AROUND RIM

Date	Mintage	G-4	VG-8	F-12	VF-20	XF-40	MS-60
1838 Sm.Stars	1,992,500	20.00	30.00	40.00	80.00	200.	1500.
1838 Lg.Stars	Inc. Ab.	10.00	15.00	20.00	40.00	75.00	880.
1838 Partial Drapery	Inc. Ab.	40.00	65.00	85.00	110.	275.	1200.
1839	1,053,115	10.00	15.00	20.00	40.00	70.00	880.
1839O	1,323,000	15.00	20.00	25.00	60.00	100.	950.
1839O Rev. 1838O		120.	300.	450.	600.	1500.	—
1840	1,358,580	10.00	15.00	20.00	40.00	70.00	880.
1840O	1,175,000	15.00	30.00	45.00	65.00	100.	1500.

DRAPERY ADDED TO LIBERTY

Date	Mintage	G-4	VG-8	F-12	VF-20	XF-40	MS-60
1840	Inc. Ab.	25.00	40.00	65.00	75.00	400.	—
1841	1,622,500	8.00	10.00	15.00	35.00	60.00	695.
1841O	2,007,500	15.00	20.00	30.00	50.00	80.00	1500.
1842	1,887,500	8.00	10.00	15.00	35.00	60.00	695.
1842O	2,020,000	15.00	20.00	30.00	50.00	80.00	—
1843	1,370,000	8.00	10.00	15.00	35.00	60.00	695.
1843O	150,000	50.00	65.00	125.	250.	800.	—
1844	72,500	25.00	40.00	70.00	150.	300.	2000.
1845	1,755,000	8.00	10.00	15.00	35.00	60.00	695.
1845O	230,000	15.00	30.00	75.00	150.	800.	—
1846	31,300	75.00	85.00	140.	250.	550.	—
1847	245,000	15.00	25.00	50.00	75.00	200.	1200.
1848	451,500	10.00	12.00	25.00	50.00	80.00	750.

ARROWS AT DATE

ARROWS AT DATE

Date	Mintage	G-4	VG-8	F-12	VF-20	XF-40	MS-60	Prf-65
1853	12,078,010	6.00	9.00	12.00	20.00	65.00	930.	9500.
1853O	1,100,000	8.00	15.00	25.00	40.00	150.	1000.	—
1854	4,470,000	6.00	10.00	15.00	25.00	65.00	1000.	11,000.
1854O	1,770,000	6.00	12.00	20.00	35.00	115.	1000.	—
1855	2,075,000	6.00	9.00	15.00	22.00	65.00	2500.	7000.

ARROWS AT DATE REMOVED

Date	Mintage	G-4	VG-8	F-12	VF-20	XF-40	MS-60	Prf-65
1856 Small Date	5,780,000	6.00	9.00	12.00	20.00	55.00	695.	6500.
1856 Large Date	Inc. Ab.	10.00	15.00	20.00	50.00	85.00	750.	—
1856O	1,180,000	7.00	11.00	14.00	23.00	65.00	750.	—
1856S	70,000	35.00	45.00	75.00	175.	300.	—	—
1857	5,580,000	6.00	9.00	12.00	22.00	55.00	695.	6500.
1857O	1,540,000	7.00	11.00	14.00	23.00	60.00	750.	—
1858	1,540,000	6.00	9.00	12.00	22.00	55.00	695.	6750.
1858O	290,000	20.00	30.00	50.00	80.00	150.	900.	—
1858S	60,000	35.00	50.00	80.00	200.	350.	—	—
1859	430,000	6.00	9.00	12.00	30.00	65.00	800.	6000.
1859O	480,000	6.00	10.00	15.00	45.00	85.00	800.	—
1859S	60,000	35.00	55.00	85.00	195.	375.	—	—
1860S	140,000	15.00	22.00	45.00	65.00	185.	—	—

TRANSITIONAL PATTERN

Date	Mintage	G-4	VG-8	F-12	VF-20	XF-40	MS-60	Prf-65
1859 Obverse Of 1859, Reverse Of 1860					—	—	—	10,000.

Mintmark

LEGEND REPLACES STARS ON OBVERSE

Date	Mintage	G-4	VG-8	F-12	VF-20	XF-40	MS-60	Prf-65
1860	607,000	6.00	12.00	18.00	30.00	55.00	525.	4000.
1860O	40,000	400.	500.	700.	1100.	2200.	—	—
1861	1,884,000	6.00	10.00	15.00	25.00	50.00	500.	4000.
1861S	172,500	20.00	25.00	45.00	80.00	175.	—	—
1862	847,550	5.00	10.00	15.00	25.00	50.00	500.	4000.
1862S	180,750	20.00	25.00	40.00	75.00	150.	—	—
1863	14,460	100.	140.	185.	225.	325.	950.	4000.
1863S	157,500	20.00	35.00	45.00	75.00	175.	1200.	—
1864	11,470	90.00	130.	175.	200.	300.	800.	4000.
1864S	230,000	15.00	20.00	30.00	50.00	140.	1100.	—
1865	10,500	115.	150.	200.	275.	350.	950.	4000.
1865S	175,000	15.00	25.00	30.00	60.00	140.	—	—
1866	8,725	125.	175.	225.	325.	400.	950.	4000.
1866S	135,000	15.00	25.00	30.00	55.00	150.	1200.	—
1867	6,625	175.	225.	300.	375.	450.	1000.	4000.
1867S	140,000	15.00	25.00	30.00	55.00	150.	1200.	—
1868	464,600	6.00	10.00	25.00	50.00	125.	600.	4000.
1868S	260,000	10.00	15.00	25.00	90.00	185.	1000.	—
1869	256,600	6.00	10.00	25.00	75.00	140.	725.	4000.
1869S	450,000	8.00	12.00	18.00	50.00	95.00	825.	—
1870	471,500	6.00	10.00	18.00	50.00	100.	450.	4000.
1870S	50,000	60.00	75.00	140.	200.	350.	3200.	—
1871	907,710	6.00	9.00	12.00	20.00	55.00	430.	4000.
1871CC	20,100	300.	400.	750.	950.	2000.	—	—
1871S	320,000	15.00	25.00	40.00	75.00	140.	1000.	—
1872	2,396,450	6.00	9.00	12.00	20.00	50.00	430.	4000.
1872CC	35,480	200.	300.	450.	600.	1200.	—	—
1872S	190,000	25.00	40.00	80.00	125.	200.	1100.	—
1873 Closed 3	1,568,600	15.00	25.00	35.00	60.00	85.00	430.	4500.
1873 Open 3	Inc. Ab.	25.00	45.00	65.00	100.	150.	—	—
1873CC	12,400	—	—	—	Only One Known		—	—

ARROWS AT DATE

Date	Mintage	G-4	VG-8	F-12	VF-20	XF-40	MS-60	Prf-65
1873	2,378,500	11.00	18.00	27.50	45.00	115.	1250.	5650.
1873CC	18,791	300.	425.	600.	800.	1500.	13,000.	—
1873S	455,000	16.00	20.00	32.00	60.00	125.	1500.	—
1874	2,940,700	11.00	18.00	27.50	45.00	115.	1250.	5650.
1874CC	10,817	650.	1200.	1800.	2200.	3000.	—	—
1874S	240,000	22.00	35.00	70.00	100.	175.	1500.	—

ARROWS AT DATE REMOVED

Date	Mintage	G-4	VG-8	F-12	VF-20	XF-40	MS-60	Prf-65
1875	10,350,700	6.00	9.00	12.00	20.00	50.00	430.	4000.
1875CC Mintmark In Wreath	4,645,000	10.00	15.00	20.00	45.00	75.00	430.	—
1875CC Mintmark Under Wreath	Inc. Ab.	12.00	18.00	30.00	50.00	85.00	430.	—
1875S Mintmark In Wreath	9,070,000	10.00	20.00	65.00	100.	150.	430.	—
1875S Mintmark Under Wreath	Inc. Ab.	6.00	9.00	12.00	25.00	60.00	430.	—
1876	11,461,150	6.00	9.00	12.00	25.00	60.00	430.	4000.
1876CC	8,270,000	6.00	9.00	12.00	28.00	60.00	430.	—
1876S	10,420,000	6.00	9.00	12.00	25.00	60.00	430.	—
1877	7,310,510	6.00	9.00	12.00	20.00	50.00	430.	4000.
1877CC	7,700,000	6.00	9.00	12.00	20.00	50.00	430.	—
1877S	2,340,000	6.00	9.00	12.00	25.00	55.00	430.	—
1878	1,678,800	6.00	9.00	12.00	20.00	55.00	430.	4000.
1878CC	200,000	20.00	25.00	40.00	65.00	150.	900.	—
1879	15,100	45.00	55.00	70.00	145.	225.	500.	4000.
1880	37,335	35.00	45.00	50.00	100.	150.	450.	4000.
1881	24,975	40.00	50.00	60.00	125.	200.	475.	4000.
1882	3,911,100	6.00	9.00	12.00	20.00	50.00	430.	4000.
1883	7,675,712	6.00	9.00	12.00	20.00	50.00	430.	4000.
1884	3,366,380	6.00	9.00	12.00	20.00	50.00	430.	4000.
1884S	564,969	10.00	15.00	20.00	35.00	95.00	450.	—
1885	2,533,427	6.00	9.00	12.00	20.00	55.00	430.	4000.
1885S	43,690	120.	150.	220.	325.	500.	3000.	—
1886	6,377,570	6.00	9.00	12.00	20.00	50.00	430.	4000.
1886S	206,524	15.00	20.00	30.00	45.00	90.00	500.	—
1887	11,283,939	6.00	9.00	12.00	20.00	50.00	430.	4000.
1887S	4,454,450	6.00	9.00	12.00	20.00	50.00	430.	—
1888	5,496,487	6.00	9.00	12.00	20.00	50.00	430.	4000.
1888S	1,720,000	6.00	9.00	12.00	20.00	55.00	430.	—
1889	7,380,711	6.00	9.00	12.00	20.00	50.00	430.	4000.
1889S	972,678	10.00	15.00	20.00	25.00	65.00	475.	—
1890	9,911,541	6.00	9.00	12.00	20.00	50.00	430.	4000.
1890S	1,423,076	8.00	15.00	20.00	40.00	70.00	475.	—
1891	15,310,600	6.00	9.00	12.00	20.00	50.00	430.	4000.
1891O	4,540,000	6.00	9.00	12.00	20.00	50.00	475.	—
1891S	3,196,116	6.00	9.00	12.00	25.00	55.00	500.	—

BARBER DIMES

After a run of more than half a century, the nation's Liberty seated silver coin designs were supplanted by the classical Liberty head designs prepared by Charles E. Barber in 1892. His signature, "B", appears at the truncation of the neck. The change was instituted, in large part, due to mounting public criticisms of the old designs.

Mintmark

NOTE: A $1.90 Numismatic value base has been assigned to Barber dimes, based on the $13.00 market price for one ounce of silver at the time these valuations were assigned. The bullion value of each coin's silver content increases or decreases approximately three-quarters cent for each 10-cent change in the bullion price, or 7.23-cents for each $1 change.

Date	Mintage	G-4	VG-8	F-12	VF-20	XF-40	AU-50	MS-60	MS-65	Prf-65
1892	12,121,245	3.50	4.00	7.00	13.00	29.00	55.00	315.	2200.	3800.
1892O	3,841,700	4.50	9.00	13.50	20.00	35.00	65.00	410.	2500.	—
1892S	990,710	30.00	46.00	60.00	87.00	115.	175.	440.	3400.	—
1893	3,340,792	4.75	10.00	16.00	24.00	43.00	85.00	410.	2400.	3800.
1893O	1,760,000	14.00	22.00	30.00	45.00	75.00	110.	535.	4400.	—
1893S	2,491,401	6.00	10.00	19.00	30.00	50.00	90.00	410.	2400.	—
1894	1,330,972	6.00	12.00	23.00	36.00	64.00	100.	440.	3150.	3800.
1894O	720,000	25.00	48.00	80.00	110.	220.	535.	3150	20,000.	—
1894S	24	—	Proof Only		—	—	—	—	—	—
1895	690,880	50.00	80.00	95.00	140.	200.	275.	1075.	6300.	4500.
1895O	440,000	125.	150.	175.	250.	360.	515.	2600	11,000.	—
1895S	1,120,000	14.00	23.00	36.00	57.00	88.00	100.	535.	3400.	—
1896	2,000,762	7.50	12.50	21.00	36.00	61.00	88.00	410.	2400.	3800.
1896O	610,000	38.00	60.00	90.00	125.	180.	250.	1275.	7600.	—
1896S	575,056	35.00	55.00	85.00	120.	175.	240.	760.	4250.	—
1897	10,869,264	2.00	3.50	6.50	12.50	32.00	45.00	315.	2200.	3800.
1897O	666,000	33.00	52.00	80.00	115.	170.	235.	1900.	8200.	—
1897S	1,342,844	7.50	13.00	21.00	46.00	70.00	105.	535.	3150.	—
1898	16,320,735	2.00	2.75	5.50	11.50	30.00	42.00	315.	2200.	3800.
1898O	2,130,000	4.50	8.00	17.50	32.00	68.00	92.00	575.	5400.	—
1898S	1,702,507	4.00	7.50	12.00	20.00	39.00	60.00	410.	3150.	—
1899	19,580,846	2.00	2.75	5.50	11.50	30.00	42.00	315.	2200.	3800.
1899O	2,650,000	4.25	8.50	16.00	30.00	57.00	85.00	410.	5400.	—
1899S	1,867,493	4.00	7.50	13.00	21.00	42.00	62.00	410.	3000.	—
1900	17,600,912	1.95	2.75	5.50	11.50	28.00	42.00	315.	2200.	3800.
1900O	2,010,000	5.50	9.00	17.50	33.00	64.00	90.00	660.	6600.	—
1900S	5,168,270	2.10	3.50	6.50	12.00	28.00	50.00	410.	3000.	—
1901	18,860,478	2.00	3.00	5.00	11.00	27.50	41.00	315.	2200.	3800.
1901O	5,620,000	2.00	3.00	6.00	17.00	38.00	80.00	660.	6000.	—
1901S	593,022	37.00	60.00	90.00	135.	200.	350.	1850	10,000.	—
1902	21,380,777	1.90	2.25	4.75	11.00	17.50	41.00	315.	2200.	3800.
1902O	4,500,000	2.75	4.00	7.00	16.00	33.00	60.00	500.	5200.	—
1902S	2,070,000	3.50	8.00	14.00	26.00	50.00	100.	600.	4850.	—
1903	19,500,755	1.90	2.75	5.00	11.00	28.00	42.00	315.	2200.	3800.
1903O	8,180,000	1.95	3.00	6.00	15.00	35.00	60.00	500.	4500.	—
1903S	613,300	27.50	45.00	60.00	100.	175.	250.	1500.	9750.	—
1904	14,601,027	2.00	2.75	5.50	11.50	30.00	45.00	315.	2200.	3800.
1904S	800,000	22.50	35.00	50.00	75.00	150.	210.	1500.	9100.	—
1905	14,552,350	1.95	2.50	5.00	11.00	28.00	42.00	315.	2200.	3800.
1905O	3,400,000	2.00	5.00	12.00	22.50	44.00	67.00	475.	3300.	—
1905S	6,855,199	2.10	3.00	6.50	14.00	32.00	60.00	475.	3300.	—
1906	19,958,406	1.90	2.00	3.00	10.00	27.00	40.00	315.	2200.	3800.
1906D	4,060,000	2.25	3.75	7.50	15.00	33.00	65.00	380.	2400.	—
1906O	2,610,000	2.75	5.50	13.00	25.00	39.00	70.00	475.	3300.	—
1906S	3,136,640	2.25	3.75	8.00	16.00	35.00	67.00	475.	3300.	—
1907	22,220,575	1.90	2.00	3.00	10.00	27.00	40.00	315.	2200.	3800.
1907D	4,080,000	2.25	3.75	7.50	15.00	33.00	65.00	500.	3400.	—
1907O	5,058,000	2.10	3.00	7.00	14.00	31.00	60.00	380.	2200.	—
1907S	3,178,470	2.00	4.00	8.00	16.00	35.00	67.00	500.	3150.	—
1908	10,600,545	1.90	2.00	4.00	10.50	28.00	41.00	315.	2200.	3800.
1908D	7,490,000	1.90	2.00	4.00	10.50	28.00	43.00	315.	2200.	—
1908O	1,789,000	3.50	6.50	13.00	22.00	37.00	70.00	475.	3150.	—
1908S	3,220,000	2.00	3.00	7.50	16.00	34.00	65.00	475.	2850.	—
1909	10,240,650	1.90	2.00	4.00	11.00	29.00	44.00	315.	2200.	3800.
1909D	954,000	3.50	6.50	15.00	30.00	55.00	90.00	500.	3150.	—
1909O	2,287,000	2.00	2.75	7.50	17.50	35.00	65.00	325.	2400.	—
1909S	1,000,000	4.50	9.00	19.00	36.00	60.00	110.	500.	3400.	—
1910	11,520,551	1.90	2.00	2.75	10.00	28.00	42.00	315.	2200.	3800.
1910D	3,490,000	2.00	2.75	5.50	12.00	31.00	65.00	500.	4100.	—
1910S	1,240,000	3.00	4.75	8.50	17.50	36.00	61.00	475.	2850.	—
1911	18,870,543	1.90	2.00	2.75	8.50	27.00	41.00	315.	2200.	3800.
1911D	11,209,000	1.90	2.00	2.75	9.00	28.00	42.00	315.	2200.	—
1911S	3,520,000	2.00	2.75	4.50	14.00	35.00	62.00	430.	2400.	—
1912	19,350,700	1.90	2.00	2.75	8.50	27.00	41.00	315.	2200.	3800.
1912D	11,760,000	1.90	2.00	2.75	8.50	27.00	41.00	315.	2300.	÷
1912S	3,420,000	1.90	2.00	3.75	13.00	33.00	55.00	430.	2400.	—
1913	19,760,622	1.90	2.00	2.75	8.50	27.00	41.00	315.	2200.	3800.
1913S	510,000	7.50	14.00	30.00	60.00	135.	225.	630.	3400.	—
1914	17,360,655	1.90	2.00	2.75	8.50	27.00	41.00	315.	2200.	4300.
1914D	11,908,000	1.90	2.00	2.75	8.50	27.00	41.00	315.	2200.	—
1914S	2,100,000	2.00	2.75	4.00	12.00	33.00	55.00	430.	2850.	—
1915	5,620,450	1.90	2.00	4.00	9.50	31.00	50.00	315.	2200.	3800.
1915S	960,000	2.75	4.00	9.00	17.50	39.00	75.00	475.	3150.	—
1916	18,490,000	1.90	2.00	2.75	8.50	27.00	41.00	315.	2200.	—
1916S	5,820,000	1.90	2.00	3.50	11.00	31.00	46.00	315.	2200.	—

MERCURY DIMES

The nation's fractional silver coin issues were redesigned in 1916 when the Barber designs were 25 years old. A. A. Weinman, whose monogram appears in the field behind the neck of the Mercury-winged head of Liberty on the obverse, designed this coin which carries a fasces on the reverse. This series offers two of the five overdates in 20th century U.S. coinage in the 1942/41 issues.

Mintmark

NOTE: A $1.50 Numismatic value base has been assigned to Mercury dimes, based on the $13.00 market price for one ounce of silver at the time these valuations were assigned. The bullion value of each coin's silver content increases or decreases approximately three-quarters cent for each 10-cent change in the bullion price, or 7.23-cents for each $1 change.

Date	Mintage	G-4	VG-8	F-12	VF-20	XF-40	MS-60	MS-65-65FSB		Prf-65
1916	22,180,080	2.00	3.25	4.00	5.00	8.00	32.00	70.00	225.	—
1916D	264,000	380.	450.	650.	875.	1200.	2600.	5250	14,000.	—
1916S	10,450,000	2.50	3.00	5.00	7.00	12.00	45.00	185.	875.	—
1917	55,230,000	—	1.50	3.00	4.00	6.00	27.50	70.00	250.	—
1917D	9,402,000	2.25	2.50	7.75	12.00	30.00	150.	450.	1750.	—
1917S	27,330,000	1.50	2.00	3.00	5.00	8.00	60.00	225.	1250.	—
1918	26,680,000	2.00	2.50	3.75	8.00	19.75	70.00	250.	725.	—
1918D	22,674,800	2.00	2.50	4.00	8.00	18.00	95.00	375.	3250.	—
1918S	19,300,000	1.50	2.00	3.00	5.50	11.00	80.00	300.	3000.	—
1919	35,740,000	1.50	2.00	3.00	4.50	7.50	38.00	110.	400.	—
1919D	9,939,000	2.50	3.25	6.00	15.00	30.00	175.	525.	2150.	—
1919S	8,850,000	2.40	2.50	6.00	15.00	29.00	200.	590.	4250.	—
1920	59,030,000	1.50	2.00	2.25	4.00	5.00	25.00	75.00	265.	—
1920D	19,171,000	1.50	2.00	2.50	6.00	13.00	100.	315.	1400.	—
1920S	13,820,000	1.50	2.00	2.50	6.00	12.00	90.00	290.	1950.	—
1921	1,230,000	19.50	27.00	60.00	115.	375.	1350.	2400.	5500.	—
1921D	1,080,000	30.00	38.00	75.00	145.	375.	1200.	2350.	5250.	—
1923	50,130,000	1.50	2.00	2.50	3.50	5.00	24.00	68.00	250.	—
1923S	6,440,000	2.00	2.50	3.75	6.50	25.00	135.	475.	2625.	—
1924	24,010,000	1.50	2.00	2.50	3.50	7.00	50.00	125.	425.	—
1924D	6,810,000	1.50	2.00	3.75	6.00	18.00	150.	450.	1500.	—
1924S	7,120,000	1.50	2.00	3.00	6.00	16.00	145.	500.	2750.	—
1925	25,610,000	1.50	1.85	2.00	3.00	5.50	35.00	115.	365.0	1.00
1925D	5,117,000	3.50	4.50	7.50	25.00	70.00	325.	825.	3250.	—
1925S	5,850,000	1.50	2.00	2.50	6.00	15.00	170.	600.	4150.	—
1926	32,160,000	1.50	1.85	2.00	3.00	4.50	24.00	65.00	210.0	1.00
1926D	6,828,000	1.50	2.00	3.00	5.00	15.00	100.	375.	1700.	—
1926S	1,520,000	6.50	8.50	11.00	23.00	67.00	525.	1600.	6500.	—
1927	28,080,000	—	1.50	2.00	2.50	4.00	24.00	65.00	210.	—
1927D	4,812,000	2.00	2.50	5.00	12.00	29.00	275.	600.	2250.	—
1927S	4,770,000	1.50	2.00	2.75	5.00	15.00	125.	425.	2500.	—
1928	19,480,000	—	1.50	2.00	2.50	4.00	25.00	55.00	175.	—
1928D	4,161,000	1.50	2.00	4.00	12.00	30.00	170.	435.	1550.	—
1928S	7,400,000	1.50	2.00	2.50	4.50	10.00	75.00	250.	850.	—
1929	25,970,000	—	1.50	2.00	2.50	3.25	20.00	60.00	175.	—
1929D	5,034,000	1.50	2.00	3.00	5.00	7.50	33.00	140.	415.	—
1929S	4,730,000	1.50	2.00	2.50	3.25.	4.00	40.00	160.	600.	—
1930	6,770,000	1.50	2.00	2.50	3.00	4.50	30.00	90.00	370.	—
1930S	1,843,000	1.50	2.50	4.00	5.50	10.00	115.	350.	975.	—
1931	3,150,000	—	2.00	2.25	3.00	7.75	60.00	145.	475.	—
1931D	1,260,000	7.00	8.00	9.00	14.50	24.00	120.	340.	850.	—
1931S	1,800,000	2.25	2.50	4.50	5.25	9.50	120.	335.	1075.	—
1934	24,080,000	—	—	—	1.50	2.50	17.00	80.	95.00	110.
1934D	6,772,000	—	—	—	1.50	5.00	70.00	240.	475.	—
1935	58,830,000	—	—	—	1.50	2.50	12.00	70.00	90.00	—
1935D	10,477,000	—	—	—	2.25	7.00	120.	360.	725.	—
1935S	15,840,000	—	—	—	1.50	2.50	35.00	170.	850.	—
1936	87,504,130	—	—	—	1.50	2.50	11.00	80.00	85.00	1400.
1936D	16,132,000	—	—	—	1.50	4.00	70.00	215.	450.	—
1936S	9,210,000	—	—	—	1.50	2.50	33.00	125.	210.	—
1937	56,865,756	—	—	—	1.50	2.50	11.00	68.00	65.00	1000.
1937D	14,146,000	—	—	—	1.50	2.50	55.00	175.	225.	—
1937S	9,740,000	—	—	—	1.50	2.50	43.00	140.	610.	—
1938	22,198,728	—	—	—	1.50	2.50	11.00	85.00	110.	850.
1938D	5,537,000	—	—	—	1.50	2.50	55.00	195.	230.	—
1938S	8,090,000	—	—	—	1.50	5.00	30.00	75.00	165.	—
1939	67,749,321	—	—	—	1.50	2.50	10.00	42.00	110.	700.
1939D	24,394,000	—	—	—	1.50	2.50	11.00	48.00	55.00	—
1939S	10,540,000	—	—	—	1.50	2.50	35.00	110.	1000.	—
1940	65,361,827	—	—	—	1.50	2.50	8.00	34.00	50.00	525.
1940D	21,198,000	—	—	—	1.50	2.50	20.00	105.	130.	—
1940S	21,560,000	—	—	—	1.50	2.50	8.50	40.00	85.00	—
1941	175,106,557	—	—	—	1.50	2.50	6.50	35.00	35.00	500.
1941D	45,634,000	—	—	—	1.50	2.50	27.00	42.00	56.00	—
1941S	43,090,000	—	—	—	1.50	1.85	11.00	22.00	36.00	—

Date	Mintage	G-4	VG-8	F-12	VF-20	XF-40	MS-60	MS-65-65FSB		Prf-65
1942/41	Unrecorded	310.	315.	330.	365.	390.	1600.	4000	11,000.	—
1942	205,432,329	—	—	—	—	1.50	6.00	35.00	70.00	500.
1942D	60,740,000	—	—	—	—	1.50	18.00	45.00	50.00	—
1942/41D	Unrecorded	310.	315.	335.	375.	430.	1800.	4250	12,500.	—
1942S	49,300,000	—	—	—	—	1.50	27.00	90.00	175.	—
1943	191,710,000	—	—	—	—	1.50	6.00	31.00	45.00	—
1943D	71,949,000	—	—	—	—	1.50	8.00	34.00	45.00	—
1943S	60,400,000	—	—	—	—	1.50	25.00	51.00	175.	—
1944	231,410,000	—	—	—	—	1.50	6.00	31.00	140.	—
1944D	62,224,000	—	—	—	—	1.50	8.00	34.00	45.00	—
1944S	49,490,000	—	—	—	—	1.50	8.00	38.50	70.00	—
1945	159,130,000	—	—	—	—	1.50	6.00	31.00	2000.	—
1945D	40,245,000	—	—	—	—	1.50	11.00	35.50	60.00	—
1945S	41,920,000	—	—	—	—	1.50	11.00	35.50	135.	—
1945S Micro	Inc.Ab.	—	—	—	—	2.00	15.00	65.00	275.	—

NOTE: All specimens listed as -65FSB are for fully struck MS-65 coins with fully split and rounded horizontal bands on the fasces.

ROOSEVELT DIMES

National sentiment following the death of President Franklin D. Roosevelt on April 12, 1945, led to the creation of the Roosevelt dime which was introduced in 1946. It was fitting that the dime be used for the Roosevelt memorial issue, as the former President was so closely associated with the March of Dimes. The designs were executed by John R. Sinnock, whose initials "JS" appear at the base of the bust. On July 23, 1965, Congress authorized the introduction of a cupro-nickel clad copper dime to replace the silver standard composition whch had gone unchanged for more than 90 years.

Mintmarks

1946 - 1964
Reverse

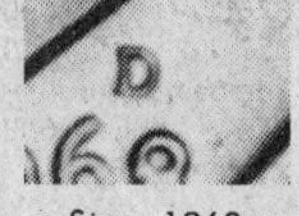

Since 1968
Obverse

NOTE: A $1.50 Numismatic value base has been assigned to silver Roosevelt dimes, based on the $13.00 market price for one ounce of silver at the time these valuations were assigned. The bullion value of each coin's silver content increases or decreases approximately three-quarters cent for each 10-cent change in the bullion price, or 7.23-cents for each $1 change.

Date	Mintage	G-4	VG-8	F-12	VF-20	XF-40	AU-50	MS-60	MS-65	Prf-65
1946	225,250,000	—	—	—	—	—	1.50	3.50	5.75	—
1946D	61,043,500	—	—	—	—	—	1.50	5.00	9.00	—
1946S	27,900,000	—	—	—	—	—	1.50	4.50	8.25	—
1947	121,520,000	—	—	—	—	—	1.50	5.00	8.25	—
1947D	46,835,000	—	—	—	—	—	1.85	8.00	16.50	—
1947S	34,840,000	—	—	—	—	—	1.50	4.50	8.80	—
1948	74,950,000	—	—	—	—	—	1.50	4.00	7.60	—
1948D	52,841,000	—	—	—	—	—	1.85	7.00	22.00	—
1948S	35,520,000	—	—	—	—	—	1.85	5.50	14.25	—
1949	30,940,000	—	—	—	—	—	7.00	15.00	29.00	—
1949D	26,034,000	—	—	—	—	—	2.25	7.50	15.00	—
1949S	13,510,000	—	—	—	—	—	7.50	35.00	60.00	—
1950	50,181,500	—	—	—	—	—	1.50	3.75	7.30	80.00
1950D	46,803,000	—	—	—	—	—	1.50	4.00	6.90	—
1950S	20,440,000	—	—	—	—	—	4.00	25.00	32.50	—
1951	102,937,602	—	—	—	—	—	1.50	4.00	6.00	80.00
1951D	56,529,000	—	—	—	—	—	1.50	4.00	7.00	—
1951S	31,630,000	—	—	—	—	—	2.75	13.00	20.00	—
1952	99,122,073	—	—	—	—	—	1.50	3.75	5.80	50.00
1952D	122,100,000	—	—	—	—	—	1.50	4.00	6.30	—
1952S	44,419,500	—	—	—	—	—	2.00	4.00	9.50	—
1953	53,618,920	—	—	—	—	—	1.50	3.50	5.60	35.00
1953D	136,433,000	—	—	—	—	—	1.50	3.50	5.00	—
1953S	39,180,000	—	—	—	—	—	1.50	3.50	5.00	—
1954	114,243,503	—	—	—	—	—	1.50	3.50	3.75	15.00
1954D	106,397,000	—	—	—	—	—	1.50	3.50	3.75	—
1954S	22,860,000	—	—	—	—	—	1.50	3.50	5.00	—
1955	12,828,381	—	—	—	—	—	1.50	3.50	5.90	15.00
1955D	13,959,000	—	—	—	—	—	1.50	3.50	6.60	—
1955S	18,510,000	—	—	—	—	—	1.50	3.50	6.60	—
1956	109,309,384	—	—	—	—	—	1.50	3.50	3.75	5.00
1956D	108,015,100	—	—	—	—	—	1.50	3.50	4.30	—
1957	161,407,952	—	—	—	—	—	1.50	3.50	3.75	3.75
1957D	113,354,330	—	—	—	—	—	1.50	3.50	5.50	—
1958	32,785,652	—	—	—	—	—	1.50	3.50	4.25	4.50
1958D	136,564,600	—	—	—	—	—	1.50	2.50	3.10	—
1959	86,929,291	—	—	—	—	—	1.50	1.80	1.90	3.75
1959D	164,919,790	—	—	—	—	—	1.50	1.80	1.90	—
1960	72,081,602	—	—	—	—	—	1.50	1.80	1.90	3.25
1960D	200,160,400	—	—	—	—	—	1.50	1.80	1.90	—
1961	96,758,244	—	—	—	—	—	1.50	1.80	1.90	2.50
1961D	209,146,550	—	—	—	—	—	1.50	1.80	1.90	—
1962	75,668,019	—	—	—	—	—	1.50	1.80	1.90	2.50
1962D	334,948,380	—	—	—	—	—	1.50	1.80	1.90	—
1963	126,725,645	—	—	—	—	—	1.50	1.80	1.90	2.50
1963D	421,476,530	—	—	—	—	—	1.50	1.80	1.90	—
1964	933,310,762	—	—	—	—	—	1.50	1.80	1.90	2.50
1964D	1,357,517,180	—	—	—	—	—	1.50	1.80	1.90	—

Commencing 1965 - See Modern Singles - Page 1897

TWENTY CENTS

This shortest lived of U. S. coins — it was actually issued in circulation quantities only in 1875 — was launched at the instigation of Western interests as the answer for change making problems in the West where cents and nickels did not circulate. Authorized by a law dated March 3, 1875, its close similarity in size and design to the quarter contributed to its demise. The coin was proportionate in weight to other silver coins being issued at the time. Congress revoked the authority for the issue on May 2, 1878.

Mintmark

Date	Mintage	G-4	VG-8	F-12	VF-20	XF-40	AU-50	MS-60	MS-65	Prf-65
1875	39,700	45.00	50.00	75.00	120.	195.	400.	2100	10,000.	6300.
1875S	1,155,000	35.00	42.00	55.00	110.	165.	350.	1400	10,000.	—
1875CC	133,290	37.00	42.00	55.00	120.	195.	350.	1700	12,000.	—
1876	15,900	60.00	75.00	110.	150.	240.	400.	2100	12,000.	7550.
1876CC	10,000				ANA Sale,1978			39,500.	—	—
1877	510	—	Proof Only		—	—	—	—	—	8750.
Impaired Proof		—	—	—	375.	475.	—	—	—	—
1878	600	—	Proof Only		—	—	—	—	—	8500.
Impaired Proof		—	—	—	375.	475.	—	—	—	—

Cleaning Coins

Coin cleaning is a very touchy subject, especially among advanced collectors. It is generally acknowledged, however, that a dirty or heavily tarnished coin is better cleaned than not, but only if the coin is properly cleaned, not polished.

There are several good coin cleaners available, some multi-purpose, others specifically suited for bronze, nickel or silver coins. Properly used, they can beautify dirty or tarnished coins, but a cleaner should never be used on a collector coin until the user has first experimented with the product on a common coin.

Rubbing or polishing a coin with any cleaner will remove the natural surface luster of the metal, and should be avoided, as should the application of any abrasive cleaning element. Valuable coins should never be cleaned except by someone experienced in using the agent, as their values can be greatly diminished through improper cleaning.

Numerical Grading

The listings in this U.S. section feature numerically assigned grade heads, which have been substituted for the traditional descriptive designations. All grades from G-4 (good) through XF-40 (extremely fine) are assigned to designate typical quality specimens in each traditional grade. The MS-60 head is equivalent to an average uncirculated designation, and coins of this quality can be expected to exhibit some tarnish, along with slight bag scratches or nicks, but there must be no overall damage. Weakly struck coins without wear also fall into this category. The MS-65 head is applied to choice quality, sharply struck coins that retain full original mint lustre, or natural toning. Their surfaces may evidence only the most minor bag markings, not serious abrasions, or rim nicks.

QUARTERS

If the production of dimes was minimal during the early years of U.S. coinage, the issue of quarters was infinitesimal. Introduced in 1796, as was the dime, the quarter was issued in only six years up to 1818, and in quantity only in 1805-07, to a combined total of some 650,000 pieces. The 1796 draped bust-small eagle type did not carry an indication of value, a trait the quarter shared with the draped bust half dime and dime issues, but the designation "25 C" was added at the base of the reverse with the introduction of the heraldic eagle design when the denomination was next minted in 1804.

Draped Bust Quarters

Date	Mintage	G-4	VG-8	F-12	VF-20	XF-40	AU-50	MS-60	MS-65
1796	6,146	3200.	4000.	5000.	7550.	15,000.	25,000.	30,000.	50,000.

HERALDIC EAGLE INTRODUCED

Date	Mintage	G-4	VG-8	F-12	VF-20	XF-40	AU-50	MS-60	MS-65
1804	6,738	425.	650.	1800.	4000.	7500.	12,500.	22,000.	45,000.
1805	121,394	175.	250.	500.	950.	2250.	4000.	3900.	8200.
1806	206,124	150.	225.	475.	950.	2150.	3800.	3900.	8200.
1806/5	Inc. Ab.	150.	225.	500.	1000.	2250.	4000.	3900.	—
1807	220,643	150.	225.	475.	950.	2150.	3800.	3900.	8200.

Liberty Cap Quarters

Date	Mintage	G-4	VG-8	F-12	VF-20	XF-40	AU-50	MS-60	MS-65
1815	89,235	65.00	80.00	100.	300.	600.	2000.	3900.	12,000.
1818	361,174	65.00	80.00	100.	300.	600.	1900.	3800.	12,000.
1818/15	Inc. Ab.	65.00	80.00	100.	300.	600.	2000.	3900.	12,000.
1819 Sm.9	144,000	65.00	80.00	90.00	250.	500.	1900.	3800.	12,000.
1819 Lg.9	Inc. Ab.	65.00	80.00	90.00	250.	500.	1900.	3800.	12,000.
1820 Sm.O	127,444	65.00	80.00	100.	185.	500.	1100.	3800.	12,000.
1820 Lg.O	Inc. Ab.	65.00	80.00	100.	185.	500.	1100.	3800.	12,000.
1821	216,851	65.00	80.00	100.	200.	500.	1100.	3800.	13,000.
1822	64,080	65.00	80.00	100.	200.	500.	1100.	3800.	13,000.
1822 25/50C.	I.A.	175.	350.	450.	800.	1400.	2000.	3800	14,000.
1823/22	17,800	1500.	6000.	7000.	10,000.	15,000.	—	—	—
			Stack's Auction, Mar. 1977			32,000.	—	Proof	—
1824	Unrecorded	65.00	80.00	100.	200.	500.	1100.	3800.	13,000.
1825/22	168,000	65.00	80.00	100.	250.	575.	1500.	3800.	12,000.
1825/23	Inc. Ab.	65.00	80.00	100.	250.	575.	1500.	3800.	12,000.
1825/24	Inc. Ab.	65.00	80.00	100.	250.	575.	1500.	3800.	12,000.
1827 Original	4,000			Stack's Auction 1977		Proof	—	27,000.	—
1827 Restrike	I.A.			Stack's Auction 1977		Proof	—	12,500.	—
1828	102,000	65.00	80.00	100.	400.	500.	1500.	3800.	12,000.
1828 25/50C.	I.A.	70.00	125.	200.	450.	550.	2000.	3900.	—

MOTTO REMOVED FROM REVERSE

Date	Mintage	G-4	VG-8	F-12	VF-20	XF-40	AU-50	MS-60	MS-65
1831 Small Letters									
	398,000	35.00	40.00	45.00	140.	250.	650.	2200.	9450.
1831 Lg.Let.	Inc. Ab.	35.00	40.00	45.00	140.	250.	650.	2200.	9450.
1832	320,000	35.00	40.00	45.00	140.	250.	650.	2200.	9450.
1833	156,000	35.00	40.00	50.00	140.	250.	650.	2200.	9450.
1834	286,000	35.00	40.00	45.00	140.	250.	650.	2200.	9450.
1835	1,952,000	35.00	40.00	45.00	140.	250.	650.	2200.	9450.
1836	472,000	35.00	40.00	45.00	140.	250.	650.	2200.	9450.
1837	252,400	35.00	40.00	45.00	140.	250.	650.	2200.	9450.
1838	832,000	35.00	40.00	45.00	140.	250.	650.	2200.	9450.

LIBERTY SEATED QUARTERS

This design was adapted to the quarter in 1838, the year after it was adopted for the lesser fractional silver issues, following the enactment of the January 18, 1837, law which reduced the weight of the coin from 104 grains to 103 1/8. The weight was again lowered to 96 grains in 1853, then increased slightly to 96.45 in 1873. Rays were added in the field around the eagle on the reverse, in addition to the arrows at the date, on the reduced weight 1853 issues. Although the arrows were retained for 1854-55, the rays were dropped. Arrows were again added at the dates in 1873-74 to mark that change.

Without Drapery

Mintmark

WITHOUT DRAPERY ON LIBERTY

Date	Mintage	G-4	VG-8	F-12	VF-20	XF-40	MS-60
1838	Inc. Ab.	15.00	20.00	25.00	50.00	160.	3150.
1839	491,146	15.00	20.00	25.00	50.00	150.	3150.
1840O	425,200	15.00	20.00	25.00	50.00	150.	3350.

DRAPERY ADDED TO LIBERTY

Date	Mintage	G-4	VG-8	F-12	VF-20	XF-40	MS-60
1840	188,127	20.00	25.00	40.00	70.00	150.	2500.
1840O	Inc. Ab.	20.00	25.00	50.00	85.00	150.	1600.
1841	120,000	50.00	75.00	100.	150.	275.	1000.
1841O	452,000	25.00	50.00	75.00	100.	200.	845.
1842 Small Date	88,000	Bowers & Ruddy Sale, Aug., 1978, Proof					32,500.
1842 Large Date	Inc. Ab.	65.00	80.00	125.	250.	350.	2000.
1842O Small Date	769,000	400.	500.	700.	1000.	2000.	—
1842O Large Date	Inc. Ab.	25.00	35.00	50.00	65.00	125.	—
1843	645,600	12.00	16.00	22.00	45.00	85.00	845.
1843O	968,000	15.00	25.00	75.00	100.00	275.	—
1844	421,200	13.00	18.00	24.00	45.00	85.00	845.
1844O	740,000	13.00	18.00	24.00	50.00	95.00	1200.
1845	922,000	12.00	16.00	22.00	45.00	85.00	845.
1846	510,000	13.00	18.00	24.00	45.00	85.00	845.
1847	734,000	12.00	16.00	22.00	45.00	85.00	845.
1847O	368,000	30.00	50.00	75.00	125.	250.	845.
1848	146,000	16.00	20.00	30.00	85.00	150.	845.
1849	340,000	16.00	20.00	30.00	45.00	100.	845.
1849O	Unrecorded	425.	600.	900.	2000.	3200.	—
1850	190,800	20.00	30.00	50.00	75.00	110.	845.
1850O	412,000	25.00	50.00	75.00	100.	175.	845.
1851	160,000	20.00	30.00	60.00	85.00	140.	845.
1851O	88,000	175.	225.	350.	500.	1100.	—
1852	177,060	25.00	40.00	60.00	85.00	140.	900.
1852O	96,000	225.	350.	450.	550.	1200.	—
1853 Recut Date	44,200	150.	175.	300.	475.	600.	3000.

Arrows at Date, With Rays, 1853 Only

ARROWS AT DATE

Date	Mintage	G-4	VG-8	F-12	VF-20	XF-40	MS-60	Prf-65
1853 Rays								
	15,210,020	10.00	15.00	20.00	32.50	125.	2250.	—
1853/4	Inc. Ab.	75.00	150.	350.	500.	1000.	4000.	—
1853O Rays								
	1,332,000	15.00	20.00	25.00	40.00	110.	3000.	—
1854	12,380,000	10.00	15.00	20.00	25.00	75.00	1575.	—
1854O	1,484,000	10.00	15.00	20.00	30.00	85.00	2500.	—
1854O Huge O								
	Inc. Ab.	150.	250.	350.	700.	1200.	—	—
1855	2,857,000	10.00	15.00	20.00	30.00	75.00	1575.	10,000.
1855O	176,000	40.00	55.00	80.00	150.	350.	1850.	—
1855S	396,400	35.00	50.00	75.00	125.	300.	1750.	—

ARROWS AT DATE REMOVED

Date	Mintage	G-4	VG-8	F-12	VF-20	XF-40	MS-60	Prf-65
1856	7,264,000	10.00	15.00	20.00	45.00	85.00	845.	4500.
1856O	968,000	20.00	30.00	45.00	65.00	140.	850.	—
1856S	286,000	35.00	55.00	75.00	160.	225.	—	—
1856S/S	Inc. Ab.	100.	150.	400.	700.	1500.	—	—
1857	9,644,000	10.00	15.00	20.00	45.00	85.00	845.	6600.
1857O	1,180,000	15.00	25.00	35.00	55.00	110.	900.	—
1857S	82,000	50.00	75.00	175.	260.	450.	—	—
1858	7,368,000	10.00	15.00	20.00	45.00	85.00	845.	6600.
1858O	520,000	20.00	30.00	45.00	65.00	140.	900.	—
1858S	121,000	30.00	35.00	150.	225.	300.	—	—
1859	1,344,000	15.00	20.00	25.00	45.00	85.00	900.	6600.
1859O	260,000	35.00	55.00	80.00	115.	225.	900.	—
1859S	80,000	50.00	85.00	135.	220.	425.	—	—
1860	805,400	15.00	20.00	25.00	45.00	85.00	900.	6600.
1860O	388,000	25.00	35.00	50.00	75.00	160.	925.	—
1860S	56,000	75.00	125.	225.	400.	600.	—	—
1861	4,854,600	10.00	15.00	20.00	45.00	85.00	850.	6600.
1861S	96,000	25.00	30.00	60.00	80.00	225.	2600.	—
1862	932,550	15.00	20.00	25.00	65.00	125.	845.	6600.
1862S	67,000	30.00	35.00	70.00	150.	300.	—	—
1863	192,060	18.00	22.00	35.00	60.00	100.	845.	6600.
1864	94,070	30.00	35.00	60.00	80.00	150.	1200.	6600.
1864S	20,000	150.	200.	350.	500.	1200.	—	—
1865	59,300	40.00	50.00	70.00	90.00	150.	845.	4100.
1865S	41,000	35.00	40.00	75.00	150.	250.	2000.	—
1866	—		Unique	—	—	—	—	—

MOTTO ABOVE EAGLE

Date	Mintage	G-4	VG-8	F-12	VF-20	XF-40	MS-60	Prf-65
1866	17,525	175.	225.	300.	400.	525.	1200.	6175.
1866S	28,000	45.00	60.00	125.	250.	425.	—	—
1867	20,625	100.	125.	175.	250.	375.	850.	6175.
1867S	48,000	40.00	55.00	100.	175.	275.	3000.	—
1868	30,000	60.00	80.00	130.	165.	275.	800.	6175.
1868S	96,000	25.00	35.00	70.00	100.	150.	1800.	—
1869	16,600	175.	225.	300.	400.	525.	1200.	6175.
1869S	76,000	30.00	40.00	75.00	115.	175.	—	—
1870	87,400	20.00	30.00	50.00	100.	175.	900.	6175.
1870CC	8,340	700.	1300.	2000.	2500.	3000.	—	—
1871	119,160	12.00	15.00	35.00	65.00	100.	900.	6175.
1871CC	10,890	450.	575.	850.	1200.	2000.	—	—
1871S	30,900	150.	270.	450.	550.	900.	2000.	—
1872	182,950	11.00	13.00	30.00	55.00	100.	800.	6175.
1872CC	22,850	210.	350.	500.	750.	2000.	—	—
1872S	83,000	150.	270.	385.	475.	750.	3500.	—
1873 Clsd.3	212,600	65.00	85.00	175.	215.	350.	—	6200.
1873 Open 3	Inc. Ab.	30.00	40.00	60.00	115.	200.	800.	—
1873CC	4,000	New England Sale, April, 1980					205,000.	—

CLOSED "3", NO ARROWS

OPEN "3", ARROWS

ARROWS AT DATE

Date	Mintage	G-4	VG-8	F-12	VF-20	XF-40	MS-60	Prf-65
1873	1,271,700	20.00	25.00	30.00	60.00	190.	2000.	10,000.

Date	Mintage	G-4	VG-8	F-12	VF-20	XF-40	MS-60	Prf-65
1873CC	12,462	400.	550.	800.	1500.	2500.	—	—
1873S	156,000	20.00	30.00	40.00	65.00	225.	2000.	—
1874	471,900	20.00	25.00	30.00	60.00	190.	2000.	10,000.
1874S	392,000	20.00	30.00	40.00	65.00	225.	2000.	—

ARROWS AT DATE REMOVED

Date	Mintage	G-4	VG-8	F-12	VF-20	XF-40	MS-60	Prf-65
1875	4,293,500	10.00	15.00	20.00	40.00	75.00	800.	6175.
1875CC	140,000	35.00	40.00	85.00	125.	275.	1400.	—
1875S	680,000	15.00	25.00	40.00	65.00	100.	800.	—
1876	17,817,150	10.00	15.00	20.00	40.00	75.00	800.	6175.
1876CC	4,944,000	10.00	15.00	25.00	45.00	85.00	800.	—
1876CC (Fine Reeding)								
	Inc. Ab.	35.00	50.00	90.00	140.	275.	800.	—
1876S	8,596,000	10.00	15.00	20.00	40.00	75.00	800.	—
1877	10,911,710	10.00	15.00	20.00	40.00	75.00	800.	6175.
1877CC	4,192,000	10.00	15.00	25.00	50.00	100.	825.	—
1877S	8,996,000	10.00	15.00	25.00	45.00	80.00	800.	—
1877S Over Horizontal S								
	Inc. Ab.	45.00	70.00	100.	140.	225.	800.	—
1878	2,260,800	9.00	15.00	20.00	40.00	75.00	800.	6175.
1878CC	996,000	15.00	20.00	30.00	50.00	90.00	800.	—
1878S	140,000	35.00	50.00	90.00	125.	225.	1500.	—
1879	14,700	65.00	75.00	100.	135.	180.	800.	6175.
1880	14,955	65.00	75.00	100.	135.	180.	800.	6175.
1881	12,975	80.00	110.	130.	165.	220.	800.	6175.
1882	16,300	80.00	110.	130.	165.	220.	800.	6175.
1883	15,439	80.00	110.	130.	165.	220.	800.	6175.
1884	8,875	100.	140.	160.	200.	265.	800.	6175.
1885	14,530	80.00	110.	130.	165.	225.	800.	6175.
1886	5,886	150.	200.	250.	300.	400.	900.	6175.
1887	10,710	80.00	110.	130.	165.	230.	800.	6175.
1888	10,833	80.00	110.	130.	165.	230.	800.	6175.
1888S	1,216,000	9.00	15.00	20.00	40.00	75.00	800.	—
1889	12,711	80.00	110.	130.	165.	200.	800.	6175.
1890	80,590	35.00	45.00	60.00	75.00	120.	800.	6175.
1891	3,920,600	9.00	15.00	20.00	40.00	75.00	800.	6175.
1891O	68,000	125.	140.	220.	400.	600.	—	—
1891S	2,216,000	10.00	15.00	20.00	45.00	75.00	800.	—

BARBER QUARTERS

Sticking with the tradition of the previous 100 years, during which time the same basic design was carried on all silver units, Barber's Liberty head design was also offered on the quarter in 1892. The larger size of this coin, coupled with the lawful requirement that an eagle be represented on all denominations above the dime, enabled the placement of an eagle on the reverse in substitution for the wreath on the new dime.

Mintmark

NOTE: A $4.50 Numismatic value base has been assigned to Barber quarters, based on the $13.00 market price for one ounce of silver at the time these valuations were assigned. The bullion value of each coin's silver content increases or decreases approximately 1.81-cents for each 10-cent change in the bullion price, or 18.09-cents for each $1 change.

Date	Mintage	G-4	VG-8	F-12	VF-20	XF-40	AU-50	MS-60	MS-65	Prf-65
1892	8,237,245	5.00	6.75	11.00	27.50	65.00	125.	475.	3200.	5400.
1892O	2,640,000	6.75	10.00	16.00	33.00	68.00	135.	575.	4100.	—
1892S	964,079	12.00	20.00	35.00	55.00	100.	175.	700.	4400.	—
1893	5,484,838	4.50	7.50	12.50	28.50	66.00	130.	535.	2850.	5400.
1893O	3,396,000	4.75	8.50	16.00	34.00	69.00	135.	630.	4100.	—
1893S	1,454,535	6.75	11.00	25.00	42.00	80.00	150.	630.	4100.	—
1894	3,432,972	4.75	8.50	13.00	29.50	67.00	130.	535.	3300.	5400.
1894O	2,852,000	5.50	9.50	20.00	37.50	72.00	140.	630.	4400.	—
1894S	2,648,821	4.75	8.50	17.50	35.00	70.00	140.	630.	4400.	—
1895	4,440,880	4.50	6.75	11.00	27.50	65.00	125.	535.	3500.	5400.
1895O	2,816,000	5.50	8.50	18.00	36.00	71.00	140.	700.	4750.	—
1895S	1,764,681	6.75	10.00	20.00	39.00	75.00	145.	630.	3650.	—
1896	3,874,762	5.00	6.75	11.00	27.50	65.00	125.	535.	3000.	5400.
1896O	1,484,000	6.75	10.00	20.00	44.00	95.00	380.	2400	14,000.	—
1896S	188,039	220.	265.	400.	600.	1100.	2300.	6000	24,000.	—
1897	8,140,731	4.50	5.50	10.00	26.00	61.00	125.	460.	3150.	5400.
1897O	1,414,800	7.25	11.50	22.00	46.00	90.00	220.	1900.	8500.	—
1897S	542,229	13.00	23.00	35.00	56.00	117.	260.	880.	4750.	—
1898	11,100,735	4.50	5.50	9.50	26.00	61.00	125.	460.	3150.	5400.
1898O	1,868,000	6.00	9.00	19.00	36.00	72.00	140.	880.	7600.	—
1898S	1,020,592	6.00	9.00	16.00	30.00	62.00	135.	585.	5700.	—
1899	12,624,846	4.50	6.75	9.50	26.00	61.00	125.	460.	3150.	5400.
1899O	2,644,000	6.75	8.50	16.50	34.00	70.00	140.	880.	6950.	—
1899S	708,000	7.50	14.00	26.50	41.00	80.00	175.	750.	4700.	—

Date	Mintage	G-4	VG-8	F-12	VF-20	XF-40	AU-50	MS-60	MS-65	Prf-65
1900	10,016,912	4.50	6.75	10.00	28.00	62.00	125.	460.	3150.	5400
1900O	3,416,000	7.00	12.00	22.00	40.00	78.00	150.	800.	7550.	—
1900S	1,858,585	5.00	6.75	11.00	28.00	62.00	130.	630.	4100.	—
1901	8,892,813	5.00	6.75	11.00	28.00	64.00	130.	460.	3150.	5400
1901O	1,612,000	12.00	19.50	40.00	70.00	132.	215.	1575.	8800.	—
1901S	72,664	600.	800.	1000.	1750.	2500.	4400	15,000.	—	—
1902	12,197,744	4.50	6.75	9.50	26.00	61.00	125.	460.	3150.	5400
1902O	4,748,000	6.75	7.75	12.00	32.00	68.00	135.	750.	4400.	—
1902S	1,524,612	8.50	13.00	21.00	40.00	80.00	150.	750.	4600.	—
1903	9,670,064	5.50	6.75	9.50	28.00	62.00	125.	460.	3150.	5400
1903O	3,500,000	6.75	8.50	12.00	33.00	72.00	150.	630.	3650.	—
1903S	1,036,000	9.50	14.00	22.00	41.00	84.00	185.	800.	5000.	—
1904	9,588,813	5.50	7.00	10.00	28.00	62.00	125.	460.	3150.	5400
1904O	2,456,000	6.00	8.50	18.00	40.00	95.00	175.	1900	10,000.	—
1905	4,968,250	5.50	6.75	10.00	28.00	63.00	125.	460.	3150.	5400.
1905O	1,230,000	7.50	12.00	22.00	42.00	105.	165.	660.	4100.	—
1905S	1,884,000	6.00	8.50	13.50	32.00	70.00	135.	630.	4100.	—
1906	3,656,435	6.00	7.50	11.50	30.00	66.00	130.	460.	3150.	5400.
1906D	3,280,000	6.25	8.50	14.00	32.00	70.00	135.	535.	3150.	—
1906O	2,056,000	6.50	9.00	15.50	35.00	74.00	145.	600.	3650.	—
1907	7,192,575	4.50	5.50	9.00	27.00	61.00	120.	460.	3150.	5400.
1907D	2,484,000	6.75	9.00	15.00	33.00	72.00	135.	600.	4100.	—
1907O	4,560,000	5.50	6.75	12.00	30.00	65.00	130.	535.	3650.	—
1907S	1,360,000	6.00	8.00	13.50	33.00	69.00	135.	700.	4400.	—
1908	4,232,545	4.50	5.50	9.00	28.00	63.00	125.	460.	3150.	5400.
1908D	5,788,000	4.50	5.00	8.50	26.00	60.00	120.	535.	3500.	—
1908O	6,244,000	4.50	5.00	8.50	26.00	60.00	120.	535.	3500.	—
1908S	784,000	7.50	12.00	20.00	38.00	80.00	175.	800.	4700.	—
1909	9,268,650	4.50	5.00	8.50	26.00	60.00	120.	460.	3150.	5400.
1909D	5,114,000	4.50	5.00	8.50	26.00	60.00	120.	535.	3500.	—
1909O	712,000	8.00	19.00	37.50	72.00	135.	195.	1300.	7900.	—
1909S	1,348,000	5.00	6.75	9.00	29.00	65.00	130.	700.	4700.	—
1910	2,244,551	4.25	5.25	9.50	30.00	66.00	130.	460.	3150.	5400.
1910D	1,500,000	6.00	9.00	16.50	36.00	75.00	135.	700.	4700.	—
1911	3,720,543	4.50	5.50	10.00	30.00	66.00	130.	460.	3150.	5400.
1911D	933,600	5.50	8.50	20.00	39.00	85.00	150.	535.	3500.	—
1911S	988,000	5.00	7.50	17.00	35.00	77.00	135.	630.	3650.	—
1912	4,400,700	4.25	5.25	9.50	28.00	63.00	125.	460.	3150.	5400.
1912S	708,000	5.50	6.75	15.00	33.00	74.00	140.	660.	4100.	—
1913	484,613	8.50	15.00	37.50	100.	300.	660.	2500.	8500.	5400.
1913D	1,450,800	8.50	10.00	17.50	37.50	80.00	140.	535.	3500.	—
1913S	40,000	215.	300.	450.	650.	1000.	2100.	5000.	—	—
1914	6,244,610	4.50	5.00	8.50	26.00	60.00	120.	460.	3150.	5400.
1914D	3,046,000	4.50	5.00	8.50	26.50	61.00	125.	500.	3500.	—
1914S	264,000	10.00	15.00	32.00	70.00	140.	275.	1500.	5700.	—
1915	3,480,450	4.50	5.00	8.50	27.00	61.00	125.	460.	3150.	5400.
1915D	3,694,000	4.50	5.00	8.50	26.50	60.00	120.	475.	3150.	—
1915S	704,000	5.50	6.50	15.00	39.00	82.00	140.	535.	3150.	—
1916	1,788,000	4.75	5.25	8.50	28.00	62.00	125.	460.	3150.	—
1916D	6,540,800	4.50	5.00	8.50	26.00	60.00	120.	475.	3150.	—

STANDING LIBERTY QUARTERS

In 1916 Hermon A. MacNeil's beautiful standing Liberty design for the quarter, which was unfortunately extremely susceptible to wear, was introduced. The devices for this coin were reworked several times in an effort to provide better wearing qualitites. The first version, minted in 1916 and early 1917, offers the date atop a raised pedestal below Liberty's feet and presents the eagle low in the field on the reverse. In 1917 the design was reworked for the first time, the most obvious change being in the positioning of the eagle with three stars beneath. This style was continued through 1924, then in 1925 a third version was created by recessing the date in the pedestal beneath Liberty's feet so that it would not wear so easily.

NOTE: A $4.00 Numismatic value base has been assigned to Standing Liberty quarters, based on the $13.00 market price for one ounce of silver at the time these valuations were assigned. The bullion value of each coin's silver content increases or decreases approximately 1.81-cents for each 10-cent change in the bullion price, or 18.09-cents for each $1 change.

Full Head Detail

Bare Breast 1916-1917

VARIETY I

Date	Mintage	G-4	VG-8	F-12	VF-20	XF-40	AU-50	MS-60	MS-65	-65FH
1916	52,000	700.	800.	1300.	1800.	2250.	2900.	3800.	7200.	17,000.
1917	8,792,000	8.00	11.00	16.50	27.50	60.00	115.	200.	1050.	2400.
1917D	1,509,200	8.00	12.00	18.50	32.00	63.00	120.	275.	1050.	3000.
1917S	1,952,000	8.00	12.00	18.50	32.00	63.00	125.	250.	1050.	3000.

Normal Head Detail

Chain Mail Clad
1917-1930

Mintmark

Overdate — 18/17S

VARIETY II

Date	Mintage	G-4	VG-8	F-12	VF-20	XF-40	AU-50	MS-60	MS-65	-65FH
1917	13,880,000	8.00	11.00	16.50	25.00	44.00	70.00	175.	1050.	2500.
1917D	6,224,400	13.00	17.50	26.00	35.00	55.00	80.00	195.	1300.	1500.
1917S	5,522,000	13.50	19.00	27.00	36.00	56.00	82.00	180.	1300.	1500.
1918	14,240,000	12.00	20.00	25.00	30.00	45.00	70.00	180.	1300.	3000.
1918D	7,380,000	15.00	20.00	30.00	45.00	75.00	120.	235.	1900.	5500.
1918S	11,072,000	14.00	16.00	17.50	29.00	47.00	80.00	175.	1400.	5800.
1918S/17	Inc. Ab.	750.	900.	1200.	1700.	2800.	5000.	9750.	25,000.	55,000.
1919	11,324,000	25.00	30.00	35.00	43.00	60.00	90.00	210.	1250.	2950.
1919D	1,944,000	40.00	60.00	95.00	125.	220.	315.	600.	3000.	13,000.
1919S	1,836,000	40.00	55.00	90.00	120.	220.	300.	550.	2650.	11,500.
1920	27,860,000	10.00	13.00	15.00	20.00	42.00	75.00	190.	1100.	2700.
1920D	3,586,400	21.00	27.50	42.00	63.00	105.	175.	270.	1800.	4800.
1920S	6,380,000	12.00	16.00	22.00	30.00	50.00	80.00	195.	1400.	6900.
1921	1,916,000	50.00	75.00	110.	140.	200.	280.	500.	1900.	3900.
1923	9,716,000	12.00	14.00	16.00	20.00	42.00	75.00	210.	1300.	4400.
1923S	1,360,000	63.00	80.00	125.	150.	220.	325.	550.	2500.	4000.
1924	10,920,000	12.00	14.00	15.00	19.00	40.00	72.00	200.	1300.	3750.
1924D	3,112,000	18.00	27.00	40.00	60.00	90.00	125.	190.	1075.	4000.
1924S	2,860,000	12.00	15.00	24.00	32.00	55.00	80.00	230.	1350.	5000.
1925	12,280,000	4.00	4.75	8.00	12.00	35.00	60.00	175.	1000.	2400.
1926	11,316,000	4.00	4.75	8.00	12.00	35.00	60.00	175.	1000.	2400.
1926D	1,716,000	6.00	9.00	13.00	30.00	60.00	90.00	175.	1000.	5500.
1926S	2,700,000	4.00	4.75	9.00	20.00	50.00	100.	230.	1650.	9000.
1927	11,912,000	4.00	4.75	8.00	12.00	35.00	60.00	175.	1000.	2400.
1927D	976,400	8.00	10.00	16.00	34.00	66.00	100.	210.	1400.	3000.
1927S	396,000	18.00	25.00	75.00	130.	500.	1000.	2500.	6800.	15,500.
1928	6,336,000	4.00	4.75	5.50	12.00	35.00	60.00	175.	1000.	2750.
1928D	1,627,600	4.75	5.25	9.00	14.00	40.00	80.00	195.	1200.	4400.
1928S	2,644,000	4.75	5.00	9.00	13.00	38.00	70.00	180.	1100.	2500.
1929	11,140,000	4.00	4.75	5.50	12.00	35.00	60.00	175.	1050.	2400.
1929D	1,358,000	4.75	5.25	6.50	15.00	42.00	85.00	195.	1075.	4600.
1929S	1,764,000	4.75	5.00	6.00	15.00	42.00	85.00	175.	1000.	2400.
1930	5,632,000	4.00	4.75	5.50	12.00	35.00	60.00	175.	1000.	2500.
1930S	1,556,000	4.75	5.00	6.00	14,00	40.00	70.00	175.	1000.	2600.

NOTE: -65FH values are for MS-65 full head pieces.

WASHINGTON QUARTERS

Offered in 1932 as a commemorative of the 200th anniversary of Washington's birth, this John Flanagan design was perpetuated as a regular issue in 1934. Flanagan, whose initials appear on the base of the bust to the right of the date, holds the distinction of being the last private artist to author a design for a regular issue U.S. coin with a precious metal content. His work survives on the cupronickel clad copper quarter introduced in 1965 which has the dual distinction of being the first clad metal issue to be placed in production — August 23 — and in circulation — November 1.

Mintmark
1932-64
Reverse

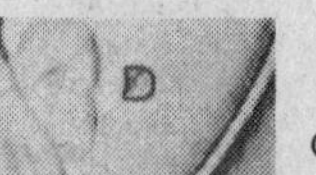

Since
1968
Obverse

NOTE: A $3.75 Numismatic value base has been assigned to silver Washington quarters, based on the $13.00 market price for one ounce of silver at the time these valuations were assigned. The bullion value of each coin's silver content increases or decreases approximately 1.81-cents for each 10-cent change in the bullion price, or 18.09-cents for each $1 change.

Date	Mintage	G-4	VG-8	F-12	VF-20	XF-40	MS-60	MS-65	Prf-65
1932	5,404,000	—	—	—	10.00	11.50	46.00	235.	—
1932D	436,800	46.00	52.00	80.00	105.	170.	950.	3900.	—
1932S	408,000	45.00	50.00	63.00	80.00	100.	450.	1700.	—
1934	31,912,052	—	—	—	3.75	4.60	57.00	49.00	—
1934D	3,527,200	—	—	—	12.00	20.00	190.	850.	—
1935	32,484,000	—	—	—	—	3.75	25.00	75.00	—
1935D	5,780,000	—	—	—	11.50	17.00	190.	850.	—
1935S	5,660,000	—	—	7.00	10.00	11.00	160.	900.	—
1936	41,303,837	—	—	—	—	3.75	21.00	77.00	800.
1936D	5,374,000	—	—	6.25	15.00	30.00	380.	1400.	—
1936S	3,828,000	—	—	—	9.50	11.50	110.	330.	—
1937	19,701,542	—	—	—	—	3.75	28.00	50.00	250.
1937D	7,189,600	—	—	—	9.50	11.00	65.00	150.	—
1937S	1,652,000	—	—	—	11.00	20.00	190.	640.	—
1938	9,480,045	—	—	—	11.00	14.00	95.00	365.	225.
1938S	2,832,000	—	—	—	10.50	11.50	95.00	245.	—
1939	33,548,795	—	—	—	—	3.75	11.00	47.00	100.
1939D	7,092,000	—	—	—	9.50	11.00	60.00	250.	—
1939S	2,628,000	—	—	—	10.00	11.50	80.00	240.	—
1940	35,715,246	—	—	—	—	3.75	12.00	32.00	90.00
1940D	2,797,600	—	—	—	10.00	12.00	90.00	290.	—
1940S	8,244,000	—	—	—	—	3.75	14.00	70.00	—
1941	79,047,287	—	—	—	—	3.75	8.25	14.50	85.00
1941D	16,714,800	—	—	—	—	3.75	25.00	50.00	—
1941S	16,080,000	—	—	—	—	3.75	25.00	50.00	—
1942	102,117,123	—	—	—	—	3.75	8.25	14.50	85.00
1942D	17,487,200	—	—	—	—	3.75	15.00	25.00	—
1942S	19,384,000	—	—	—	—	3.75	70.00	110.	—
1943	99,700,000	—	—	—	—	3.75	8.25	15.00	—
1943D	16,095,600	—	—	—	—	3.75	18.00	35.00	—
1943S	21,700,000	—	—	—	—	3.75	35.00	82.00	—
1944	104,956,000	—	—	—	—	3.75	8.25	12.50	—
1944D	14,600,800	—	—	—	—	3.75	8.50	28.50	—
1944S	12,560,000	—	—	—	—	3.75	13.00	50.00	—
1945	74,372,000	—	—	—	—	3.75	8.25	23.00	—
1945D	12,341,600	—	—	—	—	3.75	8.50	29.00	—
1945S	17,004,001	—	—	—	—	3.75	8.25	22.75	—
1946	53,436,000	—	—	—	—	3.75	6.50	11.75	—
1946D	9,072,800	—	—	—	—	3.75	8.25	16.00	—
1946S	4,204,000	—	—	—	—	3.75	8.25	12.50	—
1947	22,556,000	—	—	—	—	3.75	9.50	10.50	—
1947D	15,338,400	—	—	—	—	3.75	8.25	22.50	—
1947S	5,532,000	—	—	—	—	3.75	8.25	14.00	—
1948	35,196,000	—	—	—	—	3.75	6.50	14.50	—
1948D	16,766,800	—	—	—	—	3.75	8.25	14.50	—
1948S	15,960,000	—	—	—	—	3.75	8.25	19.75	—
1949	9,312,000	—	—	—	—	3.75	20.00	50.00	—
1949D	10,068,400	—	—	—	—	3.75	9.50	21.50	—
1950	24,971,512	—	—	—	—	3.75	6.50	11.00	80.00
1950D	21,075,600	—	—	—	—	3.75	8.25	11.00	—
1950D D/S	Inc. Ab.	8.00	15.00	30.00	45.00	125.	280.	—	—
1950S	10,284,004	—	—	—	—	3.75	8.25	24.50	—
1950S S/D	Inc. Ab.	8.00	15.00	30.00	45.00	140.	440.	—	—
1951	43,505,602	—	—	—	—	3.75	6.50	11.75	80.00
1951D	35,354,800	—	—	—	—	3.75	6.50	11.50	—
1951S	9,048,000	—	—	—	—	3.75	10.00	24.00	—
1952	38,862,073	—	—	—	—	3.75	6.50	11.50	50.00
1952D	49,795,200	—	—	—	—	3.75	6.50	11.75	—
1952S	13,707,800	—	—	—	—	3.75	6.50	19.50	—
1953	18,664,920	—	—	—	—	3.75	6.50	10.75	30.00
1953D	56,112,400	—	—	—	—	3.75	4.75	8.75	—
1953S	14,016,000	—	—	—	—	3.75	7.00	15.00	—
1954	54,645,503	—	—	—	—	3.75	6.50	7.25	17.00
1954D	42,305,500	—	—	—	—	3.75	6.50	8.75	—
1954S	11,834,722	—	—	—	—	3.75	6.50	11.00	—
1955	18,558,381	—	—	—	—	3.75	6.50	10.50	17.00
1955D	3,182,400	—	—	—	—	3.75	6.50	11.50	—
1956	44,813,384	—	—	—	—	3.75	4.75	8.75	15.00
1956D	32,334,500	—	—	—	—	3.75	4.75	8.75	—
1957	47,779,952	—	—	—	—	3.75	4.75	8.75	12.50
1957D	77,924,160	—	—	—	—	3.75	4.75	8.75	—
1958	7,235,652	—	—	—	—	3.75	4.75	9.50	15.00
1958D	78,124,900	—	—	—	—	3.75	4.75	8.25	—
1959	25,533,291	—	—	—	—	3.75	4.75	8.00	12.50
1959D	62,054,232	—	—	—	—	3.75	4.75	8.00	—
1960	30,855,602	—	—	—	—	3.75	4.75	8.00	8.50
1960D	63,000,324	—	—	—	—	3.75	4.75	7.75	—
1961	40,064,244	—	—	—	—	3.75	4.75	5.00	7.50
1961D	83,656,928	—	—	—	—	3.75	4.75	5.00	—
1962	39,374,019	—	—	—	—	3.75	4.75	5.00	7.50
1962D	127,554,756	—	—	—	—	3.75	4.75	5.00	—
1963	77,391,645	—	—	—	—	3.75	4.75	5.00	7.50
1963D	135,288,184	—	—	—	—	3.75	4.75	5.00	—
1964	564,341,347	—	—	—	—	3.75	4.75	5.00	7.50
1964D	704,135,528	—	—	—	—	3.75	4.75	5.00	—

Commencing 1965 - See Modern Singles - Page 1897

HALF DOLLARS

The half dollar was an important product of the mint during its early years, primarily because during a period of more than thirty years beginning in 1805 it was the only coin which was available for large transactions. Aside from sporadic issues of $2.50 and $5 gold pieces during the period, no other large silver or gold coins were produced from 1804 to 1838. Half dollars were issued annually during this period, excepting 1816 when a disasterous fire at the Philadelphia Mint caused a suspension of all precious metal coinage, but most were used only to transfer funds from one bank to another.

The Liberty cap design first engraved by John Reich was introduced to U.S. coinage on the 1807 half. During the period of these issues, 1807-39, the annual production of halves was so substantial that the totals generally exceeded those of the next 35 years by a significant margin. As this was the day of hand engraved dies, the die varieties for most dates are quite numerous, and the series has been extensively collected according to these varieties. In the listing which follows we have enumerated only the most popular of the over 600 known varieties.

The closing years of this type were rather historic ones. First, in 1836 the coin was converted from a lettered edge type to one with reeded edges, at the time the mint was converting to steam power, with new obverse and reverse devices being adopted, with "50 CENTS" placed beneath the the eagle in place of "50 C." Second, in 1837 the weight of the coin was lawfully reduced from 208 grains to 206¼ and the fineness raised from .8924 to .900. Third, in 1838 the designation of value on the reverse was changed to "HALF DOL." The latter year also marked the inauguration of half dollar production at New Orleans, although the 20 specimens said to have been struck do not appear in the official mint report.

Flowing Hair Half Dollars

Date	Mintage	G-4	VG-8	F-12	VF-20	XF-40	MS-60
1794	23,464	800.	1500.	2000.	3200.	5000.	—
1795	299,680	600.	750.	1350.	2000.	3450.	18,000.
1795 Recut Date							
	Inc. Ab.	600.	750.	1325.	2100.	3650.	—
1795 3 Leaves	Inc. Ab.	675.	775.	1500.	2400.	3900.	—

Draped Bust Half Dollars

Date	Mintage	G-4	VG-8	F-12	VF-20	XF-40	MS-60
1796 15 Stars	3,918	8000.	9000.	15,000.	21,000.	30,000.	—
1796 16 Stars	Inc. Ab.	8000.	9000.	15,000.	21,000.	30,000.	—
1797	Inc. Ab.	8000.	9000.	15,000.	28,000.	40,000.	—

HERALDIC EAGLE INTRODUCED

Date	Mintage	G-4	VG-8	F-12	VF-20	XF-40	MS-60
1801	30,289	100.	325.	800.	1075.	1500.	9500.
1802	29,890	85.00	300.	800.	1075.	1200.	9200.
1803 Sm. 3	188,234	80.00	150.	200.	400.	700.	9000.
1803 Lg. 3	Inc. Ab.	65.00	100.	150.	350.	650.	9000.
1805	211,722	60.00	95.00	150.	350.	650.	8900.
1805/4	Inc. Ab.	60.00	100.	200.	400.	600.	8900.
1806 Round Top 6, Large Stars							
	839,576	60.00	90.00	125.	250.	600.	8800.
1806 Round Top 6, Small Stars							
	Inc. Ab.	60.00	90.00	125.	250.	600.	8800.
1806 Pointed Top 6, Stem Not Through Claw							
	Inc. Ab.	60.00	90.00	125.	250.	750.	8800.
1806 Pointed Top 6, Stem Trhough Claw							
	Inc. Ab.	60.00	90.00	125.	250.	600.	8800.
1806/5	Inc. Ab.	65.00	105.	125.	275.	650.	8800.
1806 Over Inverted 6							
	Inc. Ab.	80.00	100.	140.	280.	675.	8800.
1807	301,076	60.00	70.00	120.	250.	600.	8800.

Liberty Cap Half Dollars

Date	Mintage	G-4	VG-8	F-12	VF-20	XF-40	MS-60
1807 Sm. Stars	750,500	25.00	30.00	37.50	75.00	160.	950.
1807 Lg. Stars	Inc. Ab.	22.00	27.50	32.50	65.00	120.	800.
1807 50/20 C.	Inc. Ab.	22.00	27.50	32.50	65.00	120.	950.
1808	1,368,600	22.00	27.50	30.00	35.00	95.00	700.
1808/7	Inc. Ab.	22.00	27.50	35.00	45.00	105.	725.
1809	1,405,810	22.00	27.50	30.00	35.00	85.00	700.
1810	1,276,276	22.00	27.50	30.00	35.00	80.00	700.
1811 Sm. 8	1,203,644	22.00	27.50	30.00	35.00	75.00	700.
1811 Lg. 8	Inc. Ab.	22.00	27.50	30.00	45.00	95.00	700.
1811 Dt. 18.11	Inc. Ab.	22.50	27.50	55.00	87.50	125.	735.
1812	1,628,059	22.00	27.50	30.00	35.00	85.00	700.
1812/11	Inc. Ab.	22.00	27.50	35.00	50.00	110.	725.
1813	1,241,903	22.00	27.50	30.00	35.00	85.00	700.
1814	1,039,075	22.00	27.50	30.00	35.00	75.00	700.
1814/13	Inc. Ab.	22.00	27.50	35.00	55.00	125.	750.
1815/12	47,150	250.	375.	450.	575.	875.	3000.
1817	1,215,567	72.00	27.50	30.00	35.00	75.00	665.
1817/13	Inc. Ab.	30.00	37.50	50.00	75.00	135.	900.
1817/14					5 Pieces Known - Rare		
1817 Dt. 181.7	Inc. Ab.	22.00	27.50	32.50	45.00	90.00	800.
1818	1,960,322	22.00	27.50	30.00	35.00	65.00	700.
1818/17	Inc. Ab.	22.00	27.50	30.00	40.00	75.00	735.
1819	2,208,000	22.00	27.50	30.00	35.00	65.00	700.
1819/18 Sm. 9	Inc. Ab.	22.00	27.50	30.00	35.00	65.00	735.
1819/18 Lg. 9	Inc. Ab.	22.00	27.50	30.00	35.00	65.00	735.
1820 Sm. Dt.	751,122	27.50	35.00	40.00	50.00	85.00	800.
1820 Lg. Dt.	Inc. Ab.	27.50	35.00	40.00	50.00	85.00	750.
1820/19	Inc. Ab.	22.00	27.50	35.00	40.00	75.00	750.
1821	1,305,797	22.00	27.50	30.00	35.00	60.00	650.
1822	1,559,573	22.00	27.50	30.00	35.00	60.00	700.
1822/1	Inc. Ab.	30.00	45.00	57.50	85.00	125.	800.
1823	1,694,200	22.00	27.50	30.00	35.00	60.00	735.
1823 Broken 3	Inc. Ab.	27.50	42.50	60.00	75.00	125.	850.
1823 Patched 3	Inc. Ab.	22.00	30.00	35.00	40.00	75.00	850.
1823 Ugly 3	Inc. Ab.	22.00	27.50	30.00	35.00	75.00	800.
1824	3,504,954	20.00	25.00	27.00	30.00	60.00	700.
1824/21	Inc. Ab.	27.00	27.50	30.00	35.00	60.00	800.
1824/Over Various Dates							
	Inc. Ab.	20.00	25.00	27.00	35.00	60.00	800.
1825	2,943,166	20.00	25.00	27.00	30.00	60.00	685.
1826	4,004,180	20.00	25.00	27.00	30.00	60.00	685.

Date	Mintage	G-4	VG-8	F-12	VF-20	XF-40	MS-60
1827 Curled 2	5,493,400	22.00	27.50	30.00	35.00	60.00	700.
1827 Square 2	Inc. Ab.	20.00	25.00	27.00	30.00	60.00	685.
1827/6	Inc. Ab.	20.00	25.00	27.00	30.00	60.00	700.
1828 Curled Base 2, No Knob	3,075,200	20.00	25.00	27.00	30.00	60.00	700.
1828 Curled Base 2, Knobbed 2	Inc. Ab.	30.00	40.00	50.00	75.00	125.	735.
1828 Small 8'S, Square Base 2, Large Letters	Inc. Ab.	20.00	25.00	27.00	30.00	60.00	685.
1828 Small 8'S, Square Base 2, Small Letters	Inc. Ab.	22.00	27.50	35.00	65.00	125.	735.
1828 Large 8'S, Square Base 2	Inc. Ab.	20.00	25.00	27.00	30.00	60.00	685.
1829	3,712,156	20.00	25.00	27.00	30.00	60.00	688.
1829/27	Inc. Ab.	20.00	25.00	27.00	30.00	65.00	725.
1830 Small 0 In Date	4,764,800	20.00	25.00	27.00	30.00	60.00	665.
1830 Large 0 In Date	Inc. Ab.	20.00	25.00	27.00	30.00	60.00	665.
1831	5,873,660	20.00	25.00	27.00	30.00	60.00	665.
1832 Sm. Lt.	4,797,000	20.00	25.00	27.00	30.00	60.00	665.
1832 Lg. Let.	Inc. Ab.	20.00	25.00	27.00	30.00	60.00	665.
1833	5,206,000	20.00	25.00	27.00	30.00	60.00	665.
1834 Small Date, Large Stars, Small Letters	6,412,004	20.00	25.00	27.00	30.00	60.00	665.
1834 Small Date, Small Stars, Small Letters	Inc. Ab.	20.00	25.00	27.00	30.00	60.00	665.
1834 Large Date, Small Letters	Inc. Ab.	20.00	25.00	27.00	30.00	60.00	665.
1834 Large Date, Large Letters	Inc. Ab.	20.00	25.00	27.00	30.00	60.00	665.
1835	5,352,006	20.00	25.00	27.00	30.00	65.00	665.
1836	6,545,000	20.00	25.00	27.00	30.00	65.00	665.
1836 50/00	Inc. Ab.	30.00	40.00	50.00	65.00	140.	700.

REEDED EDGE - 50 CENTS ON REVERSE

Date	Mintage	G-4	VG-8	F-12	VF-20	XF-40	MS-60
1836	1,200	250.	350.	475.	975.	1575.	4100.
1837	3,629,820	22.50	25.00	40.00	65.00	160.	2000.

Mintmark

HALF DOL. ON REVERSE

Date	Mintage	G-4	VG-8	F-12	VF-20	XF-40	MS-60
1838	3,546,000	22.50	27.50	40.00	70.00	160.	2100.
1838O	Est. 20	—	Stack's Sale, March, 1975, Proof				50,000.
1839	3,334,560	22.50	27.50	40.00	65.00	160.	2000.
1839O	178,976	75.00	100.	170.	310.	400.	3250.

LIBERTY SEATED HALVES

The Liberty seated half dollar series followed the same course as did the quarter series of this type. The reduction of its weight from 206¼ grains to 192 in 1853 was marked by the placing of arrows at the date on the 1853-55 issues, while rays were also present on the reverse in 1853, then arrows were again used at the date in 1873-74 to mark a weight increase to 192.9 grains.

Although the 1861-O half has a total recorded mintage of 2,532,633, only a small fraction of that quantity actually constitute U.S. issues. The mint was seized by the government of secessionist Louisiana on January 31, after 330,000 halves had been struck under the U.S. government. From then until the mint was transferred to the Confederacy in April, another 1,240,000 halves are recorded as having been struck. Before the mint's operations were closed out on May 31, another 962,633 pieces were produced, plus four trial strikings of a distinctive Confederate half dollar design which was never placed in production.

Mintmark

NOTE: A $13.00 Numismatic value base has been assigned to Liberty Seated halves, (1839-53) based on the $13.00 market price for one ounce of silver at the time these valuations were assigned. The bullion value of each coin's silver content increases or decreases approximately 3.87-cents for each 10-cent change in the bullion price, or 38.67-cents for each $1 change.

Date	Mintage	G-4	VG-8	F-12	VF-20	XF-40	MS-60
1839 No Drapery From Elbow	Inc. Ab.	30.00	35.00	60.00	145.	400.	11,000.
1839 Drapery	Inc. Ab.	13.00	20.00	25.00	45.00	75.00	800.
1840 Sm. Let.	1,435,008	13.00	20.00	22.00	40.00	65.00	800.
1840 Rev. 1838	Inc. Ab.	25.00	35.00	55.00	90.00	120.	850.
1840O	855,100	13.00	20.00	22.00	45.00	80.00	850.
1841	310,000	25.00	35.00	55.00	95.00	170.	900.
1841O	401,000	13.00	20.00	30.00	55.00	100.	900.
1842 Sm. Date	2,012,764	13.00	20.00	35.00	80.00	125.	850.
1842 Lg. Date	Inc. Ab.	13.00	20.00	22.00	40.00	65.00	850.
1842O Sm. Date	957,000	225.	275.	425.	800.	2000.	—
1842O Lg. Date	Inc. Ab.	13.00	20.00	22.00	40.00	80.00	800.
1843	3,844,000	13.00	20.00	22.00	40.00	65.00	800.
1843O	2,268,000	13.00	20.00	22.00	40.00	80.00	850.
1844	1,766,000	13.00	20.00	22.00	40.00	65.00	800.
1844O	2,005,000	13.00	20.00	22.00	40.00	80.00	850.
1845	589,000	30.00	45.00	65.00	110.	190.	950.
1845O	2,094,000	13.00	22.00	25.00	50.00	100.	1100.
1845O No Drapery	Inc. Ab.	20.00	30.00	40.00	65.00	100.	875.
1846 med.date	2,210,000	13.00	20.00	22.00	40.00	65.00	800.
1846 tall date	Inc. Ab.	13.00	20.00	22.00	40.00	65.00	800.
1846 Over Horizontal 6	Inc. Ab.	35.00	50.00	75.00	125.	160.	875.
1846O med.date	2,304,000	13.00	20.00	22.00	40.00	65.00	800.
1846O tall date	Inc. Ab.	80.00	95.00	140.	270.	380.	1200.
1847/46	1,156,000	350.	500.	750.	1250.	2000.	—
1847	Inc. Ab.	13.00	20.00	22.00	40.00	65.00	800.
1847O	2,584,000	13.00	20.00	22.00	40.00	65.00	800.
1848	580,000	30.00	45.00	65.00	110.	190.	900.
1848O	3,180,000	13.00	20.00	22.00	40.00	65.00	800.
1849	1,252,000	13.00	20.00	22.00	40.00	65.00	800.
1849O	2,310,000	13.00	20.00	22.00	40.00	65.00	800.
1850	227,000	35.00	55.00	90.00	175.	280.	800.
1850O	2,456,000	13.00	20.00	23.00	45.00	80.00	800.
1851	200,750	40.00	55.00	100.	200.	325.	950.
1851O	402,000	20.00	25.00	35.00	60.00	100.	800.
1852	77,130	65.00	80.00	125.	250.	400.	1250.
1852O	144,000	30.00	35.00	50.00	90.00	150.	800.
1853O	Unrecorded		Garrett Sale, 1979, VF 40,000.				

NOTE: A $12.50 Numismatic value base has been assigned to Liberty Seated halves, (1853-73) based on the $13.00 market price for one ounce of silver at the time these valuations were assigned. The bullion value of each coin's silver content increases or decreases approximately 3.6-cents for each 10-cent change in the bullion price, or 36-cents for each $1 change.

ARROWS AT DATE

Date	Mintage	G-4	VG-8	F-12	VF-20	XF-40	MS-60	Prf-65
1853 Rays On Reverse	3,532,708	12.50	13.50	20.00	80.00	210.	4500.	—
1853O Rays On Reverse	1,328,000	12.50	13.50	20.00	80.00	210.	4500.	—
1854	2,982,000	12.50	13.50	18.50	35.00	70.00	1375.	—
1854O	5,240,000	12.50	13.50	18.50	35.00	70.00	1375.	—
1855	759,500	12.50	13.50	18.50	35.00	70.00	1400.	12,000.
1855O	3,688,000	12.50	13.50	18.50	35.00	70.00	1375.	—
1855S	129,950	125.	175.	325.	575.	1000.	2750.	—

ARROWS AT DATE REMOVED

Date	Mintage	G-4	VG-8	F-12	VF-20	XF-40	MS-60	Prf-65
1856	938,000	12.50	13.50	18.50	25.00	57.00	850.	7550.
1856O	2,658,000	12.50	13.50	18.50	25.00	57.00	850.	—
1856S	211,000	15.00	20.00	30.00	125.	275.	1200.	—
1857	1,988,000	12.50	13.50	18.50	25.00	57.00	800.	9000.
1857O	818,000	12.50	13.50	18.50	25.00	57.00	900.	—
1857S	158,000	17.50	25.00	37.50	90.00	150.	950.	—
1858	4,226,000	12.50	13.50	18.50	25.00	57.00	800.	8000.
1858O	7,294,000	12.50	13.50	18.50	25.00	57.00	800.	—
1858S	476,000	12.50	13.50	25.00	80.00	120.	950.	—
1859	748,000	12.50	13.50	18.50	25.00	57.00	800.	8000.
1859O	2,834,000	12.50	13.50	18.50	25.00	57.00	825.	—
1859S	566,000	12.50	13.50	25.00	75.00	110.	900.	—
1860	303,700	22.00	33.00	45.00	75.00	165.	850.	8000.
1860O	1,290,000	12.50	13.50	18.50	25.00	57.00	825.	—
1860S	472,000	12.50	13.50	22.50	42.00	80.00	850.	—
1861	2,888,400	12.50	13.50	18.50	25.00	57.00	800.	8000.
1861O	2,532,633	12.50	13.50	18.50	25.00	57.00	800.	—
1861S	939,500	12.50	13.50	18.50	25.00	57.00	825.	—
1862	253,550	35.00	50.00	80.00	110.	180.	900.	8000.
1862S	1,352,000	12.50	13.50	18.50	25.00	57.00	800.	—
1863	503,660	24.00	30.00	50.00	85.00	165.	900.	8000.
1863S	916,000	12.50	13.50	18.50	25.00	57.00	800.	—
1864	379,570	24.00	30.00	50.00	85.00	165.	900.	8000.
1864S	658,000	12.50	13.50	22.00	45.00	85.00	800.	—
1865	511,900	28.00	35.00	60.00	110.	170.	900.	7550.
1865S	675,000	12.50	13.50	22.00	45.00	85.00	750.	—
1866	—	—	—	—	Proof, Unique		—	
1866S	1,054,000	40.00	65.00	100.	190.	250.	850.	—

MOTTO ABOVE EAGLE

Date	Mintage	G-4	VG-8	F-12	VF-20	XF-40	MS-60	Prf-65
1866	745,625	20.00	25.00	50.00	85.00	145.	900.	7250.
1866S	Inc. Ab.	12.50	13.50	18.50	22.00	60.00	800.	—
1867	449,925	30.00	38.00	70.00	120.	175.	1100.	7250.
1867S	1,196,000	12.50	13.50	18.50	22.00	50.00	800.	—
1868	418,200	40.00	55.00	80.00	110.	190.	1000.	7250.
1868S	1,160,000	12.50	13.50	18.50	22.00	50.00	800.	—
1869	795,900	15.00	13.50	18.50	22.00	50.00	800.	7250.
1869S	656,000	17.50	18.00	22.00	40.00	85.00	800.	—
1870	634,900	17.50	18.00	22.00	40.00	85.00	800.	7250.
1870CC	54,617	225.	300.	800.	1000.	1700.	—	—
1870S	1,004,000	20.00	25.00	35.00	50.00	90.00	850.	—
1871	1,204,560	12.50	13.50	18.50	22.00	50.00	800.	7250.
1871CC	153,950	45.00	65.00	140.	235.	500.	3500.	—
1871S	2,178,000	12.50	13.50	18.50	22.00	50.00	800.	—
1872	881,550	12.50	13.50	18.50	22.00	50.00	800.	7250.
1872CC	272,000	25.00	40.00	70.00	150.	300.	1500.	—
1872S	580,000	17.50	18.00	22.00	45.00	90.00	800.	—
1873 Closed 3								
	801,800	16.50	17.50	18.50	22.00	50.00	800.	7250.
1873 Open 3								
	Inc. Ab.	40.00	60.00	100.	170.	225.	800.	—
1873CC	122,500	45.00	65.00	125.	200.	375.	1750.	—
1873S No Arrows		5,000 Minted			No Specimens Known To Survive			

NOTE: A $12.50 Numismatic value base has been assigned to Liberty Seated halves, (1873-91) based on the $13.00 market price for one ounce of silver at the time these valuations were assigned. The bullion value of each coin's silver content increases or decreases approximately 3.62-cents for each 10-cent change in the bullion price, or 36.17-cents for each $1 change.

ARROWS AT DATE

Date	Mintage	G-4	VG-8	F-12	VF-20	XF-40	MS-60	Prf-65
1873	1,815,700	17.00	25.00	32.50	75.00	155.	2100.	12,000.
1873CC	214,560	30.00	50.00	100.	140.	200.	2300.	—
1873S	233,000	20.00	27.50	40.00	75.00	160.	2100.	—
1874	2,360,300	17.00	25.00	32.50	75.00	155.	2250.	12,000.
1874CC	59,000	80.00	110.	225.	350.	675.	2500.	—
1874S	394,000	22.50	29.00	50.00	80.00	170.	2100.	—

ARROWS AT DATE REMOVED

Date	Mintage	G-4	VG-8	F-12	VF-20	XF-40	MS-60	Prf-65
1875	6,027,500	12.50	13.50	18.50	22.00	50.00	800.	7250.
1875CC	1,008,000	12.50	13.50	22.50	32.50	60.00	800.	—
1875S	3,200,000	—	15.50	18.50	22.00	50.00	800.	—
1876	8,419,150	12.50	13.50	18.50	22.00	50.00	800.	7250.
1876CC	1,956,000	17.00	18.50	22.50	32.50	60.00	800.	—
1876S	4,528,000	12.50	13.50	18.50	22.00	50.00	800.	—
1877	8,304,510	12.50	13.50	18.50	22.00	50.00	800.	7250.
1877CC	1,420,000	12.50	17.00	22.50	32.50	60.00	800.	—
1877S	5,356,000	12.50	13.50	18.50	22.00	50.00	800.	—
1878	1,378,400	12.50	13.50	18.50	22.00	50.00	800.	7250.
1878CC	62,000	175.	280.	390.	525.	875.	3000.	—
1878S	12,000	2500.	3500.	4250.	5500.	7000.	14,000.	—

Date	Mintage	G-4	VG-8	F-12	VF-20	XF-40	MS-60	Prf-65
1879	5,900	100.	110.	125.	175.	250.	1000.	7250.
1880	9,755	85.00	95.00	110.	150.	200.	1000.	7250.
1881	10,975	80.00	90.00	105.	140.	180.	1000.	7250.
1882	5,500	100.	110.	125.	175.	250.	1000.	7250.
1883	9,039	85.00	95.00	110.	150.	200.	1000.	7250.
1884	5,275	100.	110.	125.	175.	250.	1000.	7250.
1885	6,130	95.00	105.	120.	170.	240.	1000.	7250.
1886	5,886	100.	110.	125.	175.	250.	1000.	7250.
1887	5,710	100.	110.	125.	175.	250.	1000.	7250.
1888	12,833	80.00	90.00	105.	140.	175.	1000.	7250.
1889	12,711	80.00	90.00	105.	140.	175.	1000.	7250.
1890	12,590	80.00	90.00	105.	140.	175.	1000.	7250.
1891	200,600	15.50	17.00	25.00	40.00	75.00	800.	7250.

BARBER HALVES

The Barber half is identical in design to the quarter, and was issued over the same period of time as it and the dime, excepting that none were minted in 1916.

Mintmark

NOTE: A $ 9.00 Numismatic value base has been assigned to Barber halves, based on the $13.00 market price for one ounce of silver at the time these valuations were assigned. The bullion value of each coin's silver content increases or decreases approximately 3.62-cents for each 10-cent change in the bullion price, or 36.17-cents for each $1 change.

Date	Mintage	G-4	VG-8	F-12	VF-20	XF-40	AU-50	MS-60	MS-65	Prf-65
1892	935,245	15.00	17.00	37.00	73.00	165.	250.	950.	6300.	6900.
1892O	390,000	105.	125.	175.	225.	300.	500.	1900.	6800.	—
1892S	1,029,028	90.00	110.	150.	200.	265.	450.	1700.	8000.	—
1893	1,826,792	13.50	15.00	39.00	75.00	175.	260.	900.	6300.	6900.
1893O	1,389,000	17.00	25.00	47.00	85.00	200.	300.	1400.	9800.	—
1893S	740,000	62.00	90.00	135.	190.	250.	375.	1600.	9800.	—
1894	1,148,972	10.50	13.50	38.00	74.00	175.	260.	1000.	6300.	6900.
1894O	2,138,000	13.50	15.00	41.00	77.00	180.	270.	1200.	9000.	—
1894S	4,048,690	10.50	13.50	26.00	62.00	150.	250.	1075.	8500.	—
1895	1,835,218	10.50	13.50	31.00	67.00	165.	250.	1075.	800.	6900.
1895O	1,766,000	10.50	13.50	38.00	72.00	170.	260.	1400.	9500.	—
1895S	1,108,086	17.00	26.00	48.00	90.00	190.	275.	1000.	7200.	—
1896	950,762	17.00	17.50	40.00	84.00	180.	265.	1100.	7000.	6900.
1896O	924,000	13.50	24.00	44.00	95.00	200.	280.	2900.	12,000.	—
1896S	1,140,948	50.00	70.00	95.00	145.	225.	350.	2900.	12,000.	—
1897	2,480,731	9.00	10.50	19.00	60.00	145.	250.	900.	6300.	6900.
1897O	632,000	50.00	70.00	88.00	144.	210.	600.	3500.	16,000.	—
1897S	933,900	60.00	80.00	110.	165.	235.	360.	2500.	14,500.	—
1898	2,956,735	8.00	10.50	19.00	55.00	130.	250.	900.	7500.	6900.
1898O	874,000	17.00	25.00	50.00	115.	250.	400.	1700.	11,000.	—
1898S	2,358,550	9.00	10.50	26.00	58.00	135.	260.	1400.	9800.	—
1899	5,538,846	9.00	10.50	18.00	55.00	130.	250.	900.	6300.	6900.
1899O	1,724,000	9.00	10.50	30.00	65.00	145.	260.	1575.	10,500.	—
1899S	1,686,411	9.00	10.50	25.00	60.00	135.	260.	1150.	7400.	—
1900	4,762,912	9.00	10.50	17.50	55.00	130.	250.	900.	6300.	6900.
1900O	2,744,000	9.00	10.50	19.00	57.00	135.	260.	1900.	14,000.	—
1900S	2,560,322	9.00	13.50	20.00	56.00	125.	250.	1300.	9800.	—
1901	4,268,813	9.00	10.50	18.00	56.00	130.	250.	900.	6300.	6900.
1901O	1,124,000	9.00	10.50	26.00	74.00	195.	325.	2200.	13,000.	—
1901S	847,044	17.00	18.00	50.00	120.	290.	600.	2800.	13,000.	—
1902	4,922,777	9.00	10.50	17.00	55.00	125.	250.	900.	6300.	6900.
1902O	2,526,000	9.00	10.50	18.00	57.00	130.	260.	1600.	12,500.	—
1902S	1,460,670	9.00	10.50	21.00	60.00	145.	275.	1600.	9800.	—
1903	2,278,755	9.00	10.50	20.00	59.00	142.	265.	900.	6300.	6900.
1903O	2,100,000	9.00	10.50	23.00	65.00	155.	275.	1600.	9500.	—
1903S	1,920,772	9.00	10.50	19.00	58.00	140.	260.	1450.	9200.	—
1904	2,992,670	9.00	10.50	17.50	55.00	125.	250.	900.	6300.	6900.
1904O	1,117,600	9.00	10.50	30.00	75.00	200.	300.	2800.	16,000.	—
1904S	553,038	13.50	18.00	46.00	93.00	210.	375.	2300.	13,000.	—
1905	662,727	10.00	13.50	41.00	82.00	195.	340.	1500.	8600.	6900.
1905O	505,000	13.50	18.00	45.00	92.00	200.	365.	1800.	9500.	—
1905S	2,494,000	9.00	10.50	17.50	55.00	130.	250.	1500.	9600.	—
1906	2,638,675	9.00	10.50	17.00	53.00	120.	245.	900.	6300.	6900.
1906D	4,028,000	9.00	10.50	17.00	54.00	122.	250.	950.	6300.	—
1906O	2,446,000	9.00	10.50	17.00	54.00	122.	250.	1300.	7500.	—
1906S	1,740,154	9.00	10.50	20.00	57.00	130.	260.	1200.	7600.	—
1907	2,598,575	9.00	10.50	17.00	54.00	125.	250.	900.	6300.	6900.
1907D	3,856,000	9.00	10.50	17.00	54.00	125.	250.	950.	6300.	—
1907O	3,946,000	9.00	10.50	17.00	54.00	125.	250.	1100.	7200.	—
1907S	1,250,000	9.00	10.50	17.00	56.00	130.	260.	1600.	8500.	—
1908	1,354,545	9.00	10.50	22.00	61.00	145.	275.	900.	6300.	6900.
1908D	3,280,000	9.00	10.50	17.00	53.00	120.	240.	950.	6300.	—
1908O	5,360,000	9.00	10.50	17.00	53.00	120.	240.	950.	6300.	—
1908S	1,644,828	9.00	10.50	17.00	55.00	125.	250.	1200.	7200.	—
1909	2,368,650	9.00	10.50	17.00	53.00	120.	240.	900.	6300.	6900.

Date	Mintage	G-4	VG-8	F-12	VF-20	XF-40	AU-50	MS-60	MS-65	Prf-65
1908O	5,360,000	9.00	10.50	17.00	53.00	120.	240.	950.	6300.	—
1908S	1,644,828	9.00	10.50	17.00	55.00	125.	250.	1200.	7200.	—
1909	2,368,650	9.00	10.50	17.00	53.00	120.	240.	900.	6300.	6900.
1909O	925,400	11.00	17.00	19.00	60.00	145.	275.	1850.	9500.	—
1909S	1,764,000	9.00	10.50	17.00	53.00	120.	240.	1300.	8200.	—
1910	418,551	11.00	17.00	32.00	80.00	210.	375.	1500.	7700.	6900.
1910S	1,948,000	9.00	10.50	17.00	55.00	125.	250.	1425.	7900.	—
1911	1,406,543	9.00	10.50	17.00	55.00	125.	250.	900.	6300.	6900.
1911D	695,080	11.00	17.00	19.00	60.00	150.	275.	950.	6300.	—
1911S	1,272,000	9.00	10.50	17.00	55.00	125.	250.	1075.	7700.	—
1912	1,550,700	9.00	10.50	17.00	55.00	125.	250.	900.	6300.	6900.
1912D	2,300,800	9.00	10.50	17.00	53.00	120.	240.	875.	6300.	—
1912S	1,370,000	9.00	10.50	17.00	55.00	125.	250.	1100.	7700.	—
1913	188,627	17.00	22.00	50.00	125.	250.	400.	1800.	8800.	6900.
1913D	534,000	11.00	17.00	24.00	68.00	160.	285.	1100.	6300.	—
1913S	604,000	11.00	17.00	21.00	60.00	145.	265.	1400.	8000.	—
1914	124,610	25.00	32.00	65.00	140.	275.	450.	1850.	7900.	7500.
1914S	992,000	9.00	10.50	17.00	55.00	130.	260.	1300.	7700.	—
1915	138,450	20.00	25.00	55.00	125.	250.	425.	1650.	8500.	7500.
1915D	1,170,400	9.00	10.50	17.00	53.00	120.	240.	875.	6300.	—
1915S	1,604,000	9.00	10.50	17.00	53.00	120.	240.	950.	7200.	—

WALKING LIBERTY HALVES

Designed, like the new dime introduced in 1916, by A. A. Weinman, whose monogram appears near the rim beneath the eagle's tail feathers on the reverse, this coin expresses the bold character of America in the early 1900s.

Mintmarks

NOTE: A $8.00 Numismatic value base has been assigned to Walking Liberty halves, based on the $13.00 market price for one ounce of silver at the time these valuations were assigned. The bullion value of each coin's silver content increases or decreases approximately 3.62-cents for each 10-cent change in the bullion price, or 36.17-cents for each $1 change.

MINT MARK ON OBVERSE

Date	Mintage	G-4	VG-8	F-12	VF-20	XF-40	AU-50	MS-60	MS-65	Prf-65
1916	608,000	19.00	22.00	45.00	85.00	155.	250.	575.	2500.	—
1916D	1,014,400	16.00	18.00	22.00	53.00	115.	185.	500.	2400.	—
1916S	508,000	27.00	37.00	90.00	200.	330.	500.	1150.	4750.	—
1917D	765,400	12.00	15.00	26.00	70.00	145.	275.	625.	3125.	—
1917S	952,000	12.50	16.00	30.00	120.	310.	535.	1600.	7000.	—

MINT MARK ON REVERSE

Date	Mintage	G-4	VG-8	F-12	VF-20	XF-40	AU-50	MS-60	MS-65	Prf-65
1917	12,292,000	8.25	9.00	13.00	20.00	35.00	75.00	250.	875.	—
1917D	1,940,000	9.00	14.00	18.00	50.00	140.	285.	775.	4150.	—
1917S	5,554,000	8.75	9.75	16.00	24.00	50.00	110.	375.	3150.	—
1918	6,634,000	9.00	10.00	18.00	45.00	135.	275.	545.	2750.	—
1918D	3,853,040	9.00	14.00	18.00	50.00	160.	325.	1400.	8100.	—
1918S	10,282,000	9.00	10.50	16.00	28.00	50.00	110.	425.	3150.	—
1919	962,000	12.00	15.00	27.00	100.	350.	580.	1500.	5600.	—
1919D	1,165,000	11.00	15.00	29.00	130.	390.	790.	3400.	16,000.	—
1919S	1,552,000	10.00	15.00	24.00	90.00	365.	850.	3150.	20,000.	—
1920	6,372,000	8.50	9.50	15.00	21.00	52.00	105.	310.	1475.	—
1920D	1,551,000	9.50	15.00	21.00	100.	240.	560.	2000.	8350.	—
1920S	4,624,000	8.75	11.00	17.00	40.00	115.	375.	1675.	5250.	—
1921	246,000	60.00	70.00	135.	375.	850.	1600.	3100.	8500.	—
1921D	208,000	85.00	110.	185.	390.	1050.	1700.	3400.	10,350.	—
1921S	548,000	16.00	19.00	35.00	190.	1400.	4600.	15,000.	32,500.	—
1923S	2,178,000	10.00	12.00	17.00	40.00	150.	390.	1700.	9000.	—
1927S	2,392,000	8.25	9.75	14.00	25.00	85.00	245.	1200.	6450.	—
1928S	1,940,000	9.00	10.50	15.00	30.00	100.	280.	1400.	8650.	—
1929D	1,001,200	10.00	11.00	13.00	20.00	70.00	150.	515.	2650.	—
1929S	1,902,000	9.00	10.00	13.00	19.00	65.00	150.	515.	2800.	—
1933S	1,786,000	8.00	8.50	9.25	20.00	50.00	175.	575.	2875.	—
1934	6,964,000	8.00	8.50	9.00	9.25	19.00	45.00	165.	550.	—
1934D	2,361,400	8.00	8.50	9.00	9.25	44.00	105.	335.	1125.	—
1934S	3,652,000	8.00	8.50	9.00	9.25	26.00	100.	535.	2050.	—
1935	9,162,000	8.00	8.50	9.00	9.25	18.00	28.00	80.00	275.	—
1935D	3,003,800	8.00	8.50	9.00	9.25	45.00	100.	340.	1100.	—
1935S	3,854,000	8.00	8.50	9.00	9.25	35.00	100.	415.	1250.	—

Date	Mintage	G-4	VG-8	F-12	VF-20	XF-40	AU-50	MS-60	MS-65	Prf-65
1936	12,617,901	8.00	8.50	9.00	9.25	18.00	30.00	80.00	275.	3000.
1936D	4,252,400	8.00	8.50	9.00	9.25	31.00	60.00	265.	775.	—
1936S	3,884,000	8.00	8.50	9.00	9.25	34.00	65.00	300.	960.	—
1937	9,527,728	8.00	8.50	9.00	9.25	18.00	31.00	80.00	275.	2000.
1937D	1,676,000	8.00	8.50	9.00	9.25	48.00	115.	400.	1100.	—
1937S	2,090,000	8.00	8.50	9.00	9.25	35.00	85.00	315.	1000.	—
1938	4,118,152	8.00	8.50	9.00	9.25	19.00	46.00	250.	825.	1725.
1938D	491,600	25.00	26.00	28.00	40.00	95.00	275.	800.	4025.	—
1939	6,820,808	8.00	8.50	9.00	9.25	18.00	30.00	90.00	350.	1575.
1939D	4,267,800	8.00	8.50	9.00	9.25	19.00	35.00	155.	550.	—
1939S	2,552,000	8.00	8.50	9.00	9.25	21.00	57.00	275.	975.	—
1940	9,167,279	8.00	8.50	9.00	9.25	19.00	28.00	80.00	280.	1200.
1940S	4,550,000	8.00	8.50	9.00	9.25	20.00	33.00	275.	750.	—
1941	24,207,412	8.00	8.50	9.00	9.25	12.50	19.00	80.00	235.	1100.
1941D	11,248,400	8.00	8.50	9.00	9.25	12.50	34.00	120.	385.	—
1941S	8,098,000	8.00	8.50	9.00	9.25	12.50	59.00	350.	600.	—
1942	47,839,120	8.00	8.50	9.00	9.25	12.50	19.00	80.00	235.	1100.
1942D	10,973,800	8.00	8.50	9.00	9.25	12.50	30.00	110.	375.	—
1942S	12,708,000	8.00	8.50	9.00	9.25	12.50	48.00	300.	475.	—
1943	53,190,000	8.00	8.50	9.00	9.25	12.50	19.00	80.00	235.	—
1943D	11,346,000	8.00	8.50	9.00	9.25	12.50	32.00	110.	400.	—
1943S	13,450,000	8.00	8.50	9.00	9.25	12.50	43.00	275.	450.	—
1944	28,206,000	8.00	8.50	9.00	9.25	12.50	19.00	80.00	235.	—
1944D	9,769,000	8.00	8.50	9.00	9.25	12.50	30.00	110.	375.	—
1944S	8,904,000	8.00	8.50	9.00	9.25	12.50	40.00	275.	425.	—
1945	31,502,000	8.00	8.50	9.00	9.25	12.50	19.00	80.00	235.	—
1945D	9,966,800	8.00	8.50	9.00	9.25	12.50	29.00	110.	375.	—
1945S	10,156,000	8.00	8.50	9.00	9.25	12.50	35.00	275.	410.	—
1946	12,118,000	8.00	8.50	9.00	9.25	12.50	23.00	85.00	275.	—
1946D	2,151,000	8.00	8.50	9.00	9.25	12.50	60.00	175.	330.	—
1946S	3,724,000	8.00	8.50	9.00	9.25	12.50	38.00	275.	515.	—
1947	4,094,000	8.00	8.50	9.00	9.25	12.50	41.00	135.	390.	—
1947D	3,900,600	8.00	8.50	9.00	9.25	12.50	36.00	115.	370.	—

FRANKLIN HALVES

The Franklin half, with its Liberty bell reverse reminiscent of the design carried on the sesquicentennial commemorative half of 1926, was designed by then chief mint engraver John R. Sinnock, whose initials appear on the truncation of the bust. The series was ended prematurely in 1963 when Congress called for a switch to an issue honoring President John F. Kennedy who was assassinated on November 22, 1963.

Mintmark

NOTE: A $8.00 Numismatic value base has been assigned to Franklin halves, based on the $13.00 market price for one ounce of silver at the time these valuations were assigned. The bullion value of each coin's silver content increases or decreases approximately 3.62-cents for each 10-cent change in the bullion price; or 36.17-cents for each $1 change.

Date	Mintage	G-4	VG-8	F-12	VF-20	XF-40	AU-50	MS-60	MS-65	Prf-65
1948	3,006,814	—	—	—	—	—	8.00	22.00	60.00	—
1948D	4,028,600	—	—	—	—	—	8.00	20.00	41.00	—
1949	5,614,000	—	—	—	—	—	12.50	50.00	150.	—
1949D	4,120,600	—	—	—	—	—	19.00	50.00	145.	—
1949S	3,744,000	—	—	—	—	—	70.00	225.	500.	—
1950	7,793,509	—	—	—	—	—	8.00	30.00	92.00	525.
1950D	8,031,600	—	—	—	—	—	8.00	22.00	72.00	—
1951	16,859,602	—	—	—	—	—	8.00	16.50	26.00	425.
1951D	9,475,200	—	—	—	—	—	8.00	40.00	135.	—
1951S	13,696,000	—	—	—	—	—	8.00	25.00	100.	—
1952	21,274,073	—	—	—	—	—	8.00	18.00	27.00	250.
1952D	25,395,600	—	—	—	—	—	8.00	18.00	39.00	—
1952S	5,526,000	—	—	—	—	—	8.00	35.00	85.00	—
1953	2,796,920	—	—	—	—	—	8.00	22.50	51.00	140.
1953D	20,900,400	—	—	—	—	—	8.00	16.50	24.00	—
1953S	4,148,000	—	—	—	—	—	8.00	22.50	48.00	—
1954	13,421,503	—	—	—	—	—	8.00	14.00	18.00	80.00
1954D	25,445,580	—	—	—	—	—	8.00	16.50	20.00	—
1954S	4,993,400	—	—	—	—	—	8.00	16.50	27.00	—
1955	2,876,381	—	—	—	—	—	8.00	20.00	33.00	70.00
1956	4,701,384	—	—	—	—	—	8.00	14.50	19.50	20.00
1957	6,361,952	—	—	—	—	—	8.00	16.50	19.00	13.50
1957D	19,966,850	—	—	—	—	—	8.00	12.00	15.00	—
1958	4,917,652	—	—	—	—	—	8.00	14.00	21.00	16.00
1958D	23,962,412	—	—	—	—	—	8.00	10.00	12.50	—

Date	Mintage	G-4	VG-8	F-12	VF-20	XF-40	AU-50	MS-60	MS-65	Prf-65
1959	7,349,291	—	—	—	—	—	8.00	14.00	17.00	9.00
1959D	13,053,750	—	—	—	—	—	8.00	14.00	17.00	—
1960	7,715,602	—	—	—	—	—	8.00	9.50	17.00	9.00
1960D	18,215,812	—	—	—	—	—	8.00	9.50	17.00	—
1961	11,318,244	—	—	—	—	—	8.00	9.50	11.50	9.00
1961D	20,276,442	—	—	—	—	—	8.00	9.50	10.00	—
1962	12,932,019	—	—	—	—	—	8.00	9.50	11.00	9.00
1962D	35,473,281	—	—	—	—	—	8.00	9.50	11.00	—
1963	25,239,645	—	—	—	—	—	8.00	9.50	10.00	9.00
1963D	67,069,292	—	—	—	—	—	8.00	9.50	10.00	—

KENNEDY HALVES

This young series already has an interesting history. Thus far it has been issued in three metal varieties — .900 fine silver in 1964, .400 clad silver from 1965 through 1970, and cupro-nickel clad copper commencing 1971 — and with mint marks on both the reverse (1964) and the obverse (from 1968). It also offers a 1970-D issue produced only to satisfy the collector set demand. Still, in just eight years of issue the quantity minted has exceeded the total combined production for the previous 170 years. The obverse for the coin was designed by Gilroy Roberts, whose stylized initials appear on the base of the bust, and the reverse by Frank Gasparro, whose initials appear beneath the eagle's left leg.

MINTMARKS

NOTE: A $8.00 Numismatic value base has been assigned to 1964 dated Kennedy halves, $3.75 for issues dated 1965 through 1970, based on the $13.00 market price for one ounce of silver at the time these valuations were assigned. The bullion value of each 1964 dated coin's silver content increases or decreases approximately 3.62-cents for each 10-cent change in the bullion price, or 36.17 cents for each $1 change; for later dates the movement is approximately 1.48-cents per 10-cents, or 14.79-cents per $1 change.

Date	Mintage	G-4	VG-8	F-12	VF-20	XF-40	MS-60	MS-65	Prf-65
1964	277,254,766	—	—	—	—	—	9.50	10.00	9.00
1964D	156,205,446	—	—	—	—	—	9.50	10.00	—
1965	65,879,366	—	—	—	—	—	3.75	4.50	—
1966	108,984,932	—	—	—	—	—	3.75	4.50	—
1967	295,046,978	—	—	—	—	—	3.75	4.50	—
1968D	246,951,930	—	—	—	—	—	3.00	3.75	—
1968S	3,041,506	—	—	—	—	—	—	—	4.00
1969D	129,881,800	—	—	—	—	—	3.00	3.75	—
1969S	2,934,631	—	—	—	—	—	—	—	4.00
1970D	2,150,000	—	—	—	—	—	45.00	54.00	—
1970S	2,632,810	—	—	—	—	—	—	—	10.00

Commencing 1971 - See Modern Singles - Page 1897

SILVER DOLLARS

The silver dollar provided the base from which all other coins in the nation's currency system, as established by the act of April 2, 1792, was calculated, with gold coins provided for on a ratio of 15 to 1 from this standard. In name, our dollar's origins can be traced to the early 1500s when the first large silver coins — Joachimstalers — were produced in Germany, while it was patterned after the Spanish milled dollar which predominated in the Western Hemisphere in the late 1700s.

The pure silver weight of the dollar coin was set at slightly more that 371 grains, with the total weight of the .8924 fine coin being 420 grains, or approximately the same as the prevalent standard for the Spanish milled dollar of the day. There was, however, enough of a differential to provide for a profitable trade in the export of U.S. silver dollars in favor of Spanish dollars, which could be turned into the mint for recoining at a profit.

This situation ultimately led to the suspension of silver dollar mintage in just ten years persuant to an order issued by President Thomas Jefferson on March 28, 1804. Prior to that time a quantity of 19,570 dollars had been struck using 1803 dies, but none dated 1804. The use of dies dated for the previous year early in the following year was a common practice at the time, as all dies were used until they were no longer serviceable.

Dollars dated 1804 do exist, however, there being a total of 15 known in three varieties. The first known specimen to surface was obtained from the mint by Matthew Stickney in 1843 in exchange for a coin needed for the mint cabinet. This was one of eight so-called "originals" produced in 1834-35 to insert in special presentation proof sets which had been requested by the Secretary of State. The seven so-called "restrikes," six of one variety and one of another, were produced around 1859 by mint officials intent on serving the needs of collectors who wanted specimens of the coin.

Flowing Hair Silver Dollars

Date	Mintage	G-4	VG-8	F-12	VF-20	XF-40	MS-60
1794	1,758	3500.	5500.	7500.	13,500.	17,500.	—
			Keisberg Auction Oct., 1978				57,500.
1795 2 Leaves	203,033	1100.	1400.	1950.	3450.	7400.	30,000.
1795 3 Leaves	Inc. Ab.	1100.	1400.	1950.	3450.	7400.	30,000.

Draped Bust Silver Dollars

SMALL EAGLE

Date	Mintage	G-4	VG-8	F-12	VF-20	XF-40	MS-60
1795	Inc. Ab.	900.	1400.	1600.	2500.	4100.	27,500.
1796 Small Date, Small Letters	72,920	800.	1300.	1475.	2300.	4000.	23,000.
1796 Small Date, Large Letters	Inc. Ab.	800.	1300.	1475.	2300.	4000.	23,000.
1796 Large Date, Small Letters	Inc. Ab.	800.	1300.	1475.	2300.	4000.	23,000.
1797 9 Stars Left, 7 Stars Right, Small Letters	7,776	900.	1400.	1600.	2500.	4100.	27,500.
1797 9 Stars Left, 7 Stars Right, Large Letters	Inc. Ab.	850.	1400.	1600.	2500.	4100.	25,000.
1797 10 Stars Left, 6 Stars Right	Inc. Ab.	850.	1400.	1475.	2300.	4000.	25,000.
1798 13 Stars	327,536	800.	1300.	1475.	2300.	4000.	23,000.
1798 15 Stars	Inc. Ab.	900.	1500.	1700.	2600.	4200.	23,000.

Heraldic Eagle

Date	Mintage	G-4	VG-8	F-12	VF-20	XF-40	MS-60
1798 Knob 9	Inc. Ab.	300.	375.	550.	700.	1250.	12,500.
1798 10 Arrows	Inc. Ab.	300.	375.	550.	700.	1200.	12,500.
1798 4 Berries	Inc. Ab.	300.	375.	550.	700.	1250.	12,500.
1798 5 Berries, 12 Arrows	Inc. Ab.	300.	375.	550.	700.	1250.	12,500.
1798 High 8	Inc. Ab.	300.	375.	550.	700.	1250.	12,500.
1798 13 Arrows	Inc. Ab.	300.	375.	550.	700.	1250.	12,500.
1799/98 13 Star Reverse	423,515	300.	375.	550.	700.	1250.	15,000.
1799/98 15 Star Reverse	Inc. Ab.	300.	375.	550.	700.	1250.	15,000.
1799 Irregular Date, 13 Star Reverse	Inc. Ab.	300.	375.	550.	700.	1225.	12,500.
1799 Irregular Date, 15 Star Reverse	Inc. Ab.	300.	375.	550.	700.	1225.	12,500.
1799 Perfect Date, 7 And 6 Star Obverse, No Berries	Inc. Ab.	300.	375.	550.	700.	1225.	12,500.
1799 Perfect Date, 7 And 6 Star Obverse, Small Berries	Inc. Ab.	300.	375.	550.	700.	1225.	12,500.
1799 Perfect Date, 7 And 6 Star Obverse, Medium Large Berries	Inc. Ab.	300.	375.	550.	700.	1225.	12,500.
1799 Perfect Date, 7 And 6 Star Obverse, Extra Large Berries	Inc. Ab.	300.	375.	550.	700.	1225.	12,500.
1799 8 Stars Left, 5 Stars Right On Obverse	Inc. Ab.	300.	375.	550.	700.	1225.	12,500.
1800 Liberty "R" Double Cut	220,920	300.	375.	550.	700.	1225.	12,500.
1800 States First "T" Double Cut	Inc. Ab.	300.	375.	550.	700.	1225.	12,500.
1800 Both Letters Double Cut	Inc. Ab.	300.	375.	550.	700.	1225.	12,500.
1800 United, "T" Double Cut	Inc. Ab.	300.	375.	550.	700.	1225.	12,500.
1800 Very Wide Date, Low 8	Inc. Ab.	300.	375.	550.	700.	1225.	12,500.
1800 Sm. Berries	Inc. Ab.	300.	375.	550.	700.	1225.	12,500.
1800 Dot Date	Inc. Ab.	300.	375.	550.	700.	1225.	12,500.
1800 12 Arrows	Inc. Ab.	300.	375.	550.	700.	1225.	12,500.
1800 10 Arrows	Inc. Ab.	300.	375.	550.	700.	1250.	12,500.
1800 "Americai"	Inc. Ab.	300.	375.	550.	700.	1250.	12,500.
1801	54,454	300.	375.	550.	700.	1250.	12,500.
1801	(Unrecorded)	Proof Restrike - Rare					
1802/1 Close	1250.	300.	375.	550.	700.	1200.	12,500.
1802/1 Wide	1250.	300.	375.	550.	700.	1200.	12,500.
1802 Close, Perfect Date	Inc. Ab.	300.	375.	550.	700.	1250.	12,500.
1802 Wide, Perfect Date	Inc. Ab.	300.	375.	550.	700.	1250.	12,500.
1802	(Unrecorded)	Proof Restrike - Rare					
1803 Lg. 3	85,634	300.	375.	550.	700.	1250.	12,500.
1803 Sm. 3	Inc. Ab.	300.	375.	550.	700.	1250.	12,500.
1803	(Unrecorded)	Proof Restrike - Rare					
1804	15 Known	3 Varieties. Private Sale, 1979 200,000.					

GOBRECHT PATTERNS

In anticipation of a reduction in standard for the silver dollar which would allow its reintroduction, as a similar move in 1834 had allowed the Mint to reintroduce the production of gold coins which would circulate, officials sanctioned the development of patterns for the issue. The preparation of the new designs was placed in the hands of Christian Gobrecht, who engraved the work of artists Thomas Sully (obverse) and Titian Peale (reverse).

Several patterns dated 1836 were prepared from Gobrecht's designs, in silver and copper, plain and reeded edges, with the engravers name both on and below the base of Liberty, and with the eagle both in a field of stars and plain, only one of which is normally encountered. About 1,000 examples in silver, plain edge, Gobrecht on base and with the eagle in a field of stars were struck. Several similar patterns were again prepared in 1838 and 1839 with an arc of 13 stars added to the obverse and the engravers name removed. These obverse designs are the same as were adopted for the other silver values in 1837 without the stars, and revised with stars added in 1838.

Date	Mintage	VF-20	XF-40	Proof
1836 No Stars Obverse	Est. 1000	1600.	2800.	5800.
1838 No Stars Reverse	Est. 25 (Proof Only)	2750.	2950.	7100.
1839 No Stars Reverse	Est. 300 (Proof Only)	2250.	2450.	6400.

LIBERTY SEATED DOLLARS

With the lawful content of the silver having been reduced to 412½ grains from 416, in raising the fineness to .900 to facilitate fabrication, by the new coinage law of January 18, 1837, the minting of the dollar was renewed in 1840. Production of the coin remained nominal, however, until its issue was discontinued by the coinage law of February 12, 1873, in part because enactment of the February 21, 1853, law which reduced the relative bullion contents of the fractional silver issues left the dollar, at 412½ grains, worth more than its face value.

NO MOTTO

Date	Mintage	G-4	VG-8	F-12	VF-20	XF-40	MS-60	MS-65	Prf-65
1840	61,005	95.00	110.	140.	175.	250.	1700.	—	—
1841	173,000	70.00	75.00	115.	140.	190.	1750.	6300.	—
1842	184,618	70.00	75.00	115.	140.	190.	1700.	6300.	—
1843	165,100	70.00	75.00	115.	140.	190.	1700.	6300.	—
1844	20,000	130.	155.	180.	200.	350.	1800.	—	—
1845	24,500	120.	150.	180.	200.	325.	1800.	—	—
1846	110,600	75.00	80.00	115.	140.	190.	1750.	6300.	—
1846O	59,000	110.	130.	160.	225.	400.	—	—	—
1847	140,750	75.00	80.00	115.	140.	190.	1750.	6300.	—
1848	15,000	105.	115.	150.	200.	290.	1800.	6500.	—
1849	62,600	85.00	98.00	115.	140.	200.	1750.	6300.	—
1850	7,500	150.	170.	225.	275.	400.	1700.	—	—
1850O	40,000	130.	160.	200.	350.	800.	3500.	—	—
1851	1,300	—	—	—	Rare	—	—	—	—
1852	1,100	—	—	—	Rare	—	—	—	—
1853	46,110	100.	110.	125.	160.	220.	1750.	—	—
1854	33,140	125.	160.	225.	300.	650.	1750.	—	—
1855	26,000	200.	275.	350.	450.	650.	1900.	—	15,000.
1856	63,500	125.	140.	190.	240.	350.	1800.	—	12,000.
1857	94,000	115.	130.	160.	210.	290.	1700.	—	12,000.
1858	Est. 80	—	—	—	Proof	Only	—	—	12,000.
	Impaired Proof		1600.	1850.	2150.	2750.	—	—	—
1859	256,500	90.00	100.	125.	150.	200.	1700.	6300.	12,000.
1859O	360,000	70.00	75.00	115.	140.	190.	1700.	6300.	—
1859S	20,000	115.	135.	170.	250.	450.	—	—	—
1860	218,930	90.00	100.	125.	150.	225.	1700.	6300.	12,000.
1860O	515,000	65.00	70.00	115.	140.	190.	1700.	6300.	—
1861	78,500	85.00	95.00	125.	150.	190.	1750.	6500.	12,000.
1862	12,090	220.	275.	375.	525.	700.	2200.	—	12,000.
1863	27,660	125.	150.	180.	240.	475.	1900.	6300.	12,000.
1864	31,170	125.	150.	180.	240.	450.	1700.	6300.	12,000.
1865	47,000	120.	140.	170.	225.	325.	1750.	6300.	12,000.
1866	Only 2 Known Without Motto								

Mintmark

MOTTO ADDED ON REVERSE

Date	Mintage	G-4	VG-8	F-12	VF-20	XF-40	MS-60	MS-65	Prf-65
1866	49,625	120.	140.	170.	225.	300.	1800.	6300.	12,000.
1867	47,525	110.	125.	160.	195.	260.	1800.	6300.	12,000.
1868	162,700	95.00	110.	130.	160.	200.	1700.	6300.	12,000.
1869	424,300	80.00	90.00	120.	140.	185.	1700.	6300.	12,000.
1870	416,000	80.00	90.00	120.	140.	185.	1700.	6300.	12,000.
1870CC	12,462	125.	150.	225.	300.	500.	2100.	—	—
1870S	Unrecorded		Aug. 1978 ANA Sale			VF 39,000.		—	—
1871	1,074,760	65.00	70.00	120.	140.	185.	1700.	6300.	12,000.
1871CC	1,376	400.	500.	750.	1000.	1400.	6000.	—	—
1872	1,106,450	65.00	70.00	120.	140.	185.	1700.	6300.	12,000.
1872CC	3,150	225.	275.	375.	500.	700.	3200.	—	—
1872S	9,000	90.00	110.	200.	325.	700.	2750.	—	—
1873	293,600	70.00	75.00	120.	140.	185.	1700.	6300.	12,000.
1873CC	2,300	500.	600.	900.	1100.	1700.	7500.	—	—
1873S	700				Unknown			—	—

TRADE DOLLARS

The trade dollar is the only U.S. monetary obligation that has ever been, in effect, demonetized. Although this 420 grain, .900 fine silver coin was originally authorized by the act of February 12, 1873, to compete with other trade coins of the day in the Orient, it was also provided with legal tender status. The legal tender provision was erased by a June 22, 1876, law which restricted future production of the coin to export demand.

Enactment of the coinage act of February 28, 1878, authorizing the restoration of the standard silver dollar brought an end to the production of the trade dollar, except for proofs which were struck through 1885. An act of March 3, 1887, repealed the trade dollar provisions and provided for their redemption. Under the provisions of this law $7,689,-036 of the coins were redeemed at face value for recoinage into standard dollars and subsidiary coins, with all that remained outstanding reverting to bullion value.

Mintmark

Date	Mintage	G-4	VG-8	F-12	VF-20	XF-40	MS-60	MS-65	Prf-65
1873	397,500	45.00	55.00	60.00	75.00	95.00	850.	6900.	12,000.
1873CC	124,500	50.00	55.00	60.00	75.00	110.	900.	6900.	—
1873S	703,000	45.00	55.00	60.00	70.00	95.00	850.	6900.	—
1874	987,800	40.00	45.00	60.00	65.00	95.00	850.	6900.	12,000.
1874CC	1,373,200	50.00	55.00	60.00	75.00	100.	900.	6900.	—
1874S	2,549,000	45.00	55.00	60.00	65.00	95.00	850.	6900.	—
1875	218,900	65.00	80.00	110.	150.	250.	950.	6900.	12,000.
1875CC	1,573,700	50.00	55.00	60.00	70.00	95.00	900.	6900.	—
1875S	4,487,000	45.00	55.00	60.00	65.00	95.00	850.	6900.	—
1875S/CC	Inc.Ab.	80.00	110.	230.	360.	500.	1500.	—	—
1876	456,150	45.00	55.00	60.00	65.00	95.00	850.	6900.	12,000.
1876CC	509,000	50.00	55.00	65.00	80.00	100.	900.	6900.	—
1876S	5,227,000	45.00	55.00	60.00	65.00	95.00	850.	6900.	—
1877	3,039,710	45.00	55.00	60.00	65.00	95.00	850.	6900.	12,000.
1877CC	534,000	50.00	60.00	90.00	120.	145.	950.	6900.	—
1877S	9,519,000	45.00	55.00	60.00	65.00	95.00	850.	6900.	—
1878	900			Proof Only					12,000.
	Impaired Proof		425.	465.	500.	550.	—	—	—
1878CC	97,000	95.00	140.	175.	210.	400.	2500.	—	—
1878S	4,162,000	45.00	55.00	60.00	65.00	95.00	850.	6900.	—
1879	1,541			Proof	Only				12,000.
	Impaired Proof		425.	465.	500.	550.	—	—	—
1880	1,987			Proof	Only				12,000.
	Impaired Proof		425.	465.	500.	550.	—	—	—
1881	960			Proof	Only				12,000.
	Impaired Proof		425.	465.	500.	550.	—	—	—
1882	1,097			Proof	Only				12,000.
	Impaired Proof		425.	465.	500.	550.	—	—	—
1883	979			Proof	Only				10,500.
	Impaired Proof		425.	465.	500.	550.	—	—	—
1884	10		Proof Only, Keisberg Auction, 1976						52,500.
1885	5	Proof Only, Excessively Rare							

MORGAN DOLLARS

A five year lapse in the minting of standard silver dollars was ended by enactment of a February 28, 1878, coinage law, which held the metallic content of the coin to its former standard. Issue of the standard dollar had been halted in favor of the trade dollar, a slightly heavier coin authorized on a standard designed to allow it to compete with the dollar size coins of other nations in the Orient trade.

The 1878 turn around, achieved by the silver interests who had witnessed a rapid decline in the value of their commodity, ushered in the era of the silver dollar. In the years that followed the Treasury was required to purchase and convert into dollar coins such large quantities of silver that the available supplies far exceeded the demand, even for the Silver Certificate issues which they backed.

The initial mintages were authorized by the Bland-Allison Act, and that measure was followed in 1890 by the Sherman Act, and the War Revenue Act of 1898. With the exhaustion of the government's bullion stock in 1904 production of the silver dollar was again discontinued, to be renewed in 1921 under provisions of the Pittman Act of 1918. Under the provisions of this act over 270 million Morgan dollars were melted down for export and recoinage into subsidiary coins, accounting for the several scarce issues in the Morgan series which have coinage records of a million or more pieces.

Mintmark

First Reverse - 8 Tail Feathers

7/8 Tail Feathers

Second Reverse - 7 Tail Feathers
Top Arrow Feather Straight
Concave Breast

Third Reverse - 7 Tail Feathers
Top Arrow Feather Slanted
Convex Breast

NOTE: A $19.00 Numismatic value base has been assigned to Morgan dollars, based on the $13.00 market price for one ounce of silver at the time these valuations were assigned. The bullion value of each coin's silver content increases or decreases approximately 7.74-cents for each 10-cent change in the bullion price, or 77.35-cents for each $1 change.

Date	Mintage	VG-8	F-12	VF-20	XF-40	AU-50	MS-60	MS-65	Prf-65
1878 8 Tail Feathers									
	750,000	21.00	23.00	28.00	33.00	40.00	63.00	225.	8200.
1878 7 Over 8 Tail Feathers									
	9,759,550	22.00	24.00	31.50	42.00	63.00	82.00	410.	—
1878 7 Tail Feathers, Second Reverse									
	Inc. Ab.	19.50	20.00	22.00	25.00	28.00	50.00	170.	9500.
1878 7 Tail Feathers, Third Reverse									
	Inc. Ab.	19.50	20.00	22.00	25.00	28.00	50.00	170.	—
1878S	9,744,000	19.50	20.00	21.00	22.00	23.00	47.00	70.00	—
1878CC	2,212,000	28.00	31.50	38.00	42.00	56.00	105.	200.	—
1879	14,807,100	—	—	19.00	20.00	22.00	50.00	250.	8200.
1879O	2,887,000	—	—	19.00	20.00	25.00	70.00	600.	—
1879S Second Reverse									
	9,110,000	—	—	19.00	20.00	22.00	47.00	60.00	—
1879S Third Reverse									
	Inc. Ab.	—	—	19.00	20.00	22.00	47.00	60.00	—
1879CC	756,000	38.00	44.00	78.00	225.	475.	1050.	5400.	—
1880	12,601,335	—	—	19.00	20.00	22.00	50.00	210.	8200.
1880 8/7*	Inc. Ab.	90.00	110.	175.	250.	400.	—	—	—
1880O	5,305,000	—	—	—	—	22.00	100.	660.	—
1880O 8/7*	Inc. Ab.	40.00	50.00	60.00	75.00	95.00	175.	—	—
1880S	8,900,000	—	—	19.00	20.00	22.00	47.00	60.00	—
1880S 8/7*	Inc. Ab.	—	—	—	—	—	65.00	—	—
1880CC Second Reverse									
	591,000	44.00	52.00	65.00	82.00	115.	190.	280.	—
1880/79CC Second Reverse									
	Inc. Ab.	44.00	52.00	65.00	82.00	115.	190.	280.	—
1880CC Third Reverse									
	Inc. Ab.	44.00	52.00	65.00	82.00	115.	190.	280.	—

*Die Varieties Exist For These Issues.

Date	Mintage	VG-8	F-12	VF-20	XF-40	AU-50	MS-60	MS-65	Prf-65
1880CC 8/7 Third Reverse, High 7*									
	Inc. Ab.	—	—	—	—	—	190.	—	—
1880CC 8/7 Third Reverse, Low 7									
	Inc. Ab.	—	—	—	—	—	175.	—	—
1881	9,163,975	—	—	19.00	20.00	22.00	50.00	210.	9500.
1881O	5,708,000	—	—	19.00	20.00	22.00	50.00	225.	—
1881S	12,760,000	—	—	19.00	20.00	22.00	47.00	60.00	—
1881CC	296,000	74.00	83.00	93.00	105.	135.	190.	290.	—
1882	11,101,100	—	—	19.00	20.00	22.00	50.00	210.	8200.
1882O	6,090,000	—	—	19.00	20.00	22.00	50.00	225.	—
1882O/S	Inc. Ab.	—	—	19.00	20.00	22.00	50.00	—	—
1882S	9,250,000	—	—	19.00	20.00	22.00	47.00	63.00	—
1882CC	1,133,000	28.00	31.50	38.00	42.00	50.00	105.	150.	—
1883	12,291,039	—	—	19.00	20.00	22.00	50.00	165.	8200.
1883O	8,725,000	—	—	19.00	20.00	22.00	47.00	63.00	—
1883S	6,250,000	—	—	19.00	34.00	160.	590.	3150.	—
1883CC	1,204,000	28.00	31.50	38.00	42.00	51.00	72.00	88.00	—
1884	14,070,875	—	—	19.00	20.00	22.00	70.00	245.	8200.
1884O	9,730,000	—	—	19.00	20.00	22.00	47.00	63.00	—
1884S	3,200,000	—	—	19.00	26.00	240.	1400.	16,400.	—
1884CC	1,136,000	38.00	40.00	45.00	50.00	60.00	72.00	78.00	—
1885	17,787,767	—	—	19.00	20.00	22.00	47.00	70.00	9500.
1885O	9,185,000	—	—	19.00	20.00	22.00	47.00	65.00	—
1885S	1,497,000	—	—	22.00	33.00	66.00	190.	770.	—
1885CC	228,000	138.	145.	165.	185.	225.	315.	290.	—
1886	19,963,886	19.00	20.00	—	—	22.00	47.00	54.00	6900.
1886O	10,710,000	—	—	19.00	22.00	60.00	610.	8800.	—
1886S	750,000	28.00	30.00	38.00	45.00	71.00	330.	800.	—
1887	20,290,710	—	—	19.00	20.00	22.00	47.00	57.00	8200.
1887O	11,550,000	—	—	19.00	20.00	31.50	63.00	500.	—
1887S	1,771,000	19.00	20.00	23.00	25.00	35.00	150.	350.	—
1888	19,183,833	—	—	19.00	20.00	22.00	47.00	145.	9500.
1888O	12,150,000	—	—	19.00	22.00	28.00	47.00	200.	—
1888S	657,000	29.00	33.00	52.00	63.00	81.00	315.	960.	—
1889	21,726,811	—	—	19.00	20.00	22.00	47.00	145.	8200.
1889O	11,875,000	—	—	19.00	23.00	29.00	170.	1070.	—
1889S	700,000	29.00	34.00	50.00	57.00	75.00	195.	535.	—
1889CC	350,000	145.	190.	330.	650.	1775.	7650.	27,000.	—
1890	16,802,590	—	—	19.00	20.00	24.00	47.00	235.	8200.
1890O	10,701,000	—	19.00	20.00	23.00	31.50	95.00	610.	—
1890S	8,230,373	20.00	21.00	22.00	27.00	34.00	90.00	265.	—
1890CC	2,309,041	28.00	31.50	38.00	46.00	73.00	235.	610.	—
1890CC Tail Bar Variety									
	Inc. Ab.	—	—	38.00	46.00	73.00	235.	610.	—
1891	8,694,206	19.00	20.00	21.00	24.00	50.00	215.	675.	9500.
1891O	7,954,529	19.00	20.00	21.00	24.00	50.00	190.	2200.	—
1891S	5,296,000	20.00	21.00	23.00	27.00	30.00	100.	335.	—
1891CC	1,618,000	28.00	31.50	38.00	46.00	70.00	170.	475.	—
1892	1,037,245	20.00	21.00	25.00	29.00	40.00	215.	1325.	9500.
1892O	2,744,000	20.00	21.00	25.00	29.00	40.00	280.	3275.	—
1892S	1,200,000	23.00	30.00	63.00	195.	975.	6550.	22,500.	—
1892CC	1,352,000	38.00	43.00	53.00	88.00	190.	385.	1100.	—
1893	378,792	43.00	53.00	64.00	115.	195.	675.	2575.	9500.
1893O	300,000	49.00	63.00	115.	285.	390.	1325.	15,000.	—
1893S	100,000	875.	1150.	1775.	3400.	12,500.	27,000.	69,000.	—
1893CC	677,000	46.00	62.00	140.	350.	500.	1325.	4650.	—
1894	110,972	250.	325.	380.	590.	900.	1725.	8600.	10,000.
1894O	1,723,000	21.00	24.00	28.00	39.00	90.00	685.	9450.	—
1894S	1,260,000	25.00	31.50	63.00	125.	240.	580.	1900.	—
1895	12,880		Struck Only In Proof					—	39,000
	Impaired Proof		4000.	5000.	6500.	7500.	—	—	—
1895O	450,000	52.00	65.00	140.	345.	825.	3800.	53,000.	—
1895S	400,000	72.00	95.00	175.	565.	1000.	1900.	4900.	—
1896	9,967,762	—	—	19.00	20.00	22.00	47.00	139.	9500.
1896O	4,900,000	—	—	21.00	26.00	88.00	975.	12,000.	—
1896S	5,000,000	23.00	29.00	50.00	110.	280.	1020.	2650.	—
1897	2,822,731	—	—	19.00	20.00	22.00	47.00	150.	8200.
1897O	4,004,000	—	19.00	21.00	25.00	63.00	600.	7050.	—
1897S	5,825,000	20.00	21.00	24.00	27.00	33.00	100.	365.	—
1898	5,884,735	—	—	19.00	20.00	22.00	50.00	120.	8200.
1898O	4,440,000	—	—	19.00	20.00	22.00	47.00	71.00	—
1898S	4,102,000	20.00	21.00	24.00	27.00	57.00	390.	790.	—
1899	330,846	45.00	57.00	69.00	82.00	95.00	112.	360.	9500.
1899O	12,290,000	—	—	19.00	20.00	22.00	47.00	65.00	—
1899S	2,562,000	21.00	24.00	31.50	38.00	75.00	500.	1100.	—
1900	8,880,938	—	—	19.00	20.00	22.00	47.00	140.	9500.
1900O	12,590,000	—	—	19.00	20.00	22.00	47.00	120.	—
1900O/CC*	Inc. Ab.	—	—	—	—	22.00	50.00	—	—
1900S	3,540,000	20.00	21.00	24.00	26.00	53.00	280.	700.	—
1901	6,962,813	29.00	33.00	39.00	50.00	225.	1200.	11,650.	12,000
1901O	13,320,000	—	—	19.00	20.00	22.00	47.00	150.	—
1901S	2,284,000	19.00	25.00	30.00	40.00	75.00	440.	1500.	—
1902	7,994,777	19.00	20.00	22.00	25.00	40.00	88.00	580.	9500.
1902O	8,636,000	—	—	19.00	20.00	22.00	47.00	76.00	—
1902S	1,530,000	35.00	38.00	75.00	115.	170.	480.	1150.	—
1903	4,652,755	19.00	20.00	22.00	25.00	38.00	88.00	440.	9000.
1903O	4,450,000	170.	190.	225.	265.	315.	420.	660.	—
1903S	1,241,000	24.00	29.00	50.00	170.	630.	2500.	7950.	—
1904	2,788,650	19.00	20.00	22.00	25.00	57.00	380.	2400.	8200.
1904O	3,720,000	—	—	19.00	20.00	22.00	47.00	59.00	—
1904S	2,304,000	29.00	44.00	57.00	138.	500.	1500.	5800.	—
1921	44,690,000	—	—	19.00	20.00	22.00	44.00	63.00	—
1921D	20,345,000	—	—	19.00	20.00	22.00	50.00	380.	—
1921S	21,695,000	—	—	19.00	20.00	22.00	75.00	880.	—

PEACE DOLLARS

The new Peace dollar, featuring the word PEACE on the rocky crag upon which the eagle is perched and dedicated to a world thought to be at permanent peace as a result of the war to end all wars, was designed by Anthony De Francisci, whose monogram appears below the truncated bust of Liberty. Credit for the release of this new design rests at least in part with the American Numismatic Association and Farran Zerbe, a veteran numismatist and frequent participant in government numismatic projects.

The new coin was placed in production in mid-December of 1921, with over a million pieces being produced by year end, and released on January 3, 1922. Its coinage continued uninterrupted until 1928 when the slackening of demand for the coin for circulation purposes and as backing for Silver Certificates demanded a suspension. An Agricultural Adjustment Act of May 12, 1933, and a subsequent Silver Purchase Act of 1934, calling for the receipt of silver on a war-debt account and requiring its conversion into silver dollars, caused a renewal of coinage in 1934-35.

At this point the new Silver Certificate series of 1934 was launched which certified that "one dollar in silver" backed the issue, rather than "one silver dollar" as in the past. This ended any need for the silver dollar as currency backing.

A last issue of .900 fine silver dollars was authorized on August 3, 1964, but the projected 45 million example edition was never produced. The issue of this coin had been debated by the Treasury and White House for more than a year, before a permanent delay in its production was announced on May 25, 1965. Before that happened, however, dies were prepared (presumably of the Peace dollar design) with the 1964 date, and sample production runs were carried out at the Denver Mint. No examples are known to exist, Mint officials reporting they were all destroyed.

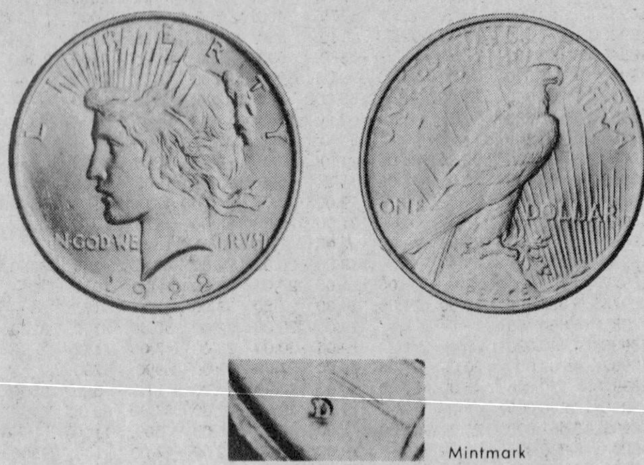

NOTE: A $19.00 Numismatic value base has been assigned to Peace dollars, based on the $13.00 market price for one ounce of silver at the time these valuations were assigned. The bullion value of each coin's silver content increases or decreases approximately 7.74-cents for each 10-cent change in the bullion price, or 77.35-cents for each $1 change.

Date	Mintage	VG-8	F-12	VF-20	XF-40	AU-50	MS-60	MS-65
1921	1,006,473	38.00	40.00	50.00	69.00	100.	600.	2650.
1922	51,737,000	—	—	—	19.00	20.00	43.00	50.00
1922D	15,063,000	—	—	—	19.00	22.00	66.00	380.
1922S	17,475,000	—	—	—	19.00	22.00	75.00	630.
1923	30,800,000	—	—	—	19.00	20.00	43.00	50.00
1923D	6,811,000	—	—	—	20.00	24.00	70.00	615.
1923S	19,020,000	—	—	—	19.00	22.00	125.	750.
1924	11,811,000	—	—	—	19.00	20.00	45.00	115.
1924S	1,728,000	19.00	21.00	23.00	31.50	50.00	260.	1600.
1925	10,198,000	—	—	—	19.00	20.00	45.00	82.00
1925S	1,610,000	19.00	20.00	22.00	28.00	40.00	345.	1260.
1926	1,939,000	19.00	20.00	23.00	25.00	37.00	66.00	365.
1926D	2,348,700	19.00	20.00	23.00	29.00	45.00	175.	820.
1926S	6,980,000	19.00	20.00	22.00	25.00	35.00	75.00	335.
1927	848,000	25.00	28.00	32.00	37.00	59.00	125.	745.
1927D	1,268,900	19.00	20.00	24.00	33.00	110.	380.	2650.
1927S	866,000	21.00	22.00	24.00	31.50	75.00	485.	1575.
1928	360,649	165.	175.	195.	240.	300.	440.	1760.
1928S	1,632,000	20.00	21.00	22.00	30.00	58.00	345.	1385.
1934	954,057	25.00	28.00	31.50	35.00	75.00	140.	795.
1934D	1,569,500	20.00	21.00	22.00	30.00	63.00	200.	1600.
1934S	1,011,000	20.00	23.00	50.00	160.	500.	3150.	10,700.
1935	1,576,000	20.00	21.00	22.00	28.00	47.00	100.	490.
1935S	1,964,000	20.00	21.00	22.00	29.00	67.00	280.	1500.

EISENHOWER DOLLARS

The new Eisenhower dollar was created to serve the immediate needs of the Nevada gaming industry, and the future needs of the vending industry. In addition to being minted for circulation in the cupro-nickel clad copper composition, silver interests were able to give the issue a tie to the dollar's historic past by providing for special limited issue uncirculated and proof editions of the coin to be offered, at premiums, in .400 fine silver. Designed by Frank Gasparro, the Eisenhower obverse is tied to an Apollo reverse which pays tribute to the nation's space program, and particularly the Apollo 11 moon landing of July 20, 1969, which commenced during the administration of President Eisenhower.

The coin exists in both high and low relief varieties. All proofs are of the high relief variety, while the uncirculated silver edition of 1971 is low relief and that of 1972 high relief. The 1971 clad metal editions and the 1972 Denver Mint issues are all low relief, while the 1972 Philadelphia issue exists in both high and low relief versions.

Cupro-Nickel Clad Copper .400 Fine Silver Composition

NOTE: A $10.75 Numismatic value has been assigned to silver Eisenhower dollars, based on the $13.00 market price for one ounce of silver at the time these valuations were assigned. The bullion value of each coin's silver content increases or decreases approximately 3.16-cents for each 10-cent change in the bullion price, or 31.63-cents for each $1 change.

Date	Mintage	MS-65
1971	47,799,000	2.80
1971D	68,587,424	2.25
1971S Silver Unc.	6,868,530	10.75
1971S Silver Prf.	4,265,234	12.25
1972	75,890,000	2.80
1972D	92,548,511	2.15
1972S Silver Unc.	2,193,056	18.00
1972S Silver Prf.	1,811,631	38.00
1973	2,000,056	16.50
1973D	2,000,000	16.50
1973S Silver Unc.	1,833,140	18.00
1973S Silver Prf.	1,005,617	160.
1973S Clad Prf.	2,769,624	7.00
1974	27,366,000	2.00
1974D	35,466,000	2.00
1974S Silver Unc.	1,720,000	18.00
1974S Silver Prf.	1,306,579	43.00
1974S Clad Prf.	2,617,350	7.00
1976 Type I	117,337,000	4.00
1976 Type II	Inc. Ab.	—
1976D Type I	103,228,274	2.40
1976D Type II	Inc. Ab.	1.75
1976S Cld.Prf.,Typ.I	2,909,369	14.00
1976S Cld.Prf.,Ty.II	4,149,730	5.00
1976S Silver Unc.	—	13.00
1976S Silver Prf.	—	13.75
1977	12,596,000	1.50
1977-D	32,983,006	1.50
1977-S Clad Prf.	3,251,152	5.00
1978	25,702,000	1.50
1978-D	33,012,890	1.50
1978S Clad Prf.	3,127,788	15.00

GOLD DOLLARS

The issue of a gold dollar unit was not authorized in the original national coinage law of 1792, although a legal tender ratio of 15 to 1 between silver and gold was specified therein. It was to materialize in 1849, under an act dated March 3, largely at the instigation of the influential gold lobby spawned by the general opposition to bank money and the California gold rush. During its 41 year life the issue was to be offered in three basic types, all of which were designed by James B. Longacre. The gold standard was .900 fine, with the first type being thicker and 2mm smaller in diameter than the others.

The gold dollar soon became a circulating coin, where the silver dollar had not, as the relative value of gold declined due to the large quantities being mined from the California fields. By the mid-1860s the ratio had begun to slide back and the issue of gold dollars abated. During the Civil War the issue was all but halted, as both silver and gold coins disappeared from circulation, a situation which prevailed until the resumption of specie payments in 1876. By that time the silver dollar was the coin of issue and the gold dollar was allowed to linger until its life was legislatively ended by an act of September 26, 1890.

Mintmark

Liberty Head

Date	Mintage	F-12	VF-20	XF-40	AU-50	MS-60
1849 Open Wreath	688,567	250.	340.	405.	480.	1000.
1849 Closed Wreath	Inc. Ab.	250.	340.	405.	480.	1000.
1849C Closed Wreath	11,634	275.	425.	650.	975.	1750.
1849C Open Wreath	Inc. Ab.		Auction '79, XF 90,000.			Rare
1849D Open Wreath	21,588	250.	575.	850.	1200.	1950.
1849O Open Wreath	215,000	250.	340.	405.	480.	1000.
1850	481,953	250.	340.	405.	480.	1000.
1850C	6,966	250.	550.	725.	1100.	2400.
1850D	8,382	250.	675.	950.	1500.	2750.
1850O	14,000	250.	340.	405.	480.	1000.
1851	3,317,671	250.	340.	405.	480.	1000.
1851C	41,267	250.	425.	550.	850.	1550.
1851D	9,882	275.	675.	950.	1500.	2750.
1851O	290,000	275.	340.	405.	480.	1000.
1852	2,045,351	250.	340.	405.	480.	1000.
1852C	9,434	275.	550.	725.	1100.	2400.
1852D	6,360	275.	675.	950.	1500.	2750.
1852O	140,000	250.	340.	405.	480.	1000.
1853	4,076,051	250.	340.	405.	480.	1000.
1853C	11,515	250.	425.	650.	975.	1750.
1853D	6,583	250.	675.	950.	1500.	2750.
1853O	290,000	250.	340.	405.	480.	1000.
1854	736,709	250.	340.	405.	480.	1000.
1854D	2,935	350.	975.	1500.	2600.	4950.
1854S	14,632	250.	340.	425.	925.	2600.

MINTMARK BELOW WREATH TIE

Small Indian Head

Date	Mintage	F-12	VF-20	XF-40	AU-50	MS-60
1854	902,736	300.	460.	850.	1800.	5000.
1855	758,269	300.	460.	850.	1800.	5000.
1855C	9,803	400.	775.	1250.	2700.	8750.
1855D	1,811	1750.	3000.	5250.	—	10,000.
1855O	55,000	350.	575.	1050.	1950.	8250.
1856S	24,600	350.	475.	900.	1800.	7500.

MINTMARK BELOW WREATH TIE

Large Indian Head

Date	Mintage	F-12	VF-20	XF-40	AU-50	MS-60	Prf-65
1856 Upright 5	1,762,936	225.	300.	330.	360.	900.	—
1856 Slant 5	Inc. Ab.	225.	300.	330.	360.	900.	—
1856D	1,460	2250.	3750.	5750.	—	14,500.	—
1857	774,789	225.	300.	330.	360.	900.	—
1857C	13,280	225.	475.	650.	1100.	2150.	—
1857D	3,533	350.	775.	1450.	1950.	3750.	—
1857S	10,000	225.	325.	355.	725.	1550.	—
1858	117,995	225.	300.	330.	360.	900.	15,000.
1858D	3,477	450.	775.	1500.	2300.	4250.	—
1858S	10,000	225.	300.	330.	575.	1200.	—
1859	168,244	225.	300.	330.	360.	900.	13,500.
1859C	5,235	225.	475.	750.	1200.	2350.	—
1859D	4,952	250.	750.	1300.	1900.	2750.	—
1859S	15,000	225.	300.	375.	950.	2250.	—
1860	36,668	225.	300.	330.	360.	900.	12,000.
1860D	1,566	2000.	3500.	5750.	—	11,500.	—
1860S	13,000	225.	325.	375.	575.	1100.	—
1861	527,499	225.	300.	330.	360.	900.	12,000.
1861D	Unrecorded	3500.	8000.	13,500.	—	22,500.	—
1862	1,361,390	225.	300.	330.	360.	900.	13,000.
1863	6,250	225.	450.	750.	1750.	4500.	12,500.
1864	5,950	225.	425.	600.	1300.	3200.	12,500.
1865	3,725	225.	425.	700.	1450.	3500.	14,000.
1866	7,130	225.	325.	425.	625.	1750.	13,500.
1867	5,250	225.	325.	400.	800.	1750.	12,500.
1868	10,525	225.	325.	350.	750.	1500.	12,500.
1869	5,925	225.	330.	375.	625.	1600.	12,500.
1870	6,335	225.	325.	375.	625.	1400.	11,500.
1870S	3,000	350.	500.	1100.	1700.	3750.	—
1871	3,930	225.	350.	500.	850.	1750.	12,000.
1872	3,530	225.	350.	500.	900.	1900.	12,000.
1873 Clsd 3	125,125	225.	300.	550.	900.	1550.	12,500.
1873 Open 3	Inc. Ab.	225.	300.	330.	360.	900.	—
1874	198,820	225.	300.	330.	360.	900.	12,750.
1875	420	—	2500.	3500.	4500.	9750.	15,000.
1876	3,245	225.	330.	375.	625.	1850.	11,000.
1877	3,920	225.	350.	550.	1100.	1950.	12,500.
1878	3,020	225.	350.	550.	1100.	1850.	12,500.
1879	3,030	225.	350.	575.	1050.	1600.	9500.
1880	1,636	225.	350.	575.	1000.	1450.	9500.
1881	7,707	225.	325.	350.	425.	1000.	9000.
1882	5,125	225.	325.	375.	500.	1000.	9500.
1883	11,007	225.	300.	330.	360.	900.	9000.
1884	6,236	225.	300.	350.	425.	1000.	9000.
1885	12,261	225.	300.	330.	360.	975.	9000.
1886	6,016	225.	325.	375.	450.	975.	9000.
1887	8,543	225.	325.	350.	400.	900.	9000.
1888	16,580	225.	300.	330.	360.	900.	9000.
1889	30,729	225.	300.	330.	360.	900.	9000.

QUARTER EAGLES

The quarter eagle or $2.50 gold piece, along with its sister multiples of $5 and $10, was authorized by the original coinage law of April 2, 1792. Its stipulated weight was 67½ grains of .916 2/3 fine gold, where it remained until the standard was changed to 64½ grains at .899225 fine by the act of June 28, 1834, the latter being subsequently revised to .900 fine by a law of January 18, 1837.

The Liberty cap type, which was designed by Robert Scot, did not carry a designation of value. The Turban head design of John Reich introduced in 1808 carried the designation "2½D." on the reverse below the eagle and proved to be the last issue for 13 years as the increasing value of gold was driving the coins from circulation as soon as they were released. A small coinage was resumed on a sporadic basis in 1821 with the coin reduced significantly in size, but maintained at the former weight and fineness standards.

The new standards specified by the law of 1834 led to the introduction of a new design featuring the Liberty band holding the hair, but with the turban removed, executed by William Kneass. This coin became a regular issue, with the quantities produced increasing significantly.

Liberty Cap

Date	Mintage	F-12	VF-20	XF-40	MS-60
1796 No Stars	963	9000.	17,000.	22,500.	50,000.
1796 Stars	432	6000.	9000.	14,000.	32,000.
1797	427	4500.	6750.	9500.	22,500.
1798	1,094	2500.	4700.	6750.	19,500.
1802 Over 1	3,035	2250.	3500.	6000.	18,000.
1804 13 Star Reverse	3,327	3400.	6500.	10,000.	19,000.
1804 14 Star Reverse	Inc. Ab.	2350.	3500.	6000.	18,000.
1805	1,781	2500.	3500.	6000.	18,000.
1806 Over 4	1,616	2500.	3500.	6000.	18,000.
1806 Over 5	Inc. Ab.	4000.	6500.	10,000.	19,000.
1807	6,812	2500.	3500.	6000.	18,000.

Turban Head

Date	Mintage	F-12	VF-20	XF-40	MS-60
1808 (20MM Dia.)	2,710	6500.	10,500.	17,500.	32,500.
1821 (18.5MM Dia.)	6,448	2500.	5000.	7500.	15,000.
1824 Over 21	2,600	2500.	4500.	7250.	14,000.
1825	4,434	2500.	4500.	7250.	14,000.
1826 Over 25	760	3500.	5500.	10,000.	18,000.
1827	2,800	2500.	4500.	7250.	13,500.
1829	3,403	2250.	4500.	7250.	13,500.
1830	4,540	2250.	4250.	7250.	13,500.
1831	4,520	1750.	3500.	5500.	13,000.
1832	4,400	1750.	3500.	5500.	13,000.
1833	4,160	1750.	3500.	5500.	13,000.
1834	4,000	3500.	7000.	12,000.	25,000.

Mintmark

Liberty Without Turban

Date	Mintage	VF-20	XF-40	AU-50	MS-60	MS-65
1834	112,234	410.	500.	875.	4300.	21,000.
1835	131,402	410.	500.	875.	4300.	21,000.
1836	547,986	410.	500.	875.	4300.	21,000.
1837	45,080	410.	500.	875.	4300.	21,000.
1838	47,030	410.	500.	875.	4300.	21,000.
1838C	7,880	450.	850.	1350.	5000.	—
1839	27,021	410.	500.	875.	4300.	21,000.
1839C	18,140	425.	750.	1350.	5000.	—
1839D	13,674	850.	1500.	3000.	7500.	—
1839O	17,781	410.	750.	1150.	4500.	21,000.

CORONET QTR. EAGLES

In 1840 the quarter eagle was redesigned by Christian Gobrecht to conform to the style of the half eagle and eagle. This design was to survive, largely unchanged, for 68 years. The series encompasses one of the more interesting regular issue U.S. coins, the 1848 CAL piece, an issue of 1,389 coins counterstamped after minting with the mark "CAL." on the reverse above the eagle to designate that they were struck from a 230 ounce shipment of gold sent to Secretary of War Marcy by Col. R. B. Mason, the military governor of California.

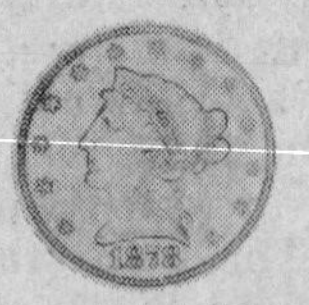

MINTMARK

Coronet Head

Date	Mintage	F-12	VF-20	XF-40	AU-50	MS-60	Prf-65
1840	18,859	200.	250.	300.	400.	750.	—
1840C	12,822	250.	350.	625.	850.	1500.	—
1840D	3,532	250.	650.	1000.	—	—	—
1840O	33,580	200.	250.	300.	375.	650.	—
1841					Stack's Sale, 1976		41,000.
1841C	10,281	200.	350.	525.	900.	1500.	—
1841D	4,164	225.	600.	1300.	2000.	3750.	—
1842	2,823	250.	450.	800.	—	—	—
1842C	6,729	225.	350.	550.	800.	1350.	—
1842D	4,643	225.	650.	1150.	1600.	3500.	—
1842O	19,800	200.	250.	300.	400.	650.	—
1843	100,546	200.	250.	300.	340.	550.	—
1843C Sm Dt	26,064	750.	1500.	2500.	—	7500.	—
1843C Lg Dt	Inc. Ab.	200.	375.	600.	900.	1350.	—
1843D	36,209	200.	500.	800.	1250.	2000.	—
1843O Sm Dt	288,002	200.	250.	300.	340.	600.	—
1843O Lg Dt	76,000	200.	250.	300.	350.	700.	—
1844	6,784	200.	350.	600.	900.	1450.	—
1844C	11,622	200.	350.	525.	800.	1250.	—
1844D	17,332	200.	500.	800.	1250.	2000.	—
1845	91,051	200.	250.	300.	350.	600.	—
1845D	19,460	200.	475.	700.	1000.	1600.	—
1845O	4,000	400.	850.	1250.	—	3500.	—
1846	21,598	200.	250.	300.	340.	600.	—
1846C	4,808	250.	600.	850.	1250.	2250.	—
1846D	19,303	300.	525.	800.	1300.	2200.	—
1846O	66,000	200.	250.	300.	350.	600.	—
1847	29,814	200.	250.	300.	340.	600.	—
1847C	23,226	250.	350.	525.	800.	1200.	—
1847D	15,784	300.	475.	800.	1250.	2000.	—
1847O	124,000	200.	250.	300.	340.	600.	
1848	7,497	300.	500.	800.	1150.	1750.	—

Enlarged

Date	Mintage	F-12	VF-20	XF-40	AU-50	MS-60	Prf-65
1848 CAL.	1,389	3500.	4500.	8000.	—	17,500.	—
1848C	16,788	250.	350.	550.	800.	1300.	—
1848D	13,771	300.	500.	800.	1400.	2500.	—
1849	23,294	200.	250.	300.	350.	600.	—
1849C	10,220	250.	350.	550.	800.	1250.	—
1849D	10,945	250.	550.	900.	1350.	2500.	—
1850	252,923	200.	250.	300.	350.	600.	—
1850C	9,148	250.	350.	550.	750.	1200.	—
1850D	12,148	250.	500.	800.	1200.	2000.	—
1850O	84,000	200.	250.	300.	350.	600.	—
1851	1,372,748	200.	250.	300.	340.	550.	—
1851C	14,923	250.	350.	500.	800.	1350.	—
1851D	11,264	250.	500.	850.	1250.	2000.	—
1851O	148,000	200.	250.	300.	340.	575.	—
1852	1,159,681	200.	250.	300.	340.	550.	—
1852C	9,772	250.	350.	575.	800.	1350.	—
1852D	4,078	250.	600.	950.	1400.	2500.	—
1852O	140,000	200.	250.	300.	350.	600.	—
1853	1,404,668	200.	250.	300.	340.	550.	—
1853D	3,178	250.	600.	950.	1400.	2250.	—
1854	596,258	200.	250.	300.	340.	550.	—
1854C	7,295	200.	350.	550.	800.	1400.	—
1854D	1,760	1000.	2000.	3500.	—	7500.	—
1854O	153,000	200.	250.	300.	350.	600.	—
1854S	246	10,000.	20,000.	30,000.	—	—	—
1855	235,480	200.	250.	300.	340.	550.	—
1855C	3,677	500.	800.	1250.	—	3000.	—
1855D	1,123	1000.	2000.	3750.	—	7500.	—
1856	384,240	200.	250.	300.	340.	550.	—
					Stack's Sale, Feb. 1977		17,000.
1856C	7,913	225.	400.	550.	800.	1500.	—
1856D	874	2000.	4000.	6000.	—	15,000.	—

Date	Mintage	F-12	VF-20	XF-40	AU-50	MS-60	Prf-65
1856O	21,100	200.	250.	325.	400.	600.	—
1856S	71,120	200.	250.	325.	400.	650.	—
1857	214,130	200.	250.	300.	340.	550.	—
1857D	2,364	250.	750.	1100.	1950.	4500.	—
1857O	34,000	200.	250.	300.	350.	600.	—
1857S	69,200	200.	250.	300.	375.	850.	—
1858	47,377	200.	250.	300.	350.	600.	25,000.
1858				Stack's Sale, Feb.,1977			12,000.
1858C	9,056	250.	350.	500.	750.	1400.	—
1859	39,444	200.	250.	300.	350.	600.	23,000.
1859D	2,244	250.	700.	1000.	1450.	2750.	—
1859S	15,200	200.	250.	300.	450.	750.	—
1860	22,675	200.	250.	300.	325.	550.	21,000.
1860C	7,469	250.	350.	575.	950.	1850.	—
1860S	35,600	200.	250.	300.	350.	650.	—
1861	1,283,878	200.	250.	300.	340.	550.	22,000.
1861S	24,000	200.	250.	300.	400.	700.	—
1862	98,543	200.	250.	300.	340.	600.	22,000.
1862 Over 1	Inc. Ab.	—	1000.	1500.	—	3500.	—
1862S	8,000	200.	250.	375.	—	1000.	—
1863	30		Bowers & Ruddy, Aug. 1978, Proof Only				36,000.
1863S	10,800	200.	250.	300.	350.	600.	—
1864	2,874	600.	1000.	2000.	—	3500.	21,000.
1865	1,545	450.	900.	1800.	—	3250.	23,000.
1865S	23,376	200.	250.	300.	350.	600.	—
1866	3,110	225.	300.	500.	700.	1250.	18,000.
1866S	38,960	200.	250.	300.	350.	600.	—
1867	3,250	225.	275.	450.	600.	950.	16,000.
1867S	28,000	200.	250.	300.	350.	600.	—
1868	3,625	250.	300.	400.	600.	1050.	16,000.
1868S	34,000	200.	250.	325.	400.	650.	—
1869	4,345	200.	250.	325.	450.	750.	16,000.
1869S	29,500	200.	250.	300.	340.	750.	—
1870	4,555	210.	260.	350.	450.	750.	15,000.
1870S	16,000	200.	250.	300.	340.	650.	—
1871	5,350	210.	275.	325.	400.	750.	15,000.
1871S	22,000	200.	250.	300.	340.	650.	—
1872	3,030	225.	275.	400.	575.	900.	15,000.
1872S	18,000	200.	250.	300.	340.	600.	—
1873 Clsd 3	178,025	200.	250.	300.	340.	550.	—
1873 Open 3	Inc. Ab.	200.	250.	300.	340.	550.	15,000.
1873S	27,000	200.	250.	300.	340.	550.	—
1874	3,940	225.	300.	375.	500.	750.	17,500.
1875	420	1500.	3000.	5500.	7250.	9000.	25,000.
1875S	11,600	200.	250.	300.	350.	600.	—
1876	4,221	210.	250.	300.	450.	900.	15,000.
1876S	5,000	210.	250.	325.	450.	1050.	—
1877	1,652	325.	450.	700.	900.	2000.	17,000.
1877S	35,400	200.	250.	300.	340.	550.	—
1878	286,260	200.	250.	300.	340.	550.	17,000.
1878S	178,000	200.	250.	300.	340.	550.	—
1879	88,990	200.	250.	300.	340.	550.	13,000.
1879S	43,500	200.	250.	300.	340.	550.	—
1880	2,996	215.	250.	325.	400.	800.	13,000.
1881	691	600.	950.	1750.	—	3500.	17,000.
1882	4,067	215.	250.	325.	400.	700.	13,000.
1883	2,002	225.	250.	400.	500.	800.	13,000.
1884	2,023	225.	250.	400.	500.	800.	13,000.
1885	887	500.	850.	1500.	—	3000.	13,000.
1886	4,088	215.	250.	300.	400.	650.	13,000.
1887	6,282	200.	250.	300.	400.	600.	13,000.
1888	16,098	200.	250.	300.	340.	550.	13,000.
1889	17,648	200.	250.	300.	340.	550.	13,000.
1890	8,813	200.	250.	300.	340.	550.	12,500.
1891	11,040	215.	250.	300.	340.	550.	12,500.
1892	2,545	215.	250.	350.	500.	800.	12,500.
1893	30,106	200.	250.	300.	340.	550.	12,500.
1894	4,122	200.	250.	325.	400.	800.	12,500.
1895	6,199	200.	250.	300.	340.	650.	12,500.
1896	19,202	200.	250.	300.	340.	550.	12,500.
1897	29,904	200.	250.	300.	340.	550.	12,500.
1898	24,165	200.	250.	300.	340.	550.	12,500.
1899	27,350	200.	250.	300.	340.	550.	12,500.
1900	67,205	200.	250.	300.	340.	550.	12,500.
1901	91,322	200.	250.	300.	340.	550.	12,500.
1902	133,733	200.	250.	300.	340.	550.	12,500.
1903	201,257	200.	250.	300.	340.	550.	12,500.
1904	160,960	200.	250.	300.	340.	550.	12,500.
1905	217,944	200.	250.	300.	340.	550.	12,500.
1906	176,490	200.	250.	300.	340.	550.	12,500.
1907	336,448	200.	250.	300.	340.	550.	12,500.

INDIAN HEAD QTR. EAGLES

This $2½ gold piece, and its sister $5 issue, has the distinction of presenting a design on which the relief is recessed below the surface of the field. It is the work of Bela Lyon Pratt.

Mintmark

Date	Mintage	VF-20	XF-40	AU-50	MS-60	MS-65	Prf-65
1908	565,057	240.	275.	300.	515.	2750.	13,000.
1909	441,899	240.	275.	300.	600.	3250.	13,000.
1910	492,682	240.	275.	300.	600.	3250.	13,000.
1911	704,191	240.	275.	300.	550.	3100.	13,000.
1911D	55,680	750.	1600.	2750.	7500.	22,000.	—
1912	616,197	240.	275.	300.	515.	3100.	13,000.
1913	722,165	240.	275.	300.	515.	3100.	13,000.
1914	240,117	240.	300.	325.	1400.	4500.	13,000.
1914D	448,000	240.	275.	300.	515.	2750.	—
1915	606,100	240.	275.	300.	515.	2750.	14,000.
1925D	578,000	240.	275.	300.	515.	2650.	—
1926	446,000	240.	275.	300.	515.	2650.	—
1927	388,000	240.	275.	300.	515.	2650.	—
1928	416,000	240.	275.	300.	515.	2650.	—
1929	532,000	240.	275.	300.	515.	2650.	—

THREE DOLLARS

Authorized on February 21, 1853, this unpopular issue survived 36 years despite the fact that more than 100,000 examples were produced only in the first year. The coin's only logical application was to purchase sheets of 3-cent stamps, the adoption of that postal rate having led to the introduction of the silver three cent piece two years earlier. The designs are by James B. Longacre.

MINTMARK BELOW WREATH TIE

Date	Mintage	F-12	VF-20	XF-40	AU-50	MS-60	Prf-65
1854	138,618	500.	1040.	1250.	1800.	3900.	—
1854D	1,120	2000.	4500.	7500.	10,000.	—	—
1854O	24,000	500.	1040.	1350.	2000.	4000.	—
1855	50,555	500.	1040.	1250.	1800.	3900.	—
1855S	6,600	550.	1040.	1500.	2200.	—	—
1856	26,010	500.	1040.	1250.	1800.	3900.	—
1856S	34,500	500.	1040.	1250.	2000.	4000.	—
1857	20,891	500.	1040.	1250.	1800.	3900.	—
1857S	14,000	510.	1040.	1300.	2000.	4200.	—
1858	2,133	550.	1100.	1500.	2200.	4500.	—
1859	15,638	500.	1040.	1250.	1800.	3900.	25,000.
1860	7,155	550.	1040.	1350.	2000.	4000.	25,000.
1860S	7,000	525.	1040.	1350.	2000.	5000.	—
1861	6,072	550.	1040.	1350.	2000.	4500.	25,000.
1862	5,785	525.	1040.	1350.	1900.	4000.	25,000.
1863	5,039	600.	1040.	1300.	2500.	5500.	25,000.
1864	2,680	600.	1040.	1500.	2500.	7000.	25,000.
1865	1,165	700.	1100.	1500.	2500.	8500.	30,000.
1866	4,030	525.	1040.	1400.	1950.	4000.	25,000.
1867	2,650	575.	1100.	1500.	2100.	4750.	25,000.
1868	4,875	525.	1040.	1250.	1900.	4000.	25,000.
1869	2,525	575.	1040.	1350.	2000.	3900.	25,000.
1870	3,535	525.	1040.	1250.	2050.	4000.	25,000.
1870S	2			Only One Specimen Known			
1871	1,330	550.	1150.	1700.	2500.	4500.	25,000.
1872	2,030	525.	1100.	1500.	2200.	4250.	25,000.
1873 Open 3	25		Proof	Only	—		44,000.
1873 Closed 3	Inc. Ab.		Restrikes	—	—	8500.	25,000.
1874	41,820	500.	1040.	1250.	1800.	3900.	25,000.
1875	20		(Proofs Only), Stack's Sale, Feb. 1979				40,000.
1876	45		(Proofs Only), Bowers & Ruddy, Nov. 1979				27,000.
1877	1,488	600.	1200.	1600.	2250.	5500.	25,000.
1878	82,324	500.	1040.	1250.	1800.	3900.	23,000.
1879	3,030	550.	1100.	1300.	2100.	4300.	22,000.
1880	1,036	550.	1200.	1500.	2250.	4500.	22,000.
1881	554	900.	1400.	2250.	3100.	6500.	25,000.
1882	1,576	550.	1100.	1300.	2000.	4000.	19,000.
1883	989	550.	1200.	1500.	2250.	4500.	24,000.
1884	1,106	550.	1100.	1400.	2000.	4100.	19,000.
1885	910	550.	1100.	1450.	2250.	4850.	24,000.
1886	1,142	550.	1200.	1400.	2000.	4100.	19,000.
1887	6,160	525.	1040.	1250.	1900.	4000.	19,000.
1888	5,291	525.	1040.	1250.	1900.	4000.	19,000.
1889	2,429	525.	1040.	1250.	1900.	3900.	19,000.

STELLA

This coin, in reality simply a pattern coin, is one of the more intriguing products of the United States Mint. Its standing is much akin to that accorded the 1856 Flying Eagle cent, which was also nothing more than a pattern, although it ultimately enjoyed a short life of active issue. While the stella never emerged as a coin-of the-realm issue, many collect it as an adjunct to the gold coinage series.

First envisioned by John A. Kasson, U.S. Minister to Austria, the stella was intended as an international coin issue which would tie our coinage to the Latin Monetary Union formed in Europe in 1865. The purpose of the LMU was to standardize coinage systems, and the stella was approximately equivalent in value to France's 20 francs, which was the base unit of the Union, along with Austria's 8 florins, Holland's 10 gulden, Italy's 20 lire and Spain's 20 pesetas.

The issue — "stella" is Latin for "star," the latter being the central feature on the reverse of the coin — materialized through the efforts of Dr. W. W. Hubbell who held the patent on the "goloid" coinage metal (gold, silver and copper in combination) used in the coins. Two types of patterns were prepared in both 1879 and 1880, a flowing hair design by Charles E. Barber and a coiled hair by George Morgan. Only the 1879 Barber flowing hair type was produced in quantity, with 400 examples being prepared for the review of Congress. A few examples of each were also struck in aluminum and copper, and in one case white metal.

Date	Type	Mintage	Proof
1879	Flowing Hair	415	60,000.
1879	Coiled Hair	10	130,000.
1880	Flowing Hair	15	85,000.
1880	Coiled Hair	10	125,000.

HALF EAGLES

The history of this denomination closely parallels that of the quarter eagle, with the legal specifications always being double those of the lesser value. The Turban head design was issued regularly, although in small quantities, however, from the time of its introduction in 1807 to 1834. The large issues of the 1830s are a direct result of the mining activities in the southeast during the period. Again, the major change in standard instituted in 1834 led to the introduction of a new design featuring the Liberty head without a turban.

Liberty Cap

Date	Mintage	F-12	VF-20	XF-40	MS-60
1795 Sm. Eagle	8,707	3500.	6500.	8500.	35,000.
1795 Lg. Eagle	Inc. Ab.	4000.	7500.	10,000.	37,000.
1796 Over 95 Small Eagle	6,196	3750.	6500.	10,000.	26,000.
1797 Over 95 Large Eagle	3,609	4200.	5250.	8500.	15,000.
1797 15 Stars, Small Eagle	Inc. Ab.	4750.	6000.	8500.	24,000.
1797 16 Stars, Small Eagle	Inc. Ab.	4750.	6250.	9500.	19,000.
1798 Sm. Eagle	24,867	—	-	Very Rare	—
1798 Large Eagle, Small 8	Inc. Ab.	950.	2750.	5000.	11,500.
1798 Large Eagle, Large 8, 13 Star Reverse	Inc. Ab.	950.	2750.	5000.	11,000.
1798 Large Eagle, Large 8, 14 Star Reverse	Inc. Ab.	1150.	2750.	5000.	12,500.
1799	7,451	950.	2500.	4750.	11,000.
1800	37,628	950.	2500.	4250.	10,000.
1802 Over 1	53,176	950.	2500.	4250.	10,000.
1803 Over 2	33,506	950.	2500.	4250.	10,000.
1804 Sm. 8	30,475	950.	2500.	4000.	10,000.
1804 Lg. 8	Inc. Ab.	950.	2500.	4000.	10,000.
1805	33,183	950.	2500.	4000.	10,000.
1806 Pointed 6	64,093	950.	2500.	4000.	9000.
1806 Round 6	Inc. Ab.	950.	2500.	4000.	9000.
1807	32,488	950.	2500.	4000.	9000.

Turban Head

Date	Mintage	F-12	VF-20	XF-40	MS-60
1807	51,605	1100.	2000.	4000.	8250.
1808	55,578	1100.	2000.	4000.	8250.
1808 Over 7	Inc. Ab.	1200.	2350.	4500.	9000.
1809 Over 8	33,875	1100.	2000.	4000.	8250.
1810 Small Date, Small 5	100,287	—	Rare	—	—
1810 Small Date, Lg. 5	Inc. Ab.	1200.	2500.	4500.	9500.
1810 Large Date, Sm. 5	Inc. Ab.	1100.	2500.	4500.	9500.
1810 Large Date, Lg. 5	Inc. Ab.	1100.	2000.	4000.	8250.
1811 Small 5	99,581	1200.	2500.	4000.	9250.
1811 Large 5	Inc. Ab.	1250.	2500.	4250.	8250.
1812	58,087	1150.	2500.	4250.	9500.

LARGE HEAD TYPE INTRODUCED

Date	Mintage	F-12	VF-20	XF-40	MS-60
1813	95,428	1300.	2500.	3500.	8500.
1814 Over 13	15,454	2200.	3500.	6500.	13,000.
1815	635	-	Very Rare	—	—
1818	48,588	2000.	3250.	4500.	9000.
1819	51,723	—	Rare	—	—
1820 Curve Base 2, Small Letters	263,806	1500.	2500.	3250.	9000.
1820 Curve Base 2, Large Letters	Inc. Ab.	1500.	2500.	3250.	9000.
1820 Square Base 2	Inc. Ab.	1350.	2500.	3000.	8500.
1821	34,641	3000.	4500.	7500.	12,000.
1822	17,796	3 Known - Very Rare		—	—
1823	14,485	3250.	4750.	8000.	14,500.
1824	17,340	—	Rare	—	—
1825 Over 21	29,060	3250.	5000.	7500.	15,000.
1825 Over 24	Inc. Ab.	-	Very Rare	—	
1826	18,069	2750.	4000.	5250.	12,000.
1827	24,913	—	Rare	—	60,000.
1828 8 Over 7	28,029	—	Rare	—	—
1828	Inc. Ab.	—	Auction '79, MS-65 110,000.		
1829 Lg. Dt.	57,442		Stack's Auction 1976, 65,000.		
1829 Sm. Dt.	Inc. Ab.		Stack's Sale, Aug. 1976, 65,000.		
1830 Sm. 5D.	126,351	1750.	2500.	5000.	10,000.
1830 Lg. 5D.	Inc. Ab.	1750.	2850.	5250.	11,500.

Date	Mintage	F-12	VF-20	XF-40	MS-60
1831	140,594	1500.	2250.	4750.	11,000.
1832 Curve Base 2, 12 Stars	157,487	—	Rare	—	—
1832 Square Base 2, 13 Stars					
	Inc. Ab.	2500.	4000.	8750.	15,000.
1833	193,630	1750.	2800.	4750.	11,000.
1834 Plain 4	50,141	1750.	2750.	4500.	11,000.
1834 Crosslet 4	Inc. Ab.	1750.	3000.	5000.	12,000.

MINTMARK ABOVE DATE

Liberty Without Turban

Date	Mintage	VF-20	XF-40	AU-50	MS-60	MS-65
1834 Plain 4	658,028	325.	475.	1100.	5500.	24,000.
1834 Crosslet 4	Inc. Ab.	450.	750.	1500.	6500.	—
1835	371,534	325.	475.	1100.	5500.	24,000.
1836	553,147	325.	475.	1100.	5500.	24,000.
1837	207,121	325.	475.	1100.	5500.	24,000.
1838	286,588	325.	475.	1100.	5500.	24,000.
1838C	17,179	800.	1750.	2500.	6000.	—
1838D	20,583	800.	1750.	2500.	7000.	—

CORONET HALF EAGLES

When this new design by Christian Gobrecht was introduced in 1839 the diameter of the coin was reduced by slightly less than 1mm. The basic design was to survive until 1908, with the motto "In God We Trust" being added above the eagle on the reverse in 1866.

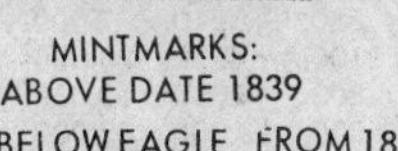

MINTMARKS:
ABOVE DATE 1839
BELOW EAGLE FROM 1840

NOTE: A $200.00 Numismatic value base has been assigned to Liberty Head half eagles, based on the $550.00 market price for one ounce of gold at the time these valuations were assigned. The bullion value of each coin's gold content increases or decreases approximately 24.19-cents for each $1 change in the bullion price.

Date	Mintage	F-12	VF-20	XF-40	MS-60	Prf-65
1839	118,143	200.	225.	350.	1800.	—
1839 Over 8 Curved Date						
	Inc. Ab.	200.	300.	600.	1800.	—
1839C	17,205	250.	450.	750.	2500.	—
1839D	18,939	250.	700.	1100.	3500.	—
1840	137,382	200.	225.	260.	1800.	—
1840C	18,992	225.	350.	550.	1950.	—
1840D	22,896	225.	600.	850.	3500.	—
1840O	40,120	200.	225.	300.	—	—
1841	15,833	200.	225.	275.	1800.	—
1841C	21,467	225.	350.	550.	1950.	—
1841D	30,495	225.	550.	800.	3000.	—
1841O	50	Only 2 Known		—		—
1842 Sm Let	27,578	200.	225.	300.	1800.	—
1842 Lg Let	Inc. Ab.	200.	225.	275.	1800.	—
1842C Sm Dt	28,184	350.	800.	1500.	4000.	—
1842C Lg Dt	Inc. Ab.	225.	350.	600.	2200.	—
1842D Sm Dt	59,608	225.	550.	800.	2750.	—
1842D Lg Dt	Inc. Ab.	250.	750.	1000.	—	—
1842O	16,400	225.	400.	550.	1800.	—
1843	611,205	200.	225.	260.	1800.	—
1843C	44,201	200.	325.	500.	1850.	—
1843D	98,452	200.	525.	800.	2600.	—
1843O Sm Let	19,075	200.	225.	350.	1800.	—
1843O Lg Let	82,000	200.	225.	300.	1800.	—
1844	340,330	200.	225.	250.	1800.	—
1844C	23,631	200.	325.	550.	2200.	—
1844D	88,982	200.	525.	800.	2800.	—
1844O	364,600	200.	225.	300.	1800.	—
1845	417,099	200.	225.	260.	1800.	—
1845D	90,629	200.	525.	800.	2750.	—
1845O	41,000	200.	225.	300.	1800.	—
1846	395,942	200.	225.	260.	1800.	—
1846C	12,995	300.	500.	700.	2200.	—
1846D	80,294	225.	550.	800.	3000.	—
1847	915,981	200.	225.	260.	1800.	—

Date	Mintage	F-12	VF-20	XF-40	MS-60	Prf-65
1847C	84,151	275.	355.	600.	1950.	—
1847D	64,405	200.	550.	800.	2750.	—
1847O	12,000	250.	400.	750.	2000.	—
1848	260,775	200.	225.	260.	1800.	—
1848C	64,472	225.	325.	550.	2000.	—
1848D	47,465	250.	550.	800.	3200.	—
1849	133,070	200.	225.	260.	1800.	—
1849C	64,823	225.	325.	550.	1850.	—
1849D	39,036	250.	550.	800.	3200.	—
1850	64,491	200.	225.	260.	1800.	—
1850C	63,591	200.	325.	550.	1850.	—
1850D	43,984	200.	550.	800.	2750.	—
1851	377,505	200.	225.	260.	1800.	—
1851C	49,176	225.	325.	550.	1850.	—
1851D	62,710	200.	550.	800.	2750.	—
1851O	41,000	200.	225.	275.	1800.	—
1852	573,901	200.	225.	260.	1800.	—
1852C	72,574	225.	325.	600.	1800.	—
1852D	91,584	225.	500.	800.	2750.	—
1853	305,770	200.	225.	250.	1800.	—
1853C	65,571	225.	350.	600.	1800.	—
1853D	89,678	200.	500.	800.	2800.	—
1854	160,675	200.	225.	250.	1800.	—
1854C	39,283	200.	325.	550.	1900.	—
1854D	56,413	200.	500.	800.	2750.	—
1854O	46,000	200.	250.	325.	1800.	—
1854S	268	—		Very Rare	—	—
1855	117,098	200.	225.	250.	1800.	—
1855C	39,788	200.	325.	600.	1850.	—
1855D	22,432	200.	550.	800.	2750.	—
1855O	11,100	250.	400.	650.	1850.	—
1855S	61,000	200.	250.	375.	1800.	—
1856	197,990	200.	225.	250.	1800.	—
1856C	28,457	250.	400.	600.	2250.	—
1856D	19,786	225.	550.	800.	3000.	—
1856O	10,000	275.	400.	800.	1900.	—
1856S	105,100	200.	225.	275.	1800.	—
1857	98,188	200.	225.	250.	1800.	—
1857C	31,360	275.	400.	600.	1850.	—
1857D	17,046	225.	550.	850.	3500.	—
1857O	13,000	200.	300.	450.	1950.	—
1857S	87,000	200.	225.	250.	1800.	—
1858	15,136	200.	225.	350.	1800.	50,000.
1858C	38,856	200.	350.	600.	1950.	—
1858D	15,362	275.	550.	900.	3500.	—
1858S	18,600	200.	225.	275.	1800.	—
1859	16,814	200.	225.	275.	1800.	25,000.
1859C	31,847	200.	325.	600.	2000.	—
1859D	10,366	250.	550.	900.	3500.	—
1859S	13,220	250.	350.	550.	1800.	—
1860	19,825	200.	225.	275.	1800.	22,000.
1860C	14,813	225.	400.	650.	2250.	—
1860D	14,635	225.	550.	850.	3500.	—
1860S	21,200	200.	250.	350.	1600.	—
1861	688,150	200.	225.	260.	1600.	20,000.
1861C	6,879	500.	800.	1500.	3000.	—
1861D	1,597	2500.	4000.	6000.	10,000.	—
1861S	18,000	200.	350.	600.	—	—
1862	4,465	250.	450.	650.	1750.	20,000.
1862S	9,500	200.	275.	500.	—	—
1863	2,472	600.	900.	1500.	3000.	20,000.
1863S	17,000	200.	350.	600.	—	—
1864	4,220	400.	600.	950.	3500.	29,000.
1864S	3,888	1000.	1500.	2000.	5000.	—
1865	1,295	600.	900.	1500.	3000.	25,000.
1865S	27,612	200.	300.	600.	—	—
1866S	9,000	200.	325.	650.	—	—

MOTTO ADDED OVER EAGLE

Date	Mintage	VF-20	XF-40	AU-50	MS-60	MS-65	Prf-65
1866	6,730	375.	700.	—	—	—	20,000.
1866S	34,920	300.	500.	—	1250.	—	—
1867	6,920	350.	700.	—	1250.	—	18,000.
1867S	29,000	225.	400.	—	—	—	—
1868	5,725	325.	600.	—	—	—	20,000.
1868S	52,000	225.	300.	—	—	—	—
1869	1,785	750.	1250.	—	—	—	20,000.
1869S	31,000	225.	400.	—	—	—	—
1870	4,035	350.	750.	—	—	—	20,000.
1870CC	7,675	2500.	3800.	7250.	—	—	—
1870S	17,000	250.	350.	—	800.	—	—
1871	3,230	400.	600.	—	1000.	—	20,000.
1871CC	20,770	600.	850.	—	—	—	—
1871S	25,000	250.	350.	500.	800.	—	—

Date	Mintage	VF-20	XF-40	AU-50	MS-60	MS-65	Prf-65
1872	1,690	750.	1250.	—	2500.	—	20,000.
1872CC	16,980	750.	1250.	1600.	—	—	—
1872S	36,400	225.	275.	—	550.	—	—
1873 Clsd 3	49,305	225.	235.	260.	395.	3400.	20,000.
1873 Open 3	63,200	225.	235.	260.	395.	3400.	—
1873CC	7,416	950.	1350.	—	2500.	—	—
1873S	31,000	225.	300.	—	650.	—	—
1874	3,508	400.	600.	—	1000.	—	25,000.
1874CC	21,198	450.	900.	2000.	3500.	—	—
1874S	16,000	250.	325.	—	—	—	—
1875	220	—	Rare	—	—	—	—
1875CC	11,828	775.	1250.	—	—	—	—
1875S	9,000	350.	750.	—	2000.	—	—
1876	1,477	650.	1100.	—	2250.	—	20,000.
1876CC	6,887	850.	1200.	—	2250.	—	—
1876S	4,000	2000.	2500.	—	—	—	—
1877	1,152	800.	1250.	—	2500.	—	20,000.
1877CC	8,680	800.	1500.	—	2750.	—	—
1877S	26,700	225.	235.	275.	450.	—	—

NOTE: Specimens of common date $5 gold coins of the period 1878 through 1908 free of surface blemishes often command substantial premiums above the prices quoted in the uncirculated column.

Date	Mintage	VF-20	XF-40	AU-50	MS-60	MS-65	Prf-65
1878	131,740	225.	235.	260.	395.	2750.	20,000.
1878CC	9,054	1750.	2700.	—	—	—	—
1878S	144,700	225.	235.	260.	395.	2750.	—
1879	301,950	225.	235.	260.	395.	2750.	18,000.
1879CC	17,281	300.	550.	700.	950.	—	—
1879S	426,200	225.	235.	260.	395.	2750.	—
1880	3,166,436	225.	235.	260.	395.	2750.	17,500.
1880CC	51,017	225.	550.	700.	950.	—	—
1880S	1,348,900	225.	235.	260.	395.	2750.	—
1881	5,708,802	225.	235.	260.	395.	2750.	16,000.
1881/80	(Inc. Ab.)			Only 2 Known		—	—
1881CC	13,886	350.	550.	700.	950.	—	—
1881S	969,000	225.	235.	260.	395.	2750.	—
1882	2,514,568	225.	235.	260.	395.	2750.	16,000.
1882CC	82,817	225.	500.	650.	950.	—	—
1882S	969,000	225.	235.	260.	395.	2750.	—
1883	233,461	225.	235.	260.	395.	2750.	16,000.
1883CC	12,958	225.	400.	650.	950.	—	—
1883S	83,200	225.	235.	260.	395.	2750.	—
1884	191,078	225.	235.	260.	395.	2750.	16,000.
1884CC	16,402	225.	500.	650.	850.	—	—
1884S	177,000	225.	235.	260.	395.	2500.	—
1885	601,506	225.	235.	260.	395.	2500.	16,000.
1885S	1,211,500	225.	235.	260.	395.	2500.	—
1886	388,432	225.	235.	260.	395.	2500.	16,000.
1886S	3,268,000	225.	235.	260.	395.	2500.	—
1887	87		Proofs Only	—	—	—	35,000.
1887S	1,912,000	225.	235.	260.	395.	2500.	—
1888	18,296	225.	235.	260.	395.	2500.	15,000.
1888S	293,900	225.	235.	260.	395.	2500.	—
1889	7,565	300.	400.	550.	800.	—	15,000.
1890	4,328	250.	400.	550.	800.	—	15,000.
1890CC	53,800	225.	550.	700.	900.	—	—
1891	61,413	225.	235.	260.	395.	—	15,000.
1891CC	208,000	225.	500.	700.	900.	—	—
1892	753,572	225.	235.	260.	395.	2500.	14,000.
1892CC	82,968	225.	600.	700.	900.	—	—
1892O	10,000	750.	1000.	1450.	2250.	—	—
1892S	298,400	225.	235.	260.	395.	2500.	—
1893	1,528,197	225.	235.	260.	395.	2500.	14,000.
1893CC	60,000	225.	600.	750.	900.	—	—
1893O	110,000	225.	300.	375.	700.	—	—
1893S	224,000	225.	235.	260.	395.	2500.	—
1894	957,955	225.	235.	260.	395.	2500.	14,000.
1894O	16,600	225.	300.	400.	750.	—	—
1894S	55,900	225.	235.	260.	395.	2500.	—
1895	1,345,936	225.	235.	260.	395.	2500.	14,000.
1895S	112,000	225.	235.	260.	395.	2500.	—
1896	59,063	225.	235.	260.	395.	2500.	14,000.
1896S	155,400	225.	235.	260.	395.	2500.	—
1897	867,883	225.	235.	260.	395.	2500.	14,000.
1897S	354,000	225.	235.	260.	395.	2500.	—
1898	633,495	225.	235.	260.	395.	2500.	14,000.
1898S	1,397,400	225.	235.	260.	395.	2500.	—
1899	1,710,729	225.	235.	260.	395.	2500.	14,000.
1899S	1,545,000	225.	235.	260.	395.	2500.	—
1900	1,405,730	225.	235.	260.	395.	2500.	14,000.
1900S	329,000	225.	235.	260.	395.	2500.	—
1901	616,040	225.	235.	260.	395.	2500.	14,000.
1901S	3,648,000	225.	235.	260.	395.	2500.	—
1902	172,562	225.	235.	260.	395.	2500.	14,000.
1902S	939,000	225.	235.	260.	395.	2500.	—
1903	227,024	225.	235.	260.	395.	2500.	14,000.
1903S	1,855,000	225.	235.	260.	395.	2500.	—
1904	392,136	225.	235.	260.	395.	2500.	14,000.
1904S	97,000	225.	235.	260.	395.	2500.	—
1905	302,308	225.	235.	260.	395.	2500.	14,000.
1905S	880,700	225.	235.	260.	395.	2500.	—
1906	348,820	225.	235.	260.	395.	2500.	14,000.
1906D	320,000	225.	235.	260.	395.	2500.	—
1906S	598,000	225.	235.	260.	395.	2500.	—
1907	626,192	225.	235.	260.	395.	2500.	14,000.
1907D	888,000	225.	235.	260.	395.	2500.	—
1908	421,874	225.	235.	260.	395.	2500.	—

INDIAN HEAD HALF EAGLES

This design by Bela L. Pratt, as was the case with the like design for the $2.50 gold piece, materialized as a direct result of President Theodore Roosevelt's interest in fathering the development of a more artistic coinage.

MINTMARK AT POINT OF FASCES

NOTE: A $240.00 Numismatic value base has been assigned to Indian Head half eagles, based on the $550.00 market price for one ounce of gold at the time these valuations were assigned. The bullion value of each coin's gold content increases or decreases approximately 24.19-cents for each $1 change in the bullion price.

Date	Mintage	VF-20	XF-40	AU-50	MS-60	MS-65	Prf-65
1908	578,012	240.	300.	380.	950.	5500.	20,000.
1908D	148,000	240.	300.	380.	950.	6000,	—
1908S	82,000	325.	550.	825.	4200.	14,500.	—
1909	627,138	240.	300.	380.	950.	5750.	20,000.
1909D	3,423,560	240.	300.	380.	910.	4400.	—
1909O	34,200	500.	1150.	2400.	13,500.	45,000.	—
1909S	297,200	240.	350.	775.	3000.	13,000.	—
1910	604,250	240.	300.	380.	950.	5750.	20,000.
1910D	193,600	240.	300.	800.	2500.	7250.	—
1910S	770,200	240.	350.	800.	3250.	13,500.	—
1911	915,139	240.	300.	380.	910.	4900.	20,000.
1911D	72,500	350.	600.	1500.	6600.	21,000.	—
1911S	1,416,000	240.	325.	600.	2200.	8300.	—
1912	790,144	240.	300.	380.	910.	5000.	18,000.
1912S	392,000	240.	350.	850.	2600.	13,000.	—
1913	916,099	240.	300.	380.	910.	5000.	20,000.
1913S	408,000	300.	425.	1550.	6500.	25,500.	—
1914	247,125	240.	300.	380.	950.	5000.	20,000.
1914D	247,000	240.	300.	380.	950.	7500.	—
1914S	263,000	240.	350.	650.	2200.	9750.	—
1915	588,075	240.	300.	380.	910.	5000.	22,000.
1915S	164,000	300.	400.	1100.	4250.	20,000.	—
1916S	240,000	240.	325.	800.	2000.	10,000.	—
1929	662,000	2000.	4000.	6000.	12,000.	25,000.	—

EAGLES

The highest denomination ($10) coin authorized by the original coinage act, this unit was not minted during the years 1805 through 1837 because it could not be maintained in circulation. The legal 15 to 1, silver to gold ratio at which it was minted had been exceeded in the world markets, meaning the nation's gold coins were undervalued in terms of silver, causing them to flow out of the country.

Liberty Cap

Date	Mintage	F-12	VF-20	XF-40	MS-60
1795	5,583	2500.	4750.	10,000.	28,000.
1796	4,146	2000.	4750.	10,000.	28,000.
1797 Sm. Eagle	3,615	2750.	4750.	10,000.	28,000.

Heraldic Eagle Introduced

Date	Mintage	F-12	VF-20	XF-40	MS-60
1797 Lg. Eagle	10,940	1950.	3000.	7500.	17,500.
1798 Over 97, 9 Stars Left, 4 Right					
	900		Auction '79, XF 17,500.		
1798 Over 97, 7 Stars Left, 6 Right					
	842		Auction '79, AU 60,000.		
1799	37,449	2000.	3750.	6500.	16,000.
1800	5,999	2250.	3750.	6500.	16,000.
1801	44,344	2000.	3750.	6500.	16,000.
1803	15,017	2250.	3750.	6500.	16,000.
1804	3,757	2750.	4500.	7750.	18,000.

CORONET EAGLES

Enactment of the 1834 law which significantly reduced the fine gold content of all U.S. gold coins enabled a resumption of eagle coinage in 1838. This signalled the first introduction of the Coronet design by Christian Gobrecht, which except for the addition of the motto "In God We Trust" over the eagle on the reverse survived until 1907.

Mintmark

NOTE: A $310.00 Numismatic value base has been assigned to Liberty Head eagles, based on the $550.00 market price for one ounce of gold at the time these valuations were assigned. The bullion value of each coin's gold content increases or decreases approximately 48.37 cents for each $1 change in the bullion price.

Date	Mintage	F-12	VF-20	XF-40	MS-60	Prf-65
1838	7,200	600.	1250.	2700.	10,500.	—
1839 Lg. Lts.	38,248	400.	700.	2300.	8000.	—

OLD STYLE (ENLARGED) NEW STYLE

NEW TYPE LIBERTY HEAD INTRODUCED

Date	Mintage	F-12	VF-20	XF-40	MS-60	Prf-65
1839 Sm. Lts.	Inc. Ab.	500.	1000.	1500.	5000.	—
1840	47,338	350.	375.	450.	4600.	—
1841	63,131	350.	375.	450.	4600.	—
1841O	2,500	400.	650.	1200.	6500.	—
1842 Sm. Dt.	81,507	350.	375.	450.	4600.	—
1842 Lg. Dt.	Inc. Ab.	350.	375.	450.	4600.	—
1842O	27,400	350.	375.	450.	4600.	—
1843	75,462	350.	375.	450.	4600.	—
1843O	175,162	350.	375.	450.	4600.	—
1844	6,361	350.	500.	450.	5500.	—
1844O	118,700	350.	375.	450.	5500.	—
1845	26,153	350.	375.	450.	5500.	—
1845O	47,500	350.	375.	450.	5500.	—
1846	20,095	350.	375.	450.	5500.	—
1846O	81,780	350.	375.	450.	5500.	—
1847	862,258	350.	375.	450.	5500.	—
1847O	571,500	350.	375.	450.	5500.	—
1848	145,484	350.	375.	450.	5500.	—
1848O	38,850	350.	375.	450.	4600.	—
1849	653,618	350.	375.	450.	4600.	—
1849O	23,900	350.	375.	450.	4600.	—
1850	291,451	350.	375.	450.	4600.	—
1850O	57,500	350.	375.	450.	4600.	—
1851	176,328	350.	375.	450.	4600.	—
1851O	263,000	350.	375.	450.	4600.	—
1852	263,106	350.	375.	450.	4600.	—
1852O	18,000	350.	375.	425.	4600.	—
1853	201,253	350.	375.	450.	4600.	—
1853O	51,000	350.	375.	450.	4600.	—
1854	54,250	350.	375.	450.	4600.	—
1854O	52,500	350.	375.	450.	4600.	—
1854S	123,826	350.	375.	450.	4600.	—
1855	121,701	350.	375.	450.	4600.	—
1855O	18,000	350.	375.	450.	4600.	—
1855S	9,000	400.	750.	1100.	5250.	—
1856	60,490	350.	375.	450.	4600.	—
1856O	14,500	350.	375.	450.	4600.	—
1856S	68,000	350.	375.	450.	4600.	—
1857	16,606	350.	375.	450.	4600.	—
1857O	5,500	550.	1000.	1750.	—	—
1857S	26,000	350.	375.	450.	4600.	—
1858	2,521	3000.	4500.	6000.	—	35,000.
1858O	20,000	350.	375.	450.	4600.	—
1858S	11,800	350.	375.	450.	4850.	—
1859	16,093	350.	375.	450.	4600.	30,000.
1859O	2,300	1275.	2350.	3500.	—	—
1859S	7,000	500.	800.	1150.	4600.	—
1860	15,105	350.	375.	450.	4600.	30,000.
1860O	11,100	350.	375.	700.	4600.	—
1860S	5,000	550.	900.	1250.	6000.	—
1861	113,233	350.	375.	450.	4600.	30,000.
1861S	15,500	350.	375.	500.	4600.	—
1862	10,995	350.	375.	450.	4600.	39,000.
1862S	12,500	350.	400.	825.	4600.	—
1863	1,248	2000.	3500.	5000.	9000.	32,500.
1863S	10,000	350.	450.	950.	—	—
1864	3,580	600.	1000.	1500.	5500.	37,500.
1864S	2,500	1250.	1650.	2000.	—	—
1865	4,005	550.	900.	1250.	5750.	30,000.
1865S	16,700	400.	825.	1200.	4750.	—
1865S Over Inverted 186						
	Inc. Ab.	New England Sale, May 1978			VF 600.	—
1866S	8,500	950.	1450.	2000.	—	—

MOTTO ADDED OVER EAGLE

Date	Mintage	VF-20	XF-40	AU-50	MS-60	MS-65	Prf-65
1866	3,780	375.	500.	800.	1200.	—	30,000.
1866S	11,500	400.	600.	850.	1400.	—	—
1867	3,140	375.	500.	—	1100.	—	30,000.
1867S	9,000	450.	650.	—	1250.	—	—
1868	10,655	375.	400.	—	800.	—	32,500.
1868S	13,500	400.	550.	650.	1000.	—	—
1869	1,855	1500.	2500.	—	4000.	—	30,000.
1869S	6,430	450.	650.	775.	1350.	—	—
1870	4,025	450.	850.	—	1250.	—	27,500.
1870CC	5,908	1700.	3600.	8000.	—	—	—
1870S	8,000	450.	600.	800.	1200.	—	—
1871	1,820	1500.	2250.	—	3500.	—	30,000.
1871CC	8,085	700.	1500.	—	2500.	—	—
1871S	16,500	400.	550.	—	950.	—	—
1872	1,650	1250.	2000.	2650.	3500.	—	27,500.
1872CC	4,600	750.	1000.	—	—	—	—
1872S	17,300	375.	500.	675.	950.	—	—
1873	825	2000.	2500.	3250.	5000.	—	36,000.
1873CC	4,543	1400.	1750.	2800.	—	—	—
1873S	12,000	375.	550.	700.	1000.	—	—

Date	Mintage	VF-20	XF-40	AU-50	MS-60	MS-65	Prf-65
1874	53,160	375.	385.	410.	650.	—	27,500.
1874CC	16,767	400.	900.	1150.	1600.	—	—
1874S	10,000	400.	650.	850.	1250.	—	—
1875	120			Garrett Sale, 1976		—	91,000.
1875CC	7,715	750.	1300.	1900.	2500.	—	—
1876	732	2250.	4000.	5500.	8500.	—	30,000.
1876CC	4,696	1200.	1750.	2200.	3500.	—	—
1876S	5,000	700.	1000.	1400.	2000.	—	—
1877	817	2500.	4500.	5250.	7500.	—	30,000.
1877CC	3,332	1700.	2250.	2750.	4000.	—	—
1877S	17,000	375.	400.	550.	650.	—	—
1878	73,800	310.	350.	410.	450.	2900.	30,000.
1878CC	3,244	1700.	2250.	2750.	4000.	—	—
1878S	26,100	310.	350.	450.	575.	—	—
1879	384,770	310.	350.	410.	450.	2900.	27,000.
1879CC	1,762	5250.	7500.	9000.	—	—	—
1879O	1,500	2500.	3500.	4600.	6000.	—	—
1879S	224,000	310.	350.	410.	450.	—	—
1880	1,644,876	310.	350.	410.	450.	2900.	25,000.
1880CC	11,190	310.	700.	800.	1400.	—	—
1880O	9,200	400.	600.	750.	1100.	—	—
1880S	506,250	310.	350.	410.	450.	2900.	—
1881	3,877,260	310.	350.	410.	450.	2900.	25,000.
1881CC	24,015	310.	450.	650.	1150.	—	—
1881O	8,350	310.	500.	650.	900.	—	—
1881S	970,000	310.	350.	410.	450.	2900.	—
1882	2,324,480	310.	350.	410.	450.	2900.	25,000.
1882CC	6,764	310.	550.	800.	1600.	—	—
1882O	10,820	310.	350.	500.	650.	—	—
1882S	132,000	310.	350.	410.	450.	2900.	—
1883	208,740	310.	350.	410.	450.	2900.	25,000.
1883CC	12,000	310.	700.	950.	1400.	—	—
1883O	800	3500.	5000.	6250.	9000.	—	—
1883S	38,000	310.	350.	410.	450.	2900.	—
1884	76,905	310.	350.	410.	450.	2900.	—
1884CC	9,925	310.	550.	850.	1400.	—	—
1884S	124,250	310.	350.	410.	450.	2900.	—
1885	253,527	310.	350.	410.	450.	2900.	25,000.
1885S	228,000	310.	350.	410.	450.	2900.	—
1886	236,160	310.	350.	410.	450.	2900.	22,000.
1886S	826,000	310.	350.	410.	450.	2900.	—
1887	53,680	310.	350.	410.	450.	2900.	22,000.
1887S	817,000	310.	350.	410.	450.	2900.	—
1888	132,996	310.	350.	410.	450.	2900.	21,000.
1888O	21,335	310.	350.	500.	850.	—	—
1888S	648,700	310.	350.	410.	450.	2900.	—
1889	4,485	400.	650.	850.	1500.	—	22,000.
1889S	425,400	310.	350.	410.	450.	2900.	—
1890	58,043	310.	350.	410.	450.	2900.	22,000.
1890CC	17,500	310.	450.	600.	950.	—	—
1891	91,868	310.	350.	410.	450.	2900.	22,000.
1891CC	103,732	310.	450.	600.	950.	—	—
1892	797,552	310.	350.	410.	450.	2900.	20,000.
1892CC	40,000	310.	600.	—	950.	—	—
1892O	28,688	310.	350.	410.	650.	—	—
1892S	115,500	310.	350.	410.	450.	2900.	—
1893	1,840,895	310.	350.	410.	450.	2900.	20,000.
1893CC	14,000	310.	450.	600.	950.	—	—
1893O	17,000	310.	350.	—	750.	—	—
1893S	141,350	310.	350.	410.	450.	2900.	—
1894	2,470,778	310.	350.	410.	450.	2900.	20,000.
1894O	107,500	310.	350.	410.	450.	2900.	—
1894S	25,000	310.	350.	410.	450.	2900.	—
1895	567,826	310.	350.	410.	450.	2900.	20,000.
1895O	98,000	310.	350.	410.	450.	2900.	—
1895S	49,000	310.	350.	410.	450.	2900.	—
1896	76,348	310.	350.	410.	450.	2900.	20,000.
1896S	123,750	310.	350.	410.	450.	2900.	—
1897	1,000,159	310.	350.	410.	450.	2900.	20,000.
1897O	42,500	310.	350.	410.	450.	2900.	—
1897S	234,750	310.	350.	410.	450.	2900.	—
1898	812,197	310.	350.	410.	450.	2900.	20,000.
1898S	473,600	310.	350.	410.	450.	2900.	—
1899	1,262,305	310.	350.	410.	450.	2900.	20,000.
1899O	37,047	310.	350.	410.	450.	2900.	—
1899S	841,000	310.	350.	410.	450.	2900.	—
1900	293,960	310.	350.	410.	450.	2900.	20,000.
1900S	81,000	310.	350.	410.	450.	2900.	—
1901	1,718,825	310.	350.	410.	450.	2900.	20,000.
1901O	72,041	310.	350.	410.	450.	2900.	—
1901S	2,812,750	310.	350.	410.	450.	2900.	—
1902	82,513	310.	350.	410.	450.	2900.	20,000.
1902S	469,500	310.	350.	410.	450.	2900.	—
1903	125,926	310.	350.	410.	450.	2900.	20,000.
1903O	112,771	310.	350.	410.	450.	2900.	—
1903S	538,000	310.	350.	410.	450.	2900.	—
1904	162,038	310.	350.	410.	450.	2900.	20,000.
1904O	108,950	310.	350.	410.	450.	2900.	—
1905	201,078	310.	350.	410.	450.	2900.	20,000.
1905S	369,250	310.	350.	410.	450.	2900.	—
1906	165,497	310.	350.	410.	450.	2900.	20,000.
1906D	981,000	310.	350.	410.	450.	2900.	—
1906O	86,895	310.	350.	410.	450.	2900.	—
1906S	457,000	310.	350.	410.	450.	2900.	—
1907	1,203,973	310.	350.	410.	450.	2900.	20,000.
1907D	1,030,000	310.	350.	410.	450.	2900.	—
1907S	210,500	310.	350.	410.	450.	2900.	—

INDIAN HEAD EAGLES

Another of the coin designs directly attributable to President Theodore Roosevelt's instigation, this issue was designed by Augustus Saint-Gaudens, America's leading sculptor of his day. The initial issues did not carry the motto "In God We Trust" because the President personally objected to its use on coins, but it was restored through Congressional pressure in 1908. Unlike the reeded edges carried on all other gold coins, excepting the Saint-Gaudens double eagle, this coin carries raised stars; 46 from 1907-11, then with the admission of Arizona and New Mexico to statehood, 48 commencing in 1912.

MINTMARK AT POINT OF FASCES

Date	Mintage	VF-20	XF-40	AU-50	MS-60	MS-65	Prf-65
1907 Wire Edge, Periods Before And After Legends	500	—	3000.	—	9500.	20,000.	—
1907 Same, Without Stars On Edge		—	Unique	—	—	—	—
1907 Rolled Edge, Periods	42	—	—	—	50,000.	—	—
1907 Without Periods	239,406	490.	525.	575.	1300.	7000.	—
1908 Without Motto	33,500	500.	600.	850.	3600.	14,500.	—
1908D Without Motto	210,000	490.	525.	650.	2100.	8500.	—

NOTE: A $490.00 Numismatic value base has been assigned to Indian Head eagles, based on the $550.00 market price for one ounce of gold at the time these valuations were assigned. The bullion value of each coin's gold content increases or decreases approximately 48.37 cents for each $1 change in the bullion price.

IN GOD WE TRUST MOTTO ADDED

Date	Mintage	VF-20	XF-40	AU-50	MS-60	MS-65	Prf-65
1908	341,486	490.	525.	575.	1100.	6000.	22,500.
1908D	836,500	490.	525.	575.	1700.	9000.	—
1908S	59,850	550.	800.	1400.	5250.	17,000.	—
1909	184,863	490.	525.	575.	1200.	6250.	22,500.
1909D	121,540	490.	525.	675.	2050.	8500.	—
1909S	292,350	490.	525.	600.	2900.	8250.	—
1910	318,704	490.	525.	575.	1050.	5500.	22,500.
1910D	2,356,640	490.	525.	575.	1050.	4500.	—
1910S	811,000	490.	525.	875.	3000.	8250.	—
1911	505,595	490.	525.	575.	1000.	4750.	22,500.
1911D	30,100	700.	1200.	2750.	9500.	30,000.	—
1911S	51,000	550.	750.	1400.	5500.	18,000.	—
1912	405,083	490.	525.	575.	1050.	5000.	22,500.
1912S	300,000	490.	550.	1400.	3750.	12,000.	—
1913	442,071	490.	525.	575.	1000.	4750.	22,500.
1913S	66,000	600.	900.	2400.	22,500.	62,000.	—
1914	151,050	490.	525.	575.	1300.	6000.	25,000.
1914D	343,500	490.	525.	575.	1250.	6500.	—
1914S	208,000	490.	525.	750.	3250.	12,000.	—
1915	351,075	490.	525.	575.	975.	4500.	25,000.
1915S	59,000	490.	525.	1700.	6000.	21,000.	—
1916S	138,500	490.	525.	850.	3250.	11,750.	—
1920S	126,500	10,000.	16,000.	24,000.	47,500.	80,000.	—
1926	1,014,000	490.	525.	575.	960.	4400.	—
1930S	96,000	3500.	5000.	9000.	16,000.	27,500.	—
1932	4,463,000	490.	525.	575.	960.	4400.	—
1933	312,500	—	15,000.	—	50,000.	—	—

CORONET DOUBLE EAGLES

The largest regular issue U.S. coin, the $20 gold piece was born as a direct result of the economic realities of the development of the California gold fields. Its standard is exactly double that of the eagle, at 516 grains .900 fine, and it was authorized by the act of March 3, 1849.

Like the other Coronet designs, this one is the work of Longacre, with the motto again being added in 1866, then a switch to a fully spelled out denomination being made in 1877. The only issue of particular note in the series is the 1861 and 1861S offering with a distinctively different reverse, distinguished by its tall, slim letters, executed by A. C. Paquet but quickly withdrawn from production.

Mintmark

NOTE: A $575.00 Numismatic value base has been assigned to Liberty Head double eagles, based on the $550.00 market price for one ounce of gold at the time these valuations were assigned. The bullion value of each coin's gold content increases or decreases approximately 96.75-cents for each $1 change in the bullion price.

Date	Mintage	VF-20	XF-40	AU-50	MS-60	MS-65	Prf-65
1849	1	Unique, In U. S. Mint Collection				—	—
1850	1,170,261	600.	790.	1000.	3200.	22,500.	—
1850O	141,000	600.	850.	1150.	3750.	—	—
1851	2,087,155	600.	790.	1000.	3000.	22,500.	—
1851O	315,000	600.	790.	1150.	3300.	—	—
1852	2,053,026	600.	790.	1000.	3000.	22,500.	—
1852O	190,000	600.	850.	1150.	3250.	—	—
1853	1,261,326	600.	790.	1000.	3000.	22,500.	—
1853O	71,000	600.	950.	1800.	3750.	—	—
1854	757,899	600.	790.	1000.	3000.	22,500.	—
1854O	3,250	Auction '79, XF 45,000.				—	—
1854S	141,468	600.	790.	1150.	4000.	—	—
1855	364,666	600.	790.	1000.	3000.	22,500.	—
1855O	8,000	1750.	3200.	5750.	10,000.	—	—
1855S	879,675	600.	790.	1000.	3000.	—	—
1856	329,878	600.	790.	1000.	3000.	22,500.	—
1856O	2,250	Stack's Sale June, 1979 XF 70,000.				—	—
1856S	1,189,750	600.	790.	1000.	3000.	22,500.	—
1857	439,375	600.	790.	1000.	3000.	22,500.	—
1857O	30,000	600.	900.	1400.	4000.	—	—
1857S	970,500	600.	790.	1000.	3000.	22,500.	—
1858	211,714	600.	790.	1000.	3000.	22,500.	—
1858O	35,250	600.	1400.	2250.	4000.	—	—
1858S	846,710	600.	790.	1000.	3000.	22,500.	—
1859	43,597	600.	950.	1550.	3500.	—	—
1859O	9,100	1750.	3000.	4250.	7250.	—	—
1859S	636,445	600.	790.	1000.	3000.	22,500.	—
1860	577,670	600.	790.	1000.	3000.	22,500.	45,000.
1860O	6,600	3000.	4000.	5250.	8000.	—	—
1860S	544,950	600.	790.	1000.	3000.	22,500.	—
1861	2,976,453	600.	790.	1000.	3000.	22,500.	50,000.
1861 Paquet Rev.	Inc. Ab.			Extremely Rare		—	—
1861O	17,741	1500.	2250.	3750.	7500.	—	—
1861S	768,000	600.	790.	1000.	3000.	22,500.	—
1861S Paquet Rev.	Inc. Ab.	Auction '79, AU 20,000.				—	—
1862	92,133	600.	800.	1100.	3500.	—	40,000.
1862S	854,173	600.	790.	1000.	3000.	22,500.	—

1861
PAQUET
REVERSE

Date	Mintage	VF-20	XF-40	AU-50	MS-60	MS-65	Prf-65
1863	142,790	600.	790.	1000.	3300.	—	45,000.
1863S	966,570	600.	790.	1000.	3000.	22,500.	—
1864	204,285	600.	790.	1000.	3300.	—	40,000.
1864S	793,660	600.	790.	1000.	3000.	22,500.	—
1865	351,200	600.	790.	1000.	3200.	—	45,000.
1865S	1,042,500	600.	790.	1000.	3000.	22,500.	—
1866S	Inc. Below	600.	1200.	1850.	4000.	—	—

MOTTO ADDED OVER EAGLE

Date	Mintage	VF-20	XF-40	AU-50	MS-60	MS-65	Prf-65
1866	698,775	580.	600.	630.	1500.	—	40,000.
1866S	842,250	580.	600.	630.	1500.	—	—
1867	251,065	580.	600.	630.	1050.	—	37,500.
1867S	920,750	580.	600.	630.	1300.	—	—
1868	98,600	580.	600.	630.	1750.	—	40,000.
1868S	837,500	580.	600.	630.	1350.	—	—
1869	175,155	580.	600.	630.	1100.	—	37,500.
1869S	686,750	580.	600.	630.	1100.	—	—
1870	155,185	580.	600.	630.	1050.	—	37,500.
1870CC	3,789	Stack's Sale, Feb. 1979, AU 28,500.					—
1870S	982,000	580.	600.	630.	1050.	—	—
1871	80,150	580.	600.	630.	1500.	—	37,500.
1871CC	17,387	1850.	2750.	3200.	4000.	—	—
1871S	928,000	580.	600.	630.	1050.	7000.	—
1872	251,880	580.	600.	630.	1050.	—	40,000.
1872CC	26,900	580.	900.	1450.	2400.	—	—
1872S	780,000	580.	600.	630.	1050.	7000.	—
1873 Closed 3							
	Est. 208,925	580.	600.	630.	1750.	—	35,000.

NOTE: Specimens of common date $20 gold coins of the period 1873 through 1928 free of surface blemishes often command substantial premiums above the prices quoted in the uncirculated column.

Date	Mintage	VF-20	XF-40	AU-50	MS-60	MS-65	Prf-65
1873 Open 3							
	Est. 1,500,900	580.	600.	630.	1050.	7000.	—
1873CC	22,410	580.	1300.	1750.	2800.	—	—
1873S	1,040,600	580.	600.	630.	1050.	7000.	—
1874	366,800	580.	600.	630.	1050.	7000.	37,500.
1874CC	115,085	580.	850.	1150.	1750.	—	—
1874S	1,214,000	580.	600.	630.	1050.	7000.	—
1875	295,740	580.	600.	630.	1050.	7000.	37,500.
1875CC	111,151	580.	800.	1200.	1800.	—	—
1875S	1,230,000	580.	600.	630.	1050.	7000.	—
1876	583,905	580.	600.	630.	1050.	7000.	55,000.
1876CC	138,441	580.	800.	900.	1250.	—	—
1876S	1,597,000	580.	600.	630.	1050.	7000.	—

TWENTY DOLLARS SPELLED OUT

Date	Mintage	VF-20	XF-40	AU-50	MS-60	MS-65	Prf-65
1877	397,670	575.	595.	630.	690.	1700.	45,000.
1877CC	42,565	730.	755.	1150.	2500.	—	—
1877S	1,735,000	575.	595.	630.	690.	1700.	—
1878	543,645	575.	595.	630.	690.	1700.	40,000.
1878CC	13,180	730.	755.	1250.	2750.	—	—
1878S	1,739,000	575.	595.	630.	690.	1700.	—
1879	207,630	575.	595.	630.	690.	1700.	40,000.
1879CC	10,708	850.	1500.	2250.	3750.	—	—
1879O	2,325	1750.	2500.	4750.	8000.	—	—
1879S	1,223,800	575.	595.	630.	690.	1700.	—
1880	51,456	575.	595.	630.	690.	1700.	37,500.
1880S	836,000	575.	595.	630.	690.	1700.	—
1881	2,260	575.	595.	630.	690.	1700.	40,000.
1881S	727,000	575.	595.	630.	690.	1700.	—
1882	630	8000.	15,000.	23,500.	35,000.	—	65,000.
1882CC	39,140	575.	800.	950.	1450.	—	—
1882S	1,125,000	575.	595.	630.	690.	1700.	—
1883	92	Stack's Sale, June 1979, Proof 92,500.					—
1883CC	59,962	575.	595.	950.	1500.	—	—
1883S	1,189,000	575.	595.	630.	690.	1700.	—
1884	71	Stack's Sale, June 1979, Proof 44,000.					—
1884CC	81,139	575.	595.	900.	1400.	—	—
1884S	916,000	575.	595.	630.	690.	1700.	—
1885	828	4500.	7500.	13,000.	25,000.	—	55,000.
1885CC	9,450	850.	1250.	1750.	3000.	—	—
1885S	683,500	575.	595.	630.	690.	1700.	—

Date	Mintage	VF-20	XF-40	AU-50	MS-60	MS-65	Prf-65
1886	1,106	5000.	10,000.	13,500.	22,000.	—	38,500.
1887	121	Stack's Sale, June 1979, Proof 37,000.					—
1887S	283,000	575.	595.	630.	690.	1500.	—
1888	226,266	575.	595.	630.	690.	—	30,000.
1888S	859,600	575.	595.	630.	690.	1500.	—
1889	44,111	575.	595.	630.	690.	—	35,000.
1889CC	30,945	730.	800.	950.	1450.	—	—
1889S	774,700	575.	595.	630.	690.	1500.	—
1890	75,995	575.	595.	630.	690.	—	35,000.
1890CC	91,209	730.	800.	900.	1400.	—	—
1890S	802,750	575.	595.	630.	690.	1500.	—
1891	1,442	2000.	3000.	4250.	7500.	—	40,000.
1891CC	5,000	1200.	1750.	2800.	5500.	—	—
1891S	1,288,125	575.	595.	630.	690.	1500.	—
1892	4,523	1200.	1750.	2400.	5000.	—	35,000.
1892CC	27,265	575.	900.	1400.	2150.	—	—
1892S	930,150	575.	595.	630.	690.	1500.	—
1893	344,339	575.	595.	630.	690.	1500.	33,000.
1893CC	18,402	575.	950.	1500.	2800.	—	—
1893S	996,175	575.	595.	630.	690.	1500.	—
1894	1,368,990	575.	595.	630.	690.	1500.	30,000.
1894S	1,048,550	575.	595.	630.	690.	1500.	—
1895	1,114,656	575.	595.	630.	690.	1500.	30,000.
1895S	1,143,500	575.	595.	630.	690.	1500.	—
1896	792,663	575.	595.	630.	690.	1500.	30,000.
1896S	1,403,925	575.	595.	630.	690.	1500.	—
1897	1,383,261	575.	595.	630.	690.	1500.	30,000.
1897S	1,470,250	575.	595.	630.	690.	1500.	—
1898	170,470	575.	595.	630.	690.	1500.	30,000.
1898S	2,575,175	575.	595.	630.	690.	1500.	—
1899	1,669,384	575.	595.	630.	690.	1500.	30,000.
1899S	2,010,300	575.	595.	630.	690.	1500.	—
1900	1,874,584	575.	595.	630.	690.	1500.	30,000.
1900S	2,459,500	575.	595.	630.	690.	1500.	—
1901	111,526	575.	595.	630.	690.	1500.	30,000.
1901S	1,596,000	575.	595.	630.	690.	1500.	—
1902	31,254	575.	595.	630.	690.	1500.	30,000.
1902S	1,753,625	575.	595.	630.	690.	1500.	—
1903	287,428	575.	595.	630.	690.	1500.	30,000.
1903S	954,000	575.	595.	630.	690.	1500.	—
1904	6,256,797	575.	595.	630.	690.	1500.	30,000.
1904S	5,134,175	575.	595.	630.	690.	1500.	—
1905	59,011	575.	595.	630.	690.	1500.	30,000.
1905S	1,813,000	575.	595.	630.	690.	1500.	—
1906	69,690	575.	595.	630.	690.	1500.	30,000.
1906D	620,250	575.	595.	630.	690.	1500.	—
1906S	2,065,750	575.	595.	630.	690.	1500.	—
1907	1,451,864	575.	595.	630.	690.	1500.	30,000.
1907D	842,250	575.	595.	630.	690.	1500.	—
1907S	2,165,800	575.	595.	630.	690.	1500.	—

SAINT- GAUDENS $20

Perhaps America's most beautiful coin, the production issues of the Augustus Saint-Gaudens double eagle pale in comparison with his original models and the rare 1907 high relief strikes which could be suitably struck up in production. The 1907 issue also includes varieties with Roman numeral dating, while the 1907 and some 1908 issues do not bear the motto "In God We Trust." The motto "E PLURIBUS UNUM" is carried on the edge. Although specimens dated 1933 were struck, none were released prior to President Franklin D. Roosevelts move in 1934 to prohibit American citizens from holding gold, so none may be legally held. This series includes one of four 20th century overdates.

NOTE: A $650.00 Numismatic value base has been assigned to Saint-Gaudens type double eagles, based on the $550.00 market price for one ounce of gold at the time these valuations were assigned. The bullion value of each coin's gold content increases or decreases approximately 96.75-cents for each $1 change in the bullion price.

ROMAN NUMERAL DATE — HIGH RELIEF

ARABIC DATE TYPE

Mintmark

Roman Numerals

Date	Mintage	VF-20	XF-40	AU-50	MS-60	MS-65	Prf-65
1907 Extremely High Relief, Plain Edge							
	Unique			—		—	—
1907 Extremely High Relief, Lettered Edge							
	Unrecorded	Stack's Sale, May 23-24 1974				—	200,000.
1907 High Relief, Roman Numerals, Plain Edge							
		Currently offered at 180,000.				—	—
1907 High Relief, Roman Numerals, Wire Rim							
	11,250	3200.	5750.	8500.	14,500.	27,500.	—
1907 High Relief, Roman Numerals, Flat Rim							
	Inc. Ab.	3200.	5750.	8500.	14,500.	28,500.	—
1907 Large Letters On Edge					Unique	—	—
1907 Small Letters On Edge							
	361,667	650.	670.	875.	1050.	2500.	—
1908	4,271,551	650.	670.	690.	950.	1750.	—
1908D	663,750	650.	670.	690.	1050.	2800.	—

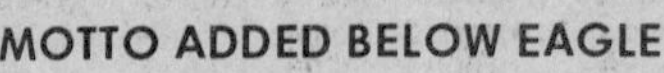

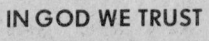

IN GOD WE TRUST MOTTO ADDED BELOW EAGLE

Date	Mintage	VF-20	XF-40	AU-50	MS-60	MS-65	Prf-65
1908	156,359	650.	670.	690.	950.	4500.	40,000.
1908D	349,500	650.	670.	690.	715.	4250.	—
1908S	22,000	800.	1200.	1500.	4500.	15,750.	—
1909 Over 8	161,282	650.	670.	975.	2300.	7750.	—
1909	Inc. Ab.	650.	670.	975.	1400.	7000.	40,000.
1909D	52,500	650.	670.	690.	715.	1900.	—
1909S	2,774,925	785.	800.	825.	950.	2300.	—
1910	482,167	650.	670.	690.	715.	2000.	40,000.
1910D	429,000	650.	670.	690.	715.	2350.	—
1910S	2,128,250	650.	670.	690.	715.	2500.	—
1911	197,350	650.	670.	690.	715.	3000.	40,000.
1911D	846,500	650.	670.	690.	715.	2100.	—
1911S	775,750	650.	670.	690.	715.	2550.	—
1912	149,824	650.	670.	900.	1150.	5500.	40,000.
1913	168,838	650.	670.	690.	1050.	2900.	40,000.
1913D	393,500	650.	670.	690.	715.	2500.	—
1913S	34,000	650.	900.	1150.	1900.	4600.	—
1914	95,320	650.	670.	690.	1050.	4900.	40,000.
1914D	453,000	650.	670.	690.	715.	2100.	—
1914S	1,498,000	650.	670.	690.	715.	2100.	—
1915	152,050	650.	670.	690.	1100.	2700.	40,000.
1915S	567,500	650.	670.	690.	715.	2300.	—
1916S	796,000	650.	670.	900.	1050.	3500.	—
1920	228,250	650.	670.	900.	1100.	3500.	—
1920S	558,000	5000.	9000.	11,750.	24,000.	44,500.	—
1921	528,500	12,500.	20,000.	27,000.	34,500.	56,500.	—
1922	1,375,500	650.	670.	690.	715.	1300.	—
1922S	2,658,000	650.	900.	1150.	1450.	4600.	—
1923	566,000	650.	670.	690.	715.	1300.	—
1923D	1,702,250	650.	900.	1050.	1350.	2100.	—
1924	4,323,500	650.	670.	690.	715.	1200.	—
1924D	3,049,500	650.	900.	1100.	2200.	8000.	—
1924S	2,927,500	650.	900.	1100.	1900.	6000.	—
1925	2,831,750	650.	670.	690.	715.	1200.	—
1925D	2,938,500	875.	1150.	1400.	3100.	8000.	—
1925S	3,776,500	875.	1150.	1400.	3000.	7000.	—
1926	816,750	650.	670.	690.	715.	1200.	—
1926D	481,000	1000.	1200.	1600.	3300.	9200.	—
1926S	2,041,500	875.	1100.	1300.	2200.	5250.	—
1927	2,946,750	650.	670.	690.	715.	1200.	—
1927D	180,000		Private Sale, Sept. 1974			175,000.	—
1927S	3,107,000	2750.	4500.	5750.	13,000.	23,000.	—
1928	8,816,000	650.	670.	875.	715.	1300.	—
1929	1,779,750	1750.	3500.	4500.	10,250.	21,000.	—
1930S	74,000	6000.	10,000.	12,750.	22,000.	35,000.	—
1931	2,938,250	4250.	7500.	10,500.	18,500.	35,000.	—
1931D	106,500	3750.	7250.	9750.	21,000.	37,500.	—
1932	1,101,750	5000.	9000.	11,250.	23,000.	45,000.	—
1933	445,500		None placed in circulation			—	—

MODERN SINGLES

Commencing with 1965 coin issues, we list only uncirculated and proof conditions. Coins in lesser conditions are numismatically valued at little over face.

Date	Cents Mintage	Unc.	Proof	Nickels Mintage	Unc.	Proof	Dimes Mintage	Unc.	Proof	Quarters Mintage	Unc.	Proof	Halves Mintage	Unc.	Proof
1965	1,497,224,900	.15	NM	136,131,380	.15	NM	1,652,140,570	.20	NM	1,819,717,540	.80	NM	Refer to Regular Date Listings		
1966	2,188.147,783	.15	NM	156,208,283	.15	NM	1,382,734,540	.20	NM	821,101,500	.80	NM			
1967	3,048,667,100	.15	NM	107,325,800	.15	NM	2,244,007,320	.20	NM	1,524,031,848	.80	NM			
1968	1,707,880,970	.15	NM	———	NM	NM	424,470,000	.20	NM	220,731,500	.80	NM			
1968D	2,886,269,600	.15	NM	91,227,880	.15	NM	480,748,280	.20	NM	101,534,000	1.00	NM			
1968S	261,311,510	.15	.25	103,437,510	.15	.40	Proof Only	NM	.75	Proof Only	NM	.75			
1969	1,136,910,000	.25	NM	———	NM	NM	145,790,000	.20	NM	176,212,000	.50	NM			
1969D	4,002,832,200	.15	NM	202,807,500	.15	NM	563,323,870	.20	NM	114,372,000	1.25	NM			
1969S	547,309,631	.15	.25	123,099,631	.15	.40	Proof Only	NM	.75	Proof Only	NM	.75			
1970	1,898,315,000	.15	NM	———	NM	NM	345,570,000	.20	NM	136,420,000	.50	NM			
1970D	2,891,438,900	.15	NM	515,485,380	.15	NM	754,942,100	.20	NM	417,341,364	.50	NM			
1970S	693,192,814	.15	.65	241,464,814	.15	.65	Proof Only	NM	1.25	Proof Only	NM	1.00			
1971	1,919,490,000	.15	NM	106,884,000	.15	NM	162,690,000	.20	NM	109,284,000	.50	NM	155,164,000	1.00	NM
1971D	2,911,045,600	.15	NM	316,144,800	.15	NM	377,914,240	.20	NM	258,634,428	.50	NM	302,097,424	1.00	NM
1971S	528,354,192	.15	.25	Proof Only	NM	1.25	Proof Only	NM	.75	Proof Only	NM	.75	Proof Only	NM	3.75
1972	2,933,255,000	.15	NM	202,036,000	.15	NM	431,540,000	.20	NM	215,048,000	.40	NM	153,180,000	.75	NM
1972D	2,665,071,400	.15	NM	351,694,600	.15	NM	330,290,000	.20	NM	311,067,732	.40	NM	141,890,000	.75	NM
1972S	380,200,104	.15	.25	Proof Only	NM	1.25	Proof Only	NM	.75	Proof Only	NM	.75	Proof Only	NM	3.75
1973	3,728,245,000	.10	NM	384,396,000	.15	NM	315,670,000	.20	NM	346,924,000	.40	NM	64,964,000	.75	NM
1973D	3,549,576,588	.10	NM	261,405,400	.15	NM	455,032,426	.20	NM	232,977,400	.40	NM	83,171,400	.75	NM
1973S	319,937,634	.15	.75	Proof Only	NM	2.25	Proof Only	NM	1.75	Proof Only	NM	1.50	Proof Only	NM	4.50
1974	4,232,140,523	.10	NM	601,752,000	.15	NM	470,248,000	.20	NM	801,456,000	.40	NM	———	.75	NM
1974D	4,235,098,000	.10	NM	277,373,000	.15	NM	571,083,000	.20	NM	353,160,300	.40	NM	———	.75	NM
1974S	412,039,228	.15	.75	Proof Only	NM	3.75	Proof Only	NM	1.50	Proof Only	NM	1.50	Proof Only	NM	4.50
1975	5,451,476,142	.10	NM	181,772,000	.15	NM	585,673,900	.20	NM	———	NM	NM	———	NM	NM
1975D	4,505,245,300	.10	NM	401,875,300	.15	NM	313,705,300	.20	NM	———	NM	NM	———	NM	NM
1975S	Proof Only	NM	11.00	Proof Only	NM	2.50	Proof Only	NM	2.50	———	NM	NM	———	NM	NM
1976	4,674,292,426	.10	NM	367,124,000	.15	NM	568,760,000	.20	NM	Refer To Bicentennial Coinage Listings					
1976D	4,221,592,455	.10	NM	563,964,147	.15	NM	695,222,774	.20	NM						
1976S	Proof Only	NM	3.50	Proof Only	NM	1.50	Proof Only	NM	1.25						
1977	4,469,930,000	.10	NM	585,376,000	.15	NM	796,930,000	.20	NM	468,556,000	.40	NM	43,598,000	.75	NM
1977D	4,149,062,300	.10	NM	297,313,460	.15	NM	376,607,228	.20	NM	258,898,212	.40	NM	31,449,106	.75	NM
1977S	Proof Only	NM	4.50	Proof Only	NM	1.50	Proof Only	NM	1.50	Proof Only	NM	1.00	Proof Only	NM	3.75
1978	5,558,605,000	.10	NM	391,308,000	.15	NM	663,980,000	.20	NM	521,452,000	.40	NM	14,350,000	.75	NM
1978D	4,280,233,400	.10	NM	313,092,780	.15	NM	282,847,540	.20	NM	287,373.152	.40	NM	13,765,799	.75	NM
1978S	Proof Only	NM	5.00	Proof Only	NM	1.35	Proof Only	NM	1.50	Proof Only	NM	1.00	Proof Only	NM	6.75

PROOF SETS

Date	Mintage	Value
1936	3,837	10,500.
1937	5,542	7000.
1938	8,045	3700.
1939	8,795	3300.
1940	11,246	2350.
1941	15,287	2250.
1942 both 5C	21,120	2650.
1942 5 coins	Inc. Ab.	2250.
1950	51,386	1150.
1951	57,500	880.
1952	81,980	530.
1953	128,800	295.
1954	233,300	170.
1955 box	378,200	140.
1955 flat pack	Inc. Ab.	135.
1956	669,384	48.00
1957	1,247,952	25.00
1958	875,652	35.00
1959	1,149,291	24.00
1960 lg. date	1,691,602	19.00
1960 sm. date	Inc. Ab.	38.00
1961	3,028,244	16.50
1962	3,218,019	16.50
1963	3,075,645	16.50
1964	3,950,762	16.50
1965 SMS*	2,360,000	6.75
1966 SMS*	2,261,583	6.75
1967 SMS*	1,863,344	12.00
1968S	3,041,509	7.75
1968 S No S 10 C	—	11,500.
1969S	2,934,631	7.75
1970S lg. date	2,632,810	17.50
1970S sm. date	Inc. Ab.	165.
1970S No S 10 C	Est. 2,200	1850.
1971S	3,224,138	5.10
1971S No S 5C	Est. 1,655	2775.
1972S	3,267,667	5.35
1973S	2,769,624	12.60
1974S	2,617,350	13.25
1975S	2,909,369	27.00
1976S 3pc.	—	21.00
1976S	4,149,730	10.75
1977S	3,251,152	11.50
1978S	3,127,788	26.50
1979S	—	24.00

*Special mint sets produced by the U.S. Mint and possessing a proof-like appearance.

MINT SETS

Date	Mintage	Value
1940-P-D-S	—	—
1941-P-D-S	—	—
1942-P-D-S Both 5C	—	—
1943-P-D-S	—	—
1944-P-D-S	—	—
1945-P-D-S	—	—
1946-P-D-S	—	1900.
1947-P-D-S (Est)	5,000	1450.
1948-P-D-S (Est.)	6,000	330.
1949-P-D-S (Est.)	5,200	1700.
1950-P-D-S	—	—
1951-P-D-S	8,654	570.
1952-P-D-S	11,499	380.
1953-P-D-S	15,538	280.
1954-P-D-S	25,599	210.
1955-P-D-S	49,656	126.
1956-P-D	45,475	80.00
1957-P-D	32,324	125.
1958-P-D	50,315	117.
1959-P-D	187,000	53.00
1960-P-D Lg. Date	260,485	40.00
1960-P-D Sm. Date	Inc. Ab.	43.00
1961-P-D	223,704	39.00
1962-P-D	385,285	38.00
1963-P-D	606,622	38.00
1964-P-D	978,157	37.00
1965	2,360,000	6.75
1966	2,261,583	6.75
1967	1,863,344	12.00
1968-P-D-S	2,105,128	6.95
1969-P-D-S	1,306,723	6.95
1970-P-D-S Lg. Date	2,150,000	58.00
1970-P-D-S Sm. Date	Inc. Ab.	60.00
1971-P-D-S	2,193,396	2.70
1972-P-D-S	2,750,000	2.65
1973-P-D-S	1,767,691	38.00
1974-P-D-S	1,975,981	5.50
1975-P-D-S	1,921,488	7.00
1976 (3 Pcs.)	—	22.00
1976	1,892,513	5.00
1977	—	6.95
1978	—	7.50
1979		6.95

The mintage figures listed above document only the Treasury produced sets, while the valuations are strictly tied to the combined values of the individual coins contained in a given set. For this reason in some instances valuations are often at considerable variance with the quantities of issue indicated. When a dash (-) appears in the mintage column no sets were reported as produced by the Treasury, all existent sets having been privately assembled. The official production figure of 20,739 reported for 1949 undoubtedly represents the combined treasury issue of mint sets for the years 1946-49.

BICENTENNIAL COINAGE

The nation's quarter, half and dollar coinage was redesigned in 1975 to provide circulation issue commemoratives of the bicentennial of the American Revolution. While the obverses of these coins retained the familiar portraits of Washington, Kennedy and Eisenhower, with the addition of commemorative — 1776 • 1976 — dual dating, the reverses were completely redesigned to feature themes reminiscent of the birth of the country.

NOTE: The Numismatic value bases for the Bicentennial Coinage are $3.00 for quarters, $4.50 for halves and $14.00 for dollars, based on the $13.00 market price for one ounce of silver at the time these valuations were assigned. The bullion value of each quarter increases or decreases approximately three-quarters of a cent for each 10-cent change in the bullion price, or 7.4-cents for each $1 change; on halves 1.48-cents for each 10-cent change, or 14.79-cents for each $1 change; on dollars 3.16-cents for each 10-cent change, or 31.36-cents for each $1 change; set of the three pieces (uncirculated or proof quality) 5.38-cents for each 10-cent change, or 53.82-cents for each $1 change.

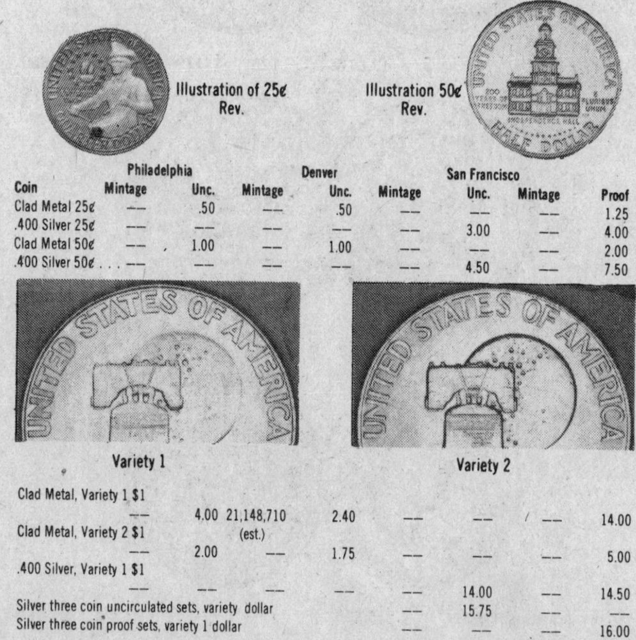

Illustration of 25¢ Rev.

Illustration 50¢ Rev.

Variety 1

Variety 2

Coin	Philadelphia Mintage	Unc.	Denver Mintage	Unc.	San Francisco Mintage	Unc.	Mintage	Proof
Clad Metal 25¢	—	.50	—	.50	—	—	—	1.25
.400 Silver 25¢	—	—	—	—	—	3.00	—	4.00
Clad Metal 50¢	—	1.00	—	1.00	—	—	—	2.00
.400 Silver 50¢	—	—	—	—	—	4.50	—	7.50
Clad Metal, Variety 1 $1	—	4.00	21,148,710 (est.)	2.40	—	—	—	14.00
Clad Metal, Variety 2 $1	—	2.00	—	1.75	—	—	—	5.00
.400 Silver, Variety 1 $1	—	—	—	—	—	14.00	—	14.50
Silver three coin uncirculated sets, variety dollar					—	15.75	—	—
Silver three coin proof sets, variety 1 dollar					—	—	—	16.00

QUARTER

Date	Event	Mintage	XF-40	AU-55	MS-60	MS-65
1893	Isabella Quarter	24,214	115.	405.	580.	1575.

DOLLAR

Date	Event	Mintage	XF-40	AU-55	MS-60	MS-65
1900	Lafayette Dollar	36,026	235.	560.	1965.	8650.

HALF DOLLARS

NOTE: A $6.25 Numismatic value base has been assigned to selected common commemorative halves, based on the $25.00 market price for one ounce of silver at the time these valuations were assigned. The bullion value of each coin's silver content increases or decreases approximately 3.62-cents for each 10-cent change in the bullion price, or 36.17-cents for each $1 change.

2x2 ADDED

Date	Event	Mintage	XF-40	AU-55	MS-60	MS-65
1921	Alabama 2X2	6,006	95.00	112.	515.	1700.
1921	Alabama	59,038	115.	200.	425.	1250.

Date	Event	Mintage	XF-40	AU-55	MS-60	MS-65
1936	Albany	17,671	125.	170.	335.	1800.

Date	Event	Mintage	XF-40	AU-55	MS-60	MS-65
1937	Antietam	18,028	175.	235.	420.	800.

Date	Event	Mintage	XF-40	AU-55	MS-60	MS-65
1935	Arkansas PDS Set	5,505	—	—	275.	450.

COMMEMORATIVES

Date	Event	Mintage	XF-40	AU-55	MS-60	MS-65
1936	Arkansas PDS Set	9,660	—	—	275.	450.
1937	Arkansas PDS Set	5,505	—	—	305.	500.
1938	Arkansas PDS Set	3,155	—	—	580.	1350.
1939	Arkansas PDS Set	2,104	—	—	1630.	2700.
	Arkansas - Type Coin	—	25.00	39.00	77.00	140.

See Also Robinson-Arkansas

Date	Event	Mintage	XF-40	AU-55	MS-60	MS-65
1936	Bay Bridge	71,424	45.00	67.50	108.	270.

1934 ADDED

Date	Event	Mintage	XF-40	AU-55	MS-60	MS-65
1934	Boone	10,007	—	58.00	124.	250.
1935	Boone - PDS Set w/1934	5,005	—	—	1715.	2600.
1935	Boone - PDS Set	2,003	—	—	315.	620.
1936	Boone - PDS Set	5,005	—	—	315.	620.
1937	Boone - PDS Set	2,506	—	—	755.	1485.
1938	Boone - PDS Set	2,100	—	—	1515.	2525.
	Boone - Type Coin	—	—	40.00	100.	190.

Date	Event	Mintage	XF-40	AU-55	MS-60	MS-65
1936	Bridgeport	25,015	60.00	73.00	170.	395.

Date	Event	Mintage	XF-40	AU-55	MS-60	MS-65
1925S	California Jubilee	86,594	70.00	95.00	190.	845.

Date	Event	Mintage	XF-40	AU-55	MS-60	MS-65
1936	Cincinnati - PDS Set	5,005	—	—	1575.	2600.
1936	Cincinnati - Type Coin	—	175.	260.	520.	840.

Date	Event	Mintage	XF-40	AU-55	MS-60	MS-65
1936	Cleveland - Great Lakes	50,030	30.00	40.00	85.00	150.

Date	Event	Mintage	XF-40	AU-55	MS-60	MS-65
1936	Columbia PDS Set	9,007	—	—	1100.	2080.
1936	Columbia - Type Coin	—	87.00	125.	335.	675.

Date	Event	Mintage	XF-40	AU-55	MS-60	MS-65
1892	Columbian Expo	950,000	6.25	7.25	26.00	157.
1893	Columbian Expo	1,550,405	6.25	8.00	23.00	157.

Date	Event	Mintage	XF-40	AU-55	MS-60	MS-65
1935	Connecticut	25,018	105.	115.	265.	600.

Date	Event	Mintage	XF-40	AU-55	MS-60	MS-65
1936	Delaware	20,993	105.	115.	265.	600.

Date	Event	Mintage	XF-40	AU-55	MS-60	MS-65
1936	Elgin	20,015	81.00	100.	230.	515.

Date	Event	Mintage	XF-40	AU-55	MS-60	MS-65
1936	Gettysburg	26,928	87.00	135.	335.	785.

STAR ADDED

Date	Event	Mintage	XF-40	AU-55	MS-60	MS-65
1922	Grant-With Star	4,256	245.	405.	845.	3375.
1922	Grant	67,405	37.50	42.00	115.	480.

Date	Event	Mintage	XF-40	AU-55	MS-60	MS-65
1928	Hawaiian	10,008	595.	1100.	1715.	4950.

Date	Event	Mintage	XF-40	AU-55	MS-60	MS-65
1935	Hudson	10,008	440.	500.	845.	1850.

Date	Event	Mintage	XF-40	AU-55	MS-60	MS-65
1924	Huguenot-Wallon	142,080	45.00	58.00	115.	500.

Date	Event	Mintage	XF-40	AU-55	MS-60	MS-65
1918	Lincoln-Illinois	100,058	37.00	54.00	95.00	280.

Date	Event	Mintage	XF-40	AU-55	MS-60	MS-65
1946	Iowa	100,057	36.00	48.00	90.00	195.

Date	Event	Mintage	XF-40	AU-55	MS-60	MS-65
1925	Lexington-Concord	162,013	26.00	38.00	85.00	170.

Date	Event	Mintage	XF-40	AU-55	MS-60	MS-65
1936	Long Island	81,826	25.00	40.00	77.00	145.

Date	Event	Mintage	XF-40	AU-55	MS-60	MS-65
1936	Lynchburg	20,013	75.00	124.	225.	580.

Date	Event	Mintage	XF-40	AU-55	MS-60	MS-65
1920	Maine	50,028	37.00	54.00	120.	495.

Date	Event	Mintage	XF-40	AU-55	MS-60	MS-65
1934	Maryland	25,015	81.00	97.00	195.	450.

2x4 ADDED

Date	Event	Mintage	XF-40	AU-55	MS-60	MS-65
1921	Missouri - 2X4	5,000	230.	250.	965.	2800.
1921	Missouri	15,428	185.	240.	935.	2600.

Date	Event	Mintage	XF-40	AU-55	MS-60	MS-65
1923S	Monroe	274,077	15.00	22.50	60.00	205.

Date	Event	Mintage	XF-40	AU-55	MS-60	MS-65
1938	New Rochelle	15,266	150.	210.	425.	925.

Date	Event	Mintage	XF-40	AU-55	MS-60	MS-65
1936	Norfolk	16,936	156.	195.	425.	1125.

Date	Event	Mintage	XF-40	AU-55	MS-60	MS-65
1926	Oregon	47,955	37.00	52.00	135.	250.
1926S	Oregon	83,055	37.00	52.00	135.	270.
1928	Oregon	6,028	50.00	89.00	305.	620.
1933D	Oregon	5,008	81.00	102.	335.	740.
1934D	Oregon	7,006	45.00	73.00	255.	590.
1936	Oregon	10,006	44.00	58.00	157.	395.
1936S	Oregon	5,006	54.00	81.00	245.	675.
1937D	Oregon	12,008	44.00	53.00	150.	310.
1938	Oregon - PDS Set	6,005	—	—	610.	1250.
1939	Oregon - PDS Set	3,004	—	—	995.	1500.
	Oregon - Type Coin	—	39.00	52.00	135.	270.

Date	Event	Mintage	XF-40	AU-55	MS-60	MS-65
1915S	Panama - Pacific	27,134	125.	445.	940.	8200.

1921 VERSION

Date	Event	Mintage	XF-40	AU-55	MS-60	MS-65
1920	Pilgrim	152,112	26.00	28.00	72.00	250.
1921	Pilgrim	20,053	52.50	73.00	195.	700.

Date	Event	Mintage	XF-40	AU-55	MS-60	MS-65
1936	Rhode Island - PDS Set	15,010	—	—	610.	1000.
1936	Rhode Island - Type Coin	—	32.00	67.50	180.	335.

Date	Event	Mintage	XF-40	AU-55	MS-60	MS-65
1937	Roanoke	29,030	52.00	81.00	180.	620.

Date	Event	Mintage	XF-40	AU-55	MS-60	MS-65
936	Robinson-Arkansas	25,265 (See Also Arkansas)	62.00	81.00	150.	420.

Date	Event	Mintage	XF-40	AU-55	MS-60	MS-65
935S	San Diego	70,132	31.00	34.00	79.00	210.
936D	San Diego	30,092	39.00	45.00	130.	310.

Date	Event	Mintage	XF-40	AU-55	MS-60	MS-65
1926	Sesquicentennial	141,120	25.00	27.50	61.00	180.
1935	Spanish Trail	10,008	435.	590.	1035.	2600.
1925	Stone Mountain	1,314,709	10.50	21.00	37.00	100.
1934	Texas	61,463	37.50	46.00	95.00	195.
1935	Texas - PDS Set	9,994	—	—	290.	600.
1936	Texas - PDS Set	8,911	—	—	290.	600.
1937	Texas - PDS Set	6,571	—	—	365.	675.
1938	Texas - PDS Set	3,775	—	—	700.	1240.
	Texas - Type Coins	—	—	—	95.00	200.
1925	Ft. Vancouver	14,994	155.	245.	640.	2075.
1927	Vermont	28,142	69.00	125.	300.	1025.
1946	B.T.W. - PDS Set	200,113	—	—	55.00	60.00
1947	B.T.W. - PDS Set	100,017	—	—	66.00	118.
1948	B.T.W. - PDS Set	8,005	—	—	110.	300.
1949	B.T.W. - PDS Set	6,004	—	—	210.	450.
1950	B.T.W. - PDS Set	6,004	—	—	163.	405.
	San Francisco Mintage 512,091					
1951	B.T.W. - PDS Set	7,004	—	—	130.	310.
	B.T.W. - Type Coin	—	9.00	13.00	18.00	19.00
	Philadelphia Mintage 510,082					
1951	Wash.-Carv. - PDS Set	10,004	—	—	73.00	130.
	Philadelphia Mintage 110,018					
1952	Wash.-Carv. - PDS Set	8,006	—	—	110.	270.
	Philadelphia Mintage 2,006,292					
1953	Wash.-Carv. - PDS Set	8,003	—	—	170.	320.
	San Francisco Mintage 108,020					
1954	Wash.-Carv. - PDS Set	12,006	—	—	79.00	112.
	San Francisco Mintage 122,024					
	Wash.-Carver - Type Coin	—	9.00	13.00	13.50	14.50
1936	Wisconsin	25,015	78.00	95.00	185.	620.
1936	York County	25,015	78.00	110.	185.	560.

GOLD DOLLARS

Date	Event	Mintage	AU-55	MS-60	MS-65
1903	Louisiana, Jefferson	17,500	360.	1000.	2100.
1903	Louisiana, Mckinley	17,500	360.	1000.	2100.
1904	Lewis and Clark Expo.	10,025	610.	2600.	5850.
1905	Lewis and Clark Expo.	10,041	610.	2600.	5850.
1915S	Pan-Pacific Expo.	15,000	320.	1265.	4700.
1916	Mckinley Memorial	9,977	310.	1000.	2075.
1917	Mckinley Memorial	10,000	320.	1070.	2275.

GOLD TWO AND A HALF DOLLARS

Date	Event	Mintage	AU-55	MS-60	MS-65
1915S	Pan-Pacific Expo.	6,749	1000.	4150.	12,750.

Date	Event	Mintage	AU-55	MS-60	MS-65
1926	Philadelphia Sesqui.	46,019	320.	650.	1345.

GOLD FIFTY DOLLARS

Date	Event	Mintage	AU-55	MS-60	MS-65
1915S	Pan-Pacific Expo., Round	483	9000.	19,000.	58,000.
1915S	Pan-Pacific Expo., Octagon	645	7000.	13,500.	45,000.

HAWAII

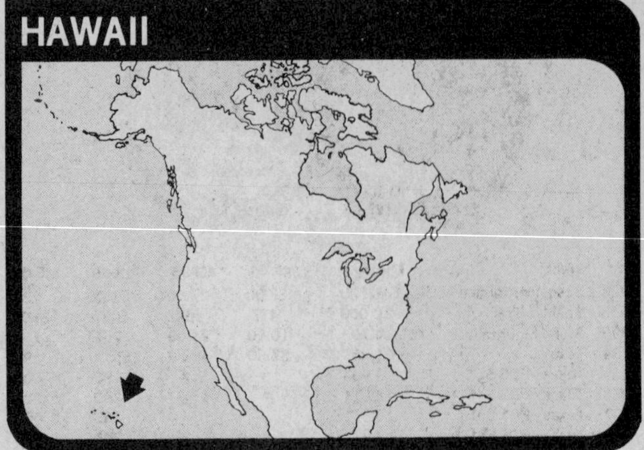

The State of Hawaii, 50th state of the United States, consists of eight main islands and numerous smaller islands of coral and volcanic origin situated in the central Pacific Ocean 2,400 miles from San Francisco. The archipelago has an area of 6,450 sq. mi. and a population of 846,900. Capital: Honolulu. The principal industries are tourism and agriculture. Cane sugar and pineapples are exported.

The islands, originally populated by Polynesians who traveled from the Society Islands, were discovered by British navigator Capt. James Cook in 1778. He named them the Sandwich Islands. King Kamehameha the Great united the islands under one kingdom (1795-1810) which endured until 1893 when Queen Liliuokalani, the gifted composer of 'Aloha Oe' and other songs was deposed and a provisional government established. This was followed by a republic which governed Hawaii until 1898 when it ceded itself to the United States. Hawaii was organized as a territory in 1900 and attained statehood on Aug. 21, 1959.

The coinage issued under the Kingdom of Hawaii is obsolete.

RULERS

Kamehameha III, 1825-54
Kamehameha IV, 1854-1863
Kamehameha V, 1863-1872
William Lunalilo, 1873-74
David Kalakaua, 1874-1891
Queen Liliuokalani, 1891-93
Provisional Govt., 1893-94
Republic, 1894-1898
Annexed to U.S., 1898-1900
Territory, 1900-1959

MONETARY SYSTEM

100 Hapa Haneri=Akahi Dala
100 Cents=1 Dollar (Dala)

CENT

COPPER

KM#	Date	Mintage	VG	Fine	VF	XF	AU	MS-60	MS-65
1a	1847 plain 4, 13 berries (6 left, 7 right)								
		.100	175.00	225.00	275.00	400.00	600.00	1250.	1750.
1b	1847 plain 4, 15 berries (8 left, 7 right)								
		Inc. Ab.	210.00	260.00	325.00	500.00	1000.	1500.	2000.
1c	1847 plain 4, 17 berries (8 left, 9 right)								
		Inc. Ab.	175.00	225.00	300.00	450.00	750.00	1350.	1850.
1d	1847 crosslet 4, 15 berries (7 left, 8 right)								
		Inc. Ab.	175.00	225.00	275.00	400.00	575.00	1250.	1750.
1e	1847 crosslet 4, 18 berries (9 left, 9 right)								
		Inc. Ab.	175.00	225.00	300.00	475.00	850.00	1400.	2000.

SOUVENIR CENT

Modern replicas of the 1847 cent have been produced in several varieties, struck of brass oroide since the late 1940's for sale to tourists as souvenirs of their visits to the islands.

5 CENTS (PATTERN)

GERMAN SILVER

KM#	Date	Mintage	VG	Fine	VF	XF	AU	MS-60	MS-65
2	1881	*200 pcs.	2500.	3000.	3500.	4500.	5500.	6500.	9000.

NOTE: All original specimens of this pattern were struck on thin nickel-silver planchets, presumably in Paris and have "MAILLECHORT" stamped on the edge. In the early 1900's deceptive replicas of the issue were produced in Canada, on thick and thin nickel and aluminum, and thin copper planchets (thick about 2.7 to 3.1mm; thin about 1.4 to 1.7 mm). The original patterns can be easily distinguished from the replicas, because on the former a small cross surmounts the crown on the reverse; on the replicas the crown is topped by a small ball.

10 CENTS (UMI KENETA)

.900 SILVER

KM#	Date	Mintage	VG	Fine	VF	XF	AU	MS-60	MS-65
3	1883	.250	25.00	35.00	75.00	275.00	600.00	1500.	2200.
	1883	26 pcs.	—	—	—	—	—	Proof	10,000.

COPPER

KM#	Date	Mintage	VG	Fine	VF	XF	AU	MS-60	MS-65
3a	1883	—	—	—	—	—	—	Proof	Unique

1/8 DOLLAR (HAPAWALU)
PATTERN

.900 SILVER

KM#	Date	Mintage	VG	Fine	VF	XF	AU	MS-60	MS-65
4	1883	20 pcs.	—	—	—	—	—	Proof	30,000.

COPPER

KM#	Date	Mintage	VG	Fine	VF	XF	AU	MS-60	MS-65
4a	1883	18 pcs.	—	—	—	—	—	Proof	7500.

1/4 DOLLAR (HAPAHA)

.900 SILVER

KM#	Date	Mintage	VG	Fine	VF	XF	AU	MS-60	MS-65
5	1883	.500	30.00	40.00	55.00	90.00	150.00	325.00	450.00
	1883/1383								
		Inc. Ab.	30.00	40.00	65.00	110.00	175.00	350.00	500.00
	1883	26 pcs.	—	—	—	—	—	Proof	10,000.

COPPER

KM#	Date	Mintage	VG	Fine	VF	XF	AU	MS-60	MS-65
5a	1883	18 pcs.	—	—	—	—	—	Proof	7500.

1/2 DOLLAR (HAPULA)

KM#	Date	Mintage	VG	Fine	VF	XF	AU	MS-60	MS-65
		.900 SILVER							
6	1883	.700	60.00	90.00	120.00	250.00	500.00	1200.	1750.
	1883	26 pcs.	—	—	—	—	—	Proof	10,000.
		COPPER							
6a	1883	18 pcs.	—	—	—	—	—	Proof	7500.

DOLLAR (AKAHI DALA)

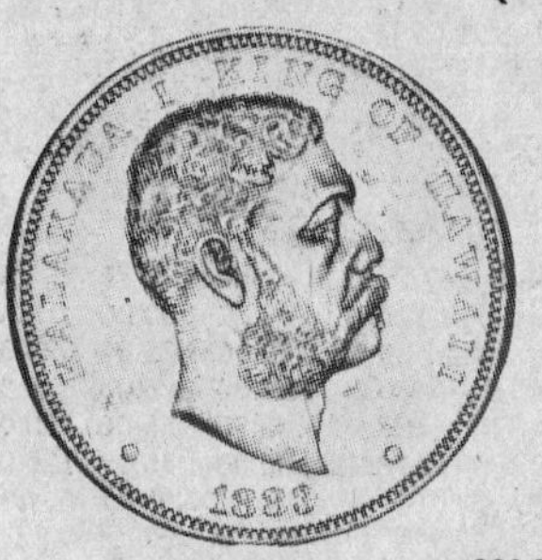

KM#	Date	Mintage	VG	Fine	VF	XF	AU	MS-60	MS-65
		.900 SILVER							
7	1883	.500	225.00	275.00	350.00	900.00	3000.	7750.	11,000.
	1883	26 pcs.	—	—	—	—	—	Proof	15,000.
		COPPER							
7a	1883	18 pcs.	—	—	—	—	—	Proof	10,000.

NOTE: Official records indicate the following quantities of the above issues were redeemed and melted: KM#1, 88,305; KM#3, 79; KM#5, 257,400; KM#6, 612,245; KM#7, 453,652. That leaves approximate net mintages of: KM#1, 11,600; KM#3, 250,000; KM#5, (regular date) 202,600, (overdate) 40,000; KM#6, 87,700; KM#7, 46,300.

LILIUOKALANI PATTERNS

NOTE: The Liliuokalai and Kaiulani patterns have no official status. They were struck at the private order of wealthy English collector Reginald Huth byPinches and Company of London and first appeared in Honolulu about 1901.

DOLLAR (AKAHI DALA)

SILVER

KM#	Date	Mintage	XF	Unc	Proof
8	1891(93)	50 pcs.	—	—	5500.

NOTE: Two recent replicas of the Liliuokalani dollar exist. One is a 32mm sterling silver piece. The originals have a 38mm diameter which copies the original obverse and reverse devices, with the word COPY added incuse near the rim on the reverse. The second is a 39mm, gold anodized aluminum piece produced for sale to tourists and featuring a representation of the obverse, with the initials RHM added in the field, in combination with the 1883 dollar reverse design.

20 DOLLARS (DALA)

GOLD

KM#	Date	Mintage	XF	Unc	Proof
9	1893	3 pcs.	—	—	65,000.

KAIULANI PATTERNS

DOLLAR

KM#	Date	Metal	Mintage	XF	Unc	Proof
10	1895 one dolphin on obverse	Silver	*20 pcs.	—	—	4500.

NOTE: Replicas exist in gold anodized aluminum featuring a representation of the obverse, with the initials RHM added in the field, in combination with the 1883 dollar reverse design.

KM#	Date	Metal	Mintage	XF	Unc	Proof
11	1895 four dolphins on obverse	Silver	*30 pcs.	—	—	4000.
11a	1895	Iron	3 pcs.	—	—	5000.
11b	1895	Copper	2 pcs.	—	—	6000.
11c	1895	Tin	Unique	—	—	7000.
11d	1895	Gold	Unique	—	—	90,000.

UNAUTHORIZED PATTERNS

1/8 DOLLAR (HAPAWALU)

KM#	Date	Metal	Mintage	XF	Unc	Proof
12	1883	Bronze	*20 pcs.	—	—	5000.
12a	1883	Nickel	—	—	—	6000.
12b	1883	Gold	Unique	—	—	35,000.
12c	1883	Platinum	Est. 3 pcs.	—	—	10,000.

1/4 DOLLAR (HAPAHA)

KM#	Date	Metal	Mintage	XF	Unc	Proof
13	1884	Bronze	—	—	—	2750.
13a	1884	Brass	Unique	—	—	3000.
13b	1884	Oride	Unique	—	—	3000.
13c	1884	Gold	—	—	—	24,000.
13d	1884	Platinum	—	—	—	6000.

1/2 DOLLAR (HAPULA)

KM#	Date	Metal	Mintage	XF	Unc	Proof
14	1884	Bronze	—	—	—	3500.
14a	1884	Gold	2 pcs.	known	—	24,000.
14b	1884	Platinum	—	—	—	7000.

NOTE: All of the patterns in this section are of spurious origin. It is thought they were produced clandestinely by a workman at the Philadelphia mint, where the original die making tools were still preserved, in the early 1900's. The "unauthorized" 1/8 dollar patterns may be distinguished from the "official" pieces by the presence of flowing "lazy" eights in the date, as contrasted to the "block" eights used on regular Hawaiian coinage.

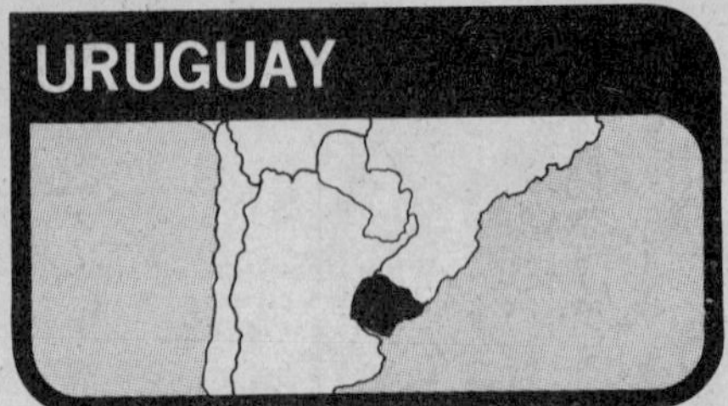

The Oriental Republic of Uruguay (so called because of its location on the east bank of the Uruguay River) is situated on the Atlantic coast of South America between Argentina and Brazil. This most advanced of South American countries has an area of 72,200 sq. mi. (186,997 sq. km.) and a population of 3.1 million. Capital: Montevideo. Uruguay's chief economic asset is its rich, rolling grassy plains. Meat, wool, hides and skins are exported.

Uruguay was discovered in 1516 by Juan Diaz de Solis, a Spaniard, but settled by the Portuguese who founded Colonia in 1680. Spain contested Portuguese possession and, after a long struggle, gained control of the country in 1778. During the general South American struggle for independence, Uruguay cast off the Spanish bond, only to be reconquered by the Portuguese from Brazil in the struggle of 1816-20. Revolt flared anew in 1825 and independence was reasserted in 1828 with the help of Argentina. The Uruguayan republic was established in 1830.

MINTMARKS

A - Paris, Berlin, Vienna
D - Lyon (France)
H - Birmingham
Mo - Mexico City
(p) Poissy, France
So - Santiago (Small O above S)

MONETARY SYSTEM

100 Centesimo = 1 Peso

Commencing 1975

1000 Old Pesos = 1 New Peso

CENTESIMO

BRONZE, 5 gm.

Y#	Date	Mintage	Fine	VF	XF	Unc
7	1869A	1.000	1.00	3.00	7.00	35.00
	1869H	1.000	1.00	3.50	7.00	27.50

COPPER-NICKEL, 5gm.

Y#	Date	Mintage	Fine	VF	XF	Unc
15	1901A	5.000	.25	.50	2.00	11.00
	1909A	5.000	.25	.50	2.00	10.00
	1924(p)	3.000	.40	.75	2.00	8.50
	1936A	2.000	.50	.80	2.00	10.00

1.5gm.

Y#	Date	Mintage	Fine	VF	XF	Unc
28	1953	5.000	.10	.15	.30	.50

ALUMINUM

Y#	Date	Mintage	Fine	VF	XF	Unc
A55	1977So	70.000	—	—	—	.15

2 CENTESIMOS

BRONZE, 10 gm.

Y#	Date	Mintage	Fine	VF	XF	Unc
8	1869A	3.000	1.00	2.50	6.00	35.00
	1869H	2.000	1.25	2.50	6.00	27.50

COPPER-NICKEL, 3.5 gm.

Y#	Date	Mintage	Fine	VF	XF	Unc
16	1901A	7.500	.30	.60	1.75	13.00
	1909A	10.000	.30	.60	1.50	6.00
	1924(p)	11.000	.30	.60	2.25	8.00
	1936A	6.500	.40	1.00	3.00	12.00
	1941So	10.000	.25	.50	1.75	6.50

COPPER, 3.5 gm.

Y#	Date	Mintage	Fine	VF	XF	Unc
16a	1943So	5.000	.25	.50	1.75	5.00
	1944So	3.500	.20	.35	1.25	4.00
	1945So	2.500	.20	.50	1.50	5.50
	1946So	2.500	.20	.50	1.50	5.50
	1947So	5.000	.20	.35	.75	3.00
	1948So	7.500	.15	.30	.60	2.00
	1949So	7.400	.15	.30	.60	2.00
	1951So	12.500	.15	.25	.50	1.75

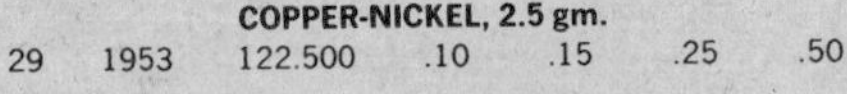

COPPER-NICKEL, 2.5 gm.

Y#	Date	Mintage	Fine	VF	XF	Unc
29	1953	122.500	.10	.15	.25	.50

NICKEL-BRASS, 2.0 gm.

Y#	Date	Mintage	Fine	VF	XF	Unc
33	1960	17.500	—	.10	.15	.40

ALUMINUM

Y#	Date	Mintage	Fine	VF	XF	Unc
B55	1977So	1000.000	—	—	.10	.20

4 CENTESIMOS

BRONZE, 20 gm.

Y#	Date	Mintage	Fine	VF	XF	Unc
9	1869A	2.000	1.50	6.00	15.00	75.00
	1869H	6.250	1.25	4.75	8.50	42.00

5 CENTESIMOS

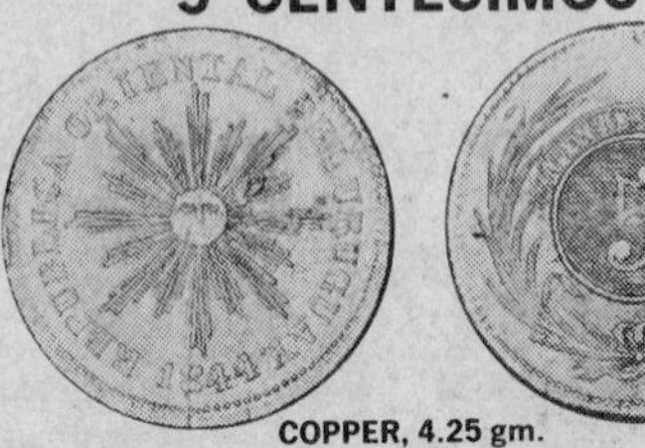

COPPER, 4.25 gm.

Y#	Date	Mintage	VG	Fine	VF	XF
1	1840	1.500	125.00	250.00	500.00	1000.
	1844/0	—	80.00	160.00	325.00	525.00
	1844	—	80.00	160.00	325.00	525.00
	1854/40	—	23.00	42.50	85.00	150.00
	1854/44	—	18.00	35.00	75.00	125.00

4.35 gm.

Y#	Date	Mintage	VG	Fine	VF	XF
1.1	1855	—	100.00	150.00	350.00	750.00

Y#	Date	Mintage	Fine	VF	XF	Unc
4	1857D	—	4.00	8.00	20.00	75.00

COPPER-NICKEL, 5.0 gm.

Y#	Date	Mintage	Fine	VF	XF	Unc
17	1901A	6.000	.20	.65	1.75	12.00
	1909A	5.000	.20	.50	1.75	12.00
	1909A	—	—	—	Proof	125.00
	1924(p)	5.000	.25	.75	3.00	10.00
	1936A	3.000	.25	.75	2.50	10.00
	1941So	26.000	.20	.50	1.25	3.50
	1941S(O)	—	—	—	Proof	200.00

COPPER,5.0 gm.

Y#	Date	Mintage	Fine	VF	XF	Unc
17a	1944So	4.000	.15	.35	.85	12.00
	1946So	2.000	.15	.30	1.50	13.00
	1947So	2.000	.15	.30	1.50	13.00
	1948So	3.000	.15	.30	1.00	12.00
	1949So	2.800	.15	.30	1.00	12.00
	1951So	15.000	.15	.30	.60	9.00

COPPER-NICKEL, 3.5 gm.

Y#	Date	Mintage	Fine	VF	XF	Unc
30	1953	81.800	.10	.15	.20	.50

NICKEL-BRASS, 3.5 gm.

34	1960	88.000	—	.10	.15	.40

ALUMINUM

C55	1977So	80.000	—	—	.10	.20

10 CENTESIMOS

2.5000 gm., .900 SILVER, .0723 oz ASW

11	1877A	3.000	BV	3.00	8.00	27.50
	1893 w/o mm	—	55.00	70.00	110.00	250.00
	1893So	1.000	BV	4.50	12.00	35.00

8 gm., ALUMINUM-BRONZE
Constitution Centennial

18	1930(a)	5.000	1.00	2.50	7.50	30.00

6 gm.

19	1936A	2.000	1.00	3.25	8.50	25.00

COPPER-NICKEL, 4.5 gm.

31	1953	28.250	.10	.15	.25	.50
	1959	10.000	.15	.25	.60	2.50

NICKEL-BRASS, 4.5 gm.

35	1960	72.500	.10	.20	.30	.40

ALUMINUM-BRONZE

Y#	Date	Mintage	Fine	VF	XF	Unc
55	1976So	127.400	—	—	—	.20
	1977So	—	—	—	—	.10

20 CENTESIMOS

COPPER
Weight 28gm, 2.75mm thick.

Y#	Date	Mintage	VG	Fine	VF	XF
2	1840	2,125	15.00	45.00	100.00	225.00

Rev: Small design.
Reduced weight 21gm, 1.75mm thick.

2.1	1843/40	—	15.00	50.00	125.00	250.00
	1844	—	50.00	125.00	250.00	575.00

Rev: Small design.

2.2	1854	—	14.00	37.50	65.00	135.00

Rev: Large design

2.3	1854	—	40.00	100.00	225.00	450.00

Y#	Date	Mintage	VG	Fine	VF	XF
2.3	1855	—	30.00	60.00	150.00	300.00

21.3 gm.

Y#	Date	Mintage	Fine	VF	XF	Unc
5	1857D	—	—	7.50	15.00	60.00

5.0000 gm., .900 SILVER, .1446 oz ASW

12	1877A	1.500	4.50	6.50	15.00	55.00
	1893/73So	.750	5.00	7.50	15.00	40.00

5.0000 gm., .800 SILVER, .1286 oz ASW

20	1920	2.500	BV	4.50	7.00	35.00

Constitution Centennial

21	1930(a)	2.500	BV	4.00	8.50	25.00

3.2000 gm., .720 SILVER, .0740 oz ASW

25	1942So	18.000	BV	BV	2.50	6.00

32	1954	10.000	BV	BV	2.25	4.50

2.5000 gm., aluminum

Y#	Date	Mintage	Fine	VF	XF	Unc
40	1965So	40.000	.10	.15	.25	.35

ALUMINUM-BRONZE

Y#	Date	Mintage	Fine	VF	XF	Unc
56	1976So	40.000	—	—	.10	.25
	1977So	—	—	—	—	.10

25 CENTESIMOS

3.0000 gm., copper-nickel

Y#	Date	Mintage	Fine	VF	XF	Unc
36	1960	48.000	.10	.25	.30	.65

40 CENTESIMOS

35.0000 gm., copper
Obv: Male sunface

Y#	Date	Mintage	VG	Fine	VF	XF
3	1844	—	55.00	95.00	275.00	500.00

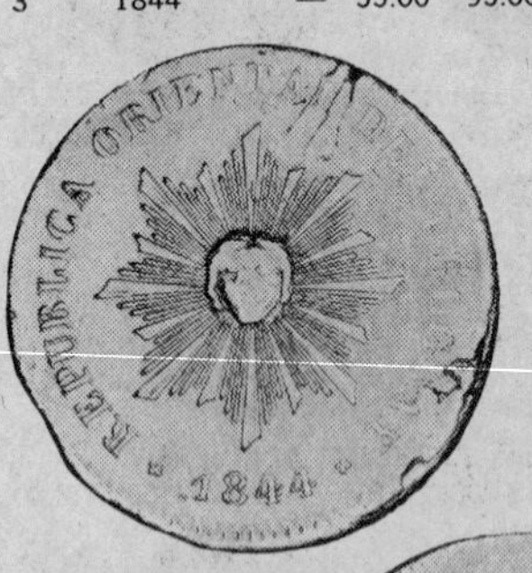

Obv: Female sunface

Y#	Date	Mintage	VG	Fine	VF	XF
3.1	1844	50 est.	125.00	250.00	550.00	800.00

NOTE: There are at least 12 different obverse and reverse die varieties known for the 40 Centesimos dated 1844.

Y#	Date	Mintage	Fine	VF	XF	Unc
6	1857D	—	6.00	9.00	25.00	100.00

50 CENTESIMOS

12.5000 gm., .900 SILVER, .3617 oz ASW

Y#	Date	Mintage	Fine	VF	XF	Unc
13	1877A	.400	BV	12.00	25.00	90.00
	1893/73SO	.500	BV	12.00	22.50	80.00
	1894	.800	BV	11.00	20.00	80.00

NOTE: 1894 has larger letters.

Y#	Date	Mintage	Fine	VF	XF	Unc
22	1916	6.000	BV	12.00	25.00	100.00
	1917	Inc. Ab.	BV	11.00	16.00	60.00

7.0000 gm., .720 SILVER, .1620 oz ASW

Y#	Date	Mintage	Fine	VF	XF	Unc
26	1943So	10.800	BV	BV	5.00	12.00

7.0000 gm., copper-nickel

Y#	Date	Mintage	Fine	VF	XF	Unc
37	1960	18.000	.15	.35	.45	.60

3.0000 gm., aluminum

Y#	Date	Mintage	Fine	VF	XF	Unc
41	1965So	50.000	.10	.15	.20	.30

ALUMINUM-BRONZE

Y#	Date	Mintage	Fine	VF	XF	Unc
57	1976So	30.000	.10	.15	.20	.30
	1977So	—	—	—	—	.15

PESO

27.0000 gm., .875 SILVER, .7596 oz ASW

Y#	Date	Mintage	Fine	VF	XF	Unc
10	1844	1,500	160.00	425.00	800.00	1600.

NOTE: Y#10 exists both with coin and medal reverse alignments.

25.5000 gm., .917 SILVER, .7518 oz ASW

Y#	Date	Mintage	Fine	VF	XF	Unc
14	1877A	.300	22.50	35.00	75.00	250.00
	1877A	—	—	—	Proof	1200.

25.0000 gm., .900 SILVER

Y#	Date	Mintage	Fine	VF	XF	Unc
14a	1878A	*.100	125.00	350.00	1000.	3000.
	1893So	.500	22.50	30.00	65.00	200.00
	1893	.600	22.50	27.50	50.00	300.00
	1895	1.000	22.50	27.50	50.00	175.00

***NOTE:** 43,200 melted after they were recovered from salt water.

23	1917	2.000	22.50	25.00	60.00	200.00

9.0000 gm., .720 SILVER, .2083 oz ASW

27	1942So	9.000	BV	BV	6.50	18.00

6.0000 gm., copper-nickel

38	1960	8.000	.25	.50	.75	1.25

3.5000 gm., aluminum-bronze

Y#	Date	Mintage	Fine	VF	XF	Unc
42	1965So	60.000	—	.10	.20	.30
	1965So	25 pcs.	—	—	Proof	—

2.0000 gm., nickel-brass

45	1968So	103.200	—	—	.10	.20
	1968So	50 pcs.	—	—	Proof	—

ALUMINUM-BRONZE

48	1969So	51.800	—	—	.10	.20

NEW PESO

ALUMINUM-BRONZE

58	1976So	65.540	.15	.25	.35	.65
	1977So	—	.15	.25	.35	.65
	1978So	—	.15	.25	.35	.65

5 PESOS

8.4850 gm., .917 GOLD, .2501 oz AGW
Constitution Centennial

24	1930(a)	*.100	165.00	175.00	225.00	250.00

NOTE: Only 14,415 were released. Remainder withheld.

ALUMINUM-BRONZE, 7 gm.

43	1965So	18.000	.15	.25	.40	.60
	1965So	25 pcs.	—	—	Proof	—

NICKEL-BRASS, 3 gm.

Y#	Date	Mintage	Fine	VF	XF	Unc
46	1968So	42.680	.10	.20	.30	.40
	1968So	50 pcs.	—	—	Proof	—

ALUMINUM-BRONZE, 3 gm.

49	1969So	42.320	—	—	.10	.20

5 NEW PESOS
(Monetary Reform)

COPPER-NICKEL-ALUMINUM
150th Anniversary of Revolutionary Movement

59	1975So	3.000	.75	.90	1.50	7.00

COPPER-ALUMINUM
250th Anniversary Founding of Montevideo

60	1976So	.300	.75	1.00	1.75	7.00

10 PESOS

12.5000 gm., .900 SILVER, .3617 oz ASW
Gaucho Heroes Sesquicentennial

Y#	Date	Mintage	Fine	VF	XF	Unc
39	1961	3.000	BV	BV	11.00	12.50
	1961	—	—	—	Proof	975.00

ALUMINUM-BRONZE, 8 gm.

Y#	Date	Mintage	Fine	VF	XF	Unc
44	1965So	18.000	.10	.15	.20	.60

NICKEL-BRASS, 4gm.

Y#	Date	Mintage	Fine	VF	XF	Unc
47	1968So	75.000	.10	.15	.20	.35
	1968So	50 pcs.	—	—	Proof	—

ALUMINUM-BRONZE, 4 gm.

Y#	Date	Mintage	Fine	VF	XF	Unc
50	1969So	25.000	.10	.15	.20	.35

20 PESOS

COPPER-NICKEL, 3.89 gm.

Y#	Date	Mintage	Fine	VF	XF	Unc
51	1970So	50.000	.10	.20	.35	.50

50 PESOS

COPPER-NICKEL, 5.25 gm.

Y#	Date	Mintage	Fine	VF	XF	Unc
52	1970So	20.000	.15	.30	.50	1.50

NICKEL-BRASS, 6 gm.
Centennial Birth Of Rodo

Y#	Date	Mintage	Fine	VF	XF	Unc
54	1971So	15.000	.15	.30	.50	2.00

100 PESOS

COPPER-NICKEL

Y#	Date	Mintage	Fine	VF	XF	Unc
A53	1973Mo	20.000	.25	.50	1.00	2.25

1000 PESOS

25.0000 gm., .900 SILVER, .7234 oz ASW
F.A.O. Issue

Y#	Date	Mintage	Fine	VF	XF	Unc
53	1969So	.500	BV	BV	22.50	25.00
	1969So	250 pcs.	—	—	Proof	—

BRONZE

Y#	Date	Mintage	Fine	VF	XF	Unc
53a	1969So	.011	—	—	—	50.00

NCLT ISSUES

PATTERNS

KM#	Date	Mintage	Identification	Mkt.Val.
1	1844	—	1 Peso,Lead	—
2	1854	—	4 Reales, Gold	—
3	1869	—	4 Centesimos, Bronze	—
4	1869	—	100 Centesimos, Silver	—
5	1869A	—	1 Centesimo, Silver, Y7a	—
6	1869H	—	1 Centesimo, Silver, Y7a	—
7	1869A	—	1 Centesimo, Gold, Y7b	—
8	1869H	—	1 Centesimo, Gold, Y7b	—
9	1869A	—	2 Centesimos, Silver, Y8a	—
10	1869H	—	2 Centesimos, Silver, Y8a	—
11	1869A	—	2 Centesimos, Gold, Y8b	—
12	1869H	—	2 Centesimos, Gold, Y8b	—
13	1869A	—	4 Centesimos, Silver, Y9a	—
14	1869H	—	4 Centesimos, Silver, Y9a	—
15	1869A	—	4 Centesimos, Gold, Y9b	—
16	1869H	—	4 Centesimos, Gold, Y9b	—
17	1870	—	10 Centesimos,Copper	—
18	1870	—	10 Centesimos, .900 Silver, Y11	—
19	1870	—	20 Centesimos, Copper,	—
20	1870	—	20 Centesimos, Silver	—
21	1870	—	50 Centesimos, .900 Silver, Y13	—
22	1870	—	50 Centesimos, Copper, Y13a	—
23	1870	—	50 Centesimos, Gold, 10mm, Y13b	—
24	1870	—	1 Peso, .900 Silver, Y14	—
25	1870	—	1 Peso, Copper, 37mm, Y14a	—
26	1870	—	1 Peso, Gold, 16mm, Y14b	—
27	1870	—	1 Peso, Copper, 16mm, Y14c	—
28	1870	—	2 Pesos,Copper	—
29	1870	—	5 Pesos,Copper	—
30	1870	—	5 Pesos,Gilded Copper	—
31	1870	—	1 Doblon, Gilded Bronze	—
32	1899	—	5 Centesimos,Nickel, No Value	—
33	1899	—	5 Centesimos, Nickel, Value Below	—
34	1899	—	10 Centesimos, Nickel, No Value	—
35	1899	—	10 Centavos, Nickel	—
36	1899	—	20 Centesimos, Nickel, No Value	—
37	1899	—	20 Centavos, Nickel	—
38	ND(1904)	—	4 Centesimos, Copper-Nickel	—
39	1916	45	50 Centesimos, Silver	—
40	1917	20	1 Peso,Silver	—
41	1942	10	20 Centesimos, Copper & Gold	—
42	1942	20	20 Centesimos, Silver & Gold	—
43	1942So	—	1 Pesos, Gold, Y27a	—
44	1943So	1 pc.	2 Centesimos, Gold, Y16b	—
45	1943So	—	50 Centesimos, Gold, Y26a	—
46	1953	100	1 Centesimo, .916 Gold, Y28a	—
47	1953	—	2 Centesimos, Aluminum, Y29a	—
48	1953	100	2 Centesimos, .916 Gold, Y29b	—
49	1953	100	5 Centesimos, .916 Gold, Y30a	—
50	1953	100	10 Centesimos, .916 Gold, Y31a	—
51	1954	100	20 Centesimos, .983 Gold, Y32a	—
52	1959	—	10 Centesimos, .916 Gold, Y31a	—
53	1960	100	2 Centesimos, Gold, Y33a	—
54	1960	100	5 Centesimos, Gold, Y34a	—
55	1960	100	10 Centesimos, Gold, Y35a	—
56	1960	100	25 Centesimos, Gold, Y36a	—
57	1960	100	50 Centesimos, Gold, Y37a	—
58	1960	—	1 Peso, Gold, Y38a	—
59	1960	100	10 Pesos, Gold	—
60	1965So	10	20 Centesimos, Copper, Y40a	—
61	1965So	—	20 Centesimos, Silver, Y40b	—
62	1965So	—	20 Centesimos, Gold, Y40c	—
63	1965So	25	50 Centesimos, Aluminum-Bronze, Y41a	—
64	1965So	10	50 Centesimos, Copper, Y41b	—
65	1965So	25	50 Centesimos, Copper-Nickel, Y41c	—
66	1965So	—	50 Centesimos, Silver, Y41d	—
67	1965So	—	50 Centesimos, Gold, Y41e	—
68	1965So	10	1 Peso, Copper, Y42a	—
69	1965So	25	1 Peso, Copper-Nickel, Y42b	—
70	1965So	—	1 Peso, Silver Y42c	—
71	1965So	—	1 Peso, Gold, Y42d	—
72	1965So	10	5 Pesos, Copper, Y43a	—
73	1965So	25	5 Pesos, Copper-Nickel, Y43b	—
74	1965So	—	5 Pesos, Silver, Y43c	—
75	1965So	—	5 Pesos, Gold, Y43d	—
76	1965So	10	10 Pesos, Copper, Y44a	—
77	1965So	—	10 Pesos, Silver, Y44b	—
78	1968So	100	1 Peso, Copper-Nickel, Y45a	—
79	1968So	1,000	1 Peso, Silver, Y45b	10.00
80	1968So	100	5 Pesos, Copper-Nickel, Y46a	—
81	1968So	1,000	5 Pesos, Silver, Y46b	12.50
82	1968So	100	10 Pesos, Copper-Nickel, Y47a	—
83	1968So	1,000	10 Pesos, Silver, Y47b	15.00
84	1968So	1,000	20 Pesos, Silver	17.50
85	1968So	1,000	50 Pesos, Silver	22.50
86	1969So	50	1 Peso, Copper-Nickel, Y48a	50.00
87	1969So	1,000	1 Peso, .900 Silver, Y48b	15.00
88	1969So	50	5 Pesos, Copper-Nickel, Y49a	45.00
89	1969So	1,000	5 Pesos, .900 Silver, Y49b	20.00
90	1969So	50	10 Pesos, Copper-Nickel, Y50a	55.00
91	1969So	—	10 Pesos, .900 Silver, Y50b	28.50
92	1969	20,000	1000 Pesos, Copper	50.00
93	1969	250	1000 Pesos, Silver	—
94	1969So	450	1000 Pesos, Gold, Y53b	—
95	1970So	3 pcs.	20 Pesos, Gold, Y51a	—
96	1970So	3 pcs.	50 Pesos, Gold, Y52a	—
97	1971So	—	50 Pesos, Copper-Nickel, Y54a	—
98	1971So	80	50 Pesos, Copper-Nickel, w/F.ORELLANA, P., Y54b	—
99	1971So	2,000	50 Pesos, Silver, Y54c	75.00
100	1971So	200	50 Pesos, Gold, Y54d	—
101	1973	—	100 Pesos, Silver, YA53a	100.00

ESSAIS (E)

Standard metals unless otherwise noted

Y#	Date	Mintage	Identification	Issue Price	Mkt Val.
E6	1856	—	40 Centesimos	—	—
E15	1924	12	1 Centesimo,Nickel	—	—
E16	1924	12	2 Centesimos,Nickel	—	—
E17	1924	12	5 Centesimos,Nickel	—	—
E18	1930	70	10 Centesimos, Bronze "Ensayo"	—	—
E18a	1930	60	10 Centesimos, Gold "Ensayo"	—	—

Y#	Date	Mintage	Identification	Issue Price	Mkt Val.
E20	1930	70	20 Centesimos,Bronze 'ENSAYO'	—	—
E20a	1930	60	20 Centesimos,Gold 'ENSAYO'	—	—
E24	1930	70	5 Pesos,Bronze 'ENSAYO'	—	—
E24a	1930	60	5 Pesos,Gold 'ENSAYO'	—	—

PIEFORTS (P)

(Double Thickness)

P—	1870	—	20 Centesimos,Copper	—	—

MINT SETS

KM#	Date	Mintage	Identification	Issue Price	Mkt. Val.
S1	1969/70(5)	—	Y48-52	—	—
S2	1969/70(5)	—	Y48-52	—	—

NOTE: KM#S1 was issued for the law no. 13,637 of Dec. 21, 1967 while S2 was issued for the 11th Assembly of the Interamerica Bank.

S3	1976(4)	—	Y55-58	—	—

PROOF SETS

STANDARD METALS

101	1953(4)	100	Y28-31	—	—
102	1968(5)	1,000	Y45b-47b,51b-52b	—	70.00
103	1968(3)	50	Y45-47	—	—
104	1968(3)	*50	Y45a-47a	—	175.00
105	1969(3)	*50	Y48a-50a	—	175.00
106	1969(3)	1,000	Y48b-50b	—	65.00
107	1969/70(5)	50 est.	Y48a-50a,51-52	—	150.00
108	1969/70(5)	1,000	Y48b-52b	—	55.00

VATICAN-PAPAL STATES

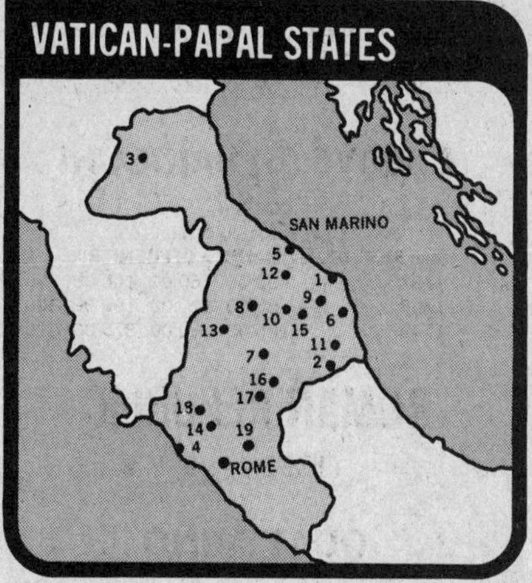

1 - Ancona
2 - Ascoli
3 - Bologna
4 - Civitavecchia
5 - Fano
6 - Fermo
7 - Foligno
8 - Gubbio
9 - Macerata
10 - Matelica
11 - Montalto
12 - Pergola
13 - Perugia
14 - Ronciglione
15 - San Severino
16 - Spoleto
17 - Terni
18 - Tivoli
19 - Viterbo

MONETARY SYSTEM

6 Quattrini = 1 Bolognino or Baiocco
5 Baiocchi = 1 Grossi
2 Grossi = 1 Giuli = 1 Paoli
3 Giuli = 3 Paoli = 1 Testone
10 Giuli = 10 Paoli = 1 Scudo
3 Scudi = 1 Doppia

ANCONA

ANCONNA

A city in the Marches, was founded by Syracusan refugees about 390 B.C. It became a semi-independent republic under papal protection in the 14th century, and a papal state in 1532. From 1797 until the formation of the United Kingdom of Italy it was part of the Roman Republic (1798-99), a papal state (1799-1808), part of the Italian Kingdom of Napoleon (1808-14), a papal state (1814-48), a part of the Roman Republic (1848-49), and a papal state (1849-60).

MINTMARKS

A - Ancona

MONETARY SYSTEM

100 Baiocchi = 1 Scudo

VN (1) BAIOCCO

COPPER

C#	Date	Year	Good	VG	Fine	VF
1	1796	XXI	7.50	15.00	35.00	50.00
	1796	XXII	7.50	15.00	35.00	50.00
	Rev: Value and mint in wreath.					
1.1	ND	XXI	7.50	15.00	35.00	50.00
	ND	XXII	7.50	15.00	35.00	50.00

DVE (2) BAIOCCHI

COPPER

2	1796	XXII	7.50	15.00	35.00	50.00
	Obv: Shield w/pointed top.					
2.1	1796	XXII	7.50	15.00	35.00	50.00

DVE E MEZZO (2-1/2) BAIOCCHI

COPPER

3	1796	10.00	20.00	40.00	55.00

ROMAN REPUBLIC

(1798-1799, 1848-1849)

BAIOCCO

CAST COPPER

Rev: A below date.

C#	Date	Mintage	VG	Fine	VF	XF
12	1849A	—	5.50	10.00	20.00	32.50

DVE (2) BAIOCCHI

COPPER
Obv: Fasces, REPUBBLICA ROMANA, mm.
Rev: Value in wreath.

C#	Date	Mintage	Good	VG	Fine	VF
6	1798 A/P	—	15.00	25.00	50.00	75.00
	1798 A/7	—	15.00	25.00	50.00	75.00
	1799 A/P	—	15.00	25.00	50.00	75.00
	1799 A/7	—	15.00	25.00	50.00	75.00

Obv: Fasces, REP. ROM. ANCONA. Rev: Value.

C#	Date	Mintage	Good	VG	Fine	VF
6a	1798	—	25.00	40.00	75.00	110.00
	1799	—	25.00	40.00	75.00	110.00

3 BAIOCCHI

CAST COPPER
Obv: Fasces, REPUBBLICA ROMANA.
Rev: Value, date, mm.

C#	Date	Mintage	VG	Fine	VF	XF
13	1848A	—	30.00	60.00	100.00	150.00

1/2 SCUDO

13.60 gm., SILVER
Obv: Arms, PIVS SEXTVS PON SILVER MA XXII.
Rev: Seated figure, AVXILIVM DE SANCTO 1778.

C#	Date	Year	Good	VG	Fine	VF
9	1778A	(1799)	80.00	150.00	200.00	250.00

NOTE: The above coin was restruck in 1799 during the siege of Ancona.

SCUDO

26.34 gm., SILVER
Obv: Arms, PIVS SEXTVS PONT M A VI.
Rev: Seated figure, AVXILIVM DE SANCTO 1780.

C#	Date	Year	Good	VG	Fine	VF
10	1780A	(1799)	65.00	120.00	250.00	400.00

NOTE: The above coin was restruck in 1799 during the siege of Ancona.

ASCOLI

A city in the Marches, was ruled by prince-bishops from Charlemagne's time until becoming a free republic in 1185. It became a papal possession in 1426.

UN (1) QUATTRINI

COPPER
Obv: Arms, PIVS SEXTVS PON M A XX.
Rev: Standing figure of Pope, S FELICIANO.

C#	Date	Mintage	VG	Fine	VF	XF
—	1794	—	7.50	15.00	25.00	50.00
	1795	—	7.50	15.00	25.00	50.00

Obv: Arms, PIVS SEXTVS PMA XXIII.
Rev: Value/ASCOLI/date.

C#	Date	Year	Good	VG	Fine	VF
1	1797	XXIII	27.50	55.00	100.00	150.00

MEZZO (1/2) BAIOCCO

Obv: Arms, PIVS SEXT P M A XXIII.
Rev: Value/ASCOLI.

C#	Date	Year	Good	VG	Fine	VF
2	1797	XXIII	30.00	60.00	100.00	150.00

VN (1) BAIOCCO

COPPER
Obv: Arms, PIVS SEXTVS P M A XXIII.
Rev: Value/ASCOLI/date.

C#	Date	Year	Good	VG	Fine	VF
3	1797	XXIII	30.00	55.00	100.00	150.00

DVE E MEZZO (2-1/2) BAIOCCHI

COPPER
Obv: Value, ASCOLI. Rev: St. Peter, legend S.P.APOSI....

C#	Date	Mintage	VG	Fine	VF	XF
4	ND	—	50.00	100.00	190.00	275.00
	1797	—	50.00	100.00	190.00	275.00

CINQVE (5) BAIOCCHI

COPPER
Obv: Value, ASCOLI.
Rev: St. Peter, leg: SANCTA DEI GENITRIX.

C#	Date	Mintage	VG	Fine	VF	XF
5	1797	—	30.00	60.00	100.00	150.00
	1798	—	55.00	110.00	190.00	300.00
	1799	—	125.00	250.00	375.00	625.00

ROMAN REPUBLIC

(1798-1799)

QUATTRINO

COPPER
Obv: Fasces divides R-R. Rev. leg: ASCOLI on two lines.

C#	Date	Mintage	VG	Fine	VF	XF
6	ND	—	75.00	125.00	200.00	300.00

MEZZO (1/2) BAIOCCO

COPPER
Obv: Fasces divides R-R. Rev. leg: ASCOLI, value.

C#	Date	Mintage	VG	Fine	VF	XF
7	ND	—	50.00	75.00	125.00	200.00

DVE (2) BAIOCCHI

COPPER
Obv. leg: REPUBLICA ROMANA, fasces.
Rev. leg: ASCOLI, value.

C#	Date	Mintage	VG	Fine	VF	XF
8	ND	—	25.00	50.00	100.00	175.00

BOLOGNA

(BOLONIA)

A city in Emilia, began as an independent commune, and after serving under various masters became a papal possession in 1506. Except for the Napoleonic period (1797-1815) and the revolutions of 1821 and 1831, it remained a papal state until 1860.

MINTMARKS

B - Bologna

QUATTRINO

COPPER

C#	Date	Mintage	VG	Fine	VF	XF
25	1778B	—	2.00	4.00	6.00	12.00

Rev.: Greek key border design

C#	Date	Mintage	VG	Fine	VF	XF
25.1	1778B	—	2.00	4.00	6.00	12.00
	1779B	—	2.00	4.00	6.00	12.00

Obv: Square shield. Rev: Leaves of wreath joined clockwise.

C#	Date	Mintage	VG	Fine	VF	XF
25.2	1778B	—	2.00	4.00	6.00	12.00
	1779B	—	2.00	4.00	6.00	12.00

Obv: Similar to C#25. Rev: Oak leaves of wreath joined counterclockwise.

C#	Date	Mintage	VG	Fine	VF	XF
25.3	1779B	—	2.50	5.00	7.00	12.00

Rev: Different leaves in wreath.

C#	Date	Mintage	VG	Fine	VF	XF
25.4	1779B	—	2.50	5.00	7.00	12.00
	1784B	—	2.50	5.00	7.00	12.00

Obv: Square Shield. Rev:Chain Border Design.

C#	Date	Mintage	VG	Fine	VF	XF
25.5	1779B	—	2.50	5.00	7.00	12.00
	1784B	—	2.50	5.00	7.00	12.00

Rev: Wreath border design.

C#	Date	Mintage	VG	Fine	VF	XF
25.6	1784B	—	2.50	5.00	7.00	12.00

Obv: Rampant lion. Rev: 5 line legend.

C#	Date	Mintage	VG	Fine	VF	XF
26	1795B	—	2.00	4.00	6.00	12.00

Obv: Date in exergue.

C#	Date	Mintage	VG	Fine	VF	XF
26.1	1796B	—	2.00	4.00	6.00	12.00

MEZZO (1/2) BAIOCCO

COPPER
Obv: Arms. Rev: Rampant lion.

C#	Date	Mintage	VG	Fine	VF	XF
27	1777B	—	2.00	4.00	7.50	12.00

Obv: 2 shields. Rev: Legend in wreath.

C#	Date	Year	VG	Fine	VF	XF
28	1781B	VII	2.00	4.00	6.00	12.00
	1784B	X	2.00	4.00	6.00	12.00

Obv: Rampant lion. Rev: 5 line legend.

C#	Date	Mintage	VG	Fine	VF	XF
29	1795B	—	2.00	4.00	6.00	12.00
	1796B	—	2.00	4.00	6.00	12.00

BAIOCCO

COPPER

C#	Date	Year	VG	Fine	VF	XF
30	1780B	VI	2.00	4.00	7.00	12.50

Obv: 2 oval shields. Rev: 4-stemmed lily, date in exergue.

C#	Date	Year	VG	Fine	VF	XF
30.1	1780	—	2.00	4.00	7.00	12.50

Obv: Value in exergue.

C#	Date	Year	VG	Fine	VF	XF
30.2	1780	—	2.00	4.00	7.00	12.50

Obv: 2 shields. Rev: Legend in wreath.

C#	Date	Year	VG	Fine	VF	XF
31	1781B	VI	2.00	4.00	7.00	12.50

C#	Date	Year	VG	Fine	VF	XF
32	1784	X	2.00	4.00	7.00	12.50

Rev: PIVS/VI/PONT/ANN.X and date in wreath.

C#	Date	Year	VG	Fine	VF	XF
32.1	1784	X	2.00	4.00	7.00	12.50

C#	Date	Mintage	VG	Fine	VF	XF
33	1795B	—	2.00	4.00	6.00	12.00
	1796B	—	2.00	4.00	6.00	12.00

2 BAIOCCHI

COPPER

C#	Date	Mintage	VG	Fine	VF	XF
34	1795B	—	2.00	4.00	6.00	12.00
	1796B	—	2.00	4.00	6.00	12.00

BILLON, 1.2-1.8gm
Obv: Bust right. Rev: St. Peter.

C#	Date	Mintage	VG	Fine	VF	XF
35	1778B	—	2.00	4.00	6.00	12.00
	1779B	—	2.00	4.00	6.00	12.00
	1784B	—	2.00	4.00	6.00	12.00
	1785B	—	2.00	4.00	6.00	12.00
	1786B	—	2.00	4.00	6.00	12.00
	1787B	—	2.00	4.00	6.00	12.00
	1788B	—	2.00	4.00	6.00	12.00
	1789B	—	2.00	4.00	6.00	12.00
	1790B	—	2.00	4.00	6.00	12.00
	1791B	—	2.00	4.00	6.00	12.00
	1792B	—	2.00	4.00	6.00	12.00
	1793B	—	2.00	4.00	6.00	12.00
	1794B	—	2.00	4.00	6.00	12.00
	1795B	—	2.00	4.00	6.00	12.00
	1796B	—	2.00	4.00	6.00	12.00

IIII BAIOCCHI

BILLON, 3-3.5gm
Obv: Keys. Rev: St. Peter.

C#	Date	Mintage	VG	Fine	VF	XF
36	1778B	—	4.00	8.00	12.00	20.00

C#	Date	Year	VG	Fine	VF	XF
37	1778B	—	2.50	5.00	10.00	15.00
	1778B	IIII	2.50	5.00	10.00	15.00
	1779B	IIII	2.50	5.00	10.00	15.00
	1785B	—	2.50	5.00	10.00	15.00
	1786B	—	2.50	5.00	10.00	15.00

C#	Date	Year	VG	Fine	VF	XF
37	1789B	—	2.50	5.00	10.00	15.00
	1790B	—	2.50	5.00	10.00	15.00
	1791B	—	2.50	5.00	10.00	15.00
	1793B	—	2.50	5.00	10.00	15.00
	1794B	—	2.50	5.00	10.00	15.00
	1795B	—	2.50	5.00	10.00	15.00
	1796B	—	2.50	5.00	10.00	15.00

5 BOLOGINI

1.321 gm., .917 SILVER

C#	Date	Mintage	VG	Fine	VF	XF
38	1777B	—	3.00	6.00	10.00	15.00

5 BAIOCCHI

1.321 gm., .917 SILVER

C#	Date	Mintage	VG	Fine	VF	XF
39	1777B	—	2.00	4.00	8.00	12.00
	1778B	—	2.00	4.00	8.00	12.00
	1779B	—	2.00	4.00	8.00	12.00
	1780B	—	2.00	4.00	8.00	12.00
	1783B	—	2.00	4.00	8.00	12.00

Obv: Arms. Rev: St. Peter.

C#	Date	Mintage	VG	Fine	VF	XF
40	1778B	—	2.00	4.50	9.00	14.00

Obv: Papal arms. Rev: City arms.

C#	Date	Mintage	VG	Fine	VF	XF
41	1778B	—	3.00	6.00	9.00	15.00
	1780B	—	2.00	4.00	6.00	12.00

Obv: Lily with value in exergue.
Rev: Arms of Bologna; date below.

C#	Date	Mintage	VG	Fine	VF	XF
—	1778	—	3.00	6.00	9.00	16.00

Obv: Lily plant. Rev: St. Peter.

C#	Date	Mintage	VG	Fine	VF	XF
42	1796B	—	3.00	6.00	9.00	16.00

10 BAIOCCHI

2.642 gm., .917 SILVER
Obv: Arms. Rev: Madonna.

C#	Date	Mintage	VG	Fine	VF	XF
43	1781B	—	2.00	4.00	7.00	15.00
	1785B	—	2.00	4.00	7.00	15.00
	1786B	—	2.00	4.50	8.00	16.00

12 BAIOCCHI

3.50 gm., .917 SILVER
Obv: Bust right. Rev: Lion.

C#	Date	Mintage	VG	Fine	VF	XF
44	1795B	—	4.00	8.00	15.00	25.00

20 BAIOCCHI

5.285 gm., .917 SILVER
Obv: Arms. Rev: Lion.

C#	Date	Mintage	VG	Fine	VF	XF
45	1777B	—	6.50	10.00	15.00	20.00
	1778B	—	2.50	6.00	12.00	15.00
	1779B	—	2.50	6.00	12.00	15.00
	1780B	—	2.50	6.00	12.00	15.00
	1786B	—	2.50	6.00	12.00	15.00
	1787B	—	2.50	6.00	12.00	15.00

NOTE: Varieties exist.

30 BAIOCCHI

7.928 gm., .917 SILVER
Obv: Bust right. Rev: Arms.

C#	Date	Year	VG	Fine	VF	XF
46	1777B	III	10.00	20.00	40.00	60.00
	1778B	IIII	10.00	20.00	40.00	60.00
	1779B	—	5.50	10.00	15.00	30.00
	1785B	—	5.50	10.00	15.00	30.00
	1786B	—	5.50	10.00	15.00	30.00
	1792B	—	5.50	10.00	15.00	30.00

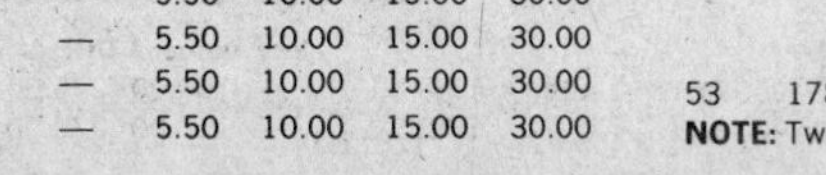

C#	Date	Mintage	VG	Fine	VF	XF
47	1782B	—	10.00	20.00	40.00	60.00

1/2 SCUDO

13.214 gm., .917 SILVER

C#	Date	Year	VG	Fine	VF	XF
48	—	ANNO III	20.00	40.00	60.00	90.00
	1778	IIII	10.00	20.00	40.00	65.00

Rev: Pius VI and St. Peter standing.

C#	Date	Mintage	VG	Fine	VF	XF
49	1784	—	10.00	20.00	40.00	60.00
	1785	—	10.00	20.00	40.00	60.00
	1795	—	10.00	20.00	40.00	60.00

C#	Date	Year	VG	Fine	VF	XF
50	1782	VIII	20.00	40.00	60.00	90.00

80 BOLOGNINI

Sede Vacante Issue

20.75 gm., .917 SILVER
Obv: Arms. Rev: St. Peter.

C#	Date	Mintage	VG	Fine	VF	XF
51	1775AN (no) I B		40.00	60.00	100.00	200.00
51a	1775ANNO IV BILAEI B	—	60.00	100.00	200.00	400.00

SCUDO

26.428 gm., .917 SILVER
Obv: Arms. Rev: St. Peter.

C#	Date	Year	VG	Fine	VF	XF
52	1777	III	40.00	60.00	100.00	200.00
	1778	IIII	40.00	60.00	90.00	175.00
	1780	VI	40.00	60.00	90.00	175.00

Obv: Bust right. Rev: Temple.

C#	Date	Year	VG	Fine	VF	XF
53	1782	VIII	40.00	65.00	120.00	200.00

NOTE: Two varieties exist.

C#	Date	Mintage	VG	Fine	VF	XF
54	1795	—	40.00	60.00	120.00	240.00

1/2 ZECCHINO

.986 GOLD 1.726gm
Obv: Arms. Rev: St. Peter.

C#	Date	Mintage	VG	Fine	VF	XF
56	1786B	—	400.00	600.00	800.00	1000.

ZECCHINO

3.452 gm., .996 GOLD
Obv: Arms. Rev: St. Peter.

C#	Date	Mintage	VG	Fine	VF	XF
57	1778B	—	200.00	350.00	500.00	750.00
	1779B	—	200.00	350.00	500.00	750.00
	1780B	—	200.00	350.00	500.00	750.00
	1786B	—	200.00	350.00	500.00	750.00
	1787B	—	200.00	350.00	500.00	750.00

.986 GOLD

C#	Date	Mintage	VG	Fine	VF	XF
58	1782B	—	350.00	600.00	850.00	1000.

2 ZECCHINI

6.904 gm., .996 GOLD

C#	Date	Mintage	VG	Fine	VF	XF
59	1786B	—	350.00	450.00	700.00	900.00
	1787B	—	350.00	450.00	700.00	900.00

5 ZECCHINI

17.26 gm., .996 GOLD

C#	Date	Year	VG	Fine	VF	XF
60	1787B	XIII	300.00	600.00	850.00	1200.

10 ZECCHINI

34.520 gm., .996 GOLD

C#	Date	Year	VG	Fine	VF	XF
61	1786B	XII	500.00	1000.	1500.	2000.
	1787B	XII	500.00	1000.	1500.	2000.

15 PAOLI - 1/2 DOPPIE

2.734 gm., .917 GOLD
Obv: Lily plant. Rev: Arms.

C#	Date	Mintage	VG	Fine	VF	XF
62	1778B	—	200.00	350.00	600.00	900.00

Rev: 2 shields.

C#	Date	Mintage	VG	Fine	VF	XF
63	1778B	—	200.00	350.00	500.00	750.00
	1779B	—	200.00	350.00	500.00	750.00
	1786B	—	175.00	300.00	350.00	400.00
	1787B	—	175.00	300.00	350.00	400.00
	1788B	—	175.00	300.00	350.00	400.00
	1791B	—	175.00	300.00	350.00	400.00

30 PAOLI - DOPPIE

5.469 gm., .917 GOLD
Obv: Lily plant. Rev: 2 shields, value: P.30.

C#	Date	Mintage	VG	Fine	VF	XF
64	1778B	—	150.00	300.00	400.00	500.00
	1779B	—	150.00	300.00	400.00	500.00
	1785B	—	150.00	300.00	400.00	500.00

Rev: No value indication

C#	Date	Mintage	VG	Fine	VF	XF
64a	1786B	—	150.00	275.00	325.00	400.00
	1787B	—	150.00	275.00	325.00	400.00
	1788B	—	150.00	275.00	325.00	400.00
	1789B	—	150.00	275.00	325.00	400.00
	1790B	—	150.00	275.00	325.00	400.00
	1791B	—	150.00	275.00	325.00	400.00
	1792B	—	150.00	275.00	325.00	400.00

Rev. value: 1 DOP.

C#	Date	Mintage	VG	Fine	VF	XF
64b	1787B	—	150.00	275.00	325.00	400.00
	1788B	—	150.00	275.00	325.00	400.00

60 PAOLI

10.938 gm., .917 GOLD
Obv: Lily plant. Rev: 2 shields, value: P.60.

C#	Date	Mintage	VG	Fine	VF	XF
65	1778B	—	350.00	450.00	600.00	800.00
	1780B	—	350.00	450.00	600.00	800.00
	1781B	—	350.00	450.00	600.00	800.00

Rev.: No value indication.

C#	Date	Mintage	VG	Fine	VF	XF
65a	1786B	—	350.00	450.00	600.00	800.00
	1787B	—	350.00	450.00	600.00	800.00
	ANNO XIII B	—	350.00	450.00	600.00	800.00

Rev. value: 2 DOP.

C#	Date	Mintage	VG	Fine	VF	XF
65b	1787B	—	350.00	450.00	600.00	800.00
	1796B	—	350.00	450.00	600.00	800.00

4 DOPPIE

21.876 gm., .917 GOLD

C#	Date	Year	VG	Fine	VF	XF
66	1786B	XII	350.00	500.00	1000.	1650.
	1787B	XIII	350.00	500.00	1000.	1650.

REVOLUTIONARY GOV'T

(1796-1797)

MEZZO (1/2) QUATTRINO

COPPER
Obv: BONON. DOCET, rampant lion. Rev: Value, date.

C#	Date	Mintage	VG	Fine	VF	XF
67	1796	—	20.00	40.00	75.00	110.00

VN (1) CARLINO

BILLON
Obv: .COMVNITAS.ET.SENATVS.BONON., arms
Rev: VN CARLINO BOLOGNE SE within wreath

C#	Date	Mintage	VG	Fine	VF	XF
67.3	ND(1796)	—	20.00	40.00	75.00	110.00

DVE (2) CARLINI

BILLON
Similar to 1 Carlino, C#67.3.

C#	Date	Mintage	VG	Fine	VF	XF
67.4	ND(1796)	—	15.00	30.00	60.00	90.00

NOTE: Exists with and without stars on reverse.

5 PAOLI

(= 1/2 Scudo)

14.50 gm., .833 SILVER

C#	Date	Mintage	VG	Fine	VF	XF
68	1796	—	35.00	60.00	85.00	145.00
	1797	—	35.00	60.00	85.00	155.00

10 PAOLI

(= Scudo)

29 gm., .833 SILVER

C#	Date	Mintage	VG	Fine	VF	XF
69	1796	—	60.00	85.00	125.00	185.00
	1797	—	60.00	85.00	125.00	185.00

C#	Date	Mintage	VG	Fine	VF	XF
69	1796	—	60.00	85.00	125.00	175.00
	1797	—	60.00	100.00	150.00	225.00

Obv: COMVNITAS. ET. SENATVS. BONON.

C#	Date	Mintage	VG	Fine	VF	XF
69a	MDCCXCVI (1796)	—	50.00	75.00	100.00	175.00

NOTE: Varieties exist.

CIVITAVECCHIA

A seaport in Latium and one of the oldest papal states, was founded by Roman emperor Trajan, destroyed by the Saracens in 812, and rebuilt by Pope Leo IV.

DVE E MEZZO (2-1/2) BAOICCHI

COPPER, 30mm
Obv: Value, CIVITAVECCHIA, date.
Rev: Bust left, leg.: S P APOSTOLORUM PRINCEPS

C#	Date	Mintage	Good	VG	Fine	VF
5	1796	—	15.00	20.00	30.00	45.00
	1797	—	15.00	20.00	30.00	45.00

25mm

C#	Date	Mintage	Good	VG	Fine	VF
5a	1797	—	12.00	16.00	32.50	45.00

CINQVE (5) BAOICCHI

COPPER
Obv. leg.: ANNO XIII 1797, value.
Rev. leg.: SANCTA DEI GENITRIX, bust of virgin Mary.

C#	Date	Mintage	Good	VG	Fine	VF
6	1797	—	15.00	20.00	40.00	60.00

ROMAN REPUBLIC

(1798-1799)

DVE (2) BAIOCCHI

COPPER
Obv: Fasces, leg: REPVBBLICA ROMANA.
Rev: Value, C, wreath.

C#	Date	Mintage	Good	VG	Fine	VF
11	ND	—	15.00	20.00	40.00	60.00

Obv: As Rev. above. Rev: As above.

C#	Date	Mintage	Good	VG	Fine	VF
12	ND	—	15.00	20.00	40.00	60.00

CLITUNNO

A department under the Roman Republic (1798-99) during the Napoleonic period.

ROMAN REPUBLIC

(1798-99)

VN (1) BAIOCCO

COPPER
Obv: Fasces, leg: REPVBBLICA ROMANA.
Rev: Value, CLITUNNO.

C#	Date	Mintage	Good	VG	Fine	VF
1	ND	—	35.00	65.00	100.00	135.00

DVE (2) BAIOCCHI

COPPER
Obv: Fasces, REPV.ROM.CLITTUNO. Rev: Value.

C#	Date	Mintage	Good	VG	Fine	VF
2	ND	—	30.00	55.00	70.00	120.00

FANO

A coastal city in the Marches, became a papal possession in 1462.

DVE E MEZZO (2-1/2) BAIOCCHI

COPPER
Obv: Value, FANO, date. Rev: Bust of St. Peter, leg: S.P.APOSTOLORUM PRINCEPS.

C#	Date	Mintage	Good	VG	Fine	VF
1	1796	—	15.00	30.00	50.00	75.00
	1797	—	15.00	25.00	40.00	70.00

CINQVE (5) BAIOCCHI

COPPER
Obv: Value, leg.: FANO, PIUS PAPA SEXTUS ANNO XXIII.
Rev: Bust of Virgin Mary, SANCTA DEI GENITRIX.

C#	Date	Mintage	Good	VG	Fine	VF
2	1797	—	15.00	30.00	45.00	70.00

FERMO

A city in the Marches, was founded as a Latin colony in 264 B.C., became a free city in 1199, and was acquired by the papacy in 1550.

MEZZO (1/2) BAICCO

COPPER

C#	Date	Year	Good	VG	Fine	VF
1	1797	XXIII	10.00	16.50	26.50	50.00
	1798	XXIII	10.00	16.50	26.50	50.00

Obv: Value, FERMANO, date.

C#	Date	Mintage	Good	VG	Fine	VF
1.1	1798	—	10.00	16.50	26.50	50.00

DVE E MEZZO (2-1/2) BAIOCCHI

COPPER
Obv: Value, FERMO, date. Rev: Bust of St. Peter left, S P APOSTOLORUM PRINCEPS.

C#	Date	Mintage	Good	VG	Fine	VF
2	1796	—	10.00	16.50	27.50	45.00
	1797	—	10.00	16.50	27.50	45.00

Rev. leg: S P PETRVS APOSTOL PRINC.

C#	Date	Mintage	Good	VG	Fine	VF
2.1	1796	—	12.50	20.00	30.00	45.00

Rev. leg: S P APOSTOLORUM PRINCDDS.

C#	Date	Mintage	Good	VG	Fine	VF
2.2	1796	—	12.50	20.00	30.00	45.00

Rev. leg: S P APOSTOLOR PRINCEPS.

C#	Date	Mintage	Good	VG	Fine	VF
2.3	1797	—	12.50	20.00	30.00	45.00

Rev. leg: S P APOST PRINCEPS.

C#	Date	Mintage	Good	VG	Fine	VF
2.4	1797	—	12.50	22.00	35.00	50.00

CINQVE (5) BAIOCCHI

COPPER

C#	Date	Mintage	Good	VG	Fine	VF
3	1797	—	10.00	15.00	22.50	40.00
	1799	—	10.00	15.00	22.50	40.00

Obv: L CHOTOTM appears below bust.

C#	Date	Mintage	Good	VG	Fine	VF
3.1	1797	—	10.00	15.00	22.50	40.00
	1799	—	10.00	15.00	22.50	40.00

Rev. value: BAIOC/CHI/CINQVE.

C#	Date	Mintage	Good	VG	Fine	VF
3.2	1799	—	10.00	15.00	22.50	40.00

SESSANTA (60) BAIOCCHI

BILLON
Obv: Arms, leg. PIVS SEXTON PONT MAXIMUS AN XXV.
Rev: Value, FERMO,date.

C#	Date	Year	Good	VG	Fine	VF
4	1799	XXV	40.00	75.00	100.00	125.00

PROVISIONAL REPUBLIC

(1798)

MEZZO (1/2) BAIOCCO

COPPER
Obv: Arms in circle, ANNO PMO REIP FIRM 1798.
Rev: Value, FERMO; wreath.

C#	Date	Mintage	Good	VG	Fine	VF
5	1798	—	7.50	15.00	25.00	40.00

ROMAN REPUBLIC

(1798-99)

VN (1) QUATRINO

COPPER
Obv.: Fasces, REPVBLICA ROMANA.
Rev: Value, FERMO.

C#	Date	Mintage	Good	VG	Fine	VF
6	1798	—	15.00	25.00	40.00	60.00
	1799	—	15.00	25.00	40.00	60.00

MEZZO (1/2) BAIOCCO

COPPER

C#	Date	Mintage	Good	VG	Fine	VF
7	1798	—	8.50	15.00	25.00	40.00

Obv: Fasces, REPVBLICA ROMANA.
Rev: Value, FERMO, wide milled border.

C#	Date	Mintage	Good	VG	Fine	VF
8	(1798)	—	6.50	10.00	20.00	30.00

VN (1) BAIOCCO

COPPER

C#	Date	Mintage	Good	VG	Fine	VF
10	1798	—	6.50	14.00	20.00	30.00

NOTE: Above coin is also found without date.

C#	Date	Mintage	Good	VG	Fine	VF
9	(1798)	—	6.50	14.00	20.00	30.00

Rev: w/o date.

C#	Date	Mintage	Good	VG	Fine	VF
9.1	(1798)	—	6.50	14.00	20.00	30.00

Obv: ANNO I, REPVBLICA ROMANA.
Rev: Value, FERM
, within wreath.

C#	Date	Mintage	Good	VG	Fine	VF
10	(1798)	—	6.50	14.00	20.00	30.00

Obv: Fasces, REPVBLIC ROMANA. Rev: Value, FERMO.

C#	Date	Mintage	Good	VG	Fine	VF
11	(1798)	—	10.00	17.50	25.00	35.00

DVE (2) BAIOCCHI

COPPER
Obv: Fasces, REPVBLIC ROMANA. Rev: Value, Date.

C#	Date	Mintage	Good	VG	Fine	VF
12	1798	—	8.50	15.00	25.00	40.00

NOTE: This coin is also found without date.

Obv: ANNO I, REPVBLICA ROMANA.

C#	Date	Mintage	Good	VG	Fine	VF
14	1798	—	8.50	15.00	25.00	40.00

NOTE: This coin is also found without date.

Obv leg.: ANNO PMO DELLA REPVB
around wreath. Rev: Similar to C#12.

C#	Date	Mintage	Good	VG	Fine	VF
13	1798	—	8.50	15.00	25.00	40.00

FOLIGNO

(FVLIGNO)

A city in Umbria, was governed by deputies of the Holy See from 1305 to 1439, and was a possession of the papacy until 1860.

QUATRINO

COPPER
Obv: Arms, PIVS SEXTVS PON M A year.
Rev: Standing figure, S. Feliciano.

C#	Date	Year	Good	VG	Fine	VF
1	(1794)	XX	20.00	40.00	60.00	100.00
	(1795)	XXI	20.00	40.00	60.00	100.00

MEZZO (1/2) BAIOCCO

COPPER
Obv: Leg. Lozenge Shaped Arms, PIUS SEXTVS PON M A, year. Rev: Value, DI FULIGNO.

C#	Date	Year	Good	VG	Fine	VF
2	(1794)	XX	25.00	35.00	55.00	85.00
	(1795)	XXI	25.00	35.00	55.00	85.00

NOTE: This coin is also found with legend as FOLIGNO instead of FVLIGNO.

Rev: With date.

C#	Date	Year	Good	VG	Fine	VF
2.1	1795	XXI	25.00	35.00	55.00	85.00

Obv: Shield Shaped Arms, Leg. PIVS SEXT P M A XXIII.
Rev: Value, FVLIGNO.

C#	Date	Year	Good	VG	Fine	VF
—	1797	XXIII	25.00	35.00	55.00	85.00
	1798	XXIII	25.00	35.00	55.00	85.00

VN (1) BAIOCCO

COPPER

C#	Date	Year	Good	VG	Fine	VF
3	(1794)	XX	15.00	25.00	40.00	60.00
	(1795)	XXI	15.00	25.00	40.00	60.00

NOTE: These coins are also found with date on reverse.Also exist with FVLIGNO instead of FOLIGNO.

C#	Date	Year	Good	VG	Fine	VF
3.1	(1794)	XX	15.00	25.00	40.00	60.00
	(1795)	XXI	15.00	25.00	40.00	60.00

NOTE: These coins are also found with date on reverse. Also exist with FVLIGNO instead of FOLIGNO.

DVE (2) BAIOCCHI

COPPER

C#	Date	Year	Good	VG	Fine	VF
4	1794	XX	15.00	25.00	40.00	70.00
	1795	XX	15.00	25.00	40.00	70.00
	1795	XXI	15.00	25.00	40.00	70.00
	1796	XXI	15.00	25.00	40.00	70.00

NOTE: These coins also exist with FOLIGNO instead of FVLIGNO.

DVE E MEZZO (2-1/2) BAIOCCHI

COPPER
Rev. leg.: S P APOSTOLORUM PRINCEPS.

C#	Date	Mintage	Good	VG	Fine	VF
5	1796	—	15.00	25.00	40.00	60.00
	1797	—	15.00	25.00	40.00	60.00

NOTE: Varieties exist with PRINCEP or PRINC instead of PRINCEPS.

CINQVE (5) BAIOCCHI

COPPER
Obv: Value Leg. FVLIGNO PIVS SEXTVS ANNO XXIII 1797.
Rev: Bust of Virgin Mary left, SANCTA DEI GENITRIX, T M below bust.

C#	Date	Mintage	Good	VG	Fine	VF
6	1797	—	15.00	25.00	40.00	70.00

ROMAN REPUBLIC

(1798-99)

QUATTRINO

COPPER

C#	Date	Mintage	Good	VG	Fine	VF
7	1798	—	12.50	25.00	40.00	70.00
	1799	—	12.50	25.00	40.00	70.00

MEZZO (1/2) BAIOCCO

COPPER
Obv: Star in circle, DE FVLIGNO.
Rev: Value, star above and below.

C#	Date	Mintage	Good	VG	Fine	VF
8	1798	—	—	—	Rare	—
	1799	—	—	—	Rare	—

GUBBIO

(EUGUBIA)

A city in Umbria, was part of the donation of Charlemagne to the pope in 774. It became a consul-governed republic in 1151, came under the dukes of Urbino in 1387, and was ceded to the pope in 1624.

MEZZO (1/2) BAIOCCO

COPPER

C#	Date	Year	Good	VG	Fine	VF
31	1789	XV	12.50	25.00	40.00	60.00
	1790	XV	12.50	25.00	40.00	60.00
	1790	XVI	4.00	8.50	15.00	30.00
	1791	XVI	4.00	8.50	15.00	30.00
	1794	XX	4.00	8.50	15.00	30.00
	1795	XX	4.00	8.50	15.00	30.00

VN (1) BAIOCCO

COPPER

C#	Date	Year	Good	VG	Fine	VF
32	1789	XV	5.00	10.00	15.00	25.00
	1790	XV	5.00	10.00	15.00	25.00
	1791	XVII	5.00	10.00	15.00	25.00
	1792	XVII	5.00	10.00	15.00	25.00
	1792	XVIII	5.00	10.00	15.00	25.00
	1793	XVIII	5.00	10.00	15.00	25.00
	1794	XX	5.00	10.00	15.00	25.00
	1795	XX	5.00	10.00	15.00	25.00

NOTE: There are several die varieties of the above coins.

DVE (2) BAIOCCHI

COPPER

Obv: Arms,Leg. PIVS SEXTVS PON M A , YEAR

C#	Date	Year	Good	VG	Fine	VF
33	1789	XV	10.00	15.00	25.00	40.00
	1790	XV.	10.00	15.00	25.00	40.00

Rev: Value DI GVBBIO within wreath.

C#	Date	Year	Good	VG	Fine	VF
33.1	1790	XVI	10.00	15.00	25.00	40.00
	1791	XVI	10.00	15.00	25.00	40.00
	1795	XXI	10.00	15.00	25.00	40.00
	1796	XXI	10.00	15.00	25.00	40.00

DVE E MEZZO
(2-1/2) BAIOCCHI

COPPER

C#	Date	Mintage	Good	VG	Fine	VF
34	1796	—	4.00	8.00	15.00	25.00

Obv.: Value, DI GVBBIO, 1796.

C#	Date	Mintage	Good	VG	Fine	VF
34a	1796	—	—	—	Rare	—

CINQVE (5) BAIOCCHI

COPPER

Obv: Value Leg. PIVS PAPA SEXTVS, YEAR.
Rev: Bust Of Virgin Mary, Leg.: SANCTA DEI GENITRIX.

C#	Date	Year	Good	VG	Fine	VF
35	1797	XXIII	10.00	15.00	25.00	40.00

ROMAN REPUBLIC

(1798-99)

MEZZO (1/2) BAIOCCO

COPPER

Obv: Value, GVBBIO.Rev: Same.

C#	Date	Mintage	Good	VG	Fine	VF
41	(1798)	—	20.00	35.00	55.00	80.00

DVE (2) BAIOCCHI

COPPER

Obv: Value, GVBBIO, 1798 within wreath.
Rev: Fasces, REPVBBLICA ROMANA.

C#	Date	Mintage	Good	VG	Fine	VF
42	1798	—	15.00	30.00	45.00	70.00
42.1	1798	—	15.00	30.00	45.00	70.00

MACERATA

A city in the Marches, was, except for a period of French occupation during the Napoleonic era, a faithful papal subject from the 13th century until the dismembering of the papal states.

CINQVE (5) BAIOCCHI

COPPER

C#	Date	Year	Good	VG	Fine	VF
1	1797	XXIII	15.00	27.50	42.50	65.00
	1798	XXIII	15.00	27.50	42.50	65.00

SESSANTA (60) BAIOCCHI

BILLON

Obv: Arms, Leg.: PIVS SEXTVS PONT MAXIMVS AN XXV.
Rev: Value, MACERATA, date.

C#	Date	Year	Good	VG	Fine	VF
2	1799	XXV	40.00	75.00	125.00	200.00

ROMAN REPUBLIC

(1798-1799)

QUATRINO

COPPER

Obv: Fasces, Leg.: A.I.D.L.I. Rev: Value, Leg.: MACER.

C#	Date	Mintage	VG	Fine	VF	XF
3	ND	—	15.00	25.00	40.00	80.00

MEZZO (1/2) BAIOCCO

COPPER

Obv: Fasces, Leg. A.I. DELLA LIB. ITAL.
Rev.: Value, Leg.: MACERATA.

C#	Date	Mintage	VG	Fine	VF	XF
4	ND	—	12.50	20.00	35.00	70.00

MATELICA

A city and papal possession in Macerata.

VN (1) QUATRINO

COPPER

Obv.: Arms Leg.: PIVS SEX P M A XXIII.
Rev.: Value, MATELICA.

C#	Date	Year	Good	VG	Fine	VF
1	1797	XXIII	25.00	45.00	75.00	120.00
	1798	XXIII	25.00	45.00	75.00	120.00

NOTE: Varieties exist with PIVS SEXT PM A XXIII and PIVS SEX P M A XIII on obverse.

MEZZO (1/2) BAIOCCO

COPPER

Obv.: Arms, Leg.: PIVS SEXT P M A XXIII.
Rev.: Value, MATELI CA.

C#	Date	Year	Good	VG	Fine	VF
2	1797	XXIII	25.00	45.00	75.00	120.00
	1798	XXIII	25.00	45.00	75.00	120.00

DVE E MEZZO
(2-1/2) BAIOCCHI

COPPER

Obv.: Value, MATELICA.
Rev: Bust of St. Peter, S P APOSTOLORVM PRINC.

C#	Date	Year	Good	VG	Fine	VF
3	1797	XXIII	25.00	45.00	75.00	120.00

CINQVE (5) BAIOCCHI

COPPER

Obv.: Value, Leg.: PIVS PAPA SEXTVS ANNO XXIII.
Rev: Bust of Virgin Mary, SANCTA DEI GENITRIX
T M below bust.

C#	Date	Year	Good	VG	Fine	VF
4	1797	XXIII	30.00	50.00	85.00	125.00

MONTALTO

A city and papal possession in the province of Ascoli, Marches.

DVE E MEZZO
(2-1/2) BAIOCCHI

COPPER

Obv: Value, MONTALTO, date. Rev: Bust of St. Peter, leg. S P APOSTOLORUM PRINCEPS.

C#	Date	Mintage	Good	VG	Fine	VF
1	1797	—	20.00	35.00	55.00	80.00

NOTE: Varieties exist with obverse legend as S P APOSTOLOR PRINCEPS, S P APOOLLORU PRINCEPS and S P APOOLORU PRINCEPS P.

CINQVE (5) BAIOCCHI

COPPER

C#	Date	Year	Good	VG	Fine	VF
2	1797	XXIII	25.00	45.00	75.00	120.00

PERGOLA

A city and papal possession in the province of Pesaro, Urbino.

MEZZO (1/2) BAIOCCO

COPPER
Obv: Arms, PIVS SEXT P M A XXIII.
Rev: Value, PERGOLA 1797.

C#	Date	Year	Good	VG	Fine	VF
1	1797	XXIII	15.00	30.00	45.00	75.00

DVE E MEZZO (2-1/2) BAIOCCHI

COPPER

C#	Date	Mintage	Good	VG	Fine	VF
2	1796	—	15.00	30.00	45.00	75.00
	1797	—	25.00	50.00	75.00	110.00

CINQVE (5) BAIOCCHI

COPPER
Obv.: Value, Leg.: PERGOLA PIVS PAPA SEXTVS. ANNO XXIII, date.
Rev: Bust of Virgin Mary, SANCTA DEI GENITRIX around, T M below bust.

C#	Date	Year	Good	VG	Fine	VF
3	1797	XXIII	20.00	45.00	65.00	100.00

ROMAN REPUBLIC

(1798-99)

MEZZO (1/2) BAIOCCO

COPPER
Obv.: Value, PERGOLA, wreath.
Rev.: Value, PERGOLA, pearled circle.

C#	Date	Mintage	Good	VG	Fine	VF
4	(1798)	—	17.50	32.50	65.00	80.00

NOTE: Two varieties exist.

Obv.: Value, PERGOLA, circle of rings.

C#	Date	Mintage	Good	VG	Fine	VF
4.1	(1798)	—	20.00	37.50	65.00	90.00

VN (1) BAIOCCO

COPPER
Obv: Value, PERGOLA 1798; rope circle around.
Rev: Value, PERGOLA; wreath around.

C#	Date	Mintage	Good	VG	Fine	VF
5	1798	—	17.50	32.50	65.00	80.00

DVE (2) BAIOCCHI

COPPER
Obv.: Fasces REPVBLICA ROMANA.
Rev.: Value, PERGOLA, date, vines.

C#	Date	Mintage	Good	VG	Fine	VF
6	1798	—	15.00	30.00	50.00	75.00

Obv.:Leg.: REPVBBLICA ROMANA. Rev.: W/O date.

C#	Date	Mintage	Good	VG	Fine	VF
6.1	(1798)	—	16.50	32.50	50.00	80.00

PERUGIA

A city in Umbria, passed under the popes in the 9th century but continued to maintain an independent existence until occupied by the French in 1797. It was seized by Austria in 1849 and annexed to Piedmont in 1860.

MEZZO (1/2) BAIOCCO

COPPER
Obv.: Arms, Leg.: PIVS SEXTVS P M A XXIII.
Rev.: Value, PERVGIA, date.

C#	Date	Year	Good	VG	Fine	VF
1	1797	XXIII	10.00	20.00	40.00	65.00

VN (1) BAIOCCO

COPPER
Obv: Arms, PIVS SEXTVS POM M A XXI.
Rev.: Value, Date, PERVSIA AVGVSTA.

C#	Date	Year	Good	VG	Fine	VF
2	1795	XXI	15.00	30.00	50.00	75.00

Obv: Arms, PIVS SEXTVS P M A XXIII.
Rev: Value, PERUGIA 1797.

C#	Date	Year	Good	VG	Fine	VF
2a	1797	XXIII	15.00	30.00	50.00	75.00

DVE (2) BAIOCCHI

COPPER

C#	Date	Year	Good	VG	Fine	VF
3	1795	XXI	15.00	25.00	45.00	75.00
	(1795)	XXI	15.00	25.00	45.00	75.00
	(1796)	XXI	15.00	25.00	45.00	75.00
	1797	XXI	15.00	25.00	45.00	75.00

Obv: Arms, PIVS SEXTVS PON M A XXIII.
Rev: Value, P.

C#	Date	Year	Good	VG	Fine	VF
3a	(1797)	XXIII	10.00	20.00	35.00	50.00
	1798	XXIII	10.00	20.00	35.00	50.00

DVE E MEZZO (2-1/2) BAIOCCHI

COPPER

C#	Date	Mintage	Good	VG	Fine	VF
4	1796	—	15.00	25.00	45.00	75.00
	1797	—	15.00	25.00	45.00	75.00

QVATTRO (4) BAIOCCHI

BILLON
Obs.: Leg.: PIVS SEXTVS PON M A XXIII, PERVGIA, date.
Rev.: Value.

C#	Date	Year	Good	VG	Fine	VF
—	1797	XXIII	15.00	25.00	45.00	75.00

CINQVE (5) BAIOCCHI

COPPER

C#	Date	Year	Good	VG	Fine	VF
5	1797	XXIII	10.00	20.00	40.00	60.00
	1798	XXIII	10.00	20.00	40.00	60.00

NOTE: Varieties exist with error in reverse legend as GENETRIX and/or obverse as PAPA PIVS instead of PIVS PAPA.

SEI (6) BAIOCCHI

BILLON
Obv.: Leg.: PIVS SEXTVS PMA XXIII, PERVGIA, date.
Rev.: Value.

C#	Date	Year	Good	VG	Fine	VF
—	1797	XXIII	20.00	40.00	65.00	100.00

OTTO (8) BAIOCCHI

BILLON

C#	Date	Year	Good	VG	Fine	VF
7	1797	XXIII	15.00	35.00	60.00	100.00

ROMAN REPUBLIC

(1798-99)

DVE (2) BAIOCCHI

COPPER

C#	Date	Mintage	Good	VG	Fine	VF
11	ND(1799)	—	12.50	25.00	45.00	65.00

Obv.: Leg.: PERVGIA A VII RE , within circle, eight stars around all.

C#	Date	Mintage	Good	VG	Fine	VF
11.1	(1799)	—	15.00	30.00	45.00	70.00

Rev. leg.: VII omitted.

C#	Date	Mintage	Good	VG	Fine	VF
11.2	(1799)	—	10.00	20.00	35.00	50.00

C#	Date	Mintage	Good	VG	Fine	VF
11.3	(1799)	—	15.00	30.00	45.00	70.00

Obv.: Fasces, Leg.: REPVBLICA ROMANA.

C#	Date	Mintage	Good	VG	Fine	VF
11.4	(1799)	—	10.00	20.00	35.00	50.00

CINQVE (5) BAIOCCHI

COPPER
C#4 is overstruck with dies for C#5

and then countermarked with a fasces.

C#	Date	Mintage	Good	VG	Fine	VF
12	(1799)	—	25.00	50.00	90.00	125.00

SCUDO

SILVER
Obv.: Eagle, PERUGIA AVII, below REPUBLICA. ROMANA. Rev.: Value Within Wreath.

C#	Date	Mintage	VG	Fine	VF	XF
13	(1799)	—	500.00	1000.	1500.	2500.

ROMAN REPUBLIC

REPUBBLICA ROMANA

(1798-1799)

NOTE: For other coins listed by Craig under this heading see Ancona and Bologna.

MINTMARKS

R - Rome

A short-lived republican movement fostered by the French Revolution, submerged the papal states in 1798-99. They reappeared in 1814, and except for the republican movement of 1848-49, maintained their authority until 1860.

MEZZO (1/2) BAIOCCO

COPPER
Obv.: Fasces Within, Leg.: REPVBLICA ROMANA.
Rev.: Value Within Wreath.

C#	Date	Mintage	Good	VG	Fine	VF
1	ND	—	4.00	7.50	12.50	20.00
	Obv: Legend REPVBBLICA ROMANA.					
1.1	ND	—	4.00	7.50	12.50	22.50

VN (1) BAIOCCO

COPPER
Obv.: Two Fasces Within Leg.: REPVNNLICA ROMANA.
Rev.: Value Within Rectangle, Year Above REPVBBLICANO below.

C#	Date	Year	Good	VG	Fine	VF
2	(1798)	Sesto(6)	25.00	45.00	60.00	100.00
	Obv: Fasces within legend REPUBLICA ROMANA. Rev: Value within wreath.					
3	ND-R	—	4.00	7.50	12.50	20.00

DVE (2) BAIOCCHI

COPPER
Obv.: Fasces, REPVBLICA ROMANA.
Rev.: Value, Date.

C#	Date	Year	Good	VG	Fine	VF
—	1798	—	4.00	7.50	12.50	20.00
	1798 with star	—	4.00	7.50	12.50	20.00
	Obv.: Eagle In Wreath, REPVBBLICA ROMANA. Rev.: Value In Triangle Of Fasces, Tear Below.					
4	(1798)	Sesto(6)	15.00	30.00	55.00	85.00
	Obv.: Crossed Flags And Fasces. Rev.: Wreath Around Fasces.					
5	(1798)	Sesto(6)	25.00	45.00	60.00	100.00
	Obv.: Fasces, REP. RPM AN 7 R in script. Rev.: 2 BIAOCCHI in triangle.					
8	(1799)	7	15.00	25.00	40.00	75.00
	Obv: Legends in Roman capitals.					
8.1	(1799)	AN VII	15.00	25.00	40.00	75.00
	Obv.: Fasces, REP ROM AN VII. Rev.: DVE BIAOCCHI in triangle.					
7	(1799)	VII	6.50	12.00	25.00	45.00
	Obv: Fasces in branches, REPVBBLICA ROMANA. Rev: Value, year, mintmark.					
6b	(1799)R	VII	6.50	12.00	25.00	45.00
	Obv. leg.: REPUBLICA ROMANA.					
6b.1	(1799)	VII	6.50	12.00	25.00	45.00
	Obv. leg.: REPVBLICA ROMANA. Rev: Value, year, mintmark.					
6b.2	(1799)R	VII	6.50	12.00	25.00	45.00
	Obv. leg: ROMANA REPVBLICA.					
6b.3	(1799)R	VII	6.50	12.00	25.00	45.00
	Obv: Fasces in branches. Rev: Value in wreath.					
6a	(1799)	—	6.50	12.00	25.00	45.00

Obv.: Fasces, REPUBBLICA ROMANA.

C#	Date	Mintage	Good	VG	Fine	VF
6	(1799)	—	6.50	12.50	25.00	45.00
	(1799)GH	—	6.50	12.50	25.00	45.00
	(1799)TM	—	6.50	12.50	25.00	45.00
	(1799)HT	—	6.50	12.50	25.00	45.00
	(1799)R	—	6.50	12.50	25.00	45.00

NOTE: Varieties exist with obverse legend as REPUBLICA, REPVBBLICA, and REPVBLICA and with rosette below fasces.

C#	Date	Mintage	Good	VG	Fine	VF
6c	(1799)	—	12.50	25.00	40.00	75.00
	(1799)TM	—	12.50	25.00	40.00	75.00

CINQVE (5) BAIOCCHI

COPPER
Obv.: Bust Of Virgin Mary, SANCTA DEI GENITRIX.
Rev.: Value.

C#	Date	Good	VG	Fine	VF
9	(1799) with star	25.00	50.00	75.00	100.00
	(1799) 3 stars	25.00	50.00	75.00	100.00
	(1799) rosette	25.00	50.00	75.00	100.00
	(1799) 3 rosettes	25.00	50.00	75.00	100.00
	(1799)TM 3 rosettes —	25.00	50.00	75.00	100.00

SCUDO

26.76 gm., .917 SILVER

Rev: Value, ROMANO

C#	Date	Year	Good	VG	Fine	VF
11	ND	—	125.00	150.00	200.00	250.00

(1848-1849)

1/2 BAIOCCO

COPPER
Obv.: Value, REPUBBLICA ROMANA, date.
Rev.: Eagle On Fasces Within Wreath, DIO E POPOLO, mm below fasces.

C#	Date	Mintage	Good	VG	Fine	VF
21	1849R	—	2.00	4.00	6.50	10.00

BAIOCCO

COPPER

C#	Date	Mintage	Good	VG	Fine	VF
22	1849R	—	2.00	4.00	6.50	10.00

3 BAIOCCHI

COPPER
Similar To C#23.1, But W/Round Top 3.

C#	Date	Mintage	Good	VG	Fine	VF
23	1849R	—	4.00	8.00	15.00	20.00

C#	Date	Mintage	Good	VG	Fine	VF
23.1	1849B	—	5.00	10.00	18.00	30.00
	1849R	—	4.00	8.00	15.00	20.00

4 BAIOCCHI

1.95 gm., .200 SILVER

C#	Date	Mintage	Good	VG	Fine	VF
24	1849B	—	5.00	10.00	18.00	30.00
	1849R	—	4.00	8.00	13.00	20.00

8 BAIOCCHI

3.90 gm., .200 SILVER

C#	Date	Mintage	Good	VG	Fine	VF
25	1849R	—	7.50	15.00	25.00	40.00

16 BAIOCCHI

7.80 gm., .200 SILVER

C#	Date	Mintage	Good	VG	Fine	VF
26	1849R	—	9.00	18.00	25.00	45.00

40 BAIOCCHI

20 gm., .200 SILVER

C#	Date	Mintage	Good	VG	Fine	VF
27	1849R	—	30.00	65.00	100.00	175.00

MEDALLIC ISSUES

SCUDO

SILVER
Obv: Eagle. Rev: ALLE SPERANZE.

C#	Date	Year	Good	VG	Fine	VF
10	—	A6	125.00	250.00	350.00	500.00
	Rev: LIBERTA ROMANA					
10a	—	AN VII	125.00	250.00	350.00	450.00
	Rev: LIBERTA ROMANA 27 PIOVOSO					
10b	ND	—	125.00	250.00	350.00	500.00

RONCIGLIONE

A town and papal possession in Latium.

TRE (3) BAIOCCHI

COPPER
Obv.: Value, RONCIGLIONE, date.
Rev.: Bust Of Virgin Mary, Lrg.: FEDELTA E RELIGIONE.

C#	Date	Mintage	Good	VG	Fine	VF
2	1799	—	30.00	60.00	80.00	135.00
	Obv: Value, RONCIGLION, date.					
2.1	1799	—	35.00	65.00	80.00	135.00
	Obv.: Value, RONCIGLIONE, date.					
2.2	1799	—	45.00	90.00	150.00	225.00

C#	Date	Mintage	Good	VG	Fine	VF
1	1799	—	110.00	120.00	225.00	350.00

SAN SEVERINO

A city and papal possession in Macerata.

VN (1) QUATRINO

COPPER
Obv.: Arms, Leg.: PIVS SEXT P M A XXIII.
Rev.: Values, S SEVERINO.

C#	Date	Year	Good	VG	Fine	VF
1	(1797)	XXIII	7.50	15.00	25.00	50.00
	1798	XXIII	7.50	15.00	25.00	50.00

MEZZO (1/2) BAIOCCO

COPPER

C#	Date	Year	Good	VG	Fine	VF
2	(1796)	XXII	7.50	15.00	25.00	45.00
	(1797)	XXII	7.50	15.00	25.00	45.00
	1797	XXIII	7.50	15.00	25.00	45.00
	1797	XXIII	7.50	15.00	25.00	45.00
	(1798)	XXIII	7.50	15.00	25.00	45.00

DVE E MEZZO (2-1/2) BAIOCCHI

COPPER

C#	Date	Mintage	Good	VG	Fine	VF
3	1796	—	10.00	20.00	35.00	50.00
	1797	—	10.00	20.00	35.00	50.00

NOTE: Varieties also exist with reverse legend as S P APOSTOLOR PRINCEPS and S P APOST PRINC.

Date error variety.

C#	Date	Mintage	Good	VG	Fine	VF
3a	1769(1796)	—	25.00	45.00	90.00	150.00

CINQVE (5) BAIOCCHI

COPPER
T. M. below bust.

C#	Date	Year	Good	VG	Fine	VF
4	1797	XXIII	15.00	25.00	45.00	65.00

SPOLETO

(SPOLETVM)

A town in Umbria, was bequeathed to Pope Gregory VII by the empress Matilda, but maintained its independence until definitely occupied by Gregory IX in 1213. In 1809 it served as the capital of the French department of Trasimene.

CINQVE (5) BAIOCCHI

COPPER
Obv.: Value Leg.: SPOLE TUM UMB PIVS PAPA. SEXTVS ANNO XXIII 1797.
Rev: Bust of Virgin Mary, SANCTA DEI GENITRIX.

C#	Date	Year	Good	VG	Fine	VF
2	1797	XXIII	40.00	80.00	110.00	140.00

SEI (6) BAIOCCHI

SILVER
Obv: SPOLETUM UMB CAP, PIVS SEXTVS P M A XXIII.
Rev.: Value.

C#	Date	Year	Good	VG	Fine	VF
—	1797-98)	XXIII	25.00	45.00	75.00	110.00

TERNI

A town in Umbria, was founded in 672 B.C. during most of the Middle Ages and up until 1860, it was a papal possession.

QVATTRO (4) BAIOCCHI

SILVER
Obv.: Terni 1797, Leg.: PIVS SEXTVS P M A XXIII.
Rev.: Value.

C#	Date	Year	Good	VG	Fine	VF
4	1797	XXIII	25.00	45.00	75.00	110.00

CINQVE (5) BAIOCCHI

COPPER
Obv.: Value, TERNI, LEG.: PIVS SEXTVS, .DATE.

Rev: Bust of Virgin Mary, SANCTA DEI GENITRIX.

C#	Date	Year	Good	VG	Fine	VF
2	1797	XXIII	30.00	50.00	75.00	125.00

SEI (6) BAIOCCHI

SILVER

6	1797	XXIII	30.00	50.00	75.00	150.00

OTTO (8) BAIOCCHI

SILVER

8	1797	XXIII	35.00	65.00	100.00	165.00

NOTE: A variety exists with obverse legend as PIVS SEXTVS P M A XXIII.

TIVOLI

A small town approximately 15 miles (24 km.) north of Rome.

CINQVE (5) BAICCHI

COPPER

Obv.: Value, TERNI, PIVS SEXTVS, date.

Rev: Bust of Virgin Mary, SANCTA DEI GENITRIX.

2	1797	XXIII	25.00	40.00	60.00	80.00

VITERBO

A city and papal possession in Latium.

MEZZO (1/2) BAIOCCO

COPPER

Obv.: Arms, Leg.: PIVS SEXTVS P M A XXIII.

Rev.: Value, VITERBO, date.

1	1797	XXIII	7.50	12.50	25.00	40.00

DVE E MEZZO (2-1/2) BAIOCCHI

COPPER, 30mm

2	1796	—	10.00	20.00	30.00	45.00
	1797	—	10.00	20.00	30.00	45.00

Rev. leg. ends: PRINC., 25-26mm

C#	Date	Mintage	Good	VG	Fine	VF
2a	1797	—	10.00	20.00	30.00	45.00
	1798	—	10.00	20.00	30.00	45.00

CINQVE (5) BAIOCCHI

COPPER

C#	Date	Year	Good	VG	Fine	VF
3	1797	XXIII	15.00	25.00	45.00	75.00

VATICAN CITY—PAPAL STATES

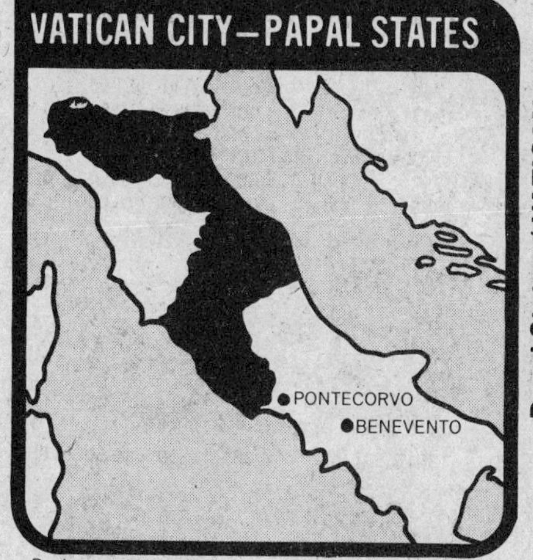

During many centuries prior to the formation of the unified Kingdom of Italy, when Italy was divided into numerous independent papal and ducal states, the Popes held temporal sovereignty over an area in central Italy comprising some 17,000 sq. mi. (44,030 sq. km.) including the city of Rome. At the time of the general unification of Italy under the Kingdom of Sardinia, 1861, the papal dominions beyond Rome were acquired by that kingdom, diminishing the Pope's sovereignty to Rome and its environs. In 1870, while France's opposition to papal dispossession was neutralized by its war with Prussia, the Italian army seized weakly defended Rome and made it the capital of Italy, thereby abrogating the last vestige of papal temporal power. In 1871, the Italian Parliament enacted the Law of Guarantees, which guaranteed a special status for the Vatican area, and spiritual freedom and a generous income for the Pope. Pope Pius IX and his successors adamantly refused to acknowledge the validity of these laws, and voluntarily "imprisoned" themselves in the Vatican. The impasse between State and Church lasted until the signing of the Lateran Treaty, Feb. 11, 1929, by which Italy recognized the sovereignty and independence of the new Vatican City state.

PAPAL STATES

PONTIFFS

Pius VI, 1775-1799
Pius VII, 1800-1823
Sede Vacante, Aug. 20-Sept. 28, 1823
Leo XII, 1823-1829
Sede Vacante, Feb. 10-Mar. 31, 1829
Pius VIII, 1829-1830
Sede Vacante, Nov. 30, 1830-Feb. 2, 1831
Gregory XVI, 1831-1846
Sede Vacante, June 1-16, 1846
Pius IX, 1846-1878

MINTMARKS

B - Bologna
R - Rome

NOTE: For similar coins dated 1775-1797 with and without 'B' mintmark see Papal City States, Bologna.

MONETARY SYSTEM

(Until 1860)

150 Quattrini = 30 Baiocchi = 6 Grossi = 4 Carlini = 3 Giulio = 3 Paoli = 1 Testone.
100 Baiocchi = 1 Scudo
30 Paoli = Doppia

QUATTRINO

C#	Date	Year	VG	Fine	VF	XF
67	1783	IX	4.00	7.50	12.50	20.00

C#	Date	Year	VG	Fine	VF	XF
	1784	IX	4.00	7.50	12.50	20.00
	1784	X	4.00	7.50	12.50	20.00
	1785	X	4.00	7.50	12.50	20.00
	1786	XII	4.00	7.50	12.50	20.00
	1787	XII	4.00	7.50	12.50	20.00

Obv: Arms, value: "UN" QUARTRINO

C#	Date	Year	VG	Fine	VF	XF
67a	1797	XXIII	6.00	10.00	18.00	26.50
	1798	XXIII	6.00	10.00	18.00	26.50
106	1801R	—	4.00	7.50	12.50	18.50
107	1802R	II	4.00	7.50	12.50	18.50

Obv. value: 'QUATTRINO'

C#	Date	Year	VG	Fine	VF	XF
107a	1816B	XVI	4.00	7.00	10.00	18.50
	1816R	XVI	4.00	7.00	10.00	18.50
	1816R	XVII	4.00	7.00	10.00	18.50
	1821B	XXII	4.00	7.00	10.00	18.50
	1821R	XXII	4.00	7.00	10.00	18.50
	1822B	XXII	4.00	7.00	10.00	18.50
107.5	1816B	XVI	8.00	15.00	22.50	30.00

Rev. value: 'QUATTRINO'

C#	Date	Year	VG	Fine	VF	XF
125.5	1824(B)	I	4.00	7.00	10.00	18.50
126	1824R	I	2.50	4.00	7.00	12.50
	1825R	II	2.50	4.00	7.00	12.50
126a	1826R	IV	2.50	4.00	7.00	12.50
135	1829R	I	3.00	5.00	8.00	15.00
144	1831R	I	2.00	4.00	7.50	15.00
144a	1835R	V	2.00	4.00	7.50	15.00
	1836B	VI	2.00	4.00	7.50	15.00
	1838R	VIII	2.00	4.00	7.50	15.00
	1839B	IX	4.00	7.50	15.00	30.00
	1839R	IX	2.00	4.00	7.50	15.00
	1840B	X	4.00	7.50	15.00	30.00
	1841R	X	3.00	6.00	10.00	17.50
	1841R	XI	2.00	4.00	7.50	15.00
	1843B	XIII	2.00	4.00	7.50	15.00

C#	Date	Year	VG	Fine	VF	XF
144a	1843R	XIII	2.00	4.00	7.50	15.00
	1844B	XIV	2.00	4.00	7.50	15.00
	1844R	XIV	2.00	4.00	7.50	15.00

C#	Date	Mintage	VG	Fine	VF	XF
164	1851R	yr.VI.090	3.00	6.00	9.00	15.00
	1854B	yr.IX.173	3.00	6.00	9.00	15.00

MEZZO (1/2) BAIOCCO

COPPER

Obv: Arms. Rev: Value in wreath.

C#	Date	Year	VG	Fine	VF	XF
68	1783	IX	3.00	6.50	9.00	15.00
	1784	X	3.00	6.50	9.00	15.00

C#	Date	Year	VG	Fine	VF	XF
68.1	1786	XII	3.00	6.50	9.00	15.00
	1788	XIV	3.00	6.50	9.00	15.00
	1789	XV	3.00	6.50	9.00	15.00
	1790	XVI	3.00	6.50	9.00	15.00
	1797	XXIII	3.00	6.50	9.00	15.00

Obv: Double date.

C#	Date	Year	VG	Fine	VF	XF
68a	1797	XXIII	4.00	8.00	15.00	25.00

Obv.: leg.: SACR. BASILIC, LATER. POSSES.

C#	Date	Year	VG	Fine	VF	XF
108	1801R	—	3.00	6.00	9.00	15.00

Varieties exist.

C#	Date	Year	VG	Fine	VF	XF
109	1802R	II	2.00	4.00	7.50	12.50

Obv. denomination: MEZZO BO. Rev: Legends in wreath.

C#	Date	Year	VG	Fine	VF	XF
109a	1816R	XVI	5.00	10.00	15.00	25.00
	1816R	XVII	5.00	10.00	15.00	25.00

C#	Date	Year	VG	Fine	VF	XF
109a.1	1816B	XVI	3.00	6.50	15.00	25.00
	1816B	XVII	3.00	6.50	15.00	25.00
	1822B	XXII	9.00	15.00	25.00	50.00
	1822R	XXII	3.00	6.50	15.00	25.00

C#	Date	Year	VG	Fine	VF	XF
127	1824B	I	6.00	10.00	17.50	35.00

C#	Date	Year	VG	Fine	VF	XF
127a	1825R	II	4.00	7.50	12.50	25.00
	1826R	III	4.00	7.50	12.50	25.00

Obv. leg: PIUS VIII PONT MAX. ANNO I

C#	Date	Year	VG	Fine	VF	XF
136	1829B	I	3.50	6.50	9.00	15.00
	1829R	I	3.50	6.50	9.00	15.00

Rev. value: MEZZO BAIOCCO ROMANO.

C#	Date	Year	VG	Fine	VF	XF
145	1831R	I	2.00	4.00	6.00	12.50
	1832B	II	4.00	7.50	12.50	25.00
	1832B	III	3.50	6.50	9.00	15.00
	1833B	III	2.00	4.00	6.00	10.00
	1834B	IV	2.00	4.00	6.00	12.50

C#	Date	Year	VG	Fine	VF	XF
145a	1835B	V	2.00	4.00	6.00	12.50
	1835R	V	2.00	4.00	6.00	12.50
	1836B	VI	2.00	4.00	6.00	12.50
	1836R	VI	2.00	4.00	6.00	12.50
	1837B	VII	2.00	4.00	6.00	12.50
	1837R	VII	3.50	6.50	9.00	15.00
	1838B	VIII	2.00	4.00	6.00	12.50
	1838R	VIII	3.50	6.50	9.00	15.00
	1839B	IX	2.00	4.00	6.00	12.50
	1839R	IX	3.50	6.50	9.00	15.00
	1840R	IX	3.50	6.50	9.00	15.00
	1840B	X	3.00	6.00	12.50	20.00
	1840R	X	2.00	4.00	6.00	12.50
	1841B	X	3.00	6.00	12.50	20.00
	1841R	XI	2.00	4.00	6.00	12.50
	1842B	XI	2.00	4.00	6.00	12.50
	1842B	XII	2.00	4.00	6.00	12.50
	1842R	XII	2.00	4.00	6.00	12.50
	1843B	XII	2.00	4.00	6.00	12.50
	1843B	XIII	2.00	4.00	6.00	12.50
	1843R	XIII	2.00	4.00	6.00	12.50
	1844B	XIII	2.00	4.00	6.00	12.50
	1844B	XIV	2.00	4.00	6.00	12.50
	1844R	XIV	2.00	4.00	6.00	12.50
	1845B	XV	2.00	4.00	6.00	12.50
	1845R	XV	2.00	4.00	6.00	12.50

C#	Date	Mintage	VG	Fine	VF	XF
165	1847B yr.II	.074	2.00	4.00	6.00	12.50
	1847R yr.II	9,000	3.50	7.50	12.50	25.00
	1848/7B yr.II	.049	2.50	5.00	9.50	15.00
	1848B yr.II	I.A.	3.50	6.00	10.00	18.50
	1848R yr.II	.644	2.00	4.00	6.00	12.50
	1848R yr.III	I.A.	2.00	4.00	6.00	12.50
	1848R yr.IIII	I.A.	3.50	6.00	10.00	18.50
	1849B yr.III	.104	2.00	4.00	6.00	12.50
	1849B yr.IV	I.A.	2.00	4.00	6.00	12.50
	1849R yr.IIII	1.921	2.00	4.00	6.00	12.50
	1849R yr.IV	I.A.	2.00	4.00	6.00	18.50

C#	Date	Mintage	VG	Fine	VF	XF
166	1850B yr.IV	.176	2.00	4.00	6.00	12.50
	1850R yr.IV					

C#	Date	Mintage	VG	Fine	VF	XF
166		5.552	2.00	4.00	6.00	12.50
	1850B yr.V	I.A.	2.00	4.00	6.00	12.50
	1850R yr.V	I.A.	2.00	4.00	6.00	12.50
	1851B yr.V					
		1.257	2.00	4.00	6.00	12.50
	1851R yr.V					
		4.001	2.00	4.00	6.00	12.50
	1851B yr.VI	I.A.	2.00	4.00	6.00	12.50
	1851R yr.VI	I.A.	2.00	4.00	6.00	12.50
	1852B yr.VI	.706	2.00	4.00	6.00	12.50

BAIOCCO

COPPER

C#	Date	Year	VG	Fine	VF	XF
69	(1782)	VIII	3.50	7.50	12.50	25.00
	(1783)	IX	3.50	7.50	12.50	25.00
	(1785)	XI	3.50	7.50	12.50	25.00
	(1787)	XIII	3.50	7.50	12.50	25.00
	(1789)	XV	3.50	7.50	12.50	25.00
	(1790)	XVI	3.50	7.50	12.50	25.00
	(1791)	XVII	3.50	7.50	12.50	25.00
	(1793)	XIX	3.50	7.50	12.50	25.00
	(1794)	XX	3.50	7.50	12.50	25.00

C#	Date	Year	VG	Fine	VF	XF
69a	(1797)	XXIII	5.00	10.00	15.00	25.00

Arabic Date

C#	Date	Year	VG	Fine	VF	XF
69b	1783	—	5.00	10.00	15.00	30.00

BILLON

C#	Date	Year	VG	Fine	VF	XF
73	1780	—	3.00	6.00	10.00	18.50
	1782	—	3.00	6.00	10.00	18.50

COPPER

Obv. denomination: VN BAIOC.

C#	Date	Year	VG	Fine	VF	XF
110	1800R	I	5.00	10.00	15.00	25.00

Obv. denomination: BAIOCCO

C#	Date	Year	VG	Fine	VF	XF
111	1801R	—	3.50	6.50	12.50	25.00

C#	Date	Year	VG	Fine	VF	XF
111.1	1801R	—	3.50	6.50	12.50	25.00

Rev: G. PASINATES S. C. below date

C#	Date	Year	VG	Fine	VF	XF
111.2	1801R	—	10.00	20.00	35.00	50.00

C#	Date	Year	VG	Fine	VF	XF
112	1802R	II	7.50	15.00	25.00	45.00
	1815B	XVI	6.00	10.00	17.50	35.00

C#	Date	Year	VG	Fine	VF	XF
112.1	1816B	XVI	6.00	10.00	17.50	35.00
	1816R	XVI	6.00	10.00	17.50	35.00
	1816B	XVII	6.00	10.00	17.50	35.00
	1816R	XVII	10.00	20.00	35.00	50.00

C#	Date	Year	VG	Fine	VF	XF
137	1829R	I	9.00	17.50	25.00	45.00

NOTE: Two varieties of edge inscription exist.

C#	Date	Year	VG	Fine	VF	XF
146	1831R	I	5.00	10.00	15.00	25.00
	1832R	I	15.00	25.00	45.00	75.00
	1832R	II	7.50	15.00	25.00	45.00

C#	Date	Year	VG	Fine	VF	XF
146a	1835B	V	2.00	4.00	6.00	12.50
	1835R	V	2.00	4.00	6.00	12.50
	1836B	VI	2.00	4.00	6.00	12.50
	1836R	VI	2.00	4.00	6.00	12.50
	1837B	VII	2.00	4.00	6.00	12.50
	1837R	VII	2.00	4.00	6.00	12.50
	1838B	VIII	15.00	25.00	45.00	75.00
	1838R	VIII	5.00	10.00	15.00	25.00
	1839R	VIII	7.50	15.00	25.00	45.00
	1839B	IX	2.00	4.00	6.00	12.50
	1839R	IX	5.00	10.00	15.00	25.00
	1840B	X	2.00	4.00	6.00	12.50
	1840R	X	2.00	4.00	6.00	12.50
	1841B	X	5.00	10.00	15.00	25.00
	1841B	XI	10.00	15.00	25.00	45.00
	1841R	XI	3.50	7.50	15.00	25.00
	1842R	XI	3.50	7.50	15.00	25.00
	1842B	XII	2.00	4.00	6.00	12.50
	1842R	XII	3.50	7.50	15.00	25.00
	1843R	XII	3.50	7.50	15.00	25.00

C#	Date	Year	VG	Fine	VF	XF
146a	1843B	XIII	3.50	7.50	15.00	25.00
	1843R	XIII	3.50	7.50	15.00	25.00
	1844B	XIII	2.00	4.00	6.00	12.50
	1844B	XIV	2.00	4.00	6.00	12.50
	1844R	XIV	2.00	4.00	6.00	12.50
	1845B	XV	2.00	4.00	6.00	12.50
	1845R	XV	3.50	7.50	15.00	25.00

C#	Date	Mintage	VG	Fine	VF	XF
167	1846B yr.I	—	6.50	12.50	20.00	35.00
	1846R yr.I					
		7.500	4.00	7.50	12.50	20.00
	1847B yr.I	.058	4.00	7.50	12.50	20.00
	1847R yr.I	.014	7.50	15.00	25.00	45.00
	1847R yr.II	I.A.	4.00	7.50	12.50	20.00
	1848R yr.II	.494	3.50	7.50	12.50	20.00
	1848R yr.III					
		I.A.	2.00	4.50	7.50	15.00
	1848R yr.IV	I.A.	2.00	4.50	7.50	15.00

NOTE: Varieties of date wording exist.

C#	Date	Mintage	VG	Fine	VF	XF
167.1	1849R yr.IV					
		1.080	2.50	5.00	10.00	17.50

C#	Date	Mintage	VG	Fine	VF	XF
168	1849B yr.IV	.061	6.50	12.50	20.00	35.00
	1850B yr.IV	.402	4.00	7.50	12.50	20.00
	1850R yr.IV					
		4.681	2.50	5.00	10.00	17.50
	1850B yr.V	I.A.	4.00	7.50	12.50	20.00
	1850R yr.V	I.A.	2.50	5.00	10.00	17.50
	1851B yr.V	.899	2.50	5.00	10.00	17.50
	1851R yr.V					
		5.706	4.00	7.50	12.50	20.00
	1851B yr.VI	I.A.	2.00	4.00	6.00	10.00
	1851R yr.VI	I.A.	4.00	7.50	12.50	20.00
	1852B yr.VI	.655	2.00	4.00	6.00	10.00
	1852R yr.VI					
		1.211	7.50	15.00	25.00	55.00
	1853R yr.VII					
		.035	7.50	15.00	25.00	55.00

2 BAIOCCHI

BILLON

Obv. Keys. Rev: Value.

C#	Date	Year	VG	Fine	VF	XF
74	1777	—	3.00	7.00	12.50	25.00
	1778	—	3.00	7.00	12.50	25.00
	1794	—	3.00	7.00	12.50	25.00
	1796	—	3.00	7.00	12.50	25.00

COPPER

C#	Date	Year	VG	Fine	VF	XF
70	(1785)	XI	3.00	7.50	15.00	30.00
	(1786)	XII	3.00	7.50	15.00	30.00
	(1787)	XIII	3.00	7.50	15.00	30.00
	!1788)	XIV	3.00	7.50	15.00	30.00
	(1789)	XV	3.00	7.50	15.00	30.00
	(1790)	XVI	3.00	7.50	15.00	30.00
	(1791)	XVII	3.00	7.50	15.00	30.00
	(1792)	XVIII	3.00	7.50	15.00	30.00
	(1793)	XIX	3.00	7.50	15.00	30.00
	(1794)	XX	3.00	7.50	15.00	30.00
	(1795)	XXI	3.00	7.50	15.00	30.00
	(1797)	XXIII	3.00	7.50	15.00	30.00
70a	(1797)	XXIII	4.00	8.00	16.00	30.00

C#	Date	Mintage	VG	Fine	VF	XF
169	1848B yr.III	.644	2.50	4.50	7.50	15.00
	1848R yr.III	.227	2.50	4.50	7.50	15.00
	1849R yr.IV	1.117	2.50	4.50	7.50	15.00

C#	Date	Mintage	VG	Fine	VF	XF
169a	1849B yr.III	—	2.50	4.00	6.00	10.00
	1849B yr.IV	—	2.50	4.50	7.50	15.00
	1850B yr.IV	—	2.50	4.50	7.50	15.00
	1850R yr.IV	3.784	2.50	4.50	7.50	15.00
	1850B yr.V	—	6.50	12.50	20.00	35.00
	1850R yr.V	I.A.	2.50	4.50	7.50	15.00
	1851B yr.V	—	2.50	4.50	7.50	15.00
	1851R yr.V	2.557	2.50	4.50	7.50	15.00
	1851B yr.VI	—	2.50	4.50	7.50	15.00
	1851R yr.VI	I.A.	2.50	4.50	7.50	15.00
	1852B yr.V	—	5.00	10.00	20.00	35.00
	1852R yr.V	1.727	4.00	7.50	15.00	25.00
	1852B yr.VI	—	2.50	4.50	7.50	15.00
	1852R yr.VI	I.A.	2.50	4.50	7.50	15.00
	1852R yr.VII	I.A.	4.00	7.50	15.00	25.00
	1853R yr.VI	1.460	4.00	7.50	15.00	25.00
	1853B yr.VII	—	3.50	7.50	15.00	25.00
	1853R yr.VII	I.A.	2.50	4.50	7.50	15.00
	1853R yr.VIII	I.A.	2.50	4.50	7.50	15.00
	1854R yr.VIII	5.000	35.00	75.00	100.00	175.00

2-1/2 BAIOCCHI

COPPER

C#	Date	Year	VG	Fine	VF	XF
71	1795	—	15.00	25.00	40.00	75.00

C#	Date	Year	VG	Fine	VF	XF
71a	1796	—	15.00	25.00	40.00	75.00

C#	Date	Year	VG	Fine	VF	XF
71b	1796	—	10.00	20.00	35.00	60.00
	1797	—	10.00	20.00	35.00	60.00

Reduced size, 25mm.

C#	Date	Year	VG	Fine	VF	XF
71c	1797	—	10.00	20.00	35.00	60.00

4 BAIOCCHI

BILLON

C#	Date	Year	VG	Fine	VF	XF
75	1777	—	7.50	15.00	25.00	50.00
	1793	—	7.50	15.00	25.00	50.00
	1794	—	7.50	15.00	25.00	50.00

GROSSO

1.3210 gm., .917 SILVER, .0389 oz ASW
Obv: Arms. Rev: Holy door.

C#	Date	Year	VG	Fine	VF	XF
82	1775	I	15.00	25.00	40.00	75.00

C#	Date	Year	VG	Fine	VF	XF
83	1777	III	5.00	10.00	17.50	30.00
	1778	III	5.00	10.00	17.50	30.00
	1778	IV	5.00	10.00	17.50	30.00
	1783	VIII	5.00	10.00	17.50	30.00

C#	Date	Year	VG	Fine	VF	XF
83a	1784	X	5.00	10.00	17.50	30.00
	1786	XXI	5.00	10.00	17.50	30.00
	1787	XIII	5.00	10.00	17.50	30.00

C#	Date	Year	VG	Fine	VF	XF
113	1815R	XVI	7.50	15.00	25.00	45.00
	1816B	XVI	15.00	25.00	40.00	75.00
	1816B	XVII	7.50	15.00	25.00	45.00
	1817B	XVII	7.50	15.00	25.00	45.00

5 BAIOCCHI

COPPER

C#	Date	Year	VG	Fine	VF	XF
72	1797	—	12.50	25.00	45.00	75.00
	1799	—	12.50	25.00	45.00	75.00

1.3430 gm., .900 SILVER, .0388 oz ASW

C#	Date	Year	VG	Fine	VF	XF
147	1835R	V	4.00	7.50	15.00	25.00
	1836B	VI	4.00	7.50	15.00	25.00
	1839R	IX	6.00	10.00	17.50	35.00
	1840B	X	4.00	7.50	15.00	25.00
	1841R	X	10.00	20.00	35.00	70.00
	1841B	XI	4.00	7.50	15.00	25.00
	1841R	XI	12.50	25.00	45.00	75.00
	1842B	XI	4.00	7.50	15.00	25.00
	1842R	XI	15.00	30.00	60.00	90.00
	1842B	XII	4.00	7.50	15.00	25.00
	1842R	XII	6.00	10.00	17.50	35.00
	1843B	XIII	6.00	10.00	17.50	35.00
	1843R	XIII	6.00	10.00	12.50	35.00
	1844B	XIII	4.00	7.50	15.00	25.00
	1844B	XIV	4.00	7.50	15.00	25.00
	1844/3R	—	7.50	15.00	25.00	50.00
	1844R	XIV	6.00	10.00	17.50	35.00
	1845B	XV	4.00	7.50	17.50	25.00
	1845R	XV	6.00	10.00	17.50	35.00
	1846R	XVI	4.00	7.50	12.50	20.00

C#	Date	Mintage	VG	Fine	VF	XF
171	1847B yr.I	2.387	6.00	10.00	20.00	40.00
	1847R yr.II	1.191	6.00	10.00	20.00	40.00
	1848R yr.II	2.122	20.00	40.00	80.00	125.00
	1849R yr.IV	.021	4.00	7.50	12.50	20.00
	1850R yr.V	.010	4.00	7.50	15.00	30.00
	1851R yr.V	.011	4.00	7.50	15.00	30.00
	1851R yr.VI	I.A.	4.00	7.50	15.00	30.00
	1852R yr.VII	.020	4.00	7.50	30.00	50.00
	1853R yr.VII	.014	4.00	7.50	30.00	50.00
	1855B yr.IX	9.200	20.00	40.00	100.00	175.00
	1855R yr.X	I.A.	20.00	40.00	55.00	100.00

1.4280 gm., .800 SILVER, .0367 oz ASW

C#	Date	Mintage	VG	Fine	VF	XF
171a	1856R yr.X	3.440	20.00	40.00	60.00	90.00
	1857R yr.XI	.023	4.00	7.50	15.00	25.00
	1858R yr.XII	1.573	4.00	7.50	15.00	25.00
	1858B yr.XIII	.224	4.00	7.50	15.00	25.00
	1858R yr.XIII	Inc. Ab.	4.00	7.50	15.00	25.00
	1859B yr.XIII					

C#	Date	Mintage	VG	Fine	VF	XF
171a		.173	4.00	7.50	15.00	25.00
	1859R yr.XIII	.083	4.00	7.50	15.00	25.00
	1860R yr.XV	.169	4.00	7.50	15.00	25.00
	1861R yr.XVI	.147	4.00	7.50	15.00	25.00
	1862R yr.XVII	.135	4.00	7.50	15.00	25.00
	1863R yr.XVIII	.044	4.00	7.50	15.00	25.00
	1864R yr.XIX	.101	4.00	7.50	15.00	25.00

1.3330 gm., .835 SILVER, .0357 oz ASW

C#	Date	Mintage	VG	Fine	VF	XF
171b	1865R yr.XIX	.106	9.00	17.50	30.00	50.00
	1865R yr.XX	I.A.	4.00	7.50	15.00	25.00
	1866R yr.XX	.040	6.00	10.00	17.50	35.00

COPPER

C#	Date	Mintage	VG	Fine	VF	XF
170	1849B yr.IV	—	5.00	8.00	15.00	25.00
	1849R yr.IV	.938	5.00	8.00	15.00	25.00
	1850B yr.IV	—	5.00	8.00	15.00	25.00
	1850R yr.IV	10.164	5.00	8.00	15.00	25.00
	1850B yr.V	—	5.00	8.00	15.00	25.00
	1850R yr.V	I.A.	5.00	8.00	15.00	25.00

Rev: Similar to C#170.

C#	Date	Mintage	VG	Fine	VF	XF
170a	1850B yr.V	—	5.00	8.00	15.00	25.00
	1850R yr.V	I.A.	5.00	8.00	15.00	25.00
	1851B yr.V	—	5.00	8.00	15.00	25.00
	1851R yr.V	7.949	5.00	7.50	15.00	25.00
	1851B yr.VI	—	4.00	7.50	15.00	25.00
	1851R yr.VI	I.A.	4.00	7.50	15.00	25.00
	1852B yr.VI	—	4.00	7.50	15.00	25.00
	1852R yr.VI	9.746	4.00	7.50	15.00	25.00
	1852B yr.VII	—	4.00	7.50	15.00	25.00
	1852R yr.VII	Inc. Ab.	4.00	7.50	15.00	25.00
	1853B yr.VII	—	4.00	7.50	15.00	25.00
	1853R yr.VII	8.428	4.00	7.50	15.00	25.00
	1853B yr.VIII	—	4.00	7.50	15.00	25.00
	1853R yr.VIII	Inc. Ab.	4.00	7.50	15.00	25.00
	1854B yr.VIII					

C#	Date	Mintage	VG	Fine	VF	XF
170a	1854R yr.VIII	1.977	9.00	17.50	35.00	55.00
	1854B yr.IX	—	4.00	7.50	15.00	25.00
	1854R yr.IX	I.A.	9.00	17.50	35.00	55.00

CARLINO

BILLON

C#	Date	Year	VG	Fine	VF	XF
76	1777	III	4.00	7.50	15.00	25.00
	1780	VI	4.00	7.50	15.00	25.00
	1792	XVII	4.00	7.50	15.00	25.00
	1794	XX	4.00	7.50	15.00	25.00
	1796	XXII	4.00	7.50	15.00	25.00

Rev: Without 'ROMANO'

C#	Date	Year	VG	Fine	VF	XF
76a	1777	III	20.00	40.00	60.00	90.00

OTTO (8) BAIOCCHI

BILLON

C#	Date	Year	VG	Fine	VF	XF
77	1793	—	5.00	10.00	20.00	35.00

GIULIO

.917 SILVER
Obv: Arms. Rev: Holy door.

C#	Date	Year	VG	Fine	VF	XF
84	1775	I	12.50	25.00	45.00	75.00

2.642 gm.
Obv: Arms. Rev: Holy church seated in clouds.

C#	Date	Year	VG	Fine	VF	XF
114	1817B	XVIII	12.50	25.00	45.00	75.00

10 BAIOCCHI

2.6870 gm., .900 SILVER, .0777 oz ASW

C#	Date	Year	VG	Fine	VF	XF
148	1836B	VI	12.50	25.00	45.00	75.00
	1836R	VI	8.00	15.00	25.00	50.00
	1839B	IX	8.00	15.00	30.00	50.00
	1839R	IX	8.00	15.00	25.00	50.00
	1841B	XI	5.00	10.00	20.00	45.00
	1841R	XI	10.00	20.00	35.00	50.00
	1842B	XI	8.00	15.00	25.00	50.00
	1842B	XII	5.00	10.00	20.00	45.00
	1842R	XII	12.50	25.00	45.00	75.00
	1843B	XIII	8.00	15.00	25.00	50.00
	1844B	XIV	8.00	15.00	25.00	50.00
	1846R	XVI	10.00	20.00	35.00	50.00

C#	Date	Mintage	VG	Fine	VF	XF
172	1847B yr.I	.011	8.00	15.00	25.00	50.00
	1847B yr.II	I.A.	8.00	15.00	25.00	50.00
	1847R yr.II	.012	4.00	7.50	15.00	25.00
	1848B yr.II	.017	10.00	20.00	40.00	75.00
	1848R yr.II	.033	4.00	7.50	15.00	25.00
	1848B yr.III	I.A.	4.00	7.50	15.00	25.00
	1848R yr.III	I.A.	4.00	7.50	15.00	25.00
	1849R yr.IIII					

C#	Date	Mintage	VG	Fine	VF	XF
172		1.274	25.00	50.00	75.00	100.00
	1850R yr.IIII	.089	4.00	7.50	15.00	30.00
	1850R yr.V	I.A.	5.00	10.00	20.00	45.00
	1852R yr.VII	.033	4.00	7.50	15.00	30.00
	1853R yr.VII	.041	4.00	7.50	15.00	30.00
	1854R yr.VIII	5.570	40.00	75.00	90.00	135.00
	1855R yr.IX	4.400	40.00	75.00	90.00	135.00
	1856R yr.X	1.140	45.00	85.00	100.00	150.00

2.8570 gm., .800 SILVER, .0734 oz ASW

C#	Date	Mintage	VG	Fine	VF	XF
172a	1858R yr.XII	2.548	4.00	7.50	15.00	25.00
	1858R yr.XIII		4.00	7.50	15.00	25.00
	1858B Yr. XIII	Inc. Ab.	4.00	7.50	15.00	25.00
	1859R yr.XIII	.088	4.00	8.00	15.00	25.00
	1860R yr.XIV	.150	10.00	20.00	40.00	60.00
	1861R yr.XVI	.327	4.00	7.50	15.00	25.00
	1862R yr.XVI	7.417	4.00	7.50	15.00	25.00
	1862R yr.XVII	Inc. Ab.	4.00	7.50	15.00	25.00
	1863R yr.XVI	—	75.00	125.00	175.00	300.00
	1863R yr.XVII	1.084	4.00	7.50	15.00	25.00
	1863R yr.XVIII	Inc. Ab.	4.00	7.50	15.00	25.00
	1864R yr.XVIII	1.147	10.00	20.00	35.00	70.00
	1864R yr.XIX	Inc. Ab.	10.00	20.00	35.00	70.00

2.6660 gm., .835 SILVER, .0715 oz ASW

C#	Date	Mintage	VG	Fine	VF	XF
172b	1865R yr.XIX	.409	8.00	15.00	30.00	45.00
	1865R yr.XX	I.A.	8.00	15.00	30.00	45.00

DODI (12) BAIOCCHI

BILLON
Obv: Keys. Rev: Value.

C#	Date	Year	VG	Fine	VF	XF
79	1793	—	20.00	35.00	65.00	90.00

DUE (2) CARLINI

BILLON

C#	Date	Year	VG	Fine	VF	XF
78	1777	III	8.00	15.00	25.00	45.00
	1780	VI	8.00	15.00	25.00	45.00
	1780	VII	8.00	15.00	25.00	45.00
	1781	VI	8.00	15.00	25.00	45.00
	1781	VIII	8.00	15.00	25.00	45.00
	(1784)	X	8.00	15.00	25.00	45.00
	(1785)	XI	8.00	15.00	25.00	45.00
	1794	XX	8.00	15.00	25.00	45.00
	1795	XX	8.00	15.00	25.00	45.00
	1796	XXI	8.00	15.00	25.00	45.00
	1796	XXII	8.00	15.00	25.00	45.00

DOPPIO (2) GIULIO

5.2850 gm., .917 SILVER, .1558 oz ASW
Obv: Legend in center. Rev: Saint on clouds.

C#	Date	Year	VG	Fine	VF	XF
85	1775	I	20.00	40.00	60.00	90.00

Obv: Arms.

C#	Date	Year	VG	Fine	VF	XF
86	1775	I	15.00	30.00	50.00	85.00

C#	Date	Year	VG	Fine	VF	XF
86a	1783	IX	6.00	10.00	20.00	40.00
	1784	IX	6.00	10.00	20.00	40.00
	1784	X	6.00	10.00	20.00	40.00
	1786	XIII	6.00	10.00	20.00	40.00
	1787	XIII	6.00	10.00	20.00	40.00
	1788	XIV	6.00	10.00	20.00	40.00
	1790	XV	6.00	10.00	20.00	40.00
	1790	XVI	6.00	10.00	20.00	40.00
	1792	XVIII	6.00	10.00	20.00	40.00
	1796	XXII	6.00	10.00	20.00	40.00

Obv: Bust right.

C#	Date	Year	VG	Fine	VF	XF
87	1776	II	12.50	25.00	40.00	75.00
	1777	II	12.50	25.00	40.00	75.00

Obv. leg: 'PISU SEXTUS' added.

C#	Date	Year	VG	Fine	VF	XF
87a	1777	IV	7.50	15.00	25.00	45.00
	1778	IV	7.50	15.00	25.00	45.00
	1779	IV	7.50	15.00	25.00	45.00
	1779	V	7.50	15.00	25.00	45.00
	1780	V	7.50	15.00	25.00	45.00
	1780	VI	7.50	15.00	25.00	45.00
	1780	VII	7.50	15.00	25.00	45.00
	1781	VII	7.50	15.00	25.00	45.00
	1782	VII	7.50	15.00	25.00	45.00
	1782	VIII	7.50	15.00	25.00	45.00
	1783	IX	7.50	15.00	25.00	45.00
	1784	IX	7.50	15.00	25.00	45.00
	1784	X	7.50	15.00	25.00	45.00

C#	Date	Year	VG	Fine	VF	XF
115	1816B	XVII	25.00	45.00	75.00	90.00
	1816B	XVIII	25.00	45.00	75.00	90.00
	1818B	XVII	10.00	20.00	40.00	65.00
	1818B	XVIII	10.00	20.00	40.00	65.00

Sede Vacante

C#	Date	Year	VG	Fine	VF	XF
122	1823B	—	30.00	60.00	85.00	110.00

20 BAIOCCHI

5.2850 gm., .917 SILVER, .1558 oz ASW

C#	Date	Year	VG	Fine	VF	XF
149	1834R	IV	10.00	20.00	40.00	75.00

5.3740 gm., .900 SILVER, .1555 oz ASW

C#	Date	Year	VG	Fine	VF	XF
150	1835B	V	8.00	15.00	30.00	55.00
	1835R	V	10.00	20.00	40.00	75.00
150	1836R	V	80.00	150.00	200.00	350.00
	1836B	VI	8.00	15.00	30.00	55.00
	1836R	VI	40.00	75.00	100.00	175.00
	1837R	VII	20.00	40.00	75.00	125.00
	1838B	VIII	8.00	15.00	30.00	55.00
	1838R	VIII	10.00	20.00	40.00	75.00
	1839R	IX	10.00	20.00	40.00	75.00
	1840B	X	8.00	15.00	30.00	55.00
	1841B	XI	8.00	15.00	30.00	55.00
	1841R	XI	10.00	20.00	40.00	75.00
	1842B	XII	25.00	45.00	75.00	110.00
	1842R	XII	10.00	20.00	40.00	75.00
	1844B	XIII	8.00	15.00	30.00	55.00
	1844R	XIII	100.00	250.00	500.00	750.00
	1844B	XIV	8.00	15.00	30.00	55.00
	1845B	XV	8.00	15.00	30.00	55.00
	1846R	XVI	10.00	20.00	40.00	75.00

C#	Date	Mintage	VG	Fine	VF	XF
173	1848R yr. II	—	10.00	20.00	40.00	75.00
	1848 yr. III	—	10.00	20.00	40.00	75.00

NOTE: Two varieties of ANNO III exist.

C#	Date	Mintage	VG	Fine	VF	XF
173	1849B yr.III	—	10.00	20.00	40.00	75.00
	1849B yr.IV	—	10.00	20.00	40.00	75.00
	1849R yr.IV	—	10.00	20.00	40.00	75.00
	1850B yr.IV	—	15.00	30.00	45.00	75.00
	1850R yr.IV	—	8.00	15.00	30.00	45.00
	1850R yr.V	—	9.00	17.50	30.00	45.00
	1851B yr.V	—	15.00	30.00	45.00	80.00
	1852B yr.VII	—	30.00	60.00	90.00	125.00
	1852R yr.VII	.010	15.00	30.00	50.00	90.00
	1853R yr.VII	.126	12.50	25.00	50.00	80.00
	1854R yr.VIII	—	10.00	20.00	40.00	75.00
	1856R yr.X	—	12.50	25.00	50.00	75.00
	1858B yr.XII	—	8.00	15.00	30.00	45.00
	1858R yr.XII	—	8.00	15.00	30.00	45.00

5.7140 gm., .800 SILVER, .1469 oz ASW

C#	Date	Mintage	VG	Fine	VF	XF
173a	1858B yr.XIII	—	8.00	12.50	25.00	45.00
	1858R yr.XIII	—	8.00	12.50	25.00	45.00
	1859B yr.XIII	.604	8.00	12.50	25.00	45.00
	1859R yr.XIII	1.104	8.00	12.50	25.00	45.00
	1859R yr.XIV	Inc. Ab.	8.00	12.50	25.00	45.00
	1860/50R	—	8.00	12.50	25.00	45.00
	1860R yr.XIV	3.656	8.00	12.50	25.00	45.00
	1860R yr.XV I.A.		8.00	12.50	25.00	45.00
	1861R yr.XV	2.987	8.00	12.50	25.00	45.00
	1861R yr.XVI	Inc. Ab.	8.00	12.50	25.00	45.00
	1862R yr.XVI	1.150	8.00	12.50	25.00	45.00
	1862R yr.XVII	Inc. Ab.	8.00	12.50	25.00	45.00
	1863R yr.XVII	3.155	8.00	12.50	25.00	45.00
	1863R yr.XVIII	Inc. Ab.	8.00	12.50	25.00	45.00
	1864R yr.XVIII	2.100	8.00	12.50	25.00	45.00
	1864R yr.XIX	Inc. Ab.	10.00	20.00	40.00	75.00
	1865R yr.XIX	7.346	8.00	12.50	25.00	45.00
	1865R yr.XX I.A.		8.00	12.50	25.00	45.00
	1866R yr.XX	5.600	8.00	12.50	25.00	45.00

VENTICINQUE (25) BAIOCCHI

BILLON

C#	Date	Year	VG	Fine	VF	XF
80	1795	XX	10.00	20.00	40.00	65.00
	1795	XXI	10.00	20.00	40.00	65.00
	1796	XXI	10.00	20.00	40.00	65.00
	1796	XXII	10.00	20.00	40.00	65.00

TESTONE (30 BAIOCCHI)

7.9280 gm., .917 SILVER, .2337 oz ASW

C#	Date	Year	VG	Fine	VF	XF
88	1785	XI	17.50	30.00	50.00	75.00
	1786	XI	17.50	30.00	50.00	75.00
	1786	XII	17.50	30.00	50.00	75.00
	1790	XV	17.50	30.00	50.00	75.00
	1790	XVI	17.50	30.00	50.00	75.00
	1796	XXII	17.50	25.00	40.00	60.00
116	1802R	III	12.50	25.00	40.00	60.00
	1803R	III	12.50	25.00	40.00	65.00
138	1830R	II	25.00	45.00	75.00	100.00

Sede Vacante

C#	Date	Year	VG	Fine	VF	XF
141	1830B	—	25.00	45.00	75.00	100.00
	1830R	—	25.00	45.00	75.00	100.00

C#	Date	Year	VG	Fine	VF	XF
151	1834R	IV	15.00	30.00	45.00	75.00

8.0610 gm., .900 SILVER, .2332 oz ASW
Rev: Value and date in wreath.

C#	Date	Year	VG	Fine	VF	XF
152	1836B	VI	30.00	50.00	75.00	100.00
	1836R	VI	50.00	75.00	100.00	150.00
	1837B	VII	30.00	50.00	75.00	100.00
	1837R	VII	50.00	75.00	100.00	150.00
	1838R	VIII	30.00	50.00	75.00	100.00
	1846R	XVI	30.00	50.00	75.00	100.00

50 BAIOCCHI

13.2140 gm., .917 SILVER, .3896 oz ASW

C#	Date	Year	VG	Fine	VF	XF
153	1832B	II	20.00	40.00	60.00	75.00
	1832R	II	25.00	45.00	60.00	85.00
	1834R	IV	25.00	45.00	60.00	85.00

NOTE: Two varieties of 1832B exist.

13.4350 gm., .900 SILVER, .3887 oz ASW
Rev: Value and date in wreath.

C#	Date	Year	VG	Fine	VF	XF
154	1835R	V	25.00	50.00	70.00	100.00
	1836B	VI	25.00	50.00	70.00	100.00
	1836R	VI	50.00	75.00	100.00	150.00
	1837B	VII	25.00	50.00	70.00	100.00
	1840B	X	50.00	75.00	100.00	150.00
	1841B	XI	25.00	50.00	70.00	100.00
	1842R	XII	50.00	75.00	100.00	150.00
	1843R	XIII	25.00	50.00	70.00	100.00
	1845R	XV	25.00	50.00	70.00	100.00
	1846R	XVI	25.00	50.00	70.00	100.00

C#	Date	Mintage	VG	Fine	VF	XF
174	1850R yr.IV	.104	25.00	50.00	70.00	100.00
	1850R yr.V	I.A.	25.00	60.00	85.00	125.00
	1853R yr.VII	.684	50.00	75.00	100.00	150.00
	1853R yr.VIII	Inc. Ab.	25.00	60.00	85.00	125.00
	1854B yr.IX	2,718	25.00	60.00	85.00	125.00
	1856B yr.X	4,226	25.00	60.00	85.00	125.00
	1857B yr.XII	8,711	50.00	75.00	100.00	150.00

1/2 SCUDO

13.2140 gm., .917 SILVER, .3896 oz ASW
Obv: Arms. Rev: Saint on clouds.

C#	Date	Year	VG	Fine	VF	XF
89	1775	I	25.00	50.00	75.00	125.00
	1775	II	25.00	50.00	75.00	125.00
	1776	II	25.00	50.00	75.00	125.00
	1777	II	25.00	50.00	75.00	125.00

Obv: Arms changed, leg: PIUS SEXTUS.

C#	Date	Year	VG	Fine	VF	XF
89a	1778	IV	20.00	40.00	60.00	100.00
	1778	V	20.00	40.00	60.00	100.00
	1779	V	20.00	40.00	60.00	100.00
	1780	V	20.00	40.00	60.00	100.00
	1780	VI	20.00	40.00	60.00	100.00
	1785	XI	20.00	40.00	60.00	100.00
	1796	XXII	20.00	40.00	60.00	100.00

C#	Date	Year	VG	Fine	VF	XF
90	1777	III	30.00	60.00	85.00	140.00

13.25 gm.
Neapolitan Occupation
Obv. leg: FERDINANDUS IV N. ET. S.R. within wreath.
Rev: Holy church standing, DEFENSORI REGLIGONIS.

C#	Date	Mintage	VG	Fine	VF	XF
101	1800R	—	500.00	1000.	1350.	1750.

C#	Date	Year	VG	Fine	VF	XF
117	1800R	I	35.00	70.00	100.00	140.00
	1802R	II	35.00	70.00	100.00	140.00
	1802R	III	35.00	70.00	100.00	140.00
	1803R	III	35.00	70.00	100.00	140.00
	1816B	XVII	35.00	70.00	100.00	140.00

Sede Vacante

C#	Date	Year	VG	Fine	VF	XF
123	1823B	—	30.00	45.00	70.00	125.00

Sede Vacante

C#	Date	Year	VG	Fine	VF	XF
132	1829B	—	35.00	65.00	100.00	150.00
	1829R	—	35.00	70.00	100.00	150.00

SESSANTA (60) BAIOCCHI

BILLON
Obv: Arms. Rev: Value.

C#	Date	Year	VG	Fine	VF	XF
81	1795	XXI	40.00	60.00	90.00	125.00
	1796	XXII	40.00	60.00	90.00	125.00
	1797	XXII	40.00	60.00	90.00	125.00
	1797	XXIII	40.00	60.00	90.00	125.00
	1799	XXV	40.00	60.00	90.00	125.00
81a	1793	XXI (error date)	75.00	100.00	140.00	200.00

SCUDO

26.4280 gm., .917 SILVER, .7792 oz ASW
Obv: Arms. Rev: Saint on clouds.

C#	Date	Year	VG	Fine	VF	XF
91	1780	VI	30.00	50.00	75.00	125.00

26.2500 gm., .917 SILVER, .7739 oz ASW
Neapolitan Occupation
Obv: FERDINANDUS IV NEAP. ET. SIC. REX within wreath.
Rev: Holy church standing, RELIGIONE DEFENSA.

C#	Date	Mintage	VG	Fine	VF	XF
102	1800R	—	575.00	1250.	1650.	2350.

Obv: FERDINANDUS IV UTR. SIC. REX within wreath.
Rev: Holy church seated, AUXILIUM DE SANCTO.

C#	Date	Mintage	VG	Fine	VF	XF
103	1800(R)	—	600.00	1000.	1350.	1750.

Obv. legend: PIVUS

C#	Date	Year	VG	Fine	VF	XF
118.1	1800R	I	30.00	50.00	75.00	125.00

Obv. legend: PIUS

C#	Date	Year	VG	Fine	VF	XF
118.2	1800R	I	50.00	100.00	140.00	200.00

C#	Date	Year	VG	Fine	VF	XF
119	1802R	II	30.00	50.00	75.00	125.00
	1802R	III	30.00	50.00	75.00	125.00
	1802R	IV	40.00	75.00	100.00	175.00
	1803R	IV	60.00	100.00	150.00	200.00
	1805R	VI	30.00	50.00	75.00	125.00
	1807R	VIII	30.00	50.00	75.00	125.00

26.4280 gm., .917 SILVER, .7792 oz ASW
Rev: Similar to C#119.

C#	Date	Year	VG	Fine	VF	XF
119.1	1815R	XVI	30.00	50.00	75.00	125.00
	1816B	XVII	30.00	50.00	75.00	125.00
	1817B	XVII	45.00	75.00	100.00	175.00
	1818B	XVIII	30.00	50.00	75.00	125.00

Obv: Bust of Pius VII right. Rev: Holy Church.

C#	Date	Year	VG	Fine	VF	XF
120	1816R	XVII	90.00	150.00	225.00	375.00

Sede Vacante

C#	Date	Mintage	VG	Fine	VF	XF
124	1823B	—	50.00	75.00	100.00	150.00

Sede Vacante

C#	Date	Mintage	VG	Fine	VF	XF
124.1	1823R	—	100.00	150.00	225.00	400.00

C#	Date	Year	VG	Fine	VF	XF
128	1825R	II	75.00	135.00	175.00	300.00
	1825B	III	75.00	135.00	175.00	300.00
	1826R	III	75.00	135.00	175.00	300.00

Rev: Long rays above Holy Church.

C#	Date	Year	VG	Fine	VF	XF
128.1	1826R	III	75.00	135.00	175.00	300.00

Sede Vacante

C#	Date	Mintage	VG	Fine	VF	XF
133	1829B	—	75.00	135.00	175.00	300.00
	1829R	—	85.00	145.00	185.00	325.00

Obv: Bust of Pius VIII. Rev: Two saints.

C#	Date	Year	VG	Fine	VF	XF
139	1830B	I	85.00	145.00	185.00	325.00
	1830R	I	75.00	135.00	175.00	300.00

Sede Vacante

C#	Date	Mintage	VG	Fine	VF	XF
142	1830B	—	75.00	145.00	185.00	325.00
	1830 Roma	—	85.00	135.00	175.00	300.00

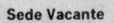

C#	Date	Year	VG	Fine	VF	XF
155	1831B	An. I	55.00	90.00	150.00	250.00
	1831R	An. I	45.00	75.00	90.00	125.00
	1833B	An. III	100.00	200.00	300.00	400.00
	1833R	An. III	55.00	90.00	140.00	200.00
	1833R	A. III	90.00	175.00	300.00	400.00
	1834R	An. IV	45.00	75.00	90.00	125.00
	1834R	A. IV	100.00	200.00	275.00	350.00

26.8710 gm., .900 SILVER, .7776 oz ASW
Obv: Similar to C#155.

C#	Date	Year	VG	Fine	VF	XF
156	1835B	V	45.00	75.00	90.00	125.00
	1835R	V	75.00	125.00	200.00	300.00
	1836R	VI	75.00	125.00	200.00	300.00
	1837R	VII	45.00	75.00	90.00	125.00
	1838B	VIII	60.00	100.00	150.00	250.00
	1838R	VIII	75.00	125.00	200.00	300.00
	1839R	VIII	75.00	125.00	200.00	300.00
	1839R	IX	75.00	125.00	200.00	300.00
	1840R	X	50.00	80.00	110.00	150.00
	1841R	XI	75.00	125.00	200.00	300.00
	1842R	XI	90.00	175.00	250.00	350.00
	1842R	XII	125.00	300.00	500.00	1000.
	1843R	XIII	45.00	75.00	90.00	125.00
	1844R	XIV	75.00	125.00	200.00	300.00
	1845R	XV	45.00	75.00	90.00	125.00
	1846R	XVI	45.00	75.00	90.00	125.00

Sede Vacante

C#	Date	Year	VG	Fine	VF	XF
162	1846R	—	90.00	150.00	200.00	300.00

Obv: W/NIC. CER. BARA below bust.
Rev: Similar to C#156.

C#	Date	Mintage	VG	Fine	VF	XF
175	1846B yr.I	2,073	60.00	90.00	125.00	200.00
	1846R yr.I	1,820	125.00	225.00	375.00	500.00
	1847B yr.II	.020	45.00	75.00	90.00	125.00
	1847R yr.II	.012	60.00	100.00	150.00	225.00
	1848R yr.II	.029	45.00	75.00	90.00	125.00
	1848R yr.III	I.A.	60.00	100.00	150.00	225.00

w/o NIC. CER. BARA below bust.
Rev: Similar to C#156.

C#	Date	Mintage	VG	Fine	VF	XF
175.1	1850R yr.IV	9,222	45.00	75.00	90.00	125.00
	1853R yr.VII	.527	45.00	75.00	90.00	125.00
	1853B yr.VIII	2,310	150.00	250.00	400.00	600.00
	1853R yr.VIII	Inc. Ab.	45.00	75.00	90.00	125.00
	1854B yr.IX	3,715	150.00	250.00	400.00	600.00
	1854R yr.IX	.146	45.00	75.00	90.00	125.00
	1856R yr.XI	1,050	100.00	200.00	300.00	400.00

1.7330 gm., .900 GOLD, .14.4mm, .0501 oz AGW

C#	Date	Mintage	Fine	VF	XF	Unc
176	1853B yr.VIII	3,306	125.00	175.00	225.00	400.00
	1853R yr.VIII	.209	90.00	125.00	175.00	200.00
	1854B yr.VIII	5,539	125.00	175.00	225.00	400.00
	1854R yr.VIII	.097	100.00	135.00	200.00	350.00
	1854R yr.IX	Inc. Ab.	100.00	135.00	200.00	350.00
	1857R yr.XII	.016	125.00	150.00	275.00	400.00

16.3mm

C#	Date	Mintage	Fine	VF	XF	Unc
176a	1858R yr.XII	.359	100.00	135.00	200.00	350.00
	1858R yr.XIII	Inc. Ab.	90.00	125.00	175.00	200.00
	1859R yr.XIII	.103	90.00	125.00	175.00	200.00
	1861R yr.XV	.084	100.00	135.00	200.00	350.00
	1861R yr.XVI	Inc. Ab.	100.00	135.00	200.00	350.00
	1862R yr.XVI	.226	100.00	135.00	200.00	350.00
	1862R yr.XVII	Inc. Ab.	100.00	135.00	200.00	350.00
	1863R yr.XVII					

C#	Date	Mintage	Fine	VF	XF	Unc
176a		.149	100.00	135.00	200.00	350.00
	1863R yr.XVIII	Inc. Ab.	100.00	135.00	200.00	350.00
	1864R yr.XIX	5,735	125.00	150.00	225.00	400.00
	1865R yr.XIX	.021	100.00	135.00	200.00	350.00

MEZZO (1/2) ZECCHINO

1.7260 gm., .998 GOLD, .0553 oz AGW
Obv: Arms, Rev: Saint on clouds

C#	Date	Year	Fine	VF	XF	Unc
92	1796	XXII	175.00	300.00	400.00	550.00

15 PAOLI

(= Mezza Doppia d'oro)

2.7300 gm., .917 GOLD, .0804 oz AGW
Obv: Lily, Rev: St. Peter

C#	Date	Year	Fine	VF	XF	Unc
94	1776	—	150.00	275.00	375.00	500.00
	1777	—	150.00	275.00	375.00	500.00
	1778	—	150.00	275.00	375.00	500.00
	1782	—	150.00	275.00	375.00	500.00
	1783	—	150.00	275.00	375.00	500.00
	1784	—	150.00	275.00	375.00	500.00
94a	1787	—	175.00	300.00	400.00	550.00

ZECCHINO

3.4520 gm., .998 GOLD, .1107 oz AGW

C#	Date	Year	Fine	VF	XF	Unc
93	1775	I	150.00	275.00	350.00	500.00
	1776	II	150.00	275.00	350.00	500.00

Obv: Arms 'PIUS SEXTUS'.

C#	Date	Year	Fine	VF	XF	Unc
93a	1783	IX	125.00	250.00	350.00	500.00
	1784	IX	125.00	250.00	350.00	500.00
	1784	X	125.00	250.00	350.00	500.00

2-1/2 SCUDI

4.3340 gm., .900 GOLD, .1254 oz AGW
Obv: Bust of Gregory XVI left.
Rev: Value and date in wreath.

C#	Date	Year	Fine	VF	XF	Unc
158	1835B	V	175.00	300.00	400.00	550.00
	1835R	V	175.00	300.00	400.00	550.00
	1836B	V	175.00	300.00	400.00	550.00
	1836B	VI	100.00	175.00	250.00	325.00
	1836R	VI	100.00	200.00	250.00	325.00
	1837R	VII	150.00	275.00	350.00	475.00
	1839R	IX	150.00	275.00	350.00	475.00
	1840B	X	100.00	200.00	250.00	325.00
	1841R	XI	175.00	300.00	400.00	600.00
	1842B	XII	100.00	200.00	250.00	325.00
	1842R	XII	200.00	350.00	500.00	700.00
	1843B	XIII	100.00	200.00	250.00	325.00
	1844B	XIII	150.00	225.00	300.00	375.00
	1845B	XV	200.00	375.00	550.00	850.00
	1845R	XV	150.00	275.00	400.00	500.00
	1846B	XVI	100.00	175.00	250.00	325.00

C#	Date	Mintage	Fine	VF	XF	Unc
177	1848R yr.II	3,197	175.00	300.00	375.00	450.00
	1853R yr.VII	.117	175.00	300.00	375.00	450.00
	1853R yr.VIII	Inc. Ab.	100.00	175.00	225.00	300.00
	1854R yr.VIII	.276	100.00	175.00	225.00	300.00
	1854B yr.IX	.032	90.00	150.00	200.00	300.00
	1854R yr.IX	Inc. Ab.	90.00	150.00	200.00	300.00
	1855R yr.IX	.059	90.00	150.00	200.00	300.00

C#	Date	Mintage	Fine	VF	XF	Unc
177	1855R yr.X	Inc. Ab.	90.00	150.00	200.00	300.00
	1856B yr.X	8,040	110.00	200.00	250.00	350.00
	1856R yr.X	.104	90.00	150.00	200.00	300.00
	1856R yr.XI	Inc. Ab.	90.00	150.00	200.00	300.00
	1857R yr.X	—	100.00	175.00	225.00	300.00
	1857R yr.XI	—	175.00	325.00	400.00	550.00
	1857B yr.XII	6,284	150.00	250.00	325.00	400.00
	1857R yr.XII	—	90.00	150.00	200.00	300.00
	1858R yr.XII	—	100.00	175.00	225.00	375.00
	1858B yr.XIII	2,787	175.00	275.00	350.00	425.00
	1858R yr.XIII	—	90.00	150.00	200.00	275.00
	1859B yr.XIII	.066	100.00	175.00	225.00	300.00
	1859R yr.XIII	—	90.00	150.00	200.00	300.00
	1859R yr.XIV	—	90.00	150.00	200.00	300.00
	1860R yr.XIV	—	90.00	150.00	200.00	300.00
	1860R yr.XV	—	90.00	150.00	200.00	300.00
	1861R yr.XV	—	90.00	150.00	200.00	300.00
	1861R yr.XVI	—	90.00	150.00	200.00	300.00
	1862R yr.XVI	—	90.00	150.00	200.00	300.00
	1862R yr.XVII	—	90.00	150.00	200.00	300.00
	1863R yr.XVII	—	90.00	150.00	200.00	300.00

30 PAOLI

(= Doppia d'oro)

5.4690 gm., .917 GOLD, .1612 oz AGW
Obv: Lily, Rev: St. Peter

C#	Date	Year	Fine	VF	XF	Unc
95	1776	—	175.00	275.00	400.00	600.00
	1777	—	125.00	175.00	275.00	400.00
	1778	—	125.00	175.00	275.00	400.00
	1779	—	125.00	175.00	275.00	400.00
	1780	—	125.00	175.00	275.00	400.00
	1781	—	125.00	175.00	275.00	400.00
	1782	—	125.00	175.00	275.00	400.00
	1783	—	125.00	175.00	275.00	400.00
	1784	—	125.00	175.00	275.00	400.00
	1785	—	125.00	175.00	275.00	400.00

C#	Date	Year	Fine	VF	XF	Unc
95a	1786	—	125.00	175.00	275.00	400.00
	1787	—	125.00	175.00	275.00	400.00
	1788	—	125.00	175.00	275.00	400.00
	1790	—	125.00	175.00	275.00	400.00
	1791	—	125.00	175.00	275.00	400.00
	1792	—	125.00	175.00	275.00	400.00
	1793	—	125.00	175.00	275.00	400.00

DOPPIA

.917 GOLD

ROME MINT

C#	Date	Year	Fine	VF	XF	Unc
121	(1800/1)	I	225.00	450.00	550.00	700.00
	(1801/2)	II	225.00	450.00	550.00	700.00
	(1802/3)	III	225.00	450.00	550.00	700.00
	(1803/4)	IV	225.00	450.00	550.00	700.00
	(1804/5)	V	225.00	450.00	550.00	700.00
	(1807/8)	VIII	225.00	450.00	550.00	700.00
	(1809/10)	X	250.00	500.00	650.00	800.00

Modified design

C#	Date	Year	Fine	VF	XF	Unc
121.1	(1815/6)	XVI	225.00	450.00	550.00	700.00
	(1817/8)	XVIII	300.00	600.00	800.00	1000.
	(1823/4)	XXIV	225.00	450.00	550.00	700.00

BOLOGNA MINT

C#	Date	Year	Fine	VF	XF	Unc
121.2	(1815/6)B	XVI	225.00	450.00	550.00	700.00
	(1816/7)B	XVII	225.00	450.00	550.00	700.00
	(1820/1)B	XXI	300.00	500.00	650.00	850.00
	(1821/2)B	XXII	225.00	450.00	550.00	700.00

Sede Vacante

C#	Date	Year	Fine	VF	XF	Unc
125	1823B	—	300.00	600.00	800.00	1000.
	1823R	—	300.00	600.00	800.00	1000.
129	(1823/4)R	I	300.00	600.00	800.00	1000.
	(1824/5)B	II	300.00	500.00	700.00	900.00
	(1824/5)R	II	300.00	600.00	800.00	1000.

Sede Vacante

C#	Date	Year	Fine	VF	XF	Unc
134	1829B	—	225.00	450.00	550.00	750.00
	1829R	—	350.00	700.00	1000.	1500.

Sede Vacante
Obv: Arms. Rev: Radiant dove.

C#	Date	Year	Fine	VF	XF	Unc
143	1830R	—	400.00	750.00	1250.	1750.

C#	Date	Year	Fine	VF	XF	Unc
157	1833R	III	300.00	600.00	750.00	1000.
	1834B	III	300.00	500.00	700.00	900.00

2 ZECCHINI

6.9040 gm., .998 GOLD, .2215 oz AGW

C#	Date	Year	Fine	VF	XF	Unc
130	1825R	III	500.00	1000.	1500.	2000.

Obv: Bust facing left.

C#	Date	Year	Fine	VF	XF	Unc
131	1828R	V	500.00	1000.	1500.	2000.

5 SCUDI

8.6680 gm., .900 GOLD, .2508 oz AGW
Obv: Bust of Gregory XVI left.
Rev: Sts. Peter and Paul, value in exergue.

C#	Date	Year	Fine	VF	XF	Unc
159	1834R	IV	1500.	3000.	3500.	4250.

C#	Date	Year	Fine	VF	XF	Unc
160	1835B	V	350.00	600.00	900.00	1100.
	1835R	V	350.00	650.00	900.00	1100.
	1836R	VI	350.00	650.00	800.00	1000.
	1837R	VI	500.00	1000.	1500.	2000.
	1837R	VII	350.00	650.00	800.00	1000.
	1838R	VII	350.00	650.00	900.00	1100.
	1838R	VIII	350.00	650.00	900.00	1100.
	1839R	VIII	450.00	900.00	1250.	1700.
	1839R	IX	450.00	900.00	1250.	1700.
	1840R	IX	450.00	900.00	1250.	1700.
	1841B	XI	500.00	800.00	1200.	2000.
	1841R	XI	350.00	650.00	900.00	1100.
	1842B	XII	350.00	600.00	900.00	1100.
	1842R	XII	350.00	650.00	900.00	1100.
	1843B	XIII	500.00	800.00	1200.	2000.
	1843R	XIII	350.00	650.00	900.00	1100.
	1845R	XV	350.00	650.00	900.00	1100.
	1846R	XVI	350.00	650.00	900.00	1100.

Sede Vacante
Obv: Arms. Rev: Radiant dove.

C#	Date	Year	Fine	VF	XF	Unc
163	1846R	—	900.00	1500.	2000.	3000.

C#	Date	Mintage	Fine	VF	XF	Unc
178	1846B yr.I	.011	350.00	650.00	900.00	1100.
	1846R yr.I	5,755	400.00	725.00	1100.	1450.
	1847R yr.II	1,399	450.00	900.00	1250.	1500.
	1848R yr.III	1,633	400.00	725.00	1000.	1350.
	1850R yr.IV	6,473	450.00	900.00	1250.	1500.
	1854R yr.IX	.104	300.00	600.00	800.00	950.00

60 PAOLI

(= Due doppia d'oro)

10.9380 gm., .917 GOLD, .3225 oz AGW

C#	Date	Year	Fine	VF	XF	Unc
96	1777	—	650.00	800.00	1200.	2000.

10 SCUDI

17.3360 gm., .900 GOLD, .5016 oz AGW

C#	Date	Year	Fine	VF	XF	Unc
161	1835B	V	400.00	650.00	800.00	1100.
	1835R	V	350.00	600.00	750.00	1000.
	1836R	V	450.00	650.00	800.00	1100.
	1836B	V	450.00	800.00	1200.	1600.
	1836R	VI	450.00	650.00	800.00	1100.
	1837R	VI	450.00	650.00	800.00	1100.
	1837R	VII	450.00	650.00	800.00	1100.
	1838R	VII	400.00	800.00	1000.	1250.
	1838R	VIII	400.00	650.00	800.00	1100.
	1839R	VIII	400.00	650.00	800.00	1100.
	1839R	IX	450.00	900.00	1250.	1600.
	1840B	X	450.00	800.00	1250.	1600.
	1840R	X	400.00	650.00	800.00	1100.
	1841R	X	400.00	650.00	800.00	1100.
	1841B	XI	400.00	650.00	800.00	1100.
	1841R	XI	400.00	650.00	800.00	1100.
	1842R	XI	400.00	800.00	1000.	1250.
	1842B	XII	400.00	650.00	800.00	1100.
	1842R	XII	400.00	650.00	800.00	1100.
	1843R	XIII	450.00	900.00	1250.	1600.
	1844R	XIV	450.00	900.00	1250.	1600.
	1845B	XV	400.00	650.00	800.00	1100.
	1845R	XV	450.00	900.00	1250.	1600.

Obv: Bust of Pius IX left.
Rev: Value and date in wreath.

C#	Date	Mintage	Fine	VF	XF	Unc
179	1850R yr.IV	5,875	800.00	1600.	2125.	2800.
	1850R yr.V	I.A.	500.00	900.00	1500.	2000.
	1856R yr.XI	2,483	800.00	1400.	1900.	2800.

DECIMAL COINAGE

100 Centesimi = 20 Soldi = 1 Lira

CENTESIMO

COPPER

C#	Date	Mintage	Fine	VF	XF	Unc
180	1866R yr.XXI	.525	3.00	5.00	8.50	17.50
	1867R yr.XXII	2.930	3.00	5.00	8.50	17.50
	1868R yr.XXII	1.960	6.50	12.50	20.00	35.00

1/2 SOLDO

(= 2-1/2 Centesimi)

COPPER

C#	Date	Mintage	Fine	VF	XF	Unc
181	1866R yr.XXI	.189	3.00	5.00	8.50	17.50
	1867R yr.XXI	7.892	1.75	2.50	5.00	10.00
	1867R yr.XXII	Inc. Ab.	1.75	2.50	5.00	10.00

SOLDO

(= 5 Centesimi)

COPPER

Obv: Small bust.

C#	Date	Mintage	Fine	VF	XF	Unc
182	1866R yr.XXI	1.280	1.75	2.50	5.00	10.00

Obv: Large bust.

C#	Date	Mintage	Fine	VF	XF	Unc
182a	1866R yr.XXI	Inc. Ab.	1.75	2.50	5.00	10.00
	1867R yr.XXI	8.544	1.75	2.50	5.00	10.00

2 SOLDI

(= 10 Centesimi)

COPPER

C#	Date	Mintage	Fine	VF	XF	Unc
183	1866R yr.XXI	3.410	2.00	4.00	8.00	17.50
	1867R yr.XXI	3.188	2.00	4.00	8.00	17.50

4 SOLDI

(= 20 Centesimi)

COPPER

C#	Date	Mintage	Fine	VF	XF	Unc
184	1866R yr.XXI	2.465	3.00	5.00	10.00	20.00
	1867R yr.XXI	2.039	3.00	5.00	10.00	20.00
	1867R yr.XXII	Inc. Ab.	3.00	5.00	10.00	20.00
	1868R yr.XXII	5.602	3.00	5.00	10.00	20.00
	1868R yr.XXIII	Inc. Ab.	3.00	5.00	10.00	20.00
	1869R yr.XXIII	2.760	3.00	5.00	10.00	20.00
	1869R yr.XXIV	Inc. Ab.	3.00	5.00	10.00	20.00

BILLON

C#	Date	Mintage	Fine	VF	XF	Unc
184a	1868 Yr. XXII	—	—	—	—	—

5 SOLDI

(= 25 Centesimi)

1.2500 gm., .835 SILVER, .0335 oz ASW

C#	Date	Mintage	Fine	VF	XF	Unc
186	1866R yr.XXI	.964	4.00	8.00	15.00	25.00
	1867R yr.XXI	1.920	4.00	8.00	12.50	20.00
	1867R yr.XXII	Inc. Ab.	4.00	8.00	12.50	20.00

10 SOLDI

(= 50 Centesimi)

2.5000 gm., .835 SILVER, .0671 oz ASW

Obv. leg: PIUS IX PON. MAX. A.....

C#	Date	Mintage	Fine	VF	XF	Unc
187	1866R yr.XXI	.292	8.00	12.50	20.00	45.00
	1867R yr.XXI	4.402	4.00	8.00	12.50	20.00
	1867R yr.XXII	Inc. Ab.	4.00	8.00	12.50	20.00
	1868R yr.XXII	8.204	4.00	8.00	12.50	20.00

Obv. leg: PIUS IX P.M.A.....

C#	Date	Mintage	Fine	VF	XF	Unc
187a	1868R yr.XXIII	Inc. Ab.	4.00	8.00	12.50	20.00
	1869R yr.XXIII	4.433	4.00	8.00	12.50	20.00
	1869R yr.XXIV	Inc. Ab.	4.00	8.00	12.50	20.00

LIRA

5.0000 gm., .835 SILVER, .1342 oz ASW

Small bust

Obv: Without ornament below bust.

C#	Date	Mintage	Fine	VF	XF	Unc
188	1866R yr.XX	7.634	45.00	75.00	125.00	300.00

Obv: With roses below bust.

C#	Date	Mintage	Fine	VF	XF	Unc
188b	1866R yr.XX	I.A.	45.00	75.00	125.00	450.00
	1866R yr.XXI	Inc. Ab.	5.00	10.00	20.00	40.00

Obv: With ornament below bust.

C#	Date	Mintage	Fine	VF	XF	Unc
188f	1866R yr.XXI	Inc. Ab.	4.50	7.50	15.00	25.00

Medium bust

C#	Date	Mintage	Fine	VF	XF	Unc
188d	1866R yr.XXI	Inc. Ab.	5.00	10.00	17.50	35.00

Obv: Large bust, PIUS IX PON. MAX. AN...

C#	Date	Mintage	Fine	VF	XF	Unc
188a	1866R yr.XXI	Inc. Ab.	5.00	7.50	15.00	25.00
	1867R yr.XXI	5.339	4.50	7.50	15.00	25.00
	1867R yr.XXII	Inc. Ab.	4.50	7.50	15.00	25.00
	1868R yr.XXII	2.050	4.50	7.50	15.00	25.00

Obv. leg: PIUS IX PON.M.A....

C#	Date	Mintage	Fine	VF	XF	Unc
188e	1868R yr.XXIII	Inc. Ab.	4.50	7.50	15.00	25.00
	1869R yr.XXIII	1.144	5.00	10.00	17.50	35.00
	1869R yr.XXIV	Inc. Ab.	5.00	10.00	17.50	35.00

2 LIRE

10.0000 gm., .835 SILVER, .2684 oz ASW

Obv. leg: PIUS IX PON MAX.A....

C#	Date	Mintage	Fine	VF	XF	Unc
189	1866R yr.XX	.367	90.00	175.00	275.00	500.00
	1866R yr.XXI	Inc. Ab.	12.50	25.00	40.00	65.00
	1867R yr.XXI	1.124	15.00	30.00	50.00	100.00
	1867R yr.XXII	Inc. Ab.	12.50	20.00	35.00	65.00
	1868R yr.XXII	.530	15.00	30.00	40.00	65.00

Obv. leg: PIUS IX PON.M.A....

C#	Date	Mintage	Fine	VF	XF	Unc
189a	1868R yr.XXIII	Inc. Ab.	15.00	30.00	50.00	100.00
	1869R yr.XXIV	.111	12.50	25.00	40.00	65.00
	1870R yr.XXIV	.183	15.00	30.00	50.00	100.00

2-1/2 LIRE

12.5000 gm., .900 SILVER, .3617 oz ASW

C#	Date	Mintage	Fine	VF	XF	Unc
190	1867R yr.XXI	.257	30.00	50.00	80.00	150.00

5 LIRE

1.6120 gm., .900 GOLD, .0466 oz AGW

C#	Date	Mintage	Fine	VF	XF	Unc
192	1866R yr.XXI	3,226	350.00	500.00	650.00	800.00
	1867R yr.XXII	3,787	400.00	600.00	750.00	1000.

2.5000 gm., .900 SILVER, .0723 oz ASW

C#	Date	Mintage	Fine	VF	XF	Unc
191	1867R yr.XXI	5,804	100.00	175.00	225.00	400.00
	1870R yr.XXIV	.010	90.00	125.00	175.00	300.00
	1870R yr.XXV	Inc. Ab.	90.00	125.00	175.00	300.00

10 LIRE

3.2250 gm., .900 GOLD, .0933 oz AGW
Obv. leg: PIUS IX PON. MAX.A....

C#	Date	Mintage	Fine	VF	XF	Unc
193	1866R yr.XXI	8,578	350.00	500.00	650.00	800.00
	1867R yr.XXI	8,570	350.00	500.00	650.00	800.00
	1867R yr.XXII	Inc. Ab.	350.00	500.00	650.00	800.00

Obv. leg: PIUS IX P.M.A.....

C#	Date	Mintage	Fine	VF	XF	Unc
193a	1869R yr.XXIV	5,945	400.00	600.00	750.00	1000.

20 LIRE

6.4510 gm., .900 GOLD, .1866 oz AGW
Plain edge, small bust

C#	Date	Mintage	Fine	VF	XF	Unc
194	1866R yr.XX	.103	500.00	650.00	800.00	1250.

Reeded edge

C#	Date	Mintage	Fine	VF	XF	Unc
194.1	1866R yr.XX I.A.		300.00	400.00	550.00	800.00
	1866R yr.XXI	Inc. Ab.	300.00	400.00	550.00	800.00
	1867R yr.XXI	.039	300.00	400.00	550.00	800.00

Medium bust

C#	Date	Mintage	Fine	VF	XF	Unc
194.2	1867R yr.XXII	Inc. Ab.	300.00	400.00	550.00	800.00
	1868R yr.XXII	.038	300.00	400.00	550.00	800.00
	1868R yr.XXIII	Inc. Ab.	300.00	400.00	550.00	800.00

Large bust

C#	Date	Mintage	Fine	VF	XF	Unc
194.3	1868R yr.XXIII	.039	300.00	400.00	550.00	800.00
	1869R yr.XXIII	.054	300.00	400.00	550.00	800.00
	1869R yr.XXIV	Inc. Ab.	300.00	400.00	550.00	800.00
	1870R yr.XXIV	.024	500.00	650.00	800.00	1250.
	1870R yr.XXV	Inc. Ab.	500.00	650.00	800.00	1250.

50 LIRE

16.1290 gm., .900 GOLD, .4667 oz AGW

C#	Date	Mintage	Fine	VF	XF	Unc
195	1868R yr.XXII	1,173	750.00	1500.	2000.	3250.
	1868R yr.XXIII	Inc. Ab.	1500.	2000.	3000.	4500.
	1870R yr.XXIV	1,459	750.00	1500.	2000.	3350.

100 LIRE

32.2580 gm., .900 GOLD, .9335 oz AGW

C#	Date	Mintage	Fine	VF	XF	Unc
196	1866R yr.XXI	1,115	1000.	1850.	2500.	3500.
	1868R yr.XXIII	440 pcs.	1500.	2500.	3500.	5000.
	1869T yr.XXIII	624 pcs.	1500.	2500.	3500.	5000.
	1869R yr.XXIV	Inc. Ab.	2500.	3500.	5000.	8000.

VATICAN CITY

ROME

The State of the Vatican City, a papal state on the right bank of the Tiber River within the boundaries of Rome, has an area of 0.17 sq. mi. (44 sq. km.) and a population of 1,000. Capital: Vatican City.

Vatican City State, comprising the Vatican, St. Peter's and extraterritorial right to Castel Gandolfo and 13 buildings in Rome, is all that remains of the extensive papal state over which the Pope exercised temporal power in central Italy. During the struggle for Italian unification, the papal states, including Rome, were forcibly incorporated into the Kingdom of Italy in 1870. The resultant confrontation of crozier and sword remained unresolved until the signing of the Lateran Treaty, Feb. 11, 1929, between the Vatican and the Kingdom of Italy which recognized the independence and sovereignty of the State of the Vatican City, defined the relationship between the government and the church within Italy, and financially compensated the Holy See for its territorial losses in 1870.

Today the Pope exercises supreme legislative, executive and judicial power within the Vatican City, and the State of the Vatican City is recognized by many nations as an independent sovereign state under the temporal jurisdiction of the Pope, even to the extent of ambassadorial exchange.

PONTIFFS

Pius XI, 1922-1939
Sede Vacante, Feb. 10 - Mar. 2, 1939
Pius XII, 1939-1958
Sede Vacante, Oct. 9 -28, 1958
John XXIII, 1958-1963
Sede Vacante, June 3 - 21,1963
Paul VI, 1963-1978
Sede Vacante, Aug. 6 - 26, 1978
John Paul I, 8/26-9/28, 1978
Sede Vacante, Sept. 28 - Oct. 16, 1978
John Paul II, 1978—

MONETARY SYSTEM

100 Centesimi = 1 Lira

5 CENTESIMI

BRONZE

Y#	Date	Mintage	Fine	VF	XF	Unc
1	1929	.010	3.00	5.00	12.50	25.00
	1930	.100	2.00	4.50	7.00	15.00
	1931	.100	2.00	4.50	7.00	15.00
	1932	.100	2.00	4.50	7.00	15.00
	1934	.100	2.00	4.50	7.00	15.00
	1935	.044	4.00	8.00	20.00	35.00
	1936	.062	2.00	4.50	7.00	15.00
	1937	.062	2.00	4.50	7.00	17.50
	1938	—	—	—	Rare	—

Jubilee

Y#	Date	Mintage	Fine	VF	XF	Unc
11	1933-34	.100	4.00	8.00	20.00	35.00

Y#	Date	Mintage	Fine	VF	XF	Unc
22	1939	.062	2.00	4.50	7.00	15.00
	1940	.062	4.00	8.00	15.00	25.00

Y#	Date	Mintage	Fine	VF	XF	Unc
22	1941	5,000	6.00	12.50	20.00	35.00

BRASS

Y#	Date	Mintage	Fine	VF	XF	Unc
31	1942	5,000	6.00	12.50	20.00	40.00
	1943	1,000	20.00	40.00	75.00	135.00
	1944	1,000	20.00	40.00	75.00	135.00
	1945	1,000	20.00	40.00	75.00	135.00
	1946	1,000	20.00	40.00	75.00	135.00

10 CENTESIMI

BRONZE

Y#	Date	Mintage	Fine	VF	XF	Unc
2	1929	.010	3.00	5.00	12.50	25.00
	1930	.090	2.00	4.50	7.00	15.00
	1931	.090	2.00	4.50	7.00	15.00
	1932	.090	2.00	4.50	7.00	15.00
	1934	.090	2.00	4.50	7.00	15.00
	1935	.090	2.00	4.50	7.00	15.00
	1936	.081	1.50	4.50	6.00	12.50
	1937	.081	2.00	4.50	7.00	15.00
	1938	—	—	—	Rare	—

Jubilee

Y#	Date	Mintage	Fine	VF	XF	Unc
12	1933-34	.090	5.00	11.50	16.00	35.00

Y#	Date	Mintage	Fine	VF	XF	Unc
23	1939	.081	3.00	5.00	12.50	25.00
	1940	.081	3.00	5.00	12.50	25.00
	1941	7,500	4.50	10.00	15.00	30.00

BRASS

Y#	Date	Mintage	Fine	VF	XF	Unc
32	1942	7,500	6.00	12.50	20.00	45.00
	1943	1,000	15.00	40.00	80.00	135.00
	1944	1,000	15.00	40.00	80.00	135.00
	1945	1,000	15.00	40.00	80.00	135.00
	1946	1,000	15.00	40.00	80.00	135.00

20 CENTESIMI

NICKEL

Y#	Date	Mintage	Fine	VF	XF	Unc
3	1929	.010	3.00	6.00	15.00	25.00
	1930	.080	2.00	4.50	7.00	15.00
	1931	.080	2.00	4.50	7.00	15.00
	1932	.080	2.00	4.50	7.00	15.00

Y#	Date	Mintage	Fine	VF	XF	Unc
3	1934	.080	2.00	4.50	7.00	15.00
	1935	9,000	9.00	20.00	45.00	100.00
	1936	.064	1.50	3.00	5.00	10.00
	1937	.064	2.00	4.50	7.00	15.00

Jubilee

Y#	Date	Mintage	Fine	VF	XF	Unc
13	1933-34	.080	5.00	10.00	15.00	25.00

Y#	Date	Mintage	Fine	VF	XF	Unc
24	1939	.064	2.00	4.50	7.00	15.00

STAINLESS STEEL

Y#	Date	Mintage	Fine	VF	XF	Unc
24a	1940	.064	1.00	2.00	3.50	4.50
	1941	.130	1.00	2.00	3.50	4.50

Y#	Date	Mintage	Fine	VF	XF	Unc
33	1942	.130	1.00	2.00	3.50	5.00
	1943	1,000	16.50	35.00	65.00	100.00
	1944	1,000	16.50	35.00	65.00	100.00
	1945	1,000	16.50	35.00	65.00	100.00
	1946	1,000	16.50	35.00	65.00	100.00

50 CENTESIMI

NICKEL

Y#	Date	Mintage	Fine	VF	XF	Unc
4	1929	.010	4.00	8.00	15.00	25.00
	1930	.080	2.00	4.50	7.00	15.00
	1931	.080	2.00	4.50	7.00	15.00
	1932	.080	2.00	4.50	7.00	15.00
	1934	.080	2.00	4.50	7.00	15.00
	1935	.014	9.00	20.00	35.00	90.00
	1936	.052	1.50	3.50	7.50	12.50
	1937	.052	2.00	4.50	7.00	15.00

Jubilee

Y#	Date	Mintage	Fine	VF	XF	Unc
14	1933-34	.080	5.00	10.00	15.00	25.00

Y#	Date	Mintage	Fine	VF	XF	Unc
25	1939	.052	2.00	4.50	7.00	15.00

STAINLESS STEEL

Y#	Date	Mintage	Fine	VF	XF	Unc
25a	1940	.052	1.00	2.00	3.50	5.00
	1941	.180	1.00	2.00	3.50	5.00

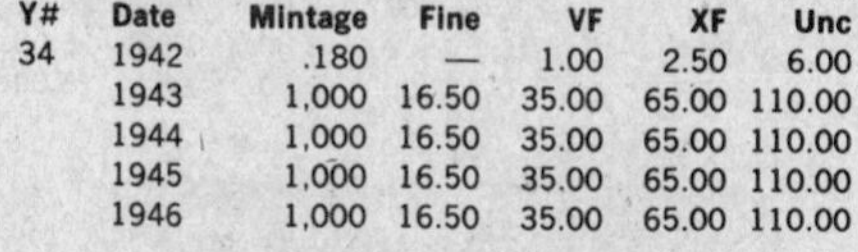

Y#	Date	Mintage	Fine	VF	XF	Unc
34	1942	.180	—	1.00	2.50	6.00
	1943	1,000	16.50	35.00	65.00	110.00
	1944	1,000	16.50	35.00	65.00	110.00
	1945	1,000	16.50	35.00	65.00	110.00
	1946	1,000	16.50	35.00	65.00	110.00

LIRA

NICKEL

Y#	Date	Mintage	Fine	VF	XF	Unc
5	1929	.010	4.00	10.00	15.00	30.00
	1930	.080	2.00	4.50	7.00	15.00
	1931	.080	2.00	4.50	7.00	15.00
	1932	.080	2.00	4.50	7.00	15.00
	1934	.080	2.00	4.50	7.00	15.00
	1935	.040	2.00	4.50	7.00	15.00
	1936	.040	2.00	4.50	7.00	15.00
	1937	.100	2.00	4.50	7.00	15.00

Jubilee, enlargement of date area

Y#	Date	Mintage	Fine	VF	XF	Unc
15	1933-34	.080	5.00	10.00	15.00	25.00

Y#	Date	Mintage	Fine	VF	XF	Unc
26	1939	.070	2.00	4.50	7.00	17.50

STAINLESS STEEL

Y#	Date	Mintage	Fine	VF	XF	Unc
26a	1940	.070	1.00	2.00	3.50	5.00
	1941	.284	1.00	2.00	3.50	5.00

Y#	Date	Mintage	Fine	VF	XF	Unc
35	1942	.284	—	—	2.50	5.00
	1943	1,000	16.50	35.00	65.00	110.00
	1944	1,000	16.50	35.00	65.00	110.00
	1945	1,000	16.50	35.00	65.00	110.00
	1946	1,000	16.50	35.00	65.00	110.00

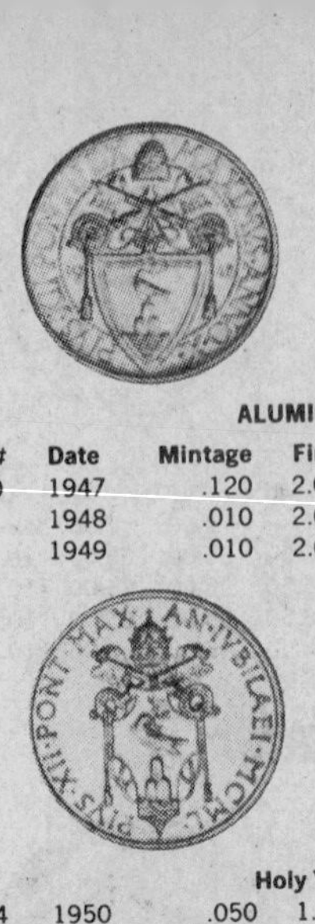

ALUMINUM

Y#	Date	Mintage	Fine	VF	XF	Unc
40	1947	.120	2.00	3.50	7.50	25.00
	1948	.010	2.00	3.50	7.50	25.00
	1949	.010	2.00	3.50	7.50	25.00

Holy Year

Y#	Date	Mintage	Fine	VF	XF	Unc
44	1950	.050	1.50	3.50	5.00	7.50

Y#	Date	Mintage	Fine	VF	XF	Unc
49	1951	.400	—	1.00	2.00	3.00
	1952	.400	—	1.00	2.00	3.00
	1953	.400	—	1.00	2.00	3.00
	1955	.010	2.00	4.00	7.50	12.50
	1956	.020	2.00	4.00	7.50	12.50
	1957	.030	2.00	4.00	7.50	12.50
	1958	.030	1.00	2.00	3.00	5.00

Y#	Date	Mintage	Fine	VF	XF	Unc
58	1959	.025	3.00	5.50	10.00	15.00
	1960	.025	4.00	10.00	17.50	30.00
	1961	.025	3.00	5.50	10.00	15.00
	1962	.025	3.00	5.50	10.00	15.00

Ecumenical Council

Y#	Date	Mintage	Fine	VF	XF	Unc
67	1962	.050	2.00	3.00	7.50	15.00

Y#	Date	Mintage	Fine	VF	XF	Unc
76	1963	.060	2.00	3.00	8.00	15.00
	1964	.060	2.00	3.00	7.50	15.00
	1965	.060	2.00	3.00	7.50	15.00

Y#	Date	Mintage	Fine	VF	XF	Unc
84	1966	.090	1.00	1.50	2.00	4.00

Fifth Year

Y#	Date	Mintage	Fine	VF	XF	Unc
92	1967	.100	1.00	1.50	2.00	4.00

F. A. O. Issue

Y#	Date	Mintage	Fine	VF	XF	Unc
100	(1968)	.100	—	.65	1.00	1.85

Y#	Date	Mintage	Fine	VF	XF	Unc
108	1969	.100	—	.50	.75	1.00

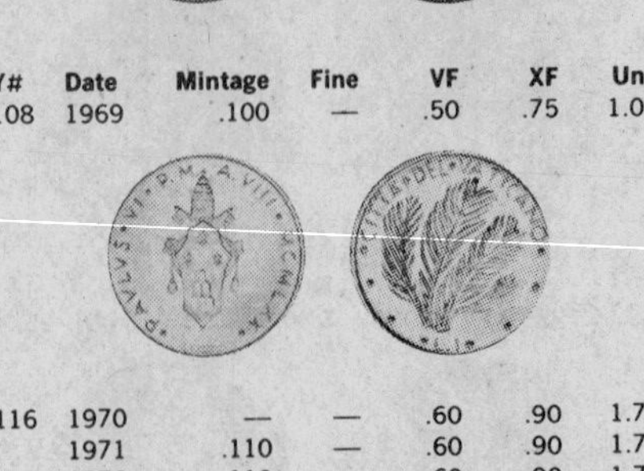

Y#	Date	Mintage	Fine	VF	XF	Unc
116	1970	—	—	.60	.90	1.75
	1971	.110	—	.60	.90	1.75
	1972	.110	—	.60	.90	1.75
	1973	—	—	.60	.90	1.75
	1974	—	—	.40	.75	1.40
	1975	.150	—	—	.75	1.40
	1976	.150	—	—	.75	1.40
	1977	.135	—	—	.60	1.40

Holy Year

Y#	Date	Mintage	Fine	VF	XF	Unc
124	1975	.180	—	—	.50	1.00

2 LIRE

NICKEL

Y#	Date	Mintage	Fine	VF	XF	Unc
6	1929	.010	4.00	7.50	15.00	35.00
	1930	.050	3.00	5.00	8.50	15.00
	1931	.050	3.00	5.00	8.50	15.00
	1932	.050	3.00	5.00	8.50	15.00
	1934	.050	3.00	5.00	8.50	15.00
	1935	.070	3.00	5.00	8.50	15.00
	1936	.010	3.00	5.00	8.50	15.00
	1937	.070	3.00	5.00	8.50	15.00

Jubilee

Y#	Date	Mintage	Fine	VF	XF	Unc
16	1933-34	.050	6.00	10.00	17.50	30.00

Y#	Date	Mintage	Fine	VF	XF	Unc
27	1939	.040	2.50	4.50	7.50	15.00

STAINLESS STEEL

Y#	Date	Mintage	Fine	VF	XF	Unc
27a	1940	.040	2.00	4.50	7.00	12.50
	1941	.270	2.00	4.50	7.00	12.50

Y#	Date	Mintage	Fine	VF	XF	Unc
36	1942	.270	2.00	4.50	7.00	12.50
	1943	1,000	15.00	35.00	65.00	110.00
	1944	1,000	15.00	35.00	65.00	110.00
	1945	1,000	15.00	35.00	65.00	110.00
	1946	1,000	16.50	40.00	75.00	110.00

ALUMINUM

Y#	Date	Mintage	Fine	VF	XF	Unc
41	1947	.070	4.00	9.00	15.00	32.50
	1948	.120	4.00	8.00	12.50	15.00
	1949	.010	4.00	8.00	12.50	15.00

Holy Year

Y#	Date	Mintage	Fine	VF	XF	Unc
45	1950	.050	2.00	3.00	4.50	8.50

Y#	Date	Mintage	Fine	VF	XF	Unc
50	1951	.400	—	1.00	2.00	3.00
	1952	.400	—	1.00	2.00	3.00
	1953	.400	—	1.00	2.00	3.00
	1955	.020	2.00	3.00	4.50	10.00
	1956	.040	2.00	3.00	4.50	10.00
	1957	.030	2.00	3.00	4.50	10.00
	1958	.030	2.00	3.00	4.50	10.00

Y#	Date	Mintage	Fine	VF	XF	Unc
59	1959	.025	3.00	5.50	10.00	17.50
	1960	.025	3.00	6.00	12.50	20.00
	1961	.025	2.00	3.00	5.00	8.00
	1962	.025	2.00	3.00	5.00	8.00

Ecumenical Council

Y#	Date	Mintage	Fine	VF	XF	Unc
68	1962	.050	1.00	2.00	3.00	5.00

Y#	Date	Mintage	Fine	VF	XF	Unc
77	1963	.060	2.00	5.00	8.00	12.50
	1964	.060	—	1.75	2.50	5.00
	1965	.060	—	1.00	2.00	3.00

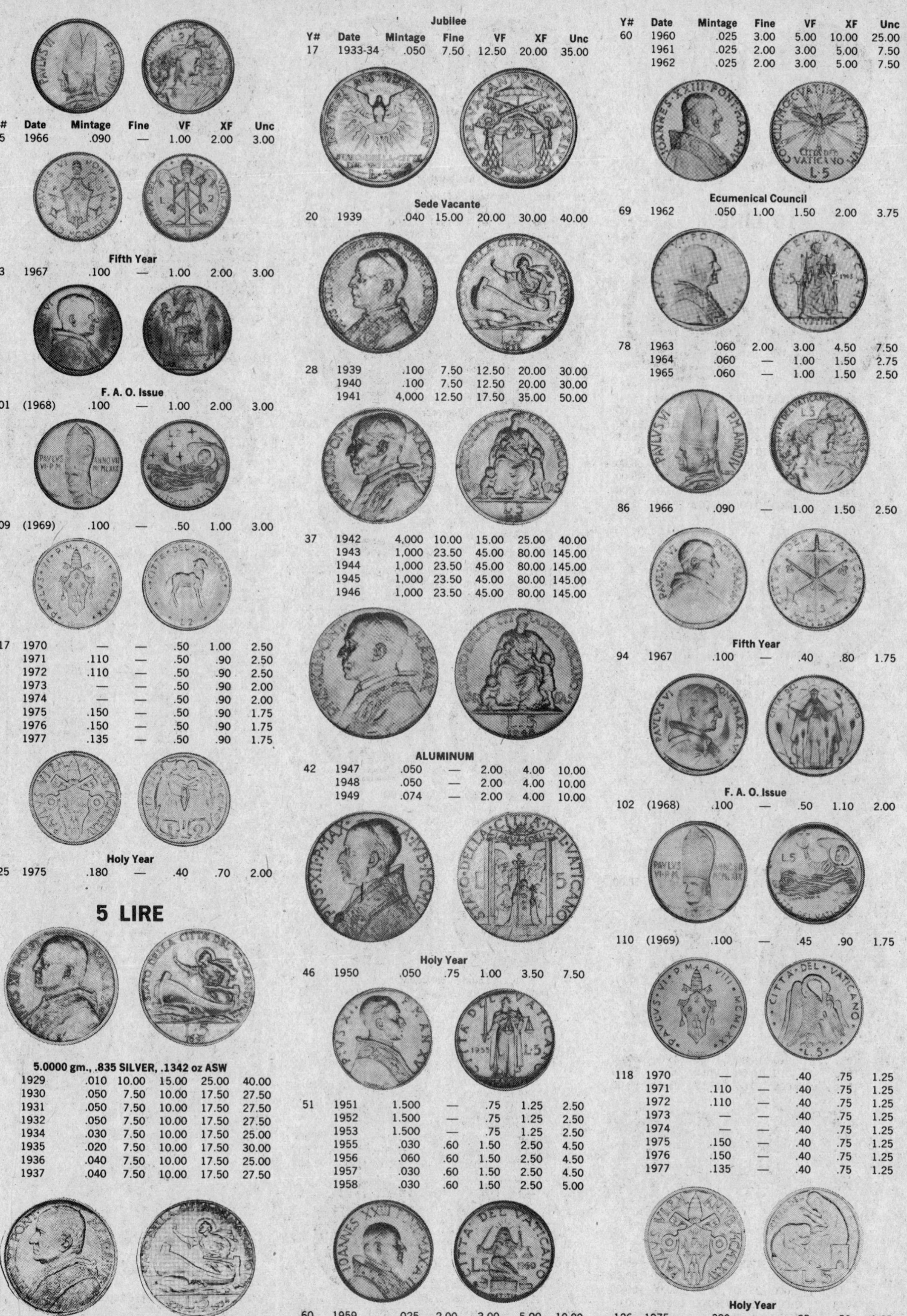

Y#	Date	Mintage	Fine	VF	XF	Unc
85	1966	.090	—	1.00	2.00	3.00
	Fifth Year					
93	1967	.100	—	1.00	2.00	3.00
	F. A. O. Issue					
101	(1968)	.100	—	1.00	2.00	3.00
109	(1969)	.100	—	.50	1.00	3.00
117	1970	—	—	.50	1.00	2.50
	1971	.110	—	.50	.90	2.50
	1972	.110	—	.50	.90	2.50
	1973	—	—	.50	.90	2.00
	1974	—	—	.50	.90	2.00
	1975	.150	—	.50	.90	1.75
	1976	.150	—	.50	.90	1.75
	1977	.135	—	.50	.90	1.75
	Holy Year					
125	1975	.180	—	.40	.70	2.00

5 LIRE

5.0000 gm., .835 SILVER, .1342 oz ASW

Y#	Date	Mintage	Fine	VF	XF	Unc
7	1929	.010	10.00	15.00	25.00	40.00
	1930	.050	7.50	10.00	17.50	27.50
	1931	.050	7.50	10.00	17.50	27.50
	1932	.050	7.50	10.00	17.50	27.50
	1934	.030	7.50	10.00	17.50	25.00
	1935	.020	7.50	10.00	17.50	30.00
	1936	.040	7.50	10.00	17.50	25.00
	1937	.040	7.50	10.00	17.50	27.50

Jubilee

Y#	Date	Mintage	Fine	VF	XF	Unc
17	1933-34	.050	7.50	12.50	20.00	35.00
	Sede Vacante					
20	1939	.040	15.00	20.00	30.00	40.00
28	1939	.100	7.50	12.50	20.00	30.00
	1940	.100	7.50	12.50	20.00	30.00
	1941	4,000	12.50	17.50	35.00	50.00
37	1942	4,000	10.00	15.00	25.00	40.00
	1943	1,000	23.50	45.00	80.00	145.00
	1944	1,000	23.50	45.00	80.00	145.00
	1945	1,000	23.50	45.00	80.00	145.00
	1946	1,000	23.50	45.00	80.00	145.00
	ALUMINUM					
42	1947	.050	—	2.00	4.00	10.00
	1948	.050	—	2.00	4.00	10.00
	1949	.074	—	2.00	4.00	10.00
	Holy Year					
46	1950	.050	.75	1.00	3.50	7.50
51	1951	1.500	—	.75	1.25	2.50
	1952	1.500	—	.75	1.25	2.50
	1953	1.500	—	.75	1.25	2.50
	1955	.030	.60	1.50	2.50	4.50
	1956	.060	.60	1.50	2.50	4.50
	1957	.030	.60	1.50	2.50	4.50
	1958	.030	.60	1.50	2.50	5.00
60	1959	.025	2.00	3.00	5.00	10.00

Y#	Date	Mintage	Fine	VF	XF	Unc
60	1960	.025	3.00	5.00	10.00	25.00
	1961	.025	2.00	3.00	5.00	7.50
	1962	.025	2.00	3.00	5.00	7.50
	Ecumenical Council					
69	1962	.050	1.00	1.50	2.00	3.75
78	1963	.060	2.00	3.00	4.50	7.50
	1964	.060	—	1.00	1.50	2.75
	1965	.060	—	1.00	1.50	2.50
86	1966	.090	—	1.00	1.50	2.50
	Fifth Year					
94	1967	.100	—	.40	.80	1.75
	F. A. O. Issue					
102	(1968)	.100	—	.50	1.10	2.00
110	(1969)	.100	—	.45	.90	1.75
118	1970	—	—	.40	.75	1.25
	1971	.110	—	.40	.75	1.25
	1972	.110	—	.40	.75	1.25
	1973	—	—	.40	.75	1.25
	1974	—	—	.40	.75	1.25
	1975	.150	—	.40	.75	1.25
	1976	.150	—	.40	.75	1.25
	1977	.135	—	.40	.75	1.25
	Holy Year					
126	1975	.380	—	.25	.50	1.25

16th Year

Y#	Date	Mintage	Fine	VF	XF	Unc
133	1978	—	—	—	—	—

10 LIRE

10.0000 gm., .835 SILVER, .2684 OZ ASW

Y#	Date	Mintage	Fine	VF	XF	Unc
8	1929	.010	12.50	17.50	25.00	45.00
	1930	.050	10.00	15.00	20.00	35.00
	1931	.050	10.00	15.00	20.00	35.00
	1932	.050	10.00	15.00	20.00	35.00
	1934	.060	10.00	15.00	20.00	35.00
	1935	.050	10.00	15.00	20.00	35.00
	1936	.040	10.00	15.00	20.00	35.00
	1937	.040	10.00	15.00	20.00	35.00

Jubilee

Y#	Date	Mintage	Fine	VF	XF	Unc
18	1933-34	.050	12.50	17.50	25.00	45.00

Sede Vacante

Y#	Date	Mintage	Fine	VF	XF	Unc
21	1939	.030	15.00	20.00	30.00	50.00

Y#	Date	Mintage	Fine	VF	XF	Unc
29	1939	.010	10.00	17.50	25.00	50.00
	1940	.010	10.00	17.50	25.00	50.00
	1941	4,000	10.00	17.50	25.00	50.00

Y#	Date	Mintage	Fine	VF	XF	Unc
38	1942	4,000	12.50	20.00	30.00	65.00
	1943	1,000	25.00	50.00	100.00	150.00
	1944	1,000	25.00	50.00	100.00	150.00
	1945	1,000	25.00	50.00	100.00	150.00
	1946	1,000	25.00	50.00	100.00	150.00

ALUMINUM

Y#	Date	Mintage	Fine	VF	XF	Unc
43	1947	.050	1.00	2.00	4.50	10.00
	1948	.050	1.00	2.00	4.00	9.00
	1949	.060	1.00	2.00	4.00	9.00

Holy Year

Y#	Date	Mintage	Fine	VF	XF	Unc
47	1950	.060	.75	1.25	2.50	6.50

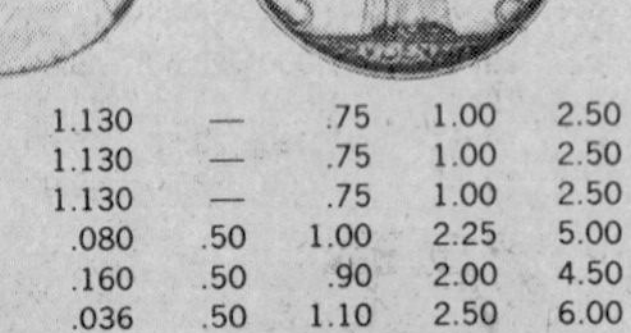

Y#	Date	Mintage	Fine	VF	XF	Unc
52	1951	1.130	—	.75	1.00	2.50
	1952	1.130	—	.75	1.00	2.50
	1953	1.130	—	.75	1.00	2.50
	1955	.080	.50	1.00	2.25	5.00
	1956	.160	.50	.90	2.00	4.50
	1957	.036	.50	1.10	2.50	6.00
	1958	.030	.50	.90	2.00	5.00

Y#	Date	Mintage	Fine	VF	XF	Unc
61	1959	.050	1.00	2.00	3.00	5.00
	1960	.050	1.00	2.00	4.00	6.50
	1961	.050	1.00	2.00	3.00	5.00
	1962	.050	1.00	2.00	3.00	5.00

Ecumenical Council

Y#	Date	Mintage	Fine	VF	XF	Unc
70	1962	.100	—	1.00	2.00	3.50

Y#	Date	Mintage	Fine	VF	XF	Unc
79	1963	.090	.25	1.00	2.00	4.00
	1964	.090	—	1.00	2.00	3.50
	1965	.090	—	1.00	2.00	3.50

Y#	Date	Mintage	Fine	VF	XF	Unc
87	1966	.100	—	.30	.75	2.00

Fifth Year

Y#	Date	Mintage	Fine	VF	XF	Unc
95	1967	.110	—	.30	.75	1.50

F. A. O. Issue

Y#	Date	Mintage	Fine	VF	XF	Unc
103	(1968)	.110	—	.40	.80	1.50

Y#	Date	Mintage	Fine	VF	XF	Unc
111	(1969)	.110	—	.30	.75	2.00

Y#	Date	Mintage	Fine	VF	XF	Unc
119	1970	—	—	.25	.55	1.50
	1971	.160	—	.25	.50	1.25
	1972	.160	—	.25	.50	1.10
	1973	—	—	.25	.50	1.10
	1974	—	—	.25	.50	1.10
	1975	.200	—	.25	.50	1.10
	1976	.200	—	.25	.50	1.10
	1977	.200	—	.25	.50	1.10

Holy Year

Y#	Date	Mintage	Fine	VF	XF	Unc
127	1975	.400	—	.25	.75	2.00

16th Year

Y#	Date	Mintage	Fine	VF	XF	Unc
134	1978	—	—	.25	.50	1.00

Obv: Similar to 100 Lire, y#146

Y#	Date	Mintage	Fine	VF	XF	Unc
143	1979	—	—	—	—	—

20 LIRE

ALUMINUM-BRONZE

Y#	Date	Mintage	Fine	VF	XF	Unc
A52	1957	.020	.50	1.25	3.00	7.00
	1958	.060	.50	1.00	2.00	3.00
62	1959	.060	.50	1.00	2.00	5.00
	1960	.050	.50	1.00	2.00	6.00
	1961	.050	.50	1.00	2.00	4.00
	1962	.050	.50	1.00	2.00	4.00

Ecumenical Council

Y#	Date	Mintage	Fine	VF	XF	Unc
71	1962	.100	.25	1.00	2.00	4.00
80	1963	.090	—	1.00	2.00	4.00
	1964	.090	—	1.00	2.00	4.00
	1965	.090	—	1.00	2.00	4.00
88	1966	.100	—	.30	.75	1.50

Fifth Year

Y#	Date	Mintage	Fine	VF	XF	Unc
96	1967	.110	—	.30	.75	1.25

F. A. O. Issue

Y#	Date	Mintage	Fine	VF	XF	Unc
104	(1968)	.105	—	.25	.75	1.50

Y#	Date	Mintage	Fine	VF	XF	Unc
112	1969	.110	—	.25	.60	1.25

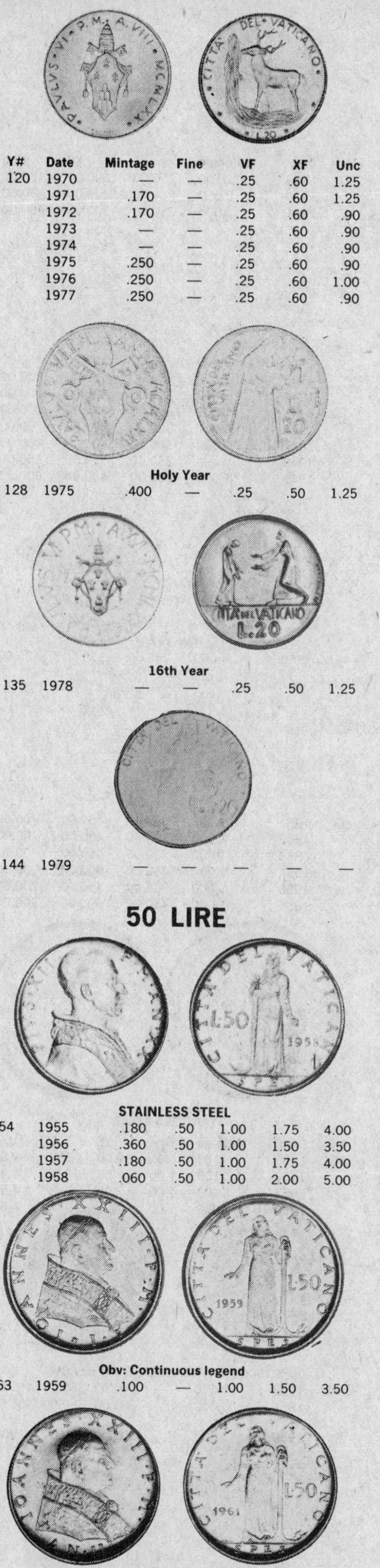

Y#	Date	Mintage	Fine	VF	XF	Unc
120	1970	—	—	.25	.60	1.25
	1971	.170	—	.25	.60	1.25
	1972	.170	—	.25	.60	.90
	1973	—	—	.25	.60	.90
	1974	—	—	.25	.60	.90
	1975	.250	—	.25	.60	.90
	1976	.250	—	.25	.60	1.00
	1977	.250	—	.25	.60	.90

Holy Year

Y#	Date	Mintage	Fine	VF	XF	Unc
128	1975	.400	—	.25	.50	1.25

16th Year

Y#	Date	Mintage	Fine	VF	XF	Unc
135	1978	—	—	.25	.50	1.25
144	1979	—	—	—	—	—

50 LIRE

STAINLESS STEEL

Y#	Date	Mintage	Fine	VF	XF	Unc
54	1955	.180	.50	1.00	1.75	4.00
	1956	.360	.50	1.00	1.50	3.50
	1957	.180	.50	1.00	1.75	4.00
	1958	.060	.50	1.00	2.00	5.00

Obv: Continuous legend

Y#	Date	Mintage	Fine	VF	XF	Unc
63	1959	.100	—	1.00	1.50	3.50

Obv: Date under bust.

Y#	Date	Mintage	Fine	VF	XF	Unc
63.1	1960	.100	—	1.00	2.50	4.00
	1961	.100	—	1.00	2.00	3.50
	1962	.100	—	1.00	2.00	3.50

Ecumenical Council

Y#	Date	Mintage	Fine	VF	XF	Unc
72	1962	.200	—	.50	1.25	3.00
81	1963	.120	—	.50	1.00	2.00
	1964	.120	—	.50	1.00	2.00
	1965	.120	—	.50	1.00	2.00
89	1966	.150	—	.50	1.00	2.00

Fifth Year

Y#	Date	Mintage	Fine	VF	XF	Unc
97	1967	.190	—	.55	1.00	2.50

F. A. O. Issue

Y#	Date	Mintage	Fine	VF	XF	Unc
105	(1968)	.190	—	.70	1.25	2.75
113	1969	.190	—	.55	1.00	2.50
121	1970	—	—	.30	.75	2.00
	1971	.700	—	.30	.75	2.00
	1972	.700	—	.30	.75	1.50
	1973	—	—	.30	.75	1.50
	1974	—	—	.30	.75	1.50
	1975	.600	—	.30	.75	1.50
	1976	.600	—	.30	.75	1.50

Holy Year

Y#	Date	Mintage	Fine	VF	XF	Unc
129	1975	.500	—	.40	1.00	2.50

Y#	Date	Mintage	Fine	VF	XF	Unc
A121	1977	.600	—	.30	.75	1.50

16th Year

Y#	Date	Mintage	Fine	VF	XF	Unc
136	1978	—	—	.25	.75	2.00

Y#	Date	Mintage	Fine	VF	XF	Unc
145	1979	—	—	—	—	—

100 LIRE

8.8000 gm., .900 GOLD, .2546 oz AGW

Y#	Date	Mintage	VF	XF	Unc
9	1929	10,000	250.00	300.00	450.00
	1930	2,621	425.00	725.00	1200.
	1931	3,343	250.00	300.00	450.00
	1932	5,073	250.00	300.00	450.00
	1934	2,533	300.00	350.00	600.00
	1935	7,015	250.00	300.00	450.00

Jubilee, - 23.5mm

Y#	Date	Mintage	VF	XF	Unc
19	1933-34	—	250.00	300.00	450.00

5.1900 gm., .900 GOLD, .1501 oz AGW
20.5mm

Y#	Date	Mintage	VF	XF	Unc
10	1936	8,239	300.00	400.00	500.00
	1937	2,000	750.00	1500.	2000.
	1938	5 or 6	—	Rare	—

Y#	Date	Mintage	VF	XF	Unc
30	1939	2,100	250.00	300.00	450.00
	1940	2,000	250.00	300.00	450.00
	1941	2,000	250.00	300.00	450.00

Y#	Date	Mintage	VF	XF	Unc
39	1942	2,000	250.00	300.00	450.00
	1943	1,000	350.00	525.00	800.00
	1944	1,000	350.00	525.00	800.00
	1945	1,000	350.00	525.00	800.00
	1946	1,000	300.00	500.00	750.00
	1947	1,000	300.00	400.00	600.00
	1948	—	250.00	350.00	450.00
	1949	1,000	300.00	400.00	600.00

Holy Year

Y#	Date	Mintage	VF	XF	Unc
48	1950	4,000	250.00	350.00	425.00

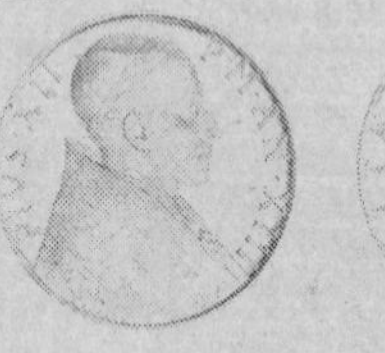
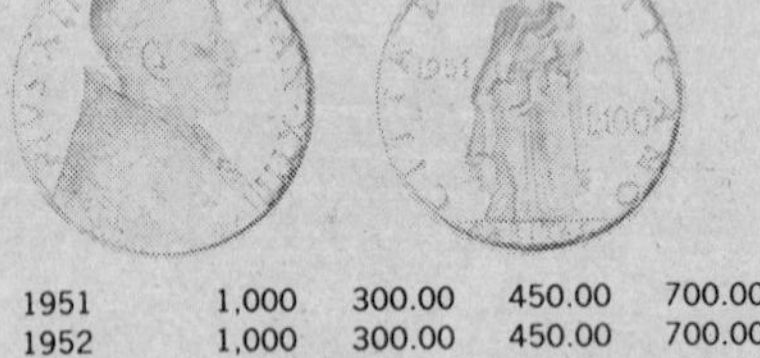

Y#	Date	Mintage	VF	XF	Unc
53	1951	1,000	300.00	450.00	700.00
	1952	1,000	300.00	450.00	700.00
	1953	1,000	300.00	450.00	700.00
	1954	1,000	450.00	600.00	900.00
	1955	1,000	300.00	450.00	700.00
	1956	1,000	450.00	600.00	900.00

STAINLESS STEEL

Y#	Date	Mintage	Fine	VF	XF	Unc
55	1955	1.30	1.00	2.00	3.00	4.50
	1956	.100	1.00	2.00	3.00	4.50
	1957	1.400	1.00	2.00	3.00	4.50
	1958	.852	1.00	2.00	3.00	4.50

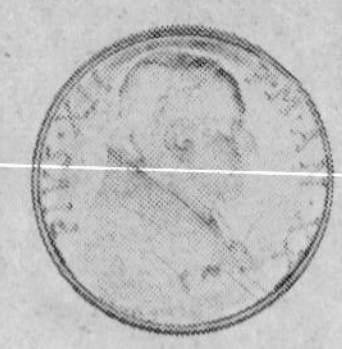

5.1900 gm., .900 GOLD, .1501 oz AGW

Y#	Date	Mintage	Fine	VF	XF	Unc
A53	1957	2,000	—	250.00	350.00	450.00
	1958	3,000	—	250.00	350.00	450.00
66	1959	3,000	—	600.00	900.00	1500.

STAINLESS STEEL

Y#	Date	Mintage	Fine	VF	XF	Unc
64	1959	.783	.25	.60	1.25	3.00

Y#	Date	Mintage	Fine	VF	XF	Unc
64.1	1960	.783	.50	1.00	2.00	3.50
	1961	.783	.50	1.00	2.00	3.50
	1962	.783	.50	1.00	2.00	3.50

Ecumenical Council

Y#	Date	Mintage	Fine	VF	XF	Unc
73	1962	1.566	—	1.00	2.00	3.50

Y#	Date	Mintage	Fine	VF	XF	Unc
82	1963	.560	.50	1.00	1.75	3.50
	1964	.560	.50	1.00	1.75	3.50
	1965	.560	.50	1.00	1.75	3.50

Y#	Date	Mintage	Fine	VF	XF	Unc
90	1966	.390	—	1.00	1.75	3.50

Fifth Year

Y#	Date	Mintage	Fine	VF	XF	Unc
98	1967	.320	—	.50	1.00	3.00

F. A. O. Issue

Y#	Date	Mintage	Fine	VF	XF	Unc
106	(1968)	.315	.25	.50	1.00	3.50

Y#	Date	Mintage	Fine	VF	XF	Unc
114	1969	.320	.25	.50	1.00	3.00

Y#	Date	Mintage	Fine	VF	XF	Unc
122	1970	—	.25	.50	1.00	2.50
	1971	.970	.25	.50	1.00	2.50
	1972	.970	.25	.50	.90	2.00
	1973	—	.25	.50	.90	2.00
	1974	—	.25	.50	.90	2.00
	1975	.808	—	—	.75	1.75
	1976	.808	—	—	.75	1.75
	1977	.819	—	—	.75	1.75

Holy Year

Y#	Date	Mintage	Fine	VF	XF	Unc
130	1975	.605	—	.60	1.25	3.50

16th Year

Y#	Date	Mintage	Fine	VF	XF	Unc
137	1978	—	—	.50	1.00	2.50

Y#	Date	Mintage	Fine	VF	XF	Unc
146	1979	—	—	—	—	—

200 LIRE

ALUMINUM-BRONZE
16th Year

Y#	Date	Mintage	Fine	VF	XF	Unc
138	1978	—	—	.75	1.50	3.00

Y#	Date	Mintage	Fine	VF	XF	Unc
147	1979	—	—	—	—	—

500 LIRE

11.0000 gm., .835 SILVER, .2953 oz ASW

Y#	Date	Mintage	Fine	VF	XF	Unc
56	1958	.020	BV	9.00	12.50	25.00

Sede Vancante

Y#	Date	Mintage	Fine	VF	XF	Unc
57	1958	.100	BV	10.00	15.00	25.00

Obv: Continuous legend

Y#	Date	Mintage	Fine	VF	XF	Unc
65	1959	.030	12.50	25.00	35.00	50.00

Obv: Date under bust

Y#	Date	Mintage	Fine	VF	XF	Unc
65.1	1960	.030	20.00	30.00	45.00	100.00
	1961	.030	BV	10.00	20.00	32.50
	1962	.030	BV	10.00	20.00	32.50

Ecumenical Council

Y#	Date	Mintage	Fine	VF	XF	Unc
74	1962	.060	BV	10.00	15.00	25.00

Sede Vacante

Y#	Date	Mintage	Fine	VF	XF	Unc
75	1963	.200	BV	10.00	15.00	25.00

Y#	Date	Mintage	Fine	VF	XF	Unc
83	1963	.070	BV	12.50	20.00	40.00
	1964	.070	BV	10.00	15.00	25.00
	1965	.070	BV	10.00	15.00	25.00

Y#	Date	Mintage	Fine	VF	XF	Unc
91	1966	.100	BV	10.00	15.00	25.00

Fifth Year

Y#	Date	Mintage	Fine	VF	XF	Unc
99	1967	.110	BV	9.00	12.50	20.00

F. A. O. Issue

Y#	Date	Mintage	Fine	VF	XF	Unc
107	(1968)	.110	BV	9.00	12.50	20.00

Y#	Date	Mintage	Fine	VF	XF	Unc
115	1969	.110	BV	9.00	12.50	20.00

Y#	Date	Mintage	Fine	VF	XF	Unc
123	1970	—	BV	BV	10.00	15.00

Y#	Date	Mintage	Fine	VF	XF	Unc
123	1971	.130	BV	BV	10.00	15.00
	1972	.130	BV	BV	10.00	15.00
	1973	—	BV	BV	10.00	15.00
	1974	—	BV	BV	10.00	15.00
	1975	.162	BV	BV	10.00	15.00
	1976	.162	BV	BV	10.00	15.00
	1977	—	BV	BV	10.00	15.00

Holy Year

Y#	Date	Mintage	Fine	VF	XF	Unc
131	1975	.200	BV	BV	9.00	15.00
132	1977	.160	BV	BV	BV	12.50

16 Th Year

Y#	Date	Mintage	Fine	VF	XF	Unc
139	1978	—	BV	BV	BV	10.00

Sede Vacante

Y#	Date	Mintage	Fine	VF	XF	Unc
140	1978	.500	BV	BV	12.50	25.00

Sede Vacante

Y#	Date	Mintage	Fine	VF	XF	Unc
141	1978	—	BV	BV	12.50	25.00
148	1979	—	—	—	—	—

1000 LIRE

.835 SILVER
Pope John Paul I

Y#	Date	Mintage	Fine	VF	XF	Unc
142	1978	—	BV	BV	12.50	25.00

NCLT ISSUES

MINT SETS

KM#	Date	Mintage	Identification	Issue Price	Mkt. Val.
S1	1929(9)	10,000	Y1-9	—	550.00
S2	1929(8)	10,000	Y1-8	—	325.00
S3	1930(9)	2,621	Y1-9	—	800.00
S4	1930(8)	50,000	Y1-8	—	125.00
S5	1931(9)	3,343	Y1-9	—	400.00
S6	1931(8)	50,000	Y1-8	—	125.00
S7	1932(9)	5,073	Y1-9	—	400.00
S8	125.00	50,000	Y1-8	—	125.00
S9	1933-34(9)	23,235	Y11-19	—	400.00
S10	1933-34(8)	50,000	Y11-18	—	175.00
SA10	1934(9)	2,533	Y1-8,10	—	800.00
SB10	1934(8)	30,000	Y1-8	—	120.00
S11	1935(9)	2,015	Y1-8,10	—	900.00
S12	1935(8)	9,000	Y1-8	—	250.00
S13	1936(9)	8,239	Y1-8,10	—	400.00
S14	1936(8)	40,000	Y1-8	—	75.00
S15	1937(9)	2,000	Y1-8,10	—	7000.
S16	1937(8)	20,000	Y1-8	—	120.00
S17	1938(3)	—	Y1-2,10	—	4500.
S18	1939(9)	2,700	Y22-27,28-30	—	500.00
S19	1939(8)	10,000	Y22-29	—	135.00
S20	1939(2)	30,000	Y20,21	—	75.00
S21	1940(9)	2,000	Y22,23,24a-30a	—	500.00
S22	1940(8)	10,000	Y22,23,24a-29a	—	135.00
S23	1941(9)	2,000	Y22,23,24a-30a	—	675.00
S24	1941(8)	4,000	Y22,23,24a-29a	—	250.00
S25	1942(9)	2,000	Y31-39	—	750.00
S26	1942(8)	4,000	Y31-38	—	350.00
S27	1943(9)	1,000	Y31-39	—	2000.
S28	1943(8)	1,000	Y31-38	—	900.00
S29	1944(9)	1,000	Y31-39	—	2000.
S30	1944(8)	1,000	Y31-38	—	900.00
S31	1945(9)	1,000	Y31-39	—	2000.
S32	1945(8)	1,000	Y31-38	—	900.00
S33	1946(9)	1,000	Y31-39	—	2000.
S34	1946(8)	1,000	Y31-38	—	950.00
S35	1947(5)	1,000	Y39-43	—	700.00
S36	1947(4)	50,000	Y40-43	—	75.00
S37	1947(2)	—	Y42-43	—	—
S38	1948(5)	5,000	Y39-43	—	350.00
S39	1948(4)	10,000	Y40-43	—	50.00
S40	1949(5)	1,000	Y39-43	—	700.00
S41	1949(4)	10,000	Y40-43	—	50.00
S42	1950(5)	20,000	Y44-48	—	350.00
S43	1950(4)	50,000	Y44-47	—	35.00
S44	1951(5)	1,000	Y49-52,53	—	650.00
S45	1951(4)	400,000	Y49-52	—	5.50
S46	1952(5)	1,000	Y49-52,53	—	650.00
S47	1952(4)	400,000	Y49-52	—	5.50
S48	1953(5)	1,000	Y49-52,53	—	650.00
S49	1953(4)	400,000	Y49-52	—	5.50
S50	1954(1)	1,000	Y53	—	1000.
S51	1955(7)	1,000	Y49-55	—	800.00
S52	1955(6)	10,000	Y49-52,54,55	—	50.00
S53	1956(7)	1,000	Y49-55	—	800.00
S54	1956(6)	10,000	Y49-52,54,55	—	50.00
S55	1957(8)	2,000	Y49-A52,A53,54,55	—	500.00
S56	1957(7)	20,000	Y49-A52,54,55	—	60.00
S57	1958(9)	3,000	Y49-A52,A53-56	—	450.00
S58	1958(8)	20,000	Y49-A52,54-56	—	60.00
S59	1958(1)	12,000	Y57	—	25.00
S60	1959(9)	25,000	Y58-66	—	1750.
S61	1959(8)	25,000	Y58-65	—	175.00
S62	1960(8)	25,000	Y58-65	—	200.00
S63	1961(8)	25,000	Y58-65	—	75.00
S64	1962(8)	25,000	Y58-65	—	75.00
S65	1962(8)	50,000	Y67-74	—	65.00
S66	1963(8)	60,000	Y76-83	—	175.00
S67	1963(1)	200,000	Y75	—	25.00
S68	1964(8)	60,000	Y76-83	—	50.00
S69	1965(8)	60,000	Y76-83	—	45.00
S70	1966(8)	90,000	Y84-91	—	35.00
S71	1967(8)	100,000	Y92-99	3.25	35.00
S72	1968(8)	100,000	Y100-107	4.20	35.00
S73	1969(8)	100,000	Y108-115	4.20	35.00
S74	1970(8)	100,000	Y116-123	5.00	25.00
S75	1971(8)	110,000	Y116-123	—	25.00
S76	1972(8)	110,000	Y116-123	6.00	20.00
S77	1973(8)	132,000	Y116-123	6.75	20.00
S78	1974(8)	132,000	Y116-123	7.25	20.00
S79	1975(8)	180,000	Y116-123	9.00	20.00
S80	1975(8)	180,000	Y124-131	—	35.00
S81	1976(7)	—	Y133-139	—	25.00
S82	1977(7)	—	—	—	30.00
S83	1978(7)	—	Y133-139	—	30.00

PROVA (P) SETS

SILVER

KM#	Date	Mintage	Identification	Issue Price	Mkt. Val.
P1	1951(4)	103	Y49a-52a	—	450.00
P2	1952(4)	103	Y49a-52a	—	450.00
P3	1953(4)	103	Y49a-52a	—	450.00
P4	1955(6)	103	Y49a-52a,54a,55a	—	675.00
P5	1956(6)	103	Y49a-52a,54a,55a	—	675.00
P6	1957(7)	103	Y49a-A52a,54A,55A	—	775.00
P7	1958(8)	103	Y49a-A52a,54a-55a,56	—	875.00
P8	1959(8)	103	Y58a-62a,63a-65a	—	875.00
P9	1960(8)	103	Y58a-62a,A63a-A65a	—	875.00
P10	1961(8)	103	Y58a-62a,A63a-A64a,A65	—	875.00
P11	1962(8)	103	Y58a-62a,A63a-A64a,A65	—	875.00
P12	1962(8)	103	Y67a-73a,74	—	875.00
P13	1963(8)	103	Y76a-82a,83	—	875.00
P14	1964(8)	103	Y76a-82a,83	—	875.00
P15	1965(8)	103	Y76a-82a,83	—	875.00
P16	1966(8)	103	Y84a-90a,91	—	875.00
P17	1967(8)	103	Y92a-98a,99	—	875.00
P18	1968(8)	103	Y100a-106a,107	—	875.00
P19	1969(8)	103	Y108a-114a,115	—	875.00
P20	1970(8)	103	Y116a-122a,123	—	875.00
P21	1971(8)	103	Y116a-122a,123	—	875.00
P22	1972(8)	103	Y116a-122a,123	—	875.00
P23	1973(8)	103	Y116a-122a,123	—	875.00
P24	1974(8)	103	Y116a-122a,123	—	875.00
P25	1975(8)	103	Y116a-122a,123	—	875.00
P26	1975(8)	103	Y124a-130a,131	—	875.00

VENEZUELA

The Republic of Venezuela ("Little Venice"), located on the northern coast of South America between Colombia and Guyana, has an area of 352,143 sq. mi. (912,050 sq. km.) and a population of 12.3 million. Capital: Caracas. Petroleum and mining provide 90 percent of Venezuela's exports although they employ less than 2 percent of the work force. Coffee, grown on 60,000 plantations, is the chief crop.

Columbus discovered Venezuela on his third voyage in 1498. Initial exploration did not reveal Venezuela to be a land of great wealth. An active pearl trade operated on the off-shore islands and slavers raided the interior in search of Indians to be sold into slavery, but no significant mainland settlements were made before 1567 when Caracas was founded. Venezuela, the home of Bolivar, was the first South American colony to revolt against Spain in 1811. Independence was attained in 1821 but not recognized by Spain until 1845. Together with Ecuador, Panama and Colombia, Venezuela was part of "Great Colombia" until 1830 when it became a sovereign and independent state.

MINTMARKS

A - Paris
(a) - Paris, privy marks only
H - Heaton, Birmingham

MONETARY SYSTEM

16 Reales = 1 Escudo

PROVINCE OF BARINAS

A province of west central Venezuela on the Apure plains.Occupied by General Jose Antonio Paez in 1817. The city of Barinas was overrun with refugees and Paez asked that all silver be turned in to be recoined into new coins to facilitate commerce and trade. The coins were made but found disfavor with Simon Bolivar who issued a decree that the coins should not circulate outside Barinas province and would be redeemed by the central goverment.

2 REALES

SILVER

C#	Date	Mintage	VG	Fine	VF
—	1817	—	—	—	—

PROVINCE OF CARACAS

1802-1821

A province surrounding the capital city of Caracas in Venezuela. The first mint in Venezuela opened here in November 1802 by the Spaniards. Coins made in 1802, 1804 and 1805. Caracas revolted on April 19, 1810 The city again surrendered to Spanish forces in July, 1812.Royalist coinage in copper and silver was issued until 1822. Five denominations were issued in that period, 2 copper and 3 silver.

1/8 REAL

COPPER, 19-25mm

C#	Date	Mintage	VG	Fine	VF
1	1802	.059	850.00	1000.	1500.
	1804	.019	850.00	1000.	1500.
	1805	.100	500.00	750.00	900.00
	1813	3,632	—	—	—
	1814	.012	500.00	750.00	900.00
1	1817	4,500	850.00	1000.	1500.
	1818	.094	225.00	300.00	450.00

1/4 REAL

COPPER, 21-26mm

C#	Date	Mintage	VG	Fine	VF
2	1802	.014	1000.	1250.	1500.
	1804	6,589	1000.	1250.	1500.
	1805	.070	600.00	900.00	1100.
	1813	.010	125.00	175.00	225.00
	1814	.040	40.00	55.00	80.00
	1816	.750	20.00	25.00	40.00

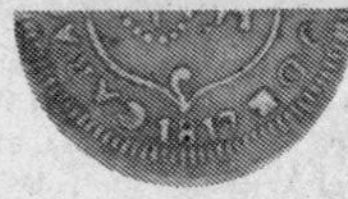
Small date

Large date

C#	Date	Mintage	VG	Fine	VF
	1817 lg.dt.	.490	20.00	25.00	40.00
	1817sm.dt.	1.640	20.00	25.00	40.00
	1818	2.240	17.50	22.00	27.50
	1821	.650	20.00	25.00	40.00

REAL

SILVER

C#	Date	Mintage	VG	Fine	VF
5	1817	6,500	1000.	1250.	1500.
	1818	.014	300.00	550.00	850.00
	1820	.011	400.00	600.00	1000.
	1821	8,000	400.00	600.00	1000.

2 REALES

SILVER, 21-25mm
Obverse without CARACAS. Reverse cross between F-7.

C#	Date	Mintage	VG	Fine	VF
6	1816	.033	250.00	350.00	450.00
	1817	.224	250.00	350.00	450.00

Obv: With CARACAS

C#	Date	Mintage	VG	Fine	VF
6.1	1817	.076	25.00	40.00	60.00
	1818	.777	25.00	40.00	60.00
	1819	1.450	25.00	40.00	60.00
	1820	.755	35.00	55.00	80.00
	1821	.110	60.00	100.00	150.00

4 REALES

SILVER, 30-32mm

C#	Date	Mintage	VG	Fine	VF
7	1819	.018	500.00	800.00	1250.
	1820	.029	500.00	800.00	1250.

COUNTERSTAMP ISSUES

1/2 PESO

COPPER
c/s: 1/2P on 1/4 Real, C#2.

C#	Date	Year	Mintage	VG	Fine	VF
—	ND	1818	—	—	—	—
		1821	—	—	—	—

PESO

COPPER
c/s: 1P on 1/4 Real, C#2.

C#	Date	Year	Mintage	VG	Fine	VF
—	ND	1818	—	—	—	—
		1821	—	—	—	—

5 PESOS

COPPER
c/s: 5P on 1/4 Real, C#2.

C#	Date	Year	Mintage	VG	Fine	VF
—	ND	1818	—	—	—	—
		1821	—	—	—	—

Royalists, Republicans, or both

REAL

SILVER
Copy of Lima cob of previous century.

C#	Date	Mintage	VG	Fine	VF
12	(1810-21)LM*	—	55.00	90.00	160.00
	(1810-21)ML*	—	55.00	90.00	160.00

2 REALES

SILVER

C#	Date	Mintage	VG	Fine	VF
13	(1810-21)LM*	—	20.00	30.00	40.00
	(1810-21)ML*	—	20.00	30.00	40.00

NOTE: Of the many actual, false and blundered dates the following have been noted 184, 231, 1816, 471, 817, 814, 751, 142, 182, 1817, 931, 781, 172, 174, 1812-1817. Bogus MM's L-M and M-L.

Royalists or Republicans

Republican Coinage 1812

19 refers to 19 April 1810, date of the Declaration of Independence.

1/8 REAL

COPPER, 24mm
CARACAS MINT

C#	Date	Mintage	VG	Fine	VF
21	1812	7,000	450.00	600.00	750.00

1/4 REAL

COPPER, 26-30mm

C#	Date	Mintage	VG	Fine	VF
22	1812	.030	65.00	100.00	150.00

1/2 REAL

SILVER, 16mm

Large 1/2

C#	Date	Mintage	VG	Fine	VF
25.1	Ano 2(1812)	.016	600.00	1200.	2000.

Small 1/2

C#	Date	Mintage	VG	Fine	VF
25.2	Ano 2(1812)	—	800.00	1500.	2750.

REAL

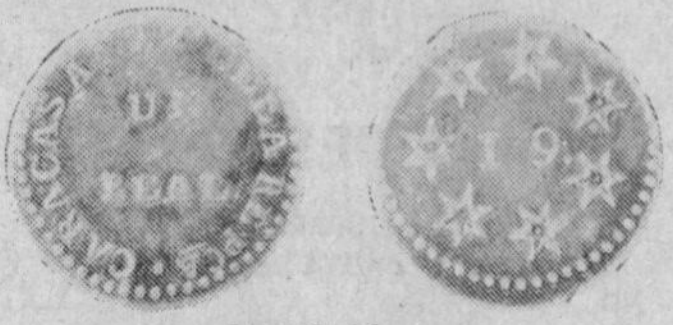

SILVER, 20mm

C#	Date	Mintage	VG	Fine	VF
26	Ano 2(1812)	.020	600.00	1000.	1500.

Under Colombia

1/4 REAL

SILVER, 11.5-15mm

C#	Date	Mintage	VG	Fine	VF
31	1821	.090	400.00	550.00	650.00
	1822	.540	150.00	200.00	250.00

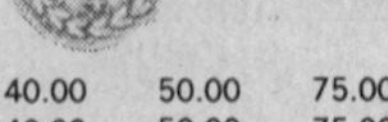

C#	Date	Mintage	VG	Fine	VF
34	1829	.750	40.00	50.00	75.00
	1830	.650	40.00	50.00	75.00

1/2 REAL

SILVER

C#	Date	Mintage	VG	Fine	VF
35	1829	1 known	—	Rare	—

2 REALES

SILVER

Obv: Without CARACAS. Rev: Cross between two rosettes.

C#	Date	Mintage	VG	Fine	VF
—	1818(1830)	.268	35.00	60.00	100.00

PROVINCE OF GUAYANA

Province in eastern Venezuela. Legislation was passed on October 26, 1813 for the making of coins to alleviate the coin shortage caused by the lack of commerece due to the isolated geographical location of the province in relation to other Spanish forces.Later this province came under British Guiana.

Royalist Issues 1813-1817

1/4 REAL

COPPER, 18-20.6mm

C#	Date	Mintage	VG	Fine	VF
40	1813	—	800.00	1200.	1750.
	1815	—	800.00	1200.	1750.

1/2 REAL

COPPER, 24-30mm

C#	Date	Mintage	VG	Fine	VF
41	1813	—	75.00	100.00	200.00
	1814	—	15.00	30.00	50.00
	1815	—	15.00	30.00	50.00
	1816	—	15.00	30.00	50.00
	1817	—	15.00	30.00	50.00

PROVINCE OF MARACAIBO

A province in northwestern Venezuela. Includes the city of Maracaibo which is on the Channel between Lake Maracaibo and the Caribbean Sea. Crude coinage made here in 1813 during War of Independence.

1/2 REAL

COPPER

C#	Date	Mintage	VG	Fine	VF
10	1813	—	350.00	450.00	600.00

REPUBLIC OF VENEZUELA

MONETARY SYSTEM

10 Reales = 1 Peso

1/2 REAL

.900 SILVER

Value shown as 1-1/2 Real, erroneously.

Y#	Date	Mintage	Fine	VF	XF
8	1858A	.040	500.00	600.00	800.00

REAL

.900 SILVER

Similar to 2 Reales, Y#10.

Y#	Date	Mintage	Fine	VF	XF
9	1858A	.042	150.00	250.00	400.00

2 REALES

.900 SILVER

Y#	Date	Mintage	Fine	VF	XF
10	1858A	.030	175.00	250.00	500.00

5 REALES

.900 SILVER

Y#	Date	Mintage	Fine	VF	XF
11	1858A	.026	350.00	600.00	900.00

10 REALES

SILVER

Y#	Date	Mintage	VF	XF	Unc
A11	1863A	—	—	—	—

NOTE: Almost entire issue remelted.

MONETARY REFORM

100 Centavos = 1 Venezolano

(1871-79)

100 Centimos = 1 Bolivar (1879-)

1/4 CENTAVO

COPPER

Y#	Date	Mintage	Fine	VF	XF
1	1843WW	3.840	6.00	12.00	20.00
	1852H	2.000	20.00	30.00	45.00

Y#	Date	Mintage	Fine	VF	XF
4	1852	4.000	12.00	17.50	30.00

1/2 CENTAVO

COPPER, 24mm

Y#	Date	Mintage	Fine	VF	XF
2	1843WW	.960	12.50	20.00	30.00
	1852H	.500	20.00	30.00	45.00

22mm

Y#	Date	Mintage	Fine	VF	XF
5	1852	1.000	12.50	20.00	30.00

CENTAVO

COPPER

Y#	Date	Mintage	Fine	VF	XF
3	1843WWYON	.480	32.00	60.00	80.00
	1852HEATON	.250	20.00	40.00	75.00

Y#	Date	Mintage	Fine	VF	XF
6	1852	.500	14.00	25.00	35.00

Plain edge, thin planchet.

Y#	Date	Mintage	Fine	VF	XF
7	1858 HEATON with LIBERTAD incuse	1.000	6.00	12.00	22.50

Engrailed edge, thick planchet.

Y#	Date	Mintage	Fine	VF	XF
7.1	1858 HEATON with LIBERTAD in relief	1.000	6.00	12.00	20.00
	1862HEATON	2.000	6.00	12.00	20.00
	1863HEATON	Inc. Ab.	6.00	12.00	20.00

COPPER-NICKEL

Y#	Date	Mintage	Fine	VF	XF
25	1876	8.000	6.00	7.50	15.00
	1877	2.000	7.50	10.00	17.50

2-1/2 CENTAVOS

COPPER-NICKEL

Y#	Date	Mintage	Fine	VF	XF
26	1876	1.500	6.00	10.00	20.00
	1877	.500	10.00	15.00	30.00

5 CENTAVOS

1.2500 gm., .835 SILVER, .0336 oz ASW

Y#	Date	Mintage	Fine	VF	XF
12	1874	.800	20.00	40.00	65.00
	1876	.520	20.00	40.00	65.00

5 CENTIMOS

COPPER-NICKEL

Y#	Date	Mintage	VF	XF	Unc
27	1896	4.000	.35	.75	4.50
	1915	2.000	.50	.75	3.00
	1921	2.000	.35	.60	3.25
	1925	2.000	.35	.60	3.25
	1927	2.000	.25	.50	3.00
	1929	2.000	.20	.50	3.00
	1936	5.000	.25	.50	3.00
	1938	6.000	.20	.50	3.00

BRASS

Y#	Date	Mintage	VF	XF	Unc
29	1944	4.000	2.00	3.00	6.00

COPPER-NICKEL

Y#	Date	Mintage	VF	XF	Unc
29a	1945	12.000	.20	.40	1.50
	1946	12.000	.20	.40	1.00
	1948	18.000	.20	.35	1.50

Y#	Date	Mintage	VF	XF	Unc
38	1958	25.000	.20	.25	.40
38.1	1964	40.000	.10	.15	.20
	1965	60.000	—	.10	.20
38.2	1971	40.000	—	—	.20

COPPER-CLAD STEEL

Y#	Date	Mintage	VF	XF	Unc
49	1974	200.000	—	—	.15
	1976	200.000	—	—	.15
	1977	—	—	—	.15

10 CENTAVOS

2.5000 gm., .835 SILVER, .0671 oz ASW

Y#	Date	Mintage	Fine	VF	XF
13	1874A	.800	40.00	60.00	110.00
	1876A	.280	40.00	60.00	120.00

COPPER-NICKEL

Y#	Date	Mintage	VF	XF	Unc
A40	1971	60.000	—	—	.25

12-1/2 CENTIMOS

COPPER-NICKEL

Y#	Date	Mintage	VF	XF	Unc
28	1896	6.000	2.00	5.00	30.00
	1925	.800	2.00	10.00	60.00
	1927	.800	2.00	5.00	30.00
	1929	.800	.30	2.00	15.00
	1936	1.200	.30	.65	5.00
	1938	1.600	.30	.65	5.00

NOTE: Varieties Exist.

BRASS

Y#	Date	Mintage	VF	XF	Unc
30	1944	.800	25.00	45.00	125.00

COPPER-NICKEL

Y#	Date	Mintage	VF	XF	Unc
30a	1945	11.200	.35	.50	1.00
	1946	9.200	.40	.60	1.25
	1948	6.000	.50	.75	1.50

Y#	Date	Mintage	VF	XF	Unc
39	1958	10.000	—	.15	.50
	1969	2.000	Not released		250.00

20 CENTAVOS

5.0000 gm., .835 SILVER, .1342 oz ASW

Y#	Date	Mintage	Fine	VF	XF
14	1874A	.400	40.00	65.00	100.00
	1876A	.140	85.00	140.00	200.00

1/5 BOLIVAR

1.0000 gm., .835 SILVER, .0268 oz ASW

Y#	Date	Mintage	Fine	VF	XF
19	1879	.130	450.00	650.00	850.00

1/4 BOLIVAR

1.2500 gm., .835 SILVER, .0336 oz ASW

Y#	Date	Mintage	Fine	VF	XF
20	1894	2.000	6.00	12.00	20.00
	1900	.400	25.00	50.00	75.00
	1901	.400	25.00	50.00	75.00
	1903	.400	20.00	30.00	50.00
	1911	.600	20.00	30.00	50.00
	1912	.800	15.00	20.00	30.00
	1919	.400	4.00	11.00	30.00
	1921	.800	3.00	6.00	15.00
	1924	.400	3.00	8.00	20.00
	1929	1.200	1.00	2.00	5.00
	1935	3.400	BV	1.25	2.00
	1936	2.800	BV	1.00	1.50
	1944	1.800	BV	1.00	1.25
	1945	8.000	BV	1.00	1.25
	1946	8.000	BV	1.00	1.25
	1948	8.640	BV	1.00	1.25

25 CENTIMOS

1.2500 gm., .835 SILVER, .0336 oz ASW

Y#	Date	Mintage	VF	XF	Unc
35	1954	36.000	BV	1.00	1.25

Y#	Date	Mintage	VF	XF	Unc
35a	1960(a)	48.000	BV	1.00	1.50

NICKEL

Y#	Date	Mintage	VF	XF	Unc
40	1965	240.000	—	.15	.30

26.8 gm., 1.18mm thick

Y#	Date	Mintage	VF	XF	Unc
50	1977	.250	—	.10	.20

26.5 gm., 1.07mm thick

Y#	Date	Mintage	VF	XF	Unc
50a	1978	120.000	—	.10	.20

50 CENTAVOS

12.5000 gm., .835 SILVER, .3356 oz ASW

Y#	Date	Mintage	Fine	VF	XF
15	1873A	.100	70.00	125.00	200.00
	1874A	.300	70.00	125.00	200.00
	1876A	.160	70.00	125.00	200.00

1/2 BOLIVAR

2.5000 gm., .835 SILVER, .0671 oz ASW

Y#	Date	Mintage	Fine	VF	XF
21	1879	.200	30.00	75.00	125.00
	1886	.300	30.00	75.00	125.00
	1887	.310	150.00	250.00	450.00
	1888	.230	450.00	650.00	1200.
	1889	.080	1200.	1500.	2200.
	1893	.500	20.00	40.00	65.00
	1900A	.600	50.00	75.00	125.00
	1900 w/o mm	—	75.00	125.00	200.00
	1901	.600	50.00	75.00	125.00
	1903	.200	60.00	100.00	175.00
	1911	.300	60.00	100.00	175.00
	1912	1.920	15.00	30.00	65.00
	1919	.400	7.50	15.00	27.50
	1921	.600	7.50	15.00	27.50
	1924	.800	7.50	15.00	27.50
	1929	.400	3.00	5.00	12.00
	1935	1.000	2.00	3.00	5.00
	1936	.600	4.00	7.00	12.00

Y#	Date	Mintage	VF	XF	Unc
21a	1944	.500	2.00	3.00	5.00
	1945	4.000	BV	BV	2.50
	1946	2.500	BV	BV	2.50

50 CENTIMOS

2.5000 gm., .835 SILVER, .0671 OZ ASW

Y#	Date	Mintage	VF	XF	Unc
36	1954	15.000	BV	BV	3.00

Y#	Date	Mintage	VF	XF	Unc
36a	1960(a)	20.000	BV	BV	3.50

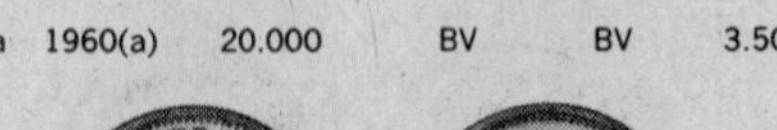

NICKEL

Y#	Date	Mintage	VF	XF	Unc
41	1965	180.000	.15	.25	.35

BOLIVAR

5.0000 gm., .835 SILVER, .1342 oz ASW

Y#	Date	Mintage	Fine	VF	XF
22	1879	.380	50.00	75.00	175.00
	1886	.050	30.00	60.00	125.00
	1887	.280	150.00	250.00	350.00
	1888	.200	160.00	275.00	375.00
	1889	.120	160.00	275.00	375.00
	1893	.500	20.00	40.00	75.00
	1900	.380	30.00	60.00	100.00
	1901	.320	30.00	60.00	100.00
	1903	.800	20.00	40.00	75.00
	1911	1.500	10.00	25.00	45.00
	1912	.820	20.00	40.00	75.00
	1919	1.000	BV	12.00	30.00
	1921	1.000	BV	5.00	20.00
	1924	1.500	BV	4.50	15.00
	1926	1.000	BV	4.50	17.50
	1929	2.500	BV	4.50	6.00
	1935	5.000	BV	4.50	6.00
	1936	5.000	BV	4.50	6.00

Y#	Date	Mintage	VF	XF	Unc
22a	1945	8.000	BV	BV	5.00

Y#	Date	Mintage	VF	XF	Unc
37	1954	13.500	BV	BV	4.50

Y#	Date	Mintage	VF	XF	Unc
37a	1960(a)	30.000	BV	BV	4.50
	1965(a)	20.000	BV	BV	4.50

NICKEL

Y#	Date	Mintage	VF	XF	Unc
42	1967	180.000	—	.50	.75

Y#	Date	Mintage	VF	XF	Unc
52	1977	200.000	—	.40	1.00

2 BOLIVARES

10.0000 gm., .835 SILVER, .2685 oz ASW

Y#	Date	Mintage	Fine	VF	XF
23	1879	.380	50.00	150.00	200.00
	1886	.240	50.00	150.00	200.00
	1887	.200	45.00	100.00	175.00
	1888	.140	50.00	150.00	200.00
	1889	.050	125.00	250.00	350.00
	1894	.250	50.00	150.00	200.00
	1900	.350	25.00	100.00	150.00
	1902	.500	25.00	100.00	150.00
	1903	.500	15.00	30.00	75.00
	1904	.500	15.00	30.00	75.00
	1905	.750	10.00	27.50	65.00
	1911	.750	10.00	27.50	65.00
	1912	.500	10.00	27.50	65.00
	1913	.210	17.50	60.00	100.00
	1919	1.000	BV	10.00	25.00
	1922	1.000	BV	10.00	25.00
	1924	1.250	BV	10.00	20.00
	1926	1.000	BV	10.00	20.00
	1929	1.500	BV	8.00	18.00
	1930	.430	BV	12.00	30.00
	1935	3.000	BV	8.00	10.00
	1936	2.500	BV	8.00	10.00

Y#	Date	Mintage	VF	XF	Unc
23a	1945	3.000	BV	BV	8.50

Y#	Date	Mintage	VF	XF	Unc
A37	1960(a)	4.000	BV	BV	8.50
	1965(a)	7.170	BV	BV	8.50

NICKEL

Y#	Date	Mintage	VF	XF	Unc
43	1967	50.000	.35	.75	1.40

VENEZOLANO

25.0000 gm., .900 SILVER, .7234 oz ASW

Y#	Date	Mintage	Fine	VF	XF
16	1876A	.035	250.00	550.00	1200.

5 BOLIVARES

25.0000 gm., .900 SILVER, .7234 oz ASW

Y#	Date	Mintage	Fine	VF	XF
24	1879	.250	25.00	75.00	175.00
	1886	.470	22.50	65.00	150.00
	1887	.500	25.00	65.00	150.00
	1888	.280	25.00	65.00	150.00
	1889	.320	25.00	75.00	175.00
	1900	.270	22.50	35.00	150.00
	1901	.090	25.00	65.00	150.00
	1902	.500	25.00	35.00	90.00
	1903	.200	25.00	35.00	90.00
	1904	.200	25.00	35.00	125.00
	1905	.300	25.00	35.00	90.00
	1910	.400	25.00	35.00	90.00
	1911	1.100	22.50	25.00	50.00
	1912	.700	22.50	25.00	50.00
	1919	.400	22.50	25.00	50.00
	1921	.500	22.50	25.00	35.00
	1924	.500	22.50	25.00	35.00
	1926	.800	22.50	25.00	35.00
	1929	.800	22.50	25.00	35.00
	1935	1.600	22.50	25.00	35.00
	1936	2.000	22.50	25.00	35.00

NICKEL

Y#	Date	Mintage	VF	XF	Unc
44	1973	20.000	1.50	2.00	4.00

Y#	Date	Mintage	VF	XF	Unc
53	1977	60.000	1.50	1.75	2.25

10 BOLIVARES

3.2258 gm., .900 GOLD, .0933 oz AGW

Y#	Date	Mintage	VF	XF	Unc
31	1930	.500	60.00	65.00	75.00

30.0000 gm., .900 SILVER, .8681 oz ASW

Y#	Date	Mintage	VF	XF	Unc
45	1973	2.000	BV	BV	30.00

20 BOLIVARES

6.4516 gm., .900 GOLD, .1867 oz AGW

Y#	Date	Mintage	VF	XF	Unc
32	1879	.041	BV	125.00	150.00
	1880	.084	BV	125.00	150.00
	1886	.500	BV	125.00	160.00
	1887	.105	BV	125.00	160.00
	1888	.081	BV	125.00	160.00
	1904	.100	BV	125.00	160.00
	1905	.100	BV	125.00	140.00
	1910(a)	.100	BV	125.00	140.00
	1911	.050	BV	135.00	175.00
	1912	.150	BV	125.00	140.00

25 BOLIVARES
(5 VENEZOLANOS)

8.0645 gm., .900 GOLD, .2333 oz AGW

Y#	Date	Mintage	VF	XF	Unc
17	1875A	.069	175.00	275.00	375.00

28.2800 gm., .925 SILVER, .8411 oz ASW
Conservation Series

Y#	Date	Mintage	VF	XF	Unc
46	1975	9,408	BV	BV	25.00
	1975	—	—	Proof	30.00

50 BOLIVARS

35.0000 gm., .925 SILVER, 1.0409 oz ASW
Conservation Series
Obv: Similar to 25 Bolivars, Y#46.

Y#	Date	Mintage	VF	XF	Unc
47	1975	.010	BV	BV	40.00
	1975	—	—	Proof	50.00

100 BOLIVARES

32.2581 gm., .900 GOLD, .9334 oz AGW

Y#	Date	Mintage	VF	XF	Unc
34	1886	4,250	BV	625.00	1100.
	1887	.028	BV	625.00	1100.
	1888	.032	BV	625.00	1100.
	1889	.023	BV	625.00	1100.

500 BOLIVARES

18.0000 gm., .900 GOLD, .5209 oz AGW
Nationalization Of Oil Industry

Y#	Date	Mintage	VF	XF	Unc
54	1975	100 pcs.	—	—	—

1000 BOLIVARES

.900 GOLD
Conservation Series

Y#	Date	Mintage	VF	XF	Unc
48	1975	3,351	BV	BV	650.00
	1975	—	—	Proof	800.00

NCLT ISSUES

ESSAIS

Standard metals unless otherwise noted

KM#	Date	Mintage	Identification	Mkt.Val.
EA11	1863E	—	10 Reales, plain edge	—
E17	1875A	—	25 Bolivares	—

MINT SETS

KM#	Date	Mintage	Identification	Issue Price	Mkt. Val.
S1	1975(2)	—	Y46,47	35.00	65.00

PROOF SETS
STANDARD METALS

KM#	Date	Mintage	Identification	Issue Price	Mkt. Val.
101	1975(2)	—	Y46,47	—	75.00

VIETNAM

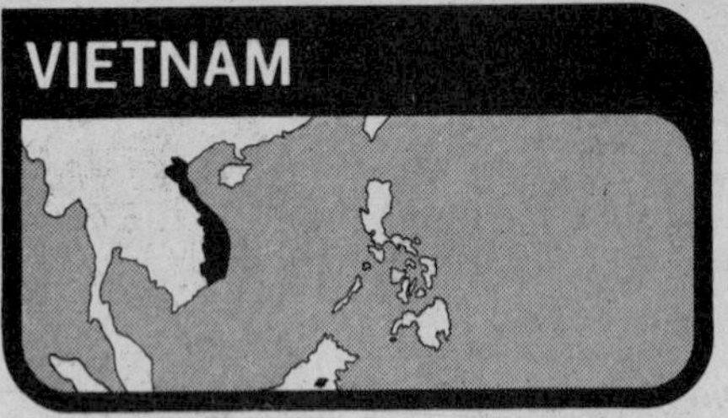

In 207 B.C. a Chinese general set up the kingdom of Nam-Viet on the Red River. This kingdom was overthrown by the Chinese under the Han Dynasty in 111B.C., whereupon the country became a Chinese province under the name of Giao-Chi, which was later changed to Annam or Dominion of the South. Chinese rule was maintained until 968, when the Vietnamese became independent until 1407 when China again invaded Vietnam. The chinese were driven out in 1428 and the country became independent and named Dai-Viet.

The former Protectorate of Annam, now part of Vietnam, had an area of 57,840 sq. mi. (141,806 sq. km.) and supported a population of about 6 million. It was bounded on the North by Tonkin and on the South by Cochin China. Former capital: Hue. Chief products of the area are silk, cinnamon and rice. There are important mineral deposits in the mountainous inland.

United Dai Viet

EMPERORS OF DAI VIET

Gia Long, 1802-1820
Minh Mang, 1820-1841
Thieu Tri, 1841-1847
Tu Duc, 1848-1883
Kien Phuc, 1883-1884
Ham Nghi, 1884-1885

Protectorate of Annam

EMPERORS OF ANNAM

Dong Khanh, 1885-1888
Than Thoi, 1888-1907
Duy Tan, 1907-1916
Khai Dinh, 1916-1925
Bao Dai, 1926-1945

REBELS

Tri Nguyen, 1831-1834
Nguyen Long, 1832-1833

IDENTIFICATION

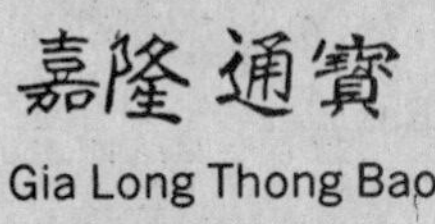

Gia Long Thong Bao

明命通寶

Minh Mang Thong Bao

紹治通寶

Thieu Tri Thong Bao

嗣德通寶

Tu Duc Thong Bao

建福通寶

Kien Phuc Thong Bao

咸宜通寶

Ham Nghi Thong Bao

同慶通寶

Dong Khanh Thong Bao

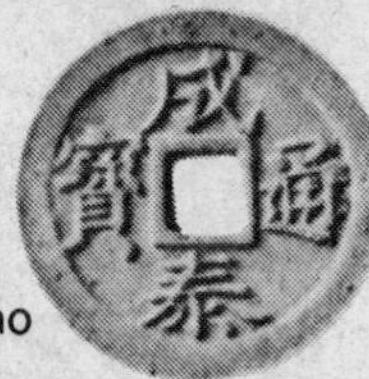

成泰通寶

Thanh Thoi Thong Bao

維新通寶

Duy Tan Thong Bao

啓定通寶

Khai Dinh Thong Bao

保大通寶

Bao Dai Thong Bao

Cyclical Dates

	庚	辛	壬	癸	甲	乙	丙	丁	戊	己
戌	1850 1910		1862 1922		1874 1934		1886 1946		1838 1898	
亥		1851 1911		1863 1923		1875 1935		1887 1947		1839 1899
子	1840 1900		1852 1912		1864 1924		1876 1936		1888 1948	
丑		1841 1901		1853 1913		1865 1925		1877 1937		1889 1949
寅	1830 1890		1842 1902		1854 1914		1866 1926		1878 1938	
卯		1831 1891		1843 1903		1855 1915		1867 1927		1879 1939
辰	1880 1940		1832 1892		1844 1904		1856 1916		1868 1928	
巳		1881 1941		1833 1893		1845 1905		1857 1917		1869 1929
午	1870 1930		1882 1942		1834 1894		1846 1906		1858 1918	
未		1871 1931		1883 1943		1835 1895		1847 1907		1859 1919
申	1860 1920		1872 1932		1884 1944		1836 1896		1848 1908	
酉		1861 1921		1873 1933		1885 1945		1837 1897		1849 1909

Cyclical dates consist of a pair of characters one of which indicates the animal associated with that year. Every 60 years, this pair of characters is repeated. The first character of a cyclical date corresponds to a character in the first row of the chart above. The second character is taken from the column at left. In this catalog where a cyclical date is used, the abbreviation CD appears before the A.D. date.

Annamese silver and gold coins were sometimes dated according to the year of the emperor's reign. In this case, simply add the year of reign to the year in which the reign began, then subtract 1. Thus the third year of Tu Duc would be 1849 (1847 plus 3 = 1850 -1 = 1849 or 1847 - 1; 1848 = 2; 1849 = 3). In this catalog the A.D. date appears in parenthesis followed by the year of reign.

NUMERALS

Column A, conventional; Column B, formal.

No.	A			B	
1	一	正	元	壹	弌
2	二			弍	貳
3	三			叁	弎
4	四			肆	
5	五			伍	
6	六			陸	
7	七			柒	
8	八			捌	
9	九			玖	
10	十			拾	什
20	十 二			拾貳	
25	五 十 二			伍拾貳	
30	十 三			拾叁	
100	百 一			佰壹	
1,000	千 一			什壹	

WEIGHT SYSTEM

COPPER AND ZINC

10 Dong (zinc) = 1 Dong (copper)
600 Dong (zinc) = 1 Quan (string of cash)
Approx. 2600 Dong (zinc) = 1 Piastre

NOTE: One dong coins in lead were also minted and were worth somewhat less than zinc dong. The dong is also called a sapeque or cash.

SILVER AND GOLD

2-1/2 Quan = 1 Lang
10 Tien (Mace) = 1 Lang (Tael)
14 to 17 Piastres (silver) = 1 Piastre (gold)
14 to 17 Lang (silver) = 1 Lang (gold)

NOTE: The piastre is also called a dollar.

The real currency of Annam consisted of copper and zinc coins similar to Chinese cash. Gold and silver coins, either circular or rectangular, were also minted, and may be divided into two classes: those intended for circulation and those intended as rewards or gifts. Both types are listed here, as they often appear in auctions. Generally the piastres and half piastres and the silver bars were intended for circulation. The gold bars enjoyed a limited circulation, and the remaining round gold and silver coins were largely non-circulating.

It should be remembered that the tien and lang are weights and not denominations. All of these gold and silver coins circulated and exchanged at the prevailing market value of the metal they contained. The relative values of the coins therefore fluctuated greatly.

The fineness of the gold and silver coins also varied considerably. Generally the gold and silver bars range from .700 to .900 fine, while the round coins were between .500 and .950 fine. The silver dragon piastres and half piastres range from .500 to .700 fine and although they were intended to be equivalent to a Mexican dollar, they normally exchanged for about 70 cents (Mexican).

Only a few of the gold and silver coins are inscribed with a weight. Therefore most must be weighed to determine their value. The following list gives the approximate weights of the various units used:

PIASTRE SYSTEM

1/4 Piastre	6.3 - 6.6 grams
1/2 Piastre	13.3 - 13.7 grams
1 Piastre	26.0 - 27.5 grams

TIEN AND LANG SYSTEM

1/2 Tien	1.8 grams
1 Tien	3.5 - 4.0 grams
2 Tien	7.0 - 7.7 grams
1/4 Lang	8.8 - 9.8 grams
3 Tien	10.5 - 11 grams
4 Tien	15.2 - 15.5 grams
5 Tien	18 - 19 grams
6 Tien	23 grams
7 Tien	25 - 26 grams
8 Tien	30.5 grams
9 Tien	34.2 grams
1 Lang	37 grams
5 Lang	185 - 191 grams
10 Lang	380 - 385 grams
50 Lang	1,915 - 1,920 grams

QUAN SYSTEM

1/2 Quan	2.5 grams
1 Quan	5.0 - 5.2 grams
1-1/2 Quan	7.5 - 8.0 grams
2 Quan	10.3 - 10.5 grams
2-1/2 Quan	13.0 - 13.5 grams
3 Quan	16 grams

NOTE: The Quan System was used only for silver bars.

FANTASIES

Large-size copper coins about 125 mm with obverse legends similar to 1 Dong as listed here, but having 8 character reverses are considered to be modern fantasies.

NOTE: Sch # are in reference to Albert Schroeder's Annam, Etudes Numismatiques or to the revised version titled Gold and Silver Coins of Annam, edited by John Novak and Bernard Permer.

Chinese/French

安南	An Nam = name of the country
大南	Dai Nam = a name for Annam
越南	Viet Nam = a name for Annam
年	Nien = year
造	Tao = made
银	Ngan = silver
金	Kim = gold
錢	Tien = a cash coin; also a weight about 3.7 grams
兩	Lang = a weight; about 37 grams
貫	Quan = a string of cash
分	Phan = a weight; about .37 grams

文 Van = a dong or cash coin

平中 Trung Binh = a name of weight standard

PROVINCES

IN TONKIN

山西 Son Tay

河内 Ha Noi

TOWN AND OUT POSTS

Noi Thang (Court Treasury) 帑内

DONG

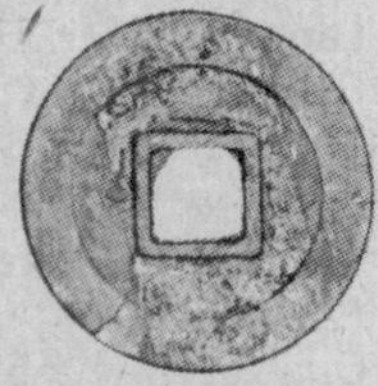

COPPER or BRASS, 24-26mm
Rev: Plain.

C#	Date	Emperor	Good	VG	Fine	VF
61.1	(1802-20)	Gia Long	1.25	2.00	3.50	6.00
	20-24mm					
61.2	(1802-20)	Gia Long	.85	1.50	2.75	4.50
	Rev: With dot.					
61.3	(1802-20)	Gia Long	2.00	3.50	5.50	9.00
	Rev: With circle.					
61.3a	(1802-20)	Gia Long	2.00	3.50	5.50	9.00
	Obv: Double rim.					
61.3b	(1802-20)	Gia Long	2.00	3.50	5.50	9.00
	Obv. & rev: Double rim.					
61.3c	(1802-20)	Gia Long	2.00	3.50	5.50	9.00
	Rev: With crescent.					
61.4	(1802-20)	Gia Long	2.75	4.50	7.50	12.50

Rev: Characters LUC PHAN in seal script.

C#	Date	Emperor	Good	VG	Fine	VF
62	(1802-20)	Gia Long	2.75	4.50	7.50	12.50

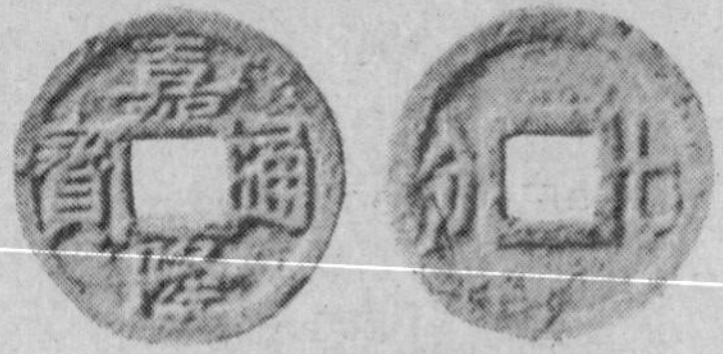

Rev: Characters THAT PHAN indicating the weight (7 phan)

C#	Date	Emperor	Good	VG	Fine	VF
63	(1802-20)	Gia Long	5.50	9.00	15.00	25.00
	ZINC **Rev: Plain**					
73	(1802-20)	Gia Long	4.50	7.50	12.50	20.00
	Rev: Characters THAT PHAN, similar to C#63.					
60	(1802-20)	Gia Long	3.50	5.50	9.00	15.00

COPPER or BRASS, 24-26mm

C#	Date	Emperor	Good	VG	Fine	VF
81.1	(1820-41)	Minh Mang	2.00	3.50	5.50	9.00
	20-24mm					
81.2	(1820-41)	Minh Mang	.75	1.25	2.00	3.50
	ZINC					
79 (83)	(1820-41)	Minh Mang	2.00	3.50	6.00	10.00

Nguy Khoi Rebellion
Obv. leg: TRI NGUYEN THONG BAO

C#	Date	Emperor	Good	VG	Fine	VF
137	(1831-34)	—	8.50	13.50	21.50	35.00

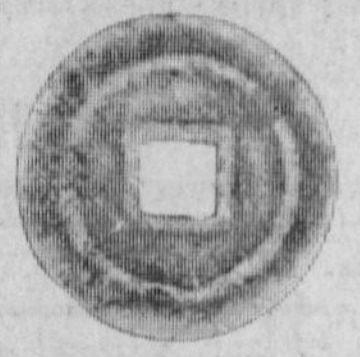

BRASS
Nung Rebellion
Obv. leg: NGUYEN LONG THONG BAO

C#	Date	Emperor	Good	VG	Fine	VF
138	(1832-33)	—	8.50	13.50	21.50	35.00
	Rev: Character XUONG					
139	(1832-33)	—	6.50	11.50	18.50	30.00

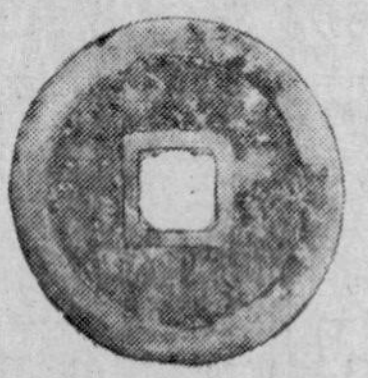

COPPER or BRASS, 24-26mm

C#	Date	Emperor	Good	VG	Fine	VF
141.1	(1841-47)	Thieu Tri	.60	1.00	1.75	3.00
	20-24mm					
141.2	(1841-47)	Thieu Tri	.60	1.00	1.75	3.00
	ZINC					
140	(1841-47)	Thieu Tri	4.50	7.50	12.50	21.50

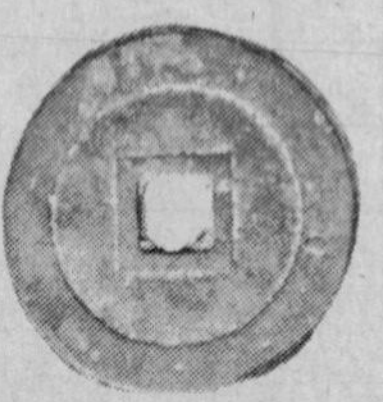

COPPER or BRASS, 24-26mm

C#	Date	Emperor	Good	VG	Fine	VF
201.1	(1848-83)	Tu Duc	1.25	2.00	3.50	6.00
	20-22mm					
201.2	(1848-83)	Tu Duc	1.25	2.00	3.50	6.00

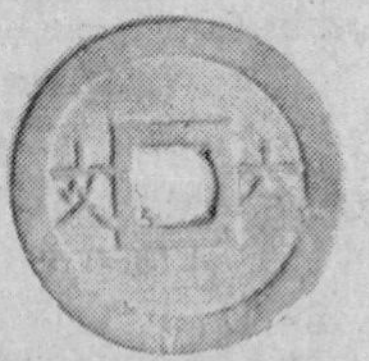

Rev: LUC VAN indicating value of six zinc Dong

C#	Date	Emperor	Good	VG	Fine	VF
202	(1848-83)	Tu Duc	1.25	2.00	3.50	6.00
	24-26mm					
202.1	(1848-83)	Tu Duc	1.25	2.00	3.50	6.00
	Rev: BAT VAN indicating value, AN NAM indicating country.					
203	(1848-83)	Tu Duc	Reported, not confirmed			
	ZINC **Rev: Plain.**					
191	(1848-83)	Tu Duc	2.00	3.50	5.50	9.00

Rev: HA NOI in two characters.

C#	Date	Emperor	Good	VG	Fine	VF
192.1	(1848-83)	Tu Duc	5.00	8.50	13.50	21.50

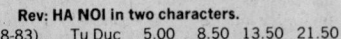

Rev: SON TAY in two characters.

C#	Date	Emperor	Good	VG	Fine	VF
192.2	(1848-83)	Tu Duc	5.00	8.50	13.50	21.50

The following coins (C#204-207) have the legend TU DUC BAO SAO obverse indicating that they were token coins.

10 DONG

COPPER or BRASS
Rev: Three characters

C#	Date	Emperor	Good	VG	Fine	VF
204	(1848-83)	Tu Duc	11.50	18.50	30.00	50.00

Rev: Four characters

C#	Date	Emperor	Good	VG	Fine	VF
204a	(1848-83)	Tu Duc	11.50	18.50	30.00	50.00

20 DONG

COPPER or BRASS

C#	Date	Emperor	Good	VG	Fine	VF
205	(1848-83)	Tu Duc	11.50	18.50	30.00	50.00

30 DONG

COPPER or BRASS

C#	Date	Emperor	Good	VG	Fine	VF
205.5	(1848-83)	Tu Duc	12.50	20.00	35.00	60.00

40 DONG

COPPER or BRASS

C#	Date	Emperor	Good	VG	Fine	VF
206	(1848-83)	Tu Duc	12.50	20.00	35.00	60.00

50 DONG

COPPER or BRASS

C#	Date	Emperor	Good	VG	Fine	VF
206.5	(1848-83)	Tu Duc	11.50	18.50	30.00	50.00

60 DONG

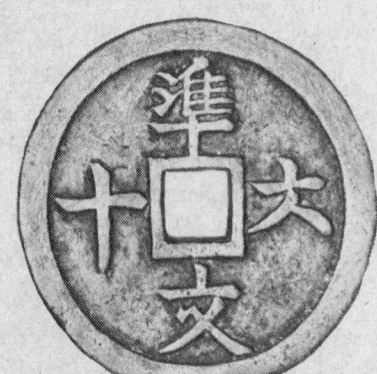

COPPER or BRASS, 49mm

C#	Date	Emperor	Good	VG	Fine	VF
207.1	(1848-83)	Tu Duc	12.50	20.00	35.00	60.00

Smaller size

C#	Date	Emperor	Good	VG	Fine	VF
207.2	(1848-83)	Tu Duc	11.50	18.50	30.00	50.00

REGULAR COINAGE RESUMED

DONG

ZINC
Obv: KIEN PHUC THONG BAO

C#	Date	Emperor	Good	VG	Fine	VF
271.1	(1883-84)	Kien Phuc	18.50	30.00	50.00	80.00

Obv: PHUC written differently

C#	Date	Emperor	Good	VG	Fine	VF
271.2	(1883-84)	Kien Phuc	18.50	30.00	50.00	80.00

COPPER or BRASS
Obv: Ham Nghi Thong Bao.
Rev: Two characters.

C#	Date	Emperor	Good	VG	Fine	VF
281	(1884-85)	Ham Nghi	35.00	60.00	100.00	165.00

24mm

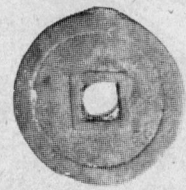

C#	Date	Emperor	Good	VG	Fine	VF
301.1	(1885-88)	Dong Khanh	2.75	4.50	7.50	12.50

26mm

C#	Date	Emperor	Good	VG	Fine	VF
301.2	(1885-88)	Dong Khanh	11.50	18.50	30.00	50.00

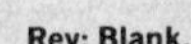

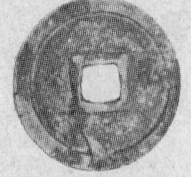

Rev: Blank.

Y#	Date	Emp.	Good	VG	Fine	VF
1	(1888-1907)	Than Thoi	2.00	3.50	5.50	9.00

Rev: LUC VAN indicating six zinc Dong value.

Y#	Date	Emp.	Good	VG	Fine	VF
—	(1888-1907)	Than Thoi	—	—	Rare	—

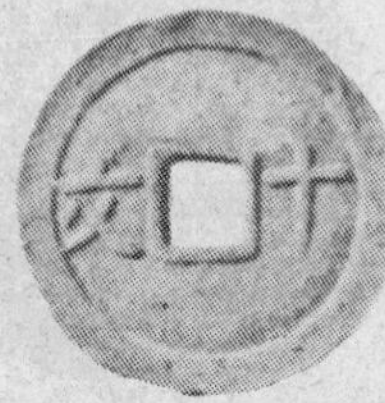

Rev: THAP VAN indicating ten zinc Dong value.

Y#	Date	Emp.	Good	VG	Fine	VF
2	(1888-1907)	Than Thoi	1.25	2.00	3.50	6.00

Y#	Date	Emp.	Good	VG	Fine	VF
3	(1907-16)	Duy Tan	1.75	2.75	4.50	7.50

Similar to Y#5.1 but cast.

Y#	Date	Emp.	Good	VG	Fine	VF
4	(1916-25)	Khai Dinh	5.50	9.00	15.00	25.00

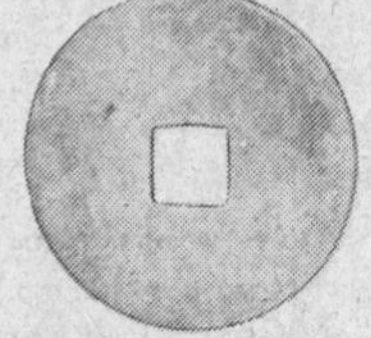

Struck, 22mm. Some pieces are uniface.

Y#	Date	Emp.	Good	VG	Fine	VF
5.1	(1916-25)	Khai Dinh	1.75	2.75	4.50	7.50

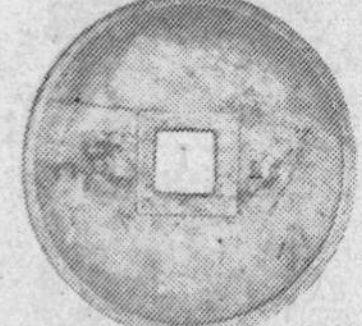

Larger size, characters slightly different.

Y#	Date	Emp.	Good	VG	Fine	VF
5.2	(1916-25)	Khai Dinh	2.00	3.50	6.00	10.00

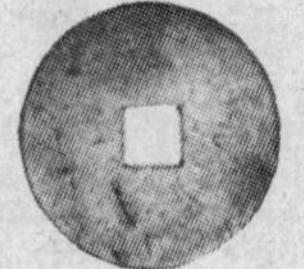

18mm

Y#	Date	Emp.	Good	VG	Fine	VF
6	(1926-45)	Bao Dai	4.50	7.50	12.50	20.00

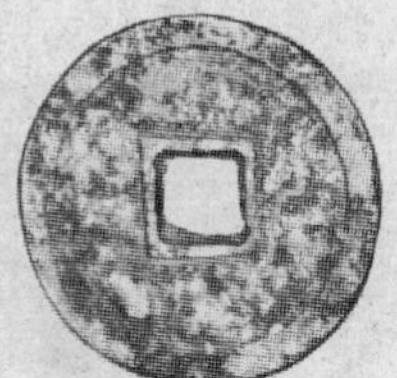

Rev: Plain, 24mm.

Y#	Date	Emp.	Good	VG	Fine	VF
6a	(1926-45)	Bao Dai	4.50	7.50	12.50	20.00

Rev: THAP VAN, 26mm.

Y#	Date	Emp.	Good	VG	Fine	VF
7	(1926-45)	Bao Dai	2.00	3.50	6.00	10.00

60 DONG

COPPER or BRASS
Obv: Similar to 1 Dong, C#202.
Rev: Circular 8 character legend.

C#	Date	Emperor	Good	VG	Fine	VF
213	—	—	—	—	—	—

Rev: 4 character legend.

C#	Date	Emperor	Good	VG	Fine	VF
215	—	—	—	—	—	—

SILVER COINS

The silver currency of Annam consisted of rectangular bars or ingots (in units of Guan and Tien and Lang) and round coins (in units of Piastres and Tien and Lang). The silver coins are listed here according to the system in which they are denominated, Piastre, Quan or Tien and Lang. Most of the coins do not carry any indication of their denomination.

Therefore one must rely on the coin's weight to know its denomination.

PIASTRE SERIES

1/4 PIASTRE

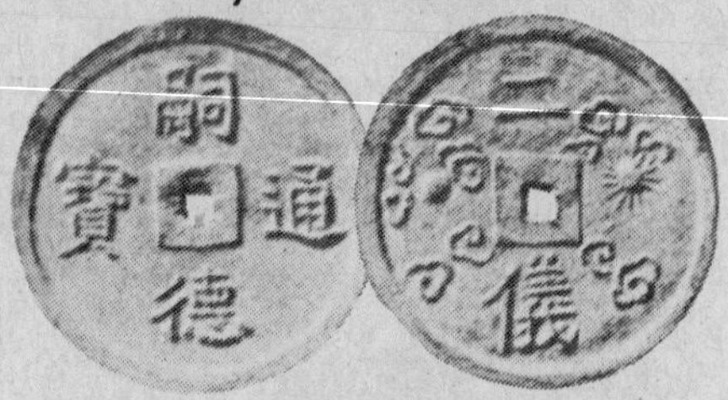

SILVER, 6.6 gm.
Rev: Two characters, sun, moon and clouds.

Sch#	Date	Emp.	VG	Fine	VF	XF
355	ND(1841-47)	Thieu Tri	42.50	85.00	175.00	250.00

Rev: Four characters.

Sch#	Date	Emp.	VG	Fine	VF	XF
420	ND(1885-89)	Dong Khanh	42.50	85.00	175.00	250.00

1/2 PIASTRE

SILVER, 13.3-13.7 gm.

Sch#	Date	Emp.	VG	Fine	VF	XF
184	ND	Minh Mang	21.50	42.50	85.00	125.00
185	(1833) Yr.14	Minh Mang	21.50	42.50	85.00	125.00

Sch#	Date	Emp.	VG	Fine	VF	XF
186	(1834) Yr.15	Minh Mang	21.50	42.50	85.00	125.00

13.3 gm.
Rev: Two dragons. Aquare hole in center.

Sch#	Date	Emp.	VG	Fine	VF	XF
239	ND(1841-47)	Thieu Tri	55.00	110.00	225.00	325.00

13.5 gm.
Rev: Small dragon.

Sch#	Date	Emp.	VG	Fine	VF	XF
260	ND(1841-47)	Thieu Tri	50.00	100.00	200.00	275.00

13.6 gm.
Rev: Large dragon.

Sch#	Date	Emp.	VG	Fine	VF	XF
259	ND(1841-47)	Thieu Tri	50.00	100.00	200.00	275.00

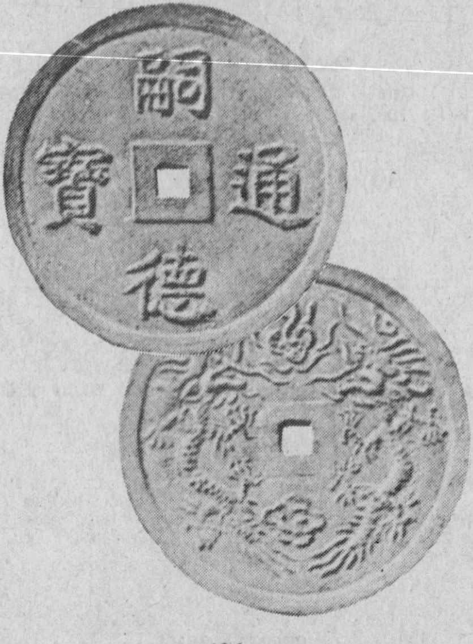

13.1 g.
Square hole in center

Sch#	Date	Emp.	VG	Fine	VF	XF
347	ND(1848-83)	Tu Duc	37.50	75.00	150.00	225.00

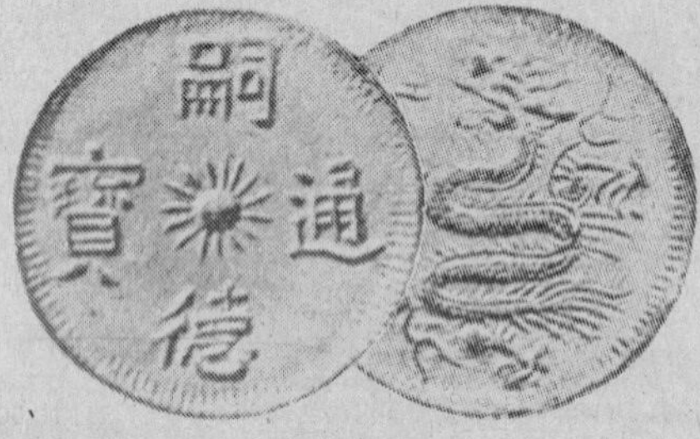

13.3 gm.

Sch#	Date	Emp.	VG	Fine	VF	XF
369	ND(1848-83)	Tu Duc	50.00	100.00	200.00	275.00

plain edge, 31mm

Sch#	Date	Emp.	VG	Fine	VF	XF
369a	ND(1848-83)	Tu Duc	55.00	110.00	225.00	325.00

12.4 gm.
Obv: Dot in center of sun.

Sch#	Date	Emp.	VG	Fine	VF	XF
370	ND(1848-83)	Tu Duc	50.00	100.00	200.00	275.00

PIASTRE

SILVER, 35mm, 26.3-26.7 gm.

Sch#	Date	Emp.	VG	Fine	VF	XF
	ND(1820-48)	Minh Mang	125.00	250.00	500.00	750.00

39-41mm

Sch#	Date	Emp.	VG	Fine	VF	XF
—	ND(1820-48)	Minh Mang	62.50	135.00	275.00	400.00
181	(1832) Yr.13	Minh Mang	62.50	135.00	275.00	400.00
182	(1833) Yr.14	Minh Mang	50.00	100.00	200.00	300.00
183	(1834) Yr.15	Minh Mang	35.00	70.00	140.00	200.00
183a	(1835) Yr.16	Minh Mang	87.50	175.00	350.00	500.00

25.8 - 26.4 gm.
Square hole in center. Rev: Two dragons.

Sch#	Date	Emp.	VG	Fine	VF	XF
238	ND(1841-47)	Thieu Tri	150.00	300.00	600.00	850.00

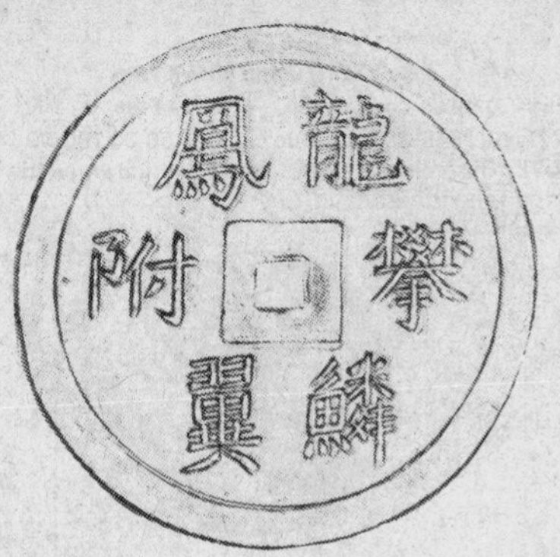

26.4 - 28.5 gm.
Obv: Two characters. Rev: Six characters.

Sch#	Date	Emp.	VG	Fine	VF	XF
244	ND(1841-47)	Thieu Tri	62.50	135.00	275.00	400.00

26.5 gm.

258	ND(1841-47)	Thieu Tri	50.00	100.00	200.00	275.00

Rev: Dragon facing opposite direction.

258a	ND(1841-47)	Thieu Tri	62.50	135.00	275.00	400.00

43mm, 26.6 gm.
Square hole in center. Rev: Two dragons.

347b	ND(1848-83)	Tu Duc	100.00	200.00	400.00	550.00

51mm

Sch#	Date	Emp.	VG	Fine	VF	XF
347c	ND(1848-83)	Tu Duc	225.00	450.00	850.00	1250.

26.2 gm.

368	ND(1848-83)	Tu Duc	55.00	110.00	225.00	325.00

26.5 gm.
Rev: Dragon and LONG VAN

371	ND(1848-83)	Tu Duc	62.50	135.00	275.00	400.00

26.3 - 26.7 gm.

371	ND(1916-25)	Khai Dinh	45.00	87.50	175.00	250.00

As above but characters heavier, flame ball smaller.

	ND(1916-25)	Khai Dinh	45.00	87.50	175.00	250.00

NOTE: The Khai Dinh Piastres have been found struck over Minh Mang Piastres.

Weight unknown

	ND(1926-45)	Bao Dai	100.00	200.00	400.00	550.00

DOLLAR SERIES

So called dollars of Tu Duc with rev. leg. 7 Mace 2 Candareens are believed to be modern fantasies by some authorities.

TIEN AND LANG SERIES

Certain coins were issued in weights from 1 Tien through 1 Lang each with a different virtue.

VIRTUES

1 Tien = Viet Tu (benignity)
2 Tien = Viet Hien (gratitude)
3 Tien = Viet Lang (kindness)
4 Tien = Viet De (respect)
5 Tien = Viet Ngai (Justice)
6 Tien = Viet Thinh (obedience)
7 Tien = Viet Hue (benevolence)
8 Tien = Viet Thuan (submissiveness)
9 Tien = Viet Nhan (humanity)
1 Lang = Viet Trung (faithfulness)

DONG

SILVER, 4.5 gm.

Sch#	Date	Emp.	VG	Fine	VF	XF
180	ND(1820-41)	Minh Mang	25.00	50.00	100.00	140.00

1.8 gm.

Sch#	Date	Emp.	VG	Fine	VF	XF
257	ND(1841-47)	Thieu Tri	25.00	50.00	100.00	140.00

1.5 gm.

367	ND(1848-83	Tu Duc	25.00	50.00	100.00	140.00

Weight unknown, 26mm.

367a	ND(1848-83)	Tu Duc	25.00	50.00	100.00	140.00

The silver dongs above were probably not intended for circulation. Beware of silver plated copper coins.

TIEN

SILVER
Weight unknown

189	ND(1820-41)	Minh Mang	25.00	50.00	100.00	140.00

3.6 gm.

250	ND(1841-47)	Minh Mang	25.00	50.00	100.00	140.00

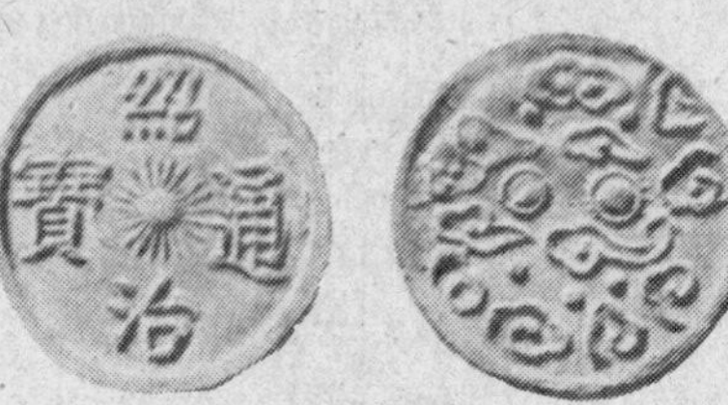

3.7 - 4.0 gm.
Obv: Four characters.
Rev: Sun, moon and five planets.

262	ND(1841-47)	Minh Mang	25.00	50.00	100.00	140.00

3.6 - 4.0 .gm.
Obv: Two characters.
Rev: Scepter and swastika.

Sch#	Date	Emp.	VG	Fine	VF	XF
264	ND(1841-47)	Minh Mang	25.00	50.00	100.00	140.00

Rev: Mirror image of above.

265	ND(1841-47)	Minh Mang	25.00	50.00	100.00	140.00

4.0 gm.
Obv: Two characters.

266	ND(1841-47)	Minh Mang	25.00	50.00	100.00	140.00

3.7 gm.
Rev: TAM DA, The Three Plenties.

267	ND(1841-47)	Minh Mang	25.00	50.00	100.00	140.00

Weight unknown
Rev: Flaming ball

	ND(1841-47)	Minh Mang	17.50	35.00	70.00	100.00

Rev: Two scepters and two swastikas.
Square hole in center.

256	ND(1841-47)	Minh Mang	25.00	50.00	100.00	140.00

3.5 gm.
Obv: Four characters

353	ND(1848-83)	Tu Duc	25.00	50.00	100.00	140.00

3.7 gm.
Rev: Sun, moon and five planets.

Sch#	Date	Emp.	VG	Fine	VF	XF
352	ND(1848-83)	Tu Duc	25.00	50.00	100.00	140.00

Weight unknown
Obv: Four characters.
Rev: NHAI DUC and two fish.

354	ND(1848-83)	Tu Duc	25.00	50.00	100.00	140.00

3.8 gm.
Rev: NGI NGHI and sun, moon and clouds.

355B	ND(1848-83)	Tu Duc	25.00	50.00	100.00	140.00

3.8 gm.
Obv: Four characters.
Rev: TAM DA, The Three Plenties.

357	ND(1848-83)	Tu Duc	25.00	50.00	100.00	140.00

3.6 gm.
Rev: Two swastikas and two scepters which look like flowers.

361	ND(1848-83)	Tu Duc	25.00	50.00	100.00	140.00

3.7 gm.
Rev: TU BAO, The Four Precious Objects.

362	ND(1848-83)	Tu Duc	25.00	50.00	100.00	140.00

3.3 gm.
Rev: The Five Precious Objects

363	ND(1848-83	Tu Duc	25.00	50.00	100.00	140.00

3.5 - 3.7 gm.
Rev: The Eight Precious Objects

364	ND(1848-83	Tu Duc	25.00	50.00	100.00	140.00

NOTE: There are three varieties of this coin based upon the placement of the symbols.

3.8 gm.
Rev: VTET TU and NHAT TIEN

Sch#	Date	Emp.	VG	Fine	VF	XF
377	ND(1848-83	Tu Duc	25.00	50.00	100.00	140.00

NOTE: This coin is one of a set of ten known as the coins of the Ten Virtues.

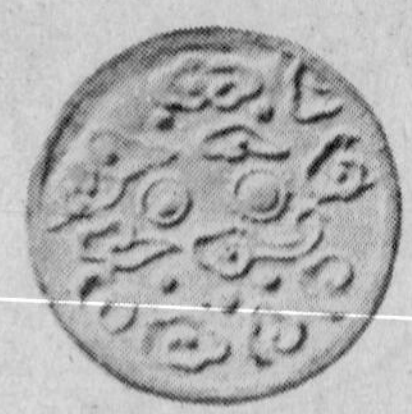

3.9 gm.
Rev: Sun, moon and five planets.

386	ND(1848-83	Tu Duc	17.50	35.00	70.00	100.00

4.0 gm.
Rev: TAM DA, The Three Plenties.

387	ND(1848-83	Tu Duc	25.00	50.00	100.00	140.00

4.1 gm.
Rev: Scepter and Swastika

388	ND(1848-83	Tu Duc	25.00	50.00	100.00	140.00

3.8 gm.
Rev: Horn

389	ND(1848-83	Tu Duc	25.00	50.00	100.00	140.00

3.5 gm.
Rev: The Five Precious Objects

390	ND(1848-83)	Tu Duc	25.00	50.00	100.00	140.00

1-1/2 TIEN

SILVER, 5.63 gm.

—	ND(1841-47)	Thieu Tri	25.00	50.00	100.00	140.00

5.2 grams
Obv: Four characters

Sch#	Date	Emp.	VG	Fine	VF	XF
358	ND(1848-83)	Tu Duc	25.00	50.00	100.00	140.00

5.3 gm.
Rev: Four different characters

Sch#	Date	Emp.	VG	Fine	VF	XF
—	ND(1848-83)	Tu Duc	25.00	50.00	100.00	140.00

2 TIEN

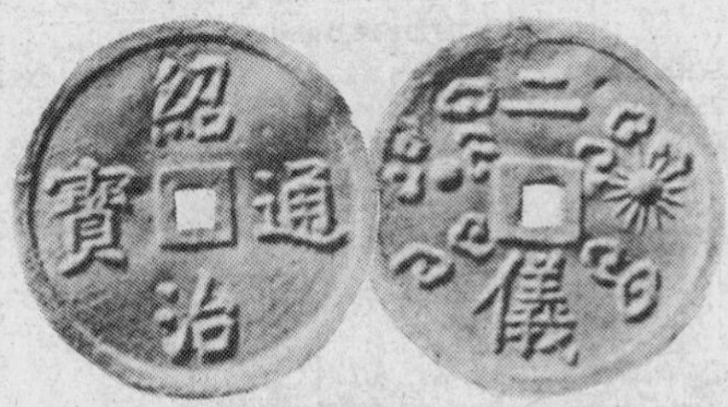

SILVER, 7.6 gm.
Rev: NGI NGHI, sun, moon and clouds.

Sch#	Date	Emp.	VG	Fine	VF	XF
251	ND(1841-47)	Thieu Tri	30.00	60.00	120.00	175.00

7.5 gm.
Rev: Two dragons

Sch#	Date	Emp.	VG	Fine	VF	XF
240	ND(1841-47)	Thieu Tri	30.00	60.00	120.00	175.00

7.6 gm.
Square hole in center. Rev: Four characters.

Sch#	Date	Emp.	VG	Fine	VF	XF
351	ND(1848-83)	Tu Duc	30.00	60.00	120.00	175.00

7.3 gm.
Rev: NHI TIEN and VIET HIEN

Sch#	Date	Emp.	VG	Fine	VF	XF
378	ND(1848-83)	Tu Duc	30.00	60.00	120.00	175.00

NOTE: One of the Ten Virtues coins.

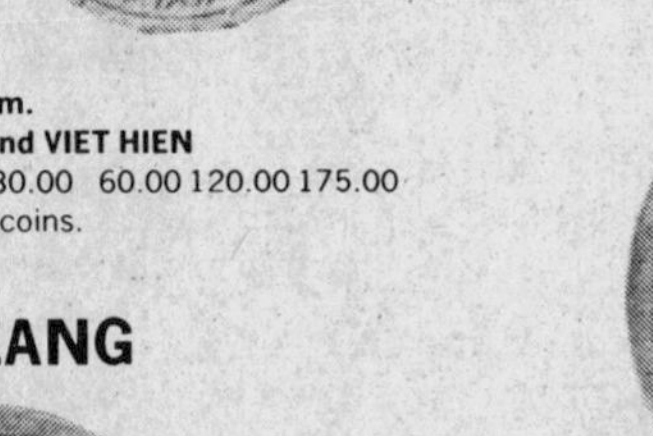

1/4 LANG

SILVER, 9.2 gm.
Obv: Four characters

Sch#	Date	Emp.	VG	Fine	VF	XF
249	ND(1841-47)	Thieu Tri	27.50	55.00	110.00	150.00

9.6 gm.
Rev: Dragon and four characters.

Sch#	Date	Emp.	VG	Fine	VF	XF
261	ND(1841-47)	Thieu Tri	45.00	87.50	175.00	250.00

9.4 gm.
Obv: Eight characters. Rev: Dragon.

Sch#	Date	Emp.	VG	Fine	VF	XF
350	ND(1848-83)	Tu Duc	27.50	55.00	110.00	150.00

9.5 - 9.8 gm.
Obv: Four characters.

Sch#	Date	Emp.	VG	Fine	VF	XF
375	ND(1848-83)	Tu Duc	27.50	55.00	110.00	150.00

8.8 gm.
* Obv: Four characters.

Sch#	Date	Emp.	VG	Fine	VF	XF
422	ND(1885-88)	Dong Khanh	27.50	55.00	110.00	150.00

3 TIEN

SILVER, 11.9 gm.
Rev: TAM THO, The Three Longevities.

Sch#	Date	Emp.	VG	Fine	VF	XF
252	ND(1841-47)	Thieu Tri	30.00	60.00	120.00	175.00

Obv: Four characters.

Sch#	Date	Emp.	VG	Fine	VF	XF
373	ND(1848-83)	Tu Duc	30.00	60.00	120.00	175.00

11.3 gm.
Rev: TAM TIEN and VIET LANG

Sch#	Date	Emp.	VG	Fine	VF	XF
379	ND(1848-83)	Tu Duc	30.00	60.00	120.00	175.00

NOTE: One of the Ten Virtue coins.

10.2 gm.
Rev: Four characters.

Sch#	Date	Emp.	VG	Fine	VF	XF
421	ND(1885-88)	Dong Khanh	35.00	70.00	140.00	200.00

4 TIEN

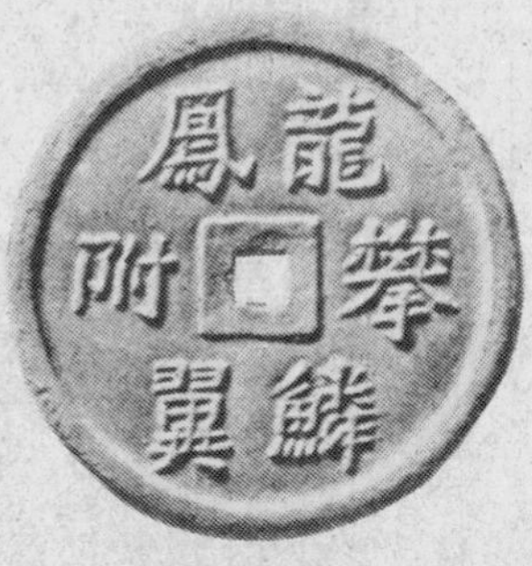

SILVER, 15.5 gm.
Obv: Two characters. Rev: Six characters.

Sch#	Date	Emp.	VG	Fine	VF	XF
246	ND(1841-47)	Thieu Tri	37.50	75.00	150.00	225.00

Rev: TU MY, clouds and trees.

Sch#	Date	Emp.	VG	Fine	VF	XF
254	ND(1841-47)	Thieu Tri	35.00	70.00	140.00	200.00

15.0 - 15.5 gm.
Obv: Four characters. Square hole in center.

351	ND(1848-83)	Tu Duc	27.50	55.00	110.00	150.00

15 gm.
Rev: TU TIEN and VIET DE

380	ND(1848-83)	Tu Duc	37.50	75.00	150.00	225.00

NOTE: One of the Ten Virtue coins.

15.3 gm.
Rev: Dragon

428	ND(1888-1907)	Than Thoi	37.50	75.00	150.00	225.00

5 TIEN

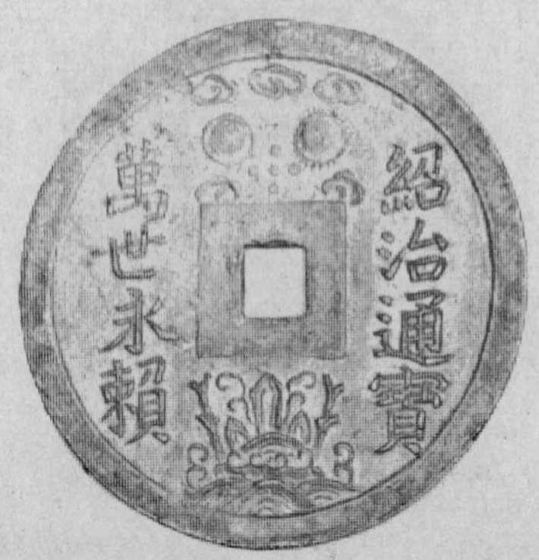

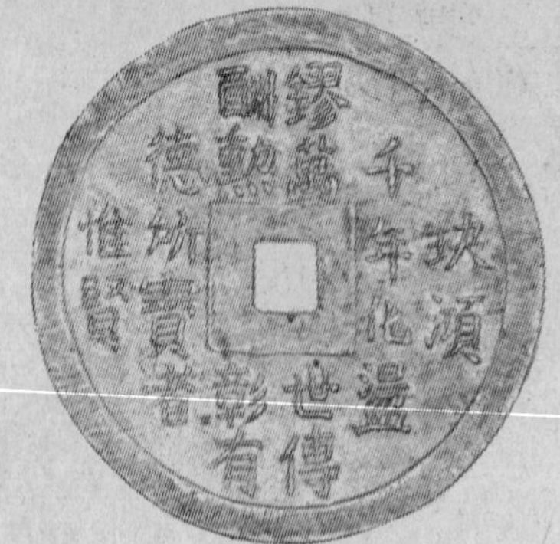

SILVER, 19 gm.
Obv. and rev: Legends

Sch#	Date	Emp.	VG	Fine	VF	XF
242	ND(1841-47)	Thieu Tri	87.50	175.00	350.00	500.00

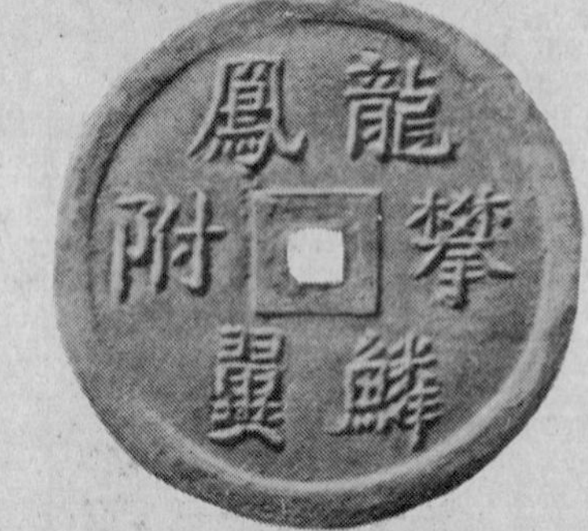

19.2 gm.
Obv: THIEU TRI and plants.

243	ND(1841-47)	Thieu Tri	67.50	135.00	275.00	400.00

18.5 - 19 gm.

247	ND(1841-47)	Thieu Tri	67.50	135.00	275.00	400.00

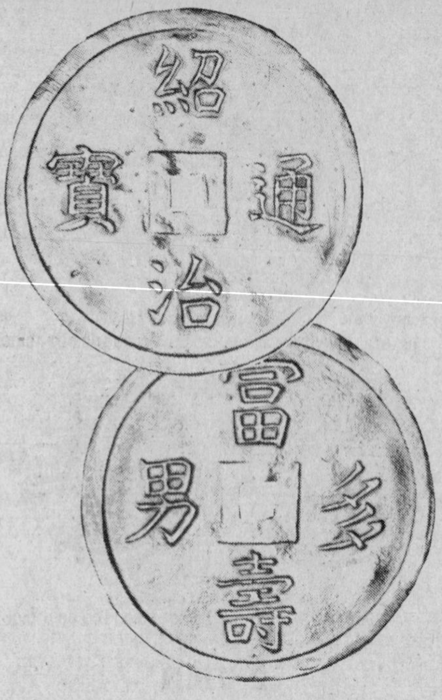

17.0 - 18.5 gm.

Sch#	Date	Emp.	VG	Fine	VF	XF
253	ND(1841-47)	Thieu Tri	67.50	135.00	275.00	400.00

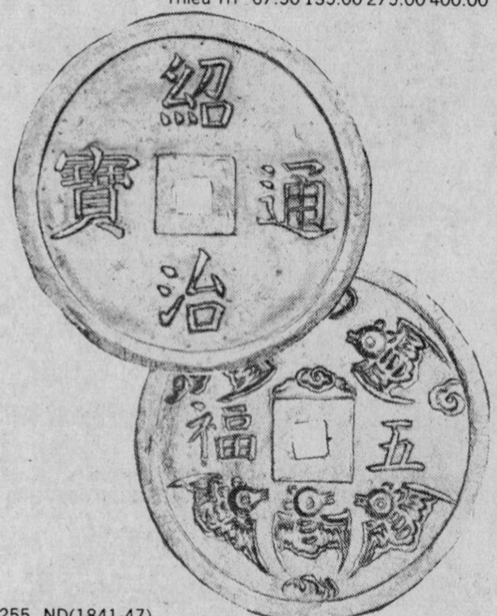

255	ND(1841-47)	Thieu Tri	55.00	110.00	225.00	325.00

19 gm.

261	ND(1841-47)	Thieu Tri	67.50	135.00	275.00	400.00

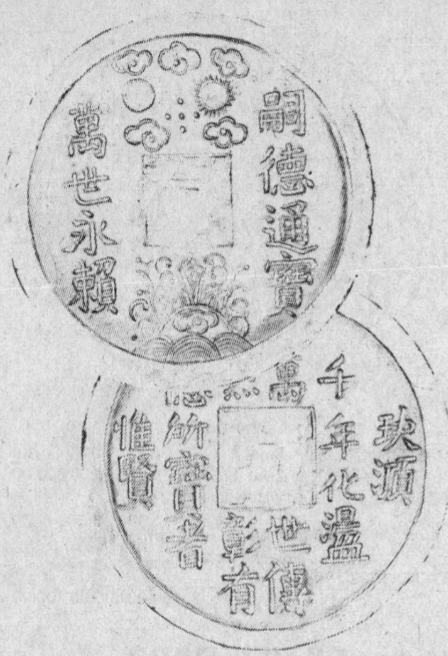

Sch#	Date	Emp.	VG	Fine	VF	XF
348	ND(1848-83)	Tu Duc	67.50	135.00	275.00	400.00

18 gm.

349	ND(1848-83)	Tu Duc	55.00	110.00	225.00	325.00

18.9 gm.

359	ND(1848-83)	Tu Duc	55.00	110.00	225.00	325.00

18.5 gm.

Sch#	Date	Emp.	VG	Fine	VF	XF
372	ND(1848-83)	Tu Duc	67.50	135.00	275.00	400.00

18.9 - 20 gm.

374	ND(1848-83)	Tu Duc	67.50	135.00	275.00	400.00

18.8 gm.
Rev: NGU TIEN and VIET NGAI.

381	ND(1848-83)	Tu Duc	67.50	135.00	275.00	400.00

NOTE: One of the Ten Virtue coins.

6 TIEN

SILVER, 23 gm.

Sch#	Date	Emp.	VG	Fine	VF	XF
382	ND(1848-83)	Tu Duc	87.50	175.00	350.00	500.00

NOTE: One of the Ten Virtue coins.

7 TIEN

SILVER, 26 gm.

383	ND(1848-83)	Tu Duc	110.00	225.00	450.00	650.00

NOTE: One of the Ten Virtue coins.

8 TIEN

SILVER, 30.5 gm.

384	ND(1848-83)	Tu Duc	135.00	275.00	550.00	800.00

NOTE: One of the Ten Virtue coins.

9 TIEN

SILVER, 34.2 gm.

Sch#	Date	Emp.	VG	Fine	VF	XF
385	ND(1848-83)	Tu Duc	175.00	350.00	700.00	1000.

NOTE: One of the Ten Virtue coins.

LANG

SILVER, 38mm, 38 gm.

Sch#	Date	Emp.	VG	Fine	VF	XF
187	ND(1820-41)	Minh Mang	100.00	200.00	400.00	550.00

40mm

Sch#	Date	Emp.	VG	Fine	VF	XF
187a	ND(1820-41)	Minh Mang	100.00	200.00	400.00	550.00

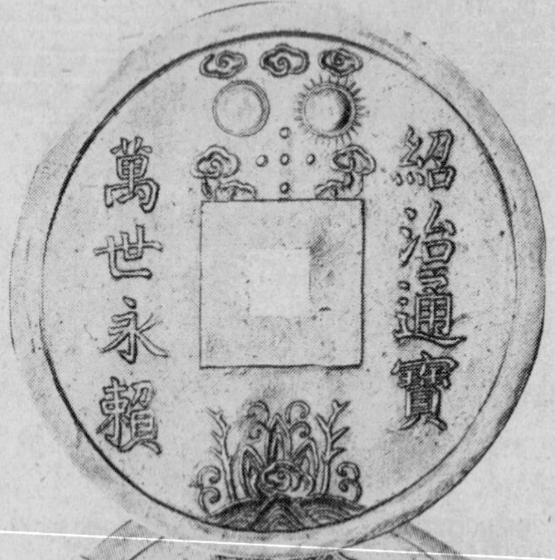

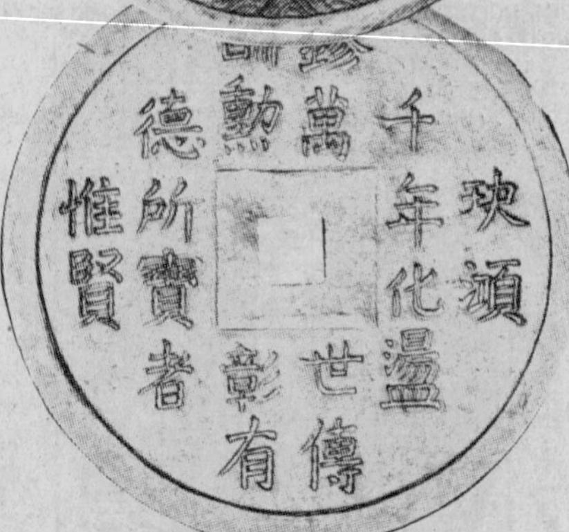

63mm, 38 - 38.8 gm.

Sch#	Date	Emp.	VG	Fine	VF	XF
241	ND(1841-47)	Thieu Tri	150.00	300.00	600.00	850.00

63mm, 37.3 gm.

Sch#	Date	Emp.	VG	Fine	VF	XF
348	ND(1848-83)	Tu Duc	150.00	300.00	600.00	850.00

37.2 gm.
Rev: Dragon and two characters.

Sch#	Date	Emp.	VG	Fine	VF	XF
371	ND(1848-83)	Tu Duc	87.50	175.00	350.00	500.00

37.4 gm.

Sch#	Date	Emp.	VG	Fine	VF	XF
376	ND(1848-83)	Tu Duc	135.00	275.00	550.00	800.00

NOTE: One of the Ten Virtue coins.

65mm, weight unknown.
Obv: 8 characters

Sch#	Date	Emp.	VG	Fine	VF	XF
431	ND(1888-1907)	Than Thoi	125.00	250.00	500.00	700.00

SILVER BARS

According to contemporary reports, the main currency of Annam, aside from Dong coins, were Piastres and silver bars. All of these bars are inscribed with their weight and many contain a date or the name of the province in which they were made.

TIEN

SILVER, 3.8 - 3.9 gm.

Sch#	Date	Emp.	VG	Fine	VF	XF
174	ND(1820-41)	Minh Mang	25.00	50.00	100.00	150.00

4.2 gm.

Sch#	Date	Emp.	VG	Fine	VF	XF
175	ND(1820-41)	Minh Mang	25.00	50.00	100.00	150.00

2 TIEN

SILVER, 8 gm.

Sch#	Date	Emp.	VG	Fine	VF	XF
176	ND(1820-41	Minh Mang	30.00	60.00	120.00	175.00

7.0 - 7.8 gm.
Court Treasury. Rev: Five characters.

Sch#	Date	Emp.	VG	Fine	VF	XF
331	ND(1848-83)	Tu Duc	30.00	60.00	120.00	175.00

7.9 gm.
Court Treasury. Rev: Error, third and fifth characters the same.

Sch#	Date	Emp.	VG	Fine	VF	XF
337	ND(1848-83)	Tu Duc	30.00	60.00	120.00	175.00

6.8 gm.
Rev: Four characters.

335	ND(1848-83)	Tu Duc	30.00	60.00	120.00	175.00

3 TIEN

SILVER, 11.6 gm.

177	ND(1820-41)	Minh Mang	45.00	87.50	175.00	250.00

10.2 gm.
Court Treasury

332	ND(1848-83)	Tu Duc	45.00	87.50	175.00	250.00

4 TIEN

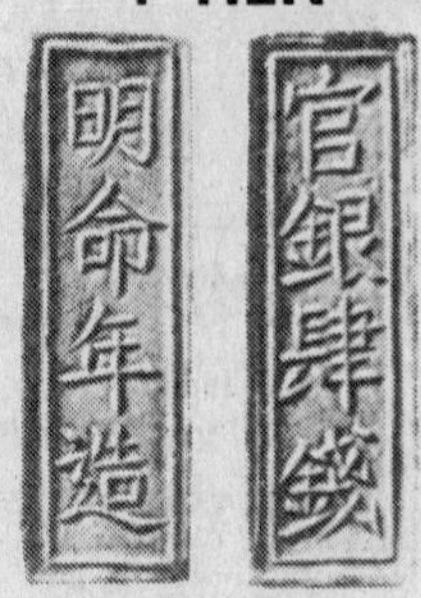

SILVER, 15.4 gm.

178	ND(1820-41)	Minh Mang	50.00	100.00	200.00	300.00

15.5 gm.
Court Treasury

236	ND(1841-47)	Thieu Tri	50.00	100.00	200.00	300.00

15 gm.
Court Treasury

333	ND(1848-83)	Tu Duc	50.00	100.00	200.00	50.00

5 TIEN

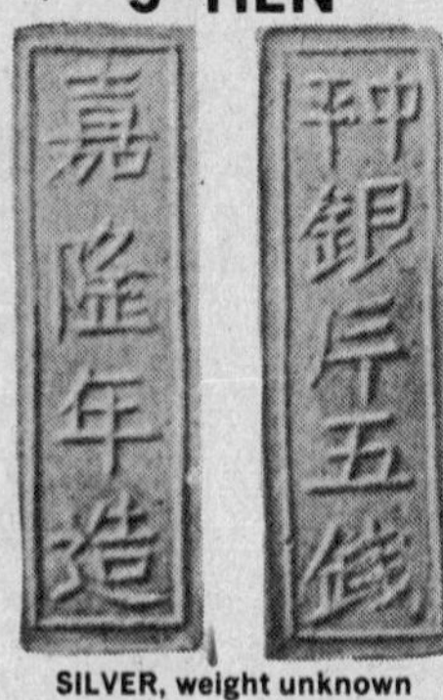

SILVER, weight unknown
Rev: Six characters

Sch#	Date	Emp.	VG	Fine	VF	XF
122	ND(1802-20)	Gia Long	62.50	125.00	250.00	350.00

19 gm.
Rev: Four characters

179	ND(1820-41	Minh Mang	62.50	125.00	250.00	350.00

19.2 gm.
Court Treasury. Rev: Five characters.

237	ND(1841-47)	Thieu Tri	62.50	125.00	250.00	350.00

19 gm.
Court Treasury

334	ND(1848-83)	Tu Duc	62.50	125.00	250.00	350.00

LANG

SILVER, 36.7 gm.
Large characters

118	ND(1802-20)	Gia Long	37.50	42.50	50.00	60.00

NOTE: Sch#118 Was Produced As A Common Form Of Bullion until the Vietnam conflict.

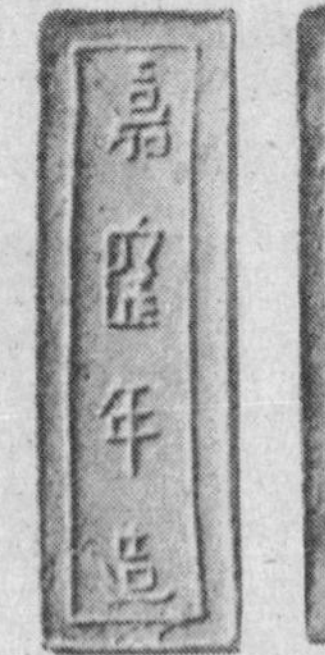

Small characters

Sch#	Date	Emp.	VG	Fine	VF	XF
119	ND(1802-20)	Gia Long	45.00	70.00	140.00	200.00

NOTE: Two varieties of edge inscriptions.

Weight unknown
Obv: Eight characters. Rev: Six characters.

—	ND(1802-20)	Gia Long	45.00	90.00	180.00	275.00

52mm, 37. - 38. gm.

169	ND(1820-41)	Minh Mang	45.00	87.50	175.00	250.00

41mm, weight unknown.

—	ND(1820-41)	Minh Mang	45.00	70.00	140.00	200.00

38 gm.

Court Treasury

Sch#	Date	Emp.	VG	Fine	VF	XF
219	ND(1841-47)	Thieu Tri	45.00	90.00	180.00	275.00

Rev: Gia Dinh Province

—	CD1844	Thieu Tri	62.50	125.00	250.00	350.00

Weight unknown
Court Treasury

320a	ND(1848-83)		37.50	42.50	50.00	60.00

NOTE: Sch#320A was produced as a common form of bullion until the Vietnam Conflict.

38 gm.
Binh Dinh province indicated on edge

320	ND(1848-83)	Tu Duc	45.00	70.00	140.00	200.00

Weight unknown
Dinh Tuong Province

320b	CD1859	Tu Duc	62.50	125.00	250.00	350.00

Rev: Phu Yen Province

320c	CD1859	Tu Duc	62.50	125.00	250.00	350.00

Province uncertain

Sch#	Date	Emp.	VG	Fine	VF	XF
323	CD1860	Tu Duc	62.50	125.00	250.00	350.00

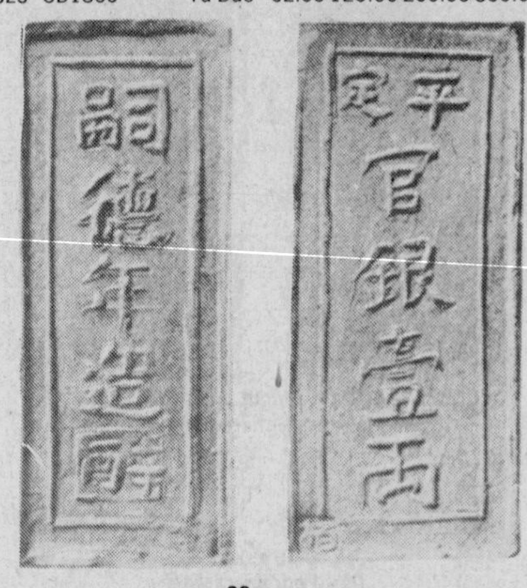

38 gm.
Obv: Date. Rev: Binh Dinh Province

321	CD1861	Tu Duc	62.50	125.00	250.00	350.00

Weight unknown
Phu Yen Province

322	CD1861	Tu Duc	62.50	125.00	250.00	350.00

37 gm.
Obv: Date. Rev: An Gian, a fort near Cambodian border.

324	CD1863	Tu Duc	87.50	175.00	350.00	500.00

37.7 gm.
Court Treasury. Very crude.
Fineness (.700) inscribed on edge.

423	ND(1885-88)	Dong Khanh	45.00	87.50	175.00	250.00

Weight unknown
Date on edge

—	CD1919	Khai Dinh	45.00	90.00	180.00	275.00
—	CD1922	Khai Dinh	45.00	90.00	180.00	275.00

5 LANG

SILVER, 181 - 191 gm.

Sch#	Date	Emp.	VG	Fine	VF	XF
170	ND(1820-41)	Minh Mang	200.00	275.00	375.00	500.00

40X92mm, 186 - 191 gm.
Court Treasury

220	ND(1841-47)	Thieu Tri	200.00	275.00	375.00	500.00

Weight unknown
Court Treasury

—	ND(1888-1907)	Than Thoi	200.00	275.00	375.00	500.00

10 LANG

NOTE: 10 Lang curved "banana" bars similar in shape to Sch#173 but, with other various markings were produced as a common form of bullion until the Vietnam Conflict. Market value for these private issues is bullion plus 10-20 percent depending on the markings.

SILVER, about 385 gm.
Coirt Treasury. Similar to sch#173.

171	CD1832	Minh Mang	400.00	450.00	500.00	600.00

Quang An Province. Similar to Sch#173.

—	CD1832	Minh Mang	400.00	450.00	500.00	600.00

Court Treasury. Similar to Sch#173.

172	CD1833	Minh Mang	400.00	450.00	500.00	600.00

Son Tay Province. Similar to Sch#173.

—	CD1833	Minh Mang	400.00	450.00	500.00	600.00

Son Tay Province

173	CD1837	Thieu Tri	400.00	450.00	500.00	600.00

42X115mm
Court Treasury. Obv. & Rev: Legends.

221	ND(1841-74)	Thieu Tri	400.00	475.00	550.00	650.00

45X120 gm. About 385 gm.

Hung Yen Province. Obv. & rev: Legends.

222	CD1844	Thieu Tri	400.00	475.00	550.00	650.00

Binh Dinh Province

223	CD1844	Thieu Tri	400.00	475.00	550.00	650.00

Quang Yen Province. Obv. & rev: Legends.

—	CD1844	Thieu Tri	400.00	475.00	550.00	650.00

San Tay Province. Similar to above.

224	CD1845	Thieu Tri	400.00	475.00	550.00	650.00

48X120mm, 385 gm.
Quang Nam Province. Similar to above.

Sch#	Date	Emp.	VG	Fine	VF	XF
225	CD1846	Thieu Tri	400.00	475.00	550.00	650.00

Son Tay Province. Similar to above.
— CD1846 Thieu Tri 400.00 475.00 550.00 650.00

46X120mm
Hung Yen Province. Similar to above.
226 CD1847 Thieu Tri 400.00 475.00 550.00 650.00

Lang Son Province. Similar to above.
227 CD1847 Thieu Tri 400.00 475.00 550.00 650.00

Bac Ninh Province. Similar to above.
228 CD1847 Thieu Tri 400.00 475.00 550.00 650.00

Son Tay Province. Similar to above.
229 CD1847 Thieu Tri 400.00 475.00 550.00 650.00

Gia Dinh. Similar to above.
230 CD1847 Thieu Tri 400.00 475.00 550.00 650.00

Weight unknown
Hung Yen Province. Similar to S#173.
— CD1844 Thieu Tri 400.00 475.00 550.00 650.00

Son Tay Province
— CD1844 Thieu Tri 400.00 475.00 550.00 650.00

34X100mm, 382.5 gm.
Court Treasury
329 (1848-83) Tu Duc 400.00 475.00 550.00 650.00

383 gm.
Son Tay. Similar to Sch#173.
330 CD1852 Tu Duc Reported, not confirmed

Thai Nguyen Province. Similar to Sch#173.
325 CD1860 Tu Duc 400.00 450.00 500.00 600.00

Binh Dinh Province. Similar to Sch#173.
326 CD1861 Tu Duc 400.00 450.00 500.00 600.00

Son Tay Province. Similar to Sch#173.
327 CD1880 Tu Duc 400.00 450.00 500.00 600.00

Nghe An Province. Similar to Sch#173.
328 CD1882 Tu Duc 400.00 450.00 500.00 600.00

20 LANG

SILVER, 49X122mm, 765.5 gm.
Court Treasury. Legends both sides framed with in orante border.

231 (1841-47) Thieu Tri — — Rare —

30 LANG

SILVER, 55X127mm, 1149 gm.
Similar to 20 Lang, Sch #231.
232 (1841-47) Thieu Tri — Rare —

40 LANG

SILVER, 60X130mm, 1528 gm.
Similar to 20 Lang, Sch#231.
233 (1841-47) Thieu Tri — — Rare —

50 LANG

SILVER, 65X140mm, 1915 gm.
Similar to 20 Lang, Sch#231.
234 ND(1841-47) Thieu Tri — — Rare —

100 LANG

SILVER, 77X160mm, 3831 gm.
Similar to 20 Lang, Sch#231.
235 ND(1841-47) Thieu Tri — — Rare —

QUAN SYSTEM

(SILVER BARS ONLY)

1/2 QUAN

SILVER, weight unknown

Sch#	Date	Emp.	VG	Fine	VF	XF
338	ND(1848-83)	Tu Duc	17.50	35.00	70.00	100.00

7/10 QUAN

SILVER, 3.5 gm.
339 ND(1848-83) Tu Duc 18.50 37.50 75.00 125.00

QUAN

SILVER, 5.0 - 5.2 gm.
340 ND(1848-83) Tu Duc 21.50 42.50 85.00 150.00

1-1/2 QUAN

SILVER, 7.5 - 8. gm.
341 ND(1848-83) Tu Duc 25.00 50.00 100.00 175.00

2 QUAN

SILVER, 10.5 gm.
342 ND(1848-83) Tu Duc 35.00 70.00 140.00 200.00

10.3 - 10.5 grams
Similar to Sch#342, but thinner characters.
345 (1848-83) Tu Duc 37.50 75.00 150.00 225.00

2-1/2 QUAN

SILVER, 13. - 13.5 gm.

Sch#	Date	Emp.	VG	Fine	VF	XF
343	(1848-83)	Tu Duc	42.50	85.00	175.00	250.00

3 QUAN

SILVER, 16 gm.
thick characters
344 (1848-83) Tu Duc 50.00 100.00 200.00 300.00

15.4 gm.
thin characters.
Obv. & rev: Double borders.
346 (1848-83) Tu Duc 50.00 100.00 200.00 300.00

GOLD COINS

The smaller gold coins and bars saw a limited circulation, mainly among the local merchants and foreign traders. The larger gold bars were used mainly for hoarding, while most of the round gold coins were intended as rewards and gifts. Many of these gold coins appear to have been struck from silver coin dies.

GOLD PIASTRE SERIES

1/4 PIASTRE

GOLD, 5.4 - 6.5 gm.
212 ND(1820-41) Minh Mang 200.00 235.00 285.00 350.00

6.4 gm.

Sch#	Date	Emp.	VG	Fine	VF	XF
425	ND(1885-88)	Dong Khanh	200.00	235.00	285.00	350.00

6.6 gm.

Sch#	Date	Emp.	VG	Fine	VF	XF
435	ND(1888-1907)	Than Thoi	200.00	235.00	285.00	350.00

1/2 PIASTRE

GOLD, 11.5 - 13.3 gm.

Sch#	Date	Emp.	VG	Fine	VF	XF
207	ND (1820-40)	Minh Mang	350.00	385.00	425.00	500.00
208	(1833) Yr.14	Minh Mang	350.00	400.00	475.00	550.00
206	(1834) Yr.15	Minh Mang	350.00	400.00	475.00	550.00

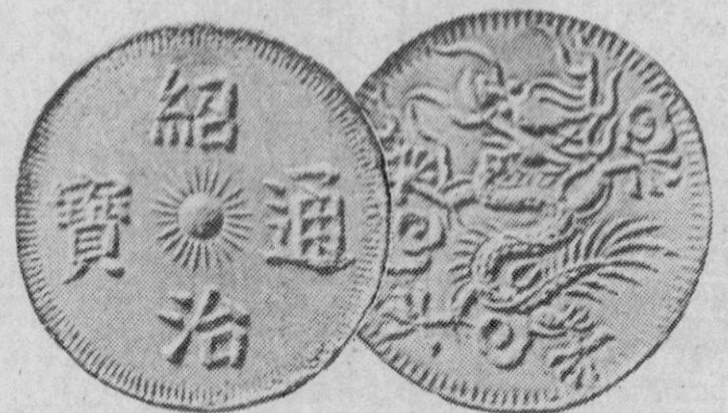

13.5 gm.
Rev: Large dragon

Sch#	Date	Emp.	VG	Fine	VF	XF
285	ND(1841-47)	Thieu Tri	350.00	400.00	475.00	550.00

Obv: Similar to Sch#285. Rev: Smaller Dragon.

Sch#	Date	Emp.	VG	Fine	VF	XF
286	ND(1841-47)	Thieu Tri	350.00	400.00	475.00	550.00

13.2 gm.

Sch#	Date	Emp.	VG	Fine	VF	XF
413	ND(1848-83)	Tu Duc	350.00	385.00	425.00	500.00

PIASTRE

GOLD, 26. - 27.5 gm.

Sch#	Date	Emp.	VG	Fine	VF	XF
207	ND (1820-40)	Minh Mang	850.00	900.00	1000.	1150.
206	(1834) Yr.15	Minh Mang	850.00	950.00	1100.	1350.
206	(1835) Yr.16	Minh Mang	850.00	950.00	1100.	1350.

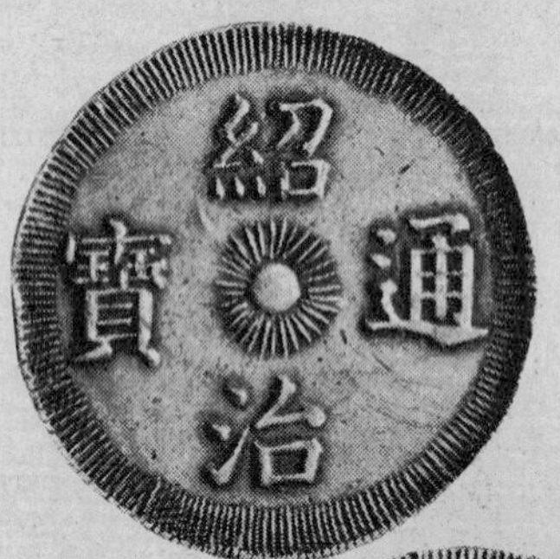

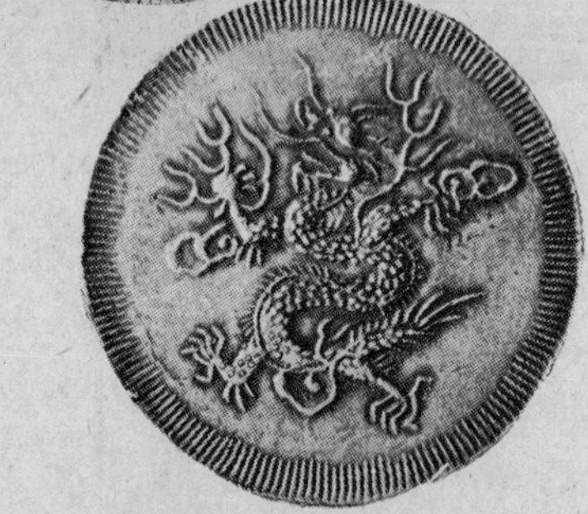

26.6 - 27 gm.

Sch#	Date	Emp.	VG	Fine	VF	XF
283	ND(1841-47)	Thieu Tri	875.00	1000.	1200.	1500.

26.75 gm.
Obv. & rev: Denticled rim.

Sch#	Date	Emp.	VG	Fine	VF	XF
278	ND(1841-47)	Thieu Tri	850.00	950.00	1100.	1350.

Rev: Dragon and no legend

Sch#	Date	Emp.	VG	Fine	VF	XF
368	ND(1848-83)	Tu Duc	875.00	1000.	1200.	1500.

26.8 gm.
Dotted rims

Sch#	Date	Emp.	VG	Fine	VF	XF
411	ND(1848-83)	Tu Duc	850.00	950.00	1100.	1350.

26.2 gm.

Sch#	Date	Emp.	VG	Fine	VF	XF
414	ND(1848-83)	Tu Duc	900.00	1100.	1250.	1500.

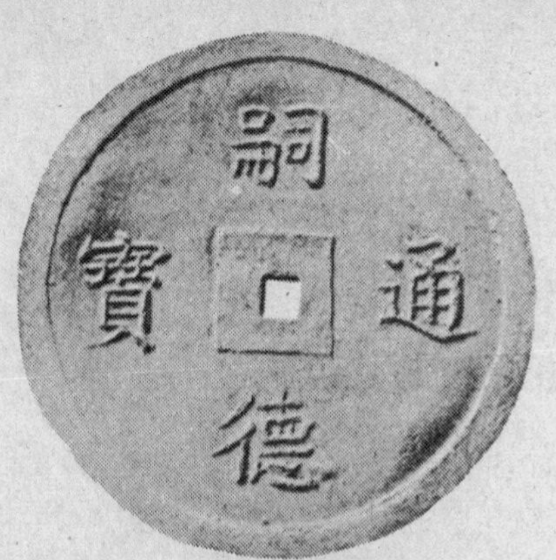

27 gm.

Sch#	Date	Emp.	VG	Fine	VF	XF
402	ND(1848-83)	Tu Duc	900.00	1100.	1250.	1500.

TIEN AND LANG SERIES

1/2 TIEN

GOLD, 1.8 gm.
Obv: Four characters. Rev: Plain.

Sch#	Date	Emp.	VG	Fine	VF	XF
257	ND(1841-47)	Thieu Tri	65.00	100.00	150.00	225.00

NOTE: Beware of gold plated copper coins.

Sch#	Date	Emp.	VG	Fine	VF	XF
424	ND(1885-88	Dong Khanh	65.00	100.00	150.00	225.00

TIEN

GOLD, 4 gm.

Sch#	Date	Emp.	VG	Fine	VF	XF
209	ND(1820-41)	Minh Mang	125.00	150.00	200.00	275.00

Rev: Flaming sun.

Sch#	Date	Emp.	VG	Fine	VF	XF
287	ND(1841-47)	Thieu Tri	125.00	165.00	225.00	300.00

3.8 gm.
Rev: Scepter and swastika.

Sch#	Date	Emp.	VG	Fine	VF	XF
288	ND(1841-47)	Thieu Tri	125.00	165.00	225.00	300.00

4.0 gm.
Rev: Guitar.

Sch#	Date	Emp.	VG	Fine	VF	XF
289	ND(1841-47)	Thieu Tri	125.00	165.00	225.00	300.00

Rev: Horn.

Sch#	Date	Emp.	VG	Fine	VF	XF
290	ND(1841-47)	Thieu Tri	125.00	165.00	225.00	300.00

3.8 gm.
Rev: Fan.

Sch#	Date	Emp.	VG	Fine	VF	XF
291	ND(1841-47)	Thieu Tri	125.00	165.00	225.00	300.00

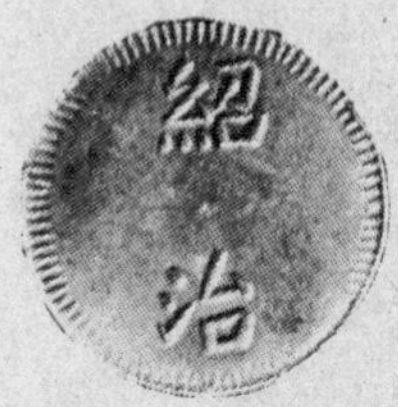

4.0 gm.
Rev: Calabash.

Sch#	Date	Emp.	VG	Fine	VF	XF
292	ND(1841-47)	Thieu Tri	125.00	165.00	225.00	300.00

4.2 gm.
Rev: Clappers.

Sch#	Date	Emp.	VG	Fine	VF	XF
293	ND(1841-47)	Thieu Tri	125.00	165.00	225.00	300.00

4.0 gm.
Rev: Books.

Sch#	Date	Emp.	VG	Fine	VF	XF
294	ND(1841-47)	Thieu Tri	125.00	165.00	225.00	300.00

3.8 gm.
Rev: TAM DA, The Three Plenties.

Sch#	Date	Emp.	VG	Fine	VF	XF
295	ND(1841-47)	Thieu Tri	125.00	165.00	225.00	300.00

Rev: NHAT NGUYEN

Sch#	Date	Emp.	VG	Fine	VF	XF
377	ND(1848-83)	Tu Duc	125.00	165.00	225.00	300.00

3.9 gm.
Obv: Four characters. Rev: NHAT NGUYEN.

Sch#	Date	Emp.	VG	Fine	VF	XF
432	ND(1888-1907)	Than Thoi	135.00	185.00	250.00	350.00

1-1/2 TIEN

GOLD, 5.6 gm.

Sch#	Date	Emp.	VG	Fine	VF	XF
406	ND(1848-83)	Tu Duc	175.00	225.00	300.00	400.00

2 TIEN

GOLD, 7.8 gm.

Sch#	Date	Emp.	VG	Fine	VF	XF
210	ND(1820-41)	Minh Mang	250.00	300.00	375.00	500.00

Obv: Four characters.

Sch#	Date	Emp.	VG	Fine	VF	XF
281	ND(1841-47)	Thieu Tri	250.00	300.00	375.00	500.00

7.3 gm.

Sch#	Date	Emp.	VG	Fine	VF	XF
378	ND(1848-83)	Tu Duc	250.00	300.00	375.00	500.00

1/4 LANG

GOLD, 9.5 - 9.85 gm.

Sch#	Date	Emp.	VG	Fine	VF	XF
375	ND(1848-83)	Tu Duc	300.00	350.00	425.00	550.00

3 TIEN

GOLD, 11 gm.

Sch# Date Emp. VG Fine VF XF
407 ND (1848-83) Tu Duc 350.00 400.00 475.00 600.00

11.3 gm.
No hole center
379 ND (1848-83) Tu Duc 350.00 400.00 475.00 600.00
NOTE: This is one of the Ten Virtues series.

10.5 gm.
Rev: Dragon, no legend.
433 ND(1888-1907)
Than Thoi 350.00 400.00 475.00 600.00

10. - 10.5 gm.
Rev: Dragon and TAM THO, The Three Longevities.
436 ND(1888-1907)
Than Thoi 350.00 400.00 475.00 600.00

4 TIEN

GOLD, 14.7 gm.
Obv: Four characters
406 ND(1848-83) Tu Duc 450.00 500.00 600.00 750.00

14.5 gm.
Rev: Two characters. Square hole in center.
409 ND(1848-83) Tu Duc 450.00 500.00 600.00 750.00

15 gm.
Rev: Four characters. No square hole in center.
380 ND(1848-83) Tu Duc 450.00 500.00 600.00 750.00
NOTE: This is one of the Ten Virtues series.

14.5 gm.
437 ND(1888-1907)
Than Thoi 475.00 550.00 675.00 850.00

5 TIEN

GOLD, 19.2 gm.
205 ND (1820-41)
Minh Mang 600.00 700.00 825.00 1000.

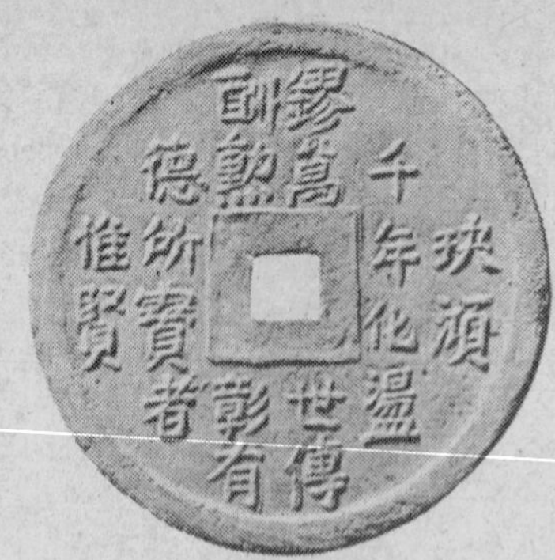

19.5 gm.
Sch# Date Emp. VG Fine VF XF
279 ND(1841-47)
Thieu Tri 650.00 750.00 900.00 1150.

18 - 20 gm.
Rev: Dragon and four characters.
374 ND(1848-83) Tu Duc 600.00 700.00 825.00 1000.

18.9 gm.
414 ND(1848-83) Tu Duc 600.00 700.00 825.00 1000.

19 gm.
405 ND(1848-83) Tu Duc 600.00 700.00 825.00 1000.

Sch# Date Emp. VG Fine VF XF
404 ND(1848-83) Tu Duc 650.00 850.00 1100. 1500.

18 gm.
Obv: Four characters.
Rev: Two characters and five bats.
410 ND (1848-83) Tu Duc 600.00 700.00 850.00 1100.

18.8 gm.
Rev: Four characters. No square hole in center.
381 ND(1848-83) Tu Duc 650.00 850.00 1100. 1400.
NOTE This is one of the Ten Virtues series.

6 TIEN

GOLD, 23 gm.
382 ND(1848-83) Tu Duc 750.00 900.00 1150. 1500.
NOTE This is one of the Ten Virtues series.

7 TIEN

GOLD, 26 gm.
383 ND(1848-83) Tu Duc 800.00 900.00 1150. 1500.
NOTE This is one of the Ten Virtues series.

8 TIEN

GOLD, 30.5 gm.
384 ND(1848-83) Tu Duc 950.00 1100. 1350. 1650.
NOTE This is one of the Ten Virtues series.

9 TIEN

GOLD, 34.2 gm.
385 ND(1848-83) Tu Duc 1100. 1250. 1450. 1750.
NOTE This is one of the Ten Virtues series.

LANG

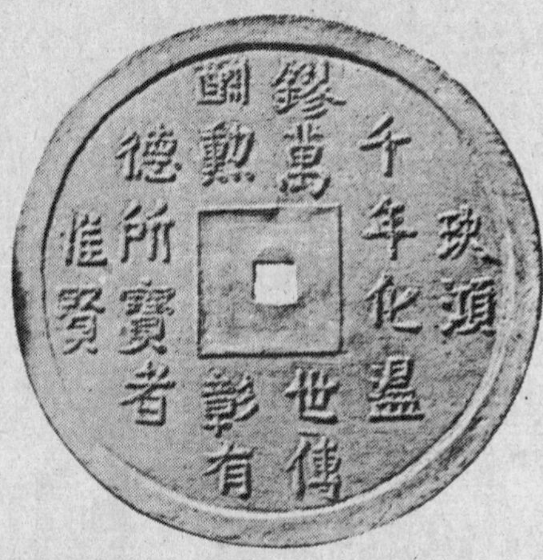

GOLD, 38 gm.
Obv: 8 characters

Sch#	Date	Emp.	VG	Fine	VF	XF
403	ND(1848-83)	Tu Duc	1200.	1350.	1500.	1850.

37. - 37.6 gm.
Rev: Dragon and two characters

Sch#	Date	Emp.	VG	Fine	VF	XF
414	ND(1848-83)	Tu Duc	1250.	1400.	1650.	2000.

37.4 grams

Sch#	Date	Emp.	VG	Fine	VF	XF
376	ND(1848-83)	Tu Duc	1200.	1350.	1500.	1850.

NOTE This is one of the Ten Virtues series.

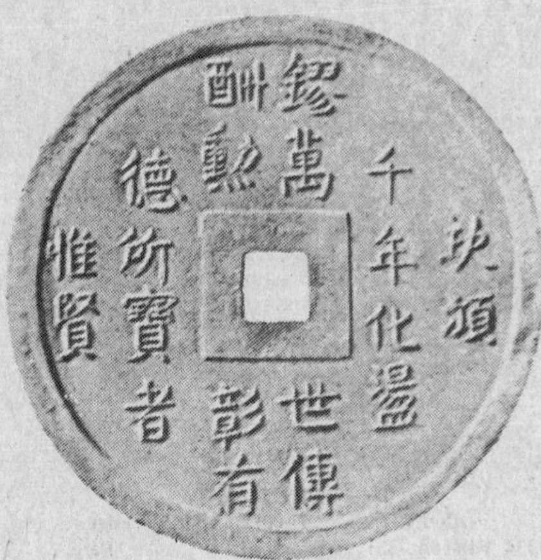

Weight unknown

Sch#	Date	Emp.	VG	Fine	VF	XF
431	ND(1888-1907)	Than Thoi	1250.	1400.	1600.	1850.

GOLD BARS

TIEN

GOLD, weight unknown

Sch#	Date	Emp.	VG	Fine	VF	XF
200	ND(1820-41)	Minh Mang	125.00	165.00	200.00	250.00

3.9 gm.
Court Treasury. Fineness (.850) inscribed on edge.

Sch#	Date	Emp.	VG	Fine	VF	XF
273	NV(1841-47)	Thieu Tri	135.00	175.00	225.00	300.00

Weight unknown
Court treasury

Sch#	Date	Emp.	VG	Fine	VF	XF
397	ND(1848-83)	Tu Duc	125.00	165.00	200.00	250.00

2 TIEN

GOLD, weight unknown

Sch#	Date	Emp.	VG	Fine	VF	XF
201	ND(1820-41)	Minh Mang	235.00	275.00	325.00	400.00

7.5 gm.
Court Treasury. Fineness (.850) on edge.

Sch#	Date	Emp.	VG	Fine	VF	XF
274	ND(1841-47)	Thieu Tri	250.00	285.00	350.00	450.00

Weight unknown
Court Treasury. Fineness (.850) on edge.

Sch#	Date	Emp.	VG	Fine	VF	XF
398	ND(1848-83)	Tu Duc	235.00	275.00	325.00	400.00

3 TIEN

GOLD, weight unknown

Sch#	Date	Emp.	VG	Fine	VF	XF
202	ND(1820-41)	Minh Mang	350.00	400.00	475.00	600.00

11.3 gm.

Sch#	Date	Emp.	VG	Fine	VF	XF
275	ND(1841-47)	Thieu Tri	350.00	425.00	500.00	650.00

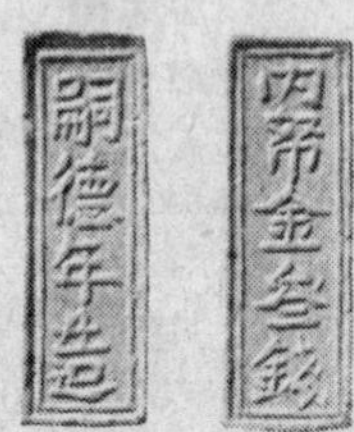

Weight unknown
Court Treasury

Sch#	Date	Emp.	VG	Fine	VF	XF
399	ND(1848-83)	Tu Duc	350.00	400.00	475.00	600.00

4 TIEN

GOLD, weight unknown

Sch#	Date	Emp.	VG	Fine	VF	XF
203	ND(1820-41)	Minh Mang	475.00	550.00	650.00	800.00

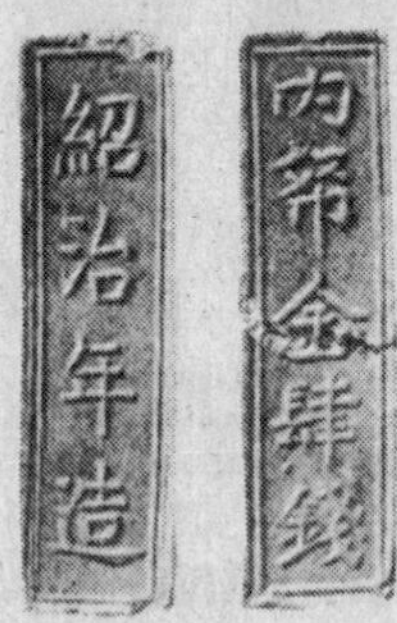

15.25 gm.
Court Treasury. Fineness (.850) on edge.

Sch#	Date	Emp.	VG	Fine	VF	XF
276	ND(1841-47)	Minh Mang	475.00	550.00	650.00	800.00

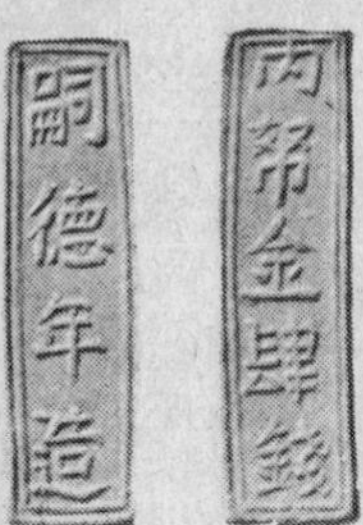

Weight unknown
Court Treasury. Fineness (.850) on edge.

Sch#	Date	Emp.	VG	Fine	VF	XF
400	ND(1848-83)	Tu Duc	475.00	550.00	650.00	800.00

5 TIEN

GOLD, weight unknown

Sch#	Date	Emp.	VG	Fine	VF	XF
204	ND(1820-41)	Minh Mang	600.00	700.00	850.00	1000.

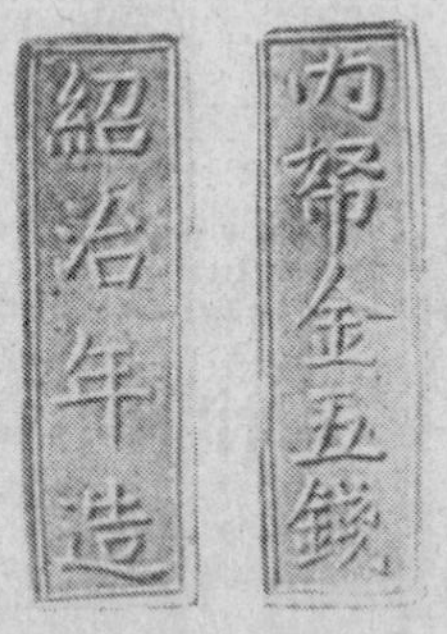

18.85 gm.
Court Treasury. Fineness (.850) on edge.

Sch#	Date	Emp.	VG	Fine	VF	XF
277	ND(1841-47)	Minh Mang	600.00	700.00	850.00	1000.

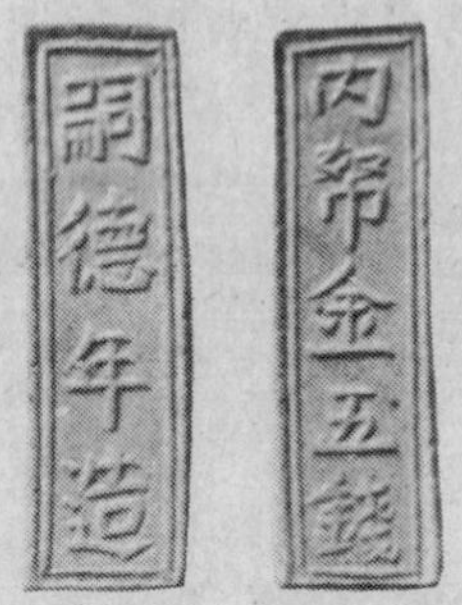

Weight unknown
Court Treasury. Fineness (.850) on edge.

Sch#	Date	Emp.	VG	Fine	VF	XF
401	ND(1848-83)	Tu Duc	600.00	700.00	850.00	1000.

LANG

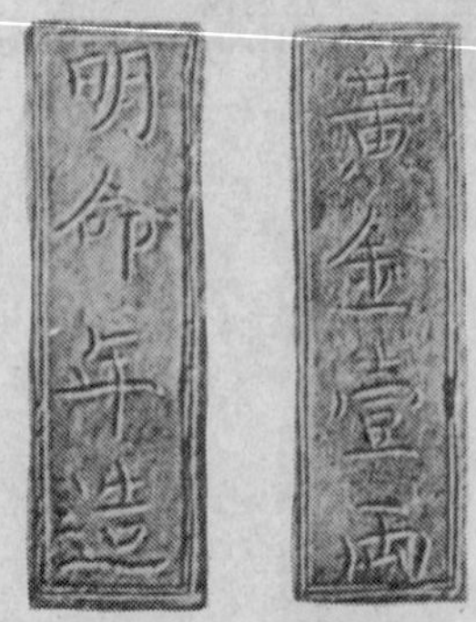

GOLD, weight unknown
Fineness (.850) on edge. Very crude.

Sch#	Date	Emp.	VG	Fine	VF	XF
190	ND(1820-41)	Minh Mang	1150.	1350.	1650.	2000.

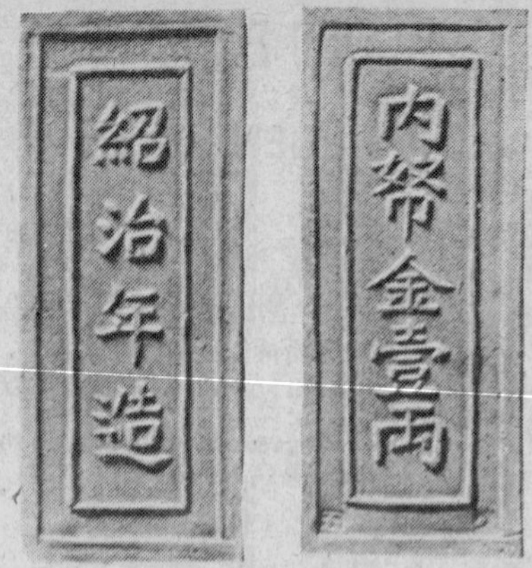

Court Treasury

Sch#	Date	Emp.	VG	Fine	VF	XF
268	ND(1841-47)	Minh Mang	1150.	1350.	1650.	2000.

Fineness (.850) on edge.

Sch#	Date	Emp.	VG	Fine	VF	XF
269	CD1843	Thieu Tri	1150.	1350.	1700.	2150.

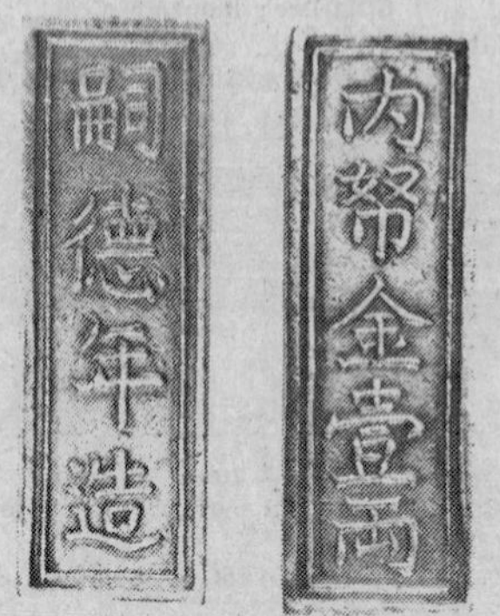

37.4 gm.
Court Treasury. Fineness (.950) on edge.

Sch#	Date	Emp.	VG	Fine	VF	XF
391	ND(1848-83)	Tu Duc	1150.	1350.	1650.	2000.

Court Treasury. Fineness (.850) on edge.

Sch#	Date	Emp.	VG	Fine	VF	XF
392	ND(1848-83)	Tu Duc	1150.	1350.	1650.	2000.

Court Treasury. Crude.

Sch#	Date	Emp.	VG	Fine	VF	XF
423	ND(1885-88)	Dong Khanh	1200.	1450.	1850.	2350.

36.1 - 36.7 gm.
Court Treasury. Fineness (.850) on edge.

Sch#	Date	Emp.	VG	Fine	VF	XF
429	ND(1888-1907)	Than Thoi	1200.	1450.	1850.	2350.

Court Treasury. Fineness (.800) on edge.

Sch#	Date	Emp.	VG	Fine	VF	XF
430	ND(1888-1907)	Than Thoi	1200.	1450.	1850.	2350.

5 LANG

GOLD, weight unknown
Fineness (.850) on edge

Sch#	Date	Emp.	VG	Fine	VF	XF
191	ND(1820-41)	Minh Mang	—	—	Rare	—

190.25 gm.
Court Treasury. Fineness (.850) on edge.

Sch#	Date	Emp.	VG	Fine	VF	XF
394	ND(1848-83)	Tu Duc	—	—	Rare	—

10 LANG

GOLD, weight unknown
Similar to Sch#173 Silver 10 Lang, Sch#173.

Court Treasury. Fineness (.850) on edge.

Sch#	Date	Emp.	VG	Fine	VF	XF
192	CD1837	Minh Mang	—	—	Rare	—

43X108mm, 382.4 gm.
Court Treasury. Fineness (.750) on edge.

Sch#	Date	Emp.	VG	Fine	VF	XF
270	ND(1841-47)	Thieu Tri	—	—	Rare	—

30x100mm, weight unknown
Fineness (.900) on edge. Rev: Four characters.
All legends engraved.

Sch#	Date	Emp.	VG	Fine	VF	XF
396	ND(1848-83)	Tu Duc	—	—	Rare	—

Bac Ninh province. Rev: Two characters (engraved) plus hallmark.

Sch#	Date	Emp.	VG	Fine	VF	XF
395	CD1849	Tu Duc	—	—	Rare	—

30 LANG

GOLD, 43X101mm, weight unknown
Obv: DAI NAM NGUYEN BAO. Fineness (.750) on edge.
Obv: and Rev: leg. framed with in ornate border.

Sch#	Date	Emp.	VG	Fine	VF	XF
193	(1840) yr.21	Thien Tri	—	—	Rare	—

40 LANG

GOLD, 43X107mm, weight unknown
Obv: DAI NAM NGUYEN BAO. Fineness (.750) on edge.
Obv: and Rev: leg. framed with in ornate border.

Sch#	Date	Emp.	VG	Fine	VF	XF
195	(1840) yr.21	Minh Mang	—	—	Rare	—

43X112mm
Obv: VIET NAM NGUYEN BAO.
Fineness (.900) on edge.

Sch#	Date	Emp.	VG	Fine	VF	XF
194	ND(1820-41)	Minh Mang	—	—	Rare	—

50 LANG

GOLD, weight unknown
Obv: 48x118mm, Viet Nam Nguyen Bao.
Fineness (.750) on edge.
Obv: and Rev: leg. framed with in ornate border.

Sch#	Date	Emp.	VG	Fine	VF	XF
196	(1837) Yr.18	Minh Mang	—	—	Rare	—

49X115mm
Obv: DAI NAM NGUYEN BAO. Fineness (.800) on edge.
Obv: and Rev: leg. framed with in ornate border.

Sch#	Date	Emp.	VG	Fine	VF	XF
197	(1838) Yr.19	Minh Mang	—	—	Rare	—

1917.35 grams
Court Treasury. Fineness (.700) on edge.

Sch#	Date	Emp.	VG	Fine	VF	XF
271	CD1843	Thieu Tri	—	—	Rare	—

100 LANG

GOLD, 59X138mm, weight unknown
Obv: VIET NAM NGUYEN BAO, small characters
Fineness (.850) on edge.
Obv: and Rev. Leg. framed within ornate border.

Sch#	Date	Emp.	VG	Fine	VF	XF
198	(1833) Yr.14	Minh Mang	—	—	Rare	—

Similar to Sch#198 but large characters on obv.

Sch#	Date	Emp.	VG	Fine	VF	XF
199	(1833)Yr. 14	Minh Mang	—	—	Rare	—

3831 gm.
Court Treasury. Fineness (.700) on edge.
Obv. and Rev. Leg. framed within ornate border.

Sch#	Date	Emp.	VG	Fine	VF	XF
272	CD1843	Thieu Tri	—	—	Rare	—

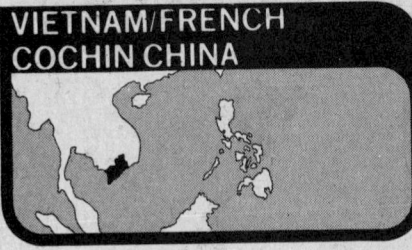

VIETNAM/FRENCH COCHIN CHINA

Cochin-China, a colony of France in Indo-China, now part of Vietnam, occupied an alluvial plain of the Mekong Delta along the South China Sea. In its colonial period, Cochin-China had an area of 24,981 sq. mi. (63,701 sq. km.) and a population of about 5 million. Capital: Saigon. The region was (and is) one of Asia's chief rice-growing areas. Fishing is also an important economic activity. French Cochin-China exported rice, fish and timber.

The region, inhabited mainly by Vietnamese, was formerly part of the ancient Khmer empire and later of the Empire of Dai Viet. It was brought under French control in 1862-67 and made a colony. The Japanese occupied the area before World War II to use as a base for the invasion of Malaya. When France regained power of the area following World War II, Cochin-China was included in the Federation of Indo-China as an autonomous republic. It was attached to Vietnam in 1949.

MINTMARKS

A - Paris
K - Bordeaux

MONETARY SYSTEM

5 Sapeques = 1 Cent
100 Cents = 1 Piastre

SAPEQUE

BRONZE
Center hole punched in France 1 Centime Y#41

Y#	Date	Mintage	Fine	VF	XF	Unc
A1	1875K	1.000	20.00	40.00	55.00	75.00

Y#	Date	Mintage	Fine	VF	XF	Unc
1	18789A	20.000	30.00	55.00	75.00	150.00

NOTE: The above coin has 2/1000 on the reverse and thus is often mistaken for a 2 Sapeque.

CENT

BRONZE

Y#	Date	Mintage	Fine	VF	XF	Unc
2	1879A	.500	7.50	16.50	40.00	100.00
	1884A	.444	12.50	40.00	75.00	125.00
	1885A	3,673	20.00	55.00	100.00	250.00
	1885A	100 pcs.	—	—	Proof	500.00

10 CENTS

2.7216 gm., .900 SILVER, .0787 oz ASW

Y#	Date	Mintage	Fine	VF	XF	Unc
3	1879A	.400	20.00	50.00	110.00	250.00
	1884A	.510	22.50	60.00	125.00	300.00
	1885A	100 pcs.	—	—	Proof	600.00

20 CENTS

5.4431 gm., .900 SILVER, .1575 oz ASW

Y#	Date	Mintage	Fine	VF	XF	Unc
4	1879A	.350	30.00	65.00	110.00	300.00
	1884A	.320	40.00	80.00	175.00	450.00
	1885A	100 pcs.	—	—	Proof	800.00

50 CENTS

13.6078 gm., .900 SILVER, .3937 oz ASW

Y#	Date	Mintage	Fine	VF	XF	Unc
5	1879A	.180	65.00	140.00	275.00	600.00
	1884A	.010	80.00	265.00	500.00	1300.
	1885A	100 pcs.	—	—	Proof	1000.

PIASTRE

27.2156 gm., .900 SILVER, .7875 oz ASW

Y#	Date	Mintage	Fine	VF	XF	Unc
6	1885A	100 pcs.	—	—	Proof	6000.

NCLT ISSUES

ESSAIS (E)

Standard metals unless otherwise noted

Y#	Date	Mintage	Identification	Issue Price	Mkt Val.
—	1878	—	1 Sapeque	—	175.00
—	—	—	1 Sapeque, as above, w/o date	—	175.00
	1879	—	1 Sapeque	—	200.00
E2	1879A	—	1 Cent	—	250.00
E3	1879A	—	10 Cents	—	350.00
E4	1879A	—	20 Cents	—	500.00
E5	1879A	—	50 Cents	—	650.00
E6	1879A	—	1 Piastre	—	6000.

Y#	Date	Mintage	Identification	Issue Price	Mkt Val.
E6	1879E	—	1 Piastre, w/o Essai	—	6000.
E6	1884A	—	1 Piastre	—	6000.

PROOF SETS

STANDARD METALS

KM#	Date	Mintage	Identification	Issue Price	Mkt. Val.
10	1885A(5)	100	Y2-6	—	9500.

VIETNAM-TONKIN

Tonkin, a former French protectorate in North Indo-China, comprises the greater part of present North Vietnam. It had an area of 44,672 sq. mi. (75,700 sq. km.) and a population of about 4 million. Capital: Hanoi. The initial value of Tonkin to France was contained in the access it afforded to the trade of China's Yunnan province.

France established a protectorate over Annam and Tonkin by the treaties of Tientsin and Hue negotiated in 1884. Tonkin was incorporated in the independent state of Vietnam (within the French Union) and upon the defeat of France by the Viet Minh became the body of North Vietnam.

MINTMARKS

(a) - Paris, privy marks only

1/600 PIASTRE

ZINC

Y#	Date	Mintage	Fine	VF	XF	Unc
1	1905 A	60.000	3.50	6.50	13.50	21.50

NOTE: Previously it had been thought that genuine specimens of this coin were 1.5mm thick while thinner pieces were counterfeits. Recent evidence however indicates that the genuine coin is about 0.8mm thick and weighs 2.5 grams while the 1.5mm thick piece is a piefort weighing about 4.8 grams.

NCLT ISSUES

ESSAIS (E)

Standard metals unless otherwise noted

Y#	Date	Mintage	Identification	Issue Price	Mkt Val.
E1	1905(a)	—	1/600 Piastre	—	135.00

PIEFORTS (P)

Double Thickness

Standard metals unless otherwise noted

Y#	Date	Mintage	Identification	Issue Price	Mkt Val.
P1	1905(a)	—	1/600 Piastre	—	350.00

VIETNAM

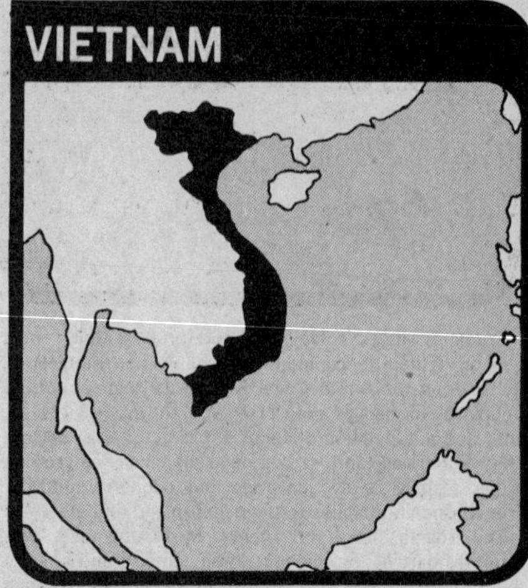

The Socialist Republic of Vietnam, located in Southeast Asia west of the South China Sea, has an area of 127,300 sq. mi. (329,707 sq. km.) and a population of 50.5 million. Capital: Hanoi. Agricultural products, coal, and mineral ores are exported.

At the start of World War II, Vietnamese Nationalists fled to China's Kwangsi provinces where Ho Chi Minh organized the Revolution to free Vietnam of French rule. The Japanese occupied Vietnam during World War II. As the end of the war drew near, they ousted the Vichy French administration and granted Vietnam independence under a puppet government headed by Bao Dai, emperor of Annam. The Bao Dai government collapsed at the end of the war, and on Sept. 2, 1945, Ho Chi Minh proclaimed the existence of an independent Vietnam consisting of Cochin-China, Annam, and Tonkin, and set up a provisional Communist goverement. France recognized the new government as a free state, but reneged and in 1949 reinstalled Bao Dai as Ruler of Vietnam and extended the regime independence within the French Union. Ho Chi Minh led a Guerrilla war in (the first Indochina war) against the French puppet state that raged on to the disastrous defeat of the French by the Viet Minh at Dien Bien Phu on May 7, 1954.

An agreement signed at Geneva on July 21, 1954, provided for a temporary division of Vietnam at the 17th parallel of latitude, between a Communist- dominated north and a U.S.-supported south. In Oct. 1955, South Vietnam deposed Bao Dai by referendum and authorized the establishment of a republic with Ngo Dinh Diem as president. The Republic of South Vietnam was proclaimed on Oct. 26, 1955, and was immediately recognized by some Western Powers.

The activities of Communists in South Vietnam led to U.S. intervention and the second Indochina war which came to a brief halt in 1973 (when a cease-fire was arranged and U.S. forces withdrawn), but didn't end until April 30, 1975, when South Vietnam surrendered unconditionally. The National Liberation front assumed power in the government of South Vietnam until July 2, 1976, when the two Vietnams were reunited as the Socialist Republic of Vietnam.

NOTE: For earlier coinage see French Indo-China.

NORTH VIETNAM

MONETARY SYSTEM

10 Xu = 1 Hao
10 Hao = 1 Dong

PROVISIONAL GOV'T

1945-1946

20 XU

ALUMINUM

Y#	Date	Mintage	Fine	VF	XF	Unc
1	1945	—	35.00	50.00	75.00	150.00

5 HAO

ALUMINUM

Value in incuse lettering

Y#	Date	Mintage	Fine	VF	XF	Unc
2	1946	—	10.00	20.00	35.00	65.00

NOTE: Common with rotated dies.

Value in raised lettering

Y#	Date	Mintage	Fine	VF	XF	Unc
2a	1946	—	4.50	8.50	13.50	20.00

DONG

ALUMINUM

Y#	Date	Mintage	Fine	VF	XF	Unc
3	1946	—	35.00	65.00	125.00	225.00

2 DONG

BRONZE

Y#	Date	Mintage	Fine	VF	XF	Unc
4	1946	—	25.00	40.00	75.00	125.00

DEMOCRATIC REPUBLIC

1954—

XU

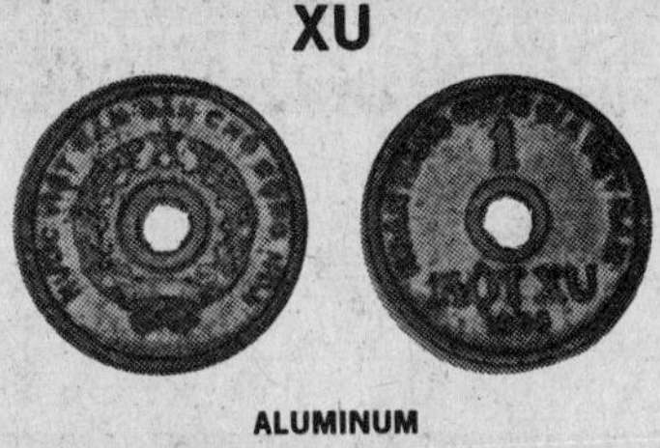

ALUMINUM

Y#	Date	Mintage	Fine	VF	XF	Unc
5	1958	—	.50	1.00	2.00	3.50

2 XU

ALUMINUM

Y#	Date	Mintage	Fine	VF	XF	Unc
6	1958	—	.50	1.00	2.00	3.50

5 XU

ALUMINUM

Y#	Date	Mintage	Fine	VF	XF	Unc
7	1958	—	.50	1.00	2.25	4.00

SOUTH VIETNAM

MINTMARKS

(a) - Paris, privy marks only

MONETARY SYSTEM

100 Xu = (Su) 1 Dong

XU

ALUMINUM

Y#	Date	Mintage	Fine	VF	XF	Unc
14	ND 1975	—	—	—	—	—

2 XU

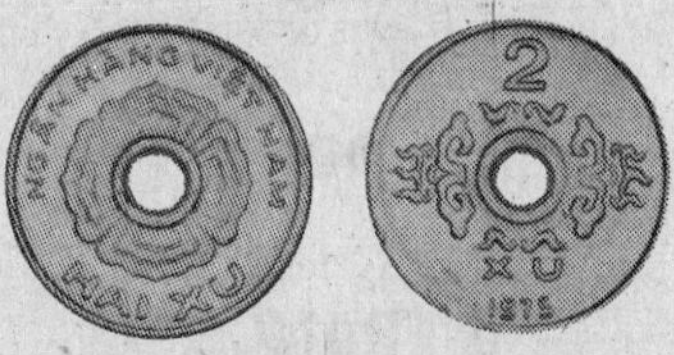

ALUMINUM

Y#	Date	Mintage	Fine	VF	XF	Unc
15	1975	—	—	—	—	—

5 XU

ALUMINUM

Y#	Date	Mintage	Fine	VF	XF	Unc
16	ND 1977	—	.10	.15	.25	.50

10 SU

ALUMINUM

Y#	Date	Mintage	Fine	VF	XF	Unc
1	1953(a)	20.000	.25	.50	.85	1.50

20 SU

ALUMINUM

Y#	Date	Mintage	Fine	VF	XF	Unc
2	1953(a)	15.000	.30	.60	1.00	2.00

50 XU

ALUMINUM

Y#	Date	Mintage	Fine	VF	XF	Unc
3	1953(a)	15.000	1.75	4.00	10.00	17.50

50 SU

ALUMINUM

Y#	Date	Mintage	Fine	VF	XF	Unc
4	1960	10.000	.25	.50	1.00	2.00

50 XU

ALUMINUM

Y#	Date	Mintage	Fine	VF	XF	Unc
6	1963	20.000	.20	.40	.75	1.75

DONG

COPPER-NICKEL

Y#	Date	Mintage	Fine	VF	XF	Unc
5	1960	105.000	.15	.25	.30	.60

Y#	Date	Mintage	Fine	VF	XF	Unc
7	1964	190.000	.15	.25	.30	.60

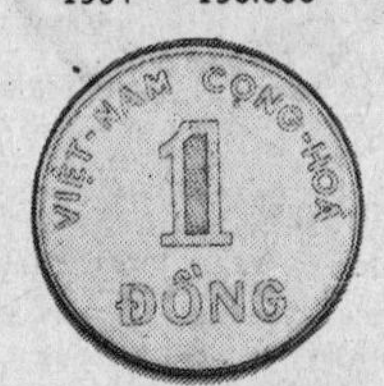

NICKEL-CLAD STEEL

Y#	Date	Mintage	Fine	VF	XF	Unc
7a	1971	—	.10	.15	.25	.50

ALUMINUM
F.A.O. Issue

Y#	Date	Mintage	Fine	VF	XF	Unc
12	1971	30.000	.10	.15	.25	.50

5 DONG

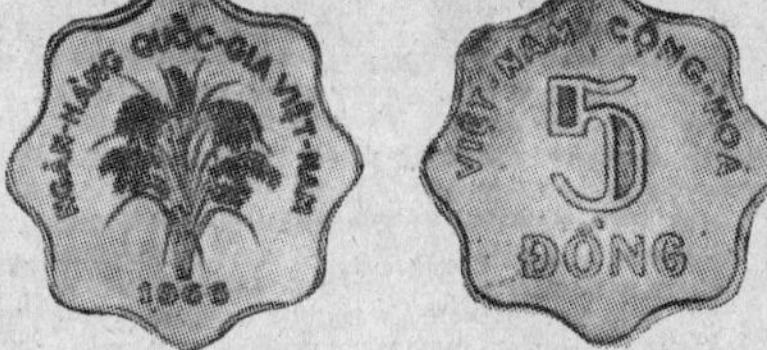

COPPER-NICKEL

Y#	Date	Mintage	Fine	VF	XF	Unc
8	1966	100.000	.15	.25	.65	1.25

NICKEL-CLAD STEEL

Y#	Date	Mintage	Fine	VF	XF	Unc
8a	1971	15.000	.15	.25	.50	.90

10 DONG

COPPER-NICKEL

Y#	Date	Mintage	Fine	VF	XF	Unc
9	1964	45.000	.20	.40	.75	1.25

NICKEL-CLAD STEEL

Y#	Date	Mintage	Fine	VF	XF	Unc
9a	1968	30.000		.15	.25	.60
	1970	50.000		.15	.25	.60

BRASS-CLAD STEEL
F.A.O. Issue

Y#	Date	Mintage	Fine	VF	XF	Unc
13	1974	30.000	.10	.15	.30	.50

20 DONG

NICKEL-CLAD STEEL

Y#	Date	Mintage	Fine	VF	XF	Unc
10	1968	—	.25	.50	1.00	2.00

F.A.O. Issue

Y#	Date	Mintage	Fine	VF	XF	Unc
11	1968	.500	.25	.50	1.00	2.00

NCLT ISSUES

ESSAIS

Standard metals unless otherwise noted

Y#	Date	Mintage	Identification	Issue Price	Mkt Val.
E1	1953(a)	1,200	10 Su	—	20.00
E2	1953(a)	1,200	20 Su	—	25.00
E3	1953(a)	1,200	50 Xu	—	30.00

PIEFORTS (P)

PIEFORTS with ESSAI (PE)

Standard metals unless otherwise noted

Y#	Date	Mintage	Identification	Issue Price	Mkt Val.
PE1	1953(a)	104	10 Su	—	90.00
PE2	1953(a)	104	20 Su	—	95.00
PE3	1953(a)	104	50 Xu	—	125.00

PATTERNS

KM#	Date	Mintage	Identification	Mkt.Val.
1	1963	—	50 Xu, Aluminum-Bronze	—
2	1963	—	50 Xu, Copper-Nickel	—

SOCIALIST REPUBLIC

1976 —

XU

ALUMINUM

Rev. leg.: NGAN HANG NHA NUOC VIET NAM.

Y#	Date	Mintage	Fine	VF	XF	Unc
8	1976	—	—	—	—	—

2 XU

ALUMINUM

Rev. leg.: NGAN HANG NHA NUOC VIET NAM.

Y#	Date	Mintage	Fine	VF	XF	Unc
9	1976	—	—	—	—	—

5 XU

ALUMINUM

Rev. leg.: NGAN HANG NHA NUOC VIET NAM.

Y#	Date	Mintage	Fine	VF	XF	Unc
10	1976	—	—	—	—	—

HAO

ALUMINUM

Y#	Date	Mintage	Fine	VF	XF	Unc
11	1976	—	—	—	—	—

2 HAO

ALUMINUM

Y#	Date	Mintage	Fine	VF	XF	Unc
12	1976	—	—	—	—	—

5 HAO

ALUMINUM

Y#	Date	Mintage	Fine	VF	XF	Unc
13	1976	—	—	—	—	—

DONG

ALUMINUM

Y#	Date	Mintage	Fine	VF	XF	Unc
14	1976	—	.10	.15	.25	.50

Listings For

VISCAYAN REPUBLIC: refer to Spain

WEST AFRICAN STS.

French West Africa, a former federation of eight French colonial territories on the northwest coast of Africa, had an area of 1,831,079 sq. mi. (4,742,495 sq. km.) and a population of about 17 million. Capital: Dakar. The constituent territories were Mauritania, Senegal, Dahomey, French Sudan, Ivory Coast, Upper Volta, Niger and French Guinea.

The members of the federation were overseas territories within the French Union until Sept. of 1958 when all but French Guinea approved the constitution of the Fifth French Republic, thereby electing to become autonomous members of the new French Community. French Guinea voted to become the fully independent Republic of Guinea. The other seven attained independence in 1960. The French West Africa territories were provided with a common currency, a practice which was continued as the monetary union of the West African States which provides a common currency to the autonomous republics of Dahomey (now Benin), Senegal, Upper Volta, Ivory Coast, Togo and Niger.

NOTE: For earlier coinage see Togo, and French West Africa.

MINTMARKS

(a) - Paris, privy marks only

MONETARY SYSTEM

100 Centimes = 1 Franc

FRANC

ALUMINUM

Y#	Date	Mintage	VF	XF	Unc
1	1961(a)	3.000	—	.10	.40
	1962(a)	2.000	—	.10	1.50
	1963(a)	4.500	—	.10	1.25
	1964(a)	5.000	—	.10	.25
	1965(a)	6.000	—	.10	.20
	1967(a)	2.500	—	.10	.20
	1970(a)	4.000	Reported, not confirmed		
	1971(a)	4.000	—	.10	.20
	1972(a)	4.000	—	.10	.20
	1973(a)	4.500	—	.10	.20
	1974(a)	—	—	.10	.20
	1975(a)	—	—	—	—
	1976(a)	8.000	—	—	—

NOTE: The 1962 and 1963 issue have the engraver general's name on the obverse.

STEEL

Y#	Date	Mintage	VF	XF	Unc
7	1976	8.000	—	—	.15
	1977	—	—	—	.15
	1978	—	—	—	—

5 FRANCS

ALUMINUM-BRONZE

Y#	Date	Mintage	VF	XF	Unc
2	1960(a)	5.000	—	.10	.35
	1962(a)	5.000	—	.10	.35
	1963(a)	—	—	.10	.35
	1965(a)	6.510	—	.10	.40
	1966(a)	6.000	Reported, not confirmed		
	1967(a)	6.010	—	.10	.30
	1968(a)	6.000	—	.10	.30
	1969(a)	8.000	—	.10	.30

Y#	Date	Mintage	VF	XF	Unc
2	1970(a)	10.005	—	.10	.30
	1971(a)	10.000	—	.10	.40
	1972(a)	5.000	—	.10	.40
	1973(a)	6.000	—	.10	.30
	1974(a)	13.326	—	.10	.30
	1975(a)	—	—	.10	.30
	1976(a)	20.010	—	.10	.30
	1977(a)	—	—	.10	.40
	1978(a)	—	—	—	—

10 FRANCS

ALUMINUM-BRONZE

Y#	Date	Mintage	VF	XF	Unc
3	1959(a)	10.000	.10	.15	.40
	1961(a)	—	.10	.15	.50
	1962(a)	—	.10	.15	.50
	1964(a)	10.000	.10	.15	.50
	1965(a)	6.000	Reported, not confirmed		
	1966(a)	6.000	.10	.15	.40
	1967(a)	3.500	.10	.15	.50
	1968(a)	6.000	.10	.15	.40
	1969(a)	7.000	.10	.15	.50
	1970(a)	7.000	.10	.15	.35
	1971(a)	8.000	.10	.15	.35
	1972(a)	5.500	.10	.15	.35
	1973(a)	3.000	.10	.15	.35
	1974(a)	10.000	.10	.15	.40
	1975(a)	—	.10	.15	.35
	1976(a)	18.000	.10	.15	.35
	1977(a)	—	—	—	—
	1978(a)	—	—	—	—

25 FRANCS

ALUMINUM-BRONZE

Y#	Date	Mintage	VF	XF	Unc
A3	1970(a)	7.000	.15	.25	.75
	1971(a)	7.000	.15	.25	1.00
	1972(a)	2.000	.25	.50	1.50
	1975(a)	—	.15	.25	.75
	1976(a)	3.365	—	—	—
	F.A.O. Issue				
7	1980a	—	—	—	—

50 FRANCS

COPPER-NICKEL
F.A.O. Issue

Y#	Date	Mintage	VF	XF	Unc
5	1972(a)	20.000	.35	.50	1.00
	1974(a)	3.000	.40	.60	1.25
	1975(a)	9.000	.35	.50	.75
	1976(a)	6.002	.35	.50	.75
	1978(a)	—	—	—	—

100 FRANCS

NICKEL

Y#	Date	Mintage	VF	XF	Unc
4	1967(a)	—	1.00	1.25	1.50
	1968(a)	25.000	1.00	1.25	1.50
	1969(a)	25.000	1.00	1.25	1.50
	1970(a)	4.510	.80	.90	1.00
	1971(a)	12.000	.50	.75	1.00
	1972(a)	5.000	.60	.75	1.00
	1973(a)	5.000	.60	.75	1.00
	1974(a)	8.500	.60	.75	1.00
	1975(a)	—	.60	.75	1.00
	1976(a)	11.575	.60	.75	1.00
	1977(a)	—	—	—	—
	1978(a)	—	—	—	—

500 FRANCS

25.0000 gm., .900 SILVER, .7234 oz ASW
10th Anniversary of Monetary Union

Y#	Date	Mintage	VF	XF	Unc
6	1972(a)	.100	—	30.00	50.00

NCLT ISSUES

ESSAIS (E)

Standard metals unless otherwise noted

Y#	Date	Mintage	Identification	Issue Price	Mkt Val.
E3	1959	—	10 Francs	—	25.00
E2	1960	—	5 Francs	—	25.00
E1	1961(a)	—	1 Franc	—	17.50
E4	1967A	—	100 Francs	—	21.50
EA3	1970A	—	25 Francs	—	18.50
E5	1972A	—	50 Francs	—	20.00
E6	1972(a)	2,000	500 Francs	5.00	100.00
E7	1976	—	1 Franc	—	18.50

Listings For

WEST GERMANY: refer to Germany

WEST IRIAN: refer to Indonesia

WEST NEW GUINEA: refer to Indonesia

WESTERN SAMOA

The Independent State of Western Samoa, located in the Pacific Ocean 1,600 miles (2,574 km.) northeast of New Zealand, has an area of 1,133 sq. mi. (2,934 sq. km.) and a population of 155,000. Capital: Apia. The economy is based on agriculture, fishing and tourism. Copra, cocoa and bananas are exported.

The Samoan group of islands was discovered by Dutch navigator Jacob Roggeveen in 1772. Great Britain, the United States and Germany established consular representation at Apia in 1847, 1853 and 1861 respectively. The conflicting interests of the three powers produced the Berlin agreement of 1889 which declared Samoa neutral and had the effect of establishing a tripartite protectorate over the islands. A further agreement, 1899, recognized the rights of the United States in those islands east of 171 deg. west longitude (American Samoa) and of Germany in the other islands (Western Samoa). New Zealand occupied Western Samoa at the start of World War I and administered it as a League of Nations mandate and U. N. trusteeship until Jan. 1, 1962, when it became an independent state.

Western Samoa is a member of the Commonwealth of Nations. The Chief Executive is Chief of State. The prime minister is the Head of Government. The present Head of State, Malietoa Tanumafili II, holds his position for life. Future Heads of State will be elected by the Legislative Assembly for five-year terms.

Western Samoa, which had used New Zealand coinage, converted to a decimal coinage in 1967.

RULERS

New Zealand, 1914-1962
Malietoa Tanumafili II, 1962 -

MONETARY SYSTEM

100 Sene = 1 Tala

SENE

BRONZE

Y#	Date	Mintage	VF	XF	Unc
1	1967	.915	.10	.15	.20
	1967	.015	—	Proof	1.75
13	1974	1.000	—	.10	.15
	.925 SILVER				
13a	1974	5,578	—	Proof	4.50

2 SENE

BRONZE

Y#	Date	Mintage	VF	XF	Unc
2	1967	.465	.10	.15	.25
	1967	.015	—	Proof	2.00

Y#	Date	Mintage	VF	XF	Unc
14	1974	1.140	.10	.15	.20
		.925 SILVER			
14a	1974	5,578	—	Proof	5.50

5 SENE

Y#	Date	Mintage	VF	XF	Unc
		COPPER-NICKEL			
3	1967	.495	.15	.25	.35
	1967	.015	—	Proof	2.25
15	1974	.856	—	—	.30
		.925 SILVER			
15a	1974	5,578	—	Proof	6.50

10 SENE

Y#	Date	Mintage	VF	XF	Unc
		COPPER-NICKEL			
4	1967	.400	.20	.35	.50
	1967	.015	—	Proof	2.50

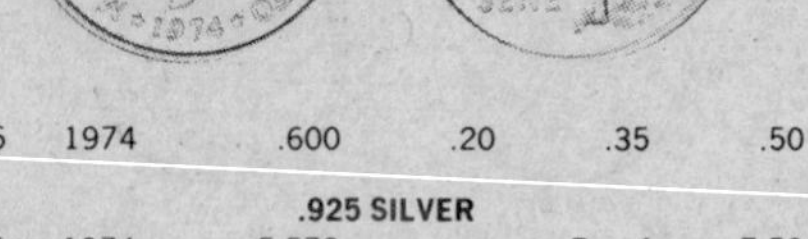

Y#	Date	Mintage	VF	XF	Unc
16	1974	.600	.20	.35	.50
		.925 SILVER			
16a	1974	5,578	—	Proof	7.50

20 SENE

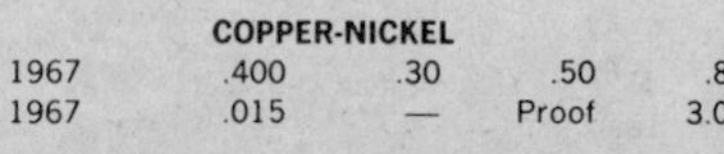

Y#	Date	Mintage	VF	XF	Unc
		COPPER-NICKEL			
5	1967	.400	.30	.50	.85
	1967	.015	—	Proof	3.00

Y#	Date	Mintage	VF	XF	Unc
17	1974	.400	.30	.50	.85
		.925 SILVER			
17a	1974	5,578	—	Proof	8.50

50 SENE

Y#	Date	Mintage	VF	XF	Unc
		COPPER-NICKEL			
6	1967	.080	.75	1.25	1.75
	1967	.015	—	Proof	3.50
18	1974	.050	.75	1.25	1.75
		.925 SILVER			
18a	1974	5,578	—	Proof	10.00

TALA

COPPER-NICKEL
Obv: Similar to 50 Sene, Y#6.

Y#	Date	Mintage	VF	XF	Unc
7	1967	.020	1.75	2.50	4.00
	1967	.015	—	Proof	10.00

75th Anniversary Death of Robert Louis Stevenson

Y#	Date	Mintage	VF	XF	Unc
8	1969	.025	2.00	3.00	6.50
	1969	1,500	—	Proof	135.00

200th Anniversary Captain Cook Voyages
Obv: Similar to Y#8

Y#	Date	Mintage	VF	XF	Unc
9	1970	.032	2.00	2.50	6.00
	1970	3,000	—	Proof	60.00

Visit Of Pope Paul VI
Obv: Similar to Y#8

Y#	Date	Mintage	VF	XF	Unc
10	1970	.035	2.00	3.00	6.00
	1970	3,000	—	Proof	50.00

Roggeveen's Pacific Voyage
Obv: Similar to Y#8

Y#	Date	Mintage	VF	XF	Unc
11	1972	.035	2.00	3.00	8.00
	1972	3,000	—	Proof	40.00

10th British Commonwealth Games
Obv: Similar to Y#8

Y#	Date	Mintage	VF	XF	Unc
12	1974	.040	2.00	2.50	5.00
		27.2500 gm., .925 SILVER, .8104 oz ASW			
12a	1974	1,500	—	Proof	175.00

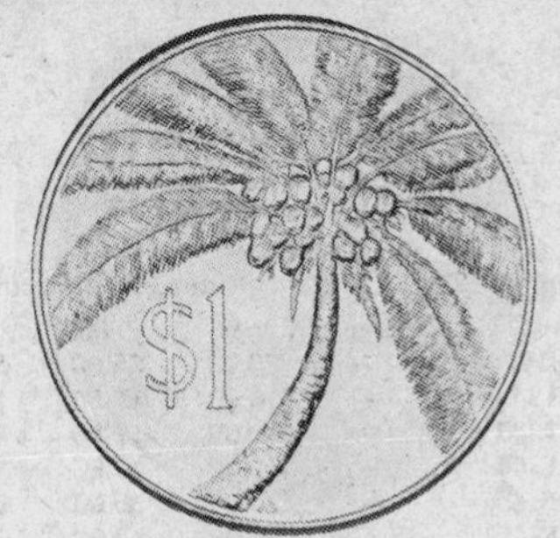

COPPER-NICKEL
Obv: Similar to 50 Sene, Y#18.

Y#	Date	Mintage	VF	XF	Unc
19	1974	.024	1.75	2.25	4.50

27.2500 gm., .925 SILVER, .8104 oz ASW

Y#	Date	Mintage	VF	XF	Unc
19a	1974	.011	—	Proof	27.50

COPPER-NICKEL
U.S. Bicentennial

Y#	Date	Mintage	VF	XF	Unc
20	1976	.040	2.00	2.50	5.00

27.2500 gm., .925 SILVER, .8104 oz ASW

Y#	Date	Mintage	VF	XF	Unc
20a	1976	4,127	—	Proof	60.00

COPPER-NICKEL
Montreal Olympics
Obv: Similar to Y#8.

Y#	Date	Mintage	VF	XF	Unc
22	1976	.040	2.00	2.50	5.00

27.2500 gm., .925 SILVER, .8104 oz ASW

Y#	Date	Mintage	VF	XF	Unc
22a	1976	6,000	—	Proof	60.00

COPPER-NICKEL
Queen's Silver Jubilee
Obv: Similar to Y#8.

Y#	Date	Mintage	VF	XF	Unc
24	1977	.025	2.00	3.00	6.00

27.2500 gm., .925 SILVER, .8104 oz ASW

Y#	Date	Mintage	VF	XF	Unc
24a	1977	6,000	—	Proof	60.00

COPPER-NICKEL
Lindbergh's New York to Paris Flight
Obv: Similar to Y#8.

Y#	Date	Mintage	VF	XF	Unc
26	1977	.020	2.00	3.00	6.00

27.2500 gm., .925 SILVER, .8104 oz ASW

Y#	Date	Mintage	VF	XF	Unc
26a	1977	5,000	—	—	50.00

COPPER-NICKEL
50th Anniversary First Transpacific Flight
Obv: Similar to Y#8.

Y#	Date	Mintage	VF	XF	Unc
28	1978	.020	1.75	2.50	8.00

27.2500 gm., .925 SILVER, .8104 oz ASW

Y#	Date	Mintage	VF	XF	Unc
28a	1978	5,000	—	—	60.00

COPPER-NICKEL
XI Commonwealth Games
Obv: Similar to Y#8.

Y#	Date	Mintage	VF	XF	Unc
30	1978	.020	2.00	3.00	6.00

27.2500 gm., .925 SILVER, .8104 oz ASW

Y#	Date	Mintage	VF	XF	Unc
30a	1978	5,000	—	Proof	45.00

COPPER-NICKEL
Bicentenary Of The Death Of Cook
Obv: Similar To Y#8

Y#	Date	Mintage	VF	XF	Unc
32	1979	5,000	—	—	5.00

27.2500 gm., .500 SILVER, .4381 oz ASW

Y#	Date	Mintage	VF	XF	Unc
32a	1979	3,000	—	—	—

10 TALA

27.2500 gm., .500 SILVER, .4381 oz ASW
Bicentenary Of The Death Of Cook

Y#	Date	Mintage	VF	XF	Unc
33	1979	3,000	—	—	20.00

27.2500 gm., .925 SILVER, .8104 oz ASW

Y#	Date	Mintage	VF	XF	Unc
33a	1979	5,000	—	Proof	45.00

100 TALA

15.5500 gm., .917 GOLD, .GOLD, .4583 oz AGW
U.S. Bicentennial

Y#	Date	Mintage	VF	XF	Unc
21	1976	2,000	— Proof only		300.00

Montreal Olympics

Y#	Date	Mintage	VF	XF	Unc
23	1976	2,500	— Proof only		300.00

Queen's Silver Jubilee

Y#	Date	Mintage	VF	XF	Unc
25	1977	2,500	— Proof only		300.00

Lindbergh's New York to Paris Flight

Y#	Date	Mintage	VF	XF	Unc
27	1977	1,000	— Proof only		300.00

50th Anniversary Transpacific Flight

Y#	Date	Mintage	VF	XF	Unc
29	1978	1,500	— Proof only		300.00

XI Commonwealth Games

Y#	Date	Mintage	VF	XF	Unc
31	1978	1,000	— Proof only		300.00

Bicentenary of the Death of Captain James Cook

Y#	Date	Mintage	VF	XF	Unc
34	1979	1,000	—	Proof only	300.00

NCLT ISSUES

MINT SETS

KM#	Date	Mintage	Identification	Issue Price	Mkt. Val.
S1	1967(6)	—	Y1-6	—	—
S2	1974(7)	10,740	Y13-19	5.30	6.50

PROOF SETS

STANDARD METALS

KM#	Date	Mintage	Identification	Issue Price	Mkt. Val.
101	1967(7)	15,000	Y1-7	10.00	15.00
102	1974(7)	5,578	Y13a-19a	53.00	70.00

YEMEN ARAB REPUBLIC

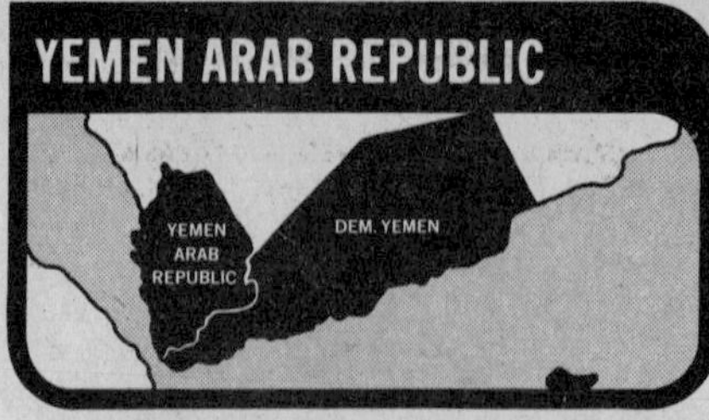

The Yemen Arab Republic, located in the southwestern corner of the Arabian Peninsula, has an area of 75,000 sq. mi. (195,000 sq. km.) and a population of 6.4 million. Capital: San'a. The industries of Yemen, one of the world's poorest countries, are agriculture and local handicrafts. Qat (a mildly narcotic leaf), coffee, cotton and rock salt are exported.

One of the oldest centers of civilization in the Near East, Yemen was once part of the Minaean Kingdom and of the ancient Kingdom of Sheba, after which it was captured successively by Egyptians, Ethiopians and Romans. It was converted to the Moslem religion in 628 A.D. and administered as a caliphate until 1538, when it came under Turkish occupation which was maintained until 1918 when autonomy was achieved through revolution.

Provoked by the harsh rule of Imam Mohammed al-Badr, last ruler of the Kingdom of Mutawwakkilite, the National Liberation Front seized control of the government on Sept. 27, 1962. Badr fled to Saudi Arabia, and to maintain a pretense of sovereignty issued a coinage for the Royalist government in exile.

RULERS

Imam Yahya, AH1322-67/AD1904-48
Imam Ahmad, AH1367-82/AD1948-62
Imam al-Badr, AH1382-88/AD1962-68
(mostly in exile)

MINT: San'a

MONETARY SYSTEM

160 Zalat = 80 Halala =
40 Buqsha = 1 Riyal

NOTE: The Riyal was called an IMADI RIYAL during the reign of Imam Yahya, and an AHMADI RIYAL during the reign of Imam Ahmad. Except for 1/2 Halala, which bears no indication of value, all of the Mutawakkilite coins bear the denomination expressed as a fraction of the Riyal.

DATING: All coins of Imam Yahya have accession date AH 1322 on obverse and actual date of issue on reverse. All coins of Imam Ahmad bear accession date AH 1367 on obverse and actual date on reverse.

NOTE: Coins struck during the Mutawakkilite kingdom, as well as the early issues of the Republic (Y-20 through Y-A25 and Y32), were struck at the mint in San'a. The San'a Mint was essentially a medieval mint, using hand-cut dies and crudely machined blanks. There is a large amount of variation from one die to the next, and literally hundreds of subtypes could be identified. Types are divided only when there are changes in the inscriptions, or major variations in the basic type, such as the use of open and closed crescents in which the ruler's name was written.

MUTAWWAKKILITE KINGDOM

1/2 HALALA (ZALAT)

BRONZE
Accession Date AH1322

Y#	Date	Mintage	VG	Fine	VF
B1	ND	—	60.00	85.00	140.00

Dated accessionally on obverse. Probably struck about 1925. Dies may have been prepared in Italy.

Obv: Crescent. Denomination not on coin.

Y#	Date	Mintage	VG	Fine	VF
1a.1	AH1341	—	Reported, not confirmed		
	1342	—	50.00	80.00	125.00

Obv: W/o crescent. Rev: Date in margin.

Y#	Date	Mintage	VG	Fine	VF
1a.2	AH1342	—	50.00	80.00	125.00

Obv: Similar to Y#1a.1. Rev: Date moved within circle.

Y#	Date	Mintage	VG	Fine	VF
1a.3	AH1340	—	20.00	35.00	50.00
	1342	—	10.00	17.50	27.50
	1343	—	10.00	17.50	27.50
	1344	—	10.00	17.50	27.50
	1345	—	20.00	35.00	50.00
	1346	—	10.00	17.50	27.50

1/80 RIYAL (=1 HALALA)

BRONZE (Yellow or Red)
Accession Date AH1322

Y#	Date	Mintage	VG	Fine	VF
2.1	AH1322 (accessional data only; w/o actual date)	—	25.00	50.00	75.00

Rev: Denomination added w/o mint name.

Y#	Date	Mintage	VG	Fine	VF
2.2	AH1330	—	8.50	15.00	25.00
	1332	—	7.50	12.50	20.00
	1333	—	7.50	12.50	20.00
	1338	—	10.00	18.00	25.00
	ND Mule	—	10.00	17.50	30.00

NOTE: The number of stars on the reverse as well as the exact arrangement of the legend, varies within each year. The mule consists of 2 obverses.

Obv: W/ 'RABB AL-ALAMIN'.
Rev: 'STRUCK AT SAN'A added.

Y#	Date	Mintage	VG	Fine	VF
2.3	AH1340	—	7.50	12.50	20.00
	1341	—	7.50	12.50	20.00

Obv: Without RABB AL-ALAMIN.
Rev: SANA below date.

Y#	Date	Mintage	VG	Fine	VF
2.4	AH1341	—	12.00	20.00	35.00
	1342	—	12.00	20.00	35.00

Obv: RABB AL-ALAMIN.

Y#	Date	Mintage	VG	Fine	VF
2.5	AH1341	—	3.00	5.50	10.00
	1342	—	3.00	5.50	10.00
	1343	—	3.00	5.50	10.00
	1344	—	3.00	5.50	10.00
	1345	—	3.00	5.50	10.00
	1346	—	3.00	5.50	10.00
	1347	—	3.00	5.50	10.00
	1348	—	3.00	5.50	10.00
	1349	—	3.00	5.50	10.00
	1350	—	3.00	5.50	10.00
	1351	—	4.00	7.00	12.50
	1352	—	4.00	7.00	12.50
	1353	—	4.00	7.00	12.50
	1358	—	7.50	12.50	22.50
	1359	—	5.00	9.00	14.00
	1360	—	5.00	9.00	14.00
	1361	—	6.00	10.00	17.50

NOTE: Number of stars on reverse varies. Some examples of 1346 show the 6 reengraved over low 6.

BRONZE
Accession Date AH1367

Y#	Date	Mintage	Fine	VF	XF
11	AH1368	—	.75	1.50	2.25
	1371	—	.60	1.00	1.65
	1372	—	.60	1.00	1.65
	1373	—	.60	1.00	1.65
	1374	—	.60	1.00	1.65
	1275 (error for 1375)				
	1382	—	10.00	17.50	30.00
		—	.50	.90	1.50
	1386/76	—	.50	.90	1.50
	1378	—	.60	1.00	1.65
	1379	—	1.00	1.75	2.75
	1380/79	—	1.00	1.75	2.75
	1380/9	—	1.00	1.75	2.75
	1381	—	.40	.75	1.10
	1381/80/78	—	.85	1.50	2.50
	1381/79	—	.85	1.50	2.50

NOTE: There is a variation in the number of stars on reverse, as follows AH1368 - 8 stars AH1371-74 and some AH1381 not overdate have 7 stars AH1375-1381 including some AH1381 not overdate, and all AH1381 overdates have 8 Stars.

NOTE: Formerly listed AH1386 is now listed as AH1386/76.

ALUMINUM

Y#	Date	Mintage	Fine	VF	XF
11a	AH1374	—	.50	1.25	2.00
	1375	—	Reported, Not Confirmed		
	1376	—	.50	1.25	2.00
	1377	—	1.25	2.00	3.25
	1378	—	.50	.65	1.00
	1379/5	—	5.00	8.00	12.50
	1379/8	—	3.00	5.00	7.50
	1379	—	3.00	5.00	7.50

NOTE: AH1374 has 7 stars, the rest have 8 stars on reverse.

Y#	Date	Mintage	Fine	VF	XF
18	AH1367 (accessional year only)				
		—	.25	.35	.60

NOTE: Y#18 and 19 were struck privately in Lebanon.

1/40 RIYAL (= 1 BUQSHA)

BRONZE (Yellow or Red)
Accession Date AH1322
Obv: W/o 'RABB AL ALAMIN'.

Y#	Date	Mintage	VG	Fine	VF
3.1	AH1341	—	6.00	10.00	16.50

Obv: W/ 'RABB AL ALAMIN' added.

Y#	Date	Mintage	VG	Fine	VF
3.2	AH1342	—	3.00	5.00	10.00
	1343	—	3.00	5.00	10.00
	1344	—	8.00	15.00	25.00
	1345	—	3.00	5.00	10.00
	1349	—	1.50	3.50	6.50
	1353	—	Reported, not confirmed		
	1358	—	2.00	4.00	7.50
	1359	—	2.00	4.00	7.50
3.2	1360	—	2.00	4.00	7.50
	1361/0	—	4.50	9.00	14.50
	1362/0	—	2.50	5.00	10.00
	1362	—	1.50	3.50	6.50
	1363	—	1.50	3.50	6.50
	1364	—	1.50	3.50	6.50
	1365/4	—	1.50	3.50	6.50
	1366	—	1.50	3.50	6.50
	1367	—	5.00	10.00	17.50

BRONZE
Accession Date AH1367

Y#	Date	Mintage	Fine	VF	XF
12	AH1368	—	1.00	2.00	3.00
	1369	—	1.25	2.50	3.50
	1370	—	.75	1.25	2.00
	1371	—	.75	1.25	2.00
	1372	—	.75	1.25	2.00
	1373	—	.75	1.25	2.00
	1374	—	.75	1.25	2.00
	1375/4	—	1.00	1.75	2.75
	1375	—	.75	1.25	2.00
	1376	—	1.00	1.75	2.75
	1377/6	—	.75	1.25	2.00
	1379/7	—	.75	1.25	2.00
	1380/79	—	1.50	2.75	4.50

ALUMINUM

Y#	Date	Mintage	Fine	VF	XF
12a	AH1374	—	1.00	1.50	2.50
	1375	—	1.00	1.50	2.50
	1376	—	1.00	1.50	2.50
	1377/6	—	1.75	3.25	6.00
	1377	—	3.50	6.00	10.00

NOTE: AH1377 plain date has 1376 instead of 1367 on obverse.

Y#	Date	Mintage	Fine	VF	XF
19	AH1367 (accessional date)				
		—	.25	.35	.60

1/20 IMADI RIYAL

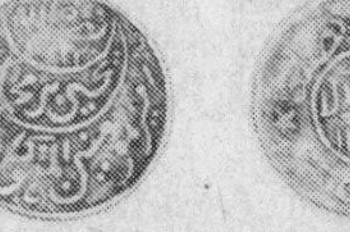

SILVER
Accession Date AH1322
Obv: Narrow crescent. Rev W/o SANA.

Y#	Date	Mintage	VG	Fine	VF
4.1	AH1337	—	12.50	20.00	35.00
	1339	—	10.00	17.50	30.00
	1340	—	10.00	17.50	30.00

NOTE: The number of stars on reverse varies.

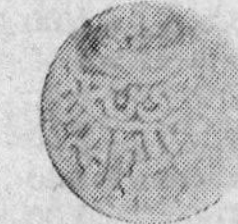

Rev: SANA below date.

Y#	Date	Mintage	VG	Fine	VF
4.2	AH1341	—	17.50	30.00	45.00

Obv: Redesigned; wide crescent.

Y#	Date	Mintage	VG	Fine	VF
4.3	AH1342	—	5.00	10.00	18.50
	1343	—	3.50	7.00	12.50
	1344	—	3.50	7.00	12.50
	1345	—	3.50	7.00	12.50
	1347	—	4.00	8.50	15.00
	1348	—	3.50	7.00	12.50
	1349	—	3.50	7.00	12.50
	1350	—	3.50	7.00	12.50
	1351	—	4.00	8.50	15.00
	1352	—	4.50	9.00	16.50
	1353	—	7.50	12.50	22.50
	1358	—	3.50	7.00	12.50
	1359	—	3.50	7.00	12.50
	1362/59	—	7.50	12.50	22.50
	1363	—	6.00	11.00	20.00
	1364/40	—	4.00	8.00	14.00
	1364	—	4.00	8.00	14.00
	1365	—	4.00	8.00	14.00
	1366/4	—	4.00	8.00	14.00
	1366	—	4.00	8.00	14.00

NOTE: Y#4.1, 4.2 and 4.3 are all without RABB AL-ALAMIN on obverse.

1/16 AHMADI RIYAL

SILVER
Accession Date AH1367
Obv: W/'AMIR AL-MU'MININ'.

Y#	Date	Mintage	Fine	VF	XF
13	AH1367	—	1.50	3.00	5.00
	1368	—	1.50	3.00	5.00
	1371	—	1.50	3.00	5.00
	1374	—	1.50	3.00	5.00

NOTE: Size of inner circle on reverse varies.

Obv: W/ 'AL-AMIR'.

Y#	Date	Mintage	Fine	VF	XF
13.1	AH1374	—	7.50	13.50	22.50

1/10 IMADI RIYAL

SILVER
Accession Date AH1322
Obv: Narrow crescent, with 'RABB al ALAMIN'.
Rev: No SANA.

Y#	Date	Mintage	VG	Fine	VF
5.1	AH1337	—	15.00	25.00	40.00

Obv: W/o 'RABB AL-ALAMIN'.

Y#	Date	Mintage	VG	Fine	VF
5.2	AH1339	—	8.50	15.00	25.00
	1340	—	8.50	15.00	25.00

Rev: SANA below date.

Y#	Date	Mintage	VG	Fine	VF
5.3	AH1341	—	12.50	20.00	30.00

Rev: SANA above date.

Y#	Date	Mintage	VG	Fine	VF
5.4	AH1342	—	12.50	20.00	30.00

Obv: w/o 'RABB AL-ALAMIN'.

Y#	Date	Mintage	VG	Fine	VF
5.5	AH1342	—	3.00	5.00	10.00
	1343	—	3.00	5.00	10.00
	1344	—	3.00	5.00	10.00
	1345	—	3.00	5.00	10.00
	1347	—	3.00	5.00	10.00
	1348	—	3.00	5.00	10.00
	1349	—	2.50	4.50	9.00
	1351	—	5.00	7.50	12.50
	1352	—	5.00	7.50	12.50
	1358/49	—	2.50	4.50	9.00
	1358	—	3.00	5.00	10.00
	1359/49	—	3.00	5.00	10.00
	1363	—	2.50	4.50	9.00
	1364/3	—	2.50	4.50	9.00
	1364	—	2.50	4.50	9.00
	1365	—	2.50	4.50	9.00
	1366/5	—	2.50	4.50	9.00

NOTE: Number of stars on reverse and arrangement of obverse inscription varies considerably.

Accession Date AH1367

Y#	Date	Mintage	VG	Fine	VF
A14	AH1370	—	—	—	—

1/8 IMADI RIYAL

SILVER
Accession Date AH1322
Rev: THUMN in place of USHR below date.

Y#	Date	Mintage	VG	Fine	VF
8	AH1339	—	100.00	150.00	225.00

1/8 AHMADI RIYAL

SILVER
Accession Date AH1367
Pentagonal planchet

Y#	Date	Mintage	Fine	VF	XF
14	AH1367	—	3.00	4.50	7.50
	1368	—	3.00	4.50	7.50
	1370	—	3.00	4.50	7.50
	1371	—	2.00	3.50	6.00
	1372	—	2.00	3.50	6.00
	1373	—	2.00	3.50	6.00
	1374	—	2.00	3.50	6.00
	1379	—	2.50	4.00	6.50
	1380	—	2.50	4.00	6.50

NOTE: Size of inner circle on reverse varies.

Hexagonal planchet

Y#	Date	Mintage	Fine	VF	XF
14a	AH1368	—	100.00	150.00	225.00

1/4 IMADI RIYAL

SILVER
Accession Date AH1322
Obv: Closed crescent. Rev: SANA below date.

Y#	Date	Mintage	VG	Fine	VF
6.1	AH1341	—	12.50	20.00	30.00
	1342	—	15.00	25.00	40.00

Obv: Open crescent with 'RABB AL-ALAMIN'.
Rev: SANA above date.

Y#	Date	Mintage	VG	Fine	VF
6.2	AH1342	—	15.00	25.00	40.00

Obv: Crescents and stars in border.

Y#	Date	Mintage	VG	Fine	VF
6.3	AH1342	—	12.50	20.00	32.50

Obv: With crescents only in border.

Y#	Date	Mintage	VG	Fine	VF
6.4	AH1342	—	12.50	20.00	32.50
	1343	—	10.00	18.00	27.50

NOTE: Number of crescents on obverse varies.

Rev: Redesigned w/ date moved to margin.

Y#	Date	Mintage	VG	Fine	VF
10	AH1343	—	7.50	12.50	20.00
	1344	—	4.25	6.50	12.50
	1345	—	4.25	6.50	12.50
	1349	—	Reported, not confirmed		
	1351	—	5.00	8.00	15.00
	1352	—	5.00	8.00	15.00
	1358	—	3.50	5.50	12.00
	1359	—	3.50	5.50	12.00
	1363	—	3.50	5.00	10.00
	1364/3	—	3.50	5.50	12.00
	1364	—	3.50	5.00	10.00
	1365/4	—	3.50	5.00	10.00
	1365	—	3.50	5.00	10.00
	1366	—	3.50	5.00	10.00

NOTE: The size of the reverse inner circle varies. Also, the number of crescents on obverse varies from 12 to 16.

1/4 AHMADI RIYAL

SILVER
Accession Date AH1367

Y#	Date	Mintage	Fine	VF	XF
15	AH1367	—	4.00	6.00	10.00
	1368	—	4.00	6.00	10.00
	1370	—	3.50	5.00	8.00
	1371/68	—	—	—	—
	1371/0	—	3.50	5.00	8.00
	1371	—	3.50	5.00	8.00
	1372	—	3.50	5.00	8.00
	1374	—	3.50	5.00	7.00
	1375/3	—	3.50	5.00	7.00
	1375	—	3.50	5.00	7.00
	1376	—	Reported, not confirmed		
	1377/5	—	3.50	5.00	8.00
	1380	—	15.00	30.00	50.00

NOTE: The size of reverse inner circle varies considerably. All dates have only the final 2 digits on the coin.

1/2 AHMADI RIYAL

SILVER
Accession Date AH1367
Rev: Closed crescent, full dates, denomination and mint name face inward.

Y#	Date	Mintage	Fine	VF	XF
16.1	AH1367	—	10.00	14.00	19.00
	1368	—	10.00	14.00	19.00

NOTE: These coins were struck over blanks punched from Maria Theresa dollars. The outer rings are reported to have circulated as currency, but this is doubtful, as they are found only counterstamped 'VOID' in Arabic.

Rev: Open crescent, full dates, denomination and mint name face inward.

Y#	Date	Mintage	Fine	VF	XF
16.2	AH1367	—	12.00	16.00	24.00
	1368	—	10.00	12.50	17.50
	1369	—	10.00	12.50	17.50
	1370	—	10.00	12.50	17.50
	1372/68	—	10.00	12.50	17.50
	1373	—	10.00	12.50	17.50

Similar to Y#16.2 w/ partial date; last two digits only.

Y#	Date	Mintage	Fine	VF	XF
16.3	AH(13)75	—	10.00	14.00	18.50

Full date; denomination and mint name face outward.

Y#	Date	Mintage	Fine	VF	XF
16.4	AH1377	—	10.00	12.50	16.00
	1378	—	10.00	12.50	16.00
	1379	—	10.00	12.50	16.00
	1380	—	30.00	40.00	50.00
	1381	—	22.50	32.50	40.00
	1382	—	12.50	16.00	25.00

IMADI RIYAL

SILVER
Accession Date AH1322

Y#	Date	Mintage	Fine	VF	XF
7	AH1344	—	18.00	22.50	27.50

NOTE: Several varieties exist, possibly struck over a number of years with frozen date.

AHMADI RIYAL

SILVER
Accession date AH1362

Y#	Date	Mintage	Fine	VF	XF
17	AH1367	—	18.00	24.00	28.00
	1370	—	18.00	24.00	28.00
	1371	—	18.00	24.00	28.00
17	1372/68	—	30.00	50.00	70.00
	1373	—	16.50	18.50	22.50
	1374	—	18.00	24.00	30.00
	1375	—	16.50	20.00	25.00
	1378	—	16.50	22.50	27.50
	1380	—	16.50	22.50	27.50

NOTE: These are found struck over Maria Theresa Talers and other foreign crowns. Most AH1373 Riyals appear to be recut from AH1372 dies, and the dates are easily confused.

NOTE: Maria Theresa Talers and Eritrea Talleros are reported to exist c/s with obv. and rev. of the 1/16 Ahmadi Riyal (Y#13), but their authenticity has not been confirmed.

GOLD 1/4 RIYAL

GOLD
Accession date AH1322

Y#	Date	Mintage	Fine	VF	XF
A10	AH(13)44	—	—	Rare	—

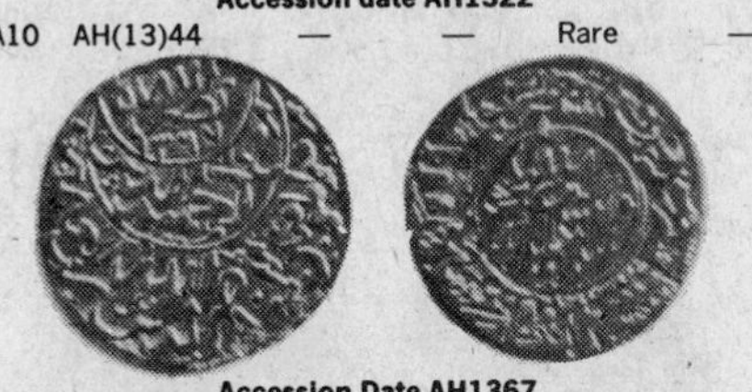

Accession Date AH1367

Y#	Date	Mintage	Fine	VF	XF
G15	AH1371	—	250.00	300.00	350.00
	1375	—	250.00	300.00	350.00
	1377/5	—	250.00	300.00	350.00

GOLD 1/2 RIYAL

GOLD
Accession Date AH1367

Y#	Date	Mintage	Fine	VF	XF
G16	AH1371	—	400.00	450.00	550.00
	1375	—	400.00	450.00	550.00
	1378	—	400.00	450.00	550.00
	1379	—	400.00	450.00	550.00
	1380	—	400.00	450.00	550.00
	1381	—	400.00	450.00	550.00

GOLD RIYAL

GOLD
Accession Date AH1322

Y#	Date	Mintage	Fine	VF	XF
G7	AH1344	—	—	850.00	1150.

Accession Date AH1367

Y#	Date	Mintage	Fine	VF	XF
G17	AH1373	—	—	—	—
	1377	—	—	600.00	750.00
	1381	—	—	600.00	750.00

NOTE: All Yemeni gold are believed to be presentation pieces.

ROYALIST GOVERNMENT

(in exile)

Imam Badr 1962-1970

RIAL

24.9200 gm., .720 SILVER, .5769 oz ASW
Sir Winston Churchill Memorial

Y#	Date	Year	Mintage	VF	XF	Unc
—	AH1385	1965	6,000	BV	17.50	20.00
	1385	1965	—	—	Proof	22.50

NOTE: The above coin probably was not intended for circulation, but specimens are known to have been distributed by the exiled monarch to Saudi and other dignitaries.

REPUBLIC

1/80 RIYAL

(= 1/2 Buqsha)

BRONZE

Y#	Date	Mintage	VF	XF	Unc
20	AH1382	—	.50	1.00	1.50

NOTE: 2 varieties exist.

Y#	Date	Mintage	VF	XF	Unc
21	AH1382	—	2.00	3.50	5.00

NOTE: 4 varieties known to exist.

1/2 BUQSHA

BRONZE

Y#	Date	Mintage	VF	XF	Unc
32	AH1382	—	3.00	5.00	8.50

COPPER-ALUMINUM

Y#	Date	Year	Mintage	VF	XF	Unc
26	AH1382	1963	10.000	.15	.20	.30

NOTE: Y#26-31 were struck at Cairo.

1/40 RIYAL (= 1 BUQSHA)

BRASS or BRONZE

Y#	Date	Mintage	VF	XF	Unc
22	AH1382	—	.75	1.00	1.50
	1383	—	1.50	2.25	3.50
	1384	—	4.00	7.50	12.50

NOTE: Dated both sides; AH1382 and AH1383 are dated AH1382 on obverse, actual date on reverse; AH1384 dated AH1384 on both sides. There are many varieties of date size, inner circle size, calligraphy, etc.

BUQSHA

COPPER-ALUMINUM

Y#	Date	Year	Mintage	VF	XF	Unc
27	AH1382	1963	10.377	.20	.30	.50

1/20 RIAL (= 2 BUQSHA)

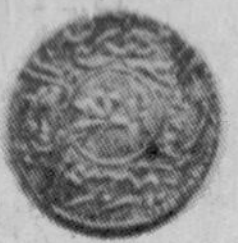

.720 SILVER
Thick variety, 1.1-1.6 gm.
Rev: Two stones in top row of wall.

Y#	Date	Mintage	VF	XF	Unc
23	AH1382	—	2.50	3.50	5.00

Thin variety, 0.6-0.9 gm.
Rev: Three stones in top row of wall.

Y#	Date	Mintage	VF	XF	Unc
23.1	AH1382	—	2.00	3.00	4.50

2 BUQSHA

COPPER-ALUMINUM

Y#	Date	Year	Mintage	VF	XF	Unc
A27	AH1382	1963	—	.25	.60	.75

1/10 RIYAL (= 4 BUQSHA)

.720 SILVER

Thick variety, 2.4-3.0 gm.
Rev: Three stones in top row of wall.

Y#	Date	Mintage	VF	XF	Unc
24	AH1382	—	2.25	2.75	5.00

Thin variety, 1.4-1.8 gm.
Rev: Four stones in top row of wall.

Y#	Date	Mintage	VF	XF	Unc
24.1	AH1382	—	2.00	2.50	4.00

5 BUQSHA

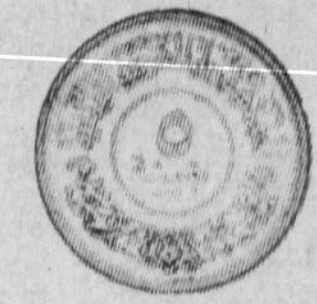

.720 SILVER

Y#	Date	Year	Mintage	VF	XF	Unc
28	AH1382	1963	1.600	1.25	1.50	2.00

2/10 RIYAL (= 8 BUQSHA)

.720 SILVER
Thick variety, 5.8-6.5 gm.

Y#	Date	Mintage	VF	XF	Unc
25	AH1382	—	5.00	6.00	9.00

Thin variety, 5.001 gm.

Y#	Date	Mintage	VF	XF	Unc
25.1	AH1382	—	—	—	—

NOTE: The weight of this coin corresponds to the proper weight of the 1/4 Riyal, but bears the denomination USHRAN (two tenths), probably in error.

1/4 RIAL (= 10 BUQSHA)

.720 SILVER
Thick variety, 6.0-7.0 gm.

Y#	Date	Mintage	VF	XF	Unc
A25	AH1382	—	20.00	27.50	37.50

Thin variety, 4.0-4.6 gm.

Y#	Date	Mintage	VF	XF	Unc
A25a	AH1382	—	20.00	27.50	37.50

10 BUQSHA

.720 SILVER

Y#	Date	Year	Mintage	VF	XF	Unc
29	AH1382	1963	1.024	2.00	2.25	2.75

20 BUQSHA

.720 SILVER

Y#	Date	Year	Mintage	VF	XF	Unc
30	AH1382	1963	1.016	4.00	5.00	6.50

RIAL

.720 SILVER

Y#	Date	Year	Mintage	VF	XF	Unc
31	AH1382	1963	4.614	8.00	9.00	10.00

DECIMAL COINAGE

100 Fils = 1 Riyal

FIL

ALUMINUM

Y#	Date	Year	Mintage	VF	XF	Unc
33	AH1394	1974	1.000	—	—	—
	1394	1974	5,024	—	Proof	—

F.A.O. Issue

Y#	Date	Year	Mintage	VF	XF	Unc
42	AH1398	1978	7,000	—	1.25	2.00

5 FILS

BRASS

Y#	Date	Year	Mintage	VF	XF	Unc
34	AH1394	1974	10.000	—	.25	.50
	1394	1974	5,024	—	Proof	—

F.A.O. Issue

Y#	Date	Year	Mintage	VF	XF	Unc
38	AH1394	1974	.500	—	—	.15

10 FILS

BRASS

Y#	Date	Year	Mintage	VF	XF	Unc
35	AH1394	1974	20.000	—	.25	.50
	1394	1974	5,024	—	Proof	—

F.A.O. Issue

Y#	Date	Year	Mintage	VF	XF	Unc
39	AH1394	1974	.200	—	—	.25

25 FILS

COPPER-NICKEL

Y#	Date	Year	Mintage	VF	XF	Unc
36	AH1394	1974	15.000	—	.30	.75
	1394	1974	5,024	—	Proof	—

F.A.O. Issue

Y#	Date	Year	Mintage	VF	XF	Unc
40	AH1394	1974	.040	—	—	.50

50 FILS

COPPER-NICKEL

Y#	Date	Year	Mintage	VF	XF	Unc
37	AH1394	1974	10.000	—	.35	1.00
	1394	1974	5,024	—	Proof	—

F.A.O. Issue

Y#	Date	Year	Mintage	VF	XF	Unc
41	AH1394	1974	.025	—	—	.75

RIYAL

12.0000 gm., .925 SILVER, .3569 oz ASW

H#	Date	Year	Mintage	XF	Unc	Proof
1	—	1969	1,500	—	—	12.50

COPPER-NICKEL
F.A.O. Issue

Y#	Date	Year	Mintage	VF	XF	Unc
43	AH1398	1978	7,000	—	5.00	8.00

2 RIYALS

25.0000 gm., .925 SILVER, .7435 oz ASW
Apollo II

H#	Date	Year	Mintage	XF	Unc	Proof
2	—	1969	1,500	—	—	27.50

Apollo II
Obv: Similar to H#2

H#	Date	Year	Mintage	XF	Unc	Proof
3	—	1969	1,500	—	—	27.50

H#	Date	Year	Mintage	XF	Unc	Proof
4	—	1969	1,500	—	—	22.50

2-1/2 RIYALS

9.0000 gm., .925 SILVER, .2676 oz ASW

H#	Date	Year	Mintage	XF	Unc	Proof
14	AH1395	1975	*.205	—	20.00	—
	AH1395	1975	*5,000	—	—	30.00

***NOTE:** Projected mintage.

5 RIYALS

4.9000 gm., .900 GOLD, .1418 oz AGW
Obv: Arms. Rev: Falcon.

Fr#	Date	Mintage	XF	Unc	Proof
10	1969	—	—	—	100.00

18.0000 gm., .925 SILVER, .5353 oz ASW

H#	Date	Year	Mintage	XF	Unc	Proof
15	AH1395	1975	*.235	—	25.00	—
	1395	1975	*5,000	—	—	30.00

***NOTE:** Projected mintage.

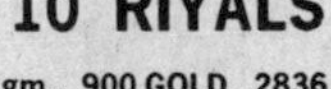

10 RIYALS

9.8000 gm., .900 GOLD, .2836 oz AGW
Rev: Gazelle.

Fr#	Date	Mintage	XF	Unc	Proof
9	1969	—	—	—	200.00

36.0000 gm., .925 SILVER, 1.0707 oz ASW
Rev: XXI. Olympiad

H#	Date	Year	Mintage	XF	Unc	Proof
16	AH1395	1975	*—	—	35.00	—
	1395	1975	*5,000	—	—	40.00

***NOTE:** Projected mintage.

15 RIYALS

54.0000 gm., .925 SILVER, 1.6061 oz ASW

H#	Date	Year	Mintage	XF	Unc	Proof
17	AH1395	1975	*.070	—	50.00	—
	1395	1975	*5,000	—	—	60.00

***NOTE:** Projected mintage.

20 RIYALS

19.6000 gm., .900 GOLD, .5672 oz AGW
Obv: Arms. Rev: Apollo 11 landing.

Fr#	Date	Mintage	XF	Unc	Proof
7	1969	—	—	—	375.00
		Rev: Camel.			
8	1969	—	—	—	375.00

H#	Date	Year	Mintage	XF	Unc	Proof
18	AH1395	1975	—	—	—	—
	1395	1975	*3,500	—	—	—

***NOTE:** Projected mintage.

25 RIYALS

.900 GOLD

H#	Date	Year	Mintage	XF	Unc	Proof
19	AH1395	1975	—	—	—	—
	1395	1975	*3,500	—	—	—

***NOTE:** Projected mintage.

30 RIYALS

29.4000 gm., .900 GOLD, .8508 oz AGW
Rev: Bust of Al-Zubairi.

Fr#	Date	Mintage	XF	Unc	Proof
6	1969	—	—	—	575.00

50 RIYALS

49.0000 gm., .900 GOLD, 1.4180 oz AGW
Rev: Lion.

Fr#	Date	Mintage	XF	Unc	Proof
5	1969	—	—	—	925.00

H#	Date	Year	Mintage	XF	Unc	Proof
20	AH1395	1975	—	—	—	—
	1395	1975	3,500	—	—	—

***NOTE:** Projected mintage.

75 RIYALS

13.6500 gm., .900 GOLD, .3950 oz ASW
Obv: Arms. Rev: XXI Olympiad.

H#	Date	Year	Mintage	XF	Unc	Proof
21	AH1395	1975	—	—	260.00	—
	1395	1975	*3,500	—	—	275.00

***NOTE:** Projected mintage.

100 RIYALS

.900 GOLD

H#	Date	Year	Mintage	XF	Unc	Proof
22	AH1395	1975	—	—	135.00	—
	1395	1975	*3,500	—	—	175.00

***NOTE:** Projected mintage.

NCLT ISSUES

MINT SETS

KM#	Date	Mintage	Identification	Issue Price	Mkt. Val.
S1	1975(4)	—	H14-17	50.00	60.00
S2	1975(5)	—	H18-22	360.00	—

PROOF SETS

STANDARD METALS

KM#	Date	Mintage	Identification	Issue Price	Mkt. Val.
101	1969(7)	—	H2,3,F5-6,8-10	375.00	1400.
102	1969(4)	1,500	H1-4	—	70.00
103	1969(3)	—	H2,3,6	78.00	300.00
104	1974(5)	20,000	Y32-36	15.00	18.00
105	1974(5)	5,024	Y33-37	—	—
106	1975(5)	*3,500	H18-22	485.00	—
107	1975(4)	*5,000	H14-17	75.00	85.00

***NOTE:** Projected mintage.

YEMEN

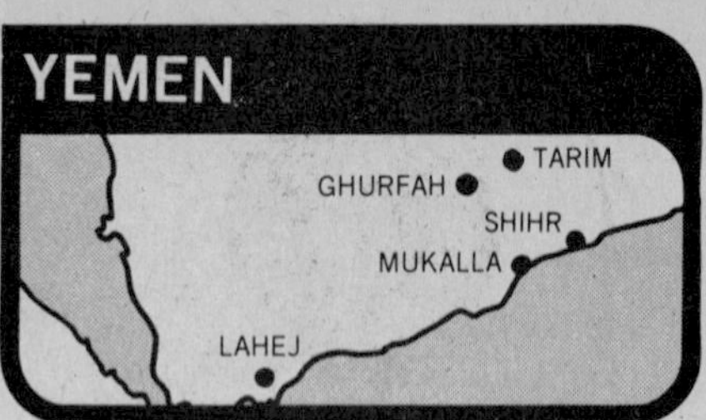

The states of Britain's former Eastern and Western Aden Protectorates, now a part of the People's Democratic Republic of Yemen, were coin issuing entities of interest to numismatists.

ADEN-PROTECTORATE STATES

GHURFAH

A city sultanate of Eastern Aden Protectorate was an oasis settlement located in the Hadramaut wadi region on the southern coast of Arabia.

RULERS

Abdat Umar bin Abdat, 1928-1939
Ubayd bin Saht bin Abdat, 1939-1945

4 CHOMSIHS

.900 SILVER

Y#	Date	Year	Mintage	Fine	VF	XF
4	AH1344	1926	5,000	25.00	40.00	60.00

8 CHOMSIHS

.900 SILVER

Y#	Date	Year	Mintage	Fine	VF	XF
6	AH1344	1926	5,000	22.50	27.50	40.00

15 CHOMSIHS

.900 SILVER

Y#	Date	Year	Mintage	Fine	VF	XF
8	AH1344	1926	.010	8.00	12.50	17.50

30 CHOMSIHS

.900 SILVER

Y#	Date	Year	Mintage	Fine	VF	XF
10	AH1344	1926	.010	12.50	17.50	25.00

45 CHOMSIHS

.900 SILVER

Y#	Date	Year	Mintage	Fine	VF	XF
11	AH1344	1926	.010	200.00	300.00	450.00

60 CHOMSIHS

.900 SILVER

12	AH1344	1926	.010	30.00	45.00	60.00

LAHEJ

A sultanate situated north of the port city of Aden, was comprised in Western Aden Protectorate located in southern Arabia near the entrance of the Red Sea. Lahej entered into a protective treaty relationship with Britain following Britain's capture of Aden in 1839.

RULERS

Ali bin Muhsin, 1849-1863
Fadi III bin Ali, 1863,1874-1898

1/2 PESSA

COPPER

1	ND	(1860)	—	12.50	20.00	30.00

2	AH1291	1896	—	15.00	25.00	35.00

The date AH1291-1874 appears on Y#2 coins and refers to the date the Sultan began his first reign.

KASADI STATE OF MUKALLA

A port, city sultanate and capital of the Quaiti state of Shihr and Mukalla in Eastern Aden Protectorate in southern Arabia, was a principal port servicing trade between the Near East and India and Java.

RULER

Salah bin Muhammad

1/2 CHOMSIHS

BRONZE

Y#	Date	Year	Mintage	VG	Fine	VF
1	AH1276	1859	—	45.00	75.00	120.00

CHOMSIHS

BRONZE

2	AH1276	1859	—	40.00	65.00	100.00

QUAITI STATE

The Quaiti State of Shihr and Mukalla was comprised in Eastern Aden Protectorate located in southern Arabia near the entrance to the Red Sea.

RULERS

Munasin bin Abdallah bin Umar
Awadh bin Umar, 1866-1909

COUNTERSTAMP ISSUES

1/4 ANNA

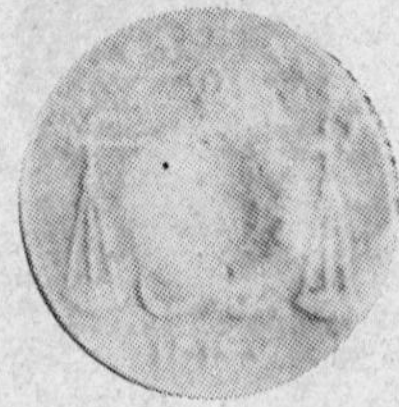

COPPER

c/s: Arabic in 10mm circle on Br. India 1/4 Anna C#592.

1.1	AH1307 (1830-33)		—	6.50	12.50	18.50

c/s: Arabic in 10mm circle on Br. India 1/4 Anna, C#867.

1.2	AH1307 (1833-58)		—	6.50	12.50	18.50

c/s: Arabic in 15mm circle on Br. India 1/4 Anna Y#7.

1.3	AH1307	1862-76	—	6.50	12.50	18.50

c/s: Arabic in 10mm circle on Mombasa 1/4 Anna, Y#1.

1.4	AH1307	AH1388	—	12.50	17.50	22.50

c/s: Arabic in 10mm circle on Zanzibar Pysa, Y#1.

1.5	AH1307	AH1299	—	12.50	17.50	22.50

1/2 ANNA

COPPER

c/s: Arabic in 15mm circle on Br. India 1/2 Anna, C#593.

2.1	AH1307	(1834)	—	13.50	20.00	25.00

c/s: Arabic in 10mm circle on Br. India 1/2 Anna, C#868.

Y#	Date	Year	Mintage	VG	Fine	VF
2.2	AH1307 (1833-45)		—	13.50	20.00	25.00

c/s: In 15mm circle on Br. India 1/2 Anna Y#8.

2.3	AH1307	1862-76	—	13.50	20.00	25.00

1/2 RUPEE

SILVER

c/s: Arabic in 10mm circle on Br. India 1/2 Rupee.

3	AH1307	—	—	17.50	20.00	25.00

c/s: Arabic in 15mm circle on Br. India 1/2 Rupee.

4	AH1307	—	—	20.00	24.00	28.00

RUPEE

c/s: Arabic in 10mm circle on Br. India Rupee, Y#5.

5	AH1307	—	—	20.00	24.00	30.00

PRICES-Single c/s on coin. Add 15 per cent for each additional c/s.

c/s: Arabic in 15mm circle on Br. India Rupee, Y#5.

6	AH1307	—	—	22.00	26.00	36.00

RYAL

SILVER

c/s: Arabic in 10mm circle on Austria MTT, Y#55.

7	AH1307	(1780)	—	40.00	45.00	55.00

c/s: Arabic in 10mm circle on Austria MTT, Y#55.

Y#	Date	Year	Mintage	VG	Fine	VF
7a	AH1307	(1780)	—	45.00	50.00	65.00

SOVEREIGN

GOLD

Y#	Date	Year	Mintage	VG	Fine	VF
7b	AH1307	1889	—	Rare	—	—

REGULAR COINAGE

5 CHOMSIHS

COPPER and BRONZE

Y#	Date	Year	Mintage	VG	Fine	VF
8	AH1315	1897	—	7.50	15.00	25.00

Y#	Date	Year	Mintage	VG	Fine	VF
9	AH1318	1900	—	6.50	12.50	20.00

1/3 RYAL

SILVER

KM#	Date	Mintage	VG	Fine	VF
10	AH1315	—	—	350.00	500.00

1/2 RYAL

SILVER

KM#	Date	Mintage	VG	Fine	VF
11	AH1316	—	—	450.00	600.00

SEIYUN & TARIM

Kathiri State of Seiyun and Tarim, a city sultanate in Eastern Aden Protectorate, was an important oasis settlement in the Hadramaut Wadi region on the southern coast of Arabia. It became a British treaty protectorate in the 1880's.

MONETARY SYSTEM

120 Chomsihs = 1 Ryal

CHOMSIH

COPPER, thin

Y#	Date	Year	Mintage	VG	Fine	VF
A1	AH1258	1842	—	10.00	17.50	27.50

3 CHOMSIHS

COPPER, thick

Y#	Date	Year	Mintage	VG	Fine	VF
A2	AH1258	1842	—	14.00	25.00	45.00

4 CHOMSIHS

SILVER

Y#	Date	Year	Mintage	Fine	VF	XF
A4	AH1270	1853	—	55.00	85.00	125.00

6 CHOMSIHS

SILVER

Y#	Date	Year	Mintage	Fine	VF	XF
1	AH1315	1897	.130	3.00	5.00	6.00

8 CHOMSIHS

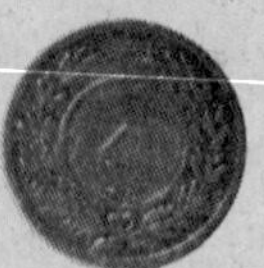

SILVER

Y#	Date	Year	Mintage	Fine	VF	XF
A5	AH1270	1853	—	55.00	85.00	125.00

12 CHOMSIHS

SILVER

Y#	Date	Year	Mintage	Fine	VF	XF
2	AH1315	1897	.070	6.00	7.50	9.00

16 CHOMSIHS

SILVER

Y#	Date	Year	Mintage	Fine	VF	XF
A6	AH1270	1853	—	65.00	100.00	140.00

24 CHOMSIHS

SILVER

Y#	Date	Year	Mintage	Fine	VF	XF
3	AH1315	1897	.030	8.00	10.00	12.50

30 CHOMSIHS

SILVER

Y#	Date	Year	Mintage	Fine	VF	XF
A3	AH1258	1842	—	100.00	150.00	250.00

YEMEN-DEM. REP.

The People's Democratic Republic of Yemen, located on the southern coast of the Arabian Peninsula, has an area of 112,000 sq. mi. (290,078 sq. km.) and a population of 1.6 million. Capital: Aden. It consists of the port city of Aden, 17 states of the former South Arabian Federation, 3 small shaikhdoms, 3 large sultanates, Quaiti, Kathiri, and Mahri, which made up the Eastern Aden Protectorate, and Socotra, the largest island in the Arabian Sea. The port of Aden is the area's most valuable natural resource. Cotton, fish, coffee and hides are exported.

Between 1200 B.C. and the 6th century A.D., what is now the People's Democratic Republic of Yemen was part of the Minaean kingdom. In subsequent years it was controlled by Persians, Egyptians and Turks. Aden, one of the cities mentioned in the Bible, had been a port for trade between the East and West for 2,000 years. British rule began in 1839 when the British East India Co. seized control to put an end to the piracy threatening trade with India. To protect their foothold in Aden, the British found it necessary to extend their control into the area known historically as the Hadramaut, and to sign protection treaties with the shaikhs of the hinterland. Eventually, 15 of the 16 Western Protectorate states, the Wahidi state of the Eastern Protectorate, and Aden Colony joined to form the Federation of South Arabia.

In 1959, Britain agreed to prepare South Arabia for full independence, which was achieved on Nov. 30, 1967, at which time South Arabia, including Aden, changed its name to the People's Republic of Southern Yemen. On Dec. 1, 1970, following the overthrowing of the new government by the National Liberation Front, Southern Yemen changed its name to the People's Democratic Republic of Yemen.

SOUTH ARABIA

MONETARY SYSTEM

1000 Fils = 1 Dinar

FILS

ALUMINUM

Y#	Date	Mintage	VF	XF	Unc
1	1964	10.000	—	.10	.15
	1964	—	—	Proof	2.00

5 FILS

BRONZE

Y#	Date	Mintage	VF	XF	Unc
2	1964	10.000	.15	.25	.40
	1964	—	—	Proof	2.50

25 FILS

COPPER-NICKEL

Y#	Date	Mintage	VF	XF	Unc
3	1964	4.000	.20	.40	.75
	1964	—	—	Proof	3.00
	1976	2.000	—	—	—

50 FILS

COPPER-NICKEL

Y#	Date	Mintage	VF	XF	Unc
4	1964	6.000	.30	.60	1.00
	1964	—	—	Proof	4.00

NCLT ISSUES

PROOF SETS

KM#	Date	Mintage	Identification	Issue Price	Mkt. Val.
101	1964(4)	10,500	Y1-4	9.90	10.00

YEMEN DEMOCRATIC REPUBLIC

MONETARY SYSTEM

1000 Fils = 1 Dinar

2-1/2 FILS

ALUMINUM

Y#	Date	Mintage	VF	XF	Unc
3	1973	20.000	.10	.15	.25

5 FILS

BRONZE

Y#	Date	Mintage	VF	XF	Unc
2	1971	2.000	.30	.60	1.00

ALUMINUM

Y#	Date	Year	Mintage	VF	XF	Unc
4	AH1393	1973	20.000	.15	.30	.50

YUGOSLAVIA

The Socialist Federal Republic of Yugoslavia, a Balkan country located on the east shore of the Adriatic Sea, has an area of 99,000 sq. mi. (256,409 km.) and a population of 21.6 million. Capital: Belgrade. The chief industries are agriculture, mining, manufacturing and tourism. Machinery, nonferrous metals, meat and fabrics are exported.

Yugoslavia was proclaimed on Dec. 1, 1918, after the union of the Kingdom of Serbia, Montenegro and the South Slav territories of Austria-Hungary; and changed its official name from the Kingdom of the Serbs, Croats and Slovenes to the Kingdom of Yugoslavia on Oct. 3, 1929. The republic is currently composed of six autonomous republics - Serbia, Croatia, Slovenia, Bosnia-Herzegovina, Macedonia and Montenegro - and two autonomous provinces within Serbia: Kosovo-Melohija and Vojvodina. The government of Yugoslavia attempted to remain neutral in World War II but, yielding to German pressure, aligned itself with the Axis powers in March of 1941; a few days later it was overthrown by revolutionary forces and its neutrality reasserted. The Nazis occupied the country on April 6, and throughout the remaining war years were resisted by a number of guerrilla armies, notably that of Marshal Josip Broz Tito. After the defeat of the Axis powers, a leftist coalition headed by Tito abolished the monarchy and, on Jan. 31, 1946, established a "people's republic."

The name Yugoslavia appears on the coinage in letters of the Cyrillic alphabet alone until formation of the Federated People's Republic of Yugoslavia in 1953, after which both the Cyrillic and Latin alphabets are employed. From 1965, the coin denomination appears in the four different languages of the federated republics in letters of both the Cyrillic and Latin alphabets.

Para ПАРА Para, Par, ПАРИ
Dinara: ДИНАРА Dinara, Dinarja, ДИНАРА

RULERS

Petar I, 1918-1921
Alexander I, 1921-1934
Petar II, 1934-1945

MINT MARKS

(a) - Paris, privy marks only
B - Belgrade Kovinca A.D.
Set special head
L - London
P - Poissy (thunderbolt)

MONETARY SYSTEM

100 Para = 1 Dinar

5 PARA

ZINC

Y#	Date	Mintage	Fine	VF	XF	Unc
1	1920	3.825	—	7.50	12.50	22.50

COPPER-ZINC

Y#	Date	Mintage	Fine	VF	XF	Unc
36	1965	—	—	—	.10	.20

Y#	Date	Mintage	Fine	VF	XF	Unc
38	1965	—	—	—	—	.15
	1973	—	—	—	—	.10
	1974	3.628	—	—	—	.10
	1975	20.272	—	—	—	.10
	1976	30.490	—	—	—	.10
	1977	—	—	—	—	.10
	1978	—	—	—	—	.10

10 PARA

ZINC

Y#	Date	Mintage	Fine	VF	XF	Unc
2	1920	58.946	—	4.00	6.00	10.00

COPPER-ZINC

Y#	Date	Mintage	Fine	VF	XF	Unc
39	1965	—	—	—	.15	.35
	1973	—	—	—	.10	.20
	1974	60.139	—	—	.10	.20
	1975	36.079	—	—	.10	.15
	1976	36.111	—	—	.10	.15
	1977	—	—	—	.10	.15
	1978	—	—	—	.10	.15

20 PARA

COPPER-ZINC

Y#	Date	Mintage	Fine	VF	XF	Unc
40	1965	—	—	—	.15	.35
	1973	—	—	—	.10	.30
	1974	31.364	—	—	.10	.30
	1975	44.683	—	—	.10	.30
	1976	33.312	—	—	.10	.30
	1977	—	—	—	.10	.30
	1978	—	—	—	.10	.30

25 PARA

NICKEL-BRONZE

Y#	Date	Mintage	Fine	VF	XF	Unc
3	1920	48.173	1.00	1.75	2.50	5.00

BRONZE

Y#	Date	Mintage	Fine	VF	XF	Unc
13	1938	160.000	1.25	2.00	3.50	7.50

50 PARA

NICKEL-BRONZE

Y#	Date	Mintage	Fine	VF	XF	Unc
4	1925	25.000	.25	.50	1.50	4.00
	1925(p)	24.500	.25	.50	1.50	4.00

ALUMINUM-BRONZE

Y#	Date	Mintage	Fine	VF	XF	Unc
14	1938	200.00	.35	.60	1.50	3.00

ZINC

Y#	Date	Mintage	Fine	VF	XF	Unc
21	1945	—	—	.40	1.50	4.00

ALUMINUM

Y#	Date	Mintage	Fine	VF	XF	Unc
25	1953	—	—	—	.10	.15

COPPER-ZINC

Y#	Date	Mintage	Fine	VF	XF	Unc
41	1965	—	—	.10	.20	.65
	1973	—	—	.10	.20	.65
	1974	.033	—	.50	1.75	2.50
	1975	10.220	—	.10	.20	.65
	1976	8.438	—	.10	.20	.65
	1977	—	—	.10	.20	.65
	1978	—	—	.10	.20	.65

DINAR

NICKEL-BRONZE

Y#	Date	Mintage	Fine	VF	XF	Unc
5	1925	37.000	.50	.80	1.50	4.50
	1925(p)	37.500	.50	.80	1.50	4.50

ALUMINUM-BRONZE

Y#	Date	Mintage	Fine	VF	XF	Unc
15	1938	100.000	.50	.75	1.00	3.00

ZINC

Y#	Date	Mintage	Fine	VF	XF	Unc
22	1945	90.000	.25	.40	1.00	2.50

ALUMINUM

Y#	Date	Mintage	Fine	VF	XF	Unc
26	1953	—	—	—	.10	.20

Y#	Date	Mintage	Fine	VF	XF	Unc
32	1963	—	—	—	.10	.15

COPPER-NICKEL

Y#	Date	Mintage	Fine	VF	XF	Unc
37	1965	—	—	.15	.30	.60

Y#	Date	Mintage	Fine	VF	XF	Unc
42	1968	—	—	.15	.30	.60

Y#	Date	Mintage	Fine	VF	XF	Unc
A45	1973	—	—	.10	.15	.40
	1974	42.724	—	.10	.15	.35
	1975	30.260	—	.10	.15	.35
	1976	22.349	—	.10	.15	.35
	1977	—	—	.10	.15	.35
	1978	—	—	.10	.15	.35

F.A.O. Issue

Y#	Date	Mintage	Fine	VF	XF	Unc
54	1976	.500	—	.10	.15	.25

2 DINARA

NICKEL-BRONZE

Y#	Date	Mintage	Fine	VF	XF	Unc
6	1925	29.500	.65	1.00	2.00	5.00
	1925(p)	25.002	.65	1.00	2.00	5.00

ALUMINUM-BRONZE, 14mm crown

Y#	Date	Mintage	Fine	VF	XF	Unc
16	1938	74.250	.50	.90	1.60	3.00

12mm crown

Y#	Date	Mintage	Fine	VF	XF	Unc
17	1938	.750	4.00	6.00	12.00	20.00

ZINC

Y#	Date	Mintage	Fine	VF	XF	Unc
23	1945	70.000	.35	.60	1.50	5.00

ALUMINUM

Y#	Date	Mintage	Fine	VF	XF	Unc
27	1953	—	—	.15	.20	.30
33	1963	—	—	.15	.20	.30

COPPER-NICKEL
F.A.O. Issue

Y#	Date	Mintage	Fine	VF	XF	Unc
43	1970	.500	—	.25	.40	1.00

Y#	Date	Mintage	Fine	VF	XF	Unc
45	1971	.500	—	.15	.30	.60
	1972	—	—	.15	.20	.40
	1973	—	—	.15	.20	.45
	1974	10.989	—	.15	.20	.40
	1975	.092	—	.45	.90	1.75
	1976	6.092	—	.15	.20	.40
	1977	—	—	.15	.20	.40
	1978	—	—	.15	.20	.40

5 DINARA

ZINC

Y#	Date	Mintage	Fine	VF	XF	Unc
24	1945	50.000	.65	.75	1.75	5.00

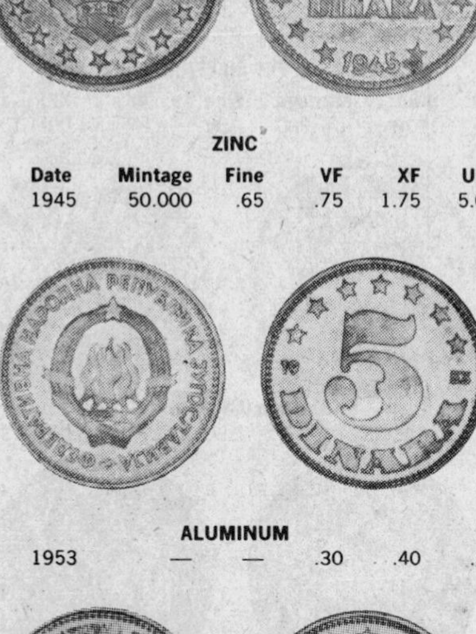

ALUMINUM

Y#	Date	Mintage	Fine	VF	XF	Unc
28	1953	—	—	.30	.40	.50
34	1963	—	—	.30	.40	.50

COPPER-NICKEL
F.A.O. Issue

Y#	Date	Mintage	Fine	VF	XF	Unc
44	1970	.500	.35	.50	.75	1.25

Regular Issue

Y#	Date	Mintage	Fine	VF	XF	Unc
46	1971	—	—	.30	.40	.60
	1972	—	—	.30	.40	.60
	1973	—	—	.50	1.00	2.00
	1974	6.054	—	.30	.40	.60
	1975	12.533	—	.30	.40	.60
	1976	4.961	—	.30	.40	.60

30th Anniversary of Nazi Defeat

Y#	Date	Mintage	Fine	VF	XF	Unc
47	1975	1.000	—	.35	.75	1.50

10 DINARA

7.0000 gm., .500 SILVER .1125 oz ASW

Y#	Date	Mintage	Fine	VF	XF	Unc
7	1931	16.000	BV	3.50	6.00	10.00
	1931(A)	4.000	3.50	5.00	8.00	15.00

NICKEL

Y#	Date	Mintage	Fine	VF	XF	Unc
18	1938	25.000	—	1.50	2.50	5.50

ALUMINUM-BRONZE

Y#	Date	Mintage	Fine	VF	XF	Unc
29	1955	—	—	.60	.75	1.00

Y#	Date	Mintage	Fine	VF	XF	Unc
35	1963	—	—	.60	.75	1.00

COPPER-NICKEL

Y#	Date	Mintage	Fine	VF	XF	Unc
A47	1976	10.550	—	.60	.75	1.25
	1977	—	—	.60	.75	1.00
	1978	—	—	.60	.75	1.00

F.A.O. Issue

Y#	Date	Mintage	Fine	VF	XF	Unc
55	1976	.500	—	—	—	1.50

20 DINARA

6.4516 gm., .900 GOLD .1867 oz AGW

Y#	Date	Mintage	Fine	VF	XF	Unc
10	1925 (a)	1,000	125.00	135.00	150.00	200.00

14.0000 gm., .500 SILVER .2250 oz ASW

Y#	Date	Mintage	Fine	VF	XF	Unc
8	1931	12.500	BV	7.00	10.00	20.00

9.0000 gm., .750 SILVER .2170 oz ASW

Y#	Date	Mintage	Fine	VF	XF	Unc
19	1938	.750	BV	6.50	7.50	10.00

ALUMINUM-BRONZE

Y#	Date	Mintage	Fine	VF	XF	Unc
30	1955	—	.75	1.25	1.50	2.00

Y#	Date	Mintage	Fine	VF	XF	Unc
A35	1963	—	.75	1.25	1.50	2.00

9.0000 gm., .925 SILVER .2676 oz ASW
25th Anniversary
Similar to 50 Dinara, Y#49.

Y#	Date	Mintage				
48	1968	.010	—	—	Proof	25.00

50 DINARA

23.3300 gm., .750 SILVER, .5626 oz ASW

Y#	Date	Mintage	Fine	VF	XF	Unc
9	1932 B w/signature at truncation					
		5.500	BV	20.00	35.00	57.50
	1932 L w/o signature at truncation					
		5.500	BV	17.50	32.50	52.50

15.0000 gm., .750 SILVER, .3617 oz ASW

Y#	Date	Mintage	Fine	VF	XF	Unc
20	1938	.200	BV	BV	11.00	13.50

ALUMINUM-BRONZE

Y#	Date	Mintage	Fine	VF	XF	Unc
31	1955	—	1.50	2.75	3.00	3.50

Y#	Date	Mintage	Fine	VF	XF	Unc
B35	1963	—	1.50	2.75	3.00	3.50

20.0000 gm., .925 SILVER, .5948 oz ASW
25th Anniversary

Y#	Date	Mintage				
49	1968	.010	—	—	Proof	35.00

100 DINARA

7.8200 gm., .900 GOLD, .2263 oz AGW
25th Anniversary

Y#	Date	Mintage	XF	Unc	Proof
50	1968	.010	—	—	150.00

10.0000 gm., .925 SILVER, .2974 oz ASW
8TH Mediterranean Games At Split

Y#	Date	Mintage	XF	Unc	Proof
57	1979	—	—	—	—

150 DINARA

12.5000 gm., .925 SILVER, .3717 oz ASW
8TH Mediterranean Games At Split.

Y#	Date	Mintage	VF	XF	Unc
58	1979	6,000	—	Proof	—

200 DINARA

15.6400 gm., .900 GOLD, .4526 oz AGW
25th Anniversary

Y#	Date	Mintage	XF	Unc	Proof
51	1968	.010	—	—	300.00

15.0000 gm., .750 SILVER, .3617 oz ASW
85th Birthday of Tito

Y#	Date	Mintage	XF	Unc	Proof
56	1977	.500	—	—	25.00

15.0000 gm., .925 SILVER, .4461 oz ASW
8TH Mediterranean Games At Split.

Y#	Date	Mintage	VF	XF	Unc
59	1979	6,000	—	Proof	—

250 DINARA

17.5000 gm., .925 SILVER, .5204 oz ASW
8TH Mediterranean Games At Split.
Obv: Similar to 200 Dinara, Y#59.

Y#	Date	Mintage	VF	XF	Unc
60	1979	6,000	—	Proof	—

300 DINARA

20.0000 gm., .925 SILVER, .5948 oz ASW
8TH Mediterranean Games At Split.
Obv: Similar to 200 dinara, Y#59

Y#	Date	Mintage	VF	XF	Unc
61	1979	6,000	—	Proof	—

350 DINARA

22.5000 gm., .925 SILVER, .6692 oz ASW
8TH Mediterranean Games At Split.
Obv: Similar to 200DINARA, Y#59.

Y#	Date	Mintage	VF	XF	Unc
62	1979	6,000	—	Proof	—

400 DINARA

25.0000 gm., .925 SILVER, .7435 oz ASW
8TH Mediterranean Games At Split.
Obv: Similar to 200 Dinara, Y#59.

Y#	Date	Mintage	VF	XF	Unc
63	1979	6,000	—	Proof	—

500 DINARA

39.1000 gm., .900 GOLD, 1.1315 oz AGW
25th Anniversary
Obv: Similar to 200 Dinara, Y#51.

Y#	Date	Mintage	XF	Unc	Proof
52	1968	.010	—	—	750.00

1000 DINARA

78.2000 gm., .900 GOLD, 2.2630 oz AGW
25th Anniversary
Obv: Similar to 200 Dinara, Y#51.

Y#	Date	Mintage	XF	Unc	Proof
53	1968	.010	—	—	1500.

1500 DINARA

8.8000 gm., .900 GOLD, .2546 oz AGW
8TH Mediterranean Games At Split.

Y#	Date	Mintage	VF	XF	Unc
64	1979	—	—	—	—

2000 DINARA

11.8000 gm., .900 GOLD, .3414 oz AGW
8TH Mediterranean Games At Split.

Y#	Date	Mintage	VF	XF	Unc
65	1979	—	—	—	—

2500 DINARA

14.7000 gm., .900 GOLD, 4254 oz AGW
8TH Mediterranean Games At Split.

Y#	Date	Mintage	VF	XF	Unc
66	1979	—	—	—	—

5000 DINARA

29.5000 gm., .900 GOLD, .8536 oz AGW
8TH Mediterranean Games At Split.

Y#	Date	Mintage	VF	XF	Unc
67	1979	—	—	—	—

TRADE COINS

DUKAT

3.4900 gm., .986 GOLD, .1106 oz AGW
Obv: Head of Alexander left; sign: KOVNICA A.D. below bust. Rev: Crowned double headed eagle.

Y#	Date	Mintage	VF	XF	Unc
A11.1	1931	2,869	BV	80.00	125.00

Obv: Sign: KOVNICI A.D. below bust.

Y#	Date	Mintage	VF	XF	Unc
A11.2	1931	Inc.Ab.	BV	125.00	180.00

Obv: Without sign. below bust.

Y#	Date	Mintage	VF	XF	Unc
A11.3	1931	Inc. Ab.	BV	125.00	180.00

Smaller lettering

Y#	Date	Mintage	VF	XF	Unc
A11.4	1931B	—	BV	125.00	180.00
	1932B	—	BV	80.00	125.00
	1933B	—	BV	150.00	225.00
	1934B	—	BV	275.00	375.00

NOTE: Issues found with countermarks by kings portrait at bottom are sword for Bosina, ear of corn for Serbia.

4 DUKATA

13.9600 gm., .986 GOLD, .4425 oz AGW
Obv. sign: KOVNICA A.D. below busts.

Y#	Date	Mintage	VF	XF	Unc
12.1	1931	51 pcs.	BV	325.00	500.00

Obv: sign: KOVNICI A.D. below busts.

Y#	Date	Mintage	VF	XF	Unc
12.2	1931	Inc.Ab.	BV	450.00	650.00

Obv: w/o sign below smaller busts.

Y#	Date	Mintage	VF	XF	Unc
12.3	1931	—	BV	Rare	—
	1932B	—	BV	325.00	500.00
	1933B	—	BV	450.00	650.00

NCLT ISSUES

MINT SETS

KM#	Date	Mintage	Identification	Issue Price	Mkt. Val.
S1	1953/55(7)	—	Y25-31	—	20.00
S2	1963(5)	—	Y32-B35	—	20.00
S3	1965(5)	—	Y37-41	—	20.00

PROOF SETS

STANDARD METALS

KM#	Date	Mintage	Identification	Issue Price	Mkt. Val.
101	1968(6)	*10,000	Y48-53	—	2750.
102	1968(4)	*10,000	Y50-53	—	2700.
103	1968(2)	*10,000	Y48-49	15.00	60.00
104	1979(7)	6,000	Y57-63	—	—

***NOTE:** Authorized mintages.

YUGOSLAVIA — CATTARO, RAGUSA, & ZARA

CATTARO

A seaport of Montenegro, Yugoslavia, occupies a ledge between the Montenegrin Mountains and an inlet of the Adriatic sea which forms one of the finest natural harbors in the world. It has at various times been occupied by Turks, Venetians, Spaniards, French, English and Austrians. It became a part of Yugoslavia in 1918. Cattaro was united to the French empire during the period of 1807-13. In 1813, while the city was besieged by Montenegrins and a British fleet, the French defenders issued an emergency cast silver coinage.

EMERGENCY

FRANC

CAST SILVER

C#	Date	Mintage	VG	Fine	VF
1	1813	—	35.00	60.00	90.00

5 FRANCS

CAST SILVER

C#	Date	Mintage	VG	Fine	VF
2	1813	—	200.00	400.00	600.00

10 FRANCS

CAST SILVER

C#	Date	Mintage	VG	Fine	VF
3	1813	—	800.00	1500.	2000.

RAGUSA

A port city on the Dalmatian coast of Yugoslavia. Upon its incorporation in Yugoslavia in 1918, its name was officially changed to Dubrovnik. Ragusa was once a great mercantile power, the merchant fleets of which sailed as far abroad as India and America. The city's present industries include oil-refining, slate mining, and the manufacture of liquers, cheese, silk, leather and soap.

The island rock of Ragusa was colonized during the 7th century by refugees from the destroyed Latin communities of Salona and Epidaurus, and a colony of Slavs. For four centuries Ragusa successfully defended itself against attacks by foreign powers, but from 1205 to 1358 recognized Venetian suzeranity. From 1358 to 1526, Ragusa was a vassal state of Hungary. The fall of Hungary in 1526 freed Ragusa, permitting it to become one of the foremost commercial powers of the Mediterranean and a leader in the development of literature and art. After this period its importance declined, due in part to the discovery of America which reduced the importance of Mediterranean ports. A measure of its former economic importance was regained during the Napoleonic Wars when the republic, by adopting a policy of neutrality (1800-1805), became the leading carrier of the Mediterranean. This favored position was terminated by French seizure in 1805. In 1814 Ragusa was annexed by Austria, remaining a part of the Austrian Empire until its incorporation in the newly formed state of Yugoslavia in 1918.

MONETARY SYSTEM

6 Soldi = 1 Grosetto
12 Grosetti = 1 Perpero
40 Grosetti = 1 Ducato
60 Grosetti = 1 Tallero

SOLDO

COPPER
Obv: Saint Blaze over wall.
Rev: Christ under stars.

C#	Date	Mintage	Fine	VF	XF
1	1689-1797 many dates & varieties				
		—	8.00	12.00	20.00

3 SOLDI

COPPER
Obv: "PROT. REIP. RHACUSINE", St. Blaze. Rev Christ.

C#	Date	Mintage	Fine	VF	XF
2	1795-99 various varieties				
		—	9.00	14.00	22.00

VI (6) GROSSETTI

BILLON
Obv: St. Blaze. Rev: Value.

C#	Date	Mintage	Fine	VF	XF
4	1801	—	20.00	30.00	50.00

PERPERO

BILLON
Obv: St. Blaze. Rev: Christ.

C#	Date	Mintage	Fine	VF	XF
5	1801-03	—	25.00	35.00	60.00

DUCATO

SILVER
Obv: Arms. Rev: St. Blaze.

C#	Date	Mintage	Fine	VF	XF
6	1797	—	25.00	35.00	60.00

DUCAT ET SEM

(= Tallero)

SILVER
Rev: Crowned arms.

C#	Date	Mintage	Fine	VF	XF
9	1751-79	—	50.00	60.00	120.00

2 DUCATI

SILVER
Obv: Bust right. Rev: Arms.

C#	Date	Mintage	Fine	VF	XF
10	1791GA	—	80.00	100.00	200.00

C#	Date	Mintage	Fine	VF	XF
11	1792GA	—	75.00	100.00	150.00
	1793GA	—	80.00	120.00	175.00
	1794GA	—	75.00	100.00	150.00
	1795GA	—	90.00	130.00	225.00

ZARA

Zara, a port and fortress in Dalmatia, was occupied by the French during the period of 1807-13. While the French defenders of the city were under siege in 1813, they issued a silver emergency coinage.

EMERGENCY FRENCH COINAGE

4 FRANCS - 60 CENTIMES

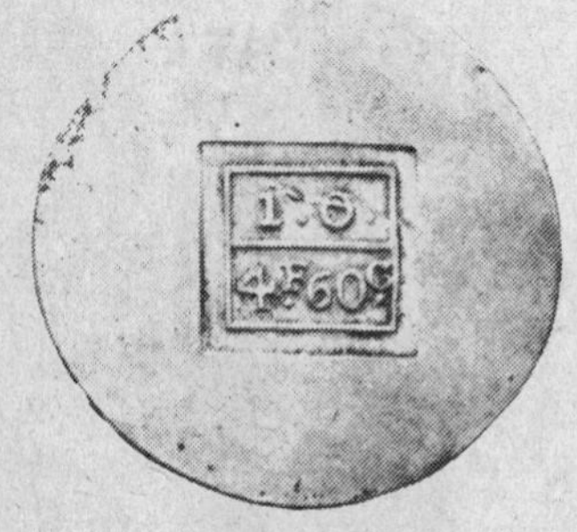

SILVER

C#	Date	Mintage	Fine	VF	XF
1	1813	—	150.00	225.00	300.00

9 FRANCS - 20 CENTIMES

SILVER

C#	Date	Mintage	Fine	VF	XF
2	1813	—	400.00	600.00	900.00

18 FRANCS - 40 CENTIMES

SILVER

Obv: Similar to 9 Francs - 20 Centimes, C#2.

C#	Date	Mintage	Fine	VF	XF
3	1813	—	1000.	1500.	2000.

YUGOSLAVIA/Croatia

Croatia, a federal republic of the Socialist Federal Republic of Yugoslavia, has an area of 21,829 sq. mi. (56,538 sq. km.) and a population of about 5 million. Capital: Zagreb.

The country was attached to the kingdom of Hungary until Dec. 1, 1918, when it joined with Serbia, Slovenia, Bosnia-Herzegovina, Macedonia and Montenegro to form the Kingdom of the Serbs, Croats and Slovenes, which changed its name to the Kingdom of Yugoslavia on Oct. 3, 1929. On April 6, 1941, Hitler, angered by the coup d' etat that overthrew the pro-Nazi regime of regent Prince Paul, sent the Nazi armies crashing across the Yugoslav borders from Germany, Hungary, Romania and Bulgaria. Within a week the army of the Balkan kingdom was prostrate and broken. Yugoslavia was dismembered to award Hitler's Balkan allies. Croatia, reconstituted as a nominal kingdom, was given to the administration of an Italian princeling, who wisely decided to remain in Italy.

The word 'kunas', derived from the Russian 'cunica' which means marten, reflects the use of furs for money in medieval eastern Europe.

1 KUNA

ZINC

Similar to 2 Kune, Y#1.

Y#	Date	Mintage	VF	XF	Unc
—	1941	—	—	Rare	—

2 KUNE

ZINC

Y#	Date	Mintage	VF	XF	Unc
1	1941	—	5.00	10.00	20.00

50 KUNA

Dated 1934, this coin is found struck in various metals. It is considered a modern fantasy issue.

500 KUNA

GOLD

Fr#	Date	Mintage	VF	XF	Unc
1	1941	170 pcs.	—	1250.	3500.

NCLT ISSUES

PATTERNS

KM#	Date	Mintage	Identification	Mkt.Val.
1	1934	—	5 Kuna, Bronze	350.00

KM#	Date	Mintage	Identification	Mkt.Val.
2	1934	—	5 Kuna, Silver	250.00
3	1941	—	25 Banica, Zinc	—
4	1941	—	50 Banica, Zinc	—
5	1941	—	1 Kuna, Silver	—
6	1941	—	2 Kuna, Silver	—
7	1941	—	500 Kuna, Aluminum	—
8	1941	—	500 Kuna, Aluminum	—

YUGOSLAVIA/Montenegro

The former independent kingdom of Montenegro, now one of the nominally autonomous federated units of Yugoslavia, was located in southeastern Europe north of Albania. As a kingdom, it had an area of 5,333 sq. mi. (13,812 sq. km.) and a population of about 250,000. Capital: Titograd. The predominantly pastoral kingdom had few industries.

Montenegro became an independent state in 1355 following the break-up of the Serb empire. During the Turkish invasion of Albania and Herzegovina in the 15th century, the Montenegrins moved their capital to the remote mountain village of Cetinje where they maintained their independence through two centuries of intermittent attack, emerging as the only one of the Balkan states not subjugated by the Turks. When World War I began, Montenegro joined with Serbia and was subsequently invaded and occupied by the Austrians. Austria withdrew upon the defeat of the Central Powers, permitting the Serbians to move in and maintain the occupation. Montenegro then joined the kingdom of the Serbs, Croats and Slovenes, which later became Yugoslavia.

The coinage, issued under the autocratic rule of Prince Nicholas, is obsolete.

RULERS

Nicholas I, as Prince, 1860-1910
as King, 1910-1918

MINTMARKS

(a) - Paris, privy marks only

MONETARY SYSTEM

100 Para = 1 Perper

PARA

BRONZE

Y#	Date	Mintage	Fine	VF	XF	Unc
1	1906	.200	5.00	12.50	22.50	35.00

Y#	Date	Mintage	Fine	VF	XF	Unc
11	1913	.100	6.00	13.50	25.00	35.00
	1914	.200	4.50	11.50	18.50	25.00

2 PARE

BRONZE

Y#	Date	Mintage	Fine	VF	XF	Unc
2	1906	.600	4.50	7.00	13.50	17.50
	1908	.250	5.00	8.00	17.50	22.50

Y#	Date	Mintage	Fine	VF	XF	Unc
12	1913	.500	4.00	7.00	13.50	17.50
	1914	.400	4.00	7.00	13.50	17.50

10 PARA

NICKEL

Y#	Date	Mintage	Fine	VF	XF	Unc
3	1906	.750	2.75	5.00	10.00	15.00
	1908	.250	4.00	6.00	12.50	17.50

Y#	Date	Mintage	Fine	VF	XF	Unc
13	1913	.200	4.00	6.00	10.00	15.00
	1914	.800	2.75	4.00	8.00	10.00

20 PARA

NICKEL

Y#	Date	Mintage	Fine	VF	XF	Unc
4	1906	.600	4.50	6.00	10.00	15.00
	1908	.400	4.50	6.00	10.00	15.00

Y#	Date	Mintage	Fine	VF	XF	Unc
14	1913	.200	6.00	8.00	12.50	17.50
	1914	.800	4.00	7.00	10.00	15.00

PERPER

5.0000 gm., .835 SILVER, .1342 oz ASW

Y#	Date	Mintage	Fine	VF	XF	Unc
5	1909(a)	.500*	8.50	15.00	25.00	35.00

Approximately 30 per cent melted.

Y#	Date	Mintage	Fine	VF	XF	Unc
15	1912	.520	10.00	17.50	30.00	40.00
	1914	.500	10.00	17.50	30.00	40.00

2 PERPERA

10.0000 gm., .835 SILVER, .2685 oz ASW

Y#	Date	Mintage	Fine	VF	XF	Unc
6	1910	.300	12.00	20.00	32.50	37.50

Y#	Date	Mintage	Fine	VF	XF	Unc
16	1914	.200	13.50	22.50	35.00	40.00

5 PERPERA

24.0000 gm., .900 SILVER, .6944 oz ASW

Y#	Date	Mintage	Fine	VF	XF	Unc
7	1909(a)	60,000*	90.00	130.00	175.00	225.00

*Approximately 50 per cent melted.

Y#	Date	Mintage	Fine	VF	XF	Unc
17	1912	40,002	90.00	130.00	175.00	225.00
	1914	20,000	100.00	150.00	200.00	250.00

10 PERPERA

3.3875 gm., .900 GOLD, .0980 oz AGW

Y#	Date	Mintage	Fine	VF	XF	Unc
8	1910	40,000	225.00	350.00	450.00	550.00

50th Year of Reign

Y#	Date	Mintage	Fine	VF	XF	Unc
18	1910	35,000	225.00	350.00	450.00	550.00

20 PERPERA

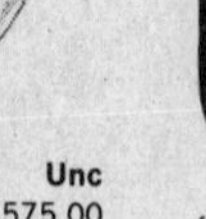

6.7751 gm., .900 GOLD, .1960 oz AGW

Y#	Date	Mintage	Fine	VF	XF	Unc
9	1910	30,000	275.00	400.00	500.00	575.00

50th Year of Reign

Y#	Date	Mintage	Fine	VF	XF	Unc
19	1910	30,000	275.00	400.00	500.00	575.00

100 PERPERA

33.8753 gm., .900 GOLD, .9802 oz AGW

Y#	Date	Mintage	Fine	VF	XF	Unc
10	1910	300 pcs.	2250.	3000.	10,000.	12,500.
	1910	—	—	—	Proof	12,500.

50th Year of Reign

Y#	Date	Mintage	Fine	VF	XF	Unc
20	1910	500 pcs.	2750.	3500.	11,000.	12,500.

YUGOSLAVIA/Serbia

Serbia, a former inland Balkan kingdom (now a federated republic of Yugoslavia) had an area of 34,116 sq. mi. (88,361 sq. km.). Capital: Belgrade.

Serbia emerged as a separate kingdom in the 12th century and attained its greatest expansion and political influence in the mid-14th century. After the Battle of Kosovo, 1389, Serbia became a vassal principality of Turkey and remained under Turkish suzeranity until it was re-established as an independent kingdom by the 1887 Treaty of Berlin. Following World War I, which had its immediate cause in the assassination of Austrian Archduke Francis Ferdinand by a Serbian nationalist, Serbia joined with the Croats and Slovenes to form the new kingdom of the South Slavs with Peter I of Serbia as king. The name of the kingdom was later changed to Yugoslavia. Invaded by Germany during World War II, Serbia emerged as a constituent republic of the Socialist Federal Republic of Yugoslavia.

RULERS

Michael, Obrenovich III
as Prince 1839-1842, 1860-1868
Milan, Obrenovich IV,
as Prince, 1868-1882
Alexander I, 1889-1902
Petar I, 1903-1918

GERMAN OCCUPATION

MINTMARKS

A - Paris
(a) - Paris, privy mark only
H - Birmingham
V - Vienna

MONETARY SYSTEM

100 Para = 1 Dinara

PARA

BRONZE

Serbia spelled СРБСКИ

Y#	Date	Mintage	VF	XF	Unc
1	1868	7.500	6.00	10.00	15.00

Third letter in Serbia is similar to 'h' with a 't' bar atop the upright.

Y#	Date	Mintage	VF	XF	Unc
1.1	1868	Inc. Ab.	12.00	20.00	30.00

2 PARE

BRONZE

Y#	Date	Mintage	VF	XF	Unc
13	1904	12.500	3.00	7.00	12.50

5 PARE

BRONZE

Y#	Date	Mintage	VF	XF	Unc
2	1868	7.420	8.00	13.00	25.00

Y#	Date	Mintage	VF	XF	Unc
7	1879	6.000	3.50	8.00	13.00

COPPER-NICKEL

Y#	Date	Mintage	VF	XF	Unc
14	1883	4.000	2.00	4.00	7.00
	1884H	3.000	2.00	7.50	15.00
	1904	8.000	1.50	3.50	6.00
	1904	Inc. Ab.	—	Proof	75.00
	1912	10.000	1.50	3.50	6.00
	1917	5.000	10.00	20.00	30.00

GOLD

Y#	Date	Mintage	VF	XF	Unc
14a	1917	—	—	—	350.00

10 PARE

BRONZE

Y#	Date	Mintage	VF	XF	Unc
3	1868	6.590	4.00	12.50	25.00

Y#	Date	Mintage	VF	XF	Unc
8	1879	9.000	4.00	7.00	10.50

COPPER-NICKEL

Y#	Date	Mintage	VF	XF	Unc
15	1883	5.000	1.75	4.00	8.00
	1884-H	6.500	1.75	4.00	8.00
	1904	—	—	Proof only	75.00
	1912	7.700	1.50	3.00	6.50
	1917	5.000	1.50	3.00	6.50

GOLD

Y#	Date	Mintage	VF	XF	Unc
15a	1917	—	—	—	500.00

20 PARE

COPPER-NICKEL

Y#	Date	Mintage	VF	XF	Unc
16	1883	2.500	2.25	8.00	15.00
	1884H	6.000	2.00	7.00	12.50
	1904	—	—	Proof only	75.00
	1912	5.650	1.75	5.00	9.50
16	1917	5.000	1.75	5.00	9.50

GOLD

Y#	Date	Mintage	VF	XF	Unc
16a	1917	—	—	—	500.00

50 PARE

2.5000 gm., .835 SILVER, .0671 oz ASW

Y#	Date	Mintage	VF	XF	Unc
4	1875	2.000	6.00	12.00	20.00

Y#	Date	Mintage	VF	XF	Unc
4a	1879	.600	8.00	15.00	25.00
	1879	—	—	Proof	250.00

Obv: With designer's signature below neck.

Y#	Date	Mintage	VF	XF	Unc
19	1904	1.400	1.75	5.00	10.00
	1912	.800	2.50	7.50	12.50
	1915(a)	9.700	2.00	4.00	8.00

Obv: Without designer's signature

Y#	Date	Mintage	VF	XF	Unc
19a	1915(a)	1.862	5.00	12.00	20.00

ZINC
German Puppet State

Y#	Date	Mintage	VF	XF	Unc
23	1942	—	4.00	9.00	15.00

DINAR

5.0000 gm., .835 SILVER, .1342 oz ASW

Y#	Date	Mintage	VF	XF	Unc
5	1875	3.000	6.00	17.50	35.50

Y#	Date	Mintage	VF	XF	Unc
5a	1879	.800	8.50	15.00	22.50
	1879	—	—	Proof	225.00

Y#	Date	Mintage	VF	XF	Unc
17	1897	4.000	5.00	10.00	15.00

Obv: With designer's signature below neck

Y#	Date	Mintage	VF	XF	Unc
20	1904	.993	4.50	10.00	25.00
	1912	8.000	4.25	8.00	15.00
	1915(a)	7.529	4.25	8.00	15.00

Obv: Without designer's signature

Y#	Date	Mintage	VF	XF	Unc
20a	1915(a)	2.312	5.00	15.00	25.00

ZINC
German Puppet State

Y#	Date	Mintage	VF	XF	Unc
24	1942	—	.75	2.00	4.50

2 DINARA

10.0000 gm., .835 SILVER, .2684 oz ASW

Y#	Date	Mintage	VF	XF	Unc
6	1875	1.000	30.00	60.00	100.00

Y#	Date	Mintage	VF	XF	Unc
6a	1879	.750	12.00	20.00	35.00
	1879	—	—	Proof	350.00

Y#	Date	Mintage	VF	XF	Unc
18	1897	1.000	10.00	15.00	22.50

Obv: With designer's signature below neck

Y#	Date	Mintage	VF	XF	Unc
21	1904	.387	10.00	12.00	15.00
	1912	.800	8.00	8.00	12.50
	1915(a)	2.502	BV	8.00	10.00

Obv: Without designer's signature

Y#	Date	Mintage	VF	XF	Unc
21a	1915(a)	.826	8.00	12.00	17.50

ZINC
German Puppet State

Y#	Date	Mintage	VF	XF	Unc
25	1942	—	1.00	2.00	5.00

5 DINARA

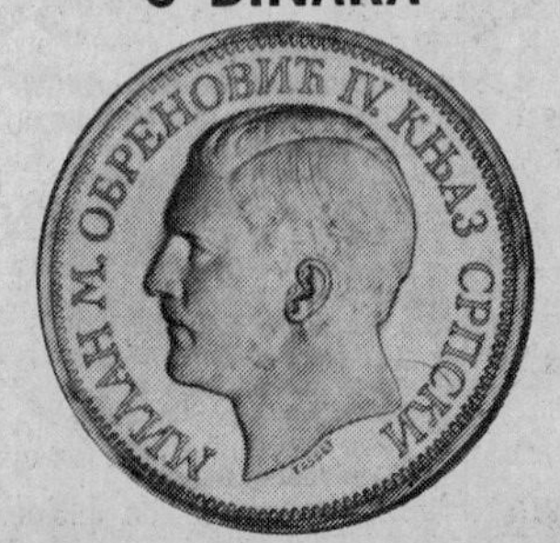

25.0000 gm., .900 SILVER, .7234 oz ASW

Y#	Date	Mintage	VF	XF	Unc
9	1879	.200	45.00	80.00	135.00
	1879	—	—	Proof	1350.

25.0000 gm., .835 SILVER, .6712 oz ASW
Karageorgevich Dynasty 100th Anniversary

22	1904	.200	45.00	75.00	125.00

1.6129 gm., .900 GOLD, .3467 oz AGW

22a	1904	4 pcs.	—	—	—

10 DINARA

3.2258 gm., .900 GOLD, .0933 oz AGW

11	1882V	.300	85.00	175.00	250.00

ZINC
German Puppet State

26	1943	1.750	3.00	5.00	9.00

20 DINARA

6.4516 gm., .900 GOLD, .1867 oz AGW
Obv: Full title in legend.

10	1879A	.050	125.00	200.00	275.00

Obv: Short title in legend.

Y#	Date	Mintage	VF	XF	Unc
12	1882V	—	135.00	150.00	200.00

Obv: Head of Petar I with cap and beard.
Rev: Value/date/arms

	1917	—	Reported, not confirmed

NCLT ISSUES

PATTERNS

KM#	Date	Mintage	Identification	Mkt.Val.
1	1882V	—	20 Dinara, Copper	225.00
2	1890	—	1 Dinar, Silver	—
3	1890	—	2 Dinara, Silver	—
4	1890	—	2 Dinara, Aluminum-Bronze	125.00
5	1890	—	2 Dinara, Gilt Bronze	125.00

The Republic of Zaire (formerly the Belgian Congo), located in the south-central part of Africa, has an area of 905,063 sq. mi. (2,344,102 sq. km.) and a population of 24.9 million. Capital: Kinshasa. The mineral-rich country produces copper, tin, diamonds, gold, zinc, cobalt and uranium.

In ancient times the territory comprising Zaire was occupied by Negrito peoples (Pygmies) pushed into the mountains by Bantu and Nilotic invaders. The interior was first explored by the American correspondent Henry Stanley, who was subsequently commissioned by King Leopold II of Belgium to conclude development treaties with the local chiefs. The Berlin conference of 1885 awarded the area to Leopold, who administered and exploited it as his private property until it was annexed to Belgium in 1908. Following the eruption of bloody independence riots in 1959, Belgium granted the Belgian Congo independence as the Republic of the Congo on June 30, 1960. The nation officially changed its name to Zaire on Oct. 27, 1971.

BELGIAN CONGO

The Belgian Congo attained independence with the distinction of being the most ill-prepared country to ever undertake self-government. Without a single doctor, lawyer or engineer, with no organized unit capable of maintaining law and order, independence disintegrated into an orgy of anarchy. Provinces seceded. Intertribal warfare erupted. Belgian troops intervened to protect Belgian citizens from retributive massacre. By 1961 four groups were fighting for political dominance. The most serious threat to the viability of the country was posed by the secession of mineral-rich Katanga province on July 11, 1960. After two and one-half years of sporadic warfare with a U.N. military force, Katanga's leaders capitulated, Jan. 14, 1963, and the rebellious province was partitioned into three provinces.

RULERS

Belgian, until 1960

MONETARY SYSTEM

100 Centimes = 1 Franc

CENTIME

COPPER

Y#	Date	Mintage	VF	XF	Unc
1	1887	.180	2.50	6.00	10.00
	1888	Inc. Ab.	1.50	4.00	10.00
15	1910	2.000	1.00	2.00	5.00
	1919	.500	1.50	3.00	8.50

2 CENTIMES

COPPER

2	1887	.130	2.50	4.00	10.00
	1888	Inc. Ab.	2.50	4.00	10.00

Y#	Date	Mintage	VF	XF	Unc
16	1910	1.500	2.50	6.00	20.00
	1919	.500	4.75	10.00	25.00

5 CENTIMES

OVERDATE

COPPER

Y#	Date	Mintage	VF	XF	Unc
3	1887	.180	4.00	10.00	22.50
	1888/87	Inc. Ab.	6.00	10.00	25.00
	1888	Inc. Ab.	1.00	6.00	12.50
	1894	.150	1.00	6.00	12.50

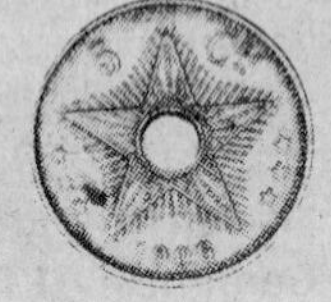

COPPER-NICKEL

Y#	Date	Mintage	VF	XF	Unc
9	1906	.100	1.75	3.50	10.00
	1908	.180	1.50	3.00	10.00

Y#	Date	Mintage	VF	XF	Unc
12	1909	1.800	4.00	6.00	50.00

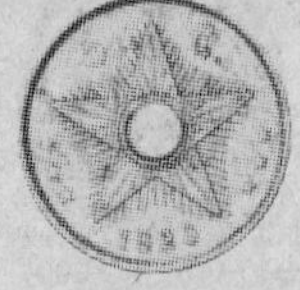

Y#	Date	Mintage	VF	XF	Unc
17	1910	6.000	1.50	2.50	5.00
	1911	5.000	1.50	2.50	5.00
	1917H	1.000	2.00	4.00	8.00
	1918H	2.000	2.00	4.00	8.00
	1919	6.850	.75	1.50	4.00
	1920	2.740	1.00	1.75	5.00
	1921	17.260	.75	1.50	4.00
	1921H	3.000	1.00	1.75	5.00
	1925	11.000	.75	1.50	4.00
	1926/5	5.770	4.50	—	—
	1926	Inc. Ab.	.75	1.75	4.00
	1927	2.000	1.00	1.75	4.00
	1928	1.500	1.25	2.00	5.00

10 CENTIMES

COPPER

Y#	Date	Mintage	VF	XF	Unc
4	1887	.040	5.00	12.50	30.00
	1888	Inc. Ab.	3.00	7.50	17.50
	1889	.100	2.00	6.00	12.50
	1894	.150	2.00	6.00	12.50

COPPER-NICKEL

Y#	Date	Mintage	VF	XF	Unc
10	1906	.100	2.00	4.00	10.00
	1908	.800	1.75	3.00	10.00

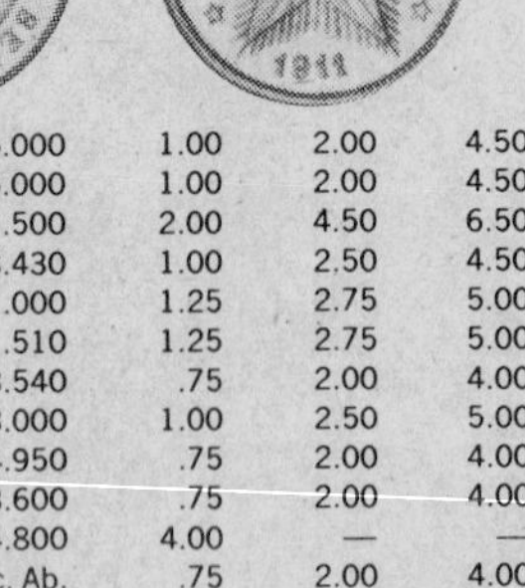

Y#	Date	Mintage	VF	XF	Unc
13	1909	1.500	3.50	6.00	50.00

Y#	Date	Mintage	VF	XF	Unc
18	1910	5.000	1.00	2.00	4.50
	1911	5.000	1.00	2.00	4.50
	1917H	.500	2.00	4.50	6.50
	1919	3.430	1.00	2.50	4.50
	1919H	1.000	1.25	2.75	5.00
	1920	1.510	1.25	2.75	5.00
	1921	13.540	.75	2.00	4.00
	1921H	3.000	1.00	2.50	5.00
	1922	14.950	.75	2.00	4.00
	1924	3.600	.75	2.00	4.00
	1925/4	4.800	4.00	—	—
	1925	Inc. Ab.	.75	2.00	4.00
	1927	2.020	.75	2.00	4.00
	1928	5.600	.75	2.00	4.00

20 CENTIMES

COPPER-NICKEL

Y#	Date	Mintage	VF	XF	Unc
11	1906	.100	3.00	7.50	10.00
	1908	.400	2.25	4.00	10.00

Y#	Date	Mintage	VF	XF	Unc
14	1909	.300	4.00	8.00	50.00

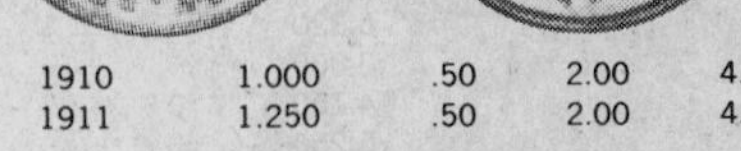

Y#	Date	Mintage	VF	XF	Unc
19	1910	1.000	.50	2.00	4.00
	1911	1.250	.50	2.00	4.00

50 CENTIMES

2.5000 gm. .835 SILVER, .0671 oz ASW

Y#	Date	Mintage	VF	XF	Unc
5	1887	.020	17.50	30.00	75.00
	1891	.060	12.50	25.00	75.00
	1894	.040	12.50	25.00	75.00
	1896	.200	12.50	22.50	75.00

NOTE: Legends on the reverses of Y#20 and Y#21 alternately in Flemish - Belgisch Congo - and French - Congo Belge - as indicated.

COPPER-NICKEL
Rev: French legend CONGO BELGE

Y#	Date	Mintage	VF	XF	Unc
20	1921	4.000	1.75	3.50	20.00
	1922	5.800	1.50	3.00	20.00
	1923	7.200	1.50	3.00	20.00
	1924	4.050	1.75	3.50	20.00
	1925	13.350	1.25	2.75	15.00
	1926/5	20.600	6.50	—	—
	1926	Inc. Ab.	1.25	1.75	15.00
	1927	7.400	1.25	3.00	20.00
	1928	7.480	1.25	3.00	15.00
	1929/7	3.810	6.50	—	—
	1929/8	Inc. Ab.	6.50	—	—
	1929	Inc. Ab.	1.50	3.00	15.00

Rev: Flemish legend BELGISCH CONGO

Y#	Date	Mintage	VF	XF	Unc
20.1	1921	4.000	1.75	3.50	20.00
	1922	5.800	1.50	3.00	15.00
	1923/1	7.200	6.50	—	—
	1923	Inc. Ab.	1.50	3.00	15.00
	1924	4.050	1.75	3.50	20.00
	1925/4	13.350	6.50	—	—
	1925	Inc. Ab.	1.25	3.00	20.00
	1926	20.600	1.25	3.00	15.00
	1927	7.400	1.25	3.00	15.00
	1928	—	1.25	3.00	15.00
	1929	3.810	1.25	3.00	15.00

FRANC

5.0000 gm. .835 SILVER, .1342 oz ASW

Y#	Date	Mintage	VF	XF	Unc
6	1887	.020	25.00	45.00	125.00
	1891	.070	22.50	40.00	125.00

Y#	Date	Mintage	VF	XF	Unc
6	1894	.070	22.50	40.00	125.00
	1896	.160	22.50	35.00	125.00

COPPER-NICKEL
Rev: French legend CONGO BELGE

Y#	Date	Mintage	VF	XF	Unc
21	1920	2.340	2.50	5.00	25.00
	1921	1.760	2.50	5.00	25.00
	1922	10.000	1.75	4.00	20.00
	1923/2	Inc.Ab.	2.25	5.00	22.50
	1923	6.180	1.75	4.00	20.00
	1924	5.320	1.75	4.00	20.00
	1925	10.000	1.50	3.50	20.00
	1926	14.750	1.50	3.50	20.00
	1927	15.250	1.50	3.50	20.00
	1928	9.250	1.50	3.75	20.00
	1929	5.000	1.75	4.00	20.00
	1930	5.000	1.75	4.00	20.00

Rev: Flemish legend BELGISCH CONGO

Y#	Date	Mintage	VF	XF	Unc
21.1	1920	2.340	2.50	5.00	25.00
	1921	1.760	2.50	5.00	25.00
	1922	10.000	1.50	3.50	20.00
	1923	6.180	1.75	4.00	20.00
	1924	5.320	1.75	4.00	20.00
	1925	10.000	1.50	3.50	20.00
	1926/5	14.750	6.50	—	—
	1926	Inc. Ab.	1.50	3.50	20.00
	1928	—	1.50	3.75	20.00
	1929	5.000	1.75	4.00	20.00
	1930	5.000	1.75	4.00	20.00

BRASS

Y#	Date	Mintage	VF	XF	Unc
22	1944	25.000	.75	2.25	5.00
	1946	15.000	1.00	2.50	6.00
	1949	15.000	1.00	2.50	3.50

2 FRANCS

10.0000 gm., .835 SILVER, .2685 oz ASW

Y#	Date	Mintage	VF	XF	Unc
7	1887	.020	50.00	75.00	190.00
	1891	.030	40.00	60.00	190.00
	1894	.080	35.00	100.00	190.00
	1896	.100	35.00	100.00	190.00

BRASS

Y#	Date	Mintage	VF	XF	Unc
24	1943	25.000	1.00	4.00	25.00

Y#	Date	Mintage	VF	XF	Unc
23	1946	25.000	1.50	2.50	4.50
	1947	19.120	1.50	2.00	3.50

5 FRANCS

25.0000 gm., .900 SILVER, .7234 oz ASW

Y#	Date	Mintage	VF	XF	Unc
8	1887	8,000	125.00	275.00	600.00
	1891	.030	125.00	275.00	600.00
	1894	.050	125.00	275.00	600.00
	1896	.110	125.00	275.00	600.00

NICKEL-BRONZE

Y#	Date	Mintage	VF	XF	Unc
26	1936	2.600	6.00	14.00	75.00
	1937	11.400	5.00	10.00	75.00

BRASS

Y#	Date	Mintage	VF	XF	Unc
25	1947	10.000	3.00	6.00	25.00
	1948	—	3.00	6.00	25.00

50 FRANCS

SILVER

Y#	Date	Mintage	VF	XF	Unc
27	1944	1.000	50.00	75.00	115.00

NCLT ISSUES

PATTERNS

KM#	Date	Mintage	Identification	Issue Price	Mkt. Val.
—	1896	—	5 Francs, .900 Silver	—	650.00

RUANDA—URUNDI

The Belgian Colony in the Congo and Ruanda-Urundi were united administratively from 1925 to 1960. Ruanda—Urundi was made a U.N. Trust territory in 1946. Coins for these 2 areas were made jointly between 1954 and 1960. Ruanda-Urundi became the Rpublic of Ruanda on June 1, 1962.

50 CENTIMES

ALUMINUM

Y#	Date	Mintage	VF	XF	Unc
29	1954	4.700	.35	.50	1.00
	1955	20.300	.15	.40	1.00

FRANC

ALUMINUM

Y#	Date	Mintage	VF	XF	Unc
30	1957	10.000	.25	.65	1.25
	1958	20.000	.25	.65	1.00
	1959	20.000	.25	.65	1.00
	1960	20.000	.25	.65	1.25

5 FRANCS

BRASS

28	1952	10.000	1.00	2.00	8.00

ALUMINUM

31	1956	10.000	.45	.75	2.00
	1958	26.110	.45	.70	1.75
	1959	3.980	.45	.70	2.00

NOTE: For later coinage see Rwanda and Burundi, Rwanda, and Burundi.

CONGO DEMOCRATIC REPUBLIC

Democratic Republic of the Congo achieved independence on June 30, 1960. It followed the same monetary system as when under the Belgians. Monetary Reform of 1967 introuced. new denominations and coins. The name of the country was changed to Zaire in 1971.

MINTMARKS

B - Brusseles, privy marks only

10 FRANKS

ALUMINUM

1	1965	100.000*	.50	1.00	1.75

***NOTE:** Most recalled and melted down.

3.1900 gm., .900 GOLD, .0923 oz AGW

Fr#	Date	Mintage	XF	Unc	Proof
5	1965	3,000*	—	—	65.00

***NOTE:** Approximately 70 per cent melted.

20 FRANKS

6.3400 gm., .900 GOLD, .1834 oz AGW

Fr#	Date	Mintage	XF	Unc	Proof
4	1965	3,000*	—	—	125.00

***NOTE:** Approximately 70 per cent melted.

25 FRANKS

8.0000 gm., .900 GOLD, .2315 oz AGW

3	1965	3,000*	—	—	150.00

***NOTE:** Approximately 70 per cent melted.

SILVER

3a	1965	2 Known	—	—	—

50 FRANKS

15.9800 gm., .900 GOLD, .4624 oz AGW

2	1965	3,000*	—	—	300.00

***NOTE:** Approximately 70 per cent melted.

100 FRANKS

32.2300 gm., .900 gold .9327 oz AGW

1	1965	3,000*	—	—	625.00

***NOTE:** Approximately 70 per cent melted.

SILVER

1a	1965	2 Known	—	—	—

MONETARY REFORM

100 Sengi = 1 Likuta
100 Makuta (plural of Likuta) = 1 Zaire

10 SENGI

ALUMINUM

Y#	Date	Mintage	VF	XF	Unc
2	1967	—	.20	.40	.75

.900 GOLD
Obv: Bust of President Mobutu.
Rev: Tiger head above crossed spears.

KM#	Date	Mintage	XF	Unc	Proof
1	1970	1,000	—	—	100.00

LIKUTA

ALUMINUM

Y#	Date	Mintage	VF	XF	Unc
3	1967	36.290	.25	.75	1.25
	1968	36.290	.25	.75	1.00
	1969	12.890	.25	.75	1.00

5 MAKUTA

COPPER-NICKEL

4	1967	1.980	1.00	1.50	2.00
	1968	1.980	1.00	1.50	2.00
	1969	.490	1.00	1.50	2.00

25 MAKUTAS

.900 GOLD
Similar to 1 Zaire, KM#4.

KM#	Date	Mintage	XF	Unc	Proof
2	1970	1,000	—	—	250.00

50 MAKUTAS

.900 GOLD
Similar to 1 Zaire, KM#4.

3	1970	1,000	—	—	500.00

ZAIRE

.900 GOLD
President Mobutu

4	1970	1,000	—	—	1000.

NCLT ISSUES

ESSAIS (E)

Standard metals unless otherwise noted

KM#	Date	Mintage	Identification	Issue Price	Mkt. Val.
E4a	1970	—	1 Zaire, Silver	—	150.00

MINT SETS

KM#	Date	Mintage	Identification	Issue Price	Mkt. Val.
S1	1970	1,000	KM1-4	1300.	1800.

KATANGA

Katanga, the southern province of the former Belgian Congo, had an area of 191,873 sq. mi. (496,951 sq. km.) and was noted for its mineral wealth.

MONETARY SYSTEM

100 Centimes = 1 Franc

FRANC

BRONZE

Y#	Date	Mintage	VF	XF	Unc
2	1961	—	.50	1.00	1.50

5 FRANCS

BRONZE

Y#	Date	Mintage	VF	XF	Unc
3	1961	—	1.50	1.75	2.00

13.3300 gm., .900 GOLD, .3857 oz AGW
Similar to Y#3.

Y#	Date	Mintage	VF	XF	Unc
1	1961	.020	BV	BV	250.00

REP. OF ZAIRE

MONETARY SYSTEM

100 Makuta = 1 Zaire

5 MAKUTA

COPPER-NICKEL

Y#	Date	Mintage	VF	XF	Unc
3	1977	—	—	—	1.00

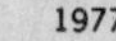

10 MAKUTA

COPPER-NICKEL

Y#	Date	Mintage	VF	XF	Unc
4	1973	5.000	—	3.00	10.00
	1975	—	—	1.50	10.00

20 MAKUTA

COPPER-NICKEL

Y#	Date	Mintage	VF	XF	Unc
5	1973	—	—	3.00	10.00
	1976	—	1.75	—	—

25 MAKUTAS

.900 GOLD

H#	Date	Mintage	XF	Unc	Proof
8	1970	1,000	—	—	—

50 MAKUTAS

.900 GOLD

H#	Date	Mintage	XF	Unc	Proof
9	1970	1,000	—	—	—

ZAIRE

.900 GOLD

H#	Date	Mintage	XF	Unc	Proof
10	1970	1,000	—	—	—

2-1/2 ZAIRES

.925 SILVER
Conservation Series

Y#	Date	Mintage	VF	XF	Unc
8	1975	3,500	BV	BV	25.00
	1975	—	—	Proof	30.00

5 ZAIRES

.925 SILVER
Conservation Series

Y#	Date	Mintage	VF	XF	Unc
9	1975	3,500	BV	35.00	40.00
	1975	—	—	Proof	50.00

100 ZAIRES

.900 GOLD
Conservation Series

Y#	Date	Mintage	VF	XF	Unc
10	1975	1,100	BV	BV	650.00
	1975	—	—	Proof	800.00

NCLT ISSUES

ESSAIS (E)

Standard metals unless otherwise noted

KM#	Date	Mintage	Identification	Issue Price	Mkt. Val.
E1	1964	—	1 Zaire, Silver	—	—

PROOF SETS

KM#	Date	Mintage	Identification	Issue Price	Mkt. Val.
101	1965(5)	*3,000	F1-5	490.00	675.00

***NOTE:** Approximately 70 per cent melted.

KM#	Date	Mintage	Identification	Issue Price	Mkt. Val.
102	1970(4)	1,000	H7-10	—	—
103	1975(2)	—	Y8,9	60.00	75.00

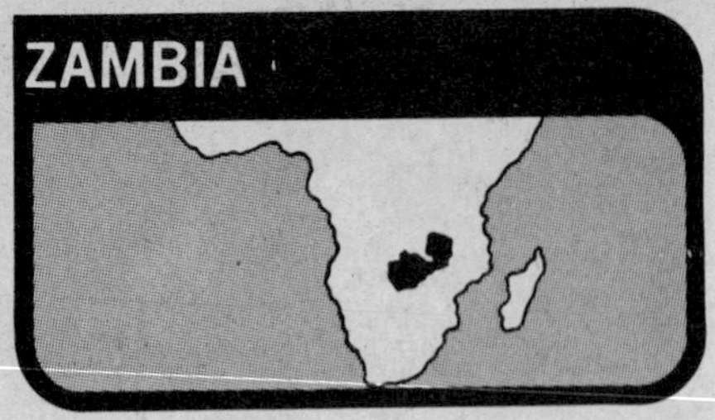

The Republic of Zambia (formerly Northern Rhodesia), a landlocked country in south-central Africa, has an area of 290,724 sq. mi. (752,972 sq. km.) and a population of 5.4 million. Capital: Lusaka. The economy of Zambia is based principally on copper, of which Zambia is the world's third largest producer. Copper, zinc, lead, cobalt and tobacco are exported.

The area that is now Zambia was brought within the British sphere of influence in 1888 by empire builder Cecil Rhodes, who obtained mining concessions in southcentral Africa from indigenous chiefs. The territory was ruled by the British South Africa Company, which Rhodes established, until 1924 when its administration was transferred to the British government as a protectorate. In 1953, Northern Rhodesia was joined with Nyasaland and the colony of Southern Rhodesia to form the Federation of Rhodesia and Nyasaland. Northern Rhodesia seceded from the Federation on Oct. 24, 1964, and became the independent Republic of Zambia. Zambia is a member of the Commonwealth of Nations. The president is Chief of State.

Zambia converted to a decimal coinage on January 16, 1969.

NOTE: For earlier coinage see Rhodesia and Nyasaland.

RULERS

British, until 1964

MONETARY SYSTEM

12 Pence = 1 Shilling
20 Shillings = 1 Pound

PENNY

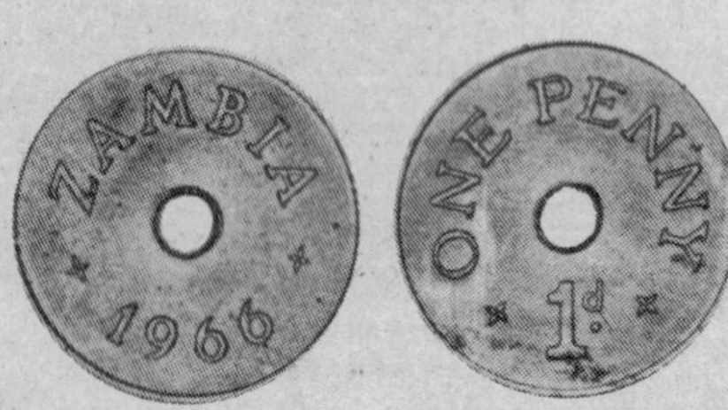

BRONZE

Y#	Date	Mintage	Fine	VF	XF	Unc
5	1966	7.200	.10	.20	.40	.75
	1966	60 pcs.	—	—	Proof	—

SIXPENCE

COPPER-NICKEL-ZINC

Y#	Date	Mintage	Fine	VF	XF	Unc
1	1964	3.500	.15	.30	.60	1.00
	1964	5,000	—	—	Proof	2.00

Y#	Date	Mintage	Fine	VF	XF	Unc
6	1966	7.200	.20	.40	.50	.75
	1966	60 pcs.	—	—	Proof	—

SHILLING

COPPER-NICKEL

Y#	Date	Mintage	Fine	VF	XF	Unc
2	1964	3.510	.35	.75	1.50	2.25
	1964	5,000	—	—	Proof	4.00

Y#	Date	Mintage	Fine	VF	XF	Unc
7	1966	5.000	.25	.40	.75	1.50
	1966	60 pcs.	—	—	Proof	—

2 SHILLINGS

COPPER-NICKEL

Y#	Date	Mintage	Fine	VF	XF	Unc
3	1964	3.770	.60	1.00	1.75	3.50
	1964	5,000	—	—	Proof	5.50
8	1966	5.000	.50	1.00	1.50	2.25
	1966	60 pcs.	—	—	Proof	—

5 SHILLINGS

COPPER-NICKEL

Y#	Date	Mintage	Fine	VF	XF	Unc
4	1965	.010	1.50	2.50	3.50	5.00
		.020	—	—	Proof	10.00

DECIMAL COINAGE

100 Ngwee = 1 Kwacha

NGWEE

BRONZE

Y#	Date	Mintage	VF	XF	Unc
9	1968	8.000	.10	.15	.25
	1968	4,000	—	Proof	2.50
	1969	16.000	.10	.15	.25
	1972	20.000	.10	.15	.25
	1978	.020	—	Proof	2.50

2 NGWEE

BRONZE

Y#	Date	Mintage	VF	XF	Unc
10	1968	29.000	.10	.20	.35
	1968	4,000	—	Proof	3.00
	1978	.020	—	Proof	2.50

5 NGWEE

COPPER-NICKEL

Y#	Date	Mintage	VF	XF	Unc
11	1968	12.000	.20	.30	.50
	1968	4,000	—	Proof	3.50
	1972	4.000	.20	.30	.50
	1978	.020	—	Proof	3.00

10 NGWEE

COPPER-NICKEL-ZINC

Y#	Date	Mintage	VF	XF	Unc
12	1968	1.000	.35	.65	1.00
	1968	4,000	—	Proof	4.00
	1972	1.000	.35	.65	1.00
	1978	.020	—	Proof	3.50

20 NGWEE

COPPER-NICKEL

Y#	Date	Mintage	VF	XF	Unc
13	1968	1.500	1.00	1.25	2.00
	1968	4,000	—	Proof	5.00
	1972	7.500	1.00	1.25	2.00
	1978	.020	—	Proof	4.00

50 NGWEE

COPPER-NICKEL
F.A.O. Issue

Y#	Date	Mintage	VF	XF	Unc
14	1969	.070	1.50	2.25	3.50

F.A.O. Issue

Y#	Date	Mintage	VF	XF	Unc
15	1972	.510	2.00	3.00	5.00

Second Republic 13th December 1972

Y#	Date	Mintage	VF	XF	Unc
16	1972	6.000	1.75	2.50	4.00
	1972	2,000	—	Proof	9.00
	1978	.020	—	Proof	7.50

KWACHA

COPPER-NICKEL
10th Anniversary of Independence

Y#	Date	Mintage	VF	XF	Unc
17	1974	500 pcs.	—	Proof	50.00

5 KWACHA

28.2800 gm., .925 SILVER, .8411 oz ASW
Conservation Series
Obv: Similar to 20 Ngwee, Y#13.

Y#	Date	Mintage	VF	XF	Unc
18	1979	—	BV	BV	25.00
	1979	.010	—	Proof	30.00

10 KWACHA

35.0000 gm., .925 SILVER, 1.0409 oz ASW
Conservation Series
Obv: Similar to 20 Ngwee, Y#13.

Y#	Date	Mintage	VF	XF	Unc
19	1979	—	BV	35.00	40.00
	1979	.010	—	Proof	50.00

200 KWACHA

33.4300 gm., .900 GOLD, .9674 oz AGW
Conservation Series
Obv: Similar to 20 Ngwee, Y#13.

Y#	Date	Mintage	VF	XF	Unc
20	1979	—	BV	BV	650.00
	1979	1,000	—	Proof	800.00

NCLT ISSUES

MINT SETS

KM#	Date	Mintage	Identification	Issue Price	Mkt. Val.
S1	1968(5)	—	Y9-13	2.00	4.50

PROOF SETS

STANDARD METALS

KM#	Date	Mintage	Identification	Issue Price	Mkt. Val.
101	1964(3)	5,000	Y1-3	—	10.00
102	1965(2)	100	Y4 (2 pcs.)	—	—
103	1966(8)	30	Y5-8 Double sets	—	—
104	1968(5)	4,000	Y9-13	10.00	16.50
105	1978(6)	20,000	Y9-13,16	21.00	21.50

Listings For

ZANZIBAR: refer to Tanzania

ZARA: refer to Yugoslavia

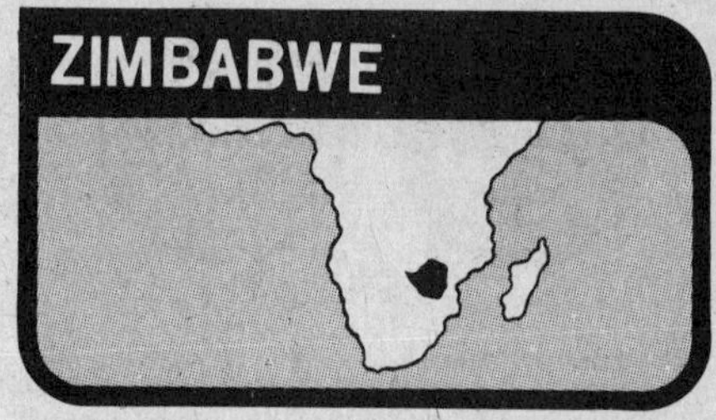

The Republic of Zimbabwe Rhodesia (formerly Southern Rhodesia), located in the east-central part of southern Africa, has an area of 150,820 sq. mi. (390,622 sq. km.) and a population of 6.7 million. Capital: Salisbury. The economy is based on agriculture and mining. Tobacco, sugar, asbestos, copper and chrome, ore and coal are exported.

The Rhodesian area, the habitat of paleolithic man, contains extensive evidence of earlier civilizations, notably the world-famous ruins of Zimbabwe, a gold-trading center that flourished about the 14th or 15th century A.D. The Portuguese of the 16th century were the first Europeans to attempt to develop south-central Africa, but it remained for Cecil Rhodes and the British South Africa Co. to open the hinterlands. Rhodes obtained a concession for mineral rights from local chiefs in 1888 and administered his African empire (named Southern Rhodesia in 1895) through the British South Africa Co. until 1923, when the British government annexed the area after the white settlers voted for existence as a separate entity, rather than for incorporation into the Union of South Africa. From Sept. of 1953 through 1963 Southern Rhodesia was joined with the British Protectorates of Northern Rhodesia and Nyasaland into a multiracial federation. When the federation was dissolved at the end of 1963, Northern Rhodesia and Nyasaland became the independent states of Zambia and Malawi.

Britain was prepared to grant independence to Southern Rhodesia but declined to do so when the politically dominant white Rhodesians refused to give assurances of representative government. On May 11, 1965, following two years of unsuccessful negotiation with the British government, Prime Minister Ian Smith issued an unilateral declaration of independence. Britain responded with economic sanctions supported by the United Nations. After further futile attempts to effect an accommodation, the Rhodesian Parliament severed all ties with Britain, and on March 2, 1970, established the Republic of Rhodesia.

On March 3, 1978, Prime Minister Ian Smith and three moderate black nationalist leaders signed an agreement providing for black majority rule. The name of the country was changed to Zimbabwe Rhodesia.

The U. S. Government and the United Nations still consider the country to be the British colony of Southern Rhodesia.

SOUTHERN RHODESIA

RULERS

George V, 1910-1936
Edward VIII, 1936
George VI, 1936-1952
Elizabeth II, 1952-1970

MONETARY SYSTEM

12 Pence = 1 Shilling
2 Shillings = 1 Florin
5 Shillings = 1 Crown
20 Shillings = 1 Pound

1/2 PENNY

COPPER-NICKEL

Y#	Date	Mintage	VF	XF	Unc
1	1934	.240	4.50	15.00	40.00
	1936	.240	17.50	40.00	150.00

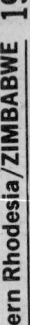

Y#	Date	Mintage	VF	XF	Unc
8	1938	.240	4.00	12.50	35.00
	1938	—	—	Proof	200.00
	1939	.480	4.00	9.00	30.00
	1939	—	—	Proof	200.00
	BRONZE				
8a	1942	.480	3.00	7.50	22.50
	1942	—	—	Proof	250.00
	1943	.960	1.75	3.50	7.50
	1944	.960	1.75	3.50	11.50

New legend: KING GEORGE THE SIXTH

Y#	Date	Mintage	VF	XF	Unc
27	1951	.480	1.25	5.00	8.00
	1952	.480	1.25	3.00	10.00
	1952	—	—	Proof	150.00

Y#	Date	Mintage	VF	XF	Unc
35	1954	.960	3.00	20.00	35.00
	1954	—	—	Proof	300.00
	1958	—	—	Proof	350.00

PENNY

COPPER-NICKEL

Y#	Date	Mintage	VF	XF	Unc
2	1934	.360	2.75	6.00	20.00
	1935	.492	3.50	10.00	40.00
	1936	1.044	1.75	5.00	25.00

Y#	Date	Mintage	VF	XF	Unc
9	1937	.908	1.00	3.00	15.00
	1937	—	—	Proof	400.00
	1938	.240	2.75	10.00	25.00
	1939	1.284	1.75	5.25	15.00
	1940	1.080	2.00	5.50	17.50
	1941	.720	2.00	5.00	15.00
	1942	.960	2.00	6.00	20.00
	BRONZE				
9a	1942	.480	15.00	35.00	80.00
	1942	—	—	Proof	300.00
	1943	3.120	2.00	5.00	13.50
	1944	2.400	2.00	5.00	15.00
	1947	3.600	2.00	5.00	10.00

New legend: KING GEORGE THE SIXTH

Y#	Date	Mintage	VF	XF	Unc
28	1949	1.440	2.00	5.00	13.50
	1950	.720	2.00	6.00	25.00
	1951	4.896	1.00	3.00	9.00
	1952	2.400	1.00	3.00	8.00

Y#	Date	Mintage	VF	XF	Unc
36	1954	.960	15.00	25.00	85.00
	1954	—	—	Proof	300.00

3 PENCE

1.4100 gm., .925 SILVER, .0419 oz ASW

Y#	Date	Mintage	VF	XF	Unc
3	1932	.688	5.00	15.00	40.00
	1932	—	—	Proof	110.00
	1934	.628	5.00	15.00	40.00
	1935	.840	5.00	15.00	40.00
	1936	1.052	5.00	17.50	45.00

Y#	Date	Mintage	VF	XF	Unc
12	1937	1.228	5.00	10.00	32.50
	1937	—	—	Proof	250.00

Obv: KING moved right of head

Y#	Date	Mintage	VF	XF	Unc
17	1939	.160	25.00	45.00	100.00
	1939	—	—	Proof	375.00
	1940	1.200	4.00	10.00	40.00
	1941	.600	7.50	20.00	45.00
	1942	2.000	4.00	10.00	35.00
	1.4100 gm., .500 SILVER, .0226 oz ASW				
17b	1944	1.600	3.00	8.00	35.00
	1945	.800	7.50	20.00	60.00
	1946	2.400	7.00	15.00	40.00
	COPPER-NICKEL				
17a	1947	8.000	1.50	3.50	8.50

New legend: KING GEORGE THE SIXTH

Y#	Date	Mintage	VF	XF	Unc
29	1948	2.000	2.00	5.00	15.00
	1949	4.000	2.00	5.00	17.50
	1951	5.600	2.00	5.00	11.50
	1952	4.800	2.00	5.00	15.00
	1952	—	—	Proof	150.00

6 PENCE

2.8300 gm., .925 SILVER, .0841 oz ASW

Y#	Date	Mintage	VF	XF	Unc
4	1932	.544	5.50	15.00	45.00
	1932	—	—	Proof	125.00
	1934	.214	10.00	25.00	100.00
	1935	.380	5.50	20.00	65.00
	1936	.675	5.50	20.00	65.00

Y#	Date	Mintage	VF	XF	Unc
13	1937	.823	7.50	20.00	50.00
	1937	—	—	Proof	250.00

Obv: KING moved right of head

Y#	Date	Mintage	VF	XF	Unc
18	1939	.200	17.00	40.00	150.00
	1939	—	—	Proof	400.00
	1940	.600	7.00	17.50	65.00
	1941	.300	10.00	30.00	75.00
	1942	1.200	5.00	15.00	45.00
	2.8300 gm., .500 SILVER, .0454 oz ASW				
18b	1944	.800	4.00	15.00	45.00
	1945	.400	65.00	100.00	200.00
	1946	1.600	10.00	25.00	60.00
	COPPER-NICKEL				
18a	1947	5.000	2.00	5.00	20.00
	1947	—	—	Proof	350.00

New legend: KING GEORGE THE SIXTH

Y#	Date	Mintage	VF	XF	Unc
30	1948	1.000	2.00	5.00	15.00
	1949	2.000	1.75	5.00	25.00
	1950	2.000	1.75	5.00	22.50
	1951	2.800	1.75	3.75	15.00
	1952	1.200	3.00	7.00	22.50

SHILLING

5.6600 gm., .925 SILVER, .1683 oz ASW

Y#	Date	Mintage	VF	XF	Unc
5	1932	.896	8.00	20.00	60.00
	1932	—	—	Proof	140.00
	1934	.333	11.50	50.00	150.00
	1935	.830	8.50	22.50	75.00
	1936	1.663	7.00	20.00	60.00

Y#	Date	Mintage	VF	XF	Unc
14	1937	1.700	10.00	22.00	55.00
	1937	—	—	Proof	275.00

Obv: KING moved right of head

Y#	Date	Mintage	VF	XF	Unc
19	1939	.420	40.00	100.00	150.00
	1939	—	—	Proof	450.00
	1940	.750	25.00	55.00	110.00
	1941	.800	30.00	65.00	120.00
	1942	2.100	8.00	17.50	50.00

5.6600 gm., .500 SILVER, .0909 oz ASW

Y#	Date	Mintage	VF	XF	Unc
19b	1944	1.600	7.50	15.00	50.00
	1946	1.700	20.00	40.00	100.00

COPPER-NICKEL

Y#	Date	Mintage	VF	XF	Unc
19a	1947	8.000	3.00	6.50	35.00

New legend: KING GEORGE THE SIXTH

Y#	Date	Mintage	VF	XF	Unc
31	1948	1.500	2.00	6.00	20.00
	1949	4.000	2.00	8.00	30.00
	1950	2.000	2.00	5.50	27.50
	1951	3.000	1.50	5.50	25.00
	1952	2.600	1.50	6.50	30.00

2 SHILLINGS

11.3100 .925 SILVER, .3363 oz ASW

Y#	Date	Mintage	VF	XF	Unc
6	1932	.498	12.50	35.00	100.00
	1932	—	—	Proof	160.00
	1934	.154	25.00	80.00	200.00
	1935	.365	15.00	35.00	100.00
	1936	.683	15.00	50.00	125.00

Y#	Date	Mintage	VF	XF	Unc
15	1937	.552	20.00	35.00	65.00
	1937	—	—	Proof	275.00

Obv: KING moved right of head

Y#	Date	Mintage	VF	XF	Unc
20	1939	.120	200.00	350.00	500.00
	1939	—	—	Proof	800.00
	1940	.525	35.00	65.00	125.00
	1941	.400	35.00	70.00	150.00
	1942	.850	20.00	35.00	75.00

11.3100 gm., .500 SILVER, .1818 oz ASW

Y#	Date	Mintage	VF	XF	Unc
20b	1944	1.300	12.50	22.50	60.00
	1946	.700	500.00	900.00	1500.

COPPER-NICKEL

Y#	Date	Mintage	VF	XF	Unc
20a	1947	3.750	5.00	10.00	55.00

New legend: KING GEORGE THE SIXTH

Y#	Date	Mintage	VF	XF	Unc
32	1948	.750	3.00	6.50	30.00
	1949	2.000	3.00	7.50	45.00
	1950	1.000	3.00	7.00	40.00
	1951	2.600	3.00	5.50	27.50
	1952	1.800	3.00	7.00	40.00

Y#	Date	Mintage	VF	XF	Unc
37	1954	.300	60.00	150.00	400.00
	1954	—	—	Proof	500.00

1/2 CROWN

14.1400 .GM., .925 SILVER, .4205 oz ASW

Y#	Date	Mintage	VF	XF	Unc
7	1932	.634	12.75	35.00	100.00
	1932	—	—	Proof	160.00
	1934	.419	15.00	45.00	150.00
	1935	.512	12.75	40.00	125.00
	1936	.518	12.75	35.00	110.00

Rev: Similar to Y#7

Y#	Date	Mintage	VF	XF	Unc
16	1937	1.174	15.00	32.50	75.00
	1937	—	—	Proof	300.00

Obv: KING moved right of head. Rev: Similar to Y#7.

Y#	Date	Mintage	VF	XF	Unc
21	1938	.400	16.00	30.00	100.00
	1939	.224	35.00	75.00	250.00
	1939	—	—	Proof	500.00
	1940	.800	12.75	25.00	65.00
	1941	1.240	12.75	20.00	45.00
	1942	2.008	12.75	20.00	55.00

14.1400 gm., .500 SILVER, .2273 oz ASW

Y#	Date	Mintage	VF	XF	Unc
21b	1944	.800	12.50	30.00	75.00
	1946	1.400	25.00	60.00	150.00

COPPER-NICKEL

Y#	Date	Mintage	VF	XF	Unc
21a	1947	6.000	5.00	10.00	22.50

New legend: KING GEORGE THE SIXTH

Y#	Date	Mintage	VF	XF	Unc
33	1948	.800	5.00	10.00	35.00
	1949	1.600	5.00	8.50	45.00
	1950	1.200	5.00	8.50	45.00
	1951	3.200	5.00	7.50	35.00
	1952	2.800	5.00	8.50	40.00
	1952	—	—	Proof	400.00

Y#	Date	Mintage	VF	XF	Unc
38	1954	1.200	15.00	40.00	75.00
	1954	—	—	Proof	450.00

CROWN

28.2800 gm., .500 SILVER, .4546 oz ASW
Cecil Rhodes Centennial

Y#	Date	Mintage	VF	XF	Unc
34	1953	.124	BV	15.00	20.00
	1953	1,500	Proof	—	125.00

NCLT ISSUES

PROOF SETS

STANDARD METALS

KM#	Date	Mintage	Identification	Issue Price	Mkt. Val.
101	1932(5)	496	Y3-7	—	500.00
102	1937(6)	40	Y9,12-16	—	1500.
103	1939(5)	10	Y17-21	—	2500.
104	1953(2)	3	Y34 double set	—	Rare
105	1954(4)	20	Y35-38	—	1000.

RHODESIA & NYASALAND

The Federation of Rhodesia and Nyasaland (or the Central African Federation), comprising the British protectorates of Northern Rhodesia and Nyasaland and the self-governing colony of Southern Rhodesia, was located in the east-central part of southern Africa. The multiracial federation had an area of about 487,000 sq. mi. (1,261,330 sq. km.) and a population of 6.8 million. Capital: Salisbury, in Southern Rhodesia.

The geographical unity of the three British possessions suggested the desirability of political and economic union as early as 1924. Despite objections by the African constituency of Northern Rhodesia and Nyasaland, who feared that African self-determination would be retarded by the dominant influence of prosperous and self-governing Southern Rhodesia, the Central African Federation was established in Sept. of 1953. As feared, the Federation was effectively and profitably dominated by the European constituency of Southern Rhodesia despite the fact that the three component countries largely retained their prefederation political structure. It was dissolved at the end of 1963, largely because of the effective opposition of the Nyasaland African Congress. Northern Rhodesia and Nyasaland became independent states in 1964. Southern Rhodesia unilaterally declared its independence the following year.

The coinage is obsolete.

NOTE: For earlier coinage see Southern Rhodesia.

RULERS

Elizabeth II, 1952-1964

MONETARY SYSTEM

12 Pence = 1 Shilling
5 Shillings = 1 Crown

1/2 PENNY

BRONZE

Y#	Date	Mintage	VF	XF	Unc
1	1955	.720	—	1.00	2.00
	1955	2,010	—	Proof	10.00
	1956	.480	—	.50	1.50
	1956	—	—	Proof	125.00
	1957	1.920	.25	.50	1.00
	1958	2.400	—	.25	1.00
	1958	—	—	Proof	125.00
	1964	1.440	—	.25	.50

PENNY

BRONZE

Y#	Date	Mintage	VF	XF	Unc
2	1955	2.040	—	1.00	4.00
	1955	2,010	—	Proof	12.50
	1956	4.800	—	.50	2.50
	1956	—	—	Proof	150.00
	1957	7.200	—	.25	2.00
	1958	2.880	—	.25	2.00
	1958	—	—	Proof	150.00
	1961	4.800	—	.25	1.00
	1962	6.000	—	—	1.00
	1963	6.000	—	—	1.00
	1963	—	—	Proof	150.00

3 PENCE

COPPER-NICKEL

Y#	Date	Mintage	VF	XF	Unc
3	1955	1.200	.50	1.50	3.00
	1955	10 pcs.	—	Proof	400.00
	1956	3.200	1.00	2.50	15.00
	1957	6.000	—	1.00	1.50
	1962	4.000	—	.50	1.50
	1963	2.000	—	.50	1.50
	1964	3.600	—	.50	1.00
	1.4100 gm., .500 SILVER, .0226 oz ASW				
3a	1955	2,000	—	Proof	15.00

6 PENCE

COPPER-NICKEL

Y#	Date	Mintage	VF	XF	Unc
4	1955	.400	2.00	5.00	15.00
	1955	10 pcs.	—	Proof	450.00
	1956	.800	2.00	5.00	25.00
	1957	4.000	1.00	1.50	3.00
	1962	2.800	1.00	1.50	4.00
	1963	.800	15.00	22.50	45.00
	2.8300 gm., .500 SILVER, .0454 oz ASW				
4a	1955	2,000	—	Proof	17.50

SHILLING

COPPER-NICKEL

Y#	Date	Mintage	VF	XF	Unc
5	1955	.200	7.50	10.00	20.00
	1955	10 pcs.	—	Proof	500.00
	1956	1.700	2.00	7.50	25.00
	1957	3.500	1.00	2.00	4.00
	5.6600 gm., .500 SILVER, .0909 oz ASW				
5a	1955	2,000	—	Proof	20.00

2 SHILLINGS

COPPER-NICKEL

Y#	Date	Mintage	VF	XF	Unc
6	1955	1.750	3.00	5.00	14.00
	1955	10 pcs.	—	Proof	750.00
	1956	1.850	1.00	2.50	7.50
	1957	1.500	2.00	4.00	11.50
	11.3100 gm., .500 SILVER, .1818 oz ASW				
6a	1955	2,000	—	Proof	25.00

1/2 CROWN

COPPER-NICKEL

Y#	Date	Mintage	VF	XF	Unc
7	1955	1.600	2.00	4.00	10.00
	1955	10 pcs.	—	Proof	700.00
	1956	.160	25.00	50.00	100.00
	1957	2.400	20.00	35.00	75.00
	14.1400 gm., .500 SILVER, .2273 oz ASW				
7a	1955	2,000	—	Proof	70.00

NOTE: For later coinage see Malawi, Rhodesia and Zambia.

NCLT ISSUES

PROOF SETS

STANDARD METALS

KM#	Date	Mintage	Identification	Issue Price	Mkt. Val.
101	1955(7)	10	Y1-7	—	2000.
102	1955(7)	2,000	Y1-2,3a-7a	—	125.00

REPUBLIC OF RHODESIA

MONETARY SYSTEM

12 Pence = 1 Shilling
20 Shillings = 1 Pound

3 PENCE

COPPER-NICKEL

Y#	Date	Mintage	VF	XF	Unc
A1	1968	2.400	.20	.35	1.00
	1968	10 pcs.	—	Proof	1500.

Rev: Error on shaft of spear.

Y#	Date	Mintage	VF	XF	Unc
—	1968	150 pcs.		(double strike)	300.00

6 PENCE = 5 CENTS

COPPER-NICKEL

Y#	Date	Mintage	VF	XF	Unc
1	1964	13.500	.20	.35	1.00
	1964	2,048	—	Proof	15.00

SHILLING = 10 CENTS

COPPER-NICKEL

Y#	Date	Mintage	VF	XF	Unc
2	1964	15.500	.30	.50	1.50
	1964	2,048	—	Proof	15.00

2 SHILLINGS = 20 CENTS

COPPER-NICKEL

Y#	Date	Mintage	VF	XF	Unc
3	1964	10.500	.60	1.00	2.50
	1964	2,048	—	Proof	17.50

2-1/2 SHILLINGS = 25 CENTS

COPPER-NICKEL

Y#	Date	Mintage	VF	XF	Unc
4	1964	11.500	1.00	1.50	4.50
	1964	2,048	—	Proof	25.00

10 SHILLINGS

3.9940 gm., .916 GOLD, .1177 oz AGW

Y#	Date	Mintage	XF	Unc	Proof
A5	1966	4,000	—	—	125.00

POUND

7.9881 gm., .916 GOLD .2354 oz AGW

Y#	Date	Mintage	XF	Unc	Proof
B5	1966	3,000	—	—	350.00

5 POUNDS

39.9403 gm., .916 GOLD, 1.1772 oz AGW

Y#	Date	Mintage	XF	Unc	Proof
C5	1966	1,000	—	—	850.00

DECIMAL COINAGE

100 Cents = 1 Dollar
(10 Shillings)

1/2 CENT

BRONZE

Y#	Date	Mintage	VF	XF	Unc
5	1970	10.000	—	.10	.15
	1970	12 pcs.	—	Proof	1200.
	1971	2.000	—	—	.20
	1972	2.000	—	.10	.20
	1975	10.001	—	.10	.15

CENT

BRONZE

Y#	Date	Mintage	VF	XF	Unc
6	1970	25.000	—	.10	.15
	1970	12 pcs.	—	Proof	1200.
	1971	15.000	—	.10	.15
	1972	10.000	—	.10	.15
	1973	5.000	—	.10	.20
	1973	25 pcs.	—	Proof	2000.
	1974	—	—	.10	.15
	1975	10.000	—	.10	.15
	1976	20.000	—	.10	.15

2-1/2 CENTS

COPPER-NICKEL

Y#	Date	Mintage	VF	XF	Unc
7	1970	4.000	.15	.25	.50
	1970	12 pcs.	—	Proof	1200.

5 CENTS

COPPER-NICKEL

Y#	Date	Mintage	VF	XF	Unc
8	1973	—	.15	.25	.40
	1973	25 pcs.	—	Proof	2000.

Y#	Date	Mintage	VF	XF	Unc
9	1975	3.500	.15	.25	.40
	1976	8.038	.15	.25	.40

10 CENTS

COPPER-NICKEL

Y#	Date	Mintage	VF	XF	Unc
10	1975	1.874	.25	.40	.75
	1976	.129	.30	.60	1.00

20 CENTS

COPPER-NICKEL

Y#	Date	Mintage	VF	XF	Unc
11	1975	—	.60	.85	1.25
	1976	1.937	.60	.85	1.25
	1977	—	—	—	—

25 CENTS

COPPER-NICKEL

Y#	Date	Mintage	VF	XF	Unc
12	1975	—	.75	1.25	2.00
	1976	1.011	.75	1.25	2.00

NCLT ISSUES

PROOF SETS

STANDARD METALS

KM#	Date	Mintage	Identification	Issue Price	Mkt. Val.
101	1964(8)	10	Y1-4 double set	—	650.00
102	1964(4)	2,040	Y1-4	—	75.00
103	1966(3)	2,000	YA5-C5	280.00	1250.
104	1970(6)	6	Y5-7 double set	—	7000.

HEJIRA DATE CHART

HEJIRA (Hijra, Hegira), the name of the Mohammedan era (A. H. = Anno Hegirae) dates back to the Christian year 622 when Mohammed "fled" from Mecca, escaping to Medina to avoid persecution from the Koreish tribesmen. Based on a lunar year the Mohammedan year is 11 days shorter.

* = Leap Year (Christian Calendar)

AH Hijra year	AD Christian Date
1174	1760, August 13
1175	1761, August 2*
1176	1762, July 28
1177	1763, July 12
1178	1764, July 1
1179	1765, June 20*
1180	1766, June 9
1181	1767, May 30
1182	1768, May 18
1183	1769, May 7*
1184	1770, April 27
1185	1771, April 16
1186	1772, April 4
1187	1773, March 25*
1188	1774, March 14
1189	1775, March 4
1190	1776, February 21
1191	1777, February 9*
1192	1778, January 30
1193	1779, January 19
1194	1780, January 8
1195	1780, December 28*
1196	1781, December 17
1197	1782, December 7
1198	1783, November 26
1199	1784, November 14*
1200	1785, November 4
1201	1786, October 24
1202	1787, October 13
1203	1788, October 2*
1204	1789, September 21
1205	1790, September 10
1206	1792, August 31
1207	1792, August 19*
1208	1793, August 9
1209	1794, July 29
1210	1795, July 18
1211	1796, July 7*
1212	1797, June 26
1213	1798, June 15
1214	1799, June 5
1215	1800, May 25
1216	1801, May 14
1217	1802, May 4
1218	1803, April 23
1219	1804, April 12*
1220	1805, April 1
1221	1806, March 21
1222	1807, March 11
1223	1808, February 28*
1224	1809, February 16
1225	1810, February 6
1226	1811, January 26
1227	1812, January 16*
1228	1813, January 4
1229	1813, December 24
1230	1814, December 14
1231	1815, December 3
1232	1816, November 21*
1233	1817, November 11
1234	1818, October 31
1235	1819, October 20
1236	1820, October 9*
1237	1821, September 28
1238	1822, September 18
1239	1823, September 7
1240	1824, August 26*
1241	1825, August 16
1242	1826, August 5
1243	1827, July 25
1244	1828, July 14
1245	1829, July 3
1246	1830, June 22
1247	1831, June 12

AH Hijra Year	AD Christian Date
1248	1832, May 31*
1249	1833, May 21
1250	1834, May 10
1251	1835, April 29
1252	1836, April 18*
1253	1837, April 7
1254	1838, March 27
1255	1839, March 17
1256	1840, March 5*
1257	1841, February 23
1258	1842, February 12
1259	1843, February 1
1260	1844, January 22*
1261	1845, January 10
1262	1845, December 30
1263	1846, December 20
1264	1847, December 9
1265	1848, November 27*
1266	1849, November 17
1267	1850, November 6
1268	1851, October 27
1269	1852, October 15*
1270	1853, October 4
1271	1854, September 24
1272	1855, September 13
1273	1856, September 1*
1274	1857, August 22
1275	1858, August 11
1276	1859, July 31
1277	1860, July 20*
1278	1861, July 9
1279	1862, June 29
1280	1863, June 18
1281	1864, June 6*
1282	1865, May 27
1283	1866, May 16
1284	1867, May 5
1285	1868, April 24*
1286	1869, April 13
1287	1870, April 3
1288	1871, March 23
1289	1872, March 11*
1290	1873, March 1
1291	1874, February 18
1292	1875, February 7
1293	1876, January 28*
1294	1877, January 16
1295	1878, January 5
1296	1878, December 26
1297	1879, December 15
1298	1890, December 4*
1299	1881, November 23
1300	1882, November 12
1301	1883, November 2
1302	1884, October 21*
1303	1885, October 10
1304	1886, September 30
1305	1887, September 19
1306	1888, September 7*
1307	1889, August 28
1308	1890, August 17
1309	1891, August 7
1310	1892, July 26*
1311	1893, July 15
1312	1894, July 5
1313	1895, June 24
1314	1896, June 12*
1315	1897, June 2
1316	1898, May 22
1317	1899, May 12
1318	1900, May 1
1319	1901, May 20
1320	1902, April 10
1321	1903, March 30
1322	1904, March 18*
1323	1905, March 8
1324	1906, February 25
1325	1907, February 14
1326	1908, February 4*
1327	1909, January 23
1328	1910, January 13

AH Hijra Year	AD Christian Date
1329	1911, January 2
1330	1911, December 22
1331	1912, December 11*
1332	1913, November 30
1333	1914, November 19
1334	1915, November 9
1335	1916, October 28*
1336	1917, October 17
1337	1918, October 7
1338	1919, September 26
1339	1920, September 15*
1340	1921, September 4
1341	1922, August 24
1342	1923, August 14
1343	1924, August 2*
1344	1925, July 22
1345	1926, July 12
1346	1927, July 1
1347	1928, July 20*
1348	1929, July 9
1349	1930, May 29
1350	1931, May 19
1351	1932, May 7*
1352	1933, April 26
1353	1934, April 16
1354	1935, April 5
1355	1936, March 24*
1356	1937, March 14
1357	1938, March 3
1358	1939, February 21
1359	1940, February 10*
1360	1941, January 29
1361	1942, January 19
1362	1943, January 8
1363	1943, December 28
1364	1944, December 17*
1365	1945, December 6
1366	1946, November 25
1367	1947, November 15
1368	1948, November 3*
1369	1949, October 24
1370	1950, October 13
1371	1951, October 2
1372	1952, September 21*
1373	1953, September 10
1374	1954, August 30
1375	1955, August 20
1376	1956, August 8*
1377	1957, July 29
1378	1958, July 18
1379	1959, July 7
1380	1960, June 25*
1381	1961, June 14
1382	1962, June 4
1383	1963, May 25
1384	1964, May 13*
1385	1965, May 2
1386	1966, April 22
1387	1967, April 11
1388	1968, May 31*
1389	1969, March 20
1390	1970, March 9
1391	1971, February 27
1392	1972, February 16*
1393	1973, February 4
1394	1974, January 25
1395	1975, January 14
1396	1976, January 3*
1397	1976, December 23*
1398	1977, December 12
1399	1978, December 2
1400	1979, November 21
1401	1980, November 9*
1402	1981, October 30
1403	1982, October 19
1404	1983, October 8
1405	1984, September 27*
1406	1985, September 16
1407	1986, September 6
1408	1987, August 26
1409	1988, August 14*